P9-DTP-704

THE RIVERSIDE
SHAKESPEARE

GENERAL AND TEXTUAL EDITOR

G. Blakemore Evans, *Harvard University*
with the assistance of
J. J. M. Tobin, *University of Massachusetts, Boston*

EDITORS

Herschel Baker, *Harvard University*

Anne Barton, *Trinity College, Cambridge*

Frank Kermode, *King's College, Cambridge*

Harry Levin, *Harvard University*

Hallett Smith, *California Institute of Technology*

Marie Edel, *Houghton Mifflin Company*

ESSAYS BY

Heather Dubrow, *University of Wisconsin, Madison*

William T. Liston, *Ball State University*

Charles H. Shattuck, *University of Illinois*

THE RIVERSIDE SHAKESPEARE

SECOND EDITION

THE COMPLETE WORKS

HOUGHTON MIFFLIN COMPANY BOSTON NEW YORK

Senior Sponsoring Editor: Dean Johnson
Editorial Assistant: Mary Furlong Healey
Senior Project Editor: Janet Young
Editorial Assistant: Elizabeth Emmons
Senior Production/Design Coordinator: Sarah Ambrose
Senior Manufacturing Coordinator: Florence Cadran
Senior Marketing Manager: Nancy Lyman

Cover design by Anthony Saizon
Cover image: Staunton portrait of Shakespeare, The Folger Shakespeare Library

Printed in the U.S.A.

Library of Congress Catalog Card Number: 96-76897

ISBN: 0–395–75490–9
9 10 11 12 13 14 15 16 17 18 19 20-DW-05 04 03

Publisher's Preface

Making the works of William Shakespeare generally available to his myriad readers has a long history. Although even the most loyal and enthusiastic of his contemporaries may not, perhaps, have allowed his writings the kind of universal esteem in which the world (and not just the English-speaking world) now holds them, they nonetheless witnessed in 1623, only seven years after his death, the publication of what is usually called "the First Folio," a collection of thirty-six plays that has furnished the basis of what we now call "the Shakespeare canon."

The editorial tradition initiated by the First Folio, itself based on a variety of different sources (authorial or scribal drafts, earlier published quarto editions of individual plays, and prompt-books or other theatrically associated manuscripts), has grown mightily and become increasingly refined and more solidly focused over the many years since Nicholas Rowe's first edited edition appeared in 1709. *The Riverside Shakespeare*, then, is only one of the latest links in a long and honorable chain of editorial and critical labors, even though it has, happily, become for most the standard one-volume Shakespeare for critical reference and for teaching. It is the cornerstone of Houghton Mifflin's college publishing program and a touchstone of quality for all the Company's efforts.

This Second Edition of *The Riverside Shakespeare* owes its existence to the hands and minds of many; it is their cooperative work that has produced the pages that follow. It is my privilege to represent all of them in introducing this new edition to the many readers who will be informed, educated, and delighted by what it contains.

Nader F. Darehshori, Chairman
Houghton Mifflin Company

Acknowledgments for the Second Edition

The Riverside Shakespeare was first published twenty-three years ago. Since then, of course, students of Shakespeare have been very busy both critically and textually, and a great deal of scholarly work has consequently been published. Something like a sea change has taken place in critical approaches, many of them relatively new approaches which see the plays and poems through eyes that focus primarily on sociological, political, new historicist, and gender-oriented values—varieties of criticism that are also often reflected in "new" theatrical productions. To meet such very real challenges, we have added an interpretive essay by Heather Dubrow entitled "Twentieth-Century Shakespeare Criticism" (see pages 27–54) and a continuation of Charles H. Shattuck's "Shakespeare's Plays in Performance: From 1660 to 1971" (Appendix A), William T. Liston's "Shakespeare's Plays in Performance: From 1970" (Appendix B). Other major additions include *The Reign of King Edward the Third* (1596; written c. 1592–5), a history play now generally accepted as, at least in part, by Shakespeare, published here for the first time in a one-volume Works since the 1870s; and *A Funeral Elegy* by W. S. (1612), a poem recently claimed for Shakespeare by Donald W. Foster. The essay "Shakespeare's Text" and the "Note on the Text" that is appended to each of the plays and poems have been thoroughly revised in the light of the many textual studies that have appeared since 1974. Also revised, updated, and enlarged are the "Chronology and Sources," "Records, Documents, and Allusions" (Appendix C), "Annals, 1552–1616" (Appendix D), and the "Selected Bibliography."

We have gone heavily into debt to a small army of generous helpers who have made this Second Edition possible. Our good friends William Bond, Philip Finkelpearl, Jonathan Hart, John Klause, and Vincent Petronella have come to our rescue when critical help was most urgently needed, and we are very grateful for their support. And to those who served as our computer-amanuenses our deepest thanks are also due: Scott Gordon, Carla Mazzio, Eric Wilson, Marie Henson, Doug Trevor, and Susannah Tobin (who, at a moment of crisis, single-handedly took over).

As always in the past, the staffs of the Widener and Houghton Libraries have been continually helpful, with special thanks due to Carolyn Fawcett. Fredric W. Wilson and Annette Fern, the Curator and Research and Reference Librarian of the Harvard Theatre Collection, were more than generous with both time and materials, placing the extraordinary richness of the collection entirely at our disposal. We are, of course, deeply indebted to Houghton Mifflin, particularly to Dean Johnson and Janet Young, both of whom have provided unstinting support (coupled with great patience). Sarah Ambrose also provided technical assistance in the book's production. We would also like to thank Susan Boulanger, who copy-edited our typescripts; Rebecca Cottingham, who proof-read new material; and Rose Corbett Gordon, who helped to assemble many of the new illustrations.

Finally, to our wives, Betty and Rosemary, who together with us suffered all of the many Second Edition birth pangs, we offer loving salutations: *Laudate uxores!*

G. Blakemore Evans
J. J. M. Tobin

Acknowledgments for the First Edition

The Textual Editor has received, over the years, much special help and advice from friends and colleagues which it is now his happy privilege to acknowledge. Dr. Marie Edel, apart from her own share in this edition, has served throughout as an unofficial general editor, and her learning, critical insight, and infallible eye for detail have placed me, *sine spe*, profoundly in her debt. Our long association has been a continuing source of pleasure to me. Professor Marvin Spevack, who used the present text as the basis for his *Complete and Systematic Concordance to the Works of Shakespeare* (6 vols., 1968–70), has been more than helpful in a variety of ways, particularly in rechecking the accuracy of the text and Textual Notes. To both these friends my gratitude goes far beyond anything I can possibly express. I am further greatly indebted to the unfailing kindness and patience of the staffs of the Houghton Library and the Harvard Theatre Collection, especially to my old friend Dr. William Bond, Director of the Houghton Library, Miss Carolyn Jakeman, Miss Katherine Pantzer, Miss Marte Shaw, and Dr. Jeanne Newlin. Miss Eva Faye Benton, English Librarian at the University of Illinois, also has my special thanks, as do Professors Michael T. Kiernan, Frederick Kiefer, and David George, each of whom in different ways assisted me at need. Finally, to my wife, who with truly Spartan endurance read aloud to me the complete text (including all the punctuation marks!), I offer once again my wondering and loving thanks for her continual support in this and all other things.

G. Blakemore Evans

Contents

COMEDIES

HISTORIES

TRAGEDIES

ROMANCES

POEMS

List of Illustrations

ILLUSTRATIONS IN THE TEXT

MAPS

MAPS

Abbreviations

F1, F2, etc. First Folio, Second Folio, etc.
O1, O2, etc. First Octavo, Second Octavo, etc.
Q1, Q2, etc. First Quarto, Second Quarto, etc.
(c) corrected state
(u) uncorrected state
conj. conjecture
ed. editor; edition
l(l). line(s)
n.s. new series
om. omit(s), omitted
o.s.d. opening stage direction
s.d(d). stage direction(s)
ser. series
sig(s). signature(s)
s.p(p). speech-prefix(es)
subs. substantially

Key to Works Cited

Reference in explanatory and textual notes is in general by last name of editor or author. Not included in the following list of works so cited are editions of individual plays or special studies referred to in the selected bibliographies appended to the "Note on the Text" following each of the plays and poems.

AEB, *Analytical and Enumerative Bibliography*
ALEXANDER, Peter, ed., *Works*, 1951
BELL, Robert, ed., Shakespeare's *Poems*, 1855
BENSON, John, *Poems: Written by Wil. Shake-speare. Gent.*, 1640
BOSWELL, James, ed., *Works*, 1821 (21 vols.)
BROOKE, Tucker, ed., *Much Ado about Nothing* (Yale), 1917
BULLEN, Arthur H., ed., *Works*, 1904–7 (10 vols.)
BULLOCH, John, *Studies on the Text of Shakespeare*, 1878
BULLOUGH, Geoffrey, *Narrative and Dramatic Sources of Shakespeare*, 1957–75 (8 vols.)
BUTLER, Samuel, ed., *Shakespeare's Sonnets*, 1899
CAMBRIDGE, *Works*, ed. W. G. Clark and W. A. Wright, 1863–66 (9 vols.); ed. W. A. Wright, 1891–93 (9 vols.)
CAPELL, Edward, ed., *Works*, [1768] (10 vols.)
CAPELL MS, Edward Capell's marked copy of Lintott's edition of Shakespeare's *Poems* (Trinity College, Cambridge)
COLLIER, John P., ed., *Works*, 1842–44 (8 vols.); 1853; 1858 (6 vols.)
COLLIER MS, Perkins' Second Folio, 1632 (Huntington Library)
COLMAN, George, ed., *Dramatick Works of Beaumont and Fletcher*, 1778 (vol. X)
COWDEN CLARKE, Charles and Mary, eds., *Works*, 1864–68 (3 vols.)
COWL, R. P. (with A. E. Morgan), *1 Henry IV* (Arden), 1939
CRAIG, William J., ed., *Works*, 1891
CRAIK, George L., *The English of Shakespeare*, 1857

Crow, John, "Editing and Emending," *Essays and Studies*, n.s., VII (1955), 1–20

Daniel, P. A., *Notes and Conjectural Emendations*, 1870

Davenant, William, *The Rivals*, 1668 (adaptation of *The Two Noble Kinsmen*)
Macbeth, 1674
The Law against Lovers (combination of *Measure for Measure* and *Much Ado about Nothing*)

Davenant-Dryden, John Dryden and William Davenant, *The Tempest: or the Enchanted Island*, 1669

Davenport, A., "Notes on *King Lear*," *N & Q*, n.s., CXCVIII (1953), 20–22

Deighton, K., ed., *Timon of Athens* (Arden), 1905

Delius, Nicolaus, ed., *Works*, 1854–60 (7 vols.); 1872 (2 vols.)

Dering MS, Sir Edward Dering, *Henry IV* (two parts combined) (Folger MS. V. b. 34), ed. G. W. Williams and G. B. Evans, 1974

Douai MS (*Twelfth Night, As You Like It, Comedy of Errors, Romeo and Juliet, Julius Caesar, Macbeth*), Douai MS. 7.87, in the Douai Public Library (see G. B. Evans, *PQ*, XLI [1962], 158–72)

Drew, Philip, "A Suggested Reading in *Measure for Measure*," *SQ*, IX (1958), 202–4

Dyce, Alexander, ed., *Works*, 1857 (6 vols.); 1864–67 (9 vols.); 1875–76 (9 vols.)
Works of Beaumont and Fletcher, 1843–46 (11 vols.)

Edwards, Thomas, *The Canons of Criticism*, 1748

ELN, *English Language Notes*

ELR, *English Literary Renaissance*

Evans, Thomas, ed., Shakespeare's *Poems*, [1775]

Ewing, Thomas, ed., Shakespeare's *Poems*, 1771

Farmer, Richard, in *Works* (Johnson-Steevens), 1773

Folger MS: (*Julius Caesar*) Folger Shakespeare Library, MS. V. a. 85 (see G.B. Evans, *JEGP*, XLI [1942], 401–17); (*Merry Wives of Windsor*) MS. V. a. 73 (see G.B. Evans in *Shakespeare, Text, and Language*, eds. B. Fabian and K. Tetzeli von Rosador [1987], 57–79)

Furness, H. H., ed., *New Variorum Edition*, 1871–1928 (vols. 1–15; vols. 16–21 by H. H. Furness, Jr.)

Gentleman, Francis, ed., *Poems Written by Shakespeare*, 1774

Gildon, Charles, ed., Shakespeare's *Poems*, 1710; 1714

Globe, ed. William G. Clark and W. A. Wright, *Works*, 1864

Halliwell, James O., ed., *Works*, 1853–65 (16 vols.)

Hanmer, Thomas, ed., *Works*, 1743–44 (6 vols.); 1745; 1770–71 (6 vols.)

Harness, William, ed., *Works*, 1825 (8 vols.)

Harrison, G. B., ed., *Works* (Penguin), 1937–56 (37 vols.)

Hart, H. C., ed., *Love's Labour's Lost* (Arden), 1906

Heath, Benjamin, *Revisal of Shakespeare's Text*, 1765

Herford, Charles H., ed., *Works*, 1899 (10 vols.)
The Two Noble Kinsmen (Temple), 1897

Hinman, Charlton, *The Printing and Proof-Reading of the First Folio of Shakespeare*, 1963 (2 vols.)

HLQ, *Huntington Library Quarterly*

Hopkinson, A. F., ed., *The Two Noble Kinsmen*, 1894

Housman, R. F., ed., *A Collection of English Sonnets*, [1835]

Hudson, Henry N., ed., *Works*, 1851–56 (11 vols.); 1880–81 (20 vols.)

Hunter, John, ed., *Macbeth*, 1870

Jarcho, Saul, "Falstaff, Kittredge, and Galen," *Perspectives in Biology and Medicine*, XXX (1987), 197–200

JEGP, *Journal of English and Germanic Philology*

Jennens, Charles, ed., *Hamlet* (1773), *Julius Caesar* (1773, 1774), *King Lear* (1770), *Macbeth* (1773), *Othello* (1773)

Johnson, Samuel, ed., *Works*, 1765 (2 eds., 8 vols.); 1768 (8 vols.)

Keightley, Thomas, ed., *Works*, 1864 (6 vols.)

KELLNER, Leon, *Restoring Shakespeare*, 1925

KITTREDGE, George L., ed., *Works*, 1936

KNIGHT, Charles, ed., *Works*, 1838–43 (8 vols.); 1842–44 (12 vols.)

KÖKERITZ, Helge, *Shakespeare's Pronunciation* (1953)

LANSDOWNE, George Granville, Lord Lansdowne, *The Jew of Venice* (adaptation of *The Merchant of Venice*); 1701

LEISI, Ernst, ed., *Measure for Measure*, 1964

LIBRARY, THE, *Transactions of the Bibliographical Society*

LINTOTT, Bernard, ed., Shakespeare's *Poems* (2 vols., [1709], [1711])

LITTLEDALE, Harold, ed., *The Two Noble Kinsmen* (New Shakespeare Society), 1876, 1885

MACMILLAN, Michael, ed., *Julius Caesar* (Arden), 1942

MALONE, Edmond, ed., *Works*, 1790 (10 vols.)

MASON, John Monck, *Comments on . . . Shakespeare's Plays*, 1785

MLR, *Modern Language Review*

MUNRO, John, ed., *Works* (The London Shakespeare), 1958 (6 vols.)

MURDEN, A. (R. Newton et al.), *Poems* [Shakespeare's] *on Several Occasions*, [1760?]

NEILSON, William A., ed., *Works*, 1906

NEILSON-HILL, *Works*, ed. W. A. Neilson and C. J. Hill, 1942

N & Q, *Notes and Queries*

O.E.D., *Oxford English Dictionary*

ONIONS, C. T., *A Shakespeare Glossary* (2nd ed. revised), 1953

OULTON, W. C., ed., Shakespeare's *Poems*, 1804 (2 vols.)

PADUA PROMPT-BOOK (*Macbeth, Measure for Measure, The Winter's Tale*) in *Shakespearean Prompt-Books of the Seventeenth Century*, ed. G. B. Evans, 1960–63 (vols. I and II)

PBSA, *Papers of the Bibliographical Society of America*

PELICAN, *Works*, general ed. Alfred Harbage (rev. 1-vol. ed.), 1969

PMLA, *Publications of the Modern Language Association of America*

PQ, *Philological Quarterly*

POPE, Alexander, ed., *Works*, 1723–25 (6 vols.); 1728 (8 vols.)

RANN, Joseph, ed., *Works*, 1786–[94] (6 vols.)

REED, Edward B., ed., *Shakespeare's Sonnets* (Yale), 1923

REED, Isaac, ed., *Works*, 1803 (21 vols.); 1813 (21 vols.)

RES, *Review of English Studies*

RIDLEY, M. R., ed., *Works* (New Temple), 1935–36 (40 vols.)

RINGLER, William, "Exit Kent," *SQ*, XI (1960), 311–17

RITSON, Joseph, *Remarks, Critical and Illustrative . . . on the Last Edition of Shakespeare*, 1778

RODERICK, Richard, *Remarks on Shakespear* (in Thomas Edwards, *Canons of Criticism*, 6th ed.), 1758

ROLFE, W. J., ed., *The Two Noble Kinsmen*, 1883

ROWE, Nicholas, ed., *Works*, 1709 (2 eds., 6 vol.); 1714 (8 vols.)

SB, *Studies in Bibliography*

SCHMIDT, Alexander, *Shakespeare-Lexicon* (2 vols., 4th ed., rev. G. Sarrazin), 1923

SEL, *Studies in English Literature 1500–1900*

SEWARD, Thomas (see THEOBALD, *Works of Beaumont and Fletcher*, 1750)

SEWELL, George, ed., Shakespeare's *Poems*, 1725; 1728

SEYMOUR, E. H., *Remarks . . . upon the Plays of Shakespeare*, 1805 (2 vols.)

SINGER, S. W., ed., *Works*, 1826 (10 vols.); 1855–56 (10 vols.)

SISSON, Charles, ed., *Works*, [1954]

SKEAT, Walter W., ed., *The Two Noble Kinsmen*, 1875

SMOCK ALLEY PROMPT-BOOK (*Hamlet, Macbeth, Othello, King Lear, Twelfth Night, A Midsummer Night's Dream, Henry VIII, 1 Henry IV, The Comedy of Errors, The Merry Wives of Windsor, The Winter's Tale*), Smock Alley Theatre, Dublin (see G. B. Evans, ed., *Shakespearean Prompt-Books of the Seventeenth Century*, 1966–96 (vols. IV–VIII)

SP, *Studies in Philology*

SQ, *Shakespeare Quarterly*

S. ST., *Shakespeare Studies*

S. SUR., *Shakespeare Survey*

STATE POEMS, *Poems on Affairs of State*, 1707

STAUNTON, Howard, ed., *Works*, 1858–60 (3 vols.)

STEEVENS, George, ed., *Works*, 1773 (with Samuel Johnson, 10 vols.); 1778 (10 vols.); 1793 (15 vols.)

SYMPSON, J. (see THEOBALD, *Works of Beaumont and Fletcher*, 1750)

THEOBALD, Lewis, ed., *Works*, 1733 (7 vols.); 1740 (8 vols.); 1757 (8 vols.)
(with Thomas Seward and J. Sympson), *Works of Beaumont and Fletcher*, 1750 (vol. X: *The Two Noble Kinsmen*)

THIRLBY, Styan (see THEOBALD, *Works*, 1733)

TILLEY, M. P., *A Dictionary of the Proverbs of England in the Sixteenth and Seventeenth Centuries*, 1950

TLS, (London) *Times Literary Supplement*

TONSON, J., *The Works of Mr. Francis Beaumont and Mr. John Fletcher*, 1711 (vol. VII)

TYRRELL, Henry, ed., *Works*, 1850–53 (4 vols.)

TYRWHITT, Thomas, *Observations and Conjectures upon Some Passages of Shakespeare*, 1766

UPTON, John, *Critical Observations on Shakespeare*, 1747

VAUGHAN, Henry H., *New Readings . . . of Shakespeare's Tragedies*, 1878–86 (3 vols.)

WALKER, William S., *Critical Examination of the Text of Shakespeare*, 1860 (3 vols.)

WARBURTON, William, ed., *Works*, 1747 (8 vols.)

WEBER, Henry, ed., *Works of Beaumont and Fletcher*, 1812 (vol. XIII)

WELLS, Stanley and Gary Taylor, et al., eds., *William Shakespeare: The Complete Works, Original Spelling Edition* (1986)
William Shakespeare: A Textual Companion (1987)

WHITE, Richard Grant, ed., *Works*, 1857–66 (12 vols.); 1883 (6 vols.)

WILSON, John Dover (with A. Quiller-Couch et al.), ed., *Works* (New Shakespeare), 1921–66 (39 vols.)

THE RIVERSIDE SHAKESPEARE

General Introduction

Harry Levin

I. THE SHAKESPEAREAN HERITAGE

Now and again the observation is offered about a great writer that he has created a world of his own. Such artificial worlds are necessarily smaller than the one we live in; otherwise they would not help us much to understand it; like a map, they locate situations by reducing them to a comprehensible scale. Lifelike and large as these representations of truth may seem to us, they are limited nonetheless by the means and motives of their creation. Yet the writers whom we regard as the very greatest have a way of surpassing limitations by convincing us that their range of perception is just as wide, and their sense of reality just as authentic, as anything that we are ever likely to encounter during the course of our own experience. So the ancients placed Homer in a unique position because his epic outlook seemed to be coextensive with the breadth and depth of the world they knew. Similarly, for the Middle Ages, all the circumstances of human existence were summed up in the luminous vision of Dante. Since then man's horizons have so enlarged and his problems have so complicated themselves that, although he still can find much beauty and significance in the poetry of Homer and Dante, they have long since ceased to serve as his active guides. Indeed, if it were not for Shakespeare, we might well doubt whether any single creative genius could have encompassed so much of the variety, the profundity, and the abundance of life as it has been lived in the modern era of civilization.

Shakespeare's works have therefore been accorded a place in our culture above and beyond their topmost place in our literature. They have been virtually canonized as humanistic scriptures, the tested residue of pragmatic wisdom, a general collection of quotable texts and usable examples. Reprinted, reedited, commented upon, and translated into most languages, they have preempted more space on the library shelves than the books of—or about—any other author. Meanwhile they have become a staple of the school and college curricula, as well as the happiest of hunting-grounds for scholars and critics. As plays they continue to meet the one decisive criterion by maintaining their importance in the dramatic repertory, all the way from Harlem to Uzbekistan, and to provide the roles that leading actors compete in when they seek to demonstrate their talents. Ever since David Garrick staged his Stratford Jubilee of 1769, Shakespeare's native town has been a shrine for literary pilgrims; more recently its festival has come to set a standard for Shakespearean productions; and now the cult has spread to transatlantic Stratfords in Ontario and Connecticut, not to mention regular performance at innumerable theatres elsewhere. If all this seems to smack too uncritically of ritual observance and traditional piety, we should be reminded that Shakespearean drama has continually renewed itself through adaptation to changing times. It has adapted not only to contemporary dress but to current issues; thus the conflicts of the Roman plays have been sharpened by the political pressures of the twentieth century.

Shakespeare showed prophetic insight into his own future when, looking back to Rome in *Julius Caesar*, he allowed his Cassius to look ahead down the centuries to come:

> How many ages hence
> Shall this our lofty scene be acted over
> In states unborn and accents yet unknown!
> (III.i.113–15)

The leading spirit among his fellow dramatists, Ben Jonson, also foresaw that triumphant survival when he prefaced Shakespeare's First Folio with the poetic tribute: "He was not of an age, but for all time!" But Jonson, who was well aware that such universality must have its basis in a firm grasp of immediacy, had begun his poem by hailing Shakespeare as the major voice of his time: "Soul of the Age!" Few of his contemporaries had been quite so magnanimous or far-seeing. The earliest critical recognition of his career had been a truculent outburst from Robert Greene, hack-writing upon his very deathbed in 1592, and denouncing Shakespeare as a young upstart for his presumption in vying with those already established playwrights whom we call the University Wits. That outburst was countered soon enough by a handsome retraction from Greene's editor, Henry Chettle, and the subsequent testimonials from Shakespeare's colleagues suggest their personal affection and professional esteem.[1] In those days, however, merely to be recognized as a playwright was to be rather an artisan than an artist; it did not carry with it any particular standing as a man of letters. His more serious literary pretensions were declared when he brought out his two narrative poems in the classical erotic vein, and when he privately circulated his sonnets, which would be published belatedly under other auspices.

As for the plays, they were the property of the producing company, which had commissioned and bought them outright at ten pounds or so apiece. So long as they were popular on the stage, it would not have been in the company's interest for them to be printed. Sooner or later slightly more than half of them found their way into print, many of these pirated and garbled, through the separate editions known as quartos. Subject to such hazards of publication and to the rigors of censorship, Shakespeare's hand was obscured by anonymity while he was young and unknown, and credited apocryphally with plays by other hands when he was older and famous. On the whole, it is surprising and fortunate that the corpus of his writing has mainly come down to us through so authoritative an edition as the First Folio. Seven years before that landmark appeared, Jonson had braved the scorn of critics for gathering up the plays he had written to date and bringing them out in folio as *Works*—a format and a title which then seemed much too pretentious for mere stage-pieces. Shakespeare's collected volume, edited by two of his fellow actors and theatrical partners, John Heminge and Henry Condell, bore a title simply indicating the disposition of its contents: *Comedies, Histories, and Tragedies*. From its appearance in 1623, seven years after his death, Shakespeare stood among England's principal authors; but through the seventeenth century he shared equal applause with the scholarly Jonson and the courtly John Fletcher; he did not emerge into the light of preeminence until Dryden signalized him as that writer who possessed "the most comprehensive soul."

The neo-classicists of the eighteenth century, emphasizing that opposition between nature and art which Shakespeare had done so much to reconcile, thought of him as a wholly natural genius who was consequently lacking in conscious artistry. The turning point in the history of his reputation came with the preface to Samuel Johnson's edition of 1765. It was Dr. Johnson who, rescuing Shakespeare from the indignity of being harshly judged by neo-classical rules, insisted on granting him the status of a classic. If his plays followed certain laws of their own, henceforth the path lay open to the discovery of those laws. But the Romantics were as eager to associate him with nature itself as their predecessors had been to distinguish his endeavors from their notions of art. Even Ben Jonson's eulogy had been, as he dryly put it, "on this side idolatry." During the later eighteenth and most of the nineteenth century, Shakespeare's interpreters practiced what Bernard Shaw liked to call "Bardolatry." They all but deified the Bard of Avon because he was the creator of so many characters who could be treated as if they were human beings—could be identified with, psychologized over, arraigned for moral judgment. Shakespeare's full-bodied realism, as opposed to the more formal characterization of continental drama, meanwhile triumphed over the barriers of verse translation. His name became a rallying cry in the campaigns for Romanticism, and his influence contributed to the self-realization of the various national literatures of Europe.

Our century, which has latterly celebrated the four-hundredth anniversary of his birth, has brought him the twelfth generation of his continuing audience. Yet, despite the ever-widening time-span, we may approach him somewhat more closely today than we could have done at intervals in the past. Historical knowledge of his period has helped to bridge the gap, while a comparative view of the drama is helping us to see his work in more extended and clarifying perspective. So much interpretation has surrounded it that we sometimes barely glimpse the forest because of the many screeds which the commentators, like his Orlando, have hung upon the trees. But commentary is useful in alerting us to assumptions or implications we might have missed, and editorial scholarship has learned to correct distortions by removing encrustations. It is the purpose of this introduction, and of the comments that herewith introduce and accompany Shakespeare's texts, to set them into their most meaningful contexts. Universal as his attraction has been, it is best understood through particulars. Though—to our advantage—his creations are relatively timeless, they would not mean so much to us if they had not been timely in their day. Nor would they have made their lasting impact, if their author had not been past master of his exacting and exciting medium, linguistic, poetic, dramatic. Since that mastery was the ripe attainment of an individual mind, we owe some attention to the man in his time before turning to the materials and techniques of his art.

[1] The passages from Greene and Chettle, together with various other biographical and critical documents referred to in this essay, are reprinted in Appendix C below.

II. THE BIOGRAPHICAL RECORD

Contrary to a fairly widespread impression, there is no special mystery about his life. Indeed it is unusually well documented, for a commoner's of his period. Unfortunately for our personal curiosity, most of this documentation takes the colorless form of entries in parish registers or municipal archives, legal instruments involving property, all too fragmentary theatrical records, and a few business letters to or about him. The biographical outline provided by more than a hundred such documents is filled in by well over fifty literary allusions to Shakespeare and his works in the published writings of contemporaries. But these details, even when they have been eked out by traditions and conjectures, scarcely combine to portray a vivid personality. Modern readers, accustomed by the Romantics to poets who lived their poems and dramatized their lives, have felt somewhat put off by the undramatic nature of the dramatist's private career. The figure of Shakespeare as a practical man of affairs, although well attested by the evidence, seemed rather too modest to occupy the lofty pedestal reared by the Bardolaters. Hence the strange proliferation of irresponsible theories proposing rival candidates for the authorship of Shakespeare's work, most of them titled and all of them colorful but none of them circumstanced to have done the job—as William Shakespeare indubitably was. His existence should not seem uneventful if we consider that its main events were the thirty-eight plays created, in rapid succession and brilliant diversity, within a span of less than twenty-five years.

The first recorded fact under the family name at Stratford-on-Avon is neither inspiring nor revealing: it is the imposition of a fine upon the poet's father for countenancing a dunghill too near the house and shop on Henley Street that would be pointed out as Shakespeare's birthplace. What would be truly significant was the son's lifelong connection with the prosperous and picturesque market town in the rich heart of rural England. He was a country boy, and he kept returning to the Warwickshire countryside, like the fabled giant who renewed his energies by touching his native soil. North of the winding Avon lay the Forest of Arden, which must have cast some shade on the woodland scenes of *As You Like It*, even though the play introduces tropical flora and fauna, and is linked by verbal associations with the Franco-Belgian Ardennes. The association that means most here, however, is the fact that Shakespeare's mother had been Mary Arden, and that her yeoman family was related to those Ardens who held large estates nearby. Her husband, John Shakespeare, son of a local tenant farmer, was by trade a glover or leatherworker. He became one of Stratford's leading citizens, was elected a burgess or member of the town council, acted as magistrate and in various civic capacities, and served a brief term as bailiff or mayor during William's infancy. Though John's fortunes declined before his death in 1601, about the time when *Hamlet* was being completed, he lived to be granted the arms and style of a gentleman, probably through the endeavors and the successes of his son.

Thus, like many good English families, the Shakespeares made the transition from the status of tradesman to that of esquire during the reign of Queen Elizabeth. The name of their eldest son William appears first on record under the date of his baptism, April 26, 1564, at the Church of the Holy Trinity, where he was to be buried just fifty-two years afterward. Since the day of his death in 1616 was (if the inscription on his monument in the church can be trusted) April 23, which is also the holiday of England's patron Saint George, it is coincidentally celebrated as Shakespeare's birthday. Because the sons of burgesses were specifically entitled to free tuition at the local grammar school, it seems most probable that he studied there, absorbing a curriculum strongly based on rhetoric, Christian ethics, and classical literature. He did not go on to attend a university; and, understandably, he would not be regarded as a man of learning by such consciously erudite humanists as Jonson and Milton. But our age is so much less devoted than theirs to the cultivation of the classics that what looked to Jonson like "small Latin and less Greek" might well strike us as a respectable grounding in the humanities. His plays show amply that he was conversant with Latin and French, plus a smattering of other foreign languages, history both ancient (notably Plutarch) and modern (the British chronicles), philosophic speculation (Montaigne), continental fiction such as Boccaccio's, earlier English poets like Chaucer and Gower—not to mention fellow Elizabethans, from the high-minded Sidney to the abusive Greene.

A writer's reading tends to reveal itself most directly through his earliest efforts, and Shakespeare's smell somewhat of the Greco-Roman lamp in their use of quotation and mythological ornament. The prototypes for academic drama, as Polonius would duly observe, were Seneca for tragedy and Plautus for comedy. It is no accident that the apprentice Shakespeare, while feeling his way toward popular dramatic forms of his own, was to experiment with the Senecan *Titus Andronicus* and the Plautine *Comedy of Errors*; and it is noteworthy that Francis Meres, when he attempted a survey of English writers in his *Palladis Tamia* of 1598, cited Shakespeare as the versatile counterpart of both Roman playwrights—also mentioning Ovid as his forerunner in the field of amorous poetry. One of the better-grounded Shakespearean rumors, coming down to us from an actor in his troupe, tells us that he taught Latin for a while as a country schoolmaster. But he has expressed his opinion of pedantry in Holofernes and *Love's Labor's Lost*. The book-learning that Shakespeare displays here and there is far less impressive, in the long run, than his fund of general information. His frame of reference is so far-ranging, and he is so concretely versed in the tricks of so many trades, that lawyers have written to prove he was trained in the law, sailors about his expert seamanship, naturalists upon his botanizing, and so on through the professions. If this be paradox, it is resolved by Fielding's remark that Shakespeare was "learned in human nature." So far as education has genuine meaning, he must be viewed as a genuinely educated man.

Some confusion seems to attend the facts regarding his marriage, but these are too meagre to encourage surmises. We know that a license was obtained on November 27, 1582, that the former Anne Hathaway was eight years his senior, and that their elder daughter Susanna was born six months later and christened on May 26, 1583. But, since the betrothal might have taken place at some previous point, we may allow the couple the benefit of ceremonies timed more casually in their day than in ours. Nor should we infer any reservations about his wife from the one bequest to her in his will: that "second-best bed" may have been hallowed by conjugal sentiments, and she was provided for otherwise through her dower rights. Given the circumstances of his calling, which inevitably centred on London and occasionally branched out into provincial tours, it could be said that he was at some pains to keep up his domestic ties with Stratford. Twin children, Hamnet and Judith, were born there in 1585; Hamnet, his only son, was to die eleven years later. Biography loses sight of Shakespeare during the interval between the birth of the twins and Greene's attack in 1592, but the latter makes it quite explicit that Shakespeare had meanwhile become a player and was already emerging as a playwright. Retrospectively it would seem clear that those crucial seven years had been fully occupied, not to say well spent, in preparing to meet the demands of the theatrical profession and to endow it with a steady sequence of its finest vehicles.

Though he is listed as having appeared in his own plays and Jonson's, we have no account of his acting. The two roles that tradition has assigned to him are secondary, though not uncongenial: the Ghost in *Hamlet* and the old servitor Adam in *As You Like It*. In any case, the fundamental certainty about Shakespeare is that he was a man of the theatre to his fingertips. No titled amateur could have conceivably handled, with such practiced and inventive skill, all the available resources of his professional medium. His craftsmanship as a dramatist was solidly backed, like Molière's, by long experience as an actor-manager—by the manager's sense of the public, as well as the actor's talent for projecting himself into other selves. During the seasons of 1592–3 the plague was making its terrible visitations; and while the London theatres were closed, Shakespeare seems to have been composing his non-dramatic Ovidian poems, *Venus and Adonis* and *The Rape of Lucrece*. When the theatres reopened, he was one of the sharers or partners in a newly organized company under the sponsorship of the Lord Chamberlain, head of the royal household. This company was to dominate the Elizabethan and the Jacobean stage (in the later period under the sponsorship of King James himself), performing publicly at the famous Globe playhouse and for smaller audiences at the Blackfriars. Along with its best-known actors, Richard Burbage and William Kemp, he received payment for presenting two plays before the Queen at court during the Christmas festivities of 1594.

The Chamberlain's Men had not infrequent occasion to offer such command performances; and after 1603, when the troupe became His Majesty's Servants, its sharers were officially treated as members of the royal household. Shakespeare made other connections with courtly circles, principally through the patronage of the dashing young Earl of Southampton, to whom he had dedicated both of his printed poems. Southampton is one of those actual personages who have been identified with the noble youth addressed in Shakespeare's sonnets. On that theme there has been—in Falstaffian disproportion—an intolerable deal of conjecture to one halfpennyworth of fact. If the sonnets constitute the key with which Shakespeare "unlocked his heart," in Wordsworth's unguarded phrase, then they have opened no secret doors; if they had done so, as Browning retorted, "the less Shakespeare he." To reread them as if they were confessions is to beg a moot question, since there is just as little external support for attempts at other identifications: the Dark Lady, the rival poet. Doubtless Shakespeare could not have dealt so movingly with love and friendship and with literary and sexual rivalry if he had not experienced them in some intimate guise. But his sonnets would differ unbelievably from his plays, and would come suspiciously close to the effusions of more subjective writers, if he had not again been exercising his gift for dramatic projection. The sonneteer's involvement, within his formal genre, is that of the dramatist with his *dramatis personae*. After all, it is he himself who assumes the identities of his characters:

> my nature is subdu'd
> To what it works in, like the dyer's hand.
> (Sonnet 111.6–7)

The advance in Shakespeare's worldly fortunes is evident from a number of business transactions. In 1597 he acquired New Place, one of the most substantial residences in Stratford. Gradually he had given up acting for writing; and by his late forties, several years before his relatively early death, he was living in retirement there. His meticulous testament, which remembers his colleagues, seems designed to perpetuate his estate through his elder daughter's progeny. But his line did not survive his grandchildren; for his many living descendants we must look to the drama. His monument, the bust in the chancel of Holy Trinity Church, is thought to be a true—if stylized—portrait. The same benignant features greet the reader from the frontispiece to the Folio. The recurrent word in the testimonials of Shakespeare's friends and acquaintances is "gentle." It characterizes an engaging but self-effacing person who, while remaining impersonal, could penetrate the minds of multitudinous personalities. Coleridge described him as "myriad-minded." Keats suggested how those many aspects must have been integrated when he spoke of "Negative Capability," that quality of sympathetic imagination, that unexampled gift of insight which enabled Shakespeare to empathize with all sorts and conditions of men. It was Keats again who threw light on the symbolic relation between an artist's *modus vivendi* and his artistic achievement, when he succinctly noted: "Shakespeare lived a life of Allegory. His works are the comments on it."

All lives are more or less allegorical, insofar as they relive the cycle of Everyman. Shakespeare's uniqueness lies in his commentary, his memorable power of individualizing those common experiences. The course of his worldly career has sometimes been subdivided into four periods, which were neatly but problematically formulated by Edward Dowden. To label the first period "In the Workshop" and the second "In the World" is cogent enough, since it merely implies an objective development from apprenticeship to maturity through the mastery of a craft. But to call the third phase "Out of the Depths" and the fourth "On the Heights" is to misread the plays by presuming that Shakespeare intended them as successive chapters in a kind of spiritual autobiography. We are less well acquainted with what went into his work than with what came out of it. That there are emotions of despair in *Hamlet* and attitudes of serenity in *The Tempest* we cannot doubt; yet he could not simply have chosen to write tragedies while he was feeling depressed and comedies when a mellower mood came upon him; there were more determining factors, as we shall see. Clearly the man who wrote *Romeo and Juliet* knew what it felt like to be in love. It may be that the author of *King Lear* had known sufferings that brought him near to madness. But, by following that line of rationalization, we reduce it to the absurd presumption that the author of *Macbeth* had committed murder. Whereas the play is an imaginative exercise, a psychological discipline which we undergo with the playwright, who—by conveying what it might feel like to be a murderer—ends by enlarging our consciousness.

III. THE HISTORICAL BACKGROUND

We can follow the development of Shakespeare's work in greater clarity if we view it as a response to, and an expression of, the proud and eventful period in which he lived and for which he constructed the principal monument. To recollect that the year of his birth marked the deaths of both Michelangelo and Calvin is to set him at the zenith of the two great formative movements in the arts and religion that they personify, the Renaissance and the Reformation. The year of his own death also bore witness to Harvey's first lectures on physiology, heralding a momentous succession of new achievements for scientific method. Putting Shakespeare beside his immediate contemporaries, we may note that he was born in the same year as Galileo and died in the same year as Cervantes. Cervantes is said to have written an epitaph for the Middle Ages by demonstrating, through the very first of modern novels, that the invention of gunpowder had exploded the institution of chivalry. Yet Shakespeare seems to have anticipated that point in *1 Henry IV*, where the antagonistic conceptions of honor advanced by Hotspur and Falstaff run parallel to the ideological argument between Don Quixote and Sancho Panza. And Shakespeare seems to have anticipated Galileo's demonstration that the earth revolves around the sun, which supported the astronomical challenge to the anthropocentric conception of the universe, when Hamlet wrote in his little metaphysical poem addressed to Ophelia:

> Doubt thou the stars are fire,
> Doubt that the sun doth move. . . . (II.ii.116–17)

But heretical doubts were still counterweighed by an orthodox belief that the human race played the central role in a cosmic spectacle, whose interpretation might be sought in the antiquated pseudo-science of astrology, as Sonnet 15 affirms in a characteristically theatrical metaphor:

> That this huge stage presenteth nought but shows
> Whereon the stars in secret influence comment.

The drama is the most social of literary forms, since it stands in so direct a relationship to its audience. Hence it presupposes certain fostering conditions, and its golden ages have been sporadic in finding their conjunctions of time and place: ancient Athens, classical France, baroque Spain, Zen Buddhist Japan, and Shakespeare's lifetime in England. We like to look back on his age as "the spacious times of great Elizabeth." The nostalgic phrase of Queen Victoria's poet laureate, Tennyson, conjures up the national cult of the Virgin Queen, with its emanations of courtly compliment and magnificent pageantry. Elizabethan men of letters vied with courtiers in paying their elaborate respects to the royal coquette, most elaborately in Spenser's *Faerie Queene*. Shakespeare was not remiss in declaring his homage, gallantly alluding to "a fair vestal throned by the west" in *A Midsummer Night's Dream* (II.i.158) and retroactively prophesying blessings for the reign of the newly christened Princess Elizabeth in *Henry VIII* (V.v). But the spaciousness of the times found surer justification in its discoveries, conquests, and hitherto unparalleled geographical expansion. "This England," of which the Bastard Faulconbridge boasts in *King John* (V.vii.112–18) and for which John of Gaunt voices his fears in *Richard II* (II.i.40 ff.), was breathlessly transforming itself from an island off the coast of Europe into a dominant sea power and an emergent colonial empire. Shakespeare was well abreast what was happening; *The Tempest* reenacts a shipwreck encountered by the Virginia Company's fleet; conversely, *Hamlet* and *Richard II* were performed on the East India Company's flagship off the coast of Sierra Leone in 1607.

The imperial trend, which had its prose epic in the voyages chronicled by Hakluyt and Purchas, brought commercial affluence in its wake. But rapidly accumulating wealth, inequitably distributed at best, was by no means a guarantee of widespread economic security; the discontented populace of Shakespeare's Roman plays and the hungry followers of Jack Cade in *2 Henry VI* lend a prefiguring voice to protests against the enclosure of common lands and other social grievances of the sixteenth century. England's main international effort, during the late Middle Ages and the early Renaissance, had been to disentangle the ties that had bound her to France since the Norman Conquest. The rhythm of Shakespeare's history plays, which is agitated by the battles of the Hundred Years' War, accelerates to its patriotic climax with the triumph of Henry V at Agincourt. The long-drawn-out civil conflict, the struggle among the barons over the kingship, had led on through the Wars of the Roses to the attrition of feudal power and the establishment of a more centralized monarchy under the house of Tudor—a consummation which Shakespeare hails at the end of *Richard III*. For him—as for the chroniclers he rather freely followed, the compendious Holinshed and especially the apologist Edward Hall—the Tudors had conjointly inherited the strongest claims of their warring predecessors, the houses of York and Lancaster. Their enthronement seemed to have been providentially ordained to foster the restoration of peace, with the attendant cultural benefits that distinguish a glorious epoch.

Loyal subjects were bound to see the whole historical sequence as the consummation of a legendary design. Shakespeare even envisages a laying-on-of-hands between the last of the Lancastrian kings, the ill-fated Henry VI, and the founder of the Tudor line, the young Earl of Richmond, later to be crowned as Henry VII. Yet the claim of the Lancasters was itself open to question, since their crown had been wrenched away from Richard II by Henry IV, practicing an admixture of force and "policy" (a word which always connotes the intrigues of Machiavellian statecraft). The situation, as Shakespeare has treated it, illustrates the division of loyalties that intensified the complications of king-making and -unmaking. Ideally, God's ruler can do no wrong; he rules by divine right, as the legitimate Richard ineffectually reminds his refractory peers. The blame for his mistakes is largely placed upon his parasitical favorites, those "caterpillars of the commonwealth" (II.iii.166). At all events, there is nothing that could morally justify his dethronement; and the scene of Richard's deposition was considered such political tinder that it was omitted from the earlier quartos of the play. Consequently Henry's rule is regarded by his enemies as a usurpation, though he is much abler than his deposed cousin, and the curse of the Plantagenets hangs heavy over the destinies of the Lancastrians. In their turn the latter yield to the brief and violent Yorkist dynasty, culminating in the nightmarish regime of the arch-usurper Richard III, from which the Tudors bring about England's happy deliverance.

Their strategy was that of the popular monarch, firmly controlling baronial factions, while commanding enthusiastic loyalty from the common people. Shakespeare's commoners are as likely to be misled by demagogues as his kings are by self-serving councillors; but when king and people strive together in mutual confidence, then they fulfill the basic Tudor principle of "commonweal." Unhappily, the ensuing era of stability and prosperity was menaced and riven by religious dissension. The English Reformation, made official at the personal behest of the sovereign, Henry VIII, broke politically with the Roman Catholic Church but did not embrace the theological doctrines of the extreme Puritans. During the short reigns of Henry's son and elder daughter, Edward VI and "Bloody Mary," Catholics and Protestants were successively persecuted, the Queen having married the King of Spain and attempted to revive Catholicism in England. The accession of Henry's younger daughter Elizabeth in 1558 reaffirmed and established the Anglican compromise, while the Tudor dynasty was guided to its culmination through her fortunate gifts, which included longevity. Thus the intellectual climate surrounding Shakespeare was one in which inherited dogmas had been forcibly questioned and strategically modified. Like all Elizabethans, he was—at least nominally—an Anglican whose forebears had been brought up in the Catholic confession. Unlike the majority of contemporary believers, he was tolerant enough to enter into the spirit of both faiths with that "wonderful philosophic impartiality" which Coleridge has discerned in his politics.

The tone of his comedies is sometimes affected by the bustle of current mercantile enterprise; even their foreign settings seem to reflect an increasingly cosmopolitan outlook. Through the resounding series of explorations, exploitations, and naval campaigns against Spain, with the western hemisphere as the grand prize, England was achieving its leadership among nations. The climactic decade of Elizabeth's reign occurred between the defeat of the Spanish Armada in 1588 (*Love's Labor's Lost* jibes at its fallen vainglory in the mock-heroic person of Don Armado) and the return of the Essex expedition from Ireland in 1599 (welcomed in triumphal expectation by the Chorus in the fifth act of *Henry V*). Shakespeare, who was even then moving through the dramatic workshop into a wider world, expressed the upsurging nationalism of those fervent years through his cycle of history plays; all but the belated *Henry VIII* were produced during that decade. But the Irish expedition proved a failure; the brilliant Earl of Essex, long the Queen's favorite, was precipitated from her favor; and, after an abortive conspiracy against her, he was beheaded in 1601. Confronted with an aging Queen, the unsettled problem of her succession, and the mounting unrest at the turn of the century, many anxious and thoughtful Englishmen had pinned their hopes upon him. Possibly Shakespeare had done so; we know that his company's revival of *Richard II*, as a possible incitement to treason, topically figured in Essex's trial. His downfall heralded the approaching transition, as did the concurrent appearance of *Hamlet*.

A modulation, deeper perhaps and sadder and wiser

than the conventionally mellow Elizabethan note, could be heard in the literature of the later fifteen-nineties, as writers turned away from sonnets to satires, cultivated their melancholia, and began to sound the depths of tragedy. It may be symptomatic, if not prophetic, that the typical protagonist of Jacobean drama is rather a disinherited prince than a self-crowned king. James I, who finally succeeded Elizabeth upon her demise in 1603, never approached her in popularity; yet, since he was already King James VI of Scotland, his accession united the crowns of both kingdoms; and, being a conscientious patron of letters, he accorded royal sponsorship to the Shakespearean troupe, as well as to the standard English Bible that perpetuates his name. Shakespeare, for his part, paid homage to the new king with *Macbeth*, not only by choosing a Scottish theme, but more specifically by recalling the legend that traced the Stuart line back to Banquo. Shakespeare's Witches predict a brighter future for the Stuarts than they were to have, and James himself stored up trouble for his successors by promoting a courtly aristocracy and alienating a more and more Puritanical middle class. But the most salient characteristic of Jacobean culture was its devotion to the pursuit of knowledge, which involved the most searching introspection and the most fanciful speculation, along with the ambitious program for science that Bacon outlined in his *Advancement of Learning*. "And New Philosophy," as Donne lamented, "calls all in doubt."

Shakespeare, of course, was a playwright and not a philosopher. Yet drama is dialectic in concrete form; the attitudes and actions of its characters would have little value or meaning if they were not based on certain philosophical premises. Shakespeare's plays are very richly charged with implicit ideas, some of which are made memorably explicit by sententious remarks or purple passages, whose purpose is to keep us well aware of the larger issues and moral implications. One of his fullest statements in this vein, the monologue of Ulysses on "degree" in *Troilus and Cressida* (I.iii.85 ff.), frames his weary Greek heroes against a backdrop as wide as the universe. But this particular universe is the traditional cosmos of Ptolemaic astronomy, where the planets revolve around the earth in concentric orbits, influencing human destiny in ways that the astrologers claimed to interpret. This macrocosm centres upon that microcosm which is man, in whose person the elements are mixed, the humors disposed, and the faculties governed to accord with a similar pattern. Hence King Lear, within his "little world of man" (III.i.10), reproduces the storm that rages upon the heath. His psychological breakdown has its external counterpart in the disintegration of his kingdom. The body politic resembles the human body; the order of physical nature is a visible mirror of the divine order. The age-old conception of a "great chain of being," extending from God through the angels toward mankind and downward to beasts, plants, and inanimate matter, links together all created things. Prospero, through his natural magic, is served by the ethereal Ariel from on high and by the bestial Caliban at the subhuman level.

Given this all-embracing continuity, every creature must adhere to its hierarchic position in order to discharge its preordained function—must, in Ulysses' words, "observe degree, priority, and place." The stars set the universal example, and it is their harmonious functioning that generates the music of the spheres. All is well with societies, families, and individuals when they do their duties and know their places. But when they stray out of orbit, Ulysses warns of disastrous consequences, shifting his comparison from the planetary to the musical plane:

> Take but degree away, untune that string,
> And hark what discord follows. Each thing meets
> In mere oppugnancy: the bounded waters
> Should lift their bosoms higher than the shores,
> And make a sop of all this solid globe. . . .

It seems unlikely that so word-conscious a writer could have penned that last line without a side-glance at the theatre where his plays were being performed; for the Globe was truly a microcosm or little world of man, an artistic replica of the whole human condition. As for its solidity, we are told in *The Tempest* (IV.i.148–58) that Prospero's pageant and "the great globe itself" have been compounded of the same insubstantial fabric, the stuff of dreams. Ulysses, having sketched his ideal world-order, visualizes its impending dissolution, and opens up a harrowing prospect of chaos and anarchy. Similarly, a number of Shakespeare's histories and his tragedies take place in a "time misord'red" (*2 Henry IV*, IV.ii.33) which the hero is called upon to set right, while his comedies revel in timeless disorder until the norms of society are restored by the happy ending. Now, as between a set of professed ideals and the observed realities of experience, there is usually some sort of gap or lag, which tends to widen during critical periods such as the Renaissance, thereby amplifying the dimensions of the tragic or the comic point of view. And if the accepted world view was founded upon an obsolete cosmology, as the scientists were impressively showing, then scholastic traditions could be undermined by experimental approaches and monarchic authority itself would soon be challenged by more democratic ideologies.

The humanism of the Renaissance, with its consciousness of historic renewal, its revivals of the classics and the fine arts, its confidence in the mind, and its embellishment of its material surroundings, was a flowering of plenitude, to be sure; but it was likewise a crisis of uncertainty. It balanced the immediacies of this world against otherworldly values; its enjoyment of the senses quickened the lively spirits of comedy; but its fullness of life was deeply grounded in the inevitability of death, which is the precondition of tragedy. The medieval vision, with its tangible hopes for an afterlife in the next world, found its fulfillment in a *Divine Comedy*. In the Middle Ages tragedies were falls of princes, like Richard II's "sad stories of the death of kings" (III.ii.156). Men's decline from prosperity to adversity taught a moral lesson by manifesting the power of providence and the transience of mere earthly glory. The fickle bitch-goddess Fortune determined the fates of captains and kings, alike with beggars and clowns, through the revolutions of her allegorical wheel. To suffer her slings and arrows had been the sanctioned course; to take arms against them was a novel and tempting alternative. To become the captain of one's fate, to make one's own fortune, to rise in the world by exerting one's will—it is through this dynamic choice that the self-reliant protagonists of Marlowe's plays attain their heroic stature. The individualism of Dr. Faustus, exploring all the available possibilities, recognizes no limits. Shakespeare reveals a more comprehensive awareness of the opposing forces that take the measure of the individual, and of the resulting interplay between character and destiny.

The exclamation of Hamlet, "What a piece of work is a man!" (II.ii.303), carries an ironic reverberation. His melancholy gaze looks up and down: skyward toward "this brave o'erhanging firmament" and earthward toward the grave. Those two portraits which he shows to the Queen illustrate man's potentialities for good and for evil. The scale ascends or descends with the spiritual and carnal aspects of his dual nature; he can aspire to be a godlike Hyperion or else can grovel like a brutal satyr. Hamlet's existential dilemma echoes the self-interrogations of Montaigne, not merely through the language of John Florio's translation but in its ambiguous balance between scepticism and faith. Though the supernatural is invoked and evoked throughout Shakespeare's work, it remains—as it doubtless should—an ultimate mystery. We are mystified with Hamlet over questions which were highly problematic in Shakespeare's day; we share the suspense over whether the Ghost is real or false, and whether it has been sent from heaven, purgatory, or hell. With Lady Macbeth we suspect that the apparition of Banquo may be a subjective phenomenon, while the "dagger of the mind" (II.i.38) might conceivably be the playwright's expressionistic device for conveying Macbeth's remorse of conscience. As for the Witches, though they foretell the outcome, they do not control it, since their prophecies are equivocations and Macbeth is free to choose at every stage. Omens and dreams portending catastrophes, though they are often greeted with disbelief, charge the air with fatality when they come true.

Most of the plays, unfolding within a Biblical frame of reference, broadly conform to the tenets of Christianity: witness the enforced conversion of Shylock the Jew. Yet *King Lear* deliberately reverts to a pre-Christian Britain, where the gods are pluralized and supplicated by pagan names, and where the enigma of their relation to men is argued back and forth: is it supernal grace or naturalistic indifference, poetic justice or cosmic irony? Moreover, the characters in the Roman plays are measured by the ethics of Stoicism. Suicide is denounced in the tragedies subject to Christian doctrine; Hamlet resists it because God's ethical canon is set against self-slaughter; and Ophelia's funeral rites are abridged because "her death was doubtful" (V.i.227). Whereas, in the environment of Rome and under the danger of humiliation, self-inflicted death can be an act of greatness, ennobling the final moments of both Cleopatra and Brutus. An anachronistic clock is mentioned in *Julius Caesar* (II.i.192), and it has been charged that Shakespeare's Romans are Elizabethans thinly disguised. Yet, in our single drawing of a contemporaneous Shakespearean production, the cast of *Titus Andronicus* is depicted in something like Roman dress. What is more important, Shakespeare has used his imagination to catch the moral atmosphere breathed by his ancient heroes. His recreation of a vital past is animated by the sense of living in a time of greatness, which is so energetically affirmed by King Henry V in his speech on Saint Crispin's Day. As the Earl of Warwick tells Henry IV, "There is a history in all men's lives" (*2 Henry IV*, III.i.80).

IV. THE LINGUISTIC MEDIUM

Among the various circumstances that made his moment so opportune for Shakespeare, the fundamental one was the state of the language, which was just ripe for his formative use of it. Language, as a means of communication, is always the key to other human relationships; as a mode of expression, it has been more incisive and effective at certain times than at others. "Words, words, words," as Hamlet wearily intimates to Polonius (II.ii.192), lose their significance when they are divorced from actuality. The increased diffusion of the printed word, during the centuries since Shakespeare wrote, has led toward inflation and devaluation. More recently, the audio-visual revolution of our time seems to be restoring the impact of the spoken word. But, though it is our great good fortune to have inherited the tongue of Shakespeare, we cannot claim that this is the dialect we speak and hear. If we are Americans, approaching him from some remove in culture as well as history, we must traverse a longer distance; yet American speech has occasionally preserved spellings, pronunciations, or turns of phrase which have not survived in British English. In any case, the primary source of confusion for the modern reader is not the rare or archaic term, which can be looked up as readily as the learned allusion, but terms which look familiar and sound strange because their meanings have shifted. Thus, when Shakespeare speaks of "conceit," he does not mean vanity, as we might; adhering to etymology more closely than we do, he means a conception or notion, or possibly the imagination itself.

To understand the difference between Shakespeare's English and ours, we must allow for the process of semantic change, which has been continually eroding or encrusting his original meaning. For example, he uses the old word *anon* for "right away," whereas in our minds it has slowed down to mean "by and by."

We miss the joke played by the Prince on Francis, in the first tavern scene of *1 Henry IV*, unless we catch the full force of that locution. The passage of time, which has weakened some expressions, has had a strengthening influence upon others. The epithet *villain*, which originally signified a member of a lower class, has acquired an undertone of hostility and immorality. On the other hand, *fellow*, which has friendly overtones for us, was insulting in Shakespeare's day. Phrases that were metaphors to him have often lost their coloring with us: since we seldom play the game of bowls, we overlook the concrete implications of "There's the rub" (an impediment on the green) or "assays of bias" (a weight on the ball). When the Germans possessively refer to *unser* (our) Shakespeare, they have at least one point in favor of their claim. The text through which they usually approach him was translated, largely by A. W. Schlegel, into the standard literary German of not much more than 150 years ago. The text of Shakespeare, as we come to know him, is separated from us by an interval of some 350 years. Linguistically, their Shakespeare is as accessible to them as, let us say, the poems of Wordsworth are to us.

To commune directly with our Shakespeare is a more demanding and more rewarding task of elucidation. His language is neither Old nor Middle English; yet it obviously differs from the current vernacular; it is what the linguists describe as Early New English. Its heyday coincided with many other creative activities of the Renaissance. The Elizabethans shared the grandiose humanistic confidence in the power of the word as an instrument of the reason. Logic and grammar stood squarely behind rhetoric, and rhetoric was the art of persuasion by words. Witness the reactions of the crowd in *Julius Caesar* to the respective speeches of Brutus and Antony: Brutus persuades them at first, but in the long run Antony proves the more persuasive. Since the stage is an unavoidably limited arena for the display of heroic action, words must be accepted as deeds, and heroes confound one another by declamation rather than by prowess. The warrior must "play the orator." Hotspur disclaims eloquence and despises poetry; yet he outtalks nearly everyone else in the play, and turns out to be its most poetical character. Comparably another valiant soldier, Othello, deprecates himself as rude in speech. His address to the Senate in Act I is not only eloquent in itself, but evocative of the verbal magic by which he has won Desdemona. He rises to epic pitch again with his monologues in Acts III and V, when he is driven by jealousy to take leave of military glory, and when on the brink of suicide he recaptures a victory out of his past.

Even Shakespeare's fools are dialecticians, like Feste in *Twelfth Night*; while it is Costard, the clown of *Love's Labor's Lost*, who enunciates the longest word in the Shakespearean glossary: *honorificabilitudinitatibus* (V.i.41). *Love's Labor's Lost* may be viewed as a virtual war of words, a campaign by the women—who habitually stand closer to nature—against the bookishness of the men, who are finally (V.ii.402 ff.) compelled to give up their cult of preciosity,

> Taffata phrases, silken terms precise,
> Three-pil'd hyperboles, spruce affection,
> Figures pedantical,

and to express their courtship in plain-spoken homespun: "In russet yeas and honest kersey noes." Accordingly, their spokesman Berowne completes his renunciation of literary artifice by protesting:

> And to begin, wench, so God help me law!
> My love to thee is sound, sans crack or flaw.

But his Rosaline, still detecting a note of courtly affectation, manages to have the last word by mockingly asking him to dispense with the French preposition:

> Sans "sans," I pray you.

The tables are turned in *Henry V*, when an English king courts a French princess by teaching her to speak plainly. There too the humorous dialects of the three captains, the Welsh Fluellen, the Scottish Jamie, and the Irish McMorris, all of them fighting together under the crown of England, resound with a patriotic zeal which is linguistic as well as political. And when the Duke of Norfolk is condemned to lifelong banishment in *Richard II*, his lament at being cut off from his native English (I.iii.159–73) gives Shakespeare a chance to salute his cherished medium.

Many languages have their valid claims to poetic euphony. However, if the criterion be expressiveness, then English has two incomparable advantages, its rich vocabulary and its flexible syntax. These it owes to the intermingling of the cultures that contributed to it, Roman and Celtic, Anglo-Saxon and Norman French. The high proportion of loan-words and phrases has endowed it, to a unique degree, with what the rhetoricians called "copiousness": a multiplicity of words to choose from, a variety of ways for saying the same thing. But if you say the same thing another way, what you are actually saying is somewhat different; you are shading it differently, so that your capacity for precise and perceptive description has been increased. Working with about 2,000 words, Racine could employ the same word for different things, and so could Shakespeare on occasion. Berowne's single line,

> Light, seeking light, doth light of light beguile,
> (*Love's Labor's Lost*, I.i.77)

uses "light" in four significations: *intellect*, seeking *wisdom*, cheats *eyesight* out of *daylight*. The paraphrase should help to explain how, with *Love's Labor's Lost*, Shakespeare freed himself from his early virtuosity. Ultimately he drew upon well over 21,000 words, probably a wider range than any other writer, which opened up immense potentialities for obtaining the right nuance, the *mot juste* in any particular situation. Now you can get along on as few as 850 words in a synthetic language, notably Basic English, where the aim is straightforward denotation, flat statement. But poetry depends on connotation, shaded suggestion, and Shakespeare's verbal shadings reflect the subtlety and the penetration of his insights.

We could illustrate the kind of resources available for his diction by citing a common instance, the official adjective *royal* deriving historically from the French through the Normans. It has not one but two synonyms: the Latin *regal*, which now and then adds weight, and the Saxon *kingly*, most emphatic of the three, since it goes beyond the Romance and the Latinate versions to the underlying Germanic substructure. English poetry borrows its strength from the Saxon, and its color from the other sources. Hopkins and Milton represent those extremes among the poets; Shakespeare so combines the elements as to produce a dramatic conflict at the stylistic level. When Horatio is admonished by Hamlet,

> Absent thee from felicity a while,
> And in this harsh world draw thy breath in pain,
> (V.ii.347–48)

the Latinate abstraction for heaven remains mysterious, opaque, and far away, while the Germanic monosyllables of the next line emphasize the grim immediacy of the present world. They also tend to retard the speed of the verse, as Pope observed and exemplified: "And ten low words oft creep in one dull line." Whereas the effect of polysyllables, as Marlowe discovered with his mouth-filling proper names ("Usumcasane and Theridamas"), is to accelerate the rhythm. Hence, in the echoing heartcry of Macbeth, the pace adjusts itself to the mood:

> No; this my hand will rather
> The multitudinous seas incarnadine,
> Making the green one red. (II.ii.58–60)

The sentence begins in immediate circumstance, when Macbeth looks down at his bloody hand; then the guilty vision of the second line swells up hyperbolically like an advancing wave, which recedes as the third line tapers off.

If vocabulary can be endlessly elaborated, syntax has been relatively simplified. Since English is not a highly inflected language, it is easy to transpose parts of speech. When Prospero refers to "the dark backward and abysm of time" (*The Tempest*, I.ii.50), he makes a substantive out of the Anglo-Saxon adverb "backward," characteristically pairing it off in a doublet with the Greco-Roman "abysm" (or abyss). Inversions of word-order, adapting to the metrical framework, occur so freely that they end by increasing the complexity and formality of the sentence-structure. Elisions like *'tis* and contractions like *o'er* may strike us as rather stilted today, and ethical datives (Hotspur's "See how this river comes *me* çranking in" [*I Henry IV*, III.i.97]) as positively Chaucerian, but they still had a colloquial ring for Shakespeare's contemporaries. The intimate singular form of the personal pronoun (*thou* and *thee*) had not yet given way to the indiscriminate plural *you*. The present tense of the verb could still command the suffixes *-est* and *-eth* in prose, though in verse these were tending to drop out. The King James Bible, which has subsequently done so much to stabilize and standardize English usage, did not appear until late in Shakespeare's career. During his lifetime there were no English grammars to lay down rules or dictionaries to restrict word-formation. This was an immeasurable boon for writers, though it has augmented the problems of their editors, particularly in the field of orthography. Shakespeare was free to experiment with the language, stimulated by its intermixture of archaisms and neologisms, at the point when it had reached its maximum of structural plasticity.

His idiom is differentiated from ours, not only by grammar and semantics, but by phonetic changes. What is known as the Great Vowel Shift, intervening a century before, had given rise to some of the existing disparities between English and continental pronunciation. The capital letter *I* had come to stand for the same typical diphthong as the interjection *ay*. The dropping of the final *-e*, which went out in the wake of Middle English, was more than the loss of an extra syllable; it left behind it a terminal stress which confirmed the iambic tendencies of English versification and brought about a shortage of unaccented feminine endings. The preterite and participial ending *-ed* is sounded at times and slurred at others by Shakespeare, according to the beat of his blank verse, as in this clause of Romeo's:

> Which the | dark night | hath so | discov | ered.

Nouns that terminate in *-tion* are normally prolonged by two syllables, as in this line from *A Midsummer Night's Dream*:

> Such tricks | hath strong | imag | ina | tion.

But certain words that have two syllables for us, notably *heaven* and *spirit*, are generally monosyllabic with Shakespeare. Others that are monosyllabic for us, conversely, may be disyllabic for him: *fire*, *hour*. Word-accent, which was not so rigidly fixed in his day, may vary with the verse-accent; simply reading the verse aloud should teach one how to pronounce *perséver* or *revénue*. Some of the rhymes may point back to the older pronunciations. If *join* accords with *line* or *sea* with *way*, then it is not difficult to imagine a contemporaneous performance of Shakespeare sounding as though it were acted in the brogue at the Abbey Theatre. In general, the vowels seem to have been purer, the gutturals firmer than in later practice.

In reading and studying Shakespeare, at best we merely approximate the actual conditions of his art. All too frequently we forget that it was designed to be projected vocally and taken in by ear, or else we find that our auditory responses are insufficiently trained or experienced. Here we find ourselves facing a matter of taste upon which criticism has been most severe, Shakespeare's puns. "A quibble," in the dictum of Dr. Johnson, "was to him the fatal Cleopatra for which he lost the world and was content to lose it." We can scarcely believe that, just because Shakespeare was fond of wordplay, he could ever have played for such high stakes. Here it seems to be Johnson who has staked too much in order to make a sweeping epigram. When Prince Hal is challenging Falstaff's tall tale, he insists: "Come, your reason, Jack, your reason." And Falstaff evades the Prince by standing upon his mock-dignity: "If reasons were as plentiful as blackberries, I would give no man a reason upon compulsion, I" (*1 Henry IV*, II.iv.205 ff.). The Elizabethan pronunciation of *reason* as *raisin* improves the joke; but it does not, in our reaction, make it funny. A pun consists, by Addison's definition, of two words that agree in sound while differing in sense. Consequently, for serious-minded men, it is a distraction. Yet Falstaff is the incarnation of frivolous-minded man, and poets put the sound before the sense whenever they search for a rhyme. For the Elizabethans, wit was a precondition of poetry, not less so when the two were brought together on a verbal plane. In the playhouse especially, the poet's aptness must have called forth a matching alertness on the part of the spectators.

Punning was not invariably comic, in the facetious sense; it could even have a tragic reverberation, as when John of Gaunt plays with his name on his deathbed. The dirge in *Cymbeline* becomes a dance of death, levelling young lovers with kings and beggars, when the refrain of the first stanza closes with a domestic pun:

> Golden lads and girls all must,
> As chimney-sweepers, come to dust.
> (IV.ii.262–63)

An audience which could feel and absorb that shock must have had both sharp hearing and mental agility. It must have been keenly aware of the uses of words in order to gain enjoyment from their calculated abuses. Shakespeare was more than a master at putting the proper word in the proper place; he could inspire some of his slower-witted characters with a gift for putting the improper word in the proper place. This device for promulgating the *mal à propos* has been named the malapropism, after the garrulous dowager in Sheridan's *Rivals*, Mrs. Malaprop. But Shakespeare seems to have inspired her too; for, as a past mistress at "abusing God's patience and the Queen's English," she was long preceded by Mistress Quickly. In such nonsense, as in Shakespeare's puns, there is unexpected pith. Dogberry, the constable of *Much Ado about Nothing*, personifies the self-importance of the petty official. When insulted, he rises to the heights of bumbling indignation: "Dost thou not suspect my place? Dost thou not suspect my years?" (IV.ii.74–75). Striving to command respect, he unwittingly reverses himself and concurs with his detractors. It is an application of the same principle when Mistress Quickly, seeking to attest her own respectability, casts suspicion on herself with an unconscious double-entendre: "Thou or any man knows where to have me, thou knave, thou!" (*1 Henry IV*, III.iii.129–30).

A Shakespearean phrase, like a musical theme, is subject to orchestration. Developed through a sequence of repetitions and variations, modulated into changing harmonies, and counterpointed with other themes, it can set forth a distinguishing pattern of thought. Sometimes a key-word, which invites careful scrutiny, illuminates the basic idea of a play: consider the preoccupation with "grief" in *Richard II*, the emphasis on "blood" in *Macbeth*, the scrutiny of "nature" in *King Lear*, the irony of "honest" in *Othello*, the amplification of "space" in *Antony and Cleopatra*, or the ambiguities of "art" in *The Tempest*. Concordances may prove useful, not merely for locating passages, but for bringing out thematic significances. In browsing through the *Oxford English Dictionary*, one is struck by the number of quotations indicating Shakespeare as the first user of a given word. It was he who introduced such ordinary words as *lonely* and *laughable*, invented such onomatopoetic vocables as *bump*, borrowed from their classical cognates *monumental* and *aerial*—not to mention *critic* and *pedant*, without which his students would be at a loss. Some of our idioms started out as his coinages: to fall to blows, to breathe one's last, to drink someone's health, to see something in the mind's eye. Unconsciously we quote *2 Henry IV* (IV.v.92) when we affirm that a wish is father to a thought. Shakespearean aphorisms have turned into proverbs: "The devil can quote scripture" and "Misery makes strange bedfellows" come, with slight modification, from *The Merchant of Venice* (I.iii.98) and *The Tempest* (II.ii.40) respectively. When we state that a boy is poor but honest or a girl fancy-free, we never give the author due credit for coining those epithets; and if we swear a mild oath by the dickens, we are likely to think of another writer than Shakespeare.

V. THE STYLISTIC TECHNIQUE

Style could be envisaged as the difference between the linguistic materials available to a writer and the individual use to which he puts them, but the line would not be easy to draw in the case of Shakespeare because he did so much to shape and extend them. We seldom refer to a Shakespearean style because, whenever the protean dramatist speaks, it is through the distinctive voices of more than a thousand characters. Every voice is so individualized—according to Pope—that, even if the speech-prefixes were removed, we should have little difficulty in identifying the speaker. Shakespeare characterizes his *dramatis personae* fully as much by their words as by their actions, yet many of their finest lines bear a family resemblance which distinguishes them further as the utterance of our greatest poet. Poetry, of course, is not necessarily delimited by metre. Shakespeare often turns to prose, with brilliant effectiveness and always for a definite reason—if only to fulfill the pedestrian function of reading a letter or interposing some document. Though there is no invariable rule, the comic scenes are frequently in prose, whereas the tragic scenes are usually in verse. Yet some of the most tragic, notably

Ophelia's mad scenes and the sleep-walking scene of Lady Macbeth, are in that special kind of distracted prose which Shakespeare reserved for moments of mental distraction, when the fragments of suppressed emotion well up from the unconscious. The Falstaffian comedy of *The Merry Wives of Windsor* is mostly prose; such histories as *King John* and *Richard II* are wholly verse.

Moreover, Shakespeare utilizes a good deal of rhyme, particularly in his earlier works; nearly half of *Love's Labor's Lost* is rhymed, in accordance with its interplay of stylistic awareness. The habit of rhyming is sloughed off more and more by the later plays: if we exclude the incidental songs and the interpolated masque, there is scarcely more than a single couplet to interrupt the blank verse of *The Tempest*. Shakespeare's lyrics, many of them set to music by such gifted Elizabethan composers as Thomas Morley, are among the most melodious outpourings of a golden age of song. They are also designed to fit succinctly into their dramatic contexts. For the most part, they add to the entertainment of the comedies; but on occasion, as with Ophelia or the Fool in *King Lear*, the pathos of the tragedies is enhanced by snatches from ballads or popular airs. The plays written in the mid-fifteen-nineties belong to what is termed Shakespeare's lyrical period. Stylistically, they employ the mellifluous rhythms, the witty conceits, and the courtly conventions that—through his two epyllia (*Venus and Adonis* and *Lucrece*) and his 154 sonnets—gained him his repute as the singer of love. Typical of their *cantabile* manner, as W. H. Auden would describe it with an apt musical term, is the set-piece of Oberon in *A Midsummer Night's Dream*: "I know a bank where the wild thyme blows . . ." (II.i.249 ff.). The dialogue that introduces Romeo to Juliet forms a sonnet and coincides with the movement of a dance. The farewell of Richard II to his queen, like the introduction of Berowne to Rosaline, is presented in stichomythy, repartee which alternates lines between two speakers:

> *Queen.* And must we be divided? must we part?
> *Richard.* Ay, hand from hand, my love, and heart from heart. (V.i.81–82)

How consciously Shakespeare handled his verbal vehicles may be inferred from a brief interchange in *As You Like It*. Rosalind and Jaques are talking, in the elegant prose that composes so much of the comedy, when Orlando enters and salutes her:

> Good day and happiness, dear Rosalind!

Whereupon Jaques makes his exit brusquely and prosaically:

> Nay then God buy you, and [i.e. if] you talk in blank verse. (IV.i.30–32)

Iambic pentameter, the Shakespearean measure, is a compromise between the strict formality of verse and the apparent formlessness of prose. It came into existence as a rough vernacular equivalent for the classical hexameter. Though it retained the traditional English stress, it abandoned rhyme; it organized and regulated the flow of natural speech within the rhythmic structure of poetry; its metrical recurrences allowed for unlimited variety in the phrasing. Shakespeare's meteoric contemporary Marlowe first established control over his medium, after a generation of awkward experiments. He developed the verse-paragraph, which was actually a periodic sentence wherein each clause corresponded with a line, building up to a rhetorical climax. "Marlowe's mighty line," as Ben Jonson labelled it, owed its sweep and resonance to its strategic deployment of polysyllables, with colorful and euphonious names to round out a terminal flourish: "And ride in triumph through Persepolis!" The declamatory rhetoric of the stentorian *Tamburlaine* is imitated in Shakespeare's histories and parodied, through Ancient Pistol, in *2 Henry IV*. Once the five-foot cadence became the regular pattern, in a succession of steady beats following unstressed syllables, it could be varied and modified. When the underlying beat was fixed in the mind, extra syllables could be accommodated or shorts and longs shifted, substituting trochees or spondees for iambs. An ever-changing syncopation could be set up between the speech rhythm and the prosodic scheme.

Shakespeare's developing mastery of his technique is graphically revealed in his treatment of the blank-verse line. The apprentice plays depend on set speeches, beginning and ending squarely with the beginning and ending of a line; subsequently these are broken up, so that speeches may end and begin again in the middle of a line. Only one percent of the lines in *The Comedy of Errors* are divided in this way; in *The Tempest* the proportion is eighty-five percent. The caesura, that traditional breathing-space within the line, falls regularly in the third foot with the early Shakespeare, but later tends to fall back farther or else to move about. Most of the early lines are end-stopped, with a pause which is generally marked by the punctuation; but the later ones tend increasingly to run over; and these enjambments range from an earlier twelve percent to a late forty-one percent. The resulting effect of limpidity, in Shakespeare's final phase, is reinforced by a tendency to use feminine endings, thereby converting the pentameter into an eleven-syllable line which terminates on the off-beat. (Wolsey's "Farewell, a long farewell to all my greatness" is not less typical for having been frequently attributed to the collaboration of Fletcher.) Here the figures are five percent at the earliest and thirty-five percent at the latest. English heroic verse was thus carried along, through the course of Shakespeare's twenty-five-year development, from its first Marlovian fluency toward its culminating Miltonic elaboration. Illustrations, however, are more convincing than either generalizations or statistics.

We can follow that evolution more clearly by contrasting a pair of passages from his earliest and his latest writing. This is Joan La Pucelle, Shakespeare's disparaging characterization of Joan of Arc, introducing herself to Charles the Dauphin in *1 Henry VI*:

Lo, whilest I waited on my tender lambs,
And to sun's parching heat display'd my cheeks,
God's Mother deigned to appear to me,
And in a vision full of majesty
Will'd me to leave my base vocation
And free my country from calamity. . . .
Resolve on this: thou shalt be fortunate
If thou receive me for thy warlike mate.
(I.ii.76 ff.)

The regularity is absolute to the point of monotony, though it has not been achieved without certain procrustean tricks of stretching out and slurring over: the definite article is omitted from the second line, and in the fifth "vocation" must be pronounced with four syllables. The verse-paragraph is built up through a sequence of lines corresponding to its component clauses, and the passage is rounded out with a sententious couplet. Note also the archaic alliterations: "whilest / waited," "country / calamity." Here, by way of comparison, is the valedictory speech of the dying Katherine of Aragon, spoken to her gentlewoman Patience in *Henry VIII*:

When I am dead, good wench,
Let me be us'd with honor. Strew me over
With maiden flowers, that all the world may know
I was a chaste wife to my grave. Embalm me,
Then lay me forth. Although unqueen'd, yet like
A queen, and daughter to a king, inter me.
I can no more. (IV.ii.167–73)

These seven lines contain five short sentences, four of them commencing and four of them concluding somewhere within the pentameter. There are three feminine endings and three enjambments—a high percentage even for a late work. The abrupt breaks and the breathless run-overs seem to echo the feelings they convey. The context lends a poignant modesty to the personal pronoun, when it becomes the unaccented eleventh syllable: "Embalm me," "inter me." The contrast between the pomposity of artificial diction and the simplicity of genuine anguish is as striking as the improvement in Shakespeare's portraiture between La Pucelle and Katherine.

Whether it be as loud as a public proclamation or as muted as a breaking heart, Shakespeare's discourse is intended to be spoken. But its appeal is visual as well as vocal, proceeding directly through the ear to the eye; hence it enables us, by listening closely, to visualize the scene. Every word is a picture, Thomas Gray suggested, exaggerating somewhat in order to make an important point. The verbal sound is completed by the pictorial image. When Berowne says,

Light, seeking light, doth light of light beguile,

his ingenuity calls our attention to the words themselves, obscuring the realities beyond them. But when Othello, approaching Desdemona's bed in V.ii, says,

Put out the light, and then put out the light,

his thought moves from the plane of words to the plane of deeds and their consequences. The actual candle, which is being extinguished, becomes a symbol of Desdemona's fated life. Othello, like Hotspur, "apprehends a world of figures," a whole new dimension of experience which Shakespeare reveals through his imagery. Like all great poets, he views the world metaphorically—or, as Hamlet would put it, "tropically." The basic trope, or figure of speech, can be illustrated by an obvious example from the Old English. Literally, we say that a ship *sails* the sea. But figuratively, speaking the language of connotation rather than denotation, we may say that the ship *ploughs* the sea. This implies a correspondence which can be stated logically:

$$\frac{\text{SHIP}}{\text{SEA}} = \frac{\text{PLOUGH}}{\text{(LAND)}}$$

The literal reality is the first term of the equation; the figurative extension is the second; and "land" is in parentheses because it is out of sight.

When the relationship is made explicit, it becomes a simile: "Even as a plough is to the land, so is a ship to the sea." Shakespeare makes frequent use of this more formal device. The messenger in the second scene of *Macbeth* reports that the opposing armies are

As two spent swimmers that do cling together
And choke their art.

But metaphor is so inherent a mode of apprehension that it has no need for the guideposts of *like* or *as*; the relationship it expresses is implicit. Rhetoricians term it the figure of transport, and indeed Shakespeare uses it to transport us from the events on the stage to a wider universe of discourse. To be sure, all language is metaphorical. We could hardly enunciate a sentence without making use of fossilized metaphors. We use *bias* as a synonym for prejudice, without remembering the weighted bowl; and when we speak of spurring someone on, we seldom think in terms of horsemanship. Yet Macbeth, who is never far from the battlefield, brings out the original force of the phrase when he soliloquizes:

I have no spur
To prick the sides of my intent, but only
Vaulting ambition, which o'erleaps itself,
And falls on th' other. (I.vii.25–28)

Here the literal meaning is an abstraction, the description of a psychological process, which is made concrete by the equestrian analogy. To sum it up in another paradigm:

$$\frac{\text{AMBITION}}{\text{INTENTION}} = \frac{\text{SPUR}}{\text{(HORSE)}}$$

But the analogy is a negative one, to which Macbeth does not adhere consistently. Ambition, instead of acting as a spur, seems to become a horse itself—or perhaps its rider—and to run away with the situation. The metaphor becomes a hyperbole, and the leap that fails by its very excess of energy becomes a portent of Macbeth's fall.

Shakespeare's vision of things is at times so vivid that it seems to leave his expression turgid, and he falls into what the classical-minded critics deplored as mixed metaphor. When Hamlet proposes "to take arms against a sea of troubles" (III.i.58), Pope replaced *sea* with the emendation *siege* to preserve the military tone. Yet the bold image of a warrior stalking, sword in hand, into the sea is not uncharacteristic of the Anglo-Saxon imagination. Since the Elizabethan poets worked from a repertory of conventionalized tropes and stock comparisons, which they adapted and recombined, they ran the continual risk of standardization. We are not altogether surprised when, at the first sight of Juliet, Romeo muses:

It seems she hangs upon the cheek of night
As a rich jewel in an Ethiop's ear. (I.v.45–46)

Juliet is to night, in other words, what the jewel is to its Ethiopian wearer. The conceit is a static one which, while personifying the night, turns Juliet into an inanimate object, an earring, a mere decoration. Like so much of the diction in the first act, this is surface embellishment, reminding us of the comedies or of the sonneteers. Yet the fundamental antithesis between light and darkness pervades the tragedy like a motif in music, and calls forth such numerous and intricate variations that the reader can best be referred to Caroline Spurgeon's essay on the subject. A simpler instance, which suggests how the same pair of opposites can be tensely dramatic rather than dazzingly poetic, is Macbeth's invocation:

Stars, hide your fires,
Let not light see my black and deep desires.
(I.iv.50–51)

The broken couplet does nothing to decorate surfaces; momentarily it peers into depths; it psychologizes Macbeth's resolve by framing it within a moral perspective. It extends the imaginative focus from what is being enacted before us to the more speculative drama that takes place in the mind's eye.

The sphere of Shakespeare's images is so vast and rich in itself that it has been investigated and charted for clues to his personal temperament. But though we can follow up associations of thought through his image-clusters, these are subordinated to his controlling purposes as a playwright. The imagery fulfills a structural and a thematic function, linking together a train of ideas or projecting a scheme of values. It enhances the strain of melancholy in *Hamlet* by dwelling on sickness and decay, and sharpens the ethical choices in *King Lear* through its emphasis on sight and blindness. The sun, a traditional emblem of kingship from the time of the Pharaohs, sheds its light on Shakespeare's procession of English kings, detaching itself from Richard II after his downfall to shine on the erstwhile Bullingbrook, now King Henry IV. Above all, the man from Stratford keeps returning to the theme of a garden; it is the norm of all that is soundest and happiest within his frame of reference. The moral of *Richard II* is pronounced by a gardener, who compares his well-tended plot with the commonwealth gone to seed (III.iv.29 ff.). The war of *Henry V* is ended when the King conquers France, "this best garden of the world" (V.ii.36). The Wars of the Roses start with a confrontation in the Temple Garden (*1 Henry VI*, II.iv), and the rebellious Cade is run to earth in a quiet Kentish garden (*2 Henry VI*, IV.x). A charming garden in Belmont resolves the urban tensions of *The Merchant of Venice*. Hamlet's blighted world is "an unweeded garden" (I.ii.135). Iago affirms the freedom of the will, and draws a microcosmic parallel, when he tells Roderigo: "Our bodies are our gardens" (*Othello*, I.iii.320).

The allegory is applied by Friar Lawrence, in *Romeo and Juliet*, when he discusses the benign and malignant properties of plants. It is acted out when Perdita in *The Winter's Tale*—or, with a pathetic difference, Ophelia—distributes flowers, or when the madness of Lear is crowned with weeds. Images are suited to the styles of the characters: Othello's parlance is full of martial pomp and circumstance. When Iago vilifies him as an old black ram (I.i.88), Iago's string of beastly epithets serves to characterize himself. With Macbeth the characteristic gesture is dressing or undressing, arming or disarming. Its significance is made clear by his preliminary question:

The Thane of Cawdor lives; why do you dress me
In borrowed robes? (I.iii.108–9)

After he has seized the crown, his disaffected thanes look upon the ensuing disorder as an almost Falstaffian spectacle:

He cannot buckle his distemper'd cause
Within the belt of rule. (V.ii.15–16)

The same note of carnal grossness—perhaps foreshadowing the drunken grooms— is intermixed with the clothing metaphor, when Lady Macbeth is urging him not to let his resolution bog down in an anticlimax:

Was the hope drunk
Wherein you dress'd yourself? Hath it slept since?
And wakes it now to look so green and pale
At what it did so freely? (I.vii.35–38)

Macbeth has felt himself restrained by a surge of pity, symbolized in the person of "a naked new-born babe" (I.vii.21)—a symbol which unites the related themes of his childlessness, Banquo's progeny, and the doomed children of Macduff. Recent critics have traced these configurations in such fascinating detail that we are sometimes tempted to read the plays as if they were metaphysical poems. But though we cannot overrate the importance of the poetry, its function is to orchestrate the drama, to integrate the words at every turn with the actions and the ideas.

VI. THE THEATRICAL SETTING

To take full advantage of reading Shakespeare, we must cultivate both the mind's ear and the mind's eye; we must learn to hear the verse spoken aloud as we read it, and also to see the drama enacted in an imaginary theatre. Experienced musicians are able to read score, to glance at the notes on a sheet of paper and know how the music will sound. Similarly, theatrical experience can teach one to look at a script and imagine what the rendition would be like. Shakespeare's plays, though they have meant so many things to so many men, are primarily scripts. The fact that they are so commonly apprehended through the printed page has caused a certain amount of misapprehension among his readers, including his critics. But with Shakespearean criticism there has been a growing effort to understand his work in its own terms, to reconstruct the means by which he gained his effects: such was the approach of Granville-Barker, who himself had been a successful actor-manager-playwright. When we open an edition of *Hamlet* at Act I, Scene 1, we are usually confronted with the designation: "Elsinore. A platform before the castle." This was supplied for the reader's convenience by eighteenth-century editors, along with such standard rubrics as "A room in the palace" for tragedy, "A battlefield" for history, or "Another part of the forest" for comedy. With few exceptions, designations of place do not appear in the quartos and folios, and many of the earliest texts make no designation of act and scene.

Shakespeare's stage itself was basically a platform. That of the Globe (as we infer from the extant specifications of a rival playhouse modelled on it, the Fortune) measured 27½ feet deep by 43 feet wide. The editions of the eighteenth century presupposed a theatre of their own time, with its proscenium framing a picture of the play's visual background, a landscape or an edifice painted in perspective on shutters or drop-curtains and wings. The theatre of the ancient Greeks had embraced two concentric circles, an orchestra (originally meaning a dancing-place) all but surrounded by an embankment of seats. Circular arrangements of this kind existed in England when the strolling players acted out their moralities and interludes upon the village green. The emphasis was horizontal, bringing the actors and the spectators together in a vital interrelationship. Modern theatres tend, by contrast, to be vertical in their thrust. The orchestra has shrunk to a pit for musicians, dividing the actors within their lighted picture-frame from the passive spectators in the darkened auditorium. The Elizabethan theatre had a horizontal basis, which it happily combined with certain vertical features. Its platform-stage was encircled on three sides by the standing spectators or groundlings (who paid a penny for admittance), so that the production—if not quite in the round—employed what today we call arena staging. The surrounding amphitheatre (apparently polygonal at the Globe) consisted of three stories, each with its gallery, like those old-fashioned inn-yards used on occasion for theatres. Admission to the galleries cost an additional penny and entitled the spectator to a seat.

Just beyond the stage rose the tiring-house, containing—as the name (attiring-house) implies—the actors' dressing rooms, and providing a conventionalized background which adapted itself to their histrionic requirements. Most of the acting had to take place downstage; but upstage there was a curtained area which could be used for discoveries, could be opened up to disclose—we can readily imagine—Ferdinand and Miranda playing at chess. Behind its curtain or arras, which was black for tragedy and particolored for comedy (a painted cloth or imitation tapestry), would be discovered the body of the slain Polonius or the sleeping Falstaff, "snorting like a horse." In back at a higher level, there was a specialized playing space indicated in the Shakespearean directions as "above" or "aloft." Thence the invisible Prospero looked down on the lovers and the conspirators; this was a battlement ("on the walls") for the history plays; from it Richard II made his punning descent, a symbolic come-down, to the "base court." There seem to have been practical upper windows, at one of which Juliet first made her most celebrated appearance, in what later came to be known as the balcony scene. Somewhere beneath the windows, to the left and right of the mainstage, were the doors for major exits and entrances. Housed at the highest level were the musicians and the instruments for other sound effects that punctuated the dramatic rhythm. Cannonades and fireworks won even more applause than the familiar hautboys (oboes) or rebecks (fiddles), and started the fire that burned down the Globe during a representation of *Henry VIII* in 1613.

The tiring-house was crowned with a small hut or turret, whence a flag and a trumpeter announced the day's performance. Though the large pit was open to the sky, most of the stage was covered by a projecting roof called the shadow or heavens, whose underside was illuminated with signs of the zodiac. The posts or pillars that supported this projection could lend themselves to the play at hand; they might have been the trees in the Forest of Arden on which Orlando hangs his verses. The stage, which stood about five feet from the ground, could be entered from underneath by a trap or traps, whose most famous use was to serve as a grave for Ophelia. Actors could be lowered from above, like the supernatural personages in *The Tempest*, or pulled upward, as when the dying Antony is lifted into Cleopatra's monument, by some sort of machine. Plays had to be performed in broad daylight, of course, between the hours of two and four or five in the afternoon. Open-air performances must have fostered a more exaggerated style of acting than that to which we have become accustomed, more dependent on sonorous elocution and stylized gesture, although it is significant that Hamlet cautions the Players against overacting. In an age when both men and women prided themselves on the extravagant design and flamboyant color of their garments, it was the actors who cut the most gorgeous figures. Appearing in the dress of their day, with certain exotic or historical touches relating to their roles, they set a modish standard: "The glass of fashion and the mould of form."

Most of the attempted reconstructions err by making the Shakespearean playhouse look like a quaint little Tudor cottage, thatched and half-timbered. Actually, we gather from the Fortune contract that the Globe may have had arches, pilasters, and other details of baroque architecture. When these were further embellished with bright hangings, costumed actors, and all the trappings of pageantry, the impression must have been spectacular. Thomas Coryat, the Jacobean traveller, found the theatres of Venice less stately than those of London, and he is corroborated by foreign observers who were impressed by English playhouses. Though their average size has been variously computed, they would seem to have held an audience of between 2,000 and 3,000. Nonetheless, the prologue to *Henry V* is somewhat apologetic:

Can this cockpit hold
The vasty fields of France? Or may we cram
Within this wooden O the very casques
That did affright the air at Agincourt?

But this was a request for "that willing suspension of disbelief, which," as Coleridge would argue, "constitutes poetic faith." As the Chorus intimates, the theatres were in the sporting districts near the cockfighting arenas and the bear-baiting pits, not to mention the stews or houses of prostitution. The Globe was located in Southwark on the Bankside, south of the river Thames and out of the city of London, where public plays were officially frowned upon. Shakespeare and his colleagues were to acquire a private playhouse indoors at Blackfriars, north of London Bridge, in 1608; and they would frequently perform before the court at Whitehall Palace and on tour elsewhere. However, their greatest successes were inalterably associated with that wooden O which lived up to so proud a title as the Globe, *theatrum mundi*. Its sign is referred to in *Hamlet* (II.ii.362) when Rosencrantz speaks of "Hercules and his load" (i.e. the world on his shoulders), and tradition recounts that its motto was *Totus mundus agit histrionem* (literally, "All the world plays the actor"). Shakespeare's rendering, "All the world's a stage," furnishes the theme for the set-piece of the melancholy Jaques in *As You Like It*, and the première of that comedy may well have marked the opening of the Globe in 1599.

Though there was no scenery, there were a good many properties: a throne or bed, for example, or a conventional hedge. Romeo evidently jumps over an "orchard wall" to hide in the Capulets' garden, and the departing Benvolio concludes that scene (II.i) by saying:

Go then, for 'tis in vain
To seek him here that means not to be found.

And the next scene—the balcony scene—begins, in the modernized text, with Romeo coming forward to say:

They jest at scars that never felt a wound.

Here the change of pronunciation obscures a rhyme which shows that the action has been continuous. Scenes do not need to be localized unless the locality forms a meaningful aspect of the situation, and then Shakespeare tells us whatever we need to know by merely dropping an appropriate word. "This is Illyria, lady," Viola is told on her first entrance in *Twelfth Night*. On the other hand, when Bullingbrook asks, "How far is it, my lord, to Berkeley now?", the reply is:

Believe me, noble lord,
I am a stranger here in Gloucestershire.
(*Richard II*, II.iii.1–3)

Shakespeare does his own scene-painting through speeches. It is King Duncan himself who sets the stage, when he arrives at Inverness as Macbeth's guest (I.vi):

This castle hath a pleasant seat, the air
Nimbly and sweetly recommends itself
Unto our gentle senses.

The picture, reflecting his own serene nobility of character, is thereupon filled in by the noble Banquo, who is likewise destined to be a victim of their host:

This guest of summer,
The temple-haunting marlet, does approve,
By his loved mansionry, that the heaven's breath
Smells wooingly here.

Banquo's delicate evocation of the swift, building its lofty nest in churches, is at odds with the omens hinted by other birds, the croaking raven and the fatal owl. It has a special effect which Sir Joshua Reynolds would compare with "repose" in painting. Repose indeed! It is there at Macbeth's castle that Duncan is to take his last repose. That temple-haunting marlet proves to be another omen of death, and we are nearer to hell's breath than to heaven's, as the clownish Porter will bring home to us in his drunken monologue next morning.

Shakespeare's numerous shifts of scene were made possible by this technique of verbal description. *Antony and Cleopatra* has no less than forty-two scenes, as it has been editorially subdivided, fifteen of them in the fourth act alone. A play which keeps shuttling back and forth between Rome and Alexandria, moving on to Athens and even to Asia Minor at one point, is far too immense to be produced with the pictorial scenery of latter-day stagecraft. But poetry can take continents in its stride, as Donne reminds us in "A Valediction: Of Weeping":

On a round ball
A workman that hath copies by, can lay
An Europe, Afric, and an Asia,
And quickly make that which was nothing all.

Time proves to be no more of an obstacle than space is for Shakespeare. In *The Winter's Tale* it is Father Time himself who offers an apologia for skipping over sixteen years, allowing the hero and heroine to grow up between the third and fourth acts. Dr. Johnson defended Shakespeare against those neoclassical critics who could not forgive him for neglecting their dogmatic unities of time and place, and the romantic Coleridge would declare that Shakespeare's plays observe the one important unity, that of feeling. Yet, as if to confound his detractors by showing them that he could solve any technical problem they put to him, he pays strict attention to all the unities in the academic *Comedy of Errors* and in the courtly *Tempest*. His dramaturgy was broad enough to comprehend both of the extremes that Polonius holds up: "scene individable, or poem unlimited; . . . the law of writ and the liberty" (II.ii.399–401).

Ben Jonson, as a professing classicist, disapproved of such liberties, believed in a more rigorous verisimilitude, and thought it implausible that a history play could

with three rusty swords,
And help of some few foot-and-half-foot words,
Fight over York and Lancaster's long jars,
And in the tiring-house bring wounds to scars.
(*Every Man in His Humor*, Prologue)

From a realistic standpoint, it is perfectly true that all theatrical illusion hinges upon a series of makeshifts: "In little room confining mighty men" (*Henry V*, Epilogue). Since there could be no question of staging a military campaign within the confines of the theatre, it had to be suggested by alarums and excursions: by ringing the bell that called men forth to arms and by sending small parties of supernumeraries across the stage, wearing counterfeit armor, bloody make-up, and the heraldic escutcheons of Lancaster or York. Trumpets and banners would help; but it was oratory that had to do the rest, with vaunts before the battle and parleys afterward, volleys of sesquipedalian verbiage. This required some cooperation on the part of the audience, a meeting of minds which the Chorus bespeaks in the Prologue to *Henry V*:

Piece out our imperfections with your thoughts.

Shakespeare seems to be reaching the limits of the dramatic medium and to be striking out toward the epic—or, more prophetically, the cinema—when his self-conscious Chorus interlinks the episodes with narrative exposition and makes his repeated appeals to the hearers' imagination:

Still be kind,
And eche [i.e. eke] out our performance with
your mind. (III.Cho.34–35)

Through the choruses of *Henry V*, Shakespeare manifests his own awareness of convention, that body of unspoken assumptions without which the theatre could not exist. Convention may be defined as a gentlemen's agreement between the actor and the spectator to take the word for the deed, to accept the symbol as the reality, and thereby to gain impressive effects with limited means. Though the Elizabethans did not follow the classical rules, it would be a serious mistake to conclude that their drama was amorphous. On the contrary, they worked with an elaborate set of conventions, which Shakespeare followed conscientiously.

French classicism, which forbade a tragic protagonist to think out loud, supplied him with a confidant invariably at hand to draw out his thoughts through conversation. This device would seem to be no less conventional—and scarcely more natural—than the Shakespearean soliloquy, which enables us to overhear a character's innermost stream of consciousness, or its briefer version, the aside. Simply to speak in verse is an artifice, after all, comparatively more artificial with rhyme than with blank verse. Shakespeare ordinarily utilizes a rhyming couplet to close a blank-verse scene. Tragedies conventionally terminate with didactic couplets pronounced by the highest-ranking figure among the survivors. It is the Prince of Verona who makes the concluding pronouncement:

For never was a story of more woe
Than this of Juliet and her Romeo.

Marked by their terminal rhymes, which were less of an interruption than a falling curtain would have been, scenes succeeded one another as actors walked on and off the Elizabethan stage. Acts were more perceptibly divided, most appropriately by music, which could be harmonized with the stage business. Act III of *A Midsummer Night's Dream* ends with the stage direction "*They sleep all the act*." That is to say, the enchanted lovers remain in sleeping postures through the musical *entr'acte* to wake up disenchanted in Act IV. There was some danger that, without a clear-cut interval, the audience might not realize when one scene was ending and the next one beginning. Hence an actor who left the stage at the end of one scene could not immediately reappear in the next. In *Richard II* a dramatically unmotivated exit is made by John of Gaunt a few lines before the end of the first scene for no other reason than that he must be onstage at the beginning of the second scene. Scholars have retroactively named this practice the law of re-entry, though it had no such name for the playwrights who practiced it. It is the intrinsic nature of conventions that they be taken for granted, without being made too explicit or codified. We can attend a film and grasp the temporal significance of a flashback or slow dissolve without giving them names.

Given the vast potentialities and the adaptable mechanisms of the Shakespearean theatre, everything hinged upon the contribution of those human beings who brought it to life. Shakespeare's career was paralleled—and fulfilled—by the development of the profession or "quality" of acting. That had been a precarious way of life, since stage-players were "glorious vagabonds," who would have been arrested as vagrants if they had not been taken into the service of some highly placed protector. Consequently, Shakespeare's troupe enjoyed the distinction of being patronized by the Lord Chamberlain, the traditional arbiter of English entertainment, and subsequently by the King himself. Inasmuch as it was a stock company, Shakespeare must have owed something to the talents of the fellow actors for whom he wrote. His leading actor, Richard Burbage (whose more flexible style superseded the popular ranting of Marlowe's tragedian, Edward Alleyn), was able to create the successive roles of Romeo, Hamlet, and Lear within the decade of their composition. Hamlet, keenly interested in matters theatrical, gives us a glimpse of a typical cast when the Players come to Elsinore:

> He that plays the king shall be welcome—his Majesty shall have tribute on me, the adventerous knight shall use his foil and target, the lover shall not sigh gratis, the humorous man shall end his part in peace, the clown shall make those laugh whose lungs are tickle a' th' sere, and the lady shall say her mind freely, or the blank verse shall halt for't. (II.ii.319–25)

The Shakespearean repertory is not so easily reduced to types as the Savoy Operas, yet Shakespeare must have had certain actors in mind for certain parts, and his characterizations may have been influenced by their personal traits. Hamlet looks askance at the improvised gags of the clown; Shakespeare took pains to write lines that suited the styles of his comedians. The principal comedian of earlier years, Will Kemp, seems to have specialized in not-so-clever servants like Peter in *Romeo and Juliet*. Presumably, he was Launce in *The Two Gentlemen of Verona* and the closely related Launcelot Gobbo in *The Merchant of Venice*, both of whom engage in dialogues with themselves (a gag which Shakespeare elaborated for Falstaff and the Porter). He was succeeded by Robert Armin, whose specialty was fools, which may explain the remarkable exfoliation of such jesters from *As You Like It* through *King Lear*. The most difficult part, from our point of view, would have been the lady, since she had to be impersonated by a boy. That may help to account for the number of shrews and viragoes in the early plays, or the fondness of heroines in the comedies for assuming—or resuming—masculine garb. The boy-actor needed the utmost that blank verse could offer, by way of feminine aura, to catch the adolescent charms of Juliet, let alone the mature seductions of Cleopatra.

Among the factors converging toward the inspiration for Shakespeare, we should not overlook that presence which has left the least record. To have great poets, said Whitman, you must have great audiences. Shakespeare's work was predicated, to a considerable degree, upon the imaginative collaboration of his Elizabethan-Jacobean audience. Doubtless it was easily amused by the slapstick of the clowns; but it must also have relished the blandishments of the lovers and subtleties of the humorous men. A large middle-class public at the Globe, a select circle in the private house at Blackfriars, and finally the court itself—all could react with enthusiasm to the same playwright. But they reacted according to their "divers capacities," as Heminge and Condell noted, in addressing the First Folio "to the great variety of readers, from the most able to him that can but spell." Shakespeare's universality—his ability to please every taste, to win "all men's suffrage," in Ben Jonson's phrase—was compounded out of his very heterogeneity, his appeal to individuals through a concrete understanding of their concerns. Normally, about half a dozen theatres were functioning in his London. At the other end of the seventeenth century, when the size of the city had doubled and was tripling, there would be no more than two or three. Already during his lifetime, as his company's acquisition of the Blackfriars portended, the democratic base for the drama was dwindling. Cut off altogether by the Puritans during the Commonwealth, and partially revived by the Restoration as an upper-class amusement, it never again came so close to so large a proportion of the people.

VII. THE ARTISTIC DEVELOPMENT

Socrates is said to have reconciled the idea of tragedy with that of comedy, and to have predicted that the two ideas would some day be realized by the same genius. But that was in the small hours of Plato's *Symposium*, when the listeners were overcome by wine or sleep, and the argument has been lost to posterity. Two thousand years afterward, when the Elizabethans blended both modes into what they called a gallimaufry or hodgepodge, they were attacked by traditionalists for juxtaposing—in Sidney's phrase—"hornpipes and funerals." Dr. Johnson would defend Shakespeare by arguing that, although his plays were neither tragedies nor comedies in the strictly classical sense, they came closer to life than either through their variety; and Victor Hugo would maintain that they distilled the very essence of modern drama by intermixing the grotesque and the sublime. The combination, by whatever name it be invoked, is an organic feature of English dramaturgy. It goes back at least as far as *The Second Shepherds' Play* of Wakefield, where the ritual of the babe in the manger is parodied by the farce of the stolen sheep. Thus the drunken Porter of *Macbeth* is no mere vulgar interpolation to tickle the groundlings; he is a quizzical commentator upon the serious action, like the Gravedigger in *Hamlet*. The clown, who enhances the merriment of *As You Like It* or *Twelfth Night* by opposing the cult of melancholy personified in Jaques or Malvolio, does not proffer comic relief in *King Lear*; he brings out the pathos by making the King "taste his folly," by joking with ill-timed persistence about Lear's fatal mistake.

The Shakespearean practice of complementing and contrasting the main plot with a secondary plot reaches its fullest development in *King Lear*. The Celtic tale about a father with kind and unkind daughters is deliberately paralleled by the episode—drawn from Sidney's *Arcadia*—of another father with kind and unkind sons, and the physical blinding of Gloucester is a commentary upon the moral blindness of Lear. Such underplots are often romantic, and always parodic, in their relation to the central theme. The underplot of *Hamlet* focuses on Laertes, another son avenging his father, after mischances brought about through Hamlet's love for Ophelia. But there is also an overplot which involves still another son avenging his father, through the military campaign of Fortinbras and the power struggle between Denmark and Norway. Such overplots are enveloping actions which frame the personal issue at a dynastic or a national level. The title-page of the Folio indicates Shakespeare's versatility by naming the principal genres of Elizabethan drama: comedy, history, tragedy. Polonius, who shares Hamlet's interest in theatrical criticism, recognizes categories as hybrid as "tragical-comical-historical-pastoral," and it would be easy to extend his list of the permutations made possible by the multiple plot. "Seneca cannot be too heavy, nor Plautus too light," continues Polonius (II.ii.396–402). We have already noted how the apprentice playwright took those Latin models in his stride and encompassed their extremes with *Titus Andronicus* and *The Comedy of Errors*.

The evolution of the English drama is deeply rooted in the liturgy of the medieval church and, beyond it, in the substratum of folklore. The hobby-horse of the primitive May-games was not altogether forgotten by Shakespeare. Certainly in his youth he must have visited the neighboring cathedral town of Coventry, still a centre for the street performance of Biblical cycles, and watched the pageant representing the Slaughter of the Innocents, where Herod rants in the manner that Hamlet describes. The scene where Lady Macduff and her children are slaughtered is more understandable, though not less terrible, in the light of that popular precedent. The members of the local gilds that put on those mysteries could not have been too unlike Bottom the Weaver and his fellow tradesmen. Shakespeare is recalling the morality plays, as they were performed by strolling actors, when he alludes to the mischief-making Vice, who marshalled the Deadly Sins with his dagger of lath (*Twelfth Night*, IV.ii.124 ff.). Falstaff is likened to that prototype for leading Prince Hal astray (*1 Henry IV*, II.iv.453), while the latter—like the prodigal hero of the moralities—is beguiled by temptation in tavern scenes. During the Tudor period these native strains converged with more self-consciously literary influences—in the Senecan tragedy of the Inns of Court and the Plautine comedy of the colleges—and were augmented by tournaments, processions, and other quasi-dramatic manifestations. By the time England's first playhouse (expressly named the Theatre) was erected in 1576, the outstanding need was for young talents who would take up playwriting as a career.

Gradually and brilliantly, during the fifteen-eighties, that requirement was met. John Lyly, adapting his ornate prose to the clever badinage of the child-actors, charmed a patrician audience with his brittle "court comedies"; Falstaff mocks at their euphuistic style in his play-acting scene (*1 Henry IV*, II.iv.398 ff.). Christopher Marlowe, at the forefront of the University Wits, caught the collective voice of the Armada decade in his tragedies of overreaching ambition; Shakespeare (who was born in the same year as Marlowe and lived twenty-three years longer) was indebted to him not only for his pioneering in blank verse but for his characterization of hero-villains like Richard III. Thomas Kyd set his stamp on the tragedy of revenge with the play that probably enjoyed the longest run and the widest influence of its author's generation; *The Spanish Tragedy*, with its father avenging a son, its play within the play, its introductory ghost, and its heroine's madness, prepared the way for *Hamlet*. Insofar as these Shakespearean prototypes had their own forerunners among the classics, they conformed roughly to the traditional five-act scheme. But the internal structure of a play, as it was analyzed by Renaissance critics, counted no more than four stages: *protasis* (introduction), *epitasis* (development), *catastasis* (crisis), and *catastrophe* (final overturn). Modern handbooks of dramatic technique, such as that of Gustav Freytag, reduce the sequence to three: exposition, climax, dénouement. This gives the Shakespearean play a pyramidal shape, which rises from Act I to Act III and falls thence to Act V. Sometimes one of the intervening acts, especially the fourth, may seem thin or else padded.

The average number in the cast of a Shakespearean comedy is eighteen, just about half as many as the thirty-five in a history, with tragedy in between at twenty-seven. It follows that comedy is constructed most tightly and history most loosely, since the one contrives and controls its *dramatis personae* while the other must take them as they emerge (and ask the players to double in lesser roles). The histories were bound to be more or less episodic, since they were expected to stick fairly close to the annals of England, as chronicled by Holinshed and others, reign by reign and year by year. Shakespeare first achieved and asserted his mastery through his cycle of plays in this genre. If we regard *King John* as its prologue and *Henry VIII* as its epilogue, it comprises further two tetralogies mainly covering the fifteenth century. The earlier and cruder tetralogy deals with the later reigns: the three parts of *Henry VI* and *Richard III*. The four remaining plays, composed later but dealing with the earlier chronology, stand together as a culmination: *Richard II*, the two parts of *Henry IV*, and *Henry V*. "All is true," the name by which Sir Henry Wotton knew *Henry VIII*, is the implicit claim of each history, even though it be colored by Tudor propaganda. Its pedagogical tendencies are underlined by its catalogues of heraldry and genealogy. Above all, like the well-known Elizabethan collection of didactic monologues in verse, it is a *Mirror for Magistrates*. Richard II proposes himself as an object lesson in how not to govern, when he enjoins his queen: "Tell thou the lamentable tale of me" (V.i.44). The delinquent Prince Hal becomes the exemplary Henry V, having learned to rule by fraternizing with his future subjects and having thereby acted out his allegorical education.

The line between the histories and the tragedies need not be quite so sharply drawn as it is by the classifications of the Folio. *Richard II* and *Richard III* could qualify as tragedies, insofar as they are unified through the persons of their weak or wicked protagonists. *King Lear* and *Macbeth* might almost be reckoned with the histories, since they somewhat marginally stem from the historical—or legendary—matter of Britain, if not of England. Shakespeare was freer to face some of the ethical issues raised in the history plays, with less political constraint and more dramatic artistry, by turning in mid-career to the matter of Rome. For the good European, the Englishman whose myth traced his cultural heritage from the line of its founder Brutus (and ultimately, through Aeneas, back to Troy), all roads—if pursued far enough—led in that direction. Rome's original Forum provided the best sounding-board for civic debate and ideological rhetoric. Shakespeare's biographical inspiration, Plutarch's *Parallel Lives of the Noble Greeks and Romans*, was the great casebook for studies in heroic virtue; Plutarch, though writing in Greek, cites the Latin *virtus*, which is rendered as "valiantness" by the translator Shakespeare depended upon, Sir Thomas North; and the concept has its Renaissance counterpart in Machiavelli's *virtù*, which in turn approximates our notions of self-reliance or individualism. In transferring his venue from the English monarchy to the Roman republic, Shakespeare shifted his emphasis from kingship to citizenship, and from the duties of the subject to the rights of the citizen.

Julius Caesar, Shakespeare's most forensic play, shows the state in danger of domination by an individual, with consequences that lead from forum to battlefield and look ahead from republican ideals toward the corruptions of empire. *Coriolanus*, set in a prior age, pits an individual against the state—so vigorously that twentieth-century audiences, protesting as loudly as the Roman populace, have rioted against its authoritarian hero. *Antony and Cleopatra*, by presenting a pair of individuals abandoning their public responsibilities in favor of their private relationship, weighs the claims of state against a love magnified to a corresponding grandeur. *Titus Andronicus* is merely a pseudo-Roman play, really an immature tragedy of revenge; and perhaps *Timon of Athens* belongs on the opposite edge of this group, for its Plutarchan origin, if not for its stark reduction of magnanimity to misanthropy. But *Antony and Cleopatra*, in its expansiveness, transcends the sphere of the Roman plays to embrace that of Shakespeare's romantic tragedies. It is not less poignant than *Romeo and Juliet* because its concern is with last love rather than first love. However, the very notion that love could be tragic material was something of an innovation with Shakespeare; the subject had been conventionally viewed as the peculiar domain of comedy. Since *Romeo and Juliet* marks a strategic turning-point in this regard, we should not be surprised that its formal and stylistic features are reminiscent of Shakespeare's early comedies, or that it is characterized in the First Quarto by the paradoxical phrase, "conceited tragedy."

If *Antony and Cleopatra* magnifies a passion to the scale of imperial war, *Troilus and Cressida* belittles the Trojan war by reducing it to the plane of cynical intrigue. A double plot, not balanced but precariously loaded on both sides, contributes to the general feeling of irresolution and disintegration. *Othello* has more in common with its Italianate predecessor, *Romeo and Juliet*, though the youthful lovers were the victims of fatality, whereas the Moor is victimized by malign human agency. The element of contrivance, of sheer stage-management on the part of Iago, is not without its faintly comic overtone. Othello lives in a world of human relations, good or bad, unlike the three tragic protagonists with whom he is commonly grouped, whose existence is a confrontation with the universe at large. Lear and Macbeth share with Hamlet, albeit to a less explicit degree, the ambivalent preoccupation with man in his pride and shame, his angelic possibilities and animal limitations. Hamlet's plight is a paradigm of man's divided condition: his personal gifts, his cosmic doubts, his oppressive mandate, his interrupted quest. Lear's downfall is all the more tragic for having been self-decreed. Blindly he must condemn himself to suffer before he can understand the sufferings of others; he must put off the trappings of majesty, submit to the rigors of nature, and be abased to the level of "unaccommodated man," a mad and naked beggar like Tom o' Bedlam. His questioning becomes a theodicy, an inquiry into the justice of God or the gods, providence or chance.

Macbeth is less reflective, a diametrical contrast with *Hamlet*, which is nearly twice as long. Yet the hero, degenerating so rapidly into a villain before our eyes, offers himself as a test case in ironic support of his declaration: "I dare do all that may become a man" (I.vii.46). Indeed he is daring enough to attempt any action. As for his conception of what is becoming to human nature, it has been fatally confused by his encounter with the Weird Sisters:

> Fair is foul, and foul is fair,
> Hover through the fog and filthy air. (I.i.11–12)

If fair looked fair and foul looked foul, if the good were always attractive and the bad as black as the devil, then there would be no serious problem of evil. But moral choice is difficult precisely because of the murky atmosphere through which men walk at the crises of their lives. Shakespeare's crudest villain happens to be a black man, Aaron the Moor in *Titus Andronicus*. It required the growth of psychological insight to portray the inherent nobility of Othello, the Moor of Venice—or, for that matter, the latent depravity of his white friend who is known as "honest Iago." The casket scene in *The Merchant of Venice* acts out the parable: "All that glisters is not gold." Again and again, in comedy as well as tragedy, the cry of disillusionment goes up, when it is discovered that the beautiful appearances have been masking the ugly realities. Such a recognition, which Aristotle termed *anagnorisis*, brings with it the special illumination that tragedy casts. The protagonist, forced to see through and look beyond the entrammelling circumstances of his life heretofore, seems to gain a momentary glimpse into the ultimate nature of things. The disparity between his expectations and what has happened to him is what we term dramatic irony.

The protagonist is not only the leading character, but (as the derivation of the word *agony* suggests) he is engaged in an *agon* or conflict. His conflict is not simply with recognizable antagonists, but with an inner self on the one hand and with the outermost forces that shape events on the other. When those events come to pass, his part in the total pattern—looking back upon it—we view as his destiny. Meanwhile speculation has been rife as to whether it could be foreseen, and here is where all the oracles come in. But though the Witches have access to foreknowledge by virtue of being supernatural creatures, this cannot help mere humans; it can only mislead Macbeth. Macbeth's position is that of the sleepless sailor, harassed by the First Witch because his wife has flouted her:

> Though his bark cannot be lost,
> Yet it shall be tempest-toss'd. (I.iii.24–25)

Though the Witches can conjure up a storm, it is the captain who steers the ship and who would be responsible for its loss. So it is with Macbeth, whose course through the dangerous seas of necessity must be charted by his own free will. Soliloquizing over each step he takes, he is fully aware of the moral implications of his own misdeeds. Since the social and natural order was conceived as so rigid a set of structures, it had to be the villain who would take the initiative of breaking through them. Both Iago and Edmund challenge man's superstitious habit of blaming the fates and affirm both his freedom and his responsibility, just as Cassius did in *Julius Caesar*:

> The fault, dear Brutus, is not in our stars,
> But in ourselves, that we are underlings.
> (I.ii.140–41)

The individualist who adopts such an attitude is willing to risk the immediate outcome. His challenge to the powers that be is bound to fail, and the mundane pattern is completed when the corpses are borne off the stage. The rest, the initiation into the last mystery, must perforce be silence. But with Richard II, whose posture of dying is so much nobler than the postures he has assumed in his heyday, we welcome the termination of our vicarious sufferings:

> Cry woe, destruction, ruin, and decay:
> The worst is death, and death will have his day.
> (III.ii.102–3)

The last act is death's day; and, both for the moribund and the survivors, the moment of leaving this world is the supreme occasion. Othello rises to a farewell gesture by reenacting one of his braver deeds. A patriarch like John of Gaunt may be visited on his deathbed with the gift of prophecy (*Richard II*, II.i.31 ff.). A thorough scoundrel, like the former Thane of Cawdor, may display redeeming qualities in the manner of his death:

> Nothing in his life
> Became him like the leaving it. He died
> As one that had been studied in his death. . . .
> (*Macbeth*, I.iv.7–9)

For a better man there would have been a fuller report, and the normal conclusion of a tragedy strikes the note of eulogy.

Tragedy is based on the stuff of history or legend—at any rate, on matters of public importance. Comedy is concerned with private matters, and derives from fiction rather than fact. Of course, the comic in Shakespeare is by no means limited to plays that have been labelled comedies. His unclassical habit of allowing clowns to associate with kings, which led to some of the most touching moments in *King Lear*, created the greatest clown of all as a boon companion for the playboy prince in *Henry IV*; and Falstaff is all the more of a creation for having had so little warrant as a historic personage. As a master of the revels, his office is highly unofficial; whereas the fool is a licensed purveyor of high spirits, the court or household jester in the plays where he appears. Given his motley garb, his cap and bells, and the bauble with which he pretends to converse, it is remarkable how many variations Shakespeare can impose on so conventionalized a role. Fools, like Feste, are obliged to be festive; but, like the equally well named Touchstone, they may also serve to authenticate or to discredit the intelligence and good will of the others. Such buffoons are shrewd professional entertainers.

> This fellow is wise enough to play the fool,
> And to do that well craves a kind of wit,

so Viola comments in *Twelfth Night* (III.i.60–61). Yet the nameless Fool of *King Lear* is a natural, a half-witted mascot, a simpleton inspired with the intuitive wisdom of nature. The fool's stock joke is to engage another character in a dialectical exchange which demonstrates that the other, though he wears no coxcomb, is no less given to folly. The classic retort is some version of *tu quoque* (you too, you're another). That demonstration comprises the gambit of Feste, when his syllogisms prove that Olivia is a greater fool than he (I.iv.66–72). He is incidentally doing his duty by chasing gloom, by persuading his mistress not to mourn. In *Hamlet* the fool is conspicuously dead; he is represented by the skull of Yorick, who was the King's jester some twenty-three years before. Though the unspoken catchword is still *tu quoque*, its exuberant cry has darkly altered into *memento mori*: you too will come to this one day.

It is not for nothing that the word *play* has the double meaning of drama and game. Comedy reverts to the playful origins of the theatre by celebrating a festival of some sort. Two of Shakespeare's titles commemorate such seasonal occasions: *A Midsummer Night's Dream* and *Twelfth Night, or What You Will*. Twelfth Night (the Feast of the Epiphany) was the high season for the presentation of plays at court, while the subtitle expresses the same desire to please the public that is advertised in the title of *As You*

Like It. In that play (IV.i) the disguised Rosalind encourages Orlando by inviting him to rehearse his suit: "Come, woo me, woo me; for now I am in a holiday humor and like enough to consent." It is this holiday humor that sets the mood and pace for Shakespearean comedy. When Orlando's protestations wax too warm, Rosalind cools them by comparing him with a clutch of unhappy lovers out of mythology, concluding with an astringent generalization: "Men have died from time to time, and worms have eaten them, but not for love." Where a tragic situation seems absolutely unique, a comic one keeps reminding us of others, referring us back from the individual to the standards and usages of society. Comedy gains its effects through the intellectual detachment of the spectator, tragedy through his emotional involvement. Empathizing with Romeo and Juliet, we may well agree with the Prince that there never was a story of more woe. Looking down with Berowne from his hiding-place aloft, we can take a detached overview of his fellow suitors as, one by one, they go through parallel speeches and motions (and of him too, shortly, when he reveals identical frailties):

> Like a demigod here sit I in the sky,
> And wretched fools' secrets heedfully o'er-eye.
> (*Love's Labor's Lost*, IV.iii.77–78)

The heroes and heroines of *Love's Labor's Lost*, having forgathered "to parley, to court, and dance" (V.ii.122), are fairly typical in their behavior. Dancing is a stylization of courtship; and, even when they are not paired off in a galliard or a coranto, the movement of the plot is a choreography. Inevitably, its resolution is marriage; in technical terms, "the catastrophe is a nuptial." Yet the happy ending of this particular play must be grimly postponed, while *The Taming of the Shrew* and *All's Well That Ends Well* are largely devoted to post-marital problems. Sooner or later Jack is bound to get Jill; but if the course of true love ran too smoothly there would be no drama. The obstacles placed in its way take the form of "errors" or "supposes," crisscrosses or mistaken identities, tangled and disentangled either by accident or by mischief, usually by an engaging combination of both. Comedy inclines toward the farcical, to the extent that it is propelled by manipulations of this kind. Puck's love-potion makes a mockery out of the convention of love at first sight. But there can be no doubt that Dan Cupid holds sway over the motivation of the comedies, even more than Machiavelli does with the histories and tragedies. Hence the heroines offer a clinching illustration for Meredith's theory of the comic spirit, whose prerequisite is the civilizing presence of womanhood. Shakespeare's women are not content to be mere cynosures; they are the pursuers of the men, as Bernard Shaw pointed out in a characteristic overstatement. The battle of the sexes becomes a banter of wits. It is a tennis game between Berowne and Rosaline, "a set of wit well played" (V.ii.29). Definitively, it is the "merry war" between Beatrice and Benedick in *Much Ado.*

Falstaff surpasses other comic figures because, in his own analysis, he is both witty in himself and the cause that wit is in other men (*2 Henry IV*, I.ii.9–10). He is not only a laughingstock but a laugher, who can enjoy the laugh on himself and turn it against the scoffers. Ben Jonson peopled his stage with laughingstocks, who thereupon became the obvious targets for his own sardonic wit. Shakespeare greeted the Jonsonian Comedy of Humors through Corporal Nym in *Henry V* and his catchphrase, "That's the humor of it." But Shakespeare's *dramatis personae* are characteristically the laughers, the wits who can poke fun and bandy it back when it is directed against them. Jonson's setting is that of New Comedy, the realistic middle-class milieu of shops and city streets. Shakespeare solves his characters' dilemmas by wafting them away from town or court into the romantic woods—another part of some forest or the enchanted island of *The Tempest*. Yet he was not unaffected by the new tendency toward satire that was in the air at the turn of the century. It invaded his artistic province with the War of the Theatres, the controversy to which Rosencrantz alludes and which has sent the Players abroad to Elsinore (*Hamlet*, II.ii.329 ff.). Hamlet himself is, among innumerable other things, a malcontent or—as Shakespeare would put it—a humorous man, like Jaques and so many of Jonson's spokesmen. The "late innovation" may have intensified the satiric thrust and the disillusioned tone of Shakespeare's so-called problem plays or bitter comedies: the mock-heroic and mock-romantic ironies of *Troilus and Cressida*, the fleshly revulsions and repressive countermeasures of *Measure for Measure*.

But even Shakespeare's sunniest comedies have some shadow hanging over them; the cakes and ale of Illyria are consumed in a house of mourning; and if the heroine does not die in *Much Ado about Nothing*, that is not the hero's fault. It seems a natural development, after Shakespeare's major tragedies, that his latest work should mark a reversion to comedy with a note of thoughtful speculation and imaginative surprise. We classify these final plays under the subspecies of Shakespearean romance, not only because their plots are traceable to continental fictions and treat of love like most of the other comedies, but because they exude a sense of strangeness; they reflect the exploratory impulse of their day in sea voyages and fabulous adventures; they invite

> a wild dedication of yourselves
> To unpath'd waters, undream'd shores.
> (*The Winter's Tale*, IV.iv.566–67)

The freshness of the experience is conveyed through the innocent eyes of the heroines, and indeed by their very names: Marina (daughter of the sea) in *Pericles*, Perdita (lost child) in *The Winter's Tale*, and Miranda (wonder) in *The Tempest*. The romances might also be classed as tragicomedies (*Cymbeline* is actually printed with the tragedies in the Folio). A tragicomedy, as distinguished from a tragedy with comic episodes, is more like a melodrama; it has its serious entanglements and its threatened deaths, particularly in its opening phase; but calamities are averted by happy endings, after stretching the long arm of coincidence. John Fletcher, presumably Shakespeare's junior collaborator in *The Two Noble Kinsmen* and his heir presumptive as chief playwright for the King's Men, won his facile success in this vein. There are signs in the romances—their increasing use of music, dance, and the spectacular devices of Stuart masques—that the drama was drawing closer to the private theatre and its courtly audience. Structurally, in registering the passage of time, the succession of generations, the recapitulation of the past, they tend toward narrative and verge upon the novelistic. Thematically much preoccupied with reconciliation, exile and return, mock-death and revival, they abound in recognition scenes. If the harvest masque in *The Tempest* is autumnal, *The Winter's Tale* is redeemed by a sheep-shearing festival in the spring. Shakespeare's playwriting career was rounded out in the mellow ripeness of craft and thought.

VIII. THE CONTINUING IMPACT

Like most tragedies, Shakespeare's are named for their heroes (when the major theme is love, the heroine is accorded a double billing). In the histories, too, the title centres on the name of the protagonist (or, at all events, the reigning monarch). Comedies, on the other hand, are titled with a proverbial expression or a generalizing phrase (*Troilus and Cressida* and *Cymbeline* are polymorphous in this respect, as in others). Comedy thus follows its traditional function of subordinating individuals to a social pattern, whereas they are dominant in tragedy. Yet that comic individualist, Falstaff, makes so large a place for himself that he plays hob with the historical values of *2 Henry IV*. From the lifetime of Shakespeare, it was recognized that the breadth and depth of his appeal were based upon his prolific capacities for the discernment and the depiction of character. His characterization was so dynamic that, by the later years of the eighteenth century, it was looked upon—almost religiously—as an act of creation. His nineteenth-century critics, whose approach was moralistic and psychological rather than theatrical, concentrated on his characters to the virtual exclusion of everything else, treating them as if they were actual people and speculating on what they did offstage. That process of introspective and rationalistic scrutiny reached its high point with the influential study of A. C. Bradley, *Shakespearean Tragedy*, published in the earliest years of the present century. More recently, a fuller understanding of Shakespeare's background and medium has prompted the ironic query of L. C. Knights's challenging pamphlet, *How Many Children Had Lady Macbeth?*

Character remains the central factor in our apprehension of Shakespeare. However, we have come to regard his characters less as independent personalities than as actors' roles, less as old friends than as second selves. The Latin plural noun used by his editors in listing them, *personae*, which is the source of our word "persons," signified masks. This was derived, in turn, from the verb *personare*, meaning "to impersonate"; originally it had meant "to sound through," with reference to the mouthpiece that amplified the actor's voice within the classical mask. A theatre of masks, such as the Commedia dell'Arte, tends to stylize personality and to depend on recurrent types. Shakespeare, in his versatility, uses this un-Shakespearean method on rare occasions, notably in the underplot of *Love's Labor's Lost*. Don Armado and Holofernes are even designated by the generic names of Braggart and Pedant in the speech-prefixes of the quarto text. When they join the low comedians in the rustic pageant of the Nine Worthies, they are treated like Ben Jonson's laughingstocks and hooted off the stage. But few of Shakespeare's comic figures are such humorless butts or one-track minds. When the laughing courtiers make cruel fun of the play within the play in *A Midsummer Night's Dream*, Theseus—who has just uttered his eloquent speech on the power of imagination—offers a defense of amateur actors which is essentially a plea to all spectators: "The best in this kind are but shadows; and the worst are no worse, if imagination amend them" (V.i.211–12).

In the Jonsonian world, human nature is masked by caricatures which, through their emphasis on typical traits, exhibit *Every Man in His Humor*. In the Shakespearean world every man is individualized, compounded of many humors, richly endowed with unsuspected qualities which are unmasked by the intervention of circumstance. Prince Hal, who has been masquerading as a prodigal son, approaches his exposure of Falstaff's cowardice with this high-spirited affirmation:

> I am now of all humors that have show'd themselves
> humors since the old days of goodman Adam to the
> pupil age of this present twelve a' clock at midnight.
> (*1 Henry IV*, II.iv.92–95)

He is conscious of flouting the laws of decorum, both dramatic and political, which require that princes shall act and talk like nobody else except princes. Yet the raffish company he consorts with is ennobling to Falstaff, just as the humbling of Lear proves to be the apotheosis of the Fool. Hal's irregular apprenticeship will make it possible for Henry V, moving incognito among his common soldiers on the eve of Agincourt, to tell them: "I think the King is but a man, as I am" (IV.i.101–2). Villains are humanized as much as heroes. The case that Cassius makes against Julius Caesar is one that is likely to touch our ideological sympathies. Richard III can blame his misshapen body, Edmund his illegitimacy, as a reason for taking so resentful and aggressive an attitude toward society. Iago likewise searches his mind for motives, though they remain so inscrutable that Coleridge has accused him of "a motiveless malignity." It has remained for our epoch to demonstrate that there can be such things as gratuitous crimes, that malignity can be a motive unto itself. Shylock is not, strictly speaking, a villain; he is a serio-comic intriguer who will justly be hoisted with his own petard. Yet his pound of flesh is a legalistic and ineffectual attempt to compensate for racial indignities which, like the prejudices against Othello, have provoked his grim revenge and do something to extenuate it.

In the mythology of popular allusion, where Romeo has become a synonym for any youthful lover and *Falstaffian* is an epithet for corpulent conviviality, Shylock has persisted more as a stereotype of the extortionate miser than an archetype of the eternal Jew. Benedick seems to have bequeathed his name—usually normalized into Benedict—to all men who have ever accepted the married condition, in spite of his own reluctance to abandon that militant bachelorhood which constitutes his characteristic stance. If an individual had not been characterized with such memorable complexity, in each of these instances, posterity might not have cared enough to simplify him into a stock type. Othello has become a byword for jealousy, popularly identified with the green-eyed monster itself. Yet everything we see and hear bears out his own description of himself as "one not easily jealous" (V.ii.345). His noble-minded lack of suspicion, as a senior officer placing trust in his subalterns and somewhat out of his element in a domestic situation, inclines him to believe Iago and therefore to feel that his love has been betrayed by Desdemona. His main fault, as Dostoevsky perceived, was to be overtrustful rather than jealous. Comparably, Hamlet has been taken to task—or, perhaps more often, sentimentalized—for an alleged inability to make up his mind. Actually, both the testimony about him and his ultimate heroism show that his hesitations are uncharacteristic. It is a measure of the baffling predicament in which he finds himself that

> the native hue of resolution
> Is sicklied o'er with the pale cast of thought.
> (III.i.84)

If Hamlet's personality seems peculiarly elusive, if his different interpreters can endow him with such widely differing characteristics, it is because his part is presented subjectively, much of it confided to us through soliloquies. His dilemmas, for the moment, seem our very own. Confronted with the suspense he faces, we cannot but share his doubts and deliberations. The example of Laertes, seeking revenge for the death of Polonius, enables Hamlet to take a more objective view of his own situation by recognizing that it is not unique:

> For by the image of my cause I see
> The portraiture of his. (V.ii.77–78)

Through some such chain of empathy, we can also put ourselves in Hamlet's place and learn to know ourselves from his experience. Our identification with Macbeth is not likely to be so complete; it would be quite impossible, if we thought of him from the outside as the hardened criminal he becomes. But no man is created a criminal type; even the hired murderers, when Macbeth compares them to dogs, respond with dignity: "We are men, my liege" (III.i.90). A man becomes whatever he decides; and, from the inside, while Macbeth takes one wrong turn after another, we share with him the anguish of every decision. Lady Macbeth seems monolithic by contrast, seemingly untouched by the moral compunctions that make his path to power so thorny. Yet her latent sense of guilt betrays itself by making her a somnambulist, condemned to recapitulate the episode of Duncan's murder over and over again. And though she gives the dire command that her husband executes, her suppressed compassion rises to the surface ambivalently at the doomed king's bedside:

> Had he not resembled
> My father as he slept, I had done't. (II.ii.12–13)

Though the absence of actresses may have limited the number and the length of feminine parts, it did not inhibit Shakespeare's gifts for feminine characterization. Witness the "infinite variety" of Cleopatra in her moods and changes, ranging from a spoiled child to an oriental despot, from a lustful gipsy to a goddess of love.

Just as these characters ask for our participation in their emotions, so they exist by virtue of Shakespeare's. Having presumably lived and felt for them all, he should not be linked with any single one of them to the exclusion of others. Yet there are certain personages who play the theatrical role of the *raisonneur*, who are spokesmen not so much for the playwright himself as for the scheme of values that frames the play. Such a personage is Menenius Agrippa, genial and tart by turns as he moderates between the plebeians and Coriolanus. Such are the royal uncles—John of Gaunt and, after his demise, Edmund of York—serving as an ethical weathervane for the rights and wrongs of Richard II. Through their comments we gain a longer and clearer perspective on the fortunes of the protagonists, who—as they recede into the middle distance—stay with us as patterns of behavior or cases of conscience, case histories or secular rituals. Their precepts have taken flight and become *geflügelte Worte*, winged words which have left the playhouse to enter into the contexts of our lives. Though we laugh at the old lady who enjoyed *Hamlet* because it contained so many familiar quotations, she was simply paying an artless tribute to Shakespeare's skill in providing human problems with usable formulations. This is reflected among the titles of modern writers, who very frequently take Shakespearean echoes as their points of departure. Aldous Huxley's satirical utopia, *Brave New World*, harks back to the last act of *The Tempest*:

> O brave new world
> That has such people in't! (V.i.183–84)

Huxley's echo is an irony; but so is Miranda's naive exclamation, which the experienced Prospero intercepts at once with the dry retort: "'Tis new to thee."

Macbeth's revulsive summary of life itself as

> a tale
> Told by an idiot, full of sound and fury,
> Signifying nothing, (V.v.26–28)

has its all too literal exemplification by William Faulkner, with Benjy's narrative in *The Sound and the Fury*. But though existence has become meaningless for Macbeth, it is replete with endless meaning for Shakespeare. In his *Pale Fire* Vladimir Nabokov goes out of his way not to quote from *Timon of Athens*; and the passage that he pointedly avoids,

> The moon's an arrant thief,
> And her pale fire she snatches from the sun,
> (IV.iii.437–38)

becomes a generalization about the literary indebtedness of lesser luminaries to Shakespeare. That he stands among our most valued possessions would go without saying, if it were not that, the more we reflect on the matter, the more we realize the large extent to which we are possessed by him.

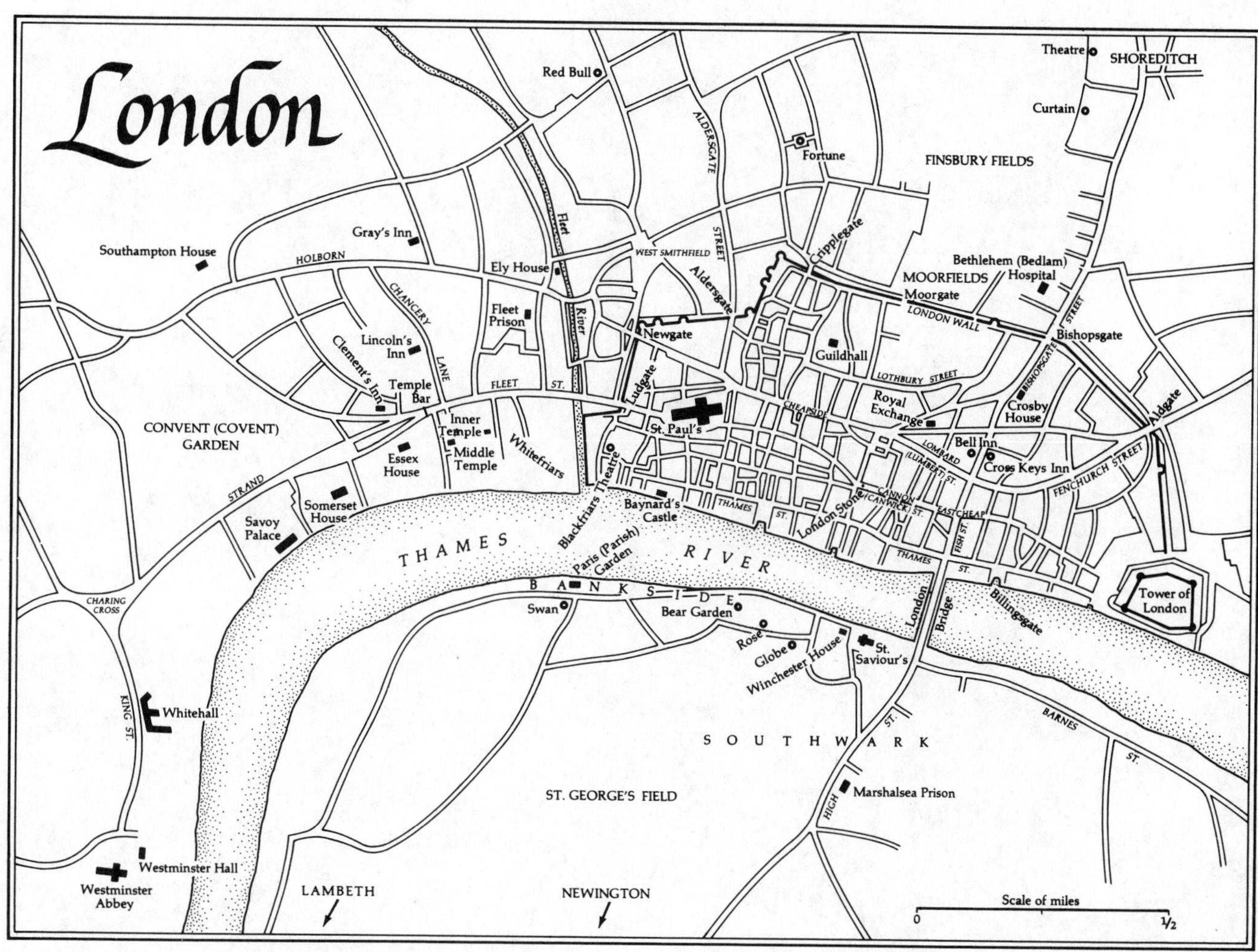

Twentieth-Century Shakespeare Criticism

Heather Dubrow

INTRODUCTION

Can this cockpit hold
The vasty fields of France? Or may we cram
Within this wooden O the very casques
That did affright the air at Agincourt?
O, pardon! since a crooked figure may
Attest in little place a million.

Henry V
(Prologue, 11–16)

If students currently studying Shakespeare had taken a course on his plays and poems in 1910 or 1950, what critical issues would they have encountered in their classrooms and in the introductions to their editions?[1] The scholarship published on Shakespeare in each of those years suggests some answers. Among the articles appearing in 1910 were "The Revision of *King Lear*," "Anachronism in Shakespeare Criticism," and "Shakespeare's *Julius Caesar* in the Light of Some Other Versions." The many titles of 1950 include "Shakespeare's Imagery: The Diabolic Images in *Othello*," "The Poetry of the Storm in *King Lear*," and "Theme and Character in *Hamlet*." After another forty years, in 1990, Shakespeareans published essays on "Dramatic Form in Shakespeare and the Jacobeans," "Shakespeare as Fetish," and "Hearing Ophelia: Gender and Tragic Discourse in *Hamlet*." These titles represent significant shifts in critical preoccupations: Notice, for example, that language and style become more important in the 1950 essays and that gender and the fetishistic misappropriation of Shakespeare concern critics in 1990. Yet our specimen titles testify as well to continuities. An essay referring to "dramatic form," for instance, might have been written in 1910 or 1950 as well as in 1990, and Shakespeare's putative revision of *King Lear* was a contested issue in the closing years of the century as well as in the opening ones. These samples from the vast array of Shakespeare criticism also demonstrate the range of problems evoked by his plays—and hence the range of questions and perspectives that students can debate today.

Repetition-with-a-difference is one of Shakespeare's favorite structural devices (witness, among many other examples, the successive characters who self-consciously play the part of king in *1 Henry IV*, including the king himself); repetition-with-a-difference also aptly describes many shifts in the topics that engage Shakespeareans. Elmer Edgar Stoll asserted in 1910 that the solution to anachronistic readings is closer attention to Shakespeare's culture, and arguments about the significance of history were also to characterize significant critical movements in the final decades of the century; yet Stoll would no doubt have taken issue with many later critics' presuppositions about Elizabethan history and the methodology for studying it. R. H. Cunnington maintained in 1910 that Shakespeare made significant changes in *King Lear,* a contention that was to be the cornerstone of certain theories about textual editing and its critical consequences towards the end of the twentieth century; yet different assumptions

[1]Many people have contributed to this essay by answering queries and reading sections of the manuscript; in particular, I thank G. Blakemore Evans (Harvard University, retired), Richard Helgerson (University of California–Santa Barbara), Clark Hulse (University of Illinois–Chicago), Richard Knowles (University of Wisconsin–Madison), Jacques Lezra (University of Wisconsin–Madison), David Loewenstein (University of Wisconsin –Madison), Phyllis Rackin (University of Pennsylvania), Donald Rowe (University of Wisconsin–Madison), J. J. M. Tobin (University of Massachusetts–Boston), and Susanne Wofford (University of Wisconsin–Madison). I am also grateful to the following Houghton Mifflin readers for their useful suggestions: Maurice Hunt (Baylor University, Texas), Grace Ioppolo (The Catholic University of America, Washington, D.C.), Lowell Johnson (Saint Olaf College, Minnesota), Ritchie Kendall (University of North Carolina at Chapel Hill), and Deborah Montouri (University of Missouri–Columbia). In addition, I would like to thank my research assistants, Amelia Nearing and Braden Hosch.

about the workings of Shakespeare's text inform debates in each of these periods. As these instances remind us, the changes in how Shakespeare is read provide a convenient microcosm of both recurrent patterns and new directions in literary criticism; so in studying Shakespeare criticism, one can investigate how and why the study of literature itself has developed.

The vastness of my topic, twentieth-century Shakespeare criticism, mandates selectivity.[2] This essay will focus largely on critical inquiry rather than scholarly research, though I refer briefly to the latter enterprise when it is particularly germane to critical developments. Since performance criticism is included in the essay on stage history and textual problems are discussed both in the Textual Introduction and in the "Note on the Text" appended to each of the plays and poems, I mention those highly significant fields only in passing. In order to avoid a mere list of names, this survey concentrates on representative figures, especially when examining Shakespeare criticism before 1970; inevitably, yet regrettably, some important Shakespeareans are omitted as a consequence of this decision, but those I do select may serve to "Attest in little place a million."

Having opened *Henry V* by announcing his attempt to encompass English history within the confines of a theatre, Shakespeare concludes the play with a choric epilogue crystallizing some of the pessimistic undertones sounded in his prologue. Telling the story of Henry V and his fellow warriors, he declares, has involved "Mangling by starts [intermittently, or with sudden movements] the full course of their glory" (Epilogue, 4). The best way to avoid mangling the glories and the limitations of twentieth-century Shakespeare criticism is to examine the challenges of telling this particular narrative. For Shakespeare criticism is vast enough to demand a selective and schematic overview—and yet complex enough to destabilize any such overview.

To begin with, critics often resist being crammed into the categories mandated by a survey. Widely and rightly identified with the study of character, A. C. Bradley nonetheless emphasizes the significance of theatrical production; distinguished (in both senses of the word) by his interest in stagecraft, Harley Granville-Barker announces the centrality of character. The newer critical methods of the final decades of the century are often seen as rejecting the formal concerns of many earlier critics, but a number of feminist analyses pivot on the connections between gender and genre. This complexity is one of the many reasons why it is dangerous merely to see Shakespeare studies, or any other field, as a collection of *-isms*. Labels like New Criticism, structuralism, feminism, and new historicism facilitate useful preliminary sketches of critical movements, but they do not represent clear-cut and definitive categories.

Similarly, whereas my division between the types of criticism written before and those written after 1970 serves important rhetorical functions, it must be interpreted with care. Most literary critics rightly agree that important changes in their field occurred during the final three decades of the century, and a further advantage of this division is that it conveniently corresponds to the first publication of *The Riverside Shakespeare* in 1974, thus permitting the third and fifth sections of this essay to extend the analyses in the original introductions to the individual plays contained in that edition. Yet criticism resists chronological as well as methodological pigeonholing. Some of the approaches associated with the end of the century had important antecedents much earlier. Furthermore, as hinted by the list of titles with which this section opened, traditional approaches are still alive and well in some quarters at the end of the century. Nor should we view either of the two periods in question as monolithic, a strategy the primary advantage of which is to facilitate the dismissal of critics of whom one disapproves. Some of the most distinguished Shakespeareans writing during the first seventy years of the century were severely attacked during their lifetimes; A. C. Bradley, for example, had many adherents and admirers, but his work hardly produced the kind of critical consensus posited by those who generalize about the past in order to reject it. Similarly, the tensions and disagreements between new historicist and feminist Shakespeareans, as well as the changes within each of those movements, call into question the pejorative commentaries on contemporary criticism that amalgamate varied methodologies and their equally diverse practitioners.

Indeed, any historical demarcation of Shakespeare criticism becomes dangerous when it tempts us to generalize dismissively about one camp or the other. In acknowledging the changes in criticism in the final thirty or so years of the twentieth century, some Shakespeareans gloss them as a tragic fall into murky French rivers of theory; others read the same divide as a comedic replacement of a weak and rigid old guard by a more vital newer generation. But whereas this essay acknowledges some pivotal differences between much of the criticism written before and that written after 1970, it challenges both of those conflicting evaluations of the changes. As I have observed, sweeping indictments of either section of the century too often neglect important distinctions in quality and aims among practitioners of a particular critical methodology. In any event, such judgments are not the purpose of this particular essay: My primary agenda is neither to praise nor to bury the authors and movements surveyed below. Writers in a range of disciplines have trenchantly challenged the possibility of wholly disinterested criticism, but whether or not one subscribes to that position, some critical texts are more disinterested than others, and I aim here for as balanced an overview as possible.

[2]Throughout this essay I am indebted to a large number of book-length studies of Shakespeare criticism; readers desiring more detailed examinations of twentieth-century Shakespeare criticism should consult the studies of it included under General Criticism in the Selected Bibliography, a listing that also provides bibliographical information about other critical texts more briefly cited in this essay.

A. C. Bradley and the Study of Character and Plot

Acute in his insights, graceful in his style, and tenacious in his pursuit of problematical issues, A. C. Bradley has been one of the most influential Shakespeare critics of this century. His analyses appear in two collections, both based on lectures he delivered at Oxford, where he held the Chair of Poetry: *Shakespearean Tragedy: Lectures on Hamlet, Othello, King Lear, Macbeth* (1904; rev. ed. 1905) and *Oxford Lectures on Poetry* (1909). Central to Bradley's work in both volumes is his emphasis on character. He stresses, however, that drama concerns not merely character as such but rather its relationship to the dramatic plot: "The centre of the tragedy . . . may be said with equal truth to lie in action issuing from character, or in character issuing in action" (*Shakespearean Tragedy*, p. 12).[3] The events of the play, in other words, are not impelled primarily by fate or chance, though Bradley acknowledges that those forces do play some role; rather, they follow logically from the nature of the protagonist. Shakespearean tragedy, Bradley observes later in the book, often involves external conflicts such as the feud in *Romeo and Juliet*, but even more important are conflicts within its tragic heroes, who typically suffer from "a fatal tendency to identify the whole being with one interest, object, passion, or habit of mind" (p. 20).

Guided by such assumptions, Bradley proceeds to examine the protagonists in the four tragedies on which he concentrates, emphasizing, for example, the nobility and trustfulness of Othello and declaring that Hamlet suffers not from the innate inability to act that some previous critics had attributed to him but rather from emotional disorders sparked by his mother's behavior. In developing these arguments, Bradley directs his attention to the aspects of character that are not specific to a given time or place, a significant contrast with the interest in history that characterizes a number of other Shakespeareans throughout the twentieth century.

Bradley's essays encompass authoritative discussions of a range of subjects besides character. He analyzes the tragic plot at length, emphasizing its culmination not merely in suffering and loss but also in reconciliation and even exultation. The issue of reconciliation was to generate lively disputes throughout the century, with critics arguing, for example, about whether *King Lear* terminates in utter despair or in some sort of rebirth. Moreover, in studying the protagonists of Shakespeare's tragedies, Bradley attempts to adjudicate a number of specific interpretive problems and cruxes; thus he marshals evidence about Hamlet's and Macbeth's ages and analyzes Hamlet's relationship to Ophelia.

Bradley is sometimes described as the culmination of nineteenth-century Shakespeare studies, but that designation may risk underestimating both the range of other influences that he orchestrates and his potential contributions to twentieth-century criticism. His theories of tragedy are evidently indebted to the Greek philosopher and rhetorician Aristotle. The study of character was central to nineteenth-century criticism, and in the genealogy of Bradley's approach to that subject one can discern in particular the English and German Romantic writers who preceded him, notably Samuel Taylor Coleridge and August Wilhelm von Schlegel. Also influential is the work of Maurice Morgann, the eighteenth-century writer who, like Bradley, tends to analyze dramatic personages as though they were real people enjoying a life outside the text. (Morgann's writing may be readily consulted in a modern edition, *Shakespearian Criticism*, edited by Daniel A. Fineman [1972]). Bradley had studied philosophy early in his life, and *Oxford Lectures on Poetry* includes an essay on Georg Wilhelm Friedrich Hegel, the nineteenth-century German philosopher whose theories of tragedy, notably his emphasis on reconciliation, lie behind some of Bradley's judgments.

A full roll call of the twentieth-century critics who write on character, often explicitly or implicitly inspired by Bradley's work, would be no less lengthy—and no less tedious—than the lists of warriors in classical epic. Again, a few specimens must suffice. Some critics have redirected the study of character by focusing on the literary and cultural backgrounds shaping particular dramatic personages. Witness, for example, Bernard Spivack's *Shakespeare and the Allegory of Evil: The History of a Metaphor in Relation to His Major Villains* (1958), which anatomizes Iago primarily by charting his antecedents in the Vice figures of medieval and early Renaissance drama. Yet others, as we will see shortly, have redefined character study by applying psychoanalytic methods. Moreover, like Bradley many twentieth-century critics have studied the structure of Shakespeare's plots, tracing questions such as the relationship among narrative lines and the workings of mirror scenes. Plotting is among the many recurrent concerns of one of the deans of Shakespeare criticism, Maynard Mack, though his approach is too eclectic to be categorized in terms of any single issue; in "*King Lear*" *in Our Time* (1965), for example, he considers plot, generic conventions, theatre history, imagery, and theme.

Despite—and because of—its impact on so many twentieth-century critics, Bradley's work was regularly attacked both by Shakespeareans writing shortly after he did and by their counterparts later in the century. Some critics have challenged his readings of particular plays and personages, notably his arguments about the nobility of Othello. Bradley's emphasis on character has also proved highly controversial. According to some of his critics, it tempts him to devote too little attention to other important aspects of the plays, such as language and stagecraft, and his focus on the aspects of character that are not specific to a given period or country prevents him from analyzing the historical and cultural issues that concern so many critics in the final decades of the twentieth century.

[3]Throughout this essay, all citations are to the latest edition identified in my text.

Bradley's critics also complain that he, like Morgann, reads Shakespeare's personages as though they had some reality outside the text; his mode of criticism was to be attacked in a witty essay by L. C. Knights entitled, "How Many Children Had Lady Macbeth?" (reprinted in Knights's *"Hamlet" and Other Shakespearean Essays* [1979]). Bradley surely opens himself to such accusations in many passages, notably his discussion of what Desdemona might have been like had she not been killed. On the other hand, *pace* Knights, in one of the several lengthy notes in *Shakespearean Tragedy*, Bradley in fact observes that, whereas Macbeth's desire for an heir is significant, we neither can know nor should care how many children he had. This declaration crystallizes differing assumptions about character and indeed representation in general: Should dramatic personages be read as rhetorical constructs confined to the text or as mimetic representations of imagined persons?

However one adjudicates the debates about Bradley's approach, it is clear that by precept and example he helped to establish premises that throughout the twentieth century have been enthusiastically embraced by some Shakespeare critics and as intensely scorned by others: Interpretations of the tragedies should focus primarily on their protagonists, rather than on characters such as Desdemona and Iago or on cultural issues, and such analyses may downplay specificities of time and place. In developing their own interpretations of Shakespearean drama, contemporary students still face the challenge of either espousing or rejecting these assumptions.

Harley Granville-Barker and the Analysis of Stagecraft

Vast and invaluable, the scholarly enterprise of unearthing and editing records of Elizabethan theatre has extended throughout the twentieth century. Although my overview of Shakespeare studies primarily addresses criticism, specimen instances of that scholarly undertaking should be noted, partly because they facilitated, indeed enabled, critical analyses of Shakespeare's theatre. For example, W. W. Greg edited *Henslowe's Diary* (1904–1908), the records of a theatre owner-manager who worked closely with Shakespeare and other playwrights; this intriguing document might well interest students in Shakespeare courses as well as scholars, for it is our principal source for information about payments to dramatists, collaboration between writers, props, receipts for productions, and so on. Other records from the Elizabethan and earlier stages have been compiled and analyzed by a range of Shakespeareans, including E. K. Chambers, Alfred Harbage, Richard Hosley, Samuel Schoenbaum, and Glynne Wickham.

Building on documents like these, throughout the twentieth century many Shakespeareans have scrutinized the conditions of the Elizabethan theatre and their impact on critical interpretation. Shakespeare the playwright, such studies remind us, was also Shakespeare the actor and "sharer" (the latter role involved being one of the principal members of an acting company and sharing its profits rather than receiving a wage): His knowledge of theatrical conditions was extensive and immediate. Some critics have analyzed the physical structure of the theatre; others have debated the composition of the audience; and yet others have attempted to reconstruct Elizabethan acting practices, debating in particular whether the mode was naturalistic, artificially formal, or some combination of or transition between those modes. The work of Alfred Harbage demonstrates the connections between such issues and critical interpretation. In *Shakespeare's Audience* (1941), for example, he maintains that the group attending plays was broad in its social composition, including a large number of shopkeepers and craftsmen but also encompassing working men and apprentices; such contentions provoked lively debate and disagreement later in the century, with Ann Jennalie Cook's *Privileged Playgoers of Shakespeare's London, 1576–1642* (1985) asserting that Shakespeare's audience included more members of social elites and fewer poor Londoners than Harbage had claimed. Other critics, including David Bevington, Muriel C. Bradbrook, John Russell Brown, Andrew Gurr, and J. L. Styan, have variously approached Shakespeare's stagecraft by tracing early modern theatrical conditions, by analyzing theatrical conventions, or by studying performances. (The essay on stage history in this volume discusses performance criticism.) Issues like these continued to spark lively debate in the final decades of the twentieth century, with the excavations of the Globe and Rose Theatres intensifying interest in stage conditions.

Probably the most influential student of Shakespeare's stagecraft, however, is Harley Granville-Barker. He was himself a playwright, director, and actor, whose wide theatrical experience included, for example, directing the distinguished British actor John Gielgud in a renowned production of *King Lear* at the Old Vic (1940). His Shakespeare criticism, some of which was originally written for an edition, was published in six volumes under the title *Prefaces to Shakespeare* (1927–1974; the sixth volume appears in the United States as *More Prefaces to Shakespeare* [1974]). He also comments extensively on Shakespeare and other playwrights in *On Dramatic Method* (1931), based on his Clark Lectures.

Granville-Barker's criticism manifests the preoccupation with character that was so common in the first part of the twentieth century. Unlike Bradley and many other students of character, however, he focuses on performance; for example, in his lengthy discussions of Shakespeare's language, he argues that the playwright conceived of verse primarily as speech, and he insists that the process of creating a play involves a collaboration between the actors and the playwright. Explicitly addressing directors as well as readers, Granville-Barker provides practical advice about issues such as when intermissions should occur and what costumes are appropriate for particular plays; in the case of *Lear*, for example, he suggests we should heed the text's emphasis on the barbarism of Lear's court. As Arthur M. Eastman observes when analyzing Granville-Barker in a useful survey entitled *A Short History of Shakespearean Criticism* (1968), "We see him in shirt-sleeves, as it were, vigorously and passionately communing with his company" (p. 324).

Granville-Barker also devotes considerable space to Elizabethan stage conditions and practices, such as the absence of women on the stage. Like many other critics writing in the first part of the twentieth century, he assumes that Shakespeare skillfully suppressed many of the problems potentially associated with casting boys in female parts; for example, he notes, as many other critics before him had done, that characters who are romantically involved with each other are relatively seldom shown on stage together in the absence of other personages. A number of Shakespeareans working in the last two decades of the century, however, were to interpret cross-dressing as a destabilization of gender categories and an introduction of homoerotic possibilities.

Granville-Barker frequently laments the probability that the differences between Elizabethan and modern theatrical conditions will distort productions. For example, he asserts that the final act of *Julius Caesar*, though skillfully constructed in terms of Elizabethan stagecraft, is likely to prove problematical on the contemporary stage. Given the inevitable differences in such conditions, Granville-Barker repeatedly warns directors of the dangers of further deviations from Elizabethan practices.

One might well claim that his preoccupation with the stage sometimes blinds Granville-Barker to complexities of the text. Witness, for example, his assertion that the Fool in *King Lear* is of relatively minor importance and provides a restoratively lightened mood. Yet his insistence as both critic and director on the significance of Elizabethan theatrical conventions and practices was a major contribution to twentieth-century Shakespeare studies.

Hardin Craig, Theodore Spencer, and the History of Ideas

Many twentieth-century Shakespeareans have practiced what might loosely be termed "historical criticism." Some do so by analyzing stage history and dramatic conventions, as we have already observed; others buttress their interpretations with historical research about the political, social, and intellectual history of Elizabethan and Jacobean England. The latter enterprise engenders pressing methodological questions that are relevant to contemporary undergraduates and graduate students when they attempt to generalize about, say, Shakespeare's attitudes to kingship or to gender. On what documents and what sectors of the culture should one concentrate, and what are the consequences of these decisions? Are texts shaped by their culture, or are they themselves the shapers of the culture? And what assumptions—or biases—do critics bring to their analyses of such questions?

In the first seventy years of the century, many Shakespeareans practicing historical criticism concentrated on the history of ideas, exploring in particular conceptions of the state and of what critics from this period often term human nature, though that very concept was also to be interrogated later in the century. E. M. W. Tillyard's *Elizabethan World Picture* (1943) is sometimes cited as representative of this type of criticism. Doing so is polemically expeditious but intellectually meretricious. Although his work was respected in some quarters and proved very useful to a number of his contemporaries, even in his own day Tillyard was accused of oversimplifying intellectual and political history. His critics alleged then, as they do now, that *The Elizabethan World Picture* is too monochromatic and, similarly, that *Shakespeare's History Plays* (1944) errs in assuming that Shakespeare wholeheartedly subscribed to and supported the so-called Tudor myth (that is, the theory that the depredations wrought by unseating Richard II, a lawful king, were gloriously resolved by the Tudor dynasty). Citing Tillyard as typical of his generation of critics is a facile way of discrediting more subtle work.

A fairer specimen of such work is Hardin Craig's *The Enchanted Glass: The Elizabethan Mind in Literature* (1935), a study that has commanded the respect of many Shakespeareans. Exemplifying the thoroughness that he explicitly advocates, Craig adduces wide research in primary sources to investigate Elizabethan attitudes toward education, science, religion, politics, logic, rhetoric, and literature itself; he also generalizes about conceptions of human nature and the propensities of "the Elizabethan mind," both common approaches among critics of his generation. In the course of these analyses, he explores texts by Shakespeare and a range of other writers, including a number of playwrights.

The Enchanted Glass both exemplifies and endorses a type of historical criticism that has been practiced by many twentieth-century Shakespeareans—and intensely criticized by many others. "The writers of the Renaissance," Craig observes in describing the viewpoint of historical criticism, "expressed the opinions of their age as these opinions had been coloured and modified by them themselves as individuals" (p. 63). This is, many literary critics would assume, an unexceptionable, even obvious, statement. Some, however, portray artists as more independent of their age, variously asserting that they are concerned with universal verities or that they transcend the limitations of a given culture. And yet other critics, especially many of those writing in the last two decades of the century, deny authors the degree of autonomy and individuality that Craig grants them. In *The Enchanted Glass* Craig also asserts that historical criticism should avoid both praise and blame in studying an earlier age. Again, many critics subscribe to this principle; others argue that such judgments are a valuable part of criticism; and still others maintain that it is impossible to avoid interested judgments, though in critics like Craig they may masquerade as objectivity.

Shakespeare, according to Craig, is deeply influenced by the prevailing concepts of his age, though he adapts them rather than mechanically echoing them. In particular, he was primarily shaped by the optimistic strains of sixteenth-century culture rather than its darker side. Having declared that what matters most about literature is an author's opinions about life, Craig proceeds to celebrate Shakespeare's wisdom rather than his literary skill: "Shakespeare's greatness is primarily a greatness of thought . . . . The world . . . has believed in the significance of what he had to say about humanity" (p. 83).

Theodore Spencer's *Shakespeare and the Nature of Man*, which was first published in 1942 but appeared in a revised edition seven years later, offers another influential and representative specimen of intellectual history. Whereas Craig devotes much of his attention to types of learning, Spencer concentrates on Renaissance ideas concerning three spheres: the cosmos, the world of nature, and the state. The period witnessed two conflicting approaches to these realms, he argues: The more optimistic, rooted in a synthesis of classical thinkers like Aristotle and Plato and of Christianity, stressed the dignity and potentiality of human beings and the order of the universe; the more pessimistic, fuelled both by the Christian emphasis on man's limitations and more recent discoveries by Machiavelli, Copernicus, and Montaigne, attacked idealistic visions of human potentialities and of the world. Like Craig, Spencer posits a major break at the end of the sixteenth century, with a significant tilt towards pessimism. *Hamlet*, he maintains, pivots on the conflict between the optimistic and pessimistic views of human beings; Troilus's distress stems partly from the challenges to his Elizabethan sense of an ordered universe.

Some telling passages in Spencer's *Shakespeare and the Nature of Man* demonstrate both liabilities and strengths in the type of criticism he and Craig practice. Spencer's assertion that *Coriolanus* "lacks reverberations" (p. 178) because it devotes little attention to cosmology or external nature invites the question of whether he is privileging certain intellectual contexts over others and in doing so neglecting many types of reverberation. In concluding the book, Spencer relates Shakespeare's era to the time the book was written, finding in twentieth-century pessimism a culmination of its sixteenth- and seventeenth-century counterpart. His suggestion that Hitler is Machiavelli's heir—possibly the first of many frightening offspring from that genealogy—demonstrates that his criticism was colored by the events leading up to World War II and by that conflict itself. Hence the book invites us to ask in what ways any critic's reading of Shakespeare's culture is impelled by responses to her or his own culture and to consider the consequences of that response.

The work of both Craig and Spencer poses yet another question about critical approaches to Shakespeare, a question that once again is germane to contemporary students attempting to analyze cultural attitudes and beliefs. As we will see, much of the criticism written towards the end of the twentieth century eschews formulations like "the mind of Renaissance man" in favor of statements about cultural anxieties and tensions. But the methodological issues raised by recent generalizations about an entire culture are cognate to a query generated by the ways Craig and Spencer discuss Shakespeare's worldview. What are the advantages—and what are the risks—of generalizing about the mind or the culture of an age as opposed to focusing on differences among its members and subcultures?

Ernest Jones and Psychoanalytic Criticism

In the later decades of the twentieth century, the psychology departments of many universities have focused on fields like cognitive science and experimental psychology to the virtual exclusion of classical psychoanalysis, mentioning Freud dismissively when they mention him at all. Feminist courses often revile him as source, symptom, and symbol of patriarchal assumptions about women. In popular culture, Freud is typically known through reductive oversimplifications of his ideas ("all men want to sleep with their mothers"). Influenced by these developments, many students respond to traditional psychoanalytic interpretations with little interest and less respect. But whether or not one ultimately subscribes to psychoanalytic readings, they do call for informed and judicious responses rather than automatic rejection. Reading Freud himself, whose works are available in a thoroughly indexed standard edition that facilitates browsing, may well be the best antidote to oversimplifications of his ideas.

Reading Freud is also a useful introduction to the psychoanalytic Shakespeare criticism written during the first seventy years of the century. While studies composed during the final three decades are often inspired by psychoanalysts other than Freud, notably Jacques Lacan, he was certainly the primary influence on work in this field earlier in the century. Freud himself mentions Shakespeare frequently, citing characters and scenes as instances of the psychological dynamics he is tracing. Among his principal contributions to Shakespeare studies is his essay "The Theme of the Three Caskets," a title referring to one of the plot strands of *The Merchant of Venice*. Having noted parallels between the three caskets with which Portia confronts her suitors and Lear's attempt to measure the love of his three daughters, Freud maintains that both these choices really represent selections among women. He proceeds to suggest that the lead casket, as well as the role of Cordelia, in fact encodes the choice of death.

For much of the twentieth century, the most influential literary critic deploying psychoanalysis was not Freud but his disciple Ernest Jones, a distinguished psychoanalyst in his own right. When Freud traces the spread of psychoanalysis in *On the History of the Psycho-analytic Movement* (1914), he singles out Jones's contributions to the growth of the movement. In many of his essays, Jones demonstrates connections between his and other disciplines, arguing for affinities with anthropological inquiry and applying ideas from his own discipline to artistic renditions of the Madonna, to the interpretation of folkloric motifs like throwing rice at weddings, and so on. Similarly, in *Hamlet and Oedipus* (1949), a study that was to prove highly influential, he deploys the tools of Freudian analysis to address the vexed issue of why Hamlet delays killing Claudius. He also extends some ideas from that book in an essay, "The Death of Hamlet's Father," published in his *Essays in Applied Psycho-analysis* (1951).

Jones's deep and often uncritical debt to Freud is manifest in the genealogy of *Hamlet and Oedipus*. As Jones reports in his preface, a footnote by Freud inspired the work; Jones originally published some of the resulting ideas in essay form in 1910. The arguments in *Hamlet and Oedipus* are grounded in the theories of classical Freudian psychoanalysis, notably the abiding significance of infantile and childhood experiences, the male child's desire to kill his father to facilitate his union with his mother, and the return of repressed memories and desires. After a useful summary and critique of previous theories, Jones develops and expands Freud's suggestion that Claudius performs the very acts Hamlet desires and fears to stage himself—killing his father and having intercourse with his mother. When Claudius actually enacts Hamlet's wishes, the old, repressed Oedipal conflicts emerge again, leaving the prince with unbearable thoughts of incest and patricide.

The author of *Hamlet and Oedipus* extends this interpretation in several directions. In Hamlet's relation to Ophelia, Jones finds the child's tendency to divide the mother into the opposing figures of saint and whore. *Julius Caesar*, he argues, is closely connected to *Hamlet* in several ways, notably in how it stages relationships between fathers and sons. Primarily, however, Jones is concerned to read Shakespeare's own character through reading his texts. Unlike Bradley, Jones stresses the problems raised by approaching dramatic characters as though they were actual people; he argues, though, that one can profitably study what one of his chapter titles terms, "The Hamlet in Shakespeare." It is no accident, Jones maintains, that 1601, the date to which many scholars assign *Hamlet*, was also the year Shakespeare's own father died. That event may well have revived in Shakespeare the forbidden drives of his childhood, which, Jones argues, lie behind the play, as do the sexual tensions revealed in Shakespeare's sonnets.

Many critics have found substantial evidence for Jones's psychoanalytic interpretations in the text; witness, for example, Hamlet's preoccupation with his mother's sexuality and his idealization of his father, which can be read as a suppression of antagonism. The impact of Jones's psychoanalytic interpretation is evident as well in the famous movie version starring Sir Laurence Olivier (1948), which features shots of a bed at several points, notably when Hamlet confronts his mother in her chamber. At the same time, Jones's interpretation has provoked the reservations generated by many other kinds of psychoanalytic readings as well. Some Shakespeareans would argue that Jones's credo about the connections between Hamlet and his creator exemplifies the dangers in the psychoanalytic tendency to see writing as the expression of repressed neuroses. Others challenge the fundamental psychoanalytic premises behind Jones's analyses, such as his emphasis on repressed childhood experiences in general and the Oedipal struggle with the father in particular. And still others maintain that the prejudices about women inherent in classical Freudian theory discredit this and other versions of it.

Despite such reservations, throughout the twentieth century certain critics have adopted and adapted classical Freudian paradigms. Norman N. Holland opens *Psychoanalysis and Shakespeare* (1966) with an overview of the work of Freud and other practitioners of the field, then proceeds to summarize psychoanalytic interpretations of specific plays, supplementing them with his own readings. C. L. Barber has had a significant impact on Shakespeare criticism because of both his own writings and the work of the many psychoanalytically oriented Shakespeareans whom he trained and, as their prefaces attest, deeply influenced. Freudian ideas are threaded through several of Barber's essays and his best known book, *Shakespeare's Festive Comedy: A Study in Dramatic Form and its Relation to Social Custom* (1959); for example, he relates Shakespeare's wordplay to Freud's arguments about the displacements involved in wit.

G. Wilson Knight and the Analysis of Image and Theme

In contrast to—and often in explicit opposition to—the study of plot, character, and stagecraft, a number of important critics during the first half of the twentieth century focused on Shakespeare's style, examining issues like diction, meter, rhetoric, and imagery. Or, to put it another way, they read a Shakespeare play as what has been termed a "dramatic poem." Such concerns were, however, anticipated long before the twentieth century, reminding us again to qualify commonplaces about the development of critical methodologies. In particular, as early as 1794, Walter Whiter's *Specimen of a Commentary on Shakspeare* prefigured the stylistic perspective that was to be adopted by G. Wilson Knight and many other twentieth-century Shakespeareans. Whiter, influenced by the philosopher John Locke's theories about the association of ideas, traces recurrent words and images; he reveals, for example, connections between *suit* (in its senses of "dress" and "petition") and *weed* (which could also refer to clothing).

Published in 1935, Caroline F. E. Spurgeon's *Shakespeare's Imagery and What It Tells Us* provides statistical counts of patterns of imagery and asserts that such patterns reveal Shakespeare's temperament. By comparing the frequency of images in his plays with their usage by other dramatists and by the essayist Francis Bacon, she argues, for instance, that Shakespeare loved the countryside and outdoor sports, felt sympathetic towards animals, and was horrified by disease. Spurgeon also charts the prevalence of a range of images in Shakespeare's canon as a whole and compares their frequency in various plays. Although many Shakespeareans acknowledge her book as a pioneering study of imagery, the work of Wolfgang Clemen is widely considered more sound. Clemen's *Development of Shakespeare's Imagery*, though published in 1951, is an expanded version of a study that appeared in Germany in 1936, one of many testaments to the contributions of German Shakespeareans during the twentieth century. *The Development of Shakespeare's Imagery* differs from Spurgeon's study in its emphasis on the relationship of an image to its dramatic context. As his title would suggest, Clemen traces the maturation of Shakespeare's language, asserting that in the early comedies the images are typically inorganic and decorative, while later they assume dramatic functions, variously foreshadowing developments in the plot, signalling distinctive characteristics of the personages who use them, and representing a line of action in their own right. In *Othello*, for example, Iago's studied behavior is manifest in his predilection for similes over metaphors; his images are static and those of Othello dynamic.

When imagery is defined broadly to encompass figurative language, the Shakespeareans who have studied it in this century are legion. Sister Miriam Joseph's *Shakespeare's Use of the Arts of Language* (1947), M. M. Mahood's *Shakespeare's Wordplay* (1957), and Robert Bechtold Heilman's *This Great Stage: Image and Structure in "King Lear"* (1948) exemplify three significant approaches. Sister Miriam Joseph roots her work in the Greek and Roman theories of rhetoric in which Shakespeare, like other members of his culture, was so thoroughly trained; she catalogues his use of the principal rhetorical figures and of patterns of argumentation. Mahood's study focuses on the pun, glossing and analyzing key passages that use it and relating Shakespeare's wordplay to Renaissance attitudes toward language. In *This Great Stage*, Heilman, influenced by the New Critical practices that we will examine shortly, traces recurrent patterns like references to sight and to nature; he relates them to central themes, parting company with the readers who interpret the play more pessimistically in his insistence that its imagistic patterns suggest that people learn through suffering.

Although so many other Shakespeareans have examined imagery, G. Wilson Knight remains one of the most—if not the most—influential practitioner of this approach. A prolific writer, Knight is the author of seven books on Shakespeare's plays and sonnets; his best known work includes *The Wheel of Fire: Interpretations of Shakespearian Tragedy* (1930; rev. ed. 1949) and *The Imperial Theme: Further Interpretations of Shakespeare's Tragedies Including the Roman Plays* (1931; rev. ed. 1951).

The prefaces to the several editions of *The Wheel of Fire* and *The Imperial Theme* and their opening chapters, entitled respectively "On the Principles of Shakespeare Interpretation" and "On Imaginative Interpretation," aptly gloss the theories in which Knight's work is rooted. Not criticism but interpretation, he argues, should be our aim; according to his rather idiosyncratic definitions, the former objectifies the work and passes judgment on it, while the second enters into it imaginatively, avoiding evaluation. In his descriptions of the identification with the author involved in that imaginative process, one may find hints of the mysticism that becomes so much more evident in his later work: "The critic is, and should be, cool and urbane, seeing the poetry he discusses not with the eyes of a lover but as an object; whereas interpretation deliberately immerses itself in its theme and speaks less from the seats of judgement than from the creative centre" (*The Imperial Theme*, p. vi). According to Knight, interpretation should focus on images and symbols; it is through images, he asserts, that action occurs and themes are developed. In the term "theme" he encompasses both the traditional literary meaning of the term and its sense in musicology. Thus in writing about *Macbeth* he draws attention to the pervasiveness of fear and relates it to patterns of darkness permeated with light or color, including the redness of blood.

This approach to *Macbeth* exemplifies several other principles governing Knight's criticism. His readings emphasize the unity in plays, which is typically produced by a central pattern of images, themes, and symbols. Often that unity depends on the interplay of opposites; thus, for example, he finds in *Hamlet* a conflict between human life and negation and in *The Winter's Tale* an opposition between maturity and evil on the one hand and young love and resurrection on the other. Because of such patterns, Knight asserts, Shakespeare's plays generally have a single "atmospheric suggestion." He finds unity not only within individual plays but also in groups of them; hence, for instance, he identifies a "hate-theme" running through many Shakespearean dramas and maintains that music and storms are the central symbols throughout the canon, with the former representing harmony and the latter discord.

In outlining his critical approach, Knight defends an emphasis on the "spatial" rather than the "temporal." The former is associated with recurrent linguistic and thematic patterns, the latter with the linearity of plot. Hugh Grady argues in his study of Shakespeare criticism, *The Modernist Shakespeare* (1991), that Knight's preference for the spatial signals his participation in modernism, a complex literary and cultural movement characteristically associated with the rejection of history and concomitant espousal of spatiality. Whether or not one accepts this thought-provoking thesis, it reminds us to trace developments in Shakespeare studies to the larger culture, not just to changing practices within the academy.

Knight's work, whatever its roots, exemplifies some dangers inherent in the pursuit of images, themes, and symbols. The neat contrasts he identifies risk oversimplifying the plays, and, similarly, by reading characters as symbols, he sometimes ignores important complexities; thus his repeated suggestion that Shakespeare's kings represent the principle of order neglects both the dangerously unruly behavior of many of these monarchs and Shakespeare's interrogations of the nature of kingship. Such intellectual fogginess, Knight's detractors rightly assert, is echoed in and encouraged by his vague and emotive language. On the other hand, his contributions to twentieth-century Shakespeare criticism are extensive. In identifying patterns of themes and images, he celebrated the achievements of certain plays that some earlier critics had considered artistic failures, notably the late romances and *Antony and Cleopatra*, and hence directed more attention to them. His readings also illuminated the artistic structure of many other plays and thus provided a model for many other Shakespeareans, including the New Critics to whom we will now turn.

Cleanth Brooks and New Criticism

So popular was New Criticism during the 1950s and 1960s that English professors typically claim it virtually took over literary studies in the American academy. This is hyperbolic, like so many assertions variously proffered by the adherents and detractors of New Criticism: Other methodologies remained popular in some circles during those decades, and even at its peak New Criticism inspired attacks as well as professions of faith. In any event, however, the movement became so controversial after its heyday that when Cleanth Brooks, one of its principal proponents, lectured on it at the University of Wisconsin in 1991, he felt compelled to assert that it was "neither a noxious disease nor a conspiracy."

Like other literary movements, New Criticism can best be understood by identifying what it reacts against. Its founders aim to reject and replace several types of criticism common in Shakespeare studies and elsewhere earlier in the century: the study of ethical values and philosophical issues through literature, the tracing of literary history, and the political criticism that was especially popular in the 1930s. The genealogy of New Criticism also encompasses the modernist emphasis on art as an impersonal object, separate from its creators. Many early proponents were members of the movement known as Agrarianism, a conservative reaction against what were seen as the abuses of modern culture. The influence of science on New Criticism is more difficult to assess, with some New Critics overtly and intensely reacting against science and technology while others attempted to import some values from those fields into literary criticism. I. A. Richards, one of the progenitors of New Criticism, declares in the preface of *Principles of Literary Criticism* (1924; rev. ed. 1926): "A book is a machine to think with" (p. 1).

New Criticism, then, involves studying the literary text as a verbal and aesthetic object—not as a key to the author's biography or psychology; a source of intellectual, political, or stage history, or a repository of ethical values. More specifically, New Critics often posit fundamental differences between non-literary and literary language. The first is straightforward, the second characterized by denseness and richness. And hence the first can and should be read for its expository content, while the second is not a repository of messages, but rather an organic artistic achievement.

This emphasis on the text as an organism helps to explain the protocols with which New Critics characteristically approach it. Their method mandates close attention to nuances of language; the term "close reading" is sometimes used synonymously with New Criticism, though it does not invariably carry such connotations. In their intense scrutiny of the text, New Critics concentrate on qualities like tone, ambiguity, and paradox, thus manifesting their delight in verbal complexity and ingenuity. They also frequently probe the workings of metaphor. The tensions produced by paradox and cognate techniques are seen not as symptoms of unresolved or uncontrolled ambivalences in the writer or culture but rather as components of overall unity. Indeed, New Critics are generally not interested in the psychology of the writer, as was Ernest Jones, or in the lineaments of a culture, as were Hardin Craig and Theodore Spencer; adopting T. S. Eliot's credo about the impersonality of art, they assume that the attitudes expressed by the text are those of a fictive speaker, not a poet. To put it another way, New Criticism is sometimes seen as a version of formalism, the methodology that studies literature by looking at aesthetic or formal characteristics such as genre, structure, and meter; but while other types of formalist analysis often generalize about literature, New Critics characteristically look closely at particular texts.

A corollary of that interest in particular texts, according to many enemies of New Criticism, is a total neglect of the interplay between literature and its political and cultural environment. Gerald Graff, whose *Professing Literature: An Institutional History* (1987) provides a useful and often iconoclastic survey of literary criticism, insists that New Criticism did not totally reject moral, social, and historical concerns but rather looked at how such issues operate within texts. One might add that, whatever the principles of New Criticism might be in theory, in practice many of its adherents did integrate into their analyses dimensions that the movement is popularly supposed to ignore. Reuben Brower, for example, was one of the deans of American New Criticism—yet in *Hero and Saint: Shakespeare and the Graeco-Roman Heroic Tradition* (1971), his interest in the relationship between classical and English literature precludes his examining Shakespearean plays as isolated entities.

How did New Criticism affect Shakespeare studies? Its principles encouraged the study of non-dramatic poetry manifesting the complexities prized by members of the movement, so Donne and other metaphysical poets became especially popular, with dramatic literature and prose receiving somewhat less attention. But Shakespeare was by no means neglected, as our titles of articles dating from 1950 would suggest. Cleanth Brooks is among the leaders of the movement; he promulgated its principles and practiced its methods in *The Well Wrought Urn: Studies in the Structure of Poetry* (1947), among other books, and the anthologies he edited or coedited, such as *Understanding Poetry* (1938; rev. ed. 1976), profoundly influenced the teaching of literature.

Brooks's essay "The Naked Babe and the Cloak of Manliness," which is included in *The Well Wrought Urn*, not only exemplifies but also explicitly advocates the application of New Critical techniques to Shakespeare. Although he acknowledges distinctions between Shakespeare's language and Donne's, Brooks also identifies similarities that justify transferring to drama techniques that the New Critics had developed in studying Donne, especially their approach to metaphor. Brooks then turns to two problematical passages spoken by Macbeth: his rendition of pity for Duncan as "a naked new-born babe, / Striding the blast, or heaven's cherubin" (I.vii.21–22) and his description of "daggers / Unmannerly breech'd with gore" (II.iii.115–16) after the murder of Duncan. Acknowledging Caroline Spurgeon's identification of images of clothing in this play, Brooks extends and deepens her argument: He relates clothing to hypocrisy, masquerade, and the assumption of unearned titles. The babe, he proceeds to demonstrate, represents not only human sympathy but also the future that Macbeth, obsessed with establishing a dynasty, wants to control but cannot. These patterns of imagery and symbolism merge at the culmination of the play, when the peregrination of Birnan wood fuses previous references to planting and clothing and Macduff reveals that he was born through a Caesarean section.

This essay stages many principles of New Criticism. Brooks's argument is rooted in his close attention to knotty language. In uncovering connections among images, he demonstrates the organic unity celebrated by practitioners of his methodology. Many previous readers had considered the apparently contradictory description of the babe a lapse and the reference to the daggers an unlikely image inviting textual emendation. Brooks, in contrast, explicates these lines in ways that suggest that ostensible dissonances really constitute a subtle and meaningful pattern; thus, like many other New Critics, he celebrates the achievements of passages that had been variously ignored and condemned by their predecessors.

As this essay has already indicated, evaluating New Criticism judiciously is difficult because of the controversy surrounding the method. In the final decades of the twentieth century, it became a scapegoat for the errors, real or imputed, of many other types of earlier criticism, with attacks on it a common, even ritualistic move in the process of establishing a different critical stance. Certainly to the extent that New Criticism does neglect history, distinguished historical studies of Shakespeare written before, during, and after the decades in which it flourished demonstrate the perils of that omission. Similarly, reading a play as a dramatic poem risks erasing the important insights of students of stagecraft. It is telling that in comparing Donne and Shakespeare, Brooks directs his attention to similarities and differences in their language rather than to the consequences of writing lyric poetry as opposed to drama; New Critics have been accused, not without justice, of obscuring the distinction between the two modes by seeing plays as dramatic poems. The New Critical celebration of artistry discourages the salutary recognition of less successfully deployed language or dubious values in the text. Despite such limitations, the continuing influence of New Criticism is evident even in the final years of the twentieth century: Many students are still trained in its methods and assumptions, often without having them identified as such. And, whatever the faults of New Criticism, that influence is by no means inevitably malignant—or totally antithetical to the concerns of the very Shakespeareans who have so passionately attacked New Criticism. Readers can still profitably borrow some of the analytical techniques of New Criticism without subscribing to problematical tenets like the impersonality of the text or the timelessness of art; strategies for close reading can even support and enrich analyses of issues like gender and politics. The rigorous scrutiny of language practiced by New Critics at their best can breed not only intellectual excitement but also a recognition of complexities and contradictions sometimes overlooked by those who scan the plays less closely in search of evidence for broad generalizations.

Other Approaches

Even a brief survey of a few approaches not encompassed in the schema of this essay again demonstrates the variety and range of Shakespeare criticism written between 1900 and 1970—and again warns us against sweeping generalizations about this era. A. C. Bradley's anatomy of Shakespeare's tragic plots exemplifies the interest in genre and in plotting that has impelled many Shakespeareans throughout the century. A number of scholars have directed their energies to genres other than tragedy. Thus critics have debated the characteristics of the so-called problem plays and even which dramas should receive that label; important studies include William Witherle Lawrence's *Shakespeare's Problem Comedies* (1931; rev. ed. 1960) and Ernest Schanzer's *The Problem Plays of Shakespeare: A Study of "Julius Caesar," "Measure for Measure," "Antony and Cleopatra"* (1963). (The continuing impact of Bradley is manifest in Lawrence's dedication of his book to the author of *Shakespearean Tragedy*.) A volume referred to earlier, C. L. Barber's *Shakespeare's Festive Comedy*, develops what was to become a widely accepted description of the plays in question: Elizabethan holiday customs and rituals, which often involve a period of saturnalian release, lie behind the structure of several Shakespearean comedies and the treatment of the tavern world in *Henry IV.* As this argument would suggest, while Barber's study exemplifies psychological and genre criticism, even more apparent is his interest in anthropology—an influence manifest as well in a number of other studies that appeared during the first seventy years of the century.

The concern for genre is related to other approaches to literary conventions and traditions that also flourished before 1970. Elmer Edgar Stoll's *Shakespeare Studies: Historical and Comparative in Method* (1927) emphasizes character but, unlike Bradley, he suggests that we must relate dramatis personae to dramatic conventions more than to the so-called realities of human behavior. Madeleine Doran, a highly influential scholar, investigates such conventions in many of her works. For example, *Endeavors of Art: A Study of Form in Elizabethan Drama* (1954) relates drama to theories about art, anatomizes several dramatic genres, and studies the treatment of character and stage practice.

Analyzing Shakespeare's relationship to literary sources and analogues can be another rewarding avenue of interpretation. Geoffrey Bullough's *Narrative and Dramatic Sources of Shakespeare* (1957–75) is an eight-volume collection of and commentary on the sources; Kenneth Muir's *Sources of Shakespeare's Plays* (1977) enumerates and analyzes the principal antecedents to these texts. A number of important books, notably David Bevington's *From "Mankind" to Marlowe: Growth of Structure in the Popular Drama of Tudor England* (1962), examine specific literary precursors and influences; Harry Levin, one of the founders of comparatist studies in the United States, positions Shakespeare's work in relation to a wide range of English and Continental analogues in *The Question of Hamlet* (1959) and in the essays collected in *Shakespeare and the Revolution of the Times: Perspectives and Commentaries* (1976).

Some critics during the first seventy years of the century uncovered Christian allusions and symbolism in Shakespeare's plays, a project that continued in subsequent decades as well. In *Shakespearean Tragedy: Its Art and Its Christian Premises* (1969), Roy W. Battenhouse explores Christian references and attitudes in several plays and *The Rape of Lucrece.* Some Shakespeareans, however, have claimed that he exaggerates their influence, and in *Shakespeare and Christian Doctrine* (1963) Roland Mushat Frye asserts that Shakespeare is relatively uninterested in theological debates and that he subordinates his discussions of them to character and plot. The debate over reading *Measure for Measure* as a Christian allegory crystallizes many arguments about such approaches to Shakespeare.

If any further proof of the challenges of categorizing critics were needed, witness the career of Northrop Frye, the prolific Canadian critic who might justly be labelled a genre critic, an anthropological critic, a formalist, a structuralist (an approach described in the next section of this essay), and so on. *Anatomy of Criticism: Four Essays* (1957) lays out Frye's agenda for literary criticism: He is dedicated to classifying its forms and types, rather than celebrating its achievements or evaluating the relative merits of particular texts. Literary criticism, he maintains, should function like other sciences. Frye is also involved in uncovering the recurrent symbols that he terms archetypes, such as images of the apocalypse. As even this brief summary would suggest, Frye draws on a wide range of sources, including the Greek rhetorician Aristotle, the Russian formalists, the psychologist Carl Jung, Christianity, and anthropological studies of myth and criticism.

The range of writers on whom Frye has published is no less wide. He focuses specifically on Shakespeare, however, in several of his works, notably *A Natural Perspective: The Development of Shakespearean Comedy and Romance* (1965); in addition, several of his other books are studded with examples from Shakespeare. Frye's interest lies not in the close scrutiny of particular texts but rather in the comprehensive discovery and classification of recurrent generic, mythic, and Christian patterns. Thus in *Anatomy of Criticism* he subdivides the main genres and modes into types that enjoy a dynamic relationship with each other and with seasonal patterns; Shakespeare, Frye suggests, offers instances of domestic comedy in the multiple marriages he portrays, of ironic comedy in the rejection of Falstaff, and of the phase of comedy that moves towards romance in plays like *A Midsummer Night's Dream* or, more surprisingly, *The Two Gentlemen of Verona.* In *A Natural Perspective* he contrasts Jonson's predilection for realistic and ironic modes with the attraction to the incredible, the stylized, and the folkloric in Shakespeare. Hence, according to Frye, the romances that Shakespeare wrote at the end of his career are a culmination of elements present elsewhere in the canon. Indeed, not the least of Frye's many contributions to Shakespeare studies is his emphasis on the comedies and romances—a fact that reminds one how many Shakespeareans during the first seventy years of the twentieth century concentrated instead on the tragedies and thus impels students of Shakespeare and Shakespeare criticism to speculate about the many reasons certain critics, certain methodologies, and certain periods may favor particular plays and genres over others.

SHAKESPEARE CRITICISM 1970–

From ancient grudge break to new mutiny,
Where civil blood makes civil hands unclean.

Romeo and Juliet
(Prologue, 3–4)

Introduction

Although the 1970s witnessed significant departures in Shakespeare criticism, the field did not experience a total and instantaneous conversion like the one enjoyed by Oliver in *As You Like It*. Older approaches, as this essay has already noted, continued to thrive in many classrooms and journals; even A. C. Bradley, one of the earliest twentieth-century critics, would have felt at home in a number of lecture halls at the end of the twentieth century, and even A. C. Bradley's mother would have felt satisfied by the amount of attention her son's ideas continued to receive in some quarters. Certain newer methodologies and issues are deeply rooted in previous criticism (witness the connections between structuralism and formalism, among many other examples); books like Sigurd Burckhardt's *Shakespearean Meanings* (1968) and Jan Kott's *Shakespeare Our Contemporary* (1964) anticipate some of the developments associated with criticism written in the 1980s and 1990s.

But such caveats are intended to moderate, not invalidate, generalizations about the significant changes in Shakespeare criticism after 1970. To begin with, on the whole Shakespeareans writing after 1970 are far more indebted to Continental theory than their predecessors had been. In particular, four French theorists, Louis Althusser, Jacques Derrida, Michel Foucault, and Jacques Lacan, profoundly influenced Shakespeare studies, as well as many other fields in literary studies. These men constitute a close-knit group biographically and intellectually—Lacan was Althusser's analyst, Althusser a philosophy tutor of both Foucault and Derrida—though they sometimes parted company, as when Derrida criticized Lacan's reading of Poe's "Purloined Letter." But the French connection should not be studied at the expense of other Continental sources. Many ideas customarily attributed to these French theorists, such as the Derridean concept of the trace mentioned below, are anticipated in the work of the German philosopher Martin Heidegger; Friedrich Nietzsche's premises lie behind some of Foucault's assertions, such as the analyses of power that were to influence new historicists so deeply.

Whatever the etiologies of the newer types of Shakespeare criticism, their physiognomies manifest changing perspectives on the author and his achievements. As we have seen, for all the other differences among them, most of the critical methodologies flourishing in the first seventy years of the century encourage their adherents to celebrate Shakespeare, whether for his insights into character, his skillful stagecraft, or his wise reinterpretations of the intellectual debates of his era. Certain studies published during the last thirty years of the century do continue to extol Shakespeare's achievements, often by imputing to him progressive social attitudes; some feminists, for example, portray him as not agent but rather antagonist of the misogyny of his age. But by and large celebration became suspect; many critics writing after 1970 instead fault Shakespeare for complicity in repressive ideologies about centralized power, about gender, and about cultural minorities. Indeed, such Shakespeareans are typically concerned to interrogate, not replicate, what they perceive as a dangerous lionizing. What functions, critics pursuing this line of inquiry demand, are served by the widespread habit in our schools and in our culture at large of turning Shakespeare into a cultural icon? As that query suggests, recent Shakespeare criticism carries with it a number of pedagogical imperatives that have themselves been the object of debate.

Another change in attitudes toward authors in general, and Shakespeare in particular, involves denial of their agency, or ability to act with some degree of free will. Whereas classical Freudian psychoanalysis paints Shakespeare, like most writers, as an unwilling and unwitting victim of his neuroses, most other types of traditional criticism assume authorial control. Variously influenced by the conviction that the author expresses the ideology of dominant groups in his culture and by the assumption that Shakespeareans should study conditions of production like the patronage system rather than the idiosyncratic habits of a particular author, many critics writing after 1970 play down Shakespeare's agency and his autonomy.

These changing views of Shakespeare's authorship and authority necessarily involve changing viewpoints on his plays. Earlier in the century, critics from a range of persuasions typically saw those texts as carefully designed and unified—well wrought urns, to borrow the title of Cleanth Brooks's most famous New Critical book. Thus Bradley presupposes that Shakespeare adeptly bodies forth consistent characters, G. Wilson Knight identifies complex patterns of images and themes, and Brooks finds artistic maturity in Macbeth's "naked babe." In the final decades of the century, some critics came to see the text as indeed skillfully designed—but by the culture for ideological ends rather than by the writer for artistic ones. Others emphasized inconsistency or fissures in the text, whether caused by the linguistic gaps that interest many adherents to newer critical methodologies or by the tensions emanating from fraught issues like gender and monarchical power. Similarly, whereas the attention to language that united earlier Shakespeareans ranging from Caroline Spurgeon to Cleanth Brooks certainly continued during the later part of the twentieth century, linguistic contradictions often came to be treated not as a source of the meaningful ironies that attracted so many New Critics but rather as a symptom of fundamental instabilities in Shakespeare, his language, or his culture.

Shakespeare's culture was also reinterpreted during the last thirty years of the twentieth century. In general, indictments of various forms of repression, notably protocolonialism and patriarchy, replaced admiration for the achievements of the Elizabethan Golden Age. And much as an earlier vision of the text as ordered and unified was challenged by an emphasis on its fissures and fault lines, so earlier analyses that posited widely shared and comfortably held Elizabethan and Jacobean attitudes were succeeded by studies that variously assumed the imposition of political and social beliefs on suppressed groups or the clash between official and subversive ideologies. Thus the dissonances that many critics had primarily associated with the seventeenth century but not the preceding one, such as a deep pessimism about human achievements and potentialities, came to be considered characteristic of both epochs.

Shifts like the ones surveyed above spurred and were spurred by comparable redefinitions of the critical enterprise. In many circles, the study of character was not only dismissed but also distrusted as a symptom of a misguided belief in the autonomy of the individual. Similarly, towards the end of the twentieth century, many practitioners of the newer critical methodologies rejected the term *identity*, which they saw as positing an intrinsic and stable essence; it became common instead to posit the concept of *subjectivity*, which typically suggests that the self is in fact an unstable entity constructed by a culture rather than by private experience. And many though by no means all Shakespeareans became more interested in Shakespeare's culture and less in subtleties of his language or in formal issues like metrics.

These shifts in what Shakespeareans studied were mirrored by shifts in the perspective from which they studied it. During the first seventy years of the century, many critics, like their predecessors in earlier centuries, praised Shakespeare for his universal insights into human nature; witness A. C. Bradley's assertion that the central issues about Shakespeare's tragic heroes are not specific to a particular country or period. As we have seen, although a commitment to Shakespeare's universality survived undaunted in some quarters, many critics towards the end of the century came to view the playwright and his texts as rooted in a particular time and place: Shakespeare the propounder of the verities of human nature was replaced by Shakespeare the producer and reproducer—or, in an alternative version, the victim—of sixteenth- and seventeenth-century assumptions about the power of the monarch, the inferiority of women, and the significance of nationalism. The very existence of an ahistorical human nature was denied by Shakespeareans and other critics, who faulted that concept for its failure to acknowledge the ways particular cultures construct—and create illusions about—subjectivity.

For all the other differences among them, many though not all of the methodologies that flourished earlier in the century charted the historical differences between their culture and the Renaissance and yet at the same time asserted a kind of emotional propinquity to Shakespeare's world. Thus, on the one hand, they emphasized the gulf that separates the sixteenth and seventeenth centuries from the twentieth, an approach facilitated when intellectual historians like Craig focus on connections between the Renaissance and Middle Ages. Yet, on the other hand, not the least aim of many critics in the earlier part of the twentieth century was to forge an imaginative identification between themselves and the author and thus to foster such an identification in the reader as well. Witness G. Wilson Knight's insistent distinction between criticism and interpretation, Freud's and Jones's tracing of common psychoanalytic patterns, and Spencer's connection of Machiavelli and Hitler. In contrast, many studies written in the final decades of the twentieth century offer a mirror image of these patterns. Rather than distinguishing Shakespeare's world from our own, such books and essays variously announce and imply fundamental connections between what is tellingly called early modern culture and the critics' own society; Shakespeare's period is seen as the site of protocapitalism, the source of twentieth-century conceptions of subjectivity and authorship, and the arena for modes of patriarchal suppression not unlike their analogues in the twentieth century. At the same time, rather than exemplifying and encouraging an imaginative identification with Shakespeare and his culture, these analyses typically mandate critical distance and detachment from the era studied. The text, according to such readings, was likely to seduce its original readers into adopting its ideology and might do the same to naive contemporary critics. One can cite exceptions and qualifications to such patterns, notably the urge to speak with the dead that Stephen Greenblatt announces at the beginning of *Shakespearean Negotiations: The Circulation of Social Energy in Renaissance England* (1988), but nonetheless these types of suspicion of the text frequently recur.

The changes I am charting are not, of course, unique to Shakespeare criticism. Comparable shifts occurred elsewhere; for example, many students of other sixteenth- and seventeenth-century texts have been engaged in reinterpreting them as sites of repression and oppression rather than artistic triumphs, reacting against what they consider the uncritical respect for that era held by earlier scholars. Viewing the term "the Renaissance" as complicit in such celebrations of artistic achievement, many scholars came to prefer the alternative formulation "early modern period." And the instability of language, the centrality of gender, and the ideological functions of the literary text all became central issues in other fields of literary criticism as well towards the end of the twentieth century. Another way of positioning the developments treated in this section of the essay is to observe that many of them are products of poststructuralism, a movement, discussed below, that emphasizes the instability of language.

An examination of the opening of Theodore Spencer's *Shakespeare and the Nature of Man*, published in 1942, can crystallize and summarize the principal changes I have been surveying:

> There are three main ways in which we can study the expression of human experience in the arts. We can study the historical—the intellectual, social and emotional—background which the artist was able to use, and out of which he grew; we can study the craft, the artistic medium, which he employed; and we can try to analyze and judge the final product in relation to what we believe to be true of human experience as a whole. (p. vii)

Many of Spencer's original readers would have accepted this statement without question and, indeed, many Shakespeareans at the end of the century would as comfortably endorse it. Yet the developments in Shakespeare criticism after 1970 have called into question virtually every idea and perspective in Spencer's statement. Whereas critics writing towards the end of the century typically second Spencer's emphasis on history, they play down the categories he terms intellectual and emotional, focusing instead on political and ideological developments. And a number of them challenge the idea that history is simply "background," preferring instead an interactive paradigm for the relationship between literary and historical texts. They typically reject the very notion of universal human experience—and reject Spencer's use of the ostensibly universal male pronoun. And they are more likely to be interested in political craftiness than artistic craft.

Structuralism, Deconstruction, and Other Linguistic Developments

Structuralism and deconstruction, two modes of criticism that flourished in the American academy in the 1970s and early 1980s even though they were grounded in theories developed much earlier on the Continent, were the harbingers of many other changes in Shakespeare criticism. An interdisciplinary movement developing from the work of the early twentieth-century linguist Ferdinand de Saussure, structuralism deploys linguistics as a model for other fields. Its practitioners are interested in studying repeated structural patterns in, say, a literary text, an anthropological rite, or an utterance; they adopt a synchronic rather than a diachronic perspective (that is, they look at patterns that recur at the same time rather than tracing historical shifts). In so doing, they are concerned to formulate general rules and to observe the workings of binaries, which are generally abstract categories like up/down or adjective/noun rather than ethical or thematic divisions like good/evil. Especially influential was Saussure's insistence that the meaning of a word is based not on any intrinsic and stable characteristic but rather on contrasts with other words (we recognize *bat* because of its difference from *hat*). The impact of structuralism on criticism of the plays was slight, but, as we will see, it had a marked effect on approaches to Shakespeare's non-dramatic poetry.

The relationship between structuralism and poststructuralism is complex and contested. Some assert that the "post" alludes to a position beyond and a rejection of structuralism. Thus structuralism is seen as positing rule-bound, orderly systems, while poststructuralism glories in the subversion of these and many other rules. Other theorists, however, stress the continuities between the two movements, noting in particular that Saussure's assertion that the meaning of one word depends on that of another word exemplifies the indeterminacies emphasized by poststructuralists. In any event, poststructuralism characteristically focuses on the instabilities of language and interpretation.

For several reasons, deconstruction, a type of poststructuralism, is even harder to define responsibly than other literary movements. Though it was originally an approach to philosophical inquiry developed by Jacques Derrida, American literary critics adapted it into a series of protocols for literary analysis that certain theorists consider a distortion of Derrida. Disagreements among adherents, as well as variations and changes in their critical practice, further complicate the process of definition; for example, deconstruction is often viewed as apolitical and/or ahistorical, and yet many critics challenge those labels and in fact deploy some aspects of deconstruction in the course of political criticism. Derrida himself glosses these contradictory descriptions of deconstruction in his repeated warnings against seeing it as monolithic.

One can, however, generalize about certain characteristics of deconstruction as it influenced literary criticism in the United States, particularly during the 1980s. Deconstruction emphasizes the instability of linguistic and philosophical systems, especially their propensity for erecting hierarchical binaries such as speech versus writing or male versus female that on closer inspection break down, with one of the opposing terms in fact containing the other. Hence literary critics tended to focus on that instability and on its manifestations in some issues targeted by Derrida, such as the relationship between speech and writing, marginality, absences and gaps, and, in particular, the trace (which may be defined as the imprint of what was present in the past or will be present in the future, or alternatively, as others would have it, as the imprint of what can never be fully present). More specifically, critics interested in deconstruction during the 1980s typically engaged in a type of close reading. Like New Critics, they scrutinized paradoxes and tensions in the text—but unlike New Critics, they viewed those elements not as contributing to a richly textured, unified whole but rather as fracturing the ostensible unity of the text and undermining its apparent meanings.

This version of deconstruction generated a small group of significant essays, several of which appear in *Shakespeare and the Question of Theory*, edited by Patricia Parker and Geoffrey Hartman (1985). One typical article in that volume, Howard Felperin's "'Tongue-tied our queen?': The Deconstruction of Presence in *The Winter's Tale*," concentrates on indeterminacies in Shakespeare's romance, maintaining that neither the innocence of Hermione's behavior nor the clarity of the oracle's pronouncements are as reliable as they would appear to be; the play exemplifies the absences and opacities that deconstruction considers intrinsic to language. On the whole, however, the kind of deconstructive analysis exemplified by this essay enjoyed only a brief and limited impact on Shakespeare studies.

Nonetheless, deconstruction remains a highly significant trace, as it were, in projects and methods that more deeply affect that field. Its influence is ap-

parent in the challenge to patriarchal hierarchies in feminism and the analysis of erased and eroded gender boundaries in gay and lesbian studies and queer theory; arguably it also informs some of the political criticism that became so influential in the final decades of the twentieth century. Like many other critical approaches, deconstruction became hybridized towards the end of the century.

Language and textuality, central concerns of structuralism and deconstruction, are at the core of other approaches to Shakespeare that flourished during the 1970s and early 1980s. Metatheatre, the study of how drama comments on itself, especially on its own theatricality, is not a new approach, but it enjoyed a resurgence of interest during that period, manifest in studies like James L. Calderwood's *Metadrama in Shakespeare's Henriad: "Richard II" to "Henry V"* (1979). Similarly, rhetoric is a longstanding concern of Shakespeareans, but the final decades of the century saw a reinterpretation of it from the perspective of newer linguistic approaches like deconstruction; witness, for example, Patricia Parker's essay, "Shakespeare and Rhetoric: 'Dilation' and 'Delation' in *Othello*" (in *Shakespeare and the Question of Theory* [1985]). Speech act theory, a mode of analysis based on the work of two philosophers, J. L. Austin and John R. Searle, studies utterances as acts, classifying them according to the type of work they do; systems of categorization differ from one practitioner to another, with Searle's schema, for example, distinguishing the acts of requesting, asserting, advising, warning, and so forth. When applied to literary criticism, speech act analysis can investigate questions such as why a particular character is repeatedly attracted to a certain type of speech act or how and why a direct speech act may conceal an indirect one; thus it is particularly well suited to the analysis of drama, as Joseph A. Porter's *Drama of Speech Acts: Shakespeare's Lancastrian Tetralogy* (1979) demonstrates.

New Historicism, Cultural Materialism, Cultural Studies, Marxism

During the last three decades of the twentieth century, Shakespeare criticism came to manifest an intense interest in historical inquiry. That much is evident; but defining and distinguishing the movements in question can be tricky. New historicism, cultural materialism, cultural studies, and Marxism all share some preoccupations; moreover, these types of criticism developed and changed so much in the final decades of the century that definitions based on only a few of their practitioners or even on the early work of a given practitioner, as opposed to essays and books written by the same person ten years later, are deceptive. Critics attacking these movements are prone to neglect such distinctions: Straw men make weak soldiers. Delineating new historicism is further complicated by the often neglected fact that its Renaissance avatar is but one version: It also encompasses significant work in American studies and other fields.

Enumerating the sources of new historicism can, however, help to craft a definition of the movement despite such complexities. Many of its early practitioners were influenced by the anthropologist Clifford Geertz; in particular, Geertz draws attention to the ways cultures deploy ideology and other symbolic systems to control their members. Also significant is the psychoanalyst Jacques Lacan, who emphasizes that subjectivity is rooted in language and is developed in relation to an often threatening Other. (The Other accrues a range of meanings in Lacan's writing; for example, he relates it to the prohibitions associated with what he terms the Law of the Father, discussed below.) The impact of Marxism differs noticeably from one new historicist to another and often from one text by the same critic to another, but in general Louis Althusser, who revised earlier Marxist models of the relationship between literary texts and the culture's economy, is another major influence. Above all, new historicism builds on the writings of Michel Foucault, whose analyses of power may be its single most important source.

The publication of Stephen Greenblatt's *Renaissance Self-Fashioning: From More to Shakespeare* in 1980 is generally seen as the inaugural moment of the new historicism. This seminal book announces a project that is central to the movement: reinterpreting the relationship between the literary text and what earlier critics might have called its historical context or background in ways that call those very divisions into question. The literary should not be privileged over the historical, new historicists maintain. Nor should history be read as a stable background: It interacts with literature and is itself a text, no less unstable and no less problematical to interpret than the traditional objects of literary inquiry. Engaged in a complexly interactive relationship with other texts, in the broadest sense of that term, the literary text is seen as being shaped by and shaping its culture. New historicists also typically study a different type of history from their predecessors: By and large they choose to examine the workings of ideology and systems of representation in lieu of the conventional concerns of political history, such as wars and treaties, or of intellectual history. Thus new historicists approach power, which is among their principal preoccupations, from a Foucauldian perspective: They devote comparatively little attention to its official manifestations, such as the passing of legislation and the formation of armies, and more to its workings through theatrical spectacles like a monarch's processions or through ideological constructions like treatises on witchcraft. And, following Foucault, they are less interested in historical continuities and more in discontinuities and ruptures.

These principles generate characteristic practices when new historicists turn to Shakespeare. To begin with, they do so often: Their emphasis on theatricality in its many senses encourages them to focus on drama. Their concern for the conditions of production generates research into the workings of the theatre; thus in *The Place of the Stage: License, Play, and Power in Renaissance England* (1988) Steven Mullaney relates the location of playhouses in the area of London suggestively known as "the liberties" to the transgressiveness of theatre. New historicists also typically address issues like what Hal's manipulations show about the workings of power, how *The Tempest* shapes and is shaped by colonialism, and why *Henry V* manifests anxieties about the Irish.

New historicist writing about Shakespeare exemplifies the rhetorical practices characteristic of the movement. Because their conception of history is based on disjunctive moments that nonetheless may reveal the totality of a culture, their work often recounts anecdotes—this is frequently seen as the signature trait of the movement, and it is certainly one of its most controversial mannerisms—with Mullaney, for example, beginning one chapter by describing the display of an executed body and another with the incarceration of two lepers. Similarly, new historicists juxtapose literary and non-literary texts to imply suggestive connections between them; in one of his best known essays, "Invisible Bullets" (included in his book *Shakespearean Negotiations* [1988]), Greenblatt plays the stagings of power in Thomas Harriot's report on Virginia against Shakespeare's portrayal of Hal. Operating from the position that criticism is not a disinterested activity but the product of the critic's own presuppositions, new historicists, like many other critics at the end of the twentieth century, incorporate autobiographical observations into their work; in *Learning to Curse: Essays in Early Modern Culture* (1990), Greenblatt writes about his education, his father, and his father's cousin, and in *Forms of Nationhood: The Elizabethan Writing of England* (1992) Richard Helgerson adduces his own position as a Californian and a Peace Corps volunteer in West Africa.

Despite these and other similarities, new historicists approach Shakespeare in significantly different ways. Some emphasize the centralized power represented by the monarch, an orientation exemplified by Jonathan Goldberg's *James I and the Politics of Literature: Jonson, Shakespeare, Donne, and Their Contemporaries* (1983); others trace the diffusion and circulation of power. Some members of the movement present Shakespeare as an exponent of the dominant views of his culture and a supporter of its powerful leaders; in *Forms of Nationhood*, for example, Helgerson argues that Shakespeare contributed to the development of a theatre that supported royalist power, though not without hints of subversion. Other critics instead emphasize his transgressiveness. Most new historicists, following Foucault, chart history in terms of large time units and seismic shifts; but in *Puzzling Shakespeare: Local Reading and Its Discontents* (1988) Leah S. Marcus relates the plays to such local events as an early seventeenth-century protest against the encroachment of royal prerogatives on the rights of London. The feminist accusation that new historicists neglect gender is true of many but by no means all studies and is less true of new historicism in the 1990s than the 1980s. One important early exception to that neglect is the discussion of Elizabeth and the figure of the Amazon in Louis Montrose's article "*A Midsummer Night's Dream* and the Shaping Fantasies of Elizabethan Culture: Gender, Power, Form" (reprinted in *Rewriting the Renaissance: The Discourses of Sexual Difference in Early Modern Europe*, ed. Margaret W. Ferguson, Maureen Quilligan, Nancy J. Vickers [1986]). And, as I have emphasized, the work of a given new historicist may change more than the enemies or even the admirers of the movement acknowledge. For example, Greenblatt defines his relationship to Marxism differently in his successive books, and the highly influential model of subversion contained and even generated by those in power, developed in his seminal essay "Invisible Bullets," was to be variously refined and rejected by him and other new historicists.

Because of the significant differences among the leading new historicists, arriving at a balanced assessment of their contributions to Shakespeare studies is difficult. Surely they redirected attention to important issues that had been slighted, though in fact not totally ignored, by many other Shakespeareans, such as colonialism and race, and through their emphasis on theatricality offered a major reinterpretation of the questions about stagecraft that had engaged earlier critics. Indubitably they encouraged critics of many persuasions to read Shakespeare's plays in relation to non-literary texts that had received more cursory attention, or none at all, earlier, such as the medical manuals that Greenblatt deploys when writing about Shakespearean comedy in "Fiction and Friction," an essay in *Shakespearean Negotiations*, or the marriage manuals he quotes in *Renaissance Self-Fashioning*. Unquestionably the movement has sparked interest in tensions in Shakespeare's culture; at its best it has done so with exemplary subtlety and has inspired fruitful historical research even by critics who are not primarily new historicists. And certainly this, like many other versions of poststructuralism, has impelled Shakespeareans to reexamine their own critical enterprise.

But new historicist Shakespearean criticism also exemplifies the problems with which the movement as a whole has rightly been charged. For all the ostensible reactions against totalizing models both in new historicism itself and in the Marxist theories that influenced it, many practitioners of this method are still prone to assume a unified and monolithic culture; the focus on the court and London at the expense of other geographical areas and other seats of power has contributed to that tendency. The new historicist emphasis on cultural tension and anxiety is an important corrective to interpretations that attribute to the plays lighthearted tones and harmonious values, but like many correctives it encourages the pendulum to swing too far in its new direction: Critical tact mandates that one observe dissonances in a culture or a particular text while at the same time acknowledging that they do not necessarily drown out or even dominate other tones and values.

Bereleigh House, Hampshire. Collection of F. Tyrwhitt-Drake

Elizabeth Tudor dominated her age in symbol and in fact, a dominance celebrated in the portrait above (by an unknown artist) commemorating the defeat of the Spanish Armada in 1588. Through the left window are seen English ships arrayed against the Spanish fleet; through the right, a storm taking savage toll of the Armada. The magnificence of the Queen's highly stylized gem-encrusted costume befits the proud occasion here signalized.

The portrait of James I, her successor, is related to a different aspect of English foreign policy. It is a detail from a larger painting, by the Indian artist Bichitr, in which James, together with the Ottoman sultan, is represented as paying homage to the Mogul emperor Jahāngīr at his court in Delhi. The likeness of James was almost certainly copied from a miniature carried to India by Sir Thomas Roe on his embassy of 1615–18 to negotiate commercial privileges for the East India Company. The figure at the bottom is a court official holding a picture of an elephant and two horses—presumably the gifts which James is imagined as offering.

Courtesy of the Smithsonian Institution, Freer Gallery of Art, Washington, D.C.

By Sir William (or Francis) Segar; reproduction courtesy of the National Gallery of Ireland

Artist unknown. National Portrait Gallery, London

By Isaac Oliver. The Folger Shakespeare Library

Many of Elizabeth's courtiers patronized the arts, and both Henry Wriothesley, third Earl of Southampton (facing page) and William Herbert, third Earl of Pembroke (left) were Shakespeare's patrons. *Venus and Adonis* and *The Rape of Lucrece* are dedicated to Southampton, and he is the man most often conjectured to be the fair youth addressed in many of Shakespeare's sonnets. Heminge and Condell dedicated the First Folio (1623) to Pembroke and his brother the Earl of Montgomery and described them as having "prosequuted both [the plays], and their Authour liuing, with so much fauour." The portrait of Southampton was painted to commemorate his imprisonment in the Tower for his part in the ill-fated Essex rebellion of 1601. Both Southampton and Robert Devereux, second Earl of Essex (above left) were condemned to death, but only Essex was executed. On the eve of the attempted rebellion the conspirators subsidized a special performance of *Richard II* (with its dangerous precedent of a king's deposition) by Shakespeare's company, the Chamberlain's Men; an investigation evidently cleared them of complicity, for no charges were brought against them.

At the upper right is a portrait of William Cecil, Baron Burghley, Elizabeth's Principal Secretary (later Lord High Treasurer) and her most trusted adviser from the beginning of her reign until his death in 1598, five years before her own.

By John de Critz the Elder. By kind permission of His Grace, the Duke of Buccleuch, K.T., Boughton House, Northamptonshire, England

PLATE 3

The subject of this curious birth-to-death painting was Sir Henry Unton (1557?–1596), diplomatist and soldier, whose family seat, at Wadley, near Faringdon, in Berkshire, is shown in parts of the picture. In a general right-to-left direction, the scenes depict his birth, his student years at Oxford, his wedding feast and masque (1580), and (above the feast) the activities of his maturity as a traveller in Italy, a general in the Netherlands, and an ambassador in France (where he died), before ending with his funeral. His typically

National Portrait Gallery, London

ostentatious tomb in the church at Faringdon is shown in the lower left corner. Of particular interest is the wedding masque. In the hall, below the banqueting chamber, is placed a consort of six musicians. The masquers, in costume, preceded by a taborer and a "truchman" (an interpreter or presenter) with a paper in his hand, represent Mercury, Diana, and six Nymphs, all in red masks, with ten Cupids (five white and five black, perhaps representing day and night) who act as torchbearers to the principals.

Victoria & Albert Museum, London/Art Resource, NY

Theodora Wilbour Fund, Museum of Fine Arts, Boston

The artifacts pictured on this page and the next, all of them from the end of the sixteenth century or the beginning of the next, reflect the widespread taste for elegance and the high refinement achieved in the arts and crafts. The exceptionally fine miniature above, by Nicholas Hilliard, shows an unknown young man holding his locket (doubtless containing a portrait of his beloved) over his heart, against a background of gold flames symbolizing the ardor of his passion. The tankard to the right is of faience with English silver mounts. Below, the wool and silk tent-stitched panel depicts French styles of dress which had become highly fashionable in England.

The Metropolitan Museum of Art, Gift of Irwin Untermyer, 1964 (64.101.1283).

Lord
IVDICIO PYLIVM GENIO SOCRATEM ARTE MARONEM
TERRA TEGIT, POPVLVS MÆRET, OLYMPVS HABET
STAY PASSENGER, WHY GOEST THOV BY SO FAST,
READ IF THOV CANST, WHOM ENVIOVS DEATH HATH PLAST
WITH IN THIS MONVMENT SHAKSPEARE: WITH WHOME,
QVICK NATVRE DIDE WHOSE NAME, DOTH DECK Y^S TOMBE,
FAR MORE, TEN COST: SIEH ALL Y^T HE HATH WRITT,
LEAVES LIVING ART, BVT PAGE, TO SERVE HIS WITT.
OBIT ANO DO 1616
ÆTATIS 53 DIE 23 AP

Holy Trinity Church, Stratford-upon-Avon Photo (c) Woodmansterne

The Shakespeare monument in Holy Trinity Church, Stratford. Only two authentically attributed and nearly contemporary representations of Shakespeare have survived: one, the Janssen bust, erected by 1623, shown above (see, further, Appendix C, Number 6B); the other, the copperplate engraving by Martin Droeshout on the title-page of the First Folio, 1623 (reproduced on page 91 of this text). The limestone bust, repainted in the nineteenth century in an attempt to recapture the original effect (auburn hair and beard, scarlet doublet, black gown, etc.), presumably depicts Shakespeare in later life. The Droeshout portrait, on the other hand, is believed to have been engraved in 1623 after some earlier sketch of Shakespeare as a younger man. The other alleged portraits, several of them more ideally pleasing, are either later in date (and in some cases derivative) or, if contemporary, of doubtful attribution as portraits of Shakespeare.

PLATE 6

Queen Elizabeth died on March 24, 1603, and her funeral, conducted with great magnificence, took place on April 28. The Lords and Ladies of the Realm and their servants, ambassadors, members of the Council, the Lord Mayor of London, the Heralds of the College of Arms, the Master of the Revels, and all the many members of the Queen's household, high and low, were in dutiful attendance, dressed in decent black. The pictures here shown are from a contemporary watercolor sketch of the whole procession, possibly by William Camden. The lower section includes some of the Children of the Chapel (the "little eyases" of *Hamlet*, II.ii.339), who had been acting with great success at the Second Blackfriars Theatre since 1600.

PLATE 7

Cultural materialism has been described as the British brand of new historicism, but the two should be distinguished. By and large, cultural materialists, rooted as they are in British traditions of Marxist criticism such as the cultural studies project at the University of Birmingham, are more overt and consistent in their deployment of Marxist models. By and large, too, cultural materialists write more about the relationship of Shakespeare studies and other types of literary criticism to their own culture than do new historicists. Some observers of both movements have traced this tendency to the cultural materialists' aim of having a political impact on their society, a hope that, according to this reading, new historicists have largely abandoned. Yet these generalizations, like so many other overviews of critical movements, immediately call for qualifications. In particular, new historicism, like many other types of criticism, became more deeply (or perhaps merely more openly) Marxist in the 1990s than it had been earlier. Futhermore, many new historicists would disagree with the assertion that they have abandoned any hope of creating or even witnessing significant political change. However one distinguishes new historicists and cultural materialists, *Political Shakespeare: Essays in Cultural Materialism*, edited by Jonathan Dollimore and Alan Sinfield (1985; rev. ed. 1994), aptly exemplifies the several aims of the latter group of critics. For instance, in one essay Sinfield, manifesting the Marxist principle that education is one of the most important, if not the most important, avenue through which a culture imposes its values, argues that the English examination system deploys Shakespeare to reinforce right-wing agendas.

Cultural studies also eludes easy definitions, in part because its adherents disagree about what type of work should be classified under this rubric. Some wish to confine the label to particular types of Marxist criticism; others are content to extend it to virtually any examination of a culture. As this debate would suggest, much new historicist and cultural materialist work might also be categorized as cultural studies. More specifically, however, practitioners of cultural studies are often though not invariably interested in race, class, and gender and in popular culture in its many manifestations—movies, advertisements, comic strips, and so on. This, like other critical movements towards the end of the twentieth century, typically challenges the boundaries between disciplines. Marjorie Garber's *Vested Interests: Cross-Dressing and Cultural Anxiety* (1992) is characteristic of a cultural studies approach to Shakespeare—and, as I will suggest, of other movements in Shakespeare studies as well. What this volume does not do is as revealing as what it does: Rather than focusing specifically on Shakespeare, as Garber's earlier books had done, this one weaves together occasional analyses of his work with allusions to cultural artifacts ranging from minstrel shows to Rudolph Valentino's movies to Elvis Presley impersonators. These juxtapositions implicitly define the principles impelling this and so many other works of cultural studies. According to its practitioners, rather than celebrating the unique achievements of Shakespeare, presented as loftily apart from the detritus of popular culture, we should scan the plays for what they reveal about his society and our own, necessarily including in our investigations material previously viewed as irrelevant to scholarly investigation.

Like Freudianism, Marxism itself is often defined reductively and dismissed resoundingly by people who do not bother to read its principal texts. Economic determinism, especially as manifested in a class system, is certainly a central component in much Marxist analysis, but the movement cannot simply be described in those terms. For, again like Freudianism, Marxism has witnessed enough disagreements among its adherents further to complicate definitions. In particular, the idea that the economic is the base on which the cultural superstructure depends was challenged by Louis Althusser's emphasis on a dynamic interplay between the economic strata of a society and what he terms its "repressive state apparatuses" like the police force and "ideological state apparatuses" like religion. Alternatively, some Marxists have focused on the workings of ideology in lieu of privileging economic causality.

Marxism had a relatively minor effect on Shakespeare studies up to about 1970—and a major one subsequently. First, some of its concepts and terms came to enjoy a wide currency even among scholars whose primary orientation is not Marxist. Hegemony, often defined as the process by which a dominant group imposes its will on other sections of the society and encourages them to misidentify their own interests with those of the dominant class, is a case in point. Even more to our purposes here, partly because of the Marxist position that the autonomous and stable self is a myth, discussions of character have become taboo in many circles. The second way Marxism has affected Shakespeare studies we have already examined: It has had a profound influence, sometimes acknowledged and sometimes covert, on new historicism, cultural materialism, and cultural studies. Both the initial failure fully to recognize its impact, especially evident in studies published in the 1980s, and the subsequent extent of that impact demonstrate the workings of hegemony within the academy itself.

Finally, of course, some important Shakespeare criticism is primarily Marxist in its orientation. The work of the German critic Robert Weimann, especially *Shakespeare and the Popular Tradition in the Theater: Studies in the Social Dimension of Dramatic Form and Function* (1978), has enjoyed a considerable vogue in both American and British Shakespeare studies. Engaged in relating medieval and Renaissance theatre to social and economic developments, Weimann propounds the theory that in both periods the stage included the *locus* and *platea*, which he variously describes as actual physical regions and modes of drama. According to Weimann, the locus, which derives from the scaffold of medieval drama, often represents a particular place and is associated with the higher members of the social order; the platea, in contrast, is physically closer to the audience and is unlocalized. Or, to put it another way, the locus is sometimes defined as the official world of history, the world of Hal's royal father; the platea is the popular and transgressive realm of Hal's second father, Falstaff. M. D. Bristol's *Shakespeare's America, America's Shakespeare* (1990) brings a Marxist perspective to the project of attacking the idealization of Shakespeare, encompassing as well many broader issues about the workings of the academy. The infusion of Marxism has had, then, the positive effect of encouraging Shakespeareans to rethink some debatable premises about their own enterprise. Yet because so many critics have adopted certain concepts without much analysis or recognition of their contested interpretations even (or especially) within Marxist theory, those ideas have themselves sometimes enjoyed the uncritical assent previously granted to concepts like character. For example, whereas informed references to the economy of sixteenth- and seventeenth-century England can be very illuminating, routine allusions to capitalism or protocapitalism in Shakespeare's culture often ignore how varied and complex that economy was. Similarly, many commentaries on hegemony could profitably be modulated to acknowledge long-standing disagreements about whether or not it involves continuing struggles. And the term *ideology* is most fruitful when one engages with Marxist and other debates about its meanings and workings (for example, does it necessarily involve deception?), rather than deploying it loosely, as some critics are prone to do.

Feminisms, Gender Studies, Gay and Lesbian Criticism, Queer Theory

Feminism and new historicism are the two primary catalysts for the changes Shakespeare criticism has witnessed since 1970. And just as any description of new historicism calls for distinctions and subdivisions, so feminism, both in general and within Shakespeare studies in particular, should be thought of in the plural, as feminisms. Only then are the range and variety of the movement, too often neglected by its detractors, apparent.

One common schema for diagramming feminism as a whole distinguishes Anglo-American and French branches, associating the former primarily with studies of women's experience and the latter with the more abstract analyses of connections between gender and language exemplified by the work of such French theorists as Hélène Cixous, Luce Irigaray, and Julia Kristeva. If one accepts this division, most feminist Shakespeare criticism falls in the Anglo-American camp; studies of the female body and of female language or its absence do, however, sometimes rely on the French feminists, and the ideas associated with them became more prominent in several studies published in the 1990s. In any event, many feminists have rejected the divide in question, citing the work of critics who cross its borders and noting its disregard for Third World brands of feminism.

Carol Thomas Neely categorizes three types of feminist inquiry in her essay "Feminist Modes of Shakespearean Criticism: Compensatory, Justificatory, Transformational" (*Women's Studies*, 9 [1981], 3–15); her system acutely summarizes some changes in the field, but for our purposes it is limited by its inevitable ignorance of developments after 1981. And any narrative of Shakespearean feminisms should be bracketed with reminders of the survival and interpenetrations of critical methodologies. Bearing these caveats in mind, however, one can extend and adapt Neely's system to sketch a broad overview of Shakespearean feminisms during the final three decades of the century. The surge of feminist criticism in the 1970s initially focused on Shakespeare's female characters, particularly the strong heroines, as Neely suggests in delineating the compensatory mode. This concern was superseded in many quarters by attention to the workings of patriarchy in Shakespeare's culture (and often, implicitly, in the critic's culture as well) and issues about the female body. In the 1990s many Shakespeareans turned to discussing gender in general, a move embraced by some feminists and condemned by others as a repetition of the erasure of women, and to redefining feminist concerns in relation to Marxism. The centrality of gender itself became contested in the 1990s, with some feminist Shakespeareans, like feminists in other fields, distrustful of privileging it over other distinctions, notably race. Moreover, during the three decades in question, many feminist Shakespeareans became increasingly concerned to reject the ahistorical generalizations about women and the female that are sometimes labeled essentialism because they presume an inherent, stable core of being; instead, such critics attempt to root their work in the specificities of, say, wet-nursing in Elizabethan and Jacobean England.

Some of the most influential Shakespearean feminist scholarship deploys object relations theory, a mode of psychoanalysis associated with John Bowlby, among others. Sometimes considered a type of neo-Freudianism, object relations theory charts developmental patterns by focusing not on the Oedipal trauma, as classic Freudianism would do, but rather on the child's interactions with objects and people in her or his environment, which often precede the Oedipal stage. Nancy Chodorow deploys the theory in a way especially relevant to feminists in *The Reproduction of Mothering: Psychoanalysis and the Sociology of Gender* (1978): She develops the argument that because male identity depends on the fraught and often unsuccessful process whereby a child distinguishes himself from a parent of the opposite sex, men are likely to suffer from recurrent fears of an engulfing mother and a repeated impulse to reject women and the feminine. In her essay "The Hand That Rocks the Cradle: Recent Gender Theories and Their Implications" (reprinted in *The (M)other Tongue: Essays in Feminist Psychoanalytic Interpretation*, edited by Shirley Nelson Garner, Claire Kahane, and Madelon Sprengnether [1985]), Coppélia Kahn explicates this model and details what she considers the limitations of Freud's writing on femininity; in an influential series of articles, she applies object relations theory to Shakespearean texts, typically revealing male fears of a dominating woman. Thus, for example, Kahn's "Absent Mother in *King Lear*" (available in *Rewriting the Renaissance*) draws attention to the lack of maternal figures in the play and the large number of negative references to women and generativity, tracing both phenomena to male fears of female domination. Another influential study, Janet Adelman's *Suffocating Mothers: Fantasies of Maternal Origin in Shakespeare's Plays, "Hamlet" to "The Tempest"* (1992) also exemplifies the impact of object relations theory. Adelman charts Shakespeare's development in terms of male fears of having originated in a threatening female body, uncovering menacing mothers in a few early plays, their disappearance in many plays written later in the 1590s, their dramatic reappearance in *Hamlet*, and the renegotiation of issues raised by these maternal figures in subsequent dramas. Thus Adelman's *Macbeth* turns on fantasies of escaping maternal power, and her *Coriolanus* constructs Volumnia as a mother who fails to nourish her son properly.

Another type of feminism might fall under the broad label *cultural critique*: In general, this version concentrates on the workings of gender in a culture, and in the case of Shakespeare it typically reads the plays as studies in patriarchy. Critics debate, however, about whether women in Shakespeare's England enjoyed an improved status, a change sometimes attributed to the influence of Protestantism and the reign of Elizabeth, or whether their position should be glossed primarily in terms of suppression and misogyny. Juliet Dusinberre's *Shakespeare and the Nature of Women* (1975) maintains that not only Shakespeare but most of his fellow playwrights held feminist attitudes; on the other hand, the historian Lisa Jardine's *Still Harping on Daughters: Women and Drama in the Age of Shakespeare* (1983) suggests that apparently strong women were often perceived, represented, and repressed as a source of threats. Critics differ, too, in defining Shakespeare's relationship to patriarchy, with some casting him as a defender of the status quo, others as a protofeminist, and others finding ambivalences throughout his career. Carol Thomas Neely's *Broken Nuptials in Shakespeare's Plays* (1985) trenchantly demonstrates that Shakespeare's interactions with patriarchy and misogyny were not univocal, varying significantly from play to play and genre to genre. His dramas in the comedic genre, Neely asserts, negotiate tensions about misogyny and the gendering of power, with female characters generally turning the men into good husbands, though at the price of accepting their domination. *Othello*, according to this reading, intensifies and reinterprets certain patterns from the comedies. Not merely Iago and Othello but all the male characters are contaminated by the anxieties with which Shakespeare's comic heroes struggle, whereas the female characters—including Emilia, whom many earlier critics had dismissed or disdained—represent a sane and sanative approach. (A version of this chapter appears in an important early anthology edited by Carolyn Ruth Swift Lenz, Gayle Greene, and Carol Thomas Neely, *The Woman's Part: Feminist Criticism of Shakespeare* [1983]). Similarly, in *Women and the English Renaissance: Literature and the Nature of Womankind, 1540–1620* (1984), Linda Woodbridge lauds Emilia for her brave insubordination. The feminist analyses within this book are useful in part because, unlike many other commentaries on Shakespeare, they position his plays within extensive analyses of non-Shakespearean drama.

Many though by no means all feminists practicing these modes of cultural critique are influenced by poststructuralism. It encourages its adherents to emphasize that linguistic systems, including the categories used to describe women and femininity, are culturally constructed and radically unstable. Karen Newman's *Fashioning Femininity and English Renaissance Drama* (1991), for example, traces slippages in descriptions of the female body; her statements about devoting more attention to constructions of femininity than to women's experience manifest the influence of poststructuralism and of approaches sometimes associated with the French feminists.

Another influential avenue of criticism is often termed *materialist feminism*. The use of "materialist" rather than "Marxist" by many of its practitioners is striking, gesturing towards both a continuing unease about Marxism and the long-standing tensions between Marxists and feminists about the priority of economics and gender respectively. But whatever label is affixed to this movement, typically its proponents are very indebted to Marxism. The first chapter of Jean E. Howard's *Stage and Social Struggle in Early Modern England* (1994) articulates key principles of materialist feminism. Thus, for example, she attacks the search for authorial agency, stating that it "eclipses the possibility of asking how gender, class, race, and social marginality or centrality impinge on the way characters are depicted as bearers of theatrical power" (p. 9). Notice how her passive voice ("are depicted") itself stages the transfer of agency away from the author. Similarly, Catherine Belsey, another prominent materialist and feminist critic, explores the potentialities of materialist feminism in her afterword to a collection edited by Valerie Wayne, *The Matter of Difference: Materialist Feminist Criticism of Shakespeare* (1991); she stresses that its orientation need not be exclusively economic. Another instance of this type of feminism is "Patriarchal Territories: The Body Enclosed," by Peter Stallybrass, an essay included in *Rewriting the Renaissance*. Borrowing the contrast between the so-called classical and grotesque bodies established by the theorist Mikhail Bakhtin, Stallybrass adapts it to discuss the workings of class and to reinterpret *Othello*.

Distinguishing gender studies from other brands of criticism, feminist and otherwise, is not always easy, in part because this term, like so many others in contemporary theory, is slippery. Its political and intellectual range is considerable: The label can be affixed to the work of reactionary critics who attempt to counter what they see as an undue attention to women with a renewed interest in male identity, to adaptations of feminism, and to the most experimental studies in queer theory. In general, though, gender studies focuses less on women and femininity per se and more on the constructions of gender, which may variously involve positions seen as male, as female, or as transgressive challenges to and elisions of those boundaries. An early version of this enterprise is Coppélia's Kahn's *Man's Estate: Masculine Identity in Shakespeare* (1981). Several studies discussed elsewhere in this essay, such as Stephen Orgel's articles on cross-dressing and Valerie Traub's *Desire and Anxiety: Circulations of Sexuality in Shakespearean Drama* (1992), exemplify more recent approaches to gender studies.

Despite the distinctions among the work surveyed above, some generalizations about the consequences of feminist criticism and related work in gender studies are possible. These approaches have encouraged Shakespeareans to read dramatic conflict less as a product of particular characters and more as a symptom of the workings of patriarchy. Thus in *Romeo and Juliet* the death of the young lovers stems neither from flaws in their own characters such as impetuosity nor from fate but rather from the inexorable operation of patriarchy, signalled early on by the fights and bawdy jokes. Feminists have also redirected attention to women characters who had been ignored by many critics or dismissively condemned by others; witness, for example, Neely's emphasis on Emilia or the many studies that find strength in Desdemona. Conversely, feminist criticism has repeatedly drawn attention to the silencing of women in Shakespearean drama, arguing in particular that the apparently harmonious resolutions on which many comedies terminate are purchased by literally and metaphorically stilling female voices. And the movement has contributed significantly to the study of gender in Tudor and Stuart England.

Despite—or because of—these and many other achievements, feminist criticism remains controversial in certain circles. The resistance to it crystallized in "Feminist Thematics and Shakespearean Tragedy," an essay Richard Levin published in *PMLA*, the journal of the Modern Language Association of America, in 1988; similar attacks were shortly to be levelled by other critics, such as Brian Vickers in *Appropriating Shakespeare: Contemporary Critical Quarrels* (1993). The intense reaction to Levin's essay sparked a lengthy group letter, a conference session, and a collection of essays assessing feminism and other recent developments in Shakespeare criticism, *Shakespeare Left and Right*, edited by Ivo Kamps (1991).

Some opponents of feminist scholarship have argued that it neglects distinctions among male and among female characters, uncritically condemning the former and celebrating the latter, and that it focuses on gender at the expense of traditional staples of literary criticism, such as generic norms. Like a number of other charges against critical movements, these accusations hold for some though by no means all work from the critics in question. Others have faulted this type of criticism for broad and hence problematical generalizations about patriarchy; certainly Tudor and Stuart culture witnessed more dissension on issues like the role of a wife or the valuation of female silence than the less acute feminist studies have acknowledged. In addition, some Shakespeareans accuse proponents of the movement of imposing their own twentieth-century political preoccupations on Shakespeare's plays, a charge that raises broad questions confronted by contemporary students. To what extent and to what ends should readers judge the values implicit and explicit in Shakespearean drama? And can they—or should they—detach themselves from their own cultures in so doing?

Gay and lesbian criticism and queer theory became a significant force in literary studies during the 1990s, and their impact on Shakespeare criticism in particular was considerable. One can distinguish the two movements by the fact that adherents of queer theory are generally more interested in the breakdown of all gender divisions; they relate sexual practices and preferences to instabilities of subjectivity, while many though not all practitioners of gay and lesbian criticism posit distinctive identities for gay men, lesbian women, and their heterosexual counterparts respectively. The term *queer*, like the use of *black* by African-Americans, also aims to challenge and unseat traditional schema of categorization: *Queer* at once attempts to recuperate what had been a pejorative term and to replace *gay* and *lesbian*, labels variously criticized for replicating heterosexist assumptions or for creating an artificial divide between men and women.

Both gay and lesbian studies and queer theory stem from a range of sources. These movements participate in the challenges to the concept of a stable identity levied by Derrida, Lacan, and many other poststructuralist theorists, and in the attacks on hierarchical categories sparked by deconstruction. In his *History of Sexuality* (1976– ; first English translation, 1979), a multivolume study left uncompleted at his death, Michel Foucault posits several radical changes in sexuality at the end of the eighteenth and beginning of the nineteenth century. Until then, he maintains, people were seen as performing certain sexual acts but not having a defined sexual identity: A man who engaged in homoerotic relationships would not have been categorized as a homosexual. After this watershed, Foucault asserts, sexual behavior came to be regulated in different ways, notably through medical discourses. Widely—and perhaps too uncritically—accepted by practitioners of gay and lesbian criticism and queer theory, this approach to historicizing sexuality was to spur many reinterpretations of Renaissance texts. Eve Kosofsky Sedgwick's concept of homosocial desire, developed in *Between Men: English Literature and Male Homosocial Desire* (1985), has also been frequently adopted by

Shakespeareans: She posits a continuum running from types of male bonding to overtly homoerotic behavior, thus again challenging neat divisions between sexual practices and preferences and providing a model for the subordination of women in the interests of male relationships.

Critics influenced by gay and lesbian and queer theory direct renewed attention to putative homoerotic relationships that previous critics had also observed, such as Antonio's friendship with Bassanio in *The Merchant of Venice*; and they scrutinize references to many other same-sex friendships in the plays, finding, for example, homoerotic overtones in Titania's closeness to her votaress and arguing more generally that the comedies often enact a rejection of homoerotic possibilities in favor of compulsory heterosexuality. In *Sodometries: Renaissance Texts, Modern Sexualities* (1992) Jonathan Goldberg traces the shifting and ambiguous erotics of the plays about Hal, attributing to Shakespeareans themselves a kind of hidden desire for that character. In essays like "Nobody's Perfect: Or, Why Did the English Stage Take Boys for Men?" (*South Atlantic Quarterly*, 88 [1989], 7–29), Stephen Orgel develops the debatable though thought-provoking proposition that Shakespeare's culture was really more threatened by heterosexual than homosexual acts.

Orgel's assertion, like several other propositions characteristic of these modes of criticism, is grounded in close examinations of cross-dressing in the plays, a topic that became important in Shakespeare studies during the 1990s. Such studies examine both the casting of boys as women and the complication of that pattern when the boy actors then disguise their assumed female gender. As I observed earlier, many critics writing during the first seventy years of the century maintain that Shakespeare effectively erases the tensions and transgressive implications latent in the practice of boys playing women; in turn feminist critics often interpret female characters assuming male garb as a strategy by which powerful and clever women assert their power. Under the influence of gay and lesbian criticism and queer theory, however, all types of cross-dressing become an often uneasy flirtation with the possibility of homoerotic relationships. This argument is developed in several essays by Orgel, such as the one cited above. Focusing particularly on the liminality of cross-dressing, Bruce R. Smith's *Homosexual Desire in Shakespeare's England: A Cultural Poetics* (1991) emphasizes the complex and varied responses that it provoked in Shakespeare's original audience. In *Desire and Anxiety: Circulations of Sexuality in Shakespearean Drama* (1992), Valerie Traub argues that critics have been too quick to associate cross-dressing with male homoerotic desire rather than acknowledging the traces, however faint, however masked, of lesbianism in Shakespeare's texts and culture.

Psychoanalytic Criticism

Freudian criticism, never uncontroversial, sustained repeated hits during the final three decades of the twentieth century. Many feminists condemned it as patriarchal; many critics committed to historicization rejected it because of its putative commitment to a stable self and to ahistorical generalizations about human nature. Nonetheless, Freudian and neo-Freudian models remained powerful in Shakespeare criticism, although often they were adapted in response to such attacks. The mode of feminist analysis based on object relations theory, which we have already explored, is a case in point: Shakespeareans using this methodology often reverse the limitations Freud attributed to women by drawing attention to the perils of male development. In addition, a number of studies composed during the period orchestrate Freudian and other approaches. Witness *The Whole Journey: Shakespeare's Power of Development* (1986), written in part by C. L. Barber and completed after his death by his former student, Richard P. Wheeler. This book negotiates connections among a wide range of approaches, including an examination of Christian elements in Shakespeare's work and culture, but it is buttressed at many points by Freudian concepts. Wheeler also relies on psychoanalytic concepts in his study *Shakespeare's Development and the Problem Comedies: Turn and Counter-Turn* (1981). The work of Marjorie Garber, to which I referred above, variously deploys and defuses Freudian concepts, frequently relating them to types of poststructuralist analysis such as deconstruction and to other psychoanalytic models. For example, in one essay in *Shakespeare's Ghost Writers: Literature as Uncanny Causality* (1987) she suggests that Freud's essay "The Theme of the Three Caskets" represses his concerns about his father's marriages, his own relationships with women, including his daughter, and his Jewishness.

In addition to their Freudian roots, the psychoanalytic Shakespeare studies written after 1970 often manifest the influence of the French psychoanalyst Jacques Lacan. Lacan himself would resist being distinguished from mainstream Freudian analysis in this way, since he repeatedly insists on his debt to Freud. Lacan is, however, even more interested in linguistic issues than was his master; especially germane to literary critics is his assertion that the unconscious works like a language. Moreover, his conception of selfhood emphasizes disruption, incompletion, and loss; one can make a persuasive case that these elements are so significant in the work of Freud himself that critics are misguided when they associate him with a stable notion of self, but it remains true that Lacan is even more preoccupied with the concept of a divided subjectivity than was Freud.

Charting Lacan's ideas is complicated by the fogginess of some of his prose, his predilection for wordplay, and the need to rely in part on reports of his teaching. In general, he posits a developmental model involving two stages, though he also describes them as coexisting orders of experience: the *Imaginary* and the *Symbolic*. The Imaginary is characterized by a dyadic unity with the mother and is prelinguistic. The Symbolic, associated with the entry into language, involves the constraints created by what Lacan terms the Law of the Father, which comprise a range of societal regulations including but not confined to the Oedipal prohibition; entering the Symbolic entails a loss of unity and wholeness. Or, to put it another way, in the Lacanian Symbolic, the self is constituted in relation to a threatening and powerful Other, which often operates through a gaze that objectifies and controls it, a concept related as well to Foucault's writing on surveillance. Lacan is at pains to emphasize, though, that even the harmony of the Imaginary stage is only apparent, since subjectivity is from the beginning associated with deception and loss.

Lacan's ideas have often been attacked, especially by his fellow psychoanalysts and by feminists; whereas some members of the latter group embrace him as a source of critiques of patriarchy, others find dangerously patriarchal assumptions inherent in his system. Despite such disputes, his impact on cinematic and literary criticism has been deep, and Shakespeare studies is no exception. New historicism, as I have already observed, borrows a Lacanian interpretation of subjectivity. Barbara Freedman's *Staging the Gaze: Postmodernism, Psychoanalysis, and Shakespearean Comedy* (1991) deploys Lacan throughout, though Freedman also draws on Renaissance theories of vision and perception and, like many Lacanians, utilizes classical Freudian ideas as well. She argues, for example, that *The Comedy of Errors* involves misrecognition in Lacan's sense and the uncanny in Freud's and relates those concepts to the divided self.

THE POEMS

Jaques. I pray you mar no more trees with writing love-songs in their barks.
Orlando. I pray you mar no moe of my verses with reading them ill-favoredly.

As You Like It
(III.ii.259–62)

The Sonnets

Are Shakespeare's sonnets arranged in the order he intended? Do they recount autobiographical experience—and if so do they demonstrate that Shakespeare had a homoerotic relationship? Is the central figure in Sonnet 94 primarily the subject of praise or the target of bitter reproof? The complexity of questions like these has generated a flood of criticism on the sonnets throughout the twentieth century and, of course, earlier as well.

Like other floods, this one has done some damage. The less successful attempts to rearrange the poems, thus restoring Shakespeare's imputed intentions, remind one of the observation that the sonnets affect otherwise sensible critics the way catnip affects otherwise sensible cats. Similarly, none of the repeated attempts to identify the principal figures in the sequence, generally called the Friend and the Dark Lady, with historical personages has won anything approaching universal agreement, and, in particular, most Shakespeareans have reacted skeptically to the historian A. L. Rowse's assertion that Aemilia Lanyer was the Dark Lady. On the other hand, the twentieth century has also witnessed incisively original responses to the questions on which this section opened, responses that exemplify both the potentialities and the problems of the various critical approaches defined in earlier sections of this essay. (A reader who has not previously examined those sections may find it useful to consult them for definitions of the critical terminology that appears below.)

The knotty syntax of many lines in these poems and the scholarly enigmas they pose both demand judicious editorial work, so the commentaries in editions of the sonnets have often proved influential. Hyder Edward Rollins's two-volume New Variorum Shakespeare *Sonnets* (1944) offers a sound overview of earlier critical problems. Given the potential significance of such editions, it is not surprising that one of the principal, if not the principal, contribution to twentieth-century criticism of the sonnets is Stephen Booth's edition, *Shakespeare's Sonnets* (1977). Influenced deeply though implicitly by the linguistic criticism of the 1970s and anticipating deconstructive moves that were to become prominent in American criticism during the next decade, Booth demonstrates the complex interplay of often contradictory meanings; he also includes brief but sane discussions of the principal controversies connected with the sonnets. The lengthy introduction of John Kerrigan's edition, *The Sonnets and A Lover's Complaint* (1986), acutely addresses many problems connected with the sequence, arguing, for example, that the current order of the poems is satisfactory; among Kerrigan's contributions is his emphasis on connections between the sonnets and "A Lover's Complaint."

Debates about the sonnets frequently center on the conditions of publication and the reliability of the edition on which later versions are necessarily based, a 1609 volume brought out by a publisher named Thomas Thorpe. Most Shakespeareans have agreed that this edition was not authorized and that hence the poems within it do not appear in the order Shakespeare intended. The critics who feel the 1609 edition is unreliable in that respect have, as I already noted, often attempted to reorder the poems; Brents Stirling's *Shakespeare Sonnet Order: Poems and Groups* (1968) is widely considered the best of these studies. But in *Captive Victors: Shakespeare's Narrative Poems and Sonnets* (1987), I argue that the very nature of this cycle militates against a narrative sequence of poems: Most of them involve meditations or obsessive repetitions rather than attempts at storytelling in the usual sense. Similarly, in my essay "'Incertainties now crown themselves assur'd': The Politics of Plotting Shakespeare's Sonnets," *Shakespeare Quarterly*, 47 (1996), 291–305, I advocate questioning the widely accepted assumption that virtually all of the first 126 poems necessarily refer to the male Friend and the subsequent lyrics to the Dark Lady: Many poems in both sections do not identify the gender of their addressee, and the contention that internal evidence indicates which lyrics involve the youth and which the Dark

Lady often rests on circular reasoning. Katherine Duncan-Jones also challenges the premises behind attempts to reorder the sequence but does so from a very different perspective: In her thought-provoking revisionist essay "Was the 1609 *Shake-speares Sonnets* Really Unauthorized?" (*Review of English Studies*, 34 [1983], 151–71), she maintains that Thorpe was a reliable printer who was unlikely to bring out a pirated edition and that the sequence in its current form does manifest structural unity. In his New Cambridge edition of these poems (1996), however, Gwynne B. Evans takes issue with Duncan-Jones's contention that Shakespeare arranged for Thorpe to publish his sonnets; he cites among other evidence the apparent absence of authorial oversight during the printing of the edition and the unlikelihood that Shakespeare would have made public the sexual relationship with the young man that the sonnets imply.

Several twentieth-century studies have explored the literary backgrounds of the collection and related it to the literary history of its period. In *The Shakespearean Moment and Its Place in the Poetry of the Seventeenth Century* (1954), Patrick Cruttwell argues that the 1590s represented a watershed in English literary history, with the sonnets enacting a movement from simple lyricism to a more critical and dramatic mode of writing. Thirty-two years later, as we will see, Joel Fineman, though influenced by different critical methods and assumptions, was also to interpret these poems as a turning point. J. W. Lever's *Elizabethan Love Sonnet* (1956; rev. ed. 1966) traces the connections between Shakespeare's sequence and the English sonnet tradition; J. B. Leishman's *Themes and Variations in Shakespeare's Sonnets* (1961; rev. ed. 1963) instead adopts a comparatist approach, positioning Shakespeare's lyrics in relation to classical and Continental treatments of their main themes and to a range of sonnets by English, French, and Italian poets.

Thematic and stylistic concerns have shaped a number of other studies. In *The Sense of Shakespeare's Sonnets* (1952), Edward Hubler studies Shakespeare's treatment of issues like the workings of love and the stewardship praised in the Biblical parable of the talents. Murray Krieger's *Window to Criticism: Shakespeare's* Sonnets *and Modern Poetics* (1964) focuses on metaphoric patterns of references to mirrors and windows; in so doing, as his title implies, he relates the poems to contemporary poetic theory, devising and defending ways of moving beyond the New Critical emphasis on the isolated poem. Before publishing his landmark edition, Stephen Booth explored the poems in *An Essay on Shakespeare's Sonnets* (1969); here he demonstrates how the extraordinary difficulties of interpreting these poems are in part at least moderated by strategies like simultaneous likeness and difference. Exemplifying the benefits of close attention to nuances of language, Anne Ferry analyzes conceptions of temporality in several authors (*All in War with Time: Love Poetry of Shakespeare, Donne, Jonson, Marvell* [1975]) and the development of concepts of interiority (*The "Inward" Language: Sonnets of Wyatt, Sidney, Shakespeare, Donne* [1983]). Helen Vendler's *Shakespeare's "Sonnets": A Commentary* (forthcoming) offers detailed poem-by-poem commentaries on the entire collection, focusing on the connections between formal considerations and meaning; in contrast to the poststructuralist interpretive emphasis on textual fissures and failures, her readings typically posit aesthetically successful resolutions to the problems confronted in these lyrics.

The linguistic criticism that enjoyed a brief vogue during the 1970s left its mark on the sonnets. Roman Jakobson, a distinguished linguist, collaborated with Lawrence G. Jones to produce a structuralist reading of Sonnet 129, *Shakespeare's Verbal Art in "Th' Expense of Spirit"* (1970); this monograph is a classic example of the potentialities and limitations of its method, on the one hand drawing attention to important grammatical and syntactical patterns that other readers had neglected and on the other privileging patterns of no significance. Structuralism and other types of linguistic analysis shape Giorgio Melchiori's *Shakespeare's Dramatic Meditations: An Experiment in Criticism* (1976), though the book is also infused with commentary on social issues, demonstrating that such concerns are not necessarily inimical to linguistic analysis, as opponents of that methodology sometimes assert.

Wordsworth declared that Shakespeare unlocked his heart in the sonnets, and ever since readers have debated what the poems reveal about that heart—and about the loins to which it apparently bears such an uneasy relationship. Until the advent of the gay and lesbian criticism, many critics either firmly denied the possibility of a homoerotic relationship between the poet and Friend, citing the conventions of male friendship in the Renaissance to explain language that might otherwise seem sexual, or broached the possibility circumspectly and hesitantly. W. H. Auden, himself gay, wrote an introduction to the poems for the Signet edition (1964; published in a revised edition with Shakespeare's other poems in 1989); even he felt impelled—or constrained—to declare that the relationship to the Friend is primarily mystical.

Practitioners of the new gay and lesbian criticism and of queer theory have, however, determinedly raised the very issue about the sonnets that so many other Shakespeareans had avoided. In 1985, Joseph Pequigney published *Such Is My Love: A Study of Shakespeare's Sonnets*, a pioneering work that not only asserts that the poems record a sexual relationship between two men but also finds in them specific references to many sexual practices. The extremity of some of Pequigney's readings may well stem from his polemical mission of emphasizing homoerotic interpretations suppressed by other critics; Bruce R. Smith's *Homosexual Desire in Shakespeare's England: A Cultural Poetics* (1991) also assumes a homoerotic relationship but is more judicious in evaluating whether particular lines and images refer to that relationship.

Recent theoretical developments also made their presence felt in several other approaches to the sonnets that appeared towards the end of the twentieth century. The reaction against idolizations of Shakespeare is exemplified by Margreta de Grazia's *Shakespeare Verbatim: The Reproduction of Authenticity and the 1790 Apparatus* (1991); when discussing the sonnets she demonstrates how a succession of editors responded to these poems in terms of their own agendas, notably changing concepts of authorship. De Grazia has also published a series of influential articles on these poems; for example, in "The Scandal of Shakespeare's Sonnets" (*Shakespeare Survey*, 46 [1993], 35–49), she interprets the relationship with the Dark Lady as threatening the social order. Lars Engle's *Shakespearean Pragmatism: Market of His Time* (1993) explores conceptions of value in the sonnets and plays from the perspective of pragmatism, a philosophical movement that had a considerable impact on literary criticism in the final decades of the century. Developed by philosophers such as Richard Rorty and adapted by literary critics such as Stanley Fish, this movement holds that apparent truths are created by the systems that promulgate and defend them rather than having a stable and prior existence.

Several characteristics associated with the criticism written after 1970—a preoccupation with subjectivity, the influence of Lacan, and a prose style that its defenders call precise and sophisticated and its detractors merely obscure—are evident in Joel Fineman's book *Shakespeare's Perjured Eye: The Invention of Poetic Subjectivity in the Sonnets* (1986). The sonnets, Fineman asserts in this important study, appeared at and helped to shape a crucial development in the history of lyric poetry; conventions of praise were exhausted, and Shakespeare reinterprets and revives them. In so doing, his book argues, Shakespeare spearheads the development of modern subjectivity.

Venus and Adonis

The continuing significance of genre for Shakespeare studies is manifest in the essays and books that approach *Venus and Adonis* in terms of its literary form. The genre with which it is primarily associated, the *epyllion* or "little epic," is not easy to define, not least because critics debate its relationship, if any, to classical analogues, and, indeed, the very existence of a cognate classical type. In any event, the poem clearly participates in a tradition of Ovidian mythological verse that also includes Marlowe's *Hero and Leander* and many other texts, and three important studies in particular have traced the ways Shakespeare adopts and adapts that tradition. William Keach's *Elizabethan Erotic Narratives: Irony and Pathos in the Ovidian Poetry of Shakespeare, Marlowe, and Their Contemporaries* (1977) directs attention to the darker side of Ovid, overlooked by many other readers. Similarly, four years later, Clark Hulse's *Metamorphic Verse: The Elizabethan Minor Epic* connected the tradition named in his title not only to Ovid but also to Petrarchism and to types of history writing; the study encompasses commentaries on both *Venus and Adonis* and *The Rape of Lucrece*. In *Shakespeare and Ovid* (1993) Jonathan Bate traces the ways *Venus and Adonis* is deeply concerned with transgressive sexuality; the influence of Ovid is especially apparent, he maintains, when Shakespeare displays the polymorphousness of desire.

Many of the complex issues *Venus and Adonis* raises crystallize in another generic question, the dilemma of whether it should be read as comic, tragic, farcical, or some hybrid of these types. Some critics interpret it as a serious moral struggle, while others insist on humorous elements. Perhaps the most judicious response is the assertion that it is ambivalent in these as in many other regards, a perspective developed by Hulse and Keach among others.

Intellectual history was a forte of traditional Renaissance scholarship, and a number of scholars have approached the poem from that perspective. They typically offer allegorical interpretations of its main characters and events, variously adducing the doctrine of the humors (a central premise of Renaissance medicine), Renaissance theories of the soul (not necessarily a Christian concept in these formulations), and Neo-Platonic comparisons of various types of love and various versions of Venus. Some studies identify Venus with passion and Adonis with reason, two coordinates with which Renaissance texts often mapped behavior, but others dispute that interpretation. For example, Heather Asals asserts that the goddess of love progresses upwards through the Platonic hierarchy, moving from mere lust to true love ("Venus and Adonis: The Education of a Goddess," *Studies in English Literature, 1500–1900*, 13 [1973], 31–51).

As the range of allegorical interpretations would suggest, critics part company on the values informing the poem, their opinions forming a spectrum from the assertion that *Venus and Adonis* delights in amoral naturalism to the claim that it is a deeply moral rejection of Venus's sensuality. Hence readings of the principal characters differ too, with Adonis's behavior variously interpreted as insufferably priggish and entirely appropriate. Interpretations of Venus often introduce parallels with other characters in Shakespeare, notably Cleopatra and the Dark Lady of the sonnets. The feasibility of such evaluations is, however, challenged by the critics who insist that allegorical readings, not psychological evaluations, are the appropriate response to the lovers in the poem. Other studies examine language, style, and tone. In one of the strongest analyses of these issues, Lucy Gent focuses on the exaggerated rhetoric of the poem and suggests that its central problem is the relationship between hyperbole and reality ("'Venus and Adonis': The Triumph of Rhetoric," *Modern Language Review*, 69 [1974], 721–29).

The Rape of Lucrece

The legend of Lucrece, the faithful Roman wife who killed herself after being raped by one of her husband's army companions, has inspired paintings and drawings by numerous artists—Botticelli, Cranach, Rembrandt, and Rowlandson, among others. Some

Lucreces are proudly defiant, others desolate. And some pictorial treatments emphasize the rape, others its political consequences. Literary critics have responded to the poem from a similar range of perspectives.

Several of those studies position *The Rape of Lucrece* in relation to other texts, literary and pictorial. As its title indicates, R. Thomas Simone's monograph *Shakespeare and "Lucrece": A Study of the Poem and Its Relation to the Plays* (1974), the only book-length study devoted specifically to Shakespeare's poem, focuses on the relationship between this text and its author's dramas. This perspective is too often ignored in studies of Shakespeare's non-dramatic poems. More specifically, a number of critics have connected the treatment of Rome in this poem and elsewhere in Shakespeare's canon; see, for example, Robert S. Miola's *Shakespeare's Rome* (1983). Incisive and thorough analyses of other literary and artistic treatments of the story appear in Ian Donaldson, *The Rapes of Lucretia: A Myth and Its Transformations* (1982). Stephanie H. Jed's *Chaste Thinking: The Rape of Lucretia and the Birth of Humanism* (1989) provides a different type of background, scrutinizing the legend of Lucrece in relation to Jed's materialist reinterpretation of humanism. Focusing on the language that renders Tarquin's psychological states, Jonathan Bate demonstrates how Shakespeare characteristically transforms Ovid's physical metamorphoses into mental ones (*Shakespeare and Ovid* [1993]).

The elaborately rhetorical language of the poem has attracted attention from many other perspectives as well; indeed, comparing critical treatments of this issue provides a synecdochic summary of changes in Shakespeare criticism and in the profession at large. Choosing a title that signals the New Critical perspective on organic unity, Robert J. Griffin analyzes the language of both *The Rape of Lucrece* and *Venus and Adonis* in "'These Contraries Such Unity Do Hold': Patterned Imagery in Shakespeare's Narrative Poems," (*Studies in English Literature, 1500–1900*, 4 [1964], 43–55). Katharine Eisaman Maus stresses the problems more than the potentialities of language in "Taking Tropes Seriously: Language and Violence in Shakespeare's *Rape of Lucrece*" (*Shakespeare Quarterly*, 37 [1986], 66–82): Having demonstrated that both the characters and the narrators approach tropes as though they were literally true, she suggests that the poem reveals the dangers of language and investigates alternative modes of representation, notably the visual. In *Captive Victors: Shakespeare's Narrative Poems and Sonnets* (1987), I draw on the modes of linguistic criticism that were popular in the 1970s; arguing that *syneciosis*, which links opposites, is the central trope of the poem, my book relates that figure to issues ranging from political rivalries to redefinitions of subjectivity. Deconstructive and psychoanalytic approaches to language are evident in Joel Fineman's article, "Shakespeare's *Will*: The Temporality of Rape." (The text is reprinted in a posthumous collection of Fineman's essays—this gifted critic died young—*The Subjectivity Effect in Western Literary Tradition: Essays Toward the Release of Shakespeare's Will* [1991]). Fineman argues that the poem, which shares many rhetorical characteristics with the sonnets, reveals the construction of Shakespeare's own subjectivity and the subjectivities of his characters: In particular, according to Fineman, *The Rape of Lucrece* contrasts a fallen and duplicitous language with a clearer one. Other linguistic studies of the poem engage with the issue of how Lucrece's hyperbolic language affects interpretations of her behavior.

As that question might suggest, feminism has generated a number of important studies of the poem and can be credited with some of the renewed interest in it. Some of the most significant of these analyses are by Coppélia Kahn. In "The Rape in Shakespeare's *Lucrece*" (*Shakespeare Studies*, 9 [1976], 45–72), she affirms that the central issue in the poem is indeed rape and suggests that that act uncovers the destructive workings of patriarchy, notably its emphasis on wifely chastity and its encouragement of proprietory male responses to women. Similarly, Nancy Vickers's reading of the poem concentrates on the dangers of the type of conventional physical description known as a blazon ("'The blazon of sweet beauty's best': Shakespeare's *Lucrece*," in *Shakespeare and the Question of Theory*, ed. Patricia Parker and Geoffrey Hartman [1985]).

The potential tensions between these studies of the politics of gender on the one hand and studies of politics in the more literal sense on the other are neatly encapsulated when one compares Vickers's essay with the equally incisive analysis by Annabel Patterson in *Reading Between the Lines* (1993). Too many critics, Patterson asserts, have focused on the rape at the expense of the central political action it generates: Brutus's overthrow of the tyrannical Tarquins and the consequent shift to republicanism. The conflict between the two approaches becomes explicit when she proceeds to fault feminists for privileging gender over more important social divisions. Patterson subordinates the concerns that feminist and other critics considered primary through a telling clause: "What delays the reader for 1,855 lines is primarily psychological and rhetorical filler" (p. 301). Notice particularly how the diminution of the issues discussed in those lines is skillfully effected through the words "delays" and "filler." Conversely, Vickers writes, "Shakespeare's poem closes as it opened, as men rhetorically compete with each other over Lucrece's body" (p. 108). The episode she describes is in fact succeeded by seven stanzas tracing Brutus's political actions; her verb "closes" positions the competition whose dangers Vickers exposes as the climax of the poem, privileging it over the political rebellion that succeeds it. One could find similarly revealing rhetoric in most of the essays and books surveyed above, reminding us that Shakespeare's critics can best be evaluated, moderated, and variously appreciated and repudiated if one scrutinizes their own writing with the analytical techniques one brings to literary texts, reading critically in more than one sense of that adverb. We should note the gaps and silences of these studies as well as what is being said overtly. And we should read them with the close attention to details of language and rhetorical strategies that the sonnets, *Venus and Adonis*, and *The Rape of Lucrece* themselves call for and reward.

CONCLUSION, OR, EXIT PURSUED BY AN EDITOR

> A savage clamor!
> Well may I get aboard! This is the chase;
> I am gone for ever. *Exit pursued by a bear.*
>
> *The Winter's Tale* (III.ii.56–58)

Some of the shifts traced in this essay are apparent in the relative attention granted to various genres at different times; for example, feminism sparked a renewed concern for the comedies towards the end of the century, while during that same period gay and lesbian studies and queer theory intensified interest in Shakespeare's sonnets. Surveying the changing critical responses to a given play can provide a different but no less valuable key to changes in Shakespeare criticism, and I have chosen *As You Like It* and *Henry V* to summarize such metamorphoses because critical responses to those two dramas are in many ways typical of developments throughout the field.

Approaches to *As You Like It* before 1970 often explored images and themes, with Caroline F. E. Spurgeon, for example, pointing out that the play contains more similes involving animals than any of its author's other comedies (*Shakespeare's Imagery and What It Tells Us* [1935]). In addition, Shakespeareans elucidated a number of scholarly issues with important critical implications, such as Shakespeare's refashioning of his principal source, Thomas Lodge's *Rosalynde* (1590). The section in Rosalie L. Colie's *Shakespeare's Living Art* (1974) that treats the play in relation to pastoral patterns exemplifies the engagement with genre in much twentieth-century Renaissance criticism. Indeed, another generic study, C. L. Barber's *Shakespeare's Festive Comedy: A Study of Dramatic Form and Its Relation to Social Custom* (1959), established an interpretation of the play that was to dominate many other critical interpretations: According to Barber, *As You Like It* exemplifies the retreat to a green world of festivity and liberty that is enacted as well in several of Shakespeare's other comedies. In that world, Orlando learns to replace Petrarchan silliness with a more mature version of loving, thanks to the wise and charming Rosalind; the union of no fewer than four pairs of lovers at the end creates and represents social harmony and reconciliation.

It is too easy, however, for critics committed to a darker reading to deny the subtleties their predecessors at their best brought to interpretations like Barber's. As Anne Barton's introduction to the play in this volume demonstrates, studies of *As You Like It* influenced by the model of festive comedy and by other traditional approaches to comedic form do not necessarily erase or misrepresent all tensions: She scrupulously notes the limitations of the new society created in Arden, reminds us that this version of pastoral is not entirely pleasant, and traces the countervailing notes represented by Touchstone and Jaques. Nor are the sexual ambiguities of the play completely overlooked by traditional critics. In *Shakespeare's Festive Comedy*, C. L. Barber himself acknowledges the homoerotic overtones in Phebe's response to Rosalind/Ganymede, though he delineates them in terms that some later critics were to find homophobic.

> She has, in effect, a girlish crush on the femininity which shows through Rosalind's disguise; the aberrant affection is happily got over when Rosalind reveals her identity and makes it manifest that Phebe has been loving a woman (p. 231).

In general, before 1970 critics typically acknowledge anxieties and tensions in the play but represent them as artistically delimited and controlled. Thus in her introduction to the play in this volume, Barton can write of its "essential optimism" and of its "insistence upon the tolerance and inclusiveness of the new society epitomized in the final dance" (pp. 366–67).

Certain concerns of earlier criticism are reinterpreted in approaches to the play after 1970, reminding us again that repetition-with-a-difference is sometimes the best description of the changes in Shakespearean criticism. Thus, for example, Barbara J. Bono cites the characteristics of pastoral in developing a feminist interpretation ("Mixed Gender, Mixed Genre in Shakespeare's *As You Like It*," in *Renaissance Genres: Essays on Theory, History, and Interpretation*, ed. Barbara Kiefer Lewalski [1986]). But more typically the criticism of the play written in the final decades of the twentieth century shifts the balances of earlier interpretations; in particular, the threats and tensions that previous critics had recognized but subordinated are seen as playing a more central role throughout *As You Like It*, not least during the apparent reconciliations on which it culminates. Many feminist readers find in the closural drive of the play not joyous reconciliation but repression: Rosalind yields power to her father and husband-to-be, metaphorically silenced much as the heroines in other comedies are literally silenced. Or perhaps indeed Rosalind never had the freedom that more optimistic critics attribute to her; Peter Erickson asserts that the green world was in fact a patriarchal world (*Patriarchal Structures in Shakespeare's Drama* [1985]). Adherents of feminism, gender studies, and gay and lesbian criticism have all engaged with the cross-dressing in the play, with Valerie Traub in particular taking Barber to task for his celebration of heterosexuality in the passage quoted above (*Desire and Anxiety: Circulations of Sexuality in Shakespearean Drama* [1992]).

Louis Montrose's "'The Place of a Brother' in *As You Like It*: Social Process and Comic Form" (*Shakespeare Quarterly*, 32 (1981), 28–54) exemplifies a new historicist approach to the tensions of this comedy. The relationship between Oliver and Orlando, Montrose maintains, is central to *As You Like It*, and so too are the material issues about inheritance and primogeniture it raises, questions that are overlooked when one approaches the text simply as a love story. Montrose sedulously notes connections between the relationships among men that he studies and male-female relationships, but his privileging of the former and of economic problems over those of gender helps to explain the continuing disagreements between new historicists and feminists. In its emphasis on the role of property in Elizabethan England, Montrose's essay also provides a textbook example of shifts in critical focus since Anne Barton contributed her introduction to this edition. According to Barton,

> There is a flurry of events at the beginning—Oliver's various attempts to rid himself of his virtuous younger brother, the banishment of Rosalind and then of Oliver himself—but these are transparently devices for getting all the major characters away from the familiar world and into the forest of Arden, rather than incidents exploited for their own sake (p. 365).

According to Montrose, however, "What happens to Orlando at home is not Shakespeare's contrivance to get him into the forest; what happens to Orlando in the forest is Shakespeare's contrivance to remedy what has happened to him at home" (p. 29).

Henry V also neatly exemplifies changes in critical perspectives. Many of the readings of it before the advent of the new historicism were influenced by E. M. W. Tillyard's formulation of the so-called Tudor myth, the doctrine that the civil wars of the fifteenth century, retribution for the sin of deposing Richard II, culminated in and were resolved by the glorious reign of the Tudor family. This reading casts Shakespeare as proponent of—or apologist for—the order and stability that were assumed to be the dominant values of his culture. And it casts the king as the idealized hero of a patriotic drama, the widespread interpretation that shapes Herschel Baker's introduction in this volume.

This is not to say, however, that such an approach to the play was universally accepted until new historicism and other recent methodologies questioned it. In *Characters of Shakespeare's Plays* (1817; rev. 1818), the nineteenth-century Romantic critic William Hazlitt, far from idealizing Hal, stresses his faults. In the subsequent century Henry Ansgar Kelly was to challenge Tillyard, substituting a thoroughly documented reinterpretation of Tudor historiography (*Divine Providence in the England of Shakespeare's Histories* [1970]). And many other twentieth-century critics acknowledged complexities and inconsistencies in the portrayal of the king, as, indeed, Baker himself does.

But even when we register such caveats, it is clear that the final decades of the century, particularly the years after 1980, witnessed four principal shifts in interpretations of *Henry V*: more attention to its cynical perspectives on politics and the resulting implications about ideology; intense interest in the presence of Scottish, Welsh, and Irish "others"; cynical reexaminations of Henry's courtship of Katherine; and reconsiderations of the theatricality of the play. These changes are mirrored in the differences between Sir Laurence Olivier's cinematic version of the play, produced to spur English patriotism during the dark days of World War II, and Kenneth Branagh's more cynical and violent film. The clergymen who appear at the beginning of the play, for instance, are comic in Olivier's version, conniving in Branagh's.

First, then, many critics attacked the premise that the play represents a straightforward celebration of royal power and monarchical heroism. In an important study of *Henry V*, Norman Rabkin borrows the philosopher Ludwig Wittgenstein's discussion of an image that can be visualized as either a duck or a rabbit but never both at once to argue that the play lends itself to two contradictory readings that cannot be reconciled: Henry as ideal Christian prince and Henry as dangerous Machiavel (*Shakespeare and the Problem of Meaning* [1981]). In "Invisible Bullets," Stephen Greenblatt cites the Henriad as evidence for the new historicist paradigm described earlier: Apparent challenges to power are seen as contained and even generated by the dominant culture for its own ends. (Rightly considered one of the most typical and influential new historicist manifestos, the essay appears in Greenblatt's *Shakespearean Negotiations: The Circulation of Social Energy in Renaissance England* [1988] and in a number of collections.) A significantly different perspective on power and ideology emerges when two of the leading English cultural materialists, Jonathan Dollimore and Alan Sinfield, argue against the monolithic oversimplifications of history that they attribute even to many of the critics who reject Tillyard; a more acute reading of the play, they maintain, stresses contradictions and tensions in its ideological agendas ("History and Ideology: The Instance of *Henry V*," in *Alternative Shakespeares*, ed. John Drakakis [1985]). Despite the salient differences among them, most of these interpretations are united by their interest in ideology. The concept has been defined and deployed in more ways than those using it sometimes acknowledge (for example, some maintain that it is an appurtenance of only the group in power, while others posit conflicting ideologies associated with lower social strata as well). But however it is interpreted, ideology has been a central topic in Shakespeare studies after 1970.

The presence of various Others has also interested students of *Henry V* during the final decades of the twentieth century. Many feminist critics have found in the courtship scene that concludes the play the type of objectification and silencing of women that they attribute to comedic closure as well. Noting Henry's appropriation of his future wife in that episode, Phyllis Rackin demonstrates how he bases his own authority on women throughout the play (*Stages of History: Shakespeare's English Chronicles* [1990]). Nationalism and its twin, the denigration of outsiders and marginalized groups, also became central topics in Shakespeare studies after about 1980, and these issues too engage a number of Shakespeareans when they approach *Henry V*; for example, in "'Vile Participation': The Amplification of Violence in the Theater of *Henry V*," (*Shakespeare Quarterly*, 42 [1991], 1–32), Joel B. Altman relates the play to contemporaneous conflicts in Ireland. Altman's title refers to theatre, and, given the post-structuralist interest in representation and the new historicist concentration on theatricality, it is not surprising that the self-conscious references to the Globe in *Henry V*, exemplified by the initial epigraph in this essay, have caught the attention of critics.

The theatre, so central a concern in *Henry V*, also provides an apt parallel to and summary of the subject of this essay. Most scholars trace the origins of the Shakespearean stage to innyards and bearbaiting arenas; some argue instead for the Roman amphitheatre. Both bearbaiting and theatrical performance might plausibly be listed as analogues to the controversies among Shakespeareans throughout the twentieth century. But the best of the books and articles they have written splendidly elucidate the complexities of Shakespearean poetry and drama. And studying the history of Shakespeare criticism can elucidate as well the dramas staged in our own classrooms when students and teachers decide what issues to discuss and what perspectives to adopt as they engage with Shakespeare.

Shakespeare's Text

G. Blakemore Evans

Most readers of Shakespeare know that Macbeth, reproached by Lady Macbeth for seeming cowardice, asserts, "I dare do all that may become a man; / Who dares do more is none" (I.vii.46–47); that Richard III, frightened by a threatening dream, insists defensively, "Richard loves Richard, that is, I am I" (V.iii.183); that Romeo in despair after receiving word of Juliet's supposed death cries out, "Is it e'en so? Then I defy you, stars!" (V.i.24); that the villain-bastard Edmund convinces himself that "Edmund the base / Shall top th' legitimate" Edgar (*King Lear*, I.ii.20–21); and that as Falstaff lay dying, about to be transported straight to Arthur's bosom, " 'a babbl'd of green fields" (*Henry V*, II.iii.16–17). What most readers are not aware of, however, is that none of these familiar lines appears in the original, basic texts in exactly the form here quoted; that, in fact, each contains one or more emended words designed to restore meaning to an otherwise corrupt passage.[1] And these are but five out of hundreds of passages in Shakespeare's plays that require some sort of editorial intervention. The different kinds and several sources of textual corruption and what such corruption may imply for the general authority of a particular text, together with an examination of the various bibliographical techniques and approaches that have been devised to recover what may be called the "true text"—these, the disease, its causes, and the proposed remedies, are among the principal subjects of the following essay.

Before we turn, however, to a consideration of the various problems involved in establishing Shakespeare's text, it will be useful to give a brief statement of what is meant when we speak of the Shakespeare canon, that is, the body of writing (plays and poems) which by general consensus is now accepted as constituting Shakespeare's "works."

So far as the plays are concerned, the bounds of the canon are, with three exceptions, laid down by the contents of the first collected edition of Shakespeare's dramatic works, published by William Jaggard in 1623 and now universally referred to as the First Folio (F1). This collection contains thirty-six plays and forms the central core of the canon. Eighteen of these plays had been published earlier in separate quarto (Q) editions of different degrees of authority, ranging in date from 1594 (*Titus Andronicus*) to 1622 (*Othello*). The remaining eighteen plays were here printed for the first time, and for these plays the First Folio is our sole authority. Since 1623 only two other plays, and two passages from a third, have been generally admitted to the canon: *Pericles*, *The Two Noble Kinsmen*, and *Sir Thomas More* (two passages only).[2] The first was attributed to Shakespeare on the title-page of the first quarto (Q1) in 1609; the second to John Fletcher and Shakespeare on the title-page of the only quarto edition in 1634. The two passages from the manuscript play *Sir Thomas More* (first printed in 1844) are now widely accepted as by Shakespeare. Indeed, one of the passages, a substantial scene of 147 lines, is believed by most to be

[1] The original, unemended readings for these passages may be consulted in the Textual Notes following each play. The passage from *King Lear* is discussed later in this essay (page 66).

[2] A fourth play, *Edward III* (c. 1592–5), has been included in this revised edition of *The Riverside*. Edward Capell, in 1760, first claimed the play for Shakespeare and recent scholarship has identified his hand in, at least, the so-called "Countess scenes" (I.ii—II.i–ii) and IV.iv (in which Prince Edward, surrounded by the French forces, refuses to surrender). Some critics, including Eliot Slater, Fred Lapides, and Richard Proudfoot, like Capell, argue for single authorship and strongly favor Shakespeare as that author. See the critical introduction and "Note on the Text" to the play.

written in Shakespeare's autograph (Hand D in the manuscript).[3] It should be observed that the inclusion of a play in the canon does not necessarily imply that it is wholly the work of Shakespeare. The questions of Shakespeare's revision of older plays by other hands or his collaboration with other writers are a source of endless disagreement among scholars. Discussion of such matters will be found in the separate critical introductions and, to some extent, in the "Note on the Text" to each play.

The canon of the poems includes *Venus and Adonis*, *The Rape of Lucrece*, the Sonnets, "The Phoenix and Turtle," and, "A Lover's Complaint." Five poems that appear elsewhere in Shakespeare's work are included in *The Passionate Pilgrim*; whether any of the unattributed poems in that collection are his is uncertain. Recently, Donald Foster has argued strongly for adding "A Funeral Elegy" by "W.S." (1612) to the canon. This poem (of 578 lines) has now been included in *The Riverside*, but any final verdict on its Shakespearean authorship must, at least for now, and perhaps indefinitely, remain open. The evidence for and against attributing "A Funeral Elegy" to Shakespeare is discussed in the critical introduction to the poem. It is now (2002) agreed that "A Funeral Elegy" is not by Shakespeare but the work of John Ford (see p. 1895).

I. THE MANUSCRIPTS, OR WHAT LIES BEHIND THE PRINTED TEXTS

The extent of corruption or uncertain authority in Shakespeare's texts will appear strange to most present-day readers, who are accustomed to accept any book they may read as reproducing exactly what the author wrote. Although their faith is in fact not always fully justified, their general assumption is relatively sound. Today there is ordinarily a direct link between the author and the published text, and the line of authority is thus continuous from author to reader. But for Elizabethan-Jacobean printed drama, with rare exceptions (especially the plays of Ben Jonson), the line from author to reader was much more tortuous, even broken. This relative dissociation of author and printed text gives rise to a basic question: What was the source, or sources, of the manuscripts from which Shakespeare's plays were set up by the printer, both the separately published plays (the quartos) and those in the First Folio (1623) collection? Until about eighty years ago no one seems to have given much serious consideration to this question, and yet the answer can tell us a great deal about a number of the problems that plague Shakespeare's text.

Unfortunately, no substantive manuscripts, either authorial or scribal, have survived for the main body of the Shakespeare canon,[4] but it is nevertheless possible from what we know of extant contemporary manuscripts of plays by other writers, and with some aid from the scene in *Sir Thomas More* generally believed to be in Shakespeare's hand, to sketch with some degree of accuracy what may be called the "fortunes" of a dramatic manuscript in the Elizabethan-Jacobean period. After an author had completed his working draft, known then as "foul papers," either he prepared a "fair copy" of it himself, presumably making last-minute changes and adjustments as he copied, or he (or his acting company) hired a professional scribe to make a clean transcript of the "foul papers," which, depending upon opportunity or the author's literary conscience, he might or might not read over to catch errors or make improvements. From what we believe we know of Shakespeare's "foul papers," learned from a study of a number of his plays thought to have been printed from such copy (e.g. *Hamlet*, Q2 and *Romeo and Juliet*, Q2)[5] and the evidence of the scene from *Sir Thomas More* (see the "Note on the Text" to that play), it is clear that his working drafts presented considerable difficulties for scribes (as later for compositors) and that the resulting text could in many significant details be inaccurate or confused. Moreover, there is essentially no evidence that Shakespeare was himself at all concerned with preserving an authoritative text of his plays for future readers. Although he most probably saw his two major poems, *Venus and Adonis* and *Lucrece*, through the press personally, visiting the printing-house daily to correct, forme by forme, the sheets as they were printed off,[6] there is no evidence to suggest that he interested himself in the publication of a single one of his plays. If he had, we may ask, why did he, after the appearance, for example, of corrupt pirated texts of *Romeo and Juliet* (Q1, 1597) and *Hamlet* (Q1, 1603) permit the so-called "good" quartos of these two plays (Q2, 1599 and 1604) to be printed from his "foul papers" instead of seeing to it that "fair copies" were provided? Or, again, why did he do nothing to see that the pirated texts of *Henry V* (Q1, 1600) and *The Merry Wives of Windsor* (Q1, 1602) were replaced by the publication of sound editions during his lifetime? Relevant here also is the question as to why he allowed so many of his plays to remain unpublished. It is true that, generally speaking, once a dramatist had completed a play and sold it to an acting company, he ceased to have any personal rights in it, the play becoming the property of the company, which thus controlled the uses to which the play could be put, including its publication. But even if this impediment was not (as some would argue) more apparent than real, it seems reasonable, considering Shakespeare's eminence in his company and hence his presumed authority, to conclude that his attitude toward his plays, once the immediate excitement of creation had worn off, was more that of a practical man of the theatre,

[3] See the discussion of Shakespeare's involvement in *Sir Thomas More* in the introduction to the specially prepared texts of these two passages included in the present edition. These texts are accompanied by photographic reproductions of the three pages believed to be in Shakespeare's autograph.

[4] The earliest extant manuscript of one of Shakespeare's canonical plays is a telescoped version of *1* and *2 Henry IV*, prepared by Sir Edward Dering about 1623 and based on the earlier quartos. See G. W. Williams and G. B. Evans, eds., *William Shakespeare, "The History of King Henry the Fourth," As Revised by Sir Edward Dering, Bart.* (Folger Facsimiles, 1974)

[5] Q2 = Second Quarto; F1 = First Folio. For definitions of "quarto" (Q) and "folio" (F) and other technical bibliographical terms used in this introduction and in the separate "Note on the Text" prefixed to the Textual Notes for each play, see the "Glossary of Selected Bibliographical Terms" (hereafter referred to as the "Glossary") following this essay.

[6] See the Glossary, under *Sheet* and *Forme*.

THE MOST LA-
mentable Romaine
Tragedie of Titus Andronicus:

As it was Plaide by the Right Ho-
nourable the Earle of *Darbie*, Earle of *Pembrooke*,
and Earle of *Suffex* their Seruants.

LONDON,
Printed by Iohn Danter, and are
to be fold by *Edward White* & *Thomas Millington*,
at the little North doore of Paules at the
figne of the Gunne,
1594.

The earliest known "good" quarto of a Shakespearean play: title-page of the First Quarto of *Titus Andronicus* (1594), from the unique copy discovered in Sweden in 1904 and now in the Folger Shakespeare Library

interested in performance and the box-office, than that of a man with deeply felt literary pretensions, like Jonson, bent on preserving his works in authoritative texts for posterity.

After the manuscript of a play became the property of an acting company, several things could (and did) happen to it. If still in author's draft form ("foul papers"), it might be annotated by the company's official book-keeper in preparation for the transcription of a "fair copy" intended for use as the company's prompt-book. If already a "fair copy" when it came into the book-keeper's hands, it would undergo a similar process. In either case, the book-keeper's attentions might include regularizing speech-prefixes, adding missing stage directions (both matters about which Shakespeare seems to have been careless, as the first *More* passage and some of the quarto and First Folio texts show), indicating properties and sound effects needed at certain points, and marking cuts in the full text (Shakespeare's plays, for example, were generally over the average length required) either to improve the pace of scenes or simply to reduce the text to actable proportions within what Shakespeare loosely called the "two hours' traffic" of the stage. Once transcribed as "fair copy" the "foul papers" seem to have been retained in the company's archives. After the "book of the play" (that is, the official prompt-book) had been prepared, it had to be licensed by the Master of the Revels before it could be publicly acted—a step which in itself often necessitated changes to meet official demands. It could then be subjected to further alterations as various matters of detail came to be ironed out in rehearsal and performance, obviously a continuing process. Later still, in an attempt to give an older play a new look, the same manuscript (or even the "foul papers") might undergo drastic and far-reaching revisions, with additions, perhaps by another hand. Thus several different manuscript versions of the same play (including possible private transcripts made at any point in the stages described above) might be simultaneously in existence and hence more or less available to serve as copy for a printed edition.

Investigation, under the leadership of A. W. Pollard, J. Dover Wilson, W. W. Greg, Fredson Bowers, and Alice Walker, has been able to distinguish five general categories of manuscripts which, it is believed, may be shown to underlie Shakespeare's printed texts. First, author's manuscript, either his final carefully prepared "fair copy" or some stage of his working draft or "foul papers." Second, a scribal transcript of either the author's "fair copy" or his "foul papers." Third, the official theatre prompt-book (itself based on a manuscript falling under one of the two preceding heads), or a scribal copy based on it. Fourth, an unauthorized manuscript derived from the play as officially staged in London, or as cut by the company for provincial touring and reported from memory (i.e., a memorial reconstruction) by one or more actors who had at one time or another taken part in the play, usually playing comparatively minor roles. The reporter(s) may occasionally have called upon some professional writer to eke out the text, as, for example, may have happened in Q1 of *Romeo and Juliet*, V.iii.224–69. Fifth, in the case of a number of the First Folio texts, a kind of mixed copy, partly printed and partly manuscript, in which the printer employed an earlier printed edition (one or more quartos) that had been corrected and in some cases augmented by collation with a presumably authoritative manuscript. Further comment on these categories will be made in the following section.

II. THE EARLY PRINTED TEXTS

(1) *The quarto editions.* Nineteen[7] of Shakespeare's plays were published individually in quarto format before the appearance of his collected plays in the First Folio (1623). Among these quarto editions it is necessary to distinguish two main classes: the "good" quartos and the "bad" quartos. A "good" quarto is one printed from an authoritative manuscript, most often some form of the author's manuscript; in Shakespeare's case, most frequently the "foul papers." There are twelve "good" quartos: *Titus Andronicus* (1594),

[7] Twenty-one, if the quarto editions of *The Troublesome Reign of John, King of England* (1591) and *The Taming of a Shrew* (1594) are considered as "bad" quartos of *King John* and *The Taming of the Shrew*. The present discussion does not treat them as such, although the view that *A Shrew* is a "bad" quarto of *The Shrew* has recently met with general acceptance (see "Note on the Text" to *The Shrew*).

Richard II (1597), *1 Henry IV* (1598),[8] *Love's Labor's Lost* (1598), *Romeo and Juliet* (Q2, 1599), *2 Henry IV* (1600), *The Merchant of Venice* (1600), *A Midsummer Night's Dream* (1600), *Much Ado about Nothing* (1600), *Hamlet* (Q2, 1604/5), *Troilus and Cressida* (1609), and *Othello* (1622).[9] Each of these (except *Othello* and perhaps *1 Henry IV*) is generally believed to have been printed from Shakespeare's "foul papers" or from some kind of transcript of the "foul papers," and each (except *Othello*) is now usually accepted as furnishing the basic text of the play. To this official list of twelve "good" quartos must here be added: (1) the quarto edition of *The Two Noble Kinsmen* (1634), a play generally accepted as a collaboration between Shakespeare and John Fletcher and probably printed in those parts now assigned to Shakespeare from his "foul papers";[10] and (2) the quarto of *Edward III* (1596) which is probably based on some kind of scribal transcript.

The class of "bad" quartos represents a very different kind of textual authority, or lack of authority. According to the most widely accepted theory,[11] what lies behind a "bad" quarto text is a manuscript based on "memorial reconstruction." For most "bad" quarto texts this theory postulates an actor (or actors) who has taken some part (usually minor) in a performance of the play, most often a provincial performance, and who attempts to reconstruct the play from memory in order to produce a version of the text for some unauthorized acting group or to sell to a not too scrupulous printer. The resulting text is, thus, at several removes from any authoritative manuscript and suffers from the characteristic weaknesses of its memorially contaminated source: misplaced scenes or groups of lines (technically called anticipations and recollections), assimilations, garbled and farced-out speeches, amateurish and frequently unmetrical verse, commonplace word substitutions and flat prosaic paraphrases, actors' expletives, and bits and pieces from analogous scenes and situations in other plays. Such texts tend to be much shortened (the "bad" quarto of *Hamlet* is about half as long as the "good" quarto), not only because of failure of memory on the part of the reporter(s) but also as a result of original cutting in the performance from which the reported text was reconstructed. Despite these shortcomings the "bad" quartos are of special value for three reasons: they sometimes preserve the correct reading at points where the "good" text has been garbled in printing (notably in *Romeo and Juliet*); they occasionally contain lines which appear to be authorial but which are wanting in the "good" text either through compositorial carelessness or because they represent later additions by the author; and they afford a number of lively descriptive stage directions which record an eyewitness view of what took place during actual performance. There are "bad" quartos of nine plays: *2* and *3 Henry VI* (called *The First Part of the Contention betwixt the Two Famous Houses of York and Lancaster*, 1594, and *The True Tragedy of Richard Duke of York*, 1595), *Richard III* (1597), *Romeo and Juliet* (1597), *Henry V* (1600), *The Merry Wives of Windsor* (1602), *Hamlet* (1603), *King Lear* (1608), and *Pericles* (1609).[12] There was also almost certainly a "bad" quarto of *Love's Labor's Lost*, but no copy of this edition has survived. The "bad" quartos of *Richard III* and *King Lear*, both of which present comparatively superior texts, pose special problems of provenience; they are, nevertheless, here included in the "bad" quarto category

THE
Firſt part of the Con-
tention betwixt the two famous Houſes of Yorke
and Lancaſter, with the death of the good
Duke Humphrey:
And the baniſhment and death of the Duke of
Suffolke, and the Tragicall end of the proud Cardinall
of *VVinchester*, vvith the notable Rebellion
of *Iacke Cade*:
And the Duke of Yorkes firſt claime vnto the Crowne.

LONDON.
Printed by Thomas Creed, for Thomas Millington,
and are to be ſold at his ſhop vnder Saint Peters
Church in Cornwall.
1594.

The "bad" quarto of the play known in the received text as *Henry VI, Part 2*: title-page of a copy of the First Quarto (1594) in the Folger Shakespeare Library

[8] An earlier edition, probably also 1598, survives in a single sheet. This edition is discussed in the "Note on the Text" to *1 Henry IV*.

[9] For a complete list of the several editions through which a number of the quarto texts ("good" and "bad") passed, see the "Note on the Text" for each play.

[10] Paul Bertram (*Shakespeare and "The Two Noble Kinsmen,"* New Brunswick, New Jersey, 1965) has gone so far as to claim the whole play as Shakespeare's. His arguments have not been generally accepted.

[11] Two other theories have been advanced to account for the generally inferior texts found in the "bad" quartos: (1) the revision theory, which explained these texts as early versions either by the author himself or by some other writer, of the final form of the play as it appeared in a "good" text; (2) the stenographic theory, which accounted for the badness of the "bad" quartos by postulating a shorthand report taken down in the theatre during performance. Neither theory is now generally accepted, although the revision theory has had a few unsuccessful recent proponents. For a recent critique of some of the arguments concerning "foul papers" and "bad/good" quartos as technical terms, see Paul Werstine, "Narratives about Printed Shakespeare Texts: 'Foul Papers' and 'Bad' Quartos," *SQ*, XLI (1990), 65–86.

[12] *Pericles* was not included in either the First Folio (1623) or the Second Folio (1632); it was first added to the so-called Folio canon in the second issue of the Third Folio (1664), in a text derived from one of the later editions (Q6) of the "bad" quarto. *Pericles* is the only play in the Shakespeare canon that is entirely dependent for its text on a "bad" quarto.

as showing evidence of some form of memorial contamination.[13]

One other quarto edition should be mentioned. When, in his *Palladis Tamia* (1598), Francis Meres published a list of six "tragedies" and six comedies by Shakespeare, he included a comedy called "Loue labours wonne." No such play, at least under that name, has come down to us, but we now know, since T. W. Baldwin's discovery in 1957, that a quarto edition of a play with that name was included in a bookseller's stock in 1603.[14]

(2) *The First Folio.* Seven years after Shakespeare's death, the printer and publisher William Jaggard and his son Isaac, in association with three other booksellers and publishers, William Aspley, John Smethwick, and Edward Blount, produced the volume now regularly called the First Folio (1623), the first collected edition of Shakespeare's plays.[15] This collection seems to have been undertaken with the advice and aid of Shakespeare's company, the King's Men, and was prefaced with a dedication to the Earls of Pembroke and Montgomery and an address "To the great Variety of Readers," both signed by two of Shakespeare's oldest acting colleagues, John Heminge and Henry Condell. It contains thirty-six plays, eighteen here printed for the first time in any form: *The Tempest, The Two Gentlemen of Verona, Measure for Measure, The Comedy of Errors, As You Like It, The Taming of the Shrew, All's Well That Ends Well, Twelfth Night, The Winter's Tale, King John, 1 Henry VI, Henry VIII, Coriolanus, Timon of Athens, Julius Caesar, Macbeth, Antony and Cleopatra,* and *Cymbeline*. For these eighteen plays the First Folio is our sole authority. For *Othello*, and for six plays which had appeared earlier only in "bad" quarto texts (*The Merry Wives of Windsor, Henry V, 2* and *3 Henry VI, Richard III,* and *King Lear*), it also gives us our most authoritative texts.

Although the several kinds of printer's copy that Jaggard, presumably with the cooperation of Heminge and Condell, assembled for the texts of the First Folio have been touched on occasionally in the preceding section, the matter of printer's copy as it applies specifically to the Folio may be briefly outlined here. For more finely drawn distinctions and the expression of conflicting opinions the reader must consult the fuller discussions in the "Note on the Text" to each of the plays.

Half the plays included in the First Folio had already been printed in some form in separate quarto editions (i.e., the "good" and "bad" quartos). Those responsible for the Folio collection made use of these earlier printed texts in roughly two ways. In some cases, they reprinted the quarto text (not necessarily from the first edition), sometimes introducing a few new readings of uncertain authority and making occasional modifications in stage directions and some more or less obvious corrections (for example, *Titus Andronicus* [with one new scene from manuscript], *1 Henry IV, Love's Labor's Lost, Romeo and Juliet, A Midsummer Night's Dream, The Merchant of Venice,* and *Much Ado about Nothing*, all from "good" quartos). As copy for other plays, they arranged for a revision and correction of a quarto text by collation with a presumably authoritative manuscript (perhaps the official prompt book), thus producing copy for the printer that was a combination of printed and manuscript material (*Richard III* and *King Lear* [from "bad" quartos], *Richard II, 1 Henry IV,* and *Troilus and Cressida* [from "good" quartos], and, in the view of many, *2 Henry IV, Hamlet,* and *Othello* [from "good" quartos]).[16] Partial use of this sort seems also to have been made of the "bad" quarto texts of *2* and *3 Henry VI* and *Henry V*. These three plays, however, are basically dependent on manuscript copy, probably "foul papers." Alone among the already published plays included in the First Folio, *The Merry Wives of Windsor* seems totally uninfluenced by its earlier ("bad") quarto edition.

The eighteen plays now first printed were based upon various types of manuscript copy. For some plays Shakespeare's "foul papers" or transcripts of his "foul papers" were drawn upon (*The Comedy of Errors, The Taming of the Shrew, All's Well That Ends Well, King John, 1 Henry VI, Antony and Cleopatra, Julius Caesar, Macbeth, Coriolanus* (but possibly from authorial "fair copy" of "foul papers"), and *Henry VIII*. The remaining plays in this group show evidence of having been set from some form of scribal copy: some from specially prepared transcripts by Ralph Crane[17] (*The Tempest* [transcribed from "foul papers" or slightly revised "fair copy"], *Two Gentlemen of Verona* [probably from "foul papers"], *The Merry Wives of Windsor* [probably from some sort of prompt-book], *Measure for Measure* [perhaps from "foul papers" or possibly a prompt-book], *The Winter's Tale* [from "foul papers" or authorial "fair copy" used as a prompt-book], *Timon of Athens* [from "foul papers"

[13] For a discussion of the special problems here involved, see the "Note on the Text" to *Richard III* and to *King Lear*.

[14] Apart from "Loue labours wonne," a number of other "lost" plays have been attributed to Shakespeare. On September 9, 1653, Humphrey Moseley entered on the Stationers' Register "The History of Cardenio, by Mr Fletcher & Shakespeare." and "Henry ye first, & Hen: the 2d. by Shakespeare, & Davenport."; and on June 28, 1660, "The History of King Stephen.", "Duke Humphrey, a Tragedy.", and "Iphis and Iantha or a marriage without a man, a Comedy.", all three being attributed to "Will: Shakespeare." Two of these plays (*Henry the First* and *Duke Humphrey*) also appear with the same attributions in John Warburton's eighteenth-century holograph list of manuscript plays, all but a very few of which (including the two above) were accidentally destroyed by his servant. Except for *Cardenio*, nothing further is known about these plays that connects them with Shakespeare, and Moseley's attributions are often of uncertain authority. In the case of *Cardenio*, we possess a drastic revision of the play published by Lewis Theobald in 1728 under the title *The Double Falsehood, or The Distress'd Lovers*, but the three manuscripts of *Cardenio* that he claimed to have owned have disappeared.

[15] The nine so-called "Pavier" quartos, printed in 1619, though with various dates, are sometimes thought of as the first attempt at a selected collection of the plays. The nine include: *The Whole Contention* (i.e., the "bad" quarto versions of 2 and *3 Henry VI*), *The Merry Wives of Windsor, Henry V, King Lear, Pericles* (all "bad" quartos), *The Merchant of Venice, A Midsummer Night's Dream*, and two apocryphal plays, *A Yorkshire Tragedy* and *Sir John Oldcastle*.

[16] For details of the most recent and frequently controversial views on the exact nature of the printer's copy for these and the other plays, discussed below, see the "Note on the Text" preceding the Textual Notes to each play.

[17] For a discussion of Crane's scribal characteristics, see the "Note on the Text" to *The Tempest* and to *The Two Gentlemen of Verona*. See also T. H. Howard-Hill, *Ralph Crane and Some Shakespeare First Folio Comedies* (1972).

or a transcript of "foul papers"], and probably *Cymbeline* [from scribal transcript in two hands at one remove from "foul papers"]). *As You Like It* is thought to be set up either from a prompt-book or from the "foul papers" annotated by the book-keeper preparatory to making the official prompt-book, and printer's copy for *Twelfth Night* appears to be a "literary" transcript probably printed from an authorial "fair copy," prompt-book, or, possibly, "foul papers."

Although the several procedures described above may fail to inspire, and rightly, great confidence in the integrity of the Folio texts, they do suggest some degree of discrimination and sense of responsibility on the part of those concerned with the First Folio collection. Even so we are scarcely able to endorse Heminge and Condell's claim (in "To the great Variety of Readers") that the texts as they are printed in the First Folio are "cur'd, and perfect of their limbes [referring to those plays earlier published in what are now considered to be "bad" quarto editions]; and all the rest, absolute in their numbers, as he [Shakespeare] conceiued them."

The textual history of Shakespeare's plays from 1623 to the end of the seventeenth century may be shortly dealt with. A second folio appeared in 1632, a third in 1663/4,[18] and a fourth in 1685, each printed from the one immediately preceding. They show a progressive modernizing and regularizing of the text, affecting not only punctuation and spelling but language and syntax as well. None of the changes so made, not even the occasional verbal corrections or additions in the Second Folio (1632), has any independent manuscript authority. Such quarto editions as appeared after 1623 were either reprints of the earlier quartos or texts derived from the First Folio, including several Restoration acting versions (*Othello*, *Hamlet*, *Julius Caesar*) which show evidence of contemporary stage practice.

(3) *The Poems. Venus and Adonis*, the first of Shakespeare's works to appear in print, was printed and published by Richard Field, in quarto, in 1593. The first quarto edition of *The Rape of Lucrece* followed in the next year (1594), again printed by Field but published by John Harrison. Both poems were printed with Shakespeare's authorization and each contains a short prose dedication to his patron, Henry Wriothesley, the young Earl of Southampton. The volume entitled *Shake-speares Sonnets* (1609), which contains also "A Lover's Complaint," once questioned but now generally accepted as by Shakespeare, was, on the other hand, most probably unauthorized. So was the small earlier miscellany of short poems by Shakespeare and others (all, however, attributed to Shakespeare) called *The Passionate Pilgrim* and published in 1599 (enlarged with more non-Shakespearean materials in 1612) by William Jaggard. The only other poem generally believed to be by Shakespeare, "The Phoenix and Turtle," was first printed among a group of commendatory verses appended to Robert Chester's *Love's Martyr* in 1601.

None of the poems appeared in the First Folio, except for three set-pieces in *Love's Labor's Lost* that were later printed as separate poems in *The Passionate Pilgrim*. The nearest thing to a collected edition before the eighteenth century was *Poems: Written by Wil. Shake-speare. Gent.* published by John Benson in 1640. It included all but eight of the sonnets (misleadingly rearranged, grouped, and titled), "A Lover's Complaint," "The Phoenix and Turtle," and the complete contents of the 1612 *Passionate Pilgrim*, together with other non-Shakespearean poems, but not *Venus and Adonis* and *Lucrece*.

III. THE HISTORY OF THE TEXT, 1700–1900

In considering the later history of Shakespeare's text it is important to draw a general distinction between the textual approach taken by editors and critics before roughly 1909, the date of A. W. Pollard's important *Shakespeare Folios and Quartos*, and the approach, based on a growing knowledge of kinds of manuscript copy and analytical bibliographical techniques, since adopted by most scholars. Valuable contributions to the better understanding of the text of individual plays had, of course, been made before Pollard's study, particularly those of P. A. Daniel, but the larger principles of textual criticism, particularly of what lay behind the printed text, were for the most part unformed. As a result, a more or less ungoverned eclecticism prevailed. To say this is not to discount the value and importance of the work done by the small army of editors who, from the time of Nicholas Rowe's edition (1709) to the great Cambridge edition of 1863–66, exercised their critical ingenuity in improving the text—as a glance at the Textual Notes to any of the plays and poems in this volume will immediately show. But their work was largely concerned with the details of emendation, made for the most part without any very clear understanding of the special conditions which had governed the production of the early printed texts.

The eighteenth century marks the beginning of what may be called the scholarly or academic approach to Shakespeare. In 1709 Nicholas Rowe produced the first edited text of the plays. Rowe was himself a dramatist and had connections with the theatre, and his edition reflects these professional interests. Unfortunately, Rowe chose to base his text on the Fourth Folio (1685), with very occasional consultation of one of the earlier folios or quartos. The result was a generally inferior text that seriously vitiated later editions for the next sixty years and more. Nevertheless, Rowe made some substantial contri-

[18] Six plays in addition to *Pericles* (*The London Prodigal*; *The Life and Death of Thomas Lord Cromwell*; *The History of Sir John Oldcastle*; *The Puritan, or The Widow of Watling Street*; *A Yorkshire Tragedy*; and *The Tragedy of Locrine*) were added in the second issue of the Third Folio (and reprinted in the Fourth) and are now commonly referred to as the "Shakespeare Apocrypha." None of the six is now accepted as Shakespeare's.

butions. To him as the first official editor of the plays we owe a large number of corrections and emendations that survive as part of any modern edition.[19] He also undertook a more or less systematic division of all the plays into acts and scenes and was the first, except for some sporadic instances in the Restoration actors' quartos, to indicate a localized setting for many of the individual scenes. Further, his edition contains the first serious attempt at a biography of Shakespeare, still an important source on certain matters, and illustrations that tell us a good deal about early eighteenth-century staging.

Shakespeare's second editor was Alexander Pope. When Pope produced his edition in 1723, he was already established as England's leading poet and *arbiter elegantiarum*. These roles he exercised much too freely to qualify in any sense as a serious editor. He pontificated on what was good or bad in the plays, marking the "good" or "moral" with inverted commas and relegating the "bad" to the bottom of the page as the illiterate interpolations of the ignorant actors and unworthy of a place in the text proper. If he did not understand a word or construction, he often changed it, and he worked assiduously to regularize Shakespeare's metre. He did, however, recover passages and scenes from some of the quartos ignored by Rowe (that is, he undertook some limited collation of the quarto texts), and he also restored to verse many passages that had been misprinted in the early editions as prose, and to prose many that had been misprinted as verse. It has been said—if unkindly, nevertheless with considerable truth—that it took over a hundred years for Shakespeare's text to recover from the well-meant but misguided ministrations of both Pope and Rowe.

In 1733 Lewis Theobald published his first edition of the plays, but before doing so he had dared to cross swords with Pope. His attack on Pope's edition, which appeared in 1726, he called *Shakespeare Restor'd*, and in it he showed in unflattering detail how basically bad Pope's edition was. Pope's answer, apart from incorporating a number of Theobald's readings in the text of his second edition (1728) and including others in a sneering appendix, was to make Theobald the hero of his first *Dunciad* (1728) as the pre-eminent type and prince of dullness and to nickname him "piddling Tibbald." From that day to this, Pope's attack has done much to obscure Theobald's remarkable capabilities as an editor, which were of a sort that Pope, as poet and critic, tended by nature to despise. Indeed, Theobald may fairly be considered the first of Shakespeare's major editors, and his contributions, particularly in felicitous emendations, are to be found everywhere in any modern text. But beyond this, he approached the editor's task with a much clearer notion than his predecessors had of what such duties entailed, and with a much wider acquaintance with other Elizabethan drama and nondramatic literature. He also had a greater respect for his author's language and syntax and a scholarly perspective foreign to Rowe and Pope.

The next three editors, Sir Thomas Hanmer (1744), William Warburton (1747), and Samuel Johnson (1765), may, so far as the history of the text is concerned, be passed over quickly. Each made occasional brilliant emendations, although Warburton is principally famous as a warning example of the danger of overingenuity in emendation and of emending where no emendation is needed. Johnson, who knew and outlined (in his "Proposals," 1756) the proper method by which a relatively sound text might be achieved, did only a bare minimum of what he rightly said should no longer be stigmatized as, in Pope's words, the "dull duty of an editor" (namely, collation and evaluation of the various early editions), instead concerning himself largely with explanatory annotation and general criticism, both of which he was especially well qualified to perform and for both of which he is still recognized as one of the great Shakespearean critics.

In 1768, quietly and pretty much unnoticed, Edward Capell brought out his text of the plays. None of his important contemporaries had a kind word to say about Capell's edition, and his two principal successors, George Steevens and Edmond Malone, denigrated it at every opportunity—and stole from it unblushingly. Later opinion, however, has more and more seen Capell as the first so-called modern editor, and his edition as an important landmark. Capell deserves the title of the first modern for a number of reasons. He was the first to put into practice, though perhaps not the first to understand, the principle of copy-text, that is, the need for choosing, in the light of the evidence, a basic substantive text and for adhering faithfully to that text. In his search for such basic texts, Capell also for the first time recognized the usual superiority of the earliest printed texts (the "good" quartos) as opposed to those texts as they appeared in the First Folio. Thus he began the trend away from the eclecticism of the earlier editors, who, failing to take a definite stand on a particular copy-text, allowed themselves considerable liberty in adopting readings from any text, early or late, that happened to appeal to their aesthetic sensibilities. Succeeding editors learned something of this cardinal rule from Capell, but in the case of a textually complex play like *Hamlet*, for example, which Capell for the first time based directly on Q2 (1604/5), no later influential text comparably faithful to Q2 was produced until Dover Wilson's edition in 1934.[20]

In a special sense Capell's was the first "pure" edited text. His predecessors, and most of his successors,

[19] Reference to the Textual Notes following each play will reveal the extent to which Rowe and his many successors have influenced the text of the present edition. For recent studies of some of Rowe's successors, see: Arthur Sherbo, *The Birth of Shakespeare Studies: Commentators from Rowe (1709) to Boswell-Malone (1821)* (East Lansing, Michigan, 1986); Peter Leary, *Lewis Theobald and the Editing of Shakespeare* (Oxford, 1990); Peter Martin, *Edmond Malone: Shakespeare Scholar* (Cambridge, 1995).

[20] Some details in the discussion of Capell I owe to an unpublished doctoral dissertation by my friend, Hymen H. Hart. Capell's commentaries and textual notes were published posthumously: *Notes and Various Readings to Shakespeare*, 3 vols. (London, 1780–83?); Vol. III is entitled *The School of Shakespeare*).

employed as printer's copy some other more or less recent edition into which they inserted their manuscript corrections.[21] This method almost inevitably perpetuated and gave a specious authority to readings from the Fourth Folio, on which Rowe, the first link in the chain, had based his 1709 edition. Capell, on the other hand, prepared a wholly new text for the printer, meticulously copied out by himself (reputedly ten times!), based on his own thorough collation of all the obtainable sixteenth- and seventeenth-century editions (quarto and folio). To Capell also belongs the credit of being the first to print a systematic textual apparatus—a remarkably full one—recording the variants from the early editions and the readings of the first five of his eighteenth-century predecessors. Nothing comparable was attempted until the Cambridge edition of 1863–66, nearly a hundred years later. The problem of chronology, an important approach to an understanding of Shakespeare's development, was first attacked by Capell, though the credit is usually given to Malone, and he was the first to attempt a serious treatment of Shakespeare's metrics. His official position as deputy-inspector of plays brought Capell into close contact with the theatre and goes far to explain his special sensitivity, continually reflected in his text, to stage business and movement. It may also explain why he was the first to understand fully the concept of the "cleared stage" as the limiting principle of Elizabethan scene division. A measure of Capell's importance may perhaps be seen in the fact that his name appears more frequently in the Textual Notes to the present edition than that of any later editor.

Capell's immediate followers, George Steevens and Edmond Malone, both produced major editions (Steevens, 1787, 1793; Malone, 1790), but textually they leaned heavily on Capell—at the same time affecting to despise him. It is, indeed, scarcely an exaggeration to say that by the end of the eighteenth century the texts of Shakespeare that went under the names of Steevens and Malone were, with some refinements in specific readings, in basic essentials the text of Edward Capell. To assert this is not to deny the importance of the work done by Steevens and Malone, especially Malone. Like Capell, who had published in what he called *The School of Shakespeare* the results of his combing of Elizabethan and Jacobean literature for Shakespeare's sources and other material that might be used to illustrate and throw new light on the plays, both men were what the wits called "black-letter editors"—that is, editors who drew on a wide reading in the popular literature of Shakespeare's time, some of which was even then still printed in the so-called gothic black-letter typeface. Unlike Capell, both Steevens and Malone wrote polished and untortured English, and their commentaries, though often owing much to Capell's notes, became widely known and were reprinted in edition after edition, culminating in the so-called First Variorum, the Boswell-Malone edition of 1821.[22] Malone, moreover, was the first to demonstrate through a careful analytical study the sole authority of the First Folio (1623) in relation to the later folios, showing that even the variant readings of the Second Folio (1632) were entirely without independent manuscript authority. He also deserves special praise for his scholarly researches into the early history of the English stage and for his careful transcriptions of early manuscript materials, some of which have since disappeared. He was also the first to publish a scholarly edition of Shakespeare's *Poems* and *Pericles* (1780), though in the *Poems* he again had Capell as his guide since he made essentially unacknowledged use of a marked copy of Lintott's 1709 edition of the *Poems* prepared by Capell for an edition of his own which he did not live to publish.

With Capell, Steevens, and Malone the text of Shakespeare had been brought about as far as the limited textual approach employed by these men could bring it, and the nineteenth century, although it produced many new editions under highly competent and learned editors (Charles Knight, J. P. Collier, Alexander Dyce, and R. G. White, especially), brought very little advance in new theory or basic techniques. The culmination of the line initiated by Capell is the great Cambridge *Shakespeare* edited by W. G. Clark and W. A. Wright, which appeared between 1863 and 1866 (with its important revision by Wright in 1891–93), a text that was to remain, especially in its one-volume Globe edition (1864), the standard for the next fifty years.

IV. SHAKESPEARE'S TEXT AND THE "NEW BIBLIOGRAPHY"

The first decade of the twentieth century marked the beginnings of what has been called the "New Bibliography." Spearheaded by men like R. B. McKerrow, A. W. Pollard, W. W. Greg, and J. Dover Wilson, a fresh and comparatively "scientific" approach to the problems presented by the text was undertaken. An important forward step was made in 1909 by Pollard, who clarified the whole problem of the quarto texts by recognizing that, when Heminge and Condell in their address "To the great Variety of Readers" in the First Folio criticized earlier printed texts of the plays as "stolne, and surreptitious copies, maimed, and deformed by the frauds and stealthes of iniurious imposters, that expos'd them," they were not thereby condemning, as had usually been supposed, all the earlier quartos, but only certain piratically published or "expos'd" quartos. These Pollard

[21] Thus Pope's edition was printed from Rowe's third (1714), Theobald's and Hanmer's from Pope's second (1728), Warburton's from Theobald's second (1740), and Johnson's partly from Warburton's (1747) and partly from Theobald's 1757 edition.

[22] As here used, the term "Variorum" means that the edition reprints all the prefaces of the earlier editors, selected studies and essays by various hands, and a great part of the annotation from Pope through Reed. Actually, all major editions had been "Variorums" in this sense since the 1773 Johnson-Steevens edition, so that the traditional term "First Variorum" as applied to the Boswell-Malone 1821 edition is a misnomer. As used today, with reference to the *New Variorum Shakespeare*, the idea of a "Variorum" has been enlarged to include an exhaustive record of all significant textual variants, emendations, source materials, and selected criticism.

designated the "bad" quartos to distinguish them from the "good" quartos, or texts published, usually with the company's permission, from authoritative manuscripts. Pollard's distinction stimulated investigation in two fruitful directions. It was supported by W. W. Greg's analysis (1910) of the quarto of *The Merry Wives of Windsor*, in which he outlined the basic essentials of the theory of "memorial reconstruction," a theory which he was able to confirm and extend in his famous monograph on Greene's *Orlando Furioso* and Peele's *Battle of Alcazar* (1923). From these beginnings rose the widespread application of the "memorial reconstruction" theory to the whole class of "bad" quartos (see, particularly, the studies of Peter Alexander, Madeleine Doran, D. L. Patrick, G. I. Duthie, and H. R. Hoppe) and a sounder understanding of the extent to which these "bad" quarto texts might be of value to an editor.

The "good" quartos, given an improved status by Pollard's distinction, came under new scrutiny with the pioneer work of Dover Wilson, both in his essay on Shakespeare's spelling forms in *Shakespeare's Hand in "Sir Thomas More"* (1923) and in his later important study *The Manuscript of Shakespeare's "Hamlet"* (1934). Thus the first serious attempts to learn exactly what kinds of manuscripts lay behind the texts of the "good" quartos and the First Folio got under way. Other important studies followed, most notably W. W. Greg, *The Editorial Problem in Shakespeare* (1942, revised 1951) and *The Shakespeare First Folio* (1955), Alice Walker, *Textual Problems of the First Folio* (1953), Fredson Bowers, *On Editing Shakespeare and the Elizabethan Dramatists* (1955) and *Bibliography and Textual Criticism* (1964), and Stanley Wells, Gary Taylor, et al., *William Shakespeare: A Textual Companion* (1987), each probing, synthesizing, and correcting earlier work and adding valuable new techniques and further detailed information.[23]

Another aspect of textual study has received a good deal of attention in more recent years: the analysis of printing-house procedures and the way in which these procedures and the habits of individual compositors may have influenced the printed text. Aside from the interest in analytical bibliography that had been increasing steadily since R. B. McKerrow's edition of Thomas Nashe (1904–10), part of the impetus for this kind of study may be said to stem from Thomas Satchell's suggestion (*The Times Literary Supplement*, 1920) that two compositors can be distinguished, through certain spelling preferences, at work on the text of the First Folio *Macbeth*. Out of this combined interest in printing-house practice and compositor study grew E. E. Willoughby's important monograph, *The Printing of the First Folio of Shakespeare* (1932), which was to remain the standard work for the next twenty-five years. Willoughby substantiated Satchell's suggestion by showing the presence of two main compositors (usually called A and B) at work throughout the First Folio, and he placed renewed emphasis on the already recognized but still largely unexplored problem of stop-press correction, those changes made in the printed text, through proof-reader and compositor, during the process of printing. This latter problem, for the quarto texts, was pursued further by Dover Wilson in his work on *Hamlet* (see above) and W. W. Greg in his monograph *The Variants in the First Quarto of "King Lear"* (1940).

In 1963 Charlton Hinman, after twenty years of unremitting work, published his monumental two-volume study, *The Printing and Proof-Reading of the First Folio of Shakespeare*. Hinman, correcting a number of serious misconceptions and errors in Willoughby's pioneer study, demonstrated by a variety of new techniques exactly how (by the method known as cast-off copy)[24] and in what order the plays in the First Folio were printed. He also established the presence of five compositors (two main compositors, A and B, and three others, C and D, who set largely in the Comedies, and E, apparently an apprentice, who worked in the Tragedies), distinguishing their work partly through an analysis of type-fonts, a technique which greatly strengthened and refined the older results arrived at through spelling tests alone.[25] In addition, Hinman was able to place the texts of all plays that depend on the First Folio for their basic copy-text (twenty-five) on a much firmer basis by offering the results of a thorough machine collation of some fifty copies of the First Folio. Allowing for the possibility of earlier proof correction of the standing type, the comparatively small number of significant press-corrections which were revealed demonstrates to what a slight extent, except in the work of Compositor E, any serious effort was made to ensure a sound text. Indeed, much of the press-correction seems to have been more concerned with the appearance of the page than with the accuracy of the text, and such substantive press-correction as was undertaken appears most frequently to have been made without consultation of the printer's copy.[26]

As a result of the impetus given by the "New Bibliography," a number of important editions of Shakespeare have appeared during the last seventy-some years. Among the most significant are J. Dover Wilson's New *Shakespeare* (1921–66), G. L. Kittredge's (1936; revised by Irving Ribner, 1971), W. A. Neilson and C. J. Hill's (1942), Peter Alexander's (1951), Hardin Craig's (1951; revised by David Bevington, 1973; fourth edition, 1992), C. J. Sisson's (1953), John Munro's (The London Shakespeare, 1958), and the individually edited volumes of the New Variorum (beginning with S. B. Hemingway's *1 Henry IV*, 1936), the New Arden (1951–82; a third Arden series was begun in 1995), the Pelican

[23] The most significant studies devoted to the textual problems of the individual plays may be found listed following the "Note on the Text" to each play.

[24] For a discussion of cast-off copy, see the Glossary under *Casting off*.

[25] Since Hinman first identified five First Folio compositors (A–E), five more (F–J) have been proposed, but the existence of F and J has been seriously questioned; F is now considered to be the same as D and J probably the same as A (see the valuable summary of the results of the more recent Folio compositor studies in Stanley Wells, Gary Taylor, et al., *William Shakespeare: A Textual Companion* [1987], 148–54).

[26] See the Glossary under *Proof correction* and *Stop-press correction*.

(1956–68; reissued in one volume, under the general editorship of Alfred Harbage, 1969), the Signet (1963–68; reissued in one volume, under the general editorship of Sylvan Barnet, 1972), the New Penguin (1967–), the New Oxford (1982– ; *Complete Works*, modern spelling [1986] and *Complete Works*, original spelling [1986]), and the New Cambridge (1984–).

V. THE EDITING OF A SHAKESPEAREAN PLAY

Some of the matters discussed in the foregoing sections may be clarified if we examine in some small detail the various steps in the editorial process as it applies to a single play: *King Lear*. *King Lear* affords an unusually complicated set of textual problems, a discussion of which will illustrate a variety of similar problems encountered individually and in varying degrees in other plays.

Let us suppose, for the sake of the present discussion, that an editor is undertaking a critical edition of *King Lear* for the first time and that he does not have ready to hand a body of earlier scholarly research on which to draw in formulating his premises. There are three early printed texts of *Lear*: Q1 (1608), Q2 (1619), and F1 (1623). Pursuing the principle of copy-text selection (i.e., choosing as the basic text that edition or manuscript which appears most nearly to represent an author's final intention), the editor must first analyze each of these editions to determine which of them best fulfills this criterion. After a complete collation and analysis of the three texts, he will find that Q2 is essentially a reprint, without independent authority, of Q1 and may thus, for the moment, be dismissed. Comparison of Q1 and F1 will reveal that these texts differ in several hundred readings and that each contains words, lines, and longer passages (Q1 a whole scene) not present in the other. Given this sort of situation, the editor must now try to determine which of these texts offers the best authority for what Shakespeare wrote. Upon careful examination, he will discover, first, that, although Q1 exhibits many of the characteristics that are associated with the "bad" quartos or memorially reported texts, other aspects of Q1 suggest direct contact at places with an authoritative manuscript, probably Shakespeare's "foul papers." Second, he will find that F1 presents a text printed from copies of both Q1 and Q2 that have been corrected and amplified by collation with an apparently authoritative manuscript, probably the official prompt-book of the King's Men.[27] The editor must now decide which of these two texts to select as the copy-text. Since Q1 gives evidence of considerable memorial contamination, he is forced to turn to F1 as the basic copy-text. But he does so without any great assurance of the ultimate authority of that text in the matter of individual readings, since the quality of the F1 text, so far as it differs from the Q1–2 text, depends upon the care and accuracy of the collator who was responsible for the preparation of the printer's copy. (A similar situation exists in *Richard III*.)

Other complicating factors remain to be considered, however. First, the question of the authority of the manuscript used by the collator from which corrections, additions, even deletions were made in preparing the Q1–2 copy for the Folio text. If, as seems likely, this manuscript was the official promptbook, a certain caution must be exercised, because such a manuscript is almost sure to contain theatrical cuts and sophisticated readings. The matter of theatrical cuts will be discussed later in more detail. Here we may simply notice two examples of sophisticated readings. When F1 in III.vii.58 and 63 reads "sticke boarish phangs" and "that sterne time" for the Q1–2 readings "rash borish phangs" and "that dearne time", most editors now feel justified in adopting the Q1–2 readings, believing, according to the principle of *lectio difficilior*, that the more commonplace F1 readings reflect a vulgarizing of Shakespeare's idiom by stage performance. In other words, although F1 offers a generally sounder text than Q1–2, its readings, where they differ from Q1–2, may arise through several agencies, only the first of which carries any authority: (1) genuine corrections made by the collator from manuscript authority, including possible revisions made by Shakespeare himself; (2) changes made by some other person (the book-keeper or the actors); (3) errors committed by the collator; (4) errors or sophistications introduced by the compositor(s) or proof-reader in the printshop.

Second, since the F1 text was, we now believe, set up from corrected and augmented printed copy (Q1 and, to a lesser degree, Q2), it is necessary to know whether the particular copies of Q1 and Q2 used by the collator were made up of corrected or uncorrected sheets. Thus at IV.ii.28, where F1 reads "My Foole vsurps my body", Q1 in the corrected state of the sheet reads "A foole vsurps my bed". In the uncorrected state, however, Q1 reads "My foote vsurps my body" and is followed in part by Q2, which reads in turn "My foote vsurps my head". A comparison of these several readings makes it clear that in this section F1 was printed from an uncorrected state of Q1, retaining "my" and "body", and that the collator caught the error in "foote" (probably from the manuscript) but either decided to allow "My" and "body" to stand (as making sufficient sense) or failed to notice them. Since the extent and kind of correction of the line in Q1 strongly suggest that the proof-corrector consulted his manuscript copy, its reading, even allowing for the ambiguous authority of that manuscript, must be accorded considerable weight. Hence, because the F1 line seems to be a combination of correction and the following of uncorrected printed copy, most modern editors choose to read the line as in Q1: "A fool usurps my bed". This is a particularly revealing example and illustrates how textual corruption can happen, and how difficult, without the kind of bibliographical evidence here

[27] The "two *Lear*" theory (i.e., that the play as it appears in Q1 and F1 must be considered as two significantly different plays and must be presented as such), a theory not here accepted, is discussed in the "Note on the Text."

fortunately present, it may be to detect it. Who, for instance, would seriously challenge the F1 reading or even that of Q2 (an obvious compositorial fudge to make better sense of "foote" by contrasting it with "head" instead of "body") were no other texts available—if, in other words, either only the text of F1 or the text of Q2 were now extant? Such a consideration should make an editor especially wary in dealing with those plays of which only one basic text has survived, such as the eighteen plays printed for the first time in F1.

This example also raises a question of the relative validity of bibliographical method. The principle here followed assumes that where the F1 text was printed from an uncorrected state of Q1 (or Q2) an editor is justified in restoring the reading of the corrected state of Q1 as more likely to represent what he believes Shakespeare wrote. Such an assumption is based upon a number of factors that make it a probable method of approaching the textual situation here involved, but obviously it cannot claim to be based on certainty. Textual analysis is not in any real sense a scientific discipline, because the essentially human element (stupidity, error, inconsistency, and simple laziness) must always be allowed for and can so easily upset the nicest calculations. It deals for the most part, aside from its most mechanical aspects, in approaches and principles based on a weighing of a variety of kinds of evidence and often reaches conclusions that allow only a measure of greater or lesser probability. Thus when an editor in the instances discussed above chooses to desert his copy-text (here F1) and read with the corrected state of Q1, he is making an editorial decision that is based not on unassailable evidence or certainty but on a method of approach that, given the evidence available, seems to him most likely to restore the author's original language. No one, it should be stressed, is more painfully conscious than the editor of how often the "principles" that he seems to lay down with an inevitable appearance of dogma, particularly in textually difficult plays like *Lear*, *Hamlet*, *Richard III*, *Othello*, and *Troilus and Cressida*, are indeed only working hypotheses and hence open to challenge on a different interpretation of the same evidence.

Another related aspect of the F1 text must be considered: the use of corrected Q2 copy for parts of the F1 text. Since Q2 is essentially a reprint of Q1, with one or two slight additions (III.vi.47, IV.vi.197), and its variants cannot lay claim to manuscript authority, where F1 reproduces a reading from its Q2 copy that differs from the reading of Q1, it may be fairly argued that the collator in preparing his Q2 copy failed to make the proper correction from the manuscript and that the Q1 reading, which has at least some manuscript authority, should be restored (see the Textual Notes at I.iv.22, 31, II.ii.65, 100, 151, etc.). Again the principle employed must be recognized as one involving only a measure of probability.

Speaking generally, an editor today, having chosen for what he considers sound reasons a particular copy-text, will adhere to that copy-text unless he sees substantial grounds for departing from it. Several examples of deliberate departure from the copy-text readings have already been cited in the preceding discussion, involving F1 sophistication or vulgarization, press variants, and faulty printer's copy. But these are all matters of substituting one early reading for another early reading that the evidence suggests has superior authority. What, however, guides the editor when he has to determine whether a passage unique to a text of such uneven authority as Q1 is indeed Shakespeare's and not rather the work of some alien hand? He may find, for instance, that the passage fits naturally into the context of surrounding lines or that it contains actual verbal links which show that at one time it was part of the original, cut in the printer's copy or accidentally (even intentionally) omitted by the compositor. For example, in I.ii, lines 95–97 are found only in Q1–2. Where F1 reads "*Glou.* He cannot bee such a Monster. *Edmond* seeke him out:", Q1–2 read "*Glost.* He cannot be such a monster. / *Bast.* Nor is not sure. / *Glost.* To his father, that so tenderly and intirely loues him, heauen and earth! *Edmund* seeke him out,". The tone of Edmund's "Nor is not sure." is perfectly in keeping with his pretended defense of Edgar in lines 85–88 ("I dare pawne downe my life for him, that he hath writ this to feele my affection to your Honor, & to no other pretence of danger." [F1]), and an editor is justified in feeling that the F1 omission is most probably the result of a theatrical cut. Even more clearly the result of an intentional cut in the prompt-book, however, is the omission in F1 of lines 16–20 toward the end of I.iii, where the first half of the additional Q1–2 line 16 ("Not to be ouerrul'd.") completes the full sense of lines 14–15, common to both F1 and Q1–2. One more example may be noted in I.iv, where, at line 137, both F1 and Q1–2 make the Fool say "Do'st thou know the difference my Boy, betweene a bitter Foole, and a sweet one [foole, Q1–2]." and Lear answers "No Lad, teach me." At this point F1 omits lines 140–155 found in Q1–2 ("*Foole.* That Lord . . . they'l be snatching;"), in the first part of which lines the Fool gives in detail the answer to the question he had posed in lines 137–38. The omission of this passage makes relative nonsense of the F1 text, and it is difficult to believe that such an omission represents an intentional theatrical cut reflecting the collator's use of a prompt-book manuscript, but it is also difficult to explain how a passage of this length could be accidentally omitted by the F1 compositor.

One substantial passage, a whole scene (IV.iii), occurs only in Q1–2, and in such a case the editor is forced to judge its authenticity on its own merits, without the aid of immediate context. The poetic quality and general context of the scene are such, however, that no editor, since Pope first included it in an edited text, has seriously questioned its Shakespearean origin. It is, moreover, the kind of scene that can be deleted without any dislocation of the plot-line, hence a natural prey for a book-keeper intent on shortening an overlong play.

Occasionally, however, an editor rejects Q1–2 additions. Such rejected readings tend to be extra-metrical single words or phrases, which, given the postulated memorial contamination of the Q1 text, are looked upon as the work of either the reporters or the actors. For instance, in I.i.45, Q1–2 read "The two great Princes *France* and *Burgundy*", where F1 reads "The Princes, *France* & *Burgundy*". To include "two great" would make the F1 line, already extra-metrical ("May be preuented now. The Princes, *France* & *Burgundy*"), completely unmanageable as a single line and necessitate its being broken into a half-line plus a full line, the half-line being left uncompleted in the middle of a speech. It is clear, moreover, that the additional Q1–2 words are in fact mere padding to substitute metrically for the omission of lines 40–45 in Q1–2. (An analogous example of F1 padding, to accommodate a cut of some lines occurring in Q1–2, may be studied in the Textual Notes to II.ii.145.) Again, in line 90 of the opening scene, the Q1–2 reading "How, nothing can come of nothing, speake againe." offers a good instance of the extra-metrical expletive common in reported texts and usually considered as an actor's trick for false emphasis. F1 reads "Nothing will come of nothing, speake againe."—a stronger and metrically better balanced line. (Compare the Q1–2 addition of "Goe to, goe to" in line 233 of this same scene.)

At this point, an editor, having determined that a critically edited text of *Lear* should, on the evidence sketched above, be based on F1 but admit a substantial number of lines found only in Q1–2, still has to face the problem of necessary emendation. In a number of instances, even with the aid of Q1–2, individual readings require editorial emendation to bring meaning to an otherwise corrupt passage. Significant emendation is made on two levels: (1) substantive (i.e. corrections concerned with the verbal texture of a passage, including also stage directions and speech-prefixes); and (2) semi-substantive (i.e., corrections concerned with punctuation, the so-called accidentals, that may be said to affect the meaning of a passage). Examples of semi-substantive emendation occur frequently in *Lear*, particularly in passages dependent on the lightly and erratically punctuated Q1 text, and may be readily studied by turning to the Textual Notes (see, for example, I.i.20–21, 127, I.iv.92, 204, II.i.14, II.ii.45–46, 51, II.iv.102, III.iv.117, III.vi.68–69, III.vii.46–47, IV.i.2, IV.ii.66, IV.iii.17–18, 19, 51, IV.vi.265–66, V.iii.51–52, 121–22). Substantive emendation is generally speaking a more complicated matter and is worth illustration here.

In I.ii.20–21, where Edmund says in F1, "*Edmond* the base / Shall to'th' Legitimate:", Q1–2 read: "*Edmund* the base shall tooth' legitimate:". Several emendations have been suggested ("Shall be the" [Pope], "Shall toe the" [Hanmer]) and a few editors have defended the F1 reading (Sisson most recently) on the grounds that it might be interpreted to mean "shall fight against" or "shall turn into"—both strained interpretations. But most editors accept, as does the present editor, Edwards' conjecture, "Shall top the legitimate"—a reading that on both graphic ("to" or "too" to "top") and associative terms (with "I grow" [line 21] and by contrast with the repeated burden of "base" that informs much of the soliloquy) fulfills the demands of the context perfectly.

Again, in II.ii.143 (a passage found only in Q1–2) the uncorrected state of Q1 reads "as basest and contaned wretches". In the corrected state "contaned" is altered to "temnest", a reading followed by Q2. The puzzling "temnest" is a nonce-word of at best questionable meaning; moreover, it is metrically unsatisfactory. Pope emended it to "the meanest" and was followed in desperation by several of his successors. Capell was the first to see that a better reading was a combination of the corrected and uncorrected states: "contemned'st". It is possible, in this case, to reconstruct perhaps how the corrected state of Q1 came to read "temnest". The proof-corrector wrote "temnest" in the margin of his proof-sheet and crossed through "taned" in the uncorrected reading "contaned"; the compositor, however, in making the correction, thought "contaned" as a whole was marked for deletion and hence did not retain the necessary "con". One further point. The form "contemnest" which the proof-corrector intended is a possible Elizabethan past participial superlative, but it does not take account of the "d" in "contaned", the presence of which in the uncorrected reading, however badly garbled that reading may be, probably reflects a "d" form in the manuscript.[28]

A final example: in IV.vi.165–67 (part of a passage found only in F1) F1 reads "Place sinnes with Gold . . . Arme it in ragges". Pope was the first to suggest reading "Plate sins with gold". He was probably led to his emendation by "Arme", since the meaning of "plate" was in Shakespeare's time "to cover with metal plates for ornament or protection," but he may also have recognized how easily a carelessly formed "t" in the English secretary hand could be misread as a secretary "c". A little later Theobald (in his second edition, 1740), adopting Pope's "Plate", emended "sinnes" to "sin", making clear for the first time the antecedent of "it" in line 167. Both Pope's and Theobald's emendations illustrate what is called the principle of *ductus literarum* (i.e. the guidance, through form or shape and number, of the letters in a word requiring emendation). Thus a compositor would be much more likely to misread "Plate" as "Place" than to misread "Plate" as "Disguise" or "Cover," either word in itself possible, though metrically awkward, if only the context of the passage is considered. Theobald, on the other hand, instead of emending "sinnes" to "sin", might have emended "it" (line 167) to "them" to make it agree with "sinnes". But it is obviously much more probable that a compositor would misread "sinne" as "sinnes" (the misreading of a singular as a plural is not uncommon in F1 and other contemporary printed texts) than that he would misread "them" as "it."

[28] Peter Blayney, however, (*The Texts of "King Lear,"* 1982) proposes, temptingly, that the compositor should have probably corrected Q1's uncorrected form "contaned" to "contemned."

The three examples just discussed illustrate most of the approaches that may, with some degree of safety, be taken to the problem of emendation, always allowing, of course, for sheer inspiration, which, though most often highly dangerous, may be on properly rare occasions the "very opening of the mouth of nature." To sum up, these approaches are: (1) through the immediate or larger context; (2) through contributory bibliographical evidence, when any is available; (3) through metrical considerations; (4) through recognizing possible compositorial misreading of the various kinds of hands practiced in the period; and (5) through the *ductus literarum*, an approach closely associated with (4).

We have now followed an editor through the principal steps he must take before he can begin to produce a critical text, modernized or old-spelling, of *King Lear*. Enough has been said to make it clear that, even when all the procedures outlined above have been conscientiously applied, much remains uncertain and problematical. That no two editors, given the diversity and complicated nature of the textual situation and the considerable element of personal editorial decision involved, would ever produce identical critical texts of *Lear* need not be a matter for surprise or alarm. It is indeed the very presence of the human element, the possibility for the exercise of individual taste and critical acumen, that has made the editing of Shakespeare such a challenge to so many scholars for the last two hundred and seventy years.

Before describing the general textual principles underlying the present edition, a recent and significant editorial development deserves notice. The editors of the New Oxford *Complete Works* (1986), Stanley Wells, Gary Taylor, John Jowett, and William Montgomery, have introduced a new approach to what are called Shakespeare's "two-text" plays, based on two interrelated postulates: (1) that Shakespeare was regularly given to revising his work; and (2) that where there are two substantially variant versions of the same play, one of which can be associated with performance by Shakespeare's company, the theatre version is to be preferred as the basic text because it preserves, so the assumption goes, Shakespeare's final revision (for example, the F1 text of *Hamlet* [1623], being theatrically connected, must be chosen as the *textus receptus* for a modern edition in preference to that of Q2 [1604/5], which was set from Shakespeare's autograph [i.e., his "foul papers"]). Anything like compelling evidence for either of these assumptions is tenuous, particularly the second. That Shakespeare occasionally revised *currente calamo* is unquestioned (e.g., in *Love's Labor's Lost*, *Romeo and Juliet*, and *A Midsummer Night's Dream)*, and that he sometimes, if rarely, added new bits of dialogue is also generally accepted (e.g. in *Hamlet* and *Lear*), but to argue that he was personally responsible for the text of a play as it finally emerged in an acting version (or versions), including cuts and most verbal variants, is a larger and much more dangerous presumption. Further discussion of these and related matters may be found in the "Note on the Text" to *2 Henry VI*, *Henry V*, *Hamlet*, and *Lear*.

VI. THE PRESENT TEXT

The present text is based on a new collation and study of the early substantive editions and consultation of all the major edited texts from Rowe's (1709) onward. Every effort consistent with critical sense has been made to adhere to the declared copy-text (see the "Note on the Text" following each of the plays and poems), and unnecessary emendation, that pricking devil, has been carefully eschewed. When the copy-text, however, resisted all reasonable attempts to make sense of it, readings from another early printed text or from other editions have, of course, been admitted, but in all such cases the emendation has been placed in square brackets to warn the reader that the text at this point is open to question. The original reading, and the source of the emended reading, will be found recorded in the Textual Notes. Obvious compositorial errors, unless the error produces a new word, are corrected without employing square brackets, but the original reading is nevertheless recorded in the Textual Notes. Square brackets have also been used to alert the reader to all added or altered material in stage directions and to distinguish words or passages that have been inserted into the basic copy-text from some other early edition which there is reason to believe preserves Shakespearean words or lines missing for one reason or another from the copy-text. The source of all such additional bracketed material is indicated in the Textual Notes, except for certain supplementary character identifications that are plain from the context, e g., "*Enter* DUKE [FREDERICK] *with* LORDS.", "*Enter* CLOWN, *Old Lady* [COUNTESS], *and* LAFEW." When the speech-prefixes for a character show more than one form in the copy-text, they have been regularized to a single form throughout; altered forms are not enclosed in square brackets, but the copy-text variations, where they seem of textual or bibliographical interest, are recorded in the Textual Notes. When a speech is assigned to a speaker different from the one designated in the copy-text, the speech-prefix is of course treated like any other emendation.

Although the present text is basically a modern-spelling text, an attempt has been made to preserve a selection of Elizabethan spelling forms that reflect, or may reflect, a distinctive contemporary pronunciation, both those that are invariant in the early printed texts and those that appear beside the spellings familiar today and so suggest possible variant pronunciations of single words. In the first category, examples may be found in such forms (including also proper names) as *haberdepois* (avoirdupois), *fift* or *sixt* (fifth or sixth), *wrack* (wreck); *Birnan* (Birnam), *Bullingbrook* (Bolingbroke), *Callice* (Calais), *Dolphin* (Dauphin), *Roan* (Rouen). In the second category: *bankrout–bankrupt*, *conster–construe*, *embassador–ambassador*, *fadom–fathom*, *incestious–incestuous*, *renowm–renown*, *vild–vile*. For words in this second category the present text, following the example of Kittredge, adopts on each occurrence the variant form that appears in the copy-text. Although the forms preserved may in many cases represent scribal or compositorial choices rather than Shakespeare's own preferences, such an approach nevertheless suggests the kind of linguistic climate in which he wrote and avoids the unhistorical and sometimes insensitive levelling that full-scale modernization (never consistent itself) imposes. It was believed, in short, that something valuable was to be gained by allowing, within limits, some of the variety and color of the originals to survive the process of modernization.

The punctuation of a modernized text presents serious problems. A frequent practice is to impose a single modern standard throughout, but this leads almost inevitably to a heavy use of semicolons and periods. The punctuation in the early texts is comparatively light, especially in the earlier quartos, and creates occasional difficulties for the modern reader, but an editor who feels, as Dr. Johnson did, that punctuation is entirely in his power, and who ignores the punctuation of the copy-text, does so at the risk of continual damage to the movement and frequently to the meaning of the lines, either verse or prose. Judging from the evidence of the insurrection scene in *Sir Thomas More* (accepted in this edition as almost certainly in Shakespeare's autograph), Shakespeare employed a punctuation so light as to be almost non-existent. This single example need not, of course, mean that he always did so, but the supposition that he favored a light and running punctuation receives considerable support from the quarto texts believed to have been set from some form of his autograph. Thus, though the punctuation in the early texts may be in good part the work of someone in the printing-house, or of a scribe, it is probably nearer to Shakespeare's intentions and nearer to the speech rhythms of the period than any later and more tightly logical system can pretend to be. In the present edition, therefore, the punctuation of the different copy-texts has been followed as closely as is consistent with clarity. In many plays this means a frequent use of the comma where modern punctuation would employ either a semicolon or a period, but the resulting freedom in the flow of the verse and the immediacy with which sentences and sentence elements are related justify such an approach. Where, however, there is danger of misreading or ambiguity in the original pointing, the punctuation has been adjusted; but all changes that seem to involve a shift in meaning are recorded in the Textual Notes.

In writing verse, Elizabethan poets made a regular distinction, usually carefully preserved in printed texts, between final *-ed* (syllabic) and *-'d* (non-syllabic) in words to which it is phonetically possible to attach both forms of the suffix. This useful distinction has been retained in verse passages, and all departures from the copy-text form are recorded in the Textual Notes.[29] In prose, however, the two forms appear to have been used indiscriminately, the choice being governed sometimes merely by the compositor's need to justify his lines. For this reason the present text has levelled all such forms in prose passages to *-'d*, except (a) in certain words where the form in *-ed* seems to have been commonly employed in colloquial usage, and (b) in the speeches of a very few characters, such as Don Armado or Fluellen, who are presented to us as affected or "outlandish" speakers.

The act and scene designations in the present text generally agree with those found in the Globe edition (1864). Where such designations are additions to the copy-text, or alterations of it, they are here enclosed in square brackets and their sources are recorded in the Textual Notes. In addition, a summary statement of the act-scene arrangement in the copy-text will be found at the beginning of the Textual Notes to each play. The scene-by-scene line-numbering is based on the lineation of verse and prose as that appears in the present text; hence it will often differ, especially in prose passages, from that found in other texts, but usually by not more than a few lines either way. A system of what is called through-line-numbering (TLN) was introduced by Charlton Hinman in his facsimile of the First Folio published in 1968. The basis of his system, which numbers the lines of each play consecutively, ignoring scene breaks, from beginning to end, is the text as it is printed in the First Folio. Thus line numbers are assigned to whatever act and scene designations occur, to stage directions, and to every line and part line (including verse run-overs but excluding turn-overs and turn-unders) that takes up what might be considered a line space in the First Folio. Where additional lines, not in the Folio, appear in a modern text edited from quarto copy-text, these additional lines are indicated by placing after the last numbered folio line a plus sign followed by the number of added lines. For example, "2225+10" indicates that, following line 2225 in the Folio numeration, the text contains ten lines found only in the quarto text. A system of block TLN notation, based on Hinman's facsimile, has been worked out as follows. At the top of each column of the text (the first page of a play excepted) may be found the numbers of the first and last lines in that column (e.g., 2403–2455). Thus a reference to line 2425 of *Hamlet* may be readily located with something approaching accuracy. Two special points need to be noticed. First, frequently in prose passages (and occasionally in verse passages) the second number in a block reappears as the first number in the next block because a prose line (or mislined verse line) in the Folio numeration has necessarily been divided between two lines in the present text. Second, where a series of lines that do not appear in F1 (and hence have no Folio line numbers) are divided between the end of one column and the beginning of the next, the lines are described thus: "1065+9 (1–3)" and "1065+9 (4–9)", indicating that a total of nine lines are involved in the non-F1 lines and that individual lines in this group may be distinguished as "1065+1", "1065+2", etc. TLN numbering for *Pericles*, *The Two Noble Kinsmen*, and *Edward III* is based on the first quarto of *Pericles* (1609), the quarto of *The Two Noble Kinsmen* (1634), and the

[29] An exception has been made in the case of *Edward III* (see the "Note on the Text").

first quarto of *Edward III* (1596). The reader should be warned that the total number of lines recorded for a play by the TLN method does not at all accurately indicate the actual number of lines of dialogue contained in the play, since such numeration includes F1 act-scene divisions and stage directions, verse runovers, and part lines, and on the other hand does not include in the final figure all the additional lines not present in the F1 text.

The Textual Notes, which follow the individual plays, are intended to serve two principal functions. First, as has already been pointed out, they are intended to document the texts in the present edition by recording the source of all emendations and additions, i.e., the authority (other early printed texts or later editions) on which the emendation or addition has been adopted. They include also a record of all changes in the punctuation of the copy-text that may be said to affect meaning significantly. New readings introduced by the present editor are designated "*ed.*" Second, the Textual Notes have been so constructed as to offer a reader all the essential information he may need to study in depth the whole textual situation as it has been outlined for him in the "Note on the Text" prefixed to the Textual Notes for each play. Thus for what may be called two-text plays (i.e., plays published first in quarto from an authoritative manuscript and later in F1 in a substantially different text) the Textual Notes record the more significant variations between the version here chosen as copy-text and the other substantive version, and for *Richard III*, *Hamlet*, *Troilus and Cressida*, *King Lear*, and *Othello*, where the choice of copy-text is more complicated than in other plays, they record all substantive variants of the second text.

Five qualifications on the inclusiveness of the Textual Notes should be pointed out here. (1) Although substantial passages of special interest are quoted from each of the "bad" quartos at appropriate places in the Textual Notes, no systematic attempt could be made to record the great mass of individual textual variants in these quartos (apart from those for *Richard III* and *Lear*, both special cases) except where such variants are cited as part of an entry concerned with a particular reading in the substantive texts. (2) Where there is more than a single edition of a quarto published before the appearance of F1 in 1623, the numerous errors or unauthoritative compositorial variants introduced into the second and all succeeding editions are in general not recorded unless they figure as part of the presentation of the development of the substantive texts. (3) The variant readings of the later folios (1632, 1663/4, 1685) and of those quartos published after F1 (1623), since they possess no independent or manuscript authority, are included only when they seem to be of special significance in the later history of the text. (4) No attempt has been made to record the many hundreds of textual emendations offered by editors and critics during the past two hundred and seventy years unless (a) one of these emendations has been adopted in the present text, or (b) the textual situation was desperate enough to warrant a selection of the proposed readings. In particular cases, some of the suggested emendations are noticed in the glossarial notes. (5) Adjustments in verse alignment are not recorded unless they affect the passage in some significant way. Although in one sense these partial exclusions in the Textual Notes constitute a limitation, in another they greatly sharpen the focus on significant readings and serve to winnow out a great deal of meaningless chaff. The reader who desires additional details may refer to the collations in the revised Cambridge *Shakespeare* (1891–93) or to the more recent volumes of the *New Variorum Shakespeare*.

The text of *The Riverside* has been used by Professor Marvin Spevack as the basis of his widely known *Complete and Systematic Concordance to the Works of Shakespeare* (9 vols., 1968–80). This invaluable concordance is the first that in any definitive sense deserves the term "complete." It lists, with context, arranged alphabetically for the works as a whole (Vols. IV–VI) and individually, without context, for each work (Vols. I–III), *all* uses of *all* words occurring in the present text of the plays and poems. It also presents, as part of Volumes I–III, separate character concordances to each play, and includes in Volume VI a number of extremely useful appendices: a Word-Frequency Index, a Reverse-Word Index, a list of Hyphenated Words alphabetized by first, second, and third elements, a list of Homographs, and a Conversion Table for through-line-numbering. The last three volumes are in the nature of complementary appendices to Volumes I–VI: Volume VII, a concordance to stage directions; Volume VIII, a concordance to the "bad" quartos, *The Taming of a Shrew*, and *The Troublesome Reign of King John*; and Volume IX, a collation of substantive variants, recording the accepted readings in eight major editions from the second Cambridge *Shakespeare* (1891–93) through *The Riverside* (1974). Professor Spevack's concordance completely supersedes the old John Bartlett *Concordance* (1894), which is far from complete; and it serves a large variety of interests (including inclusiveness) not covered by the old-spelling concordances now being published, a separate volume to each play, by T. H. Howard-Hill. In fairness to Professor Spevack, it should here be noted that the very occasional discrepancies between his concordance and the texts as now published must be laid to the present editor's belated change of mind. In Volume VI (pp. 4341–42) Professor Spevack has included a list of substantive changes; some adjustments in punctuation do not in any way affect the use of the concordance. A one-volume concordance based on Volumes IV–VI, *The Harvard Concordance to Shakespeare*, was published by Harvard University Press (1973).

Glossary of Selected Bibliographical Terms

The following definitions are intended for use with the foregoing essay and with the bibliographical "Note on the Text" preceding the Textual Notes to each play. They should be considered as general working definitions, aimed primarily at the non-specialist. For further information the reader may consult: Fredson Bowers, *Principles of Bibliographical Description* (Princeton, 1949); Philip Gaskell, *A New Introduction to Bibliography* (Oxford, 1972); Charlton Hinman, *The Printing and Proof-Reading of the First Folio of Shakespeare*, 2 vols. (Oxford, 1963); Joseph Moxon, *Mechanick Exercises on the Whole Art of Printing* (1683–84), ed. Herbert Davis and Harry Carter (London, 1958); and R. B. McKerrow, *An Introduction to Bibliography for Literary Students* (Oxford, rev. ed., 1928).

Analytical bibliography (sometimes referred to as the "New Bibliography"). Analytical bibliography (as distinguished from descriptive or merely enumerative bibliography) is concerned with the printing process (i.e. the various steps through which printer's copy passes on its way to becoming a book) and seeks to establish, so far as possible, (a) the kind and authority (source), usually manuscript (except in reprints), of the printer's copy; and (b) the extent to which the composition and printing processes may have affected the quality of the printed text. The principal matters with which an analytical bibliographer concerns himself are: (a) the method employed in composition (whether seriatim or by casting off); (b) compositor determination (i.e. determining the identity and the characteristics of the compositor or compositors responsible for setting the type); (c) analysis of the amount and accuracy of press-correction through the collation of multiple copies of the same edition; (d) analysis of the running-titles, rules, etc. to establish the possible order of imposition within the sheet, or of sheets within the book; and (e) the detection and interpretation of cancels. Most of the bibliographical terms employed above are separately defined elsewhere in the Glossary.

Broadside: usually, a single folio leaf (half the size of the basic sheet), printed on one side only, used for the publication of proclamations, ballads, and ephemera generally. Occasionally the full, unfolded sheet was used.

Cancel: a term used to describe newly set printed matter substituted for some part of the contents of a work as originally set and printed off. The leaf (or leaves) that is replaced is known as the *cancellandum* (plural *cancellanda*); the leaf (or leaves) that is substituted (necessarily reset recto and verso), as the *cancellans* (plural *cancellantes*). Very occasionally a short passage may be found cancelled by a newly set printed slip pasted over the original setting of type; thus the necessity of resetting a whole leaf is avoided.

Casting off and cast-off copy. To cast off or count off printer's copy is (a) to estimate in advance as nearly as possible how many sheets a given amount of manuscript or printed copy will require to produce a book in a chosen type-size and format (folio, quarto, octavo, or other); (b) to estimate, even more exactly, the amount of copy, page by page, that may be contained in a sheet (or sheets), inner and outer forme, thus permitting copy to be divided among two or more printing shops, or two compositors within a single shop working simultaneously, either together on the setting of one sheet or independently on different sheets, with the necessary assurance, not always justified in actual practice, that one will end where the other began. The Shakespeare First Folio (a folio-in-sixes) used setting by cast-off copy generally throughout. For a large book like the First Folio, in which each page contains two long columns of relatively small type, this method had certain definite advantages. First, it allowed two compositors to work simultaneously on each six-leaf quire (see *Folio-in-sixes*). Assuming a six-leaf quire with the pages numbered consecutively 1 through 12, one compositor could, after the copy had been cast off, begin setting page 6, working back from page 6 to page 5, from 5 to 4, finally ending by setting page 1. The second compositor could at the same time begin setting page 7, working forward to page 8 and so seriatim through page 12. Such a procedure essentially halved the time it would have taken a single compositor working serially from page 1 through 12 on the same amount of copy, and thus balanced the differential in time between the comparatively slower process of composition (type-setting) and the faster mechanical process of impression (printing off), by permitting printing to begin as soon as pages 6 and 7 (constituting the inner forme of the innermost of the three sheets employed in the quire and the first to be set up by the two compositors working simultaneously) were in type, to be followed in sequence by pages 5 and 8, 4 and 9, etc. In contrast, if the six-leaf quire were set seriatim (i.e. pages 1 through 12), printing could not begin until page 7 had been set, completing the first printable forme. Second, the technique of setting from cast-off copy considerably reduced the amount of type locked up in type-pages at any one time, since once pages 6 and 7, 5 and 8, etc. had been printed off, the type could at once be redistributed in the type cases and become available for use in setting later pages of the same quire. In the seriatim method a much larger amount of type was out of circulation for a considerably longer period. Since the quantity of a particular type-face was necessarily limited, the comparatively speedier freeing of that type for further setting was an important consideration. The use of cast-off copy was not, however, without some attendant dangers. If, in a folio-in-sixes for example, the copy had been inaccurately cast off, the compositor who was working back from page 6 to page 1 of a given quire might discover when he came to set page 1 that he had either too little or too much copy to fit the regular format of the page. Since he had no place to go, the last page of the preceding quire and the following page of the present quire being either already printed off or in the process of being so, he had to solve his problem within the limits of page 1. If his copy had been overestimated, he could employ more white space in setting up the page (allowing some extra space between speeches, setting with extra space for entries and exits, turning over verse lines, etc.). If his copy had been underestimated, he might be in deeper trouble. If by the utmost squeezing and crowding he could not accommodate his remaining material, "judicious" omission was his only recourse. How often this desperate situation arose, we do not know, but Charlton Hinman (*The Printing and Proof-Reading of the First Folio of Shakespeare*, II, 507–8) suggests such an explanation to account for the omission of an important stage direction in *Antony and Cleopatra* at V.ii.34, where the folio page, significantly the first page of quire 2z, shows other obvious evidence of crowding.

Catchword: a printer's device, derived from earlier manuscript practice, to link page to page, both within the quire and from quire to quire. It consists of setting the first word of the following page (or the beginning of the word if it is of several syllables) at the foot of the preceding page, below the text and as far to the right as the line-measure (see *Line-measure*) being employed will allow. Catchwords were considered useful both in imposition and binding procedures. A lack of agreement between the catchword and the first word on the following page is a warning signal of possible textual difficulties, involving perhaps the omission of one or more words. Abbreviated as "cw."

Collation: (a) A formula for describing the make-up of a printed book (or manuscript); for example, 4to A–H4 (i.e. a quarto, with quires signed A through H, each quire containing four leaves). (b) The word-for-word and point-for-point comparison of two texts of the same work (either printed or manuscript) made with the intention of correcting one text by reference to the other or of recording differences between the two texts.

Composition: the setting of type from printer's copy.

Compositor: one who composes or sets type from printer's copy.

Copy: see *Printer's copy*.

Copy-text: here used as defined by R. B. McKerrow: the printed edition (or manuscript) upon which an editor bases the text. W. W. Greg's more restrictive use of the term (i.e., a text chosen for its accidentals [punctuation, spelling] in preference to the use of the accidentals in a later (non-autograph) substantively revised text on the grounds that such a text is more likely to retain accidentals closer to the author's) has comparatively small relevance to Shakespeare's texts, because it is generally accepted that in large part the punctuation and spelling are compositorial (or editorial).

Edition: all copies of a book printed from the same setting of type (allowing for the differences between copies resulting from press-correction). See *State*; *Issue*; *Stop-press correction*.

Folio: (a) A printer's designation for the format of a book (applied also to the bound volume) in which the individual sheets have been folded once, across the middle of the longer side (i.e. parallel with the shorter side), thus producing two leaves for every sheet (see *Sheet*). The measurements of each leaf, depending on the size of the sheet employed, vary from approximately 15″ by 10″ (large folio) to 12″ by 8″ (small folio), with many intermediate sizes. Abbreviated as "2°" and in non-collational reference as "F". Folio volumes in Elizabethan-Jacobean times (and later) were usually gathered in fours, sixes, or eights (see *Folio-in-sixes*). Bound copies of the same book will differ in leaf measurements depending on the amount of trimming the sheets were subjected to in the process of binding (true also, of course, of bound copies in quarto, octavo, and other formats). (b) Used also (derived from manuscript terminology and abbreviated as "fol." or "f.") to designate a single leaf (as distinguished from a page) in a quire (even in books of other than folio format).

Folio-in-sixes: a book (like the Shakespeare First Folio) in folio format in which each quire is made up of three folded sheets placed one inside another at the fold so as to produce a quire of six leaves (twelve pages). In such a folio quire, leaves 1 and 6, 2 and 5, 3 and 4 will be what are called conjugate leaves, i.e. leaves which are part of the same sheet and joined at the fold. This method of production facilitated both the sewing and binding process, reducing the bulk of a folio volume's spine. The same process was used to produce a folio-in-fours (two sheets) and a folio-in-eights (four sheets).

Format: see *Folio*; *Quarto*; *Octavo*.

Forme: a term applied to type-pages once they have been imposed (see *Imposition*) and firmly locked in the "chase" (the metal rectangular frame surrounding the imposed type-pages). A forme is described as "outer" or "inner," the outer forme always containing the first page of a quire (i.e. the recto of the first leaf) in all formats (folio, quarto, octavo, etc.)

Gathering: used as synonymous with "quire" (see *Quire*).

Imposition: the correct placement of the type-pages in the forme (outer and inner). See *Forme*. In quarto format, pages 1, 4, 5, 8 would thus be imposed in the outer forme and pages 2, 3, 6, 7 in the inner forme, each set so arranged in its forme that when the sheet is correctly folded the pages will appear in the sequence 1 through 8.

Impression: any continuous press-run from one setting of type. In Elizabethan-Jacobean times an ordinance of the Stationers' Company issued in 1587 made it illegal (with rare exceptions, specially authorized) to print off more than 1250 to 1500 copies of a work from the same setting of type. The rule (not always observed) was aimed at protecting the compositors from exploitation by the master printers. Since type was regularly redistributed to the type-cases as soon as the press-run had been completed for each forme, the same type being employed in setting other parts of the same book, what we would call a new impression (or reimpression) from the original setting of type very rarely occurred at this period.

Issue: a term used to designate the republication (second issue) of what are basically the original sheets of a book, but with the addition or substitution of newly set matter (usually a cancel title-page, more rarely other reset material supplied by a cancel leaf or cancel quire). See *Cancel*.

Justifying: the process by which a compositor in setting prose (occasionally verse) might adjust his line length to fit the adopted line-measure (see *Line-measure*), thus producing an even right type-page margin. The compositor could "justify" his line by altering the amount of space between words and by variations in spelling forms (e.g. "do" or "doe", "sin" or "sinne", "felicity" or "felicitie").

Line-measure: the chosen width of a type-page, or of a column in a two-column page (hence controlling the capacity of the individual type-line), determined in advance according to book format and page design, and controlled, from page to page, by the setting on the compositor's composing-stick. See *Justifying*.

Octavo: a printer's designation for the format of a book (applied also to the bound volume) in which the individual sheets have been folded three times, the direction of all three folds repeating that used in folio and quarto format, thus producing eight leaves (sixteen pages) to a quire. Abbreviated as "8°" or "8vo" and in non-collational reference as "O". The measurements of an octavo may be taken as roughly half those of a quarto, with the proviso noted under *Folio*.

Perfecting: the impression or printing off of the second side (either outer or inner forme) of a sheet that has already been printed off on one side.

Press-correction: see *Stop-press correction*.

Printer's copy: the manuscript or printed material from which the compositor set his type-pages. When the compositor used an earlier edition of a work as copy for a new edition in the same format, he usually set it page for page (a paginary reprint). A revised edition of a work was often set from mixed copy, an earlier edition with manuscript insertions.

Proof correction (see also *Stop-press correction*). The extent and kind of correction in the Elizabethan-Jacobean printing-house is at present a matter of some dispute. The older orthodox view was that what is usually called stop-press correction or simply press-correction (i.e. corrections to the forme, the imposed type-pages, made in the process of printing off) represented essentially all the correction to which a book at this time was subjected. Recently, however, it has been suggested that stop-press correction is only the last step of several stages of correction, the earlier stages of which were conducted before the forme ever reached the press—in other words, that stop-press correction represents only the final tidying up of errors that had evaded correction in the rough proofs taken directly from the standing type (see *Standing type*) prior to its bedding in the press. This newer view has the support of Joseph Moxon's discussion of proof correction in his *Mechanick Exercises* (1683–84), a discussion that the proponents of the older view deny has any necessary bearing on the practices of the early part of the century. The truth probably lies somewhere in the middle. Under certain circumstances some books may have been corrected only after presswork began; others (possibly including the First Folio of Shakespeare) underwent proof correction in several stages, press-correction being the final step.

Quarto: a printer's designation for the format of a book (applied also to the bound volume) in which the individual sheets have been folded twice, the direction of both folds repeating that used for folio format, thus producing four leaves (eight pages). Abbreviated as "4°" or "4to" and in non-collational references as "Q". Quartos were sometimes gathered in eights, producing a quire of eight leaves (sixteen pages). The measurements of a quarto, though it gives a squarer appearance, are roughly half those of a folio, with the proviso noted under *Folio*.

Quire: (a) The sheet as folded to produce a book in folio format (two leaves, four pages), quarto format (four leaves, eight pages), etc. (b) Two or more sheets gathered one within another and so arranged as to form a bibliographical unit (e.g. quarto-in-eights, folio-in-sixes).

Recto: the front of a leaf; in an opened book (or manuscript) always the right-hand page. Abbreviated as superscript "r" following the leaf number. See *Verso*.

Running-title: a line of type, placed at the top of each page, containing the title of the work or distinguishing different sections of the work. Also called "running-head." Running-titles were not composed as part of the type-page, but inserted at the top of each type-page at the time of imposition. In this way the same set (or sets) of running-titles might be used throughout a book without the necessity of resetting.

Sheet: the basic component of a book. In Elizabethan-Jacobean times the size of the sheet varied consid-

350 The Tragedie of

hould my performance perish.
Rom. Thou hast *Ventidius* that, without the which a
Souldier and his Sword graunts scarce distinction : thou
wilt write to *Anthony*.
Ven. Ile humbly signifie what in his name,
That magicall word of Warre we haue effected,
How with his Banners, and his well paid ranks,
The nere-yet beaten Horse of Parthia,
We haue iaded out o'th Field.
Rom. Where is he now?
Ven. He purposeth to Athens, whither with what hast
The waight we must conuay with's, will permit:
We shall appeare before him. On there, passe along.
Exeunt.

Enter Agrippa at one doore, Enobarbus at another.
Agri. What are the Brothers parted?
Eno. They haue dispatcht with *Pompey*, he is gone,
The other three are Sealing. *Octauia* weepes
To part from Rome: *Cæsar* is sad, and *Lepidus*
Since *Pompey's* feast, as *Menas* saies, is troubled
With the Greene-Sicknesse.
Agri. 'Tis a Noble *Lepidus*.
Eno. A very fine one: oh, how he loues *Cæsar*.
Agri. Nay but how deerely he adores *Mark Anthony*.
Eno. *Cæsar*? why he's the Iupiter of men.
Ant. What's *Anthony*, the God of Iupiter?
Eno. Spake you of *Cæsar*? How, the non-pareill?
Agri. Oh *Anthony*, oh thou Arabian Bird!
Eno. Would you praise *Cæsar*, say *Cæsar* go no further.
Agr. Indeed he plied them both with excellent praises.
Eno. But he loues *Cæsar* best, yet he loues *Anthony*:
Hoo Hearts, Tongues, Figure,
Scribes, Bards, Poets, cannot
Thinke speake, cast, write, sing, number: hoo,
His loue to *Anthony*. But as for *Cæsar*,
Kneele downe, kneele downe, and wonder.
Agri. Both he loues.
Eno. They are his Shards, and he their Beetle, so:
This is to horse: Adieu, Noble *Agrippa*.
Agri. Good Fortune worthy Souldier, and farewell.

Enter Cæsar, Anthony, Lepidus, and Octauia.
Antho. No further Sir.
Cæsar. You take from me a great part of my selfe:
Vse me well in't. Sister, proue such a wife
As my thoughts make thee, and as my farthest Band
Shall passe on thy approofe: most Noble *Anthony*,
Let not the peece of Vertue which is set
Betwixt vs, as the Cyment of our loue
To keepe it builded, be the Ramme to batter
The Fortresse of it: for better might we
Haue lou'd without this meane, if on both parts
This be not cherisht.
Ant. Make me not offended, in your distrust.
Cæsar. I haue said.
Ant. You shall not finde,
Though you be therein curious, the lest cause
For what you seeme to feare, so the Gods keepe you,
And make the hearts of Romaines serue your ends:
We will heere part.
Cæsar. Farewell my deerest Sister, fare thee well,
The Elements be kind to thee, and make
Thy spirits all of comfort: fare thee well.
Octa. My Noble Brother.
Anth. The Aprill's in her eyes, it is Loues Spring,
And these the showers to bring it on: be cheerfull.

Octa. Sir, looke well to my Husbands house: and
Cæsar. What *Octauia*?
Octa. Ile tell you in your eare.
Ant. Her tongue will not obey her heart, nor can
Her heart informe her tougue.
The Swannes downe feather
That stands vpon the Swell at the of full Tide:
And neither way inclines.
Eno. Will *Cæsar* weepe?
Agr. He ha's a cloud in's face.
Eno. He were the worse for that were he a Horse so is
he being a man.
Agri. Why *Enobarbus*:
When *Anthony* found *Iulius Cæsar* dead,
He cried almost to roaring: And he wept,
When at Phillippi he found *Brutus* slaine.
Eno. That yeare indeed, he was trobled with a rume,
What willingly he did confound, he wail'd,
Beleeu't till I weepe too.
Cæsar. No sweet *Octauia*,
You shall heare from me still: the time shall not
Out-go my thinking on you.
Ant. Come Sir, come,
Ile wrastle with you in my strength of loue,
Looke heere I haue you, thus I let you go,
And giue you to the Gods.
Cæsar. Adieu, be happy.
Lep. Let all the number of the Starres giue light
To thy faire way.
Cæsar. Farewell, farewell. *Kisses Octauia.*
Ant. Farewell. *Trumpets sound. Exeunt.*

Enter Cleopatra, Charmian, Iras, and Alexas.
Cleo. Where is the Fellow?
Alex. Halfe afeard to come.
Cleo. Go too, go too: Come hither Sir.
Enter the Messenger as before.
Alex. Good Maiestie: *Herod* of Iury dare not looke
vpon you, but when you are well pleas'd.
Cleo. That *Herods* head, Ile haue: but how? When
Anthony is gone, through whom I might commaund it:
Come thou neere.
Mes. Most gratious Maiestie.
Cleo. Did'st thou behold *Octauia*?
Mes. I dread Queene.
Cleo. Where?
Mes. Madam in Rome, I lookt her in the face: and
saw her led betweene her Brother, and *Marke Anthony*.
Cleo. Is she as tall as me?
Mes. She is not Madam.
Cleo. Didst heare her speake? Is she shrill tongu'd or low?
Mes. Madam, I heard her speake, she is low voic'd.
Cleo. That's not so good: he cannot like her long.
Char. Like her? Oh *Isis*: 'tis impossible.
Cleo. I thinke so *Charmian*: dull of tongue, & dwarfish
What Maiestie is in her gate, remember
If ere thou look'st on Maiestie.
Mes. She creepes: her motion, & her station are as one.
She shewes a body, rather then a life,
A Statue, then a Breather.
Cleo. Is this certaine?
Mes. Or I haue no obseruance.
Cha. Three in Egypt cannot make better note.
Cleo. He's very knowing, I do perceiu't,
There's nothing in her yet.
The

Proof-page of *Antony and Cleopatra* from the First Folio (1623), sig. xx6v. It represents the uncorrected state of the page and shows the proof-reader's marks indicating corrections. All but two of the corrections here marked were duly made in the corrected state. (*The Folger Shakespeare Library*)

erably, measuring approximately from 20″ by 15″ (large folio) to 16″ by 12″ (small folio). The size of the sheets used in the Shakespeare First Folio falls between these limits, the largest known copy, after being trimmed in the process of binding, measuring 17″ by 13⅜″ (McKerrow).

Signature: (a) A printer's device for indicating the correct order of quires in a book and of the individual pages in a particular quire. The "signature," which is placed below the text at the foot of a recto page, is usually made up of (1) a symbol (usually a letter of the alphabet) which implies definite sequence and serves as an aid to the binder and (2) a numeral which indicates the exact position of that leaf within the quire and serves as an aid to the correct imposition of the type-pages in the outer and inner formes (see *Forme*) and as a guide to the folding of the printed sheet. Thus in a book printed in quarto format (having four leaves, eight pages, to a quire) the recto of the first leaf of the first quire (not including preliminary matter, which is often signed with an arbitrary symbol to distinguish it and is frequently the last part of a book to be printed) may be signed A1, the second leaf A2, and the third A3, the fourth leaf being, as a rule, unsigned. (b) Also used (abbreviated as "sig.") to refer, especially in unfoliated or unpaged books, to an individual page of a particular quire, as, for example, sig. A3ᵛ, referring to the verso of the third leaf in quire A. The word will also, unfortunately, be found used in earlier bibliographical work as a synonym for "quire" or "gathering."

Standing type: (a) Type-pages before final imposition and bedding on the press. (b) Type-pages preserved as originally set after a completed press-run.

State: (a) A term used to distinguish different copies of the same edition some of which (second state) contain cancels inserted before first publication or reset material introduced in the course of the original press-run. (b) Also used to describe the corrected and uncorrected stages resulting from proof correction of the outer and inner formes of individual sheets. In sense (a) the terms "state" and "issue" are often difficult, sometimes impossible, to distinguish.

Stop-press correction (see also *Proof correction*). Although it now seems probable that, in the production of a number of books, one or more proofs were taken from the standing type and corrections made before the type-pages were locked up in the chase and placed on the press, the only corrected proofs, with the exception of two or three non-Shakespearean examples, that have survived seem to represent proofs taken at the beginning of a press-run. While such press-proofs were being read and marked by the proof-corrector, the printing process was continued, something around an average of ten percent of the total number of sheets in the press-run being printed off (either outer or inner forme) before the corrected press-proof was returned; printing was then stopped, and corrections were made by a compositor, either with the forme still in the press or, if the required corrections were substantial enough to warrant it, by removing the forme from the press bed to the correcting stone. Once the corrections had been made, printing was resumed, but those sheets printed off while the press-proof was being corrected were not discarded. If further errors in the printed sheets were observed, the press might be stopped a second, even a third, time and the correction process repeated, thus producing a second or third state of correction in a certain number of sheets. When it came to the point of assembling copies of the book from the separate quire piles of printed sheets, corrected (abbreviated as "c") and uncorrected (abbreviated as "u") sheets were treated indiscriminately, different copies of the bound volume being made up of different chance assortments of the corrected and uncorrected states. Accidents damaging or disarranging (i.e. pieing) the type during a press-run might also result in stop-press corrections.

Verso: the back of a leaf; in an opened book (or manuscript) always the left-hand page. Abbreviated as superscript "v" following the leaf number. See *Recto*.

A sixteenth-century printing shop. From Stephen Batman, *The Doom Warning All Men to the Judgment* (1581). The printing press here shown, in all essentials typical of presses used down to the end of the eighteenth century, is being worked at "full press" (i.e. with two men), one man (right) removing from the tympan a sheet just printed off, the other inking the type-bed with the ink-balls, preparatory to the next "pull." Note (left) the "platen" (half the size of a sheet), fastened flexibly at the lower end of the large screw spindle, which, when the carriage was slid back under it, was brought down evenly and firmly on the type-bed by a strong pull of the "bar" to make the impression. In the foreground are two "piles," one of sheets already printed off in the press-run, the other of sheets still waiting to be "impressed." In the rear of the shop a compositor (right), sitting before a "case" of type, is seen setting from "copy," which is held in a copy-holder to his left. Opposite him, another compositor is either making press-corrections or setting type. (*By permission of the Harvard College Library*)

Chronology and Sources

G. Blakemore Evans

J. J. M. Tobin

The following table attempts to arrange Shakespeare's plays and poems in the order of their composition, to present the evidence for the proposed order, and, because dating sometimes depends upon the time when particular sources became available, to list the source materials for each work.

Any attempt to arrange the plays chronologically is beset with hazards and uncertainties, and, as the information in the table will make clear, the undertaking has given rise to differences of opinion among a long line of editors and critics. The first to attack the problem was Edward Capell, although the credit as pioneer is usually assigned to Edmond Malone, whose "An Attempt to Ascertain the Order in Which the Plays Attributed to Shakspeare Were Written" was published in 1778, two years before Capell's earlier chronology appeared in print. Since the time of Capell and Malone, many of whose proposed dates are no longer acceptable, other scholars have addressed themselves to the problem of chronology, and the results of their labors may be found authoritatively brought together by Sir Edmund Chambers in the first volume of his *William Shakespeare: A Study of Facts and Problems* (Oxford, 1930). The most useful general review of the evidence for dating is James G. McManaway's "Recent Studies in Shakespeare's Chronology" in Volume III of *Shakespeare Survey* (1950), but well worth consideration for the chronology of the early plays is Marco Mincoff's *Shakespeare: The First Steps* (1976), and for the entire canon the stimulating "The Canon and Chronology of Shakespeare's Plays" section (pp. 69–144) of *William Shakespeare: A Textual Companion* (1987), edited by Stanley Wells, Gary Taylor, John Jowett, and William Montgomery.

Evidence for dating may be distinguished as of two kinds: internal evidence and external evidence. Internal evidence, as the term suggests, is drawn from the texts of the plays and poems and deals for the most part in topical allusions (which if dateable may establish a *terminus a quo*, i.e., a date before which the work cannot have been written), metrical development, kinds and handling of imagery, incidence of rhyme, and vocabulary. External evidence is concerned with rather more concrete matters: dates of actual publication; entry on the Stationers' Register (cited below as *S.R.*), Henslowe's *Diary*, Francis Meres's *Palladis Tamia* (1598), Revels accounts, etc.; and allusions to, or imitations of, Shakespeare's plays or poems by contemporary writers whose work can be dated.

Even with the aid of all the known evidence it is frequently impossible to narrow the date of a play to the limits even of a particular year, although it will be noticed that the dating set forth below becomes somewhat firmer beginning with *Richard II* (1595). External evidence can generally establish a *terminus ad quem*, i.e. the date after which the work cannot have been written, but it tells us nothing definite about how long before this terminal date the work was in fact composed. It is at this point that internal evidence must be brought to bear, but internal evidence is slippery in the extreme and often susceptible of more than one interpretation. The problem is further complicated by two other factors: the possibility that Shakespeare reworked an earlier play by another writer (mixed authorship) and the possibility that a play as we now have it represents Shakespeare's reworking of his original version (revision). The claims of both mixed authorship and revision have given rise to much disagreement among critics, and consequently to further uncertainty in establishing a chronology.

The table, which for the chronology is based in great part on the work of Chambers and McManaway and more recent investigations of particular plays, is arranged, following the name of the play or poem, to give, in the first column, the most commonly accepted date or dates for that play or poem (where more than one title is assigned to the same year or years the order of listing represents the probable order of composition) and, where indicated, the date of suggested revision; and in the second column, the basic evidence for the dating, followed by a list of the proposed sources, arranged under the categories employed by Geoffrey Bullough in *Narrative and Dramatic Sources of Shakespeare* (8 vols., London, 1957–75). Shakespeare's widespread use of works by his contemporaries and of contemporary translations of classical authors is amply represented but not exhaustively so. A complete listing of Shakespeare's use of such writers as Thomas Nashe, Apuleius, Philip Sidney, Edmund Spenser, and Robert Southwell, even if possible, would require an additional volume.

TITLE	PROPOSED DATE	EVIDENCE FOR DATING; SOURCES
1 Henry VI	1589–90 (revised 1594–95)	Published in F1 (1623). Performed March 3, 1592 (marked "ne," i.e. new or, possibly, revised or relicensed by Henslowe, *Diary*). Alluded to by Nashe (*Pierce Penilesse*, August 8, 1592; see Appendix C, Number 12). Rival theories of authorship: (1) wholly by Shakespeare and revised after *2* and *3 Henry VI*; (2) reworking of an earlier play by another hand or hands (Greene, Peele, Nashe the strongest candidates). Some would place the play in any form later than *2* and *3 Henry VI*. No definite proof that the F1 text represents the play in essentially the same form as performed for Henslowe or referred to by Nashe. SOURCES: (1) Hall, *The Union of the Two Noble and Illustre Families of Lancaster and York* (1548). (2) Holinshed, *Chronicles* (2nd ed., 1587). (3) Fabyan, *Chronicle* (1559 ed.; first English version 1533). (4) Geoffrey of Monmouth, *Historia Regum Britanniae*. PROBABLE SOURCE: Sir Thomas Coningsby, *Journal of the Siege of Rouen* (MS; published 1847).
2 Henry VI	1590–91	"Bad" quarto (*The First Part of the Contention betwixt the Two Famous Houses of York and Lancaster*) entered on *S.R.* March 12, 1594; published 1594. Received text published in F1 (1623). The plague closed the theatres in London for three months in 1592, the whole of 1593, and the first half of 1594. The "bad" quarto version presumably derived from forced provincial tours and implies a date not later than the beginning of 1592 for the original play. Greene parodied a line in *3 Henry VI* (I.iv.137) before his death on September 3, 1592 (*Groatsworth of Wit*; see Appendix C, Number 8), which seems to require a still earlier date for *2 Henry VI*. As for *1 Henry VI*, authorship problems raise further diffficulties, but it seems relatively sure that the F1 texts of *2* and *3 Henry VI* are essentially the plays as performed around 1590–91. SOURCES: (1) Hall, *The Union of . . . Lancaster and York* (1548). (2) Fabyan, *Chronicle* (1559 ed.). PROBABLE SOURCES: (1) Holinshed, *Chronicles* (2nd ed., 1587). (2) Foxe, *Acts and Monuments* (1570 ed.). (3) Grafton, *Chronicle at Large* (1569). (4) Apuleius, *The Golden Ass* (tr. Adlington, 1566), for the description of the death of Jack Cade in IV.x.
3 Henry VI	1590–91	"Bad" quarto (*The True Tragedy of Richard Duke of York*) published 1595. Received text published in F1 (1623). See Greene's allusion (1592) under *2 Henry VI* above. The two parts are closely connected (both "bad" quartos were published by the same publisher) and present essentially the same problems. SOURCES: (1) Hall, *The Union of . . . Lancaster and York* (1548). (2) Holinshed, *Chronicles* (2nd ed., 1587). PROBABLE SOURCE: Foxe, *Acts and Monuments* (1570 ed.). POSSIBLE SOURCE: Baldwin, ed., *A Mirror for Magistrates* (1559).
Richard III	1592–93	"Bad" quarto entered on *S.R.* October 20, 1597; published 1597. Somewhat enlarged and revised text published in F1 (1623). Close links with *3 Henry VI* suggest that it was composed immediately after that play. Heavily influenced anonymous *King Leir* (1594). SOURCES: (1) Hall, *The Union of . . . Lancaster and York* (1548). (2) Holinshed, *Chronicles* (2nd ed., 1587). PROBABLE SOURCES: (1) Baldwin, ed., *A Mirror for Magistrates* (1559). (2) Anon., *The True Tragedy of Richard III* (c. 1591). (3) Stow, *The Chronicles of England* (1580). (4) Nashe, *Summer's Last Will and Testament*, performed 1592 (1600). (5) Apuleius, *The Golden Ass* (tr. Adlington, 1566) for the description of the deaths of the princes. (6) Seneca, *Hercules Furens*, *Octavia*, *Medea* (tr. Studley, 1566), and *Hippolytus* (tr. Studley, 1567).
Venus and Adonis	1592–93	Entered on *S.R.* April 18, 1593; published 1593. Generally thought of as being composed in 1592–93 because of the enforced suspension of theatrical performances in London as a result of the plague. A minority interpret Shake-

TITLE	PROPOSED DATE	EVIDENCE FOR DATING; SOURCES
Venus and Adonis (cont.)		speare's reference to the poem as "the first heire of my inuention" as implying that it predates any of his work in the drama, thus throwing the date of composition back into the late 1580's. SOURCES: (1) Ovid, *Metamorphoses* (tr. Golding, 1565, 1567), Bks. III, IV, X. (2) Apuleius, *The Golden Ass* (tr. Adlington, 1566) esp. Bk. VIII, chapt 32, for the fatal boar hunt. PROBABLE SOURCE: Lodge, *Scilla's Metamorphosis* (1589).
The Comedy of Errors	1592–94	Published in F1 (1623). Performed at Gray's Inn December 28, 1594 (see Appendix C, Number 14). The allusion to France "arm'd and reverted, making war against her heir" (III.ii.123–24) has generally been taken to date the play before July 9, 1593, when a truce was declared between Henry IV and the League, but it has recently been shown that comments on the struggle as still in progress appeared for several years after 1593. It is therefore possible that the Gray's Inn performance was the first (1594) and that the play with its classical source and unusual amount of legal terminology was written for that occasion. SOURCES: Plautus, (1) *Menaechmi* (English tr. by William Warner, 1595) and (2) *Amphitruo*. (3) Lyly, *Midas* (c. 1589). (4) Gascoigne, *Supposes* (1566). (5) St. Paul, Acts of the Apostles and Epistle to the Ephesians. PROBABLE SOURCE: Gower, *Confessio Amantis* (1554 ed.), Bk. VIII. POSSIBLE SOURCE: Sir Philip Sidney, *The Countess of Pembroke's Arcadia* (1590).
Edward III	1592–95	First attributed to Shakespeare by Capell in *Prolusions*, 1760; arguments are that it is all by one author and he is or is not Shakespeare, or that the play is by at least two hands, one of which is or is not Shakespeare's. Supporters of Shakespeare's role focus on the "Countess scenes" (I.ii, II.i.ii.) and IV.iv. The play was entered in the Stationers' Register 1 December 1595, providing a *terminus ad quem* for composition; it was published in 1596 as *The Raigne of King Edward the third: As it hath bin sundrie times plaied about the Citie of London* and in a second quarto edition in 1599. SOURCES: (1) Froissart, *Chronicles* (tr. Lord Berners, c. 1523–25). (2) Painter, *The Palace of Pleasure Beautified* (1575), Novel 46, "The Countesse of Salesburie." (3) Holinshed, *Chronicles* (2nd ed., 1587).
Sonnets	1593–1609	Entered on *S.R.* May 20, 1609; published 1609. The date span here suggested reflects the great range of critical opinion (Rollins, *New Variorum*, II, 73). Minority views would either push the dating back into the middle 1580's for some sonnets or see other sonnets as late as 1609. There are one or two facts and one interesting implication. Meres (before September 7, 1598) refers to Shakespeare's "sugred Sonnets among his priuate friends" (see Appendix C, Number 22), and William Jaggard printed two of the sonnets (138, 144) in the 1599 *Passionate Pilgrim*. Some of the sonnets, therefore, were in existence by 1598, a conclusion that helps not at all, since all dating theories allow this premise. More significant, perhaps, is the large number of verbal and thematic parallels that can be established between the Sonnets, the other poems, and the earlier plays (through *King John*, 1594–96), but certain of the later plays do show such parallels, including *As You Like It* (1599), *Hamlet* (1600–01) and *Troilus and Cressida* (1601–2). 107 is now generally accepted as having been composed in 1603–4, referring as it apparently does to the peaceful accession of King James. SOURCES: (1) Ovid, *Metamorphoses* (tr. Golding, 1567), esp. Bk. XV. (2) Daniel, *Delia* (1592). (3) Sidney, *Arcadia* (1590) and *Astrophel and Stella* (1591). (4) Spenser, *Ruines of Rome: By Bellay* (1591). (5) Henry Constable, *Diana* (1592, enlarged 1594). (6) Wilson, *The Arte of Rhetorique* (1553). (7) Marlowe and Chapman, *Hero and Leander* (1598). (8) Barnfield, *The Affectionate Shepherd* (1594) and *Cynthia* (1595).
The Rape of Lucrece	1593–94	Published 1594. Many verbal links have been pointed out between *Lucrece* and *Titus Andronicus* (some, though fewer, between that play and *Venus and Adonis*). SOURCES: (1) Ovid, *Fasti*, Bk. II. (2) Livy, *Historia*, Bk. I (with possible use of William Painter's tr. in *The Palace of Pleasure*, 1566). (3) Daniel, *The Complaint of Rosamond* (1592). (4) Southwell, *St. Peter's Complaint* (1595), composed several years earlier. PROBABLE SOURCE: Chaucer, *The Legend of Good Women* (lines 1680–1885).
Titus Andronicus	1593–94	Performed January 24, 1594 (Henslowe's *Diary*, where it is marked "ne," i.e. new or, possibly, revised or relicensed). Entered on *S.R.* February 6, 1594; published 1594. Listed by Meres (*Palladis Tamia*, 1598) as by Shakespeare. Rival

TITLE	PROPOSED DATE	EVIDENCE FOR DATING; SOURCES
Titus Andronicus (cont.)		theories of authorship: (1) Shakespeare's thorough rewriting, except for Act I, of an earlier play (c. 1589), probably by Peele; (2) wholly Shakespeare's. An allusion to a play on this subject in *A Knack to Know a Knave*, acted as "ne" on June 10, 1592 (Henslowe, *Diary*), must, if we accept the dates 1593–94, be interpreted as a reference to the pre-Shakespearean play. SOURCES: (1) Anon., *The History of Titus Andronicus* (known only from an eighteenth-century chapbook in the Folger Shakespeare Library). (2) Ovid, *Metamorphoses* (tr. Golding, 1567), Bk. VI. (3) Seneca, *Thyestes* (tr. Jasper Heywood, 1560). (4) Nashe, *Christ's Tears over Jerusalem* (1593). PROBABLE SOURCE: Plutarch, *Lives* (tr. North, 1579 ed.).
The Taming of the Shrew	1593–94	Entered on *S.R.* January 22, 1607; published in F1 (1623). A play called *The Taming of a Shrew* was entered on *S.R.* May 2, 1594, and published in the same year. Two general views of *A Shrew* have been held: (1) that it is a "bad" quarto text of a play that served as Shakespeare's source for *The Shrew*; (2) that *A Shrew* is a "bad" quarto version of Shakespeare's *The Shrew*. If the second view is accepted, a view that has steadily gained support in recent years, Shakespeare's play (*The Shrew*) would have to be dated not later than 1593. The performance of a play called "the tamynge of A shrowe" is recorded in Henslowe's *Diary* for June 11, 1594, at the Newington Butts theatre, where both Shakespeare's company (the Chamberlain's Men) and the Admiral's Men are believed to have been performing at this time. Significantly perhaps, Henslowe does not mark the play "ne" (i.e. new, or possibly revised or relicensed). SOURCES: (1) *A Merry Jest of a Shrewd and Curst Wife Lapped in Morel's Skin for Her Good Behavior* (c. 1550). (2) Gascoigne, *Supposes* (1566). (3) *The Taming of a Shrew* (published 1594) [see above for a different view]. (4) For the Sly framework: some version of a story that appears in P. Heuterus' *De Rebus Burgundicis* (1584; Bk. IV) that relates a very similar prank played by Philip the Good of Burgundy on a drunken countryman. Shakespeare may have got the story from a now-lost collection of tales by Richard Edwards published in 1570 (see Thomas Warton, *History of English Poetry* [1774–81], Section 52); a later fragment (c. 1620) with the title "The Waking Man's Dream" may be part of a reprint of Edwards' collection (see *Shakespeare's Library*, ed. W. C. Hazlitt [1875], IV, 406–14). A translation of Heuterus' version by Grimestone (from the French of S. Goulart) appeared in 1607.
The Two Gentlemen of Verona	1594	Published in F1 (1623). Noted by Meres (*Palladis Tamia*, 1598) as by Shakespeare. Generally admitted to be Shakespeare's earliest attempt at romantic comedy. Leech (New Arden ed.) suggests that it was composed in two stages, first stage 1592, second stage late 1593, and that it precedes *The Comedy of Errors*. The two stages, he believes, may explain some of the numerous inconsistencies in the play as we now have it. But a date earlier than 1594 remains problematical. Intriguingly, several names of the characters parallel those of Elizabethan contemporaries in Nashe's *Have With You to Saffron Walden* (1596, but in manuscript circulation three months before publication). SOURCES: (1); J. de Montemayor, *Diana* (possibly in Yonge's English tr., published 1598 but in MS sixteen years earlier). (2) Brooke, *Romeus and Juliet* (1562). (3) Lyly, *Midas* (c. 1589). PROBABLE SOURCES: (1) Elyot, *The Governor* (1531). (2) Edwards, *Damon and Pithias* (c. 1565).
Love's Labor's Lost	1594–95 (revised 1597 for court performance)	Published 1598. It seems likely that a "bad" quarto edition preceded the 1598 quarto, but no copy is extant. Meres (*Palladis Tamia*, 1598) mentions the play as Shakespeare's, coupled with what sounds like a companion play, "Loue labours wonne," of which, although we know it to have been published in quarto by 1603, no copy has survived (see T. W. Baldwin, *Shakspere's "Love's Labor's Won,"* 1957). There seems to be a reference in IV.iii.343–44 to Chapman's *Shadow of Night* (1594), which would place the play not earlier than that year. The Muscovite disguise in V.ii and Berowne's complaint in I.i.48 ("Not to see ladies") are thought to show the influence of the Gray's Inn Christmas revels of 1594–95 (see Appendix C, Number 14); and Berowne's remark in V.ii.460–62 may be taken as a reference to the ill-fated performance of *The Comedy of Errors* during those revels. Further, the song in V.ii.889–924 was probably not composed before 1597 since as seems likely it draws from Gerard's *Herbal* published in that year. This song and other revisions were probably written for the court performance (not later than Christmas of 1597) referred to on the title-page of the 1598 quarto.

TITLE	PROPOSED DATE	EVIDENCE FOR DATING; SOURCES
Love's Labor's Lost (cont.)		SOURCE: None definite; some suggested analogues with French history of the sixteenth century; probable influence of *commedia dell'arte* in plot and character types and of the Gray's Inn Christmas revels of 1594–95; song in V.ii.889–924 probably based on Gerard's *Herbal* (1597). No other of Shakespeare's plays shows so many parallels of word and phrase with Nashe's *Have With You to Saffron Walden* (1596). Don Armado's language appears to parody examples in Wilson, *The Arte of Rhetorique* (1553).
Additions to *Sir Thomas More*	1594–95	Suggested dates for the play as a whole range from 1590 to 1605, but the most widely accepted dating for the original play is 1590–93, for the revisions 1592–94 or 1600–4. Shakespeare's proposed part in the revisions is limited to a single scene (Addition II in Hand D) and a shorter passage (Addition III in Hand C). For a full discussion, see the critical Introduction to Additions II and III in this edition. SOURCES (for the play as a whole): (1) Holinshed, *Chronicles* (1587 ed.). (2) Nicholas Harpsfield, MS "Life of More" (1557–8; not published until 1932). (3) Thomas Stapleton, *Vita Thomas Moxi* (1588). (4) Foxe, *Acts and Monuments* (1570). (5) Anon. *Marriage of Wit and Science* (1568). (6) Thomas Ingelend, *The Disobedient Child* (c. 1562). (7) Richard Weaver, *Lusty Juventus* (c. 1550). (8) W. Wager (?), *The Trial of Treasure* (1567).
King John	1594–96	Published in F1 (1623). Listed by Meres (*Palladis Tamia*, 1598) as by Shakespeare. The dating problem for *King John is* exceptionally murky. Two widely different views are held about the relationship of Shakespeare's play to the anonymous two-part play called *The Troublesome Reign of John, King of England*, published in 1591: (1) *T.R.* is the principal source of *King John* (the orthodox and still most generally accepted opinion); (2) *T.R.* is a memorial imitation of Shakespeare's play (i.e. a "bad" quarto). The proponents of (2), who are few in number, would thus date *King John* not later than 1590. If they should ever prove their case, the chronology of Shakespeare's early plays would have to be reconsidered. SOURCES: (1) Anon., *The Troublesome Reign of John, King of England*, 2 pts. (published 1591) [see above for another view]. (2) Holinshed, *Chronicles* (2nd ed., 1587). PROBABLE SOURCE: Hall, *The Union of . . . Lancaster and York* (1548). POSSIBLE SOURCE: Foxe, *Acts and Monuments* (1570 ed.).
Richard II	1595	Entered on *S.R.* August 29, 1597; published 1597. Listed by Meres (*Palladis Tamia*, 1598) as by Shakespeare. Shakespeare is probably indebted to Daniel's *Civil Wars* (1595). It is possible that a performance of this play took place at the house of Sir Edward Hoby, December 9, 1595 (see Appendix C, Number 15). If the "K. Richard" of Hoby's letter is indeed Shakespeare's *Richard II*, this piece of evidence, coupled with the probable influence of Daniel, would give us the first definite year date for the composition of one of the plays. SOURCES: (1) Hall, *The Union of . . . Lancaster and York* (1548). (2) Holinshed, *Chronicles* (2nd ed., 1587). (3) Anon., *1 Richard II* (or *Thomas of Woodstock*) (c. 1592). (4) Nashe, *Christ's Tears Over Jerusalem* (1593). PROBABLE SOURCE: Daniel, *Civil Wars* (1595). POSSIBLE SOURCES: (1) Baldwin, ed., *A Mirror for Magistrates* (1559). (2) Froissart, *Chronicles* (tr. Lord Berners, c. 1523–25). (3) Lyly, *Euphues* (1578). (4) Thomas Lodge, "Truth's Complaint Over England," in *An Alarum Against Usurers* (1584). (5) Anon., *Chronicque de la Traison et Mort de Richard Deux* and (6) Jean Créton, *Histoire du Roy d'Angleterre Richard* (both of these eyewitness accounts existed only in manuscript in the 16th c., but Créton's work was certainly used by Stow in his *Chronicles* (1580).
Romeo and Juliet	1595–96	"Bad" quarto published 1597; "good" quarto published 1599. Listed by Meres (*Palladis Tamia*, 1598) as by Shakespeare. Several astrological references in the play and an allusion to the great earthquake of 1584 as having occurred eleven years earlier seem to point to 1595 or 1596. Baldwin (*Five-Act Structure*) suggests a date of 1591, between *The Two Gentlemen of Verona* and *Lucrece*, partly on the evidence of another quake in 1580. SOURCES: (1) Brooke, *The Tragical History of Romeus and Juliet* (1562). (2) Daniel, *Complaint of Rosamond* (1592). (3) John Eliot, *Ortho-epia Gallica* (1593). (4) Nashe, *Have With You to Saffron Walden* (1596).
A Midsummer Night's Dream	1595–96	Entered on *S.R.* October 8, 1600; published 1600. Listed by Meres (*Palladis Tamia*, 1598) as by Shakespeare. The play suggests special composition for a wedding, and eleven different weddings have been suggested, ranging in date from 1590 to 1600 (despite the fact that Meres's listing rules out any date

TITLE	PROPOSED DATE	EVIDENCE FOR DATING; SOURCES
A Midsummer Night's Dream (cont.)		after September 7, 1598, for the play except in a revised form). An allusion to bad summer weather (II.i.81–117) has been connected with conditions in 1594, 1595, and 1596, the most recent opinion favoring 1596. The only wedding late enough in that year is the double wedding of the daughters of the Earl of Worcester, November 8, 1596. Much of that recent criticism favors the Sir Thomas Berkeley–Elizabeth Carey wedding of February, 1596. SOURCE: No source known for the main plot; for the Pyramus and Thisby story, Ovid, *Metamorphoses* (tr. Golding, 1567), Bk. IV. PROBABLE SOURCES: (1) Chaucer, "The Knight's Tale" and "The Miller's Tale." (2) Plutarch, *Lives* (tr. North, 1579 ed.). (3) *Huon of Bordeaux* (tr. Lord Berners, c. 1533–42). (4) Scot, *Discovery of Witchcraft* (1584). (5) Nashe, *Terrors of the Night* (1594). (6) Apuleius, *The Golden Ass* (tr. Adlington, 1566). POSSIBLE SOURCES: (1) Robinson, ed., *A Handful of Pleasant Delights* (1584; for Pyramus and Thisby). (2) Preston, *Cambises* (1561). (3) Seneca, *Oedipus* (tr. Neville, 1563), *Medea* (tr. Studley, 1566), *Hippolytus* (tr. Studley, 1567). (4) Spenser, *The Shepherd's Calendar* (1579). (5) Lyly, *Gallathea* (1585). (6) Erasmus, *The Praise of Folly* (in the original Latin or tr. Thomas Challoner, 1549).
The Merchant of Venice	1596–97	Entered on *S.R.* July 22, 1598; published 1600. Listed by Meres (*Palladis Tamia*, 1598) as by Shakespeare. Among various supposed allusions in the play, only one seems unambiguous evidence for dating. I.i.27–29 refers to a ship ("wealthy *Andrew*") and there is little doubt that Shakespeare is here glancing at a Spanish vessel called the *St. Andrew*, which was captured in the Cadiz expedition of 1596. News of the capture reached England by July 30, 1596. Late 1596, or early 1597, seems, therefore, a likely date of composition. SOURCES: Marlowe, *The Jew of Malta* (c. 1589; for some details only). (2) Nashe, *Have With You to Saffron Walden* (1596). (3) Alexander Silvayn, *The Orator* (tr. L. Piot, 1596). PROBABLE SOURCES: (1) Giovanni Fiorentino, *Il Pecorone* (1558), first story of fourth day (no contemporary tr. known). (2) Masuccio, *Il Novellino* (1476), fourteenth story (no contemporary tr. known). (3) *Gesta Romanorum* (tr. Richard Robinson, 1577, 1595), story 66. POSSIBLE SOURCES: (1) Munday, *Zelauto* (1580). (2) Anon., *The Jew* (c. 1569–79; not extant).
1 Henry IV	1596–97	Entered on *S.R.* February 25, 1598; published 1598. Meres (*Palladis Tamia*, 1598) refers to "Henry the 4." as by Shakespeare. SOURCES: (1) Holinshed, *Chronicles* (2nd ed., 1587). (2) Anon., *The Famous Victories of Henry V* (c. 1586). (3) Anon., *1 Richard II* (or *Thomas of Woodstock* c. 1592). PROBABLE SOURCES: (1) Stow, *Chronicles of England* (1580). (2) Daniel, *Civil Wars* (1595). POSSIBLE SOURCE: Baldwin, ed., *A Mirror for Magistrates* (1559).
The Merry Wives of Windsor	1597 (revised c. 1600–1)	Entered on *S.R.* January 18, 1602; "bad" quarto published 1602. Received text published in F1 (1623). Until relatively recently *Merry Wives* was regularly dated 1601–2, but Hotson's suggestion that the play was originally written specially for the Garter Feast held at Westminster April 23, 1597, is being more and more strongly supported (see, however, the view of Elizabeth Schafer that the Garter references need not be to the Westminster feast of April 1597, in *N & Q* ccxxxvi (1991), 57–60). On this theory, the play was revised for the public theatre about 1600–1, and it is the revised version that lies behind the "bad" quarto, while the F1 text represents in most essentials (except for the name Broome for Brooke) the earlier "court" performance. On this view, Shakespeare wrote *Merry Wives* shortly after he began work on *2 Henry IV.* Meres (*Palladis Tamia*) does not list *Merry Wives* among Shakespeare's plays as of September 7, 1598, but a special court production might not have been known to him. SOURCES: None definite. PROBABLE SOURCES: (1) Ovid, *Metamorphoses* (tr. Golding, 1567), Bk. III. (2) J. Rathgeb's *Journal* (1602; an account of the Mompelgard visit, details of which could have been known earlier to Shakespeare). (3) Nashe, several works, including *Lenten Stuffe* (1599). POSSIBLE SOURCES: (1) Tarlton, *News Out of Purgatory* (1590). (2) Rich, *His Farewell to Military Profession* (1581). (3) Lyly, *Endimion* (1588).
2 Henry IV	1598	Entered on *S.R.* August 23, 1600; published 1600. Some traces of the name Oldcastle (the original name of Falstaff, changed, it is supposed, because of offense to the Cobham family) remain in the speech-prefixes in the early part of *2 Henry IV*; this indicates that Shakespeare must have started composition of *2 Henry IV* before Part 1 (containing the alteration to Falstaff) was entered on *S.R.* (February 25, 1598). That Part 2 was not much more than begun at

TITLE	PROPOSED DATE	EVIDENCE FOR DATING; SOURCES
2 Henry IV (cont.)		this time is suggested by the omission of "First Part" on the title-page of the 1598 quarto. Meres's reference to "Henry the 4." (*Palladis Tamia;* see above under *1 Henry IV*) is ambiguous so far as Part 2 is concerned. SOURCES: (1) Holinshed, *Chronicles* (2nd ed., 1587). (2) Anon., *The Famous Victories of Henry V* (c. 1586). PROBABLE SOURCES: (1) Hall, *The Union of . . . Lancaster and York* (1548). (2) Daniel, *Civil Wars* (1595). (3) John Eliot, *Ortho-epia Gallica* (1593). (4) Timothy Bright, *Treatise of Melancholy* (1586). POSSIBLE SOURCES: (1) Elyot, *The Governor* (1531). (2) Stow, *Chronicles of England* (1580). (3) Nicholas Harpsfield, *The Life of Sir Thomas More* (c. 1557, existed only in manuscript in 16th. c.).
Much Ado about Nothing	1598–99	Marked "to be staied" on *S.R.* August 4, 1600; registered for publication on *S.R.* August 23, 1600; published 1600. Not included by Meres (*Palladis Tamia*) as of September 7, 1598. This omission by Meres may be significant, but it need not be so, since he fails to include *The Taming of the Shrew* (1593–94). PROBABLE SOURCES: (1) Ariosto, *Orlando Furioso* (tr. Harington, 1591), Bk. V. (2) Spenser, *The Faerie Queene*, Bk. II, Canto iv (1590) and Bk. VI, Canto vii (1596), the latter for Mirabella as an element in the character of Beatrice. (3) Bandello, *Novelle*, Novella 22 (1554; no contemporary English tr. known; French tr. in Belleforest's *Histoires Tragiques*, vol. III, 1568, story 18). (4) Apuleius, *The Golden Ass* (tr. Adlington, 1566). (5) Whetstone, *The Rocke of Regard* (1576). (6) Castiglione, *The Courtier* (tr. Hoby, 1561). POSSIBLE SOURCE: Munday (?), *Fedele and Fortunio* (c. 1584).
Henry V	1599	Published in F1 (1623). Marked "to be staied" on *S.R.* August 4, 1600. A "bad" quarto text (1600) had been published by Millington and Busby before August 14, when its transfer to Thomas Pavier was entered on *S.R.* Not included by Meres (*Palladis Tamia*) as of September 7, 1598. Imitation of certain scenes in *Henry V*, and verbal echoes from it, in *1 Sir John Oldcastle* give a definite *terminus ad quem* for Shakespeare's play, since the authors (Munday, Drayton, Wilson, and Hathaway) of *1 Oldcastle* were paid for the finished play on October 16, 1599, by Henslowe (*Diary*, fol. 65). An allusion, usually taken as referring to Essex's Irish campaign, in the Chorus to Act V has been used to date the play between March 27 and September 28, 1599. This view has been challenged by W. D. Smith, who argues that the allusion is rather to Lord Mountjoy, Elizabeth's successful commander in Ireland between early 1600 and Elizabeth's death in 1603. SOURCES: (1) Holinshed, *Chronicles* (2nd ed., 1587). (2) Tacitus, *Annals*, Bks. I, II (tr. Grenewey, 1598). (3) Anon., *The Famous Victories of Henry V* (c. 1586). (4) Nashe, *Lenten Stuffe*, 1598–9 (1599). POSSIBLE SOURCES: (1) Anon., *The Battle of Agincourt* (c. 1530). (2) Daniel, *Civil Wars* (1595).
Julius Caesar	1599	Published in F1 (1623). A performance, probably at the Globe, was witnessed by a German traveller, Thomas Platter, on September 21, 1599 (see Appendix C, Number 16). Not included by Meres (*Palladis Tamia*) as of September 7, 1598. Jonson appears to paraphrase III.ii.104–5 in *Every Man Out of His Humor* (1599), as does the anonymous author of *Wisdom of Doctor Dodipoll* (1600), p. 129 (ed. Bullen). SOURCES: (1) Plutarch, *Lives* (tr. North, 1579; the lives of Caesar, Brutus, Antony, and Cicero). (2) Nashe, *Summer's Last Will and Testament*, performed 1592 (1600), *The Terrors of the Night*, 1593 (1594), and *Lenten Stuffe*, 1598–9 (1599). (3) Daniel, *Musophilus* and *Letter from Octavia* (1599). (4) Davies, *Nosce Teipsum* (1599). (5) Baldwin, *A Mirror for Magistrates* (3rd ed., 1563). POSSIBLE SOURCES: (1) Tacitus, *Annals* (tr. Grenewey, 1598). (2) Appian, *Civil Wars* (tr. W. B., 1578). (3) Pescetti, *Il Cesare* (1594). (4) Anon., *Caesar and Pompey, or Caesar's Revenge* (c. 1595).
As You Like It	1599	Published in F1 (1623). Marked "to be staied" on *S.R.* August 4, 1600. Not included by Meres (*Palladis Tamia*) as of September 7, 1598. Setting of the song "It was a lover and his lass" (V.iii.16–33), probably original to this play, was published in Thomas Morley's *First Book of Airs* (1600). SOURCES: (1) Lodge, *Rosalynde* (1590). (2) Nashe, *Pierce Penniless* (1592). PROBABLE SOURCE: Anon., *Sir Clyomon and Sir Clamydes* (c. 1570).
Hamlet	1600–1	Entered on *S.R.* July 26, 1602; "bad" quarto published 1603; "good" quarto published 1604. A play on the Hamlet story existed at least as early as 1589, probably by Thomas Kyd (see Nashe's preface to Greene's *Menaphon*, 1589 [Appendix C, Number 17]). Topical references in the play to the players'

TITLE	PROPOSED DATE	EVIDENCE FOR DATING; SOURCES
Hamlet (cont.)		"inhibition," which has arisen out of the "late innovation" (II.ii.332–33), and to the "aery of children, little eyases" (II.ii.339), have been used in dating. Two interpretations have been advanced for the "inhibition-innovation" reference: (1) that it refers to the abortive Essex rebellion of February 8, 1601; (2) that it refers to the Privy Council decree of June 22, 1600, which limited the number of playhouses in London to two and performances to twice weekly. The "little eyases" passage, since it occurs only in the F1 text and clearly comments on the so-called War of the Theatres (after the middle of 1601), may be a later addition. The two incidental allusions to Julius Caesar link closely with *Julius Caesar* (1599) and suggest that the material was still fresh in Shakespeare's mind when he turned to *Hamlet*. Gabriel Harvey's well-known reference to Shakespeare's *Hamlet* (see Appendix C, Number 18), which is usually dated before the execution of Essex (February 25, 1601), is perhaps more safely dated as not later than July 21, 1603. SOURCES: (1) It is generally agreed that the principal source was the earlier Hamlet play (now lost) referred to above. (2) Bright, *A Treatise of Melancholy* (1586). (3) Lavater, *Of Ghosts and Spirits Walking by Night* (tr. R. H., 1572). (4) Scot, *Discovery of Witchcraft* (1584). (5) Nashe, *Pierce Penilesse* (1592) and several other pamphlets including *Lenten Stuffe* (1599). (6) Montaigne, *Essays* (tr. Florio, 1603; used in MS). (7) Apuleius, *The Golden Ass* (tr. Adlington, 1566). POSSIBLE SOURCES: (1) Belleforest, *Histoires Tragiques* (vol. V, story 3, 1570; in the original, which was the source for the *Ur-Hamlet* play, or in the anonymous tr. *The History of Hamblet*, in an edition antedating the earliest now known [1608]). (2) Gabriel Harvey, *Pierce's Supererogation* (1593). The presence of Harveian diction in the texture of *Hamlet* creates an historical irony; see, again, Appendix C, No. 18.
The Phoenix and Turtle	c. 1601	Published in Robert Chester's *Love's Martyr* (1601). It seems to have been written specifically for this volume. PROBABLE SOURCE: The Song of Songs.
Twelfth Night	1601–2	Published in F1 (1623). A performance at the Middle Temple, possibly the first, described by John Manningham in his *Diary* (see Appendix C, Number 19), took place February 2, 1602. The play is probably not earlier than 1600, since the snatches of songs in II.iii seem to derive from Robert Jones's *First Book of Songs and Airs,* published in that year. There is a possible allusion to Sir Toby Belch in Jonson's *Poetaster* (III.iv.345), acted in 1601. Not included by Meres (*Palladis Tamia*) as of September 7, 1598. SOURCE: Rich, *His Farewell to Military Profession* (1581). PROBABLE SOURCES: (1) *Gl'Inganniati* (1531; no contemporary tr. known). (2) Nashe, *Have With You to Saffron Walden* (1596). POSSIBLE SOURCES: (1) Forde, *The Famous History of Parismus* (1598). (2) Gabriel Harvey, *Ciceronianus* (1577, no contemporary tr. known; for fascination with capital letters and rhetoric linked to coiffure).
Troilus and Cressida	1601–2	Entered on *S.R.* February 7, 1603; published 1609. F1 text (1623) substantially different. The reference in the Prologue to the "prologue arm'd" is generally taken as pointing to Jonson's *Poetaster* (1601), in which an "armed Prologue" appears. The character of Ajax is by some thought to be Shakespeare's parting blow at Jonson in the War of the Theatres in answer to Jonson's attack on Shakespeare's company in *Poetaster.* What appears to be a reference to Gilbert's *De Magnete* (1600) in III.ii.179 and IV.ii.104–5 may be taken to support a date after that year. SOURCES: (1) Caxton, *The Ancient History of the Destruction of Troy* (tr. of Le Fèvre; 1596 ed.). (2) Homer, *Iliads* (tr. Chapman, 1598; only Bks. I–II, VII–XI and *Achilles' Shield*). (3) Lydgate, *The Ancient History and Only True Chronicle of the Wars* [*of Troy*] (tr. of Guido delle Colonne; 1555 ed.). PROBABLE SOURCES: (1) Chaucer, *Troilus and Criseyde.* (2) Ovid, *Metamorphoses* (tr. Golding, 1567), Bks. XII, XIII. POSSIBLE SOURCES: (1) Chettle and Dekker, *Troilus and Cressida* (1599; extant only in a fragmentary MS "plot"). (2) Greene, *Planetomachia* (1585). (3) Nashe, *Summer's Last Will and Testament* (1600).
A Lover's Complaint	1602–8	*A Lover's Complaint* follows the Sonnets in Thomas Thorpe's 1609 volume which was registered on 20 May. The convention of a sonnet sequence followed by a complaint poem was in vogue in the 1590's, but the verbal links to other works by Shakespeare are to those of the early 1600's, except for a number to *Cymbeline* (1609–10). It would appear that either Shakespeare re-

TITLE	PROPOSED DATE	EVIDENCE FOR DATING; SOURCES
A Lover's Complaint (cont.)		turned to a convention already passé or revised just before publication a work he had begun several years before. SOURCES: (1) Daniel, *The Complaint of Rosamond* (1592). (2) Spenser, *The Ruines of Time* (1591). POSSIBLE SOURCES: (1) Lodge, *The Tragicall Complaint of Elstred* (1593). (2) Henry Willobie, *Willobie His Avisa* (1594).
All's Well That Ends Well	1602–3	Published in F1 (1623). Some critics believe, on the basis of different styles, that Shakespeare first wrote this play, or parts of it, as early as 1594–95, and that the F1 text represents his reworking around 1602–3. The fact that the "bed trick" here used is found also in Shakespeare's source suggests that the play is at least earlier than *Measure for Measure*, where the "bed trick" is Shakespeare's addition to the plot he borrows. SOURCES: (1) Painter, *The Palace of Pleasure* (1566–67), Novel 38 (tr. of Boccaccio). (2) Erasmus, *A Modest Meane to Marriage*, tr. N.L. (1568). (3) Apuleius, *The Golden Ass* (Adlington tr., 1566).
Measure for Measure	1604	Published in F1 (1623). Performed at court December 26, 1604. The Duke referred to in connection with the King of Hungary's peace (I.ii.1–5) has been identified with the Duke of Holstein, Queen Anne's brother, in England in 1604 to raise men in the Protestant cause against Rudolph II of Hungary. SOURCE: Whetstone, *Promos and Cassandra* (1578; a play based on Giraldi Cinthio's *Hecatommithi* [1565], Decade 8, Novella 5, and Claude Rouillet's *Philanira* [1556]). PROBABLE SOURCES: (1) Cinthio, *Epitia* (1583; no contemporary tr. known). (2) Cinthio, *Hecatommithi* (1565; no contemporary tr. known, though Whetstone included a prose version in his *Heptameron of Civil Discourses* [1582], which Shakespeare may have known). POSSIBLE SOURCE: Silvayn, *The Orator* (tr. L. Piot, 1596).
Othello	1604	Published 1622; F1 text (1623) substantially different. Performed at court November 1, 1604. Some possibility of an earlier date is suggested by what appear to be verbal borrowings from *Othello* in the "bad" quarto of *Hamlet* (1603). Stanley Wells has pointed out that Knolles *History of the Turks*, a source for I.iii., has a preface dated "the last of September 1603." SOURCES: (1) Giraldi Cinthio, *Hecatommithi* (1565), Decade 3, Novella 7 (no contemporary English tr. known; Shakespeare does not appear to have used the French tr. by Chappuys [1584]). (2) Pliny, *The History of the World* (tr. Holland, 1601). (3) Contareni, *The Commonwealth and Government of Venice* (tr. Lewkenor, 1599). (4) Apuleius, *The Golden Ass* (both in the original and in Adlington's tr. 1566). (5) Richard Knolles, *History of the Turks* (1603). POSSIBLE SOURCE: Apuleius, *Apologia* (no known contemporary tr.).
King Lear	1605	Entered on *S.R.* November 26, 1607; published 1608 in a text in many ways resembling a "bad" quarto. Received text published in F1 (1623). Performed at court December 26, 1606. The popularity of Shakespeare's play probably led to the publication (entered on *S.R.* May 14, 1594, and again May 8, 1605) of the much earlier anonymous *Chronicle History of King Leir* (c. 1590) in 1605. Since Shakespeare's play uses material from Harsnett's *Declaration of Egregious Popish Impostures*, it cannot be earlier than 1603; and the imitation of *Lear* (I.iv) by Sharpham in *The Fleer*, entered on *S.R.* May 13, 1606, affords a terminal date. SOURCES: (1) Anon., *The Chronicle History of King Leir* (c. 1590). (2) Holinshed, *Chronicles* (2nd ed., 1587). (3) Sidney, *Arcadia* (1590). (4) Spenser, *The Faerie Queene*, Bk. II, Canto x and Bk. III, Cantos ix–x (1590). (5) *Mirror for Magistrates* (ed. Higgins, 1574, 1587). (6) Harsnett, *Declaration of Egregious Popish Impostures* (1603). (7) Montaigne, *Essays* (tr. Florio, 1603). (8) Nashe, several works including *Summer's Last Will and Testament* (1600) and *Have With You to Saffron Walden* (1596). (9) Plutarch, *Lives* (tr. North, 1579); the life of Agesilaus). POSSIBLE SOURCE: Marston, *The Malcontent* (1604).
Macbeth	1606	Published in F1 (1623). Contains probable allusions to the equivocation issue at the trial of the Gunpowder Plot conspirators (January-March 1606). There is some evidence that the play was first performed before James I on August 7, 1606, in honor of the visit of King Christian of Denmark. There is also, however, some evidence suggesting that Shakespeare may have written an earlier version of *Macbeth* c. 1598. Simon Forman has left a description of a performance seen by him April 20, 1611 (see Appendix C, Number 20).

TITLE	PROPOSED DATE	EVIDENCE FOR DATING; SOURCES
Macbeth (cont.)		SOURCES: (1) Holinshed, *Chronicles* (2nd ed., 1587). (2) Seneca, *Hercules Furens Medea*, and *Agamemnon* (the second two in Studley's tr., 1566, 1565). (3) Nashe, *Christ's Tears Over Jerusalem* (1593). PROBABLE SOURCES: (1) Buchanan, *Rerum Scoticarum Historia* (1582). (2) Apuleius, *The Golden Ass* (tr. Adlington, 1566). (3) John Leslie, *De Origine, Moribus, et Rebus Gestis Scotorum* (no contemporary tr. 1578).
Antony and Cleopatra	1606–7	Entered on *S.R.* May 20, 1608; published in F1 (1623). Some influence of Shakespeare's play has been found in Daniel's revision of his *Cleopatra*, published in 1607. SOURCES: (1) Plutarch, *Lives* (tr. North, 1579; the life of Antony). (2) Appian, *Civil Wars* (tr. W. B., 1578). PROBABLE SOURCES: (1) Plutarch, *Lives* (tr. North, 1603; Simon Goulart's life of Octavius Caesar). (2) Daniel, *The Tragedy of Cleopatra* (1599 ed.). and *Letter from Octavia* (1599). (3) Apuleius, *The Golden Ass* (tr. Adlington, 1566).
Coriolanus	1607–8	Published in F1 (1623). Apart from stylistic evidence, there is little to suggest a more exact date. The reference to "the coal of fire upon the ice" (I.i.173) has been taken as alluding to the great frost of 1607–8 (see Dekker (?), *The Great Frost*, 1608), when the Thames was frozen over and pans of coals were burned on it. An allusion to Hugh Middleton's project for bringing water into London (begun in February 1609 but discussed earlier) has been detected in III.i.95–97. SOURCES: (1) Plutarch, *Lives* (tr. North, 1579; life of Coriolanus, and for proper names several other of the lives, including that of Agesilaus). (2) Averell, *A Marvellous Combat of Contrarieties* (1588; this and the two following for Menenius' fable of the belly). (3) Sidney, *An Apology for Poetry* (1595). (4) Camden, *Remains . . . Concerning Britain* (1605). PROBABLE SOURCES: (1) Livy, *Roman History* (tr. Holland, 1600). (2) Thomas and Dudley Digges, *Four Paradoxes, or Politique Discourses* (1604). (3) Jean Bodin, *Six Books of a Commonweal* (tr. Richard Knolles, 1606). (4) Edward Forset, *A Comparative Discourse of the Bodies Natural and Politique* (1606).
Timon of Athens	1607–8	Published in F1 (1623). The play was probably left unfinished by Shakespeare and never acted. Stylistic evidence places it somewhere between 1605 and 1608; some recent critics who argue for Middleton as either collaborator or reviser see the play as composed 1604–6. SOURCE: Plutarch, *Lives* (tr. North, 1579; lives of Alcibiades and Antony). POSSIBLE SOURCES: (1) Lucian, *Timon, or the Misanthrope* (no contemporary English tr. known; Latin tr. by Erasmus, 1506; Italian by Lonigo, 1536; French by Bretin, 1583). (2) Lyly, *Campaspe* (c. 1584). (3) Anon., *Timon* (c. 1602; possible relationship to Shakespeare's play much debated). (4) Jakob Gretser, *Timon: Comoedia Imitata* (no contemporary English tr., 1584).
Pericles	1607–8	Entered on *S.R.* May 20, 1608; published, in a "bad" quarto text, 1609. The play was not included among Shakespeare's collected works until the second issue of F3 (1664). A performance was seen at court by the Venetian and French ambassadors between May 1606 and November 1608. George Wilkins' little novel, *The Painful Adventures of Pericles Prince of Tyre*, based in part on this play, was published in 1608. The problem of authorship is discussed in the introduction to the play. SOURCES: (1) Gower, *Confessio Amantis* (1554 ed.). (2) Twine, *The Pattern of Painful Adventures* (1594 and 1607). POSSIBLE SOURCES: (1) Sidney, *Arcadia* (1590). (2) Silvayn, *The Orator* (tr. L. Piot, 1596).
Cymbeline	1609–10	Published in F1 (1623). Simon Forman saw a performance probably between April 20 and 30, 1611 (see Appendix C, Number 20). Metrical and stylistic evidence links *Cymbeline* with *The Winter's Tale* and *The Tempest.* SOURCES: (1) Holinshed, *Chronicles* (2nd ed., 1587). (2) *Mirror for Magistrates* (ed. Blenerhasset, 1578, and Higgins, 1587). (3) Anon., *Frederyke of Jennen* (1560 ed.; based on Boccaccio's *Decameron*). (4) Anon., *The Rare Triumphs of Love and Fortune* (1582). (5) Apuleius, *The Golden Ass* (tr. Adlington, 1566). PROBABLE SOURCE: Boccaccio, *Decameron,* Day 2, Tale 9 (no contemporary English tr. known; two in French, the one by Maçon [1545] frequently reprinted). POSSIBLE SOURCE: Anon., *Sir Clyomon and Clamydes* (c. 1570).
The Winter's Tale	1610–11	Published in F1 (1623). Simon Forman saw a performance on May 15, 1611 (see Appendix C, Number 20), and a court performance took place November 5, 1611. In IV.iv.783–91 the reference to a source probably used for *Cym-*

TITLE	PROPOSED DATE	EVIDENCE FOR DATING; SOURCES
The Winter's Tale (cont.)		*beline* (Boccaccio's *Decameron*, Day 2, Tale 9) would seem to indicate that *The Winter's Tale* is the later play. SOURCES: (1) Greene, *Pandosto, the Triumph of Time* (1588). (2) Sabie, *The Fisherman's Tale* (1594) and *Flora's Fortune* (1595). PROBABLE SOURCE: Greene, *The Second Part of Cony-Catching* (1591; for Autolycus' first trick on the Clown). POSSIBLE SOURCE: Forde, *The Famous History of Parismus* (1598).
The Tempest	1611	Published in F1 (1623). Performed at court November 1, 1611 and for the Lady Elizabeth's wedding festivities in 1612/13. The play makes use of sources not available before September 1610. SOURCES: None known for the main plot, but Shakespeare used: (1) Strachey, *True Repertory of the Wrack and Redemption of Sir Thomas Gates* (dated July 15, 1610, but not published until 1625 in *Purchas His Pilgrims*). (2) Jourdain, *A Discovery of the Bermudas* (1610). (3) [Virginia Council], *True Declaration of the Estate of the Colony in Virginia* (1610). (4) Montaigne, *Essays* (tr. Florio, 1603). (5) Ovid, *Metamorphoses*, Bk. VII (both in the original and in Golding's tr., 1567).
A Funeral Elegy by W.S.	1612	Entered in *S.R.* 13 February, 1612 by Thomas Thorpe, the publisher of *Shakespeare's Sonnets* (1609), as a book to be printed as "A funerall Elegye in memory of the late virtuous master William Peter of Whipton neare Exetour." William Peter, an Oxford-educated Devonshire gentleman, had been murdered less than three weeks earlier on 25 January. The question of whether the "W.S." on the title page is or is not William Shakespeare has inspired considerable recent controversy. The debate is fairly discussed in the Introduction to the poem. SOURCES: Samuel Daniel, *A Funeral Poem upon the Death of the late noble Earl of Devonshire* (1606). PROBABLE SOURCE: Daniel, *The Complaint of Rosamond* (1592). POSSIBLE SOURCE: Shakespeare, several plays and poems, especially *Richard II* (1595–6).
Henry VIII	1612–13	Published in F1 (1623). The Globe Theatre burned down during a performance of the play, probably the first, on June 29, 1613. An account of the play and the fire is contained in a letter (July 2, 1613) from Sir Henry Wotton to Sir Edmund Bacon (see Appendix C, Number 21A) . The question of Shakespeare's collaboration with John Fletcher in *Henry VIII* is discussed in the Introduction to the play. SOURCES: (1) Holinshed, *Chronicles* (2nd ed., 1587). (2) Foxe, *Acts and Monuments* (1570 ed.). (3) John Speed, *History of Great Britaine* (1611). PROBABLE SOURCES: (1) Samuel Rowley, *When You See Me, You Know Me* (1604). (2) Hall, *The Union of . . . Lancaster and York* (1548).
Cardenio (a lost play)	1612–13	A play called "Cardenno" or "Cardenna" was twice acted at court 1612–13 by the King's Men. It was attributed to Fletcher and Shakespeare in Humphrey Moseley's *S.R.* entry September 9, 1653. The play itself has been lost, but it is likely that Lewis Theobald's *Double Falsehood, or The Distress'd Lovers* (1728) represents a drastic reworking of the original *Cardenio.* SOURCE: Cervantes, *Don Quixote* (tr. Shelton, 1612), the story of Cardenio and Lucinda.
The Two Noble Kinsmen	1613	Entered on *S.R.* April 8, 1634; published 1634. Both the entry and the title-page describe the play as by Fletcher and Shakespeare; the question of their collaboration is discussed in the Introduction to the play. A date not earlier than 20 February 1613 is indicated for at least part of the play by the borrowing of the morris-dance in III.v from Beaumont's *Inner Temple and Gray's Inn Mask*, produced February 20 of that year. Probably referred to in *Bartholomew Fair* (1614), IV.ii. SOURCES: (1) Chaucer, "The Knight's Tale." (2) Beaumont, *Inner Temple and Gray's Inn Mask* (1613).

The opening pages of the Shakespeare First Folio (1623) are reproduced below, by kind permission of the Harvard College Library, from the copy in the Harry Elkins Widener Collection. The pages are here reduced by slightly more than one fourth; the dimensions of the original are approximately 13 by 8⅜ inches.

To the Reader.

This Figure, that thou here seest put,
It was for gentle Shakespeare cut;
Wherein the Grauer had a strife
with Nature, to out-doo the life :
O, could he but haue drawne his wit
As well in brasse, as he hath hit
His face ; the Print would then surpasse
All, that was euer writ in brasse.
But, since he cannot, Reader, looke
Not on his Picture, but his Booke.

B. I.

Mr. WILLIAM
SHAKESPEARES
COMEDIES,
HISTORIES, &
TRAGEDIES.

Publiſhed according to the True Originall Copies.

LONDON
Printed by Iſaac Iaggard, and Ed. Blount. 1623.

TO THE MOST NOBLE AND INCOMPARABLE PAIRE OF BRETHREN.

WILLIAM
Earle of Pembroke, &c. Lord Chamberlaine to the *Kings most Excellent Maiesty.*

AND

PHILIP
Earle of Montgomery, &c. Gentleman of his Maiesties Bed-Chamber. Both Knights of the most Noble Order of the Garter, and our singular good
LORDS.

Right Honourable,

WHilst we studie to be thankful in our particular, for the many fauors we haue receiued from your L.L. we are falne vpon the ill fortune, to mingle two the most diuerse things that can bee, feare, and rashnesse; rashnesse in the enterprize, and feare of the successe. For, when we valew the places your H.H. sustaine, we cannot but know their dignity greater, then to descend to the reading of these trifles: and, while we name them trifles, we haue depriu'd our selues of the defence of our Dedication. But since your L.L. haue beene pleas'd to thinke these trifles some-thing, heeretofore; and haue prosequuted both them, and their Authour liuing, with so much fauour: we hope, that (they out-liuing him, and he not hauing the fate, common with some, to be exequutor to his owne writings) you will vse the like indulgence toward them, you haue done

A 2 vnto

vnto their parent. There is a great difference, vvhether any Booke choose his Patrones, or finde them: This hath done both. For, so much were your L. L. likings of the seuerall parts, vvhen they were acted, as before they vvere published, the Volume ask'd to be yours. We haue but collected them, and done an office to the dead, to procure his Orphanes, Guardians; vvithout ambition either of selfe-profit, or fame: onely to keepe the memory of so worthy a Friend, & Fellow aliue, as was our Shakespeare, *by humble offer of his playes, to your most noble patronage. Wherein, as we haue iustly obserued, no man to come neere your L.L. but vvith a kind of religious addresse; it hath bin the height of our care, vvho are the Presenters, to make the present worthy of your H.H. by the perfection. But, there we must also craue our abilities to be considerd, my Lords. We cannot go beyond our owne powers. Country hands reach foorth milke, creame, fruites, or what they haue: and many Nations (we haue heard) that had not gummes & incense, obtained their requests with a leauened Cake. It vvas no fault to approch their Gods, by what meanes they could: And the most, though meanest, of things are made more precious, when they are dedicated to Temples. In that name therefore, we most humbly consecrate to your H.H. these remaines of your seruant* Shakespeare; *that what delight is in them, may be euer your L.L. the reputation his, & the faults ours, if any be committed, by a payre so carefull to shew their gratitude both to the liuing, and the dead, as is*

Your Lordshippes most bounden,

John Heminge.
Henry Condell.

To the great Variety of Readers.

FRom the most able, to him that can but spell: There you are number'd. We had rather you were weighd. Especially, when the fate of all Bookes depends vpon your capacities : and not of your heads alone, but of your purses. Well ! It is now publique, & you wil stand for your priuiledges wee know : to read, and censure. Do so, but buy it first. That doth best commend a Booke, the Stationer saies. Then, how odde soeuer your braines be, or your wisedomes, make your licence the same, and spare not. Iudge your sixe-pen'orth, your shillings worth, your fiue shillings worth at a time, or higher, so you rise to the iust rates, and welcome. But, what euer you do, Buy. Censure will not driue a Trade, or make the Iacke go. And though you be a Magistrate of wit, and sit on the Stage at *Black-Friers*, or the *Cock-pit*, to arraigne Playes dailie, know, these Playes haue had their triall alreadie, and stood out all Appeales ; and do now come forth quitted rather by a Decree of Court, then any purchas'd Letters of commendation.

It had bene a thing, we confesse, worthie to haue bene wished, that the Author himselfe had liu'd to haue set forth, and ouerseen his owne writings ; But since it hath bin ordain'd otherwise, and he by death departed from that right, we pray you do not envie his Friends, the office of their care, and paine, to haue collected & publish'd them ; and so to haue publish'd them, as where (before) you were abus'd with diuerse stolne, and surreptitious copies, maimed, and deformed by the frauds and stealthes of iniurious impostors, that expos'd them : euen those, are now offer'd to your view cur'd, and perfect of their limbes ; and all the rest, absolute in their numbers, as he conceiued thē. Who, as he was a happie imitator of Nature, was a most gentle expresser of it. His mind and hand went together : And what he thought, he vttered with that easinesse, that wee haue scarse receiued from him a blot in his papers. But it is not our prouince, who onely gather his works, and giue them you, to praise him. It is yours that reade him. And there we hope, to your diuers capacities, you will finde enough, both to draw, and hold you : for his wit can no more lie hid, then it could be lost. Reade him, therefore ; and againe, and againe : And if then you doe not like him, surely you are in some manifest danger, not to vnderstand him. And so we leaue you to other of his Friends, whom if you need, can bee your guides : if you neede them not, you can leade your selues, and others. And such Readers we wish him.

A 3

Iohn Heminge.
Henrie Condell.

To the memory of my beloued, The AVTHOR Mr. William Shakespeare: And what he hath left vs.

To draw no enuy (Shakespeare) on thy name,
Am I thus ample to thy Booke, and Fame:
While I confesse thy writings to be such,
As neither Man, nor Muse, can praise too much.
'Tis true, and all mens suffrage. But these wayes
Were not the paths I meant vnto thy praise:
For seeliest Ignorance on these may light,
Which, when it sounds at best, but eccho's right;
Or blinde Affection, which doth ne're aduance
The truth, but gropes, and vrgeth all by chance;
Or crafty Malice, might pretend this praise,
And thinke to ruine, where it seem'd to raise.
These are, as some infamous Baud, or Whore,
Should praise a Matron. What could hurt her more?
But thou art proofe against them, and indeed
Aboue th'ill fortune of them, or the need.
I, therefore will begin. Soule of the Age!
The applause! delight! the wonder of our Stage!
My Shakespeare, rise; I will not lodge thee by
Chaucer, or Spenser, or bid Beaumont lye
A little further, to make thee a roome:
Thou art a Moniment, without a tombe,
And art aliue still, while thy Booke doth liue,
And we haue wits to read, and praise to giue.
That I not mixe thee so, my braine excuses;
I meane with great, but disproportion'd Muses:
For, if I thought my iudgement were of yeeres,
I should commit thee surely with thy peeres,
And tell, how farre thou didst our Lily out-shine,
Or sporting Kid, or Marlowes mighty line.
And though thou hadst small Latine, and lesse Greeke,
From thence to honour thee, I would not seeke
For names; but call forth thund'ring Æschilus,
Euripides, and Sophocles to vs,
Paccuuius, Accius, him of Cordoua dead,
To life againe, to heare thy Buskin tread,
And shake a Stage: Or, when thy Sockes were on,
Leaue thee alone, for the comparison

9 A

Of all, that insolent Greece, *or haughtie* Rome
sent forth, or since did from their ashes come.
Triumph, my Britaine, *thou hast one to showe,*
To whom all Scenes of Europe *homage owe.*
He was not of an age, but for all time!
And all the Muses *still were in their prime,*
when like Apollo *he came forth to warme*
Our eares, or like a Mercury *to charme!*
Nature her selfe was proud of his designes,
And ioy'd to weare the dressing of his lines!
Which were so richly spun, and wouen so fit,
As, since, she will vouchsafe no other Wit.
The merry Greeke, *tart* Aristophanes,
Neat Terence, *witty* Plautus, *now not please;*
But antiquated, and deserted lye
As they were not of Natures family.
Yet must I not giue Nature all: Thy Art,
My gentle Shakespeare, *must enioy a part.*
For though the Poets *matter, Nature be,*
His Art doth giue the fashion. And, that he,
Who casts to write a liuing line, must sweat,
(such as thine are) and strike the second heat
Vpon the Muses *anuile: turne the same,*
(And himselfe with it) that he thinkes to frame;
Or for the lawrell, he may gaine a scorne,
For a good Poet's *made, as well as borne.*
And such wert thou. Looke how the fathers face
Liues in his issue, euen so, the race
Of Shakespeares *minde, and manners brightly shines*
In his well torned, and true-filed lines:
In each of which, he seemes to shake a Lance,
As brandish't at the eyes of Ignorance.
Sweet Swan of Auon! *what a sight it were*
To see thee in our waters yet appeare,
And make those flights vpon the bankes of Thames,
That so did take Eliza, *and our* Iames!
But stay, I see thee in the Hemisphere
Aduanc'd, and made a Constellation there!
Shine forth, thou Starre of Poets, *and with rage,*
Or influence, chide, or cheere the drooping Stage;
Which, since thy flight frō hence, hath mourn'd like night,
And despaires day, but for thy Volumes light.

BEN: IONSON.

Vpon the Lines and Life of the Famous Scenicke Poet, Maſter WILLIAM SHAKESPEARE.

Hoſe hands, which you ſo clapt, go now, and wring
You *Britaines* braue; for done are *Shakeſpeares* dayes:
His dayes are done, that made the dainty Playes,
Which made the Globe of heau'n and earth to ring.
Dry'de is that veine, dry'd is the *Theſpian* Spring,
Turn'd all to teares, and *Phœbus* clouds his rayes:
That corp's, that coffin now beſticke thoſe bayes,
Which crown'd him *Poet* firſt, then *Poets* King.
If *Tragedies* might any *Prologue* haue,
All thoſe he made, would ſcarſe make one to this:
Where *Fame*, now that he gone is to the graue
(Deaths publique tyring-houſe) the *Nuncius* is.
For though his line of life went ſoone about,
The life yet of his lines ſhall neuer out.

HVGH HOLLAND.

A CATALOGVE
of the feuerall Comedies, Hiftories, and Tragedies contained in this Volume.

COMEDIES.

HISTORIES.

TRAGEDIES.

TO THE MEMORIE

of the deceased Authour Maister W. SHAKESPEARE.

SHake-speare, *at length thy pious fellowes giue*
The world thy Workes: thy Workes, by which, out-liue
Thy Tombe, thy name must · when that stone is rent,
And Time dissolues thy Stratford *Moniment,*
Here we aliue shall view thee still. This Booke,
When Brasse and Marble fade, shall make thee looke
Fresh to all Ages: when Posteritie
Shall loath what's new, thinke all is prodegie
That is not Shake-speares*; eu'ry Line, each Verse*
Here shall reuiue, redeeme thee from thy Herse.
Nor Fire, nor cankring Age, as Naso *said,*
Of his, thy wit-fraught Booke shall once inuade.
Nor shall I e're beleeue, or thinke thee dead
(Though mist) vntill our bankrout Stage be sped
(Impossible) with some new straine t'out-do
Passions of Iuliet, *and her* Romeo*;*
Or till I heare a Scene more nobly take,
Then when thy half-Sword parlying Romans *spake.*
Till these, till any of thy Volumes rest
Shall with more fire, more feeling be exprest,
Be sure, our Shake-speare, *thou canst neuer dye,*
But crown'd with Lawrell, liue eternally.

L. Digges.

To the memorie of M. *W. Shake-speare.*

VVEE *wondred* (Shake-speare) *that thou went'st so soone*
From the Worlds-Stage, to the Graues-Tyring-roome.
Wee thought thee dead, but this thy printed worth,
Tels thy Spectators, that thou went'st but forth
To enter with applause. An Actors Art,
Can dye, and liue, to acte a second part.
That's but an Exit *of Mortalitie;*
This, a Re-entrance to a Plaudite.

I. M.

The Workes of William Shakespeare,

containing all his Comedies, Histories, and Tragedies: Truely set forth, according to their first ORJGJNALL.

The Names of the Principall Actors in all these Playes.

William Shakespeare.
Richard Burbadge.
John Hemmings.
Augustine Phillips.
William Kempt.
Thomas Poope.
George Bryan.
Henry Condell.
William Slye.
Richard Cowly.
John Lowine.
Samuell Crosse.
Alexander Cooke.
Samuel Gilburne.
Robert Armin.
William Ostler.
Nathan Field.
John Underwood.
Nicholas Tooley.
William Ecclestone.
Joseph Taylor.
Robert Benfield.
Robert Goughe.
Richard Robinson.
Iohn Shancke.
Iohn Rice.

THE TEMPEST.

Actus primus, Scena prima.

A tempestuous noise of Thunder and Lightning heard: Enter a Ship-master, and a Boteswaine.

Master.

Bote-swaine.

Botes. Heere Master: What cheere?

Mast. Good: Speake to th'Mariners: fall too't, yarely, or we run our selues a ground, bestirre, bestirre. *Exit.*

Enter Mariners.

Botes. Heigh my hearts, cheerely, cheerely my harts: yare, yare: Take in the toppe-sale: Tend to th'Masters whistle: Blow till thou burst thy winde, if roome enough.

Enter Alonso, Sebastian, Anthonio, Ferdinando, Gonzalo, and others.

Alon. Good Boteswaine haue care: where's the Master? Play the men.

Botes. I pray now keepe below.

Anth. Where is the Master, Boson?

Botes. Do you not heare him? you marre our labour, Keepe your Cabines: you do assist the storme.

Gonz. Nay, good be patient.

Botes. When the Sea is: hence, what cares these roarers for the name of King? to Cabine; silence: trouble vs not.

Gon. Good, yet remember whom thou hast aboord.

Botes. None that I more loue then my selfe. You are a Counsellor, if you can command these Elements to silence, and worke the peace of the present, wee will not hand a rope more, vse your authoritie: If you cannot, giue thankes you haue liu'd so long, and make your selfe readie in your Cabine for the mischance of the houre, if it so hap. Cheerely good hearts: out of our way I say. *Exit.*

Gon. I haue great comfort from this fellow: methinks he hath no drowning marke vpon him, his complexion is perfect Gallowes: stand fast good Fate to his hanging, make the rope of his destiny our cable, for our owne doth little aduantage: If he be not borne to bee hang'd, our case is miserable. *Exit.*

Enter Boteswaine.

Botes. Downe with the top-Mast: yare, lower, lower, bring her to Try with Maine-course. A plague——

A cry within. Enter Sebastian, Anthonio & Gonzalo.

vpon this howling: they are lowder then the weather, or our office: yet againe? What do you heere? Shal we giue ore and drowne, haue you a minde to sinke?

Sebas. A poxe o'your throat, you bawling, blasphemous incharitable Dog.

Botes. Worke you then.

Anth. Hang cur, hang, you whoreson insolent Noysemaker, we are lesse afraid to be drownde, then thou art.

Gonz. I'le warrant him for drowning, though the Ship were no stronger then a Nutt-shell, and as leaky as an vnstanched wench.

Botes. Lay her a hold, a hold, set her two courses off to Sea againe, lay her off.

Enter Mariners wet.

Mari. All lost, to prayers, to prayers, all lost.

Botes. What must our mouths be cold?

Gonz. The King, and Prince, at prayers, let's assist them, for our case is as theirs.

Sebas. I'am out of patience.

An. We are meerly cheated of our liues by drunkards, This wide-chopt-rascall, would thou mightst lye drowning the washing of ten Tides.

Gonz. Hee'l be hang'd yet,
Though euery drop of water sweare against it,
And gape at widst to glut him. *A confused noyse within.*
Mercy on vs.
We split, we split, Farewell my wife, and children,
Farewell brother: we split, we split, we split.

Anth. Let's all sinke with' King

Seb. Let's take leaue of him. *Exit.*

Gonz. Now would I giue a thousand furlongs of Sea, for an Acre of barren ground: Long heath, Browne firrs, any thing; the wills aboue be done, but I would faine dye a dry death. *Exit.*

Scena Secunda.

Enter Prospero and Miranda.

Mira. If by your Art (my deerest father) you haue
Put the wild waters in this Rore; alay them:
The skye it seemes would powre down stinking pitch,
But that the Sea, mounting to th' welkins cheeke,
Dashes the fire out. Oh! I haue suffered
With those that I saw suffer: A braue vessell

A (Who

(Who had no doubt some noble creature in her)
Dash'd all to peeces : O the cry did knocke
Against my very heart : poore soules, they perish'd.
Had I byn any God of power, I would
Haue suncke the Sea within the Earth, or ere
It should the good Ship so haue swallow'd, and
The fraughting Soules within her.
Pros. Be collected,
No more amazement : Tell your pitteous heart
there's no harme done.
Mira. O woe, the day.
Pros. No harme :
I haue done nothing, but in care of thee
(Of thee my deere one ; thee my daughter) who
Art ignorant of what thou art. naught knowing
Of whence I am : nor that I am more better
Then *Prospero*, Master of a full poore cell,
And thy no greater Father.
Mira. More to know
Did neuer medle with my thoughts.
Pros. 'Tis time
I should informe thee farther : Lend thy hand
And plucke my Magick garment from me : So,
Lye there my Art: wipe thou thine eyes, haue comfort,
The direfull spectacle of the wracke which touch'd
The very vertue of compassion in thee :
I haue with such prouision in mine Art
So safely ordered, that there is no soule
No not so much perdition as an hayre
Betid to any creature in the vessell
Which thou heardst cry, which thou saw'st sinke : Sit
For thou must now know farther. [downe,
Mira. You haue often
Begun to tell me what I am, but stopt
And left me to a bootelesse Inquisition,
Concluding, stay : not yet.
Pros. The howr's now come
The very minute byds thee ope thine eare,
Obey, and be attentiue. Canst thou remember
A time before we came vnto this Cell ?
I doe not thinke thou canst, for then thou was't not
Out three yeeres old.
Mira. Certainely Sir, I can.
Pros. By what ? by any other house, or person ?
Of any thing the Image, tell me, that
Hath kept with thy remembrance.
Mira. 'Tis farre off :
And rather like a dreame, then an assurance
That my remembrance warrants : Had I not
Fowre, or fiue women once, that tended me ?
Pros. Thou hadst ; and more *Miranda* : But how is it
That this liues in thy minde ? What seest thou els
In the dark-backward and Abisme of Time ?
Yf thou remembrest ought ere thou cam'st here,
How thou cam'st here thou maist.
Mira. But that I doe not.
Pros. Twelue yere since (*Miranda*) twelue yere since,
Thy father was the Duke of *Millaine* and
A Prince of power :
Mira. Sir, are not you my Father ?
Pros. Thy Mother was a peece of vertue, and
She said thou wast my daughter ; and thy father
Was Duke of *Millaine*, and his onely heire,
And Princesse ; no worse Issued.
Mira. O the heauens,
What fowle play had we, that we came from thence ?
Or blessed was't we did ?
Pros. Both, both my Girle.
By fowle-play (as thou saist) were we heau'd thence,
But blessedly holpe hither.
Mira. O my heart bleedes
To thinke oth' teene that I haue turn'd you to,
Which is from my remembrance, please you, farther ;
Pros. My brother and thy vncle, call'd *Anthonio* :
I pray thee marke me, that a brother should
Be so perfidious : he, whom next thy selfe
Of all the world I lou'd, and to him put
The mannage of my state, as at that time
Through all the signories it was the first,
And *Prospero*, the prime Duke, being so reputed
In dignity ; and for the liberall Artes,
Without a paralell ; those being all my studie,
The Gouernment I cast vpon my brother,
And to my State grew stranger, being transported
And rapt in secret studies, thy false vncle
(Do'st thou attend me ?)
Mira. Sir, most heedefully.
Pros. Being once perfected how to graunt suites,
how to deny them : who t'aduance, and who
To trash for ouer-topping ; new created
The creatures that were mine, I say, or chang'd 'em,
Or els new form'd 'em ; hauing both the key,
Of Officer, and office, set all hearts i'th state
To what tune pleas'd his eare, that now he was
The Iuy which had hid my princely Trunck,
And suckt my verdure out on't : Thou attend'st not ?
Mira. O good Sir, I doe.
Pros. I pray thee marke me :
I thus neglecting worldly ends, all dedicated
To closenes, and the bettering of my mind
with that, which but by being so retir'd
Ore-priz'd all popular rate : in my false brother
Awak'd an euill nature, and my trust
Like a good parent, did beget of him
A falsehood in it's contrarie, as great
As my trust was, which had indeede no limit,
A confidence sans bound. He being thus Lorded,
Not onely with what my reuenew yeelded,
But what my power might els exact. Like one
Who hauing into truth, by telling of it,
Made such a synner of his memorie
To credite his owne lie, he did beleeue
He was indeed the Duke, out o'th' Substitution
And executing th'outward face of Roialtie
With all prerogatiue : hence his Ambition growing :
Do'st thou heare ?
Mira. Your tale, Sir, would cure deafenesse.
Pros. To haue no Schreene between this part he plaid,
And him he plaid it for, he needes will be
Absolute *Millaine*, Me (poore man) my Librarie
Was Dukedome large enough : of temporall roalties
He thinks me now incapable. Confederates
(so drie he was for Sway) with King of *Naples*
To giue him Annuall tribute, doe him homage
Subiect his Coronet, to his Crowne and bend
The Dukedom yet vnbow'd (alas poore *Millaine*)
To most ignoble stooping.
Mira. Oh the heauens :
Pros. Marke his condition, and th'euent, then tell me
If this might be a brorher.
Mira. I should sinne
To thinke but Noblie of my Grand-mother,
Good

THE PLAYS

Comedies

Histories

Tragedies

Romances

The Reign of King Edward the Third

Now Widely Attributed to Shakespeare

Sir Thomas More

The Additions Ascribed to Shakespeare

The Comedy of Errors

Although *The Comedy of Errors* is the only play by Shakespeare which includes the word *comedy* in its title, critics have persistently wanted to dismiss it as a farce, unworthy of serious consideration, however great its success as a theatrical frolic. Coleridge claimed that the play was a virtual paradigm of the lesser genre: "in exactest consonance with the philosophical principles and character of farce, as distinguished from comedy and from entertainments." It would be hard to deny that *The Comedy of Errors* has some of the characteristics of farce. As Coleridge observed, the device of the identical Antipholuses which Shakespeare took from the *Menaechmi* of Plautus strains the verisimilitude usually thought appropriate to comedy. Shakespeare's insistence upon compounding this basic absurdity by inventing identical servants to wait upon the single pair of twins provided in his Latin source pushes the story still further in the direction of that cloud-cuckoo-land of farce where, by special agreement between dramatist and audience, even the wildest and most coincidental plot structures become acceptable.

Twelfth Night, a play no one has ever wished to categorize as farce, also turns in part upon the confusions generated by twins identical in appearance. Viola and Sebastian, however, are both strangers in Illyria. They are mistaken for one another, pardonably, by new acquaintances; not, as in *The Comedy of Errors*, by those who know them well. Moreover, Viola recognizes at once what has happened: "Prove true, imagination, O, prove true, / That I, dear brother, be now ta'en for you!" (III.iv.375–76). Antipholus of Syracuse, by contrast, is journeying through the world in search of his lost twin. The extraordinary things that begin to happen to him as soon as he sets foot in Ephesus constitute a virtual proclamation that his seven-year quest is over, his missing brother found. Yet for almost five acts the Syracusan Antipholus fails to reach this glaringly obvious conclusion, preferring to invoke sorcery or hallucination to explain his situation. He is not meant to seem obtuse. His reactions are simply governed here, although not in other respects, by the rules of farce rather than comedy. Similarly, Shakespeare asks his audience to accept without question the fact that the Sicilian Antipholus and Dromio each manage to disembark at Ephesus in Asia Minor wearing clothes indistinguishable from those that the native Antipholus and Dromio happen to have put on that morning. In *Twelfth Night*, Viola goes out of her way to explain that her boy's disguise is a deliberate copy in its "fashion, color, ornament" of the garb habitually worn by her lost brother. No rationalization of this kind is even attempted in *The Comedy of Errors*. Again, the latitude of farce must be invoked, even as it must when considering that hail of blows and beatings which falls upon the perplexed and innocent Dromios without, as it seems, causing them any real physical or psychological harm.

Yet despite its emphasis on plot and situational absurdity, despite the merry violence in many of the scenes, it is not really possible to contain *The Comedy of Errors* within the bounds of farce as defined by the *Oxford English Dictionary*: "a dramatic work (usually short) which has as its sole object to excite laughter." A comparison here with Shakespeare's principal source is illuminating. Although William Warner's translation of Plautus' *Menaechmi* did not appear until 1595, Shakespeare had almost certainly read the play in Latin before that date. Probably the "comedy of errors (like to Plautus his Menaechmus)" referred to as part of the disordered Christmas revels at Gray's Inn on December 28, 1594,[1] was Shakespeare's. It may well have been written, and given its initial performance, two or three years before. By Shakespearean standards, *The Comedy of Errors* is a short play, indeed the shortest in the canon, but the *Menaechmi* is very considerably shorter still. Plautus' play is also far less complex, concentrating almost entirely upon plot mistakings. Its characters are simple and rigidly type-cast. Peniculus, a parasite, is virtually summed up by his anxiety over his next free meal; Erotium, a courtesan, by the cupidity associated with her trade; while Menaechmus' wife, who is not even honored with a name of her own, is insufferably shrewish because, according to the conventions of Plautine drama, wives always are. At the end, it seems quite natural that her exasperated husband should propose to auction her off to anyone foolish enough to bid for so tiresome a commodity. Unlike Shakespeare's Adriana, she has no feelings to be considered.

Even Plautus' two brothers Menaechmus are differentiated almost entirely in terms of the situation into which each is flung. For the stranger Menaechmus Epidamnum proves to be a kind of land of the heart's desire, a place where courtesans press their favors on him gratis, banquets spread themselves for free, and total strangers press valuable gifts into his hands and decline payment. Puzzled but delighted, he welcomes this unexpected largesse of fortune. Meanwhile his twin brother is undergoing precisely the opposite experience in a familiar world of business and domestic cares which seems all at once to have run mad. Unlike Shakespeare, who was to concentrate attention on the problems of the Syracusan Antipholus, Plautus spends more time on the uncomfortable experience of the native twin than he does on the golden dream briefly enjoyed by the traveller. The Roman play is tightly constructed, lively and inventive, full of the atmosphere of a bustling harbor town. It would be difficult, however, to claim that it has any object or concern other than to turn the normal world upside down and to evoke laughter of a simple and unreflective kind.

Shakespeare retained the conventional city street of Roman comedy with its separate and stylized houses. Probably, when the play was performed at Gray's Inn, there were free-standing structures of painted canvas to represent the Phoenix, where the native Antipholus and his family live, the Porpentine for the courtesan, and the priory or abbey which becomes so important in the fifth act. This setting, with its invisible but strongly contrasted off-stage localities—the mart with its world of business and, in the opposite direction, the more open and ambiguous sea-port—made it easy for Shakespeare to preserve the classical unity of place, while building up the image of a credible and populous town. He changed its name, however, from Epidamnum to Ephesus. Ephesus, as a number of commentators have pointed out, had specific associations in Acts 19:13–29 with witchcraft and sorcery, and in Ephesians 5:22–33 with St. Paul's discussion of Christian marriage. These are both important themes in *The Comedy of Errors*.

Shakespeare may well have felt in the early 1590's that it would be a useful discipline to submit himself to the three unities, even if (as it turned out) he saw no subsequent need to employ them until he wrote *The Tempest* at the end of his career. He may also have turned to Plautus, as other Elizabethan dramatists had done before him, in order to learn something about the construction of a finely engineered dramatic plot after the more rambling organization typical of his own Henry VI plays or, possibly, of *The Two Gentlemen of Verona*.[2] If so, he did not hesitate to create for himself technical problems far exceeding anything posed by his source. By supplying twin servants, borrowed from another play by Plautus, the *Amphitruo*, to the twin masters of the *Menaechmi* and so doubling the opportunities for planned confusion he made *The Comedy of Errors* structurally as much a tour de force as one of the great Bach fugues. Even more important, he added three characters—Egeon, Luciana, and the Abbess—who have little or nothing to do with laughter.

Egeon derives not from classical comedy but from the story of Apollonius of Tyre as retold by the fourteenth-century poet John Gower in his *Confessio Amantis* (a story to which Shakespeare was to return years later for the plot of *Pericles*). The two appearances of old Egeon, at the beginning and end of *The Comedy of Errors*, not only define its time-span from morning until the sunset hour appointed for his execution: they greatly deepen the basic Plautine material in ways that often seem to anticipate *Pericles* and its successors. Parents in Roman comedy, like wives, were usually nothing but a nuisance, repressing and causing trouble for the young. Egeon cannot be fitted into such a scheme. It is true that his long opening account of the shipwreck which was the source of all his woes is faintly absurd. A family of six scattered by Fortune in a fashion at once so implausible and so ingeniously patterned announces itself fairly clearly as material for a comedy resolution. Yet it is wrong for actors to make Egeon's explanation to the Duke overtly comic. The anguish of the old man is real, even if the verse he speaks suggests delicately to a theatre audience that his loss will not prove irremediable. Later, in Act V, he addresses the son he believes to be guilty of forgetfulness and ingratitude in lines so bitter that they seem to prefigure the reproaches of Antonio in *Twelfth Night*, or even those of King Lear. Most important of all, Egeon allowed Shakespeare to open the play under the shadow of death and to keep this threat alive in the background, like a sword that has been drawn and not sheathed, until it flashes into prominence again in Act V only to dissolve before the discoveries and accords of the final scene. Death is never a serious possibility in the

[1] See Appendix B, Number 14, below.

[2] See the discussion of the date of *The Two Gentlemen of Verona* on pages 177—78.

Menaechmi, or in most of Roman comedy. Shakespeare, even at the beginning of his dramatic career, seems to have been wedded to the idea that happy endings must, to carry conviction, be won from a serious confrontation with mortality, violence, and time.

Behind the *Menaechmi*, as behind all the plays of Plautus, lay a Greek original now lost. Mistaken identity and the recovery or reunion of lost children seem to have been almost obsessive preoccupations of the New Comedy written by Menander and his contemporaries towards the end of the 4th century B.C. A response, probably, to the political and economic chaos of a Hellenistic world that was filled with displaced persons, where children were often "lost" by parents too poor or too distracted to cope with them at the time of their birth, and where free citizens could become slaves overnight, the theme has an emotional resonance in the surviving Menandrian fragments which vanished in the later, Roman adaptations. For Plautus, living in a very different and more stable world, dealing with the Greek material at second hand, these plots became little more than an approved comic formula. *The Comedy of Errors* is remarkable on a number of counts, but not least because of the way it revitalizes and gives new meaning to a seemingly outworn dramatic convention. This meaning is not really Menandrian. Between Menander's *Epitrepontes* or *Periceiromene* and Shakespeare's play there stretches not only an immense gulf of space and time but also the fact of Christianity with its stress upon the inner life. Menander's characters were psychologically more complex than their Roman descendants but it is still true that identity for them is principally a matter of establishing parentage and social class. Their quest is accomplished when they achieve the equivalent of a birth certificate. Antipholus of Syracuse, by contrast, has voluntarily left a father and a defined and satisfactory social role in order to find a missing mother and twin brother without whom he feels psychologically incomplete.

I to the world am like a drop of water,
That in the ocean seeks another drop,
Who, falling there to find his fellow forth
(Unseen, inquisitive), confounds himself.
So I, to find a mother and a brother,
In quest of them (unhappy) ah, lose myself.
(I.ii.35–40)

Discontented and uneasy, Antipholus of Syracuse declares in the first scene in which he appears that he will, as a temporary distraction, "lose myself" in the streets of Ephesus. This is exactly what happens to him, but it happens in ways that neither he nor the writers of classical comedy could possibly have anticipated.

Unlike Plautus, Shakespeare seems to have been less interested in the problems of the native twin angered by the perversity of a familiar world than he was in the more extreme situation of the traveller, especially vulnerable because far from home, who finds himself losing his own sense of self in an alien city of reputed sorcery and spells. Antipholus of Syracuse, claimed as husband by a woman he has never seen before and does not like, saluted familiarly by men whose names he does not know and by a courtesan who assumes old acquaintance, badgered about inexplicable rings and chains and gold, finds it increasingly difficult to remain sure of a personal identity which everyone, even his own servant Dromio, seems determined not to recognize. Where the equivalent character in the *Menaechmi* had thought Epidamnum bewildering but delightful, Antipholus of Syracuse comes to regard Ephesus as a nightmare country where "none but witches do inhabit" (III.ii.156). Before long his self-confidence has been so badly shaken that he is asking Luciana to give him a new identity through the transforming power of romantic love (III.ii.33–52).

Like Egeon, Luciana is a character for whom there is no analogue in Plautus. The voice of reason and tolerance in the play, sane in the midst of madness, she counters the possessiveness and jealous frenzy of her sister Adriana with counsels of generosity and patience. Her own ideal of marriage is strikingly like that of the reformed Katherina at the end of *The Taming of the Shrew*: a relationship of mutual trust in which the woman is frankly subservient to her husband, as St. Paul believed she should be, but finds her own liberty and independence within this circumscription. It does not seem to be an ideal which Luciana has had much opportunity to see in practice. Faced with a nagging and suspicious sister and a brother-in-law who is careless of his wife's feelings and quick to anger, not to mention the dubious bond between the Ephesian Dromio and his spherical Nell, Luciana has remained single rather than court "troubles of the marriage-bed" (II.i.27). At the end of the play, however, it seems to be assumed that she will marry the Syracusan Antipholus: the man who appealed to her in Act III to help him forge a new identity through union with her own.

Before this can happen, violence and disorder in Ephesus rise to a pitch that is both funny and frightening. Outsiders like Angelo the goldsmith, Balthasar the merchant, Dr. Pinch the schoolmaster, the courtesan, and finally the Duke himself are all drawn into what at first had seemed only a family affair. In the last movement of the play, images of restraint, humiliation, and death proliferate. Antipholus of Syracuse, threatened with bondage and believing that he has seen the devil in the person of the courtesan, takes sanctuary in the abbey. His brother of Ephesus, having tried to savage his own wife, is bound and cast into a dark vault. Adriana, determined to remove from the abbey the man she believes to be her husband, is betrayed by the Abbess into a demonstration of her own shrewishness and publicly shamed. Pinch is tortured by his enraged prisoner. Old Egeon, led in bonds to the place of execution, is apparently spurned by the son he has brought up, and the angry explanations of Antipholus of Ephesus are so crossed and contradicted by the testimony of other characters that the Duke can only conclude that everyone is bewitched: "I think you all have drunk of Circe's cup" (V.i.271). Words are incapable of dealing with this tangle: indeed, they make it worse. Only the stage presence of the Syracusan Antipholus, as he emerges from the abbey to confront his twin for the first time in the play, can make sense of the tangle.

After the tension and accumulated mistakings of nearly five acts, this discovery generates an enormous sense of relief. The theatre audience, of course, unlike the characters in the play, has possessed the key to the situation all along: the knowledge that there are really two Dromios and two Antipholuses in Ephesus. The one surprise is Aemilia. When the Abbess recognizes Egeon as her long-lost husband and the two Antipholuses as her sons, Shakespeare deals a shrewd blow at the seeming omniscience of the spectators. Plautus had not restored this missing bit of the puzzle. There have been no hints in Shakespeare's play that Egeon's wife was alive and living in Ephesus. The discovery that she has been there all the time, that the virtuous and reverend lady who governs the abbey and has such decided views about a wife's duty to her husband is really the mother of the twins, is comical in the fullest sense of the word. As with Egeon's initial narrative of shipwreck and loss, there is something consciously absurd about this reunion which happens not only beyond hope but beyond any expectation explicitly generated by the play. Almost always, the theatre audience laughs when Aemilia identifies Egeon, but the laughter is not the laughter of farce.

At its ending *The Comedy of Errors* admits its own artificiality, its participation in that special realm of fairy-tale where the lost are always found, while reminding the theatre audience that it has not been in complete control of the situation after all. This last scene is consciously contrived but also moving in a way that seems to anticipate the marvellous discoveries of *Cymbeline* and *The Winter's Tale*. Certainly the emotions liberated look forward to the last plays. In the final moments of the comedy, the Syracusan Dromio makes another mistake. He addresses to the Ephesian Antipholus the question he ought to ask his own Syracusan master: "shall I fetch your stuff from shipboard?" "Dromio, what stuff of mine hast thou embark'd?" the puzzled Antipholus returns. But, for the first time in the play, no altercation, no ferocious exchange of words and blows results. Instead, Antipholus of Syracuse points out gently,

> He speaks to me. I am your master, Dromio.
> Come go with us, we'll look to that anon.
> Embrace thy brother there, rejoice with him.

The basic situation of the play, the source of all the misunderstanding, remains but it has been robbed of its sting. There is no pain in this final confusion of identities and no violence, only delight: "After so long grief, such nativity!"

Anne Barton

A Renaissance performance of Terence. From Terence: *Comoediae* (Lyon, 1493). The woodcut above, from the earliest printed book containing illustrations depicting dramatic performance, is from Terence's *Phormio, or The Scheming Parasite* (I.ii). It shows the kind of staging that Shakespeare uses in *The Comedy of Errors*. At the rear of the stage, clearly marked, may be seen the "houses" of the principal characters: Demipho (left), Chremes (centre), and Dorio (right). These "houses" remain unchanged throughout the play, and the characters enter from them and exit into them, but all the action takes place on the stage in front of the "houses." For comparison with *The Comedy of Errors*, see the note at the beginning of I.i, below. *(By permission of the Harvard College Library)*

The Comedy of Errors

[Dramatis Personae

Solinus, *Duke of Ephesus*
Egeon, *a merchant of Syracuse*
Antipholus of Ephesus | *twin brothers, and sons*
Antipholus of Syracuse | *to Egeon and Aemilia*
Dromio of Ephesus | *twin brothers, and bondmen*
Dromio of Syracuse | *to the two Antipholuses*
Balthazar, *a merchant*
Angelo, *a goldsmith*
First Merchant of Ephesus, *friend to Antipholus of Syracuse*
Second Merchant of Ephesus, *to whom Angelo is a debtor*

Doctor Pinch, *a conjuring schoolmaster*

Aemilia, *wife to Egeon, an abbess at Ephesus*
Adriana, *wife to Antipholus of Ephesus*
Luciana, *her sister*
Luce, *servant to Adriana (also known as* Nell*)*
Courtezan

Jailer, Headsman, Messenger, Officers, *and other* Attendants

Scene: *Ephesus*]

ACT I, Scene I

Enter the Duke of Ephesus *with* [Egeon] *the merchant of Syracusa,* Jailer [*with* Officers], *and other* Attendants.

Ege. Proceed, Solinus, to procure my fall,
And by the doom of death end woes and all.
Duke. Merchant of Syracusa, plead no more.
I am not partial to infringe our laws;
The enmity and discord which of late
Sprung from the rancorous outrage of your Duke
To merchants, our well-dealing countrymen,
Who, wanting guilders to redeem their lives,
Have seal'd his rigorous statutes with their bloods,
Excludes all pity from our threat'ning looks:
For since the mortal and intestine jars
'Twixt thy seditious countrymen and us,
It hath in solemn synods been decreed,
Both by the Syracusians and ourselves,
To admit no traffic to our adverse towns:
Nay more, if any born at Ephesus be seen
At any Syracusian marts and fairs;
Again, if any Syracusian born
Come to the bay of Ephesus, he dies,
His goods confiscate to the Duke's dispose,
Unless a thousand marks be levied
To quit the penalty and to ransom him.
Thy substance, valued at the highest rate,
Cannot amount unto a hundred marks,
Therefore by law thou art condemn'd to die.
Ege. Yet this my comfort, when your words are done,
My woes end likewise with the evening sun.
Duke. Well, Syracusian; say in brief the cause
Why thou departedst from thy native home,
And for what cause thou cam'st to Ephesus.
Ege. A heavier task could not have been impos'd
Than I to speak my griefs unspeakable:
Yet that the world may witness that my end

Words and passages enclosed in square brackets in the text above are either emendations of the copy-text or additions to it. The Textual Notes immediately following the play cite the earliest authority for every such change or insertion and supply the reading of the copy-text wherever it is emended in this edition.

I.i. Location: The mart of Ephesus. Following classical precedent, the action of this play takes place either (a) outside three "houses," perhaps merely doors (in the centre the house of Antipholus of Ephesus, marked as the Phoenix; to either side, the house of the Courtezan, marked as the Porpentine, and the priory, marked perhaps with a cross) or (b) on the open stage generally, which then serves as a more or less unlocalized playing place, here called "The mart," i.e. the marketplace or exchange.
2. doom: judgment, sentence. 4. partial: improperly inclined.
6. outrage: violent conduct.
7. well-dealing: doing business honestly and peaceably.
8. wanting: lacking. guilders: Dutch coins, but here used in the general sense of "money."
9. seal'd . . . bloods: ratified his extremely harsh laws by payment of their lives.
11. intestine: violent, deadly. (The usual meaning, "internal," i.e. "civil," does not fit the context here.) jars: strife, quarrels.
15. admit . . . to: to permit no trade between. adverse: hostile.
17. marts. Synonymous here with *fairs*.
20. confiscate: confiscated. dispose: disposal.
21. marks. A mark was two-thirds of a pound (an amount, not a coin). 22. quit: pay.
23. Thy substance: the sum total of your wealth.

Was wrought by nature, not by vile offense,
I'll utter what my sorrow gives me leave.
In Syracusa was I born, and wed
Unto a woman, happy but for me,
And by me, had not our hap been bad:
With her I liv'd in joy; our wealth increas'd
By prosperous voyages I often made
To Epidamium, till my factor's death,
And [the] great care of goods at randon left,
Drew me from kind embracements of my spouse;
From whom my absence was not six months old
Before herself (almost at fainting under
The pleasing punishment that women bear)
Had made provision for her following me,
And soon, and safe, arrived where I was.
There had she not been long but she became
A joyful mother of two goodly sons:
And, which was strange, the one so like the other
As could not be distinguish'd but by names.
That very hour, and in the self-same inn,
A mean woman was delivered
Of such a burthen male, twins both alike.
Those, for their parents were exceeding poor,
I bought, and brought up to attend my sons.
My wife, not meanly proud of two such boys,
Made daily motions for our home return:
Unwilling I agreed. Alas! too soon
We came aboard.
A league from Epidamium had we sail'd
Before the always-wind-obeying deep
Gave any tragic instance of our harm:
But longer did we not retain much hope;
For what obscured light the heavens did grant
Did but convey unto our fearful minds
A doubtful warrant of immediate death,
Which though myself would gladly have embrac'd,
Yet the incessant weepings of my wife,
Weeping before for what she saw must come,
And piteous plainings of the pretty babes,
That mourn'd for fashion, ignorant what to fear,
Forc'd me to seek delays for them and me.
And this it was (for other means was none):
The sailors sought for safety by our boat,
And left the ship, then sinking-ripe, to us.
My wife, more careful for the latter-born,
Had fast'ned him unto a small spare mast,
Such as sea-faring men provide for storms;
To him one of the other twins was bound,
Whilst I had been like heedful of the other.
The children thus dispos'd, my wife and I,
Fixing our eyes on whom our care was fix'd,

34. **nature**: natural affection, i.e. a father's love. 38. **hap**: fortune. 41. **Epidamium**: Plautus' Epidamnum, modern Durrës (Italian Durazzo) in Albania. Shakespeare may have supposed, however, that it was in Greece; see note on line 93. **factor's**: agent's.
42. **at randon**: at random, i.e. neglected, unattended.
43. **kind**: affectionate. 52. **As**: that they. 54. **mean**: low-born.
58. **not meanly**: in no small degree. 59. **motions**: proposals.
64. **instance**: indication, sign. 67. **fearful**: full of fear.
68. **doubtful**: frightening, dreadful. 72. **plainings**: wailings.
73. **for fashion**: in imitation.
74. **delays**: ways of deferring (the execution of the death warrant, line 68). 77. **sinking-ripe**: ready to sink.
78. **careful**: full of care, anxious. **latter-born**: second-born.
84. **whom**: him on whom.

Fast'ned ourselves at either end the mast,
And floating straight, obedient to the stream,
Was carried towards Corinth, as we thought.
At length the sun, gazing upon the earth,
Dispers'd those vapors that offended us,
And by the benefit of his wished light
The seas wax'd calm, and we discovered
Two ships from far, making amain to us,
Of Corinth that, of Epidaurus this.
But ere they came—O, let me say no more!
Gather the sequel by that went before.
Duke. Nay, forward, old man, do not break off so,
For we may pity, though not pardon thee.
Ege. O, had the gods done so, I had not now
Worthily term'd them merciless to us!
For ere the ships could meet by twice five leagues,
We were encount'red by a mighty rock,
Which being violently borne [upon],
Our helpful ship was splitted in the midst;
So that, in this unjust divorce of us,
Fortune had left to both of us alike
What to delight in, what to sorrow for.
Her part, poor soul! seeming as burdened
With lesser weight, but not with lesser woe,
Was carried with more speed before the wind,
And in our sight they three were taken up
By fishermen of Corinth, as we thought.
At length, another ship had seiz'd on us,
And knowing whom it was their hap to save,
Gave healthful welcome to their shipwrack'd guests,
And would have reft the fishers of their prey,
Had not their [bark] been very slow of sail;
And therefore homeward did they bend their course.
Thus have you heard me sever'd from my bliss,
That by misfortunes was my life prolong'd,
To tell sad stories of my own mishaps.
Duke. And for the sake of them thou sorrowest for,
Do me the favor to dilate at full
What have befall'n of them and [thee] till now.
Ege. My youngest boy, and yet my eldest care,
At eighteen years became inquisitive
After his brother; and importun'd me
That his attendant—so his case was like,
Reft of his brother, but retain'd his name—
Might bear him company in the quest of him:
Whom whilst I labored of a love to see,

86. **straight**: at once.
89. **vapors that offended**: clouds that injured or assailed.
92. **making amain**: proceeding at full speed.
93. **Epidaurus**: possibly Dubrovnik on the Adriatic coast, north of Epidamnum; but if Shakespeare supposed the latter to be in Greece, he may mean here the Greek Epidaurus, not far from Corinth.
95. **that**: what. 96. **forward**: go on. 99. **Worthily**: justly.
103. **Our . . . midst**: i.e. the mast to which they were fastened was broken in half. 106. **What**: something. 107. **as**: as if.
114. **healthful**: saving. 115. **reft**: robbed.
122. **dilate at full**: relate in detail, i.e. amplify.
123. **have befall'n**: has become.
124. **youngest boy**. Lines 78 ff. have led the reader to suppose that Egeon's charge was the elder son.
127. **so . . . like**: whose situation was similar.
128. **Reft . . . name**. Although commentators have found difficulty with this line (in view of line 52), the meaning seems clear enough, i.e. Egeon, presuming his elder son lost (or dead), has conferred his name on his younger son, who is now his "eldest care" (line 124).
130. **labored . . . love**: i.e. was racked by a desire.

I hazarded the loss of whom I lov'd.
Five summers have I spent in farthest Greece,
Roaming clean through the bounds of Asia,
And coasting homeward, came to Ephesus;
Hopeless to find, yet loath to leave unsought
Or that, or any place that harbors men.
But here must end the story of my life,
And happy were I in my timely death,
Could all my travels warrant me they live.

Duke. Hapless Egeon, whom the fates have mark'd
To bear the extremity of dire mishap!
Now trust me, were it not against our laws,
Against my crown, my oath, my dignity,
Which princes, would they, may not disannul,
My soul should sue as advocate for thee:
But though thou art adjudged to the death,
And passed sentence may not be recall'd
But to our honor's great disparagement,
Yet will I favor thee in what I can;
Therefore, merchant, I'll limit thee this day
To seek thy [health] by beneficial help.
Try all the friends thou hast in Ephesus;
Beg thou, or borrow, to make up the sum,
And live: if no, then thou art doom'd to die.
Jailer, take him to thy custody.

Jail. I will, my lord.

Ege. Hopeless and helpless doth Egeon wend,
But to procrastinate his liveless end. *Exeunt*.

[Scene II]

Enter Antipholus Erotes [of Syracuse, First] Merchant [of Ephesus], *and* Dromio [of Syracuse].

[1. E.] Mer. Therefore give out you are of Epidamium,
Lest that your goods too soon be confiscate:
This very day a Syracusian merchant
Is apprehended for [arrival] here;
And not being able to buy out his life,
According to the statute of the town,
Dies ere the weary sun set in the west.
There is your money that I had to keep.

S. Ant. Go bear it to the Centaur, where we host,
And stay there, Dromio, till I come to thee.

133. **clean**: completely. **bounds**: territories.
136. **Or**: either. **harbors**: lodges.
138. **timely**: opportune or seasonable (in that he would now die happy if he believed that his sons lived).
139. **travels**: (1) journeyings; (2) travails, hardships. **warrant**: assure.
144. **would they**: even if they wanted to. **disannul**: annul, cancel.
150. **limit**: allot as a limit. (The Duke's statement sets up the time scheme of the play.)
158. **procrastinate**: postpone. **liveless**: lifeless.

I.ii. Location: The mart.
o.s.d. **Erotes**. Explained as deriving in some way (as by compositorial misreading) from Latin *erraticus* or *errans* (genitive *errantis*), "wandering" (designating the twin who is travelling in search of his brother). The F1 spelling *Errotis* at II.ii o.s.d. (see the Textual Notes) supports this conjecture. See also the note to II.i o.s.d. 5. **buy out**: ransom.
9. **Centaur**. Named from the figure on the sign over the door. Not only inns but shops had such signs; see below, I.ii.75, where we learn that the house in which Antipholus of Ephesus lives and carries on his business is called the Phoenix. **host**: lodge.

Within this hour it will be dinner-time;
Till that, I'll view the manners of the town,
Peruse the traders, gaze upon the buildings,
And then return and sleep within mine inn,
For with long travel I am stiff and weary.
Get thee away.

S. Dro. Many a man would take you at your word,
And go indeed, having so good a mean. *Exit Dromio*.

S. Ant. A trusty villain, sir, that very oft,
When I am dull with care and melancholy,
Lightens my humor with his merry jests.
What, will you walk with me about the town,
And then go to my inn and dine with me?

[1.] E. Mer. I am invited, sir, to certain merchants,
Of whom I hope to make much benefit;
I crave your pardon. Soon at five a' clock,
Please you, I'll meet with you upon the mart,
And afterward consort you till bed-time:
My present business calls me from you now.

S. Ant. Farewell till then. I will go lose myself,
And wander up and down to view the city.

[1.] E. Mer. Sir, I commend you to your own content. *Exit*.

S. Ant. He that commends me to mine own content,
Commends me to the thing I cannot get:
I to the world am like a drop of water,
That in the ocean seeks another drop,
Who, falling there to find his fellow forth
(Unseen, inquisitive), confounds himself.
So I, to find a mother and a brother,
In quest of them (unhappy), ah, lose myself.

Enter Dromio of Ephesus.

Here comes the almanac of my true date.
What now? How chance thou art return'd so soon?

E. Dro. Return'd so soon! rather approach'd too late:
The capon burns, the pig falls from the spit;
The clock hath strucken twelve upon the bell:
My mistress made it one upon my cheek:
She is so hot, because the meat is cold:
The meat is cold, because you come not home:
You come not home, because you have no stomach:
You have no stomach, having broke your fast:
But we that know what 'tis to fast and pray,
Are penitent for your default to-day.

S. Ant. Stop in your wind, sir; tell me this, I pray:
Where have you left the money that I gave you?

11. **dinner-time**: i.e. about twelve o'clock; cf. line 45.
13. **Peruse**: inspect.
18. **mean**: means, i.e. the money entrusted to him.
19. **villain**: fellow (used here good-naturedly), but with some suggestion of "villein" or "bondman." 21. **humor**: mood.
25. **benefit**: profit. 26. **Soon**: in early evening.
28. **consort**: keep company with. 30. **lose myself**: roam at will.
35. **to**: in relation to. 37. **forth**: out.
38. **Unseen, inquisitive**: unknown and eagerly inquiring. **confounds himself**: destroys itself, i.e. loses its identity. (The play is much concerned with apparent loss of identity.) 40. **unhappy**: unlucky.
41. **almanac . . . date**: i.e. indicator of my age (since he and Dromio were both born on the same day and in the same hour).
42. **How chance**: how does it come about that.
46. **made it one**: i.e. struck one o'clock. 49. **stomach**: appetite.
52. **penitent**: i.e. doing penance. **default**: fault, sin.
53. **wind**: idle talk.

E. Dro. O—sixpence that I had a' We'n'sday last
To pay the saddler for my mistress' crupper?
The saddler had it, sir, I kept it not.
S. Ant. I am not in a sportive humor now:
Tell me, and dally not, where is the money?
We being strangers here, how dar'st thou trust
So great a charge from thine own custody?
E. Dro. I pray you jest, sir, as you sit at dinner.
I from my mistress come to you in post:
If I return, I shall be post indeed,
For she will [score] your fault upon my pate:
Methinks your maw, like mine, should be your [clock],
And strike you home without a messenger.
S. Ant. Come, Dromio, come, these jests are out of season,
Reserve them till a merrier hour than this:
Where is the gold I gave in charge to thee?
E. Dro. To me, sir? Why, you gave no gold to me.
S. Ant. Come on, sir knave, have done your foolishness,
And tell me how thou hast dispos'd thy charge.
E. Dro. My charge was but to fetch you from the mart
Home to your house, the Phoenix, sir, to dinner;
My mistress and her sister stays for you.
S. Ant. Now, as I am a Christian, answer me,
In what safe place you have bestow'd my money;
Or I shall break that merry sconce of yours
That stands on tricks when I am undispos'd:
Where is the thousand marks thou hadst of me?
E. Dro. I have some marks of yours upon my pate;
Some of my mistress' marks upon my shoulders;
But not a thousand marks between you both.
If I should pay your worship those again,
Perchance you will not bear them patiently.
S. Ant. Thy mistress' marks? What mistress, slave, hast thou?
E. Dro. Your worship's wife, my mistress at the Phoenix;
She that doth fast till you come home to dinner;
And prays that you will hie you home to dinner.
S. Ant. What, wilt thou flout me thus unto my face,
Being forbid? There, take you that, sir knave.
[*Strikes Dromio.*]
E. Dro. What mean you, sir? For God sake hold your hands!
Nay, and you will not, sir, I'll take my heels.
Exit Dromio [of] Ephesus.
S. Ant. Upon my life, by some device or other
The villain is o'erraught of all my money.
They say this town is full of cozenage:
As nimble jugglers that deceive the eye,
Dark-working sorcerers that change the mind,
Soul-killing witches that deform the body,
Disguised cheaters, prating mountebanks,
And many such-like liberties of sin:
If it prove so, I will be gone the sooner.
I'll to the Centaur to go seek this slave;
I greatly fear my money is not safe. *Exit.*

ACT II, [SCENE I]

Enter ADRIANA, *wife to Antipholus Sereptus [of Ephesus], with* LUCIANA, *her sister.*

Adr. Neither my husband nor the slave return'd,
That in such haste I sent to seek his master?
Sure, Luciana, it is two a' clock.
Luc. Perhaps some merchant hath invited him,
And from the mart he's somewhere gone to dinner.
Good sister, let us dine, and never fret;
A man is master of his liberty:
Time is their master, and when they see time,
They'll go or come; if so, be patient, sister.
Adr. Why should their liberty than ours be more?
Luc. Because their business still lies out a' door.
Adr. Look when I serve him so, he takes it [ill].
Luc. O, know he is the bridle of your will.
Adr. There's none but asses will be bridled so.
Luc. Why, headstrong liberty is lash'd with woe:
There's nothing situate under heaven's eye
But hath his bound in earth, in sea, in sky.
The beasts, the fishes, and the winged fowls
Are their males' subjects and at their controls:
Man, more divine, the master of all these,
Lord of the wide world and wild wat'ry seas,
Indu'd with intellectual sense and souls,
Of more pre-eminence than fish and fowls,
Are masters to their females, and their lords:
Then let your will attend on their accords.
Adr. This servitude makes you to keep unwed.
Luc. Not this, but troubles of the marriage-bed.
Adr. But, were you wedded, you would bear some sway.
Luc. Ere I learn love, I'll practice to obey.
Adr. How if your husband start some other where?
Luc. Till he come home again, I would forbear.
Adr. Patience unmov'd! no marvel though she pause—
They can be meek that have no other cause:
A wretched soul, bruis'd with adversity,
We bid be quiet when we hear it cry;
But were we burd'ned with like weight of pain,

56. crupper: leather strap, attached to the back of a saddle and passed under the horse's tail, to prevent the saddle from slipping forwards.
61. from: out of. **63. post:** haste.
64. post: i.e. the doorpost on which tavern reckonings were marked.
65. score: mark, cut. **73. dispos'd:** deposited. **79. sconce:** head.
80. stands: insists. **undispos'd:** i.e. not in a merry mood.
81. thousand marks. Ironically, this is the exact amount needed to ransom his father. **93. God:** God's. **94. and:** if.
96. o'erraught: overreached, i.e. cheated. **97. cozenage:** cheating.
101. prating mountebanks: i.e. itinerant quack doctors crying up their remedies.
102. liberties of sin: wicked transgressors (Kittredge).

II.i. Location: Before the house of Antipholus of Ephesus.
o.s.d. Sereptus. A verbal echo of Plautus, who in the prologue to the *Menaechmi* describes the lost twin as *puer surreptus*, "the boy who was snatched away."
11. still: constantly. **out a' door:** i.e. away from home.
12. serve: treat. **15. lash'd:** (1) scourged; (2) bound.
17. his: its. **22. intellectual sense:** reason.
25. accords: assents, i.e. wishes.
30. start . . . where: go off in some other direction, i.e. after some other woman. **32. pause:** i.e. before marrying.
33. other cause: cause to be otherwise.

As much, or more, we should ourselves complain:
So thou, that hast no unkind mate to grieve thee,
With urging helpless patience would relieve me;
But if thou live to see like right bereft,
This fool-begg'd patience in thee will be left.
Luc. Well, I will marry one day, but to try.
Here comes your man, now is your husband nigh.

Enter DROMIO [OF] EPHESUS.

Adr. Say, is your tardy master now at hand?

E. Dro. Nay, he's at [two] hands with me, and that my two ears can witness.

Adr. Say, didst thou speak with him? Know'st thou his mind?

E. Dro. Ay, ay, he told his mind upon mine ear.
Beshrew his hand, I scarce could understand it.

Luc. Spake he so doubtfully, thou couldst not feel his meaning?

E. Dro. Nay, he strook so plainly, I could too well feel his blows; and withal so doubtfully, that I could scarce understand them.

Adr. But say, I prithee, is he coming home?
It seems he hath great care to please his wife.
E. Dro. Why, mistress, sure my master is horn-mad.
Adr. Horn-mad, thou villain!
E. Dro. I mean not cuckold-mad—
But sure he is stark mad:
When I desir'd him to come home to dinner,
He ask'd me for a [thousand] marks in gold:
"'Tis dinner-time," quoth I: "My gold!" quoth he.
"Your meat doth burn," quoth I: "My gold!" quoth he.
"Will you come?" quoth I: "My gold!" quoth he;
"Where is the thousand marks I gave thee, villain?"
"The pig," quoth I, "is burn'd": "My gold!" quoth he.
"My mistress, sir," quoth I: "Hang up thy mistress!
I know not thy mistress, out on thy mistress!"
Luc. Quoth who?
E. Dro. Quoth my master.
"I know," quoth he, "no house, no wife, no mistress."
So that my arrant, due unto my tongue,
I thank him, I bare home upon my shoulders:
For, in conclusion, he did beat me there.
Adr. Go back again, thou slave, and fetch him home.
E. Dro. Go back again, and be new beaten home?
For God's sake send some other messenger.

39. **helpless**: unavailing.
40. **see . . . bereft**: see yourself similarly deprived of your rights.
41. **fool-begg'd**: foolishly urged. **left**: abandoned.
45–46. **he's . . . witness**: i.e. he boxed my ears.
48. **told.** With pun on *tolled.*
49. **Beshrew**: mischief take. **understand.** With play on "stand under." 50. **doubtfully**: ambiguously. 52. **strook**: struck.
53. **doubtfully**: unsettledly (looking forward to the implied "madness" of lines 57 ff.).
57. **horn-mad**: acting like an infuriated horned animal (but Adriana is quick to suspect a reference to the horns cuckolds were supposed to have).
67. **Hang . . . mistress**: let your mistress go hang herself.
72. **my arrant**: my errand, what I have to deliver. **due . . . tongue**: which I should have carried back by means of my tongue.

Adr. Back, slave, or I will break thy pate across.
E. Dro. And he will bless that cross with other beating:
Between you I shall have a holy head.
Adr. Hence, prating peasant! fetch thy master home.
E. Dro. Am I so round with you, as you with me,
That like a football you do spurn me thus?
You spurn me hence, and he will spurn me hither:
If I last in this service, you must case me in leather.
[*Exit.*]
Luc. Fie, how impatience low'reth in your face!
Adr. His company must do his minions grace,
Whilst I at home starve for a merry look:
Hath homely age th' alluring beauty took
From my poor cheek? Then he hath wasted it.
Are my discourses dull? Barren my wit?
If voluble and sharp discourse be marr'd,
Unkindness blunts it more than marble hard.
Do their gay vestments his affections bait?
That's not my fault, he's master of my state.
What ruins are in me that can be found,
By him not ruin'd? Then is he the ground
Of my defeatures. My decayed fair
A sunny look of his would soon repair.
But, too unruly deer, he breaks the pale,
And feeds from home; poor I am but his stale.
Luc. Self-harming jealousy—fie, beat it hence!
Adr. Unfeeling fools can with such wrongs dispense:
I know his eye doth homage otherwhere,
Or else what lets it but he would be here?
Sister, you know he promis'd me a chain;
Would that alone a' love he would detain,
So he would keep fair quarter with his bed!
I see the jewel best enamelled
Will lose his beauty; yet the gold bides still
That others touch and, often touching, will
Where gold; and no man that hath a name
By falsehood and corruption doth it shame.
Since that my beauty cannot please his eye,
I'll weep what's left away, and weeping die.
Luc. How many fond fools serve mad jealousy?
Exeunt.

78. **across.** Dromio's reply quibbles on *a cross.*
79. **bless**: make happy (?) or sign with another cross (?); perhaps with a quibble on *bless* = wound, drub (from French *blesser*).
80. **holy**: (1) marked with a cross; (2) full of holes.
82. **round**: plainspoken (with quibble on "spherical").
87. **do . . . grace**: show favor to his paramours.
89. **homely age**: ugly old age.
90. **wasted**: (1) laid waste; (2) squandered.
91. **discourses**: conversations.
92. **voluble**: fluent, animated. **sharp**: witty.
94. **affections**: passions. **bait**: entice.
95. **state**: outward estate, i.e. clothes. 97. **ground**: cause.
98. **defeatures**: disfigurements. **decayed fair**: perished beauty.
100. **pale**: enclosure.
101. **from**: away from. **stale**: literally, stalking-horse; here, dupe, laughingstock. 103. **dispense**: put up. 105. **lets**: prevents.
107. **Would . . . detain**: would that he would withhold only that manifestation of love (?).
108. **So**: provided. **keep . . . with**: be true to.
109–13. **I . . . shame.** A difficult, possibly corrupt, passage. Herford explains: "The best enamelled jewel tarnishes; but the gold setting keeps its lustre however it may be worn by the touch; similarly, a man of assured reputation can commit domestic infidelity without blasting it." 116. **fond**: doting.

[Scene II]

Enter Antipholus Erotes [of Syracuse].

S. Ant. The gold I gave to Dromio is laid up
Safe at the Centaur, and the heedful slave
Is wand'red forth, in care to seek me out.
By computation and mine host's report,
I could not speak with Dromio since at first
I sent him from the mart! See, here he comes.

Enter Dromio [of] Syracusa.

How now, sir, is your merry humor alter'd?
As you love strokes, so jest with me again.
You know no Centaur? You receiv'd no gold?
Your mistress sent to have me home to dinner?
My house was at the Phoenix? Wast thou mad,
That thus so madly thou didst answer me?

S. Dro. What answer, sir? when spake I such a word?

S. Ant. Even now, even here, not half an hour since.

S. Dro. I did not see you since you sent me hence
Home to the Centaur with the gold you gave me.

S. Ant. Villain, thou didst deny the gold's receipt,
And toldst me of a mistress, and a dinner,
For which I hope thou feltst I was displeas'd.

S. Dro. I am glad to see you in this merry vein.
What means this jest? I pray you, master, tell me.

S. Ant. Yea, dost thou jeer and flout me in the teeth?
Think'st thou I jest? Hold, take thou that, and that. *Beats Dromio.*

S. Dro. Hold, sir, for God's sake! Now your jest is earnest,
Upon what bargain do you give it me?

S. Ant. Because that I familiarly sometimes
Do use you for my fool, and chat with you,
Your sauciness will jest upon my love,
And make a common of my serious hours.
When the sun shines, let foolish gnats make sport,
But creep in crannies, when he hides his beams:
If you will jest with me, know my aspect,
And fashion your demeanor to my looks,
Or I will beat this method in your sconce.

S. Dro. Sconce call you it? So you would leave battering, I had rather have it a head. And you use these blows long, I must get a sconce for my head, and insconce it too, or else I shall seek my wit in my shoulders. But I pray, sir, why am I beaten?

S. Ant. Dost thou not know?

S. Dro. Nothing, sir, but that I am beaten.

S. Ant. Shall I tell you why?

S. Dro. Ay, sir, and wherefore; for they say, every why hath a wherefore.

S. Ant. Why first—for flouting me, and then wherefore—
For urging it the second time to me.

S. Dro. Was there ever any man thus beaten out of season,
When in the why and the wherefore is neither rhyme nor reason?
Well, sir, I thank you.

S. Ant. Thank me, sir, for what?

S. Dro. Marry, sir, for this something that you gave me for nothing.

S. Ant. I'll make you amends next, to give you nothing for something. But say, sir, is it dinner-time?

S. Dro. No, sir, I think the meat wants that I have.

S. Ant. In good time, sir: what's that?

S. Dro. Basting.

S. Ant. Well, sir, then 'twill be dry.

S. Dro. If it be, sir, I pray you eat none of it.

S. Ant. Your reason?

S. Dro. Lest it make you choleric, and purchase me another dry basting.

S. Ant. Well, sir, learn to jest in good time—there's a time for all things.

S. Dro. I durst have denied that before you were so choleric.

S. Ant. By what rule, sir?

S. Dro. Marry, sir, by a rule as plain as the plain bald pate of Father Time himself.

S. Ant. Let's hear it.

S. Dro. There's no time for a man to recover his hair that grows bald by nature.

S. Ant. May he not do it by fine and recovery?

S. Dro. Yes, to pay a fine for a periwig, and recover the lost hair of another man.

S. Ant. Why is Time such a niggard of hair, being (as it is) so plentiful an excrement?

S. Dro. Because it is a blessing that he bestows on beasts, and what he hath scanted [men] in hair he hath given them in wit.

S. Ant. Why, but there's many a man hath more hair than wit.

S. Dro. Not a man of those but he hath the wit to lose his hair.

S. Ant. Why, thou didst conclude hairy men plain dealers without wit.

S. Dro. The plainer dealer, the sooner lost; yet he loseth it in a kind of jollity.

S. Ant. For what reason?

II.ii. Location: The mart.
4. computation: reckoning (of time).
22. in the teeth: to my face.
24. earnest: (1) serious; (2) money paid down to secure a bargain.
28. jest . . . love: trifle with my indulgence.
29. common: public playground.
32. aspect: (1) expression; (2) influence, favorable or unfavorable, of the planets.
34. sconce: head; but Dromio plays on the meanings "fort" (line 35, with accompanying quibble on *battering* as "beating" and "using a battering ram") and "protective covering" (line 37).
38. insconce: fortify, protect.
38–39. seek . . . shoulders: i.e. because his head will be beaten into his shoulders.
51. Marry: indeed (a weakened oath, "by the Virgin Mary").
55. wants that: lacks what. **57. In good time:** indeed.
62. choleric: irascible. Overdone meat was believed to cause an excess of the bodily fluid called choler, which produced irascibility.
63. dry basting: severe beating.
74. fine and recovery: a legal process by which an entailed estate could be converted into a fee-simple. **78. excrement:** outgrowth.
80. scanted: been niggardly of, stinted.
84–85. hath . . . hair: i.e. can manage to contract syphilis (which causes loss of hair).
86–87. plain dealers: men who deal honestly and plainly.
88. dealer: i.e. dealer with women.

S. Dro. For two—and sound ones too.
S. Ant. Nay, not sound, I pray you.
S. Dro. Sure ones then.
S. Ant. Nay, not sure, in a thing falsing.
S. Dro. Certain ones then.
S. Ant. Name them.

S. Dro. The one, to save the money that he spends in [tiring]; the other, that at dinner they should not drop in his porridge.

S. Ant. You would all this time have prov'd there is no time for all things.

S. Dro. Marry, and did, sir: namely, [e'en] no time to recover hair lost by nature.

S. Ant. But your reason was not substantial, why there is no time to recover.

S. Dro. Thus I mend it: Time himself is bald, and therefore, to the world's end, will have bald followers.

S. Ant. I knew 'twould be a bald conclusion. But soft, who wafts us yonder?

Enter ADRIANA *and* LUCIANA.

Adr. Ay, ay, Antipholus, look strange and frown,
Some other mistress hath thy sweet aspects:
I am not Adriana, nor thy wife.
The time was once, when thou unurg'd wouldst vow
That never words were music to thine ear,
That never object pleasing in thine eye,
That never touch well welcome to thy hand,
That never meat sweet-savor'd in thy taste,
Unless I spake, or look'd, or touch'd, or carv'd to thee.
How comes it now, my husband, O, how comes it,
That thou art then estranged from thyself?
Thyself I call it, being strange to me,
That, undividable incorporate,
Am better than thy dear self's better part.
Ah, do not tear away thyself from me;
For know, my love, as easy mayst thou fall
A drop of water in the breaking gulf,
And take unmingled thence that drop again,
Without addition or diminishing,
As take from me thyself and not me too.
How dearly would it touch thee to the quick,
Shouldst thou but hear I were licentious,
And that this body, consecrate to thee,
By ruffian lust should be contaminate?
Wouldst thou not spit at me, and spurn at me,
And hurl the name of husband in my face,
And tear the stain'd skin [off] my harlot brow,
And from my false hand cut the wedding-ring,
And break it with a deep-divorcing vow?
I know thou canst, and therefore see thou do it.
I am possess'd with an adulterate blot;
My blood is mingled with the crime of lust:
For if we two be one, and thou play false,
I do digest the poison of thy flesh,
Being strumpeted by thy contagion.
Keep then fair league and truce with thy true bed,
I live dis-stain'd, thou undishonored.

S. Ant. Plead you to me, fair dame? I know you not:
In Ephesus I am but two hours old,
As strange unto your town as to your talk,
Who, every word by all my wit being scann'd,
Wants wit in all one word to understand.

Luc. Fie, brother, how the world is chang'd with you:
When were you wont to use my sister thus?
She sent for you by Dromio home to dinner.

S. Ant. By Dromio?
S. Dro. By me?

Adr. By thee, and this thou didst return from him,
That he did buffet thee, and in his blows
Denied my house for his, me for his wife.

S. Ant. Did you converse, sir, with this gentlewoman?
What is the course and drift of your compact?

S. Dro. I, sir? I never saw her till this time.

S. Ant. Villain, thou liest, for even her very words
Didst thou deliver to me on the mart.

S. Dro. I never spake with her in all my life.

S. Ant. How can she thus then call us by our names,
Unless it be by inspiration?

Adr. How ill agrees it with your gravity
To counterfeit thus grossly with your slave,
Abetting him to thwart me in my mood!
Be it my wrong you are from me exempt,
But wrong not that wrong with a more contempt.
Come, I will fasten on this sleeve of thine:
Thou art an elm, my husband, I a vine,
Whose weakness, married to thy [stronger] state,
Makes me with thy strength to communicate:
If aught possess thee from me, it is dross,
Usurping ivy, brier, or idle moss,
Who, all for want of pruning, with intrusion
Infect thy sap, and live on thy confusion.

S. Ant. To me she speaks, she moves me for her theme:
What, was I married to her in my dream?
Or sleep I now and think I hear all this?
What error drives our eyes and ears amiss?
Until I know this sure uncertainty,
I'll entertain the [offer'd] fallacy.

Luc. Dromio, go bid the servants spread for dinner.

S. Dro. O for my beads! I cross me for a sinner.

The Comedy of Errors II.ii

91. sound: valid (but Antipholus' objection quibbles on the sense "healthy"). **94. falsing:** deceptive. **98. tiring:** dressing the hair.
99. porridge: soup. **108. bald:** lame, stupid.
109. soft: hold. **wafts:** beckons. **110. strange:** distant.
122. undividable: indivisibly.
123. better part: spiritually or physically the best qualities of a man; cf. III.ii.61. **125. fall:** let fall.
129. As . . . too: i.e. we are so indivisibly one that we cannot be separated without inevitable loss to each other.
130. dearly: deeply, keenly. **141. crime:** sin.

144. strumpeted: made a strumpet. **146. dis-stain'd:** unstained.
151. all: i.e. all that you have been saying. **153. use:** treat.
161. compact: plot. **169. grossly:** obviously. **170. mood:** anger.
171. exempt: separated. **172. more:** greater.
177. aught . . . me: anything (evil) hold a part in you which separates you from me. **dross:** impure matter mixed with a pure substance.
178. idle: barren, useless. **180. confusion:** ruin.
181. moves: pleads with. **for her theme:** as the subject of what she is saying.
185. know . . . uncertainty: know this to be undeniable illusion.
186. entertain: accept. **fallacy:** delusive notion.
188. beads: rosary. **cross . . . sinner:** i.e. he makes the sign of the cross to protect himself as a mere sinning mortal.

This is the fairy land. O spite of spites!
We talk with goblins, owls, and sprites;
If we obey them not, this will ensue:
They'll suck our breath, or pinch us black and blue.

Luc. Why prat'st thou to thyself, and answer'st not?
Dromio, thou [drumble,] thou snail, thou slug, thou sot!

S. Dro. I am transformed, master, am [not I]?

S. Ant. I think thou art in mind, and so am I.

S. Dro. Nay, master, both in mind and in my shape.

S. Ant. Thou hast thine own form.

S. Dro. No, I am an ape.

Luc. If thou art chang'd to aught, 'tis to an ass.

S. Dro. 'Tis true she rides me and I long for grass.
'Tis so, I am an ass, else it could never be
But I should know her as well as she knows me.

Adr. Come, come, no longer will I be a fool,
To put the finger in the eye and weep,
Whilst man and master laughs my woes to scorn.
Come, sir, to dinner. Dromio, keep the gate.
Husband, I'll dine above with you to-day,
And shrive you of a thousand idle pranks.
Sirrah, if any ask you for your master,
Say he dines forth, and let no creature enter.
Come, sister. Dromio, play the porter well.

S. Ant. Am I in earth, in heaven, or in hell?
Sleeping or waking, mad or well-advis'd?
Known unto these, and to myself disguis'd?
I'll say as they say, and persever so,
And in this mist at all adventures go.

S. Dro. Master, shall I be porter at the gate?

Adr. Ay, and let none enter, lest I break your pate.

Luc. Come, come, Antipholus, we dine too late. [*Exeunt.*]

ACT III, SCENE I

Enter ANTIPHOLUS OF EPHESUS, *his man* DROMIO [OF EPHESUS], ANGELO *the goldsmith, and* BALTHAZAR *the merchant.*

E. Ant. Good Signior Angelo, you must excuse us all,
My wife is shrewish when I keep not hours:
Say that I linger'd with you at your shop
To see the making of her carcanet,
And that to-morrow you will bring it home.
But here's a villain that would face me down
He met me on the mart, and that I beat him,
And charg'd him with a thousand marks in gold,
And that I did deny my wife and house.
Thou drunkard, thou, what didst thou mean by this?

E. Dro. Say what you will, sir, but I know what I know:
That you beat me at the mart, I have your hand to show;
If the skin were parchment, and the blows you gave were ink,
Your own handwriting would tell you what I think.

E. Ant. I think thou art an ass.

E. Dro. Marry, so it doth appear
By the wrongs I suffer, and the blows I bear.
I should kick, being kick'd, and being at that pass,
You would keep from my heels, and beware of an ass.

E. Ant. Y' are sad, Signior Balthazar, pray God our cheer
May answer my good will and your good welcome here.

Balth. I hold your dainties cheap, sir, and your welcome dear.

E. Ant. O, Signior Balthazar, either at flesh or fish,
A table full of welcome makes scarce one dainty dish.

Balth. Good meat, sir, is common; that every churl affords.

E. Ant. And welcome more common, for that's nothing but words.

Balth. Small cheer and great welcome makes a merry feast.

E. Ant. Ay, to a niggardly host and more sparing guest:
But though my cates be mean, take them in good part;
Better cheer may you have, but not with better heart.
But soft, my door is lock'd; go bid them let us in.

E. Dro. Maud, Bridget, Marian, Cic'ly, Gillian, Ginn!

S. Dro. [*Within.*] Mome, malt-horse, capon, coxcomb, idiot, patch!
Either get thee from the door, or sit down at the hatch;
Dost thou conjure for wenches, that thou call'st for such store,
When one is one too many? Go get thee from the door.

E. Dro. What patch is made our porter? My master stays in the street.

S. Dro. [*Within.*] Let him walk from whence he came, lest he catch cold on 's feet.

E. Ant. Who talks within there? Ho, open the door!

192. breath: i.e. breath of life (probably connected with the folk belief that the breath of man was his soul).
194. drumble: sluggish person, drone. **sot:** fool.
198. ape: counterfeit (aping myself).
204. put . . . weep: i.e. play the child.
207. above. The living quarters would be on the floor above the business quarters.
208. shrive you of: hear you confess and forgive you for.
209. Sirrah: term of address to inferiors.
210. forth: away from home. **213. well-advis'd:** sane.
216. at all adventures: whatever happens.

III.i. Location: Before the house of Antipholus of Ephesus.
4. carcanet: jewelled necklace.
6. face me down: maintain to my face that.

8. with: i.e. with the possession of. **9. deny:** disclaim.
17. at that pass: in that predicament.
19. sad: serious. **cheer:** fare. **20. answer:** match.
27. sparing: frugal. **28. cates:** provisions. **mean:** modest, plain.
32. Mome: blockhead. **malt-horse:** brewer's horse, i.e. heavy or stupid creature. **patch:** fool.
33. hatch: bottom half of a divided door.
34. conjure for: summon up by magic. **37. on 's:** in his.

S. Dro. [*Within.*] Right, sir, I'll tell you when, and you'll tell me wherefore.
E. Ant. Wherefore? For my dinner: I have not din'd to-day.
S. Dro. [*Within.*] Nor to-day here you must not, come again when you may.
E. Ant. What art thou that keep'st me out from the house I owe?
S. Dro. [*Within.*] The porter for this time, sir, and my name is Dromio.
E. Dro. O villain, thou hast stol'n both mine office and my name:
The one ne'er got me credit, the other mickle blame.
If thou hadst been Dromio to-day in my place,
Thou wouldst have chang'd thy face for a name, or thy name for an ass.

Enter LUCE [*within*].

Luce. [*Within.*] What a coil is there, Dromio? Who are those at the gate?
E. Dro. Let my master in, Luce.
Luce. [*Within.*] Faith, no, he comes too late,
And so tell your master.
E. Dro. O Lord, I must laugh!
Have at you with a proverb—Shall I set in my staff?
Luce. [*Within.*] Have at you with another, that's—When? can you tell?
S. Dro. [*Within.*] If thy name be called Luce—Luce, thou hast answer'd him well.
E. Ant. Do you hear, you minion? You'll let us in, I hope?
Luce. [*Within.*] I thought to have ask'd you.
S. Dro. [*Within.*] And you said no.
E. Dro. So come help: well strook! there was blow for blow.
E. Ant. Thou baggage, let me in.
Luce. [*Within.*] Can you tell for whose sake?
E. Dro. Master, knock the door hard.
Luce. [*Within.*] Let him knock till it ache.
E. Ant. You'll cry for this, minion, if I beat the door down.
Luce. [*Within.*] What needs all that, and a pair of stocks in the town?

Enter ADRIANA [*within*].

42. **owe**: own. 44. **office**: function. 45. **mickle**: much.
47. **chang'd . . . a name.** A puzzling passage. Dover Wilson suggests emending *a name* to *an aim*, i.e. a mark or target (for the blows Dromio has received); Foakes accepts his emendation and in addition reads *office* for *face* (a change supported by lines 44–45). **an ass**: i.e. the name of ass.
47 s.d. **Enter Luce within.** It seems probable that the entry of Luce here and of Adriana at line 60, although they speak from "within" and out of sight of Antipholus of Ephesus and his companions, was managed in such a way as to make them partly visible to the audience, and that they withdraw following line 64, as Dover Wilson has suggested. 48. **coil**: fuss.
51. **Have at you**: here I come at you. **set . . . staff**: take up my residence here (with a bawdy innuendo).
52. **When . . . tell**: i.e. never (a conventional phrase of derision or defiance).
54. **minion**: hussy. **hope.** No rhyming line follows. The loss of a line, supposed by Malone and others, would account for the obscurity of the next two lines. Alternatively, some editors follow Theobald in emending *hope* to *trow* (i.e. suppose), thus producing a rhyming triplet.
60. **What . . . town**: why do we put up with all this when the town provides means of punishment.

Adr. [*Within.*] Who is that at the door that keeps all this noise?
S. Dro. [*Within.*] By my troth, your town is troubled with unruly boys.
E. Ant. Are you there, wife? You might have come before.
Adr. [*Within.*] Your wife, sir knave? Go get you from the door.
E. Dro. If you went in pain, master, this knave would go sore.
Ang. Here is neither cheer, sir, nor welcome: we would fain have either.
Balth. In debating which was best, we shall part with neither.
E. Dro. They stand at the door, master, bid them welcome hither.
E. Ant. There is something in the wind, that we cannot get in.
E. Dro. You would say so, master, if your garments were thin.
Your cake here is warm within: you stand here in the cold.
It would make a man mad as a buck to be so bought and sold.
E. Ant. Go fetch me something: I'll break ope the gate.
S. Dro. [*Within.*] Break any breaking here, and I'll break your knave's pate.
E. Dro. A man may break a word with [you], sir, and words are but wind:
Ay, and break it in your face, so he break it not behind.
S. Dro. [*Within.*] It seems thou want'st breaking, out upon thee, hind!
E. Dro. Here's too much "out upon thee!"; I pray thee let me in.
S. Dro. [*Within.*] Ay, when fowls have no feathers, and fish have no fin.
E. Ant. Well, I'll break in: go borrow me a crow.
E. Dro. A crow without feather? Master, mean you so?
For a fish without a fin, there's a fowl without a feather:
If a crow help us in, sirrah, we'll pluck a crow together.
E. Ant. Go, get thee gone, fetch me an iron crow.
Balth. Have patience, sir, O, let it not be so!
Herein you war against your reputation,
And draw within the compass of suspect
Th' unviolated honor of your wife.
Once this—your long experience of [her] wisdom,
Her sober virtue, years, and modesty,
Plead on [her] part some cause to you unknown;
And doubt not, sir, but she will well excuse

61. **keeps**: continues to make.
65. **If . . . sore**: if you were in pain, then this knave she mentions would be in pain; i.e. she means you.
67. **debating**: discussing. **part**: depart.
72. **mad . . . buck.** Cf. *horn-mad*, II.i.57. **bought and sold**: imposed upon. 75. **break a word**: exchange words. 77. **hind**: slave.
80. **crow**: crowbar (with following quibble by Dromio).
83. **pluck . . . together**: pick a bone, settle accounts.
87. **suspect**: suspicion. 89. **Once this**: in short.
90. **virtue**: merit. 92. **well excuse**: explain satisfactorily.

Why at this time the doors are made against you.
Be rul'd by me, depart in patience,
And let us to the Tiger all to dinner;
And about evening come yourself alone
To know the reason of this strange restraint.
If by strong hand you offer to break in
Now in the stirring passage of the day,
A vulgar comment will be made of it;
And that supposed by the common rout
Against your yet ungalled estimation,
That may with foul intrusion enter in,
And dwell upon your grave when you are dead;
For slander lives upon succession,
For ever hous'd where it gets possession.

E. Ant. You have prevail'd. I will depart in quiet,
And in despite of mirth mean to be merry.
I know a wench of excellent discourse,
Pretty and witty; wild, and yet, too, gentle;
There will we dine. This woman that I mean,
My wife (but, I protest, without desert)
Hath oftentimes upbraided me withal:
To her will we to dinner. [*To Angelo.*] Get you home
And fetch the chain; by this I know 'tis made.
Bring it, I pray you, to the Porpentine,
For there's the house. That chain will I bestow
(Be it for nothing but to spite my wife)
Upon mine hostess there. Good sir, make haste.
Since mine own doors refuse to entertain me,
I'll knock elsewhere, to see if they'll disdain me.

Ang. I'll meet you at that place some hour hence.

E. Ant. Do so. This jest shall cost me some expense. *Exeunt.*

[Scene II]

Enter [Luciana] *with* Antipholus of Syracusa.

[*Luc.*] And may it be that you have quite forgot
A husband's office? Shall, Antipholus,
Even in the spring of love, thy love-springs rot?
Shall love, in [building], grow so [ruinous]?
If you did wed my sister for her wealth,
Then for her wealth's sake use her with more kindness:
Or if you like elsewhere, do it by stealth,
Muffle your false love with some show of blindness:
Let not my sister read it in your eye;
Be not thy tongue thy own shame's orator:
Look sweet, speak fair, become disloyalty;
Apparel vice like virtue's harbinger;
Bear a fair presence, though your heart be tainted;
Teach sin the carriage of a holy saint;
Be secret-false: what need she be acquainted?
What simple thief brags of his own [attaint]?
'Tis double wrong, to truant with your bed,
And let her read it in thy looks at board:
Shame hath a bastard fame, well managed;
Ill deeds is doubled with an evil word.
Alas, poor women, make us [but] believe
(Being compact of credit) that you love us;
Though others have the arm, show us the sleeve:
We in your motion turn, and you may move us.
Then, gentle brother, get you in again;
Comfort my sister, cheer her, call her [wife]:
'Tis holy sport to be a little vain,
When the sweet breath of flattery conquers strife.

S. Ant. Sweet mistress—what your name is else, I know not,
Nor by what wonder you do hit of mine—
Less in your knowledge and your grace you show not
Than our earth's wonder, more than earth divine.
Teach me, dear creature, how to think and speak:
Lay open to my earthy, gross conceit,
Smoth'red in errors, feeble, shallow, weak,
The folded meaning of your words' deceit.
Against my soul's pure truth why labor you,
To make it wander in an unknown field?
Are you a god? Would you create me new?
Transform me then, and to your pow'r I'll yield.
But if that I am I, then well I know
Your weeping sister is no wife of mine,
Nor to her bed no homage do I owe:
Far more, far more, to you do I decline.
O, train me not, sweet mermaid, with thy note,
To drown me in thy [sister's] flood of tears.
Sing, siren, for thyself, and I will dote;
Spread o'er the silver waves thy golden hairs,
And as a [bed] I'll take [them], and there lie,
And in that glorious supposition think
He gains by death that hath such means to die:
Let Love, being light, be drowned if she sink!

Luc. What, are you mad, that you do reason so?

S. Ant. Not mad, but mated—how, I do not know.

Luc. It is a fault that springeth from your eye.

S. Ant. For gazing on your beams, fair sun, being by.

Luc. Gaze when you should, and that will clear your sight.

93. made: fastened. **99. stirring passage:** busy traffic.
100. vulgar: public. **101. supposed:** conjectured.
102. ungalled estimation: unblemished reputation.
105. For . . . succession: i.e. one slander begets another, so that its successors (heirs) never end.
108. in . . . mirth: though I do not feel like being merry.
112. desert: my deserving it. **116. Porpentine:** porcupine.

III.ii. Location: Scene continues.
1. may: can. **3. love-springs:** tender shoots of love.
8. Muffle . . . blindness: cover up the love you faithlessly feel for another with an outward appearance that will keep it from being seen.
11. fair: courteously. **become disloyalty:** carry infidelity gracefully. **12. harbinger:** messenger. **14. carriage:** demeanor.

15. what: why.
16. What simple thief: i.e. what thief is so simple (stupid) that he. **attaint:** dishonor; or possibly, conviction of crime.
17. truant with: be unfaithful to. **18. board:** table.
19. bastard fame: sham reputation.
22. Being . . . credit: i.e. as you easily may, for we are entirely composed of credulity.
24. motion: i.e. orbit (referring to the motion of the spheres).
27. vain: false. **30. wonder:** miracle. **hit of:** hit on, guess.
32. earth's wonder. Perhaps an allusion to Queen Elizabeth, before whom the play may have been performed.
34. conceit: understanding.
36. folded: hidden. **deceit:** i.e. ambiguous, apparently misleading, meaning. **44. decline:** incline.
45. train: entice. **mermaid:** i.e. siren. **note:** music.
51. death, die. These words were frequently used with reference to sexual intercourse.
52. light: (1) wanton; (2) buoyant. Antipholus suggests that Love cannot possibly sink and thus cannot be drowned.
53. reason: argue.
54. mated: (1) amazed; (2) matched with a wife. **56. by:** near.

S. Ant. As good to wink, sweet love, as look on night.
Luc. Why call you me love? Call my sister so.
S. Ant. Thy sister's sister.
Luc. That's my sister.
S. Ant. No;
It is thyself, mine own self's better part:
Mine eye's clear eye, my dear heart's dearer heart,
My food, my fortune, and my sweet hope's aim,
My sole earth's heaven, and my heaven's claim.
Luc. All this my sister is, or else should be.
S. Ant. Call thyself sister, sweet, for I am thee:
Thee will I love and with thee lead my life;
Thou hast no husband yet, nor I no wife.
Give me thy hand.
Luc. O soft, sir, hold you still;
I'll fetch my sister to get her good will. *Exit.*

Enter Dromio [of] Syracusa.

S. Ant. Why, how now, Dromio, where run'st thou so fast?

S. Dro. Do you know me, sir? Am I Dromio? Am I your man? Am I myself?

S. Ant. Thou art Dromio, thou art my man, thou art thyself.

S. Dro. I am an ass, I am a woman's man, and besides myself.

S. Ant. What woman's man, and how besides thyself?

S. Dro. Marry, sir, besides myself, I am due to a woman: one that claims me, one that haunts me, one that will have me.

S. Ant. What claim lays she to thee?

S. Dro. Marry, sir, such claim as you would lay to your horse, and she would have me as a beast; not that, I being a beast, she would have me, but that she, being a very beastly creature, lays claim to me.

S. Ant. What is she?

S. Dro. A very reverent body: ay, such a one as a man may not speak of without he say "Sir-reverence." I have but lean luck in the match, and yet is she a wondrous fat marriage.

S. Ant. How dost thou mean a fat marriage?

S. Dro. Marry, sir, she's the kitchen wench and all grease, and I know not what use to put her to but to make a lamp of her and run from her by her own light. I warrant, her rags and the tallow in them will burn a Poland winter: if she lives till doomsday, she'll burn a week longer than the whole world.

S. Ant. What complexion is she of?

S. Dro. Swart, like my shoe, but her face nothing like so clean kept: for why? she sweats, a man may go over shoes in the grime of it.

S. Ant. That's a fault that water will mend.

S. Dro. No, sir, 'tis in grain, Noah's flood could not do it.

S. Ant. What's her name?

S. Dro. Nell, sir; but her name [and] three quarters, that's an ell and three quarters, will not measure her from hip to hip.

S. Ant. Then she bears some breadth?

S. Dro. No longer from head to foot than from hip to hip: she is spherical, like a globe; I could find out countries in her.

S. Ant. In what part of her body stands Ireland?

S. Dro. Marry, sir, in her buttocks, I found it out by the bogs.

S. Ant. Where Scotland?

S. Dro. I found it by the barrenness, hard in the palm of the hand.

S. Ant. Where France?

S. Dro. In her forehead, arm'd and reverted, making war against her heir.

S. Ant. Where England?

S. Dro. I look'd for the chalky cliffs, but I could find no whiteness in them. But I guess, it stood in her chin, by the salt rheum that ran between France and it.

S. Ant. Where Spain?

S. Dro. Faith, I saw it not; but I felt it hot in her breath.

S. Ant. Where America, the Indies?

S. Dro. O, sir, upon her nose, all o'er embellish'd with rubies, carbuncles, sapphires, declining their rich aspect to the hot breath of Spain, who sent whole armadoes of carrects to be ballast at her nose.

S. Ant. Where stood Belgia, the Netherlands?

S. Dro. O, sir, I did not look so low. To conclude, this drudge or diviner laid claim to me, call'd me Dromio, swore I was assur'd to her, told me what privy marks I had about me, as the mark of my shoulder, the mole in my neck, the great wart on my left arm, that I, amaz'd, ran from her as a witch.
And I think, if my breast had not been made of faith, and my heart of steel,
She had transform'd me to a curtal dog, and made me turn i' th' wheel.

S. Ant. Go hie thee presently, post to the road,
And if the wind blow any way from shore,
I will not harbor in this town to-night.
If any bark put forth, come to the mart,

58. wink: close the eyes.
64. My . . . claim: my sole heaven on earth and my claim on heaven hereafter. **78. besides myself:** (1) out of my mind; (2) also myself.
90. reverent: reverend, worthy (used primarily for the sake of the following quibble in *Sir-reverence*).
91. without: unless. **Sir-reverence:** save your reverence (a conventional phrase of apology before an offensive expression).
92. lean: poor.
99. doomsday: i.e. when the world was supposedly to be consumed by fire. **102. Swart:** swarthy, dark.

106. in grain: fast dyed, indelible.
109. Nell. Elsewhere she is called Luce.
110. an ell: a measure of 45 inches (with play on *a Nell*).
120. barrenness. Referring to the calluses on the palm of a kitchen drudge, or to the hand's dryness (a moist hand was thought to denote fruitfulness). Dover Wilson detects a pun on *barren ness* (i.e. promontory).
123–24. arm'd . . . heir. An allusion to the armed resistance of the Catholic Holy League to Protestant Henry of Navarre, designated heir to the French throne by Henry III in 1589.
123. arm'd and reverted: (1) in arms and revolted; (2) covered with an eruption and receding (alluding to loss of hair from venereal disease). **124. heir.** With pun on *hair*. **127. them:** i.e. her teeth.
128. rheum: mucus from the nose. **135. declining:** bending.
137. armadoes: armadas, fleets. **carrects:** carracks, galleons. **ballast:** ballasted, loaded. **140. diviner:** sorceress.
141. assur'd: betrothed. **142. of:** on.
146. curtal dog: dog with a docked tail. **turn . . . wheel:** turn the spit by running in a wheel.
147. presently: at once. **road:** roadstead, harbor.

Where I will walk till thou return to me.
If every one knows us, and we know none,
'Tis time, I think, to trudge, pack, and be gone.

S. Dro. As from a bear a man would run for life,
So fly I from her that would be my wife. *Exit.*

S. Ant. There's none but witches do inhabit here,
And therefore 'tis high time that I were hence.
She that doth call me husband, even my soul
Doth for a wife abhor. But her fair sister,
Possess'd with such a gentle sovereign grace,
Of such enchanting presence and discourse,
Hath almost made me traitor to myself;
But lest myself be guilty to self-wrong,
I'll stop mine ears against the mermaid's song.

Enter ANGELO *with the chain.*

Ang. Master Antipholus—

S. Ant. Ay, that's my name.

Ang. I know it well, sir. Lo here's the chain.
I thought to have ta'en you at the Porpentine;
The chain unfinish'd made me stay thus long.

S. Ant. What is your will that I shall do with this?

Ang. What please yourself, sir; I have made it for you.

S. Ant. Made it for me, sir! I bespoke it not.

Ang. Not once, nor twice, but twenty times you have.
Go home with it, and please your wife withal,
And soon at supper-time I'll visit you,
And then receive my money for the chain.

S. Ant. I pray you, sir, receive the money now,
For fear you ne'er see chain nor money more.

Ang. You are a merry man, sir, fare you well. *Exit.*

S. Ant. What I should think of this, I cannot tell:
But this I think, there's no man is so vain
That would refuse so fair an offer'd chain.
I see a man here needs not live by shifts,
When in the streets he meets such golden gifts.
I'll to the mart and there for Dromio stay:
If any ship put out, then straight away. *Exit.*

ACT IV, SCENE I

Enter a [SECOND] MERCHANT [OF EPHESUS, ANGELO *the*] *goldsmith, and an* OFFICER.

[*2. E.*] *Mer.* You know since Pentecost the sum is due,
And since I have not much importun'd you,
Nor now I had not, but that I am bound
To Persia, and want guilders for my voyage:
Therefore make present satisfaction,
Or I'll attach you by this officer.

153. **trudge, pack, be gone.** These words are synonymous. 160. **Possess'd with:** possessing. 163. **to:** of.
171. **bespoke:** requested. 180. **vain:** foolish.
182. **shifts:** stratagems, tricks.

IV.i. **Location:** The mart.
1. **Pentecost:** Whitsuntide. 5. **present:** immediate.
6. **attach:** arrest.

Ang. Even just the sum that I do owe to you
Is growing to me by Antipholus,
And in the instant that I met with you
He had of me a chain. At five a' clock
I shall receive the money for the same:
Pleaseth you walk with me down to his house,
I will discharge my bond, and thank you too.

Enter ANTIPHOLUS [OF] EPHESUS, DROMIO [OF EPHESUS] *from the Courtezan's.*

Off. That labor may you save; see where he comes.

E. Ant. While I go to the goldsmith's house, go thou
And buy a rope's end; that will I bestow
Among my wife and [her] confederates,
For locking me out of my doors by day.
But soft, I see the goldsmith. Get thee gone,
Buy thou a rope, and bring it home to me.

E. Dro. I buy a thousand pound a year! I buy a rope! *Exit Dromio.*

E. Ant. A man is well holp up that trusts to you:
I promised your presence and the chain,
But neither chain nor goldsmith came to me:
Belike you thought our love would last too long
If it were chain'd together, and therefore came not.

Ang. Saving your merry humor, here's the note
How much your chain weighs to the utmost charect,
The fineness of the gold, and chargeful fashion,
Which doth amount to three odd ducats more
Than I stand debted to this gentleman.
I pray you see him presently discharg'd,
For he is bound to sea, and stays but for it.

E. Ant. I am not furnish'd with the present money:
Besides, I have some business in the town.
Good signior, take the stranger to my house,
And with you take the chain, and bid my wife
Disburse the sum on the receipt thereof.
Perchance I will be there as soon as you.

Ang. Then you will bring the chain to her yourself?

E. Ant. No, bear it with you, lest I come not time enough.

Ang. Well, sir, I will. Have you the chain about you?

E. Ant. And if I have not, sir, I hope you have:
Or else you may return without your money.

Ang. Nay, come, I pray you, sir, give me the chain:
Both wind and tide stays for this gentleman,
And I, to blame, have held him here too long.

E. Ant. Good Lord! you use this dalliance to excuse
Your breach of promise to the Porpentine:

8. **growing . . . by:** due . . . from.
16. **bestow:** employ.
21. **I . . . year.** An obscure remark. Dromio may mean that in buying the rope he will be purchasing an annuity that will yield him a thousand poundings (i.e. beatings) a year. 22. **holp:** helped.
25. **Belike:** probably. 28. **utmost charect:** last carat.
29. **chargeful fashion:** expensive design or workmanship.
30. **ducats:** gold (or sometimes silver) coins of varying value, widely used in European countries. 41. **time enough:** in time.
48. **dalliance:** trifling, idle delay.

I should have chid you for not bringing it,
But like a shrew you first begin to brawl.
[*2. E.*] *Mer.* The hour steals on, I pray you, sir, dispatch.
Ang. You hear how he importunes me—the chain!
E. Ant. Why, give it to my wife, and fetch your money.
Ang. Come, come, you know I gave it you even now.
Either send the chain, or send me by some token.
E. Ant. Fie, now you run this humor out of breath.
Come, where's the chain? I pray you let me see it.
[*2. E.*] *Mer.* My business cannot brook this dalliance.
Good sir, say whe'r you'll answer me or no:
If not, I'll leave him to the officer.
E. Ant. I answer you? What should I answer you?
Ang. The money that you owe me for the chain.
E. Ant. I owe you none, till I receive the chain.
Ang. You know I gave it you half an hour since.
E. Ant. You gave me none, you wrong me much to say so.
Ang. You wrong me more, sir, in denying it.
Consider how it stands upon my credit.
[*2. E.*] *Mer.* Well, officer, arrest him at my suit.
Off. I do, and charge you in the Duke's name to obey me.
Ang. This touches me in reputation.
Either consent to pay this sum for me
Or I attach you by this officer.
E. Ant. Consent to pay thee that I never had!
Arrest me, foolish fellow, if thou dar'st.
Ang. Here is thy fee, arrest him, officer.
I would not spare my brother in this case,
If he should scorn me so apparently.
Off. I do arrest you, sir: you hear the suit.
E. Ant. I do obey thee, till I give thee bail.
But, sirrah, you shall buy this sport as dear
As all the metal in your shop will answer.
Ang. Sir, sir, I shall have law in Ephesus,
To your notorious shame, I doubt it not.

Enter DROMIO [OF] SYRACUSA *from the bay.*

S. Dro. Master, there's a bark of Epidamium
That stays but till her owner comes aboard,
And then, sir, she bears away. Our fraughtage, sir,
I have convey'd aboard, and I have bought
The oil, the balsamum, and aqua-vitae.
The ship is in her trim, the merry wind
Blows fair from land: they stay for nought at all
But for their owner, master, and yourself.
E. Ant. How now? a madman? Why, thou peevish sheep,
What ship of Epidamium stays for me?
S. Dro. A ship you sent me to, to hire waftage.

56. **send me . . . token:** send with me some object belonging to you to prove that the request comes from you. 59. **brook:** tolerate.
60. **whe'r:** whether. **answer:** satisfy, pay.
68. **stands . . . credit:** concerns my reputation for probity in business dealings. 78. **apparently:** openly. 87. **fraughtage:** cargo.
89. **balsamum:** balm. **aqua-vitae:** spirits.
90. **in her trim:** rigged and ready to sail.
93. **peevish:** silly. **sheep.** With a pun on *ship* (line 94), pronounced similarly. 95. **waftage:** passage.

E. Ant. Thou drunken slave, I sent thee for a rope,
And told thee to what purpose and what end.
S. Dro. You sent me for a rope's end as soon:
You sent me to the bay, sir, for a bark.
E. Ant. I will debate this matter at more leisure,
And teach your ears to list me with more heed.
To Adriana, villain, hie thee straight:
Give her this key, and tell her, in the desk
That's cover'd o'er with Turkish tapestry
There is a purse of ducats; let her send it.
Tell her I am arrested in the street,
And that shall bail me. Hie thee, slave, be gone!
On, officer, to prison till it come.

Exeunt [*all but Dromio of Syracuse*].

S. Dro. To Adriana! That is where we din'd,
Where Dowsabel did claim me for her husband:
She is too big, I hope, for me to compass.
Thither I must, although against my will,
For servants must their masters' minds fulfill. *Exit.*

[SCENE II]

Enter ADRIANA *and* LUCIANA.

Adr. Ah, Luciana, did he tempt thee so?
Mightst thou perceive austerely in his eye
That he did plead in earnest? yea or no?
Look'd he or red or pale, or sad or merrily?
What observation mad'st thou in this case
[Of] his heart's meteors tilting in his face?
Luc. First he denied you had in him no right.
Adr. He meant he did me none: the more my spite.
Luc. Then swore he that he was a stranger here.
Adr. And true he swore, though yet forsworn he were.
Luc. Then pleaded I for you.
Adr. And what said he?
Luc. That love I begg'd for you, he begg'd of me.
Adr. With what persuasion did he tempt thy love?
Luc. With words that in an honest suit might move.
First he did praise my beauty, then my speech.
Adr. Didst speak him fair?
Luc. Have patience, I beseech.
Adr. I cannot, nor I will not, hold me still,
My tongue, though not my heart, shall have his will.
He is deformed, crooked, old, and sere,
Ill-fac'd, worse bodied, shapeless every where;
Vicious, ungentle, foolish, blunt, unkind,
Stigmatical in making, worse in mind.
Luc. Who would be jealous then of such a one?
No evil lost is wail'd when it is gone.
Adr. Ah, but I think him better than I say,

98. **for . . . end:** i.e. to be hanged. 101. **list:** listen to.
110. **Dowsabel:** a name derived from French *douce et belle*, i.e. gentle and beautiful, here applied ironically to Nell (Luce).
111. **compass:** (1) achieve; (2) put my arm round.

IV.ii. **Location:** Before the house of Antipholus of Ephesus.
2. **austerely:** seriously.
6. **heart's meteors:** i.e. passions. **tilting:** contending.
7. **no:** i.e. any. 8. **spite:** grief, vexation.
16. **him fair:** to him courteously. 18. **his:** its.
19. **sere:** withered. 20. **shapeless:** misshapen.
22. **Stigmatical in making:** physically deformed by nature.

And yet would herein others' eyes were worse:
Far from her nest the lapwing cries away;
My heart prays for him, though my tongue do curse.

Enter Dromio [of] Syracusa.

S. Dro. Here, go: the desk, the purse! [Sweat] now, make haste!
Luc. How hast thou lost thy breath?
S. Dro. By running fast.
Adr. Where is thy master, Dromio? Is he well?
S. Dro. No, he's in Tartar limbo, worse than hell:
A devil in an everlasting garment hath him;
[One] whose hard heart is button'd up with steel;
A fiend, a fairy, pitiless and rough;
A wolf, nay worse, a fellow all in buff;
A back-friend, a shoulder-clapper, one that countermands
The passages of alleys, creeks, and narrow lands;
A hound that runs counter, and yet draws dry-foot well;
One that before the judgment carries poor souls to hell.
Adr. Why, man, what is the matter?
S. Dro. I do not know the matter, he is 'rested on the case.
Adr. What, is he arrested? Tell me at whose suit.
S. Dro. I know not at whose suit he is arrested well;
But ['a's] in a suit of buff which 'rested him, that can I tell.
Will you send him, mistress, redemption, the money in his desk?
Adr. Go fetch it, sister. (*Exit Luciana.*) This I wonder at,
[That] he unknown to me should be in debt.
Tell me, was he arrested on a band?
S. Dro. Not on a band but on a stronger thing:
A chain, a chain! Do you not [hear] it ring?
Adr. What, the chain?
S. Dro. No, no, the bell, 'tis time that I were gone:
It was two ere I left him, and now the clock strikes one.
Adr. The hours come back! that did I never [hear].
S. Dro. O yes, if any hour meet a sergeant, 'a turns back for very fear.

26. herein . . . worse: i.e. that in seeing him other women would view him even less favorably (so that he would not be attractive to them).
27. lapwing: pewit, which tries to divert attention from the nest to protect its young.
32. Tartar: Tartarean, infernal. **limbo:** loosely, hell; also a cant term for prison.
33. everlasting garment: i.e. the arresting officer's buff-leather jerkin, with a play on "suit of durance" (see IV.iii.27).
35. fairy: malevolent spirit.
37. back-friend: false friend; but also alluding to an officer's clapping a man on the back or shoulder to signify arrest. **countermands:** prohibits. **38. creeks:** narrow winding passages.
39. counter: (1) following a scent in the opposite direction to that taken by the game; (2) debtors' prison. **draws dry-foot:** tracks game by the scent of the foot.
40. judgment: legal judgment (with a quibble on "Judgment Day"). **hell:** another term for a debtors' prison. **41. matter:** cause.
42. on the case: a type of legal action, but with a quibble on *case* = container (in contrast to *matter* = contents), i.e. skin or suit of clothes (recalling "back-friend" and "shoulder-clapper").
45. 'a's: he's.
49. band: bond (but Dromio quibbles on the sense "neck-band"); cf. IV.iii.31. **56. sergeant:** arresting officer.

Adr. As if Time were in debt! How fondly dost thou reason!
S. Dro. Time is a very bankrout and owes more than he's worth to season.
Nay, he's a thief too: have you not heard men say,
That Time comes stealing on by night and day?
If ['a] be in debt and theft, and a sergeant in the way,
Hath he not reason to turn back an hour in a day?

Enter Luciana.

Adr. Go, Dromio, there's the money, bear it straight,
And bring thy master home immediately.
Come, sister, I am press'd down with conceit—
Conceit, my comfort and my injury. *Exeunt.*

[Scene III]

Enter Antipholus [of] Syracusa.

[*S. Ant.*] There's not a man I meet but doth salute me
As if I were their well-acquainted friend,
And every one doth call me by my name:
Some tender money to me, some invite me;
Some other give me thanks for kindnesses;
Some offer me commodities to buy.
Even now a tailor call'd me in his shop,
And show'd me silks that he had bought for me,
And therewithal took measure of my body.
Sure these are but imaginary wiles,
And Lapland sorcerers inhabit here.

Enter Dromio [of] Syracusa.

S. Dro. Master, here's the gold you sent me for. What, have you got the picture of old Adam new apparell'd?

S. Ant. What gold is this? What Adam dost thou mean?

S. Dro. Not that Adam that kept the Paradise, but that Adam that keeps the prison; he that goes in the calve's-skin that was kill'd for the Prodigal; he that came behind you, sir, like an evil angel, and bid you forsake your liberty.

S. Ant. I understand thee not.

S. Dro. No? Why, 'tis a plain case: he that went like a base-viol in a case of leather; the man, sir, that when gentlemen are tir'd, gives them a sob and 'rests

57. fondly: foolishly.
58. bankrout: bankrupt. **to season:** at any given moment.
65. conceit: thought, imaginings.

IV.iii. Location: The mart.
10. imaginary wiles: tricks of the imagination.
11. Lapland. Notorious for witchcraft and sorcery.
13. have . . . apparell'd: have you found the arresting officer (likened, because of his leather jerkin, to Adam clothed in beasts' skins) a new suit (with obvious pun) and thus got rid of him.
19. calve's-skin . . . Prodigal. Allusion to the story of the Prodigal Son, for whom a fatted calf was killed (see Luke 15:11–32).
20. evil angel. Perhaps an allusion (by contraries) is intended to the good angel who delivered Peter from prison (Acts 12:6–11), or (directly) to the Evil Angel in Marlowe's *Doctor Faustus*. See also lines 40–41.
25. sob: a rest given to a horse to recover its wind (with following pun on *'rests*).

them; he, sir, that takes pity on decay'd men and gives them suits of durance; he that sets up his rest to do more exploits with his mace than a morris-pike.

S. Ant. What, thou mean'st an officer?

S. Dro. Ay, sir, the sergeant of the band: he that brings any man to answer it that breaks his band; one that thinks a man always going to bed and says, "God give you good rest!"

S. Ant. Well, sir, there rest in your foolery. Is there any ships puts forth to-night? May we be gone?

S. Dro. Why, sir, I brought you word an hour since that the bark *Expedition* put forth to-night, and then were you hind'red by the sergeant to tarry for the hoy *Delay*. Here are the angels that you sent for to deliver you.

S. Ant. The fellow is distract, and so am I,
And here we wander in illusions:
Some blessed power deliver us from hence!

Enter a COURTEZAN.

Cour. Well met, well met, Master Antipholus.
I see, sir, you have found the goldsmith now.
Is that the chain you promis'd me to-day?

S. Ant. Sathan, avoid, I charge thee tempt me not.

S. Dro. Master, is this Mistress Sathan?

S. Ant. It is the devil.

S. Dro. Nay, she is worse, she is the devil's dam, and here she comes in the habit of a light wench; and thereof comes that the wenches say, "God damn me," that's as much to say, "God make me a light wench." It is written, they appear to men like angels of light, light is an effect of fire, and fire will burn: *ergo*, light wenches will burn. Come not near her.

Cour. Your man and you are marvellous merry, sir.
Will you go with me? we'll mend our dinner here.

S. Dro. Master, if [you] do, expect spoon-meat, or bespeak a long spoon.

S. Ant. Why, Dromio?

S. Dro. Marry, he must have a long spoon that must eat with the devil.

S. Ant. Avoid then, fiend, what tell'st thou me of supping?
Thou art, as you are all, a sorceress:
I conjure thee to leave me and be gone.

Cour. Give me the ring of mine you had at dinner,
Or, for my diamond, the chain you promis'd,
And I'll be gone, sir, and not trouble you.

S. Dro. Some devils ask but the parings of one's nail,
A rush, a hair, a drop of blood, a pin,
A nut, a cherry-stone;
But she, more covetous, would have a chain.
Master, be wise, and if you give it her,
The devil will shake her chain, and fright us with it.

Cour. I pray you, sir, my ring, or else the chain;
I hope you do not mean to cheat me so?

S. Ant. Avaunt, thou witch! Come, Dromio, let us go.

S. Dro. "Fly pride," says the peacock: mistress, that you know.

Exit [*with Antipholus of Syracuse*].

Cour. Now out of doubt Antipholus is mad,
Else would he never so demean himself.
A ring he hath of mine worth forty ducats,
And for the same he promis'd me a chain:
Both one and other he denies me now.
The reason that I gather he is mad,
Besides this present instance of his rage,
Is a mad tale he told to-day at dinner,
Of his own doors being shut against his entrance.
Belike his wife, acquainted with his fits,
On purpose shut the doors against his way.
My way is now to hie home to his house,
And tell his wife that, being lunatic,
He rush'd into my house, and took perforce
My ring away. This course I fittest choose,
For forty ducats is too much to lose. [*Exit.*]

[SCENE IV]

Enter ANTIPHOLUS [OF] EPHESUS *with* [*the* OFFICER].

E. Ant. Fear me not, man, I will not break away;
I'll give thee, ere I leave thee, so much money,
To warrant thee, as I am 'rested for.
My wife is in a wayward mood to-day,
And will not lightly trust the messenger,
That I should be attach'd in Ephesus;
I tell you, 'twill sound harshly in her ears.

Enter DROMIO [OF] EPHESUS *with a rope's end.*

Here comes my man: I think he brings the money.
How now, sir? have you that I sent you for?

E. Dro. Here's that, I warrant you, will pay them all.

E. Ant. But where's the money?

E. Dro. Why, sir, I gave the money for the rope.

E. Ant. Five hundred ducats, villain, for a rope?

E. Dro. I'll serve you, sir, five hundred at the rate.

E. Ant. To what end did I bid thee hie thee home?

---

27. **durance:** (1) durable cloth; (2) imprisonment. **sets . . . rest:** ventures all (continuing the pun on *'rest*, which occurs once more in line 33).
28. **mace:** club carried by a constable. **morris-pike:** kind of pike supposedly of Moorish origin.
40. **hoy:** small vessel. **angels:** gold coins worth about 10 shillings.
42. **distract:** distracted, mad.
48. **Sathan, avoid:** Satan, be off (Matthew 4:10; the Geneva Version is here quoted exactly).
52. **habit:** (1) dress; (2) demeanor, manner. **light:** wanton.
55–56. **angels of light.** See 2 Corinthians 11:14: ". . . Satan himself is transformed into an angel of light." 56. **ergo:** therefore.
57. **burn:** communicate venereal disease.
59. **Will you:** if you will. **mend:** supplement.
60. **spoon-meat:** food for infants, hence delicacies.

75. **and if:** if.
80. **Fly . . . peacock:** i.e. an accusation of dishonesty coming from a dishonest person is as out of place as a warning against pride would be from the peacock. 82. **demean:** conduct. 87. **rage:** insanity.
94. **perforce:** forcibly.

IV.iv. Location: Scene continues.
3. **warrant thee:** give you security. 5. **trust:** credit.
6. **attach'd:** arrested. 14. **at the rate:** for that amount.

E. Dro. To a rope's end, sir, and to that end am I return'd.
E. Ant. And to that end, sir, I will welcome you. [*Beats Dromio.*]

Off. Good sir, be patient.

E. Dro. Nay, 'tis for me to be patient: I am in adversity.

Off. Good now, hold thy tongue.

E. Dro. Nay, rather persuade him to hold his hands.

E. Ant. Thou whoreson, senseless villain!

E. Dro. I would I were senseless, sir, that I might not feel your blows.

E. Ant. Thou art sensible in nothing but blows, and so is an ass.

E. Dro. I am an ass indeed; you may prove it by my long ears. I have serv'd him from the hour of my nativity to this instant, and have nothing at his hands for my service but blows. When I am cold, he heats me with beating; when I am warm, he cools me with beating. I am wak'd with it when I sleep, rais'd with it when I sit, driven out of doors with it when I go from home, welcom'd home with it when I return; nay, I bear it on my shoulders, as a beggar wont her brat; and I think when he hath lam'd me, I shall beg with it from door to door.

Enter Adriana, Luciana, Courtezan, *and a schoolmaster call'd* Pinch.

E. Ant. Come go along, my wife is coming yonder.

E. Dro. Mistress, *respice finem*, respect your end, or rather, the prophecy like the parrot, "beware the rope's end."

E. Ant. Wilt thou still talk? *Beats Dromio.*

Cour. How say you now? Is not your husband mad?
Adr. His incivility confirms no less.
Good Doctor Pinch, you are a conjurer,
Establish him in his true sense again,
And I will please you what you will demand.
Luc. Alas, how fiery, and how sharp, he looks!
Cour. Mark, how he trembles in his ecstasy!
Pinch. Give me your hand, and let me feel your pulse.
E. Ant. There is my hand, and let it feel your ear. [*Strikes Pinch.*]
Pinch. I charge thee, Sathan, hous'd within this man,
To yield possession to my holy prayers,
And to thy state of darkness hie thee straight:
I conjure thee by all the saints in heaven!
E. Ant. Peace, doting wizard, peace! I am not mad.
Adr. O that thou wert not, poor distressed soul!
E. Ant. You minion, you, are these your customers?
Did this companion with the saffron face
Revel and feast it at my house to-day,
Whilst upon me the guilty doors were shut,
And I denied to enter in my house?
Adr. O husband, God doth know you din'd at home,
Where would you had remain'd until this time,
Free from these slanders and this open shame.
E. Ant. Din'd at home? Thou villain, what sayest thou?
E. Dro. Sir, sooth to say, you did not dine at home.
E. Ant. Were not my doors lock'd up, and I shut out?
E. Dro. Perdie, your doors were lock'd, and you shut out.
E. Ant. And did not she herself revile me there?
E. Dro. Sans fable, she herself revil'd you there.
E. Ant. Did not her kitchen maid rail, taunt, and scorn me?
E. Dro. Certes she did, the kitchen vestal scorn'd you.
E. Ant. And did not I in rage depart from thence?
E. Dro. In verity you did, my bones bears witness,
That since have felt the vigor of his rage.
Adr. Is't good to soothe him in these contraries?
Pinch. It is no shame; the fellow finds his vein,
And yielding to him, humors well his frenzy.
E. Ant. Thou hast suborn'd the goldsmith to arrest me.
Adr. Alas, I sent you money to redeem you,
By Dromio here, who came in haste for it.
E. Dro. Money by me? Heart and good will you might,
But surely, master, not a rag of money.
E. Ant. Went'st not thou to her for a purse of ducats?
Adr. He came to me, and I deliver'd it.
Luc. And I am witness with her that she did.
E. Dro. God and the rope-maker bear me witness
That I was sent for nothing but a rope!
Pinch. Mistress, both man and master is possess'd:
I know it by their pale and deadly looks.
They must be bound and laid in some dark room.
E. Ant. Say wherefore didst thou lock me forth to-day?
And why dost thou deny the bag of gold?

21. **Good now:** pray you.
27. **sensible in:** (1) senitive to; (2) made sensible by.
30. **ears.** With pun on *years*; i.e. Dromio is an ass for not having left Antipholus' service long ago.
38. **wont:** is accustomed to (bear).
39. **I . . . it:** i.e. all Iwill get is a beating (the usual reward of beggars).
41. **respice finem:** look to your end (with pun on *respice funem*, look to the hangman's rope).
42. **prophesy: . . . parrot.** There are references to parrots' being taught to say "rope," i.e. apparently prophesying that the hearer was destined for hanging.
47. **conjurer.** Being able to speak Latin, Pinch could conjure evil spirits. 49. **please:** pay. 50. **sharp:** angry.
51. **ecstasy:** madness.

60. **minion:** hussy. 61. **companion:** fellow. **saffron:** yellow.
64. **denied . . . in:** refused admittance to. 67. **slanders:** disgraces.
71. **Perdie:** assuredly (a weakened oath, like French *pardieu*, originally "by God"). 73. **Sans:** without.
75. **Certes:** certainly. **kitchen vestal.** Johnson explains that Luce's task was, "like that of the vestal virgins, to keep the fire burning." There is obvious irony in the bracketing of Luce with virgins.
79. **soothe:** humor.
82. **suborn'd . . . me:** induced the goldsmith to lie for you in order to have me arrested. 86. **rag:** scrap. 93. **deadly:** deathly.
94. **bound . . . room.** The regular treatment for the insane in Shakespeare's day. 95. **forth:** out.

Adr. I did not, gentle husband, lock thee forth.
E. Dro. And, gentle master, I receiv'd no gold;
But I confess, sir, that we were lock'd out.
Adr. Dissembling villain, thou speak'st false in both.
E. Ant. Dissembling harlot, thou art false in all,
And art confederate with a damned pack
To make a loathsome abject scorn of me;
But with these nails I'll pluck out these false eyes
That would behold in me this shameful sport.

Enter three or four, and offer to bind him; he strives.

Adr. O, bind him, bind him, let him not come near me.
Pinch. More company! the fiend is strong within him.
Luc. Ay me, poor man, how pale and wan he looks!
E. Ant. What, will you murther me? Thou jailer, thou,
I am thy prisoner. Wilt thou suffer them
To make a rescue?
Off. Masters, let him go:
He is my prisoner, and you shall not have him.
Pinch. Go bind this man, for he is frantic too.
[*They offer to bind Dromio of Ephesus.*]
Adr. What wilt thou do, thou peevish officer?
Hast thou delight to see a wretched man
Do outrage and displeasure to himself?
Off. He is my prisoner; if I let him go,
The debt he owes will be requir'd of me.
Adr. I will discharge thee ere I go from thee:
Bear me forthwith unto his creditor,
And knowing how the debt grows, I will pay it.
Good Master Doctor, see him safe convey'd
Home to my house. O most unhappy day!
E. Ant. O most unhappy strumpet!
E. Dro. Master, I am here ent'red in bond for you.
E. Ant. Out on thee, villain, wherefore dost thou mad me?
E. Dro. Will you be bound for nothing? Be mad, good master,
Cry "The devil!"
Luc. God help, poor souls, how idlely do they talk!
Adr. Go bear him hence. Sister, go you with me.
Exeunt. Manent Officer, Adriana, Luciana, Courtezan.
Say now, whose suit is he arrested at?
Off. One Angelo, a goldsmith. Do you know him?
Adr. I know the man; what is the sum he owes?
Off. Two hundred ducats.
Adr. Say, how grows it due?
Off. Due for a chain your husband had of him.
Adr. He did bespeak a chain for me, but had it not.
Cour. When as your husband all in rage to-day
Came to my house, and took away my ring—
The ring I saw upon his finger now—
Straight after did I meet him with a chain.
Adr. It may be so, but I did never see it.
Come, jailer, bring me where the goldsmith is,
I long to know the truth hereof at large.

Enter Antipholus [of] Syracusa, *with his rapier drawn, and* Dromio [of] Syracusa.

Luc. God for thy mercy! they are loose again.
Adr. And come with naked swords: let's call more help
To have them bound again.
Off. Away, they'll kill us.
Exeunt omnes [but Antipholus of Syracuse and Dromio of Syracuse] as fast as may be, frighted.
S. Ant. I see these witches are afraid of swords.
S. Dro. She that would be your wife now ran from you.
S. Ant. Come to the Centaur, fetch our stuff from thence;
I long that we were safe and sound aboard.

S. Dro. Faith, stay here this night, they will surely do us no harm. You saw they speak us fair, give us gold: methinks they are such a gentle nation that, but for the mountain of mad flesh that claims marriage of me, I could find in my heart to stay here still, and turn witch.

S. Ant. I will not stay to-night for all the town:
Therefore away, to get our stuff aboard. *Exeunt.*

ACT V, Scene I

Enter the [Second] Merchant *and* [Angelo] *the goldsmith.*

Ang. I am sorry, sir, that I have hind'red you,
But I protest he had the chain of me,
Though most dishonestly he doth deny it.
[*2. E.*] *Mer.* How is the man esteem'd here in the city?
Ang. Of very reverent reputation, sir,
Of credit infinite, highly belov'd,
Second to none that lives here in the city:
His word might bear my wealth at any time.
[*2. E.*] *Mer.* Speak softly, yonder, as I think, he walks.

Enter Antipholus [of Syracuse] *and* Dromio [of Syracuse] *again.*

Ang. 'Tis so; and that self chain about his neck,
Which he forswore most monstrously to have.
Good sir, draw near to me, I'll speak to him.
Signior Antipholus, I wonder much
That you would put me to this shame and trouble,
And, not without some scandal to yourself,
With circumstance and oaths so to deny
This chain which now you wear so openly.

102. pack: gang of conspirators.
111. make a rescue: forcibly remove a person from legal custody.
113 s.d. offer: make an attempt.
114. peevish: foolish. **116. displeasure:** offense.
119. discharge: pay.
121. knowing . . . grows: as soon as I know how the debt arose.
126. mad: madden. **129. idlely:** idly, irrationally.

143. at large: in full. **149. stuff:** baggage.

V.i. Location: Before a priory.
8. His . . . time: his word would be sufficient security for as much as I am worth. **10. self:** same. **11. forswore:** denied on oath.
16. circumstance: details, particulars.

Beside the charge, the shame, imprisonment,
You have done wrong to this my honest friend,
Who, but for staying on our controversy,
Had hoisted sail and put to sea to-day.
This chain you had of me, can you deny it?

S. Ant. I think I had, I never did deny it.

[*2. E.*] *Mer.* Yes, that you did, sir, and forswore it too.

S. Ant. Who heard me to deny it or forswear it?

[*2. E.*] *Mer.* These ears of mine thou know'st did hear thee;
Fie on thee, wretch, 'tis pity that thou liv'st
To walk where any honest men resort.

S. Ant. Thou art a villain to impeach me thus:
I'll prove mine honor and mine honesty
Against thee presently, if thou dar'st stand.

[*2. E.*] *Mer.* I dare, and do defy thee for a villain.
They draw.

Enter ADRIANA, LUCIANA, COURTEZAN, *and others.*

Adr. Hold, hurt him not for God sake! he is mad.
Some get within him, take his sword away:
Bind Dromio too, and bear them to my house.

S. Dro. Run, master, run, for God's sake take a house!
This is some priory, in, or we are spoil'd.
Exeunt [*Antipholus of Syracuse and Dromio of Syracuse*] *to the priory.*

Enter LADY ABBESS.

Abb. Be quiet, people. Wherefore throng you hither?

Adr. To fetch my poor distracted husband hence.
Let us come in, that we may bind him fast,
And bear him home for his recovery.

Ang. I knew he was not in his perfect wits.

[*2. E.*] *Mer.* I am sorry now that I did draw on him.

Abb. How long hath this possession held the man?

Adr. This week he hath been heavy, sour, sad,
And much different from the man he was;
But till this afternoon his passion
Ne'er brake into extremity of rage.

Abb. Hath he not lost much wealth by wrack of sea?
Buried some dear friend? Hath not else his eye
Stray'd his affection in unlawful love—
A sin prevailing much in youthful men,
Who give their eyes the liberty of gazing?
Which of these sorrows is he subject to?

Adr. To none of these, except it be the last,
Namely, some love that drew him oft from home.

Abb. You should for that have reprehended him.

Adr. Why, so I did.

Abb. Ay, but not rough enough.

Adr. As roughly as my modesty would let me.

Abb. Haply, in private.

Adr. And in assemblies too.

Abb. Ay, but not enough.

Adr. It was the copy of our conference:
In bed he slept not for my urging it;
At board he fed not for my urging it;
Alone, it was the subject of my theme;
In company I often glanced it;
Still did I tell him it was vild and bad.

Abb. And thereof came it that the man was mad.
The venom clamors of a jealous woman
Poisons more deadly than a mad dog's tooth.
It seems his sleeps were hind'red by thy railing,
And thereof comes it that his head is light.
Thou say'st his meat was sauc'd with thy upbraidings:
Unquiet meals make ill digestions,
Thereof the raging fire of fever bred,
And what's a fever but a fit of madness?
Thou say'st his sports were hind'red by thy brawls:
Sweet recreation barr'd, what doth ensue
But moody and dull melancholy,
Kinsman to grim and comfortless despair,
And at her heels a huge infectious troop
Of pale distemperatures and foes to life?
In food, in sport, and life-preserving rest
To be disturb'd, would mad or man or beast:
The consequence is then, thy jealous fits
Hath scar'd thy husband from the use of wits.

Luc. She never reprehended him but mildly,
When he demean'd himself rough, rude, and wildly.
Why bear you these rebukes, and answer not?

Adr. She did betray me to my own reproof.
Good people, enter and lay hold on him.

Abb. No, not a creature enters in my house.

Adr. Then let your servants bring my husband forth.

Abb. Neither. He took this place for sanctuary,
And it shall privilege him from your hands
Till I have brought him to his wits again,
Or lose my labor in assaying it.

Adr. I will attend my husband, be his nurse,
Diet his sickness, for it is my office,
And will have no attorney but myself,
And therefore let me have him home with me.

Abb. Be patient, for I will not let him stir
Till I have us'd the approved means I have,
With wholesome syrups, drugs, and holy prayers,
To make of him a formal man again:
It is a branch and parcel of mine oath,
A charitable duty of my order,
Therefore depart, and leave him here with me.

Adr. I will not hence, and leave my husband here;
And ill it doth beseem your holiness
To separate the husband and the wife.

Abb. Be quiet and depart, thou shalt not have him.
[*Exit.*]

Luc. Complain unto the Duke of this indignity.

18. charge: expense. **20. staying on:** delaying as a result of. **29. impeach:** accuse. **31. presently:** immediately. **34. within him:** under his guard. **36. take:** take refuge in. **37. spoil'd:** done for. **47. passion:** disorder. **48. rage:** madness. **49. wrack of:** shipwreck at. **51. Stray'd:** led astray.

62. copy . . . conference: theme of all our talk. **66. glanced:** hinted at. **67. Still:** continually. **vild:** vile. **69. venom:** venomous. **82. distemperatures:** physical disorders. **84. mad or:** madden either. **99. office:** duty (as a wife). **100. attorney:** agent. **103. approved:** proved, tested. **105. formal:** normal, sane. **106. parcel:** part.

Adr. Come go: I will fall prostrate at his feet,
And never rise until my tears and prayers
Have won his Grace to come in person hither,
And take perforce my husband from the Abbess.

[*2. E.*] *Mer.* By this I think the dial points at five.
Anon I'm sure the Duke himself in person
Comes this way to the melancholy vale,
The place of [death] and sorry execution,
Behind the ditches of the abbey here.

Ang. Upon what cause?

[*2. E.*] *Mer.* To see a reverent Syracusian merchant,
Who put unluckily into this bay
Against the laws and statutes of this town,
Beheaded publicly for his offense.

Ang. See where they come, we will behold his death.

Luc. Kneel to the Duke before he pass the abbey.

Enter the Duke of Ephesus [*attended*] *and* [Egeon] *the merchant of Syracuse, bare-head, with the* Headsman *and other* Officers.

Duke. Yet once again proclaim it publicly,
If any friend will pay the sum for him,
He shall not die, so much we tender him.

Adr. Justice, most sacred Duke, against the Abbess!

Duke. She is a virtuous and a reverend lady,
It cannot be that she hath done thee wrong.

Adr. May it please your Grace, Antipholus my husband,
Who I made lord of me and all I had,
At your important letters—this ill day
A most outrageous fit of madness took him,
That desp'rately he hurried through the street—
With him his bondman, all as mad as he—
Doing displeasure to the citizens
By rushing in their houses, bearing thence
Rings, jewels, any thing his rage did like.
Once did I get him bound, and sent him home,
Whilst to take order for the wrongs I went,
That here and there his fury had committed.
Anon, I wot not by what strong escape,
He broke from those that had the guard of him,
And with his mad attendant and himself,
Each one with ireful passion, with drawn swords,
Met us again, and madly bent on us
Chas'd us away; till raising of more aid,
We came again to bind them. Then they fled
Into this abbey, whither we pursu'd them,
And here the Abbess shuts the gates on us,
And will not suffer us to fetch him out,
Nor send him forth, that we may bear him hence.
Therefore, most gracious Duke, with thy command
Let him be brought forth, and borne hence for help.

Duke. Long since thy husband serv'd me in my wars,
And I to thee engag'd a prince's word,
When thou didst make him master of thy bed,
To do him all the grace and good I could.
Go some of you, knock at the abbey-gate,
And bid the Lady Abbess come to me:
I will determine this before I stir.

Enter a Messenger.

[*Mess.*] O mistress, mistress, shift and save yourself!
My master and his man are both broke loose,
Beaten the maids a-row, and bound the doctor,
Whose beard they have sing'd off with brands of fire,
And ever as it blaz'd, they threw on him
Great pails of puddled mire to quench the hair;
My master preaches patience to him, and the while
His man with scissors nicks him like a fool;
And sure (unless you send some present help)
Between them they will kill the conjurer.

Adr. Peace, fool, thy master and his man are here,
And that is false thou dost report to us.

Mess. Mistress, upon my life, I tell you true;
I have not breath'd almost since I did see it.
He cries for you, and vows, if he can take you,
To scorch your face, and to disfigure you.
Cry within.
Hark, hark, I hear him, mistress; fly, be gone!

Duke. Come stand by me, fear nothing. Guard with halberds!

Adr. Ay me, it is my husband! Witness you,
That he is borne about invisible:
Even now we hous'd him in the abbey here,
And now he's there, past thought of human reason.

Enter Antipholus [of Ephesus] *and* Dromio of Ephesus.

E. Ant. Justice, most gracious Duke, O, grant me justice,
Even for the service that long since I did thee,
When I bestrid thee in the wars, and took
Deep scars to save thy life; even for the blood
That then I lost for thee, now grant me justice.

Ege. Unless the fear of death doth make me dote,
I see my son Antipholus and Dromio.

E. Ant. Justice, sweet prince, against that woman there!
She whom thou gav'st to me to be my wife;
That hath abused and dishonored me,
Even in the strength and height of injury:
Beyond imagination is the wrong
That she this day hath shameless thrown on me.

Duke. Discover how, and thou shalt find me just.

E. Ant. This day, great Duke, she shut the doors upon me,
While she with harlots feasted in my house.

121. sorry: sad. **132. tender**: have a concern for.
138. important: importunate, pressing. **letters**. Possibly Adriana had been a ward of the Duke. **140. desp'rately**: recklessly.
142. displeasure: offense. **146. take order**: make reparation.
148. wot: know. **160. help**: cure.

162. engag'd: pledged. **164. grace**: favor.
170. a-row: one after another. **173. puddled**: foul.
175. nicks . . . fool: cuts his hair in a fantastic fashion, like a court jester's. **185. halberds**: long-handled spears with blades.
188. hous'd him in: drove him into.
192. bestrid: stood over (to defend when fallen).
199. abused: maltreated. **203. Discover**: reveal.
205. harlots: lewd fellows.

Duke. A grievous fault! Say, woman, didst thou so?
Adr. No, my good lord. Myself, he, and my sister
To-day did dine together: so befall my soul
As this is false he burthens me withal!
Luc. Ne'er may I look on day, nor sleep on night,
But she tells to your Highness simple truth!
Ang. O perjur'd woman! They are both forsworn:
In this the madman justly chargeth them.
E. Ant. My liege, I am advised what I say,
Neither disturbed with the effect of wine,
Nor heady-rash, provok'd with raging ire,
Albeit my wrongs might make one wiser mad.
This woman lock'd me out this day from dinner;
That goldsmith there, were he not pack'd with her,
Could witness it, for he was with me then,
Who parted with me to go fetch a chain,
Promising to bring it to the Porpentine,
Where Balthazar and I did dine together.
Our dinner done, and he not coming thither,
I went to seek him. In the street I met him,
And in his company that gentleman.
There did this perjur'd goldsmith swear me down
That I this day of him receiv'd the chain,
Which, God he knows, I saw not; for the which
He did arrest me with an officer.
I did obey, and sent my peasant home
For certain ducats; he with none return'd.
Then fairly I bespoke the officer
To go in person with me to my house.
By th' way we met
My wife, her sister, and a rabble more
Of vild confederates. Along with them
They brought one Pinch, a hungry lean-fac'd villain,
A mere anatomy, a mountebank,
A threadbare juggler and a fortune-teller,
A needy, hollow-ey'd, sharp-looking wretch,
A living dead man. This pernicious slave,
Forsooth, took on him as a conjurer,
And gazing in mine eyes, feeling my pulse,
And with no face, as 'twere, outfacing me,
Cries out, I was possess'd. Then all together
They fell upon me, bound me, bore me thence,
And in a dark and dankish vault at home
There left me and my man, both bound together,
Till gnawing with my teeth my bonds in sunder,
I gain'd my freedom; and immediately
Ran hither to your Grace, whom I beseech
To give me ample satisfaction
For these deep shames and great indignities.
Ang. My lord, in truth, thus far I witness with him:
That he din'd not at home, but was lock'd out.
Duke. But had he such a chain of thee, or no?
Ang. He had, my lord, and when he ran in here,
These people saw the chain about his neck.
[*2. E.*] *Mer*. Besides, I will be sworn these ears of mine
Heard you confess you had the chain of him,
After you first forswore it on the mart,
And thereupon I drew my sword on you;
And then you fled into this abbey here,
From whence I think you are come by miracle.
E. Ant. I never came within these abbey walls,
Nor ever didst thou draw thy sword on me;
I never saw the chain, so help me heaven;
And this is false you burthen me withal.
Duke. Why, what an intricate impeach is this!
I think you all have drunk of Circe's cup.
If here you hous'd him, here he would have been;
If he were mad, he would not plead so coldly.
You say he din'd at home; the goldsmith here
Denies that saying. Sirrah, what say you?
E. Dro. Sir, he din'd with her there, at the Porpentine.
Cour. He did, and from my finger snatch'd that ring.
E. Ant. 'Tis true, my liege, this ring I had of her.
Duke. Saw'st thou him enter at the abbey here?
Cour. As sure, my liege, as I do see your Grace.
Duke. Why, this is strange. Go call the Abbess hither.
I think you are all mated, or stark mad.
Exit one to the Abbess.
Ege. Most mighty Duke, vouchsafe me speak a word:
Haply I see a friend will save my life,
And pay the sum that may deliver me.
Duke. Speak freely, Syracusian, what thou wilt.
Ege. Is not your name, sir, call'd Antipholus?
And is not that your bondman, Dromio?
E. Dro. Within this hour I was his bondman, sir,
But he, I thank him, gnaw'd in two my cords:
Now am I Dromio, and his man, unbound.
Ege. I am sure you both of you remember me.
E. Dro. Ourselves we do remember, sir, by you;
For lately we were bound as you are now.
You are not Pinch's patient, are you, sir?
Ege. Why look you strange on me? You know me well.
E. Ant. I never saw you in my life till now.
Ege. O! grief hath chang'd me since you saw me last,
And careful hours with time's deformed hand
Have written strange defeatures in my face:
But tell me yet, dost thou not know my voice?
E. Ant. Neither.
Ege. Dromio, nor thou?
E. Dro. No, trust me, sir, nor I.
Ege. I am sure thou dost!

208–9. so . . . As: I swear by my hope of salvation that.
209. burthens: burdens, charges. **withal:** with.
214. liege: sovereign. **am advised:** know very well.
219. pack'd: in league. **221. parted with:** departed from.
231. peasant: servant. **233. fairly:** civilly. **bespoke:** requested.
239. mere anatomy: absolute skeleton. **mountebank:** quack, charlatan. **240. juggler:** sorcerer.
243. took . . . as: pretended to be.

270. impeach: accusation.
271. Circe's cup: i.e. the drink by means of which the sorceress Circe transformed men into beasts. **273. coldly:** coolly, rationally.
282. mated: confounded, stupefied.
299. careful: full of care. **deformed:** deforming.
300. defeatures: disfigurements.

E. Dro. Ay, sir, but I am sure I do not—and whatsoever a man denies, you are now bound to believe him.

Ege. Not know my voice! O time's extremity,
Hast thou so crack'd and splitted my poor tongue
In seven short years, that here my only son
Knows not my feeble key of untun'd cares?
Though now this grained face of mine be hid
In sap-consuming winter's drizzled snow,
And all the conduits of my blood froze up,
Yet hath my night of life some memory,
My wasting lamps some fading glimmer left,
My dull deaf ears a little use to hear:
All these old witnesses—I cannot err—
Tell me thou art my son Antipholus.

E. Ant. I never saw my father in my life.

Ege. But seven years since, in Syracusa, boy,
Thou know'st we parted, but perhaps, my son,
Thou sham'st to acknowledge me in misery.

E. Ant. The Duke, and all that know me in the city,
Can witness with me that it is not so.
I ne'er saw Syracusa in my life.

Duke. I tell thee, Syracusian, twenty years
Have I been patron to Antipholus,
During which time he ne'er saw Syracusa:
I see thy age and dangers make thee dote.

Enter the Abbess *with* Antipholus [of] Syracusa *and* Dromio [of] Syracusa.

Abb. Most mighty Duke, behold a man much wrong'd. *All gather to see them.*

Adr. I see two husbands, or mine eyes deceive me.

Duke. One of these men is genius to the other:
And so of these, which is the natural man,
And which the spirit? Who deciphers them?

S. Dro. I, sir, am Dromio, command him away.

E. Dro. I, sir, am Dromio, pray let me stay.

S. Ant. Egeon art thou not? or else his ghost?

S. Dro. O my old master, who hath bound him here?

Abb. Whoever bound him, I will loose his bonds,
And gain a husband by his liberty.
Speak, old Egeon, if thou be'st the man
That hadst a wife once call'd Aemilia,
That bore thee at a burthen two fair sons.
O, if thou be'st the same Egeon, speak,
And speak unto the same Aemilia!

Ege. If I dream not, thou art Aemilia.
If thou art she, tell me, where is that son
That floated with thee on the fatal raft?

Abb. By men of Epidamium he and I,
And the twin Dromio, all were taken up;
But by and by rude fishermen of Corinth
By force took Dromio and my son from them,
And me they left with those of Epidamium.
What then became of them I cannot tell;
I to this fortune that you see me in.

Duke. Why, here begins his morning story right:
These two Antipholus', these two so like,
And these two Dromios, one in semblance—
Besides her urging of her wrack at sea—
These are the parents to these children,
Which accidentally are met together.
Antipholus, thou cam'st from Corinth first?

S. Ant. No, sir, not I, I came from Syracuse.

Duke. Stay, stand apart, I know not which is which.

E. Ant. I came from Corinth, my most gracious lord—

E. Dro. And I with him.

E. Ant. Brought to this town by that most famous warrior,
Duke Menaphon, your most renowned uncle.

Adr. Which of you two did dine with me to-day?

S. Ant. I, gentle mistress.

Adr. And are not you my husband?

E. Ant. No, I say nay to that.

S. Ant. And so do I, yet did she call me so;
And this fair gentlewoman, her sister here,
Did call me brother. [*To Luciana.*] What I told you then
I hope I shall have leisure to make good,
If this be not a dream I see and hear.

Ang. That is the chain, sir, which you had of me.

S. Ant. I think it be, sir, I deny it not.

E. Ant. And you, sir, for this chain arrested me.

Ang. I think I did, sir, I deny it not.

Adr. I sent you money, sir, to be your bail,
By Dromio, but I think he brought it not.

E. Dro. No, none by me.

S. Ant. This purse of ducats I receiv'd from you,
And Dromio my man did bring them me.
I see we still did meet each other's man,
And I was ta'en for him, and he for me,
And thereupon these errors are arose.

E. Ant. These ducats pawn I for my father here.

Duke. It shall not need, thy father hath his life.

Cour. Sir, I must have that diamond from you.

E. Ant. There take it, and much thanks for my good cheer.

Abb. Renowned Duke, vouchsafe to take the pains
To go with us into the abbey here,
And hear at large discoursed all our fortunes;
And all that are assembled in this place
That by this sympathized one day's error
Have suffer'd wrong, go keep us company,
And we shall make full satisfaction.
Thirty-three years have I but gone in travail
Of you, my sons, and till this present hour
My heavy burthen [ne'er] delivered.
The Duke, my husband, and my children both,
And you the calendars of their nativity,
Go to a gossips' feast, and go with me—
After so long grief, such nativity!

Duke. With all my heart, I'll gossip at this feast.

Exeunt omnes. Manent the two Dromios and two brothers.

308. extremity: extreme rigor.
311. my . . . cares: i.e. my voice enfeebled and made discordant by care. **312. grained:** furrowed. **316. lamps:** eyes.
333. genius: attendant spirit. **335. deciphers:** distinguishes.
344. burthen: burden, birth.

387. still: continually. **398. sympathized:** shared in (by all).
405. calendars . . . nativity: i.e. the Dromios; see note to I.ii.41.
406. gossips' feast: a feast of the godparents, a baptismal feast. **go.** Some editors emend to *joy*. **407. grief:** suffering.
408. gossip: make merry.

S. Dro. Master, shall I fetch your stuff from shipboard?
E. Ant. Dromio, what stuff of mine hast thou embark'd?
S. Dro. Your goods that lay at host, sir, in the Centaur.
S. Ant. He speaks to me. I am your master, Dromio.
Come go with us, we'll look to that anon.
Embrace thy brother there, rejoice with him.
Exit [with Antipholus of Ephesus].
S. Dro. There is a fat friend at your master's house,
That kitchen'd me for you to-day at dinner:
She now shall be my sister, not my wife.
E. Dro. Methinks you are my glass, and not my brother:
I see by you I am a sweet-fac'd youth.
Will you walk in to see their gossiping?
S. Dro. Not I, sir, you are my elder.
E. Dro. That's a question; how shall we try it?
S. Dro. We'll draw cuts for the senior, till then, lead thou first.
E. Dro. Nay then thus:
We came into the world like brother and brother;
And now let's go hand in hand, not one before another.
Exeunt.

411. lay at host: were put up.

416. kitchen'd: entertained in the kitchen.

418. glass: mirror. **423. cuts:** lots.

NOTE ON THE TEXT

The only authority for the text of *The Comedy of Errors* is the First Folio (1623); all later texts are derived from that source. Although it has generally been believed that the manuscript underlying the F1 text was Shakespeare's "foul papers," and that this manuscript could not have served as the prompt-book (Greg, Foakes, Jorgensen, Wells, Taylor/Wells, Dorsch), Werstine has recently argued that as good a case may be made for considering the official prompt-book as the printer's copy as for the "foul papers." His case is clearly and closely argued, but Taylor/Wells point out that he "is perhaps prone to lay too much blame on the compositors [B,C,D], and to assume whenever compositorial error is possible it is also probable." For many of the ambiguities and inconsistencies in speech-prefixes, character names, and stage directions (sometimes lacking), Werstine is able to find parallels in one or more of the few contemporary manuscript prompt-books now extant, but this raises a question: Do any of these manuscript prompt-books retain as many vestiges of "foul papers" (not just one or two in one prompt-book or one or two in another) as the F1 text of *Errors* seems to display? Such a question suggests that the whole problem needs further study. Whether or not Werstine's arguments may be considered persuasive so far as *Errors* is concerned, his study serves to warn scholars that Greg's insistence on a prompt-book as being always basically "correct" needs to be at least somewhat revised (see also Long). Although the F1 text as a whole presents comparatively few difficulties, there is fairly frequent failure of the speech-prefixes to distinguish between the two Antipholi and the two Dromios; in addition, Luce is once called Nell (III.ii.109; also called Dowsabel [IV.i.110], but only ironically), Luciana appears as Juliana in III.ii o.s.d., and the stage directions at IV.iv.146, thought probably authorial, seem to have been mishandled by the compositor (B; see Textual Notes).

For further information, see: J. D. Wilson, ed., New Shakespeare *The Comedy of Errors* (Cambridge, 1922); W. W. Greg, *The Shakespeare First Folio* (Oxford, 1955); R. A. Foakes, ed., New Arden *The Comedy of Errors* (London, 1962); P. A. Jorgensen, ed., Pelican *The Comedy of Errors* (Baltimore, Maryland, 1969); Stanley Wells, ed., New Penguin *The Comedy of Errors* (Harmondsworth, Middlesex, 1972); W. B. Long, "'A bed / for woodstock': A Warning for the Unwary," *Medieval and Renaissance Drama in England*, II (1985), 91–118, and "Stage-Directions: A Misinterpreted Factor in Determining Textual Provenance," *Text*, II (1985), 121–34; Stanley Wells, Gary Taylor, et al., *William Shakespeare: A Textual Companion* (Oxford, 1987); Paul Werstine, "'Foul Papers' and 'Prompt-Books': Printer's Copy for Shakespeare's *Comedy of Errors*," *SB*, XLI (1988), 232–46; T. S. Dorsch, ed., New Cambridge *The Comedy of Errors* (Cambridge, 1988).

TEXTUAL NOTES

Dramatis personae: *subs. as first given in Douai MS and Rowe*

Act-scene division: *F1 marks acts and first scene of each act, except Act II (act only); other scene divisions from Rowe and later editors (see first note to each scene); present act-scene arrangement as a whole first established by Capell*

I.i

Location: *ed.*

o.s.d. **with Officers]** *Capell*

1 s.p. **Ege.]** *Rowe (subs.);* Marchant. *F1* (Mer. *or* Merch. *throughout scene*)

27 **sun]** *F2;* Sonne *F1*

38 **me]** mee too *F2*

42 **the . . . left]** *Theobald;* he . . . left *F1;* he great store of goods at randone leaving *F2*

54 **mean]** poor meane *F2*

55 **burthen male, twins]** burthen, Maletwins *F2*

60 **agreed.]** *F4 (subs.);* agreed, *F1*

63 **always-wind-obeying]** *first hyphen, Theobald*

77 **sinking-ripe]** *hyphen, F2*

102 **upon]** *Pope (after F2* up upon*);* vp *F1*

116 **bark]** *F2;* backe *F1*

123 **thee]** *F2;* they *F1*

144 **princes, . . . they,]** *Theobald;* Princes . . . they *F1*

151 **health]** *Wilson;* helpe *F1*

I.ii

I.ii] *Pope*

Location: *Cambridge*

o.s.d. **Antipholus]** *Malone;* Antipholis *F1*

o.s.d. **First]** *Dyce;* a *F1*

1 s.p. **1. E. Mer.]** *Dyce;* Mer. *F1*

4 **arrival]** *F2;* a riuall *F1 (F1 makes possible, but unlikely, sense)*

9 s.p. **S. Ant.]** *Kittredge (after Rowe, Capell; this s.p. is used throughout the present text for Antipholus of Syracuse);* Ant. *F1 (throughout this scene; in later scenes* Ant., An., Antip., Anti., S. Anti., S. Ant.*); adjustment to* S. Ant. *not generally recorded hereafter*

17 s.p. **S. Dro.]** *Kittredge (after Rowe, Capell);* Dro. *F1 (the s.p.* Dro. *occurs occasionally hereafter for* S. Dro. *in F1; adjustment to* S. Dro. *not generally further recorded)*

24, 32 s.pp. **1. E. Mer.]** *Dyce;* E. Mar. *F1*

32 s.d. **Exit.]** *Rowe;* Exeunt. *F1*

40 **(unhappy), ah,]** *ed.;* (vnhappie a) *F1;* (unhappie) *F2*

66 **clock]** *Pope;* cooke *F1*
92 **s.d. Strikes Dromio.]** *Douai MS (subs.), Collier*
94 **s.d. Exit]** *F2;* Exeunt *F1*
95 **device]** *F2;* deuise *F1*
96 **o'erraught]** *Hanmer;* ore-wrought *F1*
99 **Dark-working]** *hyphen, F2*

II.i

II.i] *Rowe;* Actus Secundus, *F1*
Location: *Dyce (after Pope)*
o.s.d. **Antipholus]** *Malone;* Antipholis *F1*
11 **a' door]** *ed. (after F4* adoor); adore *F1*
12 **ill]** *F2;* thus *F1*
22 **Indu'd]** *Rowe;* Indued *F1*
23 **pre-eminence]** *Capell;* prehemineence *F1*
45 **two]** *F2;* too *F1*
47–8 **Say . . . mind?]** *as verse, Steevens; as prose, F1*
61 **thousand]** *F2;* hundred *F1*
71–4 **I . . . there.]** *as verse, Pope; as prose, F1*
76 **s.p. E. Dro.]** *Rowe;* Dro. *F1 (the s.p.* Dro. *occurs occasionally hereafter for* E. Dro. *in] F1; adjustment to* E. Dro. *not generally further recorded)*
78 **across]** *F2;* a-crosse *F1 (perhaps to emphasize the pun in the next two lines)*
85 **s.d. Exit.]** *F2*
91 **wit?]** *F4;* wit, *F1*
107 **alone a' love]** *ed. (after Cunningham conj.);* alone, a loue *F1;* alone, alone *F2*
110–2 **yet . . . gold;]** *Alexander;* yet . . . touch, and . . . will, / Where gold *F1*
115 **what's left away,]** *Pope;* (what's left away) *F1*
116 **s.d. Exeunt.]** *F2;* Exit. *F1*

II.ii

II.ii] *Capell*
Location: *Wilson*
o.s.d. **Antipholus]** *Malone;* Antipholis *F1*
o.s.d. **Erotes]** *F2;* Errotis *F1*
3–4 **out. . . . report,]** *Rowe (after F4* report,); out . . . report. *F1*
6 **s.d. Dromio of Syracusa]** *ed. (after Rowe);* Dromio Siracusia *F1;* Dromio Siracusan *F2 (read as* Syracusa *hereafter)*
12 **didst]** *F2;* did didst *F1*
14 **s.p. S. Ant.]** *Capell (subs.);* E. Ant. *F1 (i.e. Antipholus Erotes)*
45–6 **Why . . . me.]** *as verse, Capell; as prose, F1*
47–9 **Was . . . you.]** *as verse, Rowe; as prose, F1*
80 **men]** *Theobald;* them *F1*
98 **tiring]** *Pope;* trying *F1*
102 **e'en]** *Capell conj.;* in *F1 (a Shakespearean spelling of* e'en)
136 **off]** *Hanmer;* of *F1*
146 **dis-stain'd]** *Theobald;* distain'd *F1*
156 **me?]** *Rowe;* me. *F1*
171 **wrong]** *Dyce;* wrong, *F1*
175 **stronger]** *F3;* stranger *F1*
186 **offer'd]** *Capell;* free'd *F1*
194 **drumble]** *ed.;* Dromio *F1*
195 **not I]** *Theobald;* I not *F1*
219 **s.d. Exeunt.]** *Rowe*

III.i

Location: *Pope (subs.)*
o.s.d. **Balthazar]** *F2;* Balthaser *F1*
24 **common;]** *Theobald;* common *F1*
25 **s.p. E. Ant.]** *Rowe (this s.p. is used throughout the present text for Antipholus of Ephesus);* Anti. *F1 (and later in F1* Ant., Anti., E. Ant.); *adjustment to* E. Ant. *not generally recorded hereafter*
31 **Cic'ly]** *ed.;* Cisley *F1*
32, 37, etc. **s.dd. Within.]** *Rowe*
35 **many? Go]** *F4;* many, goe *F1*
41 **not,]** *F3;* not *F1*
47, 60 **s.dd. within]** *Rowe (subs.)*
54] *Malone suggests that a following rhyming line (probably ending in* rope) *is missing*
56 **So, . . . strook!]** *Dyce (subs.);* So come helpe, well strooke, *F1*
60 **s.d. within]** *Rowe (subs.)*
75 **you]** *F2;* your *F1*
89 **this—]** *Theobald (subs., after Rowe);* this *F1*
89, 91 **her]** *Douai MS, Rowe;* your *F1*
110 **yet, too.]** *Rowe (subs.);* yet too *F1*
114 **s.d. To Angelo.]** *Cambridge*

III.ii

III.ii] *Pope*
Location: *ed. (after Wilson)*
o.s.d. **Luciana]** *F2;* Iuliana *F1*
1 **s.p. Luc.]** *Rowe;* Iulia. *F1*
4 **building]** *Theobald;* buildings *F1*
4 **ruinous]** *Theobald conj.;* ruinate *F1*
16 **attaint]** *Douai MS, Rowe;* attaine *F1*
21 **but]** *Theobald;* not *F1*
26 **wife]** *F2;* wise *F1*
46 **sister's]** *F2;* sister *F1*
49 **bed]** *F2;* bud *F1*
49 **them]** *Edwards;* thee *F1*
71–80 **Why . . . thyself?]** *as prose, Rowe; as verse, F1*
109 **and]** *Theobald;* is *F1*
126 **chalky]** *F2;* chalkle *F1*
145–6 **And . . . wheel.]** *as verse, Knight; as prose, F1*
146 **curtal]** *F2;* Curtull *F1*
157 **high]** *F4;* hie *F1*

IV.i

Location: *Wilson*
o.s.d. **Second]** *Dyce*
1, 52, etc. **s.pp. 2. E. Mer.]** *Dyce;* Mar. *F1*
17 **her]** *Douai MS, Rowe;* their *F1*
84 **s.d. Syracusa]** *ed.;* Sira. *F1 (this form and* Sir., Sirac. *have been regularly expanded as* Syracusa *in the present text)*
108 **s.d. all . . . Syracuse]** *Kittredge (after Capell)*

IV.ii

IV.ii] *Capell*
Location: *Wilson (subs., after Pope)*
6 **Of]** *F2;* Oh, *F1*
28 **s.d. Dromio of Syracusa]** *ed.;* S. Dromio *F1*
29 **Sweat]** *Wilson;* sweet *F1*
34 **One]** *F2;* On *F1*
37 **back-friend]** *hyphen, F4*
38 **alleys]** *Capell;* allies *F1*
42, 45 **'rested]** *Theobald;* rested *F1*
44–6 **I . . . desk?]** *as verse, Capell; as prose, F1*
45 **'a's]** *Clark, Glover conj.;* is *F1*
46 **mistress,]** *Theobald;* Mistris *F1*
47 **s.d. Exit Luciana.]** *placed as in Cambridge; after l. 47. F1*
47 **at,]** *Rowe;* at. *F1*
48 **That]** *F2;* Thus *F1*
51 **hear]** *F3;* here *F1*
55 **hear]** *F2;* here *F1*
58 **bankrout]** *F2;* bankerout *F1*
61 **'a]** *Staunton;* I *F1*
66 **s.d. Exeunt.]** *Rowe;* Exit. *F1*

IV.iii

IV.iii] *Capell*
Location: *Wilson*
1 **s.p. S. Ant.]** *Rowe (after F2* An.S.)
25 **'rests]** *Theobald;* rests *F1*
34 **Well . . . foolery.]** *as prose, Capell; as verse, F1*
40 **hoy]** *Pope;* Hoy *F1 (in italics)*
60 **you do,]** *F2;* do *F1*
71–6 **Some . . . it.]** *as verse, Capell (subs.); as prose, F1*
80 **s.d. with . . . Syracuse]** *Capell (subs.)*
96 **s.d. Exit.]** *F2*

IV.iv

IV.iv] *Capell*
Location: *ed. (after Wilson)*
o.s.d. **the Officer]** *Capell;* a Iailor *F1*
3 **'rested]** *Theobald;* rested *F1*
6 **Ephesus;]** *Capell (subs.);* Ephesus, *F1*
17 **s.d. Beats Dromio.]** *Douai MS, Pope*
53 **s.d. Strikes Pinch.]** *Douai MS (subs.), Dyce*
56 **straight:]** *Capell (subs.);* straight, *F1*
75 **Certes]** *Rowe;* Certis *F1*
79 **contraries]** *F2;* crontraries *F1*
107 **him.]** *F2;* him *F1*
109 **me? . . . thou,]** *Rowe;* me, . . . thou? *F1*
110–1 **I . . . rescue?]** *as verse, Pope; as prose, F1*
113 **s.d. They . . . Ephesus.]** *Cambridge*
128 **Cry "The devil!"]** *Theobald (subs.);* cry the diuell. *F1*
129 **help,]** *Theobald;* help *F1*
130 **s.d. Manent]** *Rowe;* Manet *F1; F1 s.d. after l. 131; placed as in Theobald*
146 **again.]** againe. / *Runne all out. F1 (apparently anticipating the s.d. at the end of the line)*
146 **s.d. but . . . Syracuse]** *Cambridge*

V.i

Location: *ed. (after Pope)*
o.s.d. **Second]** *Dyce*
4, 9, etc. **s.pp. 2. E. Mer.]** *Dyce;* Mar. *F1*
37 **s.d. Antipholus . . . Syracuse]** *Capell (subs.)*
38 **quiet,]** *Theobald;* quiet *F1*
45 **sour,]** *F2;* sower *F1*
77 **brawls]** *F2;* bralles *F1*
112 **s.d. Exit.]** *Hanmer (after Theobald)*
121 **death]** *F3;* depth *F1*
129 **s.d. attended]** *Capell*
138 **letters—]** *Theobald (subs.);* Letters *F1*
168 **s.p. Mess.]** *F2*
189 **s.d. Dromio]** *Rowe;* E. Dromio *F1*
195 **s.p. Ege.]** *Rowe (subs.);* Mar. Fat. *F1*
235 **By]** *F4;* By' *F1*
241 **needy . . . wretch]** needy-hollow-ey'd-sharpe-looking-wretch *F1*
245 **no face]** *Pope;* no-face *F1*
246 **all together]** *Rowe;* altogether *F1*
283, 287, etc. **s.pp. Ege.]** *Rowe (subs.);* Fa., Fath., *or* Father. *F1 (throughout rest of scene)*
305 **Ay, sir,]** I sir, *F1 (possibly we should read* I, sir?)
318 **witnesses . . . err—]** *Rowe (subs.);* witnesses, I cannot erre. *F1*
321 **Syracusa, boy,]** *Capell;* Siracusa boy *F1*
357–62 **Why . . . together.]** *placed as in Capell; these lines follow l. 346 in F1 (if we suppose a line or two lost, dealing with the "wrack," in Aemilia's speech, ll. 340–6, then the F1 order, with the Duke's speech as an aside, would make good sense)*
363 **Antipholus]** *Capell; Duke.* Antipholus *F1 (see preceding note)*
363 **first?]** *Capell;* first. *F1*
375 **s.d. To Luciana.]** *Cambridge (after Capell)*
397–9 **place . . . wrong,]** *Rowe (subs.);* place: . . . wrong. *F1*
403 **ne'er]** *Dyce;* are *F1*
406 **gossips']** *Halliwell;* Gossips *F1*
408 **s.d. Manent]** *Rowe;* Manet *F1*
414 **s.d. with . . . Ephesus]** *Theobald (subs.)*
423 **senior]** *Rowe;* Signior *F1*
426 **s.d. Exeunt.]** Exeunt. / FINIS. *F1*

The Taming of the Shrew

IN THE YEAR 1594 there was published an anonymous play entitled *The Taming of a Shrew*, now generally believed to be either a pirated and inaccurate version of Shakespeare's comedy or else a "bad" quarto of a different play, now lost, which also served Shakespeare as a source for his own *The Taming of the Shrew*. In general outline, *A Shrew* is very close to Shakespeare's play, although there are very few verbal parallels and the entire comedy is markedly inferior to the one published as Shakespeare's in the First Folio of 1623. Shakespeare's fantasy about courtship and marriage in Padua is clearly an early comedy, part of the group which also includes *The Two Gentlemen of Verona* and *The Comedy of Errors*. None of these plays is easy to date, but *The Taming of the Shrew* must have been written between 1590 and 1594. Like *The Comedy of Errors*, it displays a complete assurance of technique within limits admittedly narrower, closer to farce, than those of the comedies Shakespeare was to write later in the decade. Inventive, witty, and vital, it has come honestly by its enduring popularity in the theatre. Indeed, no other play by Shakespeare depends so heavily upon theatrical realization as opposed to mere reading. Attitudes and turns of phrase that seem archaic, or even brutal, on the printed page, have a way of becoming entirely acceptable as soon as Katherina and Petruchio are actually speaking. On the stage, unless the actor deliberately coarsens his part, Petruchio comes over far less as an aggressive male out to bully a refractory wife into total submission than he does as a man who genuinely prizes Katherina and, by exploiting an age-old and basic antagonism between the sexes, manoeuvres her into an understanding of his nature and also her own.

Shrewish wives in English drama can trace their descent from Mrs. Noah in the mystery plays, that indomitable scold who would not leave her "gossips" and get into the ark at her husband's bidding even though the whole world was drowning in the Flood. Intractable, violent, and sharp-tongued wives, some of them fond of cuckolding their husbands as well as merely ordering them about, represented a familiar comic type in Tudor interludes and farces. Roman comedy had also dealt with the termagant wife. Elizabethan dramatists who adapted plays by Plautus and Terence found it easy to graft the classical shrew onto her native counterpart. Meanwhile, outside the theatre, there was no decline in that venerable and even more extensive tradition of shrew literature which Chaucer had contributed to, as well as the more humble compilers of jest-books or of ballads like "A Merry Jest of a Shrewd and Curst Wife Lapped in Morel's Skin for Her Good Behavior" (c. 1550). Verbal similarities indicate that Shakespeare knew this particular ballad; certainly he knew others like it, in which the approved remedy for a domineering wife was physical violence, the more ingenious and excruciating the better. By comparison with the husband who binds his erring spouse, beats her, bleeds her into a state of debility, or (in the case of the ballad mentioned above) incarcerates her inside the salted skin of the dead horse Morel, Petruchio—although no Romeo—is almost a model of intelligence and humanity. His aim, moreover, is not the crude one of the traditional wife-tamer, out to pulverize the woman's will as well as, in most cases, her body. What Petruchio wants, and ends up with, is a Katherina of unbroken spirit and gaiety who has suffered only minor physical discomfort and who has learned the value of self-control and of caring about someone other than herself.

Northrop Frye once remarked that the Katherina of Act I is not really dissimilar from the Katherina of Act V: at the beginning of the comedy she is persecuting her sister Bianca, and at the end she is engaged in precisely the same activity—except that now she has learned how to do it with social approval on her side. The remark is far from representing the whole truth about Katherina's progress in the course of the comedy, but it does usefully point to the way Petruchio's "method" has harmonized and ordered the elements of a personality without doing violence to its essential selfhood. Shakespeare's sympathy with and almost uncanny understanding of women characters is one of the distinguishing features of his comedy, as opposed to that of most of his contemporaries. His heroines not only tend to overshadow their male counterparts, as Rosalind overshadows Orlando, Julia Proteus, or Viola Orsino: they adumbrate and urge throughout the play values which, with their help, will triumph in the new, more enlightened society of the end. Nevertheless, there is no hint anywhere in his work that he would have dissented from the official position of the Elizabethan church as derived from the counsel of St. Paul in his letter to the Ephesians: "Let women be subject to their husbands, as to the Lord; for the husband is the head of the woman, as Christ is the head of the church." The attitude adopted by the reformed Katherina in the last scene of the comedy is strikingly like that of Luciana rebuking her nagging and possessive sister Adriana in *The Comedy of Errors*: both women see the subservience of a wife to her husband as an in-built law of nature, not to be transgressed, and both have the force of the entire comedy behind them in their belief.

Although it lacks the essential seriousness and the poetry of *As You Like It*, *Twelfth Night*, or even *Love's Labor's Lost*, *The Taming of the Shrew* is nonetheless psychologically discerning. Petruchio comes to Padua initially because he is looking for a rich wife. At the first sight of Katherina, however, this cold, unemotional project becomes something far more complex: Kate is not only a problem to be solved, but a prize, in ways that have nothing to do with the size of her dowry. She is, in fact, a far more honest and interesting person than her apparently docile and much-admired sister Bianca, although Petruchio is the only person in Padua, at least until Act V, to see that this is true. As for Katherina herself, the stage convention which allows the actress playing the part to show plainly in her face that she falls in love with Petruchio the moment she sets eyes on him has much to recommend it. Heartily sick of a single life, not to mention all the adulation showered on Bianca, she is really more than ready to give herself to a man but, imprisoned within a set of aggressive attitudes which have become habitual, has not the faintest idea how to do so. Petruchio's strategy is perceptively designed to make her abandon a shrew's role originally adopted as a defense, not intrinsic in her nature, and to permit her to escape into freedom and love within the bonds of marriage.

The two techniques he employs are complementary. First of all, he "kills her in her own humor" (IV.i.180), "is more shrew than she" (IV.i.85–86), beating the servants, hurling dinner plates, insulting tradesmen, scolding and complaining, throwing tantrums and changing his mind with the wind. Not only does he present her in all this with a masculine version of her own unreasonable and arbitrary behavior, he forces her to experience it objectively and to realize just how impossible it is for another person to tolerate. At the same time, he goes on assuring her, despite everything she can do and say to prove the contrary, that she herself is gentle, rational, and loving: exactly the hidden qualities in her that he needs to foster and encourage. Petruchio wins in the end not because of superior force but because he succeeds in showing Katherina both the unloveliness of the false personality she has adopted and the emotional truth of the self she has submerged. The method used is not exactly Freud's, but the integrated and quietly confident Kate who wins Petruchio's wager for him at the end of the comedy is a woman who has discovered and come to terms with her own genuine nature.

There are undeniable elements of farce in the Katherina/Petruchio plot, as well as a robust glee in that age-old motif of the battle between the sexes which Shakespeare does, at moments in the play, exploit for its own, eminently theatrical, sake. Nevertheless, all the exuberance and in-fighting ultimately serves an end poles apart from the mere vindictive savagery of "The Curst Wife Lapped in Morel's Skin." It is true that by comparison with Beatrice in *Much Ado about Nothing* (1598) Katherina is a character sketched in bold, rapid strokes, with none of Beatrice's sophistication, verbal brilliance, or emotional depth. She is nonetheless an important first study for Benedick's exasperating sparring partner, another woman who shelters behind a false aggressiveness and has to be tricked into accepting a man's love. The achievement of *The Taming of the Shrew* lies more on the surface, depends more upon stage incident and rough-and-tumble than was to be the case in the comedies of the later 1590's, yet both structurally and thematically it is a remarkably consistent and skillful play. Certainly Shakespeare seems to have taken pains not only to link those ideas about role-playing and transformation which are so important in the taming plot with the parallel story of Bianca and her three suitors, but also to extend them beyond the inset play into the strangely truncated adventure of Christopher Sly.

The Bianca plot is derived from a play by George Gascoigne, *Supposes* (1566), in itself an adaptation of Ariosto's comedy *I Suppositi* (1509). Both plays declare their Plautine ancestry. They are concerned almost entirely with plot "mistaking," false "supposes" about the identity of characters and the nature of situations. Polynesta, Gascoigne's equivalent to Bianca, is a shadowy figure and, like most of her prototypes in Roman comedy, rarely appears on stage. She is really the excuse for the intrigue, more than a character in her own right. When the comedy begins, she is pregnant by her lover Erostrato, who has changed identities with his servant Dulipo in order to gain access to Polynesta. The false Erostrato, posing as a suitor to Polynesta, defeats an elderly but rich rival by means of the same ruse that Tranio employs to help Lucentio in Shakespeare's play. As in Shakespeare, the real father then puts in an unexpected appearance and is horrified to discover his own identity usurped by a perfect stranger and his son's by the servant he has raised in his house. False suppositions proliferate but all ends happily at last with Polynesta married to her seducer Erostrato and Dulipo, suddenly revealed as the long-lost son of the Gremio figure, transformed from a servant into a man of rank and fortune.

In taking over Gascoigne's plot, Shakespeare obviously intended the various "supposes" inherent in it as a complement to those in the Katherina/Petruchio story. He rejected the idea that Tranio might be other than he seemed—the favorite New Comedy motif of the child lost in infancy and reared as a servant never appealed much to Elizabethans—but made up for the loss of this particular mistake of identity by providing Bianca with a third suitor, Hortensio, and having him woo her in the disguise of a music master. Elizabethan preferences must also have been partly responsible for the fact that Bianca, unlike Polynesta, is still a virgin and a much more active and developed character than her prototype. Less predictable was Shakespeare's decision to present her as a mirror image of her elder sister Katherina. Bianca's sweet submissiveness is no more integral to her character than Kate's bad temper is to hers. Already in the scene where she is wooed by the disguised Lucentio and Hortensio she displays a deviousness and cunning which suggest that the dutiful daughter and long-suffering, patient younger sister are roles that she knows how to play, rather than indications of her true character. Once married to Lucentio, she ceases abruptly to be "sweet Bianca." At the wedding feast itself she reveals an unexpected streak of bawdry, willfulness, and arrogance. Lucentio, as it turns out, and not Petruchio, has married the shrewish sister. As for Hortensio, his headstrong widow is clearly going to drive him to experiment with Petruchio's wife-taming methods before the first week of marriage is out.

In the marriage feast which concludes *The Taming of the Shrew* all the plot material of the comedy proper is woven together in a fashion that is thematically as well as structurally masterful. Spare and elegant, almost dance-like in form, the play transforms the Roman model from which, basically, it derives into a thing of grace and sophistication. Patently designed to be watched, not read, full of game-playing and visual humor, it is perhaps the most unequivocally light-hearted of all Shakespeare's comedies, the one whose qualities lie most obviously on the surface. If it is short on poetry and deep emotion, without the power to disturb of *Twelfth Night* or *Measure For Measure*, it makes up for these deficiencies by sheer theatrical brilliance—as the theatre itself has always known. This pervading sense of symmetry and control is one of the things which make the abrupt disappearance of Christopher Sly and of the frame so elaborately set up in the Induction such a puzzle.

The idea of the play set within a frame seems to have been especially popular in the late 1580's and early 1590's. It was one way of exploring the new self-sufficiency of a stage world which had only recently become entirely secular and needed to redefine its relationship with an audience coming to the theatre now less for instruction than delight. *The Taming of a Shrew* is one of a number of plays surviving from this period which presented that audience with an image of itself in the form of one or more on-stage spectators who watch, and thereby help to distance, an illusion. In this text, Christopher Sly remains visible on stage almost to the end of the inset play, and takes a lively interest in the performance put on for his benefit. He inquires knowledgeably after the next appearance of the fool, refuses to have people sent to prison, and when it becomes necessary for the purposes of the lord's game with him that he fall asleep, he has to be plied with drink before he will remove his attention from the play. There is a certain charm about the conclusion of *A Shrew*, when Sly wakes from what he regards as the best dream he has ever had and resolves to go home and apply the lesson in shrew-taming to his own recalcitrant wife. In the theatre, directors often insert these additional Sly episodes into Shakespeare's play on the grounds that it is both illogical and unsatisfying to have him vanish without explanation after Act I and to miss out the moment when he regains his own humble identity. They may well be right.

The idea for Sly's transformation may have been suggested originally by a story (1570), now lost, by the early Elizabethan dramatist and Master of the Children of the Chapel, Richard Edwards. Shakespeare need not, however, have been dependent upon a specific source: the motif of the beggar who wakes to find himself inexplicably surrounded with wealth and comfort beyond his wildest imaginings was popular both in Europe and in the East. It is one of the tales told in *The Arabian Nights*, where the adventure-loving caliph Haroun Al Raschid engineers the trick, and it is reported that Philip the Good of Burgundy actually played a similar prank. Inherent in all versions is the return of the beggar to his original state and his conviction that all the wonders he has seen and enjoyed were only an exceptionally vivid dream. It is possible, of course, that in Shakespeare's play, as in *A Shrew*, the Sly framework continued to the end, and that the portion now missing was simply omitted from the Folio text as the result of some unexplained accident. Against this view is the fact that Shakespeare's Sly, unlike his namesake in *A Shrew*, is presented as bored with the comedy he watches from the beginning and already nodding off after the first scene. It has sometimes been suggested that Shakespeare decided to truncate the part so savagely because he discovered that he could not trust the actor who played it not to dominate the entire comedy. Hamlet is particularly scathing about clowns who persistently speak "more than is set down for them," even though "in the mean time some necessary question of the play be then to be consider'd." He calls them "villainous" (III.ii.38–45). Was the original Sly an actor of this kind, whose antics distracted attention from the inset play to such an extent that Shakespeare had to banish him from the stage as soon as possible? Alternatively, it has been argued that Sly was never intended to do more than lead the theatre audience into the play-world of Padua and, having done that, had fulfilled his function and might disappear, like the Fool in *King Lear*. Critics who are of this persuasion insist that in Shakespeare's richer and more resonant comedy it could only be disturbing to remain aware of Sly throughout, and a positive anticlimax to have to return from the wedding feast and the triumph of Petruchio and Kate to the bare heath at the end, and Sly's rueful awakening. On the whole, experimentation in the theatre with the extra dialogue from *A Shrew* (recorded in the Textual Notes below) suggests that this is not psychologically true, that Sly can lead us away from Shakespeare's Padua quite as subtly and effectively as Feste leads us from Illyria or Puck from the palace of Duke Theseus. The question of why, in the Folio text, he does not, seems likely to remain a source of controversy.

What does seem clear is that the Sly scenes, mysterious though their abbreviation is, lock into place in Shakespeare's play as part of an overall concern with transformation and questions of identity. Baptista discovers at the wedding feast that he does not recognize Kate, his own daughter, "for she is chang'd, as she had never been" (V.ii.115). Bianca too is "chang'd," although not for the better. These particular transformations have a psychological truth behind them of a kind alien to the situation comedy of Gascoigne or Plautus. Yet Shakespeare allows them to grow out of a series of more literal mistakings in the form of those multiple disguises associated with the Bianca plot and, on the outermost circle of the action, the confusion of the tinker who wakes to find he is a lord. It seems right that this ancient wish-dream of poverty translated to riches should introduce a play concerned throughout with role-playing, with the discrepancy between what people seem and what they really are. Interestingly enough, although the actors who entertain Sly in *A Shrew* are presented as bunglers, men who talk about performing a "Tragicall" or a "comodotie" and request the lord to provide them with a little vinegar to make their devil roar, their equivalents in the Folio text are men of dignity and skill. Precursors of the city-tragedians in *Hamlet*, they are honorably received by the lord, who commands that they should "want nothing that my house affords" (Induction i.104). It is difficult to say just why the players should be debased in *A Shrew*, but it is obviously fitting in Shakespeare's text that they should be what they are: magicians whose art is not confined to the stage but an integral part of life itself.

Anne Barton

The Taming of a Shrew by "J. R." (c. 1635). The program for "taming a shrew" advocated by the Father (left) in this woodcut from a broadside ballad differs sharply from the tactics employed by Petruchio: understanding and mutual forbearance as opposed to male chauvinism. (*The Folger Shakespeare Library*)

The Taming of the Shrew

[DRAMATIS PERSONAE

LORD
CHRISTOPHER SLY, *a tinker*
HOSTESS, PAGE, PLAYERS, HUNTSMEN, *and* SERVANTS
} *persons in the Induction*

BAPTISTA, *a rich gentleman of Padua*
VINCENTIO, *an old gentleman of Pisa*
LUCENTIO, *son to Vincentio, in love with Bianca*
PETRUCHIO, *a gentleman of Verona, suitor to Katherina*
GREMIO
HORTENSIO
} *suitors to Bianca*

TRANIO
BIONDELLO
} *servants to Lucentio*
GRUMIO
CURTIS
} *servants to Petruchio*
PEDANT

KATHERINA, *the shrew*
BIANCA
} *daughters to Baptista*
WIDOW

TAILOR, HABERDASHER, *and* SERVANTS *attending on Baptista and Petruchio*

SCENE: *Padua, and Petruchio's country house*]

[INDUCTION,] SCENE I

Enter beggar, CHRISTOPHERO SLY, *and* HOSTESS.

Sly. I'll pheeze you, in faith.

Host. A pair of stocks, you rogue!

Sly. Y' are a baggage, the Slys are no rogues. Look in the chronicles; we came in with Richard Conqueror. Therefore *paucas pallabris*, let the world slide. Sessa!

Host. You will not pay for the glasses you have burst?

Sly. No, not a denier. Go by, Saint Jeronimy! go to thy cold bed, and warm thee.

Host. I know my remedy; I must go fetch the [thirdborough]. [*Exit.*]

Sly. Third, or fourth, or fift borough, I'll answer him by law. I'll not budge an inch, boy; let him come, and kindly. *Falls asleep.*

Wind horns. Enter a LORD *from hunting, with his* TRAIN.

Lord. Huntsman, I charge thee, tender well my hounds
(Brach Merriman, the poor cur, is emboss'd),
And couple Clowder with the deep-mouth'd brach.
Saw'st thou not, boy, how Silver made it good
At the hedge-corner, in the coldest fault?
I would not lose the dog for twenty pound.

[1.] Hun. Why, Belman is as good as he, my lord;
He cried upon it at the merest loss,
And twice to-day pick'd out the dullest scent.
Trust me, I take him for the better dog.

Lord. Thou art a fool; if Echo were as fleet,
I would esteem him worth a dozen such.
But sup them well, and look unto them all,
To-morrow I intend to hunt again.

[1.] Hun. I will, my lord.

Lord. What's here? One dead, or drunk? See, doth he breathe?

2. Hun. He breathes, my lord. Were he not warm'd with ale,
This were a bed but cold to sleep so soundly.

Lord. O monstrous beast, how like a swine he lies!

Words and passages enclosed in square brackets in the text above are either emendations of the copy-text or additions to it. The Textual Notes immediately following the play cite the earliest authority for every such change or insertion and supply the reading of the copy-text wherever it is emended in this edition.

Ind. i. Location: Before an alehouse on a heath.
1. **I'll pheeze you.** A vague threat, equivalent to modern "I'll fix you" or "I'll do for you."
2. **A pair of stocks:** i.e. I'll have you in the stocks.
4. **Richard.** Sly's blunder for *William.*
5. **paucas pallabris:** few words (Spanish *pocas palabras*).
6. **Sessa.** Of uncertain meaning; perhaps equivalent to "let it go" (from Spanish *cesar*, "cease"). 8. **burst:** broken.
9. **denier:** copper coin worth very little. **Go . . . Jeronimy.** Sly's variation of a stock tag signifying impatient dismissal; it stemmed from a line in Kyd's *Spanish Tragedy*, "Hieronimo, beware; go by, go by," but Sly confuses Hieronimo in the play with St. Jerome (Latin Hieronymus).
9–10. **Go . . . thee.** Cf. *Lear*, III.iv.48; probably proverbial.
12. **thirdborough:** constable. The first syllable evolved from the Old English word for "peace." 13. **fift:** fifth.
14. **boy:** here, a term of contempt, applicable to either sex.
15. **kindly:** i.e. welcome. s.d. **Wind:** blow. 16. **tender:** care for.
17. **Brach:** bitch hound. In view of the repetition of the word in the next line, most editors emend, commonly either to *Broach* (= bleed) or to *Breathe* (= allow to rest). **emboss'd:** foaming at the mouth.
20. **in . . . fault:** when the scent was coldest.
23. **cried upon it:** bayed, i.e. was the first to recover the scent. **at . . . loss:** when the scent had been completely lost.

Grim death, how foul and loathsome is thine image!
Sirs, I will practice on this drunken man.
What think you, if he were convey'd to bed,
Wrapp'd in sweet clothes, rings put upon his fingers,
A most delicious banquet by his bed,
And brave attendants near him when he wakes,
Would not the beggar then forget himself?

1. Hun. Believe me, lord, I think he cannot choose.

2. Hun. It would seem strange unto him when he wak'd.

Lord. Even as a flatt'ring dream or worthless fancy.
Then take him up, and manage well the jest.
Carry him gently to my fairest chamber,
And hang it round with all my wanton pictures.
Balm his foul head in warm distilled waters,
And burn sweet wood to make the lodging sweet.
Procure me music ready when he wakes,
To make a dulcet and a heavenly sound;
And if he chance to speak, be ready straight,
And with a low submissive reverence
Say, "What is it your honor will command?"
Let one attend him with a silver basin
Full of rose-water and bestrew'd with flowers,
Another bear the ewer, the third a diaper,
And say, "Will't please your lordship cool your hands?"
Some one be ready with a costly suit,
And ask him what apparel he will wear;
Another tell him of his hounds and horse,
And that his lady mourns at his disease.
Persuade him that he hath been lunatic,
And when he says he is, say that he dreams,
For he is nothing but a mighty lord.
This do, and do it kindly, gentle sirs;
It will be pastime passing excellent,
If it be husbanded with modesty.

1. Hun. My lord, I warrant you we will play our part
As he shall think by our true diligence
He is no less than what we say he is.

Lord. Take him up gently and to bed with him,
And each one to his office when he wakes.

[*Some bear out Sly.*] *Sound trumpets.*

Sirrah, go see what trumpet 'tis that sounds.

[*Exit Servingman.*]

Belike some noble gentleman that means
(Travelling some journey) to repose him here.

Enter SERVINGMAN.

How now? who is it?

Serv. An't please your honor, players
That offer service to your lordship.

Enter PLAYERS.

Lord. Bid them come near. Now, fellows, you are welcome.

Players. We thank your honor.

Lord. Do you intend to stay with me to-night?

2. Play. So please your lordship to accept our duty.

Lord. With all my heart. This fellow I remember
Since once he play'd a farmer's eldest son.
'Twas where you woo'd the gentlewoman so well.
I have forgot your name; but sure that part
Was aptly fitted and naturally perform'd.

[*1. Play.*] I think 'twas Soto that your honor means.

Lord. 'Tis very true; thou didst it excellent.
Well, you are come to me in happy time,
The rather for I have some sport in hand,
Wherein your cunning can assist me much.
There is a lord will hear you play to-night;
But I am doubtful of your modesties,
Lest, over-eyeing of his odd behavior
(For yet his honor never heard a play),
You break into some merry passion,
And so offend him; for I tell you, sirs,
If you should smile, he grows impatient.

[*1.*] *Play.* Fear not, my lord, we can contain ourselves,
Were he the veriest antic in the world.

Lord. Go, sirrah, take them to the buttery,
And give them friendly welcome every one.
Let them want nothing that my house affords.

Exit one with the Players.

Sirrah, go you to Barthol'mew my page,
And see him dress'd in all suits like a lady;
That done, conduct him to the drunkard's chamber,
And call him madam, do him obeisance.
Tell him from me, as he will win my love,
He bear himself with honorable action,
Such as he hath observ'd in noble ladies
Unto their lords, by them accomplished;
Such duty to the drunkard let him do,
With soft low tongue and lowly courtesy,
And say, "What is't your honor will command,
Wherein your lady, and your humble wife,
May show her duty and make known her love?"
And then with kind embracements, tempting kisses,
And with declining head into his bosom,
Bid him shed tears, as being overjoyed
To see her noble lord restor'd to health,
Who for this seven years hath esteemed him
No better than a poor and loathsome beggar.

35. **image**: likeness (with reference to the ancient view that sleep was the image of death). 36. **practice**: play a joke.
38. **sweet**: perfumed. 39. **banquet**: light repast.
40. **brave**: finely dressed. 44. **worthless fancy**: empty fantasy.
48. **Balm**: anoint. 52. **straight**: immediately.
57. **diaper**: towel. 64. **is**: i.e. is indeed mad.
66. **kindly**: naturally, i.e. convincingly. 67. **passing**: surpassingly.
68. **husbanded with modesty**: managed with restraint.
73. **office**: duty. 74. **Sirrah**: ordinary form of address to inferiors.
75. **Belike**: probably. 77. **An't**: if it.

82. **duty**: expression of respect. 87. **naturally**: realistically.
88. **Soto**. A character of this name, with a role like that described by the Lord, appears in Fletcher's ***Women Pleased***, but since that play was first acted around 1620, the reference here must either be a late addition or point to a much earlier play on which Fletcher's play was based. 90. **in happy time**: opportunely.
91. **The rather for**: the more so because. 92. **cunning**: skill.
93. **will**: who will (a frequent construction).
94. **modesties**: self-control. 95. **over-eyeing of**: observing.
97. **merry passion**: fit of laughter.
101. **antic**: grotesque creature, eccentric.
102. **buttery**: store room for liquor (kept in butts) and other provisions. 104. **want**: lack. 106. **in all suits**: in every detail.
110. **honorable**: becoming, decorous.
112. **accomplished**: performed. 122. **him**: himself.

And if the boy have not a woman's gift
To rain a shower of commanded tears,
An onion will do well for such a shift,
Which in a napkin (being close convey'd)
Shall in despite enforce a watery eye.
See this dispatch'd with all the haste thou canst;
Anon I'll give thee more instructions.

Exit a Servingman.

I know the boy will well usurp the grace,
Voice, gait, and action of a gentlewoman.
I long to hear him call the drunkard husband,
And how my men will stay themselves from laughter
When they do homage to this simple peasant.
I'll in to counsel them; haply my presence
May well abate the over-merry spleen,
Which otherwise would grow into extremes.

[Exeunt.]

[SCENE II]

Enter aloft the drunkard [SLY] *with* ATTENDANTS, *some with apparel, basin and ewer, and other appurtenances, and* LORD.

Sly. For God's sake, a pot of small ale.

1. Serv. Will't please your [lordship] drink a cup of sack?

2. Serv. Will't please your honor taste of these conserves?

3. Serv. What raiment will your honor wear to-day?

Sly. I am Christophero Sly, call not me honor nor lordship. I ne'er drank sack in my life; and if you give me any conserves, give me conserves of beef. Ne'er ask me what raiment I'll wear, for I have no more doublets than backs, no more stockings than legs, nor no more shoes than feet— nay, sometime more feet than shoes, or such shoes as my toes look through the overleather.

Lord. Heaven cease this idle humor in your honor!
O that a mighty man of such descent,
Of such possessions, and so high esteem,
Should be infused with so foul a spirit!

Sly. What, would you make me mad? Am not I Christopher Sly, old Sly's son of Burton-heath, by birth a pedlar, by education a card-maker, by transmutation a bear-herd, and now by present profession a tinker? Ask Marian Hacket, the fat ale-wife of Wincot, if she know me not. If she say I am not fourteen pence on the score for sheer ale, score me up for the lying'st knave in Christendom. What! I am not bestraught. Here's—

3. Serv. O, this it is that makes your lady mourn!

2. Serv. O, this is it that makes your servants droop!

Lord. Hence comes it that your kindred shuns your house,
As beaten hence by your strange lunacy.
O noble lord, bethink thee of thy birth,
Call home thy ancient thoughts from banishment,
And banish hence these abject lowly dreams.
Look how thy servants do attend on thee,
Each in his office ready at thy beck.
Wilt thou have music? Hark, Apollo plays, *Music.*
And twenty caged nightingales do sing.
Or wilt thou sleep? We'll have thee to a couch,
Softer and sweeter than the lustful bed
On purpose trimm'd up for Semiramis.
Say thou wilt walk; we will bestrow the ground.
Or wilt thou ride? Thy horses shall be trapp'd,
Their harness studded all with gold and pearl.
Dost thou love hawking? Thou hast hawks will soar
Above the morning lark. Or wilt thou hunt?
Thy hounds shall make the welkin answer them
And fetch shrill echoes from the hollow earth.

1. Serv. Say thou wilt course, thy greyhounds are as swift
As breathed stags; ay, fleeter than the roe.

2. Serv. Dost thou love pictures? We will fetch thee straight
Adonis painted by a running brook,
And Cytherea all in sedges hid,
Which seem to move and wanton with her breath,
Even as the waving sedges play with wind.

Lord. We'll show thee Io as she was a maid,
And how she was beguiled and surpris'd,
As lively painted as the deed was done.

3. Serv. Or Daphne roaming through a thorny wood,
Scratching her legs that one shall swear she bleeds,
And at that sight shall sad Apollo weep,
So workmanly the blood and tears are drawn.

Lord. Thou art a lord, and nothing but a lord.
Thou hast a lady far more beautiful
Than any woman in this waning age.

1. Serv. And till the tears that she hath shed for thee

126. **shift**: purpose. 127. **napkin**: handkerchief.
128. **in despite**: i.e. in spite of his inability to weep.
130. **Anon**: very shortly. 131. **usurp**: assume.
136. **haply**: perhaps.
137. **spleen**: impulse, mood. Fits of laughter (as of anger) were supposed to originate in the spleen.

Ind. ii. Location: A bedchamber in the Lord's house.
o.s.d. **aloft**: i.e. in the gallery over the back of the stage.
1. **small**: weak. 2. **sack**: Spanish white wine.
3. **conserves**: sweetmeats of fruit.
7–8. **conserves of beef**: salt beef. 9. **doublets**: jackets.
12. **overleather**: upper leather. 13. **idle humor**: absurd fancy.
18. **Burton-heath**: perhaps Barton-on-the-Heath, a Warwickshire village about sixteen miles from Stratford.
19. **card-maker**: maker of cards for combing wool.
20. **bear-herd**: keeper of a tame bear.
22. **Wincot**: a small village about four miles from Stratford; the parish records indicate that Hackets were living there in the 1590's.
23. **on the score**: in debt (originally recorded by scoring or notching a stick). **sheer ale**: i.e. ale alone.
24. **score**: reckon. **lying'st . . . Christendom.** Cf. *2 Henry VI*, II.i.126. 25. **bestraught**: distracted, mad.
31. **ancient thoughts**: former reason. 35. **Apollo**: god of music.
39. **Semiramis**: legendary queen of Assyria notorious for her voluptuousness. 40. **bestrow**: bestrew (with coverings).
41. **trapp'd**: adorned. 45. **welkin**: sky. 47. **course**: hunt hares.
48. **breathed**: in full breath, in good wind. **roe**: a kind of small, fleet deer.
50. **Adonis**: the young hunter beloved of Venus and slain by a wild boar. The story is the subject of Shakespeare's *Venus and Adonis*.
51. **Cytherea**: Venus (so named from her traditional association with the island Cythera). 52. **wanton**: play amorously.
54. **Io**: a Greek maiden loved by Jupiter, who turned her into a cow in an unsuccessful attempt to conceal her from Juno.
56. **lively**: realistically.
57. **Daphne**: a nymph changed by Diana into a laurel tree to preserve her from rape by Apollo. 63. **waning**: degenerate.

Like envious floods o'errun her lovely face,
She was the fairest creature in the world,
And yet she is inferior to none.

Sly. Am I a lord, and have I such a lady?
Or do I dream? Or have I dream'd till now?
I do not sleep: I see, I hear, I speak;
I smell sweet savors, and I feel soft things.
Upon my life, I am a lord indeed,
And not a tinker, nor Christopher Sly.
Well, bring our lady hither to our sight,
And once again a pot o' th' smallest ale.

2. Serv. Will't please your mightiness to wash your hands?
O how we joy to see your wit restor'd!
O that once more you knew but what you are!
These fifteen years you have been in a dream,
Or when you wak'd, so wak'd as if you slept.

Sly. These fifteen years! by my fay, a goodly nap,
But did I never speak of all that time?

1. Serv. O yes, my lord, but very idle words,
For though you lay here in this goodly chamber,
Yet would you say ye were beaten out of door,
And rail upon the hostess of the house,
And say you would present her at the leet,
Because she brought stone jugs and no seal'd quarts.
Sometimes you would call out for Cicely Hacket.

Sly. Ay, the woman's maid of the house.

3. Serv. Why, sir, you know no house nor no such maid,
Nor no such men as you have reckon'd up,
As Stephen Sly, and old John Naps of Greece,
And Peter Turph, and Henry Pimpernell,
And twenty more such names and men as these,
Which never were, nor no man ever saw.

Sly. Now Lord be thanked for my good amends!

All. Amen.

Enter [*the* PAGE *as a*] *lady, with* ATTENDANTS.

Sly. I thank thee, thou shalt not lose by it.

Page. How fares my noble lord?

Sly. Marry, I fare well, for here is cheer enough.
Where is my wife?

Page. Here, noble lord, what is thy will with her?

Sly. Are you my wife and will not call me husband?
My men should call me "lord"; I am your goodman.

Page. My husband and my lord, my lord and husband,
I am your wife in all obedience.

Sly. I know it well. What must I call her?

Lord. Madam.

Sly. Al'ce madam, or Joan madam?

Lord. Madam, and nothing else, so lords call ladies.

Sly. Madam wife, they say that I have dream'd,
And slept above some fifteen year or more.

Page. Ay, and the time seems thirty unto me,
Being all this time abandon'd from your bed.

Sly. 'Tis much. Servants, leave me and her alone.
Madam, undress you, and come now to bed.

Page. Thrice-noble lord, let me entreat of you
To pardon me yet for a night or two;
Or if not so, until the sun be set.
For your physicians have expressly charg'd,
In peril to incur your former malady,
That I should yet absent me from your bed.
I hope this reason stands for my excuse.

Sly. Ay, it stands so that I may hardly tarry so long. But I would be loath to fall into my dreams again. I will therefore tarry in despite of the flesh and the blood.

Enter a MESSENGER.

Mess. Your honor's players, hearing your amendment,
Are come to play a pleasant comedy,
For so your doctors hold it very meet,
Seeing too much sadness hath congeal'd your blood,
And melancholy is the nurse of frenzy.
Therefore they thought it good you hear a play,
And frame your mind to mirth and merriment,
Which bars a thousand harms and lengthens life.

Sly. Marry, I will, let them play it. Is not a comonty a Christmas gambold, or a tumbling-trick?

Page. No, my good lord, it is more pleasing stuff.

Sly. What, household stuff?

Page. It is a kind of history.

Sly. Well, we'll see't. Come, madam wife, sit by my side, and let the world slip, we shall ne'er be younger. [*They all sit.*] *Flourish*.

[ACT I, SCENE I]

Enter LUCENTIO *and his man* TRANIO.

Luc. Tranio, since for the great desire I had
To see fair Padua, nursery of arts,
I am arriv'd for fruitful Lombardy,
The pleasant garden of great Italy,
And by my father's love and leave am arm'd
With his good will and thy good company,
My trusty servant, well approv'd in all,

65. envious: spiteful. **67. yet**: still, even now. **81. fay**: faith.
82. of: during. **86. house**: tavern.
87. present: bring a charge against. **leet**: manorial court (where complaints about short measure would be heard).
88. seal'd: officially stamped as a guarantee of full measure.
93. Stephen Sly. There was a Stratford citizen of this name. **Greece.** Probably an error for *Greet*, the name of a village twenty miles from Stratford.
97. amends: Sly's error for *amendment*, i.e. recovery (as in line 129).
101. Marry: why, indeed (originally the name of the Virgin Mary used as an oath). **cheer**: hospitable entertainment.
105. goodman: husband (a word in use among the lower classes).

115. abandon'd: banished.
122. In . . . incur: on peril of incurring. **130. pleasant**: merry.
132. sadness . . . blood. That melancholy thickens the blood was a long-established medical belief. **133. frenzy**: madness.
138. gambold. Perhaps Sly's blunder for *gambol* (as *comonty* is for *comedy*), but it is an old form of the word.
140. household stuff. The ordinary meaning is "house furnishings," but Sly may mean "domestic goings-on." **141. history**: story.
144 s.d. Flourish: trumpet fanfare.

I.i. Location: Padua. A street before Baptista's house.
2. nursery of arts. Padua's university, founded in the thirteenth century, was famous throughout Europe.
3. am arriv'd for: have come here on my way to. **fruitful**: fertile.
7. approv'd: tried, proved dependable.

Here let us breathe, and haply institute
A course of learning and ingenious studies.
Pisa, renowned for grave citizens,
Gave me my being and my father first,
A merchant of great traffic through the world,
Vincentio, come of the Bentivolii;
Vincentio's son, brought up in Florence,
It shall become to serve all hopes conceiv'd,
To deck his fortune with his virtuous deeds.
And therefore, Tranio, for the time I study,
Virtue and that part of philosophy
Will I apply that treats of happiness
By virtue specially to be achiev'd.
Tell me thy mind, for I have Pisa left
And am to Padua come, as he that leaves
A shallow plash to plunge him in the deep,
And with saciety seeks to quench his thirst.

Tra. *Mi perdonato*, gentle master mine;
I am, in all affected as yourself,
Glad that you thus continue your resolve
To suck the sweets of sweet philosophy.
Only, good master, while we do admire
This virtue and this moral discipline,
Let's be no Stoics nor no stocks, I pray,
Or so devote to Aristotle's checks
As Ovid be an outcast quite abjur'd.
Balk logic with acquaintance that you have,
And practice rhetoric in your common talk,
Music and poesy use to quicken you,
The mathematics, and the metaphysics,
Fall to them as you find your stomach serves you:
No profit grows where is no pleasure ta'en.
In brief, sir, study what you most affect.

Luc. Gramercies, Tranio, well dost thou advise.
If, Biondello, thou wert come ashore,
We could at once put us in readiness,
And take a lodging fit to entertain
Such friends as time in Padua shall beget.
But stay a while, what company is this?

Tra. Master, some show to welcome us to town.

Enter BAPTISTA *with his two daughters*, KATHERINA *and* BIANCA, GREMIO, *a pantaloon*, HORTENSIO, [*suitor*] *to Bianca*. LUCENTIO, TRANIO *stand by*.

Bap. Gentlemen, importune me no farther,
For how I firmly am resolv'd you know:
That is, not to bestow my youngest daughter
Before I have a husband for the elder.
If either of you both love Katherina,
Because I know you well, and love you well,
Leave shall you have to court her at your pleasure.

Gre. To cart her rather; she's too rough for me.
There, there, Hortensio, will you any wife?

Kath. [*To Baptista.*] I pray you, sir, is it your will
To make a stale of me amongst these mates?

Hor. Mates, maid, how mean you that? No mates for you,
Unless you were of gentler, milder mould.

Kath. I' faith, sir, you shall never need to fear.
Iwis it is not half way to her heart;
But if it were, doubt not her care should be
To comb your noddle with a three-legg'd stool,
And paint your face, and use you like a fool.

Hor. From all such devils, good Lord deliver us!

Gre. And me too, good Lord!

Tra. Husht, master, here's some good pastime toward;
That wench is stark mad or wonderful froward.

Luc. But in the other's silence do I see
Maid's mild behavior and sobriety.
Peace, Tranio!

Tra. Well said, master, mum, and gaze your fill.

Bap. Gentlemen, that I may soon make good
What I have said, Bianca, get you in,
And let it not displease thee, good Bianca,
For I will love thee ne'er the less, my girl.

Kath. A pretty peat! it is best
Put finger in the eye, and she knew why.

Bian. Sister, content you in my discontent.
Sir, to your pleasure humbly I subscribe;
My books and instruments shall be my company,
On them to look and practice by myself.

Luc. Hark, Tranio, thou mayst hear Minerva speak.

Hor. Signior Baptista, will you be so strange?
Sorry am I that our good will effects
Bianca's grief.

Gre. Why will you mew her up,
Signior Baptista, for this fiend of hell,
And make her bear the penance of her tongue?

Bap. Gentlemen, content ye; I am resolv'd.
Go in, Bianca. [*Exit Bianca.*]
And for I know she taketh most delight
In music, instruments, and poetry,
Schoolmasters will I keep within my house,
Fit to instruct her youth. If you, Hortensio,
Or, Signior Gremio, you, know any such,
Prefer them hither; for to cunning men

8. breathe: pause for breath, i.e. remain for a time. **institute:** embark upon. **9. ingenious:** intellectual. **11. first:** before me.
12. traffic: business.
15. become: befit. **serve:** fulfill. **conceiv'd:** i.e. entertained for him by his friends. **19. apply:** study. **23. plash:** pool.
24. saciety: satiety. **25. Mi perdonato:** pardon me.
26. affected: disposed.
31. stocks: blocks of wood, i.e. beings destitute of feelings. The pun on *stoics/stocks* was commonplace.
32. devote: devoted. **checks:** restraints.
33. As: that. **Ovid:** the Latin love-poet; the antithesis is between an ascetic regimen of serious study (Aristotle) and lighter entertainment (Ovid). **34. Balk logic:** chop logic, bandy arguments.
36. quicken: stimulate, enliven.
38. Fall to: partake of. **stomach:** appetite, inclination.
40. affect: find pleasing. **41. Gramercies:** many thanks.
42. come ashore. Like a number of other inland cities, Padua is endowed by Shakespeare with a harbor.
47 s.d. pantaloon: foolish old man (a stock character in Italian comedy).

55. cart. Disorderly women were sometimes punished by being driven through the streets in a cart.
58. stale: laughingstock (but she has also in mind the sense "harlot," suggested by Gremio's jest about carting). **mates:** rude fellows.
59. mates: husbands. **62. Iwis:** indeed. **it:** i.e. marriage.
65. paint: i.e. redden with scratches.
68. Husht: keep silent. **toward:** in view.
69. froward: perverse, refractory. **78. peat:** pet, spoiled darling.
79. Put . . . eye: i.e. weep. **and:** if.
84. Minerva: goddess of wisdom.
85. so strange: i.e. so unnatural a father.
87. mew: shut (term for caging a falcon).
88. for: for the benefit of (?) or in place of (?).
89. her . . . her: i.e. Bianca . . . Katherina's.
97. Prefer: recommend. **cunning:** skillful, able.

I will be very kind, and liberal
To mine own children in good bringing-up,
And so farewell. Katherina, you may stay,
For I have more to commune with Bianca. *Exit.*

Kath. Why, and I trust I may go too, may I not?
What, shall I be appointed hours, as though (belike)
I knew not what to take and what to leave? Ha! *Exit.*

Gre. You may go to the devil's dam; your gifts are so good, here's none will hold you. Their love is not so great, Hortensio, but we may blow our nails together, and fast it fairly out. Our cake's dough on both sides. Farewell; yet for the love I bear my sweet Bianca, if I can by any means light on a fit man to teach her that wherein she delights, I will wish him to her father.

Hor. So will I, Signior Gremio. But a word, I pray. Though the nature of our quarrel yet never brook'd parle, know now upon advice, it toucheth us both, that we may yet again have access to our fair mistress, and be happy rivals in Bianca's love, to labor and effect one thing specially.

Gre. What's that, I pray?

Hor. Marry, sir, to get a husband for her sister.

Gre. A husband! a devil.

Hor. I say, a husband.

Gre. I say, a devil. Think'st thou, Hortensio, though her father be very rich, any man is so very a fool to be married to hell?

Hor. Tush, Gremio; though it pass your patience and mine to endure her loud alarums, why, man, there be good fellows in the world, and a man could light on them, would take her with all faults, and money enough.

Gre. I cannot tell; but I had as lief take her dowry with this condition: to be whipt at the high cross every morning.

Hor. Faith, as you say, there's small choice in rotten apples. But come, since this bar in law makes us friends, it shall be so far forth friendly maintain'd till by helping Baptista's eldest daughter to a husband we set his youngest free for a husband, and then have to't afresh. Sweet Bianca, happy man be his dole! He that runs fastest gets the ring. How say you, Signior Gremio?

Gre. I am agreed, and would I had given him the best horse in Padua to begin his wooing that would thoroughly woo her, wed her, and bed her, and rid the house of her! Come on.

Exeunt ambo [*Gremio and Hortensio*]. *Manent Tranio and Lucentio.*

101. **commune:** talk over. 105. **dam:** mother. **gifts:** endowments.
106–7. **Their love:** our love of them (i.e. women).
107–8. **blow our nails:** i.e. twiddle our thumbs, wait patiently.
108. **fast . . . out:** pass the time in abstinence.
108–9. **Our cake's dough.** Proverbial expression for failure.
109. **on both sides:** for both of us. 112. **wish:** commend.
115. **brook'd parle:** tolerated discussion. **advice:** reflection.
toucheth: behooves, concerns. 124. **very:** completely.
126. **pass:** exceeds. 128. **and:** if.
132–33. **high cross:** cross set on a pedestal in a marketplace.
135–36. **bar in law:** obstacle strong enough to halt a lawsuit.
139–40. **happy . . . dole:** may his (the successful suitor's) lot be that of a happy man (proverbial).
140. **ring:** prize (alluding to the sport of running or riding at the ring, which was carried off by a lance); with play on "wedding ring."
145 s.d. **ambo:** both.

Tra. I pray, sir, tell me, is it possible
That love should of a sudden take such hold?

Luc. O Tranio, till I found it to be true,
I never thought it possible or likely.
But see, while idly I stood looking on,
I found the effect of love in idleness,
And now in plainness do confess to thee,
That art to me as secret and as dear
As Anna to the Queen of Carthage was:
Tranio, I burn, I pine, I perish, Tranio,
If I achieve not this young modest girl.
Counsel me, Tranio, for I know thou canst;
Assist me, Tranio, for I know thou wilt.

Tra. Master, it is no time to chide you now,
Affection is not rated from the heart.
If love have touch'd you, nought remains but so,
"*Redime te captum quam queas minimo.*"

Luc. Gramercies, lad. Go forward, this contents;
The rest will comfort, for thy counsel's sound.

Tra. Master, you look'd so longly on the maid,
Perhaps you mark'd not what's the pith of all.

Luc. O yes, I saw sweet beauty in her face,
Such as the daughter of Agenor had,
That made great Jove to humble him to her hand,
When with his knees he kiss'd the Cretan strond.

Tra. Saw you no more? Mark'd you not how her sister
Began to scold, and raise up such a storm
That mortal ears might hardly endure the din?

Luc. Tranio, I saw her coral lips to move,
And with her breath she did perfume the air.
Sacred and sweet was all I saw in her.

Tra. Nay, then 'tis time to stir him from his trance.
I pray, awake, sir; if you love the maid,
Bend thoughts and wits to achieve her. Thus it stands:
Her elder sister is so curst and shrewd
That till the father rid his hands of her,
Master, your love must live a maid at home,
And therefore has he closely mew'd her up,
Because she will not be annoy'd with suitors.

Luc. Ah, Tranio, what a cruel father's he!
But art thou not advis'd, he took some care
To get her cunning schoolmasters to instruct her?

Tra. Ay, marry, am I, sir; and now 'tis plotted.

Luc. I have it, Tranio.

Tra. Master, for my hand,
Both our inventions meet and jump in one.

Luc. Tell me thine first.

Tra. You will be schoolmaster,
And undertake the teaching of the maid:
That's your device.

154. **Anna:** the sister and confidante of Dido.
160. **rated:** driven away by scolding.
162. **Redime . . . minimo:** "Ransom yourself from captivity as cheaply as you can" (Terence, *Eunuchus*, I.i.29; quoted here in the version in Lily's Latin grammar). 163. **contents:** is satisfying.
165. **look'd . . . on:** i.e. spent so much of your time looking at.
168. **daughter of Agenor:** Europa, loved by Jupiter; he assumed the form of a bull to carry her off. 170. **strond:** strand, shore.
180. **curst and shrewd.** The adjectives are synonyms, both meaning here "ill-natured, shrewish."
183. **closely . . . up:** placed her in close confinement (cf. line 87).
184. **Because:** so that. 186. **advis'd:** aware. 189. **for:** by.
190. **inventions:** schemes. **jump:** agree.

Luc. It is; may it be done?
Tra. Not possible; for who shall bear your part,
And be in Padua here Vincentio's son,
Keep house and ply his book, welcome his friends,
Visit his countrymen, and banquet them?
Luc. *Basta*, content thee; for I have it full.
We have not yet been seen in any house,
Nor can we be distinguish'd by our faces
For man or master. Then it follows thus:
Thou shalt be master, Tranio, in my stead;
Keep house and port and servants, as I should.
I will some other be, some Florentine,
Some Neapolitan, or meaner man of Pisa.
'Tis hatch'd, and shall be so. Tranio, at once
Uncase thee; take my color'd hat and cloak.
When Biondello comes, he waits on thee,
But I will charm him first to keep his tongue.
Tra. So had you need.
In brief, sir, sith it your pleasure is,
And I am tied to be obedient—
For so your father charg'd me at our parting;
"Be serviceable to my son," quoth he,
Although I think 'twas in another sense—
I am content to be Lucentio,
Because so well I love Lucentio.
Luc. Tranio, be so, because Lucentio loves,
And let me be a slave, t' achieve that maid
Whose sudden sight hath thrall'd my wounded eye.

Enter BIONDELLO.

Here comes the rogue. Sirrah, where have you been?
Bion. Where have I been? Nay, how now, where are you? Master, has my fellow Tranio stol'n your clothes? or you stol'n his? or both? Pray what's the news?
Luc. Sirrah, come hither, 'tis no time to jest,
And therefore frame your manners to the time.
Your fellow Tranio here, to save my life,
Puts my apparel and my count'nance on,
And I for my escape have put on his;
For in a quarrel since I came ashore
I kill'd a man, and fear I was descried.
Wait you on him, I charge you, as becomes,
While I make way from hence to save my life.
You understand me?
Bion. Ay, sir!—[*aside*] ne'er a whit.
Luc. And not a jot of Tranio in your mouth,
Tranio is chang'd into Lucentio.
Bion. The better for him, would I were so too!
Tra. So could I, faith, boy, to have the next wish after,
That Lucentio indeed had Baptista's youngest daughter.
But, sirrah, not for my sake, but your master's, I advise
You use your manners discreetly in all kind of companies.

198. **Basta:** enough. **full:** i.e. fully planned.
203. **port:** state, style of living. 205. **meaner:** of lower class.
207. **Uncase:** undress. 211. **sith:** since.
214. **serviceable:** diligent in service.
229. **count'nance:** outward appearance.

When I am alone, why then I am Tranio;
But in all places else [your] master Lucentio.
Luc. Tranio, let's go.
One thing more rests, that thyself execute—
To make one among these wooers. If thou ask me why,
Sufficeth my reasons are both good and weighty.
Exeunt.

The Presenters above speaks.

1. Serv. My lord, you nod, you do not mind the play.
Sly. Yes, by Saint Anne, do I. A good matter, surely; comes there any more of it?
Page. My lord, 'tis but begun.
Sly. 'Tis a very excellent piece of work, madam lady; would 'twere done! *They sit and mark.*

[SCENE II]

Enter PETRUCHIO *and his man* GRUMIO.

Pet. Verona, for a while I take my leave
To see my friends in Padua, but of all
My best beloved and approved friend,
Hortensio; and I trow this is his house.
Here, sirrah Grumio, knock, I say.
Gru. Knock, sir? whom should I knock? Is there any man has rebus'd your worship?
Pet. Villain, I say, knock me here soundly.
Gru. Knock you here, sir? Why, sir, what am I, sir, that I should knock you here, sir?
Pet. Villain, I say, knock me at this gate,
And rap me well, or I'll knock your knave's pate.
Gru. My master is grown quarrelsome. I should knock you first,
And then I know after who comes by the worst.
Pet. Will it not be?
Faith, sirrah, and you'll not knock, I'll ring it.
I'll try how you can *sol*, *fa*, and sing it.
He wrings him by the ears.
Gru. Help, [masters], help, my master is mad.
Pet. Now knock when I bid you, sirrah villain!

Enter HORTENSIO.

Hor. How now, what's the matter? My old friend Grumio! and my good friend Petruchio! How do you all at Verona?
Pet. Signior Hortensio, come you to part the fray?
Con tutto [*il*] *core, ben trovato*, may I say.
Hor. *Alla nostra casa ben venuto, molto honorato signor mio Petrucio.*

248 s.d. **Presenters:** those who, by means of a prologue or an induction, introduce or present a play to the spectators.
249. **mind:** pay attention to. 254 s.d. **mark:** observe.

I.ii. **Location:** Padua. Before Hortensio's house.
4. **trow:** believe. 7. **rebus'd:** blunder for *abused*.
8, 11, 12. **me:** i.e. for me (but Grumio misunderstands, or pretends to). 16. **ring.** With play on *wring*.
19. **villain:** base-born creature.
22. **How . . . all:** i.e. how are all your family.
24. **Con . . . trovato:** with all my heart, well met.
25–26. **Alla . . . Petrucio:** welcome to our house, my most honored Signor Petruchio. (Note the spelling of the name; in Italian *ch* is pronounced *k*, and *c* before *i* like English *ch*.)

Rise, Grumio, rise, we will compound this quarrel.

Gru. Nay, 'tis no matter, sir, what he 'leges in Latin. If this be not a lawful cause for me to leave his service, look you, sir. He bid me knock him and rap him soundly, sir. Well, was it fit for a servant to use his master so, being perhaps (for aught I see) two and thirty, a peep out?
Whom would to God I had well knock'd at first,
Then had not Grumio come by the worst.

Pet. A senseless villain! Good Hortensio,
I bade the rascal knock upon your gate,
And could not get him for my heart to do it.

Gru. Knock at the gate? O heavens! Spake you not these words plain, "Sirrah, knock me here; rap me here; knock me well, and knock me soundly"? And come you now with "knocking at the gate"?

Pet. Sirrah, be gone, or talk not, I advise you.

Hor. Petruchio, patience, I am Grumio's pledge.
Why, this' a heavy chance 'twixt him and you,
Your ancient, trusty, pleasant servant Grumio.
And tell me now, sweet friend, what happy gale
Blows you to Padua here from old Verona?

Pet. Such wind as scatters young men through the world
To seek their fortunes farther than at home,
Where small experience grows. But in a few,
Signior Hortensio, thus it stands with me:
Antonio, my father, is deceas'd,
And I have thrust myself into this maze,
Happily to wive and thrive as best I may.
Crowns in my purse I have, and goods at home,
And so am come abroad to see the world.

Hor. Petruchio, shall I then come roundly to thee,
And wish thee to a shrewd ill-favor'd wife?
Thou'dst thank me but a little for my counsel;
And yet I'll promise thee she shall be rich,
And very rich. But th' art too much my friend,
And I'll not wish thee to her.

Pet. Signior Hortensio, 'twixt such friends as we
Few words suffice; and therefore, if thou know
One rich enough to be Petruchio's wife
(As wealth is burthen of my wooing dance),
Be she as foul as was Florentius' love,
As old as Sibyl, and as curst and shrowd
As Socrates' Xantippe, or a worse,
She moves me not, or not removes at least
Affection's edge in me. [Whe'er] she is as rough
As are the swelling Adriatic seas,
I come to wive it wealthily in Padua;
If wealthily, then happily in Padua.

Gru. Nay, look you, sir, he tells you flatly what his mind is. Why, give him gold enough, and marry him to a puppet or an aglet-baby, or an old trot with ne'er a tooth in her head, though she have as many diseases as two and fifty horses. Why, nothing comes amiss, so money comes withal.

Hor. Petruchio, since we are stepp'd thus far in,
I will continue that I broach'd in jest.
I can, Petruchio, help thee to a wife
With wealth enough, and young and beauteous,
Brought up as best becomes a gentlewoman.
Her only fault, and that is faults enough,
Is that she is intolerable curst
And shrowd and froward, so beyond all measure,
That were my state far worser than it is,
I would not wed her for a mine of gold.

Pet. Hortensio, peace! thou know'st not gold's effect.
Tell me her father's name, and 'tis enough;
For I will board her, though she chide as loud
As thunder when the clouds in autumn crack.

Hor. Her father is Baptista Minola,
An affable and courteous gentleman.
Her name is Katherina Minola,
Renown'd in Padua for her scolding tongue.

Pet. I know her father, though I know not her,
And he knew my deceased father well.
I will not sleep, Hortensio, till I see her,
And therefore let me be thus bold with you
To give you over at this first encounter,
Unless you will accompany me thither.

Gru. I pray you, sir, let him go while the humor lasts. A' my word, and she knew him as well as I do, she would think scolding would do little good upon him. She may perhaps call him half a score knaves or so. Why, that's nothing; and he begin once, he'll rail in his rope-tricks. I'll tell you what, sir, and she stand him but a little, he will throw a figure in her face, and so disfigure her with it, that she shall have no more eyes to see withal than a cat. You know him not, sir.

Hor. Tarry, Petruchio, I must go with thee,
For in Baptista's keep my treasure is.
He hath the jewel of my life in hold,
His youngest daughter, beautiful Bianca,
And her withholds from me [and] other more,

27. **compound**: settle. 28. **'leges**: alleges.
33. **two . . . out**: slang for "drunk" (deriving from the card game trentuno, or one and thirty; *peep* = pip, a spot on a playing card, and *a peep out* = off by one). 45. **pledge**: surety.
46. **this'**: this is. **heavy chance**: sad happening.
47. **ancient**: of long standing.
52. **in a few**: in brief. 59. **come roundly**: speak plainly.
68. **burthen**: burden, ground bass or undersong.
69. **foul**: ugly. **Florentius' love.** A reference to a story best known from Chaucer's *Canterbury Tales*, where it is assigned to the Wife of Bath. Sir Florent promises to marry an old hag if she will tell him the answer to a riddle on which his life depends. After their marriage she becomes young and beautiful. The story is told also by Chaucer's contemporary John Gower in his *Confessio Amantis*, a book that Shakespeare used as a source in another early play, *The Comedy of Errors*.
70. **Sibyl**: prophetess of Cumae to whom Apollo gave as many years of life as she could hold grains of sand in her hand. **shrowd**: shrewd, i.e. shrewish. 71. **Xantippe.** Proverbial for shrewishness.
72. **moves**: disturbs, troubles.
72–73. **or . . . me**: nor dulls in the least the keenness of my inclination (to marry her for her wealth). 78. **mind**: intention.
79. **aglet-baby**: small metal figure serving as the tag on a lacing-cord. **trot**: common prostitute. 82. **withal**: with it. 84. **that**: what.
91. **state**: estate, means.
95. **board**: accost, make advances to (literally, come alongside a ship in order to attack). **chide**: rail, brawl. *Scold* (see line 100) is synonymous. 105. **give you over**: leave you.
107. **humor**: mood, whim.
112. **rope-tricks**: blunder for *rhetorics* (an interpretation supported by *figure* in line 114) (?) or tricks that deserve hanging (?).
113. **stand**: withstand. 115. **withal**: with.
118. **keep**: keeping, custody; perhaps also with the sense of "fortified place" (cf. *dungeon keep*) or "strongroom." *Hold* in line 119 is parallel.

Suitors to her and rivals in my love;
Supposing it a thing impossible,
For those defects I have before rehears'd,
That ever Katherina will be woo'd.
Therefore this order hath Baptista ta'en,
That none shall have access unto Bianca
Till Katherine the curst have got a husband.

Gru. Katherine the curst!
A title for a maid of all titles the worst.

Hor. Now shall my friend Petruchio do me grace,
And offer me disguis'd in sober robes
To old Baptista as a schoolmaster
Well seen in music, to instruct Bianca,
That so I may by this device at least
Have leave and leisure to make love to her,
And unsuspected court her by herself.

Enter Gremio, *and* Lucentio *disguised* [*as a schoolmaster*].

Gru. Here's no knavery! See, to beguile the old
folks, how the young folks lay their heads together!
Master, master, look about you! Who goes there? ha!

Hor. Peace, Grumio, it is the rival of my love.
Petruchio, stand by a while.

Gru. A proper stripling, and an amorous!
[*They stand aside.*]

Gre. O, very well, I have perus'd the note.
Hark you, sir, I'll have them very fairly bound—
All books of love, see that at any hand—
And see you read no other lectures to her.
You understand me. Over and beside
Signior Baptista's liberality,
I'll mend it with a largess. Take your paper too,
And let me have them very well perfum'd;
For she is sweeter than perfume itself
To whom they go to. What will you read to her?

Luc. What e'er I read to her, I'll plead for you
As for my patron, stand you so assur'd,
As firmly as yourself were still in place,
Yea, and perhaps with more successful words
Than you—unless you were a scholar, sir.

Gre. O this learning, what a thing it is!

Gru. O this woodcock, what an ass it is!

Pet. Peace, sirrah!

Hor. Grumio, mum! [*Coming forward.*] God save you, Signior Gremio.

Gre. And you are well met, Signior Hortensio.
Trow you whither I am going? To Baptista Minola.
I promis'd to inquire carefully
About a schoolmaster for the fair Bianca,
And by good fortune I have lighted well

131. **grace**: a favor. 134. **seen**: versed.
141. **love**: i.e. love-suit.
143. **proper stripling**: handsome young man (ironically alluding to Gremio).
144. **note**. Evidently a memorandum from the supposed schoolmaster about books for Bianca.
145. **I'll have them**: I desire them to be, i.e. see that they are. **fairly**: handsomely. 146. **at any hand**: in any case.
147. **read . . . lectures**: teach . . . subjects.
150. **mend**: augment. **largess**: liberal gift. **paper**: i.e. the "note" of line 144. 151. **them**: i.e. the books.
156. **as**: i.e. as if. **in place**: present.
160. **woodcock**. A bird easily caught, hence proverbial for stupidity.
164. **Trow**: know.

On this young man; for learning and behavior
Fit for her turn, well read in poetry
And other books, good ones, I warrant ye.

Hor. 'Tis well; and I have met a gentleman
Hath promis'd me to help [me] to another,
A fine musician to instruct our mistress;
So shall I no whit be behind in duty
To fair Bianca, so beloved of me.

Gre. Beloved of me, and that my deeds shall prove.

Gru. And that his bags shall prove.

Hor. Gremio, 'tis now no time to vent our love;
Listen to me, and if you speak me fair,
I'll tell you news indifferent good for either.
Here is a gentleman whom by chance I met,
Upon agreement from us to his liking,
Will undertake to woo curst Katherine,
Yea, and to marry her, if her dowry please.

Gre. So said, so done, is well.
Hortensio, have you told him all her faults?

Pet. I know she is an irksome brawling scold.
If that be all, masters, I hear no harm.

Gre. No, say'st me so, friend? What countryman?

Pet. Born in Verona, old [Antonio's] son.
My father dead, my fortune lives for me,
And I do hope good days and long to see.

Gre. O sir, such a life, with such a wife, were strange;
But if you have a stomach, to't a' God's name;
You shall have me assisting you in all.
But will you woo this wild-cat?

Pet. Will I live?

Gru. Will he woo her? ay—or I'll hang her.

Pet. Why came I hither but to that intent?
Think you a little din can daunt mine ears?
Have I not in my time heard lions roar?
Have I not heard the sea, puff'd up with winds,
Rage like an angry boar chafed with sweat?
Have I not heard great ordnance in the field,
And heaven's artillery thunder in the skies?
Have I not in a pitched battle heard
Loud 'larums, neighing steeds, and trumpets' clang?
And do you tell me of a woman's tongue,
That gives not half so great a blow to hear
As will a chestnut in a farmer's fire?
Tush, tush, fear boys with bugs.

Gru. For he fears none.

Gre. Hortensio, hark.
This gentleman is happily arriv'd,
My mind presumes, for his own good and [ours].

Hor. I promis'd we would be contributors,
And bear his charge of wooing, whatsoe'er.

Gre. And so we will, provided that he win her.

Gru. I would I were as sure of a good dinner.

177. **bags**: i.e. money bags. 178. **vent**: express.
179. **fair**: courteously, civilly. 180. **indifferent**: equally.
182. **Upon . . . liking**: who, if we will meet the terms he wants (see lines 214–15).
194. **a'**: of, i.e. in. 202. **chafed**: irritated.
203. **ordnance**: cannon. 206. **'larums**: alarums, calls to arms.
208. **blow**: blasting noise.
210. **fear . . . bugs**: frighten children with bogeymen.
212. **happily**: propitiously. 215. **charge**: expense.

Enter Tranio *brave, [as Lucentio,] and* Biondello.

Tra. Gentlemen, God save you. If I may be bold,
Tell me, I beseech you, which is the readiest way
To the house of Signior Baptista Minola?
Bion. He that has the two fair daughters? is't he you mean?
Tra. Even he, Biondello.
Gre. Hark you, sir, you mean not her to—
Tra. Perhaps him and her, sir; what have you to do?
Pet. Not her that chides, sir, at any hand, I pray.
Tra. I love no chiders, sir. Biondello, let's away.
Luc. [*Aside.*] Well begun, Tranio.
Hor. Sir, a word ere you go.
Are you a suitor to the maid you talk of, yea or no?
Tra. And if I be, sir, is it any offense?
Gre. No; if without more words you will get you hence.
Tra. Why, sir, I pray, are not the streets as free
For me as for you?
Gre. But so is not she.
Tra. For what reason, I beseech you?
Gre. For this reason, if you'll know,
That she's the choice love of Signior Gremio.
Hor. That she's the chosen of Signior Hortensio.
Tra. Softly, my masters! If you be gentlemen,
Do me this right: hear me with patience.
Baptista is a noble gentleman,
To whom my father is not all unknown,
And were his daughter fairer than she is,
She may more suitors have, and me for one.
Fair Leda's daughter had a thousand wooers,
Then well one more may fair Bianca have;
And so she shall. Lucentio shall make one,
Though Paris came in hope to speed alone.
Gre. What, this gentleman will out-talk us all.
Luc. Sir, give him head, I know he'll prove a jade.
Pet. Hortensio, to what end are all these words?
Hor. Sir, let me be so bold as ask you,
Did you yet ever see Baptista's daughter?
Tra. No, sir, but hear I do that he hath two:
The one as famous for a scolding tongue,
As is the other for beauteous modesty.
Pet. Sir, sir, the first's for me, let her go by.
Gre. Yea, leave that labor to great Hercules,
And let it be more than Alcides' twelve.
Pet. Sir, understand you this of me, in sooth:
The youngest daughter, whom you hearken for,
Her father keeps from all access of suitors,
And will not promise her to any man,
Until the elder sister first be wed.
The younger then is free, and not before.
Tra. If it be so, sir, that you are the man
Must stead us all, and me amongst the rest;
And if you break the ice, and do this [feat],
Achieve the elder, set the younger free
For our access—whose hap shall be to have her
Will not so graceless be to be ingrate.
Hor. Sir, you say well, and well you do conceive,
And since you do profess to be a suitor,
You must, as we do, gratify this gentleman,
To whom we all rest generally beholding.
Tra. Sir, I shall not be slack; in sign whereof,
Please ye we may contrive this afternoon,
And quaff carouses to our mistress' health,
And do as adversaries do in law,
Strive mightily, but eat and drink as friends.
Gru., Bion. O excellent motion! Fellows, let's be gone.
Hor. The motion's good indeed, and be it so,
Petruchio, I shall be your *ben venuto*. *Exeunt.*

[ACT II, Scene I]

Enter Katherina *and* Bianca.

Bian. Good sister, wrong me not, nor wrong yourself,
To make a bondmaid and a slave of me—
That I disdain; but for these other [gawds],
Unbind my hands, I'll pull them off myself,
Yea, all my raiment, to my petticoat,
Or what you will command me will I do,
So well I know my duty to my elders.
Kath. Of all thy suitors here I charge [thee] tell
Whom thou lov'st best; see thou dissemble not.
Bian. Believe me, sister, of all the men alive
I never yet beheld that special face
Which I could fancy more than any other.
Kath. Minion, thou liest. Is't not Hortensio?
Bian. If you affect him, sister, here I swear
I'll plead for you myself, but you shall have him.
Kath. O then belike you fancy riches more:
You will have Gremio to keep you fair.
Bian. Is it for him you do envy me so?
Nay then you jest, and now I well perceive
You have but jested with me all this while.
I prithee, sister Kate, untie my hands.
Kath. If that be jest, then all the rest was so.
Strikes her.

Enter Baptista.

Bap. Why, how now, dame, whence grows this insolence?
Bianca, stand aside. Poor girl, she weeps.
Go ply thy needle, meddle not with her.
For shame, thou hilding of a devilish spirit,

217. s.d. brave: finely dressed. **224. what . . . do**: what is it to you.
236. Softly: gently. **237. right**: justice.
242. Fair Leda's daughter: Helen of Troy.
245. Paris: Trojan prince who won Helen from her husband, King Menelaus of Sparta. **came**: were to come. **speed**: succeed.
247. jade: ill-conditioned horse (not likely to finish the course).
256. Alcides' twelve: i.e. the twelve labors of Hercules (the descendant of Alcaeus). **257. sooth**: truth.
258. hearken: lie in wait. **264. stead**: help.

267. whose hap: he whose good fortune.
269. conceive: understand. **271. gratify**: reward.
272. generally: as a whole. **beholding**: beholden, indebted.
274. contrive: spend, pass (time). **275. carouses**: toasts.
276. adversaries: i.e. lawyers on opposite sides of a case.
280. ben venuto: welcome, i.e. host.

II.i. Location: Padua. Baptista's house.
3. gawds: ornaments. **12. fancy**: love. **13. Minion**: hussy.
14. affect: love. **17. fair**: finely dressed. **18. envy**: hate.
26. hilding: good-for-nothing jade.

Why dost thou wrong her that did ne'er wrong thee?
When did she cross thee with a bitter word?
Kath. Her silence flouts me, and I'll be reveng'd.
Flies after Bianca.
Bap. What, in my sight? Bianca, get thee in.
Exit [Bianca].
Kath. What, will you not suffer me? Nay, now I see
She is your treasure, she must have a husband;
I must dance barefoot on her wedding-day,
And for your love to her lead apes in hell.
Talk not to me, I will go sit and weep,
Till I can find occasion of revenge. *[Exit.]*
Bap. Was ever gentleman thus griev'd as I?
But who comes here?

Enter Gremio, Lucentio *in the habit of a mean man,* Petruchio *with* [Hortensio *as a musician, and*] Tranio [*as Lucentio*] *with his boy* [Biondello] *bearing a lute and books.*

Gre. Good morrow, neighbor Baptista.
Bap. Good morrow, neighbor Gremio. God save you, gentlemen!
Pet. And you, good sir! Pray have you not a daughter
Call'd Katherina, fair and virtuous?
Bap. I have a daughter, sir, call'd Katherina.
Gre. You are too blunt, go to it orderly.
Pet. You wrong me, Signior Gremio, give me leave.
I am a gentleman of Verona, sir,
That hearing of her beauty and her wit,
Her affability and bashful modesty,
Her wondrous qualities and mild behavior,
Am bold to show myself a forward guest
Within your house, to make mine eye the witness
Of that report which I so oft have heard.
And for an entrance to my entertainment,
I do present you with a man of mine,
[Presenting Hortensio.]
Cunning in music and the mathematics,
To instruct her fully in those sciences,
Whereof I know she is not ignorant.
Accept of him, or else you do me wrong.
His name is Litio, born in Mantua.
Bap. Y' are welcome, sir, and he, for your good sake.
But for my daughter Katherine, this I know,
She is not for your turn, the more my grief.
Pet. I see you do not mean to part with her,
Or else you like not of my company.
Bap. Mistake me not, I speak but as I find.
Whence are you, sir? What may I call your name?
Pet. Petruchio is my name, Antonio's son,
A man well known throughout all Italy.
Bap. I know him well; you are welcome for his sake.

Gre. Saving your tale, Petruchio, I pray
Let us that are poor petitioners speak too.
[Backare]! you are marvellous forward.
Pet. O, pardon me, Signior Gremio, I would fain be doing.
Gre. I doubt it not, sir; but you will curse your wooing.
[Neighbor], this is a gift very grateful, I am sure of it. To express the like kindness, myself, that have been more kindly beholding to you than any, freely give unto [you] this young scholar [*presenting Lucentio*], that hath been long studying at Rheims, as cunning in Greek, Latin, and other languages, as the other in music and mathematics. His name is Cambio; pray accept his service.

Bap. A thousand thanks, Signior Gremio. Welcome, good Cambio. [*To Tranio.*] But, gentle sir, methinks you walk like a stranger. May I be so bold to know the cause of your coming?

Tra. Pardon me, sir, the boldness is mine own,
That being a stranger in this city here,
Do make myself a suitor to your daughter,
Unto Bianca, fair and virtuous.
Nor is your firm resolve unknown to me,
In the preferment of the eldest sister.
This liberty is all that I request,
That upon knowledge of my parentage,
I may have welcome 'mongst the rest that woo,
And free access and favor as the rest;
And toward the education of your daughters,
I here bestow a simple instrument,
And this small packet of Greek and Latin books.
If you accept them, then their worth is great.
Bap. Lucentio is your name, of whence, I pray?
Tra. Of Pisa, sir, son to Vincentio.
Bap. A mighty man of Pisa; by report
I know him well. You are very welcome, sir.
Take you the lute, and you the set of books.
You shall go see your pupils presently.
Holla, within!

Enter a Servant.

Sirrah, lead these gentlemen
To my daughters, and tell them both,
These are their tutors. Bid them use them well.
[*Exit Servant with Lucentio and Hortensio, Biondello following.*]
We will go walk a little in the orchard,
And then to dinner. You are passing welcome,
And so I pray you all to think yourselves.
Pet. Signior Baptista, my business asketh haste,
And every day I cannot come to woo.
You knew my father well, and in him me,
Left soly heir to all his lands and goods,
Which I have bettered rather than decreas'd.

33–34. **dance . . . hell.** Both proverbial fates assigned to old maids.
38 s.d. **mean:** of low rank (i.e. Lucentio is in his disguise as the schoolmaster Cambio).
45. **orderly:** properly, i.e. more ceremoniously.
50. **qualities:** natural gifts.
54. **for an entrance:** as an entrance fee. **entertainment:** reception.
66. **as I find:** i.e. as the facts stand.
70. **I . . . well:** i.e. his name is well known to me.

71. **Saving:** with all respect for.
73. **Backare:** stand back (pseudo-Latin).
74. **would . . . doing:** am eager to get on with the business (*doing* is also slang for "having sexual intercourse").
86. **stranger:** foreigner. 97. **favor:** leave, permission.
102. **Lucentio . . . name.** As Baptista presumably learns from the inscriptions in the books. 104. **report:** reputation.
107. **presently:** immediately. 111. **orchard:** garden.
112. **passing:** exceedingly. 117. **soly:** solely.

Then tell me, if I get your daughter's love,
What dowry shall I have with her to wife?
Bap. After my death, the one half of my lands,
And in possession twenty thousand crowns.
Pet. And for that dowry, I'll assure her of
Her widowhood, be it that she survive me,
In all my lands and leases whatsoever.
Let specialties be therefore drawn between us,
That covenants may be kept on either hand.
Bap. Ay, when the special thing is well obtain'd,
That is, her love; for that is all in all.
Pet. Why, that is nothing; for I tell you, father,
I am as peremptory as she proud-minded;
And where two raging fires meet together,
They do consume the thing that feeds their fury.
Though little fire grows great with little wind,
Yet extreme gusts will blow out fire and all;
So I to her, and so she yields to me,
For I am rough, and woo not like a babe.
Bap. Well mayst thou woo, and happy be thy speed!
But be thou arm'd for some unhappy words.
Pet. Ay, to the proof, as mountains are for winds,
That [shake] not, though they blow perpetually.

Enter HORTENSIO [*as Litio*] *with his head broke.*

Bap. How now, my friend, why dost thou look so pale?
Hor. For fear, I promise you, if I look pale.
Bap. What, will my daughter prove a good musician?
Hor. I think she'll sooner prove a soldier,
Iron may hold with her, but never lutes.
Bap. Why then thou canst not break her to the lute?
Hor. Why no, for she hath broke the lute to me.
I did but tell her she mistook her frets,
And bow'd her hand to teach her fingering;
When, with a most impatient devilish spirit,
"Frets, call you these?" quoth she, "I'll fume with them."
And with that word she strook me on the head,
And through the instrument my pate made way,
And there I stood amazed for a while,
As on a pillory, looking through the lute,
While she did call me rascal fiddler
And twangling Jack, with twenty such vild terms,
As had she studied to misuse me so.
Pet. Now by the world, it is a lusty wench!
I love her ten times more than e'er I did.
O, how I long to have some chat with her!
Bap. Well, go with me and be not so discomfited.
Proceed in practice with my younger daughter;

122. **possession:** i.e. immediate possession.
124. **widowhood:** widow's share of the estate.
126. **specialties:** express contracts.
133. **They . . . fury:** i.e. they cancel each other out (pride meets pride). 138. **speed:** fortune. 139. **unhappy:** hateful.
140. **to the proof:** in proved (tested) armor.
141 **s.d. with . . . broke:** with a bleeding cut on his head.
146. **hold with her:** stand her usage. 147. **break:** train.
149. **frets:** bars for fingering on a lute. 150. **bow'd:** bent.
152. **fume.** With obvious play on *fret* in the sense "be vexed."
155. **amazed:** in confusion.
158. **twangling Jack:** twanging knave. **vild:** vile.
159. **As:** as if. 160. **lusty:** lively, vigorous.

She's apt to learn, and thankful for good turns.
Signior Petruchio, will you go with us,
Or shall I send my daughter Kate to you?
Pet. I pray you do. I'll attend her here,
Exit [*Baptista with Gremio, Tranio, and Hortensio*]. *Manet Petruchio.*
And woo her with some spirit when she comes.
Say that she rail, why then I'll tell her plain
She sings as sweetly as a nightingale;
Say that she frown, I'll say she looks as clear
As morning roses newly wash'd with dew;
Say she be mute, and will not speak a word,
Then I'll commend her volubility,
And say she uttereth piercing eloquence;
If she do bid me pack, I'll give her thanks,
As though she bid me stay by her a week;
If she deny to wed, I'll crave the day
When I shall ask the banes, and when be married.
But here she comes, and now, Petruchio, speak.

Enter KATHERINA.

Good morrow, Kate, for that's your name, I hear.
Kath. Well have you heard, but something hard of hearing:
They call me Katherine that do talk of me.
Pet. You lie, in faith, for you are call'd plain Kate,
And bonny Kate, and sometimes Kate the curst;
But Kate, the prettiest Kate in Christendom,
Kate of Kate-Hall, my super-dainty Kate,
For dainties are all Kates, and therefore, Kate,
Take this of me, Kate of my consolation—
Hearing thy mildness prais'd in every town,
Thy virtues spoke of, and thy beauty sounded,
Yet not so deeply as to thee belongs,
Myself am mov'd to woo thee for my wife.
Kath. Mov'd! in good time! Let him that mov'd you hither
Remove you hence. I knew you at the first
You were a moveable.
Pet. Why, what's a moveable?
Kath. A join'd-stool.
Pet. Thou hast hit it; come sit on me.
Kath. Asses are made to bear, and so are you.
Pet. Women are made to bear, and so are you.
Kath. No such jade as you, if me you mean.
Pet. Alas, good Kate, I will not burthen thee,
For knowing thee to be but young and light.

165. **apt:** willing, quick. 168. **attend:** await.
172. **clear:** cheerful, serene. 177. **pack:** be gone.
179. **deny:** refuse. **crave the day:** inquire the date.
180. **ask the banes:** have the banns read.
183. **something:** somewhat.
188. **Kate-Hall.** Kate is so well spoken of that her residence takes its name from her rather than from her family or her father.
189. **Kates.** A play on *cates*, "delicacies." Many editors read *cates*.
192. **sounded:** proclaimed (but *deeply* in the next line indicates a quibble on the sense "plumbed").
195. **in good time:** indeed, forsooth.
197. **moveable.** With pun on "piece of furniture."
198. **join'd-stool:** a stool with legs fitted into it, a good piece of joinery.
199. **bear:** carry (with following puns on "bear children" and "support a man during sexual intercourse").
201. **jade:** a horse that soon tires. 202. **burthen:** burden.
203. **For knowing:** because I know. **light:** (1) delicate, slight; (2) wanton; (3) lacking a burden in the musical sense of "having no ground bass."

Kath. Too light for such a swain as you to catch,
And yet as heavy as my weight should be.
Pet. Should be! should—buzz!
Kath. Well ta'en, and like a buzzard.
Pet. O slow-wing'd turtle, shall a buzzard take thee?
Kath. Ay, for a turtle, as he takes a buzzard.
Pet. Come, come, you wasp, i' faith you are too angry.
Kath. If I be waspish, best beware my sting.
Pet. My remedy is then to pluck it out.
Kath. Ay, if the fool could find it where it lies.
Pet. Who knows not where a wasp does wear his sting?
In his tail.
Kath. In his tongue.
Pet. Whose tongue?
Kath. Yours, if you talk of tales, and so farewell.
Pet. What, with my tongue in your tail? Nay, come again,
Good Kate; I am a gentleman—
Kath. That I'll try. *She strikes him.*
Pet. I swear I'll cuff you, if you strike again.
Kath. So may you lose your arms.
If you strike me, you are no gentleman,
And if no gentleman, why then no arms.
Pet. A herald, Kate? O, put me in thy books!
Kath. What is your crest? a coxcomb?
Pet. A combless cock, so Kate will be my hen.
Kath. No cock of mine, you crow too like a craven.
Pet. Nay, come, Kate, come; you must not look so sour.
Kath. It is my fashion when I see a crab.
Pet. Why, here's no crab, and therefore look not sour.
Kath. There is, there is.
Pet. Then show it me.
Kath. Had I a glass, I would.
Pet. What, you mean my face?
Kath. Well aim'd of such a young one.
Pet. Now, by Saint George, I am too young for you.
Kath. Yet you are wither'd.
Pet. 'Tis with cares.
Kath. I care not.
Pet. Nay, hear you, Kate. In sooth you scape not so.
Kath. I chafe you if I tarry. Let me go.
Pet. No, not a whit, I find you passing gentle:
'Twas told me you were rough and coy and sullen,
And now I find report a very liar;
For thou art pleasant, gamesome, passing courteous,
But slow in speech, yet sweet as spring-time flowers.
Thou canst not frown, thou canst not look askaunce,
Nor bite the lip, as angry wenches will,
Nor hast thou pleasure to be cross in talk;
But thou with mildness entertain'st thy wooers,
With gentle conference, soft, and affable.
Why does the world report that Kate doth limp?
O sland'rous world! Kate like the hazel-twig
Is straight and slender, and as brown in hue
As hazel-nuts, and sweeter than the kernels.
O, let me see thee walk. Thou dost not halt.
Kath. Go, fool, and whom thou keep'st command.
Pet. Did ever Dian so become a grove
As Kate this chamber with her princely gait?
O, be thou Dian, and let her be Kate,
And then let Kate be chaste, and Dian sportful!
Kath. Where did you study all this goodly speech?
Pet. It is extempore, from my mother-wit.
Kath. A witty mother! witless else her son.
Pet. Am I not wise?
Kath. Yes, keep you warm.
Pet. Marry, so I mean, sweet Katherine, in thy bed;
And therefore setting all this chat aside,
Thus in plain terms: your father hath consented
That you shall be my wife; your dowry 'greed on;
And will you, nill you, I will marry you.
Now, Kate, I am a husband for your turn,
For by this light whereby I see thy beauty,
Thy beauty that doth make me like thee well,
Thou must be married to no man but me;
For I am he am born to tame you, Kate,
And bring you from a wild Kate to a Kate
Conformable as other household Kates.

Enter BAPTISTA, GREMIO, TRANIO [*as Lucentio*].

Here comes your father. Never make denial;
I must and will have Katherine to my wife.
Bap. Now, Signior Petruchio, how speed you with my daughter?
Pet. How but well, sir? how but well?
It were impossible I should speed amiss.
Bap. Why, how now, daughter Katherine, in your dumps?
Kath. Call you me daughter? Now I promise you
You have show'd a tender fatherly regard,
To wish me wed to one half lunatic,
A madcap ruffian and a swearing Jack,

204. light: quick, elusive. **swain:** young rustic, country bumpkin.
206. buzz. Punning on *be/bee*, with the rude implication that her remark makes no more sense than a buzzing sound. **buzzard:** fool (figuratively). In line 207 the word denotes an inferior kind of hawk, in line 208 a buzzing insect (which prompts Petruchio's *wasp* in line 209). **207. turtle:** turtledove.
217. talk of tales: talk idly (with obvious pun).
223. arms: coat of arms.
224. herald: authority on heraldry. **books:** (1) heraldic registers; (2) good books, i.e. favor.
225. crest: (1) heraldic device; (2) comb, as on a cock's head. **coxcomb.** The badge of the court fool.
226. combless: gentle, with crest cut down.
227. craven: a cock that will not fight. **229. crab:** crab apple.
235. aim'd of: guessed for. **236. young:** i.e. strong.
240. scape: escape.
241. chafe: (1) irritate; (2) inflame, excite.

243. coy: disdainful.
246. But: not other than. **247. askaunce:** scornfully.
251. conference: conversation. **256. halt:** limp.
257. whom . . . command: i.e. command your servants, not me.
258. Dian: Diana, goddess of the hunt and of chastity.
261. sportful: amorous.
266. keep you warm. Alluding to the proverbial "wit enough to keep oneself warm" (cf. "sense enough to come in out of the rain"), which she implies is as much wit as he possesses.
271. nill you: will you not. **272. for your turn:** to suit you.
277. wild Kate. Perhaps with a pun on *wildcat.*
281. speed: succeed, fare. **284. in your dumps:** downcast.
285. promise: assure.

That thinks with oaths to face the matter out.
Pet. Father, 'tis thus: yourself and all the world,
That talk'd of her, have talk'd amiss of her.
If she be curst, it is for policy,
For she's not froward, but modest as the dove;
She is not hot, but temperate as the morn;
For patience she will prove a second Grissel,
And Roman Lucrece for her chastity;
And to conclude, we have 'greed so well together
That upon Sunday is the wedding-day.
Kath. I'll see thee hang'd on Sunday first.
Gre. Hark, Petruchio, she says she'll see thee hang'd first.
Tra. Is this your speeding? Nay then good night our part!
Pet. Be patient, gentlemen, I choose her for myself.
If she and I be pleas'd, what's that to you?
'Tis bargain'd 'twixt us twain, being alone,
That she shall still be curst in company.
I tell you 'tis incredible to believe
How much she loves me. O, the kindest Kate,
She hung about my neck, and kiss on kiss
She vied so fast, protesting oath on oath,
That in a twink she won me to her love.
O, you are novices! 'tis a world to see
How tame, when men and women are alone,
A meacock wretch can make the curstest shrew.
Give me thy hand, Kate, I will unto Venice
To buy apparel 'gainst the wedding-day.
Provide the feast, father, and bid the guests,
I will be sure my Katherine shall be fine.
Bap. I know not what to say, but give me your hands.
God send you joy, Petruchio, 'tis a match.
Gre., Tra. Amen, say we. We will be witnesses.
Pet. Father, and wife, and gentlemen, adieu.
I will to Venice, Sunday comes apace.
We will have rings and things, and fine array;
And kiss me, Kate, we will be married a' Sunday.
Exeunt Petruchio and Katherine [severally].
Gre. Was ever match clapp'd up so suddenly?
Bap. Faith, gentlemen, now I play a merchant's part,
And venture madly on a desperate mart.
Tra. 'Twas a commodity lay fretting by you;
'Twill bring you gain, or perish on the seas.
Bap. The gain I seek is, quiet [in] the match.
Gre. No doubt but he hath got a quiet catch.
But now, Baptista, to your younger daughter;
Now is the day we long have looked for.
I am your neighbor, and was suitor first.
Tra. And I am one that love Bianca more
Than words can witness, or your thoughts can guess.

289. face: brazen. **292. policy:** crafty purpose.
295. Grissel: patient Griselda, a model of wifely submission. Her story is told by the Clerk in Chaucer's *Canterbury Tales.*
296. Lucrece: Lucretia, who committed suicide after her rape by Sextus Tarquinius. Shakespeare told the story in *The Rape of Lucrece.*
309. vied: i.e. kept matching in an effort to go me one better.
311. a world: worth a world, matter for wonder.
313. meacock: timid. **315. 'gainst:** in preparation for.
317. fine: handsomely dressed. **325. clapp'd up:** settled.
327. mart: bargain.
328. fretting: decaying in disuse (with a play on "irritable").

Gre. Youngling, thou canst not love so dear as I.
Tra. Greybeard, thy love doth freeze.
Gre. But thine doth fry.
Skipper, stand back, 'tis age that nourisheth.
Tra. But youth in ladies' eyes that flourisheth.
Bap. Content you, gentlemen, I will compound this strife.
'Tis deeds must win the prize, and he of both
That can assure my daughter greatest dower
Shall have my Bianca's love.
Say, Signior Gremio, what can you assure her?
Gre. First, as you know, my house within the city
Is richly furnished with plate and gold,
Basins and ewers to lave her dainty hands;
My hangings all of Tyrian tapestry;
In ivory coffers I have stuff'd my crowns;
In cypress chests my arras counterpoints,
Costly apparel, tents, and canopies,
Fine linen, Turkey cushions boss'd with pearl,
Valens of Venice gold in needle-work;
Pewter and brass, and all things that belongs
To house or house-keeping. Then at my farm
I have a hundred milch-kine to the pail,
Six score fat oxen standing in my stalls,
And all things answerable to this portion.
Myself am strook in years, I must confess,
And if I die to-morrow, this is hers,
If whilst I live she will be only mine.
Tra. That "only" came well in. Sir, list to me:
I am my father's heir and only son.
If I may have your daughter to my wife,
I'll leave her houses three or four as good,
Within rich Pisa walls, as any one
Old Signior Gremio has in Padua,
Besides two thousand ducats by the year
Of fruitful land, all which shall be her jointer.
What, have I pinch'd you, Signior Gremio?
Gre. Two thousand ducats by the year of land!
[*Aside.*] My land amounts not to so much in all.—
That she shall have, besides an argosy
That now is lying in Marsellis road.
What, have I chok'd you with an argosy?
Tra. Gremio, 'tis known my father hath no less
Than three great argosies, besides two galliasses
And twelve tight galleys. These I will assure her,
And twice as much, what e'er thou off'rest next.
Gre. Nay, I have off'red all, I have no more,
And she can have no more than all I have;
If you like me, she shall have me and mine.

337. dear. With a play on "expensively."
339. Skipper: flighty fellow.
341. Content you: be calm. **compound:** settle.
342–43. he . . . That: whichever of you two.
343. assure: convey (property). **349. Tyrian:** purple or dark red.
351. arras counterpoints: tapestry counterpanes.
352. tents: bed hangings. **353. boss'd:** embossed, studded.
354. Valens: valances, fringes or short draperies edging bed canopies.
357. milch-kine . . . pail: dairy cattle.
359. all . . . portion: i.e. everything else on the same scale.
360. strook: struck, i.e. advanced.
369. ducats: Venetian gold coins.
370. jointer: jointure, marriage settlement.
371. pinch'd: discomfited. **374. argosy:** large merchant vessel.
375. Marsellis road: harbor of Marseilles.
376. chok'd: silenced. **378. galliasses:** large galleys.
379. tight: watertight, sound.

Tra. Why then the maid is mine from all the world,
By your firm promise; Gremio is outvied.
Bap. I must confess your offer is the best,
And let your father make her the assurance,
She is your own, else you must pardon me;
If you should die before him, where's her dower?
Tra. That's but a cavil; he is old, I young.
Gre. And may not young men die as well as old?
Bap. Well, gentlemen,
I am thus resolv'd: on Sunday next you know
My daughter Katherine is to be married.
Now on the Sunday following shall Bianca
Be bride to you, if you make this assurance;
If not, to Signior Gremio.
And so I take my leave, and thank you both. *Exit.*
Gre. Adieu, good neighbor. Now I fear thee not.
Sirrah, young gamester, your father were a fool
To give thee all, and in his waning age
Set foot under thy table. Tut, a toy!
An old Italian fox is not so kind, my boy. *Exit.*
Tra. A vengeance on your crafty withered hide!
Yet I have fac'd it with a card of ten.
'Tis in my head to do my master good.
I see no reason but suppos'd Lucentio
Must get a father, call'd suppos'd Vincentio;
And that's a wonder. Fathers commonly
Do get their children; but in this case of wooing,
A child shall get a sire, if I fail not of my cunning.
Exit.

ACT III, [Scene I]

Enter Lucentio [*as Cambio*], Hortensio [*as Litio*], *and* Bianca.

Luc. Fiddler, forbear, you grow too forward, sir.
Have you so soon forgot the entertainment
Her sister Katherine welcom'd you withal?
Hor. But, wrangling pedant, this is
The patroness of heavenly harmony.
Then give me leave to have prerogative,
And when in music we have spent an hour,
Your lecture shall have leisure for as much.
Luc. Preposterous ass, that never read so far
To know the cause why music was ordain'd!
Was it not to refresh the mind of man
After his studies or his usual pain?
Then give me leave to read philosophy,
And while I pause, serve in your harmony.
Hor. Sirrah, I will not bear these braves of thine.
Bian. Why, gentlemen, you do me double wrong

To strive for that which resteth in my choice.
I am no breeching scholar in the schools,
I'll not be tied to hours, nor 'pointed times,
But learn my lessons as I please myself.
And to cut off all strife, here sit we down:
Take you your instrument, play you the whiles,
His lecture will be done ere you have tun'd.
Hor. You'll leave his lecture when I am in tune?
Luc. That will be never, tune your instrument.
Bian. Where left we last?
Luc. Here, madam:
"*Hic ibat Simois; hic est* [*Sigeia*] *tellus;*
Hic steterat Priami regia celsa senis."
Bian. Conster them.
Luc. "*Hic ibat,*" as I told you before, "*Simois,*" I am Lucentio, "*hic est,*" son unto Vincentio of Pisa, "[*Sigeia*] *tellus,*" disguis'd thus to get your love, "*Hic steterat,*" and that Lucentio that comes a-wooing, "*Priami,*" is my man Tranio, "*regia,*" bearing my port, "*celsa senis,*" that we might beguile the old pantaloon.
Hor. Madam, my instrument's in tune.
Bian. Let's hear. O fie, the treble jars.
Luc. Spit in the hole, man, and tune again.
Bian. Now let me see if I can conster it: "*Hic ibat Simois,*" I know you not, "*hic est* [*Sigeia*] *tellus,*" I trust you not, "*Hic steterat Priami,*" take heed he hear us not, "*regia,*" presume not, "*celsa senis,*" despair not.
Hor. Madam, 'tis now in tune.
Luc. All but the base.
Hor. The base is right, 'tis the base knave that jars.
[*Aside.*] How fiery and forward our pedant is!
Now, for my life, the knave doth court my love:
Pedascule, I'll watch you better yet.
[*Bian.*] In time I may believe, yet I mistrust.
[*Luc.*] Mistrust it not, for sure Aeacides
Was Ajax, call'd so from his grandfather.
[*Bian.*] I must believe my master, else, I promise you,
I should be arguing still upon that doubt.
But let it rest. Now, Litio, to you:
Good master, take it not unkindly, pray,
That I have been thus pleasant with you both.
Hor. [*To Lucentio.*] You may go walk, and give me leave a while;
My lessons make no music in three parts.
Luc. Are you so formal, sir? Well, I must wait,

385. outvied: outdone. **387. let your father:** if your father will.
400. gamester. Perhaps alluding to the fact that Tranio's offer rests on a gamble, not a certainty.
402. Set . . . table: i.e. become your dependent. **a toy:** nonsense.
405. fac'd . . . ten: bluffed with only a ten-spot. **410. get:** beget.
411. See the Textual Notes for an episode in the Sly framework preserved in *The Taming of a Shrew*.

III.i. Location: Padua. Baptista's house.
6. prerogative: precedence. **8. lecture:** lesson.
9. Preposterous: reversing the natural order of things.
10. ordain'd: instituted. **12. pain:** labor, toil.
15. braves: offensive remarks.

18. breeching scholar: schoolboy liable to be flogged.
22. the whiles: for the present.
24. I . . . tune: i.e. my instrument is in tune; but Lucentio pretends to take *I* literally and *in tune* in the sense "in harmony" (with Bianca).
28–29. Hic . . . senis: "Here flowed the Simois; here is the Sigeian land; here stood the lofty palace of old Priam" (Ovid, *Heroides*, I.33–34). **30. Conster:** construe. **36. port:** demeanor.
37. pantaloon: foolish old man (Gremio). **39. jars:** is out of tune.
40. Spit . . . hole. Perhaps to tighten the peg so that the string would stay in tune longer, but the phrase may mean simply "get ready for a fresh try."
50. Pedascule: pedant (a Latin coinage, with vocative ending).
52–53. Aeacides . . . grandfather. To mislead Hortensio, Lucentio pretends to be concerned with the next line of his Latin passage. Actually, he seems now to be referring to Ovid's *Metamorphoses*, xiii.27–28. *Aeacides* = descendant of Aeacus.
58. pleasant: merry. **59. give me leave:** allow me opportunity.
60. in three parts: for three voices. **61. formal:** precise.

[*Aside.*] And watch withal, for but I be deceiv'd,
Our fine musician groweth amorous.

Hor. Madam, before you touch the instrument,
To learn the order of my fingering,
I must begin with rudiments of art,
To teach you gamouth in a briefer sort,
More pleasant, pithy, and effectual,
Than hath been taught by any of my trade;
And there it is in writing, fairly drawn.

Bian. Why, I am past my gamouth long ago.

Hor. Yet read the gamouth of Hortensio.

Bian. [*Reads.*]
"*Gamouth* I am, the ground of all accord:
A re, to plead Hortensio's passion;
B mi, Bianca, take him for thy lord,
C fa ut, that loves with all affection.
D sol re, one cliff, two notes have I,
E la mi, show pity, or I die."
Call you this gamouth? Tut, I like it not.
Old fashions please me best; I am not so nice
To [change] true rules for [odd] inventions.

Enter a MESSENGER.

[*Mess.*] Mistress, your father prays you leave your books,
And help to dress your sister's chamber up.
You know to-morrow is the wedding-day.

Bian. Farewell, sweet masters both, I must be gone. [*Exeunt Bianca and Messenger.*]

Luc. Faith, mistress, then I have no cause to stay. [*Exit.*]

Hor. But I have cause to pry into this pedant.
Methinks he looks as though he were in love;
Yet if thy thoughts, Bianca, be so humble
To cast thy wand'ring eyes on every stale,
Seize thee that list. If once I find thee ranging,
Hortensio will be quit with thee by changing. *Exit.*

[SCENE II]

Enter BAPTISTA, GREMIO, TRANIO [*as Lucentio*], KATHERINE, BIANCA, [LUCENTIO *as Cambio,*] *and others, attendants.*

Bap. [*To Tranio.*] Signior Lucentio, this is the 'pointed day,
That Katherine and Petruchio should be married,
And yet we hear not of our son-in-law.
What will be said? What mockery will it be,
To want the bridegroom when the priest attends
To speak the ceremonial rites of marriage?
What says Lucentio to this shame of ours?

Kath. No shame but mine. I must forsooth be forc'd
To give my hand oppos'd against my heart

62. but: unless. **67. gamouth:** gamut, the diatonic scale.
73. ground: basis, foundation. **accord:** harmony.
76. ut: the lowest note, now called *do.* **77. cliff:** clef, key.
80. nice: capricious, or perhaps a late use of its earlier common meaning "simple, foolish." **90. stale:** decoy, bait.
91. Seize . . . list: let him take you that will. **ranging:** inconstant.
92. be quit: be quits, get even. **changing:** i.e. loving another.

III.ii. Location: Padua. Before Baptista's house.

Unto a mad-brain rudesby full of spleen,
Who woo'd in haste, and means to wed at leisure.
I told you, I, he was a frantic fool,
Hiding his bitter jests in blunt behavior;
And to be noted for a merry man,
He'll woo a thousand, 'point the day of marriage,
Make friends, invite, and proclaim the banes,
Yet never means to wed where he hath woo'd.
Now must the world point at poor Katherine,
And say, "Lo, there is mad Petruchio's wife,
If it would please him come and marry her!"

Tra. Patience, good Katherine, and Baptista too.
Upon my life, Petruchio means but well,
Whatever fortune stays him from his word.
Though he be blunt, I know him passing wise;
Though he be merry, yet withal he's honest.

Kath. Would Katherine had never seen him though!

Exit weeping [*followed by Bianca and others*].

Bap. Go, girl, I cannot blame thee now to weep,
For such an injury would vex a very saint,
Much more a shrew of [thy] impatient humor.

Enter BIONDELLO.

Bion. Master, master, news, [old news,] and such news as you never heard of!

Bap. Is it new and old too? how may that be?

Bion. Why, is it not news to [hear] of Petruchio's coming?

Bap. Is he come?

Bion. Why, no, sir.

Bap. What then?

Bion. He is coming.

Bap. When will he be here?

Bion. When he stands where I am, and sees you there.

Tra. But say, what to thine old news?

Bion. Why, Petruchio is coming in a new hat and an old jerkin; a pair of old breeches thrice turn'd; a pair of boots that have been candle-cases, one buckled, another lac'd; an old rusty sword ta'en out of the town armory, with a broken hilt, and chapeless; with two broken points; his horse hipp'd, with an old mothy saddle and stirrups of no kindred; besides, possess'd with the glanders and like to mose in the chine, troubled with the lampass, infected with the fashions, full of windgalls, sped with spavins, ray'd with the yellows, past cure

10. rudesby: rude, boisterous fellow. **spleen:** sudden impulse.
12. frantic: mad. **13. blunt:** rude.
14. be noted for: gain a reputation as. **16. banes:** banns.
23. fortune: chance. **25. honest:** honorable. **30. old:** rare.
44. jerkin: jacket.
45. candle-cases: receptacles for candle ends (because no longer fit to wear).
48. chapeless: without a chape, the metal tip of the sheath. **points:** tagged laces for attaching hose to doublet. **hipp'd:** lame in the hip. (Most of the diseases here named are discussed in Gervase Markham's *How to Choose, Ride, Train, and Diet . . . Horses,* 1593.)
50. glanders: swellings underneath the horse's jaw.
51. mose . . . chine: suffer from a dark discharge from the nostrils (a characteristic of glanders). **lampass:** a thick, spongy skin over a horse's upper teeth, making eating almost impossible.
52. fashions: farcins, small tumors on the horse's body. **windgalls:** soft tumors generally found on the fetlock joint. **sped:** far gone.
53. spavins: a disease of the hock. **ray'd:** defiled. **yellows:** jaundice.

of the fives, stark spoil'd with the staggers, begnawn with the bots, [sway'd] in the back, and shoulder-shotten, near-legg'd before, and with a half- [cheek'd] bit and a head-stall of sheep's leather, which being restrain'd to keep him from stumbling, hath been often burst, and now repair'd with knots; one girth six times piec'd, and a woman's crupper of velure, which hath two letters for her name fairly set down in studs, and here and there piec'd with packthread.

Bap. Who comes with him?

Bion. O, sir, his lackey, for all the world caparison'd like the horse; with a linen stock on one leg, and a kersey boot-hose on the other, gart'red with a red and blue list; an old hat, and the humor of forty fancies prick'd in't for a feather: a monster, a very monster in apparel, and not like a Christian footboy or a gentleman's lackey.

Tra. 'Tis some odd humor pricks him to this fashion;
Yet oftentimes he goes but mean apparell'd.

Bap. I am glad he's come, howsoe'er he comes.

Bion. Why, sir, he comes not.

Bap. Didst thou not say he comes?

Bion. Who? that Petruchio came?

Bap. Ay, that Petruchio came.

Bion. No, sir, I say his horse comes, with him on his back.

Bap. Why, that's all one.

Bion. Nay, by Saint Jamy,
I hold you a penny,
A horse and a man
Is more than one,
And yet not many.

Enter PETRUCHIO *and* GRUMIO.

Pet. Come, where be these gallants? Who's at home?

Bap. You are welcome, sir.

Pet. And yet I come not well.

Bap. And yet you halt not.

Tra. Not so well apparell'd
As I wish you were.

Pet. Were it better I should rush in thus:
[*Pretends great excitement.*]
But where is Kate? Where is my lovely bride?
How does my father?—Gentles, methinks you frown,
And wherefore gaze this goodly company,
As if they saw some wondrous monument,
Some comet or unusual prodigy?

Bap. Why, sir, you know this is your wedding-day.
First were we sad, fearing you would not come,
Now sadder, that you come so unprovided.
Fie, doff this habit, shame to your estate,
An eye-sore to our solemn festival!

Tra. And tell us what occasion of import
Hath all so long detain'd you from your wife,
And sent you hither so unlike yourself?

Pet. Tedious it were to tell, and harsh to hear—
Sufficeth I am come to keep my word,
Though in some part enforced to digress,
Which at more leisure I will so excuse
As you shall well be satisfied with all.
But where is Kate? I stay too long from her.
The morning wears, 'tis time we were at church.

Tra. See not your bride in these unreverent robes,
Go to my chamber, put on clothes of mine.

Pet. Not I, believe me, thus I'll visit her.

Bap. But thus, I trust, you will not marry her.

Pet. Good sooth, even thus; therefore ha' done with words;
To me she's married, not unto my clothes.
Could I repair what she will wear in me,
As I can change these poor accoutrements,
'Twere well for Kate, and better for myself.
But what a fool am I to chat with you,
When I should bid good morrow to my bride,
And seal the title with a lovely kiss!
Exit [*with Grumio*].

Tra. He hath some meaning in his mad attire.
We will persuade him, be it possible,
To put on better ere he go to church.

Bap. I'll after him, and see the event of this.
Exit [*with Gremio and Attendants*].

Tra. But, sir, love concerneth us to add
Her father's liking, which to bring to pass,
As before imparted to your worship,
I am to get a man—what e'er he be,
It skills not much, we'll fit him to our turn—
And he shall be Vincentio of Pisa,
And make assurance here in Padua
Of greater sums than I have promised.
So shall you quietly enjoy your hope,
And marry sweet Bianca with consent.

Luc. Were it not that my fellow schoolmaster
Doth watch Bianca's steps so narrowly,

54. **fives:** swellings at the base of the ear. **staggers:** a disease causing a staggering gait.
55. **bots:** intestinal worms. **sway'd:** with a wrenched and depressed backbone.
56. **shoulder-shotten:** with a dislocated shoulder. **near-legg'd before:** with knock-kneed forelegs.
57. **half-cheek'd:** i.e. loose. **head-stall:** part of the bridle over the head. **sheep's leather:** i.e. leather of inferior quality. Pigskin was commonly used in fine saddlery. 58. **restrain'd:** drawn tight.
59. **burst:** broken.
60. **piec'd:** mended. **crupper:** strap fastened to the saddle and passing under the horse's tail. 61. **velure:** velvet.
66. **stock:** stocking.
67. **kersey boot-hose:** coarse woollen stocking for wearing under boots. 68. **list:** strip of cloth.
68–69. **humor . . . fancies:** i.e. some ornament of highly whimsical design. 69. **prick'd:** pinned. **for:** in place of.
72. **humor:** whim, caprice. **pricks:** spurs, incites.
83. **hold:** wager. 87. **gallants:** gentlemen.
93. **Gentles:** gentlemen.

99. **unprovided:** poorly equipped.
100. **habit:** costume. **estate:** position, station.
101. **solemn:** ceremonious. 105. **harsh:** rough.
107. **digress:** deviate (from a promise).
112. **unreverent:** disrespectful.
116. **Good sooth:** indeed. **ha':** have.
118. **repair . . . me:** change for the better what she will take on in having me for a husband. 123. **lovely:** loving.
127. **event:** outcome.
128–29. **But . . . liking.** Generally considered a crux, but the meaning may be "But, sir, love [i.e. the love-suits for Bianca's hand; cf. *love* in I.ii.141] makes us concerned to achieve her father's approval." Many editors emend *But, sir, love* to *But, sir, to love* or *But to her love*, to make easier sense and also regularize the metre.
130. **As.** Frequently emended to *As I*, again for metrical reasons.
132. **skills:** matters. 139. **narrowly:** closely.

'Twere good methinks to steal our marriage,
Which once perform'd, let all the world say no,
I'll keep mine own, despite of all the world.
Tra. That by degrees we mean to look into,
And watch our vantage in this business.
We'll overreach the greybeard, Gremio,
The narrow-prying father, Minola,
The quaint musician, amorous Litio,
All for my master's sake, Lucentio.

Enter GREMIO.

Signior Gremio, came you from the church?
Gre. As willingly as e'er I came from school.
Tra. And is the bride and bridegroom coming home?
Gre. A bridegroom, say you? 'tis a groom indeed,
A grumbling groom, and that the girl shall find.
Tra. Curster than she? why, 'tis impossible.
Gre. Why, he's a devil, a devil, a very fiend.
Tra. Why, she's a devil, a devil, the devil's dam.
Gre. Tut, she's a lamb, a dove, a fool to him!
I'll tell you, Sir Lucentio: when the priest
Should ask if Katherine should be his wife,
"Ay, by gogs-wouns," quoth he, and swore so loud,
That all amaz'd the priest let fall the book,
And as he stoop'd again to take it up,
This mad-brain'd bridegroom took him such a cuff
That down fell priest and book, and book and priest.
"Now take them up," quoth he, "if any list."
Tra. What said the wench when he rose again?
Gre. Trembled and shook; for why, he stamp'd and swore
As if the vicar meant to cozen him.
But after many ceremonies done,
He calls for wine. "A health!" quoth he, as if
He had been aboard, carousing to his mates
After a storm, quaff'd off the muscadel,
And threw the sops all in the sexton's face,
Having no other reason
But that his beard grew thin and hungerly,
And seem'd to ask him sops as he was drinking.
This done, he took the bride about the neck,
And kiss'd her lips with such a clamorous smack
That at the parting all the church did echo.
And I seeing this, came thence for very shame,
And after me I know the rout is coming.
Such a mad marriage never was before.
Hark, hark, I hear the minstrels play. *Music plays.*

Enter PETRUCHIO, KATE, BIANCA, HORTENSIO [*as Litio*], BAPTISTA, [GRUMIO, *and* TRAIN].

Pet. Gentlemen and friends, I thank you for your pains.
I know you think to dine with me to-day,
And have prepar'd great store of wedding cheer,
But so it is, my haste doth call me hence,
And therefore here I mean to take my leave.
Bap. Is't possible you will away to-night?
Pet. I must away to-day, before night come.
Make it no wonder; if you knew my business,
You would entreat me rather go than stay.
And, honest company, I thank you all
That have beheld me give away myself
To this most patient, sweet, and virtuous wife.
Dine with my father, drink a health to me,
For I must hence, and farewell to you all.
Tra. Let us entreat you stay till after dinner.
Pet. It may not be.
Gre. Let me entreat you.
Pet. It cannot be.
Kath. Let me entreat you.
Pet. I am content.
Kath. Are you content to stay?
Pet. I am content you shall entreat me stay,
But yet not stay, entreat me how you can.
Kath. Now if you love me stay.
Pet. Grumio, my horse.
Gru. Ay, sir, they be ready; the oats have eaten the horses.
Kath. Nay then,
Do what thou canst, I will not go to-day,
No, nor to-morrow—not till I please myself.
The door is open, sir, there lies your way;
You may be jogging whiles your boots are green.
For me, I'll not be gone till I please myself.
'Tis like you'll prove a jolly surly groom,
That take it on you at the first so roundly.
Pet. O Kate, content thee, prithee be not angry.
Kath. I will be angry; what hast thou to do?
Father, be quiet, he shall stay my leisure.
Gre. Ay, marry, sir, now it begins to work.
Kath. Gentlemen, forward to the bridal dinner.
I see a woman may be made a fool,
If she had not a spirit to resist.
Pet. They shall go forward, Kate, at thy command.
Obey the bride, you that attend on her.
Go to the feast, revel and domineer,
Carouse full measure to her maidenhead,
Be mad and merry, or go hang yourselves;
But for my bonny Kate, she must with me.
Nay, look not big, nor stamp, nor stare, nor fret,
I will be master of what is mine own.
She is my goods, my chattels, she is my house,
My household stuff, my field, my barn,
My horse, my ox, my ass, my any thing;
And here she stands, touch her whoever dare,

140. steal our marriage: marry secretly.
144. vantage: advantage, opportunity.
147. quaint: skilled, clever.
152. a groom indeed: (1) a fine kind of bridegroom (ironic); (2) a servingman actually.
157. fool: i.e. poor weak creature. **to:** compared with.
160. gogs-wouns: God's (Christ's) wounds.
161. amaz'd: bewildered. **163. took:** struck. **165. list:** choose.
167. for why: because.
168. cozen: cheat (by making the ceremony invalid through some irregularity). **171. aboard:** aboard ship. **173. sops:** dregs.
175. hungerly: sparsely. **181. rout:** crowd (of guests).

191. Make: consider. **193. honest:** worthy. **204. horse.** Plural.
205–6. oats . . . horses: i.e. the horses are stuffed full of oats.
211. be . . . green: i.e. get an early start (proverbial); *green* = fresh, new. **213. jolly:** overbearing.
214. roundly: outspokenly, unceremoniously.
216. what . . . do: it's no concern of yours. **217. stay:** await.
224. domineer: carouse.
228. big: threatening (said to the wedding guests, not to Katherine, whose conduct it really describes).
232. ox . . . thing. Alluding to the Tenth Commandment.

I'll bring mine action on the proudest he
That stops my way in Padua. Grumio,
Draw forth thy weapon, we are beset with thieves;
Rescue thy mistress if thou be a man.
Fear not, sweet wench, they shall not touch thee, Kate!
I'll buckler thee against a million.

Exeunt Petruchio, Katherina, [and Grumio].

Bap. Nay, let them go, a couple of quiet ones.

Gre. Went they not quickly, I should die with laughing.

Tra. Of all mad matches never was the like.

Luc. Mistress, what's your opinion of your sister?

Bian. That being mad herself, she's madly mated.

Gre. I warrant him, Petruchio is Kated.

Bap. Neighbors and friends, though bride and bridegroom wants
For to supply the places at the table,
You know there wants no junkets at the feast.
Lucentio, you shall supply the bridegroom's place,
And let Bianca take her sister's room.

Tra. Shall sweet Bianca practice how to bride it?

Bap. She shall, Lucentio. Come, gentlemen, let's go. *Exeunt.*

[ACT IV, SCENE I]

Enter GRUMIO.

Gru. Fie, fie on all tir'd jades, on all mad masters, and all foul ways! Was ever man so beaten? Was ever man so ray'd? Was ever man so weary? I am sent before to make a fire, and they are coming after to warm them. Now were not I a little pot and soon hot, my very lips might freeze to my teeth, my tongue to the roof of my mouth, my heart in my belly, ere I should come by a fire to thaw me. But I with blowing the fire shall warm myself; for considering the weather, a taller man than I will take cold. Holla, ho, Curtis!

Enter CURTIS.

Curt. Who is that calls so coldly?

Gru. A piece of ice. If thou doubt it, thou mayst slide from my shoulder to my heel with no greater a run but my head and my neck. A fire, good Curtis.

Curt. Is my master and his wife coming, Grumio?

Gru. O ay, Curtis, ay, and therefore fire, fire; cast on no water.

Curt. Is she so hot a shrew as she's reported?

Gru. She was, good Curtis, before this frost; but thou know'st winter tames man, woman, and beast; for it hath tam'd my old master and my new mistress and myself, fellow Curtis.

[*Curt.*] Away, you three-inch fool! I am no beast.

Gru. Am I but three inches? Why, thy horn is a foot, and so long am I at the least. But wilt thou make a fire, or shall I complain on thee to our mistress, whose hand (she being now at hand) thou shalt soon feel, to thy cold comfort, for being slow in thy hot office?

Curt. I prithee, good Grumio, tell me, how goes the world?

Gru. A cold world, Curtis, in every office but thine, and therefore fire. Do thy duty and have thy duty, for my master and mistress are almost frozen to death.

Curt. There's fire ready, and therefore, good Grumio, the news.

Gru. Why, "Jack, boy! ho, boy!" and as much news as wilt thou.

Curt. Come, you are so full of cony-catching!

Gru. Why, therefore fire, for I have caught extreme cold. Where's the cook? Is supper ready, the house trimm'd, rushes strew'd, cobwebs swept, the servingmen in their new fustian, [their] white stockings, and every officer his wedding garment on? Be the Jacks fair within, the Gills fair without, the carpets laid, and every thing in order?

Curt. All ready; and therefore I pray thee, news.

Gru. First, know my horse is tir'd, my master and mistress fall'n out.

Curt. How?

Gru. Out of their saddles into the dirt, and thereby hangs a tale.

Curt. Let's ha't, good Grumio.

Gru. Lend thine ear.

Curt. Here.

Gru. There. [*Strikes him.*]

Curt. This 'tis to feel a tale, not to hear a tale.

Gru. And therefore 'tis call'd a sensible tale; and this cuff was but to knock at your ear, and beseech list'ning. Now I begin: *Inprimis*, we came down a foul hill, my master riding behind my mistress—

Curt. Both of one horse?

Gru. What's that to thee?

Curt. Why, a horse.

234. bring . . . on: (1) attack; (2) bring legal action against.
239. buckler: shield. **246. wants:** are lacking. **247. For to:** to.
248. junkets: sweetmeats.

IV.i. Location: Petruchio's country house.
3. ray'd: dirtied.
6. little . . . hot: proverbial for a small person with a quick temper.
9. blowing the fire: i.e. keeping myself in a rage.
11. taller. With play on the sense "better."
19–20. fire . . . water. An allusion to the round or catch "Scotland's burning," in which the words "Fire, fire!" are followed by "Cast on water."

26. I . . . beast: i.e. don't call me your fellow, since you have just admitted that you are a beast.
27. horn: cuckold's horn. (The passage is full of indelicate jesting.)
32. hot office: task of providing heat. **37. duty:** due, reward.
41. Jack . . . boy: the first words of another catch.
43. cony-catching: trickery, evasion (perhaps with punning reference to Grumio's fondness for catches).
46. rushes. Used as floor covering.
47. fustian: coarse cloth of cotton and flax.
48. officer: household servant.
49. Jacks: (1) servingmen; (2) drinking vessels.
50. Gills: (1) maidservants; (2) small drinking vessels (*gills*). **carpets:** here, probably table coverings.
58. thereby . . . tale: there is a story connected with that.
64. sensible: (1) reasonable; (2) capable of being felt.
66. Inprimis: in the first place. **67. foul:** muddy. **69. of:** on.

Gru. Tell thou the tale. But hadst thou not cross'd me, thou shouldst have heard how her horse fell, and she under her horse; thou shouldst have heard in how miry a place, how she was bemoil'd, how he left her with the horse upon her, how he beat me because her horse stumbled, how she waded through the dirt to pluck him off me; how he swore, how she pray'd that never pray'd before; how I cried, how the horses ran away, how her bridle was burst; how I lost my crupper, with many things of worthy memory, which now shall die in oblivion, and thou return unexperienc'd to thy grave.

Curt. By this reck'ning he is more shrew than she.

Gru. Ay, and that thou and the proudest of you all shall find when he comes home. But what talk I of this? Call forth Nathaniel, Joseph, Nicholas, Philip, Walter, Sugarsop, and the rest; let their heads be slickly comb'd, their blue coats brush'd, and their garters of an indifferent knit; let them curtsy with their left legs, and not presume to touch a hair of my master's horse-tail till they kiss their hands. Are they all ready?

Curt. They are.

Gru. Call them forth.

Curt. Do you hear, ho? You must meet my master to countenance my mistress.

Gru. Why, she hath a face of her own.

Curt. Who knows not that?

Gru. Thou, it seems, that calls for company to countenance her.

Curt. I call them forth to credit her.

Enter four or five SERVINGMEN.

Gru. Why, she comes to borrow nothing of them.

Nath. Welcome home, Grumio!

Phil. How now, Grumio?

Jos. What, Grumio!

Nich. Fellow Grumio!

Nath. How now, old lad?

Gru. Welcome, you; how now, you; what, you; fellow, you—and thus much for greeting. Now, my spruce companions, is all ready, and all things neat?

Nath. All things is ready. How near is our master?

Gru. E'en at hand, alighted by this; and therefore be not—Cock's passion, silence! I hear my master.

Enter PETRUCHIO *and* KATE.

Pet. Where be these knaves? What, no man at door
To hold my stirrup, nor to take my horse?
Where is Nathaniel, Gregory, Philip?

All Serv. Here, here, sir, here, sir.

Pet. Here, sir! here, sir! here, sir! here, sir!
You loggerheaded and unpolish'd grooms!
What? no attendance? no regard? no duty?
Where is the foolish knave I sent before?

Gru. Here, sir, as foolish as I was before.

Pet. You peasant swain, you whoreson malt-horse drudge!
Did I not bid thee meet me in the park,
And bring along these rascal knaves with thee?

Gru. Nathaniel's coat, sir, was not fully made,
And Gabr'el's pumps were all unpink'd i' th' heel;
There was no link to color Peter's hat,
And Walter's dagger was not come from sheathing;
There were none fine but Adam, Rafe, and Gregory;
The rest were ragged, old, and beggarly,
Yet, as they are, here are they come to meet you.

Pet. Go, rascals, go, and fetch my supper in.
Exeunt Servants.
[*Sings.*] "Where is the life that late I led?
Where are those"—
Sit down, Kate, and welcome. Soud, soud, soud, soud!

Enter SERVANTS *with supper.*

Why, when, I say? Nay, good sweet Kate, be merry.
Off with my boots, you rogues! You villains, when?
[*Sings.*] "It was the friar of orders grey,
As he forth walked on his way"—
Out, you rogue, you pluck my foot awry.
Take that, and mend the plucking [off] the other.
[*Strikes him.*]
Be merry, Kate. Some water here; what ho!

Enter one with water.

Where's my spaniel Troilus? Sirrah, get you hence,
And bid my cousin Ferdinand come hither;
One, Kate, that you must kiss, and be acquainted with.
Where are my slippers? Shall I have some water?
Come, Kate, and wash, and welcome heartily.
You whoreson villain, will you let it fall?
[*Strikes him.*]

Kath. Patience, I pray you, 'twas a fault unwilling.

Pet. A whoreson, beetle-headed, flap-ear'd knave!
Come, Kate, sit down, I know you have a stomach.
Will you give thanks, sweet Kate, or else shall I?
What's this? Mutton?

1. Serv. Ay.

Pet. Who brought it?

Peter. I.

Pet. 'Tis burnt, and so is all the meat.

73. cross'd: interrupted. **75–76. bemoil'd:** covered with mud.
88. what: why.
91. blue coats. The regular dress for menservants.
92. indifferent knit: i.e. ordinary pattern or texture.
99. countenance: pay your respects to (with obvious pun following).
104. credit: honor (again with following pun).
118. Cock's passion: by God's (Christ's) suffering.

125. loggerheaded: blockheaded.
129. peasant swain: rascally lout. **malt-horse drudge:** slow, heavy horse, used to grind malt by working a treadmill.
133. unpink'd: without eyelets.
134. link: torch (the smoke of which could be used to blacken old hats). **135. sheathing:** having a sheath made.
136. fine: well dressed.
140–41. Where . . . those: fragment of a song no longer extant; lines 145–46 are from another.
142. Soud: an expression of impatience (?). Some editors emend to *Food*.
157. beetle-headed: blockheaded (*beetle* = a heavy tool for ramming and pounding). **158. stomach:** (1) appetite; (2) temper.

What dogs are these? Where is the rascal cook?
How durst you, villains, bring it from the dresser
And serve it thus to me that love it not?
There, take it to you, trenchers, cups, and all.
[*He throws down the table and meat and all, and beats them.*]
You heedless joltheads and unmanner'd slaves!
What, do you grumble? I'll be with you straight.
[*Exeunt Servants.*]

Kath. I pray you, husband, be not so disquiet.
The meat was well, if you were so contented.

Pet. I tell thee, Kate, 'twas burnt and dried away,
And I expressly am forbid to touch it;
For it engenders choler, planteth anger,
And better 'twere that both of us did fast,
Since of ourselves, ourselves are choleric,
Than feed it with such overroasted flesh.
Be patient, to-morrow't shall be mended,
And for this night we'll fast for company.
Come, I will bring thee to thy bridal chamber.
Exeunt.

Enter Servants *severally.*

Nath. Peter, didst ever see the like?

Peter. He kills her in her own humor.

Enter Curtis, *a servant.*

Gru. Where is he?

Curt. In her chamber, making a sermon of continency to her,
And rails, and swears, and rates, that she, poor soul,
Knows not which way to stand, to look, to speak,
And sits as one new risen from a dream.
Away, away, for he is coming hither. [*Exeunt.*]

Enter Petruchio.

Pet. Thus have I politicly begun my reign,
And 'tis my hope to end successfully.
My falcon now is sharp and passing empty,
And till she stoop, she must not be full-gorg'd,
For then she never looks upon her lure.
Another way I have to man my haggard,
To make her come, and know her keeper's call,
That is, to watch her, as we watch these kites
That bate and beat and will not be obedient.
She eat no meat to-day, nor none shall eat;
Last night she slept not, nor to-night she shall not;
As with the meat, some undeserved fault
I'll find about the making of the bed,
And here I'll fling the pillow, there the bolster,
This way the coverlet, another way the sheets.
Ay, and amid this hurly I intend
That all is done in reverend care of her,
And in conclusion, she shall watch all night,
And if she chance to nod I'll rail and brawl,
And with the clamor keep her still awake.
This is a way to kill a wife with kindness,
And thus I'll curb her mad and headstrong humor.
He that knows better how to tame a shrew,
Now let him speak; 'tis charity to shew. *Exit.*

[Scene II]

Enter Tranio [*as Lucentio*] *and* Hortensio [*as Litio*].

Tra. Is't possible, friend Litio, that Mistress Bianca
Doth fancy any other but Lucentio?
I tell you, sir, she bears me fair in hand.

[*Hor.*] Sir, to satisfy you in what I have said,
Stand by and mark the manner of his teaching.
[*They stand aside.*]

Enter Bianca [*and* Lucentio *as Cambio*].

[*Luc.*] Now, mistress, profit you in what you read?

Bian. What, master, read you? First resolve me that.

[*Luc.*] I read that I profess, the Art to Love.

Bian. And may you prove, sir, master of your art!

Luc. While you, sweet dear, prove mistress of my heart! [*They retire.*]

Hor. Quick proceeders, marry! Now tell me, I pray,
You that durst swear that your mistress Bianca
Lov'd [none] in the world so well as Lucentio.

Tra. O despiteful love, unconstant womankind!
I tell thee, Litio, this is wonderful.

Hor. Mistake no more, I am not Litio,
Nor a musician, as I seem to be,
But one that scorn to live in this disguise
For such a one as leaves a gentleman,
And makes a god of such a cullion.
Know, sir, that I am call'd Hortensio.

Tra. Signior Hortensio, I have often heard
Of your entire affection to Bianca,
And since mine eyes are witness of her lightness,
I will with you, if you be so contented,
Forswear Bianca and her love for ever.

Hor. See how they kiss and court! Signior Lucentio,
Here is my hand, and here I firmly vow
Never to woo her more, but do forswear her
As one unworthy all the former favors
That I have fondly flatter'd [her] withal.

Tra. And here I take the like unfeigned oath,
Never to marry with her though she would entreat.

163. dresser: sideboard. **165. trenchers:** wooden dishes or plates.
166. joltheads: blockheads.
167. with you straight: after you straightway (to punish you).
172. choler: the humor, or bodily fluid, that was thought to make one short-tempered. **174. of ourselves:** by our nature.
180. kills . . . humor: i.e. masters her ill temper with a worse temper.
190. sharp: hungry.
191. stoop: fly to the lure (a baited device used to recall a falcon), i.e. submit to authority.
193. man: tame. **haggard:** wild female hawk.
195. watch her: keep her from sleeping. **kites:** falcons.
196. bate and beat: flap and flutter the wings impatiently.
197. She eat: she ate. **203. intend:** pretend.

207. still: always. **211. shew:** show, i.e. reveal his method.

IV.ii. Location: Padua. Before Baptista's house.
3. bears . . . hand: treats me encouragingly (with suggestion of deceit).
6. profit you: do you make progress. **read:** study.
7. resolve: answer.
8. that: what. **Art to Love:** Ovid's *Ars Amandi.*
11. proceeders. Playing on the academic term "to proceed Master of Arts," suggested by Bianca's "master of your art."
15. wonderful: a cause for wonder. **20. cullion:** base fellow.
23. entire: unfeigned, sincere. **24. lightness:** wantonness.
31. fondly: foolishly.

Fie on her, see how beastly she doth court him!
Hor. Would all the world but he had quite forsworn!
For me, that I may surely keep mine oath,
I will be married to a wealthy widow,
Ere three days pass, which hath as long lov'd me
As I have lov'd this proud disdainful haggard.
And so farewell, Signior Lucentio.
Kindness in women, not their beauteous looks,
Shall win my love, and so I take my leave,
In resolution as I swore before. [*Exit.*]
Tra. Mistress Bianca, bless you with such grace
As 'longeth to a lover's blessed case!
Nay, I have ta'en you napping, gentle love,
And have forsworn you with Hortensio.
Bian. Tranio, you jest, but have you both forsworn me?
Tra. Mistress, we have.
Luc. Then we are rid of Litio.
Tra. I' faith, he'll have a lusty widow now,
That shall be woo'd and wedded in a day.
Bian. God give him joy!
Tra. Ay, and he'll tame her.
Bian. He says so, Tranio?
Tra. Faith, he is gone unto the taming-school.
Bian. The taming-school! what, is there such a place?
Tra. Ay, mistress, and Petruchio is the master,
That teacheth tricks eleven and twenty long,
To tame a shrew and charm her chattering tongue.

Enter BIONDELLO.

Bion. O master, master, I have watch'd so long
That I am dog-weary, but at last I spied
An ancient angel coming down the hill,
Will serve the turn.
Tra. What is he, Biondello?
Bion. Master, a mercantant, or a pedant,
I know not what, but formal in apparel,
In gait and countenance surely like a father.
Luc. And what of him, Tranio?
Tra. If he be credulous, and trust my tale,
I'll make him glad to seem Vincentio,
And give assurance to Baptista Minola,
As if he were the right Vincentio.
Take [in] your love, and then let me alone.
[*Exeunt Lucentio and Bianca.*]

Enter a PEDANT.

Ped. God save you, sir!

34. beastly: i.e. lewdly.
35. Would . . . forsworn: i.e. would that Bianca should be left an old maid, since he does not believe that she will really marry Cambio-Lucentio, whom he thinks to be a penniless musician (Bond).
45. 'longeth: belongs. **50. lusty:** spirited, vigorous.
54. he . . . taming-school. How does Tranio know this, since Hortensio has only just made his decision and has not mentioned his intention to visit Petruchio? Imperfectly adjusted revision has been suggested. See Textual Notes, line 53, for a curiously close textual parallel here with *The Taming of a Shrew.*
57. tricks . . . long: i.e. tricks that meet the need of the case; an allusion to the card game trentuno (cf. I.ii.33).
61. ancient angel: i.e. a fellow of the good old stamp. The angel was a gold coin bearing the figure of the archangel Michael.
62. serve the turn: answer our purpose.
63. marcantant: merchant (Italian *mercantante*).

Tra. And you, sir! you are welcome.
Travel you far on, or are you at the farthest?
Ped. Sir, at the farthest for a week or two,
But then up farther, and as far as Rome,
And so to Tripoli, if God lend me life.
Tra. What countryman, I pray?
Ped. Of Mantua.
Tra. Of Mantua, sir? marry, God forbid!
And come to Padua, careless of your life?
Ped. My life, sir? How, I pray? for that goes hard.
Tra. 'Tis death for any one in Mantua
To come to Padua. Know you not the cause?
Your ships are stay'd at Venice, and the Duke,
For private quarrel 'twixt your Duke and him,
Hath publish'd and proclaim'd it openly.
'Tis marvel, but that you are but newly come,
You might have heard it else proclaim'd about.
Ped. Alas, sir, it is worse for me than so,
For I have bills for money by exchange
From Florence, and must here deliver them.
Tra. Well, sir, to do you courtesy,
This will I do, and this I will advise you.
First, tell me, have you ever been at Pisa?
Ped. Ay, sir, in Pisa have I often been,
Pisa renowned for grave citizens.
Tra. Among them know you one Vincentio?
Ped. I know him not, but I have heard of him;
A merchant of incomparable wealth.
Tra. He is my father, sir, and sooth to say,
In count'nance somewhat doth resemble you.
Bion. [*Aside.*] As much as an apple doth an oyster, and all one.
Tra. To save your life in this extremity,
This favor will I do you for his sake;
And think it not the worst of all your fortunes
That you are like to Sir Vincentio.
His name and credit shall you undertake,
And in my house you shall be friendly lodg'd.
Look that you take upon you as you should;
You understand me, sir? So shall you stay
Till you have done your business in the city.
If this be court'sy, sir, accept of it.
Ped. O sir, I do, and will repute you ever
The patron of my life and liberty.
Tra. Then go with me to make the matter good.
This by the way I let you understand:
My father is here look'd for every day,
To pass assurance of a dow'r in marriage
'Twixt me and one Baptista's daughter here.
In all these circumstances I'll instruct you;
Go with me to clothe you as becomes you. *Exeunt.*

SCENE [III]

Enter KATHERINA *and* GRUMIO.

Gru. No, no, forsooth I dare not for my life.

80. goes hard: is serious. **102. all one:** no matter.
107. credit: reputation. **undertake:** assume.
109. take upon you: i.e. act your part. **113. repute:** consider.
118. pass: convey. **120. circumstances:** details.

IV.iii. Location: Petruchio's house.

Kath. The more my wrong, the more his spite appears.
What, did he marry me to famish me?
Beggars that come unto my father's door
Upon entreaty have a present alms,
If not, elsewhere they meet with charity;
But I, who never knew how to entreat,
Nor never needed that I should entreat,
Am starv'd for meat, giddy for lack of sleep,
With oaths kept waking, and with brawling fed;
And that which spites me more than all these wants,
He does it under name of perfect love;
As who should say, if I should sleep or eat,
'Twere deadly sickness, or else present death.
I prithee go, and get me some repast;
I care not what, so it be wholesome food.

Gru. What say you to a neat's foot?

Kath. 'Tis passing good, I prithee let me have it.

Gru. I fear it is too choleric a meat.
How say you to a fat tripe finely broil'd?

Kath. I like it well, good Grumio, fetch it me.

Gru. I cannot tell, I fear 'tis choleric.
What say you to a piece of beef and mustard?

Kath. A dish that I do love to feed upon.

Gru. Ay, but the mustard is too hot a little.

Kath. Why then the beef, and let the mustard rest.

Gru. Nay then I will not, you shall have the mustard,
Or else you get no beef of Grumio.

Kath. Then both or one, or any thing thou wilt.

Gru. Why then the mustard without the beef.

Kath. Go get thee gone, thou false deluding slave, *Beats him.*
That feed'st me with the very name of meat.
Sorrow on thee and all the pack of you
That triumph thus upon my misery!
Go get thee gone, I say.

Enter Petruchio *and* Hortensio *with meat.*

Pet. How fares my Kate? What, sweeting, all amort?

Hor. Mistress, what cheer?

Kath. Faith, as cold as can be.

Pet. Pluck up thy spirits, look cheerfully upon me.
Here, love, thou seest how diligent I am
To dress thy meat myself, and bring it thee.
I am sure, sweet Kate, this kindness merits thanks.
What, not a word? Nay then, thou lov'st it not;
And all my pains is sorted to no proof.
Here, take away this dish.

Kath. I pray you let it stand.

Pet. The poorest service is repaid with thanks,
And so shall mine before you touch the meat.

Kath. I thank you, sir.

Hor. Signior Petruchio, fie, you are to blame.
Come, Mistress Kate, I'll bear you company.

Pet. [*Aside.*] Eat it up all, Hortensio, if thou lovest me.—
Much good do it unto thy gentle heart!
Kate, eat apace. And now, my honey love,
Will we return unto thy father's house,
And revel it as bravely as the best,
With silken coats and caps, and golden rings,
With ruffs and cuffs, and fardingales, and things,
With scarfs and fans, and double change of brav'ry,
With amber bracelets, beads, and all this knav'ry.
What, hast thou din'd? The tailor stays thy leisure,
To deck thy body with his ruffling treasure.

Enter Tailor.

Come, tailor, let us see these ornaments;
Lay forth the gown.

Enter Haberdasher.

What news with you, sir?

[*Hab.*] Here is the cap your worship did bespeak.

Pet. Why, this was moulded on a porringer—
A velvet dish. Fie, fie, 'tis lewd and filthy.
Why, 'tis a cockle or a walnut-shell,
A knack, a toy, a trick, a baby's cap.
Away with it! come let me have a bigger.

Kath. I'll have no bigger, this doth fit the time,
And gentlewomen wear such caps as these.

Pet. When you are gentle, you shall have one too,
And not till then.

Hor. [*Aside.*] That will not be in haste.

Kath. Why, sir, I trust I may have leave to speak,
And speak I will. I am no child, no babe;
Your betters have endur'd me say my mind,
And if you cannot, best you stop your ears.
My tongue will tell the anger of my heart,
Or else my heart concealing it will break,
And rather than it shall, I will be free,
Even to the uttermost, as I please, in words.

Pet. Why, thou say'st true, it is [a] paltry cap,
A custard-coffin, a bauble, a silken pie.
I love thee well in that thou lik'st it not.

Kath. Love me, or love me not, I like the cap,
And it I will have, or I will have none.

[*Exit Haberdasher.*]

Pet. Thy gown? why, ay. Come, tailor, let us see't.
O mercy, God, what masquing stuff is here?
What's this? a sleeve? 'tis like [a] demi-cannon.
What, up and down carv'd like an apple-tart?
Here's snip and nip and cut and slish and slash,
Like to a censer in a barber's shop.
Why, what a' devil's name, tailor, call'st thou this?

Hor. [*Aside.*] I see she's like to have neither cap nor gown.

2. more: greater. **my wrong:** the wrong done to me.
5. present: immediate. **11. spites:** vexes.
13. As . . . say: as if to say. **17. neat's:** ox's.
19. choleric: productive of temper. Cf. IV.i.172. **32. very:** mere.
36. all amort: dispirited, dejected.
43. sorted . . . proof: i.e. fruitless. **44. stand:** remain.

54. bravely: finely arrayed.
56. fardingales: farthingales, hooped petticoats.
57. brav'ry: finery. **58. this knav'ry:** i.e. such tricks.
60. ruffling: gaily ruffled. **64. porringer:** porridge bowl.
65. lewd: worthless. **66. cockle:** cockleshell.
67. knack: knickknack. **trick:** trifle.
69. fit the time: agree with the present fashion.
82. custard-coffin: crust over a custard (perhaps with pun on *costard*, slang for "head").
87. masquing stuff: i.e. material fit only for a masque.
88. demi-cannon: large cannon. **89. up and down:** exactly.
91. censer: perfuming pan with a perforated lid. **92. a':** in.

Tai. You bid me make it orderly and well,
According to the fashion and the time.
Pet. Marry, and did; but if you be remember'd,
I did not bid you mar it to the time.
Go hop me over every kennel home,
For you shall hop without my custom, sir.
I'll none of it; hence, make your best of it.
Kath. I never saw a better fashion'd gown,
More quaint, more pleasing, nor more commendable.
Belike you mean to make a puppet of me.
Pet. Why, true, he means to make a puppet of thee.
Tai. She says your worship means to make a puppet of her.
Pet. O monstrous arrogance! Thou liest, thou thread, thou thimble,
Thou yard, three-quarters, half-yard, quarter, nail!
Thou flea, thou nit, thou winter-cricket thou!
Brav'd in mine own house with a skein of thread?
Away, thou rag, thou quantity, thou remnant,
Or I shall so bemete thee with thy yard
As thou shalt think on prating whilst thou liv'st!
I tell thee, I, that thou hast marr'd her gown.
Tai. Your worship is deceiv'd, the gown is made
Just as my master had direction.
Grumio gave order how it should be done.
Gru. I gave him no order, I gave him the stuff.
Tai. But how did you desire it should be made?
Gru. Marry, sir, with needle and thread.
Tai. But did you not request to have it cut?
Gru. Thou hast fac'd many things.
Tai. I have.
Gru. Face not me; thou hast brav'd many men, brave not me; I will neither be fac'd nor brav'd. I say unto thee, I bid thy master cut out the gown, but I did not bid him cut it to pieces. *Ergo*, thou liest.
Tai. Why, here is the note of the fashion to testify.
Pet. Read it.
Gru. The note lies in 's throat if he say I said so.
Tai. [*Reads.*] "*Inprimis*, a loose-bodied gown"—
Gru. Master, if ever I said loose-bodied gown, sew me in the skirts of it, and beat me to death with a bottom of brown thread. I said a gown.
Pet. Proceed.
Tai. [*Reads.*] "With a small compass'd cape"—
Gru. I confess the cape.
Tai. [*Reads.*] "With a trunk sleeve"—
Gru. I confess two sleeves.
Tai. [*Reads.*] "The sleeves curiously cut."
Pet. Ay, there's the villainy.

94. **orderly:** properly. 96. **be rememb'red:** recollect.
98. **kennel:** gutter. 102. **quaint:** beautiful, elegant.
108. **nail:** measure of $2\frac{1}{4}$ inches. 109. **nit:** egg of a louse.
110. **Brav'd:** defied. 111. **quantity:** fragment.
112. **bemete:** measure, i.e. beat. **yard:** yardstick.
113. **think on:** remember. **whilst:** as long as. 122. **fac'd:** trimmed.
124. **Face:** bully. **brav'd:** dressed splendidly. 125. **brave:** defy.
127. **Ergo:** therefore.
134. **loose-bodied gown:** loosely fitted gown (a style of dress worn by prostitutes, among others).
137. **bottom:** ball (properly, the core on which the thread was wound).
139. **compass'd:** circular. 141. **trunk sleeve:** large, wide sleeve.
143. **curiously:** elaborately.

Gru. Error i' th' bill, sir, error i' th' bill! I commanded the sleeves should be cut out, and sew'd up again, and that I'll prove upon thee, though thy little finger be arm'd in a thimble.
Tai. This is true that I say; and I had thee in place where, thou shouldst know it.
Gru. I am for thee straight. Take thou the bill, give me thy mete-yard, and spare not me.
Hor. God-a-mercy, Grumio, then he shall have no odds.
Pet. Well, sir, in brief, the gown is not for me.
Gru. You are i' th' right, sir, 'tis for my mistress.
Pet. Go take it up unto thy master's use.
Gru. Villain, not for thy life! Take up my mistress' gown for thy master's use!
Pet. Why, sir, what's your conceit in that?
Gru. O, sir, the conceit is deeper than you think for:
Take up my mistress' gown to his master's use!
O fie, fie, fie!
Pet. [*Aside.*] Hortensio, say thou wilt see the tailor paid.—
Go take it hence, be gone, and say no more.
Hor. Tailor, I'll pay thee for thy gown to-morrow,
Take no unkindness of his hasty words.
Away, I say, commend me to thy master.
Exit Tailor.
Pet. Well, come, my Kate, we will unto your father's
Even in these honest mean habiliments;
Our purses shall be proud, our garments poor,
For 'tis the mind that makes the body rich;
And as the sun breaks through the darkest clouds,
So honor peereth in the meanest habit.
What, is the jay more precious than the lark,
Because his feathers are more beautiful?
Or is the adder better than the eel,
Because his painted skin contents the eye?
O no, good Kate; neither art thou the worse
For this poor furniture and mean array.
If thou accountedst it shame, lay it on me,
And therefore frolic, we will hence forthwith,
To feast and sport us at thy father's house.
Go call my men, and let us straight to him,
And bring our horses unto Long-lane end;
There will we mount, and thither walk on foot.
Let's see, I think 'tis now some seven a' clock,
And well we may come there by dinner-time.
Kath. I dare assure you, sir, 'tis almost two,
And 'twill be supper-time ere you come there.
Pet. It shall be seven ere I go to horse.
Look what I speak, or do, or think to do,
You are still crossing it. Sirs, let't alone,
I will not go to-day, and ere I do,

150. **place where:** the right place.
151. **bill.** With quibble on its sense as a kind of weapon—a blade fixed onto a long staff. 152. **mete-yard:** measuring-stick.
157. **unto . . . use:** i.e. for whatever purpose the tailor's master can find for it (but Grumio pretends to misunderstand).
160. **conceit:** idea, meaning.
174. **peereth:** appears. **habit:** attire.
180. **furniture:** furnishing, i.e. costume.
188. **dinner-time:** i.e. around noon. 192. **Look what:** whatever.
193. **crossing:** contradicting.

It shall be what a' clock I say it is.
Hor. [*Aside.*] Why, so this gallant will command the sun. [*Exeunt.*]

[Scene IV]

Enter Tranio [*as Lucentio*], *and the* Pedant *dress'd like Vincentio,* [*booted and bare-headed*].

Tra. [Sir], this is the house, please it you that I call?
Ped. Ay, what else? And but I be deceived,
Signior Baptista may remember me
Near twenty years ago in Genoa,
Where we were lodgers at the Pegasus.
Tra. 'Tis well, and hold your own in any case
With such austerity as 'longeth to a father.

Enter Biondello.

Ped. I warrant you. But, sir, here comes your boy;
'Twere good he were school'd.
Tra. Fear you not him. Sirrah Biondello,
Now do your duty throughly, I advise you.
Imagine 'twere the right Vincentio.
Bion. Tut, fear not me.
Tra. But hast thou done thy errand to Baptista?
Bion. I told him that your father was at Venice,
And that you look'd for him this day in Padua.
Tra. Th' art a tall fellow; hold thee that to drink.
Here comes Baptista; set your countenance, sir.

Enter Baptista *and* Lucentio [*as Cambio*].

Signior Baptista, you are happily met.
[*To the Pedant.*] Sir, this is the gentleman I told you of.
I pray you stand good father to me now,
Give me Bianca for my patrimony.
Ped. Soft, son!
Sir, by your leave, having come to Padua
To gather in some debts, my son Lucentio
Made me acquainted with a weighty cause
Of love between your daughter and himself;
And for the good report I hear of you,
And for the love he beareth to your daughter,
And she to him, to stay him not too long,
I am content, in a good father's care,
To have him match'd; and if you please to like
No worse than I, upon some agreement
Me shall you find ready and willing
With one consent to have her so bestowed;
For curious I cannot be with you,
Signior Baptista, of whom I hear so well.
Bap. Sir, pardon me in what I have to say—
Your plainness and your shortness please me well.
Right true it is, your son Lucentio here
Doth love my daughter, and she loveth him,
Or both dissemble deeply their affections;
And therefore if you say no more than this,
That like a father you will deal with him,
And pass my daughter a sufficient dower,
The match is made, and all is done:
Your son shall have my daughter with consent.
Tra. I thank you, sir. Where then do you know best
We be affied and such assurance ta'en
As shall with either part's agreement stand?
Bap. Not in my house, Lucentio, for you know
Pitchers have ears, and I have many servants;
Besides, old Gremio is heark'ning still,
And happily we might be interrupted.
Tra. Then at my lodging, and it like you.
There doth my father lie; and there this night
We'll pass the business privately and well.
Send for your daughter by your servant here;
My boy shall fetch the scrivener presently.
The worst is this, that at so slender warning,
You are like to have a thin and slender pittance.
Bap. It likes me well. Cambio, hie you home,
And bid Bianca make her ready straight;
And if you will, tell what hath happened:
Lucentio's father is arriv'd in Padua,
And how she's like to be Lucentio's wife. [*Exit Lucentio.*]
Bion. I pray the gods she may with all my heart!
Tra. Dally not with the gods, but get thee gone. *Exit* [*Biondello*].

Enter Peter, [*a servant, who whispers to Tranio*].

Signior Baptista, shall I lead the way?
Welcome! one mess is like to be your cheer.
Come, sir, we will better it in Pisa.
Bap. I follow you. *Exeunt.*

Enter Lucentio [*as Cambio*] *and* Biondello.

Bion. Cambio!
Luc. What say'st thou, Biondello?
Bion. You saw my master wink and laugh upon you?
Luc. Biondello, what of that?
Bion. Faith, nothing; but h'as left me here behind to expound the meaning or moral of his signs and tokens.
Luc. I pray thee moralize them.
Bion. Then thus: Baptista is safe, talking with the deceiving father of a deceitful son.
Luc. And what of him?
Bion. His daughter is to be brought by you to the supper.

196. See the Textual Notes for an episode of the Sly framework preserved in *The Taming of a Shrew*.

IV.iv. Location: Padua. Before Baptista's house.
2. but: unless.
5. the Pegasus: i.e. an inn so named, marked by a sign displaying the winged horse of classical myth.
10. Fear you not: have no fears about. 11. throughly: thoroughly.
17. tall: clever. hold . . . drink: i.e. Tranio tips him.
18. set your countenance: look grave. 23. Soft: not so fast.
36. curious: particular about every detail.

49. affied: betrothed. 53. heark'ning still: always listening.
54. happily: haply, perchance. 55. and it like: if it please.
56. lie: lodge. 57. pass: transact.
59. scrivener: notary. presently: immediately.
61. pittance: scanty meal. 66. like: likely.
70. mess: dish. cheer: welcome, entertainment.
78. h'as: he has. 81. moralize: interpret.
82. safe: i.e. safely taken care of.

Luc. And then?

Bion. The old priest of Saint Luke's church is at your command at all hours.

Luc. And what of all this?

Bion. I cannot tell, [except] they are busied about a counterfeit assurance. Take you assurance of her, *cum privilegio ad imprimendum solum;* to th' church take the priest, clerk, and some sufficient honest witnesses.
If this be not that you look for, I have no more to say,
But bid Bianca farewell for ever and a day.

Luc. Hear'st thou, Biondello?

Bion. I cannot tarry. I knew a wench married in an afternoon as she went to the garden for parsley to stuff a rabbit, and so may you, sir. And so adieu, sir; my master hath appointed me to go to Saint Luke's to bid the priest be ready to come against you come with your appendix. *Exit.*

Luc. I may and will, if she be so contented.
She will be pleas'd, then wherefore should I doubt?
Hap what hap may, I'll roundly go about her;
It shall go hard if Cambio go without her. *Exit.*

[SCENE V]

Enter PETRUCHIO, KATE, HORTENSIO, [*and* SERVANTS].

Pet. Come on a' God's name, once more toward our father's.
Good Lord, how bright and goodly shines the moon!

Kath. The moon! the sun—it is not moonlight now.

Pet. I say it is the moon that shines so bright.

Kath. I know it is the sun that shines so bright.

Pet. Now by my mother's son, and that's myself,
It shall be moon, or star, or what I list,
Or ere I journey to your father's house.—
Go on, and fetch our horses back again.—
Evermore cross'd and cross'd, nothing but cross'd!

Hor. Say as he says, or we shall never go.

Kath. Forward, I pray, since we have come so far,
And be it moon, or sun, or what you please;
And if you please to call it a rush-candle,
Henceforth I vow it shall be so for me.

Pet. I say it is the moon.

Kath. I know it is the moon.

Pet. Nay then you lie; it is the blessed sun.

Kath. Then God be blest, it [is] the blessed sun,
But sun it is not, when you say it is not;
And the moon changes even as your mind.
What you will have it nam'd, even that it is,
And so it shall be so for Katherine.

Hor. Petruchio, go thy ways, the field is won.

91. **except:** unless. 92. **Take you assurance:** make yourself sure.
93. **cum . . . solum:** with exclusive rights to print.
103. **against:** by the time that. 104. **appendix:** addition, i.e. bride.
107. **about her:** i.e. about marrying her.

IV.v. Location: A road leading to Padua.
8. **Or ere:** before.
14. **rush-candle:** inferior candle made by dipping a rush into grease.
20. **moon . . . mind.** Under Kate's apparent acquiescence lies an ironic thrust, since the moon was thought to govern the moods of a lunatic.

Pet. Well, forward, forward, thus the bowl should run,
And not unluckily against the bias.
But soft, company is coming here.

Enter VINCENTIO.

[*To Vincentio.*] Good morrow, gentle mistress, where away?
Tell me, sweet Kate, and tell me truly too,
Hast thou beheld a fresher gentlewoman?
Such war of white and red within her cheeks!
What stars do spangle heaven with such beauty,
As those two eyes become that heavenly face?
Fair lovely maid, once more good day to thee.
Sweet Kate, embrace her for her beauty's sake.

Hor. 'A will make the man mad, to make [a] woman of him.

Kath. Young budding virgin, fair, and fresh, and sweet,
Whither away, or [where] is thy abode?
Happy the parents of so fair a child!
Happier the man whom favorable stars
Allots thee for his lovely bedfellow!

Pet. Why, how now, Kate, I hope thou art not mad.
This is a man, old, wrinkled, faded, withered,
And not a maiden, as thou say'st he is.

Kath. Pardon, old father, my mistaking eyes,
That have been so bedazzled with the sun,
That every thing I look on seemeth green;
Now I perceive thou art a reverent father.
Pardon, I pray thee, for my mad mistaking.

Pet. Do, good old grandsire, and withal make known
Which way thou travellest—if along with us,
We shall be joyful of thy company.

Vin. Fair sir, and you my merry mistress,
That with your strange encounter much amaz'd me,
My name is call'd Vincentio, my dwelling Pisa,
And bound I am to Padua, there to visit
A son of mine, which long I have not seen.

Pet. What is his name?

Vin. Lucentio, gentle sir.

Pet. Happily met, the happier for thy son.
And now by law, as well as reverent age,
I may entitle thee my loving father.
The sister to my wife, this gentlewoman,
Thy son by this hath married. Wonder not,
Nor be not grieved; she is of good esteem,
Her dowry wealthy, and of worthy birth;
Beside, so qualified as may beseem
The spouse of any noble gentleman.
Let me embrace with old Vincentio,
And wander we to see thy honest son,
Who will of thy arrival be full joyous.

Vin. But is this true, or is it else your pleasure,

24. **bowl:** ball in the game of bowls.
25. **bias:** an off-centre weight in the bowl which governs its course unless it is diverted by some obstacle; hence *against the bias* means "off its proper course." 47. **green:** young and fresh.
48. **reverent:** reverend.
54. **encounter:** manner of address, behavior.
63. **this:** this time. 64. **esteem:** reputation.
66. **so qualified:** of such qualities.

Like pleasant travellers, to break a jest
Upon the company you overtake?

Hor. I do assure thee, father, so it is.

Pet. Come go along and see the truth hereof,
For our first merriment hath made thee jealous.

Exeunt [all but Hortensio].

Hor. Well, Petruchio, this has put me in heart.
Have to my widow! and if she [be] froward,
Then hast thou taught Hortensio to be untoward. *Exit.*

[ACT V, SCENE I]

Enter BIONDELLO, LUCENTIO, *and* BIANCA; GREMIO *is out before.*

Bion. Softly and swiftly, sir, for the priest is ready.

Luc. I fly, Biondello; but they may chance to need thee at home, therefore leave us.

Bion. Nay, faith, I'll see the church a' your back, and then come back to my [master's] as soon as I can. *[Exeunt Lucentio, Bianca, and Biondello.]*

Gre. I marvel Cambio comes not all this while.

Enter PETRUCHIO, KATE, VINCENTIO, GRUMIO, *with* ATTENDANTS.

Pet. Sir, here's the door, this is Lucentio's house.
My father's bears more toward the market-place;
Thither must I, and here I leave you, sir.

Vin. You shall not choose but drink before you go.
I think I shall command your welcome here;
And by all likelihood some cheer is toward. *Knock.*

Gre. They're busy within, you were best knock louder.

PEDANT *looks out of the window.*

Ped. What's he that knocks as he would beat down the gate?

Vin. Is Signior Lucentio within, sir?

Ped. He's within, sir, but not to be spoken withal.

Vin. What if a man bring him a hundred pound or two, to make merry withal?

Ped. Keep your hundred pounds to yourself, he shall need none so long as I live.

Pet. Nay, I told you your son was well belov'd in Padua. Do you hear, sir?—to leave frivolous circumstances, I pray you tell Signior Lucentio that his father is come from Pisa, and is here at the door to speak with him.

Ped. Thou liest, his father is come from Padua and here looking out at the window.

Vin. Art thou his father?

Ped. Ay, sir, so his mother says, if I may believe her.

76. **jealous:** suspicious.
78. **froward:** refractory. 79. **untoward:** unmannerly.

V.i. **Location:** Padua. Before Lucentio's house.
o.s.d. **out before:** on the forestage.
4. **I'll . . . back:** I'll see the church over you, i.e. I'll see you into the church. 9. **bears:** lies (nautical term).
13. **cheer is toward:** entertainment is in preparation.
27. **circumstances:** matters.

Pet. [*To Vincentio.*] Why, how now, gentleman? Why, this is flat knavery, to take upon you another man's name.

Ped. Lay hands on the villain. I believe 'a means to cozen somebody in this city under my countenance.

Enter BIONDELLO.

Bion. I have seen them in the church together, God send 'em good shipping! But who is here? Mine old master Vincentio! Now we are undone and brought to nothing.

Vin. [*Seeing Biondello.*] Come hither, crack-hemp.

Bion. I hope I may choose, sir.

Vin. Come hither, you rogue. What, have you forgot me?

Bion. Forgot you? no, sir. I could not forget you, for I never saw you before in all my life.

Vin. What, you notorious villain, didst thou never see thy [master's] father, Vincentio?

Bion. What, my old worshipful old master? Yes, marry, sir—see where he looks out of the window.

Vin. Is't so indeed? *He beats Biondello.*

Bion. Help, help, help! here's a madman will murder me. *[Exit.]*

Ped. Help, son! help, Signior Baptista! *[Exit above.]*

Pet. Prithee, Kate, let's stand aside and see the end of this controversy. *[They retire.]*

Enter PEDANT [*below*] *with* SERVANTS, BAPTISTA, TRANIO [*as Lucentio*].

Tra. Sir, what are you that offer to beat my servant?

Vin. What am I, sir? Nay, what are you, sir? O immortal gods! O fine villain! A silken doublet, a velvet hose, a scarlet cloak, and a copatain hat! O, I am undone, I am undone! While I play the good husband at home, my son and my servant spend all at the university.

Tra. How now, what's the matter?

Bap. What, is the man lunatic?

Tra. Sir, you seem a sober ancient gentleman by your habit; but your words show you a madman. Why, sir, what 'cerns it you if I wear pearl and gold? I thank my good father, I am able to maintain it.

Vin. Thy father! O villain, he is a sailmaker in Bergamo.

Bap. You mistake, sir, you mistake, sir. Pray what do you think is his name?

Vin. His name! as if I knew not his name! I have brought him up ever since he was three years old, and his name is Tranio.

36. **flat:** downright. 39–40. **under my countenance:** in my person.
42. **good shipping:** fair sailing. 43. **undone:** ruined.
45–46. **crack-hemp:** gallows bird.
47. **I hope . . . choose:** i.e. I am not subject to your orders.
63. **offer:** presume. 66. **fine:** consummate.
67. **copatain:** high-crowned.
68–69. **good husband:** careful manager. 75. **cerns:** concerns.
76. **maintain:** afford.

Ped. Away, away, mad ass, his name is Lucentio, and he is mine only son, and heir to the lands of me, Signior Vincentio.

Vin. Lucentio! O, he hath murd'red his master! Lay hold on him, I charge you, in the Duke's name. O, my son, my son! Tell me, thou villain, where is my son Lucentio?

Tra. Call forth an officer.

[*Exit Servant, who returns with an Officer.*]

Carry this mad knave to the jail. Father Baptista, I charge you see that he be forthcoming.

Vin. Carry me to the jail?

Gre. Stay, officer, he shall not go to prison.

Bap. Talk not, Signior Gremio; I say he shall go to prison.

Gre. Take heed, Signior Baptista, lest you be cony-catch'd in this business. I dare swear this is the right Vincentio.

Ped. Swear if thou dar'st.

Gre. Nay, I dare not swear it.

Tra. Then thou wert best say that I am not Lucentio.

Gre. Yes, I know thee to be Signior Lucentio.

Bap. Away with the dotard, to the jail with him!

Enter Biondello, Lucentio, *and* Bianca.

Vin. Thus strangers may be hal'd and abus'd. O monstrous villain!

Bion. O, we are spoil'd and—yonder he is. Deny him, forswear him, or else we are all undone.

Exeunt Biondello, Tranio, and Pedant as fast as may be.

Luc. Pardon, sweet father. *Kneel.*
Vin. Lives my sweet son?
Bian. Pardon, dear father.
Bap. How hast thou offended?
Where is Lucentio?
Luc. Here's Lucentio,
Right son to the right Vincentio,
That have by marriage made thy daughter mine,
While counterfeit supposes blear'd thine eyne.

Gre. Here's packing, with a witness, to deceive us all!

Vin. Where is that damned villain Tranio,
That fac'd and braved me in this matter so?
Bap. Why, tell me, is not this my Cambio?
Bian. Cambio is chang'd into Lucentio.
Luc. Love wrought these miracles. Bianca's love
Made me exchange my state with Tranio,
While he did bear my countenance in the town,
And happily I have arrived at the last
Unto the wished haven of my bliss.
What Tranio did, myself enforc'd him to;
Then pardon him, sweet father, for my sake.

93. forthcoming: ready to appear (in court) when required.
99. cony-catch'd: duped.
117. supposes: suppositions, conjectures; an allusion to Gascoigne's play *Supposes* (itself based on Ariosto's *I Suppositi*), from which Shakespeare took the Lucentio-Bianca plot. **blear'd thine eyne:** hoodwinked you (*eyne* is an archaic plural of *eye*).
118. packing: conspiracy, plotting. **witness:** vengeance.
121. fac'd and braved. Cf. IV.iii.124–25.
125. state: rank and degree.

Vin. I'll slit the villain's nose, that would have sent me to the jail.

Bap. But do you hear, sir? Have you married my daughter without asking my good will?

Vin. Fear not, Baptista, we will content you, go to; but I will in to be reveng'd for this villainy. *Exit.*

Bap. And I, to sound the depth of this knavery. *Exit.*

Luc. Look not pale, Bianca, thy father will not frown. *Exeunt* [*Lucentio and Bianca*].

Gre. My cake is dough, but I'll in among the rest,
Out of hope of all but my share of the feast. [*Exit.*]
Kath. Husband, let's follow, to see the end of this ado.
Pet. First kiss me, Kate, and we will.
Kath. What, in the midst of the street?
Pet. What, art thou asham'd of me?
Kath. No, sir, God forbid, but asham'd to kiss.
Pet. Why then let's home again. Come, sirrah, let's away.
Kath. Nay, I will give thee a kiss; now pray thee, love, stay.
Pet. Is not this well? Come, my sweet Kate:
Better once than never, for never too late. *Exeunt.*

[Scene II]

Enter Baptista, Vincentio, Gremio, *the* Pedant, Lucentio, *and* Bianca; [Petruchio, Katherina, Hortensio,] Tranio, Biondello, Grumio, *and* Widow: *the servingmen with Tranio bringing in a banquet.*

Luc. At last, though long, our jarring notes agree,
And time it is, when raging war is [done],
To smile at scapes and perils overblown.
My fair Bianca, bid my father welcome,
While I with self-same kindness welcome thine.
Brother Petruchio, sister Katherina,
And thou, Hortensio, with thy loving widow,
Feast with the best, and welcome to my house.
My banket is to close our stomachs up
After our great good cheer. Pray you sit down,
For now we sit to chat as well as eat.
Pet. Nothing but sit and sit, and eat and eat!
Bap. Padua affords this kindness, son Petruchio.
Pet. Padua affords nothing but what is kind.
Hor. For both our sakes, I would that word were true.
Pet. Now, for my life, Hortensio fears his widow.
Wid. Then never trust me if I be afeard.
Pet. You are very sensible, and yet you miss my sense:
I mean Hortensio is afeard of you.

140. My . . . dough. Proverbial expression for failure. Cf. I.i.108–9.
141. Out . . . but: with hope of nothing except.

V.ii. Location: Padua. Lucentio's house.
3. scapes: escapes. **overblown:** blown over.
9. banket: banquet, i.e. light repast of sweets, fruit, and wine.
16. fears. The widow takes this word in its causative sense, "frightens."

Wid. He that is giddy thinks the world turns round.
Pet. Roundly replied.
Kath. Mistress, how mean you that?
Wid. Thus I conceive by him.
Pet. Conceives by me! how likes Hortensio that?
Hor. My widow says, thus she conceives her tale.
Pet. Very well mended. Kiss him for that, good widow.
Kath. "He that is giddy thinks the world turns round":
I pray you tell me what you meant by that.
Wid. Your husband, being troubled with a shrew,
Measures my husband's sorrow by his woe:
And now you know my meaning.
Kath. A very mean meaning.
Wid. Right, I mean you.
Kath. And I am mean indeed, respecting you.
Pet. To her, Kate!
Hor. To her, widow!
Pet. A hundred marks, my Kate does put her down.
Hor. That's my office.
Pet. Spoke like an officer. Ha' to thee, lad!
Drinks to Hortensio.
Bap. How likes Gremio these quick-witted folks?
Gre. Believe me, sir, they butt together well.
Bian. Head, and butt! an hasty-witted body
Would say your head and butt were head and horn.
Vin. Ay, mistress bride, hath that awakened you?
Bian. Ay, but not frighted me, therefore I'll sleep again.
Pet. Nay, that you shall not, since you have begun;
Have at you for a [bitter] jest or two!
Bian. Am I your bird? I mean to shift my bush,
And then pursue me as you draw your bow.
You are welcome all.
Exit Bianca [with Katherina and Widow].
Pet. She hath prevented me. Here, Signior Tranio,
This bird you aim'd at, though you hit her not;
Therefore a health to all that shot and miss'd.
Tra. O, sir, Lucentio slipp'd me like his greyhound,
Which runs himself, and catches for his master.
Pet. A good swift simile, but something currish.
Tra. 'Tis well, sir, that you hunted for yourself;
'Tis thought your deer does hold you at a bay.
Bap. O, O, Petruchio, Tranio hits you now.
Luc. I thank thee for that gird, good Tranio.
Hor. Confess, confess, hath he not hit you here?
Pet. 'A has a little gall'd me, I confess;
And as the jest did glance away from me,
'Tis ten to one it maim'd you [two] outright.

21. Roundly: frankly, plainly.
22. Thus . . . him: that's what I take him for.
29. Measures: judges. **31. very mean:** very contemptible.
32. I . . . you: i.e. I am moderate (in temper) compared with you.
35. marks. A mark was the sum of 13*s.* 4*d.* **37. Ha':** i.e. here's.
45. Have at you: I shall come at you. **bitter:** shrewd, sharp.
46. your bird: i.e. the bird you are aiming your darts at. **shift my bush:** fly to another tree (so that he will have to follow her if he intends to keep her as his target). **49. prevented:** forestalled.
52. slipp'd: unleashed.
54. swift: (1) ready-witted; (2) having reference to swiftness.
56. hold you at a bay: turn to make a stand against you (hunting term). **58. gird:** taunt; sharp, biting jest. **60. gall'd:** wounded.

Bap. Now in good sadness, son Petruchio,
I think thou hast the veriest shrew of all.
Pet. Well, I say no; and therefore [for] assurance
Let's each one send unto his wife,
And he whose wife is most obedient,
To come at first when he doth send for her,
Shall win the wager which we will propose.
Hor. Content. What's the wager?
Luc. Twenty crowns.
Pet. Twenty crowns!
I'll venture so much of my hawk or hound,
But twenty times so much upon my wife.
Luc. A hundred then.
Hor. Content.
Pet. A match! 'tis done.
Hor. Who shall begin?
Luc. That will I.
Go, Biondello, bid your mistress come to me.
Bion. I go. *Exit.*
Bap. Son, I'll be your half, Bianca comes.
Luc. I'll have no halves; I'll bear it all myself.

Enter BIONDELLO.

How now, what news?
Bion. Sir, my mistress sends you word
That she is busy, and she cannot come.
Pet. How? she is busy, and she cannot come!
Is that an answer?
Gre. Ay, and a kind one too.
Pray God, sir, your wife send you not a worse.
Pet. I hope better.
Hor. Sirrah Biondello, go and entreat my wife
To come to me forthwith. *Exit Biondello.*
Pet. O ho, entreat her!
Nay then she must needs come.
Hor. I am afraid, sir,
Do what you can, yours will not be entreated.

Enter BIONDELLO.

Now, where's my wife?
Bion. She says you have some goodly jest in hand.
She will not come; she bids you come to her.
Pet. Worse and worse; she will not come! O vild,
Intolerable, not to be endur'd!
Sirrah Grumio, go to your mistress,
Say I command her come to me. *Exit [Grumio].*
Hor. I know her answer.
Pet. What?
Hor. She will not.
Pet. The fouler fortune mine, and there an end.

Enter KATHERINA.

Bap. Now, by my holidam, here comes Katherina!
Kath. What is your will, sir, that you send for me?
Pet. Where is your sister, and Hortensio's wife?

63. good sadness: all seriousness. **65. assurance:** proof.
74. A match: agreed.
78. I'll . . . half: I'll share the wager with you. **85. hope:** expect.
93. vild: vile.
99. holidam: properly *halidom*, i.e. holiness; but, as the spelling shows, the word had come to be taken as referring to the Virgin Mary.

Kath. They sit conferring by the parlor fire.
Pet. Go fetch them hither. If they deny to come,
Swinge me them soundly forth unto their husbands.
Away, I say, and bring them hither straight.
[*Exit Katherina.*]
Luc. Here is a wonder, if you talk of a wonder.
Hor. And so it is; I wonder what it bodes.
Pet. Marry, peace it bodes, and love, and quiet life,
An aweful rule, and right supremacy;
And to be short, what not, that's sweet and happy.
Bap. Now fair befall thee, good Petruchio!
The wager thou hast won, and I will add
Unto their losses twenty thousand crowns,
Another dowry to another daughter,
For she is chang'd, as she had never been.
Pet. Nay, I will win my wager better yet,
And show more sign of her obedience,
Her new-built virtue and obedience.

Enter KATE, BIANCA, *and* WIDOW.

See where she comes, and brings your froward wives
As prisoners to her womanly persuasion.
Katherine, that cap of yours becomes you not;
Off with that bable, throw it under-foot.
[*Katherina throws down her cap.*]
Wid. Lord, let me never have a cause to sigh,
Till I be brought to such a silly pass!
Bian. Fie, what a foolish duty call you this?
Luc. I would your duty were as foolish too.
The wisdom of your duty, fair Bianca,
Hath cost me [a] hundred crowns since supper-time.
Bian. The more fool you for laying on my duty.
Pet. Katherine, I charge thee tell these head-strong women
What duty they do owe their lords and husbands.
Wid. Come, come, you're mocking; we will have no telling.
Pet. Come on, I say, and first begin with her.
Wid. She shall not.
Pet. I say she shall, and first begin with her.
Kath. Fie, fie, unknit that threat'ning unkind brow,
And dart not scornful glances from those eyes,
To wound thy lord, thy king, thy governor.
It blots thy beauty, as frosts do bite the meads,
Confounds thy fame, as whirlwinds shake fair buds,
And in no sense is meet or amiable.
A woman mov'd is like a fountain troubled,
Muddy, ill-seeming, thick, bereft of beauty,
And while it is so, none so dry or thirsty
Will deign to sip, or touch one drop of it.
Thy husband is thy lord, thy life, thy keeper,
Thy head, thy sovereign; one that cares for thee,
And for thy maintenance; commits his body
To painful labor, both by sea and land;
To watch the night in storms, the day in cold,
Whilst thou li'st warm at home, secure and safe;
And craves no other tribute at thy hands
But love, fair looks, and true obedience—
Too little payment for so great a debt.
Such duty as the subject owes the prince,
Even such a woman oweth to her husband;
And when she is froward, peevish, sullen, sour,
And not obedient to his honest will,
What is she but a foul contending rebel,
And graceless traitor to her loving lord?
I am asham'd that women are so simple
To offer war where they should kneel for peace,
Or seek for rule, supremacy, and sway,
When they are bound to serve, love, and obey.
Why are our bodies soft, and weak, and smooth,
Unapt to toil and trouble in the world,
But that our soft conditions, and our hearts,
Should well agree with our external parts?
Come, come, you froward and unable worms!
My mind hath been as big as one of yours,
My heart as great, my reason haply more,
To bandy word for word and frown for frown;
But now I see our lances are but straws,
Our strength as weak, our weakness past compare,
That seeming to be most which we indeed least are.
Then vail your stomachs, for it is no boot,
And place your hands below your husband's foot;
In token of which duty, if he please,
My hand is ready, may it do him ease.
Pet. Why, there's a wench! Come on, and kiss me, Kate.
Luc. Well, go thy ways, old lad, for thou shalt ha't.
Vin. 'Tis a good hearing when children are toward.
Luc. But a harsh hearing when women are froward.
Pet. Come, Kate, we'll to bed.
We three are married, but you two are sped.
[*To Lucentio.*] 'Twas I won the wager, though you hit the white,
And being a winner, God give you good night!
Exit Petruchio [*with Katherina*].
Hor. Now go thy ways, thou hast tam'd a curst shrow.
Luc. 'Tis a wonder, by your leave, she will be tam'd so. [*Exeunt.*]

103. deny: refuse. **104. Swinge:** whip. **me.** The ethical dative.
109. aweful rule: order commanding respect.
111. fair: good fortune. **122. bable:** bauble.
125. duty: obedience. **129. laying:** betting.
140. Confounds: ruins. **fame:** reputation. **142. mov'd:** angry.

157. peevish: obstinate, willful. **161. simple:** foolish.
166. Unapt: unfit. **167. conditions:** qualities.
169. unable worms: i.e. poor weak creatures.
170. big: haughty, arrogant.
176. Then . . . boot: Then lower your pride, for there is no help for it.
179. do him ease: give him pleasure.
182. toward: tractable, obedient. **185. sped:** done for.
186. white: centre of the target; playing on Bianca's name, which in Italian means "white." **188. shrow:** shrew.
189. See the Textual Notes for the final episodes of the Sly framework preserved in *The Taming of a Shrew.*

NOTE ON THE TEXT

The basic authority for *The Taming of the Shrew* is the First Folio (1623); all later texts are derived essentially from that source. A quarto edition based on F1 (referred to as Q in the Textual Notes) was printed in 1631.

There has been much speculation about the relation between *The Shrew* and a play entitled *A Pleasant Conceited Historie, called The taming of a Shrew,* which was published in 1594 (referred to as (Q) in the Textual Notes). The once-popular theory that *A Shrew* is the direct source of Shakespeare's play is no longer accepted. Today scholars generally hold either (a) that *A Shrew* is a "bad" quarto derived by some form of memorial imitation from *The Shrew*, or (b) that both plays are derived from a common original, the 1594 text of *A Shrew* being indeed a "bad" quarto, but a "bad" quarto of Shakespeare's source. The first alternative, originally proposed by Samuel Hickson in 1856, has been accepted by all recent editors (Morris, Oliver, Thompson, and Wells/Taylor). Textually, *A Shrew* is of little value to an editor of Shakespeare's *Shrew*, since, whether or not we accept it as a "bad" quarto of *The Shrew*, there is only some occasional verbal correspondence between the two texts. It does, however, preserve, in mangled form, a conclusion of the Sly framework and four short Sly inter-scenes, all of which are lacking in the F1 text. The conclusion and two of the inter-scenes were inserted in the text of *The Shrew* by Pope; in the present edition these three passages are included in the Textual Notes (see II.i.411, IV.iii.196, V.ii.189), together with two inter-scenes not included by Pope (see the end of the Textual Notes). Other passages from (Q) are quoted at Induction, ii.129–44, IV.ii.50–6, V.ii.136–79. Two later editions of *A Shrew* appeared in 1596 and 1607.

The F1 text gives evidence of having been printed from Shakespeare's "foul papers" (perhaps from "foul papers" which had undergone some form of revision). Since there is also evidence of a book-keeper's hand at several places in the F1 text (for example, in the use of actors' names for character names, though "Sincklo" at Induction, i.88 would appear to be authorial), it is further supposed that these "foul papers" had been annotated by a book-keeper in preparation for the production of an official prompt-book. Omissions in the stage directions and the palpable confusion in speech-prefixes at III.i.48–54 and IV.ii.4–8 make it most unlikely that the manuscript from which the F1 text was printed could itself have served as a prompt-book.

The most vexing textual problem in *The Shrew* concerns the broken Sly framework—a framework that begins brilliantly and then, except for a single inter-scene reappearance, simply disappears. *A Shrew*, on the other hand, contains not only reported versions of the opening two scenes of the Sly frame but four inter-scenes and an "epilogue" which completes the frame by returning Sly to the real world—ready now to tame his own wife. Oliver sums up his view of the problems as follows: "If, then, Shakespeare finally had an 'incomplete' Induction in his play, it would seem to mean *either* that he never had any other, *or* that, having tried the full framework, he afterwards preferred to discard part of it" (p. 29). The reasons he offers for supposing that Shakespeare purposely left the frame incomplete (open-endedness, danger of anticlimax, pp. 31–33) seem less than persuasive. And, if we admit that Shakespeare did originally complete the frame (as there seems every commonsense reason to suppose, a view ably presented by Morris, following the arguments of Wentersdorf), why must it have been Shakespeare himself who decided to do without the later inter-scenes and the "epilogue"?

Oliver argues that the copy for F1 was Shakespeare's "foul papers," which "apparently bore signs of change of mind—not only during composition (as perhaps in the false start to 4.4, . . .) but also after a period of time, whether that period extended only over months or over years" (p. 10). Morris, on the other hand, following Greg, argues that F copy was a transcript of the "foul papers," which had been lightly annotated by the book-keeper, in preparation for a prompt-book (pp. 2–12). In either case, it is very possible that the manuscript copy for F1 had been marked at some stage, perhaps because of casting problems, to indicate the omission of the *whole* framework, a decision that need have nothing to do with Shakespeare himself, and that in casting off copy for what was to become quire S of *The Shrew*, the person(s) responsible failed to notice that the Induction and the first inter-scene following I.i had been marked (perhaps unclearly) for deletion and probably realized the apparent intention to delete the frame with the now missing inter-scene only at the end of I.ii (sig. S5^v). Compositor B, who set the six folio formes (inner and outer) of quire S, began setting, as Charlton Hinman shows (vol. II, p. 447), with sig. S3^v (p. 210), commencing with line 74 of Induction ii—i.e., at a point where it may not even have been clear to him that he was dealing with anything other than a regular comic plot, or subplot, instead of a framing device. He then set S4^r, S4^v, and S3^r, thus completing a forme (inner and outer) of four pages ready for printing. He next set S2^v (p. 208, the first page of *The Shrew*). At this time, even had he wished to omit the Induction and first inter-scene, he could not do so, since the inter-scene and Induction i (from line 84) and ii were in all probability already being printed off. In any case, B would not necessarily have been conscious that the frame and inter-scenes were not meant to be included until encountering the first excised inter-scene in setting S5^v, the page he set immediately after S2^v. At this point he accepted their deletion, recognizing perhaps that the later inter-scenes were not absolutely necessary to the continuity of the larger framework. Even so, it may be objected that, since B also set the final page of *The Shrew* (sig. V1^r p. 229), he might have been expected to recall setting the Induction and would at least, although all but one of the inter-scenes had been omitted, have included the "epilogue," whether marked for deletion or not. That B failed to do so suggests either that he did not realize the need for the "epilogue" to complete the Induction frame, or that, since a delay of perhaps as much as two months occurred before he came to set the final page of *The Shrew* (Hinman, vol. II, pp. 461–62), he had simply forgotten the Induction and the one inter-scene earlier included. Such an explanation is, of course, hypothetical, but no more so than other attempts to explain away the truncated state of the text in F1.

For further information, see: Samuel Hickson, "*The Taming of the Shrew,*" *N & Q*, XXII (1850), 345–7; Peter Alexander, "*The Taming of a Shrew,*" *TLS*, 16 September 1926, p. 614, and "The Original Ending of *The Taming of the Shrew,*" *SQ*, XX (1969), 111–16; J. D. Wilson, ed., New Shakespeare *The Taming of the Shrew* (Cambridge, 1928) [the preceding studies view *A Shrew* as a "bad" quarto of *The Shrew*]; R. A. Houk, "The Evolution of *The Taming of the Shrew,*" *PMLA,* LVII (1942), 1009–38; G. I. Duthie, *The Taming of a Shrew* and *The Taming of the Shrew,*" *RES*, XIX (1943), 337–56 [the last two studies support the view that *A Shrew* and *The Shrew* are derived from a common source]; W. W. Greg, *The Shakespeare First Folio* (Oxford, 1955); J. W. Shroeder, "*The Taming of a Shrew* and *The Taming of the Shrew*: A Case Reopened," *JEGP*, LVII (1958), 424–43 [reopens the argument that *A Shrew* in its present form was one of the sources of *The Shrew*]; Richard Hosley, "Sources and Analogues of *The Taming of the Shrew,*" *Huntington Library Quarterly*, XXVII (1964), 289–308 [points out new sources and defends the spelling *Litio* against the *Li-*

cio of F2; in his Pelican edition, Hosley accepts the "bad" quarto relationship of *A Shrew* to *The Shrew*]; K. P. Wentersdorf, "The Original Ending of *The Taming of the Shrew*: A Reconsideration," *SEL,* XVIII (1978), 389–406; Brian Morris, ed., New Arden *The Taming of the Shrew* (London, 1981); H. J. Oliver, ed., New Oxford *The Taming of the Shrew* (Oxford, 1982); Ann Thompson, ed., New Cambridge *The Taming of the Shrew* (Cambridge, 1984); Stanley Wells and Gary Taylor, "No Shrew, A Shrew, and The Shrew: Internal Revision in *The Taming of the Shrew,*" in *Shakespeare, Text, and Language,* ed. Bernhard Fabian and Kurt Tetzeli von Rosador (Zurich, 1987), pp. 351–70; Stanley Wells, Gary Taylor, et al., *William Shakespeare: A Textual Companion* (Oxford, 1987).

TEXTUAL NOTES

Dramatis personae: *subs. as first given by Rowe*
Act-scene division: *none in (Q); F1 gives headings for I.i (at the beginning of the Induction), Act III (at III.i of the present text), IV.i (at IV.iii), and Act V (at V.ii); other act-scene divisions from Rowe and later editors (see first note to each scene); present act-scene arrangement as a whole first established by Steevens*

Induction, i

Induction, i] *Pope;* Actus primus. Scoena Prima. *F1*
Location: *Theobald*
o.s.d. Enter . . . Hostess.] *Kittredge (subs.);* Enter Begger and Hostes, Christophero Sly. *F1;* Enter a Tapster, beating out of his doores Slie Droonken. *(Q)*
1 s.p. Sly.] *Rowe;* Begger. *F1 (or* Beg. *throughout)*
9 Saint] *Dyce;* S. *F1*
12 thirdborough] *Theobald;* Head- / borough *F1*
12 s.d. Exit.] *Rowe; (Q) has* Exit Tapster.
17 (Brach . . . cur, is emboss'd),] *White;* Brach . . . Curre is imbost, *F1*
22, 30 s.pp. 1. Hun.] *Capell;* Hunts. *F1*
32–3 He . . . soundly.] *as verse, Rowe; as prose, F1*
73 s.d. Some . . . Sly.] *Theobald; (Q) has* Exeunt two with Slie.
74 s.d. Exit Servingman.] *Theobald*
78 s.d. Enter Players.] Enter two of the players with packs at their backs, and a boy. *(Q)*
88 s.p. 1. Play.] *Capell;* Sincklo. *F1 (the name of the actor who played this role)*
100 s.p. 1. Play.] *Capell;* Plai. *F1*
135 peasant.] *Johnson;* peasant, *F1*
138 s.d. Exeunt.] *Capell*

Induction, ii

Induction, ii] *Capell*
Location: *Theobald*
o.s.d. Enter . . . Lord.] Enter two with a table and a banquet on it, and two other, with Slie asleepe in a chaire, richlie apparelled, & the musick plaieng. *(Q)*
2, 3, 76 Will't] *F3;* Wilt *F1*
2 lordship] *Q;* Lord *F1*
18 Sly's] *Q* (Slies); Sies *F1*
23 fourteen pence] *Rowe;* xiiii.d. *F1*
25 What!] *Hanmer (subs.);* What *F1*
26 s.p. 3. Serv.] *Capell;* 3. Man. *F1 (throughout scene)*
27 s.p. 2. Serv.] *Capell;* 2 Man. *F1 (throughout scene)*
47 s.p. 1. Serv.] *Capell;* 1 Man. *F1 (throughout scene)*
73 Christopher] Christophero *F2*
98 s.d. the Page as a] *Capell; s.d. in (Q) reads:* Enter the boy in Womans attire.
100 s.p. Page.] *Capell;* Lady. *F1 (or* La. *throughout scene)*
110 Al'ce] *Capell;* Alce *F1*
129–44] *(Q) gives the following equivalent of these lines:* Lord. May it please you, your honors plaiers be come / To offer your honour a plaie. / *Slie.* A plaie *Sim,* O braue, be they my plaiers? / *Lord.* I my Lord. / *Slie.* Is there not a foole in the plaie? / *Lord.* Yes my lord. / *Slie.* When wil they plaie *Sim?* / *Lord.* Euen when it please your honor, they be readie. / *Boy.* My lord Ile go bid them begin their plaie. / *Slie.* Doo, but looke that you come againe. / *Boy.* I warrant you my lord, I wil not leaue you thus. / *Exit* boy. / *Slie.* Come *Sim,* where be the plaiers? *Sim* stand by / Me and weele flout the plaiers out of their cotes. / *Lord.* Ile cal them my lord. Hoe where are you there? / Sound Trumpets.
137 will, . . . Is] *Capell;* will let them play, it is *F1*
138 comonty] *(Q), in Induction, i, calls a comedy a* comoditie
144 s.d. They all sit.] *Malone (subs.)*
144 s.d. Flourish.] *part of o.s.d. for I.i, F1;* Sound Trumpets. *(Q)*

I.i

I.i] *Pope*
Location: *Wilson (subs., after Theobald)*
o.s.d. Tranio] *F2;* Triano *F1*
13 Vincentio] *Hanmer;* Vincentio's *F1*
14 brought] *F2;* brough *F1*
25 Mi perdonato] *Capell (reading* perdonate); Me Pardonato *F1*
26 am,] *ed.;* am *F1*
33 Ovid] *F3;* Ouid; *F1*
47 s.d. Katherina] *F2;* Katerina *F1 (occasionally throughout; the form reflects Shakespeare's pronunciation)*
47 s.d. suitor] *F2* (shuiter); sister *F1*
57 s.p. Kath.] *Rowe;* Kate. *F1 (throughout)*
57 s.d. To Baptista.] *Capell*
71 Maid's] *Rowe;* Maids *F1*
78–9 A . . . why.] *as verse, Capell; as prose, F1*
90 resolv'd] *Q;* resould *F1*
91 s.d. Exit Bianca.] *Theobald*
98 kind, and liberal] *Theobald, Hanmer;* kind and liberall, *F1*
108 cake's] *F3;* cakes *F1*
145 s.d. Manent] *Pope;* Manet *F1*
162 captum] *F2;* captam *F1*
163 contents;] *Theobald;* contents, *F1*
164 counsel's] *F2;* counsels *F1*
207 color'd] *F2;* Conlord *F1*
207 cloak.] *Pope;* cloake, *F1*
227 time.] *F2;* time *F1*
235 Ay, sir!—[aside]] *Munro (after Rowe, Dyce);* I sir, *F1 (F1 is ambiguous; most recent editors read* I, sir!)
239–44 So . . . Lucentio.] *as verse, Capell; as prose, F1*
244 your] *F2;* you *F1*
249 s.p. 1. Serv.] *Capell;* 1. Man. *F1*

I.ii

I.ii] *Capell*
Location: *Pope*
18 masters] *Theobald;* mistris *F1*
24 Con . . . trovato] *Theobald (after Rowe);* Contutti le core bene trobatto *F1*
25 ben] *F2;* bene *F1*
25 molto] *Theobald;* multo *F1*
25 honorato] *F2;* honorata *F1*
28 'leges] *Capell;* leges *F1*
34–5 Whom . . . worst.] *as verse, Rowe; as prose, F1*
46 this' a] *W. S. Walker conj.;* this a *F1*
50 young men] *F3;* yongmen *F1*
52 grows. But . . . few,] *Hanmer (subs.);* growes but . . . few. *F1*
70 Sibyl] *Theobald;* Sibell *F1*
71 Xantippe] *Theobald;* Zentippe *F1*
73 Whe'er] *ed.;* Were *F1*
74 seas,] *Rowe;* seas. *F1*
79 aglet-baby] *hyphen, Theobald*
112 rope-tricks] *hyphen, Theobald*
121 me and other] *Capell;* me. Other *F1*
137 s.d. disguised] *F2;* disgused *F1*
137 s.d. as a schoolmaster] *Wilson (subs.)*
138–9 old folks] *F2;* olde- / folkes *F1*
143 s.d. They stand aside.] *Kittredge (after Capell)*
162 s.d. Coming forward.] *Collier*
164 Minola.] *Rowe (subs.);* Minola, *F1*
172 me] *Rowe;* one *F1*
190 Antonio's] *Rowe;* Butonios *F1*
206 trumpets'] *Capell;* trumpets *F1*
209 chestnut] *Singer;* Chesse-nut *F1*
213 ours] *Thirlby conj.;* yours *F1*
227 s.d. Aside.] *Capell*
264 stead] *Capell;* steed *F1*
265 feat] *Rowe;* seeke *F1*
279 motion's] *Rowe;* motions *F1*
280 ben] *F2;* Been *F1*

II.i

II.i] *Pope*
Location: *Pope*
3 gawds] *Theobald;* goods *F1*
8 thee] *F2*
30 s.d. Bianca] *Rowe*
36 s.d. Exit.] *Rowe*
38 s.d. Hortensio . . . and] *Rowe*
42–3 And . . . virtuous?] *as verse, Capell; as prose, F1*
55 s.d. Presenting Hortensio.] *Rowe*
60 Litio] Licio *F2*
71–3 Saving . . . forward.] *as verse, Steevens (after Capell); as prose, F1*
73 Backare] *Craig;* Bacare *F1 (in italics)*
74 O . . . doing.] *as verse, Hanmer; as prose, F1*
75–6 wooing. Neighbor,] *Theobald;* wooing neighbors: *F1*
76–87 Neighbor . . . coming?] *as prose, Pope; as verse, F1*
77 it.] *Rowe (subs.);* it, *F1*
77 kindness,] *Cambridge;* kindnesse *F1*
79 you] *Capell*
79 s.d. presenting Lucentio] *Rowe*
85 s.d. To Tranio.] *Rowe*
90 a suitor] *Q;* as utor *F1*
104 Pisa; by report] *Rowe;* Pisa by report, *F1*
110 s.d. Exit . . . following.] *Capell*
131 proud-minded] *hyphen, Rowe*
141 shake] *F2;* shakes *F1*
153 strook] *Capell;* stroke *F1*
157 rascal fiddler] *Capell;* Rascall, Fidler, *F1*
168 s.d. Baptista . . . Hortensio] *Theobald (s.d. placed as in Rowe; after l. 167, F1)*
186 bonny] *F4;* bony *F1*
213–4 Who . . . tail.] *as verse, Rowe; as prose, F1*
247 askaunce] *ed. (after Capell);* a sconce *F1*
263 mother-wit] *hyphen, Rowe*
278 s.d. Tranio] *Q;* Trayno *F1 (s.d. after l. 275, F1; placed as in Pope)*
301 good night] *F3;* godnight *F1*
324 s.d. severally] *Theobald*
330 in] *Rowe;* me *F1*
354 Valens] *ed.;* Vallens *F1*
357 pail] *F2;* pale *F1*
373 s.d. Aside.] *Warburton conj.*
375 Marsellis] *F2;* Marcellus *F1*

379 **tight]** *Rowe;* tite *F1*
411] *After this line Pope inserts the first five speeches of the following Sly framework from* (*Q*); *Capell, after III.ii:* Then *Slie* speakes. / *Slie. Sim,* when will the foole come againe? / *Lord.* Heele come againe my Lord anon. / *Slie.* Gis some more drinke here, souns wheres / The Tapster, here *Sim* eate some of these things. / *Lord.* So I doo my Lord. / *Slie.* Here *Sim,* I drinke to thee. / *Lord.* My Lord heere comes the plaiers againe, / *Slie.* O braue, heers two fine gentlewomen.

III.i

III.i] *Rowe;* Actus Tertia. *F1*
Location: *Theobald*
19 **'pointed]** *Hanmer;* pointed *F1*
28 **hic]** *Q;* hie *F1 (?)*
28, 33, 42 **Sigeia]** *F2 (subs.);* sigeria *F1*
43 **steterat]** *F2;* staterat *F1*
48–50 **How . . . yet.]** *continued to Hortensio, Rowe; assigned to* Luc., *F1*
48 **s.d. Aside.]** *Capell*
51 **s.p. Bian.]** *Theobald conj.; line given as part of preceding speech, F1*
52 **s.p. Luc.]** *Theobald conj.;* Bian. *F1*
54 **s.p. Bian.]** *Theobald conj.;* Hort. *F1*
59 **s.d. To Lucentio.]** *Capell*
62 **s.d. Aside.]** *Cambridge*
73 **s.d. Reads.]** *Capell*
74 **A re]** *Q;* Are *F1*
75 **B mi]** *Pope;* Beeme *F1*
76 **C fa ut]** *Q;* Cfavt *F1*
81 **change]** *F2;* charge *F1*
81 **odd]** *Theobald;* old *F1*
82 **s.p. Mess.]** *Neilson;* Nicke. *F1 (perhaps Nicholas Tooley, who may have played the role)*
85 **s.d. Exeunt . . . Messenger.]** *Neilson*
86 **s.d. Exit.]** *Rowe*
90–1 **stale, . . . list.]** *Capell (subs.);* stale: . . . List, *F1*

III.ii

III.ii] *Pope*
Location: *Malone (after Capell)*
o.s.d. **Lucentio]** *Rowe*
1 **s.d. To Tranio.]** *Capell*
1 **'pointed]** *Pope;* pointed *F1*
13 **behavior;]** *F4;* behauiour, *F1*
14 **man,]** *Rowe;* man; *F1*
15 **'point]** *Pope;* point *F1*
26 **s.d. followed . . . others]** *Capell (subs.)*
29 **thy]** *F2*
30 **old news]** *Capell*
33 **hear]** *Q;* heard *F1*
48 **hipp'd,]** *Hanmer;* hip'd *F1*
55 **sway'd]** *Hanmer;* Waid *F1*
56 **near-legg'd]** *hyphen, Rowe*
57 **half-cheek'd]** *Singer;* halfe-chekt *F1*
82–6 **Nay . . . many.]** *as verse, Collier (after Rowe); as prose, F1*
86 **s.d. Enter . . . Grumio.]** Enter Ferando baselie attired, and a red cap on his head. (*Q*)
87–90 **Come . . . were.]** *as verse, Capell; as prose, F1*
91 **s.d. Pretends great excitement.]** *ed.*
123 **s.d. with Grumio]** *Dyce (subs.)*
127 **s.d. with . . . Attendants]** *Cambridge (subs.)*
146 **narrow-prying]** *hyphen, Pope*
153 **grumbling]** *F2;* grumlling *F1*
167–83 **Trembled . . . play.]** *as verse, Steevens (after F2); as prose, F1*
183 **s.d. Grumio, and Train]** *Capell*
199 **s.p. Gre.]** *F2;* Gra. *F1*
209 **to-morrow—]** *Sisson;* to morrow, *F1*
239 **s.d. Petruchio, Katherina]** *Rowe (subs.);* P. Ka. *F1*
239 **s.d. and Grumio]** *Capell (subs.)*

IV.i

IV.i] *Pope*
Location: *Pope*
3 **ray'd]** *Johnson;* raide *F1;* raied *Q*
26 **s.p. Curt.]** *F2;* Gru. *F1*
41 **"Jack . . . boy!"]** *quotes, Warburton*
48 **their]** *F3;* the *F1*
62 **s.d. Strikes him.]** *Rowe*
117 **s.p. Gru.]** *F3;* Gre. *F1*
129 **peasant]** *Rowe;* pezant. *F1*
139 **s.d. Exeunt Servants.]** *Theobald;* Ex. Ser. *F1*
140 **s.d. Sings.]** *Theobald*
140–1 **"Where . . . those"]** *quotes, Theobald*
142 **s.d. Enter . . . supper.]** They couer the bord and fetch in the meate. (*Q*)
145 **s.d. Sings.]** *Rowe*
148 **off]** *Rowe;* of *F1*
148 **s.d. Strikes him.]** *Rowe;* He beates them all. (*Q*)
155 **s.d. Strikes him.]** *Capell*
165 **s.d. He . . . them.]** (*Q*)
167 **s.d. Exeunt Servants.]** *Dyce*
178 **s.d. Enter Servants severally.]** Manent seruingmen and eate vp all the meate. (*Q*)
180 **s.d. Enter . . . servant.]** *placed as in Capell; after l. 181, F1*
184–7 **And . . . hither.]** *as verse, Pope; as prose, F1*
187 **s.d. Exeunt.]** *Pope*

IV.ii

IV.ii] *Steevens*
Location: *Pope, Theobald*
1 **Litio]** *Pelican;* Lisio *F1 (throughout scene)*
4 **s.p. Hor.]** *F2;* Luc. *F1*
5 **s.d. They stand aside.]** *Theobald (subs.)*
6, 8 **s.pp. Luc.]** *F2;* Hor. *F1*
7 **What . . . First]** *Theobald;* What Master reade you first, *F1*
8 **read . . . profess,]** *Rowe* (read *F4*); reade, . . . professe *F1*
10 **prove]** *F2;* ptoue *F1*
10 **s.d. They retire.]** *Theobald (subs.)*
13 **none]** *Rowe;* me *F1*
31 **her]** *F3;* them *F1*
35 **forsworn!]** *Capell;* forsworn *F1*
36 **oath,]** *Rowe;* oath. *F1*
43 **s.d. Exit.]** *Rowe*
45 **'longeth]** *Hanmer;* longeth *F1*
50–6] *With these lines cf. the curiously close equivalent in* (*Q*): [*Valeria.*] . . . But tell me my Lord, is *Ferando* married then? / *Aurel.* He is: and *Polidor* shortly shall be wed, / And he meanes to tame his wife ere long. / *Vale.* He saies so. / *Aurel.* Faith he's gon vnto the taming schoole. / *Val.* The taming schoole: why is there such a place? / *Aurel.* I: and *Ferando* is the Maister of the schoole.
53 **Tranio?]** *ed.;* Tranio. *F1*
63 **mercantant]** *ed.;* Marcantant *F1; called* marchant *in* (*Q*)
65 **countenance]** *F2;* eountenance *F1*
71 **Take]** *F2; Par.* Take *F1*
71 **in]** *Theobald;* me *F1*
71 **s.d. Exeunt . . . Bianca.]** *Rowe*
101 **s.d. Aside.]** *Rowe*

IV.iii

IV.iii] *Steevens;* Actus Quartus. Scena Prima. *F1* ((*Q*) *offers more frequent verbal links with this scene than usual*)
Location: *Capell (subs.)*
o.s.d. **Enter]** *Q;* Entor *F1*
19 **choleric]** phlegmaticke *F2*
50 **s.d. Aside.]** *Theobald*
62 **s.d. Enter Haberdasher.]** *placed as in Dyce; after l. 61, F1*
63 **s.p. Hab.]** *Rowe;* Fel. *F1*
72 **s.d. Aside.]** *Hanmer*
81 **a]** *Q*
82 **custard-coffin]** *hyphen, Warburton*
85 **s.d. Exit Haberdasher.]** *Cambridge*
86 **gown?]** *Rowe;* gowne, *F1*
88 **a]** *Q*
91 **censer]** *Rowe;* Censor *F1*
93 **s.d. Aside.]** *Theobald*
108 **yard,]** *F2;* yard *F1*
109 **winter-cricket]** *hyphen, Capell*
133, 141, etc. **s.dd. Reads.]** *Capell*
150 **where,]** *Q;* where *F1*
164 **s.d. Aside.]** *Rowe*
175 **What,]** *Theobald (after Pope);* What *F1*
181 **me.]** *F4;* me, *F1*
196 **s.d. Aside.]** *Globe*
196] *Pope here inserts part of the following Sly framework from* (*Q*); *Capell, after V.i: Slie* sleepes. / *Lord.* Whose within there? come hither sirs my Lords / A sleepe againe: go take him easily vp, / And put him in his one apparell againe, / And lay him in the place where we did find him, / Iust vnderneath the alehouse side below, / But see you wake him not in any case. / *Boy.* It shall be don my Lord come helpe to beare him / hence, *Exit.*

IV.iv

IV.iv] *Steevens*
Location: *Capell*
o.s.d. **booted and bare-headed]** *from F1 s.d. at l. 18 below:* Enter Baptista and Lucentio: Pedant booted and bare headed.
1 **Sir]** *Theobald;* Sirs *F1*
4 **Genoa,]** *Theobald;* Genoa. *F1*
5 **Where . . . Pegasus.]** *continued to Pedant, Theobald; part of Tranio's following speech, F1*
7 **'longeth]** *Hanmer;* longeth *F1*
19 **Signior]** *Capell; Tra.* Signior *F1 (repeated s.p.)*
20 **s.d. To the Pedant.]** *Capell*
64 **And, . . . will,]** *Rowe;* And . . . will *F1*
64 **happened:]** *Capell (subs.);* hapned, *F1*
66 **s.d. Exit Lucentio.]** *Nicholson conj. (in Cambridge)*
68 **s.d. Exit Biondello.]** *Cambridge;* Exit. *F1 (after l. 67)*
68 **s.d. a servant . . . Tranio]** *ed. (after Bond)*
78 **h'as]** *Hanmer;* has *F1*
91 **except]** *F2;* expect *F1*
93 **imprimendum solum]** *F2;* Imprendum solem *F1*

IV.v

IV.v] *Steevens*
Location: *Hanmer (subs.)*
o.s.d. **Hortensio]** *Q;* Hortentio *F1 (occasionally)*
o.s.d. **and Servants]** *Cambridge*
17 **then]** theu *F1*
18 **is]** *Q;* in *F1*
27 **s.d. To Vincentio.]** *Rowe*
35 **a]** *F2;* the *F1*
38 **where]** *F2;* whether *F1*
41 **Allots]** *Q;* A lots *F1*
76 **s.d. all but Hortensio]** *Cambridge*
78 **be]** *F2*

V.i

V.i] *Warburton*
Location: *Pope*
o.s.d. **Bianca]** *Q;* Bianea *F1*
5 **master's]** *Capell;* mistris *F1*
6 **s.d. Exeunt . . . Biondello.]** *Rowe;* Exit. *F1 (after l. 4)*
30 **liest,]** *F2;* liest *F1*
35 **s.d. To Vincentio.]** *Capell*
44 **brought]** *Q;* brough *F1*
45 **s.d. Seeing Biondello.]** *Rowe*
53 **master's]** *F2;* Mistris *F1*
55 **marry]** *F2;* marie *F1*
59 **s.d. Exit.]** *Capell*
60 **s.d. Exit above.]** *Capell*
62 **s.d. They retire.]** *Theobald*
62 **s.d. below]** *Capell*
74 **madman]** *Rowe;* mad man *F1*
75 **'cerns]** *Collier;* cernes *F1*
83 **Tranio]** *F2;* Tronio *F1*
91 **s.d. Exit . . . Officer.]** *ed.*
107 **s.d. Bianca]** *Q;* Biancu *F1*
110 **and—]** *Capell;* and *F1*
111 **s.d. Exeunt]** *Theobald;* Exit *F1*
139 **s.d. Lucentio and Bianca]** *Capell*
140 **dough, but]** *Q;* doug, h but *F1*
141 **s.d. Exit.]** *Rowe*
146 **No]** *Q;* Mo *F1*

V.ii

V.ii] *Steevens;* Actus Quintus. *F1*
Location: *Pope*
o.s.d. **Petruchio, Katherina, Hortensio]** *Rowe (subs.)*
2 **done]** *Rowe;* come *F1*

37 **thee,**] *F2* (*comma, Theobald*); the *F1*
40 **butt!**] *Rowe* (*subs.*); but *F1*
45 **bitter**] *Theobald conj.*; better *F1*
48 s.d. **with . . . Widow**] *Rowe* (*subs.*)
62 **two**] *Rowe*; too *F1*
62 **outright**] *F3*; out right *F1*
65 **for**] *F2*; sir *F1*
82–8 **How . . . come.**] *as verse, Rowe; as prose, F1*
89 s.d. **Enter Biondello.**] *placed as in Capell; after* can, *l. 89, F1*
96 s.d. **Grumio**] *Rowe*
105 s.d. **Exit Katherina.**] *Rowe* (*subs.*)
122 s.d. **Katherina . . . cap.**] *Rowe* (*subs.*)
128 **a**] *Capell*; fiue *F1*
130–1 **Katherine . . . husband.**] *as verse, Rowe; as prose, F1*
132 **you're**] *F3*; your *F1*
136–79] *Cf.* (*Q*): *Kate.* Then you that liue thus by your pompered wills, / Now list to me and marke what I shall say, / Theternall power that with his only breath, / Shall cause this end and this beginning frame, / Not in time, nor before time, but with time, confusd, / For all the course of yeares, of ages, moneths, / Of seasons temperate, of dayes and houres, / Are tund and stopt, by measure of his hand, / The first world was, a forme, without a forme, / A heape confusd a mixture all deformd, / A gulfe of gulfes, a body bodiles, / Where all the elements were orderles, / Before the great commander of the world, / The King of Kings the glorious God of heauen, / Who in six daies did frame his heauenly worke, / And made all things to stand in perfit course. / Then to his image he did make a man. / Olde *Adam* and from his side a sleepe, / A rib was taken, of which the Lord did make, / The woe of man so termed by *Adam* then, / Woman for that, by her came sinne to vs, / And for her sin was *Adam* doomd to die, / As *Sara* to her husband, so should we, / Obey them, loue them, keepe, and nourish them, / If they by any meanes doo want our helpes, / Laying our handes vnder theire feete to tread, / If that by that we, might procure there ease, / And for a president Ile first begin, / And lay my hand vnder my husbands feete / She laies her hand vnder her husbands feete.
136 **threat'ning**] *Q*; thretaning *F1*
186 s.d. **To Lucentio.**] *Malone*
187 s.d. **with Katherina**] *Rowe* (*subs.*)
189 s.d. **Exeunt.**] *Rowe*; FINIS. *F1*
189] *Pope here inserts the conclusion of the Sly framework from* (*Q*), *omitting the Tapster's opening speech:* Then enter two bearing of *Slie* in his / Owne apparrell againe, and leaues him / Where they found him, and then goes out. / Then enter the *Tapster.* / *Tapster.* Now that the darkesome night is ouerpast, / And dawning day apeares in cristall sky, / Now must I hast abroad: but soft whose this? / What *Slie* oh wondrous hath he laine here allnight, / Ile wake him, I thinke he's starued by this, / But that his belly was so stuft with ale, / What how *Slie,* Awake for shame. / *Slie. Sim* gis some more wine: whats all the / Plaiers gon: am not I a Lord? / *Tapster.* A Lord with a murrin: come art thou / dronken still? / *Slie.* Whose this? *Tapster,* oh Lord sirra, I haue had / The brauest dreame to night, that euer thou / Hardest in all thy life. / *Tapster.* I marry but you had best get you home, / For your wife will course you for dreming here to night, / *Slie* Will she? I know now how to tame a shrew, / I dreamt vpon it all this night till now, / And thou hast wakt me out of the best dreame / That euer I had in my life, but Ile to my / Wife presently and tame her too / And if she anger me. / *Tapster.* Nay tarry *Slie* for Ile go home with thee, / And heare the rest that thou hast dreamt to night. / *Exeunt Omnes.*
Two other Sly inter-scene passages occur in A Shrew:
(*1*) *after Scene xiv* (*not in* The Shrew): *Slie. Sim* must they be married now? / *Lord.* I my Lord. / Enter *Ferando and Kate and Sander.* / *Slie.* Looke *Sim* the foole is come againe now.
(*2*) *after the* (*Q*) *equivalent of V.i.87–95: Phylotus and Valeria* runnes away. / Then *Slie* speakes. / *Slie.* I say wele haue no sending to prison. / *Lord.* My Lord this is but the play, theyre but in iest. / *Slie.* I tell thee *Sim* wele haue no sending, / To prison thats flat: why *Sim* am not I *Don Christo Vary*? / Therefore I say they shall not go to prison. / *Lord.* No more they shall not my Lord, / They be run away. / *Slie.* Are they run away *Sim*? thats well, / Then gis some more drinke, and let them play againe. / *Lord.* Here my Lord. / *Slie* drinkes and then falls a sleepe.

A sufferer from love melancholy. From Samuel Rowlands, *The Melancholy Knight* (1615). This representation of the fashionable and prescribed posture for the suffering lover matches almost perfectly Moth's advice to the infatuated Don Armado on how to win the love of Jaquenetta: he must sing "with your hat penthouse-like o'er the shop of your eyes; with your arms cross'd on your thin-bellied doublet like a rabbit on a spit" (*Love's Labor's Lost*, III.i.17–19). Similarly in *The Two Gentlemen of Verona* (II.i.18–20), Speed knows by "special marks" that Valentine is in love, first of all, as he tells his master, because "you have learn'd . . . to wreathe your arms, like a malecontent." (*Bodleian Library, University of Oxford; Shelfmark = 4to.L.71.Art* [4])

The Two Gentlemen of Verona

THE TWO GENTLEMEN OF VERONA has the unenviable distinction of being the least loved and least regarded of Shakespeare's comedies. Even *The Comedy of Errors* and *The Taming of the Shrew* have always enjoyed a robust theatrical life. This fact has enabled them to surmount, even to mock, the disparagements of critics more concerned to praise Shakespeare's mature comedies at the expense of his early work than to distinguish the special qualities and merits of those early plays. As it happens, *The Two Gentlemen of Verona* does, when sympathetically acted and directed, possess a delicate, lyrical charm. Launce and Julia are splendid acting parts and, on the stage, the dog Crab is invariably seductive. There is some fine verse and some excellent comic invention. Nevertheless, that new critical assessment which has rehabilitated *Love's Labor's Lost* and discovered that *The Comedy of Errors* is more than knockabout farce continues to hesitate over *The Two Gentlemen of Verona*. Although there have been successful professional productions since William Poel demonstrated in 1898 and 1910 that the play could hold an audience, it is still infrequently performed. It continues to engage academic attention less for itself than as a limping forerunner of Shakespeare's developed romantic style in comedy.

There are some valid reasons for this comparative neglect. The only text of *The Two Gentlemen of Verona*, that of the First Folio, is a maze of contradictions and inconsistencies. Shakespeare seems to have been unable to make up his mind whether the main action of the play takes place in Verona, Milan, or Padua. Silvia's father wavers disconcertingly between being a Duke and an Emperor; Launce and his dog were fairly obviously an afterthought, imperfectly welded into a plot which originally employed only one comic servant; and Sir Eglamour appears to be two quite different people. The quality of the verse is extremely uneven. Most puzzling of all, the play's resolution is achieved through a movement of plot so brusque, so destructive of the relationships of the characters as they have been developed, that generations of commentators have tried to absolve Shakespeare from responsibility for Valentine's overgenerous gift of his lady Silvia to his friend Proteus, the man who had been doing his best to rape her only a moment before.

There is no real case for assuming either that Shakespeare had a collaborator at whose doorstep the awkward moments of the comedy may conveniently be laid, or that the First Folio text seriously misrepresents the lost original. Clifford Leech's theory that the play was composed in two phases, part of it written perhaps in 1592 and the rest added hastily for performance late in 1593, has more to recommend it but is still highly conjectural. Like most of Shakespeare's early work, *The Two Gentlemen of Verona* cannot be dated with any precision. The first mention of it is in Meres's list of 1598. Because of its romance elements, features which seem to anticipate *As You Like It* and *Twelfth Night*, it is generally placed after *The Comedy of Errors* and *The Taming of the Shrew* in the chronology. But recent commentators point to the fact that forests, journeys, and heroines disguised as boys had figured in earlier English comedy. There is no reason why experimentation with classical and Italian models should necessarily have preceded Shakespeare's exploration, in *The Two Gentlemen of Verona*, of the more native tradition. The play is really neither more nor less innovative than the two which have been claimed as its forerunners.

Dramatically, *The Two Gentlemen of Verona* seems in fact more tentative than either *The Comedy of Errors* or *The Taming of the Shrew*. Stanley Wells has pointed to the almost exclusive reliance of this comedy upon soliloquy, duologue, and the aside as comment. Thirteen of its twenty scenes are realized entirely in terms of these three relatively uncomplicated dramatic techniques. Where Shakespeare does attempt a more complex orchestration of voices, the result tends to be awkward and ill-sustained. Characters are left to stand about, forgotten, in uncomfortable silence as the dialogue shifts back by preference to those tête-à-tête conversations which the dramatist knew how to handle. Wells remarks that although a similar technique can be observed in some Tudor interludes, neither *The Comedy of Errors* nor *The Taming of the Shrew* is limited in this way. Both these latter comedies are assured and confident in their construction of scenes involving the interplay of three or more characters. So, for that matter, are the three Henry VI plays and *Richard III*. The contrasted failure of *The Two Gentlemen of Verona* to make a success out of anything more extended than the duet seems to suggest that it was the work of a man still more at home with narrative or lyrical verse than with drama: a man who might well have turned subsequently to the discipline of Roman comedy in order to acquire certain formal theatrical skills which he was conscious that he lacked. It is entirely possible that *The Two Gentlemen of Verona* was Shakespeare's first professional play.

Its ultimate source was the story of Felix and Felismena as told in the *Diana* of the Portuguese writer Jorge de Montemayor. The *Diana* would have been available to Shakespeare in a French translation, but he may have depended not upon it for the shadowy prototypes of Proteus, Julia, and Silvia but upon a lost play, "The history of felix & philiomena," which was performed at court by the Queen's Men in 1585. In Montemayor, the equivalent to Silvia had been conveniently killed off at the end, allowing the Proteus and Julia characters to return to their original pairing. By adding Valentine to the story, Shakespeare created the possibility of a symmetrical happy ending. At the same time, his introduction of the complementary theme of friendship betrayed greatly complicated Montemayor's original account of falsehood in love. Interestingly, Cervantes did much the same thing to the Felix and Felismena plot when he wove it into Part I of *Don Quixote*. He made Cardenio, Valentine's counterpart, an integral part of the imbroglio involving the treacherous friend Don Fernando, Cardenio's lady Luscinda, and Don Fernando's first love Dorothea. As Cervantes tells it, the story is one of unquestioned absolutes, of extreme but unexamined romantic implausibilities. As such, it raises no problems. For Shakespeare, on the other hand, working in a different medium and essentially more realistic in his attitude towards these characters, the love and friendship motifs proved less easy to reconcile.

The idea that blind love must necessarily win a victory over rational friendship (as it does, painfully, in Chaucer's "Knight's Tale") ran side by side in the Middle Ages with the contrasted idea that the wise man, however tempted, will always value friendship over love. One of these two distinct literary traditions was rooted in the code of *l'amour courtois*; the other arose from a more moralistic but equally powerful set of demands. That concentration upon the nature and accords of love characteristic of Shakespearean comedy should not be allowed to obscure the fact that most Elizabethans would have seconded the opinion of Francis Bacon in his *Essays* that friendship is a serious matter and passion a far more dangerous and ephemeral kind of commitment. Although it might seem less promising as a dramatic subject than love, friendship was in fact celebrated in a number of Elizabethan plays. Probably, Shakespeare knew Richard Edwards' *Damon and Pithias* (1565), described as "the excellent Comedy of Two the most Faithfullest Friends" and much admired by contemporaries. In Lyly's *Endimion* (1588) and Peele's *The Old Wive's Tale* (1590) he would have found a character racked by the choice between friendship and love who, because he correctly prefers friendship, is awarded love as well. There must have been other sixteenth-century plays, now lost, which derived from and extended the considerable body of non-dramatic friendship literature.

In *Endimion, The Old Wive's Tale* and, by implication, in *Damon and Pithias*, friendship and love were conceived of as warring absolutes. The Knight Eumenides in *Endimion* has only one magical wish and a difficult decision to make as to whether he should expend it on a beloved mistress or a friend. Peele's wandering knight is brought to the extreme point of raising his sword to cleave his lady in two rather than dishonor his promise to share everything obtained on his journey with his friend, before he is mercifully absolved. In *The Two Gentlemen of Verona*, by contrast, love and friendship are not rival values. Only the disordered vision of a Proteus insists that they cancel each other out.

> Methinks my zeal to Valentine is cold,
> And that I love him not as I was wont:
> O, but I love his lady too too much,
> And that's the reason I love him so little.
>
> (II.iv.203–6)

His challenging remark to Silvia, "In love / Who respects friend?", provokes a crushing reply: "All men but Proteus" (V.iv.53–54). Even the steadfast Valentine is mocked and chided when his passion temporarily deprives him of his sense of proportion and, in the braggardism of his praise of Silvia, of consideration for the feelings of a friend. His suggestion, in II.iv, that Proteus' lady Julia might just serve to carry Silvia's train is arrogant and unlovely. In order to reach the harmony of love and friendship that is proper, the "One feast, one house, one mutual happiness" of the play's conclusion, attitudes like these need to be castigated and amended.

Neither love nor friendship is allowed to establish itself in the comedy as an ideal. The servants Launce and Speed provide an ironic commentary throughout, grounding the fantasies of their masters in reality. Speed irreverently denies that Silvia's divine beauty has any objective existence, that it is any more than the result of a partial way of seeing. He pokes fun at Valentine's love melancholy, and at the consequent dulling of his perceptions. In II.i he has to explain the meaning of Silvia's letter-trick to a Valentine so absurdly far gone in a dream of love that he fails to recognize its palpable and inviting presence. On a lower, less exacting but also more honest level, the friendship between Launce and Speed echoes the bond which unites their masters. Like Proteus, Launce considers marriage, but his wooing of the milkmaid possessed of more hair than wit, more faults than hairs, and more wealth than faults, is the most loveless and practical of bargains. Launce's real devotion, his gestures of genuine self-sacrifice, are reserved for Crab, his dog.

In the comedies of John Lyly, servants and minor characters had sometimes been allowed to mimic the behavior of their betters. Shakespeare may well have learned from Lyly's technique of parallel and juxtaposition. The drama of Lyly, however, was essentially rigid and conservative. Although the sighings and posturings of a Sir Tophas at the bottom of the scale might momentarily render love ridiculous, this parody in no way qualified the celebration of Endimion's ideal love for Cynthia at the top. Plays like *Endimion* arranged their characters in a strict hierarchy. Themes of love or friendship could be refracted among the various levels without the dramatist ever suggesting, as Shakespeare had already begun to do in *The Two Gentlemen of Verona*, that the commentary provided by pages or fools might modify admiration of the more dignified central characters. Lyly would never have had the effrontery to hint that a comic servingman who volunteers to be whipped himself so that his dog will not have to pay for its social misdemeanors displays a generosity which puts a Proteus or a Valentine, for all their hyperbolic oaths, to shame.

If *The Two Gentlemen of Verona* was indeed Shakespeare's first comedy, his tendency to hand over most of the initiative and just judgment to the women in his cast of characters was already marked. Proteus is treacherous and Valentine, at least in the first half of the play, self-pitying and selfish. The Duke is mercenary and unfeeling: ready to push his daughter into marriage with a fool simply on the grounds of wealth. Even Sir Eglamour, the romantic knight faithful unto death, abruptly turns coward and abandons Silvia to her fate when they meet the outlaws in the forest. By contrast, Silvia herself remains unshakeably loyal to the lover she has chosen, whatever obstacles fortune, her father, or the scheming Proteus can invent. She is even tender of the rights and feelings of a Julia she has never met, but only heard of by report. As for Julia, the fact that she anticipates Rosalind and Viola by assuming a boy's disguise to follow her lover is really less important than the character Shakespeare has given her: intrepid and sane, witty but sensitive, capable of committing follies but also of mocking them herself. She and Launce are the only two people in the play prepared with open eyes to suffer and be humiliated for love. The parallel between them is indicated subtly in IV.iv when Launce's rhetorical question hurled at the unrepentant Crab, "How many masters would do this for his servant?", is echoed soon after by Julia's cry as she prepares to deliver Proteus' ring to Silvia, as instructed: "How many women would do such a message?"

It is primarily because of the attitudes embodied in Julia, Silvia and Launce that Shakespeare's blunder in the final scene, when without warning he gives ideal friendship precedence over love, is so disastrous. Proteus' sudden repentance and Valentine's unquestioning forgiveness are entirely acceptable. The lightning reformation of evildoers was common in Elizabethan drama. It is even possible to read into Valentine's free pardon a new maturity, a fine tempering of spirit learned during his enforced exile in the forest. The gift of Silvia to his friend, on the other hand, is an intolerable clumsiness for which Shakespeare must take the blame. A gesture that would have been perfectly appropriate in Lyly or Peele, establishing a correct priority of values as a prelude to the happy ending, it has the effect here of negating the whole previous development of the comedy. Up to this point, *The Two Gentlemen of Verona* has placed small faith in love and friendship as abstract ideals. Only the false logic of Proteus, the braggardism and self-pity of Valentine, have coined generalizations of this kind. Certainly the play has not dignified friendship at the expense of love. If anything, it has suggested that as young men grow up and find themselves as individuals, love must and should come to dominate friendship in their lives, without cancelling out the earlier bond. And Silvia herself has never been portrayed as a chattel, a mere passive prize to be awarded to her would-be rapist without regard for her own feelings and inclinations.

As it happens, Proteus is given no opportunity to take up Valentine's excessive offer: "All that was mine in Silvia I give thee." Julia, as soon as the words are spoken, sinks fainting to the ground. The discovery of the true identity of Proteus' page drastically alters the situation. Proteus himself accepts Speed's doctrine of the relativity, the subjective nature of love: "What is in Silvia's face, but I may spy / More fresh in Julia's with a constant eye?" Valentine wins Silvia as the free gift of a Duke finally able to see what everyone else has known all along—that the preferred suitor Thurio, for all his wealth, is both a coward and a fool. Even the outlaws are forgiven and restored to favor in an ending which, after its one misstep, manages to achieve not only symmetry but joy.

The Two Gentlemen of Verona is not, by Shakespearean standards, a great comedy. More patchy and unsure than any of his other plays in the genre, it suggests a Shakespeare who at this stage in his career had not yet developed the full courage of his artistic convictions. Valentine's gift of Silvia to Proteus looks very like a nervous recourse to tradition, to the practice of older dramatists. Significantly, it occurs at the point which, in any comedy, is most difficult to handle with assurance: the resolution. The play's faults of tone and structure, its various inconsistencies and contradictions, should not however be allowed to obscure its very real merits. Although some of the verse is wooden, mechanically padded out to fill the line, the man who could give Proteus his description of Orpheus' lute,

> Whose golden touch could soften steel and stones,
> Make tigers tame, and huge leviathans
> Forsake unsounded deeps to dance on sands,
> (III.ii.78–80)

was already a dramatic poet worth the marking. Even more remarkable in its way is the supple, idiosyncratic prose spoken by Launce. In the prose comedy of Lyly, all the characters had employed the same distanced and deliberately artificial idiom. The prose of Launce, like that of Falstaff and Benedick later, seems to have been created by the character himself, to represent his particular and natural style of expression.

In innumerable ways, *The Two Gentlemen of Verona* looks forward to Shakespeare's later comedies. The character of Julia and her masculine disguise, the central position of the women in the play, the serious use of the clowns as commentators, and of music, themes of travel, and the transformation of people through love, the greenwood as the place where pretenses are dropped and characters appear for what they really are, the carefully calculated mixture of prose and verse: all of these motifs and devices were to be extended and developed in succeeding plays. Most important of all, when it is true to itself the comedy insists upon both the importance and the relativity of love. It fights shy of system and abstraction in favor of a meticulous, sensitive exploration of individual situations and reactions. The central issue, how to relate friendship and love, was one that Shakespeare returned to in the Sonnets, in *The Merchant of Venice*, *Much Ado about Nothing* and, near the end of his writing life, in *The Winter's Tale*. Arguably, these later treatments are all of them more assured and consistently successful. Yet *The Two Gentlemen of Verona* has a freshness and lyrical charm all its own, an uncertain glory that is no more to be despised than that of the April day described by Proteus, wavering between brilliance and cloud.

Anne Barton

A table-book for the year 1581. Harvard College Library. This is a fine example (shown actual size) of the kind of sixteenth-century pocket tables or table-book to which Hamlet refers when he says: "My tables—meet it is I set it down / That one may smile, and smile, and be a villain!" (*Hamlet*, I.v.107–8), and to which Julia metaphorically likens Lucetta in *The Two Gentlemen of Verona* (II.vii.2–4). It was called "tables" because it was made up of a number of thick, heavily waxed (hence erasable) cardboard leaves (each a table). The example above has an almanac for the year 1581 at the beginning and is handsomely bound in a typical Elizabethan stamped leather binding. Notice the brass clasps which hold it closed. (*By permission of the Harvard College Library*)

The Two Gentlemen of Verona

The Names of All the Actors

Duke [of Milan], *father to Silvia*
Valentine, Proteus } *the two Gentlemen*
Antonio, *father to Proteus*
Thurio, *a foolish rival to Valentine*
Eglamour, *agent for Silvia in her escape*
Host, *where Julia lodges*
Outlaws, *with Valentine*

Speed, [*page*] *to Valentine*
Launce, *a clownish servant to Proteus*
Panthino, *servant to Antonio*

Julia, *beloved of Proteus*
Silvia, *beloved of Valentine*
Lucetta, *waiting-woman to Julia*

[Attendants; Musicians]

[Scene: *Verona; Milan; and a forest somewhere between Milan and Mantua*]

ACT I, Scene I

[*Enter*] Valentine, Proteus.

Val. Cease to persuade, my loving Proteus:
Home-keeping youth have ever homely wits.
Were't not affection chains thy tender days
To the sweet glances of thy honor'd love,
I rather would entreat thy company,
To see the wonders of the world abroad,
Than (living dully sluggardiz'd at home)
Wear out thy youth with shapeless idleness.
But since thou lov'st, love still, and thrive therein,
Even as I would, when I to love begin.
Pro. Wilt thou be gone? Sweet Valentine, adieu,
Think on thy Proteus, when thou, happ'ly, seest
Some rare noteworthy object in thy travel.
Wish me partaker in thy happiness
When thou dost meet good hap; and in thy danger
(If ever danger do environ thee)
Commend thy grievance to my holy prayers,
For I will be thy beadsman, Valentine.
Val. And on a love-book pray for my success?
Pro. Upon some book I love I'll pray for thee.
Val. That's on some shallow story of deep love,
How young Leander cross'd the Hellespont.
Pro. That's a deep story of a deeper love,
For he was more than over shoes in love.
Val. 'Tis true; for you are over boots in love,
And yet you never swom the Hellespont.
Pro. Over the boots? nay, give me not the boots.
Val. No, I will not; for it boots thee not.
Pro. What?
Val. To be in love—where scorn is bought with groans;
Coy looks with heart-sore sighs; one fading moment's mirth
With twenty watchful, weary, tedious nights:
If happ'ly won, perhaps a hapless gain;
If lost, why then a grievous labor won;
However—but a folly bought with wit,
Or else a wit by folly vanquished.
Pro. So, by your circumstance, you call me fool.
Val. So, by your circumstance, I fear you'll prove.
Pro. 'Tis love you cavil at, I am not Love.
Val. Love is your master, for he masters you;
And he that is so yoked by a fool,
Methinks should not be chronicled for wise.
Pro. Yet writers say: as in the sweetest bud
The eating canker dwells, so eating love
Inhabits in the finest wits of all.
Val. And writers say: as the most forward bud
Is eaten by the canker ere it blow,

Words and passages enclosed in square brackets in the text above are either emendations of the copy-text or additions to it. The Textual Notes immediately following the play cite the earliest authority for every such change or insertion and supply the reading of the copy-text wherever it is emended in this edition.

I.i. Location: Verona. A street.
2. homely: simple.
3. affection: passion (stronger than the modern meaning). tender: youthful. 8. shapeless: lacking form, aimless.
9. love still: go on loving. 12. happ'ly: haply, perchance.
13. object: sight. 15. hap: fortune.
17. Commend thy grievance: commit your trouble.
18. beadsman: one who prays in another's behalf.
19. love-book: love-manual or love story (instead of a prayer book).

22. **Leander:** youth who nightly swam the Hellespont to visit Hero. One night he drowned in his attempt, whereupon Hero threw herself into the Hellespont and drowned also. 26. **swom:** swam.
27. **give . . . boots:** i.e. do not make fun of me. 28. **boots:** profits.
31. **watchful:** wakeful. 32. **hapless:** unfortunate.
34. **However:** whichever, either way.
36. **circumstance:** detailed proof (so also at line 84).
37. **circumstance:** condition, situation. 43. **canker:** cankerworm.
44. **Inhabits:** dwells. 46. **blow:** open.

Even so by love the young and tender wit
Is turn'd to folly, blasting in the bud,
Losing his verdure, even in the prime,
And all the fair effects of future hopes.
But wherefore waste I time to counsel thee
That art a votary to fond desire?
Once more adieu. My father at the road
Expects my coming, there to see me shipp'd.

Pro. And thither will I bring thee, Valentine.

Val. Sweet Proteus, no; now let us take our leave.
To Milan let me hear from thee by letters
Of thy success in love, and what news else
Betideth here in absence of thy friend;
And I likewise will visit thee with mine.

Pro. All happiness bechance to thee in Milan.

Val. As much to you at home; and so farewell.
Exit.

Pro. He after honor hunts, I after love:
He leaves his friends, to dignify them more;
I [leave] myself, my friends, and all, for love.
Thou, Julia, thou hast metamorphis'd me,
Made me neglect my studies, lose my time,
War with good counsel, set the world at nought;
Made wit with musing weak, heart sick with thought.

[*Enter*] Speed.

Speed. Sir Proteus! 'save you! Saw you my master?

Pro. But now he parted hence to embark for Milan.

Speed. Twenty to one then he is shipp'd already,
And I have play'd the sheep in losing him.

Pro. Indeed a sheep doth very often stray,
And if the shepherd be awhile away.

Speed. You conclude that my master is a shepherd then, and I [a] sheep?

Pro. I do.

Speed. Why then my horns are his horns, whether I wake or sleep.

Pro. A silly answer, and fitting well a sheep.

Speed. This proves me still a sheep.

Pro. True; and thy master a shepherd.

Speed. Nay, that I can deny by a circumstance.

Pro. It shall go hard but I'll prove it by another.

Speed. The shepherd seeks the sheep, and not the sheep the shepherd; but I seek my master, and my master seeks not me: therefore I am no sheep.

Pro. The sheep for fodder follow the shepherd, the shepherd for food follows not the sheep; thou for wages followest thy master, thy master for wages follows not thee: therefore thou art a sheep.

Speed. Such another proof will make me cry "baa."

Pro. But dost thou hear? gav'st thou my letter to Julia?

Speed. Ay, sir; I (a lost mutton) gave your letter to her (a lac'd mutton), and she (a lac'd mutton) gave me (a lost mutton) nothing for my labor.

Pro. Here's too small a pasture for such store of muttons.

Speed. If the ground be overcharg'd, you were best stick her.

Pro. Nay, in that you are astray; 'twere best pound you.

Speed. Nay, sir, less than a pound shall serve me for carrying your letter.

Pro. You mistake; I mean the pound—a pinfold.

Speed. From a pound to a pin? fold it over and over,
'Tis threefold too little for carrying a letter to your lover.

Pro. But what said she?

[*Speed nods, and Proteus looks at him questioningly.*]

Speed. Ay.

Pro. Nod-ay—why, that's "noddy."

Speed. You mistook, sir: I say, she did nod; and you ask me if she did nod, and I say, "Ay."

Pro. And that set together is "noddy."

Speed. Now you have taken the pains to set it together, take it for your pains.

Pro. No, no, you shall have it for bearing the letter.

Speed. Well, I perceive I must be fain to bear with you.

Pro. Why, sir, how do you bear with me?

Speed. Marry, sir, the letter, very orderly, having nothing but the word "noddy" for my pains.

Pro. Beshrew me, but you have a quick wit.

Speed. And yet it cannot overtake your slow purse.

Pro. Come, come, open the matter in brief: what said she?

Speed. Open your purse, that the money and the matter may be both at once deliver'd.

Pro. Well, sir, here is for your pains. What said she?

Speed. Truly, sir, I think you'll hardly win her.

Pro. Why? couldst thou perceive so much from her?

48. blasting: withering.
49. his verdure: its fresh vigor. **prime:** early spring.
50. effects: fulfillments. **future hopes:** promise of future development. **52. fond:** foolish, doting. **53. road:** roadstead, harbor.
54. Expects: awaits. **shipp'd:** aboard. Shakespeare seems to have supposed that Verona was a seaport. **55. bring:** accompany.
58. success: fortune (good or bad).
60. visit: bestow the same benefit on.
64. friends. Often used in reference to relatives. **dignify them more:** i.e. by improving himself. **65. leave:** neglect.
66. metamorphis'd: variant form of *metamorphosed.*
67. lose: waste.
69. thought: melancholy (supposed typical of lovers).
70. 'save you: God save you. **71. parted:** departed.
72, 73. shipp'd, sheep. The pun would be obvious to the Elizabethans, who gave *ship* and *sheep* almost the same pronunciation.
75. And if: if.
79. my . . . horns: he owns my horns, i.e. he is a cuckold (referring to the notion that the husbands of unfaithful wives sprouted horns).
85. It . . . I'll: I'll fare ill indeed if I can't.
93. cry "baa": i.e. admit I am a sheep (with quibble on "say 'bah'").
94. dost thou hear: i.e. listen to me.
97. lac'd mutton: prostitute. **101. overcharg'd:** overburdened.
102. stick: stab (with sexual innuendo).
103. astray: (1) straying (like a lost sheep); (2) deviating from propriety. **104. pound you:** (1) put you in the pound; (2) beat you.
107. pinfold: enclosure for stray cattle.
108. pin. Proverbially worthless. **fold:** multiply.
112. noddy: (1) a simpleton; (2) the knave in various card games.
120. fain: willing.
120–21. bear with: (1) put up with; (2) act as bearer for.
123. Marry: indeed (originally the name of the Virgin Mary used as an oath). **orderly:** properly, duly.
125. Beshrew me: mischief take me (a weakened curse).
127. open: disclose. **133. hardly win:** have a hard time winning.
134–35. perceive . . . her: deduce that from her behavior. Speed's reply quibbles on *perceive* in the now obsolete sense "receive." (Cf. the similar possibilities for wordplay in modern *gather* or *take in.*)

Speed. Sir, I could perceive nothing at all from her; no, not so much as a ducat for delivering your letter: and being so hard to me that brought your mind, I fear she'll prove as hard to you in telling your mind. Give her no token but stones, for she's as hard as steel.

Pro. What said she? nothing?

Speed. No, not so much as "Take this for thy pains." To testify your bounty, I thank you, you have [testern'd] me; in requital whereof, henceforth carry your letters yourself: and so, sir, I'll commend you to my master.

Pro. Go, go, be gone, to save your ship from wrack,
Which cannot perish having thee aboard,
Being destin'd to a drier death on shore. [*Exit Speed.*]
I must go send some better messenger:
I fear my Julia would not deign my lines,
Receiving them from such a worthless post. *Exit.*

Scene II

Enter Julia *and* Lucetta.

Jul. But say, Lucetta, now we are alone,
Wouldst thou then counsel me to fall in love?
Luc. Ay, madam, so you stumble not unheedfully.
Jul. Of all the fair resort of gentlemen
That every day with parle encounter me,
In thy opinion which is worthiest love?
Luc. Please you repeat their names, I'll show my mind
According to my shallow simple skill.
Jul. What think'st thou of the fair Sir Eglamour?
Luc. As of a knight well-spoken, neat, and fine;
But were I you, he never should be mine.
Jul. What think'st thou of the rich Mercatio?
Luc. Well of his wealth; but of himself, so, so.
Jul. What think'st thou of the gentle Proteus?
Luc. Lord, Lord! to see what folly reigns in us!
Jul. How now? what means this passion at his name?
Luc. Pardon, dear madam, 'tis a passing shame
That I (unworthy body as I am)
Should censure thus on lovely gentlemen.
Jul. Why not on Proteus, as of all the rest?
Luc. Then thus: of many good I think him best.

137. ducat: here, a silver coin worth about 3*s.* 6*d.*
139. mind: intentions. **in telling:** when you tell her.
140. stones: jewels.
145. testern'd me: given me a testern (sixpence).
146. commend you: deliver your greetings.
148. wrack: shipwreck.
150. Being: i.e. since you are. Lines 148–50 allude to the proverb "He that is born to be hanged shall never be drowned."
151. some better messenger. This (and the episode as a whole) seems to ignore the fact that Proteus has a servant of his own, Launce. It has been suggested that the character of Launce was an afterthought in Shakespeare's composition of the play.
152. deign: accept graciously.
153. post: (1) messenger; (2) blockhead.

I.ii. Location: Verona. The garden of Julia's house.
4. resort: company. **5. parle:** talk.
12. Mercatio. The name suggests a merchant (from Italian *mercato*, "market"). **16. passion:** passionate outburst.
17. passing: surpassing. **19. censure:** pass judgment.

Jul. Your reason?
Luc. I have no other but a woman's reason:
I think him so, because I think him so.
Jul. And wouldst thou have me cast my love on him?
Luc. Ay—if you thought your love not cast away.
Jul. Why, he, of all the rest, hath never mov'd me.
Luc. Yet he, of all the rest, I think best loves ye.
Jul. His little speaking shows his love but small.
Luc. Fire that's closest kept burns most of all.
Jul. They do not love that do not show their love.
Luc. O, they love least that let men know their love.
Jul. I would I knew his mind.
Luc. Peruse this paper, madam.
Jul. "To Julia"—say, from whom?
Luc. That the contents will show.
Jul. Say, say; who gave it thee?
Luc. Sir Valentine's page; and sent, I think, from Proteus.
He would have given it you, but I, being in the way,
Did in your name receive it; pardon the fault, I pray.
Jul. Now, by my modesty, a goodly broker!
Dare you presume to harbor wanton lines?
To whisper and conspire against my youth?
Now trust me, 'tis an office of great worth,
And you an officer fit for the place.
There! take the paper; see it be return'd,
Or else return no more into my sight.
Luc. To plead for love deserves more fee than hate.
Jul. Will ye be gone?
Luc. That you may ruminate. *Exit.*
Jul. And yet I would I had o'erlook'd the letter;
It were a shame to call her back again,
And pray her to a fault for which I chid her.
What 'fool is she, that knows I am a maid,
And would not force the letter to my view!
Since maids, in modesty, say "no" to that
Which they would have the profferer construe "ay."
Fie, fie, how wayward is this foolish love,
That (like a testy babe) will scratch the nurse
And presently, all humbled, kiss the rod!
How churlishly I chid Lucetta hence,
When willingly I would have had her here!
How angerly I taught my brow to frown,
When inward joy enforc'd my heart to smile!
My penance is, to call Lucetta back
And ask remission for my folly past.
What ho! Lucetta!

[*Enter* Lucetta.]

Luc. What would your ladyship?
Jul. Is't near dinner-time?

27. mov'd: proposed marriage to.
34. this paper: i.e. the letter which in I.i Speed has assured Proteus he delivered personally to Julia. Another instance of confused plotting, unless lines 39–40 are interpreted to mean that Lucetta deceived Speed by pretending to be Julia, an interpretation which the word *broker* in line 41 makes unlikely. **39. in the way:** at hand.
41. broker: go-between. **48. more fee:** better recompense.
50. o'erlook'd: looked over, read.
52. to a fault: to commit a fault. **53. 'fool:** a fool.
58. testy: fretful. **59. presently:** immediately.
62. angerly: angrily.

Luc. I would it were,
That you might kill your stomach on your meat,
And not upon your maid.
Jul. What is't that you
Took up so gingerly?
Luc. Nothing.
Jul. Why didst thou stoop then?
Luc. To take a paper up that I let fall.
Jul. And is that paper nothing?
Luc. Nothing concerning me.
Jul. Then let it lie for those that it concerns.
Luc. Madam, it will not lie where it concerns
Unless it have a false interpreter.
Jul. Some love of yours hath writ to you in rhyme.
Luc. That I might sing it, madam, to a tune:
Give me a note, your ladyship can set.
Jul. As little by such toys as may be possible:
Best sing it to the tune of "Light o' love."
Luc. It is too heavy for so light a tune.
Jul. Heavy? belike it hath some burden then?
Luc. Ay; and melodious were it, would you sing it.
Jul. And why not you?
Luc. I cannot reach so high.
Jul. Let's see your song. [*Takes the letter.*] How now, minion?
Luc. Keep tune there still, so you will sing it out.
And yet methinks I do not like this tune.
Jul. You do not?
Luc. No, madam, 'tis too sharp.
Jul. You, minion, are too saucy.
Luc. Nay, now you are too flat,
And mar the concord with too harsh a descant:
There wanteth but a mean to fill your song.
Jul. The mean is drown'd with [your] unruly bass.
Luc. Indeed I bid the base for Proteus.
Jul. This babble shall not henceforth trouble me.
Here is a coil with protestation! [*Tears the letter.*]
Go, get you gone; and let the papers lie:
You would be fing'ring them, to anger me.
Luc. She makes it strange, but she would be best pleas'd
To be so ang'red with another letter. [*Exit.*]
Jul. Nay, would I were so ang'red with the same.
O hateful hands, to tear such loving words!
Injurious wasps, to feed on such sweet honey,
And kill the bees that yield it with your stings!
I'll kiss each several paper for amends.
Look, here is writ "kind Julia." Unkind Julia,
As in revenge of thy ingratitude,
I throw thy name against the bruising stones,
Trampling contemptuously on thy disdain.
And here is writ "love-wounded Proteus."
Poor wounded name: my bosom as a bed
Shall lodge thee till thy wound be throughly heal'd;
And thus I search it with a sovereign kiss.
But twice, or thrice, was "Proteus" written down:
Be calm, good wind, blow not a word away
Till I have found each letter in the letter,
Except mine own name; that, some whirlwind bear
Unto a ragged, fearful, hanging rock,
And throw it thence into the raging sea.
Lo, here in one line is his name twice writ,
"Poor forlorn Proteus, passionate Proteus:
To the sweet Julia"—that I'll tear away—
And yet I will not, sith so prettily
He couples it to his complaining names.
Thus will I fold them one upon another;
Now kiss, embrace, contend, do what you will.

[*Enter* LUCETTA.]

Luc. Madam,
Dinner is ready, and your father stays.
Jul. Well, let us go.
Luc. What, shall these papers lie like tell-tales here?
Jul. If you respect them, best to take them up.
Luc. Nay, I was taken up for laying them down;
Yet here they shall not lie, for catching cold.
Jul. I see you have a month's mind to them.
Luc. Ay, madam, you may say what sights you see;
I see things too, although you judge I wink.
Jul. Come, come, will't please you go? *Exeunt.*

SCENE III

Enter ANTONIO *and* PANTHINO.

Ant. Tell me, Panthino, what sad talk was that
Wherewith my brother held you in the cloister?
Pan. 'Twas of his nephew Proteus, your son.
Ant. Why, what of him?
Pan. He wond'red that your lordship
Would suffer him to spend his youth at home,
While other men, of slender reputation,
Put forth their sons to seek preferment out:

68. kill: satisfy. **stomach:** (1) appetite; (2) anger.
68, 69. meat, maid. A quibble, *meat* being pronounced as *mate.*
74. concerns: is of importance.
78. note: (1) musical note; (2) letter. **set:** (1) set to music; (2) write. Julia takes it in the sense of "set store." **79. toys:** trifles.
80. "Light o' Love": a popular tune, mentioned also in *Much Ado,* III.iv.44. **81. heavy:** serious.
82. burden: (1) bass accompaniment; (2) load.
84. reach so high: (1) sing such high notes; (2) aspire to one of such high rank. **85. minion:** hussy. **86. tune:** (1) pitch; (2) temper.
88. sharp. With quibble on the sense "pinching."
90. flat. With quibble on the sense "blunt."
91. descant: improvised harmony added to a melody.
92. mean: (1) tenor (i.e. Proteus); (2) opportunity.
93. unruly bass. With quibble on the sense "base misconduct."
94. bid . . . for: support the cause of (a figure from the game of prisoner's base), with obvious pun.
96. coil with protestation: fuss about protestations of love.
99. makes it strange: pretends to be indifferent.
101. so . . . same: i.e. I wish I still had the first letter to be so angered by. **103. wasps:** i.e. fingers.

105. several paper: separate fragment.
106. Unkind: unnatural, cruel. **107. As:** as if.
112. throughly: thoroughly.
113. search: probe, cleanse. **sovereign:** curative.
123. sith: since. **prettily:** ingeniously.
124. complaining: lamenting.
128. your father. After one other reference to her father (I.iii.4–8), Shakespeare seems to treat Julia as a wealthy orphan (see II.vii.86–87). **stays:** waits. **131. respect:** prize. **132. taken up:** rebuked.
133. for: for fear of. **134. month's mind:** strong desire.
136. wink: close my eyes.

I.iii. Location: Verona. Antonio's house.
1. sad: serious.
6. slender reputation: i.e. lower social station than yourself.
7. Put forth: send away from home. **out:** abroad.

Some to the wars, to try their fortune there;
Some to discover islands far away;
Some to the studious universities.
For any or for all these exercises
He said that Proteus, your son, was meet;
And did request me to importune you
To let him spend his time no more at home,
Which would be great impeachment to his age,
In having known no travel in his youth.
Ant. Nor need'st thou much importune me to that
Whereon this month I have been hammering.
I have consider'd well his loss of time,
And how he cannot be a perfect man,
Not being tried and tutor'd in the world:
Experience is by industry achiev'd,
And perfected by the swift course of time.
Then tell me, whither were I best to send him?
Pan. I think your lordship is not ignorant
How his companion, youthful Valentine,
Attends the Emperor in his royal court.
Ant. I know it well.
Pan. 'Twere good, I think, your lordship sent him thither:
There shall he practice tilts and tournaments,
Hear sweet discourse, converse with noblemen,
And be in eye of every exercise
Worthy his youth and nobleness of birth.
Ant. I like thy counsel; well hast thou advis'd;
And that thou mayst perceive how well I like it,
The execution of it shall make known:
Even with the speediest expedition
I will dispatch him to the Emperor's court.
Pan. To-morrow, may it please you, Don Alphonso
With other gentlemen of good esteem
Are journeying to salute the Emperor,
And to commend their service to his will.
Ant. Good company; with them shall Proteus go—

[*Enter*] PROTEUS.

And in good time! now will we break with him.
Pro. Sweet love, sweet lines, sweet life!
Here is her hand, the agent of her heart;
Here is her oath for love, her honor's pawn:
O that our fathers would applaud our loves,
To seal our happiness with their consents!
O heavenly Julia!
Ant. How now? what letter are you reading there?
Pro. May't please your lordship, 'tis a word or two
Of commendations sent from Valentine,
Deliver'd by a friend that came from him.
Ant. Lend me the letter; let me see what news.
Pro. There is no news, my lord, but that he writes

15. **impeachment:** reproach. **to his age:** when he is old.
18. **hammering:** deliberating. 21. **tried:** tested, proved.
27. **Emperor.** Another inconsistency; Valentine has gone to Milan, and in the next scene appears in the ducal court there. See the note on II.iv.76, 77, 79. 30. **practice:** perform.
31. **discourse:** conversation, talk. **converse:** associate.
32. **be . . . of:** have an opportunity to see. 42. **commend:** commit.
44. **in good time:** at the right moment (often used of people arriving opportunely). **break with:** disclose our purpose to.
47. **pawn:** pledge. 49. **seal:** ratify.
53. **commendations:** greetings.

How happily he lives, how well-belov'd
And daily graced by the Emperor;
Wishing me with him, partner of his fortune.
Ant. And how stand you affected to his wish?
Pro. As one relying on your lordship's will,
And not depending on his friendly wish.
Ant. My will is something sorted with his wish:
Muse not that I thus suddenly proceed;
For what I will, I will, and there an end.
I am resolv'd that thou shalt spend some time
With Valentinus in the Emperor's court;
What maintenance he from his friends receives,
Like exhibition thou shalt have from me.
To-morrow be in readiness to go—
Excuse it not, for I am peremptory.
Pro. My lord I cannot be so soon provided:
Please you deliberate a day or two.
Ant. Look what thou want'st shall be sent after thee.
No more of stay: to-morrow thou must go.
Come on, Panthino; you shall be employ'd
To hasten on his expedition.
[*Exeunt Antonio and Panthino.*]
Pro. Thus have I shunn'd the fire for fear of burning,
And drench'd me in the sea, where I am drown'd.
I fear'd to show my father Julia's letter,
Lest he should take exceptions to my love,
And with the vantage of mine own excuse
Hath he excepted most against my love.
O, how this spring of love resembleth
The uncertain glory of an April day,
Which now shows all the beauty of the sun,
And by and by a cloud takes all away.

[*Enter* PANTHINO.]

Pan. Sir Proteus, your [father] calls for you:
He is in haste; therefore I pray you go.
Pro. Why, this it is: my heart accords thereto,
And yet a thousand times it answers "no." *Exeunt.*

ACT II, SCENE I

Enter VALENTINE, SPEED.

Speed. Sir, your glove.
Val. Not mine: my gloves are on.
Speed. Why then this may be yours—for this is but one.
Val. Ha? let me see; ay, give it me, it's mine:
Sweet ornament that decks a thing divine—
Ah, Silvia, Silvia!
Speed. [*Shouting.*] Madam Silvia! Madam Silvia!

58. **graced:** shown favor. 60. **affected:** disposed.
63. **something sorted:** rather in agreement.
64. **Muse:** wonder, grumble. 68. **friends:** relatives.
69. **exhibition:** allowance of money.
71. **Excuse it not:** offer no excuses. **peremptory:** resolved.
72. **provided:** equipped. 74. **Look what:** whatever.
83. **excepted most against:** set most strong impediments in the way of.

II.i. Location: Milan. The Duke's palace.
1, 2. **on, one.** A common pun, encouraged by the fact that the words were similar in sound and often spelled alike (*on*).

Val. How now, sirrah?

Speed. She is not within hearing, sir.

Val. Why, sir, who bade you call her?

Speed. Your worship, sir, or else I mistook.

Val. Well—you'll still be too forward.

Speed. And yet I was last chidden for being too slow.

Val. Go to, sir; tell me, do you know Madam Silvia?

Speed. She that your worship loves?

Val. Why, how know you that I am in love?

Speed. Marry, by these special marks: first, you have learn'd, like Sir Proteus, to wreathe your arms, like a malecontent; to relish a love-song, like a robin-redbreast; to walk alone, like one that had the pestilence; to sigh, like a schoolboy that had lost his A B C; to weep, like a young wench that had buried her grandam; to fast, like one that takes diet; to watch, like one that fears robbing; to speak puling, like a beggar at Hallowmas. You were wont, when you laugh'd, to crow like a cock; when you walk'd, to walk like one of the lions; when you fasted, it was presently after dinner; when you look'd sadly, it was for want of money: and now you are metamorphis'd with a mistress, that when I look on you, I can hardly think you my master.

Val. Are all these things perceiv'd in me?

Speed. They are all perceiv'd without ye.

Val. Without me? they cannot.

Speed. Without you? nay, that's certain; for without you were so simple, none else would: but you are so without these follies, that these follies are within you, and shine through you like the water in an urinal, that not an eye that sees you but is a physician to comment on your malady.

Val. But tell me: dost thou know my lady Silvia?

Speed. She that you gaze on so as she sits at supper?

Val. Hast thou observ'd that? Even she I mean.

Speed. Why, sir, I know her not.

Val. Dost thou know her by my gazing on her, and yet know'st her not?

Speed. Is she not hard-favor'd, sir?

Val. Not so fair, boy, as well-favor'd.

Speed. Sir, I know that well enough.

Val. What dost thou know?

Speed. That she is not so fair as (of you) well favor'd.

Val. I mean that her beauty is exquisite, but her favor infinite.

Speed. That's because the one is painted, and the other out of all count.

Val. How painted? and how out of count?

Speed. Marry, sir, so painted to make her fair, that no man counts of her beauty.

Val. How esteem'st thou me? I account of her beauty.

Speed. You never saw her since she was deform'd.

Val. How long hath she been deform'd?

Speed. Ever since you lov'd her.

Val. I have lov'd her ever since I saw her, and still I see her beautiful.

Speed. If you love her, you cannot see her.

Val. Why?

Speed. Because Love is blind. O that you had mine eyes, or your own eyes had the lights they were wont to have when you chid at Sir Proteus for going ungarter'd!

Val. What should I see then?

Speed. Your own present folly, and her passing deformity: for he, being in love, could not see to garter his hose; and you, being in love, cannot see to put on your hose.

Val. Belike, boy, then you are in love—for last morning you could not see to wipe my shoes.

Speed. True, sir; I was in love with my bed. I thank you, you swing'd me for my love, which makes me the bolder to chide you for yours.

Val. In conclusion, I stand affected to her.

Speed. I would you were set, so your affection would cease.

Val. Last night she enjoin'd me to write some lines to one she loves.

Speed. And have you?

Val. I have.

Speed. Are they not lamely writ?

Val. No, boy, but as well as I can do them.

[*Enter*] Silvia.

Peace, here she comes.

Speed. [*Aside.*] O excellent motion! O exceeding puppet! Now will he interpret to her.

Val. Madam and mistress, a thousand good morrows.

Speed. [*Aside.*] O, give ye good ev'n! here's a million of manners.

Sil. Sir Valentine and servant, to you two thousand.

Speed. [*Aside.*] He should give her interest, and she gives it him.

Val. As you enjoin'd me, I have writ your letter

7. sirrah: usual form of address to an inferior.
14. Go to: an expression of remonstrance.
19. wreathe: fold. Folded arms conventionally betokened melancholy, particularly love melancholy.
20. malecontent: variant form of *malcontent*. **23. A B C:** primer.
24. watch: lie awake. **25. puling:** whiningly.
26. Hallowmas: All Saints' Day (November 1), when beggars asked for special alms.
28. lions. Possibly those kept in the Tower of London.
29. presently: immediately. **31. with:** by. **that:** so that.
34. without ye: outside you, i.e. by your external appearance.
36–37. without: unless. **37. would:** i.e. would perceive them.
39–40. urinal: glass vessel for examining urine.
48. hard-favor'd: ugly.
49. Not . . . well-favor'd. Valentine explains his meaning in lines 54–55. **52. of:** by. **55. favor:** charm, graciousness of nature.

57. out . . . count: incalculable.
60. counts of: makes account of, esteems.
63. deform'd: i.e. altered by the lover's eye, which does not view the loved one realistically. **71. lights:** sight.
73. going ungarter'd. Carelessness in dress was thought to be a sign of lovesickness. **75. passing:** exceedingly great.
82. swing'd: beat (past of *swinge*). **85. set:** seated.
94. motion: puppet show.
95. interpret: supply explanatory comment on the action (as a puppeteer did). **98. give:** i.e. God give.
100. servant: one devoted to the service of a lady (who was not pledged by accepting it).
102–3. He . . . him: i.e. he ought to outdo her (in compliments), but she outdoes him.

Unto the secret, nameless friend of yours;
Which I was much unwilling to proceed in,
But for my duty to your ladyship.

Sil. I thank you, gentle servant—'tis very clerkly done.

Val. Now trust me, madam, it came hardly off;
For being ignorant to whom it goes,
I writ at random, very doubtfully.

Sil. Perchance you think too much of so much pains?

Val. No, madam; so it stead you, I will write
(Please you command) a thousand times as much;
And yet—

Sil. A pretty period! Well—I guess the sequel;
And yet I will not name it—and yet I care not—
And yet take this again—and yet I thank you—
Meaning henceforth to trouble you no more.

Speed. [*Aside.*] And yet you will; and yet another "yet."

Val. What means your ladyship? Do you not like it?

Sil. Yes, yes; the lines are very quaintly writ,
But (since unwillingly) take them again.
Nay, take them.

Val. Madam, they are for you.

Sil. Ay, ay; you writ them, sir, at my request,
But I will none of them; they are for you.
I would have had them writ more movingly.

Val. Please you, I'll write your ladyship another.

Sil. And when it's writ, for my sake read it over,
And if it please you, so; if not, why, so.

Val. If it please me, madam, what then?

Sil. Why, if it please you, take it for your labor;
And so good morrow, servant. *Exit Silvia.*

Speed. O jest unseen, inscrutable; invisible,
As a nose on a man's face, or a weathercock on a steeple!
My master sues to her; and she hath taught her suitor,
He being her pupil, to become her tutor.
O excellent device, was there ever heard a better,
That my master being scribe, to himself should write the letter?

Val. How now, sir? What are you reasoning with yourself?

Speed. Nay, I was rhyming; 'tis you that have the reason.

Val. To do what?

Speed. To be a spokesman from Madam Silvia.

Val. To whom?

Speed. To yourself; why, she woos you by a figure.

Val. What figure?

Speed. By a letter, I should say.

Val. Why, she hath not writ to me?

Speed. What need she, when she hath made you write to yourself? Why, do you not perceive the jest?

Val. No, believe me.

Speed. No believing you indeed, sir: but did you perceive her earnest?

Val. She gave me none, except an angry word.

Speed. Why, she hath given you a letter.

Val. That's the letter I writ to her friend.

Speed. And that letter hath she deliver'd, and there an end.

Val. I would it were no worse.

Speed. I'll warrant you, 'tis as well:
"For often have you writ to her; and she in modesty,
Or else for want of idle time, could not again reply;
Or fearing else some messenger, that might her mind discover,
Herself hath taught her love himself to write unto her lover."
All this I speak in print, for in print I found it. Why muse you, sir? 'tis dinner-time.

Val. I have din'd.

Speed. Ay, but hearken, sir; though the chameleon Love can feed on the air, I am one that am nourish'd by my victuals, and would fain have meat. O, be not like your mistress—be mov'd, be mov'd. *Exeunt.*

107. **duty**: respect, submission.
108. **clerkly**: in a scholarly manner. 109. **hardly**: with difficulty.
111. **doubtfully**: uncertainly. 113. **stead**: benefit.
116. **A pretty period**: i.e. a fine point to stop your sentence, since "And yet" implies that you regret your labor for me. **Well**: very well. 118. **again**: back. 122. **quaintly**: skillfully.
141. **reasoning**: discussing. 148. **figure**: device.

Scene II

Enter Proteus, Julia.

Pro. Have patience, gentle Julia.

Jul. I must, where is no remedy.

Pro. When possibly I can, I will return.

Jul. If you turn not, you will return the sooner.
Keep this remembrance for thy Julia's sake.
[*Giving a ring.*]

Pro. Why then we'll make exchange: here, take you this.

Jul. And seal the bargain with a holy kiss.

Pro. Here is my hand for my true constancy;
And when that hour o'erslips me in the day
Wherein I sigh not, Julia, for thy sake,
The next ensuing hour some foul mischance
Torment me for my love's forgetfulness!
My father stays my coming; answer not;
The tide is now—nay, not thy tide of tears,
That tide will stay me longer than I should.
Julia, farewell! [*Exit Julia.*]
What, gone without a word?
Ay, so true love should do: it cannot speak,
For truth hath better deeds than words to grace it.

[*Enter*] Panthino.

Pan. Sir Proteus, you are stay'd for.

157. **earnest**: serious (but Valentine picks it up in the sense of "pledge"). 167. **her mind discover**: reveal her private intent.
169. **speak in print**: speak precisely.
171. **din'd**: i.e. feasted on Silvia's beauty.
172. **chameleon**. Popularly supposed to subsist on air.
174. **fain**: gladly.

II.ii. Location: Verona. Julia's house.
2. **is**: there is. 4. **turn**: prove unfaithful. 13. **stays**: waits for.
18. **hath . . . it**: is adorned better by actions than by words.

Pro. Go; I come, I come.
Alas, this parting strikes poor lovers dumb. *Exeunt.*

Scene III

Enter Launce [*leading a dog*].

Launce. Nay, 'twill be this hour ere I have done weeping; all the kind of the Launces have this very fault. I have receiv'd my proportion, like the prodigious son, and am going with Sir Proteus to the Imperial's court. I think Crab my dog be the sourest-natur'd dog that lives: my mother weeping, my father wailing, my sister crying, our maid howling, our cat wringing her hands, and all our house in a great perplexity, yet did not this cruel-hearted cur shed one tear. He is a stone, a very pibble stone, and has no more pity in him than a dog. A Jew would have wept to have seen our parting; why, my grandam, having no eyes, look you, wept herself blind at my parting. Nay, I'll show you the manner of it. This shoe is my father; no, this left shoe is my father; no, no, this left shoe is my mother; nay, that cannot be so neither; yes, it is so, it is so—it hath the worser sole. This shoe, with the hole in it, is my mother, and this my father—a vengeance on't! there 'tis. Now, sir, this staff is my sister, for, look you, she is as white as a lily and as small as a wand. This hat is Nan, our maid. I am the dog—no, the dog is himself, and I am the dog—O! the dog is me, and I am myself; ay, so, so. Now come I to my father: "Father, your blessing." Now should not the shoe speak a word for weeping; now should I kiss my father; well, he weeps on. Now come I to my mother. O that she could speak now like a [wood] woman! Well, I kiss her; why, there 'tis; here's my mother's breath up and down. Now come I to my sister; mark the moan she makes. Now the dog all this while sheds not a tear, nor speaks a word; but see how I lay the dust with my tears.

[*Enter*] Panthino.

Pan. Launce, away, away! aboard! Thy master is shipp'd, and thou art to post after with oars. What's the matter? why weep'st thou, man? Away, ass, you'll lose the tide, if you tarry any longer.

Launce. It is no matter if the tied were lost; for it is the unkindest tied that ever any man tied.

Pan. What's the unkindest tide?

Launce. Why, he that's tied here, Crab, my dog.

Pan. Tut, man, I mean thou'lt lose the flood, and in losing the flood, lose thy voyage, and in losing thy voyage, lose thy master, and in losing thy master, lose thy service, and in losing thy service—Why dost thou stop my mouth?

Launce. For fear thou shouldst lose thy tongue.

Pan. Where should I lose my tongue?

Launce. In thy tale.

Pan. In thy tail!

Launce. Lose the tide, and the voyage, and the master, and the service, and the tied! Why, man, if the river were dry, I am able to fill it with my tears; if the wind were down, I could drive the boat with my sighs.

Pan. Come; come away, man—I was sent to call thee.

Launce. Sir—call me what thou dar'st.

Pan. Wilt thou go?

Launce. Well, I will go. *Exeunt.*

II.iii. Location: Verona. A street.
2. **kind:** kindred, family.
3–4. **proportion, prodigious:** blunders for *portion* and *prodigal*.
5. **Imperial's:** blunder for *Emperor's*. (See note on I.iii.27.)
10. **pibble:** pebble.
27. **wood:** distraught (with punning reference to a wooden shoe?).
29. **up and down:** exactly. 34. **post:** hasten.

Scene IV

Enter Valentine, Silvia, Thurio, Speed.

Sil. Servant!
Val. Mistress?
Speed. Master, Sir Thurio frowns on you.
Val. Ay, boy, it's for love.
Speed. Not of you.
Val. Of my mistress then.
Speed. 'Twere good you knock'd him. [*Exit.*]
Sil. Servant, you are sad.
Val. Indeed, madam, I seem so.
Thu. Seem you that you are not?
Val. Happ'ly I do.
Thu. So do counterfeits.
Val. So do you.
Thu. What seem I that I am not?
Val. Wise.
Thu. What instance of the contrary?
Val. Your folly.
Thu. And how quote you my folly?
Val. I quote it in your jerkin.
Thu. My jerkin is a doublet.
Val. Well then I'll double your folly.
Thu. How?

Sil. What, angry, Sir Thurio? do you change color?

Val. Give him leave, madam, he is a kind of chameleon.

Thu. That hath more mind to feed on your blood than live in your air.

Val. You have said, sir.

Thu. Ay, sir, and done too—for this time.

Val. I know it well, sir; you always end ere you begin.

Sil. A fine volley of words, gentlemen, and quickly shot off.

Val. 'Tis indeed, madam, we thank the giver.

II.iv. Location: Milan. The Duke's palace.
16. **instance:** proof. 18. **quote:** observe, "read" (Schmidt).
19. **jerkin:** short coat worn over, or instead of, the doublet. Valentine takes advantage of the fact that *quote* (often spelled *cote*) and *coat* were homophones.
28. **in your air:** i.e. on the air you breathe. Thurio alludes to the belief that the chameleon lives on air (see note on II.i.172), but he also draws on the commonplace that words are air to imply that he will challenge Valentine to a duel rather than swallow more of his insults.
30. **done.** The expected contrast with Valentine's sarcastic "said," but Thurio uses it in the sense "finished," though his "for this time" implies that next time he will act.
32. **begin:** i.e. get to the point of acting.

Sil. Who is that, servant?
Val. Yourself, sweet lady, for you gave the fire. Sir Thurio borrows his wit from your ladyship's looks, and spends what he borrows kindly in your company.
Thu. Sir, if you spend word for word with me, I shall make your wit bankrupt.
Val. I know it well, sir; you have an exchequer of words and, I think, no other treasure to give your followers; for it appears by their bare liveries that they live by your bare words.
Sil. No more, gentlemen, no more; here comes my father.

[*Enter*] DUKE.

Duke. Now, daughter Silvia, you are hard beset.
Sir Valentine, your father is in good health:
What say you to a letter from your friends
Of much good news?
Val. My lord, I will be thankful
To any happy messenger from thence.
Duke. Know ye Don Antonio, your countryman?
Val. Ay, my good lord, I know the gentleman
To be of worth and worthy estimation,
And not without desert so well reputed.
Duke. Hath he not a son?
Val. Ay, my good lord, a son that well deserves
The honor and regard of such a father.
Duke. You know him well?
Val. I knew him as myself: for from our infancy
We have convers'd and spent our hours together,
And though myself have been an idle truant,
Omitting the sweet benefit of time
To clothe mine age with angel-like perfection,
Yet hath Sir Proteus (for that's his name)
Made use and fair advantage of his days;
His years but young, but his experience old;
His head unmellowed, but his judgment ripe;
And in a word (for far behind his worth
Comes all the praises that I now bestow),
He is complete in feature and in mind
With all good grace to grace a gentleman.
Duke. Beshrew me, sir, but if he make this good,
He is as worthy for an empress' love
As meet to be an emperor's counsellor.
Well, sir—this gentleman is come to me
With commendation from great potentates,
And here he means to spend his time a while.
I think 'tis no unwelcome news to you.
Val. Should I have wish'd a thing, it had been he.
Duke. Welcome him then according to his worth—
Silvia, I speak to you, and you, Sir Thurio;

37. fire: spark (which set off the "volley").
39. kindly: naturally, properly.
45. bare: threadbare. **liveries:** distinctive garments worn by a gentleman's retainers.
49. hard beset: strongly besieged (by young men).
53. happy messenger: bearer of good news.
63. convers'd: been companions. **65. Omitting:** neglecting.
70. unmellowed: i.e. without grey hairs.
73. complete: perfect. **feature:** general personal appearance.
76, 77, 79. empress' love, emperor's counsellor, great potentates. The language of these lines seems more suited to the Emperor of I.iii.27 ff. than to a Duke of Milan. With line 76 cf. V.iv.141.

For Valentine, I need not cite him to it.
I will send him hither to you presently. [*Exit.*]
Val. This is the gentleman I told your ladyship
Had come along with me, but that his mistress
Did hold his eyes lock'd in her crystal looks.
Sil. Belike that now she hath enfranchis'd them
Upon some other pawn for fealty.
Val. Nay sure, I think she holds them prisoners still.
Sil. Nay then he should be blind, and being blind,
How could he see his way to seek out you?
Val. Why, lady, Love hath twenty pair of eyes.
Thu. They say that Love hath not an eye at all.
Val. To see such lovers, Thurio, as yourself:
Upon a homely object Love can wink.
Sil. Have done, have done; here comes the gentleman. [*Exit Thurio.*]

[*Enter*] PROTEUS.

Val. Welcome, dear Proteus! Mistress, I beseech you
Confirm his welcome with some special favor.
Sil. His worth is warrant for his welcome hither,
If this be he you oft have wish'd to hear from.
Val. Mistress, it is: sweet lady, entertain him
To be my fellow-servant to your ladyship.
Sil. Too low a mistress for so high a servant.
Pro. Not so, sweet lady, but too mean a servant
To have a look of such a worthy mistress.
Val. Leave off discourse of disability.
Sweet lady, entertain him for your servant.
Pro. My duty will I boast of, nothing else.
Sil. And duty never yet did want his meed.
Servant, you are welcome to a worthless mistress.
Pro. I'll die on him that says so but yourself.
Sil. That you are welcome?
Pro. That you are worthless.

[*Enter* THURIO.]

Thu. Madam, my lord your father would speak with you.
Sil. I wait upon his pleasure. Come, Sir Thurio,
Go with me. Once more, new servant, welcome;
I'll leave you to confer of home affairs;
When you have done, we look to hear from you.
Pro. We'll both attend upon your ladyship.
[*Exeunt Silvia and Thurio.*]
Val. Now tell me: how do all from whence you came?
Pro. Your friends are well and have them much commended.
Val. And how do yours?
Pro. I left them all in health.
Val. How does your lady, and how thrives your love?

85. cite: urge. **86. presently:** at once. **88. Had:** would have.
90. Belike that: perhaps. **enfranchis'd:** released from confinement.
91. Upon . . . fealty: i.e. for some other lover's vow of faithful service. **104. entertain:** engage.
109. disability: unworthiness.
112. want his meed: lack his reward.
114. die on: die fighting against.
123. them much commended: sent their kind regards.

Pro. My tales of love were wont to weary you;
I know you joy not in a love-discourse.
Val. Ay, Proteus, but that life is alter'd now:
I have done penance for contemning Love,
Whose high imperious thoughts have punish'd me
With bitter fasts, with penitential groans,
With nightly tears, and daily heart-sore sighs,
For in revenge of my contempt of love,
Love hath chas'd sleep from my enthralled eyes,
And made them watchers of mine own heart's sorrow.
O gentle Proteus, Love's a mighty lord,
And hath so humbled me as I confess
There is no woe to his correction,
Nor to his service no such joy on earth:
Now no discourse, except it be of love;
Now can I break my fast, dine, sup, and sleep,
Upon the very naked name of love.
Pro. Enough; I read your fortune in your eye.
Was this the idol that you worship so?
Val. Even she; and is she not a heavenly saint?
Pro. No; but she is an earthly paragon.
Val. Call her divine.
Pro. I will not flatter her.
Val. O, flatter me; for love delights in praises.
Pro. When I was sick, you gave me bitter pills,
And I must minister the like to you.
Val. Then speak the truth by her; if not divine,
Yet let her be a principality,
Sovereign to all the creatures on the earth.
Pro. Except my mistress.
Val. Sweet, except not any,
Except thou wilt except against my love.
Pro. Have I not reason to prefer mine own?
Val. And I will help thee to prefer her too:
She shall be dignified with this high honor—
To bear my lady's train, lest the base earth
Should from her vesture chance to steal a kiss,
And of so great a favor growing proud,
Disdain to root the summer-swelling flow'r,
And make rough winter everlastingly.
Pro. Why, Valentine, what braggadism is this?
Val. Pardon me, Proteus, all I can is nothing
To her, whose worth [makes] other worthies nothing:
She is alone.
Pro. Then let her alone.
Val. Not for the world. Why, man, she is mine own,
And I as rich in having such a jewel
As twenty seas, if all their sand were pearl,
The water nectar, and the rocks pure gold.
Forgive me, that I do not dream on thee,
Because thou seest me dote upon my love.
My foolish rival, that her father likes
(Only for his possessions are so huge),
Is gone with her along, and I must after,
For love, thou know'st, is full of jealousy.
Pro. But she loves you?
Val. Ay, and we are betroth'd: nay more, our marriage hour,
With all the cunning manner of our flight,
Determin'd of—how I must climb her window,
The ladder made of cords, and all the means
Plotted and 'greed on for my happiness.
Good Proteus, go with me to my chamber,
In these affairs to aid me with thy counsel.
Pro. Go on before; I shall inquire you forth.
I must unto the road, to disembark
Some necessaries that I needs must use,
And then I'll presently attend you.
Val. Will you make haste?
Pro. I will. *Exit* [*Valentine*].
Even as one heat another heat expels,
Or as one nail by strength drives out another,
So the remembrance of my former love
Is by a newer object quite forgotten.
[Is it] mine [eye], or Valentinus' praise,
Her true perfection, or my false transgression,
That makes me reasonless, to reason thus?
She is fair; and so is Julia that I love
(That I did love, for now my love is thaw'd,
Which like a waxen image 'gainst a fire
Bears no impression of the thing it was).
Methinks my zeal to Valentine is cold,
And that I love him not as I was wont:
O, but I love his lady too too much,
And that's the reason I love him so little.
How shall I dote on her with more advice,
That thus without advice begin to love her?
'Tis but her picture I have yet beheld,
And that hath dazzled my reason's light;
But when I look on her perfections,
There is no reason but I shall be blind.
If I can check my erring love, I will;
If not, to compass her I'll use my skill. *Exit.*

Scene V

Enter Speed *and* Launce, [*meeting*].

Speed. Launce, by mine honesty, welcome to [Milan].

Launce. Forswear not thyself, sweet youth, for I am not welcome. I reckon this always, that a man is never undone till he be hang'd, nor never welcome to a place till some certain shot be paid and the hostess say "Welcome."

Speed. Come on, you madcap, I'll to the alehouse

137. as: that.
138. to his correction: comparable to (the woe of) his punishment.
152. principality: a celestial being, belonging to one of the nine orders of angels.
155. Except . . . love: i.e. to place any as her equal is a detraction to her. **157. prefer:** advance.
164. braggadism: braggartism, excessive praise.
165. can: i.e. can say of her.
166. To her: i.e. in comparison with her real worth.
167. alone: unique.
172. do . . . thee: seem careless of your welcome or your feelings.

175. for: because. **186. forth:** out. **187. road:** harbor.
189. presently: immediately.
192. Even . . . expels. It was thought that the application of external heat would ease the pain of a burn. **207. advice:** deliberation.
209. picture: outer show. **212. no reason but:** no doubt that.
214. compass: obtain.

II.v. Location. Milan. A street.
5. undone: ruined. **6. shot:** fee, tavern reckoning.

with you presently; where, for one shot of five pence, thou shalt have five thousand welcomes. But, sirrah, how did thy master part with Madam Julia?

Launce. Marry, after they clos'd in earnest, they parted very fairly in jest.

Speed. But shall she marry him?

Launce. No.

Speed. How then? shall he marry her?

Launce. No, neither.

Speed. What, are they broken?

Launce. No, they are both as whole as a fish.

Speed. Why then, how stands the matter with them?

Launce. Marry, thus: when it stands well with him, it stands well with her.

Speed. What an ass art thou! I understand thee not.

Launce. What a block art thou, that thou canst not! My staff understands me.

Speed. What thou say'st?

Launce. Ay, and what I do too. Look thee, I'll but lean, and my staff understands me.

Speed. It stands under thee indeed.

Launce. Why, stand-under and under-stand is all one.

Speed. But tell me true, will't be a match?

Launce. Ask my dog. If he say ay, it will; if he say no, it will; if he shake his tail and say nothing, it will.

Speed. The conclusion is then, that it will.

Launce. Thou shalt never get such a secret from me but by a parable.

Speed. 'Tis well that I get it so. But, Launce, how say'st thou that my master is become a notable lover?

Launce. I never knew him otherwise.

Speed. Than how?

Launce. A notable lubber—as thou reportest him to be.

Speed. Why, thou whoreson ass, thou mistak'st me.

Launce. Why, fool, I meant not thee, I meant thy master.

Speed. I tell thee, my master is become a hot lover.

Launce. Why, I tell thee, I care not, though he burn himself in love. If thou wilt, go with me to the alehouse; if not, thou art an Hebrew, a Jew, and not worth the name of a Christian.

Speed. Why?

Launce. Because thou hast not so much charity in thee as to go to the ale with a Christian. Wilt thou go?

Speed. At thy service. *Exeunt.*

SCENE VI

Enter PROTEUS *solus*.

Pro. To leave my Julia—shall I be forsworn?
To love fair Silvia—shall I be forsworn?
To wrong my friend, I shall be much forsworn.
And ev'n that pow'r which gave me first my oath
Provokes me to this threefold perjury.
Love bade me swear, and Love bids me forswear.
O sweet-suggesting Love, if thou hast sinn'd,
Teach me, thy tempted subject, to excuse it!
At first I did adore a twinkling star,
But now I worship a celestial sun.
Unheedful vows may heedfully be broken,
And he wants wit that wants resolved will
To learn his wit t' exchange the bad for better.
Fie, fie, unreverend tongue, to call her bad,
Whose sovereignty so oft thou hast preferr'd
With twenty thousand soul-confirming oaths.
I cannot leave to love, and yet I do;
But there I leave to love where I should love.
Julia I lose, and Valentine I lose:
If I keep them, I needs must lose myself;
If I lose them, thus find I by their loss—
For Valentine, myself; for Julia, Silvia.
I to myself am dearer than a friend,
For love is still most precious in itself,
And Silvia (witness heaven, that made her fair)
Shows Julia but a swarthy Ethiope.
I will forget that Julia is alive,
Rememb'ring that my love to her is dead;
And Valentine I'll hold an enemy,
Aiming at Silvia as a sweeter friend.
I cannot now prove constant to myself,
Without some treachery us'd to Valentine.
This night he meaneth with a corded ladder
To climb celestial Silvia's chamber-window,
Myself in counsel his competitor.
Now presently I'll give her father notice
Of their disguising and pretended flight,
Who, all enrag'd, will banish Valentine;
For Thurio, he intends, shall wed his daughter;
But, Valentine being gone, I'll quickly cross
By some sly trick blunt Thurio's dull proceeding.
Love, lend me wings to make my purpose swift,
As thou hast lent me wit to plot this drift. *Exit.*

SCENE VII

Enter JULIA *and* LUCETTA.

Jul. Counsel, Lucetta; gentle girl, assist me;

12. clos'd: (1) came to terms; (2) embraced.
18. are they broken: have they fallen out (but Launce in his reply quibbles on *broken* in the sense "in pieces").
19. whole . . . fish. A proverbial comparison.
22. stands well. One of Launce's numerous bawdy equivoques.
40. by a parable: i.e. indirectly, obscurely.
41–42. how say'st thou: what have you to say to this.
45. lubber: clumsy, stupid fellow.
47. whoreson: a term of abuse (literally, bastard).
47–48. thou mistak'st me: you mistake my meaning (but Launce replies to the sense "you misjudge me"). **55. worth:** worthy of.
58. go . . . Christian. Alluding to a "church-ale," a festival at which ale was sold to raise funds for the church.

II.vi. Location: Milan. The Duke's palace.
5. Provokes: urges, incites. **7. sweet-suggesting:** sweetly seductive.
11. Unheedful . . . heedfully: ill-considered . . . upon consideration.
12. wants: lacks. **13. learn:** teach. **14. unreverend:** irreverent.
15. preferr'd: recommend, urged.
16. soul-confirming: sworn on my soul. **17. leave:** cease.
23–24. I . . . itself. Proteus, in saying that self-love is superior to love for his friend, speaks like a villain and against the orthodox code of friendship, just as lines 25–26 show him a traitor to the code of love.
24. still: always. **35. counsel:** consultation. **competitor:** ally.
37. pretended: intended. **40. cross:** thwart. **41. blunt:** stupid.

II.vii. Location: Verona. Julia's house.

And ev'n in kind love I do conjure thee,
Who art the table wherein all my thoughts
Are visibly character'd and engrav'd,
To lesson me and tell me some good mean
How with my honor I may undertake
A journey to my loving Proteus.

Luc. Alas, the way is wearisome and long.

Jul. A true-devoted pilgrim is not weary
To measure kingdoms with his feeble steps;
Much less shall she that hath Love's wings to fly,
And when the flight is made to one so dear,
Of such divine perfection, as Sir Proteus.

Luc. Better forbear till Proteus make return.

Jul. O, know'st thou not his looks are my soul's food?
Pity the dearth that I have pined in,
By longing for that food so long a time.
Didst thou but know the inly touch of love,
Thou wouldst as soon go kindle fire with snow
As seek to quench the fire of love with words.

Luc. I do not seek to quench your love's hot fire,
But qualify the fire's extreme rage,
Lest it should burn above the bounds of reason.

Jul. The more thou dam'st it up, the more it burns:
The current that with gentle murmur glides,
Thou know'st, being stopp'd, impatiently doth rage;
But when his fair course is not hindered,
He makes sweet music with th' enamell'd stones,
Giving a gentle kiss to every sedge
He overtaketh in his pilgrimage;
And so by many winding nooks he strays
With willing sport to the wild ocean.
Then let me go, and hinder not my course:
I'll be as patient as a gentle stream,
And make a pastime of each weary step,
Till the last step have brought me to my love,
And there I'll rest, as after much turmoil
A blessed soul doth in Elysium.

Luc. But in what habit will you go along?

Jul. Not like a woman, for I would prevent
The loose encounters of lascivious men:
Gentle Lucetta, fit me with such weeds
As may beseem some well-reputed page.

Luc. Why then your ladyship must cut your hair.

Jul. No, girl, I'll knit it up in silken strings,
With twenty odd-conceited true-love knots:
To be fantastic may become a youth
Of greater time than I shall show to be.

Luc. What fashion, madam, shall I make your breeches?

Jul. That fits as well as "Tell me, good my lord,
What compass will you wear your farthingale?" 51
Why, ev'n what fashion thou best likes, Lucetta.

Luc. You must needs have them with a codpiece, madam.

Jul. Out, out, Lucetta, that will be ill-favor'd.

Luc. A round hose, madam, now's not worth a pin,
Unless you have a codpiece to stick pins on.

Jul. Lucetta, as thou lov'st me, let me have
What thou think'st meet, and is most mannerly.
But tell me, wench, how will the world repute me
For undertaking so unstaid a journey?
I fear me it will make me scandaliz'd.

Luc. If you think so, then stay at home and go not.

Jul. Nay, that I will not.

Luc. Then never dream on infamy, but go.
If Proteus like your journey when you come,
No matter who's displeas'd when you are gone:
I fear me he will scarce be pleas'd withal.

Jul. That is the least, Lucetta, of my fear:
A thousand oaths, an ocean of his tears,
And instances of infinite of love,
Warrant me welcome to my Proteus.

Luc. All these are servants to deceitful men.

Jul. Base men, that use them to so base effect!
But truer stars did govern Proteus' birth:
His words are bonds, his oaths are oracles,
His love sincere, his thoughts immaculate,
His tears pure messengers sent from his heart,
His heart as far from fraud as heaven from earth.

Luc. Pray heav'n he prove so when you come to him!

Jul. Now, as thou lov'st me, do him not that wrong,
To bear a hard opinion of his truth:
Only deserve my love by loving him,
And presently go with me to my chamber,
To take a note of what I stand in need of,
To furnish me upon my longing journey.
All that is mine I leave at thy dispose,
My goods, my lands, my reputation;
Only, in lieu thereof, dispatch me hence.
Come; answer not; but to it presently,
I am impatient of my tarriance. *Exeunt.*

ACT III, Scene I

Enter Duke, Thurio, Proteus.

Duke. Sir Thurio, give us leave, I pray, a while,
We have some secrets to confer about. [*Exit Thurio.*]
Now tell me, Proteus, what's your will with me?

Pro. My gracious lord, that which I would discover
The law of friendship bids me to conceal,
But when I call to mind your gracious favors

3. table: tablet, notebook. **4. character'd**: written.
10. measure: traverse. **18. inly**: inward. **22. qualify**: moderate..
28. enamell'd: having naturally a hard shiny surface.
32. wild ocean: open sea. **40. prevent**: forestall.
41. encounters: accostings. **42. weeds**: clothes.
46. odd-conceited: strangely devised.
47. fantastic: capricious. **become**: befit.
48. greater time: more years.
51. compass: circumference. **farthingale**: hooped petticoat.

53. codpiece: a bag-like appendage at the front of breeches.
54. ill-favor'd: uncomely. **55. round hose**: short padded breeches.
56. stick pins on. A common method of ornamenting the codpiece.
60. unstaid: unconventional.
61. scandaliz'd: disgraced (by becoming a source of scandal).
67. withal: with it. **70. infinite**: an infinity.
85. longing: prompted by longing.
86. at thy dispose: in your charge. **90. tarriance**: delay.

III.i. Location: Milan. The Duke's palace.
1. give us leave: polite form of dismissal. **4. discover**: reveal.

Done to me (undeserving as I am),
My duty pricks me on to utter that
Which else no worldly good should draw from me.
Know, worthy prince, Sir Valentine, my friend,
This night intends to steal away your daughter;
Myself am one made privy to the plot.
I know you have determin'd to bestow her
On Thurio, whom your gentle daughter hates,
And should she thus be stol'n away from you,
It would be much vexation to your age.
Thus, for my duty's sake, I rather chose
To cross my friend in his intended drift,
Than, by concealing it, heap on your head
A pack of sorrows which would press you down,
Being unprevented, to your timeless grave.

Duke. Proteus, I thank thee for thine honest care,
Which to requite, command me while I live.
This love of theirs myself have often seen,
Haply when they have judg'd me fast asleep,
And oftentimes have purpos'd to forbid
Sir Valentine her company and my court;
But fearing lest my jealous aim might err,
And so, unworthily, disgrace the man
(A rashness that I ever yet have shunn'd),
I gave him gentle looks, thereby to find
That which thyself hast now disclos'd to me.
And that thou mayst perceive my fear of this,
Knowing that tender youth is soon suggested,
I nightly lodge her in an upper tow'r,
The key whereof myself have ever kept;
And thence she cannot be convey'd away.

Pro. Know, noble lord, they have devis'd a mean
How he her chamber-window will ascend,
And with a corded ladder fetch her down;
For which the youthful lover now is gone,
And this way comes he with it presently,
Where (if it please you) you may intercept him.
But, good my lord, do it so cunningly
That my discovery be not aimed at:
For love of you, not hate unto my friend,
Hath made me publisher of this pretense.

Duke. Upon mine honor, he shall never know
That I had any light from thee of this.

Pro. Adieu, my lord, Sir Valentine is coming.
[*Exit.*]

[*Enter*] VALENTINE.

Duke. Sir Valentine, whither away so fast?

Val. Please it your Grace, there is a messenger
That stays to bear my letters to my friends,
And I am going to deliver them.

Duke. Be they of much import?

Val. The tenure of them doth but signify
My health and happy being at your court.

Duke. Nay then no matter; stay with me a while;
I am to break with thee of some affairs

18. drift: scheme.
21. Being unprevented: if they are not forestalled. **timeless:** untimely, premature. **28. jealous aim:** suspicious conjecture.
34. suggested: tempted. **42. presently:** even now.
45. discovery: disclosure. **aimed at:** guessed.
47. pretense: intention. **56. tenure:** tenor.
59. break . . . of: disclose to you.

That touch me near, wherein thou must be secret.
'Tis not unknown to thee that I have sought
To match my friend Sir Thurio to my daughter.

Val. I know it well, my lord, and sure the match
Were rich and honorable; besides, the gentleman
Is full of virtue, bounty, worth, and qualities
Beseeming such a wife as your fair daughter.
Cannot your Grace win her to fancy him?

Duke. No, trust me, she is peevish, sullen, froward,
Proud, disobedient, stubborn, lacking duty,
Neither regarding that she is my child,
Nor fearing me as if I were her father;
And may I say to thee, this pride of hers
(Upon advice) hath drawn my love from her,
And where I thought the remnant of mine age
Should have been cherish'd by her child-like duty,
I now am full resolv'd to take a wife,
And turn her out to who will take her in:
Then let her beauty be her wedding-dow'r,
For me and my possessions she esteems not.

Val. What would your Grace have me to do in
this?

Duke. There is a lady in [Milano] here
Whom I affect; but she is nice and coy,
And nought esteems my aged eloquence.
Now therefore would I have thee to my tutor
(For long agone I have forgot to court;
Besides, the fashion of the time is chang'd)
How and which way I may bestow myself
To be regarded in her sun-bright eye.

Val. Win her with gifts, if she respect not words:
Dumb jewels often in their silent kind
More than quick words do move a woman's mind.

Duke. But she did scorn a present that I sent her.

Val. A woman sometime scorns what best contents her.
Send her another; never give her o'er,
For scorn at first makes after-love the more.
If she do frown, 'tis not in hate of you,
But rather to beget more love in you.
If she do chide, 'tis not to have you gone,
For why, the fools are mad, if left alone.
Take no repulse, what ever she doth say;
For "get you gone," she doth not mean "away!"
Flatter and praise, commend, extol their graces;
Though ne'er so black, say they have angels' faces.
That man that hath a tongue, I say is no man,
If with his tongue he cannot win a woman.

Duke. But she I mean is promis'd by her friends
Unto a youthful gentleman of worth,
And kept severely from resort of men,
That no man hath access by day to her.

Val. Why then I would resort to her by night.

Duke. Ay, but the doors be lock'd, and keys kept
safe,

65. virtue: good accomplishments. **qualities:** attainments.
67. fancy: love. **68. peevish:** willful. **froward:** perverse.
73. advice: deliberation. **74. where:** whereas.
82. affect: am fond of. **nice:** difficult to please. **coy:** offish, shy.
85. agone: ago (already rare in Shakespeare's day). **forgot:** forgotten how. **87. bestow:** conduct. **89. respect:** heed.
90. kind: nature. **91. quick:** lively. **99. For why:** because.
101. For: i.e. for when she says. **103. black:** dark-complexioned.
109, 112. That: so that.

That no man hath recourse to her by night.
Val. What lets but one may enter at her window?
Duke. Her chamber is aloft, far from the ground,
And built so shelving that one cannot climb it
Without apparent hazard of his life.
Val. Why then a ladder, quaintly made of cords,
To cast up, with a pair of anchoring hooks,
Would serve to scale another Hero's tow'r,
So bold Leander would adventure it.
Duke. Now as thou art a gentleman of blood,
Advise me where I may have such a ladder.
Val. When would you use it? pray, sir, tell me that.
Duke. This very night; for Love is like a child,
That longs for every thing that he can come by.
Val. By seven a' clock I'll get you such a ladder.
Duke. But hark thee: I will go to her alone.
How shall I best convey the ladder thither?
Val. It will be light, my lord, that you may bear it
Under a cloak that is of any length.
Duke. A cloak as long as thine will serve the turn?
Val. Ay, my good lord.
Duke. Then let me see thy cloak—
I'll get me one of such another length.
Val. Why, any cloak will serve the turn, my lord.
Duke. How shall I fashion me to wear a cloak?
I pray thee let me feel thy cloak upon me.
What letter is this same? What's here? "To Silvia"?
And here an engine fit for my proceeding!
I'll be so bold to break the seal for once. [*Reads.*]
"My thoughts do harbor with my Silvia nightly,
And slaves they are to me that send them flying:
O, could their master come and go as lightly,
Himself would lodge where, senseless, they are lying!
My herald thoughts in thy pure bosom rest them,
While I, their king, that thither them importune,
Do curse the grace that with such grace hath blest them,
Because myself do want my servants' fortune.
I curse myself, for they are sent by me,
That they should harbor where their lord should be."
What's here?
"Silvia, this night I will enfranchise thee."
'Tis so; and here's the ladder for the purpose.
Why, Phaëton (for thou art Merops' son),
Wilt thou aspire to guide the heavenly car,
And with thy daring folly burn the world?
Wilt thou reach stars, because they shine on thee?
Go, base intruder, overweening slave,
Bestow thy fawning smiles on equal mates,

113. lets: hinders. **115. shelving:** projecting.
116. apparent: obvious. **117. quaintly:** skillfully.
119–20. Hero's . . . Leander. See note to I.i.22.
121. blood: good parentage. **131. turn:** purpose.
133. such another: i.e. the same.
138. engine: contrivance (i.e. the rope ladder).
140. harbor: lodge. **142. lightly:** quickly.
143. senseless: insensible. **lying:** dwelling.
145. importune: urge, order.
146. grace . . . grace: good fortune . . . favor. **147. want:** lack.
148. for: since. **151. enfranchise thee:** set you free.
153. Phaëton: Phaëthon, the son of Helios, the sun-god, who made a disastrous attempt to drive his father's chariot. A large portion of the earth was scorched before Zeus intervened and slew Phaëthon. **Merops' son.** Phaëthon's mother Clymene was the wife of Merops.
156. reach: reach for. **157. overweening:** presumptuous.
158. equal mates: women of your own rank.

And think my patience (more than thy desert)
Is privilege for thy departure hence.
Thank me for this more than for all the favors
Which (all too much) I have bestowed on thee.
But if thou linger in my territories
Longer than swiftest expedition
Will give thee time to leave our royal court,
By heaven, my wrath shall far exceed the love
I ever bore my daughter, or thyself.
Be gone, I will not hear thy vain excuse,
But as thou lov'st thy life, make speed from hence. [*Exit.*]
Val. And why not death, rather than living torment?
To die is to be banish'd from myself,
And Silvia is myself: banish'd from her
Is self from self, a deadly banishment.
What light is light, if Silvia be not seen?
What joy is joy, if Silvia be not by?
Unless it be to think that she is by,
And feed upon the shadow of perfection.
Except I be by Silvia in the night,
There is no music in the nightingale;
Unless I look on Silvia in the day,
There is no day for me to look upon.
She is my essence, and I leave to be,
If I be not by her fair influence
Foster'd, illumin'd, cherish'd, kept alive.
I fly not death, to fly his deadly doom:
Tarry I here, I but attend on death,
But fly I hence, I fly away from life.

[*Enter* PROTEUS *and*] LAUNCE.

Pro. Run, boy, run, run, and seek him out.
Launce. Soho, soho!
Pro. What seest thou?
Launce. Him we go to find. There's not a hair on 's head but 'tis a Valentine.
Pro. Valentine?
Val. No.
Pro. Who then? his spirit?
Val. Neither.
Pro. What then?
Val. Nothing.
Launce. Can nothing speak? Master, shall I strike?
Pro. Who wouldst thou strike?
Launce. Nothing.
Pro. Villain, forbear.
Launce. Why, sir, I'll strike nothing. I pray you—
Pro. Sirrah, I say forbear. Friend Valentine, a word.
Val. My ears are stopp'd and cannot hear good news,
So much of bad already hath possess'd them.

160. Is privilege for: licenses. **164. expedition:** speed.
173. deadly: deathlike. **177. shadow:** image, illusion.
182. leave: cease.
183. fair influence: beneficial effect (astrological figure).
185. I . . . doom: I do not elude death by fleeing from the Duke's sentence of death. **186. attend on:** wait.
189. Soho: a cry used in hunting the hare (note Launce's pun on *hair* in line 191).
192. Valentine. With quibble on the sense "love token."

Pro. Then in dumb silence will I bury mine,
For they are harsh, untuneable, and bad.
Val. Is Silvia dead?
Pro. No, Valentine.
Val. No Valentine indeed, for sacred Silvia.
Hath she forsworn me?
Pro. No, Valentine.
Val. No Valentine, if Silvia have forsworn me.
What is your news?

Launce. Sir, there is a proclamation that you are vanish'd.

Pro. That thou art banish'd—O, that's the news!—
From hence, from Silvia, and from me thy friend.
Val. O, I have fed upon this woe already,
And now excess of it will make me surfeit.
Doth Silvia know that I am banished?
Pro. Ay, ay; and she hath offered to the doom
(Which unrevers'd stands in effectual force)
A sea of melting pearl, which some call tears;
Those at her father's churlish feet she tender'd,
With them, upon her knees, her humble self,
Wringing her hands, whose whiteness so became them
As if but now they waxed pale for woe:
But neither bended knees, pure hands held up,
Sad sighs, deep groans, nor silver-shedding tears
Could penetrate her uncompassionate sire;
But Valentine, if he be ta'en, must die.
Besides, her intercession chaf'd him so,
When she for thy repeal was suppliant,
That to close prison he commanded her,
With many bitter threats of biding there.
Val. No more; unless the next word that thou speak'st
Have some malignant power upon my life;
If so—I pray thee breathe it in mine ear,
As ending anthem of my endless dolor.
Pro. Cease to lament for that thou canst not help,
And study help for that which thou lament'st.
Time is the nurse and breeder of all good.
Here if thou stay, thou canst not see thy love;
Besides, thy staying will abridge thy life.
Hope is a lover's staff; walk hence with that
And manage it against despairing thoughts.
Thy letters may be here, though thou art hence,
Which, being writ to me, shall be deliver'd
Even in the milk-white bosom of thy love.
The time now serves not to expostulate:
Come, I'll convey thee through the city-gate;
And ere I part with thee, confer at large
Of all that may concern thy love-affairs.
As thou lov'st Silvia (though not for thyself)
Regard thy danger, and along with me.
Val. I pray thee, Launce, and if thou seest my boy,
Bid him make haste and meet me at the North-gate.
Pro. Go, sirrah, find him out. Come, Valentine.

208. mine: i.e. my news.
225. Which . . . force: which, if not reversed, will certainly be carried out. **236. repeal:** recall from banishment.
237. close: tightly shut. **238. biding:** i.e. making her remain.
242. ending anthem: requiem. **243. that:** what.
244. study help: devise a remedy. **249. manage:** wield.
253. expostulate: discuss. **255. confer at large:** discuss at length.
257. though . . . thyself: even if not for your own sake.

Val. O my dear Silvia! Hapless Valentine!
[*Exeunt Valentine and Proteus.*]

Launce. I am but a fool, look you, and yet I have the wit to think my master is a kind of a knave; but that's all one, if he be but one knave. He lives not now that knows me to be in love, yet I am in love, but a team of horse shall not pluck that from me; nor who 'tis I love; and yet 'tis a woman; but what woman, I will not tell myself; and yet 'tis a milkmaid; yet 'tis not a maid, for she hath had gossips; yet 'tis a maid, for she is her master's maid, and serves for wages. She hath more qualities than a water-spaniel, which is much in a bare Christian. [*Pulling out a paper.*] Here is the cate-log of her condition. "*Inprimis*, She can fetch and carry." Why, a horse can do no more; nay, a horse cannot fetch, but only carry, therefore is she better than a jade. "*Item*, She can milk." Look you, a sweet virtue in a maid with clean hands.

[*Enter*] Speed.

Speed. How now, Signior Launce? what news with your mastership?

Launce. With my [master's ship]? why, it is at sea.

Speed. Well, your old vice still: mistake the word. What news then in your paper?

Launce. The blackest news that ever thou heardst.

Speed. Why, man? how black?

Launce. Why, as black as ink.

Speed. Let me read them.

Launce. Fie on thee, jolthead, thou canst not read.

Speed. Thou liest; I can.

Launce. I will try thee. Tell me this: who begot thee?

Speed. Marry, the son of my grandfather.

Launce. O illiterate loiterer! it was the son of thy grandmother. This proves that thou canst not read.

Speed. Come, fool, come; try me in thy paper.

Launce. There—and Saint Nicholas be thy speed!

Speed. [*Reads.*] "*Inprimis*, She can milk."

Launce. Ay, that she can.

Speed. "*Item*, She brews good ale."

Launce. And thereof comes the proverb: "Blessing of your heart, you brew good ale."

Speed. "*Item*, She can sew."

Launce. That's as much as to say, "Can she so?"

Speed. "*Item*, She can knit."

265. that's . . . knave: no matter, if his knavery be but slight.
270. gossips: godparents (to a child of hers).
272–73. water-spaniel. The spaniel was proverbial for fawning submissiveness.
273. bare: mere (perhaps with quibble on the sense "naked," in contrast to a spaniel's thick coat).
274. cate-log: catalogue (Launce's pronunciation). **condition:** qualities.
275. Inprimis: *Imprimis*, in the first place (signalling the beginning of a list, as *Item* distinguishes each later section).
277. jade: (1) ill-conditioned horse; (2) loose woman.
290. jolthead: blockhead. **296. loiterer:** idler, truant.
300. Saint Nicholas: patron saint of scholars. **speed:** protection, help (with a play on Speed's name).

Launce. What need a man care for a stock with a wench, when she can knit him a stock?

Speed. "*Item*, She can wash and scour."

Launce. A special virtue; for then she need not be wash'd and scour'd.

Speed. "*Item*, She can spin."

Launce. Then may I set the world on wheels, when she can spin for her living.

Speed. "*Item*, She hath many nameless virtues."

Launce. That's as much as to say "bastard virtues," that indeed know not their fathers, and therefore have no names.

Speed. Here follow her vices.

Launce. Close at the heels of her virtues.

Speed. "*Item*, She is not to be [kiss'd] fasting, in respect of her breath."

Launce. Well, that fault may be mended with a breakfast. Read on.

Speed. "*Item*, She hath a sweet mouth."

Launce. That makes amends for her sour breath.

Speed. "*Item*, She doth talk in her sleep."

Launce. It's no matter for that, so she sleep not in her talk.

Speed. "*Item*, She is slow in words."

Launce. O villain, that set this down among her vices! To be slow in words is a woman's only virtue. I pray thee out with't, and place it for her chief virtue.

Speed. "*Item*, She is proud."

Launce. Out with that too; it was Eve's legacy, and cannot be ta'en from her.

Speed. "*Item*, She hath no teeth."

Launce. I care not for that neither, because I love crusts.

Speed. "*Item*, She is curst."

Launce. Well, the best is, she hath no teeth to bite.

Speed. "*Item*, She will often praise her liquor."

Launce. If her liquor be good, she shall; if she will not, I will; for good things should be prais'd.

Speed. "*Item*, She is too liberal."

Launce. Of her tongue she cannot, for that's writ down she is slow of; of her purse she shall not, for that I'll keep shut. Now, of another thing she may, and that cannot I help. Well, proceed.

Speed. "*Item*, She hath more hair than wit, and more faults than hairs, and more wealth than faults."

Launce. Stop there; I'll have her. She was mine and not mine twice or thrice in that last article. Rehearse that once more.

Speed. "*Item*, She hath more hair than wit"—

Launce. More hair than wit? It may be; I'll prove it: the cover of the salt hides the salt, and therefore it is more than the salt; the hair that covers the wit is more than the wit, for the greater hides the less. What's next?

309. **stock**: dowry.
310. **stock**: stocking. 315. **set . . . wheels**: take life easy.
317. **nameless**: inexpressible. 323–24. **in respect**: on account.
327. **sweet mouth**: sweet tooth (with an implication of wantonness).
330. **sleep.** With play on *slip*, pronounced similarly.
337. **proud.** With secondary meaning "lascivious."
343. **curst**: shrewish. 345. **praise**: appraise, i.e. sip or taste.
348. **liberal**: bold, wanton.

Speed. "And more faults than hairs"—

Launce. That's monstrous. O that that were out!

Speed. "And more wealth than faults."

Launce. Why, that word makes the faults gracious. Well, I'll have her; and if it be a match, as nothing is impossible—

Speed. What then?

Launce. Why, then will I tell thee—that thy master stays for thee at the North-gate.

Speed. For me?

Launce. For thee? ay, who art thou? He hath stay'd for a better man than thee.

Speed. And must I go to him?

Launce. Thou must run to him, for thou hast stay'd so long that going will scarce serve the turn.

Speed. Why didst not tell me sooner? Pox of your love-letters! [*Exit.*]

Launce. Now will he be swing'd for reading my letter—an unmannerly slave, that will thrust himself into secrets. I'll after, to rejoice in the boy's correction. *Exit.*

Scene II

Enter Duke, Thurio.

Duke. Sir Thurio, fear not but that she will love you
Now Valentine is banish'd from her sight.
Thu. Since his exile she hath despis'd me most,
Forsworn my company, and rail'd at me,
That I am desperate of obtaining her.
Duke. This weak impress of love is as a figure
Trenched in ice, which with an hour's heat
Dissolves to water, and doth lose his form.
A little time will melt her frozen thoughts,
And worthless Valentine shall be forgot.

[*Enter*] Proteus.

How now, Sir Proteus? is your countryman,
According to our proclamation, gone?
Pro. Gone, my good lord.
Duke. My daughter takes his going grievously.
Pro. A little time, my lord, will kill that grief.
Duke. So I believe; but Thurio thinks not so.
Proteus, the good conceit I hold of thee
(For thou hast shown some sign of good desert)
Makes me the better to confer with thee.
Pro. Longer than I prove loyal to your Grace
Let me not live to look upon your Grace.
Duke. Thou know'st how willingly I would effect
The match between Sir Thurio and my daughter?
Pro. I do, my lord.
Duke. And also, I think, thou art not ignorant
How she opposes her against my will?

368. **gracious**: acceptable.
379. **going**: walking. 382. **swing'd**: thrashed (past of *swinge*).

III.ii. Location: Milan. The Duke's palace.
5. **That**: so that. **am desperate**: despair.
6. **impress**: impression. 7. **Trenched**: cut.
14. **grievously**: bitterly, sorrowfully. 17. **conceit**: opinion.
19. **the better**: the more readily. 26. **opposes her against**: resists.

Pro. She did, my lord, when Valentine was here.
Duke. Ay, and perversely she persevers so.
What might we do to make the girl forget
The love of Valentine, and love Sir Thurio?
Pro. The best way is to slander Valentine
With falsehood, cowardice, and poor descent,
Three things that women highly hold in hate.
Duke. Ay, but she'll think that it is spoke in hate.
Pro. Ay, if his enemy deliver it;
Therefore it must with circumstance be spoken
By one whom she esteemeth as his friend.
Duke. Then you must undertake to slander him.
Pro. And that, my lord, I shall be loath to do:
'Tis an ill office for a gentleman,
Especially against his very friend.
Duke. Where your good word cannot advantage him,
Your slander never can endamage him;
Therefore the office is indifferent,
Being entreated to it by your friend.
Pro. You have prevail'd, my lord; if I can do it
By aught that I can speak in his dispraise,
She shall not long continue love to him.
But say this weed her love from Valentine,
It follows not that she will love Sir Thurio.
Thu. Therefore, as you unwind her love from him,
Lest it should ravel and be good to none,
You must provide to bottom it on me;
Which must be done by praising me as much
As you in worth dispraise Sir Valentine.
Duke. And, Proteus, we dare trust you in this kind,
Because we know (on Valentine's report)
You are already Love's firm votary,
And cannot soon revolt and change your mind.
Upon this warrant shall you have access
Where you with Silvia may confer at large—
For she is lumpish, heavy, melancholy,
And (for your friend's sake) will be glad of you—
Where you may temper her by your persuasion
To hate young Valentine and love my friend.
Pro. As much as I can do, I will effect.
But you, Sir Thurio, are not sharp enough:
You must lay lime to tangle her desires
By wailful sonnets, whose composed rhymes
Should be full-fraught with serviceable vows.
Duke. Ay, much is the force of heaven-bred poesy.
Pro. Say that upon the altar of her beauty
You sacrifice your tears, your sighs, your heart;
Write till your ink be dry, and with your tears
Moist it again, and frame some feeling line
That may discover such integrity:
For Orpheus' lute was strung with poets' sinews,
Whose golden touch could soften steel and stones,

35. deliver: utter, speak.
36. circumstance: convincing detail. **41. very:** special.
42. advantage: profit.
44. indifferent: neutral, neither good nor bad. **49. weed:** remove.
53. provide: take care. **bottom:** wind (as on a core).
62. lumpish: spiritless. **64. Where:** whereas. **temper:** mould.
68. lime: birdlime, a sticky substance smeared on twigs to entangle small birds.
70. serviceable vows: vows expressing readiness to serve.
75. feeling: impassioned.
76. discover such integrity: reveal such single-hearted devotion.
77. sinews: nerves.

Make tigers tame, and huge leviathans
Forsake unsounded deeps to dance on sands.
After your dire-lamenting elegies,
Visit by night your lady's chamber-window
With some sweet consort; to their instruments
Tune a deploring dump—the night's dead silence
Will well become such sweet-complaining grievance.
This, or else nothing, will inherit her.
Duke. This discipline shows thou hast been in love.
Thu. And thy advice this night I'll put in practice:
Therefore, sweet Proteus, my direction-giver,
Let us into the city presently
To sort some gentlemen well skill'd in music.
I have a sonnet that will serve the turn
To give the onset to thy good advice.
Duke. About it, gentlemen!
Pro. We'll wait upon your Grace till after supper,
And afterward determine our proceedings.
Duke. Even now about it! I will pardon you.
Exeunt.

ACT IV, Scene I

Enter Valentine, Speed, *and certain* Outlaws.

1. Out. Fellows, stand fast; I see a passenger.
2. Out. If there be ten, shrink not, but down with 'em.
3. Out. Stand, sir, and throw us that you have about ye.
If not, we'll make you sit, and rifle you.
Speed. Sir, we are undone; these are the villains
That all the travellers do fear so much.
Val. My friends—
1. Out. That's not so, sir; we are your enemies.
2. Out. Peace! we'll hear him.
3. Out. Ay, by my beard, will we, for he is a proper man.
Val. Then know that I have little wealth to lose.
A man I am cross'd with adversity;
My riches are these poor habiliments,
Of which if you should here disfurnish me,
You take the sum and substance that I have.
2. Out. Whither travel you?
Val. To Verona.
1. Out. Whence came you?
Val. From Milan.
3. Out. Have you long sojourn'd there?
Val. Some sixteen months, and longer might have stay'd,
If crooked fortune had not thwarted me.
1. Out. What, were you banish'd thence?
Val. I was.
2. Out. For what offense?

79. leviathans: whales. **83. consort:** band of musicians.
84. deploring: doleful. **dump:** mournful tune.
85. grievance: sorrow. **86. inherit:** gain, obtain.
87. discipline: instruction. **91. sort:** choose.
93. onset: beginning. **95. wait upon:** attend.
97. pardon: excuse from attendance.

IV.i. Location: A forest between Milan and Mantua.
1. passenger: traveller on foot, wayfarer.
3. Stand: halt (but *sit* in line 4 plays against the sense "stand up").
10. proper: good-looking, well made. **14. disfurnish:** deprive.
22. crooked: malignant.

Val. For that which now torments me to rehearse:
I kill'd a man, whose death I much repent,
But yet I slew him manfully in fight,
Without false vantage, or base treachery.
1. Out. Why, ne'er repent it, if it were done so.
But were you banish'd for so small a fault?
Val. I was, and held me glad of such a doom.
2. Out. Have you the tongues?
Val. My youthful travel therein made me happy,
Or else I often had been miserable.
3. Out. By the bare scalp of Robin Hood's fat friar,
This fellow were a king for our wild faction!
1. Out. We'll have him. Sirs, a word.
Speed. Master, be one of them;
It's an honorable kind of thievery.
Val. Peace, villain.
2. Out. Tell us this: have you any thing to take to?
Val. Nothing but my fortune.
3. Out. Know then, that some of us are gentlemen,
Such as the fury of ungovern'd youth
Thrust from the company of aweful men.
Myself was from Verona banished
For practicing to steal away a lady,
[An] heir, and [near] allied unto the Duke.
2. Out. And I from Mantua, for a gentleman,
Who, in my mood, I stabb'd unto the heart.
1. Out. And I for such like petty crimes as these.
But to the purpose—for we cite our faults
That they may hold excus'd our lawless lives;
And partly, seeing you are beautified
With goodly shape, and by your own report
A linguist, and a man of such perfection
As we do in our quality much want—
2. Out. Indeed because you are a banish'd man,
Therefore, above the rest, we parley to you:
Are you content to be our general?
To make a virtue of necessity
And live as we do in this wilderness?
3. Out. What say'st thou? wilt thou be of our consort?
Say "ay" and be the captain of us all:
We'll do thee homage and be rul'd by thee,
Love thee as our commander and our king.
1. Out. But if thou scorn our courtesy, thou diest.
2. Out. Thou shalt not live to brag what we have offer'd.
Val. I take your offer, and will live with you,
Provided that you do no outrages

27. I . . . man. Valentine's lie is presumably meant to impress the outlaws.
32. held . . . doom: was pleased with such a sentence (i.e. to get off so easily).
33. the tongues: knowledge of foreign languages.
34. travel. Perhaps correctly *travail*, i.e. laborious study; so F1 reads, but ambiguously, since Elizabethan spelling did not distinguish the two words. **happy:** skillful.
36. friar: i.e. Friar Tuck. **37. faction:** company.
40. any . . . take to: any means of livelihood.
44. aweful: commanding respect (?) or law-abiding (?).
46. practicing: plotting. **49. mood:** anger.
56. quality: profession.
58. Therefore . . . rest: for that reason chiefly.
60. make . . . of: embrace as if by choice. **62. consort:** company.

On silly women or poor passengers.
3. Out. No, we detest such vile base practices.
Come, go with us, we'll bring thee to our crews,
And show thee all the treasure we have got;
Which, with ourselves, all rest at thy dispose.
Exeunt.

Scene II

Enter Proteus.

Pro. Already have I been false to Valentine,
And now I must be as unjust to Thurio:
Under the color of commending him,
I have access my own love to prefer—
But Silvia is too fair, too true, too holy,
To be corrupted with my worthless gifts.
When I protest true loyalty to her,
She twits me with my falsehood to my friend;
When to her beauty I commend my vows,
She bids me think how I have been forsworn
In breaking faith with Julia whom I lov'd;
And notwithstanding all her sudden quips,
The least whereof would quell a lover's hope,
Yet, spaniel-like, the more she spurns my love,
The more it grows, and fawneth on her still.

[*Enter*] Thurio, Musician[s].

But here comes Thurio. Now must we to her window,
And give some evening music to her ear.
Thu. How now, Sir Proteus, are you crept before us?
Pro. Ay, gentle Thurio, for you know that love
Will creep in service where it cannot go.
Thu. Ay, but I hope, sir, that you love not here.
Pro. Sir, but I do; or else I would be hence.
Thu. Who? Silvia?
Pro. Ay, Silvia—for your sake.
Thu. I thank you for your own. Now, gentlemen,
Let's tune, and to it lustily a while.

[*Enter at one side*] Host, Julia [*in boy's clothes, as Sebastian*].

Host. Now, my young guest, methinks you're allycholly; I pray you, why is it?
Jul. Marry, mine host, because I cannot be merry.
Host. Come, we'll have you merry: I'll bring you where you shall hear music and see the gentleman that you ask'd for.
Jul. But shall I hear him speak?
Host. Ay, that you shall.
Jul. That will be music. [*Music plays.*]
Host. Hark, hark!
Jul. Is he among these?
Host. Ay; but peace, let's hear 'em.

70. silly: defenseless. **72. crews:** bands.

IV.ii. Location: Milan. Outside the Duke's palace, under Silvia's window.
2. unjust: false. **3. color:** pretense.
9. commend: recommend, direct. **12. quips:** sharp jests, sarcasms.
20. go: walk. **27. allycholly:** blunder for *melancholy*.
32. ask'd for: inquired about.

SONG

Who is Silvia? what is she,
That all our swains commend her?
Holy, fair, and wise is she;
The heaven such grace did lend her,
That she might admired be.

Is she kind as she is fair?
For beauty lives with kindness.
Love doth to her eyes repair,
To help him of his blindness;
And, being help'd, inhabits there.

Then to Silvia let us sing,
That Silvia is excelling;
She excels each mortal thing
Upon the dull earth dwelling.
To her let us garlands bring.

Host. How now? are you sadder than you were before? How do you, man? The music likes you not.

Jul. You mistake; the musician likes me not.

Host. Why, my pretty youth?

Jul. He plays false, father.

Host. How, out of tune on the strings?

Jul. Not so; but yet so false that he grieves my very heart-strings.

Host. You have a quick ear.

Jul. Ay, I would I were deaf; it makes me have a slow heart.

Host. I perceive you delight not in music.

Jul. Not a whit, when it jars so.

Host. Hark, what fine change is in the music.

Jul. Ay; that change is the spite.

Host. You would have them always play but one thing?

Jul. I would always have one play but one thing.
But, host, doth this Sir Proteus that we talk on
Often resort unto this gentlewoman?

Host. I tell you what Launce, his man, told me: he lov'd her out of all nick.

Jul. Where is Launce?

Host. Gone to seek his dog, which to-morrow, by his master's command, he must carry for a present to his lady.

Jul. Peace, stand aside, the company parts.

Pro. Sir Thurio, fear not you, I will so plead,
That you shall say my cunning drift excels.

Thu. Where meet we?

Pro. At Saint Gregory's well.

Thu. Farewell.

[*Exeunt Thurio and Musicians.*]

[*Enter*] SILVIA [*above at her window*].

Pro. Madam, good ev'n to your ladyship.

Sil. I thank you for your music, gentlemen.
Who is that that spake?

Pro. One, lady, if you knew his pure heart's truth,
You would quickly learn to know him by his voice.

Sil. Sir Proteus, as I take it.

Pro. Sir Proteus, gentle lady, and your servant.

Sil. What's your will?

Pro. That I may compass yours.

Sil. You have your wish: my will is even this,
That presently you hie you home to bed.
Thou subtile, perjur'd, false, disloyal man,
Think'st thou I am so shallow, so conceitless,
To be seduced by thy flattery,
That hast deceiv'd so many with thy vows?
Return, return, and make thy love amends.
For me (by this pale queen of night I swear),
I am so far from granting thy request,
That I despise thee for thy wrongful suit,
And by and by intend to chide myself
Even for this time I spend in talking to thee.

Pro. I grant, sweet love, that I did love a lady;
But she is dead.

Jul. [*Aside.*] 'Twere false, if I should speak it;
For I am sure she is not buried.

Sil. Say that she be; yet Valentine thy friend
Survives; to whom (thyself art witness)
I am betroth'd; and art thou not asham'd
To wrong him with thy importunacy?

Pro. I likewise hear that Valentine is dead.

Sil. And so suppose am I; for in [his] grave
Assure thyself my love is buried.

Pro. Sweet lady, let me rake it from the earth.

Sil. Go to thy lady's grave and call hers thence,
Or at the least, in hers sepulchre thine.

Jul. [*Aside.*] He heard not that.

Pro. Madam, if your heart be so obdurate,
Vouchsafe me yet your picture for my love,
The picture that is hanging in your chamber;
To that I'll speak, to that I'll sigh and weep;
For since the substance of your perfect self
Is else devoted, I am but a shadow;
And to your shadow will I make true love.

Jul. [*Aside.*] If 'twere a substance, you would sure deceive it,
And make it but a shadow, as I am.

Sil. I am very loath to be your idol, sir;
But since your falsehood shall become you well
To worship shadows and adore false shapes,
Send to me in the morning, and I'll send it;
And so, good rest.

Pro. As wretches have o'ernight
That wait for execution in the morn.

[*Exeunt Proteus and Silvia.*]

Jul. Host, will you go?

Host. By my halidom, I was fast asleep.

Jul. Pray you, where lies Sir Proteus?

Host. Marry, at my house. Trust me, I think 'tis almost day.

43. admired: wondered at.
45. For . . . kindness: i.e. beauty without kindness dies unenjoyed, and undelighting (Johnson). **55. likes:** pleases.
65. slow: heavy. **67. jars:** is discordant.
68. fine change: delicate modulation.
76. out . . . nick: beyond all reckoning. **83. drift:** scheme.

92. compass: obtain. **95. subtile:** crafty.
96. conceitless: witless.
111. thy importunacy: your importunity, i.e. the improper urging of your own suit. **124. else:** elsewhere. **shadow:** mere nothing.
125. shadow: i.e. picture. **126. deceive:** be false to.
129. become: befit. **135. halidom:** sanctity, salvation.
136. lies: lodges.

Jul. Not so; but it hath been the longest night
That e'er I watch'd, and the most heaviest.
[*Exeunt*.]

Scene III

Enter Eglamour.

Egl. This is the hour that Madam Silvia
Entreated me to call and know her mind.
There's some great matter she'd employ me in.
Madam, madam!

[*Enter*] Silvia [*above at her window*].

Sil. Who calls?
Egl. Your servant and your friend;
One that attends your ladyship's command.
Sil. Sir Eglamour, a thousand times good morrow.
Egl. As many, worthy lady, to yourself.
According to your ladyship's impose,
I am thus early come to know what service
It is your pleasure to command me in.
Sil. O Eglamour, thou art a gentleman—
Think not I flatter, for I swear I do not—
Valiant, wise, remorseful, well accomplish'd:
Thou art not ignorant what dear good will
I bear unto the banish'd Valentine,
Nor how my father would enforce me marry
Vain Thurio, whom my very soul [abhors].
Thyself hast lov'd, and I have heard thee say
No grief did ever come so near thy heart
As when thy lady and thy true-love died,
Upon whose grave thou vow'dst pure chastity.
Sir Eglamour, I would to Valentine,
To Mantua, where I hear he makes abode;
And for the ways are dangerous to pass,
I do desire thy worthy company,
Upon whose faith and honor I repose.
Urge not my father's anger, Eglamour,
But think upon my grief, a lady's grief,
And on the justice of my flying hence,
To keep me from a most unholy match,
Which heaven and fortune still rewards with plagues.
I do desire thee, even from a heart
As full of sorrows as the sea of sands,
To bear me company, and go with me;
If not, to hide what I have said to thee,
That I may venture to depart alone.
Egl. Madam, I pity much your grievances,
Which since I know they virtuously are plac'd,
I give consent to go along with you,
Reaking as little what betideth me,
As much I wish all good befortune you.
When will you go?
Sil. This evening coming.
Egl. Where shall I meet you?
Sil. At Friar Patrick's cell,
Where I intend holy confession.
Egl. I will not fail your ladyship. Good morrow,
Gentle lady.
Sil. Good morrow, kind Sir Eglamour.
Exeunt.

Scene IV

Enter Launce [*with his dog*].

Launce. When a man's servant shall play the cur with him, look you, it goes hard: one that I brought up of a puppy; one that I sav'd from drowning, when three or four of his blind brothers and sisters went to it. I have taught him, even as one would say precisely, "Thus I would teach a dog." I was sent to deliver him as a present to Mistress Silvia from my master; and I came no sooner into the dining-chamber but he steps me to her trencher and steals her capon's leg. O, 'tis a foul thing when a cur cannot keep himself in all companies! I would have (as one should say) one that takes upon him to be a dog indeed, to be, as it were, a dog at all things. If I had not had more wit than he, to take a fault upon me that he did, I think verily he had been hang'd for't; sure as I live he had suffer'd for't. You shall judge: he thrusts me himself into the company of three or four gentleman-like dogs, under the Duke's table. He had not been there (bless the mark!) a pissing-while, but all the chamber smelt him. "Out with the dog," says one. "What cur is that?" says another. "Whip him out," says the third. "Hang him up," says the Duke. I, having been acquainted with the smell before, knew it was Crab, and goes me to the fellow that whips the dogs: "Friend," quoth I, "you mean to whip the dog?" "Ay, marry, do I," quoth he. "You do him the more wrong," quoth I, "'twas I did the thing you wot of." He makes me no more ado, but whips me out of the chamber. How many masters would do this for his servant? Nay, I'll be sworn, I have sat in the stocks for puddings he hath stol'n, otherwise he had been executed; I have stood on the pillory for geese he hath kill'd, otherwise he had suffer'd for't. Thou think'st not of this now. Nay, I remember the trick you serv'd me, when I took my leave of Madam Silvia. Did not I bid thee still mark me, and do as I do? When didst thou see me heave up my

140. **watch'd:** stayed awake. **heaviest:** grievous.

IV.iii. Location: The same, early the next morning.
o.s.d. **Eglamour.** Presumably not the Eglamour referred to in I.ii.9–11.
8. **impose:** command. 13. **remorseful:** compassionate.
14. **dear:** affectionate.
23. **Mantua.** Shakespeare here chose Mantua because he recalled that Romeus fled in exile to that city in Brooke's *Romeus and Juliet*; the detail reappears in *Romeo and Juliet*, a play for which Brooke's poem is the principal source. This is only one of a substantial number of echoes in *Two Gentlemen* from Brooke; another is the rendezvous at Friar Patrick's (Friar Lawrence's in Brooke and *Romeo and Juliet*) cell (lines 43–44 below). 24. **for:** because. 31. **still:** always.
37. **grievances:** trouble, distress. 40. **Reaking:** recking, caring.

41. **befortune:** befall.

IV.iv. The same, some hours later.
3. **of:** from. 4. **went to it:** met their death.
5. **even . . . precisely:** i.e. as one might say in the most perfect method (of dog-training). 9. **trencher:** wooden plate.
10. **keep:** behave properly.
11–12. **one that:** i.e. such a dog as.
13. **a dog at:** adept at (but the joke obviously resides in the fact that the words have their literal meaning also; so too for *pissing-while* in line 19, slang for "a short time").
19. **bless the mark:** a phrase of apology for indecorous language.
27. **wot:** know. 31. **puddings:** stomachs or intestines of animals.

leg and make water against a gentlewoman's farthingale? Didst thou ever see me do such a trick?

[*Enter*] PROTEUS, JULIA [*disguised as Sebastian*].

Pro. Sebastian is thy name? I like thee well,
And will employ thee in some service presently.
Jul. In what you please; I'll do what I can.
Pro. I hope thou wilt. [*To Launce.*] How now, you whoreson peasant,
Where have you been these two days loitering?

Launce. Marry, sir, I carried Mistress Silvia the dog you bade me.

Pro. And what says she to my little jewel?

Launce. Marry, she says your dog was a cur, and tells you currish thanks is good enough for such a present.

Pro. But she receiv'd my dog?

Launce. No indeed did she not; here have I brought him back again.

Pro. What, didst thou offer her this from me?

Launce. Ay, sir, the other squirrel was stol'n from me by the hangman's boys in the market-place; and then I offer'd her mine own, who is a dog as big as ten of yours, and therefore the gift the greater.

Pro. Go, get thee hence, and find my dog again,
Or ne'er return again into my sight.
Away, I say! stayest thou to vex me here?
[*Exit Launce.*]
A slave, that still an end turns me to shame!
Sebastian, I have entertained thee,
Partly that I have need of such a youth
That can with some discretion do my business—
For 'tis no trusting to yond foolish lout—
But chiefly for thy face and thy behavior,
Which (if my augury deceive me not)
Witness good bringing up, fortune, and truth:
Therefore know [thou], for this I entertain thee.
Go presently, and take this ring with thee,
Deliver it to Madam Silvia—
She lov'd me well deliver'd it to me.
Jul. It seems you lov'd not her, [to] leave her token:
She is dead, belike?
Pro. Not so; I think she lives.
Jul. Alas!
Pro. Why dost thou cry "alas"?
Jul. I cannot choose
But pity her.
Pro. Wherefore shouldst thou pity her?
Jul. Because methinks that she lov'd you as well
As you do love your lady Silvia:
She dreams on him that has forgot her love;
You dote on her that cares not for your love.
'Tis pity love should be so contrary;
And thinking on it makes me cry "alas!"
Pro. Well, give her that ring and therewithal
This letter; that's her chamber. Tell my lady

41. **presently:** at once.
43. **whoreson peasant.** Coarsely playful rather than genuinely abusive.
55. **squirrel:** i.e. little dog. 56. **hangman's:** fit for the hangman.
62. **still an end:** continually. 63. **entertained:** taken into service.
73. **deliver'd:** who delivered. 74. **leave:** part with.
85. **therewithal:** at the same time.

I claim the promise for her heavenly picture.
Your message done, hie home unto my chamber,
Where thou shalt find me sad and solitary. [*Exit.*]
Jul. How many women would do such a message?
Alas, poor Proteus, thou hast entertain'd
A fox to be the shepherd of thy lambs.
Alas, poor fool, why do I pity him
That with his very heart despiseth me?
Because he loves her, he despiseth me;
Because I love him, I must pity him.
This ring I gave him when he parted from me,
To bind him to remember my good will;
And now am I (unhappy messenger)
To plead for that which I would not obtain,
To carry that which I would have refus'd,
To praise his faith which I would have disprais'd.
I am my master's true confirmed love;
But cannot be true servant to my master,
Unless I prove false traitor to myself.
Yet will I woo for him, but yet so coldly
As, heaven it knows, I would not have him speed.

[*Enter*] SILVIA [*attended*].

Gentlewoman, good day; I pray you be my mean
To bring me where to speak with Madam Silvia.
Sil. What would you with her, if that I be she?
Jul. If you be she, I do entreat your patience
To hear me speak the message I am sent on.
Sil. From whom?
Jul. From my master, Sir Proteus, madam.
Sil. O, he sends you for a picture?
Jul. Ay, madam.
Sil. Ursula, bring my picture there.
Go give your master this. Tell him from me,
One Julia, that his changing thoughts forget,
Would better fit his chamber than this shadow.
Jul. Madam, please you peruse this letter—
Pardon me, madam, I have unadvis'd
Deliver'd you a paper that I should not:
This is the letter to your ladyship.
Sil. I pray thee let me look on that again.
Jul. It may not be; good madam, pardon me.
Sil. There, hold!
I will not look upon your master's lines;
I know they are stuff'd with protestations,
And full of new-found oaths, which he will break
As easily as I do tear his paper.
Jul. Madam, he sends your ladyship this ring.
Sil. The more shame for him that he sends it me;
For I have heard him say a thousand times
His Julia gave it him at his departure:
Though his false finger have profan'd the ring,
Mine shall not do his Julia so much wrong.
Jul. She thanks you.
Sil. What say'st thou?
Jul. I thank you, madam, that you tender her.
Poor gentlewoman, my master wrongs her much.
Sil. Dost thou know her?

93. **poor fool.** Referring to herself. 107. **speed:** succeed.
109. **where to speak:** where I may speak.
122. **unadvis'd:** inadvertently.
140. **tender:** regard sympathetically.

Jul. Almost as well as I do know myself.
To think upon her woes I do protest
That I have wept a hundred several times.
Sil. Belike she thinks that Proteus hath forsook her?
Jul. I think she doth; and that's her cause of sorrow.
Sil. Is she not passing fair?
Jul. She hath been fairer, madam, than she is:
When she did think my master lov'd her well,
She, in my judgment, was as fair as you;
But since she did neglect her looking-glass,
And threw her sun-expelling mask away,
The air hath starv'd the roses in her cheeks,
And pinch'd the lily-tincture of her face,
That now she is become as black as I.
Sil. How tall was she?
Jul. About my stature; for at Pentecost,
When all our pageants of delight were play'd,
Our youth got me to play the woman's part,
And I was trimm'd in Madam Julia's gown,
Which served me as fit, by all men's judgments,
As if the garment had been made for me;
Therefore I know she is about my height.
And at that time I made her weep agood,
For I did play a lamentable part.
Madam, 'twas Ariadne passioning
For Theseus' perjury and unjust flight;
Which I so lively acted with my tears
That my poor mistress, moved therewithal,
Wept bitterly; and would I might be dead
If I in thought felt not her very sorrow.
Sil. She is beholding to thee, gentle youth.
Alas, poor lady, desolate and left!
I weep myself to think upon thy words.
Here, youth, there is my purse; I give thee this
For thy sweet mistress' sake, because thou lov'st her.
Farewell.
Jul. And she shall thank you for't, if e'er you know her. [*Exit Silvia with Attendants.*]
A virtuous gentlewoman, mild and beautiful!
I hope my master's suit will be but cold,
Since she respects my mistress' love so much.
Alas, how love can trifle with itself!
Here is her picture: let me see; I think
If I had such a tire, this face of mine
Were full as lovely as is this of hers;
And yet the painter flatter'd her a little,
Unless I flatter with myself too much.
Her hair is auburn, mine is perfect yellow:
If that be all the difference in his love,
I'll get me such a color'd periwig.
Her eyes are grey as glass, and so are mine;

154. **starv'd**: nipped. 156. **black**: dark-complexioned.
158. **Pentecost**: Whitsuntide (seven weeks after Easter).
159. **pageants of delight**: delightful entertainments.
161. **trimm'd**: decked out. 165. **agood**: in earnest.
166. **lamentable**: tragic.
167–68. **Ariadne . . . flight.** King Minos' daughter Ariadne, having enabled Theseus to slay the Minotaur, fled with him from Crete, but Theseus abandoned her on the island of Naxos, where she hanged herself. 167. **passioning**: sorrowing. 168. **unjust**: faithless.
173. **beholding**: beholden, indebted. 181. **cold**: vain.
185. **tire**: headdress.

Ay, but her forehead's low, and mine's as high.
What should it be that he respects in her,
But I can make respective in myself,
If this fond Love were not a blinded god?
Come, shadow, come, and take this shadow up,
For 'tis thy rival. O thou senseless form,
Thou shalt be worshipp'd, kiss'd, lov'd, and ador'd;
And were there sense in his idolatry,
My substance should be statue in thy stead.
I'll use thee kindly for thy mistress' sake
That us'd me so; or else, by Jove I vow,
I should have scratch'd out your unseeing eyes,
To make my master out of love with thee. *Exit.*

ACT V, SCENE I

Enter EGLAMOUR.

Egl. The sun begins to gild the western sky,
And now it is about the very hour
That Silvia at Friar Patrick's cell should meet me.
She will not fail, for lovers break not hours,
Unless it be to come before their time,
So much they spur their expedition.
See where she comes.

[*Enter*] SILVIA.

Lady, a happy evening!
Sil. Amen, amen! Go on, good Eglamour,
Out at the postern by the abbey wall;
I fear I am attended by some spies.
Egl. Fear not: the forest is not three leagues off;
If we recover that, we are sure enough. *Exeunt.*

SCENE II

Enter THURIO, PROTEUS, JULIA [*disguised as Sebastian*].

Thu. Sir Proteus, what says Silvia to my suit?
Pro. O, sir, I find her milder than she was,
And yet she takes exceptions at your person.
Thu. What? that my leg is too long?
Pro. No, that it is too little.
Thu. I'll wear a boot, to make it somewhat rounder.
[*Jul.* *Aside.*] But love will not be spurr'd to what it loathes.
Thu. What says she to my face?
Pro. She says it is a fair one.
Thu. Nay then the wanton lies; my face is black.

193. **as high**: i.e. as high as hers is low. High foreheads were greatly admired. 194. **respects**: cares for.
195. **respective**: worthy of being cared for.
197. **shadow . . . shadow.** Cf. lines 124–25. **take . . . up**: (1) hold; (2) oppose, challenge. 198. **senseless**: insensible.
200. **sense**: reason. 201. **statue**: i.e. idol.

V.i. Location: Milan. An abbey.
9. **postern**: small back or side door.
12. **recover**: reach. **sure**: safe.

V.ii. Location: Milan. The Duke's palace.
3. **takes exceptions at**: objects to.
7. **spurr'd**: incited (with obvious quibble on Thurio's reference to being booted). 9. **fair**: pale.

Pro. But pearls are fair; and the old saying is,
Black men are pearls in beauteous ladies' eyes.
[*Jul.* *Aside.*] 'Tis true, such pearls as put out ladies' eyes,
For I had rather wink than look on them.
Thu. How likes she my discourse?
Pro. Ill, when you talk of war.
Thu. But well, when I discourse of love and peace.
Jul. [*Aside.*] But better indeed, when you hold [your] peace.
Thu. What says she to my valor?
Pro. O, sir, she makes no doubt of that.
Jul. [*Aside.*] She needs not, when she knows it cowardice.
Thu. What says she to my birth?
Pro. That you are well deriv'd.
Jul. [*Aside.*] True: from a gentleman to a fool.
Thu. Considers she my possessions?
Pro. O ay; and pities them.
Thu. Wherefore?
Jul. [*Aside.*] That such an ass should owe them.
Pro. That they are out by lease.
Jul. Here comes the Duke.

[*Enter*] Duke.

Duke. How now, Sir Proteus? how now, Thurio?
Which of you saw Eglamour of late?
Thu. Not I.
Pro. Nor I.
Duke. Saw you my daughter?
Pro. Neither.
Duke. Why then
She's fled unto that peasant Valentine;
And Eglamour is in her company.
'Tis true; for Friar Laurence met them both,
As he in penance wander'd through the forest;
Him he knew well, and guess'd that it was she,
But being mask'd, he was not sure of it;
Besides, she did intend confession
At Patrick's cell this even, and there she was not.
These likelihoods confirm her flight from hence:
Therefore I pray you stand not to discourse,
But mount you presently and meet with me
Upon the rising of the mountain foot
That leads toward Mantua, whither they are fled.
Dispatch, sweet gentlemen, and follow me. [*Exit.*]
Thu. Why, this it is to be a peevish girl,
That flies her fortune when it follows her.
I'll after, more to be reveng'd on Eglamour
Than for the love of reckless Silvia. [*Exit.*]
Pro. And I will follow, more for Silvia's love
Than hate of Eglamour that goes with her. [*Exit.*]
Jul. And I will follow, more to cross that love
Than hate for Silvia, that is gone for love. *Exit.*

12. **pearls**: i.e. things of great price.
13. **pearls**: cataracts.
20. **makes . . . of**: is in no uncertainty about (another double-edged reply, like line 9). 23. **deriv'd**: descended. 28. **owe**: own.
37. **Friar Laurence.** Possibly a slip for Friar Patrick; see the note on IV.iii.23. 43. **likelihoods**: indications.
49. **peevish**: silly, childish.
50. **fortune**: good fortune.
52. **reckless**: heedless, uncaring. 55. **cross**: frustrate.

Scene III

[*Enter*] Silvia, Outlaws.

1. Out. Come, come,
Be patient; we must bring you to our captain.
Sil. A thousand more mischances than this one
Have learn'd me how to brook this patiently.
2. Out. Come, bring her away.
1. Out. Where is the gentleman that was with her?
3. Out. Being nimble-footed, he hath outrun us,
But Moyses and Valerius follow him.
Go thou with her to the west end of the wood;
There is our captain. We'll follow him that's fled—
The thicket is beset, he cannot scape.
1. Out. Come, I must bring you to our captain's cave.
Fear not; he bears an honorable mind,
And will not use a woman lawlessly.
Sil. O Valentine, this I endure for thee! *Exeunt.*

Scene IV

Enter Valentine.

Val. How use doth breed a habit in a man!
This shadowy desert, unfrequented woods,
I better brook than flourishing peopled towns:
Here can I sit alone, unseen of any,
And to the nightingale's complaining notes
Tune my distresses and record my woes.
O thou that dost inhabit in my breast,
Leave not the mansion so long tenantless,
Lest growing ruinous, the building fall
And leave no memory of what it was!
Repair me with thy presence, Silvia;
Thou gentle nymph, cherish thy forlorn swain.
[*Shouts within.*]
What hallowing and what stir is this to-day?
These are my mates, that make their wills their law,
Have some unhappy passenger in chase.
They love me well; yet I have much to do
To keep them from uncivil outrages.
Withdraw thee, Valentine: who's this comes here?
[*Steps aside.*]

[*Enter*] Proteus, Silvia, Julia [*disguised as Sebastian*].

Pro. Madam, this service I have done for you
(Though you respect not aught your servant doth)
To hazard life, and rescue you from him
That would have forc'd your honor and your love.
Vouchsafe me, for my meed, but one fair look:
A smaller boon than this I cannot beg,
And less than this, I am sure you cannot give.

V.iii. Location: The forest.
3. **more**: greater. 4. **learn'd**: taught. **brook**: endure.
6. **gentleman**: i.e. Eglamour. His flight seems scarcely in character.
8. **Moyses**: variant of *Moses*.

V.iv. Location: The forest.
1. **use**: practice. 2. **desert**: deserted region. 6. **record**: sing.
7. **inhabit**: lodge. 13. **hallowing**: shouting.
15. **Have**: who have. **unhappy passenger**: unfortunate traveller.
20. **respect**: heed. 23. **meed**: reward. **fair**: kind.

Val. [*Aside.*] How like a dream is this! I see, and hear:
Love, lend me patience to forbear a while.
Sil. O miserable, unhappy that I am!
Pro. Unhappy were you, madam, ere I came;
But by my coming I have made you happy.
Sil. By thy approach thou mak'st me most unhappy.
Jul. [*Aside.*] And me, when he approacheth to your presence.
Sil. Had I been seized by a hungry lion,
I would have been a breakfast to the beast
Rather than have false Proteus rescue me.
O heaven be judge how I love Valentine,
Whose life's as tender to me as my soul!
And full as much (for more there cannot be)
I do detest false perjur'd Proteus.
Therefore be gone, solicit me no more.
Pro. What dangerous action, stood it next to death,
Would I not undergo for one calm look?
O, 'tis the curse in love, and still approv'd,
When women cannot love where they're belov'd!
Sil. When Proteus cannot love where he's belov'd!
Read over Julia's heart (thy first best love),
For whose dear sake thou didst then rend thy faith
Into a thousand oaths; and all those oaths
Descended into perjury, to love me.
Thou hast no faith left now, unless thou'dst two,
And that's far worse than none: better have none
Than plural faith, which is too much by one.
Thou counterfeit to thy true friend!
Pro. In love
Who respects friend?
Sil. All men but Proteus.
Pro. Nay, if the gentle spirit of moving words
Can no way change you to a milder form,
I'll woo you like a soldier, at arm's end,
And love you 'gainst the nature of love—force ye.
Sil. O heaven!
Pro. I'll force thee yield to my desire.
Val. [*Coming forward.*] Ruffian! let go that rude uncivil touch,
Thou friend of an ill fashion!
Pro. Valentine!
Val. Thou common friend, that's without faith or love,
For such is a friend now! treacherous man,
Thou hast beguil'd my hopes! Nought but mine eye
Could have persuaded me; now I dare not say
I have one friend alive; thou wouldst disprove me.
Who should be trusted, when one's right hand
Is perjured to the bosom? Proteus,
I am sorry I must never trust thee more,
But count the world a stranger for thy sake.
The private wound is deepest: O time most accurst!
'Mongst all foes that a friend should be the worst!
Pro. My shame and guilt confounds me.
Forgive me, Valentine; if hearty sorrow
Be a sufficient ransom for offense,
I tender't here: I do as truly suffer
As e'er I did commit.
Val. Then I am paid;
And once again I do receive thee honest.
Who by repentance is not satisfied
Is nor of heaven nor earth, for these are pleas'd;
By penitence th' Eternal's wrath's appeas'd:
And that my love may appear plain and free,
All that was mine in Silvia I give thee.
Jul. O me unhappy! [*Swoons.*]
Pro. Look to the boy.
Val. Why, boy! why, wag! how now? what's the matter? Look up; speak.
Jul. O good sir, my master charg'd me to deliver a ring to Madam Silvia, which (out of my neglect) was never done.
Pro. Where is that ring, boy?
Jul. Here 'tis; this is it. [*Shows a ring.*]
Pro. How? let me see.
Why, this is the ring I gave to Julia.
Jul. O, cry you mercy, sir, I have mistook;
This is the ring you sent to Silvia.
[*Shows another ring.*]
Pro. But how cam'st thou by this ring? At my depart
I gave this unto Julia.
Jul. And Julia herself did give it me,
And Julia herself hath brought it hither.
Pro. How? Julia?
Jul. Behold her that gave aim to all thy oaths,
And entertain'd 'em deeply in her heart.
How oft hast thou with perjury cleft the root?
O Proteus, let this habit make thee blush!
Be thou asham'd that I have took upon me
Such an immodest raiment—if shame live
In a disguise of love!
It is the lesser blot, modesty finds,
Women to change their shapes than men their minds.
Pro. Than men their minds? 'tis true. O heaven, were man
But constant, he were perfect; that one error
Fills him with faults; makes him run through all th' sins:
Inconstancy falls off ere it begins.
What is in Silvia's face, but I may spy
More fresh in Julia's with a constant eye?
Val. Come, come, a hand from either.
Let me be blest to make this happy close;
'Twere pity two such friends should be long foes.

31. **approach:** i.e. advances. 37. **tender:** dear.
42. **undergo:** undertake. **calm:** i.e. gentle.
43. **still approv'd:** ever attested by experience.
54. **respects:** considers.
57. **arm's end:** sword's point (with bawdy innuendo).
61. **fashion:** kind (perhaps with reference to the kind of friendship now fashionable; see lines 62–63).
62–63. **common . . . now:** i.e. ordinary, commonplace friend, which, as friendship is valued to-day, means one without faith or love.

73. **confounds:** destroys. 77. **commit:** transgress, sin.
78. **receive:** acknowledge, believe.
94. **cry you mercy:** I beg your pardon.
101. **gave aim to:** was the object of.
103. **root:** i.e. the bottom of the heart. 104. **habit:** garb.
106–7. **if . . . love:** if a disguise assumed for love's sake can produce shame.
113. **Inconstancy . . . begins:** an inconstant man begins to be faithless even before he has declared his love.
115. **constant:** steadfast, faithful. 117. **close:** union.

Pro. Bear witness, heaven, I have my wish for ever.
Jul. And I mine.

[*Enter*] Duke, Thurio, Outlaws.

Outlaws. A prize, a prize, a prize!
Val. Forbear, forbear, I say; it is my lord the Duke.
Your Grace is welcome to a man disgrac'd,
Banished Valentine.
Duke. Sir Valentine!
Thu. Yonder is Silvia; and Silvia's mine.
Val. Thurio, give back, or else embrace thy death;
Come not within the measure of my wrath.
Do not name Silvia thine; if once again,
[Milan] shall not hold thee. Here she stands,
Take but possession of her with a touch:
I dare thee but to breathe upon my love.
Thu. Sir Valentine, I care not for her, I;
I hold him but a fool that will endanger
His body for a girl that loves him not.
I claim her not, and therefore she is thine.
Duke. The more degenerate and base art thou
To make such means for her as thou hast done,
And leave her on such slight conditions.
Now, by the honor of my ancestry,
I do applaud thy spirit, Valentine,
And think thee worthy of an empress' love.
Know then, I here forget all former griefs,
Cancel all grudge, repeal thee home again,
Plead a new state in thy unrivall'd merit,

121. A prize: booty. **126. give back:** stand back.
127. measure: reach (i.e. of his sword).
137. make such means: use such efforts.
138. on . . . conditions: so easily. **142. griefs:** grievances.
143. repeal: recall from exile.
144. Plead . . . state: argue (that there is) a new condition of things (Leech).

To which I thus subscribe: Sir Valentine,
Thou art a gentleman and well deriv'd,
Take thou thy Silvia, for thou hast deserv'd her.
Val. I thank your Grace; the gift hath made me happy.
I now beseech you (for your daughter's sake)
To grant one boon that I shall ask of you.
Duke. I grant it (for thine own) what e'er it be.
Val. These banish'd men, that I have kept withal,
Are men endu'd with worthy qualities.
Forgive them what they have committed here,
And let them be recall'd from their exile;
They are reformed, civil, full of good,
And fit for great employment, worthy lord.
Duke. Thou hast prevail'd, I pardon them and thee;
Dispose of them as thou know'st their deserts.
Come, let us go, we will include all jars
With triumphs, mirth, and rare solemnity.
Val. And as we walk along, I dare be bold
With our discourse to make your Grace to smile.
What think you of this page, my lord?
Duke. I think the boy hath grace in him; he blushes.
Val. I warrant you, my lord—more grace than boy.
Duke. What mean you by that saying?
Val. Please you, I'll tell you as we pass along,
That you will wonder what hath fortuned.
Come, Proteus, 'tis your penance but to hear
The story of your loves discovered;
That done, our day of marriage shall be yours,
One feast, one house, one mutual happiness. *Exeunt.*

152. kept withal: lived with.
156–57. They . . . employment. An attempt to include everyone in the happy ending, but a little awkward in view of Valentine's comment in lines 14–17. **160. include all jars:** conclude all discords.
161. solemnity: festivity.
169. That: so that. **wonder:** marvel at. **fortuned:** happened.

NOTE ON THE TEXT

The sole authority for *The Two Gentlemen of Verona* is the First Folio (1623); all later texts are derived from that source. On the whole, F1 offers a sound enough text, but there is real confusion in the use of the place names Verona, Milan, and Padua (see Textual Notes, II.v.2, III.i.81, V.iv.129).

As in the case of *The Tempest,* the manuscript underlying the F1 text is believed to have been a transcript specially prepared for the printers by Ralph Crane (for whose scribal characteristics see the "Note on the Text" to *The Tempest*). The transcript differed from the copy for *The Tempest,* however, in one important respect: it employed (in common with the copy for *The Merry Wives of Windsor* and that for *The Winter's Tale,* two other probable Crane transcripts) the so-called "massed entry" technique. Under this system, the names of all the characters who are to take part in a scene are grouped together, usually in order of appearance, in a single inclusive entry direction at the opening of the scene, and no points of entry are indicated in the text for those characters in the group who actually enter later. Exits within the scene are also generally ignored. Other examples of the "massed entry" technique occur outside of Shakespeare, but no entirely satisfactory explanation of its employment has been advanced. The theory of "assembled texts," principally developed by Dover Wilson, which holds that it arose from the use of copy-text made up by assembling players' parts, is now discredited. The prevailing current view sees the practice as a misguided attempt by the scribe (or, in some cases, the author) to imitate the formal aspects of neo-classical scene division. By this convention, a new scene was indicated upon the entrance of each major character or group of characters by means of a list which included, though without the direction "Enter," first the newly entered character or characters (and, not infrequently, those who were to enter later in the scene), then those characters remaining on stage from the scene just ended; and neither points of later entry within the scene nor exits were marked. Since *The Two Gentlemen,* like *The Merry Wives* and *The Winter's Tale,* is regularly divided in F1 into acts and scenes on the usual Elizabethan principle (a new scene being indicated by a cleared stage), the "massed entry" technique produces only confusion.

There is nothing in the F1 text to suggest that the copy

behind Crane's transcript was a prompt-book. Indeed, the kind of tangle represented by the Verona-Milan-Padua difficulties would surely have been cleared up in any copy immediately associated with the stage. Crane's copy, without the "massed entries" introduced by Crane, was probably some form of Shakespeare's "foul papers" (Wells/Taylor, Schlueter).

For further information, see: J. D. Wilson, ed., New Shakespeare *The Two Gentlemen of Verona* (Cambridge, 1921); W. W. Greg, *The Shakespeare First Folio* (Oxford, 1955); Clifford Leech, ed., New Arden *The Two Gentlemen of Verona* (London, 1969); Stanley Wells, Gary Taylor, et al., *William Shakespeare: A Textual Companion* (Oxford, 1987); Kurt Schlueter, ed., New Cambridge *The Two Gentlemen of Verona* (Cambridge, 1990).

TEXTUAL NOTES

Dramatis personae: *as given in F1, following the play, with a few additions by Pope and later editors*
Proteus] *Steevens;* Protheus *F1 (throughout)*
Antonio] *Capell;* Anthonio *F1*
page] *Capell;* a clownish servant, *F1*
a clownish servant] *transferred, following Leech, from F1 description of Speed;* the like *F1*
Panthino] *Capell;* Panthion *F1*
Act-scene division: *from F1*

I.i

Location: *Wilson (after Theobald)*
o.s.d. **Enter . . . Proteus.]** *Rowe;* Valentine: Protheus, and Speed. *F1 (an example of the "massed entries" used throughout the F1 text; Speed does not actually enter until l. 69)*
2 **Home-keeping youth]** *F2;* Home-keeping-youth *F1*
13 **travel]** *F4;* trauaile *F1*
24 **over shoes]** *Rowe;* ouer-shooes *F1*
25 **over boots]** *Rowe;* ouer-bootes *F1*
57 **Milan]** *Rowe (subs.);* Millaine *F1 (generally throughout)*
65 **leave]** *Pope;* loue *F1*
65 **all,]** *Dyce;* all *F1*
69 **s.d. Enter Speed.]** *Rowe*
77 **a]** *F2*
93 **"baa."]** *Capell;* baâ. *F1 (F1 form suggests doubling of the "a" sound)*
109 **lover.]** *F2;* louer *F1*
110 **s.d. Speed . . . questioningly.]** *Sisson (subs.; after Theobald, Nicholson conj.)*
111 **Ay]** *Nicholson conj.;* I *F1*
112 **Nod-ay]** *Cambridge (subs.);* Nod-I *F1*
113–4 **You . . . "Ay."]** *as prose, Capell; as verse, F1*
123–4 **Marry . . . pains.]** *as prose, Capell; as verse, F1*
136–41 **Sir . . . steel.]** *as prose, Capell; as verse, F1*
142 **she? Nothing?]** *Cambridge;* she, nothing? *F1*
143–5 **No . . . me;]** *as prose, Capell; as verse, F1*
145 **testern'd]** *F2;* cestern'd *F1*
150 **s.d. Exit Speed.]** *Dyce*

I.ii

Location: *Capell*
5 **parle]** *Rowe;* par'le *F1*
56 **"ay"]** *Rowe (subs.);* I *F1*
66 **s.d. Enter Lucetta.]** *Rowe*
78 **set.]** *F2;* set *F1 (possibly the lack of pointing in F1 indicates an interrupted speech)*
80 **"Light o' love."]** *Theobald;* Light O, Loue. *F1*
85 **s.d. Takes the letter.]** *Kittredge (after Capell, Collier)*
93 **your]** *F2;* you *F1*
96 **s.d. Tears the letter.]** *Pope*
100 **s.d. Exit.]** *F2*
108 **bruising stones]** *F2;* bruzing-stones *F1*
126 **s.d. Enter Lucetta.]** *Pope*
137 **will't]** *Rowe;* wilt *F1*

I.iii

Location: *Theobald*
o.s.d. **Enter . . . Panthino.]** *Rowe (subs.);* Enter Antonio and Panthino. Protheus. *F1*
24 **whither]** *F2;* whether *F1*
43 **s.d. Enter Proteus.]** *F2*
50 **O]** *F2; Pro.* Oh *F1 (repeated s.p.)*
70 **readiness]** *F2;* readinesse, *F1*
77 **s.d. Exeunt . . . Panthino.]** *Rowe*
87 **s.d. Enter Panthino.]** *Rowe*
88 **father]** *F2;* Fathers *F1*
91 **s.d. Exeunt.]** Exeunt. Finis. *F1*

II.i

Location: *Pope, Theobald*
o.s.d. **Enter . . . Speed.]** *Rowe;* Enter Valentine, Speed, Siluia. *F1*
6 **s.d. Shouting.]** *Kittredge*
52–3 **well favor'd]** *F2;* well-fauourd *F1*
54–5 **I . . . infinite.]** *as prose, Capell; as verse, F1*
66–7 **I . . . beautiful.]** *as prose, Capell; as verse, F1*
79–80 **Belike . . . shoes.]** *as prose, Rowe; as verse, F1*
87–8 **Last . . . loves.]** *as prose, Pope; as verse, F1*
92 **s.d. Enter Silvia.]** *Rowe (after l. 93); placed as in Kittredge*
94, 98, 102 **s.dd. Aside.]** *Capell*
98 **ye good ev'n]** *Rowe (subs.);* ye-good-ev'n *F1*
109 **hardly off]** *F2;* hardly-off *F1*
113 **stead]** *Capell;* steed *F1*
119 **s.d. Aside.]** *Rowe*
139 **device]** *F4;* deuise *F1*
148 **woos]** *Rowe;* woes *F1 (generally)*
152–4 **What . . . jest?]** *as prose, Capell; as verse, F1*
156–7 **No . . . earnest?]** *as prose, Pope; as verse, F1*
165–8 **"For . . . lover."]** *quotes, Theobald*

II.ii

Location: *Pope, Theobald*
o.s.d. **Enter . . . Julia.]** *Rowe;* Enter Protheus, Iulia, Panthion. *F1*
5 **s.d. Giving a ring.]** *Rowe*
16 **s.d. Exit Julia.]** *Rowe*
18 **s.d. Enter Panthino.]** *Capell (after Rowe); note that the form is* Panthion *in F1 o.s.d.*

II.iii

Location: *Theobald*
o.s.d. **Enter . . . dog.]** *Pope (subs., after Rowe);* Enter Launce, Panthion. *F1*
27–8 **wood woman]** *Theobald;* would-woman *F1*
32 **s.d. Enter Panthino.]** *Capell (after Rowe); note that the form is* Panthion *in F1 o.s.d.*
33 **aboard]** *F4;* a Boord *F1*
37–8 **tied . . . unkindest tied]** *Theobald;* tide vnkindest Tide *F1*
38 **tied.]** *Pope;* tide. *F1*
40 **tied]** *Pope;* tide *F1*
49 **tail!]** *Dyce;* Taile. *F1*
51 **tied]** *Singer;* tide *F1*

II.iv

Location: *Pope, Theobald*
o.s.d. **Enter . . . Speed.]** *Rowe;* Enter Valentine, Siluia, Thurio, Speed, Duke, Protheus. *F1*
7 **s.d. Exit.]** *Cambridge*
37–40 **Yourself . . . company.]** *as prose, Pope; as verse, F1*
43–8 **I . . . father.]** *as prose, Pope; as verse, F1*
48 **s.d. Enter Duke.]** *Rowe*
86 **s.d. Exit.]** *Rowe*
97 **yourself:]** *F4;* your selfe, *F1*
99 **s.d. Exit Thurio.]** *Collier*
99 **s.d. Enter Proteus.]** *Rowe*
108 **worthy]** *F2;* worthy a *F1*
115 **s.d. Enter Thurio.]** *Collier*
121 **s.d. Exeunt . . . Thurio.]** *Rowe*
166 **makes]** *F2;* make *F1*
191 **s.d. Exit Valentine.]** *Rowe;* Exit. *F1 (after l. 190)*
196 **Is . . . praise,]** *Malone (after F2* Is it mine then, or *Valentineans* praise?); It is mine, or Valentines praise? *F1*
205 **too too]** *Rowe;* too-too *F1*
210 **dazzled]** *Rowe;* dazel'd *F1;* dazel'd so *F2*
214 **s.d. Exit.]** *F2;* Exeunt. *F1*

II.v

Location: *Theobald*
o.s.d. **meeting]** *Capell*
2 **Milan]** *Pope;* Padua *F1*
8 **Come on]** *F4;* Come-on *F1*
42 **that]** *F2;* that that *F1*
53 **wilt,]** *Knight;* wilt *F1*

II.vi

Location: *Capell (subs.)*
1–2 **Julia— . . . Silvia—]** *Wilson;* Iulia; . . . Siluia; *F1*
35 **counsel]** *Theobald;* counsaile *F1*

II.vii

Location: *Pope, Theobald*
67 **withal]** *F2;* with all *F1*
70 **of infinite]** as infinite *F2*

III.i

Location: *Theobald*
o.s.d. **Enter . . . Proteus.]** *Rowe;* Enter Duke, Thurio, Protheus, Valentine, Launce, Speed. *F1*
2 **s.d. Exit Thurio.]** *Rowe*
50 **s.d. Exit.]** *Rowe*
50 **s.d. Enter Valentine.]** *Rowe;* Enter. *F2*
81 **Milano]** *Collier MS (after Pope);* Verona *F1*
83 **nought]** *F2;* naught *F1*
139 **s.d. Reads.]** *Rowe*
144 **rest them]** *F4;* rest-them *F1*
169 **s.d. Exit.]** *F2*
173 **self,]** *F2;* selfe. *F1*
187 **s.d. Enter . . . Launce.]** *F2*
189 **Soho, soho!]** *Theobald (subs.);* So-hough, Soa hough— *F1*
212 **Silvia.]** *F4 (subs.);* Siluia, *F1*
223 **banished]** *Rowe;* banish'd *F1*
246 **Here]** *F3;* Here, *F1*
262 **s.d. Exeunt . . . Proteus.]** *Theobald;* Exeunt. *F2*
273–4 **s.d. Pulling . . . paper.]** *Rowe*
278 **milk.]** *Rowe (subs.);* milke, *F1*
279 **s.d. Enter Speed.]** *F2*
282 **master's ship]** *Theobald;* Mastership *F1*
301 **s.d. Reads.]** *Capell*
318 **"bastard virtues"]** *Rowe:* Bastard-vertues *F1 (in italics)*
321 **follow]** *F1 (c);* followes *F1 (u) (the uncorrected form should perhaps be retained)*
323 **kiss'd]** *Rowe* (kist)
333–6 **O . . . virtue.]** *as prose, Pope; as verse, F1*
338–9 **Out . . . her.]** *as prose, Pope; as verse, F1*
353 **hair]** *F1 (c);* haires *F1 (u)*

356 **that last]** *F1 (c)*; that *F1 (u)*
359 **be;]** *Theobald;* be *F1*
372 **then]** *F4;* then, *F1*
381 s.d. **Exit.]** *Capell*
384 s.d. **Exit.]** *Capell;* Exeunt. *F1*

III.ii

Location: *Capell (subs.)*
o.s.d. **Enter . . . Thurio.]** *Rowe;* Enter Duke, Thurio, Protheus. *F1*
10 s.d. **Enter Proteus.]** *Rowe*
14 **grievously.]** *Capell;* grieuously? *F1 (c)*; heauily? *F1 (u)*
85 **sweet-complaining]** *hyphen, Capell*
93 **advice]** *F2;* aduise *F1*

IV.i

Location: *Neilson-Hill*
7 **friends—]** *Pope;* friends. *F1*
34 **travel]** *F3;* trauaile *F1*
35 **been]** *F2;* beene often *F1*
47 **An . . . near]** *Theobald;* And heire and Neece, *F1*
61 **this]** the *F2*

IV.ii

Location: *Theobald (subs.)*
o.s.d. **Enter Proteus.]** *Rowe;* Enter Protheus, Thurio, Iulia, Host, Musitian, Siluia. *F1*
15 s.d. **Enter . . . Musicians.]** *Rowe; note that F1 o.s.d. has* Musitian
25 s.d. **Enter . . . Sebastian.]** *ed. (after Rowe, Capell)*
35 s.d. **Music plays.]** *Capell*
38 **hear 'em]** *F3;* heare'm *F1*
61–2 **Not . . . heart-strings.]** *as prose, Pope; as verse, F1*
71 **thing?]** *Pope;* thing. *F1*
84 s.d. **Exeunt . . . Musicians.]** *Rowe*
84 s.d. **Enter . . . window.]** *Theobald (after Rowe)*
107, 118, 126 s.dd. **Aside.]** *Pope*
113 **his]** *F2;* her *F1*
133 s.d. **Exeunt . . . Silvia.]** *Rowe;* Exeunt. *F2*
137–8 **Marry . . . day.]** *as prose, Pope; as verse, F1*
140 s.d. **Exeunt.]** *F2*

IV.iii

Location: *ed. (after Capell)*
o.s.d. **Enter Eglamour.]** *Rowe;* Enter Eglamore, Siluia. *F1*
4 s.d. **Enter . . . window.]** *Theobald*
11–2 **gentleman— . . . not—]** *Pope (subs.)*; Gentleman: / Thinke . . . flatter (for . . . not) *F1*
17 **abhors]** *Hanmer;* abhor'd *F1*
37–8 **grievances, Which]** *to ease the sense between ll. 37 and 38, Collier MS reads:* grievances, / And the most true affections that you bear; / Which
40 **Reaking]** *ed.;* Wreaking *F1*

IV.iv

Location: *ed. (after Wilson)*
o.s.d. **Enter . . . dog.]** *Pope (after Rowe)*; Enter Launce, Protheus, Iulia, Siluia. *F1*
17 **gentleman-like dogs]** *Rowe;* gentleman-like-dogs *F1*
39 s.d. **Enter . . . Sebastian.]** *ed. (after Rowe)*
43 s.d. **To Launce.]** *Johnson*
47 **jewel]** *Pope;* Iewell *F1 (F4 italicizes; Wilson suggests that the F1 capital indicates that* Jewel *is the dog's name; evidently the compositor of F4 thought so)*
52–3 **No . . . again.]** *as prose, Pope; as verse, F1*
55–8 **Ay . . . greater.]** *as prose, Pope; as verse, F1*
61 s.d. **Exit Launce.]** *Rowe (after F2* Exit., *both following l. 62); placed as in Capell*
70 **thou]** *F2;* thee *F1*
74 **to]** *F2;* not *F1*
89 s.d. **Exit.]** *F2*
107 s.d. **Enter Silvia attended.]** *Malone (after Rowe)*
149–50 **is: . . . well,]** *Rowe (subs.)*; is, . . . well; *F1*
165 **agood]** *F2;* a good *F1*
179 s.d. **Exit . . . Attendants.]** *Dyce;* Exit. *F2 (after l. 178)*
205 s.d. **Exit.]** *F2;* Exeunt. *F1*

V.i

Location: *Pope, Capell*
o.s.d. **Enter Eglamour.]** *Rowe;* Enter Eglamoure, Siluia. *F1*
7 s.d. **Enter Silvia.]** *Rowe*

V.ii

Location: *Theobald (subs.)*
o.s.d. **Enter . . . Sebastian.]** *ed. (after Rowe)*; Enter Thurio, Protheus, Iulia, Duke. *F1*
7 s.p., s.d. **Jul. Aside.]** *Boswell conj.;* Pro. *F1*
13 s.p., s.d. **Jul. Aside.]** *Rowe;* Thu. *F1*
18, 21, 24, 28 s.dd. **Aside.]** *Capell*
18 **your]** *F3;* you *F1*
30 s.d. **Enter Duke.]** *Rowe*
32 **saw]** say saw Sir *F2;* saw Sir *F4*
44 **stand]** *F2;* stand, *F1*
48 s.d. **Exit.]** *Rowe*
52 s.d. **Exit.]** *Capell*
54 s.d. **Exit.]** *Capell*
56 s.d. **Exit.]** *Capell;* Exeunt. *F1*

V.iii

Location: *Pope*
o.s.d. **Enter]** *Rowe*

V.iv

Location: *Pope*
o.s.d. **Enter Valentine.]** *Rowe;* Enter Valentine, Protheus, Siluia, Iulia, Duke, Thurio, Out-lawes. *F1*
12 s.d. **Shouts within.]** *Collier (subs.)*
18 s.d. **Steps aside.]** *Johnson*
18 s.d. **Enter . . . Sebastian.]** *ed. (after Rowe)*
26 s.d. **Aside.]** *Theobald*
32 s.d. **Aside.]** *Rowe*
49 **love]** deceive *F2*
49 **me.]** *F4 (subs.)*; me, *F1*
57 **woo]** move *F2*
57 **arm's]** *Capell;* armes *F1*
60 s.d. **Coming forward.]** *Collier MS*
63 **Treacherous]** Thou treacherous *F2*
67 **trusted]** trusted now *F2*
84 s.d. **Swoons.]** *Pope*
91 s.d. **Shows a ring.]** *ed. (after Johnson)*
95 s.d. **Shows another ring.]** *Johnson*
113 **falls off]** *F2;* falls-off *F1*
120 s.d. **Enter . . . Outlaws.]** *Rowe*
121 s.p. **Outlaws.]** *Dyce;* Out-l. *F1*
129 **Milan]** *Theobald;* Verona *F1*
144 **unrivall'd]** arrival'd *F2*
173 s.d. **Exeunt.]** Exeunt. *[list of actors]* FINIS. *F1*

Love's Labor's Lost

Love's Labor's Lost is perhaps the most relentlessly Elizabethan of all Shakespeare's plays. Filled with word games, elaborate conceits, parodies of spoken and written styles and obscure topical allusions, it continually requires—and baffles—scholarly explanation. Nothing can ever make most of the puns and witticisms of *Love's Labor's Lost* seem contemporary again. They are rooted too firmly in a specific society and moment of historical time. Hazlitt and Dr. Johnson thought the comedy wholly insignificant, a piece of linguistic self-indulgence which Shakespeare happily outgrew, and this view was shared until comparatively recently by the majority of critics. As with *Troilus and Cressida*, the rediscovery of the play seems to have originated in the postwar theatre. Despite the inaccessibility of much of the dialogue, *Love's Labor's Lost* has repeatedly demonstrated that it can communicate its quality and concerns to a modern audience which, although it may not be able to explain just why "a costard broken in a shin" (III.i.70) should be funny, responds to the freshness and brilliance of the comedy just the same. A major critical revaluation has accompanied this theatrical success. In particular, that old concern with the play as a supposed mine of concealed information about the activities and character of various prominent Elizabethans has fallen out of favor. There is, after all, not a shred of proof that Shakespeare was really satirizing Gabriel Harvey in the person of the pedant Holofernes, or that the famous crux at IV.iii.251 can be resolved through reference to a free-thinking "school of night" associated with Raleigh. Contemporary references of this kind, if and where they exist, are ultimately less important than the nature of *Love's Labor's Lost* as a complex and quite autonomous work of art.

Although the textual history of *Love's Labor's Lost* is unclear, scholars no longer regard it as a very early play. Theories that it was originally commissioned for performance outdoors in the grounds of some great country house are in many ways attractive, but remain hypothetical. Certainly it was played at court before the Queen during the Christmas revels of 1597 or 1598 and at Southampton's house to celebrate his release from prison in 1604. The Second Quarto also mentions public performances at the Globe and at Blackfriars. That the comedy was revised by Shakespeare at some point seems plain, but no agreement has ever been reached as to the date and extent of these alterations. The First Quarto of 1598 describes itself as "Newly corrected and augmented" and there are some obvious tracks in the snow registered at IV.iii.292–314 and again at V.ii.817–22 (see the Textual Notes). On the whole, a date around 1595 seems right for the main body of the play, although Shakespeare may have been tinkering with the text as late as 1597. A connection between Rosaline and the Dark Lady of the sonnets has long been recognized but, considering the notorious impossibility of arriving at a date for the sonnets, is scarcely helpful in placing the composition of *Love's Labor's Lost*. More promising are the stylistic affinities with *Romeo and Juliet*, *Richard II*, and *A Midsummer Night's Dream*. Different though they are in form and subject matter, the four plays nonetheless seem to constitute a natural group. All of them are lyrical and ornate, various and highly patterned in their verse forms. Quintessentially Elizabethan, they share a kind of linguistic exuberance and also a delight in exploring and extending their particular dramatic genres.

Between *A Midsummer Night's Dream* and *Love's Labor's Lost*, as might be expected, the connection is especially close. Both comedies belong to that small group of Shakespeare's plays for which there appears to be no narrative or dramatic source. Shakespeare could have read in the *Académie Française* of P. de la Primaudaye, translated into English in 1586, about the ideal of a league of study. Berowne, Dumaine, Longaville, Boyet, and Marcade are Anglicized versions of names belonging to actual French noblemen of the late sixteenth century. In 1578, Marguerite de Valois made a state visit with a retinue of ladies to her estranged husband Henry of Navarre, in the course of which they discussed the disposition of Aquitaine. One of Marguerite's ladies-in-waiting had a daughter, Hélène de Tournon, who seems, like Katherine's sister, to have died of love. Behind Holofernes lies a character type familiar in the *commedia dell'arte*, while Don Armado can trace his lineage back to the braggart warrior of Greek New Comedy. These few hints and suggestions do not provide much in the way of a narrative framework, and indeed the plot of *Love's Labor's Lost* is even more slender than that of *A Midsummer Night's Dream*. Action, in any sense that Aristotle would have understood, is confined to two arrivals: that of the Princess and her ladies in Act II, which destroys the Academe, and that of the messenger at the end, which destroys something even larger. Between these two very different invasions of the royal park the comedy unfolds entirely through the juxtaposition of attitudes and styles of wit, and through little, contrived shows: the masque of the Muscovites, or that Pageant of the Nine Worthies which stands in the equivalent position to the Pyramus and Thisby interlude in *A Midsummer Night's Dream*. In this play too a certain self-consciousness about comedy as a form becomes particularly striking in the fifth act.

As the title informs us from the start, love's labor will be lost, not won. In defiance of an immemorial comic convention, this play ends in partings, with the severance of people in love and not with marriage. Moreover, it draws attention to its own unorthodoxy.

> Our wooing doth not end like an old play:
> Jack hath not Gill. These ladies' courtesy
> Might well have made our sport a comedy.
> (V.ii.874–76)

Berowne's rueful comment stresses the violation of an accepted dramatic formula: "Jack shall have Jill; / Nought shall go ill; / The man shall have his mare again, and all shall be well" (*A Midsummer Night's Dream*, III.ii.461–63). Although there is hope at the end that these marriages may merely be postponed, a year, as Berowne recognizes, is "too long for a play" (V.ii.878). The gradual revelation of why this should be so, why the women must reject their suitors and demand a resolution outside the limits of comedy, is the main business of *Love's Labor's Lost*: in fact, its plot.

The scheme of the Academe, through which Navarre and his friends hope to defeat Time and live forever in the memories of men, is both misguided and untenable. It is not, however, either ludicrous or contemptible. Navarre's image of "cormorant devouring Time" (I.i.4) is near-allied to that "devouring Time" of the sonnets which blunts the lion's paws and burns the long-lived phoenix in her blood. In the sonnets Shakespeare proposes two weapons against Time: children and, more persuasively, poetry. Navarre's Academe, significantly, has nothing to do either with the begetting of children or with the perpetuation of an actual love experience in verse. Navarre's attempt to prolong life by turning his back on it, forswearing women, liberty, festivity, and rest is not only paradoxical: it represents a sterile "treason 'gainst the kingly state of youth" (IV.iii.289). Three years of youth, as Berowne knows from the start, are too precious to sacrifice in the interests of a dubious memory on earth which will not even fall due until the king and his three friends are dead. Meanwhile, there is the sobering example of that dedicated scholar Holofernes: an embodiment of the pointless learning of those pedants who may be able to name all the stars in the firmament yet "have no more profit of their shining nights / Than those that walk and wot not what they are" (I.i.90–91).

The Academe, of course, is never in any real danger of succeeding. Almost before the ink is dry on the King's new edict forbidding any converse with women, the law is violated by Costard the clown. His trespass is immediately compounded by that of Don Armado, the haughty Spaniard who informs on Costard and then proceeds to court Jaquenetta himself. In the effort to escape punishment for his offense, Costard goes through a remarkable series of linguistic gyrations. If the proclamation specified a year's imprisonment for being taken with a wench, Costard will claim she was not a wench at all, but a damsel. Told that *damsel* too is covered by the law, he tries *virgin* and *maid* in rapid succession only to discover in the end that facts are facts and cannot be altered by verbal description. Navarre consigns him to prison and a diet of bran and water. Costard's defeat here constitutes a warning to the King and his courtiers, but they are not yet ready to heed it. Only with the entrance of the Princess of France and her ladies in Act II does the dangerous falsity of the language customarily employed by Navarre and his friends come under direct attack.

The Princess and her retinue come from a world outside the confines of Navarre that is colder and more realistic than the playground of the park. They too are witty, and they like to play with words. Unlike the men, however, they play their verbal games without ever losing sight of facts and situations. When Navarre bids the Princess "welcome to the court of Navarre," she reminds him sharply that

" 'welcome' I have not yet. The roof of this court is too high to be yours, and welcome to the wide fields too base to be mine" (II.i.91–94). Although she is cheerfully willing to accept a lodging in the open air because of the King's vow, she refuses to allow him to confuse her tent with the court. Throughout the comedy the women are ruthless in their dismemberment of the airy rhetoric, the unexamined conceits and images offered by the men. The King, rashly declaring that he and the other "Muscovites" have "measur'd many miles" (V.ii.184) to have the pleasure of dancing with the Princess and her ladies, is disconcerted to be asked the precise number of inches in these miles he claims to have "measured." Berowne requests "one sweet word" with the Princess and is given "honey," "milk," and "sugar" and told to consider himself overpaid. He speaks metaphorically of his heart and its sufferings, according to the immemorial language of love, and finds that Rosaline insists upon answering him in the manner of someone about to administer the Elizabethan equivalent of a cardiogram.

This feminine literal-mindedness may be exasperating, but it is not merely perverse. The Princess and her ladies do not trust the oaths and protestations of their suitors, do not credit the sincerity of their love. In a sense, they are right to be sceptical. High-spirited and inventive though it is, the wit of Berowne, Navarre, Dumaine, and Longaville is fatally self-indulgent. It exists at too great a remove from reality, and it can be not only imperceptive but cruel. The masque of the Muscovites, the first of the two plays within the play, demonstrates that although Navarre and his friends may be in love, they are not really in love with Rosaline, Katherine, Maria, and the Princess of France as individuals. These suitors judge by courtly outsides alone, in marked contrast to the women, who seize upon manners and traits of character in talking about the men they love and distrust in equal measure. When the women mask themselves and exchange favors, their lovers are completely and ignominiously taken in. Berowne woos the Princess instead of Rosaline; Dumaine mistakes Maria for Katherine; Longaville falls into the opposite error, and the King offers the realm of Navarre to Berowne's proper lady. By the end of the masque it has become apparent that the Academe, far from being the chief obstacle to love, was only a temporary and negligible block. Far more serious and disturbing are the habitual attitudes of the men and the verbal style which expresses and defines those attitudes.

With the failure of the masque of the Muscovites, a state of impasse seems to have been reached in the comedy. It is hard to see what the King and his friends can say to convince the women of their sincerity. Certainly their attempts at eloquence only work against them, and they have already proved the frailty of vows: "If love make me forsworn, how shall I swear to love?" (IV.ii.105). At this point of stalemate, Costard enters to announce that the Pageant of the Nine Worthies is at hand. On the politic ground that it will be as well to have one show worse than that of the King and his companions, Navarre agrees to see it. The decision is crucial.

Although the actors who participate in the pageant are an unpromising lot ("The pedant, the braggart, the hedge-priest, the fool, and the boy"), their intentions are of the very best, and they are also more sensitive and vulnerable to mockery than Bottom and the rude mechanicals of *A Midsummer Night's Dream*. In this audience, however, only the women are civil, refusing to take any part in the mounting storm of hilarity by which the actors are assailed. Indeed the Princess does all she can to counteract it, encouraging the performers and thanking them courteously for their pains. Her attitude is poles apart from that of the King and his courtiers, who begin by deriding the entertainment itself and end, inexcusably, by savaging individual actors not for their performances but for being the real-life people they are. Nathaniel the curate retires in dismay while Holofernes, in the role of Judas Maccabaeus, stumbles away through the gathering darkness with the reproach, "This is not generous, not gentle, not humble" (V.ii.629). Don Armado is treated worst of all but, significantly, he is concerned less for his own humiliation than for that of Hector, the hero he represents: "The sweet war-man is dead and rotten, sweet chucks, beat not the bones of the buried. When he breathed, he was a man" (V.ii.660–62). Navarre and his friends are not only forsworn; they are betraying precisely that ideal of immortality through fame which led them to found the Academe in the first place. It is Armado, eccentric though he is, who alone defends the dignity and worth of the dead, an issue about which the King once cared passionately, but which he appears to have forgotten now.

The Pageant of the Nine Worthies, naturally evocative of death and time, seems to concentrate and draw to itself all those images of mortality which have begun to make themselves felt in the last movement of the play. Although *Love's Labor's Lost* opens under the shadow of death, the great motivation for the Academe, it subsequently banishes not merely the threat but the very idea. Even the stag killed by the Princess becomes, in the alliterative verses of Holofernes, an unreal animal and its fate just about as credible as the executions ordered by the Queen at the garden party in *Alice in Wonderland*. Not until Act V do intimations of mortality begin to rise, slowly but disturbingly, through the fabric of the play, in the form of Katherine's sudden remembrance of her dead sister, Berowne's talk of plague symptoms, or his strident comparison of Holofernes to "a death's face in a ring" (V.ii.612). By way of this gradual massing of images, the triumph of Death in the person of Marcade is prepared for artistically without losing, in the theatre, any of its emotional shock:

> I am sorry, madam, for the news I bring
> Is heavy in my tongue. The King your father—
> (V.ii.718–19)

The Princess, however, has intuitions independent of words: "Dead, for my life!" The messenger does not need to complete the sentence he began. Within a matter of seconds, the comedy is checked in full career.

Vows began the play of *Love's Labor's Lost* and vows of another kind end it. The artificial enclosure of the royal park violated now by death and time, the King and his friends accept the need to seek out a harsher and less protected world. They also accept penance for their faults. Navarre is dismissed by the Princess to "some forlorn and naked hermitage" where he is to try for twelve months "if frosts and fasts, hard lodging and thin weeds / Nip not the gaudy blossoms of your love." At the end of this period he may address her again on the basis of "these deserts": tangible proofs of constancy and endurance, not mere words and promises. Dumaine and Longaville accept similar conditions from Katherine and Maria. Berowne, the most brilliant and also the most deeply tainted of the men, receives a penance even more severe. He is sent by Rosaline to test his wit against the reality of sickness and disease, to "jest a twelvemonth in a hospital." Intellectually, Berowne is entirely aware that "to move wild laughter in the throat of death" is impossible, something that cannot be. Emotionally, this is an experience which the man who led the assault upon the Nine Worthies needs to undergo. As Rosaline points out:

> A jest's prosperity lies in the ear
> Of him that hears it, never in the tongue
> Of him that makes it; then, if sickly ears,
> Deaf'd with the clamors of their own dear groans,
> Will hear your idle scorns, continue then,
> And I will have you and that fault withal;
> But if they will not, throw away that spirit,
> And I shall find you empty of that fault.
>
> (V.ii.861–68)

Language cannot exist in a vacuum. Even on what may seem to be its most trivial and humorous levels, it is an instrument of communication between people which demands that the speaker should consider the nature and feelings of the hearer. In love, above all, this is true—but it is also true in more ordinary relationships. Gently but firmly, the men are sent away to learn something that the women have known all along: how to accommodate speech to facts and to emotional realities, as opposed to using it as a means of evasion, idle amusement, or unthinking cruelty.

It may seem surprising that a play as verbally brilliant as *Love's Labor's Lost* should end by acknowledging the defeat of the word, but then the entire comedy is built upon paradox. The illogical scheme of the Academe at the beginning, the attempt to perpetuate life by denying it, is nicely balanced by the fact that it is the messenger at the end who breaks the impasse between the ladies of France and the suitors they cannot be persuaded to take seriously. Marcade, in his mourning clothes, makes it possible for the men's proposals of marriage to be entertained and for the redemptive trials and penances to be imposed. Only by accepting the reality of death as it exists in that world of plague and star-crossed love beyond the confines of the park can the men be freed from their self-imposed bondage. It is only by being, for a little while, lost that love's labor can eventually, and fully, be won.

As though conscious of the fact that in this resolution the arts of language have been subjected to an unfriendly scrutiny, Shakespeare allows them a restitution in the final song. Gathered together for the last time, before they disperse in their separate directions, all the characters of the comedy stand silently, for once, to hear the dialogue which the two learned men have composed in praise of the owl and the cuckoo. In doing so they seem to adumbrate that new social order, fragile and transitory but harmonious and at peace with itself, which the year of trial and penances may bring.

> When daisies pied, and violets blue,
> And lady-smocks all silver-white,
> And cuckoo-buds of yellow hue
> Do paint the meadows with delight,
> The cuckoo then on every tree
> Mocks married men, for thus sings he,
> "Cuckoo;
> Cuckoo, cuckoo"—O word of fear,
> Unpleasing to a married ear!

In a sense, this song recapitulates the entire development of the comedy. It begins with the enamelled, deliberately fanciful meadows of spring, moves on to a summer of frank sensuality, "When turtles tread, and rooks and daws, / And maidens bleach their summer smocks." It ends, like the action itself, in winter-time: the season of chill and deprivation.

> When icicles hang by the wall,
> And Dick the shepherd blows his nail,
> And Tom bears logs into the hall,
> And milk comes frozen home in pail;
> When blood is nipp'd, and ways be foul,
> Then nightly sings the staring owl,
> "Tu-whit, to-who"—
> A merry note,
> While greasy Joan doth keel the pot.

Yet despite this movement from spring towards winter, each season in the lyric contains a sense of its opposite. In the halcyon months of spring and summer the cuckoo's voice keeps human beings in touch with the realities of their condition in a world of time and mutability: with the threat of love grown old and bitter, with the metamorphosis of faith into infidelity and distrust. Conversely, winter is enlivened by the merry note of the owl, a voice of unexpected and compensating cheer in a dark season. The song presents a wholeness of outlook in which fact and fancy, youth and age, life and death are held in equilibrium. The unifying effect of the music must not be underestimated, but still this harmony is essentially verbal. The problem of how to create a truly meaningful language of love may still be unresolved for the people of the play: the year of penance remains to be lived through and its outcome cannot be predicted with confidence. Nevertheless, this final lyric stands as an encouraging indication of what language can do when handled rightly, of how finely—when it is honest and also disciplined by art—it can express the truth of the human condition. The balance held in the song is one which the women of France have possessed throughout, which Navarre and his friends have yet to acquire, and it holds the door open for a vindication of the arts of language after all.

Anne Barton

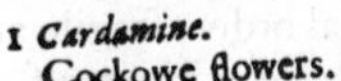

✻ *The description.*

1 THe first of the Cuckowe flowers, hath leaues at his springing vp somewhat rounde, and those that spring afterward grow iagged like the leaues of Greeke Valerian: among which riseth vp a stalke a foote long, set with the like leaues, but smaller and more iagged, resembling the leaues of Rocket. The flowers grow at the top in small bundels, white of colour, hollowe in the middle, resembling the white sweete Iohn: after which do come small chaffie huskes, or seede vessels, wherein the seede is conteined. The roote is small and threddie.

5 Milke white Ladie smockes hath stalkes rising immediately from the roote, deuiding themselues into sundrie small twiggie and hard braunches, set with leaues like those of Serpillum. The flowers growe at the top, made of fower leaues of a yellowish colour. The roote is tough and woddy, with some fibres annexed thereto.

✻ *The place.*

These kinds of Cuckowe flowers, grow not so much in waters as they do in moist medowes, and in such places as be verie often ouerflowen not onely with raine water, but also with riuers and ponds.

✻ *The time.*

These flower for the most part in Aprill and Maie, when the Cuckowe doth begin to sing her pleasant notes without stammering.

In composing the song that ends *Love's Labour's Lost*, Shakespeare may well have had in mind the passages above from John Gerard's *Herbal*, published late in 1597. Despite Gerard, he seems to treat lady-smocks and cuckoo-flowers as distinct kinds, though in assigning to the cuckoo-flower "buds of yellow hue" he borrows a detail from Gerard's description of the "Milke white Ladie smockes." *(By permission of the Harvard College Library)*

Love's Labor's Lost

[Dramatis Personae

Ferdinand, *King of Navarre*
Berowne, Longaville, Dumaine } *lords attending on the King*
Boyet, Marcade } *lords attending on the Princess of France*
Don Adriano de Armado, *a fantastical Spaniard*
Sir Nathaniel, *a curate*
Holofernes, *a schoolmaster*
Dull, *a constable*
Costard, *a clown*
Moth, *page to Armado*
Forester

The Princess of France
Rosaline, Maria, Katherine } *ladies attending on the Princess*
Jaquenetta, *a country wench*

Lords, Attendants, *etc.*

Scene: *Navarre*]

[ACT I, Scene I]

Enter Ferdinand, *King of Navarre*, Berowne, Longaville, *and* Dumaine.

King. Let fame, that all hunt after in their lives,
Live regist'red upon our brazen tombs,
And then grace us in the disgrace of death;
When spite of cormorant devouring Time,
Th' endeavor of this present breath may buy
That honor which shall bate his scythe's keen edge,
And make us heirs of all eternity.
Therefore, brave conquerors—for so you are,
That war against your own affections
And the huge army of the world's desires—
Our late edict shall strongly stand in force:
Navarre shall be the wonder of the world;
Our court shall be a little academe,
Still and contemplative in living art.
You three, Berowne, Dumaine, and Longaville,
Have sworn for three years' term to live with me,
My fellow scholars, and to keep those statutes
That are recorded in this schedule here.
Your oaths are pass'd, and now subscribe your names,
That his own hand may strike his honor down
That violates the smallest branch herein.
If you are arm'd to do, as sworn to do,
Subscribe to your deep oaths, and keep it too.

Long. I am resolved, 'tis but a three years' fast:
The mind shall banquet, though the body pine;
Fat paunches have lean pates; and dainty bits
Make rich the ribs, but bankrout quite the wits.

Dum. My loving lord, Dumaine is mortified:
The grosser manner of these world's delights
He throws upon the gross world's baser slaves;
To love, to wealth, to pomp, I pine and die,
With all these living in philosophy.

Ber. I can but say their protestation over:
So much, dear liege, I have already sworn,
That is, to live and study here three years.
But there are other strict observances:
As not to see a woman in that term,
Which I hope well is not enrolled there;
And one day in a week to touch no food,
And but one meal on every day beside,
The which I hope is not enrolled there;
And then to sleep but three hours in the night,
And not be seen to wink of all the day—

Words and passages enclosed in square brackets in the text above are either emendations of the copy-text or additions to it. The Textual Notes immediately following the play cite the earliest authority for every such change or insertion and supply the reading of the copy-text wherever it is emended in this edition.

I.i. Location: Navarre. The King's park. (The action of the play throughout takes place in the park.)
2. brazen: brass, i.e. enduring.
3. grace: honor. disgrace: disfigurement, decay.
4. spite of: in spite of. cormorant: ravenous.
5. breath: breathing-space, i.e. brief earthly life. 6. bate: dull.
9. affections: passions. 13. academe: academy.
14. living art: the art of living (i.e. the Stoic *ars vivendi*), or vital learning (David).
18. schedule: document. 19. pass'd: pledged.
22. arm'd: prepared (for the combat; cf. the martial imagery of lines 8–10). 27. bankrout: bankrupt (a variant form).
28. mortified: dead to worldly pleasures.
32. With . . . living: i.e. finding a substitute for love, wealth, and pomp (?) or living with these companions (?). 34. liege: sovereign.
43. wink of: close the eyes during.

When I was wont to think no harm all night,
And make a dark night too of half the day—
Which I hope well is not enrolled there.
O, these are barren tasks, too hard to keep,
Not to see ladies, study, fast, not sleep.
King. Your oath is pass'd to pass away from these.
Ber. Let me say no, my liege, and if you please:
I only swore to study with your Grace,
And stay here in your court for three years' space.
Long. You swore to that, Berowne, and to the rest.
Ber. By yea and nay, sir, then I swore in jest.
What is the end of study, let me know.
King. Why, that to know which else we should not know.
Ber. Things hid and barr'd (you mean) from common sense.
King. Ay, that is study's godlike recompense.
Ber. Com' on then, I will swear to study so,
To know the thing I am forbid to know:
As thus—to study where I well may dine,
When I to [feast] expressly am forbid;
Or study where to meet some mistress fine,
When mistresses from common sense are hid;
Or having sworn too hard-a-keeping oath,
Study to break it and not break my troth.
If study's gain be thus, and this be so,
Study knows that which yet it doth not know.
Swear me to this, and I will ne'er say no.
King. These be the stops that hinder study quite,
And train our intellects to vain delight.
Ber. Why? all delights are vain, but that most vain
Which, with pain purchas'd, doth inherit pain:
As, painfully to pore upon a book
To seek the light of truth, while truth the while
Doth falsely blind the eyesight of his look.
Light, seeking light, doth light of light beguile;
So ere you find where light in darkness lies,
Your light grows dark by losing of your eyes.
Study me how to please the eye indeed
By fixing it upon a fairer eye,
Who dazzling so, that eye shall be his heed,
And give him light that it was blinded by.
Study is like the heaven's glorious sun,
That will not be deep search'd with saucy looks;
Small have continual plodders ever won,
Save base authority from others' books.
These earthly godfathers of heaven's lights,
That give a name to every fixed star,
Have no more profit of their shining nights
Than those that walk and wot not what they are.
Too much to know is to know nought but fame;
And every godfather can give a name.
King. How well he's read, to reason against reading!
Dum. Proceeded well, to stop all good proceeding!
Long. He weeds the corn and still lets grow the weeding.
Ber. The spring is near when green geese are a-breeding.
Dum. How follows that?
Ber. Fit in his place and time.
Dum. In reason nothing.
Ber. Something then in rhyme.
King. Berowne is like an envious sneaping frost
That bites the first-born infants of the spring.
Ber. Well, say I am, why should proud summer boast
Before the birds have any cause to sing?
Why should I joy in any abortive birth?
At Christmas I no more desire a rose
Than wish a snow in May's new-fangled shows;
But like of each thing that in season grows.
So you, to study now it is too late,
Climb o'er the house to unlock the little gate.
King. Well, sit you out; go home, Berowne; adieu.
Ber. No, my good lord, I have sworn to stay with you;
And though I have for barbarism spoke more
Than for that angel knowledge you can say,
Yet, confident, I'll keep what I have sworn,
And bide the penance of each three years' day.
Give me the paper, let me read the same,
And to the strictest decrees I'll write my name.
King. How well this yielding rescues thee from shame!
Ber. [*Reads.*] "*Item,* That no woman shall come within a mile of my court"—Hath this been proclaim'd?
Long. Four days ago.
Ber. Let's see the penalty. [*Reads.*] "—on pain of losing her tongue." Who devis'd this penalty?
Long. Marry, that did I.

44. think no harm: i.e. sleep soundly. **47. barren**: dull, fruitless.
50. and if: if.
54. By . . . nay: (1) most earnestly (a common meaning, derived from Matthew 5:33–37); (2) equivocally, ambiguously.
57. common sense: ordinary perception.
59. Com' on. This, the quarto spelling, stresses the pun on *common sense* (line 57).
70. stops: obstacles. **71. train**: allure, entice.
73. pain: (1) labor; (2) suffering. **purchas'd**: obtained. **inherit**: possess. **76. falsely**: treacherously. **his look**: its power to see.
77. Light . . . beguile: the eye, seeking enlightenment, deprives itself of the power to see, i.e. excessive study frustrates the search for truth by making the student blind.
80. Study me: i.e. study rather (as far as I am concerned).
81. a fairer eye: i.e. a sweetheart.
82. Who dazzling so: i.e. the man (who has fixed his eye "upon a fairer eye") being thus dazzled. **heed**: guard, protection.
83. it: i.e. his eye. **86. Small**: little.
87. base: commonplace (because secondhand).
88. earthly godfathers: i.e. astronomers, who give names to stars as godparents give names to children at baptism. **91. wot**: know.
92. fame: hearsay, secondhand information.
95. Proceeded: advanced in a course of study (an academic term).
96. He . . . weeding: he pulls up the young wheat and leaves the weeds.
97. green geese: young geese, ready for sale about Whitsuntide; here, simpletons, young fools.
99. rhyme. Berowne caps Dumaine's statement with a quibbling reference to the proverbial "neither rhyme nor reason."
100. envious: malicious. **sneaping**: nipping.
101. infants: buds. **102. proud**: splendid.
107. like of: am pleased with.
109. Climb . . . gate: i.e. act without any sense of fitness, behave incongruously.
110. sit you out: don't take part (a term from cardplaying).
112. barbarism: ignorance, lack of culture.
115. bide . . . day: endure the hardship of each day of the three years.
119. Item: word preceding each part of a list or enumeration.
125. Marry: indeed (a weakened oath, "by the Virgin Mary").

Ber. Sweet lord, and why?
Long. To fright them hence with that dread penalty.
[*Ber.*] A dangerous law against gentility. [*Reads.*]
"*Item*, If any man be seen to talk with a woman within the term of three years, he shall endure such public shame as the rest of the court can possible devise."
This article, my liege, yourself must break,
For well you know here comes in embassy
The French king's daughter with yourself to speak—
A maid of grace and complete majesty—
About surrender up of Aquitaine
To her decrepit, sick, and bedred father;
Therefore this article is made in vain,
Or vainly comes th' admired Princess hither.
King. What say you, lords? Why, this was quite forgot.
Ber. So study evermore is overshot:
While it doth study to have what it would,
It doth forget to do the thing it should;
And when it hath the thing it hunteth most,
'Tis won as towns with fire—so won, so lost.
King. We must of force dispense with this decree,
She must lie here on mere necessity.
Ber. Necessity will make us all forsworn
Three thousand times within this three years' space;
For every man with his affects is born,
Not by might mast'red, but by special grace.
If I break faith, this word shall speak for me:
I am forsworn "on mere necessity."
So to the laws at large I write my name, [*Subscribes.*]
And he that breaks them in the least degree
Stands in attainder of eternal shame.
Suggestions are to other as to me;
But I believe, although I seem so loath,
I am the last that will last keep his oath.
But is there no quick recreation granted?
King. Ay, that there is. Our court you know is haunted
With a refined traveller of Spain,
A man in all the world's new fashion planted,
That hath a mint of phrases in his brain;
One who the music of his own vain tongue
Doth ravish like enchanting harmony;
A man of complements, whom right and wrong
Have chose as umpeer of their mutiny.
This child of fancy, that Armado hight,
For interim to our studies shall relate,
In high-borne words, the worth of many a knight
From tawny Spain, lost in the world's debate.
How you delight, my lords, I know not, I,
But I protest I love to hear him lie,
And I will use him for my minstrelsy.
Ber. Armado is a most illustrious wight,
A man of fire-new words, fashion's own knight.
Long. Costard the swain and he shall be our sport,
And so to study three years is but short.

Enter a Constable [DULL] *with a letter, with* COSTARD.

Dull. Which is the Duke's own person?
Ber. This, fellow. What wouldst?
Dull. I myself reprehend his own person, for I am his Grace's farborough; but I would see his own person in flesh and blood.
Ber. This is he.
Dull. Signior Arme—Arme—commends you. There's villainy abroad; this letter will tell you more.
Cost. Sir, the contempts thereof are as touching me.
King. A letter from the magnificent Armado.
Ber. How low soever the matter, I hope in God for high words.
Long. A high hope for a low heaven. God grant us patience!
Ber. To hear, or forbear hearing?
Long. To hear meekly, sir, and to laugh moderately; or to forbear both.
Ber. Well, sir, be it as the style shall give us cause to climb in the merriness.
Cost. The matter is to me, sir, as concerning Jaquenetta: the manner of it is, I was taken with the manner.
Ber. In what manner?
Cost. In manner and form following, sir, all those three: I was seen with her in the manor-house, sitting with her upon the form, and taken following her into the park, which, put together, is in manner and form following. Now, sir, for the manner—it is the manner of a man to speak to a woman; for the form—in some form.
Ber. For the following, sir?
Cost. As it shall follow in my correction, and God defend the right!
King. Will you hear this letter with attention?
Ber. As we would hear an oracle.
Cost. Such is the simplicity of man to hearken after the flesh.

128. **gentility**: courtesy. 131. **possible**: possibly.
134. **in embassy**: as an ambassador. 136. **complete**: perfect.
138. **bedred**: bedridden. 142. **overshot**: wide of the mark, in error.
146. **with fire**: i.e. by destroying them with fire.
147. **of force**: necessarily.
148. **lie**: lodge, stay. **mere**: absolute, utter.
151. **affects**: affections, passions. 152. **special grace**: divine aid.
153. **word**: motto, watchword.
155. **at large**: as a whole, in general.
157. **in attainder of**: condemned and disgraced to.
158. **Suggestions**: temptations. 161. **quick**: lively.
162–63. **haunted With**: frequented by. 166. **who**: whom.
168. **complements**: accomplishments.
169. **umpeer**: umpire. **mutiny**: discord.
170. **child of fancy**: fantastic creature. **hight**: is called.
171. **interim**: intermission, refreshing interval.
172. **high-borne**: lofty.
173. **tawny**: i.e. sunburned. **debate**: warfare.
174. **How you delight**: what delights you. 177. **wight**: person.
178. **fire-new**: newly coined.
179. **Costard**. His name means a kind of large apple; also, humorously, the head. **swain**: rustic youth. 181. **Duke's**: i.e. King's.
183. **reprehend**: blunder for *represent*.
184. **farborough**: apparently Dull's version of *thirdborough*, a petty constable. 190. **contempts**: blunder for *contents*.
191. **magnificent Armado**: grandiose or pompous Armado (the Spanish Armada was so called).
199. **style**. With play (in *climb*, line 200) on *stile*. Cf. IV.i.96–97.
202–3. **with the manner**: in the very act. 207. **form**: bench.
213. **correction**: punishment.

King. [*Reads.*] "Great deputy, the welkin's vicegerent, and sole dominator of Navarre, my soul's earth's god, and body's fost'ring patron"—

Cost. Not a word of Costard yet.

King. [*Reads.*] "So it is"—

Cost. It may be so; but if he say it is so, he is, in telling true—but so.

King. Peace!

Cost. —be to me, and every man that dares not fight!

King. No words!

Cost. —of other men's secrets, I beseech you.

King. [*Reads.*] "So it is, besieged with sable-colored melancholy, I did commend the black oppressing humor to the most wholesome physic of thy health-giving air; and as I am a gentleman, betook myself to walk: the time When? about the sixt hour, when beasts most graze, birds best peck, and men sit down to that nourishment which is called supper: so much for the time When. Now for the ground Which? which, I mean, I walk'd upon: it is ycliped thy park. Then for the place Where? where, I mean, I did encounter that obscene and most prepost'rous event that draweth from my snow-white pen the ebon-colored ink which here thou viewest, beholdest, surveyest, or seest. But to the place Where? It standeth north-north-east and by east from the west corner of thy curious-knotted garden. There did I see that low-spirited swain, that base minnow of thy mirth"—

Cost. Me?

King. [*Reads.*] "that unlettered small-knowing soul"—

Cost. Me?

King. [*Reads.*] "that shallow vassal"—

Cost. Still me?

King. [*Reads.*] "which, as I remember, hight Costard"—

Cost. O! me.

King. [*Reads.*] "sorted and consorted, contrary to thy established proclaimed edict and continent canon; which with—O, with—but with this I passion to say wherewith"—

Cost. With a wench.

King. [*Reads.*] "with a child of our grandmother Eve, a female; or for thy more sweet understanding, a woman. Him I (as my ever-esteemed duty pricks me on) have sent to thee, to receive the meed of punishment, by thy sweet Grace's officer, Anthony Dull, a man of good repute, carriage, bearing, and estimation."

Dull. Me, an't shall please you: I am Anthony Dull.

King. [*Reads.*] "For Jaquenetta (so is the weaker vessel called), which I apprehended with the aforesaid swain, I keep her as a vessel of thy law's fury, and shall, at the least of thy sweet notice, bring her to trial. Thine, in all complements of devoted and heart-burning heat of duty,

Don Adriano de Armado."

Ber. This is not so well as I look'd for, but the best that ever I heard.

King. Ay, the best for the worst. But, sirrah, what say you to this?

Cost. Sir, I confess the wench.

King. Did you hear the proclamation?

Cost. I do confess much of the hearing it, but little of the marking of it.

King. It was proclaim'd a year's imprisonment to be taken with a wench.

Cost. I was taken with none, sir, I was taken with a damsel.

King. Well, it was proclaim'd damsel.

Cost. This was no damsel neither, sir, she was a virgin.

[*King*.] It is so varied too, for it was proclaim'd virgin.

Cost. If it were, I deny her virginity; I was taken with a maid.

King. This maid will not serve your turn, sir.

Cost. This maid will serve my turn, sir.

King. Sir, I will pronounce your sentence: you shall fast a week with bran and water.

Cost. I had rather pray a month with mutton and porridge.

King. And Don Armado shall be your keeper.
My Lord Berowne, see him delivered o'er,
And go we, lords, to put in practice that
Which each to other hath so strongly sworn.

[*Exeunt King, Longaville, and Dumaine.*]

Ber. I'll lay my head to any good man's hat,
These oaths and laws will prove an idle scorn.
Sirrah, come on.

Cost. I suffer for the truth, sir; for true it is, I was taken with Jaquenetta, and Jaquenetta is a true girl, and therefore welcome the sour cup of prosperity! Affliction may one day smile again, and till then, sit thee down, sorrow! *Exeunt.*

[Scene II]

Enter Armado *and* Moth, *his page.*

Arm. Boy, what sign is it when a man of great spirit grows melancholy?

219–20. welkin's vicegerent: heaven's deputy.
225. but so: i.e. not saying much. **233. physic:** medicine.
235. sixt: sixth. **240. ycliped:** called. **241. obscene:** disgusting.
242. prepost'rous: out of place, highly indecorous.
242–43. snow-white pen: i.e. white quill.
246. curious-knotted: intricately designed. Patterned garden beds were called knots. **247. low-spirited:** base.
248. minnow: i.e. contemptible little creature.
250. unlettered: illiterate. **253. vassal:** base slave.
258. sorted: associated.
259–60. continent canon: law enforcing restraint.
260. passion: grieve. **266. meed:** reward.
272–73. weaker vessel: i.e. woman.
281. best for: best example of. **sirrah:** form of address to inferiors.
294. is so varied: provides for that variation.
298. This . . . turn: this quibbling won't get you out of your difficulty (but Costard picks up the words in a ribald sense).
302–3. mutton and porridge: mutton soup (but *mutton* was also slang for "prostitute"). **308. lay:** wager. **312. true:** honest.
315. sit thee down: i.e. settle down with me.

I.ii. o.s.d. Moth. Pronounced *mot* or *mote* by the Elizabethans and possibly intended by Shakespeare to represent the word now written *mote*, which he seems regularly to have spelled *moth*.

Moth. A great sign, sir, that he will look sad.

Arm. Why, sadness is one and the self-same thing, dear imp.

Moth. No, no, O Lord, sir, no.

Arm. How canst thou part sadness and melancholy, my tender juvenal?

Moth. By a familiar demonstration of the working, my tough signior.

Arm. Why tough signior? Why tough signior?

Moth. Why tender juvenal? Why tender juvenal?

Arm. I spoke it tender juvenal as a congruent epitheton appertaining to thy young days, which we may nominate tender.

Moth. And I tough signior as an appertinent title to your old time, which we may name tough.

Arm. Pretty and apt.

Moth. How mean you, sir? I pretty, and my saying apt? or I apt, and my saying pretty?

Arm. Thou pretty, because little.

Moth. Little pretty, because little. Wherefore apt?

Arm. And therefore apt, because quick.

Moth. Speak you this in my praise, master?

Arm. In thy condign praise.

Moth. I will praise an eel with the same praise.

Arm. What? that an eel is ingenious?

Moth. That an eel is quick.

Arm. I do say thou art quick in answers; thou heat'st my blood.

Moth. I am answer'd, sir.

Arm. I love not to be cross'd.

Moth. [*Aside.*] He speaks the mere contrary, crosses love not him.

Arm. I have promised to study three years with the Duke.

Moth. You may do it in an hour, sir.

Arm. Impossible.

Moth. How many is one thrice told?

Arm. I am ill at reck'ning, it fitteth the spirit of a tapster.

Moth. You are a gentleman and a gamester, sir.

Arm. I confess both, they are both the varnish of a complete man.

Moth. Then I am sure you know how much the gross sum of deuce-ace amounts to.

Arm. It doth amount to one more than two.

Moth. Which the base vulgar do call three.

Arm. True.

Moth. Why, sir, is this such a piece of study? Now here is three studied ere ye'll thrice wink; and how easy it is to put "years" to the word "three," and study three years in two words, the dancing horse will tell you.

Arm. A most fine figure!

Moth. [*Aside.*] To prove you a cipher.

Arm. I will hereupon confess I am in love; and as it is base for a soldier to love, so am I in love with a base wench. If drawing my sword against the humor of affection would deliver me from the reprobate thought of it, I would take Desire prisoner, and ransom him to any French courtier for a new-devis'd cur'sy. I think scorn to sigh; methinks I should outswear Cupid. Comfort me, boy: what great men have been in love?

Moth. Hercules, master.

Arm. Most sweet Hercules! More authority, dear boy, name more; and, sweet my child, let them be men of good repute and carriage.

Moth. Sampson, master; he was a man of good carriage, great carriage, for he carried the town gates on his back like a porter; and he was in love.

Arm. O well-knit Sampson, strong-jointed Sampson! I do excel thee in my rapier as much as thou didst me in carrying gates. I am in love too. Who was Sampson's love, my dear Moth?

Moth. A woman, master.

Arm. Of what complexion?

Moth. Of all the four, or the three, or the two, or one of the four.

Arm. Tell me precisely of what complexion.

Moth. Of the sea-water green, sir.

Arm. Is that one of the four complexions?

Moth. As I have read, sir, and the best of them too.

Arm. Green indeed is the color of lovers; but to have a love of that color, methinks Sampson had small reason for it. He surely affected her for her wit.

Moth. It was so, sir, for she had a green wit.

Arm. My love is most immaculate white and red.

Moth. Most maculate thoughts, master, are mask'd under such colors.

Arm. Define, define, well-educated infant.

Moth. My father's wit and my mother's tongue assist me!

Arm. Sweet invocation of a child, most pretty and pathetical!

Moth. If she be made of white and red,
Her faults will ne'er be known,
For blush in cheeks by faults are bred,
And fears by pale white shown:
Then if she fear, or be to blame,
By this you shall not know,

5. **imp**: child (literally, sprig, shoot). 7. **part**: distinguish between. 8. **juvenal**: youth. 9. **familiar**: plain. 9–10. **working**: operation. 13–14. **congruent epitheton**: suitable epithet. 15. **nominate**: call. 16. **appertinent**: appropriate. 25. **condign**: worthily deserved. 29–30. **thou . . . blood**: you anger me. 34. **crosses**: i.e. coins (many of which were stamped with crosses). 39. **told**: counted, reckoned. 42. **gamester**: gambler. 43. **varnish**: finish, gloss. 46. **deuce-ace**: a two and a one, the second lowest throw at dice. 48. **vulgar**: common people. 53. **dancing horse**. Referring to a celebrated performing horse named Morocco, who had been trained to count by tapping with his hoof.

55. **figure**: example of verbal ingenuity (but the sense "numeral" probably inspires Moth's following aside). 56. **cipher**: nonentity. 58–59. **base . . . base**: morally reprehensible . . . low-born. 60. **humor of affection**: inclination to love. 63. **a new-devis'd cur'sy**: a new way of bowing, i.e. any new fashion. **think scorn**: disdain. 64. **outswear**: conquer by swearing. 69. **carriage**: behavior (with following quibble). 70. **Sampson**: Samson. For the exploit mentioned by Moth see Judges 16:3. 78. **complexion**: (1) color of skin; (2) temperament, disposition (supposed to be determined by the proportions of the four bodily fluids or "humors"—blood, phlegm, choler, and melancholy). 88. **affected**: loved. **wit**: intelligence. 89. **green**: immature. 92. **maculate**: stained, impure. 94. **Define**: explain your meaning. 98. **pathetical**: moving, touching.

For still her cheeks possess the same
Which native she doth owe.

A dangerous rhyme, master, against the reason of white and red.

Arm. Is there not a ballet, boy, of the King and the Beggar?

Moth. The world was very guilty of such a ballet some three ages since, but I think now 'tis not to be found; or if it were, it would neither serve for the writing nor the tune.

Arm. I will have that subject newly writ o'er, that I may example my digression by some mighty president. Boy, I do love that country girl that I took in the park with the rational hind Costard. She deserves well.

Moth. [*Aside.*] To be whipt; and yet a better love than my master.

Arm. Sing, boy, my spirit grows heavy in love.

Moth. And that's great marvel, loving a light wench.

Arm. I say, sing.

Moth. Forbear till this company be past.

Enter Clown [Costard], *Constable* [Dull], *and Wench* [Jaquenetta].

Dull. Sir, the Duke's pleasure is that you keep Costard safe, and you must suffer him to take no delight nor no penance, but 'a must fast three days a week. For this damsel, I must keep her at the park; she is allow'd for the dey-woman. Fare you well.

Arm. I do betray myself with blushing. Maid.
Jaq. Man.
Arm. I will visit thee at the lodge.
Jaq. That's hereby.
Arm. I know where it is situate.
Jaq. Lord, how wise you are!
Arm. I will tell thee wonders.
Jaq. With that face?
Arm. I love thee.
Jaq. So I heard you say.
Arm. And so farewell.
Jaq. Fair weather after you!
[*Dull.*] Come, Jaquenetta, away.

Exeunt [*Dull and Jaquenetta*].

Arm. Villain, thou shalt fast for thy offenses ere thou be pardoned.

Cost. Well, sir, I hope when I do it I shall do it on a full stomach.

Arm. Thou shalt be heavily punished.

Cost. I am more bound to you than your fellows, for they are but lightly rewarded.

Arm. Take away this villain, shut him up.

Moth. Come, you transgressing slave, away.

Cost. Let me not be pent up, sir; I will fast, being loose.

Moth. No, sir, that were fast and loose; thou shalt to prison.

Cost. Well, if ever I do see the merry days of desolation that I have seen, some shall see.

Moth. What shall some see?

Cost. Nay, nothing, Master Moth, but what they look upon. It is not for prisoners to be too silent in their words, and therefore I will say nothing. I thank God I have as little patience as another man, and therefore I can be quiet. *Exit* [*with Moth*].

Arm. I do affect the very ground (which is base) where her shoe (which is baser) guided by her foot (which is basest) doth tread. I shall be forsworn (which is a great argument of falsehood) if I love. And how can that be true love, which is falsely attempted? Love is a familiar; Love is a devil; there is no evil angel but Love. Yet was Sampson so tempted, and he had an excellent strength; yet was Salomon so seduced, and he had a very good wit. Cupid's butt-shaft is too hard for Hercules' club, and therefore too much odds for a Spaniard's rapier. The first and second cause will not serve my turn; the passado he respects not, the duello he regards not: his disgrace is to be called boy, but his glory is to subdue men. Adieu, valor, rust, rapier, be still, drum, for your manager is in love; yea, he loveth. Assist me, some extemporal god of rhyme, for I am sure I shall turn sonnet. Devise, wit, write, pen, for I am for whole volumes in folio. *Exit.*

[ACT II, Scene I]

Enter the Princess of France *with three attending Ladies* [Rosaline, Maria, Katherine] *and three* Lords, [*one named* Boyet].

Boyet. Now, madam, summon up your dearest spirits;

106. native: naturally. **owe:** own. **109. ballet:** ballad.
109–10. King . . . Beggar: i.e. King Cophetua and the beggar maid with whom he fell in love, the subjects of a popular ballad. Cf. IV.i.64–66. **113. serve:** be acceptable.
116. example: give an example of. **digression:** lapse from propriety. **117. president:** precedent.
118. rational: capable of thought. **hind:** rustic (perhaps with quibble on the sense "male deer"). **121. love:** lover.
123. light: wanton.
129. penance: a blunder for *pleasance* (?) or perhaps Dull, like Costard elsewhere, is simply using a word that means the opposite of what he supposes. **'a:** he.
131. allow'd . . . dey-woman: approved to serve as dairy-woman.
136. That's hereby. It is clear from the rest of Jaquenetta's replies that some derisive sense is intended here, but the precise meaning is obscure.
140. With that face: a slang expression equivalent to "You don't say so."
146. Villain: (1) servant, peasant; (2) rascal.

148–49. on . . . stomach. With quibble on the secondary sense "with good courage." **151. fellows:** servants. **152. lightly:** slightly.
157. fast and loose: a cheating trick.
160. desolation: for *dissipation* (?) or *consolation* (?). But see note to line 129. **167. affect:** love. **170. argument:** proof.
172. familiar: attendant evil spirit, demon.
174. Salomon: Solomon.
176. butt-shaft: an arrow, without barb, for shooting at targets; often assigned to Cupid, perhaps because he was represented as a child.
177–78. first . . . cause: i.e. certain situations recognized in the code of honor as justifying a duel. Armado means that he is helpless against Cupid because Cupid will not be governed by the code.
178. passado: fencing thrust. **179. duello:** duelling code.
182. manager: expert wielder. **183. extemporal:** impromptu.
184. turn sonnet: i.e. become a sonneteer.
185. folio: i.e. the largest size of book.

II.i.1. dearest spirits: best wits.

Consider who the King your father sends,
To whom he sends, and what's his embassy:
Yourself, held precious in the world's esteem,
To parley with the sole inheritor
Of all perfections that a man may owe,
Matchless Navarre; the plea of no less weight
Than Aquitaine, a dowry for a queen.
Be now as prodigal of all dear grace
As Nature was in making graces dear,
When she did starve the general world beside
And prodigally gave them all to you.

Prin. Good Lord Boyet, my beauty, though but mean,
Needs not the painted flourish of your praise:
Beauty is bought by judgment of the eye,
Not utt'red by base sale of chapmen's tongues.
I am less proud to hear you tell my worth
Than you much willing to be counted wise
In spending your wit in the praise of mine.
But now to task the tasker: good Boyet,
You are not ignorant all-telling fame
Doth noise abroad Navarre hath made a vow,
Till painful study shall outwear three years,
No woman may approach his silent court;
Therefore to 's seemeth it a needful course,
Before we enter his forbidden gates,
To know his pleasure; and in that behalf,
Bold of your worthiness, we single you
As our best-moving fair solicitor.
Tell him, the daughter of the King of France,
On serious business craving quick dispatch,
[Importunes] personal conference with his Grace.
Haste, signify so much, while we attend,
Like humble[-visag'd] suitors, his high will.

Boyet. Proud of employment, willingly I go.

Exit Boyet.

Prin. All pride is willing pride, and yours is so.
Who are the votaries, my loving lords,
That are vow-fellows with this virtuous Duke?

[1.] Lord. [Lord] Longaville is one.

Prin. Know you the man?

[Mar.] I know him, madam; at a marriage-feast,
Between Lord Perigort and the beauteous heir
Of Jaques Falconbridge, solemnized
In Normandy, saw I this Longaville,
A man of sovereign [parts, peerless] esteem'd,
Well fitted in arts, glorious in arms;
Nothing becomes him ill that he would well.
The only soil of his fair virtue's gloss,
If virtue's gloss will stain with any soil,
Is a sharp wit match'd with too blunt a will,
Whose edge hath power to cut, whose will still wills
It should none spare that come within his power.

Prin. Some merry mocking lord belike, is't so?

[Mar.] They say so most that most his humors know.

Prin. Such short-liv'd wits do wither as they grow.
Who are the rest?

[Kath.] The young Dumaine, a well-accomplish'd youth,
Of all that virtue love for virtue loved;
Most power to do most harm, least knowing ill;
For he hath wit to make an ill shape good,
And shape to win grace though he had no wit.
I saw him at the Duke Alanson's once,
And much too little of that good I saw
Is my report to his great worthiness.

[Ros.] Another of these students at that time
Was there with him, if I have heard a truth.
Berowne they call him, but a merrier man,
Within the limit of becoming mirth,
I never spent an hour's talk withal.
His eye begets occasion for his wit,
For every object that the one doth catch
The other turns to a mirth-moving jest,
Which his fair tongue, conceit's expositor,
Delivers in such apt and gracious words
That aged ears play truant at his tales,
And younger hearings are quite ravished,
So sweet and voluble is his discourse.

Prin. God bless my ladies! are they all in love,
That every one her own hath garnished
With such bedecking ornaments of praise?

[1.] Lord. Here comes Boyet.

Enter BOYET.

Prin. Now, what admittance, lord?

Boyet. Navarre had notice of your fair approach,
And he and his competitors in oath
Were all address'd to meet you, gentle lady,
Before I came. Marry, thus much I have learnt:
He rather means to lodge you in the field,
Like one that comes here to besiege his court,
Than seek a dispensation for his oath,
To let you enter his [unpeopled] house.

Enter [FERDINAND, *King of*] *Navarre*, LONGAVILLE, DUMAINE, *and* BEROWNE, [*and* ATTENDANTS].

Here comes Navarre. [*The ladies-in-waiting mask.*]

King. Fair Princess, welcome to the court of Navarre.

5. inheritor: possessor. **6. owe**: own.
7. plea: that which is claimed. **10. dear**: costly (because scarce).
11. starve: stint, deprive. **general**: whole. **beside**: apart (from you). **14. flourish**: embellishment.
16. utt'red: offered for sale. **chapmen's**: merchants'.
17. proud: pleased. **tell**: (1) describe; (2) reckon up.
20. task the tasker: i.e. set a task for you, who have been setting one for me. **21. fame**: rumor. **23. painful**: laborious.
25. to 's: to us. **28. Bold**: confident.
29. best-moving: most eloquent. **fair**: just.
37. the votaries: those who have taken vows.
45. arts: intellectual accomplishments. **46. would**: wishes to do.
49. too . . . will: i.e. a disposition unwilling to spare others' feelings.
50. still: ever.
57. Of . . . loved: loved for his virtue by all who love virtue.
58. Most . . . ill: i.e. because of his innocence, possessed of the greatest power to do the greatest harm.
59–60. he . . . wit: his intelligence is such that it would make up for an ugly body, and his physical endowment is such that it would make up for lack of brains. **61. Duke Alanson's**: Duke of Alençon's.
62. little: short. **63. report**: testimony.
66. Berowne. Here perhaps with a play on *brown* = sombre (David).
67. becoming: decorous. **68. withal**: with.
72. conceit's expositor: fancy's interpreter.
74. play truant at: i.e. stop attending to serious matters in order to listen to. **76. voluble**: quick-witted. **80. admittance**: reception.
82. competitors: associates. **83. address'd**: made ready, prepared.
88. unpeopled: i.e. lacking the proper retinue of servants.

Prin. "Fair" I give you back again, and "welcome" I have not yet. The roof of this court is too high to be yours, and welcome to the wide fields too base to be mine.

King. You shall be welcome, madam, to my court.

Prin. I will be welcome then—conduct me thither.

King. Hear me, dear lady: I have sworn an oath.

Prin. Our Lady help my lord! he'll be forsworn.

King. Not for the world, fair madam, by my will.

Prin. Why, will shall break it, will, and nothing else.

King. Your ladyship is ignorant what it is.

Prin. Were my lord so, his ignorance were wise,
Where now his knowledge must prove ignorance.
I hear your Grace hath sworn out house-keeping:
'Tis deadly sin to keep that oath, my lord,
And sin to break it.
But pardon me, I am too sudden bold;
To teach a teacher ill beseemeth me.
Vouchsafe to read the purpose of my coming,
And suddenly resolve me in my suit.
[*Giving a paper.*]

King. Madam, I will, if suddenly I may.

Prin. You will the sooner, that I were away,
For you'll prove perjur'd if you make me stay.

Ber. Did not I dance with you in Brabant once?

Kath. Did not I dance with you in Brabant once?

Ber. I know you did.

Kath. How needless was it then
To ask the question?

Ber. You must not be so quick.

Kath. 'Tis long of you that spur me with such questions.

Ber. Your wit's too hot, it speeds too fast, 'twill tire.

Kath. Not till it leave the rider in the mire.

Ber. What time a' day?

Kath. The hour that fools should ask.

Ber. Now fair befall your mask!

Kath. Fair fall the face it covers!

Ber. And send you many lovers!

Kath. Amen, so you be none.

Ber. Nay then will I be gone.

King. Madam, your father here doth intimate
The payment of a hundred thousand crowns,
Being but the one half of an entire sum
Disbursed by my father in his wars.
But say that he, or we, as neither have,
Receiv'd that sum, yet there remains unpaid
A hundred thousand more, in surety of the which
One part of Aquitaine is bound to us,
Although not valued to the money's worth.
If then the King your father will restore
But that one half which is unsatisfied,

92. **roof . . . court:** i.e. the sky. 99. **by my will:** willingly.
104. **sworn out house-keeping:** renounced hospitality.
107. **sudden:** rashly.
110. **suddenly:** immediately. **resolve:** answer.
117. **quick:** sharp. 118. **long:** because.
123. **fair befall:** good fortune to.
128. **intimate:** suggest, discuss. 136. **valued:** equal in value.

We will give up our right in Aquitaine,
And hold fair friendship with his Majesty.
But that, it seems, he little purposeth:
For here he doth demand to have repaid
A hundred thousand crowns, and not demands,
[On] payment of a hundred thousand crowns,
To have his title live in Aquitaine;
Which we much rather had depart withal,
And have the money by our father lent,
Than Aquitaine, so gelded as it is.
Dear Princess, were not his requests so far
From reason's yielding, your fair self should make
A yielding 'gainst some reason in my breast,
And go well satisfied to France again.

Prin. You do the King my father too much wrong,
And wrong the reputation of your name,
In so unseeming to confess receipt
Of that which hath so faithfully been paid.

King. I do protest I never heard of it;
And, if you prove it, I'll repay it back,
Or yield up Aquitaine.

Prin. We arrest your word.
Boyet, you can produce acquittances
For such a sum from special officers
Of Charles his father.

King. Satisfy me so.

Boyet. So please your Grace, the packet is not come
Where that and other specialties are bound:
To-morrow you shall have a sight of them.

King. It shall suffice me; at which interview
All liberal reason I will yield unto.
Mean time receive such welcome at my hand
As honor (without breach of honor) may
Make tender of to thy true worthiness.
You may not come, fair Princess, within my gates,
But here without you shall be so receiv'd
As you shall deem yourself lodg'd in my heart,
Though so denied fair harbor in my house.
Your own good thoughts excuse me, and farewell.
To-morrow shall we visit you again.

Prin. Sweet health and fair desires consort your Grace!

King. Thy own wish wish I thee in every place.
Exit [*with Longaville, Dumaine, and Attendants*].

Ber. Lady, I will commend you to [mine own] heart.

Ros. Pray you, do my commendations—I would be glad to see it.

Ber. I would you heard it groan.

Ros. Is the fool sick?

Ber. Sick at the heart.

Ros. Alack, let it blood.

Ber. Would that do it good?

Ros. My physic says ay.

146. **depart withal:** part with. 148. **gelded:** i.e. reduced in value.
155. **unseeming to:** seeming to be unwilling to.
159. **arrest:** take as security.
164. **specialties:** special terms or documents.
167. **liberal:** gentlemanlike, generous. 173. **As:** that.
177. **consort:** attend. 184. **the fool:** the poor thing.
186. **let it blood:** bleed it. Bloodletting was a common medical treatment. 188. **physic:** medical knowledge.

Ber. Will you prick't with your eye?
Ros. No point, with my knife.
Ber. Now God save thy life!
Ros. And yours from long living!
Ber. I cannot stay thanksgiving. *Exit.*

Enter DUMAINE.

Dum. Sir, I pray you a word. What lady is that same?
Boyet. The heir of Alanson, [Katherine] her name.
Dum. A gallant lady. Monsieur, fare you well. *Exit.*

[*Enter* LONGAVILLE.]

Long. I beseech you a word. What is she in the white?
Boyet. A woman sometimes, and you saw her in the light.
Long. Perchance light in the light. I desire her name.
Boyet. She hath but one for herself, to desire that were a shame.
Long. Pray you, sir, whose daughter?
Boyet. Her mother's, I have heard.
Long. God's blessing on your beard!
Boyet. Good sir, be not offended,
She is an heir of Falconbridge.
Long. Nay, my choler is ended.
She is a most sweet lady.
Boyet. Not unlike, sir, that may be. *Exit Longaville.*

Enter BEROWNE.

Ber. What's her name in the cap?
Boyet. [Rosaline,] by good hap.
Ber. Is she wedded or no?
Boyet. To her will, sir, or so.
Ber. O, you are welcome, sir, adieu.
Boyet. Farewell to me, sir, and welcome to you. *Exit Berowne.*
Mar. That last is Berowne, the merry madcap lord.
Not a word with him but a jest.
Boyet. And every jest but a word.
Prin. It was well done of you to take him at his word.
Boyet. I was as willing to grapple as he was to board.
Kath. Two hot sheeps, marry.
Boyet. And wherefore not ships?
No sheep, sweet lamb, unless we feed on your lips.
[*Kath.*] You sheep, and I pasture: shall that finish the jest?
Boyet. So you grant pasture for me. [*Offering to kiss her.*]
[*Kath.*] Not so, gentle beast.
My lips are no common, though several they be.
Boyet. Belonging to whom?
[*Kath.*] To my fortunes and me.
Prin. Good wits will be jangling, but, gentles, agree:
This civil war of wits were much better used
On Navarre and his book-men, for here 'tis abused.
Boyet. If my observation (which very seldom lies),
By the heart's still rhetoric, disclosed with eyes,
Deceive me not now, Navarre is infected.
Prin. With what?
Boyet. With that which we lovers entitle "affected."
Prin. Your reason?
Boyet. Why, all his behaviors did make their retire
To the court of his eye, peeping thorough desire:
His heart like an agot with your print impressed,
Proud with his form, in his eye pride expressed;
His tongue, all impatient to speak and not see,
Did stumble with haste in his eyesight to be;
All senses to that sense did make their repair,
To feel only looking on fairest of fair:
Methought all his senses were lock'd in his eye,
As jewels in crystal for some prince to buy,
Who tend'ring their own worth from where they were glass'd,
Did point you to buy them, along as you pass'd;
His face's own margent did cote such amazes
That all eyes saw his eyes enchanted with gazes.
I'll give you Aquitaine and all that is his,
And you give him for my sake but one loving kiss.
Prin. Come to our pavilion—Boyet is dispos'd.
Boyet. But to speak that in words which his eye hath disclos'd.
I only have made a mouth of his eye,
By adding a tongue which I know will not lie.
[*Mar.*] Thou art an old love-monger and speakest skillfully.
[*Kath.*] He is Cupid's grandfather, and learns news of him.
[*Ros.*] Then was Venus like her mother, for her father is but grim.

190. No point: (1) it is dull; (2) by no means.
193. stay thanksgiving: take time to thank you properly.
198. and: if. **199. light . . . light:** wanton if clearly seen.
203. God's . . . beard. Jesting reference to a man's beard was thought to be insulting. **208. unlike:** unlikely.
212. or so: or something of the kind.
214. welcome to you: you are welcome to go (?).
217. take . . . word: give him word for word.
218. grapple . . . board: come to grips with him . . . attack (terms from naval warfare).
219. sheeps, ships. Elizabethan puns on these near-homonyms are numberless.
222. So: provided.
223. common: common land. **though:** inasmuch as (?). **several:** (1) private enclosed land; (2) more than one; (3) parted.
225. jangling: disputing.
227. book-men: scholars. **abused:** misapplied.
229. still rhetoric: silent eloquence. **232. affected:** being in love.
234. retire: withdrawal. **235. thorough:** through.
236. agot: agate (often carved with small figures and set into rings). **impressed:** engraved.
237. his form: the form imprinted on it, i.e. the image of the Princess.
238. to . . . see: at being able only to speak, not to see.
239. in . . . be: to participate in the sense of sight.
240. repair: resort. **241. looking:** through looking.
244. Who: which. **tend'ring:** offering, showing forth. **glass'd:** enclosed in glass. **245. point:** direct.
246. margent. Margins of books often bore commentary upon the adjoining text; hence the word is here applied to the King's looks of amazement, which comment on what his eye beholds. **cote:** variant form of *quote* (indicating the Elizabethan pronunciation), i.e. indicate.
250. dispos'd: inclined (to be merry). **254. skillfully:** as an expert.
256. her . . . grim: i.e. Boyet is no "beauty."

Boyet. Do you hear, my mad wenches?
[*Mar.*] No.
Boyet. What then, do you see?
[*Mar.*] Ay, our way to be gone.
Boyet. You are too hard for me.
Exeunt omnes.

[ACT III, SCENE I]

Enter Braggart [ARMADO] *and his Boy* [MOTH].

Arm. Warble, child, make passionate my sense of hearing.

Moth. [*Sings the song*] "Concolinel."

Arm. Sweet air! Go, tenderness of years, take this key, give enlargement to the swain, bring him festinately hither. I must employ him in a letter to my love.

Moth. Master, will you win your love with a French brawl?

Arm. How meanest thou? Brawling in French?

Moth. No, my complete master, but to jig off a tune at the tongue's end, canary to it with your feet, humor it with turning up your eyelids, sigh a note and sing a note, sometime through the throat, [as] if you swallow'd love with singing love, sometime through [the] nose, as if you snuff'd up love by smelling love; with your hat penthouse-like o'er the shop of your eyes; with your arms cross'd on your thin[-bellied] doublet like a rabbit on a spit; or your hands in your pocket like a man after the old painting; and keep not too long in one tune, but a snip and away: these are complements, these are humors, these betray nice wenches that would be betray'd without these; and make them men of note—do you note?—men that most are affected to these.

Arm. How hast thou purchased this experience?

Moth. By my [penny] of observation.

Arm. But O—but O—

Moth. "The hobby-horse is forgot."

Arm. Call'st thou my love "hobby-horse"?

Moth. No, master, the hobby-horse is but a colt, [*aside*] and your love perhaps a hackney.—But have you forgot your love?

Arm. Almost I had.

Moth. Negligent student, learn her by heart.

Arm. By heart and in heart, boy.

Moth. And out of heart, master; all those three I will prove.

Arm. What wilt thou prove?

Moth. A man, if I live; and this, "by, in, and without," upon the instant: by heart you love her, because your heart cannot come by her; in heart you love her, because your heart is in love with her; and out of heart you love her, being out of heart that you cannot enjoy her.

Arm. I am all these three.

Moth. And three times as much more—[*aside*] and yet nothing at all.

Arm. Fetch hither the swain, he must carry me a letter.

Moth. A message well sympathiz'd—a horse to be embassador for an ass.

Arm. Ha, ha? what sayest thou?

Moth. Marry, sir, you must send the ass upon the horse, for he is very slow-gaited. But I go.

Arm. The way is but short, away!

Moth. As swift as lead, sir.

Arm. The meaning, pretty ingenious?
Is not lead a metal heavy, dull, and slow?

Moth. *Minime*, honest master, or rather, master, no.

Arm. I say lead is slow.

Moth. You are too swift, sir, to say so.
Is that lead slow which is fir'd from a gun?

Arm. Sweet smoke of rhetoric!
He reputes me a cannon, and the bullet, that's he;
I shoot thee at the swain.

Moth. Thump then, and I flee. [*Exit.*]

Arm. A most acute juvenal, volable and free of grace!
By thy favor, sweet welkin, I must sigh in thy face:
Most rude melancholy, valor gives thee place.
My herald is return'd.

Enter Page [MOTH] *and Clown* [COSTARD].

Moth. A wonder, master! Here's a costard broken in a shin.

Arm. Some enigma, some riddle—come, thy l'envoy—begin.

Cost. No egma, no riddle, no l'envoy, no salve in the mail, sir. O sir, plantan, a plain plantan; no l'envoy, no l'envoy, no salve, sir, but a plantan!

Arm. By virtue thou enforcest laughter—thy

257. **mad wenches**: high-spirited girls.

III.i.1. **passionate**: impassioned, feeling.
3. **Concolinel.** Unexplained; probably the title of a song.
5. **enlargement**: freedom. 6. **festinately**: in haste.
9. **brawl**: one of the oldest of figure dances (from French *branle*).
11. **jig**: sing in the tune of a jig.
12. **canary**: dance in a very lively manner (from the name of a dance). 14. **sometime**: from time to time, at times.
17. **penthouse-like**: like a projecting roof.
18. **arms cross'd.** Folded arms betokened love melancholy.
19. **thin-bellied doublet**: (1) doublet with an unpadded belly or lower front; (2) doublet over a thin belly (suggestive of one wasted by love-longing).
22. **a snip and away**: a snatch and then on to another. **complements**: gentlemanly actions. 23. **nice**: coy.
25. **affected**: inclined.
28–29. **But . . . forgot.** The line, a lament for the passing of the good old days, occurs again in *Hamlet* (III.ii.135) and elsewhere, and was probably the refrain of a song. The hobby-horse, a dancer costumed to suggest a horse, was a favorite figure in May-games and other traditional festivities which were falling into disuse, partly because of Puritan disapproval.
30. **hobby-horse**: slang for a wanton or a prostitute.
31. **colt**: (1) a young male horse; (2) a lascivious person.
32. **hackney**: (1) riding horse; (2) prostitute (slang).
51. **sympathiz'd**: matched. 52. **embassador**: ambassador.
60. **Minime**: by no means.
65. **Thump**: i.e. make a noise like a gun going off.
66. **volable**: voluble, i.e. quick-witted.
67. **favor**: good will, leave (with a play, perhaps, on the sense "face")
68. **gives thee place**: yields its place to you.
70. **a costard . . . shin**: a head with a cut on its shin.
71. **l'envoy**: i.e. explanation; properly, a postscript to a literary composition, which sends the piece on its way to its intended readers and interprets or comments on its import (cf. lines 81–82).
72. **salve.** Possibly Costard here says *salvé* (a salute) when he means *salve* (a healing ointment); hence Armado in lines 78–79 points out that he has taken "salve for l'envoy," i.e. salutation for farewell.
73. **mail**: pouch, bag (of a seller of cures). **plantan**: plantain, a healing herb. Costard wants the common home remedy, not strange remedies with foreign names.

silly thought, my spleen; the heaving of my lungs provokes me to ridiculous smiling—O, pardon me, my stars! Doth the inconsiderate take salve for l'envoy, and the word "l'envoy" for a salve?

Moth. Do the wise think them other? is not l'envoy a salve?

Arm. No, page, it is an epilogue or discourse, to make plain
Some obscure precedence that hath tofore been sain.
I will example it:
The fox, the ape, and the humble-bee
Were still at odds, being but three.
There's the moral. Now the l'envoy.

Moth. I will add the l'envoy. Say the moral again.

Arm. The fox, the ape, and the humble-bee
Were still at odds, being but three.

Moth. Until the goose came out of door,
And stayed the odds by adding four.
Now will I begin your moral, and do you follow with my l'envoy:
The fox, the ape, and the humble-bee
Were still at odds, being but three.

Arm. Until the goose came out of door,
Staying the odds by adding four.

Moth. A good l'envoy, ending in the goose; would you desire more?

Cost. The boy hath sold him a bargain, a goose, that's flat.
Sir, your pennyworth is good, and your goose be fat.
To sell a bargain well is as cunning as fast and loose:
Let me see: a fat l'envoy—ay, that's a fat goose.

Arm. Come hither, come hither. How did this argument begin?

Moth. By saying that a costard was broken in a shin.
Then call'd you for the l'envoy.

Cost. True, and I for a plantan; thus came your argument in;
Then the boy's fat l'envoy, the goose that you bought,
And he ended the market.

Arm. But tell me, how was there a costard broken in a shin?

Moth. I will tell you sensibly.

Cost. Thou hast no feeling of it, Moth. I will speak that l'envoy:
I, Costard, running out that was safely within,
Fell over the threshold, and broke my shin.

Arm. We will talk no more of this matter.

Cost. Till there be more matter in the shin.

Arm. Sirrah Costard, I will enfranchise thee.

76. spleen. Supposedly the organ in which laughter originated.
78. inconsiderate: unthinking one, dull-witted person.
82. precedence: preceding matter. (The second half of Armado's line is redundant.) **sain:** said.
83. example: give an example of. (The example is thought by commentators to contain some topical reference, no longer clear.)
85. still: always. **at odds:** (1) quarrelling; (2) an odd number.
92. stayed the odds: (1) checked the quarrelling; (2) prevented an odd number. **four:** i.e. a fourth.
101. sold . . . goose: made a fool of him.
102. your . . . and: you got your money's worth if.
103. fast and loose: cheating. **105. argument:** topic, discussion.
113. sensibly: feelingly, with emotion. **119. matter:** pus.

Cost. O, marry me to one Frances! I smell some l'envoy, some goose, in this.

Arm. By my sweet soul, I mean setting thee at liberty, enfreedoming thy person: thou wert immured, restrained, captivated, bound.

Cost. True, true, and now you will be my purgation and let me loose.

Arm. I give thee thy liberty, set thee from durance, and in lieu thereof, impose on thee nothing but this: bear this significant [*giving a letter*] to the country maid Jaquenetta. There is remuneration, for the best ward of mine honor is rewarding my dependants. Moth, follow.

Moth. Like the sequel, I. Signior Costard, adieu.

Exit [Armado, followed by Moth].

Cost. My sweet ounce of man's flesh, my incony Jew!
Now will I look to his remuneration. Remuneration! O, that's the Latin word for three farthings: three farthings—remuneration. "What's the price of this inkle?"—"One penny."—"No, I'll give you a remuneration": why, it carries it. Remuneration: why, it is a fairer name than French crown! I will never buy and sell out of this word.

Enter BEROWNE.

Ber. O, my good knave Costard, exceedingly well met!

Cost. Pray you, sir, how much carnation ribbon may a man buy for a remuneration?

Ber. O, what is a remuneration?

Cost. Marry, sir, halfpenny farthing.

Ber. O, why then three-farthing worth of silk.

Cost. I thank your worship, God be wi' you!

Ber. O, stay, slave; I must employ thee.
As thou wilt win my favor, good my knave,
Do one thing for me that I shall entreat.

Cost. When would you have it done, sir?

Ber. O, this afternoon.

Cost. Well, I will do it, sir; fare you well.

Ber. O, thou knowest not what it is.

Cost. I shall know, sir, when I have done it.

Ber. Why, villain, thou must know first.

Cost. I will come to your worship to-morrow morning.

Ber. It must be done this afternoon. Hark, slave, it is but this:
The Princess comes to hunt here in the park,
And in her train there is a gentle lady:
When tongues speak sweetly, then they name her name,
And Rosaline they call her. Ask for her,
And to her white hand see thou do commend

122. goose: slang for "whore."
126–27. be my purgation: clear me of wrongdoing (with obvious second sense extending to *bound* and *let me loose*).
130. significant: token, sign. **132. ward:** guard.
135. incony: fine, rare. **Jew.** Used playfully.
139. inkle: a kind of linen tape.
140. it carries it: it wins the day.
141. French crown: (1) a coin; (2) bald head (caused by syphilis, often called "the French disease").
142. out . . . word: using any other word but this.
145. carnation: flesh-colored.

This seal'd-up counsel. There's thy guerdon; go.

Cost. Gardon, O sweet gardon! better than remuneration, aleven-pence-farthing better; most sweet gardon! I will do it, sir, in print. Gardon! Remuneration! *Exit.*

Ber. O, and I, forsooth, in love! I, that have been love's whip,
A very beadle to a humorous sigh,
A critic, nay, a night-watch constable,
A domineering pedant o'er the boy,
Than whom no mortal so magnificent!
This wimpled, whining, purblind, wayward boy,
This senior[-junior], giant-dwarf, Dan Cupid,
Regent of love-rhymes, lord of folded arms,
Th' anointed sovereign of sighs and groans,
Liege of all loiterers and malecontents,
Dread prince of plackets, king of codpieces,
Sole imperator and great general
Of trotting paritors (O my little heart!),
And I to be a corporal of his field,
And wear his colors like a tumbler's hoop!
What! I love, I sue, I seek a wife—
A woman, that is like a German [clock],
Still a-repairing, ever out of frame,
And never going aright, being a watch,
But being watch'd that it may still go right!
Nay, to be perjur'd, which is worst of all;
And among three to love the worst of all,
A whitely wanton with a velvet brow,
With two pitch-balls stuck in her face for eyes;
Ay, and, by heaven, one that will do the deed
Though Argus were her eunuch and her guard.
And I to sigh for her, to watch for her,
To pray for her, go to! It is a plague
That Cupid will impose for my neglect
Of his almighty dreadful little might.
Well, I will love, write, sigh, pray, sue, groan:
Some men must love my lady, and some Joan.
[*Exit.*]

169. **counsel:** private communication. **guerdon:** reward.
171. **aleven:** eleven. 172. **in print:** i.e. most exactly.
175. **beadle:** parish officer who whipped petty offenders. **humorous:** moody. 177. **pedant:** schoolmaster.
178. **magnificent:** proud, boastful.
179. **wimpled:** blindfolded. **purblind:** totally blind.
180. **senior-junior.** Perhaps with play on *Signor Junior*, i.e. Mr. Youngboy. **Dan:** sir (from Latin *dominus*, "master").
181. **folded arms.** See note on III.i.18.
184. **plackets:** slits in petticoats, i.e. women (in bawdy sense). **codpieces:** baggy appendages at the front of breeches, i.e. men (in bawdy sense).
186. **paritors:** apparitors, officers who summoned offenders to an ecclesiastical court. 187. **a corporal . . . field:** his field officer.
188. **tumbler's hoop.** Usually decorated with varicolored ribbons.
191. **Still:** ever. **frame:** order.
193. **But . . . right:** i.e. unless an eye is kept on her to see that she behaves herself. 196. **whitely:** pale, sallow.
198. **do the deed:** engage in sexual intercourse.
199. **Argus:** a monster with a hundred eyes, never all closed simultaneously. 200. **watch:** stay awake all night.
205. **my lady:** milady, i.e. a woman of gentle birth. **Joan:** stock name for a peasant wench.

[ACT IV, SCENE I]

Enter the PRINCESS, *a* FORESTER, *her Ladies* [ROSALINE, MARIA, KATHERINE], *and her* LORDS, [*among them* BOYET].

Prin. Was that the King that spurr'd his horse so hard
Against the steep-up rising of the hill?

For. I know not, but I think it was not he.

Prin. Whoe'er 'a was, 'a show'd a mounting mind.
Well, lords, to-day we shall have our dispatch;
[On] Saturday we will return to France.
Then, forester, my friend, where is the bush
That we must stand and play the murtherer in?

For. Hereby, upon the edge of yonder coppice,
A stand where you may make the fairest shoot.

Prin. I thank my beauty, I am fair that shoot,
And thereupon thou speak'st the fairest shoot.

For. Pardon me, madam, for I meant not so.

Prin. What, what? First praise me, and again say no?
O short-liv'd pride! Not fair? alack for woe!

For. Yes, madam, fair.

Prin. Nay, never paint me now;
Where fair is not, praise cannot mend the brow.
Here (good my glass), take this for telling true:
[*Giving him money.*]
Fair payment for foul words is more than due.

For. Nothing but fair is that which you inherit.

Prin. See, see, my beauty will be sav'd by merit.
O heresy in fair, fit for these days!
A giving hand, though foul, shall have fair praise.
But come, the bow: now mercy goes to kill,
And shooting well is then accounted ill.
Thus will I save my credit in the shoot:
Not wounding, pity would not let me do't;
If wounding, then it was to show my skill,
That more for praise than purpose meant to kill.
And out of question so it is sometimes:
Glory grows guilty of detested crimes,
When for fame's sake, for praise, an outward part,
We bend to that the working of the heart;
As I for praise alone now seek to spill
The poor deer's blood, that my heart means no ill.

Boyet. Do not curst wives hold that self-sovereignty
Only for praise' sake, when they strive to be
Lords o'er their lords?

Prin. Only for praise—and praise we may afford
To any lady that subdues a lord.

Enter Clown [COSTARD].

IV.i.9. **coppice:** thicket.
10. **stand:** hunter's station. **fairest:** most favorable.
16. **paint:** flatter. 17. **fair:** beauty.
18. **good my glass:** my good mirror (because he shows the Princess her face at its true value). 20. **inherit:** own.
21. **by merit:** (1) by its own deserts; (2) by my giving of gratuities.
22. **heresy.** Because the Protestant Church teaches salvation by faith, not by "merit," i.e. good works. **in fair:** with regard to beauty.
25. **then:** i.e. when it is a merciful person who is doing the shooting.
30. **out of question:** undoubtedly.
31. **Glory:** i.e. the desire for too much glory. **detested:** detestable.
36. **curst:** shrewish.

Boyet. Here comes a member of the commonwealth.
Cost. God dig-you-den all! Pray you, which is the head lady?
Prin. Thou shalt know her, fellow, by the rest that have no heads.
Cost. Which is the greatest lady, the highest?
Prin. The thickest and the tallest.
Cost. The thickest and the tallest! it is so, truth is truth.
And your waist, mistress, were as slender as my wit,
One a' these maids' girdles for your waist should be fit.
Are not you the chief woman? You are the thickest here.
Prin. What's your will, sir? what's your will?
Cost. I have a letter from Monsieur Berowne to one Lady Rosaline.
Prin. O, thy letter, thy letter! He's a good friend of mine.
Stand aside, good bearer. Boyet, you can carve,
Break up this capon.
Boyet. I am bound to serve.
This letter is mistook; it importeth none here.
It is writ to Jaquenetta.
Prin. We will read it, I swear.
Break the neck of the wax, and every one give ear.
Boyet reads. "By heaven, that thou art fair, is most infallible; true, that thou art beauteous; truth itself, that thou art lovely. More fairer than fair, beautiful than beauteous, truer than truth itself, have commiseration on thy heroical vassal! The magnanimous and most illustrate King Cophetua set eye upon the pernicious and indubitate beggar Zenelophon; and he it was that might rightly say, *Veni, vidi, vici;* which to annothanize in the vulgar—O base and obscure vulgar!—*videlicet,* He came, [saw], and overcame: he came, one; [saw], two; [overcame], three. Who came? the king. Why did he come? to see. Why did he see? to overcome. To whom came he? to the beggar. What saw he? the beggar. Who overcame he? the beggar. The conclusion is victory; on whose side? the [king's]. The captive is enrich'd; on whose side? the beggar's. The catastrophe is a nuptial; on whose side? the king's; no, on both in one, or one in both. I am the king, for so stands the comparison; thou the beggar, for so witnesseth thy lowliness. Shall I command thy love? I may. Shall I enforce thy love? I could. Shall I entreat thy love? I will. What shalt thou exchange for rags? robes; for tittles? titles; for thyself? me. Thus expecting thy reply, I profane my lips on thy foot, my eyes on thy picture, and my heart on thy every part. Thine, in the dearest design of industry,
Don Adriano de Armado.
Thus dost thou hear the Nemean lion roar
'Gainst thee, thou lamb, that standest as his prey;
Submissive fall his princely feet before,
And he from forage will incline to play.
But if thou strive, poor soul, what art thou then?
Food for his rage, repasture for his den."
Prin. What plume of feathers is he that indited this letter?
What vane? What weathercock? Did you ever hear better?
Boyet. I am much deceived but I remember the style.
Prin. Else your memory is bad, going o'er it erewhile.
Boyet. This Armado is a Spaniard that keeps here in court,
A phantasime, a Monarcho, and one that makes sport
To the Prince and his book-mates.
Prin. Thou fellow, a word.
Who gave thee this letter?
Cost. I told you: my lord.
Prin. To whom shouldst thou give it?
Cost. From my lord to my lady.
Prin. From which lord to which lady?
Cost. From my Lord Berowne, a good master of mine,
To a lady of France that he call'd Rosaline.
Prin. Thou hast mistaken his letter. Come, lords, away.
[*To Rosaline.*] Here, sweet, put up this—'twill be thine another day. [*Exeunt Princess and Train.*]
Boyet. Who is the shooter? Who is the shooter?
Ros. Shall I teach you to know?
Boyet. Ay, my continent of beauty.
Ros. Why, she that bears the bow.
Finely put off!
Boyet. My lady goes to kill horns, but if thou marry,
Hang me by the neck if horns that year miscarry.
Finely put on!
Ros. Well then I am the shooter.
Boyet. And who is your deer?

41. commonwealth: common people.
42. dig-you-den: give you good evening.
56. Break up: cut up (a technical term in carving), i.e. open. **capon:** i.e. love letter (a play on French *poulet* in the same sense).
57. mistook: mis-taken, delivered to the wrong person (so also *mistaken* in line 106). **importeth:** concerns.
59. Break . . . wax: i.e. break the seal (with continuation of the image in *capon*). **65. illustrate:** illustrious.
65–66. King . . . Zenelophon. See note on I.ii.109–10.
66. indubitate: undoubted.
68. annothanize: anatomize, i.e. explain, interpret (?) or annotate, gloss (?). **vulgar:** vernacular. **69. videlicet:** namely.
77. catastrophe: denouement, outcome.
82. exchange: obtain in exchange. **83. tittles:** jots, points.
84. expecting: awaiting. **86. industry:** zealous gallantry.
88. Nemean lion: the lion of Nemea, in Greece, slain by Hercules as the first of his twelve labors. **91. forage:** raging, ravening.
92. strive: resist. **93. repasture:** food.
94. What . . . feathers: i.e. what kind of fine bird.
95. vane: weathervane (with play on *vain*).
96. but I: if I do not. **97. erewhile:** i.e. so recently.
98. keeps: lives.
99. phantasime: one full of fantastic notions. **Monarcho:** i.e. man with a highly inflated sense of self-importance (from the nickname of a hanger-on at court who had declared that he was monarch of the world). **100. To:** for.
107. 'twill . . . day: i.e. your turn will come.
108. shooter. Many editors emend to *suitor* (then pronounced *shooter*), but Boyet already knows (from lines 53, 104–5) that the suitor is Berowne. As we know, the Princess is the shooter, and Rosaline in line 114 only says *she* is the shooter to "take a shot" at Boyet. **109. continent of:** container of all, sum of.
110. put off: answered, evaded.
112. if . . . miscarry: if there is a shortage of horns, i.e. if you don't make your husband a cuckold.

Ros. If we choose by the horns, yourself come not near.
Finely put on indeed!

Mar. You still wrangle with her, Boyet, and she strikes at the brow.

Boyet. But she herself is hit lower. Have I hit her now?

Ros. Shall I come upon thee with an old saying, that was a man when King Pippen of France was a little boy, as touching the hit it?

Boyet. So I may answer thee with one as old, that was a woman when Queen Guinover of Britain was a little wench, as touching the hit it.

Ros. [*Sings.*] Thou canst not hit it, hit it, hit it,
Thou canst not hit it, my good man.

Boyet. [*Sings.*] And I cannot, cannot, cannot,
And I cannot, another can.

Exeunt [*Rosaline and Katherine*].

Cost. By my troth, most pleasant. How both did fit it!

Mar. A mark marvellous well shot, for they both did hit [it].

Boyet. A mark! O, mark but that mark! a mark, says my lady!
Let the mark have a prick in't, to mete at, if it may be.

Mar. Wide a' the bow-hand! I' faith, your hand is out.

Cost. Indeed 'a must shoot nearer, or he'll ne'er hit the clout.

Boyet. And if my hand be out, then belike your hand is in.

Cost. Then will she get the upshoot by cleaving the [pin].

Mar. Come, come, you talk greasily, your lips grow foul.

Cost. She's too hard for you at pricks, sir, challenge her to bowl.

Boyet. I fear too much rubbing. Good night, my good owl. [*Exeunt Boyet and Maria.*]

Cost. By my soul, a swain, a most simple clown!
Lord, Lord, how the ladies and I have put him down!
O' my troth, most sweet jests, most incony vulgar wit!
When it comes so smoothly off, so obscenely as it were, so fit.
Armado [a' th' one] side—O, a most dainty man!
To see him walk before a lady and to bear her fan!
To see him kiss his hand! and how most sweetly 'a will swear!
And his page a' t' other side, that handful of wit!
Ah, heavens, it is [a] most pathetical nit!

[*Shout*] *within.*

Sola, sola! *Exit.*

[Scene II]

Enter Dull, Holofernes *the Pedant, and* Nathaniel [*from watching the hunt*].

Nath. Very reverent sport truly, and done in the testimony of a good conscience.

Hol. The deer was (as you know) *sanguis*, in blood, ripe as the pomewater, who now hangeth like a jewel in the ear of *caelo*, the sky, the welkin, the heaven, and anon falleth like a crab on the face of *terra*, the soil, the land, the earth.

Nath. Truly, Master Holofernes, the epithites are sweetly varied, like a scholar at the least; but, sir, I assure ye it was a buck of the first head.

Hol. Sir Nathaniel, *haud credo.*

Dull. 'Twas not a haud credo, 'twas a pricket.

Hol. Most barbarous intimation! yet a kind of insinuation, as it were *in via*, in way, of explication; *facere*, as it were, replication, or rather *ostentare*, to show, as it were, his inclination, after his undressed, unpolished, uneducated, unpruned, untrained, or rather unlettered, or ratherest unconfirmed fashion, to insert again my *haud credo* for a deer.

Dull. I said the deer was not a haud credo, 'twas a pricket.

Hol. Twice sod simplicity, *bis coctus!*
O thou monster Ignorance, how deformed dost thou look!

Nath. Sir, he hath never fed of the dainties that are bred in a book;
He hath not eat paper, as it were; he hath not drunk ink; his intellect is not replenished; he is only an animal, only sensible in the duller parts;
And such barren plants are set before us, that we thankful should be—

117. **still:** always. **strikes . . . brow:** (1) takes good aim; (2) taunts you with being a cuckold.
118. **lower:** i.e. in the heart. **hit her:** read her situation accurately.
119. **come upon:** riposte against.
120. **a man:** i.e. already far from new. **Pippen:** Pepin (died 768), father of Charlemagne.
121. **the hit it:** a popular catch, or round, to be sung dancing (with obvious bawdy implication).
123. **Guinover.** Guinevere, legend has it, lived even earlier than Pepin; in addition, Boyet has appropriately chosen the name of a woman famous for being unfaithful to her husband.
132. **prick:** centre of the target, bull's-eye (with a bawdy quibble). **mete at:** measure by, take aim at.
133. **Wide . . . bow-hand:** too far to the left. **out:** at fault, inaccurate.
134. **clout:** mark of cloth in the centre of the target.
136. **upshoot:** best shot. **pin:** i.e. the pin which held the clout.
137. **greasily:** grossly.
139. **rubbing:** in the game of bowls, encountering an obstacle.
142. **incony:** rare, fine.
143. **obscenely.** Whatever word Costard intends, this one describes the preceding dialogue more accurately than he knows.
144. **dainty:** refined, elegant.
146. **swear.** A line to furnish the expected rhyme is presumably lost.
148. **pathetical nit:** touching little fellow. 149. **Sola:** a hunting cry.

IV.ii.1–2. **in the testimony:** with the warrant.
3–4. **in blood:** in excellent physical condition.
4. **pomewater:** a kind of apple.
4–6. **now . . . anon:** at one moment . . . at the next.
6. **crab:** crab apple. 8. **epithites:** epithets.
10. **buck . . . head:** a deer of the fifth year, with its first fully developed antlers.
11. **Sir:** courtesy title for a priest. **haud credo:** I cannot believe it. Dull misunderstands this as an assertion that the animal was a doe of some kind. (A. L. Rowse, in the London *Times Literary Supplement*, July 18, 1952, suggests that Dull hears *haud credo* as "awd (old) gray doe.") 12. **pricket:** a deer of the second year.
13. **intimation:** intrusion.
15. **facere . . . replication:** to make . . . explanation.
18. **unconfirmed:** unconsolidated, i.e. his *fashion* is without the coherence proper to learning.
22. **Twice sod:** twice-seethed, i.e. twice-boiled (repeated in *bis coctus*), probably referring to Dull's repeating his mistake. **simplicity:** ignorance, rusticity.

Which we [of] taste and feeling are—for those parts that do fructify in us more than he.
For as it would ill become me to be vain, [indiscreet], or a fool,
So were there a patch set on learning, to see him in a school:
But *omne bene*, say I, being of an old father's mind:
Many can brook the weather that love not the wind.

Dull. You two are book-men: can you tell me by your wit
What was a month old at Cain's birth, that's not five weeks old as yet?

Hol. [Dictynna], goodman Dull, [Dictynna], goodman Dull.

Dull. What is [Dictynna]?

Nath. A title to Phoebe, to Luna, to the moon.

Hol. The moon was a month old when Adam was no more,
And raught not to five weeks when he came to five-score.
Th' allusion holds in the exchange.

Dull. 'Tis true indeed, the collusion holds in the exchange.

Hol. God comfort thy capacity! I say, th' allusion holds in the exchange.

Dull. And I say, the pollution holds in the exchange, for the moon is never but a month old; and I say beside that, 'twas a pricket that the Princess kill'd.

Hol. Sir Nathaniel, will you hear an extemporal epitaph on the death of the deer? And to humor the [ignorant, call I] the deer the Princess kill'd a pricket.

Nath. *Perge*, good Master Holofernes, *perge*, so it shall please you to abrogate squirility.

Hol. I will something affect the letter, for it argues facility.
The preyful Princess pierc'd and prick'd a pretty pleasing pricket;
Some say a sore, but not a sore, till now made sore with shooting.
The dogs did yell: put *l* to sore, then sorel jumps from thicket,
Or pricket sore, or else sorel; the people fall a-hooting.
If sore be sore, then L to sore makes fifty sores o' sorel:

Of one sore I an hundred make by adding but one more L.

Nath. A rare talent!

Dull. [*Aside*.] If a talent be a claw, look how he claws him with a talent.

[*Hol.*] This is a gift that I have, simple; simple, a foolish extravagant spirit, full of forms, figures, shapes, objects, ideas, apprehensions, motions, revolutions. These are begot in the ventricle of memory, nourish'd in the womb of [pia mater], and delivered upon the mellowing of occasion. But the gift is good in those [in] whom it is acute, and I am thankful for it.

[*Nath.*] Sir, I praise the Lord for you, and so may my parishioners, for their sons are well tutor'd by you, and their daughters profit very greatly under you. You are a good member of the commonwealth.

[*Hol.*] *Mehercle*, if their sons be [ingenious], they shall want no instruction; if their daughters be capable, I will put it to them: but *vir* [*sapit*] *qui pauca loquitur*. A soul feminine saluteth us.

Enter JAQUENETTA *and the Clown* [COSTARD].

Jaq. God give you good morrow, Master Person.

[*Hol.*] Master Person, *quasi* [pers-one]. And if one should be pierc'd, which is the one?

Cost. Marry, Master Schoolmaster, he that is likel'est to a hogshead.

[*Hol.*] Of piercing a hogshead! a good lustre of conceit in a turf of earth; fire enough for a flint, pearl enough for a swine: 'tis pretty; it is well.

Jaq. Good Master Person, be so good as read me this letter. It was given me by Costard, and sent me from Don Armado. I beseech you read it.

[*Hol.*] *Facile, precor gelida quando* [*pecus omne*] *sub umbra ruminat*, and so forth. Ah, good old Mantuan! I may speak of thee as the traveller doth of Venice:

[*Venechia, Venechia*],
Che non te [*vede*], *che non te* [*prechia*].

Old Mantuan, old Mantuan! who understandeth thee not, loves thee not. *Ut, re, sol, la, mi, fa.* Under pardon, sir, what are the contents? or rather, as Horace says in his—What, my soul, verses?

29. Which we: we who. **do fructify:** are fruitful.
31. So . . . learning: it would be putting a fool to learn (?) or it would be setting a blemish on learning (?).
32. omne bene: all's well. **an old father's mind:** the opinion of some wise man of the past.
33. brook: endure. The proverb means that one must put up with many things one does not like.
36. Dictynna: the moon (a rather rare classical name for her, appropriate in the mouth of the pedantic Holofernes). **goodman:** yeoman, or more generally any person below the rank of gentleman.
40. raught: reached.
41. Th' allusion . . . exchange: i.e. the riddle is not affected by the substitution of Adam's name for Cain's.
42. collusion: Like *pollution* (line 46), another of Dull's "mistakings," but Shakespeare seems here to be commenting on the kind of in-game that is being inflicted on Dull by Holofernes and Nathaniel.
50. extemporal: extempore. **53. Perge:** proceed.
54. abrogate squirility: abstain from scurrility (with apparent reference to *pricket* = prick it).
55. something: somewhat. **affect the letter:** use alliteration.
56. preyful: desirous of prey. **57. sore:** a deer of the fourth year.
58. sorel: a deer of the third year. **59. Or:** either.
60, 61. L. With reference to the Roman numeral for fifty.

63. talent: i.e. talon. **64. claws:** scratches, i.e. flatters.
67. motions: impulses.
68. ventricle of memory: one of three divisions of the brain, supposed to be the seat of memory.
69. pia mater: membrane surrounding the brain.
76. under you: under your instruction (with an equivoque carried on in lines 79–80). **78. Mehercle:** by Hercules. **79. want:** lack.
80. vir . . . loquitur: that man is wise who speaks little.
82. Person: i.e. Parson.
83. quasi: as if, that is. **pers-one:** i.e. pierce-one (*pierce* being pronounced *perse*).
86. likel'est: likeliest, i.e. likest. **hogshead.** "Piercing a hogshead" was slang for getting drunk.
87–88. lustre of conceit: spark of imagination.
93–94. Facile . . . ruminat. The beginning of the first eclogue of Mantuan, an Italian writer of pastorals who died in 1516. *Facile* is an error for *Fauste*, and the line may be translated: "Faustus, while all the cattle chew their cud in the cool shade." If the error is not a misprint, Shakespeare is jibing at the pedant's Latin.
97–98. Venechia . . . prechia: Venice, Venice, he who has not seen you cannot value you (a version of an Italian proverb).
100. Ut . . . fa. He sings the scale, in incorrect order. (*Ut* was the old name for modern *do*.)

[*Nath.*] Ay, sir, and very learned.

[*Hol.*] Let me hear a staff, a stanze, a verse; *lege, domine.*

[*Nath.*] [*Reads.*]

"If love make me forsworn, how shall I swear to love?
Ah, never faith could hold, if not to beauty vowed!
Though to myself forsworn, to thee I'll faithful prove;
Those thoughts to me were oaks, to thee like osiers bowed.
Study his bias leaves, and makes his book thine eyes,
Where all those pleasures live that art would comprehend.
If knowledge be the mark, to know thee shall suffice;
Well learned is that tongue that well can thee commend,
All ignorant that soul that sees thee without wonder;
Which is to me some praise that I thy parts admire.
Thy eye Jove's lightning bears, thy voice his dreadful thunder,
Which, not to anger bent, is music and sweet fire.
Celestial as thou art, O, pardon love this wrong,
That sings heaven's praise with such an earthly tongue."

Hol. You find not the apostraphas, and so miss the accent. Let me supervise the [canzonet]. [*He takes the letter.*] Here are only numbers ratified, but for the elegancy, facility, and golden cadence of poesy, *caret.* Ovidius Naso was the man. And why indeed "Naso," but for smelling out the odoriferous flowers of fancy, the jerks of invention? *Imitari* is nothing: so doth the hound his master, the ape his keeper, the tired horse his rider. But, damosella virgin, was this directed to you?

Jaq. Ay, sir, from one Monsieur Berowne, one of the strange queen's lords.

[*Hol.*] I will overglance the superscript: "To the snow-white hand of the most beauteous Lady Rosaline." I will look again on the intellect of the letter, for the nomination of the party [writing] to the person written unto: "Your ladyship's in all desired employment, Berowne." Sir [Nathaniel], this Berowne is one of the votaries with the King, and here he hath framed a letter to a sequent of the stranger queen's, which accidentally, or by the way of progression, hath miscarried. Trip and go, my sweet, deliver this paper into the royal hand of the King; it may concern much. Stay not thy compliment; I forgive thy duty. Adieu.

Jaq. Good Costard, go with me. Sir, God save your life!

Cost. Have with thee, my girl.

Exit [*with Jaquenetta*].

[*Nath.*] Sir, you have done this in the fear of God, very religiously; and as a certain father saith—

Hol. Sir, tell not me of the father, I do fear colorable colors. But to return to the verses: did they please you, Sir Nathaniel?

Nath. Marvellous well for the pen.

Hol. I do dine to-day at the father's of a certain pupil of mine, where, if (before repast) it shall please you to gratify the table with a grace, I will, on my privilege I have with the parents of the foresaid child or pupil, undertake your *bien venuto*; where I will prove those verses to be very unlearned, neither savoring of poetry, wit, nor invention. I beseech your society.

Nath. And thank you too; for society, saith the text, is the happiness of life.

Hol. And certes the text most infallibly concludes it. [*To Dull.*] Sir, I do invite you too, you shall not say me nay: *pauca verba.* Away, the gentles are at their game, and we will to our recreation.

Exeunt.

[Scene III]

Enter Berowne *with a paper in his hand, alone.*

Ber. The King he is hunting the deer: I am coursing myself. They have pitch'd a toil: I am toiling in a pitch—pitch that defiles—defile! a foul word. Well, "set thee down, sorrow!" for so they say the fool said, and so say I, and I the fool: well prov'd, wit! By the Lord, this love is as mad as Ajax. It kills sheep; it kills me, I a sheep: well prov'd again a' my side! I will not love; if I do, hang me; i' faith, I will not. O but her eye—by this light, but for her eye, I would not love her; yes, for her two eyes. Well, I do nothing in the world but lie, and lie in my throat. By heaven, I do love, and it hath taught

104. **staff, stanze.** Both words mean "stanza." **lege, domine**: read, master.
105–18. This sonnet was printed with some verbal changes in *The Passionate Pilgrim* (1599); so were the poems at IV.iii.58–71, 99–118 (the three being there numbered v, iii, and xvi respectively).
108. **to me were**: i.e. which seemed to me as strong as. **osiers**: willows.
109. **Study . . . leaves**: i.e. the student abandons his inclination (to learning).
119. **find . . . apostraphas**: disregard the marks indicating contractions. It has been suggested that Holofernes is reproving Nathaniel for reading *sings* when the metre of the last line requires *singës*, and that his technical term is therefore a blunder; but his complaint may be more general. 120. **supervise**: look over.
121. **numbers ratified**: verses metrically correct.
123. **caret**: it is lacking. 124. **Naso.** From Latin *nasus*, "nose."
125. **jerks of invention**: strokes of imagination. **Imitari**: to imitate.
130. **strange**: foreign. 131. **superscript**: address, salutation.
133. **intellect**: meaning, i.e. contents. 138. **sequent**: follower.
139–40. **by . . . progression**: in going from hand to hand.

140. **Trip and go**: a common phrase, from a favorite song to accompany dancing.
142–43. **Stay . . . compliment**: do not take time for a polite leave taking. 143. **forgive thy duty**: waive the requirement of a curtsy.
146. **Have with thee**: I'll go with you. 147. **father**: church father.
149–50. **colorable colors**: plausible excuses.
152. **for the pen**: so far as the penmanship is concerned (cf. V.ii.40); or, perhaps, considering the writer (an example of the "learned" man's condescension to the courtier). 155. **gratify**: grace.
157. **bien venuto**: welcome (Italian *ben venuto*).
163. **certes**: certainly. 165. **pauca verba**: few words.
166. **gentles**: gentlefolk.

IV.iii.1–2. **coursing**: pursuing. 2. **pitch'd a toil**: set a snare.
2–3. **toiling . . . pitch**: a quibbling reference to Rosaline's eyes, which he has called two pitch-balls (III.i.197).
4. **set thee down.** See note on I.i.315.
6. **mad as Ajax.** Ajax, maddened by the refusal of the Greek leaders to give him the slain Achilles' armor, attacked a flock of sheep, thinking they were the Greek army.
11–12. **in my throat**: i.e. profoundly.

me to rhyme and to be mallicholy; and here is part of my rhyme, and here my mallicholy. Well, she hath one a' my sonnets already: the clown bore it, the fool sent it, and the lady hath it: sweet clown, sweeter fool, sweetest lady! By the world, I would not care a pin, if the other three were in. Here comes one with a paper, God give him grace to groan! *He stands aside, [climbing into a tree].*

The KING *ent'reth [with a paper].*

King. Ay me!

Ber. [*Aside.*] Shot, by heaven! Proceed, sweet Cupid, thou hast thump'd him with thy bird-bolt under the left pap. In faith, secrets!

King. [*Reads.*]
"So sweet a kiss the golden sun gives not
To those fresh morning drops upon the rose,
As thy eye-beams, when their fresh rays have smote
The night of dew that on my cheeks down flows;
Nor shines the silver moon one half so bright
Through the transparent bosom of the deep,
As doth thy face through tears of mine give light.
Thou shin'st in every tear that I do weep,
No drop but as a coach doth carry thee;
So ridest thou triumphing in my woe.
Do but behold the tears that swell in me,
And they thy glory through my grief will show.
But do not love thyself, then thou [wilt] keep
My tears for glasses, and still make me weep.
O queen of queens, how far dost thou excel
No thought can think, nor tongue of mortal tell."
How shall she know my griefs? I'll drop the paper.
Sweet leaves, shade folly. Who is he comes here?

Enter LONGAVILLE *[with a paper]. The King steps aside.*

What, Longaville, and reading! Listen, ear.

Ber. [*Aside.*] Now in thy likeness, one more fool appear!

Long. Ay me, I am forsworn!

Ber. [*Aside.*] Why, he comes in like a perjure, wearing papers.

[*King.*] [*Aside.*] In love, I hope—sweet fellowship in shame.

Ber. [*Aside.*] One drunkard loves another of the name.

Long. Am I the first that have been perjur'd so?

Ber. [*Aside.*] I could put thee in comfort: not by two that I know.
Thou makest the triumphery, the corner-cap of society,
The shape of love's Tyburn that hangs up simplicity.

Long. I fear these stubborn lines lack power to move.
O sweet Maria, empress of my love,
These numbers will I tear, and write in prose!

Ber. [*Aside.*] O, rhymes are guards on wanton Cupid's hose:
Disfigure not his shop.

Long. This same shall go. *He reads the sonnet.*
"Did not the heavenly rhetoric of thine eye,
'Gainst whom the world cannot hold argument,
Persuade my heart to this false perjury?
Vows for thee broke deserve not punishment.
A woman I forswore, but I will prove,
Thou being a goddess, I forswore not thee.
My vow was earthly, thou a heavenly love;
Thy grace being gain'd cures all disgrace in me.
Vows are but breath, and breath a vapor is;
Then thou, fair sun, which on my earth dost shine,
Exhal'st this vapor-vow; in thee it is.
If broken then, it is no fault of mine:
If by me broke, what fool is not so wise
To lose an oath to win a paradise?"

Ber. [*Aside.*] This is the liver-vein, which makes flesh a deity,
A green goose a goddess; pure, pure [idolatry].
God amend us, God amend! we are much out a' th' way.

Enter DUMAINE *[with a paper].*

Long. By whom shall I send this?—Company? Stay. [*Steps aside.*]

Ber. [*Aside.*] "All hid, all hid," an old infant play.
Like a demigod here sit I in the sky,
And wretched fools' secrets heedfully o'er-eye.
More sacks to the mill! O heavens, I have my wish!
Dumaine transformed! four woodcocks in a dish!

Dum. O most divine Kate!

Ber. [*Aside.*] O most profane coxcomb!

Dum. By heaven, the wonder in a mortal eye!

Ber. [*Aside.*] By earth, she is not, corporal, there you lie.

Dum. Her amber hairs for foul hath amber coted.

Ber. [*Aside.*] An amber-color'd raven was well noted.

Dum. As upright as the cedar.

Ber. [*Aside.*] Stoop, I say,
Her shoulder is with child.

Dum. As fair as day.

Ber. [*Aside.*] Ay, as some days, but then no sun must shine.

13. mallicholy: melancholy. **18. in:** i.e. in the same predicament.
23. bird-bolt: blunt arrow for killing birds. See note on I.ii.176.
24. under . . . pap: i.e. in the heart.
28. night of dew: night's allowance of tears.
38. glasses: mirrors.
46. perjure: perjurer. **wearing papers.** Perjurers were sometimes punished by being exposed to public view wearing paper placards which set forth their offenses.
51. triumphery: triumvirate (an apparently unique variant of *triumviry*). **corner-cap:** three-cornered cap.
52. Tyburn: the site of public executions in London. There are many references to its triangular gallows.
56. guards: trimmings. **hose:** breeches.
57. shop: codpiece (slang). **58–71.** See the note on IV.ii.105–18.
59. whom: which. **65. grace:** favor. **68. Exhal'st:** drawest up.
71. To: as to.
72. liver-vein: the style and manner of men in love (the liver being the supposed seat of the affections).
73. green goose: young goose, i.e. gawky young girl.
74. much . . . way: gone far astray.
76. All hid. Alluding to the game of hide and seek.
79. More . . . mill: i.e. there's more to come (proverbial).
80. woodcocks. Proverbially silly birds.
84. she . . . corporal: i.e. field officer in Cupid's army (cf. III.i.187).
85. coted: quoted, i.e. set down as, caused to be regarded as. Her amber-colored hair has made amber seem ugly by comparison.
86. raven. A quibble on *foul/fowl*. **well noted:** accurately observed (ironic).
87. Stoop: stooped (perhaps also suggesting that Dumaine should come down to earth).
88. is with child: i.e. is humped.

Dum. O that I had my wish!
Long. [*Aside.*] And I had mine!
King. [*Aside.*] And mine too, good Lord!
Ber. [*Aside.*] Amen, so I had mine. Is not that a good word?
Dum. I would forget her, but a fever she
Reigns in my blood, and will rememb'red be.
Ber. [*Aside.*] A fever in your blood! why then incision
Would let her out in saucers. Sweet misprision!
Dum. Once more I'll read the ode that I have writ.
Ber. [*Aside.*] Once more I'll mark how love can vary wit.
Dum. (*Reads his sonnet.*)
"On a day—alack the day!—
Love, whose month is ever May,
Spied a blossom passing fair
Playing in the wanton air:
Through the velvet leaves the wind,
All unseen, can passage find;
That the lover, sick to death,
[Wish'd] himself the heavens' breath.
Air, quoth he, thy cheeks may blow;
Air, would I might triumph so!
But, alack, my hand is sworn
Ne'er to pluck thee from thy [thorn];
Vow, alack, for youth unmeet,
Youth so apt to pluck a sweet.
Do not call it sin in me,
That I am forsworn for thee;
Thou for whom Jove would swear
Juno but an Ethiop were,
And deny himself for Jove,
Turning mortal for thy love."
This will I send and something else more plain
That shall express my true love's fasting pain.
O would the King, Berowne, and Longaville
Were lovers too! Ill, to example ill,
Would from my forehead wipe a perjur'd note:
For none offend where all alike do dote.
Long. [*Advancing.*] Dumaine, thy love is far from charity,
That in love's grief desir'st society:
You may look pale, but I should blush, I know,
To be o'erheard and taken napping so.
King. [*Advancing.*] Come, sir, you blush; as his your case is such;
You chide at him, offending twice as much.
You do not love Maria? Longaville
Did never sonnet for her sake compile,
Nor never lay his wreathed arms athwart
His loving bosom to keep down his heart.
I have been closely shrouded in this bush
And mark'd you both, and for you both did blush.

92. **a good word**: i.e. kind. 95. **incision**: bloodletting.
96. **saucers**: bowls used to receive the blood. **misprision**: mistake.
99–118. See note on IV.ii.105–18. 102. **wanton**: frolicsome.
104. **can**: gan, i.e. began to, did. 105. **That**: so that.
116. **Ethiop**: blackamoor. 120. **fasting**: caused by abstinence.
122. **example**: furnish a precedent for.
123. **perjur'd note.** See note on IV.iii.46.
125. **charity**: Christian love.
133. **wreathed arms.** See note on III.i.18.

I heard your guilty rhymes, observ'd your fashion,
Saw sighs reek from you, noted well your passion.
"Ay me!" says one, "O Jove!" the other cries;
One, her hairs were gold, crystal the other's eyes.
[*To Longaville.*] You would for paradise break faith and troth,
[*To Dumaine.*] And Jove for your love would infringe an oath.
What will Berowne say when that he shall hear
Faith infringed, which such zeal did swear?
How will he scorn! how will he spend his wit!
How will he triumph, leap, and laugh at it!
For all the wealth that ever I did see,
I would not have him know so much by me.
Ber. Now step I forth to whip hypocrisy.
[*Descending and advancing.*]
Ah, good my liege, I pray thee pardon me!
Good heart, what grace hast thou thus to reprove
These worms for loving, that art most in love?
Your eyes do make no [coaches;] in your tears
There is no certain princess that appears;
You'll not be perjur'd, 'tis a hateful thing;
Tush, none but minstrels like of sonneting!
But are you not asham'd? Nay, are you not,
All three of you, to be thus much o'ershot?
You found his mote, the King your mote did see;
But I a beam do find in each of three.
O, what a scene of fool'ry have I seen,
Of sighs, of groans, of sorrow, and of teen!
O me, with what strict patience have I sat,
To see a king transformed to a gnat!
To see great Hercules whipping a gig,
And profound Salomon to tune a jig,
And Nestor play at push-pin with the boys,
And critic Timon laugh at idle toys!
Where lies thy grief, O, tell me, good Dumaine?
And, gentle Longaville, where lies thy pain?
And where my liege's? All about the breast!
A caudle ho!
King. Too bitter is thy jest.
Are we betrayed thus to thy over-view?
Ber. Not you by me, but I betrayed to you:
I that am honest, I that hold it sin
To break the vow I am engaged in.
I am betrayed by keeping company
With men like [you], men of inconstancy.
When shall you see me write a thing in rhyme,
Or groan for Joan, or spend a minute's time
In pruning me? When shall you hear that I

138. **reek**: smoke. 145. **spend**: employ. 148. **by**: about.
153–54. **Your . . . appears.** Alluding to the King's sonnet (IV.iii.32–33).
158. **o'ershot**: wide of the mark, in error.
159. **You**: i.e. Longaville. **his**: i.e. Dumaine's.
159,160. **mote, beam.** See Matthew 7:3–5: "And why seest thou the mote that is in thy brother's eye, but perceivest not the beam that is in thine own eye?" (Geneva). 162. **teen**: grief.
164. **gnat**: i.e. an insignificant little creature (perhaps quibbling on "moth," which was pronounced *mote* [line 159]). 165. **gig**: top.
166. **Salomon**: Solomon, proverbial for wisdom. **tune**: play.
167. **Nestor**: oldest and wisest of the Greeks in the Trojan war. **push-pin**: a child's game with pins.
168. **critic**: cynic, censorious. **Timon.** Noted for his misanthropy. **laugh . . . toys**: take pleasure in foolish trifles.
172. **caudle**: a warm, thin gruel given to the sick.
176. **engaged in**: sworn to. 181. **pruning**: preening, dressing up.

Will praise a hand, a foot, a face, an eye,
A gait, a state, a brow, a breast, a waist,
A leg, a limb—
King. Soft, whither away so fast?
A true man, or a thief, that gallops so?
Ber. I post from love; good lover, let me go.

Enter JAQUENETTA *and Clown* [COSTARD].

Jaq. God bless the King!
King. What present hast thou there?
Cost. Some certain treason.
King. What makes treason here?
Cost. Nay, it makes nothing, sir.
King. If it mar nothing neither,
The treason and you go in peace away together.
Jaq. I beseech your Grace let this letter be read:
Our person misdoubts it; 'twas treason, he said.
King. Berowne, read it over.
He [*Berowne*] *reads the letter.*
Where hadst thou it?
Jaq. Of Costard.
King. Where hadst thou it?
Cost. Of Dun Adramadio, Dun Adramadio.
[*Berowne tears the letter.*]
King. How now, what is in you? Why dost thou tear it?
Ber. A toy, my liege, a toy; your Grace needs not fear it.
Long. It did move him to passion, and therefore let's hear it.
Dum. [*Gathering up the pieces.*] It is Berowne's writing, and here is his name.
Ber. [*To Costard.*] Ah, you whoreson loggerhead, you were born to do me shame.
Guilty, my lord, guilty! I confess, I confess.
King. What?
Ber. That you three fools lack'd me fool to make up the mess.
He, he, and you—and you, my liege!—and I,
Are pick-purses in love, and we deserve to die.
O, dismiss this audience, and I shall tell you more.
Dum. Now the number is even.
Ber. True, true, we are four.
Will these turtles be gone?
King. Hence, sirs, away!
Cost. Walk aside the true folk, and let the traitors stay. [*Exeunt Costard and Jaquenetta.*]
Ber. Sweet lords, sweet lovers, O, let us embrace!
As true we are as flesh and blood can be.
The sea will ebb and flow, heaven show his face;
Young blood doth not obey an old decree.
We cannot cross the cause why we were born;
Therefore of all hands must we be forsworn.
King. What, did these rent lines show some love of thine?
Ber. Did they, quoth you? Who sees the heavenly Rosaline,
That (like a rude and savage man of Inde),
At the first op'ning of the gorgeous east,
Bows not his vassal head, and strooken blind,
Kisses the base ground with obedient breast?
What peremptory eagle-sighted eye
Dares look upon the heaven of her brow,
That is not blinded by her majesty?
King. What zeal, what fury, hath inspir'd thee now?
My love (her mistress) is a gracious moon,
She (an attending star) scarce seen a light.
Ber. My eyes are then no eyes, nor I Berowne.
O, but for my love, day would turn to night!
Of all complexions the cull'd sovereignty
Do meet as at a fair in her fair cheek,
Where several worthies make one dignity,
Where nothing wants that want itself doth seek.
Lend me the flourish of all gentle tongues—
Fie, painted rhetoric! O, she needs it not.
To things of sale a seller's praise belongs:
She passes praise, then praise too short doth blot.
A wither'd hermit, fivescore winters worn,
Might shake off fifty, looking in her eye:
Beauty doth varnish age, as if new born,
And gives the crutch the cradle's infancy.
O, 'tis the sun that maketh all things shine!
King. By heaven, thy love is black as ebony.
Ber. Is ebony like her? O [wood] divine!
A wife of such wood were felicity.
O, who can give an oath? Where is a book?
That I may swear beauty doth beauty lack,
If that she learn not of her eye to look:
No face is fair that is not full so black.
King. O paradox! Black is the badge of hell,
The hue of dungeons, and the school of night;
And beauty's crest becomes the heavens well.
Ber. Devils soonest tempt, resembling spirits of light.
O, if in black my lady's brows be deck'd,
It mourns that painting [and] usurping hair
Should ravish doters with a false aspect:
And therefore is she born to make black fair.

183. state: attitude, pose. **185. true:** honest. **186. post:** hasten. **187. present:** i.e. writing. **188. makes treason:** has treason to do. **192. person:** parson. Actually, at IV.ii.140–42 it is Holofernes, not Nathaniel, who comments on the letter, and treason is not mentioned, but there is confusion in the text at that point (see the Textual Notes). **misdoubts:** suspects. **203. mess:** group of four at table. **205. pick-purses:** i.e. cheaters. **208. turtles:** turtledoves, lovers. **214. cross . . . born:** i.e. hold out against love. **215. of all hands:** in any case.

218. rude: ignorant. **Inde:** India. **220. strooken:** struck. **222. peremptory:** determined. **eagle-sighted.** The eagle was thought to be able to gaze directly at the sun. **227. scarce . . . light:** a light hardly to be seen. **230. cull'd sovereignty:** those selected as supreme. **232. worthies:** excellencies, i.e. beauties. **dignity:** i.e. surpassing beauty. **233. wants . . . want:** is lacking . . . desire. **234. flourish:** eloquence, embellishment. **gentle:** noble. **235. painted:** artificial. **236. of sale:** for sale. **237. She . . . blot:** i.e. she exceeds anything that can be said in her praise; hence any praise of her will inevitably fall short, and be a blemish instead of an ornament. **246. book:** Bible. **248. of her eye:** i.e. from Rosaline's black eyes. **to look:** i.e. how beauty should look. **249. full so:** just as. **250. badge of hell.** Devils were regularly represented as black. **251. school of night.** Many emendations have been proposed for *school*, but the phrase may allude to a group of writers whose chief patron was Sir Walter Raleigh, a group that was called "Sir Walter Rauley's Schoole of Atheisme." **252. And beauty's crest:** but the badge of beauty (the sun?). **253. Devils . . . light.** Cf. 2 Corinthians 11:14: "Satan himself is transformed into an angel of light." **255. usurping:** i.e. false.

Her favor turns the fashion of the days,
For native blood is counted painting now;
And therefore red, that would avoid dispraise,
Paints itself black, to imitate her brow.
Dum. To look like her are chimney-sweepers black.
Long. And since her time are colliers counted bright.
King. And Ethiops of their sweet complexion crack.
Dum. Dark needs no candles now, for dark is light.
Ber. Your mistresses dare never come in rain,
For fear their colors should be wash'd away.
King. 'Twere good yours did; for, sir, to tell you plain,
I'll find a fairer face not wash'd to-day.
Ber. I'll prove her fair, or talk till doomsday here.
King. No devil will fright thee then so much as she.
Dum. I never knew man hold vile stuff so dear.
Long. Look, here's thy love [*showing his boot*], my foot and her face see.
Ber. O, if the streets were paved with thine eyes,
Her feet were much too dainty for such tread!
Dum. O vile! then as she goes what upward lies
The street should see as she walk'd overhead.
King. But what of this, are we not all in love?
Ber. O, nothing so sure, and thereby all forsworn.
King. Then leave this chat, and, good Berowne, now prove
Our loving lawful, and our faith not torn.
Dum. Ay marry, there—some flattery for this evil.
Long. O, some authority how to proceed;
Some tricks, some quillets, how to cheat the devil.
Dum. Some salve for perjury.
Ber. O, 'tis more than need.
Have at you then, affection's men-at-arms.
Consider what you first did swear unto:
To fast, to study, and to see no woman—
Flat treason 'gainst the kingly state of youth.
Say, can you fast? Your stomachs are too young,
And abstinence engenders maladies.
⟨And where that you have vow'd to study, lords,
In that each of you have forsworn his book,
Can you still dream and pore and thereon look?
For when would you, my lord, or you, or you,
Have found the ground of study's excellence
Without the beauty of a woman's face?
From women's eyes this doctrine I derive:
They are the ground, the books, the academes,
From whence doth spring the true Promethean fire.
Why, universal plodding poisons up
The nimble spirits in the arteries,
As motion and long-during action tires
The sinowy vigor of the traveller.
Now for not looking on a woman's face,
You have in that forsworn the use of eyes,
And study too, the causer of your vow.
For where is any author in the world
Teaches such beauty as a woman's eye?
Learning is but an adjunct to ourself,
And where we are, our learning likewise is.
Then when ourselves we see in ladies' eyes,
With ourselves,
Do we not likewise see our learning there?⟩
O, we have made a vow to study, lords,
And in that vow we have forsworn our books.
For when would you, my liege, or you, or you,
In leaden contemplation have found out
Such fiery numbers as the prompting eyes
Of beauty's tutors have enrich'd you with?
Other slow arts entirely keep the brain;
And therefore, finding barren practicers,
Scarce show a harvest of their heavy toil;
But love, first learned in a lady's eyes,
Lives not alone immured in the brain,
But with the motion of all elements,
Courses as swift as thought in every power,
And gives to every power a double power,
Above their functions and their offices.
It adds a precious seeing to the eye:
A lover's eyes will gaze an eagle blind.
A lover's ear will hear the lowest sound,
When the suspicious head of theft is stopp'd.
Love's feeling is more soft and sensible
Than are the tender horns of cockled snails.
Love's tongue proves dainty Bacchus gross in taste.
For valor, is not Love a Hercules,
Still climbing trees in the Hesperides?
Subtile as Sphinx, as sweet and musical
As bright Apollo's lute, strung with his hair.
And when Love speaks, the voice of all the gods
Make heaven drowsy with the harmony.
Never durst poet touch a pen to write
Until his ink were temp'red with Love's sighs:
O then his lines would ravish savage ears
And plant in tyrants mild humility.
From women's eyes this doctrine I derive:

258. **favor:** face.
259. **native blood:** natural color. **counted:** accounted, taken to be.
264. **crack:** boast. 271. **then:** i.e. at doomsday.
284. **quillets:** verbal niceties, quibbles.
286. **Have at you:** here goes. **affection's:** love's.
289. **state:** majesty, power.
292–314. These lines are a first-draft version of part of lines 315–62.
293. **book:** true book, i.e. woman's face.
296. **ground:** basis, foundation.
300. **Promethean fire:** i.e. divine fire; from the legend that Prometheus stole fire from heaven and gave it to man.
301. **up:** completely.
302. **spirits . . . arteries.** The "spirits" that were thought to give life to man—natural (seated in the liver), vital (the heart), and animal (the brain)—supposedly coursed through the arteries.
303. **long-during:** long-continued. 304. **sinowy:** sinewy, muscular.
318. **leaden:** dull.
319. **fiery numbers:** i.e. the sonnets and other poems or verses.
321. **arts:** branches of knowledge. **keep:** remain in, dwell.
329. **Above . . . offices:** over and above their usual functions (*functions* and *offices* are synonyms).
331. **gaze . . . blind.** See the note on line 222.
333. **the suspicious . . . stopp'd:** i.e. even the ears of a thief, apprehensive of danger, are deaf. 334. **sensible:** sensitive.
335. **cockled:** having a shell. With the line cf. *Venus and Adonis*, lines 1033–34.
338. **Hesperides:** i.e. the garden (as misunderstood by the Elizabethans) in which the golden apples grew, watched by the daughters of Hesperus. The last of Hercules' twelve labors was to gain possession of the fruit. 341. **voice:** i.e. responsive songs.

They sparkle still the right Promethean fire;
They are the books, the arts, the academes,
That show, contain, and nourish all the world,
Else none at all in aught proves excellent.
Then fools you were these women to forswear,
Or keeping what is sworn, you will prove fools.
For wisdom's sake, a word that all men love,
Or for love's sake, a word that loves all men,
Or for men's sake, the [authors] of these women,
Or women's sake, by whom we men are men,
[Let] us once lose our oaths to find ourselves,
Or else we lose ourselves to keep our oaths.
It is religion to be thus forsworn:
For charity itself fulfills the law,
And who can sever love from charity?

King. Saint Cupid, then! and, soldiers, to the field!

Ber. Advance your standards, and upon them, lords;
Pell-mell, down with them! but be first advis'd,
In conflict that you get the sun of them.

Long. Now to plain-dealing, lay these glozes by:
Shall we resolve to woo these girls of France?

King. And win them too; therefore let us devise
Some entertainment for them in their tents.

Ber. First, from the park let us conduct them thither;
Then homeward every man attach the hand
Of his fair mistress. In the afternoon
We will with some strange pastime solace them,
Such as the shortness of the time can shape,
For revels, dances, masks, and merry hours
Forerun fair Love, strewing her way with flowers.

King. Away, away, no time shall be omitted
That will be time, and may by us be fitted.

Ber. [*Allons! allons!*] Sow'd cockle reap'd no corn,
And justice always whirls in equal measure:
Light wenches may prove plagues to men forsworn;
If so, our copper buys no better treasure. [*Exeunt.*]

[ACT V, SCENE I]

Enter the Pedant [HOLOFERNES], *the Curate* [SIR NATHANIEL], *and* DULL.

Hol. *Satis quid sufficit.*

Nath. I praise God for you, sir. Your reasons at dinner have been sharp and sententious: pleasant without scurrility, witty without affection, audacious without impudency, learned without opinion, and strange without heresy. I did converse this *quondam* day with a companion of the King's, who is intituled, nominated, or called, Don Adriano de Armado.

Hol. *Novi* [*hominem*] *tanquam te.* His humor is lofty, his discourse peremptory, his tongue filed, his eye ambitious, his gait majestical, and his general behavior vain, ridiculous, and thrasonical. He is too picked, too spruce, too affected, too odd as it were, too peregrinate, as I may call it.

Nath. A most singular and choice epithet.

Draw out his table-book.

Hol. He draweth out the thread of his verbosity finer than the staple of his argument. I abhor such fanatical phantasimes, such insociable and point-devise companions, such rackers of ortography, as to speak "dout," fine, when he should say "doubt"; "det," when he should pronounce "debt"—*d, e, b, t,* not *d, e, t:* he clepeth a calf, "cauf"; half, "hauf"; neighbor *vocatur* "nebor"; neigh abbreviated "ne." This is abhominable—which he would call "abbominable"; it insinuateth me of [insanie]: *ne intelligis, domine?* to make frantic, lunatic.

Nath. *Laus Deo,* [*bone*] *intelligo.*

Hol. [*Bone? bone* for *bene,*] Priscian a little scratch'd, 'twill serve.

Enter Braggart [ARMADO], *Boy* [MOTH, *and* COSTARD].

Nath. *Videsne quis venit?*

Hol. *Video, et gaudeo.*

Arm. [*To Moth.*] Chirrah!

Hol. [*Quare*] chirrah, not sirrah?

Arm. Men of peace, well encount'red.

Hol. Most military sir, salutation.

Moth. [*Aside to Costard.*] They have been at a great feast of languages, and stol'n the scraps.

Cost. O, they have liv'd long on the alms-basket of words. I marvel thy master hath not eaten thee for a word, for thou art not so long by the head as

355. **loves.** Variously glossed, for example as "is a friend to," "is lovable to," "sets a value upon," "inspires with love."
361. **For . . . law.** Cf. Romans 13:8: "he that loveth another hath fulfilled the law."
366. **get . . . them:** i.e. get the sun in their eyes; hence, get the advantage of them. 367. **glozes:** pretenses, sophistries.
372. **attach:** seize.
380. **Allons:** come. **cockle:** i.e. weeds. **corn:** grain.
381. **measure:** proportion. 382. **Light:** frivolous.
383. **copper:** base coin.

V.i.1. **Satis quid sufficit:** properly, *satis (est) quod sufficit*, enough is as good as a feast. Some editors correct Holofernes' faulty Latin; others suppose a satiric intent on Shakespeare's part (see note on IV.ii.93–94). 2. **reasons:** discourses.
3. **sharp:** acute, subtle. **sententious:** pithy.
4. **affection:** affectation. **audacious:** spirited, bold (in a good sense).
5. **opinion:** self-conceit, arrogance.
6. **strange:** new, fresh. **this quondam:** the other.
7. **intituled:** entitled.
9. **Novi . . . te:** I know the man as well as I know you. **humor:** mental disposition.
10. **peremptory:** overbearing. **filed:** polished.
11. **majestical:** stately. 12. **thrasonical:** boastful.
13. **picked:** fastidious. 14. **peregrinate:** foreign.
15. **singular:** unmatched. **s.d. table-book:** notebook.
17. **staple:** fibre. **argument:** subject matter.
18. **fanatical:** extravagant. **phantasimes:** fantastic fellows. **insociable:** not companionable.
18–19. **point-devise:** extremely precise.
19. **rackers of ortography:** tormentors of orthography. Holofernes represents the group of Renaissance educators who sought to bring the spelling and pronunciation of English words as close as possible to their Latin originals. 20. **fine:** mincingly. 22. **clepeth:** calls.
23. **vocatur:** is called.
25. **it . . . insanie:** (1) it suggests insanity to me; (2) it introduces frenzy into me (i.e. it drives me frantic).
25–26. **ne intelligis, domine:** do you understand, master.
27. **Laus . . . intelligo:** God be praised, I understand well.
28–29. **Priscian . . . scratch'd:** i.e. your Latin is a little faulty. Priscian's grammars (written about the beginning of the sixth century) were considered standard.
30. **Videsne quis venit:** do you see who comes.
31. **Video, et gaudeo:** I see and rejoice. 33. **Quare:** why.
38. **alms-basket:** baskets in which scraps were collected for the poor, i.e. public charity.

honorificabilitudinitatibus: thou art easier swallow'd than a flap-dragon.

Moth. Peace, the peal begins.

Arm. [*To Holofernes.*] Monsieur, are you not lett'red?

Moth. Yes, yes, he teaches boys the horn-book. What is *a*, *b*, spell'd backward, with the horn on his head?

Hol. *Ba*, *pueritia*, with a horn added.

Moth. *Ba*, most silly sheep, with a horn. You hear his learning.

Hol. *Quis*, *quis*, thou consonant?

Moth. The last of the five vowels, if "you" repeat them; or the fift, if I.

Hol. I will repeat them—*a*, *e*, *I*—

Moth. The sheep: the other two concludes it—*o*, *U*.

Arm. Now by the salt [wave] of the Mediterraneum, a sweet touch, a quick venue of wit—snip, snap, quick and home. It rejoiceth my intellect. True wit!

Moth. Offer'd by a child to an old man: which is wit-old.

Hol. What is the figure? What is the figure?

Moth. Horns.

Hol. Thou disputes like an infant; go whip thy gig.

Moth. Lend me your horn to make one, and I will whip about your infamy, [*manu*] *cita*—a gig of a cuckold's horn.

Cost. And I had but one penny in the world, thou shouldst have it to buy gingerbread. Hold, there is the very remuneration I had of thy master, thou halfpenny purse of wit, thou pigeon-egg of discretion. O, and the heavens were so pleas'd that thou wert but my bastard, what a joyful father wouldest thou make me! Go to, thou hast it *ad dunghill*, at the fingers' ends, as they say.

Hol. O, I smell false Latin, "dunghill" for *unguem*.

Arm. Arts-man, preambulate, we will be singuled from the barbarous. Do you not educate youth at the charge-house on the top of the mountain?

Hol. Or *mons*, the hill.

Arm. At your sweet pleasure, for the mountain.

Hol. I do, *sans question*.

Arm. Sir, it is the King's most sweet pleasure and affection to congratulate the Princess at her pavilion in the posteriors of this day, which the rude multitude call the afternoon.

Hol. The posterior of the day, most generous sir, is liable, congruent, and measurable for the afternoon. The word is well cull'd, chose, sweet, and apt, I do assure you, sir, I do assure.

Arm. Sir, the King is a noble gentleman, and my familiar, I do assure ye, very good friend; for what is inward between us, let it pass. I do beseech thee remember thy courtesy; I beseech thee apparel thy head; and among other [importunate] and most serious designs, and of great import indeed too—but let that pass; for I must tell thee it will please his Grace (by the world) sometime to lean upon my poor shoulder, and with his royal finger, thus, dally with my excrement, with my mustachio; but, sweet heart, let that pass. By the world, I recount no fable: some certain special honors it pleaseth his greatness to impart to Armado, a soldier, a man of travel, that hath seen the world; but let that pass. The very all of all is—but, sweet heart, I do implore secrety—that the King would have me present the Princess (sweet chuck) with some delightful ostentation, or show, or pageant, or antic, or firework. Now, understanding that the curate and your sweet self are good at such eruptions and sudden breaking out of mirth (as it were), I have acquainted you withal, to the end to crave your assistance.

Hol. Sir, you shall present before her the Nine Worthies. Sir [Nathaniel], as concerning some entertainment of time, some show in the posterior of this day, to be [rend'red] by our [assistance,] the King's command, and this most gallant, illustrate, and learned gentleman, before the Princess, I say none so fit as to present the Nine Worthies.

Nath. Where will you find men worthy enough to present them?

Hol. Joshua, yourself; myself; and this gallant gentleman, Judas Machabeus; this swain (because of

41. honorificabilitudinitatibus: dative (or ablative) plural of a medieval Latin word meaning "the state of being loaded with honors"; "often mentioned as the longest word known" (Johnson).
42. flap-dragon: a flaming raisin floating on wine or ale, to be snapped up with the mouth. **43. peal:** peal of bells, i.e. babble of tongues.
45. lett'red: i.e. an educated man.
46. horn-book: printed sheet of paper, protected by a thin sheet of transparent horn, from which children learned their letters.
49. pueritia: childishness, child.
52. Quis: who. **consonant:** i.e. nonentity, since a consonant requires a vowel to turn it into a pronounceable syllable.
53. last. Many editors emend to *third*, but they miss the jest. Moth is answering the question "Who is a sheep?" and (as David points out) "To Moth, Holofernes remains 'you' (and thus the sheep) no matter who repeats the vowels." **54. fift:** fifth.
56. concludes it: (1) proves my contention; (2) completes the list of vowels. **57. o, U:** oh, you. **59. touch:** stroke. **venue:** thrust.
60. home: to the point aimed at.
63. wit-old. With a quibble on *wittol*, a contented cuckold.
64. figure: figure of speech. **66. disputes:** reasonest.
67. gig: top. **69. manu cita:** with ready hand.
74. halfpenny purse: tiny purse just large enough for a small coin.
79–80. [ad] unguem: to a nicety, perfectly (literally, to the nail).
81. Arts-man: scholar. **preambulate:** walk ahead (with me).
singuled: separated, singled out. **83. charge-house:** school.

86. sans: without. **88. congratulate:** give pleasure to.
91. generous: well-born.
92. liable, congruent, and measurable. All synonyms, meaning "suitable, fit."
93. chose: (well) chosen. Many editors read *choice*, following F2.
96. familiar: intimate friend. **97. inward:** confidential, private.
98. remember thy courtesy: i.e. remember that you have removed your hat (see line 35). **101. let that pass:** never mind about that.
104. excrement: outgrowth (of hair; used also of fingernails).
109. all of all: sum of all. **110. secrety:** secrecy.
111. chuck: chick (a term of endearment).
112. ostentation: spectacular show. **antic:** pageant or other entertainment with the characters in grotesque or fantastic costumes.
117–118. Nine Worthies: a group of nine famous conquerors often mentioned in literature or represented in pageants and plays. The usual list comprised three pagans, Hector of Troy, Alexander the Great, and Julius Caesar; three Jews, Joshua, David, and Judas Maccabaeus; and three Christians, King Arthur, Charlemagne, and Godfrey of Bouillon. The list varied, but Hercules and Pompey make their first recorded appearance in it in Holofernes' next speech.
123. present: represent.
126–27. Joshua . . . Machabeus. Possibly an unrevised draft, since Holofernes assigns himself no role, and Nathaniel and Armado eventually play Alexander and Hector respectively.

his great limb or joint) shall pass Pompey the Great; the page, Hercules.

Arm. Pardon, sir, error: he is not quantity enough for that Worthy's thumb, he is not so big as the end of his club.

Hol. Shall I have audience? He shall present Hercules in minority; his enter and exit shall be strangling a snake; and I will have an apology for that purpose.

Moth. An excellent device! so if any of the audience hiss, you may cry, "Well done, Hercules, now thou crushest the snake!" That is the way to make an offense gracious, though few have the grace to do it.

Arm. For the rest of the Worthies?
Hol. I will play three myself.
Moth. Thrice-worthy gentleman!
Arm. Shall I tell you a thing?
Hol. We attend.
Arm. We will have, if this fadge not, an antic. I beseech you follow.

Hol. *Via*, goodman Dull! thou hast spoken no word all this while.

Dull. Nor understood none neither, sir.
Hol. [*Allons!*] we will employ thee.
Dull. I'll make one in a dance, or so; or I will play
On the tabor to the Worthies, and let them dance the hay.
Hol. Most dull, honest Dull! to our sport; away!
Exeunt.

[SCENE II]

Enter the Ladies: [*the* PRINCESS, MARIA, KATHERINE, *and* ROSALINE].

Prin. Sweet hearts, we shall be rich ere we depart,
If fairings come thus plentifully in.
A lady wall'd about with diamonds!
Look you what I have from the loving King.
Ros. Madam, came nothing else along with that?
Prin. Nothing but this? Yes, as much love in rhyme
As would be cramm'd up in a sheet of paper,
Writ a' both sides the leaf, margent and all,
That he was fain to seal on Cupid's name.
Ros. That was the way to make his godhead wax,
For he hath been five thousand year a boy.
Kath. Ay, and a shrowd unhappy gallows too.
Ros. You'll ne'er be friends with him, 'a kill'd your sister.
Kath. He made her melancholy, sad, and heavy,
And so she died. Had she been light, like you,
Of such a merry, nimble, stirring spirit,
She might 'a' been [a] grandam ere she died.
And so may you; for a light heart lives long.
Ros. What's your dark meaning, mouse, of this light word?
Kath. A light condition in a beauty dark.
Ros. We need more light to find your meaning out.
Kath. You'll mar the light by taking it in snuff;
Therefore I'll darkly end the argument.
Ros. Look what you do, you do it still i' th' dark.
Kath. So do not you, for you are a light wench.
Ros. Indeed I weigh not you, and therefore light.
Kath. You weigh me not? O, that's you care not for me.
Ros. Great reason: for past care is still past cure.
Prin. Well bandied both, a set of wit well played.
But, Rosaline, you have a favor too?
Who sent it? and what is it?
Ros. I would you knew.
And if my face were but as fair as yours,
My favor were as great: be witness this.
Nay, I have verses too, I thank Berowne;
The numbers true, and, were the numb'ring too,
I were the fairest goddess on the ground.
I am compar'd to twenty thousand fairs.
O, he hath drawn my picture in his letter!
Prin. Any thing like?
Ros. Much in the letters, nothing in the praise.
Prin. Beauteous as ink—a good conclusion.
Kath. Fair as a text B in a copy-book.
Ros. Ware pencils [ho]! let me not die your debtor,
My red dominical, my golden letter:
O that your face were not so full of O's!
Prin. A pox of that jest! and I beshrow all shrows.

128. pass: perform. **133. have audience:** be heard.
134. Hercules in minority. Hercules' first exploit was to strangle two serpents sent by the envious Juno to destroy him in his cradle. **enter:** entrance. **147. fadge:** turn out well.
149. Via: on! (a cry of encouragement).
153. make one: be one of the party.
154. tabor: a small drum. **hay:** a country dance, something like a reel.

V.ii.2. fairings: presents.
3. A lady . . . diamonds. A description of the King's gift; similar gems are listed in extant inventories.
9. That . . . name: so that he was obliged to add Cupid's name (as witness to his vows) on an attached slip of paper. Seals were often thus attached to legal documents.
10. wax: grow (with play on the wax of the seal).
11. five thousand year. The supposed age of the world.
12. shrowd: shrewd, i.e. evilly disposed (or perhaps here used adverbially, in the sense "grievously"). **unhappy:** bringing bad luck. **gallows:** knave fit to be hanged. **15. light:** cheerful.
17. 'a': have.
19. dark: obscure, hidden. **light:** trivial, unimportant.
20. light condition: wanton nature.
22. taking . . . snuff: taking offense, with pun on snuffing a candle (*light*). **24. Look what:** whatever.
26. I . . . you: I do not weigh as much as you. (Katherine takes it in a different sense, which she explains.)
28. for . . . cure: i.e. Katherine is beyond hope of cure.
30. favor: love token.
35. numbers: metre. **numb'ring:** estimate.
37. fairs: beautiful women.
40. letters: penmanship. **praise:** i.e. content.
41. Beauteous as ink. A jibe at Rosaline's dark complexion.
42. text B. The text hand was one of the more formal of the Elizabethan styles of writing. *B* is meant, perhaps, to suggest *black*.
43. Ware pencils: i.e. beware this sketching of portraits with the finely pointed brushes used for make-up. **let . . . debtor:** i.e. I owe you one for that.
44. red dominical: the red letter used to mark Sundays on calendars. The medieval Latin name for Sunday was *dies dominica*. **golden letter.** Also used to mark Sundays. Here used quibblingly with reference to Katherine's fair complexion.
45. O's: marks left by smallpox (hence the Princess' next remark).
46. beshrow all shrows: beshrew (i.e. mischief take) all shrews.

But, Katherine, what was sent to you from fair Dumaine?
Kath. Madam, this glove.
Prin. Did he not send you twain?
Kath. Yes, madam, and moreover
Some thousand verses of a faithful lover.
A huge translation of hypocrisy,
Vildly compiled, profound simplicity.
Mar. This, and these [pearls], to me sent Longaville.
The letter is too long by half a mile.
Prin. I think no less. Dost thou not wish in heart
The chain were longer and the letter short?
Mar. Ay, or I would these hands might never part.
Prin. We are wise girls to mock our lovers so.
Ros. They are worse fools to purchase mocking so.
That same Berowne I'll torture ere I go.
O that I knew he were but in by th' week!
How I would make him fawn, and beg, and seek,
And wait the season, and observe the times,
And spend his prodigal wits in bootless rhymes,
And shape his service wholly to my device,
And make him proud to make me proud that jests!
So pair-taunt-like would I o'ersway his state
That he should be my fool and I his fate.
Prin. None are so surely caught, when they are catch'd,
As wit turn'd fool; folly, in wisdom hatch'd,
Hath wisdom's warrant and the help of school,
And wit's own grace to grace a learned fool.
Ros. The blood of youth burns not with such excess
As gravity's revolt to [wantonness].
Mar. Folly in fools bears not so strong a note
As fool'ry in the wise, when wit doth dote,
Since all the power thereof it doth apply
To prove, by wit, worth in simplicity.

Enter Boyet.

Prin. Here comes Boyet, and mirth is in his face.
Boyet. O, I am [stabb'd] with laughter! Where's her Grace?
Prin. Thy news, Boyet?
Boyet. Prepare, madam, prepare!
Arm, wenches, arm! encounters mounted are
Against your peace. Love doth approach disguis'd,
Armed in arguments—you'll be surpris'd.
Muster your wits, stand in your own defense,
Or hide your heads like cowards, and fly hence.
Prin. Saint Denis to Saint Cupid! What are they
That charge their breath against us? Say, scout, say.
Boyet. Under the cool shade of a sycamore
I thought to close mine eyes some half an hour;
When lo, to interrupt my purpos'd rest,
Toward that shade I might behold address'd
The King and his companions. Warily
I stole into a neighbor thicket by,
And overheard what you shall overhear:
That by and by disguis'd [they] will be here.
Their herald is a pretty knavish page,
That well by heart hath conn'd his embassage.
Action and accent did they teach him there:
"Thus must thou speak," and "thus thy body bear";
And ever and anon they made a doubt
Presence majestical would put him out;
"For," quoth the King, "an angel shalt thou see;
Yet fear not thou, but speak audaciously."
The boy replied, "An angel is not evil;
I should have fear'd her had she been a devil."
With that all laugh'd, and clapp'd him on the shoulder,
Making the bold wag by their praises bolder.
One rubb'd his elbow thus, and fleer'd, and swore
A better speech was never spoke before.
Another, with his finger and his thumb,
Cried, "*Via!* we will do't, come what will come."
The third he caper'd, and cried, "All goes well."
The fourth turn'd on the toe, and down he fell.
With that they all did tumble on the ground,
With such a zealous laughter, so profound,
That in this spleen ridiculous appears,
To check their folly, passion's solemn tears.
Prin. But what, but what, come they to visit us?
Boyet. They do, they do; and are apparell'd thus,
Like Muscovites or Russians, as I guess.
Their purpose is to parley, to court, and dance,
And every one his love-feat will advance
Unto his several mistress, which they'll know
By favors several which they did bestow.
Prin. And will they so? The gallants shall be task'd:
For, ladies, we will every one be mask'd,
And not a man of them shall have the grace,
Despite of suit, to see a lady's face.
Hold, Rosaline, this favor thou shalt wear,
And then the King will court thee for his dear.
Hold, take thou this, my sweet, and give me thine,
So shall Berowne take me for Rosaline.
And change you favors too, so shall your loves
Woo contrary, deceiv'd by these removes.
Ros. Come on then, wear the favors most in sight.
Kath. But in this changing, what is your intent?

51. translation: metaphor (a rhetorical term). **52. Vildly:** vilely. **simplicity:** foolishness (cf. line 78). **57. Ay . . . part.** Meaning not clear; perhaps "Yes, may I never give one of my hands to a husband who can't be more generous." **61. in . . . week:** caught for good. **64. bootless:** unavailing. **66. make him . . . jests:** make him dress himself splendidly to please me when I am only acting in jest. **67. pair-taunt-like:** i.e. holding the winning hand (from the name of a winning combination of cards in the game of post and pair). **75. note:** stigma. **82. encounters:** assailants. **mounted:** raised. **84. surpris'd:** overcome. **87. Saint Denis:** patron saint of France. **88. charge:** level (as a weapon).

92. might: could. **address'd:** directed. **95. overhear:** hear over again. **96. by and by:** soon. **98. conn'd:** learned. **embassage:** message. **101. made a doubt:** expressed fear. **102. put him out:** make him forget his lines. **107. clapp'd:** patted. **109. rubb'd his elbow.** An indication of satisfaction. **fleer'd:** grinned. **111. with . . . thumb:** i.e. snapping his fingers. **117. spleen ridiculous:** ridiculous fit of laughter. **118. solemn:** melancholy. **121. Like Muscovites.** Russian costumes were not uncommon in court masquerades. **123. love-feat:** act of courtship. **126. task'd:** put to the test. **129. suit:** pleading. **132–33. Hold . . . Rosaline.** Possibly Shakespeare's revised version of lines 130–31. **135. removes:** exchanges. **136. most in sight:** conspicuously.

Prin. The effect of my intent is to cross theirs:
They do it but in mockery merriment,
And mock for mock is only my intent.
Their several counsels they unbosom shall
To loves mistook, and so be mock'd withal
Upon the next occasion that we meet,
With visages display'd, to talk and greet.
Ros. But shall we dance, if they desire us to't?
Prin. No, to the death we will not move a foot,
Nor to their penn'd speech render we no grace,
But while 'tis spoke each turn away [her] face.
Boyet. Why, that contempt will kill the speaker's heart,
And quite divorce his memory from his part.
Prin. Therefore I do it, and I make no doubt
The rest will [ne'er] come in, if he be out.
There's no such sport as sport by sport o'erthrown,
To make theirs ours and ours none but our own;
So shall we stay, mocking intended game,
And they, well mock'd, depart away with shame.
Sound trumpet [within].
Boyet. The trumpet sounds, be mask'd; the maskers come. *[The Ladies mask.]*

Enter BLACKMOORS *with music, the Boy* [MOTH] *with a speech,* [*the* KING] *and the rest of the* LORDS *disguised [as Russians].*

Moth. "All hail, the richest beauties on the earth!"—
[Boyet]. Beauties no richer than rich taffata.
Moth. "A holy parcel of the fairest dames
The Ladies turn their backs to him.
That ever turn'd their—backs—to mortal views!"
Ber. Their "eyes," villain, their "eyes."
Moth. "That [ever] turn'd their eyes to mortal views!
Out"—
Boyet. True, out indeed.
Moth. "Out of your favors, heavenly spirits, vouchsafe
Not to behold"—
Ber. "Once to behold," rogue.
Moth. "Once to behold with your sun-beamed eyes,
—with your sun-beamed eyes"—
Boyet. They will not answer to that epithet;
You were best call it "daughter-beamed eyes."
Moth. They do not mark me, and that brings me out.
Ber. Is this your perfectness? Be gone, you rogue! *[Exit Moth.]*

139. mockery: mocking.
141. counsels: private purposes, inmost thoughts.
146. to the death: as long as we live.
147. penn'd speech: speech written out with care.
152. out: put out of his part, i.e. confused.
155. stay: remain as visitors.
157 s.d. Blackmoors: black Africans.
159. taffata: i.e. masks of taffeta. **160. parcel:** company.
172. daughter-beamed. Because they are women (quibbling on *sun* and *son*).
173. mark: pay attention to. **brings me out:** puts me off, makes me forget my lines.
174. your perfectness: i.e. the perfect mastery of your lines that you led us to expect.

Ros. What would these strangers? Know their minds, Boyet.
If they do speak our language, 'tis our will
That some plain man recount their purposes.
Know what they would.
Boyet. What would you with the Princess?
Ber. Nothing but peace, and gentle visitation.
Ros. What would they, say they?
Boyet. Nothing but peace, and gentle visitation.
Ros. Why, that they have, and bid them so be gone.
Boyet. She says, you have it, and you may be gone.
King. Say to her we have measur'd many miles,
To tread a measure with her on this grass.
Boyet. They say that they have measur'd many a mile
To tread a measure with you on this grass.
Ros. It is not so. Ask them how many inches
Is in one mile: if they have measured many,
The measure then of one is eas'ly told.
Boyet. If to come hither you have measur'd miles,
And many miles, the Princess bids you tell
How many inches doth fill up one mile.
Ber. Tell her, we measure them by weary steps.
Boyet. She hears herself.
Ros. How many weary steps
Of many weary miles you have o'ergone
Are numb'red in the travel of one mile?
Ber. We number nothing that we spend for you;
Our duty is so rich, so infinite,
That we may do it still without accompt.
Vouchsafe to show the sunshine of your face,
That we (like savages) may worship it.
Ros. My face is but a moon, and clouded too.
King. Blessed are clouds, to do as such clouds do!
Vouchsafe, bright moon, and these thy stars, to shine
(Those clouds removed) upon our watery eyne.
Ros. O vain petitioner! beg a greater matter,
Thou now requests but moonshine in the water.
King. Then in our measure do but vouchsafe one change.
Thou bid'st me beg; this begging is not strange.
Ros. Play, music, then! Nay, you must do it soon.
[Music plays.]
Not yet; no dance: thus change I like the moon.
King. Will you not dance? How come you thus estranged?
Ros. You took the moon at full, but now she's changed.
King. Yet still she is the moon, and I the man.
The music plays, vouchsafe some motion to it.

177. plain: plainspoken.
179. visitation: visit. **184. measur'd:** paced.
185. tread a measure: dance a stately dance.
200. accompt: reckoning.
203. but a moon: i.e. not a sun (the king symbol, proper to the real Princess). **clouded:** i.e. obscured by the mask. **206. eyne:** eyes.
208. moonshine . . . water: i.e. nothing (proverbial).
209. change: (1) change of the moon; (2) round or figure in dancing.
210. not strange: not foreign (though done by a supposed foreigner).
215. man: i.e. man in the moon.
216. motion. Rosaline takes this in the sense "response."

[*Ros.*] Our ears vouchsafe it.
King. But your legs should do it.
Ros. Since you are strangers, and come here by chance,
We'll not be nice; take hands. We will not dance.
King. Why take we hands then?
Ros. Only to part friends.
Curtsy, sweet hearts—and so the measure ends.
King. More measure of this measure; be not nice.
Ros. We can afford no more at such a price.
King. Price you yourselves; what buys your company?
Ros. Your absence only.
King. That can never be.
Ros. Then cannot we be bought; and so, adieu—
Twice to your visor, and half once to you.
King. If you deny to dance, let's hold more chat.
Ros. In private then.
King. I am best pleas'd with that.
[*They converse apart.*]
Ber. White-handed mistress, one sweet word with thee.
Prin. Honey, and milk, and sugar: there is three.
Ber. Nay then two treys, and if you grow so nice,
Metheglin, wort, and malmsey; well run, dice!
There's half a dozen sweets.
Prin. Seventh sweet, adieu.
Since you can cog, I'll play no more with you.
Ber. One word in secret.
Prin. Let it not be sweet.
Ber. Thou grievest my gall.
Prin. Gall! bitter.
Ber. Therefore meet.
[*They converse apart.*]
Dum. Will you vouchsafe with me to change a word?
Mar. Name it.
Dum. Fair lady—
Mar. Say you so? Fair lord—
Take that for your fair lady.
Dum. Please it you,
As much in private, and I'll bid adieu.
[*They converse apart.*]
[*Kath.*] What, was your vizard made without a tongue?
Long. I know the reason, lady, why you ask.
[*Kath.*] O for your reason! quickly, sir, I long!
Long. You have a double tongue within your mask,
And would afford my speechless vizard half.

[*Kath.*] "Veal," quoth the Dutchman. Is not veal a calf?
Long. A calf, fair lady!
[*Kath.*] No, a fair lord calf.
Long. Let's part the word.
[*Kath.*] No, I'll not be your half.
Take all and wean it, it may prove an ox.
Long. Look how you butt yourself in these sharp mocks!
Will you give horns, chaste lady? Do not so.
[*Kath.*] Then die a calf, before your horns do grow.
Long. One word in private with you ere I die.
[*Kath.*] Bleat softly then, the butcher hears you cry. [*They converse apart.*]
Boyet. The tongues of mocking wenches are as keen
As is the razor's edge invisible,
Cutting a smaller hair than may be seen;
Above the sense of sense, so sensible
Seemeth their conference, their conceits have wings
Fleeter than arrows, bullets, wind, thought, swifter things.
Ros. Not one word more, my maids, break off, break off.
Ber. By heaven, all dry-beaten with pure scoff!
King. Farewell, mad wenches, you have simple wits. *Exeunt* [*King, Lords, and Blackmoors*].
Prin. Twenty adieus, my frozen Muscovits.
Are these the breed of wits so wondered at?
Boyet. Tapers they are, with your sweet breaths puff'd out.
Ros. Well-liking wits they have—gross gross, fat fat.
Prin. O poverty in wit, kingly-poor flout!
Will they not (think you) hang themselves to-night?
Or ever but in vizards show their faces?
This pert Berowne was out of count'nance quite.
Ros. They were all in lamentable cases!
The King was weeping-ripe for a good word.
Prin. Berowne did swear himself out of all suit.
Mar. Dumaine was at my service, and his sword:
"No point," quoth I; my servant straight was mute.
Kath. Lord Longaville said I came o'er his heart,
And trow you what he call'd me?
Prin. Qualm, perhaps.

218. strangers: foreigners. **219. nice:** coy.
222. More measure: a larger amount.
227. visor: mask. The line has not been satisfactorily explained.
228. deny: refuse. **232. treys:** threes. **nice:** subtle.
233. Metheglin: a Welsh drink brewed from honey. **wort:** sweet unfermented beer. **malmsey:** a strong sweet wine.
235. cog: cheat.
237. Thou . . . gall: you are causing me pain by chafing a sore place (but the Princess picks up *gall* in the sense of "bile"—cf. "bitter as gall"). **meet:** fitting.
242. vizard: mask. **tongue.** W. J. Lawrence, in the *Times Literary Supplement*, June 7, 1923, explained that Elizabethan masks were kept in place by a tongue, or interior projection, held in the mouth.
245. double. With play on the sense "ambiguous, deceptive."
247. Veal. The Dutchman's pronunciation of "well," or the German *viel* (much). In addition to calling Longaville a calf, Katherine may be punning on *veil*, i.e. the mask, and, in the combination of *long* (line 244) and *veal*, on Longaville's name.
249. part the word: divide the word *calf* between us. **your half:** (1) half of something of which you are the other half; (2) your better half, i.e. wife. **250. wean:** i.e. raise.
251. butt: injure (with play on the horns of the ox).
252. give horns: (1) attack with horns (developing the idea in *butt*); (2) make your husband a cuckold.
259. Above . . . sense: beyond the power of sense to perceive. **sensible:** sensitive, quick-witted. **260. conference:** conversation.
263. dry-beaten: beaten soundly without bloodshed.
268. Well-liking: plump.
269. kingly-poor flout. The Princess jibes at Rosaline's pun on *liking/like king* and caps it by reversing the syllables of *li-king* into *king-ly*. **272. pert:** lively, brisk.
273. cases: (1) states; (2) costumes.
274. weeping-ripe for: ready to weep for lack of.
275. out . . . suit: past all propriety (with another play, perhaps, on costume). **277. No point.** See note on II.i.190.
279. trow you: would you believe. **Qualm:** i.e. heartburn. (Pronounced somewhat like *come*, and hence suggesting the Princess' "go" in the next line.)

Kath. Yes, in good faith.
Prin. Go, sickness as thou art!
Ros. Well, better wits have worn plain statute-caps.
But will you hear? the King is my love sworn.
Prin. And quick Berowne hath plighted faith to me.
Kath. And Longaville was for my service born.
Mar. Dumaine is mine, as sure as bark on tree.
Boyet. Madam, and pretty mistresses, give ear:
Immediately they will again be here
In their own shapes; for it can never be
They will digest this harsh indignity.
Prin. Will they return?
Boyet. They will, they will, God knows,
And leap for joy, though they are lame with blows:
Therefore change favors, and when they repair,
Blow like sweet roses in this summer air.
Prin. How blow? how blow? speak to be understood.
Boyet. Fair ladies mask'd are roses in their bud;
Dismask'd, their damask sweet commixture shown,
Are angels [vailing] clouds, or roses blown.
Prin. Avaunt, perplexity! What shall we do,
If they return in their own shapes to woo?
Ros. Good madam, if by me you'll be advis'd,
Let's mock them still, as well known as disguis'd.
Let us complain to them what fools were here,
Disguis'd like Muscovites, in shapeless gear;
And wonder what they were, and to what end
Their shallow shows and prologue vildly penn'd,
And their rough carriage so ridiculous,
Should be presented at our tent to us.
Boyet. Ladies, withdraw; the gallants are at hand.
Prin. Whip to our tents, as roes [run] o'er land.
Exeunt [Princess and Ladies].

Enter the KING *and the rest [of the* LORDS *in their proper habits].*

King. Fair sir, God save you! Where's the Princess?
Boyet. Gone to her tent. Please it your Majesty
Command me any service to her thither?
King. That she vouchsafe me audience for one word.
Boyet. I will, and so will she, I know, my lord.
Exit.
Ber. This fellow pecks up wit as pigeons pease,
And utters it again when God doth please.
He is wit's pedlar, and retails his wares
At wakes and wassails, meetings, markets, fairs:

And we that sell by gross, the Lord doth know,
Have not the grace to grace it with such show.
This gallant pins the wenches on his sleeve;
Had he been Adam, he had tempted Eve.
'A can carve too, and lisp; why, this is he
That kiss'd his hand away in courtesy;
This is the ape of form, monsieur the nice,
That when he plays at tables chides the dice
In honorable terms; nay, he can sing
A mean most meanly, and in hushering
Mend him who can. The ladies call him sweet;
The stairs as he treads on them kiss his feet.
This is the flow'r that smiles on every one,
To show his teeth as white as whalë's bone;
And consciences that will not die in debt
Pay him the due of honey-tongued Boyet.
King. A blister on his sweet tongue, with my heart,
That put Armado's page out of his part!

Enter the [PRINCESS, *ushered by* BOYET, *and her*] LADIES.

Ber. See where it comes! Behavior, what wert thou
Till this madman show'd thee? And what art thou now?
King. All hail, sweet madam, and fair time of day!
Prin. "Fair" in "all hail" is foul, as I conceive.
King. Conster my speeches better, if you may.
Prin. Then wish me better, I will give you leave.
King. We came to visit you, and purpose now
To lead you to our court; vouchsafe it then.
Prin. This field shall hold me, and so hold your vow:
Nor God, nor I, delights in perjur'd men.
King. Rebuke me not for that which you provoke:
The virtue of your eye must break my oath.
Prin. You nickname virtue; vice you should have spoke,
For virtue's office never breaks men's troth.
Now by my maiden honor, yet as pure
As the unsallied lily, I protest,
A world of torments though I should endure,
I would not yield to be your house's guest:
So much I hate a breaking cause to be
Of heavenly oaths, vow'd with integrity.
King. O, you have liv'd in desolation here,
Unseen, unvisited, much to our shame.
Prin. Not so, my lord, it is not so, I swear;
We have had pastimes here and pleasant game,

281. **plain statute-caps:** perhaps the woollen caps required by law to be worn by the London apprentices.
288. **shapes:** (1) forms; (2) clothes (cf. line 303).
289. **digest:** put up with, stomach. 292. **repair:** return.
293. **Blow:** bloom.
296. **damask:** red and white. **commixture:** complexion.
297. **vailing:** letting fall, shedding. **blown:** fully opened (cf. *full-blown*). 298. **Avaunt, perplexity:** away, riddler.
301. **as . . . disguis'd:** as much in their real persons as when they were disguised. 303. **shapeless gear:** ill-cut clothes.
309. **Whip:** dart, fly. **land:** laund, open space in a wooded area.
315. **pease:** peas.
316. **utters:** puts forth, sells. **when . . . please:** i.e. when the moment is propitious. 318. **wakes:** festivals. **wassails:** revels.

319. **by gross:** wholesale.
321. **pins . . . sleeve:** gains the favor of all the girls (?) or has all the girls hanging on his arm (?). 322. **had:** would have.
323. **carve:** i.e. woo with the most delicate courtesy. **lisp:** talk affectedly. 325. **form:** strict manners. **nice:** punctilious.
326. **tables:** backgammon. 327. **honorable:** polite.
328. **mean:** tenor. **meanly:** indifferently. **hushering:** ushering, introducing (the function of a gentleman usher).
329. **Mend:** better, improve on. 332. **whalë's:** i.e. walrus'.
337. **Behavior:** i.e. politeness, fine manners.
338. **madman:** droll fellow. 341. **Conster:** construe.
348. **virtue:** power (but the Princess picks up the word in the sense "goodness"). 349. **nickname:** misname, miscall.
350. **office:** operation. 352. **unsallied:** unsullied.

A mess of Russians left us but of late.
King. How, madam? Russians?
Prin. Ay, in truth, my lord;
Trim gallants, full of courtship and of state.
Ros. Madam, speak true. It is not so, my lord.
My lady (to the manner of the days)
In courtesy gives undeserving praise.
We four indeed confronted were with four
In Russian habit; here they stay'd an hour,
And talk'd apace; and in that hour, my lord,
They did not bless us with one happy word.
I dare not call them fools; but this I think,
When they are thirsty, fools would fain have drink.
Ber. This jest is dry to me. Gentle sweet,
Your wits makes wise things foolish. When we greet,
With eyes best seeing, heaven's fiery eye,
By light we lose light; your capacity
Is of that nature that to your huge store
Wise things seem foolish, and rich things but poor.
Ros. This proves you wise and rich, for in my eye—
Ber. I am a fool, and full of poverty.
Ros. But that you take what doth to you belong,
It were a fault to snatch words from my tongue.
Ber. O, I am yours, and all that I possess!
Ros. All the fool mine?
Ber. I cannot give you less.
Ros. Which of the vizards was it that you wore?
Ber. Where? when? what vizard? why demand you this?
Ros. There then, that vizard, that superfluous case,
That hid the worse, and show'd the better face.
King. [*Aside*.] We were descried, they'll mock us now downright.
Dum. [*Aside*.] Let us confess and turn it to a jest.
Prin. Amaz'd, my lord? Why looks your Highness sad?
Ros. Help, hold his brows, he'll sound! Why look you pale?
Sea-sick, I think, coming from Muscovy.
Ber. Thus pour the stars down plagues for perjury.
Can any face of brass hold longer out?
Here stand I, lady, dart thy skill at me,
Bruise me with scorn, confound me with a flout,
Thrust thy sharp wit quite through my ignorance,
Cut me to pieces with thy keen conceit;
And I will wish thee never more to dance,
Nor never more in Russian habit wait.
O, never will I trust to speeches penn'd,
Nor to the motion of a schoolboy's tongue,
Nor never come in vizard to my friend,
Nor woo in rhyme, like a blind harper's song!
Taffata phrases, silken terms precise,
Three-pil'd hyperboles, spruce affection,
Figures pedantical—these summer flies
Have blown me full of maggot ostentation.
I do forswear them, and I here protest,
By this white glove (how white the hand, God knows!),
Henceforth my wooing mind shall be express'd
In russet yeas and honest kersey noes.
And to begin, wench, so God help me law!
My love to thee is sound, sans crack or flaw.
Ros. Sans "sans," I pray you.
Ber. Yet I have a trick
Of the old rage. Bear with me, I am sick;
I'll leave it by degrees. Soft, let us see—
Write "Lord have mercy on us" on those three:
They are infected, in their hearts it lies;
They have the plague, and caught it of your eyes.
These lords are visited; you are not free,
For the Lord's tokens on you do I see.
Prin. No, they are free that gave these tokens to us.
Ber. Our states are forfeit, seek not to undo us.
Ros. It is not so, for how can this be true,
That you stand forfeit, being those that sue?
Ber. Peace, for I will not have to do with you.
Ros. Nor shall not, if I do as I intend.
Ber. Speak for yourselves, my wit is at an end.
King. Teach us, sweet madam, for our rude transgression
Some fair excuse.
Prin. The fairest is confession.
Were not you here but even now, disguis'd?
King. Madam, I was.
Prin. And were you well advis'd?
King. I was, fair madam.
Prin. When you then were here,
What did you whisper in your lady's ear?
King. That more than all the world I did respect her.
Prin. When she shall challenge this, you will reject her.
King. Upon mine honor, no.
Prin. Peace, peace, forbear:
Your oath once broke, you force not to forswear.
King. Despise me when I break this oath of mine.
Prin. I will, and therefore keep it. Rosaline,
What did the Russian whisper in your ear?

361. **mess**: group of four. 365. **to . . . days**: in the current fashion.
370. **happy**: felicitous.
373. **dry**: dull, stupid (with pun on "thirsty").
374. **greet**: i.e. look at. 386. **demand**: question.
389. **downright**: out and out. 391. **Amaz'd**: confounded.
392. **sound**: swoon. 395. **face of brass**: i.e. guilty self-assurance.
397. **confound**: destroy. 400. **wish**: invite.
401. **wait**: attend upon. 404. **friend**: sweetheart.
405. **like . . . song**. Harping was proverbially the resource of the blind. 406. **Taffata**: taffeta.
407. **Three-pil'd**: deep-piled, like velvet of the best quality. **affection**: affectation.
409. **blown . . . ostentation**: i.e. deposited on me their eggs, which have hatched into the maggots of vanity.
413. **russet**: rough homespun. **kersey**: coarse woollen cloth.
414. **law**: la (an interjection).
416. **Sans "sans"**: i.e. no affected foreign words. **Yet**: still. **trick**: touch. 417. **rage**: fever, infection.
419. **Lord . . . us**. The sign put on the door of a plague-stricken house.
422. **visited**: attacked by plague (the term officially used). **free**: (1) free of plague; (2) untouched by love, fancy-free.
423. **Lord's tokens**: (1) plague spots; (2) love tokens given by the lords. 424. **free**: liberal (?) or free of obligation (?).
425. **states**: estates. **undo us**: undo our forfeiture, i.e. reject our yielding of ourselves.
427. **sue**: (1) bring the suit (it is the defendant who may have to forfeit his lands, not the plaintiff); (2) plead.
434. **well advis'd**: in your right mind. 437. **respect**: value, prize.
438. **challenge**: lay claim to. 440. **force not**: i.e. find it easy.

Ros. Madam, he swore that he did hold me dear
As precious eyesight, and did value me
Above this world; adding thereto, moreover,
That he would wed me, or else die my lover.
Prin. God give thee joy of him! The noble lord
Most honorably doth uphold his word.
King. What mean you, madam? By my life, my troth,
I never swore this lady such an oath.
Ros. By heaven, you did; and to confirm it plain,
You gave me this: but take it, sir, again.
King. My faith and this the Princess I did give;
I knew her by this jewel on her sleeve.
Prin. Pardon me, sir, this jewel did she wear,
And Lord Berowne (I thank him) is my dear.
What? will you have me, or your pearl again?
Ber. Neither of either; I remit both twain.
I see the trick an't; here was a consent,
Knowing aforehand of our merriment,
To dash it like a Christmas comedy.
Some carry-tale, some please-man, some slight zany,
Some mumble-news, some trencher-knight, some Dick,
That smiles his cheek in years and knows the trick
To make my lady laugh when she's dispos'd,
Told our intents before; which once disclos'd,
The ladies did change favors; and then we,
Following the signs, woo'd but the sign of she.
Now, to our perjury to add more terror,
We are again forsworn, in will and error.
Much upon this 'tis; [*to Boyet*] and might not you
Forestall our sport, to make us thus untrue?
Do not you know my lady's foot by th' squier,
And laugh upon the apple of her eye?
And stand between her back, sir, and the fire,
Holding a trencher, jesting merrily?
You put our page out. Go, you are allow'd;
Die when you will, a smock shall be your shroud.
You leer upon me, do you? There's an eye
Wounds like a leaden sword.
Boyet. Full merrily
Hath this brave [manage], this career, been run.
Ber. Lo, he is tilting straight! Peace, I have done.

Enter Clown [COSTARD].

Welcome, pure wit, thou part'st a fair fray.

459. **either**: the two. **remit**: give up, surrender.
460. **an't**: on it, i.e. of it. **consent**: agreement, i.e. conspiracy.
462. **dash**: destroy, frustrate.
463. **carry-tale**: talebearer. **please-man**: sycophant. **zany**: clown.
464. **mumble-news**: prattler, gossip. **trencher-knight**: i.e. parasite (a trencher is a wooden platter or dish). **Dick**: silly person.
465. **smiles . . . years**: laughs his face into wrinkles.
469. **she**: i.e. each one's supposed mistress.
472. **Much . . . 'tis**: i.e. this must be substantially what happened.
474. **squier**: square, rule. Berowne means that Boyet knows well what will please the Princess.
475. **apple**: pupil. Boyet is in a position to have private jokes with the Princess. 477. **Holding a trencher**: i.e. dancing attendance.
478. **allow'd**: privileged to jest (as a fool was).
479. **smock**: woman's undergarment (either a charge of effeminacy or equivalent to saying that women will be the death of him).
481. **leaden sword**: i.e. a stage sword, unable to wound.
482. **brave**: fine. **manage**: piece of horsemanship. **career**: running, course.
483. **tilting straight**: back immediately to his verbal sparring.

Cost. O Lord, sir, they would know
Whether the three Worthies shall come in or no.
Ber. What, are there but three?
Cost. No, sir, but it is vara fine,
For every one pursents three.
Ber. And three times thrice is nine.
Cost. Not so, sir, under correction, sir, I hope it is not so.
You cannot beg us, sir, I can assure you, sir, we know what we know.
I hope, sir, three times thrice, sir—
Ber. Is not nine.
Cost. Under correction, sir, we know whereuntil it doth amount.
Ber. By Jove, I always took three threes for nine.
Cost. O Lord, sir, it were pity you should get your living by reck'ning, sir.
Ber. How much is it?
Cost. O Lord, sir, the parties themselves, the actors, sir, will show whereuntil it doth amount. For mine own part, I am, as [they] say, but to parfect one man in one poor man, Pompion the Great, sir.
Ber. Art thou one of the Worthies?
Cost. It pleas'd them to think me worthy of Pompey the Great; for mine own part, I know not the degree of the Worthy, but I am to stand for him.
Ber. Go bid them prepare.
Cost. We will turn it finely off, sir; we will take some care. *Exit.*
King. Berowne, they will shame us; let them not approach.
Ber. We are shame-proof, my lord; and 'tis some policy
To have one show worse than the King's and his company.
King. I say they shall not come.
Prin. Nay, my good lord, let me o'errule you now.
That sport best pleases that doth [least] know how:
Where zeal strives to content, and the contents
Dies in the zeal of that which it presents.
Their form confounded makes most form in mirth,
When great things laboring perish in their birth.
Ber. A right description of our sport, my lord.

Enter Braggart [ARMADO].

Arm. Anointed, I implore so much expense of thy royal sweet breath as will utter a brace of words.
[*Converses apart with the King, and delivers him a paper.*]
Prin. Doth this man serve God?

487. **vara**: very.
488. **pursents**: presents; i.e. represents. 489. **under**: subject to.
490. **beg us**: prove us fools. 494. **whereuntil**: whereunto, i.e. to how much.
496. **it . . . get**: it would be too bad if you had to earn.
501–2. **parfect**: i.e. perform or present.
502. **Pompion**: pumpkin (error for *Pompey*).
512. **policy**: wise strategy.
517–18. **the contents . . . presents**: i.e. the substance of the play is murdered by the actors in their excessive eagerness to please (which makes them undertake too ambitious a project for their talents).
521. **right**: exact. **our sport**: i.e. the Muscovite masque.

Ber. Why ask you?
Prin. 'A speaks not like a man of God his making.
Arm. That is all one, my fair, sweet, honey monarch; for I protest, the schoolmaster is exceeding fantastical, too too vain, too too vain: but we will put it (as they say) to *fortuna de la* [*guerra*]. I wish you the peace of mind, most royal couplement. *Exit.*
King. Here is like to be a good presence of Worthies: he presents Hector of Troy; the swain, Pompey the Great; the parish curate, Alexander; Armado's page, Hercules; the pedant, Judas Machabeus;
And if these four Worthies in their first show thrive,
These four will change habits, and present the other five.
Ber. There is five in the first show.
King. You are deceived, 'tis not so.
Ber. The pedant, the braggart, the hedge-priest, the fool, and the boy:
Abate throw at novum, and the whole world again
Cannot pick out five such, take each one in his vein.
King. The ship is under sail, and here she comes amain.

Enter [COSTARD *for*] *Pompey.*

Cost. "I Pompey am"—
Ber. You lie, you are not he.
Cost. "I Pompey am"—
Boyet. With libbard's head on knee.
Ber. Well said, old mocker. I must needs be friends with thee.
Cost. "I Pompey am, Pompey surnam'd the Big"—
Dum. "The Great."
Cost. It is "Great," sir.
"Pompey surnam'd the Great,
That oft in field with targe and shield did make my foe to sweat,
And travelling along this coast, I here am come by chance,
And lay my arms before the legs of this sweet lass of France."
If your ladyship would say, "Thanks, Pompey," I had done.
[*Prin.*] Great thanks, great Pompey.
Cost. 'Tis not so much worth; but I hope I was perfect. I made a little fault in "Great."
Ber. My hat to a halfpenny, Pompey proves the best Worthy.

Enter Curate [SIR NATHANIEL] *for Alexander.*

Nath. "When in the world I liv'd, I was the world's commander;
By east, west, north, and south, I spread my conquering might.
My scutcheon plain declares that I am Alisander"—
Boyet. Your nose says, no, you are not; for it stands too right.
Ber. Your nose smells "no" in [this], most tender-smelling knight.
Prin. The conqueror is dismay'd. Proceed, good Alexander.
Nath. "When in the world I liv'd, I was the world's commander"—
Boyet. Most true, 'tis right; you were so, Alisander.
Ber. Pompey the Great—
Cost. Your servant, and Costard.
Ber. Take away the conqueror, take away Alisander.
Cost. [*To Nathaniel.*] O sir, you have overthrown Alisander the conqueror! You will be scrap'd out of the painted cloth for this. Your lion, that holds his poll-axe sitting on a close-stool, will be given to Ajax; he will be the ninth Worthy. A conqueror, and afeard to speak! Run away for shame, Alisander. [*Nathaniel retires.*] There an't shall please you, a foolish mild man, an honest man, look you, and soon dash'd. He is a marvellous good neighbor, faith, and a very good bowler; but for Alisander—alas, you see how 'tis—a little o'erparted. But there are Worthies a-coming will speak their mind in some other sort.
Prin. Stand aside, good Pompey.

Enter Pedant [HOLOFERNES] *for Judas, and the Boy* [MOTH] *for Hercules.*

Hol. "Great Hercules is presented by this imp,
Whose club kill'd Cerberus, that three-headed *canus;*
And when he was a babe, a child, a shrimp,
Thus did he strangle serpents in his *manus.*
Quoniam he seemeth in minority,
Ergo I come with this apology."
[*Aside.*] Keep some state in thy exit, and vanish. [*Moth retires.*]
"Judas I am"—
Dum. A Judas!
Hol. Not Iscariot, sir.
"Judas I am, ycliped Machabeus."

526. God his: God's.
530–31. fortuna . . . guerra: the fortune of war.
532. couplement: couple. **533. presence:** assembly, company.
542. hedge-priest: illiterate priest of low status.
544. Abate . . . novum: except for a lucky throw of the dice in the game of novum (from Latin *novem,* "nine"), played by five players and having nine and five as its principal throws. The quibble here is on the presentation of nine characters by five players.
545. vein: individual character.
548. libbard's: leopard's. An allusion to Pompey's coat of arms, which would properly be on his shield; perhaps Costard is holding the shield awkwardly low.
553. targe: light shield. **559. perfect:** word-perfect.
565. right: straight (an allusion to a reputed physical characteristic of Alexander, a wry neck).
566. Your . . . this. Alexander was reputed to possess skin and breath of a "marvellous good savour" (North's Plutarch). **tender-smelling:** endowed with a sensitive sense of smell.
575–76. You . . . this. An allusion to the frequent representation of the Nine Worthies on canvases or tapestries.
576–77. lion . . . close-stool. Alexander's arms showed a lion seated in a chair and holding a battle-axe. **close-stool:** privy.
578. Ajax. With a pun on *a jakes,* i.e. a privy. Ajax, a Greek warrior, coveted the armor of the slain Achilles.
584. o'erparted: given too difficult a part.
588. imp: child (as at I.ii.5).
589. Cerberus: the three-headed dog at the entrance to Hades, whose capture was one of Hercules' tasks. **canus:** dog (properly *canis*).
591. manus: hands. **592. Quoniam:** since.
593. Ergo: therefore. **594. state:** dignity.
598. ycliped: called (as at I.i.240).

Dum. Judas Machabeus clipt is plain Judas.
Ber. A kissing traitor. How art thou prov'd Judas?
Hol. "Judas I am"—
Dum. The more shame for you, Judas.
Hol. What mean you, sir?
Boyet. To make Judas hang himself.
Hol. Begin, sir, you are my elder.
Ber. Well follow'd: Judas was hang'd on an elder.
Hol. I will not be put out of countenance.
Ber. Because thou hast no face.
Hol. What is this?
Boyet. A cittern-head.
Dum. The head of a bodkin.
Ber. A death's face in a ring.
Long. The face of an old Roman coin, scarce seen.
Boyet. The pommel of Caesar's falchion.
Dum. The carv'd-bone face on a flask.
Ber. Saint George's half-cheek in a brooch.
Dum. Ay, and in a brooch of lead.
Ber. Ay, and worn in the cap of a tooth-drawer. And now forward, for we have put thee in countenance.
Hol. You have put me out of countenance.
Ber. False, we have given thee faces.
Hol. But you have out-fac'd them all.
Ber. And thou wert a lion, we would do so.
Boyet. Therefore as he is, an ass, let him go.
And so adieu, sweet Jude! Nay, why dost thou stay?
Dum. For the latter end of his name.
Ber. For the ass to the Jude; give it him. Jud-as, away!
Hol. This is not generous, not gentle, not humble.
Boyet. A light for Monsieur Judas! It grows dark, he may stumble. [*Holofernes retires.*]
Prin. Alas, poor Machabeus, how hath he been baited!

Enter Braggart [ARMADO *for Hector*].

Ber. Hide thy head, Achilles, here comes Hector in arms.
Dum. Though my mocks come home by me, I will now be merry.
King. Hector was but a Troyan in respect of this.
Boyet. But is this Hector?
King. I think Hector was not so clean-timber'd.
Long. His leg is too big for Hector's.
Dum. More calf, certain.
Boyet. No, he is best indu'd in the small.
Ber. This cannot be Hector.
Dum. He's a god or a painter, for he makes faces.
Arm. "The armipotent Mars, of lances the almighty,
Gave Hector a gift"—
Dum. A [gilt] nutmeg.
Ber. A lemon.
Long. Stuck with cloves.
Dum. No, cloven.
Arm. Peace!—
"The armipotent Mars, of lances the almighty,
Gave Hector a gift, the heir of Ilion;
A man so breathed, that certain he would fight, yea,
From morn till night, out of his pavilion.
I am that flower"—
Dum. That mint.
Long. That columbine.
Arm. Sweet Lord Longaville, rein thy tongue.
Long. I must rather give it the rein, for it runs against Hector.
Dum. Ay, and Hector's a greyhound.
Arm. The sweet war-man is dead and rotten, sweet chucks, beat not the bones of the buried. When he breathed, he was a man. But I will forward with my device. [*To the Princess.*] Sweet royalty, bestow on me the sense of hearing.

Berowne steps forth [*to whisper to Costard and then returns to his place*].

Prin. Speak, brave Hector, we are much delighted.
Arm. I do adore thy sweet Grace's slipper.
Boyet. Loves her by the foot.
Dum. He may not by the yard.
Arm. This Hector far surmounted Hannibal. The party is gone"—
Cost. Fellow Hector, she is gone; she is two months on her way.
Arm. What meanest thou?
Cost. Faith, unless you play the honest Troyan, the poor wench is cast away. She's quick, the child brags in her belly already. 'Tis yours.
Arm. Dost thou infamonize me among potentates? Thou shalt die.
Cost. Then shall Hector be whipt for Jaquenetta that is quick by him, and hang'd for Pompey that is dead by him.
Dum. Most rare Pompey!
Boyet. Renowned Pompey!
Ber. Greater than great, great, great, great Pompey! Pompey the Huge!
Dum. Hector trembles.

599. clipt: abbreviated.
600. A kissing traitor. An allusion to the kiss by which Judas Iscariot betrayed Jesus, but perhaps also a quibble on *clipt* in the sense "embraced."
605. Begin . . . elder: i.e. hang yourself first, since you have precedence as my senior. **606. Judas . . . elder.** An old tradition.
609. What is this. Holofernes points to his face, provoking the quips which follow. All the replies allude to faces carved as ornaments on various objects. **610. cittern:** cithern, guitar.
611. bodkin: a long pin or pin-shaped ornament for the hair, or a small dagger. **612. death's face:** death's head.
613. scarce seen: worn almost indistinguishable.
614. falchion: curved sword. **615. flask:** powder flask.
616. half-cheek: profile.
618. tooth-drawer. Evidently a brooch or badge in the tooth-drawer's cap was a distinguishing mark of his dress.
623. out-fac'd them all: put all the faces out of countenance (through mockery). **629. gentle:** courteous. **humble:** kind.
632. Achilles: the best warrior on the Greek side, as Hector was on the Trojan side. **634. by me:** to me, i.e. to injure me.
636. Troyan: (1) Trojan; (2) cant term for boon companion, dissolute fellow. **respect of:** comparison with.
638. clean-timber'd: well built.
640. calf: (1) part of the leg; (2) stupid fellow, dolt.
641. indu'd: endowed, supplied. **small:** the part of the leg below the calf. **644. armipotent:** powerful in arms.
646. gilt: glazed with the yolk of an egg (an old cookery term).
652. Ilion: Troy. **653. so breathed:** in such good condition.
654. pavilion: the tent which would be used by a combatant when not engaged in fighting. **669. yard:** penis. **676. quick:** pregnant.
678. infamonize: defame.
682. that is dead: i.e. whose hopes of winning Jaquenetta have been killed.

Ber. Pompey is mov'd. More Ates, more Ates! stir them [on], stir them on!

Dum. Hector will challenge him.

Ber. Ay, if 'a have no more man's blood in his belly than will sup a flea.

Arm. By the north pole, I do challenge thee.

Cost. I will not fight with a pole like a Northren man; I'll slash, I'll do it by the sword. I bepray you let me borrow my arms again.

Dum. Room for the incens'd Worthies!

Cost. I'll do it in my shirt.

Dum. Most resolute Pompey!

Moth. Master, let me take you a button-hole lower. Do you not see Pompey is uncasing for the combat? What mean you? You will lose your reputation.

Arm. Gentlemen and soldiers, pardon me, I will not combat in my shirt.

Dum. You may not deny it; Pompey hath made the challenge.

Arm. Sweet bloods, I both may and will.

Ber. What reason have you for't?

Arm. The naked truth of it is, I have no shirt; I go woolward for penance.

Boyet. True, and it was enjoin'd him in Rome for want of linen; since when, I'll be sworn he wore none but a dishclout of Jaquenetta's, and that 'a wears next his heart for a favor.

Enter a Messenger, Monsieur MARCADE.

Marc. God save you, madam!
Prin. Welcome, Marcade,
But that thou interruptest our merriment.
Marc. I am sorry, madam, for the news I bring
Is heavy in my tongue. The King your father—
Prin. Dead, for my life!
Marc. Even so: my tale is told.
Ber. Worthies, away! the scene begins to cloud.

Arm. For mine own part, I breathe free breath. I have seen the day of wrong through the little hole of discretion, and I will right myself like a soldier. *Exeunt Worthies.*

King. How fares your Majesty?
Prin. Boyet, prepare, I will away to-night.
King. Madam, not so, I do beseech you stay.
Prin. Prepare, I say. I thank you, gracious lords,
For all your fair endeavors, and entreat,
Out of a new-sad soul, that you vouchsafe
In your rich wisdom to excuse, or hide,
The liberal opposition of our spirits,
If overboldly we have borne ourselves
In the converse of breath—your gentleness
Was guilty of it. Farewell, worthy lord!
A heavy heart bears not a humble tongue.
Excuse me so, coming too short of thanks
For my great suit so easily obtain'd.
King. The extreme parts of time extremely forms
All causes to the purpose of his speed,
And often, at his very loose, decides
That which long process could not arbitrate.
And though the mourning brow of progeny
Forbid the smiling courtesy of love
The holy suit which fain it would convince,
Yet since love's argument was first on foot,
Let not the cloud of sorrow justle it
From what it purpos'd; since to wail friends lost
Is not by much so wholesome-profitable
As to rejoice at friends but newly found.
Prin. I understand you not, my griefs are double.
Ber. Honest plain words best pierce the ear of grief,
And by these badges understand the King.
For your fair sakes have we neglected time,
Play'd foul play with our oaths. Your beauty, ladies,
Hath much deformed us, fashioning our humors
Even to the opposed end of our intents;
And what in us hath seem'd ridiculous—
As love is full of unbefitting strains,
All wanton as a child, skipping and vain,
Form'd by the eye and therefore like the eye,
Full of straying shapes, of habits, and of forms,
Varying in subjects as the eye doth roll
To every varied object in his glance;
Which parti-coated presence of loose love
Put on by us, if, in your heavenly eyes,
Have misbecom'd our oaths and gravities,
Those heavenly eyes, that look into these faults,
Suggested us to make. Therefore, ladies,
Our love being yours, the error that love makes
Is likewise yours. We to ourselves prove false,
By being once false for ever to be true
To those that make us both—fair ladies, you;
And even that falsehood, in itself a sin,
Thus purifies itself and turns to grace.
Prin. We have receiv'd your letters full of love;
Your favors, embassadors of love;
And in our maiden council rated them
At courtship, pleasant jest, and courtesy,
As bombast and as lining to the time;
But more devout than this [in] our respects

688. **Ates.** Ate was the goddess of discord and strife.
695. **Northren man:** countryman from the north, boor.
700–701. **take . . . lower:** help you take off your doublet (with quibble on the sense "humiliate you"). 701. **uncasing:** undressing.
708. **bloods:** men of fire and spirit.
711. **go woolward:** wear no linen between the woollen outer clothing and the skin.
713. **want of linen.** Boyet suggests that the reason is not penance but a shortage of shirts.
723–25. **I . . . soldier:** i.e. I now perceive my wrongdoing and will make honorable amends. (See lines 883–84.) 732. **hide:** overlook.
733. **liberal opposition:** unrestrained antagonism.
735. **converse of breath:** conversation. **gentleness:** courtesy.

737. **humble:** courteous.
739. **suit.** The King has apparently granted this.
740–41. **The extreme . . . speed:** i.e. the pressure of final moments demands quick decisions. 741. **his:** its, i.e. time's.
742. **loose:** moment of release (technical term for the discharge of an arrow). 746 **convince:** give proof of. 748. **justle:** jostle.
752. **double:** excessive (?).
754. **badges:** i.e. the plain words he is about to speak.
758. **Even . . . intents:** into the very opposite of what we intended.
760. **strains:** impulses.
763. **straying.** Perhaps an error for *strange*, arising from an authorial spelling *straing* (as in *Sir Thomas More*, Addition II, line 8).
766. **parti-coated:** dressed like a fool, in motley. **loose:** unrestrained. 768. **misbecom'd:** been unbecoming to.
770. **Suggested:** tempted. **make:** i.e. make them. Word order and syntax in lines 766–70 are strained.
780. **At:** i.e. as merely.
781. **bombast:** wool used for padding or stuffing.
782. **devout:** serious. **respects:** regard, consideration.

Have we not been, and therefore met your loves
In their own fashion, like a merriment.
Dum. Our letters, madam, show'd much more than jest.
Long. So did our looks.
Ros. We did not cote them so.
King. Now at the latest minute of the hour,
Grant us your loves.
Prin. A time methinks too short
To make a world-without-end bargain in.
No, no, my lord, your Grace is perjur'd much,
Full of dear guiltiness, and therefore this:
If for my love (as there is no such cause)
You will do aught, this shall you do for me:
Your oath I will not trust, but go with speed
To some forlorn and naked hermitage,
Remote from all the pleasures of the world;
There stay until the twelve celestial signs
Have brought about the annual reckoning.
If this austere insociable life
Change not your offer made in heat of blood;
If frosts and fasts, hard lodging and thin weeds
Nip not the gaudy blossoms of your love
But that it bear this trial, and last love;
Then at the expiration of the year,
Come challenge me, challenge me by these deserts,
And by this virgin palm now kissing thine,
I will be thine; and till that [instant] shut
My woeful self up in a mourning house,
Raining the tears of lamentation
For the remembrance of my father's death.
If this thou do deny, let our hands part,
Neither intitled in the other's heart.
King. If this, or more than this, I would deny,
To flatter up these powers of mine with rest,
The sudden hand of death close up mine eye!
Hence [hermit] then—my heart is in thy breast.
⟨*Ber.* And what to me, my love? and what to me?
Ros. You must be purged too, your sins are rack'd,
You are attaint with faults and perjury:
Therefore if you my favor mean to get,
A twelvemonth shall you spend, and never rest,
But seek the weary beds of people sick.⟩
Dum. But what to me, my love? but what to me?
A wife?
Kath. A beard, fair health, and honesty;
With threefold love I wish you all these three.
Dum. O, shall I say, I thank you, gentle wife?
Kath. Not so, my lord, a twelvemonth and a day
I'll mark no words that smooth-fac'd wooers say.
Come when the King doth to my lady come;
Then if I have much love, I'll give you some.
Dum. I'll serve thee true and faithfully till then.
Kath. Yet swear not, lest ye be forsworn again.
Long. What says Maria?
Mar. At the twelvemonth's end
I'll change my black gown for a faithful friend.
Long. I'll stay with patience, but the time is long.
Mar. The liker you; few taller are so young.
Ber. Studies my lady? Mistress, look on me,
Behold the window of my heart, mine eye,
What humble suit attends thy answer there.
Impose some service on me for thy love.
Ros. Oft have I heard of you, my Lord Berowne,
Before I saw you; and the world's large tongue
Proclaims you for a man replete with mocks,
Full of comparisons and wounding flouts,
Which you on all estates will execute
That lie within the mercy of your wit.
To weed this wormwood from your fructful brain,
And therewithal to win me, if you please,
Without the which I am not to be won,
You shall this twelvemonth term from day to day
Visit the speechless sick, and still converse
With groaning wretches; and your task shall be,
With all the fierce endeavor of your wit,
To enforce the pained impotent to smile.
Ber. To move wild laughter in the throat of death?
It cannot be, it is impossible:
Mirth cannot move a soul in agony.
Ros. Why, that's the way to choke a gibing spirit,
Whose influence is begot of that loose grace
Which shallow laughing hearers give to fools.
A jest's prosperity lies in the ear
Of him that hears it, never in the tongue
Of him that makes it; then if sickly ears,
Deaf'd with the clamors of their own dear groans,
Will hear your idle scorns, continue then,
And I will have you and that fault withal;
But if they will not, throw away that spirit,
And I shall find you empty of that fault,
Right joyful of your reformation.
Ber. A twelvemonth? Well, befall what will befall,
I'll jest a twelvemonth in an hospital.
Prin. [*To the King.*] Ay, sweet my lord, and so I take my leave.
King. No, madam, we will bring you on your way.
Ber. Our wooing doth not end like an old play:
Jack hath not Gill. These ladies' courtesy
Might well have made our sport a comedy.
King. Come, sir, it wants a twelvemonth an' a day,
And then 'twill end.
Ber. That's too long for a play.

Enter Braggart [ARMADO].

Arm. Sweet Majesty, vouchsafe me—
Prin. Was not that Hector?

786. cote: quote, i.e. interpret.
789. world-without-end. Cf. Sonnet 57.5. **791. dear:** grievous.
797–98. until . . . reckoning: i.e. one year. The "signs" are the signs of the zodiac. **801. weeds:** clothing. **802. gaudy:** gay and showy.
803. last: continue as. **805. challenge:** claim.
812. intitled: having a legal claim.
814. flatter up: pamper, coddle. **rest:** easy living.
817–22. These lines are a first-draft version of lines 837–54.
818. rack'd: extended.
834. friend: sweetheart, lover. **835. stay:** wait.
842. the world's large tongue: i.e. universal report.
844. comparisons: satirical similes. **845. estates:** classes of people.
847. fructful: fruitful. **851. still converse:** constantly associate.
853. fierce: ardent.
854. pained impotent: those made helpless by pain.
859. influence. Used in the astrological sense.
864. dear: intense, grievous. **866. withal:** along with you.
873. bring: escort.

Dum. The worthy knight of Troy.

Arm. I will kiss thy royal finger, and take leave. I am a votary; I have vow'd to Jaquenetta to hold the plough for her sweet love three year. But, most esteemed greatness, will you hear the dialogue that the two learned men have compiled in praise of the owl and the cuckoo? It should have followed in the end of our show.

King. Call them forth quickly, we will do so.

Arm. Holla! approach.

Enter all.

This side is Hiems, Winter; this Ver, the Spring; the one maintained by the owl, th' other by the cuckoo. Ver, begin.

THE SONG

[*Spring.*] When daisies pied, and violets blue,
  And lady-smocks all silver-white,
And cuckoo-buds of yellow hue
  Do paint the meadows with delight,
The cuckoo then on every tree
Mocks married men; for thus sings he,
    "Cuckoo;
Cuckoo, cuckoo"—O word of fear,
Unpleasing to a married ear!

When shepherds pipe on oaten straws,
  And merry larks are ploughmen's clocks;
When turtles tread, and rooks and daws,
  And maidens bleach their summer smocks,
The cuckoo then on every tree
Mocks married men; for thus sings he,
    "Cuckoo;
Cuckoo, cuckoo"—O word of fear,
Unpleasing to a married ear!

Winter. When icicles hang by the wall,
  And Dick the shepherd blows his nail,
And Tom bears logs into the hall,
  And milk comes frozen home in pail;
When blood is nipp'd, and ways be [foul],
Then nightly sings the staring owl,
    "Tu-whit, to-who!"—
A merry note,
While greasy Joan doth keel the pot.

When all aloud the wind doth blow,
  And coughing drowns the parson's saw,
And birds sit brooding in the snow,
  And Marian's nose looks red and raw;
When roasted crabs hiss in the bowl,
Then nightly sings the staring owl,
    "Tu-whit, to-who!"—
A merry note,
While greasy Joan doth keel the pot.

[*Arm.*] The words of Mercury are harsh after the songs of Apollo. [You that way; we this way.]

[*Exeunt omnes.*]

883–84. **hold the plough:** i.e. become a farmer.
885. **dialogue:** debate, statement of contrasting points of view.
892. **maintained:** represented. 894. **pied:** particolored.
895, 896. **lady-smocks, cuckoo-buds.** J. W. Lever, in *Review of English Studies*, n.s. III (1952), 117–20, has shown that Shakespeare may have taken these flower-names and the cuckoo association from John Gerard's *Herbal* (1597). Modern commentators have identified them variously.
901. **word of fear:** i.e. because the cuckoo's call suggests the word *cuckold*.

905. **turtles:** turtle-doves. **tread:** mate.
913. **blows his nail.** This phrase, meaning literally "blows on his finger-nails (for warmth)," had also the sense "waits patiently while he has nothing to do" (cf. *cools his heels*). Both meanings are probably present here.
920. **keel:** cool by stirring (to keep the pot from boiling over).
922. **saw:** moral platitude (in his sermon).
925. **roasted crabs:** roasted crab apples (which were added to a bowl or pot of warmed ale).

NOTE ON THE TEXT

Love's Labor's Lost was published in quarto (Q1) in 1598; the text of the First Folio (1623) is basically a reprint of Q1 (with a few corrections, mainly in speech-prefixes), which had been corrected against a theatre-related manuscript (Wells) or by the corrector's recollections of performances (Kerrigan). A second quarto (Q2), printed in 1631, is based on the F1 text. There is, therefore, no question that Q1, as the only substantive text, must be the basis of any modern edition.

There is considerable internal evidence that Q1 was set, probably throughout, from some form of Shakespeare's "foul papers," and the text it presents is unfortunately far from satisfactory. It abounds in obvious misprints and textual cruxes, and there is a good deal of inconsistency in the use of speech-prefixes and considerable confusion in the assignment of speeches to Rosaline, Katherine, and Maria and to Holofernes and Sir Nathaniel (see Textual Notes, *passim*, especially II.i, IV.ii, V.ii; see Dover Wilson [here followed], Walton, Draudt, Kerrigan, Wells/Taylor).

One other possible complication must be noticed. It has been suggested that Q1 was actually preceded by a "bad" quarto edition of which no copy is now extant. The statement "Newly corrected and augmented" on the Q1 title page is suggestively similar to the claim "Newly corrected, augmented, and amended" on the title page of the "good" quarto (1599) of *Romeo and Juliet*—there intended to repudiate the text of the earlier "bad" quarto of that play—and both quartos were printed for the same publisher, Cuthbert Burby. To what extent, if any, the postulated "bad" quarto may have affected the text of Q1 (as, for example, the "bad" quartos of both *Romeo and Juliet* and *Hamlet* can be shown to have influenced the texts of the "good" quartos of those plays) will have to remain a matter of conjecture, but that it may have done so and hence contributed in some degree to the difficulties of the Q1 text must be considered a possibility.

The complications and confusions in Q1 have led to various theories of revision, and revision there certainly was, but of exactly what kind and at what time made is not clear. At least three passages (see the text at IV.iii.292 and V.ii.132, 817) preserve what are generally agreed to be Shakespeare's first drafts of later lines (corruption from the hypothetical "bad" quarto seems a less likely explanation), and it is probable that the characters Holofernes and Sir Nathaniel and the whole Worthies business were not part of Shakespeare's original play. On the whole it seems likely that some years elapsed between Shakespeare's first draft (perhaps 1594) and the play as we now have it (probably 1597), a revision date supported by J. W. Lever, who (in 1952) argued that Shakespeare was indebted to John Gerard's *Herbal,* first published in 1597, for the opening stanza of the song sung by Spring and Winter in V.ii.894–929 ("When daisies pied, and violets blue, / And lady-smocks all silver-white, . . ."; see the relevant page from the *Herbal* reproduced on p. 212 above). Recently, however, John Kerrigan has attempted to dismiss Lever's claim (a dismissal accepted by Wells/Taylor) by pointing out that Michael Drayton, like Shakespeare born in Warwickshire, uses "lady-smock" as early as 1593 in *The Shepherd's Garland,* eclogue 8, l. 157. (Lever had argued that Gerard's *Herbal* had first given the term currency.) Kerrigan, however, fails to note that Drayton does not associate "lady-smocks" with the cuckoo or with "cuckoo-buds," merely including them in a simple list of flowers. Kerrigan also objects that Shakespeare describes "lady-smocks" as "silver-white," not, as in Gerard, "Milke white." But again, he fails to notice that *O.E.D.* (Silver, *sb.* II, 12 and 12b) associates *silver* and *white* and that Shakespeare (depending sometimes on the metrical demands of a line) uses them as essentially synonymous (see *The Rape of Lucrece,* 1405: "his beard all silver white" and Sonnet 12.4: "And sable curls [all] silver'd o'er with white"; or *A Midsummer Night's Dream,* II.i.167 "Before milk-white, now purple with love's wound" and *2 Henry IV,* V.v.48: "How ill white hairs becomes a fool and jester"). Moreover, although Kerrigan insists that the various items in this stanza tend, generally, to appear together as commonplaces of the season, he offers no other examples that concentrate so many of the components: "Spring," "lady-smocks," "cuckoo-buds of yellow hue," the "meadows," the cuckoo and its song, which Gerard says sings, in April and May, "her pleasant notes [note Shakespeare's "unpleasing"] without stammering." Thus, although we may no longer be as categorical as we have been in claiming Gerard's *Herbal* as necessarily *the* source, there still remains, I think, the good possibility (if not, indeed, probability) that Shakespeare here drew directly from Gerard.

Although, as already noted, F1 is basically nothing but a slightly corrected reprint of Q1, it contains one line—the last in the play—not found in Q1. The line may be Shakespeare's, but it may well be an unauthorized addition made with a view to clearing the stage expeditiously. The more significant F1 variants are recorded in the Textual Notes.

The spelling of the name of Armado's page raises a difficulty. Shakespeare regularly used the single spelling *moth* (and apparently the single pronunciation *mot* or *mote*; see H. Kökeritz, *Shakespeare's Pronunciation* [New Haven, 1953], p. 320) for the senses now differentiated by the spellings *moth* and *mote.* It seems highly likely that in naming the diminutive page (and also one of the fairies in *A Midsummer Night's Dream*) he intended the sense of *mote,* that is, an atom or tiny particle; if so, consistency would require modernization of the spelling in this text (cf. the treatment of the same spelling in IV.iii.159). Since, however, there is a possibility that Shakespeare was thinking primarily of the insect (likewise a diminutive creature), it has seemed best not to depart from the traditional spelling.

For further information, see: J. D. Wilson, ed., New Shakespeare *Love's Labour's Lost* (Cambridge, 1923); Richard David, ed., New Arden *Love's Labour's Lost* (London, 1951); W. W. Greg, *The Shakespeare First Folio* (Oxford, 1955); J. W. Lever, "Three Notes on Shakespeare's Plants," *RES,* n.s., III (1952), 117–29; J. K. Walton, *The Quarto Copy for the First Folio of Shakespeare* (Dublin, 1971); G. R. Price, "The Printing of *Love's Labour's Lost* (1598)," *PBSA,* LXXII (1978), 405–34, and "Textual Notes on *Love's Labour's Lost,* 1598," *AEB,* III (1979), 3–38; Paul Werstine, "Variants in the First Quarto of *Love's Labour's Lost,*" *Shakespeare Studies,* XII (1979), 34–47; Manfred Draudt, "Printer's Copy for the Quarto of *Love's Labour's Lost,*" *The Library,* 6th ser., III (1981), 119–31, and "The 'Rosaline-Katherine Tangle' in *Love's Labour's Lost,*" *The Library,* 6th ser., IV (1982), 381–96; John Kerrigan, ed., New Penguin *Love's Labour's Lost* (Harmondsworth, Middlesex, 1982), "Shakespeare at Work: The Katherine-Rosaline Tangle in *Love's Labour's Lost,*" *RES,* n.s., XXXIII (1982), 129–36, and "*Love's Labour's Lost* and Shakespearean Revision," *SQ,* XXXIII (1982) 337–9; Stanley Wells, "The Copy for the Folio Text of *Love's Labour's Lost,*" *RES,* n.s., XXXIII (1982), 137–47; Stanley Wells, Gary Taylor, et al., *William Shakespeare: A Textual Companion* (Oxford, 1987); George Hibbard, ed., New Oxford *Love's Labour's Lost* (Oxford, 1990).

TEXTUAL NOTES

Title: Love's Labor's Lost] *F3;* **A Pleasant Conceited Comedie Called Loues labors lost. As it was presented before her Highnes this last Christmas. Newly corrected and augmented By W. Shakespere.** *Q1 (title-page);* Loues Labour's lost. *F1*

Dramatis personae: *subs. as first given by Rowe*

Act-scene division: *none in Q1; F1 marks acts only (Act V being mistakenly headed* Actus Quartus.); *scene divisions from F2 (I.i) and from Rowe and later editors (see first note to each scene); present act-scene arrangement as a whole first established by Steevens*

I.i

I.i] *F2;* Actus primus. *F1*

Location: *Cambridge (after Capell); so throughout the play*

1 s.p. **King.]** *Rowe;* Ferdinand. *Q1, F1 (or* Ferd., Fer., *throughout scene)*

5 **buy]** *F2;* buy: *Q1, F1*

13 **academe]** *Q2;* Achademe *Q1, F1 (throughout)*

16 **me,]** *F2;* me: *Q1, F1*

18 **schedule]** *Rowe;* sedule *Q1;* scedule *F1*

31 **pomp]** *F1;* pome *Q1*

50 **please:]** *F4 (subs.);* please, *Q1, F1*

55 **know.]** *Alexander (after Capell);* know? *Q1, F1*

57 **barr'd]** *F4* (bar'd); bard *Q1, F1*

57 **common]** *F1;* cammon *Q1*

59 **Com' on]** Come on *F1*

62 **feast]** *Theobald;* fast *Q1, F1*

65 **hard-a-keeping]** *hyphens, Hanmer*

72 **but]** and *F1*

80 **indeed]** *F1;* in deede *Q1 (throughout, except IV.i.134)*

87 **authority]** *F1;* aucthoritie *Q1*

104 **abortive]** *F1;* abhortiue *Q1*

109 **Climb . . . gate.]** That were to clymbe ore the house to vnlocke the gate. *F1*

114 **sworn]** swore *F2*

119, 123, 128 s.dd. **Reads.]** *Pope (subs.)*

128 s.p. **Ber.]** *Theobald; speech continued to* Longaville, *Q1, F1*

128 **gentility]** *F1;* gentletie *Q1*

131 **can possible]** shall possibly *F1*

138 **bedred]** bed-rid *F1 (with Q1 form cf.* Hamlet, *I.ii.29, and* Lucrece, *l. 975)*

153 **speak]** break *F1*

155 s.d. **Subscribes.]** *Capell*

166 **One]** *F1;* On *Q1*

169 **umpeer]** umpire *F1*

172 **high-borne]** *hyphen, F1 (eds. usually adopt F3* high-born, *but cf.* high words *in l. 193)*

178 **fire-new]** *Pope;* fier new *Q1;* fire, new *F1*

180 s.d. **Enter . . . Costard.]** *arranged as in Capell* (Dull *substituted for* Constable *by Rowe);* Enter a Constable with Costard with a letter. *Q1, F1*

181 s.p. **Dull.]** *Rowe;* Constab. *Q1, F1 (or* Const., *throughout scene)*

184 **farborough]** Tharborough *F1 (the F1 form is closer to the standard form* third-borough, *but the Q1 reading is well within Dull's capacity for verbal blundering)*

190 s.p. Cost.] Rowe; Clowne. Q1, F1 (throughout scene, except ll. 222, 224)
190 contempts] F1; Contempls Q1
211 form—] Capell; forme Q1, F1
219 etc. s.dd. Reads.] Rowe
219–20 welkin's vicegerent] F1; welkis Vizgerent Q1
222 Costard] F1; Costart Q1
231 besieged] F1; besedged Q1
234 health-giving] F1; health-geuing Q1
242 prepost'rous] F1 (preposterous); propostrous Q1
242 snow-white] F1; snowhite Q1
246 curious-knotted] hyphen, Theobald
250 small-knowing] hyphen, F2
277 heart-burning] hyphen, F1
281 worst] F1; wost Q1
294 s.p. King.] from F1 Fer.; Ber. Q1
307 s.d. Exeunt . . . Dumaine.] Capell; Exeunt. F2
313 prosperity] F1; prosperie Q1
314 Affliction] F1; afflicio Q1
314–5 till . . . thee] vntill then sit F1

I.ii

I.ii] Capell
3 s.p. Moth.] Rowe; Boy. Q1, F1 (throughout scene)
4 Why,] Pope (subs.); Why? Q1, F1
14 epitheton] F2; apethaton Q1; apathaton F1
33, 56, 120 s.dd. Aside.] Hanmer
51 ye'll] Cambridge; yele Q1; you'll F1
101 blush in] ed.; blush-in Q1, F1; blushing F2
117 president] F1; presedent Q1
127 s.p. Dull.] Rowe; Constab. Q1; Const. F1
128 suffer him to] let him F1
131 dey-woman] Wilson; Day womand Q1; Day-woman F1
134 s.p. Jaq.] Rowe; Maide. Q1, F1 (throughout scene)
140 that face?] that face. Q1; what face? F1
145 s.p. Dull.] Theobald; Clo. Q1, F1
145 s.d. Dull and Jaquenetta] Theobald
148 s.p. Cost.] Rowe; Clo. Q1, F1 (throughout scene)
166 s.d. with Moth] Pope (subs.)
179 duello] F1; Duella Q1

II.i

II.i] Rowe; Actus Secunda. F1
o.s.d. one named Boyet] Kittredge
2 Consider] F1; Cosider Q1
13 s.p. Prin.] F2; Queene. Q1, F1
21–34] F1 assigns these lines to Prin.
21 all-telling] hyphen, F1
29 best-moving] hyphen, Warburton
32 Importunes] F1; Importuous Q1
34 humble-visag'd] F1 (hyphen, Pope); humble visage Q1
37–8 Who . . . Duke?] as verse, Rowe; as prose, Q1, F1
39 s.p. 1. Lord.] Capell; Lor. Q1, F1
39 Lord] Capell
40 s.p. Mar.] Rowe; 1. Lady. Q1, F1
40–2 madam; . . . solemnized] Capell; Maddame . . . solemnized. Q1, F1
44 parts, peerless] Alexander; peerelsse he is Q1; parts he is F1
53 s.p. Mar.] Rowe; Lad. Q1; Lad. 1. F1
54 short-liv'd] F1 (hyphen, Rowe); short liued Q1
56 s.p. Kath.] Rowe; 2. Lad. Q1, F1
61 Alanson's] Rowe (subs.); Alansoes Q1, F1
64 s.p. Ros.] F1 (Rossa.); 3. Lad. Q1
80 s.p. 1. Lord.] Capell; Lord. Q1; Ma. F1
88 unpeopled] F1; vnpeeled Q1
88 s.d. and Attendants] Rowe
89 Here] F1; Bo. Heere Q1 (repeated s.p.)
89 s.d. The . . . mask.] ed. (after Capell)
90 s.p. King.] Nauar. Q1, F1 (or Nau. through l. 111)
100 it, will] Capell (subs.); it will, Q1, F1
110 s.d. Giving a paper.] Collier MS (after Capell)
115–27] Katherine's speeches in these lines assigned to Rosaline, F1
116 needless] F1; needles Q1
128 s.p. King.] F1; Ferd. Q1 (through l. 167)
140 friendship] F1; faiendship Q1
142 demand] F1; pemaund Q1
144 On] Theobald; One Q1, F1
167 I will] would I F1
173–4 heart, . . . house.] F1; hart. . . . house, Q1
178 s.p. King.] F1; Na. Q1
178 s.d. with . . . Attendants] Capell (subs.)
179 mine own] Q2; my none Q1; my owne F1
180–91] Berowne's speeches in these lines assigned to Boyet in F1.
184 fool] soule F1
190 No point] No poynt Q1, F1 (both in italics)
195 Katherine] Capell conj. (Catharine); Rosalin Q1, F1
196 lady. Monsieur] Rowe (subs.); Lady Mounsir Q1; Lady, Mounsier F1
196 s.d. Enter Longaville.] Wilson (subs.)
210 Rosaline] Brae conj. (in Cambridge); Katherin Q1; Katherine F1
219 s.p. Kath.] La. Ma. F1
219 sheeps, marry.] Rowe (marry F4); Sheepes marie. Q1; Sheepes marie: F1 (continuing the rest of l. 219 to La. Ma.)
221, 222, 224 s.pp. Kath.] Wilson; La. or Lad. Q1, F1
222 s.d. Offering . . . her.] Capell
228–9 lies), . . . eyes,] Theobald; lyes / . . . eyes. Q1; lies / . . . eyes) F1
242 lock'd] F3; lokt Q1; lockt F1
245 you to] out to F1
254 s.p. Mar.] Capell; Lad. Q1; Lad. Ro. F1
255 s.p. Kath.] Capell; Lad. 2. Q1; La. Ma. F1
256 s.p. Ros.] Rowe; Lad. 3. Q1; Lad. 2. F1
257 s.p. Mar.] Rowe; Lad. Q1; La 1. F1
258 s.p. Mar.] Neilson; Lad. Q1; Lad. 2. F1

III.i

III.i] Rowe; Actus Tertius. F1
1 s.p. Arm.] Rowe; Bra. Q1, F1 (through l. 66)
3 s.p. Moth.] Rowe; Boy. Q1, F1 (throughout scene)
3 s.d. Sings . . . "Concolinel."] Wilson; Concolinel. Q1, F1 (F1 adds Song. centred above l. 1)
13 eyelids] eie F1
15 as] Theobald
16 through the] F2; through: Q1, F1
19 thin-bellied] ed.; thinbellies Q1; thinbellie F1
25 note?—] Neilson; note Q1, F1
27 penny] Hanmer; penne Q1, F1
32 s.d. aside] Nicholson conj. (in Cambridge)
35 Negligent] F1; Necligent Q1
40 and this,] Theobald; (and this) Q1, F1
47 s.d. aside] Nicholson conj. (in Cambridge)
58–9 The . . . slow?] as verse, Pope; as prose, Q1, F1
58 The] Thy F1
65 s.d. Exit.] Rowe
66 volable] voluble F1
71 l'envoy—] Johnson; Lenuoy Q1, F1
73 the mail] Malone (after Johnson; the F2); thee male Q1, F1
73 plain] F1; pline Q1
83–92 I . . . four.] om. F1
121 Frances] Capell; Francis Q1, F1
130 s.d. giving a letter] Dyce (after Capell)
134 s.d. Armado . . . Moth] Kittredge
138 remuneration] F1; remuration Q1
139 One penny.] Cambridge; i.d. Q1, F1
140–1 it. Remuneration] Theobald; it remuneration Q1, F1
171 aleven-pence-farthing] ed.; a leuenpencefarthing Q1, F1
176 critic] F1; Crietick Q1
180 senior-junior] Hanmer (after Theobald); signior Iunios Q1, F1
180 giant-dwarf] hyphen, Theobald
185 imperator] Rowe; Emperator Q1, F1
190 German] F1 (subs.); Iermane Q1
190 clock] F2; Cloake Q1, F1
196 whitely] F3; whitly Q1, F1
204 sue] F2; shue Q1, F1
205 s.d. Exit.] Rowe

IV.i

IV.i] Rowe; Actus Quartus. F1
o.s.d. among them Boyet] ed. (after Capell)
1 s.p. Prin.] Quee. Q1, F1 (subs., throughout scene)
2 steep-up rising] Hart; steepe vp rising Q1; steepe vprising F1
3 s.p. For.] Boy. F1
6 On] F1; Ore Q1 (possibly correct = or in the early sense of "before")
14 and] and then F1
18 s.d. Giving him money.] Johnson
32 praise,] Pope; praise Q1, F1
42 s.p. Cost.] Rowe; Clo. Q1, F1 (subs., throughout scene)
69 saw] F2; See Q1, F1
70 saw] Rowe; see Q1, F1
70 overcame] F3; couercame Q1, F1
75 king's] F3; King Q1, F1
82 What] F4; What, Q1, F1
87 Adriano] Q2; Adriana Q1, F1
87 Armado] F2; Armatho Q1, F1
95 vane] Rowe; vaine Q1; veine F1
101 you:] Theobald (subs.); you, Q1, F1
107 s.d. To Rosaline.] Capell
107 s.d. Exeunt . . . Train.] Theobald (subs.); Exeunt. F1
125, 127 s.dd. Sings.] Wilson
128 s.d. Exeunt . . . Katherine.] Capell; Exit. Q1, F1 (placed as in F1; after l. 126, Q1)
130 it] F4
136 pin] F2; is in Q1, F1
139 s.d. Exeunt . . . Maria.] Theobald (subs.)
142 O'] Rowe; O Q1, F1
144 Armado] F2; Armatho Q1; Armathor F1
144 a' th' one] Rowe (subs.); ath toothen Q1; ath to the F1
148 a] F2
148 s.d. Shout] F2; Shoot Q1, F1 (s.d. placed as in Capell; after Exeunt. Q1, F1)
149 Sola, sola] Capell; Sowla, sowla Q1, F1
149 s.d. Exit.] Theobald; Exeunt. Q1, F1

IV.ii

IV.ii] Pope
o.s.d. from . . . hunt] ed. (after Alexander)
3 s.p. Hol.] Rowe; Ped. Q1, F1
8 epithites] F2; epythithes Q1, F1
14–5 explication; facere,] Theobald; explication facere: Q1, F1
22–3 Twice . . . look!] as verse, Dyce; as prose, Q1, F1
28–9 And . . . he.] as verse, Hanmer; as prose, Q1, F1
29 of] Tyrwhitt conj.
30 indiscreet] F1; indistreell Q1
36, 37 Dictynna] Rowe; Dictisima . . . dictisima . . . dictima Q1, F1
40 five weeks] Rowe; fiue-weeks Q1, F1
46 pollution] Rowe; polusion Q1, F1
52 ignorant, call I] Cambridge; ignorault cald Q1; ignorant call'd F1
52 deer] Rowe; Deare: Q1; Deare, F1
54 squirility] scurilitie F1
56 preyful] Collier; prayfull Q1, F1
58 l] Capell; ell Q1, F1
59 pricket sore] Theobald; Pricket-sore Q1, F1
59 a-hooting] hyphen, Dyce
60 L] Pope; el Q1; ell F1
60 o' sorel] Wilson (after Warburton); o sorell Q1, F1
61 L] F1; l Q1
63 s.d. Aside.] Dyce (after Collier MS)
65, 78, 83, 87, 104 s.pp. Hol.] Rowe; Nath. Q1, F1
69 pia mater] Rowe; prima- / ter Q1; primater F1
71 in] F1
73, 103 s.pp. Nath.] Rowe; Holo. or Hol. Q1, F1
78 ingenious] Capell; ingenous Q1; ingenous F1
80 sapit] Q2; sapis Q1, F1
83 pers-one] Capell; Person Q1, F1; Persone F2
85 s.p. Cost.] Rowe; Clo. Q1, F1
86 likel'est] ed.; liklest Q1; likest F1

92 **Armado]** *Collier;* Armatho *Q1, F1*
93 s.p. **Hol.]** *Thirlby conj.;* Nath. *Q1, F1*
93 **pecus omne]** *Theobald;* pecas omnia *Q1, F1*
97 **Venechia, Venechia]** *Sisson;* vemchie, vencha *Q1, F1*
98 **Che . . . che]** *Sisson;* que . . . que *Q1, F1*
98 **vede]** *Malone;* vnde *Q1, F1*
98 **prechia]** *Sisson;* perreche *Q1, F1*
100 **loves thee not.]** *om. F1*
104 **stanze]** *F1;* stauze *Q1*
105 s.p. **Nath.]** *Rowe; Q1, F1 make ll. 105–18 a continuation of the preceding speech, which they assign to* Nath. *(see note on ll. 65 etc., above)*
105 s.d. **Reads.]** *Capell*
105–18 **"If . . . tongue."]** *see a slightly variant version in* The Passionate Pilgrim, V
118 **That sings]** *F1;* That singes *Q1;* To sing *Passionate Pilgrim*
119 s.p. **Hol.]** *Rowe;* Pedan. *Q1;* Ped. *F1*
120 **canzonet]** *Theobald;* cangenet *F1 (correcting Q1* cangenct; *possibly intended as one of Holofernes' mispronunciations, like* apostraphas *in l. 119)*
120–1 s.d. **He . . . letter.]** *Wilson*
121–8 **Here . . . you?]** *continued to Holofernes, Theobald; given to* Nath. *Q1, F1*
125 **invention? Imitari]** *Theobald;* inuention imitarie *Q1, F1;* invention imitary *F2*
131 s.p. **Hol.]** *Theobald;* Nath. *Q1, F1*
134 **writing]** *Rowe;* written *Q1, F1*
136–43 **Sir . . . Adieu.]** *continued to Holofernes, Theobald (see note, l. 131); assigned to* Ped. *Q1* (Per. *F1)*
136 **Nathaniel]** *Capell;* Holofernes *Q1, F1 (Theobald om.* Sir Holofernes)
144 s.p. **Jaq.]** Mayd. *Q1, F1*
146 s.d. **with Jaquenetta]** *Rowe (subs.)*
147 s.p. **Nath.]** *Rowe;* Holo. *Q1;* Hol. *F1*
149, 153, 163 s.pp. **Hol.]** Ped. *or* Peda. *Q1, F1*
154 **before]** being *F1*
164 s.d. **To Dull.]** *Theobald*

IV.iii

IV.iii] *Steevens*
20 s.d. **climbing . . . tree]** *Wilson (after Collier MS)*
20, 42, 74 s.dd. **with a paper]** *Capell*
22, 44, etc. s.dd. **Aside.]** *Johnson*
24 s.d. **Reads.]** *Theobald*
37 **wilt]** *F1;* will *Q1*
47 s.p. **King.]** *Rowe;* Long. *Q1, F1*
51 **corner-cap]** *hyphen, Rowe*
58–71 **"Did . . . paradise?"]** *see a slightly variant version in* The Passionate Pilgrim, III
68 **vapor-vow;]** *F4;* vapour-vow *Q1;* vapor vow, *Passionate Pilgrim;* vapour-vow, *F1*
71 **lose]** *F4;* loose *Q1, F1*
72 **liver-vein]** *hyphen, Rowe*
73 **idolatry]** *F1;* ydotarie *Q1*
75 s.d. **Steps aside.]** *Johnson*
85 **hairs]** *F1;* heires *Q1*
86 **amber-color'd]** *hyphen, Rowe*
97 **ode]** *F1;* Odo *Q1*
99–118 **"On . . . love."]** *see a slightly variant version in* The Passionate Pilgrim, XVI
106 **Wish'd]** *Passionate Pilgrim, F2;* Wish *Q1, F1*
106 **heavens']** *ed.;* heauens *Q1, Passionate Pilgrim, F1*
110 **thorn]** *England's Helicon, Rowe;* throne *Q1, Passionate Pilgrim, F1*
120 **true love's]** *Rowe;* trueloues *Q1;* trueloues *F1*
125, 129 s.dd. **Advancing.]** *Rowe (subs.)*
128 **o'erheard]** *F1;* ore-hard *Q1*
140 **One,]** *Malone;* One *Q1;* On *F1*
141 s.d. **To Longaville.]** *Johnson*
142 s.d. **To Dumaine.]** *Johnson*
149 s.d. **Descending and advancing.]** *Wilson (after Johnson)*
153 **coaches; . . . tears]** *Hanmer;* couches . . . teares. *Q1, F1*
159 **mote . . . mote]** *Rowe;* Moth . . . Moth *Q1, F1*
178 **men . . . men]** *S. Walker conj.;* men like men *Q1;* men, like men *F1*
180 **Joan]** *Q1 (c)* (Ione), *F1* (Ioane); Loue *Q1 (u)*
181 **me? When]** *F3;* mee when *Q1;* mee, when *F1*
195 s.d. **Berowne . . . letter.]** *Capell (subs.)*
199 s.d. **Gathering . . . pieces.]** *Capell (subs.)*
200 s.d. **To Costard.]** *Theobald*
209 s.d. **Exeunt . . . Jaquenetta.]** *Theobald*
222 **peremptory]** *F1;* peromptorie *Q1*
238 **hermit]** *F1;* Hermight *Q1*
244 **wood]** *Rowe;* word *Q1, F1*
255 **and]** *F4*
262 **black]** *F1;* blake *Q1*
264 **crack]** *Q2;* crake *Q1, F1*
273 s.d. **showing his boot]** *Wilson (subs., after Capell)*
292–314] *These lines (included in both Q1 and F1) clearly represent Shakespeare's first draft of parts of the speech which follows in ll. 315–62*
293 **book,]** *Hanmer;* Booke. *Q1, F1*
320 **beauty's]** *Rowe;* beautis *Q1;* beauties *F1*
336 **dainty Bacchus]** *F2;* daintie, Bachus *Q1, F1*
339 **Subtile]** *F1* (Subtill); Subtit *Q1*
356 **authors]** *Johnson;* authour *Q1, F1*
358 **Let]** *F2;* Lets *Q1;* Let's *F1 (om.* us)
364 **standards]** *F1;* standars *Q1*
380 **Allons! allons!]** *Theobald;* Alone alone *Q1;* Alone, alone *F1*
380 **Sow'd]** *Capell;* sowed *Q1, F1*
383 s.d. **Exeunt.]** *F1*

V.i

V.i] *Rowe;* Actus Quartus. *F1*
1 s.p. **Hol.]** *Rowe;* Pedant. *Q1, F1 (or* Ped., Peda., *throughout scene)*
2 s.p. **Nath.]** *Rowe;* Curat. *Q1, F1 (throughout scene)*
8 **Armado]** *Rowe;* Armatho *Q1, F1*
9 **hominem]** *F3;* hominum *Q1, F1*
15 **epithet]** *F3;* Epithat *Q1, F1*
18–9 **point-devise]** *hyphen, Pope*
19 **ortography]** *ed.:* ortagriphie *Q1, F1*
25 **insanie]** *Theobald;* infamie *Q1, F1*
27 **bone]** *Theobald;* bene *Q1, F1* (bene *is correct Latin, but Holofernes' comment requires an error on Sir Nathaniel's part)*
28 **Bone . . . Priscian]** *Theobald;* Bome boon for boon prescian, *Q1, F1*
29 s.d. **and Costard]** *Rowe*
31 **gaudeo]** *Q2;* gaudio *Q1, F1*
32 s.p. **Arm.]** *Rowe;* Brag. *Q1, F1 (throughout scene)*
32 s.d. **To Moth.]** *Capell*
33 **Quare]** *F2;* Quari *Q1, F1*
36 s.p. **Moth.]** *Rowe;* Boy. *Q1, F1*
36 s.d. **Aside to Costard.]** *Johnson*
38 s.p. **Cost.]** *Rowe;* Clow. *Q1, F1 (throughout scene)*
43 s.p. **Moth.]** *Rowe;* Page. *Q1, F1 (throughout scene)*
44 s.d. **To Holofernes.]** *Capell*
58 **wave]** *F1;* wane *Q1*
59 **venue]** *F2;* vene we *Q1, F1*
69 **manu cita]** *anon. conj. (in Cambridge);* vnū cita *Q1;* vnum cita *F1*
76 **wert]** *F1;* wart *Q1*
77 **dunghill]** *F4 (subs.);* dungil *Q1, F1*
79 **dunghill]** *Rowe (subs.);* dunghel *Q1, F1*
81 **preambulate]** *Cambridge;* preambulat *Q1, F1 (in italics)*
99 **importunate]** *F1;* important *Q1*
104 **mustachio]** *F1;* mustachie *Q1*
110 **secrety]** secretie *Q1;* secrecie *F1*
118 **Nathaniel]** *Capell;* Holofernes *Q1, F1*
120 **rend'red]** *F1;* rended *Q1*
120 **assistance,]** *Theobald conj.;* assistants *Q1, F1;* assistants at *F2*
126 **myself;]** *Sisson;* my selfe, *Q1, F1*
147 **antic]** *Theobald;* Antique *Q1, F1*
152 **Allons]** *Rowe;* Alone *Q1, F1*
153–4 **I'll . . . hay.]** *as verse, Dyce; as prose, Q1, F1*
155 **Most dull]** *Theobald;* Most *Dull Q1, F1*

V.ii

V.ii] *Steevens*
3–4 **A . . . King.]** *as verse, Pope; as prose, Q1, F1*
13 **ne'er]** *F1;* neare *Q1*
15–7 **And . . . died.]** *as verse, F2; as prose, Q1, F1*
17 **'a']** *Kittredge;* a *Q1, F1*
17 **been a]** *F1;* bin *Q1*
22 **You'll]** *F1;* Yole *Q1*
43 **pencils]** *Q2* (pensils); pensalls *Q1, F1*
43 **ho!]** *Hanmer;* How? *Q1, F1*
53, 57 s.pp. **Mar.]** *F1;* Marg. *Q1*
53 **pearls]** *F1;* Pearle *Q1*
65 **device]** *so Q1, F1, breaking the couplet rhyme; F2 reads the line as* And shape his service all to my behests; *Knight suggested* hests *for* deuice
67 **pair-taunt-like]** *Percy Simpson (in* TLS); perttaunt like *Q1, F1*
70 **fool; . . . hatch'd,]** *F2;* Foole, . . . hatcht: *Q1, F1*
74 **gravity's]** *Warburton;* grauities *Q1, F1*
74 **wantonness]** *F2;* wantons be *Q1, F1*
80 **stabb'd]** *F1;* stable *Q1*
82–3 **are . . . disguis'd,]** *Theobald (subs.);* are, /Against your Peace Loue doth approch, disguysd: *Q1 (Q1 pointing makes some sense but is very awkward; F1 adds comma after* Peace)
89 **sycamore]** *F1;* Siccamone *Q1*
91 **purpos'd]** *F1;* purposed *Q1*
93 **companions. Warily]** *F1* (companions:); companions warely, *Q1*
96 **they]** *F1;* thy *Q1*
118 **folly, passion's]** *Theobald;* follie pashions *Q1;* folly passions *F1*
118 **solemn]** *F1;* solembe *Q1*
120 **apparell'd]** *F1* appariled *Q1*
122 **parley]** *Rowe;* parlee *Q1, F1*
132–3 **Hold . . . Rosaline.]** *probably a revised form of ll. 130–1*
134 **too]** *F1;* two *Q1*
135 **deceiv'd]** *F1;* deceyued *Q1*
139 **mockery]** mocking *F1*
148 **her]** *F2;* his *Q1, F1*
149 **speaker's]** keepers *F1*
152 **ne'er]** *F2;* ere *Q1, F1*
156 s.d. **trumpet within]** *Capell* (Trumpets); Trom. *Q1; om. F1*
157 s.d. **The Ladies mask.]** *Johnson*
157 s.d. **the King]** *Rowe*
157 s.d. **as Russians]** *Capell (subs., after Rowe)*
158 s.p. **Moth.]** *Rowe;* Page. *Q1, F1 (subs., throughout scene)*
159 s.p. **Boyet.]** *Theobald;* Berow. *Q1, F1*
161 **their—backs—]** *Capell;* their backes *Q1, F1*
163 **ever]** *F1;* euen *Q1*
169 **sun-beamed]** *hyphen, Rowe*
170 **sun-beamed]** *hyphen, F4*
171 **epithet]** *F4 (subs.);* Epythat *Q1;* Epythite *F1*
172 **daughter-beamed]** *hyphen, F2*
174 s.d. **Exit Moth.]** *Capell*
175 **strangers]** *F1;* stranges *Q1*
178 **Princess]** *F4;* Princes *Q1, F1*
197 **travel]** *F1;* trauaile *Q1*
211 s.d. **Music plays.]** *Capell (subs.)*
212 **yet;]** *Capell;* yet *Q1, F1*
216 **The . . . it.]** *continued to the King, Theobald; assigned to* Rosa. *Q1, F1* (. . . it, *Q1;* . . . it: *F1)*
217 s.p. **Ros.]** *Theobald*
219 **nice; take hands.]** *Theobald (subs.);* nice, take handes, *Q1, F1*
222 **measure;]** *F3;* measue *Q1;* measure, *F1*
229, 237, 241, 255 s.dd. **They converse apart.]** *Capell*
230 **White-handed]** *hyphen, F4*
242, 244, 247, 248, 249, 253, 255 s.pp. **Kath.]** *Rowe;* Maria, Mari., *or* Mar. *Q1, F1*
258–9 **seen; . . . sense, so sensible]** *Theobald;* seene, . . . sense so sensible, *Q1,* (sensible:) *F1*
263 **dry-beaten]** *hyphen, Hanmer*
264 s.d. **Exeunt . . . Blackmoors.]** *Theobald (subs.);* Exe. *Q1;* Exeunt. *F1*
269 **kingly-poor]** *hyphen, Capell*

274 **weeping-ripe]** *hyphen, Rowe*
297 **vailing]** *F1;* varling *Q1*
309 **run]** *F4;* runs *Q1, F1*
309 **s.d. Princess and Ladies]** *Capell (subs.)*
309 **s.d. of . . . habits]** *Rowe (subs.)*
311–2 **Gone . . . thither?]** *as verse, Capell (F1 as irregular verse, om.* thither); *as prose, Q1*
316 **God]** Ioue *F1*
328 **hushering]** Vshering *F1*
334 **due]** dutie *F1*
336 **Armado's]** *F2;* Armathoes *Q1, F1*
336 **s.d. Princess . . . her]** *Capell (subs.)*
338 **madman]** *F1;* mad man *Q1*
338 **show'd]** *F1;* shewed *Q1*
341 **Conster]** *ed.;* Consture *Q1;* Construe *F1*
352 **unsallied]** *cf. the form* sallied *in* Hamlet *(Q2, Q1), I.ii.129;* unsullied *F1*
356 **vow'd]** *F1;* vowed *Q1*
368 **stay'd]** *F4;* stayed *Q1, F1*
374 **foolish.]** *Rowe (subs.);* foolish *Q1, F1*
375 **eye,]** *F3;* eie: *Q1, F1*
388 **show'd]** *F1;* shewed *Q1*
389, 390 **s.dd. Aside.]** *Capell*
407 **Three-pil'd]** *hyphen, F1*
407 **hyperboles]** *F1;* Hiberboles *Q1*
415 **sans]** *F1 (in italics);* sance *Q1 (in italics)*
416 **Sans]** *Tyrwhitt conj.;* Sans, *Q1, F1 (in italics)*
439–40 **Peace . . . forswear.]** *as verse, F1; as prose, Q1*
463 **carry-tale]** *hyphen, F1*
463 **zany]** *F1;* saine *Q1*
464 **mumble-news]** *hyphen, F1*
464 **trencher-knight]** *hyphen, F1*
465 **smiles]** *F1;* smyles, *Q1*
472 **s.d. to Boyet]** *Rowe (after l. 472); placed as in Theobald*
478 **allow'd]** *F3;* aloude *Q1;* alowd *F1*
481 **merrily]** *F1;* merely *Q1*
482 **manage]** *Theobald;* nuage *Q1;* manager *F1*
485 **s.p. Cost.]** *Rowe;* Clow. *Q1, F1 (or* Clowne., Clo., *throughout scene)*
490 **You . . . know.]** *as verse, Capell; as prose, Q1, F1*
501 **they]** *F1;* thy *Q1*
502–3 **Great,]** *Rowe;* great *Q1, F1*
512 **shame-proof]** *hyphen, F1*
516 **least]** *F1;* best *Q1*
523 **s.d. Converses . . . paper.]** *Capell*
530–1 **de la guerra]** *Theobald;* delaguar *Q1, F1*
532 **couplement]** *Capell (after Warburton);* cupplement *Q1, F1*
538–9 **And . . . five.]** *as verse, Rowe; as prose, Q1, F1*
545 **pick]** pricke *F1*
546 **s.d. Costard for]** *Rowe*
557 **s.p. Prin.]** *F2;* Lady. *Q1;* La. *F1*
566 **this]** *F1;* his *Q1*
566 **tender-smelling]** *hyphen, Capell*
568 **liv'd]** *Rowe;* liued *Q1, F1*
574 **s.d. To Nathaniel.]** *Capell*
579 **afeard]** *Capell;* a feard *Q1;* affraid *F1*
580 **s.d. Nathaniel retires.]** *Capell*
582 **faith]** insooth *F1*
586 **sort.]** *Rowe;* sort. *Exit Curat. Q1, F1;* Exit Clo. *F2*
588 **s.p. Hol.]** *Rowe;* Peda. *Q1, F1 (throughout scene)*
589 **three-headed]** *hyphen, F1*
594 **s.d. Aside.]** *Neilson*
594 **s.d. Moth retires.]** *Capell;* Exit Boy. *Q1, F1 (l. 594 in italics as part of Holofernes' role in Q1)*
600 **prov'd]** *F1;* proud *Q1*
606 **elder]** *F1;* Felder *Q1*
610 **cittern-head]** *hyphen, Knight*
614 **falchion]** *F1;* Fauchion *Q1*
616 **half-cheek]** *hyphen, Theobald*
623 **out-fac'd]** *F1;* outfaste *Q1*
628 **Jud-as]** *F1;* Iudas *Q1*
630 **s.d. Holofernes retires.]** *Capell*
631 **s.d. Enter]** *F1;* Eeter *Q1*
631 **s.d. Armado for Hector]** *Capell*
638 **clean-timber'd]** *hyphen, Warburton*
646 **gilt]** *F1;* gift *Q1*
654 **I . . . flower—]** *Capell (after Theobald, who included the line as part of Armado's role as Hector);* I . . . Flower. *Q1, F1 (not distinguished by italics as part of Armado's role)*
662 **When . . . man.]** *om. F1*
663 **s.d. To the Princess.]** *Steevens (after Capell)*
664 **s.d. to . . . place]** *Capell (subs.)*
667 **I . . . slipper.]** *as F1; in italics as part of Armado's role, Q1*
671 **The . . . gone—]** *as part of Armado's speech, Pope; centred as s.d. (in italics), Q1, F1*
688–9 **mov'd. More . . . on,]** *Rowe (subs.);* mooued more Ates more Atees stir them or *Q1;* moued, more Atees more Atees stirre them, or *F1*
709 **for't]** *F1;* fort *Q1*
710 **have]** *F1;* hane *Q1*
716–7 **Welcome . . . merriment.]** *as verse, Capell; as prose, Q1, F1*
717 **interruptest]** *F1;* interrnpptest *Q1*
730 **endeavors, and entreat,]** *Rowe;* endeuors and entreat: *Q1;* endeuors and entreats: *F1*
731 **new-sad soul]** *Theobald;* new sad-soule *Q1, F1*
750 **wholesome-profitable]** *S. Walker conj.;* holdsome profitable *Q1;* wholsome profitable *F1*
759 **seem'd]** *F1;* seemed *Q1*
766 **parti-coated]** *hyphen, F1*
768 **misbecom'd]** *F1;* misbecombd *Q1*
768 **gravities,]** *Capell;* grauities. *Q1, F1*
774 **both—]** *Theobald (subs.);* both *Q1;* both, *F1*
778 **embassadors]** the Ambassadors *F1*
782 **this in]** *Hanmer;* this *Q1;* these are *F1*
785 **show'd]** *F1;* shewed *Q1*
807 **instant]** *F1;* instance *Q1*
812 **intitled]** *F1;* intiled *Q1*
816 **hermit]** *Pollard conj. (in New Cambridge);* herrite *Q1;* euer *F1*
817–22] *These lines (included in both Q1 and F1) clearly represent Shakespeare's first draft of ll. 837–54*
824 **A wife?]** *continued to Dumaine, Dyce; part of Katherine's next line, Q1, F1*
828 **smooth-fac'd]** *F3;* smothfast *Q1;* smoothfac'd *F1*
845 **estates]** *F1;* estetes *Q1*
847 **fructful]** fruitfull *F1*
872 **s.d. To the King.]** *Rowe*
879 **s.p. Arm.]** *Rowe;* Brag. *Q1, F1 (throughout scene)*
894 **s.p. Spring.]** *Theobald*
895–6 **And . . . hue]** *Theobald's arrangement; lines reversed, Q1, F1*
895 **silver-white]** *hyphen, Capell*
912 **icicles]** *F1* (Isicles); Isacles *Q1*
914 **Tom]** *F1;* Thom *Q1*
916 **foul]** *F1;* full *Q1*
930 **s.p. Arm.]** *F1* (Brag.)
930–1 **The . . . Apollo.]** *these lines set in larger roman type in Q1 without s.p.*
931 **You . . . way.]** *F1*
931 **s.d. Exeunt omnes.]** *F1* (Exeunt omnes. / FINIS.); FINIS. *Q1*

A Midsummer Night's Dream

WHEN Samuel Pepys saw *A Midsummer Night's Dream* in 1662, he reacted much as Hippolyta does to "the most lamentable comedy and most cruel death of Pyramus and Thisby" as performed by Bottom and his friends. "This is the silliest stuff that ever I heard," she says (V.i.210). Pepys's judgment, confided to his diary, that this was "the most insipid ridiculous play that ever I saw in my life" was extreme. Nevertheless, condescension to the comedy as a matter of gossamer and moonshine, a charming trifle to be eked out theatrically by as much music and spectacle as possible, dominated both the criticism and the stage representations of this play from the Restoration until the second half of the twentieth century. Only comparatively recently has it become possible to see that *A Midsummer Night's Dream* is a complex and exacting work of art. An extraordinary synthesis of material which, in itself, is challengingly diverse, the play embodies in its apparent effortlessness and poise Shakespeare's entire confidence at this time in his own comic form.

Although there is no identifiable narrative or dramatic source for the plot, a good deal of general reading seems to underlie the comedy. The influence of Ovid's *Metamorphoses* is evident both in the unifying theme of transformation and in the introduction of the Pyramus and Thisby story, which Ovid had related, and which Shakespeare must have known in the original Latin as well as in Golding's popular if rather ponderous translation of 1567. Hippolyta and her husband Theseus, that humane and practical hero, figure in Chaucer's "Knight's Tale" and also in North's translation of Plutarch's *Lives of the Noble Grecians and Romans* (1579), both of them works that Shakespeare certainly knew. Bottom's transformation may have been inspired by the misfortune which overcomes Lucius in *The Golden Ass* of Apuleius, a Latin romance of the second century A.D. which existed in an early Elizabethan translation. Oberon had appeared in the old romance *Huon of Bordeaux*, and Bottom's fumbling attempt to characterize the marvellous dream he has had (IV.i.211–14) seems to depend upon a passage from St. Paul's *Epistle to the Corinthians* as it was rendered in the Bishops' Bible. The influence of St. Augustine and of some of the Renaissance Neo-Platonists has also been detected by certain recent commentators concerned to argue that in this comedy Shakespeare, for once, was handling ideas more usually associated with Spenser or with Jonson's masques at court. If, as is often supposed, *A Midsummer Night's Dream* was commissioned for a wedding celebration at Whitehall or in some great house, the presence of such literary and iconographical elements, most of them serving to define an ideal of Christian marriage, would obviously be appropriate. Unfortunately, neither a specific occasion nor the degree of Shakespeare's possible indebtedness to writers like Ficino and Pico della Mirandola has ever been satisfactorily established.

It would be a mistake, however, to regard the interwoven strands which make up the tapestry of the comedy as being predominantly literary and intellectual. By way of the title itself, and also through Theseus's suggestion that the lovers he finds sleeping in the forest might have come there early to "observe / The rite of May" (IV.i.132–33), the action of the play is associated with two traditional and distinct country festivals. Although Shakespeare cannily refuses to make any clear statement about the night or even the month of the year in which the lovers lose themselves in the forest (he was to be similarly evasive in *Twelfth Night*, despite the apparent clue provided, again, by the title), he was obviously concerned to evoke the audience's memories of holiday license and merriment, that atmosphere of madness and of magic, herb-lore and supernatural manifestations, which Elizabethans connected both with May-day and with the summer solstice. The comedy's concern with marriage and fertility is scarcely unique in Shakespeare, but the particular stress upon man's dependence on the natural world and its seasonal rhythms is at least as likely to have been dictated by the dramatist's awareness of the customs of May-day and Midsummer Eve as by any hypothetical noble wedding.

Athens, at the beginning of the play, is partly classical and partly Chaucer's somewhat quaint medieval dukedom. When the lovers return to it at the end, it seems to have transformed itself almost entirely into an Elizabethan great house. Here, despite references to Centaurs and "my kinsman Hercules" (V.i.47), Duke Theseus rules over his little kingdom more in the manner of Leicester at Kenilworth than as an antique hero. Like Athens, the wood nearby where most of the action takes place is both mythological and intensely English, alien and familiar. It is a compelling invention precisely because its true nature remains mysterious. Are its moonlit glades beneficent and beautiful, or merely frightening, the place of error and unreason? Certainly this sylvan world is complex. The fairies who attend upon Titania are, as Bottom makes clear, both spirits and common English insects and flowers. Even the moon which presides over the whole imbroglio contrives to be a simple source of light, a goddess, the subject of learned allusions to the triple Hecate, participant in an allegorical tableau in praise of Queen Elizabeth, a stage prop, and (in the rustic imagination at least) the place that an old man with a thorn-bush and a dog calls home.

Oberon and Titania, the sovereign spirits of the wood, are exotic personages who might well inhabit a court masque, or start out from the greenery of some nobleman's park to welcome Queen Elizabeth on one of her royal progresses. Shakespeare sees them as dangerous powers whose dissensions and quarrels can disorder the seasons and throw the natural world into chaos. They bless the human marriages at the end, but it should not be forgotten that they have also the power to destroy. Puck, on the other hand, is the far more homely product of rural superstition, the Robin Goodfellow of Shakespeare's Warwickshire childhood. An intruder into the more elegant fairy world, he does not belong properly to the forest at all, but to sixteenth-century village life as it was lived in dairies, orchards, and smoky cottage interiors. His victims in the play, Hermia and Lysander, Helena and Demetrius, would probably have reminded many of the members of Shakespeare's audience of equivalent characters in the court comedies of John Lyly. They are only slightly individualized, not because Shakespeare was incapable at this stage of fuller characterization, but because he obviously wished to distance the lovers, subordinating them to the total pattern of the play. Ironically, although they themselves regard each other as strikingly different, objects of passionate love or hate, all four look and behave, from the point of view of the outsider—whether Puck or the theatre audience—remarkably alike. They present a deliberately generalized picture of love's unreason, a state governed less by individual disposition than by the madness appropriate to a particular time of life as well as of the year.

Bottom and his friends, the last and in a way the most surprising of the various groups of characters assembled in the wood, are plain Elizabethan workmen. The play which they present for the delectation of Theseus and his court is also, in essence, Elizabethan. Although most of the plays, both popular and courtly, written between 1560 and the new departure signalized by Marlowe's *Tamburlaine* in 1587 have been lost, enough of them survive to indicate that in the Pyramus and Thisby interlude Shakespeare was remembering, and mocking, actual plays which had formed part of the repertory of the children's companies and of the travelling groups of adult players when he was a boy. Some of Bottom's most grotesque speeches as Pyramus are surprisingly close to lines intended to be spoken in all seriousness in *Appius and Virginia* (1564) or in Preston's *Cambises* (1561). The mechanicals themselves are deeply confused about the nature of theatrical illusion. Probably only Bottom has ever seen a professional play. Their decision to add an explanatory Prologue, and to personify Moonshine and Wall, is unfortunate but the text they have chosen to perform is in any case hilarious, even without these blundering embellishments. Shakespeare the London professional backed by an acting company gradually outstripping its rivals and soon to build a dazzling new theatre on the Bankside and acquire a royal patent, could afford to burlesque the bad plays and outmoded acting styles of the recent past.

A Midsummer Night's Dream was first printed in a quarto edition in 1600. The comedy was first mentioned by Meres in 1598, but 1595–96 is usually accepted as the date of composition. It has certain stylistic affinities with *Richard II* and *Romeo and Juliet*, plays which must have been written at about the same time. More importantly, it seems to consolidate and conclude Shakespeare's first period of experiment with comic form. The synthesizing impulse characteristic of *A Midsummer Night's Dream* not only knits together a number of different historical times and places, literary traditions, character types, and modes of thought. It manifests itself in the play's unusual variety of metres and verse forms, as well as in the tendency, remarked on by several critics, for characters to stress the richness of their encompassing dramatic world by listing its components. Egeus is not content simply to state that Lysander has exchanged love-tokens with Hermia. He names them all: "bracelets of thy hair, rings, gawds, conceits, / Knacks, trifles, nosegays, sweetmeats" (I.i.33–34). Almost all the characters are given to list-making. Oberon painstakingly itemizes every kind of wild beast that might conceivably wake Titania; Hermia and Lysander count all the obstacles that have ever threatened true love, while the fairies almost bury Bottom alive under a deluge of honey and butterflies, glow-worms, apricots and figs.

Shakespeare's friend Ben Jonson was, in many of his plays, a compulsive maker of dramatic inventories of a superficially similar kind. *Volpone*, *The Alchemist* and *Bartholomew Fair* are filled with tallies, a sea of objects which continually threaten to engulf the characters. Nothing, however, could be more different in effect from the list-making of *A Midsummer Night's Dream*. Jonson's world of things is stifling and corrupt, inanimate, man-made and man-soiled, the dusty contents of some Gothic lumber-room of the imagination: "his copper rings, / His saffron jewel, with the toad-stone in't, / Or his embroidered suit, with the cope-stitch, / Made of a hearse-cloth, or his old tilt-feather" (*Volpone*, II.v.11–14). Almost invariably, Jonson's enumerations evoke an incoherent urban world, so overcrowded that it has become impossible for human beings to walk about naturally among the detritus of a civilization out of control. By contrast, the lists in Shakespeare's comedy create the sense of a country world that is inexhaustibly rich and various, occasionally grotesque, but basically fresh, creative, and young. Moreover, where Jonson's lists are deliberately disjunctive, images of chaos, Shakespeare's relate and interact without sacrificing the individuality of the separate components. In the remarkably generous and inclusive order of *A Midsummer Night's Dream*, where Bottom can converse amiably with the fairy queen without losing a jot of his own identity, there seems to be nothing which the shaping spirit of imagination cannot use and, in some way, make relevant to the whole.

Not surprisingly, a preoccupation with the idea of imagination, and with some of its products—dreams, the illusions of love, poetry and plays—is central to this comedy. Theseus may speak somewhat slightingly of "the lunatic, the lover, and the poet," beings "of imagination all compact" whose fantasies are literally incredible: "more strange than true" (V.i.2 ff). The play as a whole takes a far more complicated view of the matter. Theseus himself, for Shakespeare as for Chaucer and Sophocles, is preeminently the hero of a daylight world of practicalities, of the active as opposed to the contemplative life. His relationship with Hippolyta in the comedy presents an image of passion steadied by the relative maturity of the people involved. There are ages of love as well as of human life and Theseus and Hippolyta represent summer as opposed to the giddy spring fancies of the couples lost in the wood. Theseus is a wise ruler and a good man, but Shakespeare makes it plain that there are other, important areas of human experience with which he is incompetent to deal. When Theseus leads the bridal couples to bed at the end of Act V with the mocking reminder that " 'tis almost fairy time" (V.i.364), he intends the remark as a last jibe at Hermia and Lysander, Helena and Demetrius: people who, in his estimation, have been led all too easily by darkness and their own fear to suppose a bush a bear (V.i.22). The joke, however, is on Theseus. It is indeed almost fairy time. In fact, Puck, Oberon, and Titania have been waiting for this moment in order to take over the palace. For a few nocturnal hours the wood infiltrates the urban world. Even so, years before, a Titania in whom Theseus apparently does not believe led him "through the glimmering night / From Perigenia, whom he ravished," and made him "with fair Aegles break his faith, / With Ariadne, and Antiopa" (II.i.77–80). The life of the self-appointed critic of imagination and the irrational is permeated by exactly those qualities he is concerned to minimize or reject. Gently, the comedy suggests that while it is certainly possible to mistake a bush for a bear, one may also err as Theseus does by confounding a genuine bear with a bush. The second mistake is, on the whole, the more dangerous.

The last act of *A Midsummer Night's Dream* is concerned principally, and even somewhat self-consciously, with the relationship between art and life, dreams and the waking world. In terms of plot, this fifth act is superfluous. Almost all the business of the comedy has been concluded at the end of Act IV: the error of Titania's vision put right and she herself reconciled with Oberon, Hermia paired off happily with Lysander and Helena with Demetrius. Theseus has not only overruled the objections of old Egeus, but insisted upon associating these marriages with his own: "Away with us to Athens. Three and three, / We'll hold a feast in great solemnity" (IV.i.184–85). This couplet has the authentic ring of a comedy conclusion. Only one expectation generated by the action remains unfulfilled: the presentation of the Pyramus and Thisby play before the Duke and his bride. Out of this single remaining bit of material, Shakespeare constructs a fifth act which seems, in effect, to take place beyond the normal, plot-defined boundaries of comedy.

The new social order which has emerged from the ordeal of the wood makes its first public appearance at the performance of the mechanicals' play. It is sensitive and hopeful. Theseus, characteristically, is condescending about the actor's art: "The best in this kind are but shadows; and the worst are no worse, if imagination amend them" (V.i.211–12). Richard Burbage would scarcely have thanked him. Such a view of the theatre overstresses the audience's lordly willingness-to-be-fooled at the expense of the power of illusion. Certainly a quite extraordinary effort of imagination would be required to extract Aristotelian pity and fear from the tragedy of Pyramus and Thisby as enacted by Bottom and Flute. The courtly audience, like the theatre audience, laughs at the ineptitudes and absurdities of the play within the play. Unlike Berowne and his friends in the equivalent scene of *Love's Labor's Lost*, however, the on-stage spectators in *A Midsummer Night's Dream* remain courteous. Most of the remarks made by Theseus, Hippolyta, and the four lovers are not heard by the preoccupied actors. Those that do penetrate, suggestions as to the proper disposition of Moonshine's lantern, dog, and bush, cries of "Well roar'd, Lion" and "Well run, Thisby," are entirely in the spirit of the performance. It was Bottom, after all, back in the rehearsal stage, who fondly imagined a success for Lion so great that the audience would intervene to request an encore: "Let him roar again." Gratifyingly, this wish-dream just about comes true. As the play proceeds, tolerance ripens into geniality, into an unforced accord between actors and spectators based upon considerations far more complex than anything articulated by Theseus. Although the artistic merit of the Pyramus and Thisby play is virtually non-existent, the performance itself is a resounding success. No feelings have been hurt, and everyone has had a thoroughly good time. Even Theseus finds that "this palpable-gross play hath well beguil'd / The heavy gait of night" (V.i.367–68).

For the theatre audience, granted a perspective wider than the one enjoyed by Theseus and the members of his court, the Pyramus and Thisby story of love thwarted by parents and the enmity of the stars consolidates and in a sense defines the happy ending of *A Midsummer Night's Dream*. It reminds us of the initial dilemma of Hermia and Lysander, and also of how their story might well have ended: with blood and deprivation. The heavy rhetoric of the interlude fairly bristles with fate and disaster, introducing into Act V a massing of images of death. The entire action of the play within the play is tragic in intention, although not in execution. Without meaning to do so, Bottom and his associates transform tragedy into farce before our eyes, converting that litany of true love crossed which was rehearsed in the very first scene by Hermia and Lysander to laughter. In doing so, they recapitulate the development of *A Midsummer Night's Dream* as a whole, reenacting its movement from potential calamity to an ending in which quick bright things come not to confusion, as once seemed inevitable, but to joy. An intelligent director can and should ensure that the on-stage audience demonstrates some awareness of the ground-bass of mortality sounding underneath the hilarity generated by Bottom's performance, that a line like Lysander's "he is dead, he is nothing" (V.i.308–9) is not lost in the merriment. Only the theatre audience, however, can capture the full resonance of the Pyramus and Thisby play.

When Theseus dismisses the actors after the Bergomask, and the members of the stage audience depart to their chambers, *A Midsummer Night's Dream* seems once again to have arrived at its ending. For the second time Theseus is given a couplet which sounds like the last lines of a play (V.i.369–70). When something like this happened at the end of Act IV it was Bottom, starting up out of his sleep, who set the comedy going again. This time it is the entrance of the fairies, but again the prolongation has nothing to do with plot. The appearance of Puck, Oberon, Titania and their train in the heart of Athens lends a symmetry to the action which would otherwise have been lacking and also gives the lie to Theseus's scepticism. Most important of all, however, is the way Puck's speech picks up and transforms precisely those ideas of death and destruction distanced through laughter in the Pyramus and Thisby play.

> Now the hungry lion roars,
> And the wolf behowls the moon;
> Whilst the heavy ploughman snores,
> All with weary task foredone.
> Now the wasted brands do glow,
> Whilst the screech-owl, screeching loud,
> Puts the wretch that lies in woe
> In remembrance of a shroud.
> Now it is the time of night
> That the graves, all gaping wide,
> Every one lets forth his sprite,
> In the church-way paths to glide.

All the images here are of sickness, toil, and death. Even the wasted brands, in context, suggest the inevitable running down of human life as it approaches the grave.

Once again, Shakespeare has adjusted the balance between art and life, reality and illusion. Puck's hungry lion is something genuinely savage, not at all the "very gentle beast, and of a good conscience" (V.i.227–28) impersonated by Snug. Even so, his talk of graves and shrouds, drudgery and exhaustion, brings the sense of mortality kept at bay in the Pyramus and Thisby interlude closer, preparing us for the true end of the comedy after so many feints and false conclusions. Puck's speech begins a modulation which will terminate, some fifty lines later, in direct address to the audience and in a player's request for applause. Actors and spectators alike will be turned out of Athens to face the workaday world. Yet Shakespeare refuses to concede that Theseus was right. In the first place, Puck's account of the terrors of the night is not final. It serves to introduce Oberon and Titania, the most fantastic characters in the play, and in their hands Puck's night fears turn into benediction and blessing. About the facts of mortality themselves the fairy king and queen can do nothing, even as Titania could do nothing to prevent the death, years before, of the votaress of her order. All they can do is to strengthen the fidelity and trust of the three pairs of lovers, to bless these marriages, and to stress the positive side of the night as a time for love and procreation as well as for death and fear. Certainly the emphasis on the fair, unblemished children to be born is not accidental, something to be explained purely in terms of the possible occasion of the play's first performance. These children summoned up by Oberon extend the comedy into the future, counteracting the artificial finality which always threatens to diminish happy endings. A beginning is made implicit in the final moments of the play, a further and wider circle.

Unlike characters in fairy-tale, Theseus and Hippolyta, Demetrius and Helena, Lysander and Hermia cannot live happily ever after. Only the qualified immortality to be obtained through offspring is available to them. It was an idea of survival in time which the Shakespeare of the sonnets came to distrust. Nevertheless, in the general atmosphere of celebration and blessing at the end of *A Midsummer Night's Dream*, it seems for the moment enough. It is only after this final coming together in Theseus' palace of the two poles of the comedy, a world of fantasy and one of fact, of immortality and of death, that Puck turns to speak to the theatre audience. Like Theseus, he describes the actors as "shadows" and sums up the play now concluded as a "weak and idle theme, / No more yielding than a dream." When John Lyly ended his court comedies with superficially similar words of deprecation and apology, he seems to have meant them literally. Shakespeare is far more devious. Images of sleep and dreams, shadows and illusions, have been used so constantly in the course of the comedy, examined and invested with such body and significance that they cannot be regarded now as simple terms of denigration and dismissal. As with that mock-apology for the author's "rough and all-unable pen" which concludes *Henry V*, Shakespeare seems to have felt able to trust his audience to take the point: to recognize the simplification, and to understand that the play has created its own reality, a reality touching our own at every point which

> More witnesseth than fancy's images,
> And grows to something of great constancy;
> But howsoever, strange and admirable. (V.i.25–27)

Anne Barton

A Midsummer Night's Dream

[Dramatis Personae

Theseus, *Duke of Athens*
Egeus, *father to Hermia*
Lysander, Demetrius } *in love with Hermia*
Philostrate, *Master of the Revels to Theseus*

Quince, *a carpenter*
Bottom, *a weaver*
Flute, *a bellows-mender*
Snout, *a tinker*
Snug, *a joiner*
Starveling, *a tailor*
} *presenting* { Prologue, Pyramus, Thisby, Wall, Lion, Moonshine

Hippolyta, *Queen of the Amazons, betrothed to Theseus*
Hermia, *daughter to Egeus, in love with Lysander*
Helena, *in love with Demetrius*
Oberon, *King of the Fairies*
Titania, *Queen of the Fairies*
Puck, *or* Robin Goodfellow
Peaseblossom, Cobweb, Moth, Mustardseed } *fairies*

Other Fairies *attending their King and Queen;* Attendants *on Theseus and Hippolyta*

Scene: *Athens, and a wood near it*]

[ACT I, Scene I]

Enter Theseus, Hippolyta, [Philostrate,] *with others.*

The. Now, fair Hippolyta, our nuptial hour
Draws on apace. Four happy days bring in
Another moon; but O, methinks, how slow
This old moon [wanes]! She lingers my desires,
Like to a step-dame, or a dowager,
Long withering out a young man's revenue.
Hip. Four days will quickly steep themselves in night;
Four nights will quickly dream away the time;
And then the moon, like to a silver bow
[New] bent in heaven, shall behold the night
Of our solemnities.
The. Go, Philostrate,
Stir up the Athenian youth to merriments,
Awake the pert and nimble spirit of mirth,
Turn melancholy forth to funerals:
The pale companion is not for our pomp.
[*Exit Philostrate.*]
Hippolyta, I woo'd thee with my sword,
And won thy love doing thee injuries;
But I will wed thee in another key,
With pomp, with triumph, and with revelling.

Enter Egeus *and his daughter* Hermia *and* Lysander *and* Demetrius.

Ege. Happy be Theseus, our renowned Duke!
The. Thanks, good Egeus. What's the news with thee?
Ege. Full of vexation come I, with complaint
Against my child, my daughter Hermia.
Stand forth, Demetrius. My noble lord,
This man hath my consent to marry her.
Stand forth, Lysander. And, my gracious Duke,
This man hath bewitch'd the bosom of my child.
Thou, thou, Lysander, thou hast given her rhymes,
And interchang'd love-tokens with my child;
Thou hast by moonlight at her window sung
With faining voice verses of faining love,
And stol'n the impression of her fantasy

Words and passages enclosed in square brackets in the text above are either emendations of the copy-text or additions to it. The Textual Notes immediately following the play cite the earliest authority for every such change or insertion and supply the reading of the copy-text wherever it is emended in this edition.

I.i. Location: Athens. The palace of Theseus.
4. **lingers:** delays the fulfillment of.
5. **step-dame:** stepmother. **dowager:** widow with property rights charged upon an estate during her lifetime.
6. **withering out:** diminishing. 11. **solemnities:** i.e. marriage rites.
13. **pert:** lively, brisk.
15. **companion:** fellow (contemptuous). **pomp:** ceremonial splendor.
16–17. **I . . . injuries.** Theseus had made war against the Amazons and taken their queen captive. 19. **triumph:** public spectacle.
31. **faining . . . faining:** (1) loving . . . longing; (2) feigning . . . feigned.
32. **stol'n . . . fantasy:** stealthily stamped your image on her imagination, i.e. made her fall in love with you.

With bracelets of thy hair, rings, gawds, conceits,
Knacks, trifles, nosegays, sweetmeats—messengers
Of strong prevailment in unhardened youth.
With cunning hast thou filch'd my daughter's heart,
Turn'd her obedience (which is due to me)
To stubborn harshness. And, my gracious Duke,
Be it so she will not here before your Grace
Consent to marry with Demetrius,
I beg the ancient privilege of Athens:
As she is mine, I may dispose of her;
Which shall be either to this gentleman,
Or to her death, according to our law
Immediately provided in that case.
The. What say you, Hermia? Be advis'd, fair maid.
To you your father should be as a god;
One that compos'd your beauties; yea, and one
To whom you are but as a form in wax,
By him imprinted, and within his power,
To leave the figure, or disfigure it.
Demetrius is a worthy gentleman.
Her. So is Lysander.
The. In himself he is;
But in this kind, wanting your father's voice,
The other must be held the worthier.
Her. I would my father look'd but with my eyes.
The. Rather your eyes must with his judgment look.
Her. I do entreat your Grace to pardon me.
I know not by what power I am made bold,
Nor how it may concern my modesty,
In such a presence here to plead my thoughts;
But I beseech your Grace that I may know
The worst that may befall me in this case,
If I refuse to wed Demetrius.
The. Either to die the death, or to abjure
For ever the society of men.
Therefore, fair Hermia, question your desires,
Know of your youth, examine well your blood,
Whether (if you yield not to your father's choice)
You can endure the livery of a nun,
For aye to be in shady cloister mew'd,
To live a barren sister all your life,
Chaunting faint hymns to the cold fruitless moon.
Thrice blessed they that master so their blood
To undergo such maiden pilgrimage;
But earthlier happy is the rose distill'd,

33. bracelets . . . hair. Hair bracelets were a common love token. **gawds:** toys, trinkets. **conceits:** ingenious trifles.
34. Knacks: knickknacks.
38. harshness: discordance, i.e. disobedience. **39. Be it so:** if.
45. Immediately: expressly. **46. Be advis'd:** consider well.
49. a form: i.e. the impression of a seal.
51. leave: i.e. leave unchanged. **disfigure:** obliterate.
54. in this kind: in this respect, i.e. as your wooer. **wanting:** lacking. **voice:** authorization, consent.
60. how . . . concern: whether it befit.
65. die the death: be put to death by judicial sentence.
68. Know . . . youth: inquire of your youthful feelings. **blood:** passions.
70. livery: dress, distinctive garb. **71. mew'd:** shut up, confined.
73. moon: i.e. Diana, the virgin goddess, whose votary Hermia would become.
75. maiden pilgrimage: i.e. journey through life as a virgin. Lines 74–75 are a saving compliment to the Virgin Queen, Elizabeth, though lines 76–78 rather diminish its effect.
76. distill'd: made into perfume. With the image in this passage cf. Sonnet 5.

Than that which withering on the virgin thorn
Grows, lives, and dies in single blessedness.
Her. So will I grow, so live, so die, my lord,
Ere I will yield my virgin patent up
Unto his lordship, whose unwished yoke
My soul consents not to give sovereignty.
The. Take time to pause, and by the next new moon—
The sealing-day betwixt my love and me
For everlasting bond of fellowship—
Upon that day either prepare to die
For disobedience to your father's will,
Or else to wed Demetrius, as he would,
Or on Diana's altar to protest
For aye austerity and single life.
Dem. Relent, sweet Hermia, and, Lysander, yield
Thy crazed title to my certain right.
Lys. You have her father's love, Demetrius,
Let me have Hermia's; do you marry him.
Ege. Scornful Lysander, true, he hath my love;
And what is mine, my love shall render him.
And she is mine, and all my right of her
I do estate unto Demetrius.
Lys. I am, my lord, as well deriv'd as he,
As well possess'd; my love is more than his;
My fortunes every way as fairly rank'd
(If not with vantage) as Demetrius';
And (which is more than all these boasts can be)
I am belov'd of beauteous Hermia.
Why should not I then prosecute my right?
Demetrius, I'll avouch it to his head,
Made love to Nedar's daughter, Helena,
And won her soul; and she, sweet lady, dotes,
Devoutly dotes, dotes in idolatry,
Upon this spotted and inconstant man.
The. I must confess that I have heard so much,
And with Demetrius thought to have spoke thereof;
But, being over-full of self-affairs,
My mind did lose it. But, Demetrius, come,
And come, Egeus, you shall go with me;
I have some private schooling for you both.
For you, fair Hermia, look you arm yourself
To fit your fancies to your father's will;
Or else the law of Athens yields you up
(Which by no means we may extenuate)
To death, or to a vow of single life.
Come, my Hippolyta; what cheer, my love?
Demetrius and Egeus, go along;
I must employ you in some business
Against our nuptial, and confer with you
Of something nearly that concerns yourselves.

77. thorn: brier rose bush.
78. single blessedness: "divine blessing accorded to a life of celibacy" (*O.E.D.*).
80. virgin patent: privilege of virginity. **89. protest:** vow.
92. crazed: cracked, flawed. **title:** claim to possession.
98. estate unto: settle or bestow upon.
99. well deriv'd: well born.
100. possess'd: endowed with wealth. **101. fairly:** handsomely.
102. with vantage: better. **106. head:** face.
110. spotted and inconstant: stained with inconstancy.
113. self-affairs: my own affairs. **116. schooling:** admonition.
117. For: as for. **look you arm:** see that you prepare.
118. fancies: affections. **120. extenuate:** mitigate.
123. go along: come with us. **125. Against:** in preparation for.
126. nearly that: that closely.

Ege. With duty and desire we follow you.
Exeunt. [*Manent Lysander and Hermia.*]
Lys. How now, my love? why is your cheek so pale?
How chance the roses there do fade so fast?
Her. Belike for want of rain; which I could well
Beteem them from the tempest of my eyes.
Lys. Ay me! for aught that I could ever read,
Could ever hear by tale or history,
The course of true love never did run smooth;
But either it was different in blood—
Her. O cross! too high to be enthrall'd to [low].
Lys. Or else misgraffed in respect of years—
Her. O spite! too old to be engag'd to young.
Lys. Or else it stood upon the choice of friends—
Her. O hell, to choose love by another's eyes!
Lys. Or if there were a sympathy in choice,
War, death, or sickness did lay siege to it,
Making it momentany as a sound,
Swift as a shadow, short as any dream,
Brief as the lightning in the collied night,
That, in a spleen, unfolds both heaven and earth;
And ere a man hath power to say "Behold!"
The jaws of darkness do devour it up:
So quick bright things come to confusion.
Her. If then true lovers have been ever cross'd,
It stands as an edict in destiny.
Then let us teach our trial patience,
Because it is a customary cross,
As due to love as thoughts and dreams and sighs,
Wishes and tears, poor fancy's followers.
Lys. A good persuasion; therefore hear me, Hermia:
I have a widow aunt, a dowager,
Of great revenue, and she hath no child.
From Athens is her house remote seven leagues;
And she respects me as her only son.
There, gentle Hermia, may I marry thee;
And to that place the sharp Athenian law
Cannot pursue us. If thou lovest me, then
Steal forth thy father's house to-morrow night;
And in the wood, a league without the town
(Where I did meet thee once with Helena
To do observance to a morn of May),
There will I stay for thee.
Her. My good Lysander,
I swear to thee, by Cupid's strongest bow,

By his best arrow with the golden head,
By the simplicity of Venus' doves,
By that which knitteth souls and prospers loves,
And by that fire which burn'd the Carthage queen
When the false Troyan under sail was seen,
By all the vows that ever men have broke
(In number more than ever women spoke),
In that same place thou hast appointed me
To-morrow truly will I meet with thee.
Lys. Keep promise, love. Look, here comes Helena.
Enter HELENA.
Her. God speed fair Helena! whither away?
Hel. Call you me fair? That fair again unsay.
Demetrius loves your fair, O happy fair!
Your eyes are lodestars, and your tongue's sweet air
More tuneable than lark to shepherd's ear
When wheat is green, when hawthorn buds appear.
Sickness is catching; O, were favor so,
[Yours would] I catch, fair Hermia, ere I go;
My ear should catch your voice, my eye your eye,
My tongue should catch your tongue's sweet melody.
Were the world mine, Demetrius being bated,
The rest I'll give to be to you translated.
O, teach me how you look, and with what art
You sway the motion of Demetrius' heart.
Her. I frown upon him; yet he loves me still.
Hel. O that your frowns would teach my smiles such skill!
Her. I give him curses; yet he gives me love.
Hel. O that my prayers could such affection move!
Her. The more I hate, the more he follows me.
Hel. The more I love, the more he hateth me.
Her. His folly, Helena, is no fault of mine.
Hel. None but your beauty; would that fault were mine!
Her. Take comfort; he no more shall see my face;
Lysander and myself will fly this place.
Before the time I did Lysander see,
Seem'd Athens as a paradise to me;
O then, what graces in my love do dwell,
That he hath turn'd a heaven unto a hell!
Lys. Helen, to you our minds we will unfold:
To-morrow night, when Phoebe doth behold
Her silver visage in the wat'ry glass,
Decking with liquid pearl the bladed grass
(A time that lovers' flights doth still conceal),
Through Athens gates have we devis'd to steal.

127. duty and desire: eagerness to serve. **s.d. Manent:** remain.
130. Belike: very likely. **131. Beteem:** afford.
135. blood: birth, hereditary station.
136. cross: vexation, thwarting.
137. misgraffed: ill grafted, i.e. badly matched.
139. friends: i.e. relatives. **143. momentany:** momentary.
145. collied: dark (literally, blackened with coal).
146. in a spleen: i.e. as if in a sudden fit of passion (?) or in a flash (?). The spleen was thought to be the seat of sudden impulsive feelings and actions. **unfolds:** reveals.
149. quick: quickly, suddenly (perhaps with additional sense of "living" or "lively," modifying *things*). **confusion:** ruin.
150. ever: always.
152. teach . . . patience: i.e. discipline ourselves to meet this trial patiently.
154. As . . . love: as much love's due. **thoughts:** melancholy moods. **155. fancy's:** love's.
156. persuasion: opinion, doctrine. **160. respects:** regards.
167. do . . . May: perform the ceremonies of May-day.
168. stay: wait.

170. arrow . . . head. According to Ovid's *Metamorphoses,* Cupid's sharp, gold-tipped arrow produced love, his blunt, lead-tipped arrow aversion. **171. simplicity:** harmlessness, innocence.
173. Carthage queen: Dido, who immolated herself on a funeral pyre after the Trojan hero Aeneas, her lover, secretly sailed away from Carthage.
182. fair . . . fair: beauty . . . fair one (with special reference to her blonde coloring). **happy:** lucky.
183. lodestars: guiding stars. **air:** melody, music.
184. tuneable: tuneful.
186. favor: attributes, features (with play on "being favored").
190. bated: excepted. **191. translated:** transformed.
192. art: skill (i.e. in magic). **193. motion:** impulse, desire.
197. affection: passion. **move:** arouse.
209. Phoebe: Diana, the moon. **210. glass:** mirror.
212. still: always.
213. Athens. Adjectival; cf. "Verona streets," *Romeo and Juliet,* III.i.89. **devis'd:** decided.

Her. And in the wood, where often you and I
Upon faint primrose beds were wont to lie,
Emptying our bosoms of their counsel [sweet],
There my Lysander and myself shall meet;
And thence from Athens turn away our eyes,
To seek new friends and [stranger companies].
Farewell, sweet playfellow, pray thou for us;
And good luck grant thee thy Demetrius!
Keep word, Lysander; we must starve our sight
From lovers' food till morrow deep midnight.

Lys. I will, my Hermia. *Exit Hermia.*
Helena, adieu:
As you on him, Demetrius dote on you!
Exit Lysander.

Hel. How happy some o'er other some can be!
Through Athens I am thought as fair as she.
But what of that? Demetrius thinks not so;
He will not know what all but he do know;
And as he errs, doting on Hermia's eyes,
So I, admiring of his qualities.
Things base and vile, holding no quantity,
Love can transpose to form and dignity.
Love looks not with the eyes but with the mind;
And therefore is wing'd Cupid painted blind.
Nor hath Love's mind of any judgment taste;
Wings, and no eyes, figure unheedy haste;
And therefore is Love said to be a child,
Because in choice he is so oft beguil'd.
As waggish boys in game themselves forswear,
So the boy Love is perjur'd every where;
For ere Demetrius look'd on Hermia's eyne,
He hail'd down oaths that he was only mine;
And when this hail some heat from Hermia felt,
So he dissolv'd, and show'rs of oaths did melt.
I will go tell him of fair Hermia's flight;
Then to the wood will he to-morrow night
Pursue her; and for this intelligence
If I have thanks, it is a dear expense.
But herein mean I to enrich my pain,
To have his sight thither and back again. *Exit.*

[Scene II]

Enter Quince *the carpenter and* Snug *the joiner and* Bottom *the weaver and* Flute *the bellows-mender and* Snout *the tinker and* Starveling *the tailor.*

Quin. Is all our company here?

Bot. You were best to call them generally, man by man, according to the scrip.

Quin. Here is the scroll of every man's name, which is thought fit, through all Athens, to play in our enterlude before the Duke and the Duchess, on his wedding-day at night.

Bot. First, good Peter Quince, say what the play treats on; then read the names of the actors; and so grow to a point.

Quin. Marry, our play is *The most lamentable comedy and most cruel death of Pyramus and Thisby.*

Bot. A very good piece of work, I assure you, and a merry. Now, good Peter Quince, call forth your actors by the scroll. Masters, spread yourselves.

Quin. Answer as I call you. Nick Bottom the weaver.

Bot. Ready. Name what part I am for, and proceed.

Quin. You, Nick Bottom, are set down for Pyramus.

Bot. What is Pyramus? a lover, or a tyrant?

Quin. A lover, that kills himself most gallant for love.

Bot. That will ask some tears in the true performing of it. If I do it, let the audience look to their eyes. I will move storms; I will condole in some measure. To the rest—yet my chief humor is for a tyrant. I could play Ercles rarely, or a part to tear a cat in, to make all split.

"The raging rocks
And shivering shocks
Shall break the locks
Of prison gates;
And Phibbus' car
Shall shine from far,
And make and mar
The foolish Fates."

This was lofty! Now name the rest of the players. This is Ercles' vein, a tyrant's vein; a lover is more condoling.

Quin. Francis Flute the bellows-mender.

Flu. Here, Peter Quince.

Quin. Flute, you must take Thisby on you.

Flu. What is Thisby? a wand'ring knight?

Quin. It is the lady that Pyramus must love.

215. **faint**: pale (?) or faintly scented (?).
216. **counsel**: inmost thought.
219. **stranger companies**: the company of strangers.
222–23. **starve . . . food**: i.e. refrain from seeing each other.
231. **admiring of**: wondering at.
232. **holding no quantity**: lacking proportion, unshapely.
233. **transpose**: change, transform. **dignity**: worth.
236. **taste**: any trace. 237. **figure**: symbolize.
240. **game**: fun, sport.
242. **eyne**: eyes (archaic even in Elizabethan English; used for the sake of rhyme). 248. **intelligence**: information.
249. **dear expense**: painful purchase, costly gain.
251. **his sight**: the sight of him.

I.ii. Location: Athens. Quince's house.
o.s.d. The names of the craftsmen are derived in one way or another from their work. Quince's name is probably a form of *quoins* or *quines*, wedge-shaped pieces of wood used in carpentry. Snug's name suggests the expert joining of pieces of wood by a maker of fine furniture. Bottom is named for the *bottom* or core on which thread is wound. Flute would repair fluted church organs as well as domestic bellows. Snout's name suggests the spout of a kettle, an article very familiar to tinkers. Starveling takes his name from the proverbial leanness of tailors ("Nine tailors make a man").
2. **You were best**: it would be best for you. **generally**. The first of Bottom's characteristic verbal blunders. Here he obviously means "individually"—just the opposite of what he says.
3. **scrip**: script, written list. 6. **enterlude**: interlude, brief play.
10. **grow . . . point**: come systematically to a conclusion.
11. **Marry**: why, indeed (originally the name of the Virgin Mary used as an oath). **lamentable**: mournful.
26. **look . . . eyes**: take care not to injure their eyes with weeping.
27. **condole**: speak pathetically, arouse pity.
28. **humor**: temperamental bent.
29. **Ercles**: Hercules. The tradition for ranting in this part grew from Seneca's *Hercules Furens*. 29–30. **tear a cat**: i.e. rant.
30. **make all split**: cause great commotion.
35. **Phibbus' car**: the chariot of Phoebus, the sun-god.
41. **condoling**: pathetic.
45. **What**: what sort of man. **wand'ring knight**: knight-errant.

Flu. Nay, faith; let not me play a woman; I have a beard coming.

Quin. That's all one; you shall play it in a mask, and you may speak as small as you will.

Bot. And I may hide my face, let me play Thisby too. I'll speak in a monstrous little voice, "Thisne! Thisne! Ah, Pyramus, my lover dear! thy Thisby dear, and lady dear!"

Quin. No, no, you must play Pyramus; and, Flute, you Thisby.

Bot. Well, proceed.

Quin. Robin Starveling the tailor.

Star. Here, Peter Quince.

Quin. Robin Starveling, you must play Thisby's mother. Tom Snout the tinker.

Snout. Here, Peter Quince.

Quin. You, Pyramus' father; myself, Thisby's father; Snug the joiner, you the lion's part. And I hope here is a play fitted.

Snug. Have you the lion's part written? Pray you, if it be, give it me, for I am slow of study.

Quin. You may do it extempore, for it is nothing but roaring.

Bot. Let me play the lion too. I will roar, that I will do any man's heart good to hear me. I will roar, that I will make the Duke say, "Let him roar again; let him roar again."

Quin. And you should do it too terribly, you would fright the Duchess and the ladies, that they would shrike; and that were enough to hang us all.

All. That would hang us, every mother's son.

Bot. I grant you, friends, if you should fright the ladies out of their wits, they would have no more discretion but to hang us; but I will aggravate my voice so that I will roar you as gently as any sucking dove; I will roar you and 'twere any nightingale.

Quin. You can play no part but Pyramus; for Pyramus is a sweet-fac'd man; a proper man as one shall see in a summer's day; a most lovely gentleman-like man: therefore you must needs play Pyramus.

Bot. Well; I will undertake it. What beard were I best to play it in?

Quin. Why, what you will.

Bot. I will discharge it in either your straw-color beard, your orange-tawny beard, your purple-in-grain beard, or your French-crown-color beard, your perfit yellow.

Quin. Some of your French crowns have no hair at all; and then you will play barefac'd. But, masters, here are your parts, and I am to entreat you, request you, and desire you, to con them by to-morrow night; and meet me in the palace wood, a mile without the town, by moonlight; there will we rehearse; for if we meet in the city, we shall be dogg'd with company, and our devices known. In the mean time I will draw a bill of properties, such as our play wants. I pray you fail me not.

Bot. We will meet, and there we may rehearse most obscenely and courageously. Take pains, be perfit; adieu.

Quin. At the Duke's oak we meet.

Bot. Enough; hold, or cut bow-strings. *Exeunt.*

47–48. **I . . . coming.** On the Elizabethan stage, female parts were played by boys. 49. **That's all one**: that makes no difference.
50. **small**: high-pitched. 51. **And**: if. 65. **fitted**: cast.
70. **that**: so that. 74. **terribly**: terrifyingly. 76. **shrike**: shriek.
81. **aggravate.** He means just the opposite. 83. **and**: as if.
86. **proper**: handsome. 90. **Well**: very well.
93. **discharge**: perform. **your.** The indefinite use, meaning vaguely "that you know of"; a colloquialism.
94–95. **purple-in-grain**: dyed a fast purple or deep red.
95. **French-crown-color**: yellowish color of a gold coin.
96. **perfit**: perfect.
97–98. **Some . . . all.** Alluding to loss of hair from the "French disease," syphilis.

99. **am to**: must. 100. **con**: learn by heart. 105. **bill**: list.
108. **obscenely.** Bottom may connect this word with *seen* and mean "without being observed," or with *scene* and mean "dramatically."
109. **perfit**: i.e. letter-perfect in your parts.
111. **hold . . . bow-strings**: an expression of uncertain meaning, from archery; perhaps equivalent to "hold to our agreement or the project is done for."

[ACT II, Scene I]

Enter a Fairy *at one door and* Robin Goodfellow [Puck] *at another.*

Puck. How now, spirit, whither wander you?

Fairy. Over hill, over dale,
Thorough bush, thorough brier,
Over park, over pale,
Thorough flood, thorough fire,
I do wander every where,
Swifter than the moon's sphere;
And I serve the Fairy Queen,
To dew her orbs upon the green.
The cowslips tall her pensioners be,
In their gold coats spots you see:
Those be rubies, fairy favors,
In those freckles live their savors.
I must go seek some dewdrops here,
And hang a pearl in every cowslip's ear.
Farewell, thou lob of spirits; I'll be gone.
Our Queen and all her elves come here anon.

Puck. The King doth keep his revels here to-night;
Take heed the Queen come not within his sight;
For Oberon is passing fell and wrath,
Because that she as her attendant hath
A lovely boy stolen from an Indian king;
She never had so sweet a changeling.
And jealous Oberon would have the child
Knight of his train, to trace the forests wild;
But she, perforce, withholds the loved boy,
Crowns him with flowers, and makes him all her joy.
And now they never meet in grove or green,

II.i. Location: A wood near Athens.
3. **Thorough**: through. 4. **pale**: enclosure.
7. **sphere.** In the Ptolemaic system of astronomy, the moon and the other heavenly bodies were thought to revolve about the earth fixed in transparent spheres. 9. **orbs**: circles, i.e. fairy rings.
10. **pensioners.** Members of the royal bodyguard were called gentlemen pensioners. 12. **favors**: love tokens. 13. **savors**: perfumes.
16. **lob**: country bumpkin. 17. **anon**: at once.
20. **passing . . . wrath**: exceedingly fierce and angry.
23. **changeling**: child exchanged for another by fairies.
25. **trace**: traverse. 26. **perforce**: forcibly.

By fountain clear, or spangled starlight sheen,
But they do square, that all their elves for fear
Creep into acorn-cups, and hide them there.
Fairy. Either I mistake your shape and making quite,
Or else you are that shrewd and knavish sprite
Call'd Robin Goodfellow. Are not you he
That frights the maidens of the villagery,
Skim milk, and sometimes labor in the quern,
And bootless make the breathless huswife churn,
And sometime make the drink to bear no barm,
Mislead night-wanderers, laughing at their harm?
Those that Hobgoblin call you, and sweet Puck,
You do their work, and they shall have good luck.
Are not you he?
Puck. Thou speakest aright;
I am that merry wanderer of the night.
I jest to Oberon and make him smile
When I a fat and bean-fed horse beguile,
Neighing in likeness of a filly foal;
And sometime lurk I in a gossip's bowl,
In very likeness of a roasted crab,
And when she drinks, against her lips I bob,
And on her withered dewlop pour the ale.
The wisest aunt, telling the saddest tale,
Sometime for three-foot stool mistaketh me;
Then slip I from her bum, down topples she,
And "tailor" cries, and falls into a cough;
And then the whole quire hold their hips and loff,
And waxen in their mirth, and neeze, and swear
A merrier hour was never wasted there.
But room, fairy! here comes Oberon.
Fairy. And here my mistress. Would that he were gone!

Enter the King of Fairies [OBERON] *at one door with his* TRAIN, *and the Queen* [TITANIA] *at another with hers.*

Obe. Ill met by moonlight, proud Titania.
Tita. What, jealous Oberon? [Fairies,] skip hence—
I have forsworn his bed and company.
Obe. Tarry, rash wanton! Am not I thy lord?
Tita. Then I must be thy lady; but I know
When thou hast stolen away from fairy land,
And in the shape of Corin sat all day,
Playing on pipes of corn, and versing love,
To amorous Phillida. Why art thou here
Come from the farthest steep of India?
But that, forsooth, the bouncing Amazon,
Your buskin'd mistress, and your warrior love,
To Theseus must be wedded, and you come
To give their bed joy and prosperity.
Obe. How canst thou thus for shame, Titania,
Glance at my credit with Hippolyta,
Knowing I know thy love to Theseus?
Didst not thou lead him through the glimmering night
From Perigenia, whom he ravished?
And make him with fair [Aegles] break his faith,
With Ariadne, and Antiopa?
Tita. These are the forgeries of jealousy;
And never, since the middle summer's spring,
Met we on hill, in dale, forest, or mead,
By paved fountain or by rushy brook,
Or in the beached margent of the sea,
To dance our ringlets to the whistling wind,
But with thy brawls thou hast disturb'd our sport.
Therefore the winds, piping to us in vain,
As in revenge, have suck'd up from the sea
Contagious fogs; which, falling in the land,
Hath every pelting river made so proud
That they have overborne their continents.
The ox hath therefore stretch'd his yoke in vain,
The ploughman lost his sweat, and the green corn
Hath rotted ere his youth attain'd a beard.
The fold stands empty in the drowned field,
And crows are fatted with the murrion flock;
The nine men's morris is fill'd up with mud,
And the quaint mazes in the wanton green,
For lack of tread, are undistinguishable.
The human mortals want their winter here;
No night is now with hymn or carol blest.
Therefore the moon (the governess of floods),

29. fountain: spring. **30. square**: quarrel. **that**: so that.
32. making: form. **33. shrewd**: mischievous.
35. villagery: village folk, peasantry.
36. quern: handmill for grinding grain.
37. bootless: unavailingly. **huswife**: housewife, woman who manages a household.
38. sometime: at times. **bear no barm**: fail to ferment (?) or go flat (?). *Barm* yeast. **47. gossip's**: garrulous old woman's.
48. crab: crab apple. **50. dewlop**: dewlap, loose skin on the neck.
51. aunt: old woman, gossip. **saddest**: soberest.
54. tailor. Probably referring to the fact that she finds herself sitting cross-legged on the floor as tailors did to sew. **cough.** Probably with a suggestion of breaking wind.
55. quire: choir, i.e. company. **loff**: laugh.
56. waxen: increase (with archaic plural ending in *-en*). **neeze**: sneeze. **57. wasted**: spent.
63. rash wanton: impetuous and willful creature.
66, 68. Corin, Phillida. Conventional names in pastoral poetry.
67. corn: oat stalks. **versing love**: making love verses.

69. steep: mountain range.
71. buskin'd: wearing buskins or half-boots.
75. Glance . . . Hippolyta: cast aspersion on my good name by accusing me with Hippolyta.
78. Perigenia: Perigouna, daughter of the brigand Sinis, whom the youthful Theseus slew on his first journey to Athens. Shakespeare took this and the following names of Theseus' mistresses from the "Life of Theseus" in North's translation of Plutarch (which, however, reads *Perigouna*).
79. Aegles: Aegle, a nymph for whose love Theseus, in some accounts, deserted Ariadne.
80. Ariadne: daughter of Minos, king of Crete. Having slain the Minotaur with her aid, Theseus fled Crete with her, but abandoned her on the voyage back to Athens. **Antiopa**: another name for the Amazon queen captured by Theseus; here obviously taken to be distinct from Hippolyta.
82. middle summer's spring: beginning of midsummer.
84. paved fountain: spring with pebbled bottom. **rushy**: edged with rushes. **85. in**: on. **margent**: margin, edge.
86. ringlets: circular dances.
87. brawls: noisy quarrels (with probably play on *brawl* as the name of a dance [French *branle*] described as "base" by contemporary writers). **90. Contagious**: noxious. **91. pelting**: paltry.
92. overborne their continents: overflowed their banks.
94. corn: grain. **95. his**: its.
97. murrion: dead of the murrain, a disease of cattle and sheep.
98. nine men's morris: i.e. the turf marked with squares on which the rustic game of this name was played.
99. quaint mazes: complicated pattern of paths to be traced rapidly by a line of boys as a sport. **wanton**: luxuriant.
101. want their winter here. A controversial passage. Perhaps it means "lack under these circumstances their proper winter season" (with an allusion in *hymn or carol* in line 102 to Christmas observances). Most editors, following Theobald, emend *here* to *cheer*.
103. Therefore. As in lines 88 and 93, this means "in consequence of the breach between us."

Pale in her anger, washes all the air,
That rheumatic diseases do abound.
And thorough this distemperature, we see
The seasons alter: hoary-headed frosts
Fall in the fresh lap of the crimson rose,
And on old Hiems' [thin] and icy crown
An odorous chaplet of sweet summer buds
Is, as in mockery, set; the spring, the summer,
The childing autumn, angry winter, change
Their wonted liveries; and the mazed world,
By their increase, now knows not which is which.
And this same progeny of evils comes
From our debate, from our dissension;
We are their parents and original.
Obe. Do you amend it then; it lies in you.
Why should Titania cross her Oberon?
I do but beg a little changeling boy,
To be my henchman.
Tita. Set your heart at rest;
The fairy land buys not the child of me.
His mother was a vot'ress of my order,
And in the spiced Indian air, by night,
Full often hath she gossip'd by my side,
And sat with me on Neptune's yellow sands,
Marking th' embarked traders on the flood;
When we have laugh'd to see the sails conceive
And grow big-bellied with the wanton wind;
Which she, with pretty and with swimming gait,
Following (her womb then rich with my young squire)
Would imitate, and sail upon the land
To fetch me trifles, and return again,
As from a voyage, rich with merchandise.
But she, being mortal, of that boy did die,
And for her sake do I rear up her boy;
And for her sake I will not part with him.
Obe. How long within this wood intend you stay?
Tita. Perchance till after Theseus' wedding-day.
If you will patiently dance in our round,
And see our moonlight revels, go with us;
If not, shun me, and I will spare your haunts.
Obe. Give me that boy, and I will go with thee.
Tita. Not for thy fairy kingdom. Fairies, away!
We shall chide downright, if I longer stay.
Exeunt [Titania and her Train].
Obe. Well; go thy way. Thou shalt not from this grove
Till I torment thee for this injury.
My gentle Puck, come hither. Thou remember'st
Since once I sat upon a promontory,
And heard a mermaid on a dolphin's back

105. **That**: so that. **rheumatic diseases**: colds, catarrh, and other such disorders characterized by a flow of watery "rheum."
106. **distemperature**: disturbance in the natural order, i.e. bad weather (perhaps with play on the sense "ill humor," harking back to the moon's "anger" in line 104). 109. **Hiems**: the god of winter.
112. **childing**: fruitful (literally, pregnant).
113. **wonted liveries**: customary apparel. **mazed**: bewildered, confused. 114. **their increase**: what they produce.
116. **debate**: disagreement, quarrelling.
117. **original**: origin. 119. **cross**: thwart.
121. **henchman**: page of honor. **Set . . . rest**: i.e. give up that notion.
127. **traders**: trading vessels. **flood**: flood tide.
129. **wanton**: amorous. 140. **round**: circular dance.
142. **spare**: stay away from. 145. **chide**: quarrel.
146. **from**: go from. 147. **injury**: affront. 149. **Since**: when.

Uttering such dulcet and harmonious breath
That the rude sea grew civil at her song,
And certain stars shot madly from their spheres,
To hear the sea-maid's music?
Puck. I remember.
Obe. That very time I saw (but thou couldst not),
Flying between the cold moon and the earth,
Cupid all arm'd. A certain aim he took
At a fair vestal throned by [the] west,
And loos'd his love-shaft smartly from his bow,
As it should pierce a hundred thousand hearts;
But I might see young Cupid's fiery shaft
Quench'd in the chaste beams of the wat'ry moon,
And the imperial vot'ress passed on,
In maiden meditation, fancy-free.
Yet mark'd I where the bolt of Cupid fell.
It fell upon a little western flower,
Before milk-white, now purple with love's wound,
And maidens call it love-in-idleness.
Fetch me that flow'r; the herb I showed thee once.
The juice of it on sleeping eyelids laid
Will make or man or woman madly dote
Upon the next live creature that it sees.
Fetch me this herb, and be thou here again
Ere the leviathan can swim a league.
Puck. I'll put a girdle round about the earth
In forty minutes. *[Exit.]*
Obe. Having once this juice,
I'll watch Titania when she is asleep,
And drop the liquor of it in her eyes;
The next thing then she waking looks upon
(Be it on lion, bear, or wolf, or bull,
On meddling monkey, or on busy ape),
She shall pursue it with the soul of love.
And ere I take this charm from off her sight
(As I can take it with another herb),
I'll make her render up her page to me.
But who comes here? I am invisible,
And I will overhear their conference.

Enter Demetrius, Helena *following him.*

Dem. I love thee not; therefore pursue me not.
Where is Lysander and fair Hermia?
The one I'll [slay]; the other [slayeth] me.
Thou toldst me they were stol'n unto this wood;
And here am I, and wode within this wood,
Because I cannot meet my Hermia.
Hence, get thee gone, and follow me no more.

151. **breath**: voice, music.
152. **rude**: rough, boisterous. **civil**: well-behaved, gentle.
157. **all**: fully, completely.
158. **vestal**: i.e. vestal virgin. The passage is a compliment to Queen Elizabeth, and may allude to some actual entertainment in her honor, such as the water pageant with which the Earl of Hertford amused her when she visited him at Elvetham in 1591. 160. **As**: as if.
162. **moon**: i.e. Diana, the virgin goddess, whose votaress the "fair vestal" is. 164. **fancy-free**: free of love-thoughts.
168. **love-in-idleness**: a name for the pansy.
171. **or . . . or**: either . . . or.
174. **leviathan**: gigantic sea-beast (see Job 41), usually identified with the whale.
176. **forty**. Used frequently as an indefinite number.
177. **watch . . . asleep**: i.e. watch for a time when I can catch her sleeping.
186. **I am invisible**. Spoken for the benefit of the audience, to explain how he can eavesdrop unseen. 192. **wode**: mad (pronounced *wood*).

Hel. You draw me, you hard-hearted adamant;
But yet you draw not iron, for my heart
Is true as steel. Leave you your power to draw,
And I shall have no power to follow you.
Dem. Do I entice you? Do I speak you fair?
Or rather do I not in plainest truth
Tell you I do not [nor] I cannot love you?
Hel. And even for that do I love you the more:
I am your spaniel; and, Demetrius,
The more you beat me, I will fawn on you.
Use me but as your spaniel; spurn me, strike me,
Neglect me, lose me; only give me leave,
Unworthy as I am, to follow you.
What worser place can I beg in your love
(And yet a place of high respect with me)
Than to be used as you use your dog?
Dem. Tempt not too much the hatred of my spirit,
For I am sick when I do look on thee.
Hel. And I am sick when I look not on you.
Dem. You do impeach your modesty too much,
To leave the city and commit yourself
Into the hands of one that loves you not;
To trust the opportunity of night,
And the ill counsel of a desert place,
With the rich worth of your virginity.
Hel. Your virtue is my privilege. For that
It is not night when I do see your face,
Therefore I think I am not in the night,
Nor doth this wood lack worlds of company,
For you in my respect are all the world.
Then how can it be said I am alone,
When all the world is here to look on me?
Dem. I'll run from thee, and hide me in the brakes,
And leave thee to the mercy of wild beasts.
Hel. The wildest hath not such a heart as you.
Run when you will; the story shall be chang'd:
Apollo flies, and Daphne holds the chase;
The dove pursues the griffin; the mild hind
Makes speed to catch the tiger—bootless speed,
When cowardice pursues and valor flies.
Dem. I will not stay thy questions. Let me go;
Or if thou follow me, do not believe
But I shall do thee mischief in the wood.
Hel. Ay, in the temple, in the town, the field,
You do me mischief. Fie, Demetrius!
Your wrongs do set a scandal on my sex.
We cannot fight for love, as men may do.
We should be woo'd, and were not made to woo.
[*Exit Demetrius.*]

195. adamant: (1) lodestone, magnet; (2) the hardest substance.
196. you . . . iron: i.e. what you draw (my heart) is not iron, but steel of the finest temper. **197. Leave:** give up.
199. fair: courteously. **206. Neglect:** ignore.
211. Tempt: try, put to the test.
214. impeach: discredit, call into question.
218. desert: deserted, unpeopled.
220. Your . . . privilege: your excellence in my eyes is my warrant for doing so. **For that:** because.
224. in my respect: as far as I am concerned. **227. brakes:** thickets.
231. Apollo . . . chase. According to the myth, Daphne, pursued by Apollo, was saved from rape by being transformed into a laurel tree.
232. griffin: fabulous monster with the body of a lion and the head of an eagle. **hind:** female of the red deer.
235. stay thy questions: delay to listen to your talk.
240. Your . . . sex. Because he forces her to be the wooer instead of the wooed.

I'll follow thee and make a heaven of hell,
To die upon the hand I love so well. [*Exit.*]
Obe. Fare thee well, nymph. Ere he do leave this grove,
Thou shalt fly him, and he shall seek thy love.

Enter Puck.

Hast thou the flower there? Welcome, wanderer.
Puck. Ay, there it is.
Obe. I pray thee give it me.
I know a bank where the wild thyme blows,
Where oxlips and the nodding violet grows,
Quite over-canopied with luscious woodbine,
With sweet musk-roses and with eglantine;
There sleeps Titania sometime of the night,
Lull'd in these flowers with dances and delight;
And there the snake throws her enamell'd skin,
Weed wide enough to wrap a fairy in;
And with the juice of this I'll streak her eyes,
And make her full of hateful fantasies.
Take thou some of it, and seek through this grove:
A sweet Athenian lady is in love
With a disdainful youth; anoint his eyes,
But do it when the next thing he espies
May be the lady. Thou shalt know the man
By the Athenian garments he hath on.
Effect it with some care, that he may prove
More fond on her than she upon her love;
And look thou meet me ere the first cock crow.
Puck. Fear not, my lord! your servant shall do so.
Exeunt.

[Scene II]

Enter Titania, *Queen of Fairies, with her* Train.

Tita. Come, now a roundel and a fairy song;
Then, for the third part of a minute, hence,
Some to kill cankers in the musk-rose buds,
Some war with rere-mice for their leathren wings
To make my small elves coats, and some keep back
The clamorous owl, that nightly hoots and wonders
At our quaint spirits. Sing me now asleep;
Then to your offices, and let me rest.

Fairies *sing.*

[*1. Fairy.*] You spotted snakes with double tongue,
Thorny hedgehogs, be not seen,
Newts and blind-worms, do no wrong,
Come not near our fairy queen.

244. upon: by. **249. blows:** blooms.
250. oxlips: flowering plant resembling the cowslip.
251. woodbine: honeysuckle.
252. musk-roses: variety of large, fragrant rose. **eglantine:** sweet-brier, another variety of rose.
253. sometime of: at some time during. **255. throws:** sheds.
256. Weed: garment. **257. streak:** anoint.
266. fond on: infatuated with.

II.ii. Location: The wood.
1. roundel: dance in a circle. **3 cankers:** cankerworms.
4. rere-mice: bats. **leathren:** leathern.
7. quaint: pretty, dainty. **8. offices:** duties. **9. double:** forked.
11. Newts: water lizards. Newts, blind-worms, and spiders (line 20) were all thought to be poisonous.

[*Cho.*] Philomele, with melody,
Sing in our sweet lullaby,
Lulla, lulla, lullaby, lulla, lulla, lullaby.
Never harm,
Nor spell, nor charm,
Come our lovely lady nigh.
So good night, with lullaby.

1. Fairy. Weaving spiders, come not here;
Hence, you long-legg'd spinners, hence!
Beetles black, approach not near;
Worm nor snail, do no offense.

[*Cho.*] Philomele, with melody, etc.

2. Fairy. Hence, away! now all is well.
One aloof stand sentinel.
[*Exeunt Fairies. Titania sleeps.*]

Enter OBERON [*and squeezes the flower on Titania's eyelids*].

Obe. What thou seest when thou dost wake,
Do it for thy true-love take;
Love and languish for his sake.
Be it ounce, or cat, or bear,
Pard, or boar with bristled hair,
In thy eye that shall appear
When thou wak'st, it is thy dear:
Wake when some vile thing is near. [*Exit.*]

Enter LYSANDER *and* HERMIA.

Lys. Fair love, you faint with wand'ring in the wood;
And to speak troth I have forgot our way.
We'll rest us, Hermia, if you think it good,
And tarry for the comfort of the day.
Her. Be't so, Lysander. Find you out a bed;
For I upon this bank will rest my head.
Lys. One turf shall serve as pillow for us both,
One heart, one bed, two bosoms, and one troth.
Her. Nay, [good] Lysander; for my sake, my dear,
Lie further off yet; do not lie so near.
Lys. O, take the sense, sweet, of my innocence!
Love takes the meaning in love's conference:
I mean, that my heart unto yours [is] knit,
So that but one heart we can make of it;
Two bosoms interchained with an oath,
So then two bosoms and a single troth.
Then by your side no bed-room me deny;
For lying so, Hermia, I do not lie.
Her. Lysander riddles very prettily.
Now much beshrew my manners and my pride,
If Hermia meant to say Lysander lied.
But, gentle friend, for love and courtesy,
Lie further off, in humane modesty;

13. **Philomele:** the nightingale. Philomela, daughter of King Pandion of Athens, was transformed into a nightingale, according to Ovid, after her rape by her brother-in-law Tereus. 21. **spinners:** spiders or (Cairncross) daddy-longlegs. 30. **ounce:** lynx. **cat:** wildcat. 31. **Pard:** leopard. 36. **troth:** truth. 42. **troth:** pledged faith. 45. **take . . . innocence:** interpret my meaning as entirely innocent. 46. **Love . . . conference:** i.e. a lover should be able to understand what is meant when he and his beloved talk together. 52. **I . . . lie:** i.e. I am not false. 53. **prettily:** ingeniously, skillfully. 54. **beshrew:** mischief take. 57. **humane:** courteous, decorous.

Such separation as may well be said
Becomes a virtuous bachelor and a maid,
So far be distant; and good night, sweet friend.
Thy love ne'er alter till thy sweet life end!
Lys. Amen, amen, to that fair prayer, say I,
And then end life when I end loyalty!
Here is my bed; sleep give thee all his rest!
Her. With half that wish the wisher's eyes be press'd! [*They sleep.*]

Enter PUCK.

Puck. Through the forest have I gone,
But Athenian found I none,
On whose eyes I might approve
This flower's force in stirring love.
Night and silence—Who is here?
Weeds of Athens he doth wear:
This is he, my master said,
Despised the Athenian maid;
And here the maiden, sleeping sound,
On the dank and dirty ground.
Pretty soul, she durst not lie
Near this lack-love, this kill-courtesy.
Churl, upon thy eyes I throw
All the power this charm doth owe.
When thou wak'st, let love forbid
Sleep his seat on thy eyelid.
So awake when I am gone,
For I must now to Oberon. *Exit.*

Enter DEMETRIUS *and* HELENA, *running.*

Hel. Stay—though thou kill me, sweet Demetrius.
Dem. I charge thee hence, and do not haunt me thus.
Hel. O, wilt thou darkling leave me? do not so.
Dem. Stay, on thy peril; I alone will go. [*Exit.*]
Hel. O, I am out of breath in this fond chase!
The more my prayer, the lesser is my grace.
Happy is Hermia, wheresoe'er she lies,
For she hath blessed and attractive eyes.
How came her eyes so bright? Not with salt tears;
If so, my eyes are oft'ner wash'd than hers.
No, no; I am as ugly as a bear;
For beasts that meet me run away for fear.
Therefore no marvel though Demetrius
Do, as a monster, fly my presence thus.
What wicked and dissembling glass of mine
Made me compare with Hermia's sphery eyne!
But who is here? Lysander! on the ground?
Dead, or asleep? I see no blood, no wound.
Lysander, if you live, good sir, awake.
Lys. [*Awaking.*] And run through fire I will for thy sweet sake.

65. **With . . . press'd:** i.e. may half of all sleep's rest (which "all" you have wished for me) be yours. 68. **approve:** test. 73. **Despised:** who despised. 79. **owe:** possess. 85. **haunt:** follow persistently. 86. **darkling:** in the dark. 87. **Stay . . . peril:** i.e. it will be dangerous for you if you don't remain here. 88. **fond:** doting, foolishly loving. 89. **my grace:** the favor I am granted. 90. **lies:** dwells. 91. **attractive:** magnetic. 97. **as a monster:** i.e. as he would fly from a monster. 99. **Made me compare:** induced me to compare my eyes. **sphery eyne:** eyes as bright as stars in their spheres.

Transparent Helena, nature shows art,
That through thy bosom makes me see thy heart.
Where is Demetrius? O, how fit a word
Is that vile name to perish on my sword!

Hel. Do not say so, Lysander, say not so.
What though he love your Hermia? Lord, what though?
Yet Hermia still loves you; then be content.

Lys. Content with Hermia? No; I do repent
The tedious minutes I with her have spent.
Not Hermia, but Helena I love.
Who will not change a raven for a dove?
The will of man is by his reason sway'd;
And reason says you are the worthier maid.
Things growing are not ripe until their season,
So I, being young, till now ripe not to reason;
And touching now the point of human skill,
Reason becomes the marshal to my will,
And leads me to your eyes, where I o'erlook
Love's stories written in Love's richest book.

Hel. Wherefore was I to this keen mockery born?
When at your hands did I deserve this scorn?
Is't not enough, is't not enough, young man,
That I did never, no, nor never can,
Deserve a sweet look from Demetrius' eye,
But you must flout my insufficiency?
Good troth, you do me wrong (good sooth, you do)
In such disdainful manner me to woo.
But fare you well; perforce I must confess
I thought you lord of more true gentleness.
O that a lady, of one man refus'd,
Should of another therefore be abus'd! *Exit.*

Lys. She sees not Hermia. Hermia, sleep thou there,
And never mayst thou come Lysander near!
For as a surfeit of the sweetest things
The deepest loathing to the stomach brings,
Or as the heresies that men do leave
Are hated most of those they did deceive,
So thou, my surfeit and my heresy,
Of all be hated, but the most of me!
And, all my powers, address your love and might
To honor Helen and to be her knight. *Exit.*

Her. [*Starting up.*] Help me, Lysander, help me! do thy best
To pluck this crawling serpent from my breast!
Ay me, for pity! what a dream was here!
Lysander, look how I do quake with fear.
Methought a serpent eat my heart away,
And you sate smiling at his cruel prey.
Lysander! what, remov'd? Lysander! lord!
What, out of hearing gone? No sound, no word?
Alack, where are you? Speak, and if you hear;

104. **Transparent:** (1) bright, radiant; (2) capable of being seen through. 109. **What though:** what does it matter if.
115. **will:** desire.
119. **point:** summit. **skill:** discernment, judgment.
121. **o'erlook:** survey, read. 123. **keen:** bitter.
127. **Deserve:** earn.
129. **Good troth, good sooth.** Both phrases mean "in very truth."
132. **gentleness:** courtesy.
133. **of:** by (so also in lines 134, 140, 142). 134. **abus'd:** ill used.
149. **eat:** ate (common preterite form, pronounced *et*).
150. **sate:** sat. **prey:** preying. 153. **and if:** if.

Speak, of all loves! I swoon almost with fear.
No? then I well perceive you are not nigh:
Either death, or you, I'll find immediately. *Exit.*

[ACT III, SCENE I]

Enter the Clowns [QUINCE, SNUG, BOTTOM, FLUTE, SNOUT, *and* STARVELING].

Bot. Are we all met?

Quin. Pat, pat; and here's a marvail's convenient place for our rehearsal. This green plot shall be our stage, this hawthorn brake our tiring-house, and we will do it in action as we will do it before the Duke.

Bot. Peter Quince!

Quin. What sayest thou, bully Bottom?

Bot. There are things in this comedy of Pyramus and Thisby that will never please. First, Pyramus must draw a sword to kill himself; which the ladies cannot abide. How answer you that?

Snout. By'r lakin, a parlous fear.

Star. I believe we must leave the killing out, when all is done.

Bot. Not a whit! I have a device to make all well. Write me a prologue, and let the prologue seem to say we will do no harm with our swords, and that Pyramus is not kill'd indeed; and for the more better assurance, tell them that I Pyramus am not Pyramus, but Bottom the weaver. This will put them out of fear.

Quin. Well; we will have such a prologue, and it shall be written in eight and six.

Bot. No; make it two more; let it be written in eight and eight.

Snout. Will not the ladies be afeard of the lion?

Star. I fear it, I promise you.

Bot. Masters, you ought to consider with your[selves], to bring in (God shield us!) a lion among ladies, is a most dreadful thing; for there is not a more fearful wild-fowl than your lion living; and we ought to look to't.

Snout. Therefore another prologue must tell he is not a lion.

Bot. Nay; you must name his name, and half his face must be seen through the lion's neck, and he himself must speak through, saying thus, or to the same defect: "Ladies," or "Fair ladies, I would wish

154. **of all loves:** for the sake of all true love.

III.i. Location: Scene continues. (Although F1 marks an act break here, III.i is obviously a continuation of II.ii, since Titania remains asleep on stage, to wake at line 129.)
2. **marvail's:** marvellous. 4. **tiring-house:** dressing room.
8. **bully:** a friendly term meaning "fine fellow."
13. **By'r lakin:** by our ladykin, i.e. the Virgin Mary. **parlous:** perilous. 14–15. **when . . . done:** after all.
24. **eight and six:** the common ballad measure of alternating eight- and six-syllable lines.
30–31. **lion among ladies.** It has been suggested that Shakespeare here alludes to an episode at a court entertainment in Scotland in 1594, when a tame lion which was to have drawn a chariot was replaced by a black African so as not to frighten the spectators.
32. **fearful:** (1) dreadful (as referring to a lion); (2) full of fear (as referring to a bird). **your.** See note on I.ii.93.
39. **defect:** blunder for *effect.*

you," or "I would request you," or "I would entreat you, not to fear, not to tremble: my life for yours. If you think I come hither as a lion, it were pity of my life. No! I am no such thing; I am a man as other men are"; and there indeed let him name his name, and tell them plainly he is Snug the joiner.

Quin. Well; it shall be so. But there is two hard things: that is, to bring the moonlight into a chamber; for you know, Pyramus and Thisby meet by moonlight.

Snout. Doth the moon shine that night we play our play?

Bot. A calendar, a calendar! Look in the almanac. Find out moonshine, find out moonshine.

Quin. Yes; it doth shine that night.

[*Bot.*] Why then may you leave a casement of the great chamber window (where we play) open; and the moon may shine in at the casement.

Quin. Ay; or else one must come in with a bush of thorns and a lantern, and say he comes to disfigure, or to present, the person of Moonshine. Then, there is another thing: we must have a wall in the great chamber; for Pyramus and Thisby (says the story) did talk through the chink of a wall.

Snout. You can never bring in a wall. What say you, Bottom?

Bot. Some man or other must present Wall; and let him have some plaster, or some loam, or some rough-cast about him, to signify wall; or let him hold his fingers thus, and through that cranny shall Pyramus and Thisby whisper.

Quin. If that may be, then all is well. Come, sit down, every mother's son, and rehearse your parts. Pyramus, you begin. When you have spoken your speech, enter into that brake; and so every one according to his cue.

Enter Robin [Puck, *behind*].

Puck. What hempen home-spuns have we swagg'ring here,
So near the cradle of the Fairy Queen?
What, a play toward? I'll be an auditor,
An actor too perhaps, if I see cause.

Quin. Speak, Pyramus. Thisby, stand forth.

Bot. "Thisby, the flowers of odious savors sweet"—

Quin. [Odorous], odorous.

Bot. —"odors savors sweet;
So hath thy breath, my dearest Thisby dear.
But hark; a voice! Stay thou but here a while,
And by and by I will to thee appear." *Exit.*

[*Puck.*] A stranger Pyramus than e'er played here. [*Exit.*]

Flu. Must I speak now?

Quin. Ay, marry, must you; for you must understand he goes but to see a noise that he heard, and is to come again.

Flu. "Most radiant Pyramus, most lily-white of hue,
Of color like the red rose on triumphant brier,
Most brisky juvenal, and eke most lovely Jew,
As true as truest horse, that yet would never tire,
I'll meet thee, Pyramus, at Ninny's tomb."

Quin. "Ninus' tomb," man. Why, you must not speak that yet. That you answer to Pyramus. You speak all your part at once, cues and all. Pyramus, enter. Your cue is past; it is "never tire."

Flu. O—"As true as truest horse, that yet would never tire."

[*Enter* Puck, *and* Bottom *with an ass's head.*]

Bot. "If I were fair, Thisby, I were only thine."

Quin. O monstrous! O strange! We are haunted. Pray, masters, fly, masters! Help!

[*Exeunt Quince, Snug, Flute, Snout, and Starveling.*]

Puck. I'll follow you, I'll lead you about a round,
Through bog, through bush, through brake, through brier:
Sometime a horse I'll be, sometime a hound,
A hog, a headless bear, sometime a fire,
And neigh, and bark, and grunt, and roar, and burn,
Like horse, hound, hog, bear, fire, at every turn. *Exit.*

Bot. Why do they run away? This is a knavery of them to make me afeard.

Enter Snout.

Snout. O Bottom, thou art chang'd! What do I see on thee?

Bot. What do you see? You see an ass-head of your own, do you? [*Exit Snout.*]

Enter Quince.

Quin. Bless thee, Bottom, bless thee! Thou art translated. *Exit.*

Bot. I see their knavery. This is to make an ass of me, to fright me, if they could; but I will not stir from this place, do what they can. I will walk up and down here, and I will sing, that they shall hear I am not afraid. [*Sings.*]

The woosel cock so black of hue,
With orange-tawny bill,
The throstle with his note so true,
The wren with little quill—

41–42. my . . . yours: I pledge my life in defense of yours.
43. were . . . life: would endanger my life.
59–60. bush of thorns. English peasants saw "the man in the moon" as bearing a bundle of sticks on his back.
60–61. disfigure: blunder for *prefigure*. **61. present:** represent.
69. rough-cast: plaster mixed with pebbles for coating the outside of buildings.
77. hempen home-spuns: uncouth rustics (literally, persons wearing home-spun cloth made of hemp). **swagg'ring:** blustering about.
79. toward: about to take place.
82. odious: blunder for *odorous*. Dogberry makes the reverse error in *Much Ado*, III.v.16: "Comparisons are odorous."

95. brisky juvenal: lively youth. **eke:** also. **Jew.** Probably suggested by the first syllable of *juvenal* and used to provide a rhyme.
98. Ninus: mythical founder of Nineveh; his wife, Semiramis, reputedly erected Babylon, the scene of the story of Pyramus and Thisbe. **103. fair:** handsome. **were:** would be.
106. about a round: roundabout. **109. fire:** will-o'-the-wisp.
116–17. an ass-head . . . own: i.e. something dreamed up inside your own asinine head. **119. translated:** transformed.
125. woosel cock: male ousel or blackbird.
127. throstle: song thrush.
128. quill: piping voice (literally, pipe made of a hollow stalk).

Tita. [*Awaking.*] What angel wakes me from my flow'ry bed?

Bot. [*Sings.*]
The finch, the sparrow, and the lark,
The plain-song cuckoo grey,
Whose note full many a man doth mark,
And dares not answer nay—

for indeed, who would set his wit to so foolish a bird? Who would give a bird the lie, though he cry "cuckoo" never so?

Tita. I pray thee, gentle mortal, sing again.
Mine ear is much enamored of thy note;
So is mine eye enthralled to thy shape;
And thy fair virtue's force (perforce) doth move me
On the first view to say, to swear, I love thee.

Bot. Methinks, mistress, you should have little reason for that. And yet, to say the truth, reason and love keep little company together now-a-days. The more the pity that some honest neighbors will not make them friends. Nay, I can gleek upon occasion.

Tita. Thou art as wise as thou art beautiful.

Bot. Not so, neither; but if I had wit enough to get out of this wood, I have enough to serve mine owe turn.

Tita. Out of this wood do not desire to go;
Thou shalt remain here, whether thou wilt or no.
I am a spirit of no common rate;
The summer still doth tend upon my state;
And I do love thee; therefore go with me.
I'll give thee fairies to attend on thee;
And they shall fetch thee jewels from the deep,
And sing while thou on pressed flowers dost sleep.
And I will purge thy mortal grossness so,
That thou shalt like an aery spirit go.
Peaseblossom! Cobweb! Moth! and Mustardseed!

Enter four Fairies [PEASEBLOSSOM, COBWEB, MOTH, *and* MUSTARDSEED].

[*Peas.*] Ready.
[*Cob.*] And I.
[*Moth.*] And I.
[*Mus.*] And I.
[*All.*] Where shall we go?

Tita. Be kind and courteous to this gentleman,
Hop in his walks and gambol in his eyes;
Feed him with apricocks and dewberries,
With purple grapes, green figs, and mulberries;
The honey-bags steal from the humble-bees,
And for night-tapers crop their waxen thighs,
And light them at the fiery glow-worm's eyes,
To have my love to bed and to arise;
And pluck the wings from painted butterflies,
To fan the moonbeams from his sleeping eyes.
Nod to him, elves, and do him courtesies.

[*Peas.*] Hail, mortal!
[*Cob.*] Hail!
[*Moth.*] Hail!
[*Mus.*] Hail!

Bot. I cry your worships mercy, heartily. I beseech your worship's name.

Cob. Cobweb.

Bot. I shall desire you of more acquaintance, good Master Cobweb. If I cut my finger, I shall make bold with you. Your name, honest gentleman?

Peas. Peaseblossom.

Bot. I pray you commend me to Mistress Squash, your mother, and to Master Peascod, your father. Good Master Peaseblossom, I shall desire you of more acquaintance too. Your name, I beseech you, sir?

Mus. Mustardseed.

Bot. Good Master Mustardseed, I know your patience well. That same cowardly, giant-like oxbeef hath devour'd many a gentleman of your house. I promise you your kindred hath made my eyes water ere now. I desire you [of] more acquaintance, good Master Mustardseed.

Tita. Come wait upon him; lead him to my bower.
The moon methinks looks with a wat'ry eye;
And when she weeps, weeps every little flower,
Lamenting some enforced chastity.
Tie up my lover's tongue, bring him silently. *Exeunt.*

[SCENE II]

Enter King of Fairies [OBERON].

Obe. I wonder if Titania be awak'd;
Then what it was that next came in her eye,
Which she must dote on in extremity.

[*Enter* PUCK.]

Here comes my messenger. How now, mad spirit?
What night-rule now about this haunted grove?

Puck. My mistress with a monster is in love.
Near to her close and consecrated bower,
While she was in her dull and sleeping hour,
A crew of patches, rude mechanicals,
That work for bread upon Athenian stalls,
Were met together to rehearse a play
Intended for great Theseus' nuptial day.
The shallowest thick-skin of that barren sort,

131. **plain-song:** melody without variations.
132–33. **Whose . . . nay.** The similarity between *cuckoo* and *cuckold* gave rise to a common jest. 135. **give . . . lie:** call a bird a liar.
136. **never so:** i.e. ever so much, continually.
140. **thy . . . force:** the power of your beauty.
146. **gleek:** gibe, jest. 151. **owe:** own.
154. **rate:** value, worth.
155. **still:** ever, always. **doth . . . state:** attends upon me as one of my retinue. 160. **grossness:** corporeal nature.
162. **Moth.** Pronounced *mote* or *mot* by the Elizabethans, and probably intended by Shakespeare to represent here the word now written *mote*, which he seems regularly to have spelled *moth*.
166. **apricocks:** apricots. 171. **have:** i.e. attend (with lights).
179. **cry . . . mercy:** beg pardon of your honors.
182. **of more acquaintance:** to be better acquainted with me.
183–84. **If . . . you.** Cobwebs were applied to cuts to inhibit bleeding.
186. **commend me:** give my regards. **Squash:** unripe pea pod.
187 **Peascod:** mature pea pod.
192. **patience:** calmness in suffering.
199. **she weeps:** i.e. causes dew. 200. **enforced:** violated.

III.ii. Location: The wood.
2. **next:** nearest, i.e. first. 3. **in extremity:** to the utmost degree.
5. **night-rule:** night activity, night sport. **haunted:** much frequented.
7. **close:** secret. 8. **dull:** drowsy.
9. **patches:** clowns, fools. **rude mechanicals:** ignorant workingmen. 10. **stalls:** street or market booths where wares were sold.
13. **thick-skin:** blockhead. **barren sort:** stupid crew.

Who Pyramus presented, in their sport,
Forsook his scene, and ent'red in a brake;
When I did him at this advantage take,
An ass's nole I fixed on his head.
Anon his Thisby must be answered,
And forth my mimic comes. When they him spy,
As wild geese that the creeping fowler eye,
Or russet-pated choughs, many in sort
(Rising and cawing at the gun's report),
Sever themselves and madly sweep the sky,
So, at his sight, away his fellows fly;
And at our stamp, here o'er and o'er one falls;
He murther cries, and help from Athens calls.
Their sense thus weak, lost with their fears thus strong,
Made senseless things begin to do them wrong,
For briers and thorns at their apparel snatch;
Some sleeves, some hats, from yielders all things catch.
I led them on in this distracted fear,
And left sweet Pyramus translated there;
When in that moment (so it came to pass)
Titania wak'd, and straightway lov'd an ass.
Obe. This falls out better than I could devise.
But hast thou yet latch'd the Athenian's eyes
With the love-juice, as I did bid thee do?
Puck. I took him sleeping (that is finish'd too)
And the Athenian woman by his side;
That when he wak'd, of force she must be ey'd.

Enter DEMETRIUS *and* HERMIA.

Obe. Stand close; this is the same Athenian.
Puck. This is the woman; but not this the man.
Dem. O, why rebuke you him that loves you so?
Lay breath so bitter on your bitter foe.
Her. Now I but chide; but I should use thee worse,
For thou (I fear) hast given me cause to curse.
If thou hast slain Lysander in his sleep,
Being o'er shoes in blood, plunge in the deep,
And kill me too.
The sun was not so true unto the day
As he to me. Would he have stolen away
From sleeping Hermia? I'll believe as soon
This whole earth may be bor'd, and that the moon
May through the centre creep, and so displease
Her brother's noontide with th' Antipodes.
It cannot be but thou hast murd'red him;
So should a murtherer look—so dead, so grim.
Dem. So should the murthered look, and so should I,
Pierc'd through the heart with your stern cruelty.

15. **scene:** playing place. 17. **nole:** noddle, head.
19. **mimic:** actor.
21. **russet-pated choughs:** grey-headed jackdaws. **in sort:** in company, together.
25. **at our stamp.** Puck's use of *our* instead of *my* has puzzled editors, as has the notion that a fairy's stamp would be frightening. (This is the first occurrence of the word in that sense recorded in the *O.E.D.*). Many editors adopt Theobald's conjecture *at a stump.*
26. **calls:** calls for. 36. **latch'd:** anointed.
40. **of force:** perforce, necessarily.
53. **whole:** solid. **be bor'd:** have a hole bored through it.
55. **her brother's:** i.e. the sun's. **with th' Antipodes:** among the people on the other side of the earth.
57. **dead:** deadly (?) or deathly pale (?).

Yet you, the murtherer, look as bright, as clear,
As yonder Venus in her glimmering sphere.
Her. What's this to my Lysander? Where is he?
Ah, good Demetrius, wilt thou give him me?
Dem. I had rather give his carcass to my hounds.
Her. Out, dog, out, cur! thou driv'st me past the bounds
Of maiden's patience. Hast thou slain him then?
Henceforth be never numb'red among men!
O, once tell true; tell true, even for my sake!
Durst thou have look'd upon him being awake?
And hast thou kill'd him sleeping? O brave touch!
Could not a worm, an adder, do so much?
An adder did it! for with doubler tongue
Than thine, thou serpent, never adder stung.
Dem. You spend your passion on a mispris'd mood.
I am not guilty of Lysander's blood;
Nor is he dead, for aught that I can tell.
Her. I pray thee, tell me then that he is well.
Dem. And if I could, what should I get therefore?
Her. A privilege never to see me more.
And from thy hated presence part I [so]:
See me no more, whether he be dead or no. *Exit.*
Dem. There is no following her in this fierce vein.
Here therefore for a while I will remain.
So sorrow's heaviness doth heavier grow
For debt that bankrout [sleep] doth sorrow owe;
Which now in some slight measure it will pay,
If for his tender here I make some stay.
Lie down [*and sleep*].
Obe. What hast thou done? Thou hast mistaken quite,
And laid the love-juice on some true-love's sight.
Of thy misprision must perforce ensue
Some true love turn'd, and not a false turn'd true.
Puck. Then fate o'errules, that one man holding troth,
A million fail, confounding oath on oath.
Obe. About the wood go swifter than the wind,
And Helena of Athens look thou find.
All fancy-sick she is and pale of cheer
With sighs of love, that costs the fresh blood dear.
By some illusion see thou bring her here.
I'll charm his eyes against she do appear.
Puck. I go, I go, look how I go,
Swifter than arrow from the Tartar's bow. [*Exit.*]
Obe. Flower of this purple dye,
Hit with Cupid's archery,
Sink in apple of his eye.
When his love he doth espy,
Let her shine as gloriously

60. **clear:** shining.
62. **What's this to:** what has all this to do with.
70. **brave touch:** noble exploit. 71. **worm:** snake, serpent.
74. **passion:** passionate outburst. **on . . . mood:** in mistaken anger.
84. **heavier.** With play on the sense "drowsier."
85. **bankrout:** bankrupt.
87. **for his tender:** until sleep offers itself (in payment of the deficit).
90. **misprision:** mistake. 92. **troth:** faith.
93. **confounding . . . oath:** invalidating one oath with another.
96. **fancy-sick:** lovesick. **cheer:** face.
97. **costs . . . dear.** Each sigh was thought to draw a drop of blood from the heart.
99. **against . . . appear:** in preparation for her coming.
101. **arrow . . . bow.** Proverbial for swiftness.

As the Venus of the sky.
When thou wak'st, if she be by,
Beg of her for remedy.

Enter PUCK.

Puck. Captain of our fairy band,
Helena is here at hand,
And the youth, mistook by me,
Pleading for a lover's fee.
Shall we their fond pageant see?
Lord, what fools these mortals be!
Obe. Stand aside. The noise they make
Will cause Demetrius to awake.
Puck. Then will two at once woo one;
That must needs be sport alone.
And those things do best please me
That befall prepost'rously.

Enter LYSANDER *and* HELENA.

Lys. Why should you think that I should woo in scorn?
Scorn and derision never come in tears.
Look when I vow, I weep; and vows so born,
In their nativity all truth appears.
How can these things in me seem scorn to you,
Bearing the badge of faith to prove them true?
Hel. You do advance your cunning more and more;
When truth kills truth, O devilish-holy fray!
These vows are Hermia's. Will you give her o'er?
Weigh oath with oath, and you will nothing weigh.
Your vows to her and me, put in two scales,
Will even weigh; and both as light as tales.
Lys. I had no judgment when to her I swore.
Hel. Nor none, in my mind, now you give her o'er.
Lys. Demetrius loves her; and he loves not you.
Dem. [*Awaking.*] O Helen, goddess, nymph, perfect, divine!
To what, my love, shall I compare thine eyne?
Crystal is muddy. O, how ripe in show
Thy lips, those kissing cherries, tempting grow!
That pure congealed white, high Taurus' snow,
Fann'd with the eastern wind, turns to a crow
When thou hold'st up thy hand. O, let me kiss
This princess of pure white, this seal of bliss!
Hel. O spite! O hell! I see you all are bent
To set against me for your merriment.
If you were civil and knew courtesy,
You would not do me thus much injury.
Can you not hate me, as I know you do,
But you must join in souls to mock me too?
If you were men, as men you are in show,
You would not use a gentle lady so;
To vow, and swear, and superpraise my parts,
When I am sure you hate me with your hearts.
You both are rivals, and love Hermia;
And now both rivals, to mock Helena.
A trim exploit, a manly enterprise,
To conjure tears up in a poor maid's eyes
With your derision! None of noble sort
Would so offend a virgin, and extort
A poor soul's patience, all to make you sport.
Lys. You are unkind, Demetrius; be not so;
For you love Hermia; this you know I know.
And here, with all good will, with all my heart,
In Hermia's love I yield you up my part;
And yours of Helena to me bequeath,
Whom I do love, and will do till my death.
Hel. Never did mockers waste more idle breath.
Dem. Lysander, keep thy Hermia; I will none.
If e'er I lov'd her, all that love is gone.
My heart to her but as guest-wise sojourn'd,
And now to Helen is it home return'd,
There to remain.
Lys. Helen, it is not so.
Dem. Disparage not the faith thou dost not know,
Lest, to thy peril, thou aby it dear.
Look where thy love comes; yonder is thy dear.

Enter HERMIA.

Her. Dark night, that from the eye his function takes,
The ear more quick of apprehension makes;
Wherein it doth impair the seeing sense,
It pays the hearing double recompense.
Thou art not by mine eye, Lysander, found;
Mine ear, I thank it, brought me to thy sound.
But why unkindly didst thou leave me so?
Lys. Why should he stay, whom love doth press to go?
Her. What love could press Lysander from my side?
Lys. Lysander's love, that would not let him bide—
Fair Helena! who more engilds the night
Than all yon fiery oes and eyes of light.
Why seek'st thou me? Could not this make thee know,
The hate I bare thee made me leave thee so?
Her. You speak not as you think. It cannot be.
Hel. Lo! she is one of this confederacy.
Now I perceive, they have conjoin'd all three
To fashion this false sport, in spite of me.
Injurious Hermia, most ungrateful maid!
Have you conspir'd, have you with these contriv'd
To bait me with this foul derision?
Is all the counsel that we two have shar'd,
The sisters' vows, the hours that we have spent,
When we have chid the hasty-footed time
For parting us—O, is all forgot?
All school-days friendship, childhood innocence?

113. fee: right, privilege. **114. fond pageant**: foolish show.
119. alone: unparalleled.
121. prepost'rously: out of the natural order.
124–25. vows . . . appears: i.e. when vows are so born, the nature of their birth makes their sincerity manifest.
127. badge: identifying mark (like the family crest or other device worn on livery to identify a gentleman's retainers).
128. advance: hold high, i.e. display. **133. tales**: lies.
141. Taurus: a mountain range in Asiatic Turkey.
142. turns . . . crow: i.e. seems black in comparison.
144. seal: pledge. **151. show**: appearance.
153. superpraise: overpraise. **parts**: qualities.
157. trim: fine. **160. extort**: wring, torture.
169. none: i.e. of her. **175. aby**: pay for, atone for.
177. his: its. **188. oes**: circles, i.e. stars.
194. in . . . me: to vex me. **195. Injurious**: insulting.
196. contriv'd: plotted. **197. bait**: torment.
198. counsel: private thoughts, confidences.

We, Hermia, like two artificial gods,
Have with our needles created both one flower,
Both on one sampler, sitting on one cushion,
Both warbling of one song, both in one key,
As if our hands, our sides, voices, and minds
Had been incorporate. So we grew together,
Like to a double cherry, seeming parted,
But yet an union in partition,
Two lovely berries moulded on one stem;
So with two seeming bodies, but one heart,
Two of the first, [like] coats in heraldry,
Due but to one, and crowned with one crest.
And will you rent our ancient love asunder,
To join with men in scorning your poor friend?
It is not friendly, 'tis not maidenly.
Our sex, as well as I, may chide you for it,
Though I alone do feel the injury.

Her. I am amazed at your [passionate] words.
I scorn you not; it seems that you scorn me.

Hel. Have you not set Lysander, as in scorn,
To follow me and praise my eyes and face?
And made your other love, Demetrius
(Who even but now did spurn me with his foot),
To call me goddess, nymph, divine and rare,
Precious, celestial? Wherefore speaks he this
To her he hates? And wherefore doth Lysander
Deny your love (so rich within his soul)
And tender me (forsooth) affection,
But by your setting on, by your consent?
What though I be not so in grace as you,
So hung upon with love, so fortunate
(But miserable most, to love unlov'd)?
This you should pity rather than despise.

Her. I understand not what you mean by this.

Hel. Ay, do! persever, counterfeit sad looks,
Make mouths upon me when I turn my back,
Wink each at other, hold the sweet jest up;
This sport, well carried, shall be chronicled.
If you have any pity, grace, or manners,
You would not make me such an argument.
But fare ye well; 'tis partly my own fault,
Which death, or absence, soon shall remedy.

Lys. Stay, gentle Helena; hear my excuse,
My love, my life, my soul, fair Helena!

Hel. O excellent!

Her. Sweet, do not scorn her so.

Dem. If she cannot entreat, I can compel.

Lys. Thou canst compel no more than she entreat.
Thy threats have no more strength than her weak [prays].
Helen, I love thee, by my life I do!
I swear by that which I will lose for thee,
To prove him false that says I love thee not.

Dem. I say I love thee more than he can do.

Lys. If thou say so, withdraw, and prove it too.

Dem. Quick, come!

Her. Lysander, whereto tends all this?

Lys. Away, you Ethiop!

Dem. No, no; he'll
Seem to break loose—take on as you would follow,
But yet come not. You are a tame man, go!

Lys. Hang off, thou cat, thou bur! Vile thing, let loose;
Or I will shake thee from me like a serpent!

Her. Why are you grown so rude? What change is this,
Sweet love?

Lys. Thy love? Out, tawny Tartar, out!
Out, loathed med'cine! O hated potion, hence!

Her. Do you not jest?

Hel. Yes, sooth; and so do you.

Lys. Demetrius, I will keep my word with thee.

Dem. I would I had your bond, for I perceive
A weak bond holds you. I'll not trust your word.

Lys. What? should I hurt her, strike her, kill her dead?
Although I hate her, I'll not harm her so.

Her. What? can you do me greater harm than hate?
Hate me, wherefore? O me, what news, my love!
Am not I Hermia? Are not you Lysander?
I am as fair now as I was erewhile.
Since night you lov'd me; yet since night you left me:
Why then, you left me (O, the gods forbid!)
In earnest, shall I say?

Lys. Ay, by my life;
And never did desire to see thee more.
Therefore be out of hope, of question, of doubt;
Be certain! nothing truer; 'tis no jest
That I do hate thee, and love Helena.

Her. O me, you juggler, you canker-blossom,
You thief of love! What, have you come by night
And stol'n my love's heart from him?

Hel. Fine, i' faith!
Have you no modesty, no maiden shame,
No touch of bashfulness? What, will you tear
Impatient answers from my gentle tongue?
Fie, fie, you counterfeit, you puppet, you!

Her. "Puppet"? Why so? Ay, that way goes the game.
Now I perceive that she hath made compare
Between our statures: she hath urg'd her height,
And with her personage, her tall personage,
Her height, forsooth, she hath prevail'd with him.
And are you grown so high in his esteem,

203. artificial: skilled in art, able to create.
208. incorporate: united in one body. **209. seeming:** apparently.
211. lovely: loving.
213–14. Two . . . crest: "we had *two of the first*, i.e. bodies, like double coats in heraldry that belong to a man and wife as *one person*, but which, like our *single heart*, have but *one crest*" (Douce).
215. rent: rend. **220. amazed:** utterly bewildered.
225. even but now: just now. **229. your love:** his love of you.
232. grace: favor. **237. sad:** serious, grave.
238. mouths: a common corruption of *mows*, "grimaces." **upon:** at.
239. hold . . . up: carry . . . on. **240. carried:** managed.
242. argument: subject matter (for jesting).
248. If . . . compel: i.e. if Hermia cannot influence you by pleas, I can do so by force. **250. prays:** prayings, prayers.

257. Ethiop: blackamoor. Hermia is a brunette.
260. Hang off: let go.
268. weak bond: i.e. Hermia's arms. Demetrius implies that Lysander is not trying very hard to break away from her.
272. what news: what is the matter.
275. Since night: i.e. last night.
282. canker-blossom: worm that destroys the bud.
288. puppet: i.e. a mere doll rather than a woman (cf. the preceding *counterfeit*), but Hermia takes it as a reference to her small stature.
292. personage: figure.

Because I am so dwarfish and so low?
How low am I, thou painted maypole? Speak!
How low am I? I am not yet so low
But that my nails can reach unto thine eyes.
Hel. I pray you, though you mock me, [gentlemen],
Let her not hurt me. I was never curst;
I have no gift at all in shrewishness;
I am a right maid for my cowardice.
Let her not strike me. You perhaps may think,
Because she is something lower than myself,
That I can match her.
Her. "Lower"? hark again.
Hel. Good Hermia, do not be so bitter with me.
I evermore did love you, Hermia,
Did ever keep your counsels, never wrong'd you;
Save that, in love unto Demetrius,
I told him of your stealth unto this wood.
He followed you; for love I followed him.
But he hath chid me hence, and threat'ned me
To strike me, spurn me, nay, to kill me too.
And now, so you will let me quiet go,
To Athens will I bear my folly back,
And follow you no further. Let me go.
You see how simple and how fond I am.
Her. Why, get you gone. Who is't that hinders you?
Hel. A foolish heart, that I leave here behind.
Her. What, with Lysander?
Hel. With Demetrius.
Lys. Be not afraid; she shall not harm thee, Helena.
Dem. No, sir; she shall not, though you take her part.
Hel. O, when she is angry, she is keen and shrewd!
She was a vixen when she went to school;
And though she be but little, she is fierce.
Her. "Little" again? Nothing but "low" and "little"?
Why will you suffer her to flout me thus?
Let me come to her.
Lys. Get you gone, you dwarf;
You minimus, of hind'ring knot-grass made;
You bead, you acorn.
Dem. You are too officious
In her behalf that scorns your services.
Let her alone; speak not of Helena,
Take not her part. For if thou dost intend
Never so little show of love to her,
Thou shalt aby it.
Lys. Now she holds me not;
Now follow, if thou dar'st, to try whose right,
Of thine or mine, is most in Helena.
Dem. Follow? Nay; I'll go with thee, cheek by jowl. [*Exeunt Lysander and Demetrius.*]

295. low: short. **300. curst:** shrewish, sharp-tongued.
302. right: real, true. **for:** with respect to.
304. something: somewhat. **305. match:** be a match for.
310. stealth: stealing away.
323. shrewd: sharp-tongued (synonymous with *curst* in line 300).
324. vixen: shrew (literally, she-fox).
329. minimus: diminutive creature. **knot-grass:** a weed that was thought to stunt the growth of animals or children.
333. intend: offer; or, possibly, pretend. **335. aby:** pay for.
338. cheek by jowl: side by side.

Her. You, mistress, all this coil is long of you.
Nay, go not back.
Hel. I will not trust you, I,
Nor longer stay in your curst company.
Your hands than mine are quicker for a fray;
My legs are longer though, to run away. [*Exit.*]
Her. I am amaz'd, and know not what to say. *Exit.*
Obe. This is thy negligence. Still thou mistak'st,
Or else commit'st thy knaveries willfully.
Puck. Believe me, king of shadows, I mistook.
Did not you tell me I should know the man
By the Athenian garments he had on?
And so far blameless proves my enterprise,
That I have 'nointed an Athenian's eyes;
And so far am I glad it so did sort,
As this their jangling I esteem a sport.
Obe. Thou seest these lovers seek a place to fight;
Hie therefore, Robin, overcast the night;
The starry welkin cover thou anon
With drooping fog as black as Acheron,
And lead these testy rivals so astray
As one come not within another's way.
Like to Lysander sometime frame thy tongue;
Then stir Demetrius up with bitter wrong;
And sometime rail thou like Demetrius;
And from each other look thou lead them thus,
Till o'er their brows death-counterfeiting sleep
With leaden legs and batty wings doth creep.
Then crush this herb into Lysander's eye;
Whose liquor hath this virtuous property,
To take from thence all error with his might,
And make his eyeballs roll with wonted sight.
When they next wake, all this derision
Shall seem a dream and fruitless vision,
And back to Athens shall the lovers wend
With league whose date till death shall never end.
Whiles I in this affair do thee employ,
I'll to my queen and beg her Indian boy;
And then I will her charmed eye release
From monster's view, and all things shall be peace.
Puck. My fairy lord, this must be done with haste,
For Night's swift dragons cut the clouds full fast,
And yonder shines Aurora's harbinger,
At whose approach, ghosts, wand'ring here and there,
Troop home to churchyards. Damned spirits all,
That in crossways and floods have burial,
Already to their wormy beds are gone.
For fear lest day should look their shames upon,

339. coil: uproar. **long of:** because of. **345. Still:** continually.
350. so far: to this extent. **352. sort:** turn out.
353. As: that. **jangling:** disputing, wrangling.
355. Hie: hasten. **356. welkin:** sky.
357. Acheron: a river of Hades; here, Hades itself.
361. wrong: insults. **365. batty:** batlike.
366. this herb: i.e. the herb that Oberon has mentioned (II.i.184) as the antidote to love-in-idleness. **367. virtuous:** powerful.
368. with his might: by its efficacy.
370. derision: laughable mockery.
371. fruitless: having no effect, inconsequential.
373. date: duration.
379. dragons: i.e. those that were supposed to draw the chariot of the goddess of night. **full:** very.
380. Aurora's harbinger: the precursor of dawn, i.e. the morning star.
382–83. Damned . . . burial. Suicides were commonly buried at crossroads; to these Puck adds those who have drowned themselves and whose bodies have not been recovered.

They willfully themselves exile from light,
And must for aye consort with black-brow'd Night.
Obe. But we are spirits of another sort.
I with the Morning's love have oft made sport,
And like a forester, the groves may tread
Even till the eastern gate, all fiery red,
Opening on Neptune with fair blessed beams,
Turns into yellow gold his salt green streams.
But notwithstanding, haste, make no delay;
We may effect this business yet ere day. [*Exit.*]
Puck. Up and down, up and down,
I will lead them up and down;
I am fear'd in field and town.
Goblin, lead them up and down.
Here comes one.

Enter Lysander.

Lys. Where art thou, proud Demetrius? Speak thou now.
Puck. Here, villain, drawn and ready. Where art thou?
Lys. I will be with thee straight.
Puck. Follow me then
To plainer ground.
[*Exit Lysander, as following the voice.*]

Enter Demetrius.

Dem. Lysander, speak again!
Thou runaway, thou coward, art thou fled?
Speak! In some bush? Where dost thou hide thy head?
Puck. Thou coward, art thou bragging to the stars,
Telling the bushes that thou look'st for wars,
And wilt not come? Come, recreant, come, thou child,
I'll whip thee with a rod. He is defil'd
That draws a sword on thee.
Dem. Yea, art thou there?
Puck. Follow my voice; we'll try no manhood here. *Exeunt.*

[*Enter* Lysander.]

Lys. He goes before me, and still dares me on.
When I come where he calls, then he is gone.
The villain is much lighter-heel'd than I;
I followed fast, but faster he did fly,
That fallen am I in dark uneven way,
And here will rest me. [*Lie down.*] Come, thou gentle day!
For if but once thou show me thy grey light,
I'll find Demetrius and revenge this spite. [*Sleeps.*]

[*Enter*] Robin [Puck] *and* Demetrius.

Puck. Ho, ho, ho! Coward, why com'st thou not?
Dem. Abide me, if thou dar'st; for well I wot
Thou run'st before me, shifting every place,
And dar'st not stand, nor look me in the face.
Where art thou now?
Puck. Come hither; I am here.
Dem. Nay then thou mock'st me. Thou shalt buy this dear,
If ever I thy face by daylight see.
Now, go thy way. Faintness constraineth me
To measure out my length on this cold bed.
By day's approach look to be visited.
[*Lies down and sleeps.*]

Enter Helena.

Hel. O weary night, O long and tedious night,
Abate thy hours! Shine, comforts, from the east,
That I may back to Athens by daylight,
From these that my poor company detest.
And sleep, that sometimes shuts up sorrow's eye,
Steal me a while from mine own company. *Sleep.*
Puck. Yet but three? Come one more;
Two of both kinds makes up four.

[*Enter* Hermia.]

Here she comes, curst and sad.
Cupid is a knavish lad,
Thus to make poor females mad.
Her. Never so weary, never so in woe,
Bedabbled with the dew and torn with briers,
I can no further crawl, no further go;
My legs can keep no pace with my desires.
Here will I rest me till the break of day.
Heavens shield Lysander, if they mean a fray!
[*Lies down and sleeps.*]
Puck. On the ground,
Sleep sound;
I'll apply,
[To] your eye,
Gentle lover, remedy.
[*Squeezing the juice on Lysander's eyes.*]
When thou wak'st,
Thou tak'st
True delight
In the sight
Of thy former lady's eye;
And the country proverb known,
That every man should take his own,
In your waking shall be shown.
Jack shall have Jill;
Nought shall go ill:
The man shall have his mare again, and all shall be well. [*Exit.*]

[ACT IV, Scene I]

Enter Queen of Fairies [Titania] *and Clown* [Bottom], *and Fairies* [Peaseblossom, Cobweb, Moth, Mustardseed, *and others, attending*]; *and the King* [Oberon] *behind them* [*unseen*].

Tita. Come sit thee down upon this flow'ry bed,

389. the Morning's love: Cephalus, a mighty hunter, and lover of Aurora; or perhaps Aurora herself. If the first, Oberon means that he has often hunted in early morning with Cephalus; if the second, he means that he has often enjoyed the pleasures of the dawn, instead of being driven off by it.
390. like: in the guise of. forester: keeper of a royal forest or hunting preserve. 402. drawn: with drawn sword.
403. straight: straightway. 404. plainer: more level.
409. recreant: coward. 412. try: test. 417. uneven: rough.
422. Abide me: face me in fight. wot: know.

429. measure . . . length: i.e. stretch out. 432. Abate: shorten.
439. curst: ill-tempered. 444. go: walk.

While I thy amiable cheeks do coy,
And stick musk-roses in thy sleek smooth head,
And kiss thy fair large ears, my gentle joy.

Bot. Where's Peaseblossom?

Peas. Ready.

Bot. Scratch my head, Peaseblossom. Where's Mounsieur Cobweb?

Cob. Ready.

Bot. Mounsieur Cobweb, good mounsieur, get you your weapons in your hand, and kill me a red-hipp'd humble-bee on the top of a thistle; and, good mounsieur, bring me the honey-bag. Do not fret yourself too much in the action, mounsieur; and, good mounsieur, have a care the honey-bag break not, I would be loath to have you overflowen with a honey-bag, signior. Where's Mounsieur Mustardseed?

Mus. Ready.

Bot. Give me your neaf, Mounsieur Mustardseed. Pray you, leave your curtsy, good mounsieur.

Mus. What's your will?

Bot. Nothing, good mounsieur, but to help Cavalery Cobweb to scratch. I must to the barber's, mounsieur; for methinks I am marvail's hairy about the face; and I am such a tender ass, if my hair do but tickle me, I must scratch.

Tita. What, wilt thou hear some music, my sweet love?

Bot. I have a reasonable good ear in music. Let's have the tongs and the bones.

[*Music. Tongs. Rural music.*]

Tita. Or say, sweet love, what thou desirest to eat.

Bot. Truly, a peck of provender; I could munch your good dry oats. Methinks I have a great desire to a bottle of hay. Good hay, sweet hay, hath no fellow.

Tita. I have a venturous fairy that shall seek
The squirrel's hoard, and fetch thee new nuts.

Bot. I had rather have a handful or two of dried peas. But, I pray you, let none of your people stir me; I have an exposition of sleep come upon me.

Tita. Sleep thou, and I will wind thee in my arms.
Fairies, be gone, and be [all ways] away.

[*Exeunt Fairies.*]

So doth the woodbine the sweet honeysuckle
Gently entwist; the female ivy so
Enrings the barky fingers of the elm.
O, how I love thee! how I dote on thee! [*They sleep.*]

IV.i. Location: Scene continues. (Again F1 marks an act break where the action is clearly continuous, the lovers remaining asleep on the stage. The F1 act division is preceded by the notation "They sleepe all the Act."; this may mean that they sleep during some kind of inter-act music, as well as into the next scene, but it need be nothing more than an inexact reference to the fact that they sleep during the first 138 lines of the next scene.)
2. amiable: lovely. **coy:** caress.
16. overflowen with: submerged by. **19. neaf:** fist.
20. leave your curtsy: i.e. put on your hat.
23. Cavalery: cavalier (form of address for a fashionable gentleman). **Cobweb.** Peaseblossom has been asked to do the scratching. This may be Shakespeare's slip or Bottom's.
29. tongs, bones: rustic musical instruments; the tongs were struck with a key (as a triangle), and the bones were rattled between the fingers (as clappers). **33. bottle:** bundle. **34. fellow:** equal.
39. exposition: blunder for *disposition*, i.e. desire, inclination.
41. all ways away: off in all directions.
42. woodbine. Obviously not the honeysuckle here (as at II.i.251). Various vines were known by this name.

Enter Robin Goodfellow [Puck].

Obe. [*Advancing.*] Welcome, good Robin. Seest thou this sweet sight?
Her dotage now I do begin to pity.
For meeting her of late behind the wood,
Seeking sweet favors for this hateful fool,
I did upbraid her, and fall out with her.
For she his hairy temples then had rounded
With coronet of fresh and fragrant flowers;
And that same dew which sometime on the buds
Was wont to swell like round and orient pearls,
Stood now within the pretty flouriets' eyes,
Like tears that did their own disgrace bewail.
When I had at my pleasure taunted her,
And she in mild terms begg'd my patience,
I then did ask of her her changeling child;
Which straight she gave me, and her fairy sent
To bear him to my bower in fairy land.
And now I have the boy, I will undo
This hateful imperfection of her eyes.
And, gentle Puck, take this transformed scalp
From off the head of this Athenian swain,
That he, awaking when the other do,
May all to Athens back again repair,
And think no more of this night's accidents
But as the fierce vexation of a dream.
But first I will release the Fairy Queen.

[*Touching her eyes.*]

Be as thou wast wont to be;
See as thou wast wont to see.
Dian's bud [o'er] Cupid's flower
Hath such force and blessed power.
Now, my Titania, wake you, my sweet queen.

Tita. My Oberon, what visions have I seen!
Methought I was enamor'd of an ass.

Obe. There lies your love.

Tita. How came these things to pass?
O, how mine eyes do loathe his visage now!

Obe. Silence a while. Robin, take off this head.
Titania, music call, and strike more dead
Than common sleep of all these [five] the sense.

Tita. Music, ho, music, such as charmeth sleep!

[*Music, still.*]

Puck. Now, when thou wak'st, with thine own fool's eyes peep.

Obe. Sound, music! [*Louder music.*] Come, my queen, take hands with me,
And rock the ground whereon these sleepers be.
Now thou and I are new in amity,
And will to-morrow midnight solemnly
Dance in Duke Theseus' house triumphantly,
And bless it to all fair prosperity.

49. favors: i.e. flowers as love gifts. **51. rounded:** encircled.
53. sometime: formerly.
54. orient pearls: i.e. the most beautiful of pearls.
55. flouriets': flowerets'. **64. scalp:** skull.
66. other: others. **68. accidents:** events, incidents.
69. fierce: excessive, wild.
73. Dian's bud: i.e. the herb of II.i.184, III.ii.366, perhaps the flower of the *agnus castus* or chaste tree, thought to preserve chastity.
82. these five: i.e. the four lovers and Bottom.
83 s.d. Music, still: i.e. soft music. **88. solemnly:** ceremoniously.
89. triumphantly: festively.

There shall the pairs of faithful lovers be
Wedded, with Theseus, all in jollity.

Puck. Fairy King, attend and mark;
I do hear the morning lark.

Obe. Then, my queen, in silence sad,
Trip we after night's shade.
We the globe can compass soon,
Swifter than the wand'ring moon.

Tita. Come, my lord, and in our flight,
Tell me how it came this night
That I sleeping here was found,
With these mortals on the ground.

Exeunt. Wind horn [within].

Enter THESEUS, [HIPPOLYTA, EGEUS,] *and all his* TRAIN.

The. Go, one of you, find out the forester,
For now our observation is perform'd,
And since we have the vaward of the day,
My love shall hear the music of my hounds.
Uncouple in the western valley, let them go.
Dispatch, I say, and find the forester.

[Exit an Attendant.]

We will, fair queen, up to the mountain's top,
And mark the musical confusion
Of hounds and echo in conjunction.

Hip. I was with Hercules and Cadmus once,
When in a wood of Crete they bay'd the bear
With hounds of Sparta. Never did I hear
Such gallant chiding; for besides the groves,
The skies, the fountains, every region near
Seem all one mutual cry. I never heard
So musical a discord, such sweet thunder.

The. My hounds are bred out of the Spartan kind;
So flew'd, so sanded; and their heads are hung
With ears that sweep away the morning dew;
Crook-knee'd, and dewlapp'd like Thessalian bulls;
Slow in pursuit; but match'd in mouth like bells,
Each under each. A cry more tuneable
Was never hollow'd to, nor cheer'd with horn,
In Crete, in Sparta, nor in Thessaly.
Judge when you hear. But soft! What nymphs are these?

Ege. My lord, this' my daughter here asleep,
And this Lysander, this Demetrius is,
This Helena, old Nedar's Helena.
I wonder of their being here together.

The. No doubt they rose up early to observe
The rite of May; and hearing our intent,
Came here in grace of our solemnity.
But speak, Egeus, is not this the day
That Hermia should give answer of her choice?

Ege. It is, my lord.

The. Go, bid the huntsmen wake them with their horns.

[Exit an Attendant.] Shout within. Wind horns. They all start up.

Good morrow, friends. Saint Valentine is past;
Begin these wood-birds but to couple now?

Lys. Pardon, my lord. *[They kneel.]*

The. I pray you all, stand up.
I know you two are rival enemies.
How comes this gentle concord in the world,
That hatred is so far from jealousy
To sleep by hate and fear no enmity?

Lys. My lord, I shall reply amazedly,
Half sleep, half waking; but, as yet, I swear,
I cannot truly say how I came here.
But, as I think—for truly would I speak,
And now I do bethink me, so it is—
I came with Hermia hither. Our intent
Was to be gone from Athens, where we might,
Without the peril of the Athenian law—

Ege. Enough, enough, my lord; you have enough.
I beg the law, the law, upon his head.
They would have stol'n away, they would, Demetrius,
Thereby to have defeated you and me:
You of your wife, and me of my consent,
Of my consent that she should be your wife.

Dem. My lord, fair Helen told me of their stealth,
Of this their purpose hither to this wood,
And I in fury hither followed them,
Fair Helena in fancy following me.
But, my good lord, I wot not by what power
(But by some power it is), my love to Hermia
(Melted as the snow) seems to me now
As the remembrance of an idle gaud,
Which in my childhood I did dote upon;
And all the faith, the virtue of my heart,
The object and the pleasure of mine eye,
Is only Helena. To her, my lord,
Was I betrothed ere I [saw] Hermia;
But like a sickness did I loathe this food;
But, as in health, come to my natural taste,
Now I do wish it, love it, long for it,
And will for evermore be true to it.

The. Fair lovers, you are fortunately met;
Of this discourse we more will hear anon.
Egeus, I will overbear your will;
For in the temple, by and by, with us
These couples shall eternally be knit.
And, for the morning now is something worn,
Our purpos'd hunting shall be set aside.
Away with us to Athens. Three and three,
We'll hold a feast in great solemnity.
Come, Hippolyta.

[Exeunt Theseus, Hippolyta, Egeus, and Train.]

95. sad: sober. **102 s.d. Wind:** blow.
104. observation: observance, May-day rites (cf. I.i.167).
105. vaward: early part. **107. Uncouple:** unleash them.
108. Dispatch: make haste. **113. bay'd:** brought to bay.
114. hounds of Sparta. Famous for hunting ability.
115. chiding: baying. **117. Seem.** Usually emended to *Seem'd*.
120. flew'd: having large chaps. **sanded:** of a sandy color.
122. dewlapp'd: having a pendulous flap of skin at the throat.
123–24. match'd . . . each: with voices of varying but harmonious pitch, like a peal of bells.
124. cry: pack of hounds. **tuneable:** melodious.
127. soft: stop. **128. this':** this is.
134. in . . . solemnity: to honor our observance of the same rites.

139. Saint Valentine. It was supposed that birds chose their mates on St. Valentine's Day.
144. jealousy: suspicion, apprehension of evil.
145. To . . hate: as to sleep side by side with a foe.
146. amazedly: perplexedly.
152. where we might: wherever we could.
153. Without the peril: beyond the dangerous reach.
157. defeated: defrauded. **163. fancy:** love.
167. idle gaud: worthless trinket. **182. for:** since.

Dem. These things seem small and undistinguishable,
Like far-off mountains turned into clouds.
Her. Methinks I see these things with parted eye,
When every thing seems double.
Hel. So methinks;
And I have found Demetrius like a jewel,
Mine own, and not mine own.
Dem. Are you sure
That we are awake? It seems to me
That yet we sleep, we dream. Do not you think
The Duke was here, and bid us follow him?
Her. Yea, and my father.
Hel. And Hippolyta.
Lys. And he did bid us follow to the temple.
Dem. Why then, we are awake. Let's follow him,
And by the way let's recount our dreams.
[*Exeunt Lovers.*]

Bot. [*Awaking.*] When my cue comes, call me, and I will answer. My next is, "Most fair Pyramus." Heigh-ho! Peter Quince! Flute the bellows-mender! Snout the tinker! Starveling! God's my life, stol'n hence, and left me asleep! I have had a most rare vision. I have had a dream, past the wit of man to say what dream it was. Man is but an ass, if he go about [t'] expound this dream. Methought I was—there is no man can tell what. Methought I was, and methought I had—but man is but [a patch'd] fool, if he will offer to say what methought I had. The eye of man hath not heard, the ear of man hath not seen, man's hand is not able to taste, his tongue to conceive, nor his heart to report, what my dream was. I will get Peter Quince to write a ballet of this dream. It shall be call'd "Bottom's Dream," because it hath no bottom; and I will sing it in the latter end of a play, before the Duke. Peradventure, to make it the more gracious, I shall sing it at her death. [*Exit.*]

[Scene II]

Enter Quince, *Thisby* [Flute], *and the rabble* [Snout, Starveling].

Quin. Have you sent to Bottom's house? Is he come home yet?

[*Star.*] He cannot be heard of. Out of doubt he is transported.

Flu. If he come not, then the play is marr'd. It goes not forward, doth it?

Quin. It is not possible. You have not a man in all Athens able to discharge Pyramus but he.

Flu. No, he hath simply the best wit of any handicraft man in Athens.

Quin. Yea, and the best person too; and he is a very paramour for a sweet voice.

Flu. You must say "paragon." A paramour is (God bless us!) a thing of naught.

Enter Snug *the joiner.*

Snug. Masters, the Duke is coming from the temple, and there is two or three lords and ladies more married. If our sport had gone forward, we had all been made men.

Flu. O sweet bully Bottom! Thus hath he lost sixpence a day during his life; he could not have scap'd sixpence a day. And the Duke had not given him sixpence a day for playing Pyramus, I'll be hang'd. He would have deserv'd it. Sixpence a day in Pyramus, or nothing.

Enter Bottom.

Bot. Where are these lads? Where are these hearts?

Quin. Bottom! O most courageous day! O most happy hour!

Bot. Masters, I am to discourse wonders; but ask me not what; for if I tell you, I am [no] true Athenian. I will tell you every thing, right as it fell out.

Quin. Let us hear, sweet Bottom.

Bot. Not a word of me. All that I will tell you is, that the Duke hath din'd. Get your apparel together, good strings to your beards, new ribands to your pumps; meet presently at the palace; every man look o'er his part; for the short and the long is, our play is preferr'd. In any case, let Thisby have clean linen; and let not him that plays the lion pare his nails, for they shall hang out for the lion's claws. And, most dear actors, eat no onions nor garlic, for we are to utter sweet breath; and I do not doubt but to hear them say, it is a sweet comedy. No more words. Away, go, away! [*Exeunt.*]

[ACT V, Scene I]

Enter Theseus, Hippolyta, *and* Philostrate, [Lords, *and* Attendants].

Hip. 'Tis strange, my Theseus, that these lovers speak of.
The. More strange than true. I never may believe

189. **parted:** out of focus.
191–92. **like . . . mine own:** like some precious thing found by accident, and hence not certainly belonging to me, though in my possession. 202. **Heigh-ho.** A yawn. 203. **God's:** God save.
207. **go about:** attempt. 209. **patch'd:** wearing motley.
210. **offer:** venture.
211–14. **The eye . . . was.** A parody of 1 Corinthians 2:9: "The eye hath not seen, and the ear hath not heard, neither have entered into the heart of man . . ." (Bishops'). 215. **ballet:** ballad.
216. **hath no bottom:** i.e. is all tangled up because it lacks a core (*bottom*). 218. **gracious:** attractive, elegant.
219. **her:** i.e. Thisbe's.

IV.ii. Location: Athens. Quince's house.
4. **transported:** carried away by the fairies.

8. **discharge:** successfully perform the role of.
14. **a thing of naught:** something wicked.
20. **sixpence a day:** i.e. as a royal pension.
20–21. **he . . . scap'd:** his reward would certainly not have been less than. 21. **And:** if. 26. **hearts:** good fellows.
29. **am . . . wonders:** have wonders to recount.
31. **right:** exactly, just. 34. **of:** from.
36. **strings.** To attach their false beards (?). **ribands:** ribbons.
37. **presently:** immediately.
39. **preferr'd:** recommended, put forward.

V.i. Location: Athens. The palace of Theseus.
1. **that:** what. 2. **may:** can.

These antic fables, nor these fairy toys.
Lovers and madmen have such seething brains,
Such shaping fantasies, that apprehend
More than cool reason ever comprehends.
The lunatic, the lover, and the poet
Are of imagination all compact.
One sees more devils than vast hell can hold;
That is the madman. The lover, all as frantic,
Sees Helen's beauty in a brow of Egypt.
The poet's eye, in a fine frenzy rolling,
Doth glance from heaven to earth, from earth to heaven;
And as imagination bodies forth
The forms of things unknown, the poet's pen
Turns them to shapes, and gives to aery nothing
A local habitation and a name.
Such tricks hath strong imagination,
That if it would but apprehend some joy,
It comprehends some bringer of that joy;
Or in the night, imagining some fear,
How easy is a bush suppos'd a bear!

Hip. But all the story of the night told over,
And all their minds transfigur'd so together,
More witnesseth than fancy's images,
And grows to something of great constancy;
But howsoever, strange and admirable.

Enter lovers, LYSANDER, DEMETRIUS, HERMIA, *and* HELENA.

The. Here come the lovers, full of joy and mirth.
Joy, gentle friends, joy and fresh days of love
Accompany your hearts!

Lys. More than to us
Wait in your royal walks, your board, your bed!

The. Come now; what masques, what dances shall we have,
To wear away this long age of three hours
Between [our] after-supper and bed-time?
Where is our usual manager of mirth?
What revels are in hand? Is there no play
To ease the anguish of a torturing hour?
Call Philostrate.

Phil. Here, mighty Theseus.

The. Say, what abridgment have you for this evening?
What masque? what music? How shall we beguile
The lazy time, if not with some delight?

Phil. There is a brief how many sports are ripe.
Make choice of which your Highness will see first.
[*Giving a paper.*]

The. [*Reads.*] "The battle with the Centaurs, to be sung
By an Athenian eunuch to the harp."
We'll none of that: that have I told my love,
In glory of my kinsman Hercules.
"The riot of the tipsy Bacchanals,
Tearing the Thracian singer in their rage."
That is an old device; and it was play'd
When I from Thebes came last a conqueror.
"The thrice three Muses mourning for the death
Of Learning, late deceas'd in beggary."
That is some satire, keen and critical,
Not sorting with a nuptial ceremony.
"A tedious brief scene of young Pyramus
And his love Thisby; very tragical mirth."
Merry and tragical? Tedious and brief?
That is hot ice and wondrous strange snow.
How shall we find the concord of this discord?

Phil. A play there is, my lord, some ten words long,
Which is as brief as I have known a play;
But by ten words, my lord, it is too long,
Which makes it tedious; for in all the play
There is not one word apt, one player fitted.
And tragical, my noble lord, it is;
For Pyramus therein doth kill himself;
Which when I saw rehears'd, I must confess,
Made mine eyes water; but more merry tears
The passion of loud laughter never shed.

The. What are they that do play it?

Phil. Hard-handed men that work in Athens here,
Which never labor'd in their minds till now;
And now have toiled their unbreathed memories
With this same play, against your nuptial.

The. And we will hear it.

Phil. No, my noble lord,
It is not for you. I have heard it over,
And it is nothing, nothing in the world;
Unless you can find sport in their intents,
Extremely stretch'd, and conn'd with cruel pain,
To do you service.

The. I will hear that play;
For never any thing can be amiss,
When simpleness and duty tender it.
Go bring them in; and take your places, ladies.
[*Exit Philostrate.*]

3. **antic:** grotesque. **fairy toys:** trifling tales about fairy doings.
5. **shaping fantasies:** fertile imaginations. **apprehend:** perceive, imagine. 6. **comprehends:** takes in, includes.
8. **compact:** formed, composed.
11. **Helen:** Helen of Troy, a paragon of beauty. **brow of Egypt:** gipsy's face. 19. **would but:** merely wishes to.
20. **comprehends . . . joy:** has no trouble including or creating in his fantasy some source of the joy.
21. **some fear:** something to be feared.
25. **More witnesseth:** gives evidence of more. **fancy's images:** ideas created by imagination.
26. **grows to:** arrives at. **constancy:** consistency, hence certainty.
27. **howsoever:** in any event. **admirable:** to be wondered at.
34. **after-supper:** light repast following supper (?).
39. **abridgment:** pastime (to abridge or shorten the time).
42. **brief:** list, abstract. **ripe:** ready for presentation.
44. **battle . . . Centaurs:** battle between the Centaurs and the Lapithae at the wedding feast of Theseus' friend Pirithous, where the Centaurs attempted to carry off the bride, Hippodamia.
47. **glory . . . kinsman.** One version of the tradition placed Hercules at the battle against the Centaurs. He and Theseus, according to Plutarch's life of the latter, were kinsmen.
48–49. **The riot . . . rage.** Orpheus, the Thracian musician, was torn to pieces by Bacchantes at the height of their orgiastic frenzy.
50. **device:** i.e. something devised for dramatic representation.
52–53. **The thrice . . . beggary.** Perhaps a topical allusion, though laments on the low estate of learning were commonplace.
54. **critical:** censorious. 55. **sorting with:** befitting.
59. **strange.** Perhaps an error, replacing some word which with *snow* would produce a "discord" similar to *hot ice.*
65. **fitted:** well cast. 74. **toiled:** taxed. **unbreathed:** unexercised.
75. **against:** in preparation for.
80. **Extremely stretch'd:** strained to the uttermost. **conn'd:** learned by heart. 83. **simpleness:** sincerity.

Hip. I love not to see wretchedness o'ercharged,
And duty in his service perishing.

The. Why, gentle sweet, you shall see no such thing.

Hip. He says they can do nothing in this kind.

The. The kinder we, to give them thanks for nothing.
Our sport shall be to take what they mistake;
And what poor duty cannot do, noble respect
Takes it in might, not merit.
Where I have come, great clerks have purposed
To greet me with premeditated welcomes;
Where I have seen them shiver and look pale,
Make periods in the midst of sentences,
Throttle their practic'd accent in their fears,
And in conclusion dumbly have broke off,
Not paying me a welcome. Trust me, sweet,
Out of this silence yet I pick'd a welcome;
And in the modesty of fearful duty
I read as much as from the rattling tongue
Of saucy and audacious eloquence.
Love, therefore, and tongue-tied simplicity
In least speak most, to my capacity.

[*Enter* PHILOSTRATE.]

Phil. So please your Grace, the Prologue is address'd.

The. Let him approach. [*Flourish trumpet.*]

Enter [QUINCE *for*] *the Prologue.*

Pro. If we offend, it is with our good will.
That you should think, we come not to offend,
But with good will. To show our simple skill,
That is the true beginning of our end.
Consider then, we come but in despite.
We do not come, as minding to content you,
Our true intent is. All for your delight
We are not here. That you should here repent you,
The actors are at hand; and, by their show,
You shall know all, that you are like to know.

The. This fellow doth not stand upon points.

Lys. He hath rid his prologue like a rough colt; he knows not the stop. A good moral, my lord: it is not enough to speak, but to speak true.

Hip. Indeed he hath play'd on this prologue like a child on a recorder—a sound, but not in government.

The. His speech was like a tangled chain; nothing impair'd, but all disorder'd. Who is next?

Enter [*with a Trumpet before them*] PYRAMUS *and* THISBY *and* WALL *and* MOONSHINE *and* LION.

Pro. Gentles, perchance you wonder at this show;
But wonder on till truth make all things plain.
This man is Pyramus, if you would know;
This beauteous lady Thisby is certain.
This man, with lime and rough-cast, doth present
Wall, that vile Wall, which did these lovers sunder;
And through Wall's chink, poor souls, they are content
To whisper. At the which let no man wonder.
This man, with lantern, dog, and bush of thorn,
Presenteth Moonshine; for if you will know,
By moonshine did these lovers think no scorn
To meet at Ninus' tomb, there, there to woo.
This grisly beast, which Lion hight by name,
The trusty Thisby, coming first by night,
Did scare away, or rather did affright;
And as she fled, her mantle she did fall,
Which Lion vile with bloody mouth did stain.
Anon comes Pyramus, sweet youth and tall,
And finds his trusty Thisby's mantle slain;
Whereat, with blade, with bloody blameful blade,
He bravely broach'd his boiling bloody breast;
And Thisby, tarrying in mulberry shade,
His dagger drew, and died. For all the rest,
Let Lion, Moonshine, Wall, and lovers twain
At large discourse, while here they do remain.

Exit [*with Pyramus,*] *Thisby, Lion, and Moonshine.*

The. I wonder if the lion be to speak.

Dem. No wonder, my lord; one lion may, when many asses do.

Wall. In this same enterlude it doth befall
That I, one [Snout] by name, present a wall;
And such a wall, as I would have you think,
That had in it a crannied hole or chink,
Through which the lovers, Pyramus and Thisby,
Did whisper often, very secretly.
This loam, this rough-cast, and this stone doth show
That I am that same wall; the truth is so;
And this the cranny is, right and sinister,
Through which the fearful lovers are to whisper.

The. Would you desire lime and hair to speak better?

Dem. It is the wittiest partition that ever I heard discourse, my lord.

85. **wretchedness o'ercharged:** feebleness overburdened.
86. **his service:** its attempt to perform due service.
88. **in this kind:** of this sort.
91. **noble respect:** generous consideration.
92. **Takes . . . merit:** judges it in relation to the abilities of the performers, not the merit of the performance. 93. **clerks:** scholars.
101. **fearful:** timorous, frightened.
105. **least:** i.e. saying least. **to my capacity:** in my opinion. In the kindly speech of Theseus, a tribute was very likely intended to the graciousness of Queen Elizabeth. Attempts have been made to identify the passage with some particular occasion.
106. **Prologue:** speaker of the prologue. **address'd:** ready.
107 s.d. **Flourish:** sound a fanfare.
108–17. **If . . . know.** The humor of the passage is in the blunders of its punctuation. 112. **despite:** ill will, defiance of your wishes.
113. **minding:** intending.
118. **stand upon points:** (1) bother about trifles; (2) heed his punctuation. 119. **rough:** unbroken.
120. **stop:** (1) reining in a horse to a quick halt; (2) period.
121. **true:** (1) the truth; (2) correctly.

123. **recorder:** wind instrument resembling a flute or flageolet.
123–24. **government:** control, management.
126. **nothing impair'd:** i.e. still unbroken (*nothing* is here, as often, adverbial, meaning "in no respect, not at all").
137. **think no scorn:** regard it as no disgrace. 139. **hight:** is called.
142. **fall:** let fall. 144. **tall:** brave. 147. **broach'd:** stabbed.
151. **At large:** at length.
154. **No wonder:** it will be no wonder if he does.
163. **right and sinister:** running right and left, i.e. horizontal.
167. **wittiest:** cleverest.

[*Enter* PYRAMUS.]

The. Pyramus draws near the wall. Silence!

Pyr. O grim-look'd night! O night with hue so black!
O night, which ever art when day is not!
O night, O night! alack, alack, alack,
I fear my Thisby's promise is forgot!
And thou, O wall, O sweet, O lovely wall,
That stand'st between her father's ground and mine!
Thou wall, O wall, O sweet and lovely wall,
Show me thy chink, to blink through with mine eyne!
[*Wall holds up his fingers.*]
Thanks, courteous wall; Jove shield thee well for this!
But what see I? No Thisby do I see.
O wicked wall, through whom I see no bliss!
Curs'd be thy stones for thus deceiving me!

The. The wall methinks, being sensible, should curse again.

Pyr. No, in truth, sir, he should not. "Deceiving me" is Thisby's cue. She is to enter now, and I am to spy her through the wall. You shall see it will fall pat as I told you. Yonder she comes.

Enter THISBY.

This. O wall, full often hast thou heard my moans,
For parting my fair Pyramus and me!
My cherry lips have often kiss'd thy stones,
Thy stones with lime and hair knit [up in thee].

Pyr. I see a voice! Now will I to the chink,
To spy and I can hear my Thisby's face.
Thisby!

This. My love thou art, my love I think.

Pyr. Think what thou wilt, I am thy lover's grace;
And, like Limander, am I trusty still.

This. And I, like Helen, till the Fates me kill.

Pyr. Not Shafalus to Procrus was so true.

This. As Shafalus to Procrus, I to you.

Pyr. O, kiss me through the hole of this vild wall!

This. I kiss the wall's hole, not your lips at all.

Pyr. Wilt thou at Ninny's tomb meet me straightway?

This. 'Tide life, 'tide death, I come without delay.
[*Exeunt Pyramus and Thisby.*]

Wall. Thus have I, Wall, my part discharged so;
And being done, thus Wall away doth go. [*Exit.*]

The. Now is the moon used between the two neighbors.

Dem. No remedy, my lord, when walls are so willful to hear without warning.

Hip. This is the silliest stuff that ever I heard.

The. The best in this kind are but shadows; and the worst are no worse, if imagination amend them.

Hip. It must be your imagination then, and not theirs.

The. If we imagine no worse of them than they of themselves, they may pass for excellent men. Here come two noble beasts in, a man and a lion.

Enter LION *and* MOONSHINE.

Lion. You, ladies, you, whose gentle hearts do fear
The smallest monstrous mouse that creeps on floor,
May now, perchance, both quake and tremble here,
When lion rough in wildest rage doth roar.
Then know that I as Snug the joiner am
A lion fell, nor else no lion's dam,
For, if I should, as lion, come in strife
Into this place, 'twere pity on my life.

The. A very gentle beast, and of a good conscience.

Dem. The very best at a beast, my lord, that e'er I saw.

Lys. This lion is a very fox for his valor.

The. True; and a goose for his discretion.

Dem. Not so, my lord; for his valor cannot carry his discretion, and the fox carries the goose.

The. His discretion, I am sure, cannot carry his valor; for the goose carries not the fox. It is well; leave it to his discretion, and let us listen to the Moon.

Moon. This lanthorn doth the horned moon present—

Dem. He should have worn the horns on his head.

The. He is no crescent, and his horns are invisible within the circumference.

Moon. This lanthorn doth the horned moon present;
Myself the man i' th' moon do seem to be.

The. This is the greatest error of all the rest. The man should be put into the lanthorn. How is it else the man i' th' moon?

Dem. He dares not come there for the candle; for, you see, it is already in snuff.

Hip. I am a-weary of this moon. Would he would change!

The. It appears, by his small light of discretion, that he is in the wane; but yet in courtesy, in all reason, we must stay the time.

170. grim-look'd: grim-looking. **182. sensible:** capable of feeling.
183. again: in return. **187. fall pat:** happen exactly.
193. and: if.
194. My . . . think. The Q1 punctuation is here retained, although it "doth not stand upon points." **195. lover's grace:** i.e. lover.
196, 197. Limander, Helen: blunders for *Leander* and *Hero*.
198. Shafalus, Procrus: blunders for *Cephalus* and *Procris*.
200. vild: vile. **203. 'Tide:** betide, come.
206. Now . . . used: i.e. Moonshine, Wall being down, will now come into play. Most editors follow Pope in emending *moon used* to *mural* [i.e. wall] *down* (which is close to the F1 reading, *morall downe*).
208–9. so . . . hear: so willing to hear (?) or so perverse as to hear (?)—in either case, with humorous allusion to the proverb "Walls have ears" (certainly true of Snout!). **209. without warning:** surreptitiously (?) or without warning the parents (?).

211. in this kind: of this profession, i.e. actors. **shadows:** likenesses, representations.
223–24. I . . . dam: i.e. only as Snug the joiner am I a lion, or even a lioness.
224. lion fell: cruel lion (but with additional sense "lionskin"—an unintentionally humorous reference to Snug's costume).
227. gentle: polite.
231. very . . . valor: i.e. more crafty (diplomatic) than courageous.
232. goose . . . discretion: i.e. more foolish than crafty.
239. lanthorn: a variant of *lantern*, influenced by the fact that lanterns usually had sides of transparent horn rather than glass; hence there is wordplay in the reference to the "horned" (i.e. crescent) moon, as well as in the jest about the cuckold's horns in the next speech.
249. for the candle: on account of the candle.
250. in snuff: (1) offended; (2) in need of snuffing.
255. stay: wait for.

Lys. Proceed, Moon.

Moon. All that I have to say is to tell you that the lanthorn is the moon, I the man i' th' moon, this thorn-bush my thorn-bush, and this dog my dog.

Dem. Why, all these should be in the lanthorn; for all these are in the moon. But silence! here comes Thisby.

Enter THISBY.

This. This is old Ninny's tomb. Where is my love?

Lion. O! [*The Lion roars. Thisby runs off.*]

Dem. Well roar'd, Lion.

The. Well run, Thisby.

Hip. Well shone, Moon. Truly, the moon shines with a good grace. [*The Lion shakes Thisby's mantle.*]

The. Well mous'd, Lion.

Enter PYRAMUS.

Dem. And then came Pyramus. [*Exit Lion.*]

Lys. And so the lion vanish'd.

Pyr. Sweet Moon, I thank thee for thy sunny beams;
I thank thee, Moon, for shining now so bright;
For by thy gracious, golden, glittering [gleams],
I trust to take of truest Thisby sight.
But stay! O spite!
But mark, poor knight,
What dreadful dole is here!
Eyes, do you see?
How can it be?
O dainty duck! O dear!
Thy mantle good,
What, stain'd with blood?
Approach, ye Furies fell!
O Fates, come, come,
Cut thread and thrum,
Quail, crush, conclude, and quell!

The. This passion, and the death of a dear friend, would go near to make a man look sad.

Hip. Beshrew my heart, but I pity the man.

Pyr. O, wherefore, Nature, didst thou lions frame?
Since lion vild hath here deflow'r'd my dear;
Which is—no, no—which was the fairest dame
That liv'd, that lov'd, that lik'd, that look'd with cheer.
Come, tears, confound,
Out, sword, and wound
The pap of Pyramus;
Ay, that left pap,
Where heart doth hop. [*Stabs himself.*]
Thus die I, thus, thus, thus.
Now am I dead,
Now am I fled;
My soul is in the sky.

269. **mous'd**: shaken, torn (like a mouse in the jaws of a cat).
276. **spite**: malicious stroke of fortune.
278. **dole**: grievous sight.
286. **thread and thrum**: warp and the loose ends of the warp; here, the complete thread (of life).
287. **Quail**: overpower. **conclude**: bring to an end. **quell**: kill.
288. **passion**: violent expression of sorrow.
289. **go . . . make**: almost succeed in making.
294. **cheer.** Almost certainly the meaning here is "countenance."
295. **confound**: destroy (me).

Tongue, lose thy light,
Moon, take thy flight, [*Exit Moonshine.*]
Now die, die, die, die, die. [*Dies.*]

Dem. No die, but an ace, for him; for he is but one.

Lys. Less than an ace, man; for he is dead, he is nothing.

The. With the help of a surgeon he might yet recover, and yet prove an ass.

Hip. How chance Moonshine is gone before Thisby comes back and finds her lover?

[*Enter* THISBY.]

The. She will find him by starlight. Here she comes, and her passion ends the play.

Hip. Methinks she should not use a long one for such a Pyramus. I hope she will be brief.

Dem. A mote will turn the balance, which Pyramus, which Thisby, is the better: he for a man, God warr'nt us; she for a woman, God bless us.

Lys. She hath spied him already with those sweet eyes.

Dem. And thus she means, *videlicet*—

This. Asleep, my love?
What, dead, my dove?
O Pyramus, arise!
Speak, speak! Quite dumb?
Dead, dead? A tomb
Must cover thy sweet eyes.
These lily lips,
This cherry nose,
These yellow cowslip cheeks,
Are gone, are gone!
Lovers, make moan;
His eyes were green as leeks.
O Sisters Three,
Come, come to me,
With hands as pale as milk;
Lay them in gore,
Since you have shore
With shears his thread of silk.
Tongue, not a word!
Come, trusty sword,
Come, blade, my breast imbrue!
[*Stabs herself.*]
And farewell, friends;
Thus Thisby ends;
Adieu, adieu, adieu. [*Dies.*]

The. Moonshine and Lion are left to bury the dead.

Dem. Ay, and Wall too.

[*Bot.*] [*Starting up.*] No, I assure you, the wall is down that parted their fathers. Will it please you to

304–5. **Tongue . . . flight.** Pyramus reverses the order of *Tongue* and *Moon*, with the result that Moonshine receives his walking orders. "Tongue, take your flight" would mean "be made dumb (by death)."
307. **No . . . ace**: not a whole die but a single face—the one-spot. **one**: (1) a single person; (2) in a class by himself.
311. **ass.** With pun on *ace.* 315. **passion**: passionate speech.
318–19. **which . . . which**: whether . . . or.
320. **warr'nt**: defend. "God warrant us" and "God bless us" were both used conventionally to ward off an evil omen, and hence here imply Demetrius' opinion of the performances.
323. **means**: laments. **videlicet**: as follows.
336. **Sisters Three**: the Fates. 340. **shore**: shorn.
344. **imbrue**: stain with blood.

see the epilogue, or to hear a Bergomask dance between two of our company?

The. No epilogue, I pray you; for your play needs no excuse. Never excuse; for when the players are all dead, there need none to be blam'd. Marry, if he that writ it had play'd Pyramus, and hang'd himself in Thisby's garter, it would have been a fine tragedy; and so it is, truly, and very notably discharg'd. But come, your Bergomask; let your epilogue alone. [*A dance.*]

The iron tongue of midnight hath told twelve.
Lovers, to bed, 'tis almost fairy time.
I fear we shall outsleep the coming morn
As much as we this night have overwatch'd.
This palpable-gross play hath well beguil'd
The heavy gait of night. Sweet friends, to bed.
A fortnight hold we this solemnity,
In nightly revels and new jollity. *Exeunt.*

Enter PUCK.

Puck. Now the hungry [lion] roars,
And the wolf [behowls] the moon;
Whilst the heavy ploughman snores,
All with weary task foredone.
Now the wasted brands do glow,
Whilst the screech-owl, screeching loud,
Puts the wretch that lies in woe
In remembrance of a shroud.
Now it is the time of night
That the graves, all gaping wide,
Every one lets forth his sprite,
In the church-way paths to glide.
And we fairies, that do run
By the triple Hecat's team
From the presence of the sun,
Following darkness like a dream,
Now are frolic. Not a mouse
Shall disturb this hallowed house.
I am sent with broom before,
To sweep the dust behind the door.

Enter King and Queen of Fairies [OBERON *and* TITANIA] *with all their* TRAIN.

Obe. Through the house give glimmering light
By the dead and drowsy fire,
Every elf and fairy sprite
Hop as light as bird from brier,
And this ditty, after me,
Sing, and dance it trippingly.

Tita. First, rehearse your song by rote,
To each word a warbling note.
Hand in hand, with fairy grace,
Will we sing, and bless this place.
[*Song and dance.*]

Obe. Now, until the break of day,
Through this house each fairy stray.
To the best bride-bed will we,
Which by us shall blessed be;
And the issue, there create,
Ever shall be fortunate.
So shall all the couples three
Ever true in loving be;
And the blots of Nature's hand
Shall not in their issue stand;
Never mole, hare-lip, nor scar,
Nor mark prodigious, such as are
Despised in nativity,
Shall upon their children be.
With this field-dew consecrate,
Every fairy take his gait,
And each several chamber bless,
Through this palace, with sweet peace,
And the owner of it blest
Ever shall in safety rest.
Trip away; make no stay;
Meet me all by break of day.
Exeunt [*Oberon, Titania, and Train*].

Puck. If we shadows have offended,
Think but this, and all is mended,
That you have but slumb'red here
While these visions did appear.
And this weak and idle theme,
No more yielding but a dream,
Gentles, do not reprehend.
If you pardon, we will mend.
And, as I am an honest Puck,
If we have unearned luck
Now to scape the serpent's tongue,
We will make amends ere long;
Else the Puck a liar call.
So, good night unto you all.
Give me your hands, if we be friends,
And Robin shall restore amends. [*Exit.*]

353. see, hear. Order reversed by Bottom. **Bergomask dance:** a rustic dance taking its name from Bergamo in Italy.
356. no excuse: no extenuation of faults. **363. told:** struck.
366. overwatch'd: stayed up too late.
367. palpable-gross: obviously dull.
368. heavy: torpid, dull. **374. foredone:** exhausted.
375. wasted . . . glow: logs have burned down into glowing embers.
381. his sprite: its ghost.
384. triple Hecat's team. Hecate ruled in three capacities: as Luna (or Cynthia) in heaven, as Diana on earth, and as Proserpina in hell. Here she is the queen of night, drawn by her team of dragons (cf. III.ii.379). **387. frolic:** merry.
390. behind: i.e. from behind. Robin Goodfellow was a household spirit, and was thus sent to clean the house in preparation for the coming of his king and queen.

405. create: created. **412. prodigious:** abnormal.
416. take his gait: go his way. **417. several:** separate.
425. That . . . here: i.e. that it is but a "midsummer night's dream."
428. No . . . but: yielding nothing more than.
430. mend: do better the next time.
433. serpent's tongue: hissing. **437. Give . . . hands:** applaud.
438. restore amends: make amends in the future.

NOTE ON THE TEXT

A Midsummer Night's Dream was first published in quarto (Q1) in 1600 by Thomas Fisher; this edition is here used as copy-text. A second quarto (Q2), set from a copy of Q1, was printed by James Roberts in 1619 with the fraudulent date 1600; it is essentially a reprint of Q1, with a few added stage directions and an occasional correction of obvious errors. The text of the First Folio (1623) was based on a copy of Q2 which had either itself served as a prompt-book or, more probably, been corrected against an official prompt-book.

Q1 displays a number of what are thought of as Shakespearean spellings and the kinds of stage directions which are generally associated with Shakespeare's "foul papers," though the text is unusually clean and may possibly have been printed from some sort of "fair copy" of the "foul papers." It has been suggested that Q1 also shows evidence of a book-keeper's hand in a few stage directions, but nothing in these directions makes it impossible to accept them as authorial notations.

The theatrical provenience behind certain aspects of the printer's copy for F1 is unquestionable (see, for example, the Textual Notes, III.ii.416, 463, IV.i.101, IV.ii o.s.d., V.i.126, 264; the omission of the double reference to God in V.i.319–20 probably points in the same direction). The two most substantial changes are both found in V.i: the substitution of Egeus for Philostrate, except in 76–81, throughout the scene, and the alternating distribution of Theseus' speech at ll. 44–60 between Lysander and Theseus. The more significant F1 variants are recorded in the Textual Notes. In the present text the excessively heavy use of phrasal commas in Q1 has been considerably lightened.

For further information, see: J. D. Wilson, ed., New Shakespeare *A Midsummer Night's Dream* (Cambridge, 1924); W. W. Greg, *The Shakespeare First Folio* (Oxford, 1955); R. K. Turner, "Printing Methods and Textual Problems in *A Midsummer Night's Dream Q1*," *SB*, XV (1962), 34–8; Madeleine Doran, ed., Pelican *A Midsummer Night's Dream* (Baltimore, Maryland, 1969); J. K. Walton, *The Quarto Copy for the First Folio of Shakespeare* (Dublin, 1971); H. F. Brooks, ed., New Arden *A Midsummer Night's Dream* (London, 1979); R. A. Foakes, ed., New Cambridge *A Midsummer Night's Dream* (Cambridge, 1984); Barbara Hodgdon, "Gaining a Father: The Role of Egeus in the Quarto and the Folio," *RES*, n.s. XVII (1986), 534–42; Stanley Wells, Gary Taylor, John Jowett, and William Montgomery, *William Shakespeare: A Textual Companion* (Oxford, 1987); Peter Holland, ed., New Oxford *A Midsummer Night's Dream* (Oxford, 1994).

TEXTUAL NOTES

Title: **A . . . Dream]** *F1*; A Midsommer nights dreame. As it hath been sundry times publickely acted, by the Right honourable, the Lord Chamberlaine his seruants. Written by William Shakespeare. *Q1 (title-page)*

Dramatis personae: *subs. as first given by Rowe*

Act-scene division: *none in Q1–2; F1 marks acts only; scene divisions from Rowe and later editors (see first note to each scene); present act-scene arrangement as a whole first established by Capell*

I.i

I.i] *Rowe;* Actus primus. *F1*
Location: *Theobald*
o.s.d. **Philostrate]** *Theobald*
4 **wanes]** *Q2, F1;* waues *Q1*
10 **New]** *Rowe;* Now *Q1–2, F1*
15 **s.d. Exit Philostrate.]** *Theobald*
19 **s.d. Lysander and Demetrius]** *F1;* Lysander and Helena, and Demetrius *Q1–2 (Helena does not enter until l. 179)*
24 **Stand forth, Demetrius.]** *Rowe; in italics as s.d., Q1–2, F1*
26 **Stand forth, Lysander.]** *Rowe; in italics as s.d., Q1–2, F1*
29 **love-tokens]** *hyphen, F1*
84 **sealing-day]** *hyphen, Capell*
113 **over-full]** *hyphen, F1*
113 **self-affairs]** *hyphen, Q2, F1*
127 **s.d. Manent . . . Hermia.]** *F1* (Manet)
132 **Ay me!]** *Dyce;* Eigh me: *Q1;* Eigh me; *Q2; om. F1;* Hermia *F2*
136 **low]** *Theobald;* loue *Q1–2, F1*
139 **friends]** merit *F1*
143 **momentany]** momentarie *F1*
159 **remote]** remou'd *F1*
187 **Yours would]** *Hanmer;* Your words *Q1–2, F1*
200 **no fault]** none *Q2, F1*
216 **sweet]** *Theobald;* sweld *Q1–2, F1 (a barely possible reading)*
219 **stranger companies]** *Theobald;* strange companions *Q1–2, F1*
224 **s.d. Exit Hermia.]** *placed as in Dyce; after l. 223, Q1–2, F1*
226 **other some]** *Hanmer;* othersome *Q1–2, F1*
237 **figure]** *Rowe;* figure, *Q1–2, F1*
247 **wood]** *Q2, F1;* wodde *Q1*

I.ii

I.ii] *Capell*
Location: *Capell*
10 **grow]** grow on *F1*
11 **Marry]** *Q2, F1;* Mary *Q1*
11–2 **The . . . Thisby.]** *distinguished as a title, Capell*
23 **gallant]** gallantly *F1*
28 **rest—yet]** *Theobald (subs.);* rest yet, *Q1–2, F1*
30–1 **split. "The]** *Theobald (subs.);* split the *Q1–2, F1*
31–8 **"The . . . Fates."]** *as verse, Johnson; as prose, Q1–2, F1*
42 **bellows-mender]** *hyphen, F1*
86 **sweet-fac'd]** *hyphen, F1*
92 **Why,]** *Q2, F1;* Why? *Q1*
93 **straw-color]** *hyphen, F1*
94 **orange-tawny]** *hyphen, F4*
94–5 **purple-in-grain]** *hyphens, Rowe*
95 **French-crown-color]** *first hyphen, F1; second hyphen, Rowe*
104 **devices]** *F3;* deuises *Q1–2, F1*

II.i

II.i] *Rowe;* Actus Secundus. *F1*
Location: *Theobald*
o.s.d. **Puck]** *Rowe*
1 **s.p. Puck.]** *Rowe;* Robin. *Q1–2, F1 (until l. 154)*
2–9 **Over . . . green.]** *arranged as in Pope; as four verse lines, Q1–2, F1*
22 **stolen]** *Q2;* stollen, *Q1;* stolne *F1*
52 **three-foot]** *hyphen, F1*
61 **s.p. Tita.]** *Capell;* Qu. *Q1–2, F1 (throughout scene)*
61 **Fairies]** *Theobald;* Fairy *Q1–2, F1*
69 **steep]** *Q2, F1;* steppe *Q1*
79 **Aegles]** *Chambers (after North's Plutarch);* Eagles *Q1–2, F1*
91 **pelting]** petty *F1*
107 **hoary-headed]** *hyphen, Rowe;* hoared headed *Q2, F1*
109 **thin]** *Tyrwhitt conj.;* chinne *Q1–2, F1*
115 **evils comes]** *F2;* euils, / Comes *Q1–2, F1*
145 **s.d. Titania . . . Train]** *Theobald*
158 **the]** *F1*
164 **fancy-free]** *hyphen, F2*
168 **love-in-idleness]** *hyphens, Capell*
176 **s.d. Exit.]** *F2*
183 **from off]** off from *Q2, F1*
183 **off]** *Q2, F1 (see preceding note);* of *Q1*
190 **slay . . . slayeth]** *Thirlby conj.;* stay . . . stayeth *Q1–2, F1 (cf.* Romeo and Juliet, *IV.i.72)*
194 **thee]** *Q2, F1;* the *Q1*
201 **nor]** *F1;* not *Q1–2*
210 **use]** doe *F1*
242 **s.d. Exit Demetrius.]** *Capell*
244 **s.d. Exit.]** *Q2, F1*
246 **s.d. Enter Puck.]** *placed as in Capell; after l. 247, Q1–2, F1*

II.ii

II.ii] *Capell*
Location: *Pelican (after Capell)*
1 **s.p. Tita.]** *Capell;* Quee. *Q1–2, F1*
4 **leathren]** *Wilson;* lethten *Q1;* leathern *Q2, F1*
9 **s.p. 1. Fairy.]** *Capell*
13, 24 **s.pp. Cho.]** *Capell*
14 **our]** your *F1*
20 **s.p. 1. Fairy.]** 2. Fairy. *F1*
25 **s.p. 2. Fairy.]** 1. Fairy. *F1*
26 **s.d. Exeunt Fairies.]** *Rowe*
26 **s.d. Titania sleeps.]** *F1* (Shee sleepes.)
26 **s.d. and . . . eyelids]** *Capell*
27 **dost]** *Q2, F1;* doest *Q1*
28 **true-love]** *hyphen, Harness*
34 **s.d. Exit.]** *Rowe*
38 **comfort]** *Q2, F1;* comfor *Q1*
39 **Be't]** *Pope;* Bet it *Q1;* Be it *Q2, F1*
43 **good]** *Q2, F1;* god *Q1*
47 **is]** *Q2, F1;* it *Q1*
48 **we can]** can you *F1*
49 **interchained]** interchanged *F1*
65 **s.d. They sleep.]** *F1*

87 s.d. **Exit.]** *F1* (Exit Demetrius.)

103 s.d. **Awaking.]** *Rowe*

119 **human]** *F4;* humane *Q1–2, F1*

145 s.d. **Starting up.]** *Capell*

152 **hearing]** *Theobald;* hearing, *Q1–2, F1*

III.i

III.i] *Rowe;* Actus Tertius. *F1*

Location: *ed. (after Wilson)*

2 **marvail's]** *Kittredge;* maruailes *Q1;* maruailous *Q2, F1*

13 **By'r lakin]** *Pope (subs.);* Berlakin *Q1;* Berlaken *Q2, F1*

16 **device]** *Q2, F1;* deuise *Q1*

29 **yourselves]** *F1;* your selfe *Q1–2*

32 **wild-fowl]** *hyphen, Pope*

51 s.p. **Snout.]** *Cambridge;* Sn. *Q1–2, F1;* Snug. *F2*

56 s.p. **Bot.]** *Q2, F1;* Cet. *Q1*

76 s.d. **behind]** *Theobald; F1 gives an earlier duplicate s.d.* Enter Pucke. *after l. 54*

82, 84, 89, 93, 102, 103 s.pp. **Bot., Flu.]** *Q1–2, F1 give as s.pp. the character names in the play-within-the-play:* Pyra., This.

83 **Odorous, odorous]** *Collier conj.;* Odours, odorous *Q1–2;* Odours, odours *F1*

88 s.p. **Puck.]** *F1;* Quin. *Q1–2*

88 s.d. **Exit.]** *Capell*

90, 98, 104 s.pp. **Quin.]** Pet. *Q2, F1*

102 s.d. **Enter . . . head.]** *Capell (after Rowe);* Enter Piramus with the Asse head. *F1 (after l. 111)*

105 s.d. **Exeunt . . . Starveling.]** *Dyce;* The Clownes all Exit. *F1*

117 s.d. **Exit Snout.]** *Dyce*

124, 129 s.dd. **Sings.]** *Pope*

126 **orange-tawny]** *hyphen, F1*

129 s.d. **Awaking.]** *Rowe (subs.)*

139–41] *Ordered as 141, 139, 140, Q2, F1*

162 s.d. **Peaseblossom . . . Mustardseed]** *Dyce; F1 om. l. 162 and has as s.d.:* Enter Pease-blossome, Cobweb, Moth, Mustardseede, and foure Fairies.

163 **Peas. Ready . . . go?]** *Dyce (after Capell); Fairies.* [*Fai. Q2, F1*] Readie: and I, and I, and I. Where shall we goe? *Q1–2, F1*

175 s.p. **Peas.]** *Dyce;* 1. Fai. *Q1–2, F1*

176 s.p. **Cob.]** *Dyce (after Capell* 2. Fairy); *continued to* 1. Fai., *Q1–2, F1*

177 s.p. **Moth.]** *Dyce;* 2. Fai. *Q1–2, F1*

178 s.p. **Mus.]** *Dyce;* 3. Fai. *Q1–2, F1*

195 **of]** *Collier*

201 s.d. **Exeunt.]** *Rowe;* Exit. *Q1–2, F1*

III.ii

III.ii] *Capell*

Location: *Pelican (after Capell)*

o.s.d. **Enter . . . Oberon.]** Enter King of Fairies, and Robin goodfellow. *Q1–2;* Enter King of Pharies, solus. *F1*

3 s.d. **Enter Puck.]** *F1 (see preceding note)*

6–7 **love. . . . bower,]** *Rowe;* loue, . . . bower. *Q1;* loue, . . . bower, *Q2, F1*

14 **sport]** *Rowe;* sport, *Q1–2, F1*

15–6 **brake; . . . take,]** *Pope;* brake, . . . take: *Q1;* brake, . . . take, *Q2, F1*

19 **mimic]** *F1;* Minnick *Q1;* Minnock *Q2*

37, 89 **love-juice]** *hyphen, Theobald*

38 s.p. **Puck.]** Rob. *Q1–2, F1 (until l. 110)*

52 **From]** *Q2, F1;* Frow *Q1*

80 **so]** *Pope*

84 **grow]** *Pope;* grow. *Q1–2;* grow: *F1*

85 **sleep]** *Rowe;* slippe *Q1;* slip *Q2, F1*

87 s.d. **and sleep]** *ed. (after Collier)*

89 **true-love's]** *hyphen, Capell*

96 **fancy-sick]** *hyphen, F2*

101 s.d. **Exit.]** *Q2, F1*

104 **eye.]** *Rowe (subs.);* eye, *Q1–2, F1*

109 **her]** *Q2, F1;* her, *Q1*

129 **devilish-holy]** *hyphen, Capell*

137 s.d. **Awaking.]** *Rowe;* Awa. *F1 (after l. 136)*

137 **perfect,]** *Q2, F1;* perfect *Q1*

159 **derision! None]** *F1 (subs.);* derision None, *Q1;* derision, none *Q2, F1*

164 **here]** *Q2, F1;* heare *Q1*

175 **aby]** abide *F1 (again at l. 335)*

199 **sisters']** *Steevens;* sisters *Q1–2, F1*

213 **first, like]** *Theobald (Folkes conj.);* first life *Q1–2, F1*

220 **passionate]** *F1*

227 **Precious,]** *Q2, F1;* Pretious *Q1*

237 **Ay, do!]** *Rowe (subs.);* I doe. *Q1;* I, do, *Q2, F1*

250 **prays]** *Capell (Theobald conj.);* praise *Q1–2, F1*

252 **thee,]** *Q2, F1;* thee; *Q1*

257 **no; he'll]** no, hee'l *Q2;* no, Sir, *F1*

260 **off]** *Q2, F1;* of *Q1*

279 **Therefore]** *Q2, F1;* Thefore *Q1*

282 **canker-blossom]** *hyphen, F3*

299 **gentlemen]** *Q2, F1;* gentleman *Q1*

338 s.d. **Exeunt . . . Demetrius.]** *F1* (Exit); Exit. *Q2*

343 s.d. **Exit.]** *Capell*

344 **Her. I . . . say.]** *om. F1 (following l. 343 F1 reads:* Enter Oberon and Pucke.)

344 s.d. **Exit.]** *Capell;* Exeunt. *Q1–2*

346 **willfully]** willingly *F1*

364 **death-counterfeiting]** *Q2, F1;* death-counterfaiting. *Q1*

383 **all,]** *Q2, F1;* all; *Q1*

385 **lest]** *F4;* least *Q1–2, F1 (a possible reading, meaning* smallest amount of)

387 **black-brow'd]** *Q2, F1 (hyphen, F3);* black browed *Q1*

394 **notwithstanding]** *Q2, F1;* notwitstanding *Q1*

395 s.d. **Exit.]** *Rowe*

402 s.p. **Puck.]** Rob. *Q1–2, F1 (throughout rest of scene)*

404 s.d. **Exit . . . voice.]** *Cambridge (after Capell)*

406 **Speak! . . . bush?]** *Capell;* Speake in some bush. *Q1–2, F1* (bush:)

406 **dost]** *Q2, F1;* doest *Q1*

412 s.d. **Enter Lysander.]** *Theobald (subs.)*

416] *Opposite this line F1 reads:* shifting places. (*presumably a prompter's note*)

418 s.d. **Lie down.]** *F1 (after l. 418); placed as in Capell*

420 s.d. **Sleeps.]** *Capell*

420 s.d. **Enter]** *F1*

426 **shalt]** *Q2, F1;* shat *Q1*

430 s.d. **Lies . . . sleeps.]** *Malone (after Rowe and Capell)*

432 **Shine, comforts,]** *Theobald;* shine comforts, *Q1;* shine comforts *Q2, F1*

438 s.d. **Enter Hermia.]** *Q2, F1 (after l. 440); placed as in Neilson*

447 s.d. **Lies . . . sleeps.]** *Dyce (after Rowe and Capell)*

451 **To]** *Rowe*

452 s.d. **Squeezing . . . eyes.]** *Rowe*

463 s.d. **Exit.]** *Rowe (following l. 463 F1 reads:* They sleepe all the Act.)

IV.i

IV.i] *Rowe;* Actus Quartus. *F1*

Location: *ed.*

o.s.d. **Peaseblossom . . . attending]** *Dyce (after Rowe)*

o.s.d. **unseen]** *Capell*

24 **marvail's]** *Kittredge;* Maruailes *Q1;* maruailous *Q2;* maruellous *F1*

29 s.d. **Music. . . . music.]** *F1 (no period after* Music)

41 **all ways]** *Theobald;* alwaies *Q1–2, F1*

41 s.d. **Exeunt Fairies.]** *Capell*

42 **woodbine . . . honeysuckle]** *Rowe;* woodbine, . . . Honisuckle, *Q1–2, F1*

45 s.d. **They sleep.]** *Capell*

45 s.d. **Enter . . . Puck.]** Enter Robin goodfellow and Oberon. *F1*

46 s.d. **Advancing.]** *Collier*

70 s.d. **Touching her eyes.]** *Capell*

71 **Be]** Be thou *F1*

73 **bud . . . flower]** *Thirlby conj.;* budde, or Cupids flower, *Q1–2, F1*

82 **sleep . . . five]** *Theobald;* sleepe: of all these, fine *Q1,* (sleepe;) *Q2, F1*

83 **ho]** *Q2, F1;* howe *Q1*

83 s.d. **Music, still.]** *F1*

84, 93 s.pp. **Puck.]** *Rowe;* Rob. *Q1–2, F1*

85 s.d. **Louder music.]** *ed. (after Wilson)*

96 **night's]** the nights *Q2, F1*

101] *After this line F1 adds s.d.:* Sleepers Lye still. (*i.e. remain lying down*)

102 s.d. **horn]** hornes *Q2, F1*

102 s.d. **within]** *Capell*

102 s.d. **Hippolyta, Egeus,]** *F1 (in reverse order)*

107 **Uncouple]** *Q2, F1;* Vncouple, *Q1*

108 s.d. **Exit an Attendant.]** *Dyce*

113 **bay'd]** *Rowe;* bayed *Q1–2, F1*

122 **Crook-knee'd]** *hyphen, F2*

128 **this']** *ed.;* this *Q1;* this is *Q2, F1*

133 **rite]** *Pope;* right *Q1–2, F1*

138 s.d. **Exit an Attendant.]** *Dyce*

138 s.d. **Shout . . . up.]** *arranged as in Kittredge;* Shoute within: they all start vp. Winde hornes. *Q1–2;* Hornes and they wake. Shout within, they all start vp. *F1*

141 s.d. **They kneel.]** *Capell (subs.)*

149–50 **—for . . . is—]** *Capell;* (for . . . speake) / And . . . is; *Q1–2, F1*

152 **might,]** *Dyce;* might *Q1;* might be *Q2, F1*

153 **law—]** *Dyce;* lawe, *Q1;* Law. *Q2, F1*

172 **saw]** *Steevens (after Rowe);* see *Q1–2, F1*

186 s.d. **Exeunt . . . Train.]** *Capell;* Exit. *Q2;* Exit Duke and Lords. *F1*

192–3 **Are . . . awake?]** *om. F1*

198–9 **Why . . . dreams.]** *as verse, Rowe; as prose, Q1–2, F1*

199 **let's]** let vs *Q2, F1*

199 s.d. **Exeunt Lovers.]** *F1* (Exit); Exit. *Q2*

200 s.p., s.d. **Bot. Awaking.]** *from F1:* Bottome wakes. / *Clo.;* Clo. *Q1–2*

205 **have]** *om. F1*

207 **t' expound]** *ed.;* expound *Q1;* to expound *Q2, F1*

209 **a patch'd]** *F1;* patcht a *Q1–2*

219 s.d. **Exit.]** *Q2, F1*

IV.ii

IV.ii] *Capell*

Location: *Capell*

o.s.d. **and the rabble]** *om. F1*

o.s.d. **Snout, Starveling]** *F1* (Snout and Starueling)

3 s.p. **Star.]** *F1;* Flut. *Q1–2*

5 s.p. **Flu.]** *Rowe;* Thys. *Q1–2, F1 (throughout scene)*

6 **forward,]** *Q2, F1;* forward. *Q1*

14 **naught]** *F2;* nought *Q1–2, F1*

30 **no]** *F1;* not *Q1–2*

45 **go,]** *Theobald;* go *Q1–2, F1*

45 s.d. **Exeunt.]** *F1*

V.i

V.i] *Rowe;* Actus Quintus. *F1*

Location: *Theobald*

o.s.d. **Philostrate]** Egeus *F1 (see l. 38)*

o.s.d. **Lords]** *F1* (and his Lords)

o.s.d. **and Attendants]** *Capell*

3 **antic]** *Q2, F1;* antique *Q1*

4 **madmen]** *Rowe;* mad men *Q1–2, F1*

5–8, 12–7] *As Wilson suggests, the mislining in Q1 (followed in Q2, F1) probably shows that Shakespeare at some stage added these lines on the poet to the original speech; on similar evidence other insertions can also be traced in the first 84 lines of the scene*

10 **madman]** *F3* (mad-man); mad man *Q1–2, F1*

30–1 **More . . . bed!]** *as verse, F2; as prose, Q1–2, F1*

34 **our]** *F1;* Or *Q1;* or *Q2*

34 **after-supper]** *hyphen, F4*

38 **Philostrate]** Egeus *F1 (all Philostrate's lines, except 76–81, are given to Egeus in F1)*

43 s.d. **Giving a paper.]** *Theobald*

44–5, 48–9, 52–3, 56–7] *These lines are assigned to* Lis. *(i.e. Lysander) in F1*

44 s.d. **Reads.]** *Theobald*

50 **device]** *Q2, F1;* deuise *Q1*

58–60 **Merry . . . discord?]** *as regular verse, Pope (om. l. 59); as irregular verse, Q1; as mixed irregular verse and prose, Q2; as prose, F1*

84 s.d. **Exit Philostrate.]** *Pope*

105 s.d. **Enter Philostrate.]** *Capell*

107 s.d. **Flourish trumpet.]** *ed.;* Flor. Trum. *F1*

107 s.d. **Quince for]** *Rowe (F1 places* Quince.

opposite Enter the Prologue.)
122 **this]** his *F1*
126 s.d. **with . . . them]** *from F1* Tawyer with a Trumpet before them. (*Tawyer was a servant in Shakespeare's company who died in 1625*)
141 **scare]** *F3;* scarre *Q1–2, F1*
145 **trusty]** *om. F1;* gentle *F2*
151 s.d. **with Pyramus]** *Cambridge* (*subs.*); *Q1–2 s.d. after l. 154* (*here placed as in F1*); *F1 s.d.:* Exit all but Wall.
156 **Snout]** *F1;* Flute *Q1–2*
168 s.d. **Enter Pyramus.]** *F1* (*after l. 169*); *placed as in Neilson*
170 **grim-look'd]** *hyphen, Theobald*
177 s.d. **Wall . . . fingers.]** *Capell*
184–7 **No . . . comes.]** *as prose, Pope; as verse, Q1–2, F1*
187 s.d. **Enter Thisby.]** *after* fall *l. 187, F1*
191 **hair]** *Q2, F1;* hayire *Q1*
191 **up in thee]** *F1;* now againe *Q1–2*
203 s.d. **Exeunt . . . Thisby.]** *Dyce*
205 s.d. **Exit.]** *Dyce;* Exit Clow. *F1* (*i.e. the Clowns: Pyramus, Thisby, and Wall*)
206 s.p. **The.]** *Rowe;* Duk. (*or* Duke.) *Q1–2, F1* (*throughout rest of scene*)
206 **moon used]** morall downe *F1* (*both readings are corrupt; some eds. read* mural down [*Pope*], *others* wall down [*Collier MS*])
210 s.p. **Hip.]** *Rowe;* Dutch. *Q1–2, F1* (*throughout rest of scene*)
217 **beasts in,]** *Rowe;* beasts, in *Q1–2, F1*
223 **as]** one *F1*
263, 328 **tomb]** *Q2* (*subs.*), *F1;* tumbe *Q1*
264 s.d. **The . . . off.]** *F1*
268 s.d. **The . . . mantle.]** *Capell*
269 s.d. **Enter Pyramus.]** *placed as in Alexander; after l. 271, Q1–2, F1*
270 s.d. **Exit Lion.]** *ed.* (*after Wilson*)
274 **gleams]** *Knight conj.;* beames *Q1–2, F1*
275 **take]** taste *F1*
299 s.d. **Stabs himself.]** *Dyce* (*after Collier MS*)
305 s.d. **Exit Moonshine.]** *Capell*
306 s.d. **Dies.]** *Capell*
311 **yet]** *om. F1*
312–3 **before]** *Rowe;* before? *Q1–2, F1*
313 s.d. **Enter Thisby.]** *F1*
318 **mote]** *Heath conj.;* moth *Q1–2, F1*
319–20 **he . . . us.]** *om. F1*
320 **warr'nt]** *Wilson;* warnd *Q1–2*
335 **leeks.]** *Q2, F1;* leekes, *Q1*
344 s.d. **Stabs herself.]** *Dyce*
347 s.d. **Dies.]** *Warburton*
351 s.p. **Bot.]** *F1;* Lyon. *Q1–2*
351 s.d. **Starting up.]** *Capell*
357 **Marry]** *Q2, F1;* Mary *Q1*
362 s.d. **A dance.]** *Rowe*
367 **palpable-gross]** *hyphen, Capell*
371 **lion]** *Rowe;* Lyons *Q1–2, F1*
372 **behowls]** *Theobald;* beholds *Q1–2, F1*
384 **Hecat's]** *Johnson;* Hecates *Q1–2, F1*
400 s.d. **Song and dance.]** *Capell*
401–22] *Called* The Song. *and not assigned to Oberon, F1*
419–20 **And . . . rest.]** *arranged as in Staunton; lines reversed in Q1–2, F1*
422 s.d. **Oberon . . . Train]** *Capell*
423 s.p. **Puck.]** *Rowe;* Robin. *Q1–2, F1*
438 s.d. **Exit.]** *Capell;* FINIS. *Q1–2, F1*

The Merchant of Venice

THE MERCHANT OF VENICE combines two folk-tales of great age. The story of the savage creditor who tries but fails to obtain a pound of human flesh as payment of a debt came originally from the East. It was widespread in Europe by the early Middle Ages. Shakespeare's immediate source for Shylock's bond was probably the first story of the fourth day in Ser Giovanni's prose collection *Il Pecorone*, written at the end of the fourteenth century and printed in Milan in 1558. There is no record of any English translation that Shakespeare could have known. He may have read the story in Italian, or he may have depended upon a lost work in English which derived from *Il Pecorone*. An anonymous play called *The Jew*, now lost, was described by Stephen Gosson in 1579 as exhibiting "the greedinesse of worldly choosers, and bloody minds of usurers." Perhaps Shakespeare knew it. The second folk-tale, that of the lover who gains his lady because he chooses the right casket among three in a riddle game, was also traditional long before it came to be exploited by Boccaccio and Gower in the fourteenth century. Probably Shakespeare drew upon the version available in the medieval *Gesta Romanorum* (translated into English in 1577) when he devised the love trial at Belmont.

Jews had been officially banished from England for three centuries, since the reign of Edward I. In the popular imagination they figured almost as mythical beasts: strange, evil beings who had once crucified Christ and might be expected to persevere in anti-Christian activities. Although a few Jews continued to inhabit Shakespeare's London, they were forced to make a secret of their race and religion. In 1594, two or three years before the probable date of composition of *The Merchant of Venice*, they achieved an unwelcome notoriety when Roderigo Lopez, a Portuguese Jew who had been Queen Elizabeth's physician, was tried and executed for his part in a supposed poisoning plot aimed against her. Marlowe's tragedy *The Jew of Malta*, originally performed about 1589, was revived at this time in an obvious attempt to capitalize on the public interest aroused by the Lopez case. The original stimulus for *The Merchant of Venice* may have come from Shakespeare's memory of the trial. More important, probably, was the influence of Marlowe's play.

Barabas, the hero-villain of *The Jew of Malta*, is a figure of fantastic evil. Half Machiavel, half Vice, a brilliant caricature more than a credible human being, he rockets from one outrage to the next within a society of Christians who are fundamentally as corrupt as he but considerably less clever. Despite their pious professions, "desire of gold" motivates all of them. Even the holy friars squabble among themselves over the possession of Barabas' enormous wealth. This wealth is the product of trade, not usury, and Barabas' attitude towards it is that of an artist and sensualist more than a miser. Although he is directly responsible for seven murders in the course of the action, not to mention poisoning an entire convent of nuns, it is surprisingly difficult for an audience to dissociate itself from this witty and inventive villain, or to feel much sympathy for his victims. Even the death of his daughter Abigail, murdered by Barabas because (like Shakespeare's Jessica) she loves a Christian and has been converted to his faith, is made to seem wryly funny the moment after it occurs. The unquestioned centre of his play, Barabas has no real rivals in Malta either in the form of other characters or of attitudes contrasted to his own. He can be condemned only in the light of values which exist outside the play he dominates.

By contrast with Barabas, Shylock is a closely observed human being, not a bogeyman to frighten children in the nursery. In the theatre, the part has always attracted actors, and it has been played in a variety of ways. Shylock has sometimes been presented as the devil incarnate, sometimes as a comic villain gabbling absurdly about ducats and daughters. He has also been sentimentalized as a wronged and suffering father nobler by far than the people who triumph over him. Roughly the same range of interpretation can be found in criticism on the play. Shakespeare's text suggests a truth more complex than any of these extremes. A sober, cautious man, as sparing of speech as he is of the ducats he has amassed by lending money at interest, Shylock has nursed a not unjustified hatred of the Christians in Venice over long years. Even the magnanimous Antonio freely confesses that he is accustomed to revile Shylock, to spit at him and kick him, when they meet on the Rialto. Treated as something inhuman, a "dog" or "cur," Shylock not unnaturally responds, when the opportunity presents itself, with tooth and claw. Behind the "merry bond" he offers Antonio there lurks an inchoate impulse towards revenge which events, unexpectedly, transform into a real possibility.

The antipathy between Shylock and the citizens of Venice is not simply racial, nor is it a matter only of the conflict between a merchant and a usurer. Shylock is an alien in a society whose religion, pleasures, aims, and attitudes are radically different from his own. Restrained and frugal by nature, he holds the expansive way of life characteristic of the Christians in contempt: their masques and music, the wealth lavished on feasts, the upkeep of great households, jewels and fine attire. Even his economical, unadorned style of speech, a style distrustful of metaphor or figurative language, sets him off from Antonio, Portia, Bassanio and their friends as much as does his plain Jewish gaberdine in a city where the merchants were accustomed to dress like princes. Although he shares their vocabulary, at least up to a point, Shylock tends to narrow its meaning. When he decides that he may accept Antonio's bond because "Antonio is a good man," Bassanio is indignant: "Have you heard any imputation to the contrary?" (I.iii.12–14). The question elicits from Shylock one of his rare laughs. For him, the word *good* has only one meaning: financial sufficiency. The moral implications which for Bassanio are primary do not count in Shylock's estimation of a man's worth. Later on in the play, it will become apparent that the word *mercy* has no meaning for him at all.

By comparison with Shylock, the Christians may at first sight appear wasteful and superficial. Bassanio makes no attempt to conceal the fact that he has squandered all his money on good living and now needs to repair his fortunes by way of a rich marriage. Although it matters that Portia is both beautiful and good, Bassanio takes himself to Belmont primarily because she is enormously wealthy, and he does not scruple to ask for yet another loan from his indulgent friend Antonio in order that he may shine there with rich gifts, liveried servants in attendance, and splendid clothes. Lorenzo loves Shylock's daughter Jessica, but also the jewels and ducats she has promised to steal from her father on the night of their elopement. Gratiano is an unabashedly worldly chatterbox and the conversation of those shadowy figures Salerio and Solanio hovers continually around the subject of wealth. Antonio's existence, apart from his irrational love of Bassanio, seems wholly bounded by his activities as a merchant. When it seems that he has lost both his friend to Portia and all his ships to Fortune he accepts the idea of death with the passivity of a man for whom life holds nothing else of interest.

Yet it would be wrong to see Shylock as the hero of *The Merchant of Venice* even in the special sense in which Barabas, for all his wickedness, is the hero of Marlowe's play. The Christians in Venice are far from perfect, but they are not hypocrites like their coreligionists of Malta and, despite their surface materialism and occasional failure to be kind, they do embody values which make Shylock's outlook seem limited and impoverished. Although usury was a relatively common financial practice in Elizabethan England, the medieval conviction that it was wrong to take interest remained emotionally powerful. For Shakespeare's audience, Antonio's policy of lending large sums of money gratis was something rapidly fading into the past, but they could respond nonetheless to the comedy's celebration of an attitude towards wealth still honored in principle if less and less frequently in practice. Shylock accumulates money for its own sake. In his hands it remains passive, inert and cold. The Christians, by contrast, transform barren metal into other and more interesting things: silks and spices, ships that venture across the world, and, at Belmont, into a way of life that is generous and vital. On each side, the ethic involved affects areas of life other than the financial.

Shylock's relations with other people are negative and suspicious—where they are not positively destructive. Both his servant Launcelot and his daughter Jessica describe his house as hell (II.ii.22–30, II.iii.2) and both flee from it to a more spacious existence. Characteristically, Shylock cannot see the human losses he has sustained apart from their economic consequences. The abrupt departure of Launcelot means, primarily, a welcome diminution in his household expenses and an equally welcome increase in those of the hated Bassanio. Speaking of Jessica's elopement, he constantly confuses the material with the personal loss, ducats with daughters, in a fashion more grotesque than pathetic. The happiest ending he can imagine for her story would be to see her "hears'd at my foot, and the ducats in her coffin" (III.i.89–90).

Among the Christians, ideas of wealth exist in a similarly close association with personal relations, but the effect is very different. Bassanio has been a spendthrift but this fault, Shakespeare suggests, is ultimately less crippling than Shylock's avarice. It is precisely because he does not fear the ominous inscription on the third casket—"Who chooseth me must give and hazard all he hath" (II.vii.16)—that Bassanio is able to win Portia. His original in *Il Pecorone* had won the lady by underhand means: one of her maids revealed to him the secret of the drugged wine which on two earlier attempts had caused him to fail the wooing test. Bassanio, by contrast, faces the riddle-game honestly. His choice of the leaden casket demonstrates that he does in fact love Portia for herself and not simply for her golden exterior. Failure to choose rightly would have condemned him to perpetual celibacy as well as to the loss of Portia and all his hopes. The risk, however, was shared. Behind Bassanio stands Antonio, the merchant who habitually entrusts his wealth to the hazard of sea-storms, rocks, and treacherous sands and who has now literally risked all he has, including his own life, to help his friend.

Most of Shakespeare's comedies involve, at some point, a journey to a place where life is heightened, of an extraordinary quality. Belmont is a locality of this kind. Portia's house lies in an indeterminate place reached across the sea, among trees and lawns and under an open sky. With its music and its riddle-game out of the past, its possession of the kind of limitless, inexplicable wealth proper to fairy-tale, it forms an obvious contrast with the crowded, urban world of Venice where money is a commodity to be counted and painfully earned. There is a sense, however, in which Belmont is really the better self of Venice: a world of clarity, order, and materialism transfigured, presided over by a lady in whom the virtues characteristic of the Christians in the comedy manifest themselves in their most complete and realized form. As generous as Antonio and as reflective, equally capable of self-sacrificing love, she has perceptions and energies, an emotional wholeness and range of response, which he lacks. It is only Portia, in her disguise as the young lawyer, who can rescue Venice from its dilemma. She does so by demonstrating the inadequacy of Shylock's attitudes to protect even the man who believes in them. Shylock will have nothing to do with the essentially Christian quality of generosity, as defined and urged by Portia in her speech on mercy. He insists upon the letter of the law, upon the kind of literal and narrow, essentially impersonal, interpretation of words characteristic of him throughout, and finds that Portia—when forced to do so—can easily turn this game against him. Her claim that Shylock's undeniable legal right to a pound of Antonio's living flesh does not entitle him to spill even a single drop of Antonio's blood, like her warning about the peril involved in the weighing, comes from a folk tradition. In Shakespeare's hands, however, it is no longer a device to be admired in itself. Portia's triumph is really an indication of the insufficiency and mechanical nature of Shylock's own values, of how unworthy they were of the trust he placed in them.

When Shylock stumbles from the court near the end of Act IV, stripped of almost everything, including his religion, it may seem as though *The Merchant of Venice* had reached its logical, if somewhat disquieting end. In terms of plot, the comedy is over. Of the two folk-tales upon which it was based, one has already come to its conclusion in Act III, with Bassanio's success in the riddle-game. Comedies usually end with marriages, but all three of the unions with which the play is concerned have been accomplished by that point: Portia and Bassanio, Nerissa and Gratiano, Jessica and Lorenzo. Act IV is concerned to conduct the other story, that of the savage creditor and the pound of flesh, to its preordained ending. Shylock himself does not reappear after the court scene, nor does Shakespeare make any attempt to smooth over the raggedness and pain of his final exit, to make it look more like a preliminary to any genuine accommodation of Shylock within the Venetian social order. Like the last act of *A Midsummer Night's Dream*, the fifth act of *The Merchant of Venice* takes place outside the normal limits of a comedy plot. The material for it is not articulated until Act IV, and it is material of an essentially thematic rather than a narrative kind.

The Merchant of Venice is a play about contrasted attitudes towards wealth and the life-styles dictated by each, but it is also a comedy which returns to that question of love and friendship and the rivalry between them which Shakespeare had first explored in *The Two Gentlemen of Verona*. There seems little point in trying to extract from the play any explicit statement that Antonio's love for Bassanio is homosexual in origin. What is clear is that Antonio's unexplained melancholy in the opening scene is somehow connected with Bassanio's recently expressed intention to seek a wife, although Antonio himself never says so directly, and although he himself is far too magnanimous to refuse to help Bassanio in his enterprise. Nevertheless, his letter sent to Belmont in Act III is emotional in ways that seem to reflect a response to the loss of Bassanio to Portia quite as much as his anxiety over what will become of him at the hands of Shylock. There is almost a sense that Antonio welcomes death as an incontrovertible proof that he has done something for Bassanio that Portia can never hope to rival, has elevated his love above hers. But he does not know Portia.

Bassanio does not tell Portia about Antonio until he has to: when Salerio arrives at Belmont with the news of their friend's deadly peril. Her response is immediate and predictable. Freely she offers Bassanio enough money to pay Antonio's debt twenty times over and dispatches him to Venice at once, postponing their wedding night: "For never shall you lie by Portia's side / With an unquiet soul" (III.ii.305–6). To Lorenzo, after Bassanio's departure, she explains her attitude towards Antonio:

in companions
That do converse and waste the time together,
Whose souls do bear an egall yoke of love,
There must be needs a like proportion
Of lineaments, of manners, and of spirit;
Which makes me think that this Antonio,
Being the bosom lover of my lord,

Must needs be like my lord. If it be so,
How little is the cost I have bestowed
In purchasing the semblance of my soul,
From out the state of hellish cruelty.
(III.iv.11–21)

This generosity, this willingness to accommodate Antonio within the newly formed husband and wife relationship, is not merely abstract. Disguised as a man of law and accompanied by Nerissa, she sets off secretly for Venice in order to make absolutely sure that Bassanio will not lose a friend as a consequence of gaining a wife.

Antonio owes his life to Portia. Bassanio could not have saved him. Yet both Bassanio and his friend say things in the course of the trial which Portia has every right to find alarming. Antonio's hidden jealousy of the "honorable wife" emerges when he bids Bassanio return to Belmont with the story of his sacrifice and death "and when the tale is told, bid her be judge / Whether Bassanio had not once a love" (IV.i.276–77). Bassanio, in his remorse, makes it clear that he values Antonio's life not only above his own, but also above that of his wife—a priority for which, as the pretended Balthazar remarks dryly, "your wife would give you little thanks" (IV.i.288). It is because she realizes that the situation must be clarified that she resorts to the ring trick: a test which forces Bassanio to weigh his obligations to his wife against those to his friend and to recognize the latent antagonism between them.

Bassanio, to do him credit, struggles hard to keep his promise to Portia and her ring. Significantly, it is Antonio who finally persuades him otherwise: "let him have the ring. / Let his deservings and my love withal / Be valued 'gainst your wive's commandement" (IV.i.449–51). Obedient to old loyalties, Bassanio yields. He is wrong to do so and, back in Belmont, Portia plagues him for it. The contretemps over the rings is funny—indeed, in the case of Gratiano and Nerissa it is little more than an excuse for some bawdy jokes—but Portia uses it for a serious purpose. In the end, Bassanio is forgiven. It was to Portia all the time, a Portia unknown to him in her man's disguise, that he gave away the ring of love. Looked at rightly, there was no betrayal at all. Yet Portia does not reveal the truth until she has brought Antonio to the point of confessing his responsibility for the quarrel, and of swearing, "My soul upon the forfeit, that your lord / Will never more break faith advisedly" (V.i.252–53). Only then does she relent, returning the ring to Bassanio through the hands of Antonio, who discovers that he has become the surety for Bassanio's faith, in a relationship which, although it does not cancel out friendship, relegates it nonetheless to a subordinate place. There is room for friendship within the house of love, but love holds the upper and controlling hand.

The hand, however, is Portia's and it is characteristically generous and full of gifts. At the same time that she gently but firmly excludes Antonio from priority of place in Bassanio's affections, she compensates him with the news that three of the ships he had given up for lost are miraculously, and richly, arrived in port. When Antonio thanks Portia he does so as if, in some mysterious way, she were the agent of his good fortune: "Sweet lady, you have given me life and living" (V.i.286). Whether this mercantile prosperity can fully compensate Antonio for the loss of Bassanio, for the fact that he must make his exit singly behind the three couples who, at the end of the scene, move off joyously to bed, the comedy does not attempt to judge. The solitude of Antonio at the end of Act V is without the tragic overtones of Shylock's last appearance but it suggests a link between the two arch-enemies after all: both are voices somehow missing in the final chord.

There are false notes in this chord, as well as some omissions. Even at Belmont, life is not perfect.

> If to do were as easy as to know what were good to do, chapels had been churches, and poor men's cottages princes' palaces. It is a good divine that follows his own instructions; I can easier teach twenty what were good to be done, than to be one of the twenty to follow mine own teaching. The brain may devise laws for the blood, but a hot temper leaps o'er a cold decree. (I.ii.12–19)

Portia's rueful assessment of human frailty is a just one. Generosity is the great principle by which the Christians try to live and yet, at Belmont, no one remembers or pities Shylock, not even Portia. During the trial itself, she seemed to forget her own eloquent celebration of mercy as soon as it came to sentencing her victim, and she does not spare him a thought now. Gratiano, the most thoughtless of the Christians, would increase Shylock's punishment if he could. His own relationship with Nerissa is a coarsened and trivialized version of the one that binds Portia and Bassanio. Lorenzo and Jessica let money slip through their hands like water, and then depend upon other people to take them in and put the situation right. Their love-duet in the night at the beginning of Act V is beautiful, but the myths they invoke are all, disturbingly, stories of infidelity and misunderstanding: Dido and Aeneas, Troilus and Cressida, Pyramus and Thisby, Medea and Jason. There is hope embodied in the new society which forms at Belmont at the end of *The Merchant of Venice*, but there is also a consciousness that while the music of the spheres, the flawless, immutable harmony of a world better than this, exists and may even be sensed on clear nights as an influence, it remains fundamentally inaudible:

Such harmony is in immortal souls,
But whilst this muddy vesture of decay
Doth grossly close it in, we cannot hear it.
(V.i.63–65)

Under circumstances like these, the best one can do is to accept and rejoice in the music of earth, transitory and imperfect though it is.

Anne Barton

The Merchant of Venice

[DRAMATIS PERSONAE

The DUKE OF VENICE
The PRINCE OF MOROCCO } *suitors to Portia*
The PRINCE OF ARRAGON }
ANTONIO, *a merchant of Venice*
BASSANIO, *his friend, suitor to Portia*
SOLANIO }
GRATIANO } *friends to Antonio and Bassanio*
SALERIO }
LORENZO, *in love with Jessica*
SHYLOCK, *a rich Jew*
TUBAL, *a Jew, his friend*

LAUNCELOT GOBBO, *a clown, servant to Shylock*
OLD GOBBO, *father to Launcelot*
LEONARDO, *servant to Bassanio*
BALTHAZAR } *servants to Portia*
STEPHANO }
PORTIA, *a rich heiress, of Belmont*
NERISSA, *her waiting-gentlewoman*
JESSICA, *daughter to Shylock*
MAGNIFICOES *of Venice*, OFFICERS *of the Court of Justice*, JAILER, SERVANTS *to Portia, and other* ATTENDANTS

SCENE: *Partly at Venice and partly at Belmont, the seat of Portia*]

[ACT I, SCENE I]

Enter ANTONIO, SALERIO, *and* SOLANIO.

Ant. In sooth, I know not why I am so sad;
It wearies me, you say it wearies you;
But how I caught it, found it, or came by it,
What stuff 'tis made of, whereof it is born,
I am to learn;
And such a want-wit sadness makes of me,
That I have much ado to know myself.
Sal. Your mind is tossing on the ocean,
There where your argosies with portly sail
Like signiors and rich burghers on the flood,
Or as it were the pageants of the sea,
Do overpeer the petty traffickers
That cur'sy to them, do them reverence,
As they fly by them with their woven wings.
Sol. Believe me, sir, had I such venture forth,
The better part of my affections would
Be with my hopes abroad. I should be still
Plucking the grass to know where sits the wind,
Piring in maps for ports and piers and roads;
And every object that might make me fear
Misfortune to my ventures, out of doubt
Would make me sad.
Sal. My wind cooling my broth
Would blow me to an ague when I thought
What harm a wind too great might do at sea.
I should not see the sandy hour-glass run
But I should think of shallows and of flats,
And see my wealthy *Andrew* [dock'd] in sand,
Vailing her high top lower than her ribs
To kiss her burial. Should I go to church
And see the holy edifice of stone,
And not bethink me straight of dangerous rocks,
Which touching but my gentle vessel's side
Would scatter all her spices on the stream,
Enrobe the roaring waters with my silks,
And in a word, but even now worth this,
And now worth nothing? Shall I have the thought
To think on this, and shall I lack the thought
That such a thing bechanc'd would make me sad?
But tell not me; I know Antonio
Is sad to think upon his merchandise.

Words and passages enclosed in square brackets in the text above are either emendations of the copy-text or additions to it. The Textual Notes immediately following the play cite the earliest authority for every such change or insertion and supply the reading of the copy-text wherever it is emended in this edition.

I.i. Location: Venice. A street.
1. **sooth:** truth. **sad:** melancholy.
5. **I . . . learn:** I have still to find out, i.e. I don't know.
9. **argosies:** large merchant ships. **portly:** stately.
10. **signiors:** gentlemen of substance.
11. **pageants:** high mobile stages used for the miracle plays and other entertainments, something like modern floats.
12. **overpeer:** tower over, look down upon.
13. **cur'sy:** curtsy, i.e. bob up and down on the waves. **do them reverence:** make obeisance to them.
15. **venture:** speculative commercial enterprise.
16. **affections:** thoughts and feelings. 17. **still:** constantly.
19. **Piring:** peering, prying. **roads:** roadsteads, anchorages.
21. **out of doubt:** undoubtedly. 26. **flats:** shoals.
27. **wealthy:** richly laden. **Andrew.** This was the name of one of two very large Spanish galleons captured by the English in the Cadiz expedition of 1596; news of the exploit created great excitement in England, and it is doubtless alluded to here.
28. **Vailing:** lowering. **high top:** topmast.
29. **kiss her burial:** do homage to her place of burial.
31. **bethink me straight:** be put in mind straightway.
32. **gentle:** noble. 35. **but even now:** i.e. just a moment ago.
38. **bechanc'd:** should it happen.

Ant. Believe me, no. I thank my fortune for it,
My ventures are not in one bottom trusted,
Nor to one place; nor is my whole estate
Upon the fortune of this present year:
Therefore my merchandise makes me not sad.
Sol. Why then you are in love.
Ant. Fie, fie!
Sol. Not in love neither? Then let us say you are sad
Because you are not merry; and 'twere as easy
For you to laugh and leap, and say you are merry
Because you are not sad. Now by two-headed Janus,
Nature hath fram'd strange fellows in her time:
Some that will evermore peep through their eyes,
And laugh like parrots at a bagpiper;
And other of such vinegar aspect
That they'll not show their teeth in way of smile
Though Nestor swear the jest be laughable.

Enter Bassanio, Lorenzo, *and* Gratiano.

Here comes Bassanio, your most noble kinsman,
Gratiano, and Lorenzo. Fare ye well,
We leave you now with better company.
Sal. I would have stay'd till I had made you merry,
If worthier friends had not prevented me.
Ant. Your worth is very dear in my regard.
I take it your own business calls on you,
And you embrace th' occasion to depart.
Sal. Good morrow, my good lords.
Bass. Good signiors both, when shall we laugh? say, when?
You grow exceeding strange. Must it be so?
Sal. We'll make our leisures to attend on yours.
Exeunt Salerio and Solanio.
Lor. My Lord Bassanio, since you have found Antonio,
We two will leave you, but at dinner-time
I pray you have in mind where we must meet.
Bass. I will not fail you.
Gra. You look not well, Signior Antonio,
You have too much respect upon the world.
They lose it that do buy it with much care.
Believe me you are marvellously chang'd.
Ant. I hold the world but as the world, Gratiano,
A stage, where every man must play a part,
And mine a sad one.
Gra. Let me play the fool,
With mirth and laughter let old wrinkles come,
And let my liver rather heat with wine

Than my heart cool with mortifying groans.
Why should a man, whose blood is warm within,
Sit like his grandsire cut in alablaster?
Sleep when he wakes? and creep into the jaundies
By being peevish? I tell thee what, Antonio—
I love thee, and 'tis my love that speaks—
There are a sort of men whose visages
Do cream and mantle like a standing pond,
And do a willful stillness entertain,
With purpose to be dress'd in an opinion
Of wisdom, gravity, profound conceit,
As who should say, "I am Sir Oracle,
And when I ope my lips let no dog bark!"
O my Antonio, I do know of these
That therefore only are reputed wise
For saying nothing; when I am very sure
If they should speak, would almost damn those ears
Which hearing them would call their brothers fools.
I'll tell thee more of this another time;
But fish not with this melancholy bait
For this fool gudgeon, this opinion.
Come, good Lorenzo. Fare ye well a while,
I'll end my exhortation after dinner.
Lor. Well, we will leave you then till dinner-time.
I must be one of these same dumb wise men,
For Gratiano never lets me speak.
Gra. Well, keep me company but two years moe,
Thou shalt not know the sound of thine own tongue.
Ant. Fare you well! I'll grow a talker for this gear.
Gra. Thanks, i' faith, for silence is only commendable
In a neat's tongue dried and a maid not vendible.
Exeunt [Gratiano and Lorenzo].
Ant. It is that—any thing now!
Bass. Gratiano speaks an infinite deal of nothing, more than any man in all Venice. His reasons are as two grains of wheat hid in two bushels of chaff; you shall seek all day ere you find them, and when you have them, they are not worth the search.
Ant. Well, tell me now what lady is the same
To whom you swore a secret pilgrimage,
That you to-day promis'd to tell me of?
Bass. 'Tis not unknown to you, Antonio,
How much I have disabled mine estate,

42. bottom: ship. **44. fortune**: chance.
50. Janus: Roman god represented with two faces looking in opposite directions.
52. peep . . . eyes: i.e. look out through eyes half closed by laughter. Cf. line 80.
53. like parrots: i.e. raucously. **bagpiper**. Bagpipe music was regarded as melancholy.
56. Nestor: the oldest and gravest of the Greek heroes at Troy.
61. prevented: forestalled.
64. embrace th' occasion: take advantage of the opportunity.
66. when . . . laugh: i.e. when shall we next have a merry time together.
67. strange: like strangers, i.e. reserved, distant.
74. respect . . . world: concern for business affairs.
80. old: typical of old age (?) or plentiful (as in IV.ii.15) (?).
81. liver. Regarded as the seat of the emotions.
82. mortifying: killing. Groans and sighs were thought to draw blood from the heart.
84. alablaster: alabaster. Stone effigies were common on tombs in churches.
85. jaundies: jaundice (thought to be caused by an excess of one of the humors, choler or yellow bile, as melancholy was by an excess of black bile).
89. cream and mantle: i.e. acquire a set expression (literally, grow a scum). **standing**: stagnant.
90. willful stillness: self-imposed and persistent silence. **entertain**: maintain. **91. opinion**: reputation. **92. conceit**: thought.
95. of these: some men. **96. therefore**: therefor, for that reason.
98–99. would . . . fools: would speak such nonsense that those who heard them would immediately call them fools and so risk damnation. The allusion is to Matthew 5:22: "And whosoever saith unto his brother, . . . Fool, shall be worthy to be punished with hell fire" (Geneva). **101. melancholy bait**: bait of melancholy.
102. gudgeon: a small fish easily caught.
104. exhortation: sermon. **108. keep**: if you keep. **moe**: more.
110. for this gear: as a consequence of all this talk of yours.
112. neat's: ox's. **vendible**: salable, i.e. marriageable.
113. It . . . now: i.e. it is as you say—or indeed whatever you care to make it. **115. reasons**: reasonable statements, sensible ideas.

By something showing a more swelling port
Than my faint means would grant continuance.
Nor do I now make moan to be abridg'd
From such a noble rate, but my chief care
Is to come fairly off from the great debts
Wherein my time something too prodigal
Hath left me gag'd. To you, Antonio,
I owe the most in money and in love,
And from your love I have a warranty
To unburthen all my plots and purposes
How to get clear of all the debts I owe.

Ant. I pray you, good Bassanio, let me know it,
And if it stand, as you yourself still do,
Within the eye of honor, be assur'd
My purse, my person, my extremest means,
Lie all unlock'd to your occasions.

Bass. In my school-days, when I had lost one shaft,
I shot his fellow of the self-same flight
The self-same way with more advised watch
To find the other forth, and by adventuring both
I oft found both. I urge this childhood proof,
Because what follows is pure innocence.
I owe you much, and like a willful youth,
That which I owe is lost, but if you please
To shoot another arrow that self way
Which you did shoot the first, I do not doubt,
As I will watch the aim, or to find both
Or bring your latter hazard back again,
And thankfully rest debtor for the first.

Ant. You know me well, and herein spend but time
To wind about my love with circumstance,
And out of doubt you do me now more wrong
In making question of my uttermost
Than if you had made waste of all I have.
Then do but say to me what I should do
That in your knowledge may by me be done,
And I am prest unto it; therefore speak.

Bass. In Belmont is a lady richly left,
And she is fair and, fairer than that word,
Of wondrous virtues. Sometimes from her eyes
I did receive fair speechless messages.
Her name is Portia, nothing undervalu'd
To Cato's daughter, Brutus' Portia.
Nor is the wide world ignorant of her worth,
For the four winds blow in from every coast
Renowned suitors, and her sunny locks
Hang on her temples like a golden fleece,
Which makes her seat of Belmont Colchis' strond,
And many Jasons come in quest of her.
O my Antonio, had I but the means
To hold a rival place with one of them,
I have a mind presages me such thrift
That I should questionless be fortunate!

Ant. Thou know'st that all my fortunes are at sea,
Neither have I money nor commodity
To raise a present sum; therefore go forth,
Try what my credit can in Venice do.
That shall be rack'd, even to the uttermost,
To furnish thee to Belmont, to fair Portia.
Go presently inquire, and so will I,
Where money is, and I no question make
To have it of my trust, or for my sake. *Exeunt.*

[Scene II]

Enter Portia *with her waiting-woman,* Nerissa.

Por. By my troth, Nerissa, my little body is a-weary of this great world.

Ner. You would be, sweet madam, if your miseries were in the same abundance as your good fortunes are; and yet for aught I see, they are as sick that surfeit with too much as they that starve with nothing. It is no mean happiness therefore to be seated in the mean: superfluity comes sooner by white hairs, but competency lives longer.

Por. Good sentences, and well pronounc'd.

Ner. They would be better if well follow'd.

Por. If to do were as easy as to know what were good to do, chapels had been churches, and poor men's cottages princes' palaces. It is a good divine that follows his own instructions; I can easier teach twenty what were good to be done, than to be one of the twenty to follow mine own teaching. The brain may devise laws for the blood, but a hot temper leaps o'er a cold decree—such a hare is madness the youth, to skip o'er the meshes of good counsel the cripple. But this reasoning is not in the fashion to choose me a husband. O me, the word choose! I may neither choose who I would, nor refuse who I dislike; so is the will of a living daughter curb'd by the will of a dead father. Is it not hard, Nerissa, that I cannot choose one, nor refuse none?

Ner. Your father was ever virtuous, and holy

124. something: somewhat (modifies *more*). Another example of this common adverbial use occurs in line 129. **swelling port:** splendid style of living. **126. to be abridg'd:** at being reduced.
127. rate: manner of living.
128. fairly: fitly, honorably; or perhaps completely (cf. line 134).
129. time: youth. **130. gag'd:** pledged.
133. unburthen: variant form of *unburden*. **136. still:** always.
137. eye: sight, view. **139. occasions:** needs.
141. his: its. **flight:** range. **142. advised:** careful, deliberate.
143. forth: out.
144. urge: put forward, bring up. **proof:** experience.
145. innocence: childish folly (?) or childlike sincerity (?).
146. like . . . youth: i.e. because I have behaved recklessly, as youth does. **148. self:** same. **150. or:** either.
151. latter hazard: second risk. **153. spend but:** only waste.
154. circumstance: elaborate reasoning.
156. making question of: questioning whether I will do.
160. prest unto: ready for.
162. fairer . . . word: what is better still. **163. Sometimes:** formerly.
165. nothing undervalu'd: in no way inferior.

171. Colchis: the country, at the eastern end of the Black Sea, where Jason won the Golden Fleece. **strond:** strand, shore.
175. thrift: thriving, success. **176. questionless:** undoubtedly.
178. commodity: merchandise. **181 rack'd:** stretched.
183. presently: immediately.
184–85. no . . . To: have no doubt that I shall.
185. of . . . sake: on my credit as a businessman, or as a friendly loan.

I.ii. Location: Belmont. Portia's house.
8. in the mean: between the extremes of too little and too much. **comes sooner by:** sooner gets. **9. competency:** moderate means.
10. sentences: maxims. **14. divine:** clergyman.
15. follows . . . instructions: practices what he preaches.
18. for the blood: to control passion.
18–19. hot temper: impetuous temperament.
20. meshes: nets, snares.
20–21. good . . . cripple: wisdom the old man incapable of action.
21–22. this . . . me: this line of reasoning is not of a kind to help me in choosing. **24–25. will . . . will:** desire . . . testament.

men at their death have good inspirations; therefore the lott'ry that he hath devis'd in these three chests of gold, silver, and lead, whereof who chooses his meaning chooses you, will no doubt never be chosen by any rightly but one who you shall rightly love. But what warmth is there in your affection towards any of these princely suitors that are already come?

Por. I pray thee over-name them, and as thou namest them, I will describe them; and according to my description level at my affection.

Ner. First, there is the Neapolitan prince.

Por. Ay, that's a colt indeed, for he doth nothing but talk of his horse, and he makes it a great appropriation to his own good parts that he can shoe him himself. I am much afeard my lady his mother play'd false with a smith.

Ner. Then is there the County Palentine.

Por. He doth nothing but frown, as who should say, "And you will not have me, choose." He hears merry tales and smiles not. I fear he will prove the weeping philosopher when he grows old, being so full of unmannerly sadness in his youth. I had rather be married to a death's-head with a bone in his mouth than to either of these. God defend me from these two!

Ner. How say you by the French lord, Monsieur Le [Bon]?

Por. God made him, and therefore let him pass for a man. In truth, I know it is a sin to be a mocker, but he! why, he hath a horse better than the Neapolitan's, a better bad habit of frowning than the Count Palentine; he is every man in no man. If a throstle sing, he falls straight a-cap'ring. He will fence with his own shadow. If I should marry him, I should marry twenty husbands. If he would despise me, I would forgive him, for if he love me to madness, I shall never requite him.

Ner. What say you then to Falconbridge, the young baron of England?

Por. You know I say nothing to him, for he understands not me, nor I him. He hath neither Latin, French, nor Italian, and you will come into the court and swear that I have a poor pennyworth in the English. He is a proper man's picture, but alas, who can converse with a dumb show? How oddly he is suited! I think he bought his doublet in Italy, his round hose in France, his bonnet in Germany, and his behavior every where.

30. whereof: among which chests.
31. chooses his meaning: i.e. guesses your father's intention correctly.
36. over-name them: name them over. With lines 36 ff. compare *The Two Gentlemen of Verona*, I.ii.7 ff. **38. level:** guess.
40. colt: i.e. young, inexperienced creature. The Neapolitans in Shakespeare's day were famous for horsemanship.
41–42. appropriation: addition. **42. good parts:** accomplishments.
45. County Palentine: Count Palatine.
47. And: if. **choose:** i.e. do what you please.
49. weeping philosopher: Heraclitus.
51–52. death's-head . . . mouth. Probably referring to the skull and cross-bones frequently cut on tombstones. **54. by:** concerning.
60. throstle: thrush. **72. is . . . picture:** is handsome in appearance.
74. suited: apparelled. **doublet:** coat, upper garment.
75. round hose: short breeches. **bonnet:** soft, cap-like hat. The satire in this passage on the international character of an English gallant's costume was a commonplace at this time.

Ner. What think you of the Scottish lord, his neighbor?

Por. That he hath a neighborly charity in him, for he borrow'd a box of the ear of the Englishman, and swore he would pay him again when he was able. I think the Frenchman became his surety and seal'd under for another.

Ner. How like you the young German, the Duke of Saxony's nephew?

Por. Very vildly in the morning, when he is sober, and most vildly in the afternoon, when he is drunk. When he is best, he is a little worse than a man, and when he is worst, he is little better than a beast. And the worst fall that ever fell, I hope I shall make shift to go without him.

Ner. If he should offer to choose, and choose the right casket, you should refuse to perform your father's will, if you should refuse to accept him.

Por. Therefore for fear of the worst, I pray thee set a deep glass of Rhenish wine on the contrary casket, for if the devil be within, and that temptation without, I know he will choose it. I will do any thing, Nerissa, ere I will be married to a spunge.

Ner. You need not fear, lady, the having any of these lords. They have acquainted me with their determinations, which is indeed to return to their home, and to trouble you with no more suit, unless you may be won by some other sort than your father's imposition depending on the caskets.

Por. If I live to be as old as Sibylla, I will die as chaste as Diana, unless I be obtain'd by the manner of my father's will. I am glad this parcel of wooers are so reasonable, for there is not one among them but I dote on his very absence, and I pray God grant them a fair departure.

Ner. Do you not remember, lady, in your father's time, a Venetian, a scholar and a soldier, that came hither in company of the Marquis of Montferrat?

Por. Yes, yes, it was Bassanio—as I think, so was he call'd.

Ner. True, madam; he, of all the men that ever my foolish eyes look'd upon, was the best deserving a fair lady.

Por. I remember him well, and I remember him worthy of thy praise.

Enter a SERVINGMAN.

How now, what news?

Serv. The four strangers seek for you, madam, to take their leave; and there is a forerunner come from a fift, the Prince of Morocco, who brings word the Prince his master will be here to-night.

82–83. became . . . another: guaranteed the Scot's payment and pledged himself to pay the Englishman with another blow (an allusion to French promises to back the Scots in their quarrels with the English). **86. vildly:** vilely. **89. And:** if.
90. fall . . . fell: befall . . . befell. **make shift:** contrive.
96. contrary: wrong. **99. spunge:** sponge.
104. sort: manner, way.
105. imposition: conditions (if they fail to choose the right casket); see II.i.38–42.
106. Sibylla: the Cumaean Sibyl. Apollo promised her that her years would equal the number of grains of sand she held in her hand.
123. four. Nerissa has named six. **strangers:** foreigners.
125. fift: fifth.

Por. If I could bid the fift welcome with so good heart as I can bid the other four farewell, I should be glad of his approach. If he have the condition of a saint, and the complexion of a devil, I had rather he should shrive me than wive me.
Come, Nerissa. Sirrah, go before.
Whiles we shut the gate upon one wooer, another knocks at the door. *Exeunt.*

[Scene III]

Enter Bassanio *with* Shylock *the Jew.*

Shy. Three thousand ducats, well.

Bass. Ay, sir, for three months.

Shy. For three months, well.

Bass. For the which, as I told you, Antonio shall be bound.

Shy. Antonio shall become bound, well.

Bass. May you stead me? Will you pleasure me? Shall I know your answer?

Shy. Three thousand ducats for three months, and Antonio bound.

Bass. Your answer to that.

Shy. Antonio is a good man.

Bass. Have you heard any imputation to the contrary?

Shy. Ho, no, no, no, no! my meaning in saying he is a good man is to have you understand me that he is sufficient. Yet his means are in supposition: he hath an argosy bound to Tripolis, another to the Indies; I understand moreover upon the Rialto, he hath a third at Mexico, a fourth for England, and other ventures he hath, squand'red abroad. But ships are but boards, sailors but men; there be land-rats and water-rats, water-thieves and land-thieves, I mean pirates, and then there is the peril of waters, winds, and rocks. The man is notwithstanding sufficient. Three thousand ducats: I think I may take his bond.

Bass. Be assur'd you may.

Shy. I will be assur'd I may; and that I may be assur'd, I will bethink me. May I speak with Antonio?

Bass. If it please you to dine with us.

Shy. Yes, to smell pork, to eat of the habitation which your prophet the Nazarite conjur'd the devil into. I will buy with you, sell with you, talk with you, walk with you, and so following; but I will not eat with you, drink with you, nor pray with you. What news on the Rialto? Who is he comes here?

Enter Antonio.

Bass. This is Signior Antonio.

Shy. [*Aside.*] How like a fawning publican he looks!
I hate him for he is a Christian;
But more, for that in low simplicity
He lends out money gratis, and brings down
The rate of usance here with us in Venice.
If I can catch him once upon the hip,
I will feed fat the ancient grudge I bear him.
He hates our sacred nation, and he rails
Even there where merchants most do congregate
On me, my bargains, and my well-won thrift,
Which he calls interest. Cursed be my tribe
If I forgive him!

Bass. Shylock, do you hear?

Shy. I am debating of my present store,
And by the near guess of my memory,
I cannot instantly raise up the gross
Of full three thousand ducats. What of that?
Tubal, a wealthy Hebrew of my tribe,
Will furnish me. But soft, how many months
Do you desire? [*To Antonio.*] Rest you fair, good signior,
Your worship was the last man in our mouths.

Ant. Shylock, albeit I neither lend nor borrow
By taking nor by giving of excess,
Yet to supply the ripe wants of my friend,
I'll break a custom. [*To Bassanio.*] Is he yet possess'd
How much ye would?

Shy. Ay, ay, three thousand ducats.

Ant. And for three months.

Shy. I had forgot—three months—[*to Bassanio*] you told me so.
Well then, your bond; and let me see—but hear you,
Methoughts you said you neither lend nor borrow
Upon advantage.

Ant. I do never use it.

Shy. When Jacob graz'd his uncle Laban's sheep—
This Jacob from our holy Abram was
(As his wise mother wrought in his behalf)

129. condition: disposition.
130. complexion . . . devil. Devils were always represented as black in Shakespeare's day.
131. shrive me: hear my confession and grant me absolution.
132. Sirrah: form of address used to inferiors.

I.iii. Location: Venice. A public place.
1. ducats: in this play, gold coins (there were also silver ducats); their value has been variously estimated, usually at something between a quarter and a half of an English pound apiece.
7. stead: assist, supply.
17. in supposition: i.e. not certainly in existence.
19. Rialto: commercial and business exchange of Venice.
21. squand'red: unwisely scattered.
29. assur'd: sure, satisfied (but Shylock takes it up in the sense "guaranteed by adequate security").
33–38. Yes . . . you. Perhaps these lines are spoken aside while Shylock "bethinks him" (see line 30).
34. Nazarite: Nazarene. *Nazarite* is the form used in both the Geneva and Bishops' versions (in Matthew 2:23). The allusion here is to Jesus' casting devils into a herd of swine (see Mark 5:1–13).
41. fawning publican. A controversial passage. Presumably Shylock regards Antonio as one who, like a publican (a tax collector for the Romans), deprives him of his rightful profits, but who now (like the publican in Luke 18:10–14 who prayed for mercy) assumes an ingratiating demeanor because he is asking a favor.
42. for: because.
43. low simplicity. Both words have good and bad meanings: *low* = (1) humble, (2) base; *simplicity* = (1) honest plainness (the opposite of duplicity), (2) folly. Shylock may be speaking straightforwardly or ironically. **45. usance:** usury.
46. upon the hip: at a disadvantage (a wrestling term).
50. thrift: thriving, profit (so also at line 90).
55. gross: total amount. **62. excess:** interest.
63. ripe: immediate. **64. possess'd:** informed.
69. Methoughts: it seemed to me (a variant of *methought*).
70. advantage: interest. **use it:** make it my practice.
71. Jacob. See Genesis 27, 30:25–43.

The third possessor; ay, he was the third—
Ant. And what of him? did he take interest?
Shy. No, not take interest, not as you would say
Directly int'rest. Mark what Jacob did:
When Laban and himself were compremis'd
That all the eanlings which were streak'd and pied
Should fall as Jacob's hire, the ewes being rank
In end of autumn turned to the rams,
And when the work of generation was
Between these woolly breeders in the act,
The skillful shepherd pill'd me certain wands,
And in the doing of the deed of kind,
He stuck them up before the fulsome ewes,
Who then conceiving did in eaning time
Fall parti-color'd lambs, and those were Jacob's.
This was a way to thrive, and he was blest;
And thrift is blessing, if men steal it not.
Ant. This was a venture, sir, that Jacob serv'd for,
A thing not in his power to bring to pass,
But sway'd and fashion'd by the hand of heaven.
Was this inserted to make interest good?
Or is your gold and silver ewes and rams?
Shy. I cannot tell, I make it breed as fast.
But note me, signior.
Ant. Mark you this, Bassanio,
The devil can cite Scripture for his purpose.
An evil soul producing holy witness
Is like a villain with a smiling cheek,
A goodly apple rotten at the heart.
O, what a goodly outside falsehood hath!
Shy. Three thousand ducats—'tis a good round sum.
Three months from twelve; then let me see, the rate—
Ant. Well, Shylock, shall we be beholding to you?
Shy. Signior Antonio, many a time and oft
In the Rialto you have rated me
About my moneys and my usances.
Still have I borne it with a patient shrug
(For suff'rance is the badge of all our tribe).
You call me misbeliever, cut-throat dog,
And spet upon my Jewish gaberdine,
And all for use of that which is mine own.
Well then, it now appears you need my help.
Go to then, you come to me, and you say,
"Shylock, we would have moneys," you say so—
You, that did void your rheum upon my beard,
And foot me as you spurn a stranger cur
Over your threshold; moneys is your suit.
What should I say to you? Should I not say,
"Hath a dog money? Is it possible
A cur can lend three thousand ducats?" Or
Shall I bend low and in a bondman's key,
With bated breath and whisp'ring humbleness,
Say this:
"Fair sir, you spet on me on Wednesday last,
You spurn'd me such a day, another time
You call'd me dog; and for these courtesies
I'll lend you thus much moneys"?
Ant. I am as like to call thee so again,
To spet on thee again, to spurn thee too.
If thou wilt lend this money, lend it not
As to thy friends, for when did friendship take
A breed for barren metal of his friend?
But lend it rather to thine enemy,
Who if he break, thou mayst with better face
Exact the penalty.
Shy. Why, look you how you storm!
I would be friends with you, and have your love,
Forget the shames that you have stain'd me with,
Supply your present wants, and take no doit
Of usance for my moneys, and you'll not hear me.
This is kind I offer.
Bass. This were kindness.
Shy. This kindness will I show.
Go with me to a notary, seal me there
Your single bond; and in a merry sport
If you repay me not on such a day,
In such a place, such sum or sums as are
Express'd in the condition, let the forfeit
Be nominated for an equal pound
Of your fair flesh, to be cut off and taken
In what part of your body pleaseth me.
Ant. Content, in faith, I'll seal to such a bond,
And say there is much kindness in the Jew.
Bass. You shall not seal to such a bond for me,
I'll rather dwell in my necessity.
Ant. Why, fear not, man, I will not forfeit it.
Within these two months, that's a month before
This bond expires, I do expect return
Of thrice three times the value of this bond.
Shy. O father Abram, what these Christians are,
Whose own hard dealings teaches them suspect
The thoughts of others! Pray you tell me this:
If he should break his day, what should I gain
By the exaction of the forfeiture?
A pound of man's flesh taken from a man
Is not so estimable, profitable neither,
As flesh of muttons, beefs, or goats. I say,
To buy his favor, I extend this friendship.
If he will take it, so, if not, adieu;

78. compremis'd: agreed (a variant form of *compromised*).
79. eanlings: new-born lambs. **pied:** variegated in color (cf. *parti-color'd* in line 88). **80. hire:** wages. **rank:** in heat.
84. pill'd: peeled. **me.** The so-called ethical dative; a colloquialism.
85. kind: nature. **87. eaning:** lambing.
88. Fall: let fall, give birth to.
91. venture . . . for: commercial enterprise with an unpredictable outcome on which Jacob risked his time as a servant.
94. inserted: put into the Bible (?) or injected into the discussion (?). **make interest good:** justify taking interest.
97–102. Mark . . . hath. Perhaps another aside.
105. beholding: beholden, indebted. **107. rated:** reviled.
110. badge: distinctive mark.
112. spet: spit. (The same form could be the past tense; see line 126.) **gaberdine:** a loose upper garment of coarse material.
113. use. With play on "usury."
115. Go to: term of remonstrance. **117. rheum:** spittle.
118. spurn: kick.
134. A breed: offspring, increase (cf. line 96). The figure continues in *barren*. One of the oldest arguments against taking interest was that it is against nature for money to breed money.
136. break: go bankrupt. **140. doit:** coin of trifling value.
143. were kindness: would be kindness (if the offer were seriously meant).
145. single bond: bond signed only by the debtor, without sureties.
149. nominated for: stipulated as. **equal:** exact.
155. dwell: remain.
163. break his day: fail to pay on the due date.
164. forfeiture: forfeit, amount stipulated as penalty.

And for my love I pray you wrong me not.
Ant. Yes, Shylock, I will seal unto this bond.
Shy. Then meet me forthwith at the notary's;
Give him direction for this merry bond,
And I will go and purse the ducats straight,
See to my house, left in the fearful guard
Of an unthrifty knave, and presently
I'll be with you. *Exit.*
Ant. Hie thee, gentle Jew.
The Hebrew will turn Christian, he grows kind.
Bass. I like not fair terms and a villain's mind.
Ant. Come on, in this there can be no dismay,
My ships come home a month before the day.
Exeunt.

[ACT II, SCENE I]

[Flourish cornets.] Enter [the PRINCE OF*]* MOROCCO, *a tawny Moor, all in white, and three or four* FOLLOWERS *accordingly, with* PORTIA, NERISSA, *and their* TRAIN.

Mor. Mislike me not for my complexion,
The shadowed livery of the burnish'd sun,
To whom I am a neighbor and near bred.
Bring me the fairest creature northward born,
Where Phoebus' fire scarce thaws the icicles,
And let us make incision for your love,
To prove whose blood is reddest, his or mine.
I tell thee, lady, this aspect of mine
Hath fear'd the valiant; by my love, I swear
The best-regarded virgins of our clime
Have lov'd it too. I would not change this hue,
Except to steal your thoughts, my gentle queen.
Por. In terms of choice I am not soly led
By nice direction of a maiden's eyes;
Besides, the lott'ry of my destiny
Bars me the right of voluntary choosing.
But if my father had not scanted me,
And hedg'd me by his wit to yield myself
His wife who wins me by that means I told you,
Yourself, renowned Prince, then stood as fair
As any comer I have look'd on yet
For my affection.
Mor. Even for that I thank you;
Therefore I pray you lead me to the caskets
To try my fortune. By this scimitar
That slew the Sophy and a Persian prince

170. **wrong me not:** do not impute evil motives to me.
175. **fearful:** arousing anxiety, i.e. untrustworthy.
177. **Hie thee:** hasten.

II.i. Location: Belmont. Portia's house.
o.s.d. **Flourish:** sound a fanfare. **cornets:** horns (not the modern brass instrument). **accordingly:** in accord, i.e. dark-skinned and dressed in white like Morocco.
2. **shadowed . . . sun:** dark distinctive dress worn by the sun's retainers, i.e. black skin. 3. **near bred:** closely related.
5. **Phoebus:** the sun-god.
7. **whose . . . reddest:** i.e. who is most courageous.
8. **aspect:** visage. 9. **fear'd:** frightened.
12. **steal your thoughts:** gain possession of your thoughts (so that they would become more favorable to me).
13. **terms:** respect. **soly:** solely. 14. **nice:** fastidious.
15. **lott'ry . . . destiny:** game of chance on which my fate depends.
17. **scanted:** restricted. 18. **wit:** wisdom.
25. **Sophy:** Shah of Persia.

That won three fields of Sultan Solyman,
I would o'erstare the sternest eyes that look,
Outbrave the heart most daring on the earth,
Pluck the young sucking cubs from the she-bear,
Yea, mock the lion when 'a roars for prey,
To win [thee], lady. But alas the while!
If Hercules and Lichas play at dice
Which is the better man, the greater throw
May turn by fortune from the weaker hand:
So is Alcides beaten by his [page],
And so may I, blind fortune leading me,
Miss that which one unworthier may attain,
And die with grieving.
Por. You must take your chance,
And either not attempt to choose at all,
Or swear before you choose, if you choose wrong
Never to speak to lady afterward
In way of marriage; therefore be advis'd.
Mor. Nor will not. Come bring me unto my chance.
Por. First, forward to the temple; after dinner
Your hazard shall be made.
Mor. Good fortune then!
To make me blest or cursed'st among men.
[Cornets.] Exeunt.

[SCENE II]

Enter the Clown [LAUNCELOT GOBBO] *alone.*

Laun. Certainly my conscience will serve me to run from this Jew my master. The fiend is at mine elbow and tempts me, saying to me, "[Gobbo], Launcelot [Gobbo], good Launcelot," or "good [Gobbo]," or "good Launcelot [Gobbo], use your legs, take the start, run away." My conscience says, "No; take heed, honest Launcelot, take heed, honest [Gobbo]," or as aforesaid, "honest Launcelot [Gobbo], do not run, scorn running with thy heels." Well, the most courageous fiend bids me pack. "*Fia!*" says the fiend; "away!" says the fiend; "for the heavens, rouse up a brave mind," says the fiend, "and run." Well, my conscience, hanging about the neck of my heart, says very wisely to me, "My honest friend Launcelot, being an honest man's son"—or rather an honest woman's son, for indeed my father did something smack, something grow to, he had a kind of taste—well, my conscience says, "Launcelot, bouge not." "Bouge," says

26. **fields:** battles. **Solyman:** Suleiman II, the Magnificent (1496?–1566). 27. **o'erstare:** outstare. 30. **'a:** he.
32. **Lichas:** the servant of Hercules (Alcides).
32–33. **play . . . Which:** throw dice to decide which.
42. **be advis'd:** take careful thought.
43. **will not:** i.e. will not violate the condition.
44. **to the temple:** i.e. to take the oath.
46. **blest or cursed'st:** most blessed or most cursed (the superlative ending affects both adjectives).

II.ii. Location: Venice. A street.
1. **serve:** allow, encourage.
9. **with thy heels:** indignantly (with obvious pun).
10. **pack:** begone. 11. **Fia:** away (properly *via*).
12. **for the heavens:** in heaven's name (with special effect in the devil's mouth).
17–18. **smack . . . taste:** i.e. his father is given to lechery.
19. **bouge:** budge.

the fiend. "Bouge not," says my conscience. "Conscience," say I, "you counsel well." "Fiend," say I, "you counsel well." To be rul'd by my conscience, I should stay with the Jew my master, who (God bless the mark) is a kind of devil; and to run away from the Jew, I should be rul'd by the fiend, who, saving your reverence, is the devil himself. Certainly the Jew is the very devil incarnation, and in my conscience, my conscience is but a kind of hard conscience, to offer to counsel me to stay with the Jew. The fiend gives the more friendly counsel: I will run, fiend; my heels are at your commandement, I will run.

Enter OLD GOBBO *with a basket.*

Gob. Master young man, you, I pray you, which is the way to Master Jew's?

Laun. [*Aside.*] O heavens, this is my true-begotten father, who being more than sand-blind, high gravel-blind, knows me not. I will try confusions with him.

Gob. Master young gentleman, I pray you, which is the way to Master Jew's?

Laun. Turn up on your right hand at the next turning, but at the next turning of all, on your left; marry, at the very next turning, turn of no hand, but turn down indirectly to the Jew's house.

Gob. Be God's sonties, 'twill be a hard way to hit. Can you tell me whether one Launcelot, that dwells with him, dwell with him or no?

Laun. Talk you of young Master Launcelot? [*Aside.*] Mark me now, now will I raise the waters. —Talk you of young Master Launcelot?

Gob. No master, sir, but a poor man's son. His father, though I say't, is an honest exceeding poor man and, God be thank'd, well to live.

Laun. Well, let his father be what 'a will, we talk of young Master Launcelot.

Gob. Your worship's friend and Launcelot, sir.

Laun. But I pray you, *ergo*, old man, *ergo*, I beseech you, talk you of young Master Launcelot.

Gob. Of Launcelot, an't please your mastership.

Laun. *Ergo*, Master Launcelot. Talk not of Master Launcelot, father, for the young gentleman, according to Fates and Destinies, and such odd sayings, the Sisters Three, and such branches of learning, is indeed deceas'd, or as you would say in plain terms, gone to heaven.

Gob. Marry, God forbid, the boy was the very staff of my age, my very prop.

Laun. [*Aside.*] Do I look like a cudgel or a hovel-post, a staff, or a prop?—Do you know me, father?

Gob. Alack the day, I know you not, young gentleman, but I pray you tell me, is my boy, God rest his soul, alive or dead?

Laun. Do you not know me, father?

Gob. Alack, sir, I am sand-blind, I know you not.

Laun. Nay, indeed if you had your eyes you might fail of the knowing me; it is a wise father that knows his own child. Well, old man, I will tell you news of your son. Give me your blessing; truth will come to light; murder cannot be hid long; a man's son may, but in the end truth will out.

Gob. Pray you, sir, stand up. I am sure you are not Launcelot, my boy.

Laun. Pray you let's have no more fooling about it, but give me your blessing. I am Launcelot, your boy that was, your son that is, your child that shall be.

Gob. I cannot think you are my son.

Laun. I know not what I shall think of that; but I am Launcelot, the Jew's man, and I am sure Margery your wife is my mother.

Gob. Her name is Margery indeed. I'll be sworn, if thou be Launcelot, thou art mine own flesh and blood. Lord worshipp'd might he be, what a beard hast thou got! Thou hast got more hair on thy chin than Dobbin my fill-horse has on his tail.

Laun. It should seem then that Dobbin's tail grows backward. I am sure he had more hair of his tail than I have of my face when I [last] saw him.

Gob. Lord, how art thou chang'd! How dost thou and thy master agree? I have brought him a present. How 'gree you now?

Laun. Well, well; but for mine own part, as I have set up my rest to run away, so I will not rest till I have run some ground. My master's a very Jew. Give him a present! give him a halter. I am famish'd in his service; you may tell every finger I have with my ribs. Father, I am glad you are come; give me your present to one Master Bassanio, who indeed gives rare new liveries. If I serve not him, I will run as far as God has any ground. O rare fortune, here comes the man. To him, father, for I am a Jew if I serve the Jew any longer.

Enter BASSANIO *with a follower or two,* [*one of them* LEONARDO].

24. **God . . . mark.** This expression, originally used to avert ill omen, was also employed, like *saving your reverence* (line 26), as a conventional apology before an offensive expression.
27–28. **incarnation:** blunder for *incarnate*. 28. **in:** by.
36. **sand-blind:** partly blind. **high:** i.e. fully (an intensive).
37. **gravel-blind.** Launcelot's coinage for the degree of poor vision between sand-blind and stone-blind. **try confusions.** Launcelot's adaptation of *try conclusions* = make experiments.
43. **marry:** indeed (originally the name of the Virgin Mary used as an oath). 45. **Be:** by. **sonties:** little saints (?).
49. **raise the waters:** stir things up (?) or induce tears (?).
53. **well to live:** with a good livelihood (a contradiction of his preceding remark; perhaps Gobbo supposes that the phrase means "in good health").
56. **Your . . . Launcelot.** Another disclaimer of the title "Master" for Launcelot. 57. **ergo:** therefore. 59. **an:** if.
61. **father:** common form of address to an old person; hence it does not reveal to Gobbo that Launcelot is his son.
63. **Sisters Three:** the Fates.

68–69. **hovel-post:** post supporting a shed.
76–77. **it . . . child.** Launcelot reverses the usual form of the proverb, "It is a wise child that knows his own father."
85–86. **child . . . be.** Alluding to second childhood.
93. **what a beard.** Gobbo mistakes Launcelot's long hair for a beard; perhaps Launcelot has bowed his head deeply.
95. **fill-horse:** shaft horse.
96–97. **grows backward:** (1) gets shorter instead of longer; (2) grows at the wrong end (referring to Gobbo's error).
103. **set . . . rest:** boldly resolved (from a term meaning "stake everything" in the card game primero).
105. **halter:** hangman's noose. 106. **tell:** count.
108. **give me:** give (see note on I.iii.84).
109. **liveries:** distinctive garb worn by a gentleman's servants.

Bass. You may do so, but let it be so hasted that supper be ready at the farthest by five of the clock. See these letters deliver'd, put the liveries to making, and desire Gratiano to come anon to my lodging. [*Exit one of his men.*]

Laun. To him, father.

Gob. God bless your worship!

Bass. Gramercy, wouldst thou aught with me?

Gob. Here's my son, sir, a poor boy—

Laun. Not a poor boy, sir, but the rich Jew's man, that would, sir, as my father shall specify—

Gob. He hath a great infection, sir, as one would say, to serve—

Laun. Indeed the short and the long is, I serve the Jew, and have a desire, as my father shall specify—

Gob. His master and he (saving your worship's reverence) are scarce cater-cousins—

Laun. To be brief, the very truth is that the Jew, having done me wrong, doth cause me, as my father, being I hope an old man, shall frutify unto you—

Gob. I have here a dish of doves that I would bestow upon your worship, and my suit is—

Laun. In very brief, the suit is impertinent to myself, as your worship shall know by this honest old man, and though I say it, though old man, yet poor man, my father.

Bass. One speak for both. What would you?

Laun. Serve you, sir.

Gob. That is the very defect of the matter, sir.

Bass. I know thee well, thou hast obtain'd thy suit.
Shylock thy master spoke with me this day,
And hath preferr'd thee, if it be preferment
To leave a rich Jew's service, to become
The follower of so poor a gentleman.

Laun. The old proverb is very well parted between my master Shylock and you, sir: you have the grace of God, sir, and he hath enough.

Bass. Thou speak'st it well. Go, father, with thy son.
Take leave of thy old master, and inquire
My lodging out.—Give him a livery
More guarded than his fellows'; see it done.

Laun. Father, in. I cannot get a service, no, I have ne'er a tongue in my head, well! [*Looking on his palm.*] If any man in Italy have a fairer table, which doth offer to swear upon a book, I shall have good fortune. Go to, here's a simple line of life! Here's a small trifle of wives! Alas, fifteen wives is nothing! Aleven widows and nine maids is a simple coming-in for one man. And then to scape drowning thrice, and to be in peril of my life with the edge of a feather-bed, here are simple scapes. Well, if Fortune be a woman, she's a good wench for this gear. Father, come, I'll take my leave of the Jew in the twinkling. *Exit Clown* [*with Old Gobbo*].

Bass. I pray thee, good Leonardo, think on this:
These things being bought and orderly bestowed,
Return in haste, for I do feast to-night
My best esteem'd acquaintance. Hie thee, go.

Leon. My best endeavors shall be done herein.

Enter GRATIANO.

Gra. Where's your master?

Leon. Yonder, sir, he walks. *Exit Leonardo.*

Gra. Signior Bassanio!

Bass. Gratiano!

Gra. I have suit to you.

Bass. You have obtain'd it.

Gra. You must not deny me; I must go with you to Belmont.

Bass. Why then you must. But hear thee, Gratiano:
Thou art too wild, too rude, and bold of voice—
Parts that become thee happily enough,
And in such eyes as ours appear not faults,
But where thou art not known, why, there they show
Something too liberal. Pray thee take pain
To allay with some cold drops of modesty
Thy skipping spirit, lest through thy wild behavior
I be misconst'red in the place I go to,
And lose my hopes.

Gra. Signior Bassanio, hear me:
If I do not put on a sober habit,
Talk with respect, and swear but now and then,
Wear prayer-books in my pocket, look demurely,
Nay more, while grace is saying hood mine eyes
Thus with my hat, and sigh and say amen,
Use all the observance of civility,
Like one well studied in a sad ostent
To please his grandam, never trust me more.

Bass. Well, we shall see your bearing.

Gra. Nay, but I bar to-night, you shall not gauge me
By what we do to-night.

Bass. No, that were pity.
I would entreat you rather to put on
Your boldest suit of mirth, for we have friends
That purpose merriment. But fare you well,
I have some business.

Gra. And I must to Lorenzo and the rest,
But we will visit you at supper-time. *Exeunt.*

121. **Gramercy:** many thanks.
125. **infection:** blunder for *affection*, i.e. desire.
131. **cater-cousins:** good friends.
134. **frutify:** blunder for *certify* (?) or *notify* (?).
137. **impertinent.** He means the opposite.
143. **defect:** blunder for *effect*, i.e. gist.
144. **suit:** (1) request; (2) livery.
146. **preferr'd thee:** put you forward, recommended you. **preferment:** being put forward, i.e. a promotion.
149. **proverb:** i.e. "He that hath the grace of God hath enough." **parted:** divided.
155. **guarded:** ornamented (with braid or the like). It has been suggested that Bassanio takes Launcelot into service as his fool, who would wear a motley coat "guarded" with yellow.
158. **table:** part of the palm of the hand.
159. **swear . . . book:** i.e. tell the truth (about the future); with play on placing the palm upon a Bible for oath-taking.
160. **simple:** plain, unremarkable (ironic).
162. **Aleven:** eleven (a variant spelling that occurs a number of times in Shakespeare's texts).
163. **simple coming-in:** modest income (with a ribald innuendo).
165. **edge . . . feather-bed:** i.e. some sexual escapade.
167. **gear:** business. 182. **Parts:** qualities.
185. **liberal:** unrestrained. 188. **misconst'red:** misconstrued.
190. **habit:** behavior, demeanor (with play on "suit"; cf. line 201).
193–94. **hood . . . hat.** Hats were worn during meals but removed during grace. 196. **sad ostent:** sober appearance.
197 **more:** again.

[SCENE III]

Enter JESSICA *and the Clown* [LAUNCELOT].

Jes. I am sorry thou wilt leave my father so.
Our house is hell, and thou, a merry devil,
Didst rob it of some taste of tediousness.
But fare thee well, there is a ducat for thee,
And, Launcelot, soon at supper shalt thou see
Lorenzo, who is thy new master's guest.
Give him this letter, do it secretly,
And so farewell. I would not have my father
See me in talk with thee.

Laun. Adieu, tears exhibit my tongue. Most beautiful pagan, most sweet Jew! if a Christian do not play the knave and get thee, I am much deceiv'd. But adieu, these foolish drops do something drown my manly spirit. Adieu!

Jes. Farewell, good Launcelot. [*Exit Launcelot.*]
Alack, what heinous sin is it in me
To be ashamed to be my father's child!
But though I am a daughter to his blood,
I am not to his manners. O Lorenzo,
If thou keep promise, I shall end this strife,
Become a Christian and thy loving wife. *Exit.*

[SCENE IV]

Enter GRATIANO, LORENZO, SALERIO, *and* SOLANIO.

Lor. Nay, we will slink away in supper-time,
Disguise us at my lodging, and return
All in an hour.

Gra. We have not made good preparation.

Sal. We have not spoke us yet of torch-bearers.

Sol. 'Tis vile, unless it may be quaintly ordered,
And better in my mind not undertook.

Lor. 'Tis now but four of clock, we have two hours
To furnish us.

Enter LAUNCELOT [*with a letter*].

Friend Launcelot, what's the news?

Laun. And it shall please you to break up this, it shall seem to signify.

Lor. I know the hand; in faith, 'tis a fair hand,
And whiter than the paper it writ on
Is the fair hand that writ.

Gra. Love-news, in faith.

Laun. By your leave, sir.

Lor. Whither goest thou?

Laun. Marry, sir, to bid my old master the Jew to sup to-night with my new master the Christian.

Lor. Hold here, take this. Tell gentle Jessica
I will not fail her, speak it privately. *Exit Clown.*
Go, gentlemen,
Will you prepare you for this masque to-night?

II.iii. Location: Venice. Shylock's house.
5. soon at supper: at supper this evening.
10. exhibit: blunder for *inhibit*. **19. manners:** character.

II.iv. Location: Venice. A street.
5. spoke . . . of: yet bespoken.
6. quaintly ordered: skillfully managed. **10. break up:** open.
19. Hold here. Synonymous with *take this*.

I am provided of a torch-bearer.

Sal. Ay, marry, I'll be gone about it straight.

Sol. And so will I.

Lor. Meet me and Gratiano
At Gratiano's lodging some hour hence.

Sal. 'Tis good we do so. *Exit* [*with Solanio*].

Gra. Was not that letter from fair Jessica?

Lor. I must needs tell thee all. She hath directed
How I shall take her from her father's house,
What gold and jewels she is furnish'd with,
What page's suit she hath in readiness.
If e'er the Jew her father come to heaven,
It will be for his gentle daughter's sake,
And never dare misfortune cross her foot,
Unless she do it under this excuse,
That she is issue to a faithless Jew.
Come go with me, peruse this as thou goest.
Fair Jessica shall be my torch-bearer. *Exeunt.*

[SCENE V]

Enter [SHYLOCK *the*] *Jew and his man that was, the Clown* [LAUNCELOT].

Shy. Well, thou shalt see, thy eyes shall be thy judge,
The difference of old Shylock and Bassanio.—
What, Jessica!—Thou shalt not gurmandize,
As thou hast done with me—What, Jessica!—
And sleep and snore, and rend apparel out—
Why, Jessica, I say!

Laun. Why, Jessica!

Shy. Who bids thee call? I do not bid thee call.

Laun. Your worship was wont to tell me I could do nothing without bidding.

Enter JESSICA.

Jes. Call you? what is your will?

Shy. I am bid forth to supper, Jessica.
There are my keys. But wherefore should I go?
I am not bid for love, they flatter me,
But yet I'll go in hate, to feed upon
The prodigal Christian. Jessica, my girl,
Look to my house. I am right loath to go;
There is some ill a-brewing towards my rest,
For I did dream of money-bags to-night.

Laun. I beseech you, sir, go. My young master doth expect your reproach.

Shy. So do I his.

Laun. And they have conspir'd together. I will not say you shall see a masque, but if you do, then it was not for nothing that my nose fell a-bleeding

24. straight: straightway, at once.
34. gentle. With pun on *Gentile*. **35. foot:** i.e. path, way.
37. faithless: unbelieving.

II.v. Location: Venice. Before Shylock's house.
o.s.d. man that was: former servant.
3. gurmandize: gormandize.
5. rend apparel out; ruin your clothes by rough use.
18. dream of money-bags. It was considered unlucky to dream of money. **to-night:** last night.
20. reproach: blunder for *approach*, i.e. coming.
24. nose fell a-bleeding. A sign of bad luck.

on Black Monday last at six a' clock i' th' morning, falling out that year on Ash We'n'sday was four year in th' afternoon.

Shy. What, are there masques? Hear you me, Jessica:
Lock up my doors, and when you hear the drum
And the vile squealing of the wry-neck'd fife,
Clamber not you up to the casements then,
Nor thrust your head into the public street
To gaze on Christian fools with varnish'd faces;
But stop my house's ears, I mean my casements;
Let not the sound of shallow fopp'ry enter
My sober house. By Jacob's staff I swear
I have no mind of feasting forth to-night;
But I will go. Go you before me, sirrah,
Say I will come.

Laun. I will go before, sir. Mistress, look out at window for all this—

There will come a Christian by,
Will be worth a Jewess' eye. [*Exit*.]

Shy. What says that fool of Hagar's offspring, ha?
Jes. His words were "Farewell, mistress!"—nothing else.
Shy. The patch is kind enough, but a huge feeder,
Snail-slow in profit, and he sleeps by day
More than the wild-cat. Drones hive not with me,
Therefore I part with him, and part with him
To one that I would have him help to waste
His borrowed purse. Well, Jessica, go in,
Perhaps I will return immediately.
Do as I bid you, shut doors after you;
Fast bind, fast find—
A proverb never stale in thrifty mind. *Exit*.
Jes. Farewell, and if my fortune be not cross'd,
I have a father, you a daughter, lost. *Exit*.

[Scene VI]

Enter [two of] the masquers, Gratiano *and* Salerio.

Gra. This is the penthouse under which Lorenzo
Desir'd us to make stand.
Sal. His hour is almost past.
Gra. And it is marvel he out-dwells his hour,
For lovers ever run before the clock.
Sal. O, ten times faster Venus' pigeons fly
To seal love's bonds new made, than they are wont
To keep obliged faith unforfeited!

25. Black Monday: Easter Monday (so called because of a particular Easter Monday, in 1360, when bitterly cold weather caused many deaths). Launcelot's nonsense in this passage derides Shylock's superstition about his dream.
30. wry-neck'd fife: fife-player (or fife played) with head twisted to one side. Like *drum* in line 29, *fife* can refer either to the instrument or to the player. **33. varnish'd faces:** i.e. masks.
35. fopp'ry: foolishness.
36. Jacob's staff. See Genesis 32:10 and Hebrews 11:21.
41. for all this: i.e. despite all that Shylock has said.
44. Hagar's offspring. Hagar was a Gentile, and Ishmael, her son by Abraham, became an outcast. **46. patch:** fool.
47. profit: improvement, proficiency.

II.vi. Location: Scene continues.
1. penthouse: projecting roof offering shelter from the weather.
5. Venus' pigeons: the doves which drew Venus' chariot.
7. obliged: pledged.

Gra. That ever holds. Who riseth from a feast
With that keen appetite that he sits down?
Where is the horse that doth untread again
His tedious measures with the unbated fire
That he did pace them first? All things that are,
Are with more spirit chased than enjoy'd.
How like a younger or a prodigal
The scarfed bark puts from her native bay,
Hugg'd and embraced by the strumpet wind!
How like the prodigal doth she return,
With over-weather'd ribs and ragged sails,
Lean, rent, and beggar'd by the strumpet wind!

Enter Lorenzo.

Sal. Here comes Lorenzo, more of this hereafter.
Lor. Sweet friends, your patience for my long abode;
Not I but my affairs have made you wait.
When you shall please to play the thieves for wives,
I'll watch as long for you then. Approach,
Here dwells my father Jew. Ho! who's within?

[*Enter*] Jessica *above* [*in boy's clothes*].

Jes. Who are you? tell me for more certainty,
Albeit I'll swear that I do know your tongue.
Lor. Lorenzo, and thy love.
Jes. Lorenzo, certain, and my love indeed,
For who love I so much? And now who knows
But you, Lorenzo, whether I am yours?
Lor. Heaven and thy thoughts are witness that thou art.
Jes. Here, catch this casket, it is worth the pains.
I am glad 'tis night, you do not look on me,
For I am much asham'd of my exchange.
But love is blind, and lovers cannot see
The pretty follies that themselves commit,
For if they could, Cupid himself would blush
To see me thus transformed to a boy.
Lor. Descend, for you must be my torch-bearer.
Jes. What, must I hold a candle to my shames?
They in themselves, good sooth, are too too light.
Why, 'tis an office of discovery, love,
And I should be obscur'd.
Lor. So are you, sweet,
Even in the lovely garnish of a boy.
But come at once,
For the close night doth play the runaway,
And we are stay'd for at Bassanio's feast.
Jes. I will make fast the doors, and gild myself
With some moe ducats, and be with you straight.
[*Exit above*.]
Gra. Now by my hood, a gentle, and no Jew.

10. untread: retrace.
14. younger: i.e. younger son. Cf. the parable of the prodigal son in Luke 15.
15. scarfed: decked with streamers (suggesting the extravagant dress of the prodigal).
16. Hugg'd . . . wind. Continuing the parallel between the ship and the prodigal; cf. *ribs* (line 18) and *beggar'd* (line 19).
21. abode: delay. **25. father:** father-in-law.
35. exchange: i.e. change into boy's clothes.
42. light: wanton (with play on "clear").
43. 'tis . . . discovery: i.e. the whole function of torch-bearing is to bring things to view. **45. garnish:** dress. **47. close:** secret.
51. gentle. With pun on *Gentile* (as at II.iv.34).

Lor. Beshrow me but I love her heartily,
For she is wise, if I can judge of her,
And fair she is, if that mine eyes be true,
And true she is, as she hath prov'd herself;
And therefore, like herself, wise, fair, and true,
Shall she be placed in my constant soul.

Enter Jessica.

What, art thou come? On, [gentlemen], away!
Our masquing mates by this time for us stay.
Exit [with Jessica and Salerio].

Enter Antonio.

Ant. Who's there?
Gra. Signior Antonio!
Ant. Fie, fie, Gratiano, where are all the rest?
'Tis nine a' clock—our friends all stay for you.
No masque to-night, the wind is come about,
Bassanio presently will go aboard.
I have sent twenty out to seek for you.
Gra. I am glad on't. I desire no more delight
Than to be under sail, and gone to-night. *Exeunt.*

[Scene VII]

[*Flourish cornets.*] *Enter* Portia *with* [*the* Prince of] Morocco *and both their* Trains.

Por. Go, draw aside the curtains and discover
The several caskets to this noble prince.
Now make your choice.
Mor. This first, of gold, who this inscription bears,
"Who chooseth me shall gain what many men desire";
The second, silver, which this promise carries,
"Who chooseth me shall get as much as he deserves";
This third, dull lead, with warning all as blunt,
"Who chooseth me must give and hazard all he hath."
How shall I know if I do choose the right?
Por. The one of them contains my picture, Prince:
If you choose that, then I am yours withal.
Mor. Some god direct my judgment! Let me see,
I will survey th' inscriptions back again.
What says this leaden casket?
"Who chooseth me must give and hazard all he hath."
Must give—for what? for lead, hazard for lead?
This casket threatens. Men that hazard all
Do it in hope of fair advantages;
A golden mind stoops not to shows of dross.
I'll then nor give nor hazard aught for lead.
What says the silver with her virgin hue?
"Who chooseth me shall get as much as he deserves."
As much as he deserves! pause there, Morocco,
And weigh thy value with an even hand.
If thou beest rated by thy estimation,
Thou dost deserve enough, and yet enough
May not extend so far as to the lady;
And yet to be afeard of my deserving
Were but a weak disabling of myself.
As much as I deserve! why, that's the lady.
I do in birth deserve her, and in fortunes,
In graces, and in qualities of breeding;
But more than these, in love I do deserve.
What if I stray'd no farther, but chose here?
Let's see once more this saying grav'd in gold:
"Who chooseth me shall gain what many men desire."
Why, that's the lady, all the world desires her.
From the four corners of the earth they come
To kiss this shrine, this mortal breathing saint.
The Hyrcanian deserts and the vasty wilds
Of wide Arabia are as throughfares now
For princes to come view fair Portia.
The watery kingdom, whose ambitious head
Spets in the face of heaven, is no bar
To stop the foreign spirits, but they come
As o'er a brook to see fair Portia.
One of these three contains her heavenly picture.
Is't like that lead contains her? 'Twere damnation
To think so base a thought; it were too gross
To rib her cerecloth in the obscure grave.
Or shall I think in silver she's immur'd,
Being ten times undervalued to tried gold?
O sinful thought! never so rich a gem
Was set in worse than gold. They have in England
A coin that bears the figure of an angel
Stamp'd in gold, but that's insculp'd upon;
But here an angel in a golden bed
Lies all within. Deliver me the key.
Here do I choose, and thrive I as I may!
Por. There take it, Prince, and if my form lie there,
Then I am yours. [*He unlocks the golden casket.*]
Mor. O hell! what have we here?
A carrion Death, within whose empty eye
There is a written scroll! I'll read the writing.
[*Reads.*] "All that glisters is not gold,
Often have you heard that told;
Many a man his life hath sold
But my outside to behold.
Gilded [tombs] do worms infold.
Had you been as wise as bold,
Young in limbs, in judgment old,
Your answer had not been inscroll'd.
Fare you well, your suit is cold."
Cold indeed, and labor lost:
Then farewell heat, and welcome frost!
Portia, adieu. I have too griev'd a heart
To take a tedious leave; thus losers part.
Exit [with his Train].

52. Beshrow: beshrew, evil befall (a weakened curse).
65. presently: at once.

II.vii. Location: Belmont. Portia's house.
1. discover: reveal. **8. all as:** equally. **12. withal:** therewith.
25. even: impartial. **26. estimation:** valuation.

30. disabling: undervaluing. **40. shrine:** image.
41. Hyrcanian: pertaining to a desolate area southeast of the Caspian Sea. **deserts:** unpopulated areas, wastes.
42. throughfares: thoroughfares.
51. rib: enclose. **cerecloth:** shroud.
53. Being . . . gold: which is worth only one tenth as much as.
56. angel: a gold coin which bore the figure of the archangel Michael treading on the dragon.
57. insculp'd upon: engraved on the surface.
63. Death: death's-head.
72. inscroll'd: set down here; i.e. you would have made a different choice and received a different answer.

Por. A gentle riddance. Draw the curtains, go.
Let all of his complexion choose me so. *Exeunt.*

[SCENE VIII]

Enter SALERIO *and* SOLANIO.

Sal. Why, man, I saw Bassanio under sail,
With him is Gratiano gone along;
And in their ship I am sure Lorenzo is not.
Sol. The villain Jew with outcries rais'd the Duke,
Who went with him to search Bassanio's ship.
Sal. He came too late, the ship was under sail,
But there the Duke was given to understand
That in a gondilo were seen together
Lorenzo and his amorous Jessica.
Besides, Antonio certified the Duke
They were not with Bassanio in his ship.
Sol. I never heard a passion so confus'd,
So strange, outrageous, and so variable
As the dog Jew did utter in the streets.
"My daughter! O my ducats! O my daughter!
Fled with a Christian! O my Christian ducats!
Justice! the law! my ducats, and my daughter!
A sealed bag, two sealed bags of ducats,
Of double ducats, stol'n from me by my daughter!
And jewels, two stones, two rich and precious stones,
Stol'n by my daughter! Justice! find the girl,
She hath the stones upon her, and the ducats."
Sal. Why, all the boys in Venice follow him,
Crying, his stones, his daughter, and his ducats.
Sol. Let good Antonio look he keep his day,
Or he shall pay for this.
Sal. Marry, well rememb'red.
I reason'd with a Frenchman yesterday,
Who told me, in the Narrow Seas that part
The French and English, there miscarried
A vessel of our country richly fraught.
I thought upon Antonio when he told me,
And wish'd in silence that it were not his.
Sol. You were best to tell Antonio what you hear,
Yet do not suddenly, for it may grieve him.
Sal. A kinder gentleman treads not the earth.
I saw Bassanio and Antonio part:
Bassanio told him he would make some speed
Of his return; he answered, "Do not so,
[Slubber] not business for my sake, Bassanio,
But stay the very riping of the time;
And for the Jew's bond which he hath of me,
Let it not enter in your mind of love.
Be merry, and employ your chiefest thoughts
To courtship, and such fair ostents of love
As shall conveniently become you there."
And even there, his eye being big with tears,
Turning his face, he put his hand behind him,

II.viii. Location: Venice. A street.
8. gondilo: gondola. **9. amorous:** loving.
12. passion: passionate outburst. **27. reason'd:** talked.
28. Narrow Seas: English Channel. **29. miscarried:** perished.
34. suddenly: without preparation.
39. Slubber: hurry over, do in a slovenly manner. **41. for:** as for.
42. enter . . . love: i.e. intrude into your thoughts of love.
44. ostents: shows. **45. conveniently:** properly.

And with affection wondrous sensible
He wrung Bassanio's hand, and so they parted.
Sol. I think he only loves the world for him.
I pray thee let us go and find him out
And quicken his embraced heaviness
With some delight or other.
Sal. Do we so. *Exeunt.*

[SCENE IX]

Enter NERISSA *and a* SERVITOR.

Ner. Quick, quick, I pray thee, draw the curtain straight;
The Prince of Arragon hath ta'en his oath,
And comes to his election presently.

[*Flourish cornets.*] *Enter* [*the* PRINCE OF] ARRAGON, *his* TRAIN, *and* PORTIA.

Por. Behold, there stand the caskets, noble Prince.
If you choose that wherein I am contain'd,
Straight shall our nuptial rites be solemniz'd;
But if you fail, without more speech, my lord,
You must be gone from hence immediately.
Ar. I am enjoin'd by oath to observe three things:
First, never to unfold to any one
Which casket 'twas I chose; next, if I fail
Of the right casket, never in my life
To woo a maid in way of marriage;
Lastly,
If I do fail in fortune of my choice,
Immediately to leave you, and be gone.
Por. To these injunctions every one doth swear
That comes to hazard for my worthless self.
Ar. And so have I address'd me. Fortune now
To my heart's hope! Gold, silver, and base lead.
"Who chooseth me must give and hazard all he hath."
You shall look fairer ere I give or hazard.
What says the golden chest? Ha, let me see:
"Who chooseth me shall gain what many men desire."
What many men desire! That many may be meant
By the fool multitude that choose by show,
Not learning more than the fond eye doth teach,
Which pries not to th' interior, but like the martlet
Builds in the weather on the outward wall,
Even in the force and road of casualty.
I will not choose what many men desire,
Because I will not jump with common spirits,
And rank me with the barbarous multitudes.
Why then to thee, thou silver treasure house,
Tell me once more what title thou dost bear:
"Who chooseth me shall get as much as he deserves."
And well said too; for who shall go about

48. sensible: evident, intense. **50. for him:** on his account.
52. quicken . . . heaviness: enliven the sorrow he clings to.

II.ix. Location: Belmont. Portia's house.
1. straight: immediately. **3. election:** choice. **presently:** at once.
19. address'd me: prepared myself. **26. By:** for.
27. fond: foolish. **28. martlet:** martin.
29. in the weather: exposed to the elements.
30. force: power. **casualty:** mischance. **32. jump:** agree.

To cozen fortune, and be honorable
Without the stamp of merit? Let none presume
To wear an undeserved dignity.
O that estates, degrees, and offices
Were not deriv'd corruptly, and that clear honor
Were purchas'd by the merit of the wearer!
How many then should cover that stand bare?
How many be commanded that command?
How much low peasantry would then be gleaned
From the true seed of honor? and how much honor
Pick'd from the chaff and ruin of the times
To be new varnish'd? Well, but to my choice:
"Who chooseth me shall get as much as he deserves."
I will assume desert. Give me a key for this,
And instantly unlock my fortunes here.

[*He unlocks the silver casket.*]

Por. Too long a pause for that which you find there.

Ar. What's here? the portrait of a blinking idiot,
Presenting me a schedule! I will read it.
How much unlike art thou to Portia!
How much unlike my hopes and my deservings!
"Who chooseth me shall have as much as he deserves"!
Did I deserve no more than a fool's head?
Is that my prize? Are my deserts no better?

Por. To offend and judge are distinct offices,
And of opposed natures.

Ar. What is here?

[*Reads.*] "The fire seven times tried this:
Seven times tried that judgment is,
That did never choose amiss.
Some there be that shadows kiss,
Such have but a shadow's bliss.
There be fools alive, iwis,
Silver'd o'er, and so was this.
Take what wife you will to bed,
I will ever be your head.
So be gone, you are sped."
Still more fool I shall appear
By the time I linger here.
With one fool's head I came to woo,
But I go away with two.
Sweet, adieu. I'll keep my oath,
Patiently to bear my wroth.

[*Exit with his Train.*]

Por. Thus hath the candle sing'd the moth.
O, these deliberate fools, when they do choose,
They have the wisdom by their wit to lose.

Ner. The ancient saying is no heresy,
Hanging and wiving goes by destiny.

Por. Come draw the curtain, Nerissa.

Enter Messenger.

Mess. Where is my lady?

Por. Here; what would my lord?

Mess. Madam, there is alighted at your gate
A young Venetian, one that comes before
To signify th' approaching of his lord,
From whom he bringeth sensible regreets:
To wit (besides commends and courteous breath),
Gifts of rich value. Yet I have not seen
So likely an embassador of love.
A day in April never came so sweet,
To show how costly summer was at hand,
As this fore-spurrer comes before his lord.

Por. No more, I pray thee. I am half afeard
Thou wilt say anon he is some kin to thee,
Thou spend'st such high-day wit in praising him.
Come, come, Nerissa, for I long to see
Quick Cupid's post that comes so mannerly.

Ner. Bassanio, Lord Love, if thy will it be!

Exeunt.

[ACT III, Scene I]

[*Enter*] Solanio *and* Salerio.

Sol. Now what news on the Rialto?

Sal. Why, yet it lives there uncheck'd that Antonio hath a ship of rich lading wrack'd on the Narrow Seas; the Goodwins I think they call the place, a very dangerous flat, and fatal, where the carcasses of many a tall ship lie buried, as they say, if my gossip Report be an honest woman of her word.

Sol. I would she were as lying a gossip in that as ever knapp'd ginger or made her neighbors believe she wept for the death of a third husband. But it is true, without any slips of prolixity, or crossing the plain highway of talk, that the good Antonio, the honest Antonio—O that I had a title good enough to keep his name company!—

Sal. Come, the full stop.

Sol. Ha, what sayest thou? Why, the end is, he hath lost a ship.

Sal. I would it might prove the end of his losses.

Sol. Let me say amen betimes, lest the devil cross my prayer, for here he comes in the likeness of a Jew.

38. **cozen**: cheat. 39. **stamp**: official seal (as on a document).
41. **estates**: status. **degrees**: ranks.
42. **deriv'd**: inherited, gained. **clear**: illustrious.
44. **cover . . . bare**: wear their hats, who must now bare their heads (in the presence of their social superiors).
45. **be . . . command**: become servants instead of masters.
46. **gleaned**: separated. 47. **seed of honor**: nobility.
48. **ruin**: refuse. 51. **assume**: claim (as my right).
55. **schedule**: paper with writing.
61–62. **To . . . natures**: i.e. the offender should not judge his own case. 68. **iwis**: certainly.
71. **I . . . head**: i.e. you will always be a fool.
72. **sped**: taken care of (in a bad sense).
73–74. **Still . . . here**: i.e. the longer I stay here, the greater fool I will appear to be. 78. **wroth**: unhappy lot (a variant of *ruth*).
80. **deliberate**: calculating.

89. **sensible regreets**: tangible greetings. 90. **breath**: speech.
91. **Yet**: up till now.
92. **likely**: promising. **embassador**: ambassador.
94. **costly**: rich, lavish.
98. **high-day**: holiday, i.e. appropriate for some special occasion.
100. **post**: messenger.

III.i. **Location**: Venice. A street.
2. **uncheck'd**: unhindered, i.e. not denied.
4. **Goodwins**: Goodwin Sands, off the mouth of the Thames.
6–7. **my gossip Report**: i.e. Dame Rumor. *Gossip*, literally "godparent," was used of a female crony or confidante and thus developed its present sense. 9. **knapp'd**: chewed.
11. **slips of prolixity**: lapses into prolixity; or perhaps (as Kittredge suggests), wordy lies (*slip* can mean "false coin").
11–12. **crossing . . . talk**: departing from plain speech.

Enter Shylock.

How now, Shylock, what news among the merchants?

Shy. You knew, none so well, none so well as you, of my daughter's flight.

Sal. That's certain. I for my part knew the tailor that made the wings she flew withal.

Sol. And Shylock for his own part knew the bird was fludge, and then it is the complexion of them all to leave the dam.

Shy. She is damn'd for it.

Sal. That's certain, if the devil may be her judge.

Shy. My own flesh and blood to rebel!

Sol. Out upon it, old carrion, rebels it at these years?

Shy. I say, my daughter is my flesh and my blood.

Sal. There is more difference between thy flesh and hers than between jet and ivory, more between your bloods than there is between red wine and Rhenish. But tell us, do you hear whether Antonio have had any loss at sea or no?

Shy. There I have another bad match. A bankrout, a prodigal, who dare scarce show his head on the Rialto; a beggar, that was us'd to come so smug upon the mart: let him look to his bond. He was wont to call me usurer, let him look to his bond. He was wont to lend money for a Christian cur'sy, let him look to his bond.

Sal. Why, I am sure if he forfeit thou wilt not take his flesh. What's that good for?

Shy. To bait fish withal—if it will feed nothing else, it will feed my revenge. He hath disgrac'd me, and hind'red me half a million, laugh'd at my losses, mock'd at my gains, scorn'd my nation, thwarted my bargains, cool'd my friends, heated mine enemies; and what's his reason? I am a Jew. Hath not a Jew eyes? Hath not a Jew hands, organs, dimensions, senses, affections, passions; fed with the same food, hurt with the same weapons, subject to the same diseases, heal'd by the same means, warm'd and cool'd by the same winter and summer, as a Christian is? If you prick us, do we not bleed? If you tickle us, do we not laugh? If you poison us, do we not die? And if you wrong us, shall we not revenge? If we are like you in the rest, we will resemble you in that. If a Jew wrong a Christian, what is his humility? Revenge. If a Christian wrong a Jew, what should his sufferance be by Christian example? Why, revenge. The villainy you teach me, I will execute, and it shall go hard but I will better the instruction.

27. wings. With play on *wing* = an ornamental flap above the upper end of the sleeve. **withal**: with.
29. fludge: fledged, ready to fly. **complexion**: natural tendency.
35–36. rebels . . . years. Solanio pretends to misunderstand: "Do you have sensual desires at your age?"
42. Rhenish: i.e. white wine. **44. match**: bargain.
44–45. bankrout: bankrupt. **46. smug**: neat, spruce.
49. for . . . cur'sy: out of Christian courtesy.
60. dimensions: bodily proportions.
69–70. his . . . his: the Christian's . . . the Jew's.
69. humility: patient endurance.

Enter a [Serving]man *from Antonio.*

[*Serv.*] Gentlemen, my master Antonio is at his house, and desires to speak with you both.

Sal. We have been up and down to seek him.

Enter Tubal.

Sol. Here comes another of the tribe; a third cannot be match'd, unless the devil himself turn Jew.

Exeunt Gentlemen [*Solanio and Salerio, with Servingman*].

Shy. How now, Tubal, what news from Genoa? Hast thou found my daughter?

Tub. I often came where I did hear of her, but cannot find her.

Shy. Why, there, there, there, there! A diamond gone, cost me two thousand ducats in Frankford! The curse never fell upon our nation till now, I never felt it till now. Two thousand ducats in that, and other precious, precious jewels. I would my daughter were dead at my foot, and the jewels in her ear! Would she were hears'd at my foot, and the ducats in her coffin! No news of them? Why, so—and I know not what's spent in the search. Why, thou loss upon loss! the thief gone with so much, and so much to find the thief, and no satisfaction, no revenge, nor no ill luck stirring but what lights a' my shoulders, no sighs but a' my breathing, no tears but a' my shedding.

Tub. Yes, other men have ill luck too. Antonio, as I heard in Genoa—

Shy. What, what, what? ill luck, ill luck?

Tub. Hath an argosy cast away, coming from Tripolis.

Shy. I thank God, I thank God. Is it true, is it true?

Tub. I spoke with some of the sailors that escap'd the wrack.

Shy. I thank thee, good Tubal, good news, good news! Ha, ha! [Heard] in Genoa?

Tub. Your daughter spent in Genoa, as I heard, one night fourscore ducats.

Shy. Thou stick'st a dagger in me. I shall never see my gold again. Fourscore ducats at a sitting, fourscore ducats!

Tub. There came divers of Antonio's creditors in my company to Venice that swear he cannot choose but break.

Shy. I am very glad of it. I'll plague him, I'll torture him. I am glad of it.

Tub. One of them show'd me a ring that he had of your daughter for a monkey.

Shy. Out upon her! Thou torturest me, Tubal. It was my turkis, I had it of Leah when I was a bachelor. I would not have given it for a wilderness of monkeys.

Tub. But Antonio is certainly undone.

Shy. Nay, that's true, that's very true. Go, Tubal,

78. match'd: found to match them.
84–85. Frankford: Frankfort, famous for its fairs.
89. hears'd: coffined. **95. a'**: of, on.
114–15. choose but break: avoid going bankrupt.
121. turkis: turquoise.

fee me an officer; bespeak him a fortnight before. I will have the heart of him if he forfeit, for were he out of Venice I can make what merchandise I will. Go, Tubal, and meet me at our synagogue; go, good Tubal, at our synagogue, Tubal.

Exeunt.

[SCENE II]

Enter BASSANIO, PORTIA, GRATIANO, [NERISSA,] *and all their* TRAINS.

Por. I pray you tarry, pause a day or two
Before you hazard, for in choosing wrong
I lose your company; therefore forbear a while.
There's something tells me (but it is not love)
I would not lose you, and you know yourself,
Hate counsels not in such a quality.
But lest you should not understand me well—
And yet a maiden hath no tongue but thought—
I would detain you here some month or two
Before you venture for me. I could teach you
How to choose right, but then I am forsworn.
So will I never be, so may you miss me,
But if you do, you'll make me wish a sin,
That I had been forsworn. Beshrow your eyes,
They have o'erlook'd me and divided me:
One half of me is yours, the other half yours—
Mine own, I would say; but if mine, then yours,
And so all yours. O, these naughty times
Puts bars between the owners and their rights!
And so though yours, not yours. Prove it so,
Let fortune go to hell for it, not I.
I speak too long, but 'tis to peize the time,
To eche it, and to draw it out in length,
To stay you from election.

Bass. Let me choose,
For as I am, I live upon the rack.

Por. Upon the rack, Bassanio! then confess
What treason there is mingled with your love.

Bass. None but that ugly treason of mistrust,
Which makes me fear th' enjoying of my love;
There may as well be amity and life
'Tween snow and fire, as treason and my love.

Por. Ay, but I fear you speak upon the rack,
Where men enforced do speak any thing.

Bass. Promise me life, and I'll confess the truth.

Por. Well then, confess and live.

Bass. Confess and love
Had been the very sum of my confession.
O happy torment, when my torturer
Doth teach me answers for deliverance!
But let me to my fortune and the caskets.

Por. Away then! I am lock'd in one of them;
If you do love me, you will find me out.

126. **fee . . . officer:** i.e. engage a sheriff's officer for me.
128. **make what merchandise:** drive what bargain.

III.ii. Location: Belmont. Portia's house.
2. **in choosing:** if you choose. 6. **quality:** manner.
15. **o'erlook'd:** bewitched. 18. **naughty:** wicked.
20. **Prove it so:** should it prove so. 22. **peize:** weigh down, retard.
23. **eche:** eke, augment.
26–27. **confess What treason.** The rack was used to extort confessions of treason. 28. **mistrust:** doubt, uncertainty.
29. **fear:** feel apprehensive about.

Nerissa and the rest, stand all aloof.
Let music sound while he doth make his choice;
Then if he lose he makes a swan-like end,
Fading in music. That the comparison
May stand more proper, my eye shall be the stream
And wat'ry death-bed for him. He may win,
And what is music then? Then music is
Even as the flourish when true subjects bow
To a new-crowned monarch; such it is
As are those dulcet sounds in break of day
That creep into the dreaming bridegroom's ear,
And summon him to marriage. Now he goes,
With no less presence, but with much more love,
Than young Alcides, when he did redeem
The virgin tribute paid by howling Troy
To the sea-monster. I stand for sacrifice;
The rest aloof are the Dardanian wives,
With bleared visages, come forth to view
The issue of th' exploit. Go, Hercules,
Live thou, I live; with much, much more dismay
I view the fight than thou that mak'st the fray.

[Here music.]

A song, the whilst Bassanio comments on the caskets to himself.

Tell me where is fancy bred,
Or in the heart or in the head?
How begot, how nourished?
[*All.*] Reply, reply.
It is engend'red in the [eyes],
With gazing fed, and fancy dies
In the cradle where it lies.
Let us all ring fancy's knell.
I'll begin it. Ding, dong, bell.
All. Ding, dong, bell.

Bass. So may the outward shows be least themselves—
The world is still deceiv'd with ornament.
In law, what plea so tainted and corrupt
But, being season'd with a gracious voice,
Obscures the show of evil? In religion,
What damned error but some sober brow
Will bless it, and approve it with a text,
Hiding the grossness with fair ornament?
There is no [vice] so simple but assumes
Some mark of virtue on his outward parts.
How many cowards, whose hearts are all as false
As stairs of sand, wear yet upon their chins
The beards of Hercules and frowning Mars,
Who inward search'd, have livers white as milk,

44. **swan-like end.** The swan was thought to sing before dying.
49. **flourish:** fanfare of trumpets.
54. **presence:** nobility of appearance.
54–57. **much . . . monster.** Hercules' motive in rescuing the Trojan princess Hesione from a sea-monster to which she was to be sacrificed was not love for her but a desire to possess the horses which Laomedon, her father, had promised him as a reward. 56. **howling:** lamenting.
58. **Dardanian:** Trojan. 59. **bleared:** weeping.
61. **Live thou:** if you live. 63. **fancy:** love.
67. **engend'red . . . eyes.** The eyes were considered the entry-port of love.
69. **In the cradle:** (1) in the eyes where it was born; (2) in infancy.
73. **be least themselves:** i.e. falsify the inner reality.
74. **still:** ever, continually. 79. **approve:** prove, confirm.
81. **simple:** unmixed. 83. **all:** just.

And these assume but valor's excrement
To render them redoubted! Look on beauty,
And you shall see 'tis purchas'd by the weight,
Which therein works a miracle in nature,
Making them lightest that wear most of it.
So are those crisped snaky golden locks,
Which [make] such wanton gambols with the wind
Upon supposed fairness, often known
To be the dowry of a second head,
The skull that bred them in the sepulchre.
Thus ornament is but the guiled shore
To a most dangerous sea; the beauteous scarf
Veiling an Indian beauty; in a word,
The seeming truth which cunning times put on
To entrap the wisest. Therefore then, thou gaudy gold,
Hard food for Midas, I will none of thee;
Nor none of thee, thou pale and common drudge
'Tween man and man; but thou, thou meagre lead,
Which rather threaten'st than dost promise aught,
Thy paleness moves me more than eloquence,
And here choose I. Joy be the consequence!

Por. [*Aside.*] How all the other passions fleet to air,
As doubtful thoughts, and rash-embrac'd despair,
And shudd'ring fear, and green-eyed jealousy!
O love, be moderate, allay thy ecstasy,
In measure rain thy joy, scant this excess!
I feel too much thy blessing; make it less,
For fear I surfeit.

Bass. What find I here?

[*Opening the leaden casket.*]

Fair Portia's counterfeit! What demigod
Hath come so near creation? Move these eyes?
Or whether, riding on the balls of mine,
Seem they in motion? Here are sever'd lips,
Parted with sugar breath; so sweet a bar
Should sunder such sweet friends. Here in her hairs
The painter plays the spider, and hath woven
A golden mesh t' entrap the hearts of men
Faster than gnats in cobwebs. But her eyes—
How could he see to do them? Having made one,
Methinks it should have power to steal both his
And leave itself unfurnish'd. Yet look how far
The substance of my praise doth wrong this shadow
In underprizing it, so far this shadow
Doth limp behind the substance. Here's the scroll,
The continent and summary of my fortune.
[*Reads.*] "You that choose not by the view,
Chance as fair, and choose as true:
Since this fortune falls to you,
Be content, and seek no new.
If you be well pleas'd with this,
And hold your fortune for your bliss,
Turn you where your lady is,
And claim her with a loving kiss."
A gentle scroll. Fair lady, by your leave,
I come by note, to give and to receive.
Like one of two contending in a prize,
That thinks he hath done well in people's eyes,
Hearing applause and universal shout,
Giddy in spirit, still gazing in a doubt
Whether those peals of praise be his or no,
So, thrice-fair lady, stand I, even so,
As doubtful whether what I see be true,
Until confirm'd, sign'd, ratified by you.

Por. You see me, Lord Bassanio, where I stand,
Such as I am. Though for myself alone
I would not be ambitious in my wish
To wish myself much better, yet for you,
I would be trebled twenty times myself,
A thousand times more fair, ten thousand times more rich,
That only to stand high in your account,
I might in virtues, beauties, livings, friends,
Exceed account. But the full sum of me
Is sum of something; which, to term in gross,
Is an unlesson'd girl, unschool'd, unpractic'd,
Happy in this, she is not yet so old
But she may learn; happier than this,
She is not bred so dull but she can learn;
Happiest of all, is that her gentle spirit
Commits itself to yours to be directed,
As from her lord, her governor, her king.
Myself, and what is mine, to you and yours
Is now converted. But now I was the lord
Of this fair mansion, master of my servants,
Queen o'er myself; and even now, but now,
This house, these servants, and this same myself
Are yours—my lord's!—I give them with this ring,
Which when you part from, lose, or give away,
Let it presage the ruin of your love,
And be my vantage to exclaim on you.

Bass. Madam, you have bereft me of all words,
Only my blood speaks to you in my veins,
And there is such confusion in my powers,

87. excrement: outgrowth (such as beards [see line 85] or fingernails), i.e. external attributes.
88. render them redoubted: make themselves feared.
91. lightest: most wanton (with obvious wordplay).
92. crisped: curled. **snaky:** long and waving (but with a suggestion of the snake's deceptive nature).
94. supposed fairness: i.e. a supposedly beautiful woman.
95. dowry: possession. **a second:** another. With lines 95–96 cf. Sonnet 68.5–8 (where *second* has its more usual meaning).
97. guiled: guileful, treacherous.
99. Indian: i.e. dark-complexioned. Elizabethans had a particular dislike for dusky skins.
102. Midas: Phrygian king who turned whatever he touched to gold.
103. common drudge: public slave (when coined).
106. Thy paleness. Stress *Thy*, to give the required contrast with *pale* as applied to silver in line 103. Many editors emend *paleness* to *plainness*, following Theobald.
109. As: such as. **doubtful:** fearful.
112. In . . . joy: pour out your joy moderately. **scant:** diminish.
115. counterfeit: portrait. **117. Or whether:** or.
118. sever'd: separated. **123. Faster:** more firmly.
126. unfurnish'd: i.e. without its mate. **look how far:** however far, as far as.
127. substance: i.e. verbal expression. **shadow:** portrait.
128. underprizing it: i.e. understating its beauty.
129. the substance: i.e. Portia herself. **130. continent:** container.
132. Chance as fair: hazard as fortunately.
140. note: authorization in writing (i.e. the scroll). **give . . . receive:** i.e. proffer a kiss and receive one in return. **141. prize:** competition.
145. his: for him. **155. account:** estimation.
156. livings: possessions. **157. account:** calculation.
158. Is . . . something: i.e. adds up to something (how little, her following lines describe). Many editors adopt the Folio reading *nothing* in place of *something*. **term in gross:** state in full.
160. Happy: fortunate. **165. from:** by.
167. But now: just now. **173. ruin:** decay.
174. vantage: opportunity. **exclaim on:** accuse, reproach.
177. powers: faculties.

As after some oration fairly spoke
By a beloved prince, there doth appear
Among the buzzing pleased multitude,
Where every something, being blent together,
Turns to a wild of nothing, save of joy
Express'd and not express'd. But when this ring
Parts from this finger, then parts life from hence;
O then be bold to say Bassanio's dead!

Ner. My lord and lady, it is now our time,
That have stood by and seen our wishes prosper,
To cry good joy. Good joy, my lord and lady!

Gra. My Lord Bassanio and my gentle lady,
I wish you all the joy that you can wish;
For I am sure you can wish none from me;
And when your honors mean to solemnize
The bargain of your faith, I do beseech you
Even at that time I may be married too.

Bass. With all my heart, so thou canst get a wife.

Gra. I thank your lordship, you have got me one.
My eyes, my lord, can look as swift as yours:
You saw the mistress, I beheld the maid;
You lov'd, I lov'd; for intermission
No more pertains to me, my lord, than you;
Your fortune stood upon the caskets there,
And so did mine too as the matter falls;
For wooing here until I sweat again,
And swearing till my very [roof] was dry
With oaths of love, at last, if promise last,
I got a promise of this fair one here
To have her love—provided that your fortune
Achiev'd her mistress.

Por. Is this true, Nerissa?

Ner. Madam, it is, so you stand pleas'd withal.

Bass. And do you, Gratiano, mean good faith?

Gra. Yes, faith, my lord.

Bass. Our feast shall be much honored in your marriage.

Gra. We'll play with them the first boy for a thousand ducats.

Ner. What, and stake down?

Gra. No, we shall ne'er win at that sport, and stake down.
But who comes here? Lorenzo and his infidel?
What, and my old Venetian friend Salerio?

Enter LORENZO, JESSICA, *and* SALERIO, *a messenger from Venice.*

Bass. Lorenzo and Salerio, welcome hither,
If that the youth of my new int'rest here
Have power to bid you welcome. By your leave,
I bid my very friends and countrymen,
Sweet Portia, welcome.

Por. So do I, my lord,
They are entirely welcome.

Lor. I thank your honor. For my part, my lord,
My purpose was not to have seen you here,
But meeting with Salerio by the way,
He did entreat me, past all saying nay,
To come with him along.

Sal. I did, my lord,
And I have reason for it. Signior Antonio
Commends him to you. [*Gives Bassanio a letter.*]

Bass. Ere I ope his letter,
I pray you tell me how my good friend doth.

Sal. Not sick, my lord, unless it be in mind,
Nor well, unless in mind. His letter there
Will show you his estate. [*Bassanio*] *open the letter.*

Gra. Nerissa, cheer yond stranger, bid her welcome.
Your hand, Salerio. What's the news from Venice?
How doth that royal merchant, good Antonio?
I know he will be glad of our success;
We are the Jasons, we have won the fleece.

Sal. I would you had won the fleece that he hath lost.

Por. There are some shrowd contents in yond same paper
That steals the color from Bassanio's cheek—
Some dear friend dead, else nothing in the world
Could turn so much the constitution
Of any constant man. What, worse and worse!
With leave, Bassanio, I am half yourself,
And I must freely have the half of any thing
That this same paper brings you.

Bass. O sweet Portia,
Here are a few of the unpleasant'st words
That ever blotted paper! Gentle lady,
When I did first impart my love to you,
I freely told you all the wealth I had
Ran in my veins: I was a gentleman;
And then I told you true. And yet, dear lady,
Rating myself at nothing, you shall see
How much I was a braggart: when I told you
My state was nothing, I should then have told you
That I was worse than nothing; for indeed
I have engag'd myself to a dear friend,
Engag'd my friend to his mere enemy,
To feed my means. Here is a letter, lady,
The paper as the body of my friend,
And every word in it a gaping wound
Issuing life-blood. But is it true, Salerio?
Hath all his ventures fail'd? What, not one hit?
From Tripolis, from Mexico, and England,
From Lisbon, Barbary, and India,
And not one vessel scape the dreadful touch
Of merchant-marring rocks?

181. blent: blended, confused.
185. be . . . say: say with confidence.
191. you . . . me: i.e. you feel no need to be wished more joy by me (than you have already wished for yourselves). **195. so:** provided.
199. intermission: delay (in falling in love).
203. sweat again: sweated repeatedly.
204. roof: i.e. roof of the mouth. **213. play:** make a wager.
215. stake down: money to cover the bet paid down in advance (but Gratiano makes a bawdy pun on the term).
221–22. If . . . power: i.e. if my place in this household, still so new, gives me the right. **223. very:** true.

225. entirely: heartily. **232. Commends him:** sends his greetings.
236. estate: condition, situation.
239. royal merchant: i.e. prince of merchants (?). Cf. IV.i.29, where the phrase seems to mean "the richest of merchants."
241. Jasons . . . fleece. Cf. I.i.169–72.
243. shrowd: shrewd, grievous. **246. constitution:** state of mind.
247. constant: steadfast. **259. state:** estate, property.
262. mere: absolute.
264. The paper . . . friend: i.e. the letter, like my friend's body, torn open. **267. hit:** successful venture.
271. merchant-marring: destructive to merchant ships.

Sal. Not one, my lord.
Besides, it should appear, that if he had
The present money to discharge the Jew,
He would not take it. Never did I know
A creature that did bear the shape of man
So keen and greedy to confound a man.
He plies the Duke at morning and at night,
And doth impeach the freedom of the state,
If they deny him justice. Twenty merchants,
The Duke himself, and the magnificoes
Of greatest port, have all persuaded with him,
But none can drive him from the envious plea
Of forfeiture, of justice, and his bond.

Jes. When I was with him I have heard him swear
To Tubal and to Chus, his countrymen,
That he would rather have Antonio's flesh
Than twenty times the value of the sum
That he did owe him; and I know, my lord,
If law, authority, and power deny not,
It will go hard with poor Antonio.

Por. Is it your dear friend that is thus in trouble?

Bass. The dearest friend to me, the kindest man,
The best-condition'd and unwearied spirit
In doing courtesies, and one in whom
The ancient Roman honor more appears
Than any that draws breath in Italy.

Por. What sum owes he the Jew?

Bass. For me, three thousand ducats.

Por. What, no more?
Pay him six thousand, and deface the bond;
Double six thousand, and then treble that,
Before a friend of this description
Shall lose a hair through Bassanio's fault.
First go with me to church and call me wife,
And then away to Venice to your friend;
For never shall you lie by Portia's side
With an unquiet soul. You shall have gold
To pay the petty debt twenty times over.
When it is paid, bring your true friend along.
My maid Nerissa and myself mean time
Will live as maids and widows. Come away!
For you shall hence upon your wedding-day.
Bid your friends welcome, show a merry cheer—
Since you are dear bought, I will love you dear.
But let me hear the letter of your friend.

[*Bass.* (*Reads.*)] "Sweet Bassanio, my ships have all miscarried, my creditors grow cruel, my estate is very low, my bond to the Jew is forfeit; and since in paying it, it is impossible I should live, all debts are clear'd between you and I, if I might but see you at my death. Notwithstanding, use your pleasure; if your love do not persuade you to come, let not my letter."

Por. O love! dispatch all business and be gone.

273. **present:** ready. **discharge:** settle his obligation to.
274. **He:** i.e. the Jew. 276. **keen:** savage. **confound:** destroy.
278. **impeach . . . state:** i.e. accuse the state of failing to support the liberties of its citizens. 280. **magnificoes:** grandees.
281. **port:** state, dignity. **persuaded:** pleaded.
282. **envious:** malicious.
293. **best-condition'd:** best-natured. **unwearied:** i.e. most unwearied. 299. **deface:** destroy. 312. **cheer:** countenance.
313. **dear bought:** obtained at a high price.
320–21. **use your pleasure:** follow your own inclination.

Bass. Since I have your good leave to go away,
I will make haste; but till I come again,
No bed shall e'er be guilty of my stay,
Nor rest be interposer 'twixt us twain. *Exeunt.*

[Scene III]

Enter [Shylock] *the Jew and* [Solanio] *and* Antonio *and the* Jailer.

Shy. Jailer, look to him, tell not me of mercy.
This is the fool that lent out money gratis.
Jailer, look to him.

Ant. Hear me yet, good Shylock.

Shy. I'll have my bond, speak not against my bond,
I have sworn an oath that I will have my bond.
Thou call'dst me dog before thou hadst a cause,
But since I am a dog, beware my fangs.
The Duke shall grant me justice. I do wonder,
Thou naughty jailer, that thou art so fond
To come abroad with him at his request.

Ant. I pray thee hear me speak.

Shy. I'll have my bond; I will not hear thee speak.
I'll have my bond, and therefore speak no more.
I'll not be made a soft and dull-ey'd fool
To shake the head, relent, and sigh, and yield
To Christian intercessors. Follow not,
I'll have no speaking, I will have my bond. *Exit Jew.*

Sol. It is the most impenetrable cur
That ever kept with men.

Ant. Let him alone,
I'll follow him no more with bootless prayers.
He seeks my life; his reason well I know:
I oft deliver'd from his forfeitures
Many that have at times made moan to me;
Therefore he hates me.

[*Sol.*] I am sure the Duke
Will never grant this forfeiture to hold.

Ant. The Duke cannot deny the course of law;
For the commodity that strangers have
With us in Venice, if it be denied,
Will much impeach the justice of the state,
Since that the trade and profit of the city
Consisteth of all nations. Therefore go.
These griefs and losses have so bated me
That I shall hardly spare a pound of flesh
To-morrow to my bloody creditor.
Well, jailer, on. Pray God Bassanio come
To see me pay his debt, and then I care not! *Exeunt.*

[Scene IV]

Enter Portia, Nerissa, Lorenzo, Jessica, *and* [Balthazar,] *a man of Portia's.*

Lor. Madam, although I speak it in your presence,

III.iii. Location: Venice. A street.
9. **naughty:** good-for-nothing. 14. **dull-ey'd:** i.e. easily put upon.
19. **kept:** dwelt. 20. **bootless:** unavailing. 26. **deny:** refuse.
27. **commodity:** commercial privileges. **strangers:** aliens.
29. **impeach . . . state.** Cf. III.ii.278. 32. **bated:** reduced.

III.iv. Location: Belmont. Portia's house.

You have a noble and a true conceit
Of godlike amity, which appears most strongly
In bearing thus the absence of your lord.
But if you knew to whom you show this honor,
How true a gentleman you send relief,
How dear a lover of my lord your husband,
I know you would be prouder of the work
Than customary bounty can enforce you.

Por. I never did repent for doing good,
Nor shall not now: for in companions
That do converse and waste the time together,
Whose souls do bear an egall yoke of love,
There must be needs a like proportion
Of lineaments, of manners, and of spirit;
Which makes me think that this Antonio,
Being the bosom lover of my lord,
Must needs be like my lord. If it be so,
How little is the cost I have bestowed
In purchasing the semblance of my soul,
From out the state of hellish cruelty.
This comes too near the praising of myself,
Therefore no more of it. [Hear] other things:
Lorenzo, I commit into your hands
The husbandry and manage of my house
Until my lord's return. For mine own part,
I have toward heaven breath'd a secret vow
To live in prayer and contemplation,
Only attended by Nerissa here,
Until her husband and my lord's return.
There is a monast'ry two miles off,
And there we will abide. I do desire you
Not to deny this imposition,
The which my love and some necessity
Now lays upon you.

Lor. Madam, with all my heart,
I shall obey you in all fair commands.

Por. My people do already know my mind,
And will acknowledge you and Jessica
In place of Lord Bassanio and myself.
So fare you well till we shall meet again.

Lor. Fair thoughts and happy hours attend on you!

Jes. I wish your ladyship all heart's content.

Por. I thank you for your wish, and am well pleas'd
To wish it back on you. Fare you well, Jessica.
Exeunt [*Jessica and Lorenzo*].
Now, Balthazar,
As I have ever found thee honest-true,
So let me find thee still. Take this same letter,
And use thou all th' endeavor of a man
In speed to [Padua]. See thou render this
Into my [cousin's] hands, Doctor Bellario,
And look what notes and garments he doth give thee,
Bring them, I pray thee, with imagin'd speed
Unto the [traject], to the common ferry
Which trades to Venice. Waste no time in words,
But get thee gone. I shall be there before thee.

Balth. Madam, I go with all convenient speed.
[*Exit.*]

Por. Come on, Nerissa, I have work in hand
That you yet know not of. We'll see our husbands
Before they think of us.

Ner. Shall they see us?

Por. They shall, Nerissa; but in such a habit
That they shall think we are accomplished
With that we lack. I'll hold thee any wager,
When we are both accoutered like young men,
I'll prove the prettier fellow of the two,
And wear my dagger with the braver grace,
And speak between the change of man and boy
With a reed voice, and turn two mincing steps
Into a manly stride; and speak of frays
Like a fine bragging youth, and tell quaint lies,
How honorable ladies sought my love,
Which I denying, they fell sick and died.
I could not do withal. Then I'll repent,
And wish, for all that, that I had not kill'd them;
And twenty of these puny lies I'll tell,
That men shall swear I have discontinued school
Above a twelvemonth. I have within my mind
A thousand raw tricks of these bragging Jacks,
Which I will practice.

Ner. Why, shall we turn to men?

Por. Fie, what a question's that,
If thou wert near a lewd interpreter!
But come, I'll tell thee all my whole device
When I am in my coach, which stays for us
At the park-gate; and therefore haste away,
For we must measure twenty miles to-day. *Exeunt.*

[Scene V]

Enter Clown [Launcelot] *and* Jessica.

Laun. Yes, truly, for look you, the sins of the father are to be laid upon the children; therefore, I promise you, I fear you. I was always plain with you, and so now I speak my agitation of the matter; therefore be a' good cheer, for truly I think you are damn'd. There is but one hope in it that can do you any good, and that is but a kind of bastard hope neither.

Jes. And what hope is that, I pray thee?

2. conceit: conception, understanding.
9. bounty: benevolence. **enforce:** urge upon. **12. waste:** spend.
13. egall: equal.
14. needs: of necessity. **proportion:** agreement, correspondence.
20. semblance: likeness, double. **my soul:** i.e. Bassanio.
25. husbandry and manage: care and management (the two nouns are near synonyms). **33. deny this imposition:** refuse this charge.
49. Padua. A famed centre for the study of civil law.
50. cousin's: kinsman's. **51. look what:** whatever.
52. imagin'd speed: speed as quick as thought.

53. traject. Explained as from Italian *traghetto,* "ferry." **common:** public. **54. trades:** plies back and forth.
56. convenient: due, appropriate. **60. a habit:** apparel.
61. accomplished: equipped.
69. quaint: skillfully contrived, elaborate.
72. do withal: help it. **74. puny:** petty, childish.
75–76. I . . . twelvemonth: I have been out of school at least a year (ironic). **77. Jacks:** ill-mannered fellows.

III.v. Location: Belmont. Portia's garden.
1–2. sins . . . children. Referring to the Second Commandment in the Second Prayer Book (1552); "and visit the sin of the father upon the children." **3. fear:** fear for.
4. agitation: blunder for *cogitation* (?).
8. neither. Emphasizing the negative implication of what precedes (= that isn't much of a hope either).

Laun. Marry, you may partly hope that your father got you not, that you are not the Jew's daughter.

Jes. That were a kind of bastard hope indeed; so the sins of my mother should be visited upon me.

Laun. Truly then I fear you are damn'd both by father and mother; thus when I shun Scylla, your father, I fall into Charybdis, your mother. Well, you are gone both ways.

Jes. I shall be sav'd by my husband, he hath made me a Christian!

Laun. Truly, the more to blame he; we were Christians enow before, e'en as many as could well live one by another. This making of Christians will raise the price of hogs. If we grow all to be pork-eaters, we shall not shortly have a rasher on the coals for money.

Enter Lorenzo.

Jes. I'll tell my husband, Launcelot, what you say. Here he [comes].

Lor. I shall grow jealious of you shortly, Launcelot, if you thus get my wife into corners!

Jes. Nay, you need not fear us, Lorenzo, Launcelot and I are out. He tells me flatly there's no mercy for me in heaven because I am a Jew's daughter; and he says you are no good member of the commonwealth, for in converting Jews to Christians, you raise the price of pork.

Lor. I shall answer that better to the commonwealth than you can the getting up of the Negro's belly; the Moor is with child by you, Launcelot.

Laun. It is much that the Moor should be more than reason; but if she be less than an honest woman, she is indeed more than I took her for.

Lor. How every fool can play upon the word! I think the best grace of wit will shortly turn into silence, and discourse grow commendable in none only but parrots. Go in, sirrah, bid them prepare for dinner.

Laun. That is done, sir, they have all stomachs!

Lor. Goodly Lord, what a wit-snapper are you! then bid them prepare dinner.

Laun. That is done too, sir, only "cover" is the word.

Lor. Will you cover then, sir?

Laun. Not so, sir, neither, I know my duty.

Lor. Yet more quarrelling with occasion! wilt thou show the whole wealth of thy wit in an instant? I pray thee understand a plain man in his plain meaning: go to thy fellows, bid them cover the table, serve in the meat, and we will come in to dinner.

Laun. For the table, sir, it shall be serv'd in; for the meat, sir, it shall be cover'd; for your coming in to dinner, sir, why, let it be as humors and conceits shall govern. *Exit Clown.*

Lor. O dear discretion, how his words are suited!
The fool hath planted in his memory
An army of good words, and I do know
A many fools, that stand in better place,
Garnish'd like him, that for a tricksy word
Defy the matter. How cheer'st thou, Jessica?
And now, good sweet, say thy opinion,
How dost thou like the Lord Bassanio's wife?

Jes. Past all expressing. It is very meet
The Lord Bassanio live an upright life,
For having such a blessing in his lady,
He finds the joys of heaven here on earth,
And if on earth he do not [merit] it,
In reason he should never come to heaven!
Why, if two gods should play some heavenly match,
And on the wager lay two earthly women,
And Portia one, there must be something else
Pawn'd with the other, for the poor rude world
Hath not her fellow.

Lor. Even such a husband
Hast thou of me as she is for [a] wife.

Jes. Nay, but ask my opinion too of that.

Lor. I will anon, first let us go to dinner.

Jes. Nay, let me praise you while I have a stomach.

Lor. No, pray thee, let it serve for table-talk;
Then howsome'er thou speak'st, 'mong other things
I shall disgest it.

Jes. Well, I'll set you forth. *Exeunt.*

[ACT IV, Scene I]

Enter the Duke, *the* Magnificoes, Antonio, Bassanio, [Salerio,] *and* Gratiano [*with others*].

Duke. What, is Antonio here?

Ant. Ready, so please your Grace.

Duke. I am sorry for thee. Thou art come to answer

11. got: begot.
16–17. Scylla . . . Charybdis. Scylla was a sea-monster and Charybdis a whirlpool in the strait between Italy and Sicily. The difficulty of avoiding one without falling prey to the other is still proverbial.
18. gone: done for, lost.
19–20. I . . . Christian. Cf. 1 Corinthians 7:14: "the unbelieving wife is sanctified by the husband."
22. enow: enough. Shakespeare uses this form only as a modifier of plural nouns; see another example in IV.i.29.
23. live . . . another: (1) dwell side by side; (2) make a living off one another. **25. rasher:** slice of bacon.
26. for money: at any price. **29. jealious:** jealous.
32. out: at odds.
41. more than reason: larger than is reasonable. Note the wordplay on *much, more, Moor.* **41–42. honest:** chaste.
44. best grace: highest excellence. **48. stomachs:** appetites.
51. cover: lay the table.
54. I . . . duty. Launcelot now takes *cover* in the sense "put on your hat." Cf. II.ix.44.

55. quarrelling with occasion: taking issue at every opportunity.
59. meat: food.
61. table. Here used in the sense "food," as is shown by *serv'd in.*
62. cover'd: i.e. served in covered dishes.
63–64. as . . . govern: as your whims and notions shall determine.
65. discretion: discrimination. **suited:** adapted to suit the occasion.
68. A many: many. **better place:** higher rank.
69. Garnish'd: furnished (with words). **tricksy:** ingenious, clever.
70. Defy: disdain, set at nought. **matter:** substance, meaning. **How cheer'st thou:** what cheer. **82. Pawn'd:** staked.
87. stomach: (1) appetite; (2) inclination.
89. howsome'er: howsoever.
90. disgest: digest. **set you forth:** (1) serve you up; (2) praise you highly.

IV.i. Location: Venice. A court of justice.
3. answer: satisfy.

A stony adversary, an inhuman wretch,
Uncapable of pity, void and empty
From any dram of mercy.
Ant. I have heard
Your Grace hath ta'en great pains to qualify
His rigorous course; but since he stands obdurate,
And that no lawful means can carry me
Out of his envy's reach, I do oppose
My patience to his fury, and am arm'd
To suffer, with a quietness of spirit,
The very tyranny and rage of his.
Duke. Go one, and call the Jew into the court.
Sal. He is ready at the door; he comes, my lord.

Enter Shylock.

Duke. Make room, and let him stand before our face.
Shylock, the world thinks, and I think so too,
That thou but leadest this fashion of thy malice
To the last hour of act, and then 'tis thought
Thou'lt show thy mercy and remorse more strange
Than is thy strange apparent cruelty;
And where thou now exacts the penalty,
Which is a pound of this poor merchant's flesh,
Thou wilt not only loose the forfeiture,
But touch'd with humane gentleness and love,
Forgive a moi'ty of the principal,
Glancing an eye of pity on his losses,
That have of late so huddled on his back,
Enow to press a royal merchant down,
And pluck commiseration of [his state]
From brassy bosoms and rough hearts of flints,
From stubborn Turks, and Tartars never train'd
To offices of tender courtesy.
We all expect a gentle answer, Jew!
Shy. I have possess'd your Grace of what I purpose,
And by our holy Sabaoth have I sworn
To have the due and forfeit of my bond.
If you deny it, let the danger light
Upon your charter and your city's freedom!
You'll ask me why I rather choose to have
A weight of carrion flesh than to receive
Three thousand ducats. I'll not answer that;
But say it is my humor, is it answer'd?
What if my house be troubled with a rat,
And I be pleas'd to give ten thousand ducats
To have it ban'd? What, are you answer'd yet?
Some men there are love not a gaping pig;
Some that are mad if they behold a cat;
And others, when the bagpipe sings i' th' nose,
Cannot contain their urine: for affection,
[Mistress] of passion, sways it to the mood
Of what it likes or loathes. Now for your answer:
As there is no firm reason to be rend'red
Why he cannot abide a gaping pig;
Why he, a harmless necessary cat;
Why he, a woollen bagpipe, but of force
Must yield to such inevitable shame
As to offend, himself being offended;
So can I give no reason, nor I will not,
More than a lodg'd hate and a certain loathing
I bear Antonio, that I follow thus
A losing suit against him. Are you answered?
Bass. This is no answer, thou unfeeling man,
To excuse the current of thy cruelty.
Shy. I am not bound to please thee with my answers.
Bass. Do all men kill the things they do not love?
Shy. Hates any man the thing he would not kill?
Bass. Every offense is not a hate at first.
Shy. What, wouldst thou have a serpent sting thee twice?
Ant. I pray you think you question with the Jew:
You may as well go stand upon the beach
And bid the main flood bate his usual height;
You may as well use question with the wolf
Why he hath made the ewe bleak for the lamb;
You may as well forbid the mountain pines
To wag their high tops, and to make no noise
When they are fretten with the gusts of heaven;
You may as well do any thing most hard
As seek to soften that—than which what's harder?—
His Jewish heart! Therefore I do beseech you
Make no moe offers, use no farther means,
But with all brief and plain conveniency
Let me have judgment and the Jew his will.
Bass. For thy three thousand ducats here is six.
Shy. If every ducat in six thousand ducats
Were in six parts, and every part a ducat,
I would not draw them, I would have my bond.
Duke. How shalt thou hope for mercy, rend'ring none?
Shy. What judgment shall I dread, doing no wrong?
You have among you many a purchas'd slave,
Which like your asses, and your dogs and mules,
You use in abject and in slavish parts,
Because you bought them. Shall I say to you,
"Let them be free! Marry them to your heirs!
Why sweat they under burthens? Let their beds
Be made as soft as yours, and let their palates
Be season'd with such viands"? You will answer,
"The slaves are ours." So do I answer you:
The pound of flesh which I demand of him
Is dearly bought as mine, and I will have it.

6. dram: i.e. smallest amount. **7. qualify:** moderate.
10. envy's: malice's. **13. tyranny:** violence, cruelty.
16. our. The "royal" plural.
18. leadest: carriest, maintainest. **fashion:** pretense.
19. act: performance.
20. remorse: pity. **strange:** extraordinary.
24. loose: release, i.e. waive; or, since *loose* and *lose* are doublets in Elizabethan spelling, Shakespeare may have intended *lose* = forget. **forfeiture:** forfeit. **26. moi'ty:** portion. **28. huddled:** crowded.
32. stubborn: unyielding. **33. offices:** acts.
35. possess'd: informed.
36. Sabaoth: for *Sabbath* (here = Saturday). *Sabaoth* (a Hebrew word) properly means "armies" or "hosts" but was frequently confused with *Sabbath*. **38. danger:** harm. **43. humor:** whim.
46. ban'd: poisoned.
47. gaping pig: roasted pig with its mouth open.

50. affection: instinctual feelings.
54–56. he . . . he . . . he: one . . . another . . . still another.
60. lodg'd: deep-seated. **62. losing:** unprofitable.
64. current: tenor, drift.
70. think: bear in mind. **question:** argue.
72. main flood: high tide. **bate:** diminish. **74. bleak:** bleat.
77. fretten: fretted. **82. conveniency:** fitness. **87. draw:** take.
92. parts: tasks. **95. burthens:** burdens. **97. season'd:** gratified.

If you deny me, fie upon your law!
There is no force in the decrees of Venice.
I stand for judgment. Answer—shall I have it?

Duke. Upon my power I may dismiss this court,
Unless Bellario, a learned doctor,
Whom I have sent for to determine this,
Come here to-day.

Sal. My lord, here stays without
A messenger with letters from the doctor,
New come from Padua.

Duke. Bring us the letters; call the messenger.

Bass. Good cheer, Antonio! what, man, courage yet!
The Jew shall have my flesh, blood, bones, and all,
Ere thou shalt lose for me one drop of blood.

Ant. I am a tainted wether of the flock,
Meetest for death; the weakest kind of fruit
Drops earliest to the ground, and so let me.
You cannot better be employ'd, Bassanio,
Than to live still and write mine epitaph.

Enter NERISSA [*dressed like a lawyer's clerk*].

Duke. Came you from Padua, from Bellario?

Ner. From both, my lord. Bellario greets your Grace. [*Presenting a letter*.]

Bass. Why dost thou whet thy knife so earnestly?

Shy. To cut the forfeiture from that bankrout there.

Gra. Not on thy sole, but on thy soul, harsh Jew,
Thou mak'st thy knife keen; but no metal can,
No, not the hangman's axe, bear half the keenness
Of thy sharp envy. Can no prayers pierce thee?

Shy. No, none that thou hast wit enough to make.

Gra. O, be thou damn'd, inexecrable dog!
And for thy life let justice be accus'd.
Thou almost mak'st me waver in my faith
To hold opinion with Pythagoras,
That souls of animals infuse themselves
Into the trunks of men. Thy currish spirit
Govern'd a wolf, who hang'd for human slaughter,
Even from the gallows did his fell soul fleet,
And whilst thou layest in thy unhallowed dam,
Infus'd itself in thee; for thy desires
Are wolvish, bloody, starv'd, and ravenous.

Shy. Till thou canst rail the seal from off my bond,
Thou but offend'st thy lungs to speak so loud.
Repair thy wit, good youth, or it will fall
To cureless ruin. I stand here for law.

Duke. This letter from Bellario doth commend
A young and learned doctor to our court.
Where is he?

Ner. He attendeth here hard by
To know your answer, whether you'll admit him.

Duke. With all my heart. Some three or four of you
Go give him courteous conduct to this place.
Mean time the court shall hear Bellario's letter.

[*Reads*.] "Your Grace shall understand that at the receipt of your letter I am very sick, but in the instant that your messenger came, in loving visitation was with me a young doctor of Rome. His name is Balthazar. I acquainted him with the cause in controversy between the Jew and Antonio the merchant. We turn'd o'er many books together. He is furnish'd with my opinion, which better'd with his own learning, the greatness whereof I cannot enough commend, comes with him, at my importunity, to fill up your Grace's request in my stead. I beseech you let his lack of years be no impediment to let him lack a reverend estimation, for I never knew so young a body with so old a head. I leave him to your gracious acceptance, whose trial shall better publish his commendation."

Enter PORTIA *for Balthazar*.

You hear the learn'd Bellario, what he writes,
And here I take it is the doctor come.
Give me your hand. Come you from old Bellario?

Por. I did, my lord.

Duke. You are welcome, take your place.
Are you acquainted with the difference
That holds this present question in the court?

Por. I am informed throughly of the cause.
Which is the merchant here? and which the Jew?

Duke. Antonio and old Shylock, both stand forth.

Por. Is your name Shylock?

Shy. Shylock is my name.

Por. Of a strange nature is the suit you follow,
Yet in such rule that the Venetian law
Cannot impugn you as you do proceed.—
You stand within his danger, do you not?

Ant. Ay, so he says.

Por. Do you confess the bond?

Ant. I do.

Por. Then must the Jew be merciful.

Shy. On what compulsion must I? tell me that.

Por. The quality of mercy is not strain'd,
It droppeth as the gentle rain from heaven
Upon the place beneath. It is twice blest:
It blesseth him that gives and him that takes.
'Tis mightiest in the mightiest, it becomes
The throned monarch better than his crown.
His sceptre shows the force of temporal power,
The attribute to awe and majesty,
Wherein doth sit the dread and fear of kings;
But mercy is above this sceptred sway,
It is enthroned in the hearts of kings,

104. Upon: by, in accordance with.
107. stays without: waits outside.
108. letters: a letter (Latin *litterae*).
114. tainted: infected with disease, sickly. **wether:** sheep (properly, a castrated ram).
118. live still: go on living. **125. hangman's:** executioner's.
128. inexecrable: that cannot be execrated enough.
129. for thy life: because you are permitted to live.
135. fell: cruel. **140. offend'st:** injurest.
142. cureless: incurable.

148. conduct: escort. **162. to . . . lack:** which will deprive him of.
165. trial: testing. **publish:** make known.
171. difference: dispute.
173. throughly: thoroughly. **cause:** case. **178. rule:** order.
180. within his danger: at his mercy.
184. strain'd: constrained, compelled.
186. is twice blest: i.e. bestows a double blessing.
191. attribute to: visible symbol of.

It is an attribute to God himself;
And earthly power doth then show likest God's
When mercy seasons justice. Therefore, Jew,
Though justice be thy plea, consider this,
That in the course of justice, none of us
Should see salvation. We do pray for mercy,
And that same prayer doth teach us all to render
The deeds of mercy. I have spoke thus much
To mitigate the justice of thy plea,
Which if thou follow, this strict court of Venice
Must needs give sentence 'gainst the merchant there.
Shy. My deeds upon my head! I crave the law,
The penalty and forfeit of my bond.
Por. Is he not able to discharge the money?
Bass. Yes, here I tender it for him in the court,
Yea, twice the sum. If that will not suffice,
I will be bound to pay it ten times o'er,
On forfeit of my hands, my head, my heart.
If this will not suffice, it must appear
That malice bears down truth. [*To the Duke.*] And I beseech you
Wrest once the law to your authority:
To do a great right, do a little wrong,
And curb this cruel devil of his will.
Por. It must not be, there is no power in Venice
Can alter a decree established.
'Twill be recorded for a precedent,
And many an error by the same example
Will rush into the state. It cannot be.
Shy. A Daniel come to judgment! yea, a Daniel!
O wise young judge, how I do honor thee!
Por. I pray you let me look upon the bond.
Shy. Here 'tis, most reverend doctor, here it is.
Por. Shylock, there's thrice thy money off'red thee.
Shy. An oath, an oath, I have an oath in heaven!
Shall I lay perjury upon my soul?
[No], not for Venice.
Por. Why, this bond is forfeit,
And lawfully by this the Jew may claim
A pound of flesh, to be by him cut off
Nearest the merchant's heart. Be merciful,
Take thrice thy money, bid me tear the bond.
Shy. When it is paid according to the tenure.
It doth appear you are a worthy judge;
You know the law, your exposition
Hath been most sound. I charge you by the law,
Whereof you are a well-deserving pillar,
Proceed to judgment. By my soul I swear
There is no power in the tongue of man
To alter me: I stay here on my bond.

195. attribute to: quality or characteristic of.
197. seasons: tempers.
201. that same prayer: i.e. the Lord's Prayer.
203. mitigate . . . plea: i.e. soften your plea for strict justice.
206. My . . head: i.e. I ask no mercy for my deeds (a rejection of Portia's "we do pray for mercy"; cf. lines 88–89).
214. bears down truth: overthrows righteousness.
215. Wrest: strain, forcibly subject.
223. Daniel. In the Apocryphal story of Susannah and the Elders, the youthful Daniel acts as judge when the Elders accuse Susannah. By the time Gratiano picks up the term (lines 333, 340 below), the parallel has become closer, for Daniel turned the tables on the accusers just as Portia has done. **235. tenure:** tenor.
242. stay . . . on: make a stand on, i.e. insist upon the fulfillment of.

Ant. Most heartily I do beseech the court
To give the judgment.
Por. Why then thus it is:
You must prepare your bosom for his knife—
Shy. O noble judge, O excellent young man!
Por. For the intent and purpose of the law
Hath full relation to the penalty,
Which here appeareth due upon the bond.
Shy. 'Tis very true. O wise and upright judge!
How much more elder art thou than thy looks!
Por. Therefore lay bare your bosom.
Shy. Ay, his breast,
So says the bond, doth it not, noble judge?
"Nearest his heart," those are the very words.
Por. It is so. Are there balance here to weigh
The flesh?
Shy. I have them ready.
Por. Have by some surgeon, Shylock, on your charge,
To stop his wounds, lest he do bleed to death.
Shy. Is it so nominated in the bond?
Por. It is not so express'd, but what of that?
'Twere good you do so much for charity.
Shy. I cannot find it, 'tis not in the bond.
Por. You, merchant, have you any thing to say?
Ant. But little; I am arm'd and well prepar'd.
Give me your hand, Bassanio, fare you well.
Grieve not that I am fall'n to this for you;
For herein Fortune shows herself more kind
Than is her custom. It is still her use
To let the wretched man outlive his wealth,
To view with hollow eye and wrinkled brow
An age of poverty; from which ling'ring penance
Of such misery doth she cut me off.
Commend me to your honorable wife,
Tell her the process of Antonio's end,
Say how I lov'd you, speak me fair in death;
And when the tale is told, bid her be judge
Whether Bassanio had not once a love.
Repent but you that you shall lose your friend,
And he repents not that he pays your debt;
For if the Jew do cut but deep enough,
I'll pay it instantly with all my heart.
Bass. Antonio, I am married to a wife
Which is as dear to me as life itself,
But life itself, my wife, and all the world,
Are not with me esteem'd above thy life.
I would lose all, ay, sacrifice them all
Here to this devil, to deliver you.
Por. Your wife would give you little thanks for that
If she were by to hear you make the offer.
Gra. I have a wife who I protest I love;
I would she were in heaven, so she could
Entreat some power to change this currish Jew.
Ner. 'Tis well you offer it behind her back,
The wish would make else an unquiet house.

248. Hath . . . to: i.e. fully authorizes.
255. balance: scales (construed as plural).
257. on your charge: at your expense.
268. still: regularly. **use:** habit, custom. **274. process:** story.
277. love: i.e. friend. **278. Repent but you:** grieve only.

Shy. [*Aside.*] These be the Christian husbands.
I have a daughter—
Would any of the stock of Barrabas
Had been her husband rather than a Christian!
—We trifle time. I pray thee pursue sentence.
Por. A pound of that same merchant's flesh is thine,
The court awards it, and the law doth give it.
Shy. Most rightful judge!
Por. And you must cut this flesh from off his breast,
The law allows it, and the court awards it.
Shy. Most learned judge, a sentence! Come prepare!
Por. Tarry a little, there is something else.
This bond doth give thee here no jot of blood;
The words expressly are "a pound of flesh."
Take then thy bond, take thou thy pound of flesh,
But in the cutting it, if thou dost shed
One drop of Christian blood, thy lands and goods
Are by the laws of Venice confiscate
Unto the state of Venice.
Gra. O upright judge! Mark, Jew. O learned judge!
Shy. Is that the law?
Por. Thyself shalt see the act;
For as thou urgest justice, be assur'd
Thou shalt have justice more than thou desir'st.
Gra. O learned judge! Mark, Jew, a learned judge!
Shy. I take this offer then; pay the bond thrice
And let the Christian go.
Bass. Here is the money.
Por. Soft,
The Jew shall have all justice. Soft, no haste.
He shall have nothing but the penalty.
Gra. O Jew! an upright judge, a learned judge!
Por. Therefore prepare thee to cut off the flesh.
Shed thou no blood, nor cut thou less nor more
But just a pound of flesh. If thou tak'st more
Or less than a just pound, be it but so much
As makes it light or heavy in the substance
Or the division of the twentith part
Of one poor scruple, nay, if the scale do turn
But in the estimation of a hair,
Thou diest, and all thy goods are confiscate.
Gra. A second Daniel! a Daniel, Jew!
Now, infidel, I have you on the hip.
Por. Why doth the Jew pause? Take thy forfeiture.
Shy. Give me my principal, and let me go.
Bass. I have it ready for thee, here it is.
Por. He hath refus'd it in the open court;
He shall have merely justice and his bond.
Gra. A Daniel, still say I, a second Daniel!
I thank thee, Jew, for teaching me that word.
Shy. Shall I not have barely my principal?
Por. Thou shalt have nothing but the forfeiture,
To be so taken at thy peril, Jew.
Shy. Why then the devil give him good of it!
I'll stay no longer question.
Por. Tarry, Jew,
The law hath yet another hold on you.
It is enacted in the laws of Venice,
If it be proved against an alien,
That by direct or indirect attempts
He seek the life of any citizen,
The party 'gainst the which he doth contrive
Shall seize one half his goods; the other half
Comes to the privy coffer of the state,
And the offender's life lies in the mercy
Of the Duke only, 'gainst all other voice:
In which predicament I say thou stand'st;
For it appears, by manifest proceeding,
That indirectly, and directly too,
Thou hast contrived against the very life
Of the defendant; and thou hast incurr'd
The danger formerly by me rehears'd.
Down therefore, and beg mercy of the Duke.
Gra. Beg that thou mayst have leave to hang thyself,
And yet thy wealth being forfeit to the state,
Thou hast not left the value of a cord;
Therefore thou must be hang'd at the state's charge.
Duke. That thou shalt see the difference of our spirit,
I pardon thee thy life before thou ask it.
For half thy wealth, it is Antonio's;
The other half comes to the general state,
Which humbleness may drive unto a fine.
Por. Ay, for the state, not for Antonio.
Shy. Nay, take my life and all, pardon not that:
You take my house when you do take the prop
That doth sustain my house; you take my life
When you do take the means whereby I live.
Por. What mercy can you render him, Antonio?
Gra. A halter gratis—nothing else, for God sake.
Ant. So please my lord the Duke and all the court
To quit the fine for one half of his goods,
I am content; so he will let me have
The other half in use, to render it
Upon his death unto the gentleman
That lately stole his daughter.
Two things provided more, that for this favor
He presently become a Christian;
The other, that he do record a gift,

296. **Barrabas:** a criminal (whose name is properly spelled *Barabbas*) whom the Jews asked Pontius Pilate to release in preference to Jesus (see Mark 15:6–15); also the villainous chief character (*Barabas*) of Marlowe's *Jew of Malta*. Here and in Marlowe the name is pronounced with main stress on the first syllable.
298. **trifle:** waste on trifles. **pursue:** proceed with.
320. **Soft:** not so fast. 321. **all:** only. 327. **just:** exact.
328. **substance:** gross weight.
329. **division:** fraction. **twentith:** twentieth.
330. **scruple:** twenty grains, a very small amount.
331. **in . . . hair:** by a hair's breadth (?) or by the weight of a hair (?).
334. **on the hip.** See I.iii.46.

346. **stay . . . question:** await no further determination of the case.
352. **contrive:** plot. 353. **seize:** take possession of.
369. **pardon:** remit (a penalty). 372. **drive:** reduce.
373. **Ay . . . Antonio:** i.e. yes, with respect to the state's portion, but not Antonio's.
376–77. **you . . . live.** Cf. Ecclesiasticus 34:23: "He that taketh away his neighbor's living, slayeth him" (Geneva; verse 22 in King James).
380–85. **So . . . daughter.** Antonio's stipulations here are not clear. The principal ambiguities lie in *quit* (line 381) and in *in use* (line 383); *quit* may mean either "remit" or "(have him) pay," and *in use* may mean either "in trust" or "to be used as a source of income." Commentators generally favor the first interpretation in each case.
387. **presently:** immediately.

Here in the court, of all he dies possess'd
Unto his son Lorenzo and his daughter.
Duke. He shall do this, or else I do recant
The pardon that I late pronounced here.
Por. Art thou contented, Jew? what dost thou say?
Shy. I am content.
Por. Clerk, draw a deed of gift.
Shy. I pray you give me leave to go from hence,
I am not well. Send the deed after me,
And I will sign it.
Duke. Get thee gone, but do it.
[*Gra*.] In christ'ning shalt thou have two god-fathers:
Had I been judge, thou shouldst have had ten more,
To bring thee to the gallows, not to the font.
Exit [*Shylock*].
Duke. Sir, I entreat you home with me to dinner.
Por. I humbly do desire your Grace of pardon,
I must away this night toward Padua,
And it is meet I presently set forth.
Duke. I am sorry that your leisure serves you not.
Antonio, gratify this gentleman,
For in my mind you are much bound to him.
Exeunt Duke and his Train.
Bass. Most worthy gentleman, I and my friend
Have by your wisdom been this day acquitted
Of grievous penalties, in lieu whereof
Three thousand ducats, due unto the Jew,
We freely cope your courteous pains withal.
Ant. And stand indebted, over and above,
In love and service to you evermore.
Por. He is well paid that is well satisfied,
And I, delivering you, am satisfied,
And therein do account myself well paid.
My mind was never yet more mercenary.
I pray you know me when we meet again;
I wish you well, and so I take my leave.
Bass. Dear sir, of force I must attempt you further.
Take some remembrance of us as a tribute,
Not as fee. Grant me two things, I pray you,
Not to deny me, and to pardon me.
Por. You press me far, and therefore I will yield.
[*To Antonio*.] Give me your gloves, I'll wear them for your sake,
[*To Bassanio*.] And for your love I'll take this ring from you.
Do not draw back your hand, I'll take no more,
And you in love shall not deny me this!
Bass. This ring, good sir, alas, it is a trifle!
I will not shame myself to give you this.
Por. I will have nothing else but only this,
And now methinks I have a mind to it.
Bass. There's more depends on this than on the value.
The dearest ring in Venice will I give you,
And find it out by proclamation;
Only for this, I pray you pardon me.

Por. I see, sir, you are liberal in offers.
You taught me first to beg, and now methinks
You teach me how a beggar should be answer'd.
Bass. Good sir, this ring was given me by my wife,
And when she put it on, she made me vow
That I should neither sell, nor give, nor lose it.
Por. That 'scuse serves many men to save their gifts,
And if your wife be not a mad woman,
And know how well I have deserv'd this ring,
She would not hold out enemy for ever
For giving it to me. Well, peace be with you!
Exeunt [*Portia and Nerissa*].
Ant. My Lord Bassanio, let him have the ring.
Let his deservings and my love withal
Be valued 'gainst your wive's commandement.
Bass. Go, Gratiano, run and overtake him;
Give him the ring, and bring him, if thou canst,
Unto Antonio's house. Away, make haste.
Exit Gratiano.
Come, you and I will thither presently,
And in the morning early will we both
Fly toward Belmont. Come, Antonio. *Exeunt.*

[Scene II]

Enter [Portia *and*] Nerissa [*disguised as before*].

Por. Inquire the Jew's house out, give him this deed,
And let him sign it. We'll away to-night,
And be a day before our husbands home.
This deed will be well welcome to Lorenzo.

Enter Gratiano.

Gra. Fair sir, you are well o'erta'en.
My Lord Bassanio upon more advice
Hath sent you here this ring, and doth entreat
Your company at dinner.
Por. That cannot be.
His ring I do accept most thankfully,
And so I pray you tell him; furthermore,
I pray you show my youth old Shylock's house.
Gra. That will I do.
Ner. Sir, I would speak with you.
[*Aside to Portia*.] I'll see if I can get my husband's ring,
Which I did make him swear to keep for ever.
Por. [*Aside to Nerissa*.] Thou mayst, I warrant.
We shall have old swearing
That they did give the rings away to men;
But we'll outface them, and outswear them too.—
Away, make haste. Thou know'st where I will tarry.
Ner. Come, good sir, will you show me to this house? [*Exeunt*.]

399. ten more: i.e. a jury of twelve. 406. gratify: reward.
407. mind: opinion. 410. lieu: return.
412. cope: match, requite. 421. attempt: urge.
436. proclamation: advertisement (by a herald).

448. For giving: because you gave.
451. wive's: wife's. commandement. Quadrisyllabic, as frequently in Shakespeare.

IV.ii. Location: Venice. A street.
6. more advice: further consideration.
15. old: plentiful (a colloquialism).

[ACT V, SCENE I]

Enter LORENZO *and* JESSICA.

Lor. The moon shines bright. In such a night as this,
When the sweet wind did gently kiss the trees,
And they did make no noise, in such a night
Troilus methinks mounted the Troyan walls,
And sigh'd his soul toward the Grecian tents,
Where Cressid lay that night.

Jes. In such a night
Did Thisby fearfully o'ertrip the dew,
And saw the lion's shadow ere himself,
And ran dismayed away.

Lor. In such a night
Stood Dido with a willow in her hand
Upon the wild sea-banks, and waft her love
To come again to Carthage.

Jes. In such a night
Medea gathered the enchanted herbs
That did renew old Aeson.

Lor. In such a night
Did Jessica steal from the wealthy Jew,
And with an unthrift love did run from Venice,
As far as Belmont.

Jes. In such a night
Did young Lorenzo swear he lov'd her well,
Stealing her soul with many vows of faith,
And ne'er a true one.

Lor. In such a night
Did pretty Jessica (like a little shrow)
Slander her love, and he forgave it her.

Jes. I would out-night you, did nobody come;
But hark, I hear the footing of a man.

Enter a MESSENGER.

Lor. Who comes so fast in silence of the night?

Mess. A friend.

Lor. A friend! what friend? your name, I pray you, friend?

Mess. Stephano is my name, and I bring word
My mistress will before the break of day
Be here at Belmont. She doth stray about
By holy crosses, where she kneels and prays
For happy wedlock hours.

Lor. Who comes with her?

Mess. None but a holy hermit and her maid.
I pray you, is my master yet return'd?

Lor. He is not, nor we have not heard from him.
But go we in, I pray thee, Jessica,
And ceremoniously let us prepare
Some welcome for the mistress of the house.

Enter Clown [LAUNCELOT].

Laun. Sola, sola! wo ha, ho! sola, sola!

Lor. Who calls?

Laun. Sola! did you see Master Lorenzo? Master Lorenzo, sola, sola!

Lor. Leave hollowing, man—here.

Laun. Sola! where, where?

Lor. Here!

Laun. Tell him there's a post come from my master, with his horn full of good news. My master will be here ere morning. [*Exit.*]

Lor. Sweet soul, let's in, and there expect their coming.
And yet no matter; why should we go in?
My friend [Stephano], signify, I pray you,
Within the house, your mistress is at hand,
And bring your music forth into the air.
[*Exit Messenger.*]
How sweet the moonlight sleeps upon this bank!
Here will we sit, and let the sounds of music
Creep in our ears. Soft stillness and the night
Become the touches of sweet harmony.
Sit, Jessica. Look how the floor of heaven
Is thick inlaid with patens of bright gold.
There's not the smallest orb which thou behold'st
But in his motion like an angel sings,
Still quiring to the young-ey'd cherubins;
Such harmony is in immortal souls,
But whilst this muddy vesture of decay
Doth grossly close it in, we cannot hear it.

[*Enter* MUSICIANS.]

Come ho, and wake Diana with a hymn,
With sweetest touches pierce your mistress' ear,
And draw her home with music. *Play Music.*

Jes. I am never merry when I hear sweet music.

Lor. The reason is, your spirits are attentive;
For do but note a wild and wanton herd
Or race of youthful and unhandled colts,
Fetching mad bounds, bellowing and neighing loud,
Which is the hot condition of their blood,
If they but hear perchance a trumpet sound,
Or any air of music touch their ears,
You shall perceive them make a mutual stand,
Their savage eyes turn'd to a modest gaze,
By the sweet power of music; therefore the poet
Did feign that Orpheus drew trees, stones, and floods;
Since nought so stockish, hard, and full of rage,
But music for the time doth change his nature.
The man that hath no music in himself,

V.i. Location: Belmont. The avenue before Portia's house.
4. **Troilus**: Trojan prince and lover of Cressida, who proved faithless to him after she had been sent from Troy to the Greek camp.
7. **Thisby**: Thisbe, beloved of Pyramus; their story is the subject of the play performed by Bottom and his fellows in *A Midsummer Night's Dream* (V.i).
10. **Dido**: queen of Carthage who loved Aeneas and was deserted by him. **willow**. The emblem of slighted love. 11. **waft**: beckoned.
13. **Medea**: an enchantress who helped Jason win the Golden Fleece.
14. **Aeson**: Jason's father, whose youth was restored by Medea's magic arts. 16. **unthrift**: prodigal. 21. **shrow**: shrew.
24. **footing**: footsteps.
31. **crosses**: wayside crosses (common both in England and in Italy).

39. **Sola**. Perhaps the imitation of a post horn (see lines 46–48).
49. **expect**: await. 51. **signify**: give notice.
57. **Become**: befit. **touches**: notes (literally, the fingering of a musical instrument). 59. **patens**: metal plates or disks.
62. **quiring**: singing in harmony. **young-ey'd**: i.e. eternally keen-sighted. 64. **muddy . . . decay**: i.e. mortal flesh.
65. **it . . . it**: man's immortal soul . . . the music of the spheres.
66. **Diana**: here, the moon-goddess.
68 s.d. **Music**: musicians (so also in line 98).
70. **spirits are attentive**: faculties are concentrated.
71. **wanton**: untrained (cf. *unhandled*, line 72). 72. **race**: herd.
77. **mutual**: common.
79. **the poet**: perhaps Ovid, who tells the story of the Thracian musician Orpheus in his *Metamorphoses*.
81. **stockish**: resembling a block of wood, i.e. unfeeling.

Nor is not moved with concord of sweet sounds,
Is fit for treasons, stratagems, and spoils;
The motions of his spirit are dull as night,
And his affections dark as [Erebus]:
Let no such man be trusted. Mark the music.

Enter Portia *and* Nerissa.

Por. That light we see is burning in my hall.
How far that little candle throws his beams!
So shines a good deed in a naughty world.

Ner. When the moon shone, we did not see the candle.

Por. So doth the greater glory dim the less:
A substitute shines brightly as a king
Until a king be by, and then his state
Empties itself, as doth an inland brook
Into the main of waters. Music, hark!

Ner. It is your music, madam, of the house.

Por. Nothing is good, I see, without respect;
Methinks it sounds much sweeter than by day.

Ner. Silence bestows that virtue on it, madam.

Por. The crow doth sing as sweetly as the lark
When neither is attended; and I think
The nightingale, if she should sing by day
When every goose is cackling, would be thought
No better a musician than the wren.
How many things by season season'd are
To their right praise and true perfection!
Peace ho! the Moon sleeps with Endymion,
And would not be awak'd. [*Music ceases.*]

Lor. That is the voice,
Or I am much deceiv'd, of Portia.

Por. He knows me as the blind man knows the cuckoo,
By the bad voice!

Lor. Dear lady, welcome home!

Por. We have been praying for our husbands' welfare,
Which speed we hope the better for our words.
Are they return'd?

Lor. Madam, they are not yet;
But there is come a messenger before,
To signify their coming.

Por. Go in, Nerissa.
Give order to my servants that they take
No note at all of our being absent hence—
Nor you, Lorenzo—Jessica, nor you.
[*A tucket sounds.*]

Lor. Your husband is at hand, I hear his trumpet.
We are no tell-tales, madam, fear you not.

Por. This night methinks is but the daylight sick,
It looks a little paler. 'Tis a day,
Such as the day is when the sun is hid.

Enter Bassanio, Antonio, Gratiano, *and their* Followers.

Bass. We should hold day with the Antipodes,
If you would walk in absence of the sun.

Por. Let me give light, but let me not be light,
For a light wife doth make a heavy husband,
And never be Bassanio so for me—
But God sort all! You are welcome home, my lord.

Bass. I thank you, madam. Give welcome to my friend;
This is the man, this is Antonio,
To whom I am so infinitely bound.

Por. You should in all sense be much bound to him,
For as I hear he was much bound for you.

Ant. No more than I am well acquitted of.

Por. Sir, you are very welcome to our house.
It must appear in other ways than words,
Therefore I scant this breathing courtesy.

Gra. [*To Nerissa.*] By yonder moon I swear you do me wrong;
In faith, I gave it to the judge's clerk.
Would he were gelt that had it, for my part,
Since you do take it, love, so much at heart.

Por. A quarrel ho already! what's the matter?

Gra. About a hoop of gold, a paltry ring
That she did give me, whose posy was
For all the world like cutler's poetry
Upon a knife, "Love me, and leave me not."

Ner. What talk you of the posy or the value?
You swore to me, when I did give [it] you,
That you would wear it till your hour of death,
And that it should lie with you in your grave.
Though not for me, yet for your vehement oaths,
You should have been respective and have kept it.
Gave it a judge's clerk! no, God's my judge,
The clerk will ne'er wear hair on 's face that had it.

Gra. He will, and if he live to be a man.

Ner. Ay, if a woman live to be a man.

Gra. Now, by this hand, I gave it to a youth,
A kind of boy, a little scrubbed boy,
No higher than thyself, the judge's clerk,
A prating boy, that begg'd it as a fee.
I could not for my heart deny it him.

Por. You were to blame, I must be plain with you,
To part so slightly with your wife's first gift,
A thing stuck on with oaths upon your finger,
And so riveted with faith unto your flesh.
I gave my love a ring, and made him swear
Never to part with it, and here he stands.
I dare be sworn for him he would not leave it,
Nor pluck it from his finger, for the wealth
That the world masters. Now, in faith, Gratiano,
You give your wife too unkind a cause of grief;
And 'twere to me I should be mad at it.

85. stratagems: deceptive tricks. **spoils:** acts of plunder.
87. Erebus: the hell of classical mythology. **91. naughty:** wicked.
97. main of waters: ocean.
99. respect: reference to other circumstances.
103. When . . . attended: i.e. when each sings alone.
107. by . . . are: are matured by favorable occasion.
109. Endymion: a shepherd loved by the moon-goddess, who caused him to be cast into a perpetual sleep in a cave on Mount Latmos.
115. Which speed: who thrive.
121 s.d. tucket: distinctive series of notes on a trumpet.

127–28. We . . . sun: i.e. if you always walked at night (when it is day on the other side of the world), we would have day then too.
129. be light: be wanton. **130. heavy:** sorrowful.
132. sort: dispose. **136. sense:** reason.
141. scant: make brief. **breathing courtesy:** utterance of welcome.
144. gelt: gelded.
148. posy: motto, sometimes in verse (*posy* = *poesy*), inscribed inside a ring. **150. leave:** part with. **156. respective:** careful.
162. scrubbed: scrubby, stunted. **174. masters:** possesses.

Bass. [*Aside.*] Why, I were best to cut my left hand off,
And swear I lost the ring defending it.
Gra. My Lord Bassanio gave his ring away
Unto the judge that begg'd it, and indeed
Deserv'd it too; and then the boy, his clerk,
That took some pains in writing, he begg'd mine,
And neither man nor master would take aught
But the two rings.
Por. What ring gave you, my lord?
Not that, I hope, which you receiv'd of me.
Bass. If I could add a lie unto a fault,
I would deny it; but you see my finger
Hath not the ring upon it, it is gone.
Por. Even so void is your false heart of truth.
By heaven, I will ne'er come in your bed
Until I see the ring!
Ner. Nor I in yours
Till I again see mine!
Bass. Sweet Portia,
If you did know to whom I gave the ring,
If you did know for whom I gave the ring,
And would conceive for what I gave the ring,
And how unwillingly I left the ring,
When nought would be accepted but the ring,
You would abate the strength of your displeasure.
Por. If you had known the virtue of the ring,
Or half her worthiness that gave the ring,
Or your own honor to contain the ring,
You would not then have parted with the ring.
What man is there so much unreasonable,
If you had pleas'd to have defended it
With any terms of zeal, wanted the modesty
To urge the thing held as a ceremony?
Nerissa teaches me what to believe—
I'll die for't but some woman had the ring!
Bass. No, by my honor, madam, by my soul,
No woman had it, but a civil doctor,
Which did refuse three thousand ducats of me,
And begg'd the ring, the which I did deny him,
And suffer'd him to go displeas'd away—
Even he that had held up the very life
Of my dear friend. What should I say, sweet lady?
I was enforc'd to send it after him,
I was beset with shame and courtesy,
My honor would not let ingratitude
So much besmear it. Pardon me, good lady,
For by these blessed candles of the night,
Had you been there, I think you would have begg'd
The ring of me to give the worthy doctor.
Por. Let not that doctor e'er come near my house.
Since he hath got the jewel that I loved,
And that which you did swear to keep for me,
I will become as liberal as you,
I'll not deny him any thing I have,
No, not my body nor my husband's bed.
Know him I shall, I am well sure of it.

199. virtue: power, efficacy. **201. contain:** retain.
205. wanted the modesty: who would have been so lacking in moderation as.
206. urge: insist on being given. **ceremony:** sacred pledge.
210. civil doctor: doctor of civil law.
226. liberal: (1) generous; (2) sexually free.

Lie not a night from home. Watch me like Argus;
If you do not, if I be left alone,
Now by mine honor, which is yet mine own,
I'll have that doctor for [my] bedfellow.
Ner. And I his clerk; therefore be well advis'd
How you do leave me to mine own protection.
Gra. Well, do you so; let not me take him then,
For if I do, I'll mar the young clerk's pen.
Ant. I am th' unhappy subject of these quarrels.
Por. Sir, grieve not you, you are welcome notwithstanding.
Bass. Portia, forgive me this enforced wrong,
And in the hearing of these many friends
I swear to thee, even by thine own fair eyes,
Wherein I see myself—
Por. Mark you but that!
In both my eyes he doubly sees himself,
In each eye, one. Swear by your double self,
And there's an oath of credit.
Bass. Nay, but hear me.
Pardon this fault, and by my soul I swear
I never more will break an oath with thee.
Ant. I once did lend my body for his wealth,
Which but for him that had your husband's ring
Had quite miscarried. I dare be bound again,
My soul upon the forfeit, that your lord
Will never more break faith advisedly.
Por. Then you shall be his surety. Give him this,
And bid him keep it better than the other.
Ant. Here, Lord Bassanio, swear to keep this ring.
Bass. By heaven, it is the same I gave the doctor!
Por. I had it of him. Pardon me, Bassanio,
For by this ring, the doctor lay with me.
Ner. And pardon me, my gentle Gratiano,
For that same scrubbed boy, the doctor's clerk,
In lieu of this last night did lie with me.
Gra. Why, this is like the mending of highways
In summer, where the ways are fair enough.
What, are we cuckolds ere we have deserv'd it?
Por. Speak not so grossly, you are all amaz'd.
Here is a letter, read it at your leisure.
It comes from Padua, from Bellario.
There you shall find that Portia was the doctor,
Nerissa there her clerk. Lorenzo here
Shall witness I set forth as soon as you,
And even but now return'd; I have not yet
Enter'd my house. Antonio, you are welcome,
And I have better news in store for you
Than you expect. Unseal this letter soon;
There you shall find three of your argosies
Are richly come to harbor suddenly.
You shall not know by what strange accident
I chanced on this letter.
Ant. I am dumb.
Bass. Were you the doctor, and I knew you not?

230. from: away from. **Argus:** a hundred-eyed monster.
237. pen. With ribald second sense.
245. double. With play on the double reflection and the sense "deceitful." **246. of credit:** to be believed.
249. wealth: welfare. **253. advisedly:** deliberately.
262. In lieu of: in return for.
263–64. this . . . enough: this development makes what was fairly bad before even worse. **266. amaz'd:** bewildered.

Gra. Were you the clerk that is to make me cuckold?
Ner. Ay, but the clerk that never means to do it,
Unless he live until he be a man.
Bass. Sweet doctor, you shall be my bedfellow—
When I am absent, then lie with my wife.
Ant. Sweet lady, you have given me life and living,
For here I read for certain that my ships
Are safely come to road.
Por. How now, Lorenzo?
My clerk hath some good comforts too for you.
Ner. Ay, and I'll give them him without a fee.
There do I give to you and Jessica,
From the rich Jew, a special deed of gift,
After his death, of all he dies possess'd of.
Lor. Fair ladies, you drop manna in the way
Of starved people.
Por. It is almost morning,
And yet I am sure you are not satisfied
Of these events at full. Let us go in,
And charge us there upon inter'gatories,
And we will answer all things faithfully.
Gra. Let it be so. The first inter'gatory
That my Nerissa shall be sworn on is,
Whether till the next night she had rather stay,
Or go to bed now, being two hours to day.
But were the day come, I should wish it dark
Till I were couching with the doctor's clerk.
Well, while I live I'll fear no other thing
So sore, as keeping safe Nerissa's ring. *Exeunt.*

286. living: possessions. **288. road:** harbor.
298. charge . . . inter'gatories: question us under oath.
306. fear: be concerned about.

NOTE ON THE TEXT

The Merchant of Venice ("or otherwise called the Iewe of Venyce"—an alternative title recorded in the Stationers' Register on July 22, 1598) was first published in quarto (Q1) in 1600 and was printed by J. Roberts for Thomas Heyes; this edition is here used as the basic text. A second quarto (Q2), set from a copy of Q1, was printed in 1619, ostensibly by J. Roberts, with the fraudulent date 1600; Roberts had no connection with Q2, which was printed by William Jaggard for Thomas Pavier.[1] The text of the First Folio (1623) was based on a slightly corrected and edited copy of Q1. A third quarto (Q3), printed from a copy of Q1, appeared in 1637.

There has been disagreement about the exact nature of the manuscript underlying Q1. It seems most reasonable to believe that it was set either from Shakespeare's "foul papers" or from a "fair copy" of these, perhaps one made by Shakespeare himself. "Fair copy" rather than the more usual "foul papers" (Mahood, however, favors extensive use of "foul papers") is suggested because the text of Q1 is remarkably clean and, with the exception of the Salarino-Salerio tangle (see below), presents few difficulties. That tangle points clearly to the use of some kind of authorial copy; so do the occasional use of variant speech-prefixes for Shylock and Launcelot and the permissive nature of several stage directions (see, for example, II.i o.s.d. and II.ii.113 s.d.). Some scholars detect slight traces of playhouse annotation, but the evidence is ambiguous, and the Salerio-Salarino confusion makes it highly unlikely that the manuscript behind Q1 could ever have served as an actual prompt-book.

The problem concerning the names Salarino and Salerio in Q1 has engaged the attention of a long line of editors. Until Dover Wilson's edition (1926), either Salerio was absorbed into Salarino or the names were taken as representing two different characters. The form *Salarino* (once *Salerino,* at II.vi o.s.d.) never occurs in the text proper but only in stage directions and speech-prefixes *(Sal., Salar., Salari.,* and once [III.i.79] *Saleri.*), and not even in these after III.i. At III.ii.219 s.d. a character with the name Salerio enters as a messenger from Antonio, whose friend he is, and this name occurs five times in the remaining lines of the scene. Wilson suggested that at this stage in the composition of the play Shakespeare made up his mind to alter the name Salarino to Salerio, neglecting, not uncharacteristically, to make the necessary adjustments in the earlier stage directions and speech-prefixes. The present text, like that of all other recent editions (except Mahood, who distinguishes between Salarino and Solanio as companions of Bassanio and Salerio as a messenger from Venice), adopts Wilson's solution.

Q2 and F1 both show a certain amount of editing: Q2 tidies the text and adds a few new unauthorized readings and some stage directions; F1 introduces several sound effects which suggest the theatre, and gets rid of a couple of oaths. Neither text, however, shows evidence of a serious attempt at correction against an independent manuscript, though it is possible that F1 was printed from a copy of Q1 which had had some direct connection with the theatre. The more significant variants in Q2 and F1 are recorded in the Textual Notes.

For further information, see: J. D. Wilson, ed., New Shakespeare *The Merchant of Venice* (Cambridge, 1926); J. R. Brown, "The Compositors of *Hamlet* Q2 and *The Merchant of Venice,*" *SB,* VII (1955), 17–40, and ed., New Arden *The Merchant of Venice* (London, 1955); W. W. Greg, *The Shakespeare First Folio* (Oxford, 1955); D. F. McKenzie, "Compositor B's Role in *The Merchant of Venice,*" *SB,* XII (1958), 75–90; J. K. Walton, *The Quarto Copy for the First Folio of Shakespeare* (Dublin, 1971); Christopher Spencer, "Shakespeare's *Merchant of Venice* in Sixty-three Editions," *SB,* XXV (1972), 86–106; Yasumasa Okamoto, "'The three Sallies' Reconsidered: A Case Study in Shakespeare's Use of Proper Names," *Shakespeare Studies* (Tokyo), XV (1976–7), 57–75; Stanley Wells, Gary Taylor, John Jowett, and William Montgomery, *William Shakespeare: A Textual Companion* (Oxford, 1987); M. M. Mahood, ed., New Cambridge *The Merchant of Venice* (Cambridge, 1987).

[1] It should be noted that the collations of Q1 and Q2 which appear in the Cambridge *Shakespeare* (Vol. II, 1863 and 1891) and in the Furness *Variorum* (1888) reverse the correct order of the two quartos.

TEXTUAL NOTES

Title: The . . . Venice] *F1;* The most excellent Historie of the Merchant of Venice. With the extreame crueltie of Shylocke the Iewe towards the sayd Merchant, in cutting a iust pound of his flesh: and the obtayning of Portia by the choyse of three chests. As it hath beene diuers times acted by the Lord Chamberlaine his Seruants. Written by William Shakespeare. *Q1 (title-page);* The comicall History of the Merchant of Venice. *Q1 (title on sig. A2ʳ)*
Dramatis personae: *subs. as first given in Q3*
Act-scene division: *none in Q1–2; F1 marks acts only; scene divisions from Rowe and later editors (see first note to each scene); present act-scene arrangement as a whole first established by Capell*

I.i

I.i] *Rowe;* Actus Primus. *F1*
Location: *Theobald*
o.s.d. Antonio] *Capell;* Anthonio *Q1–2, F1 (throughout in s.dd. and text)*
o.s.d. Salerio] *Wilson;* Salaryno *Q1–2;* Salarino *F1*
o.s.d. Solanio] *Capell;* Salanio *Q1–2, F1*
8 s.p. Sal.] *Wilson (and F1 for* Salarino*);* Salarino. *(or* Salar., Sala., Sal. *throughout scene) Q1–2, F1*
13 them, . . . reverence,] *F3 (after F1);* them . . . reuerence *Q1;* them, . . . reuerence *Q2, F1*
15 s.p. Sol.] *Capell;* Salanio. *Q1–2;* Salar. *F1*
27 dock'd] *Rowe;* docks *Q1–2, F1*
47 neither?] *Q2;* neither: *Q1, F1*
56 s.d. Lorenzo] *Rowe;* Lorenso *Q1–2, F1 (sporadically throughout, but usually* Lorenzo*)*
93 Sir] sir an *F1*
98 damn] *F4;* dam *Q1–2, F1*
112 vendible] *F1;* vendable *Q1–2*
112 s.d. Gratiano and Lorenzo] *Theobald*
113 that—] *ed. (after Collier);* that *Q1–2, F1*
114 nothing,] *Q2, F1;* nothing *Q1*
146 youth,] *Q2, F1;* youth *Q1*

I.ii

I.ii] *Rowe*
Location: *Rowe, Capell*
7 mean] smal *F1*
21 reasoning] reason *F1*
32 you] *om. Q2*
45, 60 Palentine] Palatine *Q2*
55 Bon] *Capell;* Boune *Q1–2, F1*
60 throstle] *Pope;* Trassell *Q1–2, F1*
61 a-cap'ring] *hyphen, Dyce*
77 Scottish] other *F1*
110 pray God grant] wish *F1*

I.iii

I.iii] *Rowe*
Location: *Rowe, Theobald*
19 Indies;] *F3 (subs.);* Indies, *Q1–2, F1*
19 Rialto] *F2;* Ryalta *Q1–2, F1*
21 hath,] *Theobald;* hath *Q1–2, F1*
29, 33, 41 s.pp. Shy.] *Q2;* Iew. *Q1, F1*
41 s.d. Aside.] *Rowe*
50 well-won] *Q2;* well-wone *Q1;* well-worne *F1*
59 s.d. To Antonio.] *Rowe*
59 fair,] *Rowe;* faire *Q1–2, F1*
64 s.d. To Bassanio.] *Staunton*
64–5 Is . . . would?] are you resolu'd, / How much he would haue? *Q2;* is he yet possest / How much he would? *F1*
67 s.d. To Bassanio.] *Brown*
79 eanlings] *Capell;* eanelings *Q1–2, F1*
84 pill'd] *Knight;* pyld *Q1–2;* pil'd *F1*
104 see, the rate—] *Lloyd conj. (in Cambridge);* see the rate. *Q1–2, F1*
127 day, another time] *F1* (day;); day another time, *Q1–2*
129 moneys''?] *Theobald;* moneyes. *Q1–2, F1*

II.i

II.i] *Rowe;* Actus Secundus. *F1*
Location: *Rowe, Capell*
o.s.d. Flourish cornets.] *F1 (at end of s.d.); placed as in Malone*
o.s.d. the Prince of Morocco] *Capell;* Morochus *Q1–2, F1*
9 valiant; by . . . swear] *Steevens (subs.);* valiant, (by . . . sweare) *Q1, Q2* (valiant), *F1*
10 best-regarded] *hyphen, Malone*
31 thee] *Rowe;* the *Q1–2, F1*
31 alas the while!] *Pope;* alas, the while *Q1–2, F1*
35 page] *Theobald;* rage *Q1–2, F1*
46 s.d. Cornets.] *F1 (after l. 45); placed as in Dyce*

II.ii

II.ii] *Rowe*
Location: *Rowe, Capell*
1 s.p. Laun.] *Rowe;* Clowne. *Q1–2, F1*
3, 4, 5, 8, 9 Gobbo] *Q2;* Iobbe *Q1, F1;* Job *F3*
4 Launcelot] *Rowe;* Launcelet *or* Lancelet *Q1–2, F1 (throughout)*
12 heavens,] *Collier;* heauens *Q1–2, F1*
22 well] ill *Q2*
27 incarnation] incarnal *Q2*
32 confusions] conclusions *Q2*
33 young man] *Q2;* young-man *Q1, F1*
35, 49 s.dd. Aside.] *Johnson*
36 sand-blind] *hyphen, F1*
37 gravel-blind] *hyphen, Rowe*
68 s.d. Aside.] *Collier*
74 sand-blind] *hyphen, Rowe*
75 indeed] *F1;* in deede *Q1–2*
79 murder] *F1;* muder *Q1;* Murther *Q2*
80 in the end] at the length *Q2*
91, 109 indeed] *Q2, F1;* in deede *Q1*
95 fill-horse] *Pope;* philhorse *Q1, F1;* pilhorse *Q2*
95 has] *Q2, F1;* hase *Q1*
98 last] *Q2;* lost *Q1, F1*
113 s.d. one . . . Leonardo] *ed. (after Theobald)*
118 s.d. Exit . . . men.] *Q2*
157 head, well!] head. Well, *Q2*
157–8 s.d. Looking . . . palm.] *Johnson*
162 Aleven] *Brown;* a leuen *Q1, F1;* eleuen *Q2*
163 coming-in] *hyphen, Theobald*
168 twinkling] twinkling of an eye *Q2*
168 s.d. with Old Gobbo] *Rowe (subs.)*
174 s.d. Exit Leonardo.] *placed as in Theobald; after l. 173, Q1–2, F1*
180 must.] *Q2;* must *Q1;* must: *F1*
183 faults,] *Q2;* faults *Q1;* faults; *F1*
184 known,] *F1;* knowne; *Q1;* knowne. *Q2*

II.iii

II.iii] *Capell*
Location: *Theobald*
10 s.p. Laun.] *Q2;* Clowne. *Q1, F1*
10–1 tongue. Most . . . Jew!] *Johnson (subs.);* tongue, most . . . Iewe, *Q1–2, F1*
13 something] somewhat *F1*
15 s.d. Exit Launcelot.] *Capell;* Exit. *Q2, F1 (after l. 14)*

II.iv

II.iv] *Capell*
Location: *Theobald*
o.s.d. Salerio] *Wilson;* Salaryno *Q1;* Salarino *Q2;* Slarino *F1*
o.s.d. Solanio] *Capell;* Salanio *Q1–2, F1*
5 s.p. Sal.] *Wilson (and F1 for* Salarino*;* throughout scene*);* Salari. *Q1 (or* Sal. *throughout scene);* Salar. *Q2 (throughout scene)*
9 s.d. with a letter] *F1; s.d. placed as in Q2; after l. 9, Q1, F1*
14 Love-news,] *Q2 (subs.; hyphen, F2);* Loue, newes *Q1;* Loue newes *F1*
19 here,] *F1;* heere *Q1–2*
20 privately.] *Q2;* priuatly, *Q1;* priuately: *F1*
20 s.d. Exit Clown.] *placed as in White; after l. 23, Q1–2, F1*
27 s.d. with Solanio] *Wilson (subs., after Capell)*
39 s.d. Exeunt.] *Rowe;* Exit. *Q1–2, F1*

II.v

II.v] *Capell*
Location: *Capell (after Theobald)*
o.s.d. was,] *ed.;* was *Q1, F1; Q2 s.d. reads:* Enter the Iew and Lancelet.
1 s.p. Shy.] *Q2;* Iewe. *Q1, F1*
22 together.] *Johnson;* together, *Q1–2, F1*
28 What, are there] *Q2;* What are there *Q1;* What are their *F1*
43 Jewess'] *Pope;* Iewes *Q1–2, F1*
43 s.d. Exit.] *Rowe*
47 Snail-slow] *hyphen, Q2, F1*

II.vi

II.vi] *Capell*
Location: *ed. (after Halliwell)*
o.s.d. two of] *ed.*
o.s.d. Salerio] *Wilson;* Salerino *Q1–2;* Salino *F1 (and s.p. l. 20)*
2 Desir'd] *Q2;* desired *Q1, F1*
18 over-weather'd] *Q3;* ouer-wetherd *Q1–2;* ouer-wither'd *F1*
25 Ho] *Q2;* Howe *Q1;* Hoa *F1*
25 s.d. Enter] *Capell*
25 s.d. in boy's clothes] *Rowe*
50 s.d. Exit above.] *Theobald*
58 gentlemen] *Q2, F1;* gentleman *Q1*
59 s.d. with . . . Salerio] *Wilson (after Capell)*
66 I . . . you.] *om. Q2 (which continues ll. 67–8 to Antonio)*

II.vii

II.vii] *Capell*
Location: *Rowe, Capell*
o.s.d. Flourish cornets.] *Malone (after Capell; but F1, probably in error, places* Flo. Cornets. *after Scene viii o.s.d.)*
o.s.d. the Prince of] *Capell*
17 give—] *Capell;* giue, *Q1, Q2, (c), F1;* giue *Q2 (u)*
18 threatens.] *Rowe;* threatens *Q1–2, F1*
62 s.d. He . . . casket.] *Rowe (subs.)*
65 s.d. Reads.] *Dyce*
69 tombs] *Johnson conj.;* timber *Q1–2, F1*
74 Cold] *Capell; Mor.* Cold *Q1–2, F1 (repeated s.p.)*
77 s.d. with his Train] *Dyce*

II.viii

II.viii] *Capell*
Location: *Rowe, Capell*
o.s.d. Salerio] *Wilson;* Salarino *Q1–2, F1*
o.s.d. Solanio] Salanio *Q2*
1 s.p. Sal.] *Wilson (and Q1, F1 for* Salarino*);* Salar. *Q2; so throughout scene*
39 Slubber] *Q2, F1;* slumber *Q1*

II.ix

II.ix] *Capell*
Location: *Rowe, Capell*
o.s.d. Servitor] *Q2;* Seruiture *Q1, F1*
3 s.d. Flourish cornets.] *F1 (at end of s.d.); placed as in Malone (after Capell)*
3 s.d. the Prince of] *Capell*
3 s.d. Arragon] *Q2, F1;* Arrogon *Q1*
6 rites] *Pope;* rights *Q1–2, F1*
19 me.] *Q3* (me;); me, *Q1–2, F1*
48 chaff] *Q2, F1;* chaft *Q1*
49 varnish'd] *F1;* varnist *Q1;* vernish'd *Q2*
52 s.d. He . . . casket.] *Rowe (subs.; after l. 53); placed as in Collier*
55 schedule] *F4;* shedule *Q1;* sedule *Q2;* scedule *F1*
63 s.d. Reads.] *Q2* (hee reads.)
64 judgment] *Q2;* iudement *Q1, F1*
73 Still] *Capell; Arrag.* Still *Q1–2, F1 (repeated s.p.)*
78 wroth] *Q3;* wroath *Q1–2, F1*
78 s.d. Exit . . . Train.] *Capell (subs., after Rowe)*
98 high-day] *hyphen, F1*
101 Bassanio, Lord Love,] *Rowe;* Bassanio Lord, loue *Q1–2, F1*

III.i

III.i] Rowe; Actus Tertius. F1
Location: Rowe, Theobald
o.s.d. Enter] Q2, F1
o.s.d. Solanio] Salanio Q2
o.s.d. Salerio] Wilson; Salarino Q1–2, F1
2 s.p. Sal.] Wilson (and F1 for Salarino); Salari. Q1; Salar. Q2; so throughout scene, except Saleri. at l. 79, Q1
7 gossip] gossips Q2, F1
7 Report] Q3; report Q1–2, F1
14 company!—] Capell (after F1 company!); company. Q1–2
21 s.d. Enter Shylock.] placed as in Q2; after l. 23, Q1, F1
29 flidge] fledg'd Q2, F1
69 humility? Revenge.] Rowe; humillity, reuenge? Q1–2, F1
71 example? Why, revenge.] F2; example, why reuenge? Q1–2, F1
73 s.d. Servingman] Brown; man Q1–2, F1
74 s.p. Serv.] Rowe
78 s.d. Solanio . . . Servingman] Wilson (after Capell); Q1 repeats Enter Tuball. after this exit
91 them? Why, so—] Capell (subs.); them, why so? Q1, F1; them, why so: Q2
91 what's] how much is F1
98 Genoa—] Rowe; Genowa? Q1, F1; Genoway. Q2
107 Heard] Kellner conj.; heere Q1–2; here F1
107 Genoa?] Rowe; Genowa. Q1, F1; Genoway. Q2
109 one] in one Q2
121 turkis] ed.; Turkies Q1–2, F1

III.ii

III.ii] Rowe
Location: Rowe, Capell
o.s.d. Nerissa] Capell
56 paid] Q2; payed Q1; paied F1
61 live;] Rowe; liue Q1–2, F1
62 s.d. Here music.] F1
66 s.p. All.] W. J. Lawrence conj. (in Brown); Q1–2, F1 place Replie, replie. to the right opposite l. 65
67 eyes] F1; eye Q1–2
68 dies] F4; dies: Q1–2; dies, F1
69 lies.] F1 (lies:); lies Q1; lyes, Q2
71 I'll begin it.] in roman, as if not part of the song (which is in italics), Q1–2, F1; Johnson first included it in the song
81 vice] F2; voyce Q1–2, F1
84 stairs] F4; stayers Q1–2, F1
93 make] Pope; maketh Q1–2; makes F1
108 s.d. Aside.] from Granville's version (1701)
109 rash-embrac'd] hyphen, Theobald
110 shudd'ring] F1; shyddring Q1–2
114 s.d. Opening . . . casket.] Rowe
117 whether] F1; whither Q1–2
122 t' entrap] Q2, F1 (t'intrap); tyntrap Q1
131 s.d. Reads.] Dyce
142 eyes,] Capell; eyes: Q1, F1; eyes; Q2
158 something] nothing F1
161 than] Johnson; then Q1–2, F1; then in F2
171 yours—my lord's!—] Wilson; yours, my Lords, Q1; yours, my Lord, Q2, F1
199 lov'd; for intermission] Theobald; lou'd for intermission, Q1–2, F1
201 caskets] Casket Q2
203 sweat] F3; swet Q1–2, F1
204 roof] Q2; rough Q1, F1
232 s.d. Gives . . . letter.] Theobald
236 s.d. Bassanio] Rowe
258 braggart] Pope; Braggart, Q1–2, F1
266 life-blood] hyphen, Rowe
267 hit?] Theobald; hit, Q1–2, F1
293 best-condition'd] hyphen, 1734 ed., Capell
315 s.p., s.d. Bass. (Reads.)] Rowe
327 Nor] No Q2

III.iii

III.iii] Rowe
Location: Rowe, Theobald
o.s.d. Solanio] F1; Salerio Q1; Salarino Q2
1 s.p. Shy.] Rowe; Iew. Q1–2, F1 (throughout scene)
14 dull-ey'd] hyphen, Q2
24 s.p. Sol.] F1; Sal. Q1–2

III.iv

III.iv] Rowe
Location: Rowe, Capell
o.s.d. Balthazar] Theobald
20 soul,] Q2; soule; Q1, F1
21 cruelty] misery Q2
23 Hear] Thirlby conj.; heere Q1–2, F1
44 s.d. Jessica and Lorenzo] Rowe
45 Balthazar] F2; Balthaser Q1–2, F1
46 honest-true] hyphen, Theobald
49 Padua] Theobald; Mantua Q1–2, F1
50 cousin's] Q2, F1; cosin Q1
53 traject] Rowe; Tranect Q1–2, F1
56 s.d. Exit.] Q2
63 accoutered] apparreld Q2
80 near] F3; nere Q1–2, F1

III.v

III.v] Capell
Location: Capell (subs.)
1 s.p. Laun.] Rowe; Clowne. Q1–2, F1 (throughout scene)
13 indeed] Q2, F1; in deede Q1
22 e'en] Q2, F1; in Q1 (a Shakespearean form for e'en)
28 comes.] Q2, F1; come? Q1
29 jealious] iealous Q2, F1
49 wit-snapper] hyphen, Q2, F1
70 cheer'st] F1; cherst Q1; far'st Q2
74 life,] Q2; life Q1, F1
77 merit it] Pope; meane it, it Q1, F1; meane it, then Q2
78 In] Is F1
84 a] F1
89 howsome'er] F4; how so mere Q1; howsoere Q2; how som ere F1
90 s.d. Exeunt.] F1; Exit. Q1–2

IV.i

IV.i] Rowe; Actus Quartus. F1
Location: Rowe, Capell
o.s.d. Salerio] Cambridge
o.s.d. with others] Capell (subs.)
4 inhuman] Rowe; inhumaine, Q1; inhumane, Q2, F1
22 exacts] exact'st F1
24 loose] lose F4
30 his state] Q2, F1; this states Q1
31 flints] flint Q2
35 s.p. Shy.] Rowe; Iewe. Q1–2 (until l. 183, except ll. 65, 67, 69 in Q2), F1 (until l. 206)
36 Sabaoth] Sabbath Q2, F1
50 urine: for affection,] Thirlby conj.; vrine for affection. Q1–2, F1
51 Mistress] Thirlby and Waldron conj.; Maisters Q1–2, F1
56 bagpipe,] Alexander; bagpipe: Q1, F1; Bagpipe; Q2
58 offend,] Q2; offend Q1, F1
69 What,] F3; What Q1–2, F1
74 bleak] bleate F1
75 You may] Or even F1
75 mountain] F1; mountaine of Q1–2
79 that—] Rowe (subs.); that Q1; that, Q2, F1
79 what's harder?] F1 (what harder?); what's harder: Q1–2
100 bought as mine,] ed.; bought, as mine Q1; bought, tis mine Q2, F1
118 s.d. dressed . . . clerk] Rowe
120 both, my lord. Bellario] Pope; both? my L. Bellario Q1; both, my L. Bellario Q2; both. / My Lord Bellario F1
120 s.d. Presenting a letter.] Capell
123 sole] F1 (soale); soule Q1–2
134 human] Rowe; humaine Q1; humane Q2, F1
136 whilst] Q2, F1; whilest Q1
136 dam,] Q2, F1; dam; Q1
142 cureless] endlesse F1
150 s.d. Reads.] Collier MS (Duke reades)
154, 166 s.d. Balthazar] Boswell; Balthazer Q1–2; Balthasar F1 (but Balthazar in l. 166 s.d.)
167 You] Wilson; Duke. You Q1–2, F1 (repeated s.p.)
214 s.d. To the Duke.] ed.
230 No] Q2, F1; Not Q1
239 well-deserving] hyphen, F1
250 s.p. Shy.] Q2; Iew. Q1, F1 (until l. 314), Q2 (ll. 294, 301, 304)
258 do] should F1
259 Is it so] It is not F1
263 You] Come F1
281 instantly] presently Q2
295 s.d. Aside.] Rowe
318 s.p. Shy.] Rowe; Iew. Q1–2, F1
324 off] Q2, F1; of Q1
326 tak'st] cutst Q2
329 twentith] twentieth F1
346 question] heere in question Q2
398 s.p. Gra.] Q2, F1; Shy. Q1
400 s.d. Shylock] Rowe
407 s.d. Exeunt] Capell; Exit Q1–2, F1
426 s.d. To Antonio.] Cambridge (after Capell)
427 s.d. To Bassanio.] Cambridge (after Capell)
448 s.d. Portia and Nerissa] Theobald (subs.)

IV.ii

IV.ii] Capell
Location: Capell (subs.)
o.s.d. Portia and] F1
o.s.d. disguised as before] Kittredge
13 s.d. Aside to Portia.] Capell, Pope
15 s.d. Aside to Nerissa.] Capell (subs.)
19 s.d. Exeunt.] F1

V.i

V.i] Rowe; Actus Quintus. F1
Location: Rowe, Capell
6 Cressid] Theobald; Cressed Q1, F1; Cressada Q2
18 lov'd] F1; loued Q1–2
39 s.p. Laun.] Rowe; Clowne. Q1–2, F1 (throughout scene)
41–2 Master . . . sola,] Cambridge; M. Lorenzo, & M. Lorenzo sola, Q1, F1; M. Lorenzo, M. Lorenzo, sola, Q2; M. Lorenzo, and M. Lorenza, sola, F2; M. Lorenzo, and Mrs. Lorenza, sola, F3
48 s.d. Exit.] Capell
49 Sweet soul] arranged as in Rowe, who, however, reads Sweet Love, following F2; last words of Launcelot's speech, Q1–2, F1
51 Stephano] Q2; Stephen Q1, F1
53 s.d. Exit Messenger.] Johnson
56 ears. Soft stillness] F2 (subs.); eares soft stilnes, Q1–2, F1
59 inlaid] Rowe; inlayed Q1–2, F1
62 young-ey'd] hyphen, Q3
65 it in] in it Q2, F1
65 s.d. Enter Musicians.] Malone (after Capell)
81 stockish, hard,] F1; stockish hard Q1–2
87 Erebus] F2; Terebus Q1–2; Erobus F1
106 wren] Q2, F1; Renne Q1
109 ho!] Malone (subs.); how Q1–2, F1
110 s.d. Music ceases.] F1
114 husbands' welfare] husband health Q2
121 s.d. A tucket sounds.] F1
142 s.d. To Nerissa.] Rowe
152 it] Q2, F1
157 no . . . judge,] but wel I know F1
177 s.d. Aside.] Theobald
214 had held up] did vphold Q2
223 house.] Johnson; house Q1; house, Q2, F1
230 Argus] F2; Argos Q1–2, F1
233 my] Q2, F1; mine Q1
244 himself,] Neilson; himselfe: Q1–2, F1
245 one. Swear] Rowe (subs.); one, sweare Q1–2, F1
288 road] Pope; Rode Q1–2, F1; Rodes F2; Rhodes F3
298 inter'gatories] F1; intergotories Q1–2
300 inter'gatory] F1; intergotory Q1–2
303 bed now,] Q2; bed now Q1; bed, now F1
305 Till] That Q2
307 s.d. Exeunt.] Exeunt. / FINIS. Q1–2, F1

The Merry Wives of Windsor

NO TWO COMEDIES by Shakespeare are alike, yet there is a sense in which *The Merry Wives of Windsor* is more of a play apart than any of its companions. It is true that Elizabethan England is often clearly visible beneath the disguise of Venice, Athens, the corrupt Vienna of Duke Vincentio, Messina, or even the geographically indistinct shores of Illyria. *The Merry Wives of Windsor*, however, is unique among the comedies in that it is set explicitly in an English town well known to members of Shakespeare's audience. Moreover, it set out to remind this audience of local topography and detail. Not only Windsor Castle and its great park, but Datchet Mead, the road to Frogmore, the Garter Inn, even the great oak, the sawpit nearby, and the castle ditch where Page conceals himself with Shallow and Slender were names and places possessed of an independent, contemporary existence outside Shakespeare's play. On the whole, the most successful productions of *The Merry Wives of Windsor* are those which recognize and are concerned to build up a stage picture of ordinary, middle-class life in a small country town, among innkeepers and doctors, country magistrates, parsons, citizens and their wives and children: people who exist on the periphery of a royal residence without themselves belonging to the court.

The comedy may reflect a specific occasion as well as a particular place. The Folio, although not the quarto, text refers to the necessity of putting the town in order in preparation for a visit from the Queen (V.v.43–46) and to forthcoming ceremonies at Windsor Castle connected with the Knights of the Garter (V.v.56–73). Leslie Hotson has argued that these passages indicate a first performance before Elizabeth at Westminster during the Garter Feast of April 23, 1597, one month before the newly elected knights were formally installed at Windsor. Among the noblemen named that April was the second Lord Hunsdon, Elizabeth's Lord Chamberlain and official patron of Shakespeare's company. There is a well-known theatrical tradition, first recorded by John Dennis in 1702, to the effect that Shakespeare wrote *The Merry Wives of Windsor* at royal command, because the Queen had asked for a play about Falstaff in love, and that he completed it within fourteen days. Hotson speculates that Hunsdon commissioned and paid for the first performance of the comedy as a way of thanking his sovereign for the favor she had shown him. If this is so, Shakespeare would have had to put the piece together at great speed in order to get it ready and rehearsed in the few weeks between Hunsdon's realization of the honor in store for him and the Garter Feast of April 23.

Hotson's theory is in many ways attractive, and it has the merit of explaining the presence of two passages in the Folio text which otherwise seem puzzling. One might also argue that a comedy concerned, as this one is, with the punishment of a knight whose principles and behavior contravene all the ideals of his rank would be appropriate, almost as a kind of anti-masque, at a Garter feast. Nor is Falstaff the only character in the play who inverts the values celebrated by the Order of the Garter and makes himself ridiculous in the process. The Garter motto, "*Honi soit qui mal y pense*" (evil be to him who thinks evil), applies neatly to the jealous Ford, a man who persists in seeing evil where none exists and, in the effort to prove that his own wife is unfaithful, covers himself with shame.

Acceptance of the hypothesis that *The Merry Wives of Windsor* was originally conceived as a court entertainment on the occasion of a Garter feast, and subsequently transferred to the public stage, does not necessarily involve agreement with Hotson that the first performance occurred on April 23, 1597. A number of scholars, perplexed by the problem of the play's relation to *1* and *2 Henry IV* and to *Henry V*, have preferred a date closer to the quarto edition of 1602. Falstaff appears, of course, in both the Henry IV plays and his death is reported in *Henry V*. Bardolph is present in all three of the histories as well as in *The Merry Wives of Windsor*, and so is Mistress Quickly. Pistol swaggers through both *2 Henry IV* and *Henry V*, while Justice Shallow and Nym have another existence in *2 Henry IV* and *Henry V* respectively. Hotson's date for *The Merry Wives of Windsor* would place it between the first and second parts of *Henry IV* and well before *Henry V*. Is it reasonable to suppose that Shakespeare interrupted his work on *2 Henry IV* in order to exhibit Falstaff in a wholly different dramatic context, and that Pistol, Justice Shallow, and Nym made their first appearance in the comedy and were then displayed more extensively in the later histories? For some commentators, the idea is palpably absurd; for others, it represents an entirely plausible account of what happened.

Those who regard *The Merry Wives of Windsor* as a play of 1597 and those who see it as a work composed after *Henry V* do manage to agree on one point: Falstaff's adventures in Windsor do not lock into the historical sequence at any moment that is even vaguely definable. Anne Page's suitor Fenton is disapproved of by her father on the grounds that he is "of too high a region," impoverished, and once "kept company with the wild Prince and Poins" (III.ii.72–73). The reference is tantalizing but not very helpful. Fenton himself is never mentioned in the histories and, in *The Merry Wives of Windsor* itself, the past tense implied in the verb *kept* resolutely refuses to explain itself. Not only is there no talk of rebellion and civil war in the comedy, no mention of Prince Hal apart from this one, let alone of Henry V and preparations for the invasion of France, but the throne is occupied (at least in the Folio text) by a queen. Falstaff worries at one point (IV.v.94 ff.) that he will become a laughingstock at court should the news of his discomfitures extend so far, but we are never enlightened as to his position there or the reasons behind his present sojourn at the Garter Inn. Even odder is the fact that Mistress Quickly—and just what she is doing acting as servant to a French physician in Windsor is anybody's guess—and Falstaff do not appear to know each other or to share any common memories of the Boar's Head at Eastcheap in *1 Henry IV*.

Most readers have found that Mistress Quickly, Shallow, Bardolph, Pistol, and Nym are not quite the same people as their namesakes in the histories, although they share certain characteristics and speech habits. In the case of Falstaff, the sense of disappointment has been marked. The Windsor version of Sir John seems so tame and unresourceful compared with his far greater self of Eastcheap, Shrewsbury, Gaultree, and even Gloucestershire that critics have often wanted to explain the falling-off in terms of Shakespeare's artistic dismay at having to resurrect a character he had finished with, and officially buried in *Henry V*, simply in order to comply with a not very perceptive royal command. Arguments of this kind tend to isolate character from plot and to stress the former at the expense of the latter in a way that Elizabethans (and indeed most audiences before 1850) would not have understood. In Sophocles' tragedy *Ajax*, Odysseus is a hero by virtue of exactly those qualities of rationalism and flexibility which, in Sophocles' *Philoctetes*, make him despicable. The basic outline of the character is the same in both plays, but the plots happen to be very different and Sophocles (with the later approval of Aristotle) obviously thought of character not as an end in itself but as the servant and expressive agent of plot. Aeschylus and even Euripides operated in a similar fashion, and so did medieval dramatists. Shakespeare may never have come any closer to Aristotle's *Poetics* than the version at several removes in Sidney's *Apology for Poetry* (1595), but for him too character, although developed to an extent that would have been unthinkable even in Euripides, was still largely dependent upon plot and dramatic genre. Falstaff is probably another and a lesser creature in *The Merry Wives of Windsor* than that cunning destroyer of illusions familiar in the Henry IV plays not because his creator had tired of him but because in this play he inhabits and is subject to a world of comedy, as opposed to representing a comic viewpoint in the alien but vulnerable world of historical event.

No one has ever been able to find a specific source for the plot of *The Merry Wives of Windsor*, although the tradition to which it belongs has never been in doubt. It is a *fabliau*, a merry tale dealing with sexual misadventure, and as such it has analogues in most of the literatures of the world. Probably Shakespeare derived part of the plot for *The Merchant of Venice* from the prose collection *Il Pecorone* by Ser Giovanni. He could also have found there, in the second story told on the first day, a version of the Falstaff/Ford situation that is closer than most. In the Italian story, a young law student called Bucciuolo asks his professor for advice in conducting a love affair. The lady he selects turns out to be the professor's wife, although the student (and, for a time, the professor himself) is ignorant of this fact. When the professor realizes at last that he has been teaching the student how to seduce his own wife, he raids the house, but the lady conceals her lover under a heap of wet washing. The next day, the unsuspecting student tells the professor of his narrow escape, and also of the night of illicit love which followed. The professor learns that his wife has made a second assignation with the young man for that evening, collects a band of neighbors and relations, and makes an ignominious and fruitless assault upon the pile of washing. The lover, on this occasion, had already been smuggled out of the house by the guilty wife. Publicly humiliated, a cuckold without being able to prove it, the professor goes mad. Only then does the student discover what he has done. He flees from Bologna.

This story may well have helped to shape *The Merry Wives of Windsor*. Yet the basic situation in Shakespeare's play is really very different. The Italian professor was genuinely cuckolded, but Shakespeare's Ford is merely fool enough to think he is. Bucciuolo succeeded in committing adultery but Falstaff is tricked by a pair of wives who may be merry but are also fiercely chaste. It is the would-be lover in Shakespeare who is cleverly deceived, not the husband. There are, of course, *fabliaux* in which wives intrigue against and not for their suitors, and in some of them the baffled lecher is subjected to three separate humiliations, as Falstaff is. Moreover, Lyly's *Endimion* (1588), a comedy Shakespeare almost certainly knew, had already staged the scene of a nobleman pinched and tormented by fairies—real ones, in Lyly—as a punishment for lust. Ultimately, however, *The Merry Wives of Windsor* is a strikingly independent creation: a play which extends and, in a sense, violates the calculatedly limited form of the merry tale. Although it is perhaps the lightest of Shakespeare's comedies, a play which contains no threat of death, in which nothing much is at risk and no one, not even Falstaff, is left out of the feast at the end, it presents a vivid and detailed picture of small-town society which, if it does not exactly invite the term *realism*, nonetheless cannot be dismissed as farce.

The Falstaff of the Henry IV plays is a carnival king fighting to maintain his equilibrium in a hostile world of political intrigue. When events force him out of his tavern-citadel, he discovers that as a master of illusions himself he can survive, at least for a time, in a cold climate by recognizing and turning to his own advantage the illusions—of honor, justice, military glory, or swashbuckling youth—which other people mistake for realities. The citizens of Windsor are not without some misconceptions of their own, notably about the tractability of Anne Page or, in the case of Ford, about his wife's light-mindedness, but essentially they are clear-eyed and entirely aware of the need to band together against Falstaff, the intruder from another social and moral sphere. They see in him, rightly, a threat to the established order of a community which, although far from perfect, has nonetheless a wholeness and sanity lacking in the diseased and fragmented world of *1* and *2 Henry IV*. This society is an active force in *The Merry Wives of Windsor*. Falstaff, after launching his complacent and imperceptive assault upon the virtue of Mistress Page and Mistress Ford, is passive: an unwitting victim who merely deludes himself into thinking that he is initiating events.

The comic pattern here is unusual. Although Falstaff is without the mental agility he displays in the histories, he remains a larger-than-life, mythic figure. He is the spirit of festive inconsequence: self-indulgent, amoral, anarchic, a reveller who is out to disrupt the everyday social order. This order refuses, however, to capitulate or be changed by him in the slightest. It simply closes ranks and reaffirms its original values against an outsider who, like Malvolio in *Twelfth Night*, is made ridiculous, although his sins are of a wholly different kind. The end of the play does not accord with Shakespeare's usual comic practice. Anne Page may have managed to marry the man she loves, and Ford has learned to trust his wife, but there is no sense that a new or transformed society leaves Herne's oak. All that has happened is that a pre-existing society whose values Falstaff tried and failed to subvert has triumphed, without losing its vitality or gaiety of heart.

This solidarity is the more remarkable in that it unites characters of a somewhat prickly individuality, some of whom do not even find it easy to make themselves verbally understood. Evans, the Welsh parson, is a man who "makes fritters of English" (V.v.143). Dr. Caius, the French physician, one of his rivals for the hand of Anne Page, is even less comprehensible most of the time, a foreigner engaged in a desperate grapple with the English tongue. Slender is not only bashful almost to the point of nonexistence but has a vocabulary as slight as everything else about him, while Nym has latched onto the word *humor* as though it were a diamond discovered among the pebbles on a beach and uses it to cope with all contingencies, with the result that it rapidly ceases to have any meaning whatever. Mistress Quickly is scandalized by what seem to her to be the bawdy syllables uttered by a small boy rehearsing his Latin declension, but herself habitually blunders into unconscious obscenities about which Freud might have had a good deal to say. Bardolph confuses *sentences* with *senses*, and his associate Pistol is so lost in a private linguistic fantasy, made up of scraps and borrowings from old plays, as to be virtually impossible to engage in normal conversation. Among all these characters occupied, in their several ways, in hacking and misconstruing the English language, Falstaff stands out as a man who can make words do exactly what he wants them to do. The Fords, the Pages, and the jovial Host of the Garter are verbally competent as Evans or Mistress Quickly are not, but it is only Falstaff who fully understands the resources of language and can speak in a fashion that is genuinely creative. In this play, however, as opposed to the histories, his skill gains him nothing. Almost as much as Pistol, he is a man playing with words in a vacuum, wholly out of touch with a society whose values are no less powerful because they are never clearly articulated by the people who uphold them.

It is difficult to believe that the hard-headed Falstaff of the history plays could possibly have mistaken the amateur dramatics of the Herne the Hunter scene for reality. The *fabliau* Falstaff temporarily resident in Windsor is still witty in himself, but he is also "the cause that wit is in other men" in a different and more ignominious sense. Although the actors in the play within the play have had their squabbles and differences, they unite without question at the end to dramatize the triumph of the community. Falstaff is not merely frightened: the horns he imagined he would plant on the brows of his cuckolds Ford and Page are made, quite literally, to adorn his own forehead. In punishing their victim, the citizens of Windsor not only bury past animosities and mistrusts. They also exchange their previous verbal clumsiness, their cacophony of prose styles, for a lyrical, assured, and uniform verse inconceivable as the invention of the individual characters who speak it. Amateur theatricals have a way of being unfortunate in Shakespeare, as witness the Pageant of the Nine Worthies in *Love's Labor's Lost*, or the efforts of Bottom and his friends in *A Midsummer Night's Dream*. The potentiality for chaos and mismanagement in the show of Herne the Hunter is at least as great as it was in those earlier comedies, considering the actors who participate, but the result is very different.

> Fairies, black, grey, green, and white,
> You moonshine revellers, and shades of night,
> You orphan heirs of fixed destiny,
> Attend your office and your quality. (V.v.37–40)

This is certainly not the idiom of the Mistress Quickly we know, nor do Pistol and Evans seem to suffer, in the play scene, from their customary idiosyncrasies of expression. *The Merry Wives of Windsor* is in some ways the most realistic of Shakespeare's comedies, but we are patently not meant to puzzle over the question of just which Windsor citizen wrote the dialogue for the Herne the Hunter play, let alone what speech therapist elicited performances of such unexpected skill from Evans, Pistol, and Quickly. The verse here stands as the embodiment of a social and moral order allowed, in its moment of triumph, an expression that is appropriately impersonal and communal.

In the English histories, moral judgments are difficult and equivocal. This is one reason why Falstaff can be, at least in part, successful. In the particular comic world of Windsor, on the other hand, they are fixed and unalterable poles and Falstaff, trying to run against them, is broken. Yet there is a remarkable air of geniality and good humor about the end of the play. After all, there have been two intruders from another social sphere in the little world of Windsor. Falstaff may be baffled, but Fenton wins. Exactly the play-within-the-play that undoes the fat knight provides the young courtier with the opportunity to steal away Anne Page. Unlike Falstaff, Fenton has not misprized or trampled upon the life of Windsor. Although he sought Anne Page in marriage initially because of her father's wealth, he has come to love her for herself, and he has tried to obtain her by honorable means. Failing this, he concludes a bargain with Anne herself and then asks for and obtains the forgiveness of the society he has breached. There is some comfort here for Falstaff in discovering that the Herne the Hunter play has deceived not only himself but, unexpectedly, its own masters. When Verdi came to the end of his last opera, *Falstaff*, based on Shakespeare's play, he united all the characters in a great fugal chorus. The words of the chorus are those of Boito, Verdi's librettist, not Shakespeare, but their frank and unforced admission that every man is in some sense a fool and vulnerable to the laughter of others is entirely in the spirit of the last scene of *The Merry Wives of Windsor*. And so, even more profoundly, is the enormous vitality and expansiveness of the music Verdi found at this point: music which flowers out of and celebrates the values of this comic society.

Anne Barton

Horns, the cuckold's curse. From *Roxburghe Ballads*, ed. W. Chappell, I (1869), 151. Elizabethans seemed never to tire of allusions to the horns of the cuckold, and in *The Merry Wives of Windsor*, the horn image occurs frequently. In the woodcut here, horns are everywhere: the cornuted (horned) husband appears at the upstairs lattice window; the huntsman's rousing peal issues from a horn; the house sign is a pair of antlers; and the devil tempting the wife is horned. As Master Page says of Falstaff, who has been instructed to wear a pair of antlers at the pretended assignation in Windsor Park: "No man means evil but the devil, and we shall know him by his horns" (V.ii.12–14). *(By permission of the Harvard College Library)*

The Merry Wives of Windsor

[Dramatis Personae

Sir John Falstaff
Fenton, *a gentleman*
Robert Shallow, *a country justice*
Abraham Slender, *cousin to Shallow*
Francis Ford } *gentlemen of Windsor*
George Page }
William Page, *a boy, son to Page*
Sir Hugh Evans, *a Welsh parson*
Doctor Caius, *a French physician*
Host *of the Garter Inn*
Bardolph }
Pistol } *followers of Falstaff*
Nym }

Robin, *page to Falstaff*
Peter Simple, *servant to Slender*
John Rugby, *servant to Doctor Caius*

Mistress Alice Ford
Mistress Margaret Page
Mistress Anne Page, *her daughter*
Mistress Quickly, *servant to Doctor Caius*

Servants *to Page, Ford, etc.*

Scene: *Windsor, and the neighborhood*]

ACT I, Scene I

Enter Justice Shallow, Slender, Sir Hugh Evans.

Shal. Sir Hugh, persuade me not; I will make a Star Chamber matter of it. If he were twenty Sir John Falstaffs, he shall not abuse Robert Shallow, esquire.

Slen. In the county of Gloucester, Justice of Peace and Coram.

Shal. Ay, cousin Slender, and *Custa-lorum*.

Slen. Ay, and *Rato-lorum* too; and a gentleman born, Master Parson, who writes himself *Armigero*, in any bill, warrant, quittance, or obligation, *Armigero*.

Shal. Ay, that I do, and have done any time these three hundred years.

Slen. All his successors (gone before him) hath done't; and all his ancestors (that come after him) may. They may give the dozen white luces in their coat.

Shal. It is an old coat.

Evans. The dozen white louses do become an old coat well; it agrees well, passant. It is a familiar beast to man, and signifies love.

Shal. The luce is the fresh fish, the salt fish is an old coat.

Slen. I may quarter, coz.

Shal. You may, by marrying.

Evans. It is marring indeed, if he quarter it.

Shal. Not a whit.

Evans. Yes, py'r lady. If he has a quarter of your coat, there is but three skirts for yourself, in my simple conjectures. But that is all one. If Sir John Falstaff have committed disparagements unto you, I am of the church, and will be glad to

Words and passages enclosed in square brackets in the text above are either emendations of the copy-text or additions to it. The Textual Notes immediately following the play cite the earliest authority for every such change or insertion and supply the reading of the copy-text wherever it is emended in this edition.

I.i. Location: Windsor. Before Page's house.
o.s.d. **Sir:** courtesy title for a priest.
1. **persuade:** plead with.
2. **Star Chamber.** The court of Star Chamber, composed mainly of the King's Council, was the highest civil court in England.
6. **Coram:** i.e. quorum, a justice who sat on the bench at county sessions.
7. **Custa-lorum:** i.e. *custos rotulorum*, keeper of the rolls. The principal justice in the county had custody of the records.
8. **Rato-lorum:** i.e. *rotulorum.*
10. **Armigero:** esquire; literally, one entitled to bear (heraldic) arms. **bill:** bill of exchange. **quittance:** discharge from debt.
10–11. **obligation:** contract.
16. **give:** display as an armorial bearing. **luces:** pikes (fish).
17. **coat:** coat of arms. Evans misunderstands both *coat* (as a garment) and *luces* (as *louses*).
20. **passant.** Perhaps Evans means *passing*, i.e. exceedingly; if so, he unintentionally enriches his picture of the old coat and the lice by using the heraldic term for "walking." **familiar:** (1) domestic; (2) overintimate.
22–23. **The luce . . . coat.** Shallow's meaning has not been satisfactorily explained.
24. **quarter:** add to one's coat of arms the arms of another family by placing them in one of the four sections of the escutcheon. **coz:** cousin. 28. **py'r lady:** by Our Lady.
29. **skirts:** the full lower part of some doublets.
30. **simple:** humble (with a play on "foolish").

do my benevolence to make atonements and compremises between you.

Shal. The Council shall hear it, it is a riot.

Evans. It is not meet the Council hear a riot; there is no fear of Got in a riot. The Council, look you, shall desire to hear the fear of Got, and not to hear a riot. Take your vizaments in that.

Shal. Ha! o' my life, if I were young again, the sword should end it.

Evans. It is petter that friends is the sword, and end it; and there is also another device in my prain, which peradventure prings goot discretions with it: there is Anne Page, which is daughter to Master [George] Page, which is pretty virginity.

Slen. Mistress Anne Page? She has brown hair, and speaks small like a woman.

Evans. It is that fery person for all the orld, as just as you will desire, and seven hundred pounds of moneys, and gold, and silver, is her grandsire upon his death's-bed (Got deliver to a joyful resurrections!) give, when she is able to overtake seventeen years old. It were a goot motion if we leave our pribbles and prabbles, and desire a marriage between Master Abraham and Mistress Anne Page.

Slen. Did her grandsire leave her seven hundred pound?

Evans. Ay, and her father is make her a petter penny.

Slen. I know the young gentlewoman, she has good gifts.

Evans. Seven hundred pounds, and possibilities, is goot gifts.

Shal. Well, let us see honest Master Page. Is Falstaff there?

Evans. Shall I tell you a lie? I do despise a liar as I do despise one that is false, or as I despise one that is not true. The knight Sir John is there, and I beseech you be rul'd by your well-willers. I will peat the door for Master Page. [*Knocks.*] What ho! Got pless your house here!

Page. [*Within.*] Who's there?

[*Enter*] PAGE.

Evans. Here is Got's plessing, and your friend, and Justice Shallow, and here young Master Slender, that peradventures shall tell you another tale, if matters grow to your likings.

Page. I am glad to see your worships well. I thank you for my venison, Master Shallow.

Shal. Master Page, I am glad to see you. Much good do it your good heart! I wish'd your venison better, it was ill kill'd. How doth good Mistress Page?—and I thank you always with my heart, la! with my heart.

Page. Sir, I thank you.

Shal. Sir, I thank you; by yea and no, I do.

Page. I am glad to see you, good Master Slender.

Slen. How does your fallow greyhound, sir? I heard say he was outrun on Cotsall.

Page. It could not be judg'd, sir.

Slen. You'll not confess, you'll not confess.

Shal. That he will not. 'Tis your fault, 'tis your fault; 'tis a good dog.

Page. A cur, sir.

Shal. Sir! he's a good dog, and a fair dog—can there be more said? He is good, and fair. Is Sir John Falstaff here?

Page. Sir, he is within; and I would I could do a good office between you.

Evans. It is spoke as a Christians ought to speak.

Shal. He hath wrong'd me, Master Page.

Page. Sir, he doth in some sort confess it.

Shal. If it be confess'd, it is not redress'd. Is not that so, Master Page? He hath wrong'd me, indeed he hath, at a word he hath. Believe me, Robert Shallow, esquire, saith he is wrong'd.

Page. Here comes Sir John.

[*Enter* SIR JOHN] FALSTAFF, BARDOLPH, NYM, PISTOL.

Fal. Now, Master Shallow, you'll complain of me to the King?

Shal. Knight, you have beaten my men, kill'd my deer, and broke open my lodge.

Fal. But not kiss'd your keeper's daughter?

Shal. Tut, a pin! this shall be answer'd.

Fal. I will answer it straight: I have done all this. That is now answer'd.

Shal. The Council shall know this.

Fal. 'Twere better for you if it were known in counsel. You'll be laugh'd at.

Evans. *Pauca verba;* Sir John, good worts.

Fal. Good worts? good cabbage. Slender, I broke your head; what matter have you against me?

Slen. Marry, sir, I have matter in my head against you, and against your cony-catching ras-

33–34. compremises: compromises (a variant form), settlements by arbitration.
35. The Council . . . riot. The Privy Council sitting as Star Chamber heard such cases. But Evans supposes that Shallow is talking about an ecclesiastical council or synod.
39. vizaments: Evans' version of *advisements* = considerations.
42. that . . . sword: i.e. that the quarrel be settled by the intervention of friends.
47. Mistress. Used of unmarried as well as married women.
48. small: in a high-pitched voice.
49. orld. Evans frequently (though not consistently) omits initial *w*; see *ork* (line 145), *oman* (line 227), *ord* and its variant *ort* (line 254).
50. just: precisely. **54. motion:** move, plan.
55. pribbles and prabbles: bribbles and brabbles, i.e. petty disputings.
60. is: i.e. will. **63. gifts:** qualities of mind and body.
64. possibilities: expectations (of additional inheritance).
66. honest: worthy. **71. well-willers:** well-wishers.
78. grow: develop.

83. ill: i.e. illegally (see lines 111–12 below).
87. by . . . no: most certainly (a common usage, based on Matthew 5:37). **89. fallow:** of a fawn color.
90. Cotsall: Cotswold. The Cotswolds are a range of hills in Gloucestershire.
93. fault: misfortune (with quibble on the sense "loss of scent").
100. office: service. **103. sort:** manner.
106. at a word: in short.
114. pin: trifle. **answer'd:** accounted for.
115. answer it straight: (1) account for it strictly; (2) reply to it straightway. **118–19. in counsel:** secretly, privately.
120. Pauca verba: few words.
121. worts: vegetables (a pun on Evans' pronunciation of *words*). **cabbage:** i.e. cabbage head, fool.
122. broke: cut open. **matter:** grievance, complaint.
123. Marry: indeed (originally the name of the Virgin Mary used as an oath). **matter:** issue from the wound.
124. cony-catching: cheating.

cals, Bardolph, Nym, and Pistol. [They carried me to the tavern and made me drunk, and afterward pick'd my pocket.]

Bard. You Banbury cheese!

Slen. Ay, it is no matter.

Pist. How now, Mephostophilus?

Slen. Ay, it is no matter.

Nym. Slice, I say! *Pauca, pauca.* Slice, that's my humor.

Slen. Where's Simple, my man? can you tell, cousin?

Evans. Peace, I pray you. Now let us understand. There is three umpires in this matter, as I understand: that is, Master Page (*fidelicet* Master Page) and there is myself (*fidelicet* myself) and the three party is (lastly and finally) mine host of the Garter.

Page. We three to hear it and end it between them.

Evans. Fery goot. I will make a prief of it in my note-book, and we will afterwards ork upon the cause with as great discreetly as we can.

Fal. Pistol!

Pist. He hears with ears.

Evans. The tevil and his tam! what phrase is this? "He hears with ear"? Why, it is affectations.

Fal. Pistol, did you pick Master Slender's purse?

Slen. Ay, by these gloves, did he, or I would I might never come in mine own great chamber again else, of seven groats in mill-sixpences, and two Edward shovel-boards, that cost me two shilling and two pence a-piece of Yead Miller—by these gloves.

Fal. Is this true, Pistol?

Evans. No, it is false, if it is a pick-purse.

Pist. Ha, thou mountain-foreigner! Sir John, and master mine,
I combat challenge of this latten bilbo.
Word of denial in thy *labras* here!
Word of denial! Froth and scum, thou liest!

Slen. By these gloves, then 'twas he.

Nym. Be avis'd, sir, and pass good humors.

I will say "marry trap" with you, if you run the nuthook's humor on me—that is the very note of it.

Slen. By this hat, then he in the red face had it; for though I cannot remember what I did when you made me drunk, yet I am not altogether an ass.

Fal. What say you, Scarlet and John?

Bard. Why, sir, for my part, I say the gentleman had drunk himself out of his five sentences.

Evans. It is his five senses. Fie, what the ignorance is!

Bard. And being fap, sir, was (as they say) cashier'd; and so conclusions pass'd the careers.

Slen. Ay, you spake in Latin then too: but 'tis no matter; I'll ne'er be drunk whilst I live again, but in honest, civil, godly company, for this trick. If I be drunk, I'll be drunk with those that have the fear of God, and not with drunken knaves.

Evans. So Got udge me, that is a virtuous mind.

Fal. You hear all these matters denied, gentlemen; you hear it.

[*Enter*] Anne Page [*with wine*], Mistress Ford, Mistress Page.

Page. Nay, daughter, carry the wine in, we'll drink within. [*Exit Anne Page.*]

Slen. O heaven! this is Mistress Anne Page.

Page. How now, Mistress Ford?

Fal. Mistress Ford, by my troth, you are very well met. By your leave, good mistress. [*Kisses her.*]

Page. Wife, bid these gentlemen welcome. Come, we have a hot venison pasty to dinner. Come, gentlemen, I hope we shall drink down all unkindness.

[*Exeunt all except Shallow, Slender, and Evans.*]

Slen. I had rather than forty shillings I had my Book of Songs and Sonnets here.

[*Enter*] Simple.

How now, Simple, where have you been? I must wait on myself, must I? You have not the Book of Riddles about you, have you?

Sim. Book of Riddles? Why, did you not lend it to Alice Shortcake upon All-hallowmas last, a fortnight afore Michaelmas?

Shal. Come, coz, come, coz, we stay for you. A word with you, coz; marry, this, coz: there is as

125. **carried:** took, accompanied.
128. **Banbury cheese.** Proverbially thin; a hit at Slender which indicates that his physique matches his name.
130. **Mephostophilus:** Mephistopheles, the devil in Marlowe's *Dr. Faustus.*
132. **Slice.** Another hit at Slender's thinness (?) or Nym's threat to slice the "Banbury cheese" with his sword (?) or (as suggested by the following *Pauca*) an order to Slender to cut short his remarks (?).
133. **humor:** whim, mood. 138. **fidelicet:** *videlicet*, namely.
141. **Garter:** the name of an inn in Windsor.
154. **great chamber:** hall.
155. **groats:** coins worth fourpence. **mill-sixpences:** newly introduced machine-made coins with fluted edges.
156. **Edward shovel-boards:** old broad shillings of Edward VI, worn smooth by long use and therefore convenient for the game of shovel-board. 157. **Yead:** Ed.
160. **false.** Evans takes *true* in the sense "honest."
161. **mountain-foreigner:** i.e. Welshman.
162. **latten bilbo:** sword made of a soft alloy resembling brass (a hit at Slender's cowardice and perhaps another glance at his thinness). *Bilbo* comes from the name of the Spanish city Bilbao, where fine swords were manufactured.
163. **Word . . . labras:** i.e. I call you a liar to your face (*labras* = lips).
166. **avis'd:** advised, i.e. prudent. **pass good humors:** do nothing disagreeable.
167. **marry trap:** probably an exclamation from a children's game, meaning "now you're caught."
167–68. **run . . . me:** act like the constable, i.e. accuse me of stealing.
168. **very note:** exact information.
173. **Scarlet and John.** Will Scarlet and Little John were two of Robin Hood's companions. "Scarlet" alludes to the color of Bardolph's face.
178. **fap:** drunk.
179. **cashier'd:** deprived (of his senses). **conclusions . . . careers:** inferences galloped off at full speed, i.e. he drew the wrong conclusions.
185. **udge:** Evans' version of *judge*. 192. **troth:** faith.
195. **to:** for.
199. **Book . . . Sonnets.** Probably an allusion to the book better known as Tottel's *Miscellany* (1557), a collection of poems by Wyatt, Surrey, and others.
201–2. **Book of Riddles.** Another popular but scarcely up-to-the-minute book; although not extant in any edition older than 1629, it first appeared at least as early as 1575.
204–5. **All-hallowmas . . . Michaelmas.** Simple errs: Michaelmas is September 29; All-hallowmas, or All Saints' Day, November 1.
206. **stay:** wait.

'twere a tender, a kind of tender, made afar off by Sir Hugh here. Do you understand me?

Slen. Ay, sir, you shall find me reasonable. If it be so, I shall do that that is reason.

Shal. Nay, but understand me.

Slen. So I do, sir.

Evans. Give ear to his motions: Master Slender, I will description the matter to you, if you be capacity of it.

Slen. Nay, I will do as my cousin Shallow says. I pray you pardon me; he's a Justice of Peace in his country, simple though I stand here.

Evans. But that is not the question: the question is concerning your marriage.

Shal. Ay, there's the point, sir.

Evans. Marry, is it; the very point of it—to Mistress Anne Page.

Slen. Why, if it be so, I will marry her upon any reasonable demands.

Evans. But can you affection the oman? Let us command to know that of your mouth, or of your lips; for divers philosophers hold that the lips is parcel of the mouth. Therefore precisely, can you carry your good will to the maid?

Shal. Cousin Abraham Slender, can you love her?

Slen. I hope, sir, I will do as it shall become one that would do reason.

Evans. Nay, Got's lords and his ladies, you must speak possitable, if you can carry her your desires towards her.

Shal. That you must. Will you, upon good dowry, marry her?

Slen. I will do a greater thing than that, upon your request, cousin, in any reason.

Shal. Nay, conceive me, conceive me, sweet coz; what I do is to pleasure you, coz. Can you love the maid?

Slen. I will marry her, sir, at your request; but if there be no great love in the beginning, yet heaven may decrease it upon better acquaintance, when we are married and have more occasion to know one another. I hope, upon familiarity will grow more content. But if you say, "Marry her," I will marry her; that I am freely dissolv'd, and dissolutely.

Evans. It is a fery discretion answer, save the fall is in the ord "dissolutely." The ort is (according to our meaning) "resolutely." His meaning is good.

Shal. Ay—I think my cousin meant well.

Slen. Ay, or else I would I might be hang'd, la!

Shal. Here comes fair Mistress Anne.

[*Enter* Anne Page.]

Would I were young for your sake, Mistress Anne!

Anne. The dinner is on the table. My father desires your worships' company.

Shal. I will wait on him, fair Mistress Anne.

Evans. 'Od's plessed will! I will not be absence at the grace. [*Exeunt Shallow and Evans.*]

Anne. Will't please your worship to come in, sir?

Slen. No, I thank you, forsooth, heartily; I am very well.

Anne. The dinner attends you, sir.

Slen. I am not a-hungry, I thank you, forsooth. Go, sirrah, for all you are my man, go wait upon my cousin Shallow. [*Exit Simple.*] A Justice of Peace sometime may be beholding to his friend for a man. I keep but three men and a boy yet, till my mother be dead. But what though? yet I live like a poor gentleman born.

Anne. I may not go in without your worship; they will not sit till you come.

Slen. I' faith, I'll eat nothing. I thank you as much as though I did.

Anne. I pray you, sir, walk in.

Slen. I had rather walk here, I thank you. I bruis'd my shin th' other day with playing at sword and dagger with a master of fence (three veneys for a dish of stew'd prunes) and by my troth, I cannot abide the smell of hot meat since. Why do your dogs bark so? be there bears i' th' town?

Anne. I think there are, sir, I heard them talk'd of.

Slen. I love the sport well, but I shall as soon quarrel at it as any man in England. You are afraid if you see the bear loose, are you not?

Anne. Ay indeed, sir.

Slen. That's meat and drink to me, now. I have seen Sackerson loose twenty times, and have taken him by the chain; but (I warrant you) the women have so cried and shriek'd at it, that it pass'd. But women, indeed, cannot abide 'em, they are very ill-favor'd rough things.

[*Enter* Page.]

Page. Come, gentle Master Slender, come; we stay for you.

Slen. I'll eat nothing, I thank you, sir.

Page. By cock and pie, you shall not choose, sir! come, come.

Slen. Nay, pray you lead the way.

Page. Come on, sir.

Slen. Mistress Anne, yourself shall go first.

Anne. Not I, sir, pray you keep on.

208. afar off: indirectly.
219. simple . . . here: i.e. humble though I (his kinsman) be (but with unintentional suggestion of *simple* = simple-minded).
230. parcel: part. **236. possitable:** Evans' version of *positively*.
242. conceive: understand. **243. pleasure:** please.
247. decrease: blunder for *increase*.
250. content. Many editors adopt Theobald's emendation *contempt* as more in line with Slender's mode of expression in the surrounding prose. In either case there is an echo of the proverb "Familiarity breeds contempt." **251. dissolv'd:** blunder for *resolved*.
252. dissolutely: blunder for *resolutely*.
254. fall: Evans' version of *fault*.

264. 'Od's: God's. **269. attends:** awaits.
271. sirrah: customary form of address to an inferior.
273. beholding: beholden, indebted.
275. what though: what does it matter.
284. fence: fencing. **veneys:** bouts.
285. stew'd prunes. A favorite dish in brothels, hence slang for *prostitutes*. **290. sport:** i.e. bear-baiting.
295. Sackerson: a famous bear at Paris Garden near the Globe and other theatres on the Bankside. **297. pass'd:** defied description.
299. ill-favor'd: ugly.
303. By . . . pie: a mild oath of disputed origin. **shall not choose:** must.

Slen. Truly I will not go first; truly la! I will not do you that wrong.

Anne. I pray you, sir.

Slen. I'll rather be unmannerly than troublesome. You do yourself wrong indeed la! *Exeunt.*

Scene II

Enter Evans *and* Simple [*from dinner*].

Evans. Go your ways, and ask of Doctor Caius' house which is the way; and there dwells one Mistress Quickly, which is in the manner of his nurse—or his dry nurse—or his cook—or his laundry—his washer and his wringer.

Sim. Well, sir.

Evans. Nay, it is petter yet. Give her this letter; for it is a oman that altogether's acquaintance with Mistress Anne Page; and the letter is to desire and require her to solicit your master's desires to Mistress Anne Page. I pray you be gone. I will make an end of my dinner; there's pippins and cheese to come. *Exeunt.*

Scene III

Enter Falstaff, Host, Bardolph, Nym, Pistol, [Robin, *Falstaff's*] *page.*

Fal. Mine host of the Garter!

Host. What says my bully-rook? Speak scholarly and wisely.

Fal. Truly, mine host, I must turn away some of my followers.

Host. Discard, bully Hercules, cashier; let them wag; trot, trot.

Fal. I sit at ten pounds a week.

Host. Thou'rt an emperor—Caesar, Keiser, and Pheazar. I will entertain Bardolph; he shall draw, he shall tap. Said I well, bully Hector?

Fal. Do so, good mine host.

Host. I have spoke; let him follow. [*To Bardolph.*] Let me see thee froth and [lime]. I am at a word; follow. [*Exit.*]

Fal. Bardolph, follow him. A tapster is a good trade. An old cloak makes a new jerkin; a wither'd servingman a fresh tapster. Go, adieu.

Bard. It is a life that I have desir'd. I will thrive.

I.ii. Location: Scene continues.
1. **ask of:** inquire concerning.
4. **dry nurse.** Evans means someone who looks after an adult, as opposed to a wet nurse who cares for an infant.
8. **altogether's acquaintance:** is very well acquainted.
12. **pippins:** kind of apple.

I.iii. Location: Windsor. The Garter Inn.
2. **bully-rook:** fine fellow. **scholarly:** as befits a scholar.
6. **cashier:** dismiss. 7. **wag:** go their way.
8. **I sit at:** my expenses come to. 9. **Keiser:** kaiser, emperor.
10. **Pheazar:** vizier (?) or perhaps simply a word invented by the host to rhyme with the others. **entertain:** hire. **draw:** draw liquor.
11. **tap:** serve as tapster.
14. **froth and lime.** Serving beer with a heavy froth allowed short measure; adding lime to cheap wine masked its sour taste. **I . . . word:** i.e. I am a man of action and few words.
17. **jerkin:** close-fitting jacket.

Pist. O base Hungarian wight! wilt thou the spigot wield? [*Exit Bardolph.*]

Nym. He was gotten in drink. Is not the humor conceited?

Fal. I am glad I am so acquit of this tinderbox; his thefts were too open; his filching was like an unskillful singer, he kept not time.

Nym. The good humor is to steal at a minute's rest.

Pist. "Convey," the wise it call. "Steal"? foh! a *fico* for the phrase!

Fal. Well, sirs, I am almost out at heels.

Pist. Why then let kibes ensue.

Fal. There is no remedy; I must cony-catch, I must shift.

Pist. Young ravens must have food.

Fal. Which of you know Ford of this town?

Pist. I ken the wight; he is of substance good.

Fal. My honest lads, I will tell you what I am about.

Pist. Two yards, and more.

Fal. No quips now, Pistol! Indeed I am in the waist two yards about; but I am now about no waste; I am about thrift. Briefly—I do mean to make love to Ford's wife. I spy entertainment in her. She discourses, she carves, she gives the leer of invitation. I can construe the action of her familiar style, and the hardest voice of her behavior (to be English'd rightly) is, "I am Sir John Falstaff's."

Pist. He hath studied her [well], and translated her will, out of honesty into English.

Nym. The anchor is deep. Will that humor pass?

Fal. Now, the report goes she has all the rule of her husband's purse. He hath a legend of angels.

Pist. As many devils entertain; and "To her, boy," say I.

Nym. The humor rises; it is good. Humor me the angels.

20. **Hungarian:** i.e. beggarly (from the phonetic similarity of *Hungary* and *hungry*). **wight:** person, man.
22. **gotten in drink:** conceived when his parents were drunk (an origin attributed to cowards). 23. **conceited:** ingenious.
24. **acquit:** rid. **tinderbox.** Another allusion to Bardolph's red face.
27–28. **minute's rest.** Some editors emend to *minim's rest* or *minim-rest*, the shortest rest in music, but the F1 reading is supported by Q1–2. 29. **Convey:** steal.
30. **fico:** fig (Italian), an obscene gesture to show contempt, made by thrusting the thumb between two fingers.
31. **out at heels:** i.e. out of money, but Pistol quibbles on the literal meaning. 32. **kibes:** chilblains.
33. **cony-catch:** trick fools out of their money (literally, snare rabbits).
34. **shift:** devise a stratagem.
35. **Young . . . food.** Proverbial and Biblical, with reference to the raven's habits as a voracious scavenger.
37. **ken:** know. **of substance good:** well-to-do.
43. **thrift:** profit. 44. **entertainment:** willingness to receive me.
45. **carves:** shows courtesy (?) or speaks affectedly (?). **leer:** amorous side-glance.
46–47. **construe . . . style:** i.e. interpret the informality of her behavior (with an elaborate grammatical pun that extends to *voice* and *English'd* in the following lines).
47. **hardest voice:** (1) severest expression; (2) most difficult construction. 48. **English'd:** (1) put into words; (2) translated into English.
50. **honesty:** chastity.
51. **The anchor is deep.** A crux. The phrase may mean "the scheme is firmly set" or that Falstaff is getting out of his depth (as he soon does). **Will . . . pass:** i.e. will my figure of speech pass muster.
53. **legend:** legion (a variant spelling). **angels:** gold coins, worth about 10 shillings, stamped with the figure of the archangel Michael.
54. **entertain:** take into service.

Fal. I have writ me here a letter to her; and here another to Page's wife, who even now gave me good eyes too, examin'd my parts with most judicious iliads; sometimes the beam of her view gilded my foot, sometimes my portly belly.

Pist. Then did the sun on dunghill shine.

Nym. I thank thee for that humor.

Fal. O, she did so course o'er my exteriors with such a greedy intention, that the appetite of her eye did seem to scorch me up like a burning-glass! Here's another letter to her. She bears the purse too; she is a region in Guiana, all gold and bounty. I will be cheaters to them both, and they shall be exchequers to me. They shall be my East and West Indies, and I will trade to them both. Go, bear thou this letter to Mistress Page; and thou this to Mistress Ford. We will thrive, lads, we will thrive.

Pist. Shall I Sir Pandarus of Troy become,
And by my side wear steel? Then Lucifer take all!

Nym. I will run no base humor. Here, take the humor-letter; I will keep the havior of reputation.

Fal. [*To Robin.*] Hold, sirrah, bear you these
letters tightly;
Sail like my pinnace to these golden shores.
Rogues, hence, avaunt, vanish like hailstones; go!
Trudge! Plod away i' th' hoof! Seek shelter, pack!
Falstaff will learn the [humor] of the age,
French thrift, you rogues—myself and skirted page.

[*Exeunt Falstaff and Robin.*]

Pist. Let vultures gripe thy guts! for gourd and
fullam holds,
And high and low beguiles the rich and poor.
Tester I'll have in pouch when thou shalt lack,
Base Phrygian Turk!

Nym. I have operations [in my head] which be humors of revenge.

Pist. Wilt thou revenge?

Nym. By welkin and her star!

Pist. With wit or steel?

Nym. With both the humors, I.
I will discuss the humor of this love to [Page].

Pist. And I to [Ford] shall eke unfold
How Falstaff (varlet vile)
His dove will prove, his gold will hold,
And his soft couch defile.

Nym. My humor shall not cool. I will incense [Page] to deal with poison; I will possess him with yallowness, for the revolt of mine is dangerous—that is my true humor.

Pist. Thou art the Mars of malecontents. I second thee; troop on. *Exeunt.*

Scene IV

Enter Mistress Quickly, Simple.

Quick. What, John Rugby!

[*Enter*] John Rugby.

I pray thee go to the casement, and see if you can see my master, Master Doctor Caius, coming. If he do, i' faith, and find any body in the house, here will be an old abusing of God's patience and the King's English.

Rug. I'll go watch.

Quick. Go, and we'll have a posset for't soon at night, in faith, at the latter end of a sea-coal fire. [*Exit Rugby.*] An honest, willing, kind fellow as ever servant shall come in house withal; and I warrant you, no tell-tale nor no breed-bate. His worst fault is, that he is given to prayer; he is something peevish that way; but nobody but has his fault—but let that pass. Peter Simple, you say your name is?

Sim. Ay, for fault of a better.

Quick. And Master Slender's your master?

Sim. Ay, forsooth.

Quick. Does he not wear a great round beard, like a glover's paring-knife?

Sim. No, forsooth; he hath but a little [whey]-face, with a little yellow beard, a Cain-color'd beard.

Quick. A softly-sprighted man, is he not?

Sim. Ay, forsooth; but he is as tall a man of his hands as any is between this and his head. He hath fought with a warrener.

Quick. How say you? O, I should remember him. Does he not hold up his head (as it were) and strut in his gait?

Sim. Yes indeed does he.

Quick. Well, heaven send Anne Page no worse fortune! Tell Master Parson Evans I will do what

61. iliads: oeillades, amorous glances.
66. intention: intentness of regard.
67. burning-glass: a glass which focuses the rays of the sun and produces intense heat.
69. Guiana. A possible compliment to Sir Walter Raleigh, who in 1596, on his return from his voyage to South America, published an account entitled *The Discovery of the Large, Rich, and Beautiful Empire of Guiana.*
70. cheaters: escheators, officers appointed to oversee lands forfeited to the king, called *escheats*; with play on the ordinary meaning.
71. exchequers: treasuries; the escheator was an official of the Exchequer.
75. Sir Pandarus: the uncle of Cressida, who brought her and Troilus together as lovers; from his name is derived the word *pander.*
76. And . . . steel: i.e. and I a soldier.
78. keep . . . reputation: behave in a reputable fashion.
79. tightly: skillfully. **82. pack:** be off.
84. French thrift: an economy measure, practiced in France, of having one page rather than a retinue of servingmen. **skirted:** wearing a skirted doublet, a style popular in France.
85. gripe: grip, seize. **gourd:** hollow dice. **fullam:** loaded dice.
86. high and low: the roll of the dice (?) or false dice (?). Cf. *The Winter's Tale,* V.i.207. **87. Tester:** sixpence. **pouch:** purse.
88. Phrygian Turk: a term of abuse.
89. operations: plans, schemes. **92. welkin:** heaven, sky.
95. discuss: disclose. **96. eke:** also.

98. prove: try, test. **100. incense:** incite.
101. deal with: use. **possess him:** cause him to be possessed.
102. yallowness: yellowness (a variant spelling), i.e. jealousy. **revolt of mine:** casting off of my allegiance (?).
104. the Mars: i.e. the most warlike.

I.iv. Location: Dr. Caius' house.
5. old: great, plentiful.
8. posset: hot milk curdled with ale or wine.
9. sea-coal: mineral coal as opposed to charcoal.
11. withal: with. **12. breed-bate:** mischief maker.
13–14. something peevish: somewhat silly.
22. whey-face: pallid face.
23. Cain-color'd beard. Cain was traditionally represented with a yellow or reddish beard. **24. softly-sprighted:** mild-spirited.
25–26. as . . . hands: as valiant a man.
26. between . . . head. Not satisfactorily explained; probably a disparaging witticism. **27. warrener:** gamekeeper, especially of rabbits.

I can for your master. Anne is a good girl, and I wish—

[*Enter* Rugby.]

Rug. Out alas! here comes my master.

Quick. We shall all be shent. Run in here, good young man; go into this closet. He will not stay long. [*Shuts Simple in the closet.*] What, John Rugby! John! what, John, I say! Go, John, go inquire for my master; I doubt he be not well, that he comes not home.

[*Singing.*] And down, down, adown-a, etc.

[*Enter*] Doctor Caius.

Caius. Vat is you sing? I do not like des toys. Pray you go and vetch me in my closet [*une boîte en*] *verd*, a box, a green-a box. Do intend vat I speak? A green-a box.

Quick. Ay, forsooth, I'll fetch it you. [*Aside.*] I am glad he went not in himself; if he had found the young man, he would have been horn-mad.

Caius. Fe, fe, fe, fe! *ma foi, il fait fort* [*chaud. O, je m'en*] *vois à la cour—la grande affaire.*

Quick. Is it this, sir?

Caius. Oui, mette le au mon pocket; dépêche, quickly. Vere is dat knave Rugby?

Quick. What, John Rugby! John!

Rug. Here, sir!

Caius. You are John Rugby, and you are Jack Rugby. Come, take-a your rapier, and come after my heel to the court.

Rug. 'Tis ready, sir, here in the porch.

Caius. By my trot, I tarry too long. 'Od's me! *Qu'ai-je oublié?* Dere is some simples in my closet, dat I vill not for the varld I shall leave behind.

Quick. Ay me, he'll find the young man there, and be mad!

Caius. O diable, diable! vat is in my closet? Villainy! laroon! [*Pulling Simple out.*] Rugby, my rapier!

Quick. Good master, be content.

Caius. Wherefore shall I be content-a?

Quick. The young man is an honest man.

Caius. What shall de honest man do in my closet? Dere is no honest man dat shall come in my closet.

Quick. I beseech you be not so phlegmatic. Hear the truth of it: he came of an errand to me from Parson Hugh.

Caius. Vell?

Sim. Ay, forsooth; to desire her to—

Quick. Peace, I pray you.

Caius. Peace-a your tongue.—Speak-a your tale.

Sim. To desire this honest gentlewoman, your maid, to speak a good word to Mistress Anne Page for my master in the way of marriage.

Quick. This is all indeed la! but I'll ne'er put my finger in the fire, and need not.

Caius. Sir Hugh send-a you? Rugby, [*baillez*] me some paper. Tarry you a little-a while. [*Writes.*]

Quick. [*Aside to Simple.*] I am glad he is so quiet. If he had been throughly mov'd, you should have heard him so loud and so melancholy. But notwithstanding, man, I'll do [you] your master what good I can; and the very yea and the no is, the French doctor, my master (I may call him my master, look you, for I keep his house; and I wash, wring, brew, bake, scour, dress meat and drink, make the beds, and do all myself)—

Sim. [*Aside to Quickly.*] 'Tis a great charge to come under one body's hand.

Quick. [*Aside to Simple.*] Are you avis'd o' that? You shall find it a great charge; and to be up early and down late; but notwithstanding (to tell you in your ear, I would have no words of it) my master himself is in love with Mistress Anne Page; but notwithstanding that, I know Anne's mind—that's neither here nor there.

Caius. You jack'nape, give-a this letter to Sir Hugh. By gar, it is a shallenge. I will cut his troat in de park; and I will teach a scurvy jack-a-nape priest to meddle or make—You may be gone; it is not good you tarry here. By gar, I will cut all his two stones; by gar, he shall not have a stone to throw at his dog. [*Exit Simple.*]

Quick. Alas! he speaks but for his friend.

Caius. It is no matter-a ver dat. Do not you tell-a me dat I shall have Anne Page for myself? By gar, I vill kill de Jack priest; and I have appointed mine host of de Jarteer to measure our weapon. By gar, I will myself have Anne Page.

Quick. Sir, the maid loves you, and all shall be well. We must give folks leave to prate; what the good-jer!

Caius. Rugby, come to the court with me. By gar, if I have not Anne Page, I shall turn your head out of my door. Follow my heels, Rugby.

[*Exeunt Caius and Rugby.*]

Quick. You shall have Anne—fool's-head of your own. No, I know Anne's mind for that. Never a woman in Windsor knows more of Anne's mind than I do, nor can do more than I do with her, I thank heaven.

37. shent: scolded. **41. doubt:** fear. **44. toys:** trifles.
45–46. une . . . verd: a green box.
46. intend: hear, understand (from French *entendre*).
50. horn-mad: as mad as an enraged bull.
51–52. ma . . . affaire: my word, it is very hot; I am going to the court, the great affair.
54. Oui . . . dépêche: yes, put it in my pocket; be quick about it.
59. your rapier: i.e. your master's rapier. **62. trot:** troth.
63. Qu'ai-je oublié: what have I forgotten. **simples:** medicinal herbs. **67. diable:** devil. **68. laroon:** robber (French *larron*).
70. content: calm.
75. phlegmatic. A blunder, probably for *choleric*, which in the old "humors" physiology designated the temperament diametrically opposed to the phlegmatic.

86. and need not: if I don't have to. **87. baillez:** fetch.
90. throughly mov'd: thoroughly angered.
91. melancholy: irascible (?) or a blunder like *phlegmatic* in line 75 (?).
93. the very . . . no: i.e. what is certain (see note to I.i.87).
96. dress meat: prepare food. **98. charge:** burden.
100. Are . . . that: i.e. you may well say so.
107. jack'nape: coxcomb, fop. **110. make:** have to do, interfere.
111–12. cut . . . stones: castrate him.
117. Jack: contemptuous epithet, meaning "knavish."
118. Jarteer: Garter (French *jarretière*).
118–19. measure our weapon: i.e. act as a second.
122. good-jer: expletive of uncertain origin.
126. Anne. A quibble on *Anne / an.* Mistress Quickly means that the only result of his wooing of Anne will be his being made a fool of.

Fenton. [*Within.*] Who's within there, ho?

Quick. Who's there, I trow? Come near the house, I pray you.

[*Enter*] Fenton.

Fent. How now, good woman, how dost thou?

Quick. The better that it pleases your good worship to ask.

Fent. What news? How does pretty Mistress Anne?

Quick. In truth, sir, and she is pretty, and honest, and gentle, and one that is your friend; I can tell you that by the way, I praise heaven for it.

Fent. Shall I do any good, think'st thou? shall I not lose my suit?

Quick. Troth, sir, all is in His hands above. But notwithstanding, Master Fenton, I'll be sworn on a book she loves you. Have not your worship a wart above your eye?

Fent. Yes, marry, have I, what of that?

Quick. Well, thereby hangs a tale. Good faith, it is such another Nan; but (I detest) an honest maid as ever broke bread. We had an hour's talk of that wart. I shall never laugh but in that maid's company! But, indeed, she is given too much to allicholy and musing; but for you—well—go to.

Fent. Well; I shall see her to-day. Hold, there's money for thee. Let me have thy voice in my behalf. If thou seest her before me, commend me.

Quick. Will I? I' faith, that we will; and I will tell your worship more of the wart the next time we have confidence, and of other wooers.

Fent. Well, farewell, I am in great haste now.

Quick. Farewell to your worship. [*Exit Fenton.*] Truly, an honest gentleman; but Anne loves him not; for I know Anne's mind as well as another does. Out upon't! what have I forgot? *Exit.*

ACT II, Scene I

Enter Mistress Page [*reading of a letter*].

Mrs. Page. What, have [I] scap'd love-letters in the holiday-time of my beauty, and am I now a subject for them? Let me see. [*Reads.*] "Ask me no reason why I love you, for though Love use Reason for his precisian, he admits him not for his counsellor. You are not young, no more am I; go to then, there's sympathy. You are merry, so am I; ha, ha! then there's more sympathy. You love sack, and so do I; would you desire better

132. **trow**: wonder. **Come near**: enter. 139. **honest**: chaste.
140. **gentle**: well-mannered.
150. **it . . . Nan**: i.e. what a lively Anne she is. **detest**: blunder for *protest*.
154. **allicholy**: blunder for *melancholy*. **go to**: enough (a term of rebuke). 160. **confidence**: blunder for *conference*.

II.i. Location: Windsor. Before Page's house.
2. **holiday-time**: playtime, i.e. youthful days.
4–6. **though . . . counsellor**: i.e. though Love listens to the puritanical sermons of Reason, he doesn't follow Reason's advice; in other words, the lover knows the rational objections to his course but yields to his irrational impulses nevertheless.
7. **sympathy**: agreement, congeniality. 9. **sack**: Spanish wine.

sympathy? Let it suffice thee, Mistress Page—at the least if the love of soldier can suffice—that I love thee. I will not say, pity me—'tis not a soldier-like phrase—but I say, love me. By me,

Thine own true knight,
By day or night,
Or any kind of light,
With all his might
For thee to fight,
John Falstaff."

What a Herod of Jewry is this! O wicked, wicked world! One that is well-nigh worn to pieces with age to show himself a young gallant! What an unweigh'd behavior hath this Flemish drunkard pick'd (with the devil's name!) out of my conversation, that he dares in this manner assay me? Why, he hath not been thrice in my company! What should I say to him? I was then frugal of my mirth. Heaven forgive me! Why, I'll exhibit a bill in the parliament for the putting down of men. How shall I be reveng'd on him? for reveng'd I will be! as sure as his guts are made of puddings.

[*Enter*] Mistress Ford.

Mrs. Ford. Mistress Page, trust me, I was going to your house.

Mrs. Page. And trust me, I was coming to you. You look very ill.

Mrs. Ford. Nay, I'll ne'er believe that; I have to show to the contrary.

Mrs. Page. Faith, but you do, in my mind.

Mrs. Ford. Well—I do then; yet I say I could show you to the contrary. O Mistress Page, give me some counsel!

Mrs. Page. What's the matter, woman?

Mrs. Ford. O woman—if it were not for one trifling respect, I could come to such honor!

Mrs. Page. Hang the trifle, woman, take the honor. What is it? Dispense with trifles. What is it?

Mrs. Ford. If I would but go to hell for an eternal moment or so, I could be knighted.

Mrs. Page. What? thou liest! Sir Alice Ford! These knights will hack, and so thou shouldst not alter the article of thy gentry.

Mrs. Ford. We burn daylight. Here, read, read; perceive how I might be knighted. I shall think

20. **Herod of Jewry**: i.e. a ranting villain (like Herod in the mystery plays).
23. **unweigh'd**: ill-considered. **Flemish drunkard**: i.e. one who drinks enough to rival the Flemish (proverbially heavy drinkers).
24. **with . . . name**: may the name of devil go with him (?).
24–25. **conversation**: behavior, conduct.
25. **assay**: make advances to.
27. **What . . . say**: what could I have said. 28. **exhibit**: submit.
29. **putting down**: suppression.
32. **puddings**: sausages, stuffed intestines.
36. **very ill**: i.e. not very well.
37–38. **have to show**: have evidence.
39. **in my mind**: to my way of thinking.
52. **hack.** Of uncertain meaning; possibly "attack with swords," with sexual innuendo, matching Mrs. Ford's quibble in *knighted* = (1) given the title of knight, (2) provided with a knight as lover.
53. **article . . . gentry**: character of your station.
54. **burn daylight**: waste time.

the worse of fat men, as long as I have an eye to make difference of men's liking: and yet he would not swear; [prais'd] women's modesty; and gave such orderly and well-behav'd reproof to all uncomeliness, that I would have sworn his disposition would have gone to the truth of his words; but they do no more adhere and keep place together than the hundred Psalms to the tune of "Green-sleeves." What tempest, I trow, threw this whale (with so many tuns of oil in his belly) ashore at Windsor? How shall I be reveng'd on him? I think the best way were to entertain him with hope, till the wicked fire of lust have melted him in his own grease. Did you ever hear the like?

Mrs. Page. Letter for letter; but that the name of Page and Ford differs! To thy great comfort in this mystery of ill opinions, here's the twin-brother of thy letter; but let thine inherit first, for I protest mine never shall. I warrant he hath a thousand of these letters, writ with blank space for different names (sure, more!); and these are of the second edition. He will print them, out of doubt; for he cares not what he puts into the press, when he would put us two. I had rather be a giantess, and lie under Mount Pelion. Well—I will find you twenty lascivious turtles ere one chaste man.

Mrs. Ford. Why, this is the very same: the very hand; the very words. What doth he think of us?

Mrs. Page. Nay, I know not; it makes me almost ready to wrangle with mine own honesty. I'll entertain myself like one that I am not acquainted withal; for sure unless he know some strain in me that I know not myself, he would never have boarded me in this fury.

Mrs. Ford. "Boarding," call you it? I'll be sure to keep him above deck.

Mrs. Page. So will I; if he come under my hatches, I'll never to sea again. Let's be reveng'd on him: let's appoint him a meeting, give him a show of comfort in his suit, and lead him on with a fine-baited delay, till he hath pawn'd his horses to mine host of the Garter.

Mrs. Ford. Nay, I will consent to act any villainy against him, that may not sully the chariness of our honesty. O that my husband saw this letter! it would give eternal food to his jealousy.

Mrs. Page. Why, look where he comes; and my good man too. He's as far from jealousy as I am from giving him cause, and that (I hope) is an unmeasurable distance.

Mrs. Ford. You are the happier woman.

Mrs. Page. Let's consult together against this greasy knight. Come hither. [*They retire.*]

[*Enter*] FORD [*with*] PISTOL; PAGE [*with*] NYM.

Ford. Well, I hope it be not so.

Pist. Hope is a curtal dog in some affairs.
Sir John affects thy wife.

Ford. Why, sir, my wife is not young.

Pist. He woos both high and low, both rich and poor,
Both young and old, one with another, Ford.
He loves the gallimaufry, Ford. Perpend.

Ford. Love my wife?

Pist. With liver burning hot. Prevent; or go thou
Like Sir Actaeon he, with Ringwood at thy heels—
O, odious is the name!

Ford. What name, sir?

Pist. The horn, I say. Farewell.
Take heed, have open eye, for thieves do foot by night.
Take heed, ere summer comes or cuckoo-birds do sing.
Away, Sir Corporal Nym!
Believe it, Page, he speaks sense. [*Exit.*]

Ford. [*Aside.*] I will be patient; I will find out this.

Nym. [*To Page.*] And this is true; I like not the humor of lying. He hath wrong'd me in some humors. I should have borne the humor'd letter to her; but I have a sword, and it shall bite upon my necessity. He loves your wife: there's the short and the long. My name is Corporal Nym; I speak, and I avouch; 'tis true; my name is Nym, and Falstaff loves your wife. Adieu. I love not the humor of bread and cheese [and there's the humor of it]. Adieu. [*Exit.*]

Page. "The humor of it," quoth 'a! Here's a fellow frights English out of his wits.

Ford. I will seek out Falstaff.

Page. I never heard such a drawling, affecting rogue.

Ford. If I do find it—well.

Page. I will not believe such a Cataian, though the priest o' th' town commended him for a true man.

Ford. 'Twas a good sensible fellow—well.

[*Mrs. Page and Mrs. Ford come forward.*]

57. **make difference of:** discriminate among. **liking:** physiques.
61. **gone . . . of:** supported, confirmed.
63. **hundred Psalms.** Many editors read *Hundredth Psalm* (*hundred* is a common variant of *hundredth*). **Green-sleeves:** a popular love song, still current. 67. **entertain . . . hope:** lead him on.
72. **mystery . . . opinions:** i.e. mysterious situation in which you have acquired such a questionable reputation. 77. **out of:** without.
78. **into the press.** With second meaning "under his weight."
80. **Pelion:** mountain in Thessaly which (according to one version of the Greek myth) the giants tried to pile upon its neighbor Mount Ossa.
81. **turtles:** turtledoves, proverbially faithful to their mates.
86. **entertain:** treat. 87. **withal:** with.
88. **boarded:** made advances to (a naval term, meaning to come alongside or aboard a ship, usually in order to attack).
95. **fine-baited:** subtly alluring.
98. **Nay.** Not a refusal but an expression of willingness to go farther.
99. **chariness:** scrupulous integrity.
110. **curtal:** with tail docked. 111. **affects:** loves.
115. **gallimaufry:** hodgepodge, miscellaneous assortment (term from cookery). **Perpend:** consider.
117. **liver.** The supposed seat of the passions.
118. **Actaeon:** Greek hunter who accidentally saw Diana as she was bathing, and was punished by being turned into a stag. He was killed by his own dogs. Pistol warns Ford that he is in danger of acquiring the horns of a cuckold. **Ringwood:** common name for a dog.
119. **the name:** i.e. the name of cuckold. 122. **foot:** walk.
123. **cuckoo-birds.** The cuckoo's call supposedly foretold cuckoldry.
131–32. **upon my necessity:** when I need to use it.
136. **bread and cheese:** i.e. the daily fare Falstaff has allowed him, with, Wilson suggests, some reference to the name of the cuckoo-bread flower. 139. **his:** its. 141. **affecting:** affected.
143. **If . . . well:** if I find it to be true, I'll take proper measures.
144. **Cataian:** scoundrel (literally, a person from Cathay, i.e. China).

Page. How now, Meg?

Mrs. Page. Whither go you, George, hark you?

Mrs. Ford. How now, sweet Frank, why art thou melancholy?

Ford. I melancholy? I am not melancholy. Get you home; go.

Mrs. Ford. Faith, thou hast some crotchets in thy head now. Will you go, Mistress Page?

Mrs. Page. Have with you. You'll come to dinner, George? [*Aside to Mrs. Ford*.] Look who comes yonder. She shall be our messenger to this paltry knight.

Mrs. Ford. [*Aside to Mrs. Page*.] Trust me, I thought on her. She'll fit it.

[*Enter* MISTRESS] QUICKLY.

Mrs. Page. You are come to see my daughter Anne?

Quick. Ay, forsooth; and I pray, how does good Mistress Anne?

Mrs. Page. Go in with us and see. We have an hour's talk with you.

[*Exeunt Mrs. Page, Mrs. Ford, and Mrs. Quickly*.]

Page. How now, Master Ford?

Ford. You heard what this knave told me, did you not?

Page. Yes, and you heard what the other told me?

Ford. Do you think there is truth in them?

Page. Hang 'em, slaves! I do not think the knight would offer it; but these that accuse him in his intent towards our wives are a yoke of his discarded men—very rogues, now they be out of service.

Ford. Were they his men?

Page. Marry, were they.

Ford. I like it never the better for that. Does he lie at the Garter?

Page. Ay, marry, does he. If he should intend this voyage toward my wife, I would turn her loose to him; and what he gets more of her than sharp words, let it lie on my head.

Ford. I do not misdoubt my wife; but I would be loath to turn them together. A man may be too confident. I would have nothing lie on my head. I cannot be thus satisfied.

[*Enter*] HOST.

Page. Look where my ranting host of the Garter comes. There is either liquor in his pate, or money in his purse, when he looks so merrily. How now, mine host?

Host. How now, bully-rook? thou'rt a gentleman. Cavaleiro Justice, I say!

[*Enter*] SHALLOW.

Shal. I follow, mine host, I follow. Good even and twenty, good Master Page! Master Page, will you go with us? we have sport in hand.

Host. Tell him, Cavaleiro Justice; tell him, bully-rook.

Shal. Sir, there is a fray to be fought between Sir Hugh the Welsh priest and Caius the French doctor.

Ford. Good mine host o' th' Garter, a word with you.

Host. What say'st thou, my bully-rook?

[*Ford and the Host talks*.]

Shal. [*To Page*.] Will you go with us to behold it? My merry host hath had the measuring of their weapons, and, I think, hath appointed them contrary places; for, believe me, I hear the parson is no jester. Hark, I will tell you what our sport shall be. [*They converse apart*.]

Host. Hast thou no suit against my knight, my guest-cavalier?

[*Ford*.] None, I protest; but I'll give you a pottle of burnt sack to give me recourse to him and tell him my name is [Brook]—only for a jest.

Host. My hand, bully; thou shalt have egress and regress—said I well?—and thy name shall be [Brook]. It is a merry knight. Will you go, An-heires?

Shal. Have with you, mine host.

Page. I have heard the Frenchman hath good skill in his rapier.

Shal. Tut, sir; I could have told you more. In these times you stand on distance: your passes, stoccadoes, and I know not what. 'Tis the heart, Master Page, 'tis here, 'tis here. I have seen the time, with my long sword I would have made you four tall fellows skip like rats.

Host. Here, boys, here, here! shall we wag?

Page. Have with you. I had rather hear them scold than fight. [*Exeunt Host, Shallow, and Page*.]

Ford. Though Page be a secure fool, and stands so firmly on his wive's frailty, yet I cannot put off my opinion so easily. She was in his company at Page's house; and what they made there, I know not. Well, I will look further into't, and I have a disguise to sound Falstaff. If I find her honest, I lose not my labor; if she be otherwise, 'tis labor well bestow'd. *Exit*.

154. crotchets: whims.
156. Have with you: I'll go with you (a conventional expression; see lines 221 and 231 and III.ii.92). **174. offer**: venture.
175. yoke: pair. **180. lie**: lodge. **181. intend**: propose making.
184. lie . . . head: be my own responsibility. In line 187 Ford turns the words into an allusion to the cuckold's horns.
185. misdoubt: mistrust.
194. Cavaleiro: a gentleman expert in arms, a gallant.
195–96. Good . . . twenty: i.e. many returns of the day.
208–9. contrary places: different meeting-places.
214. pottle: two-quart tankard.
215. burnt: warmed. **recourse**: access.
216. Brook. That this form of Ford's alias, preserved in the quartos, was Shakespeare's original choice is shown by the wordplay at II.ii.150–51. Its alteration to *Broom*, to which F1 testifies, was presumably made to meet the wishes of the same Lord Cobham who is thought to have forced the replacement of *Oldcastle* by *Falstaff* in the Henry IV plays; in the latter case he would have been objecting to the use of an ancestor's name, in the former to the use of his own surname.
220. An-heires. A crux. The most widely adopted emendation is Theobald's *Mynheers*, Dutch for "sirs."
225. stand: rely. **distance**: prescribed space maintained between combatants. **passes**: lunges. **226. stoccadoes**: thrusts.
229. tall: valiant. **230. wag**: be on our way.
232. scold: quarrel noisily. **233. secure**: overconfident.
233–34. stands . . . frailty: trusts his susceptible wife so firmly.
234. wive's: wife's. **put off**: dismiss from my mind.
235. She: i.e. Mrs. Ford. **236. made**: did.
238. sound: plumb, measure the depth of.

Scene II

Enter Falstaff, Pistol.

[*Pist.* I will retort the sum in equipage.]

Fal. I will not lend thee a penny.

Pist. Why then the world's mine oyster,
Which I with sword will open.

Fal. Not a penny. I have been content, sir, you should lay my countenance to pawn. I have grated upon my good friends for three reprieves for you and your coach-fellow Nym; or else you had look'd through the grate, like a geminy of baboons. I am damn'd in hell for swearing to gentlemen my friends, you were good soldiers and tall fellows; and when Mistress Bridget lost the handle of her fan, I took't upon mine honor thou hadst it not.

Pist. Didst not thou share? Hadst thou not fifteen pence?

Fal. Reason, you rogue, reason; think'st thou I'll endanger my soul gratis? At a word, hang no more about me, I am no gibbet for you. Go—a short knife and a throng!—to your manor of Pickt-hatch! Go. You'll not bear a letter for me, you rogue? You stand upon your honor! Why, thou unconfinable baseness, it is as much as I can do to keep the terms of my honor precise. I, I, I myself sometimes, leaving the fear of [God] on the left hand, and hiding mine honor in my necessity, am fain to shuffle, to hedge, and to lurch; and yet you, rogue, will ensconce your rags, your cat-a-mountain looks, your red-lattice phrases, and your bold-beating oaths, under the shelter of your honor! You will not do it? You!

Pist. I do relent. What would thou more of man?

[*Enter*] Robin.

Rob. Sir, here's a woman would speak with you.

Fal. Let her approach.

[*Enter* Mistress] Quickly.

Quick. Give your worship good morrow.

Fal. Good morrow, goodwife.

Quick. Not so, and't please your worship.

Fal. Good maid then.

Quick. I'll be sworn,
As my mother was the first hour I was born.

Fal. I do believe the swearer. What with me?

Quick. Shall I vouchsafe your worship a word or two?

Fal. Two thousand, fair woman, and I'll vouchsafe thee the hearing.

Quick. There is one Mistress Ford, sir—I pray come a little nearer this ways. I myself dwell with Master Doctor Caius—

Fal. Well, on. Mistress Ford, you say—

Quick. Your worship says very true. I pray your worship come a little nearer this ways.

Fal. I warrant thee, nobody hears—mine own people, mine own people.

Quick. Are they so? [God] bless them and make them his servants!

Fal. Well; Mistress Ford, what of her?

Quick. Why, sir, she's a good creature. Lord, Lord, your worship's a wanton! Well—heaven forgive you, and all of us, I pray—

Fal. Mistress Ford; come, Mistress Ford—

Quick. Marry, this is the short and the long of it: you have brought her into such a canaries as 'tis wonderful. The best courtier of them all (when the court lay at Windsor) could never have brought her to such a canary; yet there has been knights, and lords, and gentlemen, with their coaches; I warrant you, coach after coach, letter after letter, gift after gift; smelling so sweetly, all musk, and so rushling, I warrant you, in silk and gold, and in such alligant terms, and in such wine and sugar of the best, and the fairest, that would have won any woman's heart; and I warrant you, they could never get an eye-wink of her. I had myself twenty angels given me this morning, but I defy all angels (in any such sort, as they say) but in the way of honesty; and I warrant you, they could never get her so much as sip on a cup with the proudest of them all, and yet there has been earls, nay (which is more) pensioners, but I warrant you all is one with her.

Fal. But what says she to me? Be brief, my good she-Mercury.

Quick. Marry, she hath receiv'd your letter—for the which she thanks you a thousand times—and she gives you to notify that her husband will be absence from his house between ten and eleven.

Fal. Ten and eleven?

Quick. Ay, forsooth; and then you may come and see the picture, she says, that you wot of. Master Ford her husband will be from home. Alas, the sweet woman leads an ill life with him. He's a very

II.ii. Location: Windsor. The Garter Inn.
1. **retort:** i.e. repay. **in equipage.** Meaning uncertain; conjectures include "in military supplies," "in stolen goods," "in regular installments."
6. **lay . . . pawn:** i.e. incur debts on the strength of my patronage.
7. **grated upon:** made a nuisance of myself with.
8. **coach-fellow:** close associate (literally, a horse teamed with another in drawing a coach).
9. **grate:** i.e. grated window in a debtor's prison. **like . . . geminy:** i.e. like a pair of baboons in a cage.
13. **took't . . . honor:** swore by my honor.
18. **short . . . throng:** i.e. with a small knife suitable for cutting purses in a crowd.
18–19. **Pickt-hatch:** an area of London noted for its brothels. The houses sometimes had the lower halves (hatches) of their divided doors guarded with spikes (piked). 21. **unconfinable:** i.e. infinite.
22. **terms:** state. **precise.** Possibly punning on the meaning "puritanical."
25. **shuffle:** practice trickery. **hedge:** dodge. **lurch:** pilfer.
26–27. **cat-a-mountain:** catamount, wildcat.
27. **red-lattice phrases:** tavern talk (from the red-latticed windows that distinguished an alehouse).
28. **bold-beating.** This word, which occurs only here, has been explained as a telescoping of *bold-faced* and *browbeating*.
35. **Not so:** i.e. I am not a wife.
40. **vouchsafe:** grant the favor of (misused by Quickly).
60. **canaries.** Not certainly explained; perhaps "state of excitement," from the lively dance called the canary. 62. **lay:** was in residence.
66. **musk:** i.e. heavy perfume (based on a highly odoriferous substance secreted by the male musk-deer).
67. **rushling:** Quickly's version of *rustling*.
68. **alligant.** She may intend either *elegant* or *eloquent*.
72. **twenty angels:** i.e. as a bribe to gain access to Mistress Ford.
77. **pensioners:** gentlemen of the royal bodyguard.
80. **she-Mercury:** female messenger. The winged Mercury was the messenger of the gods. 87. **wot:** know.

jealousy man. She leads a very frampold life with him, good heart.

Fal. Ten and eleven. Woman, commend me to her, I will not fail her.

Quick. Why, you say well. But I have another messenger to your worship. Mistress Page hath her hearty commendations to you too; and let me tell you in your ear, she's as fartuous a civil modest wife, and one (I tell you) that will not miss you morning nor evening prayer, as any is in Windsor, whoe'er be the other; and she bade me tell your worship that her husband is seldom from home, but she hopes there will come a time. I never knew a woman so dote upon a man; surely I think you have charms, la; yes, in truth.

Fal. Not I, I assure thee. Setting the attraction of my good parts aside, I have no other charms.

Quick. Blessing on your heart for't!

Fal. But I pray thee tell me this: has Ford's wife and Page's wife acquainted each other how they love me?

Quick. That were a jest indeed! They have not so little grace, I hope. That were a trick indeed! But Mistress Page would desire you to send her your little page, of all loves. Her husband has a marvellous infection to the little page; and truly Master Page is an honest man. Never a wife in Windsor leads a better life than she does: do what she will, say what she will, take all, pay all, go to bed when she list, rise when she list, all is as she will; and truly she deserves it, for if there be a kind woman in Windsor, she is one. You must send her your page, no remedy.

Fal. Why, I will.

Quick. Nay, but do so then, and look you, he may come and go between you both; and in any case have a nay-word, that you may know one another's mind, and the boy never need to understand any thing; for 'tis not good that children should know any wickedness. Old folks, you know, have discretion, as they say, and know the world.

Fal. Fare thee well, commend me to them both. There's my purse, I am yet thy debtor. Boy, go along with this woman. [*Exeunt Mrs. Quickly and Robin.*] This news distracts me!

Pist. [*Aside.*] This punk is one of Cupid's carriers.
Clap on more sails, pursue; up with your fights;
Give fire! She is my prize, or ocean whelm them all!
[*Exit.*]

Fal. Say'st thou so, old Jack? go thy ways. I'll make more of thy old body than I have done. Will they yet look after thee? Wilt thou, after the expense of so much money, be now a gainer? Good body, I thank thee. Let them say 'tis grossly done, so it be fairly done, no matter.

[*Enter*] BARDOLPH.

Bard. Sir John, there's one Master [Brook] below would fain speak with you, and be acquainted with you; and hath sent your worship a morning's draught of sack.

Fal. [Brook] is his name?

Bard. Ay, sir.

Fal. Call him in. [*Exit Bardolph.*] Such [Brooks] are welcome to me, that o'erflows such liquor. Ah, ha! Mistress Ford and Mistress Page, have I encompass'd you? Go to, *via!*

[*Enter* BARDOLPH *with*] FORD [*disguised like Brook*].

Ford. [God save] you, sir!

Fal. And you, sir! Would you speak with me?

Ford. I make bold, to press with so little preparation upon you.

Fal. You're welcome. What's your will? Give us leave, drawer. [*Exit Bardolph.*]

Ford. Sir, I am a gentleman that have spent much. My name is [Brook].

Fal. Good Master [Brook], I desire more acquaintance of you.

Ford. Good Sir John, I sue for yours—not to charge you, for I must let you understand I think myself in better plight for a lender than you are; the which hath something embold'ned me to this unseason'd intrusion; for they say, if money go before, all ways do lie open.

Fal. Money is a good soldier, sir, and will on.

Ford. Troth, and I have a bag of money here troubles me. If you will help to bear it, Sir John, take all, or half, for easing me of the carriage.

Fal. Sir, I know not how I may deserve to be your porter.

Ford. I will tell you, sir, if you will give me the hearing.

Fal. Speak, good Master [Brook], I shall be glad to be your servant.

Ford. Sir, I hear you are a scholar (I will be brief with you), and you have been a man long known to me, though I had never so good means as desire to make myself acquainted with you. I shall discover a thing to you, wherein I must very much lay open mine own imperfection; but, good Sir John, as you have one eye upon my follies, as you hear them unfolded, turn another into the register of your own, that I may pass with a reproof the easier, sith you yourself know how easy it is to be such an offender.

Fal. Very well, sir, proceed.

Ford. There is a gentlewoman in this town, her husband's name is Ford.

Fal. Well, sir.

90. frampold: disagreeable.
97. fartuous: Quickly's laughable version of *virtuous*. **modest:** proper. **103–4. have charms:** employ magic spells.
106. parts: qualities. **114. of all loves:** for love's sake.
115. infection: blunder for *affection*. **119. list:** pleases.
126. nay-word: password. The first recorded use of the word, which occurs again at V.ii.5; cf. *an ayword* (= byword), *Twelfth Night*, II.iii.135. **134. distracts:** confounds (with joy).
135. punk: whore. **carriers:** messengers.
136. Clap: put. **fights:** canvas screens raised during naval action to conceal and protect the sailors. **137. prize:** booty.

142. grossly: clumsily. **143. fairly:** fortunately.
153. encompass'd you: got round you, taken you in. **via:** go on.
156–57. preparation: prearrangement, advance notice.
158–59. Give us leave. A polite dismissal. **159. drawer:** tapster.
165. charge you: put you to any expense.
168. unseason'd: unseasonable. **183. discover:** reveal.
187. register: record. **188. sith:** since.

Ford. I have long lov'd her, and I protest to you, bestow'd much on her; follow'd her with a doting observance; engross'd opportunities to meet her; fee'd every slight occasion that could but niggardly give me sight of her; not only bought many presents to give her, but have given largely to many to know what she would have given; briefly, I have pursu'd her as love hath pursu'd me, which hath been on the wing of all occasions. But whatsoever I have merited, either in my mind or in my means, meed I am sure I have receiv'd none, unless experience be a jewel—that I have purchas'd at an infinite rate, and that hath taught me to say this:

"Love like a shadow flies when substance love pursues,
Pursuing that that flies, and flying what pursues."

Fal. Have you receiv'd no promise of satisfaction at her hands?

Ford. Never.

Fal. Have you importun'd her to such a purpose?

Ford. Never.

Fal. Of what quality was your love then?

Ford. Like a fair house built on another man's ground, so that I have lost my edifice by mistaking the place where I erected it.

Fal. To what purpose have you unfolded this to me?

Ford. When I have told you that, I have told you all. Some say that, though she appear honest to me, yet in other places she enlargeth her mirth so far that there is shrewd construction made of her. Now, Sir John, here is the heart of my purpose: you are a gentleman of excellent breeding, admirable discourse, of great admittance, authentic in your place and person, generally allow'd for your many war-like, court-like, and learned preparations.

Fal. O sir!

Ford. Believe it, for you know it. There is money, spend it, spend it; spend more; spend all I have; only give me so much of your time in exchange of it, as to lay an amiable siege to the honesty of this Ford's wife. Use your art of wooing; win her to consent to you; if any man may, you may as soon as any.

Fal. Would it apply well to the vehemency of your affection, that I should win what you would enjoy? Methinks you prescribe to yourself very preposterously.

Ford. O, understand my drift. She dwells so securely on the excellency of her honor, that the folly of my soul dares not present itself; she is too bright to be look'd against. Now, could I come to her with any detection in my hand, my desires had instance and argument to commend themselves. I could drive her then from the ward of her purity, her reputation, her marriage vow, and a thousand other her defenses, which now are too too strongly embattled against me. What say you to't, Sir John?

Fal. Master [Brook], I will first make bold with your money; next, give me your hand; and last, as I am a gentleman, you shall, [and] you will, enjoy Ford's wife.

Ford. O good sir!

Fal. I say you shall.

Ford. Want no money, Sir John, you shall want none.

Fal. Want no Mistress Ford, Master [Brook], you shall want none. I shall be with her (I may tell you) by her own appointment; even as you came in to me, her assistant or go-between parted from me. I say I shall be with her between ten and eleven; for at that time the jealious rascally knave her husband will be forth. Come you to me at night, you shall know how I speed.

Ford. I am blest in your acquaintance. Do you know Ford, sir?

Fal. Hang him, poor cuckoldly knave, I know him not. Yet I wrong him to call him poor. They say the jealous wittolly knave hath masses of money, for the which his wife seems to me well-favor'd. I will use her as the key of the cuckoldly rogue's coffer, and there's my harvest-home.

Ford. I would you knew Ford, sir, that you might avoid him if you saw him.

Fal. Hang him, mechanical salt-butter rogue! I will stare him out of his wits; I will awe him with my cudgel; it shall hang like a meteor o'er the cuckold's horns. Master [Brook], thou shalt know I will predominate over the peasant, and thou shalt lie with his wife. Come to me soon at night. Ford's a knave, and I will aggravate his style; thou, Master [Brook], shalt know him for knave, and cuckold. Come to me soon at night. *[Exit.]*

Ford. What a damn'd Epicurean rascal is this! My heart is ready to crack with impatience. Who says this is improvident jealousy? My wife hath sent to him, the hour is fix'd, the match is made. Would any man have thought this? See the hell of having a false woman! My bed shall be abus'd, my coffers ransack'd, my reputation gnawn at, and I shall not only receive this villainous wrong, but stand under the adoption of abominable terms, and

196. engross'd: monopolized. **197. fee'd:** made use of, bought.
199. largely: generously.
200. what . . . given: i.e. what gifts she would like to receive.
203. meed: reward.
207–8. Love . . . pursues. The idea is proverbial.
222. enlargeth: gives scope to, extends. **223. shrewd:** malicious.
226. of great admittance: i.e. having ready entry into good society.
226–27. authentic: recognized. **227. allow'd:** acknowledged.
228–29. preparations: accomplishments. **234. amiable:** amorous.
243. securely: confidently.
245. look'd against: looked at directly (i.e. she is like the sun).

247. instance: evidence, proof.
248. ward: posture of defense in fencing.
251. embattled: arrayed. **254. and:** if. **258. Want:** lack.
265. jealious: jealous (a variant form).
266. forth: away from home. **272. wittolly:** cuckoldly.
273. for the which: for which reason. **well-favor'd:** beautiful.
275. harvest-home: time for reaping a profit.
278. mechanical: base (literally, referring to a manual worker). **salt-butter:** another contemptuous epithet, perhaps meaning "having coarse tastes" or "malodorous."
282. predominate: have the ascendancy (like a planet at the time of its greatest influence).
284. aggravate his style: expand his title (by adding the word *cuckold* to it). **287. Epicurean:** sensual.
289. improvident jealousy: rash suspicion.
295. stand under. With a play on his bearing of a cuckold's horns.

by him that does me this wrong. Terms! names! Amaimon sounds well; Lucifer, well; Barbason, well; yet they are devils' additions, the names of fiends; but Cuckold! Wittol!—Cuckold! the devil himself hath not such a name. Page is an ass, a secure ass; he will trust his wife, he will not be jealous. I will rather trust a Fleming with my butter, Parson Hugh the Welshman with my cheese, an Irishman with my aqua-vitae bottle, or a thief to walk my ambling gelding, than my wife with herself. Then she plots, then she ruminates, then she devises; and what they think in their hearts they may effect, they will break their hearts but they will effect. [God] be prais'd for my jealousy! Eleven o'clock the hour. I will prevent this, detect my wife, be reveng'd on Falstaff, and laugh at Page. I will about it; better three hours too soon than a minute too late. Fie, fie, fie! cuckold, cuckold, cuckold! *Exit.*

SCENE III

Enter CAIUS, RUGBY.

Caius. Jack Rugby!

Rug. Sir?

Caius. Vat is the clock, Jack?

Rug. 'Tis past the hour, sir, that Sir Hugh promis'd to meet.

Caius. By gar, he has save his soul, dat he is no come; he has pray his Pible well, dat he is no come. By gar, Jack Rugby, he is dead already, if he be come.

Rug. He is wise, sir; he knew your worship would kill him if he came.

Caius. By gar, de herring is no dead so as I vill kill him. Take your rapier, Jack, I vill tell you how I vill kill him.

Rug. Alas, sir, I cannot fence.

Caius. Villainy, take your rapier.

Rug. Forbear; here's company.

[*Enter*] PAGE, SHALLOW, SLENDER, HOST.

Host. [God] bless thee, bully-doctor!

Shal. [God] save you, Master Doctor Caius!

Page. Now, good Master Doctor!

Slen. Give you good morrow, sir.

Caius. Vat be all you, one, two, tree, four, come for?

Host. To see thee fight, to see thee foin, to see thee traverse, to see thee here, to see thee there, to see thee pass thy puncto, thy stock, thy reverse, thy

297. Amaimon, Lucifer, Barbason: names of devils.
298. additions: titles. **300. secure:** overconfident.
303. cheese. The Welshman's love of cheese was proverbial.
304. aqua-vitae: brandy, spirits. **walk:** i.e. exercise.
310. prevent: forestall.

II.iii. Location: A field near Windsor.
12–13. de herring . . . him: i.e. I will kill him deader than a herring. ("As dead as a herring" was proverbial.) **24. foin:** thrust.
25. traverse: shift position from side to side.
26. puncto: thrust with the point of the sword. **stock:** stoccado, thrust. **reverse:** backhand stroke.

distance, thy montant. Is he dead, my Ethiopian? Is he dead, my Francisco? Ha, bully? What says my Aesculapius? my Galien? my heart of elder? Ha? is he dead, bully-stale? is he dead?

Caius. By gar, he is de coward Jack priest of de vorld; he is not show his face.

Host. Thou art a Castalion-King-Urinal! Hector of Greece, my boy!

Caius. I pray you bear witness that me have stay six or seven, two, tree hours for him, and he is no come.

Shal. He is the wiser man, Master Doctor: he is a curer of souls, and you a curer of bodies. If you should fight, you go against the hair of your professions. Is it not true, Master Page?

Page. Master Shallow, you have yourself been a great fighter, though now a man of peace.

Shal. Bodykins, Master Page, though I now be old and of the peace, if I see a sword out, my finger itches to make one. Though we are justices and doctors and churchmen, Master Page, we have some salt of our youth in us, we are the sons of women, Master Page.

Page. 'Tis true, Master Shallow.

Shal. It will be found so, Master Page. Master Doctor Caius, I am come to fetch you home. I am sworn of the peace. You have show'd yourself a wise physician, and Sir Hugh hath shown himself a wise and patient churchman. You must go with me, Master Doctor.

Host. Pardon, guest-justice. A [word], Mounseur Mock-water.

Caius. Mock-vater? vat is dat?

Host. Mock-water, in our English tongue, is valor, bully.

Caius. By gar, then I have as much mock-vater as de Englishman. Scurvy Jack-dog priest! By gar, me vill cut his ears.

Host. He will clapper-claw thee tightly, bully.

Caius. Clapper-de-claw? vat is dat?

Host. That is, he will make thee amends.

Caius. By gar, me do look he shall clapper-de-claw me, for, by gar, me vill have it.

Host. And I will provoke him to't, or let him wag.

27. distance: keeping the prescribed space between fencers. **montant:** upward blow. **Ethiopian.** Alluding to Caius' dark complexion (?). **28. Francisco:** Frenchman.
29. Aesculapius: Greek god of medicine. **Galien:** Galen, famous Greek physician and medical authority. **heart of elder:** i.e. coward, since the elder has soft pith at its centre.
30. bully-stale: i.e. fine Master Doctor, *stale* being used for "physician" (from the sense "urine").
33. Castalion-King-Urinal. Like *stale* in *bully-stale*, *urinal* (= a vessel for the inspection of urine) is used for "physician." *Castalion* seems to be the Host's version of *Castilian* = Spanish = cowardly.
40. go . . . of: behave contrary to (from brushing an animal's hair the wrong way).
44. Bodykins: by God's little body (a weakened oath).
46. make one: join in. **48. salt:** wantonness.
58. Mock-water. A crux. Obviously connected with *stale* (line 30) and Urinal (line 33), with a play on *make-water*, implying cowardice (like *Castalion*, line 33). The Host's equation with valor (line 61) is of course ironic.
63. Jack-dog: mongrel (hence Caius' threat to "cut his ears").
65. clapper-claw: thrash. **tightly:** soundly.
70. provoke: incite, urge.

Caius. Me tank you for dat.

Host. And moreover, bully—but first, Master Guest, and Master Page, and eke Cavaleiro Slender, go you through the town to Frogmore. [*Aside to them.*]

Page. Sir Hugh is there, is he?

Host. He is there. See what humor he is in; and I will bring the doctor about by the fields. Will it do well?

Shal. We will do it.

All [*Page, Shal., Slen.*]. Adieu, good Master Doctor. [*Exeunt all but the Host, Caius, and Rugby.*]

Caius. By gar, me vill kill de priest, for he speak for a jack-an-ape to Anne Page.

Host. Let him die; [but first] sheathe thy impatience, throw cold water on thy choler. Go about the fields with me through Frogmore, I will bring thee where Mistress Anne Page is, at a farm-house a-feasting; and thou shalt woo her. Cried game? Said I well?

Caius. By gar, me dank you vor dat. By gar, I love you; and I shall procure-a you de good guest: de earl, de knight, de lords, de gentlemen, my patients.

Host. For the which I will be thy adversary toward Anne Page. Said I well?

Caius. By gar, 'tis good; vell said.

Host. Let us wag then.

Caius. Come at my heels, Jack Rugby. *Exeunt.*

ACT III, Scene I

Enter Evans, Simple.

Evans. I pray you now, good Master Slender's servingman, and friend Simple by your name, which way have you look'd for Master Caius, that calls himself Doctor of Physic?

Sim. Marry, sir, the pittie-ward, the park-ward—every way; Old Windsor way, and every way but the town way.

Evans. I most fehemently desire you you will also look that way.

Sim. I will, sir. [*Exit.*]

Evans. [Jeshu] pless my soul! how full of chollors I am and trempling of mind! I shall be glad if he have deceiv'd me. How melancholies I am! I will knog his urinals about his knave's costard when I have good opportunities for the ork. Pless my soul! [*Sings.*]

"To shallow rivers, to whose falls
Melodious birds sings madrigals;
There will we make our peds of roses,
And a thousand fragrant posies.
To shallow—"

Mercy on me! I have a great dispositions to cry. [*Sings.*]

"Melodious birds sing madrigals—
When as I sat in Pabylon—
And a thousand vagram posies.
To shallow, etc."

[*Enter* Simple.]

Sim. Yonder he is coming, this way, Sir Hugh.

Evans. He's welcome. [*Sings.*]

"To shallow rivers, to whose falls—"

Heaven prosper the right! What weapons is he?

Sim. No weapons, sir. There comes my master, Master Shallow, and another gentleman—from Frogmore, over the stile, this way.

Evans. Pray you give me my gown, or else keep it in your arms. [*Reads in a book.*]

[*Enter*] Page, Shallow, Slender.

Shal. How now, Master Parson? Good morrow, good Sir Hugh. Keep a gamester from the dice, and a good studient from his book, and it is wonderful.

Slen. [*Aside.*] Ah, sweet Anne Page!

Page. [God] save you, good Sir Hugh!

Evans. [God] pless you from his mercy sake, all of you!

Shal. What? the sword and the word? Do you study them both, Master Parson?

Page. And youthful still, in your doublet and hose, this raw rheumatic day?

Evans. There is reasons and causes for it.

Page. We are come to you to do a good office, Master Parson.

Evans. Fery well; what is it?

Page. Yonder is a most reverend gentleman, who, belike having receiv'd wrong by some person, is at most odds with his own gravity and patience that ever you saw.

Shal. I have liv'd fourscore years and upward; I never heard a man of his place, gravity, and learning, so wide of his own respect.

Evans. What is he?

Page. I think you know him: Master Doctor Caius, the renown'd French physician.

Evans. Got's will, and his passion of my heart! I had as lief you would tell me of a mess of porridge.

Page. Why?

Evans. He has no more knowledge in Hibocrates and Galen—and he is a knave besides, a cowardly knave as you would desires to be acquainted withal.

75. Frogmore: a small village near Windsor.
88. Cried game: i.e. have I promised good sport?

III.i. Location: A field near Frogmore.
5. pittie-ward: towards the Petty or Little Park.
5–6. park-ward: towards Windsor Great Park.
11. chollors: choler, anger.
14. knog: knock. **costard:** apple, i.e. head.
15. ork: work.
17–20. To . . . posies. From Marlowe's poem "Come live with me and be my love."
24. When . . . Pabylon. The first line of a metrical version of Psalm 137.
25. vagram: Evans' version of *vagrant*, with which he confuses *fragrant*. **38. studient:** student (a variant form).
44. the word: the Bible. Line 42 seems to echo Psalm 6:4: "Return, O Lord: deliver my soul: save me for thy mercies' sake" (Geneva).
46. doublet and hose: close-fitting jacket and breeches. In cold weather a cloak would ordinarily be worn over them.
54. odds: strife. **gravity:** dignity.
58. wide of: at variance with. **respect:** reputation.
65. Hibocrates: Hippocrates, famous Greek physician and writer on medicine.

Page. I warrant you, he's the man should fight with him.

Slen. [*Aside*.] O sweet Anne Page!

[*Enter*] Host, Caius, Rugby.

Shal. It appears so by his weapons. Keep them asunder; here comes Doctor Caius.

[*Evans and Caius offer to fight*.]

Page. Nay, good Master Parson, keep in your weapon.

Shal. So do you, good Master Doctor.

Host. Disarm them, and let them question. Let them keep their limbs whole and hack our English.

Caius. I pray you let-a me speak a word with your ear. Vherefore vill you not meet-a me?

Evans. [*Aside to Caius*.] Pray you use your patience in good time.

Caius. By gar, you are de coward, de Jack dog, John ape.

Evans. [*Aside to Caius*.] Pray you let us not be laughing-stocks to other men's humors. I desire you in friendship, and I will one way or other make you amends. [*Aloud*.] I will knog your [urinals] about your knave's cogscomb [for missing your meetings and appointments].

Caius. *Diable!* Jack Rugby—mine host de Jarteer—have I not stay for him to kill him? Have I not, at de place I did appoint?

Evans. As I am a Christians-soul, now look you; this is the place appointed. I'll be judgment by mine host of the Garter.

Host. Peace, I say, Gallia and Gaul, French and Welsh, soul-curer and body-curer!

Caius. Ay, dat is very good, excellant.

Host. Peace, I say! hear mine host of the Garter. Am I politic? Am I subtle? Am I a Machivel? Shall I lose my doctor? No, he gives me the potions and the motions. Shall I lose my parson? my priest? my Sir Hugh? No, he gives me the proverbs and the no-verbs. [Give me thy hand, terrestial; so.] Give me thy hand, celestial; so. Boys of art, I have deceiv'd you both; I have directed you to wrong places. Your hearts are mighty, your skins are whole, and let burnt sack be the issue. Come, lay their swords to pawn. Follow me, [lads] of peace; follow, follow, follow. [*Exit*.]

Shal. [Afore God], a mad host. Follow, gentlemen, follow.

Slen. [*Aside*.] O sweet Anne Page!

[*Exeunt Shallow, Slender, and Page*.]

Caius. Ha, do I perceive dat? Have you make-a de sot of us, ha, ha?

Evans. This is well! he has made us his vlouting-stog. I desire you that we may be friends; and let us knog our prains together to be revenge on this same scall, scurvy, cogging companion, the host of the Garter.

Caius. By gar, with all my heart. He promise to bring me where is Anne Page; by gar, he deceive me too.

Evans. Well, I will smite his noddles. Pray you follow. [*Exeunt*.]

Scene II

[*Enter*] Mistress Page, Robin.

Mrs. Page. Nay, keep your way, little gallant; you were wont to be a follower, but now you are a leader. Whether had you rather lead mine eyes, or eye your master's heels?

Rob. I had rather, forsooth, go before you like a man than follow him like a dwarf.

Mrs. Page. O, you are a flattering boy, now I see you'll be a courtier.

[*Enter*] Ford.

Ford. Well met, Mistress Page. Whither go you?

Mrs. Page. Truly, sir, to see your wife. Is she at home?

Ford. Ay, and as idle as she may hang together, for want of company. I think if your husbands were dead, you two would marry.

Mrs. Page. Be sure of that—two other husbands.

Ford. Where had you this pretty weathercock?

Mrs. Page. I cannot tell what the dickens his name is my husband had him of. What do you call your knight's name, sirrah?

Rob. Sir John Falstaff.

Ford. Sir John Falstaff!

Mrs. Page. He, he—I can never hit on 's name. There is such a league between my goodman and he! Is your wife at home indeed?

Ford. Indeed she is.

Mrs. Page. By your leave, sir. I am sick till I see her. [*Exeunt Mrs. Page and Robin*.]

Ford. Has Page any brains? Hath he any eyes? Hath he any thinking? Sure they sleep, he hath no use of them. Why, this boy will carry a letter twenty mile, as easy as a cannon will shoot point-blank twelve score. He pieces out his wive's inclination; he gives her folly motion and advantage;

68. he: i.e. Evans. **should:** who is to.
72 s.d. offer: make as if. **76. question:** discuss.
81–82. use . . . time: i.e. the occasion calls for patience.
92. stay: waited.
95. judgment by: i.e. governed by the judgment of.
97. Gallia and Gaul: Wales and France.
101. politic: crafty. **Machivel:** Machiavel, i.e. intriguer.
103. motions: purges.
105. proverbs . . . no-verbs: i.e. what I should and should not do (with perhaps some sarcastic comment on Evans' vocabulary).
106. terrestial: terrestrial (a variant form, by analogy with *celestial*).
107. art: learning. **109. issue:** outcome. **116. sot:** fool.
117–18. vlouting-stog: flouting-stock, i.e. laughingstock.
120. scall: scald, scurvy. **cogging:** dissembling.

III.ii. Location: Windsor. A street.
3. Whether. Signalling a choice of alternatives.
13. may hang together: can be and still survive.
18. weathercock. Referring probably to Robin's feathered hat; weathercocks often had a pennon attached.
25. league: friendship. **goodman:** i.e. husband.
34. twelve score: i.e. 240 yards. **pieces out:** augments.
34–35. inclination: natural disposition.
35. folly: wantonness. **motion:** prompting. **advantage:** opportunity.

and now she's going to my wife, and Falstaff's boy with her. A man may hear this show'r sing in the wind. And Falstaff's boy with her! Good plots, they are laid, and our revolted wives share damnation together. Well, I will take him, then torture my wife, pluck the borrow'd veil of modesty from the so-seeming Mistress Page, divulge Page himself for a secure and willful Actaeon; and to these violent proceedings all my neighbors shall cry aim. [*Clock heard*.] The clock gives me my cue, and my assurance bids me search—there I shall find Falstaff. I shall be rather prais'd for this than mock'd; for it is as positive as the earth is firm that Falstaff is there. I will go.

[*Enter*] PAGE, SHALLOW, SLENDER, HOST, EVANS, CAIUS, [RUGBY].

Shal., Page, etc. Well met, Master Ford.

Ford. Trust me, a good knot. I have good cheer at home, and I pray you all go with me.

Shal. I must excuse myself, Master Ford.

Slen. And so must I, sir. We have appointed to dine with Mistress Anne, and I would not break with her for more money than I'll speak of.

Shal. We have linger'd about a match between Anne Page and my cousin Slender, and this day we shall have our answer.

Slen. I hope I have your good will, father Page.

Page. You have, Master Slender, I stand wholly for you; but my wife, Master Doctor, is for you altogether.

Caius. Ay, be-gar, and de maid is love-a me. My nursh-a Quickly tell me so mush.

Host. What say you to young Master Fenton? He capers, he dances, he has eyes of youth; he writes verses, he speaks holiday, he smells April and May—he will carry't, he will carry't—'tis in his buttons—he will carry't.

Page. Not by my consent, I promise you. The gentleman is of no having. He kept company with the wild Prince and Poins; he is of too high a region, he knows too much. No, he shall not knit a knot in his fortunes with the finger of my substance. If he take her, let him take her simply. The wealth I have waits on my consent, and my consent goes not that way.

Ford. I beseech you heartily, some of you go home with me to dinner. Besides your cheer, you shall have sport; I will show you a monster. Master Doctor, you shall go, so shall you, Master Page, and you, Sir Hugh.

Shal. Well, fare you well. We shall have the freer wooing at Master Page's.

[*Exeunt Shallow and Slender*.]

Caius. Go home, John Rugby, I come anon.

[*Exit Rugby*.]

Host. Farewell, my hearts. I will to my honest knight Falstaff, and drink canary with him. [*Exit*.]

Ford. [*Aside*.] I think I shall drink in pipe-wine first with him; I'll make him dance.—Will you go, gentles?

All. Have with you to see this monster. *Exeunt.*

SCENE III

Enter MISTRESS FORD, MISTRESS PAGE.

Mrs. Ford. What, John! What, Robert!

Mrs. Page. Quickly, quickly! Is the buck-basket—

Mrs. Ford. I warrant. What, Robin, I say!

[*Enter*] SERVANTS [*with a great buck-basket*].

Mrs. Page. Come, come, come.

Mrs. Ford. Here, set it down.

Mrs. Page. Give your men the charge, we must be brief.

Mrs. Ford. Marry, as I told you before, John and Robert, be ready here hard by in the brew-house, and when I suddenly call you, come forth, and (without any pause or staggering) take this basket on your shoulders. That done, trudge with it in all haste, and carry it among the whitsters in Datchet-mead, and there empty it in the muddy ditch close by the Thames side.

Mrs. Page. You will do it?

Mrs. Ford. I ha' told them over and over, they lack no direction. Be gone, and come when you are call'd. [*Exeunt Servants*.]

Mrs. Page. Here comes little Robin.

[*Enter*] ROBIN.

Mrs. Ford. How now, my eyas-musket, what news with you?

Rob. My master, Sir John, is come in at your back door, Mistress Ford, and requests your company.

Mrs. Page. You little Jack-a-Lent, have you been true to us?

Rob. Ay, I'll be sworn. My master knows not of your being here, and hath threat'ned to put

37–38. bear . . . wind: tell that a rain shower is coming by the rising wind, i.e. tell by these tokens that trouble is imminent.
42. divulge: reveal. **43. Actaeon.** See note to II.i.118.
44. cry aim: applaud. **46. assurance:** foreknowledge.
51. knot: company. **cheer:** fare.
68. speaks holiday: talks merrily. **69. carry't:** win the day.
69–70. in his buttons. A crux; perhaps = in his very nature (as a fresh young *button*, i.e. bud).
72. having: wealth, property.
73. Prince and Poins. An allusion to *1* and *2 Henry IV*, where Falstaff is a companion of Prince Hal and Poins.
73–74. he . . . much: i.e. he comes from too rarefied a social level and is too sophisticated and worldly. **74–75. knit . . . in:** mend.
76. simply: by herself (without dowry).
81. show . . . monster. Alluding to the sort of abnormal births exhibited at fairs.

86. anon: immediately.
88. canary: a sweet wine from the Canary Islands.
89. pipe-wine: wine in the cask (with pun on *pipe* in the musical sense, suggested by a second meaning of *canary*, i.e. a lively dance).

III.iii. Location: Windsor. Ford's house.
2–3. buck-basket: basket for dirty clothes. **7. charge:** order.
10. hard: near. **14. whitsters:** bleachers of linen.
15. Datchet-mead: a meadow along the Thames near Windsor Park.
22. eyas-musket: young sparrow hawk.
27. Jack-a-Lent: a figure set up to be used as a target; here, puppet.
30–31. put . . . liberty: i.e. discharge me.

me into everlasting liberty if I tell you of it; for he swears he'll turn me away.

Mrs. Page. Thou'rt a good boy. This secrecy of thine shall be a tailor to thee, and shall make thee a new doublet and hose. I'll go hide me.

Mrs. Ford. Do so. Go tell thy master I am alone. [*Exit Robin.*] Mistress Page, remember you your cue.

Mrs. Page. I warrant thee, if I do not act it, hiss me. [*Exit.*]

Mrs. Ford. Go to then. We'll use this unwholesome humidity, this gross wat'ry pumpion. We'll teach him to know turtles from jays.

[*Enter*] FALSTAFF.

Fal. "Have I caught thee, my heavenly jewel?" Why, now let me die, for I have liv'd long enough. This is the period of my ambition. O this blessed hour!

Mrs. Ford. O sweet Sir John!

Fal. Mistress Ford, I cannot cog, I cannot prate, Mistress Ford. Now shall I sin in my wish: I would thy husband were dead. I'll speak it before the best lord, I would make thee my lady.

Mrs. Ford. I your lady, Sir John? Alas, I should be a pitiful lady!

Fal. Let the court of France show me such another. I see how thine eye would emulate the diamond. Thou hast the right arch'd beauty of the brow that becomes the ship-tire, the tire-valiant, or any tire of Venetian admittance.

Mrs. Ford. A plain kerchief, Sir John. My brows become nothing else, nor that well neither.

Fal. [By the Lord,] thou art a tyrant to say so. Thou wouldst make an absolute courtier, and the firm fixture of thy foot would give an excellent motion to thy gait in a semicircled farthingale. I see what thou wert, if Fortune thy foe were not, Nature thy friend. Come, thou canst not hide it.

Mrs. Ford. Believe me, there's no such thing in me.

Fal. What made me love thee? Let that persuade thee there's something extraordinary in thee. Come, I cannot cog and say thou art this and that, like a many of these lisping hawthorn buds, that come like women in men's apparel, and smell like Bucklersbury in simple time—I cannot; but I love thee, none but thee; and thou deserv'st it.

Mrs. Ford. Do not betray me, sir. I fear you love Mistress Page.

Fal. Thou mightst as well say I love to walk by the Counter-gate, which is as hateful to me as the reek of a lime-kill.

Mrs. Ford. Well, heaven knows how I love you, and you shall one day find it.

Fal. Keep in that mind, I'll deserve it.

Mrs. Ford. Nay, I must tell you, so you do; or else I could not be in that mind.

[*Enter* ROBIN.]

Rob. Mistress Ford, Mistress Ford! here's Mistress Page at the door, sweating, and blowing, and looking wildly, and would needs speak with you presently.

Fal. She shall not see me, I will ensconce me behind the arras.

Mrs. Ford. Pray you do so, she's a very tattling woman. [*Falstaff stands behind the arras.*]

[*Enter* MISTRESS PAGE.]

What's the matter? How now?

Mrs. Page. O Mistress Ford, what have you done? You're sham'd, y' are overthrown, y' are undone for ever!

Mrs. Ford. What's the matter, good Mistress Page?

Mrs. Page. O well-a-day, Mistress Ford, having an honest man to your husband, to give him such cause of suspicion!

Mrs. Ford. What cause of suspicion?

Mrs. Page. What cause of suspicion? Out upon you! How am I mistook in you!

Mrs. Ford. Why, alas, what's the matter?

Mrs. Page. Your husband's coming hither, woman, with all the officers in Windsor, to search for a gentleman that he says is here now in the house, by your consent, to take an ill advantage of his absence. You are undone.

Mrs. Ford. 'Tis not so, I hope.

Mrs. Page. Pray heaven it be not so, that you have such a man here; but 'tis most certain your husband's coming, with half Windsor at his heels, to search for such a one. I come before to tell you. If you know yourself clear, why, I am glad of it; but if you have a friend here, convey, convey him out. Be not amaz'd, call all your senses to you, defend your reputation, or bid farewell to your good life for ever.

Mrs. Ford. What shall I do? There is a gentleman, my dear friend; and I fear not mine own shame so much as his peril. I had rather than a thousand pound he were out of the house.

Mrs. Page. For shame, never stand "you had rather" and "you had rather." Your husband's here

41. humidity. Cf. the description of Falstaff in *1 Henry IV*, II.iv.450, as "that swoll'n parcel of dropsies." **pumpion:** pumpkin.
42. turtles: turtledoves, i.e. constant wives. **jays:** i.e. loose women.
43. Have . . . jewel. From Sidney's *Astrophel and Stella* (1591).
45. period: goal. **48. cog:** flatter.
57. ship-tire: woman's head-dress (*tire*) in the form of a ship. **tire-valiant:** another style of head-dress.
58. of Venetian admittance: which is the vogue in Venice (a leader in fashion). **62. absolute:** finished, perfect. **63. fixture:** setting.
64. semicircled farthingale: petticoat with half-hoops to hold out the skirt behind and at the sides.
64–65. what thou wert: what you would be, i.e. what a figure you would cut at court.
65. if . . . not: i.e. if Fortune had not made you a lowly citizen's wife. *Fortune thy foe* contains an allusion to a very popular ballad tune, "Fortune My Foe." **Nature thy friend:** i.e. Nature having been so bountiful in her gifts to you.
71. hawthorn buds: i.e. young dandies (see the note on III.ii.69–70).
72. Bucklersbury: a street in London off Cheapside, inhabited by herbalists.
73. simple time: i.e. midsummer, when the annual supply of fresh herbs or simples would be scenting the air as they dried.

75. betray: deceive.
78. Counter-gate: gate of the debtors' prison in London.
79. lime-kill: lime-kiln. **88. presently:** at once.
89. ensconce: hide, conceal. **90. arras:** tapestry wall-hanging.
95. undone: ruined. **100. to:** for. **116. clear:** innocent.
118. amaz'd: bewildered. **125. stand:** lose time over.

at hand, bethink you of some conveyance. In the house you cannot hide him. O, how have you deceiv'd me! Look, here is a basket; if he be of any reasonable stature, he may creep in here, and throw foul linen upon him, as if it were going to bucking; or—it is whiting-time—send him by your two men to Datchet-mead.

Mrs. Ford. He's too big to go in there. What shall I do?

Fal. [*Starting from his concealment.*] Let me see't, let me see't, O, let me see't! I'll in, I'll in. Follow your friend's counsel. I'll in.

Mrs. Page. What, Sir John Falstaff? [*Aside.*] Are these your letters, knight?

Fal. [*To Mrs. Page.*] I love thee. Help me away. —Let me creep in here. I'll never—

[*Goes into the basket; they put clothes over him.*]

Mrs. Page. Help to cover your master, boy. Call your men, Mistress Ford. You dissembling knight!

Mrs. Ford. What, John! Robert! John!

[*Exit Robin.*]

[*Enter* SERVANTS.]

Go take up these clothes here quickly. Where's the cowl-staff? Look how you drumble! Carry them to the laundress in Datchet-mead; quickly, come.

[*Enter*] FORD, PAGE, CAIUS, EVANS.

Ford. Pray you come near. If I suspect without cause, why then make sport at me, then let me be your jest, I deserve it. How now? Whither bear you this?

Serv. To the laundress, forsooth.

Mrs. Ford. Why, what have you to do whither they bear it? You were best meddle with buck-washing.

Ford. Buck! I would I could wash myself of the buck! Buck, buck, buck! ay, buck! I warrant you, buck, and of the season too, it shall appear. [*Exeunt Servants with the basket.*] Gentlemen, I have dream'd to-night; I'll tell you my dream. Here, here, here be my keys. Ascend my chambers, search, seek, find out. I'll warrant we'll unkennel the fox. Let me stop this way first. [*Locking the door.*] So, now uncape.

Page. Good Master Ford, be contented. You wrong yourself too much.

Ford. True, Master Page. Up, gentlemen, you shall see sport anon. Follow me, gentlemen. [*Exit.*]

Evans. This is fery fantastical humors and jealousies.

Caius. By gar, 'tis no the fashion of France; it is not jealous in France.

Page. Nay, follow him, gentlemen, see the issue of his search. [*Exeunt Page, Caius, and Evans.*]

Mrs. Page. Is there not a double excellency in this?

Mrs. Ford. I know not which pleases me better, that my husband is deceiv'd, or Sir John.

Mrs. Page. What a taking was he in when your husband ask'd who was in the basket!

Mrs. Ford. I am half afraid he will have need of washing, so throwing him into the water will do him a benefit.

Mrs. Page. Hang him, dishonest rascal! I would all of the same strain were in the same distress.

Mrs. Ford. I think my husband hath some special suspicion of Falstaff's being here, for I never saw him so gross in his jealousy till now.

Mrs. Page. I will lay a plot to try that, and we will yet have more tricks with Falstaff. His dissolute disease will scarce obey this medicine.

Mrs. Ford. Shall we send that foolish carrion, Mistress Quickly, to him, and excuse his throwing into the water, and give him another hope, to betray him to another punishment?

Mrs. Page. We will do it. Let him be sent for to-morrow, eight a' clock, to have amends.

[*Enter* FORD, PAGE, CAIUS, *and* EVANS.]

Ford. I cannot find him. May be the knave bragg'd of that he could not compass.

Mrs. Page. [*Aside to Mrs. Ford.*] Heard you that?

Mrs. Ford. You use me well, Master Ford, do you?

Ford. Ay, I do so.

Mrs. Ford. Heaven make you better than your thoughts!

Ford. Amen!

Mrs. Page. You do yourself mighty wrong, Master Ford.

Ford. Ay, ay; I must bear it.

Evans. If there be any pody in the house, and in the chambers, and in the coffers, and in the presses, heaven forgive my sins at the day of judgment!

Caius. Be-gar, nor I too; there is no-bodies.

Page. Fie, fie, Master Ford, are you not asham'd? What spirit, what devil suggests this imagination? I would not ha' your distemper in this kind for the wealth of Windsor Castle.

Ford. 'Tis my fault, Master Page. I suffer for it.

Evans. You suffer for a pad conscience. Your wife is as honest a omans as I will desires among five thousand, and five hundred too.

Caius. By gar, I see 'tis an honest woman.

Ford. Well, I promis'd you a dinner. Come, come, walk in the park. I pray you pardon me; I will hereafter make known to you why I have done this. Come, wife, come, Mistress Page, I pray you pardon me; pray heartly pardon me.

127. bethink: devise. **conveyance:** expedient, stratagem.
131. bucking: washing. **132. whiting-time:** bleaching time.
147. cowl-staff: pole for carrying a basket (*cowl*) between two persons. **drumble:** move sluggishly.
155–56. buck-washing: washing clothes (but Ford picks it up in the sense of "getting rid of a cuckold's horns"). **159. of the:** in.
161. to-night: last night. **163. unkennel:** uncover.
165. uncape. Meaning uncertain; possibly "unleash," i.e. start the chase. **166. be contented:** calm yourself.
180. taking: state of agitation. **186. strain:** character.
189. gross: open, obvious.
192. obey this medicine: i.e. yield to this single dose.
193. carrion: bawd, i.e. go-between, messenger (?) or piece of old flesh (?). **194. excuse:** make excuses for.
212. presses: clothes-presses. **215. suggests:** stirs up.
216. distemper: disorder (here, of mind). **in this kind:** of this sort.
224. walk . . . park: i.e. take a stroll until dinner is ready.
227. heartly: heartily.

Page. Let's go in, gentlemen, but (trust me) we'll mock him. I do invite you to-morrow morning to my house to breakfast; after, we'll a-birding together. I have a fine hawk for the bush. Shall it be so?

Ford. Any thing.

Evans. If there is one, I shall make two in the company.

Caius. If there be one or two, I shall make-a the turd.

Ford. Pray you go, Master Page.

[*Exit with Page*.]

Evans. I pray you now remembrance to-morrow on the lousy knave, mine host.

Caius. Dat is good, by gar; with all my heart!

Evans. A lousy knave, to have his gibes and his mockeries! *Exeunt*.

Scene IV

Enter Fenton, Anne Page.

Fent. I see I cannot get thy father's love,
Therefore no more turn me to him, sweet Nan.

Anne. Alas, how then?

Fent. Why, thou must be thyself.
He doth object I am too great of birth,
And that my state being gall'd with my expense,
I seek to heal it only by his wealth.
Besides these, other bars he lays before me,
My riots past, my wild societies,
And tells me 'tis a thing impossible
I should love thee but as a property.

Anne. May be he tells you true.

[*Fent*.] No, heaven so speed me in my time to come!
Albeit I will confess thy father's wealth
Was the first motive that I woo'd thee, Anne;
Yet wooing thee, I found thee of more value
Than stamps in gold, or sums in sealed bags;
And 'tis the very riches of thyself
That now I aim at.

Anne. Gentle Master Fenton,
Yet seek my father's love, still seek it, sir.
If opportunity and humblest suit
Cannot attain it, why then hark you hither!

[*They converse apart*.]

[*Enter*] Shallow, Slender, [Mistress] Quickly.

Shal. Break their talk, Mistress Quickly, my kinsman shall speak for himself.

Slen. I'll make a shaft or a bolt on't. 'Slid, 'tis but venturing.

Shal. Be not dismay'd.

Slen. No, she shall not dismay me. I care not for that, but that I am afeard.

Quick. Hark ye, Master Slender would speak a word with you.

Anne. I come to him. [*Aside*.] This is my father's choice.
O, what a world of vild ill-favor'd faults
Looks handsome in three hundred pounds a year!

Quick. And how does good Master Fenton? Pray you a word with you.

Shal. She's coming; to her, coz. O boy, thou hadst a father!

Slen. I had a father, Mistress Anne, my uncle can tell you good jests of him. Pray you, uncle, tell Mistress Anne the jest how my father stole two geese out of a pen, good uncle.

Shal. Mistress Anne, my cousin loves you.

Slen. Ay, that I do—as well as I love any woman in Gloucestershire.

Shal. He will maintain you like a gentlewoman.

Slen. Ay, that I will, come cut and long-tail, under the degree of a squire.

Shal. He will make you a hundred and fifty pounds jointure.

Anne. Good Master Shallow, let him woo for himself.

Shal. Marry, I thank you for it; I thank you for that good comfort. She calls you, coz. I'll leave you.

Anne. Now, Master Slender—

Slen. Now, good Mistress Anne—

Anne. What is your will?

Slen. My will? 'Od's heartlings, that's a pretty jest indeed! I ne'er made my will yet, I thank heaven. I am not such a sickly creature, I give heaven praise.

Anne. I mean, Master Slender, what would you with me?

Slen. Truly, for mine own part, I would little or nothing with you. Your father and my uncle hath made motions. If it be my luck, so; if not, happy man be his dole! They can tell you how things go better than I can. You may ask your father, here he comes.

[*Enter*] Page, Mistress Page.

Page. Now, Master Slender. Love him, daughter Anne.
Why, how now? What does Master Fenton here?
You wrong me, sir, thus still to haunt my house.
I told you, sir, my daughter is dispos'd of.

Fent. Nay, Master Page, be not impatient.

228. go in: i.e. accept his invitation (?).
230. a-birding: hawking with a sparrow hawk at small birds which were thus driven out of the bushes and shot.

III.iv. Location: Windsor. Before Page's house.
1. love: i.e. good will, consent. **2. turn**: direct.
3. be thyself: i.e. decide for yourself.
5. my . . . expense: my estate being wounded by my extravagance.
8. societies: companionships.
10. property: (mere) possession (with play perhaps on a stage property and a means to an end). **12. speed**: be favorable to.
16. stamps: coins.
20. opportunity: taking advantage of opportune times for your suit.
22. Break: interrupt.

24. I'll . . . on't: i.e. I may do a good job or a bad, but I'll make a stab at it (proverbial). A shaft was a slender, sharp arrow; a bolt, a thick, blunt arrow. **'Slid**: by God's eyelid (a weakened oath).
32. vild: vile (a variant form). **ill-favor'd**: ugly.
36–37. thou . . . father: i.e. be as resolute as your father must have been in approaching a woman.
46. come . . . long-tail: i.e. whatever happens (proverbial). Literally, *cut and long-tail* = animals with docked and undocked tails, i.e. all animals. **48. make**: give.
57. 'Od's heartlings: by God's little heart (a weakened oath).
64. motions: proposals. **so**: well and good.
64–65. happy . . . dole: good luck to him (who gets you) (proverbial).

Mrs. Page. Good Master Fenton, come not to my child.
Page. She is no match for you.
Fent. Sir, will you hear me?
Page. No, good Master Fenton.
Come, Master Shallow; come, son Slender, in.
Knowing my mind, you wrong me, Master Fenton.
[*Exeunt Page, Shallow, and Slender.*]
Quick. Speak to Mistress Page.
Fent. Good Mistress Page, for that I love your daughter
In such a righteous fashion as I do,
Perforce, against all checks, rebukes, and manners,
I must advance the colors of my love,
And not retire. Let me have your good will.
Anne. Good mother, do not marry me to yond fool.
Mrs. Page. I mean it not, I seek you a better husband.
Quick. That's my master, Master Doctor.
Anne. Alas, I had rather be set quick i' th' earth,
And bowl'd to death with turnips!
Mrs. Page. Come, trouble not yourself. Good Master Fenton,
I will not be your friend nor enemy.
My daughter will I question how she loves you,
And as I find her, so am I affected.
Till then farewell, sir; she must needs go in,
Her father will be angry.
Fent. Farewell, gentle mistress; farewell, Nan.
[*Exeunt Mrs. Page and Anne.*]

Quick. This is my doing now. "Nay," said I, "will you cast away your child on a fool, and a physician? Look on Master Fenton." This is my doing.

Fent. I thank thee; and I pray thee, once to-night
Give my sweet Nan this ring. There's for thy pains.

Quick. Now heaven send thee good fortune! [*Exit Fenton.*] A kind heart he hath. A woman would run through fire and water for such a kind heart. But yet I would my master had Mistress Anne; or I would Master Slender had her; or, in sooth, I would Master Fenton had her. I will do what I can for them all three, for so I have promis'd, and I'll be as good as my word, but speciously for Master Fenton. Well, I must of another errand to Sir John Falstaff from my two mistresses. What a beast am I to slack it! *Exit.*

Scene V

Enter Falstaff.

Fal. Bardolph, I say!

[*Enter*] Bardolph.

Bard. Here, sir.

Fal. Go fetch me a quart of sack, put a toast in't. [*Exit Bardolph.*] Have I liv'd to be carried in a basket like a barrow of butcher's offal? and to be thrown in the Thames? Well, [and] I be serv'd such another trick, I'll have my brains ta'en out and butter'd, and give them to a dog for a new-year's gift. The rogues slighted me into the river with as little remorse as they would have drown'd a blind bitch's puppies, fifteen i' th' litter; and you may know by my size that I have a kind of alacrity in sinking; [and] the bottom were as deep as hell, I should down. I had been drown'd, but that the shore was shelvy and shallow—a death that I abhor; for the water swells a man; and what a thing should I have been when I had been swell'd! I should have been a mountain of mummy.

[*Enter* Bardolph *with sack.*]

Bard. Here's Mistress Quickly, sir, to speak with you.

Fal. Come, let me pour in some sack to the Thames water; for my belly's as cold as if I had swallow'd snowballs for pills to cool the reins. Call her in.

Bard. Come in, woman!

[*Enter* Mistress] Quickly.

Quick. By your leave; I cry you mercy! Give your worship good morrow.

Fal. Take away these chalices. Go, brew me a pottle of sack finely.

Bard. With eggs, sir?

Fal. Simple of itself; I'll no pullet-sperm in my brewage. [*Exit Bardolph.*] How now?

Quick. Marry, sir, I come to your worship from Mistress Ford.

Fal. Mistress Ford? I have had ford enough. I was thrown into the ford; I have my belly full of ford.

Quick. Alas the day! good heart, that was not her fault. She does so take on with her men; they mistook their erection.

Fal. So did I mine, to build upon a foolish woman's promise.

Quick. Well, she laments, sir, for it, that it would yearn your heart to see it. Her husband goes this morning a-birding; she desires you once more to come to her, between eight and nine. I must carry her word quickly. She'll make you amends, I warrant you.

Fal. Well, I will visit her, tell her so. And bid her think what a man is: let her consider his frailty, and then judge of my merit.

Quick. I will tell her.

Fal. Do so. Between nine and ten, say'st thou?

80. checks: reproofs. **81. colors:** banners.
86. set: firmly planted; here probably = buried up to the neck. **quick:** alive. **87. bowl'd:** pelted. **91. affected:** inclined.
99. once: sometime. **108. speciously:** blunder for *specially.*
111. slack: be remiss in.

III.v. Location: Windsor. The Garter Inn.

3. toast: piece of toast. **9. slighted:** tossed carelessly.
10. remorse: compassion. **15. shelvy:** made of sandbanks.
18. mummy: dead flesh. **23. reins:** kidneys.
26. cry you mercy: beg your pardon.
29. pottle: half a gallon. **finely:** so as to taste well.
39. take . . . men: scold her servants.
40. erection. Quickly means *direction,* i.e. instructions; Falstaff quibbles on the word. **44. yearn:** vex, grieve.
50. his frailty: i.e. the weakness of the flesh.

Quick. Eight and nine, sir.

Fal. Well, be gone; I will not miss her.

Quick. Peace be with you, sir. [*Exit.*]

Fal. I marvel I hear not of Master [Brook]; he sent me word to stay within. I like his money well. O, here he comes.

[*Enter*] Ford [*disguised*].

Ford. Bless you, sir!

Fal. Now, Master [Brook], you come to know what hath pass'd between me and Ford's wife?

Ford. That indeed, Sir John, is my business.

Fal. Master [Brook], I will not lie to you. I was at her house the hour she appointed me.

Ford. And sped you, sir?

Fal. Very ill-favoredly, Master [Brook].

Ford. How so, sir? Did she change her determination?

Fal. No, Master [Brook], but the peaking cornuto her husband, Master [Brook], dwelling in a continual 'larum of jealousy, comes me in the instant of our encounter, after we had embrac'd, kiss'd, protested, and, as it were, spoke the prologue of our comedy; and at his heels a rabble of his companions, thither provok'd and instigated by his distemper, and, forsooth, to search his house for his wive's love.

Ford. What? While you were there?

Fal. While I was there.

Ford. And did he search for you, and could not find you?

Fal. You shall hear. As good luck would have it, comes in one Mistress Page; gives intelligence of Ford's approach; and in her invention, and Ford's wive's distraction, they convey'd me into a buck-basket.

Ford. A buck-basket?

Fal. [By the Lord], a buck-basket! Ramm'd me in with foul shirts and smocks, socks, foul stockings, greasy napkins, that, Master [Brook], there was the rankest compound of villainous smell that ever offended nostril.

Ford. And how long lay you there?

Fal. Nay, you shall hear, Master [Brook], what I have suffer'd to bring this woman to evil for your good. Being thus cramm'd in the basket, a couple of Ford's knaves, his hinds, were call'd forth by their mistress to carry me in the name of foul clothes to Datchet-lane. They took me on their shoulders; met the jealous knave their master in the door, who ask'd them once or twice what they had in their basket. I quak'd for fear, lest the lunatic knave would have search'd it; but fate (ordaining he should be a cuckold) held his hand. Well, on went he for a search, and away went I for foul clothes. But mark the sequel, Master [Brook]. I suffer'd the pangs of three several deaths: first, an intolerable fright, to be detected with a jealious rotten bell-wether; next, to be compass'd like a good bilbo in the circumference of a peck, hilt to point, heel to head; and then to be stopp'd in like a strong distillation with stinking clothes that fretted in their own grease. Think of that—a man of my kidney. Think of that—that am as subject to heat as butter; a man of continual dissolution and thaw. It was a miracle to scape suffocation. And in the height of this bath (when I was more than half stew'd in grease, like a Dutch dish) to be thrown into the Thames, and cool'd, glowing-hot, in that surge, like a horse-shoe; think of that—hissing-hot—think of that, Master [Brook].

Ford. In good sadness, sir, I am sorry that for my sake you have suffer'd all this. My suit then is desperate; you'll undertake her no more?

Fal. Master [Brook], I will be thrown into Etna, as I have been into Thames, ere I will leave her thus. Her husband is this morning gone a-birding. I have receiv'd from her another ambassy of meeting. 'Twixt eight and nine is the hour, Master [Brook].

Ford. 'Tis past eight already, sir.

Fal. Is it? I will then address me to my appointment. Come to me at your convenient leisure, and you shall know how I speed; and the conclusion shall be crown'd with your enjoying her. Adieu. You shall have her, Master [Brook]. Master [Brook], you shall cuckold Ford. [*Exit.*]

Ford. Hum! ha? Is this a vision? Is this a dream? Do I sleep? Master Ford, awake! awake, Master Ford! There's a hole made in your best coat, Master Ford. This 'tis to be married! This 'tis to have linen and buck-baskets! Well, I will proclaim myself what I am. I will now take the lecher; he is at my house. He cannot scape me; 'tis impossible he should; he cannot creep into a halfpenny purse, nor into a pepper-box. But lest the devil that guides him should aid him, I will search impossible places. Though what I am I cannot avoid, yet to be what I would not shall not make me tame. If I have horns to make one mad, let the proverb go with me: I'll be horn-mad. *Exit.*

ACT IV, Scene I

Enter Mistress Page, [Mistress] Quickly, William.

Mrs. Page. Is he at Master Ford's already, think'st thou?

67. ill-favoredly: badly.
70. peaking: sneaking (perhaps with a quibble on *peak* = point of a horn). **cornuto:** cuckold (literally, horned creature).
98. hinds: servants. **108. several:** separate. **109. with:** by.

110. bell-wether. Alluding both to Ford's clamor and to his leading a flock of followers.
111. peck: container holding a quarter of a bushel. **hilt to point.** The test of a well-tempered sword (*bilbo*) was that it could be so bent.
112. stopp'd: shut. **113. fretted:** decayed.
115. kidney: constitution. **116. dissolution:** liquefaction.
123. good sadness: all seriousness.
125. undertake: have to do with.
129. ambassy: embassy, message.
133. address me to: prepare myself for.
146. halfpenny purse: a tiny novelty purse.
152. horn-mad: as mad as an angry bull, with punning allusion to the cuckold's horns.

IV.i. Location: Windsor. A street.

Quick. Sure he is by this—or will be presently. But truly he is very courageous mad about his throwing into the water. Mistress Ford desires you to come suddenly.

Mrs. Page. I'll be with her by and by; I'll but bring my young man here to school.

[*Enter*] Evans.

Look where his master comes; 'tis a playing-day, I see. How now, Sir Hugh, no school to-day?

Evans. No; Master Slender is let the boys leave to play.

Quick. Blessing of his heart!

Mrs. Page. Sir Hugh, my husband says my son profits nothing in the world at his book. I pray you ask him some questions in his accidence.

Evans. Come hither, William; hold up your head; come.

Mrs. Page. Come on, sirrah; hold up your head. Answer your master, be not afraid.

Evans. William, how many numbers is in nouns?

Will. Two.

Quick. Truly, I thought there had been one number more, because they say, "'Od's nouns."

Evans. Peace your tattlings! What is "fair," William?

Will. *Pulcher*.

Quick. Poulcats? There are fairer things than poulcats sure.

Evans. You are a very simplicity oman; I pray you peace. What is *lapis*, William?

Will. A stone.

Evans. And what is "a stone," William?

Will. A pebble.

Evans, No; it is *lapis*. I pray you remember in your prain.

Will. *Lapis*.

Evans. That is a good William. What is he, William, that does lend articles?

Will. Articles are borrow'd of the pronoun, and be thus declin'd, *Singulariter, nominativo, hic, haec, hoc*.

Evans. *Nominativo, hig, hag, hog;* pray you mark; *genitivo, hujus*. Well, what is your accusative case?

Will. *Accusativo, hinc*.

Evans. I pray you have your remembrance, child. *Accusativo, [hung], hang, hog*.

Quick. "Hang-hog" is Latin for bacon, I warrant you.

Evans. Leave your prabbles, oman. What is the focative case, William?

Will. O—*vocativo, O*.

Evans. Remember, William, focative is *caret*.

Quick. And that's a good root.

Evans. Oman, forbear.

Mrs. Page. Peace!

Evans. What is your genitive case plural, William?

Will. Genitive case?

Evans. Ay.

Will. [*Genitivo*,] *horum, harum, horum*.

Quick. Vengeance of Jinny's case! Fie on her! never name her, child, if she be a whore.

Evans. For shame, oman.

Quick. You do ill to teach the child such words. He teaches him to "hic" and to "hac," which they'll do fast enough of themselves, and to call "horum," —fie upon you!

Evans. Oman, art thou [lunatics]? Hast thou no understandings for thy cases and the numbers of the genders? Thou art as foolish Christian creatures as I would desires.

Mrs. Page. Prithee hold thy peace.

Evans. Show me now, William, some declensions of your pronouns.

Will. Forsooth, I have forgot.

Evans. It is *qui*, [*quae*], *quod:* if you forget your *qui*'s, your [*quae*'s], and your *quod*'s, you must be preeches. Go your ways and play, go.

Mrs. Page. He is a better scholar than I thought he was.

Evans. He is a good sprag memory. Farewell, Mistress Page.

Mrs. Page. Adieu, good Sir Hugh. [*Exit Evans*.] Get you home, boy. Come, we stay too long.

Exeunt.

Scene II

Enter Falstaff, Mistress Ford,

Fal. Mistress Ford, your sorrow hath eaten up my sufferance. I see you are obsequious in your love, and I profess requital to a hair's breadth, not only, Mistress Ford, in the simple office of love, but in all the accoustrement, complement, and ceremony of it. But are you sure of your husband now?

Mrs. Ford. He's a-birding, sweet Sir John.

Mrs. Page. [*Within*.] What ho, gossip Ford! What ho!

Mrs. Ford. Step into th' chamber, Sir John. [*Exit Falstaff*.]

[*Enter*] Mistress Page.

Mrs. Page. How now, sweet heart, who's at home besides yourself?

Mrs. Ford. Why, none but mine own people.

Mrs. Page. Indeed?

4. courageous. Perhaps she means *outrageous*.
6. suddenly: at once. 9. playing-day: holiday.
11. leave: permission. 16. accidence: Latin grammar.
24. 'Od's nouns: by God's wounds (a weakened oath); with play on odd numbers (i.e. three).
28. Poulcats: polecats, fitches (slang for "prostitutes").
30. very: complete. simplicity: fool.
41. Singulariter: in the singular number. nominativo: in the nominative case. The Latin names of other cases are in lines 43, 45, 52.
53. caret: is wanting, does not occur. Quickly takes it for *carrot*.

66. hic . . . hac: hiccup . . . hack, cough (from too much to drink).
79. preeches: i.e. breeched, whipped.
82. sprag: sprack, i.e. lively, alert.

IV.ii. Windsor: Ford's house.
2. sufferance: suffering. obsequious: devoted.
5. accoustrement: accoutrement. 9. gossip: friend.

Mrs. Ford. No, certainly. [*Aside to her.*] Speak louder.

Mrs. Page. Truly, I am so glad you have nobody here.

Mrs. Ford. Why?

Mrs. Page. Why, woman, your husband is in his old lines again. He so takes on yonder with my husband; so rails against all married mankind; so curses all Eve's daughters, of what complexion soever; and so buffets himself on the forehead, crying, "Peer out, peer out!", that any madness I ever yet beheld seem'd but tameness, civility, and patience to this his distemper he is in now. I am glad the fat knight is not here.

Mrs. Ford. Why, does he talk of him?

Mrs. Page. Of none but him, and swears he was carried out, the last time he search'd for him, in a basket; protests to my husband he is now here, and hath drawn him and the rest of their company from their sport, to make another experiment of his suspicion. But I am glad the knight is not here. Now he shall see his own foolery.

Mrs. Ford. How near is he, Mistress Page?

Mrs. Page. Hard by, at street end; he will be here anon.

Mrs. Ford. I am undone! the knight is here.

Mrs. Page. Why then you are utterly sham'd, and he's but a dead man. What a woman are you? Away with him, away with him! Better shame than murther.

Mrs. Ford. Which way should he go? How should I bestow him? Shall I put him into the basket again?

[*Enter* FALSTAFF.]

Fal. No, I'll come no more i' th' basket. May I not go out ere he come?

Mrs. Page. Alas! three of Master Ford's brothers watch the door with pistols, that none shall issue out; otherwise you might slip away ere he came. But what make you here?

Fal. What shall I do? I'll creep up into the chimney.

Mrs. Ford. There they always use to discharge their birding-pieces. Creep into the kill-hole.

Fal. Where is it?

Mrs. Ford. He will seek there, on my word. Neither press, coffer, chest, trunk, well, vault, but he hath an abstract for the remembrance of such places, and goes to them by his note. There is no hiding you in the house.

Fal. I'll go out then.

[*Mrs. Page.*] If you go out in your own semblance, you die, Sir John—unless you go out disguis'd.

Mrs. Ford. How might we disguise him?

Mrs. Page. Alas the day, I know not! There is no woman's gown big enough for him; otherwise he might put on a hat, a muffler, and a kerchief, and so escape.

Fal. Good hearts, devise something; any extremity rather than a mischief.

Mrs. Ford. My maid's aunt, the fat woman of Brainford, has a gown above.

Mrs. Page. On my word, it will serve him; she's as big as he is. And there's her thrumm'd hat and her muffler too. Run up, Sir John.

Mrs. Ford. Go, go, sweet Sir John. Mistress Page and I will look some linen for your head.

Mrs. Page. Quick, quick! we'll come dress you straight. Put on the gown the while. [*Exit Falstaff.*]

Mrs. Ford. I would my husband would meet him in this shape. He cannot abide the old woman of Brainford. He swears she's a witch, forbade her my house, and hath threat'ned to beat her.

Mrs. Page. Heaven guide him to thy husband's cudgel; and the devil guide his cudgel afterwards!

Mrs. Ford. But is my husband coming?

Mrs. Page. Ay, in good sadness, is he, and talks of the basket too, howsoever he hath had intelligence.

Mrs. Ford. We'll try that; for I'll appoint my men to carry the basket again, to meet him at the door with it, as they did last time.

Mrs. Page. Nay, but he'll be here presently. Let's go dress him like the witch of Brainford.

Mrs. Ford. I'll first direct my men what they shall do with the basket. Go up, I'll bring linen for him straight. [*Exit.*]

Mrs. Page. Hang him, dishonest varlet! we cannot misuse [him] enough.
We'll leave a proof, by that which we will do,
Wives may be merry, and yet honest too:
We do not act that often jest and laugh;
'Tis old, but true: still swine eats all the draff. [*Exit.*]

[*Enter* MISTRESS FORD *with two*] SERVANTS.

Mrs. Ford. Go, sirs, take the basket again on your shoulders. Your master is hard at door. If he bid you set it down, obey him. Quickly, dispatch. [*Exit.*]

1. Serv. Come, come, take it up.

2. Serv. Pray heaven it be not full of knight again.

1. Serv. I hope not, I had lief as bear so much lead.

[*Enter*] FORD, PAGE, CAIUS, EVANS, SHALLOW.

Ford. Ay, but if it prove true, Master Page, have you any way then to unfool me again? Set down the basket, villain! Somebody call my wife. Youth in a basket! O you panderly rascals, there's a knot, a [ging], a pack, a conspiracy against me.

22. lines: fits of temper, jealous rages. **24. complexion:** type.
26. Peer out. An order to his horns to become visible.
43. What a: what kind of. **45. murther:** murder.
54. make you: are you doing. **57. use:** are accustomed.
58. kill-hole: kiln-hole, oven. **62. abstract:** list.

73–74. extremity: extreme measure.
76. Brainford: Brentford, a village near Windsor. There is an allusion (see lines 86, 98) to the notorious "witch of Brentford," who kept a tavern there. **above:** upstairs.
78. thrumm'd: made of coarse yarn.
85. shape: disguise. **97. presently:** at once.
107. still: quiet. **draff:** swill. **110. dispatch:** make haste.
113. lief as: as lief (possibly a misprint).
115. unfool me: make me a sound man.
118. knot: company. **ging:** gang. **pack:** confederacy.

Now shall the devil be sham'd. What, wife, I say! Come, come forth! Behold what honest clothes you send forth to bleaching!

Page. Why, this passes, Master Ford. You are not to go loose any longer, you must be pinion'd.

Evans. Why, this is lunatics! this is mad as a mad dog!

Shal. Indeed, Master Ford, this is not well indeed.

Ford. So say I too, sir.

[*Enter* Mistress Ford.]

Come hither, Mistress Ford, Mistress Ford, the honest woman, the modest wife, the virtuous creature, that hath the jealious fool to her husband! I suspect without cause, mistress, do I?

Mrs. Ford. Heaven be my witness you do, [and] if you suspect me in any dishonesty.

Ford. Well said, brazen-face! hold it out. Come forth, sirrah! [*Pulling clothes out of the basket*.]

Page. This passes!

Mrs. Ford. Are you not asham'd? Let the clothes alone.

Ford. I shall find you anon.

Evans. 'Tis unreasonable! Will you take up your wive's clothes? Come away.

Ford. Empty the basket, I say!

Mrs. Ford. Why, man, why?

Ford. Master Page, as I am a man, there was one convey'd out of my house yesterday in this basket. Why may not he be there again? In my house I am sure he is. My intelligence is true, my jealousy is reasonable. Pluck me out all the linen.

Mrs. Ford. If you find a man there, he shall die a flea's death.

Page. Here's no man.

Shal. By my fidelity, this is not well, Master Ford; this wrongs you.

Evans. Master Ford, you must pray, and not follow the imaginations of your own heart. This is jealousies.

Ford. Well, he's not here I seek for.

Page. No, nor no where else but in your brain.

Ford. Help to search my house this one time. If I find not what I seek, show no color for my extremity; let me for ever be your table-sport. Let them say of me, "As jealous as Ford, that search'd a hollow walnut for his wive's leman." Satisfy me once more, once more search with me.

Mrs. Ford. What ho, Mistress Page! come you and the old woman down; my husband will come into the chamber.

Ford. Old woman? What old woman's that?

Mrs. Ford. Why, it is my maid's aunt of Brainford.

Ford. A witch, a quean, an old cozening quean! Have I not forbid her my house? She comes of errands, does she? We are simple men, we do not know what's brought to pass under the profession of fortune-telling. She works by charms, by spells, by th' figure, and such daub'ry as this is, beyond our element; we know nothing. Come down, you witch, you hag you, come down, I say!

Mrs. Ford. Nay, good, sweet husband! Good gentlemen, let him [not] strike the old woman.

[*Enter* Falstaff *disguised like an old woman, and* Mistress Page *with him*.]

Mrs. Page. Come, Mother Prat, come give me your hand.

Ford. I'll prat her. Out of my door, you witch, you rag, you baggage, you poulcat, you runnion! out, out! I'll conjure you, I'll fortune-tell you!

[*Ford beats him, and he runs away*.]

Mrs. Page. Are you not asham'd? I think you have kill'd the poor woman.

Mrs. Ford. Nay, he will do it.—'Tis a goodly credit for you.

Ford. Hang her, witch!

Evans. By yea and no, I think the oman is a witch indeed. I like not when a oman has a great peard. I spy a great peard under his muffler.

Ford. Will you follow, gentlemen? I beseech you follow; see but the issue of my jealousy. If I cry out thus upon no trail, never trust me when I open again.

Page. Let's obey his humor a little further. Come, gentlemen.

[*Exeunt Ford, Page, Shallow, Caius, and Evans*.]

Mrs. Page. Trust me, he beat him most pitifully.

Mrs. Ford. Nay, by th' mass, that he did not; he beat him most unpitifully, methought.

Mrs. Page. I'll have the cudgel hallow'd and hung o'er the altar; it hath done meritorious service.

Mrs. Ford. What think you? May we, with the warrant of womanhood and the witness of a good conscience, pursue him with any further revenge?

Mrs. Page. The spirit of wantonness is sure scar'd out of him. If the devil have him not in fee-simple, with fine and recovery, he will never, I think, in the way of waste, attempt us again.

Mrs. Ford. Shall we tell our husbands how we have serv'd him?

Mrs. Page. Yes, by all means; if it be but to scrape the figures out of your husband's brains. If

119. Now . . . sham'd: i.e. now the truth will come out (alluding to the proverbial "Tell the truth and shame the devil").
122. passes: goes beyond all bounds.
135. hold it out: keep up the pretense.
140. find: unmask, reveal. **anon**: now.
148. intelligence: information.
154. wrongs you: does you dishonor.
155. you must pray: i.e. for grace to conquer your jealousy.
156. follow . . . heart. Cf. Jeremiah 13:10, "They [the Jews] follow the wicked imaginations of their own heart" (Bishops').
161–62. show . . . extremity: make no attempt to extenuate my extravagant behavior.
162. table-sport: laughingstock of the group. **164. leman**: lover.
172. quean: hussy. **cozening**: cheating.
177. by th' figure: by drawing up astrological charts (?) or, possibly, by making wax figures of her victims to induce sickness or death by sticking pins into them. **daub'ry**: imposture.
184. prat: beat (?) or practice tricks on (?).
185. runnion: ronyon, scabby woman.
196–97. cry out: give tongue (like a hound); *open* later in the sentence has the same meaning. **197. trail**: scent.
210–11. fee-simple: i.e. absolute possession.
211. fine and recovery: procedures by which an entailed estate was converted into a fee-simple. **212. waste**: spoliation.
216. scrape: erase. **figures**: figments of the imagination.

they can find in their hearts the poor unvirtuous fat knight shall be any further afflicted, we two will still be the ministers.

Mrs. Ford. I'll warrant they'll have him publicly sham'd, and methinks there would be no period to the jest, should he not be publicly sham'd.

Mrs. Page. Come, to the forge with it, then shape it. I would not have things cool. *Exeunt.*

Scene III

Enter Host *and* Bardolph.

Bard. Sir, the [Germans desire] to have three of your horses. The Duke himself will be to-morrow at court, and they are going to meet him.

Host. What duke should that be comes so secretly? I hear not of him in the court. Let me speak with the gentlemen; they speak English?

Bard. Ay, sir; I'll call [them] to you.

Host. They shall have my horses, but I'll make them pay; I'll sauce them. They have had my [house] a week at command. I have turn'd away my other guests; they must come off. I'll sauce them, come. *Exeunt.*

Scene IV

Enter Page, Ford, *Mistress* Page, *Mistress* Ford, *and* Evans.

Evans. 'Tis one of the best discretions of a oman as ever I did look upon.

Page. And did he send you both these letters at an instant?

Mrs. Page. Within a quarter of an hour.

Ford. Pardon me, wife, henceforth do what thou wilt.
I rather will suspect the sun with [cold]
Than thee with wantonness. Now doth thy honor stand,
In him that was of late an heretic,
As firm as faith.

219. **ministers:** agents. 221. **period:** fitting conclusion.
223. **to . . . it:** i.e. let us strike while the iron is hot.

IV.iii. Location: Windsor. The Garter Inn.
2. **The Duke.** This scene and IV.v.63–92 may allude to Frederick, Duke of Württemberg, who had been elected to the Order of the Garter in 1597, at the same time as Lord Hunsdon (see the introduction to the play), but *in absentia.* From 1592, when as Count Mompelgard he visited England, he exerted every possible influence at court to have himself elected a Garter knight, in the process apparently making himself a theme for laughter. Elizabeth finally yielded, for political reasons, in 1597, but not in time for Frederick to attend the investiture and installation, nor did he in fact receive his Garter insignia until after Elizabeth's death. Evidence for this identification is found in the otherwise inexplicable quarto reading *three sorts of cosen garmombles*, replaced in the Folio text by *three Cozen-Iermans* (see Textual Notes, IV.v.77), *cousin* being a form of address between ruling princes. Other alleged topical allusions have been found in the horse-stealing itself, which is not connected with the Duke.
9. **sauce them:** make it hot for them, i.e. make them pay dearly.
10. **at command:** i.e. to be ready for their use whenever they should arrive. 11. **come off:** pay up.

IV.iv. Location: Windsor. Ford's house.
1–2. **best . . . oman:** i.e. most discreet women.
3–4. **at an instant:** at the same time.

Page. 'Tis well, 'tis well, no more.
Be not as extreme in submission as in offense;
But let our plot go forward. Let our wives
Yet once again (to make us public sport)
Appoint a meeting with this old fat fellow,
Where we may take him, and disgrace him for it.

Ford. There is no better way than that they spoke of.

Page. How? to send him word they'll meet him in the park at midnight? Fie, fie, he'll never come.

Evans. You say he has been thrown in the rivers, and has been grievously peaten as an old oman. Methinks there should be terrors in him that he should not come; methinks his flesh is punish'd, he shall have no desires.

Page. So think I too.

Mrs. Ford. Devise but how you'll use him when he comes,
And let us two devise to bring him thither.

Mrs. Page. There is an old tale goes, that Herne the Hunter
(Sometime a keeper here in Windsor forest)
Doth all the winter-time, at still midnight,
Walk round about an oak, with great ragg'd horns,
And there he blasts the tree, and takes the cattle,
And [makes] milch-kine yield blood, and shakes a chain
In a most hideous and dreadful manner.
You have heard of such a spirit, and well you know
The superstitious idle-headed eld
Receiv'd and did deliver to our age
This tale of Herne the Hunter for a truth.

Page. Why, yet there want not many that do fear
In deep of night to walk by this Herne's oak.
But what of this?

Mrs. Ford. Marry, this is our device:
That Falstaff at that oak shall meet with us,
[Disguis'd like [Herne], with huge horns on his head].

Page. Well, let it not be doubted but he'll come,
And in this shape when you have brought him thither,
What shall be done with him? What is your plot?

Mrs. Page. That likewise have we thought upon, and thus:
Nan Page (my daughter) and my little son,
And three or four more of their growth, we'll dress
Like urchins, ouphes, and fairies, green and white,
With rounds of waxen tapers on their heads,
And rattles in their hands. Upon a sudden,
As Falstaff, she, and I are newly met,
Let them from forth a sawpit rush at once
With some diffused song. Upon their sight,
We two in great amazedness will fly;
Then let them all encircle him about,
And fairy-like to pinch the unclean knight;
And ask him why, that hour of fairy revel,

31. **ragg'd:** jagged, pronged.
32. **blasts the tree:** causes the tree to be blighted. **takes:** bewitches.
36. **idle-headed:** silly, crazy. **eld:** people of an earlier generation.
39. **want:** lack. 45. **shape:** disguise.
50. **urchins:** goblins. **ouphes:** elves.
54. **sawpit:** a pit over which wood is sawed.
55. **diffused:** confused, wild.

In their so sacred paths he dares to tread
In shape profane.
[Mrs.] Ford. And till he tell the truth,
Let the supposed fairies pinch him sound,
And burn him with their tapers.
Mrs. Page. The truth being known,
We'll all present ourselves; dis-horn the spirit,
And mock him home to Windsor.
Ford. The children must
Be practic'd well to this, or they'll nev'r do't.

Evans. I will teach the children their behaviors; and I will be like a jack-an-apes also, to burn the knight with my taber.

Ford. That will be excellent. I'll go buy them vizards.

Mrs. Page. My Nan shall be the queen of all the fairies,
Finely attired in a robe of white.
Page. That silk will I go buy. [*Aside.*] And in that time
Shall Master Slender steal my Nan away,
And marry her at Eton.—Go, send to Falstaff straight.
Ford. Nay, I'll to him again in name of [Brook];
He'll tell me all his purpose. Sure he'll come.
Mrs. Page. Fear not you that. Go get us properties
And tricking for our fairies.

Evans. Let us about it. It is admirable pleasures and fery honest knaveries.

[*Exeunt Page, Ford, and Evans.*]

Mrs. Page. Go, Mistress Ford,
Send Quickly to Sir John, to know his mind.
[*Exit Mrs. Ford.*]
I'll to the doctor, he hath my good will,
And none but he, to marry with Nan Page.
That Slender (though well landed) is an idiot;
And he my husband best of all affects.
The doctor is well money'd, and his friends
Potent at court. He, none but he, shall have her,
Though twenty thousand worthier come to crave her.
[*Exit.*]

Scene V

Enter Host, Simple.

Host. What wouldst thou have, boor? What, thick-skin? Speak, breathe, discuss; brief, short, quick, snap.

Sim. Marry, sir, I come to speak with Sir John Falstaff from Master Slender.

Host. There's his chamber, his house, his castle, his standing-bed and truckle-bed; 'tis painted about with the story of the Prodigal, fresh and new. Go, knock and call; he'll speak like an Anthropophaginian unto thee. Knock, I say.

Sim. There's an old woman, a fat woman, gone up into his chamber. I'll be so bold as stay, sir, till she come down. I come to speak with her indeed.

Host. Ha? a fat woman? The knight may be robb'd. I'll call. Bully-knight! bully Sir John! speak from thy lungs military. Art thou there? It is thine host, thine Ephesian, calls.

Fal. [*Above.*] How now, mine host?

Host. Here's a Bohemian-Tartar tarries the coming down of thy fat woman. Let her descend, bully, let her descend; my chambers are honorable. Fie, privacy? fie!

[*Enter*] Falstaff.

Fal. There was, mine host, an old fat woman even now with me, but she's gone.

Sim. Pray you, sir, was't not the wise woman of Brainford?

Fal. Ay, marry, was it, mussel-shell, what would you with her?

Sim. My master, sir, my Master Slender, sent to her, seeing her go thorough the streets, to know, sir, whether one Nym, sir, that beguil'd him of a chain, had the chain or no.

Fal. I spake with the old woman about it.

Sim. And what says she, I pray, sir?

Fal. Marry, she says that the very same man that beguil'd Master Slender of his chain cozen'd him of it.

Sim. I would I could have spoken with the woman herself. I had other things to have spoken with her too from him.

Fal. What are they? let us know.

Host. Ay; come; quick.

[*Sim.*] I may not conceal them, sir.

Host. Conceal them, or thou diest.

Sim. Why, sir, they were nothing but about Mistress Anne Page, to know if it were my master's fortune to have her or no.

Fal. 'Tis, 'tis his fortune.

Sim. What, sir?

Fal. To have her, or no. Go; say the woman told me so.

Sim. May I be bold to say so, sir?

Fal. Ay, sir; like who more bold?

Sim. I thank your worship. I shall make my master glad with these tidings. [*Exit.*]

Host. Thou [art] clerkly, thou art clerkly, Sir John. Was there a wise woman with thee?

Fal. Ay, that there was, mine host, one that hath taught me more wit than ever I learn'd before in my life; and I paid nothing for it neither, but was paid for my learning.

62. **sound:** soundly.
68. **like a jack-an-apes:** disguised as a monkey (but he later appears as a satyr). 70. **vizards:** masks.
75. **Eton:** a town across the Thames from Windsor.
78. **properties:** i.e. stage properties. 79. **tricking:** adornments.
87. **he:** i.e. him. **affects:** likes.

IV.v. **Location:** Windsor. The Garter Inn.
3. **snap:** sudden.
7. **truckle-bed:** trundle bed, low bed that slides under a bed of normal height (*standing-bed*).
8. **story . . . Prodigal.** See Luke 15:11–32. This parable is also associated with Falstaff in *2 Henry IV*, II.i.144–45.

9. **Anthropophaginian:** cannibal. 18. **Ephesian:** boon companion.
20. **Bohemian-Tartar:** i.e. wild man.
28. **mussel-shell:** i.e. gaping creature (resembling an open bivalve).
31. **thorough:** through. 32. **beguil'd:** cheated, robbed.
44. **conceal:** blunder for *reveal*.
54. **like . . . bold:** like the boldest. 57. **clerkly:** scholarly, wise.
61. **was paid:** was rewarded (with a beating).

[*Enter*] BARDOLPH.

Bard. Out alas, sir, cozenage! mere cozenage.

Host. Where be my horses? Speak well of them, varletto.

Bard. Run away with the cozeners; for so soon as I came beyond Eton, they threw me off from behind one of them, in a slough of mire; and set spurs and away, like three German devils, three Doctor Faustuses.

Host. They are gone but to meet the Duke, villain, do not say they be fled. Germans are honest men.

[*Enter*] EVANS.

Evans. Where is mine host?

Host. What is the matter, sir?

Evans. Have a care of your entertainments. There is a friend of mine come to town, tells me there is three cozen-germans that has cozen'd all the hosts of Readins, of Maidenhead, of Colebrook, of horses and money. I tell you for good will, look you. You are wise and full of gibes and vlouting-stocks, and 'tis not convenient you should be cozen'd. Fare you well. [*Exit*.]

[*Enter*] CAIUS.

Caius. Vere is mine host de Jarteer?

Host. Here, Master Doctor, in perplexity and doubtful dilemma.

Caius. I cannot tell vat is dat; but it is tell-a me dat you make grand preparation for a duke de Jamany. By my trot, dere is no duke that the court is know to come. I tell you for good will; adieu. [*Exit*.]

Host. Hue and cry, villain, go! Assist me, knight, I am undone! Fly, run, hue and cry, villain! I am undone! [*Exeunt Host and Bardolph*.]

Fal. I would all the world might be cozen'd, for I have been cozen'd and beaten too. If it should come to the ear of the court, how I have been transform'd, and how my transformation hath been wash'd and cudgell'd, they would melt me out of my fat drop by drop, and liquor fishermen's boots with me. I warrant they would whip me with their fine wits till I were as crestfall'n as a dried pear. I never prosper'd since I forswore myself at primero. Well, if my wind were but long enough [to say my prayers], I would repent.

[*Enter* MISTRESS] QUICKLY.

Now? whence come you?

Quick. From the two parties, forsooth.

Fal. The devil take one party and his dam the other! and so they shall be both bestow'd. I have suffer'd more for their sakes—more than the villainous inconstancy of man's disposition is able to bear.

Quick. And have not they suffer'd? Yes, I warrant; speciously one of them. Mistress Ford, good heart, is beaten black and blue, that you cannot see a white spot about her.

Fal. What tellest thou me of black and blue? I was beaten myself into all the colors of the rainbow; and I was like to be apprehended for the witch of Brainford. But that my admirable dexterity of wit, my counterfeiting the action of an old woman, deliver'd me, the knave constable had set me i' th' stocks, i' th' common stocks, for a witch.

Quick. Sir—let me speak with you in your chamber. You shall hear how things go, and, I warrant, to your content. Here is a letter will say somewhat. Good hearts, what ado here is to bring you together! Sure, one of you does not serve heaven well, that you are so cross'd.

Fal. Come up into my chamber. *Exeunt*.

SCENE VI

Enter FENTON, HOST.

Host. Master Fenton, talk not to me, my mind is heavy; I will give over all.

Fent. Yet hear me speak. Assist me in my purpose,
And (as I am a gentleman) I'll give thee
A hundred pound in gold more than your loss.

Host. I will hear you, Master Fenton, and I will (at the least) keep your counsel.

Fent. From time to time I have acquainted you
With the dear love I bear to fair Anne Page,
Who mutually hath answer'd my affection
(So far forth as herself might be her chooser)
Even to my wish. I have a letter from her
Of such contents as you will wonder at;
The mirth whereof so larded with my matter,
That neither, singly, can be manifested
Without the show of both. Fat Falstaff
Hath a great scene; the image of the jest
I'll show you here at large. Hark, good mine host:
To-night at Herne's oak, just 'twixt twelve and one,
Must my sweet Nan present the Fairy Queen;
The purpose why, is here; in which disguise,
While other jests are something rank on foot,
Her father hath commanded her to slip
Away with Slender, and with him at Eton
Immediately to marry. She hath consented.
Now, sir,
Her mother (even strong against that match

63. mere: sheer, absolute. **65. varletto**: knave.
69–70. Doctor Faustuses. Referring to the scholar-magician Faustus in Marlowe's play.
75. your entertainments: those you receive as guests.
77. cozen-germans. A pun on "cousin-germans," i.e. close relatives, and "cozening Germans."
78. Readins: Reading. Like Maidenhead and Colnbrook (*Colebrook*), it was near Windsor.
80–81. vlouting-stocks. See note on III.i.117–18; but here Evans probably means *flouts*, i.e. jibes. **81. convenient**: fitting.
85. doubtful: apprehensive. **87. Jamany**: Germany.
88. trot: troth.
90. Hue and cry: the cry raised during pursuit of a felon.
98. liquor: oil. **101. forswore myself**: cheated.
102. primero: a popular card game.

111. speciously: blunder for *specially*. **126. cross'd**: thwarted.

IV.vi. Location: Scene continues.
2. give over: abandon.
7. keep your counsel: not divulge what you tell me.
10. mutually: in return.
14. larded: intermingled. **my matter**: the part that concerns me.
17. image: idea. **18. at large**: in detail. **20. present**: represent.
22. something . . . foot: being carried out in some number.
27. even: equally.

And firm for Doctor Caius) hath appointed
That he shall likewise shuffle her away,
While other sports are tasking of their minds,
And at the dean'ry, where a priest attends,
Straight marry her. To this her mother's plot
She (seemingly obedient) likewise hath
Made promise to the doctor. Now, thus it rests:
Her father means she shall be all in white;
And in that habit, when Slender sees his time
To take her by the hand and bid her go,
She shall go with him. Her mother hath intended
(The better to [denote] her to the doctor,
For they must all be mask'd and vizarded)
That quaint in green she shall be loose enrob'd,
With ribands pendant, flaring 'bout her head;
And when the doctor spies his vantage ripe,
To pinch her by the hand, and on that token,
The maid hath given consent to go with him.

Host. Which means she to deceive, father or mother?

Fent. Both, my good host, to go along with me.
And here it rests, that you'll procure the vicar
To stay for me at church, 'twixt twelve and one,
And in the lawful name of marrying,
To give our hearts united ceremony.

Host. Well, husband your device; I'll to the vicar.
Bring you the maid, you shall not lack a priest.

Fent. So shall I evermore be bound to thee;
Besides, I'll make a present recompense. *Exeunt.*

ACT V, SCENE I

Enter FALSTAFF, [MISTRESS] QUICKLY.

Fal. Prithee no more prattling. Go, I'll hold. This is the third time; I hope good luck lies in odd numbers. Away, go. They say there is divinity in odd numbers, either in nativity, chance, or death. Away!

Quick. I'll provide you a chain, and I'll do what I can to get you a pair of horns.

Fal. Away, I say, time wears, hold up your head and mince. [*Exit Mrs. Quickly.*]

[*Enter*] FORD [*disguised*].

How now, Master [Brook]? Master [Brook], the matter will be known to-night, or never. Be you in the park about midnight, at Herne's oak, and you shall see wonders.

Ford. Went you not to her yesterday, sir, as you told me you had appointed?

Fal. I went to her, Master [Brook], as you see, like a poor old man, but I came from her, Master [Brook], like a poor old woman. That same knave Ford, her husband, hath the finest mad devil of jealousy

in him, Master [Brook], that ever govern'd frenzy. I will tell you—he beat me grievously, in the shape of a woman; for in the shape of man, Master [Brook], I fear not Goliah with a weaver's beam, because I know also life is a shuttle. I am in haste, go along with me, I'll tell you all, Master [Brook]. Since I pluck'd geese, play'd truant, and whipt top, I knew not what 'twas to be beaten till lately. Follow me, I'll tell you strange things of this knave Ford, on whom to-night I will be reveng'd, and I will deliver his wife into your hand. Follow. Strange things in hand, Master [Brook]! Follow. *Exeunt.*

SCENE II

Enter PAGE, SHALLOW, SLENDER.

Page. Come, come; we'll couch i' th' castle-ditch till we see the light of our fairies. Remember, son Slender, my [daughter].

Slen. Ay, forsooth, I have spoke with her, and we have a nay-word how to know one another. I come to her in white, and cry "mum"; she cries "budget"; and by that we know one another.

Shal. That's good too; but what needs either your "mum" or her "budget"? The white will decipher her well enough. It hath strook ten a' clock.

Page. The night is dark, light and spirits will become it well. Heaven prosper our sport! No man means evil but the devil, and we shall know him by his horns. Let's away; follow me. *Exeunt.*

SCENE III

Enter MISTRESS PAGE, MISTRESS FORD, CAIUS.

Mrs. Page. Master Doctor, my daughter is in green. When you see your time, take her by the hand, away with her to the deanery, and dispatch it quickly. Go before into the park; we two must go together.

Caius. I know vat I have to do. Adieu.

Mrs. Page. Fare you well, sir. [*Exit Caius.*] My husband will not rejoice so much at the abuse of Falstaff as he will chafe at the doctor's marrying my daughter. But 'tis no matter; better a little chiding than a great deal of heart-break.

Mrs. Ford. Where is Nan now, and her troop of fairies, and the Welsh devil [Hugh]?

Mrs. Page. They are all couch'd in a pit hard by Herne's oak, with obscur'd lights; which, at the very

30. tasking of: fully occupying. **41. quaint:** prettily.
42. ribands: ribbons. **flaring:** streaming in the wind.
51. united ceremony: union of the marriage rite.
52. husband: manage carefully. **55. present:** immediate.

V.i. Location: Scene continues.
1. hold: keep (the appointment).
3. divinity: i.e. mysterious quality or power. **8. mince:** trip it.
13. yesterday: Actually, Falstaff's last encounter was earlier the same day. **18. finest:** most consummate.

22. Goliah . . . beam. An allusion to 1 Samuel 17:7, "the shaft of his [the giant Goliath's] spear was like a weaver's beam" (Geneva). A weaver's beam is a large wooden cylinder on a loom.
23. life . . . shuttle. An allusion to Job 7:6, "My days are swifter than a weaver's shuttle."
25. pluck'd . . . top: i.e. indulged in boyhood pranks.

V.ii. Location: Outskirts of Windsor Park.
1. couch: lie hidden.
6. mum . . . budget. Mumbudget was a children's game in which silence was required. **9. decipher:** make known.
10. strook: struck.

V.iii. Location: Scene continues.
3. dispatch: conclude. **14. obscur'd:** darkened.

instant of Falstaff's and our meeting, they will at once display to the night.

Mrs. Ford. That cannot choose but amaze him.

Mrs. Page. If he be not amaz'd, he will be mock'd; if he be amaz'd, he will every way be mock'd.

Mrs. Ford. We'll betray him finely.

Mrs. Page. Against such lewdsters, and their lechery,
Those that betray them do no treachery.

Mrs. Ford. The hour draws on. To the oak, to the oak! *Exeunt.*

Scene IV

Enter Evans [*like a satyr*] *and* [*others as*] *fairies.*

Evans. Trib, trib, fairies; come, and remember your parts. Be pold, I pray you. Follow me into the pit, and when I give the watch-ords, do as I pid you. Come, come, trib, trib. *Exeunt.*

Scene V

Enter Falstaff [*with a buck's head upon him*].

Fal. The Windsor bell hath strook twelve; the minute draws on. Now the hot-bloodied gods assist me! Remember, Jove, thou wast a bull for thy Europa, love set on thy horns. O powerful love, that in some respects makes a beast a man; in some other, a man a beast. You were also, Jupiter, a swan for the love of Leda. O omnipotent love, how near the god drew to the complexion of a goose! A fault done first in the form of a beast (O Jove, a beastly fault!) and then another fault in the semblance of a fowl—think on't, Jove, a foul fault! When gods have hot backs, what shall poor men do? For me, I am here a Windsor stag, and the fattest, I think, i' th' forest. Send me a cool rut-time, Jove, or who can blame me to piss my tallow? Who comes here? My doe?

[*Enter*] Mistress Page, Mistress Ford.

Mrs. Ford. Sir John? art thou there, my deer? my male deer?

Fal. My doe with the black scut? Let the sky rain potatoes; let it thunder to the tune of "Green-sleeves," hail kissing-comfits, and snow eringoes; let there come a tempest of provocation, I will shelter me here. [*Embracing her.*]

Mrs. Ford. Mistress Page is come with me, sweet heart.

Fal. Divide me like a brib'd-buck, each a haunch. I will keep my sides to myself, my shoulders for the fellow of this walk—and my horns I bequeath your husbands. Am I a woodman, ha? Speak I like Herne the hunter? Why, now is Cupid a child of conscience, he makes restitution. As I am a true spirit, welcome! [*There is a noise of horns.*]

Mrs. Page. Alas, what noise?

Mrs. Ford. Heaven forgive our sins!

Fal. What should this be?

Mrs. Ford, Mrs. Page. Away, away! [*The two women run away.*]

Fal. I think the devil will not have me damn'd, lest the oil that's in me should set hell on fire; he would never else cross me thus.

Enter Evans [*like a satyr*], Anne Page [*and* Boys *dressed like fairies*], Pistol [*as Hobgoblin*, Mistress] Quickly [*like the Queen of Fairies; they sing a song about him and afterward speak*].

Quick. Fairies, black, grey, green, and white,
You moonshine revellers, and shades of night,
You orphan heirs of fixed destiny,
Attend your office and your quality.
Crier Hobgoblin, make the fairy Oyes.

Pist. Elves, list your names; silence, you aery toys!
Cricket, to Windsor chimneys shalt thou leap;
Where fires thou find'st unrak'd and hearths unswept,
There pinch the maids as blue as bilberry;
Our radiant Queen hates sluts and sluttery.

Fal. They are fairies, he that speaks to them shall die.
I'll wink and couch; no man their works must eye. [*Lies down upon his face.*]

Evans. Where's Bede? Go you, and where you find a maid
That ere she sleep has thrice her prayers said,
Raise up the organs of her fantasy,
Sleep she as sound as careless infancy;
But those as sleep and think not on their sins,

17. amaze: bewilder, strike panic in.
18. mock'd: (1) deceived; (2) ridiculed. **21. lewdsters:** lechers.

V.iv. Location: Windsor Park.
3. watch-ords: watchwords.

V.v. Location: Scene continues.
2. hot-bloodied: hot-blooded.
3. Jove . . . Europa. Jupiter transformed himself into a white bull to carry off the Phoenician princess Europa.
4. set on: instigated, i.e. impelled you to assume.
6–7. a swan . . . Leda. Leda, whose husband was king of Sparta, was ravished by Jupiter in the form of a swan; their children were Helen of Troy and Pollux.
8. complexion: temperament. **A fault:** a sin (with special reference to sex). **11. hot:** lustful.
14. rut-time: period of sexual excitement in deer.
15. tallow: fat of an animal. Stags grew thin in rutting time.
18. scut: tail (of a deer); slang for the female pudenda.
19. potatoes: sweet potatoes (which were thought to stimulate sexuality). **Green-sleeves.** See note to II.i.63.
20. kissing-comfits: perfumed candies, used by women to sweeten their breath. **eringoes:** candied roots of sea-holly (another supposed aphrodisiac). **21. provocation:** sexual incitement.
24. brib'd-buck: stolen deer, which poachers would hurriedly cut up after shooting; hence, a cut-up deer.
25–26. my shoulders . . . walk: my shoulders for the keeper of this forest (with punning sense that he will fight with the keeper if necessary).
27. woodman: i.e. one who knows how to take care of himself in a forest.
28. Cupid . . . conscience: i.e. Cupid is at last behaving honorably to Falstaff.
39. orphan . . . destiny. Variously explained. Fairies were supposedly of spontaneous birth and thus would be orphans by "fixed destiny."
40. Attend: heed. **office:** duty. **quality:** business.
41. Oyes: hear ye (the call of the official crier).
42. toys: things of no substance.
44. unrak'd: not raked together and banked with fuel to keep them alive during the night.
45. bilberry: blueberry. **48. wink:** shut my eyes.
51. Raise . . . fantasy: i.e. elevate her dream-producing faculties so that she will be free of nightmares. **52. careless:** free from care.

Pinch them, arms, legs, backs, shoulders, sides, and shins.

Quick. About, about;
Search Windsor Castle, elves, within and out.
Strew good luck, ouphes, on every sacred room,
That it may stand till the perpetual doom
In state as wholesome as in state 'tis fit,
Worthy the owner, and the owner it.
The several chairs of order look you scour
With juice of balm and every precious flow'r;
Each fair installment, coat, and sev'ral crest,
With loyal blazon, evermore be blest!
And nightly, meadow-fairies, look you sing,
Like to the Garter's compass, in a ring.
Th' expressure that it bears, green let it be,
More fertile-fresh than all the field to see;
And "*Honi soit qui mal y pense*" write
In em'rald tuffs, flow'rs purple, blue, and white,
Like sapphire, pearl, and rich embroidery,
Buckled below fair knighthood's bending knee:
Fairies use flow'rs for their charactery.
Away, disperse! but till 'tis one a' clock,
Our dance of custom, round about the oak
Of Herne the hunter, let us not forget.

Evans. Pray you lock hand in hand; yourselves in order set;
And twenty glow-worms shall our lanthorns be,
To guide our measure round about the tree.
But stay, I smell a man of middle-earth.

Fal. Heavens defend me from that Welsh fairy, lest he transform me to a piece of cheese!

Pist. Vild worm, thou wast o'erlook'd even in thy birth.

Quick. With trial-fire touch me his finger-end.
If he be chaste, the flame will back descend
And turn him to no pain; but if he start,
It is the flesh of a corrupted heart.

Pist. A trial, come.

Evans. Come, will this wood take fire?

[*They put the tapers to his fingers, and he starts*.]

Fal. O, O, O!

Quick. Corrupt, corrupt, and tainted in desire!
About him, fairies, sing a scornful rhyme,
And as you trip, still pinch him to your time.

THE SONG

Fie on sinful fantasy!
Fie on lust and luxury!
Lust is but a bloody fire,
Kindled with unchaste desire,
Fed in heart, whose flames aspire,
As thoughts do blow them, higher and higher.
Pinch him, fairies, mutually!
Pinch him for his villainy!
Pinch him, and burn him, and turn him about,
Till candles, and starlight, and moonshine be out.

[*Here they pinch him and sing about him. And the Doctor*] CAIUS [*comes one way, and steals away a boy in green; and*] SLENDER [*another way; he takes a boy in white; and*] FENTON [*steals Mistress Anne Page. And a noise of hunting is made within; and all the fairies run away. Falstaff pulls off his buck's head, and rises up*.]

[*Enter*] PAGE, FORD, [MISTRESS PAGE, *and* MISTRESS FORD].

Page. Nay, do not fly, I think we have watch'd you now.
Will none but Herne the hunter serve your turn?

Mrs. Page. I pray you come, hold up the jest no higher.
Now, good Sir John, how like you Windsor wives?
See you these, husband? Do not these fair yokes
Become the forest better than the town?

Ford. Now, sir, who's a cuckold now? Master [Brook], Falstaff's a knave, a cuckoldly knave; here are his horns, Master [Brook]; and, Master [Brook], he hath enjoy'd nothing of Ford's but his buck-basket, his cudgel, and twenty pounds of money, which must be paid to Master [Brook]. His horses are arrested for it, Master [Brook].

Mrs. Ford. Sir John, we have had ill luck; we could never meet. I will never take you for my love again, but I will always count you my deer.

Fal. I do begin to perceive that I am made an ass.

Ford. Ay, and an ox too; both the proofs are extant.

Fal. And these are not fairies? I was three or four times in the thought they were not fairies, and yet the guiltiness of my mind, the sudden surprise of my powers, drove the grossness of the foppery into a receiv'd belief, in despite of the teeth of all rhyme and reason, that they were fairies. See now how wit may be made a Jack-a-Lent, when 'tis upon ill employment!

Evans. Sir John Falstaff, serve Got, and leave your desires, and fairies will not pinse you.

Ford. Well said, fairy Hugh.

Evans. And leave you your jealousies too, I pray you.

Ford. I will never mistrust my wife again, till thou art able to woo her in good English.

61. several . . . order: i.e. the individual stalls assigned in St. George's Chapel, Windsor, to the members of the Order of the Garter.
63. installment: stall. **coat:** coat of arms.
64. blazon: armorial bearings.
66. Like . . . compass: i.e. like the round garter which was worn below the left knee by members of the Order.
67. expressure: imprint (literally, expression).
69. Honi . . . pense: Evil to him who evil thinks (motto of the Order of the Garter); *pense* is here disyllabic.
70. tuffs: tufts, bunches. **73. charactery:** writing.
78. lanthorns: lanterns. **79. measure:** stately dance.
80. a man of middle-earth: i.e. a mortal. "Spirits are supposed to inhabit the ethereal regions, and fairies to dwell underground; men therefore are in a middle station" (Johnson).
82. cheese. See note to II.ii.303.
83. o'erlook'd: bewitched by the "evil eye."
86. turn him to: cause him. **92. still:** continually.
94. luxury: lechery.

95. bloody fire: fire in the blood.
99. mutually: jointly, all together.
103. watch'd you: caught you in the act.
105. hold . . . higher: continue the joke no longer.
107. fair yokes: i.e. the horns.
115. arrested: seized by warrant as security.
120. ox: i.e. fool, with punning reference to the horns (line 107). **extant:** present. **123. surprise:** confounding.
124. powers: faculties. **grossness:** flagrant character, obviousness. **foppery:** dupery, deceit. **125. despite . . . teeth:** defiance.
127. Jack-a-Lent: butt (see note on III.iii.27).

Fal. Have I laid my brain in the sun and dried it, that it wants matter to prevent so gross o'er-reaching as this? Am I ridden with a Welsh goat too? Shall I have a coxcomb of frieze? 'Tis time I were chok'd with a piece of toasted cheese.

Evans. Seese is not good to give putter; your belly is all putter.

Fal. "Seese" and "putter"! Have I liv'd to stand at the taunt of one that makes fritters of English? This is enough to be the decay of lust and late-walking through the realm.

Mrs. Page. Why, Sir John, do you think, though we would have thrust virtue out of our hearts by the head and shoulders, and have given ourselves without scruple to hell, that ever the devil could have made you our delight?

Ford. What, a hodge-pudding? A bag of flax?

Mrs. Page. A puff'd man?

Page. Old, cold, wither'd, and of intolerable entrails?

Ford. And one that is as slanderous as Sathan?

Page. And as poor as Job?

Ford. And as wicked as his wife?

Evans. And given to fornications, and to taverns, and sack, and wine, and metheglins, and to drinkings and swearings and starings, pribbles and prabbles?

Fal. Well, I am your theme. You have the start of me, I am dejected. I am not able to answer the Welsh flannel; ignorance itself is a plummet o'er me. Use me as you will.

Ford. Marry, sir, we'll bring you to Windsor, to one Master [Brook] that you have cozen'd of money, to whom you should have been a pander. Over and above that you have suffer'd, I think to repay that money will be a biting affliction.

Page. Yet be cheerful, knight. Thou shalt eat a posset to-night at my house, where I will desire thee to laugh at my wife, that now laughs at thee. Tell her Master Slender hath married her daughter.

Mrs. Page. [*Aside.*] Doctors doubt that. If Anne Page be my daughter, she is, by this, Doctor Caius' wife.

[*Enter* SLENDER.]

Slen. Whoa ho, ho! father Page!

Page. Son? how now? how now, son? have you dispatch'd?

Slen. Dispatch'd? I'll make the best in Gloucestershire know on't. Would I were hang'd la, else!

Page. Of what, son?

Slen. I came yonder at Eton to marry Mistress Anne Page, and she's a great lubberly boy. If it had not been i' th' church, I would have swing'd him, or he should have swing'd me. If I did not think it had been Anne Page, would I might never stir!—and 'tis a postmaster's boy.

Page. Upon my life then, you took the wrong.

Slen. When need you tell me that? I think so, when I took a boy for a girl. If I had been married to him (for all he was in woman's apparel) I would not have had him.

Page. Why, this is your own folly. Did not I tell you how you should know my daughter by her garments?

Slen. I went to her in [white] and cried "mum," and she cried "budget," as Anne and I had appointed, and yet it was not Anne, but a postmaster's boy.

Mrs. Page. Good George, be not angry. I knew of your purpose; turn'd my daughter into [green]; and indeed she is now with the Doctor at the dean'ry, and there married.

[*Enter* CAIUS.]

Caius. Vere is Mistress Page? By gar, I am cozen'd. I ha' married oon garsoon, a boy; oon pesant, by gar. A boy! It is not Anne Page. By gar, I am cozen'd.

Mrs. Page. Why? did you take her in [green]?

Caius. Ay, be-gar, and 'tis a boy. Be-gar, I'll raise all Windsor. [*Exit.*]

Ford. This is strange. Who hath got the right Anne?

Page. My heart misgives me. Here comes Master Fenton.

[*Enter* FENTON *and* ANNE PAGE.]

How now, Master Fenton?

Anne. Pardon, good father! good my mother, pardon!

Page. Now, mistress, how chance you went not with Master Slender?

Mrs. Page. Why went you not with Master Doctor, maid?

Fent. You do amaze her. Hear the truth of it.
You would have married her most shamefully,
Where there was no proportion held in love.
The truth is, she and I (long since contracted)
Are now so sure that nothing can dissolve us.
Th' offense is holy that she hath committed,
And this deceit loses the name of craft,
Of disobedience, or unduteous title,
Since therein she doth evitate and shun

138. coxcomb: fool's cap. **frieze:** a coarse woollen cloth made in Wales. **139. piece . . . cheese.** See note on II.ii.303.
144. late-walking: keeping late hours.
151. hodge-pudding: large pork sausage.
153–54. intolerable entrails: i.e. a monstrous belly.
155. Sathan: Satan.
157. wicked . . . wife. Job's wife counselled him to curse God and die (Job 2.9).
159. metheglins: Welsh drink of fermented honey, resembling mead.
160. starings: swaggerings.
161. your theme: the object of your mirth. **start:** advantage.
162. dejected: abased, humbled.
163. flannel. Of Welsh origin. **ignorance itself:** i.e. Evans. **plummet:** plummet line, for fathoming, probably with play (suggested by *flannel* and by *frieze*, line 138) on *plumbet*, a woollen fabric.
167. should have been: were to have been.
168. that: what. **170. eat:** consume.
171. posset. See note on I.iv.8.
174. Doctors doubt that. Proverbial expression of disbelief. *Doctors* = learned men. **175. this:** this time.

181. else: if I don't. **184. lubberly:** loutish.
185. swing'd: beaten (past tense of *swinge*).
188. postmaster: master of the post-horses.
205. oon garsoon: *un garçon*, a boy.
205–6. oon pesant: *un paysan*, a peasant. **220. amaze:** confuse.
222. proportion: balance, equality. **223. contracted:** betrothed.
224. sure: i.e. firmly bound.
227. unduteous title: designation of undutifulness.
228. evitate: avoid.

A thousand irreligious cursed hours
Which forced marriage would have brought upon her.
Ford. Stand not amaz'd; here is no remedy.
In love, the heavens themselves do guide the state;
Money buys lands, and wives are sold by fate.
Fal. I am glad, though you have ta'en a special stand to strike at me, that your arrow hath glanc'd.
Page. Well, what remedy? Fenton, heaven give thee joy!
What cannot be eschew'd must be embrac'd.

235. stand: concealed position for shooting at game.

Fal. When night-dogs run, all sorts of deer are chas'd.
Mrs. Page. Well, I will muse no further. Master Fenton,
Heaven give you many, many merry days!
Good husband, let us every one go home,
And laugh this sport o'er by a country fire—
Sir John and all.
Ford. Let it be so. Sir John,
To Master [Brook] you yet shall hold your word,
For he to-night shall lie with Mistress Ford. *Exeunt.*

239. muse: complain.

NOTE ON THE TEXT

The Merry Wives of Windsor was printed in a drastically shortened, memorially reconstructed form in 1602 (Q1). This "bad" quarto was reprinted in 1619 (Q2). The full text of the play, now generally thought to be essentially the same as that from which Q1 was reported, appeared for the first time in the First Folio (1623). A third quarto (Q3), based on F1, was published in 1630.

F1 is the principal authority for any modern edition, but Q1, although it garbles, cuts (some of the cuts were probably already made in the F1 text as acted), or invents much of the dialogue, reverses III.iv and III.v, and omits IV.i and V.i–iv, furnishes several short passages perhaps accidentally omitted from F1, as well as many stage directions, suggests corrections for a number of faulty readings, and restores some oaths and the name "Brooke" ("Broome" in F1) as the original form of Ford's alias, a change, like that of "Oldcastle" to "Falstaff" in *1* and *2 Henry IV*, made in deference to, or at the demand of, Henry Brooke, Lord Cobham. Pope and Theobald first began the practice of inserting tempting bits and pieces from Q1 into the F1 text. A few such passages have been admitted into the present text; others are recorded in the Textual Notes.

The F1 text is believed to have been printed from a transcript specially prepared for the publishers by Ralph Crane (see the "Note on the Text" to *The Tempest*). Evidence of Crane's hand may be seen in the frequent parentheses, in such hyphenated forms as *drawling-affecting, carry-her, idle-headed-Eld*, and so on (not completely recorded in the Textual Notes), and perhaps most conspicuously in the consistent use of "massed entries" (on which see the "Note on the Text" to *The Two Gentlemen of Verona*). Scholars seem generally to agree that Crane based his transcript on some kind of prompt-book, but the evidence for this view is slender.

In the F1 text thirty-seven short prose passages are wrongly printed as verse. Since the play is basically in prose, they raise no difficult problems, and with a few exceptions they are not recorded in the Textual Notes. F3 (particularly in III.iii) and Pope are responsible for adjusting these passages to prose.

Except as noted above, Q1–2 are in general cited only in connection with readings of F1. The absence of Q1–2 from the sigla cited in a textual note indicates that the reading of the lemma occurs in a passage which in Q1–2 is either omitted or so differently worded that it offers no recognizable equivalent. Some longer passages from Q1–2 which differ markedly from the F1 text are included in the Textual Notes for comparison (see I.i.1–108, III.ii.8 s.d., III.iv.1–21, IV.iv.42, V.v.49–54, 84–102, 104, 169, 236–45).

A "literary" manuscript copy of *Merry Wives* (Folger MS. V.a.73), based on F2 (1632) and showing some evidence of an indirect theatrical provenience, contains the earliest *Dramatis Personae* list; a substantial number of readings anticipating John Dennis's adaptation (1702), Rowe, and later editors; a few additions; and a number of unique readings.

For further information, see: H. C. Hart, ed., Arden *Merry Wives of Windsor* (London, 1904); W. W. Greg, ed., *The Merry Wives of Windsor, 1602* (Oxford, 1910) [first full statement of the memorial reconstruction theory], and *The Shakespeare First Folio* (Oxford, 1955); J. D. Wilson, ed., New Shakespeare *The Merry Wives of Windsor* (Cambridge, 1921); Leslie Hotson, *Shakespeare Versus Shallow* (Boston, 1937); William Bracy, *"The Merry Wives of Windsor": The History and Transmission of Shakespeare's Text* (Columbia, Mo., 1952) [argues unsuccessfully against the memorial reconstruction theory]; William Green, *Shakespeare's "Merry Wives of Windsor"* (Princeton, 1962); F. T. Bowers, ed., Pelican *The Merry Wives of Windsor* (Baltimore, Maryland, 1969); H. J. Oliver, ed., New Arden *The Merry Wives of Windsor* (London, 1971); J. A. Roberts, "*The Merry Wives* Q and F: The Vagaries of Progress," *Shakespeare Studies*, VII (1975), 143–75 [useful survey of the various theories advanced to explain the interrelations between F1 and Q1–2 from the eighteenth century to date]; G. D. Johnson, "*The Merry Wives of Windsor*, Q1: Provincial Touring and Adapted Texts," *SQ*, XXXVIII (1987), 154–65; G. B. Evans, "*The Merry Wives of Windsor*: The Folger Manuscript," in *Shakespeare, Text, and Language*, ed. B. Fabian and K. Tetzeli von Rosador (Zurich, 1987), 57–79; Stanley Wells, Gary Taylor, John Jowett, and William Montgomery, *William Shakespeare: A Textual Companion* (Oxford, 1987); K. O. Irace, *Reforming the "Bad" Quartos* (Univ. of Delaware Press, 1994); T. W. Craik, ed., New Oxford *The Merry Wives of Windsor* (Oxford, 1989).

TEXTUAL NOTES

Title: The . . . Windsor] A Most pleasaunt and excellent conceited Comedie, of Syr Iohn Falstaffe, and the merrie Wiues of Windsor. Entermixed with sundrie variable and pleasing humors, of Syr Hugh the Welch Knight, Iustice Shallow, and his wise Cousin M. Slender. With the swaggering vaine of Auncient Pistoll, and Corporall Nym. By William Shakespeare. As it hath bene diuers times Acted by the right Honorable my Lord Chamberlaines seruants. Both before her Maiestie, and

else-where. *Q1 (title-page)*
Dramatis personae: *subs. as first given in Folger MS (ca. 1650) and* Rowe
Act-scene division: *from F1*

I.i

Location: *Theobald*
o.s.d. **Enter . . . Evans.]** *Rowe;* Enter Iustice Shallow, Slender, Sir Hugh Euans, Master Page, Falstoffe, Bardolph, Nym, Pistoll, Anne Page, Mistresse Ford, Mistresse Page, Simple. *F1 (an example of the "massed entries" used throughout the F1 text; all but the first three characters actually enter at later points in the scene);* Enter Iustice Shallow, Syr Hugh, Maister Page, and Slender. *Q1–2*
1–108] *Except for ll. 1–2, these opening lines appear in a different form in Q1–2: Shal.* Nere talke to me, Ile make a star-chamber matter of it. / The Councell shall know it. [*cf. l. 117*] / *Pag.* Nay good maister *Shallow* be perswaded by mee. / *Slen.* Nay surely my vncle shall not put it vp so. / *Sir Hu.* Wil you not heare reasons M. *Slenders* [*Slender Q2*]? / You should heare reasons. / *Shal.* Tho he be a knight, he shall not thinke to carrie it so away. / M. *Page* I will not be wronged. For you / Syr, I loue you, and for my cousen / He comes to looke vpon your daughter. / *Pa.* And heres my hand, and if my daughter / Like him so well as I, wee'l quickly haue it [haue't *Q2*] a match: / In the meane time let me intreat you to soiourne / Here a while. And on my life Ile vndertake / To make you friends. / *Sir Hu.* I pray you M. *Shallowes* [*Shallow Q2*] let it be so. / The matter is pud [put *Q2*] to arbitarments. / The first man is M. *Page*, videlicet M. *Page*. / The second is my selfe, videlicet my selfe. / And [*om. Q2*] the third and last man, is mine host of the gartyr. [*the last three lines are a version of ll. 138–41*] / *Enter Syr* Iohn Falstaffe, Pistoll, Bardolfe, *and* Nim. / Here is sir *Iohn* himselfe now, look you.
3 **Falstaffs]** *F2; Falstoffs F1*
28 **py'r lady]** *Capell;* per-lady *F1*
39 **vizaments]** *Capell;* viza-ments *F1*
46 **George]** *Theobald;* Thomas *F1*
72 s.d. **Knocks.]** *Rowe*
73 **Got pless]** *F2* (Got blesse); Got-plesse *F1 (these hyphenated forms, characteristic of Crane, are not generally noted)*
74 s.d. **Within.]** *Dyce*
74 s.d. **Enter Page.]** *Collier*
75 **Got's]** *F2;* go't's *F1*
108 s.d. **Enter . . . Pistol.]** *Q1–2 (subs.)*
119 **counsel]** *Q1–2;* councell *F1*
125–7 **They . . . pocket.]** *Q1–2 (first inserted, Malone)*
141 **Garter]** *Q2;* Gater *F1;* gartyr *Q1*
161 **mountain-foreigner]** *hyphen, Hanmer*
162 **latten]** *Q1–2* (laten); Latine *F1*
168–9 **that . . . note]** And there's the humor *Q1–2*
179 **careers]** *Capell (subs.);* Car-eires *F1*
180 **Latin]** *F2;* Latten *F1*
187 s.d. **Enter . . . Page.]** *Capell;* Enter Mistresse Foord, Mistresse Page, and her daughter Anne. *Q1–2*
189 s.d. **Exit Anne Page.]** *Theobald*
193 s.d. **Kisses her.]** *Q1–2* (Syr Iohn kisses her.)
197 s.d. **Exeunt . . . Evans.]** *Rowe (subs.);* Exit all, but Slender and mistresse Anne. *Q1–2*
199 s.d. **Enter Simple.]** *Rowe*
208 **afar off]** *F2;* a farre-off *F1*
227 **oman]** *Rowe* ('oman); 'o-man *F1*
236 **carry her]** *Pope;* carry-her *F1*
253 **discretion answer]** *F2;* descetion-answere *F1*
259 s.d. **Enter Anne Page.]** *Rowe*
262 **worships']** *Capell;* worships *F1*
265 s.d. **Exeunt . . . Evans.]** *Rowe*
272 s.d. **Exit Simple.]** *Theobald*
285 **prunes)]** *followng this, Wilson inserts from Q1–2:* and I with my ward / Defending my head, he hot my shin.
299 s.d. **Enter Page.]** *Q1–2*

I.ii

Location: *ed. (after Wilson)*
o.s.d. **from dinner]** *Q1–2*
8 **altogether's]** *Tyrwhitt conj.;* altogeathers *F1*

I.iii

Location: *Pope*
13 s.d. **To Bardolph.]** *Cambridge*
14 **lime]** *Q1–2* (lyme); liue *F1*
15 s.d. **Exit.]** *Q1–2*
19 s.d. **Exit.]** *Q1–2* (Exit Bardolph.)
20 **Hungarian]** gongarian *Q1–2*
21 s.d. **Exit Bardolph.]** *Q1–2 (after l. 19); placed as in Dyce*
23 **conceited?]** *following this, Theobald inserts from Q1–2:* His minde is not heroick. And theres the humor of it.
49 **well]** *Q1–2;* will *F1*
53 **He]** She *Q1–2*
53 **a legend]** legians *Q1;* Legions *Q2; most eds. read* a legion *(Rowe), but* legend *misused for* legion *occurs outside of Shakespeare*
54 **entertain;]** attend her. *Q1–2*
61 **iliads]** *ed.;* illiads *F1*
78 **reputation.]** reputation. And theres the humor of it. *Q1–2*
79 s.d. **To Robin.]** *Theobald*
83 **humor]** *Q1–2;* honor *F1*
84 **page]** *Q1–2* (Page); Page *F1 (in italics)*
84 s.d. **Exeunt . . . Robin.]** *Q1–2* (. . . the Boy.)
89–90 **I . . . revenge.]** *as prose, Pope; as verse, F1, Q1–2*
89 **in my head]** *Q1–2 (first inserted, Pope)*
95 **Page]** *Q1–2;* Ford *F1*
96 **Ford]** *Q1–2;* Page *F1*
101 **Page]** *Rann;* Ford *F1*
102–3 **yallowness . . . humor.]** Iallowes, / And theres the humor of it. *Q1–2*

I.iv

Location: *Pope*
o.s.d. **Enter . . . Simple.]** *Q1–2;* Enter Mistris Quickly, Simple, Iohn Rugby, Doctor, Caius, Fenton. *F1*
1 s.d. **Enter John Rugby.]** *Wilson*
10 s.d. **Exit Rugby.]** *Rowe*
22 **whey-face]** *Capell;* wee-face *F1 (Q1–2 refer here to* a whay coloured beard)
23 **Cain-color'd]** *hyphen, F2;* kane colored *Q1–2*
35 s.d. **Enter Rugby.]** *Rowe*
38, 63, 67 **closet]** Counting-house *Q1–2*
39 s.d. **Shuts . . . closet.]** *Rowe;* He steps into the Counting-house. *Q1–2*
43 s.d. **Singing.]** *Theobald*
43 s.d. **Enter Doctor Caius.]** *Rowe*
44 **des toys]** *F3;* des-toyes *F1*
45–6 **une boîte en]** *Hart;* vnboyteene *F1*
51–2 **chaud . . . vois]** *ed. (after Rowe);* chando, Ie man voi *F1*
52 **affaire]** *Rowe;* affaires *F1*
54 **quickly]** *Pope;* quickly *F1 (in italics)*
58 **and]** *Q1–2;* aad *F1*
68 **laroon]** *Wilson;* La-roone *F1*
68 s.d. **Pulling Simple out.]** *Theobald*
78 **Vell?]** *Neilson;* Vell. *F1*
87 **baillez]** *Theobald;* ballow *F1*
88 s.d. **Writes.]** *Q1–2* (The Doctor writes.)
89, 100 s.dd. **Aside to Simple.]** *Cambridge*
92 **you]** *Cambridge;* yoe *F1*
98 s.d. **Aside to Quickly.]** *Cambridge*
105 **that,]** *Rowe;* that *F1*
113 s.d. **Exit Simple.]** *Rowe*
125 s.d. **Exeunt . . . Rugby.]** *Rowe;* Exit Doctor. *Q1–2*
126 **Anne—fool's-head]** *Daniel conj. (subs.); An*-fooles head *F1; Anne*-fools head *F3*
131 s.d. **Within.]** *Rowe*
132 **trow]** *Rowe;* troa *F1*
133 s.d. **Enter Fenton.]** *Rowe*
154 **to.]** *Capell:* too——— *F1*
157 **me.]** *Knight;* me.——— *F1*
162 s.d. **Exit Fenton.]** *Rowe (after l. 161); placed as in Dyce*
163 **him]** *F2;* hiim *F1*

II.i

Location: *Pope*
o.s.d. **Enter . . . letter.]** *Q1–2;* Enter Mistris Page, Mistris Ford, Master Page, Master Ford, Pistoll, Nim, Quickly, Host, Shallow. *F1*
1 **I]** *Q3*
3 s.d. **Reads.]** *Capell*
20–8 **What . . . me!]** *as prose, Pope (after F3), Q1–2; as irregular verse, F1*
32 s.d. **Enter Mistress Ford.]** *Rowe*
51 **What?]** *Johnson;* What *F1*
58 **prais'd]** *Theobald;* praise *F1*
64 **trow]** *Rowe;* troa *F1*
65 **ashore]** *Capell (subs.);* a'shoare *F1*
95 **fine-baited]** *hyphen, Capell*
108 s.d. **They retire.]** *Theobald*
108 s.d. **Enter . . . Nym.]** *Rowe (after Q1–2:* Enter Ford, Page, Pistoll and Nym.)
113–5 **He . . . Perpend.]** *as verse, Pope, Q1–2; as prose, F1*
114 **Ford.]** *Rowe (subs.);* (Ford) *F1*
115 **gallimaufry, Ford. Perpend.]** *ed. (after Sisson);* Gally-mawfry (Ford) perpend. *F1*
125 s.d. **Exit.]** *Q1–2* (Exit Pistoll:)
126 s.d. **Aside.]** *Capell*
128 s.d. **To Page.]** *Hanmer*
136 **and . . . it.]** *Q1–2 (first inserted, Capell)*
137 s.d. **Exit.]** *Q1–2* (Exit Nym.)
141 **drawling, affecting]** *F2;* drawling-affecting *F1*
147 s.d. **Mrs. . . . forward.]** *Theobald*
155 **head now. Will]** *Johnson;* head, Now: will *F1*
157 s.d. **Aside . . . Ford.]** *Capell*
160 s.d. **Aside . . . Page.]** *Capell*
161 s.d. **Enter Mistress Quickly.]** *Rowe; Q1–2 enter Mrs. Quickly around l. 149*
167 s.d. **Exeunt . . . Quickly.]** *Q1–2* (Exit)
188 s.d. **Enter Host.]** *Dyce; Q1–2 enter Host and Shallow here (after* confident. *l. 187)*
189 **ranting]** ramping *Q1–2*
193–4 **gentleman. Cavaleiro]** *Hanmer (subs.);* Gentleman Caueleiro *F1; Q1–2 read ll. 193–4 as:* God blesse you my bully rookes, God blesse / Cauelera Iustice I say.
194 s.d. **Enter Shallow.]** *Dyce*
205 s.d. **Ford . . . talks.]** *Q1–2 (Q1–2 reverse order of speeches in ll. 203–5)*
206 s.d. **To Page.]** *Johnson*
211 s.d. **They converse apart.]** *Capell*
213 **guest-cavalier]** My guest, my cauellira *Q1–2*
214 s.p. **Ford.]** *Q1–2;* Shal. *F1*
216 **Brook]** *Q2 (misprinted* Rrooke *in Q1);* Broome *F1*
219 **Brook]** *Q1–2;* Broome *F1*
220 **An-heires]** *an unsolved crux; Theobald's conj.* Mynheers *is the most popular emendation*
232 s.d. **Exeunt . . . Page.]** *Rowe;* Exit Host and Shallow. *Q1–2*
240 s.d. **Exit.]** *Rowe;* Exeunt. *F1;* Exit omnes. *Q1–2*

II.ii

Location: *Pope*
o.s.d. **Enter . . . Pistol.]** *Q1–2 (subs.);* Enter Falstaffe, Pistoll, Robin, Quickly, Bardolffe, Ford. *F1*
1 **Pist. I . . . equipage.]** *Q1–2 (after l. 2); first inserted, Theobald (after l. 4); placed as in Wilson*
3–4 **Why . . . open.]** *as verse, Steevens; as prose, F1*
13–4 **Didst . . . pence?]** *as verse, Capell; as prose, F1*
22 **honor]** *Q1–2;* hononor *F1*
22 **I, I, I]** I, I *Q1–2*
23 **God]** *Q1–2;* heauen *F1*
25 **shuffle,]** *Q1–2;* shuffle: *F1*
26 **you,]** *Pope;* you *F1*
30 s.d. **Enter Robin.]** *Rowe*
32 s.d. **Enter Mistress Quickly.]** *Q1–2*

52 **God bless]** *Q1–2;* heauen-blesse *F1*
66 **gift; . . . sweetly,]** *Capell;* gift, . . . sweetly; *F1*
90 **jealousy man]** *Theobald;* iealousie-man *F1*
112 **hope.]** *Rowe (subs.);* hope, *F1*
114 **page,]** *F4;* Page *F1*
133–4 s.d. **Exeunt . . . Robin.]** *Rowe;* Exit Mistresse Quickly. *Q1–2*
135 s.d. **Aside.]** *Wilson*
137 s.d. **Exit.]** *Rowe*
138 **so, old Jack?]** *F4 (subs.);* so (old Iacke) *F1*
143 s.d. **Enter Bardolph.]** *Q1–2*
148 **Brook]** *Q1–2;* Broome *F1 (throughout scene)*
150 s.d. **Exit Bardolph.]** *Theobald*
150 **Brooks]** *Q1–2;* Broomes *F1*
153 s.d. **Enter . . . Brook.]** *Theobald (subs.);* Enter Foord disguised like Brooke. *Q1–2*
154 **God save]** *Q1–2;* 'Blesse *F1*
159 s.d. **Exit Bardolph.]** *Theobald*
204 **jewel—]** *Theobald (subs.);* Iewell, *F1*
207–8 **"Love . . . pursues."]** *marked with gnomic quotes, F1*
233 **exchange]** *Q3;* enchange *F1*
246–7 **hand, . . . themselves.]** *Rowe (subs., after F4);* hand; . . . themselues, *F1*
254 **and]** *Q1;* if *F1, Q2*
257 **I]** M. Brooke, I *Q1–2*
286 s.d. **Exit.]** *Q1–2* (Exit Falstaffe.)
295 **abominable]** *F4;* abhominable *F1*
299 **Wittol!—Cuckold!]** *Cambridge;* Wittoll, Cuckold? *F1*
309 **God]** *Q1–2;* Heauen *F1*
314 s.d. **Exit.]** *Q1–2* (Exit Ford.); Exti. *F1*

II.iii

Location: *Dyce*
o.s.d. **Enter . . . Rugby.]** *Q1–2* (Enter the Doctor and his man.); Enter Caius, Rugby, Page, Shallow, Slender, Host. *F1*
17 s.d. **Enter . . . Host.]** *Q1–2* (Enter Shallow, Page, my [*om. Q2*] Host, and Slender.)
18 **God bless]** *Q1–2;* 'Blesse *F1*
19 **God save]** *Q1–2 (in speech by Page);* 'Saue *F1*
28 **Francisco]** francoyes *Q1–2 (possibly correct = "Frenchman")*
38–9 **Doctor: he]** *F4;* Docto)rhe *F1*
57 **word]** *Q1–2*
75 s.d. **Aside to them.]** *Capell*
81 s.p. **Page, Shal., Slen.]** *Malone (the line is spoken by Shallow in Q1–2)*
81 s.d. **Exeunt . . . Rugby.]** *ed. (after Q1–2:* Exit all but the Host and Doctor.)
84 **but first]** *Q1–2*
88 **Cried game?]** *Sisson;* Cride-game, *F1;* cried game: *Q1–2*
92 **guest]** gesse *Q1;* guests *Q2*
93 **patients]** patinces *Q1*

III.i

Location: *Malone (after Pope)*
o.s.d. **Enter . . . Simple.]** *Q1–2* (Enter Syr Hugh and Simple.); Enter Euans, Simple, Page, Shallow, Slender, Host, Caius, Rugby. *F1*
10 s.d. **Exit.]** *Cambridge*
11 **Jeshu pless]** *Q1–2;* 'Plesse *F1*
16, 22, 28 s.dd. **Sings.]** *Dyce (after Pope)*
24 **When . . . Pabylon—]** There dwelt a man in Babylon, *Q1–2*
26 s.d. **Enter Simple.]** *Cambridge*
35 s.d. **Reads in a book.]** *Dyce (after Collier MS)*
35 s.d. **Enter . . . Slender.]** *Q1–2*
40 s.d. **Aside.]** *Cambridge*
41 **God save]** *Q1–2;* 'Saue *F1*
42 **God pless]** *Q1–2;* 'Plesse *F1*
42 **mercy sake]** *Capell (subs.);* mercy-sake *F1;* mercies sake *Q1–2*
70 s.d. **Aside.]** *Cambridge*
70 s.d. **Enter . . . Rugby.]** *Q1–2* (Enter Doctor and the Host, they offer to fight.)
72 s.d. **Evans . . . fight.]** *from Q1–2 (see preceding note)*
77–8 **Let . . . English.]** *given to Shallow in Q1–2, perhaps correctly*
81 s.d. **Aside to Caius.]** *Cambridge*
85 s.d. **Aside to Caius.]** *Staunton*
88 s.d. **Aloud.]** *Staunton*
88 **urinals]** *Q1–2;* Vrinal *F1*
89 **cogscomb]** cockcomes *Q1;* coxcomb *Q2*
89–90 **for . . . appointments]** *Q1–2 (first inserted, Pope)*
105–6 **Give . . . so.]** *Q1–2* (Giue . . . hand terestial, / So); *first inserted, Theobald, who punctuates subs. as here*
106 **hand, celestial; so.]** *Theobald (subs., after Rowe);* hand (Cellestiall) so: *F1;* hand celestiall: / So *Q1–2*
110 **lads]** *Q1–2;* Lad *F1*
111 s.d. **Exit.]** *Q1–2* (Exit Host.)
112 **Afore God]** *Q1–2;* Trust me *F1*
114 s.d. **Aside.]** *Cambridge*
114 s.d. **Exeunt . . . Page.]** *Rowe (who, however, includes the Host; Neilson first om. the Host)*
120 **scall, . . . companion,]** *Capell (subs.);* scall scuruy-cogging-companion *F1*
126 s.d. **Exeunt.]** *Pope;* Exit omnes *Q1–2*

III.ii

Location: *Theobald (after Pope)*
o.s.d. **Enter . . . Robin.]** *Rowe;* Mist. Page, Robin, Ford, Page, Shallow, Slender, Host, Euans, Caius. *F1*
8 s.d. **Enter Ford.]** *Q1–2* (Enter M. Foord.); *Q1–2 begin the scene with Ford's entry and offer the following lines in place of ll. 1–59: Enter M. Foord. / For.* The time drawes on he shuld come to my house, / Well wife, you had best worke closely, / Or I am like to goe beyond your cunning: / I now wil seek my guesse that comes [guests that come *Q2*] to dinner, / And in good time see where they all are come. / *Enter Shallow, Page, host, Slender, Doctor, and sir Hugh.* / By my faith a knot well met: your welcome all. [*cf. l. 51*] / *Pa.* I thanke you good M. *Ford.* / *For.* Welcome good M. *Page,* / I would your daughter were here. / *Pa.* I thank you sir, she is very well at home.
29 s.d. **Exeunt . . . Robin.]** *Rowe*
33 **mile, as easy]** *F4;* mile as easie, *F1*
44–5 s.d. **Clock heard.]** *Capell*
49 s.d. **Enter . . . Rugby.]** *Capell (after Q1–2, which like F1 fail to enter Rugby here)*
70 **buttons]** betmes *Q1–2*
73 **Poins]** *F3* (Poinz); Pointz *F1; Q1–2 om. the whole reference to the Prince and Poins*
84 **fare you well]** God be with you *Q1–2*
85 s.d. **Exeunt . . . Slender.]** *Q1–2* (Exit)
86 s.d. **Exit Rugby.]** *Capell*
88 s.d. **Exit.]** *Q1–2* (Exit host.)
89 s.d. **Aside.]** *Johnson*

III.iii

Location: *Pope*
o.s.d. **Enter . . . Page.]** *Capell;* Enter M. Ford, M. Page, Seruants, Robin, Falstaffe, Ford, Page, Caius, Euans. *F1;* Enter Mistresse Ford, with two of her men, and a great buck basket. *Q1–2*
4 s.d. **Enter . . . buck-basket.]** *Capell (after Q1–2; see preceding note)*
15 **Datchet-mead]** *Rowe;* Dotchet Mead *F1*
20 s.d. **Exeunt Servants.]** *Folger MS, Johnson;* Exit seruant. *Q1–2*
21 s.d. **Enter Robin.]** *Rowe*
37 s.d. **Exit Robin.]** *Rowe*
39 s.d. **Exit.]** *Rowe*
42 s.d. **Enter Falstaff.]** *Q1–2* (Enter Sir Iohn.)
43–4 **"Have . . . jewel?"]** *Q1–2 om.* thee *as in Sidney's original line*
48–9 **prate, . . . Now]** *F4 (subs.);* prate (Mist. Ford) now *F1*
50 **dead.]** *Theobald (subs.);* dead, *F1*
56 **beauty]** bent *Q1–2*
61 **By the Lord]** *Q1–2*
61 **tyrant]** traitor *Q1–2*
65 **foe were not,]** *F2;* foe, were not *F1*
69 **thee]** *Q1–2;* thee. *F1*
84 s.d. **Enter Robin.]** *Capell;* Within. *F2*
92 s.d. **Falstaff . . . arras.]** *Q1–2*
92 s.d. **Enter Mistress Page.]** *Q1–2 (before Falstaff hides himself); placed as in F2*
111 **'Tis . . . hope.]** Speak louder. But I hope tis not true Mistris Page. *Q1–2*
125 **For shame]** Gode [Gods *Q2*] body woman *Q1–2*
136 s.d. **Starting . . . concealment.]** *Capell*
139 s.d. **Aside.]** *Q1–2*
141 s.d. **To Mrs. Page.]** *Malone conj.*
141 **thee.]** thee, and none but thee: *Q1–2*
142 s.d. **Goes . . . him.]** *from Q1–2 s.d.:* Sir Iohn goes into the basket, they put cloathes ouer him, the two men carries it away: Foord meetes it, and all the rest, Page, Doctor, Priest, Slender, Shallow.
145 s.d. **Exit Robin.]** *Malone*
145 s.d. **Enter Servants.]** *Capell*
148 s.d. **Enter . . . Evans.]** *Folger MS, Rowe (see l. 142 above for Q1–2)*
151 **now?]** now who goes heare? *Q1–2*
160 s.d. **Exeunt . . . basket.]** *Rowe (see l. 142 above for Q1–2)*
164 s.d. **Locking the door.]** *Capell*
169 s.d. **Exit.]** *Capell*
170 **This]** By Ieshu these *Q1–2*
175 s.d. **Exeunt . . . Evans.]** *Capell;* Exit omnes. *Q1–2*
193 **foolish]** *F2;* foolishion *F1*
198 s.d. **Enter . . . Evans.]** *Rowe;* Enter all. *Q1–2*
201 s.d. **Aside . . . Ford.]** *Capell*
202 **You . . . you?]** I, I, peace. *Q1–2 (as a separate speech for Mrs. Ford; Theobald inserts these words at the beginning of the F1 speech)*
210 **If]** By Ieshu if *Q1–2*
220 **omans]** *Capell* ('omans); o'mans *F1 (so generally)*
227 **me.]** *following this speech Q1–2 read: Sir Hu.* By so kad vdgme, M. *Fordes* [*Foord Q2*] is / Not in his right wittes:
230 **after,]** *Theobald;* after *F1*
237 **turd.]** tird: / *Sir. Hu.* In your teeth for shame. *Q1–2*
238 s.d. **Exit with Page.]** *Wilson*
241 **with all]** *F2;* withall *F1*

III.iv

Q1–2 reverse the order of Scenes iv and v
Location: *Pope (subs.)*
o.s.d. **Enter . . . Page.]** *Rowe;* Enter Fenton, Anne, Page, Shallow, Slender, Quickly, Page, Mist. Page. *F1;* Enter M. Fenton, Page [Anne Page *Q2*], and mistresse Quickly. *Q1–2*
1–21] *These lines are replaced in Q1–2 by the following essentially different lines: Fen:* Tell me sweet *Nan,* how doest thou yet resolue, / Shall foolish *Slender* haue thee to his wife? / Or one as wise as he, the learned Doctor? / Shall such as they enioy thy maiden hart? / Thou knowst that I haue alwaies loued thee deare, / And thou hast oft times swore the like to me. / *An:* Good M. *Fenton,* you may assure your selfe / My hart is setled vpon none but you, / Tis as my father and my mother please: / Get their consent, you quickly shall haue mine. / *Fen:* Thy father thinks I loue thee for his wealth, / Tho I must needs confesse at first that drew me, / But since thy vertues wiped that trash away, / I loue thee *Nan,* and so deare is it set, / That whilst I liue, I nere shall thee forget. / *Quic:* Godes pitie here comes her father. [*In Q1–2 the rough equivalent of ll. 22–66 follows the exit of Mrs. Page (with Page, who has remained on stage) about l. 94.*]
12 s.p. **Fent.]** *Q3*
21 s.d. **They converse apart.]** *Capell*
21 s.d. **Enter . . . Quickly.]** *Rowe*
31 s.d. **Aside.]** *Capell*
58 **heaven]** God *Q1–2*
66 s.d. **Enter . . . Page.]** *Rowe;* Enter M. Page his wife, M. Shallow, and Slender. *Q1–2*
74 **Fenton]** *Q3;* Fenter *F1*
76 s.d. **Exeunt . . . Slender.]** *Rowe; in Q1–2 instead of exiting* they whisper.
88 **yourself.]** *Warburton (subs.);* your selfe *F1*

94 s.d. **Exeunt . . . Anne.**] *Rowe*
102 s.d. **Exit Fenton.**] *Q1–2* (*after the equivalent of l. 100*); *placed as in Dyce*
111 s.d. **Exit.**] *Rowe;* Exeunt *F1*
121 **surge**] *Pope;* serge *F1*

III.v

Location: *Pope*
o.s.d. **Enter Falstaff.**] *Q1* (Enter Sir Iohn Falstaffe); Enter Falstaffe, Bardolfe, Quickly, Ford. *F1;* Enter Sir Iohn Falstaffe and Bardolfe. *Q2*
1 s.d. **Enter Bardolph.**] *Wilson*
4 s.d. **Exit Bardolph.**] *Theobald*
6, 13 **and**] *Q1;* if *F1, Q2*
9 **slighted**] slided *Q1–2*
18 **mummy.**] money. Now is the Sacke brewed? *Q1–2*
18 s.d. **Enter . . . sack.**] *Dyce* (*after Theobald*)
25 s.d. **Enter Mistress Quickly.**] *Q1–2*
31 **pullet-sperm**] *F2;* Pullet-Spersme *F1;* pullets sperme *Q1–2*
32 s.d. **Exit Bardolph.**] *Capell*
56 s.d. **Exit.**] *Q1–2* (Exit mistresse Quickly.)
57 **Brook**] *Q1–2;* Broome *F1* (*throughout scene*)
59 s.d. **Enter Ford disguised.**] *Dyce* (*after F2*); Enter Brooke. *Q1–2*
60 **Bless**] God saue *Q1–2*
70 **cornuto**] *F2;* Curnuto *F1*
83 **good luck**] God *Q1–2*
89 **By the Lord**] *Q1–2;* Yes: *F1*
108 **several**] egregious *Q1–2*
138 s.d. **Exit.**] *Q1–2* (Exit Falstaffe.)
152 s.d. **Exit.**] *Rowe;* Exeunt. *F1;* Exit omnes. *Q1–2*

IV.i

Scene om. Q1–2
Location: *Capell*
o.s.d. **Enter . . . William.**] Enter Mistris Page, Quickly, William, Euans. *F1*
8 s.d. **Enter Evans.**] *Rowe* (*after l. 10*); *placed as in Neilson*
9 **playing-day**] *hyphen, F4*
28–9 **Poulcats . . . poulcats**] *F2;* Powlcats . . . Powlcats *F1*
43 **hujus**] *F2;* huius *F1*
47 **hung**] *Pope;* hing *F1*
48 **Latin**] *F3;* latten *F1*
52 **O—**] *Capell;* O, *F1*
61 **Genitivo**] *Folger MS, Singer;* Genitiue *F1*
62 **Jinny's**] *Kittredge;* Ginyes *F1*
69 **lunatics**] *Folger MS, Capell;* Lunaties *F1*
77 **quae**] *Folger MS, Pope;* que *F1*
78 **quae's**] *Pope;* Ques *F1*
84–5 s.d. **Exit Evans.**] *Steevens* (*subs.*)

IV.ii

Location: *Pope*
o.s.d. **Enter . . . Ford.**] Enter Falstaffe, Mist. Ford, Mist. Page, Seruants, Ford, Page, Caius, Euans, Shallow. *F1;* Enter misteris Ford and her two men. *Q1–2* (*followed by the equivalent of ll. 108–10, before the entry of Falstaff*)
9 s.d. **Within.**] *Rowe*
11 **into th' chamber**] behind the arras *Q1–2*
11 s.d. **Exit Falstaff.**] *Rowe;* He steps behind the arras. *Q1–2*
11 s.d. **Enter Mistress Page.**] *Q1–2* (*after l. 10*); *placed as in Rowe*
16 s.d. **Aside to her.**] *Dyce* (*after Theobald*)
22 **lines**] vaine *Q1–2* (*Theobald's* lunes *is frequently adopted by eds.*)
48 s.d. **Enter Falstaff.**] *Rowe*
66 s.p. **Mrs. Page.**] *Malone;* Mist. Ford. *F1*
73 **Good hearts**] For Gods sake *Q1–2*
75–6 **aunt . . . Brainford**] Aunt Gillian of Brainford *Q1–2*
83 s.d. **Exit Falstaff.**] *F2* (Exit.)
99 **direct**] *Q3;* direct direct *F1*
101 s.d. **Exit.**] *Capell*
103 **him**] *F2*
107 **draff**] *Capell;* draugh *F1*
107 s.d. **Exit.**] *Capell*
107 s.d. **Enter . . . Servants.**] *Capell* (*subs.*); *for Q1–2 see note on o.s.d.*
110 s.d. **Exit.**] *Capell*
113 **lief as**] as leife *F2*
113 s.d. **Enter . . . Shallow.**] *Rowe;* Enter M. Ford, Page, Priest [Hugh *Q2*], Shallow, the two men carries the basket, and Ford meets it. *Q1–2*
116–7 **Youth . . . basket!**] You youth in a basket, come out here, *Q1–2*
118 **ging**] *F2;* gin *F1*
119 **What,**] *Hanmer* (*after Theobald*); What *F1*
126 **this**] *Q3;* thi *F1*
128 s.d. **Enter Mistress Ford.**] *Theobald* (*after l. 125*); *placed as in Dyce*
133 **Heaven . . . do,**] I Gods my record do you. *Q1–2*
133 **and if**] *Q1;* if *F1, Q2*
136 s.d. **Pulling . . . basket.**] *Rowe; in Q1–2 Ford says:* Pull out the cloathes, search.
139 **clothes**] *F2;* cloths *F1*
141 **'Tis unreasonable**] Ieshu plesse me *Q1–2*
142 **Come**] *Rowe;* Come, *F1*
145] *Preceding this speech of Ford's, Q1–2 read:* Sir Hu. By [By *om. Q2*] so kad vdge me, tis verie necessarie / He were put in pethlem.
145 **a man**] an honest man *Q1–2*
170 **maid's aunt**] maidens [maids *Q2*] Ant, Gillian *Q1–2*
172 s.p. **Ford**] *om. Q1*
181 **not**] *Q3*
181 s.d. **Enter . . . him.**] *Q1–2*
184 **prat her**] *Steevens;* Prat-her *F1*
186 s.d. **Ford . . . away.**] *Q1–2* (*part of s.d. at l. 181*); *placed as in Neilson*
192 **By . . . no**] By Ieshu *Q1–2*
199 **his**] her *Q1–2*
200 s.d. **Exeunt . . . Evans.**] *Dyce;* Exit omnes. *Q1–2*
201 **Trust me**] By my Troth *Q1–2*
210 **him.**] *F4* (*subs.*); him, *F1*

IV.iii

Location: *Pope*
1 **Germans desire**] *Capell;* Germane desires *F1;* three Gentlemen *Q1–2*
7 **them**] *Q1–2;* him *F1*
9 **house**] *Q1–2;* houses *F1*

IV.iv

Location: *Pope*
7 **cold**] *Rowe;* gold *F1*
28 **Herne**] Horne *Q1–2* (*throughout; possibly, as in the Brook-Broom substitution, the original name*)
33 **makes**] *F2;* make *F1*
41 **device**] *F3;* deuise *F1*
42] *At this point Q1–2 explain why the meeting must take place in the park:* Now for that Falstaffe hath bene so deceiued, / As that he dares not venture to the house, / Weele send him word to meet vs in the field,
43 **Disguis'd . . . head.**] *Q1–2* (Disguised like Horne, with huge horns on his head,); *first inserted by Theobald, who also includes the preceding line* (Weele . . . field,); *Malone as here*
45 **shape**] *F2;* shape, *F1*
61 s.p. **Mrs. Ford.**] *Rowe;* Ford. *F1*
62 **him**] *F2;* him, *F1*
71 **My . . . fairies**] my daughter *Anne*, / Shall like a litle Fayrie be disguised *Q1–2* (*Page speaking*)
73 s.d. **Aside.**] *Pope*
81 s.d. **Exeunt . . . Evans.**] *Rowe*
83 **Quickly**] *Theobald;* quickly *F1* (*not in italics as a proper name*)
83 s.d. **Exit Mrs. Ford.**] *Rowe*
90 s.d. **Exit.**] *F2;* Exit omnes. *Q1–2*

IV.v

Location: *Pope*
o.s.d. **Enter Host and Simple.**] *Q1–2;* Enter Host, Simple, Falstaffe, Bardolfe, Euans, Caius, Quickly. *F1*
2 **thick-skin**] *hyphen, Q1–2*
19 s.d. **Above.**] *Theobald* (*from Q2* he speakes aboue.)
23 s.d. **Enter Falstaff.**] *Q1–2* (Enter Sir Iohn.; *after l. 25*); *placed as in Theobald*
44 s.p. **Sim.**] *Folger MS, Rowe;* Fal. *F1*
54 **Ay, sir; like**] *F1* (I Sir: like); I tike *Q1–2*
56 s.d. **Exit.**] *Q2*
57 **Thou art**] *Q1–2;* Thou are *F1*
58 **John. Was**] *Rowe* (*subs.*); Iohn) was *F1*
59 **Ay . . . was**] *F1* (I . . . was); Marry was there *Q1–2*
62 s.d. **Enter Bardolph.**] *Q1–2*
70 **Faustuses**] *F2;* Faustasses *F1*
72 s.d. **Enter Evans.**] *Q1–2; in Q1–2 the order of entry for Evans and Caius* (*see l. 82*) *is reversed*
77 **three cozen-germans**] three Cozen-Iermans *F1;* three sorts of cosen garmombles *Q1–2*
82 s.d. **Exit.**] *Q1–2*
82 s.d. **Enter Caius.**] *Q1–2* (Enter Doctor.)
87 **duke de Jamany**] Germaine Duke *Q1–2*
89 s.d. **Exit.**] *Q1–2*
90, 91 **Hue**] *Rowe;* Huy *F1*
92 s.d. **Exeunt . . . Bardolph.**] *Capell;* Exit. *Q1–2*
103 **to . . . prayers**] *Q1–2; first inserted, Pope*
103 s.d. **Enter Mistress Quickly.**] *Q1–2* (*after l. 104*); *placed as in Theobald*
117 **Brainford.**] *Theobald* (*subs.*); Brainford, *F1*

IV.vi

Location: *ed.* (*after Wilson*)
16–7 **Fat . . . scene.**] Wherein fat Falstaffe had a mightie scare, *Q1–2*
39 **denote**] *Capell;* deuote *F1*
41 **green**] red *Q1–2*

V.i

Scene om. Q1–2
Location: *ed.* (*after Wilson*)
o.s.d. **Enter . . . Quickly.**] *Rowe;* Enter Falstaffe, Quickly, and Ford. *F1*
8 s.d. **Exit Mrs. Quickly.**] *Rowe* (*after l. 7*); *placed as in Capell*
8 s.d. **Enter Ford disguised.**] *Dyce* (*after Rowe*)

V.ii

Scene om. Q1–2
Location: *Wilson*
3 **my daughter**] *F2;* my *F1*

V.iii

Scene om. Q1–2
Location: *ed.* (*after Pelican*)
6 s.d. **Exit Caius.**] *Rowe* (*after l. 6*); *placed as in Capell*
12 **Hugh**] *Capell;* Herne *F1*

V.iv

Scene om. Q1–2
Location: *Capell* (*after Pope*)
o.s.d. **like a satyr**] *Q1–2* (*see V.v.36 s.d. below*)
o.s.d. **others as**] *Capell* (*subs.*)

V.v

In Q1–2 the dialogue for this scene contains only occasional echoes of the F1 text and omits all reference to the Garter Feast and the Queen
Location: *ed.* (*after Wilson*)
o.s.d. **Enter . . . him.**] *Q1–2* (sir Iohn); Enter Falstaffe, Mistris Page, Mistris Ford, Euans, Anne Page, Fairies, Page, Ford, Quickly, Slender, Fenton, Caius, Pistoll. *F1*
1 **strook**] *Capell;* stroke *F1*
15 s.d. **Enter . . . Ford.**] *Q1–2*
20 **hail kissing-comfits**] *Rowe;* haile-kissing Comfits *F1*
21 s.d. **Embracing her.**] *Capell*
29 s.d. **There . . . horns.**] *Q1–2* (There is a noise of hornes, the two women run away.)
33 s.d. **The . . . away.**] *Q1–2* (*see preceding note*)
34–6 **I . . . thus.**] *as prose, Pope; as verse, F1*
36 s.d. **Enter . . . speak.**] *Q1–2* (*with addition*

of Anne Page [*ed.* (*after Alexander*)] *and* Pistol as Hobgoblin [*Dyce*]; Enter Fairies. *F1*

48 s.d. **Lies . . . face.]** *Rowe*

49–54 **Evans. Where's . . . shins.]** *Q1–2 assign Evans two speeches of direction to the "Fairies," one perhaps substituting for Pistol's speech (ll. 42–6); Pistol has no part in the Q1–2 scene: Sir Hu.* Come hither *Peane*, go to the countrie houses, / And when you finde a slut that lies a sleepe, / And all her dishes foule, and roome vnswept, / With your long nailes pinch her till she crie, / And sweare to mend her sluttish huswiferie. / *Fai.* I warrant you I will performe your will. / *Hu.* Where is [Wher's *Q2*] *Pead?* go you & see where Brokers sleep, / And Foxe-eyed Seriants with their mase, / Goe laie the Proctors in the street, / And pinch the lowsie Seriants face: / Spare none of these when they are [th' are *Q2*] a bed, / But such whose nose lookes plew and red.

62 **balm, . . . flow'r;]** *Rowe* (*subs.*); Balme; . . . flowre, *F1*

65 **nightly, meadow-fairies]** *Capell;* Nightly-meadow-Fairies *F1*

66–7 **ring. . . . bears,]** *Rowe* (*subs.*); ring, . . . beares: *F1*

68 **More]** *F2;* Mote *F1*

70 **em'rald tuffs]** *Kittredge* (tufts; *hyphen dropped, Capell*); Emrold-tuffes *F1*

71 **sapphire, pearl]** *Theobald;* Saphire-pearle *F1*

80 **middle-earth]** *hyphen, Dyce*

81 **Heavens defend]** God Blesse *Q1–2*

81–2 **Heavens . . . cheese!]** *as prose, Pope; as verse, F1*

84–102] *Cf. the Q1–2 version of these lines: Quic.* Looke euery one about this round. / And if that any here be found, / For his presumption in this place, / Spare neither legge, arme, head, nor face. / *Sir Hu.* See I haue spied one by good luck, / His bodie man, his head a buck. / *Fal.* God send me good fortune now, and I care not. / *Quic.* Go strait, and do as I command, / And take a Taper in your hand, / And set it to his fingers endes, / And if you see it him offends, / And that he starteth at the flame, / Then is he mortall, know his name: / If with an F. it doth begin, / Why then be shure he is [hee's *Q2*] full of sin. / About it then, and know the truth, / Of this same metamorphised [metamorphosed *Q2*] youth. / *Sir Hu.* Giue me the Tapers, I will try / And if that he loue venery. / *They put the Tapers* [*Torches Q2*] *to his fingers, and he starts.* / *Sir Hu.* It is [Tis *Q2*] right indeed, he is full of lecheries and iniquitie. / *Quic.* A little distant from him stand, / And euery one take hand in hand, / And compasse him within a ring, / First pinch him well, and after sing.

88 s.d. **They . . . starts.]** *Q1–2* (Torches *Q2*)

92] *Following this line Theobald inserts from Q1–2: Sir Hu.* It is [Tis *Q2*] right indeed, he is full of lecheries and iniquitie.

102 s.d. **Here . . . up.]** *Q1–2* (*with* green . . . white [*Theobald*] *substituted for Q1–2's* red . . . greene; *Q1–2 also describe Anne Page as* being in white)

102 s.d. **Enter . . . Ford.]**, *Capell* (*after Rowe*); And enters M. Page M. Ford, and their wiues, M. Shallow, and Sir Hugh. *Q1–2*

104 **Will . . . turn?]** *Q1–2 give Falstaff a speech which reads like an answer to this query: Fal.* Horne the hunter quoth you: am I a ghost? / Sblood the Fairies hath made a ghost of me: / What [What, *Q2*] hunting at this time at night? / Ile lay my life the mad Prince of *Wales* / Is stealing his fathers Deare. How now who haue / we here, what is all *Windsor* stirring? Are you there?

110 **Brook]** *Q1–2;* Broome *F1* (*throughout scene*)

169] *Following this line Theobald inserts from Q1–2: Mi. For.* Nay husband let that go to make amends, / Forgiue that sum, and so weele all be friends. / *For.* Well here is my hand, all's forgiuen at last.; *and Keightley adds also the following speech from Q1–2: Fal.* It hath cost me well, / I haue bene well pinched and washed.

174 s.d. **Aside.]** *Theobald*

176 s.d. **Enter Slender.]** *Q1–2; in Q1–2 the order of entry for Slender and Caius* (*see l. 203*) *is reversed*

182 **what,]** *F2;* what *F1*

197 **white]** *Rowe;* greene *F1;* red *Q1–2*

199] *Following this line Theobald inserts from Q1–2: Sir. Hu.* Ieshu M. *Slender*, cannot you see but marrie boyes? / *Pa.* O I am vext at hart, what shal I do?

201 **green]** *Rowe;* white *F1*

203 s.d. **Enter Caius.]** *Q1–2* (Enter the Doctor.)

208 **green]** *Pope;* white *F1*

209 **be-gar . . . Be-gar]** *hyphens, ed.*

210 s.d. **Exit.]** *Capell*

214 s.d. **Enter . . . Page.]** *Q1–2*

232 **state;]** *Rowe;* state, *F1*

236–8 **Well . . . chas'd.]** *as verse, Rowe* (*after F4*); *as prose, F1*

236–45] *Cf. the concluding lines in Q1–2: Mi. For.* Come mistris *Page*, Ile be bold with you, / Tis pitie to part loue that is so true. / *Mis. Pa.* Altho that I haue missed in my intent, / Yet I am glad my husbands match was crossed, / Here M. *Fenton*, take her, and God giue thee ioy. / *Sir. Hu:* Come M. *Page*, you must needs agree. / *Fo.* I yfaith [Ifaith *Q2*] sir come, you see your wife is wel [wel *om. Q2*] pleased: / *Pa.* I cannot tel, and yet my hart's well eased, / And yet it doth me good the Doctor missed. / Come hither *Fenton*, and come hither daughter, / Go too you might haue stai'd for my good will, / But since your choise is made of one you loue, / Here take her *Fenton*, & both happie proue. / *Sir. Hu.* I wil also [also *om. Q2*] dance & eat plums at your weddings. / *Ford.* All parties pleased, now let vs in to feast, / And laugh at *Slender*, and the Doctors ieast. / He hath got the maiden, each of you a boy / To waite vpon you, so God giue you ioy, / And sir *Iohn Falstaffe* now shal you keep your word, / For *Brooke* this night shall lye with mistris *Ford.* (*Pope first inserted Sir Hugh's* I wil . . . weddings. *after l. 237*)

243 **so. Sir John,]** *Theobald* (*subs.*); so (Sir *Iohn:*) *F1*

245 s.d. **Exeunt.]** Exeunt / FINIS. *F1;* Exit omnes. / FINIS. *Q1–2*

Much Ado about Nothing

WHEN BERLIOZ, in 1861, turned *Much Ado about Nothing* into an opera, he retitled it *Béatrice et Bénédict*. He omitted Don John entirely and replaced Dogberry and Verges with a comic musician named Somarone. Claudio, Hero, and Don Pedro he kept, but purely as the agents who trick Beatrice and Benedick into matrimony. In the opera, the course of Hero's and Claudio's love is quite smooth and, also, patently subordinate to the bickerings and dissension of the rival pair. Berlioz' emphasis on Beatrice and Benedick at the expense of what is, strictly speaking, the main plot of Shakespeare's comedy is familiar: a reflection of the way actors, audiences, and readers have tended to react for several hundred years. Even King Charles I, in his personal copy of Shakespeare's Second Folio, altered the play's title as Berlioz did, proclaiming his own interest in the witty lovers rather than their romantic opposites. Shakespeare himself cannot have been unaware of the disproportionate amount of interest generated by the subplot. More important, however, is the fact that he obviously meant each plot to interconnect with and gain interest from the other. Taken by itself, without the vital undercurrent of the Beatrice and Benedick story, the relationship between Hero and Claudio seems flat and thin. On the other hand, Beatrice and Benedick cannot really sustain the play by themselves. Musically splendid though it is, Berlioz' opera is nonetheless a demonstration of the extent to which their odd and intensely individual agreement is impoverished as soon as you separate it from that skein of villainy, deceit, and misunderstanding which Don Pedro's bastard brother weaves about the more conventional lovers in Shakespeare's comedy. A Beatrice who has no need to ask Benedick to "Kill Claudio" (IV.i.289), forcing him to choose abruptly between his old world of male friendships and the new world of love, cannot fully reveal either her own nature or the depth of her lover's commitment.

In its basic outline, the Hero and Claudio plot is of great age, tracing its ancestry back to the romance literature of ancient Greece. It seems, however, to have acquired an especial popularity during the Renaissance. In constructing his own version of this archetypal story of the lady falsely accused of unchastity, cast off by her lover, and after many vicissitudes restored to him again, Shakespeare probably had at least four non-dramatic variants of the tale somewhere in mind. Ariosto's account, in Canto V of *Orlando Furioso*, of how the Scottish princess Genevra was mistaken for her maid Dalinda, seen keeping a tryst with another man, and so abandoned by her own love Ariodante, would have been available to him in Sir John Harington's translation of 1591. He must also have known Spenser's sombre version, the story of Phedon, Claribell, and the false Philemon in Book II of *The Faerie Queene* (1590), as well as that of Timbreo and Fenicia in Bandello's twenty-second novella (1554), translated into French and adapted generally by Belleforest in his *Histoires Tragiques* of 1574. George Whetstone drew upon both Bandello and Ariosto in his related tale of Rinaldo and Giletta, included in his collection *The Rock of Regard* (1576). There were also several plays, in French, Latin, and Italian, based upon this plot. In 1585, an anonymous Elizabethan dramatist (possibly Anthony Munday) produced a version of the most famous of these, Pasqualigo's *Il Fedele* (1579), under the title *Fedele and Fortunio*. Shakespeare almost certainly knew this play.

Although the essential shape of the story remains the same through all these different tellings, it was in fact subject to variation and also to marked changes in interpretation. Usually, although by no means always, the villain of the piece is the lover's friend: a man treacherously in love with the lady himself who slanders her in order to break off the match. The injured heroine is commonly a fiancée, less usually a wife. In at least one version, that of Spenser, she does actually die. More often, her death is merely symbolic: the prelude to a joyous reunion with her lover, disabused at last of his belief that she was untrue. In a significant number of cases, the lover is blamed quite specifically for the ease with which he gave credence to the false report, and for yielding himself to jealousy without sifting the matter thoroughly. Most versions deal, to some extent, with a conflict between love and friendship in which the more fiery and irrational force of love overthrows not only a former bond of trust but the integrity of a personality.

In *Much Ado about Nothing* Shakespeare transferred the rivalry between love and friendship to a position slightly outside the main imbroglio. Don John, the source of a misunderstanding that comes close to being fatal, has no interest whatever in Hero herself. A man incapable of any genuine human relationship, he is not even Claudio's friend, let alone his rival in love. Don John is a malcontent pure and simple, a man who might say with the cold duke in Thurber's story *The Thirteen Clocks*: "We all have faults, and mine is doing wickedness." Certainly, Shakespeare makes no attempt to provide him with even the kind of fairy-tale motivation that Oliver has for practicing against the life of his younger brother in *As You Like It*. The fact that Don John was born a bastard becomes an all-sufficient explanation of why it is that he is treacherous, scheming, savage, and morose. A thing of darkness, out of step with his society, he hates the children of light simply because they generate radiance in a world he prefers to see dark. This is why he plans to wreck the intended marriage of Claudio and Hero. He has nothing to gain personally from such a tactic, except the pleasure of annoying his brother, grieving Claudio, turning laughter to tears, and reducing everyone around him to the state of misery and gloom in which he languishes himself. A plot mechanism more than a complex character in his own right, Don John appears in the play as a kind of anti-comic force, the official enemy of all happy endings.

Much Ado about Nothing represents a variant on the more usual Shakespearean comic pattern of a journey from an urban to a rural, an ordinary to a heightened world, and back again. All the action of the play takes place in Messina, but it is a town temporarily lifted out of its normal habits and atmosphere by the fact that it happens to be filled with glamorous strangers resting there for a time after a triumphant military campaign, and by the sense of gaiety and elation attendant upon a newly concluded peace. Don Pedro, the prince, comes from Aragon. Benedick hails from Padua, while Claudio is a Florentine. The three are old friends, however, as well as comrades in arms. Moreover, they are quite at home in Messina. Don Pedro has stayed with Leonato before. Claudio has an uncle in the town, and he had his eye on Hero before he went off to war. Beatrice and Benedick appear to have been insulting one another joyously for years.

In the Messina of the comedy, masked faces, revels, and dances are the order of the day. Apart from Dogberry and his associates, this is a courtly world enjoying a period of carnival. Some of the deceits, like the one that brings Beatrice and Benedick together, are harmless and even beneficent. Others are not. The general atmosphere, however, is conducive to eavesdropping, mistaken identity, game-playing, and conversations reported wrongly, even as it is to music, feasting, and marriage. Claudio's wooing of Hero seems almost like an expected and conventional response to the times: an acknowledgment that, when wars are over, it is advisable to begin replenishing a population diminished by bullets and swords. Certainly, Claudio's courtship of Hero is of the most formal and socially proper kind. He takes her wealth and position as Leonato's only child into careful account, seeks the advice and approbation of his prince before embarking on the match, and behaves in every way like a sober, prudent man contracting a dynastic alliance in which the charms of the lady matter, of course, but scarcely inspire in him the recklessness of a Romeo. A man does not allow his prince, however respected, to propose marriage for him in disguise unless he sees that marriage in social more than in personal terms. This, however, is what Claudio does. Only when Don Pedro has secured the consent of both the lady and her father does the prospective bridegroom speak to Hero himself. With the war happily ended, Claudio feels that the time is right for matrimony and for begetting an heir. His practicality in this respect is not exactly held against him, but it does explain the ease with which he believes Don John's slanders, and the unconsidered violence with which he shames Hero and casts her off. Essentially, Claudio is a man who thinks he has been duped in a bargain, not a Troilus whose whole world shatters around him because he has to recognize that the goddess of his idolatry is false.

Hero too is docile and passive. She welcomes the alliance with Claudio, but there is no suggestion that she has been pining with love for the young Florentine while he has been away at the war. When it is falsely reported that Don Pedro is interested in her himself, she seems entirely willing to accept the prince as a suitor, despite the discrepancy in their ages. Like Claudio, presumably, she thinks it is high time she got married. Beatrice tells her that she has a right to her own judgment in such matters (II.i.52–6) but Hero's will conforms entirely to her father's. Elizabethans must have detected a certain irony in the name Shakespeare bestowed upon this singularly dutiful daughter. In Greek mythology, Hero was the lady beloved of Leander, who broke her religious vows in order to enjoy a clandestine love affair with him. When, through the enmity of the gods, Leander was drowned while swimming the Hellespont one night to a secret meeting with her, Hero killed herself. Shakespeare knew Marlowe's great narrative poem on the subject and, in *As You Like It*, quoted a line from it: "Who ever lov'd that lov'd not at first sight?" It would be hard to imagine an attitude further away from the caution and circumspection of Claudio's Hero.

The affairs of these two lovers, often conducted through third parties, are inveterately public. The rupture between them, when it comes, is public too. Claudio denounces Hero in church, on their wedding day, before a crowd of people, and with the backing of the prince. Even Leonato, Hero's own father, is convinced. In the bitterest speech of the comedy, he begs his own child at least to have the decency to die, and tries to prevent anyone from reviving her. The friar has some difficulty in persuading him that this condemnation may be too hasty. Apart from the friar, only Beatrice and Benedick suspect, from the first, that Hero is really innocent and the prince and Claudio misled. Beatrice, in particular, reacts violently against Claudio's public denunciation of her cousin: "What, bear her in hand until they come to take hands, and then with public accusation, uncover'd slander, unmitigated rancor—O God, that I were a man! I would eat his heart in the market-place" (IV.i.303–7). Her indignation is, in a sense, just but it also serves to indicate the distance between her own intensely personal attachment to Benedick and the more formal, outward bond which unites Claudio and Hero. Claudio's atonement when the truth is known, even his reunion with Hero, are wholly consistent with the nature of this plot: his penitence before Hero's tomb in V.iii is again public, a ritual demonstration of sorrow, and he gets his lady back only because he agrees to ally himself, sight unseen, with another daughter of Leonato's house.

Much Ado about Nothing is usually dated 1598. There is no specific source for the Beatrice and Benedick underplot, but it is important to remember that several years earlier, in *The Taming of the Shrew*, Shakespeare had already experimented with the idea of an unconventional couple who arrive at love and understanding by way of insult and aggression. Like Katherina and Petruchio before them, Beatrice and Benedick use protestations of enmity and distaste to conceal a powerful, underlying attraction. There is a suggestion in the text that these "two bears" were once, at some indeterminate past time, in love with each other (II.i.280–82). Shakespeare does not say why the relationship broke down but, in the comedy itself, each one is obsessed with and continually talking about the other in a manner which makes it clear from the start that their animosity is a cloak for feelings of a very different kind. This is why they can be tricked with such ease. All that the conspirators have to do is to suggest to each that the other has yielded first, has taken the first step towards an admission and acknowledgment of love, and all defenses crumble. Both Beatrice and Benedick, for all their surface gaiety, their scorn of the married state, are essentially lonely people. They are older than Claudio and Hero, and in danger of finding themselves imprisoned for life within a set of attitudes and social responses which, though witty and amusing, are nonetheless inhibiting and sterile. Neither can break these self-imposed fetters without help from outside. When this help arrives, they turn joyously to one another with a freedom and a depth of engagement lacking in the relationship of Hero and Claudio.

In several important respects, Beatrice and Benedick are prototypes of the witty lovers in Restoration comedy: source characters for that impressive line of skirmishing gallants and ladies which extends from Etherege and the early comedies of Dryden to Congreve's Mirabell and Millamant in *The Way of the World*. Like their Restoration descendants, they converse by preference in prose: a prose sharply distinguished from the blank-verse rhapsodies of the younger pair of lovers. Their wit is imaginative and easy, but it is also analytic: a yoking together of judgment and fancy which, again, looks forward to the period of Charles II. Essentially, Beatrice and Benedick are—like Mirabell and Millamant, or Etherege's Dorimant and Harriet—romantics who need to keep this weakness dark. For all its surface aggression, its deflationary quality, their wit is really defensive: a way of protecting a self that they know to be vulnerable. Beatrice savages Benedick in public, and mocks him behind his back, because she cannot help thinking about him and needs to camouflage this interest. Benedick defends the bachelor state, inveighs against women and even against the courtly art of music, affecting a spirit of bluff, masculine camaraderie on all social occasions, in order to fend off alternative ways of thinking and feeling. Like Restoration lovers, Beatrice and Benedick use wit to distance emotions which they recognize as potentially dangerous. They cling to the society of their own sex because there they feel safe, but they cannot resist launching provocative shafts of ridicule or inquiry into the enemy's terrain.

Although Beatrice has no evidence to advance against the damning account of how Don Pedro, Don John and Claudio actually saw Hero talk with a ruffian at her chamber window after midnight, she never for an instant believes that her cousin is guilty. Her logic here is that of the instincts and the heart, but it happens to be entirely right. Benedick, understandably, is slower to commit himself to the defense of Hero, although from the first he is puzzled by the charge against her. He makes an important decision, however, when he does not leave the church with Claudio, Don Pedro, and the bastard, as might be expected. He chooses, instead, to remain behind with Hero, Leonato, the friar, and Beatrice. In doing so, he breaks with that little all-male society of soldiers which has hitherto claimed his allegiance. He behaves in this seemingly uncharacteristic fashion although he and Beatrice have not yet, in fact, reached an understanding, simply because he is beginning to see the world through different eyes. Leonato, in the last scene of all, will claim: "The sight whereof I think you had from me, / From Claudio, and the Prince" (V.iv.25–26). This is true, however, only in the sense that had it not been for the conspiracy, Benedick would never have been able to liberate and admit responses buried deep inside himself.

At the end of the play, Claudio and Don Pedro are still inflicting upon Benedick their somewhat heavy-handed badinage about "the savage bull" and "the married man." For them, the capitulation of the confirmed bachelor is primarily a matter for laughter and self-congratulation, even as it was in the first scene of Act V when, with Hero newly "dead," they indulged their "gossip-like humor" (V.i.186) on the same subject, in order to raise their spirits, and found Benedick icily still and unresponsive. There is no evil in Claudio and the prince, but there is something schoolboyish and immature. The flight of Don John from Messina, together with Borachio's confession of the plot against Hero, relieves Benedick of the necessity of turning his sword against his former friend, but it is important that he should have accepted Beatrice's passionate and impulsive commission. We in the audience never really believe that Benedick will "kill Claudio." Law and justice in Messina are, to put it mildly, inefficient, but it is nonetheless evident, even in the scene where the challenge is formally delivered, that Hero's innocence will shortly be vindicated without any help from Benedick. What his engagement in her cause demonstrates is the new priority in his life of love, and the extent to which this love supersedes and cancels out older ties. As for Beatrice, the woman who pretended, early in the comedy, that she could not imagine why anyone should think her life incomplete without a man, a mere "clod of wayward marl" (II.i.62–63), she finds herself in Act IV wishing no fewer than three times "that I were a man." Her appeal to Benedick to do what, as a woman, she cannot herself manage, and her gratitude to him, represent, on her part, as radical a transformation of attitude as does his challenge to Claudio.

Virtually all of Shakespeare's comedies involve some kind of confrontation with death before the characters are allowed to win through to the happiness of the final scene. *Much Ado about Nothing* enacts this movement through darkness to light in a particularly striking way. The penultimate scene takes place before the monument of Leonato, the supposed burial place of Hero. The characters involved all wear mourning and they carry tapers to lighten the gloom of the place. The scene occurs at night, but once the dirge for Hero has been sung, the sun rises at once.

> Good morrow, masters, put your torches out.
> The wolves have preyed, and look, the gentle day,
> Before the wheels of Phoebus, round about
> Dapples the drowsy east with spots of grey.
> (V.iii.24–27)

As an indication of the turning point of the comedy, the moment when it begins to move irreversibly towards joy, Don Pedro's description of the new dawn could scarcely be clearer in its effect. Yet there is a sense in which the threat of death and disaster in this play has never possessed the kind of seriousness or urgency which it has, for instance, in *The Merchant of Venice* or *Measure for Measure*. This is partly because the wickedness of Don John is so fantastic and oddly remote, and partly because it is no sooner committed than revealed. It is only a matter of time before someone more intelligent than Dogberry and his ancient and most quiet watch hears Borachio's confession and understands the truth.

A town which appears to manage quite nicely despite the fact that its police force spends its time on duty sleeping, and would require another police force to prevent its halberds from being stolen by frisky citizens, is scarcely a town where evil flourishes. The ineptitudes of Dogberry and his partner Verges are not merely funny in themselves: they reassure the theatre audience that comedy remains in control of the action, even when the potential for tragedy seems greatest. Dogberry's linguistic muddles are also important in the light of the play's treatment of language and the multiple meanings of words. When Beatrice, early in Act V, makes the word *foul* jump through an astonishing series of hoops as part of her teasing refusal to give Benedick a kiss, her lover complains: "Thou hast frighted the word out of his right sense, so forcible is thy wit" (V.ii.55–56). Benedick's comment is both rueful and admiring. Both he and Beatrice are adept at verbal game-playing, although her skill, arguably, is even greater than his. Certainly the wit of both is a conscious exploration of the resources and also the illogicalities of language. Dogberry too is a character who customarily frights words out of their proper meaning. In the course of the comedy, he contrives to strike terror into the words *redemption*, *excommunication*, *suspect*, *opinioned*, *tedious*, and *blunt*, to list only a few of his victims. He does so, of course, not because he is witty but because he is ignorant. A man with an exaggerated idea of his own merits and importance—"I am a wise fellow, and which is more, an officer, and which is more, a householder, and which is more, as pretty a piece of flesh as any is in Messina" (IV.ii.80–82)—he relies upon language to overawe and impress the people with whom he deals. To some extent, his verbal habits seem to have rubbed off on his associates: Verges gets himself into some terrible linguistic tangles, and even the watch, although content in general with the simplest kind of speech, run headlong into the word *deformed* as though it were a kind of brier-patch. Only Dogberry, however, consistently misemploys the grandest words he can think of as a way of magnifying himself.

Frequently, Dogberry lunges at a glittering and distant term and misses. The result is a glorious collection of non-words, bastard compounds which hover bewilderingly on the edge of sense: *decerns*, *suffigance*, *dissembly*, or *vigitant*. Verbal mistaking of this kind is associated, on the whole, only with the most dim-witted of Shakespeare's clowns. There is, nevertheless, something almost touching about Dogberry's unrequited passion for words in a play in which other characters possess a mastery of language that is positively dazzling. The suggestion that he is a man who "hath had losses" (IV.ii.84) is made only once, and not elaborated on by Shakespeare, but it is enough to explain the compulsion behind his speech style. Dogberry is a man who has, at some time in the past, suffered heavy financial and social setbacks. He has struggled onto his feet again, owns his own house, and has two gowns "and every thing handsome about him" (IV.ii.85–86), but the doubt and the insecurity remain and cannot be banished. This is why he deals so constantly in self-magnification, bullies Verges, and becomes positively obsessed with the fact that he has publicly been described as an ass. Words are his one defense against the possibility that he may be slighted or misprized by the world. He uses them to keep the reality of his self and his situation at bay. The activity is familiar. Beatrice and Benedick happen to be masters of a linguistic game whose first principles Dogberry has never been able to grasp, but for them too words have been a way of keeping people at a distance, of protecting and isolating a vulnerable inner self. Shakespeare never allows the paragons of wit to share a scene with the man who declares that "Comparisons are odorous" (III.v.16), but he makes it clear that, for all the surface dissimilarity, there is an affinity between them.

Anne Barton

Matrimony. From Cesare Ripa, *Iconologia* (1603). "In time the savage bull doth bear the yoke," quips Don Pedro, quoting inaccurately a line from Kyd's *Spanish Tragedy*, in answer to Benedick's vigorous flouting of the suggestion that he, too, will some day "look pale with love" and become a "married man" (*Much Ado*, I.i.245–68)—as, of course, he eventually does. Not only does the emblem above show the yoke, it includes also another common symbol of marriage—the clog, a heavy piece of wood attached to the leg or neck to prevent escape. Bertram makes the allusion clear when, as his wife Helena enters, he jibes: "Here comes my clog" (*All's Well*, II.v.53). (*By permission of the Harvard College Library*)

Much Ado about Nothing

[DRAMATIS PERSONAE

DON PEDRO, *Prince of Arragon*
DON JOHN, *his bastard brother*
CLAUDIO, *a young lord of Florence*
BENEDICK, *a young lord of Padua*
LEONATO, *governor of Messina*
ANTONIO, *his brother*
BALTHASAR, *attendant on Don Pedro*
CONRADE, BORACHIO } *followers of Don John*
FRIAR FRANCIS

DOGBERRY, *a constable*
VERGES, *a headborough*
SEXTON
BOY

HERO, *daughter to Leonato*
BEATRICE, *niece to Leonato*
MARGARET, URSULA } *gentlewomen attending on Hero*

MESSENGERS, WATCH, LORD, ATTENDANTS, *etc*

SCENE: *Messina*]

[ACT I, SCENE I]

Enter LEONATO, *governor of Messina*, HERO *his daughter, and* BEATRICE *his niece, with a* MESSENGER.

Leon. I learn in this letter that Don [Pedro] of Arragon comes this night to Messina.

Mess. He is very near by this, he was not three leagues off when I left him.

Leon. How many gentlemen have you lost in this action?

Mess. But few of any sort, and none of name.

Leon. A victory is twice itself when the achiever brings home full numbers. I find here that Don [Pedro] hath bestow'd much honor on a young Florentine call'd Claudio.

Mess. Much deserv'd on his part, and equally remembr'ed by Don Pedro. He hath borne himself beyond the promise of his age, doing in the figure of a lamb the feats of a lion. He hath indeed better bett'red expectation than you must expect of me to tell you how.

Leon. He hath an uncle here in Messina will be very much glad of it.

Mess. I have already deliver'd him letters, and there appears much joy in him, even so much that joy could not show itself modest enough without a badge of bitterness.

Leon. Did he break out into tears?

Mess. In great measure.

Leon. A kind overflow of kindness. There are no faces truer than those that are so wash'd. How much better is it to weep at joy than to joy at weeping!

Beat. I pray you, is Signior Mountanto return'd from the wars or no?

Mess. I know none of that name, lady. There was none such in the army of any sort.

Leon. What is he that you ask for, niece?

Hero. My cousin means Signior Benedick of Padua.

Mess. O, he's return'd, and as pleasant as ever he was.

Beat. He set up his bills here in Messina, and challeng'd Cupid at the flight, and my uncle's fool, reading the challenge, subscrib'd for Cupid, and challeng'd him at the burbolt. I pray you, how

Words and passages enclosed in square brackets in the text above are either emendations of the copy-text or additions to it. The Textual Notes immediately following the play cite the earliest authority for every such change or insertion and supply the reading of the copy-text wherever it is emended in this edition.

I.i. Location: Messina. Before Leonato's house.
6. **action**: battle.
7. **sort**: rank (so also in line 33). **name**: reputation, prominence.
14. **figure**: appearance. 16. **bett'red**: surpassed.
18. **will**: who will (a frequent construction).
22. **modest**: moderate.
23. **badge of bitterness**: sign of sorrow. Leonato's next question translates these words into literal terms. 26. **kind**: natural.
30. **Mountanto**. From Italian *montanto*, a fencing term meaning an upward blow or thrust. 37. **pleasant**: jocular.
39. **bills**: public notices.
40. **at the flight**: to an archery contest. Perhaps she means that Benedick proclaimed himself immune to love.
41. **fool**: jester. It has been suggested that perhaps Beatrice means herself, and is referring obliquely to an earlier romantic encounter with Benedick. See lines 61–64 and II.i.278–82. **subscrib'd for**: made an undertaking on behalf of.
42. **burbolt**: bird-bolt, a blunt-headed arrow for shooting birds at short distance. The bird-bolt was allowed to fools and children as being less dangerous than the barbed long-distance arrow, and was frequently assigned to Cupid, perhaps because he was represented as a child.

many hath he kill'd and eaten in these wars? But how many hath he kill'd? for indeed I promis'd to eat all of his killing.

Leon. Faith, niece, you tax Signior Benedick too much, but he'll be meet with you, I doubt it not.

Mess. He hath done good service, lady, in these wars.

Beat. You had musty victual, and he hath holp to eat it. He is a very valiant trencherman, he hath an excellent stomach.

Mess. And a good soldier too, lady.

Beat. And a good soldier to a lady, but what is he to a lord?

Mess. A lord to a lord, a man to a man, stuff'd with all honorable virtues.

Beat. It is so indeed, he is no less than a stuff'd man. But for the stuffing—well, we are all mortal.

Leon. You must not, sir, mistake my niece. There is a kind of merry war betwixt Signior Benedick and her; they never meet but there's a skirmish of wit between them.

Beat. Alas, he gets nothing by that. In our last conflict four of his five wits went halting off, and now is the whole man govern'd with one; so that if he have wit enough to keep himself warm, let him bear it for a difference between himself and his horse, for it is all the wealth that he hath left to be known a reasonable creature. Who is his companion now? he hath every month a new sworn brother.

Mess. Is't possible?

Beat. Very easily possible. He wears his faith but as the fashion of his hat: it ever changes with the next block.

Mess. I see, lady, the gentleman is not in your books.

Beat. No, and he were, I would burn my study. But I pray you, who is his companion? Is there no young squarer now that will make a voyage with him to the devil?

Mess. He is most in the company of the right noble Claudio.

Beat. O Lord, he will hang upon him like a disease; he is sooner caught than the pestilence, and the taker runs presently mad. God help the noble Claudio! If he have caught the Benedick, it will cost him a thousand pound ere 'a be cur'd.

Mess. I will hold friends with you, lady.

Beat. Do, good friend.

Leon. You will never run mad, niece.

Beat. No, not till a hot January.

Mess. Don Pedro is approach'd.

Enter Don Pedro, Claudio, Benedick, Balthasar, *and* [Don] John *the Bastard.*

D. Pedro. Good Signior Leonato, are you come to meet your trouble? The fashion of the world is to avoid cost, and you encounter it.

Leon. Never came trouble to my house in the likeness of your Grace, for trouble being gone, comfort should remain; but when you depart from me, sorrow abides and happiness takes his leave.

D. Pedro. You embrace your charge too willingly. I think this is your daughter.

Leon. Her mother hath many times told me so.

Bene. Were you in doubt, sir, that you ask'd her?

Leon. Signior Benedick, no, for then were you a child.

D. Pedro. You have it full, Benedick. We may guess by this what you are, being a man. Truly the lady fathers herself. Be happy, lady, for you are like an honorable father.

Bene. If Signior Leonato be her father, she would not have his head on her shoulders for all Messina, as like him as she is.

Beat. I wonder that you will still be talking, Signior Benedick, nobody marks you.

Bene. What, my dear Lady Disdain! are you yet living?

Beat. Is it possible disdain should die while she hath such meet food to feed it as Signior Benedick? Courtesy itself must convert to disdain, if you come in her presence.

Bene. Then is courtesy a turncoat. But it is certain I am lov'd of all ladies, only you excepted; and I would I could find in my heart that I had not a hard heart, for truly I love none.

Beat. A dear happiness to women, they would else have been troubled with a pernicious suitor. I thank God and my cold blood, I am of your humor for that: I had rather hear my dog bark at a crow than a man swear he loves me.

Bene. God keep your ladyship still in that mind! so some gentleman or other shall scape a predestinate scratch'd face.

Beat. Scratching could not make it worse, and 'twere such a face as yours were.

44–45. promis'd . . . killing: i.e. predicted that he wouldn't kill anyone. **46. tax:** take to task, censure. **47. meet:** even, quits. **50. musty:** stale. **holp:** helped. **51. trencherman:** good eater. **52. stomach:** appetite. **54. to:** in comparison with. **58–59. stuff'd man:** i.e. a dummy, not a real man. **59–60. for . . . mortal:** as for his character—well, we all have our faults. **66. five wits.** Usually listed as memory, fantasy, judgment, imagination, and common wit. **halting:** limping. **68. wit . . . warm.** Proverbial for minimal intelligence. **69. difference:** a variation in a coat of arms to distinguish a junior member or branch of a family from the chief line. **71. known:** recognized as. **72–73. sworn brother:** friend with whom he has exchanged vows of lifelong fidelity. **75. faith:** loyalty. **77. block:** wooden mould for shaping hats; hence, fashion. **79. books:** i.e. good books, favor. **80. and:** if. **82. squarer:** quarreller. **88. presently:** immediately. **90. 'a:** he.

91. hold friends: keep on friendly terms (so as not to incur your wrath). **93. run mad:** i.e. "catch the Benedick." **98. cost:** expense. **encounter:** go to meet. **103. embrace your charge:** welcome your burden. **109. have it full:** are well answered, have got back as good as you gave. **111. fathers herself:** shows who her father is (by her resemblance to him). **114. his head:** i.e. with its marks of age. **116. still:** always. **122. convert:** change. **128. dear happiness:** great stroke of good fortune. **131. humor for that:** inclination in that respect. **134. scape:** escape. **134–35. predestinate:** foreordained, inevitable (for anyone who marries Beatrice). **137. were:** i.e. is (the verb has been attracted into the subjunctive by the preceding *'twere*).

Bene. Well, you are a rare parrot-teacher.

Beat. A bird of my tongue is better than a beast of yours.

Bene. I would my horse had the speed of your tongue, and so good a continuer. But keep your way a' God's name, I have done.

Beat. You always end with a jade's trick, I know you of old.

D. Pedro. That is the sum of all: Leonato—Signior Claudio and Signior Benedick—my dear friend Leonato hath invited you all. I tell him we shall stay here at the least a month, and he heartily prays some occasion may detain us longer. I dare swear he is no hypocrite, but prays from his heart.

Leon. If you swear, my lord, you shall not be forsworn. [*To Don John*.] Let me bid you welcome, my lord, being reconcil'd to the Prince your brother: I owe you all duty.

D. John. I thank you. I am not of many words, but I thank you.

Leon. Please it your Grace lead on?

D. Pedro. Your hand, Leonato, we will go together. *Exeunt. Manent Benedick and Claudio.*

Claud. Benedick, didst thou note the daughter of Signior Leonato?

Bene. I noted her not, but I look'd on her.

Claud. Is she not a modest young lady?

Bene. Do you question me, as an honest man should do, for my simple true judgment? or would you have me speak after my custom, as being a profess'd tyrant to their sex?

Claud. No, I pray thee speak in sober judgment.

Bene. Why, i' faith, methinks she's too low for a high praise, too brown for a fair praise, and too little for a great praise; only this commendation I can afford her, that were she other than she is, she were unhandsome, and being no other but as she is, I do not like her.

Claud. Thou thinkest I am in sport. I pray thee tell me truly how thou lik'st her.

Bene. Would you buy her, that you inquire after her?

Claud. Can the world buy such a jewel?

Bene. Yea, and a case to put it into. But speak you this with a sad brow? or do you play the flouting Jack, to tell us Cupid is a good hare-finder and Vulcan a rare carpenter? Come, in what key shall a man take you to go in the song?

Claud. In mine eye, she is the sweetest lady that ever I look'd on.

Bene. I can see yet without spectacles, and I see no such matter. There's her cousin, and she were not possess'd with a fury, exceeds her as much in beauty as the first of May doth the last of December. But I hope you have no intent to turn husband, have you?

Claud. I would scarce trust myself, though I had sworn the contrary, if Hero would be my wife.

Bene. Is't come to this? In faith, hath not the world one man but he will wear his cap with suspicion? Shall I never see a bachelor of threescore again? Go to, i' faith, and thou wilt needs thrust thy neck into a yoke, wear the print of it, and sigh away Sundays. Look, Don Pedro is return'd to seek you.

Enter Don Pedro.

D. Pedro. What secret hath held you here, that you follow'd not to Leonato's?

Bene. I would your Grace would constrain me to tell.

D. Pedro. I charge thee on thy allegiance.

Bene. You hear, Count Claudio, I can be secret as a dumb man; I would have you think so; but on my allegiance, mark you this, on my allegiance, he is in love. With who? Now that is your Grace's part. Mark how short his answer is: with Hero, Leonato's short daughter.

Claud. If this were so, so were it utt'red.

Bene. Like the old tale, my lord: "It is not so, nor 'twas not so, but indeed, God forbid it should be so."

Claud. If my passion change not shortly, God forbid it should be otherwise.

D. Pedro. Amen, if you love her, for the lady is very well worthy.

Claud. You speak this to fetch me in, my lord.

D. Pedro. By my troth, I speak my thought.

Claud. And in faith, my lord, I spoke mine.

Bene. And by my two faiths and troths, my lord, I spoke mine.

Claud. That I love her, I feel.

D. Pedro. That she is worthy, I know.

Bene. That I neither feel how she should be lov'd, nor know how she should be worthy, is the opinion that fire cannot melt out of me; I will die in it at the stake.

D. Pedro. Thou wast ever an obstinate heretic in the despite of beauty.

138. **rare**: excellent. **parrot-teacher**: i.e. one who says the same thing over and over.
139–40. **A bird . . . yours**: i.e. a bird taught to speak like me would be better than an animal taught to speak like you, for he would say nothing. 142. **so . . . continuer**: (were) so tireless.
144. **jade's trick.** A jade is an ill-conditioned horse, likely to drop out of a race before the end, as Benedick here lamely drops out of the contest of wits.
146. **That . . . all.** Don Pedro and Leonato have been conversing aside.
155. **being**: since you are.
164. **noted her not**: didn't observe her in particular.
169. **tyrant**: one pitiless and cruel. 171. **low**: short.
183. **sad**: serious. 183–84. **flouting Jack**: mocking fellow.
184–85. **to . . . carpenter**: i.e. by saying something as obviously wide of the truth as that Cupid has sharp eyes, or calling Vulcan a carpenter. (Cupid was blind, Vulcan the blacksmith of the gods.)
186. **go . . . song**: sing in harmony with you.

198–99. **wear . . . suspicion.** An allusion to the popular jest that a cuckold (husband of an unfaithful wife) grew horns.
202. **Sundays**: i.e. the day a husband would be expected to spend with his wife.
213. **part**: speaking part (namely, to ask "With who?").
215. **If . . . utt'red**: i.e. if it were true and I had told him so in confidence, he would have violated my confidence in just this manner.
216. **old tale.** Apparently some form of the Bluebeard story. In an eighteenth-century version cited by Furness, a lady who has discovered the bodies of the victims describes her experience, under the fiction that she is recalling a dream, and at intervals the murderer, who is among the listeners, interjects the words here quoted.
223. **fetch me in**: trick me, take me in.
235. **despite**: despising, contempt.

Claud. And never could maintain his part but in the force of his will.

Bene. That a woman conceiv'd me, I thank her; that she brought me up, I likewise give her most humble thanks; but that I will have a rechate winded in my forehead, or hang my bugle in an invisible baldrick, all women shall pardon me. Because I will not do them the wrong to mistrust any, I will do myself the right to trust none; and the fine is (for the which I may go the finer), I will live a bachelor.

D. Pedro. I shall see thee, ere I die, look pale with love.

Bene. With anger, with sickness, or with hunger, my lord, not with love. Prove that ever I lose more blood with love than I will get again with drinking, pick out mine eyes with a ballad-maker's pen, and hang me up at the door of a brothel-house for the sign of blind Cupid.

D. Pedro. Well, if ever thou dost fall from this faith, thou wilt prove a notable argument.

Bene. If I do, hang me in a bottle like a cat, and shoot at me, and he that hits me, let him be clapp'd on the shoulder, and call'd Adam.

D. Pedro. Well, as time shall try:
"In time the savage bull doth bear the yoke."

Bene. The savage bull may, but if ever the sensible Benedick bear it, pluck off the bull's horns, and set them in my forehead, and let me be vildly painted, and in such great letters as they write "Here is good horse to hire," let them signify under my sign, "Here you may see Benedick the married man."

Claud. If this should ever happen, thou wouldst be horn-mad.

D. Pedro. Nay, if Cupid have not spent all his quiver in Venice, thou wilt quake for this shortly.

Bene. I look for an earthquake too then.

D. Pedro. Well, you will temporize with the hours. In the mean time, good Signior Benedick, repair to Leonato's, commend me to him, and tell him I will not fail him at supper, for indeed he hath made great preparation.

Bene. I have almost matter enough in me for such an embassage, and so I commit you—

Claud. To the tuition of God. From my house—if I had it—

D. Pedro. The sixt of July. Your loving friend, Benedick.

Bene. Nay, mock not, mock not. The body of your discourse is sometime guarded with fragments, and the guards are but slightly basted on neither. Ere you flout old ends any further, examine your conscience, and so I leave you. *Exit.*

Claud. My liege, your Highness now may do me good.

D. Pedro. My love is thine to teach; teach it but how,
And thou shalt see how apt it is to learn
Any hard lesson that may do thee good.

Claud. Hath Leonato any son, my lord?

D. Pedro. No child but Hero, she's his only heir.
Dost thou affect her, Claudio?

Claud. O my lord,
When you went onward on this ended action,
I look'd upon her with a soldier's eye,
That lik'd, but had a rougher task in hand
Than to drive liking to the name of love.
But now I am return'd, and that war-thoughts
Have left their places vacant, in their rooms
Come thronging soft and delicate desires,
All prompting me how fair young Hero is,
Saying I lik'd her ere I went to wars.

D. Pedro. Thou wilt be like a lover presently,
And tire the hearer with a book of words.
If thou dost love fair Hero, cherish it,
And I will break with her, and with her father,
And thou shalt have her. Was't not to this end
That thou began'st to twist so fine a story?

Claud. How sweetly you do minister to love,
That know love's grief by his complexion!
But lest my liking might too sudden seem,
I would have salv'd it with a longer treatise.

236–37. **in . . . will:** i.e. by willful obstinacy (not by rational argument). Willful adherence to heterodox opinion was the essential element of heresy.
240–41. **that . . . forehead:** i.e. that I should wear a cuckold's horns. A rechate (or recheat) is a series of notes sounded (*winded*) on the horn for calling the hounds together.
241–42. **hang . . . baldrick:** i.e. carry my horn not in the usual place on the usual strap (*baldrick*) but where no strap is seen (because none is present)—on my forehead.
242. **shall pardon me:** must excuse me from. 245. **fine:** end.
250. **Prove:** if you can show.
250–52. **I . . . drinking.** It was a common belief that sighing (characteristic of lovers) consumed the blood, but that wine generated fresh blood. 252. **a ballad-maker's pen.** An instrument of satire.
254. **sign.** Inns, shops, etc. were identified by painted signs.
256. **notable argument:** outstanding example in discussions of the topic.
257. **bottle:** wicker case. Sometimes a cat was suspended in such a container as a target for archers.
259. **Adam.** Probably an allusion to Adam Bell, an archer celebrated in ballads for his skill. 260. **try:** test, show.
261. **In . . . yoke.** Inaccurately quoted from Kyd's *The Spanish Tragedy*, II.i.3.
262–63. **sensible:** rational. 264. **vildly:** vilely, wretchedly.
270. **horn-mad:** mad as a horned beast, stark mad (with the common allusion to cuckold's horns).
271–72. **spent . . . quiver:** used up all his arrows (with play following on *quiver* = tremble).
272. **Venice.** Noted at the time for its licentiousness.
273. **I . . . too:** i.e. it will take an earthquake as well.
274. **temporize:** come to terms, compromise.
276. **commend me:** present my compliments.
279. **matter:** substance, i.e. intelligence.
280. **and . . . you.** A conventional form of words which Claudio and Don Pedro jeer at by extending it into a stock complimentary closing for a letter.
281. **tuition:** protection. 283. **sixt:** sixth.
286. **guarded with fragments:** trimmed with odds and ends (a metaphor from dressmaking, looking back to *body* in the sense "bodice," and continued in *basted on*; but suggesting also that Don Pedro can guard his serious concerns from exposure by talking inanities when it suits him).
287. **the guards . . . neither:** the trimmings are very insecurely stitched on too (i.e. they have little connection with what is being said).
288. **flout:** mock, jeer at. **old ends:** (1) old tags (= the *fragments* of line 286); (2) conventional closings (of letters).
288–89. **examine your conscience:** i.e. consider whether you have ever been guilty of the same thing. 296. **affect:** love.
297. **ended action:** campaign now ended. 301. **now I:** now that I.
306. **presently:** any moment now.
307. **book of words:** whole book of lover's set speeches.
309. **break with:** broach the subject to.
311. **twist:** spin. 313. **his complexion:** its outward appearance.
315. **salv'd:** smoothed, i.e. put a better face on. **treatise:** discourse.

D. Pedro. What need the bridge much broader than the flood?
The fairest grant is the necessity.
Look what will serve is fit: 'tis once, thou lovest,
And I will fit thee with the remedy.
I know we shall have revelling to-night;
I will assume thy part in some disguise,
And tell fair Hero I am Claudio,
And in her bosom I'll unclasp my heart,
And take her hearing prisoner with the force
And strong encounter of my amorous tale;
Then after to her father will I break,
And the conclusion is, she shall be thine.
In practice let us put it presently. *Exeunt.*

[SCENE II]

Enter LEONATO *and an old man* [ANTONIO], *brother to Leonato,* [*meeting*].

Leon. How now, brother, where is my cousin, your son? Hath he provided this music?

Ant. He is very busy about it. But, brother, I can tell you strange news that you yet dreamt not of.

Leon. Are they good?

Ant. As the [event] stamps them, but they have a good cover; they show well outward. The Prince and Count Claudio, walking in a thick-pleach'd alley in mine orchard, were thus much overheard by a man of mine. The Prince discover'd to Claudio that he lov'd my niece your daughter, and meant to acknowledge it this night in a dance; and if he found her accordant, he meant to take the present time by the top, and instantly break with you of it.

Leon. Hath the fellow any wit that told you this?

Ant. A good sharp fellow. I will send for him, and question him yourself.

Leon. No, no, we will hold it as a dream till it appear itself; but I will acquaint my daughter withal, that she may be the better prepar'd for an answer, if peradventure this be true. Go you and tell her of it. [*Several persons cross the stage.*] Cousins, you know what you have to do. O, I cry you mercy, friend, go you with me, and I will use your skill. Good cousin, have a care this busy time. *Exeunt.*

[SCENE III]

Enter [DON] JOHN *the Bastard and* CONRADE, *his companion.*

Con. What the good-year, my lord, why are you thus out of measure sad?

D. John. There is no measure in the occasion that breeds, therefore the sadness is without limit.

Con. You should hear reason.

D. John. And when I have heard it, what blessing brings it?

Con. If not a present remedy, at least a patient sufferance.

D. John. I wonder that thou (being, as thou say'st thou art, born under Saturn) goest about to apply a moral medicine to a mortifying mischief. I cannot hide what I am: I must be sad when I have cause, and smile at no man's jests; eat when I have stomach, and wait for no man's leisure; sleep when I am drowsy, and tend on no man's business; laugh when I am merry, and claw no man in his humor.

Con. Yea, but you must not make the full show of this till you may do it without controlment. You have of late stood out against your brother, and he hath ta'en you newly into his grace, where it is impossible you should take true root but by the fair weather that you make yourself. It is needful that you frame the season for your own harvest.

D. John. I had rather be a canker in a hedge than a rose in his grace, and it better fits my blood to be disdain'd of all than to fashion a carriage to rob love from any. In this (though I cannot be said to be a flattering honest man) it must not be denied but I am a plain-dealing villain. I am trusted with a muzzle, and enfranchis'd with a clog, therefore I have decreed not to sing in my cage. If I had my mouth, I would bite; if I had my liberty, I would do my liking. In the mean time let me be that I am, and seek not to alter me.

Con. Can you make no use of your discontent?

D. John. I make all use of it, for I use it only. Who comes here?

Enter BORACHIO.

317. The fairest . . . necessity: the best gift is the one that fills the need of the occasion.
318. Look what: whatever. **'tis once:** i.e. the simple fact is.
323. in . . . unclasp: to her private hearing I'll disclose the contents (*unclasp* = open the book) of.

I.ii. Location: Leonato's house.
1. cousin. Used of aunt, uncle, niece, or nephew, as well as of cousin in the modern sense. **7. event:** outcome.
7–8. stamps . . . cover. Antonio uses the figure of news printed and bound in a book.
9–10. thick-pleach'd alley: walk bordered with bushes or small trees and overarched with their densely entwined boughs.
10. orchard: garden. **11. discover'd:** revealed.
14. accordant: consenting. **15. top:** forelock.
17. wit: intelligence.
21. appear itself: make itself evident (as a face). **withal:** with it.
25. cry you mercy: beg your pardon.

I.iii. Location: Leonato's house.
1. What the good-year. An unexplained expletive.
2. out of measure: immoderately. **4. breeds:** causes it
5. hear: listen to. **8. present:** immediate.
9. sufferance: endurance.
11. born under Saturn: born when the planet Saturn was predominant, hence supposedly morose (cf. *saturnine*).
11–12. goest . . . mischief: dost endeavor to cure a deadly ill by means of moralizing platitudes.
16. tend on: attend to. **17. claw:** flatter, humor.
18. humor: whims. **20. controlment:** restraint.
21. stood out: rebelled. **22. grace:** favor. **25. frame:** create.
27. canker: wild rose (considered a weed).
28. blood: mood, temper.
29. fashion a carriage: counterfeit a behavior.
32–33. trusted . . . muzzle: trusted as a muzzled dog is trusted, i.e. not trusted at all.
33. enfranchis'd: given my freedom. **clog:** a heavy block of wood attached to an animal to restrict its movement.
34. decreed: made up my mind.
40 s.d. Borachio. Spanish *borracho* means "drunkard."

What news, Borachio?

Bora. I came yonder from a great supper. The Prince your brother is royally entertain'd by Leonato, and I can give you intelligence of an intended marriage.

D. John. Will it serve for any model to build mischief on? What is he for a fool that betroths himself to unquietness?

Bora. Marry, it is your brother's right hand.

D. John. Who, the most exquisite Claudio?

Bora. Even he.

D. John. A proper squire! And who, and who? which way looks he?

Bora. Marry, one Hero, the daughter and heir of Leonato.

D. John. A very forward March-chick! How came you to this?

Bora. Being entertain'd for a perfumer, as I was smoking a musty room, comes me the Prince and Claudio, hand in hand in sad conference. I whipt me behind the arras, and there heard it agreed upon that the Prince should woo Hero for himself, and having obtain'd her, give her to Count Claudio.

D. John. Come, come, let us thither, this may prove food to my displeasure. That young start-up hath all the glory of my overthrow. If I can cross him any way, I bless myself every way. You are both sure, and will assist me?

Con. To the death, my lord.

D. John. Let us to the great supper, their cheer is the greater that I am subdu'd. Would the cook were a' my mind! Shall we go prove what's to be done?

Bora. We'll wait upon your lordship. *Exeunt.*

[ACT II, SCENE I]

Enter LEONATO, [ANTONIO] *his brother*, HERO *his daughter, and* BEATRICE *his niece*, [MARGARET, URSULA,] *and a* KINSMAN.

Leon. Was not Count John here at supper?

Ant. I saw him not.

Beat. How tartly that gentleman looks! I never can see him but I am heart-burn'd an hour after.

Hero. He is of a very melancholy disposition.

Beat. He were an excellent man that were made just in the midway between him and Benedick: the one is too like an image and says nothing, and the other too like my lady's eldest son, evermore tattling.

Leon. Then half Signior Benedick's tongue in Count John's mouth, and half Count John's melancholy in Signior Benedick's face—

Beat. With a good leg and a good foot, uncle, and money enough in his purse, such a man would win any woman in the world, if 'a could get her good will.

Leon. By my troth, niece, thou wilt never get thee a husband, if thou be so shrewd of thy tongue.

Ant. In faith, she's too curst.

Beat. Too curst is more than curst. I shall lessen God's sending that way, for it is said, "God sends a curst cow short horns"—but to a cow too curst he sends none.

Leon. So, by being too curst, God will send you no horns.

Beat. Just, if he send me no husband, for the which blessing I am at him upon my knees every morning and evening. Lord, I could not endure a husband with a beard on his face, I had rather lie in the woollen!

Leon. You may light on a husband that hath no beard.

Beat. What should I do with him? dress him in my apparel and make him my waiting-gentlewoman? He that hath a beard is more than a youth, and he that hath no beard is less than a man; and he that is more than a youth is not for me, and he that is less than a man, I am not for him; therefore I will even take sixpence in earnest of the berrord, and lead his apes into hell.

Leon. Well then, go you into hell.

Beat. No, but to the gate, and there will the devil meet me like an old cuckold with horns on his head, and say, "Get you to heaven, Beatrice, get you to heaven, here's no place for you maids." So deliver I up my apes, and away to Saint Peter. For the heavens, he shows me where the bachelors sit, and there live we as merry as the day is long.

Ant. [*To Hero.*] Well, niece, I trust you will be rul'd by your father.

Beat. Yes, faith, it is my cousin's duty to make cur'sy and say, "Father, as it please you." But yet for all that, cousin, let him be a handsome fellow, or else make another cur'sy and say, "Father, as it please me."

Leon. Well, niece, I hope to see you one day fitted with a husband.

47. What . . . fool: what kind of fool is he.
49. Marry: indeed (originally the name of the Virgin Mary used as an oath).
52. proper squire: handsome young fellow (spoken sneeringly).
56. forward: precocious. **March-chick:** chick which has hatched prematurely. **58. entertain'd for:** hired as.
59. smoking: refreshing the air of (by burning some aromatic substance). **60. sad:** serious. **61. arras:** tapestry wall-hanging.
66. displeasure: anger, hatred. **start-up:** upstart.
67. cross: thwart (with following quibble on the sense "make the sign of the cross"). **69. sure:** loyal, to be counted on.
73. prove: try, discover. **75. wait upon:** attend.

II.i. Location: Leonato's house.
3. tartly. Modern idiom would require the adjectival form.
4. am heart-burn'd: suffer from heartburn (caused by Don John's sour looks).

9. my . . . son: i.e. a spoiled child. **19. shrewd:** sharp, satirical.
20. curst: ill-tempered; here, sharp-tongued; in line 23, vicious, savage.
27. Just: precisely, just so. **if . . . husband.** She implies that God, in sending her a husband, would also send horns—i.e. that her husband would certainly be a cuckold.
30–31. in the woollen: between woollen blankets, without sheets.
40. in earnest: as advance payment. **berrord:** bear-ward, one who keeps and trains bears (and sometimes apes).
41. lead . . . hell. The proverbial fate of old maids.
48. For the heavens: so far as heaven is concerned. **bachelors:** unmarried persons of either sex. **53. cur'sy:** curtsy.

Beat. Not till God make men of some other mettle than earth. Would it not grieve a woman to be overmaster'd with a piece of valiant dust? to make an account of her life to a clod of wayward marl? No, uncle, I'll none. Adam's sons are my brethren, and truly I hold it a sin to match in my kinred.

Leon. Daughter, remember what I told you. If the Prince do solicit you in that kind, you know your answer.

Beat. The fault will be in the music, cousin, if you be not woo'd in good time. If the Prince be too important, tell him there is measure in every thing, and so dance out the answer. For hear me, Hero: wooing, wedding, and repenting, is as a Scotch jig, a measure, and a cinquepace; the first suit is hot and hasty, like a Scotch jig, and full as fantastical; the wedding, mannerly-modest, as a measure, full of state and ancientry; and then comes repentance, and with his bad legs falls into the cinquepace faster and faster, till he sink into his grave.

Leon. Cousin, you apprehend passing shrewdly.

Beat. I have a good eye, uncle, I can see a church by daylight.

Leon. The revellers are ent'ring, brother, make good room. [*They put on their masks.*]

Enter Prince [Don] Pedro, Claudio, *and* Benedick, *and* [Don] John, [*and* Borachio *as maskers, with a Drum*].

D. Pedro. Lady, will you walk about with your friend?

Hero. So you walk softly, and look sweetly, and say nothing, I am yours for the walk, and especially when I walk away.

D. Pedro. With me in your company?

Hero. I may say so when I please.

D. Pedro. And when please you to say so?

Hero. When I like your favor, for God defend the lute should be like the case!

D. Pedro. My visor is Philemon's roof, within the house is Jove.

Hero. Why then your visor should be thatch'd.

D. Pedro. Speak low if you speak love. [*They move aside.*]

[*Bora.*] Well, I would you did like me.

Marg. So would not I for your own sake, for I have many ill qualities.

[*Bora.*] Which is one?

Marg. I say my prayers aloud.

[*Bora.*] I love you the better; the hearers may cry amen.

Marg. God match me with a good dancer!

[*Bora.*] Amen.

Marg. And God keep him out of my sight when the dance is done! Answer, clerk.

[*Bora.*] No more words; the clerk is answer'd. [*They move aside.*]

Urs. I know you well enough, you are Signior Antonio.

Ant. At a word, I am not.

Urs. I know you by the waggling of your head.

Ant. To tell you true, I counterfeit him.

Urs. You could never do him so ill-well, unless you were the very man. Here's his dry hand up and down. You are he, you are he.

Ant. At a word, I am not.

Urs. Come, come, do you think I do not know you by your excellent wit? Can virtue hide itself? Go to, mum, you are he. Graces will appear, and there's an end. [*They move aside.*]

Beat. Will you not tell me who told you so?

Bene. No, you shall pardon me.

Beat. Nor will you not tell me who you are?

Bene. Not now.

Beat. That I was disdainful, and that I had my good wit out of the "Hundred Merry Tales"—well, this was Signior Benedick that said so.

Bene. What's he?

Beat. I am sure you know him well enough.

Bene. Not I, believe me.

Beat. Did he never make you laugh?

Bene. I pray you, what is he?

Beat. Why, he is the Prince's jester, a very dull fool; only his gift is in devising impossible slanders. None but libertines delight in him, and the commendation is not in his wit, but in his villainy, for he both pleases men and angers them, and then they laugh at him and beat him. I am sure he is in the fleet; I would he had boarded me.

Bene. When I know the gentleman, I'll tell him what you say.

Beat. Do, do, he'll but break a comparison or two on me, which peradventure, not mark'd, or not laugh'd at, strikes him into melancholy, and then

60. mettle: substance. **63. marl:** clay.
64–65. match . . . kinred: i.e. marry within the forbidden degrees of relationship; *kinred* = kindred.
70. in good time: with propriety (with obvious pun).
71. important: importunate, pressing. **measure:** (1) moderation; (2) slow, stately dance.
74. cinquepace: lively dance (trisyllabic). **75. full:** fully, quite.
76. mannerly-modest: becomingly moderate in tempo.
77. state and ancientry: traditional stateliness.
81. apprehend passing shrewdly: perceive with unusual sharpness.
85 s.d. Drum: drummer.
87. friend. Often used in the sense "lover," and perhaps so here.
88. softly: gently. **94. favor:** face.
94–95. God . . . case: i.e. God forbid that your face should not be handsomer than your mask.
96. visor: mask. **Philemon's roof.** Philemon and his wife Baucis entertained Jove in their peasant cottage, unaware of his identity (Ovid, *Metamorphoses*, viii).
98. thatch'd: (1) roofed with thatch (as peasant cottages generally were); (2) bearded.
102. ill: bad.
110. Answer, clerk: i.e. say amen (= so be it) again. It was the duty of the parish clerk to say the responses at church services.
114. At: in.
117. do . . . ill-well: imitate his imperfections so perfectly.
118. dry hand. A sign of age. **118–19. up and down:** exactly.
122. virtue: excellence (of any kind). **123. mum:** silence.
124. an end: no more to be said.
130. Hundred Merry Tales: a popular collection of jests and tales, first published in 1526. **137. dull:** stupid.
138. only his gift: i.e. his only talent. **impossible:** incredible.
139. libertines: i.e. those who reject the customary restraints upon thought and behavior. **140. villainy:** satiric rudeness.
143. fleet: i.e. company drifting about the room. **boarded:** come alongside (a ship) to attempt an attack on it; here, tried his wit on.
146. break a comparison: crack a joke.

there's a partridge wing sav'd, for the fool will eat no supper that night. [*Music for the dance begins.*] We must follow the leaders.

Bene. In every good thing.

Beat. Nay, if they lead to any ill, I will leave them at the next turning.

Dance. [*Then*] *exeunt* [*all but Don John, Borachio, and Claudio*].

D. John. Sure my brother is amorous on Hero, and hath withdrawn her father to break with him about it. The ladies follow her, and but one visor remains.

Bora. And that is Claudio. I know him by his bearing.

D. John. Are not you Signior Benedick?

Claud. You know me well, I am he.

D. John. Signior, you are very near my brother in his love. He is enamor'd on Hero. I pray you dissuade him from her, she is no equal for his birth. You may do the part of an honest man in it.

Claud. How know you he loves her?

D. John. I heard him swear his affection.

Bora. So did I too, and he swore he would marry her to-night.

D. John. Come let us to the banquet.

Exeunt. Manet Claudio.

Claud. Thus answer I in name of Benedick,
But hear these ill news with the ears of Claudio.
'Tis certain so, the Prince woos for himself.
Friendship is constant in all other things
Save in the office and affairs of love;
Therefore all hearts in love use their own tongues.
Let every eye negotiate for itself,
And trust no agent; for beauty is a witch
Against whose charms faith melteth into blood.
This is an accident of hourly proof,
Which I mistrusted not. Farewell therefore Hero!

Enter BENEDICK.

Bene. Count Claudio?

Claud. Yea, the same.

Bene. Come, will you go with me?

Claud. Whither?

Bene. Even to the next willow, about your own business, County. What fashion will you wear the garland of? about your neck, like an usurer's chain? or under your arm, like a lieutenant's scarf? You must wear it one way, for the Prince hath got your Hero.

Claud. I wish him joy of her.

Bene. Why, that's spoken like an honest drovier; so they sell bullocks. But did you think the Prince would have serv'd you thus?

Claud. I pray you leave me.

Bene. Ho, now you strike like the blind man. 'Twas the boy that stole your meat, and you'll beat the post.

Claud. If it will not be, I'll leave you. *Exit.*

Bene. Alas, poor hurt fowl, now will he creep into sedges. But that my Lady Beatrice should know me, and not know me! The Prince's fool! hah, it may be I go under that title because I am merry. Yea, but so I am apt to do myself wrong. I am not so reputed. It is the base (though bitter) disposition of Beatrice that puts the world into her person, and so gives me out. Well, I'll be reveng'd as I may.

Enter the Prince [DON PEDRO].

D. Pedro. Now, signior, where's the Count? Did you see him?

Bene. Troth, my lord, I have play'd the part of Lady Fame. I found him here as melancholy as a lodge in a warren. I told him, and I think I told him true, that your Grace had got the good will of this young lady, and I off'red him my company to a willow-tree, either to make him a garland, as being forsaken, or to bind him up a rod, as being worthy to be whipt.

D. Pedro. To be whipt? What's his fault?

Bene. The flat transgression of a schoolboy, who being overjoy'd with finding a bird's nest, shows it his companion, and he steals it.

D. Pedro. Wilt thou make a trust a transgression? The transgression is in the stealer.

Bene. Yet it had not been amiss the rod had been made, and the garland too, for the garland he might have worn himself, and the rod he might have bestow'd on you, who (as I take it) have stol'n his bird's nest.

D. Pedro. I will but teach them to sing, and restore them to the owner.

Bene. If their singing answer your saying, by my faith you say honestly.

D. Pedro. The Lady Beatrice hath a quarrel to you. The gentleman that danc'd with her told her she is much wrong'd by you.

Bene. O, she misus'd me past the endurance of

151. **leaders:** i.e. of the dance.
163–64. **very . . . love:** a very close friend of my brother's
171. **banquet:** light repast of sweets, fruit, and wine.
176. **office:** business. 177. **all:** let all.
180. **Against whose charms:** in the face of whose spells. **blood:** passion.
181. **accident . . . proof:** occurrence of a sort that takes place every hour. 182. **mistrusted:** suspected.
187. **next:** nearest. **willow.** The emblem of unrequited love.
188. **County:** count. 189. **garland:** i.e. of willow.
191. **one way:** one way or another.
194. **drovier:** drover, cattle dealer.

198. **blind man.** The particular story has not been identified. In the Spanish romance *Lazarillo de Tormes,* the hero steals a sausage from his master, a blind beggar, and is so severely punished by him that, in revenge, he causes the blind man to jump against a stone pillar.
200. **post:** pillar (but with a quibble on the sense "messenger").
202–3. **creep into sedges:** i.e. find himself a hiding-place, as an injured bird seeks refuge in the rushes along a river bank.
207. **base (though bitter):** low, yet capable of stinging its victim (?). The locution is not very natural, and Johnson conjectured that we should read *base, the bitter.*
208–9. **puts . . . person:** i.e. assumes that everyone is of her opinion.
209. **gives me out:** represents me. 213. **Troth:** in truth.
214. **Lady Fame:** Dame Rumor.
215. **lodge . . . warren:** burrow in a rabbit warren. Rabbits were proverbially melancholy.
222. **flat:** simple, silly.
225. **a trust:** i.e. the placing of one's trust in a person.
230. **bestow'd:** i.e. used 232. **them:** i.e. the nestlings.
234. **answer:** correspond to. 236. **to:** with.
239. **misus'd:** abused.

a block; an oak but with one green leaf on it would have answer'd her. My very visor began to assume life, and scold with her. She told me, not thinking I had been myself, that I was the Prince's jester, that I was duller than a great thaw, huddling jest upon jest with such impossible conveyance upon me that I stood like a man at a mark, with a whole army shooting at me. She speaks poniards, and every word stabs. If her breath were as terrible as her terminations, there were no living near her, she would infect to the north star. I would not marry her, though she were endow'd with all that Adam had left him before he transgress'd. She would have made Hercules have turn'd spit, yea, and have cleft his club to make the fire too. Come, talk not of her; you shall find her the infernal Ate in good apparel. I would to God some scholar would conjure her, for certainly, while she is here, a man may live as quiet in hell as in a sanctuary, and people sin upon purpose, because they would go thither; so indeed all disquiet, horror, and perturbation follows her.

Enter CLAUDIO *and* BEATRICE, [LEONATO *and* HERO].

D. Pedro. Look here she comes.

Bene. Will your Grace command me any service to the world's end? I will go on the slightest arrand now to the Antipodes that you can devise to send me on; I will fetch you a toothpicker now from the furthest inch of Asia, bring you the length of Prester John's foot, fetch you a hair off the great Cham's beard, do you any embassage to the Pigmies, rather than hold three words' conference with this harpy. You have no employment for me?

D. Pedro. None, but to desire your good company.

Bene. O God, sir, here's a dish I love not, I cannot endure my Lady Tongue. *Exit.*

D. Pedro. Come, lady, come, you have lost the heart of Signior Benedick.

Beat. Indeed, my lord, he lent it me awhile, and I gave him use for it, a double heart for his single one. Marry, once before he won it of me with false dice, therefore your Grace may well say I have lost it.

240. **but . . . it:** i.e. with the slightest vestige of life in it.
244. **a great thaw.** When impassable roads would prevent the usual activities and pastimes. **huddling:** piling up.
245. **impossible conveyance:** incredible adeptness.
246. **at a mark:** set up as a target. 249. **terminations:** terms, words.
250. **north star.** Supposedly the remotest star.
252. **left:** bestowed upon.
253. **Hercules . . . spit.** Omphale forced the captive Hercules to put on women's clothes and spin among her maids. Turning the spit was work of a far more menial order.
256. **Ate:** goddess of mischief and discord. **scholar:** i.e. one familiar with the Latin formulas for exorcising evil spirits.
264. **arrand:** errand.
268. **Prester John:** a legendary Far Eastern ruler who was both emperor and Christian priest (*Prester* is a shortened form of *Presbyter*, i.e. priest).
269. **Cham:** Khan of Tartary, ruler of the Mongols. **Pigmies.** Supposed to inhabit the mountains of India.
271. **harpy:** i.e. creature of prey; literally a mythical monster with the face and trunk of a woman and the wings and claws of a bird. In heraldry the harpy was assigned to one who had committed manslaughter (= Beatrice's crime!). 279. **use:** usury, interest.
280. **false:** loaded.

D. Pedro. You have put him down, lady, you have put him down.

Beat. So I would not he should do me, my lord, lest I should prove the mother of fools. I have brought Count Claudio, whom you sent me to seek.

D. Pedro. Why, how now, Count, wherefore are you sad?

Claud. Not sad, my lord.

D. Pedro. How then? sick?

Claud. Neither, my lord.

Beat. The Count is neither sad, nor sick, nor merry, nor well; but civil count, civil as an orange, and something of that jealous complexion.

D. Pedro. I' faith, lady, I think your blazon to be true, though I'll be sworn, if he be so, his conceit is false. Here, Claudio, I have woo'd in thy name, and fair Hero is won. I have broke with her father, and his good will obtain'd. Name the day of marriage, and God give thee joy!

Leon. Count, take of me my daughter, and with her my fortunes. His Grace hath made the match, and all grace say amen to it.

Beat. Speak, Count, 'tis your cue.

Claud. Silence is the perfectest heralt of joy; I were but little happy, if I could say how much! Lady, as you are mine, I am yours. I give away myself for you, and dote upon the exchange.

Beat. Speak, cousin, or (if you cannot) stop his mouth with a kiss, and let not him speak neither.

D. Pedro. In faith, lady, you have a merry heart.

Beat. Yea, my lord, I thank it—poor fool, it keeps on the windy side of care. My cousin tells him in his ear that he is in her heart.

Claud. And so she doth, cousin.

Beat. Good Lord, for alliance! Thus goes every one to the world but I, and I am sunburnt. I may sit in a corner and cry "Heigh-ho for a husband!"

D. Pedro. Lady Beatrice, I will get you one.

Beat. I would rather have one of your father's getting. Hath your Grace ne'er a brother like you? Your father got excellent husbands, if a maid could come by them.

D. Pedro. Will you have me, lady?

Beat. No, my lord, unless I might have another for working-days. Your Grace is too costly to wear every day. But I beseech your Grace pardon me, I was born to speak all mirth and no matter.

D. Pedro. Your silence most offends me, and to be merry best becomes you, for out a' question, you were born in a merry hour.

Beat. No, sure, my lord, my mother cried, but

284. **put him down:** got the better of him (with following quibble by Beatrice).
294. **civil:** (1) grave, serious; (2) Seville (a homophone); oranges of Seville are bitter.
295. **something:** somewhat, to some degree. **jealous complexion:** i.e. yellow, the color associated with jealousy.
296. **blazon:** description. 297. **so:** i.e. jealous. **conceit:** idea.
304. **all grace:** i.e. the grace of God. 306. **heralt:** herald.
315. **windy:** windward, i.e. safe.
318–19. **goes . . . world:** i.e. everyone gets married.
319. **sunburnt:** i.e. unattractive.
320. **Heigh-ho . . . husband:** the title of a ballad.
323. **getting:** begetting. 330. **matter:** substance, sense.

then there was a star danc'd, and under that was I born. Cousins, God give you joy!

Leon. Niece, will you look to those things I told you of?

Beat. I cry you mercy, uncle. By your Grace's pardon. *Exit Beatrice.*

D. Pedro. By my troth, a pleasant-spirited lady.

Leon. There's little of the melancholy element in her, my lord. She is never sad but when she sleeps, and not ever sad then; for I have heard my daughter say, she hath often dreamt of unhappiness, and wak'd herself with laughing.

D. Pedro. She cannot endure to hear tell of a husband.

Leon. O, by no means, she mocks all her wooers out of suit.

D. Pedro. She were an excellent wife for Benedick.

Leon. O Lord, my lord, if they were but a week married, they would talk themselves mad.

D. Pedro. County Claudio, when mean you to go to church?

Claud. To-morrow, my lord. Time goes on crutches till love have all his rites.

Leon. Not till Monday, my dear son, which is hence a just sevennight, and a time too brief too, to have all things answer my mind.

D. Pedro. Come, you shake the head at so long a breathing, but I warrant thee, Claudio, the time shall not go dully by us. I will in the interim undertake one of Hercules' labors, which is, to bring Signior Benedick and the Lady Beatrice into a mountain of affection th' one with th' other. I would fain have it a match, and I doubt not but to fashion it, if you three will but minister such assistance as I shall give you direction.

Leon. My lord, I am for you, though it cost me ten nights' watchings.

Claud. And I, my lord.

D. Pedro. And you too, gentle Hero?

Hero. I will do any modest office, my lord, to help my cousin to a good husband.

D. Pedro. And Benedick is not the unhopefullest husband that I know. Thus far can I praise him: he is of a noble strain, of approv'd valor, and confirm'd honesty. I will teach you how to humor your cousin, that she shall fall in love with Benedick, and I, with your two helps, will so practice on Benedick that, in despite of his quick wit and his queasy stomach, he shall fall in love with Beatrice. If we can do this, Cupid is no longer an archer; his glory shall be ours, for we are the only love-gods. Go in with me, and I will tell you my drift. *Exeunt.*

344. ever: always.
345. unhappiness: "some amusing roguery or other" (Kittredge).
350. suit: courtship. **355–56. go to church:** marry.
360. a just sevennight: exactly a week.
361. answer my mind: correspond with my wishes.
363. breathing: interval, delay. **369. minister:** furnish, supply.
372. watchings: lying awake. **379. approv'd:** tested.
382. practice on: scheme against.
383. in despite of: notwithstanding.
383–84. his queasy stomach: i.e. his squeamishness about partaking of love. **387. drift:** intent.

[Scene II]

Enter [Don] John *and* Borachio.

D. John. It is so, the Count Claudio shall marry the daughter of Leonato.

Bora. Yea, my lord, but I can cross it.

D. John. Any bar, any cross, any impediment will be med'cinable to me. I am sick in displeasure to him, and whatsoever comes athwart his affection ranges evenly with mine. How canst thou cross this marriage?

Bora. Not honestly, my lord, but so covertly that no dishonesty shall appear in me.

D. John. Show me briefly how.

Bora. I think I told your lordship a year since, how much I am in the favor of Margaret, the waiting-gentlewoman to Hero.

D. John. I remember.

Bora. I can, at any unseasonable instant of the night, appoint her to look out at her lady's chamber-window.

D. John. What life is in that, to be the death of this marriage?

Bora. The poison of that lies in you to temper. Go you to the Prince your brother; spare not to tell him that he hath wrong'd his honor in marrying the renown'd Claudio—whose estimation do you mightily hold up—to a contaminated stale, such a one as Hero.

D. John. What proof shall I make of that?

Bora. Proof enough to misuse the Prince, to vex Claudio, to undo Hero, and kill Leonato. Look you for any other issue?

D. John. Only to despite them, I will endeavor any thing.

Bora. Go then, find me a meet hour to draw Don Pedro and the Count Claudio alone, tell them that you know that Hero loves me, intend a kind of zeal both to the Prince and Claudio—as in love of your brother's honor, who hath made this match, and his friend's reputation, who is thus like to be cozen'd with the semblance of a maid—that you have discover'd thus. They will scarcely believe this without trial. Offer them instances, which shall bear no less likelihood than to see me at her chamber-window, hear me call Margaret Hero, hear Margaret term me Claudio; and bring them to see this the very night before the intended wedding—for in the mean time I will so fashion the matter that Hero shall be absent—and there shall appear such seeming truth of Hero's disloyalty, that

II.ii. Location: Leonato's house.
1. shall: is going to. **3. cross:** thwart.
5. med'cinable: medicinal, healing.
5–6. displeasure to: anger against.
6–7. comes . . . affection: goes contrary to his desires.
7. ranges evenly: runs parallel. **11. briefly:** quickly.
21. lies in: depends upon. **temper:** mix.
24. estimation: worth.
25. contaminated stale: common prostitute.
28. misuse: deceive. **vex:** torment. **35. intend:** pretend.
39. cozen'd: deceived. **semblance:** outward appearance.
41. instances: proofs.
44. term me Claudio. Apparently a slip. Many editors emend to *Borachio* (following Theobald).

jealousy shall be call'd assurance, and all the preparation overthrown.

D. John. Grow this to what adverse issue it can, I will put it in practice. Be cunning in the working this, and thy fee is a thousand ducats.

Bora. Be you constant in the accusation, and my cunning shall not shame me.

D. John. I will presently go learn their day of marriage. *Exeunt.*

[Scene III]

Enter Benedick *alone.*

Bene. Boy!

[*Enter* Boy.]

Boy. Signior?

Bene. In my chamber-window lies a book, bring it hither to me in the orchard.

Boy. I am here already, sir. *Exit.*

Bene. I know that, but I would have thee hence, and here again. I do much wonder that one man, seeing how much another man is a fool when he dedicates his behaviors to love, will, after he hath laugh'd at such shallow follies in others, become the argument of his own scorn by falling in love—and such a man is Claudio. I have known when there was no music with him but the drum and the fife, and now had he rather hear the tabor and the pipe; I have known when he would have walk'd ten mile afoot to see a good armor, and now will he lie ten nights awake carving the fashion of a new doublet; he was wont to speak plain and to the purpose (like an honest man and a soldier), and now is he turn'd ortography—his words are a very fantastical banquet, just so many strange dishes. May I be so converted and see with these eyes? I cannot tell; I think not. I will not be sworn but love may transform me to an oyster, but I'll take my oath on it, till he have made [an] oyster of me, he shall never make me such a fool. One woman is fair, yet I am well; another is wise, yet I am well; another virtuous, yet I am well; but till all graces be in one woman, one woman shall not come in my grace. Rich she shall be, that's certain; wise, or I'll none; virtuous, or I'll never cheapen her; fair, or I'll never look on her; mild, or come not near me; noble, or not I for an angel; of good discourse, an excellent musician, and her hair shall be of what color it please God. Hah! the Prince and Monsieur Love. I will hide me in the arbor.

[*Withdraws.*]

Enter Prince [Don Pedro], Leonato, Claudio. *Music* [*within*].

D. Pedro. Come, shall we hear this music?
Claud. Yea, my good lord. How still the evening is,
As hush'd on purpose to grace harmony!
D. Pedro. See you where Benedick hath hid himself?
Claud. O, very well, my lord. The music ended,
We'll fit the [hid]-fox with a pennyworth.

Enter Balthasar *with Music.*

D. Pedro. Come, Balthasar, we'll hear that song again.
Balth. O good my lord, tax not so bad a voice
To slander music any more than once.
D. Pedro. It is the witness still of excellency
To put a strange face on his own perfection.
I pray thee sing, and let me woo no more.
Balth. Because you talk of wooing, I will sing,
Since many a wooer doth commence his suit
To her he thinks not worthy, yet he woos,
Yet will he swear he loves.
D. Pedro. Nay, pray thee come,
Or if thou wilt hold longer argument,
Do it in notes.
Balth. Note this before my notes:
There's not a note of mine that's worth the noting.
D. Pedro. Why, these are very crotchets that he speaks—
Note notes, forsooth, and nothing. [*Air.*]

Bene. Now, divine air! now is his soul ravish'd! Is it not strange that sheep's guts should hale souls out of men's bodies? Well, a horn for my money when all's done.

The Song

[*Balth.*] Sigh no more, ladies, sigh no more,
Men were deceivers ever,
One foot in sea, and one on shore,
To one thing constant never.
Then sigh not so, but let them go,
And be you blithe and bonny,
Converting all your sounds of woe
Into hey nonny nonny.

49. jealousy: suspicion. **assurance:** certainty.
49–50. preparation: i.e. for the wedding.
53. ducats: continental gold coins, variously valued (but Borachio's reward is clearly to be a large one). **56. presently:** at once.

II.iii. Location: Leonato's garden.
4. orchard: garden.
5. I . . . already: i.e. I'll be back before you know I've gone.
11. argument: subject.
14. tabor: small drum. The tabor and pipe were used for social merriment, in contrast to the martial drum and fife.
16. armor: suit of armor. **17. carving:** planning.
18. doublet: close-fitting jacket.
20. turn'd ortography: i.e. become a faddist in language.
31. I'll none: I'll have none of her. **cheapen:** bargain for.
33. for an angel: (1) though she be an angel; (2) for ten shillings (involving a play on *noble* as the name of another coin, worth two thirds as much as an angel).
34–35. hair . . . God: i.e. if she satisfies all these requirements, I won't stipulate what color her hair must be.
39. grace harmony: do honor to music.
42. hid-fox. An allusion to a children's game; cf. *Hamlet*, IV.ii.30–31: "Hide fox, and all after." **pennyworth:** a good bargain, i.e. more than he bargained for.
44. tax: task. **47. To . . . on:** i.e. not to admit.
48. woo: entreat. **54. notes:** i.e. musical notes.
56. crotchets: (1) whims; (2) quarter notes in music.
57. nothing. With homophonic pun on *noting*.
59. sheep's guts: violin or lute strings. **hale:** draw, drag.
60. horn: i.e. hunting horn (but an audience always alive to the cuckold jest would have found the remark comically incongruous in Benedick's mouth).

Sing no more ditties, sing no moe,
Of dumps so dull and heavy;
The fraud of men was ever so,
Since summer first was leavy.
Then sigh not so, etc.

D. Pedro. By my troth, a good song.

Balth. And an ill singer, my lord.

D. Pedro. Ha, no, no, faith, thou sing'st well enough for a shift.

Bene. And he had been a dog that should have howl'd thus, they would have hang'd him, and I pray God his bad voice bode no mischief. I had as live have heard the night-raven, come what plague could have come after it.

D. Pedro. Yea, marry, dost thou hear, Balthasar? I pray thee get us some excellent music; for to-morrow night we would have it at the Lady Hero's chamber-window.

Balth. The best I can, my lord. *Exit Balthasar.*

D. Pedro. Do so, farewell. Come hither, Leonato. What was it you told me of to-day, that your niece Beatrice was in love with Signior Benedick?

Claud. [*Aside.*] O ay, stalk on, stalk on, the fowl sits.—I did never think that lady would have lov'd any man.

Leon. No, nor I neither, but most wonderful that she should so dote on Signior Benedick, whom she hath in all outward behaviors seem'd ever to abhor.

Bene. Is't possible? Sits the wind in that corner?

Leon. By my troth, my lord, I cannot tell what to think of it but that she loves him with an enrag'd affection; it is past the infinite of thought.

D. Pedro. May be she doth but counterfeit.

Claud. Faith, like enough.

Leon. O God! counterfeit? There was never counterfeit of passion came so near the life of passion as she discovers it.

D. Pedro. Why, what effects of passion shows she?

Claud. [*Aside.*] Bait the hook well, this fish will bite.

Leon. What effects, my lord? She will sit you—you heard my daughter tell you how.

Claud. She did indeed.

D. Pedro. How, how, I pray you? You amaze me, I would have thought her spirit had been invincible against all assaults of affection.

Leon. I would have sworn it had, my lord, especially against Benedick.

Bene. I should think this a gull, but that the white-bearded fellow speaks it. Knavery cannot sure hide himself in such reverence.

Claud. [*Aside.*] He hath ta'en th' infection. Hold it up.

D. Pedro. Hath she made her affection known to Benedick?

Leon. No, and swears she never will. That's her torment.

Claud. 'Tis true indeed, so your daughter says. "Shall I," says she, "that have so oft encount'red him with scorn, write to him that I love him?"

Leon. This says she now when she is beginning to write to him, for she'll be up twenty times a night, and there will she sit in her smock till she have writ a sheet of paper. My daughter tells us all.

Claud. Now you talk of a sheet of paper, I remember a pretty jest your daughter told [us of].

Leon. O, when she had writ it, and was reading it over, she found "Benedick" and "Beatrice" between the sheet?

Claud. That.

Leon. O, she tore the letter into a thousand halfpence; rail'd at herself, that she should be so immodest to write to one that she knew would flout her. "I measure him," says she, "by my own spirit, for I should flout him, if he writ to me, yea, though I love him, I should."

Claud. Then down upon her knees she falls, weeps, sobs, beats her heart, tears her hair, prays, curses: "O sweet Benedick! God give me patience!"

Leon. She doth indeed, my daughter says so; and the ecstasy hath so much overborne her that my daughter is sometime afeard she will do a desperate outrage to herself. It is very true.

D. Pedro. It were good that Benedick knew of it by some other, if she will not discover it.

Claud. To what end? he would make but a sport of it, and torment the poor lady worse.

D. Pedro. And he should, it were an alms to hang him. She's an excellent sweet lady, and (out of all suspicion) she is virtuous.

Claud. And she is exceeding wise.

D. Pedro. In every thing but in loving Benedick.

Leon. O my lord, wisdom and blood combating in so tender a body, we have ten proofs to one that blood hath the victory. I am sorry for her, as I have just cause, being her uncle and her guardian.

D. Pedro. I would she had bestow'd this dotage on me, I would have daff'd all other respects, and made her half myself. I pray you tell Benedick of it, and hear what 'a will say.

Leon. Were it good, think you?

Claud. Hero thinks surely she will die, for she says she will die if he love her not, and she will die ere she make her love known, and she will die if he woo her, rather than she will bate one breath of her accustom'd crossness.

70. moe: more (in number). **71. dumps:** mournful tunes.
73. leavy: leafy. **78. for a shift:** to make do.
82. live: lief. **night-raven:** a bird, variously identified, whose cry presaged disaster.
92–93. stalk . . . sits: walk stealthily, the bird has settled (in a bush).
98. Sits . . . corner: is that how the wind blows.
100. enrag'd: mad with passion.
101. infinite: infinity, boundlessness. **106. discovers:** reveals.
107. effects: manifestations. **110. sit you:** sit (a colloquialism).
118. gull: trick. **121–22. Hold it up:** keep it up.

132. smock: undergarment.
140–41. halfpence: i.e. very small bits. **151. ecstasy:** madness.
153. outrage: act of violence. **158. alms:** good deed.
159. out of: beyond. **163. blood:** natural feeling.
168. dotage: doting.
169. daff'd: doffed, put aside. **respects:** considerations.
170. half myself: i.e. my wife. **176. bate:** abate.
177. crossness: perversity.

D. Pedro. She doth well. If she should make tender of her love, 'tis very possible he'll scorn it, for the man (as you know all) hath a contemptible spirit.

Claud. He is a very proper man.

D. Pedro. He hath indeed a good outward happiness.

Claud. Before God, and in my mind, very wise.

D. Pedro. He doth indeed show some sparks that are like wit.

Claud. And I take him to be valiant.

D. Pedro. As Hector, I assure you, and in the managing of quarrels you may say he is wise, for either he avoids them with great discretion, or undertakes them with a most Christian-like fear.

Leon. If he do fear God, 'a must necessarily keep peace; if he break the peace, he ought to enter into a quarrel with fear and trembling.

D. Pedro. And so will he do, for the man doth fear God, howsoever it seems not in him by some large jests he will make. Well, I am sorry for your niece. Shall we go seek Benedick, and tell him of her love?

Claud. Never tell him, my lord. Let her wear it out with good counsel.

Leon. Nay, that's impossible, she may wear her heart out first.

D. Pedro. Well, we will hear further of it by your daughter, let it cool the while. I love Benedick well, and I could wish he would modestly examine himself, to see how much he is unworthy so good a lady.

Leon. My lord, will you walk? Dinner is ready.

Claud. [*Aside.*] If he do not dote on her upon this, I will never trust my expectation.

D. Pedro. [*Aside.*] Let there be the same net spread for her, and that must your daughter and her gentlewomen carry. The sport will be, when they hold one an opinion of another's dotage, and no such matter; that's the scene that I would see, which will be merely a dumb show. Let us send her to call him in to dinner.

[*Exeunt Don Pedro, Claudio, and Leonato.*]

Bene. [*Coming forward.*] This can be no trick: the conference was sadly borne; they have the truth of this from Hero; they seem to pity the lady. It seems her affections have their full bent. Love me? why, it must be requited. I hear how I am censur'd; they say I will bear myself proudly, if I perceive the love come from her; they say too that she will rather die than give any sign of affection. I did never think to marry. I must not seem proud; happy are they that hear their detractions, and can put them to mending. They say the lady is fair; 'tis a truth, I can bear them witness; and virtuous; 'tis so, I cannot reprove it; and wise, but for loving me; by my troth, it is no addition to her wit, nor no great argument of her folly, for I will be horribly in love with her. I may chance have some odd quirks and remnants of wit broken on me, because I have rail'd so long against marriage; but doth not the appetite alter? A man loves the meat in his youth that he cannot endure in his age. Shall quips and sentences and these paper bullets of the brain awe a man from the career of his humor? No, the world must be peopled. When I said I would die a bachelor, I did not think I should live till I were married. Here comes Beatrice. By this day, she's a fair lady. I do spy some marks of love in her.

Enter BEATRICE.

Beat. Against my will I am sent to bid you come in to dinner.

Bene. Fair Beatrice, I thank you for your pains.

Beat. I took no more pains for those thanks than you take pains to thank me. If it had been painful, I would not have come.

Bene. You take pleasure then in the message?

Beat. Yea, just so much as you may take upon a knive's point, and choke a daw withal. You have no stomach, signior, fare you well. *Exit.*

Bene. Ha! "Against my will I am sent to bid you come in to dinner"—there's a double meaning in that. "I took no more pains for those thanks than you took pains to thank me"—that's as much as to say, "Any pains that I take for you is as easy as thanks." If I do not take pity of her, I am a villain; if I do not love her, I am a Jew. I will go get her picture. *Exit.*

[ACT III, SCENE I]

Enter HERO *and two gentlewomen,* MARGARET *and* URSLEY.

Hero. Good Margaret, run thee to the parlor,
There shalt thou find my cousin Beatrice
Proposing with the Prince and Claudio.
Whisper her ear, and tell her I and Ursley
Walk in the orchard, and our whole discourse
Is all of her. Say that thou overheardst us,
And bid her steal into the pleached bower,
Where honeysuckles, ripened by the sun,
Forbid the sun to enter, like favorites

179. **tender:** offer. 180. **contemptible:** contemptuous.
182. **proper:** handsome.
183–84. **hath . . . happiness:** is fortunate in his appearance.
189. **Hector.** The greatest of the Trojan warriors.
198. **large:** broad, indelicate.
202. **good counsel:** i.e. giving herself good advice. 210. **walk:** go.
215. **carry:** undertake.
216–17. **no such matter:** nothing of the kind exists.
218. **merely . . . show:** entirely pantomime (because with no occasion for satiric exchange they will have nothing to say).
221. **sadly borne:** seriously conducted.
223. **have . . . bent:** are at full stretch.
229–30. **their detractions:** unfavorable criticisms of themselves.
230. **put . . . mending:** i.e. apply themselves to correcting their faults.
232. **reprove:** disprove, deny. 236. **quirks:** jests.
240. **sentences:** maxims.
240–41. **paper . . . brain:** verbal ammunition.
241–42. **career . . . humor:** course of his inclination.
255. **daw:** jackdaw. 256. **stomach:** appetite.

III.i. **Location:** Leonato's garden.
o.s.d. **Ursley:** variant form of *Ursula.* 3. **Proposing:** talking.

Made proud by princes, that advance their pride
Against that power that bred it. There will she hide her,
To listen our propose. This is thy office;
Bear thee well in it, and leave us alone.
Marg. I'll make her come, I warrant you, presently. [*Exit.*]
Hero. Now, Ursula, when Beatrice doth come,
As we do trace this alley up and down,
Our talk must only be of Benedick.
When I do name him, let it be thy part
To praise him more than ever man did merit.
My talk to thee must be how Benedick
Is sick in love with Beatrice. Of this matter
Is little Cupid's crafty arrow made,
That only wounds by hearsay.

Enter BEATRICE [*behind*].

Now begin,
For look where Beatrice like a lapwing runs
Close by the ground, to hear our conference.
Urs. The pleasant'st angling is to see the fish
Cut with her golden oars the silver stream,
And greedily devour the treacherous bait;
So angle we for Beatrice, who even now
Is couched in the woodbine coverture.
Fear you not my part of the dialogue.
Hero. Then go we near her, that her ear lose nothing
Of the false sweet bait that we lay for it.

[*They advance to the bower.*]

No, truly, Ursula, she is too disdainful,
I know her spirits are as coy and wild
As haggards of the rock.
Urs. But are you sure
That Benedick loves Beatrice so entirely?
Hero. So says the Prince and my new-trothed lord.
Urs. And did they bid you tell her of it, madam?
Hero. They did entreat me to acquaint her of it,
But I persuaded them, if they lov'd Benedick,
To wish him wrastle with affection,
And never to let Beatrice know of it.
Urs. Why did you so? Doth not the gentleman
Deserve as full as fortunate a bed
As ever Beatrice shall couch upon?
Hero. O god of love! I know he doth deserve
As much as may be yielded to a man;
But nature never fram'd a woman's heart
Of prouder stuff than that of Beatrice.
Disdain and scorn ride sparkling in her eyes,
Misprising what they look on, and her wit
Values itself so highly that to her
All matter else seems weak. She cannot love,
Nor take no shape nor project of affection,

12. listen our propose: listen to our conversation.
23. only . . . hearsay: wounds by hearsay only.
30. woodbine coverture: honeysuckle bower. **35. coy**: shy.
36. haggards . . . rock: mature female hawks snared in their mountain habitats, hence very difficult to tame.
42. wish him wrastle: advise him to wrestle.
45. as full as: fully as. **52. Misprising**: undervaluing, despising.
54. All matter else: i.e. what anyone else has to say.
55. take . . . affection: formulate any mental image or idea of what love is.

She is so self-endeared.
Urs. Sure I think so,
And therefore certainly it were not good
She knew his love, lest she'll make sport at it.
Hero. Why, you speak truth. I never yet saw man,
How wise, how noble, young, how rarely featur'd,
But she would spell him backward. If fair-fac'd,
She would swear the gentleman should be her sister;
If black, why, Nature, drawing of an antic,
Made a foul blot; if tall, a lance ill-headed;
If low, an agot very vildly cut;
If speaking, why, a vane blown with all winds;
If silent, why, a block moved with none.
So turns she every man the wrong side out,
And never gives to truth and virtue that
Which simpleness and merit purchaseth.
Urs. Sure, sure, such carping is not commendable.
Hero. No, not to be so odd, and from all fashions,
As Beatrice is, cannot be commendable.
But who dare tell her so? If I should speak,
She would mock me into air; O, she would laugh me
Out of myself, press me to death with wit.
Therefore let Benedick, like cover'd fire,
Consume away in sighs, waste inwardly.
It were a better death than die with mocks,
Which is as bad as die with tickling.
Urs. Yet tell her of it, hear what she will say.
Hero. No, rather I will go to Benedick,
And counsel him to fight against his passion,
And truly I'll devise some honest slanders
To stain my cousin with. One doth not know
How much an ill word may empoison liking.
Urs. O, do not do your cousin such a wrong.
She cannot be so much without true judgment—
Having so swift and excellent a wit
As she is priz'd to have—as to refuse
So rare a gentleman as Signior Benedick.
Hero. He is the only man of Italy,
Always excepted my dear Claudio.
Urs. I pray you be not angry with me, madam,
Speaking my fancy: Signior Benedick,
For shape, for bearing, argument, and valor,
Goes foremost in report through Italy.
Hero. Indeed he hath an excellent good name.
Urs. His excellence did earn it, ere he had it.
When are you married, madam?
Hero. Why, every day to-morrow. Come go in,
I'll show thee some attires, and have thy counsel
Which is the best to furnish me to-morrow.

56. self-endeared: full of self-love.
60. How: however. **rarely featur'd**: excellent in face and form.
61. spell him backward: i.e. say the reverse of him, turn his merits into faults. **63. black**: dark. **antic**: grotesque figure.
65. agot: agate; here, a small figure incised in agate for a seal or a ring. **70. simpleness**: sincerity. **purchaseth**: deserve.
72. from all fashions: contrary to all accepted behavior.
76. press . . . death. Accused felons who refused to plead either guilty or not guilty were pressed to death by heavy weights.
78. Consume . . . sighs. An allusion to the belief that each sigh cost the heart one drop of blood. **84. honest**: harmless.
90. priz'd: esteemed. **92. only**: i.e. very best.
96. argument: skills in conversation.
97. report: reputation (so also *name*, line 98).
101. every day to-morrow: i.e. to-morrow I shall be able to say that I am married every day.

Urs. [*Aside.*] She's limed, I warrant you. We have caught her, madam.
Hero. [*Aside.*] If it prove so, then loving goes by haps:
Some Cupid kills with arrows, some with traps.
[*Exeunt Hero and Ursula.*]
Beat. [*Coming forward.*] What fire is in mine ears? Can this be true?
Stand I condemn'd for pride and scorn so much?
Contempt, farewell, and maiden pride, adieu!
No glory lives behind the back of such.
And, Benedick, love on, I will requite thee,
Taming my wild heart to thy loving hand.
If thou dost love, my kindness shall incite thee
To bind our loves up in a holy band;
For others say thou dost deserve, and I
Believe it better than reportingly. *Exit.*

[Scene II]

Enter Prince [Don Pedro], Claudio, Benedick, *and* Leonato.

D. Pedro. I do but stay till your marriage be consummate, and then go I toward Arragon.

Claud. I'll bring you thither, my lord, if you'll vouchsafe me.

D. Pedro. Nay, that would be as great a soil in the new gloss of your marriage as to show a child his new coat and forbid him to wear it. I will only be bold with Benedick for his company, for from the crown of his head to the sole of his foot, he is all mirth. He hath twice or thrice cut Cupid's bow-string, and the little hangman dare not shoot at him. He hath a heart as sound as a bell, and his tongue is the clapper, for what his heart thinks, his tongue speaks.

Bene. Gallants, I am not as I have been.

Leon. So say I, methinks you are sadder.

Claud. I hope he be in love.

D. Pedro. Hang him, truant, there's no true drop of blood in him to be truly touch'd with love. If he be sad, he wants money.

Bene. I have the toothache.

D. Pedro. Draw it.

Bene. Hang it!

Claud. You must hang it first, and draw it afterwards.

D. Pedro. What? sigh for the toothache?

Leon. Where is but a humor or a worm.

Bene. Well, every one [can] master a grief but he that has it.

Claud. Yet say I, he is in love.

D. Pedro. There is no appearance of fancy in him, unless it be a fancy that he hath to strange disguises—as to be a Dutchman to-day, a Frenchman to-morrow, or in the shape of two countries at once, as a German from the waist downward, all slops, and a Spaniard from the hip upward, no doublet. Unless he have a fancy to this foolery, as it appears he hath, he is no fool for fancy, as you would have it appear he is.

Claud. If he be not in love with some woman, there is no believing old signs. 'A brushes his hat a' mornings; what should that bode?

D. Pedro. Hath any man seen him at the barber's?

Claud. No, but the barber's man hath been seen with him, and the old ornament of his cheek hath already stuff'd tennis-balls.

Leon. Indeed he looks younger than he did, by the loss of a beard.

D. Pedro. Nay, 'a rubs himself with civet. Can you smell him out by that?

Claud. That's as much as to say, the sweet youth's in love.

[*D. Pedro.*] The greatest note of it is his melancholy.

Claud. And when was he wont to wash his face?

D. Pedro. Yea, or to paint himself? for the which I hear what they say of him.

Claud. Nay, but his jesting spirit, which is now crept into a lute-string, and now govern'd by stops.

D. Pedro. Indeed that tells a heavy tale for him. Conclude, conclude, he is in love.

Claud. Nay, but I know who loves him.

D. Pedro. That would I know too. I warrant one that knows him not.

Claud. Yes, and his ill conditions, and in despite of all, dies for him.

D. Pedro. She shall be buried with her face upwards.

104. limed: caught, like a bird entangled in birdlime.
105. haps: chance.
107. What . . . ears. Alluding to the folk belief that being talked about in one's absence causes one's ears to burn.
110. No . . . such: nothing good is said about such a person when his back is turned.
112. Taming . . . hand. Beatrice has been termed a "haggard" and now acknowledges the justness of the epithet by her use of another image from falconry. **114. band:** bond.
116. better than reportingly: on better evidence than mere rumor.

III.ii. Location: Leonato's house.
3. bring: escort. **4. vouchsafe:** allow.
8. be bold with: take the liberty of asking.
11. hangman: i.e. rogue (with play on Cupid as torturer, a role played also by the public hangman). **16. sadder:** more serious.
18–19. there's . . . him: he hasn't enough natural feeling.
20. wants: lacks.
21. toothache. Lovers were commonly supposed to suffer from toothaches, but Benedick may only be inventing an excuse for his changed appearance. **23. Hang it:** confound it.
24–25. hang . . . afterwards. Alluding to the execution of traitors, who were hanged, cut down while still alive, drawn (disembowelled), and quartered.
27. humor . . . worm. Toothaches were supposedly caused by abnormal secretions or by actual worms in the teeth.
31. fancy: love (with following quibble). **36. slops:** loose breeches.
37. no doublet: i.e. with his doublet completely covered by a cloak.
46. old . . . cheek: i.e. his beard.
50. civet: perfume derived from the civet cat.
51. smell him out: discover his true nature (with obvious play on the literal sense).
52. sweet. With quibble on the sense "perfumed."
54. greatest note: most conspicuous mark.
56, 57. wash, paint: i.e. with cosmetics.
59–60. now crept. Some editors emend to *new-crept* (following Boas) in view of the second *now* in the sentence.
60. lute-string. The lute commonly provided the accompaniment for love songs. **govern'd by stops:** regulated by frets (on the fingerboard of the lute), i.e. subjected to restraints.
66. Yes: i.e. she does know him. **ill conditions:** bad characteristics.
68–69. She . . . upwards. Sexual double-entendre, taking off from a quibble on Claudio's *dies* in the sense "experiences sexual climax."

Bene. Yet is this no charm for the toothache. Old signior, walk aside with me, I have studied eight or nine wise words to speak to you, which these hobby-horses must not hear.

[*Exeunt Benedick and Leonato.*]

D. Pedro. For my life, to break with him about Beatrice.

Claud. 'Tis even so. Hero and Margaret have by this play'd their parts with Beatrice, and then the two bears will not bite one another when they meet.

Enter [DON] JOHN *the Bastard.*

D. John. My lord and brother, God save you!

D. Pedro. Good den, brother.

D. John. If your leisure serv'd, I would speak with you.

D. Pedro. In private?

D. John. If it please you, yet Count Claudio may hear, for what I would speak of concerns him.

D. Pedro. What's the matter?

D. John. [*To Claudio.*] Means your lordship to be married to-morrow?

D. Pedro. You know he does.

D. John. I know not that, when he knows what I know.

Claud. If there be any impediment, I pray you discover it.

D. John. You may think I love you not; let that appear hereafter, and aim better at me by that I now will manifest. For my brother, I think he holds you well, and in dearness of heart hath holp to effect your ensuing marriage—surely suit ill spent and labor ill bestow'd.

D. Pedro. Why, what's the matter?

D. John. I came hither to tell you, and circumstances short'ned (for she has been too long a-talking of), the lady is disloyal.

Claud. Who, Hero?

D. John. Even she—Leonato's Hero, your Hero, every man's Hero.

Claud. Disloyal?

D. John. The word is too good to paint out her wickedness. I could say she were worse; think you of a worse title, and I will fit her to it. Wonder not till further warrant. Go but with me to-night, you shall see her chamber-window ent'red, even the night before her wedding-day. If you love her then, to-morrow wed her; but it would better fit your honor to change your mind.

Claud. May this be so?

D. Pedro. I will not think it.

D. John. If you dare not trust that you see, confess not that you know. If you will follow me, I will show you enough, and when you have seen more, and heard more, proceed accordingly.

Claud. If I see any thing to-night why I should not marry her, to-morrow in the congregation, where I should wed, there will I shame her.

D. Pedro. And as I woo'd for thee to obtain her, I will join with thee to disgrace her.

D. John. I will disparage her no farther till you are my witnesses. Bear it coldly but till midnight, and let the issue show itself.

D. Pedro. O day untowardly turn'd!

Claud. O mischief strangely thwarting!

D. John. O plague right well prevented! So will you say when you have seen the sequel. [*Exeunt.*]

[SCENE III]

Enter DOGBERRY *and his compartner* [VERGES] *with the* WATCH.

Dog. Are you good men and true?

Verg. Yea, or else it were pity but they should suffer salvation, body and soul.

Dog. Nay, that were a punishment too good for them, if they should have any allegiance in them, being chosen for the Prince's watch.

Verg. Well, give them their charge, neighbor Dogberry.

Dog. First, who think you the most desartless man to be constable?

1. Watch. Hugh Oatcake, sir, or George Seacole, for they can write and read.

Dog. Come hither, neighbor Seacole. God hath blest you with a good name. To be a well-favor'd man is the gift of fortune, but to write and read comes by nature.

2. Watch. Both which, Master Constable—

Dog. You have: I knew it would be your answer. Well, for your favor, sir, why, give God thanks, and make no boast of it, and for your writing and reading, let that appear when there is no need of such vanity. You are thought here to be the most senseless and fit man for the constable of the watch; therefore bear you the lanthorn. This is your charge: you shall comprehend all vagrom men; you are to bid any man stand, in the Prince's name.

2. Watch. How if 'a will not stand?

Dog. Why then take no note of him, but let him go, and presently call the rest of the watch together, and thank God you are rid of a knave.

Verg. If he will not stand when he is bidden, he is none of the Prince's subjects.

73. hobby-horses: i.e. buffoons (from the name of a performer in the morris-dance whose costume and antics suggested a horse).
74. For: upon. **81. Good den:** good evening.
94. discover: reveal. **96. aim better at:** judge better of.
98. well: in high esteem. **dearness:** affection.
102–3. circumstances short'ned: without unnecessary details.
103–4. has . . . of: i.e. is not worth even the short time we have spent in mentioning her. **109. paint out:** depict.
112. warrant: proof (is shown). **119. that:** what.

129. coldly: calmly. **131. untowardly turn'd:** perversely altered.

III.iii. Location: A street.
1. true: loyal.
3. salvation: blunder for *damnation.* Dogberry's and Verges' words frequently mean precisely the opposite of what the speaker intends; witness *allegiance* (line 5), *desartless* (line 9), *senseless* (line 23).
14. well-favor'd: good-looking. **19. favor:** appearance.
24. lanthorn: variant form of *lantern* (by popular etymology from the fact that lanterns often had sides made of transparent sheets of horn).
25. comprehend: i.e. apprehend. **vagrom:** i.e. vagrant.
26. stand: stop.

Dog. True, and they are to meddle with none but the Prince's subjects. You shall also make no noise in the streets; for, for the watch to babble and to talk, is most tolerable, and not to be endur'd.

[2.] *Watch*. We will rather sleep than talk, we know what belongs to a watch.

Dog. Why, you speak like an ancient and most quiet watchman, for I cannot see how sleeping should offend; only have a care that your bills be not stol'n. Well, you are to call at all the alehouses, and bid those that are drunk get them to bed.

[2.] *Watch*. How if they will not?

Dog. Why then let them alone till they are sober. If they make you not then the better answer, you may say they are not the men you took them for.

[2.] *Watch*. Well, sir.

Dog. If you meet a thief, you may suspect him, by virtue of your office, to be no true man; and for such kind of men, the less you meddle or make with them, why, the more is for your honesty.

[2.] *Watch*. If we know him to be a thief, shall we not lay hands on him?

Dog. Truly by your office you may, but I think they that touch pitch will be defil'd. The most peaceable way for you, if you do take a thief, is to let him show himself what he is, and steal out of your company.

Verg. You have been always call'd a merciful man, partner.

Dog. Truly, I would not hang a dog by my will, much more a man who hath any honesty in him.

Verg. If you hear a child cry in the night, you must call to the nurse and bid her still it.

[2.] *Watch*. How if the nurse be asleep and will not hear us?

Dog. Why then depart in peace, and let the child wake her with crying, for the ewe that will not hear her lamb when it baes will never answer a calf when he bleats.

Verg. 'Tis very true.

Dog. This is the end of the charge: you, constable, are to present the Prince's own person. If you meet the Prince in the night, you may stay him.

Verg. Nay, by'r lady, that I think 'a cannot.

Dog. Five shillings to one on't, with any man that knows the [statues], he may stay him; marry, not without the Prince be willing, for indeed the watch ought to offend no man, and it is an offense to stay a man against his will.

Verg. By'r lady, I think it be so.

Dog. Ha, ah ha! Well, masters, good night. And there be any matter of weight chances, call up me. Keep your fellows' counsels and your own, and good night. Come, neighbor.

[2.] *Watch*. Well, masters, we hear our charge. Let us go sit here upon the church-bench till two, and then all to bed.

Dog. One word more, honest neighbors. I pray you watch about Signior Leonato's door, for the wedding being there to-morrow, there is a great coil to-night. Adieu! Be vigitant, I beseech you.

Exeunt [Dogberry and Verges].

Enter BORACHIO *and* CONRADE.

Bora. What, Conrade!

[2.] *Watch*. [*Aside*.] Peace, stir not.

Bora. Conrade, I say!

Con. Here, man, I am at thy elbow.

Bora. Mass, and my elbow itch'd; I thought there would a scab follow.

Con. I will owe thee an answer for that, and now forward with thy tale.

Bora. Stand thee close then under this penthouse, for it drizzles rain, and I will, like a true drunkard, utter all to thee.

[2.] *Watch*. [*Aside*.] Some treason, masters, yet stand close.

Bora. Therefore know I have earn'd of Don John a thousand ducats.

Con. Is it possible that any villainy should be so dear?

Bora. Thou shouldst rather ask if it were possible any villainy should be so rich; for when rich villains have need of poor ones, poor ones may make what price they will.

Con. I wonder at it.

Bora. That shows thou art unconfirm'd. Thou knowest that the fashion of a doublet, or a hat, or a cloak, is nothing to a man.

Con. Yes, it is apparel.

Bora. I mean the fashion.

Con. Yes, the fashion is the fashion.

Bora. Tush, I may as well say the fool's the fool. But seest thou not what a deformed thief this fashion is?

[2.] *Watch*. [*Aside*.] I know that Deformed; 'a has been a vile thief this seven year; 'a goes up and down like a gentleman. I remember his name.

Bora. Didst thou not hear somebody?

Con. No, 'twas the vane on the house.

Bora. Seest thou not, I say, what a deformed thief this fashion is, how giddily 'a turns about all the hot-bloods between fourteen and five-and-thirty, sometimes fashioning them like Pharaoh's soldiers in the reechy painting, sometime like god Bel's priests in the old church-window, sometime

33. meddle: have to do. **36. tolerable:** for *intolerable*.
38. belongs to: are the duties of.
41. bills: hooked blades fastened on long poles.
46–47. make . . . answer: . . . don't then agree to go home.
51. true: honest. **53. is:** it is.
57. they . . . defil'd. A commonplace, derived from the Apocryphal book Ecclesiasticus (13:1). **64. more:** for *less*. **66. still:** quiet.
75. present: represent. **79. statues:** i.e. statutes.
80. without: unless.

94. coil: fuss, to-do. **vigitant:** i.e. vigilant.
99. Mass: by the Mass. **100. scab:** scurvy fellow.
103. penthouse: a kind of porch structure, projecting from the main building.
104–5. like . . . all. Referring to the Latin tag "In vino veritas."
107. stand close: keep concealed. **111. dear:** costly.
113. villainy: i.e. one wanting villainy to be committed.
117. unconfirm'd: inexperienced.
119. is . . . man: i.e. does not make the man.
124. deformed thief: ill-formed thief (because fashion assumes such fantastic shapes [lines 133–38] and robs men of their money by changing so often). **134. reechy:** smoky, dirty.
135. Bel's priests. An allusion to the Apocryphal story of Bel (Baal) and the Dragon.

like the shaven Hercules in the smirch'd worm-eaten tapestry, where his codpiece seems as massy as his club?

Con. All this I see, and I see that the fashion wears out more apparel than the man. But art not thou thyself giddy with the fashion too, that thou hast shifted out of thy tale into telling me of the fashion?

Bora. Not so neither, but know that I have to-night woo'd Margaret, the Lady Hero's gentlewoman, by the name of Hero. She leans me out at her mistress' chamber-window, bids me a thousand times good night—I tell this tale vildly, I should first tell thee how the Prince, Claudio, and my master, planted and plac'd and possess'd by my master Don John, saw afar off in the orchard this amiable encounter.

Con. And thought they Margaret was Hero?

Bora. Two of them did, the Prince and Claudio, but the devil my master knew she was Margaret; and partly by his oaths, which first possess'd them, partly by the dark night, which did deceive them, but chiefly by my villainy, which did confirm any slander that Don John had made, away went Claudio enrag'd; swore he would meet her as he was appointed next morning at the temple, and there, before the whole congregation, shame her with what he saw o'er-night, and send her home again without a husband.

[2.] Watch. We charge you, in the Prince's name, stand!

[1.] Watch. Call up the right Master Constable. We have here recover'd the most dangerous piece of lechery that ever was known in the commonwealth.

[2.] Watch. And one Deformed is one of them; I know him, 'a wears a lock.

Con. Masters, masters—

2. Watch. You'll be made bring Deformed forth, I warrant you.

Con. Masters—

[2. Watch.] Never speak, we charge you; let us obey you to go with us.

Bora. We are like to prove a goodly commodity, being taken up of these men's bills.

Con. A commodity in question, I warrant you. Come, we'll obey you. *Exeunt.*

[SCENE IV]

Enter HERO *and* MARGARET *and* URSULA.

Hero. Good Ursula, wake my cousin Beatrice, and desire her to rise.

Urs. I will, lady.

Hero. And bid her come hither.

Urs. Well. [*Exit.*]

Marg. Troth, I think your other rebato were better.

Hero. No, pray thee, good Meg, I'll wear this.

Marg. By my troth 's not so good, and I warrant your cousin will say so.

Hero. My cousin's a fool, and thou art another. I'll wear none but this.

Marg. I like the new tire within excellently, if the hair were a thought browner; and your gown's a most rare fashion, i' faith. I saw the Duchess of Milan's gown that they praise so.

Hero. O, that exceeds, they say.

Marg. By my troth 's but a night-gown [in] respect of yours: cloth a' gold and cuts, and lac'd with silver, set with pearls, down sleeves, side sleeves, and skirts, round underborne with a bluish tinsel; but for a fine, quaint, graceful, and excellent fashion, yours is worth ten on't.

Hero. God give me joy to wear it, for my heart is exceeding heavy.

Marg. 'Twill be heavier soon by the weight of a man.

Hero. Fie upon thee, art not asham'd?

Marg. Of what, lady? of speaking honorably? Is not marriage honorable in a beggar? Is not your lord honorable without marriage? I think you would have me say, "saving your reverence, a husband." And bad thinking do not wrest true speaking, I'll offend nobody. Is there any harm in "the heavier for a husband"? None, I think, and it be the right husband and the right wife; otherwise 'tis light, and not heavy. Ask my Lady Beatrice else, here she comes.

Enter BEATRICE.

Hero. Good morrow, coz.

Beat. Good morrow, sweet Hero.

Hero. Why, how now? Do you speak in the sick tune?

Beat. I am out of all other tune, methinks.

Marg. Clap 's into "Light a' love"; that goes without a burden. Do you sing it, and I'll dance it.

136. shaven Hercules. This allusion has not been identified; probably the reference is to the Omphale episode (see note to II.i.253).
137. codpiece: the bag-like flap at the front of men's breeches.
139–40. fashion . . . man: i.e. clothes are more often discarded because the fashion has changed than because they are worn-out.
142. shifted. With a quibble on the meaning "changed (clothing)."
150. possess'd: informed. **151. amiable:** loving.
166. right Master. By mistaken analogy with such honorifics as "right honorable" and "right worshipful."
167. recover'd: for *discovered.* **168. lechery:** for *treachery* (?).
170. lock: i.e. a love-lock of hair. **176. obey.** He means *command.*
177. commodity: goods. **178. taken up:** (1) taken on credit; (2) arrested. **bills:** (1) bonds; (2) pikes.
179. in question: (1) questionable; (2) about to be tried at law.

III.iv. Location: Hero's apartment in Leonato's house.
5. Well: very well. **6. rebato:** stiff collar supporting a ruff.
9. 's: it is. **13. tire:** headdress. **within:** in the inner room.
17. exceeds: is beyond comparison.
18. night-gown: dressing gown.
18–19. in respect of: compared with.
19. cuts: slashed openings, showing the fabric underneath. **lac'd:** trimmed. **20. down sleeves:** long tight sleeves.
20–21. side sleeves: wide ornamental sleeves hanging open from the shoulder.
21. round underborne: lined around the bottom of the skirt.
22. quaint: elegant. **30. in:** i.e. even in.
32. saving your reverence: a phrase of apology before an improper expression.
33. And bad: if bawdy. **wrest:** twist, misinterpret.
37. light. Punning on the meaning "wanton."
38. else: i.e. if this isn't true.
42. sick tune: i.e. voice of a sick person.
44. Clap 's: let's shift. **Light a' love:** a popular song.
45. burden: bass undersong (but with punning reference to "weight of a man").

Beat. Ye light a' love with your heels! then if your husband have stables enough, you'll see he shall lack no barns.

Marg. O illegitimate construction! I scorn that with my heels.

Beat. 'Tis almost five a' clock, cousin, 'tis time you were ready. By my troth, I am exceeding ill. Heigh-ho!

Marg. For a hawk, a horse, or a husband?

Beat. For the letter that begins them all, H.

Marg. Well, and you be not turn'd Turk, there's no more sailing by the star.

Beat. What means the fool, trow?

Marg. Nothing I, but God send every one their heart's desire!

Hero. These gloves the Count sent me, they are an excellent perfume.

Beat. I am stuff'd, cousin, I cannot smell.

Marg. A maid, and stuff'd! There's goodly catching of cold.

Beat. O, God help me, God help me, how long have you profess'd apprehension?

Marg. Ever since you left it. Doth not my wit become me rarely?

Beat. It is not seen enough, you should wear it in your cap. By my troth, I am sick.

Marg. Get you some of this distill'd *carduus benedictus*, and lay it to your heart; it is the only thing for a qualm.

Hero. There thou prick'st her with a thistle.

Beat. *Benedictus*! why *benedictus*? You have some moral in this *benedictus*.

Marg. Moral? no, by my troth I have no moral meaning, I meant plain holy-thistle. You may think perchance that I think you are in love. Nay, by'r lady, I am not such a fool to think what I list, nor I list not to think what I can, nor indeed I cannot think, if I would think my heart out of thinking, that you are in love, or that you will be in love, or that you can be in love. Yet Benedick was such another, and now is he become a man. He swore he would never marry, and yet now in despite of his heart he eats his meat without grudging; and how you may be converted I know not, but methinks you look with your eyes as other women do.

Beat. What pace is this that thy tongue keeps?

Marg. Not a false gallop.

Enter URSULA.

Urs. Madam, withdraw, the Prince, the Count, Signior Benedick, Don John, and all the gallants of the town are come to fetch you to church.

Hero. Help to dress me, good coz, good Meg, good Ursula. [*Exeunt.*]

[SCENE V]

Enter LEONATO *and the Constable* [DOGBERRY] *and the Headborough* [VERGES].

Leon. What would you with me, honest neighbor?

Dog. Marry, sir, I would have some confidence with you that decerns you nearly.

Leon. Brief, I pray you, for you see it is a busy time with me.

Dog. Marry, this it is, sir.

Verg. Yes, in truth it is, sir.

Leon. What is it, my good friends?

Dog. Goodman Verges, sir, speaks a little [off] the matter; an old man, sir, and his wits are not so blunt as, God help, I would desire they were, but in faith, honest as the skin between his brows.

Verg. Yes, I thank God I am as honest as any man living, that is an old man, and no honester than I.

Dog. Comparisons are odorous—*palabras*, neighbor Verges.

Leon. Neighbors, you are tedious.

Dog. It pleases your worship to say so, but we are the poor Duke's officers; but truly, for mine own part, if I were as tedious as a king, I could find in my heart to bestow it all of your worship.

Leon. All thy tediousness on me, ah?

Dog. Yea, and 'twere a thousand pound more than 'tis, for I hear as good exclamation on your worship as of any man in the city, and though I be but a poor man, I am glad to hear it.

Verg. And so am I.

Leon. I would fain know what you have to say.

Verg. Marry, sir, our watch to-night, excepting your worship's presence, ha' ta'en a couple of as arrant knaves as any in Messina.

Dog. A good old man, sir, he will be talking; as they say, "When the age is in, the wit is out." God help us, it is a world to see! Well said, i' faith,

47. Ye . . . heels: i.e you are light-heeled (slang for "unchaste").
49. barns. With pun on *bairns*, "children."
51. with my heels: contemptuously.
56. H. With pun on *ache*, which was pronounced *aitch* in Shakespeare's day.
57. turn'd Turk: i.e. abandoned your faith (which was that you would never fall in love).
58. no . . . star: no more navigating by the north star, i.e. no more trusting to anything. **59. trow:** I wonder.
64. I am stuff'd: i.e. I have a cold (with bawdy pun by Margaret following).
68. profess'd apprehension: made wit your profession.
71–72. wear . . . cap: i.e. as a fool does his coxcomb.
73–74. carduus benedictus: blessed (or holy) thistle, a medicinal herb.
78. moral: hidden meaning. **83. list:** please.
87. a man: i.e. like other men.
89–90. eats . . . grudging: i.e. has an appetite like any other man.
94. a false gallop: (1) a canter; (2) running on untruthfully.

III.v. Location: Leonato's house.
o.s.d. Headborough: petty constable.
2. confidence: for *conference*.
3. decerns: for *concerns*. **nearly:** intimately.
9. Goodman: regular title for one just below the rank of gentleman.
12. honest . . . brows. A proverbial comparison.
16. odorous: for *odious*. **palabras:** a shortening of Spanish *pocas palabras*, "few words." **20. poor Duke's.** He intends *Duke's poor*.
22. of: on. **24. and:** even if.
25. exclamation: for *acclamation* (?). Dogberry's word is an unfortunate choice, since it normally meant "accusation" or "reproach."
30. to-night: last night. **excepting:** for *respecting*. Dogberry here intends a polite phrase meaning "If I may speak of such things without offending your worship," but he says something far different.
34. When . . . out: an adaptation of the proverb "When ale is in, wit is out."
35. it . . . see: a proverbial phrase equivalent to "It is wonderful to behold"; but Dogberry seems to mean "What a world we live in."

neighbor Verges. Well, God's a good man; and two men ride of a horse, one must ride behind. An honest soul, i' faith, sir, by my troth he is, as ever broke bread; but God is to be worshipp'd; all men are not alike, alas, good neighbor!

Leon. Indeed, neighbor, he comes too short of you.

Dog. Gifts that God gives.

Leon. I must leave you.

Dog. One word, sir. Our watch, sir, have indeed comprehended two aspicious persons, and we would have them this morning examin'd before your worship.

Leon. Take their examination yourself, and bring it me. I am now in great haste, as it may appear unto you.

Dog. It shall be suffigance.

Leon. Drink some wine ere you go; fare you well.

[*Enter a* MESSENGER.]

Mess. My lord, they stay for you to give your daughter to her husband.

Leon. I'll wait upon them, I am ready.

[*Exeunt Leonato and Messenger.*]

Dog. Go, good partner, go, get you to Francis Seacole, bid him bring his pen and inkhorn to the jail. We are now to examination these men.

Verg. And we must do it wisely.

Dog. We will spare for no wit, I warrant you. Here's that shall drive some of them to a non-come; only get the learned writer to set down our excommunication, and meet me at the jail. [*Exeunt.*]

[ACT IV, SCENE I]

Enter Prince [DON PEDRO, DON JOHN *the*] *Bastard,* LEONATO, FRIAR [FRANCIS], CLAUDIO, BENEDICK, HERO, *and* BEATRICE [*with* ATTENDANTS].

Leon. Come, Friar Francis, be brief—only to the plain form of marriage, and you shall recount their particular duties afterwards.

Friar. You come hither, my lord, to marry this lady.

Claud. No.

Leon. To be married to her. Friar, you come to marry her.

Friar. Lady, you come hither to be married to this count.

Hero. I do.

Friar. If either of you know any inward impediment why you should not be conjoin'd, I charge you on your souls to utter it.

Claud. Know you any, Hero?

Hero. None, my lord.

Friar. Know you any, Count?

Leon. I dare make his answer, none.

Claud. O, what men dare do! What men may do! What men daily do, not knowing what they do!

Bene. How now! interjections? Why then, some be of laughing, as, ah, ha, he!

Claud. Stand thee by, friar. Father, by your leave,
Will you with free and unconstrained soul
Give me this maid, your daughter?

Leon. As freely, son, as God did give her me.

Claud. And what have I to give you back whose worth
May counterpoise this rich and precious gift?

D. Pedro. Nothing, unless you render her again.

Claud. Sweet Prince, you learn me noble thankfulness.
There, Leonato, take her back again.
Give not this rotten orange to your friend,
She's but the sign and semblance of her honor.
Behold how like a maid she blushes here!
O, what authority and show of truth
Can cunning sin cover itself withal!
Comes not that blood as modest evidence
To witness simple virtue? Would you not swear,
All you that see her, that she were a maid,
By these exterior shows? But she is none:
She knows the heat of a luxurious bed;
Her blush is guiltiness, not modesty.

Leon. What do you mean, my lord?

Claud. Not to be married,
Not to knit my soul to an approved wanton.

Leon. Dear my lord, if you, in your own proof,
Have vanquish'd the resistance of her youth,
And made defeat of her virginity—

Claud. I know what you would say. If I have known her,
You will say, she did embrace me as a husband,
And so extenuate the 'forehand sin.
No, Leonato,
I never tempted her with word too large,
But as a brother to his sister, show'd
Bashful sincerity and comely love.

Hero. And seem'd I ever otherwise to you?

Claud. Out on thee seeming! I will write against it:
You seem to me as Dian in her orb,
As chaste as is the bud ere it be blown;

36. God's . . . man: God is good (proverbial).
37. of a horse: on one horse.
39. God . . . worshipp'd: i.e. we must praise God for whatever he sees fit to bestow (?).
46. comprehended: for *apprehended.* **aspicious:** for *suspicious.*
52. suffigance: for *sufficient.* **56. wait upon:** attend.
62. non-come: shortened form of *non compos mentis,* "not of sound mind," but Dogberry seems to intend *nonplus.*
63–64. excommunication: for *examination,* or (perhaps) *communication.*

IV.i. Location: A church.
12. inward: secret, private.

21–22. some . . . he. Grammars classified the interjections according to the emotions they expressed; Benedick's sample is quoted from Lily's Latin grammar.
28. counterpoise: balance, be equivalent to. **30. learn:** teach.
35. authority: authenticity.
37. modest evidence: evidence of modesty. **41. luxurious:** lustful.
44. approved: proved. **45. proof:** i.e. test or trial of her.
50. extenuate: lessen, excuse. **'forehand sin:** i.e. premarital sex relations. **52. large:** broad, immodest.
56. thee seeming: i.e. you in your mere appearance (of good).
57. Dian: Diana, emblematic of virginity. **orb:** sphere. Diana, in one of her aspects, was the moon-goddess.
58. be blown: open.

But you are more intemperate in your blood
Than Venus, or those pamp'red animals
That rage in savage sensuality.
Hero. Is my lord well, that he doth speak so wide?
Leon. Sweet Prince, why speak not you?
D. Pedro. What should I speak?
I stand dishonor'd, that have gone about
To link my dear friend to a common stale.
Leon. Are these things spoken, or do I but dream?
D. John. Sir, they are spoken, and these things are true.
Bene. This looks not like a nuptial.
Hero. "True"! O God!
Claud. Leonato, stand I here?
Is this the Prince? is this the Prince's brother?
Is this face Hero's? are our eyes our own?
Leon. All this is so, but what of this, my lord?
Claud. Let me but move one question to your daughter,
And by that fatherly and kindly power
That you have in her, bid her answer truly.
Leon. I charge thee do so, as thou art my child.
Hero. O God defend me, how am I beset!
What kind of catechizing call you this?
Claud. To make you answer truly to your name.
Hero. Is it not Hero? Who can blot that name
With any just reproach?
Claud. Marry, that can Hero,
Hero itself can blot out Hero's virtue.
What man was he talk'd with you yesternight
Out at your window betwixt twelve and one?
Now if you are a maid, answer to this.
Hero. I talk'd with no man at that hour, my lord.
D. Pedro. Why then are you no maiden. Leonato,
I am sorry you must hear. Upon mine honor,
Myself, my brother, and this grieved count
Did see her, hear her, at that hour last night
Talk with a ruffian at her chamber-window,
Who hath indeed, most like a liberal villain,
Confess'd the vile encounters they have had
A thousand times in secret.
D. John. Fie, fie, they are not to be named, my lord,
Not to be spoke of;
There is not chastity enough in language
Without offense to utter them. Thus, pretty lady,
I am sorry for thy much misgovernment.
Claud. O Hero! what a Hero hadst thou been,
If half thy outward graces had been placed
About thy thoughts and counsels of thy heart!
But fare thee well, most foul, most fair! Farewell,
Thou pure impiety and impious purity!
For thee I'll lock up all the gates of love,
And on my eyelids shall conjecture hang,
To turn all beauty into thoughts of harm,
And never shall it more be gracious.
Leon. Hath no man's dagger here a point for me?
[*Hero swoons*.]
Beat. Why, how now, cousin, wherefore sink you down?
D. John. Come, let us go. These things, come thus to light,
Smother her spirits up.
[*Exeunt Don Pedro, Don John, and Claudio*.]
Bene. How doth the lady?
Beat. Dead, I think. Help, uncle!
Hero, why, Hero! Uncle! Signior Benedick! Friar!
Leon. O Fate! take not away thy heavy hand,
Death is the fairest cover for her shame
That may be wish'd for.
Beat. How now, cousin Hero?
Friar. Have comfort, lady.
Leon. Dost thou look up?
Friar. Yea, wherefore should she not?
Leon. Wherefore? why, doth not every earthly thing
Cry shame upon her? could she here deny
The story that is printed in her blood?
Do not live, Hero, do not ope thine eyes;
For did I think thou wouldst not quickly die,
Thought I thy spirits were stronger than thy shames,
Myself would, on the rearward of reproaches,
Strike at thy life. Griev'd I, I had but one?
Chid I for that at frugal nature's frame?
O, one too much by thee! Why had I one?
Why ever wast thou lovely in my eyes?
Why had I not with charitable hand
Took up a beggar's issue at my gates,
Who smirched thus and mir'd with infamy,
I might have said, "No part of it is mine;
This shame derives itself from unknown loins"?
But mine, and mine I lov'd, and mine I prais'd,
And mine that I was proud on, mine so much
That I myself was to myself not mine,
Valuing of her—why, she, O she is fall'n
Into a pit of ink, that the wide sea
Hath drops too few to wash her clean again,
And salt too little which may season give
To her foul tainted flesh!
Bene. Sir, sir, be patient.
For my part I am so attir'd in wonder,
I know not what to say.
Beat. O, on my soul, my cousin is belied!
Bene. Lady, were you her bedfellow last night?
Beat. No, truly, not, although until last night,
I have this twelvemonth been her bedfellow.
Leon. Confirm'd, confirm'd! O, that is stronger made

62. **wide:** wide of the mark, far from the truth.
64. **gone about:** endeavored. 65. **stale:** whore.
73. **move:** propose. 74. **kindly:** natural.
79. **answer . . . name:** tell truthfully by what name you should be called (?) or acknowledge that the name you have been called ("common stale") belongs to you (?).
82. **Hero itself:** the name Hero (now the name of an unchaste woman).
89. **grieved:** aggrieved, wronged. 92. **liberal:** gross, licentious.
99. **much misgovernment:** great misconduct.
102. **thoughts and counsels:** i.e. secret thoughts (hendiadys).
105. **For thee:** because of my experience with you.
106. **conjecture:** suspicion. 108. **be gracious:** seem beautiful.
112. **spirits:** vital forces. 122. **blood:** blushes.
125. **shames:** feelings of shame.
126. **on . . . reproaches:** after reproaching you.
128. **frame:** design (with respect to the number of my offspring).
138. **I . . . mine:** i.e. that I was nothing to myself.
139. **Valuing of her:** since I valued her so exclusively.
142. **season give:** act as a preservative, i.e. as a restorative.
144. **attir'd:** wrapped.

Which was before barr'd up with ribs of iron!
Would the two princes lie, and Claudio lie,
Who lov'd her so, that speaking of her foulness,
Wash'd it with tears? Hence from her, let her die.
Friar. Hear me a little,
For I have only been silent so long,
And given way unto this course of fortune,
By noting of the lady. I have mark'd
A thousand blushing apparitions
To start into her face, a thousand innocent shames
In angel whiteness beat away those blushes,
And in her eye there hath appear'd a fire
To burn the errors that these princes hold
Against her maiden truth. Call me a fool,
Trust not my reading, nor my observations,
Which with experimental seal doth warrant
The tenure of my book; trust not my age,
My reverence, calling, nor divinity,
If this sweet lady lie not guiltless here
Under some biting error.
Leon. Friar, it cannot be.
Thou seest that all the grace that she hath left
Is that she will not add to her damnation
A sin of perjury; she not denies it.
Why seek'st thou then to cover with excuse
That which appears in proper nakedness?
Friar. Lady, what man is he you are accus'd of?
Hero. They know that do accuse me, I know none.
If I know more of any man alive
Than that which maiden modesty doth warrant,
Let all my sins lack mercy! O my father,
Prove you that any man with me convers'd
At hours unmeet, or that I yesternight
Maintain'd the change of words with any creature,
Refuse me, hate me, torture me to death!
Friar. There is some strange misprision in the princes.
Bene. Two of them have the very bent of honor,
And if their wisdoms be misled in this,
The practice of it lives in John the Bastard,
Whose spirits toil in frame of villainies.
Leon. I know not. If they speak but truth of her,
These hands shall tear her; if they wrong her honor,
The proudest of them shall well hear of it.
Time hath not yet so dried this blood of mine,
Nor age so eat up my invention,
Nor fortune made such havoc of my means,
Nor my bad life reft me so much of friends,
But they shall find, awak'd in such a kind,
Both strength of limb, and policy of mind,
Ability in means, and choice of friends,
To quit me of them throughly.
Friar. Pause awhile,
And let my counsel sway you in this case.
Your daughter here the [princes] left for dead,
Let her awhile be secretly kept in,
And publish it that she is dead indeed.
Maintain a mourning ostentation,
And on your family's old monument
Hang mournful epitaphs, and do all rites
That appertain unto a burial.
Leon. What shall become of this? what will this do?
Friar. Marry, this well carried shall on her behalf
Change slander to remorse; that is some good.
But not for that dream I on this strange course,
But on this travail look for greater birth:
She dying, as it must be so maintain'd,
Upon the instant that she was accus'd,
Shall be lamented, pitied, and excus'd
Of every hearer; for it so falls out
That what we have we prize not to the worth
Whiles we enjoy it, but being lack'd and lost,
Why then we rack the value; then we find
The virtue that possession would not show us
Whiles it was ours. So will it fare with Claudio:
When he shall hear she died upon his words,
Th' idea of her life shall sweetly creep
Into his study of imagination,
And every lovely organ of her life
Shall come apparell'd in more precious habit,
More moving, delicate, and full of life,
Into the eye and prospect of his soul,
Than when she liv'd indeed. Then shall he mourn,
If ever love had interest in his liver,
And wish he had not so accused her;
No, though he thought his accusation true.
Let this be so, and doubt not but success
Will fashion the event in better shape
Than I can lay it down in likelihood.
But if all aim but this be levell'd false,
The supposition of the lady's death
Will quench the wonder of her infamy.
And if it sort not well, you may conceal her,
As best befits her wounded reputation,
In some reclusive and religious life,
Out of all eyes, tongues, minds, and injuries.
Bene. Signior Leonato, let the friar advise you,
And though you know my inwardness and love

156–58. I . . . lady. I have kept silence so long, allowing these events to take their free course, only because I have been occupied in observing the lady (?). The passage has difficulties and may be textually corrupt (see the Textual Notes).
166–67. experimental . . . book: the seal of experience guarantees as genuine the conclusions I have drawn from my reading (of her face). *Tenure* = tenor, import. **175. proper:** its own.
182. unmeet: improper. **183. change:** exchange.
184. Refuse: renounce, cast off. **185. misprision:** misapprehension.
186. the very bent of: a perfect inclination toward.
188. practice: plotting. **189. frame:** contriving.
194. eat: eaten. **invention:** power of devising (retaliation); cf. *policy of mind*, line 198. **197. kind:** manner, degree.
198. policy of mind: shrewdness in contriving.
200. quit . . . throughly: settle my account with them thoroughly.
205. mourning ostentation: show of mourning.
209. become of: result from. **210. carried:** managed.
213. travail: labor (in the double sense of "effort" and "pain of childbirth"). **220. rack:** stretch. **223. upon:** as a result of.
225. study of imagination: imaginative study, i.e. musing, reverie.
226. organ . . . life: aspect of her as she was when she lived.
229. prospect: view.
231. interest in: any claim upon (a legal term). **liver.** The supposed seat of the passion of love.
234. success: the happy working out (of my plan).
235. event: outcome.
236. lay . . . likelihood: suggest its probable consequences.
237. if . . . false: if we miss our aim in every other respect.
240. sort: turn out.
242. reclusive: retired, secluded (as a religious recluse).
243. injuries: insults.
245. inwardness and love: close friendship (hendiadys).

Is very much unto the Prince and Claudio,
Yet, by mine honor, I will deal in this
As secretly and justly as your soul
Should with your body.

Leon. Being that I flow in grief,
The smallest twine may lead me.

Friar. 'Tis well consented; presently away,
For to strange sores strangely they strain the cure.
Come, lady, die to live; this wedding-day
Perhaps is but prolong'd, have patience and endure.

Exit [with all but Benedick and Beatrice].

Bene. Lady Beatrice, have you wept all this while?

Beat. Yea, and I will weep a while longer.

Bene. I will not desire that.

Beat. You have no reason, I do it freely.

Bene. Surely I do believe your fair cousin is wrong'd.

Beat. Ah, how much might the man deserve of me that would right her!

Bene. Is there any way to show such friendship?

Beat. A very even way, but no such friend.

Bene. May a man do it?

Beat. It is a man's office, but not yours.

Bene. I do love nothing in the world so well as you—is not that strange?

Beat. As strange as the thing I know not. It were as possible for me to say I lov'd nothing so well as you, but believe me not; and yet I lie not: I confess nothing, nor I deny nothing. I am sorry for my cousin.

Bene. By my sword, Beatrice, thou lovest me.

Beat. Do not swear and eat it.

Bene. I will swear by it that you love me, and I will make him eat it that says I love not you.

Beat. Will you not eat your word?

Bene. With no sauce that can be devis'd to it. I protest I love thee.

Beat. Why then God forgive me!

Bene. What offense, sweet Beatrice?

Beat. You have stay'd me in a happy hour, I was about to protest I lov'd you.

Bene. And do it with all thy heart.

Beat. I love you with so much of my heart that none is left to protest.

Bene. Come, bid me do any thing for thee.

Beat. Kill Claudio.

Bene. Ha, not for the wide world.

Beat. You kill me to deny it. Farewell.

Bene. Tarry, sweet Beatrice.

Beat. I am gone, though I am here; there is no love in you. Nay, I pray you let me go.

Bene. Beatrice—

Beat. In faith, I will go.

Bene. We'll be friends first.

Beat. You dare easier be friends with me than fight with mine enemy.

Bene. Is Claudio thine enemy?

Beat. Is 'a not approv'd in the height a villain, that hath slander'd, scorn'd, dishonor'd my kinswoman? O that I were a man! What, bear her in hand until they come to take hands, and then with public accusation, uncover'd slander, unmitigated rancor—O God, that I were a man! I would eat his heart in the market-place.

Bene. Hear me, Beatrice—

Beat. Talk with a man out at a window! a proper saying!

Bene. Nay, but, Beatrice—

Beat. Sweet Hero, she is wrong'd, she is sland'red, she is undone.

Bene. Beat—

Beat. Princes and counties! Surely a princely testimony, a goodly count, Count Comfect, a sweet gallant surely! O that I were a man for his sake! or that I had any friend would be a man for my sake! But manhood is melted into cur'sies, valor into compliment, and men are only turn'd into tongue, and trim ones too. He is now as valiant as Hercules that only tells a lie, and swears it. I cannot be a man with wishing, therefore I will die a woman with grieving.

Bene. Tarry, good Beatrice. By this hand, I love thee.

Beat. Use it for my love some other way than swearing by it.

Bene. Think you in your soul the Count Claudio hath wrong'd Hero?

Beat. Yea, as sure as I have a thought or a soul.

Bene. Enough, I am engag'd, I will challenge him. I will kiss your hand, and so I leave you. By this hand, Claudio shall render me a dear account. As you hear of me, so think of me. Go comfort your cousin. I must say she is dead; and so farewell. *[Exeunt.]*

[Scene II]

Enter the Constables [Dogberry *and* Verges] *and the Town Clerk* [*or* Sexton] *in gowns,* [*and the* Watch *with* Conrade *and*] Borachio.

Dog. Is our whole dissembly appear'd?

Verg. O, a stool and a cushion for the sexton.

Sex. Which be the malefactors?

Dog. Marry, that am I and my partner.

Verg. Nay, that's certain, we have the exhibition to examine.

249. Being that: since. **flow in:** am dissolved in (?) or am afloat on (?).
252. For . . . cure: strange diseases require strange and desperate cures. **254. prolong'd:** postponed. **264. even:** level, easy.
269. As strange: as much a stranger (playing on Benedick's use of *strange*). **275. eat it:** go back on your oath.
280. protest: declare (but Beatrice pretends to take it in the sense of "object," as she uses it herself in line 287).
283. in . . . hour: at just the right moment, opportunely.
291. deny: refuse. **293. am gone:** have left you (in spirit).

301. approv'd: proved. **height:** highest degree.
303–4. bear . . . hand: deceive her with false hopes.
305. uncover'd: unconcealed, open. **315. counties:** counts.
316. count: (1) the title: (2) legal indictment; (3) story. **Comfect:** comfit, sweetmeat. **317. for his sake:** i.e. to deal with him.
321. trim: fine. **331. engag'd:** bound by a pledge.
333. render . . . account: make a very costly settlement with me.

IV.ii. Location: A prison.
o.s.d. **gowns:** robes of office. **1. dissembly:** for *assembly.*
5. exhibition: possibly for *commission*, but *exhibition* could mean "an allowance of money"; in either case Verges blunders.

Sex. But which are the offenders that are to be examin'd? Let them come before Master Constable.

Dog. Yea, marry, let them come before me. What is your name, friend?

Bora. Borachio.

Dog. Pray write down Borachio. Yours, sirrah?

Con. I am a gentleman, sir, and my name is Conrade.

Dog. Write down Master Gentleman Conrade. Masters, do you serve God?

Both [*Con., Bora.*]. Yea, sir, we hope.

Dog. Write down, that they hope they serve God; and write God first, for God defend but God should go before such villains! Masters, it is prov'd already that you are little better than false knaves, and it will go near to be thought so shortly. How answer you for yourselves?

Con. Marry, sir, we say we are none.

Dog. A marvellous witty fellow, I assure you, but I will go about with him. Come you hither, sirrah; a word in your ear, sir. I say to you, it is thought you are false knaves.

Bora. Sir, I say to you, we are none.

Dog. Well, stand aside. 'Fore God, they are both in a tale. Have you writ down, that they are none?

Sex. Master Constable, you go not the way to examine; you must call forth the watch that are their accusers.

Dog. Yea, marry, that's the eftest way; let the watch come forth. Masters, I charge you in the Prince's name accuse these men.

1. Watch. This man said, sir, that Don John, the Prince's brother, was a villain.

Dog. Write down Prince John a villain. Why, this is flat perjury, to call a prince's brother villain.

Bora. Master Constable—

Dog. Pray thee, fellow, peace. I do not like thy look, I promise thee.

Sex. What heard you him say else?

2. Watch. Marry, that he had receiv'd a thousand ducats of Don John for accusing the Lady Hero wrongfully.

Dog. Flat burglary as ever was committed.

Verg. Yea, by mass, that it is.

Sex. What else, fellow?

1. Watch. And that Count Claudio did mean, upon his words, to disgrace Hero before the whole assembly, and not marry her.

Dog. O villain! thou wilt be condemn'd into everlasting redemption for this.

Sex. What else?

[*1. and 2.*] *Watch.* This is all.

Sex. And this is more, masters, than you can deny. Prince John is this morning secretly stol'n away. Hero was in this manner accus'd, in this very manner

12. sirrah: form of address to inferiors. **19. defend:** forbid.
25. witty: clever, cunning. **26. go about with:** outmaneuver.
31. in a tale: agreed on the same lie.
36. eftest. It is clear that he means something like "easiest" or "quickest," but not what word he may be mangling.
54. upon his words: on the basis of his accusation.
57. redemption. He means the opposite.

refus'd, and upon the grief of this suddenly died. Master Constable, let these men be bound, and brought to Leonato's. I will go before and show him their examination. [*Exit.*]

[*Dog.*] Come let them be opinion'd.

Verg. Let them be in the hands—

[*Con.*] [Off,] coxcomb!

Dog. God's my life, where's the sexton? Let him write down the Prince's officer coxcomb. Come, bind them. Thou naughty varlet!

[*Con.*] Away, you are an ass, you are an ass.

Dog. Dost thou not suspect my place? Dost thou not suspect my years? O that he were here to write me down as ass! But, masters, remember that I am an ass; though it be not written down, yet forget not that I am an ass. No, thou villain, thou art full of piety, as shall be prov'd upon thee by good witness. I am a wise fellow, and which is more, an officer, and which is more, a householder, and which is more, as pretty a piece of flesh as any is in Messina, and one that knows the law, go to, and a rich fellow enough, go to, and a fellow that hath had losses, and one that hath two gowns, and every thing handsome about him. Bring him away. O that I had been writ down an ass! *Exeunt.*

[ACT V, SCENE I]

Enter LEONATO *and his brother* [ANTONIO].

Ant. If you go on thus, you will kill yourself,
And 'tis not wisdom thus to second grief
Against yourself.
Leon. I pray thee cease thy counsel,
Which falls into mine ears as profitless
As water in a sieve. Give not me counsel,
Nor let no comforter delight mine ear
But such a one whose wrongs do suit with mine.
Bring me a father that so lov'd his child,
Whose joy of her is overwhelm'd like mine,
And bid him speak of patience;
Measure his woe the length and breadth of mine,
And let it answer every strain for strain,
As thus for thus, and such a grief for such,
In every lineament, branch, shape, and form;
If such a one will smile and stroke his beard,
And, sorrow wag, cry "hem!" when he should groan,
Patch grief with proverbs, make misfortune drunk
With candle-wasters, bring him yet to me,
And I of him will gather patience.
But there is no such man, for, brother, men

63. refus'd: renounced. **67. opinion'd:** for *pinioned.*
70. God's: God save. **72. naughty:** wicked.
74. suspect: for *respect.* **79. piety:** for *impiety.*
82. as . . . flesh: as fine a fellow.

V.i. Location: Near Leonato's house.
2. second: aid. **6. delight:** try to please. **7. suit with:** match.
11. Measure his woe: let his woe equal in its dimensions.
12. strain: strong feeling.
16. And, sorrow wag: and, letting sorrow go hang. Many editors emend to *Bid sorrow wag* (after Capell), i.e. bid sorrow be off.
17. drunk: i.e. insensible.
18. candle-wasters: those who sit up late over books; here, those who write moral treatises, and by extension, their good advice itself.

Can counsel and speak comfort to that grief
Which they themselves not feel, but tasting it,
Their counsel turns to passion, which before
Would give preceptial med'cine to rage,
Fetter strong madness in a silken thread,
Charm ache with air, and agony with words.
No, no, 'tis all men's office to speak patience
To those that wring under the load of sorrow,
But no man's virtue nor sufficiency
To be so moral when he shall endure
The like himself. Therefore give me no counsel,
My griefs cry louder than advertisement.
Ant. Therein do men from children nothing differ.
Leon. I pray thee peace. I will be flesh and blood,
For there was never yet philosopher
That could endure the toothache patiently,
However they have writ the style of gods,
And made a push at chance and sufferance.
Ant. Yet bend not all the harm upon yourself;
Make those that do offend you suffer too.
Leon. There thou speak'st reason; nay, I will do so.
My soul doth tell me Hero is belied,
And that shall Claudio know; so shall the Prince,
And all of them that thus dishonor her.

Enter Prince [Don Pedro] *and* Claudio.

Ant. Here comes the Prince and Claudio hastily.
D. Pedro. Good den, good den.
Claud. Good day to both of you.
Leon. Hear you, my lords—
D. Pedro. We have some haste, Leonato.
Leon. Some haste, my lord! Well, fare you well, my lord.
Are you so hasty now? well, all is one.
D. Pedro. Nay, do not quarrel with us, good old man.
Ant. If he could right himself with quarrelling,
Some of us would lie low.
Claud. Who wrongs him?
Leon. Marry, thou dost wrong me, thou dissembler, thou—
Nay, never lay thy hand upon thy sword,
I fear thee not.
Claud. Marry, beshrew my hand,
If it should give your age such cause of fear.
In faith, my hand meant nothing to my sword.
Leon. Tush, tush, man, never fleer and jest at me;
I speak not like a dotard nor a fool,
As under privilege of age to brag
What I have done being young, or what would do
Were I not old. Know, Claudio, to thy head,
Thou hast so wrong'd mine innocent child and me
That I am forc'd to lay my reverence by,
And with grey hairs and bruise of many days,
Do challenge thee to trial of a man.
I say thou hast belied mine innocent child!
Thy slander hath gone through and through her heart,
And she lies buried with her ancestors—
O, in a tomb where never scandal slept,
Save this of hers, fram'd by thy villainy!
Claud. My villainy?
Leon. Thine, Claudio, thine, I say.
D. Pedro. You say not right, old man.
Leon. My lord, my lord,
I'll prove it on his body, if he dare,
Despite his nice fence and his active practice,
His May of youth and bloom of lustihood.
Claud. Away, I will not have to do with you.
Leon. Canst thou so daff me? Thou hast kill'd my child.
If thou kill'st me, boy, thou shalt kill a man.
Ant. He shall kill two of us, and men indeed;
But that's no matter, let him kill one first.
Win me and wear me, let him answer me.
Come follow me, boy; come, sir boy, come follow me.
Sir boy, I'll whip you from your foining fence,
Nay, as I am a gentleman, I will.
Leon. Brother—
Ant. Content yourself. God knows I lov'd my niece,
And she is dead, slander'd to death by villains,
That dare as well answer a man indeed
As I dare take a serpent by the tongue.
Boys, apes, braggarts, Jacks, milksops!
Leon. Brother Anthony—
Ant. Hold you content. What, man! I know them, yea,
And what they weigh, even to the utmost scruple—
Scambling, outfacing, fashion-monging boys,
That lie and cog and flout, deprave and slander,
Go anticly, and show outward hideousness,
And speak [off] half a dozen dang'rous words,
How they might hurt their enemies—if they durst—
And this is all.
Leon. But, brother Anthony—
Ant. Come, 'tis no matter;
Do not you meddle, let me deal in this.
D. Pedro. Gentlemen both, we will not wake your patience.
My heart is sorry for your daughter's death;
But on my honor she was charg'd with nothing

24. preceptial: comprised of precepts. **26. air:** breath, i.e. words.
28. wring: writhe. **29. sufficiency:** ability.
30. moral: full of moral sentiments. **32. advertisement:** counsel.
37. style of gods: language worthy of gods (who are above human suffering).
38. a push at: an onslaught against (?), or an expression of contempt toward (*push* being a common form of *pish*) (?), (an expression of contempt). **sufferance:** suffering.
49. all is one: it does not matter.
52. Some of us. He means Don Pedro and Claudio.
55. beshrew: curse. **57. to:** i.e. in grasping. **58. fleer:** jeer.
62. head: face.

66. trial . . . man: i.e. text (or combat) worthy of a man.
75. nice fence: dextrous fencing (probably with a sneer in *nice* at the new Italian fashion of duelling with rapier and dagger in place of the older native half-sword and dagger; cf. line 84).
76. lustihood: bodily vigor. **78. daff:** doff, i.e. thrust aside.
80. men indeed: true men (cf. line 89).
82. Win . . . wear me: i.e. if he wants to have me, he'll have to overcome me first (a proverbial phrase used as a summons to action). **answer me:** meet me in response to my challenge.
84. foining: thrusting.
87. Content yourself: i.e. don't try to stop me.
94. Scambling: contentious. **outfacing:** insolent. **fashion-monging:** following the fashions, foppish.
95. cog: cheat. **deprave:** vilify.
96. Go anticly: go about fantastically dressed. **outward hideousness:** a threatening appearance. **97. dang'rous:** arrogant, threatening.
102. wake your patience: i.e. test your patience further, add to your troubles.

But what was true, and very full of proof.
Leon. My lord, my lord—
D. Pedro. I will not hear you.
Leon. No? Come, brother, away! I will be heard.
Ant. And shall, or some of us will smart for it.

Exeunt ambo [*Leonato and Antonio*].

Enter BENEDICK.

D. Pedro. See, see, here comes the man we went to seek.

Claud. Now, signior, what news?

Bene. Good day, my lord.

D. Pedro. Welcome, signior, you are almost come to part almost a fray.

Claud. We had lik'd to have had our two noses snapp'd off with two old men without teeth.

D. Pedro. Leonato and his brother. What think'st thou? Had we fought, I doubt we should have been too young for them.

Bene. In a false quarrel there is no true valor. I came to seek you both.

Claud. We have been up and down to seek thee, for we are high-proof melancholy, and would fain have it beaten away. Wilt thou use thy wit?

Bene. It is in my scabbard, shall I draw it?

D. Pedro. Dost thou wear thy wit by thy side?

Claud. Never any did so, though very many have been beside their wit. I will bid thee draw, as we do the minstrels, draw to pleasure us.

D. Pedro. As I am an honest man, he looks pale. Art thou sick, or angry?

Claud. What, courage, man! What though care kill'd a cat, thou hast mettle enough in thee to kill care.

Bene. Sir, I shall meet your wit in the career, and you charge it against me. I pray you choose another subject.

Claud. Nay then give him another staff, this last was broke cross.

D. Pedro. By this light, he changes more and more. I think he be angry indeed.

Claud. If he be, he knows how to turn his girdle.

Bene. Shall I speak a word in your ear?

Claud. God bless me from a challenge!

Bene. [*Aside to Claudio.*] You are a villain. I jest not; I will make it good how you dare, with what you dare, and when you dare. Do me right; or I will protest your cowardice. You have kill'd a sweet lady, and her death shall fall heavy on you. Let me hear from you.

Claud. Well, I will meet you, so I may have good cheer.

D. Pedro. What, a feast, a feast?

Claud. I' faith, I thank him, he hath bid me to a calve's-head and a capon, the which if I do not carve most curiously, say my knife's naught. Shall I not find a woodcock too?

Bene. Sir, your wit ambles well, it goes easily.

D. Pedro. I'll tell thee how Beatrice prais'd thy wit the other day. I said thou hadst a fine wit. "True," said she, "a fine little one." "No," said I, "a great wit." "Right," says she, "a great gross one." "Nay," said I, "a good wit." "Just," said she, "it hurts nobody." "Nay," said I, "the gentleman is wise." "Certain," said she, "a wise gentleman." "Nay," said I, "he hath the tongues." "That I believe," said she, "for he swore a thing to me on Monday night, which he forswore on Tuesday morning. There's a double tongue, there's two tongues." Thus did she an hour together trans-shape thy particular virtues, yet at last she concluded with a sigh, thou wast the proper'st man in Italy.

Claud. For the which she wept heartily and said she car'd not.

D. Pedro. Yea, that she did, but yet for all that, and if she did not hate him deadly, she would love him dearly. The old man's daughter told us all.

Claud. All, all, and, moreover, God saw him when he was hid in the garden.

D. Pedro. But when shall we set the savage bull's horns on the sensible Benedick's head?

Claud. Yea, and text underneath, "Here dwells Benedick the married man"?

Bene. Fare you well, boy, you know my mind. I will leave you now to your gossip-like humor. You break jests as braggards do their blades, which, God be thank'd, hurt not. My lord, for your many courtesies I thank you. I must discontinue your company. Your brother the bastard is fled from Messina. You have among you kill'd a sweet and innocent lady. For my Lord Lack-beard there, he and I shall meet, and till then peace be with him. [*Exit.*]

D. Pedro. He is in earnest.

Claud. In most profound earnest, and I'll warrant you, for the love of Beatrice.

D. Pedro. And hath challeng'd thee?

Claud. Most sincerely.

109 s.d. **ambo**: both. 118. **doubt**: fear.
123. **high-proof**: at a high level of.
128. **beside their wit**: out of their minds.
129. **minstrels**. Who are bidden to draw their bows across the strings of their instruments.
135. **in the career**: at full speed (an expression from jousting).
136. **charge**: direct, level. 138. **staff**: lance.
139. **broke cross**: broken crosswise, athwart his opponent's shield. Claudio means that Benedick has performed wretchedly in this first exchange.
142. **he knows . . . girdle**. Proverbial, but of uncertain meaning; generally explained as meaning "it's up to him to get himself into a better frame of mind; I shall make no effort to placate him" (*girdle* = belt). 147. **Do me right**: give me satisfaction.
147–8. **protest**: proclaim.
151–52. **so . . . cheer**: so long as I may have good cheer.
155, 157. **calve's-head, capon, woodcock**. Types of stupidity.
156. **curiously**: daintily. **naught**: worthless.
158. **your . . . easily**: your wit moves smoothly like an ambling horse (i.e. it shows no mettle or fire like a horse at the gallop).
162. **gross**: coarse. 164. **hurts nobody**: i.e. has no bite.
165–66. **a wise gentleman**. One of the established uses of this phrase was in an ironic sense.
166. **hath the tongues**: is a master of languages.
170–71. **trans-shape**: distort. 172. **proper'st**: handsomest.
177. **and if**: if. **deadly**: mortally.
179–80. **God . . . garden**. This reference to the action of III.i contains also an echo of Genesis 3:8.
181–84. **But . . . man**. Benedick is put on notice that his lordly assertion at I.i.262–68 has not been forgotten.
187. **braggards**: braggarts, i.e. those better at boasting of their prowess than of demonstrating it.

D. Pedro. What a pretty thing man is when he goes in his doublet and hose and leaves off his wit!

Enter Constables [DOGBERRY *and* VERGES, *and the* WATCH *with*] CONRADE *and* BORACHIO.

Claud. He is then a giant to an ape, but then is an ape a doctor to such a man.

D. Pedro. But soft you, let me be. Pluck up, my heart, and be sad. Did he not say my brother was fled?

Dog. Come you, sir. If justice cannot tame you, she shall ne'er weigh more reasons in her balance. Nay, and you be a cursing hypocrite once, you must be look'd to.

D. Pedro. How now? two of my brother's men bound? Borachio one!

Claud. Hearken after their offense, my lord.

D. Pedro. Officers, what offense have these men done?

Dog. Marry, sir, they have committed false report; moreover they have spoken untruths; secondarily, they are slanders; sixt and lastly, they have belied a lady; thirdly, they have verified unjust things; and to conclude, they are lying knaves.

D. Pedro. First, I ask thee what they have done; thirdly, I ask thee what's their offense; sixt and lastly, why they are committed; and to conclude, what you lay to their charge.

Claud. Rightly reason'd, and in his own division, and by my troth there's one meaning well suited.

D. Pedro. Who have you offended, masters, that you are thus bound to your answer? This learned constable is too cunning to be understood. What's your offense?

Bora. Sweet Prince, let me go no farther to mine answer: do you hear me, and let this count kill me. I have deceiv'd even your very eyes. What your wisdoms could not discover, these shallow fools have brought to light, who in the night overheard me confessing to this man how Don John your brother incens'd me to slander the Lady Hero, how you were brought into the orchard, and saw me court Margaret in Hero's garments, how you disgrac'd her when you should marry her. My villainy they have upon record, which I had rather seal with my death than repeat over to my shame. The lady is dead upon mine and my master's false accusation; and briefly, I desire nothing but the reward of a villain.

D. Pedro. Runs not this speech like iron through
your blood?

200. **goes . . . wit:** i.e. forgets to put on his good sense along with his clothes.
201. **a giant to:** i.e. much larger than (*to* = in comparison with).
202. **doctor:** scholar, learned man. 203. **soft you:** wait a minute.
203–4. **Pluck . . . heart:** collect yourself, my mind.
204. **sad:** serious.
207. **reasons:** i.e. legal cases (Dogberry seems to have confused *reasons* and *causes*). Perhaps *reasons* quibbles on *raisins*, which it closely resembled in pronunciation. **balance:** scale.
212. **Hearken after:** inquire into. 217. **slanders:** i.e. slanderers.
218. **verified:** affirmed as true (but perhaps a blunder for *testified*).
225. **well suited:** i.e. in several garbs.
227. **bound . . . answer:** bound over for trial (perhaps with puns on *bound* in the senses "pinioned" and "on the way").
236. **incens'd:** incited. 242. **upon:** as a result of.

Claud. I have drunk poison whiles he utter'd it.
D. Pedro. But did my brother set thee on to this?
Bora. Yea, and paid me richly for the practice of it.
D. Pedro. He is compos'd and fram'd of treachery,
And fled he is upon this villainy.
Claud. Sweet Hero, now thy image doth appear
In the rare semblance that I lov'd it first.

Dog. Come, bring away the plaintiffs. By this time our sexton hath reform'd Signior Leonato of the matter; and, masters, do not forget to specify, when time and place shall serve, that I am an ass.

Verg. Here, here comes Master Signior Leonato, and the sexton too.

Enter LEONATO, *his brother* [ANTONIO], *and the* SEXTON.

Leon. Which is the villain? Let me see his eyes,
That when I note another man like him
I may avoid him. Which of these is he?
Bora. If you would know your wronger, look on
me.
Leon. Art thou the slave that with thy breath
hast kill'd
Mine innocent child?
Bora. Yea, even I alone.
Leon. No, not so, villain, thou beliest thyself.
Here stand a pair of honorable men,
A third is fled, that had a hand in it.
I thank you, princes, for my daughter's death;
Record it with your high and worthy deeds.
'Twas bravely done, if you bethink you of it.
Claud. I know not how to pray your patience,
Yet I must speak. Choose your revenge yourself,
Impose me to what penance your invention
Can lay upon my sin; yet sinn'd I not,
But in mistaking.
D. Pedro. By my soul, nor I,
And yet, to satisfy this good old man,
I would bend under any heavy weight
That he'll enjoin me to.
Leon. I cannot bid you bid my daughter live—
That were impossible—but I pray you both,
Possess the people in Messina here
How innocent she died, and if your love
Can labor aught in sad invention,
Hang her an epitaph upon her tomb,
And sing it to her bones, sing it to-night.
To-morrow morning come you to my house,
And since you could not be my son-in-law,
Be yet my nephew. My brother hath a daughter,
Almost the copy of my child that's dead,
And she alone is heir to both of us.
Give her the right you should have giv'n her cousin,
And so dies my revenge.
Claud. O noble sir!
Your overkindness doth wring tears from me.
I do embrace your offer, and dispose
For henceforth of poor Claudio.

248. **practice:** execution. 253. **plaintiffs:** blunder for *defendants.*
254. **reform'd:** for *informed.* 255. **specify:** for *testify* (?).
266. **honorable:** of distinguished rank. 273. **Impose:** subject.
281. **Possess:** inform.
290. **heir to both.** Antonio's son (mentioned in I.ii.1–2) has apparently been forgotten. 291. **should:** were to.

Leon. To-morrow then I will expect your coming,
To-night I take my leave. This naughty man
Shall face to face be brought to Margaret,
Who I believe was pack'd in all this wrong,
Hir'd to it by your brother.

Bora. No, by my soul she was not,
Nor knew not what she did when she spoke to me,
But always hath been just and virtuous
In any thing that I do know by her.

Dog. Moreover, sir, which indeed is not under white and black, this plaintiff here, the offender, did call me ass. I beseech you let it be rememb'red in his punishment. And also, the watch heard them talk of one Deformed. They say he wears a key in his ear and a lock hanging by it, and borrows money in God's name, the which he hath us'd so long and never paid that now men grow hard-hearted and will lend nothing for God's sake. Pray you examine him upon that point.

Leon. I thank thee for thy care and honest pains.

Dog. Your worship speaks like a most thankful and reverent youth, and I praise God for you.

Leon. There's for thy pains.

Dog. God save the foundation!

Leon. Go, I discharge thee of thy prisoner, and I thank thee.

Dog. I leave an arrant knave with your worship, which I beseech your worship to correct yourself, for the example of others. God keep your worship! I wish your worship well. God restore you to health! I humbly give you leave to depart, and if a merry meeting may be wish'd, God prohibit it! Come, neighbor. [*Exeunt Dogberry and Verges*.]

Leon. Until to-morrow morning, lords, farewell.

Ant. Farewell, my lords, we look for you to-morrow.

D. Pedro. We will not fail.

Claud. To-night I'll mourn with Hero.

Leon. [*To the Watch.*] Bring you these fellows on.
—We'll talk with Margaret,
How her acquaintance grew with this lewd fellow.
Exeunt [*severally*].

[Scene II]

Enter Benedick *and* Margaret, [*meeting*].

Bene. Pray thee, sweet Mistress Margaret, deserve well at my hands by helping me to the speech of Beatrice.

Marg. Will you then write me a sonnet in praise of my beauty?

Bene. In so high a style, Margaret, that no man living shall come over it, for in most comely truth thou deservest it.

Marg. To have no man come over me? Why, shall I always keep below stairs?

Bene. Thy wit is as quick as the greyhound's mouth, it catches.

Marg. And yours as blunt as the fencer's foils, which hit, but hurt not.

Bene. A most manly wit, Margaret, it will not hurt a woman. And so I pray thee call Beatrice; I give thee the bucklers.

Marg. Give us the swords, we have bucklers of our own.

Bene. If you use them, Margaret, you must put in the pikes with a vice, and they are dangerous weapons for maids.

Marg. Well, I will call Beatrice to you, who I think hath legs. *Exit Margaret.*

Bene. And therefore will come.
[*Sings.*] "The god of love,
That sits above,
And knows me, and knows me,
How pitiful I deserve"—

I mean in singing; but in loving, Leander the good swimmer, Troilus the first employer of pandars, and a whole bookful of these quondam carpet-mongers, whose names yet run smoothly in the even road of a blank verse, why, they were never so truly turn'd over and over as my poor self in love. Marry, I cannot show it in rhyme; I have tried. I can find out no rhyme to "lady" but "baby," an innocent rhyme; for "scorn," "horn," a hard rhyme; for "school," "fool," a babbling rhyme: very ominous endings. No, I was not born under a rhyming planet, nor I cannot woo in festival terms.

Enter Beatrice.

Sweet Beatrice, wouldst thou come when I call'd thee?

Beat. Yea, signior, and depart when you bid me.

Bene. O, stay but till then!

Beat. "Then" is spoken; fare you well now. And yet ere I go, let me go with that I came, which

297. naughty: wicked. **299. pack'd:** involved as a conspirator.
303. by: concerning. **304–5. under . . . black:** in writing.
308–9. key . . . it. Dogberry's transmutation of the *lock* of III.iii.170.
310. in God's name: i.e. like a professional beggar (who commonly used this phrase). **us'd:** made a practice.
316. reverent. Perhaps another blunder, but *reverent* was commonly used in the sense "reverend" (see V.iv.123).
318. God . . . foundation: a phrase used by those who received alms from a charitable foundation.
321–22. I . . . yourself. Dogberry here makes use of locutions which, contrary to his intention, permit the interpretation that he is calling Leonato a knave and urging him to reform.
326. prohibit. One last example of Dogberry saying precisely the opposite of what he means. **332. lewd:** low, worthless.

V.ii. Location: Leonato's orchard.

7. come over: (1) exceed: (2) get across (pointing to a quibble on *style / stile* in line 6). Margaret then plays on a third sense, with characteristic ribaldry. **in . . . comely truth:** (1) in good truth; (2) by virtue of your beauty.
10. keep: dwell, stay. **below stairs:** i.e. in the servants' quarters.
17. give . . . bucklers: i.e. give up (*buckler* = a kind of shield).
21. pikes: spikes in the centre of a shield. **vice:** screw.
26–29. The first lines of a contemporary song.
29. How . . . deserve: how much I deserve pity (but Benedick twists the meaning to "how pitifully small my deserts are").
30. Leander. Who swam the Hellespont nightly to see his love Hero.
31. Troilus. Whose union with Cressida was arranged by her uncle Pandarus. **32. quondam:** of former days.
32–33. carpet-mongers. Knights who avoided military service were contemptuously called carpet knights. Benedick's use of the term for storied lovers of old implies that they were contemptible performers compared with himself.
38. innocent: childish. **hard:** (1) harsh, unpleasant (because associated with the idea of the cuckold's horn); (2) solid.
41. festival terms: elevated language suitable for a special occasion.
47. that I came: what I came for.

is, with knowing what hath pass'd between you and Claudio.

Bene. Only foul words—and thereupon I will kiss thee.

Beat. Foul words is but foul wind, and foul wind is but foul breath, and foul breath is noisome; therefore I will depart unkiss'd.

Bene. Thou hast frighted the word out of his right sense, so forcible is thy wit. But I must tell thee plainly, Claudio undergoes my challenge, and either I must shortly hear from him, or I will subscribe him a coward. And I pray thee now tell me, for which of my bad parts didst thou first fall in love with me?

Beat. For them all together, which maintain'd so politic a state of evil that they will not admit any good part to intermingle with them. But for which of my good parts did you first suffer love for me?

Bene. Suffer love! a good epithite! I do suffer love indeed, for I love thee against my will.

Beat. In spite of your heart, I think. Alas, poor heart, if you spite it for my sake, I will spite it for yours, for I will never love that which my friend hates.

Bene. Thou and I are too wise to woo peaceably.

Beat. It appears not in this confession; there's not one wise man among twenty that will praise himself.

Bene. An old, an old instance, Beatrice, that liv'd in the time of good neighbors. If a man do not erect in this age his own tomb ere he dies, he shall live no longer in monument than the bell rings and the widow weeps.

Beat. And how long is that, think you?

Bene. Question: why, an hour in clamor and a quarter in rheum; therefore is it most expedient for the wise, if Don Worm (his conscience) find no impediment to the contrary, to be the trumpet of his own virtues, as I am to myself. So much for praising myself, who I myself will bear witness is praiseworthy. And now tell me, how doth your cousin?

Beat. Very ill.

Bene. And how do you?

Beat. Very ill too.

Bene. Serve God, love me, and mend. There will I leave you too, for here comes one in haste.

Enter Ursula.

Urs. Madam, you must come to your uncle, yonder's old coil at home. It is prov'd my Lady Hero hath been falsely accus'd, the Prince and Claudio mightily abus'd, and Don John is the author of all, who is fled and gone. Will you come presently?

Beat. Will you go hear this news, signior?

Bene. I will live in thy heart, die in thy lap, and be buried in thy eyes; and moreover I will go with thee to thy uncle's. *Exeunt.*

[Scene III]

Enter Claudio, *Prince* [Don Pedro], *and three or four with tapers.*

Claud. Is this the monument of Leonato?

[*A*] *Lord.* It is, my lord.

[*Claud.* *Reading out of a scroll.*]

Epitaph

"Done to death by slanderous tongues
Was the Hero that here lies.
Death, in guerdon of her wrongs,
Gives her fame which never dies.
So the life that died with shame
Lives in death with glorious fame."

Hang thou there upon the tomb,
[*Hangs up the scroll.*]
Praising her when I am [dumb].
Now, music, sound, and sing your solemn hymn.

Song

Pardon, goddess of the night,
Those that slew thy virgin knight,
For the which, with songs of woe,
Round about her tomb they go.
Midnight, assist our moan,
Help us to sigh and groan,
Heavily, heavily.
Graves, yawn and yield your dead,
Till death be uttered,
Heavily, heavily.

[*Claud.*] Now, unto thy bones good night!
Yearly will I do this rite.

D. Pedro. Good morrow, masters, put your torches out.
The wolves have preyed, and look, the gentle day,
Before the wheels of Phoebus, round about
Dapples the drowsy east with spots of grey.
Thanks to you all, and leave us. Fare you well.

53. noisome: ill-smelling.
55–56. his right sense: (1) its senses, its right mind; (2) its correct meaning. **57. undergoes:** is subject to.
58–59. subscribe: formally proclaim.
63. politic: shrewdly managed.
65. suffer: (1) experience; (2) suffer from.
66. epithite: epithet, i.e. expression.
73. It . . . confession: your wisdom is not shown by this declaration that you are wise.
76. instance: proverb, maxim (i.e. that a wise man does not praise himself).
77. time . . . neighbors: good old days when neighbors were willing to speak well of one another.
82. Question: that is the question. **clamor:** sound (of the bell).
83. rheum: tears (of the widow).
84. Don . . . conscience. It was a commonplace to describe the conscience as a gnawing worm. **85. trumpet:** trumpeter.

96. old coil: great confusion, much ado. **98. abus'd:** deceived.
100. presently: immediately.
102. die. Used with the common sexual implication.

V.iii. Location: A churchyard.
5. guerdon: recompense. **12. goddess . . . night.** See note to IV.i.57.
18. Heavily: mournfully.
19. yield your dead: i.e. so that they too may "assist our moan."
20. uttered: fully expressed, i.e. adequately lamented.
25. have preyed: i.e. have finished their night's preying.
26. Before . . . Phoebus: i.e. preceding the chariot of the sun.

Claud. Good morrow, masters—each his several way.
D. Pedro. Come let us hence, and put on other weeds,
And then to Leonato's we will go.
Claud. And Hymen now with luckier issue speed 's
Than this for whom we rend'red up this woe.
Exeunt.

[Scene IV]

Enter Leonato, Benedick, [Beatrice,] Margaret, Ursula, *old man* [Antonio], Friar [Francis], Hero.

Friar. Did I not tell you she was innocent?
Leon. So are the Prince and Claudio, who accus'd her
Upon the error that you heard debated.
But Margaret was in some fault for this,
Although against her will, as it appears
In the true course of all the question.
Ant. Well, I am glad that all things sorts so well.
Bene. And so am I, being else by faith enforc'd
To call young Claudio to a reckoning for it.
Leon. Well, daughter, and you gentlewomen all,
Withdraw into a chamber by yourselves,
And when I send for you, come hither masked.
The Prince and Claudio promis'd by this hour
To visit me. You know your office, brother:
You must be father to your brother's daughter,
And give her to young Claudio. *Exeunt Ladies.*
Ant. Which I will do with confirm'd countenance.
Bene. Friar, I must entreat your pains, I think.
Friar. To do what, signior?
Bene. To bind me, or undo me—one of them.
Signior Leonato, truth it is, good signior,
Your niece regards me with an eye of favor.
Leon. That eye my daughter lent her, 'tis most true.
Bene. And I do with an eye of love requite her.
Leon. The sight whereof I think you had from me,
From Claudio, and the Prince. But what's your will?
Bene. Your answer, sir, is enigmatical,
But for my will, my will is your good will
May stand with ours, this day to be conjoin'd
In the state of honorable marriage,
In which, good friar, I shall desire your help.
Leon. My heart is with your liking.
Friar. And my help.
Here comes the Prince and Claudio.

Enter Prince [Don Pedro] *and* Claudio *and two or three other.*

D. Pedro. Good morrow to this fair assembly.
Leon. Good morrow, Prince; good morrow, Claudio;
We here attend you. Are you yet determined
To-day to marry with my brother's daughter?
Claud. I'll hold my mind were she an Ethiope.
Leon. Call her forth, brother, here's the friar ready. [*Exit Antonio.*]
D. Pedro. Good morrow, Benedick. Why, what's the matter,
That you have such a February face,
So full of frost, of storm, and cloudiness?
Claud. I think he thinks upon the savage bull.
Tush, fear not, man, we'll tip thy horns with gold,
And all Europa shall rejoice at thee,
As once Europa did at lusty Jove,
When he would play the noble beast in love.
Bene. Bull Jove, sir, had an amiable low,
And some such strange bull leapt your father's cow,
And got a calf in that same noble feat
Much like to you, for you have just his bleat.

Enter Brother [Antonio], Hero, Beatrice, Margaret, Ursula, [*the ladies masked*].

Claud. For this I owe you: here comes other reck'nings.
Which is the lady I must seize upon?
[*Ant.*] This same is she, and I do give you her.
Claud. Why then she's mine. Sweet, let me see your face.
Leon. No, that you shall not till you take her hand,
Before this friar, and swear to marry her.
Claud. Give me your hand before this holy friar—
I am your husband if you like of me.
Hero. [*Unmasking.*] And when I liv'd, I was your other wife,
And when you lov'd, you were my other husband.
Claud. Another Hero!
Hero. Nothing certainer:
One Hero died defil'd, but I do live,
And surely as I live, I am a maid.
D. Pedro. The former Hero! Hero that is dead!
Leon. She died, my lord, but whiles her slander liv'd.
Friar. All this amazement can I qualify,
When after that the holy rites are ended,
I'll tell you largely of fair Hero's death.
Mean time let wonder seem familiar,
And to the chapel let us presently.
Bene. Soft and fair, friar. Which is Beatrice?
Beat. [*Unmasking.*] I answer to that name. What is your will?

30. weeds: clothes.
32. Hymen: the god of marriage. **with . . . speed 's:** favor us with better fortune.

V.iv. Location: Leonato's house.
3. Upon: because of. **debated:** publicly discussed.
5. against her will: unintentionally.
6. question: judicial examination. **7. sorts:** turn out.
8. faith: i.e. his pledge to Beatrice. **14. office:** function, role.
17. confirm'd: steadfast, i.e. serious. **countenance:** demeanor.
20. undo: (1) ruin; (2) unbind.

36. yet: still.
43. savage bull. Another reference to Benedick's complacent statement at I.i.262–68. **45. Europa:** Europe.
46. Europa: a Phoenician princess whom Jove, in the form of a white bull, carried off from her native land.
48. amiable low: winning voice.
52. owe you: i.e. will repay you later.
52–53. other reck'nings: other accounts (that I must settle first).
59. like of: like, are willing to take.
63. defil'd: disgraced, slandered. **67. qualify:** moderate.
69. largely: fully, in detail.
70. let . . . familiar: accept these amazing events as natural.

Bene. Do not you love me?
Beat. Why, no, no more than reason.
Bene. Why then your uncle and the Prince and Claudio
Have been deceived. They swore you did.
Beat. Do not you love me?
Bene. Troth, no, no more than reason.
Beat. Why then my cousin, Margaret, and Ursula
Are much deceiv'd, for they did swear you did.
Bene. They swore that you were almost sick for me.
Beat. They swore that you were well-nigh dead for me.
Bene. 'Tis no such matter. Then you do not love me?
Beat. No, truly, but in friendly recompense.
Leon. Come, cousin, I am sure you love the gentleman.
Claud. And I'll be sworn upon't that he loves her,
For here's a paper written in his hand,
A halting sonnet of his own pure brain,
Fashion'd to Beatrice.
Hero. And here's another
Writ in my cousin's hand, stol'n from her pocket,
Containing her affection unto Benedick.

Bene. A miracle! here's our own hands against our hearts. Come, I will have thee, but by this light, I take thee for pity.

Beat. I would not deny you, but by this good day, I yield upon great persuasion, and partly to save your life, for I was told you were in a consumption.

[*Bene.*] Peace, I will stop your mouth. [*Kissing her.*]

D. Pedro. How dost thou, Benedick the married man?

Bene. I'll tell thee what, Prince: a college of wit-crackers cannot flout me out of my humor. Dost thou think I care for a satire or an epigram? No, if a man will be beaten with brains, 'a shall wear nothing handsome about him. In brief, since I do purpose to marry, I will think nothing to any purpose that the world can say against it, and therefore never flout at me for what I have said against it; for man is a giddy thing, and this is my conclusion. For thy part, Claudio, I did think to have beaten thee, but in that thou art like to be my kinsman, live unbruis'd, and love my cousin.

Claud. I had well hop'd thou wouldst have denied Beatrice, that I might have cudgell'd thee out of thy single life, to make thee a double-dealer, which out of question thou wilt be, if my cousin do not look exceeding narrowly to thee.

Bene. Come, come, we are friends. Let's have a dance ere we are married, that we may lighten our own hearts and our wives' heels.

Leon. We'll have dancing afterward.

Bene. First, of my word; therefore play, music. Prince, thou art sad, get thee a wife, get thee a wife. There is no staff more reverent than one tipp'd with horn.

Enter MESSENGER.

Mess. My lord, your brother John is ta'en in flight,
And brought with armed men back to Messina.

Bene. Think not on him till to-morrow. I'll devise thee brave punishments for him. Strike up, pipers. *Dance.* [*Exeunt.*]

91–92. our . . . hearts: i.e. our own written testimony to prove our hearts guilty as charged. **99. How . . . man.** Cf. I.i.267–68.
100. college: company, assemblage.

101. wit-crackers: jokesters (cf. *crack a joke*).
103–4. if . . . him: if a man is going to allow himself to be beaten up by wit, he will never dare wear good clothes; i.e. if a man allows ridicule to dictate his actions, he will deprive himself of many desirable things. **108. giddy:** fickle, changeable.
108–9. my conclusion: the position I have finally come to.
114. double-dealer: (1) married man (cf. *single man*); (2) unfaithful husband. **115. out of question:** without doubt.
116. narrowly: closely. **121. of:** on.
123. reverent: reverend, honorable.
124. horn. The cuckold joke once more.
128. brave: capital, fine.

NOTE ON THE TEXT

Much Ado about Nothing was first published in quarto in 1600 by Andrew Wise and William Aspley; this edition (Q) is here used as copy-text. The First Folio text (1623) was printed from a copy of Q into which had been introduced some stage directions from a manuscript prompt-book (see, for example, Textual Notes, II.i.85, II.iii.36). The textual changes found in F1 are of the kind largely attributable to compositorial tinkering or error and cannot be accorded any authority, though something like stage censorship may lie behind the F1 omissions at III.ii.34–37 and IV.ii.17–20. Only the more significant F1 variants are recorded in the Textual Notes.

The considerable confusions in Q (particularly in the speech-prefixes for Antonio and for Dogberry, Verges, and the Watch) and the many indefinite and vaguely descriptive stage directions point clearly to Shakespeare's "foul papers" as the copy-text. As further evidence of "foul papers," it may be noticed that the opening stage direction of I.i introduces a character called "Innogen" as Leonato's wife (referred to again at the beginning of II.i as "his wife") who has no speaking part in the play; presumably Shakespeare, following his source in Bandello's *Novelle*, at one time intended to include Hero's mother in his version of the story. It has been suggested that the "foul papers" had received a few additions to the stage directions by a book-keeper, perhaps as a preliminary to having a "fair copy" transcribed for the official prompt-book (see the opening stage directions of I.ii and II.i), but the evidence for a second hand is very slight.

Dover Wilson's elaborate revision theory, advanced in 1923 to explain some of the obvious difficulties and confusions in Q, has never been generally accepted, and recent bibliographical work, showing that Q was set from cast-off copy by a single compositor, has gone far to discredit it entirely.

For further information, see: J. D. Wilson, ed., New Shakespeare *Much Ado about Nothing* (Cambridge, 1923); W. W.

Greg, *The Shakespeare First Folio* (Oxford, 1955); W. C. Ferguson, "The Compositors of *Henry IV, Part 2, Much Ado about Nothing, The Shoemakers' Holiday,* and *The First Part of the Contention,*" *SB,* XIII (1960), 19–29; J.H. Smith, "The Composition of the Quarto of *Much Ado about Nothing,*" *SB,* XVI (1963), 9–26; Charlton Hinman, ed., *Much Ado about Nothing* (1600) [facsimile of Q] (Oxford, 1971); J. K. Walton, The *Quarto Copy for the First Folio of Shakespeare* (Dublin, 1971); Stanley Wells, "Editorial Treatment of Foul-Paper Texts: *Much Ado about Nothing* as Test Case," *RES,* XXXI (1980), 1–16; A. R. Humphreys, New Arden *Much Ado about Nothing* (London, 1981); F. H. Mares, New Cambridge *Much Ado about Nothing* (Cambridge, 1981); Stanley Wells, Gary Taylor, et al., *William Shakespeare: A Textual Companion* (Oxford, 1987).

TEXTUAL NOTES

Title: **Much . . . Nothing]** Much adoe about Nothing. As it hath been sundrie times publikely acted by the right honourable, the Lord Chamberlaine his seruants. Written by William Shakespeare. *Q1 (title-page)*
Dramatis personae: *subs. as first given in Rowe*
Act-scene division: *none in Q; F1, except for I.i, marks only acts; other scene divisions from Rowe and later editors (see first note to each scene); present act-scene arrangement as a whole first established by Capell*

I.i

I.i] *F1*
Location: *Pope*
o.s.d. **Messina]** Messina, Innogen his wife *Q, F1 (Innogen has no lines in the play and appears only once again, in II.i o.s.d. as* his wife; *first om. by Theobald)*
1, 10 **Pedro]** *Rowe;* Peter *Q, F1*
50 **victual]** *F1;* vittaile *Q*
51 **eat]** ease *F1*
65 **that.]** *F1;* that, *Q*
71 **creature.]** *F1;* creature, *Q*
89 **Benedick]** *F2;* Benedict *Q, F1*
92 **Do,]** *Theobald;* Do *Q, F1*
96 **are you]** you are *F1*
138 **parrot-teacher]** *hyphen, F2*
146–7 **Leonato—. . . Benedick—]** *Theobald;* Leonato, . . . Benedicke, *Q;* Leonato, . . . Benedicke; *F1*
154 s.d. **To Don John.]** *Hanmer*
172 **high]** *F3;* hie *Q, F1*
203 s.d. **Enter Don Pedro.]** *Hanmer;* Enter don Pedro, Iohn the bastard. *Q, F1*
210–2 **so . . . allegiance,]** *Nicholson conj. (in Cambridge);* so (but . . . allegiance) *Q, F1*
227 **spoke]** speake *F1*
281 **house—]** *Capell (subs.);* house *Q;* house, *F1*
301 **war-thoughts]** *F1;* warre-thoughts, *Q*
302 **vacant,]** *Capell;* vacant: *Q, F1*
309–10 **and . . . her.]** *om. F1*

I.ii

I.ii] *Capell*
Location: *Capell (subs.)*
o.s.d. **Antonio]** *Rowe*
o.s.d. **meeting]** *Cambridge*
3 s.p. **Ant.]** *Rowe;* Old *Q, F1 (throughout scene)*
7 **event]** *F2;* euents *Q, F1*
9 **thick-pleach'd]** *hyphen, Theobald*
24 s.d. **Several . . . stage.]** *Theobald (subs.)*
26 **skill]** *F1;* shill *Q*

I.iii

I.iii] *Capell*
Location: *Theobald (subs.)*
o.s.d. **Don]** *Rowe;* sir *Q, F1*
1 **good-year]** *hyphen, Malone*
8 **at least]** yet *F1*
33 **muzzle]** *F4* (muzzel); mussell *Q, F1*
39 **make]** will make *F1*
40 s.d. **Enter Borachio.]** *placed as in Dyce; after l. 41, Q, F1*
49 **Marry]** *F2;* Mary *Q, F1 (generally)*
49 **brother's]** *F1;* bothers *Q*
54 **one]** on *F1*
69 **me?]** *F1;* me. *Q*

II.i

II.i] *Rowe;* Actus Secundus. *F1*
Location: *Pope*
o.s.d. **his brother]** *Rowe (subs.);* his brother, his wife *Q, F1*
o.s.d. **Margaret, Ursula,]** *Rowe*
2 s.p. **Ant.]** *Rowe;* brother *Q, F1 (until l. 114)*
50 s.d. **To Hero.]** *Rowe*
60 **mettle]** *Wilson;* mettal *Q, F1*
66 **you.]** *Rowe (subs.);* you, *Q, F1*
76 **mannerly-modest]** *hyphen, Theobald*
77 **ancientry]** *Johnson;* aunchentry *Q, F1*
85 s.d. **They . . . masks.]** *Capell (subs.)*
85 **s.d. Prince Don Pedro]** *Rowe (subs.);* prince, Pedro *Q, F1*
85 s.d. **Don John, and Borachio]** *Wilson;* Balthasar, or dumb Iohn. *Q, F1*
85 s.d. **as . . . Drum]** *after F1:* Maskers with a drum.
88 **So]** *F1;* So, *Q*
91 **company?]** *Rowe;* company. *Q, F1*
99 s.d. **They move aside.]** *ed. (after Hanmer)*
100, 103, 105 s.pp. **Bora.]** *Wilson;* Bene. *Q, F1*
108, 111 s.pp. **Bora.]** *Wilson;* Balth. *Q, F1*
111, 124 s.dd. **They move aside.]** *ed. (after Capell)*
113 **Antonio]** *Pope;* Anthonio *Q, F1*
117 **ill-well]** *hyphen, Theobald*
150 s.d. **Music . . . begins.]** *Capell (subs.); F1 gives* Musicke for the dance. *after l. 153*
154 s.d. **Then . . . Claudio.]** *Steevens (subs.);* exeunt *Q, F1*
183 **Claudio?]** *Rowe;* Claudio. *Q, F1*
198 **blind man]** *Rowe;* blindman *Q, F1*
210 s.d. **Enter . . . Pedro.]** *from F1:* Enter the Prince.; Enter the Prince, Hero, Leonato. Iohn and Borachio, and Conrade. *Q*
223, 231 **bird's]** *Rowe;* birds *Q, F1*
244 **that]** and that *F1*
261 s.d. **Leonato and Hero]** *F1 (subs.)*
300 **obtain'd.]** *Theobald (subs.);* obtained, *Q, F1*
314 **it—]** *Wilson;* it, *Q, F1*
320 **"Heigh-ho . . . husband!"]** *quotes, Staunton*
326 s.p. **D. Pedro.]** *Rowe (subs.);* Prince *Q, F1 (throughout rest of scene)*
374 **too,]** *Rowe;* too *Q;* to *F1*
387 s.d. **Exeunt.]** *F2;* exit. *Q, F1*

II.ii

II.ii] *Capell*
Location: *Cambridge (after Theobald)*
o.s.d. **Don]** *Rowe*
37 **in]** in a *F1*
38–9 **match, . . . maid—]** *Capell (after Rowe);* match) . . . maid, *Q, F1*
44 **Margaret]** *F1;* Marg. *Q*
57 s.d. **Exeunt.]** *Rowe;* exit *Q, F1*

II.iii

II.iii] *Capell*
Location: *Theobald*
1 s.d. **Enter Boy.]** *Collier*
25 **an]** *F1;* and *Q*
36 s.d. **Withdraws.]** *Theobald*
36 s.d. **Claudio]** Claudio and Iacke Wilson *F1 (i.e. the actor who played Balthasar; F1 omits Q's entry for Balthasar at l. 42)*
36 s.d. **within]** *Neilson*
42 **hid-fox]** *Warburton;* kid-foxe *Q, F1 (a reading defended by some eds.)*
42 s.d. **Balthasar]** *Neilson;* Balthaser *Q (for F1 see second note on l. 36 s.d.)*
43 **Balthasar]** *F1;* Balthaser *Q*
57 s.d. **Air.]** *Capell*
62 s.p. **Balth.]** *Capell*
92 s.d. **Aside.]** *Johnson*
108, 121, 211, 213 s.dd. **Aside.]** *Theobald*
135 **us of]** *F1;* of vs *Q*
190 **say]** see *F1*
199 **seek]** see *F1*
208 **unworthy]** vnworthy to haue *F1*
219 s.d. **Exeunt . . . Leonato.]** *Capell (after F1* Exeunt.)
220 s.d. **Coming forward.]** *Theobald (subs.)*

III.i

III.i] *Rowe;* Actus Tertius. *F1*
Location: *Theobald*
o.s.d. **Ursley]** Vrsula *F1*
12 **propose]** purpose *F1*
14 s.d. **Exit.]** *F2*
23 s.d. **behind]** *Steevens; s.d. placed as in Cambridge; after l. 25, Q; after l. 23, F1*
33 s.d. **They . . . bower.]** *Steevens*
38 **new-trothed]** *hyphen, Theobald*
58 **she'll]** she *F1*
60 **featur'd]** *F1;* featured *Q*
61 **fair-fac'd]** *F1 (hyphen, F4);* faire faced *Q*
63 **antic]** *F1* (anticke); antique *Q*
96 **bearing,]** *F4;* bearing *Q, F1*
104, 105 s.dd. **Aside.]** *Capell*
104 **limed]** tane *F1*
106 s.d. **Exeunt . . . Ursula.]** *Capell (after Rowe);* Exit. *F1*
107 s.d. **Coming forward.]** *Theobald (subs.)*
111 **on]** *Q (c), F1;* one *Q (u)*

III.ii

III.ii] *Pope*
Location: *Theobald*
1 s.p. **D. Pedro.]** *Rowe (subs.);* Prince *Q,* (or Prin.) *F1 (throughout scene)*
28 **can]** *Pope;* cannot *Q, F1*
34–7 **or . . . doublet.]** *om. F1*
39 **it]** it to *F1*
54 s.p. **D. Pedro.]** *F1* (Prin.); Bene. *Q*
73 s.d. **Exeunt . . . Leonato.]** *Theobald*
79 s.d. **Don]** *Rowe*
80 s.p. **D. John.]** *Rowe (subs.);* Bastard *Q, F1 (or* Bast. *throughout scene)*
88 s.d. **To Claudio.]** *Rowe*
97–8 **brother, I . . . heart]** *Rowe;* brother (I . . . heart) *Q, F1*
114 **her then,]** *Hanmer;* her, then *Q, F1*
124 **her,]** *Alexander (after Capell);* her *Q, F1*
129 **midnight]** night *F1*
134 s.d. **Exeunt.]** *F2*

III.iii

III.iii] *Capell*
Location: *Pope*
37, 44, 49, 54, 67, 88 s.pp. **2. Watch.]** *Rowe;* Watch *Q, F1*
79 **statues]** *F1;* statutes *Q*
86 **fellows']** *Hanmer;* fellowes *Q, F1*
94 s.d. **Dogberry and Verges]** *Pope*
96, 106 s.pp. **2. Watch.]** *Capell;* Watch *Q, F1*
96 s.d. **Aside.]** *Rowe*
108 **Don]** *F1;* Dun *Q*
125 s.p. **2. Watch.]** *Wilson;* Watch *Q, F1*
125 s.d. **Aside.]** *Capell*
127 **gentleman]** *F2;* gentle man *Q, F1*
164, 169 s.pp. **2. Watch.]** *Wilson;* Watch 1 *Q, F1*
166 s.p. **1. Watch.]** *Wilson;* Watch 2 *Q, F1*
175 s.p. **2. Watch.]** *ed. (after Theobald* 1. Watch.); *speech continued to Conrade, Q, F1*
175 **you;]** *Wilson (subs.);* you, *Q, F1*

III.iv

III.iv] *Capell*
Location: *Theobald*
5 **s.d. Exit.]** *Hanmer*
18 **in]** *F1*; it *Q*
32–3 **"saving ... husband."]** *quotes, Cambridge*
48 **see]** looke *F1*
54 **Heigh-ho!]** *Dyce*; hey ho. *Q, F1*
80 **holy-thistle]** *hyphen, Rowe*
99 **s.d. Exeunt.]** *Rowe*

III.v

III.v] *Capell*
Location: *Theobald*
2 **s.p. Dog.]** *Rowe*; Const. Dog. *Q, F1* (*or* Con. Do., Const. Do., Constable *until l. 57*)
7 **s.p. Verg.]** *Rowe*; Headb. *Q, F1* (*or* Head. *until l. 60*)
9 **off]** *Capell conj.*; of *Q, F1*
24 **and 'twere]** *F1*; and't twere *Q*
24 **pound]** times *F1*
33 **talking;]** *Capell*; talking *Q, F1*
39 **worshipp'd;]** *Rowe*; worshipt, *Q, F1*
53 **s.d. Enter a Messenger.]** *Rowe*
56 **s.d. Exeunt ... Messenger.]** *Capell* (*after Rowe*); exit *Q, F1* (*following l. 52*)
59 **examination]** examine *F1*
62 **non-come]** *hyphen, F1*
64 **s.d. Exeunt.]** *F1*

IV.i

IV.i] *Rowe*; Actus Quartus. *F1*
Location: *Pope*
o.s.d. **with Attendants]** *Staunton* (*subs.*)
4 **s.p. Friar.]** *Rowe*; Fran. *Q, F1*
20 **not ... do!]** *om. F1*
29 **s.p. D. Pedro.]** *Rowe* (*subs.*); Prince *Q* (*here misprinted* Princn), *F1* (*throughout scene*)
53 **show'd]** *Rowe*; shewed *Q, F1*
56 **seeming!]** *Collier* (*after Knight*); seeming, *Q, F1*
56 **it:]** *Theobald*; it, *Q, F1*
68 **"True"!]** *F3* (*quotes, Wilson*); True, *Q, F1*
77 **me,]** *F2*; me *Q, F1*
109 **s.d. Hero swoons.]** *Hanmer*
112 **s.d. Exeunt ... Claudio.]** *Rowe*
120 **why,]** *Theobald*; why *Q, F1*
127 **Griev'd]** *F1*; Grieued *Q*
133 **smirched]** smeered *F1*
133 **mir'd]** *F1*; mired *Q*
136 **lov'd]** *F1*; loued *Q*
137–9 **on, ... her—]** *Rowe* (*subs.*; on, *F2*); on ... mine: ... her, *Q, F1*
144 **attir'd]** *Pope*; attired *Q, F1*
144–6 **Sir ... say.]** *as verse, Pope; as prose, Q, F1*
148 **truly, not,]** *Sisson*; truly, not *Q*; truly: not *F1*
153 **lov'd]** *F1*; loued *Q*
155–8 **Hear ... mark'd]** *as verse, Pope* (*after Rowe*); *as prose, Q, F1* (*in Q these lines fall at the bottom of sig. G1, where, in order to squeeze them in, G1ᵛ, as part of the inner forme, being already printed off* (*the result of printing from cast-off copy*), *the compositor had to set them as prose, even so extending the usual number of lines per page by two; he may, indeed, have been forced to omit some of the MS text, thus leaving the passage difficult to explain satisfactorily*)
158 **lady.]** *Rowe* (*subs.*); lady, *Q, F1*
158 **mark'd]** *F2*, markt, *Q*; markt. *F1*
161 **beat]** beare *F1*
180 **mercy!]** *F1* (mercy.); mercie, *Q*
190 **not.]** *F1* (not:); not, *Q*
202 **princes ... dead,]** *Theobald*; princesse (left for dead,) *Q*; Princesse (left for dead) *F1*
228 **moving,]** *F2*; moouing *Q, F1*
254 **s.d. with ... Beatrice]** *Rowe* (*subs.*)
271 **not; ... not:]** *F4* (*subs.*); not, ... not, *Q, F1*
275 **swear]** sweare by it *F1*
306 **rancor—]** *Rowe*; rancour? *Q, F1*
314 **Beat—]** *Theobald*; Beat? *Q, F1*
319 **compliment]** *Rowe*; complement *Q, F1*
336 **s.d. Exeunt.]** *F2*

IV.ii

IV.ii] *Capell*
Location: *Theobald*
o.s.d. **or Sexton]** *Capell* (*subs.*)
o.s.d. **and the Watch ... and]** *Capell* (*after Rowe*); *s.d. in Q, F1 reads:* Enter the Constables, Borachio, and the Towne clearke in gownes.
1 **s.p. Dog.]** *Capell*; Keeper *Q, F1* (*an error for* Kemp, *the actor who played Dogberry; see l. 9 below*)
2 **s.p. Verg.]** *Capell*; Cowley *Q, F1* (*or* Couley *throughout scene; Cowley was the actor who played Verges*)
4 **s.p. Dog.]** *Capell*; Andrew *Q, F1* (*another error for Kemp, perhaps from his role as a Merry Andrew or Fool*)
9 **s.p. Dog.]** *Capell*; Kemp *Q, F1* (*or* Ke., Kem. *throughout rest of scene*)
17–20 **Con., Bora. Yea ... villains!]** *om. F1*
17 **s.p. Con., Bora.]** *Capell*
51 **by]** by th' *F1*
59 **s.p. 1. and 2. Watch.]** *ed.*; Watch *Q, F1*
66 **s.d. Exit.]** *Theobald*
67 **s.p. Dog.]** *Rowe*; Constable *Q, F1*
68–9 **in the hands— / Con. Off, coxcomb!]** *Warburton* (*reading* in hand.); in the hands of Coxcombe. *Q, F1*
72 **them.]** *F3* (*subs.*); them, *Q*; them *F1*
73 **s.p. Con.]** *Rowe*; Couley *Q, F1*
87 **s.d. Exeunt.]** *Rowe*; exit. *Q, F1*

V.i

V.i] *Rowe*; Actus Quintus. *F1*
Location: *ed.* (*after Pope*)
1 **s.p. Ant.]** *Rowe*; Brother *Q, F1* (*throughout scene*)
6 **comforter]** comfort *F1*; comfort els *F2*
6 **ear]** *Dyce*; eare, *Q, F1*
16 **And, sorrow]** *Johnson*; And sorrow, *Q, F1*
46 **s.p. D. Pedro.]** *Rowe* (*subs.*); Prince *Q, F1* (*throughout scene*)
47 **lords—]** *Capell*; Lords? *Q, F1*
87 **lov'd]** *F1*; loued *Q*
96 **anticly]** *F3* (antickly); antiquely *Q, F1*
97 **off]** *Theobald*; of *Q, F1*
98 **enemies— ... durst—]** *ed.*; enemies, ... durst, *Q*; enemies, ... durst. *F1*
108 **No?]** *Capell*; No *Q, F1*
109 **s.d. ambo]** *F1*; amb. *Q* (*s.d. placed as in Rowe; after l. 108, Q, F1*)
109 **s.d. Enter Benedick.]** *after l. 107, F1*
115 **lik'd]** *Q, F1* (likt); like *F2*
117 **brother.]** *F4* (*subs.*); brother *Q*; brother, *F1*
123 **high-proof]** *hyphen, Theobald*
126 **Dost]** *F4*; Doest *Q, F1*
132 **What,]** *F1*; What *Q*
136 **me.]** *F4* (me:); me, *Q, F1*
145 **s.d. Aside to Claudio.]** *Cambridge*
169 **there's]** *F1*; theirs *Q*
182 **on]** *F1*; one *Q*
193 **s.d. Exit.]** *Rowe*
200 **s.d. Dogberry ... with]** *Hanmer*
203 **up,]** *Steevens*; vp *Q, F1*
206 **s.p. Dog.]** *Rowe*; Const. *Q, F1* (*throughout scene*)
257 **s.p. Verg.]** *Rowe*; Con. 2 *Q, F1*
263 **thou]** thou thou *F1*
293 **overkindness]** *F1*; ouer kindnesse *Q*
300 **Hir'd]** *Pope*; Hyred *Q*; Hired *F1*
316 **reverent]** reuerend *F1*
327 **s.d. Exeunt ... Verges.]** *Cambridge* (*placed as in Rowe*); Exeunt. *F1* (*after l. 328*)
331 **s.d. To the Watch.]** *Cambridge*
331–2 **Bring ... fellow.]** *as verse, Pope; as prose, Q, F1*
332 **s.d. severally]** *Theobald*

V.ii

V.ii] *Capell*
Location: *Brooke*
o.s.d. **meeting]** *Capell*
9 **me? Why,]** *Rowe*; me, why *Q, F1*
23 **s.d. Margaret]** *F3*; Margarite *Q, F1*
26 **s.d. Sings.]** *Pope*
26–9 **The ... deserve—]** *as verse, Capell; as prose, Q, F1*
41 **nor]** for *F1*
41 **s.d. Enter Beatrice.]** *placed as in F1; after l. 43, Q*
86 **myself.]** *Rowe* (*subs.*); my selfe *Q, F1*
88 **praiseworthy]** *F4* ; praise worthie *Q, F1*
104 **uncle's]** *Malone*; vncles *Q, F1*
104 **s.d. Exeunt.]** *F1*; exit. *Q*

V.iii

V.iii] *Capell*
Location: *Kittredge*
2 **s.p. A Lord.]** *Cambridge*; Lord *Q, F1*
3 **s.p. s.d. Claud. Reading ... scroll.]** *Capell*
9–10 **Hang ... dumb.]** *distinguished as not part of the Epitaph, Capell*
9 **s.d. Hangs ... scroll.]** *Kittredge* (*after Capell*)
10 **dumb]** *F1* (dombe); dead *Q*
11 **Now]** *Capell*; Claudio Now *Q, F1* (*repeated s.p.*)
17 **groan,]** *Capell* (*after Theobald*); grone. *Q, F1*
21 **Heavily, heavily.]** Heauenly, heauenly. *F1*
22 **s.p. Claud.]** *Rowe*; Lo. *Q, F1*
23 **rite]** *Pope*; right *Q, F1*
24, 30 **s.pp. D. Pedro.]** *Rowe* (*subs.*); Prince *Q, F1*
32 **speed 's]** *Thirlby conj.*; speeds *Q, F1*

V.iv

V.iv] *Capell*
Location: *Pope*
o.s.d. **Beatrice]** *Capell*
o.s.d. **Antonio]** *Rowe*
5 **will, ... appears]** *Capell* (will, *Theobald*); will ... appeares, *Q, F1*
7 **s.p. Ant.]** *Rowe*; Old *Q, F1* (*throughout scene*)
7 **sorts]** sort *F1*
33 **Here ... Claudio.]** *om. F1*
34 **s.p. D. Pedro.]** *Rowe* (*subs.*); Prince *Q, F1* (*throughout scene*)
39 **s.d. Exit Antonio.]** *Theobald*
40 **Benedick]** *F1*; Bened. *Q*
50 **And]** A *F1*
51 **s.d. the ladies masked]** *Kittredge* (*subs., after Theobald*)
54 **s.p. Ant.]** *Theobald*; Leo. *Q, F1*
60 **s.d. Unmasking.]** *Rowe*
61 **lov'd]** *F1*; loued *Q*
73 **s.d. Unmasking.]** *Capell*
78 **cousin,]** *Rowe*; cosin *Q, F1*
88 **Fashion'd]** *Rowe*: Fashioned *Q, F1*
98 **s.p. Bene.]** *Thirlby conj.*; Leon. *Q, F1*
98 **s.d. Kissing her.]** *Theobald*
121 **play,]** *Pope*; plaie *Q, F1*
121 **music.]** *F1*; musicke, *Q*
123 **reverent]** reuerend *F1*
129 **s.d. Exeunt.]** *Rowe*; FINIS. *Q, F1*

As You Like It

Thomas Lodge's romance *Rosalynde or Euphues' Golden Legacy* (1590), Shakespeare's source for *As You Like It*, is one of the minor classics of Elizabethan prose. Lodge himself was a borrower. A fourteenth-century poem, *The Tale of Gamelyn*, underlies his own story, although it was Lodge who expanded and altered what had originally been an exclusively masculine tale about outlaws and revengeful brothers into a pastoral concerned chiefly with love. There is no equivalent to Shakespeare's Jaques, or to Touchstone, Audrey, or William, in *Rosalynde*, but all the other main characters are there at least in outline, some of them under the same names. The plot of *As You Like It* is also derived almost entirely from Lodge, although Shakespeare made it more obviously a family affair. His Duke Frederick and Duke Senior are brothers, which they are not in Lodge, and his Celia and Rosalind, as a result, are first cousins. Shakespeare also mitigated the violence of his source. In *Rosalynde*, three men are actually killed during the wrestling match; Aliena has to be rescued, at some cost in terms of bloodshed and death, from outlaws who intend to deliver her as an unwittingly incestuous gift to her own lecherous father; and at the end this father is slain in battle. There are no deaths in *As You Like It*, no hint of incest, and the only blood spilled (Orlando's and that of Charles the wrestler and his two anonymous opponents) has a distanced, fairy-tale quality. There are no outlaws either, only banished courtiers sufficiently tender-hearted to worry about preying upon the deer in the forest, let alone upon other human beings; and the usurping duke, Celia's father, never reaches the fatal battlefield because an old religious man meets and peaceably converts him on the way.

In *Love's Labor's Lost* and *A Midsummer Night's Dream* earlier, Shakespeare had experimented with the reduction of plot entanglement, actual story line, to a minimum. *As You Like It* too is a play which stresses "Words above action, matter above words," as Ben Jonson once urged, although the effect produced is not at all like that of Jonsonian comedy. There is a flurry of events at the beginning—Oliver's various attempts to rid himself of his virtuous younger brother, the banishment of Rosalind and then of Oliver himself—but these are transparently devices for getting all the major characters away from the familiar world and into the forest of Arden, rather than incidents exploited for their own sake. Near the end, another little explosion of events precipitates four marriages and releases all the exiles from their pastoral life. In between, Shakespeare seems to go out of his way to avoid generating suspense. Celia and Oliver, Audrey and Touchstone have agreed to marry almost before we realize what is happening. Rosalind has only to abandon her disguise as Ganymede —and there is no reason on the level of plot why she should not do this as soon as she is safe in Arden—for Orlando to declare himself and Phebe to recognize that she must be content with her faithful Silvius after all.

As You Like It replaces a developing intrigue, of the kind exemplified by *Much Ado about Nothing* or *Twelfth Night*, with a structure of cunningly juxtaposed characters and attitudes which Shakespeare has elaborated until it becomes a substitute for plot. As the days go by in Arden, two or more characters meet, converse and part, to be succeeded on the stage by another group of people concerned to explore a different, but related, point of view. Without being in the least undramatic, as Jonson's early comedies often were, *As You Like It* is singularly still at the centre in a way that focuses attention upon ideas and thematic material. Unlike the Elizabethan Jonson, Shakespeare refuses to legislate or even to take sides in the various rivalries the comedy sets up: between court and country, nature and fortune, youth and age, realism and romanticism, inherent nobility and the virtue that is acquired, the active and the contemplative life, laughter and melancholy. These polarities, the subject of ceaseless debate and meditation, tend to be identified with particular characters, but the comedy as a whole is far more interested in doing justice to the complexity of the argument than in prescribing correct choices.

No society, if it is honest with itself, can pretend that these antinomies do not exist. Equally, no society can have any true cohesion or self-respect if it does not try to accommodate them all, fairly, within its total structure. Rosalind is extraordinarily important in *As You Like It*, as central and dominating a figure in her fashion as Hamlet is in his own, very different play, because in her these warring opposites are reconciled and live at peace without for an instant losing their force or individuality. Like Jaques, Rosalind knows that human beings die and that worms eat them. Like old Corin, she is aware that even the most passionate love diminishes with time, and like Touchstone, that lovers are objectively ridiculous and their airiest flights grounded in the senses. She knows these things immediately and emotionally, not merely in the abstract, and yet they do not sour her gaiety or trivialize the essential seriousness of her commitment to Orlando. Speculative and thoughtful, she is nonetheless able to give a positive shape to her own existence and to that of several other people as well. Detached but involved, she laughs at herself as much as she does at Phebe, Silvius, or Jaques, yet manages to be gentle and generous to them and perceptive in her own affairs. Life is at best imperfect, even in Arden, but Rosalind suggests that there are ways of living it well and to some purpose, despite the pessimism of Jaques. This is why she matters so much in the play, and why the resolution of the plot, such as it is, is placed almost entirely in her hands.

As You Like It was one of four plays which the Lord Chamberlain's Men formally requested to be stayed from publication in 1600. Presumably, the confidence implied by the title was justified: the play was popular with Elizabethan audiences and the actors wanted to retain their profitable monopoly of the text. *As You Like It* is absent from Meres's list of 1598, so that 1599 seems likely as the date of its composition. By then, Shakespeare had already written at least seven comedies, most of them built upon the idea of two localities, one heightened and more remarkable than the other. Like Belmont, Navarre, the wood in *The Two Gentlemen of Verona* or *A Midsummer Night's Dream*, Arden is a place set apart from the ordinary world. It is emphatically not a paradise. Winter, cold winds and rain, the penalty incurred by the Old Testament Adam, come to it. Some of its native inhabitants are churlish and stupid. Yet the forest is essentially a good place, not because it possesses limitless wealth or supernatural power, but simply because in Arden fortune does not oppress and stifle nature. People are free here, as they are not in the nervous court of Duke Frederick, to realize their own potentialities. Worldly assets and success cease to matter. In the forest, judgments are made only in terms of what people really are. Some characters, like Orlando and Rosalind, gain from the opportunity. Others do not.

The idea that sophisticated people, suddenly made part of a rustic life of which previously they had the most distant and imperfect knowledge, may discover truths obscured or undisclosed in the court is a very old one. Pastoral is a complex and enduring form, not because it is escapist, but because it is basically tough: it is a way of testing both the self and the assumptions of ordinary, urban society. *As You Like It* is a pastoral in this sense. It begins with a disordered society, a corrupt court in which violence and broken ribs are considered entertaining and men like Le Beau have to hide their own intuitive sense of justice under a foppish mask; where Oliver, simply because he is an elder son, can treat his servants and younger brother like animals. It moves from this nightmare world into Arden, an exile which is really a liberation, where ideas and relationships can be honestly examined. Long after such a masculine impersonation is necessary, Rosalind clings to the part of Ganymede because of the freedom it allows her. In her boy's disguise, she escapes (for a time) the limitations of being a woman, Duke Senior's daughter, the conscious object of Orlando's love. She learns a great deal about herself, about Orlando, and about love itself which she could not have done within the normal conventions of society. This knowledge is, in a sense, the gift of the forest but it can only come to full fruition in the world outside. Sooner or later, Rosalind must stop play-acting, must reveal herself to Orlando in her own person, and recognize the fact that Hymen, the god of marriage, presides not over the fields and woods but over the town (V.iv.141–46).

There is some truth in Jaques' accusation that Duke Senior and his companions in exile are as much usurpers in a world whose natural balance they have disturbed as Duke Frederick himself. Arden is not a place where people who are not really farmers or goat-herds can live permanently, however useful it may be as a temporary refuge. At the end, most of the characters return joyously to an urban world which, thanks to what they have learned during their banishment, they will transform. The pattern here is one that is standard in pastoral literature, and one of the sources of its enduring fascination. Shakespeare must have known Spenser's particularly haunting version of it in Book VI of *The Faerie Queene*. He returned to it himself in *Cymbeline*, *The Winter's Tale*, and *The Tempest*. *As You Like It*, however, stands out among the other plays of Shakespeare which might be described, at least in part, as pastorals by its essential optimism and by its insistence upon the tolerance and inclusiveness of the new society epitomized in the final dance.

It is true that there are some ungainly participants in this concluding ritual. The elephantine caperings of Audrey are no more "seemly" than they ever were. More important, the relativism, the sceptical attitude of Touchstone remains unchanged. Like all Shakespeare's fools, Touchstone is a corruptor of words. Language itself is one of his main preoccupations, and he likes to bewilder simple souls like Corin by demonstrating the superiority of words over facts. It is entirely characteristic of Touchstone that he does not care on which side of a question he argues. In fact, he reverses himself twice in the course of the court-versus-country dispute with Corin. What matters to him is a denial of the single, objective nature of reality: the reality believed in by men like Corin who earn what they eat, get what they wear, owe no man hate, envy no man's happiness, and never question either the values implied by these attitudes or the words used to express them. Corin is finally silenced by Touchstone's "courtly" wit. He is not, however, exactly defeated. He and the fool simply represent antithetical ways of looking at the world. Neither perspective is advanced as a model. Corin's simplicity is obviously limited, but then so is the willful complication of Touchstone's verbal kingdom.

Shakespeare's fools are usually solitaries, men who can comment on society in the way they do partly because they themselves are set apart, free of domestic entanglement or even of a personal past. Touchstone is unusual in that he does not merely talk about getting married: he actually does it, pressing in among the other "country copulatives" at the end to accept the social bond of matrimony. The bride of this man for whom words are all-important is a girl unable to comprehend or make effective use of even the simplest verbal constructs. In the first scene in which she appears, Audrey manages to misunderstand the words *poetical*, *features*, *honest*, and *foul* in rapid succession. Her mistakings are comic, but her relationship to Touchstone gives them a special significance. Audrey cannot find meanings for words; Touchstone can find too many. Both, however, are "sure together, / As the winter to foul weather" (V.iv.135–36) because when it comes to the point of choice, of action, they fall back upon appetite, non-verbal sense experience of the kind that man shares with the brute creation. Both characters make us laugh, Audrey unwittingly, Touchstone because it is his profession, but there is in both cases a fundamental misadjustment between language and fact. Certainly Touchstone does not represent a point of view to be trusted in this play, as Feste or Lear's fool do in theirs. Although the scepticism of Touchstone does distinguish gold from dross in a whole series of different encounters—with Le Beau, with Jaques, with Corin, Rosalind, and Orlando—the agent is in no sense to be confused either in nature or quality with what it is there to verify or expose. The touchstone identifies the gold: it is not in itself a precious substance. The man totally without illusions is ultimately as much a fool as his romantic opposite, Silvius. Even the most skillful use of words, the most intelligent awareness of the multiple nature of reality, if it is without commitment or generosity, leads in the end to a rigid and reductive kind of behavior, imprisoning man within the skin of the animal.

There are two important absentees from the final dance, as well as two erratic performers. Orlando's faithful servant Adam is simply too old to help initiate the new social order. Silently, he has vanished from the play. As for Jaques, although he is present in the final scene, he is adamant in his refusal to join the dance. It is one of the few absolutely just and perceptive decisions he announces in the course of the comedy. A man unbalanced in his pessimism, delighting in his own melancholy and unsociability, Jaques has hitherto dealt in judgments that were somehow incomplete or askew. Oliver confounded men with beasts but Jaques, in his reported soliloquy on the herd-abandoned deer, makes the opposite mistake of interpreting animal behavior as though it were human. Throughout Act II he clings perversely to prose and discordant sounds while all around him the play is lifting into verse and song. As the comedy progresses, he continues to fare badly. Only Jaques fails to recognize that, in their encounter in the forest, Touchstone has cleverly parodied his own style:

> And then he drew a dial from his poke,
> And looking on it, with lack-lustre eye,
> Says very wisely, "It is ten a' clock.
> Thus we may see," quoth he, "how the world wags.
> 'Tis but an hour ago since it was nine,
> And after one hour more 'twill be eleven,
> And so from hour to hour, we ripe and ripe,
> And then from hour to hour, we rot and rot;
> And thereby hangs a tale." (II.vii.20–28)

These melancholy certainties which Jaques so admires are platitudes of the most obvious kind. Even without the Duke's barbed reminder that Jaques' own libertine past scarcely qualifies him to scourge vice in others, it would be hard to see what value a satirist could have who relied upon moralizings so dusty.

Jaques' famous account of the seven ages of man, for all its verbal poise and inventiveness, is also a set piece which, for Elizabethans, must have verged on the banal. Moreover, it is generalized and demonstrably untrue. Orlando, as Touchstone is quick to point out, may be absurd when he hangs love sonnets on trees. There is still far more value in his relationship with Rosalind than Jaques accounts for in his dismissal of man as lover. Again, Jaques reduces old age to "second childishness and mere oblivion, / Sans teeth, sans eyes, sans taste, sans every thing" (II.vii.165–66). The words are no sooner spoken than Orlando enters bearing old Adam: a man enfeebled by his years, dependent now upon a younger life, but also the living image of all that Jaques has left out of his type picture: loyal, honest, and discriminating. His age has its own kind of value, "frosty but kindly," and the tenderness of Orlando, as well as the respect paid Adam by Duke Senior, ridicules Jaques' despair. With Orlando and Rosalind, Jaques makes even less headway. Orlando flatly declines the satirist's invitation to join him in a verbal assault upon the world "and all our misery": "I will chide no breather in the world but myself, against whom I know most faults" (III.ii.278–81). Rosalind, even more crushingly, points out that Jaques' ideal of silent unresponsiveness is one realized by the average fence-post (IV.i.8–9).

Throughout *As You Like It* Jaques has functioned less as the representative of a valid point of view than as a measure of the essential sanity and balance of those characters who stand closer than he to the centre of the play. He too is a kind of touchstone, testing the strength of that optimism and faith in the future characteristic of Rosalind, Orlando, Celia, and Duke Senior with his continual reminders of mortality and decay. None of them attempt to deny the facts of death and time, but all reject the hopelessness of Jaques: the notion that life is without purpose or meaning because it finishes in the grave. The new society forged in Arden is not flawless. Nevertheless, the final dance is a triumph, an image of harmony, and its movements, disciplined and artful though they are, are flexible enough to accommodate the awkwardness of the goat-girl and the fool. Jaques is respectful of what has been achieved, yet he insists at the end that there is a world elsewhere, beyond the scope of comedy. This is why he casts in his lot with the penitent Duke Frederick, a man who is still asking questions, as opposed to celebrating a resolution. Jaques' response here is, for once, justifiable. He is right to remind us that the comic dance, for all its generosity, its vigor and grace, cannot hope to contain all aspects of human experience.

"The truest poetry is the most feigning." This is what Touchstone tells an uncomprehending Audrey (III.iii.19–20). On her, as might be expected, the paradox is lost. What the fool is playfully gesturing towards is the orthodox Aristotelianism of Sidney's *Apology for Poetry* (1580). The most quintessential, and most truthful, poetry is that which is most clearly imaginary, which mirrors an ideal world of absolutes rather than an untidy world of fact. This, of course, is the argument by which Aristotle originally tried to vindicate poets and painters against Plato's dismissal of them as liars: mere copyists at secondhand of a world of sense which is itself nothing but an inferior imitation. Characteristically, Touchstone no sooner summons up Sidney's position than he proceeds to undercut and confuse it. Lovers are given to addressing their ladies in verse. What is the objective value of the promises they make in this form? By the time Touchstone has finished ringing the changes on that ambiguous word *feigning*, a wiser head than Audrey's might well be perplexed. Poetry is left in an uncertain position, partly redeemed from Plato's charge—picked up by Elizabethan Puritans—that it was an art of lies, partly called into question.

Touchstone's juggling with the counters of truth and falsehood, in their relation to reality and the imagination, is immensely relevant to *As You Like It* as a whole. This is a comedy which emphasizes its own dependence upon artifice and convention, upon openly literary modes. It goes far beyond Lodge in this respect. At a number of points, the psychology is unequivocally that of fairy-tale. Oliver, like any wicked witch, hates his brother Orlando simply because he is good and people like him. Duke Frederick banishes Rosalind for much the same non-reason. Both wicked brothers are converted in a flash, while Oliver and Celia give themselves to each other so suddenly that even Rosalind and Orlando are startled. With the exception of Rosalind, most of the characters resolve themselves when looked at closely into familiar Elizabethan types: the melancholy traveller, the fool, the scornful shepherdess and adoring swain, the romantic lover, the rustic, the good brother and the bad. Shakespeare changed the name of Lodge's Rosader to Orlando probably because he wished to remind his audience of Ariosto's hero in *Orlando Furioso* (English translation 1591): a man who runs mad in the woods for love of his lady Angelica. He reduced the character Lodge had called Adam Spencer to Adam, pure and simple, thus increasing the suggestion of primal old age: fundamental and original humanity. The informing mode of the play is pastoral, with all that the word implies of distance and fabrication. Lions and palm trees do not ordinarily exist in chilly northern forests, but then Arden cannot be located on any map. It is a place associated with the English Robin Hood ballads, but also with classical legends of the Golden World, while the folk ritual of killing the stag and enveloping the successful hunter in its skin (IV.ii) awakens echoes as old as some of the cave paintings at Lascaux.

Yet it would be a mistake to think of *As You Like It* only as a fairy-tale, a fantasy of love and game-playing in the open air. The comedy is essentially serious, concerned to examine the nature of people, emotions, and ideas. It capitalizes, as the title announces from the start, upon the familiarity and resonance possessed by certain character types and situations and moves through them to an analysis of experience which Philip Sidney would almost certainly have found insufficiently didactic: overgenerous in its attitudes and in its admission of the relativity of judgment. In *As You Like It*, however, the most feigning poetry is indeed the truest in a sense different from the one outlined in Sidney's *Apology*: out of artifice, out of convention frankly admitted as such, Shakespeare has gradually elicited a complex and subtle vision of reality.

Anne Barton

As You Like It

[Dramatis Personae

Duke Senior, *living in banishment*
Duke Frederick, *his brother, and usurper of his dominions*
Amiens, Jaques } *lords attending on the banished Duke*
Le Beau, *a courtier attending upon Duke Frederick*
Charles, *wrestler to Duke Frederick*
Oliver, Jaques, Orlando } *sons of Sir Rowland de Boys*
Adam, Dennis } *servants to Oliver*

Touchstone, *a clown*
Sir Oliver Martext, *a vicar*
Corin, Silvius } *shepherds*
William, *a country fellow, in love with Audrey*
A person representing Hymen

Rosalind, *daughter to the banished Duke*
Celia, *daughter to Duke Frederick*
Phebe, *a shepherdess*
Audrey, *a country wench*

Lords, Pages, Foresters, *and* Attendants

Scene: *Oliver's house; Duke Frederick's court; and the forest of Arden*]

ACT I, Scene I

Enter Orlando *and* Adam.

Orl. As I remember, Adam, it was upon this fashion bequeath'd me by will but poor a thousand crowns, and, as thou say'st, charg'd my brother, on his blessing, to breed me well; and there begins my sadness. My brother Jaques he keeps at school, and report speaks goldenly of his profit. For my part, he keeps me rustically at home, or (to speak more properly) stays me here at home unkept; for call you that keeping for a gentleman of my birth, that differs not from the stalling of an ox? His horses are bred better, for besides that they are fair with their feeding, they are taught their manage, and to that end riders dearly hir'd; but I (his brother) gain nothing under him but growth, for the which his animals on his dunghills are as much bound to him as I. Besides this nothing that he so plentifully gives me, the something that nature gave me his countenance seems to take from me. He lets me feed with his hinds, bars me the place of a brother, and as much as in him lies, mines my gentility with my education. This is it, Adam, that grieves me, and the spirit of my father, which I think is within me, begins to mutiny against this servitude. I will no longer endure it, though yet I know no wise remedy how to avoid it.

Enter Oliver.

Adam. Yonder comes my master, your brother.

Orl. Go apart, Adam, and thou shalt hear how he will shake me up.

Oli. Now, sir, what make you here?

Orl. Nothing. I am not taught to make any thing.

Oli. What mar you then, sir?

Orl. Marry, sir, I am helping you to mar that which God made, a poor unworthy brother of yours, with idleness.

Oli. Marry, sir, be better employ'd, and be naught a while.

Orl. Shall I keep your hogs and eat husks with

Words and passages enclosed in square brackets in the text above are either emendations of the copy-text or additions to it. The Textual Notes immediately following the play cite the earliest authority for every such change or insertion and supply the reading of the copy-text wherever it is emended in this edition.

I.i. Location. The garden of Oliver's house.
2, 3. bequeath'd, charg'd. The understood subject is *he*, i.e. Orlando's father. **2. poor a:** a poor.
4. on his blessing: i.e. on pain of losing his blessing. **breed me:** bring me up. **5–6. keeps at school:** maintains at the university.
6. goldenly: in glowing terms. **profit:** progress.
7. rustically: like a peasant; cut off from civilized society.
8. stays: detains. **8–9. unkept:** without proper maintenance.
12. fair: in fine physical condition.
13. manage: manege, paces and movements of a trained horse. **dearly:** at great expense. **16. bound:** indebted.
18. countenance: behavior, or (ironically) favor, patronage.
19. hinds: farm laborers. **bars me:** excludes me from.
21. mines: undermines. **with my education:** by the way I am brought up. **28. shake me up:** berate me (cf. *blow me up*).
29. make you: are you doing (but Orlando quibbles on the more usual sense of *make*).
31. mar. Commonly used in antithesis to *make*, as in *Othello*, I.v.4: "It makes us, or it mars us."
32. Marry: why, indeed (originally the name of the Virgin Mary used as an oath).
35. be naught: a mild curse, equivalent to "Go to the devil."

them? What prodigal portion have I spent, that I should come to such penury?

Oli. Know you where you are, sir?

Orl. O, sir, very well; here in your orchard.

Oli. Know you before whom, sir?

Orl. Ay, better than him I am before knows me. I know you are my eldest brother, and in the gentle condition of blood you should so know me. The courtesy of nations allows you my better, in that you are the first born, but the same tradition takes not away my blood, were there twenty brothers betwixt us. I have as much of my father in me as you, albeit I confess your coming before me is nearer to his reverence.

Oli. What, boy! [*Strikes him.*]

Orl. Come, come, elder brother, you are too young in this. [*Collaring him.*]

Oli. Wilt thou lay hands on me, villain?

Orl. I am no villain; I am the youngest son of Sir Rowland de Boys. He was my father, and he is thrice a villain that says such a father begot villains. Wert thou not my brother, I would not take this hand from thy throat till this other had pull'd out thy tongue for saying so. Thou hast rail'd on thyself.

Adam. Sweet masters, be patient, for your father's remembrance, be at accord.

Oli. Let me go, I say.

Orl. I will not till I please. You shall hear me. My father charg'd you in his will to give me good education. You have train'd me like a peasant, obscuring and hiding from me all gentleman-like qualities. The spirit of my father grows strong in me, and I will no longer endure it; therefore allow me such exercises as may become a gentleman, or give me the poor allottery my father left me by testament, with that I will go buy my fortunes.

Oli. And what wilt thou do? beg, when that is spent? Well, sir, get you in. I will not long be troubled with you; you shall have some part of your will. I pray you leave me.

Orl. I will no further offend you than becomes me for my good.

Oli. Get you with him, you old dog.

Adam. Is "old dog" my reward? Most true, I have lost my teeth in your service. God be with my old master, he would not have spoke such a word.

Exeunt Orlando, Adam.

Oli. Is it even so? Begin you to grow upon me? I will physic your rankness, and yet give no thousand crowns neither. Holla, Dennis!

Enter DENNIS.

Den. Calls your worship?

Oli. Was not Charles, the Duke's wrastler, here to speak with me?

Den. So please you, he is here at the door, and importunes access to you.

Oli. Call him in. [*Exit Dennis.*] 'Twill be a good way; and to-morrow the wrastling is.

Enter CHARLES.

Cha. Good morrow to your worship.

Oli. Good Monsieur Charles, what's the new news at the new court?

Cha. There's no news at the court, sir, but the old news: that is, the old Duke is banish'd by his younger brother the new Duke, and three or four loving lords have put themselves into voluntary exile with him, whose lands and revenues enrich the new Duke; therefore he gives them good leave to wander.

Oli. Can you tell if Rosalind, the Duke's daughter, be banish'd with her father?

Cha. O no; for the Duke's daughter, her cousin, so loves her, being ever from their cradles bred together, that [she] would have follow'd her exile, or have died to stay behind her. She is at the court, and no less belov'd of her uncle than his own daughter, and never two ladies lov'd as they do.

Oli. Where will the old Duke live?

Cha. They say he is already in the forest of Arden, and a many merry men with him; and there they live like the old Robin Hood of England. They say many young gentlemen flock to him every day, and fleet the time carelessly, as they did in the golden world.

Oli. What, you wrastle to-morrow before the new Duke?

Cha. Marry, do I, sir; and I came to acquaint you with a matter. I am given, sir, secretly to understand that your younger brother, Orlando, hath a disposition to come in disguis'd against me to try a fall. To-morrow, sir, I wrastle for my credit, and he that escapes me without some broken limb shall acquit him well. Your brother is but young and tender, and for your love I would be loath to foil him, as I must for my own honor if he come in; therefore out of my love to you, I came hither to acquaint you withal, that either

37–39. Shall . . . penury. An allusion to the parable of the prodigal son (Luke 15:11–32), who, having wasted his portion of his father's possessions, was forced to become a swineherd and envied the hogs their husks.
40. where: i.e. in whose presence (but Orlando again quibbles).
41. orchard: garden.
44–45. gentle . . . blood: feeling proper to gentle birth.
46. courtesy of nations: generally accepted convention; here, the custom of primogeniture. **allows:** acknowledges.
50–51. your . . . reverence: i.e. your being my senior gives you a better claim to the respect which was due him.
54. young in this: i.e. inexperienced in fighting.
56. villain: person of low birth (not the sense Oliver intended).
63. be patient: control yourselves. **70. qualities:** accomplishments.
72. exercises: occupations, training. **73. allottery:** portion.
78. your will: what you want.
85. grow upon me: i.e. get so big that you crowd me.

86. physic your rankness: administer a dose that will cure your overgrowth. **89. wrastler:** wrestler. **95. morrow:** morning.
104. leave: permission. **110. to stay:** at being forced to stay.
114. forest of Arden. The setting of much of the action of Lodge's *Rosalynde*, where it signifies the forest of Ardennes in present-day Belgium, Luxembourg, and France; but Shakespeare (and his audience) would doubtless have in mind as well the forest of Arden in Warwickshire. **118. fleet:** pass. **carelessly:** free from care.
118–19. the golden world: the Golden Age, i.e. the primal age of innocence and ease. **126. fall:** bout.
127. credit: professional reputation. **128. shall:** must.
130. foil: defeat. **132. withal:** therewith.

you might stay him from his intendment, or brook such disgrace well as he shall run into, in that it is a thing of his own search, and altogether against my will.

Oli. Charles, I thank thee for thy love to me, which thou shalt find I will most kindly requite. I had myself notice of my brother's purpose herein, and have by underhand means labor'd to dissuade him from it; but he is resolute. I'll tell thee, Charles, it is the stubbornest young fellow of France, full of ambition, an envious emulator of every man's good parts, a secret and villainous contriver against me his natural brother; therefore use thy discretion—I had as lief thou didst break his neck as his finger. And thou wert best look to't; for if thou dost him any slight disgrace, or if he do not mightily grace himself on thee, he will practice against thee by poison, entrap thee by some treacherous device, and never leave thee till he hath ta'en thy life by some indirect means or other; for I assure thee (and almost with tears I speak it) there is not one so young and so villainous this day living. I speak but brotherly of him, but should I anatomize him to thee as he is, I must blush and weep, and thou must look pale and wonder.

Cha. I am heartily glad I came hither to you. If he come to-morrow, I'll give him his payment. If ever he go alone again, I'll never wrastle for prize more. And so God keep your worship! *Exit.*

[*Oli.*] Farewell, good Charles. Now will I stir this gamester. I hope I shall see an end of him; for my soul (yet I know not why) hates nothing more than he. Yet he's gentle, never school'd and yet learned, full of noble device, of all sorts enchantingly belov'd, and indeed so much in the heart of the world, and especially of my own people, who best know him, that I am altogether mispris'd. But it shall not be so long, this wrastler shall clear all. Nothing remains but that I kindle the boy thither, which now I'll go about. *Exit.*

Scene II

Enter Rosalind *and* Celia.

Cel. I pray thee, Rosalind, sweet my coz, be merry.

Ros. Dear Celia—I show more mirth than I am mistress of, and would you yet [I] were merrier? Unless you could teach me to forget a banish'd father, you must not learn me how to remember any extraordinary pleasure.

Cel. Herein I see thou lov'st me not with the full weight that I love thee. If my uncle, thy banish'd father, had banish'd thy uncle, the Duke my father, so thou hadst been still with me, I could have taught my love to take thy father for mine; so wouldst thou, if the truth of thy love to me were so righteously temper'd as mine is to thee.

Ros. Well, I will forget the condition of my estate, to rejoice in yours.

Cel. You know my father hath no child but I, nor none is like to have; and truly when he dies, thou shalt be his heir; for what he hath taken away from thy father perforce, I will render thee again in affection. By mine honor, I will, and when I break that oath, let me turn monster. Therefore, my sweet Rose, my dear Rose, be merry.

Ros. From henceforth I will, coz, and devise sports. Let me see—what think you of falling in love?

Cel. Marry, I prithee do, to make sport withal. But love no man in good earnest, nor no further in sport neither, than with safety of a pure blush thou mayst in honor come off again.

Ros. What shall be our sport then?

Cel. Let us sit and mock the good huswife Fortune from her wheel, that her gifts may henceforth be bestow'd equally.

Ros. I would we could do so; for her benefits are mightily misplac'd, and the bountiful blind woman doth most mistake in her gifts to women.

Cel. 'Tis true, for those that she makes fair she scarce makes honest, and those that she makes honest she makes very ill-favoredly.

Ros. Nay, now thou goest from Fortune's office to Nature's. Fortune reigns in gifts of the world, not in the lineaments of Nature.

Enter Clown [Touchstone].

Cel. No; when Nature hath made a fair creature, may she not by Fortune fall into the fire? Though Nature hath given us wit to flout at Fortune, hath not Fortune sent in this fool to cut off the argument?

Ros. Indeed there is Fortune too hard for Nature,

133. brook: endure.
135. search: seeking. **140. underhand:** indirect.
143. emulator: rival. **144. parts:** qualities.
145. contriver: schemer. **natural:** own. **146. lief:** willingly.
147. thou . . . look: you had better give serious attention.
149. grace . . . thee: gain honor at your expense.
150. practice: plot, act treacherously.
155. brotherly: i.e. with brotherly reticence about his vices.
156. anatomize: dissect, lay open.
161. go alone: walk without help.
164. stir: stir up (to compete in the wrestling). **gamester:** sportive fellow. **166. gentle:** of gentlemanly character.
167. device: devising, purposes. **of all sorts:** by people of every rank. **168. enchantingly:** as if by enchantment.
171. mispris'd: despised. **172. clear:** settle. **kindle:** incite.
173. thither: i.e. to court, for the wrestling.

I.ii. Location: Lawn before the Duke's palace.
1. sweet my coz: my dear cousin.

3–4. am mistress of: have at my command, i.e. actually feel.
6. learn: instruct. **11. so:** provided that.
14. righteously temper'd: rightly compounded.
15. estate: state, circumstances. **20. perforce:** by force.
25. sports: amusements. **28. safety:** safeguard. **pure:** innocent.
29. come off: escape.
31. huswife: housewife, manager of household affairs. The conventional image of Fortune with her wheel is playfully altered (by the adjective *good*) to a domestic picture of an industrious matron at her spinning wheel. Cf. *the false huswife Fortune* in *Antony and Cleopatra,* IV.xv.44, where *huswife* = hussy.
38. honest: chaste. **39. ill-favoredly:** ugly. **40. office:** function.
41. gifts . . world: i.e. wealth, power, and the like, as contrasted with beauty and intelligence, the gifts of Nature. This distinction was an Elizabethan commonplace.
42 s.d. Touchstone. The audience does not learn the Clown's name until II.iv.19. **45. flout:** mock, jeer.
47. argument: discussion, witty exchange.

when Fortune makes Nature's natural the cutter-off of Nature's wit.

Cel. Peradventure this is not Fortune's work neither, but Nature's, who perceiveth our natural wits too dull to reason of such goddesses, [and] hath sent this natural for our whetstone; for always the dullness of the fool is the whetstone of the wits. How now, wit, whither wander you?

Touch. Mistress, you must come away to your father.

Cel. Were you made the messenger?

Touch. No, by mine honor, but I was bid to come for you.

Ros. Where learn'd you that oath, fool?

Touch. Of a certain knight, that swore by his honor they were good pancakes, and swore by his honor the mustard was naught. Now I'll stand to it, the pancakes were naught, and the mustard was good, and yet was not the knight forsworn.

Cel. How prove you that, in the great heap of your knowledge?

Ros. Ay, marry, now unmuzzle your wisdom.

Touch. Stand you both forth now. Stroke your chins, and swear by your beards that I am a knave.

Cel. By our beards (if we had them) thou art.

Touch. By my knavery (if I had it) then I were. But if you swear by that that is not, you are not forsworn. No more was this knight, swearing by his honor, for he never had any; or if he had, he had sworn it away before ever he saw those pancakes or that mustard.

Cel. Prithee, who is't that thou mean'st?

Touch. One that old Frederick, your father, loves.

[*Cel.*] My father's love is enough to honor him enough. Speak no more of him, you'll be whipt for taxation one of these days.

Touch. The more pity that fools may not speak wisely what wise men do foolishly.

Cel. By my troth, thou sayest true; for since the little wit that fools have was silenc'd, the little foolery that wise men have makes a great show. Here comes Monsieur [Le] Beau.

Enter Le Beau.

Ros. With his mouth full of news.

Cel. Which he will put on us, as pigeons feed their young.

Ros. Then shall we be news-cramm'd.

Cel. All the better; we shall be the more marketable. *Bon jour*, Monsieur Le Beau. What's the news?

Le Beau. Fair princess, you have lost much good sport.

Cel. Sport! of what color?

Le Beau. What color, madam? How shall I answer you?

Ros. As wit and fortune will.

Touch. Or as the Destinies decrees.

Cel. Well said—that was laid on with a trowel.

Touch. Nay, if I keep not my rank—

Ros. Thou losest thy old smell.

Le Beau. You amaze me, ladies. I would have told you of good wrastling, which you have lost the sight of.

Ros. Yet tell us the manner of the wrastling.

Le Beau. I will tell you the beginning; and if it please your ladyships, you may see the end, for the best is yet to do, and here where you are, they are coming to perform it.

Cel. Well, the beginning, that is dead and buried.

Le Beau. There comes an old man and his three sons—

Cel. I could match this beginning with an old tale.

Le Beau. Three proper young men, of excellent growth and presence.

Ros. With bills on their necks, "Be it known unto all men by these presents."

Le Beau. The eldest of the three wrastled with Charles, the Duke's wrastler, which Charles in a moment threw him, and broke three of his ribs, that there is little hope of life in him. So he serv'd the second, and so the third. Yonder they lie, the poor old man, their father, making such pitiful dole over them that all the beholders take his part with weeping.

Ros. Alas!

Touch. But what is the sport, monsieur, that the ladies have lost?

Le Beau. Why, this that I speak of.

Touch. Thus men may grow wiser every day. It is the first time that ever I heard breaking of ribs was sport for ladies.

Cel. Or I, I promise thee.

Ros. But is there any else longs to see this broken music in his sides? Is there yet another dotes upon rib-breaking? Shall we see this wrastling, cousin?

Le Beau. You must if you stay here, for here is the place appointed for the wrastling, and they are ready to perform it.

Cel. Yonder sure they are coming. Let us now stay and see it.

Flourish. Enter Duke [Frederick], Lords, Orlando, Charles, *and* Attendants.

49. natural: idiot, simpleton.
56. wit . . . you. Celia turns to her purpose an expression ordinarily addressed to one who was talking too much or not to the point, or giving other such evidence that his wits were deserting him. For another example see IV.i.166, "Wit, whither wilt?" (i.e. whither wilt thou go?). **65. naught:** bad. **67. forsworn:** perjured.
85. taxation: censure, slander. **88. troth:** faith.
93. put: force.
96–97. more marketable. As a fowl fattened by forced feeding would be.

101. color: sort.
106. with a trowel. Deliberately ambiguous: (1) with telling force; (2) unsubtly. Touchstone blandly ignores the second possibility.
107. rank: i.e. status as a witty jester. Rosalind puns on the sense "bad-smelling." **109. amaze:** bewilder. **115. to do:** to be done.
120. I . . . tale: i.e. that isn't a very original beginning. The motif of the father with three sons is common in folktales.
121. proper: handsome. **123. bills:** placards.
124. these presents: this present document (with obvious pun on *presence*). **128. that:** so that. **130. dole:** lamentation.
141–42. broken music: i.e. noisy breaking of ribs. Rosalind twists to her own purposes a term used of music arranged for instruments of more than one kind.
148 s.d. Flourish: trumpet fanfare (announcing an important personage).

Duke F. Come on. Since the youth will not be entreated, his own peril on his forwardness.

Ros. Is yonder the man?

Le Beau. Even he, madam.

Cel. Alas, he is too young! yet he looks successfully.

Duke F. How now, daughter and cousin? are you crept hither to see the wrastling?

Ros. Ay, my liege, so please you give us leave.

Duke F. You will take little delight in it, I can tell you, there is such odds in the man. In pity of the challenger's youth I would fain dissuade him, but he will not be entreated. Speak to him, ladies, see if you can move him.

Cel. Call him hither, good Monsieur Le Beau.

Duke F. Do so; I'll not be by.

Le Beau. Monsieur the challenger, the princess calls for you.

Orl. I attend them with all respect and duty.

Ros. Young man, have you challeng'd Charles the wrastler?

Orl. No, fair princess; he is the general challenger. I come but in, as others do, to try with him the strength of my youth.

Cel. Young gentleman, your spirits are too bold for your years. You have seen cruel proof of this man's strength. If you saw yourself with your eyes, or knew yourself with your judgment, the fear of your adventure would counsel you to a more equal enterprise. We pray you for your own sake to embrace your own safety, and give over this attempt.

Ros. Do, young sir, your reputation shall not therefore be mispris'd. We will make it our suit to the Duke that the wrastling might not go forward.

Orl. I beseech you, punish me not with your hard thoughts, wherein I confess me much guilty to deny so fair and excellent ladies any thing. But let your fair eyes and gentle wishes go with me to my trial; wherein if I be foil'd, there is but one sham'd that was never gracious; if kill'd, but one dead that is willing to be so. I shall do my friends no wrong, for I have none to lament me; the world no injury, for in it I have nothing. Only in the world I fill up a place, which may be better supplied when I have made it empty.

Ros. The little strength that I have, I would it were with you.

Cel. And mine, to eke out hers.

Ros. Fare you well; pray heaven I be deceiv'd in you!

Cel. Your heart's desires be with you!

Cha. Come, where is this young gallant that is so desirous to lie with his mother earth?

Orl. Ready, sir, but his will hath in it a more modest working.

Duke F. You shall try but one fall.

Cha. No, I warrant your Grace, you shall not entreat him to a second, that have so mightily persuaded him from a first.

Orl. You mean to mock me after; you should not have mock'd me before. But come your ways.

Ros. Now Hercules be thy speed, young man!

Cel. I would I were invisible, to catch the strong fellow by the leg. *Wrastle.*

Ros. O excellent young man!

Cel. If I had a thunderbolt in mine eye, I can tell who should down. [*Charles is thrown.*] *Shout.*

Duke F. No more, no more.

Orl. Yes, I beseech your Grace, I am not yet well breath'd.

Duke F. How dost thou, Charles?

Le Beau. He cannot speak, my lord.

Duke F. Bear him away. What is thy name, young man?

Orl. Orlando, my liege, the youngest son of Sir Rowland de Boys.

Duke F. I would thou hadst been son to some man else:
The world esteem'd thy father honorable,
But I did find him still mine enemy.
Thou shouldst have better pleas'd me with this deed
Hadst thou descended from another house.
But fare thee well, thou art a gallant youth.
I would thou hadst told me of another father.
Exit Duke [*with Train and Le Beau*].

Cel. Were I my father, coz, would I do this?

Orl. I am more proud to be Sir Rowland's son,
His youngest son, and would not change that calling
To be adopted heir to Frederick.

Ros. My father lov'd Sir Rowland as his soul,
And all the world was of my father's mind.
Had I before known this young man his son,
I should have given him tears unto entreaties,
Ere he should thus have ventur'd.

Cel. Gentle cousin,
Let us go thank him, and encourage him.
My father's rough and envious disposition
Sticks me at heart. Sir, you have well deserv'd.
If you do keep your promises in love
But justly as you have exceeded all promise,
Your mistress shall be happy.

Ros. Gentleman,
[*Giving him a chain from her neck.*]

150. entreated: persuaded (to desist). **his own . . . forwardness:** i.e. let him assume the risk for his own rashness.
151. yonder. A demonstrative pronoun, not an adverb.
153–54. successfully: like a winner. **157. liege:** sovereign.
159. odds: disparity, i.e. superiority. **the man:** i.e. Charles.
160. fain: gladly.
175–76. If . . . judgment: i.e. if you used your powers of observation and your judgment on yourself.
177. fear: danger. **your adventure:** your venture, the risk you are taking. **178. equal:** commensurate with your powers.
181. therefore: on that account. **mispris'd:** despised.
183–84. punish . . . thoughts: don't think ill of me if I refuse to withdraw. **184. wherein:** with reference to which.
188. gracious: in favor, esteemed. **196. eke out:** supplement.
197–98. deceiv'd in you: i.e. mistaken about your chances.

203. modest working: decorous operation (Orlando is playing on the sexual implications of line 201).
209. come your ways: come along and begin.
210. be thy speed: aid you, give you success.
218. well breath'd: i.e. warmed up. **226. still:** ever, always.
231. do this: behave thus. **233. calling:** name.
238. unto: in addition to. **241. envious:** malicious.
242. Sticks: stabs.
244. But justly as: to the same degree in which. **promise:** expectation (of success in the wrestling match).

Wear this for me: one out of suits with Fortune,
That could give more, but that her hand lacks means.
Shall we go, coz?
  Cel. Ay. Fare you well, fair gentleman.
  Orl. Can I not say, I thank you? My better parts
Are all thrown down, and that which here stands up
Is but a quintain, a mere liveless block.
  Ros. He calls us back. My pride fell with my fortunes,
I'll ask him what he would. Did you call, sir?
Sir, you have wrastled well, and overthrown
More than your enemies.
  Cel. Will you go, coz?
  Ros. Have with you.—Fare you well.
Exit [with Celia].
  Orl. What passion hangs these weights upon my tongue?
I cannot speak to her, yet she urg'd conference.

Enter LE BEAU.

O poor Orlando! thou art overthrown,
Or Charles, or something weaker, masters thee.
  Le Beau. Good sir, I do in friendship counsel you
To leave this place. Albeit you have deserv'd
High commendation, true applause, and love,
Yet such is now the Duke's condition
That he misconsters all that you have done.
The Duke is humorous—what he is indeed
More suits you to conceive than I to speak of.
  Orl. I thank you, sir; and pray you tell me this:
Which of the two was daughter of the Duke,
That here was at the wrastling?
  Le Beau. Neither his daughter, if we judge by manners,
But yet indeed the [smaller] is his daughter.
The other is daughter to the banish'd Duke,
And here detain'd by her usurping uncle
To keep his daughter company, whose loves
Are dearer than the natural bond of sisters.
But I can tell you that of late this Duke
Hath ta'en displeasure 'gainst his gentle niece,
Grounded upon no other argument
But that the people praise her for her virtues,
And pity her for her good father's sake;
And on my life his malice 'gainst the lady
Will suddenly break forth. Sir, fare you well.
Hereafter, in a better world than this,
I shall desire more love and knowledge of you.
  Orl. I rest much bounden to you; fare you well.
[Exit Le Beau.]

246. one . . . Fortune: one whose petitions to Fortune are rejected (?) or one who no longer wears the livery of Fortune, i.e. one cast out of Fortune's favor (?). **247. could:** would wish to.
251. quintain: wooden figure used as a target in tilting. **liveless:** lifeless.
256. Have with you: let us go together.
257. passion: violent emotion.
258. urg'd conference: invited conversation.
260. Or: either. **264. condition:** state of mind.
265. misconsters: misconstrues.
266. humorous: temperamental, given to shifting moods or notions.
279. argument: reason, grounds.
284. in . . . world: i.e. when circumstances are more favorable.
286. bounden: indebted.

Thus must I from the smoke into the smother,
From tyrant Duke unto a tyrant brother.
But heavenly Rosalind! *Exit.*

SCENE III

Enter CELIA *and* ROSALIND.

Cel. Why, cousin, why, Rosalind! Cupid have mercy, not a word?

Ros. Not one to throw at a dog.

Cel. No, thy words are too precious to be cast away upon curs, throw some of them at me. Come lame me with reasons.

Ros. Then there were two cousins laid up, when the one should be lam'd with reasons, and the other mad without any.

Cel. But is all this for your father?

Ros. No, some of it is for my child's father. O how full of briers is this working-day world!

Cel. They are but burs, cousin, thrown upon thee in holiday foolery; if we walk not in the trodden paths, our very petticoats will catch them.

Ros. I could shake them off my coat; these burs are in my heart.

Cel. Hem them away.

Ros. I would try, if I could cry "hem" and have him.

Cel. Come, come, wrastle with thy affections.

Ros. O, they take the part of a better wrastler than myself!

Cel. O, a good wish upon you! you will try in time, in despite of a fall. But turning these jests out of service, let us talk in good earnest. Is it possible, on such a sudden, you should fall into so strong a liking with old Sir Rowland's youngest son?

Ros. The Duke my father lov'd his father dearly.

Cel. Doth it therefore ensue that you should love his son dearly? By this kind of chase, I should hate him, for my father hated his father dearly; yet I hate not Orlando.

Ros. No, faith, hate him not, for my sake.

Cel. Why should I not? Doth he not deserve well?

Enter DUKE [FREDERICK] *with* LORDS.

Ros. Let me love him for that, and do you love

287. from . . . smother: i.e. out of the frying pan into the fire.

I.iii. Location: The Duke's palace.
6. reasons: explanations (of your silence).
11. my child's father: i.e. Orlando. In her love melancholy Rosalind is dreaming of the future.
14. holiday foolery. In retort to *working-day world*, line 12 (Wilson).
18. Hem them away: i.e. cough them away, like any other choking obstruction in the throat or chest.
19–20. cry . . . him: win him merely by clearing my throat (with a play on *hem* and *him*).
22. take . . . of: (1) side with; (2) require the agency of.
25. in despite of: notwithstanding the danger of.
25–26. turning . . . service: dismissing this levity.
31. therefore ensue: follow as a consequence.
32. By . . . chase: by pursuing this course of argument.
33. dearly: intensely.
36–37. deserve well: i.e. well deserve to be hated (but Rosalind pretends to misunderstand).

him because I do. Look, here comes the Duke.
Cel. With his eyes full of anger.
Duke F. Mistress, dispatch you with your safest haste,
And get you from our court.
Ros. Me, uncle?
Duke F. You, cousin.
Within these ten days if that thou beest found
So near our public court as twenty miles,
Thou diest for it.
Ros. I do beseech your Grace
Let me the knowledge of my fault bear with me:
If with myself I hold intelligence,
Or have acquaintance with mine own desires;
If that I do not dream, or be not frantic
(As I do trust I am not), then, dear uncle,
Never so much as in a thought unborn
Did I offend your Highness.
Duke F. Thus do all traitors:
If their purgation did consist in words,
They are as innocent as grace itself.
Let it suffice thee that I trust thee not.
Ros. Yet your mistrust cannot make me a traitor.
Tell me whereon the [likelihood] depends.
Duke F. Thou art thy father's daughter, there's enough.
Ros. So was I when your Highness took his dukedom,
So was I when your Highness banish'd him.
Treason is not inherited, my lord,
Or if we did derive it from our friends,
What's that to me? my father was no traitor.
Then, good my liege, mistake me not so much
To think my poverty is treacherous.
Cel. Dear sovereign, hear me speak.
Duke F. Ay, Celia, we stay'd her for your sake,
Else had she with her father rang'd along.
Cel. I did not then entreat to have her stay,
It was your pleasure and your own remorse.
I was too young that time to value her,
But now I know her. If she be a traitor,
Why, so am I. We still have slept together,
Rose at an instant, learn'd, play'd, eat together,
And wheresoe'er we went, like Juno's swans,
Still we went coupled and inseparable.
Duke F. She is too subtile for thee, and her smoothness,
Her very silence, and her patience

Speak to the people, and they pity her.
Thou art a fool; she robs thee of thy name,
And thou wilt show more bright and seem more virtuous
When she is gone. Then open not thy lips:
Firm and irrevocable is my doom
Which I have pass'd upon her; she is banish'd.
Cel. Pronounce that sentence then on me, my liege,
I cannot live out of her company.
Duke F. You are a fool. You, niece, provide yourself;
If you outstay the time, upon mine honor,
And in the greatness of my word, you die.
Exit Duke [with Lords].
Cel. O my poor Rosalind, whither wilt thou go?
Wilt thou change fathers? I will give thee mine.
I charge thee be not thou more griev'd than I am.
Ros. I have more cause.
Cel. Thou hast not, cousin,
Prithee be cheerful. Know'st thou not the Duke
Hath banish'd me, his daughter?
Ros. That he hath not.
Cel. No, hath not? Rosalind lacks then the love
Which teacheth thee that thou and I am one.
Shall we be sund'red? shall we part, sweet girl?
No, let my father seek another heir.
Therefore devise with me how we may fly,
Whither to go, and what to bear with us,
And do not seek to take your change upon you,
To bear your griefs yourself, and leave me out;
For by this heaven, now at our sorrows pale,
Say what thou canst, I'll go along with thee.
Ros. Why, whither shall we go?
Cel. To seek my uncle in the forest of Arden.
Ros. Alas, what danger will it be to us,
Maids as we are, to travel forth so far!
Beauty provoketh thieves sooner than gold.
Cel. I'll put myself in poor and mean attire,
And with a kind of umber smirch my face;
The like do you. So shall we pass along
And never stir assailants.
Ros. Were it not better,
Because that I am more than common tall,
That I did suit me all points like a man?
A gallant curtle-axe upon my thigh,
A boar-spear in my hand, and—in my heart
Lie there what hidden woman's fear there will—
We'll have a swashing and a martial outside,
As many other mannish cowards have
That do outface it with their semblances.
Cel. What shall I call thee when thou art a man?

41. your safest haste: i.e. utmost speed, since in speed lies your safety.
42. cousin. Used of aunts, uncles, nieces, and nephews, as well as cousins in the modern sense.
47. hold intelligence: am in communication.
49. If that: if. **frantic:** raving mad. **53. purgation:** exoneration.
54. grace: virtue. **57. likelihood:** supposition that it is likely.
62. friends: relatives.
64. good my liege: my good lord duke (*liege* = sovereign).
65. To: as to. **67. stay'd her:** kept her here.
68. rang'd: roamed.
70. remorse: pity, compassion (prompted by conscience).
71. that time: at that time. The line suggests that some considerable time has passed since Duke Senior was banished. This is not the impression conveyed by I.i, but cf. II.i.2. **73. still:** always.
74. at an instant: at the same moment.
75. Juno's swans. Swans were associated with Venus, not Juno.
77. subtile: subtle, cunning.

80. name: i.e. due praise.
81. show: appear. **virtuous:** filled with admirable qualities.
83. doom: judgment, sentence.
87. provide yourself: make your preparations.
89. in . . . word: upon my word as duke. **91. change:** exchange.
102. change: i.e. of fortune. **110. provoketh:** arouses.
111. mean: lowly. **112. umber:** brown pigment.
116. suit: dress. **all points:** in every respect.
117. curtle-axe: short sword.
120. swashing: blustering, swashbuckling.
121. mannish: pretending manly courage.
122. outface it: boldly carry off a situation. **semblances:** (mere) appearances.

Ros. I'll have no worse a name than Jove's own page,
And therefore look you call me Ganymed.
But what will you [be] call'd?
Cel. Something that hath a reference to my state:
No longer Celia, but Aliena.
Ros. But, cousin, what if we assay'd to steal
The clownish fool out of your father's court?
Would he not be a comfort to our travel?
Cel. He'll go along o'er the wide world with me;
Leave me alone to woo him. Let's away,
And get our jewels and our wealth together,
Devise the fittest time and safest way
To hide us from pursuit that will be made
After my flight. Now go [we in] content
To liberty, and not to banishment. *Exeunt.*

ACT II, Scene I

Enter Duke Senior, Amiens, *and two or three* Lords, *like foresters.*

Duke S. Now, my co-mates and brothers in exile,
Hath not old custom made this life more sweet
Than that of painted pomp? Are not these woods
More free from peril than the envious court?
Here feel we not the penalty of Adam,
The seasons' difference, as the icy fang
And churlish chiding of the winter's wind,
Which when it bites and blows upon my body
Even till I shrink with cold, I smile and say,
"This is no flattery: these are counsellors
That feelingly persuade me what I am."
Sweet are the uses of adversity,
Which like the toad, ugly and venomous,
Wears yet a precious jewel in his head;
And this our life, exempt from public haunt,
Finds tongues in trees, books in the running brooks,
Sermons in stones, and good in every thing.
Ami. I would not change it. Happy is your Grace,
That can translate the stubbornness of fortune
Into so quiet and so sweet a style.
Duke S. Come, shall we go and kill us venison?
And yet it irks me the poor dappled fools,
Being native burghers of this desert city,
Should in their own confines with forked heads

125. **Ganymed:** Ganymede, the boy whom Jupiter made cupbearer to the gods. 128. **Aliena:** the estranged one (Latin). 129. **assay'd:** attempted. 133. **woo:** coax, persuade. 137. **content:** contentment.

II.i. Location: The forest of Arden.
o.s.d. **like:** in the guise of. 2. **old:** long-continued. 3. **painted:** artificial, specious. 4. **envious:** malicious, spiteful. 5. **feel we not:** i.e. we do not suffer seriously from. Many editors emend *not* to *but* (after Theobald). 5–6. **penalty . . . difference.** In Eden it was perpetual spring. 6. **as:** such as. 7. **churlish:** rough, rude. 11. **feelingly:** through my senses. 12. **uses:** benefits. 13–14. **toad . . . head.** A widespread belief. The jewel was supposed to have great curative power against disease. 14. **his:** its. 15. **exempt:** cut off. **public haunt:** the society of men. 19. **translate:** transform. 22. **irks:** distresses. **fools:** innocents (expressive of affectionate pity). 23. **desert:** uninhabited by men, "unpeopled" (III.ii.126). 24. **confines:** territories. **forked heads:** two-pronged hunting arrows.

Have their round haunches gor'd.
1. Lord. Indeed, my lord,
The melancholy Jaques grieves at that,
And in that kind swears you do more usurp
Than doth your brother that hath banish'd you.
To-day my Lord of Amiens and myself
Did steal behind him as he lay along
Under an oak, whose antique root peeps out
Upon the brook that brawls along this wood,
To the which place a poor sequest'red stag,
That from the hunter's aim had ta'en a hurt,
Did come to languish; and indeed, my lord,
The wretched animal heav'd forth such groans
That their discharge did stretch his leathern coat
Almost to bursting, and the big round tears
Cours'd one another down his innocent nose
In piteous chase; and thus the hairy fool,
Much marked of the melancholy Jaques,
Stood on th' extremest verge of the swift brook,
Augmenting it with tears.
Duke S. But what said Jaques?
Did he not moralize this spectacle?
1. Lord. O yes, into a thousand similes.
First, for his weeping into the needless stream:
"Poor deer," quoth he, "thou mak'st a testament
As worldlings do, giving thy sum of more
To that which had too [much]." Then being there alone,
Left and abandoned of his velvet [friends]:
"'Tis right," quoth he, "thus misery doth part
The flux of company." Anon a careless herd,
Full of the pasture, jumps along by him
And never stays to greet him. "Ay," quoth Jaques,
"Sweep on, you fat and greasy citizens,
'Tis just the fashion. Wherefore do you look
Upon that poor and broken bankrupt there?"
Thus most invectively he pierceth through
The body of [the] country, city, court,
Yea, and of this our life, swearing that we
Are mere usurpers, tyrants, and what's worse,
To fright the animals and to kill them up
In their assign'd and native dwelling-place.
Duke S. And did you leave him in this contemplation?
2. Lord. We did, my lord, weeping and commenting
Upon the sobbing deer.

26. **Jaques.** Pronounced as a dissyllable throughout. 30. **along:** stretched out. 31. **antique:** ancient. 32. **brawls:** noisily courses. 33. **sequest'red:** separated from the herd. 39. **Cours'd:** pursued (a hunting metaphor, picked up by *chase,* line 40). 41. **marked of:** observed by. 42. **extremest verge:** very edge of the bank. 44. **moralize:** interpret morally or symbolically. 46. **needless:** having no need (of additional water). 48. **worldlings:** mortals; worldly men. **sum of more:** additional amount. 50. **of:** by. **velvet:** i.e. in flourishing condition. There is perhaps an allusion to the so-called "velvet" on the antlers of deer during the stage of rapid growth, as well as to the rich clothing of "worldlings." 51. **'Tis right:** just so. **part:** depart from. 52. **flux:** continuous stream. **Anon:** just then; presently. **careless:** carefree. 56. **just:** exactly. 57. **broken:** ruined. 58. **invectively:** in abusive language. 61. **mere:** out-and-out. **what's worse:** whatever may be worse. 62. **up:** off (intensive).

Duke S. Show me the place.
I love to cope him in these sullen fits,
For then he's full of matter.
1. Lord. I'll bring you to him straight. *Exeunt.*

Scene II

Enter Duke [Frederick] *with* Lords.

Duke F. Can it be possible that no man saw them?
It cannot be. Some villains of my court
Are of consent and sufferance in this.
1. Lord. I cannot hear of any that did see her.
The ladies, her attendants of her chamber,
Saw her a-bed, and in the morning early
They found the bed untreasur'd of their mistress.
2. Lord. My lord, the roynish clown, at whom so oft
Your Grace was wont to laugh, is also missing.
Hisperia, the princess' gentlewoman,
Confesses that she secretly o'erheard
Your daughter and her cousin much commend
The parts and graces of the wrastler
That did but lately foil the sinowy Charles,
And she believes, where ever they are gone,
That youth is surely in their company.
Duke F. Send to his brother; fetch that gallant hither.
If he be absent, bring his brother to me;
I'll make him find him. Do this suddenly;
And let not search and inquisition quail
To bring again these foolish runaways. *Exeunt.*

Scene III

Enter Orlando *and* Adam, [*meeting*].

Orl. Who's there?
Adam. What, my young master? O my gentle master,
O my sweet master, O you memory
Of old Sir Rowland! Why, what make you here?
Why are you virtuous? Why do people love you?
And wherefore are you gentle, strong, and valiant?
Why would you be so fond to overcome
The bonny priser of the humorous Duke?
Your praise is come too swiftly home before you.
Know you not, master, to [some] kind of men
Their graces serve them but as enemies?
No more do yours. Your virtues, gentle master,
Are sanctified and holy traitors to you.

67. cope: deal with, converse with. **sullen:** melancholy.
68. matter: substance, good sense. **69. straight:** straightway.

II.ii. Location: The Duke's palace.
3. Are . . . in: i.e. have connived at. **8. roynish:** scurvy, paltry.
13. parts and graces: talents and accomplishments.
14. sinowy: sinewy. **19. suddenly:** quickly.
20. inquisition: inquiry. **quail:** slacken. **21. again:** back.

II.iii. Location: Before Oliver's house.
3. memory: reminder. **4. make you:** are you doing.
5. virtuous: full of good qualities. **7. fond:** foolish. **to:** as to.
8. bonny priser: strapping prize-fighter. **humorous:** capricious.
11. graces: virtues. **12. more:** i.e. better.

O, what a world is this, when what is comely
Envenoms him that bears it!
[*Orl.*] Why, what's the matter?
Adam. O unhappy youth,
Come not within these doors! Within this roof
The enemy of all your graces lives.
Your brother—no, no brother, yet the son
(Yet not the son, I will not call him son)
Of him I was about to call his father—
Hath heard your praises, and this night he means
To burn the lodging where you use to lie,
And you within it. If he fail of that,
He will have other means to cut you off;
I overheard him, and his practices.
This is no place, this house is but a butchery;
Abhor it, fear it, do not enter it.
[*Orl.*] Why, whither, Adam, wouldst thou have me go?
Adam. No matter whither, so you come not here.
Orl. What, wouldst thou have me go and beg my food?
Or with a base and boist'rous sword enforce
A thievish living on the common road?
This I must do, or know not what to do;
Yet this I will not do, do how I can.
I rather will subject me to the malice
Of a diverted blood and bloody brother.
Adam. But do not so. I have five hundred crowns,
The thrifty hire I sav'd under your father,
Which I did store to be my foster-nurse,
When service should in my old limbs lie lame,
And unregarded age in corners thrown.
Take that, and He that doth the ravens feed,
Yea, providently caters for the sparrow,
Be comfort to my age! Here is the gold,
All this I give you, let me be your servant.
Though I look old, yet I am strong and lusty;
For in my youth I never did apply
Hot and rebellious liquors in my blood,
Nor did not with unbashful forehead woo
The means of weakness and debility;
Therefore my age is as a lusty winter,
Frosty, but kindly. Let me go with you,
I'll do the service of a younger man
In all your business and necessities.
Orl. O good old man, how well in thee appears
The constant service of the antique world,
When service sweat for duty, not for meed!
Thou art not for the fashion of these times,
Where none will sweat but for promotion,
And having that do choke their service up
Even with the having. It is not so with thee.

23. use: are accustomed. **26. practices:** treacherous plots.
27. place: dwelling place. **butchery:** slaughterhouse.
32. boist'rous: violent. **35. do . . . can:** whatever happens to me.
37. diverted blood: disaffected kinship.
39. thrifty . . . sav'd: money I thriftily saved from my wages.
41. When . . . lame: when my duties as a servant would be performed haltingly because of my aged limbs. **42. thrown:** be thrown.
43–44. He . . . sparrow. Alluding to such Biblical passages as Job 38:41, Luke 12:6, 24. **47. lusty:** vigorous.
49. rebellious: injurious to health.
53. kindly: (1) natural; (2) pleasant. **57. constant:** faithful.
58. sweat: sweated. **meed:** reward.

But, poor old man, thou prun'st a rotten tree,
That cannot so much as a blossom yield
In lieu of all thy pains and husbandry.
But come thy ways, we'll go along together,
And ere we have thy youthful wages spent,
We'll light upon some settled low content.

Adam. Master, go on, and I will follow thee
To the last gasp, with truth and loyalty.
From [seventeen] years till now almost fourscore
Here lived I, but now live here no more.
At seventeen years many their fortunes seek,
But at fourscore it is too late a week;
Yet fortune cannot recompense me better
Than to die well, and not my master's debtor.
Exeunt.

Scene IV

Enter Rosalind *for Ganymed,* Celia *for Aliena, and Clown, alias* Touchstone.

Ros. O Jupiter, how [weary] are my spirits!

Touch. I care not for my spirits, if my legs were not weary.

Ros. I could find in my heart to disgrace my man's apparel and to cry like a woman; but I must comfort the weaker vessel, as doublet and hose ought to show itself courageous to petticoat; therefore courage, good Aliena.

Cel. I pray you bear with me, I cannot go no further.

Touch. For my part, I had rather bear with you than bear you. Yet I should bear no cross if I did bear you, for I think you have no money in your purse.

Ros. Well, this is the forest of Arden.

Touch. Ay, now am I in Arden, the more fool I. When I was at home, I was in a better place, but travellers must be content.

Enter Corin *and* Silvius.

Ros. Ay, be so, good Touchstone. Look you, who comes here, a young man and an old in solemn talk.

Cor. That is the way to make her scorn you still.

Sil. O Corin, that thou knew'st how I do love her!

Cor. I partly guess; for I have lov'd ere now.

Sil. No, Corin, being old, thou canst not guess,
Though in thy youth thou wast as true a lover
As ever sigh'd upon a midnight pillow.
But if thy love were ever like to mine—
As sure I think did never man love so—
How many actions most ridiculous
Hast thou been drawn to by thy fantasy?

Cor. Into a thousand that I have forgotten.

Sil. O, thou didst then never love so heartily!
If thou remember'st not the slightest folly
That ever love did make thee run into,
Thou hast not lov'd;
Or if thou hast not sat as I do now,
Wearing thy hearer in thy mistress' praise,
Thou hast not lov'd;
Or if thou hast not broke from company
Abruptly, as my passion now makes me,
Thou hast not lov'd.
O Phebe, Phebe, Phebe! *Exit.*

Ros. Alas, poor shepherd, searching of [thy wound],
I have by hard adventure found mine own.

Touch. And I mine. I remember when I was in love, I broke my sword upon a stone, and bid him take that for coming a-night to Jane Smile; and I remember the kissing of her batler and the cow's dugs that her pretty chopp'd hands had milk'd; and I remember the wooing of a peascod instead of her, from whom I took two cods, and giving her them again, said with weeping tears, "Wear these for my sake." We that are true lovers run into strange capers; but as all is mortal in nature, so is all nature in love mortal in folly.

Ros. Thou speak'st wiser than thou art ware of.

Touch. Nay, I shall ne'er be ware of mine own wit till I break my shins against it.

Ros. Jove, Jove! this shepherd's passion
Is much upon my fashion.

Touch. And mine, but it grows something stale with me.

Cel. I pray you, one of you question yond man,
If he for gold will give us any food;
I faint almost to death.

Touch. Holla! you clown!

Ros. Peace, fool, he's not thy kinsman.

Cor. Who calls?

Touch. Your betters, sir.

Cor. Else are they very wretched.

Ros. Peace, I say. Good even to [you], friend.

Cor. And to you, gentle sir, and to you all.

Ros. I prithee, shepherd, if that love or gold
Can in this desert place buy entertainment,
Bring us where we may rest ourselves and feed.
Here's a young maid with travel much oppressed,
And faints for succor.

Cor. Fair sir, I pity her,
And wish, for her sake more than for mine own,
My fortunes were more able to relieve her;
But I am shepherd to another man,

65. lieu of: return for.
68. low content: lowly contented state. **74. a week:** i.e. a time.

II.iv. Location: The forest of Arden.
6. weaker vessel: i.e. woman (see 1 Peter 3:7). **doublet and hose:** jacket and breeches. **9. cannot go no.** Elizabethan double negative.
12. cross: (1) burden; (2) the device stamped on a penny.
20. solemn: serious. **31. fantasy:** fanciful love-thoughts.
38. Wearing: wearying. **44. searching of:** probing.
45. hard adventure: ill chance. **48. a-night:** at night.
49. batler: a club for beating clothes while washing them.
50. chopp'd: chapped.
51. peascod: pea pod; but here apparently the whole plant. Country swains thought that peascods presented to and worn by their mistresses brought good luck in their wooing. There is, Wilson suggests, a bawdy undertone in the lines as a whole, turning on *peascod* and *codpiece*. **52. whom, her.** Both words refer to the pea plant.
55. mortal: subject to death. **56. mortal:** i.e. humanly faulty.
57. ware: aware. Touchstone then quibbles on the sense "wary."
61. upon: after. **62. something:** somewhat.
66. clown: country fellow. Rosalind quibbles on the sense "jester."
68. wretched: low in rank and means.
72. entertainment: accommodation.
75. faints for succor: is faint for lack of aid (i.e. food).

And do not shear the fleeces that I graze.
My master is of churlish disposition,
And little reaks to find the way to heaven
By doing deeds of hospitality.
Besides, his cote, his flocks, and bounds of feed
Are now on sale, and at our sheep-cote now
By reason of his absence there is nothing
That you will feed on; but what is, come see,
And in my voice most welcome shall you be.

Ros. What is he that shall buy his flock and pasture?

Cor. That young swain that you saw here but erewhile,
That little cares for buying any thing.

Ros. I pray thee, if it stand with honesty,
Buy thou the cottage, pasture, and the flock,
And thou shalt have to pay for it of us.

Cel. And we will mend thy wages. I like this place,
And willingly could waste my time in it.

Cor. Assuredly the thing is to be sold.
Go with me; if you like upon report
The soil, the profit, and this kind of life,
I will your very faithful feeder be,
And buy it with your gold right suddenly. *Exeunt.*

Scene V

Enter Amiens, Jaques, *and others.*

Song

[*Ami.*] Under the greenwood tree
Who loves to lie with me,
And turn his merry note
Unto the sweet bird's throat,
Come hither, come hither, come hither!
Here shall he see
No enemy
But winter and rough weather.

Jaq. More, more, I prithee more.

Ami. It will make you melancholy, Monsieur Jaques.

Jaq. I thank it. More, I prithee more. I can suck melancholy out of a song, as a weasel sucks eggs. More, I prithee more.

Ami. My voice is ragged, I know I cannot please you.

Jaq. I do not desire you to please me, I do desire you to sing. Come, more, another stanzo. Call you 'em stanzos?

Ami. What you will, Monsieur Jaques.

Jaq. Nay, I care not for their names, they owe me nothing. Will you sing?

Ami. More at your request than to please myself.

Jaq. Well then, if ever I thank any man, I'll thank you; but that they call compliment is like th' encounter of two dog-apes; and when a man thanks me heartily, methinks I have given him a penny, and he renders me the beggarly thanks. Come, sing; and you that will not, hold your tongues.

Ami. Well, I'll end the song. Sirs, cover the while; the Duke will drink under this tree. He hath been all this day to look you.

Jaq. And I have been all this day to avoid him. He is too disputable for my company. I think of as many matters as he, but I give heaven thanks, and make no boast of them. Come, warble, come.

Song *All together here.*

Who doth ambition shun,
And loves to live i' th' sun,
Seeking the food he eats,
And pleas'd with what he gets,
Come hither, come hither, come hither!
Here shall he see
[No enemy
But winter and rough weather].

Jaq. I'll give you a verse to this note, that I made yesterday in despite of my invention.

Ami. And I'll sing it.

[*Jaq.*] Thus it goes:

If it do come to pass
That any man turn ass,
Leaving his wealth and ease
A stubborn will to please,
Ducdame, ducdame, ducdame!
Here shall he see
Gross fools as he,
And if he will come to me.

Ami. What's that "ducdame"?

79. do . . . graze: i.e. am not the owner who profits from the shearing of the sheep I graze. **80. churlish:** miserly.
81. reaks: recks, cares.
83. cote: cottage. **bounds of feed:** areas in which he has grazing rights.
87. in my voice: as far as my word carries weight.
88. What: who. **89. erewhile:** a short time ago.
91. stand: be consonant. **93. to pay:** i.e. the money to pay.
94. mend: increase. **95. waste:** spend. **99. feeder:** servant.
100. suddenly: speedily.

II.v. Location: The forest.
3. turn: adapt, i.e. attune. **15. ragged:** raspy.
18. stanzo: stanza.

21–22. they . . . nothing. Debtors signed their names in the lender's record book. **26. compliment:** formal courtesy.
27. dog-apes: baboons.
29. beggarly: i.e. excessive, like those of an effusively grateful beggar.
31. cover: set the table. **31–32. the while:** meanwhile.
33. look: look for. **35. disputable:** fond of argument.
39. live . . . sun: i.e. live a free open-air life. **46. note:** tune.
47. in . . . invention: notwithstanding my lack of imagination.
50–57. If . . . me. Jaques' stanza serves as a realistic, if cynical, antidote to the outright romanticism of Amiens' song. Such undercutting of the romantic attitude is an important function of Jaques' role throughout.
54. Ducdame. Trisyllabic. Not satisfactorily explained, despite numerous ingenious suggestions, e.g. that it is related to Latin *duc ad me*, "lead (him) to me"; to Welsh *dewch da mi*, "come to me"; or to Gipsy *dukrā me*, a fortuneteller's cry to attract customers. The last of these is temptingly appropriate for an invitation to a gipsy existence in the forest and would clarify the reference in line 61 to "all the first-born of Egypt," i.e. all highborn persons who have adopted a gipsy life; but there is no evidence that an audience could have recognized any such derivation. *Ducdame* may well be a meaningless invented word; when Jaques tells Amiens that it serves "to call fools into a circle" (lines 59–60), probably part of his meaning is that only fools will draw round to ask what it means.
57. And if: if only.

Jaq. 'Tis a Greek invocation, to call fools into a circle. I'll go sleep, if I can; if I cannot, I'll rail against all the first-born of Egypt.

Ami. And I'll go seek the Duke, his banket is prepar'd. *Exeunt.*

Scene VI

Enter Orlando *and* Adam.

Adam. Dear master, I can go no further. O, I die for food! Here lie I down, and measure out my grave. Farewell, kind master.

Orl. Why, how now, Adam? no greater heart in thee? Live a little, comfort a little, cheer thyself a little. If this uncouth forest yield any thing savage, I will either be food for it, or bring it for food to thee. Thy conceit is nearer death than thy powers. For my sake be comfortable, hold death a while at the arm's end. I will here be with thee presently, and if I bring thee not something to eat, I will give thee leave to die; but if thou diest before I come, thou art a mocker of my labor. Well said, thou look'st cheerly, and I'll be with thee quickly. Yet thou liest in the bleak air. Come, I will bear thee to some shelter, and thou shalt not die for lack of a dinner if there live any thing in this desert. Cheerly, good Adam! *Exeunt.*

Scene VII

[*A table set out.*] *Enter* Duke Senior, [Amiens,] *and* Lord[s], *like outlaws.*

Duke S. I think he be transform'd into a beast,
For I can no where find him like a man.
1. Lord. My lord, he is but even now gone hence;
Here was he merry, hearing of a song.
Duke S. If he, compact of jars, grow musical,
We shall have shortly discord in the spheres.
Go seek him, tell him I would speak with him.

Enter Jaques.

1. Lord. He saves my labor by his own approach.
Duke S. Why, how now, monsieur, what a life is this,
That your poor friends must woo your company?
What, you look merrily!
Jaq. A fool, a fool! I met a fool i' th' forest,
A motley fool. A miserable world!
As I do live by food, I met a fool,
Who laid him down, and bask'd him in the sun,
And rail'd on Lady Fortune in good terms,
In good set terms, and yet a motley fool.
"Good morrow, fool," quoth I. "No, sir," quoth he,
"Call me not fool till heaven hath sent me fortune."
And then he drew a dial from his poke,
And looking on it, with lack-lustre eye,
Says very wisely, "It is ten a' clock.
Thus we may see," quoth he, "how the world wags.
'Tis but an hour ago since it was nine,
And after one hour more 'twill be eleven,
And so from hour to hour, we ripe and ripe,
And then from hour to hour, we rot and rot;
And thereby hangs a tale." When I did hear
The motley fool thus moral on the time,
My lungs began to crow like chanticleer,
That fools should be so deep contemplative;
And I did laugh sans intermission
An hour by his dial. O noble fool!
A worthy fool! Motley's the only wear.
Duke S. What fool is this?
Jaq. O worthy fool! One that hath been a courtier,
And says, if ladies be but young and fair,
They have the gift to know it; and in his brain,
Which is as dry as the remainder biscuit
After a voyage, he hath strange places cramm'd
With observation, the which he vents
In mangled forms. O that I were a fool!
I am ambitious for a motley coat.
Duke S. Thou shalt have one.
Jaq. It is my only suit—
Provided that you weed your better judgments
Of all opinion that grows rank in them
That I am wise. I must have liberty
Withal, as large a charter as the wind,
To blow on whom I please, for so fools have;
And they that are most galled with my folly,
They most must laugh. And why, sir, must they so?
The why is plain as way to parish church:
He that a fool doth very wisely hit
Doth very foolishly, although he smart,
[Not to] seem senseless of the bob; if not,
The wise man's folly is anatomiz'd
Even by the squand'ring glances of the fool.

59. Greek. This word could be used of any unintelligible utterance, or, more specifically, of sharpers' cant.
61. first-born of Egypt. See note to line 54. *First-born* would suggest in particular the elder of the two dukes. The phrase itself is a Biblical echo, from the account of the death of all the first-born of Egypt in Exodus 11–12.
62. banket: banquet, i.e. light repast of fruit, sweetmeats, and wine.

II.vi. Location: The forest.
5. comfort: take heart. (So also *be comfortable* in line 9.)
6. uncouth: strange, wild. **8. conceit:** imagination.
11. presently: immediately. **13–14. Well said:** well done.
14. cheerly: cheerful.

II.vii. Location: The forest.
2. like: in the form of.
5. compact of jars: composed entirely of discords.
6. discord . . . spheres. It was thought that a ravishingly beautiful harmony was produced by the movement of the crystal spheres in which, according to the Ptolemaic system, the planets and stars revolved round the earth. It was inaudible to human ears.

13. motley: wearing motley, the parti-colored costume of professional jesters. **17. set:** forthright, outspoken.
19. Call . . . fortune. An allusion to the proverb "Fortune favors fools." **20. dial:** portable sundial. **poke:** pocket, pouch.
23. wags: goes on its way. **29. moral:** moralize.
30. crow: i.e. with laughter. **chanticleer:** a cock.
31. deep: profoundly. **32. sans:** without. **34. wear:** costume.
39. dry. Dryness of the brain was supposedly connected with good memory. **remainder biscuit:** stale hardtack. **41. vents:** utters.
44. suit: (1) petition; (2) clothing (cf. line 34). **46. rank:** wild.
48. Withal: also. **charter:** privilege, license.
50. galled: rubbed on a sensitive spot.
53. He . . . hit: he that is wittily attacked by a fool.
54. Doth: acts, behaves.
55. senseless of: insensible to. **bob:** jibe, taunt.
56. anatomiz'd: dissected, laid bare.
57. squand'ring glances: random hits.

Invest me in my motley; give me leave
To speak my mind, and I will through and through
Cleanse the foul body of th' infected world,
If they will patiently receive my medicine.

Duke S. Fie on thee! I can tell what thou wouldst do.

Jaq. What, for a counter, would I do but good?

Duke S. Most mischievous foul sin, in chiding sin:
For thou thyself hast been a libertine,
As sensual as the brutish sting itself,
And all th' embossed sores, and headed evils,
That thou with license of free foot hast caught,
Wouldst thou disgorge into the general world.

Jaq. Why, who cries out on pride
That can therein tax any private party?
Doth it not flow as hugely as the sea,
Till that the weary very means do ebb?
What woman in the city do I name,
When that I say the city-woman bears
The cost of princes on unworthy shoulders?
Who can come in and say that I mean her,
When such a one as she, such is her neighbor?
Or what is he of basest function,
That says his bravery is not on my cost,
Thinking that I mean him, but therein suits
His folly to the mettle of my speech?
There then! how then? what then? Let me see wherein
My tongue hath wrong'd him; if it do him right,
Then he hath wrong'd himself. If he be free,
Why then my taxing like a wild goose flies,
Unclaim'd of any man. But who [comes] here?

Enter ORLANDO *[with his sword drawn].*

Orl. Forbear, and eat no more.

Jaq. Why, I have eat none yet.

Orl. Nor shalt not, till necessity be serv'd.

Jaq. Of what kind should this cock come of?

Duke S. Art thou thus bolden'd, man, by thy distress?
Or else a rude despiser of good manners,
That in civility thou seem'st so empty?

Orl. You touch'd my vein at first. The thorny point
Of bare distress hath ta'en from me the show
Of smooth civility; yet am I inland bred,
And know some nurture. But forbear, I say,
He dies that touches any of this fruit
Till I and my affairs are answered.

Jaq. And you will not be answer'd with reason,
I must die.

Duke S. What would you have? Your gentleness shall force,
More than your force move us to gentleness.

Orl. I almost die for food, and let me have it.

Duke S. Sit down and feed, and welcome to our table.

Orl. Speak you so gently? Pardon me, I pray you.
I thought that all things had been savage here,
And therefore put I on the countenance
Of stern command'ment. But what e'er you are
That in this desert inaccessible,
Under the shade of melancholy boughs,
Lose and neglect the creeping hours of time;
If ever you have look'd on better days,
If ever been where bells have knoll'd to church,
If ever sate at any good man's feast,
If ever from your eyelids wip'd a tear,
And know what 'tis to pity, and be pitied,
Let gentleness my strong enforcement be,
In the which hope I blush, and hide my sword.

Duke S. True is it that we have seen better days,
And have with holy bell been knoll'd to church,
And sat at good men's feasts, and wip'd our eyes
Of drops that sacred pity hath engend'red;
And therefore sit you down in gentleness,
And take upon command what help we have
That to your wanting may be minist'red.

Orl. Then but forbear your food a little while,
Whiles, like a doe, I go to find my fawn,
And give it food. There is an old poor man,
Who after me hath many a weary step
Limp'd in pure love; till he be first suffic'd,
Oppress'd with two weak evils, age and hunger,
I will not touch a bit.

Duke S. Go find him out,
And we will nothing waste till you return.

Orl. I thank ye, and be blest for your good comfort! *[Exit.]*

Duke S. Thou seest we are not all alone unhappy:
This wide and universal theatre
Presents more woeful pageants than the scene
Wherein we play in.

Jaq. All the world's a stage,
And all the men and women merely players;
They have their exits and their entrances,
And one man in his time plays many parts,
His acts being seven ages. At first the infant,

63. counter: a disk or coin of no value, used in computation. Jaques humorously adapts a betting formula: "I'll wager a counter you can't tell me . . ." **66. sting:** lust.
67. embossed: swollen. **headed evils:** sores that have come to a head.
68. license . . . foot: i.e. the privilege of living like a libertine (uncontrolled). **69. general:** whole.
70. pride: ostentation and extravagance.
71. tax: take to task, censure. **private party:** particular individual.
73. the weary very means: i.e. the source itself, becoming exhausted (?). Various emendations have been proposed, e.g. *wearer's* for *weary.*
75. city-woman: citizen's wife.
79. basest function: lowest office or rank.
80. bravery: splendid dress. **on my cost:** at my expense.
81. suits: (1) dresses; (2) makes conformable.
82. mettle: substance, tenor. **84. right:** justice.
85. free: innocent.
94. vein: condition, state of mind. **at first:** i.e. in the first explanation you suggested.
96. smooth: mild. **inland bred:** i.e. reared in a centre of civilized behavior, not on the wild or rustic outskirts.
97. nurture: education, good training. **99. answered:** satisfied.
100. And: if. **reason.** With a pun on *raisin* (then closer in pronunciation to *reason* than now). The fruits on the table may well have included grapes.
102. force: press home, urge. **104. for food:** i.e. for lack of food.
109. command'ment: command, authority. **114. knoll'd:** rung.
115. sate: sat.
118. enforcement: compulsion. **125. upon command:** at your will.
126. wanting: need. **132. weak:** enfeebling.
134. waste: consume.
137. This . . . theatre. Thought to be a reference to the Globe theatre, built in 1599, and its motto, *Totus mundus agit histrionem* (The whole world plays the actor).

Mewling and puking in the nurse's arms.
Then the whining schoolboy, with his satchel
And shining morning face, creeping like snail
Unwillingly to school. And then the lover,
Sighing like furnace, with a woeful ballad
Made to his mistress' eyebrow. Then a soldier,
Full of strange oaths, and bearded like the pard,
Jealous in honor, sudden, and quick in quarrel,
Seeking the bubble reputation
Even in the cannon's mouth. And then the justice,
In fair round belly with good capon lin'd,
With eyes severe and beard of formal cut,
Full of wise saws and modern instances;
And so he plays his part. The sixt age shifts
Into the lean and slipper'd pantaloon,
With spectacles on nose, and pouch on side,
His youthful hose, well sav'd, a world too wide
For his shrunk shank, and his big manly voice,
Turning again toward childish treble, pipes
And whistles in his sound. Last scene of all,
That ends this strange eventful history,
Is second childishness, and mere oblivion,
Sans teeth, sans eyes, sans taste, sans every thing.

Enter Orlando *with* Adam.

Duke S. Welcome. Set down your venerable burthen,
And let him feed.
Orl. I thank you most for him.
Adam. So had you need,
I scarce can speak to thank you for myself.
Duke S. Welcome, fall to. I will not trouble you
As yet to question you about your fortunes.
Give us some music, and, good cousin, sing.

Song

[*Ami.*] Blow, blow, thou winter wind,
Thou art not so unkind
As man's ingratitude;
Thy tooth is not so keen,
Because thou art not seen,
Although thy breath be rude.
Heigh-ho, sing heigh-ho! unto the green holly,
Most friendship is feigning, most loving mere folly.
[Then] heigh-ho, the holly!
This life is most jolly.

Freeze, freeze, thou bitter sky,
That dost not bite so nigh
As benefits forgot;
Though thou the waters warp,
Thy sting is not so sharp
As friend remember'd not.
Heigh-ho, sing, etc.

Duke S. If that you were the good Sir Rowland's son,
As you have whisper'd faithfully you were,
And as mine eye doth his effigies witness
Most truly limn'd and living in your face,
Be truly welcome hither. I am the Duke
That lov'd your father. The residue of your fortune,
Go to my cave and tell me. Good old man,
Thou art right welcome as thy [master] is.
Support him by the arm. Give me your hand,
And let me all your fortunes understand. *Exeunt.*

ACT III, Scene I

Enter Duke [Frederick], Lords, *and* Oliver.

Duke F. Not see him since? Sir, sir, that cannot be.
But were I not the better part made mercy,
I should not seek an absent argument
Of my revenge, thou present. But look to it:
Find out thy brother, wheresoe'er he is;
Seek him with candle; bring him dead or living
Within this twelvemonth, or turn thou no more
To seek a living in our territory.
Thy lands and all things that thou dost call thine
Worth seizure do we seize into our hands,
Till thou canst quit thee by thy brother's mouth
Of what we think against thee.
Oli. O that your Highness knew my heart in this!
I never lov'd my brother in my life.
Duke F. More villain thou. Well, push him out of doors,
And let my officers of such a nature
Make an extent upon his house and lands.
Do this expediently, and turn him going. *Exeunt.*

Scene II

Enter Orlando [*with a paper*].

Orl. Hang there, my verse, in witness of my love,
And thou, thrice-crowned queen of night, survey
With thy chaste eye, from thy pale sphere above,

144. Mewling: crying. **puking:** vomiting.
148. Sighing like furnace: i.e. emitting sighs as a furnace emits smoke.
150. bearded . . . pard: with long mustaches like the feelers of the leopard or panther.
151. Jealous in honor: jealously protective of his honor. **sudden:** rash.
154. with . . . lin'd. Perhaps with satiric reference to the bribing of judges with capons.
156. saws: maxims. **modern instances:** trite illustrations.
157. sixt: sixth.
158. pantaloon: foolish old man (from the name of a stock character in Italian comedy). **163. his:** its. **164. history:** chronicle play.
165. mere: utter. **167. burthen:** burden.
180. holly. An emblem of mirth.
187. warp: freeze (?) or contort by freezing (?).

192. faithfully: with assurances of good faith.
193. effigies: likeness, image. **194. limn'd:** portrayed.

III.i. Location: The Duke's palace.
2. better: i.e. greater. **made:** made of. **3. argument:** subject.
6. with candle. An allusion to the parable in Luke 15:8 which describes how a woman who has lost a coin lights a candle and diligently searches the house until she has found it.
7. turn: return. **11. quit:** acquit. **mouth:** testimony.
15. More villain thou. The irony of this charge nicely points up the parallel between Oliver and Duke Frederick.
16. of . . . nature: whose duty it is to see to such matters.
17. extent: seizure by writ.
18. expediently: quickly. **turn him going:** get him on his way.

III.ii. Location: The forest.
2. thrice-crowned queen: i.e. the divinity who ruled on earth as Diana, in the heavens as Cynthia the moon-goddess, and in the underworld as Hecate or Proserpina.

Thy huntress' name that my full life doth sway.
O Rosalind, these trees shall be my books,
And in their barks my thoughts I'll character,
That every eye which in this forest looks
Shall see thy virtue witness'd every where.
Run, run, Orlando, carve on every tree
The fair, the chaste, and unexpressive she. *Exit.*

Enter CORIN *and Clown* [TOUCHSTONE].

Cor. And how like you this shepherd's life, Master Touchstone?

Touch. Truly, shepherd, in respect of itself, it is a good life; but in respect that it is a shepherd's life, it is naught. In respect that it is solitary, I like it very well; but in respect that it is private, it is a very vild life. Now in respect it is in the fields, it pleaseth me well; but in respect it is not in the court, it is tedious. As it is a spare life (look you) it fits my humor well; but as there is no more plenty in it, it goes much against my stomach. Hast any philosophy in thee, shepherd?

Cor. No more but that I know the more one sickens the worse at ease he is; and that he that wants money, means, and content is without three good friends; that the property of rain is to wet and fire to burn; that good pasture makes fat sheep; and that a great cause of the night is lack of the sun; that he that hath learn'd no wit by nature, nor art, may complain of good breeding, or comes of a very dull kindred.

Touch. Such a one is a natural philosopher. Wast ever in court, shepherd?

Cor. No, truly.

Touch. Then thou art damn'd.

Cor. Nay, I hope.

Touch. Truly, thou art damn'd, like an ill-roasted egg, all on one side.

Cor. For not being at court? Your reason.

Touch. Why, if thou never wast at court, thou never saw'st good manners; if thou never saw'st good manners, then thy manners must be wicked, and wickedness is sin, and sin is damnation. Thou art in a parlous state, shepherd.

Cor. Not a whit, Touchstone. Those that are good manners at the court are as ridiculous in the country as the behavior of the country is most mockable at the court. You told me you salute not at the court but you kiss your hands; that courtesy would be uncleanly if courtiers were shepherds.

Touch. Instance, briefly; come, instance.

Cor. Why, we are still handling our ewes, and their fells you know are greasy.

Touch. Why, do not your courtier's hands sweat? And is not the grease of a mutton as wholesome as the sweat of a man? Shallow, shallow. A better instance, I say; come.

Cor. Besides, our hands are hard.

Touch. Your lips will feel them the sooner. Shallow again. A more sounder instance, come.

Cor. And they are often tarr'd over with the surgery of our sheep; and would you have us kiss tar? The courtier's hands are perfum'd with civet.

Touch. Most shallow man! thou worm's-meat, in respect of a good piece of flesh indeed! Learn of the wise, and perpend: civet is of a baser birth than tar, the very uncleanly flux of a cat. Mend the instance, shepherd.

Cor. You have too courtly a wit for me, I'll rest.

Touch. Wilt thou rest damn'd? God help thee, shallow man! God make incision in thee, thou art raw.

Cor. Sir, I am a true laborer: I earn that I eat, get that I wear, owe no man hate, envy no man's happiness, glad of other men's good, content with my harm, and the greatest of my pride is to see my ewes graze and my lambs suck.

Touch. That is another simple sin in you, to bring the ewes and the rams together, and to offer to get your living by the copulation of cattle; to be bawd to a bell-wether, and to betray a she-lamb of a twelvemonth to a crooked-pated old cuckoldly ram, out of all reasonable match. If thou beest not damn'd for this, the devil himself will have no shepherds; I cannot see else how thou shouldst scape.

Cor. Here comes young Master Ganymed, my new mistress's brother.

Enter ROSALIND [*with a paper, reading*].

Ros. "From the east to western Inde,
No jewel is like Rosalind.
Her worth, being mounted on the wind,
Through all the world bears Rosalind.
All the pictures fairest lin'd

4. Thy huntress'. It was a commonplace to represent Diana's maiden votaries as her companions in the hunt, of which she was patron.
6. character: inscribe. Orlando is making literal Duke Senior's metaphor of "tongues in trees" (II.i.16); cf. also line 127 below.
8. virtue: excellence. **10. unexpressive:** inexpressible.
13. in . . . itself: considered in and for itself.
14. in respect that: with regard to the fact that, in so far as.
15. naught: bad. **16. private:** lonely.
17. vild: vile, wretched. **20. humor:** fancy.
21. stomach: inclination (with play on the sense "appetite").
29. wit: knowledge. **art:** study. **30. complain:** lament the lack.
32. natural: born (with play on the sense "fool").
37–38. damn'd . . . side: ruined, like an egg roasted in the ashes that when opened proves to be done on one side but still raw on the other.
41. manners: (1) deportment; (2) morals. **44. parlous:** perilous.
49. but you kiss: without kissing.

52. Instance: proof. **briefly:** quickly.
53. still: always. **54. fells:** skins.
61. more sounder. Double comparatives were common in Elizabethan usage.
62. tarr'd over. Tar was applied to the sores and cuts of sheep.
64. civet: perfume derived from the civet cat.
66. in respect of: in comparison with. **67. perpend:** consider.
68. flux: secretion. **Mend:** improve.
70. rest: stop, argue no further. Touchstone then quibbles on the sense "remain, continue."
72. make incision: i.e. to let out his folly, as a surgeon let out "bad" blood. **raw:** untutored, simple; with a play on the sense "sore" (hence requiring surgery). **73. that:** what.
75–76. content . . . harm: patient in my own misfortune.
78. simple: (1) foolish; (2) unadulterated, out-and-out.
79. offer: undertake.
82. cuckoldly: i.e. horned, as cuckolds supposedly were (?) or like one who cuckolds, i.e. lecherous (?). **out of:** beyond the limits of, contrary to. **83. match:** (1) correspondence, likeness; (2) mating.
84. the devil . . . shepherds: it will be because the devil refuses to have shepherds in hell. **85. scape:** escape. **88. Inde:** Indies.
92. fairest. There is play on two senses of *fair*, "beautiful" and "blonde." Lines 92–93 say that all other beautiful women are ugly, all other blondes dark-complexioned, in comparison with (*to*) Rosalind. Blonde beauty was the Elizabethan ideal. See Rosalind's disparagement of Phebe's looks in III.v.46–47. **lin'd:** drawn.

Are but black to Rosalind.
Let no face be kept in mind
But the fair of Rosalind."

Touch. I'll rhyme you so eight years together, dinners and suppers and sleeping-hours excepted. It is the right butter-women's rank to market.

Ros. Out, fool!

Touch. For a taste:
If a hart do lack a hind,
Let him seek out Rosalind.
If the cat will after kind,
So be sure will Rosalind.
Wint'red garments must be lin'd,
So must slender Rosalind.
They that reap must sheaf and bind,
Then to cart with Rosalind.
Sweetest nut hath sourest rind,
Such a nut is Rosalind.
He that sweetest rose will find,
Must find love's prick and Rosalind.
This is the very false gallop of verses; why do you infect yourself with them?

Ros. Peace, you dull fool, I found them on a tree.

Touch. Truly, the tree yields bad fruit.

Ros. I'll graff it with you, and then I shall graff it with a medlar. Then it will be the earliest fruit i' th' country; for you'll be rotten ere you be half ripe, and that's the right virtue of the medlar.

Touch. You have said; but whether wisely or no, let the forest judge.

Enter CELIA *with a writing.*

Ros. Peace,
Here comes my sister reading, stand aside.

Cel. [*Reads.*]
"Why should this [a] desert be?
For it is unpeopled? No!
Tongues I'll hang on every tree,
That shall civil sayings show:
Some, how brief the life of man
Runs his erring pilgrimage,
That the stretching of a span
Buckles in his sum of age;
Some, of violated vows
'Twixt the souls of friend and friend;
But upon the fairest boughs,

Or at every sentence end,
Will I 'Rosalinda' write,
Teaching all that read to know
The quintessence of every sprite
Heaven would in little show.
Therefore heaven Nature charg'd
That one body should be fill'd
With all graces wide-enlarg'd.
Nature presently distill'd
Helen's cheek, but not [her] heart,
Cleopatra's majesty,
Atalanta's better part,
Sad Lucretia's modesty.
Thus Rosalind of many parts
By heavenly synod was devis'd,
Of many faces, eyes, and hearts,
To have the touches dearest priz'd.
Heaven would that she these gifts should have,
And I to live and die her slave."

Ros. O most gentle Jupiter, what tedious homily of love have you wearied your parishioners withal, and never cried, "Have patience, good people!"

Cel. How now? back, friends! Shepherd, go off a little. Go with him, sirrah.

Touch. Come, shepherd, let us make an honorable retreat, though not with bag and baggage, yet with scrip and scrippage. *Exit* [*with Corin*].

Cel. Didst thou hear these verses?

Ros. O yes, I heard them all, and more too, for some of them had in them more feet than the verses would bear.

Cel. That's no matter; the feet might bear the verses.

Ros. Ay, but the feet were lame, and could not bear themselves without the verse, and therefore stood lamely in the verse.

Cel. But didst thou hear without wondering how thy name should be hang'd and carv'd upon these trees?

Ros. I was seven of the nine days out of the wonder before you came; for look here what I found on a palm tree. I was never so berhym'd since Pythagoras' time, that I was an Irish rat, which I can hardly remember.

96. **together:** without intermission.
98. **the right . . . market:** i.e. precisely like dairy-women riding along one behind another at the same pace on their way to market.
100. **taste:** sample.
101. **hart . . . hind:** (1) male deer . . . female deer; (2) man . . . woman. (The verses are a series of double entendres.)
103. **will after kind:** will behave in accordance with its nature (proverbial). 105. **Wint'red:** readied for winter use.
108. **to cart.** The harvest was transported on farm-carts, but Touchstone is alluding here to the practice of exposing disreputable women to public derision by driving them about the town in carts.
113. **very false gallop:** true canter (suggesting effortlessly regular movement, hence a mechanical and monotonous effect).
117. **graff:** graft. What follows is a triple pun: "with *yew*, and *afterward* with a *medlar*"; "with *you*, and *in that case* with a *meddler*." The medlar is an apple-like fruit that is not ready to eat until it is on the verge of decay.
120. **right virtue:** characteristic quality. 126. **For:** because.
130. **his erring:** its wandering.
131. **span:** distance from the tip of the thumb to the tip of the little finger of a spread hand. 132. **Buckles in:** encompasses.

139. **quintessence:** ultimate essence; highest perfection. **sprite:** spirit.
140. **in little:** in small space; probably with reference to man as microcosm or miniature universe.
143. **wide-enlarg'd:** extended to the fullest (?) or hitherto dispersed at large, i.e. gathered from everywhere (?). 144. **presently:** at once.
145. **Helen's cheek:** Helen of Troy's beauty. **her heart:** i.e. her falseness in love.
147. **Atalanta's better part:** i.e. her fleetness of foot (see lines 276–77 below), as contrasted with her greed. Hippomenes defeated her in a race, and thus won her as his bride, by dropping in her way three golden apples which she paused thrice to pick up.
148. **modesty:** scrupulous chastity. The story of Lucretia's rape and suicide is told by Shakespeare in *The Rape of Lucrece*.
152. **touches:** features, traits. 153. **would:** desired.
155. **Jupiter.** Many editors read *pulpiter* (first suggested by Spedding).
156. **withal:** with. 159. **sirrah:** form of address to inferiors.
161. **not . . . baggage:** i.e. not with as much equipment as a retreating army would carry.
162. **scrip and scrippage:** a pouch and its contents.
166. **bear:** permit (with following pun on the sense "carry").
170. **without:** (1) without the help of; (2) outside.
173. **should be:** came to be.
176–77. **Pythagoras' time.** An allusion to the Pythagorean doctrine of transmigration of souls.
177. **that:** when. **Irish rat.** Alluding to an old belief that Irish enchanters could rhyme rats and other animals to death.

Cel. Trow you who hath done this?

Ros. Is it a man?

Cel. And a chain, that you once wore, about his neck. Change you color?

Ros. I prithee who?

Cel. O Lord, Lord, it is a hard matter for friends to meet; but mountains may be remov'd with earthquakes, and so encounter.

Ros. Nay, but who is it?

Cel. Is it possible?

Ros. Nay, I prithee now, with most petitionary vehemence, tell me who it is.

Cel. O wonderful, wonderful, and most wonderful wonderful! and yet again wonderful, and after that, out of all hooping!

Ros. Good my complexion, dost thou think, though I am caparison'd like a man, I have a doublet and hose in my disposition? One inch of delay more is a South-sea of discovery. I prithee tell me who is it quickly, and speak apace. I would thou couldst stammer, that thou mightst pour this conceal'd man out of thy mouth, as wine comes out of a narrow-mouth'd bottle, either too much at once, or none at all. I prithee take the cork out of thy mouth that I may drink thy tidings.

Cel. So you may put a man in your belly.

Ros. Is he of God's making? What manner of man? Is his head worth a hat? or his chin worth a beard?

Cel. Nay, he hath but a little beard.

Ros. Why, God will send more, if the man will be thankful. Let me stay the growth of his beard, if thou delay me not the knowledge of his chin.

Cel. It is young Orlando, that tripp'd up the wrastler's heels, and your heart, both in an instant.

Ros. Nay, but the devil take mocking. Speak sad brow and true maid.

Cel. I' faith, coz, 'tis he.

Ros. Orlando?

Cel. Orlando.

Ros. Alas the day, what shall I do with my doublet and hose? What did he when thou saw'st him? What said he? How look'd he? Wherein went he? What makes he here? Did he ask for me? Where remains he? How parted he with thee? And when shalt thou see him again? Answer me in one word.

Cel. You must borrow me Gargantua's mouth first; 'tis a word too great for any mouth of this age's size. To say ay and no to these particulars is more than to answer in a catechism.

Ros. But doth he know that I am in this forest and in man's apparel? Looks he as freshly as he did the day he wrastled?

Cel. It is as easy to count atomies as to resolve the propositions of a lover. But take a taste of my finding him, and relish it with good observance. I found him under a tree, like a dropp'd acorn.

Ros. It may well be call'd Jove's tree, when it drops [such] fruit.

Cel. Give me audience, good madam.

Ros. Proceed.

Cel. There lay he, stretch'd along, like a wounded knight.

Ros. Though it be pity to see such a sight, it well becomes the ground.

Cel. Cry "holla" to [thy] tongue, I prithee; it curvets unseasonably. He was furnish'd like a hunter.

Ros. O ominous! he comes to kill my heart.

Cel. I would sing my song without a burthen; thou bring'st me out of tune.

Ros. Do you not know I am a woman? when I think, I must speak. Sweet, say on.

Enter Orlando *and* Jaques.

Cel. You bring me out. Soft, comes he not here?

Ros. 'Tis he. Slink by, and note him.

Jaq. I thank you for your company, but, good faith, I had as lief have been myself alone.

Orl. And so had I; but yet for fashion sake I thank you too for your society.

Jaq. God buy you, let's meet as little as we can.

Orl. I do desire we may be better strangers.

Jaq. I pray you mar no more trees with writing love-songs in their barks.

Orl. I pray you mar no moe of my verses with reading them ill-favoredly.

Jaq. Rosalind is your love's name?

Orl. Yes, just.

Jaq. I do not like her name.

Orl. There was no thought of pleasing you when she was christen'd.

Jaq. What stature is she of?

Orl. Just as high as my heart.

Jaq. You are full of pretty answers; have you not been acquainted with goldsmiths' wives, and conn'd them out of rings?

179. Trow you: have you any idea.
181. And a chain: i.e. yes, it is a man, and one with a chain.
185. remov'd with: moved by.
189–190. petitionary vehemence: urgent entreaty.
193. out of: beyond. **hooping:** whooping, i.e. power to utter.
194. Good my complexion: have mercy on my temperament, i.e. on my woman's impatient curiosity.
195. caparison'd: decked out (ordinarily used of a horse's ornamental trappings).
196–97. is . . . discovery: will seem as long as the time needed to explore the South Seas.
205. of God's making: i.e. not of the tailor's making (the usual antithesis). **210. stay:** await.
214–15. sad . . . maid: seriously and truly.
221. Wherein went he: how was he dressed.
222. makes he: is he doing.
225. Gargantua's mouth. Rabelais' giant swallowed five pilgrims in a salad.
228. catechism: catechizing.
230. freshly: fresh, youthfully vigorous.
232. atomies: atoms, minute specks. **233. propositions:** questions.
234. relish it: enhance its flavor. **good observance:** close attention.
236. Jove's tree: i.e. the oak, the king of trees, as the eagle, also connected with Jove, is the king of birds.
238. audience: hearing, attention. **240. along:** full length.
244. holla: stop.
244–45. curvets unseasonably: frisks about at the wrong time.
245. furnish'd: dressed, equipped.
246. heart. With pun on *hart* (and so spelled in F1).
247. burthen: burden, ground-bass, repeated undersong.
248. bring'st: puttest. **251. bring me out:** put me off, confuse me.
257. God buy you: God be with you; goodbye. **261. moe:** more.
262. ill-favoredly: in an unattractive way, badly.
264. just: just so, exactly.
271–72. conn'd . . . rings: i.e. memorized the mottoes or "posies" (i.e. poesies) engraved on rings.

Orl. Not so; but I answer you right painted cloth, from whence you have studied your questions.

Jaq. You have a nimble wit; I think 'twas made of Atalanta's heels. Will you sit down with me? and we two will rail against our mistress the world, and all our misery.

Orl. I will chide no breather in the world but myself, against whom I know most faults.

Jaq. The worst fault you have is to be in love.

Orl. 'Tis a fault I will not change for your best virtue. I am weary of you.

Jaq. By my troth, I was seeking for a fool when I found you.

Orl. He is drown'd in the brook; look but in, and you shall see him.

Jaq. There I shall see mine own figure.

Orl. Which I take to be either a fool or a cipher.

Jaq. I'll tarry no longer with you. Farewell, good Signior Love.

Orl. I am glad of your departure. Adieu, good Monsieur Melancholy. [*Exit Jaques.*]

Ros. [*Aside to Celia.*] I will speak to him like a saucy lackey, and under that habit play the knave with him.—Do you hear, forester?

Orl. Very well. What would you?

Ros. I pray you, what is't a' clock?

Orl. You should ask me what time o' day; there's no clock in the forest.

Ros. Then there is no true lover in the forest, else sighing every minute and groaning every hour would detect the lazy foot of Time as well as a clock.

Orl. And why not the swift foot of Time? Had not that been as proper?

Ros. By no means, sir. Time travels in divers paces with divers persons. I'll tell you who Time ambles withal, who Time trots withal, who Time gallops withal, and who he stands still withal.

Orl. I prithee, who doth he trot withal?

Ros. Marry, he trots hard with a young maid between the contract of her marriage and the day it is solemniz'd. If the interim be but a se'nnight, Time's pace is so hard that it seems the length of seven year.

Orl. Who ambles Time withal?

Ros. With a priest that lacks Latin, and a rich man that hath not the gout; for the one sleeps easily because he cannot study, and the other lives merrily because he feels no pain; the one lacking the burthen of lean and wasteful learning, the other knowing no burthen of heavy tedious penury. These Time ambles withal.

Orl. Who doth he gallop withal?

Ros. With a thief to the gallows; for though he go as softly as foot can fall, he thinks himself too soon there.

Orl. Who stays it still withal?

Ros. With lawyers in the vacation; for they sleep between term and term, and then they perceive not how Time moves.

Orl. Where dwell you, pretty youth?

Ros. With this shepherdess, my sister; here in the skirts of the forest, like fringe upon a petticoat.

Orl. Are you native of this place?

Ros. As the cony that you see dwell where she is kindled.

Orl. Your accent is something finer than you could purchase in so remov'd a dwelling.

Ros. I have been told so of many; but indeed an old religious uncle of mine taught me to speak, who was in his youth an inland man, one that knew courtship too well, for there he fell in love. I have heard him read many lectures against it, and I thank God I am not a woman, to be touch'd with so many giddy offenses as he hath generally tax'd their whole sex withal.

Orl. Can you remember any of the principal evils that he laid to the charge of women?

Ros. There were none principal, they were all like one another as halfpence are, every one fault seeming monstrous till his fellow-fault came to match it.

Orl. I prithee recount some of them.

Ros. No; I will not cast away my physic but on those that are sick. There is a man haunts the forest, that abuses our young plants with carving "Rosalind" on their barks; hangs odes upon hawthorns, and elegies on brambles; all, forsooth, [deifying] the name of Rosalind. If I could meet that fancy-monger, I would give him some good counsel, for he seems to have the quotidian of love upon him.

Orl. I am he that is so love-shak'd, I pray you tell me your remedy.

Ros. There is none of my uncle's marks upon you. He taught me how to know a man in love; in which cage of rushes I am sure you [are] not prisoner.

Orl. What were his marks?

Ros. A lean cheek, which you have not; a blue eye and sunken, which you have not; an unquestionable spirit, which you have not; a beard neglected, which you have not (but I pardon you for that, for simply your having in beard is a younger broth-

273. **right:** true, genuine.
273–74. **painted cloth.** The cheapest type of wall-hanging, customarily decorated with scenes and mottoes, and thus another source of clichés. 280. **breather:** living person.
290. **cipher:** zero (punning on a second sense of *figure*), nonentity.
296. **habit:** guise. 299. **a' clock:** by (of) the clock.
304. **detect:** reveal. 310. **withal:** with.
313. **hard:** with an uneasy pace (the discomfort of the pace making the ride seem long). 315. **se'nnight:** week.
323. **wasteful:** consuming.

328. **go as softly:** walk as slowly.
332. **term:** session. 339. **cony:** rabbit. 340. **kindled:** born.
342. **purchase:** acquire. **remov'd:** remote.
344. **religious:** belonging to a religious order.
346. **courtship:** (1) the ways of court life; (2) wooing.
348. **touch'd:** tainted. 349. **generally:** universally.
358. **physic:** knowledge of medicine.
364. **fancy-monger:** dealer in love.
365. **quotidian:** an ague with daily attacks of chills and fever.
371. **cage of rushes:** i.e. insubstantial prison, easy to escape from.
373. **blue:** i.e. with dark circles caused by weeping and lack of sleep.
374–75. **unquestionable:** disinclined to converse.
377. **simply:** frankly. **your having in:** what you own in the way of.

er's revenue); then your hose should be ungarter'd, your bonnet unbanded, your sleeve unbutton'd, your shoe untied, and every thing about you demonstrating a careless desolation. But you are no such man; you are rather point-device in your accoustrements, as loving yourself, than seeming the lover of any other.

Orl. Fair youth, I would I could make thee believe I love.

Ros. Me believe it? You may as soon make her that you love believe it, which I warrant she is apter to do than to confess she does. That is one of the points in the which women still give the lie to their consciences. But in good sooth, are you he that hangs the verses on the trees, wherein Rosalind is so admir'd?

Orl. I swear to thee, youth, by the white hand of Rosalind, I am that he, that unfortunate he.

Ros. But are you so much in love as your rhymes speak?

Orl. Neither rhyme nor reason can express how much.

Ros. Love is merely a madness, and I tell you, deserves as well a dark house and a whip as madmen do; and the reason why they are not so punish'd and cur'd is, that the lunacy is so ordinary that the whippers are in love too. Yet I profess curing it by counsel.

Orl. Did you ever cure any so?

Ros. Yes, one, and in this manner. He was to imagine me his love, his mistress; and I set him every day to woo me. At which time would I, being but a moonish youth, grieve, be effeminate, changeable, longing and liking, proud, fantastical, apish, shallow, inconstant, full of tears, full of smiles; for every passion something, and for no passion truly any thing, as boys and women are for the most part cattle of this color; would now like him, now loathe him; then entertain him, then forswear him; now weep for him, then spit at him; that I drave my suitor from his mad humor of love to a living humor of madness, which was, to forswear the full stream of the world, and to live in a nook merely monastic. And thus I cur'd him, and this way will I take upon me to wash your liver as clean as a sound sheep's heart, that there shall not be one spot of love in't.

379. bonnet unbanded: hat without a band around the crown, a fashion described by Stubbes in *The Anatomy of Abuses* as "unseemly (I will not say how assy)."
381. careless: i.e. heedless of appearance.
382. point-device: very correct.
383. accoustrements: accoutrements.
389. apter: readier. **390. still:** regularly.
391. consciences: inmost thoughts, "hearts." **sooth:** truth.
400. merely a: an utter.
401. dark . . . whip. The common treatment for the insane.
404. profess: claim to have skill in.
410. moonish: given to changing moods. **be effeminate:** act like a woman. **411. fantastical:** fanciful, capricious.
412. apish: affected. **416. entertain:** welcome, admit.
418. drave: drove. **humor:** whim.
419. living humor: actual state.
421. merely monastic: exactly like a hermit.
422. liver. The supposed seat of the passions.
423. sound sheep's heart. Perhaps suggesting that Orlando, by being freed of love, will be reduced to one of the stupidest of animals.

Orl. I would not be cur'd, youth.

Ros. I would cure you, if you would but call me Rosalind, and come every day to my cote and woo me.

Orl. Now, by the faith of my love, I will. Tell me where it is.

Ros. Go with me to it, and I'll show it you; and by the way, you shall tell me where in the forest you live. Will you go?

Orl. With all my heart, good youth.

Ros. Nay, you must call me Rosalind. Come, sister, will you go? *Exeunt.*

Scene III

Enter Clown [Touchstone], Audrey; *and* Jaques [*behind*].

Touch. Come apace, good Audrey; I will fetch up your goats, Audrey. And how, Audrey? am I the man yet? Doth my simple feature content you?

Aud. Your features, Lord warrant us! what features?

Touch. I am here with thee and thy goats as the most capricious poet, honest Ovid, was among the Goths.

Jaq. [*Aside.*] O knowledge ill-inhabited, worse than Jove in a thatch'd house!

Touch. When a man's verses cannot be understood, nor a man's good wit seconded with the forward child, understanding, it strikes a man more dead than a great reckoning in a little room. Truly, I would the gods had made thee poetical.

Aud. I do not know what "poetical" is. Is it honest in deed and word? Is it a true thing?

Touch. No, truly; for the truest poetry is the most feigning, and lovers are given to poetry; and what they swear in poetry may be said as lovers they do feign.

Aud. Do you wish then that the gods had made me poetical?

Touch. I do, truly; for thou swear'st to me thou art honest. Now if thou wert a poet, I might have some hope thou didst feign.

Aud. Would you not have me honest?

Touch. No, truly, unless thou wert hard-favor'd; for honesty coupled to beauty is to have honey a sauce to sugar.

425. would not: do not wish to be. Rosalind then picks up *would* in the ordinary sense.

III.iii. Location: The forest.
3. feature: form and appearance. **5. warrant:** protect.
5–6. what features? To Audrey the noun is simply unintelligible.
8. capricious: ingenious, full of witty conceits; with play on Latin *caper*, "he-goat," which further suggests the sense "goatish, lascivious." **9. Goths.** Pronounced *goats.*
10. ill-inhabited: meanly lodged.
11. Jove . . . house. Jupiter and Mercury, disguised, stayed as guests in the lowly cottage of Baucis and Philemon.
13–14. forward: precocious.
15. great . . . room: exorbitant bill for food in a small, mean tavern. Some find here an allusion to Christopher Marlowe's death at the hands of Ingram Frizer in 1593 in a quarrel over a tavern bill.
18. honest: honorable, true. **20. feigning:** based on imagination.
26. honest: chaste. **29. hard-favor'd:** ugly.

Jaq. [*Aside.*] A material fool!

Aud. Well, I am not fair, and therefore I pray the gods make me honest.

Touch. Truly, and to cast away honesty upon a foul slut were to put good meat into an unclean dish.

Aud. I am not a slut, though I thank the gods I am foul.

Touch. Well, prais'd be the gods for thy foulness! sluttishness may come hereafter. But be it as it may be, I will marry thee; and to that end I have been with Sir Oliver Martext, the vicar of the next village, who hath promis'd to meet me in this place of the forest and to couple us.

Jaq. [*Aside.*] I would fain see this meeting.

Aud. Well, the gods give us joy!

Touch. Amen. A man may, if he were of a fearful heart, stagger in this attempt; for here we have no temple but the wood, no assembly but horn-beasts. But what though? Courage! As horns are odious, they are necessary. It is said, "Many a man knows no end of his goods." Right! many a man has good horns, and knows no end of them. Well, that is the dowry of his wife, 'tis none of his own getting. Horns? even so. Poor men alone? No, no, the noblest deer hath them as huge as the rascal. Is the single man therefore bless'd? No, as a wall'd town is more worthier than a village, so is the forehead of a married man more honorable than the bare brow of a bachelor; and by how much defense is better than no skill, by so much is a horn more precious than to want.

Enter Sir Oliver Martext.

Here comes Sir Oliver. Sir Oliver Martext, you are well met. Will you dispatch us here under this tree, or shall we go with you to your chapel?

Sir Oli. Is there none here to give the woman?

Touch. I will not take her on gift of any man.

Sir Oli. Truly, she must be given, or the marriage is not lawful.

Jaq. [*Discovering himself.*] Proceed, proceed. I'll give her.

Touch. Good even, good Master What-ye-call't; how do you, sir? You are very well met. God 'ild you for your last company. I am very glad to see you. Even a toy in hand here, sir. Nay, pray be cover'd.

Jaq. Will you be married, motley?

Touch. As the ox hath his bow, sir, the horse his curb, and the falcon her bells, so man hath his desires; and as pigeons bill, so wedlock would be nibbling.

Jaq. And will you (being a man of your breeding) be married under a bush like a beggar? Get you to church, and have a good priest that can tell you what marriage is. This fellow will but join you together as they join wainscot; then one of you will prove a shrunk panel, and like green timber warp, warp.

Touch. [*Aside.*] I am not in the mind but I were better to be married of him than of another, for he is not like to marry me well; and not being well married, it will be a good excuse for me hereafter to leave my wife.

Jaq. Go thou with me, and let me counsel thee.

[*Touch.*] Come, sweet Audrey,
We must be married, or we must live in bawdry.
Farewell, good Master Oliver: not
"O sweet Oliver,
O brave Oliver,
Leave me not behind thee;"
but
"Wind away,
Be gone, I say,
I will not to wedding with thee."

[*Exeunt Jaques, Touchstone, and Audrey.*]

Sir Oli. 'Tis no matter; ne'er a fantastical knave of them all shall flout me out of my calling. *Exit.*

Scene IV

Enter Rosalind *and* Celia.

Ros. Never talk to me, I will weep.

Cel. Do, I prithee, but yet have the grace to consider that tears do not become a man.

Ros. But have I not cause to weep?

Cel. As good cause as one would desire, therefore weep.

Ros. His very hair is of the dissembling color.

Cel. Something browner than Judas's. Marry, his kisses are Judas's own children.

Ros. I' faith, his hair is of a good color.

Cel. An excellent color. Your chestnut was ever the only color.

Ros. And his kissing is as full of sanctity as the touch of holy bread.

32. **material:** full of "matter" or good sense. 36. **foul:** ugly.
43. **Sir:** courtesy title for a priest. 49. **stagger:** hesitate, waver.
50–51. **horn-beasts.** With allusion to the horns of the cuckolded husband. 51. **what though:** what of that. **As:** though.
52. **necessary:** inevitable.
53. **knows . . . goods:** thinks his wealth inexhaustible.
54. **knows . . . them:** isn't aware of their points coming into view on his forehead. 55. **dowry:** i.e. what his wife brings him.
56. **getting.** With play on "begetting," with reference to his wife's children. 58. **rascal:** young, lean deer, hence inferior.
62. **defense:** skill in self-defense. 63. **want:** i.e. lack one.
65. **dispatch:** i.e. marry. 71 s.d. **Discovering:** revealing.
75. **'ild:** yield, i.e. reward. **your last company.** Referring to their earlier meeting (II.vii.12 ff.).
76. **Even . . . hand:** first a trifling matter is being undertaken.
77. **be cover'd:** put on your hat. Touchstone speaks as if to a social inferior who has respectfully bared his head.

79. **bow:** yoke.
85–86. **tell . . . is:** instruct you in the responsibilities of marriage (as the ignorant Sir Oliver cannot).
90–91. **not . . . better:** not sure but that it would be better for me.
97. **married:** i.e. properly in church. **in bawdry:** i.e. in sin.
99–101. **O . . . thee.** From a ballad of the 1580's, now lost; but lines 103–5 may be Touchstone's improvisation. 103. **Wind:** wander, go.
106. **fantastical:** full of ridiculous notions.

III.iv. **Location:** The forest.
7. **of . . . color:** i.e. red—like Judas Iscariot's, according to tradition.
8. **Something:** somewhat.
9. **Judas's own children:** i.e. traitorous, like the kiss with which Judas betrayed Jesus. 11. **Your.** The indefinite use; a colloquialism.
14. **holy bread:** ordinary leavened bread which was blessed after the Eucharist and given to non-communicants.

Cel. He hath bought a pair of cast lips of Diana. A nun of winter's sisterhood kisses not more religiously, the very ice of chastity is in them.

Ros. But why did he swear he would come this morning, and comes not?

Cel. Nay certainly there is no truth in him.

Ros. Do you think so?

Cel. Yes, I think he is not a pick-purse nor a horse-stealer, but for his verity in love, I do think him as concave as a cover'd goblet or a worm-eaten nut.

Ros. Not true in love?

Cel. Yes, when he is in—but I think he is not in.

Ros. You have heard him swear downright he was.

Cel. "Was" is not "is." Besides, the oath of [a] lover is no stronger than the word of a tapster; they are both the confirmer of false reckonings. He attends here in the forest on the Duke your father.

Ros. I met the Duke yesterday, and had much question with him. He ask'd me of what parentage I was. I told him of as good as he, so he laugh'd and let me go. But what talk we of fathers, when there is such a man as Orlando?

Cel. O, that's a brave man! he writes brave verses, speaks brave words, swears brave oaths, and breaks them bravely, quite traverse, athwart the heart of his lover, as a puisne tilter, that spurs his horse but on one side, breaks his staff like a noble goose. But all's brave that youth mounts and folly guides. Who comes here?

Enter CORIN.

Cor. Mistress and master, you have oft inquired
After the shepherd that complain'd of love,
Who you saw sitting by me on the turf,
Praising the proud disdainful shepherdess
That was his mistress.

Cel. Well; and what of him?

Cor. If you will see a pageant truly play'd
Between the pale complexion of true love
And the red glow of scorn and proud disdain,
Go hence a little, and I shall conduct you,
If you will mark it.

Ros. O, come, let us remove,
The sight of lovers feedeth those in love.
Bring us to this sight, and you shall say
I'll prove a busy actor in their play. *Exeunt.*

15. cast: cast-off; i.e. one whom he kissed might think that his lips had once belonged to Diana, the goddess of chastity.
16. of winter's sisterhood: i.e. devoted to cold and barren chastity.
23. verity: truthfulness.
24. concave: hollow. **cover'd goblet.** A goblet would have its cover on only when not in use, hence empty. **36. question:** conversation.
38. what: why.
40. brave: excellent, splendid (but used with irony and some suggestion of the related word *bravado* [= boasting without intention of action]). **42. traverse:** awry.
43. puisne: inexperienced (literally, younger). **44. staff:** spear.
45. noble goose: young, foolish courtier.
52. pageant: drama, scene.
53. pale. Every sigh was thought to draw a drop of blood from the heart. **56. will mark:** desire to witness.

SCENE V

Enter SILVIUS *and* PHEBE.

Sil. Sweet Phebe, do not scorn me, do not, Phebe;
Say that you love me not, but say not so
In bitterness. The common executioner,
Whose heart th' accustom'd sight of death makes hard,
Falls not the axe upon the humbled neck
But first begs pardon. Will you sterner be
Than he that dies and lives by bloody drops?

Enter, [behind,] ROSALIND, CELIA, *and* CORIN.

Phe. I would not be thy executioner;
I fly thee for I would not injure thee.
Thou tell'st me there is murder in mine eye:
'Tis pretty, sure, and very probable,
That eyes, that are the frail'st and softest things,
Who shut their coward gates on atomies,
Should be called tyrants, butchers, murtherers!
Now I do frown on thee with all my heart,
And if mine eyes can wound, now let them kill thee.
Now counterfeit to swound; why, now fall down,
Or if thou canst not, O, for shame, for shame,
Lie not, to say mine eyes are murtherers!
Now show the wound mine eye hath made in thee;
Scratch thee but with a pin, and there remains
Some scar of it; lean upon a rush,
The cicatrice and capable impressure
Thy palm some moment keeps; but now mine eyes,
Which I have darted at thee, hurt thee not,
Nor I am sure there is no force in eyes
That can do hurt.

Sil. O dear Phebe,
If ever (as that ever may be near)
You meet in some fresh cheek the power of fancy,
Then shall you know the wounds invisible
That love's keen arrows make.

Phe. But till that time
Come not thou near me; and when that time comes,
Afflict me with thy mocks, pity me not,
As till that time I shall not pity thee.

Ros. [*Advancing.*] And why, I pray you? Who might be your mother,
That you insult, exult, and all at once,
Over the wretched? What though you have no beauty—
As, by my faith, I see no more in you
Than without candle may go dark to bed—
Must you be therefore proud and pitiless?
Why, what means this? why do you look on me?
I see no more in you than in the ordinary
Of nature's sale-work. 'Od's my little life,
I think she means to tangle my eyes too!

III.v. Location: The forest.
5. Falls: lets fall. **6. But first begs:** without first asking.
7. dies and lives: spends his whole life and thus earns his whole living.
9. for: because. **11. pretty:** clever (ironic). **sure:** surely.
17. counterfeit to swound: pretend to swoon.
23. cicatrice: i.e. mark. **capable impressure:** perceptible impression. **29. fresh:** young and beautiful. **fancy:** love.
33. mocks: ridicule. **36. all at once:** i.e. in the same breath.
38–39. no . . . bed: i.e. not enough beauty to lighten the dark.
43. sale-work: run-of-the-mill products. **'Od's:** God save.
44. tangle: ensnare.

No, faith, proud mistress, hope not after it.
'Tis not your inky brows, your black silk hair,
Your bugle eyeballs, nor your cheek of cream
That can entame my spirits to your worship.
You foolish shepherd, wherefore do you follow her,
Like foggy south, puffing with wind and rain?
You are a thousand times a properer man
Than she a woman. 'Tis such fools as you
That makes the world full of ill-favor'd children.
'Tis not her glass, but you that flatters her,
And out of you she sees herself more proper
Than any of her lineaments can show her.
But, mistress, know yourself, down on your knees,
And thank heaven, fasting, for a good man's love;
For I must tell you friendly in your ear,
Sell when you can, you are not for all markets.
Cry the man mercy, love him, take his offer;
Foul is most foul, being foul to be a scoffer.
So take her to thee, shepherd. Fare you well.

Phe. Sweet youth, I pray you chide a year together,
I had rather hear you chide than this man woo.

Ros. He's fall'n in love with your foulness—and she'll fall in love with my anger. If it be so, as fast as she answers thee with frowning looks, I'll sauce her with bitter words.—Why look you so upon me?

Phe. For no ill will I bear you.

Ros. I pray you do not fall in love with me,
For I am falser than vows made in wine.
Besides, I like you not. If you will know my house,
'Tis at the tuft of olives here hard by.
Will you go, sister? Shepherd, ply her hard.
Come, sister. Shepherdess, look on him better,
And be not proud; though all the world could see,
None could be so abus'd in sight as he.
Come, to our flock. *Exit [with Celia and Corin].*

Phe. Dead shepherd, now I find thy saw of might,
"Who ever lov'd that lov'd not at first sight?"

Sil. Sweet Phebe—

Phe. Hah! what say'st thou, Silvius?

Sil. Sweet Phebe, pity me.

Phe. Why, I am sorry for thee, gentle Silvius.

Sil. Where ever sorrow is, relief would be.
If you do sorrow at my grief in love,
By giving love, your sorrow and my grief
Were both extermin'd.

Phe. Thou hast my love; is not that neighborly?

Sil. I would have you.

Phe. Why, that were covetousness.
Silvius, the time was that I hated thee;
And yet it is not that I bear thee love,
But since that thou canst talk of love so well,
Thy company, which erst was irksome to me,
I will endure; and I'll employ thee too.
But do not look for further recompense
Than thine own gladness that thou art employ'd.

Sil. So holy and so perfect is my love,
And I in such a poverty of grace,
That I shall think it a most plenteous crop
To glean the broken ears after the man
That the main harvest reaps. Loose now and then
A scatt'red smile, and that I'll live upon.

Phe. Know'st thou the youth that spoke to me yerwhile?

Sil. Not very well, but I have met him oft,
And he hath bought the cottage and the bounds
That the old carlot once was master of.

Phe. Think not I love him, though I ask for him;
'Tis but a peevish boy—yet he talks well—
But what care I for words? Yet words do well
When he that speaks them pleases those that hear.
It is a pretty youth—not very pretty—
But sure he's proud—and yet his pride becomes him.
He'll make a proper man. The best thing in him
Is his complexion; and faster than his tongue
Did make offense, his eye did heal it up.
He is not very tall—yet for his years he's tall;
His leg is but so so—and yet 'tis well;
There was a pretty redness in his lip,
A little riper and more lusty red
Than that mix'd in his cheek; 'twas just the difference
Betwixt the constant red and mingled damask.
There be some women, Silvius, had they mark'd him
In parcels as I did, would have gone near
To fall in love with him; but for my part
I love him not, nor hate him not; and yet
Have more cause to hate him than to love him,
For what had he to do to chide at me?
He said mine eyes were black and my hair black,
And, now I am rememb'red, scorn'd at me.
I marvel why I answer'd not again.
But that's all one; omittance is no quittance.
I'll write to him a very taunting letter,
And thou shalt bear it; wilt thou, Silvius?

47. bugle eyeballs: eyes like shiny black beads. **cream:** yellow.
48. entame: subdue. **your worship:** worship of you.
50. south: south wind (which in England brings fog and rain). **wind and rain:** i.e. sighs and tears. **51. properer:** handsomer.
54. glass: mirror. **55. out of you:** i.e. with you as her mirror.
59. friendly: as a friend. **61. Cry . . . mercy:** beg the man's pardon.
62. Foul . . . scoffer: i.e. an ugly woman is seen at her worst when, ugly though she is, she scoffs at proffered love.
64. together: without intermission. **69. sauce:** rebuke sharply.
78. could see: should be able to look (on you).
79. abus'd in sight: deceived by his eyes.
81. Dead shepherd: i.e. Marlowe (died 1593); line 82 is quoted from his *Hero and Leander* (I.176), published in 1598. **find . . . might:** perceive the force of your saying.
86. Where . . . be: i.e. wherever sorrow is felt, a desire to give relief should follow. **89. Were both extermin'd:** would both be banished.
90. is . . . neighborly: i.e. doesn't that follow from the fact that I am your neighbor (and hence, with reference to Christ's second commandment, am bound as a good Christian to love you).
91. covetousness. Referring to the Mosaic tenth commandment, "Thou shalt not covet . . . anything that is thy neighbor's." Phebe thus makes it appear that she is following the Biblical injunctions, while Silvius is breaking them.
93. yet . . . that: the time has not yet come when.
95. erst: once, before. **100. poverty of grace:** dearth of favor.
103–104. Loose . . . scatt'red: let fly . . . random (a figure from archery). **105. yerwhile:** erewhile, just now.
107. bounds: pasturage. **108. carlot:** peasant.
123. constant: uniform. **mingled damask:** mixture of red and white.
125. In parcels: part by part, in detail.
125–26. gone . . . fall: come close to falling.
129. what . . . do: what business had he.
131. am rememb'red: recall.
133. omittance . . . quittance: failure to assert a claim does not imply renunciation of the claim (legal proverb); i.e. I am still entitled to reply.

Sil. Phebe, with all my heart.
Phe. I'll write it straight;
The matter's in my head and in my heart.
I will be bitter with him and passing short.
Go with me, Silvius. *Exeunt.*

ACT IV, SCENE I

Enter ROSALIND *and* CELIA *and* JAQUES.

Jaq. I prithee, pretty youth, let me [be] better acquainted with thee.

Ros. They say you are a melancholy fellow.

Jaq. I am so; I do love it better than laughing.

Ros. Those that are in extremity of either are abominable fellows, and betray themselves to every modern censure worse than drunkards.

Jaq. Why, 'tis good to be sad and say nothing.

Ros. Why then 'tis good to be a post.

Jaq. I have neither the scholar's melancholy, which is emulation; nor the musician's, which is fantastical; nor the courtier's, which is proud; nor the soldier's, which is ambitious; nor the lawyer's, which is politic; nor the lady's, which is nice; nor the lover's, which is all these: but it is a melancholy of mine own, compounded of many simples, extracted from many objects, and indeed the sundry contemplation of my travels, in which [my] often rumination wraps me in a most humorous sadness.

Ros. A traveller! By my faith, you have great reason to be sad. I fear you have sold your own lands to see other men's; then to have seen much, and to have nothing, is to have rich eyes and poor hands.

Jaq. Yes, I have gain'd my experience.

Enter ORLANDO.

Ros. And your experience makes you sad. I had rather have a fool to make me merry than experience to make me sad—and to travel for it too!

Orl. Good day and happiness, dear Rosalind!

Jaq. Nay then God buy you, and you talk in blank verse.

Ros. Farewell, Monsieur Traveller: look you lisp and wear strange suits; disable all the benefits of your own country; be out of love with your nativity, and almost chide God for making you that countenance you are; or I will scarce think you have swam in a gundello. [*Exit Jaques.*] Why, how now, Orlando, where have you been all this while? You a lover! And you serve me such another trick, never come in my sight more.

Orl. My fair Rosalind, I come within an hour of my promise.

Ros. Break an hour's promise in love! He that will divide a minute into a thousand parts, and break but a part of the thousand part of a minute in the affairs of love, it may be said of him that Cupid hath clapp'd him o' th' shoulder, but I'll warrant him heart-whole.

Orl. Pardon me, dear Rosalind.

Ros. Nay, and you be so tardy, come no more in my sight. I had as lief be woo'd of a snail.

Orl. Of a snail?

Ros. Ay, of a snail; for though he comes slowly, he carries his house on his head; a better jointure I think than you make a woman. Besides, he brings his destiny with him.

Orl. What's that?

Ros. Why, horns! which such as you are fain to be beholding to your wives for. But he comes arm'd in his fortune, and prevents the slander of his wife.

Orl. Virtue is no horn-maker; and my Rosalind is virtuous.

Ros. And I am your Rosalind.

Cel. It pleases him to call you so; but he hath a Rosalind of a better leer than you.

Ros. Come, woo me, woo me; for now I am in a holiday humor, and like enough to consent. What would you say to me now, and I were your very very Rosalind?

Orl. I would kiss before I spoke.

Ros. Nay, you were better speak first, and when you were gravell'd for lack of matter, you might take occasion to kiss. Very good orators when they are out, they will spit, and for lovers lacking (God warn us!) matter, the cleanliest shift is to kiss.

Orl. How if the kiss be denied?

Ros. Then she puts you to entreaty, and there begins new matter.

Orl. Who could be out, being before his belov'd mistress?

Ros. Marry, that should you if I were your mistress, or I should think my honesty ranker than my wit.

Orl. What, of my suit?

Ros. Not out of your apparel, and yet out of your suit. Am not I your Rosalind?

138. passing short: exceedingly curt.

IV.i. Location: The forest.
5. are . . . of: go to extremes in.
7. modern censure: ordinary judgment.
8. sad: sober-minded. Rosalind then quibbles on the sense "heavy."
11. emulation: envy. **12. fantastical:** highly fanciful.
14. politic: shrewd, calculated. **nice:** delicate, fastidious.
16. simples: ingredients. **17. objects:** sights, observations.
17–18. sundry contemplation of: contemplation of various details during (?) or various ways of thinking about (?).
18–19. in . . . rumination: in which (melancholy) my frequent meditation. **19. humorous:** moody.
29. travel. With pun on *travail*, "labor."
31. God buy you: goodbye. **and:** if.
34. lisp: speak affectedly. **disable:** disparage.
36. nativity: birth, i.e. nationality.
38. swam . . . gundello: ridden in a gondola, i.e. seen Venice (a very popular resort of foreign travellers). **46. thousand:** thousandth.
48. clapp'd . . . shoulder: i.e. struck him in the back (with his arrow). Cf. *clapp'd i' th' clout* (hit the bull's-eye), *2 Henry IV*, III.ii.46.
49. heart-whole: not wounded in the heart.
55–56. jointure: marriage settlement.
59. horns: i.e. cuckold's horns. **fain:** obliged.
60. beholding: beholden, indebted.
61. arm'd . . . fortune: already equipped for his future. **prevents:** forestalls. **slander:** ill repute. **67. of . . . leer:** better-looking.
74. gravell'd: stuck, at a loss. **76. out:** i.e. out of "matter."
77. warn: warrant, protect. **cleanliest shift:** cleverest device (with a play in *cleanliest* on kissing versus spitting).
84. honesty: chastity. **ranker:** more corrupt.

Orl. I take some joy to say you are, because I would be talking of her.

Ros. Well, in her person, I say I will not have you.

Orl. Then in mine own person, I die.

Ros. No, faith, die by attorney. The poor world is almost six thousand years old, and in all this time there was not any man died in his own person, *videlicet*, in a love-cause. Troilus had his brains dash'd out with a Grecian club, yet he did what he could to die before, and he is one of the patterns of love. Leander, he would have liv'd many a fair year though Hero had turn'd nun, if it had not been for a hot midsummer night; for, good youth, he went but forth to wash him in the Hellespont, and being taken with the cramp was drown'd; and the foolish chroniclers of that age found it was—Hero of Sestos. But these are all lies: men have died from time to time, and worms have eaten them, but not for love.

Orl. I would not have my right Rosalind of this mind, for I protest her frown might kill me.

Ros. By this hand, it will not kill a fly. But come, now I will be your Rosalind in a more coming-on disposition; and ask me what you will, I will grant it.

Orl. Then love me, Rosalind.

Ros. Yes, faith, will I, Fridays and Saturdays and all.

Orl. And wilt thou have me?

Ros. Ay, and twenty such.

Orl. What sayest thou?

Ros. Are you not good?

Orl. I hope so.

Ros. Why then, can one desire too much of a good thing? Come, sister, you shall be the priest, and marry us. Give me your hand, Orlando. What do you say, sister?

Orl. Pray thee marry us.

Cel. I cannot say the words.

Ros. You must begin, "Will you, Orlando"—

Cel. Go to! Will you, Orlando, have to wife this Rosalind?

Orl. I will.

Ros. Ay, but when?

Orl. Why, now, as fast as she can marry us.

Ros. Then you must say, "I take thee, Rosalind, for wife."

Orl. I take thee, Rosalind, for wife.

Ros. I might ask you for your commission, but I do take thee, Orlando, for my husband. There's a girl goes before the priest, and certainly a woman's thought runs before her actions.

Orl. So do all thoughts, they are wing'd.

Ros. Now tell me how long you would have her after you have possess'd her.

Orl. For ever and a day.

Ros. Say "a day," without the "ever." No, no, Orlando, men are April when they woo, December when they wed; maids are May when they are maids, but the sky changes when they are wives. I will be more jealous of thee than a Barbary cock-pigeon over his hen, more clamorous than a parrot against rain, more new-fangled than an ape, more giddy in my desires than a monkey. I will weep for nothing, like Diana in the fountain, and I will do that when you are dispos'd to be merry. I will laugh like a hyen, and that when thou art inclin'd to sleep.

Orl. But will my Rosalind do so?

Ros. By my life, she will do as I do.

Orl. O, but she is wise.

Ros. Or else she could not have the wit to do this; the wiser, the waywarder. Make the doors upon a woman's wit, and it will out at the casement; shut that, and 'twill out at the key-hole; stop that, 'twill fly with the smoke out at the chimney.

Orl. A man that had a wife with such a wit, he might say, "Wit, whither wilt?"

Ros. Nay, you might keep that check for it, till you met your wive's wit going to your neighbor's bed.

Orl. And what wit could wit have to excuse that?

Ros. Marry, to say she came to seek you there. You shall never take her without her answer, unless you take her without her tongue. O, that woman that cannot make her fault her husband's occasion, let her never nurse her child herself, for she will breed it like a fool!

Orl. For these two hours, Rosalind, I will leave thee.

Ros. Alas, dear love, I cannot lack thee two hours!

Orl. I must attend the Duke at dinner. By two a' clock I will be with thee again.

Ros. Ay, go your ways, go your ways; I knew what you would prove; my friends told me as much, and I thought no less. That flattering tongue of yours won me. 'Tis but one cast away, and so come death! Two a' clock is your hour?

Orl. Ay, sweet Rosalind.

Ros. By my troth, and in good earnest, and so God mend me, and by all pretty oaths that are not

94. **attorney:** proxy.
94–95. **The poor . . . old.** This was the view of some Biblical commentators.
97. **videlicet:** namely. **Troilus:** the lover of Cressida, who proved faithless to him.
98. **brains . . . club.** Troilus died of a wound inflicted by Achilles' spear. Rosalind makes his end, and Leander's, as unromantic as possible.
98–99. **did . . . before:** i.e. vainly did his utmost to die earlier of frustrated love. 100. **patterns:** models.
105. **found:** gave the verdict (the customary term for the handing down of a verdict by a coroner's jury). 109. **right:** real.
138. **for your commission:** i.e. by what authority you presume to take her (since no one has given her away).
140. **goes before:** anticipates.
150–51. **Barbary cock-pigeon:** a kind of pigeon originally from the Barbary coast of Africa; but the term *Barbary* was also more widely applied to Eastern non-Christians, particularly Moslems, and is suggestive here of the vigilance of Eastern husbands in secluding their wives from other men.
152. **against:** before. **new-fangled:** delighted by novelty.
153. **giddy:** variable.
154. **Diana . . . fountain.** There may be some specific reference here; but the figure of Diana was probably common in garden fountains.
156. **hyen:** hyena. 161. **Make:** make fast, bar.
166. **Wit, whither wilt.** See note to I.ii.56. 168. **wive's:** wife's.
174–75. **her husband's occasion:** a chance to put her husband in the wrong. 179. **lack:** do without.
189. **pretty:** pleasant-sounding, inoffensive.

dangerous, if you break one jot of your promise, or come one minute behind your hour, I will think you the most pathetical break-promise, and the most hollow lover, and the most unworthy of her you call Rosalind, that may be chosen out of the gross band of the unfaithful; therefore beware my censure, and keep your promise.

Orl. With no less religion than if thou wert indeed my Rosalind; so adieu.

Ros. Well, Time is the old justice that examines all such offenders, and let Time try. Adieu.

Exit [Orlando].

Cel. You have simply misus'd our sex in your love-prate. We must have your doublet and hose pluck'd over your head, and show the world what the bird hath done to her own nest.

Ros. O coz, coz, coz, my pretty little coz, that thou didst know how many fathom deep I am in love! But it cannot be sounded; my affection hath an unknown bottom, like the bay of Portugal.

Cel. Or rather, bottomless—that as fast as you pour affection in, [it] runs out.

Ros. No, that same wicked bastard of Venus that was begot of thought, conceiv'd of spleen, and born of madness, that blind rascally boy that abuses every one's eyes because his own are out, let him be judge how deep I am in love. I'll tell thee, Aliena, I cannot be out of the sight of Orlando. I'll go find a shadow, and sigh till he come.

Cel. And I'll sleep. *Exeunt.*

Scene II

Enter Jaques *and* Lords *[as] foresters.*

Jaq. Which is he that kill'd the deer?

[1.] *Lord.* Sir, it was I.

Jaq. Let's present him to the Duke like a Roman conqueror, and it would do well to set the deer's horns upon his head, for a branch of victory. Have you no song, forester, for this purpose?

[2.] *Lord.* Yes, sir.

Jaq. Sing it. 'Tis no matter how it be in tune, so it make noise enough. *Music.*

Song

[2. *Lord.*] What shall he have that kill'd the deer?
His leather skin and horns to wear.
Then sing him home.
The rest shall bear this burthen.

192. pathetical: pitiable, miserable. **195. gross:** entire.
197. religion: faithfulness. **200. try:** determine.
201. simply: stupidly (?) or utterly (?). **misus'd:** abused, slandered.
202–4. We . . . nest: i.e. we must expose you as a member of the sex that you have defamed. There is an allusion to the proverb "It is a foul bird that fouls its own nest." **211. bastard of Venus:** Cupid.
212. thought: melancholy. **spleen:** caprice, waywardness.
213. abuses: deludes. **214. his . . . out:** he himself is blind.
217. shadow: shady place.

IV.ii. Location: The forest. This short scene is introduced to indicate the passing of the specified two hours between Scenes i and iii.
8. how . . . tune: whether you sing it on key (?) or whether the tune be good or bad (?).
12 s.d. bear this burthen: i.e. sing the words "Then sing him home" as a ground-bass or undersong throughout (?). On the stage direction see the Textual Notes. **13. Take . . . scorn:** do not disdain.
14. crest: (1) heraldic device; (2) something growing on the head.

Take thou no scorn to wear the horn,
It was a crest ere thou wast born;
Thy father's father wore it,
And thy father bore it.
The horn, the horn, the lusty horn
Is not a thing to laugh to scorn. *Exeunt.*

Scene III

Enter Rosalind *and* Celia.

Ros. How say you now? Is it not past two a' clock? And here much Orlando!

Cel. I warrant you, with pure love and troubled brain, he hath ta'en his bow and arrows and is gone forth—to sleep. Look who comes here.

Enter Silvius.

Sil. My errand is to you, fair youth,
My gentle Phebe did bid me give you this.
[Gives a letter.]
I know not the contents, but as I guess
By the stern brow and waspish action
Which she did use as she was writing of it,
It bears an angry tenure. Pardon me,
I am but as a guiltless messenger.

Ros. Patience herself would startle at this letter,
And play the swaggerer: bear this, bear all!
She says I am not fair, that I lack manners;
She calls me proud, and that she could not love me
Were man as rare as phoenix. 'Od's my will,
Her love is not the hare that I do hunt;
Why writes she so to me? Well, shepherd, well,
This is a letter of your own device.

Sil. No, I protest, I know not the contents,
Phebe did write it.

Ros. Come, come, you are a fool,
And turn'd into the extremity of love.
I saw her hand, she has a leathern hand,
A freestone-colored hand. I verily did think
That her old gloves were on, but 'twas her hands;
She has a huswive's hand—but that's no matter.
I say she never did invent this letter,
This is a man's invention and his hand.

Sil. Sure it is hers.

Ros. Why, 'tis a boisterous and a cruel style,
A style for challengers. Why, she defies me,
Like Turk to Christian. Women's gentle brain
Could not drop forth such giant-rude invention,
Such Ethiop words, blacker in their effect
Than in their countenance. Will you hear the letter?

Sil. So please you, for I never heard it yet;
Yet heard too much of Phebe's cruelty.

Ros. She Phebes me. Mark how the tyrant writes.

IV.iii. Location: The forest.
11. tenure: tenor. **17. phoenix.** Supposedly unique.
23. turn'd: brought. **25. freestone-colored:** brownish-yellow.
35. Ethiop: black. **36. countenance:** physical appearance.
39. Phebes me: behaves like Phebe towards me, i.e. addresses me in cruel words.

(*Read.*) "Art thou god to shepherd turn'd,
That a maiden's heart hath burn'd?"
Can a woman rail thus?
Sil. Call you this railing?
Ros. (*Read.*)
"Why, thy godhead laid apart,
Warr'st thou with a woman's heart?"
Did you ever hear such railing?
"Whiles the eye of man did woo me,
That could do no vengeance to me."
Meaning me a beast.
"If the scorn of your bright eyne
Have power to raise such love in mine,
Alack, in me what strange effect
Would they work in mild aspect?
Whiles you chid me, I did love;
How then might your prayers move?
He that brings this love to thee
Little knows this love in me;
And by him seal up thy mind,
Whether that thy youth and kind
Will the faithful offer take
Of me, and all that I can make,
Or else by him my love deny,
And then I'll study how to die."
Sil. Call you this chiding?
Cel. Alas, poor shepherd!
Ros. Do you pity him? No, he deserves no pity. Wilt thou love such a woman? What, to make thee an instrument, and play false strains upon thee? not to be endur'd! Well, go your way to her (for I see love hath made thee a tame snake) and say this to her: that if she love me, I charge her to love thee; if she will not, I will never have her unless thou entreat for her. If you be a true lover, hence, and not a word; for here comes more company. *Exit Silvius*

Enter OLIVER.

Oli. Good morrow, fair ones. Pray you (if you know)
Where in the purlieus of this forest stands
A sheep-cote fenc'd about with olive-trees?
Cel. West of this place, down in the neighbor bottom,
The rank of osiers by the murmuring stream
Left on your right hand brings you to the place.
But at this hour the house doth keep itself,
There's none within.
Oli. If that an eye may profit by a tongue,
Then should I know you by description—
Such garments and such years. "The boy is fair,
Of female favor, and bestows himself
Like a ripe sister; the woman low,
And browner than her brother." Are not you
The owner of the house I did inquire for?
Cel. It is no boast, being ask'd, to say we are.
Oli. Orlando doth commend him to you both,
And to that youth he calls his Rosalind
He sends this bloody napkin. Are you he?
Ros. I am. What must we understand by this?
Oli. Some of my shame, if you will know of me
What man I am, and how, and why, and where
This handkercher was stain'd.
Cel. I pray you tell it.
Oli. When last the young Orlando parted from you
He left a promise to return again
Within an hour, and pacing through the forest,
Chewing the food of sweet and bitter fancy,
Lo what befell! He threw his eye aside,
And mark what object did present itself
Under an old oak, whose boughs were moss'd with age
And high top bald with dry antiquity:
A wretched ragged man, o'ergrown with hair,
Lay sleeping on his back; about his neck
A green and gilded snake had wreath'd itself,
Who with her head nimble in threats approach'd
The opening of his mouth; but suddenly
Seeing Orlando, it unlink'd itself,
And with indented glides did slip away
Into a bush, under which bush's shade
A lioness, with udders all drawn dry,
Lay couching, head on ground, with cat-like watch
When that the sleeping man should stir; for 'tis
The royal disposition of that beast
To prey on nothing that doth seem as dead.
This seen, Orlando did approach the man,
And found it was his brother, his elder brother.
Cel. O, I have heard him speak of that same brother,
And he did render him the most unnatural
That liv'd amongst men.
Oli. And well he might so do,
For well I know he was unnatural.
Ros. But to Orlando: did he leave him there,
Food to the suck'd and hungry lioness?
Oli. Twice did he turn his back, and purpos'd so;
But kindness, nobler ever than revenge,
And nature, stronger than his just occasion,
Made him give battle to the lioness,
Who quickly fell before him, in which hurtling
From miserable slumber I awaked.
Cel. Are you his brother?
Ros. Was't you he rescu'd?
Cel. Was't you that did so oft contrive to kill him?
Oli. 'Twas I; but 'tis not I. I do not shame
To tell you what I was, since my conversion
So sweetly tastes, being the thing I am.

44. laid apart: put aside (for human shape). **48. vengeance:** harm.
50. eyne: eyes (archaic even in Elizabethan English; used here for the sake of rhyme). **53. aspect:** looks.
58. seal . . . mind: i.e. send your decision in a letter.
59. youth and kind: youthful nature.
68. instrument: (1) tool; (2) musical instrument.
76. purlieus: cleared land bordering a forest.
78. neighbor bottom: neighboring dell.
79. rank of osiers: row of willows.
86. female favor: feminine features. **bestows:** conducts.
87. ripe: mature, i.e. elder. **low:** short.

93. napkin: handkerchief. **103. what object:** what a sight.
111. unlink'd: uncoiled. **112. indented:** undulating.
114. udders . . . dry. Hence hungry.
122. render him: depict him as. **unnatural:** devoid of natural feeling. Cf. *nature* (= natural affection) in line 129.
125. to: with regard to.
128. kindness: feeling proper to his (human) kind.
129. just occasion: chance to get even. **131. hurtling:** commotion.
134. contrive: plan, devise ways.

Ros. But for the bloody napkin?
Oli. By and by.
When from the first to last betwixt us two
Tears our recountments had most kindly bath'd,
As how I came into that desert place—
[In] brief, he led me to the gentle Duke,
Who gave me fresh array and entertainment,
Committing me unto my brother's love,
Who led me instantly unto his cave,
There stripp'd himself, and here upon his arm
The lioness had torn some flesh away,
Which all this while had bled; and now he fainted,
And cried in fainting upon Rosalind.
Brief, I recover'd him, bound up his wound,
And after some small space, being strong at heart,
He sent me hither, stranger as I am,
To tell this story, that you might excuse
His broken promise, and to give this napkin,
Dy'd in [his] blood, unto the shepherd youth
That he in sport doth call his Rosalind.
[*Rosalind faints.*]

Cel. Why, how now, Ganymed, sweet Ganymed?
Oli. Many will swoon when they do look on blood.
Cel. There is more in it. Cousin Ganymed!
Oli. Look, he recovers.
Ros. I would I were at home.
Cel. We'll lead you thither.
I pray you, will you take him by the arm?
Oli. Be of good cheer, youth. You a man?
You lack a man's heart.

Ros. I do so, I confess it. Ah, sirrah, a body would think this was well counterfeited! I pray you tell your brother how well I counterfeited. Heigh-ho!

Oli. This was not counterfeit, there is too great testimony in your complexion that it was a passion of earnest.

Ros. Counterfeit, I assure you.

Oli. Well then, take a good heart and counterfeit to be a man.

Ros. So I do; but i' faith, I should have been a woman by right.

Cel. Come, you look paler and paler. Pray you draw homewards. Good sir, go with us.

Oli. That will I, for I must bear answer back
How you excuse my brother, Rosalind.

Ros. I shall devise something; but I pray you commend my counterfeiting to him. Will you go?
Exeunt.

ACT V, Scene I

Enter Clown [Touchstone] *and* Audrey.

Touch. We shall find a time, Audrey, patience, gentle Audrey.

138. **for:** i.e. what about.
140. **recountments:** stories told to each other.
150. **Brief:** in brief. **recover'd:** revived.
159. **Cousin.** In her excitement Celia forgets that Rosalind is supposed to be her brother.
165. **I do so.** She lacks a man's heart in two senses not suspected by Oliver. 170–71. **passion of earnest:** genuine seizure.

Aud. Faith, the priest was good enough, for all the old gentleman's saying.

Touch. A most wicked Sir Oliver, Audrey, a most vile Martext. But, Audrey, there is a youth here in the forest lays claim to you.

Aud. Ay, I know who 'tis; he hath no interest in me in the world. Here comes the man you mean.

Enter William.

Touch. It is meat and drink to me to see a clown. By my troth, we that have good wits have much to answer for; we shall be flouting; we cannot hold.

Will. Good ev'n, Audrey.

Aud. God ye good ev'n, William.

Will. And good ev'n to you, sir.

Touch. Good ev'n, gentle friend. Cover thy head, cover thy head; nay, prithee be cover'd. How old are you, friend?

Will. Five and twenty, sir.

Touch. A ripe age. Is thy name William?

Will. William, sir.

Touch. A fair name. Wast born i' the forest here?

Will. Ay, sir, I thank God.

Touch. "Thank God"—a good answer. Art rich?

Will. Faith, sir, so, so.

Touch. "So, so" is good, very good, very excellent good; and yet it is not, it is but so, so. Art thou wise?

Will. Ay, sir, I have a pretty wit.

Touch. Why, thou say'st well. I do now remember a saying, "The fool doth think he is wise, but the wise man knows himself to be a fool." The heathen philosopher, when he had a desire to eat a grape, would open his lips when he put it into his mouth, meaning thereby that grapes were made to eat and lips to open. You do love this maid?

Will. I do, [sir].

Touch. Give me your hand. Art thou learned?

Will. No, sir.

Touch. Then learn this of me: to have, is to have. For it is a figure in rhetoric that drink, being pour'd out of a cup into a glass, by filling the one doth empty the other. For all your writers do consent that *ipse* is he: now, you are not *ipse*, for I am he.

Will. Which he, sir?

Touch. He, sir, that must marry this woman. Therefore, you clown, abandon—which is in the vulgar leave—the society—which in the boorish is company—of this female—which in the common is woman; which together is, abandon the society of this female, or, clown, thou perishest; or to thy better

V.i. Location: The forest.
8–9 interest in: claim to. **10. clown:** country yokel.
12. shall: must. **flouting:** making sport. **hold:** hold back, refrain. **14. God ye:** God give you.
16. Cover thy head: William has respectfully removed his hat.
27. good, very good. Touchstone is punning on another meaning of *so, so:* "just so; very good."
33–35. heathen . . . mouth. Capell suggests that this notion occurs to Touchstone because William is standing with his mouth open, gaping at him in bewilderment. The inference is that Audrey is no grape for William's swallowing.
43. your writers: authorities (the indefinite *your,* as in III.iv.12). **ipse:** he himself.

understanding, diest; or (to wit) I kill thee, make thee away, translate thy life into death, thy liberty into bondage. I will deal in poison with thee, or in bastinado, or in steel; I will bandy with thee in faction; I will o'errun thee with [policy]; I will kill thee a hundred and fifty ways: therefore tremble and depart.

Aud. Do, good William.

Will. God rest you merry, sir. *Exit.*

Enter Corin.

Cor. Our master and mistress seeks you. Come away, away!

Touch. Trip, Audrey, trip, Audrey! I attend, I attend. *Exeunt.*

Scene II

Enter Orlando *and* Oliver.

Orl. Is't possible that on so little acquaintance you should like her? that but seeing, you should love her? and loving, woo? and wooing, she should grant? and will you persever to enjoy her?

Oli. Neither call the giddiness of it in question, the poverty of her, the small acquaintance, my sudden wooing, nor [her] sudden consenting; but say with me, I love Aliena; say with her that she loves me; consent with both that we may enjoy each other. It shall be to your good; for my father's house and all the revenue that was old Sir Rowland's will I estate upon you, and here live and die a shepherd.

Enter Rosalind.

Orl. You have my consent. Let your wedding be to-morrow; thither will I invite the Duke and all 's contented followers. Go you and prepare Aliena; for look you, here comes my Rosalind.

Ros. God save you, brother.

Oli. And you, fair sister. [*Exit.*]

Ros. O my dear Orlando, how it grieves me to see thee wear thy heart in a scarf!

Orl. It is my arm.

Ros. I thought thy heart had been wounded with the claws of a lion.

Orl. Wounded it is, but with the eyes of a lady.

Ros. Did your brother tell you how I counterfeited to sound when he show'd me your handkercher?

52. to wit: namely. **53. translate:** change.
54–55. bastinado: beating with a stick.
55. bandy: vie, contend. **faction:** factious spirit.
56. o'errun: overwhelm. **policy:** craftiness.
59. God . . . merry. A common form of greeting or leavetaking.

V.ii. Location: The forest.
4. persever: persevere. **5. giddiness:** dizzying speed.
6. sudden: swift. **11. estate:** bestow as an estate.
15. all 's: all his. **contented:** ready, willing.
17. brother: (prospective) brother-in-law.
18. sister. Oliver is presumably entering into the supposed Ganymed's pretense of being Rosalind.
20. heart . . . scarf. Rosalind pretends to assume that any bandage (*scarf*) worn by Orlando must cover the part that he has long proclaimed wounded—his heart—and further that he has been wearing it on his sleeve. **26. sound:** swoon.

Orl. Ay, and greater wonders than that.

Ros. O, I know where you are. Nay, 'tis true. There was never any thing so sudden but the fight of two rams, and Caesar's thrasonical brag of "I came, saw, and [overcame]." For your brother and my sister no sooner met but they look'd; no sooner look'd but they lov'd; no sooner lov'd but they sigh'd; no sooner sigh'd but they ask'd one another the reason; no sooner knew the reason but they sought the remedy: and in these degrees have they made a pair of stairs to marriage, which they will climb incontinent, or else be incontinent before marriage. They are in the very wrath of love, and they will together. Clubs cannot part them.

Orl. They shall be married to-morrow; and I will bid the Duke to the nuptial. But O, how bitter a thing it is to look into happiness through another man's eyes! By so much the more shall I to-morrow be at the height of heart-heaviness, by how much I shall think my brother happy in having what he wishes for.

Ros. Why then to-morrow I cannot serve your turn for Rosalind?

Orl. I can live no longer by thinking.

Ros. I will weary you then no longer with idle talking. Know of me then (for now I speak to some purpose) that I know you are a gentleman of good conceit. I speak not this that you should bear a good opinion of my knowledge, insomuch I say I know you are; neither do I labor for a greater esteem than may in some little measure draw a belief from you, to do yourself good, and not to grace me. Believe then, if you please, that I can do strange things. I have, since I was three year old, convers'd with a magician, most profound in his art, and yet not damnable. If you do love Rosalind so near the heart as your gesture cries it out, when your brother marries Aliena, shall you marry her. I know into what straits of fortune she is driven, and it is not impossible to me, if it appear not inconvenient to you, to set her before your eyes to-morrow, human as she is, and without any danger.

Orl. Speak'st thou in sober meanings?

Ros. By my life I do, which I tender dearly, though I say I am a magician. Therefore put you in your best array, bid your friends; for if you will

29. where you are: what you mean.
31. thrasonical: vaunting. Thraso is a braggart soldier in Terence's *Eunuchus*.
37. degrees. With a pun on the meaning "steps." **pair:** flight.
38–39. incontinent: immediately (with following pun on the sense "unchaste"). **40. wrath:** rage, passionate ardor.
41. Clubs. Regularly used for breaking up street fights.
43. bid: invite. **52–53. to some purpose:** with serious intent.
54. conceit: understanding. **55. insomuch:** inasmuch as.
58. grace: do honor to. **60. convers'd:** associated.
61. not damnable: i.e. not a practicer of black magic, which involved trafficking with evil spirits and invited damnation.
62. gesture: bearing. **63. cries it out:** plainly reveals.
66. inconvenient: unfitting.
67–68. human . . . danger: i.e. in her own person, not a spirit in her shape who might endanger Orlando's soul (cf. the apparition of Helen in Marlowe's *Doctor Faustus*). **69. sober:** serious.
70. tender dearly: value highly.
71. though . . . magician: i.e. though I endanger my life by saying openly that I practice magic (some forms of which were punishable by death).

be married to-morrow, you shall; and to Rosalind, if you will.

Enter Silvius *and* Phebe.

Look, here comes a lover of mine and a lover of hers.

Phe. Youth, you have done me much ungentleness,
To show the letter that I writ to you.

Ros. I care not if I have. It is my study
To seem despiteful and ungentle to you.
You are there followed by a faithful shepherd—
Look upon him, love him; he worships you.

Phe. Good shepherd, tell this youth what 'tis to love.

Sil. It is to be all made of sighs and tears,
And so am I for Phebe.

Phe. And I for Ganymed.

Orl. And I for Rosalind.

Ros. And I for no woman.

Sil. It is to be all made of faith and service,
And so am I for Phebe.

Phe. And I for Ganymed.

Orl. And I for Rosalind.

Ros. And I for no woman.

Sil. It is to be all made of fantasy,
All made of passion, and all made of wishes,
All adoration, duty, and observance,
All humbleness, all patience, and impatience,
All purity, all trial, all observance;
And so am I for Phebe.

Phe. And so am I for Ganymed.

Orl. And so am I for Rosalind.

Ros. And so am I for no woman.

Phe. If this be so, why blame you me to love you?

Sil. If this be so, why blame you me to love you?

Orl. If this be so, why blame you me to love you?

Ros. Why do you speak too, "Why blame you me to love you?"

Orl. To her that is not here, nor doth not hear.

Ros. Pray you no more of this, 'tis like the howling of Irish wolves against the moon. [*To Silvius.*] I will help you if I can. [*To Phebe.*] I would love you if I could.—To-morrow meet me all together. [*To Phebe.*] I will marry you, if ever I marry woman, and I'll be married to-morrow. [*To Orlando.*] I will satisfy you, if ever I satisfied man, and you shall be married to-morrow. [*To Silvius.*] I will content you, if what pleases you contents you, and you shall be married to-morrow. [*To Orlando.*] As you love Rosalind, meet. [*To Silvius.*] As you love Phebe, meet. And as I love no woman, I'll meet. So fare you well; I have left you commands.

Sil. I'll not fail, if I live.

Phe. Nor I.

Orl. Nor I. *Exeunt.*

77. **ungentleness:** discourtesy.
79. **study:** diligent endeavor. 80. **despiteful:** cruel.
96. **observance:** devoted service.
98. **trial:** being tested, proving one's constancy. **observance.** Some editors, taking this repetition as an error, emend to *obedience.*
106–7. **Why . . . to.** Emended by some editors to *Who . . . to,* to accord with Orlando's reply.

Scene III

Enter Clown [Touchstone] *and* Audrey.

Touch. To-morrow is the joyful day, Audrey, to-morrow will we be married.

Aud. I do desire it with all my heart; and I hope it is no dishonest desire to desire to be a woman of the world. Here come two of the banish'd Duke's pages.

Enter two Pages.

1. Page. Well met, honest gentleman.

Touch. By my troth, well met. Come, sit, sit, and a song.

2. Page. We are for you, sit i' th' middle.

1. Page. Shall we clap into't roundly, without hawking or spitting or saying we are hoarse, which are the only prologues to a bad voice?

2. Page. I' faith, i' faith, and both in a tune, like two gipsies on a horse.

Song

It was a lover and his lass,
With a hey, and a ho, and a hey nonino,
That o'er the green corn-field did pass,
In spring time, the only pretty [ring] time,
When birds do sing, hey ding a ding, ding,
Sweet lovers love the spring.

Between the acres of the rye,
With a hey, and a ho, and a hey nonino,
These pretty country folks would lie,
In spring time, etc.

This carol they began that hour,
With a hey, and a ho, and a hey nonino,
How that a life was but a flower,
In spring time, etc.

And therefore take the present time,
With a hey, and a ho, and a hey nonino,
For love is crowned with the prime,
In spring time, etc.

Touch. Truly, young gentlemen, though there was no great matter in the ditty, yet the note was very untuneable.

1. Page. You are deceiv'd, sir, we kept time, we lost not our time.

Touch. By my troth, yes; I count it but time lost to hear such a foolish song. God buy you, and God mend your voices! Come, Audrey. *Exeunt.*

V.iii. **Location:** The forest.
4. **dishonest:** immodest. 4–5. **woman . . . world:** married woman.
10. **We . . . you:** i.e. that suits us.
11. **clap into't roundly:** strike into it briskly.
13. **only:** i.e. only proper, i.e. customary.
14. **in a tune:** (1) in unison; (2) keeping in time. Both here and in the next line *a* = one. 18. **corn-field:** wheatfield.
19. **ring time:** season for weddings.
22. **Between . . . rye:** i.e. on the unploughed strips separating the planted fields. 30. **take:** seize for enjoyment.
32. **prime:** springtime. 35. **ditty:** words. **note:** music.
36. **untuneable:** untuneful.
39. **yes:** i.e. yes, you did lose (waste) your time.

Scene IV

Enter Duke Senior, Amiens, Jaques, Orlando, Oliver, Celia.

Duke S. Dost thou believe, Orlando, that the boy
Can do all this that he hath promised?

Orl. I sometimes do believe, and sometimes do not,
As those that fear they hope, and know they fear.

Enter Rosalind, Silvius, *and* Phebe.

Ros. Patience once more, whiles our compact is urg'd:
You say, if I bring in your Rosalind,
You will bestow her on Orlando here?

Duke S. That would I, had I kingdoms to give with her.

Ros. And you say you will have her, when I bring her.

Orl. That would I, were I of all kingdoms king.

Ros. You say you'll marry me, if I be willing?

Phe. That will I, should I die the hour after.

Ros. But if you do refuse to marry me,
You'll give yourself to this most faithful shepherd?

Phe. So is the bargain.

Ros. You say that you'll have Phebe, if she will?

Sil. Though to have her and death were both one thing.

Ros. I have promis'd to make all this matter even:
Keep you your word, O Duke, to give your daughter;
You, yours, Orlando, to receive his daughter;
Keep you your word, Phebe, that you'll marry me,
Or else, refusing me, to wed this shepherd;
Keep your word, Silvius, that you'll marry her
If she refuse me; and from hence I go
To make these doubts all even.

Exeunt Rosalind and Celia.

Duke S. I do remember in this shepherd boy
Some lively touches of my daughter's favor.

Orl. My lord, the first time that I ever saw him
Methought he was a brother to your daughter.
But, my good lord, this boy is forest-born,
And hath been tutor'd in the rudiments
Of many desperate studies by his uncle,
Whom he reports to be a great magician,
Obscured in the circle of this forest.

Enter Clown [Touchstone] *and* Audrey.

Jaq. There is sure another flood toward, and these couples are coming to the ark. Here comes a pair of very strange beasts, which in all tongues are call'd fools.

Touch. Salutation and greeting to you all!

Jaq. Good my lord, bid him welcome. This is the motley-minded gentleman that I have so often met in the forest. He hath been a courtier, he swears.

Touch. If any man doubt that, let him put me to my purgation. I have trod a measure, I have flatt'red a lady, I have been politic with my friend, smooth with mine enemy, I have undone three tailors, I have had four quarrels, and like to have fought one.

Jaq. And how was that ta'en up?

Touch. Faith, we met, and found the quarrel was upon the seventh cause.

Jaq. How seventh cause? Good my lord, like this fellow.

Duke S. I like him very well.

Touch. God 'ild you, sir, I desire you of the like. I press in here, sir, amongst the rest of the country copulatives, to swear and to forswear, according as marriage binds and blood breaks. A poor virgin, sir, an ill-favor'd thing, sir, but mine own; a poor humor of mine, sir, to take that that no man else will. Rich honesty dwells like a miser, sir, in a poor house, as your pearl in your foul oyster.

Duke S. By my faith, he is very swift and sententious.

Touch. According to the fool's bolt, sir, and such dulcet diseases.

Jaq. But for the seventh cause—how did you find the quarrel on the seventh cause?

Touch. Upon a lie seven times remov'd (bear your body more seeming, Audrey), as thus, sir. I did dislike the cut of a certain courtier's beard. He sent me word, if I said his beard was not cut well, he was in the mind it was: this is call'd the Retort Courteous. If I sent him word again, it was not well cut, he would send me word he cut it to please himself: this is call'd the Quip Modest. If again, it was not well cut, he disabled my judgment: this is call'd the Reply Churlish. If again, it was not well cut, he would answer I spake not true: this is call'd the Reproof Valiant. If again, it was not well cut, he would say I lie: this is call'd the Countercheck Quarrelsome; and so to Lie Circumstantial and the Lie Direct.

Jaq. And how oft did you say his beard was not well cut?

Touch. I durst go no further than the Lie Circumstantial, nor he durst not give me the Lie Direct; and so we measur'd swords and parted.

Jaq. Can you nominate in order now the degrees of the lie?

V.iv. Location: The forest.
4. **fear they hope**: fear they are merely hoping (without prospect of fulfillment). 5. **urg'd**: put forward. 8. **had I**: even if I had.
18. **even**: smooth, unobstructed by difficulty.
26. **do remember**: am reminded (of).
27. **lively**: lifelike. **touches**: aspects, details. **favor**: appearance.
32. **desperate**: dangerous.
34. **Obscured**: hidden; with a possible allusion in *Obscured in the circle* to the magic circle within which a magician was supposed safe during his dealing with spirits. 35. **toward**: on the way.

43–44. **put . . . purgation**: challenge me to clear myself (of the charge of lying). 44. **measure**: a slow, stately dance.
46. **undone**: bankrupted (by running up huge bills and failing to pay).
47. **like . . . fought**: almost had to fight. 48. **ta'en up**: settled.
54. **desire . . . like**: wish you the same.
56. **copulatives**: people about to marry. 57. **blood**: passion.
58. **humor**: whim. 60. **honesty**: chastity.
62–63. **swift and sententious**: ready-witted and pithy.
64. **fool's bolt**. Alluding to the proverb "A fool's bolt [arrow] is soon shot."
65. **dulcet diseases**: pleasing discomfort. A jester's shafts of wit are entertaining but can strike painfully home.
69. **more seeming**: in a more seemly fashion.
69–70. **dislike**: find fault with. 75. **Modest**: moderate.
76. **disabled**: belittled, declared incompetent.
80. **Countercheck**: counter-rebuff, contradiction.
81. **Circumstantial**: indirect.
87. **measur'd swords**: i.e. prepared for duelling.
88. **nominate**: name over.

Touch. O sir, we quarrel in print, by the book—as you have books for good manners. I will name you the degrees. The first, the Retort Courteous; the second, the Quip Modest; the third, the Reply Churlish; the fourth, the Reproof Valiant; the fift, the Countercheck Quarrelsome; the sixt, the Lie with Circumstance; the seventh, the Lie Direct. All these you may avoid but the Lie Direct; and you may avoid that too, with an If. I knew when seven justices could not take up a quarrel, but when the parties were met themselves, one of them thought but of an If, as, "If you said so, then I said so"; and they shook hands and swore brothers. Your If is the only peacemaker; much virtue in If.

Jaq. Is not this a rare fellow, my lord? He's as good at any thing, and yet a fool.

Duke S. He uses his folly like a stalking-horse, and under the presentation of that he shoots his wit.

Enter HYMEN, ROSALIND, *and* CELIA. *Still music.*

Hym. Then is there mirth in heaven,
When earthly things made even
Atone together.
Good Duke, receive thy daughter,
Hymen from heaven brought her,
Yea, brought her hither,
That thou mightst join [her] hand with his
Whose heart within his bosom is.

Ros. [*To Duke Senior.*] To you I give myself, for I am yours.
[*To Orlando.*] To you I give myself, for I am yours.

Duke S. If there be truth in sight, you are my daughter.

Orl. If there be truth in sight, you are my Rosalind.

Phe. If sight and shape be true,
Why then my love adieu!

Ros. I'll have no father, if you be not he;
I'll have no husband, if you be not he;
Nor ne'er wed woman, if you be not she.

Hym. Peace ho! I bar confusion,
'Tis I must make conclusion
Of these most strange events.
Here's eight that must take hands
To join in Hymen's bands,
If truth holds true contents.
[*To Orlando and Rosalind.*]
You and you no cross shall part;
[*To Oliver and Celia.*]
You and you are heart in heart;
[*To Phebe.*]
You to his love must accord,

Or have a woman to your lord;
[*To Touchstone and Audrey.*]
You and you are sure together,
As the winter to foul weather.—
Whiles a wedlock-hymn we sing,
Feed yourselves with questioning;
That reason wonder may diminish
How thus we met, and these things finish.

SONG

Wedding is great Juno's crown,
O blessed bond of board and bed!
'Tis Hymen peoples every town,
High wedlock then be honored.
Honor, high honor, and renown
To Hymen, god of every town!

Duke S. O my dear niece, welcome thou art to me,
Even daughter, welcome, in no less degree.

Phe. I will not eat my word, now thou art mine,
Thy faith my fancy to thee doth combine.

Enter Second Brother [JAQUES DE BOYS].

Jaq. de B. Let me have audience for a word or two.
I am the second son of old Sir Rowland,
That bring these tidings to this fair assembly.
Duke Frederick, hearing how that every day
Men of great worth resorted to this forest,
Address'd a mighty power, which were on foot
In his own conduct, purposely to take
His brother here, and put him to the sword;
And to the skirts of this wild wood he came;
Where, meeting with an old religious man,
After some question with him, was converted
Both from his enterprise and from the world,
His crown bequeathing to his banish'd brother,
And all their lands restor'd to [them] again
That were with him exil'd. This to be true,
I do engage my life.

Duke S. Welcome, young man;
Thou offer'st fairly to thy brothers' wedding:
To one his lands withheld, and to the other
A land itself at large, a potent dukedom.
First, in this forest let us do those ends
That here were well begun and well begot;
And after, every of this happy number,
That have endur'd shrewd days and nights with us,
Shall share the good of our returned fortune,
According to the measure of their states.

90. **by the book:** according to established rules. There were, in fact, such books, hardly less fantastic than Touchstone's "lie seven times remov'd." One which may be glanced at here is Vincent Saviolo's *Practice of the Rapier and Dagger* (1594–5), the second part of which treats of "Honor and Honorable Quarrels," with a section headed "Of the manner and diversity of Lies." 99. **take up:** settle.
102. **swore brothers:** i.e. became sworn brothers, pledged to the mutual loyalty proper to actual brothers.
106. **stalking-horse:** any deceptive cover used by a game-stalker to get within shooting distance of his quarry.
107. **under . . . that:** i.e. using his assumed folly as a protective disguise. 107 s.d. **Hymen:** god of marriage. **Still:** soft.
108. **mirth:** joy. 110. **Atone:** are at one, accord.
130. **If . . . contents:** i.e. if truth is true. 131. **cross:** disagreement.
133. **accord:** assent.
134. **to:** for.
135. **sure together:** securely joined. 138. **Feed:** satisfy.
139. **reason:** rational explanation.
141. **Juno's.** Juno was the goddess of marriage.
144. **High:** solemn.
148. **Even . . . degree:** i.e. you are no whit less welcome to me than a daughter. 150. **combine:** unite.
156. **Address'd:** made ready, levied. **power:** army.
157. **In . . . conduct:** under his personal command.
161. **question:** conversation. 166. **engage:** pledge.
167. **Thou offer'st fairly:** you bring handsome gifts.
169. **A land . . . large:** a whole country in itself. The restoration of the dukedom to Rosalind's father means that her husband will be the next duke.
170. **do those ends:** bring to a conclusion those purposes.
171. **begot:** conceived. 172. **every:** every one.
173. **shrewd:** sorely difficult. 175. **states:** rank.

Mean time, forget this new-fall'n dignity,
And fall into our rustic revelry.
Play, music, and you brides and bridegrooms all,
With measure heap'd in joy, to th' measures fall.
Jaq. Sir, by your patience.—If I heard you rightly,
The Duke hath put on a religious life,
And thrown into neglect the pompous court?
Jaq. de B. He hath.
Jaq. To him will I. Out of these convertites
There is much matter to be heard and learn'd.
[*To Duke Senior.*] You to your former honor I bequeath,
Your patience and your virtue well deserves it;
[*To Orlando.*] You to a love, that your true faith doth merit;
[*To Oliver.*] You to your land, and love, and great allies;
[*To Silvius.*] You to a long and well-deserved bed;
[*To Touchstone.*] And you to wrangling, for thy loving voyage
Is but for two months victuall'd.—So to your pleasures,
I am for other than for dancing measures.
Duke S. Stay, Jaques, stay.
Jaq. To see no pastime I. What you would have
I'll stay to know at your abandon'd cave. *Exit.*
Duke S. Proceed, proceed. We'll begin these rites,
As we do trust they'll end, in true delights.
[*A dance.*] *Exeunt* [*all but Rosalind*].

176. new-fall'n: newly acquired. **178. music:** musicians.
180. patience: indulgence, permission.
182. pompous: ceremonious. **184. convertites:** converts.

[EPILOGUE]

Ros. It is not the fashion to see the lady the epilogue; but it is no more unhandsome than to see the lord the prologue. If it be true that good wine needs no bush, 'tis true that a good play needs no epilogue. Yet to good wine they do use good bushes; and good plays prove the better by the help of good epilogues. What a case am I in then, that am neither a good epilogue, nor cannot insinuate with you in the behalf of a good play! I am not furnish'd like a beggar, therefore to beg will not become me. My way is to conjure you, and I'll begin with the women. I charge you, O women, for the love you bear to men, to like as much of this play as please you; and I charge you, O men, for the love you bear to women (as I perceive by your simp'ring, none of you hates them), that between you and the women the play may please. If I were a woman I would kiss as many of you as had beards that pleas'd me, complexions that lik'd me, and breaths that I defied not; and I am sure, as many as have good beards, or good faces, or sweet breaths, will for my kind offer, when I make curtsy, bid me farewell. *Exit.*

Epi. 2. unhandsome: unfitting.
3–4. good . . . bush. Proverbial. The ivy bush was formerly the vintner's sign. **7. case:** predicament.
8. insinuate: ingratiate myself. **10. furnish'd:** dressed, equipped.
11. conjure: earnestly charge.
18. If . . . woman. Women's parts were played by boys.
19. lik'd: pleased. **20. defied:** disliked.
23. bid me farewell: i.e. by applauding.

NOTE ON THE TEXT

The First Folio (1623) is our only authority for *As You Like It*; all later texts are derived from that source. Critics are agreed that (1) the printer's copy for *As You Like It*, Fl, was not a Shakespearean holograph; and (2) the Fl text is clean and essentially sound, showing no signs of significant revision (*pace* Wilson). But here agreement ends. Knowles argues that the Fl copy was either a prompt-book (so Greg), a transcript from the prompt-book (so Latham), or a transcript of the "foul papers," partially annotated by the book-keeper as copy for the official prompt-book; Wells/Taylor are similarly uncertain, suggesting that "the copy was either the prompt-book or a literary transcript, either from the prompt-book itself or the foul papers." A theatrical provenience is supported by the act and scene divisions in the Fl text and probably by the imperative stage directions at I.ii.212, 215; II.v.37; IV.ii.12; V.iv.107.

For further information, see: J. D. Wilson, ed., New Shakespeare *As You Like It* (Cambridge, 1926; rev. 1947); W. W. Greg, *The Shakespeare First Folio* (Oxford, 1955); Agnes Latham, ed., New Arden *As You Like It* (London, 1975); Richard Knowles, ed., New Variorum *As You Like It* (New York, 1977); Stanley Wells, Gary Taylor, et al., *William Shakespeare: A Textual Companion* (Oxford, 1987); Alan Brissenden, ed., New Oxford *As You Like It* (Oxford, 1993).

TEXTUAL NOTES

Dramatis personae: *subs. as first given by Rowe; an earlier list, which describes Duke Senior as* **Ferdinand Old duke of Burgundy,** *appears in the Douai MS*
Act-scene division: *from Fl*

I.i

Location: *Rowe, Pope*
52 What,] *Theobald;* **What** *Fl*
52 s.d. Strikes him.] *White*
54 s.d. Collaring him.] *Johnson*
93 s.d. Exit Dennis.] *Johnson*
109 she] *F3;* **hee** *Fl*
151, 167 device] *F3;* **deuise** *Fl*
156 anatomize] *F3;* **anathomize** *Fl*
163 s.p. Oli.] *F2*

I.ii

Location: *Capell (after Rowe)*
4 I] *Rowe*
31 huswife] *Capell;* **houswife** *Fl*
53 and] *Malone*
57 s.p. Touch.] *Malone;* **Clow.** *Fl (throughout)*
81 mean'st] *Rowe;* **means't** *Fl*
83 s.p. Cel.] *Theobald;* **Ros.** *Fl*
84 s.d. Exeunt] *Rowe (subs.);* **Ex.** *Fl*
87 wise men] *F3;* **Wisemen** *Fl*
91 Le] *F2;* **the** *Fl*
91 Beau] *Steevens;* **Beu** *Fl (throughout, except in s.d. following l. 91)*
97 Bon jour] *Rowe (subs.);* **Boon-iour** *Fl*
149 s.p. Duke F.] *Malone;* **Duke.** *Fl (throughout)*
149–56 Come . . . wrastling.] *as prose, Pope; as verse, Fl*
208 You . . . after;] *Cambridge, following Theobald, suggests reading* **And you . . . after, (i.e. If you . . . after,)** *on the suppo-*

sition that the compositor took And *to be part of the speech-prefix* Orland.; *though not necessary, the emendation makes for easier sense*
215 s.d. **Charles is thrown.]** *Rowe*
230 s.d. **with . . . Beau]** *Capell (subs.)*
242 **deserv'd.]** *Pope (subs.)*; deseru'd, *F1*
243 **love]** *Singer*; loue; *F1*; love, *F2*
244 **all]** all in *F2*
245 s.d. **Giving . . . neck.]** *Theobald*
251 **quintain]** *Theobald*; quintine *F1*
256 s.d. **with Celia]** *Rowe (subs.)*
272 **smaller]** *Malone*; taller *F1*
286 s.d. **Exit Le Beau.]** *Capell*
289 **Rosalind]** *Rowe*; Rosaline *F1 (through II.v; Compositor D's spelling)*

I.iii

Location: *Theobald (subs.)*
1–2 **Why . . . word?]** *as prose, Rowe; as verse, F1*
12 **working-day]** *hyphen, Rowe*
42 **uncle?]** *Capell*; Vncle. *F1*
52 **traitors:]** *Theobald (subs.)*; Traitors, *F1*
57 **likelihood]** *F2*; likelihoods *F1*
78 **her]** *F2*; per *F1*
82 **lips:]** *Pope*; lips *F1*; lips, *F2*
83 **doom]** *Rowe*; doombe *F1*
89 s.d. **with Lords]** *Malone (subs.)*; &c. *F1*
126 **be]** *F2*; by *F1*
131 **travel]** *F3*; trauaile *F1*
133 **woo]** *F2* (wooe); woe *F1 (sporadically throughout)*
137 **we in]** *F2*; in we *F1*

II.i

Location: *Theobald (after Rowe)*
6 **fang]** *Johnson*; phange *F1*
18 **I . . . it.]** *Upton suggested giving these words to Duke Senior and has been followed by many eds.*
18 **it. Happy]** *Rowe (subs.)*; it, happy *F1*
31 **antique]** *Pope*; anticke *F1*
45 **similes]** *Steevens*; similies *F1*
49 **much]** *F2*; must *F1*
50 **friends]** *Rowe*; friend *F1*
59 **the]** *F2*

II.ii

Location: *Rowe (subs.)*

II.iii

Location: *Capell (after Rowe)*
o.s.d. **meeting]** *Capell*
10 **some]** *F2*; seeme *F1*
16 s.p. **Orl.]** *F2; continued to Adam, F1*
29 s.p. **Orl.]** *F2*; Ad. *F1*
35 **can.]** *F3* (can:); can, *F1*
39 **sav'd]** *Rowe*; saued *F1*
46 **servant.]** *Theobald (subs.)*; seruant, *F1*
71 **seventeen]** *Rowe*; seauentie *F1*

II.iv

Location: *Theobald (after Rowe)*
1 **weary]** *Theobald*; merry *F1*
19 **so,]** *Rowe*; so *F1*
33 **heartily!]** *Dyce (after F4)*; hartily, *F1*
38 **Wearing]** Wearying *F2 (adopted by some eds.)*
44 **shepherd!]** *F2*; Shepheard *F1*
44 **thy]** *Rowe*; they *F1*; their *F2*
44 **wound]** *F2*; would *F1*
48 **a-night]** *hyphen, Collier*
69 **you]** *F2*; your *F1*
74 **travel]** *F3*; trauaile *F1*
81 **reaks]** *ed.*; wreakes *F1*
83 **Besides,]** *Rowe*; Besides *F1*

II.v

Location: *Capell (after Rowe)*
1 s.p. **Ami.]** *Capell*
12–4, 17–9, 34–7, 46–7] *as prose, Pope; as irregular verse, F1*
26 **compliment]** *Pope*; complement *F1*
44–5 **No . . . weather.]** *from ll. 7–8 above*; &c. *F1*
49 s.p. **Jaq.]** *F2*; Amy. *F1*

II.vi

Location: *Capell (after Rowe)*
1–18] *as prose, Pope; as irregular verse, F1*
14, 18 **cheerly]** *F4*; cheerely *F1*

II.vii

Location: *Capell (after Rowe)*
o.s.d. **A . . . out.]** *Rowe*
o.s.d. **Amiens]** *Capell*
o.s.d. **Lords]** *Rowe*; Lord *F1*
38 **brain]** *F2*; braiue *F1*
48 **Withal]** *F2*, Wiithall *F1*
55 **Not to]** *Theobald*
56 **wise man's]** *Rowe*; Wise-mans *F1*
56 **anatomiz'd]** *F3*; anathomiz'd *F1*
64 **sin]** *F2*; fin *F1*
75 **city-woman]** *hyphen, Pope*
83 **then! . . . what then?]** *Wilson (after Theobald)*; then, how then, what then, *F1*
87 **any man. But]** *F2*; any. man But *F1 (Furness claims that some copies of F1 have been corrected, but Hinman records no corrected state)*
87 **comes]** *F2*; come *F1*
87 s.d. **with . . . drawn]** *Douai MS, Theobald*
100–1 **and . . . die.]** *as prose, Capell; as verse, F1*
135 s.d. **Exit.]** *Rowe*
167–8 **Welcome . . . feed.]** *as verse, Pope; as prose, F1*
174 s.p. **Ami.]** *Johnson*
182 **Then]** *Rowe*; The *F1*
198 **master]** *F2*; masters *F1*

III.i

Location: *Rowe (subs.)*

III.ii

Location: *Rowe*
o.s.d. **with a paper]** *Capell*
27 **good]** *F2*; pood *F1*
32–3 **Such . . . shepherd?]** *as prose, Pope; as verse, F1*
87 s.d. **with . . . reading]** *Capell*
89 **Rosalind]** *Kittredge points out that F1 here, and through l. 112, spells the name as* Rosalinde *to emphasize the pronunciation*
92 **lin'd]** *Pope*; Linde *F1*
97 **sleeping-hours]** *hyphen, Dyce*
125 s.d. **Reads.]** *Dyce*
125 **a desert be?]** *Rowe*; Desert bee, *F1*
128 **show]** *F4*; shoe *F1*
135 **boughs]** *Rowe*; bowes *F1*
143 **wide-enlarg'd.]** *Rowe (subs.; hyphen, Dyce)*; wide enlarg'd, *F1*
145 **her]** *Douai MS, Rowe*; his *F1*
148 **Lucretia's]** *F4*; Lucrecia's *F1*
158 **now?]** *Theobald*; now *F1*; now! *F2*
158 **back,]** *Dyce*; backe *F1*
162 s.d. **with Corin]** *Rowe (subs.)*
196 **hose]** a hose *F2*
227 **size.]** *F3 (subs.)*; size, *F1*
237 **such]** *Capell*; forth *F1*; forth such *F2*
244 **thy]** *Rowe*; the *F1*
246 **heart]** *Rowe*; Hart *F1*
294 s.d. **Exit Jaques.]** *Douai MS, Rowe*
295 s.d. **Aside to Celia.]** *Capell*
347 **lectures]** *F3*; Lectors *F1*; Lecturs *F2*
363 **deifying]** *F2*; defying *F1*
371 **are]** *F2*; art *F1*
382 **point-device]** *hyphen, Theobald*

III.iii

Location: *Capell (after Rowe)*
o.s.d. **behind]** *Collier*
2 **Audrey?]** *Capell*; Audrey *F1*
7 **goats]** *Munro*; Goats, *F1*
10, 32, 46 s.dd. **Aside.]** *Johnson*
14–5 **God 'ild]** *Theobald (after F2* godild); goddild *F1*
56–7 **Horns? . . . alone?]** *Theobald (subs., after Rowe)*; hornes, euen so poore men alone: *F1*
67 s.p. **Sir Oli.]** *Rowe*; Ol. *F1 (throughout)*
71 s.d. **Discovering himself.]** *Johnson*
90 s.d. **Aside.]** *Capell*
90 **mind]** *Capell*; minde, *F1*
96 s.p. **Touch.]** *F2* (Clo.); Ol. *F1*
99–105 **O . . . thee.]** *subs. as verse, Warburton conj.; as prose, F1*
105 s.d. **Exeunt . . . Audrey.]** *Capell*
107 s.d. **Exit.]** *Capell*; Exeunt. *F1*

III.iv

Location: *Capell (after Rowe)*
5–14 **As . . . bread.]** *as prose, Pope; as irregular verse, F1*
30 **a]** *F2*

III.v

Location: *Rowe (implied)*
1 **Phebe;]** *Rowe*; Phebe *F1*; Phebe, *F3*
7 s.d. **behind]** *Collier (after Capell)*
9 **thee]** *ed.*; thee, *F1*
10 **eye:]** *F4 (subs.)*; eye, *F1*
11 **pretty,]** *Theobald*; pretty *F1*
17 **why,]** *Theobald*; why *F1*
20 **thee;]** thee, *F1*
22 **lean]** Leane but *F2*
35 s.d. **Advancing.]** *Capell*
37 **have]** *F2*; hau *F1*
37 **beauty—]** *Pope (subs.)*; Beauty *F1*
66–70 **He's . . . me?]** *as prose, Pope; as irregular verse, F1*
80 s.d. **with . . . Corin]** *Hanmer (subs.)*
88 **love,]** *F4*; loue *F1*
108 **carlot]** *Steevens*; Carlot *F1 (in italics, as a proper name)*
128 **Have]** I haue *F2*
134 **taunting]** *F4*; tanting *F1*

IV.i

Location: *Rowe*
1 **be]** *F2*
6 **abominable]** *F3*; abhominable *F1*
18 **my]** *F2*; by *F1*
19 **rumination]** *Rowe (the comma is very faint in F4)*; rumination, *F1*
29 **travel]** *F3*; trauaile *F1*
38 s.d. **Exit Jaques.]** *Dyce*; Exit. *F2 (after l. 32)*
49 **heart-whole]** *F4*; heart hole *F1*
55 **jointure]** *F2*; ioyncture *F1*
69 **holiday]** *Capell*; holy-day *F1*
97 **love-cause]** *hyphen, Theobald*
105 **chroniclers]** *F2*; Chronoclers *F1*
105 **was—]** *Theobald (subs.)*; was *F1*
106 **Sestos]** *F2*; Cestos *F1*
138 **I . . . commission,]** *as prose, Pope; as verse, F1*
200 s.d. **Orlando]** *Rowe*
210 **it]** *F2*; in *F1*

IV.ii

Location: *Capell (after Rowe)*
o.s.d. **as]** *Malone*
2 s.p. **1. Lord.]** *Malone (after Capell)*; Lord. *F1*
7 s.p. **2. Lord.]** *Malone (after Capell)*; Lord. *F1*
10 s.p. **2. Lord.]** *C. J. Hill (in Riverside Six Plays)*
12 s.d. **The . . . burthen.]** *as s.d., Theobald; as concluding part of l. 12, F1*

IV.iii

Location: *Capell (after Rowe)*
1–5 **How . . . here.]** *as prose, Pope; as verse, F1*
5 **forth—to]** *Capell*; forth / To *F1*
5 s.d. **Enter Silvius.]** *placed as in Pope; after* brain, *l. 4, F1*
7 **did]** *om. F2*
7 s.d. **Gives a letter.]** *Johnson (subs.)*
34 **giant-rude]** *hyphen, Capell*
44 **apart]** *F2*; a part *F1*
73 **lover,]** *F4*; louer *F1*
78 **bottom,]** *Rowe*; bottom *F1*
87 **the]** But the *F2*
105 **top]** *F2*; top, *F1*
142 **In]** *F2*; I *F1*
155 **his]** *F2*; this *F1*
156 s.d. **Rosalind faints.]** *Pope*
165 **I . . . it.]** *as prose, Pope; as verse, F1*
170 **a]** *om. F2*

V.i

Location: *Rowe*
10 **clown.]** *F4 (subs.)*; Clowne, *F1*
22 **Wast]** *Pope*; Was't *F1*

32 **wise man]** *F4;* wiseman *F1*
37 **sir]** *F2;* sit *F1*
56 **policy]** *F2;* police *F1*
58 **Do,]** *F4;* Do *F1*
59 **merry,]** *F4;* merry *F1*

V.ii

Location: *Capell (after Rowe)*
7 **her]** *Douai MS, Rowe*
13–6 **You . . . Rosalind.]** *as prose, Pope; as verse, F1*
18 **s.d. Exit.]** *Capell*
32 **overcame]** *F2;* ouercome *F1*
46 **heart-heaviness]** *hyphen, Rowe*
56 **are]** *F2;* arc *F1*
67 **human]** *Rowe;* humane *F1*
110 **s.d. To Silvius.]** *Douai MS, Capell*
111 **s.d. To Phebe.]** *Douai MS, Johnson*
112 **all together]** *F4;* altogether *F1*
113 **s.d. To Phebe.]** *Pope*
114 **s.d. To Orlando.]** *Pope*
116 **s.d. To Silvius.]** *Pope*
118 **s.d. To Orlando.]** *Johnson*
119 **s.d. To Silvius.]** *Douai MS, Johnson*

V.iii

Location: *Capell (after Rowe)*
16 **It was]** Twas *Morley (in* First Booke of Ayres, *1600)*
17 **hey, and]** haye with *Morley, Adv. MS 5.2.14, fol. 18 (in National Library, Edinburgh)*
18 **corn-field]** corne fields *Morley*
19 **In]** *Knight (after Adv. MS), Morley;* In the *F1*
19 **ring]** *Steevens conj. and Morley, Adv. MS;* rang *F1*
20 **a ding, ding]** ading ading *Morley, Adv. MS*
23, 27, 31 **hey, and]** hay, with *Morley*
24 **folks]** fooles *Morley, Adv. MS*
24 **would]** did *Adv. MS*
30–3 **And . . . etc.]** *Johnson's arrangement (as in Morley and Adv. MS); in F1 these lines follow l. 21*
30 **And . . . time]** Then prettie louers take the time *Morley, Adv. MS*
36 **untuneable.]** *F2;* vntunable *F1*

V.iv

Location: *Capell (after Rowe)*
25 **s.d. Exeunt]** *Hanmer;* Exit *F1*
34 **s.d. Enter . . . Audrey.]** *placed as in Rowe; after l. 33, F1*
81 **to]** *F2* (to the); ro *F1*
114 **her]** *F3;* his *F1*
116 **s.d. To Duke Senior.]** *Douai MS, Rowe*
117 **s.d. To Orlando.]** *Douai MS, Rowe*
121 **adieu!]** *Theobald;* adieu *F1;* adiev. *F2*
130 **s.d. To . . . Rosalind.]** *Johnson*
131 **s.d. To . . . Celia.]** *Johnson*
132 **s.d. To Phebe.]** *Johnson*
134 **s.d. To . . . Audrey.]** *Johnson*
148 **daughter,]** *F4;* daughter *F1*
150 **s.d. Jaques de Boys]** *Rowe*
151, 183 **s.pp. Jaq. de B.]** *Rowe;* 2. Bro. *F1*
164 **them]** *Douai MS, Rowe;* him *F1*
171 **were]** *F2;* vvete *F1*
186 **s.d. To Duke Senior.]** *Rowe*
186 **bequeath,]** *Rowe;* bequeath *F1;* bequeath; *F2*
188 **s.d. To Orlando.]** *Rowe*
189 **s.d. To Oliver.]** *Rowe*
190 **s.d. To Silvius.]** *Rowe*
191 **s.d. To Touchstone.]** *Rowe*
197 **rites]** *Rowe;* rights *F1*
198 **trust they'll end,]** *Pope;* trust, they'l end *F1*
198 **s.d. A dance.]** *Capell*
198 **s.d. Exeunt.]** *Craig;* Exit *F1*
198 **s.d. all but Rosalind]** *ed.*

Epilogue

Epilogue] *so titled by Theobald*
23 **s.d. Exit.]** Exit. / FINIS. *F1*

"It was a lover and his lass." From the unique copy of Thomas Morley's *First Book of Airs, or Little Short Songs* (1600) in the Folger Shakespeare Library. This setting by Thomas Morley (1557–1603) of "It was a lover and his lass" (*As You Like It*, V.iii.16–33) is one of the very few contemporary settings for a Shakespearean lyric that have survived. The melody is scored in the upper staff, the lute accompaniment in the lower staff. A setting without words for a song called "O mistress mine" in Morley's *First Book of Consort Lessons* (1599) may be for Shakespeare's lyric in *Twelfth Night* (II.iii. 39–52). There are also contemporary settings for "Where the bee sucks" and "Full fadom five" in *The Tempest*; these are by Robert Johnson, one of the Musicians of the Lute to James I, and may have been specially written for the court performance of *The Tempest* in 1613 in honor of the marriage of the Lady Elizabeth, James I's daughter, to the Elector Palatine.

Twelfth Night

TWELFTH NIGHT, OR WHAT YOU WILL is the only play for which Shakespeare provided an alternative title. As with *Much Ado about Nothing*, *As You Like It*, and *All's Well That Ends Well*, his other late Elizabethan comedies, the title as a whole is more serious than its offhand and casual manner would suggest. The word *will* possessed for Elizabethans its modern sense of "wish" or "inclination," and this is its primary significance here: an airy invitation to reader or audience to rechristen the comedy according to individual taste and reaction. (King Charles I was one of those who responded: he insisted upon describing it, in his personal copy of the Second Folio, as *Malvolio*.) Elizabethans, however, also used the noun *will* for irrational desire, passion (often physical) uncontrolled by judgment. Shakespeare puns elaborately on the word in several of his sonnets to the Dark Lady. In this sense, the comedy is indeed about what people—Olivia, Orsino, Antonio, Malvolio, and even Viola—"will," the frightening suddenness with which "the pales and forts of reason," as Hamlet termed them, may be swept away by a kind of emotional thunderstorm.

The first mention of *Twelfth Night* comes from the diary of the lawyer John Manningham. "At our feast," he noted, "we had a play called 'Twelve Night, or What You Will,' much like the Comedy of Errors, or Menechmi in Plautus, but most like and near to that in Italian called *Inganni*." The feast in question here was Candlemas, February 2, 1602, and the place was the Middle Temple. Probably this was not the first performance of the comedy. On stylistic grounds, and also from the evidence provided by certain topical allusions contained within it, a date of 1600 or 1601 seems more likely. Leslie Hotson, in his book *The First Night of "Twelfth Night,"* has attempted to place the first performance more precisely. He believes that Shakespeare wrote the play at royal command in honor of the state visit of Don Virginio Orsino, Duke of Bracciano, and that it was first presented on Twelfth Night (January 6) in 1601. As it happened, news of Orsino's projected visit did not reach England until December 26, 1600. Hotson's theory implies that Shakespeare wrote the comedy, and that the Lord Chamberlain's Men somehow managed to learn their parts and rehearse for a performance at court, within a space of ten or eleven days. This seems hard to believe. Hotson also argues that this original audience was meant to recognize Olivia as Queen Elizabeth, Orsino as the visiting Italian Duke, and Malvolio as the pompous Comptroller of the Royal Household, Sir William Knollys. The comedy as a whole set out to compliment the visitor from Italy, flatter the aging queen, and bait an unpopular court official. Again, the theory seems forced and implausible. It is difficult to believe that either Elizabeth or her foreign guest would have welcomed the association with Olivia and Orsino, given the folly of both characters and the extent to which they are humiliated in the course of the action. As for Malvolio, to identify him with a real individual and suggest that this is the key to the character is to limit his function and impact and sadly to inhibit that complexity of response which an audience normally feels towards him in the theatre.

Even if the comedy received its first performance on Twelfth Night, Shakespeare is most unlikely to have given it this name purely for so accidental and ephemeral a reason. Within the play itself there are no specific references to the Feast of the Epiphany, the twelfth and culminating day of the Christmas season. The action, from Viola's arrival on the seacoast of Illyria to the discoveries of the final scene, seems to occupy about three months. This is the length of time that Antonio claims to have known the youth Sebastian and that Cesario, by "his" own testimony, has served the Duke. Shakespeare could easily have made it clear, had he wished, that Sir Toby's disorderly revel in the third scene of Act II was a Twelfth Night celebration, but he did not. Probably, he deliberately avoided any such pinpointing of the time of year because he wished to draw the attention of his audience to the Twelfth Night theme in ways that were more pervasive and subtle.

Epiphany was originally a major Christian feast, even more important than Christmas. It commemorated not only the coming of the Magi with gifts to Bethlehem, but two later events in the life of Christ: his baptism, and the miracle at Cana. Human nature being what it is, it was perhaps inevitable that a celebration which initially was wholly pious should, with time, alter its complexion, attracting to itself in the process a good deal of the license and even the specific customs of the pagan Saturnalia. Before long, the Church found itself struggling to suppress what had gradually become a kind of annual orgy within sacred precincts: the celebration of a world turned ritually upside down. The effort was, in part, successful. By the end of the fifteenth century the riotous Feast of Fools, now associated with Epiphany, had at least been driven out of the church itself and forced to adopt less overtly blasphemous forms. In secular society, however, especially in the Inns of Court and the universities and in princely gatherings, it continued to flourish during Shakespeare's lifetime. If he christened a comedy *Twelfth Night*, it seems reasonable to assume that he intended that title to summon up images of Epiphany as it was kept in his own time: a period of holiday abandon in which the normal rules and order of life were suspended or else deliberately inverted, in which serious issues and events mingled perplexingly with revelry and apparent madness. This, in effect, is the atmosphere in Illyria: a country where everyone (except, perhaps, Feste) is very much in earnest, but also a little insane.

Manningham was not wholly imperceptive in pointing out the resemblance between *Twelfth Night* and *Inganni*. In 1537 there was published an Italian comedy of disguise and mistaken identity called *Gl'Ingannati*. It reappeared throughout the century in a number of different adaptations and languages (sometimes called *Inganni*) and left its mark on at least one work of English fiction known to Shakespeare: Barnabe Rich's prose tale "Apolonius and Silla" in his collection entitled *Rich His Farewell to Military Profession* (1581). *Gl'Ingannati* involves a brother and sister parted by accident and eventually reunited; its heroine disguises herself as a boy and finds that she has to pay court to an embarrassingly susceptible lady in the name of the master she herself loves. These are things that happen in *Twelfth Night* too, and yet neither *Gl'Ingannati* nor any of the works that derive from it can really be regarded as a source for Shakespeare's play. *Gl'Ingannati* and all its tribe are heavily indebted to Plautine comedy: they are slick, fast-moving, unemotional, and certainly unpoetic, concerned primarily with plot and intrigue. In general shape, let alone in tone and spirit, they are worlds away from *Twelfth Night*. There is no more reason to suppose that Shakespeare was thinking of *Gl'Ingannati* or any of its descendants when he conceived his own play than that *The Comedy of Errors* or *The Two Gentlemen of Verona* earlier borrowed from this source in creating the dilemma of the two Antipholuses or Julia's reluctant embassy to Silvia in her boy's disguise. This is plot material of the most ownerless and ancient kind: the very stuff of Comedy since Menander.

The words "Twelfth Night" not only suggest a carnival world; they warn an audience that it is not to ask too many awkward questions about the miraculous resemblance of boy and girl twins who, on the stage, will almost invariably look less than identical. Nor are we to question love at first sight, a duke who accepts as his wife a servant he thought, only five minutes before, was a boy, or the feasibility of persuading a man that he can make his fortune forever by way of yellow stockings and crossed garters. In a world that is ritually upside down, almost anything can happen. There is a sense in which Sir Toby Belch is the master of these disorderly revels, a man literally intoxicated throughout most of the play, for whom Time in its logical, workaday aspect has simply ceased to exist: "To be up after midnight and to go to bed then, is early; so that to go to bed after midnight is to go to bed betimes" (II.iii.7–9). As a kind of carnival, or temporary, king, Sir Toby rules his sector of Olivia's household according to the rules of holiday inconsequence. His chief enemy, of course, is Malvolio. Olivia's steward is not only dedicated to work, sobriety, and regular hours: he insists that all the world should follow his example, that there should be no cakes and ale, no tang of ginger on the tongue, and no relaxation of discipline in man's progress from cradle to grave. He has no use for folly, whether it is that of Feste the professional, or Fabian's low taste for the sport of bear-baiting, or the nightly songs and carousals of Sir Toby and his companion Aguecheek.

Toby himself is a parasite sponging off a young and wealthy niece. He uses this position to deceive and profit from the ridiculous ambitions of a hanger-on of his own, Sir Andrew Aguecheek. In the final scene he will turn viciously on this supposed friend: "Will you help?—an ass-head and a coxcomb and a knave, a thin-fac'd knave, a gull!" (V.i.206–7). There is nothing lovely, or even honest, about Sir Toby's riotous little court. Yet a theatre audience will always, at least up to the point of Malvolio's incarceration in the dark house in Act IV, support Sir Toby, Sir Andrew, Maria, Feste, and Fabian in their plot against the steward. In the study it is possible to be more soft-hearted. To watch *Twelfth Night* on the stage, however, is to participate and delight in a heightened world temporarily free from Time and normal responsibility. At a party where everyone is joyously drunk, Malvolio is the guest who insists on remaining cold sober, who reads long lectures on temperance to everyone else, and threatens to summon the police. As such, he is our enemy as well as Sir Toby's, not only because he tries to suppress music and revelry which we find entertaining, but because we recognize that, in his view, we ought not to be indulging ourselves by going to the theatre at all. This is why his downfall, in its early stages, is so delicious. Yellow-stockinged and cross-gartered, trying to learn how to smile, Malvolio has become the unconscious victim of precisely that irrational spirit of holiday which he so despises. He has harbored a private folly all along—his conceit, born of self-love and isolation, that Olivia adores him—and when his enemies employ it against him, his behavior becomes at least as mad as theirs.

Madness in Illyria is by no means confined to Sir Toby, his entourage, and the deceived Malvolio. The very first scene of the comedy introduces Orsino, a nobleman committed to a course of wild extravagancy, in the Elizabethan sense of that word. He is bound up within a fiction, a dream of romantic passion, in which the voyage itself is really more important than its specific goal. *Twelfth Night* is not Jonsonian comedy. Whatever some critics may say, the lovelorn Orsino is not a figure of fun. Indeed, the verse he speaks at the beginning of the play is seductively beautiful: intense, metaphoric, and imaginative. Only by the slightest touches—the way his hunting image, for instance, threatens to overbalance into an Actaeon/cuckold joke which the speaker certainly does not intend—does Shakespeare hint at something that Feste, later, will make explicit: the fact that Orsino's love-melancholy is essentially sterile and self-induced, a state of mind dependent upon that very absence and lack of response from Olivia which it affects to lament.

On the whole, Olivia will suffer greater humiliation than Orsino in the course of the comedy, although her lack of self-knowledge is no more acute than his. She is described from the beginning in words that evoke a complex response:

> The element itself, till seven years' heat,
> Shall not behold her face at ample view;
> But like a cloistress she will veiled walk,
> And water once a day her chamber round
> With eye-offending brine; all this to season
> A brother's dead love, which she would keep fresh
> And lasting in her sad remembrance. (I.i.25–31)

The underlying image here is homely, even a little grotesque. Like a housewife who carefully turns a piece of pickled meat once a day in its brine bath, Olivia intends through salt tears to preserve the memory of her dead brother beyond the normal span of grief. There is something forced and abnormal about such mourning, but there is also—as Orsino's reaction makes clear—something noble. Like the King of Navarre and his courtiers in *Love's Labor's Lost*, Olivia is engaged in a war against Time and human forgetfulness. In her case, the struggle takes the form not of a league of study but of resistance to that natural psychological process by which, gradually, we cease to grieve for the dead. The attempt fails, even as the Academe fails. Olivia finds that she "cannot cross the cause why we were born" (*Love's Labor's Lost*, IV.iii.214). At the first sight of Cesario she abandons her veil and, in rapid succession after that, her tears, her rites of memory, her pride, and even her modesty. It is right and proper, in accord with all the laws of comedy, that this should happen, that Sebastian ultimately should fill up the place of the dead brother in Olivia's heart. Seven years is a long time, and youth is very short. The world, as Benedick observed, "must be peopled" (*Much Ado about Nothing*, II.iii.242). Yet Olivia's ignominious collapse, while necessary, is also sad. Man has his glimpses of the ideal, whether of love or of fidelity to the dead. Not even in Illyria, however, can such ideals be sustained.

In the comedies that he wrote before *Twelfth Night*, Shakespeare had created a number of fantasy worlds, places that never were on sea or land, where life has some of the qualities of a dream. He invented Portia's house over the sea at Belmont, with its riddle-game, its music, and its limitless wealth; the forests of *As You Like It*, *The Two Gentlemen of Verona*, and *A Midsummer Night's Dream*; the withdrawn, artificially enclosed park of *Love's Labor's Lost*. Even in *The Comedy of Errors*, *The Taming of the Shrew*, *The Merry Wives of Windsor*, and *Much Ado about Nothing*, there are shadowy traces of this pattern of movement from an ordinary world to a second, somehow magical, environment in which characters are transformed, but which they must leave at the end of the comedy to take up the burden of the everyday. The people who set out from Arden, Navarre, Oberon's wood, Windsor Great Park, or the nightmare house of Petruchio are not quite the same as those who, briefly, have sojourned there. Their experiences in this second, heightened world have altered them, usually for the better. It is clear, however, that their future lies in a harsher, more realistic society, subject to imperfection, death, human limitation, and Time, which we accept as an image of our own.

In the final romances, Shakespeare abandoned this comic pattern. *The Tempest* is the only play which even approximates to it, and it does so in a very peculiar sense indeed. The characters of the last plays are continually travelling, but the places from which they set out, to which they journey, and to which they return are all equally marvellous. There is no distinction in this particular sense between Tharsus, Tyre, and Mytilene in *Pericles*, between Sicily and Bohemia in *The Winter's Tale*, between Cymbeline's court and the forest to which Imogen flees. It is, in fact, the second world entirely that we meet in the last plays: the world of the mythical and the strange. People may be transformed within it, but their transformation no longer depends upon their experience of an extraordinary place where the demands of life as they know it are, for a time, suspended and which they must leave at the end.

In ways that go beyond the implications of its title, *Twelfth Night* is a kind of Janus-faced play, mediating between the early comedies and the last romances. Viola's disguise as Cesario recalls the masculine impersonations of Julia and Rosalind. Yet in her strange passivity, her insistence upon enduring events rather than creating them, she is like Perdita and Miranda, Marina and Imogen. The theme of mistaken identity, that confusion between twins which finally gives Sebastian to Olivia, Viola to Orsino, Shakespeare had exploited years before in *The Comedy of Errors*. Its emotional quality in *Twelfth Night*, however, prefigures the highly charged reunions of *Pericles* and *The Winter's Tale*. With respect to the idea of two comic worlds, one of them heightened, the other an analogue to our own reality, *Twelfth Night* also seems to strike a balance between the practice of early and of late Shakespearean comedy. Viola and Sebastian are shipwrecked into Illyria, even as (metaphorically at least) Hermia, Helena, Demetrius, and Lysander were shipwrecked into the forest by the harsh laws of society, or Bassanio fled the poverty of his condition in Venice in search of the Golden Fleece at Belmont. But the *Twelfth Night* characters remain in Illyria; they do not return. Nor do we gain any sense of what Messaline, the place from which they say they have come, is like. Any contrasts between the heightened and the ordinary must be found within Illyria itself.

Both Viola and Sebastian, the two intruders from the sea, accept Illyria more or less as they find it. They may be momentarily baffled by the topsy-turvy world of the revels: both yield themselves to the current without even trying, as Malvolio tries, to alter its course. Sebastian cheerfully marries a woman he doesn't know, and who may well be mad, simply because she is lovely and lays passionate claim to him. Viola, once committed to her role as Orsino's page, conscientiously does whatever she is told, however painful, without trying to impose her own will upon events. She is careful to keep at arm's length from the love-crazed Olivia, but essentially she plays a waiting game, believing that Time "must untangle this, not I" (II.ii.40). When circumstances provide her with virtual proof that her twin brother is not only alive but the source of considerable confusion and misunderstanding in Illyria, she not only makes no attempt to explain, let alone find him: she sits almost unnaturally still, leaving the wretched Antonio to flounder in an agony of mind, and her own love Orsino to entertain the most murderous suspicions and intents. Hopelessly entangled herself in the rough-and-tumble world of the underplot, deceived by the false challenge of Sir Toby, terrified by the bare prospect of combat with Sir Andrew, her efforts are all to evade action rather than, like Rosalind, to initiate it. Even her boy's disguise operates not as a liberation but merely as a way of going underground in a difficult situation, of waiting to see what Time will bring. This attitude, as it turns out, is the best she could have adopted. By surrendering herself unquestioningly to the madness of Illyria, by remaining aware but passive, she contrives to win Olivia for her brother, redeem Antonio's life, and marry Orsino herself. Time does untangle the knot without her help: she was right to believe, against all chance and probability, that tempests might be kind, and salt waves fresh in love (III.iv.384).

Time, however, is a twofold entity in *Twelfth Night*. Even Viola, for all her faith in Time as a redemptive and beneficent force, can see that it has another face. When she tells Orsino about that supposed sister who never told her love, but sat "like Patience on a monument, / Smiling at grief" (II.iv.114–15), until it was too late, or agrees with him sadly that women are indeed like summer roses which "die, even when they to perfection grow" (II.iv.41), her words are filled with a bitter consciousness that for her too the months are passing and slowly diminishing her beauty and her youth, hidden in a boy's disguise. The chief spokesman in the play for this second, realistic kind of Time is not, however, Viola but Feste. Feste is not only a wise fool, a man in complete intellectual and emotional control of himself, who has chosen the part of professional jester: he operates throughout the comedy as a truth-teller who reminds the other characters that holiday, by its very nature, is not eternal. It is Feste who points out to the revellers that the future is uncertain, laughter momentary, and youth "a stuff will not endure" (II.iii.52). He tells Olivia something she does not want to hear, that "beauty's a flower" (I.v.52), and suggests ominously beneath his seeming lightness that "pleasure will be paid, one time or another" (II.iv.70–71). An isolated figure, with no discernible loyalties, involvements, or private life, he seems to be as much (or as little) at home in Orsino's house as in Olivia's. In both he remains watchful, observant, and essentially detached.

Elizabethans would naturally have expected Feste to be heavily involved in the plot against Malvolio, not only because he had a personal grudge against the steward, but because such behavior was appropriate to a fool. Real-life fools, if they had sufficient wit, were much given to the perpetration of practical jokes, as witness some of the stories told in *A Nest of Ninnies* (1605), that scarifying anthology compiled by Robert Armin, the actor who originally played Feste. Shakespeare, however, keeps Feste apart from the gulling of Malvolio until the Sir Topas scene, just before the end. This, of course, is the scene in which it is first intimated that the spirit of carnival may be about to break. Even Sir Toby can scent the morning air. He begins to worry that they have gone too far by imprisoning Malvolio in the dark house, and wishes that they "were well rid of this knavery" (IV.ii.67–68). In Act V images of death and violence proliferate. Antonio appears bound, anguished, and facing the prospect of execution. His presence summons up the memory of war and destruction, that sea-fight in which Orsino's young nephew had been maimed for life. Maddened by jealousy, Orsino himself threatens to kill Cesario. Sir Toby and Sir Andrew, having narrowly escaped serious injury at the hands of Sebastian, arrive on the scene covered with blood and calling for a surgeon. The party, as it seems, is over. Suddenly sober and disillusioned, Sir Andrew wishes pathetically that he were at home. Two broken revellers, even their friendship destroyed, they vanish from the stage, not to reappear. Maria does not appear either, to give us any indication of how she feels about her marriage-bargain with Sir Toby. As for Malvolio, he intrudes briefly upon the scene of joy at the end, without understanding any of it, and departs as a figure of violence, threatening revenge upon this society in which he is an alien.

At the end of *Twelfth Night*, the two kinds of Time which have coexisted throughout the comedy suddenly diverge. They are used to distinguish a world of fiction from one of fact. For Viola and Orsino, Olivia and Sebastian, there will be no awakening from the dream, no need to leave a heightened realm. The clock by which they live is that of fairy-tale: beneficent, unhurried, and admittedly unreal. Shakespeare goes out of his way to stress the formal, distanced quality of their story at its conclusion. This is why Sebastian and Viola, twins parted for only three months, put one another through a question-and-answer test of the most artificial kind, why Viola (unlike Rosalind) does not return to her girl's clothes. Orsino simply accepts a woman he has never, in fact, seen. Olivia accepts as husband a stranger she has mistaken for someone else. These resolutions and accords are powerful and emotionally charged, but they are also deliberately playlike and literary, not to be confused with the way of the world as we know it to be. Olivia and Sebastian, Viola and Orsino confront us at the end less as representatives of a new society than as people who, by the special dispensation of Comedy, have been allowed to escape from death and time.

There is a disturbingly large number of important absentees in the ending of *Twelfth Night*, more than in any other Shakespearean comedy. Sir Andrew, Sir Toby, Maria, and Malvolio do not participate in this happy ending. Antonio is present, but seems to have no part to play. Feste is absent too during the revelations and explanations, but he seems (characteristically) to understand and accept what has happened when he reappears to end the comedy. We in the theatre audience have also to face expulsion from Illyria, along with Sir Andrew and Sir Toby, Maria and the steward. Our revels, too, have ended. It is the task of Feste in his final song to tell us this, and to build a bridge from that remote, enchanted place where the two romantic couples remain forever to the very different world outside the theatre which is our own. Like Jaques' summary of the seven ages of life from cradle to grave, Feste's account of man's inexorable progress from a child's holiday realm of irresponsibility and joy into age, vice, disillusionment, and death draws upon an old, didactic tradition. Its basic pessimism is informed and sweetened, however, not only by the music to which it is set, but by the tolerance and acceptance of Feste himself. Precisely because of his anonymity and aloofness in the play now ended, he can be trusted to speak for all mankind, and not simply for himself. There is nothing that can be done about those harsh facts of existence to which Feste points, any more than about the wind and the rain. They must simply be endured. Like childhood happiness, all comedies come to an end. The great and consoling difference lies in the fact that one can, after all, as Feste points out, return to the theatre: and there, "we'll strive to please you every day."

Anne Barton

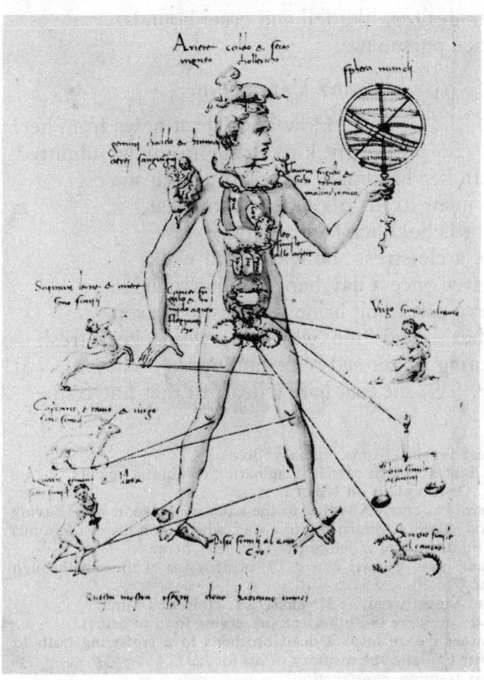

Man and the zodiac. From *Grilandus Inventum Libri IV*, MS Harvard College Library, 1506–8. Sir Toby, in answer to Sir Andrew's proposal for "some revels," says, "What shall we do else? were we not born under Taurus?" Sir Andrew asks: "Taurus? That's sides and heart." And Sir Toby rejoins: "No, sir, it is legs and thighs. Let me see thee caper" (*Twelfth Night*, I.iii.137–41). Shakespeare's reference is to the commonly held belief (by no means dead today) that individual parts of man's body were under the particular influence of one or another of the twelve signs of the zodiac. In the drawing here reproduced, which details the scheme, the relation of man (microcosm) to the universe (macrocosm) is emphasized by the "sphaera mundi" that the youth holds in his left hand.

Both Sir Toby and Sir Andrew are wrong according to the standard manuals (Taurus governing neck and throat, and Leo, sides and heart), but a minority view agreed with Sir Toby. Obviously Shakespeare is out for fun, not "science," and Sir Toby's choice of Taurus, instead of Sagittarius or Aquarius, probably is intended to carry a bawdy allusion as applied to legs and thighs. Nor does Shakespeare miss the opportunity for a play on "caper" and "Capricorn," the goat, which, as the picture indicates, governs the knees. (*By permission of the Harvard College Library*)

Twelfth Night, or What You Will

[Dramatis Personae

Orsino, *Duke of Illyria*
Sebastian, *brother to Viola*
Antonio, *a sea captain, friend to Sebastian*
Sea Captain, *friend to Viola*
Valentine } *gentlemen attending on the Duke*
Curio
Sir Toby Belch, *uncle to Olivia*
Sir Andrew Aguecheek
Malvolio, *steward to Olivia*

Fabian } *servants to Olivia*
Feste, *a clown*

Olivia, *a rich countess*
Viola, *sister to Sebastian*
Maria, *Olivia's gentlewoman*

Lords, Priests, Sailors, Officers, Musicians, Gentlewoman, Servant, *and other* Attendants

Scene: *A city in Illyria, and the sea-coast near it*]

ACT I, Scene I

Enter Orsino, *Duke of Illyria*, Curio, *and other* Lords; [Musicians *attending*].

Duke. If music be the food of love, play on,
Give me excess of it; that surfeiting,
The appetite may sicken, and so die.
That strain again, it had a dying fall;
O, it came o'er my ear like the sweet sound
That breathes upon a bank of violets,
Stealing and giving odor. Enough, no more,
'Tis not so sweet now as it was before.
O spirit of love, how quick and fresh art thou,
That notwithstanding thy capacity
Receiveth as the sea, nought enters there,
Of what validity and pitch soe'er,
But falls into abatement and low price
Even in a minute. So full of shapes is fancy
That it alone is high fantastical.

Cur. Will you go hunt, my lord?

Duke. What, Curio?

Cur. The hart.

Duke. Why, so I do, the noblest that I have.
O, when mine eyes did see Olivia first,
Methought she purg'd the air of pestilence!
That instant was I turn'd into a hart,
And my desires, like fell and cruel hounds,
E'er since pursue me.

Enter Valentine.

How now, what news from her?

Val. So please my lord, I might not be admitted,
But from her handmaid do return this answer:
The element itself, till seven years' heat,
Shall not behold her face at ample view;
But like a cloistress she will veiled walk,
And water once a day her chamber round
With eye-offending brine; all this to season
A brother's dead love, which she would keep fresh
And lasting in her sad remembrance.

Duke. O, she that hath a heart of that fine frame

Words and passages enclosed in square brackets in the text above are either emendations of the copy-text or additions to it. The Textual Notes immediately following the play cite the earliest authority for every such change or insertion and supply the reading of the copy-text wherever it is emended in this edition.

I.i. Location: The Duke's palace.
o.s.d. Illyria: a country extending along the east coast of the Adriatic, in large part approximating modern Jugoslavia.
1. music . . . love. Cf. *Antony and Cleopatra*, II.v. 1–2, "music, moody food / Of us that trade in love." The whole speech is concerned, using a figure of nausea (surfeiting), with the insatiable, but paradoxically quickly sated, quality of love as Orsino here sees it—a kind of glutton that devours dainties only to vomit them up. In a real sense, the play is about a rectification of this view of love.
3. appetite: i.e. love's appetite for music.
4. fall: cadence.
9. quick: lively, vigorous. **fresh:** keen.
10. capacity: power to take in.
12. validity: value. **pitch:** high worth (a term from falconry, designating the highest point of a hawk's flight; or perhaps *validity and pitch* is better taken as a hendiadys, meaning "high valuation."
13. abatement: depreciation. **price:** esteem.
14. shapes: fanciful forms. **fancy:** love.
15. it . . . fantastical: it carries imagination to unique heights.
16. hart. Orsino plays on *heart.*
20–22. turn'd . . . me. Alluding to the story of Actaeon who, having seen Diana naked, was turned into a stag, whereupon his own hounds hunted him down and killed him. **21. fell:** fierce.
25. element: sky. **heat:** course (?) or progress of the sun through the zodiac (?).
26. ample: unrestricted. **27. cloistress:** cloistered nun.
29. season: preserve (with play on preserving food in brine).
30. A brother's dead love: a dead brother's love (referring both to her love for him and the memory of his for her).
32. frame: framing, construction.

To pay this debt of love but to a brother,
How will she love when the rich golden shaft
Hath kill'd the flock of all affections else
That live in her; when liver, brain, and heart,
These sovereign thrones, are all supplied and fill'd
Her sweet perfections with one self king!
Away before me to sweet beds of flow'rs,
Love-thoughts lie rich when canopied with bow'rs.

Exeunt.

Scene II

Enter Viola, *a* Captain, *and* Sailors.

Vio. What country, friends, is this?
Cap. This is Illyria, lady.
Vio. And what should I do in Illyria?
My brother he is in Elysium.
Perchance he is not drown'd—what think you, sailors?
Cap. It is perchance that you yourself were saved.
Vio. O my poor brother! and so perchance may he be.
Cap. True, madam, and to comfort you with chance,
Assure yourself, after our ship did split,
When you, and those poor number saved with you,
Hung on our driving boat, I saw your brother,
Most provident in peril, bind himself
(Courage and hope both teaching him the practice)
To a strong mast that liv'd upon the sea;
Where like [Arion] on the dolphin's back,
I saw him hold acquaintance with the waves
So long as I could see.
Vio. For saying so, there's gold.
Mine own escape unfoldeth to my hope,
Whereto thy speech serves for authority,
The like of him. Know'st thou this country?
Cap. Ay, madam, well, for I was bred and born
Not three hours' travel from this very place.
Vio. Who governs here?
Cap. A noble duke, in nature as in name.
Vio. What is his name?
Cap. Orsino.
Vio. Orsino! I have heard my father name him.
He was a bachelor then.

34. golden shaft: Cupid's gold-tipped arrow, which caused love. He had also a lead-tipped arrow, which produced loathing.
35. affections else: other emotions (than love) (?) or other loves (?).
36. liver . . . heart. The supposed seats of the passions (and especially love), thought or judgment, and the feelings or sentiments respectively.
37. supplied. Synonymous with *fill'd*.
37–38. and . . . perfections: and her sweet perfections filled.
38. one self king: one and the same lord, the person whom she loves wholly.

I.ii. Location: The sea-coast.
4. Elysium: i.e. heaven. The classical name is used to play on *Illyria*.
5–6. Perchance . . . perchance: perhaps . . . by mere chance.
8. chance: i.e. a favorable possibility. **11. driving**: drifting.
12. Most provident: showing great foresight.
14. liv'd: i.e. remained afloat.
15. Arion . . . back. Arion, a Greek poet and musician, on a voyage from Sicily to Greece charmed dolphins with his singing and playing on the lyre. When he leaped overboard to escape murder by the sailors, he was saved by a dolphin on whose back he rode to shore.
19. unfoldeth: discloses.
21. like of him: i.e. chance that he escaped likewise.

Cap. And so is now, or was so very late;
For but a month ago I went from hence,
And then 'twas fresh in murmur (as you know
What great ones do, the less will prattle of)
That he did seek the love of fair Olivia.
Vio. What's she?
Cap. A virtuous maid, the daughter of a count
That died some twelvemonth since, then leaving her
In the protection of his son, her brother,
Who shortly also died; for whose dear love,
They say, she hath abjur'd the [company]
And [sight] of men.
Vio. O that I serv'd that lady,
And might not be delivered to the world
Till I had made mine own occasion mellow
What my estate is!
Cap. That were hard to compass,
Because she will admit no kind of suit,
No, not the Duke's.
Vio. There is a fair behavior in thee, captain,
And though that nature with a beauteous wall
Doth oft close in pollution, yet of thee
I will believe thou hast a mind that suits
With this thy fair and outward character.
I prithee (and I'll pay thee bounteously)
Conceal me what I am, and be my aid
For such disguise as haply shall become
The form of my intent. I'll serve this duke;
Thou shalt present me as an eunuch to him,
It may be worth thy pains; for I can sing
And speak to him in many sorts of music
That will allow me very worth his service.
What else may hap, to time I will commit,
Only shape thou thy silence to my wit.
Cap. Be you his eunuch, and your mute I'll be;
When my tongue blabs, then let mine eyes not see.
Vio. I thank thee. Lead me on. *Exeunt.*

Scene III

Enter Sir Toby [Belch] *and* Maria.

Sir To. What a plague means my niece to take the death of her brother thus? I am sure care's an enemy to life.

Mar. By my troth, Sir Toby, you must come in earlier a' nights. Your cousin, my lady, takes great exceptions to your ill hours.

32. murmur: rumor.
42–44. might . . . is: that my position in life (*estate*) might not be revealed to the world until the moment is ripe for me.
44. compass: achieve. **46. not**: not even.
47. behavior: appearance and conduct, the "outward character" of line 51. **54. become**: be suitable to.
55. form . . . intent: nature of my purpose (with *form* in the sense of "shape" looking back to *disguise*, line 54).
56. as an eunuch: i.e. as a *castrato* or male soprano singer; thus her high voice will not be incongruous with her male disguise. Actually, Viola becomes his page.
59. allow . . . service: cause me to be acknowledged as worthy to serve him. **61. shape**: fashion. **wit**: plan, device.
62. mute: i.e. silent servant (suggested by *eunuch*, both being servants in the Turkish court).

I.iii. Location: Olivia's house.
5. a': of. **cousin**: kinswoman.

Sir To. Why, let her except before excepted.

Mar. Ay, but you must confine yourself within the modest limits of order.

Sir To. Confine? I'll confine myself no finer than I am. These clothes are good enough to drink in, and so be these boots too; and they be not, let them hang themselves in their own straps.

Mar. That quaffing and drinking will undo you. I heard my lady talk of it yesterday; and of a foolish knight that you brought in one night here to be her wooer.

Sir To. Who, Sir Andrew Aguecheek?

Mar. Ay, he.

Sir To. He's as tall a man as any's in Illyria.

Mar. What's that to th' purpose?

Sir To. Why, he has three thousand ducats a year.

Mar. Ay, but he'll have but a year in all these ducats. He's a very fool and a prodigal.

Sir To. Fie, that you'll say so! He plays o' th' viol-de-gamboys, and speaks three or four languages word for word without book, and hath all the good gifts of nature.

Mar. He hath indeed, almost natural; for besides that he's a fool, he's a great quarreller; and but that he hath the gift of a coward to allay the gust he hath in quarrelling, 'tis thought among the prudent he would quickly have the gift of a grave.

Sir To. By this hand, they are scoundrels and substractors that say so of him. Who are they?

Mar. They that add moreov'r, he's drunk nightly in your company.

Sir To. With drinking healths to my niece. I'll drink to her as long as there is a passage in my throat, and drink in Illyria. He's a coward and a coystrill that will not drink to my niece till his brains turn o' th' toe like a parish-top. What, wench! *Castiliano vulgo!* for here comes Sir Andrew Agueface.

Enter Sir Andrew [Aguecheek].

Sir And. Sir Toby Belch! How now, Sir Toby Belch?

Sir To. Sweet Sir Andrew!

Sir And. Bless you, fair shrew.

Mar. And you too, sir.

Sir To. Accost, Sir Andrew, accost.

Sir And. What's that?

Sir To. My niece's chambermaid.

[*Sir And.*] Good Mistress Accost, I desire better acquaintance.

Mar. My name is Mary, sir.

Sir And. Good Mistress Mary Accost—

Sir To. You mistake, knight. "Accost" is front her, board her, woo her, assail her.

Sir And. By my troth, I would not undertake her in this company. Is that the meaning of "accost"?

Mar. Fare you well, gentlemen.

Sir To. And thou let part so, Sir Andrew, would thou mightst never draw sword again.

Sir And. And you part so, mistress, I would I might never draw sword again. Fair lady, do you think you have fools in hand?

Mar. Sir, I have not you by th' hand.

Sir And. Marry, but you shall have—and here's my hand.

Mar. Now, sir, thought is free. I pray you bring your hand to th' butt'ry-bar, and let it drink.

Sir And. Wherefore, sweetheart? What's your metaphor?

Mar. It's dry, sir.

Sir And. Why, I think so. I am not such an ass but I can keep my hand dry. But what's your jest?

Mar. A dry jest, sir.

Sir And. Are you full of them?

Mar. Ay, sir, I have them at my fingers' ends. Marry, now I let go your hand, I am barren.

Exit Maria.

Sir To. O knight, thou lack'st a cup of canary. When did I see thee so put down?

Sir And. Never in your life I think, unless you see canary put me down. Methinks sometimes I have no more wit than a Christian or an ordinary man has; but I am a great eater of beef, and I believe that does harm to my wit.

Sir To. No question.

7. **except before excepted.** A quibble on the legal phrase *exceptis excipiendis* = with the exceptions aforesaid. Sir Toby apparently means that Olivia's objections are an old story and that she is welcome to go on making them.
9. **modest:** moderate. **order:** orderly conduct.
10. **confine.** Quibbling on the sense "dress." 12. **and:** if.
14. **undo you:** be the ruin of you.
18. **Aguecheek.** Suggestive of a thin, pale face, like that of a man with ague. 20. **tall:** valiant, stalwart.
23–24. **he'll . . . ducats:** i.e. he'll run though his estate in a year (at the rate he's going). 24. **very:** true, utter.
26. **viol-de-gamboys:** *viola da gamba* ("leg-viol"), the bass of the viol family. 27. **without book:** by memory.
29. **almost natural:** almost like a "natural" or halfwit.
31. **gust:** relish, gusto. 34–35. **substractors:** i.e. detractors.
40. **coystrill:** knave.
42. **parish-top.** Parishes kept large tops for the amusement and exercise of their people in winter; they were made to spin by means of whips.
42–43. **Castiliano vulgo.** Meaning uncertain; perhaps Maria is urged to act with the proverbial gravity and decorum of the Castilians to impress Sir Andrew.
43. **Agueface.** Perhaps a slip on Shakespeare's part which was later received into the text as an intentional jest.

49. **Accost:** address (her). Sir Toby's gloss (lines 56–57) includes the several suggestive connotations of the word.
51. **chambermaid:** lady in waiting. In a household like Olivia's such a term does not imply low social position. Maria is clearly a gentlewoman.
57. **board:** approach closely (as in boarding a ship in naval warfare). **assail:** i.e. attack with offers of love. Both *board* and *assail* illustrate the common practice of applying the language of war to amorous activity.
58. **undertake:** have to do (a word frequently used in a bawdy sense).
61. **And . . . so:** i.e. if you let her go thus.
65. **have . . . hand:** are dealing with fools.
67. **Marry:** indeed (a weakened oath," by the Virgin Mary"). **you shall have.** An unfortunate choice of words.
69. **thought is free:** i.e. I may think what I like (proverbial); an unreassuring answer to his question in lines 64–65.
70. **butt'ry-bar:** entrance to the buttery, the room where butts of ale and wine were stored and from which drinks were dispensed.
73. **dry:** (1) thirsty; (2) lacking in moisture (a dry hand was associated with age and impotence).
74–75. **I . . . dry.** Alluding to a proverb to the effect that even a fool knows enough to come in out of the rain.
76. **dry jest:** (1) ironic joke; (2) barren old laughingstock.
78. **at . . . ends:** (1) in readiness; (2) held by my hand.
79. **barren:** i.e. destitute of dry jests.
80. **canary:** a sweet wine from the Canary Islands.
81. **put down:** confounded, overcome.
83. **put me down:** make me drunk.
85–86. **I . . . wit.** This reflects a current belief.

Sir And. And I thought that, I'd forswear it. I'll ride home to-morrow, Sir Toby.

Sir To. *Pourquoi*, my dear knight?

Sir And. What is "*pourquoi*"? Do, or not do? I would I had bestow'd that time in the tongues that I have in fencing, dancing, and bear-baiting. O had I but follow'd the arts!

Sir To. Then hadst thou had an excellent head of hair.

Sir And. Why, would that have mended my hair?

Sir To. Past question, for thou seest it will not [curl by] nature.

Sir And. But it becomes [me] well enough, does't not?

Sir To. Excellent, it hangs like flax on a distaff; and I hope to see a huswife take thee between her legs, and spin it off.

Sir And. Faith, I'll home to-morrow, Sir Toby. Your niece will not be seen, or if she be, it's four to one she'll none of me. The Count himself here hard by woos her.

Sir To. She'll none o' th' Count. She'll not match above her degree, neither in estate, years, nor wit; I have heard her swear't. Tut, there's life in't, man.

Sir And. I'll stay a month longer. I am a fellow o' th' strangest mind i' th' world; I delight in masques and revels sometimes altogether.

Sir To. Art thou good at these kickshawses, knight?

Sir And. As any man in Illyria, whatsoever he be, under the degree of my betters, and yet I will not compare with an old man.

Sir To. What is thy excellence in a galliard, knight?

Sir And. Faith, I can cut a caper.

Sir To. And I can cut the mutton to't.

Sir And. And I think I have the back-trick simply as strong as any man in Illyria.

Sir To. Wherefore are these things hid? Wherefore have these gifts a curtain before 'em? Are they like to take dust, like Mistress Mall's picture? Why dost thou not go to church in a galliard, and come home in a coranto? My very walk should be a jig. I would not so much as make water but in a sink-a-pace. What dost thou mean? Is it a world to hide virtues in? I did think by the excellent constitution of thy leg, it was form'd under the star of a galliard.

Sir And. Ay, 'tis strong; and it does indifferent well in a [dun-]color'd stock. Shall we [set] about some revels?

Sir To. What shall we do else? were we not born under Taurus?

Sir And. Taurus? That['s] sides and heart.

Sir To. No, sir, it is legs and thighs. Let me see thee caper. Ha, higher! Ha, ha, excellent! *Exeunt.*

Scene IV

Enter Valentine, *and* Viola *in man's attire.*

Val. If the Duke continue these favors towards you, Cesario, you are like to be much advanc'd; he hath known you but three days, and already you are no stranger.

Vio. You either fear his humor or my negligence, that you call in question the continuance of his love. Is he inconstant, sir, in his favors?

Val. No, believe me.

Enter Duke, Curio, *and* Attendants.

Vio. I thank you. Here comes the Count.

Duke. Who saw Cesario, ho?

Vio. On your attendance, my lord, here.

Duke. Stand you awhile aloof. Cesario,
Thou know'st no less but all. I have unclasp'd
To thee the book even of my secret soul.
Therefore, good youth, address thy gait unto her,
Be not denied access, stand at her doors,
And tell them, there thy fixed foot shall grow
Till thou have audience.

Vio. Sure, my noble lord,
If she be so abandon'd to her sorrow
As it is spoke, she never will admit me.

Duke. Be clamorous, and leap all civil bounds,
Rather than make unprofited return.

Vio. Say I do speak with her, my lord, what then?

Duke. O then, unfold the passion of my love,

88. **forswear**: swear off. 90. **Pourquoi**: why.
92. **bestow'd**: employed. **tongues**: languages.
94. **follow'd the arts**: applied myself to learning.
97. **mended**: improved.
98–99. **it . . . nature.** Sir Toby's jest takes advantage of the phonetic similarity of *tongues* and *tongs* (= curling-tongs) and of a second meaning of *arts*, "artificial methods."
102. **distaff**: three-foot cleft staff used in spinning wool or flax.
103–4. **huswife . . . off.** With second meaning involving *huswife* (housewife) in the sense "hussy, whore" and a reference to loss of hair from venereal disease.
107. **hard by**: near by.
110. **above her degree**: with her superior. **estate**: social position.
115. **kickshawses**: elegant trifles (the singular *kickshaws* is an anglicization of French *quelque chose*).
118. **under . . . betters**: except for those that excel me.
119. **old man**: experienced man, expert (?).
120. **galliard**: a lively dance in triple time.
121. **cut a caper**: execute a leap. Sir Toby's reply quibbles on *caper* as a condiment often served with mutton.
123. **back-trick**: steps taken backwards in the galliard.
127. **like**: likely. **take**: gather. **Mistress Mall's picture.** A topical allusion has been suspected, but the reference is probably general (*Mall* = Moll). Pictures were often protected from fading by curtains; see I.v.233.
129. **coranto**: a quick running dance. **should**: would.

130–31. **sink-a-pace**: cinquepace (French *cinque-pas*), a dance resembling the galliard.
132. **virtues**: talents, accomplishments. There is probably an allusion here to Jesus' parable of the talents (Matthew 25:14–30).
133. **star . . . galliard**: i.e. a star favorable to dancing. Cf. Beatrice's "There was a star danc'd, and under that was I born" (*Much Ado*, II.i.335). 134. **indifferent**: moderately. 135. **stock**: stocking.
138. **Taurus**: the zodiacal sign that according to a few authorities controls "legs and thighs" (line 140), but neck and throat according to the majority. See the illustration on p. 407 for the signs commonly associated with the legs.
139. **sides and heart.** Sir Andrew errs as usual; the sign for this region is Leo.

I.iv. **Location**: The Duke's palace.
5. **his humor . . . negligence**: change of mood on his part or neglect of duty on mine.
11. **On your attendance**: waiting to attend upon you.
12. **you.** Addressed to all except Viola-Cesario.
15. **address thy gait**: go.
18. **audience**: a hearing (of the Duke's love-suit).
21. **civil bounds**: i.e. bounds of good manners.
22. **unprofited**: profitless.

Surprise her with discourse of my dear faith;
It shall become thee well to act my woes:
She will attend it better in thy youth
Than in a nuntio's of more grave aspect.

Vio. I think not so, my lord.

Duke. Dear lad, believe it;
For they shall yet belie thy happy years,
That say thou art a man. Diana's lip
Is not more smooth and rubious; thy small pipe
Is as the maiden's organ, shrill and sound,
And all is semblative a woman's part.
I know thy constellation is right apt
For this affair. Some four or five attend him—
All, if you will; for I myself am best
When least in company. Prosper well in this,
And thou shalt live as freely as thy lord,
To call his fortunes thine.

Vio. I'll do my best
To woo your lady. [*Aside.*] Yet a barful strife!
Whoe'er I woo, myself would be his wife. *Exeunt.*

Scene V

Enter Maria *and* Clown [Feste].

Mar. Nay, either tell me where thou hast been, or I will not open my lips so wide as a bristle may enter, in way of thy excuse. My lady will hang thee for thy absence.

Clo. Let her hang me! He that is well hang'd in this world needs to fear no colors.

Mar. Make that good.

Clo. He shall see none to fear.

Mar. A good lenten answer. I can tell thee where that saying was born, of "I fear no colors."

Clo. Where, good Mistress Mary?

Mar. In the wars, and that may you be bold to say in your foolery.

Clo. Well, God give them wisdom that have it; and those that are fools, let them use their talents.

Mar. Yet you will be hang'd for being so long absent, or to be turn'd away—is not that as good as a hanging to you?

Clo. Many a good hanging prevents a bad marriage; and for turning away, let summer bear it out.

Mar. You are resolute then?

Clo. Not so, neither, but I am resolv'd on two points—

Mar. That if one break, the other will hold; or if both break, your gaskins fall.

Clo. Apt, in good faith, very apt. Well, go thy way, if Sir Toby would leave drinking, thou wert as witty a piece of Eve's flesh as any in Illyria.

Mar. Peace, you rogue, no more o' that. Here comes my lady. Make your excuse wisely, you were best. [*Exit.*]

Enter Lady Olivia *with* Malvolio [*and* Attendants].

Clo. Wit, and't be thy will, put me into good fooling! Those wits that think they have thee do very oft prove fools; and I that am sure I lack thee, may pass for a wise man. For what says Quinapalus? "Better a witty fool than a foolish wit."—God bless thee, lady!

Oli. Take the fool away.

Clo. Do you not hear, fellows? Take away the lady.

Oli. Go to, y' are a dry fool; I'll no more of you. Besides, you grow dishonest.

Clo. Two faults, madonna, that drink and good counsel will amend; for give the dry fool drink, then is the fool not dry; bid the dishonest man mend himself: if he mend, he is no longer dishonest; if he cannot, let the botcher mend him. Any thing that's mended is but patch'd; virtue that transgresses is but patch'd with sin, and sin that amends is but patch'd with virtue. If that this simple syllogism will serve, so; if it will not, what remedy? As there is no true cuckold but calamity, so beauty's a flower. The lady bade take away the fool, therefore I say again, take her away.

Oli. Sir, I bade them take away you.

Clo. Misprision in the highest degree! Lady, "*Cucullus non facit monachum*": that's as much to say as I wear not motley in my brain. Good madonna, give me leave to prove you a fool.

Oli. Can you do it?

Clo. Dexteriously, good madonna.

Oli. Make your proof.

Clo. I must catechize you for it, madonna. Good my mouse of virtue, answer me.

25. **Surprise:** overpower. **dear:** loving, heartfelt.
27. **attend:** heed, give ear to. 28. **nuntio's:** messenger's.
30. **yet:** as yet. 32. **rubious:** ruby-red. **pipe:** throat.
33. **shrill and sound:** high and clear (uncracked).
34. **semblative:** resembling. **part:** role (cf. *act*, line 26).
35. **constellation:** i.e. nature (as determined by position of the stars at one's birth). 39. **freely:** generously.
41. **barful strife:** i.e. an endeavor to which there is (for me) a serious impediment.

I.v. Location: Olivia's house.
o.s.d. **Feste.** This name is known only from II.iv.11.
6. **fear no colors.** Proverbial for "fear nothing" (*colors* = worldly deceptions). Feste puns on *collars* = hangman's nooses.
9. **lenten:** meagre (in wit).
12. **In the wars.** Maria quibbles on *colors* in the sense "military standards."
15. **talents:** (1) natural abilities; (2) talons (with a pun on *fools* / *fowls*). 17. **turn'd away.** With a play on *turned off* = hanged.
20. **for:** as for. **let . . . out:** let the fact that summer is coming make it endurable.
23. **points.** Maria's rejoinder quibbles on the sense "laces supporting the breeches or hose." 25. **gaskins:** breeches.
26–27: **go thy way:** run along.
27–28. **thou . . . Illyria:** i.e. you'd make him a good match.
32. **and't:** if it. 32–33. **good fooling:** good form for jesting.
33. **thee:** i.e. wit. 35. **Quinapalus.** Feste's invention.
41. **Go to:** a conventional phrase of reproof. **dry:** dull, stale.
42. **dishonest:** wanton, wicked.
43. **madonna:** my lady (Italian *mia donna*). 45. **mend:** reform.
46–47. **let . . . him:** let him be mended by someone who can do the job (*botcher* = one who mends shoes or clothes, a cobbler or a tailor).
48–49. **virtue . . . virtue.** Feste warns that he, like all men, will be imperfect after he reforms, as he was before. *Patch'd* plays on Feste's motley, the conventional parti-colored dress for jesters.
50. **so:** well and good.
51. **what remedy:** i.e. there's nothing more I can say or do.
51–52. **As . . . flower.** A difficult passage. Dover Wilson explains: "Olivia has wedded calamity by taking her vow, and has proved herself a fool, since women are proverbially unfaithful to their weeds and beauty fades like the flower."
55. **Misprision:** mistaking one thing for another.
56. **Cucullus . . . monachum:** the cowl does not make the monk.
60. **Dexteriously:** dexterously (a true variant, not Feste's coinage).
62–63. **Good . . . virtue:** my good virtuous mouse. The transposition in *Good my* is common in forms of address (e.g. *good my lord*).

Oli. Well, sir, for want of other idleness, I'll bide your proof.

Clo. Good madonna, why mourn'st thou?

Oli. Good fool, for my brother's death.

Clo. I think his soul is in hell, madonna.

Oli. I know his soul is in heaven, fool.

Clo. The more fool, madonna, to mourn for your brother's soul, being in heaven. Take away the fool, gentlemen.

Oli. What think you of this fool, Malvolio? doth he not mend?

Mal. Yes, and shall do till the pangs of death shake him. Infirmity, that decays the wise, doth ever make the better fool.

Clo. God send you, sir, a speedy infirmity, for the better increasing your folly! Sir Toby will be sworn that I am no fox, but he will not pass his word for twopence that you are no fool.

Oli. How say you to that, Malvolio?

Mal. I marvel your ladyship takes delight in such a barren rascal. I saw him put down the other day with an ordinary fool that has no more brain than a stone. Look you now, he's out of his guard already. Unless you laugh and minister occasion to him, he is gagg'd. I protest I take these wise men that crow so at these set kind of fools no better than the fools' zanies.

Oli. O, you are sick of self-love, Malvolio, and taste with a distemper'd appetite. To be generous, guiltless, and of free disposition, is to take those things for bird-bolts that you deem cannon-bullets. There is no slander in an allow'd fool, though he do nothing but rail; nor no railing in a known discreet man, though he do nothing but reprove.

Clo. Now Mercury indue thee with leasing, for thou speak'st well of fools!

Enter Maria.

Mar. Madam, there is at the gate a young gentleman much desires to speak with you.

Oli. From the Count Orsino, is it?

Mar. I know not, madam. 'Tis a fair young man, and well attended.

Oli. Who of my people hold him in delay?

Mar. Sir Toby, madam, your kinsman.

Oli. Fetch him off, I pray you, he speaks nothing but madman; fie on him! [*Exit Maria.*] Go you, Malvolio; if it be a suit from the Count, I am sick, or

64. other idleness: any other way of wasting time.
71. being: when it is.
74. mend: equivalent to "become a better fool"; Olivia uses it in the sense "become a more amusing fool," Malvolio in the sense "become more and more foolish."
80. fox: crafty fellow. **pass:** pledge. **84. with:** by.
86. out . . . guard: without a witty riposte (a figure from fencing).
87. minister occasion: give opportunity, provide openings.
88. protest: declare, avow.
89. set kind: artificial sort. **fools' zanies:** fools' fools. A zany (a character in the *commedia dell'arte*) was a clown's attendant who aped his master on stage.
90. of: with. **self-love.** The key to Malvolio's character.
91. distemper'd: unhealthy. **92. free:** open.
93. bird-bolts: blunt-headed arrows for shooting birds. The passage has reference to the proverb "A fool's bolt is soon shot."
94. allow'd: given license to speak his mind.
95. known discreet: of recognized judgment.
97. Mercury: god of guile and trickery. **leasing:** lying.
107. madman: i.e. mad talk.

not at home—what you will, to dismiss it. (*Exit Malvolio.*) Now you see, sir, how your fooling grows old, and people dislike it.

Clo. Thou hast spoke for us, madonna, as if thy eldest son should be a fool; whose skull Jove cram with brains! for—here he comes—

Enter Sir Toby.

one of thy kin has a most weak *pia mater*.

Oli. By mine honor, half drunk. What is he at the gate, cousin?

Sir To. A gentleman.

Oli. A gentleman? What gentleman?

Sir To. 'Tis a gentleman here—a plague o' these pickle-herring! How now, sot?

Clo. Good Sir Toby!

Oli. Cousin, cousin, how have you come so early by this lethargy?

Sir To. Lechery! I defy lechery. There's one at the gate.

Oli. Ay, marry, what is he?

Sir To. Let him be the devil and he will, I care not; give me faith say I. Well, it's all one. *Exit.*

Oli. What's a drunken man like, fool?

Clo. Like a drown'd man, a fool, and a madman. One draught above heat makes him a fool, the second mads him, and a third drowns him.

Oli. Go thou and seek the crowner, and let him sit o' my coz; for he's in the third degree of drink, he's drown'd. Go look after him.

Clo. He is but mad yet, madonna, and the fool shall look to the madman. [*Exit.*]

Enter Malvolio.

Mal. Madam, yond young fellow swears he will speak with you. I told him you were sick; he takes on him to understand so much, and therefore comes to speak with you. I told him you were asleep; he seems to have a foreknowledge of that too, and therefore comes to speak with you. What is to be said to him, lady? he's fortified against any denial.

Oli. Tell him he shall not speak with me.

Mal. H'as been told so; and he says he'll stand at your door like a sheriff's post, and be the supporter to a bench, but he'll speak with you.

Oli. What kind o' man is he?

Mal. Why, of mankind.

Oli. What manner of man?

Mal. Of very ill manner: he'll speak with you, will you or no.

Oli. Of what personage and years is he?

111. old: i.e. stale (cf. line 41).
115. pia mater: brain (properly, the membrane enveloping the brain).
116. What: what sort of man.
120–21. a plague . . . pickle-herring. Sir Toby thus excuses a belch.
121. sot: fool. **124. lethargy:** stupor.
129. give me faith. As protection in confrontation with the devil. **it's all one:** no matter.
132. above heat: i.e. above the point of feeling a pleasant warmth.
134. crowner: coroner.
134–35. sit . . . coz: i.e. hold an inquest on my kinsman.
141. therefore: for that very reason. **147. H'as:** he has.
148. sheriff's post: a decorative post set up outside the sheriff's office.
151. of mankind: of the human race, i.e. just an ordinary man.
155. personage: physical appearance.

Mal. Not yet old enough for a man, nor young enough for a boy; as a squash is before 'tis a peascod, or a codling when 'tis almost an apple. 'Tis with him in standing water, between boy and man. He is very well-favor'd, and he speaks very shrewishly. One would think his mother's milk were scarce out of him.

Oli. Let him approach. Call in my gentlewoman.

Mal. Gentlewoman, my lady calls. *Exit.*

Enter Maria.

Oli. Give me my veil; come throw it o'er my face.
We'll once more hear Orsino's embassy.

Enter [Viola].

Vio. The honorable lady of the house, which is she?

Oli. Speak to me, I shall answer for her. Your will?

Vio. Most radiant, exquisite, and unmatchable beauty—I pray you tell me if this be the lady of the house, for I never saw her. I would be loath to cast away my speech; for besides that it is excellently well penn'd, I have taken great pains to con it. Good beauties, let me sustain no scorn; I am very comptible, even to the least sinister usage.

Oli. Whence came you, sir?

Vio. I can say little more than I have studied, and that question's out of my part. Good gentle one, give me modest assurance if you be the lady of the house, that I may proceed in my speech.

Oli. Are you a comedian?

Vio. No, my profound heart; and yet (by the very fangs of malice I swear) I am not that I play. Are you the lady of the house?

Oli. If I do not usurp myself, I am.

Vio. Most certain, if you are she, you do usurp yourself; for what is yours to bestow is not yours to reserve. But this is from my commission; I will on with my speech in your praise, and then show you the heart of my message.

Oli. Come to what is important in't. I forgive you the praise.

Vio. Alas, I took great pains to study it, and 'tis poetical.

Oli. It is the more like to be feign'd, I pray you keep it in. I heard you were saucy at my gates, and allow'd your approach rather to wonder at you than to hear you. If you be not mad, be gone. If you have reason, be brief. 'Tis not that time of moon with me to make one in so skipping a dialogue.

Mar. Will you hoist sail, sir? Here lies your way.

Vio. No, good swabber, I am to hull here a little longer. Some mollification for your giant, sweet lady. Tell me your mind—I am a messenger.

Oli. Sure you have some hideous matter to deliver, when the courtesy of it is so fearful. Speak your office.

Vio. It alone concerns your ear. I bring no overture of war, no taxation of homage; I hold the olive in my hand; my words are as full of peace as matter.

Oli. Yet you began rudely. What are you? What would you?

Vio. The rudeness that hath appear'd in me have I learn'd from my entertainment. What I am, and what I would, are as secret as maidenhead: to your ears, divinity; to any other's, profanation.

Oli. Give us the place alone, we will hear this divinity. [*Exeunt Maria and Attendants.*] Now, sir, what is your text?

Vio. Most sweet lady—

Oli. A comfortable doctrine, and much may be said of it. Where lies your text?

Vio. In Orsino's bosom.

Oli. In his bosom? In what chapter of his bosom?

Vio. To answer by the method, in the first of his heart.

Oli. O, I have read it; it is heresy. Have you no more to say?

Vio. Good madam, let me see your face.

Oli. Have you any commission from your lord to negotiate with my face? You are now out of your text; but we will draw the curtain, and show you the picture. Look you, sir, such a one I was this present. [*Unveiling.*] Is't not well done?

Vio. Excellently done, if God did all.

Oli. 'Tis in grain, sir, 'twill endure wind and weather.

Vio. 'Tis beauty truly blent, whose red and white
Nature's own sweet and cunning hand laid on.

157. squash: unripe pea pod. **157–58. peascod:** pea pod.
158. codling: unripe apple.
159. in standing water: i.e. at the turn of the tide.
160. well-favor'd: handsome. **shrewishly:** ill-temperedly, sharply.
172–73. cast away: waste (by delivering it to the wrong person).
174. con: memorize. **175. comptible:** sensitive, susceptible.
176. least sinister usage: slightest uncivil treatment.
179. out . . . part: not in my lines. **180. modest:** befitting.
182. comedian: actor (continuing the theatrical metaphor of line 179).
183. my profound heart: my very wise lady (?).
186. do . . . myself: am not an impostor.
187–88. usurp yourself: possess yourself wrongfully (by refusing to give yourself to a husband).
189. from my commission: i.e. beyond my instructions.
192. forgive you: excuse you from. **197. keep it in:** do not utter it.
199. not mad: i.e. not utterly mad (?). Some editors emend to *but mad* (Staunton conjecture).
200. reason: your wits. **time of moon.** Certain phases of the moon were supposed to have a bad influence, particularly on lunacy.
201. make one: take part. **skipping:** flighty.
203. swabber. Continuing Maria's nautical metaphor. A swabber was a petty officer charged with keeping the decks clean. **hull:** drift with sails furled.
204. mollification: appeasement. **your giant.** Referring ironically to Maria, who is apparently diminutive (see II.v.13, III.ii.66), and alluding to giants as guardians of ladies in romantic tales.
205. Tell . . . mind. Assigned by many editors (following Warburton) to Olivia.
207. when . . . fearful: i.e. when what should be the courteous manner of its introduction is so threatening (?). **office:** business.
209. taxation of homage: demand for tribute.
211. matter: significant meaning.
215. entertainment: manner of reception.
216. maidenhead: virginity.
220. what . . . text. Picking up *divinity* (line 217), Olivia suggests that Viola-Cesario is going to proceed like a preacher in setting forth the text of a sermon. She continues this figure, with Viola's cooperation, through line 228. **222. comfortable:** full of comfort.
226. by the method: according to the accepted form in beginning a sermon. **232. out of:** wandering from.
234. such . . . present. Olivia begins as if displaying a portrait of herself painted at an earlier time, then ends with "at the present time" (*this present*).
236. if . . . all: if it is all natural (unaided by cosmetics).
237. 'Tis in grain: it is fast-dyed, i.e. it won't wash off.
239. blent: blended. **240. cunning:** skilled.

Lady, you are the cruell'st she alive
If you will lead these graces to the grave,
And leave the world no copy.

Oli. O, sir, I will not be so hard-hearted; I will give out divers schedules of my beauty. It shall be inventoried, and every particle and utensil labell'd to my will: as, *item*, two lips, indifferent red; *item*, two grey eyes, with lids to them; *item*, one neck, one chin, and so forth. Were you sent hither to praise me?

Vio. I see you what you are, you are too proud;
But if you were the devil, you are fair.
My lord and master loves you. O, such love
Could be but recompens'd, though you were crown'd
The nonpareil of beauty.

Oli. How does he love me?

Vio. With adorations, fertile tears,
With groans that thunder love, with sighs of fire.

Oli. Your lord does know my mind, I cannot love him,
Yet I suppose him virtuous, know him noble,
Of great estate, of fresh and stainless youth;
In voices well divulg'd, free, learn'd, and valiant,
And in dimension, and the shape of nature,
A gracious person. But yet I cannot love him.
He might have took his answer long ago.

Vio. If I did love you in my master's flame,
With such a suff'ring, such a deadly life,
In your denial I would find no sense,
I would not understand it.

Oli. Why, what would you?

Vio. Make me a willow cabin at your gate,
And call upon my soul within the house;
Write loyal cantons of contemned love,
And sing them loud even in the dead of night;
Hallow your name to the reverberate hills,
And make the babbling gossip of the air
Cry out "Olivia!" O, you should not rest
Between the elements of air and earth
But you should pity me!

Oli. You might do much.
What is your parentage?

Vio. Above my fortunes, yet my state is well:
I am a gentleman.

Oli. Get you to your lord.
I cannot love him; let him send no more—
Unless (perchance) you come to me again
To tell me how he takes it. Fare you well.
I thank you for your pains. Spend this for me.

Vio. I am no fee'd post, lady; keep your purse;
My master, not myself, lacks recompense.
Love make his heart of flint that you shall love,
And let your fervor like my master's be
Plac'd in contempt! Farewell, fair cruelty. *Exit.*

Oli. "What is your parentage?"
"Above my fortunes, yet my state is well:
I am a gentleman." I'll be sworn thou art;
Thy tongue, thy face, thy limbs, actions, and spirit
Do give thee fivefold blazon. Not too fast! soft, soft!
Unless the master were the man. How now?
Even so quickly may one catch the plague?
Methinks I feel this youth's perfections
With an invisible and subtle stealth
To creep in at mine eyes. Well, let it be.
What ho, Malvolio!

Enter Malvolio.

Mal. Here, madam, at your service.

Oli. Run after that same peevish messenger,
The [County's] man. He left this ring behind him,
Would I or not. Tell him I'll none of it.
Desire him not to flatter with his lord,
Nor hold him up with hopes: I am not for him.
If that the youth will come this way to-morrow,
I'll give him reasons for't. Hie thee, Malvolio.

Mal. Madam, I will. *Exit.*

Oli. I do I know not what, and fear to find
Mine eye too great a flatterer for my mind.
Fate, show thy force: ourselves we do not owe;
What is decreed must be; and be this so. [*Exit.*]

ACT II, Scene I

Enter Antonio *and* Sebastian.

Ant. Will you stay no longer? nor will you not that I go with you?

Seb. By your patience, no. My stars shine darkly over me. The malignancy of my fate might perhaps distemper yours; therefore I shall crave of you your leave, that I may bear my evils alone. It were a bad recompense for your love, to lay any of them on you.

241–43. Lady . . . copy. Reminiscent of the argument in Shakespeare's first seventeen sonnets. **241. she:** woman.
243. copy: i.e. a child inheriting your beauty. Olivia plays on the sense "transcript, record."
245 schedules: itemized lists, inventories.
246. particle and utensil: particular and item. **labell'd:** attached.
247. item: a term (= also) usually preceding each item after the first (signalled by *imprimis* = in the first place) in a list, but sometimes, as here, preceding the first as well. **indifferent:** moderately.
249. praise. With a quibble on "appraise."
251. if: even if. **the devil.** The supreme example of pride.
253. Could . . . though: could be no more than evenly repaid even though. **254. nonpareil:** one that has no equal.
255. fertile: abundant, ever-flowing. **259. stainless:** unstained.
260. In . . . divulg'd: well reputed by general opinion (*voices*).
261. dimension . . . nature: form and physique.
262. gracious person: pleasing figure of a man.
264. flame: passion. **265. deadly:** death-like.
268. willow cabin: hut of willow boughs. Willow was the symbol of unrequited love. **269. my soul:** i.e. Olivia.
270. cantons: cantos, songs. **contemned:** despised, scornfully rejected. **272. Hallow:** halloo, shout. **reverberate:** resounding.
273. babbling . . . air: echo.
275. Between . . . earth: i.e. anywhere on the face of the earth.
276. But: but that. **278. state:** condition.

284. fee'd post: messenger who should be tipped.
286. Love . . . love: may love give a heart of flint to the man you fall in love with. **288. cruelty:** cruel person.
293. give . . . blazon: i.e. proclaim you a gentleman five times over as surely as if they were coats of arms. A blazon is a heraldic description of armorial bearings. **soft:** stay.
298. creep . . . eyes. It was a conventional idea that love entered through the eyes.
300. peevish: pettish, childish. **301. County's:** Count's, i.e. Duke's.
303. flatter with: encourage. **306. Hie:** hasten.
308–9. fear . . . mind: am afraid I shall find that my eyes (i.e. senses) have seduced my mind. **310. owe:** own, control.

II.i. Location: The sea-coast.
3. patience: sufferance.
4. malignancy: virulent condition, (1) in its medical sense = deadly contagion, (2) in its astrological sense = evil stellar influence.
5. distemper: infect.

Ant. Let me yet know of you whither you are bound.

Seb. No, sooth, sir; my determinate voyage is mere extravagancy. But I perceive in you so excellent a touch of modesty, that you will not extort from me what I am willing to keep in; therefore it charges me in manners the rather to express myself. You must know of me then, Antonio, my name is Sebastian, which I call'd Rodorigo; my father was that Sebastian of Messaline, whom I know you have heard of. He left behind him myself and a sister, both born in an hour. If the heavens had been pleas'd, would we had so ended! But you, sir, alter'd that, for some hour before you took me from the breach of the sea was my sister drown'd.

Ant. Alas the day!

Seb. A lady, sir, though it was said she much resembled me, was yet of many accounted beautiful; but though I could not with such estimable wonder overfar believe that, yet thus far I will boldly publish her: she bore a mind that envy could not but call fair. She is drown'd already, sir, with salt water, though I seem to drown her remembrance again with more.

Ant. Pardon me, sir, your bad entertainment.

Seb. O good Antonio, forgive me your trouble.

Ant. If you will not murther me for my love, let me be your servant.

Seb. If you will not undo what you have done, that is, kill him whom you have recover'd, desire it not. Fare ye well at once; my bosom is full of kindness, and I am yet so near the manners of my mother, that upon the least occasion more mine eyes will tell tales of me. I am bound to the Count Orsino's court. Farewell. *Exit.*

Ant. The gentleness of all the gods go with thee!
I have many enemies in Orsino's court,
Else would I very shortly see thee there.
But come what may, I do adore thee so
That danger shall seem sport, and I will go. *Exit.*

SCENE II

Enter VIOLA *and* MALVOLIO *at several doors.*

Mal. Were you not ev'n now with the Countess Olivia?

11. sooth: truly (shortened form of *in sooth*). **determinate:** intended. **12. mere extravagancy:** utter vagabondage.
13. touch: feeling.
14. willing . . . in: desirous of keeping secret. **it charges me:** it is incumbent on me.
15. in manners: by the requirements of good manners, in courtesy.
18. Messaline. Not identified.
19. in an hour: within the same hour.
22. breach . . . sea: breaking waves, surf.
27. such estimable wonder: estimation reflecting so much admiration.
28. publish: proclaim. **29. envy:** i.e. even malice.
33. your bad entertainment: the humble hospitality I have offered you. **35. murther me:** i.e. be the cause of my death.
38. recover'd: rescued.
39–40. kindness: natural feeling, i.e. a brother's grief.
40–41. yet . . . mother: i.e. still so newly a man. Such apologies by men for womanish tears are numerous in Shakespeare.

II.ii. Location: A street.
o.s.d. several: separate.

Vio. Even now, sir; on a moderate pace I have since arriv'd but hither.

Mal. She returns this ring to you, sir. You might have sav'd me my pains, to have taken it away yourself. She adds moreover, that you should put your lord into a desperate assurance she will none of him. And one thing more, that you be never so hardy to come again in his affairs, unless it be to report your lord's taking of this. Receive it so.

Vio. She took the ring of me, I'll none of it.

Mal. Come, sir, you peevishly threw it to her; and her will is, it should be so return'd. If it be worth stooping for, there it lies, in your eye; if not, be it his that finds it. *Exit.*

Vio. I left no ring with her. What means this lady?
Fortune forbid my outside have not charm'd her!
She made good view of me; indeed so much
That methought her eyes had lost her tongue,
For she did speak in starts distractedly.
She loves me sure, the cunning of her passion
Invites me in this churlish messenger.
None of my lord's ring? Why, he sent her none.
I am the man! If it be so, as 'tis,
Poor lady, she were better love a dream.
Disguise, I see thou art a wickedness
Wherein the pregnant enemy does much.
How easy is it for the proper-false
In women's waxen hearts to set their forms!
Alas, [our] frailty is the cause, not we,
For such as we are made [of,] such we be.
How will this fadge? My master loves her dearly,
And I (poor monster) fond as much on him;
And she (mistaken) seems to dote on me.
What will become of this? As I am man,
My state is desperate for my master's love;
As I am woman (now alas the day!),
What thriftless sighs shall poor Olivia breathe!
O time, thou must untangle this, not I,
It is too hard a knot for me t' untie. [*Exit.*]

SCENE III

Enter SIR TOBY *and* SIR ANDREW.

Sir To. Approach, Sir Andrew. Not to be a-bed

3. on: at. **6. to have taken:** by taking.
8. desperate assurance: certainty without hope of change.
9. hardy: bold.
11. taking of this: i.e. reception of Olivia's message of rejection.
14. so return'd: i.e. thrown back at you.
15. in your eye: in plain view.
18. forbid . . . not. Modern idiom would omit *not.*
19. made . . . me: examined me closely.
20. lost: i.e. made her lose.
21. in starts: by fits and starts. **distractedly:** disjointedly.
23. in: by means of, through.
28. the pregnant enemy: the devil, always ready (to take advantage of our evil for his own evil ends).
29. proper-false: i.e. men who are handsome but false.
30. waxen: i.e. impressionable. The image is from sealing. **set their forms:** stamp their images. **31. frailty:** human weakness.
32. such . . . of: i.e. frail flesh. **33. fadge:** work out, come off.
34. monster: i.e. being both a man and woman. **fond:** dote.
39. thriftless: unprofitable.

II.iii. Location: Olivia's house.

after midnight is to be up betimes, and "*deliculo surgere*," thou know'st—

Sir And. Nay, by my troth, I know not; but I know, to be up late is to be up late.

Sir To. A false conclusion. I hate it as an unfill'd can. To be up after midnight and to go to bed then, is early; so that to go to bed after midnight is to go to bed betimes. Does not our lives consist of the four elements?

Sir And. Faith, so they say, but I think it rather consists of eating and drinking.

Sir To. Th' art a scholar; let us therefore eat and drink. Marian, I say, a stoup of wine!

Enter CLOWN.

Sir And. Here comes the fool, i' faith.

Clo. How now, my hearts? Did you never see the picture of "we three"?

Sir To. Welcome, ass. Now let's have a catch.

Sir And. By my troth, the fool has an excellent breast. I had rather than forty shillings I had such a leg, and so sweet a breath to sing, as the fool has. In sooth, thou wast in very gracious fooling last night, when thou spok'st of Pigrogromitus, of the Vapians passing the equinoctial of Queubus. 'Twas very good, i' faith. I sent thee sixpence for thy leman; hadst it?

Clo. I did impeticos thy gratillity; for Malvolio's nose is no whipstock. My lady has a white hand, and the Mermidons are no bottle-ale houses.

Sir And. Excellent! Why, this is the best fooling, when all is done. Now a song.

Sir To. Come on, there is sixpence for you. Let's have a song.

Sir And. There's a testril of me too. If one knight give a—

Clo. Would you have a love-song, or a song of good life?

Sir To. A love-song, a love-song.

Sir And. Ay, ay. I care not for good life.

Clown sings.

O mistress mine, where are you roaming?
O, stay and hear, your true-love's coming,

That can sing both high and low.
Trip no further, pretty sweeting;
Journeys end in lovers meeting,
Every wise man's son doth know.

Sir And. Excellent good, i' faith.

Sir To. Good, good.

Clown [*sings*].

What is love? 'Tis not hereafter;
Present mirth hath present laughter;
What's to come is still unsure.
In delay there lies no plenty,
Then come kiss me sweet and twenty;
Youth's a stuff will not endure.

Sir And. A mellifluous voice, as I am true knight.

Sir To. A contagious breath.

Sir And. Very sweet and contagious, i' faith.

Sir To. To hear by the nose, it is dulcet in contagion. But shall we make the welkin dance indeed? Shall we rouse the night-owl in a catch that will draw three souls out of one weaver? Shall we do that?

Sir And. And you love me, let's do't. I am dog at a catch.

Clo. By'r lady, sir, and some dogs will catch well.

Sir And. Most certain. Let our catch be "Thou knave."

Clo. "Hold thy peace, thou knave," knight? I shall be constrain'd in't to call thee knave, knight.

Sir And. 'Tis not the first time I have constrain'd one to call me knave. Begin, fool. It begins, "Hold thy peace."

Clo. I shall never begin if I hold my peace.

Sir And. Good, i' faith. Come, begin.

Catch sung.

Enter MARIA.

Mar. What a caterwauling do you keep here! If my lady have not call'd up her steward Malvolio and bid him turn you out of doors, never trust me.

Sir To. My lady's a Cataian, we are politicians, Malvolio's a Peg-a-Ramsey, and [*sings*] "Three merry men be we." Am not I consanguineous? Am I not of

2. betimes: in good season.
2–3. deliculo surgere. From a well-known Latin maxim, *Diluculo surgere saluberrimum est*, "to get up at dawn is very healthful."
4. by my troth: on my word. **7. can:** tankard.
10. four elements: earth, water, air, and fire, supposed the constituents of all created things.
13. Th' art a scholar: i.e. I'll accept your authority on that point.
14. stoup: large drinking-cup.
17. picture of "we three": i.e. a picture of two fools or ass-heads inscribed "we three," the viewer being the third.
18. catch: round. **20. breast:** i.e. breath, voice.
21. leg: graceful bow or obeisance (?) or fine leg for dancing (?). Relevance uncertain. **22. gracious:** delightful.
23–24. Pigrogromitus . . . Queubus. Feste's mock scholarship.
24. equinoctial: equator. **25. leman:** sweetheart.
26. impeticos: impetticoat, i.e. pocket (?) or, possibly, spend on a woman (?). **gratillity:** little tip (invented diminutive of *gratuity*).
27. whipstock: whip handle, i.e. whip. The apparent meaning is that Malvolio's nose is stuck into everything but is no real deterrent. **has . . . hand:** is gently bred (?) or has ladylike tastes (?).
28. Mermidons. Presumably a tavern, with a sign displaying Myrmidons (Achilles' troop). **bottle-ale houses:** i.e. low-class taverns.
33. testril: sixpence (invented diminutive of *tester*; Sir Andrew seems to be aping Feste, with absurd effect).
35–36. of good life: conducive to virtue, edifying.

42. sweeting: sweet one. **43. in lovers meeting:** when lovers meet.
49. still: ever, always.
51. sweet and twenty: sweet and twenty more times sweet. *Twenty* is used as an intensive.
54. contagious breath: (1) catchy song; (2) bad breath.
56–57. To . . . contagion: if we could both hear and smell with our noses, we could call it sweetly stinking.
57. welkin: heavens, i.e. heavenly bodies.
58–59. draw three souls. It was a conventional notion that music could draw the soul from the body. These three singers will have three times that effect. **weaver.** Weavers were supposedly given to singing psalms.
60. dog: i.e. very good, expert. **62. By'r lady:** by Our Lady.
63–64. "Thou knave." The words of the catch are: "Hold thy peace, thou knave; and I prithee hold thy peace." Each singer in turn thus calls another a knave.
67–68. constrain'd . . . knave: compelled someone to challenge me to a duel (but as usual Sir Andrew's form of words is unfortunate).
72. keep: keep up.
75. Cataian: Cathayan (i.e., Chinese); slang for one whose word cannot be trusted (?). **politicians:** schemers, intriguers.
76. Peg-a-Ramsey. A term of contempt, alluding to a character in a coarse ballad.
76–77. "Three . . . we." A fragment of an old song.

her blood? Tilly-vally! Lady! [*Sings.*] "There dwelt a man in Babylon, lady, lady."

Clo. Beshrew me, the knight's in admirable fooling.

Sir And. Ay, he does well enough if he be dispos'd, and so do I too. He does it with a better grace, but I do it more natural.

Sir To. [*Sings.*] "O' the twelf day of December"—

Mar. For the love o' God, peace!

Enter MALVOLIO.

Mal. My masters, are you mad? Or what are you? Have you no wit, manners, nor honesty, but to gabble like tinkers at this time of night? Do ye make an alehouse of my lady's house, that ye squeak out your coziers' catches without any mitigation or remorse of voice? Is there no respect of place, persons, nor time in you?

Sir To. We did keep time, sir, in our catches. Sneck up!

Mal. Sir Toby, I must be round with you. My lady bade me tell you, that though she harbors you as her kinsman, she's nothing allied to your disorders. If you can separate yourself and your misdemeanors, you are welcome to the house; if not, and it would please you to take leave of her, she is very willing to bid you farewell.

Sir To. [*Sings.*] "Farewell, dear heart, since I must needs be gone."

Mar. Nay, good Sir Toby.

Clo. [*Sings.*] "His eyes do show his days are almost done."

Mal. Is't even so?

Sir To. [*Sings.*] "But I will never die."

Clo. Sir Toby, there you lie.

Mal. This is much credit to you.

Sir To. [*Sings.*] "Shall I bid him go?"

Clo. [*Sings.*] "What and if you do?"

Sir To. [*Sings.*] "Shall I bid him go, and spare not?"

Clo. [*Sings.*] "O no, no, no, no, you dare not."

Sir To. [*To Clown.*] Out o' tune, sir! ye lie. [*To Malvolio.*] Art any more than a steward? Dost thou think because thou art virtuous there shall be no more cakes and ale?

Clo. Yes, by Saint Anne, and ginger shall be hot i' th' mouth too.

Sir To. Th' art i' th' right. Go, sir, rub your chain with crumbs. A stope of wine, Maria!

Mal. Mistress Mary, if you priz'd my lady's favor at any thing more than contempt, you would not give means for this uncivil rule. She shall know of it, by this hand. *Exit.*

Mar. Go shake your ears.

Sir And. 'Twere as good a deed as to drink when a man's a-hungry, to challenge him the field, and then to break promise with him, and make a fool of him.

Sir To. Do't, knight. I'll write thee a challenge, or I'll deliver thy indignation to him by word of mouth.

Mar. Sweet Sir Toby, be patient for to-night. Since the youth of the Count's was to-day with my lady, she is much out of quiet. For Monsieur Malvolio, let me alone with him. If I do not gull him into an ayword, and make him a common recreation, do not think I have wit enough to lie straight in my bed. I know I can do it.

Sir To. Possess us, possess us, tell us something of him.

Mar. Marry, sir, sometimes he is a kind of puritan.

Sir And. O, if I thought that, I'd beat him like a dog!

Sir To. What, for being a puritan? Thy exquisite reason, dear knight?

Sir And. I have no exquisite reason for't, but I have reason good enough.

Mar. The dev'l a puritan that he is, or any thing constantly but a time-pleaser, an affection'd ass, that cons state without book, and utters it by great swarths; the best persuaded of himself, so cramm'd (as he thinks) with excellencies, that it is his grounds of faith that all that look on him love him; and on that vice in him will my revenge find notable cause to work.

Sir To. What wilt thou do?

Mar. I will drop in his way some obscure epistles of love, wherein by the color of his beard, the shape of his leg, the manner of his gait, the expressure of his

78. Tilly-vally! Lady!: fiddle-faddle, lady indeed! Perhaps Sir Toby is annoyed by Maria's "my lady" instead of "your cousin" as elsewhere.
78–79. There . . . lady. The first line of the *Ballad of Constant Susanna*, with the song's "burden" (*lady, lady*) added.
80. Beshrew me: a mild oath (originally = curse me).
81–82. dispos'd: inclined to mirth.
83. natural: (1) naturally; (2) like a fool.
84. "O' . . . December." The opening line of another ballad (*twelf* = twelfth). **87. honesty**: decorum, decency.
90. coziers': cobblers'. **mitigation or remorse**: i.e. softening.
91. respect: regard. **94. Sneck up**: go hang.
95. round: plain-spoken.
96. harbors you: allows you residence.
97. nothing allied: no kin at all.
102. Farewell . . . gone. From the ballad *Corydon's Farewell to Phillis*. The subsequent lines sung by Sir Toby and Feste are slightly adapted to the occasion.
107. Sir . . . lie. It seems likely that Feste sings this line too.
110. and if: if.
113. Out o' tune: i.e. false (quibbling on *false* as in "a false note," but with intended meaning "lying"); like the following *ye lie*, a reference to Feste's "you dare not [bid him go]."
116. cakes and ale. Proverbial for revelry.
117. ginger. A common addition to ale.
119–20. rub . . . crumbs: i.e. polish your steward's chain (a reminder of his position as a servant). **120. stope**: stoup.
123. give means: i.e. provide drinks. **rule**: course of conduct.
125. Go . . . ears. Implying that Malvolio is an ass.
127. field: i.e. duelling-ground.
134. let . . . him: leave him to me. **gull**: befool.
135. an ayword: a byword or proverb (*ay* = ever). The F1 form is here retained, since Shakespeare seems to have been the first to use the phrase and its etymology is doubtful. Editors (following Rowe) usually read *a nayword*, a form that occurs twice in *The Merry Wives of Windsor*, where, however, the sense required seems to be "password." **common recreation**: general laughingstock.
138. Possess: tell, inform.
140. puritan: i.e. one who professes to be extremely precise in morals; frequently (as Malvolio has just shown himself to be), one who is complacent about his own moral superiority and highly censorious of the lapses or fancied lapses of others. Apparently Sir Andrew in lines 140–42 takes Maria to be charging him with being a member of the Puritan party in the Anglican Church, and Maria in line 147 rejects the idea. **143. exquisite**: ingenious.
148. constantly: consistently, steadily. **time-pleaser**: self-seeking flatterer. **affection'd**: full of affectation.
149. cons . . . book: commits to memory the speech and behavior of the great. **utters**: (1) repeats; (2) discharges.
150. swarths: swaths, i.e. masses. **the best . . . himself**: having the highest opinion of himself. **151–52. grounds of faith**: firm belief.
157. expressure: expressive quality.

eye, forehead, and complexion, he shall find himself most feelingly personated. I can write very like my lady your niece; on a forgotten matter we can hardly make distinction of our hands.

Sir To. Excellent, I smell a device.

Sir And. I have't in my nose too.

Sir To. He shall think by the letters that thou wilt drop that they come from my niece, and that she's in love with him.

Mar. My purpose is indeed a horse of that color.

Sir And. And your horse now would make him an ass.

Mar. Ass, I doubt not.

Sir And. O, 'twill be admirable!

Mar. Sport royal, I warrant you. I know my physic will work with him. I will plant you two, and let the fool make a third, where he shall find the letter; observe his construction of it. For this night, to bed, and dream on the event. Farewell. *Exit.*

Sir To. Good night, Penthesilea.

Sir And. Before me, she's a good wench.

Sir To. She's a beagle true-bred, and one that adores me. What o' that?

Sir And. I was ador'd once too.

Sir To. Let's to bed, knight. Thou hadst need send for more money.

Sir And. If I cannot recover your niece, I am a foul way out.

Sir To. Send for money, knight; if thou hast her not i' th' end, call me cut.

Sir And. If I do not, never trust me, take it how you will.

Sir To. Come, come, I'll go burn some sack, 'tis too late to go to bed now. Come, knight, come, knight. *Exeunt.*

Scene IV

Enter Duke, Viola, Curio, *and others.*

Duke. Give me some music. Now good morrow, friends.
Now, good Cesario, but that piece of song,
That old and antique song we heard last night;

159. feelingly personated: exactly represented.
161. hands: handwriting.
170. Ass. A quibble on *as / ass* (= Sir Andrew).
173. physic: medicine.
174. fool . . . third. Actually it is not Feste but Fabian who makes the third (see II.v). Maria's words imply that Feste is no longer present. He last speaks at lines 117–18; perhaps Malvolio waves him out as he leaves at line 124.
175. construction: interpretation. **176. event:** outcome.
177. Penthesilea: queen of the Amazons (an ironical allusion to Maria's size).
178. Before me: i.e. on my soul (formed on the pattern of such oaths as *before God* and *before heaven*). **197. beagle:** small hunting-dog.
181. I . . . too. A line that suddenly, as elsewhere in Shakespeare, reveals the human being in a hitherto ridiculous figure of fun.
184. recover: win (with a suggestion of making good on his expenditure, as in *recover a debt*).
185. foul way out: wretchedly out of pocket.
187. cut: a horse with a docked tail.
190. burn some sack: prepare some warm sack (Spanish wine) and sugar.
II.iv. Location: The Duke's palace.
2. but: just (let us have). **3. antique:** quaint.

Methought it did relieve my passion much,
More than light airs and recollected terms
Of these most brisk and giddy-paced times.
Come, but one verse.

Cur. He is not here, so please your lordship, that should sing it.

Duke. Who was it?

Cur. Feste the jester, my lord, a fool that the Lady Olivia's father took much delight in. He is about the house.

Duke. Seek him out, and play the tune the while.
[*Exit Curio.*] *Music plays.*
Come hither, boy. If ever thou shalt love,
In the sweet pangs of it remember me;
For such as I am, all true lovers are,
Unstaid and skittish in all motions else,
Save in the constant image of the creature
That is belov'd. How dost thou like this tune?

Vio. It gives a very echo to the seat
Where Love is thron'd.

Duke. Thou dost speak masterly.
My life upon't, young though thou art, thine eye
Hath stay'd upon some favor that it loves.
Hath it not, boy?

Vio. A little, by your favor.

Duke. What kind of woman is't?

Vio. Of your complexion.

Duke. She is not worth thee then. What years, i' faith?

Vio. About your years, my lord.

Duke. Too old, by heaven. Let still the woman take
An elder than herself, so wears she to him;
So sways she level in her husband's heart.
For, boy, however we do praise ourselves,
Our fancies are more giddy and unfirm,
More longing, wavering, sooner lost and worn,
Than women's are.

Vio. I think it well, my lord.

Duke. Then let thy love be younger than thyself,
Or thy affection cannot hold the bent;
For women are as roses, whose fair flow'r
Being once display'd, doth fall that very hour.

Vio. And so they are; alas, that they are so!
To die, even when they to perfection grow!

Enter Curio *and* Clown.

5. light: trivial (?) or quick in tempo (?). **recollected.** Meaning uncertain; variously explained as "refined," "studied," "farfetched," and so on.
18. Unstaid and skittish: giddy and fickle. **motions else:** other thoughts and feelings.
21–22. gives . . . thron'd: i.e. it expresses what the heart feels.
22. masterly: like one who has had experience (of love).
24. stay'd upon: attended (?) or lingered upon (?). **favor:** face.
25. by your favor: if you please (a polite phrase), but with obvious quibbles on "near your face" and "thanks to you."
26. complexion: appearance, good looks.
29. still: ever, always.
30. wears: adapts herself (like a garment adjusting itself to the wearer).
31. sways: (1) holds sway; (2) swings. **level:** in perfect balance.
33. fancies: loves. **unfirm:** fickle.
34. worn: spent. **35. think it well:** think so too.
37. hold the bent: maintain its fullness and intensity (as a bow is kept bent to its full extent under high tension).
39. display'd: fully opened. **41. even when:** just when.

Duke. O fellow, come, the song we had last night.
Mark it, Cesario, it is old and plain.
The spinsters and the knitters in the sun,
And the free maids that weave their thread with bones,
Do use to chaunt it. It is silly sooth,
And dallies with the innocence of love,
Like the old age.

Clo. Are you ready, sir?

Duke. Ay, prithee sing. *Music.*

THE SONG

[*Clo.*] Come away, come away, death,
And in sad cypress let me be laid.
[Fly] away, [fly] away, breath,
I am slain by a fair cruel maid.
My shroud of white, stuck all with yew,
O, prepare it!
My part of death, no one so true
Did share it.

Not a flower, not a flower sweet
On my black coffin let there be strown.
Not a friend, not a friend greet
My poor corpse, where my bones
shall be thrown.
A thousand thousand sighs to save,
Lay me, O, where
Sad true lover never find my grave,
To weep there.

Duke. There's for thy pains.

Clo. No pains, sir, I take pleasure in singing, sir.

Duke. I'll pay thy pleasure then.

Clo. Truly, sir, and pleasure will be paid, one time or another.

Duke. Give me now leave to leave thee.

Clo. Now the melancholy god protect thee, and the tailor make thy doublet of changeable taffata, for thy mind is a very opal. I would have men of such constancy put to sea, that their business might be every thing and their intent every where, for that's it that always makes a good voyage of nothing. Farewell. *Exit.*

Duke. Let all the rest give place.
[*Curio and Attendants retire.*]

Once more, Cesario,
Get thee to yond same sovereign cruelty.
Tell her, my love, more noble than the world,
Prizes not quantity of dirty lands;
The parts that fortune hath bestow'd upon her,
Tell her, I hold as giddily as fortune;
But 'tis that miracle and queen of gems
That nature pranks her in attracts my soul.

Vio. But if she cannot love you, sir?

Duke. [I] cannot be so answer'd.

Vio. Sooth, but you must.
Say that some lady, as perhaps there is,
Hath for your love as great a pang of heart
As you have for Olivia. You cannot love her;
You tell her so. Must she not then be answer'd?

Duke. There is no woman's sides
Can bide the beating of so strong a passion
As love doth give my heart; no woman's heart
So big, to hold so much; they lack retention.
Alas, their love may be call'd appetite,
No motion of the liver, but the palate,
That suffer surfeit, cloyment, and revolt,
But mine is all as hungry as the sea,
And can digest as much. Make no compare
Between that love a woman can bear me
And that I owe Olivia.

Vio. Ay, but I know—

Duke. What dost thou know?

Vio. Too well what love women to men may owe;
In faith, they are as true of heart as we.
My father had a daughter lov'd a man
As it might be perhaps, were I a woman,
I should your lordship.

Duke. And what's her history?

Vio. A blank, my lord; she never told her love,
But let concealment like a worm i' th' bud
Feed on her damask cheek; she pin'd in thought,
And with a green and yellow melancholy
She sate like Patience on a monument,
Smiling at grief. Was not this love indeed?
We men may say more, swear more, but indeed
Our shows are more than will; for still we prove
Much in our vows, but little in our love.

Duke. But died thy sister of her love, my boy?

Vio. I am all the daughters of my father's house,

42. **fellow**: here, a familiar term of address to one of lower station (without derogatory implication).
44. **spinsters**: spinning-women.
45. **free**: carefree. **weave ... bones**: make bone or thread lace with bone bobbins.
46. **Do use**: are accustomed. **silly sooth**: simple truth.
47. **dallies**: plays lovingly.
48. **Like ... age**: as in the good old days.
51. **Come away**: come hither.
52. **cypress**: i.e. a coffin of cypress wood, or a bier covered with cypress boughs. Cypress trees, like yews (line 55), were often planted in graveyards and were emblematic of death.
57–58. **My ... it**: i.e. I had to enact alone my role of dying, unsupported by one of equal constancy.
70–71. **pleasure ... another**: i.e. indulgence exacts payment sooner or later. 72. **leave to leave**: permission to take leave of.
73. **the melancholy god**: i.e. the god to whom you pay your devotion. Feste clearly implies that Orsino's melancholy is a self-indulgence.
74. **doublet**: close-fitting jacket. **changeable taffata**: taffeta (thin silk) woven of threads of different colors, so that its color shifts with movement.
75–78. **I ... nothing.** Intended ironically; men of such changeable mind arrive at no destination and bring nothing home.
79. **give place**: withdraw.

80. **sovereign cruelty**: supremely cruel person, "cruell'st she alive" (I.v.241). 83. **parts**: worldly goods.
84. **hold ... fortune**: esteem as lightly as fortune does (which could sweep them away in a moment).
85. **miracle ... gems**: i.e. her beauty.
86. **nature.** As contrasted with fortune. **pranks**: adorns.
90. **for your love**: for love of you.
92. **be answer'd**: accept your answer.
93–103. **There ... Olivia.** True to his changeable nature, the Duke now contradicts the opinion he voiced in lines 32–35.
94. **bide**: endure. 96. **retention**: power of retaining.
98. **No ... liver**: no impulse of the liver, i.e. not the passion of true love. **the palate**: i.e. a motion of the palate, a sensual appetite.
99. **suffer**: experience. **cloyment**: satiety. **revolt**: revulsion of appetite. Cf. lines 98–101 with Orsino's opening speech in I.i; there is considerable irony in what he here attributes to women's love and what to his own. 103. **owe**: bear.
112. **damask**: pink and white, like a damask rose.
113. **green and yellow**: pale and sallow.
114. **sate**: sat. **like ... monument**: like a sculptured figure of Patience on a tomb.
117. **more than will**: greater than our desire. **still**: ever, always.

And all the brothers too—and yet I know not.
Sir, shall I to this lady?
Duke. Ay, that's the theme,
To her in haste; give her this jewel; say
My love can give no place, bide no denay. *Exeunt.*

Scene V

Enter Sir Toby, Sir Andrew, *and* Fabian.

Sir To. Come thy ways, Signior Fabian.

Fab. Nay, I'll come. If I lose a scruple of this sport, let me be boil'd to death with melancholy.

Sir To. Wouldst thou not be glad to have the niggardly rascally sheep-biter come by some notable shame?

Fab. I would exult, man. You know he brought me out o' favor with my lady about a bear-baiting here.

Sir To. To anger him we'll have the bear again, and we will fool him black and blue, shall we not, Sir Andrew?

Sir And. And we do not, it is pity of our lives.

Enter Maria.

Sir To. Here comes the little villain. How now, my metal of India?

Mar. Get ye all three into the box-tree; Malvolio's coming down this walk. He has been yonder i' the sun practicing behavior to his own shadow this half hour. Observe him, for the love of mockery; for I know this letter will make a contemplative idiot of him. Close, in the name of jesting! [*The men hide themselves.*] Lie thou there [*throws down a letter*]; for here comes the trout that must be caught with tickling. *Exit.*

Enter Malvolio.

Mal. 'Tis but fortune, all is fortune. Maria once told me she did affect me, and I have heard herself come thus near, that should she fancy, it should be one of my complexion. Besides, she uses me with a more exalted respect than any one else that follows her. What should I think on't?

Sir To. Here's an overweening rogue!

Fab. O, peace! Contemplation makes a rare

turkey-cock of him. How he jets under his advanc'd plumes!

Sir And. 'Slight, I could so beat the rogue!

Sir To. Peace, I say!

Mal. To be Count Malvolio!

Sir To. Ah, rogue!

Sir And. Pistol him, pistol him!

Sir To. Peace, peace!

Mal. There is example for't: the Lady of the Strachy married the yeoman of the wardrobe.

Sir And. Fie on him, Jezebel!

Fab. O, peace! now he's deeply in. Look how imagination blows him.

Mal. Having been three months married to her, sitting in my state—

Sir To. O, for a stone-bow, to hit him in the eye!

Mal. Calling my officers about me, in my branch'd velvet gown; having come from a day-bed, where I have left Olivia sleeping—

Sir To. Fire and brimstone!

Fab. O, peace, peace!

Mal. And then to have the humor of state; and after a demure travel of regard—telling them I know my place as I would they should do theirs—to ask for my kinsman Toby—

Sir To. Bolts and shackles!

Fab. O, peace, peace, peace! Now, now.

Mal. Seven of my people, with an obedient start, make out for him. I frown the while, and perchance wind up my watch, or play with my—some rich jewel. Toby approaches; curtsies there to me—

Sir To. Shall this fellow live?

Fab. Though our silence be drawn from us with cars, yet peace.

Mal. I extend my hand to him thus, quenching my familiar smile with an austere regard of control—

Sir To. And does not Toby take you a blow o' the lips then?

Mal. Saying, "Cousin Toby, my fortunes, having

124. give . . . denay: yield no ground and endure no denial.

II.v. Location: Olivia's garden.
1. Come thy ways: come along.
2. Nay. Implying that Sir Toby need not urge. **scruple**: tiniest bit.
3. boil'd . . . melancholy. With a pun on *boil / bile* (pronounced alike). Black bile was the cause of melancholy.
5. sheep-biter: i.e. malicious sneak.
8. bear-baiting. A type of entertainment that Malvolio would naturally disapprove of (with some reason).
10. fool: mock. **black and blue**: i.e. thoroughly (used figuratively with *fool* instead of the usual *beat*).
12. it . . . lives: "life won't be worth living" (Kittredge).
14. metal of India: i.e. gold; here = girl worth her weight in gold.
17. behavior: courtly manners.
19–20. make . . . him: make him sit and daydream like an idiot staring into space. **20. Close**: keep hidden.
22. tickling: (1) stroking under the gills (trout were actually taken by this means); (2) flattery.
24. she: i.e. Olivia. **did affect**: was fond of.
25. fancy: fall in love. **27. follows her**: is in her service.
29. overweening: arrogant, presumptuous.
30. Contemplation. Looking back to lines 19–20.

31. jets: struts. **advanc'd**: raised. **33. 'Slight**: by God's light.
39. example: precedent. **39–40. Lady . . . Strachy.** Not certainly identified.
40. yeoman . . . wardrobe: servant in charge of clothing and linen in a nobleman's household.
41. Jezebel: the cruel and arrogant wife of Ahab, king of Israel (the application of the word to Malvolio is typical of Sir Andrew).
43. blows him: puffs him up. **45. state**: chair of state (as Count).
46. stone-bow: crossbow that shot stones instead of arrows.
47. officers: household staff. **branch'd**: figured with a pattern of leaves or flowers. **48. day-bed**: couch.
52. have . . . state: i.e. adopt the manner of the great.
53. after . . . regard: having gravely allowed my eyes to travel from one to another. **telling**: indicating to.
58. with . . . start: in obedient haste.
59. make out: sally forth.
60. my— . . . jewel. Malvolio is on the verge of saying "my chain" (his insignia of office as steward) but catches himself in time.
63–64. with cars. The general meaning is clearly "by main force." *Cars* is sometimes explained as meaning "carts" (with citation of III.ii.59–60, "oxen and wain-ropes cannot hale them together"), but Shakespeare elsewhere uses *car* only in the sense *chariot*, usually with reference to the sun-god's chariot; Johnson therefore proposed emending to *carts*. Possibly a reference to some form of torture is intended; the line would then mean "it is torture to remain silent" and would present a witty reversal of the usual purpose of torture, which is to draw speech from the silent. The emendation most often adopted, however, is Hanmer's *by th' ears*, which implies reluctance or resistance on the part of what is drawn.
66. familiar: friendly. **austere . . . control**: look of stern authority.
67. take: give.

cast me on your niece, give me this prerogative of speech"—

Sir To. What, what?

Mal. "You must amend your drunkenness."

Sir To. Out, scab!

Fab. Nay, patience, or we break the sinews of our plot!

Mal. "Besides, you waste the treasure of your time with a foolish knight"—

Sir And. That's me, I warrant you.

Mal. "One Sir Andrew"—

Sir And. I knew 'twas I, for many do call me fool.

Mal. What employment have we here?

[*Taking up the letter.*]

Fab. Now is the woodcock near the gin.

Sir To. O, peace, and the spirit of humors intimate reading aloud to him!

Mal. By my life, this is my lady's hand. These be her very c's, her u's, and her t's, and thus makes she her great P's. It is, in contempt of question, her hand.

Sir And. Her c's, her u's, and her t's: why that?

Mal. [*Reads.*] "To the unknown belov'd, this, and my good wishes":—her very phrases! By your leave, wax. Soft! And the impressure her Lucrece, with which she uses to seal. 'Tis my lady. To whom should this be?

Fab. This wins him, liver and all.

Mal. [*Reads.*]

"Jove knows I love,
But who?
Lips, do not move;
No man must know."

"No man must know." What follows? The numbers alter'd! "No man must know." If this should be thee, Malvolio?

Sir To. Marry, hang thee, brock!

Mal. [*Reads.*]

"I may command where I adore,
But silence, like a Lucrece knife,
With bloodless stroke my heart doth gore;
M. O. A. I. doth sway my life."

Fab. A fustian riddle!

Sir To. Excellent wench, say I.

Mal. "M. O. A. I. doth sway my life." Nay, but first let me see, let me see, let me see.

Fab. What dish a' poison has she dress'd him!

Sir To. And with what wing the [staniel] checks at it!

Mal. "I may command where I adore." Why, she may command me: I serve her, she is my lady. Why, this is evident to any formal capacity, there is no obstruction in this. And the end—what should that alphabetical position portend? If I could make that resemble something in me! Softly! M. O. A. I.—

Sir To. O ay, make up that. He is now at a cold scent.

Fab. Sowter will cry upon't for all this, though it be as rank as a fox.

Mal. M—Malvolio; M—why, that begins my name.

Fab. Did not I say he would work it out? The cur is excellent at faults.

Mal. M—but then there is no consonancy in the sequel that suffers under probation: A should follow, but O does.

Fab. And O shall end, I hope.

Sir To. Ay, or I'll cudgel him, and make him cry O!

Mal. And then I comes behind.

Fab. Ay, and you had any eye behind you, you might see more detraction at your heels than fortunes before you.

Mal. M. O. A. I. This simulation is not as the former; and yet, to crush this a little, it would bow to me, for every one of these letters are in my name. Soft, here follows prose. [*Reads.*] "If this fall into thy hand, revolve. In my stars I am above thee, but be not afraid of greatness. Some are [born] great, some [achieve] greatness, and some have greatness thrust upon 'em. Thy Fates open their hands, let thy blood and spirit embrace them, and to inure thyself to what thou art like to be, cast thy humble slough and appear fresh. Be opposite with a kinsman, surly with servants; let thy tongue tang arguments of state; put thyself into the trick of singularity. She thus advises thee that sighs for thee. Remember who commended thy yellow stock-

74. scab: scurvy fellow. **82. employment**: business.
83. woodcock. A proverbially stupid bird, easily caught. **gin**: trap, snare (short form of *engine* = contrivance). **84. humors**: caprice.
87. c's . . . t's. Malvolio has unwittingly spelled out *cut*, slang for the female pudenda. The "joke" is compounded by *great P's*, line 88.
88. great: capital. **in . . . question**: beyond dispute.
91–92. By your leave: with your permission (addressed to the seal as he breaks it).
92. Soft: not so fast, wait a moment. **impressure**: device impressed on the wax. **Lucrece**: i.e. a figure of the virtuous Roman matron Lucretia, who stabbed herself after her rape by Tarquin—an emblem of chastity. **93. uses**: is accustomed.
95. wins: conquers. **liver**: i.e. his love.
100–101. The numbers alter'd: the metre changed.
103. brock: badger, i.e. stinker.
108. fustian: worthless, nonsensical.
112. What: what a. **dress'd**: prepared.
113. wing: flight, i.e. speed. **staniel**: inferior hawk. **checks**: is diverted from its proper quarry by an inferior prey, i.e. is led astray.
117. formal capacity: normal understanding.
118. obstruction: obstacle, difficulty.
119. alphabetical position: arrangement of letters.
121. O, ay. Sir Toby seems to echo two of the letters that Malvolio has just read (*ay* is spelled *I*, as usual, in F1). **make up that**: piece that together, work that out.
121–22. cold scent: faint, hence difficult, trail.
123. Sowter: a hound's name; literally, cobbler, i.e. bungler. **cry upon't**: give tongue as if he had found the scent.
123–24. though . . . fox: though the deception is as easy to smell out as a stinking (*rank*) fox.
128. excellent at faults: not put off the trail by breaks in the scent (with ironic implication that he is very likely to pick up a false scent).
129. consonancy: agreement, correspondence.
130. sequel: i.e. following letter(s). **suffers**: endures, stands up. **probation**: testing, examination. **132. O**: i.e. a hangman's noose.
137. detraction: defamation.
139. simulation: representation, disguised meaning.
140. crush: force. **bow to**: (1) yield its meaning to; (2) point to, indicate. **143. revolve**: consider.
144. stars: fortunes, i.e. rank and wealth.
146–47. open their hands: i.e. are ready to give.
147. let . . . them: i.e. welcome their gifts with the whole force of your being. *Blood and spirit* = either "body and soul" or "passion and mettle." **148. inure**: accustom.
148–49. cast . . . slough: cast off your lowly demeanor. The figure is of a snake sloughing off its old skin. **149. opposite**: quarrelsome.
150. tang: sound loud with.
151. arguments of state: political topics, matters of statecraft. **trick**: custom, habit.
151–52. put . . . singularity: cultivate individuality, adopt eccentric habits.

ings, and wish'd to see thee ever cross-garter'd: I say, remember. Go to, thou art made if thou desir'st to be so; if not, let me see thee a steward still, the fellow of servants, and not worthy to touch Fortune's fingers. Farewell. She that would alter services with thee,

The Fortunate-Unhappy."

Daylight and champian discovers not more. This is open. I will be proud, I will read politic authors, I will baffle Sir Toby, I will wash off gross acquaintance, I will be point-devise the very man. I do not now fool myself, to let imagination jade me; for every reason excites to this, that my lady loves me. She did commend my yellow stockings of late, she did praise my leg being cross-garter'd, and in this she manifests herself to my love, and with a kind of injunction drives me to these habits of her liking. I thank my stars, I am happy. I will be strange, stout, in yellow stockings, and cross-garter'd, even with the swiftness of putting on. Jove and my stars be prais'd! Here is yet a postscript. [*Reads.*] "Thou canst not choose but know who I am. If thou entertain'st my love, let it appear in thy smiling; thy smiles become thee well. Therefore in my presence still smile, dear my sweet, I prithee." Jove, I thank thee. I will smile, I will do every thing that thou wilt have me. *Exit.*

Fab. I will not give my part of this sport for a pension of thousands to be paid from the Sophy.

Sir To. I could marry this wench for this device—

Sir And. So could I too.

Sir To. And ask no other dowry with her but such another jest.

Enter MARIA.

Sir And. Nor I neither.

Fab. Here comes my noble gull-catcher.

Sir To. Wilt thou set thy foot o' my neck?

Sir And. Or o' mine either?

Sir To. Shall I play my freedom at tray-trip, and become thy bond-slave?

Sir And. I' faith, or I either?

Sir To. Why, thou hast put him in such a dream, that when the image of it leaves him he must run mad.

Mar. Nay, but say true, does it work upon him?

Sir To. Like aqua-vitae with a midwife.

Mar. If you will then see the fruits of the sport, mark his first approach before my lady. He will come to her in yellow stockings, and 'tis a color she abhors, and cross-garter'd, a fashion she detests; and he will smile upon her, which will now be so unsuitable to her disposition, being addicted to a melancholy as she is, that it cannot but turn him into a notable contempt. If you will see it, follow me.

Sir To. To the gates of Tartar, thou most excellent devil of wit!

Sir And. I'll make one too. *Exeunt.*

ACT III, SCENE I

Enter VIOLA, *and* CLOWN [*with a tabor*].

Vio. 'Save thee, friend, and thy music! Dost thou live by thy tabor?

Clo. No, sir, I live by the church.

Vio. Art thou a churchman?

Clo. No such matter, sir. I do live by the church; for I do live at my house, and my house doth stand by the church.

Vio. So thou mayst say the [king] lies by a beggar, if a beggar dwells near him; or the church stands by thy tabor, if thy tabor stand by the church.

Clo. You have said, sir. To see this age! A sentence is but a chev'ril glove to a good wit. How quickly the wrong side may be turn'd outward!

Vio. Nay, that's certain. They that dally nicely with words may quickly make them wanton.

Clo. I would therefore my sister had had no name, sir.

Vio. Why, man?

Clo. Why, sir, her name's a word, and to dally with that word might make my sister wanton. But indeed, words are very rascals since bonds disgrac'd them.

Vio. Thy reason, man?

Clo. Troth, sir, I can yield you none without words, and words are grown so false, I am loath to prove reason with them.

Vio. I warrant thou art a merry fellow, and car'st for nothing.

154. cross-garter'd: wearing the garters crossed at the back so that in front they pass both above and below the knee.
156. still: always (so also in line 177).
158. alter services: exchange duties, i.e. make you master and myself your servant.
160. champian: champaign, open country. **discovers:** reveals.
161. open: evident, obvious. **proud:** lofty. **politic authors:** writers on political science.
162. baffle: treat with disdain. **wash off:** rid myself of. **gross:** low. **163. point-devise:** correctly in every detail, precisely.
164. I . . . me: I am not foolishly allowing imagination to trick me.
165. every . . . this: every piece of evidence urges this conclusion.
170. happy: blessed by fortune. **strange:** distant, reserved. **stout:** haughty.
172, 178. Jove. Here and elsewhere (III.iv.74–75, 82, and particularly IV.ii.11), possibly a replacement for an original *God*, to comply with the anti-profanity statute of 1606.
175. entertain'st: acceptest. **181. Sophy:** the Shah of Persia.
187. gull-catcher: tricker of credulous fools.
188. set. . . neck: i.e. as a symbol of conquest.
190. play: gamble. **tray-trip:** a game of dice in which the best throw was three (*tray = trey*).
196. aqua-vitae: brandy or other spirits.

205. Tartar: Tartarus, hell. **207. make one:** go along.

III.i. Location: Olivia's garden.
o.s.d. tabor: small drum.
1. 'Save: God save. **music.** Feste probably has also a pipe (played with the help of one hand while the tabor was beaten with the other).
3. live by: earn a living by. Feste quibbles on "dwell near."
4. churchman: man in holy orders.
8. So . . . beggar: in the same fashion you could say what would be taken to mean "the king lies with a beggar." (Similarly, *stands by*, line 9, could be taken to mean "is supported by.")
11–12. A sentence: any utterance.
12. chev'ril: kidskin (soft and pliable).
14. dally nicely: play sophistically.
15. make them wanton: allow them to get out of hand.
19. dally: toy amorously.
20. wanton: unchaste. Dover Wilson suggests a pun on *want one*, i.e. lack a (good) name.
21. bonds disgrac'd them. Quibbling on *bonds* as (1) sworn statements (in place of a man's plain word or promise); (2) fetters (betokening criminality).
25. reason: "the reasonableness of any proposition" (Kittredge).
26–27. car'st for nothing: dost not worry about anything. Feste then proceeds to play on other meanings of *care*.

Clo. Not so, sir, I do care for something; but in my conscience, sir, I do not care for you. If that be to care for nothing, sir, I would it would make you invisible.

Vio. Art not thou the Lady Olivia's fool?

Clo. No, indeed, sir, the Lady Olivia has no folly. She will keep no fool, sir, till she be married, and fools are as like husbands as pilchers are to herrings, the husband's the bigger. I am indeed not her fool, but her corrupter of words.

Vio. I saw thee late at the Count Orsino's.

Clo. Foolery, sir, does walk about the orb like the sun, it shines every where. I would be sorry, sir, but the fool should be as oft with your master as with my mistress. I think I saw your wisdom there.

Vio. Nay, and thou pass upon me, I'll no more with thee. Hold, there's expenses for thee.

Clo. Now Jove, in his next commodity of hair, send thee a beard!

Vio. By my troth, I'll tell thee, I am almost sick for one—[*aside*] though I would not have it grow on my chin. Is thy lady within?

Clo. Would not a pair of these have bred, sir?

Vio. Yes, being kept together, and put to use.

Clo. I would play Lord Pandarus of Phrygia, sir, to bring a Cressida to this Troilus.

Vio. I understand you, sir. 'Tis well begg'd.

Clo. The matter, I hope, is not great, sir—begging but a beggar: Cressida was a beggar. My lady is within, sir. I will conster to them whence you come; who you are, and what you would, are out of my welkin—I might say "element," but the word is overworn. *Exit.*

Vio. This fellow is wise enough to play the fool,
And to do that well craves a kind of wit.
He must observe their mood on whom he jests,
The quality of persons, and the time;
And like the haggard, check at every feather
That comes before his eye. This is a practice
As full of labor as a wise man's art;
For folly that he wisely shows is fit,
But wise [men], folly-fall'n, quite taint their wit.

Enter Sir Toby *and* Andrew.

Sir To. 'Save you, gentleman.

Vio. And you, sir.

Sir And. *Dieu vous garde, monsieur.*

Vio. *Et vous aussi; votre serviteur.*

Sir And. I hope, sir, you are, and I am yours.

Sir To. Will you encounter the house? My niece is desirous you should enter, if your trade be to her.

Vio. I am bound to your niece, sir; I mean she is the list of my voyage.

Sir To. Taste your legs, sir, put them to motion.

Vio. My legs do better understand me, sir, than I understand what you mean by bidding me taste my legs.

Sir To. I mean, to go, sir, to enter.

Vio. I will answer you with gait and entrance—but we are prevented.

Enter Olivia *and* Gentlewoman.

Most excellent accomplish'd lady, the heavens rain odors on you!

Sir And. That youth's a rare courtier—"rain odors," well.

Vio. My matter hath no voice, lady, but to your own most pregnant and vouchsafed ear.

Sir And. "Odors," "pregnant," and "vouchsafed"; I'll get 'em all three all ready.

Oli. Let the garden door be shut, and leave me to my hearing. [*Exeunt all but Olivia and Viola.*] Give me your hand, sir.

Vio. My duty, madam, and most humble service.

Oli. What is your name?

Vio. Cesario is your servant's name, fair princess.

Oli. My servant, sir? 'Twas never merry world
Since lowly feigning was call'd compliment.
Y' are servant to the Count Orsino, youth.

Vio. And he is yours, and his must needs be yours:
Your servant's servant is your servant, madam.

Oli. For him, I think not on him. For his thoughts,
Would they were blanks, rather than fill'd with me.

28–29. **in my conscience**: to let you into a secret.
30. **I . . . invisible.** Viola ought to be invisible, by Feste's process of thought, since if he cares for something and does not care for Viola, then Viola is nothing.
34. **pilchers**: pilchards, small fish resembling herring.
37. **late**: recently.
38. **orb**: earth, as the centre about which the sun courses (*walks*) in the Ptolemaic system. 39. **but**: unless.
41. **your wisdom.** An ironic form of address on the model of *your honor* or *your worship*.
42. **pass upon me**: fence with me (using sharp words as your weapon).
43. **Hold**: take this. **expenses**: something for you to spend.
44–45. **Jove . . . beard.** Feste follows the usual practice of one who received alms by invoking God's blessing on the giver.
44. **commodity**: consignment, lot.
47. **one**: a beard, i.e. a man (Orsino).
48. **my chin.** The stress belongs on *my*.
49. **pair of these**: i.e. two coins. **bred**: multiplied.
50. **put to use**: loaned at interest.
51. **Pandarus**: Cressida's uncle, and the go-between in her love affair with Troilus.
54. **The matter**: i.e. the amount begged.
55. **Cressida . . . beggar.** Alluding to the tradition stemming from Henryson's *Testament of Cresseid* that Cressida became a leper and a beggar. 56. **conster**: construe, explain.
58. **welkin, element.** *Element* in the sense "sky" is synonymous with *welkin*, but it can have other senses as well, as of course it has in the phrase *out of my element* (= here "outside the range of my information"). Feste gives a final example of how words can be made "wanton."
60. **play the fool.** Feste, like Touchstone in *As You Like It*, is a shrewd, sharp person who makes his living by playing the fool; he is not, like the Fool in *King Lear*, a "natural" or halfwit.
61. **wit**: intelligence. 62. **their mood**: the mood of those.
63. **quality**: character.
64. **haggard**: a hawk taken in maturity and hence difficult to train. **check.** See the note on II.v.113.
65. **practice**: exercise of skill. 66. **art**: skill.
67. **wisely shows**: assumes judiciously. **fit**: proper.
68. **folly-fall'n**: lapsed into folly. **taint**: discredit.
71. **Dieu . . . monsieur**: God keep you, sir.
72. **Et . . . serviteur**: And you too; your servant.
74. **encounter.** Pedantry for "enter."
75. **trade**: business. The word suggests to Viola a trading voyage.
76. **I . . . to**: i.e. my destination is.
77. **list**: limit, utmost point. 78. **Taste**: i.e. make trial of, test.
79. **understand me**: stand under me, hold me up.
82. **gait and entrance**: going and entering (answering to *go* and *enter* in line 81); with a play on "gate and entrance."
83. **prevented**: anticipated. 88. **hath no voice**: cannot be spoken.
89. **pregnant and vouchsafed**: receptive and graciously bestowed.
91. **all ready**: i.e. all ready for use in future conversation.
93. **hearing**: audience, interview.
98. **'Twas . . . world**: life has never been as pleasant (proverbial).
99. **lowly feigning**: pretending humility, i.e. calling oneself "your servant." **was call'd**: was first called, began to be called.
103. **For**: as for.

Vio. Madam, I come to whet your gentle thoughts
On his behalf.
Oli. O, by your leave, I pray you:
I bade you never speak again of him;
But would you undertake another suit,
I had rather hear you to solicit that
Than music from the spheres.
Vio. Dear lady—
Oli. Give me leave, beseech you. I did send,
After the last enchantment you did here,
A ring in chase of you; so did I abuse
Myself, my servant, and I fear me you.
Under your hard construction must I sit,
To force that on you in a shameful cunning
Which you knew none of yours. What might you think?
Have you not set mine honor at the stake,
And baited it with all th' unmuzzled thoughts
That tyrannous heart can think? To one of your receiving
Enough is shown; a cypress, not a bosom,
Hides my heart. So let me hear you speak.
Vio. I pity you.
Oli. That's a degree to love.
Vio. No, not a grize; for 'tis a vulgar proof
That very oft we pity enemies.
Oli. Why then methinks 'tis time to smile again.
O world, how apt the poor are to be proud!
If one should be a prey, how much the better
To fall before the lion than the wolf! *Clock strikes.*
The clock upbraids me with the waste of time.
Be not afraid, good youth, I will not have you,
And yet when wit and youth is come to harvest,
Your wife is like to reap a proper man.
There lies your way, due west.
Vio. Then westward-ho!
Grace and good disposition attend your ladyship!
You'll nothing, madam, to my lord by me?
Oli. Stay!
I prithee tell me what thou think'st of me.
Vio. That you do think you are not what you are.
Oli. If I think so, I think the same of you.

106. **by your leave:** a polite phrase of interruption: "please say no more" (so also *Give me leave*, line 111).
110. **music . . . spheres.** A reference to the notion that the revolution of the spheres in which the heavenly bodies were fixed produced ravishing music, inaudible to human ears.
112. **enchantment you did:** charm you worked, spell you cast.
113. **abuse:** dishonor. 115. **construction:** interpretation.
116. **To force:** for forcing.
118. **at the stake.** The figure in 118–19 is from bear-baiting; Olivia's honor is set upon by Cesario's thoughts as the bear is set upon by dogs to tear and worry it.
120. **tyrannous:** cruel. **receiving:** power to apprehend.
121. **cypress:** a nearly transparent black fabric.
123. **degree:** step; *grize* in line 124 is a synonym.
124. **'tis . . . proof:** i.e. everybody knows from experience.
126. **then:** i.e. if you are my enemy. **smile:** i.e. abandon love and its pangs. 127. **apt:** ready. 128. **should be:** were to be.
129. **lion . . . wolf:** i.e. Orsino . . . Cesario.
131. **have you:** have you for a husband. 133. **proper:** worthy.
134. **due west:** i.e. where the sun disappears from sight; a clear dismissal. **westward-ho:** the cry of watermen on the Thames when they were about to put off westward.
135. **good disposition:** a tranquil mind.
139. **That . . . what you are:** i.e. that you are mistaken in supposing you are in love with a man, not a woman.
140. **If . . . you.** Presumably she interprets his remark as meaning that she is mad but doesn't know it.

Vio. Then think you right: I am not what I am.
Oli. I would you were as I would have you be.
Vio. Would it be better, madam, than I am?
I wish it might, for now I am your fool.
Oli. [*Aside.*] O, what a deal of scorn looks beautiful
In the contempt and anger of his lip!
A murd'rous guilt shows not itself more soon
Than love that would seem hid: love's night is noon.—
Cesario, by the roses of the spring,
By maidhood, honor, truth, and every thing,
I love thee so, that maugre all thy pride,
Nor wit nor reason can my passion hide.
Do not extort thy reasons from this clause,
For that I woo, thou therefore hast no cause;
But rather reason thus with reason fetter:
Love sought is good, but given unsought is better.
Vio. By innocence I swear, and by my youth,
I have one heart, one bosom, and one truth,
And that no woman has, nor never none
Shall mistress be of it, save I alone.
And so adieu, good madam, never more
Will I my master's tears to you deplore.
Oli. Yet come again; for thou perhaps mayst move
That heart which now abhors, to like his love.
Exeunt.

Scene II

Enter Sir Toby, Sir Andrew, *and* Fabian.

Sir And. No, faith, I'll not stay a jot longer.

Sir To. Thy reason, dear venom, give thy reason.

Fab. You must needs yield your reason, Sir Andrew.

Sir And. Marry, I saw your niece do more favors to the Count's servingman than ever she bestow'd upon me. I saw't i' th' orchard.

Sir To. Did she see [thee] the while, old boy? tell me that.

Sir And. As plain as I see you now.

Fab. This was a great argument of love in her toward you.

Sir And. 'Slight! will you make an ass o' me?

Fab. I will prove it legitimate, sir, upon the oaths of judgment and reason.

Sir To. And they have been grand-jurymen since before Noah was a sailor.

Fab. She did show favor to the youth in your sight

144. **now . . . fool:** i.e. you have put me into a foolish position (in a sense that she cannot guess). 145. **deal:** large amount.
148. **love's . . . noon:** love's attempted secrecy is like broad daylight to everybody else. 151. **maugre:** in spite of. 153. **Nor:** neither.
153–54. **Do . . . cause:** do not wrest reasons for not loving me from this proposition: that because I woo, you have no cause to accept my love.
155. **rather . . . fetter:** instead bind together these two reasons (to accept my love).
156. **Love . . . better.** Olivia will receive a love that she sued for, which is good; Cesario will receive a love for which he did not have to sue, which is better. 162. **deplore:** lament, describe.

III.ii. Location: Olivia's house.
2. **venom:** venomous one. 7. **orchard:** garden.
11. **argument:** evidence. 14. **oaths:** i.e. sworn testimony.
16. **grand-jurymen:** i.e. experts in evaluating evidence.

only to exasperate you, to awake your dormouse valor, to put fire in your heart, and brimstone in your liver. You should then have accosted her, and with some excellent jests, fire-new from the mint, you should have bang'd the youth into dumbness. This was look'd for at your hand, and this was balk'd. The double gilt of this opportunity you let time wash off, and you are now sail'd into the north of my lady's opinion, where you will hang like an icicle on a Dutchman's beard, unless you do redeem it by some laudable attempt either of valor or policy.

Sir And. And't be any way, it must be with valor, for policy I hate. I had as lief be a Brownist as a politician.

Sir To. Why then build me thy fortunes upon the basis of valor. Challenge me the Count's youth to fight with him, hurt him in eleven places—my niece shall take note of it, and assure thyself, there is no love-broker in the world can more prevail in man's commendation with woman than report of valor.

Fab. There is no way but this, Sir Andrew.

Sir And. Will either of you bear me a challenge to him?

Sir To. Go, write it in a martial hand, be curst and brief. It is no matter how witty, so it be eloquent and full of invention. Taunt him with the license of ink. If thou thou'st him some thrice, it shall not be amiss; and as many lies as will lie in thy sheet of paper, although the sheet were big enough for the bed of Ware in England, set 'em down. Go about it. Let there be gall enough in thy ink, though thou write with a goose-pen, no matter. About it.

Sir And. Where shall I find you?

Sir To. We'll call thee at the cubiculo. Go.

Exit Sir Andrew.

Fab. This is a dear manikin to you, Sir Toby.

Sir To. I have been dear to him, lad, some two thousand strong, or so.

Fab. We shall have a rare letter from him; but you'll not deliver't?

Sir To. Never trust me then; and by all means stir on the youth to an answer. I think oxen and wain-ropes cannot hale them together. For Andrew, if he were open'd and you find so much blood in his liver as will clog the foot of a flea, I'll eat the rest of th' anatomy.

Fab. And his opposite, the youth, bears in his visage no great presage of cruelty.

Enter MARIA.

Sir To. Look where the youngest wren of [nine] comes.

Mar. If you desire the spleen, and will laugh yourselves into stitches, follow me. Yond gull Malvolio is turn'd heathen, a very renegado; for there is no Christian that means to be sav'd by believing rightly can ever believe such impossible passages of grossness. He's in yellow stockings.

Sir To. And cross-garter'd?

Mar. Most villainously; like a pedant that keeps a school i' th' church. I have dogg'd him like his murtherer. He does obey every point of the letter that I dropp'd to betray him. He does smile his face into more lines than is in the new map, with the augmentation of the Indies; you have not seen such a thing as 'tis. I can hardly forbear hurling things at him. I know my lady will strike him. If she do, he'll smile, and take't for a great favor.

Sir To. Come bring us, bring us where he is.

Exeunt omnes.

SCENE III

Enter SEBASTIAN *and* ANTONIO.

Seb. I would not by my will have troubled you,
But since you make your pleasure of your pains,
I will no further chide you.

Ant. I could not stay behind you. My desire
(More sharp than filed steel) did spur me forth,
And not all love to see you (though so much
As might have drawn one to a longer voyage)

19. dormouse: i.e. sleepy. **22. fire-new:** brand-new.
24. balk'd: neglected, let slip.
25. double gilt: double plating with gold; perhaps referring to Sir Andrew's double opportunity to prove his love and valor.
26. north: i.e. cold regions (of disfavor).
27–28. icicle . . . beard. Perhaps an allusion to William Barentz, a Dutchman who travelled to the Arctic in 1596–97 and wrote an account of his experiences which was entered in the Stationers' Register in June 1598 (earliest extant edition, 1609).
29. policy: cunning, strategy.
31. Brownist: a follower of Robert Browne, founder of the Congregationalist sect. **32. politician:** contriver, schemer.
33. build me: build (a colloquialism); cf. *Challenge me*, line 34.
37. love-broker: go-between in love matters.
38. report: reputation. **42. curst:** bad-tempered, insulting.
43. so: provided that, so long as.
44. invention: imagination. (Sir Toby is being intentionally contradictory in lines 43–44.)
44–45. with . . . ink: i.e. with the freedom that writing affords (arising in this case from its comparative safety).
45. If . . . him. *Thou* instead of *you* was the form of address used to friends and to social inferiors, hence an insult to a comparative stranger.
47–48. bed of Ware. This bed (which may be seen in the Victoria and Albert Museum, London) is eleven feet square.
49. gall: (1) an ingredient of ink; (2) acrimony.
50. goose-pen: quill pen made from a goose feather (with an implication that the letter will be couched in foolish terms).
52. call thee: call for you. **cubiculo:** little chamber.
53. dear . . . you: puppet dear to you (referring to Sir Toby's manipulation of him). **54. dear:** expensive.

58. then: i.e. if I don't. **59–60. wain-ropes:** wagon ropes.
60. hale: drag.
61. blood . . . liver. Cowards were thought to have white (bloodless) livers.
63. anatomy: a medical term meaning either "body" or "skeleton." In view of Sir Andrew's thinness, Sir Toby may intend the latter.
64. opposite: adversary.
66. youngest . . . nine: i.e. the very smallest of wrens.
68. the spleen: extreme mirth. The spleen was regarded as the source of immoderate or uncontrollable laughter. **69. gull:** dupe.
70. renegado: renegade, i.e. renouncer of his religion.
72–73. such . . . grossness: such obviously impossible expressions (as the letter contains).
75. pedant: schoolmaster (the point of the reference to his holding a school in the church is unexplained). **78. betray:** expose, ensnare.
79–80. lines . . . Indies. Probably referring to a map prepared by Edward Wright, Richard Hakluyt, and John Davis, and printed in 1600. It was the first English map based on Mercator's projection, and therefore showed North America (*the Indies*) as proportionately larger than in earlier maps. It is crisscrossed by numerous rhumb lines.

III.iii. Location: A street.
6. all: entirely, only.

But jealousy what might befall your travel,
Being skilless in these parts; which to a stranger,
Unguided and unfriended, often prove
Rough and unhospitable. My willing love,
The rather by these arguments of fear,
Set forth in your pursuit.

Seb. My kind Antonio,
I can no other answer make but thanks,
And thanks; and ever oft good turns
Are shuffled off with such uncurrent pay;
But were my worth as is my conscience firm,
You should find better dealing. What's to do?
Shall we go see the reliques of this town?

Ant. To-morrow, sir; best first go see your lodging.

Seb. I am not weary, and 'tis long to night;
I pray you let us satisfy our eyes
With the memorials and the things of fame
That do renown this city.

Ant. Would you'd pardon me.
I do not without danger walk these streets.
Once in a sea-fight 'gainst the Count his galleys
I did some service, of such note indeed,
That were I ta'en here, it would scarce be answer'd.

Seb. Belike you slew great number of his people?

Ant. Th' offense is not of such a bloody nature,
Albeit the quality of the time and quarrel
Might well have given us bloody argument.
It might have since been answer'd in repaying
What we took from them, which for traffic's sake
Most of our city did. Only myself stood out,
For which if I be lapsed in this place
I shall pay dear.

Seb. Do not then walk too open.

Ant. It doth not fit me. Hold, sir, here's my purse.
In the south suburbs at the Elephant
Is best to lodge. I will bespeak our diet,
Whiles you beguile the time, and feed your knowledge
With viewing of the town. There shall you have me.

Seb. Why I your purse?

Ant. Haply your eye shall light upon some toy
You have desire to purchase; and your store
I think is not for idle markets, sir.

Seb. I'll be your purse-bearer, and leave you
For an hour.

Ant. To th' Elephant.

Seb. I do remember. *Exeunt.*

Scene IV

Enter Olivia *and* Maria.

Oli. [*Aside.*] I have sent after him; he says he'll come.
How shall I feast him? What bestow of him?
For youth is bought more oft than begg'd or borrow'd.
I speak too loud.—
Where's Malvolio? He is sad and civil,
And suits well for a servant with my fortunes.
Where is Malvolio?

Mar. He's coming, madam, but in very strange manner. He is sure possess'd, madam.

Oli. Why, what's the matter? does he rave?

Mar. No, madam, he does nothing but smile. Your ladyship were best to have some guard about you, if he come, for sure the man is tainted in 's wits.

Oli. Go call him hither.

Enter Malvolio.

I am as mad as he,
If sad and merry madness equal be.
How now, Malvolio?

Mal. Sweet lady, ho, ho.

Oli. Smil'st thou? I sent for thee upon a sad occasion.

Mal. Sad, lady? I could be sad. This does make some obstruction in the blood, this cross-gartering, but what of that? If it please the eye of one, it is with me as the very true sonnet is, "Please one, and please all."

[*Oli.*] Why, how dost thou, man? What is the matter with thee?

Mal. Not black in my mind, though yellow in my legs. It did come to his hands, and commands shall be executed. I think we do know the sweet Roman hand.

Oli. Wilt thou go to bed, Malvolio?

Mal. To bed? Ay, sweet heart, and I'll come to thee.

Oli. God comfort thee! Why dost thou smile so, and kiss thy hand so oft?

Mar. How do you, Malvolio?

Mal. At your request! Yes, nightingales answer daws.

8. jealousy: suspicion, anxiety. **9. skilless in**: unfamiliar with.
15. And . . . turns. A much-emended line. Sense can be made of it by taking *ever oft* as "it has always been true that frequently," but the awkwardness of this and the metrical deficiency of the line strongly suggest corruption. Most editors adopt Theobald's *And thanks, and ever thanks; and oft good turns.*
16. shuffled off: shrugged off. **uncurrent pay**: payment in worthless money, i.e. mere thanks. An uncurrent coin is one not accepted as legal tender.
17. worth: wealth. **conscience**: awareness (of my indebtedness).
19. reliques: relics of the past, ancient monuments (see line 23).
24. renown: make famous. **26. Count his**: Count's.
28. it . . . answer'd: it would be difficult for me to make a defense.
29. Belike: probably. **31. quality**: i.e. circumstances.
32. bloody argument: occasion for bloodshed.
34. for traffic's sake: in order to resume trading.
36. lapsed: caught napping, taken by surprise (literally, slipped).
38. fit: behoove. **39. Elephant**: the name of an inn.
40. bespeak our diet: order our food.
42. have me: know where to find me.
44. Haply: perchance. **toy**: trifle. **45. store**: supply of money.
46. idle markets: luxuries.

III.iv. Location: Olivia's garden.
1. he . . . come. In view of lines 57–58, this apparently means "if he says he'll come."
5. sad: sober, serious (so also in line 18). **civil**: seemly, decorous.
6. suits: accords. **9. possess'd**: i.e. possessed of an evil spirit.
10. rave: talk incoherently. **13. tainted**: infected, disordered.
23. sonnet: poem. **Please . . . all**: i.e. if I please you, I please everyone I care to please (the first line and refrain of a popular ballad published in 1592).
26–27. Not . . . legs. Meaning not entirely clear. *To wear yellow hose* meant "to be jealous," and Malvolio may mean "Though I wear yellow on my legs, my thoughts are not black, i.e. I don't wear yellow because I am jealous." His main intent, of course, is to call attention to the stockings.
28. Roman hand. The Italian script, resembling our own, which was beginning to replace the English or secretary hand.
35–36. At . . . daws: i.e. am I to notice a question from you? O, certainly, a nightingale should answer a crow. (Malvolio is being "surly with servants," as instructed.)

Mar. Why appear you with this ridiculous boldness before my lady?

Mal. "Be not afraid of greatness": 'twas well writ.

Oli. What mean'st thou by that, Malvolio?

Mal. "Some are born great"—

Oli. Ha?

Mal. "Some achieve greatness"—

Oli. What say'st thou?

Mal. "And some have greatness thrust upon them."

Oli. Heaven restore thee!

Mal. "Remember who commended thy yellow stockings"—

Oli. Thy yellow stockings?

Mal. "And wish'd to see thee cross-garter'd."

Oli. Cross-garter'd?

Mal. "Go to, thou art made, if thou desir'st to be so"—

Oli. Am I made?

Mal. "If not, let me see thee a servant still."

Oli. Why, this is very midsummer madness.

Enter SERVANT.

Serv. Madam, the young gentleman of the Count Orsino's is return'd. I could hardly entreat him back. He attends your ladyship's pleasure.

Oli. I'll come to him. [*Exit Servant.*] Good Maria, let this fellow be look'd to. Where's my cousin Toby? Let some of my people have a special care of him. I would not have him miscarry for the half of my dowry.

Exit [*with Maria*].

Mal. O ho, do you come near me now? No worse man than Sir Toby to look to me! This concurs directly with the letter: she sends him on purpose, that I may appear stubborn to him; for she incites me to that in the letter. "Cast thy humble slough," says she; "be opposite with a kinsman, surly with servants; let thy tongue [tang] with arguments of state; put thyself into the trick of singularity"; and consequently sets down the manner how: as a sad face, a reverend carriage, a slow tongue, in the habit of some sir of note, and so forth. I have lim'd her, but it is Jove's doing, and Jove make me thankful! And when she went away now, "Let this fellow be look'd to"; "fellow"! not "Malvolio," nor after my degree, but "fellow." Why, every thing adheres together, that no dram of a scruple, no scruple of a scruple, no obstacle, no incredulous or unsafe circumstance—What can be said? Nothing that can be can come between me and the full prospect of my hopes. Well, Jove, not I, is the doer of this, and he is to be thank'd.

Enter TOBY, FABIAN, *and* MARIA.

Sir To. Which way is he, in the name of sanctity? If all the devils of hell be drawn in little, and Legion himself possess'd him, yet I'll speak to him.

Fab. Here he is, here he is. How is't with you, sir?

[*Sir To.*] How is't with you, man?

Mal. Go off, I discard you. Let me enjoy my private. Go off.

Mar. Lo, how hollow the fiend speaks within him! Did not I tell you? Sir Toby, my lady prays you to have a care of him.

Mal. Ah ha, does she so?

Sir To. Go to, go to; peace, peace, we must deal gently with him. Let me alone. How do you, Malvolio? How is't with you? What, man, defy the devil! Consider, he's an enemy to mankind.

Mal. Do you know what you say?

Mar. La you, and you speak ill of the devil, how he takes it at heart! Pray God he be not bewitch'd!

Fab. Carry his water to th' wise woman.

Mar. Marry, and it shall be done to-morrow morning if I live. My lady would not lose him for more than I'll say.

Mal. How now, mistress?

Mar. O Lord!

Sir To. Prithee hold thy peace, this is not the way. Do you not see you move him? Let me alone with him.

Fab. No way but gentleness, gently, gently. The fiend is rough, and will not be roughly us'd.

Sir To. Why, how now, my bawcock? How dost thou, chuck?

Mal. Sir!

Sir To. Ay, biddy, come with me. What, man, 'tis not for gravity to play at cherry-pit with Sathan. Hang him, foul collier!

Mar. Get him to say his prayers, good Sir Toby, get him to pray.

Mal. My prayers, minx!

Mar. No, I warrant you, he will not hear of godliness.

56. midsummer madness. Proverbial; the midsummer moon was traditionally associated with insanity. **59. attends:** awaits.
61. fellow: man (used of a servant or social inferior, without contemptuous sense). **63. miscarry:** come to harm.
64. come near: begin to understand.
67. stubborn: rude, harsh. **incites:** encourages.
71. consequently: thereafter. **72. reverend:** dignified.
73. slow tongue: deliberate manner of speaking. **habit . . . note:** attire of a kind suitable for a distinguished gentleman.
74. lim'd: caught as with birdlime (a sticky substance spread on bushes to ensnare small birds).
77. fellow. Malvolio takes the word to mean "companion." **after my degree:** according to my place, i.e. "steward."
78. adheres together: hangs together.
79. dram: small quantity (one-eighth of a fluid ounce). **scruple:** (1) doubt; (2) smallest quantity (one-third of a dram).
80. incredulous: incredible. **unsafe:** uncertain.
82. prospect: range, scope.
84. in . . . sanctity: in the name of all that is holy.
85. drawn in little: contracted into small compass (so that they could all find room in Malvolio's bosom). **Legion.** Alluding to Mark 5:8–9: "For he [Jesus] said unto him, Come out of the man, thou unclean spirit. And he asked him, What is thy name? And he answered, saying, My name is Legion: for we are many" (Geneva).
89. discard: cast off, want nothing to do with.
89–90. private: privacy. **91. hollow:** deep, resounding (adverbial).
93. have . . . of: be attentive to, take care of.
96. Let me alone: leave him to me. **97. defy:** renounce.
100. La you: an exclamation. **and:** if, when.
101. bewitch'd. Demoniac possession was sometimes attributed to witchcraft. **102. water:** urine (for analysis).
109. move him: make him angry.
111. rough: violent. **us'd:** treated.
112. bawcock: fine fellow (from French *beau coq*).
113. chuck: chick (a term of endearment).
115. biddy: child's name for a chicken.
116. gravity: a grave man. **cherry-pit:** a child's game in which cherry stones are thrown into a hole. Sir Toby provokingly talks to Malvolio as if he were a child and at the same time warns him that his soul is in danger.
117. foul collier: filthy coal-miner. Devils were always represented as coal-black, and they worked in hell-pit.
120. minx: impudent woman.

Mal. Go hang yourselves all! You are idle shallow things, I am not of your element. You shall know more hereafter. *Exit.*

Sir To. Is't possible?

Fab. If this were play'd upon a stage now, I could condemn it as an improbable fiction.

Sir To. His very genius hath taken the infection of the device, man.

Mar. Nay, pursue him now, lest the device take air, and taint.

Fab. Why, we shall make him mad indeed.

Mar. The house will be the quieter.

Sir To. Come, we'll have him in a dark room and bound. My niece is already in the belief that he's mad. We may carry it thus, for our pleasure and his penance, till our very pastime, tir'd out of breath, prompt us to have mercy on him; at which time we will bring the device to the bar and crown thee for a finder of madmen. But see, but see.

Enter Sir Andrew.

Fab. More matter for a May morning.

Sir And. Here's the challenge, read it. I warrant there's vinegar and pepper in't.

Fab. Is't so saucy?

Sir And. Ay, is't! I warrant him. Do but read.

Sir To. Give me. [*Reads.*] "Youth, whatsoever thou art, thou art but a scurvy fellow."

Fab. Good, and valiant.

Sir To. [*Reads.*] "Wonder not, nor admire not in thy mind, why I do call thee so, for I will show thee no reason for't."

Fab. A good note, that keeps you from the blow of the law.

Sir To. [*Reads.*] "Thou com'st to the Lady Olivia, and in my sight she uses thee kindly. But thou liest in thy throat, that is not the matter I challenge thee for."

Fab. Very brief, and to exceeding good sense—less.

Sir To. [*Reads.*] "I will waylay thee going home, where if it be thy chance to kill me"—

Fab. Good.

Sir To. [*Reads.*] "Thou kill'st me like a rogue and a villain."

Fab. Still you keep o' th' windy side of the law; good.

Sir To. [*Reads.*] "Fare thee well, and God have mercy upon one of our souls! He may have mercy upon mine, but my hope is better, and so look to thyself. Thy friend as thou usest him, and thy sworn enemy, Andrew Aguecheek." If this letter move him not, his legs cannot. I'll give't him.

Mar. You may have very fit occasion for't; he is now in some commerce with my lady, and will by and by depart.

Sir To. Go, Sir Andrew, scout me for him at the corner of the orchard like a bum-baily. So soon as ever thou seest him, draw, and as thou draw'st, swear horrible; for it comes to pass oft that a terrible oath, with a swaggering accent sharply twang'd off, gives manhood more approbation than ever proof itself would have earn'd him. Away!

Sir And. Nay, let me alone for swearing. *Exit.*

Sir To. Now will not I deliver his letter; for the behavior of the young gentleman gives him out to be of good capacity and breeding; his employment between his lord and my niece confirms no less. Therefore this letter, being so excellently ignorant, will breed no terror in the youth; he will find it comes from a clodpole. But, sir, I will deliver his challenge by word of mouth, set upon Aguecheek a notable report of valor, and drive the gentleman (as I know his youth will aptly receive it) into a most hideous opinion of his rage, skill, fury, and impetuosity. This will so fright them both that they will kill one another by the look, like cockatrices.

Enter Olivia *and* Viola.

Fab. Here he comes with your niece. Give them way till he take leave, and presently after him.

Sir To. I will meditate the while upon some horrid message for a challenge.

[*Exeunt Sir Toby, Fabian, and Maria.*]

Oli. I have said too much unto a heart of stone,
And laid mine honor too unchary on't.
There's something in me that reproves my fault;
But such a headstrong potent fault it is
That it but mocks reproof.

Vio. With the same havior that your passion bears
Goes on my master's griefs.

Oli. Here, wear this jewel for me, 'tis my picture.

123. idle: foolish.
124. I . . . element: i.e. I do not belong to your earthy level. **know more**: hear about this.
129. genius: governing principle of his being (literally, attendant spirit).
131–32. take . . . taint: (1) be exposed to (noxious) air and corrupt; (2) become known and be spoiled.
135–36. dark . . . bound. A common treatment at this time for the insane. **137. carry it**: keep it going.
140. bar: i.e. bar of judgment.
142. matter . . . morning: material for a May-day comedy.
145. saucy: (1) highly spiced; (2) insolent.
146. I warrant him: I guarantee he (Cesario) will be taken care of.
150. admire: marvel.
153–54. A . . . law: i.e. a carefully worded challenge, that safeguards you from a charge of slander.
156–57. in thy throat: in the most heinous degree.
164. windy side: windward, i.e. safe (because, as before, the abuse is too feeble to be defamatory, but perhaps also because *like a rogue and a villain* can be taken to modify *me*, not *thou*).
169. Thy . . . him: your friend insofar as you behave in a friendly fashion toward him.
171. move him: stir him up (with following quibble).
173. fit: convenient. **174. commerce**: dealing, business.
174–75. will . . . depart: is on the verge of departing.
176. scout me: keep watch.
177. bum-baily: petty sheriff's officer who arrested for debt.
180–81. gives . . . approbation: gives valor a higher reputation, i.e. gives a man a higher reputation for valor.
181. proof: actual trial, performance.
183. let . . . swearing: have no fears about my ability to swear.
185. gives him out: declares him. **186. capacity**: ability.
189. find: detect, see.
190. clodpole: knucklehead (variant form of *clodpoll*).
193. youth: i.e. inexperience. **aptly receive it**: readily credit the report.
196. cockatrices: basilisks, fabulous serpents that were supposedly able to kill by their glance alone.
197–98. Give them way: stay out of their way.
198. presently: immediately.
202. laid: hazarded. **unchary**: carelessly.
204. potent: powerful. **206. havior**: behavior.
208. jewel. Used of any product of the jeweller's art; here a brooch or locket with Olivia's picture set in it.

Refuse it not, it hath no tongue to vex you;
And I beseech you come again to-morrow.
What shall you ask of me that I'll deny,
That honor, sav'd, may upon asking give?

Vio. Nothing but this—your true love for my master.

Oli. How with mine honor may I give him that
Which I have given to you?

Vio. I will acquit you.

Oli. Well, come again to-morrow. Fare thee well.
A fiend like thee might bear my soul to hell. [*Exit.*]

Enter Toby *and* Fabian.

Sir To. Gentleman, God save thee!

Vio. And you, sir.

Sir To. That defense thou hast, betake thee to't. Of what nature the wrongs are thou hast done him, I know not; but thy intercepter, full of despite, bloody as the hunter, attends thee at the orchard-end. Dismount thy tuck, be yare in thy preparation, for thy assailant is quick, skillful, and deadly.

Vio. You mistake, sir, I am sure; no man hath any quarrel to me. My remembrance is very free and clear from any image of offense done to any man.

Sir To. You'll find it otherwise, I assure you; therefore, if you hold your life at any price, betake you to your guard; for your opposite hath in him what youth, strength, skill, and wrath can furnish man withal.

Vio. I pray you, sir, what is he?

Sir To. He is knight, dubb'd with unhatch'd rapier, and on carpet consideration, but he is a devil in private brawl. Souls and bodies hath he divorc'd three, and his incensement at this moment is so implacable, that satisfaction can be none but by pangs of death and sepulchre. Hob, nob, is his word; give't or take't.

Vio. I will return again into the house, and desire some conduct of the lady. I am no fighter. I have heard of some kind of men that put quarrels purposely on others, to taste their valor. Belike this is a man of that quirk.

Sir To. Sir, no; his indignation derives itself out of a very [competent] injury; therefore get you on, and give him his desire. Back you shall not to the house, unless you undertake that with me which with as much safety you might answer him; therefore on, or strip your sword stark naked; for meddle you must, that's certain, or forswear to wear iron about you.

Vio. This is as uncivil as strange. I beseech you do me this courteous office, as to know of the knight what my offense to him is. It is something of my negligence, nothing of my purpose.

Sir To. I will do so. Signior Fabian, stay you by this gentleman till my return. *Exit Toby.*

Vio. Pray you, sir, do you know of this matter?

Fab. I know the knight is incens'd against you, even to a mortal arbitrement, but nothing of the circumstance more.

Vio. I beseech you, what manner of man is he?

Fab. Nothing of that wonderful promise, to read him by his form, as you are like to find him in the proof of his valor. He is indeed, sir, the most skillful, bloody, and fatal opposite that you could possibly have found in any part of Illyria. Will you walk towards him? I will make your peace with him if I can.

Vio. I shall be much bound to you for't. I am one that had rather go with sir priest than sir knight. I care not who knows so much of my mettle. *Exeunt.*

Enter Toby *and* Andrew.

Sir To. Why, man, he's a very devil, I have not seen such a firago. I had a pass with him, rapier, scabbard, and all; and he gives me the stuck in with such a mortal motion that it is inevitable; and on the answer, he pays you as surely as your feet hits the ground they step on. They say he has been fencer to the Sophy.

Sir And. Pox on't, I'll not meddle with him.

Sir To. Ay, but he will not now be pacified. Fabian can scarce hold him yonder.

Sir And. Plague on't, and I thought he had been valiant, and so cunning in fence, I'd have seen him damn'd ere I'd have challeng'd him. Let him let the matter slip, and I'll give him my horse, grey Capilet.

Sir To. I'll make the motion. Stand here, make a good show on't; this shall end without the perdition of souls. [*Aside.*] Marry, I'll ride your horse as well as I ride you.

Enter Fabian *and* Viola.

212. sav'd: i.e. without injury to itself, safely.
215. acquit: waive all claim to.
217. like thee: in your likeness. **might:** i.e. could without resistance from me.
220. That defense: whatever skill in fencing.
222. intercepter: ambusher. **despite:** contempt and hatred.
223. bloody . . . hunter: i.e. as intent on bloodshed as the hunting dog tracking down its prey.
224. Dismount thy tuck: draw your rapier. **yare:** ready, brisk.
227. quarrel to: reason to quarrel with. **remembrance:** memory.
230. price: value. **231. opposite:** adversary.
233. withal: with.
235. unhatch'd: unhacked, undented (i.e. never used in battle).
236. on carpet consideration. A carpet knighthood was one not given on the battlefield for services performed there, hence often one given for political reasons; *consideration* suggests a bought knighthood.
240. Hob, nob: have it, have it not; i.e. "give't or take't." **word:** motto. **242. conduct:** protective escort.
244. taste: make trial of.
247. competent: sufficient. **249. that:** i.e. a duel.
251. strip . . . naked: draw your sword now (and fight with me). **meddle:** have to do, be involved. Cf. line 280, where *not meddle with* = have nothing to do with.
252. forswear . . . you: renounce your right to wear a sword.
254. know of: ascertain from. **255. of:** arising from.
256. purpose: intention.
261. to . . . arbitrement: to a point requiring settlement by a duel to the death. **264–65. read . . . form:** judge him by his appearance.
271. sir priest. Priests were often addressed by the courtesy title *sir.*
272. mettle: temperament.
274. firago: virago. Schmidt suggests that Sir Toby uses this word, applicable only to a woman (its original meaning is "acting like a man"), as a linguistic joke on Sir Andrew, who has not studied languages (I.iii.92–93); if so, there is a joke on Sir Toby also. **pass:** bout.
275. gives me: gives. **stuck in:** stoccado (or stoccato), thrust.
277. answer: return hit. **pays:** repays.
283. and . . . been: if I had supposed he was.
287. Capilet: a name meaning "little horse." It is typical of Sir Andrew's imagination that he should name a little horse "little horse."
288. motion: offer. **288–89. make . . . show:** put a good face.
289–90. perdition of souls: loss of lives.

[*To Fabian.*] I have his horse to take up the quarrel. I have persuaded him the youth's a devil.

Fab. He is as horribly conceited of him; and pants and looks pale, as if a bear were at his heels.

Sir To. [*To Viola.*] There's no remedy, sir, he will fight with you for 's oath sake. Marry, he hath better bethought him of his quarrel, and he finds that now scarce to be worth talking of; therefore draw, for the supportance of his vow. He protests he will not hurt you.

Vio. [*Aside.*] Pray God defend me! A little thing would make me tell them how much I lack of a man.

Fab. Give ground if you see him furious.

Sir To. Come, Sir Andrew, there's no remedy, the gentleman will for his honor's sake have one bout with you. He cannot by the duello avoid it; but he has promis'd me, as he is a gentleman and a soldier, he will not hurt you. Come on, to't.

Sir And. Pray God he keep his oath!

Enter ANTONIO.

Vio. I do assure you, 'tis against my will.
[*They draw.*]

Ant. Put up your sword. If this young gentleman
Have done offense, I take the fault on me;
If you offend him, I for him defy you.

Sir To. You, sir? Why, what are you?

Ant. One, sir, that for his love dares yet do more
Than you have heard him brag to you he will.

Sir To. Nay, if you be an undertaker, I am for you.
[*They draw.*]

Enter OFFICERS.

Fab. O good Sir Toby, hold! here come the officers.

Sir To. [*To Antonio.*] I'll be with you anon.
[*Steps aside to avoid the Officers.*]

Vio. Pray, sir, put your sword up, if you please.

Sir And. Marry, will I, sir; and for that I promis'd you, I'll be as good as my word. He will bear you easily, and reins well.

1. Off. This is the man, do thy office.

2. Off. Antonio, I arrest thee at the suit of Count Orsino.

Ant. You do mistake me, sir.

1. Off. No, sir, no jot. I know your favor well,
Though now you have no sea-cap on your head.
Take him away, he knows I know him well.

Ant. I must obey. [*To Viola.*] This comes with seeking you;
But there's no remedy, I shall answer it.
What will you do, now my necessity
Makes me to ask you for my purse? It grieves me
Much more for what I cannot do for you
Than what befalls myself. You stand amaz'd,
But be of comfort.

2. Off. Come, sir, away.

Ant. I must entreat of you some of that money.

Vio. What money, sir?
For the fair kindness you have show'd me here,
And part being prompted by your present trouble,
Out of my lean and low ability
I'll lend you something. My having is not much;
I'll make division of my present with you.
Hold, there's half my coffer.

Ant. Will you deny me now?
Is't possible that my deserts to you
Can lack persuasion? Do not tempt my misery,
Lest that it make me so unsound a man
As to upbraid you with those kindnesses
That I have done for you.

Vio. I know of none,
Nor know I you by voice or any feature.
I hate ingratitude more in a man
Than lying, vainness, babbling, drunkenness,
Or any taint of vice whose strong corruption
Inhabits our frail blood.

Ant. O heavens themselves!

2. Off. Come, sir, I pray you go.

Ant. Let me speak a little. This youth that you see here
I snatch'd one half out of the jaws of death,
Reliev'd him with such sanctity of love,
And to his image, which methought did promise
Most venerable worth, did I devotion.

1. Off. What's that to us? The time goes by; away!

Ant. But O, how vild an idol proves this god!
Thou hast, Sebastian, done good feature shame.
In nature there's no blemish but the mind;
None can be call'd deform'd but the unkind.
Virtue is beauty, but the beauteous evil
Are empty trunks o'erflourish'd by the devil.

1. Off. The man grows mad, away with him! Come, come, sir.

Ant. Lead me on. *Exit* [*with Officers*].

Vio. Methinks his words do from such passion fly
That he believes himself; so do not I.
Prove true, imagination, O, prove true,
That I, dear brother, be now ta'en for you!

292. take up: settle.
294. He . . . him: i.e. the youth has as dreadful a conception of Sir Andrew. **297. for 's:** for his.
298. bethought . . . quarrel: considered the grounds for his challenge.
300. supportance: upholding. **protests:** solemnly promises.
307. duello: the code of duelling.
318. undertaker: i.e. one who takes up a challenge for another.
320. be . . . anon: be back right away.
322–23. that . . . you: i.e. the horse Capilet (about which of course Viola knows nothing). **324. easily:** smoothly.
325. office: duty, function. **329. favor:** face.
333. answer it: i.e. make what defense I can.

337. amaz'd: bewildered. **343. part:** in part.
344. ability: means. **345. My having:** what I possess.
346. present: ready money.
347. coffer: store of wealth (literally, strong-box).
349. lack persuasion: fail to persuade you. **tempt:** try too far.
350. unsound: unhealthy (used figuratively).
355. vainness: vanity. **babbling:** foolish, loose talk.
356. any . . . vice: the taint of any fault.
360. one . . . death: out of the jaws of death which had half-swallowed him. **361. such.** Used here with intensive force.
362. his image: what he appeared to be (with play on *image* in the sense "religious statue").
363. venerable worth: worthiness of veneration. **365. vild:** vile.
366. Thou . . . shame. Alluding to the belief that physical beauty is a reflection of spiritual beauty. **feature:** physical form.
368. unkind: unnatural. The unnatural quality with which he is charging the supposed Sebastian is of course ingratitude.
370. trunks o'erflourish'd: (1) chests covered over with elaborate carvings; (2) bodies made externally beautiful.
374. so . . . I: I do not believe myself, i.e. I don't quite dare to believe what all this suggests to me (that my brother is alive).

Sir To. Come hither, knight; come hither, Fabian; we'll whisper o'er a couplet or two of most sage saws.

Vio. He nam'd Sebastian. I my brother know
Yet living in my glass; even such and so
In favor was my brother, and he went
Still in this fashion, color, ornament,
For him I imitate. O, if it prove,
Tempests are kind and salt waves fresh in love.
[*Exit.*]

Sir To. A very dishonest paltry boy, and more a coward than a hare. His dishonesty appears in leaving his friend here in necessity, and denying him; and for his cowardship, ask Fabian.

Fab. A coward, a most devout coward, religious in it.

Sir And. 'Slid, I'll after him again, and beat him.

Sir To. Do, cuff him soundly, but never draw thy sword.

Sir And. And I do not— [*Exit.*]

Fab. Come, let's see the event.

Sir To. I dare lay any money 'twill be nothing yet. *Exeunt.*

ACT IV, Scene I

Enter Sebastian *and* Clown.

Clo. Will you make me believe that I am not sent for you?

Seb. Go to, go to, thou art a foolish fellow,
Let me be clear of thee.

Clo. Well held out, i' faith! No, I do not know you, nor I am not sent to you by my lady, to bid you come speak with her, nor your name is not Master Cesario, nor this is not my nose neither: nothing that is so is so.

Seb. I prithee vent thy folly somewhere else,
Thou know'st not me.

Clo. Vent my folly! He has heard that word of some great man, and now applies it to a fool. Vent my folly! I am afraid this great lubber the world will prove a cockney. I prithee now ungird thy strangeness, and tell me what I shall vent to my lady. Shall I vent to her that thou art coming?

Seb. I prithee, foolish Greek, depart from me.
There's money for thee. If you tarry longer,
I shall give worse payment.

Clo. By my troth, thou hast an open hand. These wise men that give fools money get themselves a good report—after fourteen years' purchase.

Enter Andrew, Toby, *and* Fabian.

Sir And. Now, sir, have I met you again? There's for you. [*Strikes Sebastian.*]

Seb. Why, there's for thee, and there, and there. [*Strikes Sir Andrew.*] Are all the people mad? [*Draws his dagger.*]

Sir To. Hold, sir, or I'll throw your dagger o'er the house. [*Seizes Sebastian's arm.*]

Clo. This will I tell my lady straight; I would not be in some of your coats for twopence. [*Exit.*]

Sir To. Come on, sir, hold!

Sir And. Nay, let him alone. I'll go another way to work with him; I'll have an action of battery against him, if there be any law in Illyria. Though I strook him first, yet it's no matter for that.

Seb. Let go thy hand.

Sir To. Come, sir, I will not let you go. Come, my young soldier, put up your iron; you are well flesh'd. Come on.

Seb. I will be free from thee. [*Breaks away and draws his sword.*] What wouldst thou now?
If thou dar'st tempt me further, draw thy sword.

Sir To. What, what? Nay then I must have an ounce or two of this malapert blood from you. [*Draws.*]

Enter Olivia.

Oli. Hold, Toby, on thy life I charge thee hold!

Sir To. Madam—

Oli. Will it be ever thus? Ungracious wretch,
Fit for the mountains and the barbarous caves,
Where manners ne'er were preach'd! Out of my sight!
Be not offended, dear Cesario.
Rudesby, be gone!
[*Exeunt Sir Toby, Sir Andrew, and Fabian.*]
I prithee, gentle friend,
Let thy fair wisdom, not thy passion, sway
In this uncivil and unjust extent
Against thy peace. Go with me to my house,
And hear thou there how many fruitless pranks
This ruffian hath botch'd up, that thou thereby
Mayst smile at this. Thou shalt not choose but go;

378. saws: sayings, maxims.
379–80. I . . . glass: I know that the appearance of my brother is still alive every time I look in a mirror (i.e. I am the living image of my brother). **381–82. went Still in:** always wore.
383. prove: prove true. **385. dishonest:** dishonorable.
385–86. more a coward: more cowardly.
391. 'Slid: by God's eyelid. **394. And:** if.
395. event: outcome.
396. yet: now as before (?) or nevertheless (?) or after all (?).

IV.i. Location: Before Olivia's house.
4. clear: rid. **5. held out:** persisted in.
10. vent thy folly: utter your foolish talk. *Vent* was in common use, and it is hard to understand why Feste chooses to think it affected.
14. lubber: clumsy stupid fellow, lout.
15. cockney: overnice, effeminate fellow.
15–16. ungird thy strangeness: put off your pretense of being a stranger. **18. Greek:** i.e. jester.

23. report: reputation. **after . . . purchase:** i.e. provided they give generously enough. "Fourteen years' purchase" would be a high price for a piece of land, since the ordinary purchase price was based on twelve years' rental.
28. Hold: stop. **30. straight:** straightway, at once.
31. be . . . coats: i.e. be in the shoes of some of you.
33–34. go . . . him: get at him in another way.
34. action of battery: a lawsuit for assault and battery.
35. strook: struck (a common variant).
37. Let . . . hand: let go of me.
38–39. Come, my . . . flesh'd. Addressed ironically, some commentators believe, to Sir Andrew (who would then have "flesh'd" or used for the first time in battle his "unhatch'd rapier" [III.iv.235]). But it is far from evident that Sir Andrew has drawn his "iron," and certainly it is Sebastian whom Sir Toby is intent on restraining from line 28 on. If these words are addressed to him, as seems far more likely, *you are well flesh'd* = you have had a sufficient taste of combat.
44. malapert: impudent, saucy. **47. Ungracious:** graceless.
51. Rudesby: unmannerly fellow. **52. fair:** clear, equitable.
53. uncivil: barbarous (cf. lines 48–49). **unjust:** unlawful. **extent:** show of violence. **55. fruitless:** idle.
56. botch'd up: patched together, clumsily contrived.

Do not deny. Beshrew his soul for me,
He started one poor heart of mine, in thee.
Seb. What relish is in this? How runs the stream?
Or I am mad, or else this is a dream.
Let fancy still my sense in Lethe steep;
If it be thus to dream, still let me sleep!
Oli. Nay, come, I prithee. Would thou'dst be rul'd by me!
Seb. Madam, I will.
Oli. O, say so, and so be! *Exeunt.*

Scene II

Enter Maria *and* Clown.

Mar. Nay, I prithee put on this gown and this beard, make him believe thou art Sir Topas the curate, do it quickly. I'll call Sir Toby the whilst. [*Exit.*]

Clo. Well, I'll put it on, and I will dissemble myself in't, and I would I were the first that ever dissembled in such a gown. I am not tall enough to become the function well, nor lean enough to be thought a good studient; but to be said an honest man and a good house-keeper goes as fairly as to say a careful man and a great scholar. The competitors enter.

Enter Toby [*and* Maria].

Sir To. Jove bless thee, Master Parson.

Clo. *Bonos dies*, Sir Toby: for as the old hermit of Prague, that never saw pen and ink, very wittily said to a niece of King Gorboduc, "That that is is"; so I, being Master Parson, am Master Parson; for what is "that" but "that," and "is" but "is"?

Sir To. To him, Sir Topas.

Clo. What ho, I say! Peace in this prison!

Sir To. The knave counterfeits well; a good knave.

Mal. (*Within.*) Who calls there?

Clo. Sir Topas the curate, who comes to visit Malvolio the lunatic.

Mal. Sir Topas, Sir Topas, good Sir Topas, go to my lady.

Clo. Out, hyperbolical fiend! how vexest thou this man! Talkest thou nothing but of ladies?

Sir To. Well said, Master Parson.

Mal. Sir Topas, never was man thus wrong'd. Good Sir Topas, do not think I am mad; they have laid me here in hideous darkness.

Clo. Fie, thou dishonest Sathan! I call thee by the most modest terms, for I am one of those gentle ones that will use the devil himself with courtesy. Say'st thou that house is dark?

Mal. As hell, Sir Topas.

Clo. Why, it hath bay windows transparent as barricadoes, and the [clerestories] toward the south north are as lustrous as ebony; and yet complainest thou of obstruction?

Mal. I am not mad, Sir Topas, I say to you this house is dark.

Clo. Madman, thou errest. I say there is no darkness but ignorance, in which thou art more puzzled than the Egyptians in their fog.

Mal. I say this house is as dark as ignorance, though ignorance were as dark as hell; and I say there was never man thus abus'd. I am no more mad than you are; make the trial of it in any constant question.

Clo. What is the opinion of Pythagoras concerning wild-fowl?

Mal. That the soul of our grandam might happily inhabit a bird.

Clo. What think'st thou of his opinion?

Mal. I think nobly of the soul, and no way approve his opinion.

Clo. Fare thee well. Remain thou still in darkness. Thou shalt hold th' opinion of Pythagoras ere I will allow of thy wits, and fear to kill a woodcock lest thou dispossess the soul of thy grandam. Fare thee well.

Mal. Sir Topas, Sir Topas!

Sir To. My most exquisite Sir Topas!

Clo. Nay, I am for all waters.

Mar. Thou mightst have done this without thy beard and gown, he sees thee not.

Sir To. To him in thine own voice, and bring me word how thou find'st him. I would we were well rid of this knavery. If he may be conveniently deliver'd, I would he were, for I am now so far in offense with

58. Beshrew. Here much closer to its original sense "curse" than in II.iii.80.
59. He . . . thee: "He that offends thee, attacks one of my hearts, or as the ancients expressed it, half my heart" (Johnson). There may also be a glancing play on *hart*, suggested by *started*.
60. relish: taste, i.e. quality, nature. **61. Or:** either.
62. fancy: imagination. **Lethe:** the river of forgetfulness in the underworld.

IV.ii. Location: Olivia's house.
2. Sir Topas. Shakespeare may have borrowed the name from Chaucer's "Rime of Sir Thopas" in *The Canterbury Tales*. On *Sir* see the note to III.iv.271. **3. the whilst:** in the meantime.
4. dissemble: disguise.
5–6. dissembled: created a false impression, concealed his true nature.
6. tall. The sense here is probably "large, well-fleshed," in contrast to *lean*, line 7. Feste seems to be glancing jestingly at two traditional notions, that clerics are given to the pleasures of the table and that scholars lead ascetic lives.
6–7. become . . . well: grace the priestly office.
8. studient: scholar (a variant form of *student*, not Feste's invention). Most scholars were churchmen. **said:** known as.
8–9. good house-keeper: good manager of his household.
9. goes as fairly: sounds as well. **careful:** highly regardful of his duties. **10. competitors:** partners, confederates.
12. Bonos dies: for *bonus dies*, good day.
12–13. hermit of Prague. Now that Feste is a priest, the authority he invents is a man of religion. **13. wittily:** cleverly.
14. Gorboduc: a legendary king of England.

25. hyperbolical: vehement (a rhetorical term, meaning "exaggerated in style"). **fiend:** i.e. the devil by whom Malvolio is possessed.
32. modest: moderate. **34. house:** i.e. room.
37. barricadoes: barricades. **clerestories:** windows in the upper wall. **39. obstruction:** shutting out of light.
43. puzzled: greatly perplexed.
44. Egyptians . . . fog. An allusion to Exodus 10:22, "And Moses stretched forth his hand toward heaven; and there was a black darkness in all the land of Egypt three days" (Geneva).
48–49. constant question: topic for rational discourse.
50–51. Pythagoras . . . wild-fowl. Referring to the Pythagorean doctrine of transmigration of souls.
52. happily: haply, perchance.
59. allow . . . wits: grant that you are sane. **woodcock.** Proverbial for its stupidity.
62. exquisite: consummately accomplished.
63. for all waters: i.e. ready for anything (a phrase of unknown origin). **68. deliver'd:** set free.
69. far in offense: deeply in disgrace.

my niece that I cannot pursue with any safety this sport [t'] the upshot. Come by and by to my chamber.

Exit [*with Maria*].

Clo. [*Sings.*]

"Hey, Robin, jolly Robin,
Tell me how thy lady does."

Mal. Fool!

Clo. "My lady is unkind, perdie."

Mal. Fool!

Clo. "Alas, why is she so?"

Mal. Fool, I say!

Clo. "She loves another"—Who calls, ha?

Mal. Good fool, as ever thou wilt deserve well at my hand, help me to a candle, and pen, ink, and paper. As I am a gentleman, I will live to be thankful to thee for't.

Clo. Master Malvolio?

Mal. Ay, good fool.

Clo. Alas, sir, how fell you besides your five wits?

Mal. Fool, there was never man so notoriously abus'd; I am as well in my wits, fool, as thou art.

Clo. But as well! Then you are mad indeed, if you be no better in your wits than a fool.

Mal. They have here propertied me, keep me in darkness, send ministers to me, asses, and do all they can to face me out of my wits.

Clo. Advise you what you say; the minister is here. —Malvolio, Malvolio, thy wits the heavens restore! Endeavor thyself to sleep, and leave thy vain bibble babble.

Mal. Sir Topas!

Clo. Maintain no words with him, good fellow.—Who, I, sir? Not I, sir. God buy you, good Sir Topas.—Marry, amen.—I will, sir, I will.

Mal. Fool, fool, fool, I say!

Clo. Alas, sir, be patient. What say you, sir? I am shent for speaking to you.

Mal. Good fool, help me to some light and some paper. I tell thee I am as well in my wits as any man in Illyria.

Clo. Well-a-day that you were, sir!

Mal. By this hand, I am. Good fool, some ink, paper, and light; and convey what I will set down to my lady. It shall advantage thee more than ever the bearing of letter did.

Clo. I will help you to't. But tell me true, are you not mad indeed, or do you but counterfeit?

Mal. Believe me I am not, I tell thee true.

Clo. Nay, I'll ne'er believe a madman till I see his brains. I will fetch you light and paper and ink.

Mal. Fool, I'll requite it in the highest degree. I prithee be gone.

Clo. [*Sings.*]

I am gone, sir,
And anon, sir,
I'll be with you again;
In a trice,
Like to the old Vice,
Your need to sustain;

Who with dagger of lath,
In his rage and his wrath,
Cries, ah, ha! to the devil;
Like a mad lad,
Pare thy nails, dad.
Adieu, goodman devil. *Exit.*

Scene III

Enter Sebastian.

[*Seb.*] This is the air, that is the glorious sun,
This pearl she gave me, I do feel't and see't,
And though 'tis wonder that enwraps me thus,
Yet 'tis not madness. Where's Antonio then?
I could not find him at the Elephant,
Yet there he was, and there I found this credit,
That he did range the town to seek me out.
His counsel now might do me golden service,
For though my soul disputes well with my sense,
That this may be some error, but no madness,
Yet doth this accident and flood of fortune
So far exceed all instance, all discourse,
That I am ready to distrust mine eyes,
And wrangle with my reason that persuades me
To any other trust but that I am mad,
Or else the lady's mad; yet if 'twere so,
She could not sway her house, command her followers,
Take and give back affairs, and their dispatch,
With such a smooth, discreet, and stable bearing
As I perceive she does. There's something in't
That is deceivable. But here the lady comes.

71. upshot: conclusion (the decisive shot in an archery contest).
72–73. Hey . . . does. These lines, with 75, 77, 79, are from an old song, a version of which is attributed to Sir Thomas Wyatt.
75. perdie: indeed (a weakened oath, like French *pardieu*, literally "by God").
86. besides: out of. **five wits.** Usually listed as common wit (common sense), fantasy, memory, judgment, and imagination.
87–88. notoriously abus'd: egregiously misused.
91. propertied me: i.e. stowed me away like a piece of furniture (perhaps with play on stage properties).
93. face . . . wits: brazenly deny that I am sane.
94. Advise you: consider well.
95–97. Malvolio . . . babble. Feste here impersonates Sir Topas again, and in his next speech takes both parts in a dialogue between Sir Topas and himself. **96. Endeavor thyself:** strive.
100. God buy you: God be with you, goodby.
104. shent: rebuked. **108. Well-a-day:** alas.
111. advantage: benefit.

123. trice: moment.
124. Vice: the comic character in the morality plays and interludes, in which he often beat the Devil with his "dagger of lath" and threatened to trim his long nails with it. Feste here compares himself to the Vice (whose role was an ancestor of the Clown's role), and his impudent remarks to the devil by whom Malvolio is supposedly possessed are by implication addressed to Malvolio himself.
131. goodman devil. A final insult to Malvolio, who is addressed by the title proper for those below the rank of gentleman.

IV.iii. Location: Olivia's garden.
6. was: had been. **found this credit:** learned that they believed as follows. **7. range:** go about.
9. my soul . . . sense: i.e. my reason and my senses both maintain (*disputes with* = "argues together with").
11. accident . . . fortune: chance occurrence and (i.e. which is a) brimming over of good fortune.
12. instance: example, precedent. **discourse:** reasoning, logic.
15. trust: belief, conviction.
17. sway: rule, manage. **followers:** servants.
18. Take . . . dispatch: i.e. take business in hand and give instructions for its prompt execution. *Take* governs *affairs*; *give back* governs *dispatch*. **19. discreet:** judicious. **21. deceivable:** deceptive.

Enter Olivia *and* Priest.

Oli. Blame not this haste of mine. If you mean well,
Now go with me, and with this holy man,
Into the chantry by; there, before him,
And underneath that consecrated roof,
Plight me the full assurance of your faith,
That my most jealious and too doubtful soul
May live at peace. He shall conceal it
Whiles you are willing it shall come to note,
What time we will our celebration keep
According to my birth. What do you say?
Seb. I'll follow this good man, and go with you,
And having sworn truth, ever will be true.
Oli. Then lead the way, good father, and heavens so shine
That they may fairly note this act of mine! *Exeunt.*

ACT V, Scene I

Enter Clown *and* Fabian.

Fab. Now as thou lov'st me, let me see his letter.

Clo. Good Master Fabian, grant me another request.

Fab. Any thing.

Clo. Do not desire to see this letter.

Fab. This is to give a dog and in recompense desire my dog again.

Enter Duke, Viola, Curio, *and* Lords.

Duke. Belong you to the Lady Olivia, friends?

Clo. Ay, sir, we are some of her trappings.

Duke. I know thee well; how dost thou, my good fellow?

Clo. Truly, sir, the better for my foes and the worse for my friends.

Duke. Just the contrary: the better for thy friends.

Clo. No, sir, the worse.

Duke. How can that be?

Clo. Marry, sir, they praise me, and make an ass of me. Now my foes tell me plainly I am an ass; so that by my foes, sir, I profit in the knowledge of myself, and by my friends I am abus'd; so that, conclusions to be as kisses, if your four negatives make your two affirmatives, why then the worse for my friends and the better for my foes.

Duke. Why, this is excellent.

Clo. By my troth, sir, no; though it please you to be one of my friends.

Duke. Thou shalt not be the worse for me, there's gold.

Clo. But that it would be double-dealing, sir, I would you could make it another.

Duke. O, you give me ill counsel.

Clo. Put your grace in your pocket, sir, for this once, and let your flesh and blood obey it.

Duke. Well, I will be so much a sinner to be a double-dealer. There's another.

Clo. *Primo, secundo, tertio,* is a good play, and the old saying is, the third pays for all. The triplex, sir, is a good tripping measure, or the bells of Saint Bennet, sir, may put you in mind—one, two, three.

Duke. You can fool no more money out of me at this throw. If you will let your lady know I am here to speak with her, and bring her along with you, it may awake my bounty further.

Clo. Marry, sir, lullaby to your bounty till I come again. I go, sir, but I would not have you to think that my desire of having is the sin of covetousness; but as you say, sir, let your bounty take a nap, I will awake it anon. *Exit.*

Enter Antonio *and* Officers.

Vio. Here comes the man, sir, that did rescue me.
Duke. That face of his I do remember well,
Yet when I saw it last, it was besmear'd
As black as Vulcan in the smoke of war.
A baubling vessel was he captain of,
For shallow draught and bulk unprizable,
With which such scathful grapple did he make
With the most noble bottom of our fleet,
That very envy, and the tongue of loss,
Cried fame and honor on him. What's the matter?
1. Off. Orsino, this is that Antonio
That took the *Phoenix* and her fraught from Candy,
And this is he that did the *Tiger* board,
When your young nephew Titus lost his leg.

24. chantry: a small private chapel where mass was sung daily for the souls of the dead. **by:** near by.
26. Plight: pledge. The ceremony in question here is the betrothal, regarded as a binding contract; the marriage will be solemnized later (lines 30–31).
27. jealious: mistrustful (variant form of *jealous*). **doubtful:** apprehensive.
29. Whiles: until. **come to note:** become publicly known.
30. What: at which. **31. birth:** rank, social position.

V.i. Location: Before Olivia's house.
6–7. This . . . again. Manningham in his *Diary* (in which the Middle Temple performance of *Twelfth Night* is recorded; see the introduction) relates a similar incident involving Queen Elizabeth and a Dr. Bullein, her kinsman, the owner of the dog. But whether Shakespeare knew of the incident is uncertain. **20. abus'd:** deceived.
20–23. so . . . foes. This jest has never been satisfactorily paraphrased. Dover Wilson's explication may be given as one of many: "a kiss is made by four lips (contraries or negatives) brought together by two ardent mouths (affirmatives); if conclusions are like this, says Feste, then the conclusion that I am not an ass is only half the value of the conclusion that I am one."
29. But: except for the fact. **double-dealing:** (1) duplicity; (2) giving two coins.
32. Put . . . pocket: (1) pocket up (set aside) your virtue; (2) let your Grace dip into your purse (with further sense in *grace* of "favor" or "generosity").
33. flesh and blood: frail human nature. **it:** i.e. the "ill counsel."
36. Primo, secundo, tertio. Perhaps with reference to a game of dice, perhaps to a child's game.
37. the third . . . all. Proverbial; cf. "The third time's the charm."
37–38. triplex: triple time in music.
39. Saint Bennet: Saint Benedict; possibly alluding to the London parish church of St. Bennet Hithe on Paul's Wharf, just across the Thames from the Globe.
41. fool: (1) befool, cheat; (2) obtain by your jester's wit.
42. throw: (1) time; (2) throw of the dice.
53. Vulcan: the smith of the gods, blackened by the smoky fire in his smithy. **54. baubling:** trifling, toylike.
55. For . . . unprizable: valueless because of its shallow draught and small size. For another *bauble / shallow / bulk* cluster see *Troilus and Cressida,* I.iii.34–37. **56. scathful:** damaging.
57. bottom: ship.
58. envy: enmity, i.e. (we) his enemies. **loss:** i.e. the losers.
61. fraught: freight, cargo. **from Candy:** returning from Candia (Crete).

Here in the streets, desperate of shame and state,
In private brabble did we apprehend him.

Vio. He did me kindness, sir, drew on my side,
But in conclusion put strange speech upon me.
I know not what 'twas but distraction.

Duke. Notable pirate, thou salt-water thief!
What foolish boldness brought thee to their mercies
Whom thou in terms so bloody and so dear
Hast made thine enemies?

Ant. Orsino, noble sir,
Be pleas'd that I shake off these names you give me.
Antonio never yet was thief or pirate,
Though I confess, on base and ground enough,
Orsino's enemy. A witchcraft drew me hither:
That most ingrateful boy there by your side
From the rude sea's enrag'd and foamy mouth
Did I redeem; a wrack past hope he was.
His life I gave him, and did thereto add
My love, without retention or restraint,
All his in dedication. For his sake
Did I expose myself (pure for his love)
Into the danger of this adverse town,
Drew to defend him when he was beset;
Where being apprehended, his false cunning
(Not meaning to partake with me in danger)
Taught him to face me out of his acquaintance,
And grew a twenty years removed thing
While one would wink; denied me mine own purse,
Which I had recommended to his use
Not half an hour before.

Vio. How can this be?

Duke. When came he to this town?

Ant. To-day, my lord; and for three months before,
No int'rim, not a minute's vacancy,
Both day and night did we keep company.

Enter OLIVIA *and* ATTENDANTS.

Duke. Here comes the Countess, now heaven walks on earth.
But for thee, fellow—fellow, thy words are madness.
Three months this youth hath tended upon me,
But more of that anon. Take him aside.

Oli. What would my lord, but that he may not have,
Wherein Olivia may seem serviceable?
Cesario, you do not keep promise with me.

Vio. Madam—

Duke. Gracious Olivia—

Oli. What do you say, Cesario? Good my lord—

Vio. My lord would speak, my duty hushes me.

Oli. If it be aught to the old tune, my lord,
It is as fat and fulsome to mine ear
As howling after music.

Duke. Still so cruel?

Oli. Still so constant, lord.

Duke. What, to perverseness? You uncivil lady,
To whose ingrate and unauspicious altars
My soul the faithfull'st off'rings have breath'd out
That e'er devotion tender'd! What shall I do?

Oli. Even what it please my lord, that shall become him.

Duke. Why should I not (had I the heart to do it),
Like to th' Egyptian thief at point of death,
Kill what I love? (a savage jealousy
That sometime savors nobly), but hear me this:
Since you to non-regardance cast my faith,
And that I partly know the instrument
That screws me from my true place in your favor,
Live you the marble-breasted tyrant still.
But this your minion, whom I know you love,
And whom, by heaven I swear, I tender dearly,
Him will I tear out of that cruel eye,
Where he sits crowned in his master's spite.
Come, boy, with me, my thoughts are ripe in mischief.
I'll sacrifice the lamb that I do love,
To spite a raven's heart within a dove.

Vio. And I most jocund, apt, and willingly,
To do you rest, a thousand deaths would die.

Oli. Where goes Cesario?

Vio. After him I love
More than I love these eyes, more than my life,
More by all mores than e'er I shall love wife.
If I do feign, you witnesses above
Punish my life for tainting of my love!

Oli. Ay me, detested! how am I beguil'd!

Vio. Who does beguile you? who does do you wrong?

Oli. Hast thou forgot thyself? Is it so long?
Call forth the holy father.

Duke. Come, away!

Oli. Whither, my lord? Cesario, husband, stay.

Duke. Husband?

Oli. Ay, husband. Can he that deny?

Duke. Her husband, sirrah?

64. desperate . . . state: i.e. with reckless disregard of disgrace and danger. *Shame* refers perhaps to his involvement in a street brawl, *state* to his dangerous position as a public enemy.
65. brabble: brawl.
66. drew . . . side: drew his sword in my defense.
67. put . . . me: spoke very strangely to me.
68. but distraction: unless it was insanity.
69. Notable: notorious.
71. in terms: in a manner. **dear:** grievous.
73. Be pleas'd: permit.
75. base and ground. The nouns are synonyms.
79. wrack: wreck. **81. retention:** reservation.
83. pure: solely. **84. Into:** to. **adverse:** hostile.
87. Not . . . partake: having no intention of sharing.
88. face . . . acquaintance: deny brazenly that he knew me.
89–90. grew . . . wink: in the twinkling of an eye became as distant as if we had not seen each other for twenty years.
91. recommended: commended, committed.
95. vacancy: gap, interval.
101. but . . . have: i.e. except what I cannot give him (i.e. her love).
102. seem serviceable: show her duty.
109. fat and fulsome: gross and distasteful.
112. uncivil: inhumane.
113. ingrate: ungrateful. **unauspicious:** unpropitious.
115. tender'd: offered.
118. Egyptian thief. Referring to an episode in Heliodorus' *Ethiopica*, in which Thyamis, an Egyptian robber captain who has taken Chariclea captive and fallen in love with her, finds himself in danger of death at his enemies' hands and attempts to kill Chariclea first.
120. savors nobly: has a noble quality about it.
121. non-regardance: disregard, neglect. **faith:** constancy.
122. that. Repeating the sense of *Since*, line 121.
123. screws: forces. **124. marble-breasted:** stony-hearted.
125. minion: darling. **126. tender:** regard.
128. in . . . spite: in defiance of his master. **132. apt:** ready.
133. do you rest: give you peace. **136. mores:** (such) comparisons.
138. tainting . . . love: bringing my love into discredit.
139. detested: renounced, rejected.
145. sirrah: form of address to an inferior.

Vio. No, my lord, not I.
Oli. Alas, it is the baseness of thy fear
That makes thee strangle thy propriety.
Fear not, Cesario, take thy fortunes up,
Be that thou know'st thou art, and then thou art
As great as that thou fear'st.

Enter PRIEST.

O, welcome, father!
Father, I charge thee by thy reverence
Here to unfold, though lately we intended
To keep in darkness what occasion now
Reveals before 'tis ripe, what thou dost know
Hath newly pass'd between this youth and me.
Priest. A contract of eternal bond of love,
Confirm'd by mutual joinder of your hands,
Attested by the holy close of lips,
Strength'ned by interchangement of your rings,
And all the ceremony of this compact
Seal'd in my function, by my testimony;
Since when, my watch hath told me, toward my grave
I have travell'd but two hours.
Duke. O thou dissembling cub! what wilt thou be
When time hath sow'd a grizzle on thy case?
Or will not else thy craft so quickly grow,
That thine own trip shall be thine overthrow?
Farewell, and take her, but direct thy feet
Where thou and I (henceforth) may never meet.
Vio. My lord, I do protest—
Oli. O, do not swear!
Hold little faith, though thou hast too much fear.

Enter SIR ANDREW.

Sir And. For the love of God, a surgeon! Send one presently to Sir Toby.

Oli. What's the matter?

Sir And. H'as broke my head across, and has given Sir Toby a bloody coxcomb too. For the love of God, your help! I had rather than forty pound I were at home.

Oli. Who has done this, Sir Andrew?

Sir And. The Count's gentleman, one Cesario. We took him for a coward, but he's the very devil incardinate.

Duke. My gentleman, Cesario?

Sir And. 'Od's lifelings, here he is! You broke my head for nothing, and that that I did, I was set on to do't by Sir Toby.

Vio. Why do you speak to me? I never hurt you.
You drew your sword upon me without cause,
But I bespake you fair, and hurt you not.

Enter TOBY *and* CLOWN.

Sir And. If a bloody coxcomb be a hurt, you have hurt me. I think you set nothing by a bloody coxcomb. Here comes Sir Toby halting—you shall hear more. But if he had not been in drink, he would have tickled you othergates than he did.

Duke. How now, gentleman? how is't with you?

Sir To. That's all one. H'as hurt me, and there's th' end on't. Sot, didst see Dick surgeon, sot?

Clo. O, he's drunk, Sir Toby, an hour agone; his eyes were set at eight i' th' morning.

Sir To. Then he's a rogue, and a passy-measures [pavin]. I hate a drunken rogue.

Oli. Away with him! Who hath made this havoc with them?

Sir And. I'll help you, Sir Toby, because we'll be dress'd together.

Sir To. Will you help?—an ass-head and a coxcomb and a knave, a thin-fac'd knave, a gull!

Oli. Get him to bed, and let his hurt be look'd to.

[*Exeunt Clown, Fabian, Sir Toby, and Sir Andrew.*]

Enter SEBASTIAN.

Seb. I am sorry, madam, I have hurt your kinsman,
But had it been the brother of my blood,
I must have done no less with wit and safety.
You throw a strange regard upon me, and by that
I do perceive it hath offended you.
Pardon me, sweet one, even for the vows
We made each other but so late ago.
Duke. One face, one voice, one habit, and two persons,
A natural perspective, that is and is not!
Seb. Antonio, O my dear Antonio!
How have the hours rack'd and tortur'd me,
Since I have lost thee!
Ant. Sebastian are you?
Seb. Fear'st thou that, Antonio?
Ant. How have you made division of yourself?
An apple, cleft in two, is not more twin
Than these two creatures. Which is Sebastian?
Oli. Most wonderful!
Seb. Do I stand there? I never had a brother;

147. strangle thy propriety: i.e. disown your identity as my husband.
148. take . . . up: receive your fortune.
150. that thou fear'st: i.e. Orsino. **153. occasion**: necessity.
155. newly: recently. **157. joinder**: joining. **158. close**: union.
161. Seal'd: ratified, attested. **in my function**: i.e. by my authority as priest.
165. a grizzle: grey hair. **case**: skin (of a fox); Orsino is thus calling Viola-Cesario a fox-cub.
167. trip: attempt to trip up (or trap) another.
170. protest: avow, swear. **171. Hold little**: keep a little.
173. presently: immediately.
175. H'as . . . across: he has given me a cut on the head.
176. coxcomb: head (with a suggestion of the cap traditionally worn by the professional fool in its applicability to Sir Toby and Sir Andrew).
182. incardinate. Apparently Sir Andrew's slip for *incarnate*.
184. 'Od's lifelings: by God's little lives.
189. bespake you fair: spoke courteously to you.
191. set nothing by: regard as nothing. **192. halting**: limping.
193. But if: if only. **in drink**: drunk. **tickled**: chastised.
194. othergates: otherwise. **196. That's all one**: no matter.
196–97. there's . . . on't: that's that. **197. Sot**: fool.
199. set: extinguished (as in *the sun sets*), i.e. closed.
200–201. passy-measures pavin. Naylor explains *passy-measures* (from Italian *passamezzo*) as a dance tune with "strains" consisting of eight bars each (hence suggested to Sir Toby by Feste's "set at eight"). The pavin or pavan(e) was a slow and stately dance. Sir Toby obviously expects no speedy aid from Dick surgeon.
204–5. be dress'd: have our wounds cared for.
206–7. coxcomb: fool. **207. gull**: dupe.
211. with . . . safety: i.e. with due regard for my own safety.
212. throw . . . me: look at me as if I were a stranger.
216. habit: dress.
217. natural perspective: i.e. an optical illusion produced by nature, not by a perspective glass (an optical device that makes the viewer see an object differently). **that . . . not**: i.e. that must be an illusion and yet is not.

Nor can there be that deity in my nature
Of here and every where. I had a sister,
Whom the blind waves and surges have devour'd.
Of charity, what kin are you to me?
What countryman? What name? What parentage?
Vio. Of Messaline; Sebastian was my father,
Such a Sebastian was my brother too;
So went he suited to his watery tomb.
If spirits can assume both form and suit,
You come to fright us.
Seb. A spirit I am indeed,
But am in that dimension grossly clad
Which from the womb I did participate.
Were you a woman, as the rest goes even,
I should my tears let fall upon your cheek,
And say, "Thrice welcome, drowned Viola!"
Vio. My father had a mole upon his brow.
Seb. And so had mine.
Vio. And died that day when Viola from her birth
Had numb'red thirteen years.
Seb. O, that record is lively in my soul!
He finished indeed his mortal act
That day that made my sister thirteen years.
Vio. If nothing lets to make us happy both
But this my masculine usurp'd attire,
Do not embrace me till each circumstance
Of place, time, fortune, do cohere and jump
That I am Viola—which to confirm,
I'll bring you to a captain in this town,
Where lie my maiden weeds; by whose gentle help
I was preserv'd to serve this noble count.
All the occurrence of my fortune since
Hath been between this lady and this lord.
Seb. [*To Olivia.*] So comes it, lady, you have been mistook;
But Nature to her bias drew in that.
You would have been contracted to a maid,
Nor are you therein, by my life, deceiv'd,
You are betroth'd both to a maid and man.
Duke. Be not amaz'd, right noble is his blood.
If this be so, as yet the glass seems true,
I shall have share in this most happy wrack.
[*To Viola.*] Boy, thou hast said to me a thousand times
Thou never shouldst love woman like to me.
Vio. And all those sayings will I over swear,
And all those swearings keep as true in soul
As doth that orbed continent the fire
That severs day from night.
Duke. Give me thy hand,
And let me see thee in thy woman's weeds.
Vio. The captain that did bring me first on shore
Hath my maid's garments. He upon some action
Is now in durance, at Malvolio's suit,
A gentleman, and follower of my lady's.
Oli. He shall enlarge him; fetch Malvolio hither.
And yet, alas, now I remember me,
They say, poor gentleman, he's much distract.

Enter Clown *with a letter, and* Fabian.

A most extracting frenzy of mine own
From my remembrance clearly banish'd his.
How does he, sirrah?

Clo. Truly, madam, he holds Belzebub at the stave's end as well as a man in his case may do. H'as here writ a letter to you; I should have given't you to-day morning. But as a madman's epistles are no gospels, so it skills not much when they are deliver'd.

Oli. Open't and read it.

Clo. Look then to be well edified when the fool delivers the madman. [*Reads madly.*] "By the Lord, madam"—

Oli. How now, art thou mad?

Clo. No, madam, I do but read madness. And your ladyship will have it as it ought to be, you must allow *vox*.

Oli. Prithee read i' thy right wits.

Clo. So I do, madonna; but to read his right wits is to read thus; therefore perpend, my princess, and give ear.

Oli. [*To Fabian.*] Read it you, sirrah.

Fab. (*Reads.*) "By the Lord, madam, you wrong me, and the world shall know it. Though you have put me into darkness, and given your drunken cousin rule over me, yet have I the benefit of my senses as well as your ladyship. I have your own letter that induc'd me to the semblance I put on; with the which I doubt not but to do myself much right, or you much shame. Think of me as you please. I leave my duty a little unthought of, and speak out of my injury.
The madly-us'd Malvolio."

Oli. Did he write this?

Clo. Ay, madam.

Duke. This savors not much of distraction.

Oli. See him deliver'd, Fabian, bring him hither. [*Exit Fabian.*]
My lord, so please you, these things further thought on,

227. deity: divine attribute. **228. here . . . where:** omnipresence.
229. blind: ruthless. **230. Of charity:** (tell me) out of kindness.
234. suited: dressed.
237. in . . . clad: clothed in that corporeal frame.
238. participate: share existence with.
239. as . . . even: i.e. as (is likely since) all the rest accords. A common type of ellipsis; for another example see line 265.
246. lively: vivid. **249. lets:** hinders.
252. cohere: agree. **jump:** coincide, agree.
255. Where: at whose house. **weeds:** clothes.
260. Nature . . . that: i.e. your nature was true to its own bent when you fell in love with one who is the perfect likeness of me.
261. contracted: betrothed.
263. maid: virgin (here applied to a man).
264. amaz'd: astounded, dazed (a much stronger word than in modern usage).
265. glass: i.e. the "natural perspective" of line 217.
269. over: again.
271. As . . . fire: i.e. as the sun's sphere keeps the fire. *Continent* = container.

275. action: legal charge. **276. durance:** prison.
278. enlarge: release. **279. remember me:** recall.
280. distract: distracted, out of his wits.
281. extracting frenzy: i.e. madness that took other things out of my mind. **282. his:** i.e. remembrance of his frenzy.
284–85. holds . . . end: keeps the devil (who possesses him) at a distance. "To hold the devil at stave's end" was proverbial.
287–88. a madman's . . . gospels: i.e. a madman's letters are not to be taken as gospel truth (with play on the reading of appointed passages from the epistles and the gospels in a church service).
288. it . . . much: it doesn't matter much.
291. delivers: presents, speaks the words of.
294. And: if. **296. vox:** voice, i.e. dramatic reading.
299. perpend: consider. **307. the which:** i.e. the letter (as proof).
309. my duty: the duty I owe you as your servant.
315. deliver'd: released.

To think me as well a sister as a wife,
One day shall crown th' alliance on't, so please you,
Here at my house and at my proper cost.
Duke. Madam, I am most apt t' embrace your offer.
[*To Viola*.] Your master quits you; and for your service done him,
So much against the mettle of your sex,
So far beneath your soft and tender breeding,
And since you call'd me master for so long,
Here is my hand—you shall from this time be
Your master's mistress.
Oli. A sister! you are she.

Enter [Fabian *with*] Malvolio.

Duke. Is this the madman?
Oli. Ay, my lord, this same.
How now, Malvolio?
Mal. Madam, you have done me wrong,
Notorious wrong.
Oli. Have I, Malvolio? No.
Mal. Lady, you have. Pray you peruse that letter.
You must not now deny it is your hand;
Write from it if you can, in hand or phrase,
Or say 'tis not your seal, not your invention.
You can say none of this. Well, grant it then,
And tell me, in the modesty of honor,
Why you have given me such clear lights of favor,
Bade me come smiling and cross-garter'd to you,
To put on yellow stockings, and to frown
Upon Sir Toby and the lighter people;
And acting this in an obedient hope,
Why have you suffer'd me to be imprison'd,
Kept in a dark house, visited by the priest,
And made the most notorious geck and gull
That e'er invention play'd on? Tell me why!
Oli. Alas, Malvolio, this is not my writing,
Though I confess much like the character;
But out of question 'tis Maria's hand.
And now I do bethink me, it was she
First told me thou wast mad. Then cam'st in smiling,
And in such forms which here were presuppos'd
Upon thee in the letter. Prithee be content.
This practice hath most shrewdly pass'd upon thee;
But when we know the grounds and authors of it,
Thou shalt be both the plaintiff and the judge
Of thine own cause.
Fab. Good madam, hear me speak,
And let no quarrel nor no brawl to come
Taint the condition of this present hour,
Which I have wond'red at. In hope it shall not,
Most freely I confess, myself and Toby
Set this device against Malvolio here,
Upon some stubborn and uncourteous parts
We had conceiv'd against him. Maria writ
The letter at Sir Toby's great importance,
In recompense whereof he hath married her.
How with a sportful malice it was follow'd
May rather pluck on laughter than revenge,
If that the injuries be justly weigh'd
That have on both sides pass'd.
Oli. Alas, poor fool, how have they baffled thee!
Clo. Why, "some are born great, some achieve greatness, and some have greatness thrown upon them." I was one, sir, in this enterlude—one Sir Topas, sir, but that's all one. "By the Lord, fool, I am not mad." But do you remember? "Madam, why laugh you at such a barren rascal? And you smile not, he's gagg'd." And thus the whirligig of time brings in his revenges.
Mal. I'll be reveng'd on the whole pack of you. [*Exit*.]
Oli. He hath been most notoriously abus'd.
Duke. Pursue him, and entreat him to a peace;
He hath not told us of the captain yet.
When that is known, and golden time convents,
A solemn combination shall be made
Of our dear souls. Mean time, sweet sister,
We will not part from hence. Cesario, come—
For so you shall be while you are a man;
But when in other habits you are seen,
Orsino's mistress, and his fancy's queen.
Exeunt [*all but Clown*].

Clown sings.

When that I was and a little tine boy,
With hey ho, the wind and the rain,
A foolish thing was but a toy,
For the rain it raineth every day.

But when I came to man's estate,
With hey ho, etc.
'Gainst knaves and thieves men shut their gate,
For the rain, etc.

But when I came, alas, to wive,
With hey ho, etc.
By swaggering could I never thrive,
For the rain, etc.

317. think . . . wife: regard me as favorably as a sister-in-law as you would have as a wife.
318. crown . . . on't: i.e. see the performance of the two weddings that will create that relationship. **319. proper cost:** own expense.
320. apt: ready. **321. quits:** frees, withdraws all claim to.
322. mettle: disposition.
332. from it: differently. **hand or phrase:** handwriting or phraseology. **333. invention:** composition.
335. in . . . honor: with the sense of propriety of an honorable person. **336. clear lights:** i.e. sure signs.
339. lighter: lesser. **343. geck:** fool.
344. invention: devising. **347. out of:** beyond.
349. cam'st: cam'st thou.
350. which: as. **presuppos'd:** suggested beforehand.
352. shrewdly: grievously. **pass'd upon:** imposed upon.
358. wond'red: marvelled.
361. Upon: (which) in consequence of. **stubborn:** rude, haughty. **parts:** acts. **362. conceiv'd:** devised.
363. importance: importunity.
365. sportful: jesting. **follow'd:** carried through.
366. pluck on: draw on, induce.
369. baffled thee: put you down.
372. enterlude: interlude, i.e. comedy.
376. whirligig of time: i.e. time's circling course. A whirligig is a spinning top or toy.
379. He . . . abus'd. Olivia thus repeats Malvolio's own judgment at IV.ii.87–88. **381. captain.** See lines 253–56, 274–77.
382. convents: suits. **383. combination:** marriage.
389. tine: tiny. Cf. with lines 389 ff. the song in *King Lear*, III.ii.74–77, in which the variant spelling *tine* again appears.
391. A . . . toy: i.e. my mischief was not taken seriously.
395. 'Gainst . . . gate: i.e. my mischief caused men to shut their doors against me as a knave and a thief.
399. swaggering: bullying, blustering.

But when I came unto my beds,
  With hey ho, etc.
With toss-pots still had drunken heads,
  For the rain, etc.

401. unto my beds: to old age (?) **403. toss-pots:** drunkards.

A great while ago the world begun,
  [With] hey ho, etc.
But that's all one, our play is done,
  And we'll strive to please you every day.
[*Exit.*]

NOTE ON THE TEXT

The First Folio (1623) is our only authority for *Twelfth Night;* all later texts are derived from that source. There is now general agreement that the printer's copy for the F1 text was a "literary" transcript (see the notation *"Finis, Actus primus."*; this form of *"Finis."*, adopted also for Acts II and IV, is not found in manuscripts with theatrical provenience). The exact nature of the kind of manuscript behind the scribal copy, however, remains open to question: (1) the prompt-book or a transcript of the prompt-book (Chambers, Wilson, Greg); (2) scribal transcript of Shakespeare's "foul papers" (Turner, Lothian/Craik, Donno); (3) Shakespeare's own papers, perhaps a "fair copy" (more likely than the prompt-book; Warren/Wells [1994]). Wells/Taylor (1987) sum up the situation: It is "impossible to be confident about the scribe's own copy." Donno notes the possibility that the scribe, if other than Shakespeare, was Ralph Crane (see "Note on the Text" to *The Tempest).*

The F1 text is unusually clean and presents few significant problems to the editor. The play is carefully divided into acts and scenes, though the cleared stage at III.iv.272 suggests the possibility that a new scene should have been marked at that point (the present text, however, adheres to the F1 division); there is also the Viola/Violenta confusion at I.v.166 s.d., which, as Dover Wilson points out, suggests a possible link with *All's Well* (III.v o.s.d.), where another Violenta suddenly turns up, although she has no lines in the scene (or later). The mildness of the profanity in such a role as Sir Toby's is probably the result of a book-keeper's attempt to meet the provisions of the anti-profanity act of 1606 (Chambers).

For further information, see E. K. Chambers, *William Shakespeare,* 2 vols. (Oxford, 1930); J. D. Wilson, ed., New Shakespeare *Twelfth Night* (Cambridge, 1930; rev. 1949); W. W. Greg, *The Shakespeare First Folio* (Oxford, 1955); R. K. Turner, "The Text of *Twelfth Night," SQ,* XXVI (1975), 128–38; J. M. Lothian and T. W. Craik, eds., New Arden *Twelfth Night* (London, 1975); E. S. Donno, ed., New Cambridge *Twelfth Night* (Cambridge, 1985); Stanley Wells, Gary Taylor, et al., *William Shakespeare: A Textual Companion* (Oxford, 1987); Roger Warren and Stanley Wells, eds., *Twelfth Night* (Oxford, 1994).

TEXTUAL NOTES

Title: **Twelfth]** Twelfe *Fl*
Dramatis personae: *subs. as first given in Douai MS and Rowe*
Act-scene division: *from Fl*

I.i

Location: *Rowe (subs.)*
o.s.d. **Musicians attending]** *Malone (after Rowe)*
10–1 **capacity . . . sea,]** *Rowe;* capacitie, . . . Sea. *Fl*
22 s.d. **Enter Valentine.]** *placed as in Dyce; after l. 22, Fl*
38 **self]** selfe same *F2*

I.ii

Location: *Capell*
15 **Arion]** *Pope;* Orion *Fl*
23 **travel]** *F3;* trauaile *Fl*
40–1 **company And sight]** *Hanmer;* sight / And company *Fl*

I.iii

Location: *Rowe*
7 **except]** *Hanmer;* except, *Fl*
17 **wooer.]** *F2;* woer *Fl*
43 s.d. **Aguecheek]** *Malone*
52 s.p. **Sir And.]** *F2* (An.); Ma. *Fl*
52 **Accost]** *Rowe;* accost *Fl*
55 **Mary Accost]** *Rowe;* Mary, accost *Fl*
57 **woo]** *F2* (wooe); woe *Fl (frequently)*
90, 91 **Pourquoi]** *Rowe (subs.);* Pur-quoy *and* purquoy *Fl*
99 **curl by]** *Theobald;* coole my *Fl*
100 **me]** *F2;* we *Fl*
100 **does't]** *Rowe;* dost *Fl*
107 **Count]** *F2;* Connt *Fl*
115 **kickshawses]** *F3;* kicke-chawses *Fl*
129 **coranto]** *Rowe;* Carranto *Fl*
131 **dost]** *F3;* dooest *Fl*
135 **dun-color'd]** *Collier MS;* dam'd colour'd *Fl*
135 **set]** *Rowe;* sit *Fl*
139 **That's]** *F3;* That *Fl*

I.iv

Location: *Rowe (subs.)*

I.v

Location: *Rowe*
9 **lenten]** *Douai MS, Rowe;* lenton *Fl*
17 **away—]** *Dyce;* away: *Fl*
31 s.d. **Exit.]** *Pope*
31 s.d. **and Attendants]** *Staunton (after Capell)*
88 **wise men]** *F3;* Wisemen *Fl*
92 **guiltless]** *F3;* guitlesse *Fl*
107 s.d. **Exit Maria.]** *Capell*
114 **for— . . . comes—]** *Cambridge;* for . . . comes. *Fl*
120 **here—]** *Steevens;* heere. *Fl*
131 **madman]** *Rowe;* madde man *Fl*
138 s.d. **Exit.]** *Rowe*
147 **H'as]** *Staunton;* Ha's *Fl*
166 s.d. **Viola]** *F2;* Violenta *Fl*
166 **beauty—]** *Rowe;* beau- / tie. *Fl*
184 **fangs]** *Rowe;* phangs *Fl*
210 **olive]** *Rowe;* Olyffe *Fl*
219 s.d. **Exeunt . . . Attendants.]** *Capell*
234–5 s.d. **Unveiling.]** *Rowe*
245 **schedules]** *Rowe;* scedules *Fl*
257 **him,]** *F3;* him *Fl*
301 **County's]** *Capell;* Countes *Fl*
311 s.d. **Exit.]** *Rowe;* Finis, Actus primus. *Fl*

II.i

Location: *Capell*

II.ii

Location: *Capell*
3 **sir;]** *Rowe;* sir, *Fl*
20 **That]** That sure *F2*
25 **man! If]** *Rowe (subs.);* man, if *Fl*
29 **proper-false]** *hyphen, Malone*
31 **our]** *F2;* O *Fl*
32 **made of,]** *Thirlby conj.;* made, if *Fl*
41 s.d. **Exit.]** *Rowe*

II.iii

Location: *Rowe*
1 **a-bed]** *hyphen, Rowe*
3 **know'st—]** *Theobald;* know'st. *Fl*
17 **"we three"]** *quotes, Cambridge*
22 **In sooth]** *Theobald;* Insooth *Fl*
25, 31 **sixpence]** *Theobald (subs.);* sixe pence *Fl*
25 **leman]** *Theobald;* Lemon *Fl*
34 **give a—]** *F2;* giue a *Fl*
40 **true-love's]** *Rowe (hyphen, Capell);* true loues *Fl*
46 s.d. **sings]** *Cambridge*
65 **knight?]** *Capell;* knight. *Fl*
76 s.d. **sings]** *Wilson*
78 **Tilly-vally!]** *Capell;* tilly vally. *Fl*
78 **Lady!]** *F2;* Ladie, *Fl*
78, 84 s.dd. **Sings.]** *Rowe*
84 **O']** *W. S. Walker conj.;* O *Fl*
102, 104, 106 s.dd. **Sings.]** *Hanmer*
102, 104, 106] *Quotes, Theobald*
109, 110, 111, 112 s.dd. **Sings.]** *Rowe*
113 s.d. **To Clown.]** *Collier conj.*
114 s.d. **To Malvolio.]** *Collier conj.*
143 **What,]** *Rowe;* What *Fl*

151 **grounds]** ground *F2*
179 **true-bred]** *hyphen, Theobald*

II.iv

Location: *Rowe* (*subs.*)
3 **antique]** *Pope;* Anticke *F1*
14 s.d. **Exit Curio.]** *Pope*
22 **masterly.]** *Rowe;* masterly, *F1*
50 **Ay, prithee]** *Warburton* (*subs.*); I prethee *F1*
51 s.p. **Clo.]** *Capell*
53 **Fly away, fly]** *Rowe;* Fye away, fie *F1*
60 **strown]** *Rowe;* strewne *F1*
79 s.d. **Curio . . . retire.]** *Cambridge*
82–3 **lands; . . . her,]** *Pope* (her, *F2*); lands, . . . her: *F1*
88 **I]** *Hanmer;* It *F1*
96 **much;]** *Rowe;* much, *F1*

II.v

Location: *Pope*
14 **metal]** *Malone;* Mettle *F1;* Nettle *F2*
20 **Close,]** *Rowe;* Close *F1*
20–1 **jesting! Lie]** *Theobald;* ieasting, lye *F1*
20–1 s.d. **The . . . themselves.]** *Capell*
21 s.d. **Throws . . . letter.]** *Theobald*
53 **travel]** *F4;* trauaile *F1*
60 **my—]** *Collier;* my *F1*
82 s.d. **Taking . . . letter.]** *Rowe*
87, 89 **c's . . . u's . . . t's]** *Wilson;* C's . . . *V*'s . . . T's *F1* (*the italic capital V is ambiguous and could stand for either* U *or* V; *F3 first gives a capital* U)
90, 96, 103, 143 s.dd. **Reads.]** *Capell*
96–9 **"Jove . . . know."]** *as verse, Capell* (*after Hanmer*); *as prose, F1*
98 **Lips,]** *Capell MS;* Lips *F1*
105 **knife,]** *F2;* knife: *F1*
113 **staniel]** *Hanmer;* stallion *F1*
119–20 **portend? . . . me!]** *Capell* (*after Rowe*); portend, . . . me? *F1*
121 **O ay]** *Rowe* (*subs.*); O I *F1*
139 **M. O. A. I.]** *F2;* M, O, A, I. *F1*
143–59 **In . . . Fortunate-Unhappy."]** *as part of the letter, Capell* (*after F3, Hanmer*); *not distinguished by italics as part of the letter, F1*
145 **born]** *Douai MS, Rowe;* become *F1*
145 **achieve]** *F2;* atcheeues *F1*
148 **be,]** *Rowe;* be: *F1*
155 **remember.]** *Rowe* (*subs.*); remember, *F1*
159–60 **The . . . Daylight]** *Capell* (*after Hanmer*); tht [the *F2*] fortunate vnhappy daylight *F1*
161 **politic]** *F2;* pollticke *F1*
163 **point-devise]** *hyphen, Capell*
174 s.d. **Reads.]** *Collier*
177 **dear]** *F2;* deero *F1* (*Daniel conj.* dear, O)
196 **aqua-vitae]** *F2;* Aqua vite *F1*
207 s.d. **Exeunt.]** Exeunt / Finis Actus secundus *F1*

III.i

Location: *Pope*
o.s.d. **with a tabor]** *Malone*
8 **king]** *F2;* King s *F1*
47 s.d. **aside]** *Cambridge*
66 **wise man's]** *Hanmer;* Wise-mans *F1*
68 **wise men, folly-fall'n]** *Capell* (*after Theobald conj.*); wisemens folly falne *F1*
71 **vous]** *Rowe;* vou *F1*
72 **aussi;]** *Theobald* (*after Rowe*); ousie *F1*
72 **votre]** *Johnson;* vostre *F1*
82 **gait]** *Johnson* (*subs.*); gate *F1*
91 **all ready]** *Malone;* already *F1*
93 s.d. **Exeunt . . . Viola.]** *Rowe* (*subs.*)
99 **compliment]** *Pope;* complement *F1*
112 **here]** *Thirlby conj.;* heare *F1*
142 **were]** *Pope;* were, *F1*
145 s.d. **Aside.]** *Staunton* (*after Capell*)
145–6 **beautiful . . . lip!]** *Rowe* (*subs.*); beautifull? . . . lip, *F1*

III.ii

Location: *Rowe*
8 **thee]** *F3*
16 **grand-jurymen]** *Dyce;* grand Iurie men *F1*
57 **deliver't?]** *Dyce;* deliuer't. *F1*
66 **nine]** *Theobald;* mine *F1*
70 **renegado]** *Rowe;* Renegatho *F1*

III.iii

Location: *Rowe*
o.s.d. **Antonio]** *Hanmer;* Anthonio *F1* (*throughout scene*)
8 **travel]** *F2;* rrauell *F1*
15–6 **And . . . pay;]** *om. F2–4*

III.iv

Location: *Capell*
1 s.d. **Aside.]** *Neilson*
8–9 **He's . . . madam.]** *as prose, Pope; as verse, F1*
15 **merry]** *F3;* metry *F1;* mercy *F2*
20–5 **Sad . . . thee?]** *as prose, Pope; as verse, F1*
20 **Sad, lady?]** *Theobald;* Sad Lady, *F1*
24 s.p. **Oli.]** *F2;* Mal. *F1*
24 **dost]** *F3* (do'st); doest *F1*
55 **let]** *F2;* ler *F1*
60 s.d. **Exit Servant.]** *Capell*
63 s.d. **with Maria]** *Capell* (*subs.*)
70 **tang]** *F2;* langer *F1*
88 s.p. **Sir To.]** *anon. conj.* (*in Cambridge*); *line continued to Fabian, F1*
137 **thus,]** *Capell;* thus *F1*
147, 150, etc. s.dd. **Reads.]** *Rowe*
158 **sense—less]** *Dyce;* sence-lesse *F1*
171 **If]** *Hanmer;* To. If *F1* (*repeated s.p.*)
173 **You]** *F2;* Yon *F1*
173 **fit]** *F2;* sit *F1*
200 s.d. **Exeunt . . . Maria.]** *Capell*
217 s.d. **Exit.]** *F2*
220 **thee]** *F2;* the *F1*
237 **brawl]** *F3;* brall *F1*
247 **competent]** *F4;* computent *F1*
281–2 **Ay . . . yonder.]** *as prose, Capell; as verse, F1*
290 s.d. **Aside.]** *Theobald*
292 s.d. **To Fabian.]** *Douai MS, Rowe*
296 s.d. **To Viola.]** *Douai MS, Capell*
302 s.d. **Aside.]** *Capell*
311 s.d. **They draw.]** *Rowe*
318 s.d. **They draw.]** *Cambridge*
320 s.d. **To Antonio.]** *Capell*
320 s.d. **Steps . . . Officers.]** *ed.* (*after Wilson*)
326 **Antonio]** *Rowe;* Anthonio *F1*
332 s.d. **To Viola.]** *Collier*
334–5 **do, . . . purse?]** *Dyce;* do: . . . purse. *F1*
355 **babbling,]** *Steevens;* babling *F1*
372 s.d. **with Officers]** *Theobald*
375 **prove true]** *F2;* proue ttue *F1*
384 s.d. **Exit.]** *F2*
394 s.d. **Exit.]** *Theobald*
396 s.d. **Exeunt.]** *Rowe;* Exit *F1*

IV.i

Location: *Capell* (*subs.*)
10–1 **I . . . me.]** *as verse, Capell; as prose, F1*
17–20 **I . . . payment.]** *as verse, Capell; as prose, F1*
22 **wise men]** *Rowe;* Wise- / men *F1*
25 s.d. **Strikes Sebastian.]** *Douai MS, Rowe*
27 s.d. **Strikes Sir Andrew.]** *Douai MS, Rowe*
27 s.d. **Draws his dagger.]** *ed.* (*after Collier*)
29 s.d. **Seizes Sebastian's arm.]** *ed.* (*after Rowe, following l. 32*); *placed as in Wilson*
31 s.d. **Exit.]** *Rowe*
35 **strook]** *F3;* stroke *F1*
41 s.d. **Breaks . . . sword.]** *ed.* (*after Capell, Collier MS*)
44 s.d. **Draws.]** *Steevens* (*after Rowe*)
51 s.d. **Exeunt . . . Fabian.]** *Capell* (*after Rowe*)

IV.ii

Location: *Rowe*
3 s.d. **Exit.]** *Theobald*
6 **in such]** *F2; F1 accidentally repeats* in *before* such
10 s.d. **and Maria]** *Theobald*
14 **Gorboduc]** *Pope;* Gorbodacke *F1*
20 s.p., s.d. **Mal. (Within.)]** *F1 gives separate s.d.* Maluolio within. *and then s.p.*
37 **clerestories]** *Blakeway conj.* (*in Boswell*); cleere stores *F1;* cleare stones *F2*
60 **soul]** house *F2*
71 **t' the]** *ed.;* the *F1*
71 s.d. **with Maria]** *Theobald*
71, 119 s.dd. **Sings.]** *Rowe*
119 **gone]** *F2;* goue *F1*
131 **goodman]** *Capell;* good man *F1*

IV.iii

Location: *Capell*
1 s.p. **Seb.]** *F2*
4 **Antonio]** *Hanmer;* Anthonio *F1*
35 s.d. **Exeunt.]** Exeunt. / Finis Actus Quartus. *F1*

V.i

Location: *Capell*
10 **dost]** *F3* (do'st); doest *F1*
49 s.d. **Antonio]** *Rowe;* Anthonio *F1* (*throughout scene*)
104 **Madam—]** *ed.;* Madam; *F1*
118 **thief . . . death,]** *Collier;* theefe, . . . death *F1*
123 **favor,]** *Capell;* fauour: *F1*
139 **me,]** *Rowe;* me *F1*
154 **ripe,]** *Cambridge* (*after Pope*); ripe: *F1*
182 **incardinate]** *F2;* incardinatc *F1*
194 **othergates]** *Capell;* other gates *F1*
196 **H'as]** *Rowe;* has *F1*
200–1 **passy-measures pavin]** *Malone;* passy measures panyn *F1*
206 **help?—]** *Malone;* helpe *F1*
208 s.d. **Exeunt . . . Andrew.]** *Dyce*
244 **died]** *F2* (di'd); dide *F1*
250 **attire,]** *Capell;* attyre: *F1*
259 s.d. **To Olivia.]** *Rowe*
267 s.d. **To Viola.]** *Rowe*
271 **continent the fire]** *Rowe;* Continent, the fire, *F1*
285 **H'as]** *Rowe;* has *F1*
291 s.d. **Reads madly.]** *Alexander*
301 s.d. **To Fabian.]** *Rowe*
311 **madly-us'd]** *hyphen, Steevens*
315 s.d. **Exit Fabian.]** *Capell*
321 s.d. **To Viola.]** *Rowe*
324 **long,]** *Pope;* long: *F1*
326 **sister!]** *Dyce;* sister, *F1*
326 s.d. **Fabian with]** *Capell*
359 **confess, myself]** *Theobald;* confesse my selfe, *F1*
373 **Lord, fool]** *Rowe;* Lotd Foole *F1* (Lord *F2*)
378 s.d. **Exit.]** *Rowe*
388 s.d. **all but Clown]** *Dyce* (*subs.*)
405 **begun]** *Rowe;* begon *F1*
406 **With]** *F2*
408 s.d. **Exit.]** *Rowe;* FINIS. *F1*

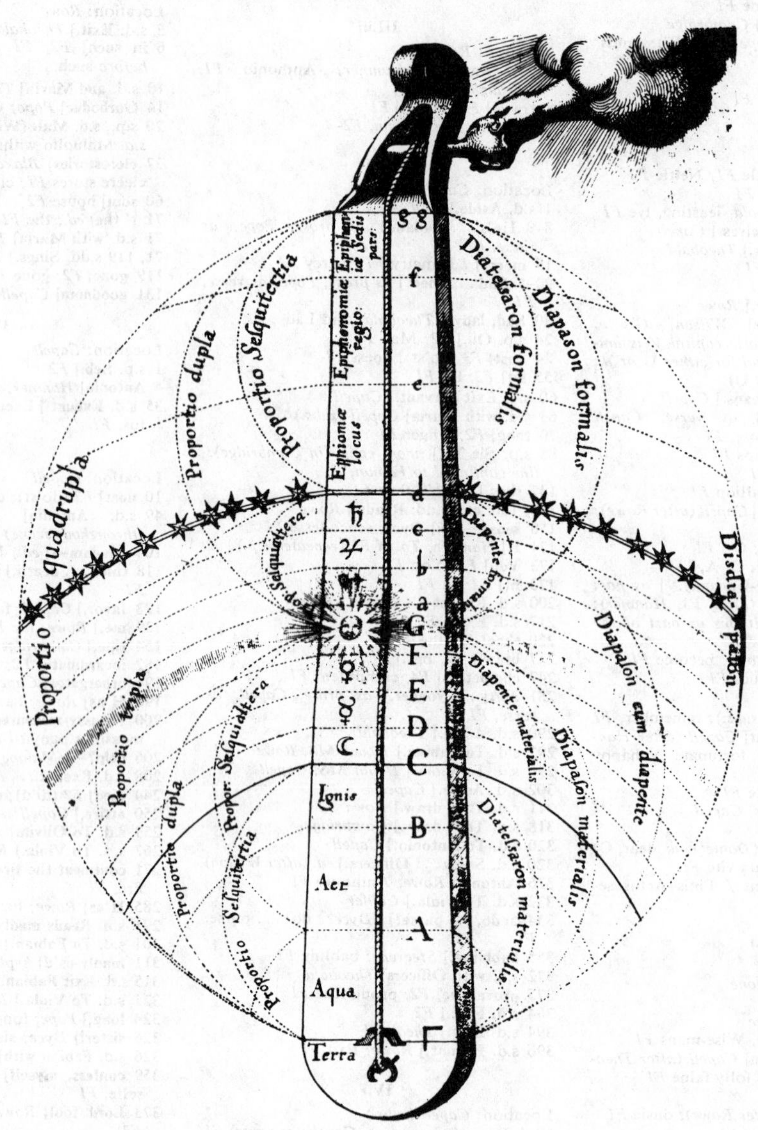

The universe as God's stringed instrument. From Robert Fludd, *Utriusque Cosmi Historia* (1617–19). The metaphor of the universe as a giant musical instrument, a divine harmony, was a commonplace of Renaissance thought. Here the hand of God is represented as tuning the universe so that the delicate harmonic relations are exactly maintained. As Ulysses, in his famous speech on order and degree and the chaos that results when these principles of harmonic subordination are violated, says: "Take but degree away, untune that string, / And hark what discord follows" (*Troilus and Cressida*, I.iii.109–10). Fludd's diagram also illustrates the principal outlines of the Ptolemaic system (see Plate 10), with the Earth as the centre of the universe. Note particularly the central and commanding position of the Sun, referred to by Ulysses as "the glorious planet Sol / In noble eminence enthron'd and spher'd / Amidst the other [planets]" (lines 89–91), through which it links the heavenly diapason with the material diapason. (*By permission of the Harvard College Library*)

Troilus and Cressida

MORE THAN ANY OTHER PLAY by Shakespeare, *Troilus and Cressida* is the discovery of the twentieth century. Its unconventional form, neither comedy, tragedy, history, nor satire, its intellectualism, savagery, and disillusion speak forcefully to contemporary audiences naturally sceptical about ideas of honor, nobility, and military glory. There is no record of any performance of this play before 1898. Since the Second World War it has scarcely left the stage, despite the large cast required for its performance and the considerable technical problems involved. Critics continue to disagree about the tone and meaning of *Troilus and Cressida*. The modern theatre has decided firmly, and surely rightly, that the play is a brilliant but scarifying vision of a world in pieces, all value and coherence gone. Despite its energy and wit, the picture of man which it presents is pessimistic almost to the point of nihilism.

On the evidence of the Stationers' Register, *Troilus and Cressida* was in existence by February 1603, although it may have been written a year or two earlier. The 1603 entry grants permission to James Roberts to print, "when he hath gotten sufficient aucthority for yt, The booke of Troilus and Cresseda, as yt is acted by my lord Chamberlens Men." Perhaps this authority (probably the permission of Shakespeare and his fellow shareholders at the Globe) was not forthcoming or perhaps the entry was a blocking entry; in any case the play did not appear in print until 1609, in a quarto edition published not by Roberts but by two partners named Richard Bonian and Henry Walley. Although they duly registered their manuscript (on January 28, 1609), they almost certainly had no legal title to it, a fact which they tried to brazen out in a preface congratulating prospective readers on their good fortune in gaining access to a work which "by the grand possessors' wills" would never have escaped.

The 1609 quarto is mysterious in ways that go beyond the problem of how Bonian and Walley secured the forbidden text. When printing began, a title-page was provided which described *Troilus and Cressida* as a play "acted by the King's Majesty's servants at the Globe." This claim accords with the specific mention of professional performances in the 1603 Stationers' Register entry. During the course of printing, however, a decision was made to replace this title-page by another, in which the reference to actors and theatre was suppressed. Moreover, following this second title-page an address to the reader was inserted which hailed *Troilus and Cressida* as "a new play, never stal'd with the stage, never clapper-claw'd with the palms of the vulgar" and urged the reader not to "like this the less for not being sullied with the smoky breath of the multitude."[1]

No satisfactory explanation of this contradiction has yet been given, although a number of hypotheses have been advanced. Were Bonian and Walley simply correcting an initial error? If so, Roberts had made the same mistake in 1603. In any case, why should a hard-working man of the theatre like Shakespeare compose a full-length drama not intended for the stage which he also declined to release for publication? It has been suggested that the play was intended for the Globe, put into rehearsal, and then withdrawn before the first performance because it proved too difficult; alternatively, that it was written for a single private

[1] For the entire address, as well as the wording of both title-pages, see the Textual Notes.

performance either at Whitehall or for the lawyers at one of the Inns of Court and was considered unsuitable for the general public. Neither theory seems convincing in the light of Shakespeare's artistic practicality, his canny sense of what a given company of actors could manage, and also his ability to please the most diverse tastes with the same play.

Nevill Coghill has argued that *Troilus and Cressida* was originally acted at the Globe but that for a later, Inns of Court performance Shakespeare added a mocking, cynical prologue and epilogue designed to protect his work against possible sneers from a more sophisticated, critical audience accustomed to the metaphysical urbanities of Donne's *Songs and Sonnets*. According to Coghill, the publishers were appealing directly to this audience when they devised their preface and second title-page. They pretended that the addition of a prologue and epilogue made *Troilus and Cressida* a new play and one that was the particular property of the lawyers. As it happens there is textual evidence in the First Folio version to suggest that originally Pandarus made his final exit in V.iii and that his re-entry to speak the epilogue was an afterthought. The prologue, on the other hand, was printed for the first time in the Folio; it does not appear in the 1609 quarto at all. Elizabethan publishers were no paragons of truth-telling. All the same, it seems hard to believe that Bonian and Walley would have gone to the trouble and expense of cancelling their title-page after printing had begun in order to announce, purely on the basis of a prologue which they were not even offering their readers and a brief epilogue which they were, that this was a fashionable new play substantially different from the one seen at the Globe.

Although Coghill's argument is ultimately unsatisfactory, it is interesting as an example of the lengths to which some critics have gone in the attempt to demonstrate that *Troilus and Cressida*, looked at properly, is really a straightforward tragedy and not a "problem play" at all. Coghill contends that once stripped of its sardonic and "misleading" prologue and epilogue, *Troilus and Cressida* becomes the play seen at the Globe: a drama about good but doomed Trojans suffering at the hands of nasty but victorious Greeks. Like G. Wilson Knight, he believes in the Trojans as heroes, the keepers of important human values tragically destroyed by an adverse fate. It is difficult to see how a mere prologue and epilogue could distort the whole character of a play, especially a play as clear and unequivocal in its sympathies as Coghill believes this one to be. The truth is that the prologue, with its abrupt shifts of tone and style, its dizzying blend of celebration and mockery, the grandiloquent and the deliberately off-hand, is a microcosm of the play it serves to introduce: a finely judged preparation for the mixed and unclassifiable experience to come. Pandarus' epilogue, by contrast, is monolithic and brutal. But it too has a structural relevance. Calculatedly shocking though it is, a theatrically brilliant last twist of the knife, it can nonetheless stand as a logical conclusion requiring no external excuse: the final step in that inexorable coarsening of action and characters evident throughout Act V. Dryden appraised the situation here more justly than Coghill and other modern critics of his persuasion. When, in 1679, Dryden set himself to convince an audience that *Troilus and Cressida* was an unmistakable tragedy, a dignified lament for Troy, he did more than merely jettison Shakespeare's prologue and epilogue. He rewrote the whole play.

The seventeenth-century editors of *Troilus and Cressida* are of small help in establishing its genre. Both the first and the corrected title-page of the 1609 quarto describe it as a "history." The preface, on the other hand, insists vigorously that it is "passing full of the palm comical; for it is a birth of . . . [that] brain that never undertook anything comical vainly." The First Folio editors, just to make the confusion complete, designed for it a place in the midst of the tragedy section, transferring it to a makeshift position between the Histories and the Tragedies only as the result of some undetermined emergency while the book was going through the press. *Troilus and Cressida* is by no means the only play of its period to be classified in a random and contradictory fashion. For Shakespeare and his contemporaries, the terms *comedy*, *history*, and *tragedy* were vaguer and less precise than they became for Dryden. All the same, one can see why this particular play invited difference of opinion. Certainly the fence-sitting position it occupies in the First Folio, although apparently the result of practical rather than esthetic uncertainties, proved to be prophetic.

To the three categories proposed by the original editors the twentieth century has added a fourth: satire. O. J. Campbell has made out a case for *Troilus and Cressida* as a play deriving from the temporary vogue for satire so marked in the last years of Elizabeth's reign. He accepts the idea of performance at one of the Inns of Court and proceeds to develop from this premise a series of parallels associating Shakespeare's play with the non-dramatic satires of writers like Marston, and with the early humor comedies of Ben Jonson. There are, undoubtedly, satiric elements in *Troilus and Cressida* (although the notion that Achilles is a malicious portrait of Elizabeth's truant favorite, the Earl of Essex, is firmly to be discounted). Yet the end of the play scarcely "leaves the audience suffused with cynical amusement" in the way Campbell suggests. Tragic pity and fear may manifest themselves only fitfully in *Troilus and Cressida*, but they are present all the same. The death of Hector is as horrifying as anything Shakespeare ever wrote, the final appearance of Cassandra has the spine-chilling quality of high tragedy, and even the young lovers of the title—flawed though they are—make undeniable emotional demands upon an audience. It is simply not possible to watch this play with unbroken intellectual detachment.

Campbell's idea that *Troilus and Cressida* belongs to the same breed as Jonson's *Every Man Out of His Humor* and *Cynthia's Revels*, that it is a work dedicated to the service of moral education, ridiculing Trojan sensuality and Greek individualism, has the merit of seeing that Shakespeare did not side with Priam and his sons. On the other hand, the comparison with Jonson only points up the absence in Shakespeare's play of any spokesman-character like Jonson's Asper, Crites, or Horace: conservative and well-balanced men of righteousness and moral sense who guide the just judgment of the theatre audience at the same time that they ridicule and correct the aberrant humors of the comedy. The fact that no one character or group of characters in *Troilus and Cressida* can be regarded as being either morally or structurally central is one of the problems of the play. Here, critics like L. C. Knights, A. P. Rossiter, Una Ellis-Fermor, and W. R. Elton would seem to be more accurate when they point to the stubborn relativism of the work, its presentation of a society in which fixed or objective values no longer operate. Elizabethan orthodoxies may be mouthed from time to time by the characters. Ulysses' speech on degree in I.iii has long been regarded as the cornerstone of the "Elizabethan world-picture," evidence of Shakespeare's fundamental conservatism. Looked at in context, however, this speech reveals itself as an adroit stringing together of pious platitudes: a piece of rhetoric which is applauded by all but to which no one, least of all Ulysses himself, pays the smallest practical attention. The abortive scheme to stir Achilles into action by making him jealous of Ajax is, in fact, a further violation of "degree, priority, and place." It derives from a disabused pragmatism of the kind advocated by Thomas Hobbes. As Elton has said, absolutes of good or evil are grotesquely out of place in this world. People and things, no matter how elevated they may sound, all come to the marketplace to be weighed and priced according to a fluctuating standard dependent upon laws of supply and demand, and the condition of the market at a given moment of time.

Neither tragedy nor satire, celebration nor parody, *Troilus and Cressida* is innovatory and experimental, yet assured. Its intellectualism does not diminish its emotional force. In the theatre it demands a dazzling variety of response from its audience, a combination of detachment and involvement, sympathy and criticism, more exacting than is usual with Shakespeare. In part the complexity which characterizes the play springs from its subject matter and from the ironies generated by the audience's detailed foreknowledge of the destiny reserved for each character. The myth of Troy was already vast and susceptible of widely divergent interpretation in the Athens of Euripides. Shakespeare received it further augmented by all the commentary and literary reworkings of the Middle Ages and early Renaissance. In writing his own play he almost certainly drew upon Chaucer's *Troilus and Criseyde* for the love story, although his own approach to the three principals was far less indulgent than Chaucer's. Probably he also knew Henryson's *Testament of Cresseid*, a fifteenth-century Scottish poem which deals movingly with the fortunes of Cressida after she has been abandoned by Diomed. For the Trojan war and its heroes he was in part dependent upon translations of Homer. The first installment of Chapman's had appeared in 1598, and there was also available Arthur Hall's translation of ten books. Virgil's *Aeneid* and the material scattered through Ovid's *Metamorphoses* which deals with Troy must also have been in his mind. But he drew upon medieval as well as classical sources, primarily upon Caxton's compendium translated from the French, the *Recuyell of the Histories of Troy*, with some consultation also of Lydgate's moralizing version of the war in his *Troy Book*. There is evidence of the existence of several earlier Elizabethan plays dealing with the story of Troilus and Cressida, but all have been lost, so that there is no way of telling what influence (if any) they exerted on Shakespeare when he came to construct his own account.

More speculative, but tantalizing, is the possible influence of Euripides. In play after play Euripides took up the matter of Troy. Elizabethans knew many of these plays, in translations and adapted versions. If Shakespeare himself ever encountered the *Orestes* he would have found there an attitude towards the myth strikingly like his own. For Euripides too, the Trojan war was an expense of spirit in a waste of shame. His Helen is a vain and light-minded flirt, manifestly not worth a fraction of the trouble she has caused, and the other "heroes" are similarly debased. Everywhere, Euripides measures the epic grandeur of the story against the unlovely reality of these events and people when seen up close. Like Shakespeare's, his play is brilliant and savage, without any clear-cut moral or structural centre. It is also mixed in form, a combination of tragedy, comedy, and satire so extreme that until recently it was as much an embarrassment to the classicists as *Troilus and Cressida* was to the Shakespeareans of the eighteenth and nineteenth centuries.

Among Shakespeare's own plays, *Hamlet* seems closely associated with *Troilus and Cressida*. Although these two plays, written about the same time, are radically different in tone and structure, they share a predilection for images of disease and physical corruption. They are also alike in exploring the hiatus between a character's words and actions, between the verbal formulation of intent and subsequent behavior. Oaths and vows are essentially an attempt to order and dictate the future by linguistic means. In *Troilus and Cressida* they exist only to be broken. Because Shakespeare does not let us forget for an instant how this story will end, the verbal contract entered into by Troilus, Pandarus, and Cressida in III.ii becomes positively hideous in its irony. Achilles, too, vows to Queen Hecuba and Polyxena that he will not go out to battle on the day which follows the single combat between Ajax and Hector. When Patroclus is killed, Achilles sweeps aside his oath. Even Thersites takes pains to remind us of the bitter end of Diomedes' pact with Cressida when he describes Diomedes as one who "will spend his mouth and promise like Brabbler the hound, but when he performs, astronomers foretell it: . . . the sun borrows of the moon when Diomed keeps his word" (V.i.90–94).

This derisory treatment of promises simply concentrates the general idea, even more widespread in this play than it is in *Hamlet*, of the irrelevance of words to deeds. Ulysses may analyze the malaise which distempers all the Greek host in traditional and lofty terms; he tries to correct it through a sordid, Machiavellian stratagem which Nestor can describe in terms of two mastiffs snarling over a bone. Hector, in the Trojan council scene, demonstrates irrefutably that Helen "is not worth what she doth cost the keeping," then ignores his own reasoning and votes to continue the war. Cressida tells Troilus that she will be "a woeful Cressid 'mongst the merry Greeks," but begins to play the coquette the moment she sets foot in the Greek camp. There is a sense in which Troilus' contemptuous dismissal of Cressida's letter as "Words, words, mere words" near the end of the play (V.iii.108) applies to all the rhetoric and oratory in it.

The words of objective observers, as Ulysses tells Achilles in III.iii, are not only the source of a man's reputation: they are the only means by which he can be confirmed in his private estimation of himself. Ulysses seems to regard this state of affairs with complacency. The play as a whole is less approving. Indeed, most of those verbal descriptions through which value is established prove to be false visions, without substance in reality. When, in III.i, Pandarus is told that the palace musicians play for Lord Paris and for his companion, "the mortal Venus, the heart-blood of beauty, love's invisible soul," he replies: "Who? my cousin Cressida?" The right answer, of course, is Helen. Pandarus is an old fool, filled with misplaced family pride, and yet his mistake is not incomprehensible. The Helen of the play is no goddess, no Platonic essence of Beauty. She is not even Homer's troubled plaything of the gods, so lovely that the mere sight of her walking by momentarily justified the entire war for the elders at the Skaian gates. An idle, pretty girl in Shakespeare, she likes to amuse herself by counting the hairs on Troilus' chin and can express a languorous opinion that "this love will undo us all" without reflecting that, in all seriousness, it might. In Marlowe's *Dr. Faustus*, Helen had been celebrated as a deity who "launched a thousand ships, / And burnt the topless towers of Ilium." For Shakespeare—and he deliberately echoed Marlowe's line—she is the source not only of destruction but debasement, a woman valueless in herself who has "turn'd crown'd kings to merchants." Cressida, whatever Pandarus may think and Troilus falsely urge upon her, comes no closer to being an ideal: "love's invisible soul." The formula itself is a distorted invention, not a reflection of truth. Yet it is for empty words like these that Troy will burn.

A similar and comic discrepancy between reputation and fact creates the impasse of I.iii where Aeneas, bearing Hector's challenge to the Greeks, inquires elaborately how he may find "that god in office, guiding men . . . the high and mighty Agamemnon." As it happens, the man he has singled out as an informant is Agamemnon himself: an Agamemnon considerably less godlike and awe-inspiring in the flesh than in the hyperbolic language of Aeneas. Just so, the heroic stature of Achilles about which everyone but Thersites talks seems to be a verbal chimera. Pompously invited, in IV.v, to feast his eyes on the splendors of Achilles' physique, Hector finds that the briefest perusal will do quite nicely. When Achilles at last takes the field and engages Hector, he has to accept the clemency of his foe. He does manage to kill Hector in their second encounter, but only through recourse to treachery, in an unfair fight. Achilles' instructions to his Myrmidons after the butchery ensure, however, that what was really a scene from the abattoir will be blazoned to the world in epic terms. This, as it seems, is how myths originate.

No Homeric reputation emerges from this play unscathed. Even Hector betrays the hopes invested in him at the beginning of the play. In the Trojan council he perversely turns his back on the truth he sees, merely because he is besotted with a cozening idea of honor and glory to be won. Worse still, his death is the result of his own greed. Hector's magnanimity, his generosity in battle to a wounded or retreating adversary, has been stressed throughout the play; indeed, this characteristic of his has been one of the few things which have rescued the war from Thersites' descriptions of it as the mere "clapper-clawing" of animals. Hector's chivalry is not proof, however, against the temptation provided by the Greek in splendid armor who crosses his path in V.vi. In order to possess this armor, he brutally kills a man who was only trying to run away. It is while Hector is gloating over his spoils, defenseless and unprepared, that Achilles catches his advantage.

In the love plot, Troilus may be more constant than Cressida: he is equally flawed. Although in the Trojan council he advances the proposition, "I take to-day a wife," it remains the illustration for an argument only. He never mentions marriage to Cressida and this silence, in a world where Chaucer's courtly-love convention does not obtain, seems strange. Fatally self-absorbed from the start, Troilus idealizes his own sensuality and, in the process, omits to notice what kind of person his beloved really is. For all their exaltation, Troilus' lines anticipating the bliss of union with Cressida in III.ii reduce love to a matter of appetite. "Love's thrice-repured nectar" may seem far removed from "the fragments, scraps, the bits and greasy relics / Of her o'er-eaten faith" which he will summon up in V.ii. The paradisal banquet has given place to the disgusting remnants, the unlovely litter of the morning after. But in both cases, before and after her treachery, Cressida is regarded by her lover principally as matter for ingestion, an object to be devoured by the senses. As the knowing presence of Pandarus continually reminds us.

The systematic undercutting and diminution of every other principal character leaves one, uncomfortably enough, to face Thersites as the one man who assesses the situation correctly. An allowed fool of the most savage kind, Thersites has only two functions in the play: to observe and to rail. He is there to remind us that love is lechery, that man is an animal, the body a sink of filth and diseases, and the human intellect a bad joke. A voice more than a person, he operates almost in the manner of a chemical agent: the addition of one dram of Thersites will turn any situation instantly into mud. If he believes that there may be some other country in which men are not wholly taken up with war and lechery, he gives no sign of it. The human condition, in his view, is faithfully mirrored in the events and personalities of the Trojan war.

No audience, at first, puts much faith in his scabrous evaluation of the loves and wars of Troy. The voice is too obviously distorted, the imagination too foul, and his own position too ignominious. In his early scenes Thersites is consistently the object of physical abuse, beaten and kicked. Yet as the play unfolds he gains both independence and a disconcerting strength. The very idea of an armed Hector seriously inquiring of Thersites on the field of battle "Art thou of blood and honor?" is absurd in a way that diminishes Hector, not Thersites. By the end, although one scarcely rejoices as he does over his discoveries, it is hard to challenge his sweeping indictment of both sides. The weakness of Cressida, the overwrought sensuality of Troilus, and the lip-smacking services of Pandarus have betrayed Love. Paris is a selfish voluptuary, Ajax a lout, and Menelaus so obviously a figure of fun that no one, not even the courteous Hector, can resist laughing at him to his face. The rationalism of Ulysses is hollow and ineffective. Only an accident, the death of Patroclus in battle, gets Achilles out of his tent and into his armor: not Ulysses' stratagem. Achilles' heroic stature is a fraud. Even Hector has looked truth in the eye and then dishonored both it and the knightly generosity of which he seemed the embodiment. Agamemnon is a nonentity and Helen, for all the poetry lavished on her, a trivial fool. Men may talk like gods. They end up behaving like those beasts to which Thersites so persistently compares them.

Argumentative and intensely verbal, almost self-consciously intellectual, *Troilus and Cressida* moves towards a position of profound scepticism. The play which contains, in Ulysses' speech on order, Shakespeare's most elaborate presentation of the medieval great chain of being, finishes by portraying a chaos which can no longer be remedied by traditional means. Accepted ideas of degree and rule, of personal honor, reputation, and love, do not, in this society, require reaffirmation so much as radical redefinition. Even the mode of speech favored by the characters is shown to be dangerously inappropriate and misjudged. In *The Language Poets Use*, Winifred Nowottny has argued that simile, a process of likening stable, defined objects to one another without ever suggesting that their identity merges in a new creation, is a figure particularly suited to the description of a familiar, ordered world. Metaphor, by contrast, is creative and exploratory: a way of mapping a fluid, uncertain reality for which there are, as yet, no categories or fixed terms. *Troilus and Cressida*, although concerned with disintegration and change, stands out among Shakespeare's plays by not employing metaphor as its dominant figure of speech. Simile, extended comparisons introduced by *like*, or *as*, or some other formal indication of parallel, seems to be the preferred idiom of both Greece and Troy. Characters often play at simile-making, as Troilus and Cressida do in their vows, or Thersites when he tries to decide to which of the many possible base or animal forms malicious wit may most effectively liken Menelaus. The speeches of Ulysses are a tissue of analogy and seemingly judicial parallel. In every case, despite the surface logic, nothing is really discovered about the focal term in the comparison. Essentially an instrument of analysis, simile as it is used in this play merely obscures identity and evades truth. When Achilles says that his mind is troubled, "like a fountain stirred," when Ajax declares that he hates proud men "as I do hate the engend'ring of toads," or Troilus pictures Cressida as a pearl embedded in India, to be reached by way of "this sailing Pandar," simile is being employed falsely to describe a world whose values are not stable, a world of chaos and relativity with which only metaphor can cope.

There are right and wrong ways of ordering the complexities of human experience at a given moment of time. In *Troilus and Cressida* the only order which ultimately passes muster and stands firm would seem to be the artistic order of the play itself. Although Shakespeare concedes much (too much, as far as earlier critics were concerned) to the formless and unorthodox in the structuring of his five acts, the logic of the play is nevertheless far more effective and impressive than anything Ulysses represents. Individual characters may be bewilderingly inconsistent; their dramatic treatment is not. Silently, through the juxtaposition and contrast of different characters and ideas, through the placing of scenes and the implicit comment they make upon one another, an order is affirmed which envelops and, in a sense, contradicts the nihilism of the action. The distortions of epic celebration, the inadequacy of simile as a way of anatomizing situations demanding a flexible, intuitive language, do not prevent Shakespeare from demonstrating that words, rightly used, can be the sensitive and precise registers of experience. Ultimately, Thersites' reductivist view of man is refuted by the simple fact that *Troilus and Cressida* exists. The disorder of the subject is not, as in so many twentieth-century works, reflected in its structure. This sense of mastery and control over difficult material is why, for all its pessimism and savagery, the experience of *Troilus and Cressida* is finally exhilarating. Despite the bleakness of the ending and the bitter prophecies of Pandarus, this great play dismisses its audience fundamentally reassured.

Anne Barton

The History of Troilus and Cressida

[DRAMATIS PERSONAE

PRIAM, *King of Troy*
HECTOR, TROILUS, PARIS, DEIPHOBUS, HELENUS — *his sons*
MARGARELON, *a bastard son of Priam*
AENEAS, ANTENOR — *Trojan commanders*
CALCHAS, *a Trojan priest, taking part with the Greeks*
PANDARUS, *uncle to Cressida*
ALEXANDER, *servant to Cressida*
SERVANT *and* BOY *to Troilus*
SERVANT *to Paris*

AGAMEMNON, *the Greek general*
MENELAUS, *his brother*
NESTOR, ULYSSES, ACHILLES, AJAX, DIOMEDES, PATROCLUS — *Greek commanders*
THERSITES, *a deformed and scurrilous Greek*
SERVANT *to Diomedes*

HELEN, *wife to Menelaus*
ANDROMACHE, *wife to Hector*
CASSANDRA, *daughter to Priam, a prophetess*
CRESSIDA, *daughter to Calchas*

TROJAN *and* GREEK SOLDIERS, *and* ATTENDANTS

SCENE: *Troy, and the Greek camp before it*]

[THE PROLOGUE

In Troy, there lies the scene. From isles of Greece
The princes orgillous, their high blood chaf'd,
Have to the port of Athens sent their ships
Fraught with the ministers and instruments
Of cruel war. Sixty and nine, that wore
Their crownets regal, from th' Athenian bay
Put forth toward Phrygia, and their vow is made
To ransack Troy, within whose strong immures
The ravish'd Helen, Menelaus' queen,
With wanton Paris sleeps—and that's the quarrel.
To Tenedos they come,
And the deep-drawing [barks] do there disgorge
Their warlike fraughtage. Now on Dardan plains
The fresh and yet unbruised Greeks do pitch
Their brave pavilions. Priam's six-gated city,
Dardan and Timbria, Helias, Chetas, Troien,
And [Antenorides], with massy staples
And corresponsive and fulfilling bolts
[Sperr] up the sons of Troy.
Now expectation, tickling skittish spirits,
On one and other side, Troyan and Greek,
Sets all on hazard—and hither am I come,
A prologue arm'd, but not in confidence
Of author's pen or actor's voice, but suited
In like conditions as our argument,
To tell you, fair beholders, that our play

Words and passages enclosed in square brackets in the text above are either emendations of the copy-text or additions to it. The Textual Notes immediately following the play cite the earliest authority for every such change or insertion and supply the reading of the copy-text wherever it is emended in this edition.

Pro. 2. orgillous: proud (variant of *orgulous*). Note that the Prologue contains no reference to the Troilus and Cressida story. **high blood:** (1) noble lineage; (2) temperament readily fired by honorable exploits.
4. Fraught: freighted, loaded. Cf. *fraughtage* (= cargo) in line 13. **ministers:** soldiers (who operate the "instruments" or weapons).
6. crownets: coronets.
7. Phrygia: in Elizabethan usage, the land of the Trojans.
8. immures: walls, defenses.
11. Tenedos: an island off the northwest coast of Asia Minor, close to Troy; here described as the naval base of the Greek invasion.
12. deep-drawing: low in the water (because of their heavy cargo).
13. Dardan: Trojan (from the name of Dardanus, ancestor of the Trojan kings).
15. brave: splendid. **pavilions:** large peaked tents.
16–17. Dardan . . . Antenorides. The names of the six gates of Troy.
17–18. massy . . . bolts: i.e. heavy, solid sockets into which correspondingly heavy and solid bolts fitted.
19. Sperr up: lock up (defensively) with bolts and bars.
23. arm'd: in armor. Lines 23–25 are usually taken as a stroke at Ben Jonson, who in *Poetaster* (1601) introduces an "armed prologue," suggesting his own embattled position in the War of the Theatres then at its height. If so, *confidence* signifies overconfidence or arrogance, the attitude for which Jonson was most often attacked. The characterization of Ajax is thought by some to be a further attack on Jonson.
24–25. suited . . . argument: i.e. dressed to match our (martial) subject matter.

Leaps o'er the vaunt and firstlings of those broils,
Beginning in the middle; starting thence away
To what may be digested in a play.
Like or find fault, do as your pleasures are,
Now good or bad, 'tis but the chance of war.]

[ACT I, SCENE I]

Enter PANDARUS *and* TROILUS.

Tro. Call here my varlet, I'll unarm again.
Why should I war without the walls of Troy,
That find such cruel battle here within?
Each Troyan that is master of his heart,
Let him to field, Troilus, alas, hath none.

Pan. Will this gear ne'er be mended?

Tro. The Greeks are strong, and skillful to their strength,
Fierce to their skill, and to their fierceness valiant,
But I am weaker than a woman's tear,
Tamer than sleep, fonder than ignorance,
Less valiant than the virgin in the night,
And skilless as unpractic'd infancy.

Pan. Well, I have told you enough of this. For my part, I'll not meddle nor make no farther. He that will have a cake out of the wheat must tarry the grinding.

Tro. Have I not tarried?

Pan. Ay, the grinding; but you must tarry the bolting.

Tro. Have I not tarried?

Pan. Ay, the bolting; but you must tarry the leavening.

Tro. Still have I tarried.

Pan. Ay, to the leavening, but here's yet in the word "hereafter" the kneading, the making of the cake, the heating the oven, and the baking; nay, you must stay the cooling too, or ye may chance burn your lips.

Tro. Patience herself, what goddess e'er she be,
Doth lesser blench at suff'rance than I do.
At Priam's royal table do I sit,
And when fair Cressid comes into my thoughts—
So, traitor, then she comes when she is thence.

Pan. Well, she look'd yesternight fairer than ever I saw her look, or any woman else.

Tro. I was about to tell thee—when my heart,
As wedged with a sigh, would rive in twain,
Lest Hector or my father should perceive me,
I have (as when the sun doth light a-scorn)
Buried this sigh in wrinkle of a smile,
But sorrow that is couch'd in seeming gladness
Is like that mirth fate turns to sudden sadness.

Pan. And her hair were not somewhat darker than Helen's—well, go to!—there were no more comparison between the women! But for my part, she is my kinswoman; I would not, as they term it, praise her, but I would somebody had heard her talk yesterday as I did. I will not dispraise your sister Cassandra's wit, but—

Tro. O Pandarus! I tell thee, Pandarus—
When I do tell thee there my hopes lie drown'd,
Reply not in how many fadoms deep
They lie indrench'd. I tell thee I am mad
In Cressid's love; thou answer'st she is fair,
Pourest in the open ulcer of my heart
Her eyes, her hair, her cheek, her gait, her voice,
Handlest in thy discourse, O, that her hand,
In whose comparison all whites are ink
Writing their own reproach; to whose soft seizure
The cygnet's down is harsh, and spirit of sense
Hard as the palm of ploughman. This thou tell'st me,
As true thou tell'st me, when I say I love her,
But saying thus, in stead of oil and balm,
Thou lay'st in every gash that love hath given me
The knife that made it.

Pan. I speak no more than truth.

Tro. Thou dost not speak so much.

Pan. Faith, I'll not meddle in it, let her be as she is; if she be fair, 'tis the better for her; and she be not, she has the mends in her own hands.

Tro. Good Pandarus! How now, Pandarus?

Pan. I have had my labor for my travail; ill thought on of her, and ill thought [on] of you; gone between and between, but small thanks for my labor.

Tro. What, art thou angry, Pandarus? What, with me?

Pan. Because she's kin to me, therefore she's not so fair as Helen. And she were [not] kin to me, she would be as fair a' Friday as Helen is on Sunday.

27. vaunt: beginnings (originally a prefix = "first part of," like *van-* in *vanguard*). **firstlings:** first fruits (synonymous with *vaunt*).
28. Beginning . . . middle: i.e. after seven years' siege (see I.iii.12); probably alluding to the fact that epic poems traditionally (since the *Iliad*) leap "into the middle of things" (*in medias res*).

I.i. Location: Troy. Before Priam's palace.
1. varlet: page or servant to a knight.
5. hath none. Because he has given his heart to Cressida.
6. gear: business. **7, 8. to:** in addition to, or in proportion to.
10. fonder: more foolish.
14. not . . . nor . . . no. Elizabethan multiple negative, implying simple negation. **meddle nor make.** A proverbial phrase (*make* = do, undertake).
15. cake: a kind of bread, flattened and shaped, baked hard on both sides. **17–18. bolting:** sifting.
20–21. leavening: fermenting (of the dough).
27. what . . . be: however much a goddess she is.
28. lesser . . . suff'rance: i.e. flinch more under suffering. *Lesser* apparently carries the sense "worse" or "with less fortitude."
31. So . . . thence: i.e. I am a traitor to say "when she comes," for by saying so I admit that she is sometimes absent from my thoughts. Most editors emend (after Rowe) to *When she comes! When is she thence?*

35. As wedged: as if cleft (as by a wedge). **rive:** split.
37. a-scorn: in mockery (?). The image seems to be of the sun gleaming momentarily through the clouds, deceptively promising fair weather. Most editors emend (after Rowe) to *a storm.*
39. is couch'd: lies low or hidden.
41. And: if. **hair . . . darker.** Blonde beauty was the Elizabethan ideal. **42. go to:** enough said.
42–43. no more comparison: (they are) not to be compared (Cressida is so superior to Helen). **47. wit:** powers of intellect.
50. fadoms: fathoms. **55. that her hand:** that hand of hers.
56. In whose comparison: in comparison with which.
57. to: in comparison with. **seizure:** clasp.
58. cygnet's: young swan's. **spirit of sense:** i.e. spirit of the sense of touch or feeling. The spirits of the senses, in Elizabethan physiology, were subtle vapors, transmitted through the nerves (thought of as hollow tubes), and believed to be the intermediaries between man's body and soul.
65. speak so much: tell the whole truth (with the implication that the whole truth about Cressida's beauty can never be told).
68. has . . . hands: (1) must make the best of it (proverbial); (2) has the remedy (i.e. cosmetics) available. **70. travail:** pains, efforts.
70–71. thought on of: thought of by.
76. as fair . . . Sunday: i.e. as beautiful at her plainest as Helen in her Sunday best.

But what [care] I? I care not and she were a blackamoor, 'tis all one to me.

Tro. Say I she is not fair?

Pan. I do not care whether you do or no. She's a fool to stay behind her father, let her to the Greeks; and so I'll tell her the next time I see her. For my part, I'll meddle nor make no more i' th' matter.

Tro. Pandarus—

Pan. Not I.

Tro. Sweet Pandarus—

Pan. Pray you speak no more to me, I will leave all as I found it, and there an end.

Exit. Sound alarum.

Tro. Peace, you ungracious clamors! peace, rude sounds!
Fools on both sides, Helen must needs be fair,
When with your blood you daily paint her thus.
I cannot fight upon this argument;
It is too starv'd a subject for my sword.
But Pandarus—O gods! how do you plague me!
I cannot come to Cressid but by Pandar,
And he's as teachy to be woo'd to woo,
As she is stubborn-chaste against all suit.
Tell me, Apollo, for thy Daphne's love,
What Cressid is, what Pandar, and what we:
Her bed is India, there she lies, a pearl;
Between our Ilium and where she [resides],
Let it be call'd the wild and wand'ring flood,
Ourself the merchant, and this sailing Pandar
Our doubtful hope, our convoy, and our bark.

Alarum. Enter Aeneas.

Aene. How now, Prince Troilus, wherefore not a-field?

Tro. Because not there. This woman's answer sorts,
For womanish it is to be from thence.
What news, Aeneas, from the field to-day?

Aene. That Paris is returned home and hurt.

Tro. By whom, Aeneas?

Aene. Troilus, by Menelaus.

Tro. Let Paris bleed, 'tis but a scar to scorn;
Paris is gor'd with Menelaus' horn. *Alarum.*

Aene. Hark what good sport is out of town to-day.

Tro. Better at home, if "would I might" were "may."
But to the sport abroad—are you bound thither?

81. stay . . . father: remain (here) after her father is gone. Cressida's father Calchas, forewarned by the Delphic oracle that Troy would be defeated, had defected to the Greeks.
88 s.d. alarum: trumpet call to arms.
92. upon this argument: in defense of this cause.
93. starv'd: thin, empty (of sustenance).
96. teachy: quick to take offense, touchy (variant of *tetchy*).
98. for . . . love: for the sake of your love of Daphne (a nymph who was turned into a laurel or bay tree to escape Apollo's importunate love). **99. we:** I.
101. Ilium. This name, usually in its Greek form *Ilion*, is used throughout for Priam's palace, hence to be distinguished from Troy, for which it is properly a poetic name.
104. convoy: protective escort, conductor.
105. Troilus. Dissyllabic throughout, except at V.ii.161 (see the note there). **106. sorts:** is appropriate.
111. a scar to scorn: (1) a wound too slight to be taken seriously; (2) a wound given in return for scorn.
112. Menelaus' horn: i.e. the cuckold's horn that Paris himself has scornfully given Menelaus.

Aene. In all swift haste.

Tro. Come go we then together. *Exeunt.*

[Scene II]

Enter Cressid *and her man* [Alexander].

Cres. Who were those went by?

Alex. Queen Hecuba and Helen.

Cres. And whither go they?

Alex. Up to the eastern tower,
Whose height commands as subject all the vale,
To see the battle. Hector, whose patience
Is as a virtue fix'd, to-day was mov'd:
He chid Andromache and strook his armorer,
And like as there were husbandry in war,
Before the sun rose he was harness'd light,
And to the field goes he; where every flower
Did as a prophet weep what it foresaw
In Hector's wrath.

Cres. What was his cause of anger?

Alex. The noise goes, this: there is among the Greeks
A lord of Troyan blood, nephew to Hector,
They call him Ajax.

Cres. Good; and what of him?

Alex. They say he is a very man *per se* and stands alone.

Cres. So do all men, unless th' are drunk, sick, or have no legs.

Alex. This man, lady, hath robb'd many beasts of their particular additions: he is as valiant as the lion, churlish as the bear, slow as the elephant; a man into whom nature hath so crowded humors that his valor is crush'd into folly, his folly sauc'd with discretion. There is no man hath a virtue that he hath not a glimpse of, nor any man an attaint but he carries some stain of it. He is melancholy without cause, and merry against the hair; he hath the joints of every thing, but every thing so out of joint that he is a gouty Briareus, many hands and no use, or purblind Argus, all eyes and no sight.

Cres. But how should this man, that makes me smile, make Hector angry?

I.ii. Location: Troy. A street.
5. Is . . . fix'd: is (ordinarily) a constant quality. **mov'd:** angry.
6. strook: struck (a common variant).
7. husbandry: careful management, thrift (with play on the sense "tillage" developing in *harness'd* and *field* in lines 8–9).
8. harness'd light: dressed in armor swiftly. **12. noise:** rumor.
13. nephew. Actually Ajax, according to the tradition followed in this play, was Hector's first cousin; see the note on II.ii.73.
15. man per se: man in a class by himself (for excellence).
20. particular additions: special attributes or descriptive titles.
22. humors: temperamental bents.
23. sauc'd: flavored, spiced. The context, however, implies a more even mixture of "folly" and "discretion," and Theobald's conjecture *forc'd* (another culinary term, meaning "stuffed,") is attractive.
25. glimpse: flash, i.e. trace. **attaint:** vice.
26. stain: tincture, slight admixture.
27. against the hair: contrary to his natural disposition (or to the particular occasion); equivalent to *against the grain.* **joints:** limbs.
28–29. a gouty Briareus: i.e. a man with a hundred hands (such as the giant Briareus was reputed to have), all disabled by gout.
29. purblind Argus: i.e. a man with a hundred eyes (such as Argus was reputed to have), all sightless.

Alex. They say he yesterday cop'd Hector in the battle and strook him down, the disdain and shame whereof hath ever since kept Hector fasting and waking.

[*Enter* PANDARUS.]

Cres. Who comes here?

Alex. Madam, your uncle Pandarus.

Cres. Hector's a gallant man.

Alex. As may be in the world, lady.

Pan. What's that? what's that?

Cres. Good morrow, uncle Pandarus.

Pan. Good morrow, cousin Cressid. What do you talk of? Good morrow, Alexander. How do you, cousin? When were you at Ilium?

Cres. This morning, uncle.

Pan. What were you talking of when I came? Was Hector arm'd and gone ere ye came to Ilium? Helen was not up, was she?

Cres. Hector was gone, but Helen was not up.

Pan. E'en so; Hector was stirring early.

Cres. That were we talking of, and of his anger.

Pan. Was he angry?

Cres. So he says here.

Pan. True, he was so; I know the cause too. He'll lay about him to-day, I can tell them that, and there's Troilus will not come far behind him. Let them take heed of Troilus; I can tell them that too.

Cres. What, is he angry too?

Pan. Who, Troilus? Troilus is the better man of the two.

Cres. O Jupiter, there's no comparison.

Pan. What, not between Troilus and Hector? Do you know a man if you see him?

Cres. Ay, if I ever saw him before and knew him.

Pan. Well, I say Troilus is Troilus.

Cres. Then you say as I say, for I am sure he is not Hector.

Pan. No, nor Hector is not Troilus in some degrees.

Cres. 'Tis just to each of them; he is himself.

Pan. Himself? alas, poor Troilus, I would he were!

Cres. So he is.

Pan. Condition I had gone barefoot to India.

Cres. He is not Hector.

Pan. Himself? no! he's not himself. Would 'a were himself! Well, the gods are above, time must friend or end. Well, Troilus, well, I would my heart were in her body. No, Hector is not a better man than Troilus.

Cres. Excuse me.

Pan. He is elder.

Cres. Pardon me, pardon me.

Pan. Th' other's not come to't. You shall tell me another tale when th' other's come to't. Hector shall not have his [wit] this year.

Cres. He shall not need it if he have his own.

Pan. Nor his qualities.

Cres. No matter.

Pan. Nor his beauty.

Cres. 'Twould not become him, his own's better.

Pan. You have no judgment, niece. Helen herself swore th' other day that Troilus, for a brown favor (for so 'tis, I must confess)—not brown neither—

Cres. No, but brown.

Pan. Faith, to say truth, brown and not brown.

Cres. To say the truth, true and not true.

Pan. She prais'd his complexion above Paris.

Cres. Why, Paris hath color enough.

Pan. So he has.

Cres. Then Troilus should have too much: if she prais'd him above, his complexion is higher than his. He having color enough, and the other higher, is too flaming a praise for a good complexion. I had as lieve Helen's golden tongue had commended Troilus for a copper nose.

Pan. I swear to you, I think Helen loves him better than Paris.

Cres. Then she's a merry Greek indeed.

Pan. Nay, I am sure she does. She came to him th' other day into the compass'd window—and you know he has not past three or four hairs on his chin—

Cres. Indeed a tapster's arithmetic may soon bring his particulars therein to a total.

Pan. Why, he is very young, and yet will he, within three pound, lift as much as his brother Hector.

Cres. Is he so young a man and so old a lifter?

Pan. But to prove to you that Helen loves him: she came and puts me her white hand to his cloven chin—

Cres. Juno have mercy! how came it cloven?

Pan. Why, you know 'tis dimpled. I think his smiling becomes him better than any man in all Phrygia.

Cres. O, he smiles valiantly.

Pan. Does he not?

Cres. O yes, and 'twere a cloud in autumn.

Pan. Why, go to then. But to prove to you that Helen loves Troilus—

Cres. Troilus will stand to the proof, if you'll prove it so.

33. cop'd: met and fought with. **34. disdain:** ignominy.
43. cousin: kinswoman; here, niece.
65. before and knew. There is a bawdy quibble on *before* (= from the front) and *knew* (= had sexual intercourse with).
71. he: i.e. each one.
74. Condition: on that condition (i.e. to make Troilus himself again); continues Pandarus' preceding speech. **had:** would have.
76. 'a: he.
78. friend or end: bring him to a happy condition or kill him (proverbial). **heart:** feelings.
81. Excuse me: i.e. I disagree; so *Pardon me* in line 83.

86. this year: i.e. ever (indefinite use).
93. for a brown favor: considering that he has a dark complexion.
98. above: beyond that of.
102. his . . . his: i.e. Troilus' . . . Paris'. **higher:** more highly colored, ruddier. **104. as lieve:** just as soon.
106. copper nose: red nose resulting from intemperance.
109. merry Greek: person of loose life (slang); the phrase, ordinarily having nothing to do with Greeks, is peculiarly apposite here.
111. compass'd window: semicircular bay-window.
112. past: more than.
113. tapster's arithmetic: i.e. reckoning of the easiest sort. A tapster scored drinks one at a time on a board; the score never got very high before payment was demanded.
117. old: experienced. **lifter:** (a) weight lifter; (b) thief; perhaps with the further sense "fornicator" (cf. *stand to the proof*, line 129, where *stand*, as frequently, has a bawdy implication).
119. puts me: puts (a colloquialism). **cloven:** cleft.
126. and: as if (so also *an'* in lines 173, 175). **cloud in autumn:** i.e. one that threatens a storm, unlike a summer cloud.

Pan. Troilus! why, he esteems her no more than I esteem an addle egg.

Cres. If you love an addle egg as well as you love an idle head, you would eat chickens i' th' shell.

Pan. I cannot choose but laugh to think how she tickled his chin. Indeed she has a marvell's white hand, I must needs confess.

Cres. Without the rack.

Pan. And she takes upon her to spy a white hair on his chin.

Cres. Alas, poor chin! many a wart is richer.

Pan. But there was such laughing! Queen Hecuba laugh'd that her eyes ran o'er.

Cres. With millstones.

Pan. And Cassandra laugh'd.

Cres. But there was a more temperate fire under the pot of her eyes. Did her eyes run o'er too?

Pan. And Hector laugh'd.

Cres. At what was all this laughing?

Pan. Marry, at the white hair that Helen spied on Troilus' chin.

Cres. And't had been a green hair, I should have laugh'd too.

Pan. They laugh'd not so much at the hair as at his pretty answer.

Cres. What was his answer?

Pan. Quoth she, "Here's but two and fifty hairs on your chin—and one of them is white."

Cres. This is her question.

Pan. That's true, make no question of that. "Two and fifty hairs," quoth he, "and one white. That white hair is my father, and all the rest are his sons." "Jupiter," quoth she, "which of these hairs is Paris my husband?" "The fork'd one," quoth he, "pluck't out, and give it him." But there was such laughing! and Helen so blush'd, and Paris so chaf'd, and all the rest so laugh'd, that it pass'd.

Cres. So let it now, for it has been a great while going by.

Pan. Well, cousin, I told you a thing yesterday, think on't.

Cres. So I do.

Pan. I'll be sworn 'tis true; he will weep you an' 'twere a man born in April. *Sound a retreat.*

Cres. And I'll spring up in his tears an' 'twere a nettle against May.

Pan. Hark, they are coming from the field. Shall we stand up here and see them as they pass toward Ilion? Good niece, do, sweet niece Cressida.

Cres. At your pleasure.

Pan. Here, here, here's an excellent place, here we may see most bravely. I'll tell you them all by their names as they pass by, but mark Troilus above the rest.

Enter AENEAS [*and passes over the stage*].

Cres. Speak not so loud.

Pan. That's Aeneas; is not that a brave man? He's one of the flowers of Troy, I can tell you. But mark Troilus; you shall see anon.

Cres. Who's that?

Enter ANTENOR [*and passes over the stage*].

Pan. That's Antenor. He has a shrowd wit, I can tell you, and he's man good enough. He's one o' th' soundest judgments in Troy, whosoever, and a proper man of person. When comes Troilus? I'll show you Troilus anon. If he see me, you shall see him nod at me.

Cres. Will he give you the nod?

Pan. You shall see.

Cres. If he do, the rich shall have more.

Enter HECTOR [*and passes over the stage*].

Pan. That's Hector, that, that, look you, that; there's a fellow! Go thy way, Hector! There's a brave man, niece. O brave Hector! look how he looks! There's a countenance! Is't not a brave man?

Cres. O, a brave man!

Pan. Is 'a not? It does a man['s] heart good. Look you what hacks are on his helmet! Look you yonder, do you see? Look you there, there's no jesting; there's laying on, take't off who will, as they say. There be hacks!

Cres. Be those with swords?

Pan. Swords! any thing, he cares not; and the devil come to him, it's all one. By God's lid, it does one's heart good. Yonder comes Paris, yonder comes Paris.

Enter PARIS [*and passes over the stage*].

Look ye yonder, niece; is't not a gallant man too, is't not? Why, this is brave now. Who said he came hurt home to-day? He's not hurt. Why, this will do Helen's heart good now, ha? Would I could see Troilus now! You shall see Troilus anon.

Cres. Who's that?

Enter HELENUS [*and passes over the stage*].

134. idle: empty, foolish (applied both to Pandarus' head and Troilus'), with play on *addle/idle*. **136. marvell's:** marvellous.
138. Without the rack: i.e. without being put to the torture.
141. is richer: i.e. has more hairs in it.
144. millstones. Proverbially shed by those too hard-hearted to shed tears. Here the point seems to be that there was nothing to make anyone laugh hard enough to cry.
150. Marry: why (originally an oath, "by the Virgin Mary").
162. his sons. Priam's sons traditionally numbered fifty; presumably the "fork'd" hair of line 164 is counted as two.
164. fork'd: (1) bifurcated; (2) horned (implying the likelihood that Paris, like Menelaus, will be made a cuckold by Helen).
165. give it him. With a quibble on "present him with horns."
166. so chaf'd: became so angry.
167. pass'd: was beyond description.
174 s.d. retreat: trumpet signal for withdrawal of forces.
176. nettle. Cressida twists the proverbial "April showers bring May flowers," perhaps also with a pun on *tears/tares* in line 175. **against:** in anticipation of.

182. bravely: admirably, capitally. Cf. Pandarus' application of the adjectival form to Aeneas, Hector, and Troilus below.
188. anon: presently, at once.
190. shrowd: sharp, biting (variant of *shrewd*).
192. whosoever: i.e. bar none.
193. proper . . . person: fine-looking man.
196. give . . . nod: i.e. call you fool (or noddy).
198. rich . . . more: i.e. one already rich (in folly) will be made richer.
205. hacks: dents, scars.
207. laying . . . will: i.e. a vigorous dealing of blows, whatever anyone may say to the contrary. The phrase *lay on* regularly attracts the phrase *take off.* **210. and:** if.
211. all one: all the same to him. **By God's lid:** by God's eyelid (a mild oath).

Pan. That's Helenus. I marvel where Troilus is. That's Helenus. I think he went not forth to-day. That's Helenus.

Cres. Can Helenus fight, uncle?

Pan. Helenus? no. Yes, he'll fight indifferent well. I marvel where Troilus is. Hark, do you not hear the people cry "Troilus"? Helenus is a priest.

Cres. What sneaking fellow comes yonder?

Enter Troilus [*and passes over the stage*].

Pan. Where? Yonder? That's Deiphobus. 'Tis Troilus! There's a man, niece! Hem! Brave Troilus, the prince of chivalry!

Cres. Peace, for shame, peace!

Pan. Mark him, note him. O brave Troilus! Look well upon him, niece. Look you how his sword is bloodied, and his helm more hack'd than Hector's, and how he looks, and how he goes! O admirable youth! he never saw three and twenty. Go thy way, Troilus, go thy way! Had I a sister were a grace, or a daughter a goddess, he should take his choice. O admirable man! Paris? Paris is dirt to him, and I warrant Helen, to change, would give an eye to boot.

[*Enter* Common Soldiers *and pass over the stage.*]

Cres. Here comes more.

Pan. Asses, fools, dolts! chaff and bran, chaff and bran! porridge after meat! I could live and die in the eyes of Troilus. Ne'er look, ne'er look, the eagles are gone; crows and daws, crows and daws! I had rather be such a man as Troilus than Agamemnon and all Greece.

Cres. There is amongst the Greeks Achilles, a better man than Troilus.

Pan. Achilles! a drayman, a porter, a very camel.

Cres. Well, well.

Pan. Well, well! Why, have you any discretion? have you any eyes? do you know what a man is? Is not birth, beauty, good shape, discourse, manhood, learning, gentleness, virtue, youth, liberality, and suchlike, the spice and salt that season a man?

Cres. Ay, a minc'd man, and then to be bak'd with no date in the pie, for then the man's date is out.

Pan. You are such a woman, a man knows not at what ward you lie.

220. **he**: i.e. Troilus. 223. **indifferent**: moderately.
233. **helm**: helmet. 234. **goes**: walks.
236. **a grace**: one of the three Graces.
237. **take his choice**: have her if he chose.
239. **to change**: to be able to exchange (Paris for Troilus). **to boot**: into the bargain. 242. **porridge**: soup.
242–43. **in the eyes of**: in the sight of, either looking at or being looked at by (Troilus).
249. **drayman**: one who drives a dray (brewer's cart).
253. **discourse**: wit in conversation.
256. **minc'd man.** Cressida means that if he is made up of so many different ingredients he resembles nothing so much as a meat pie; perhaps with a suggestion that the meat is tainted to require so much "spice and salt" to disguise the taste.
256–57. **bak'd . . . out.** Dates were one of the commonest ingredients of Elizabethan cookery, and the implication here is that a pie without dates is no proper pie. Cressida's showing that the pie contains no dates rests on the quibble in *date is out*: (1) date is wanting; (2) time is past, i.e. Troilus is out of date (and hence not a man for Cressida).
258. **such**: so unpredictable.
259. **ward**: posture of defense (a term from fencing). Note the revealing language of physical conflict with which Cressida (through line 270) describes her attitude toward men.

Cres. Upon my back, to defend my belly, upon my wit, to defend my wiles, upon my secrecy, to defend mine honesty, my mask, to defend my beauty, and you, to defend all these; and at all these wards I lie, at a thousand watches.

Pan. Say one of your watches.

Cres. Nay, I'll watch you for that; and that's one of the chiefest of them too. If I cannot ward what I would not have hit, I can watch you for telling how I took the blow—unless it swell past hiding, and then it's past watching.

Pan. You are such another!

Enter [*Troilus*'] Boy.

Boy. Sir, my lord would instantly speak with you.

Pan. Where?

Boy. At your own house, there he unarms him.

Pan. Good boy, tell him I come. [*Exit Boy.*] I doubt he be hurt. Fare ye well, good niece.

Cres. Adieu, uncle.

Pan. I will be with you, niece, by and by.

Cres. To bring, uncle?

Pan. Ay, a token from Troilus.

Cres. By the same token, you are a bawd.

[*Exit Pandarus.*]

Words, vows, gifts, tears, and love's full sacrifice,
He offers in another's enterprise,
But more in Troilus thousandfold I see
Than in the glass of Pandar's praise may be;
Yet hold I off. Women are angels, wooing:
Things won are done, joy's soul lies in the doing.
That she belov'd knows nought that knows not this:
Men prize the thing ungain'd more than it is.
That she was never yet that ever knew
Love got so sweet as when desire did sue.
Therefore this maxim out of love I teach:
Achievement is command; ungain'd, beseech;

261–62. **secrecy . . . honesty.** Cressida here seems to imply that her reputation for chastity (*honesty*) depends upon her ability to keep her own counsel.
262. **mask.** Elizabethan ladies wore silk masks to protect their faces from sun and wind.
263–64. **at a thousand watches**: in a thousand ways guarding (watching) myself (from attack).
265. **watches**: i.e. night watches (with bawdy innuendo).
266–67. **Nay . . . too**: i.e. no, I will keep an eye on you in such a situation as one of the greatest threats to my security.
268. **watch . . . telling**: guard against your revealing.
270. **watching**: concealing (by guarding the secret).
271. **You . . . another**: equivalent to modern "you're a one."
276. **doubt**: fear.
279. **To bring.** Cressida's enigmatic rejoinder has been much discussed. *Be with* (line 278) could mean not only "visit" but also "be even with," and there was an expression *be with you to bring*, in which *to bring* meant something like "with a vengeance." Possibly therefore Cressida means "Is that a threat?" On the other hand, she may be saying simply, "To bring something?" (the sense to which Pandarus replies), with the hint that she expects him to return with something from Troilus.
281. **bawd**: procurer or pander (implying that the token is a bribe).
286. **wooing**: being wooed. The active participle with passive sense was common; cf. "the house is building," an example still current.
287. **doing**: process of achieving (with bawdy play on the sense "having sexual intercourse").
289. **Men . . . is**: i.e. men value the sexual object more in anticipation than in realization.
290–91. **That . . . sue**: the woman never lived who did not know that love granted (to a man) is less sweet (to him) than love desired.
292. **out of**: derived from.
293. **Achievement . . . beseech**: i.e. physical consummation once attained makes a man a tyrant; withheld, it makes him a suppliant.

Then though my heart's content firm love doth bear,
Nothing of that shall from mine eyes appear.
Exit [with Alexander].

[SCENE III]

[Sennet.] Enter AGAMEMNON, NESTOR, ULYSSES, DIOMEDES, MENELAUS, *with others.*

Agam. Princes:
What grief hath set these jaundies o'er your cheeks?
The ample proposition that hope makes
In all designs begun on earth below
Fails in the promis'd largeness. Checks and disasters
Grow in the veins of actions highest rear'd,
As knots, by the conflux of meeting sap,
Infects the sound pine, and diverts his grain
Tortive and errant from his course of growth.
Nor, princes, is it matter new to us
That we come short of our suppose so far
That after seven years' siege yet Troy walls stand,
Sith [every] action that hath gone before,
Whereof we have record, trial did draw
Bias and thwart, not answering the aim
And that unbodied figure of the thought
That gave't surmised shape. Why then, you princes,
Do you with cheeks abash'd behold our works,
And call them shames which are indeed nought else
But the protractive trials of great Jove
To find persistive constancy in men?
The fineness of which metal is not found
In fortune's love; for then the bold and coward,
The wise and fool, the artist and unread,
The hard and soft, seem all affin'd and kin;
But in the wind and tempest of her frown,
Distinction, with a broad and powerful fan,
Puffing at all, winnows the light away,
And what hath mass or matter, by itself
Lies rich in virtue and unmingled.

Nest. With due observance of [thy] godlike seat,
Great Agamemnon, Nestor shall apply
Thy latest words. In the reproof of chance
Lies the true proof of men: the sea being smooth,
How many shallow bauble boats dare sail
Upon her [patient] breast, making their way
With those of nobler bulk!
But let the ruffian Boreas once enrage
The gentle Thetis, and anon behold
The strong-ribb'd bark through liquid mountains cut,
Bounding between the two moist elements,
Like Perseus' horse. Where's then the saucy boat
Whose weak untimber'd sides but even now
Corrivall'd greatness? Either to harbor fled,
Or made a toast for Neptune. Even so
Doth valor's show and valor's worth divide
In storms of fortune; for in her ray and brightness
The herd hath more annoyance by the breeze
Than by the tiger; but when the splitting wind
Makes flexible the knees of knotted oaks,
And flies fled under shade, why then the thing of courage,
As rous'd with rage, with rage doth sympathize,
And with an accent tun'd in self-same key
Retires to chiding fortune.

Ulyss. Agamemnon,
Thou great commander, nerves and bone of Greece,
Heart of our numbers, soul and only sprite
In whom the tempers and the minds of all
Should be shut up, hear what Ulysses speaks.
Besides th' applause and approbation
The which, [*to Agamemnon*] most mighty for thy place and sway,
[*To Nestor.*] And thou most reverend for [thy] stretch'd-out life,
I give to both your speeches, which were such
As Agamemnon and the hand of Greece
Should hold up high in brass, and such again

294. **content . . . bear**: the form and body of my heart carries the firm impress of love.

I.iii. Location: The Greek camp. Before Agamemnon's tent.
o.s.d. **Sennet**: series of trumpet notes signalling the entrance or exit of a procession or important person.
2. **jaundies**: jaundice (considered at this time as a plural). Both Agamemnon and Nestor speak repetitive commonplaces concealed in high-sounding and opaque language.
3. **proposition**: offer.
6. **highest rear'd**: aimed at the highest goal (cf. *aim*, line 15).
7. **conflux**: flowing together. Used by Shakespeare only here; so also *Tortive* (line 9), *protractive* (line 20), *persistive* (line 21), and other Latinisms in Agamemnon's vocabulary.
8. **Infects**: infect (Elizabethan third person plural in *-s*, or singular by proximity to *sap*, line 7). **his**: its (Shakespeare's almost invariable form of the neuter possessive pronoun).
9. **Tortive and errant**: twisted and wandering. **course**: natural direction. 11. **suppose**: expectation, estimate.
13. **Sith**: since. 14. **trial**: attempted performance.
15. **Bias and thwart**: awry and crosswise (cf. *tortive and errant*, line 9). 18. **works**: actions, deeds.
20. **protractive trials**: long-drawn-out testings.
21. **persistive**: persisting, enduring.
22. **metal**: i.e. constancy (using a metaphor for the refining of gold).
23. **In fortune's love**: i.e. when fortune smiles (cf. *frown*, line 26).
24. **artist**: scholar. 25. **affin'd**: joined by affinity, closely related.
27. **Distinction**: discrimination. **fan**: basket-shaped device for winnowing grain.
28. **light**: things of no "mass or matter" (line 29), i.e. chaff.
30. **virtue**: quality. **unmingled.** Quadrisyllabic.

31. **observance of**: deference to. **seat**: throne.
32. **apply**: illustrate with examples.
33. **reproof**: confutation, rebuffing. 34. **proof**: test, proving.
35. **shallow bauble boats**: flat-bottomed toy boats.
38. **Boreas**: the north wind.
39. **Thetis**: a sea-nymph, mother of Achilles, here representing the sea itself, probably by a long-standing confusion with Tethys, wife of Oceanus. 41. **two moist elements**: water and air.
42. **Perseus' horse.** Pegasus, the winged horse, which belonged to Bellerophon, was regularly associated with Perseus in Elizabethan references. **saucy**: presumptuous.
43. **untimber'd sides**: sides not supported with strong timbers (cf. *strong-ribb'd*, line 40). 44. **Corrivall'd**: vied with.
45. **toast**: a tasty morsel (alluding to pieces of toasted bread floated in a flagon of liquor). **Neptune**: god of the sea, here = the sea itself.
46. **Doth.** Singular verb preceding a plural subject. **valor's show**: the mere appearance of valor.
47. **In . . . fortune**: when fortune frowns. 48. **breeze**: gadfly.
51. **fled**: are fled. **shade**: shelter. **thing of courage**: courageous creature.
52. **As . . . sympathize**: being itself roused to rage reacts sympathetically with the rage of the elements.
54. **Retires**: returns, i.e. answers (?). Of the several emendations proposed, most editors adopt *retorts* (Dyce conjecture).
55. **nerves**: sinews. 56. **numbers**: armies. **sprite**: spirit.
57. **tempers**: temperaments, dispositions.
58. **shut up**: contained as in a single body.
61. **stretch'd-out life.** Nestor is described by Homer as "third-ag'd" (Chapman's translation, *Iliad*, I, 249).
62. **such**: i.e. of such quality and significance.
63. **and . . . Greece.** This phrase has caused much difficulty, but if *and* is taken in the sense "who is," the meaning is perfectly clear. With *hand* cf. *nerves and bone* in line 55.

As venerable Nestor, hatch'd in silver,
Should with a bond of air strong as the axle-tree
On which heaven rides, knit all the Greekish ears
To his experienc'd tongue, yet let it please both,
Thou great, and wise, to hear Ulysses speak.
[*Agam.* Speak, prince of Ithaca, and be't of less expect
That matter needless, of importless burthen,
Divide thy lips, than we are confident,
When rank Thersites opes his mastic jaws,
We shall hear music, wit, and oracle.]
[*Ulyss.*] Troy, yet upon his bases, had been down,
And the great Hector's sword had lack'd a master,
But for these instances:
The specialty of rule hath been neglected,
And look how many Grecian tents do stand
Hollow upon this plain, so many hollow factions.
When that the general is not like the hive
To whom the foragers shall all repair,
What honey is expected? Degree being vizarded,
Th' unworthiest shows as fairly in the mask.
The heavens themselves, the planets, and this centre
Observe degree, priority, and place,
Insisture, course, proportion, season, form,
Office, and custom, in all line of order;
And therefore is the glorious planet Sol
In noble eminence enthron'd and spher'd
Amidst the other; whose med'cinable eye
Corrects the [ill aspects] of [planets evil],
And posts like the commandment of a king,
Sans check, to good and bad. But when the planets
In evil mixture to disorder wander,
What plagues and what portents, what mutiny!

65. hatch'd in silver: engraved in silver (referring to Nestor's white hair).
66. bond of air: i.e. his words, to which the listeners' ears are tied. **axle-tree:** axis. **67. rides:** turns, revolves.
70–74. be't . . . oracle. A typically wordy, involved, and negative way for Agamemnon to say: when Ulysses speaks we can expect good sense and sound counsel as certainly as we can anticipate discord, railing, and lies when Thersites speaks. **70. expect:** expectation.
71. burthen: tenor.
73. rank: corrupt, coarse, foul. **mastic.** Probably connected with *mastix* (= a scourge), hence "abusive."
74. oracle: i.e. truth. **75. bases:** foundations.
77. But: except, if it were not. **instances:** reasons, facts.
78. specialty of rule: the prerogative of command which belongs to the ruler. **neglected:** disregarded, not properly respected.
79–80. look . . . factions: i.e. there are precisely as many empty pretenses of individual authority as there are tents on this plain. *Look how many* = however many, just as many. The first *Hollow* in line 80 may be intrusive; if not, it must mean "empty at the moment."
81. like the hive: i.e. the centre to which all energy is directed and from which all order emanates. The bee-state analogy was a favorite with the Elizabethans; cf. *Henry V*, I.ii.187–204.
82. foragers: workers (drones), all those subordinate to the "general" or ruler.
83–84. Degree . . . mask: i.e. when persons of various degrees are masked, the lowest is undistinguishable from the highest.
85. this centre: i.e. the earth (the centre of the Ptolemaic universe).
87. Insisture: steady continuance. **proportion:** relationship.
88. Office: proper function or service. **custom:** established practice. **89. Sol:** the sun (the king of planets).
90. spher'd: set in a sphere.
91. other: others. **med'cinable:** healing, restorative.
92. ill . . . evil: threatening glances of malign planets (i.e. their individual way of looking upon the earth). Some editors prefer the Q reading *influence of evil planets*, where *influence* = the unceasing effect of the planets on man and all other sublunary things, supposedly through a material emanation from them (*O.E.D.*).
93. posts: speeds. **94. Sans:** without.
95. evil mixture: threatening conjunction.
96. portents: (bad) omens.

What raging of the sea, shaking of earth!
Commotion in the winds! frights, changes, horrors
Divert and crack, rend and deracinate
The unity and married calm of states
Quite from their fixure! O, when degree is shak'd,
Which is the ladder of all high designs,
The enterprise is sick. How could communities,
Degrees in schools, and brotherhoods in cities,
Peaceful commerce from dividable shores,
The primogenity and due of birth,
Prerogative of age, crowns, sceptres, laurels,
But by degree stand in authentic place?
Take but degree away, untune that string,
And hark what discord follows. Each thing [meets]
In mere oppugnancy: the bounded waters
Should lift their bosoms higher than the shores,
And make a sop of all this solid globe;
Strength should be lord of imbecility,
And the rude son should strike his father dead;
Force should be right, or rather, right and wrong
(Between whose endless jar justice resides)
Should lose their names, and so should justice too!
Then every thing include itself in power,
Power into will, will into appetite,
And appetite, an universal wolf
(So doubly seconded with will and power),
Must make perforce an universal prey,
And last eat up himself. Great Agamemnon,
This chaos, when degree is suffocate,
Follows the choking,
And this neglection of degree it is
That by a pace goes backward with a purpose
It hath to climb. The general's disdain'd
By him one step below, he by the next,
That next by him beneath; so every step,
Exampled by the first pace that is sick
Of his superior, grows to an envious fever

99. Divert: turn awry. **deracinate:** tear up by the roots.
101. fixure: fixed position, stability. **degree:** the principle of proper subordination.
103. The enterprise: i.e. any undertaking.
104. Degrees: academic rank. **brotherhoods:** trade guilds, corporations. **105. dividable:** dividing (?) or divided, separated (?).
106. primogenity . . . birth: the rights of the eldest-born.
107. laurels: i.e. high distinctions.
108. authentic place: position of acknowledged authority.
109. untune that string. The Elizabethans thought of the universe as a great musical instrument tuned by the hand of God, of which order, or degree, was an attribute. See the illustration on p. 442.
111. mere oppugnancy: absolute opposition.
112. Should: would (as a result); so in lines 114, 115, 116, 118.
113. sop: a toast, or cake, floated in liquor.
114. Strength . . . imbecility: physical strength would always dominate physical weakness (as in the example in line 115). *Imbecility* (used only here by Shakespeare) did not yet refer to mental weakness.
115. rude: violent, brutal (with some underlying sense of "unmannerly").
117. Between . . . resides: i.e. justice, by securing the right, stands as a shield against the continual onslaughts of the wrong.
118. names: i.e. their identity.
119. include itself in: would become one with.
120. will . . . appetite: uncontrolled desire or lust, which finds expression in an all-devouring appetite.
123. perforce: of necessity. **prey:** act of preying, devouring.
125. suffocate: suffocated, strangled.
126. choking: the act of suffocation.
128. by a pace: step by step (Johnson), as the next sentence describes.
131. step. Meaning now the person on the step, not the step itself.
132. Exampled: given a precedent. **first pace:** i.e. the person next below the general. **sick:** i.e. distempered by disdain.

Of pale and bloodless emulation,
And 'tis this fever that keeps Troy on foot,
Not her own sinews. To end a tale of length,
Troy in our weakness stands, not in her strength.
Nest. Most wisely hath Ulysses here discover'd
The fever whereof all our power is sick.
Agam. The nature of the sickness found, Ulysses,
What is the remedy?
Ulyss. The great Achilles, whom opinion crowns
The sinow and the forehand of our host,
Having his ear full of his airy fame,
Grows dainty of his worth, and in his tent
Lies mocking our designs. With him Patroclus
Upon a lazy bed the livelong day
Breaks scurril jests,
And with ridiculous and [awkward] action,
Which, slanderer, he imitation calls,
He pageants us. Sometime, great Agamemnon,
Thy topless deputation he puts on,
And like a strutting player, whose conceit
Lies in his hamstring, and doth think it rich
To hear the wooden dialogue and sound
'Twixt his stretch'd footing and the scaffolage,
Such to-be-pitied and o'er-wrested seeming
He acts thy greatness in; and when he speaks,
'Tis like a chime a-mending, with terms [unsquar'd],
Which from the tongue of roaring Typhon dropp'd
Would seem hyperboles. At this fusty stuff
The large Achilles, on his press'd bed lolling,
From his deep chest laughs out a loud applause,
Cries, "Excellent! 'tis Agamemnon right!
Now play me Nestor, hem, and stroke thy beard,
As he being dress'd to some oration."
That's done, as near as the extremest ends
Of parallels, as like as Vulcan and his wife;
Yet god Achilles still cries, "Excellent!
'Tis Nestor right. Now play him me, Patroclus,
Arming to answer in a night alarm."
And then forsooth the faint defects of age
Must be the scene of mirth; to cough and spit,
And with a palsy fumbling on his gorget,
Shake in and out the rivet; and at this sport
Sir Valor dies; cries, "O, enough, Patroclus,
Or give me ribs of steel! I shall split all
In pleasure of my spleen." And in this fashion,
All our abilities, gifts, natures, shapes,
Severals and generals of grace exact,
Achievements, plots, orders, preventions,
Excitements to the field, or speech for truce,
Success or loss, what is or is not, serves
As stuff for these two to make paradoxes.
Nest. And in the imitation of these twain—
Who, as Ulysses says, opinion crowns
With an imperial voice—many are infect.
Ajax is grown self-will'd, and bears his head
In such a rein, in full as proud a place
As broad Achilles; keeps his tent like him,
Makes factious feasts, rails on our state of war,
Bold as an oracle, and sets Thersites,
A slave whose gall coins slanders like a mint,
To match us in comparisons with dirt,
To weaken [or] discredit our exposure,
How rank soever rounded in with danger.
Ulyss. They tax our policy, and call it cowardice,
Count wisdom as no member of the war,
Forestall prescience, and esteem no act
But that of hand. The still and mental parts,
That do contrive how many hands shall strike
When fitness calls them on, and know by measure
Of their observant toil the enemies' weight—
Why, this hath not a finger's dignity.
They call this bed-work, mapp'ry, closet-war,
So that the ram that batters down the wall,

134. pale . . . emulation. Pallor was traditionally associated with envy personified, and also with the chills that alternated with fever (cf., e.g., *agues pale* in *Venus and Adonis*, line 739). *Emulation* = jealous rivalry.
135. on foot: standing. **136. tale of length:** long tale.
138. discover'd: revealed. **139. power:** army.
143. sinow . . . forehand: i.e. foremost in strength (*sinow* is a variant form of *sinew*).
144. his airy fame: i.e. talk of his prowess. Like line 66, an allusion to the commonplace that words are breath and breath is air.
145. dainty . . . worth: oversolicitous of his (self-supposed) value.
147. Upon . . . bed: lazily upon a bed.
151. pageants: mimics (as in a theatrical exhibition).
152. topless deputation: supreme office (as general).
153. strutting player. Cf. *Macbeth*, V.v.24–25.
153–54. conceit . . . hamstring: intelligence is located in his leg muscles (literally, the tendons at the back of the knee); with a play on *conceit* in the modern sense.
154. rich: something magnificent, admirable.
155–56. wooden . . . scaffolage: i.e. the echoing noise of his mighty strides on the boards of the stage (*scaffolage* is a variant of *scaffoldage*).
157. to-be-pitied . . . seeming: pitifully overstrained mimicry.
159. chime a-mending: the cacophony produced by chimes while being retuned or repaired. **terms unsquar'd:** ill-fitting expressions. Literally, *unsquar'd* = untrimmed (as applied to building stones).
160. from: i.e. even from. **Typhon:** a giant with a hundred heads (mouths).
161. fusty: mouldy, stale. Unfortunately, there are no grounds for relating the word to *fustian*, "bombastic," which would suit the context admirably.
162. press'd: weighed down (with "large Achilles").
164. right: exactly. **165. hem:** clear your throat.
166. As . . . to: as if he were about to begin.
168. wife: Venus. Vulcan was misshapen and lame.

172. forsooth: in truth. **faint:** feeble.
174. palsy: tremorous. **gorget:** armor for protecting the throat.
175. rivet: metal bolt fastening the gorget.
176. Sir Valor: Achilles (ironic).
178. spleen. The supposed seat of fits of laughter.
180. Severals . . . exact: (our) individual and general qualities of unexceptionable excellence (?). The phrase *of grace exact* has been variously explained and emended.
181. preventions: precautions.
182. Excitements: urgings, exhortations.
184. paradoxes: ways of treating a subject to make the truth appear absurd or the absurd appear like the truth.
186–87. crowns . . . voice: adjudges supreme.
187. infect: infected, diseased.
189. In . . . rein: as haughtily (like a proud-spirited horse bridling).
190. broad: physically large. **keeps:** stays in.
191. state: council.
192. Bold . . . oracle: as confident as if he were the source of truth.
193. gall: rancor. **like a mint:** as fast as a mint coins money.
194. in comparisons: by analogies ("false" implied).
195. our exposure: i.e. as exposed as we are.
196. How . . . danger: however thickly (*rank*) we are hemmed in by danger. **197. policy:** prudent conduct of affairs.
198. member: part, element.
199. Forestall prescience: obstruct attempts to exercise foresight.
199–200. esteem . . . hand: value no performance that is not merely physical. **200. still:** quiet (as opposed to the violent).
202. fitness: suitable occasion. **measure:** computation.
203. observant toil: laborious observation. **weight:** strength.
204. not . . . dignity: no greater worth than a finger has in relation to the whole body.
205. bed-work: "planning out action and war, as a man might do on his pillow" (Theobald). **mapp'ry:** mere drawing of charts and diagrams. **closet-war:** war for the study; cf. *closet-drama*.
206. ram: i.e. battering-ram.

The Folger Shakespeare Library

By permission of the Harvard College Library

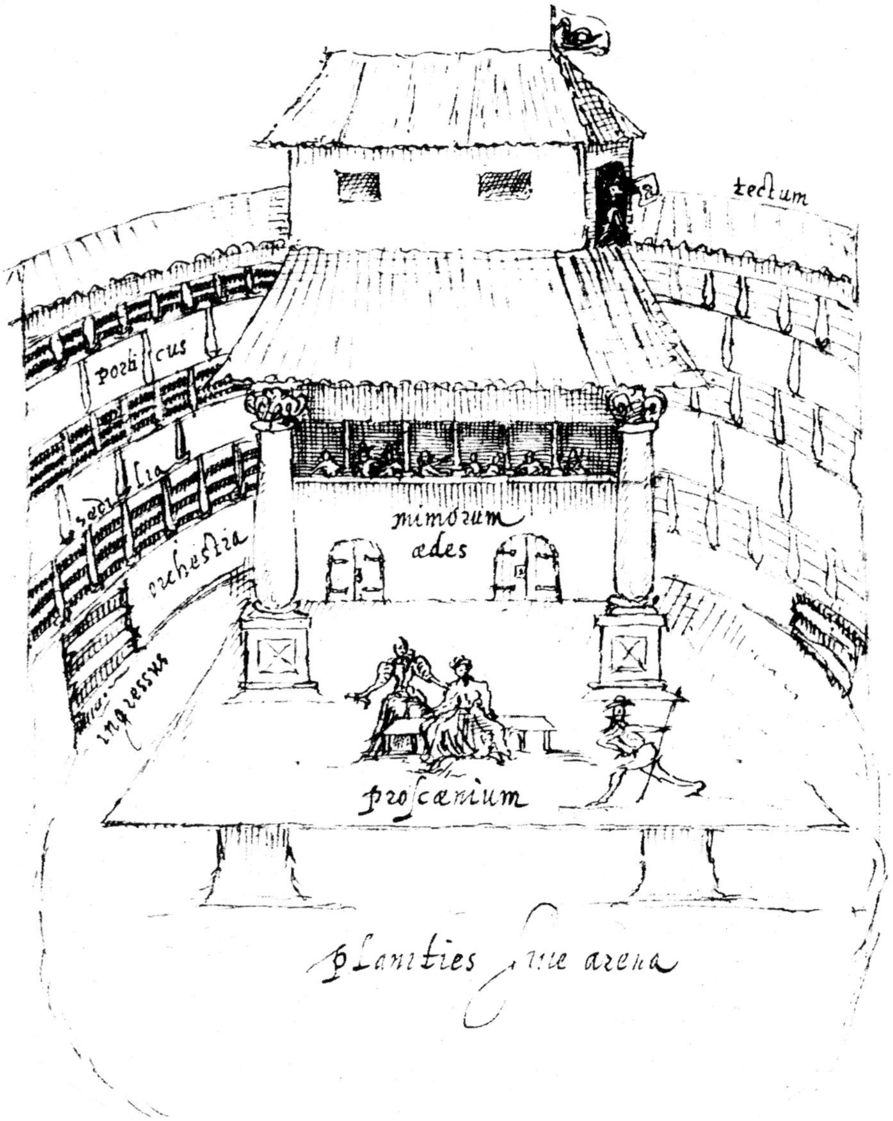

University Library, Utrecht

(Above) Johannes de Witt's sketch of the Swan Theatre (c. 1596; preserved in an early copy by his friend Arend van Buchell) is the only Elizabethan representation we possess of the interior of a public theatre. Its larger outlines confirm other kinds of contemporary evidence: the circular (or polygonal) structure, open to the sky, with three tiers of galleries, the uppermost roofed; the spectators' entrances ("*ingressus*"); the raised platform stage (wider than deep) projecting into the "yard" ("*planities siue arena*"), with two pillars supporting a roof (the "heavens") that covered the rear of the stage, and with standing-room on three sides for the "groundlings"; the tiring-house ("*mimorum aedes*"); and the "hut," from which a flag was flown during the times of performance and a trumpeter announced the beginning (on the third call) of a play. In certain details, however, the drawing is controversial, particularly in its depiction of the rear stage wall (the "scene").

The two stages shown to the left are from the title-pages of William Alabaster's *Roxana*, 1632 (upper), and Nathaniel Richards' *Messalina*, 1640. The *Roxana* stage is interesting for the curtains at the rear (perhaps concealing an inner playing area), the groundlings standing in the yard and other spectators seated above the stage (as in De Witt), and the railing surrounding the stage (as at the Globe). The *Messalina* stage also has curtains (in this case decorated with figures) and a stage railing, but adds what appears to be a curtained upper playing level and a trapdoor in the centre of the stage.

The pen-and-ink sketch shown above is the earliest known illustration (perhaps as early as 1594–95) of a scene from one of Shakespeare's plays. The artist (possibly, though probably not, Henry Peacham) has confused the action of the moment in *Titus Andronicus*, Act I: Tamora is apparently pleading with Titus to spare two of her sons, not one, and Aaron the Moor, with drawn sword in hand, is taking a more active part than his mute role in Act I allows him. Note particularly the mixture of more or less Roman costumes on the principal figures with the Elizabethan military garb on the two guards behind Titus, who also hold most un-Roman halberds. The illustration at the left (from G. Borgetto, *The Devil's Legend*, 1595) depicts two characters from the Italian *commedia dell'arte*: the Capitano (left) and the Zany. Both are associated with and may have influenced such Elizabethan comic figures as Falstaff and Parolles (who, like the Capitano, are descendants of the Roman comedy *miles gloriosus* or boasting soldier) and Costard or Launce (types of the rustic clown) and Touchstone or Feste (types of the professional fool).

The engraving opposite (c. 1662), later adapted to serve as frontispiece to Francis Kirkman's *The Wits, or Sport upon Sport* (1672), includes the earliest published depiction of Shakespearean characters, Sir John Falstaff and Mistress Quickly. Note also the stage lighting (by candelabra and footlights) and the upper curtained area, presumably a playing place, with spectators on either side.

PLATE 10

The Folger Shakespeare Library

The Folger Shakespeare Library

On these two pages are shown contemporary portraits of eight well-known Elizabethan-Jacobean actors. Six of them were members of Shakespeare's company, the Lord Chamberlain's (later the King's) Men and are listed in the First Folio (1623) as among the "Principall Actors in all these Playes." William Kemp (above, left, with a taborer) and Robert Armin (above, right) were famous comedians, Kemp being associated with the roles of Costard, Bottom, Peter (in *Romeo and Juliet*), Dogberry, and possibly Falstaff; Armin with Feste and the Fool in *King Lear*. (Kemp's portrait is from his *Nine Days' Wonder*, 1600, an account of his celebrated hundred-mile morris-dance from London to Norwich in that year; Armin's is from the title-page of his play *The Two Maids of More-Clacke*, 1609). William Sly and John Lowin (below, centre and right) are more shadowy figures, though there is a tradition that Lowin created the role of Henry VIII, having "his instructions from Mr. Shakespeare himself." Nathan Field (below, left) joined the King's Men about 1615, having been a boy actor in the Queen's Revels.

Edward Alleyn (right centre) was the leading actor of the Admiral's Men. He was famous as Tamburlaine, Barabas (in Marlowe's *The Jew of Malta*), and Faustus, and his acting style is perhaps glanced at in the role of Lucianus in the play-within-the-play in *Hamlet*. He was closely associated with the theatrical business ventures of Philip Henslowe, his father-in-law, and was the founder of Dulwich College.

By permission of the Trustees of Dulwich Picture Gallery

By permission of the Trustees of Dulwich Picture Gallery

By permission of the Trustees of Dulwich Picture Gallery

Ashmolean Museum, Oxford

(Above) Richard Burbage (c. 1567–1619), whose father James built The Theatre, the first London playhouse, in 1576, was the leading actor in the Chamberlain's-King's Men from the organization of the company in 1594 until shortly before his death. He created many of the greatest roles in Shakespeare's plays, including Richard III, Romeo, Hamlet, Othello, and Lear. Two well-known epitaphs survive; the shorter, "Exit Burbage." An extract from the longer runs: "Hee's gone & with him what a world are dead, / Which he reuiud, to be reuiued soe. / No more young Hamlett, ould Heironymoe. / Kind Leer, the greued Moore, and more beside, / That liued in him, haue now for euer dy'de."

The little sketch to the right depicts Richard Tarlton, a low comedian of the preceding generation, who died in 1588, but whose reputation continued to live well into the seventeenth century.

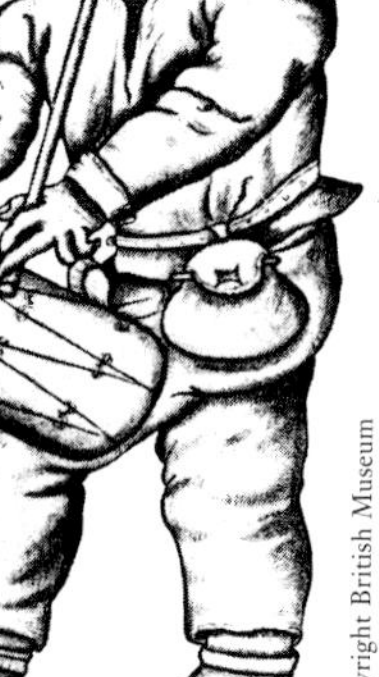

The Huntington Library, San Marino, California

Fishmongers' Company, London

Two examples of London street pageantry are shown here: above, one of the seven triumphal arches erected to welcome King James I on his first state progress through the City, in 1604 (from Stephen Harrison, *Arches of Triumph*, 1604); at left, the Fishmongers' Float, one of six in Anthony Munday's pageant for the Lord Mayor's Show of 1616. The print opposite (from *Scarron's Comical Romance of a Company of Stage Players*, 1676) shows two scenes familiar in the provinces: the arrival of a group of strolling players at an inn and their later performance on a bare platform stage in the village square. Such a company in Shakespeare's England, however, would not have included an actress; this is a French troupe.

PLATE 14

These three drawings are by the well-known scenic artist and costume designer Inigo Jones (1573–1652), who during the first four decades of the seventeenth century produced sumptuous and very costly court masques and entertainments for James I and Charles I. Unlike plays in the public theatres, the court masques employed very sophisticated scenery, set behind a proscenium arch similar to that in use today. The setting above was designed for William Davenant's masque *Britannia Triumphans* (1638). It shows the use of moveable wings (three on each side), so arranged as to suggest perspective, and a painted backdrop picturing "London afar off." The two figures at the right were drawn for the same masque and represent a ballad singer and a man playing the "tongs and key" (who recalls Bottom's liking for "the tongs and the bones" in *A Midsummer Night's Dream*, IV.i.28–29).

For the great swinge and rudeness of his poise,
They place before his hand that made the engine,
Or those that with the fineness of their souls
By reason guide his execution.
Nest. Let this be granted, and Achilles' horse
Makes many Thetis' sons. [*Tucket.*]
Agam. What trumpet? Look, Menelaus.
Men. From Troy.

[*Enter* AENEAS.]

Agam. What would you 'fore our tent?
Aene. Is this great Agamemnon's tent, I pray you?
Agam. Even this.
Aene. May one that is a herald and a prince
Do a fair message to his kingly eyes?
Agam. With surety stronger than Achilles' arm,
'Fore all the Greekish heads, which with one voice
Call Agamemnon head and general.
Aene. Fair leave and large security. How may
A stranger to those most imperial looks
Know them from eyes of other mortals?
Agam. How?
Aene. Ay,
I ask, that I might waken reverence,
And bid the cheek be ready with a blush
Modest as morning when she coldly eyes
The youthful Phoebus.
Which is that god in office, guiding men?
Which is the high and mighty Agamemnon?
Agam. This Troyan scorns us, or the men of Troy
Are ceremonious courtiers.
Aene. Courtiers as free, as debonair, unarm'd,
As bending angels; that's their [fame] in peace.
But when they would seem soldiers, they have galls,
Good arms, strong joints, true swords, and, great Jove's accord,
Nothing so full of heart. But peace, Aeneas,
Peace, Troyan, lay thy finger on thy lips!
The worthiness of praise distains his worth,
If that the prais'd himself bring the praise forth;
But what the repining enemy commends,
That breath fame blows, that praise, sole pure, transcends.
Agam. Sir, you of Troy, call you yourself Aeneas?
Aene. Ay, Greek, that is my name.
Agam. What's your affairs, I pray you?
Aene. Sir, pardon, 'tis for Agamemnon's ears.
Agam. He hears nought privately that comes from Troy.

207. swinge: impetus. **rudeness:** rough violence. **his poise:** its weight. **208. place before:** prefer above.
209. fineness . . . souls: subtlety of their "mental parts" (line 200).
210. his execution: its operation.
211–12. Achilles' horse . . . sons: i.e. Achilles' horse is worth as much as many Achilleses (sons of Thetis, Achilles' mother).
212 s.d. Tucket: distinctive series of notes on a trumpet.
219. fair: courteous.
220. surety: security. **221. 'Fore:** in the presence of.
224. looks: glances (of the eyes).
227. waken reverence: i.e. prepare to be reverent.
229. morning: i.e. Aurora, goddess of the dawn.
235. debonair: gentle, meek. **236. fame:** reputation.
237. galls: spirits resenting injuries.
238. great Jove's accord: great Jove consenting.
239. Nothing . . . heart: nothing has greater courage than they.
241. distains his worth: taints its value.
243. repining: begrudging. **244. sole:** completely, utterly.

Aene. Nor I from Troy come not to whisper with him.
I bring a trumpet to awake his ear,
To set his [sense] on [the] attentive bent,
And then to speak.
Agam. Speak frankly as the wind,
It is not Agamemnon's sleeping hour.
That thou shalt know, Troyan, he is awake,
He tells thee so himself.
Aene. Trumpet, blow [loud],
Send thy brass voice through all these lazy tents,
And every Greek of mettle, let him know,
What Troy means fairly shall be spoke aloud.
Sound trumpet.
We have, great Agamemnon, here in Troy
A prince call'd Hector—Priam is his father—
Who in [this] dull and long-continued truce
Is resty grown. He bade me take a trumpet,
And to this purpose speak: kings, princes, lords!
If there be one among the fair'st of Greece
That holds his honor higher than his ease,
And [seeks] his praise more than he fears his peril,
That knows his valor, and knows not his fear,
That loves his mistress more than in confession
With truant vows to her own lips he loves,
And dare avow her beauty and her worth
In other arms than hers—to him this challenge!
Hector, in view of Troyans and of Greeks,
Shall make it good, or do his best to do it:
He hath a lady, wiser, fairer, truer,
Than ever Greek did couple in his arms,
And will to-morrow with his trumpet call,
Midway between your tents and walls of Troy,
To rouse a Grecian that is true in love.
If any come, Hector shall honor him;
If none, he'll say in Troy when he retires,
The Grecian dames are sunburnt, and not worth
The splinter of a lance. Even so much.
Agam. This shall be told our lovers, Lord Aeneas.
If none of them have soul in such a kind,
We left them all at home. But we are soldiers,
And may that soldier a mere recreant prove,
That means not, hath not, or is not in love!
If then one is, or hath, [or] means to be,
That one meets Hector; if none else, I am he.
Nest. Tell him of Nestor, one that was a man
When Hector's grandsire suck'd. He is old now,
But if there be not in our Grecian [mould]
A noble man that hath no spark of fire

251. trumpet. Used both of the instrument and the player.
252. set . . . bent: make him bend an attentive ear.
253. frankly: freely. **258. mettle:** spirit, courage.
259. fairly: honorably. **263. resty:** sluggish (from lack of action).
265. fair'st: most illustrious. **267. praise:** honorable reputation.
269–70. in . . . loves: i.e. in avowal made with idle vows to the lips of her whom he loves.
272. In . . . hers: i.e. not in his mistress' arms but in armor.
276. couple . . . arms: embrace (with sexual implication).
280. honor him: i.e. engage him in combat.
282. sunburnt. A sunburned skin was not a mark of beauty to the Elizabethans. **283. splinter:** breaking.
285. soul . . . kind: such a spirit. **287. mere recreant:** utter traitor.
288. means not, hath not: doesn't intend to be, or has not been.
292. suck'd: was a baby at the breast.
293–94. not . . . no. Modern usage would require the omission of *no*.
293. mould: characteristic cast, native constitution. Cf. lines 349–50. Most editors prefer *host*, an easier but flatter reading.

To answer for his love, tell him from me
I'll hide my silver beard in a gold beaver,
And in my vambrace put my withered brawns,
And meeting him [will] tell him that my lady
Was fairer than his grandam, and as chaste
As may be in the world. His youth in flood,
I'll prove this troth with my three drops of blood.
Aene. Now heavens forfend such scarcity of [youth]!
Ulyss. Amen.
[*Agam.*] Fair Lord Aeneas, let me touch your hand;
To our pavilion shall I lead you, sir.
Achilles shall have word of this intent,
So shall each lord of Greece, from tent to tent.
Yourself shall feast with us before you go,
And find the welcome of a noble foe.
[*Exeunt. Manent Ulysses and Nestor.*]
Ulyss. Nestor!
Nest. What says Ulysses?
Ulyss. I have a young conception in my brain,
Be you my time to bring it to some shape.
Nest. What is't?
Ulyss. [This 'tis:]
Blunt wedges rive hard knots; the seeded pride
That hath to this maturity blown up
In rank Achilles must or now be cropp'd,
Or shedding, breed a nursery of like evil,
To overbulk us all.
Nest. Well, and how?
Ulyss. This challenge that the gallant Hector sends,
However it is spread in general name,
Relates in purpose only to Achilles.
Nest. True, the purpose is perspicuous as substance,
Whose grossness little characters sum up;
And in the publication make no strain
But that Achilles, were his brain as barren
As banks of Libya (though, Apollo knows,
'Tis dry enough), will with great speed of judgment,
Ay, with celerity, find Hector's purpose
Pointing on him.
Ulyss. And wake him to the answer, think you?
Nest. Why, 'tis most meet; who may you else oppose
That can from Hector bring those honors off,
If not Achilles? Though't be a sportful combat,
Yet in the trial much opinion dwells;
For here the Troyans taste our dear'st repute
With their fin'st palate; and trust to me, Ulysses,
Our imputation shall be oddly pois'd
In this vild action, for the success,
Although particular, shall give a scantling
Of good or bad unto the general,
And in such indexes (although small pricks
To their subsequent volumes) there is seen
The baby figure of the giant mass
Of things to come at large. It is suppos'd
He that meets Hector issues from our choice,
And choice (being mutual act of all our souls)
Makes merit her election, and doth boil
(As 'twere from forth us all) a man distill'd
Out of our virtues, who miscarrying,
What heart receives from hence a conquering part
To steel a strong opinion to themselves?
[Which entertain'd, limbs are his instruments,
In no less working than are swords and bows
Directive by the limbs.]
Ulyss. Give pardon to my speech:
Therefore 'tis meet Achilles meet not Hector.
Let us like merchants first show foul wares,
And think perchance they'll sell; if not,
The lustre of the better shall exceed
By showing the worse first. Do not consent
That ever Hector and Achilles meet,
For both our honor and our shame in this
Are dogg'd with two strange followers.
Nest. I see them not with my old eyes, what are they?
Ulyss. What glory our Achilles shares from Hector,
Were he not proud, we all should share with him.
But he already is too insolent;
And it were better parch in Afric sun
Than in the pride and salt scorn of his eyes,
Should he scape Hector fair. If he were foil'd,

295. answer for: testify to. **296. beaver:** face guard of a helmet.
297. vambrace: i.e. vantbrace, armor for the front part of the arm. **brawns:** muscles; here, arms.
300. His . . . flood: he being at the height of youthful strength.
301. troth: truth. **302. forfend:** forbid.
313. Be . . . time: act as a midwife (as for a woman whose "time" has come).
316. Blunt . . . knots: proverbial (referring to "knots" in timber). **seeded:** run to seed.
317. blown up: become overexpanded and ready to burst (like the seed pod of a plant past full bloom).
318. rank: puffed-up, swollen. **or:** either. **cropp'd:** cut off.
319. shedding: scattering its seeds. **nursery:** training ground.
320. overbulk: overwhelm. **and how:** what then follows?
324–25. perspicuous . . . up: as clearly to be seen as great wealth, the quantity of which may be expressed in a few small figures.
326. in the publication: when it is proclaimed publicly. **make no strain:** have no doubt.
328. banks of Libya: sandbanks of the Libyan desert.
329. dry. A dry brain was equated with dullness.
332. wake him: rouse himself.
336. in . . . dwells: in the combat (seen as a test of relative merit) the question of reputation is importantly involved.
337–38. taste . . . palate: i.e. are putting to the test our best by means of their best (*dear'st repute* = Achilles; *fin'st palate* = Hector).
339. Our imputation: the honor or discredit imputed to us. **oddly pois'd:** i.e. unjustly or wrongly weighed (because quite disproportionate to the cause).
340. vild: paltry (variant of *vile*). **success:** outcome (good or bad).
341. particular: belonging to an individual. **give a scantling:** i.e. be taken as a sample (of what is to come).
342. general: the whole army. **343. indexes:** tables of contents.
343–44. small . . . volumes: slight indicators of the content that follows. *Subsequent* is accented on the second syllable.
345. baby figure: embryonic form. **346. is:** will be.
349. election: basis of selection.
351. miscarrying: losing to his opponent.
352. conquering part: share of victory.
353. steel . . . themselves: i.e. attach firmly to themselves a conviction of their prowess.
354–56. limbs . . . limbs: limbs become its instruments of (victorious) action, no less responsive to it than swords and bows are subject to direction by the limbs.
357. Therefore 'tis meet: for this very reason it is proper.
358. foul: poor in quality.
360. lustre . . . exceed: the comparative fineness of the superior wares will be enhanced.
364. strange followers: i.e. unexpected or surprising corollaries.
369. better parch: better to scorch. **370. salt:** bitter, corroding.
371. scape Hector fair: escape from Hector with victory.

Why then we do our main opinion crush
In taint of our best man. No, make a lott'ry,
And by device let blockish Ajax draw
The sort to fight with Hector; among ourselves
Give him allowance for the better man,
For that will physic the great Myrmidon,
Who broils in loud applause, and make him fall
His crest that prouder than blue Iris bends.
If the dull brainless Ajax come safe off,
We'll dress him up in voices; if he fail,
Yet go we under our opinion still
That we have better men. But hit or miss,
Our project's life this shape of sense assumes:
Ajax employ'd plucks down Achilles' plumes.

Nest. Now, Ulysses, I begin to relish thy advice,
And I will give a taste thereof forthwith
To Agamemnon. Go we to him straight.
Two curs shall tame each other; pride alone
Must [tarre] the mastiffs on, as 'twere a bone.

Exeunt.

[ACT II, SCENE I]

Enter AJAX *and* THERSITES.

Ajax. Thersites!

Ther. Agamemnon, how if he had biles—full, all over, generally?

Ajax. Thersites!

Ther. And those biles did run—say so—did not the general run then? Were not that a botchy core?

Ajax. Dog!

Ther. Then would come some matter from him; I see none now.

Ajax. Thou bitch-wolf's son, canst thou not hear? Feel then. [*Strikes him.*]

Ther. The plague of Greece upon thee, thou mongrel beef-witted lord!

Ajax. Speak then, thou [whinid'st] leaven, speak; I will beat thee into handsomeness.

Ther. I shall sooner rail thee into wit and holiness, but I think thy horse will sooner con an oration without book than thou learn [a] prayer without book. Thou canst strike, canst thou? A red murrion a' thy jade's tricks!

Ajax. Toadstool! learn me the proclamation.

Ther. Dost thou think I have no sense, thou strikest me thus?

Ajax. The proclamation!

Ther. Thou art proclaim'd fool, I think.

Ajax. Do not, porpentine, do not, my fingers itch.

Ther. I would thou didst itch from head to foot; and I had the scratching of thee, I would make thee the loathsomest scab in Greece. When thou art forth in the incursions, thou strikest as slow as another.

Ajax. I say, the proclamation!

Ther. Thou grumblest and railest every hour on Achilles, and thou art as full of envy at his greatness as Cerberus is at Proserpina's beauty, ay, that thou bark'st at him.

Ajax. Mistress Thersites!

Ther. Thou shouldst strike him.

Ajax. Cobloaf!

[*Ther.*] He would pun thee into shivers with his fist, as a sailor breaks a biscuit.

[*Ajax.*] [*Beating him.*] You whoreson cur!

[*Ther.*] Do! do! thou stool for a witch! ay, do! do! thou sodden-witted lord! Thou hast no more brain than I have in mine elbows, an asinico may tutor thee. You scurvy valiant ass! thou art here but to thrash Troyans, and thou art bought and sold among those of any wit, like a barbarian slave. If thou use to beat me, I will begin at thy heel, and tell what thou art by inches, thou thing of no bowels, thou!

Ajax. You dog!

Ther. You scurvy lord!

Ajax. [*Beating him.*] You cur!

Ther. Mars his idiot! Do, rudeness, do, camel, do, do.

[*Enter* ACHILLES *and* PATROCLUS.]

372–73. our . . . taint: destroy our general reputation by the dishonor. **374. by device:** by a trick. **blockish:** stupid, dull-witted. **375. sort:** lot. **376. Give . . . for:** acknowledge him as. **377. physic:** act as a medicinal purge to. **great Myrmidon:** Achilles. The Myrmidons, a people of Thessaly, were special followers of Achilles. **378. broils:** bakes (as in the sunshine), with a strong suggestion of being overcooked. **378–79. fall His crest:** i.e. bow his pride. *Crest* = the tuft of feathers on a bird's head; here, the plumes on Achilles' helmet (cf. *plumes* in line 385). **379. blue Iris.** The messenger of Juno, here used for the rainbow, with which she was identified; perhaps "blue" as associated with the sky; but cf. *Lucrece*, line 1587: "Blue circles streamed, like rainbows in the sky." **bends:** arches. **381. voices:** words of praise. **383. hit or miss:** win or lose, either way (earliest use of this phrase). **384. life:** success. **this . . . assumes:** takes on this semblance of rational meaning. **388. straight:** straightway. **390. tarre . . . on:** set the dogs fighting against each other.

II.i. Location: The Greek camp.
2. biles: boils (a variant form).
6. botchy: ulcerous. **core:** boil (properly, the hard mass of tissue at the centre of a boil); perhaps with play on *corps* = body.
8. matter: (a) meaning; (b) pus.
12. plague of Greece. Perhaps referring to a plague visited by Apollo on the Greeks (described in the *Iliad*, Bk. I).
13. mongrel. Ajax was part Greek and part Trojan. **beef-witted:** stupid as an ox.
14. whinid'st: mouldiest (variant of *vinewed'st*). **leaven:** a batch of fermenting dough, here associated with the Biblical "leaven of maliciousness and wickedness," 1 Corinthians, 5:8 (Geneva).

15. handsomeness: (1) proper manners; (2) proper shape (alluding to Thersites' physical deformity).
17–18. con . . . book: learn a speech by heart.
19. murrion: plague (variant of *murrain*). **a':** on.
20. jade's tricks. A jade was a bad-tempered horse and his "tricks" were rearing and kicking.
21. Toadstool. Referring to Thersites as (1) poisonous, (2) deformed in shape, (3) an upstart. **learn me:** find out for me the tenor of (see lines 90–91). **22. sense:** feeling. **26. porpentine:** porcupine.
28. and: if.
30. incursions: military encounters. **another:** anyone else.
34. Cerberus: the three-headed dog that was porter-guardian of the underworld. **Proserpina:** queen of the underworld. **that:** so that.
36. Mistress. Implying cowardice (?) or a termagant's tongue (?).
38. Cobloaf: a little loaf made with a round head (Minsheu).
39. pun . . . shivers: pound you into fragments.
41. whoreson: term of general abuse (literally, son of a whore).
42. stool . . . witch: privy used by a witch, hence especially stinking; probably suggested by the common Elizabethan pun on *Ajax/a jakes* (= privy). **43. sodden-witted:** boiled-brained, stupid.
44. asinico: blockhead; literally, little ass (Spanish).
45. scurvy valiant: scabby vainglorious.
46. bought and sold: treated like a piece of merchandise.
47. use: continue. **49. bowels:** tender feeling, mercy.
53. Mars his idiot: Mars's fool, creature good only for brainless violence.

Achil. Why, how now, Ajax, wherefore do ye thus?
How now, Thersites, what's the matter, man?

Ther. You see him there? Do you?

Achil. Ay, what's the matter?

Ther. Nay, look upon him.

Achil. So I do. What's the matter?

Ther. Nay, but regard him well.

Achil. Well? why, so I do.

Ther. But yet you look not well upon him, for whosomever you take him to be, he is Ajax.

Achil. I know that, fool.

Ther. Ay, but that fool knows not himself.

Ajax. Therefore I beat thee.

Ther. Lo, lo, lo, lo, what modicums of wit he utters! his evasions have ears thus long. I have bobb'd his brain more than he has beat my bones. [I] will buy nine sparrows for a penny, and his *pia mater* is not worth the ninth part of a sparrow. This lord, Achilles, Ajax, who wears his wit in his belly and his guts in his head, [I'll] tell you what I say of him.

Achil. What?

Ther. I say, this Ajax—

[*Ajax offers to strike him.*]

Achil. Nay, good Ajax.

Ther. Has not so much wit—

Achil. Nay, I must hold you.

Ther. As will stop the eye of Helen's needle, for whom he comes to fight.

Achil. Peace, fool!

Ther. I would have peace and quietness, but the fool will not—he there, that he! Look you there.

Ajax. O thou damn'd cur! I shall—

Achil. Will you set your wit to a fool's?

Ther. No, I warrant you, the fool's will shame it.

Patr. Good words, Thersites.

Achil. What's the quarrel?

Ajax. I bade the vile owl go learn me the tenor of the proclamation, and he rails upon me.

Ther. I serve thee not.

Ajax. Well, go to, go to.

Ther. I serve here voluntary.

Achil. Your last service was suff'rance, 'twas not voluntary; no man is beaten voluntary. Ajax was here the voluntary, and you as under an impress.

Ther. E'en so; a great deal of your wit, too, lies in your sinews, or else there be liars. Hector shall have a great catch, and ['a] knock [out] either of your brains; 'a were as good crack a fusty nut with no kernel.

Achil. What, with me too, Thersites?

Ther. There's Ulysses and old Nestor, whose wit was mouldy ere [your] grandsires had nails [on their toes], yoke you like draught-oxen, and make you plough up the wars.

Achil. What? what?

Ther. Yes, good sooth. To, Achilles! to, Ajax! to—

Ajax. I shall cut out your tongue.

Ther. 'Tis no matter, I shall speak as much as thou afterwards.

Patr. No more words, Thersites, peace!

Ther. I will hold my peace when Achilles' [brach] bids me, shall I?

Achil. There's for you, Patroclus.

Ther. I will see you hang'd like clatpoles ere I come any more to your tents. I will keep where there is wit stirring, and leave the faction of fools. *Exit.*

Patr. A good riddance.

Achil. Marry, this, sir, is proclaim'd through all our host:
That Hector, by the [fift] hour of the sun,
Will with a trumpet 'twixt our tents and Troy
To-morrow morning call some knight to arms
That hath a stomach, and such a one that dare
Maintain—I know not what, 'tis trash. Farewell.

Ajax. Farewell. Who shall answer him?

Achil. I know not, 'tis put to lott'ry. Otherwise,
He knew his man.

Ajax. O, meaning you? I will go learn more of it. [*Exeunt.*]

[Scene II]

Enter Priam, Hector, Troilus, Paris, *and* Helenus.

Pri. After so many hours, lives, speeches spent,
Thus once again says Nestor from the Greeks:
"Deliver Helen, and all damage else—
As honor, loss of time, travail, expense,
Wounds, friends, and what else dear that is consum'd
In hot digestion of this cormorant war—
Shall be strook off." Hector, what say you to't?

Hect. Though no man lesser fears the Greeks than I
As far as toucheth my particular,
Yet, dread Priam,
There is no lady of more softer bowels,
More spungy to suck in the sense of fear,
More ready to cry out, "Who knows what follows?"

64. whosomever: whosoever.
65. I . . . fool. Thersites quibbles on "I know that fool."
67. Therefore . . . thee: i.e. I beat you because I am not a fool (?) or I stoop to beat you because I don't know my own superiority (?).
69. his . . . long: i.e. his attempts to get out of it are asinine. **bobb'd**: thumped. **70. will**: can.
71. pia mater: i.e. brain (properly, the membrane that covers the brain). **73–74. wears . . . head**: probably proverbial.
86. set . . . to: match your wits with.
88. Good words: i.e. speak temperately (from Plautus, *bona verba*).
93. go to: interjection expressing disapproval or protest.
94, 96. voluntary. Adverbial.
95. suff'rance: the endurance of something imposed (with play on the sense "suffering pain").
97. impress: (a) impressment, conscription; (b) imprint (of Ajax' blows). **98. E'en so**: true.
100. and 'a: if he. **100–101. either . . . brains**: the brains of either one of you (Achilles or Ajax).
101. 'a . . . good: it would be as much worth his while to.
109. To: i.e. to it (as if urging on draught oxen).
111. as much: i.e. as much sense.
114. brach: bitch dog. Cf. *masculine whore* applied to Patroclus in V.i.17. **117. clatpoles**: blockheads, dolts (variant of *clotpolls*).
122. fift: fifth. **125. a stomach**: courage (appetite for a fight).

II.ii. Location: Troy. Priam's palace.
4. travail: painful labor.
6. cormorant: gluttonous, devouring (from the large voracious sea-bird of that name). **9. my particular**: my personal concerns.
11. more softer bowels: tenderer feelings (the Elizabethan double comparative was used for emphasis).
12. spungy: absorbent (variant of *spongy*).

Than Hector is. The wound of peace is [surety],
[Surety] secure, but modest doubt is call'd
The beacon of the wise, the tent that searches
To th' bottom of the worst. Let Helen go.
Since the first sword was drawn about this question,
Every tithe soul, 'mongst many thousand dismes,
Hath been as dear as Helen; I mean, of ours.
If we have lost so many tenths of ours,
To guard a thing not ours nor worth to us
(Had it our name) the value of one ten,
What merit's in that reason which denies
The yielding of her up?

Tro. Fie, fie, my brother!
Weigh you the worth and honor of a king
So great as our dread father's in a scale
Of common ounces? Will you with compters sum
The past-proportion of his infinite,
And buckle in a waist most fathomless
With spans and inches so diminutive
As fears and reasons? Fie, for godly shame!

Hel. No marvel though you bite so sharp [at] reasons,
You are so empty of them. Should not our father
Bear the great sway of his affairs with reason,
Because your speech hath none that tell him so?

Tro. You are for dreams and slumbers, brother priest,
You fur your gloves with reason. Here are your reasons:
You know an enemy intends you harm;
You know a sword employ'd is perilous,
And reason flies the object of all harm.
Who marvels then, when Helenus beholds
A Grecian and his sword, if he do set
The very wings of reason to his heels
And fly like chidden Mercury from Jove,
Or like a star disorb'd? Nay, if we talk of reason,
[Let's] shut our gates and sleep. Manhood and honor

Should have hare hearts, would they but fat their thoughts
With this cramm'd reason; reason and respect
Make livers pale and lustihood deject.

Hect. Brother, she is not worth what she doth cost
The keeping.

Tro. What's aught but as 'tis valued?

Hect. But value dwells not in particular will,
It holds his estimate and dignity
As well wherein 'tis precious of itself
As in the prizer. 'Tis mad idolatry
To make the service greater than the god,
And the will dotes that is attributive
To what infectiously itself affects,
Without some image of th' affected merit.

Tro. I take to-day a wife, and my election
Is led on in the conduct of my will,
My will enkindled by mine eyes and ears,
Two traded pilots 'twixt the dangerous [shores]
Of will and judgment: how may I avoid
(Although my will distaste what it elected)
The wife I chose? There can be no evasion
To blench from this and to stand firm by honor.
We turn not back the silks upon the merchant
When we have soil'd them, nor the remainder viands
We do not throw in unrespective sieve,
Because we now are full. It was thought meet
Paris should do some vengeance on the Greeks.
Your breath with full consent bellied his sails;
The seas and winds, old wranglers, took a truce,
And did him service; he touch'd the ports desir'd,

14. wound . . . surety: i.e. the danger of peace lies in a sense of security.
15. secure: careless, overconfident. **modest doubt**: a reasonable measure of wariness.
16. beacon: warning light (like a fire set on a hilltop). **tent**: probe (medical).
19. tithe . . . dismes: (literally) tenth . . : tenths, The meaning of lines 19–20 has been much debated. Deighton's explanation is most widely accepted: "The meaning seems to be not that every tenth soul *only*, but every soul *that has been taken as a tithe by war* is as dear as Helen, and of such tithes there have been many thousands."
23. Had . . . name: i.e. even if Helen were a Trojan. **one ten**: one "tithe," i.e. a single Trojan life.
28. compters: counters (variant form), tokens, false coins. **sum**: add up, total.
29. past-proportion: immeasurability.
31. spans: i.e. hand spans, the distance between the extended thumb and little finger (reckoned as nine inches).
33. bite . . . at: talk so cuttingly of. **reasons.** Perhaps with a quibble on *raisins* (pronounced similarly); snapping up burning raisins floating in a glass of wine was an Elizabethan pastime.
34. Should . . . father: should our father *not*.
36. tell him so: i.e. tell him how (to conduct his affairs with reason).
37. dreams and slumbers. Cf. *bed-work*, I.iii.205.
38. fur . . . reason: i.e. employ your kind of reason to secure a comfortable life for yourself. *Fur* means "line with fur." Troilus goes on to charge Helenus with rationalizing his counsel of prudence.
41. object . . . harm: sight of anything dangerous.
45. Mercury: Jove's messenger, who was pictured as wearing shoes with wings on the heels.
46. star disorb'd: star cast out of its proper orb or sphere, i.e. shooting star.
48. Should: would certainly. **hare**: timid.
49. cramm'd. A transferred modifier, rightly describing the thoughts, which are compared to fowl fattened for market by overfeeding. **respect**: cautious consideration (of consequences).
50. livers pale. A white (*bloodless*) liver was symbolic of cowardice. **lustihood**: bodily vigor. **deject**: dejected, abated.
51–52. what . . . keeping: her keep, her living expenses.
52. What's . . . valued: what gives worth to anything except the value at which someone esteems it.
53. particular will: the arbitrary preference of any single person.
54. dignity: worth. **55. wherein . . . itself**: in its intrinsic value.
56. the prizer: i.e. the value placed on it by someone who prizes it.
57. To . . . god: i.e. to pay greater honor to a thing than in its essential nature it is worth.
58. dotes: is mad. **is attributive**: pays tribute.
59. infectiously. This may refer to the will (behaving as if diseased) or to the object of esteem (given supposed value by contagion from the will's valuation of it). **affects**: likes, admires.
60. image: appearance (within itself).
61. I . . . wife. Troilus sets up a hypothetical analogy. **election**: choice. **62. led . . . will**: guided by my desire.
64. traded pilots: intermediaries constantly going back and forth.
65. judgment: the rational faculty (as opposed to *will*). **avoid**: get rid of. **66. distaste**: (come to) dislike.
67. evasion: contrived excuse, subterfuge.
68. blench: turn aside. **and**: and at the same time.
70. remainder viands: food left uneaten.
71. unrespective sieve: i.e. the refuse basket, into which only worthless (*unrespective* = unregarded) things are thrown (?). Perhaps *unrespective* in the sense "unregarding" is a transferred modifier, rightly describing those who throw away the food.
73. vengeance. Paris had gone to Greece to avenge the Greeks' refusal to return Priam's sister Hesione (the "old aunt" of line 77), taken captive by Hercules and given by him to Telamon, king of Salamis. Telamon was Ajax' father, and according to the medieval and Renaissance tradition followed in this play Hesione was his mother. His relationship to Hector becomes of dramatic interest in IV.v.
74. breath: i.e. approving speeches or votes (again the commonplace that words are air). **bellied**: filled out, distended.
75. old wranglers: long-time opponents or quarrellers.

And for an old aunt whom the Greeks held captive,
He brought a Grecian queen, whose youth and freshness
Wrinkles Apollo's, and makes pale the morning.
Why keep we her? The Grecians keep our aunt.
Is she worth keeping? Why, she is a pearl,
Whose price hath launch'd above a thousand ships,
And turn'd crown'd kings to merchants.
If you'll avouch 'twas wisdom Paris went—
As you must needs, for you all cried "Go, go"—
If you'll confess [he] brought home worthy prize—
As you must needs, for you all clapp'd your hands,
And cried "Inestimable!"—why do you now
The issue of your proper wisdoms rate,
And do a deed that never Fortune did,
Beggar the estimation which you priz'd
Richer than sea and land? O theft most base,
That we have stol'n what we do fear to keep!
But thieves unworthy of a thing so stol'n,
That in their country did them that disgrace
We fear to warrant in our native place!

Cassandra. [*Within.*] Cry, Troyans, cry!
Pri. What noise? what shrike is this?
Tro. 'Tis our mad sister, I do know her voice.
Cas. [*Within.*] Cry, Troyans!
Hect. It is Cassandra.

Enter CASSANDRA *raving* [*with her hair about her ears*].

Cas. Cry, Troyans, cry! lend me ten thousand eyes,
And I will fill them with prophetic tears.
Hect. Peace, sister, peace!
Cas. Virgins and boys, mid-age and wrinkled [eld],
Soft infancy, that nothing canst but cry,
Add to my clamors! Let us pay betimes
A moi'ty of that mass of moan to come.
Cry, Troyans, cry! practice your eyes with tears!
Troy must not be, nor goodly Ilion stand.
Our fire-brand brother Paris burns us all.
Cry, Troyans, cry! a Helen and a woe!
Cry, cry! Troy burns, or else let Helen go. *Exit.*
Hect. Now, youthful Troilus, do not these high strains
Of divination in our sister work
Some touches of remorse? or is your blood
So madly hot that no discourse of reason,
Nor fear of bad success in a bad cause,
Can qualify the same?
Tro. Why, brother Hector,
We may not think the justness of each act
Such and no other than event doth form it,
Nor once deject the courage of our minds
Because Cassandra's mad. Her brain-sick raptures
Cannot distaste the goodness of a quarrel
Which hath our several honors all engag'd
To make it gracious. For my private part,
I am no more touch'd than all Priam's sons;
And Jove forbid there should be done amongst us
Such things as might offend the weakest spleen
To fight for and maintain.
Par. Else might the world convince of levity
As well my undertakings as your counsels,
But I attest the gods, your full consent
Gave wings to my propension, and cut off
All fears attending on so dire a project.
For what, alas, can these my single arms?
What propugnation is in one man's valor
To stand the push and enmity of those
This quarrel would excite? Yet I protest,
Were I alone to pass the difficulties,
And had as ample power as I have will,
Paris should ne'er retract what he hath done,
Nor faint in the pursuit.
Pri. Paris, you speak
Like one besotted on your sweet delights.
You have the honey still, but these the gall;
So to be valiant, is no praise at all.
Par. Sir, I propose not merely to myself
The pleasures such a beauty brings with it,
But I would have the soil of her fair rape
Wip'd off, in honorable keeping her.
What treason were it to the ransack'd queen,
Disgrace to your great worths, and shame to me,
Now to deliver her possession up
On terms of base compulsion! Can it be
That so degenerate a strain as this
Should once set footing in your generous bosoms?

79. Wrinkles Apollo's: makes Apollo's youth and freshness look aged by comparison. **morning:** i.e. rosy dawn.
82. price: value. **launch'd . . . ships.** There is no necessary connection with Marlowe's *Doctor Faustus* ("Was this the face that launch'd a thousand ships?"); there is a classical source in Lucian's *Dialogue of the Dead*, and Marlowe was not alone in drawing from it. But Shakespeare elsewhere quotes Marlowe and borrows from his work.
83. turn'd . . . merchants. An echo of Matthew 13:45: "Again, the kingdome of heaven is like unto a marchant man, seeking goodly pearls: which when he had found one precious pearl, went and sold all he had, and bought it" (Geneva). **84. avouch:** affirm.
89. issue . . . rate: repudiate the outcome of your own good judgments.
90. do . . . did: i.e. be more inconstant than even Fortune herself.
91. Beggar . . . which: esteem as worthless what.
93. That: in that.
95–96. That . . . place: who gave the Greeks in their own country a disgrace that we are now afraid to ratify.
97. Cry: weep and lament. **shrike:** shriek (variant form).
104. eld: old age. **105. canst:** can do. **106. betimes:** in advance.
107. moi'ty: portion. **moan:** lamentation.
108. practice . . . tears: accustom your eyes to weeping.
110. fire-brand brother Paris. The reference is to Hecuba's dream, when she was pregnant with Paris, that she would be delivered of a fire-brand which would be the destruction of Troy.
115. remorse: compunction.
116. discourse of reason: faculty of reason, reason itself.
117. success: outcome. **118. qualify:** moderate.
119–20. We . . . it: i.e. we must not judge the propriety of every action by its result (*event*). **121. once deject:** ever abate.
122. brain-sick raptures: mad, ecstatic fits.
123. distaste: make unpalatable.
124. our . . . engag'd: the honor of each of us bound by oath.
125. gracious: righteous. **126. touch'd:** affected. **all:** any of.
128. spleen: temper. **130. convince:** convict.
132. attest the gods: call the gods to witness.
133. propension: inclination.
134. attending on: i.e. which might accompany.
135. can . . . arms: can my unaided arms do.
136. propugnation. defense. **137. push and enmity:** hostile onset.
139. pass: experience, go through with.
141. retract: disavow, wish undone.
142. faint: weary, lose heart. **143. besotted:** doting.
145. So: under such circumstances.
146. propose . . . myself: set before my mind, have in view.
148. her fair rape: the abduction of her fair self (?).
150. ransack'd: carried off as plunder.
152. deliver . . . up: return her, having once possessed her.
154. strain: impulse. **155. once:** for a moment. **generous:** noble.

There's not the meanest spirit on our party
Without a heart to dare, or sword to draw,
When Helen is defended; nor none so noble
Whose life were ill bestow'd, or death unfam'd,
Where Helen is the subject. Then I say,
Well may we fight for her whom we know well
The world's large spaces cannot parallel.
Hect. Paris and Troilus, you have both said well,
And on the cause and question now in hand
Have gloz'd, but superficially, not much
Unlike young men, whom Aristotle thought
Unfit to hear moral philosophy.
The reasons you allege do more conduce
To the hot passion of distemp'red blood
Than to make up a free determination
'Twixt right and wrong; for pleasure and revenge
Have ears more deaf than adders to the voice
Of any true decision. Nature craves
All dues be rend'red to their owners: now,
What nearer debt in all humanity
Than wife is to the husband? If this law
Of nature be corrupted through affection,
And that great minds, of partial indulgence
To their benumbed wills, resist the same,
There is a law in each well-order'd nation
To curb those raging appetites that are
Most disobedient and refractory.
If Helen then be wife to Sparta's king,
As it is known she is, these moral laws
Of nature and of nations speak aloud
To have her back return'd. Thus to persist
In doing wrong extenuates not wrong,
But makes it much more heavy. Hector's opinion
Is this in way of truth; yet ne'er the less,
My spritely brethren, I propend to you
In resolution to keep Helen still,
For 'tis a cause that hath no mean dependance
Upon our joint and several dignities.
Tro. Why, there you touch'd the life of our design!
Were it not glory that we more affected
Than the performance of our heaving spleens,
I would not wish a drop of Troyan blood
Spent more in her defense. But, worthy Hector,

She is a theme of honor and renown,
A spur to valiant and magnanimous deeds,
Whose present courage may beat down our foes,
And fame in time to come canonize us,
For I presume brave Hector would not lose
So rich advantage of a promis'd glory
As smiles upon the forehead of this action
For the wide world's revenue.
Hect. I am yours,
You valiant offspring of great Priamus.
I have a roisting challenge sent amongst
The dull and factious nobles of the Greeks
Will [strike] amazement to their drowsy spirits.
I was advertis'd their great general slept,
Whilst emulation in the army crept:
This I presume will wake him. *Exeunt.*

[SCENE III]

Enter THERSITES *solus.*

[*Ther.*] How now, Thersites? What, lost in the labyrinth of thy fury? Shall the elephant Ajax carry it thus? He beats me, and I rail at him. O worthy satisfaction! Would it were otherwise: that I could beat him, whilst he rail'd at me. 'Sfoot, I'll learn to conjure and raise devils, but I'll see some issue of my spiteful execrations. Then there's Achilles, a rare enginer! If Troy be not taken till these two undermine it, the walls will stand till they fall of themselves. O thou great thunder-darter of Olympus, forget that thou art Jove, the king of gods, and, Mercury, lose all the serpentine craft of thy caduceus, if ye take not that little little less than little wit from them that they have, which short-arm'd ignorance itself knows is so abundant scarce, it will not in circumvention deliver a fly from a spider, without drawing their massy irons and cutting the web! After this, the vengeance on the whole camp! or rather, the Neapolitan bone-ache! for that methinks is the curse depending on those that war for a placket. I have said my prayers, and devil Envy say amen. What ho! my Lord Achilles!

156. **party:** side.
158. **When . . . defended:** when it is a question of defending Helen.
159. **bestow'd:** employed. 165. **gloz'd:** commented.
166. **Aristotle:** The mention of Aristotle in ancient Troy is, of course, an anachronism. The reference is to a passage in the *Nicomachean Ethics* (I,3). 168–69. **conduce To:** tend towards.
169. **distemp'red blood:** diseased appetite. 170. **free:** unbiased.
172. **more . . . adders.** There was a tradition that the adder could make itself deaf by laying one ear on the ground and inserting its tail in the other. Cf. Psalm 58:4–5: "like the deaf adder that stoppeth his ear. Which heareth not the voice of the enchanter, though he be most expert in charming" (Geneva).
173. **Nature:** i.e. natural law, *jus naturae*; joined in line 180 with *jus gentium*, the law of nations or civil law. **craves:** requires.
177. **affection:** passion (as opposed to reason).
178. **that.** Repeating the sense of *If* (line 176). **of partial:** out of a biased (or self-interested).
179. **benumbed:** i.e. rendered insensitive to right by passion.
185. **aloud:** loudly. 187. **extenuates:** mitigates.
189. **in . . . truth:** considered in terms of abstract right.
190. **spritely:** spirited.
190–91. **propend . . . resolution:** incline to your resolve.
192–93. **cause . . . dignities:** i.e. cause upon which our combined and individual honors depend in no slight measure. 194. **life:** heart.
195. **glory:** honor, fame. **affected:** aimed at.
196. **performance . . . spleens:** carrying out of our angry impulses.

199. **theme of:** subject encouraging.
201. **Whose present courage:** the bravery of which in the present time.
202. **canonize:** memorialize (us) as heroes (accented on the second syllable; so also *revenue*, line 206, and *advertis'd*, line 211).
205. **smiles . . . action.** The image seems to have been suggested by the idea of seizing time (favorable opportunity) by the forelock; cf. III.iii.146 ff. 208. **roisting:** boisterous. 210. **Will:** which will.
211. **advertis'd:** informed 212. **emulation:** factious envy.

II.iii. **Location:** The Greek camp. Before Achilles' tent.
2. **carry it:** bear off the honors, have the advantage.
5. **'Sfoot:** by God's foot (mild oath).
8. **enginer:** contriver, strategist (variant of *engineer*).
10. **thunder-darter.** With reference to one of Jove's titles, *Jupiter Tonans* (= thundering).
12. **serpentine . . . caduceus.** The caduceus was the wand bearing two intertwined serpents which was carried by Mercury, who was also associated with cunning and deception; hence *serpentine craft.*
14. **short-arm'd ignorance:** i.e. ignorance such that almost everything is beyond its grasp.
17. **massy irons:** massive swords (which they use in place of intelligence).
18–19. **Neapolitan bone-ache:** syphilis (believed to have originated in Naples). 19–20. **depending on:** hanging over.
20. **placket:** woman (literally, a slit or opening in a petticoat).

Patr. [*Within.*] Who's there? Thersites? Good Thersites, come in and rail.

Ther. If I could 'a' rememb'red a gilt counterfeit, thou [wouldst] not have slipp'd out of my contemplation. But it is no matter, thyself upon thyself! The common curse of mankind, folly and ignorance, be thine in great revenue! Heaven bless thee from a tutor, and discipline come not near thee! Let thy blood be thy direction till thy death; then if she that lays thee out says thou art a fair corse, I'll be sworn and sworn upon't she never shrouded any but lazars. Amen.

[*Enter* PATROCLUS.]

Where's Achilles?

Patr. What, art thou devout? Wast thou in prayer?

Ther. Ay, the heavens hear me!

Patr. Amen.

Enter ACHILLES.

Achil. Who's there?

Patr. Thersites, my lord.

Achil. Where? where? O, where? Art thou come? Why, my cheese, my digestion, why hast thou not serv'd thyself in to my table so many meals? Come, what's Agamemnon?

Ther. Thy commander, Achilles. Then tell me, Patroclus, what's Achilles?

Patr. Thy lord, Thersites. Then tell me, I pray thee, what's Thersites?

Ther. Thy knower, Patroclus. Then tell me, Patroclus, what art thou?

Patr. Thou must tell that knowest.

Achil. O, tell, tell.

Ther. I'll decline the whole question: Agamemnon commands Achilles, Achilles is my lord, I am Patroclus' knower, and Patroclus is a fool.

[*Patr.* You rascal!

Ther. Peace, fool, I have not done.

Achil. He is a privileg'd man. Proceed, Thersites.

Ther. Agamemnon is a fool, Achilles is a fool, Thersites is a fool, and, as aforesaid, Patroclus is a fool.]

Achil. Derive this; come.

Ther. Agamemnon is a fool to offer to command Achilles, Achilles is a fool to be commanded [of Agamemnon], Thersites is a fool to serve such a fool, and this Patroclus is a fool positive.

Patr. Why am I a fool?

Ther. Make that demand of the prover, it suffices me thou art. Look you, who comes here?

Enter AGAMEMNON, ULYSSES, NESTOR, DIOMED, AJAX, *and* CALCHAS.

Achil. Come, Patroclus, I'll speak with nobody. Come in with me, Thersites. [*Exit.*]

Ther. Here is such patchery, such juggling, and such knavery! All the argument is a whore and a cuckold, a good quarrel to draw emulous factions and bleed to death upon. [Now the dry suppeago on the subject, and war and lechery confound all!] [*Exit.*]

Agam. Where is Achilles?

Patr. Within his tent, but ill dispos'd, my lord.

Agam. Let it be known to him that we are here.
He [shent] our messengers, and we lay by
Our appertainings, visiting of him.
Let him be told so, lest perchance he think
We dare not move the question of our place,
Or know not what we are.

Patr. I shall say so to him. [*Exit.*]

Ulyss. We saw him at the opening of his tent,
He is not sick.

Ajax. Yes, lion-sick, sick of proud heart. You may call it melancholy, if you will favor the man; but by my head, 'tis pride. But why, why? Let him show us a cause. [A word, my lord.] [*Takes Agamemnon aside.*]

Nest. What moves Ajax thus to bay at him?

Ulyss. Achilles hath inveigled his fool from him.

Nest. Who, Thersites?

Ulyss. He.

Nest. Then will Ajax lack matter, if he have lost his argument.

Ulyss. No, you see he is his argument that has his argument, Achilles.

Nest. All the better, their fraction is more our wish than their faction. But it was a strong composure a fool could disunite.

Ulyss. The amity that wisdom knits not, folly may easily untie.

[*Enter* PATROCLUS.]

Here comes Patroclus.

Nest. No Achilles with him.

25. **'a':** have.
25–27. **If . . . contemplation:** i.e. he has been "praying" for Ajax and Achilles, forgetting the worthless Patroclus (= *gilt counterfeit*, i.e. a coin made of base metal gilded over).
26. **slipp'd.** With a play on *slip* = a counterfeit coin.
27. **thyself upon thyself.** Thersites calls down upon Patroclus the worst plague he can imagine—Patroclus himself.
29. **great revenue:** generous incoming quantities. **bless:** i.e. preserve. 30. **blood:** lust, violent passion. 32. **corse:** corpse.
33. **lazars:** lepers. 41. **cheese.** Supposed an aid to digestion.
48. **Thy knower:** one who knows you for what you really are.
52. **decline . . . question:** state in order all the points of the subject; a technical grammatical term, like *Derive* (line 61) and *positive* (line 65).
57. **privileg'd man:** i.e. a man given license to rail, just as an "allow'd fool," like Feste in *Twelfth Night*, was permitted to speak his mind with relative impunity.
61. **Derive this:** show how this follows. 62. **offer:** undertake.
65. **fool positive:** absolute fool (without any reason outside himself for being so).
67. **Make that demand:** ask that question. **of the prover:** i.e. of yourself (the one who can prove it positively). Many editors prefer the simpler F1 reading *to the Creator*.
69. **Come.** Omitted in F1, probably rightly.
71. **patchery:** trickery, hypocrisy (?).
72–73. **whore . . . cuckold:** i.e. Helen and Menelaus.
73. **draw:** attract.
74. **suppeago:** serpigo, a disfiguring skin disease.
77. **ill dispos'd:** ill; with possible play on "unfavorably inclined."
78. **we.** The royal plural. 79. **shent:** abused, berated.
79–80. **lay . . . appertainings:** waive the honor properly due to us.
82. **move the question:** insist upon the rights.
86. **lion-sick.** The lion, as king of beasts, was traditionally proud.
87–88. **melancholy . . . pride:** "i.e. not a 'humour' but a deadly sin" (A. Walker).
94–95. **matter . . . argument:** i.e. he will lack subject matter if he has lost the theme of his railing.
96–97. **he . . . Achilles:** i.e. he has a new theme for railing—Achilles, the man who took his former theme, Thersites.
98–99. **fraction . . . faction:** division . . . alliance.
99. **strong composure:** firm alliance (spoken ironically).
101. **amity:** union.

Ulyss. The elephant hath joints, but none for courtesy; his legs are legs for necessity, not for flexure.

Patr. Achilles bids me say he is much sorry,
If any thing more than your sport and pleasure
Did move your greatness and this noble state
To call upon him. He hopes it is no other
But for your health and your disgestion sake,
An after-dinner's breath.

Agam. Hear you, Patroclus:
We are too well acquainted with these answers,
But his evasion, wing'd thus swift with scorn,
Cannot outfly our apprehensions.
Much attribute he hath, and much the reason
Why we ascribe it to him; yet all his virtues,
Not virtuously on his own part beheld,
Do in our eyes begin to lose their gloss,
Yea, like fair fruit in an unwholesome dish,
Are like to rot untasted. Go and tell him
We come to speak with him, and you shall not sin
If you do say we think him over-proud
And under-honest, in self-assumption greater
Than in the note of judgment; and worthier than himself
Here tend the savage strangeness he puts on,
Disguise the holy strength of their command,
And underwrite in an observing kind
His humorous predominance; yea, watch
His [pettish lines], his ebbs, [his] flows, [as] if
The passage and whole [carriage of this action]
Rode on his tide. Go tell him this, and add,
That if he overhold his price so much,
We'll none of him; but let him, like an engine
Not portable, lie under this report:
"Bring action hither, this cannot go to war."
A stirring dwarf we do allowance give
Before a sleeping giant. Tell him so.

Patr. I shall, and bring his answer presently.

[*Exit.*]

Agam. In second voice we'll not be satisfied,
We come to speak with him. Ulysses, [enter you].

[*Exit Ulysses.*]

Ajax. What is he more than another?

Agam. No more than what he thinks he is.

Ajax. Is he so much? Do you not think he thinks himself a better man than I am?

Agam. No question.

Ajax. Will you subscribe his thought, and say he is?

Agam. No, noble Ajax, you are as strong, as valiant, as wise, no less noble, much more gentle, and altogether more tractable.

Ajax. Why should a man be proud? how doth pride grow? I know not what pride is.

Agam. Your mind is the clearer, [Ajax,] and your virtues the fairer. He that is proud eats up himself. Pride is his own glass, his own trumpet, his own chronicle, and whatever praises itself but in the deed, devours the deed in the praise.

Enter ULYSSES.

Ajax. I do hate a proud man, as I do hate the engend'ring of toads.

Nest. [*Aside.*] And yet he loves himself. Is't not strange?

Ulyss. Achilles will not to the field to-morrow.

Agam. What's his excuse?

Ulyss. He doth rely on none,
But carries on the stream of his dispose
Without observance or respect of any,
In will peculiar and in self-admission.

Agam. Why will he not upon our fair request
Untent his person and share th' air with us?

Ulyss. Things small as nothing, for request's sake only,
He makes important. Possess'd he is with greatness,
And speaks not to himself but with a pride
That quarrels at self-breath. Imagin'd worth
Holds in his blood such swoll'n and hot discourse
That 'twixt his mental and his active parts
Kingdom'd Achilles in commotion rages,
And batters down himself. What should I say?
He is so plaguy proud that the death-tokens of it
Cry "No recovery."

Agam. Let Ajax go to him.
Dear lord, go you and greet him in his tent.
'Tis said he holds you well, and will be led
At your request a little from himself.

Ulyss. O Agamemnon, let it not be so!
We'll consecrate the steps that Ajax makes

105–6. elephant . . . flexure. It was traditionally believed, despite Aristotle, that the elephant had no knee-joints and had to sleep standing up, leaning against a tree. **109. state:** noble retinue.
110–11. no other But: for no other reason except.
111. disgestion: digestion (variant form).
112. breath: breathing, exercise.
115. apprehensions: understanding (of the truth); with sense also of "capture, arrest." An example of the plural use of an abstract noun when it relates to more than one person; modern usage requires the singular. For another example see III.ii.174.
116. attribute: reputation, honor.
118. on . . . beheld: viewed by himself.
120. unwholesome: foul, dirty.
125. note of judgment: quality that is characteristic of judgment.
126. tend: wait upon. **savage strangeness:** rude aloofness.
128–29. underwrite . . . predominance: i.e. subscribe to his capricious assumption of superior authority by their deference.
130. pettish lines: ill-tempered behavior (*line* = course of action). Many editors accept Hanmer's emendation *lunes* (= fits of madness, influenced by the moon). The Q reading *course, and time* lends some support to the F1 reading here adopted.
131. passage . . . action: whole success of this undertaking (the siege of Troy). Note that *passage, carriage,* and *Rode* (line 132) are all part of the image of transport by sea.
133. overhold his price: overestimate his value.
134–35. engine Not portable: war machine too heavy to transport.
135. lie . . . report: suffer the stigma of this pronouncement.
137. allowance: approbation. **139. presently:** at once.
140. second voice: someone speaking for him.

143. No . . . is. This may be taken in two ways: (1) his worth lies only in his self-estimation; (2) he is as worthy as he thinks he is (as a covert rebuke to Ajax, who, of course, takes the statement in the first sense).
147. subscribe: endorse.
155. glass: mirror (self-reflecting). **trumpet:** i.e. praiser.
156. chronicle: record. **praises . . . deed:** praises itself in any way except by silently doing the deed. **158. engend'ring:** copulation.
164. dispose: inclination.
166. In . . . self-admission: in accordance with what he himself desires and approves.
169. for . . . only: merely because they are requested of him.
170. Possess'd. With reference to being possessed by the devil, in this case pride (= *greatness*).
172. quarrels at self-breath: find fault even with what he says of himself (as inadequate to his greatness). **173. blood:** passions.
175. Kingdom'd Achilles: i.e. Achilles seen as a microcosm of a regal state caught in civil war; cf. *Julius Caesar,* II.i.67–69.
177. plaguy: confoundedly, pestilently. **death-tokens:** plague spots (betokening death).
181. from himself: i.e. away from his characteristic arrogance.

When they go from Achilles. Shall the proud lord
That bastes his arrogance with his own seam,
And never suffers matter of the world
Enter his thoughts, save such as doth revolve
And ruminate himself, shall he be worshipp'd
Of that we hold an idol more than he?
No! this thrice worthy and right valiant lord
Shall not so [stale] his palm, nobly acquir'd,
Nor, by my will, assubjugate his merit,
As amply [titled] as Achilles' is,
By going to Achilles.
That were to enlard his fat-already pride,
And add more coals to Cancer when he burns
With entertaining great Hyperion.
This lord go to him! Jupiter forbid,
And say in thunder, "Achilles go to him."

Nest. [*Aside to Diomedes.*] O, this is well. He rubs the vein of him.

Dio. [*Aside to Nestor.*] And how his silence drinks up his applause!

Ajax. If I go to him, with my armed fist
I'll [pash] him o'er the face.

Agam. O no, you shall not go.

Ajax. And he be proud with me, I'll pheese his pride.
Let me go to him.

Ulyss. Not for the worth that hangs upon our quarrel.

Ajax. A paltry, insolent fellow!

Nest. [*Aside.*] How he describes himself!

Ajax. Can he not be sociable?

Ulyss. [*Aside.*] The raven chides blackness.

Ajax. I'll [let] his [humors] blood.

Agam. [*Aside.*] He will be the physician that should be the patient.

Ajax. And all men were of my mind—

Ulyss. [*Aside.*] Wit would be out of fashion.

Ajax. 'A should not bear it so, 'a should eat swords first. Shall pride carry it?

Nest. [*Aside.*] And 'twould, you'd carry half.

[*Ulyss.*] [*Aside.*] 'A would have ten shares. I will knead him, I'll make him supple. He's not yet through warm.

Nest. [*Aside.*] Force him with [praises]—pour in, pour [in], his ambition is dry.

Ulyss. [*To Agamemnon.*] My lord, you feed too much on this dislike.

Nest. Our noble general, do not do so.

Dio. You must prepare to fight without Achilles.

Ulyss. Why, 'tis this naming of him does him harm.
Here is a man—but 'tis before his face,
I will be silent.

Nest. Wherefore should you so?
He is not emulous, as Achilles is.

Ulyss. Know the whole world, he is as valiant—

Ajax. A whoreson dog, that shall palter with us thus!
Would he were a Troyan!

Nest. What a vice were it in Ajax now—

Ulyss. If he were proud—

Dio. Or covetous of praise—

Ulyss. Ay, or surly borne—

Dio. Or strange, or self-affected!

Ulyss. Thank the heavens, lord, thou art of sweet composure.
Praise him that gat thee, she that gave thee suck;
Fam'd be thy tutor, and thy parts of nature
Thrice fam'd beyond, [beyond] all erudition;
But he that disciplin'd thine arms to fight,
Let Mars divide eternity in twain,
And give him half; and for thy vigor,
Bull-bearing Milo his addition yield
To sinowy Ajax. I will not praise thy wisdom,
Which like a [bourn], a pale, a shore, confines
[Thy] spacious and dilated parts. Here's Nestor,
Instructed by the antiquary times;
He must, he is, he cannot but be wise.
But pardon, father Nestor, were your days
As green as Ajax', and your brain so temper'd,
You should not have the eminence of him,
But be as Ajax.

Ajax. Shall I call you father?

Nest. Ay, my good son.

Dio. Be rul'd by him, Lord Ajax.

185. seam: fat, lard.
187–88. revolve And ruminate. The verbs are synonymous, meaning "to turn over and over in the mind."
189. Of: by. **idol more:** greater object of worship.
191. stale his palm: cheapen his honors.
192. assubjugate: debase.
193. As . . . is: having a name as great as Achilles'.
196–97. add . . . Hyperion: i.e. intensify the heat of what is already hot in its own nature. The sun (*Hyperion*) enters into Cancer (a sign of the zodiac associated with heat) on June 21, the beginning of summer. **200. rubs . . . him:** tickles his desire for praise.
203. pash: smash.
205. pheese: do for, settle the business of (*O.E.D.*).
207. hangs . . . quarrel: is involved in our quarrel with the Trojans.
211. raven chides blackness: i.e. the pot calls the kettle black.
212. let . . . blood: purge his fantasies of greatness by bleeding them. *Let blood* is a medical term for bleeding a patient.
215, 219. And: if.
217. bear it so: get away with it in such a manner; cf. "carry it," line 218.
217–18. eat swords first: be stabbed before that should be permitted to happen.
220. 'A . . . shares: i.e. he is too proud to share but could qualify for all (*ten shares* = the whole).
221–22. through warm: thoroughly warmed up.
223. Force: stuff. **224. dry:** thirsty.
225. this dislike: i.e. Achilles' aloofness.
228. this naming of him: i.e. the continual reference to Achilles as though he were the Greeks' sole hope. **does him harm:** has this bad effect. **231. emulous:** covetous of praise, envious.
233. palter: trifle, play fast and loose.
238. surly borne: of arrogant bearing.
239. strange: unfriendly, distant. **self-affected:** in love with himself.
240. composure: composition (in mind and body).
241. gat: got, i.e. begot.
242. parts of nature: natural endowments.
243. beyond all erudition: above all learning; i.e. Ajax's natural endowments are such that they far surpass anything that learning could add to them (with ironical double sense).
244. But he: but for him.
245. eternity: i.e. his eternal fame as a warrior.
247. Bull-bearing . . . yield: let Milo yield his title "bull-bearing." Milo, a famous athlete of Crotona, carried a four-year-old bull on his shoulders forty yards, killed it with one blow of his fist, and ate the bull, all in one day.
248. sinowy: sinewy, muscular. **I will not:** I will forbear to (but again with ironic second sense).
249. bourn: boundary. **pale:** fence.
250. spacious . . . parts: ample and extensive qualities.
251. antiquary: ancient (first recorded use as an adjective).
254. green: youthful. **so temper'd:** i.e. at a correspondingly youthful stage of development.
255. eminence of: superiority over.

Ulyss. There is no tarrying here, the hart Achilles
Keeps thicket. Please it our great general
To call together all his state of war.
Fresh kings are come to Troy; to-morrow
We must with all our main of power stand fast;
And here's a lord—come knights from east to west,
And [cull] their flower, Ajax shall cope the best.
Agam. Go we to council. Let Achilles sleep:
Light boats sail swift, though greater hulks draw deep. *Exeunt.*

[ACT III, SCENE I]

[*Music sounds within.*] *Enter* PANDARUS [*and a* SERVANT].

Pan. Friend, you! pray you a word. Do you not follow the young Lord Paris?

Serv. Ay, sir, when he goes before me.

Pan. You depend upon him, I mean.

Serv. Sir, I do depend upon the Lord.

Pan. You depend upon a notable gentleman; I must needs praise him.

Serv. The Lord be prais'd!

Pan. You know me, do you not?

Serv. Faith, sir, superficially.

Pan. Friend, know me better, I am the Lord Pandarus.

Serv. I hope I shall know your honor better!

Pan. I do desire it.

Serv. You are in the state of grace.

Pan. Grace? Not so, friend, honor and lordship are my titles. What music is this?

Serv. I do but partly know, sir, it is music in parts.

Pan. Know you the musicians?

Serv. Wholly, sir.

Pan. Who play they to?

Serv. To the hearers, sir.

Pan. At whose pleasure, friend?

Serv. At mine, sir, and theirs that love music.

Pan. Command, I mean, [friend].

Serv. Who shall I command, sir?

Pan. Friend, we understand not one another; I am too courtly and thou too cunning. At whose request do these men play?

Serv. That's to't indeed, sir. Marry, sir, at the request of Paris my lord, who is there in person; with him, the mortal Venus, the heart-blood of beauty, love's invisible soul.

Pan. Who? my cousin Cressida?

Serv. No, sir, Helen. Could not you find out that by her attributes?

Pan. It should seem, fellow, thou hast not seen the Lady Cressid. I come to speak with Paris from the Prince Troilus. I will make a complimental assault upon him, for my business seethes.

Serv. Sodden business! there's a stew'd phrase indeed!

Enter PARIS *and* HELEN [*attended*].

Pan. Fair be to you, my lord, and to all this fair company! fair desires, in all fair measure, fairly guide them! Especially to you, fair queen, fair thoughts be your fair pillow!

Helen. Dear lord, you are full of fair words.

Pan. You speak your fair pleasure, sweet queen. Fair prince, here is good broken music.

Par. You have broke it, cousin; and by my life you shall make it whole again—you shall piece it out with a piece of your performance. Nell, he is full of harmony.

Pan. Truly, lady, no.

Helen. O sir—

Pan. Rude, in sooth, in good sooth, very rude.

Par. Well said, my lord, well, you say so in fits.

Pan. I have business to my lord, dear queen. My lord, will you vouchsafe me a word?

Helen. Nay, this shall not hedge us out, we'll hear you sing, certainly.

Pan. Well, sweet queen, you are pleasant with me. But marry thus, my lord: my dear lord and most esteem'd friend, your brother Troilus—

Helen. My Lord Pandarus, honey-sweet lord—

Pan. Go to, sweet queen, go to—commends himself most affectionately to you—

Helen. You shall not bob us out of our melody. If you do, our melancholy upon your head!

Pan. Sweet queen, sweet queen, that's a sweet queen—i' faith—

Helen. And to make a sweet lady sad is a sour offense.

Pan. Nay, that shall not serve your turn, that shall it not, in truth la! Nay, I care not for such words, no, no. And, my lord, he desires you, that if the King

260. state: council.
262. main of power: principal strength. This line seems to ignore the truce and the single combat set for the next day.
263. come knights: let knights come.
264. cull their flower: choose out the best of them. **cope the best:** encounter with the best on equal terms.
266. hulks: large unwieldy vessels.

III.i. Location: Troy. Priam's palace.
2. follow: i.e. serve. **3. goes:** walks.
4. You . . . him: a conceited way of saying, "you are his servant."
5. Lord: (1) master; (2) God (with the same quibble in line 8).
13. know . . . better. With a quibble on "see you become a better man" (continued in the next exchange).
15. state of grace: spiritual state necessary to salvation. Pandarus takes it as referring to social rank and replies that he is not entitled to be addressed as "your Grace" (used to one of royal blood) but only as "your honor" and "your lordship."
18. in parts: having a different scoring for each voice or instrument.
30. to't: to the point (in contrast to "too courtly").

33. love's invisible soul: i.e. the quintessence of love made visible in her only.
36. her attributes: i.e. the qualities I have just ascribed to her.
39. complimental assault: ceremonial attack.
40. seethes: boils, i.e. is urgent. The Servant derides the word with his *Sodden* (= boiled) and *stew'd*, both implying connection with stews, i.e. brothels, and the sweating treatment for venereal disease.
43. Fair: i.e. fair fortune.
49. broken music: music, particularly of a courtly nature, employing several different varieties of instruments.
50. broke: interrupted. **cousin:** familiar term of address among social equals, not necessarily implying actual kinship.
51. piece it out: mend it. **56. Rude:** unpolished, amateurish.
57. in fits: by fits, when the humor takes you (?); perhaps with play on "in musical strains."
60. hedge us out: deprive us (by a subterfuge).
62. pleasant: merry, jocose.
66. Go to: an expression of remonstrance. **68. bob:** cheat.
75. care not for: pay no heed to.

call for him at supper, you will make his excuse.

Helen. My Lord Pandarus—

Pan. What says my sweet queen, my very very sweet queen?

Par. What exploit's in hand? Where sups he to-night?

Helen. Nay, but, my lord—

Pan. What says my sweet queen? My cousin will fall out with you.

Helen. You must not know where he sups.

Par. I'll lay my life, with my disposer Cressida.

Pan. No, no! no such matter, you are wide. Come, your disposer is sick.

Par. Well, I'll make 's excuse.

Pan. Ay, good my lord. Why should you say Cressida? No, your [poor] disposer's sick.

Par. I spy!

Pan. You spy? what do you spy?—Come, give me an instrument.—Now, sweet queen.

Helen. Why, this is kindly done.

Pan. My niece is horribly in love with a thing you have, sweet queen.

Helen. She shall have it, my lord, if it be not my Lord Paris.

Pan. He? no! she'll none of him. They two are twain.

Helen. Falling in, after falling out, may make them three.

Pan. Come, come, I'll hear no more of this, I'll sing you a song now.

Helen. Ay, ay, prithee now. By my troth, sweet [lord], thou hast a fine forehead.

Pan. Ay, you may, you may.

Helen. Let thy song be love. This love will undo us all. O Cupid, Cupid, Cupid!

Pan. Love? ay, that it shall, i' faith.

Par. Ay, good now, love, love, nothing but love.

[*Pan.* In good troth, it begins so.] [*Sings.*]

"Love, love, nothing but love, still love,
still more!
For O, love's bow
Shoots buck and doe.
The [shaft confounds]
Not that it wounds,
But tickles still the sore.
These lovers cry, O ho, they die!
Yet that which seems the wound to kill,
Doth turn O ho! to ha, ha, he!
So dying love lives still.
O ho! a while, but ha, ha, ha!
O ho! groans out for ha, ha, ha!—hey ho!"

Helen. In love, i' faith, to the very tip of the nose.

Par. He eats nothing but doves, love, and that breeds hot blood, and hot blood begets hot thoughts, and hot thoughts beget hot deeds, and hot deeds is love.

Pan. Is this the generation of love—hot blood, hot thoughts, and hot deeds? Why, they are vipers. Is love a generation of vipers? Sweet lord, who's a-field to-day?

Par. Hector, Deiphobus, Helenus, Antenor, and all the gallantry of Troy. I would fain have arm'd to-day, but my Nell would not have it so. How chance my brother Troilus went not?

Helen. He hangs the lip at something. You know all, Lord Pandarus.

Pan. Not I, honey-sweet queen. I long to hear how they sped to-day. You'll remember your brother's excuse?

Par. To a hair.

Pan. Farewell, sweet queen.

Helen. Commend me to your niece.

Pan. I will, sweet queen. [*Exit.*] *Sound a retreat.*

Par. They're come from the field. Let us to
Priam's hall
To greet the warriors. Sweet Helen, I must woo you
To help unarm our Hector. His stubborn buckles,
With [these] your white enchanting fingers touch'd,
Shall more obey than to the edge of steel,
Or force of Greekish sinews. You shall do more
Than all the island kings—disarm great Hector.

Helen. 'Twill make us proud to be his servant,
Paris!
Yea, what he shall receive of us in duty
Gives us more palm in beauty than we have,
Yea, overshines ourself.

Par. Sweet, above thought I love [thee]! *Exeunt.*

[Scene II]

Enter Pandarus, *Troilus'* Man, [*meeting*].

Pan. How now, where's thy master? At my cousin Cressida's?

Man. No, sir, [he] stays for you to conduct him thither.

[*Enter* Troilus.]

Pan. O, here he comes! How now, how now?

84–85. My . . . you: my cousin (i.e. Paris; cf. line 50) will be annoyed with you if you don't stop interrupting.
87. lay: wager. **my disposer Cressida.** Meaning uncertain; probably a courtly turn of phrase meaning that he is always at her disposal or command. **90. make 's:** make his.
93. I spy. Alluding to the children's game of that name.
102. twain: i.e. at odds; cf. *falling out*, line 103.
103–4. Falling . . . three: i.e. sexual relations, after a lover's quarrel, may result in a child, thus making two into three.
108. fine forehead. Considered a mark of manly beauty, though the reference here probably carries some kind of bawdy implication.
109. you may: go on, keep it up. **113. good now:** if you please.
118–20. The shaft . . . sore: i.e. Love's arrow does not kill what it wounds but it continues to irritate the wound. There is probably a play on *sore* = a buck of the fourth year; cf. line 117.
121. cry, O ho: i.e. sigh. **die.** Here and in *dying* (= by dying) in line 124 the word has its sexual sense "experience orgasm."

128. doves. Doves or pigeons were believed to be especially amorous. **love:** i.e. Helen.
129. hot blood: lustful feelings. **131. generation:** progeny.
132. they are vipers. Probably with reference to Acts 28:3: "And when Paul had gathered a number of sticks, and laid them on the fire, there came a viper out of the heat, and leapt on his hand" (Geneva).
133. generation of vipers. Cf., among other New Testament passages, Matthew 23:33: "O serpents, the generation of vipers, how should ye escape the damnation of hell?" (Geneva).
136. gallantry: gallants. **139. hangs the lip:** sulks.
142. sped: succeeded, prospered.
154. island kings: the Greek leaders.
157. Gives . . . palm: affords greater preeminence to us.

III.ii. Location: Troy. Calchas' garden.
3. stays: waits.

Tro. Sirrah, walk off. [*Exit Man.*]
Pan. Have you seen my cousin?
Tro. No, Pandarus, I stalk about her door,
Like to a strange soul upon the Stygian banks
Staying for waftage. O, be thou my Charon,
And give me swift transportance to these fields
Where I may wallow in the lily-beds
Propos'd for the deserver! O gentle Pandar,
From Cupid's shoulder pluck his painted wings,
And fly with me to Cressid!

Pan. Walk here i' th' orchard, I'll bring her straight. [*Exit.*]

Tro. I am giddy; expectation whirls me round;
Th' imaginary relish is so sweet
That it enchants my sense; what will it be,
When that the wat'ry palates taste indeed
Love's thrice-repured nectar? Death, I fear me,
Sounding destruction, or some joy too fine,
Too subtile, potent, tun'd too sharp in sweetness
For the capacity of my ruder powers.
I fear it much, and I do fear besides
That I shall lose distinction in my joys,
As doth a battle, when they charge on heaps
The enemy flying.

[*Enter* Pandarus.]

Pan. She's making her ready, she'll come straight. You must be witty now: she does so blush, and fetches her wind so short, as if she were fray'd with a spirit. I'll fetch her. It is the prettiest villain, she fetches her breath as short as a new-ta'en sparrow. [*Exit.*]

Tro. Even such a passion doth embrace my bosom:
My heart beats thicker than a feverous pulse,
And all my powers do their bestowing lose,
Like vassalage at [unawares] encount'ring
The eye of majesty.

Enter Pandar *and* Cressid.

Pan. Come, come, what need you blush? Shame's a baby. Here she is now, swear the oaths now to her that you have sworn to me. [*Cressida draws backward.*] What, are you gone again? You must be watch'd ere you be made tame, must you? Come your ways, come your ways; and you draw backward, we'll put you i' th' fills. Why do you not speak to her? Come, draw this curtain, and let's see your picture. Alas the day, how loath you are to offend daylight! And 'twere dark you'd close sooner. So, so, rub on and kiss the mistress. How now, a kiss in fee-farm? Build there, carpenter, the air is sweet. Nay, you shall fight your hearts out ere I part you—the falcon as the tercel, for all the ducks i' th' river. Go to, go to.

Tro. You have bereft me of all words, lady.

Pan. Words pay no debts, give her deeds; but she'll bereave you a' th' deeds too, if she call your activity in question. What, billing again? Here's "In witness whereof the parties interchangeably"—Come in, come in, I'll go get a fire. [*Exit.*]

Cres. Will you walk in, my lord?

Tro. O Cressid, how often have I wish'd me thus!

Cres. Wish'd, my lord? The gods grant—O my lord!

Tro. What should they grant? What makes this pretty abruption? What too curious dreg espies my sweet lady in the fountain of our love?

Cres. More dregs than water, if my [fears] have eyes.

Tro. Fears make devils of cherubins, they never see truly.

Cres. Blind fear that seeing reason leads finds safer footing than blind reason stumbling without fear. To fear the worst oft cures the worse.

Tro. O, let my lady apprehend no fear. In all Cupid's pageant there is presented no monster.

Cres. Nor nothing monstrous neither?

Tro. Nothing but our undertakings, when we vow to weep seas, live in fire, eat rocks, tame tigers; thinking it harder for our mistress to devise imposition enough than for us to undergo any difficulty impos'd. This [is] the monstruosity in love, lady, that the will is infinite and the execution confin'd, that the desire is boundless and the act a slave to limit.

Cres. They say all lovers swear more performance than they are able, and yet reserve an ability that

6. Sirrah: form of address to an inferior. **walk off:** leave us.
8. stalk: walk restlessly.
9. Stygian banks: the shore of the lake called Styx, traditionally listed as one of the four rivers of the underworld.
10. Charon: the ferryman of Hell, who for a fee gave transportation (*waftage*) to the souls of the dead across Styx.
11. fields: the Elysian fields, the pagan heaven and a part of hell, to which the souls of the good were transported after death. It was thought of as a place of great sensuous delight; cf. "wallow in the lily-beds," line 12. The lily image is both Virgilian and Biblical (Song of Solomon). **13. Propos'd for:** promised to.
16. orchard: garden.
21. wat'ry palates: senses (= tastes) watering with anticipation.
23. Sounding destruction: swooning disintegration.
24. subtile: rarefied (variant of *subtle*).
27. distinction . . . joys: the power of distinguishing between greater and lesser pleasures. **29. flying:** in flight.
31. witty: clever in small talk (to put Cressida at her ease).
32. fray'd . . . spirit: frightened by a ghost.
33. villain. Like *wretch*, used as a term of endearment.
36. thicker: faster.
37. powers . . . lose: faculties, mental and physical, lose their use.
38–39. vassalage . . . majesty: vassal(s) . . . king. Cf. *gallantry* in III.1.136. **40. what:** for what reason, why.
43. watch'd. To "watch" a hawk was to prevent it from sleeping in order to tame it.
44. Come your ways: come along.
46. fills: shafts (as of a horse-drawn wagon).
47. curtain: i.e. the veil Cressida is wearing. Curtains were hung in front of pictures. **49. close:** (1) come to terms; (2) come together.
49–50. rub . . . mistress. A metaphor from bowling, describing the action of the bowl as it rolls (*rubs*) on its way to touch (*kiss*) the Jack or small ball (*mistress*).
50. in fee-farm: i.e. of unlimited duration. *Fee-farm* = a grant of lands in fee, i.e. in perpetuity.
52. falcon . . . tercel: the female as well as the male hawk.
56–57. bereave . . . question: i.e. she'll wear you out physically. *In question* = into the matter.
58. "In . . . interchangeably": the formula for concluding indentures signed between two parties. The implied image of lips as seals is a common one.
65. abruption: breaking off. **too curious dreg:** speck of dirt (i.e. bad omen) overscrupulously imagined.
69. make . . . cherubins: i.e. can distort good into evil.
71. seeing: clear-eyed.
74–75. In . . . monster: i.e. nothing like a monster (i.e. a frightening figure) takes part in Cupid's masque or procession. Spenser, however, describes a "Masque of Cupid" (*Faerie Queene*, III.xii.3–26) in which many "monsters" appear (Danger, Fear, Suspect, Fury, Cruelty, etc.), and earlier examples of Cupid's court offer similar "monsters." **77. undertakings:** vows, promises.
81. monstruosity: monstrosity, i.e. something unnatural.
85. able: capable of.

they never perform; vowing more than the perfection of ten, and discharging less than the tenth part of one. They that have the voice of lions and the act of hares, are they not monsters?

Tro. Are there such? Such are not we. Praise us as we are tasted, allow us as we prove. Our head shall go bare till merit [crown it]. No [perfection] in reversion shall have a praise in present; we will not name desert before his birth, and being born, his addition shall be humble. Few words to fair faith. Troilus shall be such to Cressid as what envy can say worst shall be a mock for his truth, and what truth can speak truest not truer than Troilus.

Cres. Will you walk in, my lord?

[*Enter* PANDARUS.]

Pan. What, blushing still? Have you not done talking yet?

Cres. Well, uncle, what folly I commit, I dedicate to you.

Pan. I thank you for that; if my lord get a boy of you, you'll give him me. Be true to my lord; if he flinch, chide me for it.

Tro. You know now your hostages: your uncle's word and my firm faith.

Pan. Nay, I'll give my word for her too. Our kindred, though they be long ere they be woo'd, they are constant being won. They are burs, I can tell you, they'll stick where they are thrown.

Cres. Boldness comes to me now, and brings me heart.
Prince Troilus, I have lov'd you night and day
For many weary months.
Tro. Why was my Cressid then so hard to win?
Cres. Hard to seem won; but I was won, my lord,
With the first glance that ever—pardon me,
If I confess much, you will play the tyrant.
I love you now, but till now not so much
But I might master it. In faith I lie,
My thoughts were like unbridled children grown
Too headstrong for their mother. See, we fools!
Why have I blabb'd? Who shall be true to us,
When we are so unsecret to ourselves?
But though I lov'd you well, I woo'd you not,
And yet, good faith, I wish'd myself a man,
Or that we women had men's privilege
Of speaking first. Sweet, bid me hold my tongue,
For in this rapture I shall surely speak
The thing I shall repent. See, see, your silence,
[Cunning] in dumbness, from my weakness draws
My very soul of counsel! Stop my mouth.
Tro. And shall, albeit sweet music issues thence.
[*Kisses her.*]
Pan. Pretty, i' faith.

86–87. perfection of ten: performance of ten perfect lovers.
88. voice . . . hares: i.e. roar out their promises like the king of beasts and perform like the timorous and cowardly hare. Lions and hares are proverbially contrasted. **91. allow us:** give us approbation.
92–93. perfection in reversion: promise of future perfection.
94. addition: title of honor.
97. mock . . . truth: ridiculing of his faithfulness.
106. flinch: prove untrue. **121. But:** but that.
130. rapture: delirious state (earliest use in this sense).
133. soul of counsel: innermost feelings.

Cres. My lord, I do beseech you pardon me,
'Twas not my purpose thus to beg a kiss.
I am asham'd. O heavens, what have I done!
For this time will I take my leave, my lord.
Tro. Your leave, sweet Cressid!
Pan. Leave! And you take leave till to-morrow morning—
Cres. Pray you content you.
Tro. What offends you, lady?
Cres. Sir, mine own company.
Tro. You cannot shun yourself.
Cres. Let me go and try.
I have a kind of self resides with you;
But an unkind self, that itself will leave
To be another's fool. I would be gone.
Where is my wit? I know not what I speak.
Tro. Well know they what they speak that speak so wisely.
Cres. Perchance, my lord, I show more craft than love,
And fell so roundly to a large confession,
To angle for your thoughts, but you are wise,
Or else you love not; for to be wise and love
Exceeds man's might; that dwells with gods above.
Tro. O that I thought it could be in a woman—
As, if it can, I will presume in you—
To feed for [aye] her lamp and flames of love,
To keep her constancy in plight and youth,
Outliving beauties outward, with a mind
That doth renew swifter than blood decays!
Or that persuasion could but thus convince me
That my integrity and truth to you
Might be affronted with the match and weight
Of such a winnowed purity in love!
How were I then uplifted! but alas,
I am as true as truth's simplicity,
And simpler than the infancy of truth.
Cres. In that I'll war with you.
Tro. O virtuous fight,
When right with right wars who shall be most right!
True swains in love shall in the world to come
Approve their truth by Troilus. When their rhymes,
Full of protest, of oath and big compare,

141. And: if. **143. content you:** be still.
148–50. I have . . . fool: i.e. half of me is yours, but an unnatural half, that will thus desert its other half to become your fool (or dupe).
154. roundly: outspoken, frankly.
155. wise: i.e. too wise to be taken in by such "craft."
156. Or . . . not. In view of the next line and a half, *Or else* creates difficulty. It has been emended in various ways (e.g. *And then* [Capell]) or given strained interpretations (e.g. "or in other words" [Staunton]), but the confusion is probably Shakespeare's, who from time to time corners himself syntactically in this way.
156–57. to . . . above. A saying popular in various wordings; the ultimate source is Publilius Syrus (*Amare et sapere vix deo conceditur,* "To love and be wise is scarcely granted to a god").
161. in . . . youth: in youthful condition (hendiadys), i.e. unchanged by the passage of time.
162. beauties outward: external marks of beauty.
163. blood decays: the physical attributes decline.
166. affronted: faced, balanced. **match and weight:** equal amount.
168. uplifted: exalted in spirit.
169. simplicity: purity, state of being unmixed.
170. infancy of truth: i.e. truth at its most pure.
171. war: i.e. vie as an equal. **173. True:** constant.
174. Approve . . . Troilus: use Troilus as a touchstone for proving their faithfulness.
175. protest: protestations (of love). **big compare:** i.e. comparisons of their love with things of great magnitude.

Wants similes, truth tir'd with iteration,
As true as steel, as plantage to the moon,
As sun to day, as turtle to her mate,
As iron to adamant, as earth to th' centre,
[Yet] after all comparisons of truth
(As truth's authentic author to be cited)
"As true as Troilus" shall crown up the verse,
And sanctify the numbers.

Cres. Prophet may you be!
If I be false, or swerve a hair from truth,
When time is old [and] hath forgot itself,
When water-drops have worn the stones of Troy,
And blind oblivion swallow'd cities up,
And mighty states characterless are grated
To dusty nothing, yet let memory,
From false to false among false maids in love,
Upbraid my falsehood! When th' have said as false
As air, as water, wind, or sandy earth,
As fox to lamb, or wolf to heifer's calf,
Pard to the hind, or step-dame to her son,
Yea, let them say, to stick the heart of falsehood,
"As false as Cressid."

Pan. Go to, a bargain made, seal it, seal it, I'll be the witness. Here I hold your hand, here my cousin's. If ever you prove false one to another, since I have taken such pain to bring you together, let all pitiful goers-between be call'd to the world's end after my name; call them all Pandars. Let all constant men be Troiluses, all false women Cressids, and all brokers-between Pandars! Say, amen.

Tro. Amen.

Cres. Amen.

Pan. Amen. Whereupon I will show you a chamber, which bed, because it shall not speak of your pretty encounters, press it to death. Away!

Exeunt [Troilus and Cressida].

And Cupid grant all tongue-tied maidens here
Bed, chamber, Pandar to provide this gear! *Exit.*

[Scene III]

Enter Ulysses, Diomed, Nestor, Agamemnon, [Ajax, Menelaus, *and*] Calchas. [*Flourish.*]

Cal. Now, princes, for the service I have done,
Th' advantage of the time prompts me aloud
To call for recompense. Appear it to [your] mind,
That through the sight I bear in things to [come],
I have abandon'd Troy, left my possession,
Incurr'd a traitor's name, expos'd myself
From certain and possess'd conveniences
To doubtful fortunes, sequest'ring from me all
That time, acquaintance, custom, and condition
Made tame and most familiar to my nature;
And here, to do you service, am become
As new into the world, strange, unacquainted.
I do beseech you, as in way of taste,
To give me now a little benefit
Out of those many regist'red in promise,
Which you say live to come in my behalf.

Agam. What wouldst thou of us, Troyan? Make demand.

Cal. You have a Troyan prisoner call'd Antenor,
Yesterday took; Troy holds him very dear.
Oft have you (often have you thanks therefore)
Desir'd my Cressid in right great exchange,
Whom Troy hath still denied, but this Antenor,
I know, is such a wrest in their affairs
That their negotiations all must slack,
Wanting his manage, and they will almost
Give us a prince of blood, a son of Priam,
In change of him. Let him be sent, great princes,
And he shall buy my daughter; and her presence
Shall quite strike off all service I have done,
In most accepted pain.

Agam. Let Diomedes bear him,
And bring us Cressid hither; Calchas shall have
What he requests of us. Good Diomed,
Furnish you fairly for this interchange;
Withal bring word if Hector will to-morrow
Be answered in his challenge: Ajax is ready.

Dio. This shall I undertake, and 'tis a burthen
Which I am proud to bear. *Exit [with Calchas].*

[*Enter*] Achilles *and* Patroclus [*and*] *stand in* [*the door of*] *their tent.*

Ulyss. Achilles stands i' th' entrance of his tent.
Please it our general pass strangely by him,
As if he were forgot, and, princes all,
Lay negligent and loose regard upon him.
I will come last; 'tis like he'll question me
Why such unplausive eyes are bent, why turn'd on him?

176. Wants similes: run out of comparisons.
177. plantage: vegetation (earliest use).
178. turtle: turtledove (emblematic of constancy).
179. adamant: loadstone, magnet. **as earth . . . centre:** as objects on the surface of the earth to the centre of the earth. Cf. IV.ii.103–5. The earth was believed to be a "great magnet" with a core of homogeneous matter (see William Gilbert, *De Magnete*, 1600, Bk. I, Chap. 17). **181. authentic author:** authoritative source or prototype.
183. numbers: measures, verses.
188. characterless: i.e. without any written records left.
190. false maids in love: maids who are false in love.
191. th': they. **194. Pard:** panther or leopard.
195. stick: pierce, stab.
202. constant. The immediate context demands *inconstant*, but Shakespeare has allowed his knowledge of the story's outcome to take precedence.
208. chamber, which bed. Most editors insert *with a bed* (Hanmer) after *chamber*; but that Pandarus in the context should think of a chamber as essentially a bed is not out of character.
208–9. because . . . death. Alluding to pressing to death with weights as the penalty for persons arraigned for felony who refused to plead.
210. maidens: virgins (of either sex). **211. gear:** equipment.

III.iii. Location: The Greek camp.
2. Th' advantage . . . time: this propitious moment.
4. sight: spiritual vision, second sight.
5. my possession: all I own.
7. From: in exchange for. **certain:** secure.
8. sequest'ring: separating. **10. tame:** domestic.
12. new: new-born. **strange:** foreign. **13. taste:** foretaste.
20. therefore: therefor, for it.
21. in . . . exchange: in exchange for someone of high rank.
23. wrest: tuning key (producing harmony or order).
25. Wanting his manage: lacking his directing hand.
27. change of: exchange for. **29. strike off:** cancel out.
30. most accepted pain: i.e. labors that you have found highly acceptable. **34. Withal:** furthermore.
35. Be answered in: meet the answerer of. **36. burthen:** burden.
39. strangely: as if he were a stranger.
41. Lay . . . regard: i.e. look at him negligently and carelessly.
43. unplausive: disapproving.

If so, I have derision medicinable
To use between your strangeness and his pride,
Which his own will shall have desire to drink.
It may do good, pride hath no other glass
To show itself but pride; for supple knees
Feed arrogance and are the proud man's fees.
Agam. We'll execute your purpose, and put on
A form of strangeness as we pass along.
So do each lord, and either greet him not,
Or else disdainfully, which shall shake him more
Than if not look'd on. I will lead the way.
Achil. What comes the general to speak with me?
You know my mind, I'll fight no more 'gainst Troy.
Agam. What says Achilles? Would he aught with us?
Nest. Would you, my lord, aught with the general?
Achil. No.
Nest. Nothing, my lord.
Agam. The better.
[*Exeunt Agamemnon and Nestor*.]
Achil. Good day, good day.
Men. How do you? how do you? [*Exit*.]
Achil. What, does the cuckold scorn me?
Ajax. How now, Patroclus?
Achil. Good morrow, Ajax.
Ajax. Ha?
Achil. Good morrow.
Ajax. Ay, and good next day too. *Exit.*
Achil. What mean these fellows? Know they not Achilles?
Patr. They pass by strangely. They were us'd to bend,
To send their smiles before them to Achilles,
To come as humbly as they us'd to creep
To holy altars.
Achil. What, am I poor of late?
'Tis certain, greatness, once fall'n out with fortune,
Must fall out with men too. What the declin'd is,
He shall as soon read in the eyes of others
As feel in his own fall; for men, like butterflies,
Show not their mealy wings but to the summer,
And not a man, for being simply man,
Hath any honor, but honor for those honors
That are without him, as place, riches, and favor—
Prizes of accident as oft as merit,
Which when they fall, as being slippery standers,
The love that lean'd on them as slippery too,
Doth one pluck down another, and together
Die in the fall. But 'tis not so with me,
Fortune and I are friends. I do enjoy
At ample point all that I did possess,
Save these men's looks, who do methinks find out
Some thing not worth in me such rich beholding
As they have often given. Here is Ulysses,
I'll interrupt his reading.
How now, Ulysses?
Ulyss. Now, great Thetis' son!
Achil. What are you reading?
Ulyss. A strange fellow here
Writes me that man, how dearly ever parted,
How much in having, or without or in,
Cannot make boast to have that which he hath,
Nor feels not what he owes, but by reflection;
As when his virtues, aiming upon others,
Heat them, and they retort that heat again
To the first [giver].
Achil. This is not strange, Ulysses.
The beauty that is borne here in the face
The bearer knows not, but commends itself
To others' eyes; nor doth the eye itself,
That most pure spirit of sense, behold itself,
Not going from itself; but eye to eye opposed,
Salutes each other with each other's form;
For speculation turns not to itself,
Till it hath travell'd and is [mirror'd] there
Where it may see itself. This is not strange at all.
Ulyss. I do not strain at the position—
It is familiar—but at the author's drift,
Who in his circumstance expressly proves
That no man is the lord of any thing,
Though in and of him there be much consisting,
Till he communicate his parts to others;
Nor doth he of himself know them for aught,
Till he behold them formed in th' applause
Where th' are extended; who like an arch reverb'rate
The voice again, or like a gate of steel,
Fronting the sun, receives and renders back
His figure and his heat. I was much rapt in this,
And apprehended here immediately
Th' unknown Ajax.
Heavens, what a man is there! A very horse,
That has he knows not what. Nature, what things there are
Most [abject] in regard, and dear in use!
What things again most dear in the esteem,
And poor in worth! Now shall we see to-morrow—
An act that very chance doth throw upon him—
Ajax renown'd! O heavens, what some men do,
While some men leave to do!

44–45. I . . . pride: i.e. I can reply that it is scorn (*derision*) of his arrogance that causes the aloofness, and this will have the effect of curing his arrogance.
47–48. no . . . pride: no mirror to view itself in except an answering pride (the *strangeness* of line 45).
49. fees: assumed perquisites. **50. We'll.** The royal plural.
55. What: why. **69. next day.** Quibbling on *morrow* = to-morrow.
71. us'd: accustomed.
73. us'd. Perhaps an error for *use* = are accustomed.
75. fall'n out: out of favor (with reference to Fortune's wheel).
79. mealy: powdery. **82. without:** external to.
84. slippery standers: of uncertain footing.
85. love that lean'd: admiration that depended.
89. At ample point: i.e. at the top of Fortune's wheel.
91. rich beholding: noble observance.
96. Writes me: writes (a colloquialism). **how . . . parted:** however richly endowed with virtues. **97. having:** possessions.
99. owes: owns, possesses. **by reflection:** i.e. by the value placed on his virtues by others. **101. retort:** turn back, return.
106. most . . . sense. See note on I.i.58. Sight was considered the highest of the five senses.
107. Not . . . itself: unless it goes out from itself. **eye to eye opposed:** i.e. one man's eye looking upon another man's eye.
109. speculation: sight. **112. strain at:** find difficulty in.
113. drift: aim, tenor.
114. circumstance: argument. **115. lord:** master, possessor.
119. formed in: given form or substance by.
120. Where: i.e. of those to whom (providing the implied antecedent of the following *who*). **123. rapt:** caught up.
125. unknown: i.e. because his excellences are not yet seen by others.
128. abject . . . use: mean in estimation and valuable in practice.
133. leave to do: leave undone.

How some men creep in skittish Fortune's hall,
Whiles others play the idiots in her eyes!
How one man eats into another's pride,
While pride is fasting in his wantonness!
To see these Grecian lords!—why, even already
They clap the lubber Ajax on the shoulder,
As if his foot were on brave Hector's breast,
And great Troy shriking.
Achil. I do believe it, for they pass'd by me
As misers do by beggars, neither gave to me
Good word nor look. What, are my deeds forgot?
Ulyss. Time hath, my lord, a wallet at his back,
Wherein he puts alms for oblivion,
A great-siz'd monster of ingratitudes.
Those scraps are good deeds past, which are devour'd
As fast as they are made, forgot as soon
As done. Perseverance, dear my lord,
Keeps honor bright; to have done is to hang
Quite out of fashion, like a rusty mail
In monumental mock'ry. Take the instant way,
For honor travels in a strait so narrow,
Where one but goes abreast. Keep then the path,
For emulation hath a thousand sons
That one by one pursue. If you give way,
Or [hedge] aside from the direct forthright,
Like to an ent'red tide, they all rush by
And leave you [hindmost];
[Or like a gallant horse fall'n in first rank,
Lie there for pavement to the abject [rear],
O'errun and trampled on.] Then what they do in present,
Though less than yours in [past], must o'ertop yours;
For Time is like a fashionable host
That slightly shakes his parting guest by th' hand,
And with his arms outstretch'd as he would fly,
Grasps in the comer. The welcome ever smiles,
And farewell goes out sighing. Let not virtue seek
Remuneration for the thing it was;
For beauty, wit,
High birth, vigor of bone, desert in service,
Love, friendship, charity, are subjects all
To envious and calumniating Time.
One touch of nature makes the whole world kin,
That all with one consent praise new-born gawds,
Though they are made and moulded of things past,
And [give] to dust, that is a little gilt,
More laud than gilt o'erdusted.
The present eye praises the present object.
Then marvel not, thou great and complete man,
That all the Greeks begin to worship Ajax;
Since things in motion sooner catch the eye
[Than] what stirs not. The cry went once on thee,
And still it might, and yet it may again,
If thou wouldst not entomb thyself alive
And case thy reputation in thy tent,
Whose glorious deeds but in these fields of late
Made emulous missions 'mongst the gods themselves,
And drave great Mars to faction.
Achil. Of this my privacy
I have strong reasons.
Ulyss. But 'gainst your privacy
The reasons are more potent and heroical.
'Tis known, Achilles, that you are in love
With one of Priam's daughters.
Achil. Ha? known?
Ulyss. Is that a wonder?
The providence that's in a watchful state
Knows almost every [grain of Pluto's gold],
Finds bottom in th' uncomprehensive depth,
Keeps place with thought and almost, like the gods,
Do thoughts unveil in their dumb cradles.
There is a mystery (with whom relation
Durst never meddle) in the soul of state,
Which hath an operation more divine
Than breath or pen can give expressure to.
All the commerce that you have had with Troy
As perfectly is ours as yours, my lord,
And better would it fit Achilles much
To throw down Hector than Polyxena.
But it must grieve young Pyrrhus now at home,
When fame shall in our islands sound her trump,
And all the Greekish girls shall tripping sing,
"Great Hector's sister did Achilles win,
But our great Ajax bravely beat down him."
Farewell, my lord; I as your lover speak:
The fool slides o'er the ice that you should break.
[*Exit*.]

134. creep: move so as to attract no notice. **skittish:** fickle.
135. play . . . eyes: i.e. make fools of themselves to attract her attention.
137. fasting . . . wantonness: abstaining out of capriciousness (?) or arrogance (?). **141. shriking:** shrieking (variant form).
145. wallet . . . back. Such a wallet appears in a number of earlier sources (e.g. Spenser's *Faerie Queene*, VI.viii.23–24), but is there symbolic of things man would be glad to forget, not his good deeds.
146. alms for oblivion: good deeds to be forgotten.
147. monster: i.e. Time.
150. Perseverance. Accented on the second syllable. **dear my:** my dear (a common type of transposition).
152–53. rusty . . . mock'ry: a suit of armor grown rusty from disuse set up as a mocking trophy of past action.
153. Take . . . way: move forward continually.
155. one . . . abreast: i.e. men must walk in single file. **Keep . . . path:** maintain your place on the path against competitors (*O.E.D.*, *v.*, 33b). **158. forthright:** straight path.
161–63. Or . . . on. These lines, which add little and disturb the metre, may represent a first thought later cancelled by Shakespeare.
162. abject rear: inferior rear ranks.
167. as . . . fly. The image suggests the fickleness of time; cf. the Latin tag *Tempus fugit* (= time flies).
172. vigor of bone: physical strength.
175. One . . . kin: i.e. there is one natural trait that all men share.
176. gawds: toys, trifles. **178. a little gilt:** thinly gilded over.
179. gilt o'erdusted: true gold obscured with dust.
181. complete: perfect. **184. cry:** applause.
187. case: enclose (as in a coffin, dead and buried).
189. Made . . . themselves: i.e. caused the very gods to take part in the battles in emulation.
190. drave . . . faction: drove . . . taking sides. Possibly a reference to the *Iliad*, Bk. V, where Mars interferes on the side of the Trojans.
192. heroical: becoming to a hero.
194. one . . . daughters: i.e. Polyxena.
196. providence: foresight. Cf. *prescience*, I.iii.199.
197. Pluto: god of the underworld; perhaps here confused, as elsewhere, even in antiquity, with Plutus, god of riches.
198. uncomprehensive: incomprehensible.
199–200. Keeps . . . cradles: keeps abreast of what is being thought and can even anticipate it before it is uttered.
201–2. with . . . meddle: i.e. of which no report can be given.
205. commerce: dealings.
209. must: will certainly. **Pyrrhus:** Achilles' son, called also Neoptolemus. **214. lover:** friend, well-wisher.
215. The fool . . . break. Meaning uncertain; perhaps, "The fool (Ajax) seems to be getting away with an apparently dangerous game, which you should take action to stop."

Patr. To this effect, Achilles, have I mov'd you.
A woman impudent and mannish grown
Is not more loath'd than an effeminate man
In time of action. I stand condemn'd for this;
They think my little stomach to the war,
And your great love to me, restrains you thus.
Sweet, rouse yourself, and the weak wanton Cupid
Shall from your neck unloose his amorous fold,
And like [a] dewdrop from the lion's mane,
Be shook to air.

Achil. Shall Ajax fight with Hector?

Patr. Ay, and perhaps receive much honor by him.

Achil. I see my reputation is at stake,
My fame is shrowdly gor'd.

Patr. O then beware!
Those wounds heal ill that men do give themselves.
Omission to do what is necessary
Seals a commission to a blank of danger,
And danger like an ague subtly taints
Even then when they sit idly in the sun.

Achil. Go call Thersites hither, sweet Patroclus.
I'll send the fool to Ajax and desire him
T' invite the Troyan lords after the combat
To see us here unarm'd. I have a woman's longing,
An appetite that I am sick withal,
To see great Hector in his weeds of peace,
To talk with him, and to behold his visage,
Even to my full of view.

Enter THERSITES.

A labor sav'd!

Ther. A wonder!

Achil. What?

Ther. Ajax goes up and down the field, asking for himself.

Achil. How so?

Ther. He must fight singly to-morrow with Hector, and is so prophetically proud of an heroical cudgelling that he raves in saying nothing.

Achil. How can that be?

Ther. Why, 'a stalks up and down like a peacock—a stride and a stand; ruminates like an hostess that hath no arithmetic but her brain to set down her reckoning; bites his lip with a politic regard, as who should say there were wit in this head and 'twould out—and so there is; but it lies as coldly in him as fire in a flint, which will not show without knocking. The man's undone for ever, for if Hector break not his neck i' th' combat, he'll break't himself in vainglory. He knows not me. I said, "Good morrow, Ajax"; and he replies, "Thanks, Agamemnon." What think you of this man that takes me for the general? He's grown a very land-fish, languageless, a monster. A plague of opinion! a man may wear it on both sides, like a leather jerkin.

Achil. Thou must be my ambassador [to him], Thersites.

Ther. Who, I? Why, he'll answer nobody; he professes not answering. Speaking is for beggars; he wears his tongue in 's arms. I will put on his presence, let Patroclus make demands to me; you shall see the pageant of Ajax.

Achil. To him, Patroclus. Tell him I humbly desire the valiant Ajax to invite the [most] valorous Hector to come unarm'd to my tent, and to procure safe-conduct for his person of the magnanimous and most illustrious six-or-seven-times-honor'd captain-general of the army, Agamemnon, [et cetera]. Do this.

Patr. Jove bless great Ajax!

Ther. Hum?

Patr. I come from the worthy Achilles—

Ther. Ha?

Patr. Who most humbly desires you to invite Hector to his tent—

Ther. Hum?

Patr. And to procure safe-conduct from Agamemnon.

Ther. Agamemnon?

Patr. Ay, my lord.

Ther. Ha?

Patr. What say you to't?

Ther. God buy you, with all my heart.

Patr. Your answer, sir.

Ther. If to-morrow be a fair day, by aleven of the clock it will go one way or other. Howsoever, he shall pay for me ere he has me.

Patr. Your answer, sir.

Ther. Fare ye well, with all my heart.

Achil. Why, but he is not in this tune, is he?

Ther. No; but [he's] out of tune thus. What music will be in him when Hector has knock'd out his brains, I know not; but I am sure none, unless the fiddler Apollo get his sinews to make catlings on.

Achil. Come, thou shalt bear a letter to him straight.

Ther. Let me bear another to his horse, for that's the more capable creature.

Achil. My mind is troubled, like a fountain stirr'd,
And I myself see not the bottom of it.

[*Exeunt Achilles and Patroclus.*]

Ther. Would the fountain of your mind were clear again, that I might water an ass at it! I had rather be a tick in a sheep than such a valiant ignorance. [*Exit.*]

218. effeminate: unmanly. **220. stomach to:** appetite for.
223. fold: embrace.
228. shrowdly gor'd: sorely (variant form of *shrewdly*) wounded (as by an animal's horn).
231. Seals . . . danger: i.e. licenses danger to do as it pleases. The reference is to a warrant with blanks to be filled in at the recipient's pleasure. **238. withal:** with. **239. weeds:** garments.
252. hostess: hostess of an inn.
254. politic regard: an appearance of being judicious.
257. knocking: striking. **258. his:** i.e. Ajax'.
263. land-fish: a fish that lives on land, hence an unnatural creature (*O.E.D.*); cf. *monster* later in the line.
264. opinion: reputation.
268–69. professes: makes a particular point of.
270. in 's: in his. **271. presence:** demeanor, bearing.
293. God buy you: God be with you, i.e. goodby.
295. aleven: eleven (a characteristic Shakespearean spelling).
296. Howsoever: whichever way.
297. pay . . . has me: i.e. pay dearly before he has the better of me.
301. out of tune: completely disordered (unharmonious).
303–4. fiddler Apollo. Apollo was the god of music.
304. make catlings on: make lute strings (made of catgut) of.
307. capable: intelligent.
311. might . . . ass. Even an ass would refuse to drink the present muddy water. **312. valiant ignorance:** vainglorious fool.

[ACT IV, SCENE I]

Enter at one door AENEAS [*with a torch*]; *at another,* PARIS, DEIPHOBUS, ANTENOR, DIOMED *the Grecian,* [*and others*] *with torches.*

Par. See ho! who is that there?
Dei. It is the Lord Aeneas.
Aene. Is the Prince there in person?
Had I so good occasion to lie long
As [you], Prince Paris, nothing but heavenly business
Should rob my bed-mate of my company.
Dio. That's my mind too. Good morrow, Lord Aeneas.
Par. A valiant Greek, Aeneas, take his hand,
Witness the process of your speech, wherein
You told how Diomed, a whole week by days,
Did haunt you in the field.
Aene. Health to you, valiant sir,
During all question of the gentle truce;
But when I meet you arm'd, as black defiance
As heart can think or courage execute.
Dio. The one and other Diomed embraces.
Our bloods are now in calm, and, so long, health!
[But] when contention and occasion meet,
By Jove I'll play the hunter for thy life,
With all my force, pursuit, and policy.
Aene. And thou shalt hunt a lion that will fly
With his face backward. In humane gentleness,
Welcome to Troy! now, by Anchises' life,
Welcome indeed! By Venus' hand I swear,
No man alive can love in such a sort
The thing he means to kill, more excellently.
Dio. We sympathize. Jove, let Aeneas live,
If to my sword his fate be not the glory,
A thousand complete courses of the sun!
But in mine emulous honor let him die,
With every joint a wound, and that to-morrow!
Aene. We know each other well.
Dio. We do, and long to know each other worse.
Par. This is the most despiteful gentle greeting,
The noblest hateful love, that e'er I heard of.
What business, lord, so early?
Aene. I was sent for to the King, but why, I know not.
Par. His purpose meets you; 'twas to bring this Greek
To Calchas' house, and there to render him,
For the enfreed Antenor, the fair Cressid.
Let's have your company, or if you please,
Haste there before us. I constantly believe
(Or rather call my thought a certain knowledge)
My brother Troilus lodges there to-night.
Rouse him and give him note of our approach,
With the whole quality wherefore. I fear
We shall be much unwelcome.
Aene. That I assure you.
Troilus had rather Troy were borne to Greece
Than Cressid borne from Troy.
Par. There is no help.
The bitter disposition of the time
Will have it so. On, lord, we'll follow you.
Aene. Good morrow, all. [*Exit.*]
Par. And tell me, noble Diomed—faith, tell me true,
Even in soul of sound good-fellowship—
Who, in your thoughts, deserves fair Helen best,
Myself, or Menelaus?
Dio. Both alike.
He merits well to have her that doth seek her,
Not making any scruple of her soil,
With such a hell of pain and world of charge;
And you as well to keep her that defend her,
Not palating the taste of her dishonor,
With such a costly loss of wealth and friends.
He like a puling cuckold would drink up
The lees and dregs of a flat tamed piece;
You like a lecher out of whorish loins
Are pleas'd to breed out your inheritors.
Both merits pois'd, each weighs nor less nor more,
But he as he, the heavier for a whore.
Par. You are too bitter to your country-woman.
Dio. She's bitter to her country. Hear me, Paris:
For every false drop in her bawdy veins,
A Grecian's life hath sunk; for every scruple
Of her contaminated carrion weight,
A Troyan hath been slain. Since she could speak,
She hath not given so many good words breath
As for her Greeks and Troyans suff'red death.
Par. Fair Diomed, you do as chapmen do,
Dispraise the thing that they desire to buy,
But we in silence hold this virtue well,
We'll not commend what we intend to sell.
Here lies our way. *Exeunt.*

[SCENE II]

Enter TROILUS *and* CRESSIDA.

Tro. Dear, trouble not yourself, the morn is cold.

IV.i. Location: Troy. A street.
9. **process:** course, tenor.
10. **a whole . . . days:** every day for a week.
12. **During . . . of:** in all our talk during. 19. **policy:** cunning.
20–21. **lion . . . backward:** i.e. if he retreats, Aeneas will retreat like the lion, without turning his back in flight. His failure to reject the idea that he might retreat under any circumstances is perhaps a courteous gesture to Diomedes as a guest.
22, 23. **Anchises, Venus.** Aeneas' father and mother.
26. **We sympathize:** I am of the same mind.
37. **meets you:** is here before you. 41. **constantly:** firmly.
45. **quality wherefore:** occasion of it.
49. **disposition . . . time:** state of present affairs.
53. **in soul:** in the spirit. 57. **soil:** moral stain, dishonor.
58. **world of charge:** tremendous cost.
60. **palating the taste:** tasting the (foul) taste.
63. **flat tamed piece:** (1) opened cask of dead wine, (2) stale used-up whore. 65. **inheritors:** descendants.
67. **he as he:** i.e. one as the other.
71. **scruple:** smallest unit of weight.
72. **carrion:** rotten, putrefied (as a dead body).
76. **chapmen:** buyers, hagglers.
77. **Dispraise . . . buy.** Cf. Proverbs 20:14: "It is naught, it is naught, sayeth the buyer: but when he is gone apart, he boasteth" (Geneva).
78–79. **But . . . sell:** i.e. we think there is great virtue in silence and will not commend (like cheap hawkers) what we intend to sell (at the highest cost, our lives if necessary). Some editors emend *not* to *but* (after Jackson's conjecture in Cambridge) for easier sense: we'll commend only what we want to dispose of (not Helen). Cf. Sonnet 21.14, "I will not praise that purpose not to sell."

IV.ii. Location: Troy. The court of Calchas' house.

Cres. Then, sweet my lord, I'll call mine uncle down,
He shall unbolt the gates.
Tro. Trouble him not;
To bed, to bed. Sleep kill those pretty eyes,
And give as soft attachment to thy senses
As infants empty of all thought!
Cres. Good morrow then.
Tro. I prithee now to bed.
Cres. Are you a-weary of me?
Tro. O Cressida! but that the busy day,
Wak'd by the lark, hath rous'd the ribald crows,
And dreaming night will hide our joys no longer,
I would not from thee.
Cres. Night hath been too brief.
Tro. Beshrew the witch! with venomous wights she stays
As tediously as hell, but flies the grasps of love
With wings more momentary-swift than thought.
You will catch cold and curse me.
Cres. Prithee tarry,
You men will never tarry.
O foolish Cressid! I might have still held off,
And then you would have tarried. Hark, there's one up.
Pan. [*Within.*] What's all the doors open here?
Tro. It is your uncle.

[*Enter* PANDARUS.]

Cres. A pestilence on him! now will he be mocking.
I shall have such a life!
Pan. How now, how now, how go maidenheads?
Here, you maid! where's my cousin Cressid?
Cres. Go hang yourself, you naughty mocking uncle!
You bring me to do—and then you flout me too.
Pan. To do what, to do what? let her say what.
What have I brought you to do?
Cres. Come, come, beshrew your heart, you'll ne'er be good,
Nor suffer others.

Pan. Ha, ha! Alas, poor wretch! a poor [*capocchia*]! hast not slept to-night? Would he not, a naughty man, let it sleep? A bugbear take him!

Cres. Did not I tell you? Would he were knock'd i' th' head! *One knocks.*
Who's that at door? Good uncle, go and see.
My lord, come you again into my chamber.
You smile and mock me, as if I meant naughtily.
Tro. Ha, ha!
Cres. Come, you are deceived, I think of no such thing. *Knock.*
How earnestly they knock! Pray you come in.
I would not for half Troy have you seen here.
Exeunt [*Troilus and Cressida*].

Pan. Who's there? What's the matter? Will you beat down the door? How now, what's the matter?

[*Enter* AENEAS.]

Aene. Good morrow, lord, good morrow.
Pan. Who's there? My Lord Aeneas! By my troth,
I knew you not. What news with you so early?
Aene. Is not Prince Troilus here?
Pan. Here? what should he do here?
Aene. Come, he is here, my lord, do not deny him.
It doth import him much to speak with me.

Pan. Is he here, say you? It's more than I know, I'll be sworn. For my own part, I came in late. What should he do here?

Aene. Who!—nay then. Come, come, you'll do him wrong ere you are ware. You'll be so true to him, to be false to him. Do not you know of him, but yet go fetch him hither, go.

[*Enter* TROILUS.]

Tro. How now, what's the matter?
Aene. My lord, I scarce have leisure to salute you,
My matter is so rash. There is at hand
Paris your brother, and Deiphobus,
The Grecian Diomed, and our Antenor
Deliver'd to [us]; and [for him] forthwith,
Ere the first sacrifice, within this hour,
We must give up to Diomedes' hand
The Lady Cressida.
Tro. Is it so concluded?
Aene. By Priam and the general state of Troy.
They are at hand and ready to effect it.
Tro. How my achievements mock me!
I will go meet them; and, my Lord Aeneas,
We met by chance, you did not find me here.
Aene. Good, good, my lord, the secrets of neighbor Pandar
Have not more gift in taciturnity.
Exeunt [*Troilus and Aeneas*].

Pan. Is't possible? No sooner got but lost? The devil take Antenor! the young prince will go mad. A plague upon Antenor! I would they had broke 's neck!

Enter CRESSID.

[*Cres.*] How now? what's the matter? who was here?
Pan. Ah, ah!
Cres. Why sigh you so profoundly? Where's my lord? Gone? Tell me, sweet uncle, what's the matter?
Pan. Would I were as deep under the earth as I am above!
Cres. O the gods! what's the matter?
Pan. Pray thee get thee in. Would thou hadst ne'er been born! I knew thou wouldest be his death. O poor gentleman! A plague upon Antenor!

4. kill: put to rest (by closing). **5. attachment:** imprisonment.
9. ribald: scurrilous, irreverent.
12. Beshrew: curses on. **venomous wights:** people who dislike each other. **24. maid:** (1) waiting-woman; (2) maiden, virgin.
26. do: (1) act; (2) have sexual relations (slang).
30. suffer others: allow others (to be good).
31. capocchia: simpleton, innocent (Italian).
33. bugbear: hobgoblin.

50. import: concern. **54. Who:** stop, hold (a form of *ho*).
56. to: as to. **know of him:** i.e. admit that he is here.
60. rash: urgent. **67. state:** council of state.
73. Have . . . taciturnity: are no more characterized by a proper silence (than I will be).

Cres. Good uncle, I beseech you, on my knees [I beseech you], what's the matter?

Pan. Thou must be gone, wench, thou must be gone; thou art chang'd for Antenor. Thou must to thy father, and be gone from Troilus. 'Twill be his death, 'twill be his bane, he cannot bear it.

Cres. O you immortal gods! I will not go.

Pan. Thou must.

Cres. I will not, uncle. I have forgot my father,
I know no touch of consanguinity;
No kin, no love, no blood, no soul so near me
As the sweet Troilus. O you gods divine,
Make Cressid's name the very crown of falsehood,
If ever she leave Troilus! Time, force, and death,
Do to this body what extremes you can;
But the strong base and building of my love
Is as the very centre of the earth,
Drawing all things to it. I'll go in and weep.

Pan. Do, do.

Cres. Tear my bright hair, and scratch my praised cheeks,
Crack my clear voice with sobs, and break my heart,
With sounding Troilus. I will not go from Troy.
[*Exeunt.*]

[Scene III]

Enter Paris, Troilus, Aeneas, Deiphobus, Antenor, Diomedes.

Par. It is great morning, and the hour prefix'd
For her delivery to this valiant Greek
Comes fast upon. Good my brother Troilus,
Tell you the lady what she is to do,
And haste her to the purpose.

Tro. Walk into her house.
I'll bring her to the Grecian presently;
And to his hand when I deliver her,
Think it an altar, and thy brother Troilus
A priest there off'ring to it his own heart. [*Exit.*]

Par. I know what 'tis to love,
And would, as I shall pity, I could help!
Please you walk in, my lords. *Exeunt.*

[Scene IV]

Enter Pandarus *and* Cressida.

Pan. Be moderate, be moderate.

Cres. Why tell you me of moderation?
The grief is fine, full, perfect, that I taste,
And violenteth in a sense as strong
As that which causeth it. How can I moderate it?
If I could temporize with my affections,

Or brew it to a weak and colder palate,
The like allayment could I give my grief:
My love admits no qualifying dross,
No more my grief, in such a precious loss.

Enter Troilus.

Pan. Here, here, here he comes. [Ah], sweet ducks!

Cres. O Troilus, Troilus! [*Embracing him.*]

Pan. What a pair of spectacles is here! Let me embrace too. "O heart," as the goodly saying is,
"O heart, heavy heart,
Why sigh'st thou without breaking?"
where he answers again,
"Because thou canst not ease thy smart
By friendship nor by speaking."
There was never a truer rhyme. Let us cast away nothing, for we may live to have need of such a verse. We see it, we see it. How now, lambs?

Tro. Cressid, I love thee in so strain'd a purity
That the blest gods, as angry with my fancy,
More bright in zeal than the devotion which
Cold lips blow to their deities, take thee from me.

Cres. Have the gods envy?

Pan. Ay, ay, ay, ay, 'tis too plain a case.

Cres. And is it true that I must go from Troy?

Tro. A hateful truth.

Cres. What, and from Troilus too?

Tro. From Troy and Troilus.

Cres. Is't possible?

Tro. And suddenly, where injury of chance
Puts back leave-taking, justles roughly by
All time of pause, rudely beguiles our lips
Of all rejoindure, forcibly prevents
Our lock'd embrasures, strangles our dear vows
Even in the birth of our own laboring breath.
We two, that with so many thousand sighs
Did buy each other, must poorly sell ourselves
With the rude brevity and discharge of one.
Injurious time now with a robber's haste
Crams his rich thiev'ry up, he knows not how.
As many farewells as be stars in heaven,
With distinct breath and consign'd kisses to them,
He fumbles up into a loose adieu;
And scants us with a single famish'd kiss,
Distasted with the salt of broken tears.

Aene. (*Within.*) My lord, is the lady ready?

Tro. Hark, you are call'd. Some say the Genius [so]
Cries ["come"] to him that instantly must die.
—Bid them have patience, she shall come anon.

93. bane: death (properly, by poison).
97. touch of consanguinity: feeling of blood relationship.
104–5. centre . . . it. See the note on III.ii.179.
109. sounding: uttering.

IV.iii. Location: Troy. Before Calchas' house.
1. great morning: broad daylight. **6. presently:** at once.

IV.iv. Location: Calchas' house.
3. fine: refined, pure.
4. violenteth: rages with violence. **sense:** emotional feeling.
6. affections: emotions, passions.

7. it: i.e. the affections (viewed as a whole). **palate:** taste.
10. in . . . loss: in the loss of so precious an object.
14. pair of spectacles: two (sad) sights (with play on "eye-glasses").
21. rhyme. No source is known for these verses.
23. We see it: i.e. we can see such a situation coming, alas.
24. strain'd: refined. **25. fancy:** love.
26. bright in zeal: burning in ardor. **33. suddenly:** immediately.
34. Puts back leave-taking: forestalls farewells.
36. rejoindure: (1) answering farewells; (2) being rejoined (in a kiss).
37. embrasures: embraces.
43. he . . . how: helter-skelter, without discrimination.
45. With . . . them: each separately uttered and ratified with an accompanying kiss. **46. loose:** casual.
48. Distasted: made bitter.
50. Genius. Each man was believed to have his own attendant spirit who presided over his destiny from birth to death.

Pan. Where are my tears? Rain, to lay this wind,
or my heart will be blown up by [th' root]. [*Exit.*]
Cres. I must then to the Grecians?
Tro. No remedy.
Cres. A woeful Cressid 'mongst the merry Greeks!
When shall we see again?
Tro. Hear me, love. Be thou but true of heart—
Cres. I true? How now? what wicked deem is this?
Tro. Nay, we must use expostulation kindly,
For it is parting from us.
I speak not "be thou true" as fearing thee,
For I will throw my glove to Death himself
That there is no maculation in thy heart;
But "be thou true" say I to fashion in
My sequent protestation: be thou true,
And I will see thee.
Cres. O, you shall be expos'd, my lord, to dangers
As infinite as imminent! but I'll be true.
Tro. And I'll grow friend with danger. Wear this sleeve.
Cres. And you this glove. When shall I see you?
Tro. I will corrupt the Grecian sentinels,
To give thee nightly visitation.
But yet be true.
Cres. O heavens, "be true" again?
Tro. Hear why I speak it, love.
The Grecian youths are full of quality;
[Their loving well compos'd with gift of nature,
Flowing] and swelling o'er with arts and exercise.
How novelty may move, and parts with [person],
Alas, a kind of godly jealousy
(Which I beseech you call a virtuous sin)
Makes me afeard.
Cres. O heavens, you love me not.
Tro. Die I a villain then!
In this I do not call your faith in question
So mainly as my merit. I cannot sing,
Nor heel the high lavolt, nor sweeten talk,
Nor play at subtile games—fair virtues all,
To which the Grecians are most prompt and pregnant—
But I can tell that in each grace of these
There lurks a still and dumb-discoursive devil
That tempts most cunningly, but be not tempted.
Cres. Do you think I will?
Tro. No,
But something may be done that we will not,
And sometimes we are devils to ourselves,
When we will tempt the frailty of our powers,
Presuming on their changeful potency.
Aene. (*Within.*) Nay, good my lord!
Tro. Come kiss, and let us part.
Par. (*Within.*) Brother Troilus!
Tro. Good brother, come you hither,
And bring Aeneas and the Grecian with you.
Cres. My lord, will you be true?
Tro. Who, I? Alas, it is my vice, my fault:
Whiles others fish with craft for great opinion,
I with great truth catch mere simplicity;
Whilst some with cunning gild their copper crowns,
With truth and plainness I do wear mine bare.
Fear not my truth: the moral of my wit
Is "plain and true"; there's all the reach of it.

[*Enter* Aeneas, Paris, Antenor, Deiphobus, *and* Diomedes.]

Welcome, Sir Diomed! Here is the lady
Which for Antenor we deliver you.
At the port, lord, I'll give her to thy hand,
And by the way possess thee what she is.
Entreat her fair, and, by my soul, fair Greek,
If e'er thou stand at mercy of my sword,
Name Cressid, and thy life shall be as safe
As Priam is in Ilion.
Dio. Fair Lady Cressid,
So please you, save the thanks this prince expects.
The lustre in your eye, heaven in your cheek,
Pleads your fair usage, and to Diomed
You shall be mistress, and command him wholly.
Tro. Grecian, thou dost not use me courteously,
To shame the seal of my petition to thee
In praising her. I tell thee, lord of Greece,
She is as far high-soaring o'er thy praises
As thou unworthy to be call'd her servant.
I charge thee use her well, even for my charge;
For by the dreadful Pluto, if thou dost not,
Though the great bulk Achilles be thy guard,
I'll cut thy throat.
Dio. O, be not mov'd, Prince Troilus.

53. Rain . . . wind: i.e. tears to allay this sighing.
54. my . . . root. It was believed that sighing shortened life by drawing blood from the heart. Pandarus ludicrously inflates his sighs into a gale that threatens to uproot his heart as if it were a tree.
56. merry Greeks. See the note on I.ii.109.
59. deem: surmise, thought.
61. it: i.e. the opportunity to "use expostulation."
62. fearing thee: doubting your faith. **63. throw . . . to:** challenge.
64. maculation: stain of inconstancy.
65. fashion in: prepare the way for.
70, 71. sleeve, glove. Common love tokens, though a sleeve was commonly given by the woman. Both men's and women's sleeves were detachable. **72. corrupt:** bribe.
73. To: in order to. **nightly:** at night.
76. quality: admirable qualities.
77–78. Their . . . exercise: i.e. in their pursuit of love they have the advantage of fine natural endowments, increased to overflowing by acquired graces in which they are well practiced.
79. novelty: the new manner (of their wooing). **parts with person:** accomplishments in addition to good looks.
80. godly jealousy. A Biblical echo; see 2 Corinthians 11:2: "For I am jealous over you, with godly jealousy" (Geneva).
86. high lavolt. The lavolta was a dance for two persons, requiring a good deal of bounding (hence "high").
88. prompt and pregnant: inclined and ready.
90. dumb-discoursive: communicating without speech.
96. will tempt: insist upon tempting. **frailty:** susceptibility.
97. Presuming . . . potency: relying presumptuously on their strength, which is in fact very unstable.
103. craft: cunning. **opinion:** reputation, approbation.
104. I . . . simplicity: "my use of bare truth wins for me the character of a plain, simple man" (Deighton).
107. moral . . . wit: the maxim that expresses my mind.
108. all the reach: the whole extent. **111. port:** city gate.
112. possess thee: explain to you.
113. Entreat: treat. **fair:** courteously, honorably.
117. So please: if it please.
122–23. shame . . . her: i.e. disdain to ratify my request by praising her (in those terms), i.e. fail to "entreat her fair" by addressing her at once as a professed lover (the *servant* of line 125). Many editors unnecessarily adopt Theobald's emendation of *seal* to *zeal*.
126. use: treat. **even . . . charge:** i.e. on the basis of my demand alone. **128. great bulk:** huge-framed. **129. mov'd:** angry.

Let me be privileg'd by my place and message,
To be a speaker free. When I am hence,
I'll answer to my lust, and know you, lord,
I'll nothing do on charge. To her own worth
She shall be priz'd; but that you say, "Be't so,"
I speak it in my spirit and honor, "No."
Tro. Come, to the port. I'll tell thee, Diomed,
This brave shall oft make thee to hide thy head.
Lady, give me your hand, and as we walk,
To our own selves bend we our needful talk.
[*Exeunt Troilus, Cressida, and Diomedes. Sound trumpet.*]
Par. Hark, Hector's trumpet!
Aene. How have we spent this morning!
The Prince must think me tardy and remiss,
That swore to ride before him to the field.
Par. 'Tis Troilus' fault. Come, come, to field with him.
[[*Dei.*] Let us make ready straight.
Aene. Yea, with a bridegroom's fresh alacrity
Let us address to tend on Hector's heels.
The glory of our Troy doth this day lie
On his fair worth and single chivalry.] *Exeunt.*

[SCENE V]

Enter AJAX *armed*, ACHILLES, PATROCLUS, AGAMEMNON, MENELAUS, ULYSSES, NESTOR, *etc.*

Agam. Here art thou in appointment fresh and fair,
Anticipating time. With starting courage,
Give with thy trumpet a loud note to Troy,
Thou dreadful Ajax, that the appalled air
May pierce the head of the great combatant,
And hale him hither.
Ajax. Thou, trumpet, there's my purse.
Now crack thy lungs, and split thy brazen pipe.
Blow, villain, till thy sphered bias cheek
Outswell the colic of puff'd Aquilon;
Come, stretch thy chest, and let thy eyes spout blood;
Thou blowest for Hector. [*Trumpet sounds.*]
Ulyss. No trumpet answers.
Achil. 'Tis but early days.

[*Enter* DIOMED *and* CRESSID.]

Agam. Is not yond Diomed, with Calchas' daughter?
Ulyss. 'Tis he, I ken the manner of his gait,
He rises on the toe. That spirit of his
In aspiration lifts him from the earth.
Agam. Is this the Lady Cressid?
Dio. Even she.
Agam. Most dearly welcome to the Greeks, sweet lady. [*Kisses her.*]
Nest. Our general doth salute you with a kiss.
Ulyss. Yet is the kindness but particular,
'Twere better she were kiss'd in general.
Nest. And very courtly counsel. I'll begin.
So much for Nestor. [*Kisses her.*]
Achil. I'll take that winter from your lips, fair lady;
Achilles bids you welcome. [*Kisses her.*]
Men. I had good argument for kissing once.
Patr. But that's no argument for kissing now,
For thus popp'd Paris in his hardiment,
And parted thus you and your argument. [*Kisses her.*]
Ulyss. O deadly gall, and theme of all our scorns,
For which we lose our heads to gild his horns!
Patr. The first was Menelaus' kiss, this, mine;
Patroclus kisses you. [*Kisses her again.*]
Men. O, this is trim!
Patr. Paris and I kiss evermore for him.
Men. I'll have my kiss, sir. Lady, by your leave.
Cres. In kissing, do you render or receive?
Patr. Both take and give.
Cres. I'll make my match to live,
The kiss you take is better than you give;
Therefore no kiss.
Men. I'll give you boot, I'll give you three for one.
Cres. You are an odd man, give even or give none.
Men. An odd man, lady? Every man is odd.
Cres. No, Paris is not, for you know 'tis true
That you are odd, and he is even with you.
Men. You fillip me a' th' head.
Cres. No, I'll be sworn.
Ulyss. It were no match, your nail against his horn.
May I, sweet lady, beg a kiss of you?
Cres. You may.
Ulyss. I do desire it.
Cres. Why, beg then.
Ulyss. Why then for Venus' sake, give me a kiss
When Helen is a maid again and his.
Cres. I am your debtor, claim it when 'tis due.
Ulyss. Never's my day, and then a kiss of you.

130. place and message: office and errand, i.e. status as an ambassador.
132. answer . . . lust: be answerable (on the battlefield) for what I please to do (?). *Lust* = pleasure, desire.
133. To: in accordance with. **137. brave:** defiance.
140. spent: used up. **146. address:** make ready.
148. single chivalry: knightly prowess as shown in single combat.

IV.v. Location: The Greek camp. Lists set out.
1. appointment: equipment (suitable to a knight).
2. starting courage: rousing spirit.
3. trumpet: (probably) trumpeter (as in line 6).
4. dreadful: inspiring dread.
6. hale: pull (alluding to the notion, already seen in I.iii.66–68, that words or sounds tie the hearer's ear to the speaker or source of the sound).
7. brazen pipe: i.e. the trumpeter's throat; "brazen" by transference from the instrument.
8. villain: fellow (not derogatory). **sphered bias cheek:** cheek puffed out like a weighted bowl (used in the game of bowls).
9. colic . . . Aquilon: i.e. the tremendously distended cheeks of puffing Aquilon (Greek name for Boreas, the north wind). The comparison is drawn from the representations of Boreas and other winds in the corners of old maps, to which Ajax ludicrously adds the roundness of a belly distended by the wind of colic.
11. for: to summon.

13. yond: yonder man.
20. but particular: limited only to one (playing on *general*).
24. winter: i.e. the cold lips of ancient Nestor.
26. good argument: good reason, i.e. Helen.
28. thus . . . hardiment: in this manner Paris popped in his bold stroke (with bawdy equivoque).
30. theme . . . scorns: the subject that has brought scorn upon all of us. **33. this is trim:** a fine thing (ironic).
37. I'll . . . live: I'll wager my life that (?).
40. boot: something in addition.
41. odd: (1) singular, strange; (2) single (because he has lost his wife Helen).
45. fillip . . . head: snap your fingernail against my head, i.e. twit me for my cuckold's horns. **No . . . sworn:** no, indeed, I don't imply any such thing. **50. his:** i.e. Menelaus'.

Dio. Lady, a word. I'll bring you to your father.
[*Exit with Cressida.*]
Nest. A woman of quick sense.
Ulyss. Fie, fie upon her!
There's language in her eye, her cheek, her lip,
Nay, her foot speaks; her wanton spirits look out
At every joint and motive of her body.
O, these encounterers, so glib of tongue,
That give a coasting welcome ere it comes,
And wide unclasp the tables of their thoughts
To every ticklish reader! set them down
For sluttish spoils of opportunity,
And daughters of the game. *Flourish.*
All. The Troyans' trumpet.

Enter all of Troy: [HECTOR *armed*, PARIS, AENEAS, HELENUS, TROILUS, *and* ATTENDANTS].

Agam. Yonder comes the troop.
Aene. Hail, all the state of Greece! What shall be done
To him that victory commands? or do you purpose
A victor shall be known? Will you the knights
Shall to the edge of all extremity
Pursue each other, or shall they be divided
By any voice or order of the field?
Hector bade ask.
Agam. Which way would Hector have it?
Aene. He cares not, he'll obey conditions.
Agam. 'Tis done like Hector.
[*Achil.*] But securely done,
A little proudly, and great deal misprising
The knight oppos'd.
Aene. If not Achilles, sir,
What is your name?
Achil. If not Achilles, nothing.
Aene. Therefore Achilles, but what e'er, know this:
In the extremity of great and little,
Valor and pride excel themselves in Hector,
The one almost as infinite as all,
The other blank as nothing. Weigh him well,
And that which looks like pride is courtesy.
This Ajax is half made of Hector's blood,
In love whereof, half Hector stays at home;
Half heart, half hand, half Hector comes to seek
This blended knight, half Troyan and half Greek.

Achil. A maiden battle then? O, I perceive you.
[*Enter* DIOMEDES.]
Agam. Here is Sir Diomed. Go, gentle knight,
Stand by our Ajax. As you and Lord Aeneas
Consent upon the order of their fight,
So be it, either to the uttermost,
Or else a breath. The combatants being kin
Half stints their strife before their strokes begin.
[*Ajax and Hector enter the lists.*]
[*Ulyss.* They are oppos'd already.]
[*Agam.*] What Troyan is that same that looks so heavy?
Ulyss. The youngest son of Priam, a true knight,
Not yet mature, yet matchless, firm of word,
Speaking [in] deeds, and deedless in his tongue,
Not soon provok'd, nor being provok'd soon calm'd;
His heart and hand both open and both free,
For what he has he gives, what thinks he shows,
Yet gives he not till judgment guide his bounty,
Nor dignifies an impare thought with breath;
Manly as Hector, but more dangerous,
For Hector in his blaze of wrath subscribes
To tender objects, but he in heat of action
Is more vindicative than jealous love.
They call him Troilus, and on him erect
A second hope, as fairly built as Hector.
Thus says Aeneas, one that knows the youth
Even to his inches, and with private soul
Did in great Ilion thus translate him to me.
Alarum. [*Hector and Ajax fight.*]
Agam. They are in action.
Nest. Now, Ajax, hold thine own!
Tro. Hector, thou sleep'st,
Awake thee!
Agam. His blows are well dispos'd. There, Ajax!
Trumpets cease.
Dio. You must no more.
Aene. Princes, enough, so please you.
Ajax. I am not warm yet, let us fight again.
Dio. As Hector pleases.
Hect. Why then will I no more.
Thou art, great lord, my father's sister's son,
A cousin-german to great Priam's seed;
The obligation of our blood forbids
A gory emulation 'twixt us twain.
Were thy commixtion Greek and Troyan so
That thou couldst say, "This hand is Grecian all,
And this is Troyan; the sinews of this leg
All Greek, and this all Troy; my mother's blood

54. quick sense: lively wit (but the words also mean "wanton sensuality," which accords with Ulysses' judgment).
57. motive: moving part (a sense found only in Shakespeare, according to *O.E.D.*). **59. a coasting:** an (amorous) approach.
60. wide . . . thoughts: i.e. open wide the book of their minds (*tables* = tablets). **61. ticklish:** prurient, lustful.
62. sluttish . . . opportunity: "corrupt wenches, of whose chastity every opportunity may make prey" (Johnson).
63. the game: sexual sport. **65. state:** nobility.
65–66. What . . . commands: i.e. how shall the victor be honored. The phrasing is Biblical; cf. 1 Samuel 17:26: "What shall be done to the man that killeth this Philistim, and taketh away the shame from Israel?" (Geneva). **67. Will you:** is it your will.
69. divided: separated (if the combat becomes dangerous).
73. securely: overconfidently.
74. misprising: undervaluing, i.e. scorning.
77. what e'er: whoever you may be.
78. In . . . little: i.e. at the two extremes on the scale of magnitude.
79. excel: outdo, surpass.
83. Ajax . . . blood. See the note on II.ii.73.

87. maiden battle: a fight not carried to a bloody outcome.
90. order of: rules governing. **92. breath:** gentle exercise.
95. heavy: sad.
98. Speaking . . . tongue: i.e. he acts rather than talks about acting.
100. free: generous; so also in line 139.
103. impare: unconsidered (Lat. *imparatus*).
105–6. subscribes . . . objects: i.e. shows the "vice of mercy" (V.iii.37) to those (such as defeated opponents) who arouse his pity (*tender objects* = objects of tenderness).
107. vindicative: vindictive, vengeful.
111. to his inches: i.e. minutely, intimately. **with private soul:** in personal confidence. **112. translate:** interpret.
116. dispos'd: placed. **121. cousin-german:** first cousin.
124. so: ordered in such a way.

Runs on the dexter cheek, and this sinister
Bounds in my father's": by Jove multipotent,
Thou shouldst not bear from me a Greekish member
Wherein my sword had not impressure made
[Of our rank feud]; but the just gods gainsay
That any [drop] thou borrow'dst from thy mother,
My sacred aunt, should by my mortal sword
Be drained! Let me embrace thee, Ajax.
By him that thunders, thou hast lusty arms!
Hector would have them fall upon him thus.
Cousin, all honor to thee!
Ajax. I thank thee, Hector.
Thou art too gentle and too free a man.
I came to kill thee, cousin, and bear hence
A great addition earned in thy death.
Hect. Not Neoptolemus so mirable,
On whose bright crest Fame with her loud'st Oyes
Cries, "This is he," could promise to himself
A thought of added honor torn from Hector.
Aene. There is expectance here from both the sides,
What further you will do.
Hect. We'll answer it:
The issue is embracement. Ajax, farewell.
Ajax. If I might in entreaties find success,
As seld I have the chance, I would desire
My famous cousin to our Grecian tents.
Dio. 'Tis Agamemnon's wish, and great Achilles
Doth long to see unarm'd the valiant Hector.
Hect. Aeneas, call my brother Troilus to me,
And signify this loving interview
To the expecters of our Troyan part;
Desire them home. Give me thy hand, my cousin.
I will go eat with thee and see your knights.

[Agamemnon *and the rest come forward.*]

Ajax. Great Agamemnon comes to meet us here.
Hect. The worthiest of them tell me name by name;
But for Achilles, my own searching eyes
Shall find him by his large and portly size.
Agam. Worthy all arms! as welcome as to one
That would be rid of such an enemy.
[But that's no welcome. Understand more clear,
What's past and what's to come is strew'd with husks
And formless ruin of oblivion;
But in this extant moment, faith and troth,
Strain'd purely from all hollow bias-drawing,
Bids thee, with most divine integrity,]
From heart of very heart, great Hector, welcome.
Hect. I thank thee, most imperious Agamemnon.
Agam. [*To Troilus.*] My well-fam'd lord of Troy, no less to you.
Men. Let me confirm my princely brother's greeting:
You brace of warlike brothers, welcome hither.
Hect. Who must we answer?
Aene. The noble Menelaus.
Hect. O, you, my lord? By Mars his gauntlet, thanks!
Mock not [that I] affect th' untraded [oath],
Your quondam wife swears still by Venus' glove.
She's well, but bade me not commend her to you.
Men. Name her not now, sir, she's a deadly theme.
Hect. O, pardon, I offend.
Nest. I have, thou gallant Troyan, seen thee oft,
Laboring for destiny, make cruel way
Through ranks of Greekish youth, and I have seen thee,
As hot as Perseus, spur thy Phrygian steed,
Despising many forfeits and subduements,
When thou hast hung [thy] advanced sword i' th' air,
Not letting it decline on the declined,
That I have said to some my standers-by
"Lo Jupiter is yonder, dealing life!"
And I have seen thee pause and take thy breath,
When that a ring of Greeks have [hemm'd] thee in,
Like an Olympian wrestling. This have I seen,
But this thy countenance, still lock'd in steel,
I never saw till now. I knew thy grandsire,
And once fought with him. He was a soldier good,
But, by great Mars, the captain of us all,
Never like thee. O, let an old man embrace thee,
And, worthy warrior, welcome to our tents.
Aene. 'Tis the old Nestor.
Hect. Let me embrace thee, good old chronicle,
That hast so long walk'd hand in hand with time.
Most reverend Nestor, I am glad to clasp thee.
Nest. I would my arms could match thee in contention,
[As they contend with thee in courtesy].
Hect. I would they could.
Nest. Ha!
By this white beard, I'd fight with thee to-morrow.
Well, welcome, welcome!—I have seen the time.
Ulyss. I wonder now how yonder city stands
When we have here her base and pillar by us.
Hect. I know your favor, Lord Ulysses, well.
Ah, sir, there's many a Greek and Troyan dead
Since first I saw yourself and Diomed
In Ilion, on your Greekish embassy.
Ulyss. Sir, I foretold you then what would ensue.
My prophecy is but half his journey yet,

128. dexter: right. **sinister:** left (here accented on the second syllable). **129. multipotent:** all-powerful.
132. rank: intemperate. **gainsay:** forbid.
136. him that thunders: Jove. **137. thus:** i.e. in a friendly embrace.
141. great addition: title of honor.
142. Neoptolemus so mirable: i.e. Achilles so worthy of admiration. As Johnson suggests, Shakespeare seems to have taken Neoptolemus as Achilles' family name because his son was called Pyrrhus Neoptolemus. **143. Oyes:** hear ye (from French *oyez*).
156. expecters . . . part: i.e. those of our Trojan side who are waiting to learn the outcome. **162. portly:** imposing.
163. Worthy all arms: worthy of all honor belonging to the profession of a knight. **as to:** i.e. as you can be to.
169. Strain'd . . . bias-drawing: rendered free of all insincere deviations from straightforward truth. *Bias-drawing* = the curved course of a bowl weighted on one side. **170. divine:** godlike.
172. imperious: imperial.
178. untraded: unfamiliar (i.e. not worn out by frequent usage).
179. quondam: former.
184. Laboring for destiny: i.e. like an agent of fate (in ending lives).
186. Perseus. See the note on I.iii.42.
187. Despising . . . subduements: disdaining to slay or subjugate many (who had been overcome in combat). Cf. lines 105–6.
188. advanced: raised.
194. Olympian: i.e. one of the gods, dwellers on Mount Olympus. **wrastling:** wrestling (variant form). **195. still:** always hitherto.
202. chronicle: storehouse of history.
210. I . . . time: i.e. the time has been (when I would have fought with you). **213. favor:** countenance.

For yonder walls that pertly front your town,
Yon towers, whose wanton tops do buss the clouds,
Must kiss their own feet.
Hect. I must not believe you.
There they stand yet, and modestly I think
The fall of every Phrygian stone will cost
A drop of Grecian blood. The end crowns all,
And that old common arbitrator, Time,
Will one day end it.
Ulyss. So to him we leave it.
Most gentle and most valiant Hector, welcome!
After the general, I beseech you next
To feast with me and see me at my tent.
Achil. I shall forestall thee, Lord Ulysses, thou!
Now, Hector, I have fed mine eyes on thee;
I have with exact view perus'd thee, Hector,
And quoted joint by joint.
Hect. Is this Achilles?
Achil. I am Achilles.
Hect. Stand fair, I pray thee, let me look on thee.
Achil. Behold thy fill.
Hect. Nay, I have done already.
Achil. Thou art too brief. I will the second time,
As I would buy thee, view thee limb by limb.
Hect. O, like a book of sport thou'lt read me o'er;
But there's more in me than thou understand'st.
Why dost thou so oppress me with thine eye?
Achil. Tell me, you heavens, in which part of his body
Shall I destroy him—whether there, or there, or there?—
That I may give the local wound a name,
And make distinct the very breach whereout
Hector's great spirit flew. Answer me, heavens!
Hect. It would discredit the blest gods, proud man,
To answer such a question. Stand again.
Think'st thou to catch my life so pleasantly
As to prenominate in nice conjecture
Where thou wilt hit me dead?
Achil. I tell thee, yea.
Hect. Wert thou an oracle to tell me so,
I'd not believe thee. Henceforth guard thee well,
For I'll not kill thee there, nor there, nor there,
But by the forge that [stithied] Mars his helm,
I'll kill thee every where, yea, o'er and o'er.
You wisest Grecians, pardon me this brag.
His insolence draws folly from my lips,
But I'll endeavor deeds to match these words,
Or may I never—
Ajax. Do not chafe thee, cousin,
And you, Achilles, let these threats alone,
Till accident or purpose bring you to't.
You may have every day enough of Hector,

219. **pertly front**: boldly serve as a front to. 220. **buss**: kiss.
222. **modestly**: at a modest estimate, without exaggeration.
224. **The end crowns all.** A version of the Latin *Finis coronat opus*, "the end crowns the work." 232. **perus'd**: thoroughly surveyed.
233. **quoted**: scrutinized. 235. **fair**: i.e. still.
239. **like . . . sport**: i.e. as material for a game, deciding by what rules of combat he may be killed.
248. **Stand again**: i.e. let me view you again.
249. **pleasantly**: easily.
250. **prenominate**: name in advance of the fact. **nice**: precise.
255. **stithied**: forged.

If you have stomach. The general state, I fear,
Can scarce entreat you to be odd with him.
Hect. I pray you let us see you in the field;
We have had pelting wars since you refus'd
The Grecians' cause.
Achil. Dost thou entreat me, Hector?
To-morrow do I meet thee, fell as death;
To-night all friends.
Hect. Thy hand upon that match.
Agam. First, all you peers of Greece, go to my tent;
There in the full convive we. Afterwards,
As Hector's leisure and your bounties shall
Concur together, severally entreat him.
[Beat loud the taborins,] let the trumpets blow,
That this great soldier may his welcome know.
Exeunt [*all but Troilus and Ulysses*].
Tro. My Lord Ulysses, tell me, I beseech you,
In what place of the field doth Calchas keep?
Ulyss. At Menelaus' tent, most princely Troilus.
There Diomed doth feast with him to-night,
Who neither looks upon the heaven nor earth,
But gives all gaze and bent of amorous view
On the fair Cressid.
Tro. Shall I, sweet lord, be bound to you so much,
After we part from Agamemnon's tent,
To bring me thither?
Ulyss. You shall command me, sir.
But gentle tell me, of what honor was
This Cressida in Troy? Had she no lover there
That wails her absence?
Tro. O, sir, to such as boasting show their scars
A mock is due. Will you walk on, my lord?
She was belov'd, [she lov'd]; she is, and doth:
But still sweet love is food for fortune's tooth.
Exeunt.

[ACT V, SCENE I]

Enter ACHILLES *and* PATROCLUS.

Achil. I'll heat his blood with Greekish wine to-night,
Which with my scimitar I'll cool to-morrow.
Patroclus, let us feast him to the height.
Patr. Here comes Thersites.

Enter THERSITES.

Achil. How now, thou [core] of envy?
Thou crusty batch of nature, what's the news?

264. **stomach**: the inclination. **general state**: the Greek leaders.
265. **be odd**: be at odds, i.e. meet in combat.
267. **pelting**: paltry, slight. **refus'd**: renounced.
269. **fell**: ruthless, terrible. 272. **in . . . we**: we all feast together.
274. **severally entreat**: individually invite him (to visit you).
275. **taborins**: a kind of drums, struck with a single stick.
278. **keep**: dwell. 282. **bent**: inclination. 284. **bound**: indebted.
287. **gentle**: in courtesy. **honor**: position, reputation.
290–91. **to . . . due**: those who boast of their wounds justly incur derision. Troilus thus indirectly admits that he is the lover in question.
293. **fortune's**: i.e. ill fortune's.

V.i. Location: The Greek camp. Before Achilles' tent.
4. **core.** See the note on II.i.6.
5. **crusty batch of nature**: scabbed lump of nature's dough (a metaphor from baking bread; cf. *cobloaf*, II.i.38). Some editors, following Theobald, emend *batch* to *botch* (= ulcer or sore).

Ther. Why, thou picture of what thou seemest, and idol of idiot-worshippers, here's a letter for thee.

Achil. From whence, fragment?

Ther. Why, thou full dish of fool, from Troy.

Patr. Who keeps the tent now?

Ther. The surgeon's box, or the patient's wound.

Patr. Well said, adversity! and what needs [these] tricks?

Ther. Prithee be silent, [boy], I profit not by thy talk. Thou art said to be Achilles' male varlot.

Patr. Male varlot, you rogue! What's that?

Ther. Why, his masculine whore. Now the rotten diseases of the south, the guts-griping, ruptures, [catarrhs,] loads a' gravel in the back, lethargies, cold palsies, raw eyes, dirt-rotten livers, whissing lungs, bladders full of imposthume, sciaticas, lime-kills i' th' palm, incurable bone-ache, and the rivell'd fee-simple of the tetter, take and take again such preposterous discoveries!

Patr. Why, thou damnable box of envy, thou, what means thou to curse thus?

Ther. Do I curse thee?

Patr. Why, no, you ruinous butt, you whoreson indistinguishable cur, no.

Ther. No? why art thou then exasperate, thou idle immaterial skein of sleave-silk, thou green sarcenet flap for a sore eye, thou tossel of a prodigal's purse, thou? Ah, how the poor world is pest'red with such water-flies, diminutives of nature!

Patr. Out, gall!

Ther. Finch-egg!

Achil. My sweet Patroclus, I am thwarted quite
From my great purpose in to-morrow's battle.
Here is a letter from Queen Hecuba,
A token from her daughter, my fair love,
Both taxing me and gaging me to keep
An oath that I have sworn. I will not break it.
Fall Greeks, fail fame, honor or go or stay,
My major vow lies here; this I'll obey.
Come, come, Thersites, help to trim my tent;
This night in banqueting must all be spent.
Away, Patroclus! [*Exeunt Achilles and Patroclus.*]

Ther. With too much blood and too little brain, these two may run mad, but, if with too much brain and too little blood they do, I'll be a curer of madmen. Here's Agamemnon, an honest fellow enough, and one that loves quails, but he has not so much brain as ear-wax; and the goodly transformation of Jupiter there, his [brother,] the bull, the primitive statue and oblique memorial of cuckolds, a thrifty shoeing-horn in a chain, [hanging] at his [brother's] leg—to what form but that he is, should wit larded with malice, and malice fac'd with wit, turn him to? To an ass, were nothing, he is both ass and ox; to an ox, were nothing, [he is] both ox and ass. To be a [dog], a moile, a cat, a fitchook, a toad, a lezard, an owl, a puttock, or a herring without a roe, I would not care; but to be Menelaus, I would conspire against destiny. Ask me [not] what I would be if I were not Thersites, for I care not to be the louse of a lazar, so I were not Menelaus. Hey-day! sprites and fires!

Enter AGAMEMNON, [HECTOR, TROILUS, AJAX,] ULYSSES, NESTOR, [MENELAUS,] *and* DIOMED, *with lights.*

Agam. We go wrong, we go wrong.

Ajax. No, yonder 'tis,
There where we see the lights.

Hect. I trouble you.

Ajax. No, not a whit.

[*Enter* ACHILLES.]

Ulyss. Here comes himself to guide you.

Achil. Welcome, brave Hector, welcome, princes all.

Agam. So now, fair Prince of Troy, I bid good night.
Ajax commands the guard to tend on you.

6–7. picture . . . idiot-worshippers: i.e. you look like a man, but you are only an image of a man, and of a man who is an idiot.
8. fragment: crust (following the metaphor of line 5).
9. full . . . fool: container brimming over with foolishness (with a pun on *fool/full* and a play on *fool* as the name of a dessert made of custard, a trifle).
10. Who . . now. Perhaps an indication that Ajax has been aping Achilles' arrogant behavior (cf. V.iv.14–15). Its principal purpose seems to be the opportunity it gives Thersites for his pun on *tent* (= surgical probe) in the next line.
12. adversity: i.e. one who talks at cross-purposes (referring to the quibble on *tent*).
15. varlot: attendant (variant form of *varlet*). Cf. *boy* in line 14.
18. south. The south wind was traditionally associated with disease, but the reference here is probably to Italy, specifically Naples (see the note on II.iii.18–19).
18–23. guts-griping . . . tetter. This "preposterous" catalogue of diseases arising from sexual license apparently draws on a passage in Greene's *Planetomachia*, 1585 (ed. Grosart, V, 103–4) listing "peculiar diseases" associated with the planet Venus.
19. loads . . . back: kidney stones. **lethargies:** comatose states.
20. whissing: wheezing. **21. imposthume:** abscesses.
21–22. lime-kills . . . palm: i.e. the burning sensation of psoriasis of the palm. *Lime-kills* is a variant spelling of *lime-kilns* (operated at exceedingly high heat).
22–23. rivell'd . . . tetter: shrivelled perpetual legacy of eczema, ringworm, etc. **23. take:** afflict, plague (used of diseases).
23–24. preposterous discoveries: revelations of perversion (such as the relationship that Thersites alleges between Achilles and Patroclus).
26. means thou: meanest thou (colloquial elision).
28. ruinous butt: broken-down wine cask.
29. indistinguishable: shapeless, deformed.
30. exasperate: exasperated.
31. immaterial . . . sleave-silk: worthless (because unwoven) loose knot of raw, untwisted silk. **sarcenet:** fine silk cloth of taffeta weave. **32. tossel:** tassel. **33. pest'red:** overrun.
35. gall: blister, or oak-gall (a round excrescence).
36. Finch-egg. Perhaps extending the idea of *diminutives of nature*; the finch was a very small bird and would lay a very small egg.
41. taxing . . . gaging: i.e. enjoining . . . binding.
48. blood: passion, irrational impulses.
50–51. I'll . . . madmen. The point is that the contingency just mentioned is an impossibility. **52. quails:** prostitutes (slang).
53–54. goodly . . . bull. With ironic reference to Jupiter's taking the form of a bull in order to carry off Europa; Menelaus resembles the metamorphosed Jupiter only in being horned.
54. primitive statue: prototype, prime example.
55. oblique. Not satisfactorily explained; possibly referring to the slanting horns of the cuckold.
55–56. thrifty . . . leg: i.e. a serviceable tool ready to Agamemnon's hand. One kind of horn leads Shakespeare to another.
57. larded: interlarded.
58. fac'd: lined. Most editors adopt the F1 reading *forced* (= stuffed), perhaps correctly.
61. moile: mule (variant form). **fitchook:** fitch, polecat (variant of *fitchew*). **lezard:** lizard (variant form).
62. puttock: chicken-hawk, kite. **herring . . . roe:** i.e. a herring of the least valuable sort.
63. care: mind (so *care . . . be* in line 65 = wouldn't mind being). **to be:** if I had to be (or, perhaps, to escape being).
65. lazar: leper.
66. sprites and fires. Referring to those entering with torches (like will-o'-the-wisps); *sprites* = spirits. **72. to:** that will.

Hect. Thanks and good night to the Greeks' general.
Men. Good night, my lord.
Hect. Good night, sweet Lord Menelaus.
Ther. Sweet draught! "Sweet," quoth 'a! Sweet sink, sweet sewer.
Achil. Good night and welcome, both [at once], to those
That go or tarry.
Agam. Good night.
Exeunt Agamemnon, Menelaus.
Achil. Old Nestor tarries; and you too, Diomed,
Keep Hector company an hour or two.
Dio. I cannot, lord, I have important business,
The tide whereof is now. Good night, great Hector.
Hect. Give me your hand.
Ulyss. [*Aside to Troilus.*] Follow his torch, he goes to Calchas' tent.
I'll keep you company.
Tro. Sweet sir, you honor me.
Hect. And so good night.
[*Exit Diomedes, Ulysses and Troilus following.*]
Achil. Come, come, enter my tent.
Exeunt [*Achilles, Hector, Ajax, and Nestor*].
Ther. That same Diomed's a false-hearted rogue, a most unjust knave. I will no more trust him when he leers than I will a serpent when he hisses. He will spend his mouth and promise, like Brabbler the hound, but when he performs, astronomers foretell it: it is prodigious, there will come some change; the sun borrows of the moon when Diomed keeps his word. I will rather leave to see Hector than not to dog him. They say he keeps a Troyan drab, and uses the traitor Calchas' tent. I'll after—nothing but lechery! all incontinent varlots! [*Exit.*]

[Scene II]

Enter Diomed.

Dio. What, are you up here, ho? Speak!
Cal. [*Within.*] Who calls?
Dio. Diomed. Calchas, I think. Where's your daughter?
Cal. [*Within.*] She comes to you.

[*Enter* Troilus *and* Ulysses *at a distance; after them,* Thersites.]

Ulyss. Stand where the torch may not discover us.

Enter Cressid.

Tro. Cressid comes forth to him.
Dio. How now, my charge?
Cres. Now, my sweet guardian, hark, a word with you. [*Whispers.*]
Tro. Yea, so familiar?
Ulyss. She will sing any man at first sight.
Ther. And any man may sing her, if he can take her cliff; she's noted.
Dio. Will you remember?
[*Cres.*] Remember? yes.
Dio. Nay, but do then,
And let your mind be coupled with your words.
Tro. What shall she remember?
Ulyss. List!
Cres. Sweet honey Greek, tempt me no more to folly.
Ther. Roguery!
Dio. Nay then—
Cres. I'll tell you what—
Dio. Fo, fo, come, tell a pin. You are forsworn.
Cres. In faith, I cannot. What would you have me do?
Ther. A juggling trick—to be secretly open.
Dio. What did you swear you would bestow on me?
Cres. I prithee do not hold me to mine oath,
Bid me do any thing but that, sweet Greek.
Dio. Good night.
Tro. Hold, patience.
Ulyss. How now, Troyan?
Cres. Diomed—
Dio. No, no, good night, I'll be your fool no more.
Tro. Thy better must.
Cres. Hark a word in your ear.
Tro. O plague and madness!
Ulyss. You are moved, Prince, let us depart, I pray,
Lest your displeasure should enlarge itself
To wrathful terms. This place is dangerous,
The time right deadly. I beseech you go.
Tro. Behold, I pray you.
Ulyss. Now, good my lord, go off;
You flow to great [distraction]. Come, my lord.
Tro. I prithee stay.
Ulyss. You have not patience, come.
Tro. I pray you stay. By hell and all hell's torments,
I will not speak a word.
Dio. And so good night.
Cres. Nay, but you part in anger.
Tro. Doth that grieve thee?
O withered truth!
Ulyss. How now, my lord?
Tro. By Jove
I will be patient.
Cres. Guardian! Why, Greek!

75. draught: privy. **76. sink:** cesspool.
77. at once: at the same time. **83. tide:** right time.
89. unjust: false. **90. leers:** looks seductively.
91–92. Brabbler the hound. ***Brabbler*** **is here confused with** ***babbler,*** i.e. one who like an ill-trained dog "spends his mouth," promising much and performing little. **93. prodigious:** portentous, an omen.
93–94. sun . . . moon: i.e. natural order is reversed.
95. leave to see: give up seeing. **96. drab:** whore.
98. incontinent varlots: sexually promiscuous rogues.
V.ii. Location: The Greek camp. Before Calchas' tent.

9. sing . . . sight: i.e. Cressida is "familiar," like an expert sight reader of music, with any man on first acquaintance.
11. cliff: (1) clef, key; (2) pudenda. **noted:** notorious, with play on musical notation. **22. tell a pin:** don't trifle.
24. secretly open. "Juggling" with two senses of *open,* "unsecret" and "yielding access."
38. wrathful terms: angry words, i.e. an open quarrel.
40. Behold: go on watching.
41. flow: are carried as on the swelling tide of your emotions. **great:** full, complete.

Dio. Fo, fo, [adieu,] you palter.
Cres. In faith, I do not. Come hither once again.
Ulyss. You shake, my lord, at something; will you go?
You will break out.
Tro. She strokes his cheek.
Ulyss. Come, come.
Tro. Nay, stay; by Jove I will not speak a word.
There is between my will and all offenses
A guard of patience. Stay a little while.
Ther. How the devil Luxury, with his fat rump and potato finger, tickles [these] together! Fry, lechery, fry!
Dio. [But] will you then?
Cres. In faith I will lo, never trust me else.
Dio. Give me some token for the surety of it.
Cres. I'll fetch you one. *Exit.*
Ulyss. You have sworn patience.
Tro. Fear me not, my lord.
I will not be myself, nor have cognition
Of what I feel; I am all patience.

Enter CRESSID.

Ther. Now the pledge, now, now, now!
Cres. Here, Diomed, keep this sleeve.
Tro. O beauty, where is thy faith?
Ulyss. My lord—
[*Tro.* I will be patient, outwardly I will.]
[*Cres.*] You look upon that sleeve, behold it well.
He lov'd me—O false wench!—Give't me again.
Dio. Whose was't?
Cres. It is no matter now I ha't again.
I will not meet with you to-morrow night.
I prithee, Diomed, visit me no more.
Ther. Now she sharpens. Well said, whetstone!
Dio. I shall have it.
Cres. What, this?
Dio. Ay, that.
Cres. O all you gods! O pretty, pretty pledge!
Thy master now lies thinking on his bed
Of thee and me, and sighs, and takes my glove,
And gives memorial dainty kisses to it,
As I kiss thee. Nay, do not snatch it from me.
He that takes that doth take my heart withal.
Dio. I had your heart before, this follows it.
Tro. I did swear patience.
[*Cres.*] You shall not have it, Diomed, faith, you shall not.
I'll give you something else.
Dio. I will have this. Whose was it?
Cres. It is no matter.
Dio. Come, tell me whose it was.
Cres. 'Twas one's that lov'd me better than you will.
But now you have it, take it.
Dio. Whose was it?

48. palter: equivocate. **53. will:** desire (to speak and act).
55. Luxury: lechery (one of the Seven Deadly Sins).
56. potato finger: finger inciting to lust, potatoes being regarded as an aphrodisiac. **59. lo:** an exclamation equivalent to *indeed.*
60. for the surety: as an assurance.
63. cognition: rational apprehension. **72. ha't:** have it.
80. memorial: commemorative. **dainty:** delightful.

Cres. By all Diana's waiting-women yond,
And by herself, I will not tell you whose.
Dio. To-morrow will I wear it on my helm,
And grieve his spirit that dares not challenge it.
Tro. Wert thou the devil, and wor'st it on thy horn,
It should be challeng'd.
Cres. Well, well, 'tis done, 'tis past. And yet it is not;
I will not keep my word.
Dio. Why then farewell,
Thou never shalt mock Diomed again.
Cres. You shall not go. One cannot speak a word
But it straight starts you.
Dio. I do not like this fooling.
Ther. Nor I, by Pluto; but that that likes not you pleases me best.
Dio. What, shall I come? The hour—
Cres. Ay, come—O Jove!—do come.—I shall be plagued.
Dio. Farewell till then.
Cres. Good night. I prithee come.
[*Exit Diomedes.*]
Troilus, farewell! one eye yet looks on thee,
But with my heart the other eye doth see.
Ah, poor our sex! this fault in us I find,
The error of our eye directs our mind.
What error leads must err; O then conclude,
Minds sway'd by eyes are full of turpitude. *Exit.*
Ther. A proof of strength she could not publish more,
Unless she said, "My mind is now turn'd whore."
Ulyss. All's done, my lord.
Tro. It is.
Ulyss. Why stay we then?
Tro. To make a recordation to my soul
Of every syllable that here was spoke.
But if I tell how these two did [co-act],
Shall I not lie in publishing a truth?
Sith yet there is a credence in my heart,
An esperance so obstinately strong,
That doth invert th' attest of eyes and ears,
As if those organs [had deceptious] functions,
Created only to calumniate.
Was Cressid here?
Ulyss. I cannot conjure, Troyan.
Tro. She was not, sure.
Ulyss. Most sure she was.
Tro. Why, my negation hath no taste of madness.

91. Diana's waiting-women: i.e. the stars (*Diana* = the moon).
101. starts you: impels you to abrupt action. **102. likes:** pleases.
105. I . . . plagued. Equivalent to her "I shall have such a life!" at IV.ii.22.
107–8. one . . . see: i.e. Cressida still has Troilus' image in her mind's eye, but the eye of her heart (reacting to passion of the moment) prefers Diomedes. **109. poor our:** our poor.
113. proof . . . more: she could not offer a stronger proof (of her "conclusion").
116–17. make . . . Of: fix firmly in my memory.
119. lie . . . truth: i.e. declare as true something that only seems (to my senses) to be true.
120. credence: faith, belief. **121. esperance:** hope.
122. invert: change to the contrary. **123. deceptious:** deceiving.
125. conjure: call up spirits, i.e. raise a false Cressida.
127. negation: refusal to believe.

Ulyss. Nor mine, my lord; Cressid was here but now.
Tro. Let it not be believ'd for womanhood!
Think we had mothers, do not give advantage
To stubborn critics, apt without a theme
For depravation, to square the general sex
By Cressid's rule. Rather think this not Cressid.
Ulyss. What hath she done, Prince, that can [soil] our mothers?
Tro. Nothing at all, unless that this were she.
Ther. Will 'a swagger himself out on 's own eyes?
Tro. This she? no, this is Diomed's Cressida.
If beauty have a soul, this is not she;
If souls guide vows, if vows be sanctimonies,
If sanctimony be the gods' delight,
If there be rule in unity itself,
This was not she. O madness of discourse,
That cause sets up with and against itself!
Bi-fold authority, where reason can revolt
Without perdition, and loss assume all reason
Without revolt. This is, and is not, Cressid!
Within my soul there doth conduce a fight
Of this strange nature, that a thing inseparate
Divides more wider than the sky and earth,
And yet the spacious breadth of this division
Admits no orifex for a point as subtle
As Ariachne's broken woof to enter.
Instance, O instance, strong as Pluto's gates,
Cressid is mine, tied with the bonds of heaven;
Instance, O instance, strong as heaven itself,
The bonds of heaven are slipp'd, dissolv'd, and loos'd,
And with another knot, [five]-finger-tied,
The fractions of her faith, orts of her love,
The fragments, scraps, the bits and greasy relics
Of her o'er-eaten faith, are given to Diomed.
Ulyss. May worthy Troilus be half attached
With that which here his passion doth express?
Tro. Ay, Greek, and that shall be divulged well
In characters as red as Mars his heart
Inflam'd with Venus. Never did young man fancy
With so eternal and so fix'd a soul.
Hark, Greek: as much [as] I do Cressid love,
So much by weight hate I her Diomed.
That sleeve is mine that he'll bear on his helm.
Were it a casque compos'd by Vulcan's skill,
My sword should bite it. Not the dreadful spout
Which shipmen do the hurricano call,
Constring'd in mass by the almighty sun,
Shall dizzy with more clamor Neptune's ear,
In his descent, than shall my prompted sword
Falling on Diomed.
Ther. He'll tickle it for his concupy.
Tro. O Cressid! O false Cressid! false, false, false!
Let all untruths stand by thy stained name,
And they'll seem glorious.
Ulyss. O, contain yourself;
Your passion draws ears hither.

Enter AENEAS.

Aene. I have been seeking you this hour, my lord.
Hector by this is arming him in Troy;
Ajax, your guard, stays to conduct you home.
Tro. Have with you, Prince. My courteous lord, adieu.
Farewell, revolted fair! and, Diomed,
Stand fast, and wear a castle on thy head!
Ulyss. I'll bring you to the gates.
Tro. Accept distracted thanks.

Exeunt Troilus, Aeneas, and Ulysses.

Ther. Would I could meet that rogue Diomed! I would croak like a raven, I would bode, I would bode. Patroclus will give me any thing for the intelligence of this whore. The parrot will not do more for an almond than he for a commodious drab. Lechery, lechery, still wars and lechery, nothing else holds fashion. A burning devil take them! *Exit.*

[SCENE III]

Enter HECTOR *and* ANDROMACHE.

And. When was my lord so much ungently temper'd

129. for: for the sake of. **130. Think:** remember that.
131–32. apt . . . depravation: always ready, even when they have no grounds for denigration.
132–33. square . . . rule: measure all women by the yardstick of Cressida's behavior.
136. Will . . . eyes: will he bluster himself out of believing what he has just seen with his own eyes. *On* = of.
139. sanctimonies: sacred things.
140. sanctimony: sanctity of life and character.
141. If . . . unity: i.e. if one is one and not dividable into two.
142. discourse: reason.
143. That . . . up: that sets up a contest (or debate).
144. Bi-fold: double, ambiguous (first recorded use).
144–46. where . . . revolt: i.e. where reason can revolt against itself (i.e. deny the senses' evidence that this is Cressida) without loss (*perdition*) of reason, and where loss of reason (inability to trust the senses) can, without revolt against reason, arrogate to itself the appearance of the highest (*all*) reason (belief that this is not Cressida).
147. there . . . fight: a battle is joined (the only recorded non-transitive use of *conduce*).
148. this: i.e. the following. **inseparate:** indivisible.
151. orifex: aperture (erroneous variant of *orifice*). **subtle:** delicate, fine.
152. Ariachne's broken woof: i.e. a fragment of a spider's web. *Ariachne* appears to be Shakespeare's error for the name of Arachne, who according to Ovid (*Metamorphoses*, VI, 1–145) was turned into a spider by Pallas for daring to challenge her successfully in a weaving contest. **155. Instance:** proof, evidence.
157. five-finger-tied: i.e. tied by human hands (referring to the physical contact Troilus has just witnessed between Diomedes and Cressida) as opposed to the "bonds of heaven" of lines 154, 156.
158. orts: leavings, scraps.
160. o'er-eaten: that she has sickened of.
161–62. May . . . With: can it be that worthy Troilus half believes (literally, is half possessed by). *Troilus* is trisyllabic here for the only time in the play: the anomaly has led some editors to insert *but* before *half*. **165. fancy:** love. **168. by weight:** precisely.
170. casque: helmet. **Vulcan's skill.** Vulcan was armorer to the gods. **171. spout:** waterspout.
173. Constring'd in mass: compressed into a dense body.
175. prompted: sword driven by the will to destroy.
177. He'll tickle it: Troilus will tickle Diomedes' helmet (?) or Diomedes will tickle it (i.e. be tickled) (?). *Tickle* is of course used in ironic understatement. **Concupy.** Shakespeare's coinage, presumably meaning either "concupiscence" or "concubine" (= Cressida).
181. passion: lamentation.
185. Have with you: let us go together. **186. revolted:** traitorous.
187. castle: i.e. a helmet giving more than ordinary protection.
191. bode: prophesy. The croaking of ravens was looked upon as a portent of evil.
192. the intelligence: news. **194. commodious:** accommodating.
195–96. burning devil: i.e. venereal disease.

V.iii. Location: Troy. Before Priam's palace.
1. ungently temper'd: unkindly disposed.

To stop his ears against admonishment?
Unarm, unarm, and do not fight to-day.
Hect. You train me to offend you, get you in.
By all the everlasting gods, I'll go!
And. My dreams will sure prove ominous to the day.
Hect. No more, I say.

Enter CASSANDRA.

Cas. Where is my brother Hector?
And. Here, sister, arm'd, and bloody in intent.
Consort with me in loud and dear petition,
Pursue we him on knees; for I have dreamt
Of bloody turbulence, and this whole night
Hath nothing been but shapes and forms of slaughter.
Cas. O, 'tis true.
Hect. Ho! bid my trumpet sound!
[*Cas.*] No notes of sally, for the heavens, sweet brother.
Hect. Be gone, I say, the gods have heard me swear.
Cas. The gods are deaf to hot and peevish vows;
They are polluted off'rings, more abhorr'd
Than spotted livers in the sacrifice.
And. O, be persuaded! do not count it holy
[To hurt by being just; it is as lawful,
For we would give much, to [use] violent thefts,
And rob in the behalf of charity.]
[*Cas.*] It is the purpose that makes strong the vow,
But vows to every purpose must not hold;
Unarm, sweet Hector.
Hect. Hold you still, I say;
Mine honor keeps the weather of my fate.
Life every man holds dear, but the dear man
Holds honor far more precious-dear than life.

Enter TROILUS.

How now, young man, meanest thou to fight to-day?
And. Cassandra, call my father to persuade.
Exit Cassandra.
Hect. No, faith, young Troilus, doff thy harness, youth,
I am to-day i' th' vein of chivalry.
Let grow thy sinews till their knots be strong,
And tempt not yet the brushes of the war.
Unarm thee, go, and doubt thou not, brave boy,
I'll stand to-day for thee and me and Troy.
Tro. Brother, you have a vice of mercy in you,
Which better fits a lion than a man.
Hect. What vice is that? Good Troilus, chide me for it.
Tro. When many times the captive Grecian falls,
Even in the fan and wind of your fair sword,
You bid them rise and live.

Hect. O, 'tis fair play.
Tro. Fool's play, by heaven, Hector.
Hect. How now? how now?
Tro. For th' love of all the gods,
Let's leave the hermit pity with our mother,
And when we have our armors buckled on,
The venom'd vengeance ride upon our swords,
Spur them to ruthful work, rein them from ruth.
Hect. Fie, savage, fie!
Tro. Hector, then 'tis wars.
Hect. Troilus, I would not have you fight to-day.
Tro. Who should withhold me?
Not fate, obedience, nor the hand of Mars
Beck'ning with fiery truncheon my retire,
Not Priamus and Hecuba on knees,
Their eyes o'ergalled with recourse of tears,
Nor you, my brother, with your true sword drawn,
Oppos'd to hinder me, should stop my way,
[But by my ruin].

Enter PRIAM *and* CASSANDRA.

Cas. Lay hold upon him, Priam, hold him fast,
He is thy crutch. Now if thou lose thy stay,
Thou on him leaning, and all Troy on thee,
Fall all together.
Pri. Come, Hector, come, go back.
Thy wife hath dreamt, thy mother hath had visions,
Cassandra doth foresee, and I myself
Am like a prophet suddenly enrapt
To tell thee that this day is ominous:
Therefore come back.
Hect. Aeneas is a-field,
And I do stand engag'd to many Greeks,
Even in the faith of valor, to appear
This morning to them.
Pri. Ay, but thou shalt not go.
Hect. I must not break my faith.
You know me dutiful, therefore, dear sir,
Let me not shame respect, but give me leave
To take that course by your consent and voice,
Which you do here forbid me, royal Priam.
Cas. O Priam, yield not to him.
And. Do not, dear father.
Hect. Andromache, I am offended with you,
Upon the love you bear me, get you in.
Exit Andromache.
Tro. This foolish, dreaming, superstitious girl
Makes all these bodements.
Cas. O, farewell, dear Hector.
Look how thou diest, look how thy eye turns pale.
Look how thy wounds do bleed at many vents,
Hark how Troy roars, how Hecuba cries out,
How poor Andromache shrills her dolors forth.
Behold, [distraction], frenzy, and amazement,
Like witless antics, one another meet,

4. train: draw, induce. **9. dear:** loving. **16. peevish:** foolish.
17. abhorr'd: abhorrent.
20. hurt . . . just: to commit injury by observing your vow.
21. For . . . much: because we would like to give generously.
23. purpose: i.e. the quality of the cause.
24. vows . . . hold: not all vows should be held inviolate.
26. keeps the weather: keeps to windward, i.e. takes precedence.
27. dear man: man who is held dear; noble man.
34. brushes: encounters.
37. vice of mercy: fault of being merciful.
38. lion. The lion, according to Pliny, spared any adversary that made submission to it. **40. captive:** conquered.

48. ruthful . . . ruth: woeful . . . mercy.
49. then 'tis wars: i.e. it is an attitude proper to war.
53. truncheon: marshal's baton or staff. **retire:** withdrawal.
55. recourse: repeated coursing or flowing. **58. ruin:** death.
62. Fall all: i.e. all will fall. **65. enrapt:** inspired.
69. faith of valor: the honor proper to a man of courage.
73. shame respect: disgrace the respect (due to you).
80. Makes . . . bodements: is the cause of all these prophecies of disaster. **84. dolors:** griefs. **86. antics:** fools.

And all cry, Hector! Hector's dead! O Hector!

Tro. Away, away.

Cas. Farewell; yet soft: Hector, I take my leave. Thou dost thyself and all our Troy deceive. [*Exit.*]

Hect. You are amaz'd, my liege, at her exclaim. Go in and cheer the town. We'll forth and fight, Do deeds worth praise, and tell you them at night.

Pri. Farewell, the gods with safety stand about thee!

[*Exeunt severally Priam and Hector.*] *Alarum.*

Tro. They are at it, hark! Proud Diomed, believe, I come to lose my arm, or win my sleeve.

Enter PANDAR.

Pan. Do you hear, my lord? Do you hear?

Tro. What now?

Pan. Here's a letter come from yond poor girl.

Tro. Let me read.

Pan. A whoreson tisick, a whoreson rascally tisick so troubles me, and the foolish fortune of this girl, and what one thing, what another, that I shall leave you one a' th's days; and I have a rheum in mine eyes too, and such an ache in my bones, that unless a man were curs'd, I cannot tell what to think on't. What says she there?

Tro. Words, words, mere words, no matter from the heart;
Th' effect doth operate another way.

[*Tearing the letter.*]

Go, wind, to wind, there turn and change together.
My love with words and errors still she feeds,
But edifies another with her deeds. *Exeunt* [*severally*].

[SCENE IV]

[*Alarum.*] *Enter* THERSITES. *Excursions.*

Ther. Now they are clapper-clawing one another; I'll go look on. That dissembling abominable varlet, Diomed, has got that same scurvy doting foolish [young] knave's sleeve of Troy there in his helm. I would fain see them meet, that that same young Troyan ass, that loves the whore there, might send that Greekish whoremasterly villain with the sleeve back to the dissembling luxurious drab, of a sleeveless arrant. A' th' t' other side, the policy of those crafty swearing rascals, that stale old mouse-eaten dry cheese, Nestor, and that same dog-fox, Ulysses, is not prov'd worth a blackberry. They set me up, in policy, that mongril cur, Ajax, against that dog of as bad a kind, Achilles; and now is the cur Ajax prouder than the cur Achilles, and will not arm to-day; whereupon the Grecians began to proclaim barbarism, and policy grows into an ill opinion.

[*Enter* DIOMED, *and* TROILUS *following.*]

Soft, here comes sleeve and t' other.

Tro. Fly not, for shouldst thou take the river Styx, I would swim after.

Dio. Thou dost miscall retire.
I do not fly, but advantageous care
Withdrew me from the odds of multitude.
Have at thee!

Ther. Hold thy whore, Grecian!—now for thy whore, Troyan!—now the sleeve, now the sleeve!

[*Exeunt Troilus and Diomedes fighting.*]

Enter HECTOR.

Hect. What art [thou], Greek? Art thou for Hector's match?
Art thou of blood and honor?

Ther. No, no, I am a rascal, a scurvy railing knave, a very filthy rogue.

Hect. I do believe thee, live. [*Exit.*]

Ther. God-a-mercy, that thou wilt believe me, but a plague break thy neck—for frighting me! What's become of the wenching rogues? I think they have swallow'd one another. I would laugh at that miracle—yet in a sort lechery eats itself. I'll seek them. *Exit.*

[SCENE V]

Enter DIOMED *and* SERVANT.

Dio. Go, go, my servant, take thou Troilus' horse,
Present the fair steed to my lady Cressid.
Fellow, commend my service to her beauty;
Tell her I have chastis'd the amorous Troyan,
And am her knight by proof.

Serv. I go, my lord. [*Exit.*]

Enter AGAMEMNON.

Agam. Renew, renew! The fierce Polydamas
Hath beat down Menon; bastard Margarelon
Hath Doreus prisoner,
And stands Colossus-wise, waving his beam,

89. **yet soft:** i.e. pause a moment.
91. **amaz'd:** stunned (speechless). **exclaim:** outcries.
101. **tisick:** a severe cough or asthma (variant of *phthisic*).
103. **leave you:** i.e. die.
104. **a' th's:** of these. **rheum:** mucous discharge.
105. **ache . . . bones.** Implying syphilis.
106. **curs'd:** under a witch's malediction.
109. **Th' effect . . . way:** i.e. her actions give the lie to what she says.
112. **edifies:** profits, supports.

V.iv. **Location:** Plains between Troy and the Greek camp.
o.s.d. **Excursions:** sallies. 1. **clapper-clawing:** thrashing, mauling.
2. **abominable.** Supposedly derived from *ab homine*, "not like a man," hence "unnatural."
4. **knave's . . . Troy:** i.e. knave of Troy's (Troilus') sleeve. **in:** on.
7. **whoremasterly:** fornicating. 8. **luxurious:** lecherous.
8–9. **sleeveless arrant:** futile errand (variant form of *errand*).
9. **policy:** stratagem.
9–10. **crafty swearing:** i.e. given to making crafty or deceptive statements (like the plan to smoke Achilles out of his tent by paying court to Ajax).
11. **dog-fox:** male fox (a symbol of craft). 12. **set me:** set.
13. **mongril:** mongrel. Used (as at II.i.13) with reference to Ajax' mixed parentage.
16. **began.** Most editors adopt Rowe's emendation *begin.* **proclaim barbarism:** declare a state of anarchy.
17. **policy:** polity, organized government. **grows . . . opinion:** begins to be looked upon with disfavor.
20. **miscall retire:** i.e. misinterpret my moving back (as retreat).
21. **advantageous care:** concern to find an advantageous position.
27. **blood:** noble descent.
31. **God-a-mercy:** an exclamation expressing thanks (literally, God have mercy, i.e. God reward you). 35. **in a sort:** in a kind of way.

V.v. **Location:** Scene continues.
9. **beam:** lance.

Upon the pashed corses of the kings
Epistrophus and Cedius; Polyxenes is slain,
Amphimachus and Thoas deadly hurt,
Patroclus ta'en or slain, and Palamedes
Sore hurt and bruised. The dreadful Sagittary
Appalls our numbers. Haste we, Diomed,
To reinforcement, or we perish all.

Enter NESTOR.

Nest. Go bear Patroclus' body to Achilles,
And bid the snail-pac'd Ajax arm for shame.
There is a thousand Hectors in the field:
Now here he fights on Galathe his horse,
And there lacks work; anon he's there afoot,
And there they fly or die, like scaling sculls
Before the belching whale; then is he yonder,
And there the strawy Greeks, ripe for his edge,
Fall down before him like a mower's swath.
Here, there, and every where, he leaves and takes,
Dexterity so obeying appetite
That what he will he does, and does so much
That proof is call'd impossibility.

Enter ULYSSES.

Ulyss. O, courage, courage, princes! Great Achilles
Is arming, weeping, cursing, vowing vengeance.
Patroclus' wounds have rous'd his drowsy blood,
Together with his mangled Myrmidons,
That noseless, handless, hack'd and chipp'd, come to him,
Crying on Hector. Ajax hath lost a friend,
And foams at mouth, and he is arm'd and at it,
Roaring for Troilus, who hath done to-day
Mad and fantastic execution,
Engaging and redeeming of himself
With such a careless force, and forceless care,
As if that [luck], in very spite of cunning,
Bade him win all.

Enter AJAX.

[*Ajax.*] Troilus, thou coward Troilus! *Exit.*
Dio. Ay, there, there.
Nest. So, so, we draw together. *Exit.*

Enter ACHILLES.

Achil. Where is this Hector?
Come, come, thou boy-queller, show thy face,
Know what it is to meet Achilles angry.

10. pashed corses: battered corpses.
14. Sagittary: "a marvellous beast" that had accompanied King Epistrophus to Troy (not the same Epistrophus of line 11); it was half man, half horse, and "shot right well with a bowe" (Caxton).
15. Appalls our numbers: dismays our soldiers.
22. scaling sculls: scattering shoals of fish.
26. leaves and takes: i.e. leaves the dead and attacks the living (?) or spares some and kills others as he chooses (?).
29. proof . . . impossibility: i.e. the accomplished fact is deemed an impossibility.
39. Engaging: pawning (forming with *redeeming* a commercial metaphor).
40. careless force: confident strength. **forceless care:** i.e. recklessness (?) or effortless skill (?).
44. draw together: begin to act as a team.
45. boy-queller: boy-killer (referring, with exaggeration, to his killing of Patroclus).

Hector, where's Hector? I will none but Hector. *Exeunt.*

[SCENE VI]

Enter AJAX.

[*Ajax.*] Troilus, thou coward Troilus, show thy head!

Enter DIOMED.

[*Dio.*] Troilus, I say, where's Troilus?
Ajax. What wouldst thou?
Dio. I would correct him.
Ajax. Were I the general, thou shouldst have my office
Ere that correction. Troilus, I say, what, Troilus!

Enter TROILUS.

Tro. O traitor Diomed! turn thy false face, thou traitor,
And pay thy life thou owest me for my horse.
Dio. Ha, art thou there?
Ajax. I'll fight with him alone. Stand, Diomed.
Dio. He is my prize, I will not look upon.
Tro. Come both you cogging Greeks, have at you both! [*Exeunt fighting.*]

[*Enter* HECTOR.]

Hect. Yea, Troilus? O, well fought, my youngest brother!

Enter ACHILLES.

[*Achil.*] Now do I see thee, ha! Have at thee, Hector! [*They fight.*]
Hect. Pause if thou wilt.
Achil. I do disdain thy courtesy, proud Troyan.
Be happy that my arms are out of use;
My rest and negligence befriends thee now,
But thou anon shalt hear of me again;
Till when, go seek thy fortune. *Exit.*
Hect. Fare thee well.
I would have been much more a fresher man,
Had I expected thee. How now, my brother?

Enter TROILUS.

Tro. Ajax hath ta'en Aeneas! Shall it be?
No, by the flame of yonder glorious heaven,
He shall not carry him; I'll be ta'en too,
Or bring him off. Fate, hear me what I say!
I reak not though I end my life to-day. *Exit.*

Enter one in armor.

Hect. Stand, stand, thou Greek, thou art a goodly mark.

V.vi. Location: Scene continues.
4–5. thou . . . correction: i.e. I would yield you my generalship sooner than the privilege of chastising him. **9. Stand:** stand aside.
10. look upon: be an onlooker.
11. cogging: cheating (applicable only to Diomedes). **have at you:** here I come at you (a stock expression of warning).
14. if thou wilt: if you wish. Hector is offering a favor, not asking one.
23. flame: i.e. the sun. **24. carry:** defeat.
25. bring him off: rescue him.
26. reak: care (variant form of *reck*). **27. mark:** target.

No? wilt thou not? I like thy armor well;
I'll frush it and unlock the rivets all,
But I'll be master of it. [*Exit one in armor.*] Wilt thou not, beast, abide?
Why then fly on, I'll hunt thee for thy hide. *Exit.*

[SCENE VII]

Enter ACHILLES *with* MYRMIDONS.

[*Achil.*] Come here about me, you my Myrmidons,
Mark what I say. Attend me where I wheel;
Strike not a stroke, but keep yourselves in breath,
And when I have the bloody Hector found,
Empale him with your weapons round about,
In fellest manner execute your arms.
Follow me, sirs, and my proceedings eye,
It is decreed Hector the great must die. *Exeunt.*

Enter THERSITES; MENELAUS [*and*] PARIS [*fighting*].

Ther. The cuckold and the cuckold-maker are at it. Now, bull! now, dog! 'Loo, Paris, 'loo! Now my double-henn'd Spartan! 'Loo, Paris, 'loo! The bull has the game, ware horns ho!

Exeunt Paris and Menelaus.

Enter Bastard [MARGARELON].

Mar. Turn, slave, and fight.
Ther. What art thou?
Mar. A bastard son of Priam's.
Ther. I am a bastard too, I love bastards. I am bastard begot, bastard instructed, bastard in mind, bastard in valor, in every thing illegitimate. One bear will not bite another, and wherefore should one bastard? Take heed, the quarrel's most ominous to us. If the son of a whore fight for a whore, he tempts judgment. Farewell, bastard. [*Exit.*]
Mar. The devil take thee, coward! *Exit.*

[SCENE VIII]

Enter HECTOR.

Hect. Most putrefied core, so fair without,
Thy goodly armor thus hath cost thy life.
Now is my day's work done, I'll take [good] breath.
Rest, sword, thou hast thy fill of blood and death.
[*Puts off his helmet and hangs his shield behind him.*]

29. **frush:** batter.

V.vii. Location: Scene continues.
2. **wheel:** range around the battlefield. 5. **Empale:** fence.
6. **execute your arms:** employ your weapons.
10. **bull:** i.e. Menelaus (the horned one). Thersites talks in terms of bull-baiting with dogs, the sort of entertainment Londoners were familiar with at Paris Garden. **'Loo:** a cry to urge on the dogs (i.e. Paris).
11. **double-henn'd Spartan:** i.e. Menelaus is henned by Helen and "double-henn'd" because Helen has played false (= *double*). Many editors prefer F1 *sparrow* to *Spartan*; the phrase then refers to Paris, who is a lecher (the sparrow was proverbially a lascivious bird) with two wives, Oenone (whom he deserted) and Helen.
21. **for a whore:** i.e. for Helen. 22. **tempts:** invites.

V.viii. Location: Scene continues.
1. **core:** i.e. the body inside the armor.

Enter ACHILLES *and* MYRMIDONS.

Achil. Look, Hector, how the sun begins to set,
How ugly night comes breathing at his heels;
Even with the vail and dark'ning of the sun,
To close the day up, Hector's life is done.
Hect. I am unarm'd, forgo this vantage, Greek.
Achil. Strike, fellows, strike, this is the man I seek. [*Hector falls.*]
So, Ilion, fall thou next! Come, Troy, sink down!
Here lies thy heart, thy sinews, and thy bone.
On, Myrmidons, and cry you all amain,
"Achilles hath the mighty Hector slain!" *Retreat.*
Hark, a retire upon our Grecian part.
[*Myr.*] The Troyans' trumpet sound the like, my lord.
Achil. The dragon wing of night o'erspreads the earth,
And stickler-like the armies separates.
My half-supp'd sword that frankly would have fed,
Pleas'd with this dainty bait, thus goes to bed.
[*Sheathes his sword.*]
Come tie his body to my horse's tail,
Along the field I will the Troyan trail. *Exeunt.*

[SCENE IX]

[*Sound retreat. Shout.*] *Enter* AGAMEMNON, AJAX, MENELAUS, NESTOR, DIOMED, *and the rest, marching.*

Agam. Hark, hark, what [shout] is this?
Nest. Peace, drums!
Soldiers. (*Within.*) Achilles! Achilles! Hector's slain! Achilles!
Dio. The bruit is, Hector's slain, and by Achilles.
Ajax. If it be so, yet bragless let it be,
Great Hector was as good a man as he.
Agam. March patiently along; let one be sent
To pray Achilles see us at our tent.
If in his death the gods have us befriended,
Great Troy is ours, and our sharp wars are ended.
Exeunt.

[SCENE X]

Enter AENEAS, PARIS, ANTENOR, DEIPHOBUS.

Aene. Stand ho! yet are we masters of the field.

Enter TROILUS.

Tro. Never go home, here starve we out the night—
Hector is slain.
All. Hector! the gods forbid!
Tro. He's dead, and at the murtherer's horse's tail,

7. **vail:** descent.
14 s.d. **Retreat:** trumpet signal for the withdrawal of forces (= *retire*, line 15). 18. **stickler-like:** like an umpire.
19. **frankly:** freely, generously.
20. **dainty bait:** light meal or snack.

V.ix. Location: Scene continues.
4. **bruit:** noise, rumor. 10. **sharp:** bitter.

V.x. Location: Scene continues.
2. **starve . . . night:** let us pass the night here in the killing cold (in preference to breaking the news to Troy; see lines 15–21).

In beastly sort, dragg'd through the shameful field.
Frown on, you heavens, effect your rage with speed!
Sit, gods, upon your thrones, and smile at Troy!
I say, at once, let your brief plagues be mercy,
And linger not our sure destructions on!

Aene. My lord, you do discomfort all the host.

Tro. You understand me not that tell me so.
I do not speak of flight, of fear, of death,
But dare all imminence that gods and men
Address their dangers in. Hector is gone.
Who shall tell Priam so, or Hecuba?
Let him that will a scritch-owl aye be call'd
Go in to Troy and say [there,] "Hector's dead!"
There is a word will Priam turn to stone,
Make wells and Niobes of the maids and wives,
Cold statues of the youth, and in a word,
Scare Troy out of itself. [But march away.
Hector is dead;] there is no more to say.
Stay yet. You [vile] abominable tents,
Thus proudly [pight] upon our Phrygian plains,
Let Titan rise as early as he dare,
I'll through and through you! and, thou great-siz'd coward,
No space of earth shall sunder our two hates.
I'll haunt thee like a wicked conscience still,
That mouldeth goblins swift as frenzy's thoughts.
Strike a free march. To Troy with comfort go;
Hope of revenge shall hide our inward woe.

Enter PANDARUS.

7. smile: mock. In view of lines 6, 8–9, many editors emend *smile at* to *smite at* (Warburton) or *smite all* (Hanmer).
13. imminence: threats of impending disaster.
14. Address . . . in: level their threats with.
16. scritch-owl: screech-owl.
19. Niobes. Niobe wept herself into a stone after her fourteen children were slaughtered by Apollo and Diana. 24. pight: pitched.
26. coward: i.e. Achilles, because he did not kill Hector in fair fight.
30. comfort: reassurance.

Pan. But hear you, hear you!

Tro. Hence, broker, lackey! [*Strikes him.*] Ignominy, shame
Pursue thy life, and live aye with thy name!

Exeunt all but Pandarus.

Pan. A goodly medicine for my aching bones! O world, world, [world!] thus is the poor agent despis'd! O [traders] and bawds, how earnestly are you set a-work, and how ill requited! Why should our endeavor be so lov'd and the performance so loath'd? What verse for it? What instance for it? Let me see:

Full merrily the humble-bee doth sing,
Till he hath lost his honey and his sting;
And being once subdu'd in armed tail,
Sweet honey and sweet notes together fail.

Good traders in the flesh, set this in your painted cloths:

As many as be here of Pandar's hall,
Your eyes, half out, weep out at Pandar's fall;
Or if you cannot weep, yet give some groans,
Though not for me, yet for [your] aching bones.
Brethren and sisters of the hold-[door] trade,
Some two months hence my will shall here be made.
It should be now, but that my fear is this,
Some galled goose of Winchester would hiss.
Till then I'll sweat and seek about for eases,
And at that time bequeath you my diseases. [*Exit.*]

33. broker: go-between, bawd. lackey: servant, slave.
37. traders: i.e. "traders in the flesh," line 45.
40. instance: example, case in point.
43. subdu'd . . . tail: having his sting removed (with sexual implication).
45–46. painted cloths: cheap wall-hangings painted with scenes and mottoes. 47. hall: guild, fraternity.
48. half out: i.e. already half blind from venereal disease.
51. hold-door trade: prostitution.
54. galled: (1) offended; (2) having venereal sores. goose of Winchester: prostitute (so called because the brothels in Southwark were under the jurisdiction of the Bishop of Winchester).
55. sweat. Sweating was one of the treatments for venereal disease.

NOTE ON THE TEXT

The textual situation in *Troilus and Cressida,* despite the efforts that have been made to clarify it in the last sixty years, is still uncertain and confused. Two "good" texts of ambiguously related authority exist: the quarto (Q), of which there are two states (distinguished in the second state by a new title page and a publisher's "Epistle," author unknown; see the Textual Notes), printed in 1609 by George Eld for Richard Bonian and Henry Walley; and the First Folio (F1) text (1623).

The exact provenience of both Q and F1 is open to question, and there is some difference of opinion among editors about which text should be chosen as copy-text. Whichever text is used, there are over 300 verbal variants, not including added or omitted passages, between Q and F1. Such being the case, how do we account for such considerable difference? Here, of course, is the nub of the textual problem. Some critics (Alexander, Williams, Greg) believe that Q was printed from a transcript ("fair copy") made by Shakespeare himself from his "foul papers" (rough draft) and that he revised stylistically in the process of copying; Walker, reverting to a view proposed by Chambers in 1930, denies the revision theory and Shakespeare's hand in the transcript of the "foul papers" behind Q (Fl being printed from a copy of Q corrected by collation with the "foul papers") and argues that the many verbal differences between Q and F1 are for the most part the result of a mixture of scribal, collational, or compositional errors, the difficulty (affecting the scribal transcript behind Q and the printer's copy for Fl) experienced in deciphering Shakespeare's hand in the "foul papers," and, in F1, some editorial and compositorial sophistication of a kind not uncommon in F1 texts (a non-revision theory no longer accepted). Other critics, though on different grounds, argue for a double revision by Shakespeare: (a) Hillebrand asserts that Shakespeare revised first in the transcript of the "foul papers" from which he believes Q was set, then, later, and more heavily, in the "foul papers," this second revision furnishing the printer's copy for the F1 text; (b) Taylor, and, with some reservations, Muir, premise that Q was set directly from a transcript of the "foul papers" made by Shakespeare, in which, in copying, he made some revisions, and from which, in turn, a scribal copy was made to function as a prompt-book (perhaps for performance at the Inns of Court, as suggested by Alexander), a preliminary prompt-book that later underwent a second revision (also by Shakespeare) and became the company's official prompt-book for Globe performances and the manuscript against which Q was collated to produce printer's copy for the F1 text. Palmer finds the evidence for the provenience of both Q and F1 copy ambiguous. He suggests that printer's copy for Q could have been either authorial (i.e., Shakespeare's "foul papers") or scribal; nevertheless, he accepts Q as copy-text because "we know only that F was (largely) printed from Q" (p. 16), and he believes that F1 "variants need not be given that respect which might, in theory [that F1 was printed from a copy of Q collated with an authoritative manuscript], have been their due" (p. 10), since "occasionally the F reading, in a part of the text which *ex hypothesi* is set from Q, displays a graphic error of the kind normally to be expected in setting from MS" (p. 10; see IV.iv.41–2, V.ii.173, V.x.20).

The present text accepts Q as its copy-text because (a) it is now generally agreed that the printer's copy for Q was either Shakespeare's "foul papers" or a transcript (perhaps Shakespearean) of the "foul papers," and (b) the nature of the copy behind the F1 text is, as outlined above, of more ambiguous provenience (i.e., depending upon what kind of manuscript was used to "correct" and amplify the copy of Q that finally served as the printer's copy). Using Q as its copy-text, then, the present text admits, in addition to the Prologue found only in F1, 44 lines or half-lines unique to F1, but otherwise adopts F1 readings only where they seem significantly superior to the equivalent Q readings. Whichever text (Q or F1) an editor chooses as copy-text, however, the result will inevitably be eclectic. How different eclectically edited texts of *Troilus and Cressida* can be may be judged by comparing the relatively recent editions of Walker, Muir, Palmer, Wells/Taylor, and the present Riverside text. Taking their treatment of Act I as a basis for comparison, Walker and Muir, although, like Palmer and Riverside, they take Q as copy-text, both read with F1 against Q some 49 times, where Palmer reads with F1 some 32 times, and Riverside some 29 times; Wells/Taylor, who use F1 as copy-text, privilege F1 against Q some 55 times.

Because of the comparatively ambiguous authority of Q and F1, the Textual Notes record all significant variants between the Q and F1 texts. Readers are thus in a position to study the evidence and form their own judgment. I.i.1–92 survives in F1 in two settings of type; they are referred to in the Textual Notes as "first setting" and "second setting."

For further information, see: Peter Alexander, *"Troilus and Cressida,* 1609," *The Library,* IX (1928), 267–86; E. K. Chambers, *William Shakespeare* (Oxford, 1930), Vol. I, 438–49; Philip Williams, "Shakespeare's *Troilus and Cressida:* The Relationship of Quarto and Folio," *SB,* III (1950–51), 131–43; H. N. Hillebrand, ed., New Variorum *Troilus and Cressida* (Philadelphia, 1953); Alice Walker, *Textual Problems of the First Folio* (Cambridge, 1953), and ed., New Shakespeare *Troilus and Cressida* (Cambridge, 1957); W. W. Greg, *The Shakespeare First Folio* (Oxford, 1955); E. A. J. Honigmann, *The Stability of Shakespeare's Text* (London, 1965), and "The Date and Revision of *Troilus and Cressida,*" in *Textual Criticism and Literary Interpretation,* ed., Jerome McGann (Chicago, 1985), pp. 38–54; J. M. Nosworthy, *Shakespeare's Occasional Plays* (London, 1965); J. K. Walton, *The Quarto Copy for the First Folio of Shakespeare* (Dublin, 1971); Gary Taylor, *"Troilus and Cressida,* Bibliography, Performance, and Interpretation," *Shakespeare Studies,* XV (1982), 99–136; Kenneth Muir, ed., New Oxford *Troilus and Cressida* (Oxford, 1982); Kenneth Palmer, ed., New Arden *Troilus and Cressida* (London, 1982); Stanley Wells, Gary Taylor, et al., *William Shakespeare: A Textual Companion* (Oxford, 1987); K. T. Bjelland, "Variants as Epistemological Shifts: A Proposed Methodology for Recovering the Two Texts of Shakespeare's *Troilus and Cressida,*" *PBSA,* LXXXVIII (1994), 53–78.

TEXTUAL NOTES

Title: **The . . . Cressida]** The Historie of Troylus and Cresseida. As it was acted by the Kings Maiesties seruants at the Globe. Written by William Shakespeare. *Q (title-page, first state);* The Famous Historie of Troylus and Cresseid. Excellently expressing the beginning of their loues, with the conceited wooing of Pandarus Prince of Licia. Written by William Shakespeare. *Q (title-page, second state);* The Tragedie of Troylus and Cressida. *F1*

The second state of Q contains the following advertisement: A neuer writer, to an euer reader. News. Eternall reader, you haue heere a new play, neuer stal'd with the Stage, neuer clapper-clawd with the palmes of the vulger, and yet passing full of the palme comicall; for it is a birth of your braine, that neuer vnder-tooke any thing commicall, vainely: And were but the vaine names of commedies changde for the titles of Commodities, or of Playes for Pleas; you should see all those grand censors, that now stile them such vanities, flock to them for the maine grace of their grauities: especially this authors Commedies, that are so fram'd to the life, that they serue for the most common Commentaries, of all the actions of our liues, shewing such a dexteritie, and power of witte, that the most displeased with Playes, are pleasd with his Commedies. And all such dull and heauy-witted worldlings, as were neuer capable of the witte of a Commedie, comming by report of them to his representations, haue found that witte there, that they neuer found in them-selues, and haue parted better wittied then they came: feeling an edge of witte set vpon them, more then euer they dreamd they had braine to grinde it on. So much and such sauored salt of witte is in his Commedies, that they seeme (for their height of pleasure) to be borne in that sea that brought forth *Venus.* Amongst all there is none more witty then this: And had I time I would comment vpon it, though I know it needs not, (for so much as will make you thinke your testerne well bestowd) but for so much worth, as euen poore I know to be stuft in it. It deserues such a labour, as well as the best Commedy in *Terence* or *Plautus.* And beleeue this, that when hee is gone, and his Commedies out of sale, you will scramble for them, and set vp a new English Inquisition. Take this for a warning, and at the perrill of your pleasures losse, and Iudgements, refuse not, nor like this the lesse, for not being sullied, with the smoaky breath of the multitude; but thanke fortune for the scape it hath made amongst you. Since by the grand possessors wills I beleeue you should haue prayd for them rather then beene prayd. And so I leaue all such to bee prayd for (for the states of their wits healths) that will not praise it, *Vale.*

Dramatis personae: *subs. as given in Capell, following Rowe*

Act-scene division: *none in Q; only I.i marked in F1; other act-scene divisions by Rowe and later editors (see first note to each scene); present act-scene arrangement as a whole first established by Dyce*

Prologue

From F1; om. Q
8 **immures]** *F2;* emures *F1*
12 **barks]** *F2;* Barke *F1*
17 **Antenorides]** *Theobald;* Antenonidus *F1*
19 **Sperr]** *Theobald;* Stirre *F1*
31 **good]** *Kittredge;* good, *F1*

I.i

I.i] *F1*
Location: *Capell (after Theobald)*
3 **within?]** *F1;* within, *Q*
5 **field,]** *F1;* field *Q*
15 **must]** must needes *F1*
20–1 **leavening]** leau'ning *F1 (first setting);* leau'ing *F1 (second setting)*
24 **"hereafter"]** *Dyce;* here- / after, *Q, F1*
25 **heating]** heating of *F1 (second setting)*
26 **ye]** *ed.;* yea *Q (cf. I.ii.48 Q, F1);* you *F1*
26 **burn]** to burne *F1*

28 suff'rance] Kittredge; suffrance Q; sufferance F1
30 thoughts—] Rowe; thoughts, Q, F1
31 comes] comes, F1
32 Well,] F1; Well Q
34 thee—] Capell; thee Q; thee, F1
36 me,] Rowe; me: Q, F1
37 a-scorn] F1; a scorne Q
45 her] it F1
46 Cassandra's] F1; Cassandraes Q
48 Pandarus!] F1; Pandarus Q
51–2 mad . . . love;] F1 (subs.); madde: . . . loue? Q
53 heart] Theobald; heart: Q; heart, F1
55 discourse,] Malone; discourse: Q; discourse. F1
58 sense] F1; sence: Q
66 in it] in't F1
70 travail] Collier; trauell Q, F1
71 on] F1
75 not] F1 (second setting)
76 a'] on F1
77 care] F1
80 s.p. Pan.] Troy. F1 (second setting)
82 her. For] F1 (subs.); her for Q
90 Helen] F1; Helleu Q
94 me!] Rowe; me Q; me? F1
96 woo] Theobald; woe Q, F1 (generally)
97 stubborn-chaste] Theobald; stubborne, chast, Q, F1
98 Daphne's] F1; Daphues Q
101 resides] F2; reides Q; recides F1
105 a-field] F2 (subs.); a field Q, F1
115 abroad—] Rowe; abrode Q; abroad, F1

I.ii

I.ii] Capell
Location: Capell (after Theobald)
o.s.d. Alexander] Theobald
1 s.p. Alex.] Malone; Man. Q, F1 (throughout scene)
6 chid] chides F1
8 light] F2; lyte Q, F1
17 th' are] ed.; the are Q; they are F1
29 purblind] purblinded F1
33 strook] F2; stroke Q, F1
34 disdain] disdaind F1
36 s.d. Enter Pandarus.] F1
45 Ilium] F1; Illum Q
48 ye] F2; yea Q, F1
51 so;] F1; so, Q
69 nor] not F1
71 just . . . them;] Johnson (subs.; F4 just); iust, . . . them Q, F1
72 Himself?] F1; Himselfe, Q
78 end.] F1 (subs.); end Q
84, 85 other's] Rowe; others Q, F1
84 come] F1; eome Q
86 wit] Rowe; will Q, F1
101 much:] Rowe (subs.); much, Q, F1
115 will he] F1: will hc O
116 lift] F1; liste Q
117 he so] he is so F1
121 Why . . . dimpled.] as prose, Pope; as verse, Q, F1
124 valiantly] F1; valianty Q
129 the] F2; thee Q, F1
139 hair] F1; heare Q (sporadically; not hereafter recorded)
146 a more] more F1
147 pot] F1; por Q
157 hairs] F1; heires Q (sporadically; not hereafter recorded)
164 pluck't] F3; pluckt Q, F1
168 for it] For is F1
172 do] does F1
179 Ilion] Illium F1
179 Cressida] F1; Cresseida Q (throughout, except at III.ii.2 and IV.v.288)
184, 189, 198, 212, 218, 226, 239 s.dd. and . . . stage] Rowe (subs.)
187 tell] om. F1
191 man] a man F1
192 judgments] iudgement F1
194 him] him him F1
198 have] haue, F1
199–200 that; there's] Pope (subs.); that, thers Q; that there's F1
200 fellow!] Rowe; fellow Q; fellow. F1
203 a brave] braue F1
204 man's] F1; man Q
206 there's] Pope; thers Q; om. F1
207 will] ill F1
210 thing,] Rowe; thing Q, F1
212 s.d. Enter Paris] placed as in Capell; after l. 209, Q, F1
217 see] om. F1
223 indifferent] F2; indifferent, Q, F1
223 well.] Rowe (subs.); well, Q, F1
231 note] not F1
233–4 and how he] following these words the F1 text ceases to be essentially a reprint of Q (see "Note on the Text")
235 never] ne're F1
237 choice] F1; choiee Q
239 an eye] money F1
239 s.d. Enter Common Soldiers] F1
240 comes] come F1
242 in the] i'th' F1
247 amongst] among F1
251 Why,] F4; why Q, F1
254–5 such-like] so forth F1
255 season] seasons F1
257 date is] dates F1
258 a woman] another woman F1
258 a man] one F1
263 lie, at] lye at, at F1
267 too] F1; two Q
270 it's] F1; its Q
271 s.d. Troilus'] Capell
274 there . . . him] om. F1
275 s.d. Exit Boy.] Capell
278 I will be] Cambridge; I wilbe Q; Ile be F1
279 uncle?] Hudson; vncle: Q; Vnkle. F1
281 s.d. Exit Pandarus.] F1
287, 290] Marked with gnomic quotes, Q
288 nought] F1; naught Q
289 prize] F1; price Q
294] Marked with gnomic quotes and in italics, Q, F1
294 Then] That F1
294 content] Contents F1
295 s.d. with Alexander] ed.

I.iii

I.iii] Capell
Location: Capell (after Rowe)
o.s.d. Sennet.] F1
2 these jaundies o'er] (o'er, Kittredge for Q ore); the Iaundies on F1
6 rear'd,] Cambridge; reard, Q, F1
8 Infects] Infect F1
13 every] F1; euer Q
19 call them shames] thinke them shame, F1
19 nought] F1; naught Q
27 broad] lowd F1
28 winnows] F1; winnowss Q
29 matter, by itself] Hanmer; matter by it selfe, Q, F1
31 thy] F1; the Q
31 godlike] godly F1
36 patient] F1; ancient Q
40 strong-ribb'd] hyphen, Pope
44 Corrivall'd] Co-riual'd F1
48 breeze] ed. (after Dyce); Bryze Q; Brieze F1
55 nerves] nerue F1 (in support of Q reading cf. V.viii.12)
56 sprite] spirit F1
58 speaks.] Rowe; speakes, Q, F1
59 th'] the F1
60 s.d. to Agamemnon] Rowe
60–1 for . . . reverend] F1; (for . . . reuerend) Q
61 s.d. To Nestor.] Rowe
61 thy] F1; the Q
61 stretch'd-out] hyphen, F1
67 On] In F1
67 heaven . . . Greekish] the Heauens ride, knit all Greekes F1
70–4 Agam. Speak . . . oracle.] F1
70 expect] Rowe (subs.); expect: F1
72 lips, than] Pope; lips; then F1
75 s.p. Ulyss.] F1
75 bases] basis F1
86 priority,] F1; prioritie Q
87 Insisture] F1; In sisture Q
92 ill . . . evil] F1; influence of euill Planets Q
94 check,] F1; check Q
102 of] to F1
106 primogenity] primogenitiue F1
110 meets] F1; melts Q
117 (Between . . . resides)] in italics, Q
117 resides] F2; recides Q, F1
118 their] her F1
119 include] includes F1
127 it is] is it F1
128 with] in F1
137 stands] liues F1
143 sinow] sinew F1
144 airy] ayery F1
149 awkward] F1; sillie Q
156 scaffolage] F1; scoaffollage Q
157 to-be-pitied] hyphens, F2
157 o'er-wrested] Pope; ore-rested Q, F1
159 unsquar'd] F1; vnsquare Q
161 seem] seemes F1
164 right] iust F1
165 hem] hum F1
176 Valor] F1; valour Q
176–8 "O . . . spleen."] quotes, Johnson (after Pope)
179 natures,] F1; natures Q
188 self-will'd] F1; selfe-wild Q
190 keeps] and keepes F1
195 or] anon. conj. (in Cambridge); our Q; and F1
199 Forestall] F1; Forstall Q
202 calls] call F1
203 enemies'] Warburton; enemies Q, F1
205 closet-war] hyphen F1
207 swinge] swing F1
209 fineness] F1; finesse Q
212 s.d. Tucket.] F1
214 s.d. Enter Aeneas.] F1
219 eyes] eares F1
223 security.] F1; security, Q
228 bid] on F1
231 god in office,] Rowe; god, in office Q; God in office F1
236 fame] F1; same Q
238 great] om. F1
238 accord,] F1; accord Q
242 that the] that he F1
244 praise, sole pure,] Capell; praise sole pure Q, F1
247 affairs] affayre F1
249 nought] F1; naught Q
250 with] om. F1
252 sense on the] F1; seat on that Q
256 loud] F1; alowd Q
262 this] F1; his Q
262 long-continued] hyphen, F1
263 resty] rusty F1
265 among] among'st F1
267 And] That F1
267 seeks] F1; feeds Q (seeds ed. conj.)
269–70 confession . . . loves,] Pope; confession, (With . . . loues) Q, F1
276 couple] compasse F1
289 or] F1; a Q
290 I am] Ile be F1
293 mould] F1; hoste Q
294 A . . . no] One . . . one F1
295 me] Cambridge; me. Q; me, F1
297 vambrace] Vantbrace F1
297 my withered brawns] this wither'd brawne F1
298 will] F1
301 prove] pawne F1
301 troth] truth F1
302 forfend] Kittredge; for-fend Q; forbid F1
302 youth] F1; men Q
304 s.p. Agam.] F1; speech continued to Ulysses, Q
305 sir] first F1
309 s.d. Exeunt . . . Nestor.] F1 (Manet; Manent F2)
315 This 'tis:] F1
324 True] om. F1
324 as] euen as F1
327 Achilles, . . . barren] F1; Achilles weare his braine, as barren, Q
328–9 (though . . . enough)] in italics (except Apollo), Q
333 Why] Yes F1
334 those honors] his Honor F1

336 the] this *F1*
340 vild] wilde *F1*
352 receives . . . a] from hence receyues the *F1*
354–6 Which . . . limbs.] *F1*
354 are] *F2;* are in *F1*
356 speech:] *F1;* speech? *Q*
358 first . . . wares] shew our fowlest Wares *F1*
360–1 shall . . . first.] yet to shew, / Shall shew the better. *F1*
363–4 For . . . followers.] *as verse, F1; as prose, Q*
367 share] weare *F1*
369 it] we *F1*
372 do] did *F1*
374 device] *F1;* deuise *Q*
376 for the better] as the worthier *F1*
386 advice] *F1;* aduise *Q*
387 thereof] of it *F1*
390 tarre] *F1;* arre *Q*
390 a] their *F1*

II.i

II.i] *Rowe*
Location: *Rowe*
2 biles—full,] *Rowe;* biles, full, *Q;* Biles (ful) *F1*
5 run—say so—] *Rowe;* run (say so), *Q;* runne, say so; *F1*
6 then] *om. F1*
8 would] there would *F1*
11 s.d. Strikes him.] *F1*
13 beef-witted] *hyphen, F1*
14 thou] you *F1*
14 whinid'st] *F1;* vnsalted *Q*
17 con] *F1;* cunne *Q*
17–8 without book] *om. F1*
18 a] *F1*
19 murrion] Murren *F1*
19 a' thy] *Sisson;* ath thy *Q;* o'th thy *F1*
21 Toadstool] Toads stoole *F1*
23 strikest] strik'st *F1*
25 fool] a foole *F1*
26 porpentine] *F1;* Porpentin *Q*
27 foot;] *anon. conj. (in Cambridge);* foote, *Q, F1*
28 of thee] *F1;* of the *Q*
29 loathsomest] lothsom'st *F1*
29–30 When . . . another.] *om. F1*
32 grumblest] *F1;* gromblest *Q*
38 Ajax. Cobloaf!] *F1;* Aiax Coblofe, *Q (in italics, as part of Thersites' preceding line)*
39, 41, 42 s.pp. Ther. . . . Ajax. . . . Ther.] *F1; ll. 39–42 (through* do!*) continued to Thersites, Q (see preceding note and l. 42 below)*
41 s.d. Beating him.] *Pope*
42 do! thou . . . ay,] *A. Walker;* do? / *Aiax.* Thou . . . witch: / *Ther.* I, *Q;* do. / *Aia.* Thou . . . Witch. / *Ther.* I, *F1*
43 sodden-witted] *hyphen, F1*
44 thee.] *F1;* thee, *Q*
44 You] Thou *F1*
45 thrash] thresh *F1*
52 s.d. Beating him.] *Rowe*
54 s.d. Enter . . . Patroclus.] *F1*
55 ye thus] you this *F1*
62 Well?] *Kittredge;* Well, *Q, F1*
62 so I do] I do so *F1*
64 whosomever] *Kittredge;* who some euer *Q, F1*
65 that,] *Rowe;* that *Q, F1*
70 I] *F1;* It *Q*
74 I'll] *F1;* I *Q*
76 Ajax—] *F1;* Aiax. *Q*
76 s.d. Ajax . . . him.] *Rowe*
85 damn'd] *F1;* damned *Q*
87 the] for a *F1*
88 Thersites] *F1;* Thesites *Q*
90 the] thee *F1*
90 tenor] tenure *F1*
95 suff'rance] *Kittredge;* suffrance *Q;* sufferance *F1*
98 so;] *Knight (after Rowe);* so, *Q, F1*
100 and . . . out] *Cambridge conj.;* and knocke at *Q;* if he knocke out *F1*
101 brains] *F1;* beains *Q*
101 'a] he *F1*
103 too, Thersites?] *F4;* to Thersites. *Q;* to Thersites? *F1*
105 your] *Theobald;* their *Q, F1*
105–6 on their toes] *F1*
106 draught-oxen] *hyphen, F1*
107 wars] warre *F1*
109 To . . . Ajax!] *Theobald;* to Achilles, to Aiax, *Q, F1*
113 peace] *om. F1*
114 brach] *Rowe;* brooch *Q, F1*
117 clatpoles] Clotpoles *F1*
122 fift] *F1;* first *Q*
126 Maintain—] *Hanmer;* Maintaine *Q, F1*
130 s.d. Exeunt.] *Pope;* Exit. *F1*

II.ii

II.ii] *Capell*
Location: *Rowe*
3 damage] *F1;* domage *Q*
4 travail] *F1;* trauell *Q*
7 strook] *Capell;* stroke *Q, F1*
9 toucheth] touches *F1*
14–5 surety, Surety] *F1;* surely / Surely *Q*
17 worst.] *F1;* worst *Q*
24 merit's] *F1;* merits *Q*
26 king] *Craig;* King: *Q;* King *F1 (but followed by a parenthesis)*
27 father's] *anon. conj. (in Cambridge);* fathers *Q;* Father *F1*
28 compters] Counters *F1*
29 past-proportion] *hyphen, Johnson*
30 in] *F1;* in, *Q*
30 waist] *Johnson;* waste *Q, F1*
31 diminutive] *F1;* dyminutue *Q*
33 at] *F1;* of *Q*
34 them.] *Rowe;* them *Q;* them, *F1*
34 father] *F1;* father; *Q*
35 reason] reasons *F1*
36 tell] tells *F1*
38 reasons:] *Pope (subs.);* reasons *Q, F1*
43 Grecian] *F1;* Gretian *Q*
45, 46] *Lines transposed, F1*
47 Let's] *F1;* Sets *Q*
48 hare] hard *F1*
50 Make] Makes *F1*
51–2 Brother . . . keeping.] *as verse, Theobald (after F1); as prose, Q*
52 keeping] holding *F1*
56 mad] made *F1*
58 attributive] inclineable *F1*
64 shores] *F1;* shore *Q*
67 chose] *F1;* choose *Q*
70 soil'd] spoyl'd *F1*
71 unrespective] *F1;* vnrespectue *Q*
71 sieve] *Johnson;* siue *Q;* same *F1*
72 full.] *F1;* full, *Q*
74 with] of *F1*
75 truce,] *F1;* ttuce: *Q*
79 pale] stale *F1*
82 launch'd] *F1;* lansh't *Q*
86 he] *F1;* be *Q*
86 worthy] Noble *F1*
87 all clapp'd] *F1;* all, clapt *Q*
90 never fortune] Fortune neuer *F1*
94 stol'n,] *F1;* stolne: *Q*
97, 99 s.dd. Within.] *Theobald*
97 shrike] shreeke *F1*
100 Cassandra] *F1;* Crssandra *Q*
100 s.d. with . . . ears] *F1; s.d. after l. 96, Q, F1; placed as in Theobald*
104 eld] *Theobald conj.;* elders *Q;* old *F1*
105 canst] can *F1*
106 clamors] clamour *F1*
122 mad.] *Rowe (subs.);* madde, *Q, F1*
178–9 minds, . . . indulgence . . . wills,] *Rowe;* mindes . . . indulgence, . . . wills *Q, F1*
180 well-order'd] well-ordred *F1*
182 refractory] *F2;* refracturie *Q, F1*
185 nations] Nation *F1*
210 strike] *F1;* shrike *Q*

II.iii

II.iii] *Capell*
Location: *Rowe, Theobald*
1 s.p. Ther.] *Hanmer*
4 satisfaction! Would] *Craig;* satisfaction, would *Q, F1*
8 enginer] *F1;* inginer *Q*
12 ye] thou *F1*
15 abundant] *F1;* aboundant *Q*
16 their] the *F1*
18 Neapolitan] *Johnson (in a note);* Neopolitan *Q; om. F1*
19 depending] dependant *F1*
23 s.d. Within.] *anon. conj. (in Cambridge)*
25 'a'] *Kittredge;* a *Q;* haue *F1*
26 wouldst] *F1;* couldst *Q*
32 art] *F1;* art not *Q*
32 corse] *Capell;* course *Q;* coarse *F1*
33 s.d. Enter Patroclus.] *F1 (after l. 22); placed after anon. conj. (in Cambridge)*
35 prayer] a prayer *F1*
37 Patr. Amen.] *om. F1*
40 O, where?] *om. F1*
40 come?] *F1;* come *Q*
42 in to] *Capell;* into *Q, F1*
47 Thersites] thy selfe *F1*
50 must] maist *F1*
50 knowest] know'st *F1*
55–60 Patr. You . . . fool.] *F1*
61 this; come.] *Rowe;* this? come? *Q, F1*
63–4 of Agamemnon] *F1* (Agamemon)
65 this] *om. F1*
67 of the prover] to the Creator *F1*
68 s.d. Diomed] Diomedes *F1 (this variation frequent in F1 s.dd.; not hereafter recorded); s.d. after l. 66, F1*
68 s.d. Calchas] *Pope;* Calcas *Q;* Chalcas *F1*
69 Come] *om. F1*
70 s.d. Exit.] *F1*
72–3 whore . . . cuckold] Cuckold . . . Whore *F1*
73 emulous] emulations, *F1*
74–5 Now . . . all!] *F1*
75 s.d. Exit.] *Theobald*
79 shent] *Theobald;* sate *Q;* sent *F1*
80 appertainings] appertainments *F1*
80 him.] *F1* (him:); him *Q*
81 so, lest] of, so *F1*
83 say so] so say *F1*
83 s.d. Exit.] *Rowe*
86 lion-sick] *hyphen, F4*
87 you will] will *F1*
88 'tis] it is *F1*
88 a] the *F1*
89 A . . . lord.] *F1*
89 s.d. Takes Agamemnon aside.] *Capell (subs.)*
92 Who,] *F1;* Who *Q*
96 argument] *F1;* argument, *Q*
97 argument,] *F3;* argument *Q, F1*
99 their] *F1;* theit *Q*
99 composure] counsell that *F1*
101 knits not,] knits, not *F1*
102 s.d. Enter Patroclus.] *F1*
104 him.] him? *F1*
105–6 The . . . flexure.] *as prose, Malone; as verse, Q, F1*
106 legs are] legge are *F1*
106 flexure] flight *F1*
111 disgestion] digestion *F1*
112 after-dinner's] *hyphen and apostrophe, Rowe*
112 Hear] *F1;* Heere *Q*
114 wing'd] *F2;* winged *Q, F1*
118 on] of *F1*
120 Yea] Yea, and *F1*
120 unwholesome] unholdsome *F1*
122 come] came *F1*
124 self-assumption] *hyphen, F1*
126 tend] tends *F1*
126–7 on, Disguise] *F1;* on / Disguise, *Q*
130 pettish lines, . . . his flows, as] *F1;* course, and time, . . . and flowes, and *Q*
131 carriage . . . action] *F1;* streame of his commencement, *Q*
136 "Bring . . . war."] *quotes, Hanmer*
139 s.d. Exit.] *Rowe*
141 enter you] *F1;* entertaine *Q*
141 s.d. Exit Ulysses.] *F1*
144 much?] *F3;* much: *Q;* much, *F1*
152 pride] it *F1*
153 Ajax] *F1*
156 whatever] *Rowe;* what euer *Q, F1*
158 do hate the] hate the *F1*
160 s.d. Aside.] *Capell*

160 **And]** *om. F1*
166 **self-admission]** *hyphen, F4*
168 **th']** the *F1*
169 **request's]** *Pope;* requests *Q, F1*
172 **self-breath]** *hyphen, F1*
172 **worth]** wroth *F1*
176 **down himself]** gainst it selfe *F1*
177 **death-tokens]** *hyphen, F3*
180 **led]** *F1;* lead *Q*
187 **doth]** doe *F1*
191 **Shall]** Must *F1*
191 **stale]** *Rowe;* staule *Q, F1*
193 **titled]** *F1;* liked *Q*
193 **is,]** is: *F1*
194 **Achilles.]** *Rowe (subs.);* Achilles, *Q, F1*
195 **fat-already]** *hyphen, Capell;* fat already, *F1*
200 **s.d. Aside to Diomedes.]** *Johnson (subs.)*
201 **s.d. Aside to Nestor.]** *Johnson (subs.)*
201 **his]** this *F1*
202–3 **If . . . face.]** *as verse, Rowe; as prose Q, F1*
203 **pash]** *F1;* push *Q*
205 **he]** a *F1*
209, 211, 213, 216, 219, 220, 223 **s.dd. Aside.]** *Capell*
212 **let his humors]** *F1;* tell his humorous *Q*
215 **of]** a *F1*
219 **'twould]** *F1;* two'od *Q*
220 **s.p. Ulyss.]** *F1;* Aiax. *Q (Q gives* 'A would . . . warm. *to Ajax)*
220–2 **I will . . . warm.]** *assigned to Ajax, F1*
223 **praises]** *F1;* praiers *Q*
224 **in]** *F1*
225 **s.d. To Agamemnon.]** *Capell*
226 **so.]** *F1;* so? *Q*
227 **You]** *F1;* Yon *Q*
228 **does]** doth *F1*
229 **man—]** *Rowe;* man *Q;* man, *F1*
233–4 **A . . . Troyan!]** *as verse, Pope; as prose, Q, F1*
233 **with us thus]** thus with vs *F1*
239 **self-affected]** *hyphen, F3*
241 **gat]** got *F1*
242 **Fam'd]** Fame *F1*
242–3 **nature . . . all]** *F1;* nature, / Thrice fam'd beyond all thy *Q*
244 **thine]** thy *F1*
246 **half; . . . vigor,]** *Rowe;* halfe, . . . vigour: *Q;* halfe, . . . vigour, *F1*
249 **bourn]** *F1;* boord *Q*
250 **Thy]** *F1;* This *Q*
254 **Ajax']** *Hanmer;* Aiax *Q, F1*
257 **s.p. Nest.]** Vlis. *F1*
258 **here,]** *F1;* here *Q*
259 **great]** *om. F1*
263 **lord—]** *Capell;* Lord *Q;* Lord, *F1*
264 **cull]** *F1;* call *Q*
266 **sail]** may saile *F1*
266 **hulks]** bulkes *F1*

III.i

III.i] *Rowe*
Location: *Capell (subs.)*
o.s.d. Music sounds within.] *F1 (after* Exeunt. *at end of II.iii); placed as in Rowe*
o.s.d. and a Servant] *F1*
1 **you not]** not you *F1*
3 **s.p. Serv.]** *F1;* Man. *Q (throughout scene)*
6 **notable]** noble *F1*
6 **gentleman;]** *F1 (subs.);* gentleman *Q*
15 **grace.]** *Warburton;* grace? *Q, F1*
17 **titles]** title *F1*
25 **friend]** *F1*
28 **thou]** thou art *F1*
31 **who is]** who's *F1*
32 **heart-blood]** *hyphen, Rowe*
34 **Who?]** *F1;* Who *Q*
35 **not you]** you not *F1*
37 **thou]** that thou *F1*
38 **Cressid.]** *from F1* Cressida.; Cressid *Q*
39 **complimental]** *Johnson;* complementall *Q, F1*
40 **seethes]** *F1;* seeth's *Q*
41 **there's]** *F1;* theirs *Q*
42 **s.d. Helen]** Helena *F1*
42 **s.d. attended]** *Theobald*
44–5 **company! . . . them!]** *Theobald (subs.);* company, . . . them, *Q;* company: . . . them, *F1*
52 **Nell, he]** *F1; Nel.* he *Q (Q may intend* Nel. *as s.p.)*
57 **lord,]** Lord: *F1*
58 **lord, dear queen.]** *F1 (subs.);* Lord deere Queene? *Q*
63 **lord:]** *Theobald (subs.);* Lord *Q;* Lord, *F1*
65, 141 **honey-sweet]** *hyphen, F4*
66–7 **Go . . . you—]** *as prose, Capell; as verse, Q, F1*
68–9 **You . . . head!]** *as prose, Hanmer; as verse, Q, F1*
71 **queen—i' faith—]** *Collier;* Queene I faith—*Q, F1*
77 **supper, you]** *F1;* super. You *Q*
79 **queen, my]** *F1;* Queenem, y *Q*
87 **I'll . . . life,]** *om. F1*
87 **life,]** *Theobald;* life *Q*
90 **make 's]** *Capell conj.;* makes *Q;* make *F1*
92 **poor disposer's]** *F1;* disposers *Q*
93 **spy.]** *F1;* spie? *Q*
95 **instrument.]** *Johnson;* instrument, *Q;* Instrument *F1*
97 **horribly]** horrible *F1*
102 **twain]** *F1;* tawine *Q*
107 **prithee now.]** *F1 (subs.);* prethee, now *Q*
108 **lord]** *F1;* lad *Q*
114 **Pan. In . . . so.]** *F1*
114 **s.d. Sings.]** *Capell (subs.)*
115 **still love]** *om. F1*
116 **bow]** *F4;* bow. *Q;* Bow, *F1*
118 **shaft confounds]** *F1;* shafts confound *Q*
128 **doves,]** *F3;* doues *Q, F1*
133 **a-field]** *Warburton (after Rowe);* a field *Q, F1*
135 **Deiphobus]** Deiphoebus *F1*
135 **Antenor]** *Pope;* Anthenor *Q, F1 (frequently; not hereafter recorded)*
147 **s.d. Exit.]** *Rowe*
147 **s.d. retreat.]** *F1;* retreat? *Q*
148 **They're]** *F1;* Their *Q*
148 **the]** *om. F1*
151 **these]** *F1;* this *Q*
157 **have,]** *Pope;* haue. *Q;* haue: *F1*
159 **s.p. Par.]** *om. F1*
159 **Sweet,]** *Rowe;* Sweet *Q, F1*
159 **thee]** *F1;* her *Q*

III.ii

III.ii] *Capell*
Location: *ed.*
o.s.d. Troilus' Man] *F1;* Troylus, man *Q*
o.s.d. meeting] *Capell*
3 **he]** *F1*
4 **s.d. Enter Troilus.]** *F1*
6 **s.d. Exit Man.]** *Kittredge (after Capell)*
9 **to]** *om. F1*
11 **these]** those *F1*
13 **Pandar]** Pandarus *F1 (this variation frequent in F1 s.dd.; not hereafter recorded)*
17 **s.d. Exit.]** *F1* (Exit Pandarus.)
22 **thrice-repured]** *hyphen, Collier;* thrice reputed *F1*
22 **Death,]** *F4;* Death *Q, F1*
22 **me,]** *White (after Rowe);* me *Q, F1*
24 **subtile]** *F1;* subtill *Q*
24 **tun'd]** and *F1*
29 **s.d. Enter Pandarus.]** *F1*
31 **now:]** *Wilson (after Pope);* now, *Q, F1*
32 **fray'd]** *Capell;* fraid *Q, F1*
32 **spirit]** sprite *F1*
34 **as short]** so short *F1*
34 **s.d. Exit.]** *F1* (Exit Pand.)
38 **unawares]** *F1;* vnwares *Q*
39 **s.d. with]** *Capell;* and *Q, F1*
39 **s.d. Cressid]** Cressida *F1 (this variation frequent in F1 s.dd.; not hereafter recorded)*
40 **Come . . . blush?]** *as prose, Pope; as verse, Q, F1*
42 **s.d. Cressida draws backward.]** *White*
47 **day,]** *F1;* day? *Q*
52 **you—the]** *A. Walker;* you. The *Q, F1*
52 **tercel,]** *F1;* tercell: *Q*
56 **a' th']** 'oth' *F1*
58 **"In . . . interchangeably"]** *quotes, Hanmer*
58 **interchangeably"—]** *Rowe;* interchangeably. *Q, F1*
59 **s.d. Exit.]** *F2*
61 **Cressid]** *Kittredge;* Cressed *Q;* Cressida *F1*
62 **grant—]** *Pope;* graunt? *Q, F1*
67 **fears]** *Pope;* teares *Q, F1*
72 **safer]** safe *F1*
74–5 **O . . . monster.]** *as prose, Pope; as verse, Q, F1*
76 **Nor]** Not *F1*
76 **neither?]** *F1;* neither *Q*
81 **is]** *F1*
92 **crown it. No perfection]** *F1* (it:); louer part no affection *Q*
99 **s.d. Enter Pandarus.]** *F1*
110 **be woo'd]** *Q* (woed); are wooed *F1*
114 **lov'd]** *F1;* loued *Q*
114–5 **Prince . . . months.]** *as verse, Rowe; as prose, Q, F1 (l. 113 also as prose, F1)*
118 **glance . . . me—]** *Rowe;* glance; that euer pardon me *Q,* (me,) *F1*
120 **till now not]** not till now *F1*
122 **unbridled]** *F3;* vnbrideled *Q, F1*
122 **grown]** *F2;* grone *Q;* grow *F1*
123 **See, we fools!]** *Theobald;* see wee fooles, *Q, F1*
126 **woo'd]** *Rowe;* woed *Q, F1*
132 **Cunning]** *Pope;* Comming *Q, F1*
133 **very . . . counsel!]** soule of counsell from me. *F1*
133 **counsel]** *F1;* councell *Q*
134 **s.d. Kisses her.]** *Rowe (subs.)*
148 **resides]** *F2;* recids *Q;* recides *F1*
150–1 **I . . . speak.]** Where is my wit? / I would be gone: I speake I know not what. *F1*
152 **that speak]** that speakes *F1*
154 **confession,]** *F1;* confession. *Q*
157 **might;]** *Capell;* might *Q;* might, *F1*
160 **aye]** *F1;* age *Q*
160 **love,]** *F2;* loue. *Q, F1*
161 **youth,]** *F1;* youth. *Q*
167 **purity]** puriritie *F1*
173 **truth]** *Kittredge;* trueth *Q;* truths *F1*
174 **Troilus.]** *Rowe (subs.);* Troylus, *Q, F1*
176 **Wants similes, truth]** *F1;* Wants simele's truth *Q*
180 **Yet]** *F1*
180 **truth]** *ed.;* truth. *Q;* truth, *F1*
181 **truth's]** *Rowe;* truths *Q, F1*
185 **and]** *F1;* or *Q*
191 **th' have]** they'aue *F1*
192 **wind, or]** as Winde, as *F1*
193 **or]** as *F1*
198 **witness.]** *Rowe;* witnes *Q, F1*
200 **pain]** paines *F1*
201 **goers-between]** *hyphen, Rowe*
202, 204 **Pandars]** *Pope;* Panders *Q, F1*
203 **brokers-between]** *hyphen, Theobald*
209 **s.d. Troilus and Cressida]** *Capell; s.d. om. F1*
211 **Pandar]** *Pope;* Pander *Q;* and Pander *F1*
211 **s.d. Exit.]** Exeunt. *F1*

III.iii

III.iii] *Capell*
Location: *Rowe*
o.s.d. Ajax] *Theobald*
o.s.d. Menelaus, and] *F1*
o.s.d. Calchas] *Rowe;* Chalcas *Q, F1*
o.s.d. Flourish.] *F1*
1 **done]** done you *F1*
3 **your]** *F1*
4 **come]** *F4 (supported by Caxton);* loue *Q, F1*
17 **demand.]** *Rowe;* demand? *Q, F1*
31 **Calchas]** *Rowe;* Calcas *Q, F1 (generally; not hereafter recorded)*
35 **answered]** answer'd *F1*
37 **s.d. with Calchas]** *Capell (subs.)*
37 **s.d. Enter]** *F1*
37 **s.d. stand]** *om. F1*
37 **s.d. the door of]** *Neilson*
39 **pass]** to passe *F1*
42–3 **me . . . him?]** *F1* (me,); me. / . . . him, *Q*
43 **unplausive]** *F1;* vnpaulsiue *Q*
61 **s.d. Exeunt . . . Nestor.]** *Capell*

63 **s.d. Exit.]** *Capell*
66 **Ajax.]** *F4;* Aiax? *Q, Fl*
67 **Ha?]** *Rowe;* Ha: *Q;* Ha. *Fl*
69 **s.d. Exit.]** *Capell;* Exeunt. *Q, Fl*
70 **fellows?]** *Fl;* fellowes *Q*
81 **but honor]** but honour'd *Fl*
88 **friends.]** *Theobald (subs.);* friends, *Q, Fl*
88 **enjoy]** *Fl;* enioy: *Q*
90 **out]** *Fl;* out: *Q*
91 **Some thing]** Something *Fl*
100 **aiming]** shining *Fl*
102 **giver]** *Fl;* giuers *Q*
105–6 **To . . . itself,]** *om. Fl*
110 **mirror'd]** *Singer MS, Collier MS;* married *Q, Fl*
110 **there]** *Fl;* there? *Q*
112 **at]** it at *Fl*
115 **man]** may *Fl*
116 **be]** is *Fl*
118 **aught,]** *Fl* (ought,); aught: *Q*
119 **th' applause]** *Fl* (th' applause,); the applause. *Q*
120 **th' are]** they are *Fl*
121 **steel]** *Pope;* steele: *Q;* steele, *Fl*
124 **immediately]** *F2;* immediately, *Q;* immediately: *Fl*
125 **Th']** The *Fl*
127 **what. Nature,]** *Fl;* what / Nature *Q*
127 **are]** *F2;* are. *Q, Fl*
128 **abject]** *Fl;* obiect *Q*
129 **esteem,]** *Fl;* esteeme: *Q*
130–1 **to-morrow— . . . him—]** *Cambridge;* to morrow, . . . him *Q;* to morrow, . . . him? *Fl*
137 **fasting]** feasting *Fl*
140 **on]** *Fl;* one *Q*
141 **shriking]** shrinking *Fl*
146–7 **oblivion, . . . ingratitudes.]** *Hanmer (reading* ingratitude); obliuion: . . . ingratitudes, *Q;* obliuion: . . . ingratitudes: *Fl*
152 **mail]** *Pope;* male *Q, Fl*
154 **narrow,]** *Fl;* narrow: *Q*
155 **one]** *Fl;* on *Q*
155 **abreast.]** *F3 (period, Pope, subs.);* a brest, *Q, Fl*
158 **hedge aside]** *Fl;* turne a side *Q*
158 **forthright]** *F4 (subs.);* forth right *Q, Fl*
160 **hindmost]** *Fl;* him, most *Q*
161–3 **Or . . . on.]** *Fl*
162 **abject rear,]** *Hanmer;* abiect, neere *Fl*
164 **past]** *Fl;* passe *Q*
169 **farewell]** farewels *Fl*
169 **Let]** O let *Fl*
178 **give]** *Thirlby conj.;* goe *Q, Fl*
183 **sooner]** begin to *Fl*
184 **Than]** *Fl* (Then); That *Q*
184 **stirs not]** not stirs *Fl*
184 **once]** out *Fl*
194 **known?]** *Fl;* knowne. *Q*
197 **grain . . . gold]** *Fl;* thing *Q*
198 **th']** *Fl;* the *Q*
198 **depth]** deepes *Fl*
210 **our islands]** her Iland *Fl*
215 **s.d. Exit.]** *Pope*
219 **this;]** *Fl;* this *Q*
224 **a]** *Fl*
225 **air]** ayrie ayre *Fl*
233 **they]** we *Fl*
241 **s.d. Enter Thersites.]** *placed as in Globe; after* sav'd! *l. 241, Q; after l. 239, Fl*
251 **'a]** he *Fl*
255 **this]** his *Fl*
259 **break't]** *Fl;* breakt *Q*
259 **vainglory]** *Fl (subs.);* vaine glory *Q*
266 **to him]** *Fl*
270 **on his]** on hit *Fl*
271 **demands]** his demands *Fl*
274 **most]** *Fl*
276 **magnanimous]** magnanimious *Fl*
277 **six-or-seven-times-honor'd]** *hyphens, Capell*
277 **captain-general]** *Hanmer;* Captaine Generall *Q;* Captaine, Generall *Fl*
278 **army,]** *comma from F4;* armie. *Q;* Grecian Armie *Fl*
278 **et cetera.]** *Fl* (&c.)
287 **safe-conduct]** *hyphen, Capell*
295 **aleven]** *ed.;* a leuen *Q;* eleuen *Fl*
295 **of the]** a *Fl*
299 **ye]** you *Fl*
301 **he's]** *Fl*
301 **of]** a *Fl*
306 **bear]** carry *Fl*
309 **s.d. Exeunt . . . Patroclus.]** *Capell*
312 **s.d. Exit.]** *Capell*

IV.i

IV.i] *Rowe*
Location: *Rowe, Theobald*
o.s.d. with a torch] *Fl*
o.s.d. Antenor] *Pope;* Autemor *Q;* Anthenor *Fl*
o.s.d. and others] *Malone*
5 **you]** *Fl;* your *Q*
6 **bed-mate]** *hyphen, Fl*
8 **Greek . . . hand,]** *Fl (subs.);* Greeke Aeneas take his hand. *Q*
9 **wherein]** within; *Fl*
10 **a]** in a *Fl*
16 **and, so long,]** *Rowe (subs.);* and so long *Q, Fl*
17 **But]** *Fl;* Lul'd *Q*
17 **meet]** meetes *Fl*
21 **backward. . . . gentleness,]** *Theobald;* back-ward, in humane gentlenesse: *Q, Fl*
30 **to-morrow!]** *Capell;* to morrow— *Q;* to morrow. *Fl*
33 **despiteful]** despightful'st *Fl*
34–5 **The . . . early?]** *as verse, Fl; as prose, Q*
37 **'twas]** it was *Fl*
38 **Calchas']** *Pope;* Calcho's *Q;* Calcha's *Fl*
38 **him,]** *Fl;* him: *Q*
41 **believe]** doe thinke *Fl*
45 **wherefore]** whereof *Fl*
46–8 **That . . . Troy.]** *as verse, Fl; as prose, Q*
51 **s.d. Exit.]** *Fl* (Exit Aeneas)
53 **soul]** the soule *Fl*
54 **deserves . . . best]** merits . . . most *Fl*
57 **soil]** soylure *Fl*
61 **friends.]** *Fl* (friends:); friends, *Q*
66 **nor less]** no lesse *Fl*
67 **the]** which *Fl*
70 **false]** *Fl;* falfe *Q*
77 **they]** you *Fl*
79–80 **We'll . . . way.]** *as verse, Fl; as prose, Q*

IV.ii

IV.ii] *Pope*
Location: *ed. (after Capell)*
7 **now,]** *Theobald:* now *Q, Fl*
7 **a-weary]** *Capell (subs.);* a weary *Q, Fl*
10 **joys]** eyes *Fl*
13 **tediously]** hidiously *Fl*
14 **momentary-swift]** *hyphen, Pope;* momentary, swift *Fl*
17 **off]** *Fl;* of *Q*
19 **s.d. Within.]** *Fl*
19 **What's]** *Fl;* Whats *Q*
20 **s.d. Enter Pandarus.]** *Fl*
23–4 **How . . . Cressid?]** *as prose, Pope; as verse, Q, Fl*
24 **Here]** Heare *Fl*
27–8 **To . . . do?]** *as prose, Pope; as verse, Q, Fl*
29–30 **Come . . . others.]** *as verse, Capell; as prose, Q, Fl*
31 **capocchia]** *Theobald;* chipochia *Q, Fl*
34 **s.d. One knocks.]** *placed as in Capell; after l. 35, Q; after l. 33, Fl*
39 **s.d. Knock.]** *placed as in Capell; after l. 40, Q, Fl*
41 **s.d. Troilus and Cressida]** *Capell*
43 **s.d. Enter Aeneas.]** *Rowe*
45 **there?]** *Pope;* there *Q, Fl*
45 **Aeneas!]** *Collier;* Aeneas: *Q;* Aeneas? *Fl*
45–6 **Who's . . . early?]** *as verse, Pope; as prose, Q, Fl*
48 **Here?]** *Fl;* Here, *Q*
51 **It's]** *Kittredge;* its *Q;* 'tis *Fl*
52 **sworn. For]** *Fl (subs.);* sworne / For *Q*
54 **Who!—nay then.]** *Capell (after Rowe);* Who, nay then! *Q;* Who, nay then: *Fl*
55 **you are]** y'are *Fl*
57 **s.d. Enter Troilus.]** *Fl*
63 **us . . . him]** *Fl;* him, and *Q*
66 **so concluded]** concluded so *Fl*
72 **neighbor Pandar]** nature *Fl*
73 **s.d. Troilus and Aeneas]** *Capell*
74 **lost?]** *Hanmer;* lost, *Q;* lost: *Fl*
77 **s.d. Enter Cressid.]** Enter Cress. *Q* (Cress. *serving as s.p.);* Enter Pandarus and Cressid. *Fl (after l. 73)*
78 **s.p. Cres.]** *Fl*
79 **Ah, ah!]** Ah, ha! *Fl*
85 **Pray thee]** Prythee *Fl*
86 **wouldest]** would'st *Fl*
88–9 **I beseech you]** *Fl*
101 **force]** orce *Fl*
102 **extremes]** extremitie *Fl*
105 **I'll]** I will *Fl*
109 **s.d. Exeunt.]** *Fl*

IV.iii

IV.iii] *Capell*
Location: *ed. (after Theobald)*
2 **For]** Of *Fl*
9 **own]** *om. Fl*
9 **s.d. Exit.]** *Capell*
12 **lords.]** *Fl;* Lords? *Q*

IV.iv

IV.iv] *Capell*
Location: *ed.*
3 **full, perfect]** full perfect *Fl*
4 **violenteth]** no lesse *Fl*
6 **affections]** affection *Fl*
9 **dross]** crosse *Fl*
10 **s.d. Enter Troilus.]** *after l. 9, Fl*
11 **Ah]** *Johnson;* a *Q, Fl*
12 **ducks]** ducke *Fl*
13 **s.d. Embracing him.]** *Malone (after Capell)*
16–7 **"O . . . breaking."]** *as verse, Pope; as prose, Q, Fl*
17 **sigh'st]** sighest *Fl*
19–20 **"Because . . . speaking."]** *as verse, Pope; as prose, Q, Fl*
24 **strain'd]** strange *Fl*
27 **deities]** *Fl;* dieties *Q*
34 **back . . . by]** *Fl;* back, leaue taking, iussles roughly by: *Q*
40–1 **ourselves . . . one.]** *Pope;* our selues: . . . one, *Q;* our selues, . . . our *Fl*
42 **time]** time; *Fl*
44 **heaven,]** *Fl;* heauen. *Q*
48 **Distasted]** Distasting *Fl*
50 **Genius]** *Fl* (genius); Genius *Q (in italics)*
50 **so]** *Fl*
51 **"come"]** *Fl (quotes, Hanmer);* so *Q*
53 **tears? Rain]** *Fl* (raine,); teares raine *Q*
54 **th' root]** *Alexander;* my throate *Q;* the root *Fl*
54 **s.d. Exit.]** *Theobald*
57 **When . . . again?]** *assigned to Troilus, Fl*
58 **me,]** me my *Fl*
58 **heart—]** *Rowe;* heart. *Q, Fl*
64 **there is]** there's *Fl*
70 **Wear]** *Fl;* were *Q*
75 **it, love.]** *F3 (subs.);* it loue, *Q;* it; Loue: *Fl*
77–8 **Their . . . Flowing]** *Fl* (Flawing *Fl;* Flowing *F2*)
79 **novelty]** nouelties *Fl*
79 **person,]** *Fl* (person.; *comma, F3);* portion, *Q*
82 **afeard]** *Capell;* a feard *Q;* affraid *Fl*
87 **subtile]** *F3;* subtill *Q, Fl*
101] *Following this line Fl reads* Exit.
102 **Who, I?]** *Fl (comma, Capell);* Who I, *Q*
106 **wear]** *Fl;* were *Q*
108 **"plain and true"]** *quotes, Johnson*
108 **s.d. Enter . . . Diomedes.]** *Malone (after Rowe);* Enter the Greekes. *Fl* (after l. 108)
112 **is.]** *Fl;* is *Q*
116 **Ilion.]** *F3;* Illion? *Q, Fl*
119 **usage]** visage *Fl*
122–3 **to thee In]** towards, / I *Fl*
131 **free.]** *F2* (free;); free? *Q, Fl*
132 **you]** my *Fl*
133 **charge.]** *Fl* (charge:); charge, *Q*
135 **I]** Ile *Fl*
136 **port.]** *Fl;* port *Q*
139 **s.d. Exeunt . . . Diomedes.]** *Ritson conj.*
139 **s.d. Sound trumpet.]** *Fl*

140 Hark,] *F1;* Harke *Q*
142 to the] in the *F1*
143] *Following this line F1 reads* Exeunt.
144–8 Dei. Let . . . chivalry.] *F1*
144 s.p. Dei.] *Ritson conj.;* Dio. *F1*
148 s.d. Exeunt.] Exeu. *Q (after l. 143); om. F1*

IV.v

IV.v] *Capell*
Location: *Capell (after Rowe)*
o.s.d. Nestor] *Theobald;* Nester, Calcas *Q;* Nestor, Calcas *F1*
5–6 May . . . hither.] *as verse, F1; as prose, Q*
11 s.d. Trumpet sounds.] *Hanmer*
12 s.d. Enter . . . Cressid.] *F4 (from F2* Enter Dio. Cres.)
13 yond] yong *F1*
15 toe] *F1;* too *Q*
18, 23, 25, 29 s.dd. Kisses her.] *Collier MS (subs.)*
20–3 Yet . . . Nestor.] *as verse, Pope; as prose, Q, F1*
29 And . . . argument.] *om. F1*
33 Patroclus] *F1;* Patrolus *Q*
33 s.d. Kisses her again.] *Collier MS (subs.)*
38–9 The . . . kiss.] *as verse, Pope; as prose, Q, F1*
43 not] *F1;* nor *Q*
48 then.] then? *F1*
49 kiss] *Kittredge;* kisse, *Q;* kisse: *F1*
50 his.] *Capell;* his— *Q, F1*
53 s.d. Exit with Cressida.] *Dyce (after Pope)*
55 language] a language *F1*
60 unclasp] *F1;* vnclapse *Q*
61 ticklish] tickling *F1*
63 s.d. Flourish.] *after following entry direction in F1*
64 Troyans'] *Theobald;* Troyans *Q, F1*
64 s.d. Hector . . . Attendants] *F1 (*armed *Capell;* Troilus *Rowe); s.d. after l. 63, Q, F1; placed as in Alexander*
65 the] you *F1*
69 they] *om. F1*
70–1 field? . . . ask.] *Rowe;* field, . . . aske? *Q;* field: . . . aske? *F1*
73 s.p. Achil.] *A. Walker (after Theobald conj.); speech continued to Agamemnon, Q, F1*
74 misprising] disprising *F1*
77–8 this: . . . little,] *Pope (subs.);* this, . . . little: *Q, F1*
81 nothing. Weigh] *F1 (subs.);* nothing, way *Q*
85 seek] *F1;* seeke: *Q*
86 then?] *F1;* then, *Q*
87 s.d. Enter Diomedes.] *Pope*
88 Sir] sir, *F1*
89 Aeneas] *F1;* Eneas *Q*
92 breath] breach *F1*
93 s.d. Ajax . . . lists.] *Capell*
94 Ulyss. They . . . already.] *F1*
95 s.p. Agam.] *F1;* Vlisses: *Q (in italics; perhaps intended as a vocative, with l. 95 as the last line of Agamemnon's speech in the Q arrangement)*
96 knight,] Knight; they call him Troylus; *F1 (the F1 addition occurs again at l. 108 in both F1 and Q)*
97 matchless,] *F1;* matchlesse *Q*
98 in] *F1*
103 impare] impaire *F1*
112 s.d. Hector . . . fight.] *Rowe*
116 dispos'd.] *Rowe (subs.);* dispo'd, *Q;* dispos'd *F1*
121 cousin-german] *hyphen, Pope*
124 commixtion] commixion *F1*
126 so] *Pope;* so, *Q, F1*
132 Of . . . feud;] *F1*
133 drop] *F1;* day *Q*
142 Neoptolemus] *F2;* Neoptolymus *Q, F1*
143 Oyes] *Dyce;* (O yes) *Q, F1*
144 could] could'st *F1*
158 s.d. Agamemnon . . . forward.] *Rowe;* Enter Agamemnon and the rest. *F1*
161 my] mine *F1*
163 all] of *F1*
165–70 But . . . integrity,] *F1*
169 bias-drawing] *hyphen, Theobald*
173 s.d. To Troilus.] *Rowe*
177 lord?] *Capell;* Lord, *Q, F1*
178 that . . . oath] *F1;* thy affect, the vntraded earth) *Q*
179 quondam] *F1;* quandom *Q*
179 glove.] *F3 (subs.);* gloue, *Q;* Gloue *F1*
187 Despising many] And seene thee scorning *F1*
188 thy] *F1;* th' *Q (probably intended as an elided form of* thy)
190 to some] vnto *F1*
190 standers-by] *hyphen, Rowe*
193 hemm'd] *F1;* shrupd *Q*
199 O] *om. F1*
206 As . . . courtesy.] *F1*
220 Yon] Yond *F1*
235 pray thee] prythee *F1*
241 dost] *Rowe;* doost *Q;* doest *F1*
252 an] the *F1*
255 stithied] *F1;* stichied *Q*
263 have] *om. F1*
272 we] you *F1*
274 him.] *F1;* him *Q*
274–5 him. Beat . . . taborins] *F1;* him / To taste your bounties *Q*
276 s.d. all . . . Ulysses] *Malone (after Rowe)*
281 upon . . . nor] on heauen, nor on *F1*
284 you] thee *F1*
287 But] As *F1*
292 belov'd, she lov'd;] *F1;* beloued my Lord, *Q*

V.i

V.i] *Rowe*
Location: *Rowe (subs.)*
2 scimitar] *Rowe;* Cemitar *Q, F1*
4 core] *F1;* curre *Q*
6 seemest] seem'st *F1*
7 idiot-worshippers] *hyphen, F1*
12 needs] need *F1*
12 these] *F1;* this *Q*
14 boy] *F1;* box *Q*
15 said] thought *F1*
18 the guts-griping,] *Capell (comma, F4);* the guts griping *Q;* guts-griping *F1*
19 catarrhs,] *F1*
19 in the] i'th' *F1*
20–3 raw . . . tetter,] and the like, *F1*
20 dirt-rotten] *Pope;* durtrotten *Q*
23 preposterous] prepostrous *F1*
26 means] mean'st *F1*
29 no] *om. F1*
30 No?] *F1;* No *Q*
31 sleave-silk] *Collier (hyphen, Dyce);* sleiue silke *Q;* Sleyd silke *F1*
31 sarcenet] *F1;* sacenet *Q*
32 tossel] *F2;* toslell *Q;* tassell *F1*
32–3 purse, thou? Ah] *F3 (subs.);* purse-thou ah *Q;* purse thou: Ah *F1*
36 Finch-egg] *hyphen, Theobald*
38 in to-morrow's] *F1 (*to morrowes); into morrowes *Q*
47 s.d. Exeunt . . . Patroclus.] *Hanmer;* Exit. *F1*
51 Here's] *F1;* her's *Q*
54 brother,] *F1;* be *Q*
56 hanging] *F1*
56 brother's] *F1;* bare *Q*
58 fac'd] *ed.;* faced *Q;* forced *F1*
60 he is] *F1;* her's *Q*
61 dog] *F1;* day *Q*
61 moile] Mule *F1*
61 fitchook] *Kittredge;* Fichooke *Q;* Fitchew *F1*
64 not] *F1*
66 Menelaus.] *F1;* Menelaus— *Q*
66 Hey-day] Hoy-day *F1*
66 sprites] spirits *F1*
66 s.d. Hector, Troilus, Ajax] *Theobald;* Hector, Aiax *F1*
66 s.d. Menelaus] *Capell*
67–8 We . . . you.] *as verse, Capell; as prose, Q, F1*
67 'tis,] *F1;* tis *Q*
68 lights] light *F1*
69 s.d. Enter Achilles.] *F1*
71 now,] *Capell;* now *Q, F1*
71 good night] *F1 (subs.);* God night *Q*
73 Greeks'] *Theobald;* Greekes *Q, F1*
76 sewer] *Rowe;* sure *Q, F1*
77–8 Good . . . tarry.] *as verse, Theobald; as prose, Q, F1*
77 at once] *F1*
79 s.d. Exeunt Agamemnon, Menelaus.] *om. F1*
80 too, Diomed,] *F1 (subs.);* to Diomed. *Q*
85 s.d. Aside to Troilus.] *Capell (after Rowe)*
85–6 Follow . . . company.] *as verse, F1; as prose, Q*
87 s.d. Exit . . . following.] *Capell*
87 s.d. Achilles . . . Nestor] *Capell (after Hanmer*
88 false-hearted] *hyphen, F1*
93 it] that it *F1*
93 sun] *F1;* Sonne *Q*
98 varlots] Varlets *F1*
98 s.d. Exit.] *Hanmer;* Exeunt *F1*

V.ii

V.ii] *Rowe*
Location: *Capell (after Rowe)*
2, 4 s.pp. Cal.] *Rowe;* Chal. *Q, F1*
2, 4 s.dd. Within.] *Hanmer*
3 Diomed. Calchas, I think.] *Rowe (subs.;* Calchas *F4);* Diomed, Chalcas I thinke *Q;* Diomed, Chalcas (I thinke) *F1*
3 your] you *F1*
4 s.d. Enter . . . Ulysses] *F1*
4 s.d. at . . . Thersites] *Capell*
5 s.d. Enter Cressid.] *placed as in F1; after* him. *l. 6, Q*
7 s.d. Whispers.] *Rowe*
10–1 sing . . . cliff] finde . . . life *F1*
13 s.p. Cres.] *F2;* Cal. *Q, F1*
13 Remember?] *F1;* Remember *Q*
16 shall] should *F1*
18 Greek,] *F1;* Greeke *Q*
22 come,] *Theobald;* come *Q;* eome *F1*
22 pin.] *Johnson;* pin *Q;* pin, *F1*
22 forsworn.] a forsworne.— *F1*
24 trick—] *Collier;* tricke *Q;* tricke, *F1*
27 do] does not *F1*
29 Hold,] *F1;* Hold *Q*
34 a] one *F1*
36 pray] pray you *F1*
40 Now] Nay *F1*
41 distraction] *F1;* distruction *Q*
42 prithee] pray thee *F1*
43 all hell's] hell *F1*
46 How now, my] Why, how now *F1*
48 adieu,] *F1* ~
50–1 You . . . out.] *as verse, F2; as prose, Q, F1*
56 these] *F1*
58 But] *F1*
62 my] sweete *F1*
64 s.d. Cressid.] *F1;* Cress. *Q*
68 Tro. I . . . will.] *F1*
69 s.p. Cres.] *F1;* Troy: *Q*
71 was't] *F1;* wast *Q*
72 ha't] haue't *F1*
78 on] in *F1*
81 Nay . . . me.] *continued to Cressida, Thirlby conj.; given to Diomedes, Q, F1 (a strained sense can be made out of the original; see Honigmann, pp. 81–2)*
82 doth take] rakes *F1*
85 s.p. Cres.] *F1; speech continued to Troilus, Q*
89 one's] *Johnson;* on's *Q;* one *F1*
91 By] *F1;* And by *Q*
98–101 Why . . . you.] *as verse, F1; as prose, Q*
102 you] me *F1*
106 s.d. Exit Diomedes.] *Capell;* Exit. *F1 (after* then. *l. 106)*
112 Minds . . . turpitude.] *F1; with gnomic quotes, Q*
113 strength] *F1;* strength, *Q*
114 said] say *F1*
118 co-act] *F4;* Court *Q;* coact *F1*
122 th' attest] that test *F1*
123 had deceptious] *F1;* were deceptions *Q*
126 not,] *Theobald;* not *Q, F1*
134 soil] *F1;* spoile *Q*

136 **'a]** he *F1*
139 **be sanctimonies]** are sanctimonie *F1*
142 **was]** is *F1*
143 **up]** vp, *F1*
143 **itself!]** *Capell* (*after Pope*); it selfe *Q*; thy selfe *F1*
144 **Bi-fold]** By foule *F1*
152 **Ariachne's]** *F1*; Ariathna's *Q* (*u*); Ariachna's *Q* (*c*)
157 **five-finger-tied]** *F1* (*hyphens, Pope*); finde finger tied *Q*
159 **relics]** *Dyce*; reliques *Q, F1*
160 **given]** bound *F1*
167 **as]** *F2*
167 **Cressid]** Cressida *F1*
169 **on]** in *F1*
173 **sun]** Fenne *F1*
181 **s.d. Aeneas]** *F1*; Eneas *Q*
189 **s.d. Aeneas]** *F1*; Eeneas *Q*
196 **s.d. Exit.]** *om. F1*

V.iii

V.iii] *Rowe*
Location: *Capell* (*after Theobald*)
4 **in]** gone *F1*
5 **all]** *om. F1*
7 **brother]** *F1*; brothet *Q*
8 **intent]** *F1*; intenr *Q*
14 **s.p. Cas.]** *F1*; Cres. *Q*
15 **Be gone]** *F4*; Begon *Q, F1*
20–2 **To . . . charity.]** *F1*
21 **lawful,]** *Tyrwhitt conj.*; lawfull: *F1*
21 **give . . . use]** *Tyrwhitt conj.*; count giue much to as *F1*
23 **s.p. Cas.]** *F1*; *speech continued to Andromache, Q*
27 **dear]** *F3*; deere *Q, F1*
28 **precious-dear]** *hyphen, F3*; precious, deere, *F1*
29 **meanest]** mean'st *F1*
31 **No, faith,]** *Theobald* (*after F4*); No faith *Q, F1*
45 **mother]** Mothers *F1*
58 **But . . . ruin.]** *F1*
67 **a-field]** *F3*; a field *Q, F1*
82 **do]** doth *F1*
84 **dolors]** dolour *F1*
85 **distraction]** *F1*; destruction *Q*
86 **antics]** *F1*; antiques *Q*
89 **yet]** yes *F1*
90 **s.d. Exit.]** *F1*
93 **worth]** of *F1*
94 **s.d. Exeunt . . . Hector.]** *Malone* (*after Capell*)
104 **a' th's]** o'th's *F1*
109 **s.d. Tearing the letter.]** *Rowe*
110 **Go, wind,]** *Capell* (*after Theobald*); Go winde *Q, F1*
112] *Following this line F1 adds:* Pand. Why, but heare you? / Troy. Hence brother lackie; ignomie and shame / Pursue thy life, and liue aye with thy name.; *these lines are found in a slightly different version in Q at V.x.32–4 (see the text) and are repeated (reading, as in Q,* broker, *for* brother) *in F1 at the same point*
112 **s.d. severally]** *Malone*

V.iv

V.iv] *Rowe*
Location: *Rowe* (*subs.*)
o.s.d. **Alarum.]** *F1* (A Larum.; *preceding* Exeunt. *at V.iii.112*); *placed as in Rowe*
o.s.d. **Excursions.]** in excursion. *F1*
2 **abominable]** *F4*; abhominable *Q, F1*
4 **young]** *F1*
9 **arrant]** errant *F1*
9 **A' th' t' other]** *ed.* (*after Rowe*); Ath'tother *Q*; O'th'tother *F1*
10 **stale]** stole *F1*
17 **s.d. Enter . . . following.]** *Capell* (*from F1 s.d.* Enter Diomed and Troylus.)
18 **t' other]** *Rowe*; tother *Q*; th'other *F1*
19–20 **Fly . . . after.]** *as verse, F1*; *as prose, Q*
24–5 **Hold . . . sleeve!]** *as prose, F1*; *as verse, Q*
25 **s.d. Exeunt . . . fighting.]** *Capell* (*after Rowe*)
26 **thou]** *F1*
30 **s.d. Exit.]** *Rowe*

V.v

V.v] *Capell*
Location: *ed.* (*after Rowe*)
o.s.d. **Servant]** Seruants *F1*
5 **s.p. Serv.]** *F1*; Man. *Q*
5 **s.d. Exit.]** *Hanmer*
5 **s.d. Enter Agamemnon.]** *placed as in F1*; *after* proof. *l. 5, Q*
6 **Polydamas]** Polidamus *F1*
9 **Colossus-wise]** *hyphen, F1*
10 **kings]** *Hanmer*; Kings: *Q, F1*
11 **Epistrophus]** *Steevens*; Epistropus *Q, F1*
11 **Cedius]** *Capell*; Cedus *Q, F1*
11 **Polyxenes]** *Dyce*; Polixines *Q, F1*
12 **Thoas]** *Pope*; Thous *Q, F1*
21 **afoot]** *F3*; a foote *Q, F1*
22 **scaling]** scaled *F1*
24 **strawy]** straying *F1*
25 **a]** the *F1*
34 **him,]** *Rowe*; him. *Q*; him; *F1*
35 **Hector.]** *F1*; Hector, *Q*
41 **luck]** *F1*; lust *Q*
43 **s.p. Ajax.]** *F1*; *Q treats* Enter Aiax. *as s.p.*
47 **s.d. Exeunt.]** *Capell*; Exit. *Q, F1*

V.vi

V.vi] *Capell*
Location: *ed.* (*after Rowe*)
1 **s.p. Ajax.]** *F1*; *Q treats* Enter Aiax. *as s.p.*
1 **s.d. Diomed]** *F1*; Diom. *Q*
2 **s.p. Dio.]** *F1*; *Q treats* Enter Diom. *as s.p.*
5 **what, Troilus!]** *Hanmer*; what Troylus. *Q*; what Troylus? *F1*
11 **s.d. Exeunt fighting.]** *Rowe*; Exit Troylus. *F1*
11 **s.d. Enter Hector.]** *F1*
12 **Troilus?]** *F1*; Troylus, *Q*
13 **s.p. Achil.]** *F1*; *Q treats* Enter Achil: *as s.p.*
13 **ha!]** *om. F1*
13 **s.d. They fight.]** *Rowe* (*subs.*)
24 **him;]** *F1* (*subs.*); him *Q*
26 **reak]** *ed.*; wreake *Q, F1*
26 **I end]** thou end *F1*
30 **s.d. Exit . . . armor.]** *ed.* (*after A. Walker*)

V.vii

V.vii] *Capell*
Location: *ed.* (*after Rowe*)
1 **s.p. Achil.]** *F1*
6 **execute]** *F1*; execut *Q*
6 **arms]** arme *F1*
8 **s.d. Exeunt.]** *Pope*; Exit. *Q, F1*
8 **s.d. fighting]** *Capell*
9 **cuckold . . . cuckold-maker]** *F1* (*subs.*); cuck-old . . . cuck-old-maker *Q*
10 **dog!]** *Rowe* (*subs.*); dogge *Q*; dogge, *F1*
10, 11 **'Loo, Paris, 'loo! . . . 'Loo, Paris, 'loo!]** *F4* (*subs. but with semicolon after first* 'loo); lowe, *Paris* lowe, . . . lowe *Paris*, lowe *Q*; lowe; *Paris* lowe; . . . lowe *Paris*, lowe; *F1*
11 **double-henn'd]** *hyphen, Pope*
11 **Spartan]** sparrow *F1*
12 **s.d. Exeunt]** *Hanmer*; Exit *Q, F1*
12 **s.d. Menelaus]** *F1*; Menelus *Q*
12 **s.d. Margarelon]** *Capell*
13, 15, 23 **s.pp. Mar.]** *Capell*; Bast. *Q, F1*
16–7 **am bastard]** am a Bastard *F1*
20 **quarrel's]** *F1*; quarrells *Q*
22 **s.d. Exit.]** *Capell*
23 **s.d. Exit.]** Exeunt. *F1*

V.viii

V.viii] *Dyce*
Location: *ed.* (*after Rowe*)
3 **good]** *F1*; my *Q*
4 **s.d. Puts . . . him.]** *Malone* (*after Capell*)
4 **s.d. Myrmidons]** his Myrmidons *F1*
5 **Look]** *F1*; Loke *Q*
6 **ugly]** *F1*; ougly *Q*
6 **heels;]** *Rowe* (*subs.*); heeles *Q*; heeles, *F1*
7 **dark'ning]** darking *F1*
10 **s.d. Hector falls.]** *Capell*
11 **thou next! Come]** thou: now *F1*
13 **and]** *om. F1*
13 **amain]** a maine *F1*
15 **retire]** retreat *F1*
15 **part]** *F1*; prat *Q*
16 **s.p. Myr.]** *Rowe*; One: *Q*; Gree. *F1*
16 **Troyans' trumpet sound]** Troian Trumpets sounds *F1*
19 **half-supp'd]** *hyphen, Pope*
20 **bait,]** *comma, F3*; baite: *Q*; bed; *F1*
20 **s.d. Sheathes his sword.]** *Capell* (*subs.*)

V.ix

V.ix] *Dyce*
Location: *ed.* (*after Rowe*)
o.s.d. **Sound retreat. Shout.]** *F1*
o.s.d. **Diomed]** *F1*; Diom: *Q*
1 **shout]** *F1*
1 **this]** that *F1*
3 **s.p. Soldiers.]** *Neilson*; Sould: *Q*; Sold. *F1*
3 **s.d. Within.]** *om. F1*
3, 4 **Hector's]** *F1*; Hectors *Q*
3 **slain! Achilles!]** *Pope*; slaine Achilles. *Q*; slaine, Achilles. *F1*
6 **as . . . man]** a man as good *F1*

V.x

V.x] *Dyce*
Location: *ed.* (*after Rowe*)
o.s.d. **Deiphobus]** *F2*; Diephobus *Q*; Deiphoebus *F1*
1 **field.]** *ed.*; field, *Q, F1*
1 **s.d. Enter Troilus.]** *after l. 2, F1*
2 **Never . . . night—]** *F1 continues line to Aeneas, but assigns to Troilus* Hector is slaine. *in l. 3*
5 **beastly]** *F1*; bestly *Q*
8 **say,]** *Theobald*; say *Q, F1*
12 **fear,]** *F1*; feare *Q*
16 **scritch-owl]** *ed.*; scrich-ould *Q*; screech-oule *F1* (*no hyphen*)
17 **in to]** *F1*; into *Q*
17 **there, "Hector's]** *F1* (*subs.*); their Hectors *Q*
20 **Cold]** *Pope*; Could *Q*; Coole *F1*
21 **Scare]** *F3*; Scarre *Q, F1*
21–2 **But . . . dead;]** *F1*
23 **yet.]** *F1* (*subs.*); yet *Q*
23 **vile]** *F1*; proud *Q*
23 **abominable]** *F4*; abhominable *Q, F1*
23 **tents,]** *F1*; tents: *Q*
24 **pight]** *F1*; pitcht *Q*
26 **great-siz'd]** *hyphen, Pope*
29 **frenzy's]** *Pope*; frienzes *Q*; frensies *F1*
30 **march. To Troy]** *ed.*; march, to Troy *Q*; march to Troy, *F1*
32 **hear you, hear]** *F1*; here you, here *Q*
33 **s.d. Strikes him.]** *Rowe*
33 **Ignominy,]** ignomy, and *F1*
34 **s.d. Exeunt . . . Pandarus.]** Exeunt. *F1*
35 **my]** mine *F1*
36 **world, world!]** *F1*; world— *Q*
37 **traders]** *Craig conj.*; traitors *Q, F1*
38 **a-work]** *F1* (aworke); a worke *Q*
39 **lov'd]** desir'd *F1*
39 **loath'd]** *F1*; loathed *Q*
41 **humble-bee]** *hyphen, Pope*
46 **cloths]** *Rowe*; cloathes *Q, F1*
47 **Pandar's]** *Rowe*; Pandars *Q*; Panders *F1* (*not in italics as a proper name*)
50 **your]** *F1*; my *Q*
51 **hold-door]** *F1*; hold-ore *Q*
54 **galled]** *F1*; gauled *Q*
56 **s.d. Exit.]** *Rowe*; Exeunt. / FINIS. *F1*; FINIS. *Q*

All's Well That Ends Well

THE PLOT OF *All's Well That Ends Well* is a tissue of traditional folk motifs. The story of the abandoned wife who performs a seemingly impossible series of tasks in order to regain her husband is at least as old as the myth of Eros and Psyche. It has analogues in many of the literatures of the world. The hero or heroine who achieves great good fortune by knowing how to cure the sickness of the king when everyone else has failed, the bed-trick, the exchange of rings, and the association of virginity with magical power are all story elements with reverberations originating far back in the past. In shaping them into a dramatic plot, Shakespeare was strongly influenced by the story of Giletta of Narbona, told as the ninth story of the third day in Boccaccio's *Decameron*. It is possible that he read the Italian original, but his chief source was probably the English translation, in William Painter's collection *The Palace of Pleasure* (1566–67, 1575).

Giletta of Narbona is the daughter of a wealthy and celebrated physician. She falls in love with Beltramo, the only son of the noble count by whom her father is employed. The count dies and Beltramo goes to Paris as a ward of the French king, who is suffering from an apparently incurable disease. When Giletta's own father also dies, she follows Beltramo to Paris, heals the king with the help of a remedy she has inherited, and then claims Beltramo as her reward. Beltramo himself is horrified by the idea, and even the king is reluctant to agree to a marriage so unequal. He keeps his word to Giletta, however, and Beltramo is forced to yield. Immediately after the wedding, Beltramo flees to Italy and enters the service of the Florentines against the Sienese. Giletta, an unhappy virgin wife, remains for a time in Rossiglione, where she wins the love and respect of all her husband's subjects. Hearing, however, of Beltramo's bitter jest, that he would consent to live with his wife when she possessed herself of a ring from which he was never parted and came to him with their son in her arms, conditions impossible (as he thought) to fulfill, she disguises herself as a pilgrim and journeys to Florence. There, discovering that Beltramo is paying court to the daughter of an impoverished gentlewoman of the city, she persuades the two women to help her. The daughter exacts Beltramo's ring as the price of her surrender, and Giletta then, for some time, secretly supplies her place in Beltramo's bed. When she is sure she is pregnant, she puts an end to these nocturnal meetings, rewards the gentlewoman and her daughter, and sends them out of Florence. Beltramo returns to Rossiglione where, some time later, Giletta suddenly appears to confront him with the ring and twin sons so like their father that Beltramo cannot help but recognize them as his own. All the courtiers and ladies of Rossiglione plead that Giletta should be accepted, and Beltramo, "perceiving her constant mind and good wit, and the two fair young boys," gladly agrees: he sets up a great feast and "from that time forth he loved and honored her as his dear spouse and wife."

As told by Boccaccio and Painter, this story has a simple shape and a clarity which are satisfying and wholly unproblematic. Everyone, even the king, is agreed at the beginning that Giletta, though wealthy, is too low-born to be Countess of Rossiglione. In her first attempt, made as the physician's daughter, she fails to win anything more than the outward appearance of rank. Subsequently, while administering Beltramo's estates, and then in Florence, she demonstrates an innate aristocracy of wit and enterprise so compelling that it annihilates the class barrier. She wins over Beltramo's household and subjects, then Beltramo himself, through sheer intellect and resourcefulness. No one in the story blames Beltramo for his initial repudiation. The king forced him into a demeaning marriage, and it rests entirely with Giletta to prove by her "diligence" that there might be something to recommend such a misalliance after all. It is true that the reader wants Giletta to succeed, but no blame attaches itself to Beltramo for being hard to persuade. Only through sheer intelligence, and by demonstrating that she can give her husband sons who inherit his face as well as his name, can Giletta make herself Beltramo's equal, his wife in fact and not in law only.

As usual, Shakespeare greatly compressed the time-span of Boccaccio's story, reducing it to a more manageably dramatic compass. He also made some significant changes in the situation and characters of the two protagonists. Helena, unlike Giletta, is poor as well as low-born, and she lacks the total self-sufficiency and some of the cunning of her prototype. Bertram, her reluctant husband, stands convicted of faults considerably more damning than Beltramo's aristocratic pride. He is callow and insensitive, a lecher, an oath-breaker, and a liar, who not only misprizes Helena but makes other serious mistakes of judgment as well. Shakespeare also added four major characters for whom there were no equivalents in his source; the old Countess of Rossillion, Lafew, Parolles, and the fool Lavatch. All four have one thing in common: they operate in their different ways, throughout the comedy, to raise Helena in our estimation and to degrade Bertram. The play that results has sacrificed the simplicity and clear emotional emphasis of the folk-tale from which it derives. Indeed it seems positively to stress the incompatibility between characters who are sophisticated and complex and a plot which is neither of these things. Like its successor *Measure for Measure*, *All's Well That Ends Well* often seems to be questioning its own story material and, particularly in the final scene, to look ironically at its own title and at the very nature of comedy.

It is virtually axiomatic in comedy since the time of Menander that when a young man or woman wishes to marry purely for love, overleaping disparities of birth, wealth, and position, the older generation represented by fathers, mothers, uncles, and guardians will strenuously oppose such an attempted infringement of the laws of established society. *All's Well That Ends Well*, with no help whatever from its source, insists upon inverting this pattern. Boccaccio's king, though grateful for his cure, did not relish bestowing Beltramo upon a rich physician's daughter. Shakespeare's King, by contrast, is warmly approving of the match, even though Helena, unlike Giletta, is not only a commoner but poor. The old lord Lafew, the most eminent of the King's courtiers, also adopts the attitude that nothing can be too good for her. Most surprising of all, the old Countess of Rossillion, Bertram's mother, greets the news that her only son has been married to her waiting gentlewoman with unfeigned delight. In this play it is the old who are generous and flexible in their social attitudes while the young—Bertram, Parolles, and (according to one view) the young lords whose constraint and inner fear at the prospect of being chosen by Helena are mocked by Lafew—tend to be class-conscious snobs.

All's Well That Ends Well is a play filled with nostalgia for the past, concerned to evoke the remembrance of better times. Rossillion, where the action begins and ends, is an almost Chekhovian backwater, elegiac and autumnal, a world preserved in amber. It derives its character chiefly from the old Countess, from the shrewd and "unhappy" fool favored by her late husband, and from memories of the dead: Bertram's father, or that wonder-working physician Gerard de Narbon whose skill, ultimately, was not proof against his own mortality. It is understandable, to some extent, that young Bertram should be impatient to leave this place, even as it is understandable that he should experience an initial psychological shock when told he must marry a girl he has known there all his life as a dependent, a kind of inferior sister. Yet neither Paris nor Florence, the two places to which he tries to escape, functions for him as that heightened, more extraordinary world familiar in so many of Shakespeare's comedies. In neither is he transformed.

In Paris as at Rossillion, the Golden Age lies in the past. The King is old and fretful, a man who has outlived his health, his friends, and his pleasure in living. The court which surrounds him is hard-headed and rational and Lafew summarizes its ordinary way of thinking when he complains, from the standpoint of an older generation, that

> They say miracles are past, and we have our philosophical persons, to make modern and familiar, things supernatural and causeless. Hence is it that we make trifles of terrors, ensconcing ourselves into seeming knowledge, when we should submit ourselves to an unknown fear. (II.iii.1–6)

Into this sceptical, hard-headed world comes Helena, offering something quite alien to it, in the form of a miraculous cure, and demanding a fairy-tale marriage as her reward. The cure, achieved by way of a secret transmitted to her from the past, is unexpectedly successful. The marriage is not. Bertram refuses to accommodate himself to the archetypal story pattern, to recognize any return of the Golden Age. A struggle develops between the demands of romance, or comic form, and the stubborn resistance set up by a realistic, everyday world in which merit is not always rewarded, or even recognized for what it is. In this world, unicorns do not exist to testify to the mystic power of virginity, and Prince Charming is likely to prefer the fashionably dressed elder sisters to beauty in rags. Love itself is not simply the servant of a fantastic plot, but a matter of complex adjustments within the personality.

From Paris, Bertram flees to Florence, a place to which his thoughts inclined him even before Helena's arrival. Like the other young lords, he is susceptible for all his rationalism to the glamour of war, and the

Florentines and the Sienese are, as the King puts it, "by th' ears" (I.ii.1). The phrase suggests a dogfight more than it does an epic combat out of the pages of chivalry, but the noble youth of France are still eager to go and fight on either side of this dispute, purely for the sake of personal honor. Honor is an important word in *All's Well That Ends Well* generally, but it is also one that takes some hard, Falstaffian knocks. The King of France will have nothing to do himself with the Italian imbroglio, for hard-headed political reasons, nor does he care if his courtiers join the Florentines or the Sienese. The First Lord tells the Duke of Florence at the beginning of Act III, after he has heard (but the theatre audience has not) "the fundamental reasons of this war," that "Holy seems the quarrel / Upon your Grace's part; black and fearful / On the opposer," and the words are recognizably a parody of what anyone involved in any war, for whatever reason, always says. Basically, Italy is a kind of gymnasium where the youth of France may exercise idle limbs and minds and indulge the only romanticism in which they still believe. The conflict itself ends in a peace treaty of an unspecified kind, after the usual quantity of bloodshed and embarrassing accidents: "There was excellent command—to charge in with our horse upon our own wings, and to rend our own soldiers!" (III.vi.48–50). Helena comes close to echoing Falstaff's words at Shrewsbury, although the emotion which prompts them is very different, when she laments that "honor but of danger wins a scar, / As oft it loses all" (III.ii.121–22). Moreover, as Lavatch points out (IV.v.94–101), even honor's scar may be ambiguous. The velvet patch on the face of the returning warrior may conceal wounds inflicted by syphilis rather than the sword.

Although Lafew, the King, and the old Countess fondly remember an age in which martial honor was something tangible and significant, it seems to have declined now into a matter of game-playing and mere words. Honor is not the only quality to be trivialized in this way. Shakespeare is concerned throughout to contrast a vanished world of the past in which words were subordinate to facts with a debased, present-day society in which language has become an empty and often a lying substitute for deeds. The King remembers and praises Bertram's father, his dead friend, as a man whose "tongue obey'd his hand" (I.ii.41). This proper subservience of speech to behavior tends now to be reversed or else, even more disturbingly, there is simply no connection at all between what people say and what they think and do. The King, Lafew, and the Countess constantly stress the rightful primacy of facts and intrinsic qualities over misleading verbal descriptions. All these members of an older generation know what the King later tries to tell Bertram, that

> Good alone
> Is good, without a name; vileness is so:
> The property by what it is should go,
> Not by the title. (II.iii.128–31)

"The mere word's a slave," he goes on, trying to make Bertram see that the fact that Helena is young, wise, and fair matters far more than the superficial social description of her as "a poor physician's daughter." He wastes his breath, however, on a young man whose best friend and greatest influence is called, entirely accurately, Parolles.

Parolles is an embodiment of that discrepancy between words and deed which plays so important a part in the play as a whole. The glorious, swashbuckling past upon which he lives, dines out at ordinaries, and attracts rich young patrons like Bertram is nothing but a verbal construct. He is really a parasite and a coward, sheltering behind a facade of language and fine clothes. He talks constantly of honor but has none, of guns and drums and wounds but in fact is timorous as a mouse. Parolles descends from a venerable line of braggart warriors, talkers and not doers, who originate with Aristophanes and then swagger their way through Menander, Plautus, and Terence into Elizabethan comedy. Shakespeare had already experimented with the *miles gloriosus* type in Don Armado, Ancient Pistol, and (with a difference) Falstaff. Parolles, however, is the most severely criticized of them all. He bears a heavy weight of moral blame for encouraging Bertram to corrupt "a well-derived nature" (III.ii.88), for upholding snobbery and vice. Lafew is entirely accurate when he declares that "there can be no kernel in this light nut; the soul of this man is his clothes" (II.v.43–44). Here, as elsewhere in the comedy, an extravagance of dress concealing emptiness or corruption within is used as a variant on the theme of fine words cloaking innate baseness. It is the way of the world that, for a time, the deception should pass, that Parolles should convince Bertram with words and clothes, while "virtue's steely bones / Looks bleak i' th' cold wind" (I.i.103–4). Lafew, Helena, Lavatch, and the Countess are never deceived by him, however, and ultimately he is subjected to a public exposure and humiliation that is crushing in a manner more usually associated with the "comical satires" of Ben Jonson than with Shakespeare. At the end, this "manifold linguist" is forced ignominiously into the position that Helena has maintained gracefully all along: "Simply the thing I am / Shall make me live" (IV.iii.333–34).

Helena herself is prized by the older generation not only because they recognize her intrinsic worth, but because she is a living example of the attitudes of the past. Certainly she makes her distrust of disembodied words plain from the start. In her imagination, the court to which Bertram has been despatched is a place of verbal conceits, "Of pretty, fond, adoptious christendoms" (I.i.174) which dress love up in fashionable disguises, losing the substance in the show. Left behind at Rossillion, she worries with some cause about what may happen to Bertram there and laments, characteristically, that "wishing well had not a body in't, / Which might be felt" (I.i.181–82). In Paris, she achieves the man she loves through an action, the healing of the King, and then discovers that her victory is hollow, a matter of words alone. She is only "the shadow of a wife . . . The name, and not the thing" (V.iii.307–8). Defeated and self-accusing, she attires herself as a pilgrim and makes her way towards Saint Jaques le Grand. Unlike Giletta, who intended quite specifically to find her husband and accomplish the task set, Helena seems to arrive in Florence more by accident than purpose. Once there, however, she proceeds to make the same use of Diana and her mother that Giletta had done, and with the same success. It is at this point that problems of a kind non-existent in Boccaccio's story rear themselves in Shakespeare's play.

Although some scholars have tried to identify *All's Well That Ends Well* with the mysterious *Love's Labor's Won*, a play mentioned by Meres in 1598 among the other early comedies of Shakespeare, its whole quality and verbal character really argue for a date around 1602–3, after *Hamlet* and *Troilus and Cressida* and just before *Measure for Measure*. The verse of *All's Well That Ends Well*—compressed, elliptical, abstract, often tortuous and obscure—is very different from the fluid, concrete, and playful language of the early comedies but, in some respects, like that of *Troilus and Cressida* and *Measure for Measure*. Even more important, the comedy ends by using the folk-motif of the bed-trick to force a clash between those opposing elements of fairy-tale and realism, of romance motivation and psychological probability, which have existed in so uneasy a harmony throughout. In the final scene of *All's Well That Ends Well*, romance wins a kind of pyrrhic victory, even as it does, again through the bed-trick, in a blatantly fictional last act of *Measure for Measure* a year later. Both victories are disturbing, because they raise in a particularly acute and deliberate fashion doubts as to the validity of comedy as an image of truth.

Bertram pays adulterous court to Diana with vows and false promises which she recognizes as such: "therefore your oaths / Are words and poor conditions, but unseal'd" (IV.ii.29–30). Back in France, he will deny that he ever made them. Helena, by contrast, takes words which Bertram originally intended only as a formula, a heightened way of declaring that he would never accept her as his wife, and interprets them literally. She forces language to become fact and confronts Bertram at the end not with words but with two talismanic things: the ring and the child she has conceived. Thematically, in terms of the debate between words and deeds which has been sustained throughout the play, this resolution is entirely right and proper. Psychologically, and in dramatic terms, it is difficult in ways that Shakespeare seems to have wanted to emphasize rather than to conceal.

In Boccaccio's story, Giletta is never believed to be dead. She reappears at Rossiglione after a long absence but not, as Helena seems to do, from the grave. Helena's supposed death is credited by other characters in the play on the best evidence: letters received from her at Saint Jaques le Grand describing her grief and illness and finally, confirmation of her decease from "the rector of the place" (IV.iii.58–59). Critics who do not like Helena often point out that she has apparently not only concocted a monstrous lie in these letters but, apparently, has bribed the rector to forge a death certificate. Helena's "death," however, will not bear investigation in such literal terms, any more than will Hermione's in *The Winter's Tale*, and for much the same reasons. Helena dies so that Diana in the final scene can expound her riddle, "one that's dead is quick" (V.iii.303), and so that the transformation of Helena herself from a condition of nothingness—a "ghost," a "shadow," a wife in name alone—into a condition replete with life and joy may be as striking as possible. There is a powerful emotionalism in the last scene of this play. It derives, however, from an accord which, unlike the wholly consistent ending of *The Winter's Tale*, seems to ignore and leave unresolved the major issues of the play.

By introducing Helena's mock-death and resurrection, Shakespeare debased Bertram in a way for which there was no precedent in his source. In Boccaccio, the poor gentlewoman and her daughter remained in Florence after helping Giletta. Diana and her mother, on the other hand, appear in Rossillion to remind Bertram that he has sworn to marry Diana after his wife's death, and to claim fulfillment now of that promise. Bertram's behavior in these straits is very like that of Angelo when faced with Isabella and Mariana at the end of *Measure for Measure*: he turns and twists, lies and calumniates, providing an entirely realistic demonstration of just how far he can go in prevarication and meanness. The revelation of Helena, her fairy-tale task accomplished, clears him of a murder charge, but it does not elicit from him anything but the most perfunctory indication of acceptance and apology. Shakespeare might easily have made Bertram eloquent here, but he did not choose to. He was perhaps too conscious of the fact that the second winning of Bertram, although more arduous, nonetheless belongs to exactly the same world of fairy-tale and romance as the first. In terms of psychological truth, there is no more reason for Bertram to accept Helena because of the bed-trick than because of the miraculous healing of the King. This second clash between realism and fable, the old world and the new, is suggested but comes to no issue. Instead, the entire scene gradually fades away and becomes dim, retreating visibly into the realm of romance.

The character of the verse of *All's Well That Ends Well* alters markedly in the last fifty lines of the play. It becomes simple, direct, and archaic: the transparent language of riddle-games and fables. Most of it is further distanced by being cast in the form of rhyming couplets whose inevitability of sound and rhythm help to characterize the larger inevitability of the archetypal happy ending. Diana plays with the situation like a good fairy about to restore a princess who vanished long ago, teasing the baffled King, enjoying mystification for its own sake. By the time Helena appears with her two talismans, the ring and the unborn child, the comedy has loosed its moorings and floated off into a poignant, but attenuated, world of unbelief. Blithely, the King turns to Diana and enjoins her to select any husband she fancies from among the nobles of his court. One might think that the misfortunes of

Helena would make him wary of this particular matrimonial method, but no one moves to break the spell. Only in the odd conditional introduced into the King's final couplet, the unexpectedly tentative "seems" and "if," is a shadow of doubt allowed to return:

> All yet seems well, and if it end so meet,
> The bitter past, more welcome is the sweet.

The title of the comedy itself, referred to now by the King as it was previously, but more confidently, by Helena herself (IV.iv.33–36,V.i.25), was proverbial. Like the proverbs continually employed in a perverse and contradictory fashion by the bitter fool Lavatch—traditional bits of lore existing uneasily in a world grown too complex for such simplifications—it serves as a gentle reminder that fairy-tales, ultimately, are not true.

Anne Barton

The table of the heart. From Geffrey Whitney. A *Choice of Emblems* (1586). When Helena in *All's Well* (I.i.94–95) describes how she sits and draws Bertram's "arched brows, his hawking eye, his curls, / In our heart's table," she is referring metaphorically to the idea expressed in the emblem above, which shows a man inscribing the lineaments of his friend on a wax tablet held against the friend's heart. So too, Hamlet, when he exclaims, "My tables—meet it is I set it down / That one may smile, and smile, and be a villain!" (*Hamlet*, I.v.107–8), is literally applying Whitney's advice, in the verses accompanying the emblem, to record "His wordes and deedes, that beares the face of frende," though in Hamlet's case the "friend" is his bitter enemy Claudius. For a picture of a contemporary pocket "tables" or table-book, see p. 180. (*By permission of the Harvard College Library*)

All's Well That Ends Well

[Dramatis Personae

King of France
Duke of Florence
Bertram, *Count of Rossillion*
Lafew, *an old lord*
Parolles, *a parasitical follower of Bertram*
Two French Lords *(the brothers Dumaine), in the Florentine service*
Rinaldo, *a steward* } *servants to the Countess of Rossillion*
Lavatch, *a clown* }
Page }

Gentleman, *an astringer*
Countess of Rossillion, *mother to Bertram*
Helena, *a gentlewoman protected by the Countess*
An old Widow *of Florence*
Diana, *daughter to the Widow*
Violenta } *neighbors and friends to the Widow*
Mariana }

Lords, Officers, Soldiers, *etc., French and Florentine*

Scene: *Rossillion; Paris; Florence; Marseilles*]

ACT I, Scene I

Enter young Bertram, *Count of Rossillion, his mother* [*the* Countess of Rossillion], *and* Helena, Lord Lafew, *all in black.*

Count. In delivering my son from me, I bury a second husband.

Ber. And I in going, madam, weep o'er my father's death anew; but I must attend his Majesty's command, to whom I am now in ward, evermore in subjection.

Laf. You shall find of the King a husband, madam; you, sir, a father. He that so generally is at all times good must of necessity hold his virtue to you, whose worthiness would stir it up where it wanted rather than lack it where there is such abundance.

Count. What hope is there of his Majesty's amendment?

Laf. He hath abandon'd his physicians, madam, under whose practices he hath persecuted time with hope, and finds no other advantage in the process but only the losing of hope by time.

Count. This young gentlewoman had a father—O, that "had," how sad a passage 'tis!—whose skill was almost as great as his honesty; had it stretch'd so far, would have made nature immortal, and death should have play for lack of work. Would for the King's sake he were living! I think it would be the death of the King's disease.

Laf. How call'd you the man you speak of, madam?

Count. He was famous, sir, in his profession, and it was his great right to be so—Gerard de Narbon.

Laf. He was excellent indeed, madam. The King very lately spoke of him admiringly and mourningly. He was skillful enough to have liv'd still, if knowledge could be set up against mortality.

Ber. What is it, my good lord, the King languishes of?

Laf. A fistula, my lord.

Ber. I heard not of it before.

Words and passages enclosed in square brackets in the text above are either emendations of the copy-text or additions to it. The Textual Notes immediately following the play cite the earliest authority for every such change or insertion and supply the reading of the copy-text wherever it is emended in this edition.

I.i. Location: Rossillion. The Count's palace. (Shakespeare's *Rossillion* is an anglicized form of *Rousillon*, the name of a former province of southern France, just north of the eastern end of the Pyrenees.)
1. **In . . . husband**: The Countess means (in the courtly language that she and Lafew use in this scene and elsewhere) that her son's departure from home causes her as much sorrow as her husband's death; but it has often been pointed out that in her form of words and especially the several possible meanings of *deliver* (not only "send" but also "give birth to" and "liberate") can be found the germ of themes—birth and death, growing up and the relationship between the generations—that are to assume great importance in the play. 4. **attend**: heed, obey.
5. **to . . . ward**: whose ward I now am. On the old Count's death the King has become the guardian of his son (as a minor) and his estates. **evermore in subjection**: i.e. whose subject I shall always be (but the words suggest also his impatience at being still under authority). 6. **of**: in. 7. **generally**: universally, i.e. to one and all.
8. **hold**: maintain, be consistent in extending.
9. **stir . . . wanted**: arouse goodness even in one who lacked it.

11–12. **amendment**: recovery.
13. **He . . . physicians**. A reversal of the usual "His physicians have abandoned him (i.e. given up hope of his recovery)."
14. **practices**: professional ministrations.
14–15. **persecuted . . . hope**: afflicted his days (with painful treatments) in hope of cure (?). Alternatively, *persecuted* (used nowhere else by Shakespeare) may mean simply "followed out, spent."
18. **passage**: expression, i.e. word (with additional suggestion of "passing away"). 19. **honesty**: integrity, honor.
19–20. **stretch'd so far**: i.e. been as great as his "honesty" (which was absolute). 21. **should**: would certainly.
27. **his great right**: i.e. his right by reason of his greatness.
30. **still**: forever. 34. **fistula**: a kind of ulcer.

Laf. I would it were not notorious. Was this gentlewoman the daughter of Gerard de Narbon?

Count. His sole child, my lord, and bequeath'd to my overlooking. I have those hopes of her good that her education promises her dispositions she inherits, which makes fair gifts fairer; for where an unclean mind carries virtuous qualities, there commendations go with pity: they are virtues and traitors too. In her they are the better for their simpleness; she derives her honesty, and achieves her goodness.

Laf. Your commendations, madam, get from her tears.

Count. 'Tis the best brine a maiden can season her praise in. The remembrance of her father never approaches her heart but the tyranny of her sorrows takes all livelihood from her cheek. No more of this, Helena; go to, no more, lest it be rather thought you affect a sorrow than to have—

Hel. I do affect a sorrow indeed, but I have it too.

Laf. Moderate lamentation is the right of the dead, excessive grief the enemy to the living.

Count. If the living be enemy to the grief, the excess makes it soon mortal.

Ber. Madam, I desire your holy wishes.

Laf. How understand we that?

Count. Be thou blest, Bertram, and succeed thy father
In manners as in shape! Thy blood and virtue
Contend for empire in thee, and thy goodness
Share with thy birthright! Love all, trust a few,
Do wrong to none. Be able for thine enemy
Rather in power than use, and keep thy friend
Under thy own life's key. Be check'd for silence,
But never tax'd for speech. What heaven more will,
That thee may furnish, and my prayers pluck down,
Fall on thy head!—Farewell, my lord.
'Tis an unseason'd courtier, good my lord,
Advise him.

Laf. He cannot want the best
That shall attend his love.

Count. Heaven bless him!
Farewell, Bertram.

Ber. The best wishes that can
Be forged in your thoughts be servants to you!

[*Exit Countess.*]

[*To Helena.*] Be comfortable to my mother, your mistress,
And make much of her.

Laf. Farewell, pretty lady,
You must hold the credit of your father.

[*Exeunt Bertram and Lafew.*]

Hel. O, were that all! I think not on my father,
And these great tears grace his remembrance more
Than those I shed for him. What was he like?
I have forgot him. My imagination
Carries no favor in't but Bertram's.
I am undone, there is no living, none,
If Bertram be away. 'Twere all one
That I should love a bright particular star
And think to wed it, he is so above me.
In his bright radiance and collateral light
Must I be comforted, not in his sphere.
Th' ambition in my love thus plagues itself:
The hind that would be mated by the lion
Must die for love. 'Twas pretty, though a plague,
To see him every hour, to sit and draw
His arched brows, his hawking eye, his curls,
In our heart's table—heart too capable

36. I . . . notorious: I wish it were not so settled a fact that everyone knows of it. **39. overlooking:** supervision.
40. education: upbringing.
40–41. her dispositions she inherits: her inborn traits and tendencies. Modern idiom would require *the* for *her*.
41. which . . . fairer: which (i.e. education) enhances fine natural qualities.
42. unclean mind: i.e. bad nature. **virtuous qualities:** acquired excellences, benefits of good training.
43. go with pity: are mingled with regret. **traitors.** Because "the advantages of education enable an ill mind to go further in wickedness than it would have done without them" (Warburton).
44. simpleness: being unmixed (with vice).
45. derives: inherits. **achieves:** attains by her own efforts.
48. season: preserve (a culinary image). **50. tyranny:** severity.
51. livelihood: (1) liveliness, animation; (2) means of living, i.e. blood.
52. Helena. Elsewhere in the dialogue the heroine's name is invariably *Helen* (F1 *Hellen*), though the longer form occurs several times in the stage directions. **go to:** a stock expression of reproof or remonstrance.
53. affect . . . have. The Countess does not mean that Helena will be suspected of hypocritically pretending a grief she has never felt (the first use of *affect* in this sense recorded in *O.E.D.* is from 1661), but that she will be suspected of making an outward show of grief in excess of what she now (after a lapse of time) feels. The situation strongly recalls *Hamlet*, I.ii.68 ff., where Gertrude urges Hamlet to put off his external show of mourning. **have—.** The F1 dash, here retained, is a puzzle. The sense of the sentence is complete (although modern idiom would require *than have it* in place of *than to have*), as Helena's reply, picking up the contrast between *affect* and *have*, confirms. A similar dash at I.iii.153 has been interpreted as signalling a pause for a reply that is slow to come, and the same explanation might serve here.
54. I . . . too. Like Hamlet, Helena acknowledges that she does make outward show of sorrow but asserts that the show is not in excess of what she feels. Not until lines 79 ff. do we learn that the sorrow is not for her father.
55. right: rightful due. Lafew's speech continues the parallel with *Hamlet* (I.ii.87 ff.). **57. be . . . grief:** i.e. resist excessive grief.
57–58. the excess . . . mortal: it soon dies of its own excess.
60. How . . . that. The reason for this remark is obscure; some commentators suggest that the line is misplaced in F1, others that Lafew considers Bertram's request an impolite interruption.
61–70. Be . . . head. With these lines cf. Polonius' advice to Laertes (*Hamlet*, I.iii.57–81).
62. manners: behavior, moral conduct. **blood and virtue:** inherited and acquired good qualities (synonymous with *birthright* and *goodness* in the second half of the sentence).
63. Contend for empire: vie for rule.
64. Share: divide the rule. **Love:** behave amiably to.
65. able for: competent to deal with.
66. in power: in capability, potentially.
66–67. keep . . . key: safeguard your friend's life as you safeguard your own. **67. check'd:** rebuked.
68. tax'd for speech: taken to task for excessive or injudicious talk.
69. furnish: supply advantageously. **pluck:** draw.
71. unseason'd: unripe.
72–73. He . . . love. Variously interpreted; perhaps "He shall not lack the best advice that my good will toward him can produce."
75. forged: shaped, devised. **be . . . you:** be at your command, i.e. be realized. **76. comfortable:** serviceable.
77. make . . . her: pay her great respect, devote yourself to her.
78. hold the credit: maintain the high reputation. **79. on:** of.
80. grace his remembrance. Because they are taken by others to be a tribute to him (?). **more.** Because more numerous (?).
81. shed. Past tense.
83. Carries no favor: contains no face (perhaps with play on "wears no love-token"). **85–86. 'Twere . . . That:** it is just as if.
88. collateral: indirect; here, shining from a different sphere. The heavenly bodies, supposedly revolving in concentric spheres, were said to move collaterally. **90. ambition:** loftiness of aim.
91. hind: female deer. **94. hawking:** keen, piercing.
95. table: drawing-board. Cf. Sonnet 24.1–2: "My heart hath play'd the painter and hath stell'd / Thy beauty's form in table of my heart." **capable:** receptive of impressions, susceptible.

Of every line and trick of his sweet favor.
But now he's gone, and my idolatrous fancy
Must sanctify his reliques. Who comes here?

Enter Parolles.

[*Aside.*] One that goes with him. I love him for his sake,
And yet I know him a notorious liar,
Think him a great way fool, soly a coward;
Yet these fix'd evils sit so fit in him,
That they take place when virtue's steely bones
Looks bleak i' th' cold wind. Withal, full oft we see
Cold wisdom waiting on superfluous folly.

Par. 'Save you, fair queen!

Hel. And you, monarch!

Par. No.

Hel. And no.

Par. Are you meditating on virginity?

Hel. Ay. You have some stain of soldier in you; let me ask a question. Man is enemy to virginity; how may we barricado it against him?

Par. Keep him out.

Hel. But he assails, and our virginity though valiant, in the defense yet is weak. Unfold to us some warlike resistance.

Par. There is none. Man, setting down before you, will undermine you and blow you up.

Hel. Bless our poor virginity from underminers and blowers-up! Is there no military policy how virgins might blow up men?

Par. Virginity being blown down, man will quicklier be blown up. Marry, in blowing him down again, with the breach yourselves made, you lose your city. It is not politic in the commonwealth of nature to preserve virginity. Loss of virginity is rational increase, and there was never virgin [got] till virginity was first lost. That you were made of is metal to make virgins. Virginity, by being once lost, may be ten times found; by being ever kept, it is ever lost. 'Tis too cold a companion; away with't!

Hel. I will stand for't a little, though therefore I die a virgin.

Par. There's little can be said in't, 'tis against the rule of nature. To speak on the part of virginity is to accuse your mothers, which is most infallible disobedience. He that hangs himself is a virgin; virginity murthers itself, and should be buried in highways out of all sanctified limit, as a desperate offendress against nature. Virginity breeds mites, much like a cheese, consumes itself to the very paring, and so dies with feeding his own stomach. Besides, virginity is peevish, proud, idle, made of self-love, which is the most inhibited sin in the canon. Keep it not, you cannot choose but lose by't. Out with't! Within [t' one] year it will make itself two, which is a goodly increase, and the principal itself not much the worse. Away with't!

Hel. How might one do, sir, to lose it to her own liking?

Par. Let me see. Marry, ill, to like him that ne'er it likes. 'Tis a commodity will lose the gloss with lying: the longer kept, the less worth. Off with't while 'tis vendible; answer the time of request. Virginity, like an old courtier, wears her cap out of fashion, richly suited, but unsuitable—just like the brooch and the toothpick, which [wear] not now. Your date is better in your pie and your porridge than in your cheek; and your virginity, your old virginity, is like one of our French wither'd pears, it looks ill, it eats drily, marry, 'tis a wither'd pear; it was formerly better, marry, yet 'tis a wither'd pear. Will you any thing with it?

Hel. Not my virginity yet: [. . .]
There shall your master have a thousand loves,
A mother, and a mistress, and a friend,

96. **trick:** characteristic trait or expression. 97. **fancy:** love.
98. **sanctify his reliques:** worship whatever reminders of him remain.
s.d. **Parolles.** The name means "words" (French *paroles*), with an appropriateness that quickly becomes evident.
99. **love:** am well disposed toward.
101. **a great way:** largely a. **soly:** solely, wholly.
102. **fix'd evils:** firmly established vices. **sit . . . him:** fit him so becomingly (the first occurrence of the clothing imagery with which Parolles is associated).
103. **take place:** find acceptance (?) or take precedence (?).
104. **Looks.** Shakespeare frequently uses a verb in *-s* with a noun that is plural in form but may be taken as singular in sense. **Withal:** therewith, i.e. in consequence of this.
105. **Cold . . . superfluous:** unprovided . . . enjoying superabundance; or (more specifically) naked . . . overdressed.
106. **'Save:** God save. **queen.** An inflated form of address such as a courtier might use to his lady.
107. **monarch.** A match for *queen.*
108. **No:** i.e. I am no monarch.
109. **And no:** i.e. nor am I a queen. 111. **stain:** tinge, trace.
118. **setting down before:** laying siege to. The military figure, continued for some lines, gives good opportunity for bawdy quibbles.
121. **policy:** stratagem, craft.
124. **Marry:** to be sure (originally an oath, "by the Virgin Mary").
126. **politic:** expedient.
128. **rational increase:** (1) judicious increase; (2) increase of rational beings. **got:** begotten. 129. **That:** that which.
130. **metal:** substance.
131. **may . . . found:** i.e. may be the means of creating ten more virgins.

133. **stand for't:** defend it.
136. **on the part:** in behalf. 137. **infallible:** certain.
138. **He . . . virgin:** i.e. a suicide and a virgin adopt the same course.
139. **murthers:** murders.
140. **sanctified limit:** boundaries of consecrated ground.
143. **his:** its (Shakespeare's all but invariable form). **stomach.** With second sense "arrogance."
145. **inhibited:** prohibited. **canon:** ecclesiastical law (?) or Scriptures (?). **Keep:** hoard.
146. **Out with't:** put it out at interest. 147. **t' one:** the one, a single.
152–53. **ill . . . likes:** i.e. one would have to do ill, by liking a man who does not like virginity.
153. **will:** that will. **gloss:** look of newness.
154. **lying:** being kept unsold.
155. **answer . . . request:** offer it while it is in demand.
157. **suited:** dressed (?) or (referring to *cap*) adorned (?). **unsuitable:** not adapted to the time, unfashionable.
158. **brooch.** Long a fashionable ornament for hats. **toothpick.** The use of toothpicks, a foreign invention, was for a time an affectation of travellers, who sometimes displayed their toothpicks in their hats. **wear not:** are not worn.
159. **Your.** The indefinite use, as in "Your worm is your only emperor for diet" (*Hamlet*, IV.iii.21), but used here with continual suggestion of the personal sense. Helena's "Not *my* virginity yet" vigorously rejects that implication. **date:** (1) the fruit (a very common ingredient in Elizabethan cookery); (2) age or sign of age.
161. **ill:** unappetizing. 162. **eats drily:** tastes dry.
163–64. **Will you:** will you do.
165. **Not . . . yet:** not with my virginity yet (?) or my virginity isn't a withered pear yet (?). Perhaps incomplete; there is an apparent gap in sense before the next line.
166. **There:** i.e. at court (as appears at line 177).
167. **mistress:** lady whom he serves. **friend:** sweetheart, mistress. The terms of amorous address in Helena's catalogue in lines 167–73 are abundantly paralleled in the conventional love poetry of Shakespeare's day.

A phoenix, captain, and an enemy,
A guide, a goddess, and a sovereign,
A counsellor, a traitress, and a dear;
His humble ambition, proud humility;
His jarring concord, and his discord dulcet;
His faith, his sweet disaster; with a world
Of pretty, fond, adoptious christendoms
That blinking Cupid gossips. Now shall he—
I know not what he shall—God send him well!
The court's a learning place, and he is one—

Par. What one, i' faith?

Hel. That I wish well. 'Tis pity—

Par. What's pity?

Hel. That wishing well had not a body in't,
Which might be felt, that we, the poorer born,
Whose baser stars do shut us up in wishes,
Might with effects of them follow our friends,
And show what we alone must think, which never
Returns us thanks.

Enter PAGE.

Page. Monsieur Parolles, my lord calls for you. [*Exit.*]

Par. Little Helen, farewell. If I can remember thee, I will think of thee at court.

Hel. Monsieur Parolles, you were born under a charitable star.

Par. Under Mars, I.

Hel. I especially think, under Mars.

Par. Why under Mars?

Hel. The wars hath so kept you under that you must needs be born under Mars.

Par. When he was predominant.

Hel. When he was retrograde, I think rather.

Par. Why think you so?

Hel. You go so much backward when you fight.

Par. That's for advantage.

Hel. So is running away, when fear proposes the safety. But the composition that your valor and fear makes in you is a virtue of a good wing, and I like the wear well.

Par. I am so full of businesses, I cannot answer thee acutely. I will return perfect courtier, in the which my instruction shall serve to naturalize thee, so thou wilt be capable of a courtier's counsel, and understand what advice shall thrust upon thee, else thou diest in thine unthankfulness, and thine ignorance makes thee away. Farewell. When thou hast leisure, say thy prayers; when thou hast none, remember thy friends. Get thee a good husband, and use him as he uses thee. So farewell. [*Exit.*]

Hel. Our remedies oft in ourselves do lie,
Which we ascribe to heaven. The fated sky
Gives us free scope, only doth backward pull
Our slow designs when we ourselves are dull.
What power is it which mounts my love so high,
That makes me see, and cannot feed mine eye?
The mightiest space in fortune nature brings
To join like likes, and kiss like native things.
Impossible be strange attempts to those
That weigh their pains in sense, and do suppose
What hath been cannot be. Who ever strove
To show her merit, that did miss her love?
The King's disease—my project may deceive me,
But my intents are fix'd, and will not leave me. *Exit.*

[SCENE II]

Flourish cornets. Enter the KING OF FRANCE *with letters,* [LORDS,] *and divers* ATTENDANTS.

King. The Florentines and Senoys are by th' ears,
Have fought with equal fortune, and continue
A braving war.

1. Lord. So 'tis reported, sir.

King. Nay, 'tis most credible; we here receive it
A certainty, vouch'd from our cousin Austria,
With caution, that the Florentine will move us
For speedy aid; wherein our dearest friend

168. **phoenix:** i.e. nonpareil (the phoenix was unique). **captain:** general (cf. "our great captain's captain [i.e. Desdemona]," *Othello,* II.i.74). 172. **jarring:** discordant. **dulcet:** harmonious.
173. **sweet disaster:** dear misfortune.
174. **adoptious christendoms:** adopted nicknames or pet names (*christendoms* = Christian names, hence familiar names generally).
175. **blinking:** i.e. blind. **gossips:** stands sponsor for, bestows (*gossip* as a noun = godparent, who gives names at baptism).
176. **send him well:** grant him good fortune.
182. **might be felt:** could be perceived by the senses. **that:** so that.
183. **baser stars:** lower fortunes. **shut . . . wishes:** limit us to mere wishing.
184. **with . . . them:** i.e. by means of our corporealized wishes.
185. **show . . . think:** make manifest what we can in fact only think.
186. **Returns us thanks:** wins us gratitude.
196. **under:** down, in an inferior position.
197. **predominant:** ascendant, in his position of greatest influence.
198. **retrograde:** moving backward (referring to a planet's apparent movement in a direction opposite to that of the zodiac).
201. **advantage:** strategic gain.
203. **composition:** compound, mixture (with quibble on "truce," "terms for ending the fighting").
204. **virtue . . . wing:** characteristic excellence of a good wing, i.e. rapid flight.
205. **wear:** practice, fashion. The choice of this word suggests that *wing* (line 204) quibbles on the sense "decorative flap of material at the shoulder"; some commentators suppose that Parolles is wearing such wings.

207. **perfect:** complete.
208. **which:** i.e. courtly behavior. **naturalize:** familiarize. **so:** provided that.
209. **capable:** receptive (with bawdy wordplay that takes in *understand, thrust,* and *diest* and makes plain what the subject of the "instruction" will be).
211–12. **makes thee away:** puts an end to you.
212. **leisure:** opportunity.
213–14. **when . . . friends.** Precisely what Parolles means by this has not been satisfactorily explained. 214. **use:** treat.
217. **fated:** instrumental to destiny. 219. **dull:** sluggish.
220. **mounts . . . high:** raises my desire to so lofty an object.
221. **makes me see:** enables me to perceive so distant an object (?). **cannot . . . eye:** will not allow my eye to feed on it.
222. **The mightiest . . . fortune:** i.e. persons separated by the greatest disparity of fortune. **brings:** causes.
223. **like likes:** as if they were alike in fortune. **native things:** creatures of the same origin. 224. **strange:** extraordinary.
225. **That . . . sense:** who make a commonsense judgment of the difficulties (i.e. the likelihood of success) of the "strange attempts" (?) or who calculate the painful cost to themselves (?).
225–26. **do . . . be:** i.e. deem impossible what in fact resolute men have done before (?). 227. **miss:** fail to achieve.

I.ii. Location: Paris. The King's palace.
o.s.d. **Flourish:** sound a fanfare. **cornets:** horns (not the modern brass instruments).
1. **Senoys:** Sienese. **by th' ears:** at odds, quarrelling.
3. **braving:** marked by mutual defiance. 4. **we.** The royal plural.
5. **our cousin Austria:** my fellow sovereign the Duke of Austria.
6. **the Florentine:** the Florentines (?) or (like *Florence* in line 12) the Duke of Florence (?). **move:** press, entreat.

Prejudicates the business, and would seem
To have us make denial.
1. Lord. His love and wisdom,
Approv'd so to your Majesty, may plead
For amplest credence.
King. He hath arm'd our answer,
And Florence is denied before he comes.
Yet for our gentlemen that mean to see
The Tuscan service, freely have they leave
To stand on either part.
2. Lord. It well may serve
A nursery to our gentry, who are sick
For breathing and exploit.
King. What's he comes here?

Enter Bertram, Lafew, *and* Parolles.

1. Lord. It is the Count [Rossillion], my good lord,
Young Bertram.
King. Youth, thou bear'st thy father's face;
Frank Nature, rather curious than in haste,
Hath well compos'd thee. Thy father's moral parts
Mayst thou inherit too! Welcome to Paris.
Ber. My thanks and duty are your Majesty's.
King. I would I had that corporal soundness now
As when thy father and myself in friendship
First tried our soldiership! He did look far
Into the service of the time, and was
Discipled of the bravest. He lasted long,
But on us both did haggish age steal on,
And wore us out of act. It much repairs me
To talk of your good father. In his youth
He had the wit which I can well observe
To-day in our young lords; but they may jest
Till their own scorn return to them unnoted
Ere they can hide their levity in honor.
So like a courtier, contempt nor bitterness
Were in his pride or sharpness; if they were,
His equal had awak'd them, and his honor,
Clock to itself, knew the true minute when
Exception bid him speak, and at this time
His tongue obey'd his hand. Who were below him
He us'd as creatures of another place,
And bow'd his eminent top to their low ranks,
Making them proud of his humility,
In their poor praise he humbled. Such a man
Might be a copy to these younger times;
Which followed well, would demonstrate them now
But goers backward.
Ber. His good remembrance, sir,
Lies richer in your thoughts than on his tomb.
So in approof lives not his epitaph
As in your royal speech.
King. Would I were with him! He would always say—
Methinks I hear him now; his plausive words
He scatter'd not in ears, but grafted them,
To grow there and to bear—"Let me not live"—
This his good melancholy oft began,
On the catastrophe and heel of pastime,
When it was out—"Let me not live," quoth he,
"After my flame lacks oil, to be the snuff
Of younger spirits, whose apprehensive senses
All but new things disdain; whose judgments are
Mere fathers of their garments; whose constancies
Expire before their fashions." This he wish'd.
I, after him, do after him wish too,
Since I nor wax nor honey can bring home,
I quickly were dissolved from my hive,
To give some laborers room.
2. Lord. You're loved, sir;
They that least lend it you shall lack you first.
King. I fill a place, I know't. How long is't, Count,
Since the physician at your father's died?
He was much fam'd.
Ber. Some six months since, my lord.
King. If he were living, I would try him yet.—
Lend me an arm.—The rest have worn me out
With several applications. Nature and sickness
Debate it at their leisure. Welcome, Count,
My son's no dearer.
Ber. Thank your Majesty. *Exeunt. Flourish.*

10. **Approv'd so:** so fully proved.
11. **arm'd our answer:** made me determine on an adverse answer (i.e. hostile, hence armed); with further suggestion that the refusal will be proof against pleas.
13. **for:** as for, with respect to. **see:** i.e. take part in.
15. **stand . . . part:** fight on either side.
15–16. **Serve A nursery:** serve as a training school.
16. **sick:** pining. 17. **breathing:** exercise.
20. **Frank:** bountiful. **curious:** working with careful skill.
21. **parts:** qualities. 25. **As:** that I had.
26–27. **look far Into:** become deeply experienced in (?) or have profound insight into (?).
27–28. **was Discipled of:** was taught by (?) or had as followers (?).
29. **on . . . on.** A not uncommon type of redundancy. **haggish:** repulsive. 30. **act:** action, activity. **repairs:** restores, refreshes.
34. **return . . . unnoted:** comes to be scornfully ignored (?).
35. **hide . . . honor:** submerge their levity in honorable action (?).
36. **courtier:** representative of true courtesy.
36–37. **contempt . . . sharpness:** there was no contempt in his pride, no wounding asperity in his keenness of wit.
38. **equal:** i.e. equal in rank.
39. **Clock to itself:** i.e. requiring no external cue. **true:** exact.
40. **Exception:** taking exception, disapproval.
41. **obey'd his hand:** said no more than his hand was willing to maintain. **Who:** those who.
42. **us'd as:** treated like. **of another place:** i.e. not of lower rank.
43. **top:** head.
45. **In . . . humbled.** A much-debated passage; perhaps "(which [i.e. humility]) he assumed in praise of (i.e. to do honor to) their poor selves." (The redundancy in "humbled his humility" would not be exceptional.)
46. **copy:** model, example to be followed (as in *copy-text*).
48. **goers backward:** regressive, inferior to him.
50. **So . . . epitaph:** i.e. the praise inscribed on his tomb is nowhere else so surely confirmed. 53. **plausive:** praiseworthy.
54. **scatter'd not:** did not merely strew casually.
55. **bear:** bear fruit.
57. **catastrophe:** conclusion (synonymous with *heel*).
58. **out:** at an end (perhaps with play on "out at heel," but also leading into the candle figure that follows).
59. **snuff:** (1) burnt end of wick (which keeps the lower part of the wick from burning properly); (2) source of offense.
60. **apprehensive:** quick to seize upon ideas, hence capricious, inconstant.
62. **Mere . . . garments:** i.e. productive of nothing but new modes of dress.
63. **Expire . . . fashions:** shift even more quickly than fashions change.
64. **after him . . . after him:** surviving him . . . in agreement with his view. 65. **nor . . . nor:** neither . . . nor.
66. **dissolved:** separated, departed.
67. **laborers:** i.e. workers, not drones.
68. **lend it you:** give you love. **lack:** miss, feel the want of.
74. **with several applications:** each with a different treatment.
75. **Debate . . . leisure:** fight it out in their own good time.

[Scene III]

Enter Countess, Steward [Rinaldo], *and* Clown [Lavatch].

Count. I will now hear. What say you of this gentlewoman?

Stew. Madam, the care I have had to even your content, I wish might be found in the calendar of my past endeavors, for then we wound our modesty, and make foul the clearness of our deservings, when of ourselves we publish them.

Count. What does this knave here? Get you gone, sirrah. The complaints I have heard of you I do not all believe. 'Tis my slowness that I do not, for I know you lack not folly to commit them, and have ability enough to make such knaveries yours.

Clo. 'Tis not unknown to you, madam, I am a poor fellow.

Count. Well, sir.

Clo. No, madam, 'tis not so well that I am poor, though many of the rich are damn'd, but if I may have your ladyship's good will to go to the world, Isbel the woman and [I] will do as we may.

Count. Wilt thou needs be a beggar?

Clo. I do beg your good will in this case.

Count. In what case?

Clo. In Isbel's case and mine own. Service is no heritage, and I think I shall never have the blessing of God till I have issue a' my body; for they say barnes are blessings.

Count. Tell me thy reason why thou wilt marry.

Clo. My poor body, madam, requires it. I am driven on by the flesh, and he must needs go that the devil drives.

Count. Is this all your worship's reason?

Clo. Faith, madam, I have other holy reasons, such as they are.

Count. May the world know them?

Clo. I have been, madam, a wicked creature, as you and all flesh and blood are, and indeed I do marry that I may repent.

Count. Thy marriage, sooner than thy wickedness.

Clo. I am out a' friends, madam, and I hope to have friends for my wive's sake.

Count. Such friends are thine enemies, knave.

Clo. Y' are shallow, madam—in great friends, for the knaves come to do that for me which I am a-weary of. He that ears my land spares my team, and gives me leave to inn the crop. If I be his cuckold, he's my drudge. He that comforts my wife is the cherisher of my flesh and blood; he that cherishes my flesh and blood loves my flesh and blood; he that loves my flesh and blood is my friend: *ergo*, he that kisses my wife is my friend. If men could be contented to be what they are, there were no fear in marriage, for young Charbon the puritan and old Poysam the papist, howsome'er their hearts are sever'd in religion, their heads are both one: they may jowl horns together like any deer i' th' herd.

Count. Wilt thou ever be a foul-mouth'd and calumnious knave?

Clo. A prophet I, madam, and I speak the truth the next way:

For I the ballad will repeat,
Which men full true shall find:
Your marriage comes by destiny,
Your cuckoo sings by kind.

Count. Get you gone, sir, I'll talk with you more anon.

Stew. May it please you, madam, that he bid Helen come to you. Of her I am to speak.

Count. Sirrah, tell my gentlewoman I would speak with her—Helen, I mean.

Clo. [*Sings.*]

"Was this fair face the cause," quoth she,
"Why the Grecians sacked Troy?
Fond done, done fond,
Was this King Priam's joy?"
With that she sighed as she stood,
With that she sighed as she stood,
And gave this sentence then:
"Among nine bad if one be good,

I.iii. Location: Rossillion. The Count's palace.
3–4. **even your content:** measure up to your wishes, serve you to your complete satisfaction. 4. **calendar:** record.
6. **make . . . clearness:** sully the brightness.
9. **sirrah:** form of address used to inferiors. **all:** entirely. Dover Wilson (following Maxwell's conjecture) reads *if I do not all believe,*—a very attractive emendation. 18. **go . . . world:** marry.
19. **woman:** i.e. servingwoman. **do . . . may:** do the best we can (doubtless with quibble on *do* in its frequent slang sense "have sexual intercourse").
23. **case.** With another bawdy quibble; the Clown's talk is full of equivoques.
23–24. **Service . . . heritage.** Proverbial, signifying that a servant's lot brings him in very little to bequeath to his heirs.
24–25. **have . . . God:** have anything to show that God has blessed me.
25. **a':** of. **barnes:** bairns, children.
29–30. **he . . . drives.** Another proverb.
32. **other holy reasons.** "He reminds the Countess that his first 'reason' is to be found in the marriage service" (Dover Wilson); but at the same time he perpetrates ribald puns in *holy* and *reasons* (= *raisings*, a near homophone in Shakespeare's pronunciation).
37. **repent:** i.e. reform, make my sexual activity lawful. The Countess' reply alludes to the proverb "Marry in haste and repent at leisure." 40. **wive's:** wife's.
42. **Y' are . . . friends:** you have a superficial understanding of true friendship (?). In Shakespeare's texts *in* is sometimes a variant spelling of *e'en*, and many editors follow Hanmer in reading *e'en* here, perhaps rightly. 44. **ears:** ploughs.
45. **inn:** harvest, get in.
49. **ergo:** therefore (signalling a logical conclusion).
50–51. **what they are:** i.e. cuckolds.
52. **Charbon, Poysam.** The names have been interpreted as derived from *chair bonne* (good flesh) and *poisson* (fish), hence appropriate, respectively, for the puritan, who rejected the ordinance of fasting, and the papist, who followed it.
52–53. **howsome'er:** howsoever, however widely.
54. **both one:** identical (in bearing horns, the mark of the cuckold). The statement about hearts and heads, as Hunter points out, comically inverts the proverb "Hearts may agree though heads differ." **jowl:** knock, bump. 56. **ever:** always.
59. **next:** nearest, most direct. Prophets spoke by immediate divine inspiration.
62–63. **Your . . . kind.** A parallel to these lines has been pointed out in a ballad of 1577, and perhaps they were a commonplace.
63. **by kind:** in accordance with its nature. The cuckoo's call was conventionally regarded as announcing to married men that they were cuckolds (see *Love's Labor's Lost,* V.ii.898–902), and this line says in effect that cuckoldry is part of the course of nature.
69. **Helen.** This suggests to the Clown Helen of Troy, a good example of what he has been talking about, and he extends his argument in the song. No source is extant, but lines 80–81 indicate that the stanza adapts some ballad known to the audience.
70. **she.** Perhaps Hecuba, wife of King Priam of Troy and mother of Paris. 72. **Fond:** foolishly.
73. **this:** i.e. Paris, who stole Helen from her husband, King Menelaus of Sparta, and thus caused the Trojan war.
76. **sentence:** judgment (?) or maxim (?).

Among nine bad if one be good,
There's yet one good in ten."

Count. What, one good in ten? You corrupt the song, sirrah.

Clo. One good woman in ten, madam, which is a purifying a' th' song. Would God would serve the world so all the year! we'd find no fault with the tithe-woman if I were the parson. One in ten, quoth 'a? And we might have a good woman born but [or] every blazing star or at an earthquake, 'twould mend the lottery well; a man may draw his heart out ere 'a pluck one.

Count. You'll be gone, sir knave, and do as I command you.

Clo. That man should be at woman's command, and yet no hurt done! Though honesty be no puritan, yet it will do no hurt; it will wear the surplice of humility over the black gown of a big heart. I am going, forsooth. The business is for Helen to come hither. *Exit.*

Count. Well, now.

Stew. I know, madam, you love your gentlewoman entirely.

Count. Faith, I do. Her father bequeath'd her to me, and she herself, without other advantage, may lawfully make title to as much love as she finds. There is more owing her than is paid, and more shall be paid her than she'll demand.

Stew. Madam, I was very late more near her than I think she wish'd me. Alone she was, and did communicate to herself her own words to her own ears; she thought, I dare vow for her, they touch'd not any stranger sense. Her matter was, she lov'd your son. Fortune, she said, was no goddess, that had put such difference betwixt their two estates; Love no god, that would not extend his might only where qualities were level; [Diana no] queen of virgins, that would suffer her poor knight surpris'd without rescue in the first assault or ransom afterward. This she deliver'd in the most bitter touch of sorrow that e'er I heard virgin exclaim in, which I held my duty speedily to acquaint you withal, sithence in the loss that may happen, it concerns you something to know it.

Count. You have discharg'd this honestly, keep it to yourself. Many likelihoods inform'd me of this before, which hung so tott'ring in the balance that I could neither believe nor misdoubt. Pray you leave me. Stall this in your bosom, and I thank you for your honest care. I will speak with you further anon. *Exit Steward.*

Enter HELEN.

Even so it was with me when I was young.
If ever we are nature's, these are ours. This thorn
Doth to our rose of youth rightly belong;
Our blood to us, this to our blood is born.
It is the show and seal of nature's truth,
Where love's strong passion is impress'd in youth.
By our remembrances of days foregone,
Such were our faults, or then we thought them none.
Her eye is sick on't; I observe her now.

Hel. What is your pleasure, madam?

Count. You know, Helen,
I am a mother to you.

Hel. Mine honorable mistress.

Count. Nay, a mother,
Why not a mother? When I said "a mother,"
Methought you saw a serpent. What's in "mother,"
That you start at it? I say I am your mother,
And put you in the catalogue of those
That were enwombed mine. 'Tis often seen
Adoption strives with nature, and choice breeds
A native slip to us from foreign seeds.
You ne'er oppress'd me with a mother's groan,
Yet I express to you a mother's care.
God's mercy, maiden! does it curd thy blood
To say I am thy mother? What's the matter,
That this distempered messenger of wet,
The many-color'd Iris, rounds thine eye?
—Why, that you are my daughter?

Hel. That I am not.

Count. I say I am your mother.

Hel. Pardon, madam;

80–83. You . . . song. The song must have reversed the proportion—one bad in ten (referring to the ten surviving sons of Priam). The Clown points out that his version refers to women, not to men, and thus purifies the original, which had no good women in it.
85. tithe-woman: tenth woman (cf. *tithe-pig*). The tithe or tenth part of the farm produce was the parson's due.
85–86. quoth 'a: did he say (a tag implying scorn).
86. And: if. **or**: ere, before.
87. blazing star: comet; or new star (nova), one of which had been announced by Tycho Brahe as recently as 1572.
87–88. mend the lottery: improve the chances of drawing a winner in the lottery of marriage. **89. pluck**: draw.
93–95. Though . . . heart: i.e. though honesty (the Clown is presumably still referring to himself—"this respectable person") is not overstrict in moral matters, still it will do no harm; it will conceal its proud spirit under an appearance of meek obedience. The final image alludes to Calvinist ministers who conformed to law by wearing the surplice, but with the black Geneva gown under it.
102. herself: in herself. **advantage.** In view of the financial figure employed by the Countess, this word is probably used in its sense of "interest (on money)." **103. make title**: lay claim.
105. demand: ask (not "ask peremptorily," as in modern usage).
106. late: recently.
109–10. any stranger sense: the ears of anyone else.
110. matter: theme. **112. estates**: stations in life.
113. extend his might: exercise his power. **only**: except.
114. level: even, equal.
115. suffer . . . surpris'd: permit her unfortunate devotee to be taken captive. **117. deliver'd**: uttered. **touch**: note, strain.
118. exclaim: complain, lament.
119. withal: with (commonly used at the end of a clause, as here). **sithence**: since. **120. something**: in some measure.
124. tott'ring: wavering. **125. misdoubt**: doubt.
126. Stall: enclose, shut up. **129. these**: i.e. these pangs of love.
131. blood: natural instincts and emotions, especially "love's strong passion" (line 133). **132. show**: outward sign.
133. impress'd. Continuing the figure in *seal*.
135. or . . . none: i.e. or perhaps "faults" is the wrong word, for we did not then consider them faults.
136. on't: of it, i.e. with it. **I . . . now**: i.e. now I understand what her looks mean. **145. strives with**: vies with, rivals.
145–46. choice . . . seeds: i.e. we choose a scion grown from foreign seeds to implant in our own stock, and it becomes as much a part of the plant as if it had sprung from it.
147. groan: i.e. in childbirth.
151. distempered. Used both of emotional disturbance and stormy weather.
152. Iris: goddess of the rainbow. **rounds**: encircles. With lines 151–52 cf. *Lucrece*, lines 1586–87, "And round about her tear-distained eye / Blue circles stream'd, like rainbows in the sky."
153. That . . . not. Helena takes advantage of the fact that *daughter* has the second meaning "daughter-in-law." (On the dash at the beginning of line 153, see the note on I.i.53.)

The Count Rossillion cannot be my brother:
I am from humble, he from honored name;
No note upon my parents, his all noble.
My master, my dear lord he is, and I
His servant live, and will his vassal die.
He must not be my brother.

Count. Nor I your mother?

Hel. You are my mother, madam; would you were—
So that my lord your son were not my brother—
Indeed my mother! Or were you both our mothers,
I care no more for than I do for heaven,
So I were not his sister. Can 't no other,
But, I your daughter, he must be my brother?

Count. Yes, Helen, you might be my daughter-in-law.
God shield you mean it not! "daughter" and "mother"
So strive upon your pulse. What, pale again?
My fear hath catch'd your fondness! Now I see
The myst'ry of your [loneliness], and find
Your salt tears' head, now to all sense 'tis gross:
You love my son. Invention is asham'd,
Against the proclamation of thy passion,
To say thou dost not: therefore tell me true,
But tell me then 'tis so; for look, thy cheeks
Confess it, [t' one] to th' other, and thine eyes
See it so grossly shown in thy behaviors
That in their kind they speak it. Only sin
And hellish obstinacy tie thy tongue,
That truth should be suspected. Speak, is't so?
If it be so, you have wound a goodly clew;
If it be not, forswear't; howe'er, I charge thee,
As heaven shall work in me for thine avail,
To tell me truly.

Hel. Good madam, pardon me!

Count. Do you love my son?

Hel. Your pardon, noble mistress!

Count. Love you my son?

Hel. Do not you love him, madam?

Count. Go not about; my love hath in't a bond
Whereof the world takes note. Come, come, disclose

157. **note**: mark of distinction. **parents**: forebears.
162. **So**: provided.
163. **both our mothers**: the mother of us both.
164. **I . . . heaven.** Helena seems at first to use *care for* in the sense "mind" ("I wouldn't mind that") but shifts in mid-career with retroactive effect, so that at the end she has said, "I would value that as I value heaven." 165. **Can 't no other**: can it not be otherwise.
168. **shield**: defend, i.e. forbid. The *not* at the end of the sentence would ordinarily strengthen the negative sense already present; but perhaps the Countess is being deliberately ambiguous (as in line 170) in order to see what Helena can be brought to say before she knows that the Countess is not hostile. 169. **strive upon**: agitate.
170. **My . . . fondness.** This can mean "my apprehensiveness has caught out your foolishness" or "my concern has perceived your love." 171. **loneliness**: seclusion from people.
172. **head**: source. **sense**: perception. **gross**: obvious.
173. **Invention**: ability to find plausible answers.
174. **Against**: in the face of. **thy.** Note the shift to the familiar form, continued to the end of the speech.
176. **then**: in that case (i.e. if you tell me true).
179. **in their kind**: in the way natural to them.
181. **suspected**: doubted, rendered suspect.
182. **wound . . . clew**: wound up a fine ball of thread (proverbial, with ironic sense; but the Countess may again be playing the ironic against the literal sense).
183. **forswear't**: affirm that it is untrue. **Howe'er**: whichever it is, in either case. 188. **Go not about**: don't evade.
189. **Whereof . . . note**: which society recognizes.

The state of your affection, for your passions
Have to the full appeach'd.

Hel. Then I confess
Here on my knee, before high heaven and you,
That before you, and next unto high heaven,
I love your son.
My friends were poor, but honest, so's my love.
Be not offended, for it hurts not him
That he is lov'd of me; I follow him not
By any token of presumptuous suit,
Nor would I have him till I do deserve him,
Yet never know how that desert should be.
I know I love in vain, strive against hope;
Yet in this captious and intenible sieve
I still pour in the waters of my love
And lack not to lose still. Thus Indian-like,
Religious in mine error, I adore
The sun, that looks upon his worshipper,
But knows of him no more. My dearest madam,
Let not your hate encounter with my love
For loving where you do; but if yourself,
Whose aged honor cites a virtuous youth,
Did ever in so true a flame of liking
Wish chastely, and love dearly, that your Dian
Was both herself and Love, O then give pity
To her whose state is such that cannot choose
But lend and give where she is sure to lose;
That seeks not to find that her search implies,
But riddle-like lives sweetly where she dies.

Count. Had you not lately an intent—speak truly—
To go to Paris?

Hel. Madam, I had.

Count. Wherefore? tell true.

Hel. I will tell truth, by grace itself I swear.
You know my father left me some prescriptions
Of rare and prov'd effects, such as his reading
And manifest experience had collected
For general sovereignty; and that he will'd me

190. **affection**: feelings. 191. **appeach'd**: informed against you.
193. **before you**: more than (I love) you. **next unto**: second only to.
195. **friends**: relatives, family. **honest**: honorable.
197–98. **I . . . suit**: I do not pursue him with any manifestations of presumptuous love (?).
201. **hope**: expectation, what can reasonably be looked for.
202. **captious**: readily receptive (probably with added sense of "capacious"). **intenible**: unretentive.
203. **still pour**: go on pouring.
204. **lack . . . still**: (1) don't fail to go on losing it; (2) have no dearth of love to go on pouring away. **Indian-like.** Probably referring to American Indians.
208. **encounter with**: stand against, oppose.
210. **aged honor**: honorable old age. **cites**: testifies to.
211. **liking**: love.
212. **that**: so that. **Dian**: Diana, goddess of chastity.
213. **Love**: i.e. Venus. 214. **such that**: such as.
216. **that . . . implies**: what causes her search (Schmidt), i.e. the object of her search.
217. **riddle-like**: paradoxically (referring to the following words) (?) or with her secret unguessed (?). The *flame of liking* of line 211, and the paradoxes of lines 212–13 and this line, suggest what Donne calls the "phoenix riddle" as Shakespeare treats it in "The Phoenix and Turtle." The passage is also reminiscent of Viola's description of a woman's concealed love in *Twelfth Night*, II.iv.110–15.
220. **grace**: God's grace.
223. **manifest experience**: experience of what is evident to the eye, i.e. clinical experience, in contrast to *reading* (line 222) (?). The usual gloss for *manifest* is, however, "widely known" or "notable."
224. **for general sovereignty**: for universal efficacy. **will'd me**: desired me.

In heedfull'st reservation to bestow them,
As notes whose faculties inclusive were
More than they were in note. Amongst the rest,
There is a remedy, approv'd, set down,
To cure the desperate languishings whereof
The King is render'd lost.
Count. This was your motive
For Paris, was it? speak.
Hel. My lord your son made me to think of this;
Else Paris, and the medicine, and the King,
Had from the conversation of my thoughts
Happily been absent then.
Count. But think you, Helen,
If you should tender your supposed aid,
He would receive it? He and his physicians
Are of a mind; he, that they cannot help him,
They, that they cannot help. How shall they credit
A poor unlearned virgin, when the schools,
Embowell'd of their doctrine, have left off
The danger to itself?
Hel. There's something in't
More than my father's skill, which was the great'st
Of his profession, that his good receipt
Shall for my legacy be sanctified
By th' luckiest stars in heaven, and would your honor
But give me leave to try success, I'd venture
The well-lost life of mine on his Grace's cure
By such a day, an hour.
Count. Dost thou believe't?
Hel. Ay, madam, knowingly.
Count. Why, Helen, thou shalt have my leave and love,
Means and attendants, and my loving greetings
To those of mine in court. I'll stay at home
And pray God's blessing into thy attempt.
Be gone to-morrow, and be sure of this,
What I can help thee to thou shalt not miss. *Exeunt.*

ACT II, [Scene I]

Enter the King, *with divers young* Lords *taking leave for the Florentine war,* [Bertram] *Count Rossillion, and* Parolles. *Flourish cornets.*

225. **In . . . them:** to put them away and keep them with the utmost care (for use in special cases). *Bestow* = stow away, treasure up. It can also mean "give" and "employ" (senses that some give it here), but Shakespeare regularly uses *reservation* in the sense "holding back," "keeping to oneself." See II.i.108 below.
226–27. **As . . . note:** as prescriptions for remedies which had more extensive curative properties than had yet been observed.
228. **approv'd:** proved, tested.
230. **render'd lost:** reported to be dying.
234. **conversation:** interchange, give-and-take.
235. **Happily:** haply, perhaps.
236. **your supposed aid:** the aid you envisage or propose.
238. **of a mind:** in agreement. **help:** cure.
241. **Embowell'd:** disembowelled, drained.
241–42. **left . . . itself:** abandoned the disease to its own course.
244. **receipt:** recipe, prescription.
245. **sanctified:** blessed. 246. **luckiest:** most benignant.
247. **try success:** test what the outcome will be.
248. **well-lost . . . mine:** i.e. my life which, if my venture fails, will be lost in a good cause. 249. **such a:** a specified.
250. **knowingly:** with full awareness of what I am doing.
254. **into:** upon. 256. **miss:** lack.
II.i. Location: Paris. The King's palace.

King. Farewell, young lords, these warlike principles
Do not throw from you; and you, my lords, farewell.
Share the advice betwixt you; if both gain all,
The gift doth stretch itself as 'tis receiv'd,
And is enough for both.
1. Lord. 'Tis our hope, sir,
After well-ent'red soldiers, to return
And find your Grace in health.
King. No, no, it cannot be; and yet my heart
Will not confess he owes the malady
That doth my life besiege. Farewell, young lords,
Whether I live or die, be you the sons
Of worthy Frenchmen. Let higher Italy
(Those bated that inherit but the fall
Of the last monarchy) see that you come
Not to woo honor, but to wed it, when
The bravest questant shrinks. Find what you seek,
That fame may cry you loud. I say farewell.
[*2.*] *Lord.* Health, at your bidding, serve your Majesty!
King. Those girls of Italy, take heed of them.
They say our French lack language to deny
If they demand. Beware of being captives
Before you serve.
Both [*Lords*]. Our hearts receive your warnings.
King. Farewell.—Come hither to me.
[*The King retires apart with some Lords.*]
1. Lord. O my sweet lord, that you will stay behind us!
Par. 'Tis not his fault, the spark.
2. Lord. O, 'tis brave wars!
Par. Most admirable! I have seen those wars.
Ber. I am commanded here, and kept a coil with,
"Too young" and "the next year" and "'tis too early."
Par. And thy mind stand to't, boy, steal away bravely.
Ber. I shall stay here the forehorse to a smock,
Creaking my shoes on the plain masonry,

1. **warlike principles:** military precepts. The King is taking leave of two groups, those who go to aid the Florentines and those who go to aid the Sienese (see I.ii.13–15).
3. **Share:** divide. **gain all:** wish to take advantage of the whole of it. 4. **receiv'd:** accepted.
6. **After well-ent'red soldiers:** when we have become properly initiated soldiers. 9. **owes:** possesses.
10. **besiege.** The King thinks of his illness as another form of warfare.
11. **be you:** show yourselves.
12. **worthy.** A transferred modifier, properly referring to *sons.* **higher Italy:** the nobles of Italy (?) or mountainous Tuscany (?).
13. **Those . . . fall:** those excepted who have merely fallen heir to places left empty by the collapse (?). The passage is variously interpreted and *the last monarchy* (line 14) variously identified.
15. **wed it:** i.e. achieve it, make it your own.
16. **questant:** seeker, i.e. mere wooer.
17. **cry you loud:** acclaim you loudly. 21. **demand:** ask.
21–22. **captives . . . serve.** Both words belong both to the language of war and the language of love; here the first refers to love, the second to war.
24. **sweet.** Used by the Elizabethans often as *dear* is used today; but here probably an affectation.
25. **spark:** spirited young man. **brave:** splendid.
26. **seen:** had experience of.
27. **commanded here:** ordered to remain here. **kept . . . with:** fussed over.
29. **And:** if. **stand to't:** is resolute. **bravely:** as would be fitting, becomingly.
30. **forehorse . . . smock:** teamed up (like the leading horse of a team) with a female. Perhaps the picture in his mind is of leading the lady in a dance, hence the particular complaint in the next line.
31. **plain:** smooth.

Till honor be bought up, and no sword worn
But one to dance with! By heaven, I'll steal away.

1. Lord. There's honor in the theft.

Par. Commit it, Count.

2. Lord. I am your accessary, and so farewell.

Ber. I grow to you, and our parting is a tortur'd body.

1. Lord. Farewell, captain.

2. Lord. Sweet Monsieur Parolles!

Par. Noble heroes! my sword and yours are kin. Good sparks and lustrous, a word, good metals: you shall find in the regiment of the Spinii one Captain Spurio, [with] his cicatrice, an emblem of war, here on his sinister cheek; it was this very sword entrench'd it. Say to him I live, and observe his reports for me.

[1.] Lord. We shall, noble captain.

Par. Mars dote on you for his novices!

[Exeunt Lords.]

What will ye do?

Ber. Stay the King.

Par. Use a more spacious ceremony to the noble lords; you have restrain'd yourself within the list of too cold an adieu. Be more expressive to them, for they wear themselves in the cap of the time, there do muster true gait; eat, speak, and move under the influence of the most receiv'd star, and though the devil lead the measure, such are to be follow'd. After them, and take a more dilated farewell.

Ber. And I will do so.

Par. Worthy fellows, and like to prove most sinewy swordmen. *Exeunt [Bertram and Parolles].*

Enter LAFEW. *[The* KING *comes forward.]*

Laf. *[Kneeling.]* Pardon, my lord, for me and for my tidings.

King. I'll see thee to stand up.

Laf. Then here's a man stands that has brought his pardon.
I would you had kneel'd, my lord, to ask me mercy,
And that at my bidding you could so stand up.

King. I would I had, so I had broke thy pate,
And ask'd thee mercy for't.

Laf. Good faith, across!
But, my good lord, 'tis thus: will you be cur'd
Of your infirmity?

King. No.

Laf. O, will you eat
No grapes, my royal fox? Yes, but you will
My noble grapes, and if my royal fox
Could reach them. I have seen a medicine
That's able to breathe life into a stone,
Quicken a rock, and make you dance canary
With spritely fire and motion, whose simple touch
Is powerful to araise King Pippen, nay,
To give great Charlemain a pen in 's hand
And write to her a love-line.

King. What her is this?

Laf. Why, Doctor She! My lord, there's one arriv'd,
If you will see her. Now by my faith and honor,
If seriously I may convey my thoughts
In this my light deliverance, I have spoke
With one, that in her sex, her years, profession,
Wisdom, and constancy, hath amaz'd me more
Than I dare blame my weakness. Will you see her—
For that is her demand—and know her business?
That done, laugh well at me.

King. Now, good Lafew,
Bring in the admiration, that we with thee
May spend our wonder too, or take off thine
By wond'ring how thou took'st it.

Laf. Nay, I'll fit you,
And not be all day neither. *[Goes to the door.]*

King. Thus he his special nothing ever prologues.

Laf. Nay, come your ways.

Enter HELEN.

King. This haste hath wings indeed.

Laf. Nay, come your ways;
This is his Majesty, say your mind to him.
A traitor you do look like, but such traitors
His Majesty seldom fears. I am Cressid's uncle,

32. Till . . . up: until others have monopolized all the available honor. **33. one . . . with**: i.e. one worn for ornament, not use.
34. theft. A play on *steal*, continued in *Commit* and *accessary*.
35. grow: have become attached.
36–37. a tortur'd body: as painful as the rending of a body by torture. This speech comes oddly from Bertram and is perhaps misassigned.
41. metals: (1) swords(men); (2) mettlesome fellows. For the Elizabethans, *metal* and *mettle* were variants of the same word.
43. Spurio. The Italian word for "spurious."
44. sinister: left. **45. observe his reports**: take note of his reply.
47. novices: young devotees.
49. Stay the King: attend (or support) the King. Some editors read *Stay;* (following F2), explained either as a telegraphic "Stay here; King's orders" or as "Stop talking; the King is approaching." Dover Wilson supposes that lines 50–60 are intended for the King's ear as he slowly comes forward with his attendants.
50. ceremony: courtesy. **51. list**: boundary, limit.
52. expressive: outgoing.
53. wear . . . time: are conspicuous ornaments of the fashionable world. **54. muster true gait**: exhibit the true (courtly) bearing.
55. receiv'd: accepted, fashionable. **56. measure**: dance.
57. dilated: expansive (synonymous with *spacious*, line 50).
59. like: likely. **61. Pardon**: i.e. indulgence.
62. I'll . . . up: i.e. let me see you rise. (The infinitive with *to* was common after verbs of perceiving.) Many editors emend *see* to *fee* (Theobald) or *sue* (Staunton conjecture).
63. brought his pardon: i.e. brought something that will win your indulgence.

66. broke thy pate: i.e. given you a blow on the head that brought blood.
67. across. "A word . . . used when any pass of wit miscarries" (Johnson). In tilting, a proper blow was delivered with the spear's point, not with the spear held athwart the adversary.
69–70. will . . . fox: i.e. do you pretend lack of interest in a cure because you suppose that a cure is beyond your reach (an allusion to Aesop's fable of the fox and the grapes). **71. and if**: if.
72. medicine. This word can mean "physician" and perhaps does so here.
74. Quicken: give life to. **canary**: a particularly energetic dance.
75. simple: mere (but perhaps with suggestion of its sense "medicinal herb").
76. Is . . . Pippen: i.e. has the potency to bring back to life a man who has been dead for centuries. The Frankish king Pepin, father of Charlemagne, died in 768.
82. light deliverance: frivolous manner of reporting.
83. profession: what she professes to be able to do.
85. blame my weakness: lay to my enfeebled faculties (?) or to my susceptibility (?). **88. admiration**: marvel.
89. spend: expend. **take off**: take away, dispel (with following play on *take* in another sense, "receive into the mind, conceive").
90. fit: accommodate, furnish.
92. special nothing: remarkable trifle.
93. come your ways: come along.
97. Cressid's uncle: i.e. Pandarus, who brought Cressida and Troilus together.

That dare leave two together; fare you well. *Exit.*
King. Now, fair one, does your business follow us?
Hel. Ay, my good lord.
Gerard de Narbon was my father,
In what he did profess, well found.
King. I knew him.
Hel. The rather will I spare my praises towards him,
Knowing him is enough. On 's bed of death
Many receipts he gave me; chiefly one,
Which as the dearest issue of his practice,
And of his old experience th' only darling,
He bade me store up, as a triple eye,
Safer than mine own two, more dear. I have so,
And hearing your high Majesty is touch'd
With that malignant cause wherein the honor
Of my dear father's gift stands chief in power,
I come to tender it, and my appliance,
With all bound humbleness.
King. We thank you, maiden,
But may not be so credulous of cure,
When our most learned doctors leave us, and
The congregated college have concluded
That laboring art can never ransom nature
From her inaidible estate; I say we must not
So stain our judgment, or corrupt our hope,
To prostitute our past-cure malady
To empirics, or to dissever so
Our great self and our credit, to esteem
A senseless help when help past sense we deem.
Hel. My duty then shall pay me for my pains.
I will no more enforce mine office on you,
Humbly entreating from your royal thoughts
A modest one, to bear me back again.
King. I cannot give thee less, to be call'd grateful.
Thou thought'st to help me, and such thanks I give
As one near death to those that wish him live.
But what at full I know, thou know'st no part,
I knowing all my peril, thou no art.
Hel. What I can do can do no hurt to try,
Since you set up your rest 'gainst remedy.

99. **follow**: i.e. have as its object.
102. **well found**: found to be skilled.
106. **dearest issue**: (1) most precious product; (2) favorite child (equivalent to *only* [= chief, supreme] *darling* in line 107).
107. **old**: long. 108. **triple**: third.
109. **Safer**: with greater attention to its security.
110. **touch'd**: infected.
111. **cause**: disease. **honor**: quality for which it is esteemed, particular efficacy. 112. **chief**: chiefly, particularly.
113. **my appliance**: my skill in administering it.
114. **bound**: dutiful. 116. **leave**: abandon hope for.
117. **congregated college**: assembled society of physicians.
118. **laboring art**: the efforts of human skill (here specifically medical science). 119. **inaidible estate**: incurable condition.
120. **stain**: pervert. 121. **prostitute**: basely submit.
122. **empirics**: quacks (accented on the first syllable).
123. **credit**. Usually explained as "reputation," but Schmidt's "belief, faith" seems superior in the context. The King's concern in this passage is his own integrity.
123–24. **esteem . . . deem**: trust to a highly unlikely remedy when I consider any remedy at all to be beyond reason.
125. **My duty**: i.e. my sense that I have performed my duty.
126. **enforce mine office**: press my professional services.
128. **A modest one**: a moderately favorable one (?) or one acknowledging that I have not impaired my modesty (?). 131. **live**: to live.
132. **no part**: in no degree, not at all.
135. **set . . . rest**: stake everything (a term from the game of primero), i.e. are resolved at all costs.

He that of greatest works is finisher
Oft does them by the weakest minister:
So holy writ in babes hath judgment shown,
When judges have been babes; great floods have flown
From simple sources; and great seas have dried
When miracles have by the great'st been denied.
Oft expectation fails, and most oft there
Where most it promises; and oft it hits
Where hope is coldest, and despair most [fits].
King. I must not hear thee; fare thee well, kind maid,
Thy pains not us'd must by thyself be paid.
Proffers not took reap thanks for their reward.
Hel. Inspired merit so by breath is barr'd.
It is not so with Him that all things knows
As 'tis with us that square our guess by shows;
But most it is presumption in us when
The help of heaven we count the act of men.
Dear sir, to my endeavors give consent,
Of heaven, not me, make an experiment.
I am not an imposture that proclaim
Myself against the level of mine aim,
But know I think, and think I know most sure,
My art is not past power, nor you past cure.
King. Art thou so confident? Within what space
Hop'st thou my cure?
Hel. The greatest grace lending grace,
Ere twice the horses of the sun shall bring
Their fiery torcher his diurnal ring,
Ere twice in murk and occidental damp
Moist Hesperus hath quench'd her sleepy lamp,
Or four and twenty times the pilot's glass
Hath told the thievish minutes how they pass,
What is infirm from your sound parts shall fly,
Health shall live free, and sickness freely die.
King. Upon thy certainty and confidence
What dar'st thou venter?
Hel. Tax of impudence,
A strumpet's boldness, a divulged shame,

138–39. **holy . . . babes**. See Matthew 11:25: "thou hast hid these things from the wise and men of understanding, and hast opened them unto babes" (Geneva). Perhaps Shakespeare has in mind Daniel's triumphant defense of Susanna against the judgment of the Elders, to which he refers in *The Merchant of Venice*, IV.i.
139–40. **great . . . sources**. Perhaps alluding to Moses' smiting of the rock in Horeb (Exodus 17:1–7).
140–41. **great . . . denied**. Probably a reference to the parting of the Red Sea to permit the departure of the Israelites from Egypt (Exodus 15); *the great'st* then = Pharoah.
142. **fails**: is disappointed. Johnson points out that line 142 has no rhyming line; possibly there is a lacuna after line 141.
143. **hits**: proves true.
148. **Inspired**: bestowed by the breath of God. **breath**: human breath, i.e. words.
150. **square**: regulate, shape. **shows**: appearances.
152. **count**: account. 154. **experiment**: trial.
155. **imposture**: impostor.
155–56. **proclaim . . . aim**: i.e. announce an intention not in accordance with my actual one. *Level* = direction.
158. **My . . . power**: what I profess is not past my power to perform.
160. **The greatest . . . grace**: with God's help.
161. **horses . . . sun**: horses that draw the sun-god's chariot.
161–62. **bring . . . his diurnal ring**: bring . . . to the end of his daily circuit.
164. **Hesperus**: the evening star (actually Venus; hence, perhaps, the use of *her* rather than the expected *his*). 165. **glass**: hourglass.
166. **thievish**. Because in their passage they steal away life.
168. **freely**: of its own accord.
170. **venter**: venture, hazard. **Tax of impudence**: accusation of shamelessness. 171. **divulged**: exposed, made public.

Traduc'd by odious ballads; my maiden's name
Sear'd otherwise; ne worse of worst—extended
With vildest torture, let my life be ended.

King. Methinks in thee some blessed spirit doth speak
His powerful sound within an organ weak;
And what impossibility would slay
In common sense, sense saves another way.
Thy life is dear, for all that life can rate
Worth name of life in thee hath estimate:
Youth, beauty, wisdom, courage, all
That happiness and prime can happy call.
Thou this to hazard needs must intimate
Skill infinite, or monstrous desperate.
Sweet practicer, thy physic I will try,
That ministers thine own death if I die.

Hel. If I break time, or flinch in property
Of what I spoke, unpitied let me die,
And well deserv'd. Not helping, death's my fee,
But if I help, what do you promise me?

King. Make thy demand.

Hel. But will you make it even?

King. Ay, by my sceptre and my hopes of [heaven].

Hel. Then shalt thou give me with thy kingly hand
What husband in thy power I will command.
Exempted be from me the arrogance
To choose from forth the royal blood of France,
My low and humble name to propagate
With any branch or image of thy state;
But such a one thy vassal, whom I know
Is free for me to ask, thee to bestow.

King. Here is my hand, the premises observ'd,
Thy will by my performance shall be serv'd.
So make the choice of thy own time, for I,
Thy resolv'd patient, on thee still rely.
More should I question thee, and more I must—
Though more to know could not be more to trust—
From whence thou cam'st, how tended on, but rest
Unquestion'd welcome and undoubted blest.—
Give me some help here ho!—If thou proceed
As high as word, my deed shall match thy deed.

Flourish. Exeunt.

173. Sear'd otherwise: branded in other ways, i.e. with other shameful names. **ne . . . worst:** nor would this be worse than what is worst (i.e. dishonor). **extended:** stretched out (as on the rack) (?) or lingered out (?). 174. **vildest:** vilest.
177–78. what . . . way: what common sense would reject as impossible, reason declares feasible on other grounds.
179–80. rate . . . life: value as worthy of being called "life."
180. hath estimate: must be accounted present.
182. happiness and prime: good fortune and youth.
183. Thou . . . hazard: that you are willing to risk all this. **intimate:** argue.
184. monstrous desperate: (that you are) horribly reckless.
185. physic: medicine.
187. break time: fail to perform within the specified time (of two days). **flinch in property:** fall short in some particular.
189. Not helping: if I do not cure you.
191. make it even: fulfill it.
195. Exempted: far removed.
198. image: likeness, copy (?). Hunter suggests that *branch or image* refers to family trees with portraits hanging from the various branches. **state:** high place.
201. premises observ'd: conditions fulfilled.
204. resolv'd: with mind made up. **still:** ever.
207. tended on: attended.
208. Unquestion'd: (1) in advance of being asked these questions; (2) unquestionably. **210. word:** promise.

[Scene II]

Enter Countess *and* Clown.

Count. Come on, sir, I shall now put you to the height of your breeding.

Clo. I will show myself highly fed and lowly taught. I know my business is but to the court.

Count. To the court! Why, what place make you special, when you put off that with such contempt? But to the court!

Clo. Truly, madam, if God have lent a man any manners, he may easily put it off at court. He that cannot make a leg, put off 's cap, kiss his hand, and say nothing, has neither leg, hands, lip, nor cap; and indeed such a fellow, to say precisely, were not for the court; but for me, I have an answer will serve all men.

Count. Marry, that's a bountiful answer that fits all questions.

Clo. It is like a barber's chair that fits all buttocks: the pin-buttock, the quatch-buttock, the brawn-buttock, or any buttock.

Count. Will your answer serve fit to all questions?

Clo. As fit as ten groats is for the hand of an attorney, as your French crown for your taffety punk, as Tib's rush for Tom's forefinger, as a pancake for Shrove Tuesday, a morris for May-day, as the nail to his hole, the cuckold to his horn, as a scolding quean to a wrangling knave, as the nun's lip to the friar's mouth, nay, as the pudding to his skin.

Count. Have you, I say, an answer of such fitness for all questions?

Clo. From below your duke to beneath your constable, it will fit any question.

Count. It must be an answer of most monstrous size that must fit all demands.

Clo. But a trifle neither, in good faith, if the learned should speak truth of it. Here it is, and all that belongs to't. Ask me if I am a courtier: it shall do you no harm to learn.

Count. To be young again, if we could, I will be a fool in question, hoping to be the wiser by your answer.

II.ii. Location: Rossillion. The Count's palace.
1–2. put . . . height: make a thorough trial. The Countess is referring to the Clown's errand to the court.
2. your breeding: (the results of) your upbringing.
3–4. highly . . . taught. "Better fed than taught" was a proverbial description of a child reared overindulgently. The Clown probably implies that he will do well at court because his "breeding" has been that of the pampered young courtiers.
5–6. make you special: do you rate as choice. **6. put off:** dismiss.
9. put it off: pull it off, make a go of it.
10. make a leg: bend his knee, make obeisance. **put off:** take off.
13. for: as for.
17. like . . . chair. A common comparison for what suits all comers. In the following line *pin* = pointed; *quatch* perhaps = broad and flat; *brawn* = fleshy or fatty. **21. ten groats:** forty pence.
22. French crown: (1) a coin; (2) bald head (resulting from syphilis, commonly called "the French disease"). **taffety punk:** taffeta-clad prostitute.
23. Tib's rush: i.e. a ring made by twisting a rush, for a love-token or for use in a mock marriage. *Tib* is a stock name for a country wench. **pancake.** Traditional fare for Shrove Tuesday, the day before the beginning of Lent.
24. morris: morris-dance (a traditional feature of May-games).
25, 27. his: its. **26. quean:** hussy. **27. pudding:** sausage.
30–31. below . . . constable. Probably with bawdy innuendo.
34. But . . . neither: on the contrary it is a mere trifle.

I pray you, sir, are you a courtier?

Clo. O Lord, sir!—There's a simple putting off. More, more, a hundred of them.

Count. Sir, I am a poor friend of yours that loves you.

Clo. O Lord, sir!—Thick, thick, spare not me.

Count. I think, sir, you can eat none of this homely meat.

Clo. O Lord, sir!—Nay, put me to't, I warrant you.

Count. You were lately whipt, sir, as I think.

Clo. O Lord, sir!—Spare not me.

Count. Do you cry, "O Lord, sir!" at your whipping, and "Spare not me"? Indeed your "O Lord, sir!" is very sequent to your whipping; you would answer very well to a whipping, if you were but bound to't.

Clo. I ne'er had worse luck in my life in my "O Lord, sir!" I see things may serve long, but not serve ever.

Count. I play the noble huswife with the time,
To entertain it so merrily with a fool.

Clo. O Lord, sir!—Why, there't serves well again.

Count. [An] end, sir; to your business: give Helen this,
And urge her to a present answer back.
Commend me to my kinsmen and my son.
This is not much.

Clo. Not much commendation to them.

Count. Not much employment for you. You understand me?

Clo. Most fruitfully, I am there before my legs.

Count. Haste you again. *Exeunt.*

[Scene III]

Enter Count [Bertram], Lafew, *and* Parolles.

Laf. They say miracles are past, and we have our philosophical persons, to make modern and familiar, things supernatural and causeless. Hence is it that we make trifles of terrors, ensconcing ourselves into seeming knowledge, when we should submit ourselves to an unknown fear.

41. O Lord, sir. "A ridicule on that foolish expletive of speech then in vogue at court" (Warburton). It evades an answer to a yes-or-no question by appearing to deprecate either reply. **putting off:** evasion. **45. Thick:** quick. **spare not me:** i.e. keep them coming.
46–47. homely meat: plain food.
54. is . . . to: follows very logically from. "O Lord, sir" during a whipping would be a plea for mercy (quite the opposite of "Spare not me").
55. answer . . . to: (1) have a very good answer to; (2) be a very appropriate subject for.
56. bound to't: (1) required to answer; (2) tied to a post for a whipping.
60. I . . . time: I am employing my time in a worthy manner indeed.
64. present: immediate.
65. Commend me: give my loving greetings.
70. fruitfully. The word *understand* routinely elicits a bawdy quibble from the Clown. **71. again:** back.

II.iii. Location: Paris. The King's palace.
2. modern: commonplace.
3. causeless: i.e. inexplicable in terms of natural law.
4. terrors: i.e. occurrences that should inspire awe. **ensconcing . . . into:** sheltering . . . in.
6. unknown fear: awe in the face of the unknown.

Par. Why, 'tis the rarest argument of wonder that hath shot out in our latter times.

Ber. And so 'tis.

Laf. To be relinquish'd of the artists—

Par. So I say, both of Galen and Paracelsus.

Laf. Of all the learned and authentic fellows—

Par. Right, so I say.

Laf. That gave him out incurable—

Par. Why, there 'tis, so say I too.

Laf. Not to be help'd—

Par. Right, as 'twere a man assur'd of a—

Laf. Uncertain life, and sure death.

Par. Just, you say well; so would I have said.

Laf. I may truly say it is a novelty to the world.

Par. It is indeed; if you will have it in showing, you shall read it in what-do-ye-call there.

[*Pointing to a ballad in Lafew's hand.*]

Laf. [*Reading the title.*] "A showing of a heavenly effect in an earthly actor."

Par. That's it I would have said, the very same.

Laf. Why, your dolphin is not lustier. 'Fore me, I speak in respect—

Par. Nay, 'tis strange, 'tis very strange, that is the brief and the tedious of it, and he's of a most facinerious spirit that will not acknowledge it to be the—

Laf. Very hand of heaven.

Par. Ay, so I say.

Laf. In a most weak—

Par. And debile minister, great power, great transcendence, which should indeed give us a further use to be made than alone the recov'ry of the King, as to be—

Laf. Generally thankful.

Enter King, Helen, *and* Attendants.

Par. I would have said it; you say well. Here comes the King.

Laf. *Lustick*, as the Dutchman says. I'll like a maid the better whilst I have a tooth in my head. Why, he's able to lead her a coranto.

7. rarest: most extraordinary. **argument:** theme, subject.
8. latter: recent, modern.
9. And so 'tis. This is Bertram's only speech until after the entrance of the other lords at line 51. It has been conjectured that Shakespeare, after beginning the scene, altered his intention to have Bertram present from the start, and that Bertram should make his entrance with the other lords.
10. relinquish'd . . . artists: given up by the learned (physicians).
11. both . . . Paracelsus: i.e. both those who follow the traditional doctrine of Galen (Greek physician of the second century A.D. who in Shakespeare's day was still the preeminent medical authority) and those who favor the new methods of Paracelsus (Swiss-born alchemist and physician [1493–1541] who had undertaken to reform the Galenic system). Some editors would add these words to Lafew's next speech, limiting Parolles again to mere assent.
12. authentic fellows: i.e. duly qualified members of the society of physicians. **16. help'd:** cured. **19. Just:** exactly.
21. in showing: visible, i.e. set forth in print.
26. lustier: more vigorous and sportive. Commentators suggest a pun on *Dauphin* (regularly spelled *Dolphin* in Shakespeare's texts). **'Fore me:** i.e. on my soul (a form of oath derived from such expressions as *'fore God* [line 45] and *'fore heaven*).
29. brief . . . tedious: short . . . long. Parolles suddenly gets into his stride with this speech and follows it up in his next, turning the tables on Lafew. Some editors reassign the speeches, to Lafew's advantage. **facinerious:** extremely wicked (variant of *facinorous*).
34. debile minister: feeble agent. **38. Generally:** universally.
41. Lustick: lusty. **42. tooth . . . head:** i.e. a taste (for girls).
43. coranto: a lively dance.

Par. *Mort du vinaigre!* is not this Helen?
Laf. 'Fore God, I think so.
King. Go call before me all the lords in court.
Sit, my preserver, by thy patient's side,
And with this healthful hand, whose banish'd sense
Thou hast repeal'd, a second time receive
The confirmation of my promis'd gift,
Which but attends thy naming.

Enter three or four LORDS.

Fair maid, send forth thine eye. This youthful parcel
Of noble bachelors stand at my bestowing,
O'er whom both sovereign power and father's voice
I have to use. Thy frank election make;
Thou hast power to choose, and they none to forsake.
Hel. To each of you one fair and virtuous mistress
Fall, when Love please! Marry, to each but one!
Laf. I'd give bay Curtal and his furniture,
My mouth no more were broken than these boys',
And writ as little beard.
King. Peruse them well.
Not one of those but had a noble father.
Hel. Gentlemen,
Heaven hath through me restor'd the King to health.
All. We understand it, and thank heaven for you.
Hel. I am a simple maid, and therein wealthiest
That I protest I simply am a maid.
Please it your Majesty, I have done already.
The blushes in my cheeks thus whisper me,
"We blush that thou shouldst choose; but be refused,
Let the white death sit on thy cheek for ever,
We'll ne'er come there again."
King. Make choice and see,
Who shuns thy love shuns all his love in me.
Hel. Now, Dian, from thy altar do I fly,
And to imperial Love, that god most high,
Do my sighs stream. (*She addresses her to a Lord.*) Sir, will you hear my suit?
1. Lord. And grant it.
Hel. Thanks, sir; all the rest is mute.
Laf. I had rather be in this choice than throw ames-ace for my life.
Hel. [*To a second Lord.*] The honor, sir, that flames in your fair eyes,
Before I speak, too threat'ningly replies.
Love make your fortunes twenty times above
Her that so wishes, and her humble love!
2. Lord. No better, if you please.
Hel. My wish receive,
Which great Love grant, and so I take my leave.
Laf. Do all they deny her? And they were sons of mine, I'd have them whipt, or I would send them to th' Turk to make eunuchs of.
Hel. [*To a third Lord.*] Be not afraid that I your hand should take,
I'll never do you wrong for your own sake.
Blessing upon your vows, and in your bed
Find fairer fortune, if you ever wed!
Laf. These boys are boys of ice, they'll none have [her]. Sure they are bastards to the English, the French ne'er got 'em.
Hel. [*To a fourth Lord.*] You are too young, too happy, and too good,
To make yourself a son out of my blood.
4. Lord. Fair one, I think not so.
Laf. There's one grape yet; I am sure thy father drunk wine—but if thou be'st not an ass, I am a youth of fourteen. I have known thee already.
Hel. [*To Bertram.*] I dare not say I take you, but I give
Me and my service, ever whilst I live,
Into your guiding power.—This is the man.
King. Why then, young Bertram, take her, she's thy wife.
Ber. My wife, my liege? I shall beseech your Highness,
In such a business, give me leave to use
The help of mine own eyes.
King. Know'st thou not, Bertram,
What she has done for me?
Ber. Yes, my good lord,
But never hope to know why I should marry her.
King. Thou know'st she has rais'd me from my sickly bed.
Ber. But follows it, my lord, to bring me down
Must answer for your raising? I know her well;
She had her breeding at my father's charge—
A poor physician's daughter my wife! Disdain
Rather corrupt me ever!

44. Mort du vinaigre: a pseudo-French oath (= death of the vinegar) of obscure origin, presumably referring to the Crucifixion. Parolles' amazement shows that he has not yet learned the means of the King's cure. **48. healthful**: healthy. **sense**: power of feeling.
49. repeal'd: called back (carrying on the figure in *banish'd*).
51. attends: awaits.
53. stand . . . bestowing: are in my power to give. A guardian had authority to marry his ward to any woman of equal rank. Helen, of course, does not meet this condition.
55. frank election: free choice. **56. forsake**: i.e. refuse.
58. to . . . one: only one to each (but with the private meaning "to all except one").
59. Curtal. The name means "having a docked tail." **furniture**: trappings.
60. My . . . broken: if my teeth showed no more gaps (perhaps with the same reference to sensual appetite as in line 42) (?) or if I were no more broken to the bit (?) or if my voice were no more broken (?).
61. writ: (if I) claimed title to. **67. protest**: avow.
69. whisper: whisper to. **70. be**: if you are.
77. all . . . mute: i.e. I have no further words for you. There are two schools of thought about Helena's exchanges with the young lords. Some commentators take Lafew's comments at lines 86–88, 93–95 at face value and suppose that the lords, though they make politely acquiescent replies, show by their demeanor their disdain of Helen. The scene can certainly be played in this way, but the weight of the lines themselves seems to favor the view that Lafew, out of earshot, misinterprets the reason for Helena's speedy passing from one to another.
79. ames-ace: two aces (the lowest throw at dice). Lafew is making a jocular understatement: "I'd rather make a losing throw with my life at stake."
80–81. honor . . . threat'ningly. Susceptible of two interpretations: that the pride of rank which he displays threatens refusal, or that the honor his look pays Helena (i.e. his evident willingness to be chosen, or his obvious admiration) threatens embarrassment to one who has made another choice.
83. so wishes: pronounces this wish.
84. No . . . please: I wish for no one better than you if you will have me. **receive**: accept.
86. Do . . . her. Helena's exchanges with the lords cannot be heard by the others. **95. got**: begot.
99–100. There's . . . wine: "There is one yet into whom his father put good blood" (Johnson). "Good wine makes good blood" was proverbial. **101. known**: come to know, i.e. seen through.
106. liege: sovereign. **110. hope**: expect.
114. breeding: upbringing. **charge**: expense.
115–16. Disdain . . . ever: let the consequences of my disdain rather spoil my fortunes forever.

King. 'Tis only title thou disdain'st in her, the which
I can build up. Strange is it that our bloods,
Of color, weight, and heat, pour'd all together,
Would quite confound distinction, yet stands off
In differences so mighty. If she be
All that is virtuous—save what thou dislik'st,
A poor physician's daughter—thou dislik'st
Of virtue for the name. But do not so.
From lowest place [when] virtuous things proceed,
The place is dignified by th' doer's deed.
Where great additions swell 's, and virtue none,
It is a dropsied honor. Good alone
Is good, without a name; vileness is so:
The property by what [it] is should go,
Not by the title. She is young, wise, fair,
In these to nature she's immediate heir;
And these breed honor. That is honor's scorn,
Which challenges itself as honor's born,
And is not like the sire. Honors thrive,
When rather from our acts we them derive
Than our foregoers. The mere word's a slave
Debosh'd on every tomb, on every grave
A lying trophy, and as oft is dumb
Where dust and damn'd oblivion is the tomb
Of honor'd bones indeed. What should be said?
If thou canst like this creature as a maid,
I can create the rest. Virtue and she
Is her own dower; honor and wealth from me.
Ber. I cannot love her, nor will strive to do't.
King. Thou wrong'st thyself, if thou shouldst strive to choose.
Hel. That you are well restor'd, my lord, I'm glad.
Let the rest go.
King. My honor's at the stake, which to defeat,
I must produce my power. Here, take her hand,
Proud scornful boy, unworthy this good gift,
That dost in vile misprision shackle up
My love and her desert; that canst not dream,
We poising us in her defective scale,
Shall weigh thee to the beam; that wilt not know
It is in us to plant thine honor where
We please to have it grow. Check thy contempt;
Obey our will, which travails in thy good;
Believe not thy disdain, but presently
Do thine own fortunes that obedient right
Which both thy duty owes and our power claims,
Or I will throw thee from my care for ever
Into the staggers and the careless lapse
Of youth and ignorance; both my revenge and hate
Loosing upon thee, in the name of justice,
Without all terms of pity. Speak, thine answer.
Ber. Pardon, my gracious lord; for I submit
My fancy to your eyes. When I consider
What great creation and what dole of honor
Flies where you bid it, I find that she, which late
Was in my nobler thoughts most base, is now
The praised of the King, who so ennobled,
Is as 'twere born so.
King. Take her by the hand,
And tell her she is thine; to whom I promise
A counterpoise—if not to thy estate
A balance more replete.
Ber. I take her hand.
King. Good fortune and the favor of the King
Smile upon this contract, whose ceremony
Shall seem expedient on the now-born brief,
And be perform'd to-night. The solemn feast
Shall more attend upon the coming space,
Expecting absent friends. As thou lov'st her,
Thy love's to me religious; else, does err.
Exeunt. Lafew and Parolles stay behind, commenting of this wedding.
Laf. Do you hear, monsieur? A word with you.
Par. Your pleasure, sir?
Laf. Your lord and master did well to make his recantation.
Par. Recantation? My lord? My master?
Laf. Ay; is it not a language I speak?
Par. A most harsh one, and not to be understood without bloody succeeding. My master?
Laf. Are you companion to the Count Rossillion?
Par. To any count, to all counts: to what is man.

117. title: i.e. lack of title. Cf. *name* (i.e. lack of name) in line 124.
119. Of . . . heat. Modifies *distinction* (line 120); *Of* = in respect of.
120. stands off: stand separated. **125. proceed:** issue.
127. additions: honorific titles and other marks of distinction.
128. dropsied: i.e. unhealthily swollen. **alone:** of itself, by its own essential nature. **129. vileness is so:** vileness is vile of itself.
130. property: quality. **go:** i.e. be accepted.
132. In . . . heir: she inherits these qualities directly from nature.
133. honor's scorn: i.e. an object of contempt in the eyes of the truly honorable. **134. challenges:** makes claims for.
138. Debosh'd: debauched, debased. **139. trophy:** memorial.
140. damn'd: damnable, hateful.
141. honor'd bones indeed: i.e. the remains of men who had truly possessed honor.
143. Virtue and she: she herself with her natural endowments of youth, wisdom, and beauty (line 130) and her honorable attainments.
145. strive to do't: attempt to do so.
146. strive to choose: endeavor to make your own choice, i.e. to follow your own wishes.
149. at the stake: under attack (a figure from bear-baiting). **which:** i.e. which attack.
152. misprision: (1) scorn; (2) error, taking one thing for another. Sometimes spelled, and probably pronounced, *misprison*; hence the following *shackle up*. **154. We.** The royal plural.
154–55. We . . . beam: I, adding my weight to her overlight (*defective* = deficient) side of the balance, shall outweigh your side and send it up to the cross-beam. The figure of the balance recurs at lines 175–76.
156. in us: in my royal power. **158. travails in:** labors for.
159. Believe not: do not credit, i.e. do not be governed by. **presently:** at once.
160. Do . . . right: do your fortunes justice by yielding that obedience.
163. staggers . . . lapse. These words may mean "giddiness and heedless downward course" or "sick confusion and reckless ruin" (Dyce emended *careless* to *cureless* for "irreparable ruin"). *Of youth and ignorance* (line 164) supports the milder reading, but the rest of the sentence accords with the bleaker prediction.
166. all . . . pity: any concessions to mercy. **168. fancy:** liking.
169. great creation: creating of greatness. **dole:** dealing out.
170. which late: who a short time ago. **171. base:** low in station.
175–76. A counterpoise . . . replete: an equal weight, if not a weight even heavier than your possessions come to.
179. Shall . . . brief. A much-debated line; perhaps "shall show itself speedily (*expedient* = expeditious) in the wake of this just-completed contract." **180. solemn:** ceremonial.
181. more attend: wait longer. **space:** time.
182. Expecting absent friends: awaiting relatives who are not now here.
183. to me: in my interpretation. **religious:** i.e. directed toward the proper object of worship. **does err:** strays from the truth, is sinful or idolatrous. **s.d. Lafew . . . wedding.** An unusual type of stage direction; possibly Shakespeare broke off work on the scene at this point and left a memorandum to guide himself when he resumed.
191. succeeding: sequel, consequences.

Laf. To what is count's man. Count's master is of another style.

Par. You are too old, sir; let it satisfy you, you are too old.

Laf. I must tell thee, sirrah, I write man; to which title age cannot bring thee.

Par. What I dare too well do, I dare not do.

Laf. I did think thee, for two ordinaries, to be a pretty wise fellow. Thou didst make tolerable vent of thy travel; it might pass: yet the scarfs and the bannerets about thee did manifoldly dissuade me from believing thee a vessel of too great a burthen. I have now found thee. When I lose thee again, I care not; yet art thou good for nothing but taking up, and that thou'rt scarce worth.

Par. Hadst thou not the privilege of antiquity upon thee—

Laf. Do not plunge thyself too far in anger, lest thou hasten thy trial; which if—Lord have mercy on thee for a hen! So, my good window of lettice, fare thee well. Thy casement I need not open, for I look through thee. Give me thy hand.

Par. My lord, you give me most egregious indignity.

Laf. Ay, with all my heart, and thou art worthy of it.

Par. I have not, my lord, deserv'd it.

Laf. Yes, good faith, ev'ry dram of it, and I will not bate thee a scruple.

Par. Well, I shall be wiser.

Laf. Ev'n as soon as thou canst, for thou hast to pull at a smack a' th' contrary. If ever thou be'st bound in thy scarf and beaten, thou shall find what it is to be proud of thy bondage. I have a desire to hold my acquaintance with thee, or rather my knowledge, that I may say in the default, "He is a man I know."

Par. My lord, you do me most insupportable vexation.

Laf. I would it were hell-pains for thy sake, and my poor doing eternal; for doing I am past, as I will by thee, in what motion age will give me leave. *Exit.*

Par. Well, thou hast a son shall take this disgrace off me, scurvy, old, filthy, scurvy lord! Well, I must be patient, there is no fettering of authority. I'll beat him, by my life, if I can meet him with any convenience, and he were double and double a lord. I'll have no more pity of his age than I would have of—I'll beat him, and if I could but meet him again.

Enter Lafew.

Laf. Sirrah, your lord and master's married, there's news for you. You have a new mistress.

Par. I most unfeignedly beseech your lordship to make some reservation of your wrongs. He is my good lord; whom I serve above is my master.

Laf. Who? God?

Par. Ay, sir.

Laf. The devil it is that's thy master. Why dost thou garter up thy arms a' this fashion? Dost make hose of thy sleeves? Do other servants so? Thou wert best set thy lower part where thy nose stands. By mine honor, if I were but two hours younger, I'd beat thee. Methink'st thou art a general offense, and every man should beat thee. I think thou wast created for men to breathe themselves upon thee.

Par. This is hard and undeserv'd measure, my lord.

Laf. Go to, sir, you were beaten in Italy for picking a kernel out of a pomegranate. You are a vagabond and no true traveller. You are more saucy with lords and honorable personages than the commission of your birth and virtue gives you heraldry. You are not worth another word, else I'd call you knave. I leave you. *Exit.*

Enter [Bertram] *Count Rossillion.*

Par. Good, very good, it is so then. Good, very good, let it be conceal'd awhile.

Ber. Undone, and forfeited to cares for ever!

194. man: servant.
196. let . . . you: i.e. don't force me to take action.
198. write man: style myself "man," claim manhood.
200. What . . . not do: i.e. what I have all too much courage for, your age inhibits me from doing.
201. ordinaries: meals. **202. make . . . of:** talk passably about.
203, 204. scarfs, bannerets. Scarfs were often worn by soldiers, but Parolles, to judge by various references to his attire, evidently goes in for excessively showy adornment. His streamers suggest to Lafew pennants on a ship; hence his figure of a vessel in line 205. Cf. *The Merchant of Venice*, II.vi.14–15, where a "scarfed bark" conversely brings to mind a young gallant.
205. burthen: cargo (variant of *burden*).
206. found thee: found you out, seen through you (with following quibble).
207. taking up. The meaning may be "contradicting," "berating," or "taking into custody," and there is a final quibble on "picking up" (in contrast to *lose*, line 206).
209. privilege of antiquity: license permitted to old age.
212. hasten thy trial: be (tested and) found out sooner.
213. hen: coward (?). **lettice:** lattice. Lafew calls Parolles a lattice window because he has seen through him; perhaps also his scarfs and bannerets suggest latticework and advertise his character as red-lattice windows advertised taverns, of which they were a regular feature.
214. Thy . . . open. The casement was made of wood. Perhaps there is a play on *case* = body.
222. bate: abate, remit. **scruple:** the smallest unit of weight, one-third of a dram.
223. be wiser. Parolles means something like "I'll avoid dotards in future," but Lafew replies to the simple sense "grow wiser."
225. pull . . . contrary: swallow a fair amount of the opposite quality.
227. hold: continue.
229. in the default: when you default (or fail). Lafew takes it for granted that that day will come. Cf. line 212, where he assumes that Parolles' *trial* (testing) will result in his being found wanting.

232. I . . . sake. Lafew adopts the verbal pattern of one who has been thanked for a kindness and who replies that he has done far less than the recipient deserves.
233. my poor doing: i.e. my very inadequate vexing of you. Lafew here picks up Parolles' *do* (line 230), then (in *for doing*) plays on the word in its slang sexual sense. **will:** i.e. will now pass.
234. in . . . leave: with whatever gait or speed my advanced age permits (alluding to Parolles' stress on his "antiquity").
235–36. shall . . . me: i.e. on whom I will retaliate.
238–39. with any convenience: on any suitable occasion.
239. and: even if.
245. make . . . wrongs: keep your affronts in some degree to yourself (Schmidt). **245–46. my good lord:** i.e. my patron.
250. garter . . . arms. Presumably Parolles has tied a scarf around each arm.
254. Methink'st. The impersonal verb *methinks* (= it seems to me) is here treated as personal, drawn into the second person singular by attraction of the following *thou*, as if with the sense "thou seemest to me." **general offense:** public nuisance.
256. breathe . . . thee: get their exercise by beating you.
257. measure: meting out of judgment, i.e. treatment.
258–59. you . . . pomegranate. The point seems to be that people find Parolles so worthy of beating that they beat him on the slightest pretext. **261. commission:** warrant.
262. gives you heraldry: entitles you to be.

Par. What's the matter, sweet heart?
Ber. Although before the solemn priest I have sworn,
I will not bed her.
Par. What, what, sweet heart?
Ber. O my Parolles, they have married me!
I'll to the Tuscan wars, and never bed her.
Par. France is a dog-hole, and it no more merits
The tread of a man's foot. To th' wars!
Ber. There's letters from my mother; what th' import is,
I know not yet.
Par. Ay, that would be known. To th' wars, my boy, to th' wars!
He wears his honor in a box unseen,
That hugs his kicky-wicky here at home,
Spending his manly marrow in her arms,
Which should sustain the bound and high curvet
Of Mars's fiery steed. To other regions!
France is a stable, we that dwell in't jades,
Therefore to th' war!
Ber. It shall be so. I'll send her to my house,
Acquaint my mother with my hate to her,
And wherefore I am fled; write to the King
That which I durst not speak. His present gift
Shall furnish me to those Italian fields
Where noble fellows strike. Wars is no strife
To the dark house and the [detested] wife.
Par. Will this *capriccio* hold in thee, art sure?
Ber. Go with me to my chamber, and advise me.
I'll send her straight away. To-morrow,
I'll to the wars, she to her single sorrow.
Par. Why, these balls bound, there's noise in it. 'Tis hard!
A young man married is a man that's marr'd;
Therefore away, and leave her bravely; go.
The King has done you wrong; but hush, 'tis so.
Exeunt.

[Scene IV]

Enter Helena *and* Clown.

Hel. My mother greets me kindly. Is she well?

Clo. She is not well, but yet she has her health. She's very merry, but yet she is not well; but thanks be given, she's very well, and wants nothing i' th' world; but yet she is not well.

Hel. If she be very well, what does she ail that she's not very well?

Clo. Truly, she's very well indeed, but for two things.

Hel. What two things?

Clo. One, that she's not in heaven, whither God send her quickly! the other, that she's in earth, from whence God send her quickly!

Enter Parolles.

Par. Bless you, my fortunate lady!

Hel. I hope, sir, I have your good will to have mine own good [fortunes].

Par. You had my prayers to lead them on, and to keep them on, have them still. O, my knave, how does my old lady?

Clo. So that you had her wrinkles and I her money, I would she did as you say.

Par. Why, I say nothing.

Clo. Marry, you are the wiser man; for many a man's tongue shakes out his master's undoing. To say nothing, to do nothing, to know nothing, and to have nothing, is to be a great part of your title, which is within a very little of nothing.

Par. Away, th' art a knave.

Clo. You should have said, sir, "Before a knave th' art a knave," that's "Before me th' art a knave." This had been truth, sir.

Par. Go to, thou art a witty fool, I have found thee.

Clo. Did you find me in yourself, sir, [*Parolles nods.*] or were you taught to find me? [*Parolles shakes his head.*] The search, sir, was profitable, and much fool may you find in you, even to the world's pleasure and the increase of laughter.

Par. A good knave, i' faith, and well fed.
Madam, my lord will go away to-night,
A very serious business calls on him.
The great prerogative and rite of love,
Which, as your due, time claims, he does acknowledge,
But puts it off to a compell'd restraint;
Whose want, and whose delay, is strew'd with sweets,
Which they distill now in the curbed time,
To make the coming hour o'erflow with joy,
And pleasure drown the brim.
Hel. What's his will else?
Par. That you will take your instant leave a' th' King,
And make this haste as your own good proceeding,

276. **letters:** a letter (Latin *litterae*).
279. **in . . . unseen.** With sexual innuendo.
280. **kicky-wicky.** Apparently Shakespeare's invention.
281. **Spending:** expending, using up. **his manly marrow:** the essence of his manliness.
282. **curvet:** a difficult leap in which all four legs are off the ground.
284. **jades:** inferior horses.
289. **His present gift:** the gift he has just made me.
290. **furnish me to:** equip me for.
292. **To:** compared with. **dark house.** Perhaps this = dismal house, but probably the reference is to a madhouse (the mad were often kept in darkness) and Bertram means that living with Helena would drive him crazy. In *Twelfth Night* the room where Malvolio is confined is called a dark house (see IV.ii.34, 41; V.i.342).
293. **capriccio:** caprice (Italian). 295. **straight:** at once.
296. **single:** (1) solitary; (2) husbandless.
297. **these . . . it:** i.e. this shows spirit. *Balls* = tennis balls.
298. **A young . . . marr'd.** Proverbial. 299. **bravely.** As at II.i.29.

II.iv. Location: Paris. The King's palace.
1. **kindly:** affectionately.
2. **well.** The Clown quibbles on the Elizabethan sense "in heaven."

4. **wants:** lacks. 6. **what:** in what, how. 24. **man's:** servant's.
26. **title:** worth.
29–30. **You . . . knave.** The Clown plays on the oath *before me* (= on my soul; see II.iii.26). He says, in effect, "You're another."
33. **in yourself.** Parolles unwarily takes this to mean "by your own efforts." 36. **pleasure:** merriment.
38. **well fed:** i.e. better fed than taught (see the note on II.ii.3).
42. **time:** the occasion. 43. **puts . . . to:** delays it because of.
44. **Whose want:** the lack of which (rite). **sweets:** fragrant flowers. Parolles uses an elaborate figure based on the distillation of perfume.
45. **they:** i.e. the want and the delay. **curbed time:** time of restraint; Hunter suggests that there is also a reference to the flask or *cucurbita* of the still.
47. **else:** besides. 49. **make:** represent.

Strength'ned with what apology you think
May make it probable need.

Hel. What more commands he?

Par. That having this obtain'd, you presently
Attend his further pleasure.

Hel. In every thing I wait upon his will.

Par. I shall report it so. *Exit Parolles.*

Hel. I pray you. Come, sirrah. *Exeunt.*

[Scene V]

Enter Lafew *and* Bertram.

Laf. But I hope your lordship thinks not him a soldier.

Ber. Yes, my lord, and of very valiant approof.

Laf. You have it from his own deliverance.

Ber. And by other warranted testimony.

Laf. Then my dial goes not true. I took this lark for a bunting.

Ber. I do assure you, my lord, he is very great in knowledge, and accordingly valiant.

Laf. I have then sinn'd against his experience, and transgress'd against his valor, and my state that way is dangerous, since I cannot yet find in my heart to repent. Here he comes. I pray you make us friends, I will pursue the amity.

Enter Parolles.

Par. [*To Bertram.*] These things shall be done, sir.

Laf. Pray you, sir, who's his tailor?

Par. Sir!

Laf. O, I know him well, I, sir, he, sir, 's a good workman, a very good tailor.

Ber. [*Aside to Parolles.*] Is she gone to the King?

Par. She is.

Ber. Will she away to-night?

Par. As you'll have her.

Ber. I have writ my letters, casketed my treasure,
Given order for our horses, and to-night,
When I should take possession of the bride,
[End] ere I do begin.

Laf. A good traveller is something at the latter end of a dinner, but [one] that lies three thirds, and uses a known truth to pass a thousand nothings with, should be once heard and thrice beaten. God save you, captain.

Ber. Is there any unkindness between my lord and you, monsieur?

Par. I know not how I have deserv'd to run into my lord's displeasure.

Laf. You have made shift to run into't, boots and spurs and all, like him that leapt into the custard; and out of it you'll run again, rather than suffer question for your residence.

Ber. It may be you have mistaken him, my lord.

Laf. And shall do so ever, though I took him at 's prayers. Fare you well, my lord, and believe this of me: there can be no kernel in this light nut; the soul of this man is his clothes. Trust him not in matter of heavy consequence; I have kept of them tame, and know their natures. Farewell, monsieur, I have spoken better of you than you have or will to deserve at my hand, but we must do good against evil. [*Exit.*]

Par. An idle lord, I swear.

Ber. I think so.

Par. Why, do you not know him?

Ber. Yes, I do know him well, and common speech
Gives him a worthy pass. Here comes my clog.

Enter Helena.

Hel. I have, sir, as I was commanded from you,
Spoke with the King, and have procur'd his leave
For present parting; only he desires
Some private speech with you.

Ber. I shall obey his will.
You must not marvel, Helen, at my course,
Which holds not color with the time, nor does
The ministration and required office
On my particular. Prepar'd I was not
For such a business; therefore am I found
So much unsettled. This drives me to entreat you
That presently you take your way for home,
And rather muse than ask why I entreat you,
For my respects are better than they seem,
And my appointments have in them a need
Greater than shows itself at the first view
To you that know them not. This to my mother.
[*Giving a letter.*]

50. apology: explanation.
51. make . . . need: make your alleged need for haste plausible.
52. presently: immediately.
53. Attend . . . pleasure: wait upon him to hear his further command.
54. wait upon: am ready to serve.

II.v: Location: Paris. The King's palace.
3. valiant approof: proved valor. **4. deliverance:** report.
6. dial: clock.
6–7. took . . . bunting. "To take a bunting for a lark" was proverbial for mistakenly ascribing worth to what is worthless. The bunting resembles the lark but lacks the lark's beautiful song. Lafew reverses the proverb but with tongue in cheek.
9. accordingly: correspondingly.
10–12. I . . . repent. Lafew adopts the language of religious confession.
16. who's his tailor. Suggesting that Parolles is no more than the product of his tailor's skill.
18. I . . . well. Lafew pretends to take Parolles' reply for the name of the tailor.
28. A good traveller: a man who has travelled widely, i.e. a man with many tales to tell.
36. made shift: contrived.
37. like . . . custard. "It was a Foolery practis'd at City-Entertainments, whilst the Jester or Zany was in Vogue, for him to leap into a large deep Custard" (Theobald).
38. you'll run: you wish to run.
38–39. suffer . . . residence: tolerate inquiry as to why you are in it.
40. mistaken him: misjudged him (or, perhaps, mistaken him for someone else). Lafew quibbles on "taken his actions amiss."
45. heavy: serious. **kept . . . tame:** had some of them in my household (*tame* = domesticated).
47. have . . . deserve: have deserved or intend to deserve (?). Singer's conjecture *have or* [i.e. either] *wit or will to deserve* is tempting.
48. do . . . evil: return good for evil.
50. I think so. Singer's emendation *I think not so* would make the following remarks easier to account for.
52–53. common . . . pass: general report esteems him a worthy man.
53. clog: trammel; literally, a heavy block of wood attached to an animal to restrict its liberty of movement. Cf. *ball-and-chain* as slang for a wife. **56. present parting:** immediate departure.
59. holds . . . with: does not match, is not in keeping with. **time:** occasion.
59–61. nor . . . particular: i.e. nor does it permit the performance of the duty incumbent upon me as a private person (i.e. as a husband).
65. muse: wonder. **66. respects:** considerations, i.e. reasons.
67. appointments: purposes, affairs.

'Twill be two days ere I shall see you, so
I leave you to your wisdom.
Hel. Sir, I can nothing say,
But that I am your most obedient servant.
Ber. Come, come, no more of that.
Hel. And ever shall
With true observance seek to eke out that
Wherein toward me my homely stars have fail'd
To equal my great fortune.
Ber. Let that go.
My haste is very great. Farewell; hie home.
Hel. Pray, sir, your pardon.
Ber. Well, what would you say?
Hel. I am not worthy of the wealth I owe,
Nor dare I say 'tis mine; and yet it is;
But like a timorous thief, most fain would steal
What law does vouch mine own.
Ber. What would you have?
Hel. Something, and scarce so much; nothing indeed.
I would not tell you what I would, my lord.
Faith, yes:
Strangers and foes do sunder, and not kiss.
Ber. I pray you stay not, but in haste to horse.
Hel. I shall not break your bidding, good my lord.
[*Ber.*] Where are my other men, monsieur?—Farewell. *Exit* [*Helena*].
Go thou toward home, where I will never come
Whilst I can shake my sword or hear the drum.
Away, and for our flight.
Par. Bravely, *coraggio!* [*Exeunt.*]

ACT III, [SCENE I]

Flourish. Enter the DUKE OF FLORENCE, *the two French* [LORDS], *with a troop of soldiers.*

Duke. So that from point to point now have you heard
The fundamental reasons of this war,
Whose great decision hath much blood let forth
And more thirsts after.
1. Lord. Holy seems the quarrel
Upon your Grace's part; black and fearful
On the opposer.
Duke. Therefore we marvel much our cousin France
Would in so just a business shut his bosom
Against our borrowing prayers.
[*2. Lord.*] Good my lord,
The reasons of our state I cannot yield
But like a common and an outward man

74. **observance**: devoted service. **eke out**: piece out; add to.
75. **homely stars**: i.e. humble birth. 77. **hie**: hasten.
79. **owe**: possess. 81. **fain**: gladly. 87. **stay**: delay.
92. **Bravely**: splendidly done, bravo. *Coraggio* (Italian "courage") apparently has much the same sense here.

III.i. Location: Florence. The Duke's palace.
3. **decision**: war to decide the issue. 4. **Holy**: righteous.
6. **opposer**: opposer's. 8. **bosom**: heart.
9. **borrowing prayers**: entreaties for aid.
10. **yield**: produce, furnish.
11. **But . . . man**: except like a member of the general public on the outside.

That the great figure of a council frames
By self-unable motion, therefore dare not
Say what I think of it, since I have found
Myself in my incertain grounds to fail
As often as I guess'd.
Duke. Be it his pleasure.
[*1. Lord.*] But I am sure the younger of our nature,
That surfeit on their ease, will day by day
Come here for physic.
Duke. Welcome shall they be;
And all the honors that can fly from us
Shall on them settle.—You know your places well;
When better fall, for your avails they fell.
To-morrow to th' field. *Flourish.* [*Exeunt.*]

[SCENE II]

Enter COUNTESS *and* CLOWN.

Count. It hath happen'd all as I would have had it, save that he comes not along with her.

Clo. By my troth, I take my young lord to be a very melancholy man.

Count. By what observance, I pray you?

Clo. Why, he will look upon his boot and sing, mend the ruff and sing, ask questions and sing, pick his teeth and sing. I know a man that had this trick of melancholy [sold] a goodly manor for a song.

Count. Let me see what he writes, and when he means to come. [*Opening a letter.*]

Clo. I have no mind to Isbel since I was at court. Our old [ling] and our Isbels a' th' country are nothing like your old ling and your Isbels a' th' court. The brains of my Cupid's knock'd out, and I begin to love, as an old man loves money, with no stomach.

Count. What have we here?

Clo. [E'en] that you have there. *Exit.*

[*Count. Reads*] *a letter.* "I have sent you a daughter-in-law; she hath recover'd the King, and undone me. I have wedded her, not bedded her, and sworn to make the 'not' eternal. You shall hear I am run away; know it before the report come. If there be breadth enough in the world, I will hold a long distance. My duty to you.

Your unfortunate son,
Bertram."

12. **figure**: shape, scheme. **frames**: constructs.
13. **self-unable motion**: his own inadequate conjectures (*motion* = motion of the mind, thought).
16. **guess'd**: made a guess (not "guessed right"). **Be . . . pleasure**: i.e. let us simply say that it is his will. 17. **nature**: temperament.
18. **surfeit on.** Equivalent to "are fed up with, are sick of," but with the metaphorical sense less faded. It was a commonplace that both in the body politic and in individuals the self-indulgent life of peace-time led to disorders that were cured by the bloodletting of war.
20. **that . . . us**: i.e. that are in my power to bestow.
22. **better fall**: better places fall vacant. **fell**: will have fallen.

III.ii. Location: Rossillion. The Count's palace.
1. **all**: entirely. 3. **troth**: faith. 5. **observance**: observation.
7. **mend**: adjust. **ruff**: ruffle, turned-over portion at the top of a boot.
7–8. **pick his teeth.** A fashionable affectation; see the note on I.i.158.
13. **old ling**: salt cods (a bawdy pun: *salt* = lascivious; *cod* = male sex organ). 14–15. **The brains . . . out**: my love is done for.
16. **stomach**: appetite. 20. **recover'd**: cured.
22. **not.** Probably punning on *knot*.

This is not well, rash and unbridled boy,
To fly the favors of so good a king,
To pluck his indignation on thy head
By the misprising of a maid too virtuous
For the contempt of empire.

Enter CLOWN.

Clo. O madam, yonder is heavy news within between two soldiers and my young lady!

Count. What is the matter?

Clo. Nay, there is some comfort in the news, some comfort. Your son will not be kill'd so soon as I thought he would.

Count. Why should he be kill'd?

Clo. So say I, madam, if he run away, as I hear he does. The danger is in standing to't; that's the loss of men, though it be the getting of children. Here they come will tell you more; for my part, I only hear your son was run away. [*Exit.*]

Enter HELEN *and two Gentlemen*, [*the French* LORDS].

[*2. Lord.*] 'Save you, good madam.
Hel. Madam, my lord is gone, for ever gone.
[*1. Lord.*] Do not say so.
Count. Think upon patience. Pray you, gentlemen,
I have felt so many quirks of joy and grief
That the first face of neither on the start
Can woman me unto't. Where is my son, I pray you?
[*1. Lord.*] Madam, he's gone to serve the Duke of
Florence.
We met him thitherward, for thence we came;
And after some dispatch in hand at court,
Thither we bend again.
Hel. Look on his letter, madam, here's my pass-
port.

[*Reads.*] "When thou canst get the ring upon my finger, which never shall come off, and show me a child begotten of thy body that I am father to, then call me husband; but in such a 'then' I write a 'never.'"

This is a dreadful sentence.
Count. Brought you this letter, gentlemen?
1. [*Lord*]. Ay, madam,
And for the contents' sake are sorry for our pains.
Count. I prithee, lady, have a better cheer;
If thou engrossest all the griefs are thine,
Thou robb'st me of a moi'ty. He was my son,
But I do wash his name out of my blood,
And thou art all my child. Towards Florence is he?
[*1. Lord.*] Ay, madam.
Count. And to be a soldier?
[*1. Lord.*] Such is his noble purpose, and believe't,
The Duke will lay upon him all the honor
That good convenience claims.
Count. Return you thither?
[*2. Lord.*] Ay, madam, with the swiftest wing of
speed.
Hel. [*Reads.*] "Till I have no wife, I have nothing
in France."
'Tis bitter.
Count. Find you that there?
Hel. Ay, madam.
[*2. Lord.*] 'Tis but the boldness of his hand haply,
Which his heart was not consenting to.
Count. Nothing in France, until he have no wife!
There's nothing here that is too good for him
But only she, and she deserves a lord
That twenty such rude boys might tend upon,
And call her hourly mistress. Who was with him?
[*2. Lord.*] A servant only, and a gentleman
Which I have sometime known.
Count. Parolles, was it not?
[*2. Lord.*] Ay, my good lady, he.
Count. A very tainted fellow, and full of wicked-
ness.
My son corrupts a well-derived nature
With his inducement.
[*2. Lord.*] Indeed, good lady,
The fellow has a deal of that too much,
Which holds him much to have.
Count. Y' are welcome, gentlemen.
I will entreat you, when you see my son,
To tell him that his sword can never win
The honor that he loses. More I'll entreat you
Written to bear along.
[*1. Lord.*] We serve you, madam,
In that and all your worthiest affairs.
Count. Not so, but as we change our courtesies.
Will you draw near? *Exit* [*with Lords*].
Hel. "Till I have no wife, I have nothing in France."
Nothing in France, until he has no wife!
Thou shalt have none, Rossillion, none in France;
Then hast thou all again. Poor lord, is't I
That chase thee from thy country, and expose
Those tender limbs of thine to the event
Of the none-sparing war? And is it I
That drive thee from the sportive court, where thou
Wast shot at with fair eyes, to be the mark
Of smoky muskets? O you leaden messengers,
That ride upon the violent speed of fire,
Fly with false aim, move the still-peering air

30. **pluck**: draw down. 31. **misprising**: scorning.
32. **empire**: i.e. an emperor. 33. **heavy**: sad.
41. **standing to't**: i.e. not running away (with a bawdy equivoque which indicates that *be kill'd* in line 37 plays on the sexual sense of *die*).
42. **getting**: begetting. 48. **Think upon patience**: control yourself.
49. **quirks**: sudden strokes.
50. **face**: appearance. **on the start**: with startling suddenness.
51. **woman me unto't**: make me respond like a (weak) woman, i.e. with tears. 53. **thitherward**: on his way thither.
56. **passport**: voucher, written confirmation.
61. **sentence**: judicial sentence.
64. **have . . . cheer**: do not look so sad.
65. **If thou engrossest**: if you monopolize. **are**: that are.
66. **moi'ty**: share, half. 68. **all my**: my only.

72. **convenience**: propriety, what is fitting. 77. **haply**: perhaps.
90–91. **has . . . have**: has altogether too much power of persuasion, which proves very advantageous to him.
97. **but . . . courtesies**: i.e. except as I repay your courtesies with mine (*change* = exchange). 98. **draw near**: come with me.
101. **Rossillion.** Helena appropriately designates her husband by the title that sums up what he has in France.
104. **event**: all that occurs, i.e. accidents, hazards.
108. **leaden messengers**: i.e. bullets.
110. **still-peering.** A controversial reading. If correct, it could mean "always looking on" or "looking on unmoved"; or *peering* may represent a shortened form of *appearing* and the compound may mean "motionless in appearance" or "always presenting itself (as a mark)." But most apposite would be a reference to the air's invulnerability, and editors usually adopt the emendation *still-piecing* = constantly closing itself up again (an anonymous conjecture first recorded by Steevens). Many other emendations have been proposed.

That sings with piercing, do not touch my lord.
Whoever shoots at him, I set him there;
Whoever charges on his forward breast,
I am the caitiff that do hold him to't;
And though I kill him not, I am the cause
His death was so effected. Better 'twere
I met the ravin lion when he roar'd
With sharp constraint of hunger; better 'twere
That all the miseries which nature owes
Were mine at once. No, come thou home, Rossillion,
Whence honor but of danger wins a scar,
As oft it loses all. I will be gone.
My being here it is that holds thee hence.
Shall I stay here to do't? No, no, although
The air of paradise did fan the house,
And angels offic'd all. I will be gone,
That pitiful rumor may report my flight
To consolate thine ear. Come night, end day!
For with the dark, poor thief, I'll steal away. *Exit.*

[Scene III]

Flourish. Enter the Duke of Florence, *[*Bertram, *Count of] Rossillion, Drum and Trumpets, Soldiers,* Parolles.

Duke. The general of our horse thou art, and we,
Great in our hope, lay our best love and credence
Upon thy promising fortune.
Ber. Sir, it is
A charge too heavy for my strength, but yet
We'll strive to bear it for your worthy sake
To th' extreme edge of hazard.
Duke. Then go thou forth,
And Fortune play upon thy prosperous helm
As thy auspicious mistress!
Ber. This very day,
Great Mars, I put myself into thy file;
Make me but like my thoughts, and I shall prove
A lover of thy drum, hater of love. *Exeunt omnes.*

[Scene IV]

Enter Countess *and* Steward.

Count. Alas! and would you take the letter of her?

111. sings. Referring to the whistling sound made by the passage of the bullet, but with implication that the air, far from being injured, sings for joy. **with piercing:** when it is pierced.
113. forward: (1) in the front ranks; (2) advancing; (3) facing the enemy. **114. caitiff:** base wretch. **hold:** force.
117. ravin: ravening.
119. nature owes: flesh is heir to (*owes* = owns).
121–22. Whence . . . all: i.e. from the war, where one can win at best no more than a scar, and often loses everything.
126. offic'd all: performed all the household duties.
127. pitiful: compassionate.
129. thief, steal. Cf. II.i.33–35.

III.iii. Location: Florence. Before the Duke's palace.
o.s.d. Drum and Trumpets: drummer and trumpeters.
2. Great . . . hope: expecting a highly favorable issue (an image of pregnancy). **lay:** wager (but Bertram quibbles on the sense "place, load"). **6. edge of hazard:** limit of danger.
7. helm: helmet. **9. file:** line of soldiers, i.e. ranks.

III.iv. Location: Rossillion. The Count's palace.

Might you not know she would do as she has done
By sending me a letter? Read it again.
[*Stew. Reads*] *letter.*
"I am Saint Jaques' pilgrim, thither gone.
Ambitious love hath so in me offended
That barefoot plod I the cold ground upon
With sainted vow my faults to have amended.
Write, write, that from the bloody course of war
My dearest master, your dear son, may hie.
Bless him at home in peace, whilst I from far
His name with zealous fervor sanctify.
His taken labors bid him me forgive;
I, his despiteful Juno, sent him forth
From courtly friends, with camping foes to live,
Where death and danger dogs the heels of worth.
He is too good and fair for death and me,
Whom I myself embrace to set him free."
[*Count.*] Ah, what sharp stings are in her mildest words!
Rinaldo, you did never lack advice so much
As letting her pass so. Had I spoke with her,
I could have well diverted her intents,
Which thus she hath prevented.
Stew. Pardon me, madam,
If I had given you this at overnight,
She might have been o'erta'en; and yet she writes,
Pursuit would be but vain.
Count. What angel shall
Bless this unworthy husband? He cannot thrive,
Unless her prayers, whom heaven delights to hear
And loves to grant, reprieve him from the wrath
Of greatest justice. Write, write, Rinaldo,
To this unworthy husband of his wife.
Let every word weigh heavy of her worth,
That he does weigh too light. My greatest grief,
Though little he do feel it, set down sharply.
Dispatch the most convenient messenger.
When haply he shall hear that she is gone,
He will return, and hope I may that she,
Hearing so much, will speed her foot again,
Led hither by pure love. Which of them both

4–17. I . . . free. These lines make a sonnet in the Shakespearean form.
4. Saint Jaques' pilgrim: a pilgrim to the shrine of St. James, presumably (in view of the references in III.v.34, 95 to "Saint Jaques le Grand" and "great Saint Jaques") to the famous shrine at Compostela in northwestern Spain. It is never made clear why Helena's route should in III.v bring her to Florence. *Jaques*, as elsewhere in Shakespeare, is dissyllabic.
7. sainted vow. This may mean "vow to the saint (James)" or simply "sacred." **my . . . amended:** to cause my sins to be pardoned (modifying not *vow* but *barefoot . . . vow*).
8. course. Perhaps with a play on *curse*.
10. Bless him: make him happy. **in peace:** (1) removed from war; (2) unvexed by a "detested wife" (II.iii.292).
11. sanctify: invoke blessing upon. **12. taken:** undertaken.
13. despiteful: cruel. **Juno.** It was Juno's hostility that caused Hercules to undertake his labors (cf. line 12).
17. Whom: i.e. death. **embrace:** (1) undergo; (2) welcome; (3) receive as a lover (in place of Bertram).
19. lack . . . much: show such poor judgment.
22. prevented: forestalled. **23. at overnight:** yesterday evening.
27. whom. Apparently referring first to Helena (as the object of *hear*) and then to her prayers (as the object of *grant*).
29. greatest justice: i.e. the supreme Judge.
30. unworthy . . . wife: husband unworthy of his wife.
32. weigh too light: (1) consider inadequate; (2) judge too lightly. **greatest:** extreme. **33. sharply:** so as to make it keenly felt.
34. convenient: fit. **35. When haply:** perhaps when.

Is dearest to me, I have no skill in sense
To make distinction. Provide this messenger.
My heart is heavy, and mine age is weak;
Grief would have tears, and sorrow bids me speak.
Exeunt.

[SCENE V]

A tucket afar off. Enter old WIDOW *of Florence, her daughter* [DIANA], VIOLENTA, *and* MARIANA, *with other* CITIZENS.

Wid. Nay, come, for if they do approach the city, we shall lose all the sight.

Dia. They say the French count has done most honorable service.

Wid. It is reported that he has taken their great'st commander, and that with his own hand he slew the Duke's brother. [*Tucket.*] We have lost our labor, they are gone a contrary way. Hark! you may know by their trumpets.

Mar. Come, let's return again and suffice ourselves with the report of it. Well, Diana, take heed of this French earl. The honor of a maid is her name, and no legacy is so rich as honesty.

Wid. I have told my neighbor how you have been solicited by a gentleman his companion.

Mar. I know that knave, hang him! one Parolles, a filthy officer he is in those suggestions for the young earl. Beware of them, Diana; their promises, enticements, oaths, tokens, and all these engines of lust, are not the things they go under. Many a maid hath been seduc'd by them, and the misery is, example, that so terrible shows in the wrack of maidenhood, cannot for all that dissuade succession, but that they are lim'd with the twigs that threatens them. I hope I need not to advise you further, but I hope your own grace will keep you where you are, though there were no further danger known but the modesty which is so lost.

Dia. You shall not need to fear me.

Enter HELEN [*habited like a pilgrim*].

Wid. I hope so. Look here comes a pilgrim. I know she will lie at my house; thither they send one another. I'll question her. God save you, pilgrim, whither are bound?

Hel. To Saint Jaques le Grand.
Where do the palmers lodge, I do beseech you?
Wid. At the Saint Francis here beside the port.
Hel. Is this the way? *A march afar.*
Wid. Ay, marry, is't. Hark you, they come this way.
If you will tarry, holy pilgrim,
But till the troops come by,
I will conduct you where you shall be lodg'd,
The rather for I think I know your hostess
As ample as myself.
Hel. Is it yourself?
Wid. If you shall please so, pilgrim.
Hel. I thank you, and will stay upon your leisure.
Wid. You came I think from France?
Hel. I did so.
Wid. Here you shall see a countryman of yours
That has done worthy service.
Hel. His name, I pray you?
Dia. The Count Rossillion. Know you such a one?
Hel. But by the ear, that hears most nobly of him.
His face I know not.
Dia. Whatsome'er he is,
He's bravely taken here. He stole from France,
As 'tis reported, for the King had married him
Against his liking. Think you it is so?
Hel. Ay, surely, mere the truth, I know his lady.
Dia. There is a gentleman that serves the Count
Reports but coarsely of her.
Hel. What's his name?
Dia. Monsieur Parolles.
Hel. O, I believe with him.
In argument of praise, or to the worth
Of the great Count himself, she is too mean
To have her name repeated. All her deserving
Is a reserved honesty, and that
I have not heard examin'd.
Dia. Alas, poor lady,
'Tis a hard bondage to become the wife
Of a detesting lord.
Wid. I [warr'nt,] good creature, wheresoe'er she is,
Her heart weighs sadly. This young maid might do her
A shrewd turn, if she pleas'd.

39. I . . . sense: I am unable on the basis of what I feel.
41–42. My . . . speak. Contrast these lines with III.ii.49–51.
42. bids me speak: i.e. governs my words.
III.v. Location: Outside the walls of Florence.
o.s.d. tucket: series of trumpet notes. **Violenta.** No lines are assigned to a character so named, and Helena's speech at the end of the scene makes it clear that the Widow has only two companions. Perhaps Shakespeare abandoned an original intention to add a character or, alternatively, to call the Widow's daughter by this name. **5. their:** i.e. the Sienese'.
10. return again: go back, return home.
12. her name: her reputation (?) or the name of maid(en), i.e. virgin (?). **13. honesty:** chastity.
17. officer: agent. **suggestions:** solicitings. **for:** on behalf of.
19. oaths: vows. **tokens:** presents, bribes. **engines of lust:** devisings to serve lust.
20. go under: masquerade as. **22. wrack:** ruin.
23. dissuade succession: stop others from following the same course.
24. lim'd . . . twigs: i.e. caught in the trap. Birds were caught by means of birdlime, a sticky substance, smeared on the twigs of bushes.
26. grace: virtue.
26–28. though . . . lost: i.e. even if there were not the further danger of pregnancy. **29. fear:** fear for.
30. hope so. Modern idiom would require *hope not.*
31. lie: lodge. **32. question:** speak to.
33. are bound: are you bound (perhaps by analogy with the corresponding singular construction *art bound,* where *art* represents a telescoping of *art thou*).
35. palmers: pilgrims (strictly speaking, those returning from the Holy Land, who brought back palm leaves as tokens).
36. Saint Francis: i.e. an inn with a figure of the saint for its sign. **port:** city gate. **43. ample:** amply, well.
44. please so: i.e. be good enough to let me be your hostess.
45. stay . . . leisure: await your convenience.
51. Whatsome'er: whatever sort of man.
52. bravely taken: excellently regarded. **53. for:** because.
55. mere the truth: absolutely true.
57. coarsely: harshly, slightingly. **58. believe:** agree.
59. In . . . praise: with respect to her own praiseworthiness. **to:** in comparison with. **61. repeated:** spoken.
61–62. All . . . honesty: her sole merit is a carefully guarded chastity.
63. examin'd: questioned. **67. weighs sadly:** is heavy.
68. shrewd: hurtful. **turn.** Frequently used with sexual implication.

Hel. How do you mean?
May be the amorous Count solicits her
In the unlawful purpose.
Wid. He does indeed,
And brokes with all that can in such a suit
Corrupt the tender honor of a maid.
But she is arm'd for him, and keeps her guard
In honestest defense.

Drum and Colors. Enter [Bertram] *Count Rossillion,* Parolles, *and the whole army.*

Mar. The gods forbid else!
Wid. So, now they come.
That is Antonio, the Duke's eldest son,
That, Escalus.
Hel. Which is the Frenchman?
Dia. He,
That with the plume; 'tis a most gallant fellow.
I would he lov'd his wife. If he were honester
He were much goodlier. Is't not a handsome gentleman?
Hel. I like him well.
Dia. 'Tis pity he is not honest. Yond's that same knave
That leads him to these places. Were I his lady,
I would poison that vile rascal.
Hel. Which is he?
Dia. That jack-an-apes with scarfs. Why is he melancholy?
Hel. Perchance he's hurt i' th' battle.
Par. Lose our drum! Well.
Mar. He's shrewdly vex'd at something. Look, he has spied us.
Wid. Marry, hang you!
Mar. And your courtesy, for a ring-carrier!
Exeunt [*Bertram, Parolles, and army*].
Wid. The troop is past. Come, pilgrim, I will bring you
Where you shall host. Of enjoin'd penitents
There's four or five, to great Saint Jaques bound,
Already at my house.
Hel. I humbly thank you.
Please it this matron and this gentle maid
To eat with us to-night, the charge and thanking
Shall be for me, and to requite you further,
I will bestow some precepts of this virgin
Worthy the note.
Both. We'll take your offer kindly. *Exeunt.*

[Scene VI]

Enter [Bertram] *Count Rossillion and the* [*two*] *French* [Lords].

[*2. Lord.*] Nay, good my lord, put him to't; let him have his way.

[*1. Lord.*] If your lordship find him not a hilding, hold me no more in your respect.

[*2. Lord.*] On my life, my lord, a bubble.

Ber. Do you think I am so far deceiv'd in him?

[*2. Lord.*] Believe it, my lord, in mine own direct knowledge, without any malice, but to speak of him as my kinsman, he's a most notable coward, an infinite and endless liar, an hourly promise-breaker, the owner of no one good quality worthy your lordship's entertainment.

[*1. Lord.*] It were fit you knew him, lest reposing too far in his virtue, which he hath not, he might at some great and trusty business in a main danger fail you.

Ber. I would I knew in what particular action to try him.

[*1. Lord.*] None better than to let him fetch off his drum, which you hear him so confidently undertake to do.

[*2. Lord.*] I, with a troop of Florentines, will suddenly surprise him; such I will have, whom I am sure he knows not from the enemy. We will bind and hoodwink him so, that he shall suppose no other but that he is carried into the leaguer of the adversaries, when we bring him to our own tents. Be but your lordship present at his examination, if he do not, for the promise of his life, and in the highest compulsion of base fear, offer to betray you, and deliver all the intelligence in his power against you, and that with the divine forfeit of his soul upon oath, never trust my judgment in any thing.

[*1. Lord.*] O, for the love of laughter, let him fetch his drum; he says he has a stratagem for't. When your lordship sees the bottom of [his] success in't, and to what metal this counterfeit lump of [ore] will be melted, if you give him not John Drum's entertainment, your inclining cannot be remov'd. Here he comes.

Enter Parolles.

[*2. Lord.*] O, for the love of laughter, hinder not the honor of his design. Let him fetch off his drum in any hand.

71. brokes: does business (ordinarily used of a middleman, but here of the principal himself).
73. guard: ward, posture of defense (a technical term in weaponry).
74. honestest defense: utmost defense of virginity. **s.d. Colors:** flagbearer. **else:** that it should be otherwise.
79. honester: more honorable in his behavior.
82. Yond: that one, the one there (demonstrative pronoun).
85. jack-an-apes: monkey. **89. shrewdly:** sorely.
92. courtesy: bow or salute. **ring-carrier:** go-between who brings presents or promises of marriage.
94. host: lodge. **enjoin'd penitents:** i.e. persons vowed to a pilgrimage as penance for their sins. **97. Please it:** if it please.
98. charge: cost.
100. precepts: i.e. good advice. **of:** upon.
101. Worthy the note: worth listening to.
102. take: accept. **kindly:** gratefully.

III.vi. Location: Camp before Florence.
1. to't: to the test. **3. hilding:** base wretch.
5. a bubble: i.e. empty and worthless despite his external glitter.
9. as: as if he were. **notable:** egregious.
12. entertainment: maintenance, patronage.
15. trusty: requiring trustworthiness.
23. surprise him: take him captive. **25. hoodwink:** blindfold.
26. leaguer: camp.
30–31. deliver . . . power: report all the information at his command.
36. bottom: i.e. full extent.
37. counterfeit. A displaced modifier, rightly describing *ore.* **ore.** Perhaps "gold," by confusion with the heraldic term *or.*
38–39. John Drum's entertainment: being beaten away from the door, i.e. ignominious dismissal (found also with *Jack* or *Tom* in place of *John*). **39. inclining:** liking, partiality.
43. in any hand: by all means.

Ber. How now, monsieur? This drum sticks sorely in your disposition.

[*1. Lord.*] A pox on't, let it go, 'tis but a drum.

Par. But a drum! Is't but a drum? A drum so lost! There was excellent command—to charge in with our horse upon our own wings, and to rend our own soldiers!

[*1. Lord.*] That was not to be blam'd in the command of the service; it was a disaster of war that Caesar himself could not have prevented, if he had been there to command.

Ber. Well, we cannot greatly condemn our success. Some dishonor we had in the loss of that drum, but it is not to be recover'd.

Par. It might have been recover'd.

Ber. It might, but it is not now.

Par. It is to be recover'd. But that the merit of service is seldom attributed to the true and exact performer, I would have that drum or another, or *hic jacet.*

Ber. Why, if you have a stomach, to't, monsieur: if you think your mystery in stratagem can bring this instrument of honor again into his native quarter, be magnanimious in the enterprise and go on; I will grace the attempt for a worthy exploit. If you speed well in it, the Duke shall both speak of it, and extend to you what further becomes his greatness, even to the utmost syllable of your worthiness.

Par. By the hand of a soldier, I will undertake it.

Ber. But you must not now slumber in it.

Par. I'll about it this evening, and I will presently pen down my dilemmas, encourage myself in my certainty, put myself into my mortal preparation; and by midnight look to hear further from me.

Ber. May I be bold to acquaint his Grace you are gone about it?

Par. I know not what the success will be, my lord, but the attempt I vow.

Ber. I know th' art valiant, and to the possibility of thy soldiership will subscribe for thee. Farewell.

Par. I love not many words. *Exit.*

[*2. Lord.*] No more than a fish loves water. Is not this a strange fellow, my lord, that so confidently seems to undertake this business, which he knows is not to be done, damns himself to do, and dares better be damn'd than to do't?

[*1. Lord.*] You do not know him, my lord, as we do. Certain it is that he will steal himself into a man's favor, and for a week escape a great deal of discoveries, but when you find him out, you have him ever after.

Ber. Why, do you think he will make no deed at all of this that so seriously he does address himself unto?

[*2. Lord.*] None in the world, but return with an invention, and clap upon you two or three probable lies. But we have almost emboss'd him, you shall see his fall to-night; for indeed he is not for your lordship's respect.

[*1. Lord.*] We'll make you some sport with the fox ere we case him. He was first smok'd by the old Lord Lafew. When his disguise and he is parted, tell me what a sprat you shall find him, which you shall see this very night.

[*2. Lord.*] I must go look my twigs. He shall be caught.

Ber. Your brother he shall go along with me.

[*2. Lord.*] As't please your lordship. I'll leave you. [*Exit.*]

Ber. Now will I lead you to the house, and show you
The lass I spoke of.
[*1. Lord.*] But you say she's honest.
Ber. That's all the fault. I spoke with her but once,
And found her wondrous cold, but I sent to her,
By this same coxcomb that we have i' th' wind,
Tokens and letters which she did re-send,
And this is all I have done. She's a fair creature;
Will you go see her?
[*1. Lord.*] With all my heart, my lord. *Exeunt.*

[Scene VII]

Enter Helen *and* Widow.

Hel. If you misdoubt me that I am not she,
I know not how I shall assure you further
But I shall lose the grounds I work upon.
Wid. Though my estate be fall'n, I was well born,
Nothing acquainted with these businesses,
And would not put my reputation now
In any staining act.
Hel. Nor would I wish you.
First give me trust, the Count he is my husband,
And what to your sworn counsel I have spoken
Is so from word to word; and then you cannot,

44–45. sticks . . . disposition: is a sore point with you (cf. *a thorn in one's flesh*), keeps you in an irritated state of mind.
46. A pox on't: plague take it. **49. wings:** flanks.
51–52. That . . . service: i.e. the orders for the action were not to blame for that. **52. disaster:** mischance.
55–56. we . . . success: i.e. we came out pretty well (*success* = outcome). **60. But that:** were it not that.
62–63. hic jacet: here lies (opening words of an epitaph), i.e. I would die in the attempt. **65. mystery:** skill.
67. magnanimious: great-hearted, valiant (variant of *magnanimous*).
68. grace: do honor to. **speed:** succeed. **70. becomes:** befits.
74. presently: at once.
75. dilemmas: perplexities (as opposed to the *certainty* of line 76). It is uncertain whether Parolles is planning to work out his plan of attack or to prepare himself for possible death (so *mortal preparation* in line 76 may mean either readying his death-dealing weapons or taking the sacrament); the latter would give him the better opportunity for solemn posturing. **82. possibility:** full capacity, utmost.
83. subscribe: vouch. **88. damns:** condemns.

92. escape . . . discoveries: to a great extent escape being revealed for what he is. **94. make no deed:** perform no part.
98. probable: plausible.
99. emboss'd: closed round, cornered (used of a hunted animal).
101. respect: regard. **103. case:** skin. **smok'd:** smelled out.
105. sprat: contemptible creature (literally, a kind of small fish).
107. look my twigs: collect my twigs for liming (see the note on III.v. 24), i.e. prepare the trap.
114. have . . . wind: are to the windward of, i.e. are stalking from an advantageous position which prevents his scenting us.
115. re-send: send back.

III.vii. Location: Florence. The Widow's house.
3. But . . . upon: i.e. without cutting the ground from under my feet (by publicly revealing my identity).
4. my . . . fall'n: my fortunes have declined. **8. trust:** credence.
9. counsel: secrecy. **10. so . . . to word:** true in every word.

By the good aid that I of you shall borrow,
Err in bestowing it.
Wid. I should believe you,
For you have show'd me that which well approves
Y' are great in fortune.
Hel. Take this purse of gold,
And let me buy your friendly help thus far,
Which I will over-pay and pay again
When I have found it. The Count he woos your daughter,
Lays down his wanton siege before her beauty,
[Resolv'd] to carry her. Let her in fine consent,
As we'll direct her how 'tis best to bear it.
Now his important blood will nought deny
That she'll demand. A ring the County wears,
That downward hath succeeded in his house
From son to son, some four or five descents,
Since the first father wore it. This ring he holds
In most rich choice; yet in his idle fire,
To buy his will, it would not seem too dear,
Howe'er repented after.
Wid. Now I see
The bottom of your purpose.
Hel. You see it lawful then. It is no more
But that your daughter, ere she seems as won,
Desires this ring; appoints him an encounter;
In fine, delivers me to fill the time,
Herself most chastely absent. After,
To marry her, I'll add three thousand crowns
To what is pass'd already.
Wid. I have yielded.
Instruct my daughter how she shall persever,
That time and place with this deceit so lawful
May prove coherent. Every night he comes
With musics of all sorts, and songs compos'd
To her unworthiness. It nothing steads us
To chide him from our eaves, for he persists
As if his life lay on't.
Hel. Why then to-night
Let us assay our plot, which if it speed,
Is wicked meaning in a lawful deed,
And lawful meaning in a lawful act,
Where both not sin, and yet a sinful fact.
But let's about it. [*Exeunt.*]

11. By: with respect to. **13. approves:** proves.
15. thus far: to this point.
16. over-pay . . . again: pay again twice over, double.
17. found it: i.e. received from you the help I still require.
19. carry: conquer. **in fine:** in the end.
20. bear it: manage the business.
21. important blood: importunate passion.
26. choice: estimation. **his idle fire:** the mad folly of his passion.
27. his will: (the object of) his lust.
29. bottom: full extent.
35. To marry her: to provide her with a dowry.
37. persever: carry on the scheme (variant of *persevere*).
39. coherent: suitable, in accord.
40. musics: groups of musicians.
41. To her unworthiness: to her, who is not his social equal (?) or toward her undoing (?) or much to her disrepute (with the neighbors) (?). **nothing steads us:** avails us not at all.
44. assay: try.
45, 46. meaning: intention (wicked on Bertram's part, lawful on Helena's).
47. both not sin: i.e. their mutual act is lawful intercourse between husband and wife. **sinful fact:** sinful deed (with respect to Bertram's intention).

ACT IV, [Scene I]

Enter [Second] French [Lord] *with five or six other* Soldiers *in ambush.*

[2.] *Lord.* He can come no other way but by this hedge-corner. When you sally upon him, speak what terrible language you will. Though you understand it not yourselves, no matter; for we must not seem to understand him, unless some one among us, whom we must produce for an interpreter.

1. Sold. Good captain, let me be th' interpreter.

[2.] *Lord.* Art not acquainted with him? Knows he not thy voice?

1. Sold. No, sir, I warrant you.

[2.] *Lord.* But what linsey-woolsey hast thou to speak to us again?

1. Sold. E'en such as you speak to me.

[2.] *Lord.* He must think us some band of strangers i' th' adversary's entertainment. Now he hath a smack of all neighboring languages; therefore we must every one be a man of his own fancy, not to know what we speak one to another; so we seem to know, is to know straight our purpose: choughs' language, gabble enough, and good enough. As for you, interpreter, you must seem very politic. But couch ho, here he comes, to beguile two hours in a sleep, and then to return and swear the lies he forges. [*They stand aside.*]

Enter Parolles.

Par. Ten a' clock: within these three hours 'twill be time enough to go home. What shall I say I have done? It must be a very plausive invention that carries it. They begin to smoke me, and disgraces have of late knock'd too often at my door. I find my tongue is too foolhardy, but my heart hath the fear of Mars before it, and of his creatures, not daring the reports of my tongue.

[2.] *Lord.* [*Aside.*] This is the first truth that e'er thine own tongue was guilty of.

Par. What the devil should move me to undertake the recovery of this drum, being not ignorant of the impossibility, and knowing I had no such purpose? I must give myself some hurts, and say I got them in exploit. Yet slight ones will not carry it. They will say, "Came you off with so little?" And great ones I dare not give; wherefore what's the instance? Tongue, I must put you into a butter-woman's mouth

IV.i. Location: Outside the Florentine camp.
11. linsey-woolsey: cloth made of linen and wool, hence a mixture or medley (of words). **14. strangers:** foreigners.
15. entertainment: service.
16. smack: taste, smattering.
17. to know: knowing, understanding.
19. know: see effected, achieve. **straight:** at once. **choughs' language:** i.e. the chattering of jackdaws that have been taught to speak.
20. gabble . . . enough: enough gabble is all we need.
21. politic: cunning. **couch:** conceal yourselves.
22. beguile: while away. **a sleep:** a nap.
26. plausive: plausible. **27. disgraces:** insults, humiliations.
30. his creatures: i.e. soldiers.
30–31. not . . . tongue: i.e. afraid to perform what my tongue utters.
40. what's the instance. This may mean either "what evidence can suffice?" or "what motive can I have had?" (repeating the question with which the speech begins).
41. butter-woman: dairy-woman (presumably garrulous).

and buy myself another of Bajazeth's mule, if you prattle me into these perils.

[2.] *Lord.* [*Aside.*] Is it possible he should know what he is, and be that he is?

Par. I would the cutting of my garments would serve the turn, or the breaking of my Spanish sword.

[2.] *Lord.* [*Aside.*] We cannot afford you so.

Par. Or the baring of my beard, and to say it was in stratagem.

[2.] *Lord.* [*Aside.*] 'Twould not do.

Par. Or to drown my clothes, and say I was stripp'd.

[2.] *Lord.* [*Aside.*] Hardly serve.

Par. Though I swore I leapt from the window of the citadel—

[2.] *Lord.* [*Aside.*] How deep?

Par. Thirty fadom.

[2.] *Lord.* [*Aside.*] Three great oaths would scarce make that be believ'd.

Par. I would I had any drum of the enemy's. I would swear I recover'd it.

[2.] *Lord.* [*Aside.*] You shall hear one anon.

Par. A drum now of the enemy's—
Alarum within.

[2.] *Lord.* *Throca movousus, cargo, cargo, cargo.*

All. *Cargo, cargo, cargo, villianda par corbo, cargo.*

Par. O, ransom, ransom! [*They seize him.*] Do not hide mine eyes. [*They blindfold him.*]

[*1. Sold. as*] *Interpreter.* *Boskos thromuldo boskos.*

Par. I know you are the Muskos' regiment,
And I shall lose my life for want of language.
If there be here German, or Dane, Low Dutch,
Italian, or French, let him speak to me,
I'll discover that which shall undo the Florentine.

Interp. *Boskos vauvado.* I understand thee, and can speak thy tongue. *Kerelybonto,* sir, betake thee to thy faith, for seventeen poniards are at thy bosom.

Par. O!

Interp. O, pray, pray, pray! *Manka revania dulche.*

[2.] *Lord.* *Oscorbidulchos volivorco.*

Interp. The general is content to spare thee yet,
And hoodwink'd as thou art, will lead thee on
To gather from thee. Haply thou mayst inform
Something to save thy life.

Par. O, let me live,
And all the secrets of our camp I'll show,
Their force, their purposes; nay, I'll speak that
Which you will wonder at.

Interp. But wilt thou faithfully?

Par. If I do not, damn me.

Interp. *Acordo linta.*
Come on, thou [art] granted space.
Exit [*with Parolles guarded*].
A short alarum within.

[2.] *Lord.* Go tell the Count Rossillion, and my brother,
We have caught the woodcock, and will keep him muffled
Till we do hear from them.

[2.] *Sold.* Captain, I will.

[2.] *Lord.* 'A will betray us all unto ourselves:
Inform on that.

[2.] *Sold.* So I will, sir.

[2.] *Lord.* Till then I'll keep him dark and safely lock'd. *Exeunt.*

[Scene II]

Enter Bertram *and the maid called* Diana.

Ber. They told me that your name was Fontibell.

Dia. No, my good lord, Diana.

Ber. Titled goddess,
And worth it, with addition! But, fair soul,
In your fine frame hath love no quality?
If the quick fire of youth light not your mind,
You are no maiden, but a monument.
When you are dead, you should be such a one
As you are now; for you are cold and stern,
And now you should be as your mother was
When your sweet self was got.

Dia. She then was honest.

Ber. So should you be.

Dia. No;
My mother did but duty, such, my lord,
As you owe to your wife.

Ber. No more a' that.
I prithee do not strive against my vows.
I was compell'd to her, but I love thee
By love's own sweet constraint, and will for ever
Do thee all rights of service.

Dia. Ay, so you serve us
Till we serve you; but when you have our roses,
You barely leave our thorns to prick ourselves,
And mock us with our bareness.

Ber. How have I sworn!

Dia. 'Tis not the many oaths that makes the truth,
But the plain single vow that is vow'd true.
What is not holy, that we swear not by,
But take the High'st to witness. Then pray you tell me,

42. Bajazeth's mule. Bajazeth is a Turkish name, and the Turks used mules extensively, but no one has explained satisfactorily why Parolles should use this phrase, though what he signifies by it is clear enough. Some editors emend *mule* to *mute* (Warburton conjecture), citing *Henry V*, I.ii.231–32, "our grave, / Like Turkish mute, shall have a tongueless mouth." **45. that:** what.
48. afford you so: allow you that, let you off so easily.
49. baring: shaving off.
58. fadom: fathom (plural). A fathom is a measure of six feet.
64. s.d. Alarum: call to arms. **69. Muskos':** Muscovites' (?).
73. discover: reveal.
75–76. betake . . . faith: i.e. say your prayers.
81. hoodwink'd. A play on "taken in" is just possible (earliest use recorded in *O.E.D.*, 1610). **lead thee on:** take you to another place.
82. gather: obtain information.
86. faithfully: truthfully (with sharp irony provided by the second sense "loyally").

88. space: a reprieve.
90. woodcock. A proverbially foolish bird, easily caught. **muffled:** blindfolded. **93. Inform on:** report.

IV.ii. Location: Florence. The Widow's house.
2. Titled goddess: bearing a goddess' name. That the goddess was the patroness of virgins seems to escape Bertram's notice.
3. worth: worthy of. **addition:** (1) augmentation; (2) added titles of honor. **4. quality:** power, operation. **5. quick:** lively, vital.
6. monument: effigy (stone, not flesh and blood).
14. vows. In view of lines 12–13, this probably refers to his vows to live apart from Helena, not to his marriage vows.
18. serve. With sexual implication. **19. barely:** bare, exposed.
22. single: (1) one (in contrast to *many*); (2) sincere.

If I should swear by Jove's great attributes
I lov'd you dearly, would you believe my oaths
When I did love you ill? This has no holding,
To swear by Him whom I protest to love
That I will work against Him; therefore your oaths
Are words and poor conditions, but unseal'd—
At least in my opinion.
Ber. Change it, change it!
Be not so holy-cruel. Love is holy,
And my integrity ne'er knew the crafts
That you do charge men with. Stand no more off,
But give thyself unto my sick desires,
Who then recovers. Say thou art mine, and ever
My love, as it begins, shall so persever.
Dia. I see that men make rope's in such a scarre,
That we'll forsake ourselves. Give me that ring.
Ber. I'll lend it thee, my dear; but have no power
To give it from me.
Dia. Will you not, my lord?
Ber. It is an honor 'longing to our house,
Bequeathed down from many ancestors,
Which were the greatest obloquy i' th' world
In me to lose.
Dia. Mine honor's such a ring,
My chastity's the jewel of our house,
Bequeathed down from many ancestors,
Which were the greatest obloquy i' th' world
In me to lose. Thus your own proper wisdom
Brings in the champion Honor on my part,
Against your vain assault.
Ber. Here, take my ring!
My house, mine honor, yea, my life, be thine,
And I'll be bid by thee.
Dia. When midnight comes, knock at my chamber-window;
I'll order take my mother shall not hear.
Now will I charge you in the band of truth,
When you have conquer'd my yet maiden bed,
Remain there but an hour, nor speak to me.
My reasons are most strong, and you shall know them
When back again this ring shall be deliver'd;
And on your finger in the night I'll put
Another ring, that what in time proceeds
May token to the future our past deeds.
Adieu till then, then fail not. You have won
A wife of me, though there my hope be done.
Ber. A heaven on earth I have won by wooing thee. [*Exit.*]
Dia. For which live long to thank both heaven and me!
You may so in the end.
My mother told me just how he would woo,
As if she sate in's heart. She says all men
Have the like oaths. He had sworn to marry me
When his wife's dead; therefore I'll lie with him
When I am buried. Since Frenchmen are so braid,
Marry that will, I live and die a maid.
Only in this disguise I think't no sin
To cozen him that would unjustly win. *Exit.*

[Scene III]

Enter the two French [Lords] *and some two or three* Soldiers.

[*1. Lord.*] You have not given him his mother's letter?

[*2. Lord.*] I have deliv'red it an hour since. There is something in't that stings his nature; for on the reading it he chang'd almost into another man.

[*1. Lord.*] He has much worthy blame laid upon him for shaking off so good a wife and so sweet a lady.

[*2. Lord.*] Especially he hath incurr'd the everlasting displeasure of the King, who had even tun'd his bounty to sing happiness to him. I will tell you a thing, but you shall let it dwell darkly with you.

[*1. Lord.*] When you have spoken it, 'tis dead, and I am the grave of it.

[*2. Lord.*] He hath perverted a young gentlewoman here in Florence, of a most chaste renown, and this night he fleshes his will in the spoil of her honor. He hath given her his monumental ring, and thinks himself made in the unchaste composition.

[*1. Lord.*] Now God delay our rebellion! As we are ourselves, what things are we!

25. Jove's. Perhaps (as elsewhere) a replacement for *God's* in conformity with a statute of 1606 which forbade profane use of God's name.
27. ill: wickedly, in a way unsanctioned by religion. **holding:** binding power (?) or consistency (?).
30. words: mere words. **poor . . . unseal'd:** invalid contracts, without the seal that would give them binding force.
32. so holy-cruel: cruel by reason of your religious scruples.
36. Who then recovers: which then recover. For the form of the verb see the note on I.i.104.
38. I . . . scarre. A notable crux, here reprinted unchanged. See the Textual Notes.
42. honor . . . house: i.e. a symbol of family honor (*'longing* = belonging). **45. honor:** chastity.
49–50. your . . . part: i.e. Honor, called in by Bertram to defend his refusal, instead becomes Diana's champion in defense of her refusal. *Proper* = pertaining to oneself; *part* = side.
53. be . . . thee: do whatever you ask.
55. order: measures. **56. band:** bond, obligation.
62. that . . . proceeds: which no matter what may happen in the future (*what* = whatever).

65. of: in. **my . . . done:** my hope of marriage is destroyed (with second meaning, Dover Wilson suggests, of "my hope of aiding Helena is accomplished"). **70. sate:** sat.
71. had: would have (?). Some editors read *has* (following Grant White), perhaps rightly, since in V.iii. Diana alleges that Bertram made such a promise (lines 139–41) and Parolles confirms the charge (lines 262–64). **73. braid:** braided, plaited, i.e. deceitful.
74. Marry: let those marry. **75. disguise:** pretense.
76. cozen: cheat. **unjustly:** dishonorably.

IV.iii. Location: The Florentine camp.
4. stings his nature. Rinaldo has known how to carry out the Countess' instructions in III.iv.31–33. **6. worthy:** well-deserved.
11. darkly: in secrecy. **14. perverted:** corrupted.
15. renown: reputation.
16. fleshes his will: feeds his lust (a figure from hunting; to flesh a dog (or a hawk) was to give him a piece of meat from the prey he had hunted down). **spoil:** (1) quarry, "kill"; (2) laying waste, destruction.
17. monumental: i.e. serving as a token or reminder of who and what he is.
18. made: a made man. **composition:** compact, bargain.
19. God . . . rebellion. Schmidt's gloss is "God make us slow to sin," but *rebellion* here (as often elsewhere) probably refers specifically to urgent sexual appetite (as a rebel against the government of reason), and *delay* may mean "allay, assuage." Dover Wilson, conjecturing that the manuscript read *Godde lay,* emended *delay* to *lay* (= exorcise, as in *lay a spirit*), a reading that involves a bawdy equivoque.

[*2. Lord.*] Merely our own traitors. And as in the common course of all treasons, we still see them reveal themselves, till they attain to their abhorr'd ends; so he that in this action contrives against his own nobility in his proper stream o'erflows himself.

[*1. Lord.*] Is it not meant damnable in us, to be trumpeters of our unlawful intents? We shall not then have his company to-night?

[*2. Lord.*] Not till after midnight; for he is dieted to his hour.

[*1. Lord.*] That approaches apace. I would gladly have him see his company anatomiz'd, that he might take a measure of his own judgments, wherein so curiously he had set this counterfeit.

[*2. Lord.*] We will not meddle with him till he come; for his presence must be the whip of the other.

[*1. Lord.*] In the mean time, what hear you of these wars?

[*2. Lord.*] I hear there is an overture of peace.

[*1. Lord.*] Nay, I assure you a peace concluded.

[*2. Lord.*] What will Count Rossillion do then? Will he travel higher, or return again into France?

[*1. Lord.*] I perceive by this demand, you are not altogether of his counsel.

[*2. Lord.*] Let it be forbid, sir, so should I be a great deal of his act.

[*1. Lord.*] Sir, his wife some two months since fled from his house. Her pretense is a pilgrimage to Saint Jaques le Grand; which holy undertaking with most austere sanctimony she accomplish'd; and there residing, the tenderness of her nature became as a prey to her grief; in fine, made a groan of her last breath, and now she sings in heaven.

[*2. Lord.*] How is this justified?

[*1. Lord.*] The stronger part of it by her own letters, which makes her story true, even to the point of her death. Her death itself, which could not be her office to say is come, was faithfully confirm'd by the rector of the place.

[*2. Lord.*] Hath the Count all this intelligence?

[*1. Lord.*] Ay, and the particular confirmations, point from point, to the full arming of the verity.

[*2. Lord.*] I am heartily sorry that he'll be glad of this.

21–25. Merely . . . himself: i.e. we are out-and-out betrayers of our own natures to evil. And we are traitors to ourselves in a second way: we reveal our self-treachery to others. Just as we see it happen that political traitors give themselves away, thus achieving their shameful deaths, so Bertram, who is plotting treason against his own nobleness of nature, by his own talk (*in his proper stream*) reveals his treason (and will reap dishonor). (Not all commentators accept this interpretation.) **26. meant damnable:** damnably minded (?).
29–30. dieted . . . hour: restricted to his appointed time (and so unable to meet us earlier). This is better in context than "limited to a single hour."
32. company: companion. **anatomiz'd:** dissected, laid open.
34. curiously: carefully, artfully. **counterfeit:** fake gem.
35–36. him . . . he . . . his: i.e. Parolles . . . Bertram . . . Bertram's.
40. Nay: nay, more.
42. higher: farther (?). See the note on ***higher Italy***, II.i.12.
43. demand: question.
44. of his counsel: in his confidence.
45–46. a great . . . act: in great part his accessory in the deed (with a quibble in *act* on *counsel / council*).
48. pretense: intention. **50. sanctimony:** piety.
52. in fine: in the end (?) or to sum up (?).
54. justified: verified. **58. office:** function.
59. rector: priest, or (less probably) governor.
62. arming: strengthening against attack, i.e. irrefutable proof.

[*1. Lord.*] How mightily sometimes we make us comforts of our losses!

[*2. Lord.*] And how mightily some other times we drown our gain in tears! The great dignity that his valor hath here acquir'd for him shall at home be encount'red with a shame as ample.

[*1. Lord.*] The web of our life is of a mingled yarn, good and ill together: our virtues would be proud, if our faults whipt them not, and our crimes would despair, if they were not cherish'd by our virtues.

Enter a MESSENGER.

How now? where's your master?

[*Mess.*] He met the Duke in the street, sir, of whom he hath taken a solemn leave. His lordship will next morning for France. The Duke hath offer'd him letters of commendations to the King.

[*2. Lord.*] They shall be no more than needful there, if they were more than they can commend.

Enter [BERTRAM] *Count Rossillion.*

[*1. Lord.*] They cannot be too sweet for the King's tartness. Here's his lordship now. How now, my lord, is't not after midnight?

Ber. I have to-night dispatch'd sixteen businesses, a month's length a-piece, by an abstract of success: I have congied with the Duke, done my adieu with his nearest; buried a wife, mourn'd for her, writ to my lady mother I am returning, entertain'd my convoy, and between these main parcels of dispatch [effected] many nicer needs. The last was the greatest, but that I have not ended yet.

[*2. Lord.*] If the business be of any difficulty, and this morning your departure hence, it requires haste of your lordship.

Ber. I mean the business is not ended, as fearing to hear of it hereafter. But shall we have this dialogue between the fool and the soldier? Come, bring forth this counterfeit module, h'as deceiv'd me like a double-meaning prophesier.

[*2. Lord.*] Bring him forth, h'as sate i' th' stocks all night, poor gallant knave. [*Exeunt Soldiers.*]

Ber. No matter, his heels have deserv'd it, in usurping his spurs so long. How does he carry himself?

[*2. Lord.*] I have told your lordship already: the stocks carry him. But to answer you as you would be

68. dignity: honor. **70. encount'red:** met, opposed.
71. web: fabric. **73. whipt:** chastened. **crimes:** sins.
74. cherish'd: looked after tenderly.
77. solemn: ceremonious, formal. **will:** i.e. will set out.
78. offer'd: tendered.
81. if . . . commend: even if they commended him more highly than they possibly can. **82. for:** i.e. to offset.
86. by . . . success: by a successful summary proceeding (Schmidt). Some editors connect the phrase with the next sentence and explain: "to give a summary of my successes" or "to give a summary of the successive items." **87. congied with:** taken leave of.
89–90. entertain'd my convoy: engaged my travel aides (?) or hired means of conveyance (?).
90. between . . . dispatch: i.e. in the intervals of winding up these major pieces of business. **91. nicer:** more delicate.
99. module: model (of soldiership). **h'as:** he has.
99–100. double-meaning prophesier: i.e. ambiguous oracle.
102. gallant: showy, flamboyant (?).
103–4. usurping his spurs: wrongfully wearing spurs (symbolic of knightly valor).
104. carry: conduct (with following quibble).

understood, he weeps like a wench that had shed her milk. He hath confess'd himself to Morgan, whom he supposes to be a friar, from the time of his remembrance to this very instant disaster of his setting i' th' stocks; and what think you he hath confess'd?

Ber. Nothing of me, has 'a?

[*2. Lord.*] His confession is taken, and it shall be read to his face. If your lordship be in't, as I believe you are, you must have the patience to hear it.

Enter [SOLDIERS *and*] PAROLLES, *with* [*First Soldier as*] *his* INTERPRETER.

Ber. A plague upon him! Muffled! He can say nothing of me.

[*1. Lord.*] Hush, hush! Hoodman comes! *Porto-tartarossa.*

Interp. He calls for the tortures. What will you say without 'em?

Par. I will confess what I know without constraint. If ye pinch me like a pasty, I can say no more.

Interp. *Bosko chimurcho.*

[*1. Lord.*] *Boblibindo chicurmurco.*

Interp. You are a merciful general. Our general bids you answer to what I shall ask you out of a note.

Par. And truly, as I hope to live.

Interp. [*Reads.*] "First demand of him, how many horse the Duke is strong." What say you to that?

Par. Five or six thousand, but very weak and unserviceable. The troops are all scatter'd, and the commanders very poor rogues, upon my reputation and credit and as I hope to live.

Interp. Shall I set down your answer so?

Par. Do, I'll take the sacrament on't, how and which way you will.

Ber. All's one to him. What a past-saving slave is this!

[*1. Lord.*] Y' are deceiv'd, my lord, this is Monsieur Parolles, the gallant militarist—that was his own phrase—that had the whole theoric of war in the knot of his scarf, and the practice in the chape of his dagger.

[*2. Lord.*] I will never trust a man again for keeping his sword clean, nor believe he can have every thing in him by wearing his apparel neatly.

Interp. Well, that's set down.

Par. "Five or six thousand horse," I said—I will say true—"or thereabouts," set down, for I'll speak truth.

[*1. Lord.*] He's very near the truth in this.

Ber. But I con him no thanks for't, in the nature he delivers it.

Par. "Poor rogues," I pray you say.

Interp. Well, that's set down.

Par. I humbly thank you, sir. A truth's a truth, the rogues are marvellous poor.

Interp. [*Reads.*] "Demand of him, of what strength they are afoot." What say you to that?

Par. By my troth, sir, if I were to live this present hour, I will tell true. Let me see: Spurio, a hundred and fifty; Sebastian, so many; Corambus, so many; Jaques, so many; Guiltian, Cosmo, Lodowick, and Gratii, two hundred fifty each; mine own company, Chitopher, Vaumond, Bentii, two hundred fifty each; so that the muster-file, rotten and sound, upon my life, amounts not to fifteen thousand pole, half of the which dare not shake the snow from off their cassocks, lest they shake themselves to pieces.

Ber. What shall be done to him?

[*1. Lord.*] Nothing, but let him have thanks. Demand of him my condition, and what credit I have with the Duke.

Interp. Well, that's set down. [*Reads.*] "You shall demand of him, whether one Captain Dumaine be i' th' camp, a Frenchman; what his reputation is with the Duke; what his valor, honesty, and expertness in wars; or whether he thinks it were not possible with well-weighing sums of gold to corrupt him to a revolt." What say you to this? What do you know of it?

Par. I beseech you let me answer to the particular of the inter'gatories. Demand them singly.

Interp. Do you know this Captain Dumaine?

Par. I know him. 'A was a botcher's prentice in Paris, from whence he was whipt for getting the shrieve's fool with child, a dumb innocent, that could not say him nay.

Ber. Nay, by your leave, hold your hands—though I know his brains are forfeit to the next tile that falls.

Interp. Well, is this captain in the Duke of Florence's camp?

Par. Upon my knowledge, he is, and lousy.

[*1. Lord.*] Nay, look not so upon me; we shall hear of your [lordship] anon.

Interp. What is his reputation with the Duke?

Par. The Duke knows him for no other but a poor officer of mine, and writ to me this other day to turn him out a' th' band. I think I have his letter in my pocket.

Interp. Marry, we'll search.

107–8. **shed her milk:** i.e. accidentally spilled the milk she was taking to market.
109–10. **the time . . . remembrance:** as far back as he can remember.
110. **instant disaster:** present stroke of misfortune.
118. **Hoodman:** the blindfold player in blind man's buff (which is therefore also called hoodman blind).
123. **pinch . . . pasty.** Referring to pinching together the top and bottom crusts of a pasty (meat pie).
127. **note:** list, memorandum. 130. **horse:** horsemen.
136–37. **how . . . will:** i.e. according to any rite you prefer. This comes close to saying "I'll swear by whatever you hold sacred."
138. **All's . . . him:** it's all the same to him. 142. **theoric:** theory.
143. **chape:** metal tip of the scabbard. 145. **clean:** polished.
146. **neatly:** elegantly.
152. **con . . . thanks:** feel no gratitude to him. *Con* (used only in this idiom) means literally "know." **nature:** fashion, manner.

160–61. **live . . . hour.** The sense is "live *only* this present hour"; editors disagree as to whether emendation is necessary and, if it is, what form it should take.
162. **so many:** as many, the same number.
166. **muster-file:** total roll. **rotten and sound:** diseased and able-bodied.
167. **pole:** poll, heads. 169. **cassocks:** military cloaks.
172. **condition:** character.
179. **well-weighing:** (1) heavy; (2) persuasive.
180. **corrupt . . . revolt:** suborn him to commit treason.
182. **particular:** individual items.
185. **botcher's:** cobbler's or clothes-mender's.
187. **shrieve's fool:** mental defective in the official care of the sheriff. **innocent:** idiot.
190–91. **his . . . falls:** i.e. such a liar is subject to sudden death at any moment.
194. **lousy:** i.e. a contemptible fellow.

Par. In good sadness, I do not know. Either it is there, or it is upon a file with the Duke's other letters in my tent.

Interp. Here 'tis, here's a paper. Shall I read it to you?

Par. I do not know if it be it or no.

Ber. Our interpreter does it well.

[*1. Lord.*] Excellently.

Interp. [*Reads.*] "Dian, the Count's a fool, and full of gold"—

Par. That is not the Duke's letter, sir; that is an advertisement to a proper maid in Florence, one Diana, to take heed of the allurement of one Count Rossillion, a foolish idle boy, but for all that very ruttish. I pray you, sir, put it up again.

Interp. Nay, I'll read it first, by your favor.

Par. My meaning in't, I protest, was very honest in the behalf of the maid; for I knew the young Count to be a dangerous and lascivious boy, who is a whale to virginity, and devours up all the fry it finds.

Ber. Damnable both-sides rogue!

Interp. [*Reads the*] *letter.*

"When he swears oaths, bid him drop gold, and take it;
After he scores, he never pays the score.
Half won is match well made; match, and well make it;
He ne'er pays after-debts, take it before,
And say a soldier, Dian, told thee this:
Men are to mell with, boys are not to kiss;
For count of this, the Count's a fool, I know it,
Who pays before, but not when he does owe it.
Thine, as he vow'd to thee in thine ear,
Parolles."

Ber. He shall be whipt through the army with this rhyme in 's forehead.

[*2. Lord.*] This is your devoted friend, sir, the manifold linguist and the armipotent soldier.

Ber. I could endure any thing before but a cat, and now he's a cat to me.

Interp. I perceive, sir, by [the] general's looks, we shall be fain to hang you.

Par. My life, sir, in any case! Not that I am afraid to die, but that my offenses being many, I would repent out the remainder of nature. Let me live, sir, in a dungeon, i' th' stocks, or any where, so I may live.

Interp. We'll see what may be done, so you confess freely; therefore once more to this Captain

Dumaine. You have answer'd to his reputation with the Duke, and to his valor; what is his honesty?

Par. He will steal, sir, an egg out of a cloister. For rapes and ravishments he parallels Nessus. He professes not keeping of oaths; in breaking 'em he is stronger than Hercules. He will lie, sir, with such volubility, that you would think truth were a fool. Drunkenness is his best virtue, for he will be swine-drunk, and in his sleep he does little harm, save to his bed-clothes about him; but they know his conditions, and lay him in straw. I have but little more to say, sir, of his honesty. He has every thing that an honest man should not have; what an honest man should have, he has nothing.

[*1. Lord.*] I begin to love him for this.

Ber. For this description of thine honesty? A pox upon him for me, he's more and more a cat.

Interp. What say you to his expertness in war?

Par. Faith, sir, h'as led the drum before the English tragedians. To belie him I will not, and more of his soldiership I know not, except in that country he had the honor to be the officer at a place there call'd Mile-end, to instruct for the doubling of files. I would do the man what honor I can, but of this I am not certain.

[*1. Lord.*] He hath out-villain'd villainy so far, that the rarity redeems him.

Ber. A pox on him, he's a cat still.

Interp. His qualities being at this poor price, I need not to ask you if gold will corrupt him to revolt.

Par. Sir, for a cardecue he will sell the fee-simple of his salvation, the inheritance of it, and cut th' entail from all remainders, and a perpetual succession for it perpetually.

Interp. What's his brother, the other Captain Dumaine?

[*2. Lord.*] Why does he ask him of me?

Interp. What's he?

Par. E'en a crow a' th' same nest; not altogether so great as the first in goodness, but greater a great deal in evil. He excels his brother for a coward, yet his brother is reputed one of the best that is. In a

203. In good sadness: in all seriousness.
213. advertisement: admonition, warning. **proper:** respectable.
214. take heed: be wary.
216. ruttish: lustful. **up again:** back in the pocket.
217. favor: leave. **221. fry:** young fish.
224. scores: incurs a debt, obtains goods on credit. **score:** bill.
225. Half . . . made: a match well started (i.e. with all the conditions clearly set forth and agreed to in advance) is a match halfway to success. *Match* may mean a game, a bargain, or the coming together of a man and a woman.
226. after-debts: debts payable after the goods have been taken.
228. mell: meddle (in sexual sense). **229. count of:** pay heed to.
230. pays before: i.e. can be made to pay in advance. **when . . . it:** after he has incurred the debt. **234. in:** i.e. attached to.
236. manifold linguist: speaker of many languages. **armipotent:** mighty in action. **238. cat:** i.e. object of aversion.
240. fain: obliged.
242–43. would . . . nature: want the rest of my natural life to repent in.

250. an egg . . . cloister: "anything, however trifling, from any place, however holy" (Johnson).
251. Nessus: the Centaur who attempted to rape Hercules' wife Dejanira and was killed by him. The Centaurs, half man and half horse, figure in myth as ravishers of the women of the Lapithae.
252. professes . . . of: makes a regular practice of not keeping.
252–53. in . . . Hercules. The parallelism is not in the breaking of oaths but in the strength.
257. they: i.e. his attendants. **conditions:** habits.
261. nothing: not at all.
266–67. led . . . tragedians: i.e. all his knowledge of the drum (symbolic of war) consists in his having beaten it at the head of a troupe of English actors (to announce their entry into a village or a playing place).
270. Mile-end: Mile-end Green, a large open area to the east of London, where the citizens received elementary military training. **doubling of files.** The simplest of drill exercises.
274. rarity: peerlessness of his performance.
278. cardecue: French coin worth a quarter of a French crown (*quart d'écu*), about two shillings.
278–81. sell . . . perpetually: i.e. renounce forever salvation for himself, his heirs, and his heirs' heirs to the end of the line. Fee-simple is the nearest thing in English property law to absolute and perpetual possession; an entail is a provision establishing that an estate is to pass successively to a series of predetermined heirs; remainders are certain residual property rights.
282. What's: what kind of man is.

retreat he outruns any lackey; marry, in coming on he has the cramp.

Interp. If your life be sav'd, will you undertake to betray the Florentine?

Par. Ay, and the captain of his horse, Count Rossillion.

Interp. I'll whisper with the general, and know his pleasure.

Par. [*Aside.*] I'll no more drumming, a plague of all drums! Only to seem to deserve well, and to beguile the supposition of that lascivious young boy the Count, have I run into this danger. Yet who would have suspected an ambush where I was taken?

Interp. There is no remedy, sir, but you must die. The general says, you that have so traitorously discover'd the secrets of your army, and made such pestiferous reports of men very nobly held, can serve the world for no honest use; therefore you must die. Come, headsman, off with his head.

Par. O Lord, sir, let me live, or let me see my death!

Interp. That shall you, and take your leave of all your friends. [*Unblinding him.*] So, look about you. Know you any here?

Ber. Good morrow, noble captain.

[*2. Lord.*] God bless you, Captain Parolles.

[*1. Lord.*] God save you, noble captain.

[*2. Lord.*] Captain, what greeting will you to my Lord Lafew? I am for France.

[*1. Lord.*] Good captain, will you give me a copy of the sonnet you writ to Diana in behalf of the Count Rossillion? And I were not a very coward, I'd compel it of you, but fare you well.

Exeunt [*Bertram and Lords*].

Interp. You are undone, captain, all but your scarf; that has a knot on't yet.

Par. Who cannot be crush'd with a plot?

Interp. If you could find out a country where but women were that had receiv'd so much shame, you might begin an impudent nation. Fare ye well, sir, I am for France too. We shall speak of you there.

Exit [*with Soldiers*].

Par. Yet am I thankful. If my heart were great,
'Twould burst at this. Captain I'll be no more,
But I will eat and drink, and sleep as soft
As captain shall. Simply the thing I am
Shall make me live. Who knows himself a braggart,
Let him fear this; for it will come to pass
That every braggart shall be found an ass.
Rust sword, cool blushes, and, Parolles, live
Safest in shame! Being fool'd, by fool'ry thrive!
There's place and means for every man alive.
I'll after them. *Exit.*

290. lackey: running servant. **coming on:** advancing.
292. undertake: engage yourself.
299–300. beguile the supposition: deceive the opinion, create a false impression in the mind.
304–5. discover'd: revealed.
306. pestiferous: pernicious. **very nobly held:** esteemed very noble.
317. will you: do you desire to send. **318. for:** off to.
328. impudent: shameless.
334. make me live: gain me a livelihood.
338. in shame: by shameful means. **fool'd:** made a fool of.

[Scene IV]

Enter Helen, Widow, *and* Diana.

Hel. That you may well perceive I have not wrong'd you,
One of the greatest in the Christian world
Shall be my surety; 'fore whose throne 'tis needful,
Ere I can perfect mine intents, to kneel.
Time was, I did him a desired office,
Dear almost as his life, which gratitude
Through flinty Tartar's bosom would peep forth,
And answer thanks. I duly am inform'd
His Grace is at Marsellis, to which place
We have convenient convoy. You must know
I am supposed dead. The army breaking,
My husband hies him home, where heaven aiding,
And by the leave of my good lord the King,
We'll be before our welcome.

Wid. Gentle madam,
You never had a servant to whose trust
Your business was more welcome.

Hel. Nor [you], mistress,
Ever a friend whose thoughts more truly labor
To recompense your love. Doubt not but heaven
Hath brought me up to be your daughter's dower,
As it hath fated her to be my motive
And helper to a husband. But O, strange men,
That can such sweet use make of what they hate,
When saucy trusting of the cozen'd thoughts
Defiles the pitchy night; so lust doth play
With what it loathes for that which is away—
But more of this hereafter. You, Diana,
Under my poor instructions yet must suffer
Something in my behalf.

Dia. Let death and honesty
Go with your impositions, I am yours
Upon your will to suffer.

Hel. Yet, I pray you:
But with the word the time will bring on summer,
When briers shall have leaves as well as thorns,
And be as sweet as sharp. We must away:
Our waggon is prepar'd, and time revives us.

IV.iv. Location: Florence. The Widow's house.
6. which gratitude: gratitude for which.
7. Through . . . bosom: even from the stony heart of a Tartar.
8. answer: respond with.
9. Marsellis: Marseilles.
10. convenient: suitable. **11. breaking:** disbanding.
14. before our welcome: i.e. before we are expected.
19. brought me up: raised me up (Dover Wilson).
20. motive: means.
23. saucy: lascivious. **cozen'd:** cheated, deluded (referring both to the general delusiveness of lust and to Bertram's delusion about the identity of his sexual partner).
24. Defiles . . . night. A reversal of the proverbial "He that touches pitch will be defiled."
25. for: in the place of, taking it to be.
27. yet: still for a time (repeated in line 30).
28. death and honesty: an honest death, a death that leaves virtue intact.
30. Upon your will: at your will, as you determine.
31. with . . . summer: i.e. with the promise that the time of further suffering will lead on to a time of fulfillment (?). The line, especially *with the word*, has been variously interpreted and much emended. It should be noted that *word* is used in the sense "promise" at II.i.210.
32. leaves: petals. **33. sweet:** fragrant.
34. time revives us: the interval of rest has restored us (?) or the coming time will give us new life (?).

All's well that ends well! still the fine's the crown;
What e'er the course, the end is the renown. *Exeunt.*

[SCENE V]

Enter CLOWN, *old Lady* [COUNTESS], *and* LAFEW.

Laf. No, no, no, your son was misled with a snipt-taffata fellow there, whose villainous saffron would have made all the unbak'd and doughy youth of a nation in his color. Your daughter-in-law had been alive at this hour, and your son here at home, more advanc'd by the King than by that red-tail'd humble-bee I speak of.

Count. I would I had not known him; it was the death of the most virtuous gentlewoman that ever nature had praise for creating. If she had partaken of my flesh, and cost me the dearest groans of a mother, I could not have ow'd her a more rooted love.

Laf. 'Twas a good lady, 'twas a good lady. We may pick a thousand sallets ere we light on such another herb.

Clo. Indeed, sir, she was the sweet marjorom of the sallet, or rather the herb of grace.

Laf. They are not herbs, you knave, they are nose-herbs.

Clo. I am no great Nebuchadnezzar, sir, I have not much skill in [grass].

Laf. Whether dost thou profess thyself—a knave or a fool?

Clo. A fool, sir, at a woman's service, and a knave at a man's.

Laf. Your distinction?

Clo. I would cozen the man of his wife and do his service.

Laf. So you were a knave at his service indeed.

Clo. And I would give his wife my bauble, sir, to do her service.

Laf. I will subscribe for thee, thou art both knave and fool.

Clo. At your service.

Laf. No, no, no.

Clo. Why, sir, if I cannot serve you, I can serve as great a prince as you are.

Laf. Who's that? a Frenchman?

Clo. Faith, sir, 'a has an English [name], but his fisnomy is more hotter in France than there.

Laf. What prince is that?

Clo. The black prince, sir, alias the prince of darkness, alias the devil.

Laf. Hold thee, there's my purse. I give thee not this to suggest thee from thy master thou talk'st of; serve him still.

Clo. I am a woodland fellow, sir, that always lov'd a great fire, and the master I speak of ever keeps a good fire. But sure he is the prince of the world; let his nobility remain in 's court. I am for the house with the narrow gate, which I take to be too little for pomp to enter. Some that humble themselves may, but the many will be too chill and tender, and they'll be for the flow'ry way that leads to the broad gate and the great fire.

Laf. Go thy ways, I begin to be a-weary of thee, and I tell thee so before, because I would not fall out with thee. Go thy ways, let my horses be well look'd to, without any tricks.

Clo. If I put any tricks upon 'em, sir, they shall be jades' tricks, which are their own right by the law of nature. *Exit.*

Laf. A shrewd knave and an unhappy.

Count. So 'a is. My lord that's gone made himself much sport out of him. By his authority he remains here, which he thinks is a patent for his sauciness, and indeed he has no pace, but runs where he will.

Laf. I like him well, 'tis not amiss. And I was about to tell you, since I heard of the good lady's death, and that my lord your son was upon his return home, I mov'd the King my master to speak in the behalf of my daughter, which in the minority of them both, his Majesty, out of a self-gracious remembrance, did first propose. His Highness hath promis'd me to do it, and to stop up the displeasure he hath conceiv'd against your son, there is no fitter matter. How does your ladyship like it?

Count. With very much content, my lord, and I wish it happily effected.

Laf. His Highness comes post from Marsellis, of as able body as when he number'd thirty. 'A will be

35. All's . . . well. Proverbial. **the fine's the crown.** Also proverbial (*fine* = end); cf. *Troilus and Cressida*, IV.v.224, "the end crowns all," and the Latin *Finis coronat opus*, "the end crowns the work."
36. the renown: i.e. what determines the praise.

IV.v. Location: Rossillion. The Count's palace.
1. with: by.
1–2. snipt-taffata: wearing a garment of taffeta slashed to show a rich lining of contrasting color, i.e. showy.
2. saffron. Alluding to a fad for wearing ruffs and collars stiffened with saffron-colored starch. Saffron was also much used for coloring pastry; hence the figure from baking in line 3.
6. red-tail'd. Perhaps a further reference to Parolles' brilliant garments, but the bumble-bee is called "red-hipp'd" in *A Midsummer Night's Dream*, IV.i.111–12.
6–7. humble-bee: a wild bee with a particularly loud buzz.
11. dearest: most intense, sorest.
14. sallets: herbs or greens for salads. **16. marjorom:** marjoram.
17. herb of grace: rue (called herb of grace because its name was identified with *rue* = repentance).
18. herbs: i.e. salad herbs as distinguished from "nose-herbs," planted in gardens for their fragrance. Dover Wilson emends *not herbs* to *knot-herbs* = herbs for planting in garden knots (elaborately patterned beds).
21. grass. With a pun on *grace*, then pronounced similarly. For Nebuchadnezzar, the king of Babylon who "did eat grass as the oxen," see Daniel 4. **22. Whether:** which of the two.
28. service. Bawdy wordplay on *service* and *serve* was very common.
30. bauble: fool's rod of office (with a bawdy innuendo).
32. subscribe: vouch.

40. fisnomy: face (variant of *physiognomy*). **more hotter.** Perhaps alluding to the facial sores of syphilis (the "French disease").
42. black prince. "An English name" (line 39) because it was the nickname of Edward III's eldest son Edward, the father of Richard II.
45. suggest: lure.
49. prince . . . world. See John 12:31. The Biblical language continues in the references to heaven and hell in lines 50–55; cf. Matthew 7:13–14. **53. chill and tender:** sensitive to cold and comfort-loving.
56. Go thy ways: go along.
57. before: i.e. before I get thoroughly tired of you.
61. jades' tricks: (1) contemptible tricks; (2) tricks played on jades (ill-trained and ill-natured horses).
63. shrewd: biting, bitter. **unhappy:** morose, discontented.
66. patent: license.
67. has no pace: will not observe the reins (a figure from horse training). **68. 'tis not amiss:** there's no harm done.
73. a self-gracious remembrance: his own kindly thoughtfulness.
80. post: at utmost speed.

here to-morrow, or I am deceiv'd by him that in such intelligence hath seldom fail'd.

Count. It rejoices me, that I hope I shall see him ere I die. I have letters that my son will be here to-night. I shall beseech your lordship to remain with me till they meet together.

Laf. Madam, I was thinking with what manners I might safely be admitted.

Count. You need but plead your honorable privilege.

Laf. Lady, of that I have made a bold charter, but I thank my God it holds yet.

Enter CLOWN.

Clo. O madam, yonder's my lord your son with a patch of velvet on 's face. Whether there be a scar under't or no, the velvet knows, but 'tis a goodly patch of velvet. His left cheek is a cheek of two pile and a half, but his right cheek is worn bare.

Laf. A scar nobly got, or a noble scar, is a good liv'ry of honor; so belike is that.

Clo. But it is your carbinado'd face.

Laf. Let us go see your son I pray you. I long to talk with the young noble soldier.

Clo. Faith, there's a dozen of 'em, with delicate fine hats, and most courteous feathers, which bow the head, and nod at every man. *Exeunt.*

ACT V, [SCENE I]

Enter HELEN, WIDOW, *and* DIANA, *with two* ATTENDANTS.

Hel. But this exceeding posting day and night
Must wear your spirits low; we cannot help it.
But since you have made the days and nights as one,
To wear your gentle limbs in my affairs,
Be bold you do so grow in my requital
As nothing can unroot you.

Enter a [GENTLEMAN, *an*] *astringer.*

In happy time!
This man may help me to his Majesty's ear,
If he would spend his power. God save you, sir.

82. **him:** a man, one. 83. **intelligence:** information.
84. **that . . . shall:** that I can hope to.
88–89. **thinking . . . admitted:** i.e. trying to think of a polite way to obtain that favor.
90–91. **honorable privilege:** privilege due your honored self.
92. **of . . . charter:** i.e. I have stretched it to the limit.
95. **patch of velvet.** Used to cover a facial wound. **scar:** i.e. wound.
97–98. **two . . . half.** The thickest velvet was three-piled; the Clown invents a quality between that and two-piled. 100. **belike:** probably.
101. **carbinado'd:** carbonadoed, slashed (used of meat scored for broiling); here alluding to surgical treatment of syphilitic sores on the face.

V.i. Location: Marseilles. A street.
1. **posting:** speedy travelling. 4. **wear:** weary.
5. **bold:** confident. **requital:** debt (literally, repayment).
6 s.d. **astringer:** falconer (strictly speaking, a trainer of goshawks, a large, short-winged variety of hawk). It is not clear why his profession should be stated, since it has no bearing on the action and is never mentioned in the dialogue. Many editors therefore omit the designation, or emend it to *a stranger* (F3), i.e. a foreigner (or possibly an authorial memorandum that this gentleman is not one who has appeared earlier). **In happy time:** most opportune.
8. **spend:** expend, use.

Gent. And you.
Hel. Sir, I have seen you in the court of France.
Gent. I have been sometimes there.
Hel. I do presume, sir, that you are not fall'n
From the report that goes upon your goodness,
And therefore goaded with most sharp occasions,
Which lay nice manners by, put you to
The use of your own virtues, for the which
I shall continue thankful.
Gent. What's your will?
Hel. That it will please you
To give this poor petition to the King,
And aid me with that store of power you have
To come into his presence.
Gent. The King's not here.
Hel. Not here, sir?
Gent. Not indeed.
He hence remov'd last night, and with more haste
Than is his use.
Wid. Lord, how we lose our pains!
Hel. All's well that ends well yet,
Though time seem so adverse and means unfit.
I do beseech you, whither is he gone?
Gent. Marry, as I take it, to Rossillion,
Whither I am going.
Hel. I do beseech you, sir,
Since you are like to see the King before me,
Commend the paper to his gracious hand,
Which I presume shall render you no blame,
But rather make you thank your pains for it.
I will come after you with what good speed
Our means will make us means.
Gent. This I'll do for you.
Hel. And you shall find yourself to be well thank'd,
What e'er falls more. We must to horse again.
Go, go, provide. [*Exeunt.*]

[SCENE II]

Enter CLOWN *and* PAROLLES.

Par. Good Master Lavatch, give my Lord Lafew this letter. I have ere now, sir, been better known to you, when I have held familiarity with fresher clothes; but I am now, sir, muddied in Fortune's mood, and smell somewhat strong of her strong displeasure.

Clo. Truly, Fortune's displeasure is but sluttish if it smell so strongly as thou speak'st of. I will hence-

13. **From . . . goodness:** from the goodness that current report ascribes to you. 14. **sharp:** urgent. **occasions:** necessities.
15. **lay . . . by:** put aside scrupulous politeness. **put:** press.
24. **use:** custom. 31. **Commend:** commit.
32. **presume:** venture to say.
35. **Our . . . means:** our resources will secure us ways of achieving.

V.ii. Location: Rossillion. Before the Count's palace.
1. **Lavatch.** This is the only occurrence of the Clown's name in the dialogue.
4. **mood:** i.e. bad mood (synonymous with *displeasure* in line 5). Note the play in *muddied / mood*, which apparently suggests to the Clown a further play on *moat*; this would explain his references below to fish (since moats served as fish ponds) and to excrement (since sewage was discharged into the moat).
6. **displeasure.** The Clown seems to use this word as interchangeable with *mood* and hence with *moat*. Fortune is sluttish in not keeping her moat cleaned out, and the Clown will therefore eat none of her fish.

forth eat no fish of Fortune's butt'ring. Prithee allow the wind.

Par. Nay, you need not to stop your nose, sir; I spake but by a metaphor.

Clo. Indeed, sir, if your metaphor stink, I will stop my nose, or against any man's metaphor. Prithee get thee further.

Par. Pray you, sir, deliver me this paper.

Clo. Foh, prithee stand away. A paper from Fortune's close-stool to give to a nobleman! Look here he comes himself.

Enter LAFEW.

Here is a purr of Fortune's, sir, or of Fortune's cat—but not a musk-cat—that has fall'n into the unclean fishpond of her displeasure, and as he says, is muddied withal. Pray you, sir, use the carp as you may, for he looks like a poor, decay'd, ingenious, foolish, rascally knave. I do pity his distress in my [similes] of comfort, and leave him to your lordship. [*Exit.*]

Par. My lord, I am a man whom Fortune hath cruelly scratch'd.

Laf. And what would you have me to do? 'Tis too late to pare her nails now. Wherein have you play'd the knave with Fortune that she should scratch you, who of herself is a good lady, and would not have knaves thrive long under [her]? There's a cardecue for you. Let the justices make you and Fortune friends; I am for other business.

Par. I beseech your honor to hear me one single word.

Laf. You beg a single penny more. Come, you shall ha't; save your word.

Par. My name, my good lord, is Parolles.

Laf. You beg more than "word" then. Cox my passion! give me your hand. How does your drum?

Par. O my good lord, you were the first that found me!

Laf. Was I, in sooth? And I was the first that lost thee.

Par. It lies in you, my lord, to bring me in some grace, for you did bring me out.

Laf. Out upon thee, knave! Dost thou put upon me at once both the office of God and the devil? one

brings thee in grace, and the other brings thee out. [*Trumpets sound.*] The King's coming, I know by his trumpets. Sirrah, inquire further after me. I had talk of you last night; though you are a fool and a knave, you shall eat. Go to, follow.

Par. I praise God for you. [*Exeunt.*]

[SCENE III]

Flourish. Enter KING, *old Lady* [COUNTESS], LAFEW, *the two French* LORDS, *with* ATTENDANTS.

King. We lost a jewel of her, and our esteem
Was made much poorer by it; but your son,
As mad in folly, lack'd the sense to know
Her estimation home.

Count. 'Tis past, my liege,
And I beseech your Majesty to make it
Natural rebellion, done i' th' blade of youth,
When oil and fire, too strong for reason's force,
O'erbears it, and burns on.

King. My honor'd lady,
I have forgiven and forgotten all,
Though my revenges were high bent upon him,
And watch'd the time to shoot.

Laf. This I must say—
But first I beg my pardon—the young lord
Did to his Majesty, his mother, and his lady
Offense of mighty note; but to himself
The greatest wrong of all. He lost a wife
Whose beauty did astonish the survey
Of richest eyes, whose words all ears took captive,
Whose dear perfection hearts that scorn'd to serve
Humbly call'd mistress.

King. Praising what is lost
Makes the remembrance dear. Well, call him hither,
We are reconcil'd, and the first view shall kill
All repetition. Let him not ask our pardon,
The nature of his great offense is dead,
And deeper than oblivion we do bury
Th' incensing relics of it. Let him approach
A stranger, no offender; and inform him
So 'tis our will he should.

Gent. I shall, my liege. [*Exit.*]

King. What says he to your daughter? Have you spoke?

Laf. All that he is hath reference to your Highness.

8–9. allow the wind: keep to the windward of me.
17. close-stool: predecessor of the water-closet.
19. purr: piece of dung (with quibble on "cat's purr"). The play on *purr* continues in *knave* (lines 24, 30, 32), since it was the name given to the jack in the card-game of post and pair.
20. musk-cat: musk-deer, the animal from which perfumers obtained musk.
22. withal: with it, in consequence. **carp:** (1) a fish (said by Hunter to have been bred in manured fishponds); (2) carper, chatterer.
23. ingenious. Out of place in the series, and not satisfactorily explained; possibly an error for *ingenerous*, "ignoble."
24–25. pity . . . comfort: show my compassion for his misery in my comforting similes, i.e. in saying that he is *like* a knave, not that he *is* a knave.
33. cardecue. See the note on IV.iii.278. **justices:** justices of the peace, who were empowered to relieve the worthy poor.
40. more than "word": i.e. "words" (a jest on Parolles' name).
40–41. Cox my passion: a weakened oath derived from an original "by God's (Christ's) suffering."
42, 44. found, lost. Cf. II.iii.205–6. **44. sooth:** truth.
46–47. in some grace: into some favor. Lafew answers with a quibble.

52. inquire . . . me: come to see me later.

V.iii. Location: Rossillion. The Count's palace.
1. of: in. **our esteem:** my own worth.
3. As . . . folly: carrying folly to the point of madness.
4. Her estimation home: her worth to the full.
6. rebellion. Line 7 shows that the rebellion is of the passions against the reason, not of the youth against external authority. Cf. *God delay our rebellion*, IV.iii.19. **blade:** green shoot, i.e. immaturity, callowness. Theobald proposed reading *blaze*, Sisson *blood* (= passion).
10. high bent: bent to the utmost (a figure from archery).
11. watch'd the time: vigilantly waited for the right moment.
14. of mighty note: egregious.
16. astonish the survey: dazzle the sight.
17. richest eyes: eyes that had seen most.
22. repetition: reviewing of past wrongs.
25. incensing . . . it: reminders of it that would inflame my anger.
26. A stranger: i.e. one whose past is a closed book.
29. hath reference to: is submitted for decision to, is at the disposal of.

King. Then shall we have a match. I have letters sent me
That sets him high in fame.

Enter COUNT BERTRAM.

Laf. He looks well on't.
King. I am not a day of season,
For thou mayst see a sunshine and a hail
In me at once. But to the brightest beams
Distracted clouds give way, so stand thou forth,
The time is fair again.
Ber. My high-repented blames,
Dear sovereign, pardon to me.
King. All is whole,
Not one word more of the consumed time.
Let's take the instant by the forward top;
For we are old, and on our quick'st decrees
Th' inaudible and noiseless foot of time
Steals ere we can effect them. You remember
The daughter of this lord?
Ber. Admiringly, my liege. At first
I stuck my choice upon her, ere my heart
Durst make too bold a herald of my tongue;
Where the impression of mine eye infixing,
Contempt his scornful perspective did lend me,
Which warp'd the line of every other favor,
Scorn'd a fair color, or express'd it stol'n,
Extended or contracted all proportions
To a most hideous object. Thence it came
That she whom all men prais'd, and whom myself,
Since I have lost, have lov'd, was in mine eye
The dust that did offend it.
King. Well excus'd.
That thou didst love her, strikes some scores away
From the great compt; but love that comes too late,
Like a remorseful pardon slowly carried,
To the great sender turns a sour offense,
Crying, "That's good that's gone." Our rash faults
Make trivial price of serious things we have,
Not knowing them until we know their grave.
Oft our displeasures, to ourselves unjust,
Destroy our friends, and after weep their dust;
Our own love waking cries to see what's done,
While shameful hate sleeps out the afternoon.
Be this sweet Helen's knell, and now forget her.
Send forth your amorous token for fair Maudlin.
The main consents are had, and here we'll stay
To see our widower's second marriage-day.
[*Count.*] Which better than the first, O dear heaven, bless!
Or, ere they meet, in me, O nature, cesse!
Laf. Come on, my son, in whom my house's name
Must be digested; give a favor from you
To sparkle in the spirits of my daughter,
That she may quickly come. [*Bertram gives a ring.*]
By my old beard,
And ev'ry hair that's on't, Helen, that's dead,
Was a sweet creature; such a ring as this,
The last that e'er I took her leave at court,
I saw upon her finger.
Ber. Hers it was not.
King. Now pray you let me see it; for mine eye,
While I was speaking, oft was fasten'd to't.
This ring was mine, and when I gave it Helen,
I bade her, if her fortunes ever stood
Necessitied to help, that by this token
I would relieve her. Had you that craft to reave her
Of what should stead her most?
Ber. My gracious sovereign,
Howe'er it pleases you to take it so,
The ring was never hers.
Count. Son, on my life,
I have seen her wear it, and she reckon'd it
At her live's rate.
Laf. I am sure I saw her wear it.
Ber. You are deceiv'd, my lord, she never saw it.
In Florence was it from a casement thrown me,
Wrapp'd in a paper, which contain'd the name
Of her that threw it. Noble she was, and thought
I stood engag'd; but when I had subscrib'd
To mine own fortune, and inform'd her fully
I could not answer in that course of honor
As she had made the overture, she ceas'd
In heavy satisfaction, and would never
Receive the ring again.
King. Plutus himself,
That knows the tinct and multiplying med'cine,
Hath not in nature's mystery more science

32. of season: i.e. of any one season, of settled weather.
35. Distracted . . . way: i.e. clouds break and give way (*Distracted* [= broken] is proleptic). **stand thou forth:** (1) come forth (from the place where you shelter from the storm); (2) come forward.
36. time: weather. **high-repented:** bitterly repented.
37. whole: well.
39. take . . . top: take time by the forelock, grasp the opportunity while we can (proverbial). Opportunity was represented as bald behind. **45. stuck:** fixed.
47. Where: i.e. in my heart. **the impression . . . eye:** the image (of Lafew's daughter) received by my eye. It was a commonplace that love entered the heart by way of the eye.
48. perspective: optical glass that distorts whatever is seen through it.
49. favor: face.
50. Scorn'd: made mock of. **express'd it stol'n:** i.e. declared it painted. **52. object:** sight. **53. she:** i.e. Helena.
56. scores: debits. **57. great compt:** total account.
58. remorseful: compassionate. **slowly carried:** i.e. arriving too late.
59. turns . . . offense. Like milk turning sour or food going bad.
61. Make . . . of: place a trifling value on.
62. know their grave: i.e. lose them irrevocably.
64. weep their dust: weep over their ashes.
66. sleeps . . . afternoon: rests peacefully after its hateful work.
68. Maudlin: form of *Magdalen*.
72. cesse: cease (an archaic form, used for the sake of rhyme).
74. digested: absorbed.
79. last: last time. **took her leave:** took leave of her.
85. Necessitied to: in need of. **86. reave:** despoil.
87. stead: help.
90–91. reckon'd . . . rate: valued it as highly as her life (*live's* = life's).
96. engag'd: pledged (to her) (?). It has been suggested that the F1 spelling *ingag'd* may mean *not gaged* or may be an error for *ungag'd*, i.e. not pledged to anyone else.
96–97. subscrib'd . . . fortune: i.e. told her of my situation.
98–99. I . . . overture: i.e. I could not in honor accept the invitation that she had tendered in honor.
100. heavy satisfaction: sorrowful conviction that no other course was open.
101. Plutus: the god of riches, i.e. the being most knowledgeable about gold.
102. tinct . . . med'cine: i.e. the "grand elixir" or "philosopher's stone," sought by the alchemists as the means of turning base metals to gold (*tinct* = tincture). Cf. *Antony and Cleopatra*, I.v.36–37, "that great med'cine hath / With his tinct gilded thee."
103. more science: deeper knowledge.

Than I have in this ring. 'Twas mine, 'twas Helen's,
Whoever gave it you. Then if you know
That you are well acquainted with yourself,
Confess 'twas hers, and by what rough enforcement
You got it from her. She call'd the saints to surety
That she would never put it from her finger,
Unless she gave it to yourself in bed,
Where you have never come, or sent it us
Upon her great disaster.

Ber. She never saw it.

King. Thou speak'st it falsely, as I love mine honor,
And mak'st [conjectural] fears to come into me,
Which I would fain shut out. If it should prove
That thou art so inhuman—'twill not prove so;
And yet I know not: thou didst hate her deadly,
And she is dead, which nothing but to close
Her eyes myself could win me to believe,
More than to see this ring. Take him away.
[*Guards seize Bertram.*]
My fore-past proofs, howe'er the matter fall,
Shall [tax] my fears of little vanity,
Having vainly fear'd too little. Away with him!
We'll sift this matter further.

Ber. If you shall prove
This ring was ever hers, you shall as easy
Prove that I husbanded her bed in Florence,
Where yet she never was. [*Exit guarded.*]

Enter a GENTLEMAN, [*the astringer*].

King. I am wrapp'd in dismal thinkings.

Gent. Gracious sovereign,
Whether I have been to blame or no, I know not.
Here's a petition from a Florentine,
Who hath for four or five removes come short
To tender it herself. I undertook it,
Vanquish'd thereto by the fair grace and speech
Of the poor suppliant, who by this I know
Is here attending. Her business looks in her
With an importing visage, and she told me,
In a sweet verbal brief, it did concern
Your Highness with herself.

[*King. Reads*] *a letter.* "Upon his many protestations to marry me when his wife was dead, I blush to say it, he won me. Now is the Count Rossillion a widower, his vows are forfeited to me, and my honor's paid to him. He stole from Florence, taking no leave, and I follow him to his country for justice. Grant it me, O King, in you it best lies; otherwise a seducer flourishes, and a poor maid is undone.
Diana Capilet."

Laf. I will buy me a son-in-law in a fair, and toll for this. I'll none of him.

King. The heavens have thought well on thee, Lafew,
To bring forth this discov'ry. Seek these suitors.
Go speedily, and bring again the Count.
[*Exeunt some Attendants.*]
I am afeard the life of Helen, lady,
Was foully snatch'd.

Count. Now, justice on the doers!

Enter BERTRAM [*guarded*].

King. I wonder, sir, [sith] wives are monsters to you,
And that you fly them as you swear them lordship,
Yet you desire to marry. What woman's that?

Enter WIDOW, DIANA.

Dia. I am, my lord, a wretched Florentine,
Derived from the ancient Capilet.
My suit, as I do understand, you know,
And therefore know how far I may be pitied.

Wid. I am her mother, sir, whose age and honor
Both suffer under this complaint we bring,
And both shall cease, without your remedy.

King. Come hither, Count, do you know these women?

Ber. My lord, I neither can nor will deny
But that I know them. Do they charge me further?

Dia. Why do you look so strange upon your wife?

Ber. She's none of mine, my lord.

Dia. If you shall marry,
You give away this hand, and that is mine;
You give away heaven's vows, and those are mine;
You give away myself, which is known mine;
For I by vow am so embodied yours,
That she which marries you must marry me,
Either both or none.

Laf. Your reputation comes too short for my daughter, you are no husband for her.

Ber. My lord, this is a fond and desp'rate creature,
Whom sometime I have laugh'd with. Let your Highness
Lay a more noble thought upon mine honor
Than for to think that I would sink it here.

King. Sir, for my thoughts, you have them ill to friend
Till your deeds gain them; fairer prove your honor
Than in my thought it lies.

Dia. Good my lord,
Ask him upon his oath, if he does think

105–7. **if . . . hers.** The sense of this seems to be: "If you know anything at all, you know that it is her ring; confess it."
112. **Upon . . . disaster:** in the event of some dire misfortune.
114. **conjectural fears:** dreadful surmises.
121–23. **My . . . little:** however this matter turns out, the evidence I already have shows that my fears cannot be censured as foolish; the folly lies in my not having been apprehensive enough.
128. **dismal:** ill-boding.
131. **removes:** stopping places on a royal progress. **come short:** failed to arrive in time. 133. **Vanquish'd:** won.
134. **by this:** by this time. 135. **looks:** shows itself.
136. **importing:** (1) full of import; (2) urgent.
137. **verbal brief:** summary statement.
142. **his . . . me:** I am entitled to performance of what he vowed.
148. **in a fair:** at a fair (implying that even in a place where misrepresentation of merchandise is routine he can buy his daughter a better husband than Bertram).
148–49. **toll for:** i.e. pay a tax for the privilege of selling. Merchandise to be sold in a market had to be entered in the toll-book for a fee.
151. **these suitors.** The King has been told of only one suitor.
155. **sith:** since.
156. **that.** Replacing a second *sith*; a frequent Elizabethan usage. **swear them lordship:** i.e. speak your marriage vows.
164. **both:** i.e. age and honor. 170. **this hand:** i.e. Bertram's.
178. **fond and desp'rate:** foolish and reckless. 181. **sink:** debase.
182. **you . . . friend:** they are not at all friendly.
183. **gain them:** win their friendship.

He had not my virginity.
King. What say'st thou to her?
Ber. She's impudent, my lord,
And was a common gamester to the camp.
Dia. He does me wrong, my lord; if I were so,
He might have bought me at a common price.
Do not believe him. O, behold this ring,
Whose high respect and rich validity
Did lack a parallel; yet for all that
He gave it to a commoner a' th' camp,
If I be one.
Count. He blushes, and 'tis hit.
Of six preceding ancestors, that gem,
Conferr'd by testament to th' sequent issue,
Hath it been owed and worn. This is his wife,
That ring's a thousand proofs.
King. Methought you said
You saw one here in court could witness it.
Dia. I did, my lord, but loath am to produce
So bad an instrument. His name's Parolles.
Laf. I saw the man to-day, if man he be.
King. Find him, and bring him hither.
[*Exit an Attendant.*]
Ber. What of him?
He's quoted for a most perfidious slave,
With all the spots a' th' world tax'd and debosh'd,
Whose nature sickens but to speak a truth.
Am I or that or this for what he'll utter,
That will speak any thing?
King. She hath that ring of yours.
Ber. I think she has. Certain it is I lik'd her,
And boarded her i' th' wanton way of youth.
She knew her distance, and did angle for me,
Madding my eagerness with her restraint,
As all impediments in fancy's course
Are motives of more fancy, and in fine,
Her [inf'nite cunning,] with her modern grace,
Subdu'd me to her rate. She got the ring,
And I had that which any inferior might
At market-price have bought.
Dia. I must be patient.
You that have turn'd off a first so noble wife,
May justly diet me. I pray you yet
(Since you lack virtue, I will lose a husband)
Send for your ring, I will return it home,
And give me mine again.
Ber. I have it not.
King. What ring was yours, I pray you?
Dia. Sir, much like
The same upon your finger.
King. Know you this ring? This ring was his of late.
Dia. And this was it I gave him, being a-bed.
King. The story then goes false, you threw it him
Out of a casement.
Dia. I have spoke the truth.

Enter PAROLLES.

Ber. My lord, I do confess the ring was hers.
King. You boggle shrewdly, every feather starts you.
Is this the man you speak of?
Dia. Ay, my lord.
King. Tell me, sirrah—but tell me true, I charge you,
Not fearing the displeasure of your master,
Which on your just proceeding I'll keep off—
By him and by this woman here what know you?

Par. So please your Majesty, my master hath been an honorable gentleman. Tricks he hath had in him, which gentlemen have.

King. Come, come, to th' purpose. Did he love this woman?

Par. Faith, sir, he did love her, but how?

King. How, I pray you?

Par. He did love her, sir, as a gentleman loves a woman.

King. How is that?

Par. He lov'd her, sir, and lov'd her not.

King. As thou art a knave, and no knave. What an equivocal companion is this!

Par. I am a poor man, and at your Majesty's command.

Laf. He's a good drum, my lord, but a naughty orator.

Dia. Do you know he promis'd me marriage?

Par. Faith, I know more than I'll speak.

King. But wilt thou not speak all thou know'st?

Par. Yes, so please your Majesty. I did go between them as I said, but more than that, he lov'd her, for indeed he was mad for her, and talk'd of Sathan and of Limbo and of Furies and I know not what. Yet I was in that credit with them at that time that I knew of their going to bed, and of other motions, as promising her marriage, and things which would derive me ill will to speak of; therefore I will not speak what I know.

King. Thou hast spoken all already, unless thou canst say they are married. But thou art too fine in thy evidence, therefore stand aside.
This ring you say was yours?
Dia. Ay, my good lord.
King. Where did you buy it? Or who gave it you?
Dia. It was not given me, nor I did not buy it.
King. Who lent it you?
Dia. It was not lent me neither.

187. impudent: shameless.
192. high respect: high place in his regard. **validity:** value.
195. 'tis hit: that went home, she has hit the mark. **196. Of:** by.
198. owed: possessed.
199–200. Methought . . . it. Diana has not said this.
205. quoted for: set down as.
206. With . . . debosh'd: i.e. accused of being corrupted with all the vices there are (*debosh'd* is a variant spelling of *debauched*).
207. sickens . . . truth: is made sick by telling a truth.
208. or . . . or: either . . . or. **for:** in consequence of.
211. boarded: made advances to.
212. knew her distance: knew how to keep tantalizingly out of reach (?). **213. Madding:** maddening, i.e. inflaming.
214. fancy's: love's. **215. motives:** causes, sources.
216. modern: commonplace.
217. Subdu'd . . . rate: made me submit to her price.
219. be patient: keep my self-control.
221. diet: restrict, deprive (?).
232. boggle: shy, take fright. **shrewdly:** violently, excessively. **starts you:** makes you jump. **237. By:** about.
250. companion: fellow.
253. drum: drummer. **naughty:** execrable.
260. Sathan: Satan. **262. that:** such.
263. motions: things urged. **268. fine:** hairsplitting.

King. Where did you find it then?
Dia. I found it not.
King. If it were yours by none of all these ways,
How could you give it him?
Dia. I never gave it him.
Laf. This woman's an easy glove, my lord, she goes off and on at pleasure.
King. This ring was mine, I gave it his first wife.
Dia. It might be yours or hers for aught I know.
King. Take her away, I do not like her now,
To prison with her; and away with him.
Unless thou tell'st me where thou hadst this ring,
Thou diest within this hour.
Dia. I'll never tell you.
King. Take her away.
Dia. I'll put in bail, my liege.
King. I think thee now some common customer.
Dia. By Jove, if ever I knew man, 'twas you.
King. Wherefore hast thou accus'd him all this while?
Dia. Because he's guilty, and he is not guilty.
He knows I am no maid, and he'll swear to't;
I'll swear I am a maid, and he knows not.
Great King, I am no strumpet, by my life;
I am either maid, or else this old man's wife.
[*Pointing to Lafew*.]
King. She does abuse our ears. To prison with her!
Dia. Good mother, fetch my bail. [*Exit Widow*.]
Stay, royal sir.
The jeweller that owes the ring is sent for,
And he shall surety me. But for this lord,
Who hath abus'd me, as he knows himself,
Though yet he never harm'd me, here I quit him.
He knows himself my bed he hath defil'd,
And at that time he got his wife with child.
Dead though she be, she feels her young one kick.
So there's my riddle: one that's dead is quick—
And now behold the meaning.

Enter Widow *and* Helen.

King. Is there no exorcist
Beguiles the truer office of mine eyes?
Is't real that I see?
Hel. No, my good lord,
'Tis but the shadow of a wife you see,
The name, and not the thing.
Ber. Both, both. O, pardon!
Hel. O my good lord, when I was like this maid,
I found you wondrous kind. There is your ring,
And look you, here's your letter. This it says:
"When from my finger you can get this ring,
And [are] by me with child, etc." This is done.
Will you be mine now you are doubly won?
Ber. If she, my liege, can make me know this clearly,
I'll love her dearly, ever, ever dearly.
Hel. If it appear not plain and prove untrue,
Deadly divorce step between me and you!
O my dear mother, do I see you living?
Laf. Mine eyes smell onions, I shall weep anon. [*To Parolles*.] Good Tom Drum, lend me a handkercher. So, I thank thee; wait on me home, I'll make sport with thee. Let thy curtsies alone, they are scurvy ones.
King. Let us from point to point this story know,
To make the even truth in pleasure flow.
[*To Diana*.] If thou beest yet a fresh uncropped flower,
Choose thou thy husband, and I'll pay thy dower,
For I can guess that by thy honest aid
Thou kept'st a wife herself, thyself a maid.
Of that and all the progress, more and less,
Resolvedly more leisure shall express.
All yet seems well, and if it end so meet,
The bitter past, more welcome is the sweet. *Flourish*.

[EPILOGUE]

[*King*. *Advancing*.] The king's a beggar, now the play is done;
All is well ended, if this suit be won,
That you express content; which we will pay,
With strife to please you, day exceeding day.
Ours be your patience then, and yours our parts;
Your gentle hands lend us, and take our hearts.
Exeunt omnes.

286. common customer: prostitute. **287. knew:** knew carnally.
299. quit: (1) acquit; (2) pay back.
303. quick: (1) alive; (2) pregnant. **304. exorcist:** conjurer.

309. like: i.e. taking the place of.
315. make . . . clearly: prove to me that this is true.
318. Deadly divorce: divorcing death. **322. So:** very good.
326. even: plain.
331. Of . . . less: the course of that and everything, both greater and smaller details.
332. Resolvedly: in a fashion that will resolve all questions.
Epi. 3. express content: i.e. applaud. **4. strife:** striving, effort.

NOTE ON THE TEXT

The First Folio (1623) is the sole authority for *All's Well That Ends Well;* all later texts are derived from that source. Among the F1 texts, that of *All's Well* is one of the worst printed and least satisfactory. Occasional permissive or other authorial stage directions and frequent variations in speech-prefixes (particularly those designating the Countess, the French Lords, and Bertram), not to mention other confusions and a character called Violenta in III.v o.s.d., who is either a ghost character or, as Hunter suggests, represents Shakespeare's first thought as the name for Diana (note the unusual descriptive reference to Diana in the o.s.d. to IV.ii: "Enter Bertram and the maid called Diana."), indicate clearly enough that some stage of Shakespeare's "foul papers" underlies the F1 text, but whether that text was set directly from the "foul papers" or from some kind of transcript of them (which would explain the general absence of characteristic Shakespearean spellings in F1; but see the Textual Notes, II.v.29, III.ii.18, 126) is a debatable question, with probability in favor of a direct use of the "foul papers." The hand of a book-keeper has been seen by some scholars in a few directions calling for stage noises and in the use of "G." and "E." (supposed to represent actors' initials, possibly Gough and Ecclestone) to distinguish, not consistently nor always accurately, the two French Lords (i.e., the brothers Dumaine). If this view is correct, though Bowers, for example, argues that at least the "G." and "E." speech-prefixes are Shakespeare's work, it points to nothing more than a preliminary rough annotation of the "foul papers"; certainly, the manuscript from which F1 was printed could never have served as an official prompt-book.

For further information, see: J. D. Wilson, ed., New Shakespeare *All's Well That Ends Well* (Cambridge, 1929) [Wilson's elaborate revision theory is no longer generally accepted]; W. W. Greg, *The Shakespeare First Folio* (Oxford, 1955); G. K. Hunter, ed., New Arden *All's Well That Ends Well* (London, 1959); Alice Walker, "Six Notes on *All's Well That Ends Well,*" *SQ,* XXXIII (1982), 339–42; F. T. Bowers, "Foul Papers, Compositor B, and the Speech-Prefixes of *All's Well That Ends Well,*" *SB,* XXXII (1979), 60–81, and "Shakespeare at Work: The Foul Papers of *All's Well That Ends Well,*" in *English Renaissance Studies,* ed. John Crow (Oxford, 1980); Russell Fraser, ed., New Cambridge *All's Well That Ends Well* (Cambridge, 1985); Stanley Wells, Gary Taylor, et al., *William Shakespeare: A Textual Companion* (Oxford, 1987); Gary Taylor, "'Praestat difficilior lectio': *All's Well That Ends Well* and *Richard III,*" *Renaissance Studies,* II (1988), 27–46; Susan Snyder, ed., New Oxford *All's Well That Ends Well* (Oxford, 1994).

TEXTUAL NOTES

Title: All's . . . Well] *F3;* Alls Well, that Ends Well *F1*
Dramatis personae: *subs. as first given by Rowe*
Act-scene division: *F1 marks acts only, except for I.i; other scene divisions from Rowe and later editors (see first note to each scene); present act-scene arrangement as a whole first established by Capell*

I.i

Location: *Cambridge*
1 s.p. **Count.]** *Rowe;* Mother. *F1 (or* Mo. *throughout scene)*
3 s.p. **Ber.]** *Rowe;* Ros. *F1 (throughout scene)*
73–8 **Heaven . . . father.]** *as verse, ed.; as prose, F1*
75 **forged]** *ed. (after Malone);* forg'd *F1 (the F1 line is extremely crowded,* thoughts *being reduced to* thoghts)
75 s.d. **Exit Countess.]** *Neilson-Hill;* Exit. *F2 (after* Bertram. *l. 74)*
76 s.d. **To Helena.]** *Nicholson conj. (in Cambridge; other eds., following Rowe, include ll. 74–5 as addressed to Helena)*
78 s.d. **Exeunt . . . Lafew.]** *Rowe*
79 **all!]** *Capell (after Rowe);* all, *F1*
87 **me.]** *Rowe (subs.);* me *F1*
93 **hour,]** *Pope;* houre *F1*
99 s.d. **Aside.]** *Cambridge*
113 **barricado]** *Rowe;* barracado *F1*
128 **got]** *F2;* goe *F1*
142 **paring]** *Rowe;* payring *F1*
147 **t' one]** *ed.;* ten *F1*
155 **request.]** *F4;* request, *F1*
158 **wear]** *Capell (after Rowe);* were *F1*
165 **yet: . . . .]** *some words or lines seem to be missing here*
170 **traitress]** *F2;* Traitoresse *F1*
172 **jarring . . . discord]** *F4;* iarring, . . . discord, *F1*
177 **one—]** *Rowe;* one. *F1*
187 s.d. **Exit.]** *Theobald*
209 **counsel]** *F2;* councell *F1*
215 s.d. **Exit.]** *F2*
223 **like likes]** *F4;* like, likes *F1*

I.ii

I.ii] *Capell*
Location: *Capell (after Pope)*
o.s.d. **Lords]** *Capell*
3 s.p. **1. Lord.]** *Rowe;* 1. Lo. G. *F1 (throughout scene; G. is perhaps an actor's initial)*
4–5 **it A certainty,]** *Capell;* it, / A certaintie *F1*
15, 67 s.pp. **2. Lord.]** *Rowe;* 2. Lo. E. *and* L. 2. E. *F1* (E. *is perhaps an actor's initial)*
18 **Rossillion]** *F2;* Rosignoll *F1*
52 **him!]** *F2 (subs.);* him *F1*
76 s.d. **Exeunt.]** *Rowe;* Exit *F1*

I.iii

I.iii] *Capell*
Location: *Pope, Capell (subs.)*
10 **believe.]** *F4 (subs.);* beleeue, *F1*
19 **I will]** *F2;* w will *F1*
42 **madam—]** *Alexander;* Madam *F1*
60–4 **For . . . kind.]** *as verse, Rowe (subs.); as prose, F1*
67 **you.]** *Theobald (subs.);* you, *F1*
75] *The repetition of this line is indicated in F1 by* bis *following l. 74*
76–9 **And . . . ten.]** *as verse, Rowe; as prose, F1*
85 **tithe-woman]** *hyphen, Theobald*
86 **or]** *Capell;* ore *F1*
90 **be gone]** *F2;* begone *F1*
95 **black gown]** *F3;* blacke-Gowne *F1*
114 **level; Diana no]** *Theobald;* leuell, *F1*
128 **Even]** *Singer; Old Cou.* Euen *F1 (repeated s.p.)*
130 **belong;]** *Theobald;* belong *F1*
134 **foregone]** *Rowe;* forgon *F1*
137 s.p. **Count.]** *Rowe;* Ol. Cou. *F1 (or* Old Cou. *through l. 167)*
161 **madam;]** *Rowe;* Madam, *F1*
171 **loneliness]** *Theobald;* louelinesse *F1*
177 **t' one]** *Hunter;* 'ton tooth *F1*
183 **forswear't; howe'er]** *F3 (subs.);* forsweare't how ere *F1*
189 **disclose]** *F3;* disclose: *F1*
202 **intenible]** *F2;* intemible *F1 (some recent eds., following Nicholson's conj. [in Cambridge], read* inteemible, *the F1* -tem- *being a variant of* teem [= *to pour out]; neither* intenible *nor* inteemible *is recorded apart from this passage)*
202 **sieve]** *F3;* Siue. *F1*
204 **lose]** *F4;* loose *F1*
231 **it? speak.]** *Steevens;* it, speake? *F1*
248 **well-lost]** *hyphen, Pope*
249 **an]** and *F2*
255 **Be gone]** *F3;* Begon *F1*

II.i

II.i] *Rowe;* Actus Secundus. *F1*
Location: *Capell*
o.s.d. **Count Rossillion]** *ed.;* Count, Rosse *F1;* Count Rosse *F2*
3 **you;]** *Rowe (subs.);* you, *F1*
3 **gain all,]** *Johnson;* gaine, all *F1*
5 s.p. **1. Lord.]** *Rowe;* Lord. G. *F1*
12 **Frenchmen]** *Warburton;* French men *F1*
18 s.p. **2. Lord.]** *Rowe;* L.G. *F1*
22 s.p. **Both Lords.]** *Capell (subs.);* Bo. *F1*
23 s.d. **The . . . Lords.]** *ed. (after Capell)*
24 s.p. **1. Lord.]** *Rowe;* 1. Lo. G. *F1 (until l. 46)*
25 **fault,]** *F3;* fault *F1*
25 s.p. **2. Lord.]** *Rowe;* 2. Lo. E. *F1 (throughout scene)*
30 **forehorse]** *F3;* for-horse *F1*
40 **kin.]** *Rowe (subs.);* kinne, *F1*
43 **with . . . an]** *Theobald;* his sicatrice, with an *F1*
46 s.p. **1. Lord.]** *Rowe;* Lo. G. *F1*
47 s.d. **Exeunt Lords.]** *Theobald (after l. 49); placed as in Capell*
60 s.d. **Bertram and Parolles]** *Capell*
60 s.d. **The . . . forward.]** *Hunter (after Collier MS)*
61 s.d. **Kneeling.]** *Johnson*
70 **will]** *Knight;* will, *F1*
79 **Doctor She]** *White;* doctor she *F1*
81 **convey]** *Rowe;* conuay *F1*
91 s.d. **Goes to the door.]** *Sisson*
97 **Cressid's]** *Pope;* Cresseds *F1*
109 **two, more dear.]** *Steevens;* two: more deare *F1*
144 **fits]** *Theobald conj.;* shifts *F1*
155 **imposture]** *Capell;* Impostrue *F1;* Impostor *F3*
171 **shame,]** *Capell (Johnson conj.);* shame *F1*
173 **otherwise;]** *Capell;* otherwise, *F1*
173 **ne]** no *F2*
173 **worst—]** *Alexander (after Wilson);* worst *F1*
192 **heaven]** *Thirlby conj.;* helpe *F1*
210 s.d. **Exeunt.]** *F2;* Exit. *F1*

II.ii

II.ii] *Capell*
Location: *Pope, Capell*
1 s.p. **Count.]** *Rowe;* Lady. *F1 (or* La. *throughout scene)*
13 **court;]** *Rowe;* Court, *F1*
40 **I]** *F3; La.* I *F1 (repeated s.p.)*
60–1 **I . . . fool.]** *as verse, Knight; as prose, F1*
63 **An]** *Rowe;* And *F1*
63 **sir;]** *Rowe (after F3, which places a semicolon after* end); sir *F1*
70 **legs]** *F2;* legegs *F1*

II.iii

II.iii] *Capell*
Location: *Pope, Capell (subs.)*
1 s.p. **Laf.]** Ol. Laf. *F1 (or* Old Laf. *until l. 184, except* Ol. Lord., *l. 99)*
2 **familiar,]** *Theobald;* familiar *F1*
9 s.p. **Ber.]** *Rowe;* Ros. *F1*
11 **say,]** *Rowe;* say *F1*
21 **indeed;]** *Capell (subs.);* indeede *F1*
22 **what-do-ye-call]** *hyphens, Glover conj.*
22 s.d. **Pointing . . . hand.]** *ed. (after Wilson)*
23 s.d. **Reading the title.]** *Alexander*
25 **it]** *Steevens;* it, *F1*
26 **dolphin]** *Theobald;* Dolphin *F1 (it is just possible that the reference is to the French Dauphin)*
26 **'Fore]** *Capell;* fore *F1*

41 **Lustick]** *F3;* Lustique *F1*
43 **coranto]** *Rowe (subs.);* Carranto *F1*
44 **Mort du vinaigre]** *Rowe;* Mor du vinager *F1*
45 **'Fore]** *Pope;* Fore *F1*
57 **mistress]** *Rowe;* Mistris; *F1*
60 **boys']** *Capell;* boyes *F1*
63–4 **Gentlemen . . . health.]** *as verse, Capell (after Theobald); as prose, F1*
70 **choose; . . . refused,]** *Rann;* choose, . . . refused; *F1*
75 **imperial Love]** *Pope;* imperial loue *F1;* imperiall Ioue *F2;* impartiall Iove *F3*
76 **s.d. She . . . Lord.]** *placed as in Wilson; after l. 62, F1*
78–9 **I . . . life.]** *as prose, Pope; as verse. F1*
80, 89, 96 **s.dd. To a second Lord., etc.]** *Capell*
84 **better,]** *Rowe;* better *F1*
94 **her]** *F2;* heere *F1*
96 **s.p. Hel.]** *F3;* La. *F1*
102 **s.d. To Bertram.]** *Rowe*
125 **place when]** *Thirlby conj.;* place, whence *F1*
128–9 **alone . . . name;]** *Capell (subs.);* a lone, / Is good without a name? *F1*
130 **it is]** *F2;* is is *F1*
133, 134 **honor's]** *Rowe;* honours *F1*
137 **word's]** *F2;* words, *F1*
138 **grave]** *Knight (after Steevens);* graue: *F1*
140–1 **tomb . . . indeed.]** *Theobald;* Tombe. . . . indeed, *F1*
168 **eyes.]** *Rowe;* eies, *F1*
175 **counterpoise— . . . estate]** *ed. (after Globe);* counterpoize: . . . estate, *F1*
179 **now-born]** *Rowe;* now borne *F1*
201 **ordinaries,]** *F3 (subs.);* ordinaries: *F1*
213 **hen!]** *F3 (subs.);* hen, *F1*
249 **dost]** *Rowe;* dooest *F1*
267 **s.p. Ber.]** *Rowe;* Ros. *F1 (throughout rest of scene)*
268 **sweet heart]** *F4;* sweet-heart *F1*
280 **kicky-wicky]** *hyphen, Theobald;* kicksie wicksie *F2*
283 **regions!]** *Capell;* Regions, *F1*
292 **detested]** *Rowe;* detected *F1*
294 **advise]** *F3;* aduice *F1;* advize *F2*
300 **s.d. Exeunt.]** *Rowe;* Exit *F1*

II.iv

II.iv] *Capell*
Location: *Pope, Capell*
16 **fortunes]** *Heath conj.;* fortune *F1*
33 **s.d. Parolles nods.]** *Sisson*
34 **s.d. Parolles . . . head.]** *Sisson*
35 **The]** *Rowe;* Clo. The *F1 (repeated s.p.)*
56 **you. Come]** *Theobald;* you come *F1*
56 **s.d. Exeunt.]** *Pope;* Exit *F1*

II.v

II.v] *Capell*
Location: *Pope, Capell*
15 **s.d. To Bertram.]** *Capell*
20 **s.d. Aside to Parolles.]** *Rowe*
27 **End]** *Collier MS;* And *F1*
28 **traveller]** *F3;* Trauailer *F1*
29 **one]** *Rowe;* on *F1*
31 **heard]** *F2;* hard *F1*
48 **s.d. Exit.]** *Rowe*
69 **s.d. Giving a letter.]** *Rowe*
89 **Ber. Where . . . Farewell.]** *Theobald conj.;* Where are my other men? Monsieur, farwell. *F1 (continued to Helena)*
89 **s.d. Exit Helena.]** *Theobald conj., after F1* Exit *following a line assigned to Helena (see preceding note)*
90 **Go]** *Theobald conj.;* Ber. Go *F1*
92 **s.d. Exeunt.]** *Rowe*

III.i

III.i] *Rowe;* Actus Tertius. *F1*
Location: *Pope, Capell*
o.s.d. **French Lords]** *Rowe;* Frenchmen *F1*
9 **s.p. 2. Lord.]** *Rowe;* French E. *F1*
12 **council]** *F3;* Counsaile *F1*
13 **self-unable]** *hyphen, F4*
17 **s.p. 1. Lord.]** *Cambridge;* Fren. G. *F1*
23 **to th']** *F2* (to the); to'th the *F1*
23 **s.d. Exeunt.]** *Rowe*

III.ii

III.ii] *Pope*
Location: *Pope, Capell*
9 **sold]** *F3;* hold *F1*
10 **s.p. Count.]** *Rowe;* Lad. *F1 (or* La. *throughout rest of scene, except* Old. La., *l. 64)*
11 **s.d. Opening a letter.]** *Capell*
13 **ling]** *F2;* Lings *F1*
18 **E'en]** *Theobald;* In *F1*
19 **s.p., s.d. Count. Reads]** *Rowe*
44 **s.d. Exit.]** *Capell*
44 **s.d. the French Lords]** *Neilson (subs.)*
45, 73, 77, 84, 86, 89 **s.pp. 2. Lord.]** *Kittredge;* French E. *or* Fren. E. *F1*
47, 52, 69, 70, 95 **s.pp. 1. Lord.]** *Kittredge;* French G. *or* Fren. G. *F1*
48 **patience.]** *F3 (subs.);* patience, *F1*
57 **s.d. Reads.]** *Capell*
62 **s.p. 1. Lord.]** *Kittredge;* 1. G. *F1*
65 **engrossest]** *F4;* engrossest, *F1*
74 **s.d. Reads.]** *Rowe (subs.)*
74–5 **"Till . . . France."]** *as prose, Capell; as verse, F1*
77–8 **'Tis . . . to.]** *as verse, ed.; as prose. F1*
84–5 **A . . . known.]** *as verse, Pope; as prose, F1*
88 **well-derived]** *hyphen, Pope*
89–96 **Indeed . . . affairs.]** *as verse, Capell; as prose, F1*
90 **that]** *Rowe;* that, *F1*
98 **s.d. with Lords]** *Neilson (after Rowe)*
117 **ravin]** *Capell;* rauine *F1*
126 **angels]** *F2;* Angles *F1*

III.iii

III.iii] *Capell*
Location: *Capell (after Pope, Theobald)*

III.iv

III.iv] *Capell*
Location: *Pope, Capell*
1 **s.p. Count.]** *Rowe;* La. *F1 (throughout scene)*
4 **s.p., s.d. Stew. Reads]** *Collier (after Capell)*
7 **have]** *F2;* hane *F1*
10 **peace, whilst]** *F3;* peace. Whilst *F1*
18 **s.p. Count.]** *Capell*

III.v

III.v] *Capell*
Location: *Capell (after Pope)*
o.s.d. **Diana]** *Rowe*
1–15 **Nay . . . companion.]** *as prose, Pope; as irregular verse, F1*
7 **s.d. Tucket.]** *Capell*
8 **way.]** ways *may be the reading of some copies of F1, but other copies clearly read* way:
21 **is,]** *Rowe;* is *F1*
29 **s.d. habited . . . pilgrim]** *Capell (after Rowe)*
33 **are]** are you *F2*
34 **le]** *F3;* la *F1*
66 **warr'nt]** *ed. (after Globe);* write *F1*
76 **Antonio]** *F2;* Anthonio *F1*
82 **Yond's]** *Rowe;* yonds *F1*
92 **s.d. Exeunt . . . army.]** *Rowe (subs.);* Exit. *F1*

III.vi

III.vi] *Capell*
Location: *Capell (subs.)*
o.s.d. **and . . . Lords]** *Rowe;* and the Frenchmen, as at first *F1*
1, 5, 7, 41, 85 **s.pp. 2. Lord.]** *Capell;* Cap. E. *F1*
3, 13, 19, 46, 51, 90 **s.pp. 1. Lord.]** *Capell;* Cap. G. *F1*
6 **Do . . . him?]** *as prose, Pope; as verse, F1*
22 **s.p. 2. Lord.]** *Cambridge;* C. E. *F1*
34 **s.p. 1. Lord.]** *Cambridge (Rowe in error);* Cap. G. *F1*
36 **his]** *Rowe;* this *F1*
37 **metal]** *F4;* mettle *F1*
37 **ore]** *Theobald* (oar); ours *F1*
39 **inclining]** *F2;* inelining *F1 (?)*
48 **command—]** *Rowe (subs.);* command, *F1*
82–3 **I . . . Farewell.]** *as prose, Pope; as verse, F1*
97, 107 **s.pp. 2. Lord.]** *Rowe;* Cap. E. *F1*
102 **s.p. 1. Lord.]** *Rowe;* Cap. G. *F1*
109 **s.p. 2. Lord.]** *Rowe;* Cap. G. *F1*
109 **s.d. Exit.]** *Theobald*
111, 117 **s.pp. 1. Lord.]** *Rowe;* Cap. E. *F1*

III.vii

III.vii] *Capell*
Location: *Theobald*
19 **Resolv'd]** *Collier (Egerton MS);* Resolue *F1*
34 **After,]** *Hunter;* after *F1;* after this *F2*
41 **steads]** *F4;* steeds *F1*
48 **s.d. Exeunt.]** *Rowe*

IV.i

IV.i] *Rowe;* Actus Quartus. *F1*
Location: *Capell*
o.s.d. **Second French Lord]** *Cambridge;* one of the Frenchmen *F1*
1 **s.p. 2. Lord.]** *Cambridge;* 1. Lord E. *F1*
7 **captain]** *F3;* Captaiue *F1*
8, 11, etc. **s.pp. 2. Lord.]** *Cambridge;* Lor. E., Lo. E., *or* L. E. *F1*
19 **choughs']** *Dyce;* Choughs *F1;* Chough's *F3*
23 **s.d. They stand aside.]** *Collier (subs.)*
32 **s.d. Aside.]** *Rowe*
42 **Bajazeth's]** *F2 (subs.);* Baiazeths *F1*
44, 48, etc. **s.dd. Aside.]** *Pope*
61, 64 **enemy's]** *Malone;* enemies *F1*
67 **s.d. They seize him.]** *Hunter (after Rowe)*
67 **s.d. They blindfold him.]** *Hunter (after Rowe)*
68 **s.p. 1. Sold. as Interpreter.]** *Kittredge (after Capell);* Inter. *F1*
69 **Muskos']** *Capell;* Muskos *F1*
88 **art]** *F3;* are *F1*
88 **s.d. with Parolles guarded]** *Capell*
91, 94 **s.pp. 2. Sold.]** *Capell;* Sol. *F1*
95 **s.d. Exeunt.]** *Rowe;* Exit *F1*

IV.ii

IV.ii] *Pope*
Location: *Capell, Theobald*
6 **monument.]** *F2 (subs.);* monument *F1*
28, 29 **Him . . . Him]** *Neilson;* him . . . him *F1*
32 **holy-cruel]** *hyphen, Theobald*
38 **make . . . scarre]** *so F1; no satisfactory explanation or emendation has been offered; Daniel's reading* may rope 's in such a snare *is perhaps the best*
42 **'longing]** *Rowe;* longing *F1*
57 **maiden bed]** *Theobald;* maiden-bed *F1*
66 **s.d. Exit.]** *F2*

IV.iii

IV.iii] *Pope*
Location: *Capell (after Theobald)*
o.s.d. **Lords]** *Rowe;* Captaines *F1*
1, 6, etc. (except ll. 82, 125) **s.pp. 1. Lord.]** *Rowe;* Cap. G. *F1*
2 **letter?]** *Rowe;* letter. *F1*
3, 8, etc. (except ll. 315, 317) **s.pp. 2. Lord.]** *Rowe;* Cap. E. *F1*
19 **rebellion!]** *Hanmer (after Rowe);* rebellion *F1*
24–5 **nobility, . . . stream]** *Theobald;* nobility . . . streame, *F1*
32 **anatomiz'd]** *Rowe;* anathomiz'd *F1*
76 **s.p. Mess.]** *Neilson;* Ser. *F1*
82 **s.p. 1. Lord.]** *Rowe;* Ber. *F1;* Cap. G. *F3*
91 **effected]** *F3;* affected *F1*
99 **h'as]** *Rowe;* ha's *F1*
101 **h'as]** *Rowe;* ha's *F1*
102 **s.d. Exeunt Soldiers.]** *Capell (after* forth, *l. 101); placed by ed.*
115 **s.d. Soldiers and]** *Capell (subs.)*
115 **s.d. First Soldier as]** *Capell (subs.)*
118 **Hush, hush!]** *assigned to 1. Lord, Walker conj.; continued to Bertram, F1*

125 s.p. **1. Lord.**] *Rowe*; Cap. *F1*
129, 158, 175, 211 s.dd. **Reads.**] *Cambridge (after Capell)*
138 **All's . . . him.**] *assigned to Bertram, Capell; continued to Parolles, F1*
196 **lordship**] *Pope*; Lord *F1*
223 s.d. **Reads the letter.**] *Rowe (subs.)*; Let. *F1*
236 **armipotent**] *Capell*; army-potent *F1*
239 **the**] *F3*; your *F1*
266 **h'as**] *Rowe*; ha's *F1*
278 **cardecue**] *F2*; Cardceue *F1*
298 s.d. **Aside.**] *Rowe*
312 s.d. **Unblinding him.**] *Rowe*
315, 317 s.pp. **2. Lord.**] *Rowe*; Lo. E. *F1*
322 s.d. **Bertram and Lords**] *Capell*
329 s.d. **with Soldiers**] *Cambridge*

IV.iv

IV.iv] *Capell*
Location: *Pope*
3 **'fore**] *F2 (subs.)*; for *F1*
9 **Marsellis**] *F2*; Marcellae *F1*
16 **you**] *F4*; your *F1*
35 **fine's**] *Theobald*; fines *F1*

IV.v

IV.v] *Capell*
Location: *Pope, Capell*
8 s.p. **Count.**] *Rowe*; La. *F1 (or* Lady. *throughout scene)*
21 **grass**] *Rowe*; grace *F1*
39 **name**] *Rowe*; maine *F1*
45 **of**] *F3*; off *F1*
80 **Marsellis**] *F2*; Marcellus *F1*
84 **It**] *F3*; Ir *F1*
99–100 **A . . . that.**] *as prose, Pope; as verse, F1*
102–3 **Let . . . soldier.**] *as prose, Pope; as verse, F1*

V.i

V.i] *Rowe*; Actus Quintus. *F1*
Location: *Capell*
6 s.d. **Enter . . . astringer.**] *ed. (from F3 s.d.* Enter a Gentleman a stranger.); Enter a gentle Astringer. *F1 (after line 6; placed as in Kittredge)*
38 s.d. **Exeunt.**] *F2*

V.ii

V.ii] *Pope*
Location: *Pope, Cambridge*
1 **Master**] *Neilson*; M^r *F1*
8 **allow**] *F2*; alow *F1*
19 **Here**] *Theobald*; *Clo.* Heere *F1 (repeated s.p.)*
20 **musk-cat**] *Theobald*; Muscat *F1*
25 **similes**] *Theobald*; smiles *F1*
25 s.d. **Exit.**] *Capell*
32 **her**] *F2*
40 **"word"**] *quotes, Cambridge*
44 **in sooth**] *Johnson*; insooth *F1*
48 **Dost**] *Rowe*; doest *F1*
51 s.d. **Trumpets sound.**] *Theobald (subs.)*
51 **coming,**] *Rowe*; comming *F1*
55 s.d. **Exeunt.**] *Rowe*

V.iii

V.iii] *Pope*
Location: *Capell (subs.)*
o.s.d. **Countess**] *Rowe*
4 s.p. **Count.**] *Rowe*; Old La. *F1 (throughout scene, except l. 195)*
25 **relics**] *F3*; reliques *F1*
27 s.d. **Exit.**] *Capell*
36 **high-repented**] *hyphen, Pope*
44 **liege.**] *Rowe*; Liege, *F1*
54 **lov'd,**] *F2*; lou'd; *F1*
58–9 **carried, . . . sender**] *Theobald*; carried . . . sender, *F1*
71 s.p. **Count.**] *Theobald; lines continued to the King, F1*
72 **meet, . . . nature,**] *Rowe*; meete in me, O Nature *F1*
76 s.d. **Bertram . . . ring.**] *Hanmer*
101 **Plutus**] *Rowe*; Platus *F1*
113 **falsely,**] *Rowe*; falsely: *F1*
114 **conjectural**] *F2*; connecturall *F1*
115 **out.**] *F4 (subs.)*; out, *F1*
116–7 **inhuman— . . . not:**] *Rowe (subs.)*; inhumane, . . . not, *F1*
120 s.d. **Guards seize Bertram.**] *Rowe*
122 **tax**] *F2*; taze *F1*
127 s.d. **Exit guarded.**] *Rowe*
127 s.d. **the astringer**] *ed. (see V.i.6 s.d.)*
139 s.p., s.d. **King. Reads**] *Rowe*
143 **honor's**] *Rowe*; honors *F1*
148 **toll**] *Rowe*; toule *F1*
151 **discov'ry.**] *Rowe*; discou'rie, *F1*
152 s.d. **Exeunt some Attendants.**] *Capell*
154 s.d. **guarded**] *Capell; s.d. placed as in Capell; after l. 152, F1*
155 **sith**] *Dyce*; sir *F1*
157 s.d. **Diana**] *Rowe*; Diana, and Parrolles *F1 (Parolles is later entered by F1 at l. 230)*
183 **them; fairer**] *Theobald conj.*; them fairer: *F1*
204 s.d. **Exit an Attendant.**] *Dyce*
204 s.p. **Ber.**] *Rowe*; Ros. *F1 (throughout rest of scene)*
207 **sickens . . . truth.**] *Hanmer (subs.)*; sickens: . . . truth, *F1*
216 **inf'nite cunning**] *Hunter (after Walker conj.)*; insuite comming *F1*
217 **rate.**] *F3 (subs.)*; rate, *F1*
228 **a-bed**] *Rowe*; a bed *F1*
245 **gentleman**] *Rowe*; Gent. *F1*
249 **knave.**] *Rowe (subs.)*; knaue, *F1*
259 **that,**] *F3*; that *F1*
276 **him.**] *Rowe*; him, *F1*
293 s.d. **Pointing to Lafew.**] *Rowe*
295 s.d. **Exit Widow.**] *Pope (after l. 295); placed as in Craig*
313 **are**] *Rowe*; is *F1*
321 s.d. **To Parolles.**] *Rowe*
321 **Good . . . handkercher.**] *as prose, Capell; as verse, F1*
327 s.d. **To Diana.**] *Rowe*
332 **Resolvedly**] *F4*; Resolduedly *F1*

Epilogue

Epilogue] *so titled by Rowe*
1 s.p., s.d. **King. Advancing.**] *Capell (after Pope)*
4 **strife**] *F2*; strift *F1 (a possible form, but not occurring elsewhere in Shakespeare)*
6 s.d. **Exeunt omnes.**] Exeunt omn. / FINIS. *F1*

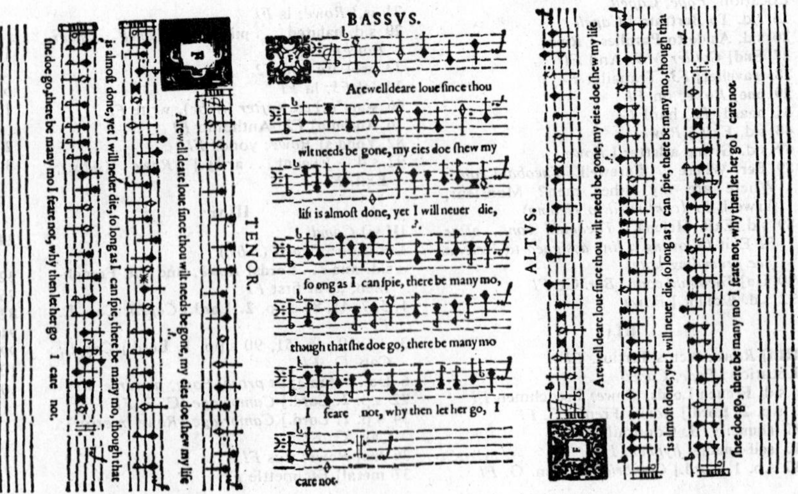

A three-part song. From Robert Jones, *The First Book of Songs and Airs* (1600). This is a three-part (tenor, alto, bass) setting of the first stanza of an old song called "Corydon's Farewell to Phyllis." Sir Toby and Feste alternately sing snatches of the first two stanzas in *Twelfth Night* (II.iii.102–12). Whether they used the present melody (published shortly before the play was first performed) cannot be determined. (*The Folger Shakespeare Library*)

Measure for Measure

MEASURE FOR MEASURE was performed at court on December 26, 1604, and probably was written earlier in that year. It is the last of Shakespeare's comedies. After it come *Othello*, *King Lear*, *Macbeth*, *Antony and Cleopatra*, *Coriolanus*, and *Timon of Athens*: an unbroken progression of tragedies halted only with the composition of *Pericles* in 1607–8. *Pericles* and its three successors among the romances are not tragedies, but neither are they plays which seem to fit into the category of comedy as we understand it in Shakespeare's earlier work. In tone and structure they constitute a race apart: a new and different species of play. *Measure for Measure* stands then as the end of a development, the last word spoken in a particular kind of dramatic investigation which seems to have begun in the early 1590's and which extended itself through some eleven comedies before reaching this terminus. The play itself has some of the qualities of a farewell: a sense of dissatisfaction with its own dramatic mode, concentrated in its notoriously troublesome final scene, and a predominant harshness of tone, a savagery even in its clowning. Frequently, it has been classed as a "dark" comedy, or as a "problem play." Certainly the shadow of the tragedies Shakespeare was to write after *Measure for Measure* seems to hang over it. Much of the action takes place in a prison, and the comedy as a whole is obsessed with the idea of death.

Measure for Measure is the only one of Shakespeare's twelve comedies which can be said to have aroused as much disagreement over interpretation as any of the great tragedies. The language of the play is particularly rich in religious imagery and reference and, of the major characters, one makes her first appearance as a novice in a convent, while another spends most of his time acting the part of a holy friar. Ideas of Christian mercy, atonement, chastity, and sin are constantly invoked. A passage from Christ's Sermon on the Mount in Matthew's gospel seems to underlie, not simply Shakespeare's shaping of the Angelo story, but the entire play: "Judge not, that ye be not judged. For with what judgment ye judge, ye shall be judged: and with what measure ye mete, it shall be measured unto you again" (Geneva). Not surprisingly, attempts have sometimes been made to see *Measure for Measure* as a Christian allegory. The Duke takes his role as the deputy of God on earth, a prince bearing the sword of heaven, with the utmost seriousness, but not even he goes as far as those commentators who have insisted upon identifying him quite literally with Christ. This theory, taken to its logical extreme, produces readings of the play in which Isabella comes to represent Man's Soul (or else the Church), with Lucio functioning as a rather shabby Satan. On the whole, doctrinaire Christian interpretations of this kind are unactable without drastic cutting and distortion of individual roles. More important, they have a way of reducing one of Shakespeare's most profound and disturbing plays to a collection of pious and undramatic platitudes.

The story of the corrupt governor who perverts justice in order to gratify his own lust, the central plot element in *Measure for Measure*, exists in a great many versions and in a variety of European languages. Shakespeare undoubtedly knew the story of Juriste, Epitia, and her brother Vico as told by Cinthio in his prose collection *Hecatommithi* (1565). Cinthio also completed a dramatic version of the story, a tragicomedy called *Epitia* after its heroine, published in Italy in 1583. Shakespeare may have seen it. The most important influence on *Measure for Measure*, however, was undoubtedly the English *Promos and Cassandra* (1578), a two-part play by George Whetstone. Whetstone himself drew upon Cinthio's *novella*, and possibly upon a sixteenth-century Latin play, *Philanira*. As in all other known versions before Shakespeare, Cassandra, the Isabella character, does in fact sleep with the unjust judge in order to save the life of her brother. (In some stories it is her husband who is in danger.) There is no real equivalent for Shakespeare's disguised Duke, although Whetstone's plot does contain a virtuous king who appears in Part II to redress Cassandra's wrongs. Most important of all, there is no hint of a Mariana. Reparation is made at the end by a marriage between Cassandra and Promos, the man who has treated her so badly.

Whetstone's play raises no problems of interpretation. It is a straightforward moral drama, perfectly summed up by the description provided on the title-page:

> The Right Excellent and famous Historye, of *Promos* and *Cassandra*: Devided into two Commicall Discourses, In the fyrste parte is showne, the unsufferable abuse, of a lewde Magistrate: The vertuous behaviours of a chaste Ladye: the uncontrowled leawdness of a favoured Curtisan. And the undeserved estimation of a pernicious Parasyte. In the second parte is discoursed, the perfect magnanimitye of a noble Kinge, in checking Vice and favouring Vertue: Wherein is showne, the Ruyne and overthrowe, of dishonest practises: with the advauncement of upright dealing.

It is worth noting, in view of the claim still often made for Isabella as an unexamined absolute, a girl who could not possibly have behaved better in an agonizing situation, that Whetstone's Cassandra does sacrifice herself for her brother but is still described as a "chaste Ladye" and her behavior as "vertuous." To say categorically that Shakespeare's heroine ought to have emulated Cassandra (and, for that matter, all her predecessors in the same predicament) by yielding to Angelo, in the knowledge that the sin would be cancelled out by the circumstances of victimization and constraint, would obviously be to create yet another simplification of a decision which Shakespeare presents as complex. Yet the argument that Elizabethans (as opposed to our permissive twentieth-century society) must necessarily have endorsed Isabella's attitude in the prison scene with Claudio because they believed that fornication, on whatever grounds, involved the perdition of the soul, is simply not borne out by *Promos and Cassandra*. Nor, for that matter, is it a view sanctioned by *Measure for Measure*.

Shakespearean comedy is in general deeply distrustful of absolutes, of characters who attempt to guide their lives according to rigid (and usually unexamined) ideals of conduct. *Measure for Measure* is no exception. Angelo's absolute of icy self-control is suspect from the beginning; it is an idea, not a fact, and it gives way entirely as soon as he faces a real temptation. There is an ironic correctness, however, in the fact that it is Isabella who brings him down. She is a kindred spirit, another virtuous absolutist. Like calls to like between them, and it is precisely this affinity which, as he senses himself, makes her so deadly to him: "O cunning enemy, that to catch a saint, / With saints dost bait thy hook" (II.ii.179–80). Beneath the sober and inflexible deportment of the lawgiver lurks a frustrated sensualist. Beneath the habit of the nun there is a narrow-minded but passionate girl afflicted with an irrational terror of sex which she has never admitted to herself. In collision over Claudio's fate, these two absolutists elicit from each other the unacknowledged and destructive aspects of their respective personalities. Angelo plunges into depravity, Isabella merely into hysteria and intolerance.

In the course of the play both undergo a painful process of education. By the end, Angelo stands humiliated and exposed before everyone: convicted of hypocrisy, avarice, lust, and a criminal perversion of justice. His only wish is for death. Isabella, the girl who could not bring herself even to name her brother's sin directly in her initial interview with Angelo, is brought to the point of urging another woman to behave like Juliet, and also consents to make, in public, a false declaration of her own loss of virginity. The Isabella who kneels beside Mariana in the final scene to beg for the life of Angelo is a different person from the chilly maiden who had to be coaxed by Lucio into pleading her brother's cause with any vigor, or from the terrified virgin who turned on Claudio like a Fury when he ventured to suggest that death might be worse than an enforced loss of chastity. Like Angelo, she has arrived at a new and juster knowledge of herself and also, by implication, of a world of compromise and imperfection which has, at least to some extent, to be accepted on its own terms.

Society in Vienna is demonstrably corrupt, but energetic. It looks, in fact, all too familiar: a recognizable image of almost any big city. When Angelo and his partner Escalus, as justices, try to set it right they become enmeshed in a web of detail. The wrong (if there was one) done to Elbow's wife cannot be disentangled from two stewed prunes—the others having been eaten—in a threepenny fruit-dish which was not china but was a good dish all the same. Justice as an abstract concept, which is how Angelo sees it, wants nothing to do with an inn-room called the Bunch of Grapes, with its low chair and its fire in winter, nor with Master Caper's four suits of peach-colored satin, as yet unpaid for, nor with young Master Rash and his commodity of brown paper and old ginger. Yet it is only by entering into this concrete world of individualized instances, of stubborn particularity, that anything like justice can be done. Angelo soon becomes exasperated when asked to make sense of the Froth/Elbow/Pompey imbroglio, and leaves the court, "hoping you'll find good cause to whip them all." It is not a very constructive approach. His far more diffident colleague Escalus, left alone to make sense of the matter, is patient and intuitive. The sheer stupidity of Constable Elbow makes a conviction impossible (much as it did in the analogous case of Mistress Quickly, Falstaff, and the Lord Chief Justice in *2 Henry IV*), but Escalus does reach the bottom of the matter. He has to turn Pompey loose, for lack of evidence, with nothing more than a warning, but he knows how to deal with him on the next encounter, and he has uncovered at least one civic abuse, in the form of those householders who pay Elbow to do their job for them, which can be set right.

Vienna is certainly in need of more magistrates like Escalus. What it emphatically does not require are draconic, inhuman laws of the kind that Angelo, with the Duke's sanction, attempts to enforce. The view that the Duke is a character who exists on a plane different from that of everyone else in the play, a personification of Christian Providence and not really a human being, is not easy to sustain from the text. It becomes particularly implausible in the theatre. What an audience actually sees is a man who has delivered up his authority to another man—and a man he has reason to suspect—in order that this surrogate should bear the opprobrium of reactivating certain harsh statutes which the Duke himself has let slip. He is a false friar, not a real one, but this does not prevent him from playing upon the credulity of his victims and hearing confession. He also tends to play upon people's emotions, displaying a kind of scientific curiosity as to how they will behave under stress. He even devises special tests for them in which pressure can be applied to points he knows, or guesses, are weak. So, he torments Isabella by withholding from her the information that her brother is really alive. Most baffling of all, he carefully arranges a bed-trick, the substitution of Mariana for Isabella, which is not only a sin in the eyes of the Church; in terms of Elizabethan common law it represents a union considerably more dubious (even without taking into account the fraud involved) than the *de praesenti* contract which allows Claudio to claim perfectly correctly, in secular terms, that Juliet "is fast my wife" (I.ii.147).

If the Duke is an image of Providence, there would seem to be chaos in heaven. Certainly, error and miscalculation are rife in his plot. In the second scene of Act IV, he talks to the Provost in terms of complete confidence about Claudio's pardon: "As near the dawning, Provost, as it is, / You shall hear more ere morning" (94–95). While the Provost reads Angelo's message, the Duke indulges in some rather complacent rhyming couplets: "This is his pardon, purchas'd by such sin / For which the pardoner himself is in" (108–9). Angelo has not, however, sent a pardon, only a reaffirmation of the original order for Claudio's execution. Providence, if that is what the Duke is, finds itself at this juncture seriously embarrassed. Clutching at straws, he decides that the long-term prisoner Barnardine must die in place of Claudio. The trouble with this is that Barnardine, understandably enough, happens not to like the idea. He sees no reason why he should suddenly go to the block at a moment convenient for the Duke's purposes, and says so. Indeed, like Juliet in an earlier scene, he interrupts the Duke in mid-sentence, then turns on his heel and departs. It is the Provost who finds a solution to the dilemma by way of the conveniently dead pirate Ragozine.

Like Angelo and Isabella, the Duke is a virtuous absolutist. He is in fact a kind of comic dramatist: a man trying to impose the order of art upon a reality which stubbornly resists such schematization. As such, he is continually being surprised by the unpredictability, not to mention rank insubordination, of his elected cast of characters. Angelo and Isabella, Barnardine, Juliet and Claudio get out of control; they do things that are not in their parts as conceived by the Duke and, as they do so, they force upon him a series of hasty rearrangements and patchings: rewritings of the script characterized by their makeshift quality. Reality in Vienna resists patterning. It can and should be cleaned up a bit, as Escalus tries to do, but essentially it remains its own vigorous, untidy self. Barnardine refuses to die at the moment required by the scenario. Claudio is won over by the rhetorical persuasion of the Duke's speech, "Be absolute for death" (III.i.5–41) but soon after is fighting for life on any terms as though he had never spoken to the friar. Angelo promises one thing and then, unexpectedly, tries to write his own fourth act. Moreover, there is one character for whom there is no place in the design as the Duke sees it, but who nonetheless refuses to get off the stage. Lucio does nothing at all for the Duke's godlike detachment, his pretense of being above ordinary human emotions and responses. He clings like a burr, breathing into the ear of the supposed friar all the scandal that this somewhat irresponsible disguise has made possible. In the final scene, where the Duke's role as a manipulator of action is most apparent, Lucio threatens continually to divert or interrupt the unfolding of the plot. He has to be shouted down before the scene can proceed as planned. With all his faults, he stands here as a man instinctively opposed to the artificial ordering of a dramatist duke. In his presence, the resolution imposed upon the comedy in its last moments looks even odder and more perfunctory than it might otherwise have done.

The long and notoriously difficult last scene of *Measure for Measure* seems to offer a strong hint as to why this was the last comedy Shakespeare ever wrote. As a comic dramatist, remaking reality in the arbitrary image of art, conducting events towards the happy ending required by this particular form, the Duke suggests an obvious parallel with Shakespeare himself. There is something forced and blatantly fictional about the Duke's ultimate disposition of people and events—and so there is about Shakespeare's. The Duke refuses to admit failure, but Shakespeare seems perversely to stress the hollowness, in a sense the falsehood, of the happy ending of this comedy. He suddenly imposes upon a play which hitherto has probed uncomfortably deep into the dark places of society and the human mind, which has been essentially realistic, an ending which is that of fairy-tale: conventional, suspect in its very tidiness, full of pyschological gaps and illogicalities.

There is, after all, nothing to prepare one for a marriage between the Duke and Isabella. There have been no love passages of even the shyest and most inarticulate kind between them. She has never expressed any dissatisfaction with her original choice of a religious life, nor has the Duke retracted his statement at the beginning of the play that he, personally, is impervious to love: "Believe not that the dribbling dart of love / Can pierce a complete bosom" (I.iii.2–3). When he abruptly asks her to "be mine" (characteristically choosing the worst possible moment to do so, when Isabella is wholly taken up with Claudio, restored to her beyond hope) and when he tells her, "I have a motion much imports your good," what seems to confront us is not an emotional reality, but simply an obeisance to the laws of comic form. It is in effect an outbreak of that pairing-off disease so prevalent in the fifth acts of Elizabethan comedy which here openly declares itself as such. The situation is not made more credible by the fact that, even as Angelo has uttered no word of love or acceptance to the faithful Mariana, so Isabella says nothing whatever in response to the Duke's proposal of marriage. Like the theatre audience, presumably, she is dumb with surprise.

Almost all of Shakespeare's comedies before *Measure for Measure* end with the formation of what Northrop Frye has called a "new society." This society is never flawless, but it is based upon tolerance and self-knowledge and it faces the future with optimism. In the dance at the end of *As You Like It* or *Much Ado about Nothing*, in the blessing of the marriage beds in *A Midsummer Night's Dream*, or the last of the entertainments in *Love's Labor's Lost*—that dialogue between the Owl and the Cuckoo where everyone, at last, has learned to listen courteously—we see the play projecting itself into the future, beyond the formal limits of its fifth act. There is continuity and promise, not simply arbitrary resolution. *Measure for Measure*, by contrast, does not really create anything that can be understood as a new society. Of the three marriages set up in its final moments, only the previous bond between Claudio and Juliet has any reality for us. The other two are ciphers. Most important of all, the play has admitted in its fifth act that it is only a play, a false geometry.

Measure for Measure departs from the norm of Shakespearean comedy in another important way. Most of its predecessors had been structured upon the idea of two contrasted localities of which one was heightened and more extraordinary than the other. The shape of the comedy was dictated by a journey from one realm into the other with, usually, a return to the normal world either implied or actually accomplished at the end. Almost all of *Measure for Measure*, however, takes place in Vienna: a city which is an image of the ordinary, the sordidly everyday. There is only one other place in the comedy. With its music and its gentle melancholy, its sense of isolation from an urban society which has passed it by, Mariana's moated grange seems to stand in the same relation to Vienna as Belmont to Venice, the wood to Duke Theseus' Athens, or Arden to the court of Duke Frederick. The great difference lies in the fact that the grange is not at all a place where people come and are transformed. It is a sealed-off enclosure, consciously thin in texture: literary and artificial. Mariana is taken away from it and transported to Vienna, a world to which she does not belong. A kind of fairy-tale princess, the mechanism of a happy ending unlikely in more realistic terms, she is made to take Isabella's place in Angelo's bed—an imaginary character substituting for a real one—and then to force a resolution which is contradictory and psychologically improbable, no matter how gratifying it may be in terms of the symmetry of plot.

Mariana is the only absolutist character in the play who escapes criticism. Her undeviating single-mindedness, the obsessive emotionalism which Tennyson explored so brilliantly in "Mariana" and "Mariana in the South" are, in Shakespeare, simply the servants of plot. Because of Mariana, there is a happy ending. It is an ending, however, which seems to create as many problems as it solves. Isabella, kneeling beside Mariana at the close, begs for Angelo's life on the grounds that

> My brother had but justice,
> In that he did the thing for which he died;
> For Angelo,
> His act did not o'ertake his bad intent,
> And must be buried but as an intent
> That perish'd by the way. (V.i.448–53)

It is hard to make sense of this argument. At best, it is special pleading of an illogical kind. That Angelo has not slept with Isabella, as he intended, is true. He has, however, slept with Mariana outside the bonds of holy matrimony, even as Claudio did with Juliet. How, then, can Isabella claim that her brother "had but justice" when he has died (as she thinks) for exactly the same sin, fornication on a pre-contract, committed by Angelo with Mariana?

There seems to be a desperate, and surely deliberate, confusion of values in *Measure for Measure*. Isabella perhaps speaks more truly than she knows when she says, in Act II, that the laws of heaven often seem oddly incompatible with those of society: "'Tis set down so in heaven, but not in earth" (II.iv.50). There is in this play an unresolved conflict between religious and secular law, between absolutes and anarchy, between a necessary but sterile order and a vigorous but suspect world of self-gratification and individualism. There is also a clash between fairy-tale and realism, the simplifications of plot and the horrifying complexities of character. In the midst of all this, Mariana seems like an exile from a land of fiction. Her moated grange is like Isabella's nunnery, or Angelo's impossible court of justice, in that it too deals with absolutes: with clear-cut black and white. It will not bear close examination of the kind urged elsewhere in the play. As for the Duke, an absolutist of an artistic as opposed to a moral, religious, or emotional kind, he appears to embody some of the problems of a Shakespeare now seemingly disillusioned with that art of comedy which, in the past, had served him so well.

Anne Barton

Pressing to death. From the title-page of the anonymous *The Life and Death of Griffin Flood Informer* (1623). This barbarous form of execution was resorted to for felons who refused to plead and was practiced as late as 1736. The so-called Press-yard in old Newgate Prison was the original scene of such tortures. With this woodcut before us, we can better understand the full force of Lucio's anguished protest when he is ordered by the Duke to marry a prostitute whom he has got with child: "Marrying a punk, my lord, is pressing to death, whipping, and hanging" (*Measure for Measure*, V.i.522–23). (*The Folger Shakespeare Library*)

Measure for Measure

The Names of All the Actors

Vincentio, *the Duke*
Angelo, *the Deputy*
Escalus, *an ancient lord*
Claudio, *a young gentleman*
Lucio, *a fantastic*
Two other like Gentlemen
Provost
Thomas } *two friars*
Peter }
[Justice]
[Varrius]
Elbow, *a simple constable*

Froth, *a foolish gentleman*
[Pompey,] *clown*, [*servant to Mistress Overdone*]
Abhorson, *an executioner*
Barnardine, *a dissolute prisoner*
[Servant]

Isabella, *sister to Claudio*
Mariana, *betrothed to Angelo*
Juliet, *beloved of Claudio*
Francisca, *a nun*
Mistress Overdone, *a bawd*

[Lords, Officers, Citizens, Boy, *and* Attendants]

The Scene: *Vienna* [*and its environs*]

ACT I, Scene I

Enter Duke, Escalus, Lords, [*and* Attendants].

Duke. Escalus.
Escal. My lord.
Duke. Of government the properties to unfold
Would seem in me t' affect speech and discourse,
Since I am put to know that your own science
Exceeds, in that, the lists of all advice
My strength can give you. Then no more remains
But that, to your sufficiency, as your worth is able,
And let them work. The nature of our people,
Our city's institutions, and the terms
For common justice, y' are as pregnant in
As art and practice hath enriched any
That we remember. There is our commission,
From which we would not have you warp. Call hither,
I say, bid come before us Angelo.
[*Exit an Attendant*.]
What figure of us think you he will bear?
For you must know, we have with special soul
Elected him our absence to supply,
Lent him our terror, dress'd him with our love,
And given his deputation all the organs
Of our own pow'r. What think you of it?
Escal. If any in Vienna be of worth
To undergo such ample grace and honor,
It is Lord Angelo.

Enter Angelo.

Duke. Look where he comes.
Ang. Always obedient to your Grace's will,
I come to know your pleasure.
Duke. Angelo:
There is a kind of character in thy life,
That to th' observer doth thy history

Words and passages enclosed in square brackets in the text above are either emendations of the copy-text or additions to it. The Textual Notes immediately following the play cite the earliest authority for every such change or insertion and supply the reading of the copy-text wherever it is emended in this edition.

I.i. Location: Vienna. The Duke's palace.
3. **Of . . . unfold**: to expound the qualities required for governing well.
4. **seem . . . discourse**: i.e. make me appear to be fond of talking for its own sake.
5. **put to know**: forced to recognize. **science**: expert knowledge.
6. **lists**: boundaries. 7. **strength**: capability.
8–9. **But . . . work.** A crux that has inspired many emendations, none satisfactory. To provide a referent for *them*, commentators have explained *sufficiency . . . worth* as "authority . . . qualifications" (or "qualifications . . . authority"), but in fact both words probably mean "qualifications." There is now wide agreement that a lacuna exists after *sufficiency*, or, less probably, after *able*.
9–11. **The nature . . . justice**: i.e. our social, political, and judicial usages. *Terms* probably means "modes of procedure." The Duke shifts in this sentence to the "royal" plural.
11. **pregnant**: ready, i.e. well versed. 12. **art**: study, theory.
14. **warp**: deviate.
16. **What . . . bear**: i.e. how do you think he will represent me as my deputy. The figure is of the royal likeness stamped on wax or metal, to validate a seal or a coin.
17. **soul**: conviction (that the choice is right) (?).
18. **Elected . . . supply**: chosen him to fill my place in my absence.
19. **Lent . . . love**: i.e. bestowed on him the royal attributes that inspire terror and those that inspire love. Cf. the list of the "servants" of kings in *Henry VIII*, V.v.48: "peace, plenty, love, truth, terror."
20. **his deputation**: to him as my deputy. **organs**: instruments.
23. **undergo**: sustain, bear up.
27. **character**: writing, i.e. clear indication.
28–29. **to . . . unfold**: i.e. enables an observer to predict what your future behavior will be. This is Johnson's explanation, strongly supported by *2 Henry IV*, III.i.80–85.

Fully unfold. Thyself and thy belongings
Are not thine own so proper as to waste
Thyself upon thy virtues, they on thee.
Heaven doth with us as we with torches do,
Not light them for themselves; for if our virtues
Did not go forth of us, 'twere all alike
As if we had them not. Spirits are not finely touch'd
But to fine issues; nor Nature never lends
The smallest scruple of her excellence,
But like a thrifty goddess, she determines
Herself the glory of a creditor,
Both thanks and use. But I do bend my speech
To one that can my part in him advertise.
Hold therefore, Angelo:
In our remove be thou at full ourself.
Mortality and mercy in Vienna
Live in thy tongue and heart. Old Escalus,
Though first in question, is thy secondary.
Take thy commission.

Ang. Now, good my lord,
Let there be some more test made of my mettle
Before so noble and so great a figure
Be stamp'd upon it.

Duke. No more evasion.
We have with a leaven'd and prepared choice
Proceeded to you; therefore take your honors.
Our haste from hence is of so quick condition
That it prefers itself, and leaves unquestion'd
Matters of needful value. We shall write to you,
As time and our concernings shall importune,
How it goes with us, and do look to know
What doth befall you here. So fare you well.
To th' hopeful execution do I leave you
Of your commissions.

Ang. Yet give leave, my lord,
That we may bring you something on the way.

Duke. My haste may not admit it,
Nor need you (on mine honor) have to do

With any scruple. Your scope is as mine own,
So to enforce or qualify the laws
As to your soul seems good. Give me your hand,
I'll privily away. I love the people,
But do not like to stage me to their eyes;
Though it do well, I do not relish well
Their loud applause and aves vehement;
Nor do I think the man of safe discretion
That does affect it. Once more fare you well.

Ang. The heavens give safety to your purposes!

Escal. Lead forth and bring you back in happiness!

Duke. I thank you. Fare you well. *Exit.*

Escal. I shall desire you, sir, to give me leave
To have free speech with you; and it concerns me
To look into the bottom of my place.
A pow'r I have, but of what strength and nature
I am not yet instructed.

Ang. 'Tis so with me. Let us withdraw together,
And we may soon our satisfaction have
Touching that point.

Escal. I'll wait upon your honor. *Exeunt.*

Scene II

Enter Lucio *and two other* Gentlemen.

Lucio. If the Duke with the other dukes come not to composition with the King of Hungary, why then all the dukes fall upon the King.

1. Gent. Heaven grant us its peace, but not the King of Hungary's!

2. Gent. Amen.

Lucio. Thou conclud'st like the sanctimonious pirate, that went to sea with the Ten Commandements, but scrap'd one out of the table.

2. Gent. "Thou shalt not steal"?

Lucio. Ay, that he raz'd.

1. Gent. Why, 'twas a commandement to command the captain and all the rest from their functions; they

29. **belongings:** qualities, attributes (the *virtues* of line 31).
30. **proper:** exclusively. **waste:** expend.
34. **all alike:** precisely the same.
35. **finely touch'd:** excellently endowed (with play on testing gold for fineness by means of a touchstone). 36. **issues:** purposes, ends.
37. **scruple:** a very small unit of weight.
38. **determines:** allots (to). 39. **glory:** proud due.
40. **use:** interest.
41. **can . . . advertise:** can instruct that part of me now vested in him, i.e. knows more about how to govern than I can tell him (cf. lines 5–7). *Advertise* is accented on the second syllable.
42. **Hold:** i.e. maintain your worthiness (?) or take this (the document, as in lines 13, 47) (?).
43. **remove:** absence. **at full.** Perhaps with play on *part* in line 41.
44. **Mortality and mercy:** i.e. authority to pronounce sentence of death and freedom to temper justice with mercy. Cf. *terror . . . love* in line 19.
45. **tongue and heart.** With reference to *Mortality* and *mercy* respectively. 46. **first in question:** i.e. first appointed.
48. **mettle.** In Elizabethan English *mettle* and *metal* were variants of the same word, with primary meaning "substance." Here the sense now spelled *metal* carries on the coining imagery of lines 16, 35–36.
51. **leaven'd:** i.e. pervaded by the gradual working of judgment (like the action of yeast in dough).
53. **so quick condition:** so urgent a nature.
54. **prefers:** advances, gives priority to. **unquestion'd:** undiscussed, uninvestigated.
56. **our concernings:** matters of concern to us. **importune:** urge, require. 57. **look to know:** expect to be informed of.
59. **hopeful.** A transferred modifier, rightly describing the Duke's expectations.
61. **bring . . . way:** escort you some distance on your way.

64. **scruple:** misgiving. **scope:** freedom to act; here, breadth of authority (a word that occurs five times in this play).
65. **enforce or qualify:** i.e. apply with greater or lesser severity.
67–72. **I . . . it:** Usually taken to allude to King James's dislike of effusive English crowds. See II.iv.24–30.
68. **stage me:** make public show of myself.
69. **do well:** i.e. show their good will.
70. **aves:** acclamations (Latin *ave*, "hail," connected with acclaim of Caesar). 71. **safe discretion:** sound judgment.
72. **does affect:** is fond of. 73. **give safety to:** protect, safeguard.
77. **free:** frank.
78. **look . . . place:** determine how far my duties and authority extend. 82. **satisfaction:** dispelling of uncertainty.
83. **wait upon:** attend, accompany.

I.ii. Location: A street.
2. **composition:** agreement, treaty.
4. **its.** With the exception of one occurrence in *2 Henry VI* (III.ii.393), this is Shakespeare's earliest recorded use of *its*, in a total of eleven. Elsewhere, save for an occasional appearance of *it* (as in *King Lear*, I.iv.216), he uses *his* as the possessive form of *it*.
7. **sanctimonious.** The earliest example of the modern ironic sense listed in *O.E.D.*; the word's only other occurrence in Shakespeare—*sanctimonious ceremonies* in *The Tempest*, IV.i.16—shows the original straightforward meaning "marked by sanctity."
8. **Commandements.** A variant spelling, perhaps here (as often in verse) quadrisyllabic.
9. **table:** tablet (referring to the tablets of stone on which the Ten Commandments were traditionally represented).
11. **raz'd:** erased, "scrap'd out."
13. **functions:** professional duties. Leisi sees an extended wordplay on *steal/stale* (= urinate), *functions*, and *put forth*.

put forth to steal. There's not a soldier of us all, that in the thanksgiving before meat, do relish the petition well that prays for peace.

2. Gent. I never heard any soldier dislike it.

Lucio. I believe thee; for I think thou never wast where grace was said.

2. Gent. No? a dozen times at least.

1. Gent. What? in metre?

Lucio. In any proportion, or in any language.

1. Gent. I think, or in any religion.

Lucio. Ay, why not? Grace is grace, despite of all controversy; as for example, thou thyself art a wicked villain, despite of all grace.

1. Gent. Well; there went but a pair of shears between us.

Lucio. I grant; as there may between the lists and the velvet. Thou art the list.

1. Gent. And thou the velvet—thou art good velvet; thou'rt a three-pil'd piece, I warrant thee. I had as lief be a list of an English kersey as be pil'd, as thou art pil'd, for a French velvet. Do I speak feelingly now?

Lucio. I think thou dost; and indeed with most painful feeling of thy speech. I will, out of thine own confession, learn to begin thy health; but, whilst I live, forget to drink after thee.

1. Gent. I think I have done myself wrong, have I not?

2. Gent. Yes, that thou hast; whether thou art tainted or free.

Enter Bawd [MISTRESS OVERDONE].

Lucio. Behold, behold, where Madam Mitigation comes!

[*1. Gent.*] I have purchas'd as many diseases under her roof as come to—

2. Gent. To what, I pray?

Lucio. Judge.

2. Gent. To three thousand dolors a year.

1. Gent. Ay, and more.

Lucio. A French crown more.

1. Gent. Thou art always figuring diseases in me; but thou art full of error, I am sound.

Lucio. Nay, not (as one would say) healthy; but so sound as things that are hollow. Thy bones are hollow; impiety has made a feast of thee.

1. Gent. How now, which of your hips has the most profound sciatica?

Mrs. Ov. Well, well; there's one yonder arrested and carried to prison was worth five thousand of you all.

2. Gent. Who's that, I pray thee?

Mrs. Ov. Marry, sir, that's Claudio, Signior Claudio.

1. Gent. Claudio to prison? 'tis not so.

Mrs. Ov. Nay, but I know 'tis so. I saw him arrested; saw him carried away; and which is more, within these three days his head to be chopp'd off.

Lucio. But after all this fooling, I would not have it so. Art thou sure of this?

Mrs. Ov. I am too sure of it; and it is for getting Madam Julietta with child.

Lucio. Believe me, this may be. He promis'd to meet me two hours since, and he was ever precise in promise-keeping.

2. Gent. Besides, you know, it draws something near to the speech we had to such a purpose.

1. Gent. But most of all agreeing with the proclamation.

Lucio. Away! let's go learn the truth of it.

Exit [*with Gentlemen*].

Mrs. Ov. Thus, what with the war, what with the sweat, what with the gallows, and what with poverty, I am custom-shrunk.

Enter Clown [POMPEY].

How now? what's the news with you?

Pom. Yonder man is carried to prison.

Mrs. Ov. Well; what has he done?

Pom. A woman.

Mrs. Ov. But what's his offense?

Pom. Groping for trouts in a peculiar river.

Mrs. Ov. What? is there a maid with child by him?

17. **dislike:** express dislike of. 22. **proportion:** form.
24–26. **Grace . . . grace.** Lucio shifts the sense of *grace* to "God's grace": grace remains grace despite all the debates about its nature—just as, to cite a parallel, in you villainy remains villainy despite the availability of grace.
27. **Well.** Often used to show that note has been taken of an insult; cf. line 60.
27–28. **there . . . us:** we are cut from the same cloth (proverbial).
29. **lists:** selvages, plain strips along the edge (from the basic sense "boundaries" seen in I.i.6).
32. **three-pil'd:** having a pile or nap of triple thickness.
33. **lief:** willingly. **kersey:** plain woollen fabric (named for Kersey in Suffolk, where it was first made). **pil'd.** Lucio plays on *piled*, "napped," and *pilled*, "bald." Loss of hair was an effect of the treatment for syphilis, which was called the "French disease"—hence *French velvet* in line 34.
34. **speak feelingly:** speak to the purpose, i.e. touch the quick; but Lucio quibbles on "speak painfully" (i.e. because his mouth is affected by the lesions of venereal disease).
38. **begin thy health:** begin drinking to your health.
39. **forget . . . thee:** remember not to drink out of your glass.
40. **done myself wrong:** i.e. laid myself open to that.
43. **tainted:** infected (in which case he has "done himself wrong" in a different sense).
44. **Mitigation.** So called because she allays sexual desire.
50. **dolors:** (1) pains; (2) dollars (continental coins).
52. **French crown:** (1) French gold coin; (2) bald head (in consequence of the "French disease").
53. **figuring:** (1) reckoning (with reference to the preceding lines); (2) imagining.
56. **sound:** resounding. **Thy . . . hollow.** Another effect of syphilis.
58. **How now.** Probably addressed to Mrs. Overdone; "How now" is a casual greeting, and sciatica (another supposed effect of venereal disease) is elsewhere associated with bawds.
60. **one yonder:** a man back there (not limited to what is in view).
61. **carried:** conducted.
64. **Marry:** indeed (originally the name of the Virgin Mary used as an oath).
70. **after . . . fooling:** to return to seriousness.
77–78. **draws . . . purpose:** fits fairly closely with the conversation we had about that situation (i.e. the relation between Claudio and Juliet? or the increasing rigor of law enforcement?).
79–80. **proclamation.** Apparently the public announcement of the revived penalty for fornication.
83. **sweat:** sweating sickness, a form of the plague (which had been rampant in 1603 and until the middle of 1604).
84. **custom-shrunk:** short on customers.
86. **Yonder man.** This cannot be anyone but Claudio, since later we hear repeatedly that he is the first and still the only victim of the new dispensation. Mrs. Overdone's ignorance of his arrest (an event which she herself has announced shortly before), together with other obvious discrepancies, has been made the basis of various theories of revision.
87. **done.** Pompey quibbles on the slang sense "copulated" (a sense to which Mrs. Overdone's name is related).
90. **peculiar:** private (i.e. where fishing is against the law).

Pom. No; but there's a woman with maid by him. You have not heard of the proclamation, have you?

Mrs. Ov. What proclamation, man?

Pom. All houses in the suburbs of Vienna must be pluck'd down.

Mrs. Ov. And what shall become of those in the city?

Pom. They shall stand for seed. They had gone down too, but that a wise burgher put in for them.

Mrs. Ov. But shall all our houses of resort in the suburbs be pull'd down?

Pom. To the ground, mistress.

Mrs. Ov. Why, here's a change indeed in the commonwealth! What shall become of me?

Pom. Come; fear not you; good counsellors lack no clients. Though you change your place, you need not change your trade; I'll be your tapster still. Courage! there will be pity taken on you. You that have worn your eyes almost out in the service, you will be consider'd.

Mrs. Ov. What's to do here, Thomas tapster? Let's withdraw.

Pom. Here comes Signior Claudio, led by the Provost to prison; and there's Madam Juliet. *Exeunt.*

Enter PROVOST, CLAUDIO, JULIET, OFFICERS.

Claud. Fellow, why dost thou show me thus to th' world?
Bear me to prison, where I am committed.

Prov. I do it not in evil disposition,
But from Lord Angelo by special charge.

Claud. Thus can the demigod, Authority,
Make us pay down for our offense by weight
The words of heaven: on whom it will, it will;
On whom it will not, so; yet still 'tis just.

[*Enter*] LUCIO *and two* GENTLEMEN.

Lucio. Why, how now, Claudio? whence comes this restraint?

Claud. From too much liberty, my Lucio, liberty:
As surfeit is the father of much fast,
So every scope by the immoderate use
Turns to restraint. Our natures do pursue,
Like rats that ravin down their proper bane,
A thirsty evil, and when we drink we die.

Lucio. If I could speak so wisely under an arrest, I would send for certain of my creditors; and yet, to say the truth, I had as lief have the foppery of freedom as the mortality of imprisonment. What's thy offense, Claudio?

Claud. What but to speak of would offend again.

Lucio. What, is't murder?

Claud. No.

Lucio. Lechery?

Claud. Call it so.

Prov. Away, sir, you must go.

Claud. One word, good friend. Lucio, a word with you.

Lucio. A hundred! if they'll do you any good.
Is lechery so look'd after?

Claud. Thus stands it with me: upon a true contract
I got possession of Julietta's bed.
You know the lady; she is fast my wife,
Save that we do the denunciation lack
Of outward order. This we came not to,
Only for propagation of a dow'r
Remaining in the coffer of her friends,
From whom we thought it meet to hide our love
Till time had made them for us. But it chances
The stealth of our most mutual entertainment
With character too gross is writ on Juliet.

Lucio. With child, perhaps?

Claud. Unhappily, even so.
And the new deputy now for the Duke—
Whether it be the fault and glimpse of newness,
Or whether that the body public be
A horse whereon the governor doth ride,
Who, newly in the seat, that it may know
He can command, lets it straight feel the spur;
Whether the tyranny be in his place,
Or in his eminence that fills it up,
I stagger in—but this new governor

92. **with maid.** Playing on *maid* = young fish (suggested by the trouts of line 90).
95. **houses:** i.e. houses of prostitution. **suburbs.** The site of the London brothels (which were thus beyond the reach of city regulations). 96. **pluck'd:** pulled.
99. **stand for seed:** remain standing to assure the continuance of prostitution (like grain left uncut to provide seed for another season), with a bawdy equivoque.
100. **put . . . them:** intervened in their behalf (?) or made an offer for their purchase (?).
112. **What's to do here:** what to-do is this. **Thomas tapster.** A stock name for a tapster; but Shakespeare may have changed his mind about Pompey's name.
120. **the demigod, Authority.** Reflecting the Elizabethan view of earthly rulers and magistrates as God's vicegerents.
121–22. **pay . . . heaven.** The oddness of *pay down . . . the words of heaven* has provoked various emendations. Johnson conjectured a lacuna between the two lines. If a period is placed after *weight,* lines 120–21 make a complete sentence; *pay down by weight* = pay the precise amount due.
122. **words of heaven.** Explained as a reference to Romans 9:15: "I will have mercy on him to whom I will show mercy" (Geneva).
123. **so:** similarly, i.e. it will not. **still:** always, in every case.
124. **whence . . . restraint.** This is inconsistent with lines 60 ff., where Lucio learns of Claudio's arrest and its cause.
127. **scope:** freedom (see note on I.i.64).
129. **ravin . . . bane]** devour greedily their own special poison (i.e. ratsbane).
130. **A thirsty . . . die.** Rat poison does not kill directly; it makes the rat thirsty, and taking water is fatal. So too much liberty stimulates lust, and the satisfying of lust incurs death.
132. **send . . . creditors:** i.e. take steps to bring about my own arrest.
133. **foppery:** folly.
134. **mortality:** being subject to death (?) or deadliness (?). Most editors from Rowe onward emend to *morality,* "moralizing talk," which provides an apt antithesis to *foppery* in the sense "idle talk." Shakespeare never uses the word *morality* elsewhere, but he does not use *mortality* in the precise sense required here either.
144. **look'd after:** kept watch upon.
145. **a true contract.** Claudio and Juliet have declared themselves husband and wife in the presence of witnesses. Under the common law such a declaration created a valid marriage (*sponsalia per verba de praesenti*), but the church required a religious ceremony before such a marriage could be consummated without incurring a penalty.
147. **fast:** firmly bound (perhaps with reference to making a contract of marriage by handfasting or joining hands).
148. **denunciation:** public announcement.
150. **propagation:** breeding, bringing to birth. Many editors adopt Malone's conjecture *prorogation,* i.e. delay; but figures of breeding and pregnancy are frequent in the play. 151. **friends:** relatives.
153. **made . . . us:** won them to our side.
155. **character:** writing, letters. **gross:** large, obvious.
158. **Whether . . . newness:** i.e. whether it is the sudden brilliance (*glimpse*) of his new honor that is to blame.
162. **straight:** straightway. 163. **in his place:** inherent in his office.
164. **eminence:** distinction, superiority.
165. **stagger in:** am at a loss to decide.

Awakes me all the enrolled penalties
Which have, like unscour'd armor, hung by th' wall
So long that nineteen zodiacs have gone round
And none of them been worn; and for a name
Now puts the drowsy and neglected act
Freshly on me—'tis surely for a name.

Lucio. I warrant it is; and thy head stands so tickle on thy shoulders that a milkmaid, if she be in love, may sigh it off. Send after the Duke, and appeal to him.

Claud. I have done so, but he's not to be found.
I prithee, Lucio, do me this kind service:
This day my sister should the cloister enter,
And there receive her approbation.
Acquaint her with the danger of my state;
Implore her, in my voice, that she make friends
To the strict deputy; bid herself assay him.
I have great hope in that; for in her youth
There is a prone and speechless dialect,
Such as move men; beside, she hath prosperous art
When she will play with reason and discourse,
And well she can persuade.

Lucio. I pray she may; as well for the encouragement of the like, which else would stand under grievous imposition, as for the enjoying of thy life, who I would be sorry should be thus foolishly lost at a game of tick-tack. I'll to her.

Claud. I thank you, good friend Lucio.

Lucio. Within two hours.

Claud. Come, officer, away! *Exeunt.*

Scene [III]

Enter Duke *and* Friar Thomas.

Duke. No; holy father, throw away that thought;
Believe not that the dribbling dart of love
Can pierce a complete bosom. Why I desire thee
To give me secret harbor, hath a purpose
More grave and wrinkled than the aims and ends
Of burning youth.

Fri. T. May your Grace speak of it?

Duke. My holy sir, none better knows than you
How I have ever lov'd the life removed,
And held in idle price to haunt assemblies
Where youth, and cost, witless bravery keeps.
I have deliver'd to Lord Angelo
(A man of stricture and firm abstinence)
My absolute power and place here in Vienna,
And he supposes me travell'd to Poland
(For so I have strew'd it in the common ear,
And so it is receiv'd). Now, pious sir,
You will demand of me why I do this.

Fri. T. Gladly, my lord.

Duke. We have strict statutes and most biting laws
(The needful bits and curbs to headstrong weeds),
Which for this fourteen years we have let slip,
Even like an o'ergrown lion in a cave,
That goes not out to prey. Now, as fond fathers,
Having bound up the threat'ning twigs of birch,
Only to stick it in their children's sight
For terror, not to use, in time the rod
[Becomes] more mock'd than fear'd; so our decrees,
Dead to infliction, to themselves are dead,
And liberty plucks justice by the nose;
The baby beats the nurse, and quite athwart
Goes all decorum.

Fri. T. It rested in your Grace
To unloose this tied-up justice when you pleas'd:
And it in you more dreadful would have seem'd
Than in Lord Angelo.

Duke. I do fear—too dreadful;
Sith 'twas my fault to give the people scope,
'Twould be my tyranny to strike and gall them
For what I bid them do; for we bid this be done,
When evil deeds have their permissive pass,

166. **Awakes me:** awakes (a colloquialism). The figure is continued in *drowsy*, line 170. 167. **unscour'd:** unpolished, i.e. rusty.
168. **zodiacs . . . round:** i.e. years have passed.
169. **worn:** i.e. used (continuing the parallel between penalties and armor; cf. *puts . . . on*, lines 170–71). **for a name:** for the sake of his reputation. 172. **tickle:** unstable, precariously attached.
173–74. **a milkmaid . . . off:** i.e. the merest breath of wind (a lovesick milkmaid's sigh) will blow it off (?). But the combination of *milkmaid* and *head* suggests a common play on *head* = maidenhead (as in IV.ii.5), and the passage may be an elliptical way of saying "a milkmaid, if her virginity were as unstable as your head, would lose it with her first sigh of love." 178. **approbation:** probation, novice's status.
180. **in my voice:** i.e. as persuasively as I would.
181. **assay him:** make trial of him (?) or assail him with words (?). Probably both senses are present: try how he will respond to your urging.
183. **prone:** eager, ready (?) or apt, expressive (?). Some commentators take the word to suggest the prostrate or bowed posture of supplication, but Shakespeare never uses *prone* in the sense of "recumbent."
184. **move.** Plural after a singular noun modified by two adjectives; for another example see III.i.126–27.
187–88. **encouragement . . . like:** giving comfort to offenders like yourself. 188. **which:** who (as often).
188–89. **stand . . . imposition:** be subject to very serious accusation.
190–91. **tick-tack:** a game resembling backgammon, scored by means of pegs set into holes; here, sexual intercourse.

I.iii. **Location:** A friary.
2. **dribbling:** falling too feebly to pierce its mark.
3. **complete:** fully defended (as if in complete armor, hence invulnerable).

5. **wrinkled:** i.e. befitting one of mature years.
8. **removed:** secluded, private. 9. **in idle price:** as of trifling value.
10. **cost:** lavish expenditure. **bravery:** display. Many editors improve the metre by inserting *a* before *witless bravery*. **keeps:** maintains. The verb in *–s* with a plural subject is common in Shakespeare.
12. **stricture:** strictness, keeping a tight rein (on oneself).
15. **strew'd:** scattered (an image from sowing seed). **common:** general. 16. **receiv'd:** accepted, believed.
17. **demand:** ask (without the modern note of peremptoriness).
20. **weeds.** A type of lawlessness, because of their rank growth and resistance to control. Almost all editors, however, find the metaphor too mixed even for Shakespeare, and emend—most often to *steeds* (Theobald), which fits well with *bits and curbs*, but is unlikely to have been mistaken for *weeds* by a compositor. More attractive is *wills* (S. Walker), which with *curb* produces a figure found elsewhere in Shakespeare, e.g. in *The Merchant of Venice*, IV.i.215–17, where *law*, *curb* (verb), and *will* are found in conjunction.
21. **fourteen.** Cf. *nineteen zodiacs* in I.ii.168. The discrepancy could have arisen from a confusion of *xiv* and *xix* in the manuscript. **let slip:** allowed to go lax, i.e. left unapplied.
22. **o'ergrown:** grown too fat, hence inactive.
23. **fond:** foolish, doting.
25. **it:** i.e. the switch made up of the twigs.
28. **Dead . . . dead:** since they are not enforced, are as if non-existent.
29. **liberty:** license. **plucks . . . nose.** An action indicating the highest degree of contempt and defiance.
30. **athwart:** contrary, topsyturvey.
31. **decorum:** appropriateness of behavior.
32. **tied-up:** leashed (but also recalling the bound-up birch twigs).
33. **dreadful:** inspiring a proper terror of punishment (cf. *terror* in line 26 and, as a royal attribute, in I.i.19). 35. **Sith:** since.
36. **strike and gall.** Recalling respectively "twigs of birch" and "bits and curbs" (*gall* = chafe, cause physical irritation).
37. **we . . . done:** i.e. it is tantamount to ordering that a thing be done.

And not the punishment. Therefore indeed, my father,
I have on Angelo impos'd the office,
Who may, in th' ambush of my name, strike home,
And yet my nature never in the fight
To do in slander. And to behold his sway,
I will, as 'twere a brother of your order,
Visit both prince and people; therefore I prithee
Supply me with the habit, and instruct me
How I may formally in person bear
Like a true friar. Moe reasons for this action
At our more leisure shall I render you;
Only, this one: Lord Angelo is precise;
Stands at a guard with envy; scarce confesses
That his blood flows; or that his appetite
Is more to bread than stone: hence shall we see
If power change purpose: what our seemers be.
Exeunt.

Scene [IV]

Enter Isabel *and* Francisca, *a nun.*

Isab. And have you nuns no farther privileges?
Fran. Are not these large enough?
Isab. Yes, truly; I speak not as desiring more,
But rather wishing a more strict restraint
Upon the sisterhood, the votarists of Saint Clare.
Lucio. (*Within.*) Ho! Peace be in this place!
Isab. Who's that which calls?
Fran. It is a man's voice. Gentle Isabella,
Turn you the key, and know his business of him;
You may, I may not; you are yet unsworn.
When you have vow'd, you must not speak with men
But in the presence of the prioress;
Then if you speak, you must not show your face,
Or if you show your face, you must not speak.
He calls again; I pray you answer him. [*Exit.*]
Isab. Peace and prosperity! Who is't that calls?

[*Enter* Lucio.]

Lucio. Hail, virgin, if you be, as those cheek-roses
Proclaim you are no less! Can you so stead me
As bring me to the sight of Isabella,
A novice of this place, and the fair sister
To her unhappy brother Claudio?
Isab. Why "her unhappy brother"? let me ask,
The rather for I now must make you know
I am that Isabella, and his sister.
Lucio. Gentle and fair, your brother kindly greets you.
Not to be weary with you, he's in prison.
Isab. Woe me! for what?
Lucio. For that which, if myself might be his judge,
He should receive his punishment in thanks:
He hath got his friend with child.
Isab. Sir, make me not your story.
Lucio. 'Tis true.
I would not—though 'tis my familiar sin
With maids to seem the lapwing, and to jest,
Tongue far from heart—play with all virgins so.
I hold you as a thing enskied, and sainted,
By your renouncement an immortal spirit,
And to be talk'd with in sincerity,
As with a saint.
Isab. You do blaspheme the good in mocking me.
Lucio. Do not believe it. Fewness and truth, 'tis thus:
Your brother and his lover have embrac'd.
As those that feed grow full, as blossoming time
That from the seedness the bare fallow brings
To teeming foison, even so her plenteous womb
Expresseth his full tilth and husbandry.
Isab. Some one with child by him? My cousin Juliet?
Lucio. Is she your cousin?
Isab. Adoptedly, as school-maids change their names
By vain though apt affection.
Lucio. She it is.
Isab. O, let him marry her.
Lucio. This is the point.
The Duke is very strangely gone from hence;
Bore many gentlemen (myself being one)
In hand, and hope of action; but we do learn
By those that know the very nerves of state,
His [givings]-out were of an infinite distance
From his true-meant design. Upon his place,
And with full line of his authority,
Governs Lord Angelo, a man whose blood
Is very snow-broth; one who never feels
The wanton stings and motions of the sense;

41. in th' ambush: under cover. **home:** to the target.
42. nature: i.e. person (contrasted with *name*).
43. do in slander: put in disrepute.
45. prince: the one who has sovereign power, i.e. Angelo.
47. formally: in external appearance and demeanor. **bear:** comport (myself).
48–49. Moe . . . more: more in number . . . greater in amount.
50. precise: punctiliously correct in manners and morals; in Shakespeare's day, often applied to Puritans.
51. Stands . . . with: maintains a wary defense against (a fencing term). **envy:** malice.
52–53. that . . . stone: i.e. that he has any sensual desires.
54. If . . . be: i.e. whether possession of power will alter intention, and whether certain persons are what they seem to be.

I.iv. Location: A nunnery.
o.s.d. Isabel. Although commentators on the play always refer to its heroine as Isabella, that form of her name appears only five times in the dialogue (three times in this scene), *Isabel* five times as often, though only twice in the stage directions. There is a similar variation of *Juliet / Julietta.* **2. large:** liberal.
5. Saint Clare: thirteenth-century foundress of an order of nuns (the Franciscan "poor Clares") having a rule of extreme austerity.
17. stead: help.

25. weary: wearisome. **29. friend:** sweetheart.
30. story: i.e. theme for jesting or deception.
32. lapwing: This bird misled predators about the whereabouts of its young by fluttering about at some distance from the nest.
34. enskied: dwelling in heaven.
38. You . . . me: in mockingly calling me a saint you blaspheme against the true saints.
39. Fewness and truth: to speak briefly and truthfully.
42. seedness: state or time of being sown.
43. foison: abundance, i.e. harvest. **plenteous:** fruitful.
44. tilth: tillage. **husbandry:** (1) tillage; (2) husband's duties. Cf. Sonnet 3.5–6. **47. change:** exchange.
48. vain: idle, i.e. producing no change in their relationship. **apt:** i.e. natural to their age.
51–52. Bore . . . action: i.e. misled them about his intentions so that they kept expecting to see military action; a telescoping of *bore in hand* (= deluded) and *bore in hope* (= maintained in expectation).
53. nerves: sinews, i.e. inner workings. **state:** policy.
56. full line: free range (as of a tether so long that it imposes no restraint).
58. snow-broth: melted snow. **59. motions:** urgings.

But doth rebate and blunt his natural edge
With profits of the mind: study and fast.
He (to give fear to use and liberty,
Which have for long run by the hideous law,
As mice by lions) hath pick'd out an act,
Under whose heavy sense your brother's life
Falls into forfeit; he arrests him on it,
And follows close the rigor of the statute,
To make him an example. All hope is gone,
Unless you have the grace by your fair prayer
To soften Angelo. And that's my pith
Of business 'twixt you and your poor brother.

Isab. Doth he so seek his life?

Lucio. H'as censur'd him
Already, and as I hear, the Provost hath
A warrant for 's execution.

Isab. Alas, what poor ability's in me
To do him good!

Lucio. Assay the pow'r you have.

Isab. My power? Alas, I doubt—

Lucio. Our doubts are traitors,
And makes us lose the good we oft might win,
By fearing to attempt. Go to Lord Angelo,
And let him learn to know, when maidens sue,
Men give like gods; but when they weep and kneel,
All their petitions are as freely theirs
As they themselves would owe them.

Isab. I'll see what I can do.

Lucio. But speedily.

Isab. I will about it straight;
No longer staying but to give the Mother
Notice of my affair. I humbly thank you.
Commend me to my brother. Soon at night
I'll send him certain word of my success.

Lucio. I take my leave of you.

Isab. Good sir, adieu. *Exeunt [severally].*

ACT II, Scene I

Enter Angelo, Escalus, *and* Servants, Justice.

Ang. We must not make a scarecrow of the law,
Setting it up to fear the birds of prey,
And let it keep one shape, till custom make it
Their perch and not their terror.

Escal. Ay, but yet
Let us be keen, and rather cut a little,
Than fall, and bruise to death. Alas, this gentleman,
Whom I would save, had a most noble father!
Let but your honor know
(Whom I believe to be most strait in virtue)

60. rebate. Synonymous with *blunt*. **edge:** keenness of desire.
62. use and liberty: license that has become customary.
64. act: law. **65. heavy sense:** severe tenor.
70–71. my . . . business: the heart of my errand.
72. H'as censur'd: he has passed judgment.
82. their petitions: the things they sue for. **83. owe:** own.
88. Commend me: give my loving greetings. **Soon at night:** early this evening.
89. certain . . . success: definite word of the outcome.

II.i. Location: A court of justice.
2. fear: frighten. **5. keen:** sharp.
6. fall. Like bludgeons or heavy weights. **bruise:** i.e. crush.
8. know: consider and decide.

That in the working of your own affections,
Had time coher'd with place, or place with wishing,
Or that the resolute acting of [your] blood
Could have attain'd th' effect of your own purpose,
Whether you had not sometime in your life
Err'd in this point which now you censure him,
And pull'd the law upon you.

Ang. 'Tis one thing to be tempted, Escalus,
Another thing to fall. I not deny
The jury, passing on the prisoner's life,
May in the sworn twelve have a thief or two
Guiltier than him they try. What's open made to justice,
That justice seizes. What knows the laws
That thieves do pass on thieves? 'Tis very pregnant,
The jewel that we find, we stoop and take't,
Because we see it; but what we do not see
We tread upon, and never think of it.
You may not so extenuate his offense
For I have had such faults; but rather tell me,
When I, that censure him, do so offend,
Let mine own judgment pattern out my death,
And nothing come in partial. Sir, he must die.

Enter Provost.

Escal. Be it as your wisdom will.

Ang. Where is the Provost?

Prov. Here, if it like your honor.

Ang. See that Claudio
Be executed by nine to-morrow morning.
Bring him his confessor, let him be prepar'd,
For that's the utmost of his pilgrimage.

[Exit Provost.]

Escal. Well; heaven forgive him! and forgive us all!
Some rise by sin, and some by virtue fall;
Some run from brakes of ice and answer none,
And some condemned for a fault alone.

Enter Elbow, Froth, *Clown* [Pompey], Officers.

Elb. Come, bring them away. If these be good people in a commonweal that do nothing but use their

10. affections: desires.
12. that: i.e. if (repeating the conditional sense of *Had time*, line 11). **blood:** passions. **13. effect:** effectuation, fulfillment.
14. had not: would not have.
15. which: for which. **censure:** condemn.
20. thief. Often used in the more general sense "criminal."
21. open: manifest.
22. What . . . laws: how can the laws take cognizance.
23. pregnant: readily perceived, obvious. **28. For:** because.
30. judgment: sentence (decreed for Claudio). **pattern out:** be the precedent for. **31. come in partial:** be admitted in my favor.
33. like: please. **35. prepar'd:** given spiritual preparation.
36. utmost . . . pilgrimage: limit of his life's journey.
39. brakes of ice. A famous crux. Attempts to relate the phrase to punishment in hell (cf. III.i.121–22), taking *brakes* as "cages" or "means of confinement," are unpersuasive, since it is clearly the inequalities of temporal justice that Escalus is talking about. Many editors adopt Rowe's *brakes of vice*, meaning "thickets (i.e. a multiplicity) of crimes," which provides the expected contrast with *a fault alone*, "a single fault." Others follow Collier in reading "breaks of ice." In its literal sense this image lacks the element of moral responsibility that the context requires; but ice is symbolic of virginity (cf. *the very ice of chastity* in *As You Like It*, III.iv.18; *as chaste as ice* in *Hamlet*, III.i.140), and the reference may be to breaches of virginity, with *fault* in line 40 meaning "a mere crack," i.e. a slighter sexual offense. **answer none:** i.e. are not called to account.
41. away: along, this way.
42–43. use . . . houses: practice their improprieties in brothels.

abuses in common houses, I know no law. Bring them away.

Ang. How now, sir, what's your name? and what's the matter?

Elb. If it please your honor, I am the poor Duke's constable, and my name is Elbow. I do lean upon justice, sir, and do bring in here before your good honor two notorious benefactors.

Ang. Benefactors? Well; what benefactors are they? Are they not malefactors?

Elb. If it please your honor, I know not well what they are; but precise villains they are, that I am sure of, and void of all profanation in the world that good Christians ought to have.

Escal. This comes off well. Here's a wise officer.

Ang. Go to; what quality are they of? Elbow is your name? [*A pause.*] Why dost thou not speak, Elbow?

Pom. He cannot, sir; he's out at elbow.

Ang. What are you, sir?

Elb. He, sir! A tapster, sir; parcel-bawd; one that serves a bad woman; whose house, sir, was (as they say) pluck'd down in the suburbs; and now she professes a hot-house; which, I think, is a very ill house too.

Escal. How know you that?

Elb. My wife, sir, whom I detest before heaven and your honor—

Escal. How? thy wife?

Elb. Ay, sir; whom I thank heaven is an honest woman.

Escal. Dost thou detest her therefore?

Elb. I say, sir, I will detest myself also, as well as she, that this house, if it be not a bawd's house, it is pity of her life, for it is a naughty house.

Escal. How dost thou know that, constable?

Elb. Marry, sir, by my wife, who, if she had been a woman cardinally given, might have been accus'd in fornication, adultery, and all uncleanliness there.

Escal. By the woman's means?

Elb. Ay, sir, by Mistress Overdone's means; but as she spit in his face, so she defied him.

Pom. Sir, if it please your honor, this is not so.

Elb. Prove it before these varlets here, thou honorable man, prove it.

Escal. Do you hear how he misplaces?

Pom. Sir, she came in great with child; and longing (saving your honors' reverence) for stew'd pruins. Sir, we had but two in the house, which at that very distant time stood, as it were, in a fruit-dish, a dish of some threepence—your honors have seen such dishes; they are not china dishes, but very good dishes.

Escal. Go to, go to; no matter for the dish, sir.

Pom. No indeed, sir, not of a pin; you are therein in the right. But to the point. As I say, this Mistress Elbow, being (as I say) with child, and being great-bellied, and longing (as I said) for pruins; and having but two in the dish (as I said), Master Froth here, this very man, having eaten the rest (as I said) and (as I say) paying for them very honestly; for, as you know, Master Froth, I could not give you three-pence again.

Froth. No indeed.

Pom. Very well; you being then (if you be remembred) cracking the stones of the foresaid pruins—

Froth. Ay, so I did indeed.

Pom. Why, very well; I telling you then (if you be rememb'red) that such a one and such a one were past cure of the thing you wot of, unless they kept very good diet, as I told you—

Froth. All this is true.

Pom. Why, very well then—

Escal. Come; you are a tedious fool. To the purpose: what was done to Elbow's wife, that he hath cause to complain of? Come me to what was done to her.

Pom. Sir, your honor cannot come to that yet.

Escal. No, sir, nor I mean it not.

Pom. Sir, but you shall come to it, by your honor's leave. And I beseech you, look into Master Froth here, sir; a man of fourscore pound a year; whose father died at Hallowmas. Was't not at Hallowmas, Master Froth?

Froth. All-hallond eve.

Pom. Why, very well; I hope here be truths. He, sir, sitting (as I say) in a lower chair, sir—'twas in the Bunch of Grapes, where indeed you have a delight to sit, have you not?

Froth. I have so, because it is an open room and good for winter.

46. matter: i.e. complaints.
47–48. poor Duke's constable. Elbow intends to depreciate himself, not the Duke.
48. lean upon. Probably a blunder for *uphold* or some such word that means the opposite of what he says; cf. *benefactors* for *malefactors* in line 50.
54. precise. This word has been used of Angelo in I.iii.50. It is not clear whether Elbow is blundering ("morally strict villain") or not ("neither more nor less than a villain"); certainly *profanation* is his blunder; but the whole sentence ironically recalls the Duke's comment on Angelo's icy, almost inhuman virtue.
57. comes off well: is well said.
58. Go to: a conventional phrase of rebuke, equivalent to "come, come" (spoken, of course, to Elbow). **quality:** occupation or station.
61. out at elbow: (1) impoverished (in his wits?); (2) rendered speechless (*out*) at the sound of his name.
62. What: of what quality (as in line 58).
63. parcel-bawd: a part-time bawd. The word *bawd* was used of men as well as women.
65–66. she . . . hot-house: i.e. her profession is the operation of a bath-house (but *professes* already had the meaning "falsely professes," and many brothels masqueraded as bath-houses).
69. detest: blunder for *attest* or *protest*, "avow."
77. pity . . . life: a very sad thing for her. Again Elbow says something other than what he intends. **naughty:** wicked.
80. cardinally: blunder for *carnally.*
82. means. Elbow takes this to mean "instrument, agent," i.e. the procurer Pompey.
88. misplaces: i.e. transposes *varlets* (= rascals) and *honorable men.*
90. saving . . . reverence: conventional phrase of apology preceding an expression that may give offense. **stew'd pruins.** Stewed prunes were a favorite dish in brothels; hence the term became a slang designation for prostitutes.
92. distant: blunder for *instant* (*instant time* = precise moment).
96. pin. Proverbial for worthlessness, but here with an equivoque, like *point* in the next line. Pompey's speeches are full of such ribaldry.
111. the thing . . . of: you-know-what; here, venereal disease.
112. good diet: strict regimen.
117. Come me: come (a colloquialism); but Pompey replies to the sense "let me come," with a bawdy quibble on *come.*
124. Hallowmas: All Saints' Day, November 1.
126. All-hallond eve: the day before Hallowmas.
128. lower chair. Not satisfactorily explained.
129. Bunch of Grapes. Rooms in taverns were often given names.
131. open: public (where a fire would be kept burning in winter).

Pom. Why, very well then; I hope here be truths.

Ang. This will last out a night in Russia
When nights are longest there. I'll take my leave,
And leave you to the hearing of the cause,
Hoping you'll find good cause to whip them all.

Escal. I think no less. Good morrow to your lordship. *Exit [Angelo].*
Now, sir, come on. What was done to Elbow's wife, once more?

Pom. Once, sir? There was nothing done to her once.

Elb. I beseech you, sir, ask him what this man did to my wife.

Pom. I beseech your honor, ask me.

Escal. Well, sir, what did this gentleman to her?

Pom. I beseech you, sir, look in this gentleman's face. Good Master Froth, look upon his honor; 'tis for a good purpose. Doth your honor mark his face?

Escal. Ay, sir, very well.

Pom. Nay, I beseech you mark it well.

Escal. Well, I do so.

Pom. Doth your honor see any harm in his face?

Escal. Why, no.

Pom. I'll be suppos'd upon a book, his face is the worst thing about him. Good then; if his face be the worst thing about him, how could Master Froth do the constable's wife any harm? I would know that of your honor.

Escal. He's in the right, constable. What say you to it?

Elb. First, and it like you, the house is a respected house; next, this is a respected fellow; and his mistress is a respected woman.

Pom. By this hand, sir, his wife is a more respected person than any of us all.

Elb. Varlet, thou liest! thou liest, wicked varlet! The time is yet to come that she was ever respected with man, woman, or child.

Pom. Sir, she was respected with him before he married with her.

Escal. Which is the wiser here: Justice or Iniquity? Is this true?

Elb. O thou caitiff! O thou varlet! O thou wicked Hannibal! I respected with her before I was married to her? If ever I was respected with her, or she with me, let not your worship think me the poor Duke's officer. Prove this, thou wicked Hannibal, or I'll have mine action of batt'ry on thee.

Escal. If he took you a box o' th' ear, you might have your action of slander too.

Elb. Marry, I thank your good worship for it. What is't your worship's pleasure I shall do with this

wicked caitiff?

Escal. Truly, officer, because he hath some offenses in him that thou wouldst discover if thou couldst, let him continue in his courses till thou know'st what they are.

Elb. Marry, I thank your worship for it. Thou seest, thou wicked varlet, now, what's come upon thee. Thou art to continue now, thou varlet, thou art to continue.

Escal. Where were you born, friend?

Froth. Here in Vienna, sir.

Escal. Are you of fourscore pounds a year?

Froth. Yes, and't please you, sir.

Escal. So. [*To Pompey.*] What trade are you of, sir?

Pom. A tapster, a poor widow's tapster.

Escal. Your mistress' name?

Pom. Mistress Overdone.

Escal. Hath she had any more than one husband?

Pom. Nine, sir; Overdone by the last.

Escal. Nine? Come hither to me, Master Froth. Master Froth, I would not have you acquainted with tapsters; they will draw you, Master Froth, and you will hang them. Get you gone, and let me hear no more of you.

Froth. I thank your worship. For mine own part, I never come into any room in a tap-house, but I am drawn in.

Escal. Well; no more of it, Master Froth. Farewell. [*Exit Froth.*] Come you hither to me, Master Tapster. What's your name, Master Tapster?

Pom. Pompey.

Escal. What else?

Pom. Bum, sir.

Escal. Troth, and your bum is the greatest thing about you, so that in the beastliest sense you are Pompey the Great. Pompey, you are partly a bawd, Pompey, howsoever you color it in being a tapster, are you not? Come, tell me true, it shall be the better for you.

Pom. Truly, sir, I am a poor fellow that would live.

Escal. How would you live, Pompey? by being a bawd? What do you think of the trade, Pompey? is it a lawful trade?

Pom. If the law would allow it, sir.

Escal. But the law will not allow it, Pompey; nor it shall not be allow'd in Vienna.

Pom. Does your worship mean to geld and splay all the youth of the city?

Escal. No, Pompey.

137. whip them all: i.e. find them all guilty. Whipping was a common penalty for bawds and prostitutes.
138. think no less: expect that will be the outcome.
155. suppos'd: blunder for *depos'd*, i.e. sworn. **book:** Bible.
162. and it like: if it please. **respected:** blunder for *suspected* (and so several times in lines 163–76). **165. By this hand.** A common oath.
172. Justice or Iniquity. Elbow and Pompey are referred to in terms of stock characters in the morality plays. **174. caitiff:** wretch.
175. Hannibal: blunder for *cannibal*, i.e. savage; but the pairing of the names of the celebrated generals Pompey and Hannibal would not go unnoted.
179. batt'ry: blunder for *slander*, as Escalus points out obliquely.
180. took: struck.
186. discover: expose.
191. continue. Dover Wilson suggests that Elbow confuses this with *contain*, i.e. be sexually continent. But perhaps he simply confuses the word with its opposite, as elsewhere.
202. Overdone . . . last. With a bawdy quibble deriving from *do* = copulate.
205. draw: deplete, drain dry; with a play on Froth's name and the drawing of liquor, and a second quibble (signalled by *hang* in line 206) on "disembowel" or, alternatively, "drag to execution" (*draw* was used in both senses in judicial sentences).
206. will hang them: will be the cause of their being hanged (?) or will have no recourse but to say "Hang them!" (?).
210. drawn in: (1) attracted to enter; (2) cheated.
217–18. your . . . about you. Probably with a reference to the fashion of wearing thickly padded trunk-hose.
220. color: try to put a better appearance on.
223. would live: want to earn a living. **230. splay:** spay.

Pom. Truly, sir, in my poor opinion, they will to't then. If your worship will take order for the drabs and the knaves, you need not to fear the bawds.

Escal. There is pretty orders beginning, I can tell you: it is but heading and hanging.

Pom. If you head and hang all that offend that way but for ten year together, you'll be glad to give out a commission for more heads. If this law hold in Vienna ten year, I'll rent the fairest house in it after threepence a bay. If you live to see this come to pass, say Pompey told you so.

Escal. Thank you, good Pompey; and in requital of your prophecy, hark you: I advise you let me not find you before me again upon any complaint whatsoever; no, not for dwelling where you do. If I do, Pompey, I shall beat you to your tent, and prove a shrewd Caesar to you; in plain-dealing, Pompey, I shall have you whipt. So for this time, Pompey, fare you well.

Pom. I thank your worship for your good counsel; [*aside*] but I shall follow it as the flesh and fortune shall better determine.

Whip me? No, no, let carman whip his jade,
The valiant heart's not whipt out of his trade. *Exit.*

Escal. Come hither to me, Master Elbow; come hither, Master Constable. How long have you been in this place of constable?

Elb. Seven year and a half, sir.

Escal. I thought, by the readiness in the office, you had continu'd in it some time. You say seven years together?

Elb. And a half, sir.

Escal. Alas, it hath been great pains to you. They do you wrong to put you so oft upon't. Are there not men in your ward sufficient to serve it?

Elb. Faith, sir, few of any wit in such matters. As they are chosen, they are glad to choose me for them. I do it for some piece of money, and go through with all.

Escal. Look you bring me in the names of some six or seven, the most sufficient of your parish.

Elb. To your worship's house, sir?

Escal. To my house. Fare you well. [*Exit Elbow.*] What's a' clock, think you?

Just. Eleven, sir.

Escal. I pray you home to dinner with me.

Just. I humbly thank you.

Escal. It grieves me for the death of Claudio,
But there's no remedy.

234. take order for: see to. **237. heading:** beheading.
240. commission: mandate. **241. after:** at the rate of.
242. bay: portion of a house lying under one gable or between two party walls.
248–49. beat ... Caesar. Alluding to Pompey's defeat by Caesar at Pharsalus in 48 B.C. *Shrewd* = harsh.
255. carman: carter. **jade:** worthless horse.
261. readiness: proficiency.
266. put ... upon't: make you serve so many times. The constable was elected annually. **267. sufficient:** suitably qualified.
269–70. choose ... them: i.e. engage me as their deputy (an ironic reminder of the Duke's deputizing of Angelo). **270. piece:** coin.
277. Eleven, sir. The Justice's brief entry into the dialogue after nearly 300 lines of silence has been variously explained as an afterthought (see the rather awkward attachment of his name to the opening stage direction) and as evidence of revision.
278. dinner. The Elizabethan dinner was at midday.

Just. Lord Angelo is severe.
Escal. It is but needful.
Mercy is not itself, that oft looks so;
Pardon is still the nurse of second woe.
But yet, poor Claudio; there is no remedy.
Come, sir. *Exeunt.*

Scene II

Enter Provost, Servant.

Serv. He's hearing of a cause; he will come straight.
I'll tell him of you.
Prov. Pray you do. [*Exit Servant.*] I'll know
His pleasure, may be he will relent. Alas,
He hath but as offended in a dream!
All sects, all ages smack of this vice, and he
To die for't!

Enter Angelo.

Ang. Now, what's the matter, Provost?
Prov. Is it your will Claudio shall die to-morrow?
Ang. Did not I tell thee yea? Hadst thou not order?
Why dost thou ask again?
Prov. Lest I might be too rash.
Under your good correction, I have seen
When, after execution, judgment hath
Repented o'er his doom.
Ang. Go to; let that be mine.
Do you your office, or give up your place,
And you shall well be spar'd.
Prov. I crave your honor's pardon.
What shall be done, sir, with the groaning Juliet?
She's very near her hour.
Ang. Dispose of her
To some more fitter place; and that with speed.

[*Enter* Servant.]

Serv. Here is the sister of the man condemn'd
Desires access to you.
Ang. Hath he a sister?
Prov. Ay, my good lord, a very virtuous maid,
And to be shortly of a sisterhood,
If not already.
Ang. Well; let her be admitted. [*Exit Servant.*]
See you the fornicatress be remov'd.
Let her have needful but not lavish means;
There shall be order for't.

Enter Lucio *and* Isabella.

Prov. 'Save your honor!
Ang. Stay a little while. [*To Isabella.*] Y' are welcome; what's your will?

283. Mercy ... so: i.e. to extend mercy too often is to prove unmerciful in the long run (since it encourages wrongdoers).

II.ii. Location: Angelo's house.
4. He: i.e. Claudio. **in a dream:** i.e. without conscious intent.
5. sects: classes. **vice:** sin.
10. Under: subject to. **seen:** known cases.
12. doom: sentence. **mine:** my responsibility.
16. Dispose of her: arrange for her to go. **25. 'Save:** God save.

Isab. I am a woeful suitor to your honor,
Please but your honor hear me.
Ang. Well; what's your suit?
Isab. There is a vice that most I do abhor,
And most desire should meet the blow of justice;
For which I would not plead, but that I must;
For which I must not plead, but that I am
At war 'twixt will and will not.
Ang. Well; the matter?
Isab. I have a brother is condemn'd to die;
I do beseech you let it be his fault,
And not my brother.
Prov. [*Aside.*] Heaven give thee moving graces!
Ang. Condemn the fault, and not the actor of it?
Why, every fault's condemn'd ere it be done.
Mine were the very cipher of a function,
To fine the faults whose fine stands in record,
And let go by the actor.
Isab. O just but severe law!
I had a brother then. Heaven keep your honor!
Lucio. [*Aside to Isabella.*] Give't not o'er so. To him again, entreat him,
Kneel down before him, hang upon his gown;
You are too cold. If you should need a pin,
You could not with more tame a tongue desire it;
To him, I say!
Isab. Must he needs die?
Ang. Maiden, no remedy.
Isab. Yes; I do think that you might pardon him,
And neither heaven nor man grieve at the mercy.
Ang. I will not do't.
Isab. But can you if you would?
Ang. Look what I will not, that I cannot do.
Isab. But might you do't, and do the world no wrong,
If so your heart were touch'd with that remorse
As mine is to him?
Ang. He's sentenc'd; 'tis too late.
Lucio. [*Aside to Isabella.*] You are too cold.
Isab. Too late? Why, no; I that do speak a word
May call it again. Well, believe this,
No ceremony that to great ones 'longs,
Not the king's crown, nor the deputed sword,
The marshal's truncheon, nor the judge's robe,
Become them with one half so good a grace
As mercy does.
If he had been as you, and you as he,
You would have slipp'd like him, but he, like you,
Would not have been so stern.
Ang. Pray you be gone.
Isab. I would to heaven I had your potency,
And you were Isabel! Should it then be thus?
No; I would tell what 'twere to be a judge,
And what a prisoner.
Lucio. [*Aside to Isabella.*] Ay, touch him; there's the vein.
Ang. Your brother is a forfeit of the law,
And you but waste your words.
Isab. Alas, alas!
Why, all the souls that were were forfeit once,
And He that might the vantage best have took
Found out the remedy. How would you be
If He, which is the top of judgment, should
But judge you as you are? O, think on that,
And mercy then will breathe within your lips,
Like man new made.
Ang. Be you content, fair maid,
It is the law, not I, condemn your brother.
Were he my kinsman, brother, or my son,
It should be thus with him: he must die to-morrow.
Isab. To-morrow? O, that's sudden! Spare him, spare him!
He's not prepar'd for death. Even for our kitchens
We kill the fowl of season. Shall we serve heaven
With less respect than we do minister
To our gross selves? Good, good my lord, bethink you:
Who is it that hath died for this offense?
There's many have committed it.
Lucio. [*Aside to Isabella.*] Ay, well said.
Ang. The law hath not been dead, though it hath slept.
Those many had not dar'd to do that evil
If the first that did th' edict infringe
Had answer'd for his deed. Now 'tis awake,
Takes note of what is done, and like a prophet
Looks in a glass that shows what future evils,
Either now, or by remissness new conceiv'd,
And so in progress to be hatch'd and born,
Are now to have no successive degrees,
But here they live, to end.
Isab. Yet show some pity.
Ang. I show it most of all when I show justice;
For then I pity those I do not know,
Which a dismiss'd offense would after gall,

35. let . . . fault: let his fault be condemned.
40. fine . . . fine: impose a penalty upon . . . penalty.
45. a pin: i.e. the merest trifle. **49. might:** could.
52. Look what: whatsoever. **54. remorse:** pity.
59. ceremony: symbolic appurtenance. **'longs:** belongs.
60. deputed sword: i.e. sword of justice, symbolizing an authority deputed by God.
61. marshal's truncheon: military commander's staff of office.
62. grace: appropriateness.
65–66. he . . . not: he would not, like you.
67. potency: power, authority to act. **69. tell:** i.e. let people see.
70. there's the vein: that's the right style; but also with reference to finding a vein in bloodletting, as *touch* suggests (cf. *As You Like It*, II.vii.94, "you touch'd my vein at first").
74. vantage: advantage. **76. top of judgment:** supreme judge.
78. breathe within: (1) come to life within; (2) breathe forth from within.
79. Like . . . made. Explained by Malone as referring to man newly created, but by most commentators as referring to man made new by God's redeeming mercy; suggesting also the transformation of Angelo into a different man. **Be you content:** i.e. be satisfied that further objection is vain.
81. kinsman. Often used of a relative more remote than a brother or sister, who in turn was more remote than a parent or a child. The nouns in this line are thus in ascending order.
83. sudden: (too) soon.
85. of season: i.e. of the proper degree of maturity. **serve.** With a quibble on serving food. **86. respect:** thoughtful care.
87. gross: corporal. **bethink you:** consider.
93. answer'd: paid. **94. prophet:** fortune-teller.
95. glass: prospective glass or magic crystal.
96. Either . . . conceiv'd: i.e. both those that are already conceived and those that will be conceived if lax enforcement of law (*remissness*) continues. **98. have . . . degrees:** propagate themselves no further.
99. here: i.e. in the potential offenders. Many editors emend to *ere* (following Hanmer) or *where* (Malone).
102. dismiss'd: forgiven. **gall:** injure.

And do him right that, answering one foul wrong,
Lives not to act another. Be satisfied;
Your brother dies to-morrow; be content.
Isab. So you must be the first that gives this sentence,
And he, that suffers. O, it is excellent
To have a giant's strength; but it is tyrannous
To use it like a giant.
Lucio. [*Aside to Isabella.*] That's well said.
Isab. Could great men thunder
As Jove himself does, Jove would never be quiet,
For every pelting, petty officer
Would use his heaven for thunder,
Nothing but thunder! Merciful heaven,
Thou rather with thy sharp and sulphurous bolt
Splits the unwedgeable and gnarled oak
Than the soft myrtle; but man, proud man,
Dress'd in a little brief authority,
Most ignorant of what he's most assur'd
(His glassy essence), like an angry ape
Plays such fantastic tricks before high heaven
As makes the angels weep; who, with our spleens,
Would all themselves laugh mortal.
Lucio. [*Aside to Isabella.*] O, to him, to him, wench! he will relent.
He's coming; I perceive't.
Prov. [*Aside.*] Pray heaven she win him!
Isab. We cannot weigh our brother with ourself.
Great men may jest with saints; 'tis wit in them,
But in the less foul profanation.
Lucio. [*Aside to Isabella.*] Thou'rt i' th' right, girl, more o' that.
Isab. That in the captain's but a choleric word,
Which in the soldier is flat blasphemy.
Lucio. [*Aside to Isabella.*] Art avis'd o' that? more on't.
Ang. Why do you put these sayings upon me?
Isab. Because authority, though it err like others,
Hath yet a kind of medicine in itself,
That skins the vice o' th' top. Go to your bosom,
Knock there, and ask your heart what it doth know
That's like my brother's fault. If it confess
A natural guiltiness such as is his,
Let it not sound a thought upon your tongue
Against my brother's life.
Ang. [*Aside.*] She speaks, and 'tis
Such sense that my sense breeds with it.—Fare you well.
Isab. Gentle my lord, turn back.
Ang. I will bethink me. Come again to-morrow.
Isab. Hark how I'll bribe you. Good my lord, turn back.
Ang. How? bribe me?
Isab. Ay, with such gifts that heaven shall share with you.
Lucio. [*Aside to Isabella.*] You had marr'd all else.
Isab. Not with fond sicles of the tested gold,
Or stones, whose rate are either rich or poor
As fancy values them; but with true prayers,
That shall be up at heaven, and enter there
Ere sun-rise, prayers from preserved souls,
From fasting maids, whose minds are dedicate
To nothing temporal.
Ang. Well; come to me to-morrow.
Lucio. [*Aside to Isabella.*] Go to; 'tis well. Away!
Isab. Heaven keep your honor safe!
Ang. [*Aside.*] Amen!
For I am that way going to temptation,
Where prayers cross.
Isab. At what hour to-morrow
Shall I attend your lordship?
Ang. At any time 'fore noon.
Isab. 'Save your honor!
[*Exeunt Isabella, Lucio, and Provost.*]
Ang. From thee: even from thy virtue.
What's this? what's this? Is this her fault, or mine?
The tempter, or the tempted, who sins most, ha?
Not she; nor doth she tempt; but it is I
That, lying by the violet in the sun,
Do as the carrion does, not as the flow'r,
Corrupt with virtuous season. Can it be
That modesty may more betray our sense
Than woman's lightness? Having waste ground enough,
Shall we desire to raze the sanctuary

103. right: justice.
107. that suffers: (the first) that undergoes the penalty.
109. like a giant: i.e. without restraint. If (as Isabella's next speech suggests) there is an allusion here to the giants who warred against the gods, the phrase would mean "without the divine attribute of mercy."
110. great men: men in high place. **111. be quiet:** have any quiet.
112. pelting: paltry. **officer:** official.
115. bolt. The damage done by lightning was formerly attributed to thunderbolts.
116. Splits: for *splitst.* A frequent type of simplification for euphony; cf. *exists,* III.i.20. **118. brief:** short-lived.
119. assur'd: assured of.
120. glassy essence: i.e. man's essential being or rational soul, which, mirror-like (*glassy*), will show the man who contemplates it what he is. *Glassy* has probably the additional sense of "fragile, highly susceptible of damage." **like . . . ape.** The point is that men who undertake to act like gods make as ludicrous (or as sad) a spectacle as apes imitating what they have seen men do.
122. with our spleens: if they had spleens like us. The spleen was regarded as the seat of laughter as well as of irascibility.
123. themselves laugh mortal: laugh themselves into a resemblance of mortals, i.e. laugh as much at men as men laugh at apes (?).
125. coming: coming round, beginning to yield.
126. cannot . . . ourself: refuse to judge ourselves and other men by the same standard.
127. may: can with impunity. **jest with:** treat with levity.
130. captain: general. **choleric:** angry.
131. blasphemy: defamation.
132. Art avis'd o': are you informed of, have you discovered.
133. put . . . upon: apply . . . to.

136. skins . . . top: causes a new skin to grow over the sore.
136–41. Go . . . life. The same argument for mercy that Escalus put forward in II.i.8–16.
141–42. 'tis Such sense: its import is such.
142. my sense breeds: my sensual desire multiplies.
143. Gentle my lord: my noble lord. **147. that:** as.
148. had . . . else: would have spoiled everything otherwise (i.e. if you had used *bribe* in the normal sense).
149. fond: foolish, i.e. foolishly valued. **sicles:** shekels, i.e. coins. **tested:** i.e. purest (as confirmed by the touchstone).
150. rate are. The context establishes a collective sense for *rate*; hence the plural verb. **153. preserved:** kept safe from the world.
159. cross: thwart, i.e. impede.
160. 'fore noon. Note that this implies a change in the hour of Claudio's execution (see II.i.33–34), but the Provost is given no change of instruction.
167. Corrupt: putrefy. **virtuous season:** season or weather that has power (*virtue*) to make things grow (perhaps with play on *season* = preservative). **168. sense:** sensual nature.
169. lightness: wantonness.

And pitch our evils there? O fie, fie, fie!
What dost thou? or what art thou, Angelo?
Dost thou desire her foully for those things
That make her good? O, let her brother live!
Thieves for their robbery have authority
When judges steal themselves. What, do I love her,
That I desire to hear her speak again?
And feast upon her eyes? What is't I dream on?
O cunning enemy, that to catch a saint,
With saints dost bait thy hook! Most dangerous
Is that temptation that doth goad us on
To sin in loving virtue. Never could the strumpet,
With all her double vigor, art and nature,
Once stir my temper; but this virtuous maid
Subdues me quite. Ever till now,
When men were fond, I smil'd and wond'red how.
Exit.

Scene III

Enter Duke [*disguised as a friar*] *and* Provost, [*meeting*].

Duke. Hail to you, Provost! so I think you are.
Prov. I am the Provost. What's your will, good friar?
Duke. Bound by my charity and my blest order,
I come to visit the afflicted spirits
Here in the prison. Do me the common right
To let me see them, and to make me know
The nature of their crimes, that I may minister
To them accordingly.
Prov. I would do more than that, if more were needful.

Enter Juliet.

Look, here comes one; a gentlewoman of mine,
Who, falling in the flaws of her own youth,
Hath blister'd her report. She is with child,
And he that got it, sentenc'd; a young man
More fit to do another such offense
Than die for this.
Duke. When must he die?
Prov. As I do think, to-morrow.
[*To Juliet.*] I have provided for you. Stay a while,
And you shall be conducted.
Duke. Repent you, fair one, of the sin you carry?
Jul. I do; and bear the shame most patiently.
Duke. I'll teach you how you shall arraign your conscience,

And try your penitence, if it be sound,
Or hollowly put on.
Jul. I'll gladly learn.
Duke. Love you the man that wrong'd you?
Jul. Yes, as I love the woman that wrong'd him.
Duke. So then it seems your most offenseful act
Was mutually committed?
Jul. Mutually.
Duke. Then was your sin of heavier kind than his.
Jul. I do confess it, and repent it, father.
Duke. 'Tis meet so, daughter, but lest you do repent
As that the sin hath brought you to this shame,
Which sorrow is always toward ourselves, not heaven,
Showing we would not spare heaven as we love it,
But as we stand in fear—
Jul. I do repent me as it is an evil,
And take the shame with joy.
Duke. There rest.
Your partner, as I hear, must die to-morrow,
And I am going with instruction to him.
Grace go with you, *Benedicite!* *Exit.*
Jul. Must die to-morrow? O injurious love,
That respites me a life whose very comfort
Is still a dying horror!
Prov. 'Tis pity of him. *Exeunt.*

Scene IV

Enter Angelo.

Ang. When I would pray and think, I think and pray
To several subjects. Heaven hath my empty words,
Whilst my invention, hearing not my tongue,
Anchors on Isabel; heaven in my mouth,
As if I did but only chew his name,
And in my heart the strong and swelling evil
Of my conception. The state, whereon I studied,
Is like a good thing, being often read,
Grown [sere] and tedious; yea, my gravity,
Wherein (let no man hear me) I take pride,
Could I, with boot, change for an idle plume,
Which the air beats for vain. O place, O form,
How often dost thou with thy case, thy habit,

171. pitch our evils. Variously explained as "cast our offensive waste matter" or "erect our privies." Those who prefer the second explanation cite *Henry VIII*, II.i.67, "Nor build our evils on the graves of great men," but no certain evidence for *evils* = privies has been found.
175–76. Thieves . . . themselves. Cf. II.i.18–23.
183. art and nature: i.e. her artifice as a prostitute added to her sexual appeal as a woman.
184. stir my temper: disturb my mental composure.
185. Subdues: overcomes. **186. fond:** infatuated.

II.iii. Location: A prison.
3. charity: obligation to perform works of Christian charity.
5. the common right: i.e. the right of all persons in holy orders.
6. make me know: inform me.
11. flaws: sudden gusts (of passion).
12. blister'd her report: blighted her reputation. **13. got:** begot.
21. arraign: accuse, bring to trial.

23. hollowly: not sincerely. **28. heavier:** graver.
31. As that: because (so also *as* in lines 33–35).
33. spare heaven: i.e. relieve by your repentance the sorrow felt in heaven for sin. **36. There rest:** continue in that frame of mind.
40. love. The result of love, her pregnancy, is presumably what saves her from execution. Many editors adopt Hanmer's emendation *law*.
42. still: ever.

II.iv. Location: Angelo's house.
2. several: separate.
3. invention: imagination.
4–5. heaven . . . his name. *His name* could of course mean "its name" (see the note on I.ii.4), but it seems more likely that *heaven* has here displaced an earlier *God*, in accordance with the statute of 1606 prohibiting the use of God's name in stage performances; so also in line 45, and perhaps elsewhere in the play where the context affords no clue.
6, 7. swelling, conception. Another pregnancy figure.
7. The state: statecraft, politics.
9. sere: arid. **gravity:** dignified demeanor.
11. boot: advantage.
12. for vain: for vanity (with pun on *for vane*). **place . . . form:** rank . . . dignity.

Wrench awe from fools, and tie the wiser souls
To thy false seeming! Blood, thou art blood.
Let's write "good angel" on the devil's horn,
'Tis not the devil's crest.

Enter SERVANT.

How now? who's there?

Serv. One Isabel, a sister, desires access to you.

Ang. Teach her the way. [*Exit Servant.*] O heavens!
Why does my blood thus muster to my heart,
Making both it unable for itself,
And dispossessing all my other parts
Of necessary fitness?
So play the foolish throngs with one that swounds,
Come all to help him, and so stop the air
By which he should revive; and even so
The general subject to a well-wish'd king
Quit their own part, and in obsequious fondness
Crowd to his presence, where their untaught love
Must needs appear offense.

Enter ISABELLA.

How now, fair maid?

Isab. I am come to know your pleasure.

Ang. That you might know it, would much better please me
Than to demand what 'tis. Your brother cannot live.

Isab. Even so. Heaven keep your honor!

Ang. Yet may he live a while; and it may be
As long as you or I. Yet he must die.

Isab. Under your sentence?

Ang. Yea.

Isab. When, I beseech you? that in his reprieve,
Longer or shorter, he may be so fitted
That his soul sicken not.

Ang. Ha? fie, these filthy vices! It were as good
To pardon him that hath from nature stol'n
A man already made, as to remit
Their saucy sweetness that do coin heaven's image
In stamps that are forbid. 'Tis all as easy
Falsely to take away a life true made
As to put metal in restrained means
To make a false one.

Isab. 'Tis set down so in heaven, but not in earth.

15. **Blood . . . blood:** i.e. under the external trappings lie the basic passions common to all men.
16. **Let's write:** i.e. say that we write. **good angel.** With a play on Angelo's name.
17. **'Tis . . . crest:** it is no true mark of his identity (as a heraldic crest is), i.e. it doesn't make an angel of him.
20. **muster to:** assemble in. 21. **it:** i.e. the heart.
24. **swounds:** faints.
26–30. **and . . . offense.** Apparently an allusion to a visit made by James I in March 1604 to the Royal Exchange in London, where a tremendous throng got out of control and nearly overwhelmed him.
27. **subject:** body of subjects.
28. **Quit . . . part:** leave their proper functions. **obsequious fondness:** foolish eagerness to pay homage. 29. **untaught:** ignorant.
40. **fitted:** equipped, prepared.
43–44. **him . . . made:** i.e. a murderer. 44. **remit:** pardon.
45. **saucy sweetness:** lascivious pleasure.
45–46. **coin . . . forbid:** i.e. beget children unlawfully. The image is of counterfeiting coins (*stamps*). 46. **all as:** just as.
48. **metal.** With the same double sense of *metal* / *mettle* as at I.i.48. **restrained:** forbidden.
50. **'Tis . . . earth:** i.e. divine law forbids them equally, but in earthly law murder is more heinous.

Ang. Say you so? Then I shall pose you quickly.
Which had you rather, that the most just law
Now took your brother's life, [or,] to redeem him,
Give up your body to such sweet uncleanness
As she that he hath stain'd?

Isab. Sir, believe this,
I had rather give my body than my soul.

Ang. I talk not of your soul; our compell'd sins
Stand more for number than for accompt.

Isab. How say you?

Ang. Nay, I'll not warrant that; for I can speak
Against the thing I say. Answer to this:
I (now the voice of the recorded law)
Pronounce a sentence on your brother's life;
Might there not be a charity in sin
To save this brother's life?

Isab. Please you to do't,
I'll take it as a peril to my soul,
It is no sin at all, but charity.

Ang. Pleas'd you to do't at peril of your soul,
Were equal poise of sin and charity.

Isab. That I do beg his life, if it be sin,
Heaven let me bear it! You granting of my suit,
If that be sin, I'll make it my morn-prayer
To have it added to the faults of mine,
And nothing of your answer.

Ang. Nay, but hear me,
Your sense pursues not mine. Either you are ignorant,
Or seem so [craftily]; and that's not good.

Isab. Let [me] be ignorant, and in nothing good,
But graciously to know I am no better.

Ang. Thus wisdom wishes to appear most bright
When it doth tax itself; as these black masks
Proclaim an enshield beauty ten times louder
Than beauty could, displayed. But mark me:
To be received plain, I'll speak more gross:
Your brother is to die.

Isab. So.

Ang. And his offense is so, as it appears,
Accountant to the law upon that pain.

Isab. True.

Ang. Admit no other way to save his life
(As I subscribe not that, nor any other,
But in the loss of question), that you, his sister,
Finding yourself desir'd of such a person,
Whose credit with the judge, or own great place,
Could fetch your brother from the manacles

51. **pose:** put a question to (shortened form of *appose*).
58. **Stand . . . accompt:** are recorded but are not charged against our account.
59–60. **I'll . . . say:** i.e. I don't necessarily subscribe to that view; I can assert any position in order to test you.
64. **Please you:** if you are willing. Isabella thinks he is talking about the possible guilt involved in pardoning Claudio.
68. **Were:** there would be. **poise:** weight.
73. **nothing.** Perhaps adverbial, "in no way." **your answer:** what you are answerable for.
74. **Your . . . mine:** i.e. you don't follow my meaning.
77. **graciously:** by God's grace.
79. **tax itself:** charge itself (with ignorance). **these black masks.** The generic use: "the black masks that women wear."
80. **enshield:** enshielded, shielded from view.
82. **received:** understood. **gross:** obviously, plainly.
86. **Accountant:** accountable. **pain:** penalty.
90. **in . . . question:** to avoid lack of matter for argument, i.e. for the sake of discussion (?). Singer's proposed change of *loss* to *loose* (= freedom) is tempting.

Of the all-[binding] law; and that there were
No earthly mean to save him, but that either
You must lay down the treasures of your body
To this supposed, or else to let him suffer—
What would you do?
Isab. As much for my poor brother as myself:
That is, were I under the terms of death,
Th' impression of keen whips I'ld wear as rubies,
And strip myself to death, as to a bed
That longing have been sick for, ere I'ld yield
My body up to shame.
Ang. Then must your brother die.
Isab. And 'twere the cheaper way:
Better it were a brother died at once,
Than that a sister, by redeeming him,
Should die for ever.
Ang. Were not you then as cruel as the sentence
That you have slander'd so?
Isab. Ignomy in ransom and free pardon
Are of two houses: lawful mercy
Is nothing kin to foul redemption.
Ang. You seem'd of late to make the law a tyrant,
And rather prov'd the sliding of your brother
A merriment than a vice.
Isab. O, pardon me, my lord, it oft falls out,
To have what we would have, we speak not what we mean.
I something do excuse the thing I hate,
For his advantage that I dearly love.
Ang. We are all frail.
Isab. Else let my brother die,
If not a fedary, but only he,
Owe and succeed thy weakness.
Ang. Nay, women are frail too.
Isab. Ay, as the glasses where they view themselves,
Which are as easy broke as they make forms.
Women? Help heaven! men their creation mar
In profiting by them. Nay, call us ten times frail,
For we are soft as our complexions are,
And credulous to false prints.
Ang. I think it well;
And from this testimony of your own sex
(Since I suppose we are made to be no stronger

97. **him**: i.e. Claudio. 100. **the terms**: sentence.
103. **longing have.** If the text is correct, *have* = I have. Of the various emendations proposed, Sisson's *long I have* is perhaps the best.
105. **the cheaper way**: a better bargain.
106. **at once**: once (and then proceeded to eternal life).
108. **die for ever**: incur damnation.
110. **slander'd so**: i.e. accused of the same thing (cruelty).
111. **Ignomy**: ignominy (a frequent variant).
112. **two houses**: different families.
113. **nothing**: in no way. Cf. *something* (= somewhat) in line 119.
114. **of late**: not long ago. 115. **prov'd**: argued.
116. **A merriment**: something to be taken lightly.
121. **frail**: morally weak, unable to resist temptation.
122. **fedary**: confederate, i.e. one guilty of the same offense.
123. **Owe and succeed**: possess and hold by succession. **thy weakness**: this frailty you speak of (but with an unintended second meaning).
126. **make forms**: (1) reflect images (as referring to mirrors); (2) produce children (as referring to women). The comparison of virginity to glass is a commonplace.
127. **men . . . mar.** Since it is women who create them.
129. **complexions**: constitutions, physical and mental.
130. **credulous**: readily receptive. **false prints.** A recurrence of the figure of lines 45–49. **think it well**: hold the same opinion.

Than faults may shake our frames), let me be bold.
I do arrest your words. Be that you are,
That is a woman; if you be more, you're none;
If you be one (as you are well express'd
By all external warrants), show it now,
By putting on the destin'd livery.
Isab. I have no tongue but one; gentle my lord,
Let me entreat you speak the former language.
Ang. Plainly conceive, I love you.
Isab. My brother did love Juliet,
And you tell me that he shall die for't.
Ang. He shall not, Isabel, if you give me love.
Isab. I know your virtue hath a license in't,
Which seems a little fouler than it is,
To pluck on others.
Ang. Believe me, on mine honor,
My words express my purpose.
Isab. Ha? little honor to be much believ'd,
And most pernicious purpose! Seeming, seeming!
I will proclaim thee, Angelo, look for't!
Sign me a present pardon for my brother,
Or with an outstretch'd throat I'll tell the world aloud
What man thou art.
Ang. Who will believe thee, Isabel?
My unsoil'd name, th' austereness of my life,
My vouch against you, and my place i' th' state,
Will so your accusation overweigh,
That you shall stifle in your own report,
And smell of calumny. I have begun,
And now I give my sensual race the rein.
Fit thy consent to my sharp appetite,
Lay by all nicety and prolixious blushes
That banish what they sue for. Redeem thy brother
By yielding up thy body to my will,
Or else he must not only die the death,
But thy unkindness shall his death draw out
To ling'ring sufferance. Answer me to-morrow,
Or by the affection that now guides me most,
I'll prove a tyrant to him. As for you,
Say what you can: my false o'erweighs your true.
Exit.

133. **Than**: than that.
134. **arrest your words**: hold you to what you have said. **that**: what.
135. **be more**: i.e. insist on keeping your chastity. **none**: no women (in terms of what you have just said of them).
136. **express'd**: shown to be. 137. **warrants**: assurances.
138. **putting . . . livery**: i.e. accepting the role that women are born to. 139. **tongue**: language.
145. **license**: allowed freedom.
146. **seems . . . fouler**: looks . . . uglier.
147. **pluck on**: draw on, tempt. 148. **purpose**: true intent.
151. **proclaim thee**: denounce you publicly.
152. **present**: immediate.
153. **with . . . aloud.** This faintly ludicrous image of a cock crowing loudly shows the pitch of Isabella's excited indignation. The rhetorical fitness of the hexameter line has been pointed out.
154. **What**: what manner of. 156. **vouch**: sworn statement.
157. **overweigh**: outweigh.
158. **in . . . report**: in your own story (implying that it has polluted or poisoned the air) (?) or, with respect to your own reputation (?).
160. **race**: strain. **the rein**: free rein.
162. **nicety**: fastidious reserve. **prolixious**: prolix, i.e. excessive, tiresome. This word (ordinarily applied to language), taken with the next line, ironically recalls Claudio's hope that Isabella will succeed by virtue of her youth's "prone and speechless dialect / Such as move men" (I.ii.183–84).
166. **unkindness**: unnaturalness (as a woman and as a sister).
167. **sufferance**: suffering (by torture).
168. **affection**: passion.

Isab. To whom should I complain? Did I tell this,
Who would believe me? O perilous mouths,
That bear in them one and the self-same tongue,
Either of condemnation or approof,
Bidding the law make curtsy to their will,
Hooking both right and wrong to th' appetite,
To follow as it draws! I'll to my brother.
Though he hath fall'n by prompture of the blood,
Yet hath he in him such a mind of honor
That had he twenty heads to tender down
On twenty bloody blocks, he'ld yield them up,
Before his sister should her body stoop
To such abhorr'd pollution.
Then, Isabel, live chaste, and, brother, die;
More than our brother is our chastity.
I'll tell him yet of Angelo's request,
And fit his mind to death, for his soul's rest. *Exit.*

ACT III, Scene I

Enter Duke [*disguised as a friar*], Claudio, *and* Provost.

Duke. So then you hope of pardon from Lord Angelo?
Claud. The miserable have no other medicine
But only hope:
I have hope to live, and am prepar'd to die.
Duke. Be absolute for death: either death or life
Shall thereby be the sweeter. Reason thus with life:
If I do lose thee, I do lose a thing
That none but fools would keep. A breath thou art,
Servile to all the skyey influences,
That dost this habitation where thou keep'st
Hourly afflict. Merely, thou art death's fool,
For him thou labor'st by thy flight to shun,
And yet run'st toward him still. Thou art not noble,
For all th' accommodations that thou bear'st
Are nurs'd by baseness. Thou'rt by no means valiant,
For thou dost fear the soft and tender fork
Of a poor worm. Thy best of rest is sleep,
And that thou oft provok'st, yet grossly fear'st

171. **Did I**: if I were to.
174. **Either . . . approof**: i.e. now condemning, now sanctioning.
175. **make curtsy**: bow, make obeisance.
176. **Hooking.** Cf. *Anchor* in line 4. 177. **draws**: drags.
178. **prompture**: urging. 179. **mind of honor**: honorable mind.

III.i. Location: The prison.
5. **absolute for death**: certain that you must die.
9. **Servile to**: the slave of. **skyey influences**: influence of the stars (supposedly a physical emanation or flow, hence the name).
10. **dost.** The subject is *influences*. A singular verb with such a subject is common enough; here it has been attracted into the second person by the surrounding matter. **habitation**: (1) the earth; (2) the body. **keep'st**: dwellest.
11. **Merely**: utterly. **fool**: plaything. 13. **still**: continually.
14. **accommodations**: comforts, sophistications of civilized life. Cf. *King Lear*, III.iv.106–8, "unaccommodated man is no more but . . . a poor, bare, fork'd animal . . . ." **bear'st**. The meaning may be "possessest" or, more narrowly, "wearest," which would make clothing the dominant idea in *accommodations* (as in the *Lear* passage); but *bear'st* also suggests bearing a child (in two senses) and leads to the next image.
15. **nurs'd by baseness**: fed by lowly means. Cf. *Antony and Cleopatra*, V.ii.7–8, "which sleeps, and never palates more the dung, / The beggar's nurse and Caesar's." 17. **worm**: snake.
18. **grossly**: stupidly.

Thy death, which is no more. Thou art not thyself,
For thou exists on many a thousand grains
That issue out of dust. Happy thou art not,
For what thou hast not, still thou striv'st to get,
And what thou hast, forget'st. Thou art not certain,
For thy complexion shifts to strange effects,
After the moon. If thou art rich, thou'rt poor,
For like an ass, whose back with ingots bows,
Thou bear'st thy heavy riches but a journey,
And death unloads thee. Friend hast thou none,
For thine own bowels, which do call thee [sire],
The mere effusion of thy proper loins,
Do curse the gout, sapego, and the rheum
For ending thee no sooner. Thou hast nor youth nor age,
But as it were an after-dinner's sleep,
Dreaming on both, for all thy blessed youth
Becomes as aged, and doth beg the alms
Of palsied eld; and when thou art old and rich,
Thou hast neither heat, affection, limb, nor beauty,
To make thy riches pleasant. What's yet in this
That bears the name of life? Yet in this life
Lie hid moe thousand deaths; yet death we fear
That makes these odds all even.
Claud. I humbly thank you.
To sue to live, I find I seek to die,
And seeking death, find life. Let it come on.
Isab. [*Within.*] What ho! Peace here; grace and good company!
Prov. Who's there? Come in, the wish deserves a welcome.
Duke. Dear sir, ere long I'll visit you again.
Claud. Most holy sir, I thank you.

Enter Isabella.

Isab. My business is a word or two with Claudio.
Prov. And very welcome. Look, signior, here's your sister.
Duke. Provost, a word with you.
Prov. As many as you please.
Duke. Bring [me] to hear [them] speak, where I may be conceal'd. [*Exeunt Duke and Provost.*]
Claud. Now, sister, what's the comfort?
Isab. Why,
As all comforts are: most good, most good indeed.

19. **not thyself**: not your own, not self-contained and independent.
20. **exists.** See the note on II.ii.116. **grains**: seeds.
23. **certain**: stable, of fixed character.
24. **complexion**: physical and mental constitution. **effects**: manifestations.
25. **After the moon**: (1) influenced by the moon; (2) resembling the moon, constantly changing.
26. **ingots**: bars of precious metal.
29. **bowels**: i.e. offspring. 30. **mere**: very. **proper**: own.
31. **sapego**: serpigo, a disfiguring skin disease. **rheum**: catarrh, running eyes, and other disorders associated with excess bodily fluid.
32. **nor youth**: neither youth.
33–34. **an after-dinner's . . . both.** "Our life . . . resembles our dreams after dinner [i.e. the noonday meal], when the events of the morning are mingled with the designs of the evening" (Johnson).
35. **as aged**: as if aged, i.e. no different from age (since young men must beg for money from their elders, just as feeble old men must look to younger men for physical assistance) (?). The passage may be corrupt and has been variously emended. 36. **eld**: old age.
37. **heat**: vigor, vitality. It was thought that in old age the blood became cold and thick. **affection**: passion. **limb**: i.e. proper use of any bodily member.
41. **makes . . . even**: i.e. removes all these ills. 42. **To sue**: suing.

Lord Angelo, having affairs to heaven,
Intends you for his swift ambassador,
Where you shall be an everlasting leiger;
Therefore your best appointment make with speed,
To-morrow you set on.
Claud. Is there no remedy?
Isab. None, but such remedy as, to save a head,
To cleave a heart in twain.
Claud. But is there any?
Isab. Yes, brother, you may live;
There is a devilish mercy in the judge,
If you'll implore it, that will free your life,
But fetter you till death.
Claud. Perpetual durance?
Isab. Ay, just, perpetual durance, a restraint,
[Though] all the world's vastidity you had,
To a determin'd scope.
Claud. But in what nature?
Isab. In such a one as, you consenting to't,
Would bark your honor from that trunk you bear,
And leave you naked.
Claud. Let me know the point.
Isab. O, I do fear thee, Claudio, and I quake,
Lest thou a feverous life shouldst entertain,
And six or seven winters more respect
Than a perpetual honor. Dar'st thou die?
The sense of death is most in apprehension,
And the poor beetle that we tread upon
In corporal sufferance finds a pang as great
As when a giant dies.
Claud. Why give you me this shame?
Think you I can a resolution fetch
From flow'ry tenderness? If I must die,
I will encounter darkness as a bride,
And hug it in mine arms.
Isab. There spake my brother; there my father's grave
Did utter forth a voice. Yes, thou must die:
Thou art too noble to conserve a life
In base appliances. This outward-sainted deputy,
Whose settled visage and deliberate word
Nips youth i' th' head, and follies doth [enew]
As falcon doth the fowl, is yet a devil;
His filth within being cast, he would appear
A pond as deep as hell.
Claud. The prenzie Angelo?
Isab. O, 'tis the cunning livery of hell,
The damned'st body to invest and cover
In prenzie guards! Dost thou think, Claudio,
If I would yield him my virginity,
Thou mightst be freed!
Claud. O heavens, it cannot be.
Isab. Yes, he would give't thee, from this rank offense,
So to offend him still. This night's the time
That I should do what I abhor to name,
Or else thou diest to-morrow.
Claud. Thou shalt not do't.
Isab. O, were it but my life,
I'd throw it down for your deliverance
As frankly as a pin.
Claud. Thanks, dear Isabel.
Isab. Be ready, Claudio, for your death to-morrow.
Claud. Yes. Has he affections in him,
That thus can make him bite the law by th' nose,
When he would force it? Sure it is no sin,
Or of the deadly seven it is the least.
Isab. Which is the least?
Claud. If it were damnable, he being so wise,
Why would he for the momentary trick
Be perdurably fin'd? O Isabel!
Isab. What says my brother?
Claud. Death is a fearful thing.
Isab. And shamed life a hateful.
Claud. Ay, but to die, and go we know not where;
To lie in cold obstruction, and to rot;
This sensible warm motion to become
A kneaded clod; and the delighted spirit
To bathe in fiery floods, or to reside
In thrilling region of thick-ribbed ice;
To be imprison'd in the viewless winds
And blown with restless violence round about
The pendant world; or to be worse than worst

56. affairs to: business with. **58. leiger**: resident ambassador.
59. appointment: preparation. **60. set on**: set forth.
66. durance: confinement. **67. just**: exactly.
68. vastidity: vastness (apparently Shakespeare's coinage).
69. a determin'd scope: fixed limits, i.e. the ever-present consciousness of the means by which he had gained his life.
71. bark: strip off (as bark from a tree). **trunk**: body (with play on "tree trunk"). **73. fear**: fear for.
74. feverous life. Cf. "life's fitful fever," *Macbeth*, III.ii.23. **entertain**: cherish, cling to. **75. respect**: regard, value.
77. apprehension: i.e. the idea of it (literally, "taking hold").
78–80. the poor . . . dies: i.e. as for the physical pain of death, a giant feels proportionately no greater pain than a beetle feels.
81. a resolution fetch: achieve resoluteness of mind.
82. flow'ry tenderness: soothing flowers of rhetoric.
88. In base appliances: by applying ignoble remedies. **outward-sainted**: outwardly saintly.
89. settled visage: composed and unaltering expression.
90. Nips . . . head. The image is of a falcon striking its prey; it continues in *enew* = drive prey into the water (*in-eau*) or covert.
92. cast. Variously explained as "vomited," "calculated" (as in *casting accounts*), "examined for diagnosis" (as in *casting urine*), etc. But in view of *pond* in line 93, the likeliest meaning is "cleared out," as mud and refuse is cleared out of a ditch or pond and cast up on the bank (*O.E.D.*, *v.*, 28, 29).
93. pond. The linking of a dirty pond and a hypocritical "settled visage" (line 89) occurs again in *The Merchant of Venice*, I.i.88–89, where men desirous of a reputation for "wisdom, gravity, profound conceit" are said to assume "visages" that "cream and mantle like a standing [stagnant] pool."
93, 96. prenzie. A word found nowhere else, and not satisfactorily explained. Among the many emendations, the two most favored by editors have been *princely* (F2) and *precise* (Tieck conjecture in Cambridge). Some proposed readings, e.g. *proxy* (Bulloch conjecture in Cambridge), fit one line but not the other, and some editors adopt different readings in the two lines.
94. livery: distribution of clothing to retainers. **95. invest**: clothe.
96. guards: trimmings, external trappings. **Dost thou think**: i.e. can you believe.
99–100. give't . . . still: grant you freedom, in return for my foul offense, to go on offending in the same fashion.
104. deliverance: liberation from prison.
105. As . . . pin: as freely as I would throw away a pin.
108. bite . . . nose: flout the law. An ironic reversal of the "biting laws" of I.iii.19; cf. also I.iii.29. **109. force**: enforce.
113. trick: trifle. **114. perdurably fin'd**: punished eternally.
118. obstruction: darkness (as in *Twelfth Night*, IV.iii.39) (?). More often explained as stoppage of blood, i.e. cessation of all vital activity.
119. sensible warm motion: i.e. body endowed with feeling and heat and movement.
120. kneaded: reduced to a common mass (*O.E.D.*). **delighted**: having (capacity for) delight (?) or now experiencing delight (?).
122. thrilling: piercingly cold. **123. viewless**: invisible.
124–25. blown . . . world. Cf. the punishment of sexual offenders in Dante's *Inferno*, Canto V. **124. restless**: never-resting.
125. pendant: hanging in space.

Of those that lawless and incertain thought
Imagine howling—'tis too horrible!
The weariest and most loathed worldly life
That age, ache, [penury], and imprisonment
Can lay on nature is a paradise
To what we fear of death.

Isab. Alas, alas!

Claud. Sweet sister, let me live.
What sin you do to save a brother's life,
Nature dispenses with the deed so far,
That it becomes a virtue.

Isab. O you beast!
O faithless coward! O dishonest wretch!
Wilt thou be made a man out of my vice?
Is't not a kind of incest, to take life
From thine own sister's shame? What should I think?
Heaven shield my mother play'd my father fair!
For such a warped slip of wilderness
Ne'er issu'd from his blood. Take my defiance!
Die, perish! Might but my bending down
Reprieve thee from thy fate, it should proceed.
I'll pray a thousand prayers for thy death,
No word to save thee.

Claud. Nay, hear me, Isabel.

Isab. O fie, fie, fie!
Thy sin's not accidental, but a trade.
Mercy to thee would prove itself a bawd,
'Tis best that thou diest quickly.

Claud. O, hear me, Isabella!

[*Enter* Duke *disguised as a friar.*]

Duke. Vouchsafe a word, young sister, but one word.

Isab. What is your will?

Duke. Might you dispense with your leisure, I would by and by have some speech with you. The satisfaction I would require is likewise your own benefit.

Isab. I have no superfluous leisure; my stay must be stolen out of other affairs; but I will attend you a while. [*Walks apart.*]

Duke. Son, I have overheard what hath pass'd between you and your sister. Angelo had never the purpose to corrupt her; only he hath made an assay of her virtue to practice his judgment with the disposition of natures. She (having the truth of honor in her) hath made him that gracious denial which he is most glad to receive. I am confessor to Angelo, and I know this to be true; therefore prepare yourself to death. Do not satisfy your resolution with hopes that are fallible, to-morrow you must die; go to your knees, and make ready.

Claud. Let me ask my sister pardon. I am so out of love with life that I will sue to be rid of it.

Duke. Hold you there! Farewell. [*Exit Claudio.*] Provost, a word with you.

[*Enter* Provost.]

Prov. What's your will, father?

Duke. That now you are come, you will be gone. Leave me a while with the maid. My mind promises with my habit, no loss shall touch her by my company.

Prov. In good time. *Exit.*

Duke. [*Turning to Isabella.*] The hand that hath made you fair hath made you good; the goodness that is cheap in beauty makes beauty brief in goodness; but grace, being the soul of your complexion, shall keep the body of it ever fair. The assault that Angelo hath made to you, fortune hath convey'd to my understanding; and but that frailty hath examples for his falling, I should wonder at Angelo. How will you do to content this substitute, and to save your brother?

Isab. I am now going to resolve him. I had rather my brother die by the law than my son should be unlawfully born. But O, how much is the good Duke deceiv'd in Angelo! If ever he return, and I can speak to him, I will open my lips in vain, or discover his government.

Duke. That shall not be much amiss; yet, as the matter now stands, he will avoid your accusation: he made trial of you only. Therefore fasten your ear on my advisings: to the love I have in doing good a remedy presents itself. I do make myself believe that you may most uprighteously do a poor wrong'd lady a merited benefit; redeem your brother from the angry law; do no stain to your own gracious person; and much please the absent Duke, if peradventure he shall ever return to have hearing of this business.

Isab. Let me hear you speak farther. I have spirit to do any thing that appears not foul in the truth of my spirit.

Duke. Virtue is bold, and goodness never fearful. Have you not heard speak of Mariana, the sister of Frederick, the great soldier who miscarried at sea?

Isab. I have heard of the lady, and good words went with her name.

Duke. She should this Angelo have married; was

126. lawless . . . thought: unrestrained and dubious conjecture.
127. Imagine. On the plural form see the note on I.ii.84.
134. dispenses with: excuses.
137. made a man: i.e. given life (with a play on "conceived" or "born"). **140. shield**: defend.
141. warped: deviating from what is natural, deformed, perverted. **slip of wilderness**: shoot of a wild stock.
142. defiance: rejection, declaration of enmity.
143. Might . . . down: even if a mere bow from me could.
148. accidental: a chance happening. **trade**: established practice.
149. prove . . . bawd: procure further sexual indulgence for you.
153. dispense with: forgo. **158. attend**: await.
162. only he hath: he has only. **assay**: test.
163. disposition: manner of thought and behavior.
164. truth: integrity. **165. gracious**: virtuous.
167. to death: for death.
173. Hold you there: continue in that resolution.
178. habit: friar's gown.
179. In good time. A phrase of acquiescence, "very well."
181–82. the goodness . . . in beauty: the kindness that beauty is free with (?).
182. makes . . . goodness: makes virtue short-lived in beauty.
183. complexion: makeup, nature.
186. but that: except for the fact that. **hath examples**: furnishes precedents. **falling.** This word, taken with Angelo's name, has prompted the suggestion that an allusion to the fallen angels is intended. **188. substitute**: deputy.
189. resolve him: give him a definite answer. **193. discover**: expose.
194. government: conduct.
196–97. avoid . . . only: i.e. get round your accusation by saying that he was merely testing you. **206. foul**: ugly. **208. fearful**: timid.
210. miscarried: was lost.
213. She . . . married. The closest modern rendering would be "Her was this Angelo to have married." Nominative for accusative in emphatic initial position is not unusual.

affianc'd to her [by] oath, and the nuptial appointed; between which time of the contract and limit of the solemnity, her brother Frederick was wrack'd at sea, having in that perish'd vessel the dowry of his sister. But mark how heavily this befell to the poor gentlewoman: there she lost a noble and renown'd brother, in his love toward her ever most kind and natural; with him, the portion and sinew of her fortune, her marriage-dowry; with both, her combinate-husband, this well-seeming Angelo.

Isab. Can this be so? Did Angelo so leave her?

Duke. Left her in her tears, and dried not one of them with his comfort; swallow'd his vows whole, pretending in her discoveries of dishonor; in few, bestow'd her on her own lamentation, which she yet wears for his sake; and he, a marble to her tears, is wash'd with them, but relents not.

Isab. What a merit were it in death to take this poor maid from the world! What corruption in this life, that it will let this man live! But how out of this can she avail?

Duke. It is a rupture that you may easily heal; and the cure of it not only saves your brother, but keeps you from dishonor in doing it.

Isab. Show me how, good father.

Duke. This forenam'd maid hath yet in her the continuance of her first affection; his unjust unkindness (that in all reason should have quench'd her love) hath (like an impediment in the current) made it more violent and unruly. Go you to Angelo, answer his requiring with a plausible obedience, agree with his demands to the point; only refer yourself to this advantage: first, that your stay with him may not be long; that the time may have all shadow and silence in it; and the place answer to convenience. This being granted in course—and now follows all—we shall advise this wrong'd maid to stead up your appointment, go in your place. If the encounter acknowledge itself hereafter, it may compel him to her recompense; and here, by this is your brother sav'd, your honor untainted, the poor Mariana advantag'd, and the corrupt deputy scal'd. The maid will I frame, and make fit for his attempt. If you think well to carry this as you may, the doubleness of the benefit defends the deceit from reproof. What think you of it?

Isab. The image of it gives me content already, and I trust it will grow to a most prosperous perfection.

Duke. It lies much in your holding up. Haste you speedily to Angelo; if for this night he entreat you to his bed, give him promise of satisfaction. I will presently to Saint Luke's; there, at the moated grange, resides this dejected Mariana. At that place call upon me, and dispatch with Angelo, that it may be quickly.

Isab. I thank you for this comfort. Fare you well, good father. *Exit.* [*Manet Duke.*]

[Scene II]

Enter Elbow, *Clown* [Pompey], Officers.

Elb. Nay, if there be no remedy for it but that you will needs buy and sell men and women like beasts, we shall have all the world drink brown and white bastard.

Duke. O heavens, what stuff is here?

Pom. 'Twas never merry world since of two usuries the merriest was put down, and the worser allow'd by order of law; a furr'd gown to keep him warm; and furr'd with fox and lambskins too, to signify that craft, being richer than innocency, stands for the facing.

Elb. Come your way, sir. Bless you, good father friar.

Duke. And you, good brother father. What offense hath this man made you, sir?

Elb. Marry, sir, he hath offended the law; and, sir, we take him to be a thief too, sir, for we have found upon him, sir, a strange picklock, which we have sent to the deputy.

Duke. Fie, sirrah, a bawd, a wicked bawd!
The evil that thou causest to be done,
That is thy means to live. Do thou but think
What 'tis to cram a maw or clothe a back
From such a filthy vice; say to thyself,

214. affianc'd . . . oath. The contract between Angelo and Mariana, unlike that between Claudio and Juliet, appears to have been *sponsalia per verba de futuro*, a betrothal which could be cancelled by mutual consent or broken for cause by either party at any time before the marriage was solemnized. Mariana's alleged unchastity (line 227) would have been adequate cause if the allegation had been true. Sexual intercourse between a betrothed pair created a valid marriage at common law. **the nuptial appointed:** the wedding day set.
215–16. limit . . . solemnity: day set for solemnizing the marriage.
221. natural: i.e. brotherly. **sinew:** i.e. strength, mainstay.
222–23. her combinate-husband: the man bound by oath to be her husband. **226. swallow'd:** retracted (cf. *eat one's words*).
227. pretending . . . dishonor: alleging she had been discovered to be unchaste. **in few:** in short.
227–28. bestow'd her on: gave her over to (with ironic play on "gave her in marriage to").
229. wears: makes her habit. **a marble:** i.e. impervious.
234. avail: benefit.
235. rupture: breach (with play on the medical sense, as indicated by *heal* and *cure*).
240–41. unjust unkindness: unnatural degree of faithlessness.
244. plausible obedience: convincing pretense of obedience.
245. to the point: in every detail. **refer yourself to:** commit yourself to, i.e. impose (?) or rely on (?).
246. advantage: favorable condition. **247. shadow:** darkness.
247, 248. time, place. It has been suggested that these words are transposed. **249. all:** i.e. the heart of the matter.
250. stead up: fulfill in your stead.
251. encounter: sexual encounter (as often; cf. line 83).
251–52. acknowledge itself: make itself known (by Mariana's pregnancy).

255. scal'd: weighed (and found wanting). **frame:** shape, prepare.
259. image: i.e mental image, idea.
261. holding up: sustaining, ability to carry it through.
264. moated: surrounded by a ditch (not necessarily filled with water). **grange:** country house.
265. dejected: (1) low-spirited; (2) humbled.
266. dispatch: settle affairs. **269 s.d. Manet:** remains.

III.ii. Location: Scene continues.
3. bastard: sweet Spanish wine (with obvious pun).
5. 'Twas . . . world: things have never gone well (proverbial).
5–6. two usuries: i.e. lending money at interest and fornication, both of which produce increase.
7. furr'd gown. Associated with usurers.
8. fox and lambskins. Most editors read *on* for *and*, for closer agreement with *facing* (line 10).
9–10. stands . . . facing: sanctions the trimming (with a bawdy equivoque).
11–12. father friar. *Friar* = brother. The Duke answers Elbow's blunder in kind.
15. the law: i.e. not me but the law (a literal-minded reply).
16. take. With a quibble on "arrest." A precise equivalent would be *apprehend*. **17. picklock:** skeleton key. **22. maw:** stomach.

From their abominable and beastly touches
I drink, I eat, [array] myself, and live.
Canst thou believe thy living is a life,
So stinkingly depending? Go mend, go mend.

Pom. Indeed, it does stink in some sort, sir; but yet, sir, I would prove—

Duke. Nay, if the devil have given thee proofs for sin,
Thou wilt prove his. Take him to prison, officer.
Correction and instruction must both work
Ere this rude beast will profit.

Elb. He must before the deputy, sir, he has given him warning. The deputy cannot abide a whoremaster. If he be a whoremonger, and comes before him, he were as good go a mile on his errand.

Duke. That we were all, as some would seem to be,
From our faults, as faults from seeming, free!

Enter LUCIO.

Elb. His neck will come to your waist—a cord, sir.

Pom. I spy comfort, I cry bail. Here's a gentleman, and a friend of mine.

Lucio. How now, noble Pompey? What, at the wheels of Caesar? Art thou led in triumph? What, is there none of Pygmalion's images newly made woman to be had now, for putting the hand in the pocket and extracting [it] clutch'd? What reply? Ha? What say'st thou to this tune, matter, and method? Is't not drown'd i' th' last rain? Ha? What say'st thou, Trot? Is the world as it was, man? Which is the way? Is it sad, and few words? or how? The trick of it?

Duke. Still thus, and thus; still worse!

Lucio. How doth my dear morsel, thy mistress? Procures she still? Ha?

Pom. Troth, sir, she hath eaten up all her beef, and she is herself in the tub.

Lucio. Why, 'tis good; it is the right of it; it must be so. Ever your fresh whore and your powder'd bawd, an unshunn'd consequence; it must be so. Art going to prison, Pompey?

Pom. Yes, faith, sir.

Lucio. Why, 'tis not amiss, Pompey. Farewell. Go say I sent thee thither. For debt, Pompey? or how?

Elb. For being a bawd, for being a bawd.

Lucio. Well, then imprison him. If imprisonment be the due of a bawd, why, 'tis his right. Bawd is he doubtless, and of antiquity too; bawd-born. Farewell, good Pompey. Commend me to the prison, Pompey. You will turn good husband now, Pompey, you will keep the house.

Pom. I hope, sir, your good worship will be my bail.

Lucio. No indeed will I not, Pompey, it is not the wear. I will pray, Pompey, to increase your bondage. If you take it not patiently, why, your mettle is the more. Adieu, trusty Pompey. Bless you, friar.

Duke. And you.

Lucio. Does Bridget paint still, Pompey? Ha?

Elb. Come your ways, sir, come.

Pom. You will not bail me then, sir?

Lucio. Then, Pompey, nor now. What news abroad, friar? what news?

Elb. Come your ways, sir, come.

Lucio. Go to kennel, Pompey, go. [*Exeunt Elbow, Pompey, and Officers.*] What news, friar, of the Duke?

Duke. I know none. Can you tell me of any?

Lucio. Some say he is with the Emperor of Russia; other some, he is in Rome; but where is he, think you?

Duke. I know not where; but wheresoever, I wish him well.

Lucio. It was a mad fantastical trick of him to steal from the state, and usurp the beggary he was never born to. Lord Angelo dukes it well in his absence; he puts transgression to't.

Duke. He does well in't.

Lucio. A little more lenity to lechery would do no harm in him. Something too crabbed that way, friar.

Duke. It is too general a vice, and severity must cure it.

Lucio. Yes, in good sooth, the vice is of a great kindred; it is well allied; but it is impossible to extirp it quite, friar, till eating and drinking be put down. They say this Angelo was not made by man and woman after this downright way of creation. Is it true, think you?

Duke. How should he be made then?

Lucio. Some report a sea-maid spawn'd him; some, that he was begot between two stock-fishes. But it is certain that when he makes water his urine is con-

24. **abominable.** Supposedly derived from *ab homine*, "alien to man, inhuman," a sense here reinforced by *beastly*.
29. **prove:** i.e. try to prove, argue.
30. **proofs for:** arguments in support of. 31. **prove:** turn out to be.
32. **Correction:** punishment. **both work:** operate together, make their joint effect felt. Probably *work* in I.i.9 has the same meaning.
37. **he . . . errand:** i.e. things will go hard with him.
38–39. **That . . . free:** would that we were all free of faults, as some make themselves appear, and that faults were free of dissembling. Many editors adopt the F2 reading *Free from* in place of *From* (line 39); this improves the metre but does not alter the sense.
40. **come . . . waist:** come to the condition of your waist, i.e. be encircled by a cord.
43–44. **at . . . triumph.** Cf. II.i.248–49. The historical Pompey was never led in triumph by Caesar, though his sons were.
45–46. **Pygmalion's . . . woman.** Alluding to the legend of the sculptor Pygmalion's female statue that came to life; with a play on *become a woman* in the sense "lose one's virginity."
47. **clutch'd:** i.e. grasping a coin.
49. **drown'd . . . rain:** i.e. out of fashion (?).
50. **Trot:** old bawd (ordinarily applied to a woman).
50–51. **Which . . . way:** how does the world go. *The trick of it* (line 52) is another way of saying the same thing. 51. **sad:** melancholy.
56. **eaten . . . beef:** worn out all her prostitutes.
57. **tub:** (1) pickling-tub (for beef); (2) sweating-tub (for treating venereal disease).
59. **fresh . . . powder'd:** (1) young; (2) not preserved . . . (1) made-up; (2) pickled, corned.
60. **unshunn'd:** unshunnable (i.e. the young whore inevitably turns into the old bawd).

68. **antiquity:** long standing.
69. **Commend.** Playing on the senses "give my regards to" and "commit." 70. **husband:** master of a household.
71. **keep the house:** (1) manage the household; (2) stay indoors.
75. **wear:** fashion. 76. **mettle:** (1) spirit; (2) metal, i.e. shackles.
77. **trusty:** faithful. 80. **Come your ways:** come along.
82. **Then:** i.e. neither then.
93. **usurp the beggary.** It is not clear why Lucio should say this.
95. **puts transgression to't:** applies extreme measures to lawbreaking.
98. **crabbed:** harsh. 99. **general:** common. 101. **sooth:** truth.
101–2. **great kindred:** (1) large family; (2) good family (*well allied*, line 102, has the same meanings). 102. **extirp:** extirpate.
105. **this.** The generic use, as in II.iv.79. **downright:** plain, ordinary (with a play on "horizontal").
107. **should he be:** is he said to have been.
108. **sea-maid:** mermaid. 109. **stock-fishes:** dried cod.

geal'd ice, that I know to be true; and he is a motion generative, that's infallible.

Duke. You are pleasant, sir, and speak apace.

Lucio. Why, what a ruthless thing is this in him, for the rebellion of a codpiece to take away the life of a man! Would the Duke that is absent have done this? Ere he would have hang'd a man for the getting a hundred bastards, he would have paid for the nursing a thousand. He had some feeling of the sport; he knew the service, and that instructed him to mercy.

Duke. I never heard the absent Duke much detected for women, he was not inclin'd that way.

Lucio. O, sir, you are deceiv'd.

Duke. 'Tis not possible.

Lucio. Who? not the Duke? Yes, your beggar of fifty; and his use was to put a ducat in her clack-dish. The Duke had crotchets in him. He would be drunk too, that let me inform you.

Duke. You do him wrong, surely.

Lucio. Sir, I was an inward of his. A shy fellow was the Duke, and I believe I know the cause of his withdrawing.

Duke. What, I prithee, might be the cause?

Lucio. No, pardon; 'tis a secret must be lock'd within the teeth and the lips. But this I can let you understand, the greater file of the subject held the Duke to be wise.

Duke. Wise? Why, no question but he was.

Lucio. A very superficial, ignorant, unweighing fellow.

Duke. Either this is envy in you, folly, or mistaking. The very stream of his life, and the business he hath helm'd, must, upon a warranted need, give him a better proclamation. Let him be but testimonied in his own bringings-forth, and he shall appear to the envious a scholar, a statesman, and a soldier. Therefore you speak unskillfully; or, if your knowledge be more, it is much dark'ned in your malice.

Lucio. Sir, I know him, and I love him.

Duke. Love talks with better knowledge, and knowledge with [dearer] love.

Lucio. Come, sir, I know what I know.

Duke. I can hardly believe that, since you know not what you speak. But if ever the Duke return (as

our prayers are he may), let me desire you to make your answer before him. If it be honest you have spoke, you have courage to maintain it. I am bound to call upon you, and I pray you your name?

Lucio. Sir, my name is Lucio, well known to the Duke.

Duke. He shall know you better, sir, if I may live to report you.

Lucio. I fear you not.

Duke. O, you hope the Duke will return no more; or you imagine me too unhurtful an opposite. But indeed I can do you little harm; you'll forswear this again.

Lucio. I'll be hang'd first; thou art deceiv'd in me, friar. But no more of this. Canst thou tell if Claudio die to-morrow, or no?

Duke. Why should he die, sir?

Lucio. Why? For filling a bottle with a tun-dish. I would the Duke we talk of were return'd again. This ungenitur'd agent will unpeople the province with continency. Sparrows must not build in his house-eaves, because they are lecherous. The Duke yet would have dark deeds darkly answer'd, he would never bring them to light. Would he were return'd! Marry, this Claudio is condemn'd for untrussing. Farewell, good friar, I prithee pray for me. The Duke (I say to thee again) would eat mutton on Fridays. He's now past it, yet (and I say to thee) he would mouth with a beggar, though she smelt brown bread and garlic. Say that I said so. Farewell. *Exit.*

Duke. No might nor greatness in mortality
Can censure scape; back-wounding calumny
The whitest virtue strikes. What king so strong
Can tie the gall up in the slanderous tongue?
But who comes here?

Enter Escalus, Provost, *and* [Officers *with*] *Bawd* [Mistress Overdone].

Escal. Go, away with her to prison.

Mrs. Ov. Good my lord, be good to me, your honor is accounted a merciful man. Good my lord.

Escal. Double and treble admonition, and still forfeit in the same kind! This would make mercy swear and play the tyrant.

Prov. A bawd of eleven years' continuance, may it please your honor.

111. motion: puppet.
112. generative: male (?). Many editors adopt Theobald's *ungenerative* (= sexless); cf. *ungenitur'd* in line 174. **infallible:** certain.
113. pleasant: jocose. **apace:** rapidly, i.e. heedlessly.
115. codpiece: baggy appendage at the front of breeches; hence slang for "penis." **118. nursing:** rearing.
121–22. detected for: accused of.
125. your. The indefinite use (but comically applicable, if Lucio but knew it, to the person he is addressing). **126. use:** custom.
126–27. clack-dish: beggar's bowl with a wooden cover that could be "clacked" to attract the attention of passers-by.
127. crotchets: whims, odd notions. **129. wrong:** injustice.
130. inward: intimate. **shy:** warily reserved (*O.E.D.*). Used by Shakespeare only here and at V.i.54, where the context helps to define its sense. **132. withdrawing:** departure, i.e. absence.
136. greater . . . subject: majority of his subjects.
139. unweighing: injudicious. **141. envy:** malice.
142. stream: course.
143. helm'd: steered, directed. **upon . . . need:** if a warrant were needed.
143–44. give . . . proclamation: proclaim him a better man (than you allow).
145. bringings-forth: achievements. **to the envious:** even to the malicious. **147. unskillfully:** in ignorance.

156–57. If . . . spoke: if what you have said is true.
157. I am bound: it is my duty. **165. opposite:** opponent.
166. forswear: deny on oath. **172. tun-dish:** funnel.
174. ungenitur'd: incapable of sex (see the note on line 112). **agent:** deputy. **175. Sparrows.** Proverbially lecherous.
177. darkly: secretly.
179. untrussing: untying the laces that fastened hose to doublet, i.e. undressing.
181. I . . . again. Here and in lines 182 (*and . . . thee*) and 184 (*Say . . . so*) Lucio brashly underlines his slanders to show his lack of concern about having them reported to the Duke.
181–82. eat . . . Fridays: eat forbidden meat, i.e. have recourse to prostitutes. *Mutton* is slang for "whore"; cf. *beef* in line 56.
183. smelt: smelt of.
183–84. brown bread: bread made of flour with most of the bran left in it, hence soon musty. **185. mortality:** humankind.
186. back-wounding: backbiting. **187. whitest:** purest.
188. tie . . . up: restrain the bitterness (or venom).
193–94. forfeit . . . kind: found guilty of the same offense.
194–95. make . . . tyrant: turn mercy itself to cruelty (with allusion to the raging and ranting of conventional tyrants, notably Herod, in early drama).

Mrs. Ov. My lord, this is one Lucio's information against me. Mistress Kate Keepdown was with child by him in the Duke's time; he promis'd her marriage. His child is a year and a quarter old come Philip and Jacob. I have kept it myself; and see how he goes about to abuse me!

Escal. That fellow is a fellow of much license; let him be call'd before us. Away with her to prison! Go to, no more words. [*Exeunt Officers with Mistress Overdone.*] Provost, my brother Angelo will not be alter'd, Claudio must die to-morrow. Let him be furnish'd with divines, and have all charitable preparation. If my brother wrought by my pity, it should not be so with him.

Prov. So please you, this friar hath been with him, and advis'd him for th' entertainment of death.

Escal. Good even, good father.

Duke. Bliss and goodness on you!

Escal. Of whence are you?

Duke. Not of this country, though my chance is now
To use it for my time. I am a brother
Of gracious order, late come from the [See],
In special business from his Holiness.

Escal. What news abroad i' th' world?

Duke. None, but that there is so great a fever on goodness, that the dissolution of it must cure it. Novelty is only in request, and, as it is, as dangerous to be ag'd in any kind of course, as it is virtuous to be constant in any undertaking. There is scarce truth enough alive to make societies secure, but security enough to make fellowships accurs'd. Much upon this riddle runs the wisdom of the world. This news is old enough, yet it is every day's news. I pray you, sir, of what disposition was the Duke?

Escal. One that, above all other strifes, contended especially to know himself.

Duke. What pleasure was he given to?

Escal. Rather rejoicing to see another merry, than merry at any thing which profess'd to make him rejoice; a gentleman of all temperance. But leave we him to his events, with a prayer they may prove prosperous, and let me desire to know how you find Claudio prepar'd. I am made to understand that you have lent him visitation.

Duke. He professes to have receiv'd no sinister measure from his judge, but most willingly humbles himself to the determination of justice; yet had he fram'd to himself (by the instruction of his frailty) many deceiving promises of life, which I (by my good leisure) have discredited to him, and now is he resolv'd to die.

Escal. You have paid the heavens your function, and the prisoner the very debt of your calling. I have labor'd for the poor gentleman to the extremest shore of my modesty, but my brother-justice have I found so severe, that he hath forc'd me to tell him he is indeed Justice.

Duke. If his own life answer the straitness of his proceeding, it shall become him well; wherein if he chance to fail, he hath sentenc'd himself.

Escal. I am going to visit the prisoner. Fare you well.

Duke. Peace be with you!

[*Exeunt Escalus and Provost.*]

He who the sword of heaven will bear
Should be as holy as severe;
Pattern in himself to know,
Grace to stand, and virtue go;
More nor less to others paying
Than by self-offenses weighing.
Shame to him whose cruel striking
Kills for faults of his own liking!
Twice treble shame on Angelo,
To weed my vice, and let his grow!
O, what may man within him hide,
Though angel on the outward side!
How may likeness made in crimes,
Making practice on the times,
To draw with idle spiders' strings
Most ponderous and substantial things!
Craft against vice I must apply.

202. Philip and Jacob: the Feast of St. Philip and St. James, May 1. This was also May-day, celebrated with traditional festivities that were the occasion of much sexual license. **204. license**: licentiousness.
207. brother: i.e. colleague in office, cf. *brother-justice*, line 252.
209. charitable: required by Christian charity.
210. wrought . . . pity: exercised his function as compassionately as I.
213. entertainment: acceptance.
218. for my time: to serve my particular occasion.
219. late: recently. **the See**: the Holy See, Rome.
223. the dissolution . . . cure it: i.e. goodness can get rid of the disease only by dying.
224. Novelty . . . request: newfangledness alone is in demand. **as . . . as**: as things stand, (it is) as. **225. ag'd**: settled, constant.
226. constant. Many editors, following Staunton, emend to *inconstant*, so that *virtuous* (line 225) means "deemed virtuous by the new scale of values." But the F1 reading makes excellent sense: "constancy is now as dangerous as it is in actuality virtuous." **truth.** Perhaps meaning here "keeping one's plain word," in contrast to the following *security*, "giving security to bind an obligation." The sentence could then mean "There is hardly enough integrity left alive to make friendships possible, but enough security demanded to make commercial partnerships burdensome."
228–29. upon this riddle: after this paradoxical fashion.
231. disposition: inclination, temperament.
232. strifes: strivings, endeavors.
236. which profess'd: whose declared purpose was.
237. temperance: moderation.
237–38. his events: the outcome of his affairs.
240–41. lent him visitation: bestowed a visit upon him.
242–43. sinister measure: unjust treatment.
244. determination: decision.
245. fram'd to himself: formed in his mind.
245–46. instruction . . . frailty: prompting of natural human weakness. **246–47. by . . . leisure**: as time gave me opportunity.
248. resolv'd to die: resolute for death.
249. You . . . function. Recalling the Duke's remarks in I.i.29 ff.
250. the very . . . calling: what you are obligated as a friar to give him. **252. shore**: limit. **modesty**: propriety.
255–56. answer . . . proceeding: matches the strictness of his official acts (cf. line 262).
261. sword of heaven: i.e. authority to execute justice (the "deputed sword" of II.ii.60).
263. Pattern . . . know: to find a precedent (for his judgment of others) in his judgment of his own behavior (?).
264. Grace . . . go: (to find in himself) grace to stand firm and virtue to go forward (?) or grace to stand firm if virtue fail (in others) (?).
265–66. More . . . weighing: allotting neither more nor less to others than is determined by weighing his own offenses. Cf. II.ii.126.
270. my vice: i.e. another's sin.
272. angel. Another play on Angelo's name.
273–76. How . . . things. Not satisfactorily explained. A major obstacle is the meaning of *likeness made in crimes*. Line 274 means "practicing deception on the world." The language of lines 275–76 is clear in itself, but not its grammatical or logical relation to what precedes. Lever's theory that two lines are missing after line 274 may well be correct.

With Angelo to-night shall lie
His old betrothed (but despised);
So disguise shall by th' disguised
Pay with falsehood false exacting,
And perform an old contracting. *Exit.*

ACT IV, Scene I

Enter Mariana, *and* Boy *singing.*

Song

Take, O, take those lips away,
That so sweetly were forsworn,
And those eyes, the break of day,
Lights that do mislead the morn;
But my kisses bring again, bring again,
Seals of love, but seal'd in vain, seal'd in vain.

Enter Duke [*disguised as a friar*].

Mari. Break off thy song, and haste thee quick away.
Here comes a man of comfort, whose advice
Hath often still'd my brawling discontent. [*Exit Boy.*]
I cry you mercy, sir, and well could wish
You had not found me here so musical.
Let me excuse me, and believe me so,
My mirth it much displeas'd, but pleas'd my woe.

Duke. 'Tis good; though music oft hath such a charm
To make bad good, and good provoke to harm.
I pray you tell me, hath any body inquir'd for me here to-day? Much upon this time have I promis'd here to meet.

Mari. You have not been inquir'd after. I have sat here all day.

Enter Isabel.

Duke. I do constantly believe you. The time is come even now. I shall crave your forbearance a little. May be I will call upon you anon for some advantage to yourself.

Mari. I am always bound to you. *Exit.*

Duke. Very well met, and well come.
What is the news from this good deputy?

Isab. He hath a garden circummur'd with brick,
Whose western side is with a vineyard back'd;
And to that vineyard is a planched gate,
That makes his opening with this bigger key.

281. **falsehood:** deception, illusion.

IV.i. Location: The moated grange at St. Luke's.
1–6 **Take . . . vain.** See "Note on the Text."
2. **were forsworn:** swore falsely (to be true).
4. **mislead the morn:** i.e. make morning think that the sun has risen.
9. **brawling:** clamorous. 10. **cry you mercy:** beg your pardon.
12. **excuse me:** excuse myself (by saying).
13. **My . . . woe:** i.e. it was a song to ease my grief, not to make me merry.
14. **charm:** magic spell.
15. **make bad good:** make evil attractive. 17. **upon:** about.
21. **constantly:** assuredly.
22. **crave . . . little:** ask you to withdraw for a short time.
25. **bound to you:** in your debt.
26. **well come:** a common variant of *welcome,* and here paralleling *well met.*
28. **circummur'd:** walled about.
30. **planched:** made of planks.

This other doth command a little door,
Which from the vineyard to the garden leads;
There have I made my promise upon the heavy
Middle of the night to call upon him.

Duke. But shall you on your knowledge find this way?

Isab. I have ta'en a due and wary note upon't.
With whispering and most guilty diligence,
In action all of precept, he did show me
The way twice o'er.

Duke. Are there no other tokens
Between you 'greed concerning her observance?

Isab. No; none but only a repair i' th' dark,
And that I have possess'd him my most stay
Can be but brief; for I have made him know
I have a servant comes with me along,
That stays upon me, whose persuasion is
I come about my brother.

Duke. 'Tis well borne up.
I have not yet made known to Mariana
A word of this. What ho, within! come forth!

Enter Mariana.

I pray you be acquainted with this maid,
She comes to do you good.

Isab. I do desire the like.

Duke. Do you persuade yourself that respect you?

Mari. Good friar, I know you do, and have found it.

Duke. Take then this your companion by the hand,
Who hath a story ready for your ear.
I shall attend your leisure, but make haste,
The vaporous night approaches.

Mari. Will't please you walk aside?
Exit [*with Isabella*].

Duke. O place and greatness! millions of false eyes
Are stuck upon thee. Volumes of report
Run with these false, and most contrarious quest
Upon thy doings; thousand escapes of wit
Make thee the father of their idle dream,
And rack thee in their fancies.

Enter Mariana *and* Isabella.

Welcome, how agreed?

37. **wary:** careful, attentive.
39. **In . . . precept:** i.e. with explanatory gestures.
41. **her observance:** the conditions she is to observe.
42. **repair:** coming.
43. **possess'd:** informed. **most:** longest possible.
46. **stays upon:** waits for. **persuasion:** belief. Cf. *persuade yourself,* line 52.
47. **borne up:** sustained, carried on. Cf. *holding up,* III.i.261.
52. **respect you:** have concern for your welfare.
53. **found it:** had proof of it. Editors have repaired the metrical deficiency of this line by inserting a word (*oft, so,* or *I*) before *have.*
57. **vaporous.** Night mists were considered noxious.
59–64. **O . . . fancies.** Most commentators agree that these lines, not appropriate to the context, were originally part of the Duke's soliloquy at III.i.185–88, perhaps preceding line 185.
60. **stuck:** fixed, fastened. **Volumes:** quantities. **report:** rumor.
61. **these false:** i.e. these false (= distorting) eyes. **contrarious.** A word (probably adverbial here) of many shades of meaning; the sense here may be that the rumormongers are hostile or perverse, that the rumors are false or inconsistent with one another or adverse, or all of these. **quest:** give tongue (like hunting dogs when they sight their quarry). 62. **escapes:** scapes, transgressions.
63. **idle dream:** foolish fantasy.
64. **rack:** stretch on the rack, i.e. distort, tear apart.

Isab. She'll take the enterprise upon her, father,
If you advise it.

Duke. It is not my consent,
But my entreaty too.

Isab. Little have you to say
When you depart from him, but soft and low,
"Remember now my brother."

Mari. Fear me not.

Duke. Nor, gentle daughter, fear you not at all.
He is your husband on a pre-contract:
To bring you thus together 'tis no sin,
Sith that the justice of your title to him
Doth flourish the deceit. Come, let us go,
Our corn's to reap, for yet our tithe's to sow.

Exeunt.

Scene II

Enter Provost *and Clown* [Pompey].

Prov. Come hither, sirrah; can you cut off a man's head?

Pom. If the man be a bachelor, sir, I can; but if he be a married man, he's his wive's head, and I can never cut off a woman's head.

Prov. Come, sir, leave me your snatches, and yield me a direct answer. To-morrow morning are to die Claudio and Barnardine. Here is in our prison a common executioner, who in his office lacks a helper. If you will take it on you to assist him, it shall redeem you from your gyves; if not, you shall have your full time of imprisonment, and your deliverance with an unpitied whipping, for you have been a notorious bawd.

Pom. Sir, I have been an unlawful bawd time out of mind, but yet I will be content to be a lawful hangman. I would be glad to receive some instruction from my fellow partner.

Prov. What ho, Abhorson! Where's Abhorson there?

Enter Abhorson.

Abhor. Do you call, sir?

Prov. Sirrah, here's a fellow will help you to-morrow in your execution. If you think it meet, compound with him by the year, and let him abide here with you; if not, use him for the present and dismiss him. He cannot plead his estimation with you; he hath been a bawd.

Abhor. A bawd, sir? fie upon him, he will discredit our mystery.

Prov. Go to, sir, you weigh equally; a feather will turn the scale. *Exit.*

Pom. Pray, sir, by your good favor—for surely, sir, a good favor you have, but that you have a hanging look—do you call, sir, your occupation a mystery?

Abhor. Ay, sir, a mystery.

Pom. Painting, sir, I have heard say, is a mystery; and your whores, sir, being members of my occupation, using painting, do prove my occupation a mystery; but what mystery there should be in hanging, if I should be hang'd, I cannot imagine.

Abhor. Sir, it is a mystery.

Pom. Proof.

Abhor. Every true man's apparel fits your thief. If it be too little for your thief, your true man thinks it big enough; if it be too big for your thief, your thief thinks it little enough; so every true man's apparel fits your thief.

Enter Provost.

Prov. Are you agreed?

Pom. Sir, I will serve him; for I do find your hangman is a more penitent trade than your bawd: he doth oft'ner ask forgiveness.

Prov. You, sirrah, provide your block and your axe to-morrow, four a' clock.

Abhor. Come on, bawd, I will instruct thee in my trade; follow.

Pom. I do desire to learn, sir; and I hope, if you have occasion to use me for your own turn, you shall find me yare; for truly, sir, for your kindness, I owe you a good turn.

Prov. Call hither Barnardine and Claudio.

Exeunt [*Abhorson and Pompey*].

Th' one has my pity; not a jot the other,
Being a murtherer, though he were my brother.

Enter Claudio.

Look, here's the warrant, Claudio, for thy death.

66. **not**: not only.
67. **Little . . . say**: say little (*have you* is imperative).
69. **Fear me not**: i.e. have no fears about my management of it.
71. **husband . . . pre-contract**: i.e. affianced husband. Cf. Claudio's "true contract" (I.ii.145), which made him Juliet's actual husband.
73. **title to him**: right to possess him.
74. **flourish**: make fair, justify.
75. **Our . . . sow**: our grain is still to be reaped, for the seed that will produce our tithe dues isn't even sown yet, i.e. we have work to do before we can enjoy the fruits of our endeavor.

IV.ii. Location: The prison.
4. **wive's**: wife's. Cf. Ephesians 5:23: "For the husband is the wive's head" (Geneva). 5. **head**: i.e. maidenhead.
6. **leave me**: leave, cease (a colloquialism). **snatches**: quibbles.
9. **common**: public. **office**: duties.
11. **gyves**: shackles; here (apparently), imprisonment.
12. **deliverance**: release. 13. **unpitied**: pitiless, severe.
19. **Abhorson**. A telescoping of *abhor* and *whoreson*.
23. **execution**. In view of the context the sense may be "execution of official duties" rather than "judicial killing," but for an executioner the distinction is academic.
24. **compound**: come to an agreement. **abide**: lodge.
25. **present**: immediate occasion.
26. **estimation**: worthiness, claim to consideration.
29. **mystery**: skilled craft. 32–33. **favor . . . favor**: leave . . . face.
33–34. **a hanging look**: (1) a melancholy expression; (2) the look of a hangman.
37. **your**. The indefinite use (as also in lines 43 ff.).
43–47. **Every . . . thief**. Abhorson begins his proof by showing that a thief is a "fitter" of clothes, hence a tailor, hence a member of a mystery. Presumably he would continue by arguing that thieves are "members of [his] occupation" (picking up Pompey's argument in line 37), and that his occupation is therefore a mystery. The argument from clothes is doubtless related to the fact that the clothes of an executed man were the due of the executioner.
43. **true man**: honest man (regularly used in antithesis to *thief*).
45. **big enough**: i.e. a big enough loss.
46. **thinks . . . enough**: i.e. doesn't think much of it.
51. **ask forgiveness**. The executioner always asked forgiveness of the condemned man.
57. **use . . . turn**: (1) make use of my professional expertise to serve your own purpose; (2) employ me for your own hanging (commonly called "turning off"). 58. **yare**: nimble, adroit.
59. **a good turn**. Referring to the proverbial "one good turn deserves another," but with play on *turn* in its senses of "sexual satisfaction" and "hanging" (as in line 57).

'Tis now dead midnight, and by eight to-morrow
Thou must be made immortal. Where's Barnardine?
Claud. As fast lock'd up in sleep as guiltless labor
When it lies starkly in the traveller's bones.
He will not wake.
Prov. Who can do good on him?
Well, go, prepare yourself. [*Knocking within.*] But hark, what noise?
Heaven give your spirits comfort! [*Exit Claudio.*] By and by.—
I hope it is some pardon or reprieve
For the most gentle Claudio.

Enter DUKE [*disguised as a friar*].

Welcome, father.
Duke. The best and wholesom'st spirits of the night
Envelop you, good Provost! Who call'd here of late?
Prov. None since the curfew rung.
Duke. Not Isabel?
Prov. No.
Duke. They will then ere't be long.
Prov. What comfort is for Claudio?
Duke. There's some in hope.
Prov. It is a bitter deputy.
Duke. Not so, not so; his life is parallel'd
Even with the stroke and line of his great justice.
He doth with holy abstinence subdue
That in himself which he spurs on his pow'r
To qualify in others. Were he meal'd with that
Which he corrects, then were he tyrannous,
But this being so, he's just. [*Knocking within.*] Now are they come. [*Exit Provost.*]
This is a gentle Provost: seldom when
The steeled jailer is the friend of men.
[*Knocking within.*]
How now? what noise? That spirit's possess'd with haste
That wounds th' unsisting postern with these strokes.

[*Enter* PROVOST.]

Prov. There he must stay until the officer
Arise to let him in; he is call'd up.
Duke. Have you no countermand for Claudio yet,
But he must die to-morrow?
Prov. None, sir, none.
Duke. As near the dawning, Provost, as it is,
You shall hear more ere morning.
Prov. Happily
You something know, yet I believe there comes
No countermand; no such example have we.
Besides, upon the very siege of justice
Lord Angelo hath to the public ear
Profess'd the contrary.

Enter a MESSENGER.

This is his [Lordship's] man.
[*Duke.*] And here comes Claudio's pardon.

Mess. My lord hath sent you this note, and by me this further charge: that you swerve not from the smallest article of it, neither in time, matter, or other circumstance. Good morrow; for as I take it, it is almost day.

Prov. I shall obey him. [*Exit Messenger.*]
Duke. [*Aside.*] This is his pardon, purchas'd by such sin
For which the pardoner himself is in.
Hence hath offense his quick celerity,
When it is borne in high authority.
When vice makes mercy, mercy's so extended,
That for the fault's love is th' offender friended.
Now, sir, what news?

Prov. I told you: Lord Angelo (belike) thinking me remiss in mine office, awakens me with this unwonted putting-on, methinks strangely, for he hath not us'd it before.

Duke. Pray you let's hear.

[*Prov. Reads*] *the letter.*

"Whatsoever you may hear to the contrary, let Claudio be executed by four of the clock, and in the afternoon Barnardine. For my better satisfaction, let me have Claudio's head sent me by five. Let this be duly perform'd, with a thought that more depends on it than we must yet deliver. Thus fail not to do your office, as you will answer it at your peril." What say you to this, sir?

Duke. What is that Barnardine who is to be executed in th' afternoon?

Prov. A Bohemian born; but here nurs'd up and bred, one that is a prisoner nine years old.

Duke. How came it that the absent Duke had not either deliver'd him to his liberty or executed him? I have heard it was ever his manner to do so.

Prov. His friends still wrought reprieves for him; and indeed his fact, till now in the government of Lord Angelo, came not to an undoubtful proof.

Duke. It is now apparent?

Prov. Most manifest, and not denied by himself.

Duke. Hath he borne himself penitently in prison? How seems he to be touch'd?

64. eight. Cf. *four* in line 53. The discrepancy has been taken to indicate careless revision, but possibly it is for Barnardine, who is also to die in the morning (line 7–8), that the block and axe are to be ready at four.
67. starkly: stiffly. A transferred modifier, rightly describing the "traveller." **traveller's**: laborer's (*travel* and *travail* were still variant spellings of a single word). Cf. Ecclesiastes 5:12, "The sleep of him that travaileth is sweet" (Geneva; "a laboring man" in King James). **68. do good on**: bestow a benefit on, aid.
70. By and by: coming; just a minute (called out to the one who knocks).
73. best . . . spirits. Contrasted with the harmful vapors alluded to in IV.i.57. **79–80. is . . . with**: runs precisely parallel with.
80. stroke. Synonymous with *line* in the image evoked by *parallel'd*. But *stroke* also recalls the *cruel striking* of Angelo's justice as it has been described in III.ii.267, and perhaps *stroke and line* has the second meaning "headsman's stroke and hangman's rope."
83. qualify: abate. **meal'd**: stained.
86. gentle: kindly. **seldom when**: it rarely happens that.
87. steeled: hardened.
89. unsisting: shortened form of *unassisting* (?). Of several proposed emendations the best are *unshifting* (Capell) and *resisting* (Collier). **postern**: small door.

95. Happily: haply, perhaps.
97. example: precedent. **98. siege**: seat.
110. his quick celerity. Explained as "its lively speed" in order to clear the phrase of the charge of tautology, but cf. *swift celerity* in V.i.394. **115. belike**: I suppose. **117. putting-on**: pressure.
122. satisfaction: assurance. **125. deliver**: declare, make known.
130. here: i.e. in Vienna.
131. is . . . old: has been a prisoner for nine years.
135. wrought: managed to obtain. **136. fact**: deed, i.e. crime.
141. touch'd: affected.

Prov. A man that apprehends death no more dreadfully but as a drunken sleep, careless, reakless, and fearless of what's past, present, or to come; insensible of mortality, and desperately mortal.

Duke. He wants advice.

Prov. He will hear none. He hath evermore had the liberty of the prison; give him leave to escape hence, he would not. Drunk many times a day, if not many days entirely drunk. We have very oft awak'd him, as if to carry him to execution, and show'd him a seeming warrant for it; it hath not mov'd him at all.

Duke. More of him anon. There is written in your brow, Provost, honesty and constancy; if I read it not truly, my ancient skill beguiles me; but in the boldness of my cunning, I will lay myself in hazard. Claudio, whom here you have warrant to execute, is no greater forfeit to the law than Angelo who hath sentenc'd him. To make you understand this in a manifested effect, I crave but four days' respite; for the which you are to do me both a present and a dangerous courtesy.

Prov. Pray, sir, in what?

Duke. In the delaying death.

Prov. Alack, how may I do it, having the hour limited, and an express command, under penalty, to deliver his head in the view of Angelo? I may make my case as Claudio's, to cross this in the smallest.

Duke. By the vow of mine order I warrant you, if my instructions may be your guide. Let this Barnardine be this morning executed, and his head borne to Angelo.

Prov. Angelo hath seen them both, and will discover the favor.

Duke. O, death's a great disguiser, and you may add to it. Shave the head, and tie the beard, and say it was the desire of the penitent to be so bar'd before his death. You know the course is common. If any thing fall to you upon this, more than thanks and good fortune, by the saint whom I profess, I will plead against it with my life.

Prov. Pardon me, good father, it is against my oath.

Duke. Were you sworn to the Duke, or to the deputy?

Prov. To him, and to his substitutes.

Duke. You will think you have made no offense, if the Duke avouch the justice of your dealing?

Prov. But what likelihood is in that?

Duke. Not a resemblance, but a certainty; yet since I see you fearful, that neither my coat, integrity, nor persuasion can with ease attempt you, I will go further than I meant, to pluck all fears out of you. Look you, sir, here is the hand and seal of the Duke; you know the character, I doubt not, and the signet is not strange to you.

Prov. I know them both.

Duke. The contents of this is the return of the Duke. You shall anon over-read it at your pleasure; where you shall find, within these two days he will be here. This is a thing that Angelo knows not, for he this very day receives letters of strange tenor, perchance of the Duke's death, perchance entering into some monastery, but by chance nothing of what is writ. Look, th' unfolding star calls up the shepherd. Put not yourself into amazement how these things should be; all difficulties are but easy when they are known. Call your executioner, and off with Barnardine's head. I will give him a present shrift, and advise him for a better place. Yet you are amaz'd, but this shall absolutely resolve you. Come away, it is almost clear dawn. *Exeunt.*

Scene III

Enter Clown [Pompey].

Pom. I am as well acquainted here as I was in our house of profession. One would think it were Mistress Overdone's own house, for here be many of her old customers. First, here's young Master Rash, he's in for a commodity of brown paper and old ginger, ninescore and seventeen pounds, of which he made five marks ready money. Marry, then ginger was not much in request, for the old women were all dead. Then is there here one Master Caper, at the suit of Master Three-pile the mercer, for some four suits of peach-color'd satin, which now peaches him a beggar. Then have we here young Dizzy, and young Master Deep-vow, and Master Copper-spur, and Master Starve-lackey the rapier and dagger man, and young Drop-heir that kill'd lusty Pudding, and Master Forthlight the tilter, and brave Master Shoe-tie the great traveller, and wild Half-can that stabb'd Pots, and I think forty more, all great doers

142–43. apprehends . . . as: conceives of death as no more dreadful than.
143. careless: without anxiety. **reakless:** reckless, unconcerned.
145. insensible of mortality: with no feeling about what death means (?). **desperately mortal:** without hope of escaping execution (?) or in a desperate state of mortal sin (?).
146. wants advice: lacks (spiritual) counsel.
156. lay . . . hazard: risk my all.
159–60. in . . . effect: through concrete evidence, by a clear demonstration.
160. four days' respite. Cf. *two days* in line 198. It is difficult to account for *four*. **161. present:** immediate. **166. limited:** fixed.
168. cross: go contrary to.
169. warrant you: guarantee you against harm.
172–73. discover the favor: recognize the face.
175. tie. Not satisfactorily explained. Many editors emend to *trim* or *dye*. **178. fall to:** befall. **upon:** in consequence of.
186. avouch: confirm, uphold. **justice:** justness.
188. resemblance: probability (?).

190. attempt: tempt. **193. character:** handwriting.
203. writ: i.e. written here (?). **unfolding star:** morning star, whose appearance tells the shepherd that it is time to release his sheep from the fold. **204. amazement:** perplexity.
209. absolutely resolve you: dispel your doubts completely.

IV.iii. Location: Scene continues.
1. am . . . acquainted: have as wide an acquaintance.
5. a commodity . . . ginger. A moneylender could circumvent the statute limiting interest on loans to ten percent by forcing a borrower to take a substantial part of the loan in some "commodity" at a valuation determined by the lender. Rash has had to agree to a valuation of 197 pounds on merchandise which on resale has brought little more than three pounds (a mark was two-thirds of a pound).
8. old women. Traditionally fond of ginger. The sentence has been taken as a reference to the heavy plague mortality in 1603.
9, Caper: i.e. frolic. The names of the prisoners are more or less suggestive of their particular bents.
10. Three-pile. See the note on I.ii.32.
11. peaches him: accuses him (of being).
16. Forthlight. Perhaps an error for *Forthright*, i.e. straight ahead (as a tilter, or jouster, might ride). **brave:** showily dressed.
17. Shoe-tie . . . traveller. Gaudy decorations on shoes were a foreign importation.

in our trade, and are now "for the Lord's sake."

Enter ABHORSON.

Abhor. Sirrah, bring Barnardine hither.

Pom. Master Barnardine! You must rise and be hang'd, Master Barnardine!

Abhor. What ho, Barnardine!

Bar. (*Within.*) A pox o' your throats! Who makes that noise there? What are you?

Pom. Your friends, sir, the hangman. You must be so good, sir, to rise, and be put to death.

Bar. [*Within.*] Away, you rogue, away! I am sleepy.

Abhor. Tell him he must awake, and that quickly too.

Pom. Pray, Master Barnardine, awake till you are executed, and sleep afterwards.

Abhor. Go in to him, and fetch him out.

Pom. He is coming, sir, he is coming. I hear his straw rustle.

Enter BARNARDINE.

Abhor. Is the axe upon the block, sirrah?

Pom. Very ready, sir.

Bar. How now, Abhorson? What's the news with you?

Abhor. Truly, sir, I would desire you to clap into your prayers; for look you, the warrant's come.

Bar. You rogue, I have been drinking all night, I am not fitted for't.

Pom. O, the better, sir; for he that drinks all night, and is hang'd betimes in the morning, may sleep the sounder all the next day.

Enter DUKE [*disguised as a friar*].

Abhor. Look you, sir, here comes your ghostly father. Do we jest now, think you?

Duke. Sir, induc'd by my charity, and hearing how hastily you are to depart, I am come to advise you, comfort you, and pray with you.

Bar. Friar, not I; I have been drinking hard all night, and I will have more time to prepare me, or they shall beat out my brains with billets. I will not consent to die this day, that's certain.

Duke. O sir, you must; and therefore I beseech you
Look forward on the journey you shall go.

Bar. I swear I will not die to-day for any man's persuasion.

Duke. But hear you—

Bar. Not a word. If you have any thing to say to me, come to my ward; for thence will not I to-day. *Exit.*

Enter PROVOST.

Duke. Unfit to live, or die; O gravel heart!
After him, fellows, bring him to the block.
[*Exeunt Abhorson and Pompey.*]

Prov. Now, sir, how do you find the prisoner?

Duke. A creature unprepar'd, unmeet for death;
And to transport him in the mind he is
Were damnable.

Prov. Here in the prison, father,
There died this morning of a cruel fever
One Ragozine, a most notorious pirate,
A man of Claudio's years; his beard and head
Just of his color. What if we do omit
This reprobate till he were well inclin'd,
And satisfy the deputy with the visage
Of Ragozine, more like to Claudio?

Duke. O, 'tis an accident that heaven provides!
Dispatch it presently, the hour draws on
Prefix'd by Angelo. See this be done,
And sent according to command, whiles I
Persuade this rude wretch willingly to die.

Prov. This shall be done, good father, presently.
But Barnardine must die this afternoon;
And how shall we continue Claudio,
To save me from the danger that might come
If he were known alive?

Duke. Let this be done:
Put them in secret holds, both Barnardine and Claudio.
Ere twice the sun hath made his journal greeting
To yond generation, you shall find
Your safety manifested.

Prov. I am your free dependant.

Duke. Quick, dispatch, and send the head to Angelo. *Exit* [*Provost*].
Now will I write letters to Angelo
(The Provost, he shall bear them), whose contents
Shall witness to him I am near at home;
And that by great injunctions I am bound
To enter publicly. Him I'll desire
To meet me at the consecrated fount,
A league below the city; and from thence,
By cold gradation and weal-balanc'd form,
We shall proceed with Angelo.

Enter PROVOST [*with Ragozine's head*].

Prov. Here is the head, I'll carry it myself.

Duke. Convenient is it. Make a swift return,
For I would commune with you of such things
That want no ear but yours.

Prov. I'll make all speed. *Exit.*

19. **"for . . . sake"**: the cry with which prisoners, who had to supply their own food and other necessities, besought the charity of those who passed by their barred windows. 27. **to**: as to.
41. **clap into**: speedily begin. 46. **betimes**: early.
48. **ghostly**: spiritual. 55. **billets**: blocks of wood, clubs.
63. **ward**: cell. 64. **gravel**: stony.

68. **transport him**: send him to the next world.
73. **omit**: pass over. 74. **well inclin'd**: in a proper state of mind.
77. **accident**: event.
78. **Dispatch it presently**: put it into execution at once.
79. **Prefix'd**: set in advance. 84. **continue**: keep.
87. **holds**: cells. 88. **journal**: daily.
89. **yond generation**: i.e. men outside the prison, on whom the sunlight falls (?). Some editors adopt Rowe's *yonder generation* (to mend the metre); others follow Hanmer in reading *th' under generation*, meaning either "people under the sun" or "people in the Antipodes" (so that lines 88 would mean either "before two days are past" or "before two nights are past").
91. **free dependant**: willing follower.
93. **Angelo.** Since in V.i the Duke enters the city with Varrius, it is conjectured that *Angelo* is an error for *Varrius*, picked up inadvertently from the end of line 92.
96. **by great injunctions**: for compelling reasons (?).
98. **fount**: spring.
100. **cold gradation**: coolly reasoned steps (?). **weal-balanc'd form**: formalities required by considerations of state (?). Most editors follow Rowe in reading *well-balanced form*, "all due formalities."
101. **with**: in the affair of, against. 103. **Convenient**: fitting.
105. **want**: require.

Isab. (*Within.*) Peace, ho, be here!
Duke. The tongue of Isabel. She's come to know
If yet her brother's pardon be come hither.
But I will keep her ignorant of her good,
To make her heavenly comforts of despair,
When it is least expected.

Enter Isabella.

Isab. Ho, by your leave!
Duke. Good morning to you, fair and gracious daughter.
Isab. The better, given me by so holy a man.
Hath yet the deputy sent my brother's pardon?
Duke. He hath releas'd him, Isabel, from the world,
His head is off, and sent to Angelo.
Isab. Nay, but it is not so.
Duke. It is no other.
Show your wisdom, daughter, in your close patience.
Isab. O, I will to him, and pluck out his eyes!
Duke. You shall not be admitted to his sight.
Isab. Unhappy Claudio! Wretched Isabel!
Injurious world! Most damned Angelo!
Duke. This nor hurts him, nor profits you a jot.
Forbear it therefore, give your cause to heaven.
Mark what I say, which you shall find
By every syllable a faithful verity.
The Duke comes home to-morrow—nay, dry your eyes—
One of our covent, and his confessor,
Gives me this instance: already he hath carried
Notice to Escalus and Angelo,
Who do prepare to meet him at the gates,
There to give up their pow'r. If you can pace your wisdom
In that good path that I would wish it go,
And you shall have your bosom on this wretch,
Grace of the Duke, revenges to your heart,
And general honor.
Isab. I am directed by you.
Duke. This letter then to Friar Peter give;
'Tis that he sent me of the Duke's return.
Say, by this token, I desire his company
At Mariana's house to-night. Her cause and yours
I'll perfect him withal, and he shall bring you
Before the Duke; and to the head of Angelo
Accuse him home and home. For my poor self,
I am combined by a sacred vow,
And shall be absent. Wend you with this letter.
Command these fretting waters from your eyes
With a light heart; trust not my holy order

110. **of**: out of. 111. **it**: i.e. comfort.
118. **close patience**: silent fortitude. 121. **Unhappy**: unfortunate.
124. **give**: commit, entrust.
128. **covent**: convent, religious house. **and**: i.e. who is.
129. **instance**: evidence.
132. **pace your wisdom**: teach your wisdom to go (a figure from riding).
133. **go.** Some such expression as *do so* must be understood after this word—a not uncommon type of ellipsis.
134. **have your bosom**: have your desire fulfilled.
137. **Peter.** Probably Shakespeare had in mind the friar of I.iii but had forgotten that he is there named Thomas.
141. **perfect him withal**: fully acquaint him with.
142. **head**: i.e. face. 143. **home and home**: to the utmost.
144. **combined**: bound (cf. *combinate-husband*, III.i.222–23).
146. **fretting**: corrosive.

If I pervert your course. Who's here?

Enter Lucio.

Lucio. Good even. Friar, where's the Provost?
Duke. Not within, sir.

Lucio. O pretty Isabella, I am pale at mine heart to see thine eyes so red; thou must be patient. I am fain to dine and sup with water and bran; I dare not for my head fill my belly; one fruitful meal would set me to't. But they say the Duke will be here to-morrow. By my troth, Isabel, I lov'd thy brother. If the old fantastical Duke of dark corners had been at home, he had liv'd. [*Exit Isabella.*]

Duke. Sir, the Duke is marvellous little beholding to your reports, but the best is, he lives not in them.

Lucio. Friar, thou knowest not the Duke so well as I do; he's a better woodman than thou tak'st him for.

Duke. Well; you'll answer this one day. Fare ye well.

Lucio. Nay, tarry, I'll go along with thee. I can tell thee pretty tales of the Duke.

Duke. You have told me too many of him already, sir, if they be true; if not true, none were enough.

Lucio. I was once before him for getting a wench with child.

Duke. Did you such a thing?

Lucio. Yes, marry, did I; but I was fain to forswear it. They would else have married me to the rotten medlar.

Duke. Sir, your company is fairer than honest. Rest you well.

Lucio. By my troth, I'll go with thee to the lane's end. If bawdy talk offend you, we'll have very little of it. Nay, friar, I am a kind of bur, I shall stick. *Exeunt.*

Scene IV

Enter Angelo *and* Escalus.

Escal. Every letter he hath writ hath disvouch'd other.

Ang. In most uneven and distracted manner. His actions show much like to madness, pray heaven his wisdom be not tainted! And why meet him at the gates, and [redeliver] our authorities there?

Escal. I guess not.

Ang. And why should we proclaim it in an hour before his ent'ring, that if any crave redress of injustice, they should exhibit their petitions in the street?

148. **pervert**: direct wrongly.
149. **Good even.** A striking discrepancy.
151. **pale . . . heart.** Grief was thought to draw blood from the heart.
152. **fain**: obliged. 153. **bran**: coarse brown bread.
153–54. **for my head**: i.e. for fear of being beheaded.
157. **of dark corners.** Cf. Lucio's earlier allegations of the Duke's secret lechery. 159. **beholding**: beholden, indebted.
160. **he . . . them**: i.e. they do not describe him.
162. **woodman**: forester, i.e. hunter (of women).
163. **answer**: be held answerable.
174. **medlar**: an apple-like fruit that was not edible until it had begun to rot. 175. **fairer**: more amusing.

IV.iv. Location: Angelo's house.
1. **disvouch'd**: disavowed. 3. **uneven**: irregular.
5. **wisdom . . . tainted**: reason . . . impaired.
7. **guess not**: cannot guess.
8. **in an hour**: "leaving a clear hour" (Lever).

Escal. He shows his reason for that: to have a dispatch of complaints, and to deliver us from devices hereafter, which shall then have no power to stand against us.

Ang. Well; I beseech you let it be proclaim'd betimes i' th' morn. I'll call you at your house. Give notice to such men of sort and suit as are to meet him.

Escal. I shall, sir. Fare you well.

Ang. Good night. *Exit* [*Escalus*].
This deed unshapes me quite, makes me unpregnant
And dull to all proceedings. A deflow'red maid!
And by an eminent body that enforc'd
The law against it! But that her tender shame
Will not proclaim against her maiden loss,
How might she tongue me! Yet reason dares her no,
For my authority bears of a credent bulk,
That no particular scandal once can touch
But it confounds the breather. He should have liv'd,
Save that his riotous youth with dangerous sense
Might in the times to come have ta'en revenge,
By so receiving a dishonor'd life
With ransom of such shame. Would yet he had liv'd!
Alack, when once our grace we have forgot,
Nothing goes right—we would, and we would not.
Exit.

Scene V

Enter Duke [*in his own habit*] *and* Friar Peter.

Duke. These letters at fit time deliver me.
[*Giving letters.*]
The Provost knows our purpose and our plot.
The matter being afoot, keep your instruction,
And hold you ever to our special drift,
Though sometimes you do blench from this to that,
As cause doth minister. Go call at Flavio's house,
And tell him where I stay. Give the like notice
To Valentius, Rowland, and to Crassus,
And bid them bring the trumpets to the gate.
But send me Flavius first.

Fri. P. It shall be speeded well. [*Exit.*]

Enter Varrius.

Duke. I thank thee, Varrius, thou hast made good haste.
Come, we will walk. There's other of our friends
Will greet us here anon. My gentle Varrius!
Exeunt.

12. **dispatch:** speedy settlement. **devices:** contrived charges.
17. **sort:** rank. **suit:** following (?) or service at court (?).
20. **unpregnant:** unready, unapt.
22. **body:** person. **enforc'd:** executed rigorously.
23. **But that:** were it not that.
24. **her maiden loss:** the loss of her virginity.
25. **tongue:** i.e. denounce. **dares her no.** Not satisfactorily explained, but the sense is clear: reason forbids it.
26. **bears of a:** bears a (cf. *allow of*, *accept of*, etc.). Some editors read *bears a* for metrical reasons. **credent bulk:** massive credibility, great power to win belief.
27. **no particular scandal:** no scandal whatever (*particular* = single, as in V.i.243).
28. **But . . . breather:** without destroying the one who uttered it. **should:** would. 29. **sense:** passion (?) or perceptiveness (?).
31. **By:** at, for.

IV.v. Location: Fields outside the town.
1. **deliver me:** deliver for me. 3. **keep:** keep to, follow.
4. **drift:** course, intention. 5. **blench:** turn aside.
6. **minister:** give occasion. 9. **trumpets:** trumpeters.

Scene VI

Enter Isabella *and* Mariana.

Isab. To speak so indirectly I am loath.
I would say the truth, but to accuse him so,
That is your part. Yet I am advis'd to do it,
He says, to veil full purpose.

Mari. Be rul'd by him.

Isab. Besides, he tells me that if peradventure
He speak against me on the adverse side,
I should not think it strange, for 'tis a physic
That's bitter to sweet end.

Enter [Friar] Peter.

Mari. I would Friar Peter—

Isab. O, peace, the friar is come.

Fri. P. Come, I have found you out a stand most fit,
Where you may have such vantage on the Duke,
He shall not pass you. Twice have the trumpets sounded;
The generous and gravest citizens
Have hent the gates, and very near upon
The Duke is ent'ring; therefore hence away!
Exeunt.

ACT V, Scene I

[*Flourish.*] *Enter* Duke, Varrius, Lords, Angelo, Escalus, Lucio, [Provost, Officers,] Citizens *at several doors.*

Duke. My very worthy cousin, fairly met!
Our old and faithful friend, we are glad to see you.

Ang., Escal. Happy return be to your royal Grace!

Duke. Many and hearty thankings to you both.
We have made inquiry of you, and we hear
Such goodness of your justice, that our soul
Cannot but yield you forth to public thanks,
Forerunning more requital.

Ang. You make my bonds still greater.

Duke. O, your desert speaks loud, and I should wrong it
To lock it in the wards of covert bosom,
When it deserves with characters of brass
A forted residence 'gainst the tooth of time
And razure of oblivion. Give [me] your hand,
And let the subject see, to make them know
That outward courtesies would fain proclaim

IV.vi. Location: A street near the city gate.
3. **advis'd:** well-advised. 10. **stand:** place to stand.
11. **have . . . on:** be in so favorable a position for accosting.
13. **generous and gravest:** noblest and worthiest (the superlative ending of *gravest* governs both adjectives).
14. **hent:** taken places at. **very near upon:** at just about this time.

V.i. Location: The city gate.
1. **cousin.** Form of address by a sovereign to one of his lords.
6. **goodness:** good reports.
7. **yield . . . thanks:** i.e. offer you public thanks.
8. **more requital:** greater reward. **bonds:** obligations.
10. **wards:** cells. **covert bosom:** private thoughts and feelings.
11. **characters:** letters, inscription.
12. **forted:** fortified. **tooth of time.** Time devours all things.
13. **razure:** obliteration. 15. **fain:** gladly.

Favors that keep within. Come, Escalus,
You must walk by us on our other hand;
And good supporters are you.

Enter [FRIAR] PETER *and* ISABELLA.

Fri. P. Now is your time: speak loud, and kneel before him.
Isab. Justice, O royal Duke! Vail your regard
Upon a wrong'd—I would fain have said a maid!
O worthy Prince, dishonor not your eye
By throwing it on any other object,
Till you have heard me in my true complaint,
And given me justice, justice, justice, justice!
Duke. Relate your wrongs. In what? By whom? Be brief.
Here is Lord Angelo shall give you justice;
Reveal yourself to him.
Isab. O worthy Duke,
You bid me seek redemption of the devil.
Hear me yourself; for that which I must speak
Must either punish me, not being believ'd,
Or wring redress from you. Hear me, O hear me, here.
Ang. My lord, her wits, I fear me, are not firm.
She hath been a suitor to me for her brother,
Cut off by course of justice—
Isab. By course of justice!
Ang. And she will speak most bitterly and strange.
Isab. Most strange! but yet most truly will I speak:
That Angelo's forsworn, is it not strange?
That Angelo's a murtherer, is't not strange?
That Angelo is an adulterous thief,
An hypocrite, a virgin-violator,
Is it not strange? and strange?
Duke. Nay, it is ten times strange.
Isab. It is not truer he is Angelo
Than this is all as true as it is strange;
Nay, it is ten times true, for truth is truth
To th' end of reck'ning.
Duke. Away with her! Poor soul,
She speaks this in th' infirmity of sense.
Isab. O Prince, I conjure thee, as thou believ'st
There is another comfort than this world,
That thou neglect me not, with that opinion
That I am touch'd with madness. Make not impossible
That which but seems unlike; 'tis not impossible
But one the wicked'st caitiff on the ground,
May seem as shy, as grave, as just, as absolute
As Angelo. Even so may Angelo,
In all his dressings, caracts, titles, forms,
Be an arch-villain. Believe it, royal Prince,
If he be less, he's nothing, but he's more,
Had I more name for badness.
Duke. By mine honesty,
If she be mad, as I believe no other,
Her madness hath the oddest frame of sense,
Such a dependancy of thing on thing,
As e'er I heard in madness.
Isab. O gracious Duke,
Harp not on that; nor do not banish reason
For inequality, but let your reason serve
To make the truth appear, where it seems hid,
And hide the false seems true.
Duke. Many that are not mad
Have sure more lack of reason. What would you say?
Isab. I am the sister of one Claudio,
Condemn'd upon the act of fornication
To lose his head, condemn'd by Angelo.
I (in probation of a sisterhood)
Was sent to by my brother; one Lucio
As then the messenger—
Lucio. That's I, and't like your Grace.
I came to her from Claudio, and desir'd her
To try her gracious fortune with Lord Angelo,
For her poor brother's pardon.
Isab. That's he indeed.
Duke. [*To Lucio.*] You were not bid to speak.
Lucio. No, my good lord,
Nor wish'd to hold my peace.
Duke. I wish you now then.
Pray you take note of it; and when you have
A business for yourself, pray heaven you then
Be perfect.
Lucio. I warrant your honor.
Duke. The warrant's for yourself; take heed to't.
Isab. This gentleman told somewhat of my tale—
Lucio. Right.
Duke. It may be right, but you are i' the wrong
To speak before your time. Proceed.
Isab. I went
To this pernicious caitiff deputy—
Duke. That's somewhat madly spoken.
Isab. Pardon it,
The phrase is to the matter.
Duke. Mended again. The matter; proceed.
Isab. In brief, to set the needless process by—
How I persuaded, how I pray'd, and kneel'd,
How he refell'd me, and how I replied

16. **keep**: dwell.
18. **supporters.** A heraldic term, designating the figures at either side of the shield. 20. **Vail your regard**: bend your look.
28. **Reveal yourself**: i.e. disclose your suit. 44. **all as**: just as.
47. **sense**: intellect, reason. 48. **conjure**: adjure. 51. **Make**: deem.
52. **unlike**: unlikely.
53. **one the wicked'st**: the most wicked (an old idiom). **caitiff**: wretch.
54. **shy.** See the note on III.ii.130. **absolute**: without defect.
56. **dressings . . . forms**: robes of office, insignia, titles, ceremonies.
58. **If . . . nothing**: i.e. he could be less a villain than he is, yet wicked.
59. **more**: i.e. worse (than *arch-villain*).
61. **frame of sense**: rational form.
62. **dependancy . . . thing**: logical order. 64. **that**: i.e. madness.
64–65. **do . . . inequality**: i.e. do not declare my reason gone because of discrepancy (between her report of Angelo and the general report) (?). This interpretation seems preferable to those that take *reason* as referring to the Duke's reason and *inequality* as "injustice" or "partiality" or "disparity" (between Isabella's status and Angelo's); it permits Isabella a more respectful address to her sovereign and furnishes an effective contrast rather than mere repetition in *reason / your reason*: "Do not adjudge me lacking in reason, but rather employ your own reason to find out the truth."
67. **hide**: remove from sight. **seems**: that seems.
70. **upon**: in consequence of. 72. **probation**: novitiate.
79. **wish'd**: asked, bidden (cf. *desir'd* in line 75). **wish you now**: bid you now to do so.
81. **A business for yourself**: a matter in which you are involved.
82. **perfect**: fully prepared. **warrant**: assure. The Duke quibbles on the sense "warrant for arrest."
90. **to the matter**: to the point, germane.
91. **Mended**: i.e. speaking sanely. **The matter**: get to the point (since you say it is to the point).
92. **set . . . by**: omit unnecessary details of the story.
93. **persuaded**: pleaded. 94. **refell'd**: refuted.

(For this was of much length)—the vild conclusion
I now begin with grief and shame to utter.
He would not, but by gift of my chaste body
To his concupiscible intemperate lust,
Release my brother; and after much debatement,
My sisterly remorse confutes mine honor,
And I did yield to him; but the next morn betimes,
His purpose surfeiting, he sends a warrant
For my poor brother's head.
Duke. This is most likely!
Isab. O that it were as like as it is true!
Duke. By heaven, fond wretch, thou know'st not what thou speak'st,
Or else thou art suborn'd against his honor
In hateful practice. First, his integrity
Stands without blemish; next, it imports no reason
That with such vehemency he should pursue
Faults proper to himself. If he had so offended,
He would have weigh'd thy brother by himself,
And not have cut him off. Some one hath set you on;
Confess the truth, and say by whose advice
Thou cam'st here to complain.
Isab. And is this all?
Then, O you blessed ministers above,
Keep me in patience, and with ripened time
Unfold the evil which is here wrapp'd up
In countenance! Heaven shield your Grace from woe,
As I, thus wrong'd, hence unbelieved go!
Duke. I know you'ld fain be gone. An officer!
To prison with her! Shall we thus permit
A blasting and a scandalous breath to fall
On him so near us? This needs must be a practice.
Who knew of your intent and coming hither?
Isab. One that I would were here, Friar Lodowick.
Duke. A ghostly father, belike. Who knows that Lodowick?
Lucio. My lord, I know him, 'tis a meddling friar.
I do not like the man; had he been lay, my lord,
For certain words he spake against your Grace
In your retirement, I had swing'd him soundly.
Duke. Words against me? This' a good friar, belike!
And to set on this wretched woman here
Against our substitute! Let this friar be found.
Lucio. But yesternight, my lord, she and that friar,
I saw them at the prison. A saucy friar,
A very scurvy fellow.
Fri. P. Blessed be your royal Grace!
I have stood by, my lord, and I have heard
Your royal ear abus'd. First, hath this woman
Most wrongfully accus'd your substitute,
Who is as free from touch or soil with her
As she from one ungot.
Duke. We did believe no less.
Know you that Friar Lodowick that she speaks of?
Fri. P. I know him for a man divine and holy,
Not scurvy, nor a temporary meddler,
As he's reported by this gentleman;
And on my trust, a man that never yet
Did (as he vouches) misreport your Grace.
Lucio. My lord, most villainously, believe it.
Fri. P. Well; he in time may come to clear himself;
But at this instant he is sick, my lord,
Of a strange fever. Upon his mere request,
Being come to knowledge that there was complaint
Intended 'gainst Lord Angelo, came I hither,
To speak as from his mouth, what he doth know
Is true and false; and what he with his oath
And all probation will make up full clear,
Whensoever he's convented. First, for this woman,
To justify this worthy nobleman,
So vulgarly and personally accus'd,
Her shall you hear disproved to her eyes,
Till she herself confess it.
Duke. Good friar, let's hear it.
[*Isabella is carried off guarded.*]
Do you not smile at this, Lord Angelo?
O heaven, the vanity of wretched fools!
Give us some seats. Come, cousin Angelo,
In this I'll be impartial. Be you judge
Of your own cause.

Enter MARIANA [*veiled*].

Is this the witness, friar?
First, let her show [her] face, and after speak.
Mari. Pardon, my lord, I will not show my face
Until my husband bid me.
Duke. What, are you married?
Mari. No, my lord.
Duke. Are you a maid?
Mari. No, my lord.
Duke. A widow then?
Mari. Neither, my lord.
Duke. Why, you are nothing then: neither maid, widow, nor wife?
Lucio. My lord, she may be a punk; for many of them are neither maid, widow, nor wife.
Duke. Silence that fellow. I would he had some cause
To prattle for himself.
Lucio. Well, my lord.
Mari. My lord, I do confess I ne'er was married,
And I confess besides I am no maid.
I have known my husband, yet my husband
Knows not that ever he knew me.

95. vild: vile (a variant form). **100. remorse**: pity.
105. fond: foolish. **107. practice**: conspiracy.
108. it . . . reason: it is irrational. **109. pursue**: persecute.
110. proper to himself: that he himself possessed.
111. weigh'd . . . himself. Cf. II.ii.126, III.ii.265–66.
115. ministers: angels. **117. Unfold**: unwrap, disclose.
118. In countenance: in the Duke's authority (?) or by the Duke's allowance (?). **122. blasting**: blighting (like a destructive wind).
127. meddling. Perhaps (as often) with an implication of sexual impropriety; cf. *saucy* (line 135), which can mean both "impudent" and "lecherous." **130. swing'd**: beaten (from *swinge*).
131. This': this is. **139. abus'd**: deceived.
141. touch or soil: impure contact.

142. ungot: unbegotten.
145. temporary meddler: meddler in temporal affairs.
148. as he vouches: i.e. as Lucio affirms.
152. Upon . . . request: solely at his request.
153. Being . . . knowledge: since he had learned.
157. probation: proof. **158. convented**: summoned.
160. vulgarly: publicly. **164. vanity**: folly.
166. be impartial: not take part. **176. Neither**: nor that either.
179. punk: prostitute.
181–82. some . . . himself: some necessity to speak in his own defense.
186. known: known carnally.

Lucio. He was drunk then, my lord, it can be no better.

Duke. For the benefit of silence, would thou wert so too!

Lucio. Well, my lord.

Duke. This is no witness for Lord Angelo.

Mari. Now I come to't, my lord.
She that accuses him of fornication,
In self-same manner doth accuse my husband,
And charges him, my lord, with such a time
When I'll depose I had him in mine arms
With all th' effect of love.

Ang. Charges she moe than me?

Mari. Not that I know.

Duke. No? You say your husband.

Mari. Why, just, my lord, and that is Angelo,
Who thinks he knows that he ne'er knew my body,
But knows he thinks that he knows Isabel's.

Ang. This is a strange abuse. Let's see thy face.

Mari. My husband bids me, now I will unmask.
[*Unveiling.*]
This is that face, thou cruel Angelo,
Which once thou swor'st was worth the looking on;
This is the hand which, with a vow'd contract,
Was fast belock'd in thine; this is the body
That took away the match from Isabel,
And did supply thee at thy garden-house
In her imagin'd person.

Duke. Know you this woman?

Lucio. Carnally, she says.

Duke. Sirrah, no more!

Lucio. Enough, my lord.

Ang. My lord, I must confess I know this woman,
And five years since there was some speech of marriage
Betwixt myself and her; which was broke off,
Partly for that her promised proportions
Came short of composition, but in chief
For that her reputation was disvalued
In levity. Since which time of five years
I never spake with her, saw her, nor heard from her,
Upon my faith and honor.

Mari. Noble Prince,
As there comes light from heaven, and words from breath,
As there is sense in truth, and truth in virtue,
I am affianc'd this man's wife as strongly
As words could make up vows; and, my good lord,
But Tuesday night last gone, in 's garden-house,
He knew me as a wife. As this is true,
Let me in safety raise me from my knees,
Or else for ever be confixed here,
A marble monument!

Ang. I did but smile till now.
Now, good my lord, give me the scope of justice,
My patience here is touch'd. I do perceive
These poor informal women are no more
But instruments of some more mightier member
That sets them on. Let me have way, my lord,
To find this practice out.

Duke. Ay, with my heart,
And punish them to your height of pleasure.
Thou foolish friar, and thou pernicious woman,
Compact with her that's gone, think'st thou thy oaths,
Though they would swear down each particular saint,
Were testimonies against his worth and credit
That's seal'd in approbation? You, Lord Escalus,
Sit with my cousin; lend him your kind pains
To find out this abuse, whence 'tis deriv'd.
There is another friar that set them on,
Let him be sent for.

Fri. P. Would he were here, my lord, for he indeed
Hath set the women on to this complaint.
Your Provost knows the place where he abides,
And he may fetch him.

Duke. Go, do it instantly. [*Exit Provost.*]
And you, my noble and well-warranted cousin,
Whom it concerns to hear this matter forth,
Do with your injuries as seems you best,
In any chastisement. I for a while will leave you;
But stir not you till you have well determin'd
Upon these slanderers.

Escal. My lord, we'll do it throughly.
Exit [*Duke*].
Signior Lucio, did not you say you knew that Friar Lodowick to be a dishonest person?

Lucio. *Cucullus non facit monachum:* honest in nothing but in his clothes, and one that hath spoke most villainous speeches of the Duke.

Escal. We shall entreat you to abide here till he come, and enforce them against him. We shall find this friar a notable fellow.

Lucio. As any in Vienna, on my word.

Escal. Call that same Isabel here once again, I would speak with her. [*Exit an Attendant.*] Pray you, my lord, give me leave to question, you shall see how I'll handle her.

Lucio. Not better than he, by her own report.

Escal. Say you?

Lucio. Marry, sir, I think if you handled her privately she would sooner confess; perchance publicly she'll be asham'd.

Enter DUKE [*in his friar's habit*], PROVOST, [OFFICERS *with*] ISABELLA.

Escal. I will go darkly to work with her.

197. **with . . . time**: with committing the offense at the very time.
198. **depose**: testify on oath. 199. **effect**: manifestations.
200. **moe**: more (persons). 202. **just**: just so, exactly.
210. **fast belock'd**. See note on I.ii.147.
211. **match**: appointed meeting (but also with reference to the marriage thus consummated).
212. **supply thee**: (1) fill her place with you; (2) satisfy your wants.
219. **for that**: because. **proportions**: portion, dowry.
220. **composition**: the agreed amount. 221. **disvalued**: debased.
222. **levity**: lightness, wantonness.
232. **confixed**: firmly fixed. 233. **marble**: immovable.
234. **scope**: full authority. 235. **touch'd**: wounded, i.e. tried beyond its limit. 236. **informal**: distracted.
242. **Compact**: leagued. 243. **each particular**: every single.
245. **seal'd in approbation.** "Angelo's faith has been tried, approved, and sealed in testimony of that approbation, and . . . is no more to be called in question" (Johnson). 255. **forth**: to the end, thoroughly.
256. **with your injuries**: with respect to the wrongs done you.
258. **determin'd**: reached a judgment. 259. **throughly**: thoroughly.
262. **Cucullus . . . monachum**: the hood does not make the monk (proverbial). Lucio does not know how truly he speaks.
266. **enforce them**: put them strongly. 267. **notable**: notorious.
271. **give.** Probably with conditional sense: "if you will give."
278. **darkly**: secretly, cunningly.

Lucio. That's the way; for women are light at midnight.

Escal. Come on, mistress. Here's a gentlewoman denies all that you have said.

Lucio. My lord, here comes the rascal I spoke of, here with the Provost.

Escal. In very good time. Speak not you to him till we call upon you.

Lucio. Mum.

Escal. Come, sir, did you set these women on to slander Lord Angelo? They have confess'd you did.

Duke. 'Tis false.

Escal. How! know you where you are?

Duke. Respect to your great place! and let the devil
Be sometime honor'd for his burning throne!
Where is the Duke? 'tis he should hear me speak.

Escal. The Duke's in us; and we will hear you speak:
Look you speak justly.

Duke. Boldly, at least. But O, poor souls,
Come you to seek the lamb here of the fox,
Good night to your redress! Is the Duke gone?
Then is your cause gone too. The Duke's unjust
Thus to retort your manifest appeal,
And put your trial in the villain's mouth
Which here you come to accuse.

Lucio. This is the rascal; this is he I spoke of.

Escal. Why, thou unreverend and unhallowed friar,
Is't not enough thou hast suborn'd these women
To accuse this worthy man, but in foul mouth,
And in the witness of his proper ear,
To call him villain, and then to glance from him
To th' Duke himself, to tax him with injustice?
Take him hence; to th' rack with him! We'll touze you
Joint by joint, but we will know his purpose.
What? "unjust"?

Duke. Be not so hot. The Duke
Dare no more stretch this finger of mine than he
Dare rack his own. His subject am I not,
Nor here provincial. My business in this state
Made me a looker-on here in Vienna,
Where I have seen corruption boil and bubble,
Till it o'errun the stew; laws for all faults,
But faults so countenanc'd, that the strong statutes
Stand like the forfeits in a barber's shop,
As much in mock as mark.

Escal. Slander to th' state!
Away with him to prison.

Ang. What can you vouch
Against him, Signior Lucio? Is this the man
That you did tell us of?

Lucio. 'Tis he, my lord.
Come hither, goodman bald-pate, do you know me?

Duke. I remember you, sir, by the sound of your voice; I met you at the prison, in the absence of the Duke.

Lucio. O, did you so? And do you remember what you said of the Duke?

Duke. Most notedly, sir.

Lucio. Do you so, sir? And was the Duke a flesh-monger, a fool, and a coward, as you then reported him to be?

Duke. You must, sir, change persons with me, ere you make that my report. You indeed spoke so of him, and much more, much worse.

Lucio. O thou damnable fellow! Did not I pluck thee by the nose for thy speeches?

Duke. I protest I love the Duke as I love myself.

Ang. Hark how the villain would close now, after his treasonable abuses!

Escal. Such a fellow is not to be talk'd withal. Away with him to prison! Where is the Provost? Away with him to prison! Lay bolts enough upon him. Let him speak no more. Away with those giglets too, and with the other confederate companion!

[*The Provost lays hands on the Duke.*]

Duke. Stay, sir, stay a while.

Ang. What, resists he? Help him, Lucio.

Lucio. Come, sir, come, sir, come, sir; foh, sir, why, you bald-pated, lying rascal, you must be hooded, must you? Show your knave's visage, with a pox to you! Show your sheep-biting face, and be hang'd an hour! Will't not off? [*Pulls off the friar's hood.*]

Duke. Thou art the first knave that e'er mad'st a duke.
First, Provost, let me bail these gentle three.
[*To Lucio.*] Sneak not away, sir, for the friar and you
Must have a word anon.—Lay hold on him.

Lucio. This may prove worse than hanging.

Duke. [*To Escalus.*] What you have spoke I pardon. Sit you down,
We'll borrow place of him.—Sir, by your leave.

[*Takes Angelo's seat.*]

Hast thou or word, or wit, or impudence,
That yet can do thee office? If thou hast,
Rely upon it till my tale be heard,

279–80. light at midnight: i.e. wanton in the dark.
290. 'Tis false. Equivocal: apparently a denial that he set the women on, but actually a denial that Angelo has been slandered, i.e. charged falsely.
292–93. let . . . throne. The Duke ironically extends the principle to its logical conclusion. **296. justly**: truthfully.
298. Come you: if you come.
301. retort: throw back, refuse to accept. **manifest**: obviously just.
302–3. the villain's mouth Which: the mouth of the villain whom.
308. in . . . ear: in his own hearing. **309. glance**: ricochet.
311. touze: tear, jerk. **313. hot**: hasty.
316. provincial: subject to local religious authority.
319. stew: (1) pot; (2) brothel. **320. countenanc'd**: tolerated.
321. forfeits . . . shop. Usually explained as extracted teeth (barber-surgeons also pulled teeth), which like disused laws have lost their power to bite. But the comparison is forced and gives a weak sense for line 322. More likely is the earlier explanation that barbers hung up in their shops, which were often thronged, a list of penalties for various kinds of misbehavior. Hart (*Notes and Queries*, July 1908, p. 64) cites from *Plain Percival*: "Speake a bloody word in a Barbers shop, you make a forfet" (quoted by Lever).

322. As . . . mark: i.e. as often broken as observed.
326. goodman: term of address, here ironic, to one below the rank of a gentleman. **bald-pate.** Lucio supposes that there is a tonsure under the Duke's hood. **341. protest**: affirm.
342. close: come to terms. **347. giglets**: wantons.
348. confederate companion: i.e. Friar Peter.
354. Show . . . face. Probably alluding to the fable of the wolf in sheep's clothing.
354–55. hang'd an hour. Presumably a jocular version of "hanged"; examples of "hanged awhile" have been cited. For another reference to the hanging of an animal, see *The Merchant of Venice*, IV.i.133–35, "Thy currish spirit / Govern'd a wolf, who hang'd for human slaughter, / Even from the gallows did his fell soul fleet. . . ."
357. gentle three: i.e. Isabella, Mariana, and Friar Peter.
362. We'll. The royal plural.

And hold no longer out.
Ang. O my dread lord,
I should be guiltier than my guiltiness,
To think I can be undiscernible,
When I perceive your Grace, like pow'r divine,
Hath look'd upon my passes. Then, good Prince,
No longer session hold upon my shame,
But let my trial be mine own confession.
Immediate sentence then, and sequent death,
Is all the grace I beg.
Duke. Come hither, Mariana.
Say: wast thou e'er contracted to this woman?
Ang. I was, my lord.
Duke. Go take her hence, and marry her instantly.
Do you the office, friar, which consummate,
Return him here again. Go with him, Provost.
Exeunt [Angelo, Mariana, Friar Peter, Provost].
Escal. My lord, I am more amaz'd at his dishonor
Than at the strangeness of it.
Duke. Come hither, Isabel,
Your friar is now your prince. As I was then
Advertising and holy to your business,
Not changing heart with habit, I am still
Attorneyed at your service.
Isab. O, give me pardon,
That I, your vassal, have employ'd and pain'd
Your unknown sovereignty!
Duke. You are pardon'd, Isabel;
And now, dear maid, be you as free to us.
Your brother's death I know sits at your heart;
And you may marvel why I obscur'd myself,
Laboring to save his life, and would not rather
Make rash remonstrance of my hidden pow'r
Than let him so be lost. O most kind maid,
It was the swift celerity of his death,
Which I did think with slower foot came on,
That brain'd my purpose. But peace be with him!
That life is better life, past fearing death,
Than that which lives to fear. Make it your comfort,
So happy is your brother.

Enter Angelo, Mariana, [Friar] Peter, Provost.

Isab. I do, my lord.
Duke. For this new-married man approaching here,
Whose salt imagination yet hath wrong'd
Your well-defended honor, you must pardon
For Mariana's sake; but as he adjudg'd your brother—
Being criminal, in double violation
Of sacred chastity and of promise-breach,
Thereon dependant, for your brother's life—
The very mercy of the law cries out
Most audible, even from his proper tongue,
"An Angelo for Claudio, death for death!"
Haste still pays haste, and leisure answers leisure;
Like doth quit like, and *Measure* still *for Measure.*
Then, Angelo, thy fault's thus manifested;
Which though thou wouldst deny, denies thee vantage.
We do condemn thee to the very block
Where Claudio stoop'd to death, and with like haste.
Away with him!
Mari. O my most gracious lord,
I hope you will not mock me with a husband!
Duke. It is your husband mock'd you with a husband.
Consenting to the safeguard of your honor,
I thought your marriage fit; else imputation,
For that he knew you, might reproach your life,
And choke your good to come. For his possessions,
Although by [confiscation] they are ours,
We do enstate and widow you with all,
To buy you a better husband.
Mari. O my dear lord,
I crave no other, nor no better man.
Duke. Never crave him, we are definitive.
Mari. [*Kneeling.*] Gentle my liege—
Duke. You do but lose your labor.
Away with him to death! [*To Lucio.*] Now, sir, to you.
Mari. O my good lord! Sweet Isabel, take my part!
Lend me your knees, and all my life to come
I'll lend you all my life to do you service.
Duke. Against all sense you do importune her.
Should she kneel down in mercy of this fact,
Her brother's ghost his paved bed would break,
And take her hence in horror.
Mari. Isabel!
Sweet Isabel, do yet but kneel by me.
Hold up your hands, say nothing; I'll speak all.
They say best men are moulded out of faults,
And for the most, become much more the better
For being a little bad; so may my husband.
O Isabel! will you not lend a knee?
Duke. He dies for Claudio's death.
Isab. [*Kneeling.*] Most bounteous sir:
Look, if it please you, on this man condemn'd
As if my brother liv'd. I partly think
A due sincerity governed his deeds,
Till he did look on me. Since it is so,
Let him not die. My brother had but justice,
In that he did the thing for which he died;

370. **passes**: transgressions. 383. **Advertising**: attentive. **holy**: devoted. 384. **habit**: attire. 385. **Attorneyed at**: acting as agent in.
386. **pain'd**: given trouble to. 388. **free to**: i.e. quick to pardon.
392. **rash remonstrance**: quick manifestation.
394. **swift celerity**. See the note on IV.ii.110.
396. **brain'd**: dashed out the brains of, brought to a shattering end.
399. **So**: thus, in this way. 401. **salt**: lecherous.
403. **adjudg'd**: condemned.
405–6. **promise-breach . . . for**: breaking his promise, conditional on the former action, to save. Strict syntax would require *promise* in place of *promise-breach*.
407. **very mercy**. Angelo's crime is such that not only justice but mercy itself demands his death. 408. **proper**: own.

410. **Haste . . . haste**: haste is always repaid with haste.
411. **quit**: requite, retaliate with. **Measure . . . Measure.** Cf. Matthew 7:2: "with what judgment ye judge, ye shall be judged, and with what measure ye mete, it shall be measured unto you again" (Geneva).
413. **though . . . deny**: even if you wished to deny it (which Angelo does not wish to do). **vantage**: i.e. a lesser penalty than was imposed on Claudio.
417. **mock . . . husband**: i.e. tantalize me by offering, and then immediately withdrawing, the gift of a husband.
420. **imputation**: imputation of sin.
424. **enstate . . . you**: i.e. endow you by virtue of a widow's rights.
427. **we are definitive**: my decision is final.
428. **liege**: sovereign.
433. **all sense**: rationality and natural feeling.
434. **in . . . fact**: to beg mercy for this crime.
435. **his paved bed**: the stone paving above his grave.

For Angelo,
His act did not o'ertake his bad intent,
And must be buried but as an intent
That perish'd by the way. Thoughts are no subjects,
Intents but merely thoughts.

Mari. Merely, my lord.

Duke. Your suit's unprofitable; stand up, I say.
I have bethought me of another fault.
Provost, how came it Claudio was beheaded
At an unusual hour?

Prov. It was commanded so.

Duke. Had you a special warrant for the deed?

Prov. No, my good lord; it was by private message.

Duke. For which I do discharge you of your office;
Give up your keys.

Prov. Pardon me, noble lord,
I thought it was a fault, but knew it not,
Yet did repent me, after more advice,
For testimony whereof, one in the prison,
That should by private order else have died,
I have reserv'd alive.

Duke. What's he?

Prov. His name is Barnardine.

Duke. I would thou hadst done so by Claudio.
Go fetch him hither, let me look upon him.
[*Exit Provost.*]

Escal. I am sorry, one so learned and so wise
As you, Lord Angelo, have still appear'd,
Should slip so grossly, both in the heat of blood
And lack of temper'd judgment afterward.

Ang. I am sorry that such sorrow I procure,
And so deep sticks it in my penitent heart
That I crave death more willingly than mercy:
'Tis my deserving, and I do entreat it.

Enter Barnardine *and* Provost, Claudio [*muffled*], Julietta.

Duke. Which is that Barnardine?

Prov. This, my lord.

Duke. There was a friar told me of this man.
Sirrah, thou art said to have a stubborn soul
That apprehends no further than this world,
And squar'st thy life according. Thou'rt condemn'd,
But for those earthly faults, I quit them all,
And pray thee take this mercy to provide
For better times to come. Friar, advise him,
I leave him to your hand. What muffled fellow's that?

Prov. This is another prisoner that I sav'd,
Who should have died when Claudio lost his head,
As like almost to Claudio as himself.
[*Unmuffles Claudio.*]

Duke. [*To Isabella.*] If he be like your brother, for his sake
Is he pardon'd, and for your lovely sake,
Give me your hand, and say you will be mine,
He is my brother too. But fitter time for that.
By this Lord Angelo perceives he's safe;
Methinks I see a quick'ning in his eye.
Well, Angelo, your evil quits you well.
Look that you love your wife; her worth worth yours.
I find an apt remission in myself;
And yet here's one in place I cannot pardon.
[*To Lucio.*] You, sirrah, that knew me for a fool, a coward,
One all of luxury, an ass, a madman,
Wherein have I so deserv'd of you,
That you extol me thus?

Lucio. Faith, my lord, I spoke it but according to the trick. If you will hang me for it, you may; but I had rather it would please you I might be whipt.

Duke. Whipt first, sir, and hang'd after.
Proclaim it, Provost, round about the city,
If any woman wrong'd by this lewd fellow
(As I have heard him swear himself there's one
Whom he begot with child), let her appear,
And he shall marry her. The nuptial finish'd,
Let him be whipt and hang'd.

Lucio. I beseech your Highness do not marry me to a whore. Your Highness said even now I made you a duke; good my lord, do not recompense me in making me a cuckold.

Duke. Upon mine honor, thou shalt marry her.
Thy slanders I forgive, and therewithal
Remit thy other forfeits. Take him to prison,
And see our pleasure herein executed.

Lucio. Marrying a punk, my lord, is pressing to death, whipping, and hanging.

Duke. Slandering a prince deserves it.
[*Exeunt Officers with Lucio.*]
She, Claudio, that you wrong'd, look you restore.
Joy to you, Mariana! Love her, Angelo!
I have confess'd her, and I know her virtue.
Thanks, good friend Escalus, for thy much goodness,
There's more behind that is more gratulate.
Thanks, Provost, for thy care and secrecy,
We shall employ thee in a worthier place.
Forgive him, Angelo, that brought you home
The head of Ragozine for Claudio's,
Th' offense pardons itself. Dear Isabel,
I have a motion much imports your good,
Whereto if you'll a willing ear incline,
What's mine is yours, and what is yours is mine.
So bring us to our palace, where we'll show
What's yet behind, that['s] meet you all should know.
[*Exeunt.*]

453. no subjects: i.e. not answerable to authority.
463. knew it not: was not certain of it.
464. more advice: further consideration.
471. still: always (heretofore). **473. temper'd:** balanced.
481. apprehends: understands. **482. squar'st:** shapest.
483. quit: remit. **492. Give:** if you will give.

495. quick'ning: renewal of life.
496. quits you well: (1) is well rewarded; (2) is requited with good (in contrast to "measure for measure").
497. her . . . yours: making your worth equal to hers (?).
498. apt remission: readiness to pardon.
499. in place: at hand, before me. **501. luxury:** lechery.
505. trick: fashion. **519. therewithal:** in addition.
522–23. pressing to death. One accused of felony who refused to plead guilty or not guilty was secured on his back and weights were piled on him in increasing number until he pleaded or died.
527. confess'd her: been her confessor.
529. behind: beyond, i.e. to come (so also in line 539).
532–34. Forgive . . . itself. This distinction between the offender and the offense recalls II.ii.34–41.
535. a motion: something to propose.
538. bring: accompany. **show:** make known.

NOTE ON THE TEXT

The First Folio (1623) is the only authority for *Measure for Measure*; all later texts are derived from that source. It is believed that the FI text was printed from a transcript, probably, like the printer's copy for the first three plays in F1, by Ralph Crane (for whose scribal characteristics see the "Note on the Text" to *The Tempest*). Even though the evidence for Crane's hand is not as strong as, for example, in *The Tempest*, the fairly heavy use of parentheses, a number of hyphenated forms, and an occasional "Jonsonian elision" (see Textual Notes, III.i.4, IV.iii.149) point in his direction, as do the act-scene division and the presence of a list of dramatis personae. The source of the transcript is also uncertain. W. W. Greg favors copy based on Shakespeare's "foul papers," but it is likewise possible that the scribe used a prompt-book and omitted the usual prompt-notations associated with theatre copy. There are, at any rate, no confusions in the F1 text serious enough to rule out a prompt-copy source; and the absence of a substantial number of exit directions cannot be considered a serious stumbling block, since, on the whole, prompters were not overly concerned about getting characters off the stage.

Dover Wilson's ingenious theory of abridgement and later expansion (1922), evolved to explain the curious mixture of prose and verse passages in the play, is no longer generally accepted, but his suggestion that the role of Lucio (in II.ii and V.i) has at some stage in the composition been "fattened" is probably correct, and his repudiation of I.ii.1–84 as an un-Shakespearean interpolation has most recently (1987) been accepted by Taylor/Wells (Gibbons disagrees, however [1991]), who further suggest that the author of these lines (as of IV.i.1–25; see below) was Thomas Middleton, who had been called in, after Shakespeare's death, to rework parts of the play and that Shakespeare's lines 85–92, in which Mistress Overdone appears to be ignorant of information she herself has earlier volunteered (lines 60–73), though probably marked for omission, somehow found their way into the transcript from which F1 was set up. The detailed evidence for attributing the reworking to Middleton may be examined in Jowett/Taylor's long essay, "'With New Additions'" in *Shakespeare Reshaped* (1993). In IV.i.1–6, the song that opens the scene ("Take, O, take those lips away,") together with a second inferior stanza, in which, as a reversal, a lover addresses his mistress, also appears in *The Bloody Brother* V.ii (c. 1619–24) by Fletcher and others, a play that may have belonged to the King's Men, Shakespeare's company. Most critics, most recently Gibbons, consider the first stanza of this song lyric to be by Shakespeare, but Alice Walker (following a suggestion of Frank O'Connor's in *The Road to Stratford*, 1948) and Taylor/Wells argue that the song and lines 7–25 were, like I.ii.1–84, interpolated after Shakespeare's death, the song being then borrowed from *The Bloody Brother* in the process of revision. The Oxford editors, though wisely retaining IV.i as in F1, offer an interesting reconstruction (in *Complete Works* 1986, p. 924) of what the text would have been like if, indeed, its opening (1–25) were originally not a part of the scene by placing IV.i.59–64 ("O place . . . fancies.") immediately after Escalus' exit at III.ii.260, continuing with IV.i.26–58, then inserting the Duke's soliloquy from III.ii.261–82, followed by IV.i.64–75 ("Welcome, . . . sow."). This hypothetical arrangement obviates the frequently voiced objection that the Duke's soliloquy in IV.i.59–64 does not afford Isabella sufficient time to explain the situation and the Duke's proposed remedy to Mariana—an objection that, however, mistakes real time for theatre time.

For further information, see: J. D. Wilson, ed., New Shakespeare *Measure for Measure* (Cambridge, 1922); W. W. Greg, *The Shakespeare First Folio* (Oxford, 1955); J. W. Lever, ed., New Arden *Measure for Measure* (London, 1965); Gary Taylor "*Measure for Measure*: IV.ii.41–46," *SQ*, XXIX (1978), 419–21; Mark Eccles, ed., New Variorum *Measure for Measure* (New York, 1980); Alice Walker, "The Text of *Measure for Measure*," in *RES*, n.s. XXXIV (1983), 1–20; Stanley Wells, Gary Taylor, John Jowett, and William Montgomery, *William Shakespeare: A Textual Companion* (Oxford, 1987); Brian Gibbons, ed., New Cambridge *Measure for Measure* (Cambridge, 1991); John Jowett and Gary Taylor, "'With New Additions': Theatrical Interpolation in *Measure for Measure*," in Gary Taylor and John Jowett, *Shakespeare Reshaped, 1606–1623* (Oxford, 1993).

TEXTUAL NOTES

Dramatis personae: ***subs. as given in F1, following the play, with a few additions by Rowe and later editors***

Act-scene division: ***from F1, with the following exceptions: I.iii, iv (numbered I.iv, v in F1, which divides I.ii into two scenes, with the break after l. 115); III.ii (no scene division in F1); see first note to each scene; present act-scene arrangement as a whole first established by Dyce***

I.i

Location: ***Theobald (after Pope)***
o.s.d. and Attendants] ***Capell***
15 s.d. Exit an Attendant.] ***Capell***
35 touch'd] ***F2;*** **touch'd** ***F1***
75 s.d. Exit.] ***placed as in F2; after l. 74, F1***

I.ii

Location: ***Rowe***
12 Why,] ***Pope;*** **Why?** ***F1***
15 relish] ***F3;*** **rallish** ***F1***
32 three-pil'd piece] ***Rowe;*** **three pild-peece** ***F1***
46 s.p. 1. Gent.] ***Theobold; continued to Lucio, F1***
46–7 I . . . to—] ***as prose, Pope; as verse, F1***
60 s.p. Mrs. Ov.] **Bawd.** ***F1 (subs. throughout)***
76 promise-keeping] ***hyphen, F2***
81 s.d. with Gentlemen] ***Capell (subs.)***
84 s.d. Enter Clown] ***placed as in Dyce (after Capell); after l. 85, F1***
86 s.p. Pom.] ***Dyce;*** **Clo.** ***F1 (subs. throughout)***
115] ***Following this line F1 inserts*** **Scena Tertia.** ***before entry of Provost, etc.; no scene break observed in Padua First Folio prompt-book, Rowe***
115 s.d. Enter . . . Officers.] ***Dyce (after Rowe; implied in Padua prompt-book);*** **Enter Prouost, Claudio, Iuliet, Officers, Lucio, & 2. Gent.** ***F1***
123 s.d. Enter . . . Gentlemen.] ***Padua prompt-book, Dyce (after Davenant); F1 is ambiguous (see preceding note) about whether only the Second Gentleman or both Gentlemen re-enter here; Padua prompt-book gives only*** **Gent** ***(also ambiguous); F2 reads*** **two Gent.**
125 liberty:] ***Rowe (subs.);*** **Liberty** ***F1***
150 propagation] ***F2;*** **propogation** ***F1***
185 reason] ***Pope;*** **reason,** ***F1***

I.iii

I.iii] ***Rowe;*** **Scena Quarta.** ***F1***
Location: ***ed. (after Wilson)***
3 Why] ***Rowe;*** **why,** ***F1***
10 cost,] **cost, and** ***F2***
14 travell'd] ***Rowe;*** **trauaild** ***F1***
27 Becomes] ***Pope (after Davenant)***
54 s.d. Exeunt.] ***F2;*** **Exit.** ***F1***

I.iv

I.iv] ***Rowe;*** **Scena Quinta.** ***F1***
Location: ***Rowe***
2, 7 s.pp. Fran.] ***Capell;*** **Nun.** ***F1***
5 sisterhood] ***F2;*** **Sisterstood** ***F1***
14 s.d. Exit.] ***Rowe***
15 s.d. Enter Lucio.] ***Rowe***
17 stead] ***Rowe;*** **steed** ***F1***
54 givings-out] ***Rowe (subs.);*** **giuing-out** ***F1***
55 true-meant] ***hyphen, Pope***
61 fast.] ***F2;*** **fast** ***F1***
63 run by] ***Rowe;*** **run-by** ***F1***
72 so seek] ***Rowe;*** **so, / Seeke** ***F1***
72 H'as] ***Theobald;*** **Has** ***F1***
90 s.d. severally] ***ed.***

II.i

Location: ***Wilson***
12 your] ***Rowe (after Davenant);*** **our** ***F1***
20 sworn twelve] ***Rowe;*** **sworne-twelue** ***F1***
36 s.d. Exit Provost.] ***Rowe***
38 Some . . . fall;] ***in italics, F1***

59 s.d. A pause.] *ed.* (*suggested by line arrangement in F1*)
63 parcel-bawd] *hyphen, Theobald*
65 suburbs] *F2;* Suborbs *F1*
65 sir,] *F2;* Sir? *F1*
90 honors'] *Capell;* honors *F1*
94 china dishes] *Rowe* (*subs.*); China-dishes *F1*
98 great-bellied] *hyphen, Capell*
126 All-hallond eve] *Rowe* (*after F2*); Allhallond-Eue *F1*
138 s.d. Exit Angelo.] *Theobald;* Exit. *F1* (*after l. 137*)
160 right, constable. What] *ed.;* right (Constable) what *F1*
197 s.d. To Pompey.] *Rowe*
212 s.d. Exit Froth.] *Rowe*
253 s.d. aside] *Staunton*
275 s.d. Exit Elbow.] *Rowe*

II.ii

Location: *Johnson*
2 s.d. Exit Servant.] *Capell*
17 s.d. Enter Servant.] *Padua prompt-book, Capell*
22 s.d. Exit Servant.] *Theobald*
36 s.d. Aside.] *Collier*
37 it?] *Rowe;* it. *F1*
43, 56, etc. s.dd. Aside to Isabella.] *Collier* (*after Johnson*)
58 it] it backe *F2*
59 'longs] *Theobald;* longs *F1*
87 gross selves] *F4;* grosse-selues *F1*
102 gall,] *Craig;* gaule *F1*
125 s.d. Aside.] *Collier*
141, 157 s.dd. Aside.] *Johnson*
149 tested gold] *Rowe;* tested-gold *F1*
153 sun-rise] *hyphen, Theobald*
160 'fore noon] *Rowe;* 'fore-noone *F1*
161 s.d. Exeunt . . . Provost.] *Capell* (*after Rowe*); Exeunt. *F2*
163 most,] *Kittredge;* most? *F1*
183 art] *Pope;* Art, *F1*

II.iii

Location: *Rowe*
o.s.d. disguised . . . friar] *Rowe* (*subs.*)
o.s.d. meeting] *ed.* (*after Dyce*)
17 s.d. To Juliet.] *Theobald*
26 offenseful] *F2;* offence full *F1*
34 fear—] *Capell;* feare. *F1*

II.iv

Location: *Capell*
9 sere] *Heath conj.* (*after Hanmer*); feard *F1*
17 s.d. Enter Servant.] *placed as in Theobald; after l. 17, F1*
19 s.d. Exit Servant.] *Capell* (*after Johnson*)
30 s.d. Enter Isabella.] *placed as in Johnson; after l. 30, F1*
48 metal] *Theobald;* mettle *F1*
53 or] *Rowe* (*after Davenant*); and *F1*
75 craftily] *Rowe* (*after Davenant*); crafty *F1*
76 me] *F2*
94 all-binding law] *Johnson;* all-building-Law *F1*
122–3 he, Owe] *Theobald* (*subs.*); he / Owe, *F1*
158 report] *F2;* reporr *F1*
185] *Line marked with gnomic quotes, F1*

III.i

Location: *Rowe*
o.s.d. disguised . . . friar] *Collier* (*subs.*)
4 I have] *Capell;* I'haue *F1*
9 skyey influences] *F4;* skyie-influences *F1*
29 thee sire] *F4;* thee, fire *F1*
44 s.d. Within.] *Capell*
47 s.d. Enter Isabella.] *placed as in Dyce; after l. 43, F1*
52 me . . . them] *Steevens conj.* (*after Davenant*); them . . . me *F1; for ll. 52–3 F2 reads:* Bring them to speake, where I may be conceal'd, yet heare them.
53 s.d. Exeunt . . . Provost.] *Rowe;* Exeunt. *F2*
55 indeed.] *F4* (*subs.*); indeede, *F1*
68 Though . . . had,] *Rowe;* Through . . . had *F1*
88 outward-sainted] *hyphen, Pope*
90 enew] *Keightley;* emmew *F1*
93, 96 prenzie] Princely *F2; among other emendations suggested,* precise (*Tieck conj. in Cambridge*) *and* puny (*Drew conj. in SQ*) *are perhaps the best*
95 damned'st] *F2;* damnest *F1*
98 freed!] *Staunton;* freed? *F1*
99 thee,] *Capell;* thee; *F1*
99 offense,] *Hanmer;* offence *F1*
129 penury] *F2;* periury *F1*
150 s.d. Enter . . . friar.] *Capell* (*subs.*); Duke steps in. *F2*
159 s.d. Walks apart.] *Capell*
173 s.d. Exit Claudio.] *Capell;* Exit. *F2* (*after l. 172*)
174 s.d. Enter Provost.] *Capell* (*before l. 174*); *placed as in Dyce*
180 s.d. Turning to Isabella.] *Wilson*
191 born] *F3;* borne *F1*
198 advisings: . . . good] *Pope;* aduisings, . . . good; *F1*
214 by] *F2*
250 stead] *Rowe;* steed *F1*
264 moated grange] *F4;* moated-Grange *F1*
269 s.d. Manet Duke.] *ed.*

III.ii

III.ii] *Capell* (*after Pope*); *F1* (*followed by the Padua prompt-book*) *correctly continues the scene without a new entry for the Duke*
Location: *ed.* (*after Wilson*)
24 abominable] *F3;* abhominable *F1*
25 eat, array] *Theobald* (*Bishop conj.*); eate away *F1*
28–9 Indeed . . . prove—] *as prose, Pope; as verse, F1*
39 seeming,] *ed.;* seeming *F1*
40 waist—] *Dyce* (waist *Johnson*); wast, *F1*
47 it] *Rowe*
68 bawd-born] *F3* (*hyphen, Steevens*); Baud borne *F1*
76 bondage. . . . patiently,] *Theobald* (*subs.*); bondage . . . patiently: *F1*
85–6 s.d. Exeunt . . . Officers.] *Rowe;* Exeunt. *F2*
145 bringings-forth] *hyphen, Dyce*
151 dearer] *Hanmer;* deare *F1*
183–4 brown bread] *Rowe;* browne-bread *F1*
189 s.d. Officers with] *Dyce* (*after Hanmer*)
206–7 s.d. Exeunt . . . Overdone.] *Rowe* (*subs.*)
219 See] *Theobald;* Sea *F1*
224 and, . . . is,] *Alexander;* and . . . is *F1*
232–3 One . . . himself.] *as prose, Capell; as verse, F1*
255–7 If . . . himself.] *as prose, Pope; as verse, F1*
260 s.d. Exeunt . . . Provost.] *Capell;* Exit. *F2*

IV.i

Location: *Cambridge* (*after Theobald*)
3 eyes, . . . day,] *Rowe;* eyes: . . . day *F1*
9 s.d. Exit Boy.] *Capell*
37 upon't.] *Rowe* (*subs.*); vpon't, *F1*
49 s.d. Enter Mariana.] *placed as in Rowe; after l. 48, F1*
58 Will't] *Steevens;* Wilt *F1*
58 s.d. with Isabella] *Rowe* (*subs.*)
64 s.d. Enter . . . Isabella.] *placed as in Johnson; after l. 64, F1*
75 tithe's] *Pope;* Tithes *F1*

IV.ii

Location: *Rowe*
3–5 If . . . head.] *as prose, Pope; as verse, F1*
44–7 If . . . thief.] *continued to Abhorson, Capell; assigned to Clo., F1*
58 yare] *Theobald;* y'are *F1*
60 s.d. Exeunt . . . Pompey.] *Capell;* Exit. *F1* (*after l. 59*)
69 s.d. Knocking within.] *Rowe* (*subs.*)
70 s.d. Exit Claudio.] *Capell*
70 by.] *F4* (*subs.*); by, *F1*
72 s.d. Enter . . . friar.] *placed as in Dyce; F1 s.d.* (Enter Duke.) *after l. 72*
85 s.d. Knocking within.] *Padua prompt-book* (Knock), *Rowe* (*subs.*)
85 s.d. Exit Provost.] *Theobald* (*subs.*)
87 s.d. Knocking within.] *Dyce* (*after Collier*)
89 s.d. Enter Provost.] *Theobald* (*subs.*)
95 Happily] *F3;* Happely *F1*
100 This . . . man.] *continued to Provost, Tyrwhitt conj.; assigned to* Duke., *F1*
100 Lordship's] *Rowe;* Lords *F1*
101 s.p. Duke.] *Tyrwhitt conj.;* Pro. *F1*
102–6 My . . . day.] *as prose, Pope; as verse, F1*
107 s.d. Exit Messenger.] *Rowe*
108 s.d. Aside.] *Johnson*
113 fault's] *Rowe;* faults *F1*
115–8 I . . . before.] *as prose, Pope; as verse, F1*
117 putting-on] *hyphen, Dyce*
119 s.p., s.d. Prov. Reads] *Rowe*
130–1 A . . . old.] *as prose, Pope; as verse, F1*
143 reakless] *ed.;* wreaklesse *F1*
169–73 By . . . favor.] *as prose, Pope; as verse, F1*
170 guide.] *F4* (*subs.*); guide, *F1*
176 bar'd] *Malone* (bared); bar'de *F1*
198 find, . . . days] *Theobald* (*after Rowe*); finde . . . daies, *F1*
210 s.d. Exeunt.] *Pope;* Exit. *F1*

IV.iii

Location: *ed.* (*after Rowe*)
7 Marry, then] *Dyce;* marrie then, *F1*
17 Shoe-tie] *Capell* (*subs.*); Shootie *F1*
18 Pots] *as proper name, Rowe; not in italics, F1*
19 "for . . . sake."] *quotes, Dyce*
26–7 Your . . . death.] *as prose, Pope; as verse, F1*
28 s.d. Within.] *Theobald*
39–40 How . . . you?] *as prose, Pope; as verse, F1*
43–4 You . . . for't.] *as prose, Pope; as verse, F1*
65 s.d. Exeunt . . . Pompey.] *Capell*
92 s.d. Exit Provost.] *Pope;* Exit. *F1* (*after l. 91*)
101 s.d. with Ragozine's head] *Dyce* (*Padua prompt-book calls for a prop head*)
149 Good . . . Provost?] *as prose, Hudson; as verse, F1*
149 Good even] *Rowe;* Good'euen *F1*
158 s.d. Exit Isabella.] *Theobald*
165–6 Nay . . . Duke.] *as prose, Pope; as verse, F1*
172–4 Yes . . . medlar.] *as prose, Pope; as verse, F1*

IV.iv

Location: *Capell*
3 manner.] *Rowe;* manner, *F1*
6 redeliver] *Capell;* re- / liuer *F1*
19 s.d. Exit Escalus.] *Capell;* Exit. *F1* (*after l. 18*)
32 liv'd] *F2;* liued *F1*

IV.v

Location: *Pope*
o.s.d. in . . . habit] *Rowe*
1 s.d. Giving letters.] *Johnson*
2 plot.] *F4* (*subs.*); plot, *F1*
6 Flavio's] *ed.* (*Theobald conj.*); Flauia's *F1*
8 Valentius] *Pope;* Valencius *F1*
10 s.d. Exit.] *Theobald*

IV.vi

Location: *Capell*
4 veil] *Malone;* vaile *F1*

V.i

Location: *Capell*
o.s.d. Flourish.] *ed.* (*from Padua prompt-book*)
o.s.d. Escalus] *F2;* Esculus *F1*
o.s.d. Provost, Officers] *Capell* (*subs.*)
13 me] *F3;* we *F1*
41 virgin-violator] *hyphen, Theobald*
54 absolute] *F4;* absolute: *F1*
78 s.d. To Lucio.] *Rowe*
159 nobleman] *F2;* Noble man *F1*

162 s.d. **Isabella . . . guarded.**] *Theobald* (*after l. 167*); *placed as in Capell*
167 s.d. **veiled**] *Rowe; s.d. placed as in Wilson; after l. 167, F1*
168 **her**] *F2;* your *F1*
181–2 **Silence . . . himself.**] *as verse, Capell; as prose, F1*
206 s.d. **Unveiling.**] *Rowe*
215 **Enough**] *F2;* Enoug *F1*
219 **promised**] *Rowe;* promis'd *F1*
227 **affianc'd**] *Rowe;* affianced *F1*
253 s.d. **Exit Provost.**] *Capell*
259 **My . . . throughly.**] *as verse, Wilson; as prose, F1*
259 s.d. **Exit Duke.**] *Capell;* Exit. *F1* (*after* slanderers. *l. 259*)
270 s.d. **Exit an Attendant.**] *Dyce* (*after Capell*)
277 s.d. **in . . . habit**] *Pope* (*subs.*)
277 s.d. **Officers with**] *Capell* (*after Theobald*)
281–2 **Come . . . said.**] *as prose, F3; as verse, F1*
283–4 **My . . . Provost.**] *as prose, Pope; as verse, F1*
295 **speak:**] *F4;* speake, *F1*
298 **fox,**] *Dyce;* Fox; *F1;* Fox? *F2*
317 **looker-on**] *hyphen, Pope*
325–6 **'Tis . . . me?**] *as verse, ed.* (*after Pope*); *as prose, F1*
348 s.d. **The . . . Duke.**] *Johnson*
355 s.d. **Pulls . . . hood.**] *Rowe*
358 s.d. **To Lucio.**] *Johnson*
361 s.d. **To Escalus.**] *Rowe*
362 s.d. **Takes Angelo's seat.**] *Neilson* (*after Capell*)
379 s.d. **Exeunt . . . Provost.**] *Pope* (*after Rowe*); *Exit. F1*
384 **Not . . . habit,**] *Rowe;* (Not . . . habit) *F1*
399 s.d. **Mariana**] *Rowe;* Maria *F1*
411 **for**] *italics, Capell*
418 **husband.**] *Rowe;* husband, *F1*
423 **confiscation**] *F2;* confutation *F1*
428 s.d. **Kneeling.**] *Johnson*
429 s.d. **To Lucio.**] *Johnson*
443 s.d. **Kneeling.**] *Rowe*
449 **died**] *F2* (di'd); dide *F1*
453–4 **subjects, Intents**] *Wilson;* subiects / Intents, *F1;* subjects; / Intents, *F4*
469 s.d. **Exit Provost.**] *Johnson*
472 **grossly**] *F2;* grosselie *F1*
477 s.d. **muffled**] *Dyce* (*after Capell*)
489 s.d. **Unmuffles Claudio.**] *Capell* (*subs.*)
490 s.d. **To Isabella.**] *Johnson*
491 **sake,**] *Rowe;* sake *F1*
497 **yours.**] *F2;* yours *F1*
500 s.d. **To Lucio.**] *Rowe*
501 **madman**] *Rowe;* mad man *F1*
522–3 **Marrying . . . hanging.**] *as prose, Pope; as verse, F1*
524 s.d. **Exeunt . . . Lucio.**] *Dyce*
539 **that's**] *F2;* that *F1*
539 s.d. **Exeunt.**] *Rowe;* FINIS. *F1* (*after list of actors*)

Hector, Ajax, and Thersites. From the title-pages of Thomas Heywood's *The Iron Age, Parts 1 and 2* (1632). The combat of Hector and Ajax here pictured (left) is in marked contrast to their chivalric encounter in *Troilus and Cressida* (IV.v). Hector's boulder may be found in Homer (*Iliad*, Book VII), but Ajax' "farre greater stone" (Chapman's translation) has been replaced with a tree torn up by its roots (a detail perhaps original with Heywood, who had earlier used it in his *Troia Britannica*, 1609). In the second woodcut (only part of which is reproduced) notice Thersites' unabashedly Elizabethan costume, with rapier, boots, and spurs, typical of the mixed costuming tradition of the period. (*By permission of the Harvard College Library*)

Henry VI, Parts 1, 2, and 3

THE THREE HENRY VI PLAYS ascribed to Shakespeare in the Folio of 1623 have prompted much more scholarship than admiration. Indeed, the first, which had not appeared in print before, was esteemed so little that until fairly recent times it was virtually excluded from the canon. Warburton and other eighteenth-century editors, repelled by its coarse depiction of Joan of Arc and by its alleged inelegance of style, assumed that Shakespeare could not have written such a sorry thing; and despite Johnson's warning that "from mere inferiority nothing can be inferred," Edmond Malone's influential *Dissertation on the Three Parts of Henry VI* (1787) led most subsequent commentators either to assign the play to someone else or to regard Shakespeare's part in it as small and unimportant. Thus its authorship has been ascribed, on such evidence as style and use of sources, to a dizzying list of candidates: to Greene, to Greene assisted by Peele and Shakespeare, to Peele and Shakespeare working as a team, to a syndicate comprising Marlowe, Peele, Nashe, Shakespeare, and certain unknown writers. The names of Chapman, Drayton, Kyd, and Lodge have also crept into the discussion. The other two plays in the trilogy had been first printed almost thirty years before: Part 2 as *The First Part of the Contention betwixt the two famous Houses of Yorke and Lancaster* (1594) and Part 3 as *The true Tragedie of Richard Duke of Yorke . . . as it was sundrie times acted by the Right Honourable the Earle of Pembrooke his seruants* (1595). Each was reprinted in 1600, and in 1619 they appeared together as *The Whole Contention betweene the two Famous Houses, Lancaster and Yorke*. These quarto texts, however, vary so strikingly from the versions printed in the Folio of 1623 that they were long thought to be old plays that Shakespeare had revised (as Malone had argued); only in recent years have they come to be generally regarded as reported texts or "bad" quartos of Shakespeare's works as they were first presented and, with minor alterations, exhumed by Heminge and Condell for publication in the Folio.

The evidence that bears upon and therefore complicates the authorship and date of Part 1 also involves Parts 2 and 3. Although in our present state of knowledge we cannot be certain of the circumstances under which these works were written and produced, any meaningful conjecture must rest upon the facts that follow:

(1) On March 3, 1592, Philip Henslowe, manager of the Rose theatre, recorded in his diary the presentation by Lord Strange's men of a "ne" (i.e. new) play, "Harey the vj." It was repeated fourteen times by June 19, shortly after which all the theatres were closed by an outbreak of the plague.

(2) In *Pierce Penniless*, which was entered in the Stationers' Register on August 8, 1592, and published soon thereafter, Nashe wrote that it would have "joyed brave Talbot, the terror of the French, to think that after he had lain two hundred years in his tomb he should triumph again on the stage, and have his bones new embalmed with the tears of ten thousand spectators at least (at several times) who in the tragedian that represents his person imagine they behold him fresh bleeding." The allusion would seem to fit *1 Henry VI*, in which Talbot plays a leading part.

(3) Shortly before his death on September 3, 1592, Greene, in *A Groatsworth of Wit*, warned certain of his fellow playwrights—presumably Marlowe,

Nashe, and Peele—about "an upstart crow, beautified with our feathers, that with his *tiger's heart wrapp'd in a player's hide* supposes he is as well able to bombast out a blank verse as the best of you; and being an absolute *Johannes fac totum*, is in his own conceit the only Shake-scene in a country." The allusion to Shakespeare is reinforced by the parody of a line in *3 Henry VI* (I.iv.137), which appears also in *The True Tragedy*: "O tiger's heart wrapt in a woman's hide."

Efforts to align these data and to ascertain their relevance to the three Henry VI plays in the Folio have led to a staggering mass of inference, interpretation, and conjecture. To rehearse all of this material, some of it extremely knotty, would be inappropriate here, but even a small sampling will indicate its scope. It has been suggested, for example, that Greene's misquotation from Part 3 makes it impossible to identify "Harey the vj" with *1 Henry VI*, since otherwise we must assume that the entire trilogy had been brought before the public between March 1592 (when the Henslowe play was "new") and the following June (when all theatrical production was halted by the plague); that Greene, ill and crotchety and jealous of a younger man's success, was only sneering at Shakespeare's pretensions as an actor; that Greene was charging Shakespeare with plagiarizing his and his associates' work, in which case *2* and *3 Henry VI* should be regarded as unauthorized adaptations of *The Contention* and *The True Tragedy*, and *1 Henry VI* either as a potboiler intended as a prologue to the plays that had been pilfered or (in Malone's words) as "the entire or nearly the entire production of some ancient dramatist"; that *1 Henry VI*, hastily thrown together to exploit the rival Pembroke troupe's success with *2* and *3 Henry VI*, was begun by Greene and Nashe and completed by Shakespeare (perhaps with Nashe's aid) for presentation by Strange's men in 1592; that Greene had blocked out the whole trilogy and written much of it when Nashe was called in to provide the first act of Part 1, Peele to supply certain things in Parts 2 and 3, and Shakespeare to touch up all three plays; that since Shakespeare was probably connected with Pembroke's troupe as early as 1592, "Harey the vj," which belonged to Strange's men, could not have been his work; that since *The Contention* and *The True Tragedy*—the latter certainly and the former probably belonging to Pembroke's men—contain many borrowings from Part 1, all three plays must have been in the Pembroke repertory, and therefore the Strange troupe's "Harey the vj" could not have been Part 1; that *The Contention* and *The True Tragedy*, formerly the property of Pembroke's men, were somehow acquired by Strange's men and revised by Shakespeare (who was a member of their troupe) as Parts 2 and 3 in 1592, when he also touched up an old Talbot play that Greene had written about 1589 and revised in 1591.

With some notable exceptions, modern scholars are agreed that *The Contention* and *The True Tragedy* are corrupt memorial reconstructions, not sources, of *2* and *3 Henry VI*. Thus Malone's once widely shared opinion that Shakespeare reworked a pair of older plays has now been generally abandoned for Peter Alexander's view that *2* and *3 Henry VI* are Shakespeare's own creation, and that the two quartos are reported texts which were pieced together from memory and perhaps from actors' parts in the possession of former members of the Pembroke troupe. In short, mutilation has replaced revision as a principle of explanation. But if Alexander (and Madeleine Doran working independently of him) have enabled us to redefine the problem, the problem still remains, and the precise connection between the six related works—"Harey the vj," the two quartos of 1594–95, and the three Henry VI plays ascribed to Shakespeare in the Folio of 1623—is still a matter of dispute. Perhaps, as certain scholars think, Shakespeare wrote *2* and *3 Henry VI* for Pembroke's men and then, encouraged by their success, prefaced them with a revision of "Harey the vj" that had somehow been secured from Strange's men. On the other hand, it is tempting to believe, with A. S. Cairncross, that *1 Henry VI* (which is unrelated to "Harey the vj") preceded Parts 2 and 3 in point of composition, that all three plays were written about 1590 for Pembroke's men or for their predecessors, and that they are mainly if not entirely Shakespeare's work. But unless new data come to light such educated guesses must take the place of knowledge.

Fortunately, the sources of these plays do not pose so many problems. The fact that different parts of *1 Henry VI* seem to draw on different works—for example, the Joan of Arc material in I.ii and V.iv from the second (1587) edition of Holinshed and certain details about the unruly servingmen in I.iii and III.i from Richard Fabyan's *Chronicle* (1559 ed.)—has been advanced as proof that several writers were involved; but it is easier to assume that here as elsewhere Shakespeare consulted various books and took from each what he most liked or needed. Thus in *1 Henry VI* Bullough finds traces of Holinshed and Geoffrey of Monmouth's *Historia Regum Britanniae*; in *2 Henry VI*, of Foxe's *Acts and Monuments*, Grafton's *Chronicle at Large* (for the spurious miracle of St. Albans in II.i), and Holinshed; and in *3 Henry VI*, of *A Mirror for Magistrates*. Despite these and other signs of Shakespeare's varied reading, the major source for all three plays is Edward Hall's *Union of the Two Noble and Illustre Families of Lancaster and York* (1548).

This famous book exemplifies the notion—as old as Augustine's *City of God*—that history, which seems to reel from one disaster to another, reveals a steady moral purpose because its course is set by God. To be sure, most fifteenth-century chroniclers had buttressed their political aspirations and attachments with deific sanctions. For example, Thomas Walsingham, the last of the line of historians produced by the great Benedictine monastery of St. Albans, was so incorrigibly hostile to Richard II and so sympathetic to Henry IV that he records the rise of the House of Lancaster as preordained by God; and John Hardyng, a shifty politician whose last patron was Richard, Duke of York, and whose clumsily versified chronicle represents almost the nadir of fifteenth-century historiography, views the savage Yorkists as instruments of providence. Compared to these, Polydore Vergil marks a real advance. This learned Italian, whose *Historia Anglica* was commissioned by Henry VII, divorced the interpretation of recent English history from partisan politics to advance the no less providential but more objective notion of divine justice as impartially punishing sin and rewarding virtue. But it was Edward Hall who most insistently depicted the triumphs of the house of Tudor and of the English Reformation as reciprocal signs of God's benign control. Like the Book of Genesis and the *Aeneid*, his *Union* tells the story of a people that, under divine guidance, fulfills its destiny. Hall's subject, like Shakespeare's in eight of the ten plays that he wrote on English history, is England in the fifteenth century, when two great ducal houses were competing for the throne. Dealing as it does with crime and retribution, with disorder and misrule, the *Union* is diffuse and episodic; but it generates real power, and its climax is impressive: the accession of the Lancastrian Earl of Richmond as Henry VII and his marriage to a daughter of the house of York are, as Hall presents them, blessings sent by God. From this union of the red rose with the white, peace descended "out of heaven into England" and the House of Tudor was secured upon the throne. Thus Hall had a double purpose: to expound the providential theme that "as by discord great things decay and fall to ruin, so the same by concord be revived and erected," and to celebrate the glories of the Tudors. Like many other writers of his age, Hall considered politics to be a branch of morals.

That Shakespeare, near the start of his career, should have been attracted to this patriotic theme is not at all surprising, and that it so clearly underlies the three parts of Henry VI and their sequel *Richard III* reinforces the conjecture that these four plays—the so-called first tetralogy—were conceived and written by one man. Shakespeare himself implies as much when, in the epilogue to *Henry V*, he speaks of the tumultuous events of Henry VI's reign "Which oft our stage hath shown"; and Johnson, who knew nothing about critical bibliography but had an ample fund of common sense, pointed to the fact that all three Henry VI plays are built upon a "series of transactions" that laces them together. Viewed as a cycle on the political disorders of fifteenth-century England, they have more merit than some of their detractors, including Coleridge and Hazlitt, have been willing to concede. For a young writer to undertake so big a subject as fifty years of English history required both skill and valor; and if the skill is sometimes lacking, the valor certifies his bold intention. Indeed, the bold intention, which imparts an almost epic sweep and power to plays so anecdotal and diffuse, may be said almost to justify the flaws. If Shakespeare, in the strength and plumage of his youth, had taken fewer chances he would not have done so much.

The audacity of youth is everywhere apparent: in the big, unwieldy canvas filled with an enormous cast of characters, in the convolutions of the plot, in the pageantry and violent action, in sheer theatricality. But it is most apparent in the style, which tends towards high and sometimes tedious declamation. Normally, all the characters speak alike, and their undifferentiated speech—a blank verse in which the unit is the single line stuffed with epithets and adorned with Latin tags and classical allusions—owes much to Seneca and Marlowe. It often gets beyond control, as in the imagistic chaos of the opening lines of *1 Henry VI* and in the bombast that Greene (of all people) saw fit to ridicule. More often, however, it is merely strident and inflated, and heavy in its metronomic beat:

> Is Talbot slain, the Frenchmen's only scourge,
> Your kingdom's terror and black Nemesis?
> O, were mine eyeballs into bullets turn'd,
> That I in rage might shoot them at your faces!
> O, that I could but call these dead to life,
> It were enough to fright the realm of France!
> Were but his picture left amongst you here,
> It would amaze the proudest of you all.
> Give me their bodies, that I may bear them hence
> And give them burial as beseems their worth.
> (IV.vii.77–86)

This kind of language, the basic idiom of these plays, continually approaches oratory. We hear it, for example, when Talbot baits the French before Bordeaux (Part 1, IV.ii), when York defends his title to the throne (Part 2, II.iii), even when Young Clifford soliloquizes on his fate (Part 3, II.vi). An even stiffer formalism appears in the monotonous stichomythy of King Edward's wooing (Part 3, III.ii), in the almost ritualistic comments on the carnage wrought at Towton (Part 3, II.v), and in the antiphonal couplets that Talbot and his son exchange before they die (Part 1, IV.v–vi). When, occasionally, Shakespeare goes beyond this sort of thing we are duly gratified. The prose of the Jack Cade scenes in Part 2, like all of Shakespeare's prose, reveals an ear so sharp that the language, in its supple, idiomatic precision, sounds not written but transcribed. Sometimes, too, the verse reminds us of Shakespeare's later work in its concentrated power, as when Young Clifford comes upon his slaughtered father:

> O, let the vile world end,
> And the premised flames of the last day
> Knit earth and heaven together!
> Now let the general trumpet blow his blast,
> Particularities and petty sounds
> To cease! Wast thou ordain'd, dear father,
> To lose thy youth in peace, and to achieve
> The silvery livery of advised age,
> And in thy reverence, and thy chair-days, thus
> To die in ruffian battle? (Part 2, V.ii.40–49)

These plays, so long derided or condemned, reveal an arc of structure. The action of Part 1, which carries through Parts 2 and 3, is the long, slow fall of England from the funeral of the warrior-king Henry V, through the erosion of his French conquests, the decline of royal power, and the resulting civil broils that spread to civil war. In depicting these events Shakespeare does not hammer so relentlessly as Hall on the theme that Henry's troubled reign was in expiation for Bullingbrook's usurpation of the throne in 1399; but none the less he deals in cause and consequence, relating circumstance to character and presenting not a random string of episodes but the moral consequences of disorder. "No simple man that sees / This jarring discord of nobility," says Exeter as events are moving inexorably towards Talbot's overthrow,

> This shouldering of each other in the court,
> This factious bandying of their favorites,
> But that it doth presage some ill event.
> 'Tis much, when sceptres are in children's hands;
> But more, when envy breeds unkind division:
> There comes the ruin, there begins confusion.
> (Part 1, IV.i.187–94)

To mould a theme like this requires a shaping hand, and therefore no one should read these plays to learn what really happened in the fifteenth century. Shakespeare manipulates his data in a way that no historian would approve; he telescopes, distorts, and rearranges "facts"; he even fabricates whole episodes to reinforce his own interpretation of the things he found in Hall and Holinshed. The reason for such license is apparent: beneath the busy, sometimes cluttered surface of the action he directs the movements of events to underscore his theme. This theme, which dominates the tetralogy, may be stated as the loss of national identity and national purpose through the evils of disorder and their restoration through the advent of the Tudors.

Even *1 Henry VI*, which is so loose and anecdotal that Bullough calls it "not so much a Chronicle play as a fantasia on historical themes," is adjusted to this end. At the very opening of the play the pageantry of Henry V's funeral is disrupted by the bickering of the dead king's brothers and by the news that Henry's French possessions—the trophies of his splendid reign—are slipping from control. The double motif thus proclaimed—internal dissension that dissipates the power of England—gains momentum as the play proceeds upon its sometimes helter-skelter way. At home, the rivalry of the Lord Protector Gloucester and the Bishop of Winchester, who exploit the weakness of the youthful Henry VI, is like "a viperous worm / That gnaws the bowels of the commonwealth" (III.i.72–73). Abroad, brave Talbot, once the terror of the French, is ill supported and betrayed by his allies, and so, unable to withstand the witch and strumpet Joan of Arc, he falls.

There are two main links between the bustling action of Part 1 and the plays that follow. First, in the famous Temple Garden scene (II.iv)—which many early scholars considered one of Shakespeare's contributions to the work that he had undertaken to revise—the fateful problem of succession is announced in the quarrel between Richard Plantagenet, Duke of York, and the Lancastrian Earl of Somerset. Warwick's choric comment on their altercation is prophetic of the ruin to come:

> this brawl to-day,
> Grown to this faction in the Temple Garden,
> Shall send between the Red Rose and the White
> A thousand souls to death and deadly night.
> (II.iv.124–27)

Second, although Henry VI's betrothal, through his unscrupulous agent Suffolk, to Margaret of Anjou provides a kind of cadence for Part 1, it also supplies both circumstance and motive for Part 2. Involving as it does the breach of Henry's contract with Joan of Armagnac and the surrender of yet more territory in France, it indicates the spreading moral blight that saps and finally destroys the royal power; by linking Henry with the she-wolf Margaret (who succeeds the fallen Joan of Arc as England's evil star) it portends new dangers for the throne; and by preparing for the intrigue between Margaret and Suffolk it generates a major motif of the plot in the succeeding play. As Part 1 closes with the prospects of a splendid royal wedding and a patched-up peace with France, Suffolk's declaration of his dark intentions suggests that mounting troubles are in store for England:

> Margaret shall now be Queen, and rule the King;
> But I will rule both her, the King, and realm.
> (V.v.107–8)

Part 2 is like its predecessor in its linear, episodic structure, but it is much more soundly built. For one thing, the lightly sketched but vivid episodes with which the play is dotted—the Duchess of Gloucester's incantation scene (I.iv), the spurious miracle of St. Albans (II.i), the contest between Horner and his man (III.i), Suffolk's execution (IV.i), and Iden's capture of Jack Cade (IV.x)—are, unlike the encounter between Talbot and the Countess of Auvergne in Part 1 (II.iii), not merely anecdotal but organic to the plot. For another, all the complicated strands of intrigue converge upon the rise of Richard, Duke of York, whose career gives shape and movement to the play. Thus such potentially disparate elements as Margaret's love affair with Suffolk, Cardinal Beaufort's hatred of his nephew Gloucester, the fall of Gloucester and his wife, and Cade's rebellion are brought into alignment and contribute to the one main thrust of action. Such unity, achieved through the most drastic rearrangement of historical data, is assisted by the bold, broad strokes with which the play unfolds. For example, in some two hundred fifty lines the opening scene moves from the pomp and glitter of the Queen's reception at the English court, to Gloucester's angry comments on King Henry's "shameful" league and "fatal" marriage, to Beaufort's and Buckingham's design to "hoise Duke Humphrey from his seat," to Salisbury's hope to save the realm by making peace between the warring factions, and so to York's soliloquy, with which the scene is closed. This soliloquy serves a triple function: it reveals York's brutal strength of purpose, it gives us his realistic views on politics, and it voices his intention

The Scene of the History Plays
SCOTLAND
Berwick
Warkworth Castle
NORTHUMBERLAND
CUMBERLAND
DURHAM
Kendal
YORKSHIRE
Gaultree Forest
York
Towton
Ferrybridge
Wakefield
Pontefract (Pomfret)
Humbleton (Holmedon) Hill
Ravenspur (Ravenspurgh)
Doncaster
LANCASHIRE
IRELAND
ENGLAND
WALES
Conway
Flint Castle
CHESHIRE
Chester
DERBY
NOTTINGHAM
LINCOLN
Harlech (Barkloughly) Castle
Newark
Swineshead (Swinsted) Abbey
Shrewsbury
SHROPSHIRE
Market Bosworth
Sutton Coldfield
Leicester
Lynn
NORFOLK
Bridgnorth
Ludlow
Coventry
Hinckley
Kenilworth (Killingworth) Castle
Warwick
Daventry (Daintry)
Cambridge
Mortimer's Cross
Wye
Worcester
Kimbolton
Bury St. Edmunds
Haverfordwest
Brecknock
Tewkesbury
Northampton
BEDFORD
Milford Haven
Gloucester
OXFORD
Stony Stratford
SUFFOLK
Monmouth
COTSWOLDS
Cirencester
Oxford
Dunstable
Pleshey (Plashy)
Berkeley Castle
HERTFORD
St. Albans
Thames R.
ESSEX
King's Langley
Barnet
Windsor
London
Bristol (Bristow)
WILTSHIRE
BERKSHIRE
Chertsey
Eltham
Gadshill
Rochester
Basingstoke
GOODWIN SANDS
SOMERSET
HAMPSHIRE
SURREY
KENT
Salisbury
Winchester
Weald of Kent
Dover
DEVON
Southampton
Calais (Callice)
DORSET
SUSSEX
Guines (Guynes)
Ardres
CORNWALL
ARTOIS
Agincourt
Crécy (Cressy)
ENGLISH CHANNEL
Somme R.
PICARDY
Harfleur (Harflew)
Rouen (Roan)
NORMANDY
Seine R.
Paris
MAINE
BRITTANY
FRANCE
ORLEANAIS
Orléans
ANJOU
POITOU
Poitiers (Poictiers)

to "raise aloft the milk-white rose" and "grapple with the house of Lancaster" for possession of the throne. In another hundred lines Scene ii presents that ambitious and "presumptuous dame, ill-nurtur'd Eleanor," and so, with all the main components of the plot set forth, the play speeds on its way.

Despite the miasma of intrigue that envelops and at times obscures the plot, *2 Henry VI* maintains a driving pace and describes two simple but related actions: the fall of Gloucester and the rise of York. By the close of Act I Gloucester's wife has been detected in her evil machinations; and within another act Gloucester himself has been maneuvered by his foes, in cynical and uneasy alliance, toward the doom that, as he himself points out, is but the "prologue" to England's "plotted tragedy":

> Beauford's red sparkling eyes blab his heart's malice,
> And Suffolk's cloudy brow his stormy hate;
> Sharp Buckingham unburthens with his tongue
> The envious load that lies upon his heart;
> And dogged York, that reaches at the moon,
> Whose overweening arm I have pluck'd back,
> By false accuse doth level at my life.
> And you, my sovereign lady, with the rest,
> Causeless have laid disgraces on my head,
> And with your best endeavor have stirr'd up
> My liefest liege to be mine enemy. (III.i.154–64)

Following Gloucester's death in Act III there is a realignment of the evil forces that have brought about his fall: Beaufort dies in "black despair"; at the instigation of the commoners Suffolk is banished from the realm and then summarily executed, so that Margaret is deprived of her ally and paramour; and thus York, though not yet free to make his bold attempt upon the throne, moves closer to his goal. Cade's abortive undertaking, a mirror-image of the horrors of rebellion which supplies the busy doings of Act IV, at last gives York the chance to "pluck the crown from feeble Henry's head." The battle of St. Albans, in Act V, provides a victory for the house of York, of course, and a conclusion for the play, but not the end of England's bloody woe. While York, flanked by his sons Edward and Richard (both future kings of England) and by the powerful Nevilles, prepares to reap the harvest he has sown, Queen Margaret and the battered Lancastrians escape to fight another day. What horrors lie ahead are indicated when Young Clifford takes his savage oath of vengeance:

> York not our old men spares;
> No more will I their babes. Tears virginal
> Shall be to me even as the dew to fire,
> And beauty, that the tyrant oft reclaims,
> Shall to my flaming wrath be oil and flax.
> Henceforth I will not have to do with pity.
> Meet I an infant of the house of York,
> Into as many gobbets will I cut it
> As wild Medea young Absyrtus did;
> In cruelty will I seek out my fame. (V.ii.51–60)

The swirling action of Part 3, which almost baffles summary, may be regarded as an emblem of the confusion that engulfs a kingdom torn by civil war. By the freest use of his materials Shakespeare had imposed a certain moral and dramaturgic structure on Parts 1 and 2, building the first on Talbot's fall as a sign of England's waning might and the second on the rise of York as the herald of disaster. But in Part 3 disaster has arrived, sweeping everything before it and obliterating such distinctions and conventions as give meaning to experience. When not merely chivalric codes but even elemental decencies are trampled on, men survive—if indeed they do survive—through the shameless use of power, reinforced with vulpine cunning. While the Yorkists and Lancastrians lurch from crime to crime, England—the hero of the trilogy—is brought almost to ruin.

3 Henry VI is a play of battles, each more savage than the last. The Lancastrian victory at Wakefield is embellished by Young Clifford's idiot revenge on York's son, little Rutland, and followed by York's own execution (or rather murder) as he stands upon a molehill with a crown of paper on his head. This famous scene (which contains the line parodied by Greene in his *Groatsworth of Wit*) attains a violence so intense that horror yields to pity. By an artful variation, the Yorkist triumph at Towton is counterpointed first by King Henry's invocation of a pastoral innocence and then by the almost ritualistic presentation of a son who has killed his father and of a father who has killed his son. Acts III and IV, which embrace ten years of complicated history and are therefore more documentary in design, present the topsy-turvy politics of a world where lust, deceit, and guile are the only modes of action. Although the battles in Act V provide a fitting close of a play whose theme is chaos, Henry's valediction, just before his murder in the Tower, reminds us that England's agony will not be ended with his death, for the murderer he confronts is Richard, Duke of Gloucester. This monster, destined to be the last, most fearful of the Yorkist kings, will have to be endured before England finally earns its right to peace on Bosworth Field.

In a trilogy more notable for bold effects and violent action than for subtlety of characterization the emergence of Richard, toward the middle of Part 3, is of great importance. Henry VI does not dominate the plays that bear his name. At the start, he, a boy-king, is overshadowed by the valiant Talbot; in Part 2 he is a kind of plaintive one-man chorus on the struggle being waged for lawless power; in Part 3 he is more pious and articulate but no less plaintive as he is being crushed by evil that he cannot control. Later, in *Richard II*, Shakespeare turned such weakness into drama, but at this stage of his career he could merely verbalize Henry's ineffectual woe. With Richard it is otherwise. With our first glimpse of him—a "heap of wrath, foul indigested lump" (V.i.157)—we feel and fear his power, and with his first soliloquy we recognize a new advance in Shakespeare's art. He speaks in his own voice, not in the stiff, forensic verse that almost all the other characters share. Even when

Margaret bids farewell to Suffolk and when York, weeping for his murdered son, denounces his tormentors, their language is contrived for declamation: it serves a public function, and in a sense it insulates the speakers within a web of rhetoric. When Richard comes upon the scene, however, the very movement of his speech, quite apart from what he says, reveals the man behind the voice: mocking, clever, cruel, and supple.

> Why, I can smile, and murther whiles I smile,
> And cry "Content" to that which grieves my heart,
> And wet my cheeks with artificial tears,
> And frame my face to all occasions.
> I'll drown more sailors than the mermaid shall,
> I'll slay more gazers than the basilisk,
> I'll play the orator as well as Nestor,
> Deceive more slily than Ulysses could,
> And, like a Sinon, take another Troy.
> I can add colors to the chameleon,
> Change shapes with Proteus for advantages,
> And set the murtherous Machevil to school.
> Can I do this, and cannot get a crown?
> Tut, were it farther off, I'll pluck it down.
> (III.ii.182–95)

Already, it is clear, *Richard III* was taking shape in Shakespeare's mind. If the Henry VI plays had served no other purpose, it would have been enough that they supplied him an apprenticeship and prepared him for that great event.

Herschel Baker

"Edward's Sacred Blood"

The Descendants of Edward III

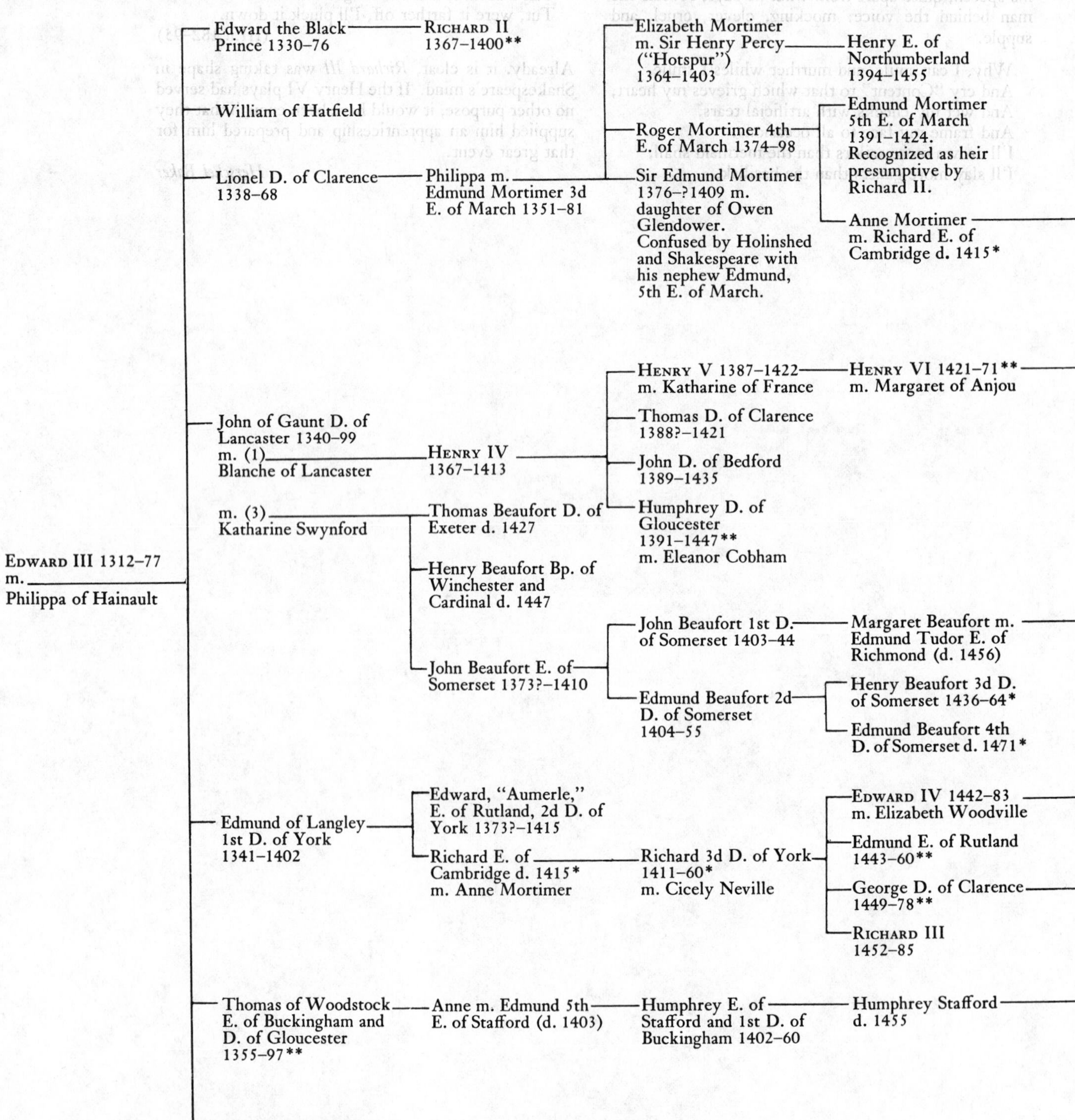

Edward III 1312–77 m. Philippa of Hainault
Edward the Black Prince 1330–76
Richard II 1367–1400**
William of Hatfield
Lionel D. of Clarence 1338–68
Philippa m. Edmund Mortimer 3d E. of March 1351–81
Elizabeth Mortimer m. Sir Henry Percy ("Hotspur") 1364–1403
Henry E. of Northumberland 1394–1455
Roger Mortimer 4th E. of March 1374–98
Edmund Mortimer 5th E. of March 1391–1424. Recognized as heir presumptive by Richard II.
Sir Edmund Mortimer 1376–?1409 m. daughter of Owen Glendower. Confused by Holinshed and Shakespeare with his nephew Edmund, 5th E. of March.
Anne Mortimer m. Richard E. of Cambridge d. 1415*
John of Gaunt D. of Lancaster 1340–99
m. (1) Blanche of Lancaster
Henry IV 1367–1413
Henry V 1387–1422 m. Katharine of France
Henry VI 1421–71** m. Margaret of Anjou
Thomas D. of Clarence 1388?–1421
John D. of Bedford 1389–1435
Humphrey D. of Gloucester 1391–1447** m. Eleanor Cobham
m. (3) Katharine Swynford
Thomas Beaufort D. of Exeter d. 1427
Henry Beaufort Bp. of Winchester and Cardinal d. 1447
John Beaufort E. of Somerset 1373?–1410
John Beaufort 1st D. of Somerset 1403–44
Margaret Beaufort m. Edmund Tudor E. of Richmond (d. 1456)
Edmund Beaufort 2d D. of Somerset 1404–55
Henry Beaufort 3d D. of Somerset 1436–64*
Edmund Beaufort 4th D. of Somerset d. 1471*
Edmund of Langley 1st D. of York 1341–1402
Edward, "Aumerle," E. of Rutland, 2d D. of York 1373?–1415
Richard E. of Cambridge d. 1415* m. Anne Mortimer
Richard 3d D. of York 1411–60* m. Cicely Neville
Edward IV 1442–83 m. Elizabeth Woodville
Edmund E. of Rutland 1443–60**
George D. of Clarence 1449–78**
Richard III 1452–85
Thomas of Woodstock E. of Buckingham and D. of Gloucester 1355–97**
Anne m. Edmund 5th E. of Stafford (d. 1403)
Humphrey E. of Stafford and 1st D. of Buckingham 1402–60
Humphrey Stafford d. 1455
William of Windsor

THE KINGS AND QUEENS OF ENGLAND

Richard II 1377–99
Henry IV 1399–1413
Henry V 1413–22
Henry VI 1422–61
Edward IV 1461–83
Richard III 1483–85
Henry VII 1485–1509
Henry VIII 1509–47
Edward VI 1547–53
Mary 1553–58
Elizabeth 1558–1603
James I 1603–25

SOME PRINCIPAL EVENTS

1399	Deposition of Richard II
1403	Battle of Shrewsbury
1415	Battle of Agincourt
1420	Treaty of Troyes
1431	Execution of Joan of Arc
1450	Cade's Rebellion
1455	First Battle of St. Albans
1460	Battle of Wakefield
1461	Second Battle of St. Albans
1471	Battle of Tewkesbury
1485	Battle of Bosworth Field
1520	Field of the Cloth of Gold

Richard 3d D. of York 1411–60*; husband of Cicely Neville and father of EDWARD IV and RICHARD III

Edward Prince of Wales 1453–71**

Henry Tudor E. of Richmond, HENRY VII 1457–1509

EDWARD V 1470–83**

Richard D. of York 1472–83**

Elizabeth m. HENRY VII 1457–1509

Arthur 1486–1502 m. Katherine of Aragon

HENRY VIII 1491–1547 m. (1) Katherine of Aragon — MARY 1516–58
m. (2) Anne Boleyn* — ELIZABETH 1533–1603
m. (3) Jane Seymour — EDWARD VI 1537–53

Edward E. of Warwick 1475–99*

Margaret Countess of Salisbury 1473–1541*

Margaret m. James IV of Scotland — James V of Scotland — Mary Queen of Scots 1542–87* — JAMES I of England, VI of Scotland

Henry Stafford 2d D. of Buckingham 1454?–83* — Edward 3d D. of Buckingham 1478–1521*

*Executed
**Murdered
Many persons of no significance to Shakespeare's history plays are omitted.

The First Part of Henry the Sixth

[Dramatis Personae

King Henry the Sixth
Duke of Gloucester, *uncle to the King, and Protector*
Duke of Bedford, *uncle to the King, and Regent of France*
Thomas Beauford, *Duke of Exeter* — *great-uncles to the King*
Henry Beauford, *Bishop of Winchester, and afterwards Cardinal* — *great-uncles to the King*
John Beauford, *Earl, afterwards Duke, of Somerset*
Richard Plantagenet, *son of Richard, late Earl of Cambridge, afterwards Duke of York*
Earl of Warwick
Earl of Salisbury
Earl of Suffolk
Lord Talbot, *afterwards Earl of Shrewsbury*
John Talbot, *his son*
Edmund Mortimer, *Earl of March*
Sir John Falstaff
Sir William Lucy
Sir William Glansdale
Sir Thomas Gargrave
Mayor of London
Woodvile, *Lieutenant of the Tower*
Vernon, *of the White Rose or York faction*
Basset, *of the Red Rose or Lancaster faction*

Lawyer
Jailers, *to Mortimer*

Charles, *Dolphin, and afterwards King, of France*
Reignier, *Duke of Anjou, and titular King of Naples*
Duke of Burgundy
Duke of Alanson
Bastard of Orleance
Governor of Paris
Master Gunner *of Orleance, and his* Son
General *of the French forces in Bordeaux*
French Sergeant
Porter
Shepherd, *father to Joan de Pucelle*

Margaret, *daughter to Reignier, afterwards married to King Henry*
Countess of Auvergne
Joan de Pucelle, *also called Joan of Aire*

Fiends *appearing to Joan de Pucelle*

Lords, Warders *of the Tower*, Papal Legate, Ambassadors, Heralds, Officers, Soldiers, Messengers, *and* Attendants, *English and French*

Scene: *England and France*]

Act I, Scene I

Dead march. Enter the Funeral of King Henry the Fift, *attended on by the* Duke of Bedford, *Regent of France, the* Duke of Gloucester, *Protector, the* Duke of Exeter, [*the* Earl of] Warwick, *the* Bishop of Winchester, *and the* Duke of Somerset; [Heralds, *etc*.].

Bed. Hung be the heavens with black, yield day to night!
Comets, importing change of times and states,
Brandish your crystal tresses in the sky,
And with them scourge the bad revolting stars
That have consented unto Henry's death:
King Henry the Fift, too famous to live long!
England ne'er lost a king of so much worth.
Glou. England ne'er had a king until his time:
Virtue he had, deserving to command;
His brandish'd sword did blind men with his beams;
His arms spread wider than a dragon's wings;
His sparkling eyes, replete with wrathful fire,
More dazzled and drove back his enemies
Than midday sun fierce bent against their faces.
What should I say? his deeds exceed all speech:
He ne'er lift up his hand but conquered.

Words and passages enclosed in square brackets in the text above are either emendations of the copy-text or additions to it. The Textual Notes immediately following the play cite the earliest authority for every such change or insertion and supply the reading of the copy-text wherever it is emended in this edition.

I.i. Location: Westminster Abbey.
o.s.d. **Dead march:** funeral march. **Fift:** Fifth.
1. **Hung . . . black.** Alluding to the fact that the "heavens"—a roof or canopy projecting over the stage—were draped in black for the presentation of a tragedy. 2. **importing:** signifying, foretelling.
3. **Brandish:** flourish, flash. **crystal tresses:** i.e. shining tails.
4. **revolting:** rebelling, i.e. traitorous.
5. **consented unto:** i.e. conspired to bring about.
9. **Virtue:** merit, power. 10. **his:** its.
16. **lift:** lifted. **but conquered:** without conquering.

Exe. We mourn in black, why mourn we not in blood?
Henry is dead, and never shall revive.
Upon a wooden coffin we attend,
And death's dishonorable victory
We with our stately presence glorify,
Like captives bound to a triumphant car.
What? shall we curse the planets of mishap
That plotted thus our glory's overthrow?
Or shall we think the subtile-witted French
Conjurers and sorcerers, that, afraid of him,
By magic verses have contriv'd his end?
Win. He was a king blest of the King of kings.
Unto the French the dreadful Judgment Day
So dreadful will not be as was his sight.
The battles of the Lord of hosts he fought;
The Church's prayers made him so prosperous.
Glou. The Church? where is it? Had not churchmen pray'd,
His thread of life had not so soon decay'd.
None do you like but an effeminate prince,
Whom like a schoolboy you may overawe.
Win. Gloucester, what e'er we like, thou art Protector,
And lookest to command the Prince and realm.
Thy wife is proud, she holdeth thee in awe,
More than God or religious churchmen may.
Glou. Name not religion, for thou lov'st the flesh,
And ne'er throughout the year to church thou go'st
Except it be to pray against thy foes.
Bed. Cease, cease these jars and rest your minds in peace.
Let's to the altar. Heralds, wait on us.
In stead of gold, we'll offer up our arms,
Since arms avail not now that Henry's dead.
Posterity, await for wretched years,
When at their mothers' moist'ned eyes babes shall suck,
Our isle be made a nourish of salt tears,
And none but women left to wail the dead.
Henry the Fift, thy ghost I invocate:
Prosper this realm, keep it from civil broils,
Combat with adverse planets in the heavens!
A far more glorious star thy soul will make
Than Julius Caesar or bright—

Enter a MESSENGER.

Mess. My honorable lords, health to you all!
Sad tidings bring I to you out of France,
Of loss, of slaughter, and discomfiture:
Guienne, Champaigne, Rheims, Orleance,
Paris, Guysors, Poictiers, are all quite lost.
Bed. What say'st thou, man, before dead Henry's corse?
Speak softly, or the loss of those great towns
Will make him burst his lead and rise from death.
Glou. Is Paris lost? is Roan yielded up?
If Henry were recall'd to life again,
These news would cause him once more yield the ghost.
Exe. How were they lost? what treachery was us'd?
Mess. No treachery, but want of men and money.
Amongst the soldiers this is muttered,
That here you maintain several factions;
And whilst a field should be dispatch'd and fought,
You are disputing of your generals.
One would have ling'ring wars with little cost;
Another would fly swift, but wanteth wings;
A third thinks, without expense at all,
By guileful fair words peace may be obtain'd.
Awake, awake, English nobility!
Let not sloth dim your honors new begot.
Cropp'd are the flower-de-luces in your arms,
Of England's coat one half is cut away. [*Exit.*]
Exe. Were our tears wanting to this funeral,
These tidings would call forth her flowing tides.
Bed. Me they concern, Regent I am of France.
Give me my steeled coat, I'll fight for France.
Away with these disgraceful wailing robes!
Wounds will I lend the French in stead of eyes,
To weep their intermissive miseries.

Enter to them another MESSENGER.

[*2.*] *Mess.* Lords, view these letters full of bad mischance.
France is revolted from the English quite,
Except some petty towns of no import.
The Dolphin Charles is crowned king in Rheims;
The Bastard of Orleance with him is join'd;

19. wooden: i.e. insensible, useless. **22. car**: chariot.
27. verses: incantations, spells. **32. prosperous**: successful.
37. Protector. According to Hall (Bullough, III, 44), the dying Henry V named his brother John, Duke of Bedford (together with Philip, Duke of Burgundy), "regent of the realme of Fraunce" and his brother Humphrey, Duke of Gloucester, "Protector of England duryng the minoritie of my child." His heir, Henry VI, was nine months old when he succeeded to the throne in 1422.
39. wife: Eleanor Cobham, first the mistress and then the second wife of Gloucester, whom he married in 1428 after his first wife, Jacqueline of Hainault, had been captured by Philip, Duke of Burgundy. **holdeth . . . awe**: overawes you. Eleanor's pride and ambition are emphasized in *2 Henry VI*. **44. jars**: discords.
48. await for: look out for, expect.
50. nourish: nurse (French *nourrice*).
52. invocate: call upon, invoke (as a saint).

60–61. Guienne . . . Poictiers. One of many departures from historical fact in this play. Two of the places named—Orleans and Poitiers—had never been in English hands, and the others were not recaptured by the French until long after the period represented.
60. Champaigne: Compiègne. **Orleance**: Orleans.
62. corse: corpse. **64. lead**: leaden coffin.
65. Roan: Rouen, the capital of Normandy.
71. several: separate, i.e. divisive.
72. field: (1) combat force; (2) battle. **73. of**: about.
75. wanteth: lacks.
80. flower-de-luces: fleur-de-lis ("lily flower"), national emblem of France. Through the marriage (1308) of Edward II with Isabella, daughter of Philip IV of France, English sovereigns had claimed the French throne for almost a hundred years, and by the Treaty of Troyes (1420) Henry V at last secured the title "King of England and Heir of France," leaving his father-in-law Charles VI in actual possession of the crown (see *Henry V*, V.ii). It was Charles VII's accession to the throne of France in 1422, shortly after the death of Henry V, that led to the renewed hostilities with England which are the subject of this play. **80, 81. arms, coat**: coat of arms.
86. wailing robes: mourning garments.
88. To weep: i.e. to weep blood (from the wounds, instead of tears from the eyes). **intermissive**: i.e. now resumed after an interval.
92. Dolphin: Dauphin, after 1349 the title of the heir apparent of the French king; in this play, Charles (1403–61), who succeeded his father in 1422. Actually, his coronation at Rheims (as Charles VII) did not occur until 1429, seven years after the time represented in this scene.
93. Bastard: Jean, Count Dunois (1403?–1468), illegitimate son of Louis, Duke of Orleans, and thus nephew of King Charles VI; later an associate of Joan of Arc in her spectacular campaign against the English.

[Reignier], Duke of Anjou, doth take his part;
The Duke of Alanson flieth to his side. *Exit.*
Exe. The Dolphin crowned king? All fly to him?
O, whither shall we fly from this reproach?
Glou. We will not fly but to our enemies' throats.
Bedford, if thou be slack, I'll fight it out.
Bed. Gloucester, why doubt'st thou of my forwardness?
An army have I muster'd in my thoughts,
Wherewith already France is overrun.

Enter another MESSENGER.

[*3.*] *Mess.* My gracious lords, to add to your laments,
Wherewith you now bedew King Henry's hearse,
I must inform you of a dismal fight
Betwixt the stout Lord Talbot and the French.
Win. What? Wherein Talbot overcame, is't so?
3. Mess. O no; wherein Lord Talbot was o'erthrown.
The circumstance I'll tell you more at large.
The tenth of August last this dreadful lord,
Retiring from the siege of Orleance,
Having full scarce six thousand in his troop,
By three and twenty thousand of the French
Was round encompassed, and set upon.
No leisure had he to enrank his men;
He wanted pikes to set before his archers;
In stead whereof sharp stakes pluck'd out of hedges
They pitched in the ground confusedly,
To keep the horsemen off from breaking in.
More than three hours the fight continued,
Where valiant Talbot above human thought
Enacted wonders with his sword and lance:
Hundreds he sent to hell, and none durst stand him;
Here, there, and every where, enrag'd he slew.
The French exclaim'd, the devil was in arms;
All the whole army stood agaz'd on him.
His soldiers, spying his undaunted spirit,
"A Talbot! a Talbot!" cried out amain,
And rush'd into the bowels of the battle.
Here had the conquest fully been seal'd up,
If Sir John Falstaff had not play'd the coward.
He, being in the vaward, plac'd behind
With purpose to relieve and follow them,
Cowardly fled, not having struck one stroke.
Hence grew the general wrack and massacre;
Enclosed were they with their enemies.
A base Wallon, to win the Dolphin's grace,
Thrust Talbot with a spear into the back,
Whom all France with their chief assembled strength
Durst not presume to look once in the face.
Bed. Is Talbot slain then? I will slay myself
For living idly here in pomp and ease,
Whilst such a worthy leader, wanting aid,
Unto his dastard foemen is betray'd.
3. Mess. O no, he lives, but is took prisoner,
And Lord Scales with him, and Lord Hungerford.
Most of the rest slaughter'd or took likewise.
Bed. His ransom there is none but I shall pay:
I'll hale the Dolphin headlong from his throne,
His crown shall be the ransom of my friend;
Four of their lords I'll change for one of ours.
Farewell, my masters, to my task will I.
Bonfires in France forthwith I am to make,
To keep our great Saint George's feast withal.
Ten thousand soldiers with me I will take,
Whose bloody deeds shall make all Europe quake.
3. Mess. So you had need, for Orleance is besieg'd;
The English army is grown weak and faint;
The Earl of Salisbury craveth supply,
And hardly keeps his men from mutiny,
Since they, so few, watch such a multitude. [*Exit.*]
Exe. Remember, lords, your oaths to Henry sworn:
Either to quell the Dolphin utterly,
Or bring him in obedience to your yoke.
Bed. I do remember it, and here take my leave,
To go about my preparation. *Exit Bedford.*
Glou. I'll to the Tower with all the haste I can,
To view th' artillery and munition,
And then I will proclaim young Henry king.
Exit Gloucester.
Exe. To Eltam will I, where the young King is,
Being ordain'd his special governor,
And for his safety there I'll best devise. *Exit.*
Win. Each hath his place and function to attend:
I am left out; for me nothing remains.
But long I will not be Jack out of office.
The King from Eltam I intend to send,
And sit at chiefest stern of public weal. *Exeunt.*

95. Alanson: Alençon. **105. dismal:** unlucky.
106. Lord Talbot: John Talbot, first Earl of Shrewsbury (1388?–1453), the most celebrated English warrior of his day. After 1427 a valued associate of John, Duke of Bedford, he was captured by Joan of Arc in 1429 and imprisoned for two years. Following his release he became an ally of Philip of Burgundy, and his reputation mounted until he, together with his son, was killed in action at Castillon.
109. at large: in detail.
110–40. The tenth . . . face. This episode actually occurred at the battle of Patay, some six weeks after the siege of Orleans had been raised by Joan of Arc in May 1429. **112. full scarce:** barely.
116. pikes: ironbound, sharpened stakes set in the earth before archers for protection against advancing horsemen.
126. agaz'd on: astounded at. **128. amain:** strongly.
130. seal'd up: completed.
131. Falstaff: i.e. Sir John Fastolfe (c. 1378–1459), a Norfolk landowner who served with notable success under Henry V and then the Duke of Bedford, rose to the governorship of Anjou and Maine in 1423, and acquired great wealth and power after his return to England. Although he was esteemed by his contemporaries, here and elsewhere in the play Shakespeare, like the Tudor chroniclers whom he followed, depicts him as a coward. This unflattering and erroneous view of Fastolfe derived ultimately from the fifteenth-century *Chronique* of Monstrelet. He is not to be confused with the Sir John Falstaff of the Henry IV plays (to whom Shakespeare originally gave the name Oldcastle).
132. vaward: vanguard. **135. wrack:** destruction.
137. Wallon: Walloon, an inhabitant of what is now southern Belgium.
154. Saint George's feast: April 23. St. George was the patron saint of England and also of the Order of the Garter.
159. Salisbury: Thomas de Montacute, fourth Earl of Salisbury (1388–1428), a stalwart of the English who lost his life while leading the siege of Orleans (see I.iv).
167. Tower: Tower of London, long used as both a royal palace and an arsenal.
170. Eltam: Eltham, a town southeast of London, formerly the site of a royal palace. **175. Jack . . . office:** i.e. an unemployed nobody.
177. at chiefest stern: in position of control.

[Scene II]

Sound a flourish. Enter Charles [*the Dolphin*], Alanson, *and* Reignier, *marching with Drum and Soldiers.*

Char. Mars his true moving, even as in the heavens,
So in the earth, to this day is not known.
Late did he shine upon the English side;
Now we are victors, upon us he smiles.
What towns of any moment but we have?
At pleasure here we lie near Orleance;
Otherwhiles the famish'd English, like pale ghosts,
Faintly besiege us one hour in a month.

Alan. They want their porridge and their fat bull-beeves:
Either they must be dieted like mules
And have their provender tied to their mouths,
Or piteous they will look, like drowned mice.

Reig. Let's raise the siege; why live we idly here?
Talbot is taken, whom we wont to fear;
Remaineth none but mad-brain'd Salisbury,
And he may well in fretting spend his gall—
Nor men nor money hath he to make war.

Char. Sound, sound alarum! We will rush on them.
Now for the honor of the forlorn French!
Him I forgive my death that killeth me,
When he sees me go back one foot or fly. *Exeunt.*

Here alarum; they are beaten back by the English with great loss. Enter Charles, Alanson, *and* Reignier.

Char. Who ever saw the like? What men have I!
Dogs! cowards! dastards! I would ne'er have fled,
But that they left me midst my enemies.

Reig. Salisbury is a desperate homicide,
He fighteth as one weary of his life.
The other lords, like lions wanting food,
Do rush upon us as their hungry prey.

Alan. Froissard, a countryman of ours, records
England all Olivers and Rolands bred
During the time Edward the Third did reign.
More truly now may this be verified,
For none but Samsons and Goliases
It sendeth forth to skirmish. One to ten!
Lean raw-bon'd rascals! who would e'er suppose
They had such courage and audacity?

I.ii. Location: France. Before Orleans.
o.s.d. flourish: fanfare of trumpets. **Reignier:** René (1409–80), Duke of Anjou and Lorraine and titular King of Naples and Sicily, whose daughter Margaret married (1445) Henry VI of England. His appearance here (as well as at II.i and III.ii) is unhistorical. **Drum:** drummer.
1–2. Mars . . . known. The notoriously eccentric orbit of the planet Mars was not explained until Johannes Kepler published his *Astronomia Nova de Motibus Stellae Martis* in 1609.
7. Otherwhiles: at times, from time to time.
14. wont: were accustomed.
16. spend his gall: exhaust his anger. **17. Nor:** neither.
18. alarum: call to arms. **19. forlorn:** lost (ironical).
28. their hungry prey: prey of their hunger.
29. Froissard: Jean Froissart (1333?–?1400), author of a splendid *Cronique* that treats the history of France and England in the fourteenth century.
30. Olivers and Rolands. Oliver and Roland were the most renowned of Charlemagne's twelve peers.
33. Samsons and Goliases. For the exploits of Samson and Goliath, Biblical characters of legendary strength, see Judges 13–16 and 1 Samuel 17. **35. rascals:** lean, inferior deer.

Char. Let's leave this town, for they are hare-brain'd slaves,
And hunger will enforce them to be more eager.
Of old I know them; rather with their teeth
The walls they'll tear down than forsake the siege.

Reig. I think by some odd gimmors or device
Their arms are set, like clocks, still to strike on;
Else ne'er could they hold out so as they do.
By my consent, we'll even let them alone.

Alan. Be it so.

Enter the Bastard of Orleance.

Bast. Where's the Prince Dolphin? I have news for him.

Char. Bastard of Orleance, thrice welcome to us.

Bast. Methinks your looks are sad, your cheer appal'd.
Hath the late overthrow wrought this offense?
Be not dismay'd, for succor is at hand:
A holy maid hither with me I bring,
Which by a vision sent to her from heaven
Ordained is to raise this tedious siege,
And drive the English forth the bounds of France.
The spirit of deep prophecy she hath,
Exceeding the nine sibyls of old Rome:
What's past and what's to come she can descry.
Speak, shall I call her in? Believe my words,
For they are certain and unfallible.

Char. Go call her in. [*Exit Bastard.*] But first, to try her skill,
Reignier, stand thou as Dolphin in my place;
Question her proudly, let thy looks be stern.
By this means shall we sound what skill she hath.

Enter Joan [de] Pucelle [*and* Bastard].

Reig. Fair maid, is't thou wilt do these wondrous feats?

Puc. Reignier, is't thou that thinkest to beguile me?
Where is the Dolphin? Come, come from behind,
I know thee well, though never seen before.
Be not amaz'd, there's nothing hid from me;
In private will I talk with thee apart.
Stand back, you lords, and give us leave a while.

Reig. She takes upon her bravely at first dash.

Puc. Dolphin, I am by birth a shepherd's daughter,
My wit untrain'd in any kind of art.
Heaven and our Lady gracious hath it pleas'd
To shine on my contemptible estate.
Lo, whilest I waited on my tender lambs,
And to sun's parching heat display'd my cheeks,
God's Mother deigned to appear to me,
And in a vision full of majesty

41. gimmors: gimmals, mechanical joints.
42. still: always, repeatedly.
48. cheer appal'd: countenance made pale. **54. forth:** out of.
56. nine sibyls. The sibyls—inspired women revered by the ancients for their alleged gift of prophecy—were often represented as five in number (as by Michelangelo on the ceiling of the Sistine Chapel); Shakespeare was perhaps confused by the story of the Cumaean sibyl's offering nine books of oracular utterances to Tarquin, king of Rome.
63. sound: ascertain.
64 s.d. Pucelle: the Maid (of Orleans), Joan of Arc.
71. takes . . . dash: plays her part splendidly from the first.
73. wit: mind.

Will'd me to leave my base vocation
And free my country from calamity.
Her aid she promis'd, and assur'd success;
In complete glory she reveal'd herself;
And whereas I was black and swart before,
With those clear rays which she infus'd on me
That beauty am I blest with which you may see.
Ask me what question thou canst possible,
And I will answer unpremeditated;
My courage try by combat, if thou dar'st,
And thou shalt find that I exceed my sex.
Resolve on this: thou shalt be fortunate
If thou receive me for thy warlike mate.

Char. Thou hast astonish'd me with thy high terms.
Only this proof I'll of thy valor make,
In single combat thou shalt buckle with me;
And if thou vanquishest, thy words are true,
Otherwise I renounce all confidence.

Puc. I am prepar'd; here is my keen-edg'd sword,
Deck'd with [five] flower-de-luces on each side,
The which at Touraine, in Saint Katherine's churchyard,
Out of a great deal of old iron I chose forth.

Char. Then come a' God's name, I fear no woman.

Puc. And while I live, I'll ne'er fly from a man.

Here they fight, and Joan de Pucelle overcomes.

Char. Stay, stay thy hands! Thou art an Amazon,
And fightest with the sword of Deborah.

Puc. Christ's Mother helps me, else I were too weak.

Char. Whoe'er helps thee, 'tis thou that must help me:
Impatiently I burn with thy desire;
My heart and hands thou hast at once subdu'd.
Excellent Pucelle, if thy name be so,
Let me thy servant and not sovereign be.
'Tis the French Dolphin sueth to thee thus.

Puc. I must not yield to any rites of love,
For my profession's sacred from above.
When I have chased all thy foes from hence,
Then will I think upon a recompense.

Char. Mean time look gracious on thy prostrate thrall.

Reig. My lord, methinks, is very long in talk.

Alan. Doubtless he shrives this woman to her smock,
Else ne'er could he so long protract his speech.

Reig. Shall we disturb him, since he keeps no mean?

Alan. He may mean more than we poor men do know:
These women are shrewd tempters with their tongues.

Reig. My lord, where are you? What devise you on?

85. **infus'd:** poured. 91. **Resolve on:** make up your mind to.
93. **high terms:** lofty claims. 94. **proof:** test.
95. **buckle:** contend. 102. **a':** in, by.
104. **Amazon:** one of a fabulous race of female warriors.
105. **Deborah:** Hebrew prophetess who successfully led her people against their Canaanite oppressors. See Judges 4, 5.
108. **thy desire:** desire for you. 111. **servant:** professed lover.
119. **shrives . . . smock:** i.e. makes love to her.
121. **mean:** moderation. 123. **shrewd:** malicious, mischievous.
124. **devise:** decide.

Shall we give o'er Orleance, or no?

Puc. Why, no, I say. Distrustful recreants,
Fight till the last gasp; I'll be your guard.

Char. What she says I'll confirm. We'll fight it out.

Puc. Assign'd am I to be the English scourge.
This night the siege assuredly I'll raise:
Expect Saint Martin's summer, halcyons' days,
Since I have entered into these wars.
Glory is like a circle in the water,
Which never ceaseth to enlarge itself,
Till by broad spreading it disperse to nought.
With Henry's death the English circle ends,
Dispersed are the glories it included.
Now am I like that proud insulting ship
Which Caesar and his fortune bare at once.

Char. Was Mahomet inspired with a dove?
Thou with an eagle art inspired then.
Helen, the mother of great Constantine,
Nor yet Saint Philip's daughters, were like thee.
Bright star of Venus, fall'n down on the earth,
How may I reverently worship thee enough?

Alan. Leave off delays, and let us raise the siege.

Reig. Woman, do what thou canst to save our honors;
Drive them from Orleance and be immortaliz'd.

Char. Presently we'll try; come, let's away about it.
No prophet will I trust, if she prove false. *Exeunt.*

[Scene III]

Enter Gloucester *with his* Servingmen [*in blue coats*].

Glou. I am come to survey the Tower this day;
Since Henry's death, I fear, there is conveyance.
Where be these warders, that they wait not here?
Open the gates, 'tis Gloucester that calls.

1. Warder. [*Within.*] Who's there, that knocks so imperiously?

1. Serv. It is the noble Duke of Gloucester.

2. Warder. [*Within.*] Whoe'er he be, you may not be let in.

1. Serv. Villains, answer you so the Lord Protector?

131. **Saint Martin's summer:** Indian summer. St. Martin's Day is November 11. **halcyons' days:** i.e. unseasonably fine weather. According to the ancients the sea became calm around the winter solstice so that the halcyon (kingfisher) could nest upon it.
138–39. **Now . . . once.** According to North's translation of Plutarch, when the timorous commander of a ship carrying Caesar, incognito, across the stormy Adriatic ordered the vessel to return to port, the distinguished passenger said, "Good fellow, be of good cheare, and forwardes hardily, feare not, for thou hast Caesar & his fortune with thee." 138. **insulting:** proudly exultant.
140. **Mahomet . . . dove.** The founder of Islam was said to have been inspired by a dove who whispered in his ear.
142. **Helen:** mother of the Emperor Constantine (who made Christianity the religion of the Roman Empire in 313) and reputedly the discoverer of the True Cross and the Holy Sepulchre.
143. **Saint Philip's daughters:** the four "virgins, which did prophesy," mentioned in Acts 21:9. 149. **Presently:** immediately.

I.iii. **Location:** London. Before the Tower gates.
o.s.d. **blue coats.** Customarily worn by servingmen.
2. **conveyance:** trickery.

1. Warder. [*Within.*] The Lord protect him! so we answer him.
We do no otherwise than we are will'd.
Glou. Who willed you? or whose will stands but mine?
There's none Protector of the realm but I.—
Break up the gates, I'll be your warrantize.
Shall I be flouted thus by dunghill grooms?

Gloucester's men rush at the Tower gates, and Woodvile the Lieutenant speaks within.

Woodv. What noise is this? What traitors have we here?
Glou. Lieutenant, is it you whose voice I hear?
Open the gates, here's Gloucester that would enter.
Woodv. Have patience, noble Duke, I may not open,
The Cardinal of Winchester forbids.
From him I have express commandement
That thou nor none of thine shall be let in.
Glou. Faint-hearted Woodvile, prizest him 'fore me?
Arrogant Winchester, that haughty prelate,
Whom Henry, our late sovereign, ne'er could brook?
Thou art no friend to God or to the King.
Open the gates, or I'll shut thee out shortly.
Servingmen. Open the gates unto the Lord Protector,
Or we'll burst them open, if that you come not quickly.

Enter to the Protector at the Tower gates WINCHESTER *and his* MEN *in tawny coats.*

Win. How now, ambitious [Humphrey], what means this?
Glou. Peel'd priest, dost thou command me to be shut out?
Win. I do, thou most usurping proditor,
And not Protector, of the King or realm.
Glou. Stand back, thou manifest conspirator,
Thou that contrivedst to murther our dead lord,
Thou that giv'st whores indulgences to sin.
I'll canvass thee in thy broad cardinal's hat,
If thou proceed in this thy insolence.
Win. Nay, stand thou back, I will not budge a foot:
This be Damascus, be thou cursed Cain,
To slay thy brother Abel, if thou wilt.
Glou. I will not slay thee, but I'll drive thee back.

10. will'd: commanded. **13. warrantize:** guarantee.
14 s.d. Woodvile: Richard Woodville (died c. 1441), a loyal Lancastrian whose descendants rose to wealth and power as supporters of the House of York after his granddaughter Elizabeth married Edward IV in 1464.
19. Cardinal of Winchester. An apparent mistake. At III.i.53 and in the opening stage direction of IV.i Beaufort is called a bishop, and at V.i.28 ff. he is spoken of as a newly created cardinal. Actually he received his red hat in 1427. **24. brook:** endure.
28 s.d. tawny coats. Customarily worn by the attendants of a great ecclesiastic. **30. Peel'd:** shaven, tonsured. **31. proditor:** traitor.
34–35. Thou . . . sin. In 1426 Gloucester charged Beaufort with various crimes, including a conspiracy against the late king when he was Prince of Wales. As Bishop of Winchester Beaufort enjoyed the revenues from the brothels in Bankside, the disreputable area south of the Thames where such theatres as the Rose and the Globe were erected in Shakespeare's time.
36. canvass: toss in a canvas sheet, belabor.
39. Damascus . . . Cain. In medieval legend the site of Damascus was thought to be the place where Cain had murdered Abel.

Thy scarlet robes as a child's bearing-cloth
I'll use to carry thee out of this place.
Win. Do what thou dar'st, I beard thee to thy face.
Glou. What? am I dar'd and bearded to my face?
Draw, men, for all this privileged place—
Blue coats to tawny coats! Priest, beware your beard,
I mean to tug it and to cuff you soundly.
Under my feet I stamp thy cardinal's hat;
In spite of Pope or dignities of church,
Here by the cheeks I'll drag thee up and down.
Win. Gloucester, thou wilt answer this before the Pope.
Glou. Winchester goose, I cry, "A rope! a rope!"
Now beat them hence, why do you let them stay?
Thee I'll chase hence, thou wolf in sheep's array.
Out, tawny-coats! Out, scarlet hypocrite!

Here Gloucester's men beat out the Cardinal's men, and enter in the hurly-burly the MAYOR OF LONDON *and his* OFFICERS.

May. Fie, lords, that you, being supreme magistrates,
Thus contumeliously should break the peace!
Glou. Peace, Mayor, thou know'st little of my wrongs.
Here's Beauford, that regards nor God nor king,
Hath here distrain'd the Tower to his use.
Win. Here's Gloucester, a foe to citizens,
One that still motions war and never peace,
O'ercharging your free purses with large fines;
That seeks to overthrow religion
Because he is Protector of the realm,
And would have armor here out of the Tower,
To crown himself king and suppress the Prince.
Glou. I will not answer thee with words, but blows.

Here they skirmish again.

May. Nought rests for me in this tumultuous strife
But to make open proclamation.
Come, officer, as loud as e'er thou canst,
Cry.

[*Off.*] All manner of men assembled here in arms this day against God's peace and the King's, we charge and command you, in his Highness' name, to repair to your several dwelling-places, and not to wear, handle, or use any sword, weapon, or dagger, henceforward, upon pain of death.

Glou. Cardinal, I'll be no breaker of the law;
But we shall meet, and break our minds at large.
Win. Gloucester, we'll meet to thy cost, be sure:
Thy heart-blood I will have for this day's work.
May. I'll call for clubs, if you will not away.
This cardinal's more haughty than the devil.

42. bearing-cloth: christening robe. **44. beard:** openly defy.
46. privileged place. As a royal residence the Tower was one of the places where the use of weapons was forbidden.
48. tug. To pull a man's beard was the deadliest of insults.
50. dignities: dignitaries.
53. Winchester goose: slang term for a venereal disease (see note to lines 34–35 above). **A rope:** a halter to hang him.
61. distrain'd: confiscated. **63. still motions:** continually stirs up.
64. your free purses: your purses freely.
81. break our minds: disclose our intentions.
84. clubs: i.e. assistance. "Prentices and clubs" was the rallying cry for the London apprentices.

Glou. Mayor, farewell; thou dost but what thou mayst.
Win. Abominable Gloucester, guard thy head,
For I intend to have it ere long.
Exeunt, [several ways, Gloucester and Winchester with their Servingmen].
May. See the coast clear'd, and then we will depart.
Good God, these nobles should such stomachs bear!
I myself fight not once in forty year. *Exeunt.*

[Scene IV]

Enter the Master Gunner *of Orleance and his* Boy.

M. Gun. Sirrah, thou know'st how Orleance is besieg'd,
And how the English have the suburbs won.
Boy. Father, I know, and oft have shot at them,
Howe'er unfortunate I miss'd my aim.
M. Gun. But now thou shalt not. Be thou rul'd by me.
Chief master gunner am I of this town,
Something I must do to procure me grace.
The Prince's espials have informed me
How the English, in the suburbs close intrench'd,
[Wont] through a secret grate of iron bars
In yonder tower to overpeer the city,
And thence discover how with most advantage
They may vex us with shot or with assault.
To intercept this inconvenience,
A piece of ord'nance 'gainst it I have plac'd,
And even these three days have I watch'd
If I could see them.
Now do thou watch, for I can stay no longer.
If thou spy'st any, run and bring me word,
And thou shalt find me at the Governor's. *Exit.*
Boy. Father, I warrant you, take you no care,
I'll never trouble you, if I may spy them. *Exit.*

Enter Salisbury *and* Talbot, [Sir William Glansdale, Sir Thomas Gargrave,] *on the turrets, with others.*

Sal. Talbot, my life, my joy, again return'd?
How wert thou handled, being prisoner?
Or by what means gots thou to be releas'd?
Discourse, I prithee, on this turret's top.
Tal. The Earl of Bedford had a prisoner
Call'd the brave Lord Ponton de Santrailles,
For him was I exchang'd and ransomed.
But with a baser man of arms by far
Once in contempt they would have barter'd me;
Which I, disdaining, scorn'd, and craved death
Rather than I would be so pill'd esteem'd:
In fine, redeem'd I was as I desir'd.

90. stomachs: fighting dispositions.

I.iv. Location: France. Orleans.
1. Sirrah: customary term of address to an inferior.
7. grace: honor, distinction. 8. espials: spies.
14. inconvenience: mischief, harm.
15. ord'nance: ordnance (a sense only later differentiated by spelling from *ordinance*). 25. gots: gottest.
33. pill'd: despoiled, impoverished.

But O, the treacherous Falstaff wounds my heart,
Whom with my bare fists I would execute,
If I now had him brought into my power.
Sal. Yet tell'st thou not how thou wert entertain'd.
Tal. With scoffs and scorns and contumelious taunts.
In open market-place produc'd they me
To be a public spectacle to all:
Here, said they, is the terror of the French,
The scarecrow that affrights our children so.
Then broke I from the officers that led me,
And with my nails digg'd stones out of the ground
To hurl at the beholders of my shame.
My grisly countenance made others fly,
None durst come near for fear of sudden death.
In iron walls they deem'd me not secure;
So great fear of my name 'mongst them were spread
That they suppos'd I could rend bars of steel,
And spurn in pieces posts of adamant;
Wherefore a guard of chosen shot I had
That walk'd about me every minute while;
And if I did but stir out of my bed,
Ready they were to shoot me to the heart.
Enter the Boy *with a linstock.*
Sal. I grieve to hear what torments you endur'd,
But we will be reveng'd sufficiently.
Now it is supper-time in Orleance:
Here, through this grate, I count each one,
And view the Frenchmen how they fortify.
Let us look in, the sight will much delight thee.
Sir Thomas Gargrave, and Sir William Glansdale,
Let me have your express opinions,
Where is best place to make our batt'ry next?
Gar. I think at the North Gate, for there stands lords.
Glan. And I here, at the bulwark of the bridge.
Tal. For aught I see, this city must be famish'd,
Or with light skirmishes enfeebled.
Here they shoot, and Salisbury falls down [together with Gargrave].
Sal. O Lord, have mercy on us, wretched sinners!
Gar. O Lord, have mercy on me, woeful man!
Tal. What chance is this that suddenly hath cross'd us?
Speak, Salisbury; at least, if thou canst, speak.
How far'st thou, mirror of all martial men?
One of thy eyes and thy cheek's side struck off!
Accursed tower! accursed fatal hand
That hath contriv'd this woeful tragedy!
In thirteen battles Salisbury o'ercame;

38. entertain'd: treated.
52. spurn: kick. adamant: i.e. the hardest substance imaginable.
53. chosen shot: selected musketeers.
54. every minute while: i.e. continually
56 s.d. linstock: stick to hold the gunner's match.
64. express: precise.
68. must be famish'd: will have to be starved out.
74. mirror: example.
75. One . . . off. A detail supplied by Hall (Bullough, III, 55): "the wynsonne of the Master gonner, perceived men lokyng out at the wyndowe, toke his matche, as his father had taught hym, whiche was gone doune to dinner, and fired the gonne, whiche brake & shevered the yron barres of the grate, whereof one strake therle so strongly on the hed, that it stroke away one of his iyes and the side of his cheke."

Henry the Fift he first train'd to the wars;
Whilst any trump did sound, or drum struck up,
His sword did ne'er leave striking in the field.
Yet liv'st thou, Salisbury? Though thy speech doth fail,
One eye thou hast to look to heaven for grace;
The sun with one eye vieweth all the world.
Heaven, be thou gracious to none alive,
If Salisbury wants mercy at thy hands!
Bear hence his body, I will help to bury it.
Sir Thomas Gargrave, hast thou any life?
Speak unto Talbot, nay, look up to him.
Salisbury, cheer thy spirit with this comfort,
Thou shalt not die whiles—
He beckons with his hand and smiles on me,
As who should say, "When I am dead and gone,
Remember to avenge me on the French."
Plantagenet, I will, and like thee, [Nero,]
Play on the lute, beholding the towns burn:
Wretched shall France be only in my name.

Here an alarum, and it thunders and lightens.

What stir is this? what tumult's in the heavens?
Whence cometh this alarum, and the noise?

Enter a Messenger.

Mess. My lord, my lord, the French have gather'd head.
The Dolphin, with one Joan de Pucelle join'd,
A holy prophetess new risen up,
Is come with a great power to raise the siege.

Here Salisbury lifteth himself up and groans.

Tal. Hear, hear how dying Salisbury doth groan!
It irks his heart he cannot be reveng'd.
Frenchmen, I'll be a Salisbury to you.
Pucelle or puzzel, Dolphin or dogfish,
Your hearts I'll stamp out with my horse's heels,
And make a quagmire of your mingled brains.
Convey me Salisbury into his tent,
And then we'll try what these dastard Frenchmen dare.

Alarum. Exeunt [bearing out the bodies].

[Scene V]

Here an alarum again, and Talbot *pursueth the* Dolphin, *and driveth him. Then enter* Joan de Pucelle, *driving Englishmen before her, [and exit after them]. Then enter* Talbot.

Tal. Where is my strength, my valor, and my force?
Our English troops retire, I cannot stay them;
A woman clad in armor chaseth them.

86. wants: lacks. **91. whiles:** until.
95. Plantagenet. Salisbury's family name was Montacute, but he was distantly related to the royal family. See note to II.iv o.s.d. **Nero.** According to Suetonius, the emperor Nero ordered certain parts of Rome put to the torch, and as he watched the fire he sang of the sack of Ilium. **97. only in:** at the very sound of.
100. gather'd head: assembled armed forces. **103. power:** army.
107. puzzel: slut, drab. Note the pun with *Pucelle*, and also that between *Dolphin* and *dogfish* (small shark).
I.v. Location: Scene continues.

Enter Pucelle.

Here, here she comes. I'll have a bout with thee;
Devil or devil's dam, I'll conjure thee.
Blood will I draw on thee—thou art a witch—
And straightway give thy soul to him thou serv'st.

Puc. Come, come, 'tis only I that must disgrace thee.

Here they fight.

Tal. Heavens, can you suffer hell so to prevail?
My breast I'll burst with straining of my courage,
And from my shoulders crack my arms asunder,
But I will chastise this high-minded strumpet.

They fight again.

Puc. Talbot, farewell, thy hour is not yet come.
I must go victual Orleance forthwith.

A short alarum: then enter the town with soldiers.

O'ertake me if thou canst, I scorn thy strength.
Go, go, cheer up thy hungry-starved men;
Help Salisbury to make his testament.
This day is ours, as many more shall be. *Exit.*

Tal. My thoughts are whirled like a potter's wheel,
I know not where I am, nor what I do.
A witch by fear, not force, like Hannibal,
Drives back our troops and conquers as she lists:
So bees with smoke and doves with noisome stench
Are from their hives and houses driven away.
They call'd us for our fierceness English dogs,
Now, like to whelps, we crying run away.

A short alarum.

Hark, countrymen, either renew the fight,
Or tear the lions out of England's coat;
Renounce your soil, give sheep in lions' stead:
Sheep run not half so treacherous from the wolf,
Or horse or oxen from the leopard,
As you fly from your oft-subdued slaves.

Alarum. Here another skirmish.

It will not be, retire into your trenches.
You all consented unto Salisbury's death,
For none would strike a stroke in his revenge.
Pucelle is ent'red into Orleance
In spite of us, or aught that we could do.
O would I were to die with Salisbury!
The shame hereof will make me hide my head.

Exit Talbot. Alarum; retreat.

[Scene VI]

Flourish. Enter on the walls Pucelle, [Charles *the*] *Dolphin,* Reignier, Alanson, *and Soldiers.*

Puc. Advance our waving colors on the walls,
Rescu'd is Orleance from the English!
Thus Joan de Pucelle hath perform'd her word.

12. But I will: if I do not. **high-minded:** arrogant.
16. hungry-starved: dying of hunger.
21. Hannibal. According to Livy, the Carthaginian leader routed the Roman army by tying blazing faggots to the horns of oxen.
22. lists: pleases. **28. coat:** coat of arms.
29. soil: native country. **give:** display (as in a heraldic emblem).
35. his revenge: revenge of him.
39 s.d. retreat: trumpet signal to recall a pursuing force.
I.vi. Location: Scene continues.
1. Advance: raise.

Char. Divinest creature, Astraea's daughter,
How shall I honor thee for this success?
Thy promises are like Adonis' garden,
That one day bloom'd and fruitful were the next.
France, triumph in thy glorious prophetess!
Recover'd is the town of Orleance.
More blessed hap did ne'er befall our state.

Reig. Why ring not out the bells aloud throughout the town?
Dolphin, command the citizens make bonfires,
And feast and banquet in the open streets,
To celebrate the joy that God hath given us.

Alan. All France will be replete with mirth and joy,
When they shall hear how we have play'd the men.

Char. 'Tis Joan, not we, by whom the day is won;
For which I will divide my crown with her,
And all the priests and friars in my realm
Shall in procession sing her endless praise.
A statelier pyramis to her I'll rear
Than Rhodope's [of] Memphis ever was.
In memory of her when she is dead,
Her ashes, in an urn more precious
Than the rich-jewell'd coffer of Darius,
Transported shall be at high festivals
Before the kings and queens of France.
No longer on Saint Denis will we cry,
But Joan de Pucelle shall be France's saint.
Come in, and let us banquet royally,
After this golden day of victory. *Flourish. Exeunt.*

ACT II, Scene I

Enter a [French] Sergeant *of a band, with two* Sentinels.

Serg. Sirs, take your places and be vigilant.
If any noise or soldier you perceive
Near to the walls, by some apparent sign
Let us have knowledge at the court of guard.

[*1.*] *Sent.* Sergeant, you shall. [*Exit Sergeant.*]
Thus are poor servitors,
When others sleep upon their quiet beds,
Constrain'd to watch in darkness, rain, and cold.

Enter Talbot, Bedford, *and* Burgundy, [*and forces*] *with scaling-ladders.*

Tal. Lord Regent, and redoubted Burgundy,
By whose approach the regions of Artois,
Wallon, and Picardy are friends to us,
This happy night the Frenchmen are secure,
Having all day carous'd and banqueted:
Embrace we then this opportunity
As fitting best to quittance their deceit
Contriv'd by art and baleful sorcery.

Bed. Coward of France, how much he wrongs his fame,
Despairing of his own arm's fortitude,
To join with witches and the help of hell!

Bur. Traitors have never other company.
But what's that Pucelle whom they term so pure?

Tal. A maid, they say.

Bed. A maid? and be so martial?

Bur. Pray God she prove not masculine ere long,
If underneath the standard of the French
She carry armor as she hath begun.

Tal. Well, let them practice and converse with spirits.
God is our fortress, in whose conquering name
Let us resolve to scale their flinty bulwarks.

Bed. Ascend, brave Talbot, we will follow thee.

Tal. Not all together. Better far, I guess,
That we do make our entrance several ways;
That, if it chance the one of us do fail,
The other yet may rise against their force.

Bed. Agreed. I'll to yond corner.

Bur. And I to this.

Tal. And here will Talbot mount, or make his grave.
Now, Salisbury, for thee, and for the right
Of English Henry, shall this night appear
How much in duty I am bound to both.

Cry: "Saint George!" "A Talbot!"
[*The English scale the walls.*]

[*1.*] *Sent.* Arm, arm! the enemy doth make assault!

The French leap o'er the walls in their shirts. Enter, several ways, Bastard, Alanson, Reignier, *half ready and half unready.*

Alan. How now, my lords? what, all unready so?

Bast. Unready? Ay, and glad we scap'd so well.

Reig. 'Twas time, I trow, to wake and leave our beds,
Hearing alarums at our chamber-doors.

Alan. Of all exploits since first I follow'd arms,
Ne'er heard I of a warlike enterprise
More venturous or desperate than this.

Bast. I think this Talbot be a fiend of hell.

Reig. If not of hell, the heavens sure favor him.

Alan. Here cometh Charles, I marvel how he sped.

Enter Charles *and* Joan [de Pucelle].

Bast. Tut, holy Joan was his defensive guard.

4. Astraea: goddess of Justice, who forsook the world when it became corrupt.
6. Adonis' garden: mythical garden noted for fertility; perhaps an allusion to a famous episode in Spenser's *Faerie Queene*, Book III, Canto vi. **21. pyramis:** pyramid.
22. Rhodope: renowned Greek courtesan alleged to have married the king of Egypt, who built one of the most beautiful of the pyramids for her. **Memphis:** ancient city on the Nile.
25. Darius: Persian king whose jewelled treasure chest was used by Alexander the Great to carry Homer's poems on his campaigns.
28. Saint Denis: patron saint of France.

II.i. Location: Before Orleans.
3. apparent: plain, unmistakable. **4. court of guard:** guardroom.
7 s.d. Burgundy: Philip the Good, Duke of Burgundy (1396–1467), who became an ally of the English by the Treaty of Troyes (1420) and was named co-regent of France (together with John, Duke of Bedford) by the dying Henry V (see note to I.i.37). After 1435 Philip shifted his allegiance to Charles VII.

11. secure: unsuspecting, overconfident.
14. quittance: requite. **15. art:** i.e. magic.
16. Coward of France: i.e. the Dauphin. **fame:** reputation.
25. practice: plot, scheme. **30. several:** different.
38 s.d. ready: dressed. According to Hall (Bullough, III, 53–54), the incident on which this scene is based actually occurred at Le Mans in May 1428, a year before the siege of Orleans. **41. trow:** believe.
48. sped: fared.

Char. Is this thy cunning, thou deceitful dame?
Didst thou at first, to flatter us withal,
Make us partakers of a little gain,
That now our loss might be ten times so much?
Puc. Wherefore is Charles impatient with his friend?
At all times will you have my power alike?
Sleeping or waking, must I still prevail,
Or will you blame and lay the fault on me?
Improvident soldiers, had your watch been good,
This sudden mischief never could have fall'n.
Char. Duke of Alanson, this was your default,
That, being captain of the watch to-night,
Did look no better to that weighty charge.
Alan. Had all your quarters been as safely kept
As that whereof I had the government,
We had not been thus shamefully surpris'd.
Bast. Mine was secure.
Reig. And so was mine, my lord.
Char. And for myself, most part of all this night,
Within her quarter and mine own precinct
I was employ'd in passing to and fro,
About relieving of the sentinels.
Then how, or which way, should they first break in?
Puc. Question, my lords, no further of the case,
How or which way. 'Tis sure they found some place
But weakly guarded, where the breach was made.
And now there rests no other shift but this,
To gather our soldiers, scatter'd and dispers'd,
And lay new platforms to endamage them.

Alarum. Enter [an English] SOLDIER *crying,* "A Talbot! a Talbot!" *They fly, leaving their clothes behind.*

Sold. I'll be so bold to take what they have left.
The cry of Talbot serves me for a sword,
For I have loaden me with many spoils,
Using no other weapon but his name. *Exit.*

[SCENE II]

Enter TALBOT, BEDFORD, BURGUNDY, *[a* CAPTAIN, *and others], their Drums beating a dead march.*

Bed. The day begins to break, and night is fled,
Whose pitchy mantle over-veil'd the earth.
Here sound retreat, and cease our hot pursuit.
Retreat.
Tal. Bring forth the body of old Salisbury,
And here advance it in the market-place,
The middle centure of this cursed town.
Now have I paid my vow unto his soul;
For every drop of blood was drawn from him
There hath at least five Frenchmen died to-night.
And that hereafter ages may behold

What ruin happened in revenge of him,
Within their chiefest temple I'll erect
A tomb, wherein his corpse shall be interr'd;
Upon the which, that every one may read,
Shall be engrav'd the sack of Orleance,
The treacherous manner of his mournful death,
And what a terror he had been to France.
But, lords, in all our bloody massacre,
I muse we met not with the Dolphin's grace,
His new-come champion, virtuous Joan of [Aire],
Nor any of his false confederates.
Bed. 'Tis thought, Lord Talbot, when the fight began,
Rous'd on the sudden from their drowsy beds,
They did amongst the troops of armed men
Leap o'er the walls for refuge in the field.
Bur. Myself, as far as I could well discern
For smoke and dusky vapors of the night,
Am sure I scar'd the Dolphin and his trull,
When arm in arm they both came swiftly running,
Like to a pair of loving turtle-doves
That could not live asunder day or night.
After that things are set in order here,
We'll follow them with all the power we have.

Enter a MESSENGER.

Mess. All hail, my lords! which of this princely train
Call ye the warlike Talbot, for his acts
So much applauded through the realm of France?
Tal. Here is the Talbot, who would speak with him?
Mess. The virtuous lady, Countess of Auvergne,
With modesty admiring thy renown,
By me entreats, great lord, thou wouldst vouchsafe
To visit her poor castle where she lies,
That she may boast she hath beheld the man
Whose glory fills the world with loud report.
Bur. Is it even so? Nay, then I see our wars
Will turn unto a peaceful comic sport,
When ladies crave to be encount'red with.
You may not, my lord, despise her gentle suit.
Tal. Ne'er trust me then; for when a world of men
Could not prevail with all their oratory,
Yet hath a woman's kindness overrul'd;
And therefore tell her I return great thanks,
And in submission will attend on her.
Will not your honors bear me company?
Bed. No, truly, 'tis more than manners will;
And I have heard it said, unbidden guests
Are often welcomest when they are gone.
Tal. Well then, alone (since there's no remedy)
I mean to prove this lady's courtesy.
Come hither, captain. (*Whispers.*) You perceive my mind?

50. cunning: skill (with magic).
61. to-night: last night. **68. her:** i.e. Joan's.
75. shift: plan, device. **77. platforms:** plans.

II.ii. Location: Within the town of Orleans.
o.s.d. dead march. For Salisbury.
3. retreat: trumpet signal for withdrawal of forces.
5. advance: raise (on a bier). **6. centure:** cincture, belt.
8. was: that was.

12–13. Within . . . interr'd. Actually, as Hall records (Bullough, III, 56), Salisbury's body "was conveyed into England, with al funerall and pompe, and buried at Bissam by his progenitors."
19. muse: wonder. **28. trull:** whore. **33. power:** forces.
41. lies: lives. **47. gentle:** courteous.
54. manners will: etiquette allows. **58. prove:** test.

Capt. I do, my lord, and mean accordingly.
Exeunt.

[Scene III]

Enter Countess [of Auvergne *and her* Porter].

Count. Porter, remember what I gave in charge,
And when you have done so, bring the keys to me.
Port. Madam, I will. *Exit.*
Count. The plot is laid. If all things fall out right,
I shall as famous be by this exploit
As Scythian Tomyris by Cyrus' death.
Great is the rumor of this dreadful knight,
And his achievements of no less account;
Fain would mine eyes be witness with mine ears
To give their censure of these rare reports.

Enter Messenger *and* Talbot.

Mess. Madam,
According as your ladyship desir'd,
By message crav'd, so is Lord Talbot come.
Count. And he is welcome. What? is this the man?
Mess. Madam, it is.
Count. Is this the scourge of France?
Is this the Talbot, so much fear'd abroad
That with his name the mothers still their babes?
I see report is fabulous and false.
I thought I should have seen some Hercules,
A second Hector, for his grim aspect
And large proportion of his strong-knit limbs.
Alas, this is a child, a silly dwarf!
It cannot be this weak and writhled shrimp
Should strike such terror to his enemies.
Tal. Madam, I have been bold to trouble you;
But since your ladyship is not at leisure,
I'll sort some other time to visit you. [*Going.*]
Count. What means he now? Go ask him whither he goes.
Mess. Stay, my Lord Talbot, for my lady craves
To know the cause of your abrupt departure.
Tal. Marry, for that she's in a wrong belief,
I go to certify her Talbot's here.

Enter Porter *with keys.*

Count. If thou be he, then art thou prisoner.
Tal. Prisoner? to whom?
Count. To me, blood-thirsty lord;
And for that cause I train'd thee to my house.
Long time thy shadow hath been thrall to me,

For in my gallery thy picture hangs;
But now the substance shall endure the like,
And I will chain these legs and arms of thine,
That hast by tyranny these many years
Wasted our country, slain our citizens,
And sent our sons and husbands captivate.
Tal. Ha, ha, ha!
Count. Laughest thou, wretch? Thy mirth shall turn to moan.
Tal. I laugh to see your ladyship so fond
To think that you have aught but Talbot's shadow
Whereon to practice your severity.
Count. Why? art not thou the man?
Tal. I am indeed.
Count. Then have I substance too.
Tal. No, no, I am but shadow of myself.
You are deceiv'd, my substance is not here;
For what you see is but the smallest part
And least proportion of humanity.
I tell you, madam, were the whole frame here,
It is of such a spacious lofty pitch,
Your roof were not sufficient to contain't.
Count. This is a riddling merchant for the nonce:
He will be here, and yet he is not here.
How can these contrarieties agree?
Tal. That will I show you presently.
Winds his horn. Drums strike up;
a peal of ordinance.

Enter Soldiers.

How say you, madam? Are you now persuaded
That Talbot is but shadow of himself?
These are his substance, sinews, arms, and strength,
With which he yoketh your rebellious necks,
Razeth your cities, and subverts your towns,
And in a moment makes them desolate.
Count. Victorious Talbot, pardon my abuse.
I find thou art no less than fame hath bruited,
And more than may be gathered by thy shape.
Let my presumption not provoke thy wrath,
For I am sorry that with reverence
I did not entertain thee as thou art.
Tal. Be not dismay'd, fair lady, nor misconster
The mind of Talbot, as you did mistake
The outward composition of his body.
What you have done hath not offended me;
Nor other satisfaction do I crave,
But only, with your patience, that we may
Taste of your wine and see what cates you have,
For soldiers' stomachs always serve them well.
Count. With all my heart, and think me honored
To feast so great a warrior in my house. *Exeunt.*

60. mean: i.e. intend to act.

II.iii. Location: Auvergne. The Countess' castle.
1. gave in charge: commanded.
6. Tomyris: Scythian queen who killed Cyrus the Great in battle and preserved his head in a wineskin filled with blood.
10. censure: judgment, opinion.
19, 20. Hercules, Hector. Men of legendary strength.
21. proportion: size. **23. writhled:** wrinkled. **27. sort:** choose.
31. Marry: indeed (originally the name of the Virgin Mary used as an oath). **for that:** because. **32. certify:** inform.
35. train'd: enticed.
36. shadow . . . me: i.e. I have held your picture prisoner.

42. captivate: taken captive. **45. fond:** foolish.
53. proportion of humanity: part of the man. **55. pitch:** height.
57. riddling merchant: dealer in riddles. **for the nonce:** for the occasion (a meaningless line-filler).
60. presently: immediately. **s.d. Winds:** sounds.
65. subverts: overturns. **67. abuse:** deception.
68. fame: report. **bruited:** announced.
72. entertain: receive. **73. misconster:** misconstrue.
78. patience: permission. **79. cates:** delicacies.

[Scene IV]

Enter Richard Plantagenet, Warwick, Somerset, Pole [Earl of Suffolk], *and others* [Vernon *and a* Lawyer].

Plan. Great lords and gentlemen, what means this silence?
Dare no man answer in a case of truth?
Suf. Within the Temple Hall we were too loud,
The garden here is more convenient.
Plan. Then say at once if I maintain'd the truth;
Or else was wrangling Somerset in th' error?
Suf. Faith, I have been a truant in the law,
And never yet could frame my will to it,
And therefore frame the law unto my will.
Som. Judge you, my Lord of Warwick, then between us.
War. Between two hawks, which flies the higher pitch,
Between two dogs, which hath the deeper mouth,
Between two blades, which bears the better temper,
Between two horses, which doth bear him best,
Between two girls, which hath the merriest eye—
I have perhaps some shallow spirit of judgment;
But in these nice sharp quillets of the law,
Good faith, I am no wiser than a daw.
Plan. Tut, tut, here is a mannerly forbearance.
The truth appears so naked on my side
That any purblind eye may find it out.
Som. And on my side it is so well apparell'd,
So clear, so shining, and so evident,
That it will glimmer through a blindman's eye.
Plan. Since you are tongue-tied and so loath to speak,
In dumb significants proclaim your thoughts:
Let him that is a true-born gentleman
And stands upon the honor of his birth,
If he suppose that I have pleaded truth,
From off this brier pluck a white rose with me.
Som. Let him that is no coward nor no flatterer,
But dare maintain the party of the truth,
Pluck a red rose from off this thorn with me.
War. I love no colors; and without all color
Of base insinuating flattery,
I pluck this white rose with Plantagenet.
Suf. I pluck this red rose with young Somerset,
And say withal, I think he held the right.
Ver. Stay, lords and gentlemen, and pluck no more,

II.iv. Location: London. The Temple Garden (in the precincts of the Middle Temple and Inner Temple, two of the Inns of Court housing the legal societies of London, so named because the buildings had earlier belonged to the Knights Templars).
o.s.d. **Plantagenet**: nickname for Geoffrey of Anjou, father of Henry II and thus founder of the dynasty that ruled England from 1154 until the advent of the Tudors in 1485. The name, later associated with all the members of this royal house, was apparently first used by Richard, Duke of York, in order to emphasize his royal lineage and thus bolster his claim to the throne against the Lancastrian branch of the family. 3. **were**: would be.
11. **pitch**: flight (a term from falconry). 12. **mouth**: voice.
14. **bear him**: carry himself.
17. **nice**: precise. **quillets**: subtleties. 18. **daw**: jackdaw.
21. **purblind**: dim-sighted. 26. **significants**: signs.
29. **pleaded**: argued (one of a number of legal terms in this scene).
32. **party**: side. 34. **colors**: pretenses, pretexts.
38. **withal**: besides.

Till you conclude that he upon whose side
The fewest roses are cropp'd from the tree
Shall yield the other in the right opinion.
Som. Good Master Vernon, it is well objected;
If I have fewest, I subscribe in silence.
Plan. And I.
Ver. Then for the truth and plainness of the case,
I pluck this pale and maiden blossom here,
Giving my verdict on the white rose side.
Som. Prick not your finger as you pluck it off,
Lest, bleeding, you do paint the white rose red,
And fall on my side so against your will.
Ver. If I, my lord, for my opinion bleed,
Opinion shall be surgeon to my hurt,
And keep me on the side where still I am.
Som. Well, well, come on, who else?
Law. Unless my study and my books be false,
The argument you held was wrong in you; [*To Somerset.*]
In sign whereof I pluck a white rose too.
Plan. Now, Somerset, where is your argument?
Som. Here in my scabbard, meditating that
Shall dye your white rose in a bloody red.
Plan. Mean time your cheeks do counterfeit our roses;
For pale they look with fear, as witnessing
The truth on our side.
Som. No, Plantagenet;
'Tis not for fear, but anger, that thy cheeks
Blush for pure shame to counterfeit our roses,
And yet thy tongue will not confess thy error.
Plan. Hath not thy rose a canker, Somerset?
Som. Hath not thy rose a thorn, Plantagenet?
Plan. Ay, sharp and piercing, to maintain his truth,
Whiles thy consuming canker eats his falsehood.
Som. Well, I'll find friends to wear my bleeding roses,
That shall maintain what I have said is true,
Where false Plantagenet dare not be seen.
Plan. Now, by this maiden blossom in my hand,
I scorn thee and thy fashion, peevish boy.
Suf. Turn not thy scorns this way, Plantagenet.
Plan. Proud Pole, I will, and scorn both him and thee.
Suf. I'll turn my part thereof into thy throat.
Som. Away, away, good William de la Pole!
We grace the yeoman by conversing with him.
War. Now, by God's will, thou wrong'st him, Somerset;
His grandfather was Lionel Duke of Clarence,
Third son to the third Edward, King of England.

43. **objected**: urged.
44. **subscribe**: submit. 52. **opinion**: judgment, conviction.
53. **Opinion**: public opinion, reputation, honor.
60. **that**: that which. 62. **counterfeit**: imitate.
68. **canker**: cankerworm, grub. 70. **his**: its.
76. **fashion**: kind, sort. **peevish boy**: sullen youngster.
78. **Pole**: family name of the Duke of Suffolk.
79. **turn . . . throat**: throw the slanders back into the throat from which they came.
81. **yeoman**: freeholder below the rank of gentleman.
83–84. **His . . . England.** Lionel was actually Richard's maternal great-great-grandfather; but Edward III's fifth son, Edmund, Duke of York, was Richard's paternal grandfather. He could thus claim descent from Edward III through both his parents.

Spring crestless yeomen from so deep a root?
Plan. He bears him on the place's privilege,
Or durst not for his craven heart say thus.
Som. By Him that made me, I'll maintain my words
On any plot of ground in Christendom.
Was not thy father, Richard Earl of Cambridge,
For treason executed in our late king's days?
And by his treason, stand'st not thou attainted,
Corrupted, and exempt from ancient gentry?
His trespass yet lives guilty in thy blood,
And till thou be restor'd, thou art a yeoman.
Plan. My father was attached, not attainted,
Condemn'd to die for treason, but no traitor;
And that I'll prove on better men than Somerset,
Were growing time once ripened to my will.
For your partaker Pole, and you yourself,
I'll note you in my book of memory,
To scourge you for this apprehension.
Look to it well, and say you are well warn'd.
Som. Ah, thou shalt find us ready for thee still;
And know us by these colors for thy foes,
For these my friends in spite of thee shall wear.
Plan. And, by my soul, this pale and angry rose,
As cognizance of my blood-drinking hate,
Will I for ever and my faction wear,
Until it wither with me to my grave,
Or flourish to the height of my degree.
Suf. Go forward, and be chok'd with thy ambition!
And so farewell until I meet thee next. *Exit.*
Som. Have with thee, Pole. Farewell, ambitious Richard. *Exit.*
Plan. How I am brav'd, and must perforce endure it!
War. This blot that they object against your house
Shall be [wip'd] out in the next parliament,
Call'd for the truce of Winchester and Gloucester;
And if thou be not then created York,
I will not live to be accounted Warwick.
Mean time, in signal of my love to thee,
Against proud Somerset and William Pole,
Will I upon thy party wear this rose.
And here I prophesy: this brawl to-day,
Grown to this faction in the Temple Garden,
Shall send between the Red Rose and the White
A thousand souls to death and deadly night.
Plan. Good Master Vernon, I am bound to you
That you on my behalf would pluck a flower.
Ver. In your behalf still will I wear the same.

85. crestless: without a coat of arms.
86. bears . . . privilege: takes advantage of the fact that this is a privileged place, where weapons are forbidden. Actually, the Temple Garden, unlike the Tower (I.iii.46), enjoyed no such privilege.
91. late king's: i.e. Henry V's. **92. attainted:** disgraced.
93. exempt: excluded.
96. attached, not attainted: arrested, not convicted. This is an important distinction, for normally the heirs of a nobleman attainted for treason were "exempt from ancient gentry" and stripped of all their rights. Richard's statement is true: his father, the Earl of Cambridge, had been summarily executed for treason without a bill of attainder (see *Henry V*, II.ii).
99. Were . . . will: if I ever have the chance.
100. For: as for. **partaker:** supporter.
102. apprehension: opinion. **104. still:** always.
108. cognizance: badge. **111. degree:** rank.
114. Have with thee: let's go. **115. brav'd:** defied, insulted.
116. object: allege.
118. Call'd . . . of: summoned to make peace between.

Law. And so will I.
Plan. Thanks, [gentlemen].
Come, let us four to dinner. I dare say
This quarrel will drink blood another day. *Exeunt.*

[Scene V]

Enter Mortimer, *brought in a chair, and* Jailers.

Mor. Kind keepers of my weak decaying age,
Let dying Mortimer here rest himself.
Even like a man new haled from the rack,
So fare my limbs with long imprisonment;
And these grey locks, the pursuivants of death,
Nestor-like aged, in an age of care,
Argue the end of Edmund Mortimer.
These eyes, like lamps whose wasting oil is spent,
Wax dim, as drawing to their exigent;
Weak shoulders, overborne with burthening grief,
And pithless arms, like to a withered vine
That droops his sapless branches to the ground.
Yet are these feet, whose strengthless stay is numb
(Unable to support this lump of clay),
Swift-winged with desire to get a grave,
As witting I no other comfort have.
But tell me, keeper, will my nephew come?
[*1.*] *Keeper.* Richard Plantagenet, my lord, will come.
We sent unto the Temple, unto his chamber,
And answer was return'd that he will come.
Mor. Enough; my soul shall then be satisfied.
Poor gentleman, his wrong doth equal mine.
Since Henry Monmouth first began to reign,
Before whose glory I was great in arms,
This loathsome sequestration have I had;
And even since then hath Richard been obscur'd,
Depriv'd of honor and inheritance.
But now, the arbitrator of despairs,
Just Death, kind umpire of men's miseries,
With sweet enlargement doth dismiss me hence.
I would his troubles likewise were expir'd,
That so he might recover what was lost.

Enter Richard [Plantagenet].

[*1.*] *Keeper.* My lord, your loving nephew now is come.
Mor. Richard Plantagenet, my friend, is he come?
Plan. Ay, noble uncle, thus ignobly us'd,
Your nephew, late-despised Richard, comes.

II.v. Location: London. The Tower.
5. pursuivants: heralds.
6. Nestor-like: i.e. extremely old, like Nestor, one of the Grecian leaders at the siege of Troy.
7. Argue: indicate. **Edmund Mortimer.** A mistake, adopted from the chroniclers, for Sir John Mortimer, who, after several years in prison, was executed in 1424 for urging his cousin Edmund Mortimer's claim to the throne. Edmund, fifth Earl of March and great-grandson of Lionel, Duke of Clarence, had been recognized as heir presumptive by Richard II in 1398. Although an object of suspicion during the early years of the Lancastrian revolution, he served honorably with Henry V in France and died in 1425 as Lord Lieutenant of Ireland. **9. exigent:** end. **11. pithless:** weak.
13. stay: support. **16. witting:** knowing.
22. his wrong: the wrong done to him.
23. Henry Monmouth: i.e. Henry V.
25. sequestration: imprisonment. **30. enlargement:** release.
36. late-despised: lately treated with contempt.

Mor. Direct mine arms I may embrace his neck,
And in his bosom spend my latter gasp.
O, tell me when my lips do touch his cheeks,
That I may kindly give one fainting kiss.
And now declare, sweet stem from York's great stock,
Why didst thou say, of late thou wert despis'd?
Plan. First, lean thine aged back against mine arm,
And in that ease, I'll tell thee my disease.
This day, in argument upon a case,
Some words there grew 'twixt Somerset and me;
Among which terms he us'd his lavish tongue
And did upbraid me with my father's death;
Which obloquy set bars before my tongue,
Else with the like I had requited him.
Therefore, good uncle, for my father's sake,
In honor of a true Plantagenet,
And for alliance sake, declare the cause
My father, Earl of Cambridge, lost his head.
Mor. That cause, fair nephew, that imprison'd me
And hath detain'd me all my flow'ring youth
Within a loathsome dungeon, there to pine,
Was cursed instrument of his decease.
Plan. Discover more at large what cause that was,
For I am ignorant and cannot guess.
Mor. I will, if that my fading breath permit
And death approach not ere my tale be done.
Henry the Fourth, grandfather to this king,
Depos'd his nephew Richard, Edward's son,
The first begotten, and the lawful heir
Of Edward king, the third of that descent;
During whose reign the Percies of the north,
Finding his usurpation most unjust,
Endeavor'd my advancement to the throne.
The reason mov'd these warlike lords to this
Was, for that (young Richard thus remov'd,
Leaving no heir begotten of his body)
I was the next by birth and parentage;
For by my mother I derived am
From Lionel Duke of Clarence, third son
To King Edward the Third; whereas he
From John of Gaunt doth bring his pedigree,
Being but fourth of that heroic line.
But mark: as in this haughty great attempt
They labored to plant the rightful heir,
I lost my liberty, and they their lives.
Long after this, when Henry the Fift
(Succeeding his father Bullingbrook) did reign,
Thy father, Earl of Cambridge then, deriv'd
From famous Edmund Langley, Duke of York,
Marrying my sister that thy mother was,
Again, in pity of my hard distress,
Levied an army, weening to redeem
And have install'd me in the diadem.
But as the rest, so fell that noble earl,
And was beheaded. Thus the Mortimers,
In whom the title rested, were suppress'd.

38. latter: final. **44. disease:** trouble, grievance.
53. for alliance sake: for the sake of our relationship. Richard's mother, Anne, was Edmund's sister. **59. Discover:** divulge.
64. nephew: kinsman (here, cousin). **67. whose:** i.e. Henry IV's.
70. mov'd: which moved. **71. for that:** because.
74. mother. Actually, his paternal grandmother (Philippa, daughter of Lionel, Duke of Clarence). **88. weening:** thinking.

Plan. Of which, my lord, your honor is the last.
Mor. True; and thou seest that I no issue have,
And that my fainting words do warrant death.
Thou art my heir; the rest I wish thee gather;
But yet be wary in thy studious care.
Plan. Thy grave admonishments prevail with me.
But yet methinks, my father's execution
Was nothing less than bloody tyranny.
Mor. With silence, nephew, be thou politic.
Strong fixed is the house of Lancaster,
And like a mountain, not to be remov'd.
But now thy uncle is removing hence,
As princes do their courts, when they are cloy'd
With long continuance in a settled place.
Plan. O uncle, would some part of my young years
Might but redeem the passage of your age!
Mor. Thou dost then wrong me, as that slaughterer doth
Which giveth many wounds when one will kill.
Mourn not, except thou sorrow for my good,
Only give order for my funeral.
And so farewell, and fair be all thy hopes,
And prosperous be thy life in peace and war! *Dies.*
Plan. And peace, no war, befall thy parting soul!
In prison hast thou spent a pilgrimage,
And like a hermit overpass'd thy days.
Well, I will lock his counsel in my breast,
And what I do imagine, let that rest.
Keepers, convey him hence, and I myself
Will see his burial better than his life.
Exeunt [Keepers, bearing out the body of Mortimer].
Here dies the dusky torch of Mortimer,
Chok'd with ambition of the meaner sort;
And for those wrongs, those bitter injuries,
Which Somerset hath offer'd to my house,
I doubt not but with honor to redress.
And therefore haste I to the parliament,
Either to be restored to my blood,
Or make my will th' advantage of my good. *Exit.*

ACT III, SCENE I

Flourish. Enter KING, EXETER, GLOUCESTER, WINCHESTER, WARWICK, SOMERSET, SUFFOLK, RICHARD PLANTAGENET, *[and others]. Gloucester offers to put up a bill; Winchester snatches it, tears it.*

Win. Com'st thou with deep premeditated lines,
With written pamphlets studiously devis'd?
Humphrey of Gloucester, if thou canst accuse,
Or aught intend'st to lay unto my charge,
Do it without invention, suddenly,

95. warrant: certify. **96. gather:** infer.
117. overpass'd: passed, spent.
123. with: by. **meaner sort:** those of lower rank (i.e. the Lancastrians). **128. blood:** hereditary rights.
129. make . . . good: make my desire the means whereby I'll reach my goal.

III.i. Location: London. The Parliament House.
o.s.d. bill: written statement. **1. lines:** i.e. of writing.
5. invention: deliberate preparation. **suddenly:** extempore.

As I with sudden and extemporal speech
Purpose to answer what thou canst object.
Glou. Presumptuous priest, this place commands my patience,
Or thou shouldst find thou hast dishonor'd me.
Think not, although in writing I preferr'd
The manner of thy vile outrageous crimes,
That therefore I have forg'd, or am not able
Verbatim to rehearse the method of my pen.
No, prelate, such is thy audacious wickedness,
Thy lewd, pestiferous, and dissentious pranks,
As very infants prattle of thy pride.
Thou art a most pernicious usurer,
Froward by nature, enemy to peace,
Lascivious, wanton, more than well beseems
A man of thy profession and degree;
And for thy treachery, what's more manifest?
In that thou laidst a trap to take my life,
As well at London Bridge as at the Tower.
Beside, I fear me, if thy thoughts were sifted,
The King, thy sovereign, is not quite exempt
From envious malice of thy swelling heart.
Win. Gloucester, I do defy thee. Lords, vouchsafe
To give me hearing what I shall reply.
If I were covetous, ambitious, or perverse,
As he will have me, how am I so poor?
Or how haps it I seek not to advance
Or raise myself, but keep my wonted calling?
And for dissension, who preferreth peace
More than I do, except I be provok'd?
No, my good lords, it is not that offends,
It is not that that hath incens'd the Duke:
It is because no one should sway but he,
No one, but he, should be about the King;
And that engenders thunder in his breast,
And makes him roar these accusations forth.
But he shall know I am as good—
Glou. As good?
Thou bastard of my grandfather!
Win. Ay, lordly sir; for what are you, I pray,
But one imperious in another's throne?
Glou. Am I not Protector, saucy priest?
Win. And am not I a prelate of the Church?
Glou. Yes, as an outlaw in a castle keeps
And useth it to patronage his theft.
Win. Unreverent Gloucester!
Glou. Thou art reverent
Touching thy spiritual function, not thy life.

7. **object:** urge in accusation.
8. **this place:** i.e. in Parliament, with the King presiding.
10. **preferr'd:** set forth, explained. At the Parliament that met at Leicester in 1426 Gloucester, according to Hall (Bullough, III, 49–50), brought against the Bishop of Winchester various charges of misconduct, including an attempted ambush of the Protector as he was journeying toward Eltham for consultation with the King.
13. **Verbatim:** orally. **method:** summary of the contents of a document. 15. **lewd:** wicked. **pestiferous:** deadly. 16. **As:** that.
31. **haps:** happens. 35. **that:** that which.
42. **grandfather:** John of Gaunt, from whose liaison with Katherine Swynford the mighty Beaufort family sprang. Following Gaunt's marriage to his mistress in 1396, their children were legitimized by an act of Parliament, and they and their descendants were powerful through the fifteenth century. Margaret Beaufort, daughter of Winchester's nephew John (the Duke of Somerset of this play), was the mother of Henry VII. 47. **keeps:** dwells.
48. **patronage:** protect.

Win. Rome shall remedy this.
[Glou.] Roam thither then.
War. My lord [*to Winchester*], it were your duty to forbear.
Som. Ay, [so] the Bishop be not overborne.
Methinks my lord should be religious,
And know the office that belongs to such.
War. Methinks his lordship should be humbler,
It fitteth not a prelate so to plead.
Som. Yes, when his holy state is touch'd so near.
War. State holy or unhallow'd, what of that?
Is not his Grace Protector to the King?
Plan. [*Aside.*] Plantagenet, I see, must hold his tongue,
Lest it be said, "Speak, sirrah, when you should;
Must your bold verdict enter talk with lords?"
Else would I have a fling at Winchester.
King. Uncles of Gloucester and of Winchester,
The special watchmen of our English weal,
I would prevail, if prayers might prevail,
To join your hearts in love and amity.
O, what a scandal is it to our crown
That two such noble peers as ye should jar!
Believe me, lords, my tender years can tell,
Civil dissension is a viperous worm
That gnaws the bowels of the commonwealth.
A noise within, "Down with the tawny-coats!"
What tumult's this?
War. An uproar, I dare warrant,
Begun through malice of the Bishop's men.
A noise again, "Stones! stones!"

Enter Mayor [of London, *attended*].

May. O my good lords, and virtuous Henry,
Pity the city of London, pity us!
The Bishop and the Duke of Gloucester's men,
Forbidden late to carry any weapon,
Have fill'd their pockets full of pebble stones;
And, banding themselves in contrary parts,
Do pelt so fast at one another's pate
That many have their giddy brains knock'd out;
Our windows are broke down in every street,
And we, for fear, compell'd to shut our shops.

Enter [Servingmen *of both parties,*] *in skirmish, with bloody pates.*

King. We charge you, on allegiance to ourself,
To hold your slaught'ring hands and keep the peace.
Pray, uncle Gloucester, mitigate this strife.
1. Serv. Nay, if we be forbidden stones, we'll fall to it with our teeth.
2. Serv. Do what ye dare, we are as resolute.
Skirmish again.
Glou. You of my household, leave this peevish broil,

58. **when . . . near:** i.e. when his position as a churchman is concerned.
63. **bold verdict:** insolent opinion. **enter talk:** engage in discussion. 66. **weal:** common good. 70. **jar:** quarrel.
71. **tender years.** Actually, Henry VI was five years old at the time of the events represented.
77. **London.** Actually, the meeting of Parliament represented in this scene was at Leicester. See note to line 10 above.
92. **peevish:** childish.

And set this unaccustom'd fight aside.
3. Serv. My lord, we know your Grace to be a man
Just and upright; and, for your royal birth,
Inferior to none but to his Majesty;
And ere that we will suffer such a prince,
So kind a father of the commonweal,
To be disgraced by an inkhorn mate,
We and our wives and children all will fight,
And have our bodies slaught'red by thy foes.
1. Serv. Ay, and the very parings of our nails
Shall pitch a field when we are dead. *Begin again.*
Glou. Stay, stay, I say!
And if you love me, as you say you do,
Let me persuade you to forbear a while.
King. O, how this discord doth afflict my soul!
Can you, my Lord of Winchester, behold
My sighs and tears, and will not once relent?
Who should be pitiful, if you be not?
Or who should study to prefer a peace,
If holy churchmen take delight in broils?
War. Yield, my Lord Protector, yield, Winchester,
Except you mean with obstinate repulse
To slay your sovereign and destroy the realm.
You see what mischief, and what murther too,
Hath been enacted through your enmity.
Then be at peace, except ye thirst for blood.
Win. He shall submit, or I will never yield.
Glou. Compassion on the King commands me stoop,
Or I would see his heart out ere the priest
Should ever get that privilege of me.
War. Behold, my Lord of Winchester, the Duke
Hath banish'd moody discontented fury,
As by his smoothed brows it doth appear.
Why look you still so stern and tragical?
Glou. Here, Winchester, I offer thee my hand.
King. Fie, uncle Beauford, I have heard you preach
That malice was a great and grievous sin;
And will not you maintain the thing you teach,
But prove a chief offender in the same?
War. Sweet King! the Bishop hath a kindly gird.
For shame, my Lord of Winchester, relent!
What, shall a child instruct you what to do?
Win. Well, Duke of Gloucester, I will yield to thee;
Love for thy love and hand for hand I give.
Glou. [*Aside.*] Ay, but, I fear me, with a hollow heart.—
See here, my friends and loving countrymen,
This token serveth for a flag of truce
Betwixt ourselves and all our followers.
So help me God, as I dissemble not!
Win. [*Aside.*] So help me God, as I intend it not!
King. O loving uncle, kind Duke of Gloucester,
How joyful am I made by this contract!
Away, my masters, trouble us no more,

99. inkhorn mate: i.e. scribbler.
103. pitch a field: fight a battle. **110. prefer:** propose.
121. privilege: advantage. **123. moody:** haughty.
131. kindly gird: proper rebuke. **138. This token:** i.e. handshake.
144. masters: here, a term of condescension.

But join in friendship, as your lords have done.
1. Serv. Content, I'll to the surgeon's.
2. Serv. And so will I.
3. Serv. And I will see what physic the tavern affords. *Exeunt* [*Servingmen, Mayor, etc.*].
War. Accept this scroll, most gracious sovereign,
Which in the right of Richard Plantagenet
We do exhibit to your Majesty.
Glou. Well urg'd, my Lord of Warwick; for, sweet prince,
And if your Grace mark every circumstance,
You have great reason to do Richard right,
Especially for those occasions
At Eltam Place I told your Majesty.
King. And those occasions, uncle, were of force:
Therefore, my loving lords, our pleasure is
That Richard be restored to his blood.
War. Let Richard be restored to his blood,
So shall his father's wrongs be recompens'd.
Win. As will the rest, so willeth Winchester.
King. If Richard will be true, not that alone
But all the whole inheritance I give
That doth belong unto the house of York,
From whence you spring by lineal descent.
Plan. Thy humble servant vows obedience
And humble service till the point of death.
King. Stoop then and set your knee against my foot,
And in reguerdon of that duty done,
I girt thee with the valiant sword of York:
Rise, Richard, like a true Plantagenet,
And rise created princely Duke of York.
Plan. And so thrive Richard as thy foes may fall!
And as my duty springs, so perish they
That grudge one thought against your Majesty!
All. Welcome, high prince, the mighty Duke of York!
Som. [*Aside.*] Perish, base prince, ignoble Duke of York!
Glou. Now will it best avail your Majesty
To cross the seas and to be crown'd in France.
The presence of a king engenders love
Amongst his subjects and his loyal friends,
As it disanimates his enemies.
King. When Gloucester says the word, King Henry goes,
For friendly counsel cuts off many foes.
Glou. Your ships already are in readiness.
Sennet. Flourish. Exeunt. Manet Exeter.
Exe. Ay, we may march in England, or in France,
Not seeing what is likely to ensue.
This late dissension grown betwixt the peers

147. physic: remedy. **150. exhibit:** present. **152. And if:** if.
154. occasions: reasons. **156. of force:** strong, compelling.
158. blood: hereditary rights (as heir to the Earl of Cambridge).
169. reguerdon: reward.
170. girt: gird. **York.** The King restores to Richard not only the earldom of Cambridge (which he inherited from his father) but also the dukedom of York (which he inherited from his father's elder brother, who had been killed at Agincourt).
175. grudge one thought: i.e. harbor one grudging thought.
179. cross the seas. Actually, Henry VI did not go to France until 1430, four years after the events represented in this scene.
185 s.d. Sennet: trumpet notes to signal the arrival or departure of a procession.

Burns under feigned ashes of forg'd love,
And will at last break out into a flame:
As fest'red members rot but by degree,
Till bones and flesh and sinews fall away,
So will this base and envious discord breed.
And now I fear that fatal prophecy
Which in the time of Henry nam'd the Fift
Was in the mouth of every sucking babe,
That Henry born at Monmouth should win all,
And Henry born at Windsor lose all:
Which is so plain that Exeter doth wish
His days may finish ere that hapless time. *Exit.*

Scene II

Enter Pucelle, *disguis'd, with four* Soldiers *with sacks upon their backs.*

Puc. These are the city-gates, the gates of Roan,
Through which our policy must make a breach.
Take heed, be wary how you place your words,
Talk like the vulgar sort of market men
That come to gather money for their corn.
If we have entrance, as I hope we shall,
And that we find the slothful watch but weak,
I'll by a sign give notice to our friends,
That Charles the Dolphin may encounter them.

[*1.*] *Sol.* Our sacks shall be a mean to sack the city,
And we be lords and rulers over Roan,
Therefore we'll knock. *Knock.*

Watch. [*Within.*] *Qui là?*

Puc. *Paysans, la pauvre gens de France,*
Poor market folks that come to sell their corn.

Watch. Enter, go in, the market bell is rung.

Puc. Now, Roan, I'll shake thy bulwarks to the ground. *Exeunt* [*to the town*].

Enter Charles, Bastard, Alanson, [Reignier, *and forces*].

Char. Saint Denis bless this happy stratagem!
And once again we'll sleep secure in Roan.

Bast. Here ent'red Pucelle and her practisants.
Now she is there, how will she specify
Here is the best and safest passage in?

Reig. By thrusting out a torch from yonder tower,
Which once discern'd, shows that her meaning is,
No way to that, for weakness, which she ent'red.

Enter Pucelle *on the top, thrusting out a torch burning.*

Puc. Behold, this is the happy wedding torch
That joineth Roan unto her countrymen,
But burning fatal to the Talbonites! [*Exit.*]

Bast. See, noble Charles, the beacon of our friend,
The burning torch in yonder turret stands.

Char. Now shine it like a comet of revenge,
A prophet to the fall of all our foes!

Reig. Defer no time, delays have dangerous ends,
Enter and cry "The Dolphin!" presently,
And then do execution on the watch.
Alarum. [*Exeunt.*]

An alarum. [*Enter*] Talbot *in an excursion.*

Tal. France, thou shalt rue this treason with thy tears,
If Talbot but survive thy treachery.
Pucelle, that witch, that damned sorceress,
Hath wrought this hellish mischief unawares,
That hardly we escap'd the pride of France. *Exit.*

An alarum. Excursions. Bedford *brought in sick in a chair. Enter* Talbot *and* Burgundy *without; within,* Pucelle, Charles, Bastard, [Alanson,] *and* Reignier, *on the walls.*

Puc. Good morrow, gallants, want ye corn for bread?
I think the Duke of Burgundy will fast
Before he'll buy again at such a rate.
'Twas full of darnel; do you like the taste?

Bur. Scoff on, vile fiend and shameless courtezan!
I trust ere long to choke thee with thine own,
And make thee curse the harvest of that corn.

Char. Your Grace may starve, perhaps, before that time.

Bed. O, let no words, but deeds, revenge this treason!

Puc. What will you do, good greybeard? Break a lance,
And run a-tilt at Death within a chair?

Tal. Foul fiend of France, and hag of all despite,
Encompass'd with thy lustful paramours!
Becomes it thee to taunt his valiant age,
And twit with cowardice a man half dead?
Damsel, I'll have a bout with you again,
Or else let Talbot perish with this shame.

Puc. Are ye so hot, sir? Yet, Pucelle, hold thy peace,
If Talbot do but thunder, rain will follow.
They [*the English*] *whisper together in council.*
God speed the parliament! Who shall be the speaker?

Tal. Dare ye come forth and meet us in the field?

Puc. Belike your lordship takes us then for fools,
To try if that our own be ours or no.

Tal. I speak not to that railing Hecate,
But unto thee, Alanson, and the rest.
Will ye, like soldiers, come and fight it out?

189. **forg'd:** false.
194. **fatal prophecy.** According to Hall (Bullough, III, 42–43), when Henry V was informed of the birth of his son at Windsor, "whether he fantasied some old blind prophesy, or had some foreknowledge, or els judged of his sonnes fortune, he sayd to the lord Fitzheugh his trusty Chamberlein these words. 'My lorde, I Henry borne at Monmoth shall small tyme reigne & much get, & Henry borne at Wyndsore shall long reigne and al lese, but as God will so be it.'"

III.ii. Location: France. Before Rouen. (The story of the capture of Rouen, as represented in this scene, is fictitious. The city was not relinquished by the English until 1449.) 2. **policy:** trickery.
5. **corn:** grain. 7. **that:** if. 10. **mean:** means.
13–14. **Qui . . . France:** "Who's there?" "Peasants, poor French folk." 20. **practisants:** fellow conspirators.
25. **to:** i.e. is comparable to.

31. **shine it:** may it shine. 34. **presently:** immediately.
35 s.d. **excursion:** sally, sortie. 39. **unawares:** unexpectedly.
40. **pride:** i.e. princes. 44. **darnel:** weeds.
46. **thine own:** i.e. your own bread.
50. **greybeard.** Actually, John, Duke of Bedford, did not die until 1435 (at the age of forty-five), some four years after he had presided over the execution of Joan of Arc.
51. **run . . . chair:** joust with Death from your invalid's chair.
52. **of all despite:** most despicable.
64. **Hecate:** goddess of witchcraft.

Alan. Signior, no.
Tal. Signior, hang! Base muleters of France!
Like peasant footboys do they keep the walls,
And dare not take up arms like gentlemen.
Puc. Away, captains, let's get us from the walls,
For Talbot means no goodness by his looks.
God buy, my lord, we came but to tell you
That we are here. *Exeunt from the walls.*
Tal. And there will we be too, ere it be long,
Or else reproach be Talbot's greatest fame!
Vow, Burgundy, by honor of thy house,
Prick'd on by public wrongs sustain'd in France,
Either to get the town again, or die:
And I, as sure as English Henry lives
And as his father here was conqueror,
As sure as in this late-betrayed town
Great Cordelion's heart was buried,
So sure I swear to get the town, or die.
Bur. My vows are equal partners with thy vows.
Tal. But ere we go, regard this dying prince,
The valiant Duke of Bedford. Come, my lord,
We will bestow you in some better place,
Fitter for sickness and for crazy age.
Bed. Lord Talbot, do not so dishonor me:
Here will I sit before the walls of Roan
And will be partner of your weal or woe.
Bur. Courageous Bedford, let us now persuade you.
Bed. Not to be gone from hence; for once I read
That stout Pendragon in his litter sick
Came to the field and vanquished his foes.
Methinks I should revive the soldiers' hearts,
Because I ever found them as myself.
Tal. Undaunted spirit in a dying breast!
Then be it so. Heavens keep old Bedford safe!
And now no more ado, brave Burgundy,
But gather we our forces out of hand,
And set upon our boasting enemy.
Exit [with Burgundy and forces into the town].

An alarum. Excursions. Enter SIR JOHN FALSTAFF *and a* CAPTAIN.

Capt. Whither away, Sir John Falstaff, in such haste?
Fal. Whither away? to save myself by flight.
We are like to have the overthrow again.
Capt. What? will you fly, and leave Lord Talbot?
Fal. Ay,
All the Talbots in the world, to save my life. *Exit.*
Capt. Cowardly knight, ill fortune follow thee!
Exit [into the town].

Retreat. Excursions. PUCELLE, ALANSON, *and* CHARLES *[enter from the town and] fly.*

Bed. Now, quiet soul, depart when heaven please,
For I have seen our enemies' overthrow.
What is the trust or strength of foolish man?
They that of late were daring with their scoffs
Are glad and fain by flight to save themselves.
Bedford dies, and is carried in by two in his chair.

An alarum. Enter TALBOT, BURGUNDY, *and the rest.*

Tal. Lost, and recovered in a day again!
This is a double honor, Burgundy;
Yet heavens have glory for this victory!
Bur. Warlike and martial Talbot, Burgundy
Enshrines thee in his heart, and there erects
Thy noble deeds as valor's monuments.
Tal. Thanks, gentle Duke. But where is Pucelle now?
I think her old familiar is asleep.
Now where's the Bastard's braves, and Charles his glikes?
What, all amort? Roan hangs her head for grief
That such a valiant company are fled.
Now will we take some order in the town,
Placing therein some expert officers,
And then depart to Paris to the King,
For there young Henry with his nobles lie.
Bur. What wills Lord Talbot pleaseth Burgundy.
Tal. But yet before we go, let's not forget
The noble Duke of Bedford late deceas'd,
But see his exequies fulfill'd in Roan.
A braver soldier never couched lance,
A gentler heart did never sway in court;
But kings and mightiest potentates must die,
For that's the end of human misery. *Exeunt.*

SCENE III

Enter CHARLES, BASTARD, ALANSON, PUCELLE, *[and forces].*

Puc. Dismay not, princes, at this accident,
Nor grieve that Roan is so recovered:
Care is no cure, but rather corrosive,
For things that are not to be remedied.
Let frantic Talbot triumph for a while,
And like a peacock sweep along his tail;
We'll pull his plumes and take away his train,
If Dolphin and the rest will be but rul'd.
Char. We have been guided by thee hitherto,
And of thy cunning had no diffidence;
One sudden foil shall never breed distrust.
Bast. Search out thy wit for secret policies,
And we will make thee famous through the world.
Alan. We'll set thy statue in some holy place,
And have thee reverenc'd like a blessed saint.

68. muleters: muleteers, mule drivers.
73. God buy: God be with you (good-by).
81. father . . . conqueror. Henry V had captured Rouen, after a long siege, in 1419.
83. Cordelion's heart. Holinshed records that Richard I, who died in 1199, requested that his heart be buried in Rouen as a token of his affection for that city. On his sobriquet *Coeur-de-Lion* see the note to *King John*, I.i.54. **89. crazy:** broken, decrepit.
95. Pendragon: the legendary Uther Pendragon, father of King Arthur. **102. out of hand:** immediately.

114. fain: eager.
121. gentle: noble. **122. familiar:** attendant demon.
123. braves: boasts. **glikes:** gleeks, scoffs.
124. amort: downcast, prostrated. **133. exequies:** funeral rites.
134. couched: lowered to the position of attack.

III.iii. Location: Plains near Rouen.
1. Dismay: lose courage.
10. diffidence: distrust, suspicion. **11. foil:** repulse.
12. policies: stratagems, tricks.

Employ thee then, sweet virgin, for our good.
Puc. Then thus it must be, this doth Joan devise:
By fair persuasions, mix'd with sug'red words,
We will entice the Duke of Burgundy
To leave the Talbot and to follow us.
Char. Ay, marry, sweeting, if we could do that,
France were no place for Henry's warriors,
Nor should that nation boast it so with us,
But be extirped from our provinces.
Alan. For ever should they be expuls'd from France,
And not have title of an earldom here.
Puc. Your honors shall perceive how I will work
To bring this matter to the wished end.
Drum sounds afar off.
Hark, by the sound of drum you may perceive
Their powers are marching unto Paris-ward.
Here sound an English march.
There goes the Talbot, with his colors spread,
And all the troops of English after him.
French march.
Now in the rearward comes the Duke and his.
Fortune in favor makes him lag behind.
Summon a parley, we will talk with him.
Trumpets sound a parley.

[*Enter the* Duke of Burgundy *and forces.*]

Char. A parley with the Duke of Burgundy!
Bur. Who craves a parley with the Burgundy?
Puc. The princely Charles of France, thy countryman.
Bur. What say'st thou, Charles? for I am marching hence.
Char. Speak, Pucelle, and enchant him with thy words.
Puc. Brave Burgundy, undoubted hope of France,
Stay, let thy humble handmaid speak to thee.
Bur. Speak on, but be not over-tedious.
Puc. Look on thy country, look on fertile France,
And see the cities and the towns defac'd
By wasting ruin of the cruel foe.
As looks the mother on her lowly babe
When death doth close his tender-dying eyes,
See, see the pining malady of France!
Behold the wounds, the most unnatural wounds,
Which thou thyself hast given her woeful breast.
O, turn the edged sword another way,
Strike those that hurt, and hurt not those that help.
One drop of blood drawn from thy country's bosom
Should grieve thee more than streams of foreign gore.
Return thee therefore with a flood of tears,
And wash away thy country's stained spots.
Bur. Either she hath bewitch'd me with her words,
Or nature makes me suddenly relent.
Puc. Besides, all French and France exclaims on thee,
Doubting thy birth and lawful progeny.
Who join'st thou with, but with a lordly nation
That will not trust thee but for profit's sake?
When Talbot hath set footing once in France
And fashion'd thee that instrument of ill,
Who then but English Henry will be lord,
And thou be thrust out like a fugitive?
Call we to mind, and mark but this for proof:
Was not the Duke of Orleance thy foe?
And was he not in England prisoner?
But when they heard he was thine enemy,
They set him free without his ransom paid,
In spite of Burgundy and all his friends.
See then, thou fight'st against thy countrymen
And join'st with them will be thy slaughter-men.
Come, come, return; return, thou wandering lord!
Charles and the rest will take thee in their arms.
Bur. [*Aside.*] I am vanquished. These haughty words of hers
Have batt'red me like roaring cannon-shot,
And made me almost yield upon my knees.—
Forgive me, country, and sweet countrymen,
And, lords, accept this hearty kind embrace.
My forces and my power of men are yours.
So farewell, Talbot, I'll no longer trust thee.
Puc. [*Aside.*] Done like a Frenchman—turn and turn again!
Char. Welcome, brave Duke, thy friendship makes us fresh.
Bast. And doth beget new courage in our breasts.
Alan. Pucelle hath bravely play'd her part in this,
And doth deserve a coronet of gold.
Char. Now let us on, my lords, and join our powers,
And seek how we may prejudice the foe. *Exeunt.*

Scene IV

Enter the King, Gloucester, Winchester, [*Richard Plantagenet, now* Duke of] York, Suffolk, Somerset, Warwick, Exeter, [Vernon, Basset, *and others*]. *To them, with his Soldiers,* Talbot.

Tal. My gracious prince, and honorable peers,
Hearing of your arrival in this realm,
I have a while given truce unto my wars,
To do my duty to my sovereign;
In sign whereof, this arm, that hath reclaim'd
To your obedience fifty fortresses,
Twelve cities, and seven walled towns of strength,
Beside five hundred prisoners of esteem,
Lets fall his sword before your Highness' feet,
And with submissive loyalty of heart

19–20. We . . . us. Actually, the Duke of Burgundy did not desert his English allies until 1435, four years after the death of Joan of Arc.
24. extirped: rooted out. **34. favor:** i.e. to us (the French).
35. Summon a parley: sound a trumpet to request negotiations.
57. country's stained spots: stained country's spots.
60. exclaims on: denounces. **61. progeny:** descent.

67. fugitive: renegade.
69. Was . . . foe. Actually, Charles, Duke of Orleans, who had been captured at Agincourt in 1415, was not released until 1440, five years after the Duke of Burgundy had shifted his allegiance to the French.
75. them: them who.
85. Done . . . again. Perhaps an allusion to the conversion, in 1593, of Henry of Navarre to Catholicism after he had long been aided by the English as a Protestant claimant to the throne of France.
91. prejudice: hurt.

III.iv. Location: Paris. The palace.
4. duty: homage. **8. esteem:** i.e. exalted rank.

Ascribes the glory of his conquest got
First to my God and next unto your Grace. [*Kneels.*]
King. Is this the Lord Talbot, uncle Gloucester,
That hath so long been resident in France?
Glou. Yes, if it please your Majesty, my liege.
King. Welcome, brave captain and victorious lord!
When I was young (as yet I am not old),
I do remember how my father said
A stouter champion never handled sword.
Long since we were resolved of your truth,
Your faithful service, and your toil in war;
Yet never have you tasted our reward,
Or been reguerdon'd with so much as thanks,
Because till now we never saw your face.
Therefore stand up, and for these good deserts
We here create you Earl of Shrewsbury,
And in our coronation take your place.
Sennet. Flourish. Exeunt. Manent Vernon and Basset.
Ver. Now, sir, to you, that were so hot at sea,
Disgracing of these colors that I wear
In honor of my noble Lord of York,
Dar'st thou maintain the former words thou spak'st?
Bas. Yes, sir, as well as you dare patronage
The envious barking of your saucy tongue
Against my lord the Duke of Somerset.
Ver. Sirrah, thy lord I honor as he is.
Bas. Why, what is he? as good a man as York.
Ver. Hark ye; not so; in witness, take ye that.
Strikes him.
Bas. Villain, thou knowest the law of arms is such
That whoso draws a sword, 'tis present death,
Or else this blow should broach thy dearest blood.
But I'll unto his Majesty, and crave
I may have liberty to venge this wrong,
When thou shalt see I'll meet thee to thy cost.
Ver. Well, miscreant, I'll be there as soon as you,
And after meet you, sooner than you would.
Exeunt.

ACT IV, SCENE I

Enter KING, GLOUCESTER, WINCHESTER, YORK, SUFFOLK, SOMERSET, WARWICK, TALBOT, *and* GOVERNOR [OF PARIS,] EXETER, [*and others*].

Glou. Lord Bishop, set the crown upon his head.
Win. God save King Henry, of that name the sixt!
Glou. Now, Governor of Paris, take your oath:
[*Governor kneels.*]
That you elect no other king but him;
Esteem none friends but such as are his friends,
And none your foes but such as shall pretend
Malicious practices against his state.
This shall ye do, so help you righteous God!
[*Exeunt Governor and Train.*]

Enter FALSTAFF.

Fal. My gracious sovereign, as I rode from Callice,
To haste unto your coronation,
A letter was deliver'd to my hands,
Writ to your Grace from th' Duke of Burgundy.
[*Presents it.*]
Tal. Shame to the Duke of Burgundy and thee!
I vow'd, base knight, when I did meet thee next,
To tear the Garter from thy craven's leg,
[*Plucking it off.*]
Which I have done, because (unworthily)
Thou wast installed in that high degree.
Pardon me, princely Henry, and the rest.
This dastard, at the battle of Poictiers,
When (but in all) I was six thousand strong
And that the French were almost ten to one,
Before we met, or that a stroke was given,
Like to a trusty squire did run away;
In which assault we lost twelve hundred men;
Myself and divers gentlemen beside
Were there surpris'd and taken prisoners.
Then judge, great lords, if I have done amiss;
Or whether that such cowards ought to wear
This ornament of knighthood, yea or no?
Glou. To say the truth, this fact was infamous
And ill beseeming any common man,
Much more a knight, a captain, and a leader.
Tal. When first this order was ordain'd, my lords,
Knights of the Garter were of noble birth,
Valiant and virtuous, full of haughty courage,
Such as were grown to credit by the wars;
Not fearing death, nor shrinking for distress,
But always resolute in most extremes.
He then, that is not furnish'd in this sort,
Doth but usurp the sacred name of knight,
Profaning this most honorable order,
And should (if I were worthy to be judge)
Be quite degraded, like a hedge-born swain
That doth presume to boast of gentle blood.
King. Stain to thy countrymen, thou hear'st thy doom!

15. liege: sovereign.
18–19. I . . . sword. Historically an impossibility, since Henry V died when his son was nine months old. **20. resolved:** convinced.
26–27. We . . . place. Actually, Talbot did not receive his earldom until 1442, eleven years after Henry VI's coronation.
28–31. Now . . . spak'st. The circumstances of this quarrel are more fully explained at IV.i.89–97. **32. patronage:** uphold, defend.
39. draws a sword: i.e. in the king's court, which was a privileged place. **present:** immediate.
40. broach . . . blood: draw your life blood.

IV.i. Location: Paris. The palace. (Despite the Folio act break, this scene seems to be continuous with III.iv.)
1. set . . . head. This scene, though dramatically effective, is historically grotesque. When Henry VI was crowned at Paris in 1431, Talbot, who had been captured at Patay, was still a prisoner of the French, Exeter was dead, and Gloucester was in England.

4. elect: accept, acknowledge. **6. pretend:** intend.
13–47. Shame . . . death. Hall's account of this episode (Bullough, III, 59–60) differs in significant details: "From this battaill [of Patay], departed without any stroke striken, sir John Fastolffe, the same yere for his valiauntnes elected into the ordre of the Garter. For whiche cause the Duke of Bedford, in a great anger, toke from hym the Image of saienct George, and his Garter, but afterward, by meane of frendes, and apparant causes of good excuse by hym alledged, he was restored to the order again, against the mynd of the lorde Talbot."
15. Garter: i.e. the badge of the Order of the Garter, a blue velvet ribbon worn below the left knee.
19. dastard: coward. **Poictiers.** Many editors emend to *Patay*.
30. fact: deed. **35. haughty courage:** lofty spirit.
36. credit: fame, estimation.
38. most extremes: greatest extremities.
39. furnish'd . . . sort: thus endowed.
43. degraded: reduced in rank. **hedge-born swain:** base-born rustic.
45. doom: judgment, sentence.

Be packing therefore, thou that wast a knight;
Henceforth we banish thee, on pain of death.
[*Exit Falstaff.*]
And now, Lord Protector, view the letter
Sent from our uncle Duke of Burgundy.
Glou. What means his Grace, that he hath chang'd his style?
No more but plain and bluntly "To the King"?
Hath he forgot he is his sovereign?
Or doth this churlish superscription
Pretend some alteration in good will?
What's here? [*Reads.*] "I have, upon especial cause,
Mov'd with compassion of my country's wrack,
Together with the pitiful complaints
Of such as your oppression feeds upon,
Forsaken your pernicious faction
And join'd with Charles, the rightful King of France."
O monstrous treachery! can this be so?
That in alliance, amity, and oaths,
There should be found such false dissembling guile?
King. What? doth my uncle Burgundy revolt?
Glou. He doth, my lord, and is become your foe.
King. Is that the worst this letter doth contain?
Glou. It is the worst, and all, my lord, he writes.
King. Why then Lord Talbot there shall talk with him,
And give him chastisement for this abuse.
How say you, my lord? are you not content?
Tal. Content, my liege? Yes. But that I am prevented,
I should have begg'd I might have been employ'd.
King. Then gather strength and march unto him straight.
Let him perceive how ill we brook his treason,
And what offense it is to flout his friends.
Tal. I go, my lord, in heart desiring still
You may behold confusion of your foes. [*Exit.*]

Enter VERNON *and* BASSET.

Ver. Grant me the combat, gracious sovereign.
Bas. And me, my lord, grant me the combat too.
York. This is my servant, hear him, noble prince.
Som. And this is mine, sweet Henry, favor him.
King. Be patient, lords, and give them leave to speak.
Say, gentlemen, what makes you thus exclaim?
And wherefore crave you combat? or with whom?
Ver. With him, my lord, for he hath done me wrong.
Bas. And I with him, for he hath done me wrong.
King. What is that wrong whereof you both complain?
First let me know, and then I'll answer you.
Bas. Crossing the sea from England into France,
This fellow here, with envious carping tongue,
Upbraided me about the rose I wear,
Saying the sanguine color of the leaves
Did represent my master's blushing cheeks,
When stubbornly he did repugn the truth
About a certain question in the law
Argu'd betwixt the Duke of York and him;
With other vile and ignominious terms:
In confutation of which rude reproach,
And in defense of my lord's worthiness,
I crave the benefit of law of arms.
Ver. And that is my petition, noble lord.
For though he seem with forged quaint conceit
To set a gloss upon his bold intent,
Yet know, my lord, I was provok'd by him,
And he first took exceptions at this badge,
Pronouncing that the paleness of this flower
Bewray'd the faintness of my master's heart.
York. Will not this malice, Somerset, be left?
Som. Your private grudge, my Lord of York, will out,
Though ne'er so cunningly you smother it.
King. Good Lord, what madness rules in brainsick men,
When for so slight and frivolous a cause
Such factious emulations shall arise!
Good cousins both, of York and Somerset,
Quiet yourselves, I pray, and be at peace.
York. Let this dissension first be tried by fight,
And then your Highness shall command a peace.
Som. The quarrel toucheth none but us alone,
Betwixt ourselves let us decide it then.
York. There is my pledge, accept it, Somerset.
Ver. Nay, let it rest where it began at first.
Bas. Confirm it so, mine honorable lord.
Glou. Confirm it so? Confounded be your strife,
And perish ye, with your audacious prate!
Presumptuous vassals, are you not asham'd
With this immodest clamorous outrage
To trouble and disturb the King and us?
And you, my lords, methinks you do not well
To bear with their perverse objections;
Much less to take occasion from their mouths
To raise a mutiny betwixt yourselves.
Let me persuade you take a better course.
Exe. It grieves his Highness. Good my lords, be friends.
King. Come hither, you that would be combatants:
Henceforth I charge you, as you love our favor,
Quite to forget this quarrel, and the cause.
And you, my lords: remember where we are—

49. uncle. The houses of Lancaster and Burgundy were allied through the marriage (1423) of John, Duke of Bedford (Henry VI's uncle), and Anne of Burgundy (Duke Philip's sister).
50. style: form of address.
53. churlish superscription: insolent form of address (on the outside of the letter). **54. Pretend:** indicate.
56. wrack: destruction. **69. abuse:** deception.
71. prevented: forestalled. **76. still:** always.
78. combat: i.e. permission to fight.

90. envious: malicious. **91. rose:** i.e. the red rose of Lancaster.
92. sanguine: blood-red. **leaves:** petals. **94. repugn:** reject.
100. law of arms: right to defend one's honor in personal combat.
102. forged quaint conceit: false ingenious phrases.
103. gloss: good appearance.
106. flower: i.e. the white rose of York. **107. Bewray'd:** showed.
111. brainsick: foolish.
113. factious emulations: partisan dissensions.
114. cousins: kinsmen.
120. pledge: i.e. the glove or gauntlet that York flings down as a gage. **123. Confounded:** destroyed.
126. immodest: immoderate. **129. objections:** accusations.

In France, amongst a fickle, wavering nation.
If they perceive dissension in our looks,
And that within ourselves we disagree,
How will their grudging stomachs be provok'd
To willful disobedience, and rebel!
Beside, what infamy will there arise,
When foreign princes shall be certified
That for a toy, a thing of no regard,
King Henry's peers and chief nobility
Destroy'd themselves, and lost the realm of France!
O, think upon the conquest of my father,
My tender years, and let us not forgo
That for a trifle that was bought with blood!
Let me be umpeer in this doubtful strife.
I see no reason, if I wear this rose,
[Putting on a red rose.]
That any one should therefore be suspicious
I more incline to Somerset than York:
Both are my kinsmen, and I love them both.
As well they may upbraid me with my crown,
Because, forsooth, the King of Scots is crown'd.
But your discretions better can persuade
Than I am able to instruct or teach;
And therefore, as we hither came in peace,
So let us still continue peace, and love.
Cousin of York, we institute your Grace
To be our regent in these parts of France;
And, good my Lord of Somerset, unite
Your troops of horsemen with his bands of foot,
And like true subjects, sons of your progenitors,
Go cheerfully together and digest
Your angry choler on your enemies.
Ourself, my Lord Protector, and the rest,
After some respite, will return to Callice;
From thence to England, where I hope ere long
To be presented, by your victories,
With Charles, Alanson, and that traitorous rout.
Flourish. Exeunt. Manent York, *Warwick, Exeter, Vernon.*

War. My Lord of York, I promise you, the King
Prettily, methought, did play the orator.
York. And so he did, but yet I like it not,
In that he wears the badge of Somerset.
War. Tush, that was but his fancy, blame him not.
I dare presume, sweet prince, he thought no harm.
York. And if I [wist] he did—but let it rest,
Other affairs must now be managed.
Exeunt. Manet Exeter.

Exe. Well didst thou, Richard, to suppress thy voice;
For had the passions of thy heart burst out,
I fear we should have seen decipher'd there
More rancorous spite, more furious raging broils,
Than yet can be imagin'd or suppos'd.
But howsoe'er, no simple man that sees
This jarring discord of nobility,

141. **grudging stomachs**: unruly tempers.
144. **certified**: informed. 145. **toy**: trifle.
150. **That . . . that**: for a trifle that which. 151. **umpeer**: umpire.
162–63. **Cousin . . . France.** Actually, John, Duke of Bedford, was regent at the time. 167. **digest**: dissipate.
170. **respite**: rest. 180. **And . . . wist**: if I knew.
184. **decipher'd**: displayed.

This shouldering of each other in the court,
This factious bandying of their favorites,
But that it doth presage some ill event.
'Tis much, when sceptres are in children's hands;
But more, when envy breeds unkind division:
There comes the ruin, there begins confusion. *Exit.*

[Scene II]

Enter Talbot *with Trump and Drum before Burdeaux.*

Tal. Go to the gates of Burdeaux, trumpeter,
Summon their general unto the wall.

[Trumpet] sounds. Enter General *[and others] aloft.*

English John Talbot, captains, [calls] you forth,
Servant in arms to Harry King of England,
And thus he would: Open your city-gates,
Be humble to us, call my sovereign yours,
And do him homage as obedient subjects,
And I'll withdraw me and my bloody power.
But if you frown upon this proffer'd peace,
You tempt the fury of my three attendants,
Lean famine, quartering steel, and climbing fire,
Who in a moment even with the earth
Shall lay your stately and air-braving towers,
If you forsake the offer of their love.
[Gen.] Thou ominous and fearful owl of death,
Our nation's terror and their bloody scourge!
The period of thy tyranny approacheth.
On us thou canst not enter but by death;
For I protest we are well fortified,
And strong enough to issue out and fight.
If thou retire, the Dolphin, well appointed,
Stands with the snares of war to tangle thee.
On either hand thee there are squadrons pitch'd,
To wall thee from the liberty of flight;
And no way canst thou turn thee for redress,
But death doth front thee with apparent spoil,
And pale destruction meets thee in the face.
Ten thousand French have ta'en the sacrament
To rive their dangerous artillery
Upon no Christian soul but English Talbot.
Lo, there thou stand'st, a breathing valiant man,
Of an invincible unconquer'd spirit!
This is the latest glory of thy praise
That I thy enemy due thee withal;
For ere the glass, that now begins to run,
Finish the process of his sandy hour,
These eyes, that see thee now well colored,

190. **bandying**: contending. **favorites**: followers.
191. **event**: outcome. 193. **envy**: malice. **unkind**: unnatural.

IV.ii. Location: France. Before Bordeaux.
o.s.d. **Trump**: trumpeter. **Burdeaux**: Bordeaux. Although in this act Talbot is shown dying in a vain attempt to take Bordeaux, he actually overran that city, as well as the whole Bordelais, before he fell at Castillon in 1453—twenty-two years after the coronation of Henry VI that is represented in the previous scene.
11. **quartering**: butchering.
13. **air-braving**: heaven-defying, i.e. lofty. 17. **period**: end.
21. **appointed**: equipped.
23. **either hand thee**: both sides of you.
26. **front**: confront. **apparent spoil**: obvious destruction.
29. **rive**: cause to burst, discharge. 34. **due**: endue.
37. **well colored**: i.e. in health.

Shall see thee withered, bloody, pale, and dead.
Drum afar off.
Hark, hark, the Dolphin's drum, a warning bell,
Sings heavy music to thy timorous soul,
And mine shall ring thy dire departure out.
Exit [with others above].

Tal. He fables not, I hear the enemy.
Out, some light horsemen, and peruse their wings.
O negligent and heedless discipline!
How are we park'd and bounded in a pale,
A little herd of England's timorous deer,
Maz'd with a yelping kennel of French curs!
If we be English deer, be then in blood,
Not rascal-like, to fall down with a pinch,
But rather, moody-mad; and, desperate stags,
Turn on the bloody hounds with heads of steel,
And make the cowards stand aloof at bay.
Sell every man his life as dear as mine,
And they shall find dear deer of us, my friends.
God and Saint George, Talbot and England's right,
Prosper our colors in this dangerous fight! *[Exeunt.]*

[SCENE III]

Enter a MESSENGER *that meets York. Enter* YORK *with Trumpet and many Soldiers.*

York. Are not the speedy scouts return'd again
That dogg'd the mighty army of the Dolphin?

Mess. They are return'd, my lord, and give it out
That he is march'd to Burdeaux with his power
To fight with Talbot. As he march'd along,
By your espials were discovered
Two mightier troops than that the Dolphin led,
Which join'd with him and made their march for Burdeaux. *[Exit.]*

York. A plague upon that villain Somerset,
That thus delays my promised supply
Of horsemen, that were levied for this siege!
Renowned Talbot doth expect my aid,
And I am louted by a traitor villain
And cannot help the noble chevalier.
God comfort him in this necessity!
If he miscarry, farewell wars in France!

Enter another Messenger [SIR WILLIAM LUCY].

[Lucy.] Thou princely leader of our English strength,
Never so needful on the earth of France,
Spur to the rescue of the noble Talbot,
Who now is girdled with a waist of iron
And hemm'd about with grim destruction.
To Burdeaux, warlike Duke! to Burdeaux, York!
Else farewell Talbot, France, and England's honor!

41. departure: i.e. death.
43. peruse their wings: reconnoitre their flanks.
44. discipline: tactics.
45. park'd . . . pale: enclosed and fenced in.
47. Maz'd: dazed. **48. in blood:** in good condition, vigorous.
49. rascal-like: like worthless deer. **pinch:** bite, nip.
50. moody-mad: dangerously incensed.

IV.iii. Location: France. Plains in Gascony.
13. louted: made a fool of, mocked.

York. O God, that Somerset, who in proud heart
Doth stop my cornets, were in Talbot's place!
So should we save a valiant gentleman
By forfeiting a traitor and a coward.
Mad ire and wrathful fury makes me weep,
That thus we die, while remiss traitors sleep.

[Lucy.] O, send some succor to the distress'd lord!

York. He dies, we lose; I break my warlike word;
We mourn, France smiles; we lose, they daily get;
All long of this vile traitor Somerset.

[Lucy.] Then God take mercy on brave Talbot's soul,
And on his son young John, who two hours since
I met in travel toward his warlike father!
This seven years did not Talbot see his son,
And now they meet where both their lives are done.

York. Alas, what joy shall noble Talbot have
To bid his young son welcome to his grave?
Away! vexation almost stops my breath,
That sund'red friends greet in the hour of death.
Lucy, farewell, no more my fortune can,
But curse the cause I cannot aid the man.
Maine, Blois, Poictiers, and Tours, are won away,
Long all of Somerset and his delay.
Exit [with his Soldiers].

[Lucy.] Thus while the vulture of sedition
Feeds in the bosom of such great commanders,
Sleeping neglection doth betray to loss
The conquest of our scarce-cold conqueror,
That ever-living man of memory,
Henry the Fift. Whiles they each other cross,
Lives, honors, lands, and all, hurry to loss.

[SCENE IV]

Enter SOMERSET *with his army, [a* CAPTAIN *of Talbot's with him].*

Som. It is too late, I cannot send them now.
This expedition was by York and Talbot
Too rashly plotted. All our general force
Might with a sally of the very town
Be buckled with. The over-daring Talbot
Hath sullied all his gloss of former honor
By this unheedful, desperate, wild adventure.
York set him on to fight and die in shame,
That, Talbot dead, great York might bear the name.

Capt. Here is Sir William Lucy, who with me
Set from our o'ermatch'd forces forth for aid.

Som. How now, Sir William, whither were you sent?

Lucy. Whither, my lord? from bought and sold Lord Talbot,
Who, ring'd about with bold adversity,

25. stop my cornets: hold back my squadrons of horse.
30. distress'd: in difficulties. **33. long of:** on account of.
41. vexation: anguish. **43. can:** is able to do.
50. scarce-cold conqueror. At the time represented in this scene Henry V had been dead thirty-one years.
51. ever-living . . . memory: man of ever-living memory.

IV.iv. Location: Scene continues.
4. the very town: i.e. only the garrison (without additional military support). **5. buckled with:** successfully resisted.

Cries out for noble York and Somerset
To beat assailing death from his weak [legions];
And whiles the honorable captain there
Drops bloody sweat from his war-wearied limbs,
And, in advantage ling'ring, looks for rescue,
You, his false hopes, the trust of England's honor,
Keep off aloof with worthless emulation.
Let not your private discord keep away
The levied succors that should lend him aid,
While he, renowned noble gentleman,
Yield up his life unto a world of odds.
Orleance the Bastard, Charles, Burgundy,
Alanson, [Reignier], compass him about,
And Talbot perisheth by your default.

Som. York set him on, York should have sent him aid.

Lucy. And York as fast upon your Grace exclaims,
Swearing that you withhold his levied host,
Collected for this expedition.

Som. York lies; he might have sent, and had the horse.
I owe him little duty, and less love,
And take foul scorn to fawn on him by sending.

Lucy. The fraud of England, not the force of France,
Hath now entrapp'd the noble-minded Talbot:
Never to England shall he bear his life,
But dies, betray'd to fortune by your strife.

Som. Come go, I will dispatch the horsemen straight;
Within six hours they will be at his aid.

Lucy. Too late comes rescue, he is ta'en or slain;
For fly he could not, if he would have fled;
And fly would Talbot never, though he might.

Som. If he be dead, brave Talbot, then adieu!

Lucy. His fame lives in the world, his shame in you. *Exeunt.*

[SCENE V]

Enter TALBOT *and his son* [JOHN].

Tal. O young John Talbot, I did send for thee
To tutor thee in stratagems of war,
That Talbot's name might be in thee reviv'd,
When sapless age and weak unable limbs
Should bring thy father to his drooping chair.
But O malignant and ill-boding stars!
Now thou art come unto a feast of death,
A terrible and unavoided danger;
Therefore, dear boy, mount on my swiftest horse,
And I'll direct thee how thou shalt escape
By sudden flight. Come, dally not, be gone.

John. Is my name Talbot? and am I your son?
And shall I fly? O, if you love my mother,
Dishonor not her honorable name
To make a bastard and a slave of me!

19. in advantage ling'ring: trying to maintain such strength as the situation affords (?). **21. worthless emulation:** unworthy rivalry. **35. take foul scorn:** regard it as disgraceful.

IV.v. Location: France. A field of battle near Bordeaux.
8. unavoided: unavoidable.

The world will say, he is not Talbot's blood,
That basely fled when noble Talbot stood.

Tal. Fly, to revenge my death, if I be slain.

John. He that flies so will ne'er return again.

Tal. If we both stay, we both are sure to die.

John. Then let me stay, and, father, do you fly.
Your loss is great, so your regard should be;
My worth unknown, no loss is known in me.
Upon my death the French can little boast;
In yours they will, in you all hopes are lost.
Flight cannot stain the honor you have won,
But mine it will, that no exploit have done.
You fled for vantage, every one will swear;
But if I bow, they'll say it was for fear.
There is no hope that ever I will stay,
If the first hour I shrink and run away.
Here on my knee I beg mortality,
Rather than life preserv'd with infamy.

Tal. Shall all thy mother's hopes lie in one tomb?

John. Ay, rather than I'll shame my mother's womb.

Tal. Upon my blessing I command thee go.

John. To fight I will, but not to fly the foe.

Tal. Part of thy father may be sav'd in thee.

John. No part of him but will be shame in me.

Tal. Thou never hadst renown, nor canst not lose it.

John. Yes, your renowned name. Shall flight abuse it?

Tal. Thy father's charge shall clear thee from that stain.

John. You cannot witness for me, being slain.
If death be so apparent, then both fly.

Tal. And leave my followers here to fight and die?
My age was never tainted with such shame.

John. And shall my youth be guilty of such blame?
No more can I be severed from your side
Than can yourself yourself in twain divide.
Stay, go, do what you will, the like do I;
For live I will not if my father die.

Tal. Then here I take my leave of thee, fair son,
Born to eclipse thy life this afternoon.
Come, side by side, together live and die,
And soul with soul from France to heaven fly. *Exeunt.*

[SCENE VI]

Alarum. Excursions, wherein Talbot's son [JOHN] *is hemm'd about, and* TALBOT *rescues him.*

Tal. Saint George and victory! fight, soldiers, fight!
The Regent hath with Talbot broke his word,
And left us to the rage of France his sword.
Where is John Talbot? Pause, and take thy breath;
I gave thee life, and rescu'd thee from death.

22. regard: i.e. concern for yourself.
28. vantage: military advantage. **32. mortality:** death.
41. abuse: dishonor. **46. age:** lifetime.

IV.vi. Location: Scene continues.
2. Regent: i.e. the Duke of York (see IV.i.162–63).

John. O, twice my father, twice am I thy son!
The life thou gav'st me first was lost and done,
Till with thy warlike sword, despite of fate,
To my determin'd time thou gav'st new date.

Tal. When from the Dolphin's crest thy sword struck fire,
It warm'd thy father's heart with proud desire
Of bold-fac'd victory. Then leaden age,
Quicken'd with youthful spleen and warlike rage,
Beat down Alanson, Orleance, Burgundy,
And from the pride of Gallia rescued thee.
The ireful Bastard Orleance, that drew blood
From thee, my boy, and had the maidenhood
Of thy first fight, I soon encountered,
And interchanging blows I quickly shed
Some of his bastard blood, and in disgrace
Bespoke him thus: "Contaminated, base,
And misbegotten blood I spill of thine,
Mean and right poor, for that pure blood of mine
Which thou didst force from Talbot, my brave boy."
Here, purposing the Bastard to destroy,
Came in strong rescue. Speak, thy father's care:
Art thou not weary, John? How dost thou fare?
Wilt thou yet leave the battle, boy, and fly,
Now thou art seal'd the son of chivalry?
Fly, to revenge my death when I am dead;
The help of one stands me in little stead.
O, too much folly is it, well I wot,
To hazard all our lives in one small boat!
If I to-day die not with Frenchmen's rage,
To-morrow I shall die with mickle age.
By me they nothing gain and if I stay,
'Tis but the short'ning of my life one day.
In thee thy mother dies, our household's name,
My death's revenge, thy youth, and England's fame:
All these, and more, we hazard by thy stay;
All these are sav'd if thou wilt fly away.

John. The sword of Orleance hath not made me smart;
These words of yours draw life-blood from my heart.
On that advantage, bought with such a shame,
To save a paltry life and slay bright fame,
Before young Talbot from old Talbot fly
The coward horse that bears me fall and die!
And like me to the peasant boys of France,
To be shame's scorn and subject of mischance!
Surely, by all the glory you have won,
And if I fly, I am not Talbot's son.
Then talk no more of flight, it is no boot;
If son to Talbot, die at Talbot's foot.

Tal. Then follow thou thy desp'rate sire of Crete,
Thou Icarus; thy life to me is sweet.
If thou wilt fight, fight by thy father's side,
And commendable prov'd, let's die in pride. *Exeunt.*

9. **determin'd:** having a definite limit. **date:** limit.
13. **youthful spleen:** the eagerness of youth. 15. **Gallia:** France.
25. **purposing:** as I purposed. 29. **seal'd:** confirmed, certified.
32. **wot:** know. 35. **mickle:** great. 48. **like:** liken.
51. **And if:** if. 52. **boot:** advantage, profit.
54–55. **sire . . . Icarus.** Alluding to the desperate attempt of Daedalus and his son Icarus to escape from King Minos of Crete by means of wings that they had made. Daedalus got away in safety, but Icarus flew so high that the wax with which the wings were fastened to his shoulders was melted by the sun, and he fell into the sea and was drowned.

[SCENE VII]

Alarum. Excursions. Enter old TALBOT *led* [*by a* SERVANT].

Tal. Where is my other life? mine own is gone.
O, where's young Talbot? where is valiant John?
Triumphant Death, smear'd with captivity,
Young Talbot's valor makes me smile at thee.
When he perceiv'd me shrink and on my knee,
His bloody sword he brandish'd over me,
And like a hungry lion did commence
Rough deeds of rage and stern impatience;
But when my angry guardant stood alone,
Tend'ring my ruin and assail'd of none,
Dizzy-ey'd fury and great rage of heart
Suddenly made him from my side to start
Into the clust'ring battle of the French;
And in that sea of blood my boy did drench
His overmounting spirit; and there died
My Icarus, my blossom, in his pride.

Enter [SOLDIERS] *with* JOHN TALBOT *borne.*

Serv. O my dear lord, lo where your son is borne!

Tal. Thou antic Death, which laugh'st us here to scorn,
Anon, from thy insulting tyranny,
Coupled in bonds of perpetuity,
Two Talbots, winged through the lither sky,
In thy despite shall scape mortality.
O thou whose wounds become hard-favored Death,
Speak to thy father ere thou yield thy breath!
Brave Death by speaking, whether he will or no;
Imagine him a Frenchman, and thy foe.
Poor boy, he smiles, methinks, as who should say,
Had Death been French, then Death had died to-day.
Come, come, and lay him in his father's arms,
My spirit can no longer bear these harms.
Soldiers, adieu! I have what I would have,
Now my old arms are young John Talbot's grave. *Dies.*

Enter CHARLES, ALANSON, BURGUNDY, BASTARD, *and* PUCELLE [*with forces*].

Char. Had York and Somerset brought rescue in,
We should have found a bloody day of this.

Bast. How the young whelp of Talbot's, raging wood,
Did flesh his puny sword in Frenchmen's blood!

Puc. Once I encount'red him, and thus I said:
"Thou maiden youth, be vanquish'd by a maid!"

IV.vii. Location: Scene continues.
3. **smear'd with captivity:** i.e. although (I am) stained by defeat (?).
9. **guardant:** guardian.
10. **Tend'ring my ruin:** anxiously protecting me in my fall.
13. **battle:** army, forces. 14. **drench:** drown.
18. **antic:** i.e. grinning like a clown, as in the pictorial representations of the *danse macabre*. 21. **lither:** yielding.
23. **become . . . Death:** make hideous Death attractive.
25. **Brave:** defy. 35. **wood:** mad.
36. **flesh:** use for the first time in battle.

But with a proud majestical high scorn
He answer'd thus: "Young Talbot was not born
To be the pillage of a giglot wench."
So rushing in the bowels of the French,
He left me proudly, as unworthy fight.
Bur. Doubtless he would have made a noble knight.
See where he lies inhearsed in the arms
Of the most bloody nurser of his harms!
Bast. Hew them to pieces, hack their bones asunder,
Whose life was England's glory, Gallia's wonder.
Char. O no, forbear! for that which we have fled
During the life, let us not wrong it dead.

Enter LUCY [*attended*, HERALD *of the French preceding*].

Lucy. Herald, conduct me to the Dolphin's tent,
To know who hath obtain'd the glory of the day.
Char. On what submissive message art thou sent?
Lucy. Submission, Dolphin? 'tis a mere French word;
We English warriors wot not what it means.
I come to know what prisoners thou hast ta'en,
And to survey the bodies of the dead.
Char. For prisoners ask'st thou? Hell our prison is.
But tell me whom thou seek'st.
Lucy. But where's the great Alcides of the field,
Valiant Lord Talbot, Earl of Shrewsbury,
Created, for his rare success in arms,
Great Earl of Washford, Waterford, and Valence,
Lord Talbot of Goodrig and Urchinfield,
Lord Strange of Blackmere, Lord Verdon of Alton,
Lord Cromwell of Wingfield, Lord Furnival of Sheffield,
The thrice-victorious Lord of Falconbridge,
Knight of the noble Order of Saint George,
Worthy Saint Michael, and the Golden Fleece,
Great marshal to Henry the Sixt
Of all his wars within the realm of France?
Puc. Here's a silly stately style indeed!
The Turk, that two and fifty kingdoms hath,
Writes not so tedious a style as this.
Him that thou magnifi'st with all these titles
Stinking and fly-blown lies here at our feet.
Lucy. Is Talbot slain, the Frenchmen's only scourge,
Your kingdom's terror and black Nemesis?
O, were mine eyeballs into bullets turn'd,
That I in rage might shoot them at your faces!
O, that I could but call these dead to life,
It were enough to fright the realm of France!
Were but his picture left amongst you here,

41. giglot: wanton. **45. inhearsed:** coffined.
46. nurser . . . harms: fosterer of his power to injure (the French).
60. Alcides: Hercules, who was descended from Alcaeus.
61–71. Valiant . . . France. This list of Talbot's titles, once thought to have been copied from the description of his tomb in Rouen in Richard Crompton's *Mansion of Magnanimity* (1599) and therefore to prove that Shakespeare had revised the play long after its original composition, appears also in Roger Cotton's *Armor of Proof* (1596). E. K. Chambers has suggested (*William Shakespeare*, I, 293) that it had perhaps been made long familiar by the tales of English travellers.
63. Washford: Wexford (in Ireland). **72. style:** list of titles.
73. The Turk: the Grand Turk, the sultan.
78. Nemesis: goddess of retributive justice.

It would amaze the proudest of you all.
Give me their bodies, that I may bear them hence
And give them burial as beseems their worth.
Puc. I think this upstart is old Talbot's ghost,
He speaks with such a proud commanding spirit.
For God's sake let him have ['em]; to keep them here,
They would but stink, and putrefy the air.
Char. Go take their bodies hence.
Lucy. I'll bear them hence; but from their ashes shall be rear'd
A phoenix that shall make all France afeard.
Char. So we be rid of them, do with ['em] what thou wilt.
And now to Paris in this conquering vein,
All will be ours, now bloody Talbot's slain. *Exeunt.*

[ACT V,] SCENE [I]

Sennet. Enter KING, GLOUCESTER, *and* EXETER.

King. Have you perus'd the letters from the Pope,
The Emperor, and the Earl of Arminack?
Glou. I have, my lord, and their intent is this:
They humbly sue unto your Excellence
To have a godly peace concluded of
Between the realms of England and of France.
King. How doth your Grace affect their motion?
Glou. Well, my good lord, and as the only means
To stop effusion of our Christian blood,
And stablish quietness on every side.
King. Ay, marry, uncle, for I always thought
It was both impious and unnatural
That such immanity and bloody strife
Should reign among professors of one faith.
Glou. Beside, my lord, the sooner to effect
And surer bind this knot of amity,
The Earl of Arminack, near knit to Charles,
A man of great authority in France,
Proffers his only daughter to your Grace
In marriage, with a large and sumptuous dowry.
King. Marriage, uncle? Alas, my years are young;
And fitter is my study and my books
Than wanton dalliance with a paramour.
Yet call th' embassadors, and as you please,
So let them have their answers every one.

84. amaze: throw into confusion.
93. phoenix: fabulous bird that every five hundred years died upon a funeral pyre of its own construction and then was reborn from its ashes.

V.i. Location: London. The palace.
1–2. Have . . . Arminack. Another anachronism. The events alluded to here—the intervention (1435) of the Emperor Sigismund and the Pope in a futile effort to secure a truce, and the abortive negotiations (1442–43) for a marriage between Henry VI and the daughter of the Duke of Armagnac—occurred long before the death of Talbot (1453).
7. affect their motion: like their proposal. **13. immanity:** ferocity.
20. dowry. According to Hall (Bullough, III, 70–71), Armagnac's offer of a princely dower for his daughter—including not only "silver hilles, and golden mountaines" but also "the whole duchie of Acquitayn or Guyen"—was so attractive that the agents of Henry VI "concluded the mariage, and by proxie affied the young Lady." The match was blocked, however, when Charles VII, in retaliation, seized Armagnac and his daughter.
21. my . . . young. Actually, Henry was twenty-one at the time.

I shall be well content with any choice
Tends to God's glory and my country's weal.

Enter WINCHESTER [*in cardinal's habit*] *and three* AMBASSADORS, [*one of them a* PAPAL LEGATE].

Exe. What, is my Lord of Winchester install'd,
And call'd unto a cardinal's degree?
Then I perceive that will be verified
Henry the Fift did sometime prophesy:
"If once he come to be a cardinal,
He'll make his cap co-equal with the crown."

King. My lords ambassadors, your several suits
Have been consider'd and debated on.
Your purpose is both good and reasonable;
And therefore are we certainly resolv'd
To draw conditions of a friendly peace,
Which by my Lord of Winchester we mean
Shall be transported presently to France.

Glou. [*To the Ambassador from Arminack.*] And for the proffer of my lord your master,
I have inform'd his Highness so at large,
As liking of the lady's virtuous gifts,
Her beauty, and the value of her dower,
He doth intend she shall be England's queen.

King. In argument and proof of which contract,
Bear her this jewel, pledge of my affection.
And so, my Lord Protector, see them guarded
And safely brought to Dover, wherein shipp'd,
Commit them to the fortune of the sea.

Exeunt [*all but Winchester and Legate*].

Win. Stay, my lord legate, you shall first receive
The sum of money which I promised
Should be delivered to his Holiness
For clothing me in these grave ornaments.

Leg. I will attend upon your lordship's leisure.

[*Exit.*]

Win. Now Winchester will not submit, I trow,
Or be inferior to the proudest peer.
Humphrey of Gloucester, thou shalt well perceive
That neither in birth, or for authority,
The Bishop will be overborne by thee.
I'll either make thee stoop and bend thy knee,
Or sack this country with a mutiny. *Exit.*

SCENE [II]

Enter CHARLES, BURGUNDY, ALANSON, BASTARD, REIGNIER, *and* JOAN [DE PUCELLE, *with forces*].

Char. These news, my lords, may cheer our drooping spirits:
'Tis said the stout Parisians do revolt,
And turn again unto the warlike French.

Alan. Then march to Paris, royal Charles of France,
And keep not back your powers in dalliance.

Puc. Peace be amongst them if they turn to us,
Else ruin combat with their palaces!

Enter SCOUT.

Scout. Success unto our valiant general,
And happiness to his accomplices!

Char. What tidings send our scouts? I prithee speak.

Scout. The English army, that divided was
Into two parties, is now conjoin'd in one,
And means to give you battle presently.

Char. Somewhat too sudden, sirs, the warning is,
But we will presently provide for them.

Bur. I trust the ghost of Talbot is not there.
Now he is gone, my lord, you need not fear.

Puc. Of all base passions, fear is most accurs'd.
Command the conquest, Charles, it shall be thine,
Let Henry fret, and all the world repine.

Char. Then on, my lords, and France be fortunate!

Exeunt.

[SCENE III]

Alarum. Excursions. Enter JOAN DE PUCELLE.

Puc. The Regent conquers, and the Frenchmen fly.
Now help, ye charming spells and periapts,
And ye choice spirits that admonish me
And give me signs of future accidents. *Thunder.*
You speedy helpers, that are substitutes
Under the lordly Monarch of the North,
Appear, and aid me in this enterprise.

Enter FIENDS.

This speedy and quick appearance argues proof
Of your accustom'd diligence to me.
Now, ye familiar spirits, that are cull'd
Out of the powerful regions under earth,
Help me this once, that France may get the field.

They walk, and speak not.

O, hold me not with silence over-long!
Where I was wont to feed you with my blood,
I'll lop a member off and give it you
In earnest of a further benefit,
So you do condescend to help me now.

They hang their heads.

No hope to have redress? My body shall
Pay recompense, if you will grant my suit.

They shake their heads.

Cannot my body nor blood-sacrifice
Entreat you to your wonted furtherance?
Then take my soul—my body, soul, and all,
Before that England give the French the foil.

They depart.

27. Tends: which tends. **31. sometime:** once.
40. presently: immediately. **49. shipp'd:** embarked.
62. mutiny: open revolt.

V.ii. Location: France. Plains in Anjou.
5. powers: forces. **dalliance:** idle delay.

7. ruin combat with: let ruin destroy. **9. accomplices:** allies.

V.iii. Location: France. Before Angiers.
2. periapts: amulets. **3. admonish:** warn.
4. accidents: events. **5. substitutes:** agents.
6. Monarch . . . North: i.e. the devil, who, with his attendant demons, was thought to inhabit northern regions. **8. quick:** in living form.
12. get the field: win the battle. **15. member:** limb.
16. earnest: advance payment.
21. wonted furtherance: customary assistance. **23. foil:** defeat.

See, they forsake me! Now the time is come
That France must vail her lofty-plumed crest
And let her head fall into England's lap.
My ancient incantations are too weak,
And hell too strong for me to buckle with:
Now, France, thy glory droopeth to the dust. *Exit.*

Excursions. BURGUNDY *and* YORK *[enter and] fight hand to hand. French fly.* [PUCELLE *is brought in captive.*]

York. Damsel of France, I think I have you fast:
Unchain your spirits now with spelling charms,
And try if they can gain your liberty.
A goodly prize, fit for the devil's grace!
See how the ugly witch doth bend her brows,
As if, with Circe, she would change my shape!

Puc. Chang'd to a worser shape thou canst not be.

York. O, Charles the Dolphin is a proper man,
No shape but his can please your dainty eye.

Puc. A plaguing mischief light on Charles and thee!
And may ye both be suddenly surpris'd
By bloody hands, in sleeping on your beds!

York. Fell banning hag, enchantress, hold thy tongue!

Puc. I prithee give me leave to curse a while.

York. Curse, miscreant, when thou com'st to the stake. *Exeunt.*

Alarum. Enter SUFFOLK *with* MARGARET *in his hand.*

Suf. Be what thou wilt, thou art my prisoner. *Gazes on her.*
O fairest beauty, do not fear nor fly,
For I will touch thee but with reverend hands.
I kiss these fingers for eternal peace,
And lay them gently on thy tender side.
Who art thou? say, that I may honor thee.

Mar. Margaret my name, and daughter to a king,
The King of Naples, whoso'er thou art.

Suf. An earl I am, and Suffolk am I call'd.
Be not offended, nature's miracle,
Thou art allotted to be ta'en by me;
So doth the swan her downy cygnets save,
Keeping them prisoner underneath [her] wings.
Yet, if this servile usage once offend,
Go, and be free again, as Suffolk's friend. *She is going.*
O, stay! [*Aside.*] I have no power to let her pass,
My hand would free her, but my heart says no.
As plays the sun upon the glassy streams,
Twinkling another counterfeited beam,
So seems this gorgeous beauty to mine eyes.
Fain would I woo her, yet I dare not speak:
I'll call for pen and ink, and write my mind.
Fie, De la Pole, disable not thyself.
Hast not a tongue? Is she not here?
Wilt thou be daunted at a woman's sight?
Ay; beauty's princely majesty is such,
'Confounds the tongue and makes the senses rough.

Mar. Say, Earl of Suffolk—if thy name be so—
What ransom must I pay before I pass?
For I perceive I am thy prisoner.

Suf. [*Aside.*] How canst thou tell she will deny thy suit,
Before thou make a trial of her love?

Mar. Why speak'st thou not? What ransom must I pay?

Suf. [*Aside.*] She's beautiful; and therefore to be wooed:
She is a woman; therefore to be won.

Mar. Wilt thou accept of ransom, yea or no?

Suf. [*Aside.*] Fond man, remember that thou hast a wife,
Then how can Margaret be thy paramour?

Mar. I were best to leave him, for he will not hear.

Suf. [*Aside.*] There all is marr'd; there lies a cooling card.

Mar. He talks at randon; sure the man is mad.

Suf. [*Aside.*] And yet a dispensation may be had.

Mar. And yet I would that you would answer me.

Suf. [*Aside.*] I'll win this Lady Margaret. For whom?
Why, for my king. Tush, that's a wooden thing!

Mar. He talks of wood; it is some carpenter.

Suf. [*Aside.*] Yet so my fancy may be satisfied,
And peace established between these realms.
But there remains a scruple in that too;
For though her father be the King of Naples,
Duke of Anjou and Maine, yet is he poor,
And our nobility will scorn the match.

Mar. Hear ye, captain? Are you not at leisure?

Suf. [*Aside.*] It shall be so, disdain they ne'er so much.
Henry is youthful and will quickly yield.—
Madam, I have a secret to reveal.

Mar. [*Aside.*] What though I be enthrall'd, he seems a knight,
And will not any way dishonor me.

Suf. Lady, vouchsafe to listen what I say.

25. vail: lower.
31. spirits: i.e. attendant demons. **spelling charms:** charms that cast a spell, incantations.
35. Circe: enchantress who, according to Homer, enticed her victims into her palace and then transformed them into beasts.
37. proper: handsome. **38. dainty:** fastidious.
40. surpris'd: captured. **42. Fell banning:** fierce cursing.
44 s.d. Suffolk. William de la Pole, fourth Earl and first Duke of Suffolk (1396–1450), served with such distinction in France that after Salisbury's death he was named commander of the English forces; but when Joan of Arc's successes led to his decline, he returned to England (1431), married Salisbury's widow (who was perhaps Geoffrey Chaucer's granddaughter), and emerged as leader of the group that, in opposition to Gloucester, sought peace with France. In 1444 he arranged Henry VI's marriage with Margaret of Anjou, and after escorting her to England became her principal ally in contriving Gloucester's fall. There is no historical foundation for his love affair with Margaret, which Shakespeare makes one of the principal motifs of *2 Henry VI*. **48. for:** in token of.
52. King of Naples. This is the Reignier of earlier scenes; see note to I.ii o.s.d. **55. allotted:** destined. **59. friend:** lover.

63. counterfeited: i.e. reflected. **67. disable:** disparage.
69. a woman's sight: the sight of a woman.
71. 'Confounds: that it confounds. **rough:** dull.
78–79. She's . . . won. A quasi-proverbial expression; cf. *Titus Andronicus*, II.i.82–83; *Richard III*, I.ii.227–28. **81. Fond:** foolish.
84. cooling card: something that cools one's ardor or disappoints one's hopes; a check, deterrent. **85. randon:** random.
86. dispensation: special permission from the Pope.
89. wooden: useless, stupid (referring either to his scheme or to the King). **91. fancy:** love. **93. scruple:** objection.
101. enthrall'd: captured, made prisoner.

Mar. [*Aside.*] Perhaps I shall be rescu'd by the French,
And then I need not crave his courtesy.
Suf. Sweet madam, give me hearing in a cause.
Mar. [*Aside.*] Tush, women have been captivate ere now.
Suf. Lady, wherefore talk you so?
Mar. I cry you mercy, 'tis but *quid* for *quo*.
Suf. Say, gentle Princess, would you not suppose
Your bondage happy, to be made a queen?
Mar. To be a queen in bondage is more vile
Than is a slave in base servility;
For princes should be free.
Suf. And so shall you,
If happy England's royal king be free.
Mar. Why, what concerns his freedom unto me?
Suf. I'll undertake to make thee Henry's queen,
To put a golden sceptre in thy hand,
And set a precious crown upon thy head,
If thou wilt condescend to be my—
Mar. What?
Suf. His love.
Mar. I am unworthy to be Henry's wife.
Suf. No, gentle madam, I unworthy am
To woo so fair a dame to be his wife
And have no portion in the choice myself.
How say you, madam, are ye so content?
Mar. And if my father please, I am content.
Suf. Then call our captains and our colors forth,
And, madam, at your father's castle walls
We'll crave a parley, to confer with him.

Sound [a parley]. Enter REIGNIER *on the walls.*

See, Reignier, see, thy daughter prisoner!
Reig. To whom?
Suf. To me.
Reig. Suffolk, what remedy?
I am a soldier, and unapt to weep,
Or to exclaim on fortune's fickleness.
Suf. Yes, there is remedy enough, my lord.
Consent, and for thy honor give consent,
Thy daughter shall be wedded to my king,
Whom I with pain have wooed and won thereto;
And this her easy-held imprisonment
Hath gain'd thy daughter princely liberty.
Reig. Speaks Suffolk as he thinks?
Suf. Fair Margaret knows
That Suffolk doth not flatter, face, or feign.
Reig. Upon thy princely warrant, I descend
To give thee answer of thy just demand.
[*Exit from the walls.*]
Suf. And here I will expect thy coming.

Trumpets sound. Enter REIGNIER [*below*].

Reig. Welcome, brave Earl, into our territories!
Command in Anjou what your honor pleases.
Suf. Thanks, Reignier, happy for so sweet a child,
Fit to be made companion with a king.
What answer makes your Grace unto my suit?
Reig. Since thou dost deign to woo her little worth
To be the princely bride of such a lord,
Upon condition I may quietly
Enjoy mine own, the country Maine and Anjou,
Free from oppression or the stroke of war,
My daughter shall be Henry's, if he please.
Suf. That is her ransom; I deliver her,
And those two counties I will undertake
Your Grace shall well and quietly enjoy.
Reig. And I again, in Henry's royal name,
As deputy unto that gracious king,
Give thee her hand, for sign of plighted faith.
Suf. Reignier of France, I give thee kingly thanks,
Because this is in traffic of a king.
[*Aside.*] And yet methinks I could be well content
To be mine own attorney in this case.—
I'll over then to England with this news,
And make this marriage to be solemniz'd.
So farewell, Reignier! set this diamond safe
In golden palaces, as it becomes.
Reig. I do embrace thee, as I would embrace
The Christian prince, King Henry, were he here.
Mar. Farewell, my lord! Good wishes, praise, and prayers
Shall Suffolk ever have of Margaret. *She is going.*
Suf. Farewell, sweet madam! But hark you, Margaret,
No princely commendations to my king?
Mar. Such commendations as becomes a maid,
A virgin, and his servant, say to him.
Suf. Words sweetly plac'd and [modestly] directed.
But, madam, I must trouble you again,
No loving token to his Majesty?
Mar. Yes, my good lord, a pure unspotted heart,
Never yet taint with love, I send the King.
Suf. And this withal. *Kiss her.*
Mar. That for thyself; I will not so presume
To send such peevish tokens to a king.
[*Exeunt Reignier and Margaret.*]
Suf. O, wert thou for myself! but, Suffolk, stay,
Thou mayest not wander in that labyrinth,
There Minotaurs and ugly treasons lurk.
Solicit Henry with her wondrous praise;
Bethink thee on her virtues that surmount,
[And] natural graces that extinguish art;
Repeat their semblance often on the seas,
That, when thou com'st to kneel at Henry's feet,
Thou mayest bereave him of his wits with wonder.
Exit.

107. captivate: taken prisoner.
109. cry you mercy: beg your pardon. **quid for quo:** tit for tat, i.e. retaliation for Suffolk's muttering to himself.
111. to be: i.e. if you were to be.
142. face: pretend (i.e. show a false face). **145. expect:** await.
148. for: in the possession of. **158. counties:** domains of a count.
164. in . . . king: in a king's business.
166. mine own attorney: advocate on my own behalf.
170. as it becomes: as befits it. **176. commendations:** greetings.
183. taint: tainted. **186. peevish:** silly.
188. labyrinth: a maze built by Daedalus (see note to IV.vi.54–55) for King Minos of Crete, who confined in it the Minotaur, a monster born of the union of Queen Pasiphaë with a bull.
193. Repeat their semblance: recall their image.

[SCENE IV]

Enter YORK, WARWICK, SHEPHERD, PUCELLE [*guarded*].

York. Bring forth that sorceress condemn'd to burn.
Shep. Ah, Joan, this kills thy father's heart outright!
Have I sought every country far and near,
And now it is my chance to find thee out,
Must I behold thy timeless cruel death?
Ah, Joan, sweet daughter Joan, I'll die with thee!
Puc. Decrepit miser! base ignoble wretch!
I am descended of a gentler blood.
Thou art no father nor no friend of mine.
Shep. Out, out! My lords, and please you, 'tis not so,
I did beget her, all the parish knows.
Her mother liveth yet, can testify
She was the first fruit of my bach'lorship.
War. Graceless, wilt thou deny thy parentage?
York. This argues what her kind of life hath been,
Wicked and vile, and so her death concludes.
Shep. Fie, Joan, that thou wilt be so obstacle!
God knows thou art a collop of my flesh,
And for thy sake have I shed many a tear.
Deny me not, I prithee, gentle Joan.
Puc. Peasant, avaunt!—You have suborn'd this man
Of purpose to obscure my noble birth.
Shep. 'Tis true, I gave a noble to the priest
The morn that I was wedded to her mother.
Kneel down and take my blessing, good my girl.
Wilt thou not stoop? Now cursed be the time
Of thy nativity! I would the milk
Thy mother gave thee, when thou suck'st her breast,
Had been a little ratsbane for thy sake!
Or else, when thou didst keep my lambs a-field,
I wish some ravenous wolf had eaten thee!
Dost thou deny thy father, cursed drab?
O, burn her, burn her! hanging is too good. *Exit.*
York. Take her away, for she hath liv'd too long,
To fill the world with vicious qualities.
Puc. First let me tell you whom you have condemn'd:
Not me begotten of a shepherd swain,
But issued from the progeny of kings;
Virtuous and holy, chosen from above,
By inspiration of celestial grace,
To work exceeding miracles on earth.
I never had to do with wicked spirits.
But you, that are polluted with your lusts,
Stain'd with the guiltless blood of innocents,
Corrupt and tainted with a thousand vices,
Because you want the grace that others have,
You judge it straight a thing impossible
To compass wonders but by help of devils.
No, misconceived! Joan of Aire hath been
A virgin from her tender infancy,
Chaste, and immaculate in very thought,
Whose maiden blood, thus rigorously effus'd,
Will cry for vengeance at the gates of heaven.
York. Ay, ay; away with her to execution!
War. And hark ye, sirs: because she is a maid,
Spare for no faggots, let there be enow.
Place barrels of pitch upon the fatal stake,
That so her torture may be shortened.
Puc. Will nothing turn your unrelenting hearts?
Then, Joan, discover thine infirmity,
That warranteth by law to be thy privilege.
I am with child, ye bloody homicides!
Murther not then the fruit within my womb,
Although ye hale me to a violent death.
York. Now heaven forfend, the holy maid with child?
War. The greatest miracle that e'er ye wrought!
Is all your strict preciseness come to this?
York. She and the Dolphin have been juggling.
I did imagine what would be her refuge.
War. Well, go to, we'll have no bastards live,
Especially since Charles must father it.
Puc. You are deceiv'd, my child is none of his,
It was Alanson that enjoy'd my love.
York. Alanson, that notorious Machevile?
It dies, and if it had a thousand lives.
Puc. O, give me leave, I have deluded you,
'Twas neither Charles nor yet the duke I nam'd,
But Reignier, King of Naples, that prevail'd.
War. A married man! that's most intolerable.
York. Why, here's a girl! I think she knows not well
(There were so many) whom she may accuse.
War. It's sign she hath been liberal and free.
York. And yet forsooth she is a virgin pure.
Strumpet, thy words condemn thy brat and thee.
Use no entreaty, for it is in vain.
Puc. Then lead me hence; with whom I leave my curse:
May never glorious sun reflex his beams
Upon the country where you make abode;
But darkness and the gloomy shade of death
Environ you, till mischief and despair
Drive you to break your necks or hang yourselves!
Exit [*guarded*].

V.iv. Location: France. Camp of the Duke of York in Anjou.
4. now . . . out: now that I have happened to discover you.
5. timeless: untimely. **7. miser:** wretch.
8. gentler: nobler. **9. friend:** relative.
13. first . . . bach'lorship: i.e. conceived out of wedlock.
15. argues: indicates, implies. **17. obstacle:** obstinate.
18. collop: slice. **23. noble:** gold coin worth *6s. 8d.*
29. ratsbane: rat poison. **35. qualities:** tricks (?).
46. want: lack.

47. straight: straightway, immediately.
49. misconceived: mistaken ones.
52. rigorously effus'd: cruelly shed. **56. enow:** enough.
60–61. discover . . . privilege: reveal your pregnancy, which, by law, will save you from execution. A pregnant woman condemned to death could petition for a stay of execution until her child was born. Shakespeare could have found this detail in Holinshed (Bullough, III, 77).
67. preciseness: propriety. **68. juggling:** i.e. misbehaving.
69. refuge: defense.
74. Machevile: Niccolò Machiavelli (1469–1527), Florentine writer and statesman who, as author of *Il Principe* (The Prince), became notorious for expounding political immorality and cynicism. The allusion to him here is of course anachronistic.
82. liberal: loose, wanton. **87. reflex:** reflect.

York. Break thou in pieces and consume to ashes,
Thou foul accursed minister of hell!

Enter [*Winchester, now*] CARDINAL [BEAUFORD, *attended*].

Car. Lord Regent, I do greet your Excellence
With letters of commission from the King.
For know, my lords, the states of Christendom,
Mov'd with remorse of these outrageous broils,
Have earnestly implor'd a general peace
Betwixt our nation and the aspiring French;
And here at hand the Dolphin and his train
Approacheth, to confer about some matter.

York. Is all our travail turn'd to this effect?
After the slaughter of so many peers,
So many captains, gentlemen, and soldiers,
That in this quarrel have been overthrown
And sold their bodies for their country's benefit,
Shall we at last conclude effeminate peace?
Have we not lost most part of all the towns,
By treason, falsehood, and by treachery,
Our great progenitors had conquered?
O Warwick, Warwick, I foresee with grief
The utter loss of all the realm of France.

War. Be patient, York. If we conclude a peace,
It shall be with such strict and severe covenants,
As little shall the Frenchmen gain thereby.

Enter CHARLES, ALANSON, BASTARD, REIGNIER, [*and others*].

Char. Since, lords of England, it is thus agreed
That peaceful truce shall be proclaim'd in France,
We come to be informed by yourselves
What the conditions of that league must be.

York. Speak, Winchester, for boiling choler chokes
The hollow passage of my poison'd voice,
By sight of these our baleful enemies.

Car. Charles, and the rest, it is enacted thus:
That, in regard King Henry gives consent,
Of mere compassion and of lenity,
To ease your country of distressful war
And suffer you to breathe in fruitful peace,
You shall become true liegemen to his crown.
And, Charles, upon condition thou wilt swear
To pay him tribute and submit thyself,
Thou shalt be plac'd as viceroy under him,
And still enjoy thy regal dignity.

Alan. Must he be then as shadow of himself?
Adorn his temples with a coronet,
And yet, in substance and authority,
Retain but privilege of a private man?
This proffer is absurd and reasonless.

Char. 'Tis known already that I am possess'd
With more than half the Gallian territories,
And therein reverenc'd for their lawful king.
Shall I, for lucre of the rest unvanquish'd,
Detract so much from that prerogative
As to be call'd but viceroy of the whole?
No, lord ambassador, I'll rather keep
That which I have than, coveting for more,
Be cast from possibility of all.

York. Insulting Charles, hast thou by secret means
Us'd intercession to obtain a league,
And, now the matter grows to compremise,
Stand'st thou aloof upon comparison?
Either accept the title thou usurp'st,
Of benefit proceeding from our king,
And not of any challenge of desert,
Or we will plague thee with incessant wars.

Reig. [*Aside to Charles*.] My lord, you do not well in obstinacy
To cavil in the course of this contract.
If once it be neglected, ten to one
We shall not find like opportunity.

Alan. [*Aside to Charles*.] To say the truth, it is your policy
To save your subjects from such massacre
And ruthless slaughters as are daily seen
By our proceeding in hostility,
And therefore take this compact of a truce,
Although you break it when your pleasure serves.

War. How say'st thou, Charles? Shall our condition stand?

Char. It shall;
Only reserv'd, you claim no interest
In any of our towns of garrison.

York. Then swear allegiance to his Majesty,
As thou art knight, never to disobey
Nor be rebellious to the crown of England,
Thou, nor thy nobles, to the crown of England.
[*Charles and his party give tokens of fealty*.]
So, now dismiss your army when ye please;
Hang up your ensigns, let your drums be still,
For here we entertain a solemn peace. *Exeunt*.

[SCENE] V

Enter SUFFOLK *in conference with the* KING, GLOUCESTER, *and* EXETER.

King. Your wondrous rare description, noble Earl,
Of beauteous Margaret hath astonish'd me.
Her virtues, graced with external gifts,
Do breed love's settled passions in my heart,
And like as rigor of tempestuous gusts

93. Thou . . . hell. This represents the contemporary English view of Joan. Hall (Bullough, III, 61) describes her as "a shepherdes daughter, a chamberlein in an hostrie, and a beggers brat: whiche blindyng the wittes of the French nacion, by revelacions, dreames & phantasticall visions, made them beleve thyngs not to be supposed, and to geve faithe to thynges impossible. For surely, if credite maie be geven to the actes of the Clergie, openly done, and commonly shewed, this woman was not inspired with the holy ghoste, nor sent from God, (as the Frenchmen beleve) but an enchanteresse, an orgayne of the devill, sent from Sathan, to blind the people and brynge them in unbelife." **120. choler:** anger. **124. in regard:** since. **125. Of:** out of. **mere:** pure. **128. liegemen:** subjects. **134. coronet:** small crown indicating a rank lower than sovereignty.

139. Gallian: French.
141–43. Shall . . . whole: i.e. to make sure that part of my domain is unmolested shall I be reduced to the status of viceroy for the whole. **lucre:** gain.
149. grows to compremise: is on the point of arbitration.
150. comparison: i.e. of the articles of the proposed truce.
152. Of benefit: as a favor. **159. policy:** astute course.
168. towns of garrison: fortified towns.

V.v. Location: London. The palace.

Provokes the mightiest hulk against the tide,
So am I driven by breath of her renown,
Either to suffer shipwrack, or arrive
Where I may have fruition of her love.

Suf. Tush, my good lord, this superficial tale
Is but a preface of her worthy praise.
The chief perfections of that lovely dame
(Had I sufficient skill to utter them)
Would make a volume of enticing lines,
Able to ravish any dull conceit;
And, which is more, she is not so divine,
So full replete with choice of all delights,
But with as humble lowliness of mind
She is content to be at your command—
Command, I mean, of virtuous chaste intents,
To love and honor Henry as her lord.

King. And otherwise will Henry ne'er presume.
Therefore, my Lord Protector, give consent
That Marg'ret may be England's royal queen.

Glou. So should I give consent to flatter sin.
You know, my lord, your Highness is betroth'd
Unto another lady of esteem.
How shall we then dispense with that contract,
And not deface your honor with reproach?

Suf. As doth a ruler with unlawful oaths,
Or one that at a triumph, having vow'd
To try his strength, forsaketh yet the lists
By reason of his adversary's odds.
A poor earl's daughter is unequal odds,
And therefore may be broke without offense.

Glou. Why, what, I pray, is Margaret more than that?
Her father is no better than an earl,
Although in glorious titles he excel.

Suf. Yes, my lord, her father is a king,
The King of Naples and Jerusalem,
And of such great authority in France
As his alliance will confirm our peace,
And keep the Frenchmen in allegiance.

Glou. And so the Earl of Arminack may do,
Because he is near kinsman unto Charles.

Exe. Beside, his wealth doth warrant a liberal dower,
Where Reignier sooner will receive than give.

Suf. A dow'r, my lords? disgrace not so your king,
That he should be so abject, base, and poor,
To choose for wealth and not for perfect love.
Henry is able to enrich his queen,
And not to seek a queen to make him rich:
So worthless peasants bargain for their wives,
As market men for oxen, sheep, or horse.
Marriage is a matter of more worth
Than to be dealt in by attorneyship.
Not whom we will, but whom his Grace affects,
Must be companion of his nuptial bed.
And therefore, lords, since he affects her most,
Most of all these reasons bindeth us
In our opinions she should be preferr'd.
For what is wedlock forced, but a hell,
An age of discord and continual strife?
Whereas the contrary bringeth bliss,
And is a pattern of celestial peace.
Whom should we match with Henry, being a king,
But Margaret, that is daughter to a king?
Her peerless feature, joined with her birth,
Approves her fit for none but for a king.
Her valiant courage and undaunted spirit
(More than in women commonly is seen)
Will answer our hope in issue of a king;
For Henry, son unto a conqueror,
Is likely to beget more conquerors,
If with a lady of so high resolve
(As is fair Margaret) he be link'd in love.
Then yield, my lords, and here conclude with me
That Margaret shall be Queen, and none but she.

King. Whether it be through force of your report,
My noble Lord of Suffolk, or for that
My tender youth was never yet attaint
With any passion of inflaming [love],
I cannot tell; but this I am assur'd,
I feel such sharp dissension in my breast,
Such fierce alarums both of hope and fear,
As I am sick with working of my thoughts.
Take therefore shipping, post, my lord, to France,
Agree to any covenants, and procure
That Lady Margaret do vouchsafe to come
To cross the seas to England and be crown'd
King Henry's faithful and anointed queen.
For your expenses and sufficient charge,
Among the people gather up a tenth.
Be gone, I say, for till you do return,
I rest perplexed with a thousand cares.
And you, good uncle, banish all offense.
If you do censure me by what you were,
Not what you are, I know it will excuse
This sudden execution of my will.
And so conduct me where, from company,
I may revolve and ruminate my grief. *Exit.*

Glou. Ay, grief, I fear me, both at first and last.
Exit Gloucester [with Exeter].

Suf. Thus Suffolk hath prevail'd, and thus he goes,
As did the youthful Paris once to Greece,
With hope to find the like event in love,
But prosper better than the Troyan did.
Margaret shall now be Queen, and rule the King;
But I will rule both her, the King, and realm. *Exit.*

15. conceit: imagination.
27. another lady: i.e. the daughter of the Earl of Armagnac.
31. triumph: tournament. **32. lists:** tournament ground.
42. As: that. **46. warrant:** ensure.
56. attorneyship: proxy. **57. affects:** desires.
59. since: i.e. the fact that.
65. pattern: model, example. **68. feature:** figure.
80. for that: because. **81. attaint:** infected.
87. post: hasten. **92. charge:** money.
93. gather . . . tenth: levy a tax of ten percent on incomes.
97. censure . . . were: judge me as when you yourself were young and passionate. **100. from company:** i.e. alone.
104. Paris: a son of Priam, king of Troy, whose abduction of Helen, wife of King Menelaus of Sparta, led to the Trojan war.
105. event: outcome.

NOTE ON THE TEXT

There is little or no general agreement on anything connected with *1 Henry VI*, particularly regarding the questions of authorship, genesis, and manuscript source for the F1 text.

The copy underlying the F1 text has been variously identified: (a) as collaborative "foul papers" (Wilson, Taylor/Jowett); (b) as a scribal copy of Shakespeare's "foul papers" (Cairncross); and (c) as Shakespeare's "fair copy" (Hattaway). Judging by the inconsistency in the use of speech-prefixes, the misplacing of some stage directions and the absence of others, and the possible implications of the confused act and scene divisions of the last two acts, it is highly unlikely that the printer's copy for F1, despite what appear to be a few book-keeper's annotations, could ever have served as a prompt-book.

As noted above, two other, partly related questions plague any discussion of *1 Henry VI*: (a) the problem of authorship, and (b) its date of composition relative to *2* and *3 Henry VI*. Some critics (e.g., Alexander, Cairncross, Bevington, and, most recently, Hattaway) claim *1 Henry VI* as essentially Shakespeare's unaided work; others (e.g., Hart, Chambers, Greg, Kittredge, Wilson, Taylor/Jowett, and the present editor) believe that the play, taking into account its various verse styles and uneven dramatic and poetic quality—all of which change from scene to scene and even within the same scene—was originally a collaborative work that was revised, with some additions, by Shakespeare. Among those most frequently proposed as furnishing the groundwork for Shakespeare's revisions are Robert Greene, George Peele (whose styles are often difficult to distinguish), and Thomas Nashe. Setting Nashe aside for the moment, Hart and Dover Wilson favor Greene over Peele (as does the present editor), Chambers favors Peele over Greene, and Wells/Taylor recognize two non-Shakespearean hands at work but prefer to call them simply "X" and "Y." Only a single scene (II.iv), almost unanimously, has been accepted as wholly Shakespeare's. Nevertheless, in the other twenty-six scenes some critics find Shakespeare's unaided hand in IV.i–iv (Hart; Wells/Taylor, IV.ii–vii.32). Dover Wilson, however, except for II.iv, allows Shakespeare only one other unaided scene (IV.v) and one part scene (II.v, except lines 74–92) and finds Shakespeare revising an underlying Greene text in some eleven scenes, whereas Wells/Taylor admit Shakespeare as a reviser only in IV.iii.33–96; they agree, however, in assigning the whole of Act I to Nashe (Hart largely to Greene, with some Shakespeare in I.i and I.iv; Chambers mostly to Peele, with possible Shakespeare in I.i and I.iii). It must now be obvious that no general consensus (aside from II.iv) can ever be achieved on the extent of Shakespeare's role in the composition of *1 Henry VI*.

The dating of *1 Henry VI* is also a matter of considerable dispute. Many scholars believe that *1 Henry VI*, regardless of authorship, was composed after *2* and *3 Henry VI* and therefore generally accept the well-known entry in Philip Henslowe's *Diary* ("ne—Rd at harey the vi the 3 of marche 1591 [i.e. 1592, new style] . . . . iij^li xvj^s 8^d") as referring to *1 Henry VI* in essentially the same form as that later printed in F1 (1623)—largely on the grounds that it appears to show some knowledge of *2* and *3 Henry VI*, while those plays seem to be ignorant of what went on in *1 Henry VI*, evidence that can in good part be otherwise explained. Others argue that *1 Henry VI* was written first (c. 1589–90, before Parts 1 and 2) and accept it as either (a) a play wholly by Shakespeare (Alexander, Bevington, Hattaway); (b) a play by three other hands, in which Shakespeare had some share (see above; Taylor/Jowett); or (c) a play originally by hands other than Shakespeare's, which Greene began to fashion into a kind of prologue to *2* and *3 Henry VI*, just before the break-up of the Strange-Admiral alliance before May 1591, a revision completed early in 1592 (before Greene's death on 3 September 1592) by Shakespeare when he was revising Parts 2 and 3 for, as Wilson suggests, the company recently formed around Richard Burbage (a chronology outlined in the present editor's review of Wilson's New Shakespeare *1–3 Henry VI*). Alexander suggests that two pieces of evidence strongly support, if not in fact prove, an early date for *1 Henry VI*: (a) a substantial number of what appear to be echoes of the play in *The Troublesome Raigne of Iohn King of England* published in 1591; (b) fifteen echoes of the play in the "bad" quartos of *2* and *3 Henry VI* (i.e. *The First part of the Contention betwixt the two famous Houses of Yorke and Lancaster* [1594] and *The true Tragedie of Richard Duke of Yorke* [1595]).

The F2 text contains an unusually large number of variant readings. These, although they are without any claim to authority, are recorded in the Textual Notes.

For further information see: H. C. Hart, ed., Arden *1 Henry VI* (London, 1909; rev. 1930); A. Gaw, *The Origin and Development of "1; Henry VI,"* (Univ. of South Carolina Studies, I, (1926): Peter Alexander, *Shakespeare's "Henry VI" and "Richard III"* (Cambridge, 1929); E. K. Chambers, *William Shakespeare*, 2 vols. (Oxford, 1930); J. D. Wilson, ed., New Shakespeare *1–3 Henry VI* (Cambridge, 1952; reviewed by G. B. Evans, *SQ*, IV [1952], 84–92); W. W. Greg, *The Shakespeare First Folio* (Oxford, 1955); Philip Williams, "New Approaches to Textual Problems in Shakespeare," *SB*, VIII (1956), 3–13; A. S. Cairncross, ed., New Arden *1 Henry VI* (London, 1962); Stanley Wells, Gary Taylor, John Jowett, and William Montgomery, *William Shakespeare: A Textual Companion* (Oxford, 1987); Michael Hattaway, ed., New Cambridge *1 Henry VI* (Cambridge, 1990); David Bevington, ed., *Complete Works of Shakespeare* (New York, 1992).

TEXTUAL NOTES

Title: **Sixth**] Sixt *F1*

Dramatis personae: *subs. as first given in Rowe*

Act-scene division: *F1 designates I.i, II.i, III.i–iv, IV.i as in the present text, and then marks the present V.i, ii as IV.ii, iii and the present V.v as Act V; other act-scene divisions from Pope and Capell (see first note to each scene); present act-scene arrangement as a whole first established by Capell (in whose edition, however, the heading for IV.vi is erroneously repeated for IV.vii)*

I.i

Location: *Theobald*

o.s.d. **Gloucester**] *Rowe;* Gloster *F1* (*see l. 37*)

o.s.d. **Heralds, etc.**] *Malone*

24 **glory's**] *Rowe;* Glories *F1*

37 **Gloucester**] *Cambridge;* Gloster *F1* (*through III.i and at V.i.58; elsewhere* Gloucester); Gloucester *first used throughout text and s.pp. (as here) in Cambridge*

45 **Heralds,**] *Pope;* Heralds *F1*

48 **Posterity,**] *Capell;* Posteritie *F1*

76 **third**] third man *F2*

80 **arms,**] *Pope;* Armes *F1*

81 s.d. **Exit.**] *Wilson*

89 s.p. **2. Mess.**] *Rowe;* Mess. *F1*

94 **Reignier**] *Rowe;* Reynold *F1*

96 **crowned**] *Rowe;* crown'd *F1*

103 s.p. **3. Mess.**] *Rowe.* Mes. *F1*

121 **human**] *F4;* humane *F1*

131 **Falstaff**] Fastolfe *Theobald* (*and most eds.*)

132 **vaward**] *Rowe;* Vauward *F1*

161 s.d. **Exit.**] *Wilson*

176 **send**] **steal** ***Mason conj.***

177 s.d. **Exeunt.**] *Cambridge;* Exit. *F1*

I.ii

I.ii] *Capell*
Location: *Theobald (after Pope)*
o.s.d **Reignier]** *F4;* Reigneir *F1 (frequently through III.ii)*
29 **Froissard]** *Reed;* Froysard *F1*
30 **bred]** *Rowe;* breed *F1*
37 **hare-brain'd]** *Dyce;* hayre-brayn'd *F1*
47 **s.p. Char.]** *Capell;* Dolph. *F1 (throughout scene)*
60 **s.d. Exit Bastard.]** *Capell*
63 **s.d. de Pucelle]** *ed. (after Rowe);* Puzel *F1 (the regular spelling through III.i)*
63 **s.d. and Bastard]** *Malone*
65 **s.p. Puc.]** *Rowe;* Puzel. *F1 (through III.i, except* Ioane. *at II.i.54, 72)*
99 **five]** *Steevens conj. (after Holinshed);* fine *F1*
113 **rites]** *Pope;* rights *F1*
131 **halcyons']** *ed.;* Halcyons *F1;* Halcyon *F3*
132 **entered]** *Malone;* entred *F1*

I.iii

I.iii] *Capell*
Location: *Hanmer (after Pope, Theobald)*
o.s.d. **in blue coats]** *Malone (after Capell)*
4 **Gloucester]** *Rowe;* Gloster *F1* (trisyllabic form needed)
5, 7, 9 **s.dd. Within.]** *Malone*
6, 8 **s.pp. 1. Serv.]** *Malone (after Capell);* Glost. 1. Man. *and* 1. Man. *F1*
6 **Gloucester]** *Pope;* Gloster *F1 (trisyllabic form needed)*
29 **Humphrey]** *Theobald;* Vmpheir *F1 (in italics)*
30 **Peel'd]** *Boswell;* Piel'd *F1*
62 **Gloucester]** *Cambridge;* Gloster *F1 (trisyllabic form needed)*
74 **s.p. Off.]** *Hanmer*
82 **cost]** deare cost *F2*
87 **Abominable]** *F3;* Abhominable *F1*
88 **s.d. several . . . Servingmen]** *Dyce (after Capell)*

I.iv

I.iv] *Capell*
Location: *Pope*
10 **Wont]** *Tyrwhitt conj.;* Went *F1*
22 **s.d. Sir William . . . Gargrave]** *Capell*
28 **Santrailles]** *Capell;* Santrayle *F1*
29 **ransomed]** *Rowe;* ransom'd *F1*
33 **pill'd]** *Capell;* pil'd *F1*
69 **s.d. shoot]** *Rowe;* shot *F1*
69 **s.d. together with Gargrave]** *Hanmer (subs.)*
95 **like thee, Nero]** *Malone;* like thee *F1* Nero like will *F2*
101 **Pucelle]** *Rowe;* Puzel *F1*
107 **Pucelle]** *Theobald;* Puzel *F1*
107 **puzzel]** *Capell;* Pussel *F1*
111 **s.d. bearing . . . bodies]** *Theobald (subs.)*

I.v.

I.v.] *Capell*
Location: *ed. (after Wilson)*
o.s.d. **and . . . them]** *Dyce (subs.)*
6 **thee— . . . witch—]** *Dyce;* thee, . . . Witch, *F1*

I.vi

I.vi] *Capell*
Location: *ed. (after Wilson)*
o.s.d. **Flourish.]** *placed as in Collier; after* retreat. *I.v. 39 s.d., F1*
2 **English!]** English wolves: *F2*
4 **s.p. Char.]** *Capell;* Dolph. *F1 (throughout scene)*
4 **Astraea's]** *F2 (reading* bright Astraea's*);* Astrea's *F1*
22 **of]** *Capell conj.;* or *F1*
26 **Transported]** *F4;* Transported, *F1*

II.i

Location: *Theobald (after Pope)*
o.s.d. **French]** *Capell*
5 **s.p. 1. Sent.]** *Capell;* Sent. *F1*
5 **s.d. Exit Sergeant.]** *Johnson*
7 **s.d. and forces]** *Capell*
7 **s.d. scaling-ladders.]** *Wilson;* scaling Ladders: Their Drummes beating a Dead March. *F1 (see below, II.ii o.s.d.)*
17 **arm's]** *Johnson;* armes *F1*
29 **all together]** *Rowe;* altogether *F1*
37 **s.d. Cry . . . Talbot!"]** *placed subs. as in Capell; after l. 38, F1*
37 **s.d. The . . . walls.]** *Theobald (subs., after l. 38); placed subs. as in Capell*
38 **s.p. 1. Sent.]** *ed.;* Sent. *F1*
38 **s.d. ready]** *Pope;* ready, *F1*
48 **s.d. de Pucelle]** *ed. (after Capell)*
54, 72 **s.pp. Puc.]** *Rowe;* Ioane. *F1*
77 **them.]** *Capell;* them. / Exeunt. *F1*
77 **s.d. an English]** *Capell;* a *F1*

II.ii

II.ii] *Capell*
Location: *Capell (after Theobald)*
o.s.d. **a . . . others]** *Capell*
o.s.d. **their . . . march]** *placed as in Pelican (after Wilson conj.); end of s.d. at II.i.7 in F1*
20 **Aire]** *ed. conj., Cairncross;* Acre *F1 (Holinshed reads* Are*; cf. V.iv.49)*
38 **Auvergne]** *Rowe;* Ouergne *F1*
59 **s.d. Whispers.]** *placed as in Johnson; after l. 59, F1*
59 **mind?]** *Dyce;* minde. *F1*

II.iii

II.iii] *Capell*
Location: *Pope*
o.s.d. **and her Porter]** *Pope*
4 **laid.]** *Pope (subs.);* layd, *F1*
16 **abroad]** *Johnson;* abroad? *F1*
27 **s.d. Going.]** *Capell*
44 **thou,]** *Theobald;* thou *F1*

II.iv

II.iv] *Capell*
Location: *Pope*
o.s.d. **Pole]** *Kittredge;* Poole *F1*
o.s.d. **Vernon]** *Hanmer*
o.s.d. **and a Lawyer]** *Ritson conj.*
1 **s.p. Plan.]** *Rowe;* Yorke. *F1 (throughout scene)*
57 **s.d. To Somerset.]** *Rowe*
78 **Pole]** *Hanmer;* Poole *F1 (throughout scene)*
117 **wip'd]** *F2;* whipt *F1*
126 **Red Rose]** *Rowe;* Red-Rose *F1*
131 **gentlemen]** *anon. conj. (in Cambridge);* gentle *F1;* gentle Sir *F2*

II.v

II.v] *Capell*
Location: *Capell (subs.)*
3 **rack]** *Pope;* Wrack *F1*
18, 33 **s.pp. 1. Keeper.]** *Capell;* Keeper. *F1*
35 **s.p. Plan.]** *Rowe;* Rich. *F1 (throughout scene)*
36 **late-despised]** *hyphen, Capell*
71 **Richard]** King Richard *F2*
75 **third]** the third *F2*
78 **fourth]** the fourth *F2*
84 **Cambridge then,]** *J. C. Maxwell conj. (privately);* Cambridge, then *F1*
118 **counsel]** *F2;* Councell *F1*
121 **s.d. Exeunt . . . Mortimer.]** *Capell (subs.);* Exit. *F1*
129 **my will]** my ill *Theobald;* mine ill *Cairncross*

III.i

Location: *Capell (after Pope)*
o.s.d. **and others]** *Malone (after Capell)*
41 **good—]** *F2;* good. *F1*
51 **s.p. Glou.]** *Hanmer;* Warw. *F1*
52 **s.p. War.]** *Hanmer; line continued to Warwick, F1 (see preceding note)*
52 **s.d. to Winchester]** *Hanmer*
53 **so]** *Cairncross;* see *F1*
61 **s.d. Aside.]** *Hanmer*
74 **What]** *Capell; King.* What *F1 (repeated s.p.)*
75 **s.d. of London attended]** *Capell*
80 **pebble]** *F3;* peeble *F1*
85 **s.d. Servingmen . . . parties]** *Capell (subs.)*
88 **Pray]** *F4;* Pray' *F1*
136 **s.d. Aside.]** *Collier*
141 **s.d. Aside.]** *Pope*
142 **Gloucester]** *Cambridge;* Gloster *F1 (trisyllabic form needed)*
147 **s.d. Servingmen, Mayor, etc.]** *Capell (subs.)*
162 **that]** *F2;* that all *F1*
177 **s.d. Aside.]** *Rowe*
198 **lose]** *F2 (reading* should lose*);* loose *F1*

III.ii

Location: *Capell (after Pope)*
o.s.d. **Pucelle]** *Rowe;* Pucell *F1 (throughout rest of play, except* Ione *in V.ii o.s.d.)*
10 **s.p. 1. Sol.]** *Capell;* Souldier. *F1*
13 **s.d. Within.]** *Capell*
13 **Qui là?]** *Sisson;* Che la. *F1*
17 **s.d. to the town]** *Capell (subs.)*
17 **s.d. Reignier, and forces]** *Cambridge (after Capell)*
21–2 **specify . . . in?]** *Rowe (subs.);* specifie? . . . in. *F1*
28 **s.d. Exit.]** *Cambridge*
35 **s.d. Exeunt.]** *Cambridge (after Capell)*
35 **s.d. Enter]** *Capell*
40 **s.d. Burgundy]** *Rowe;* Burgonie *F1 (throughout scene)*
40 **s.d. Alanson]** *Hanmer (subs.; but om. Reignier from the s.d.)*
41 **Good]** *F3;* God *F1*
59 **s.d. the English]** *Cambridge (after Capell)*
59 **s.d. council]** *Theobald (1757);* counsell *F1*
82 **late-betrayed]** *hyphen, Theobald*
103 **s.d. with . . . forces]** *Capell (subs.)*
109 **s.d. into the town]** *Dyce*
109 **s.d. enter . . . and]** *Malone*
111 **enemies']** *Theobald;* Enemies *F1*
137 **human]** *Rowe;* humane *F1*

III.iii

Location: *Dyce (after Capell)*
o.s.d. **and forces]** *Capell*
19 **Burgundy]** *Rowe;* Burgonie *F1 (throughout scene)*
35 **s.d. Enter . . . Burgundy]** *Rowe*
35 **s.d. and forces]** *Capell*
46 **foe.]** *Pope;* Foe, *F1*
48 **eyes,]** *F2;* Eyes. *F1*
78 **s.d. Aside.]** *Dyce*
85 **s.d. Aside.]** *Capell*

III.iv

Location: *Capell (after Pope)*
o.s.d. **Richard . . . of]** *ed. (after Kittredge)*
o.s.d. **Vernon . . . others]** *Capell*
12 **s.d. Kneels.]** *Cambridge*
27 **s.d. Manent]** *F2;* Manet *F1*
39 **whoso]** *Rowe;* who so *F1*

IV.i

Location: *Wilson (after Capell)*
o.s.d. **Governor . . . Exeter]** *Rowe (subs.);* Gouernor Exeter. *F1*
s.d. **and others]** *Malone (after Capell)*
3 **s.d. Governor kneels.]** *Capell*
8 **s.d. Exeunt . . . Train.]** *Capell*
12 **s.d. Presents it.]** *Capell (subs.)*
14 **thee]** *F2;* the *F1*
15 **s.d. Plucking it off.]** *Capell*
19 **Poictiers]** Patay *Capell conj. (from Holinshed; followed by most eds.)*
26 **there]** *F2;* thete *F1*
47 **s.d. Exit Falstaff.]** *Wilson (after F2)*
48 **Lord]** my Lord *F2*
55 **s.d. Reads.]** *Rowe*
77 **s.d. Exit.]** *Rowe*
77 **s.d. Basset]** *F2;* Bassit *F1*
93 **cheeks,]** *Capell;* cheekes: *F1*
112 **slight]** *F2;* sligh̄r *F1*
151 **umpeer]** *ed.;* Vmper *F1*
152 **s.d. Putting . . . rose.]** *Johnson*
172 **presented.]** *Theobald;* presented *F1*
173 **s.d. Flourish.]** *placed as in Theobald; after l. 181, F1*
173 **s.d. Manent]** *F3;* Manet *F1*
180 **I wist]** *Capell;* I wish *F1; Wilson's* iwis

(= indeed) is tempting, and OED *offers contemporary examples of* wis *corrupted to* wish, *but the emphatic position the word would be given in the present context seems false for this period and contrasts with Shakespeare's three acknowledged uses*
180 did—] *Pope;* did. *F1*

IV.ii

IV.ii] *Capell*
Location: *from F1 o.s.d.*
2 s.d. Trumpet] *Capell*
2 s.d. and others] *Malone*
3 calls] *F2;* call *F1*
12 even] *F2;* eeuen *F1*
15 s.p. Gen.] *Theobald;* Cap. *F1*
34 due] *Theobald;* dew *F1*
41 s.d. with others above] *ed. (after Malone)*
50 moody-mad] *hyphen, Capell*
56 s.d. Exeunt.] *F2*

IV.iii

IV.iii] *Capell*
Location: *Capell*
5 Talbot. . . . along,] *F2;* Talbot . . . along. *F1*
8 s.d. Exit.] *Cairncross*
16 s.d. Sir William Lucy] *Theobald*
17, 30, etc. s.pp. Lucy.] *Theobald;* 2. Mes. *or* Mes. *F1*
20 waist] *Steevens;* waste *F1*
36 travel] *F3;* trauaile *F1*
38 lives] *F1 not clear, possibly* lines; lives *F2*
46 s.d. with his Soldiers] *Cambridge (after Collier)*
49 loss] *Pope;* losse: *F1*

IV.iv

IV.iv] *Capell*
Location: *ed. (after Wilson)*
o.s.d. a . . . him] *Capell (subs.)*
13 lord?] *F3;* Lord, *F1*
16 legions] *Rowe;* Regions *F1*
26 Burgundy] and Burgundie *F2*
27 Reignier] *Rowe;* Reignard *F1*
46 world,] *F4;* world. *F1*

IV.v

IV.v] *Capell*
Location: *Theobald (after Pope)*
o.s.d. John] *Malone*
55 s.d. Exeunt.] *F2;* Exit. *F1*

IV.vi

IV.vi] *Capell*
Location: *ed. (after Wilson)*
18 encountered] *F3;* encountred *F1*
26 Speak,] *F4;* Speake *F1*
36 gain] *Knight;* gaine, *F1*
55 Icarus;] *Capell (after Theobald);* Icarus, *F1*
57 s.d. Exeunt.] *Rowe;* Exit. *F1*

IV.vii

IV.vii] *Pope*
Location: *ed. (after Wilson)*
o.s.d. by a Servant] *Capell (subs.)*
16 s.d. Soldiers] *Capell*
18 antic] *F3;* antique *F1*
32] *Following this line F2 begins* Actus Quintus, Scaena Prima.
32 s.d. with forces] *Malone (after Capell)*
36 puny sword] *Rowe;* punie-sword *F1*
50 s.d. attended . . . preceding] *Capell*
67 thrice-victorious] *hyphen, Knight*
70 Henry] our King Henry *F2*
89 'em] *Theobald;* him *F1*
94 'em] *Malone;* him *F1;* them *F2*
96 s.d. Exeunt.] *Rowe;* Exit. *F1*

V.i

V.i] *Capell;* Scena secunda. *F1*
Location: *Capell (subs.)*
27 s.d. in cardinal's habit] *Capell*
27 s.d. one . . . Legate] *Kittredge (after Capell)*
41 s.d. To . . . Arminack.] *M. Edel (after Capell, at l. 47)*
50 s.d. all . . . Legate] *Cambridge (after Capell)*
55, 62 s.dd. Exit.] *Collier MS*

V.ii

V.ii] *Capell;* Scoena Tertia. *F1*
Location: *Capell (after Pope)*
s.d. with forces] *Capell (subs.)*

V.iii

V.iii] *Capell*
Location: *Malone (after Capell)*
13 silence] *F2;* silenee *F1*
25 lofty-plumed] *hyphen, Johnson*
29 s.d. enter and] *ed.*
29 s.d. Pucelle . . . captive.] *Malone (subs.)*
43 a while] *F3;* awhile *F1*
50 thou? say] *Pope;* thou, say? *F1*
57 her] *F2;* his *F1*
60, 84, 86, 98 s.dd. Aside.] *Dyce*
65 woo] *F2;* woe *F1 (throughout scene)*
75, 78, 81, 91 s.dd. Aside.] *Pope*
101, 104, 107 s.dd. Aside.] *Theobald*
130 s.d. a parley] *Capell*
139 easy-held] *hyphen, Rowe*
144 s.d. Exit . . . walls.] *Capell*
145 s.d. below] *Capell*
165 s.d. Aside.] *Rowe*
179 modestly] *F2;* modestie *F1*
186 s.d. Exeunt . . . Margaret.] *Capell*
190 wondrous] *F3;* wonderous *F1*
192 And] *Capell;* Mad *F1*

V.iv

V.iv] *Capell*
Location: *Capell*
o.s.d. guarded] *Capell*
10 so,] *F2;* so *F1*
28 suck'st] suck'dst *F2*
32 Dost] *F3;* Doest *F1*
49 No, misconceived!] *Steevens (comma, F4);* No misconceyued, *F1*
52 maiden blood] *Theobald;* Maiden-blood *F1*
58 torture] *F2;* tortute *F1*
58 shortened] *Pope;* shortned *F1*
60 discover] *F3;* discouet *F1*
61 warranteth] *F2;* wartanteth *F1*
91 s.d. guarded] *Theobald*
93 s.d. Winchester, now] *Pelican*
93 s.d. Beauford, attended] *Capell; s.d. placed as in Pope; after l. 91, F1*
102 travail] *Steevens;* trauell *F1*
102 effect?] *Rowe;* effect, *F1*
115 s.d. and others] *Capell*
123 s.p. Car.] *Capell;* Win. *F1*
145 have than,] *Cambridge;* haue, than *F1*
155 s.d. Aside to Charles.] *Capell*
159 s.d. Aside to Charles.] *Collier (after Capell)*
172 s.d. Charles . . . fealty.] *Johnson*

V.v

V.v] *Capell;* Actus Quintus. *F1*
Location: *Capell (subs.)*
39 lord] good Lord *F2*
55 Marriage] But marriage *F2*
62 wedlock] *F2;* wedloeke *F1*
62 forced,] *F2;* forced? *F1*
64 bringeth] bringeth forth *F2*
82 love] *F2;* Ioue *F1*
102 s.d. with Exeter] *Hanmer (subs.)*
108 s.d. Exit.] Exit / FINIS. *F1*

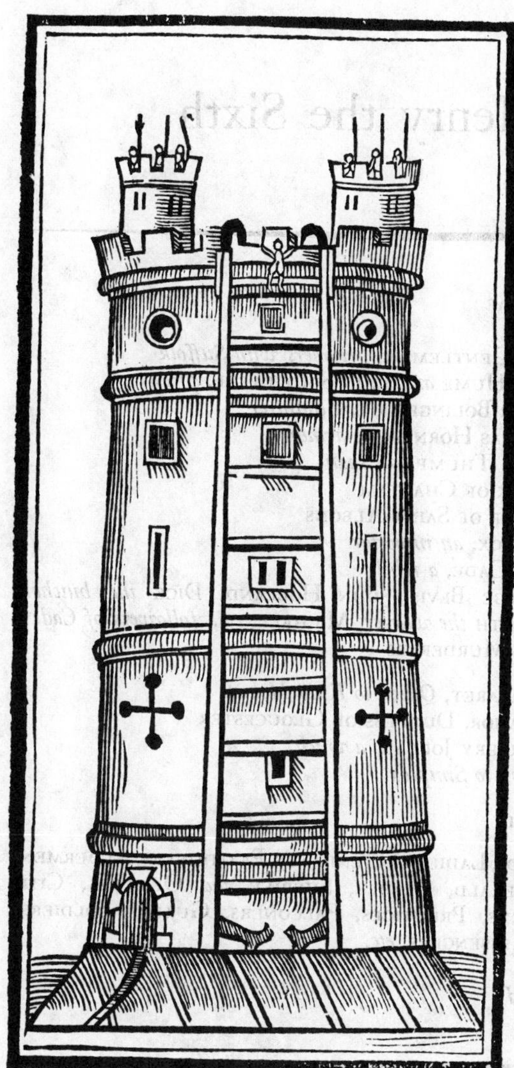

A scaling ladder. From Robert Ward, *Animadversions of War* (1639). This picture of a scaling ladder may be somewhat fanciful but it illustrates none the less the principle behind that "engine of war." Sheltered both within and behind the structure, a sizable force of besiegers could approach right up to the walls of a city, avoiding the shot, rocks, and molten lead directed at them by the city's defenders. The scaling ladders employed in *1 Henry VI* (II.i), when the English forces under Talbot surprise the city of Orleans and capture it from the French, were presumably of simpler form, probably nothing more than ordinary ladders. *(By permission of the Huntington Library, San Marino, California)*

The Second Part of Henry the Sixth

[Dramatis Personae

King Henry the Sixth
Humphrey, *Duke of Gloucester, his uncle*
Cardinal Beauford, *Bishop of Winchester, great-uncle to the King*
Richard Plantagenet, *Duke of York*
Edward *and* Richard, *his sons*
Duke of Somerset
Duke of Suffolk
Duke of Buckingham
Lord Clifford
Young Clifford, *his son*
Earl of Salisbury
Earl of Warwick
Lord Scales
Lord Say
Sir Humphrey Stafford, *and* William Stafford, *his brother*
Sir John Stanley
Vaux
Matthew Goffe
Alexander Iden, *a Kentish gentleman*
Lieutenant, Shipmaster, *and* Master's Mate, *and* Walter Whitmore
Two Gentlemen, *prisoners with Suffolk*
John Hume *and* John Southwell, *priests*
Roger Bolingbrook, *a conjurer*
Thomas Horner, *an armorer*
Peter Thump, *his man*
Clerk of Chartam
Mayor of Saint Albons
Simpcox, *an impostor*
Jack Cade, *a rebel*
George Bevis, John Holland, Dick *the butcher*, Smith *the weaver*, Michael, *etc., followers of Cade*
Two Murderers

Margaret, *Queen to King Henry*
Eleanor, Duchess of Gloucester
Margery Jordan, *a witch*
Wife *to Simpcox*

Spirit

Lords, Ladies, Attendants, Petitioners, Aldermen, Herald, Beadle, Sheriff *and* Officers, Citizens, Prentices, Falconers, Guards, Soldiers Messengers, *etc.*

Scene: *England*]

ACT I, Scene I

Flourish of trumpets: then hoboys. Enter King [Henry], Duke Humphrey [of Gloucester], Salisbury, Warwick, *and* [Cardinal] Beauford, *on the one side; the* Queen, Suffolk, York, Somerset, *and* Buckingham, *on the other.*

Suf. As by your high imperial Majesty
I had in charge at my depart for France,
As procurator to your Excellence,
To marry Princess Margaret for your Grace;
So in the famous ancient city Tours,
In presence of the Kings of France and Sicil,
The Dukes of Orleance, Calaber, Bretagne, and Alanson,
Seven earls, twelve barons, and twenty reverend bishops,
I have perform'd my task, and was espous'd;
And humbly now upon my bended knee,
In sight of England and her lordly peers,
Deliver up my title in the Queen
To your most gracious hands, that are the substance
Of that great shadow I did represent:
The happiest gift that ever marquess gave,
The fairest queen that ever king receiv'd.
King. Suffolk, arise. Welcome, Queen Margaret,
I can express no kinder sign of love
Than this kind kiss. O Lord, that lends me life,

Words and passages enclosed in square brackets in the text above are either emendations of the copy-text or additions to it. The Textual Notes immediately following the play cite the earliest authority for every such change or insertion and supply the reading of the copy-text wherever it is emended in this edition.

I.i. Location: London. The palace.
o.s.d. **Flourish**: fanfare. **hoboys**: oboes.
2. **had in charge**: was commissioned.
3. **procurator**: agent, deputy.
6. **Sicil**: Sicily, of which René, Margaret's father, was titular king.
7. **Orleance**: Orleans. **Calaber**: Calabria, a region in southern Italy. **Alanson**: Alençon. 9. **espous'd**: betrothed (as your deputy).
18. **kinder**: more natural. 19. **kind**: affectionate.

Lend me a heart replete with thankfulness!
For thou hast given me in this beauteous face
A world of earthly blessings to my soul,
If sympathy of love unite our thoughts.

Queen. Great King of England, and my gracious lord,
The mutual conference that my mind hath had,
By day, by night, waking and in my dreams,
In courtly company, or at my beads,
With you, mine alder-liefest sovereign,
Makes me the bolder to salute my king
With ruder terms, such as my wit affords
And overjoy of heart doth minister.

King. Her sight did ravish, but her grace in speech,
Her words yclad with wisdom's majesty,
Makes me from wond'ring fall to weeping joys,
Such is the fullness of my heart's content.
Lords, with one cheerful voice welcome my love.

All. (*Kneel.*) Long live Queen Margaret, England's happiness! *Flourish.*

Queen. We thank you all.

Suf. My Lord Protector, so it please your Grace,
Here are the articles of contracted peace
Between our sovereign and the French King Charles,
For eighteen months concluded by consent.

Glou. (*Reads.*) "*Inprimis*, It is agreed between the French King Charles, and William de la Pole, Marquess of Suffolk, ambassador for Henry King of England, that the said Henry shall espouse the Lady Margaret, daughter unto Reignier King of Naples, Sicilia, and Jerusalem, and crown her Queen of England ere the thirtieth of May next ensuing. *Item*, [It is further agreed between them,] that the duchy of Anjou and the county of Maine shall be releas'd and deliver'd [over] to the King her father"—

[*Duke Humphrey lets it fall.*]

King. Uncle, how now?

Glou. Pardon me, gracious lord,
Some sudden qualm hath struck me at the heart,
And dimm'd mine eyes, that I can read no further.

King. Uncle of Winchester, I pray read on.

Car. [*Reads.*] "*Item*, It is further agreed between them, that the [duchy] of Anjou and [the county of] Maine shall be releas'd and deliver'd over to the King her father, and she sent over of the King of England's own proper cost and charges, without having any dowry."

King. They please us well. Lord Marquess, kneel down.
We here create thee the first Duke of Suffolk,
And girt thee with the sword. Cousin of York,
We here discharge your Grace from being Regent
I' th' parts of France, till term of eighteen months
Be full expir'd. Thanks, uncle Winchester,
Gloucester, York, Buckingham, Somerset,
Salisbury, and Warwick;
We thank you all for this great favor done
In entertainment to my princely queen.
Come, let us in, and with all speed provide
To see her coronation be perform'd.

Exeunt King, Queen, and Suffolk. Manent the rest, [stayed by Gloucester].

Glou. Brave peers of England, pillars of the state,
To you Duke Humphrey must unload his grief,
Your grief, the common grief of all the land.
What? did my brother Henry spend his youth,
His valor, coin, and people, in the wars?
Did he so often lodge in open field,
In winter's cold and summer's parching heat,
To conquer France, his true inheritance?
And did my brother Bedford toil his wits,
To keep by policy what Henry got?
Have you yourselves, Somerset, Buckingham,
Brave York, Salisbury, and victorious Warwick,
Receiv'd deep scars in France and Normandy?
Or hath mine uncle Beauford and myself,
With all the learned Council of the realm,
Studied so long, sat in the Council-house
Early and late, debating to and fro
How France and Frenchmen might be kept in awe,
And hath his Highness in his infancy
Crowned in Paris in despite of foes?
And shall these labors and these honors die?
Shall Henry's conquest, Bedford's vigilance,
Your deeds of war, and all our counsel die?
O peers of England, shameful is this league,
Fatal this marriage, cancelling your fame,
Blotting your names from books of memory,
Rasing the characters of your renown,
Defacing monuments of conquer'd France,
Undoing all, as all had never been!

Car. Nephew, what means this passionate discourse,
This peroration with such circumstance?
For France, 'tis ours; and we will keep it still.

Glou. Ay, uncle, we will keep it, if we can;
But now it is impossible we should.
Suffolk, the new-made duke that rules the roast,
Hath given the duchy of Anjou, and Maine,

25. mutual conference: intimate communication.
27. at my beads: i.e. while saying prayers with the rosary.
28. alder-liefest: dearest of all. **31. minister**: supply.
33. yclad: clad.
39. Protector: i.e. Gloucester. Actually, his protectorship had been formally annulled in 1429, when Henry VI was crowned at Westminster at the age of eight.
43. Inprimis: imprimis, in the first place. **49. Item**: also.
55. that: so that. **60. of**: at. **61. proper**: personal.
64. We . . . Suffolk. Actually, the title was conferred on Suffolk in 1448, four years after the time represented in this scene.
65. girt: gird. **Cousin**: kinsman.
72. entertainment to: reception of.
75–146. Brave . . . long. When the terms of Henry's marriage were revealed, says Hall (Bullough, III, 103), they "semed to many, bothe infortunate, and unprofitable to the realme of England, and that for many causes. First the kyng with her [i.e. Margaret] had not one peny, and for the fetchyng of her, the Marques of Suffolke, demaunded a whole fiftene, in open parliament: also for her mariage, the Duchie of Anjow, the citee of Mauns, and the whole countie of Mayne, were delivered and released to Kyng Reyner her father, whiche countries were the very stayes, and backestandes to the Duchy of Normandy. Furthermore for this mariage, the Earle of Arminacke, toke suche great displeasure, that he became utter enemy to the realme of Englande and was the chief cause, that the Englishmen, wer expulsed out of the whole duchie of Acquitayne, and lost bothe the countreis of Gascoyn and Guyen."
78. my brother Henry: Henry V.
82. inheritance. For the English claim to the French throne see the note to *1 Henry VI*, I.i.80. **84. policy**: administrative skill.
92. awe: obedience. **100. books of memory**: i.e. chronicles.
101. Rasing the characters: erasing the records.
106. still: always. **109. rules the roast**: domineers.

Unto the poor King Reignier, whose large style
Agrees not with the leanness of his purse.

Sal. Now by the death of Him that died for all,
These counties were the keys of Normandy.
But wherefore weeps Warwick, my valiant son?

War. For grief that they are past recovery;
For were there hope to conquer them again,
My sword should shed hot blood, mine eyes no tears.
Anjou and Maine? myself did win them both.
Those provinces these arms of mine did conquer,
And are the cities that I got with wounds
Deliver'd up again with peaceful words?
Mort Dieu!

York. For Suffolk's duke, may he be suffocate,
That dims the honor of this warlike isle!
France should have torn and rent my very heart
Before I would have yielded to this league.
I never read but England's kings have had
Large sums of gold and dowries with their wives,
And our King Henry gives away his own,
To match with her that brings no vantages.

Glou. A proper jest, and never heard before,
That Suffolk should demand a whole fifteenth
For costs and charges in transporting her!
She should have stay'd in France, and starv'd in France,
Before—

Car. My Lord of Gloucester, now ye grow too hot:
It was the pleasure of my lord the King.

Glou. My Lord of Winchester, I know your mind.
'Tis not my speeches that you do mislike,
But 'tis my presence that doth trouble ye;
Rancor will out. Proud prelate, in thy face
I see thy fury. If I longer stay,
We shall begin our ancient bickerings.
Lordings, farewell, and say, when I am gone,
I prophesied France will be lost ere long.
Exit Humphrey.

Car. So, there goes our Protector in a rage.
'Tis known to you he is mine enemy;
Nay more, an enemy unto you all,
And no great friend, I fear me, to the King.
Consider, lords, he is the next of blood,
And heir-apparent to the English crown.
Had Henry got an empire by his marriage,
And all the wealthy kingdoms of the west,
There's reason he should be displeas'd at it.
Look to it, lords, let not his smoothing words
Bewitch your hearts. Be wise and circumspect.
What though the common people favor him,

111. **large style**: imposing title.
119. **Anjou . . . both.** An inaccuracy. Richard Neville, Earl of Warwick and Salisbury (1428–71), "the Kingmaker," first saw military service at the battle of St. Albans (1455), the event with which this play concludes. He is probably confused here with his father-in-law Richard Beauchamp, Earl of Warwick, who died in 1439, and whose title, descending first to his own son, was not conferred upon Neville until 1449. 123. **Mort Dieu**: by God's (Christ's) death.
131. **vantages**: profit, i.e. dowry.
133. **whole fifteenth**: tax of fifteen percent on income from land. In *1 Henry VI*, V.v.93, Suffolk had been authorized by the King to "gather up a tenth." 145. **Lordings**: gentlemen.
151. **next of blood.** Gloucester was the eldest living uncle of the then childless king.
154. **wealthy . . . west.** Perhaps an anachronistic allusion to America.
155. **he**: i.e. Gloucester. 156. **smoothing**: flattering.

Calling him "Humphrey, the good Duke of Gloucester,"
Clapping their hands, and crying with loud voice,
"Jesu maintain your royal Excellence!"
With "God preserve the good Duke Humphrey!"
I fear me, lords, for all this flattering gloss,
He will be found a dangerous Protector.

Buck. Why should he then protect our sovereign,
He being of age to govern of himself?
Cousin of Somerset, join you with me,
And all together, with the Duke of Suffolk,
We'll quickly hoise Duke Humphrey from his seat.

Car. This weighty business will not brook delay,
I'll to the Duke of Suffolk presently. *Exit Cardinal.*

Som. Cousin of Buckingham, though Humphrey's pride
And greatness of his place be grief to us,
Yet let us watch the haughty Cardinal;
His insolence is more intolerable
Than all the princes in the land beside.
If Gloucester be displac'd, he'll be Protector.

Buck. Or thou or I, Somerset, will be [Protector],
Despite Duke Humphrey or the Cardinal.
Exeunt Buckingham and Somerset.

Sal. Pride went before, ambition follows him.
While these do labor for their own preferment,
Behooves it us to labor for the realm.
I never saw but Humphrey Duke of Gloucester
Did bear him like a noble gentleman.
Oft have I seen the haughty Cardinal,
More like a soldier than a man o' th' church,
As stout and proud as he were lord of all,
Swear like a ruffian, and demean himself
Unlike the ruler of a commonweal.
Warwick, my son, the comfort of my age,
Thy deeds, thy plainness, and thy house-keeping,
Hath won the greatest favor of the commons,
Excepting none but good Duke Humphrey;
And, brother York, thy acts in Ireland,
In bringing them to civil discipline,
Thy late exploits done in the heart of France
When thou wert Regent for our sovereign,
Have made thee fear'd and honor'd of the people;
Join we together, for the public good,
In what we can to bridle and suppress
The pride of Suffolk and the Cardinal,
With Somerset's and Buckingham's ambition;
And as we may, cherish Duke Humphrey's deeds
While they do tend the profit of the land.

War. So God help Warwick, as he loves the land
And common profit of his country!

163. **flattering gloss**: attractive appearance.
166. **age.** At the time represented in this scene Henry VI was twenty-four and had long since assumed the royal power.
169. **hoise**: hoist. 170. **brook**: permit.
171. **presently**: immediately. 173. **grief**: grievance.
175. **insolence**: pride. 176. **all**: that of all. 178. **Or**: either.
180. **Pride**: i.e. the Cardinal. **ambition**: i.e. Buckingham and Somerset. 187. **as**: as if. 188. **demean**: behave.
191. **house-keeping**: hospitality.
193. **Excepting none but**: (greatest) except for their favor to.
194. **brother**: i.e. brother-in-law. York's wife was Salisbury's sister Cicely. **acts in Ireland.** An anachronism. York was appointed the King's lieutenant in Ireland in 1447, two years after the events represented in this scene. He did not return to England until 1450.

York. And so says York—[*aside*] for he hath greatest cause.
Sal. Then let's make haste away, and look unto the main.
War. Unto the main? O father, Maine is lost!
That Maine which by main force Warwick did win,
And would have kept so long as breath did last!
Main chance, father, you meant, but I meant Maine,
Which I will win from France, or else be slain.
Exeunt Warwick and Salisbury. Manet York.
York. Anjou and Maine are given to the French,
Paris is lost, the state of Normandy
Stands on a tickle point now they are gone.
Suffolk concluded on the articles,
The peers agreed, and Henry was well pleas'd
To change two dukedoms for a duke's fair daughter.
I cannot blame them all, what is't to them?
'Tis thine they give away, and not their own.
Pirates may make cheap pennyworths of their pillage
And purchase friends and give to courtezans,
Still revelling like lords till all be gone;
While as the silly owner of the goods
Weeps over them, and wrings his hapless hands,
And shakes his head, and trembling stands aloof,
While all is shar'd and all is borne away,
Ready to starve, and dare not touch his own.
So York must sit, and fret, and bite his tongue,
While his own lands are bargain'd for and sold.
Methinks the realms of England, France, and Ireland
Bear that proportion to my flesh and blood
As did the fatal brand Althaea burnt
Unto the Prince's heart of Calydon.
Anjou and Maine both given unto the French!
Cold news for me; for I had hope of France,
Even as I have of fertile England's soil.
A day will come when York shall claim his own,
And therefore I will take the Nevils' parts,
And make a show of love to proud Duke Humphrey,
And, when I spy advantage, claim the crown,
For that's the golden mark I seek to hit.
Nor shall proud Lancaster usurp my right,
Nor hold the sceptre in his childish fist,
Nor wear the diadem upon his head,
Whose church-like humors fits not for a crown.
Then, York, be still awhile, till time do serve.
Watch thou, and wake when others be asleep,
To pry into the secrets of the state,
Till Henry, surfeiting in joys of love
With his new bride and England's dear-bought queen,

207. greatest cause: i.e. as head of the rival house to Lancaster.
208. main: i.e. principal concern (with a pun on *main*, a term from the dice game called hazard, and on *Maine*, the French province).
216. tickle: precarious. **217. concluded on**: agreed to.
221. thine: i.e. York's.
222. make . . . of: i.e. sell for almost nothing.
225. While as: while. **silly**: helpless. **233. proportion**: relation.
234. fatal brand. Told by the Fates that her son Meleager would die when a brand then burning in the fire was consumed, Althaea snatched forth the brand and saved it until, years later, she caused his death by throwing it back into the fire.
235. Prince's . . . Calydon: heart of the Prince of Calydon (Meleager).
240. take . . . parts: i.e. ally myself with Salisbury and his son.
242. advantage: opportunity. **243. mark**: the center of a target.
244. proud Lancaster: i.e. Henry VI.
247. church-like humors: pious disposition.

And Humphrey with the peers be fall'n at jars:
Then will I raise aloft the milk-white rose,
With whose sweet smell the air shall be perfum'd,
And in my standard bear the arms of York,
To grapple with the house of Lancaster;
And force perforce I'll make him yield the crown,
Whose bookish rule hath pull'd fair England down.
Exit York.

[SCENE II]

Enter DUKE HUMPHREY [OF GLOUCESTER] *and his wife* ELEANOR [THE DUCHESS].

Duch. Why droops my lord, like over-ripen'd corn
Hanging the head at Ceres' plenteous load?
Why doth the great Duke Humphrey knit his brows,
As frowning at the favors of the world?
Why are thine eyes fix'd to the sullen earth,
Gazing on that which seems to dim thy sight?
What seest thou there? King Henry's diadem,
Enchas'd with all the honors of the world?
If so, gaze on, and grovel on thy face,
Until thy head be circled with the same.
Put forth thy hand, reach at the glorious gold.
What, is't too short? I'll lengthen it with mine,
And having both together heav'd it up,
We'll both together lift our heads to heaven,
And never more abase our sight so low
As to vouchsafe one glance unto the ground.
Glou. O Nell, sweet Nell, if thou dost love thy lord,
Banish the canker of ambitious thoughts!
And may that thought, when I imagine ill
Against my king and nephew, virtuous Henry,
Be my last breathing in this mortal world!
My troublous dreams this night doth make me sad.
Duch. What dream'd my lord? Tell me, and I'll requite it
With sweet rehearsal of my morning's dream.
Glou. Methought this staff, mine office-badge in court,
Was broke in twain (by whom I have forgot,
But, as I think, it was by th' Cardinal),
And on the pieces of the broken wand
Were plac'd the heads of Edmund Duke of Somerset,
And William de la Pole, first Duke of Suffolk.
This was my dream, what it doth bode God knows.
Duch. Tut, this was nothing but an argument
That he that breaks a stick of Gloucester's grove
Shall lose his head for his presumption.
But list to me, my Humphrey, my sweet duke:
Methought I sate in seat of majesty

253. at jars: into contention.
258. force perforce: by violent compulsion.
259. bookish: scholarly, i.e. tame.

I.ii. Location: London. The Duke of Gloucester's house.
2. Ceres' plenteous load: i.e. rich harvest. Ceres was the goddess of agriculture. **8. Enchas'd**: decorated. **18. canker**: ulcer.
22. this night: i.e. last night.
24. morning's dream. It was an ancient superstition that morning dreams were true.
25. mine office-badge: symbol of my authority as Protector.
32. argument: proof. **36. sate**: sat.

In the cathedral church of Westminster,
And in that chair where kings and queens were crown'd,
Where Henry and Dame Margaret kneel'd to me,
And on my head did set the diadem.

Glou. Nay, Eleanor, then must I chide outright.
Presumptuous dame, ill-nurtur'd Eleanor,
Art thou not second woman in the realm?
And the Protector's wife, belov'd of him?
Hast thou not worldly pleasure at command
Above the reach or compass of thy thought?
And wilt thou still be hammering treachery,
To tumble down thy husband and thyself
From top of honor to disgrace's feet?
Away from me, and let me hear no more!

Duch. What, what, my lord? are you so choleric
With Eleanor, for telling but her dream?
Next time I'll keep my dreams unto myself,
And not be check'd.

Glou. Nay, be not angry, I am pleas'd again.

Enter MESSENGER.

Mess. My Lord Protector, 'tis his Highness' pleasure
You do prepare to ride unto Saint Albons,
Where as the King and Queen do mean to hawk.

Glou. I go. Come, Nell, thou wilt ride with us?

Duch. Yes, my good lord, I'll follow presently.

Exit Humphrey [*with Messenger*].

Follow I must, I cannot go before
While Gloucester bears this base and humble mind.
Were I a man, a duke, and next of blood,
I would remove these tedious stumbling-blocks,
And smooth my way upon their headless necks;
And, being a woman, I will not be slack
To play my part in Fortune's pageant.
Where are you there? Sir John! Nay, fear not, man,
We are alone, here's none but thee and I.

Enter HUME.

Hume. Jesus preserve your royal Majesty!

Duch. What say'st thou? Majesty? I am but Grace.

Hume. But, by the grace of God and Hume's advice,
Your Grace's title shall be multiplied.

Duch. What say'st thou, man? Hast thou as yet conferr'd
With Margery Jordan, the cunning witch,
With Roger Bolingbrook, the conjurer?
And will they undertake to do me good?

Hume. This they have promised, to show your Highness
A spirit rais'd from depth of under ground,
That shall make answer to such questions
As by your Grace shall be propounded him.

Duch. It is enough, I'll think upon the questions.
When from Saint Albons we do make return,
We'll see these things effected to the full.
Here, Hume, take this reward. Make merry, man,
With thy confederates in this weighty cause.

Exit Eleanor.

Hume. Hume must make merry with the Duchess' gold;
Marry, and shall. But how now, Sir John Hume?
Seal up your lips, and give no words but mum;
The business asketh silent secrecy.
Dame Eleanor gives gold to bring the witch;
Gold cannot come amiss, were she a devil.
Yet have I gold flies from another coast—
I dare not say from the rich Cardinal
And from the great and new-made Duke of Suffolk;
Yet I do find it so; for, to be plain,
They, knowing Dame Eleanor's aspiring humor,
Have hired me to undermine the Duchess,
And buzz these conjurations in her brain.
They say, "A crafty knave does need no broker,"
Yet am I Suffolk and the Cardinal's broker.
Hume, if you take not heed, you shall go near
To call them both a pair of crafty knaves.
Well, so it stands; and thus, I fear, at last
Hume's knavery will be the Duchess' wrack,
And her attainture will be Humphrey's fall.
Sort how it will, I shall have gold for all. *Exit.*

[SCENE III]

Enter three or four PETITIONERS, [PETER] *the Armorer's man being one.*

1. Petit. My masters, let's stand close. My Lord Protector will come this way by and by, and then we may deliver our supplications in the quill.

2. Petit. Marry, the Lord protect him, for he's a good man! Jesu bless him!

Enter SUFFOLK *and* QUEEN.

Peter. Here 'a comes, methinks, and the Queen with him. I'll be the first, sure.

2. Petit. Come back, fool. This is the Duke of Suffolk and not my Lord Protector.

Suf. How now, fellow? wouldst any thing with me?

1. Petit. I pray, my lord, pardon me, I took ye for my Lord Protector.

Queen. [*Reading.*] "To my Lord Protector"? Are your supplications to his lordship? Let me see them. What is thine?

38. chair: the coronation chair containing the ancient Stone of Scone, which Edward I brought from Scotland in 1296.
42. ill-nurtur'd: ill-bred. **47. hammering:** devising.
54. check'd: rebuked.
57. Saint Albons: St. Albans (the Roman Verulam), a town some twenty miles north of London. **58. Where as:** where.
60. presently: immediately.
70. Majesty. An anachronism. "Your Majesty" was a title first used by the Tudors.

88. Marry: indeed (originally the name of the Virgin Mary used as an oath). **93. flies:** that flies. **coast:** direction.
97. aspiring humor: ambitious nature. **100. broker:** agent.
105. wrack: destruction.
106. attainture: conviction (and disgrace). **107. Sort:** turn out.

I.iii. Location: London. The palace.
3. in the quill: i.e. all together. **6. 'a:** he.

1. Petit. Mine is, and't please your Grace, against John Goodman, my Lord Cardinal's man, for keeping my house, and lands, and wife and all, from me.

Suf. Thy wife too? that's some wrong indeed. What's yours? What's here? [*Reads.*] "Against the Duke of Suffolk, for enclosing the commons of Melford." How now, sir knave?

2. Petit. Alas, sir, I am but a poor petitioner of our whole township.

Peter. [*Giving his petition.*] Against my master, Thomas Horner, for saying that the Duke of York was rightful heir to the crown.

Queen. What say'st thou? Did the Duke of York say he was rightful heir to the crown?

Peter. That my [master] was? No, forsooth; my master said that he was, and that the King was an usurper.

Suf. Who is there? (*Enter Servant.*) Take this fellow in, and send for his master with a pursuivant presently. We'll hear more of your matter before the King.

Exit [*Servant with Peter*].

Queen. And as for you, that love to be protected
Under the wings of our Protector's grace,
Begin your suits anew, and sue to him.

Tear the supplication.

Away, base cullions! Suffolk, let them go.

All [*Petitioners*]. Come, let's be gone. *Exeunt.*

Queen. My Lord of Suffolk, say, is this the guise,
Is this the fashions in the court of England?
Is this the government of Britain's isle,
And this the royalty of Albion's king?
What, shall King Henry be a pupil still
Under the surly Gloucester's governance?
Am I a queen in title and in style,
And must be made a subject to a duke?
I tell thee, Pole, when in the city Tours
Thou ran'st a-tilt in honor of my love
And stol'st away the ladies' hearts of France,
I thought King Henry had resembled thee
In courage, courtship, and proportion;
But all his mind is bent to holiness,
To number Ave-Maries on his beads;
His champions are the prophets and apostles,
His weapons holy saws of sacred writ,
His study is his tilt-yard, and his loves
Are brazen images of canonized saints.
I would the college of the Cardinals
Would choose him Pope and carry him to Rome,
And set the triple crown upon his head—
That were a state fit for his holiness.

21. commons: common land, the enclosure of which by landlords was the cause of mounting complaint by their tenants.
22. Melford: Long Melford, town in the county of Suffolk.
26–27. for . . . crown. In Hall (Bullough, III, 105), from whom Shakespeare drew the episode of the armorer and his man, the question of York's loyalty is not raised at all.
34. pursuivant: junior official attendant on a herald, messenger.
40. cullions: wretches (Italian *coglioni*, testicles).
42. guise: custom. **48. style:** title.
51. ran'st a-tilt: took part in a tournament. Hall reports (Bullough, I, 102) that when Suffolk went to France to arrange Henry's marriage with Margaret "there wer triumphaunt Justes, costly feastes, and delicate banquettes" to celebrate the nuptials.
54. courtship: courtliness of manner. **proportion:** physical grace.
64. state: status.

Suf. Madam, be patient. As I was cause
Your Highness came to England, so will I
In England work your Grace's full content.

Queen. Beside the haughty Protector, have we Beauford
The imperious churchman, Somerset, Buckingham,
And grumbling York; and not the least of these
But can do more in England than the King.

Suf. And he of these that can do most of all
Cannot do more in England than the Nevils:
Salisbury and Warwick are no simple peers.

Queen. Not all these lords do vex me half so much
As that proud dame, the Lord Protector's wife:
She sweeps it through the court with troops of ladies,
More like an empress than Duke Humphrey's wife.
Strangers in court do take her for the Queen.
She bears a duke's revenues on her back,
And in her heart she scorns our poverty.
Shall I not live to be aveng'd on her?
Contemptuous base-born callot as she is,
She vaunted 'mongst her minions t' other day,
The very train of her worst wearing gown
Was better worth than all my father's lands,
Till Suffolk gave two dukedoms for his daughter.

Suf. Madam, myself have lim'd a bush for her,
And plac'd a choir of such enticing birds
That she will light to listen to the lays,
And never mount to trouble you again.
So let her rest; and, madam, list to me,
For I am bold to counsel you in this.
Although we fancy not the Cardinal,
Yet must we join with him and with the lords,
Till we have brought Duke Humphrey in disgrace.
As for the Duke of York, this late complaint
Will make but little for his benefit.
So one by one we'll weed them all at last,
And you yourself shall steer the happy helm.

Sound a sennet. Enter the King, Duke Humphrey [of Gloucester], Cardinal, Buckingham, York, [Somerset,] Salisbury, Warwick, *and the* Duchess [of Gloucester].

King. For my part, noble lords, I care not which,
Or Somerset or York, all's one to me.

York. If York have ill demean'd himself in France,
Then let him be denay'd the regentship.

Som. If Somerset be unworthy of the place,
Let York be Regent, I will yield to him.

War. Whether your Grace be worthy, yea or no,
Dispute not that; York is the worthier.

74. Salisbury . . . peers. This remark anticipates the decisive part played by the powerful Neville family in the ensuing struggles between the Yorkists and Lancastrians. Salisbury was the son and Warwick ("the Kingmaker") the grandson of Sir Ralph Neville (created first Earl of Westmorland by Richard II in 1397) and his second wife Joan Beaufort (a daughter of John of Gaunt and a sister of the Cardinal). On the Beaufort family see note to *1 Henry VI*, III.i.42.
75–87. Not . . . daughter. Actually, Eleanor, Duchess of Gloucester, had been accused of witchcraft and banished from the court in 1441, four years before Queen Margaret came to England.
83. Contemptuous: contemptible. **callot:** callet, strumpet.
88. lim'd: covered with birdlime, a sticky substance used to catch birds. **89. enticing birds:** decoys.
97. late complaint: i.e. of Peter the armorer's man against his master.
100 s.d. sennet: trumpet call announcing a procession.
104. denay'd: refused.

Car. Ambitious Warwick, let thy betters speak.
War. The Cardinal's not my better in the field.
Buck. All in this presence are thy betters, Warwick.
War. Warwick may live to be the best of all.
Sal. Peace, son, and show some reason, Buckingham,
Why Somerset should be preferr'd in this.
Queen. Because the King, forsooth, will have it so.
Glou. Madam, the King is old enough himself
To give his censure. These are no women's matters.
Queen. If he be old enough, what needs your Grace
To be Protector of his Excellence?
Glou. Madam, I am Protector of the realm,
And at his pleasure will resign my place.
Suf. Resign it then and leave thine insolence.
Since thou wert king—as who is king but thou?—
The commonwealth hath daily run to wrack,
The Dolphin hath prevail'd beyond the seas,
And all the peers and nobles of the realm
Have been as bondmen to thy sovereignty.
Car. The commons hast thou rack'd, the clergy's bags
Are lank and lean with thy extortions.
Som. Thy sumptuous buildings and thy wive's attire
Have cost a mass of public treasury.
Buck. Thy cruelty in execution
Upon offenders hath exceeded law,
And left thee to the mercy of the law.
Queen. Thy sale of offices and towns in France,
If they were known, as the suspect is great,
Would make thee quickly hop without thy head.
Exit Humphrey. [*The Queen lets fall her fan.*]
Give me my fan. What, minion, can ye not?
She gives the Duchess a box on the ear.
I cry you mercy, madam; was it you?
Duch. Was't I? yea, I it was, proud Frenchwoman.
Could I come near your beauty with my nails,
I could set my ten commandements in your face.
King. Sweet aunt, be quiet, 'twas against her will.
Duch. Against her will, good king? Look to't in time,
She'll hamper thee, and dandle thee like a baby.
Though in this place most master wear no breeches,
She shall not strike Dame Eleanor unreveng'd.
Exit Eleanor.
Buck. Lord Cardinal, I will follow Eleanor,
And listen after Humphrey, how he proceeds.
She's tickled now; her fume needs no spurs,
She'll gallop far enough to her destruction.
Exit Buckingham.

117. **censure**: judgment.
125. **Dolphin**: Dauphin, title of the heir apparent to the French throne. Charles VII is so called here because the English considered Henry VI the rightful king of France.
128. **rack'd**: impoverished by extortion. 130. **wive's**: wife's.
131. **treasury**: treasure. 136. **suspect**: suspicion.
139. **cry you mercy**: beg your pardon.
142. **ten commandements**: i.e. ten fingers.
144. **Against her will**: unintentional.
146. **most master**: the one most masterful, i.e. the Queen.
149. **listen after**: inquire about.
150. **tickled**: irritated. **fume**: smoke, i.e. fury.

Enter HUMPHREY [OF GLOUCESTER].

Glou. Now, lords, my choler being overblown
With walking once about the quadrangle,
I come to talk of commonwealth affairs.
As for your spiteful false objections,
Prove them, and I lie open to the law;
But God in mercy so deal with my soul
As I in duty love my king and country!
But to the matter that we have in hand.
I say, my sovereign, York is meetest man
To be your Regent in the realm of France.
Suf. Before we make election, give me leave
To show some reason, of no little force,
That York is most unmeet of any man.
York. I'll tell thee, Suffolk, why I am unmeet:
First, for I cannot flatter thee in pride;
Next, if I be appointed for the place,
My Lord of Somerset will keep me here
Without discharge, money, or furniture,
Till France be won into the Dolphin's hands.
Last time, I danc'd attendance on his will
Till Paris was besieg'd, famish'd, and lost.
War. That can I witness, and a fouler fact
Did never traitor in the land commit.
Suf. Peace, headstrong Warwick!
War. Image of pride, why should I hold my peace?

Enter [HORNER *the*] *armorer and his man* [PETER, *guarded*].

Suf. Because here is a man accused of treason.
Pray God the Duke of York excuse himself!
York. Doth any one accuse York for a traitor?
King. What mean'st thou, Suffolk? tell me, what are these?
Suf. Please it your Majesty, this is the man
That doth accuse his master of high treason.
His words were these: that Richard Duke of York
Was rightful heir unto the English crown
And that your Majesty was an usurper.
King. Say, man, were these thy words?

Hor. And't shall please your Majesty, I never said nor thought any such matter. God is my witness, I am falsely accus'd by the villain.

Peter. By these ten bones, my lords [*holding up his hands*], he did speak them to me in the garret one night, as we were scouring my Lord of York's armor.

York. Base dunghill villain and mechanical,
I'll have thy head for this thy traitor's speech.
I do beseech your royal Majesty,
Let him have all the rigor of the law.

Hor. Alas, my lord, hang me if ever I spake the words. My accuser is my prentice, and when I did correct him for his fault the other day, he did vow upon his knees he would be even with me. I have good witness of this; therefore I beseech your Majesty, do not cast away an honest man for a villain's accusation.

152. **overblown**: blown over, dissipated. 162. **election**: choice.
166. **for**: because.
169. **discharge**: financial settlement. **furniture**: military equipment.
171. **Last time.** See *1 Henry VI*, IV.iii. 173. **fact**: deed, crime.
193. **mechanical**: menial. 202. **cast away**: destroy.

King. Uncle, what shall we say to this in law?
Glou. This doom, my lord, if I may judge:
Let Somerset be Regent o'er the French,
Because in York this breeds suspicion;
And let these have a day appointed them
For single combat in convenient place,
For he hath witness of his servant's malice.
This is the law, and this Duke Humphrey's doom.
Som. I humbly thank your royal Majesty.
Hor. And I accept the combat willingly.

Peter. Alas, my lord, I cannot fight; for God's sake pity my case. The spite of man prevaileth against me. O Lord, have mercy upon me! I shall never be able to fight a blow. O Lord, my heart!

Glou. Sirrah, or you must fight, or else be hang'd.

King. Away with them to prison; and the day of combat shall be the last of the next month. Come, Somerset, we'll see thee sent away.

Flourish. Exeunt.

[Scene IV]

Enter the witch [Margery Jordan], *the two priests* [Hume *and* Southwell], *and* Bolingbrook.

Hume. Come, my masters, the Duchess, I tell you, expects performance of your promises.

Boling. Master Hume, we are therefore provided. Will her ladyship behold and hear our exorcisms?

Hume. Ay, what else? fear you not her courage.

Boling. I have heard her reported to be a woman of an invincible spirit; but it shall be convenient, Master Hume, that you be by her aloft, while we be busy below; and so I pray you go in God's name, and leave us. (*Exit Hume.*) Mother Jordan, be you prostrate and grovel on the earth. [*She lies down upon her face.*] John Southwell, read you; and let us to our work.

Enter Eleanor [the Duchess] *aloft*, [Hume *following*].

Duch. Well said, my masters, and welcome all. To this gear, the sooner the better.

Boling. Patience, good lady, wizards know their times.
Deep night, dark night, the silent of the night,
The time of night when Troy was set on fire,
The time when screech-owls cry and ban-dogs howl,
And spirits walk, and ghosts break up their graves,
That time best fits the work we have in hand.
Madam, sit you and fear not. Whom we raise,
We will make fast within a hallow'd verge.

Here do the ceremonies belonging, and make the circle; Bolingbrook or Southwell reads, "Conjuro te, etc." *It thunders and lightens terribly; then the Spirit riseth.*

Spir. *Adsum.*
M. Jord. Asmath,
By the eternal God, whose name and power
Thou tremblest at, answer that I shall ask;
For, till thou speak, thou shalt not pass from hence.
Spir. Ask what thou wilt. That I had said, and done!
Boling. "First of the King: what shall of him become?" [*Reading out of a paper.*]
Spir. The duke yet lives that Henry shall depose;
But him out-live, and die a violent death.
[*As the Spirit speaks, Bolingbrook writes the answer.*]
Boling. "[Tell me] what [fate awaits] the Duke of Suffolk?"
Spir. By water shall he die, and take his end.
Boling. "What shall [betide] the Duke of Somerset?"
Spir. Let him shun castles.
Safer shall he be upon the sandy plains
Than where castles mounted stand.
Have done, for more I hardly can endure.
Boling. Descend to darkness and the burning lake!
False fiend, avoid!

Thunder and lightning. Exit Spirit [*sinking down again*].

Enter the Duke of York *and the* Duke of Buckingham *with their* Guard, [Sir Humphrey Stafford *as Captain,*] *and break in.*

York. Lay hands upon these traitors and their trash.
Beldam, I think we watch'd you at an inch.
What, madam, are you there? The King and commonweal
Are deeply indebted for this piece of pains.
My Lord Protector will, I doubt it not,
See you well guerdon'd for these good deserts.
Duch. Not half so bad as thine to England's king,
Injurious duke, that threatest where's no cause.
Buck. True, madam, none at all. What call you this?
Away with them, let them be clapp'd up close,
And kept asunder. You, madam, shall with us.
Stafford, take her to thee.
[*Exeunt, above, Duchess and Hume guarded.*]
We'll see your trinkets here all forthcoming.
All away! *Exit* [*Guard with Jordan, Southwell, etc.*].
York. Lord Buckingham, methinks you watch'd her well.
A pretty plot, well chosen to build upon!
Now pray, my lord, let's see the devil's writ.
What have we here? *Reads.*

204. doom: judgment.
217. Sirrah: customary form of address to an inferior.

I.iv. Location: London. Gloucester's garden.
4. exorcisms: conjurations. **13. Well said:** well done.
14. To this gear: on with the business.
18. ban-dogs: dogs chained up, either to guard a house or because of their ferocity.
22. make . . . verge: confine within a magic circle. **s.d. ceremonies belonging:** i.e. the ritual pertaining to the conjurations, such as drawing a magic circle and repeating formulas of incantation. **Conjuro te:** I conjure you.

23. Adsum: I am here.
24. Asmath: the name of the conjured fiend, perhaps a misprint for *Asnath*, an anagram for *Sathan* (Satan). **26. that:** what.
28. That: would that. **40. False:** treacherous. **avoid:** depart.
42. Beldam: hag. **at an inch:** closely.
46. guerdon'd: rewarded.
50. clapp'd up close: imprisoned closely.
53. trinkets: trash. **forthcoming:** given into legal custody.
56. plot: (1) trick; (2) plot of ground.

"The duke yet lives that Henry shall depose;
But him out-live, and die a violent death."
Why, this is just
"*Aio [te,] Aeacida, Romanos vincere posse.*"
Well, to the rest:
"Tell me what fate awaits the Duke of Suffolk?"
"By water shall he die, and take his end."
"What shall betide the Duke of Somerset?"
"Let him shun castles;
Safer shall he be upon the sandy plains
Than where castles mounted stand."
Come, come, my lords, these oracles
Are hardly attain'd, and hardly understood.
The King is now in progress towards Saint Albons,
With him the husband of this lovely lady.
Thither goes these news, as fast as horse can carry them—
A sorry breakfast for my Lord Protector.

Buck. Your Grace shall give me leave, my Lord of York,
To be the post, in hope of his reward.

York. At your pleasure, my good lord. Who's within there, ho?

Enter a Servingman.

Invite my Lords of Salisbury and Warwick
To sup with me to-morrow night. Away! *Exeunt.*

[ACT II, Scene I]

Enter the King, Queen [*with her hawk on her fist*], Protector [Gloucester], Cardinal, *and* Suffolk, *with* Falc'ners *hallowing*.

Queen. Believe me, lords, for flying at the brook,
I saw not better sport these seven years' day;
Yet by your leave, the wind was very high,
And ten to one, old Joan had not gone out.

King. But what a point, my lord, your falcon made,
And what a pitch she flew above the rest!
To see how God in all his creatures works!
Yea, man and birds are fain of climbing high.

Suf. No marvel, and it like your Majesty,
My Lord Protector's hawks do tow'r so well;
They know their master loves to be aloft,
And bears his thoughts above his falcon's pitch.

Glou. My lord, 'tis but a base ignoble mind
That mounts no higher than a bird can soar.

Car. I thought as much, he would be above the clouds.

Glou. Ay, my Lord Cardinal, how think you by that?
Were it not good your Grace could fly to heaven?

King. The treasury of everlasting joy.

Car. Thy heaven is on earth, thine eyes and thoughts
Beat on a crown, the treasure of thy heart,
Pernicious Protector, dangerous peer,
That smooth'st it so with king and commonweal!

Glou. What, Cardinal? is your priesthood grown peremptory?
Tantaene animis caelestibus irae?
Churchmen so hot? Good uncle, hide such malice;
With such holiness can you do it?

Suf. No malice, sir, no more than well becomes
So good a quarrel and so bad a peer.

Glou. As who, my lord?

Suf. Why, as you, my lord,
An't like your lordly Lord's Protectorship.

Glou. Why, Suffolk, England knows thine insolence.

Queen. And thy ambition, Gloucester.

King. I prithee peace,
Good queen, and whet not on these furious peers,
For blessed are the peacemakers on earth.

Car. Let me be blessed for the peace I make
Against this proud Protector with my sword!

Glou. [*Aside to Cardinal.*] Faith, holy uncle, would't were come to that!

Car. [*Aside to Gloucester.*] Marry, when thou dar'st.

Glou. [*Aside to Cardinal.*] Make up no factious numbers for the matter,
In thine own person answer thy abuse.

Car. [*Aside to Gloucester.*] Ay, where thou dar'st not peep. And if thou dar'st,
This evening, on the east side of the grove.

King. How now, my lords?

Car. Believe me, cousin Gloucester,
Had not your man put up the fowl so suddenly,
We had had more sport. [*Aside to Gloucester.*] Come with thy two-hand sword.

Glou. True, uncle.

[*Car.*] [*Aside to Gloucester.*] Are ye advis'd? The east side of the grove.

Glou. [*Aside to Cardinal.*] Cardinal, I am with you.

King. Why, how now, uncle Gloucester?

Glou. Talking of hawking; nothing else, my lord.
[*Aside to Cardinal.*] Now by God's Mother, priest, I'll shave your crown for this,
Or all my fence shall fail.

Car. [*Aside to Gloucester.*] *Medice, teipsum*—
Protector, see to't well, protect yourself.

King. The winds grow high, so do your stomachs, lords.

61. just: precisely.
62. Aio . . . posse: "I say that you, descendant of Aeacus, the Romans can conquer," the ambiguous answer given by the Pythian Apollo to Pyrrhus. **71. hardly attain'd:** with difficulty obtained.

II.i. Location: St. Albans.
1. flying . . . brook: hawking for waterfowl (a form of falconry favored by the nobility).
4. old . . . out: i.e. the old hawk (named Joan) would not have flown in such a high wind.
5. point: place from which to swoop upon the prey.
6. pitch: height. **8. fain:** fond.
10. My . . . hawks. Gloucester's badge was a falcon with a maiden's head, which explains the gibes that follow. **tow'r:** wheel and rise until the proper "point" is reached.

20. Beat on: i.e. ponder.
22. smooth'st: flatterest.
24. Tantaene . . . irae: "Is there such anger in heavenly minds" (*Aeneid*, i.11). **31. insolence:** pride.
33. whet: sharpen, encourage.
39. Make . . . matter: i.e. do not involve your unruly supporters in the quarrel. **40. abuse:** offense, insult.
44. put . . . fowl: i.e. raised the game. **47. advis'd:** agreed.
51. fence: skill in fencing. **Medice, teipsum:** "Physician, [heal] thyself" (Luke 4:23). **53. stomachs:** angry tempers.

How irksome is this music to my heart!
When such strings jar, what hope of harmony?
I pray, my lords, let me compound this strife.

Enter one crying, "A miracle!"

Glou. What means this noise?
Fellow, what miracle dost thou proclaim?
One. A miracle, a miracle!
Suf. Come to the King and tell him what miracle.
One. Forsooth, a blind man at Saint Albon's shrine,
Within this half hour, hath receiv'd his sight,
A man that ne'er saw in his life before.
King. Now God be prais'd, that to believing souls
Gives light in darkness, comfort in despair!

Enter the Mayor of Saint Albons *and his* Brethren, [*with music*,] *bearing the man* [Simpcox] *between two in a chair*, [*Simpcox's* Wife *and others following*].

Car. Here comes the townsmen on procession,
To present your Highness with the man.
King. Great is his comfort in this earthly vale,
Although by his sight his sin be multiplied.
Glou. Stand by, my masters. Bring him near the King,
His Highness' pleasure is to talk with him.
King. Good fellow, tell us here the circumstance,
That we for thee may glorify the Lord.
What, hast thou been long blind and now restor'd?
Simp. Born blind, and't please your Grace.
Wife. Ay indeed was he.
Suf. What woman is this?
Wife. His wife, and't like your worship.
Glou. Hadst thou been his mother, thou couldst have better told.
King. Where wert thou born?
Simp. At Berwick in the north, and't like your Grace.
King. Poor soul, God's goodness hath been great to thee.
Let never day nor night unhallowed pass,
But still remember what the Lord hath done.
Queen. Tell me, good fellow, cam'st thou here by chance
Or of devotion, to this holy shrine?
Simp. God knows, of pure devotion, being call'd
A hundred times and oft'ner, in my sleep,
By good Saint Albon, who said, "Simon, come;
Come offer at my shrine, and I will help thee."
Wife. Most true, forsooth; and many time and oft
Myself have heard a voice to call him so.
Car. What, art thou lame?
Simp. Ay, God Almighty help me!
Suf. How cam'st thou so?
Simp. A fall off of a tree.
Wife. A plum-tree, master.
Glou. How long hast thou been blind?
Simp. O, born so, master.
Glou. What, and wouldst climb a tree?
Simp. But that in all my life, when I was a youth.
Wife. Too true, and bought his climbing very dear.
Glou. Mass, thou lov'dst plums well, that wouldst venture so.
Simp. Alas, good master, my wife desired some damsons,
And made me climb, with danger of my life.
Glou. A subtile knave, but yet it shall not serve.
Let me see thine eyes. Wink now; now open them.
In my opinion yet thou seest not well.
Simp. Yes, master, clear as day, I thank God and Saint Albon.
Glou. Say'st thou me so? What color is this cloak of?
Simp. Red, master, red as blood.
Glou. Why, that's well said. What color is my gown of?
Simp. Black, forsooth, coal-black as jet.
King. Why then, thou know'st what color jet is of?
Suf. And yet, I think, jet did he never see.
Glou. But cloaks and gowns, before this day, a many.
Wife. Never, before this day, in all his life.
Glou. Tell me, sirrah, what's my name?
Simp. Alas, master, I know not.
Glou. What's his name?
Simp. I know not.
Glou. Nor his?
Simp. No indeed, master.
Glou. What's thine own name?
Simp. Saunder Simpcox, and if it please you, master.
Glou. Then, Saunder, sit there, the lying'st knave
In Christendom. If thou hadst been born blind,
Thou mightst as well have known all our names, as thus
To name the several colors we do wear.
Sight may distinguish of colors; but suddenly
To nominate them all, it is impossible.
My lords, Saint Albon here hath done a miracle;
And would ye not think [his] cunning to be great,
That could restore this cripple to his legs again?
Simp. O master, that you could!
Glou. My masters of Saint Albons, have you not
Beadles in your town, and things call'd whips?
May. Yes, my lord, if it please your Grace.
Glou. Then send for one presently.
May. Sirrah, go fetch the beadle hither straight.
Exit [*one*].

56. compound: settle.
57–160. Shakespeare found the spurious miracle of St. Albans in John Foxe's *Acts and Monuments* (1583), where it is introduced (Bullough, III, 127) as "reported as well by the penne of syr Thomas More, as also by M. William Tindall, the true Apostle of these our latter dayes, to the intent to see and note, not only the craftye working of false miracles in the clergye, but also that the prudent discretion of this high and mighty prince, the fore sayd Duke Humfrey, may geve us better to understand what man he was."
61. Albon: Alban, allegedly the first British martyr, executed (304?) in the Roman town Verulam (later renamed St. Albans) for protecting Christian converts. **66. on:** in.
69. by . . . multiplied: i.e. he will be subject to more temptation.
75. and: if. **78. like:** please.
81. Berwick: town and fortress on the Scottish border at the mouth of the River Tweed. **83. unhallowed:** unblessed.
84. still: always.
97. But that: i.e. only that one.
99. Mass: by the Mass. **103. Wink:** close both eyes.
128. nominate: call by name.
134. Beadles: officers who administered corporal punishment.
136. presently: immediately.

Glou. Now fetch me a stool hither by and by. [*A stool brought.*] Now, sirrah, if you mean to save yourself from whipping, leap me over this stool and run away.

Simp. Alas, master, I am not able to stand alone;
You go about to torture me in vain.

Enter a BEADLE *with whips.*

Glou. Well, sir, we must have you find your legs. Sirrah beadle, whip him till he leap over that same stool.

Bead. I will, my lord. Come on, sirrah, off with your doublet quickly.

Simp. Alas, master, what shall I do? I am not able to stand.

After the Beadle hath hit him once, he leaps over the stool and runs away; and they follow and cry, "A miracle!"

King. O God, seest thou this, and bearest so long?
Queen. It made me laugh to see the villain run.
Glou. Follow the knave, and take this drab away.
Wife. Alas, sir, we did it for pure need.
Glou. Let them be whipt through every market town,
Till they come to Berwick, from whence they came.

Exeunt [*Wife, Beadle, Mayor, etc.*].

Car. Duke Humphrey has done a miracle to-day.
Suf. True; made the lame to leap and fly away.
Glou. But you have done more miracles than I:
You made in a day, my lord, whole towns to fly.

Enter BUCKINGHAM.

King. What tidings with our cousin Buckingham?
Buck. Such as my heart doth tremble to unfold:
A sort of naughty persons, lewdly bent,
Under the countenance and confederacy
Of Lady Eleanor, the Protector's wife,
The ringleader and head of all this rout,
Have practic'd dangerously against your state,
Dealing with witches and with conjurers,
Whom we have apprehended in the fact,
Raising up wicked spirits from under ground,
Demanding of King Henry's life and death,
And other of your Highness' Privy Council,
As more at large your Grace shall understand.
Car. And so, my Lord Protector, by this means
Your lady is forthcoming yet at London.
[*Aside to Gloucester.*] This news, I think, hath turn'd your weapon's edge;
'Tis like, my lord, you will not keep your hour.
Glou. Ambitious churchman, leave to afflict my heart.
Sorrow and grief have vanquish'd all my powers;
And vanquish'd as I am, I yield to thee,
Or to the meanest groom.
King. O God, what mischiefs work the wicked ones,
Heaping confusion on their own heads thereby!
Queen. Gloucester, see here the tainture of thy nest,
And look thyself be faultless, thou wert best.
Glou. Madam, for myself, to heaven I do appeal,
How I have lov'd my king and commonweal;
And for my wife, I know not how it stands.
Sorry I am to hear what I have heard.
Noble she is; but if she have forgot
Honor and virtue, and convers'd with such
As, like to pitch, defile nobility,
I banish her my bed and company,
And give her as a prey to law and shame,
That hath dishonored Gloucester's honest name.
King. Well, for this night we will repose us here;
To-morrow toward London back again,
To look into this business thoroughly,
And call these foul offenders to their answers,
And poise the cause in justice' equal scales,
Whose beam stands sure, whose rightful cause prevails.

Flourish. Exeunt.

[SCENE II]

Enter YORK, SALISBURY, *and* WARWICK.

York. Now, my good Lords of Salisbury and Warwick,
Our simple supper ended, give me leave
In this close walk to satisfy myself
In craving your opinion of my title,
Which is infallible, to England's crown.
Sal. My lord, I long to hear it at full.
War. Sweet York, begin; and if thy claim be good,
The Nevils are thy subjects to command.
York. Then thus:
Edward the Third, my lords, had seven sons:
The first, Edward the Black Prince, Prince of Wales;
The second, William of Hatfield; and the third,
Lionel Duke of Clarence; next to whom
Was John of Gaunt, the Duke of Lancaster;
The fift was Edmund Langley, Duke of York;
The sixt was Thomas of Woodstock, Duke of Gloucester;
William of Windsor was the seventh and last.
Edward the Black Prince died before his father,
And left behind him Richard, his only son,
Who after Edward the Third's death reign'd as king
Till Henry Bullingbrook, Duke of Lancaster,
The eldest son and heir of John of Gaunt,
Crown'd by the name of Henry the Fourth,
Seiz'd on the realm, depos'd the rightful king,
Sent his poor queen to France, from whence she came,
And him to Pomfret; where, as all you know,
Harmless Richard was murthered traitorously.

140. me: for me, at my bidding.
160. You . . . fly. An ironic allusion to the Queen's dowry that Suffolk had arranged.
163. A sort . . . bent: a gang of disreputable people wickedly disposed.
164. Under . . . confederacy: with the protection and even the complicity. **167. practic'd:** plotted. **169. fact:** act.
175. forthcoming: in custody.
177. hour: appointment (for the duel previously arranged).

181. meanest: lowest.
191. convers'd: consorted. **200. poise:** weigh.

II.ii. Location: London. The Duke of York's garden.
3. close walk: private path.

War. Father, the Duke hath told the truth;
Thus got the house of Lancaster the crown.
York. Which now they hold by force and not by right;
For Richard, the first son's heir, being dead,
The issue of the next son should have reign'd.
Sal. But William of Hatfield died without an heir.
York. The third son, Duke of Clarence, from whose line
I claim the crown, had issue, Philippe, a daughter,
Who married Edmund Mortimer, Earl of March;
Edmund had issue, Roger Earl of March;
Roger had issue, Edmund, Anne, and Eleanor.
Sal. This Edmund, in the reign of Bullingbrook,
As I have read, laid claim unto the crown,
And but for Owen Glendower, had been king,
Who kept him in captivity till he died.
But, to the rest.
York. His eldest sister, Anne,
My mother, being heir unto the crown,
Married Richard Earl of Cambridge, who was
To Edmund Langley, Edward the Third's fift [son,] son.
By her I claim the kingdom. She was heir
To Roger Earl of March, who was the son
Of Edmund Mortimer, who married Philippe,
Sole daughter unto Lionel Duke of Clarence;
So, if the issue of the elder son
Succeed before the younger, I am king.
War. What plain proceedings is more plain than this?
Henry doth claim the crown from John of Gaunt,
The fourth son, York claims it from the third;
Till Lionel's issue fails, his should not reign.
It fails not yet, but flourishes in thee,
And in thy sons, fair slips of such a stock.
Then, father Salisbury, kneel we together,
And in this private plot be we the first
That shall salute our rightful sovereign
With honor of his birthright to the crown.
Both. Long live our sovereign Richard, England's king!
York. We thank you, lords. But I am not your king
Till I be crown'd, and that my sword be stain'd
With heart-blood of the house of Lancaster;
And that's not suddenly to be perform'd,
But with advice and silent secrecy.
Do you as I do in these dangerous days:
Wink at the Duke of Suffolk's insolence,
At Beauford's pride, at Somerset's ambition,
At Buckingham, and all the crew of them,
Till they have snar'd the shepherd of the flock,
That virtuous prince, the good Duke Humphrey.
'Tis that they seek; and they in seeking that
Shall find their deaths, if York can prophesy.
Sal. My lord, break we off; we know your mind at full.
War. My heart assures me that the Earl of Warwick
Shall one day make the Duke of York a king.
York. And, Nevil, this I do assure myself,
Richard shall live to make the Earl of Warwick
The greatest man in England but the King. *Exeunt.*

[SCENE III]

Sound trumpets. Enter the KING *and State: [the* QUEEN, GLOUCESTER, YORK, SUFFOLK, *and* SALISBURY,*] with* GUARD, *to banish the Duchess. [Enter, guarded, the* DUCHESS OF GLOUCESTER, MARGERY JORDAN, SOUTHWELL, HUME, *and* BOLINGBROOK.]

King. Stand forth, Dame Eleanor Cobham, Gloucester's wife:
In sight of God and us, your guilt is great;
Receive the sentence of the law for [sins]
Such as by God's book are adjudg'd to death.
You four, from hence to prison back again;
From thence, unto the place of execution.
The witch in Smithfield shall be burnt to ashes,
And you three shall be strangled on the gallows.
You, madam, for you are more nobly born,
Despoiled of your honor in your life,
Shall, after three days' open penance done,
Live in your country here in banishment,
With Sir John Stanley, in the Isle of Man.
Duch. Welcome is banishment, welcome were my death.
Glou. Eleanor, the law, thou seest, hath judged thee;
I cannot justify whom the law condemns.
[*Exeunt Duchess and other prisoners, guarded.*]
Mine eyes are full of tears, my heart of grief.
Ah, Humphrey, this dishonor in thine age
Will bring thy head with sorrow to the ground!
I beseech your Majesty give me leave to go;
Sorrow would solace, and mine age would ease.
King. Stay, Humphrey Duke of Gloucester! Ere thou go,
Give up thy staff. Henry will to himself
Protector be, and God shall be my hope,
My stay, my guide, and lanthorn to my feet;
And go in peace, Humphrey, no less belov'd
Than when thou wert Protector to thy king.

39–42. This . . . died. Here, as in *1 Henry IV* (see note to I.i.38) and in the chroniclers whom Shakespeare followed, Edmund Mortimer, fifth Earl of March, who was named heir presumptive to the throne by Richard II, is confused with his uncle Edmund, brother of the fourth Earl, who married Glendower's daughter. The statement that Glendower kept Edmund "in captivity till he died" seems to be Shakespeare's own addition. **53. proceedings:** succession.
56. his: i.e. John of Gaunt's **58. slips:** cuttings.
60. plot: ground.
62. birthright: hereditary right by the law of primogeniture.
68. advice: deliberation. **70. Wink at:** close your eyes to.

II.iii. Location: London. A hall of justice.
3–4. sins . . . death. A typical Old Testament injunction against witches is that in Exodus 22:18.
8. strangled . . . gallows. Hall's account (Bullough, III, 101–2) is somewhat different: "Margery Jordayne was brent in Smithfelde, & Roger Bolyngbroke was drawen & quartered at Tiborne, takyng upon his death, that there was never no suche thyng [as the alleged conspiracy] by theim ymagined, John Hum had his pardon, & Southwel died in the toure before execution: the duke of Gloucester, toke all these thynges paciently, and saied litle." **9. for:** because.
13. Sir John Stanley. Actually, Sir Thomas Stanley. **Isle of Man:** island off the northwest coast of England. **21. would:** would have.
25. lanthorn: lantern.

Queen. I see no reason why a king of years
Should be to be protected like a child.
God and King Henry govern England's realm.
Give up your staff, sir, and the King his realm.
Glou. My staff? Here, noble Henry, is my staff.
As willingly do I the same resign
As ere thy father Henry made it mine;
And even as willingly at thy feet I leave it
As others would ambitiously receive it.
Farewell, good King; when I am dead and gone,
May honorable peace attend thy throne!
Exit Gloucester.

Queen. Why, now is Henry king and Margaret queen,
And Humphrey Duke of Gloucester scarce himself,
That bears so shrewd a maim: two pulls at once—
His lady banish'd, and a limb lopp'd off.
This staff of honor raught, there let it stand,
Where it best fits to be, in Henry's hand.
Suf. Thus droops this lofty pine and hangs his sprays,
Thus Eleanor's pride dies in her youngest days.
York. Lords, let him go. Please it your Majesty,
This is the day appointed for the combat,
And ready are the appellant and defendant,
The armorer and his man, to enter the lists,
So please your Highness to behold the fight.
Queen. Ay, good my lord; for purposely therefore
Left I the court, to see this quarrel tried.
King. A' God's name see the lists and all things fit;
Here let them end it, and God defend the right!
York. I never saw a fellow worse bestead,
Or more afraid to fight, than is the appellant,
The servant of this armorer, my lords.

Enter at one door [HORNER] *the armorer and his* NEIGHBORS, *drinking to him so much that he is drunk; and he enters with a Drum before him and his staff with a sand-bag fastened to it; and at the other door* [PETER,] *his man, with a Drum and sand-bag, and* PRENTICES *drinking to him.*

1. Neigh. Here, neighbor Horner, I drink to you in a cup of sack; and fear not, neighbor, you shall do well enough.

2. Neigh. And here, neighbor, here's a cup of charneco.

3. Neigh. And here's a pot of good double beer, neighbor. Drink, and fear not your man.

Hor. Let it come, i' faith, and I'll pledge you all, and a fig for Peter!

1. Pren. Here, Peter, I drink to thee, and be not afraid.

2. Pren. Be merry, Peter, and fear not thy master. Fight for credit of the prentices.

Peter. I thank you all. Drink, and pray for me, I pray you, for I think I have taken my last draught in this world. Here, Robin, and if I die, I give thee my aporn; and, Will, thou shalt have my hammer; and here, Tom, take all the money that I have. O Lord bless me, I pray God, for I am never able to deal with my master, he hath learnt so much fence already.

Sal. Come, leave your drinking, and fall to blows. Sirrah, what's thy name?

Peter. Peter, forsooth.

Sal. Peter? What more?

Peter. Thump.

Sal. Thump? Then see thou thump thy master well.

Hor. Masters, I am come hither, as it were, upon my man's instigation, to prove him a knave and myself an honest man; and touching the Duke of York, I will take my death, I never meant him any ill, nor the King, nor the Queen; and therefore, Peter, have at thee with a downright blow!

York. Dispatch. This knave's tongue begins to double.
Sound, trumpets, alarum to the combatants!
[*Alarum.*] *They fight, and Peter* [*hits him on the head and*] *strikes him down.*

Hor. Hold, Peter, hold! I confess, I confess treason. [*He dies.*]

York. Take away his weapon. Fellow, thank God, and the good wine in thy master's way.

Peter. [*He kneels down.*] O God, have I overcome mine enemies in this presence? O Peter, thou hast prevail'd in right!

King. Go, take hence that traitor from our sight,
For by his death we do perceive his guilt,
And God in justice hath reveal'd to us
The truth and innocence of this poor fellow,
Which he had thought to have murther'd wrongfully.
Come, fellow, follow us for thy reward.
Sound a flourish. Exeunt.

[SCENE IV]

Enter DUKE HUMPHREY [OF GLOUCESTER] *and his* MEN *in mourning cloaks.*

Glou. Thus sometimes hath the brightest day a cloud,
And after summer evermore succeeds
Barren winter, with his wrathful nipping cold;
So cares and joys abound, as seasons fleet.
Sirs, what's a' clock?
Servant. Ten, my lord.
Glou. Ten is the hour that was appointed me
To watch the coming of my punish'd duchess.
Uneath may she endure the flinty streets,

28. of years: i.e. of legal age.
41. bears . . . maim: endures such a grievous mutilation. **pulls:** pluckings, loppings-off. **43. raught:** snatched.
49. appellant: challenger. **52. therefore:** therefor. **54. A':** in.
56. bestead: prepared. **58 s.d. Drum:** drummer.
60. sack: dry Spanish wine.
63. charneco: sweet Portuguese wine.
64. double: i.e. exceptionally strong.
66. Let it come: i.e. let the toast be drunk.
67. fig: sign of contempt made by thrusting the thumb between the fingers.

75. aporn: apron. **78. fence:** skill in fencing.
88. take my death: take my oath on pain of death.
91. double: speak thick, stammer.
92. alarum: call to arms, signal to begin fighting.
104. Which: whom.

II.iv. Location: London. A street. **8. Uneath:** scarcely.

To tread them with her tender-feeling feet.
Sweet Nell, ill can thy noble mind abrook
The abject people gazing on thy face,
With envious looks laughing at thy shame,
That erst did follow thy proud chariot-wheels
When thou didst ride in triumph through the streets.
But soft, I think she comes, and I'll prepare
My tear-stain'd eyes to see her miseries.

Enter the Duchess [of Gloucester, *barefoot*], *in a white sheet*, [*and verses written on her back and pinned on*,] *and a taper burning in her hand, with* [Sir John Stanley,] *the* Sheriff, *and* Officers.

Servant. So please your Grace, we'll take her from the sheriff.
Glou. No, stir not for your lives, let her pass by.
Duch. Come you, my lord, to see my open shame?
Now thou dost penance too. Look how they gaze!
See how the giddy multitude do point
And nod their heads, and throw their eyes on thee!
Ah, Gloucester, hide thee from their hateful looks,
And in thy closet pent up, rue my shame,
And ban thine enemies, both mine and thine.
Glou. Be patient, gentle Nell, forget this grief.
Duch. Ah, Gloucester, teach me to forget myself;
For whilest I think I am thy married wife,
And thou a prince, Protector of this land,
Methinks I should not thus be led along,
Mail'd up in shame, with papers on my back,
And follow'd with a rabble that rejoice
To see my tears and hear my deep-fet groans.
The ruthless flint doth cut my tender feet,
And when I start, the envious people laugh,
And bid me be advised how I tread.
Ah, Humphrey, can I bear this shameful yoke?
Trowest thou that e'er I'll look upon the world,
Or count them happy that enjoys the sun?
No; dark shall be my light, and night my day;
To think upon my pomp shall be my hell.
Sometime I'll say, I am Duke Humphrey's wife,
And he a prince, and ruler of the land;
Yet so he rul'd, and such a prince he was,
As he stood by, whilest I, his forlorn duchess,
Was made a wonder and a pointing-stock
To every idle rascal follower.
But be thou mild, and blush not at my shame,
Nor stir at nothing, till the axe of death
Hang over thee, as sure it shortly will;
For Suffolk, he that can do all in all
With her that hateth thee and hates us all,
And York and impious Beauford, that false priest,
Have all lim'd bushes to betray thy wings,
And fly thou how thou canst, they'll tangle thee.
But fear not thou, until thy foot be snar'd,
Nor never seek prevention of thy foes.
Glou. Ah, Nell, forbear! thou aimest all awry.
I must offend before I be attainted;
And had I twenty times so many foes,
And each of them had twenty times their power,
All these could not procure me any scathe
So long as I am loyal, true, and crimeless.
Wouldst have me rescue thee from this reproach?
Why, yet thy scandal were not wip'd away,
But I in danger for the breach of law.
Thy greatest help is quiet, gentle Nell.
I pray thee sort thy heart to patience,
These few days' wonder will be quickly worn.

Enter a Herald.

Her. I summon your Grace to his Majesty's parliament,
Holden at Bury the first of this next month.
Glou. And my consent ne'er ask'd herein before?
This is close dealing. Well, I will be there.
[*Exit Herald*.]
My Nell, I take my leave; and, Master Sheriff,
Let not her penance exceed the King's commission.
Sher. And't please your Grace, here my commission stays;
And Sir John Stanley is appointed now
To take her with him to the Isle of Man.
Glou. Must you, Sir John, protect my lady here?
Stan. So am I given in charge, may't please your Grace.
Glou. Entreat her not the worse in that I pray
You use her well. The world may laugh again,
And I may live to do you kindness if
You do it her. And so, Sir John, farewell!
Duch. What, gone, my lord, and bid me not farewell?
Glou. Witness my tears, I cannot stay to speak.
Exit Gloucester [*with his Men*].
Duch. Art thou gone too? All comfort go with thee,
For none abides with me. My joy is death;
Death, at whose name I oft have been afeard,
Because I wish'd this world's eternity.
Stanley, I prithee go, and take me hence,
I care not whither, for I beg no favor;
Only convey me where thou art commanded.
Stan. Why, madam, that is to the Isle of Man,
There to be us'd according to your state.
Duch. That's bad enough, for I am but reproach;
And shall I then be us'd reproachfully?
Stan. Like to a duchess, and Duke Humphrey's lady,
According to that state you shall be us'd.
Duch. Sheriff, farewell, and better than I fare,
Although thou hast been conduct of my shame.
Sher. It is my office, and, madam, pardon me.

10. abrook: endure.
11. abject: low, common. **12. envious:** spiteful.
23. hateful: full of hate. **24. closet:** private apartment.
25. ban: curse. **31. Mail'd:** wrapped.
33. deep-fet: deep-fetched. **35. start:** flinch.
36. advised: careful. **38. Trowest thou:** do you think.
46. pointing-stock: butt.
57. seek prevention: i.e. try to foil by anticipating.
59. attainted: condemned for treason or felony. **62. scathe:** harm.
68. sort: fit, adapt. **69. worn:** i.e. forgotten.
71. Bury: Bury St. Edmunds, town in the county of Suffolk. The Parliament at Bury did not actually meet until 1447, six years after the Duchess of Gloucester's disgrace. **73. close:** underhand.
81. Entreat: treat.
95. state: status, rank (but Eleanor quibbles on the sense "condition"). **101. conduct:** guide.

Duch. Ay, ay, farewell, thy office is discharg'd.
Come, Stanley, shall we go?
Stan. Madam, your penance done, throw off this sheet,
And go we to attire you for our journey.
Duch. My shame will not be shifted with my sheet.
No, it will hang upon my richest robes,
And show itself, attire me how I can.
Go, lead the way, I long to see my prison. *Exeunt.*

[ACT III, SCENE I]

Sound a sennet. [*Enter two* HERALDS *before. Then*] *enter* KING, QUEEN, CARDINAL, SUFFOLK, YORK, BUCKINGHAM, SALISBURY, *and* WARWICK *to the parliament.*

King. I muse my Lord of Gloucester is not come;
'Tis not his wont to be the hindmost man,
What e'er occasion keeps him from us now.
Queen. Can you not see? or will ye not observe
The strangeness of his alter'd countenance?
With what a majesty he bears himself,
How insolent of late he is become,
How proud, how peremptory, and unlike himself?
We know the time since he was mild and affable,
And if we did but glance a far-off look,
Immediately he was upon his knee,
That all the court admir'd him for submission;
But meet him now, and, be it in the morn,
When every one will give the time of day,
He knits his brow and shows an angry eye,
And passeth by with stiff unbowed knee,
Disdaining duty that to us belongs.
Small curs are not regarded when they grin,
But great men tremble when the lion roars,
And Humphrey is no little man in England.
First note that he is near you in descent,
And should you fall, he is the next will mount.
Me seemeth then it is no policy,
Respecting what a rancorous mind he bears
And his advantage following your decease,
That he should come about your royal person,
Or be admitted to your Highness' Council.
By flattery hath he won the commons' hearts;
And when he please to make commotion,
'Tis to be fear'd they all will follow him.
Now 'tis the spring, and weeds are shallow-rooted;
Suffer them now, and they'll o'ergrow the garden,
And choke the herbs for want of husbandry.
The reverent care I bear unto my lord
Made me collect these dangers in the Duke.
If it be fond, call it a woman's fear;
Which fear, if better reasons can supplant,
I will subscribe, and say I wrong'd the Duke.
My Lord of Suffolk, Buckingham, and York,
Reprove my allegation if you can,
Or else conclude my words effectual.
Suf. Well hath your Highness seen into this duke;
And, had I first been put to speak my mind,
I think I should have told your Grace's tale.
The Duchess by his subornation,
Upon my life, began her devilish practices;
Or if he were not privy to those faults,
Yet, by reputing of his high descent,
As next the King he was successive heir,
And such high vaunts of his nobility,
Did instigate the bedlam brain-sick Duchess
By wicked means to frame our sovereign's fall.
Smooth runs the water where the brook is deep,
And in his simple show he harbors treason.
The fox barks not when he would steal the lamb.
No, no, my sovereign, Gloucester is a man
Unsounded yet and full of deep deceit.
Car. Did he not, contrary to form of law,
Devise strange deaths for small offenses done?
York. And did he not, in his protectorship,
Levy great sums of money through the realm
For soldiers' pay in France, and never sent it,
By means whereof the towns each day revolted?
Buck. Tut, these are petty faults to faults unknown,
Which time will bring to light in smooth Duke Humphrey.
King. My lords, at once: the care you have of us
To mow down thorns that would annoy our foot
Is worthy praise; but shall I speak my conscience,
Our kinsman Gloucester is as innocent
From meaning treason to our royal person
As is the sucking lamb or harmless dove.
The Duke is virtuous, mild, and too well given
To dream on evil or to work my downfall.
Queen. Ah, what's more dangerous than this fond affiance!
Seems he a dove? his feathers are but borrow'd,
For he's disposed as the hateful raven.
Is he a lamb? his skin is surely lent him,
For he's inclin'd as is the ravenous wolves.
Who cannot steal a shape that means deceit?
Take heed, my lord, the welfare of us all
Hangs on the cutting short that fraudful man.

Enter SOMERSET.

Som. All health unto my gracious sovereign!
King. Welcome, Lord Somerset. What news from France?
Som. That all your interest in those territories
Is utterly bereft you: all is lost.

107. shifted: changed.

III.i. Location: Bury St. Edmunds. The abbey.
1. muse: wonder. **9. since:** when. **12. That:** so that.
14. give . . . day: say good morning.
18. grin: show the teeth, snarl.
19. lion. Heraldic emblem of the kings of England.
23–24. Me . . . bears: i.e. I therefore think it not prudent, considering his rancor. **29. make commotion:** i.e. lead an insurrection.
35. collect: perceive. **36. fond:** foolish.

38. subscribe: concur. **40. Reprove:** disprove.
41. effectual: decisive. **45. subornation:** instigation.
48. reputing: boasting. **51. bedlam:** crazy.
54. simple show: innocent appearance.
57. Unsounded: undisclosed. **64. to:** compared to.
74. affiance: confidence.
76. he's disposed as: he has the nature of.
79. that means deceit. Modifies *Who.*
84–85. That . . . lost. Somerset's report, though accurate, is anachronistic, for it concerns events that occurred several years after the time represented in this scene.

King. Cold news, Lord Somerset; but God's will be done!
York. [*Aside*.] Cold news for me; for I had hope of France
As firmly as I hope for fertile England.
Thus are my blossoms blasted in the bud,
And caterpillars eat my leaves away;
But I will remedy this gear ere long,
Or sell my title for a glorious grave.

Enter GLOUCESTER.

Glou. All happiness unto my lord the King!
Pardon, my liege, that I have stay'd so long.
Suf. Nay, Gloucester, know that thou art come too soon,
Unless thou wert more loyal than thou art.
I do arrest thee of high treason here.
Glou. Well, Suffolk, thou shalt not see me blush
Nor change my countenance for this arrest;
A heart unspotted is not easily daunted.
The purest spring is not so free from mud
As I am clear from treason to my sovereign.
Who can accuse me? Wherein am I guilty?
York. 'Tis thought, my lord, that you took bribes of France,
And being Protector, stay'd the soldiers' pay,
By means whereof his Highness hath lost France.
Glou. Is it but thought so? What are they that think it?
I never robb'd the soldiers of their pay,
Nor ever had one penny bribe from France.
So help me God, as I have watch'd the night,
Ay, night by night, in studying good for England.
That doit that e'er I wrested from the King,
Or any groat I hoarded to my use,
Be brought against me at my trial day!
No; many a pound of mine own proper store,
Because I would not tax the needy commons,
Have I dispursed to the garrisons,
And never ask'd for restitution.
Car. It serves you well, my lord, to say so much.
Glou. I say no more than truth, so help me God!
York. In your protectorship you did devise
Strange tortures for offenders, never heard of,
That England was defam'd by tyranny.
Glou. Why, 'tis well known that, whiles I was Protector,
Pity was all the fault that was in me;
For I should melt at an offender's tears,
And lowly words were ransom for their fault.
Unless it were a bloody murtherer,
Or foul felonious thief that fleec'd poor passengers,
I never gave them condign punishment.

91. **gear**: business.
94. **stay'd**: delayed. 105. **stay'd**: kept back.
110. **watch'd the night**: stayed awake all night.
112. **doit**: small coin of little value.
113. **groat**: coin worth fourpence.
115. **proper store**: personal funds.
117. **dispursed**: disbursed, paid out. 123. **That**: so that.
124. **whiles**: whilst. 126. **should**: would.
127. **their**: i.e. offenders'. 129. **passengers**: wayfarers.
130. **condign**: just, i.e. as severe as they deserved.

Murther indeed, that bloody sin, I tortur'd
Above the felon or what trespass else.
Suf. My lord, these faults are easy, quickly answer'd;
But mightier crimes are laid unto your charge,
Whereof you cannot easily purge yourself.
I do arrest you in his Highness' name,
And here commit you to my Lord Cardinal
To keep, until your further time of trial.
King. My Lord of Gloucester, 'tis my special hope
That you will clear yourself from all suspense.
My conscience tells me you are innocent.
Glou. Ah, gracious lord, these days are dangerous:
Virtue is chok'd with foul ambition,
And charity chas'd hence by rancor's hand;
Foul subornation is predominant,
And equity exil'd your Highness' land.
I know their complot is to have my life;
And if my death might make this island happy,
And prove the period of their tyranny,
I would expend it with all willingness.
But mine is made the prologue to their play;
For thousands more, that yet suspect no peril,
Will not conclude their plotted tragedy.
Beauford's red sparkling eyes blab his heart's malice,
And Suffolk's cloudy brow his stormy hate;
Sharp Buckingham unburthens with his tongue
The envious load that lies upon his heart;
And dogged York, that reaches at the moon,
Whose overweening arm I have pluck'd back,
By false accuse doth level at my life.
And you, my sovereign lady, with the rest,
Causeless have laid disgraces on my head,
And with your best endeavor have stirr'd up
My liefest liege to be mine enemy.
Ay, all of you have laid your heads together—
Myself had notice of your conventicles—
And all to make away my guiltless life.
I shall not want false witness to condemn me,
Nor store of treasons to augment my guilt.
The ancient proverb will be well effected:
"A staff is quickly found to beat a dog."
Car. My liege, his railing is intolerable.
If those that care to keep your royal person
From treason's secret knife and traitors' rage
Be thus upbraided, chid, and rated at,
And the offender granted scope of speech,
'Twill make them cool in zeal unto your Grace.
Suf. Hath he not twit our sovereign lady here
With ignominious words, though clerkly couch'd,
As if she had suborned some to swear
False allegations to o'erthrow his state?
Queen. But I can give the loser leave to chide.

132. **Above . . . else**: i.e. more than any other crime.
133. **easy**: slight.
140. **suspense**: i.e. uncertainty as to your innocence.
145. **subornation**: instigation to perjury. 146. **exil'd**: exiled from.
149. **prove the period**: mark the end.
160. **accuse**: accusation. **level**: aim.
164. **liefest liege**: dearest sovereign.
166. **conventicles**: secret meetings. 168. **want**: lack.
178. **twit**: twitted.
179. **clerkly couch'd**: cleverly phrased.

Glou. Far truer spoke than meant. I lose indeed;
Beshrew the winners, for they play'd me false!
And well such losers may have leave to speak.
Buck. He'll wrest the sense and hold us here all day.
Lord Cardinal, he is your prisoner.
Car. Sirs, take away the Duke, and guard him sure.
Glou. Ah, thus King Henry throws away his crutch
Before his legs be firm to bear his body.
Thus is the shepherd beaten from thy side,
And wolves are gnarling who shall gnaw thee first.
Ah, that my fear were false, ah, that it were!
For, good King Henry, thy decay I fear.
Exit Gloucester [with the Cardinal's Men].
King. My lords, what to your wisdoms seemeth best,
Do or undo, as if ourself were here.
Queen. What, will your Highness leave the parliament?
King. Ay, Margaret; my heart is drown'd with grief,
Whose flood begins to flow within mine eyes;
My body round engirt with misery—
For what's more miserable than discontent?
Ah, uncle Humphrey, in thy face I see
The map of honor, truth, and loyalty;
And yet, good Humphrey, is the hour to come
That e'er I prov'd thee false or fear'd thy faith.
What low'ring star now envies thy estate,
That these great lords, and Margaret our queen,
Do seek subversion of thy harmless life?
Thou never didst them wrong, nor no man wrong;
And as the butcher takes away the calf,
And binds the wretch, and beats it when it strays,
Bearing it to the bloody slaughter-house,
Even so remorseless have they borne him hence;
And as the dam runs lowing up and down,
Looking the way her harmless young one went,
And can do nought but wail her darling's loss,
Even so myself bewails good Gloucester's case
With sad unhelpful tears, and with dimm'd eyes
Look after him, and cannot do him good,
So mighty are his vowed enemies.
His fortunes I will weep, and 'twixt each groan
Say, "Who's a traitor, Gloucester he is none."
Exit [with Buckingham, Salisbury, and Warwick].
Queen. Free lords, cold snow melts with the sun's hot beams:
Henry my lord is cold in great affairs,
Too full of foolish pity; and Gloucester's show
Beguiles him as the mournful crocodile
With sorrow snares relenting passengers;
Or as the snake roll'd in a flow'ring bank,
With shining checker'd slough, doth sting a child
That for the beauty thinks it excellent.
Believe me, lords, were none more wise than I—
And yet herein I judge mine own wit good—
This Gloucester should be quickly rid the world,
To rid us from the fear we have of him.
Car. That he should die is worthy policy,
But yet we want a color for his death.
'Tis meet he be condemn'd by course of law.
Suf. But, in my mind, that were no policy:
The King will labor still to save his life,
The commons haply rise, to save his life;
And yet we have but trivial argument,
More than mistrust, that shows him worthy death.
York. So that, by this, you would not have him die.
Suf. Ah, York, no man alive so fain as I!
York. 'Tis York that hath more reason for his death.
But, my Lord Cardinal, and you, my Lord of Suffolk,
Say as you think, and speak it from your souls:
Were't not all one, an empty eagle were set
To guard the chicken from a hungry kite,
As place Duke Humphrey for the King's Protector?
Queen. So the poor chicken should be sure of death.
Suf. Madam, 'tis true; and were't not madness then,
To make the fox surveyor of the fold?
Who being accus'd a crafty murtherer,
His guilt should be but idly posted over,
Because his purpose is not executed.
No; let him die, in that he is a fox,
By nature prov'd an enemy to the flock,
Before his chaps be stain'd with crimson blood,
As Humphrey, prov'd by reasons, to my liege.
And do not stand on quillets how to slay him;
Be it by gins, by snares, by subtlety,
Sleeping, or waking, 'tis no matter how,
So he be dead; for that is good deceit
Which mates him first that first intends deceit.
Queen. Thrice-noble Suffolk, 'tis resolutely spoke.
Suf. Not resolute, except so much were done,
For things are often spoke and seldom meant;
But that my heart accordeth with my tongue,
Seeing the deed is meritorious,
And to preserve my sovereign from his foe,
Say but the word, and I will be his priest.
Car. But I would have him dead, my Lord of Suffolk,
Ere you can take due orders for a priest.
Say you consent, and censure well the deed,
And I'll provide his executioner,
I tender so the safety of my liege.
Suf. Here is my hand, the deed is worthy doing.
Queen. And so say I.
York. And I; and now we three have spoke it,
It skills not greatly who impugns our doom.

184. **Beshrew**: curse.
192. **gnarling**: snarling. 222. **Who's**: whoever is.
223. **Free**: noble, magnanimous.
226. **mournful crocodile**. The crocodile was thought to lure its victims with its show of pretended grief. 229. **slough**: skin.

236. **color**: pretext. 239. **still**: continually.
240. **haply**: perhaps. 241. **argument**: evidence.
242. **mistrust**: suspicion. 244. **fain**: gladly.
248. **empty**: i.e. hungry. 249. **kite**: scavenger bird, a kind of hawk.
255. **idly posted over**: foolishly ignored.
260. **prov'd**: i.e. an enemy. 261. **quillets**: subtle disputes.
262. **gins**: traps. 265. **mates**: subdues.
269. **that**: i.e. to show that.
272. **be his priest**: i.e. perform the last offices for him.
275. **censure well**: approve.
277. **tender so**: am so solicitous about.
281. **It . . . doom**: i.e. it does not much matter who questions our decision.

Enter a POST.

Post. Great lords, from Ireland am I come amain,
To signify that rebels there are up
And put the Englishmen unto the sword.
Send succors, lords, and stop the rage betime,
Before the wound do grow uncurable;
For being green, there is great hope of help. [*Exit.*]

Car. A breach that craves a quick expedient stop!
What counsel give you in this weighty cause?

York. That Somerset be sent as Regent thither:
'Tis meet that lucky ruler be employ'd—
Witness the fortune he hath had in France.

Som. If York, with all his far-fet policy,
Had been the Regent there in stead of me,
He never would have stay'd in France so long.

York. No, not to lose it all, as thou hast done.
I rather would have lost my life betimes
Than bring a burthen of dishonor home
By staying there so long till all were lost.
Show me one scar character'd on thy skin:
Men's flesh preserv'd so whole do seldom win.

Queen. Nay then, this spark will prove a raging fire,
If wind and fuel be brought to feed it with.
No more, good York; sweet Somerset, be still.
Thy fortune, York, hadst thou been Regent there,
Might happily have prov'd far worse than his.

York. What, worse than nought? nay, then a shame take all!

Som. And, in the number, thee that wishest shame!

Car. My Lord of York, try what your fortune is.
Th' uncivil kerns of Ireland are in arms,
And temper clay with blood of Englishmen.
To Ireland will you lead a band of men,
Collected choicely, from each county some,
And try your hap against the Irishmen?

York. I will, my lord, so please his Majesty.

Suf. Why, our authority is his consent,
And what we do establish he confirms.
Then, noble York, take thou this task in hand.

York. I am content. Provide me soldiers, lords,
Whiles I take order for mine own affairs.

Suf. A charge, Lord York, that I will see perform'd.
But now return we to the false Duke Humphrey.

Car. No more of him; for I will deal with him
That henceforth he shall trouble us no more.
And so break off, the day is almost spent;
Lord Suffolk, you and I must talk of that event.

York. My Lord of Suffolk, within fourteen days
At Bristow I expect my soldiers,
For there I'll ship them all for Ireland.

Suf. I'll see it truly done, my Lord of York.

Exeunt. Manet York.

York. Now, York, or never, steel thy fearful thoughts,
And change misdoubt to resolution;
Be that thou hop'st to be, or what thou art
Resign to death; it is not worth th' enjoying.
Let pale-fac'd fear keep with the mean-born man,
And find no harbor in a royal heart.
Faster than spring-time show'rs comes thought on thought,
And not a thought but thinks on dignity.
My brain, more busy than the laboring spider,
Weaves tedious snares to trap mine enemies.
Well, nobles, well; 'tis politicly done,
To send me packing with an host of men:
I fear me you but warm the starved snake,
Who, cherish'd in your breasts, will sting your hearts.
'Twas men I lack'd, and you will give them me;
I take it kindly. Yet be well assur'd
You put sharp weapons in a madman's hands.
Whiles I in Ireland nourish a mighty band,
I will stir up in England some black storm
Shall blow ten thousand souls to heaven or hell;
And this fell tempest shall not cease to rage
Until the golden circuit on my head,
Like to the glorious sun's transparent beams,
Do calm the fury of this mad-bred flaw.
And for a minister of my intent,
I have seduc'd a headstrong Kentishman,
John Cade of Ashford,
To make commotion, as full well he can,
Under the title of John Mortimer.
In Ireland have I seen this stubborn Cade
Oppose himself against a troop of kerns,
And fought so long, till that his thighs with darts
Were almost like a sharp-quill'd porpentine;
And in the end being rescued, I have seen
Him caper upright like a wild Morisco,
Shaking the bloody darts as he his bells.
Full often, like a shag-hair'd crafty kern,
Hath he conversed with the enemy,
And undiscover'd come to me again,
And given me notice of their villainies.
This devil here shall be my substitute;
For that John Mortimer, which now is dead,
In face, in gait, in speech, he doth resemble.
By this I shall perceive the commons' mind,
How they affect the house and claim of York.
Say he be taken, rack'd, and tortured,
I know no pain they can inflict upon him
Will make him say I mov'd him to those arms.
Say that he thrive, as 'tis great like he will,
Why then from Ireland come I with my strength,
And reap the harvest which that rascal sow'd.
For Humphrey being dead, as he shall be,
And Henry put apart, the next for me. *Exit.*

281 s.d. Post: messenger.
282. amain: at full speed. **285. betime:** promptly.
287. green: fresh. **293. far-fet:** far-fetched, i.e. deep.
300. character'd: inscribed. **306. happily:** haply, perhaps.
310. uncivil kerns: uncivilized light-armed Irish soldiers.
311. temper: moisten. **320. take order for:** arrange.
328. Bristow: Bristol, city near the mouth of the Severn estuary, long a major port. **331. fearful:** timid.
340. tedious: intricate. **343. starved:** stiff with cold.
350. Shall: that shall. **352. circuit:** circlet, i.e. crown.
354. mad-bred: i.e. created by the mad mismanagement of affairs by Henry. **flaw:** squall.
359. John Mortimer. For Cade's absurd claim to descent from the powerful house of Mortimer see IV.ii.136–46.
363. porpentine: porcupine.
365. Morisco: morris, a vigorous dance common in pageants and May-day games. **366. he:** i.e. the morris dancer.
372. For that: because. **375. affect:** favor.
379. great like: very likely.

[Scene II]

Enter two or three [Murderers] *running over the stage, from the murther of Duke Humphrey.*

1. Mur. Run to my Lord of Suffolk; let him know
We have dispatch'd the Duke, as he commanded.
2. Mur. O that it were to do! What have we done?
Didst ever hear a man so penitent?

Enter Suffolk.

1. Mur. Here comes my lord.
Suf. Now, sirs, have you dispatch'd this thing?
1. Mur. Ay, my good lord, he's dead.
Suf. Why, that's well said. Go, get you to my house,
I will reward you for this venturous deed.
The King and all the peers are here at hand.
Have you laid fair the bed? Is all things well,
According as I gave directions?
1. Mur. 'Tis, my good lord.
Suf. Away, be gone. *Exeunt.*

Sound trumpets. Enter the King, *the* Queen, Cardinal, Suffolk, Somerset, *with* Attendants.

King. Go call our uncle to our presence straight.
Say we intend to try his Grace to-day,
If he be guilty, as 'tis published.
Suf. I'll call him presently, my noble lord. *Exit.*
King. Lords, take your places; and I pray you all
Proceed no straiter 'gainst our uncle Gloucester
Than from true evidence of good esteem
He be approv'd in practice culpable.
Queen. God forbid any malice should prevail,
That faultless may condemn a nobleman!
Pray God he may acquit him of suspicion!
King. I thank thee, [Meg], these words content me much.

Enter Suffolk.

How now? Why look'st thou pale? Why tremblest thou?
Where is our uncle? What's the matter, Suffolk?
Suf. Dead in his bed, my lord; Gloucester is dead.
Queen. Marry, God forfend!
Car. God's secret judgment. I did dream to-night
The Duke was dumb and could not speak a word.
King sounds.
Queen. How fares my lord? Help, lords, the King is dead.
Som. Rear up his body, wring him by the nose.
Queen. Run, go, help, help! O Henry, ope thine eyes!
Suf. He doth revive again. Madam, be patient.
King. O heavenly God!
Queen. How fares my gracious lord?
Suf. Comfort, my sovereign! gracious Henry, comfort!
King. What, doth my Lord of Suffolk comfort me?
Came he right now to sing a raven's note,
Whose dismal tune bereft my vital pow'rs;
And thinks he that the chirping of a wren,
By crying comfort from a hollow breast,
Can chase away the first-conceived sound?
Hide not thy poison with such sug'red words.
Lay not thy hands on me; forbear, I say!
Their touch affrights me as a serpent's sting.
Thou baleful messenger, out of my sight!
Upon thy eyeballs murderous tyranny
Sits in grim majesty, to fright the world.
Look not upon me, for thine eyes are wounding.
Yet do not go away. Come, basilisk,
And kill the innocent gazer with thy sight;
For in the shade of death I shall find joy;
In life but double death, now Gloucester's dead.
Queen. Why do you rate my Lord of Suffolk thus?
Although the Duke was enemy to him,
Yet he most Christian-like laments his death;
And for myself, foe as he was to me,
Might liquid tears or heart-offending groans
Or blood-consuming sighs recall his life,
I would be blind with weeping, sick with groans,
Look pale as primrose with blood-drinking sighs,
And all to have the noble Duke alive.
What know I how the world may deem of me,
For it is known we were but hollow friends?
It may be judg'd I made the Duke away,
So shall my name with slander's tongue be wounded,
And princes' courts be fill'd with my reproach.
This get I by his death. Ay me, unhappy,
To be a queen, and crown'd with infamy!
King. Ah, woe is me for Gloucester, wretched man!
Queen. Be woe for me, more wretched than he is.
What, dost thou turn away and hide thy face?
I am no loathsome leper, look on me.
What? art thou like the adder waxen deaf?
Be poisonous too, and kill thy forlorn queen.
Is all thy comfort shut in Gloucester's tomb?
Why then Dame [Margaret] was ne'er thy joy.
Erect his statuë and worship it,
And make my image but an alehouse sign.
Was I for this nigh wrack'd upon the sea,
And twice by awkward wind from England's bank
Drove back again unto my native clime?
What boded this, but well forewarning wind
Did seem to say, "Seek not a scorpion's nest,
Nor set no footing on this unkind shore"?
What did I then, but curs'd the gentle gusts,
And he that loos'd them forth their brazen caves,

III.ii. Location: Bury St. Edmunds. A room of state.
3. to do: still to be done, i.e. undone.
17. published: publicly proclaimed.
18. presently: immediately. **20. straiter:** more rigorously.
21. of good esteem: i.e. creditable.
22. approv'd in: proved guilty of. **30. forfend:** forbid.
31. to-night: last night. **32 s.d. sounds:** swoons.

40. right now: just now, a moment ago.
52. basilisk: fabulous serpent whose glance was alleged to cause death.
56. rate: upbraid.
61. blood-consuming sighs. It was long believed that each sigh drew a drop of blood from the heart; cf. *blood-drinking sighs* in line 63.
76. like . . . deaf. It was another ancient superstition that adders were deaf. See Psalms 58:4–5. **waxen:** grown.
83. awkward: contrary. **bank:** shore.
89. he: him, i.e. Aeolus, god of the winds. **forth:** out of.

And bid them blow towards England's blessed shore,
Or turn our stern upon a dreadful rock?
Yet Aeolus would not be a murtherer,
But left that hateful office unto thee.
The pretty vaulting sea refus'd to drown me,
Knowing that thou wouldst have me drown'd on shore
With tears as salt as sea, through thy unkindness.
The splitting rocks cow'r'd in the sinking sands,
And would not dash me with their ragged sides,
Because thy flinty heart, more hard than they,
Might in thy palace perish [Margaret].
As far as I could ken thy chalky cliffs,
When from thy shore the tempest beat us back,
I stood upon the hatches in the storm;
And when the dusky sky began to rob
My earnest-gaping sight of thy land's view,
I took a costly jewel from my neck,
A heart it was, bound in with diamonds,
And threw it towards thy land. The sea receiv'd it,
And so I wish'd thy body might my heart.
And even with this I lost fair England's view,
And bid mine eyes be packing with my heart,
And call'd them blind and dusky spectacles,
For losing ken of Albion's wished coast.
How often have I tempted Suffolk's tongue
(The agent of thy foul inconstancy)
To sit and [witch] me, as Ascanius did
When he to madding Dido would unfold
His father's acts commenc'd in burning Troy!
Am I not witch'd like her? or thou not false like him?
Ay me, I can no more! Die, [Margaret!]
For Henry weeps that thou dost live so long.

Noise within. Enter WARWICK, [SALISBURY,] *and many* COMMONS.

War. It is reported, mighty sovereign,
That good Duke Humphrey traitorously is murd'red
By Suffolk and the Cardinal Beauford's means.
The commons, like an angry hive of bees
That want their leader, scatter up and down,
And care not who they sting in his revenge.
Myself have calm'd their spleenful mutiny,
Until they hear the order of his death.

King. That he is dead, good Warwick, 'tis too true,
But how he died God knows, not Henry.
Enter his chamber, view his breathless corpse,
And comment then upon his sudden death.

War. That shall I do, my liege. Stay, Salisbury,
With the rude multitude till I return.

[*Exit Warwick; then Salisbury with the Commons.*]

King. O Thou that judgest all things, stay my thoughts,
My thoughts that labor to persuade my soul
Some violent hands were laid on Humphrey's life!
If my suspect be false, forgive me, God,
For judgment only doth belong to thee.
Fain would I go to chafe his paly lips
With twenty thousand kisses, and to drain
Upon his face an ocean of salt tears,
To tell my love unto his dumb deaf trunk,
And with my fingers feel his hand unfeeling.
But all in vain are these mean obsequies,

Bed put forth [*with the body of Gloucester in it. Enter* WARWICK.]

And to survey his dead and earthy image,
What were it but to make my sorrow greater?

War. Come hither, gracious sovereign, view this body.

King. That is to see how deep my grave is made,
For with his soul fled all my worldly solace;
For seeing him, I see my life in death.

War. As surely as my soul intends to live
With that dread King that took our state upon him,
To free us from his Father's wrathful curse,
I do believe that violent hands were laid
Upon the life of this thrice-famed duke.

Suf. A dreadful oath, sworn with a solemn tongue!
What instance gives Lord Warwick for his vow?

War. See how the blood is settled in his face.
Oft have I seen a timely-parted ghost,
Of ashy semblance, meagre, pale, and bloodless,
Being all descended to the laboring heart,
Who, in the conflict that it holds with death,
Attracts the same for aidance 'gainst the enemy,
Which with the heart there cools and ne'er returneth
To blush and beautify the cheek again.
But see, his face is black and full of blood,
His eyeballs further out than when he lived,
Staring full ghastly, like a strangled man;
His hair uprear'd, his nostrils stretch'd with struggling;
His hands abroad display'd, as one that grasp'd
And tugg'd for life, and was by strength subdu'd.
Look, on the sheets his hair, you see, is sticking,
His well-proportion'd beard made rough and rugged,
Like to the summer's corn by tempest lodged.
It cannot be but he was murd'red here,

94. vaulting: bounding. **100. perish:** destroy.
101. ken: discern. **111. be packing:** take flight.
112. spectacles: instruments of vision, i.e. eyes.
113. Albion's: England's.
115. agent. Suffolk had been Henry's "procurator" in arranging Margaret's marriage.
116. witch: bewitch. **Ascanius:** son of Aeneas, whose wooing of Dido, Queen of Carthage, is related in Virgil's *Aeneid*, i.657–60. In Virgil, however, it is Cupid in the form of Ascanius who stirs the amorous queen.
117. madding: becoming frantic (with love). **126. want:** lack.
127. his revenge: revenge for him.
128. spleenful mutiny: angry insurrection. **129. order:** manner.
133. comment . . . upon: explain.

139. suspect: suspicion.
141. paly: pale. **146. obsequies:** duties for the dead.
154. King: i.e. Christ. **state:** condition (of humanity).
159. instance: proof.
161. timely-parted ghost: i.e. the corpse of one who has died a natural death. **163. Being all descended:** i.e. all the blood having descended.
165. the same: i.e. the blood. **aidance:** aid.
170. strangled man. Hall (Bullough, III, 107) is less certain of the cause of Gloucester's death: "The duke the night after his emprisonement, was found dedde in his bed, and his body shewed to the lordes and commons, as though he had died of a palsey or empostome: but all indifferent persons well knewe, that he died of no natural death but of some violent force: some judged hym to be strangled: some affirme, that a hote spitte was put in at his foundement: other write, that he was stiffeled or smoldered betwene twoo fetherbeddes."
172. abroad display'd: i.e. spread out. **176. lodged:** beaten down.

The least of all these signs were probable.
Suf. Why, Warwick, who should do the Duke to death?
Myself and Beauford had him in protection,
And we, I hope, sir, are no murtherers.
War. But both of you were vowed Duke Humphrey's foes,
And you [*to Cardinal*], forsooth, had the good Duke to keep.
'Tis like you would not feast him like a friend,
And 'tis well seen he found an enemy.
Queen. Then you belike suspect these noblemen
As guilty of Duke Humphrey's timeless death.
War. Who finds the heifer dead and bleeding fresh,
And sees fast by a butcher with an axe,
But will suspect 'twas he that made the slaughter?
Who finds the partridge in the puttock's nest
But may imagine how the bird was dead,
Although the kite soar with unbloodied beak?
Even so suspicious is this tragedy.
Queen. Are you the butcher, Suffolk? where's your knife?
Is Beauford term'd a kite? where are his talons?
Suf. I wear no knife to slaughter sleeping men,
But here's a vengeful sword, rusted with ease,
That shall be scoured in his rancorous heart
That slanders me with murther's crimson badge.
Say, if thou dar'st, proud Lord of Warwickshire,
That I am faulty in Duke Humphrey's death.
[*Exeunt Cardinal, Somerset, and others*.]
War. What dares not Warwick, if false Suffolk dare him?
Queen. He dares not calm his contumelious spirit,
Nor cease to be an arrogant controller,
Though Suffolk dare him twenty thousand times.
War. Madam, be still—with reverence may I say—
For every word you speak in his behalf
Is slander to your royal dignity.
Suf. Blunt-witted lord, ignoble in demeanor!
If ever lady wrong'd her lord so much,
Thy mother took into her blameful bed
Some stern untutor'd churl; and noble stock
Was graft with crab-tree slip, whose fruit thou art
And never of the Nevils' noble race.
War. But that the guilt of murther bucklers thee,
And I should rob the deathsman of his fee,
Quitting thee thereby of ten thousand shames,
And that my sovereign's presence makes me mild,
I would, false murd'rous coward, on thy knee
Make thee beg pardon for thy passed speech,
And say it was thy mother that thou meant'st,
That thou thyself wast born in bastardy;
And after all this fearful homage done,
Give thee thy hire and send thy soul to hell,
Pernicious blood-sucker of sleeping men!
Suf. Thou shalt be waking while I shed thy blood,
If from this presence thou dar'st go with me.
War. Away even now, or I will drag thee hence.
Unworthy though thou art, I'll cope with thee,
And do some service to Duke Humphrey's ghost.
Exeunt [*Suffolk and Warwick*].
King. What stronger breastplate than a heart untainted!
Thrice is he arm'd that hath his quarrel just;
And he but naked, though lock'd up in steel,
Whose conscience with injustice is corrupted.
A noise within.
Queen. What noise is this?

Enter SUFFOLK *and* WARWICK *with their weapons drawn*.

King. Why, how now, lords? your wrathful weapons drawn
Here in our presence? Dare you be so bold?
Why, what tumultuous clamor have we here?
Suf. The trait'rous Warwick, with the men of Bury,
Set all upon me, mighty sovereign.

Enter SALISBURY.

Sal. [*To the Commons within*.] Sirs, stand apart, the King shall know your mind.—
Dread lord, the commons send you word by me,
Unless Lord Suffolk straight be done to death,
Or banished fair England's territories,
They will by violence tear him from your palace,
And torture him with grievous ling'ring death.
They say, by him the good Duke Humphrey died;
They say, in him they fear your Highness' death;
And mere instinct of love and loyalty,
Free from a stubborn opposite intent,
As being thought to contradict your liking,
Makes them thus forward in his banishment.
They say, in care of your most royal person,
That if your Highness should intend to sleep,
And charge that no man should disturb your rest
In pain of your dislike, or pain of death,
Yet notwithstanding such a strait edict,
Were there a serpent seen, with forked tongue,
That slily glided towards your Majesty,
It were but necessary you were wak'd,
Lest being suffer'd in that harmful slumber,
The mortal worm might make the sleep eternal.
And therefore do they cry, though you forbid,
That they will guard you, whe'er you will or no,
From such fell serpents as false Suffolk is;
With whose envenomed and fatal sting,
Your loving uncle, twenty times his worth,
They say is shamefully bereft of life.
Commons. (*Within*.) An answer from the King, my Lord of Salisbury!
Suf. 'Tis like the commons, rude unpolish'd hinds,

178. probable: sufficient proof. **187. timeless:** untimely.
191. puttock's: kite's. **202. faulty:** guilty.
205. controller: censorious critic. **213. stern:** rough.
214. slip: cutting. **216. bucklers:** shields.
217. deathsman: executioner. **218. Quitting:** ridding.
221. passed: uttered. **224. fearful homage:** craven submission.
225. hire: reward.

230. cope with: encounter, i.e. fight. **250. mere:** pure.
251. Free . . . intent: i.e. not prompted by mere antagonism.
258. strait: strict.
262. being suffer'd: if you were allowed to continue.
263. mortal worm: deadly serpent. **265. whe'er:** whether.
266. fell: cruel. **268. his:** i.e. Suffolk's.
271. like: probable (ironic).

Could send such message to their sovereign.
But you, my lord, were glad to be employ'd,
To show how quaint an orator you are;
But all the honor Salisbury hath won
Is, that he was the lord embassador
Sent from a sort of tinkers to the King.

[*Commons*.] (*Within*.) An answer from the King, or we will all break in!

King. Go, Salisbury, and tell them all from me,
I thank them for their tender loving care;
And had I not been cited so by them,
Yet did I purpose as they do entreat;
For sure, my thoughts do hourly prophesy
Mischance unto my state by Suffolk's means.
And therefore by His majesty I swear,
Whose far-unworthy deputy I am,
He shall not breathe infection in this air
But three days longer, on the pain of death.

[*Exit Salisbury*.]

Queen. O Henry, let me plead for gentle Suffolk!

King. Ungentle queen, to call him gentle Suffolk!
No more, I say! If thou dost plead for him,
Thou wilt but add increase unto my wrath.
Had I but said, I would have kept my word;
But when I swear, it is irrevocable.
If after three days' space thou here be'st found
On any ground that I am ruler of,
The world shall not be ransom for thy life.
Come, Warwick, come, good Warwick, go with me,
I have great matters to impart to thee.

Exit [*with Warwick*].

Queen. Mischance and sorrow go along with you!
Heart's discontent and sour affliction
Be playfellows to keep you company!
There's two of you, the devil make a third,
And threefold vengeance tend upon your steps!

Suf. Cease, gentle queen, these execrations,
And let thy Suffolk take his heavy leave.

Queen. Fie, coward woman and soft-hearted wretch!
Hast thou not spirit to curse thine enemy?

Suf. A plague upon them! wherefore should I curse them?
Would curses kill, as doth the mandrake's groan,
I would invent as bitter searching terms,

As curst, as harsh, and horrible to hear,
Deliver'd strongly through my fixed teeth,
With full as many signs of deadly hate,
As lean-fac'd Envy in her loathsome cave.
My tongue should stumble in mine earnest words,
Mine eyes should sparkle like the beaten flint,
Mine hair be fix'd an end, as one distract;
Ay, every joint should seem to curse and ban;
And even now my burthen'd heart would break,
Should I not curse them. Poison be their drink!
Gall, worse than gall, the daintiest that they taste!
Their sweetest shade a grove of cypress trees!
Their chiefest prospect murd'ring basilisks!
Their softest touch as smart as lizards' stings!
Their music frightful as the serpent's hiss,
And boding screech-owls make the consort full!
All the foul terrors in dark-seated hell—

Queen. Enough, sweet Suffolk, thou torment'st thyself,
And these dread curses, like the sun 'gainst glass,
Or like an overcharged gun, recoil,
And turns the force of them upon thyself.

Suf. You bade me ban, and will you bid me leave?
Now by the ground that I am banish'd from,
Well could I curse away a winter's night,
Though standing naked on a mountain top,
Where biting cold would never let grass grow,
And think it but a minute spent in sport.

Queen. O, let me entreat thee cease. Give me thy hand,
That I may dew it with my mournful tears;
Nor let the rain of heaven wet this place
To wash away my woeful monuments.
O, could this kiss be printed in thy hand,
That thou mightst think upon these by the seal,
Through whom a thousand sighs are breath'd for thee!
So get thee gone, that I may know my grief,
'Tis but surmis'd whiles thou art standing by,
As one that surfeits thinking on a want.
I will repeal thee, or, be well assur'd,
Adventure to be banished myself;
And banished I am, if but from thee.
Go, speak not to me; even now be gone.
O, go not yet! Even thus two friends condemn'd
Embrace, and kiss, and take ten thousand leaves,
Loather a hundred times to part than die.
Yet now farewell, and farewell life with thee!

Suf. Thus is poor Suffolk ten times banished,
Once by the King, and three times thrice by thee.
'Tis not the land I care for, wert thou thence;
A wilderness is populous enough,
So Suffolk had thy heavenly company:
For where thou art, there is the world itself,
With every several pleasure in the world;

274. quaint: skillful. **277. sort:** gang.
279–97. Go . . . life. In treating Suffolk's banishment Shakespeare characteristically suppresses some of the details in Hall's account (Bullough, III, 112): "When kyng Henry perceived, that the commons wer thus stomacked and bent against the Quenes dearlynge William Duke of Suffolke, he playnly sawe that neither glosyng wolde serve, nor dissumulacion coulde appeace the continual clamor of the importunate commons: Wherfore to begyn a shorte pacificacion in so long a broyle: Firste he sequestred the lord Say, beyng threasorer of Englande, and other the Dukes adherentes, from theire offices, and authoritie, and after banished and put in exile the duke of Suffolke, as the abhorred tode, and common noysaunce of the Realme of Englande, for the terme of .v. yeres: meanyng by this exile, to appease the furious rage of the outragious people, and that pacified, to revocate him into his olde estate, as the Quenes chefe frende & counsailer."
281. cited: incited, urged. **284. Mischance:** disaster.
285. His: i.e. God's. **287. breathe infection in:** infect.
289. gentle: noble. **293. but said:** i.e. without oath.
306. heavy: mournful.
310. mandrake's groan. It was thought that the mandrake, an herb with a forked root supposed to resemble a man, uttered a shriek when uprooted which killed the hearer or drove him mad.

312. curst: malignant. **313. fixed:** clenched.
318. an: on. **distract:** mad. **319. ban:** curse.
323. cypress: tree associated with graveyards and therefore regarded as dismal. **324. prospect:** view. **325. smart:** sharp.
327. consort: group of musicians. **333. leave:** cease.
342. woeful monuments: signs of grief, i.e. teartains.
344. these: i.e. lips. **seal:** imprint.
348. surfeits: gluts oneself. **want:** famine.
349. repeal thee: obtain your recall. **350. Adventure:** venture.
363. several: separate.

And where thou art not, desolation.
I can no more: live thou to joy thy life;
Myself no joy in nought but that thou liv'st.

Enter VAUX.

Queen. Whither goes Vaux so fast? What news, I prithee?
Vaux. To signify unto his Majesty
That Cardinal Beauford is at point of death;
For suddenly a grievous sickness took him,
That makes him gasp, and stare, and catch the air,
Blaspheming God and cursing men on earth.
Sometime he talks as if Duke Humphrey's ghost
Were by his side; sometime he calls the King,
And whispers to his pillow as to him
The secrets of his overcharged soul;
And I am sent to tell his Majesty
That even now he cries aloud for him.
Queen. Go tell this heavy message to the King.
Exit [*Vaux*].
Ay me! what is this world! what news are these!
But wherefore grieve I at an hour's poor loss,
Omitting Suffolk's exile, my soul's treasure?
Why only, Suffolk, mourn I not for thee,
And with the southern clouds contend in tears,
Theirs for the earth's increase, mine for my sorrows?
Now get thee hence, the King, thou know'st, is coming.
If thou be found by me, thou art but dead.
Suf. If I depart from thee, I cannot live,
And in thy sight to die, what were it else
But like a pleasant slumber in thy lap?
Here could I breathe my soul into the air,
As mild and gentle as the cradle-babe
Dying with mother's dug between its lips;
Where, from thy sight, I should be raging mad,
And cry out for thee to close up mine eyes,
To have thee with thy lips to stop my mouth;
So shouldst thou either turn my flying soul,
Or I should breathe it so into thy body,
And then it liv'd in sweet Elysium.
To die by thee were but to die in jest,
From thee to die were torture more than death.
O, let me stay, befall what may befall!
Queen. Away! though parting be a fretful corrosive,
It is applied to a deathful wound.
To France, sweet Suffolk! Let me hear from thee;
For wheresoe'er thou art in this world's globe,
I'll have an Iris that shall find thee out.
Suf. I go.
Queen. And take my heart with thee.
[*She kisseth him.*]
Suf. A jewel, lock'd into the woefull'st cask
That ever did contain a thing of worth.
Even as a splitted bark, so sunder we;

369. **point of death.** Actually, Beaufort died (April 1447) some six weeks after Gloucester's murder and three years before Suffolk's banishment.
381. **at . . . loss:** i.e. at Beaufort's death, since he was old and already near his end. 382. **Omitting:** ignoring.
403. **fretful corrosive:** painful remedy.
404. **applied:** suitable. **deathful:** deadly.
407. **Iris:** Juno's messenger. 409. **cask:** casket.

This way fall I to death.
Queen. This way for me. *Exeunt* [*severally*].

[SCENE III]

Enter the KING, SALISBURY, *and* WARWICK *to the* CARDINAL *in bed*, [*raving and staring as if he were mad*].

King. How fares my lord? Speak, Beauford, to thy sovereign.
Car. If thou beest death, I'll give thee England's treasure,
Enough to purchase such another island,
So thou wilt let me live, and feel no pain.
King. Ah, what a sign it is of evil life,
Where death's approach is seen so terrible!
War. Beauford, it is thy sovereign speaks to thee.
Car. Bring me unto my trial when you will.
Died he not in his bed? Where should he die?
Can I make men live, whe'er they will or no?
O, torture me no more, I will confess.
Alive again? Then show me where he is,
I'll give a thousand pound to look upon him.
He hath no eyes, the dust hath blinded them.
Comb down his hair; look, look, it stands upright,
Like lime-twigs set to catch my winged soul.
Give me some drink, and bid the apothecary
Bring the strong poison that I bought of him.
King. O thou eternal Mover of the heavens,
Look with a gentle eye upon this wretch!
O, beat away the busy meddling fiend
That lays strong siege unto this wretch's soul,
And from his bosom purge this black despair!
War. See how the pangs of death do make him grin!
Sal. Disturb him not, let him pass peaceably.
King. Peace to his soul, if God's good pleasure be!
Lord Card'nal, if thou think'st on heaven's bliss,
Hold up thy hand, make signal of thy hope.
[*The Cardinal dies.*]
He dies, and makes no sign. O God, forgive him!
War. So bad a death argues a monstrous life.
King. Forbear to judge, for we are sinners all.
Close up his eyes, and draw the curtain close,
And let us all to meditation. *Exeunt.*

[ACT IV, SCENE I]

Alarum [*within*]. *Ord'nance goes off* [*like as it were a*] *fight at sea. Enter* LIEUTENANT, [*a* SHIPMASTER *and his* MATE, WALTER WHITMORE,] *and others;* [*with them*] SUFFOLK, [*disguised, and other* GENTLEMEN, *prisoners*].

Lieu. The gaudy, blabbing, and remorseful day

III.iii. Location: London. The Cardinal's bedchamber.
2. **treasure:** i.e. the wealth that Beaufort had accumulated through his avarice and rapacity. 4. **So:** if. 9. **he:** i.e. Gloucester.
16. **lime-twigs:** twigs smeared with birdlime.

IV.i. Location: The coast of Kent.
o.s.d. **Ord'nance:** ordnance (a sense only later differentiated orthographically from *ordinance*).
1. **blabbing:** i.e. revealing secrets of the dark.

Is crept into the bosom of the sea;
And now loud-howling wolves arouse the jades
That drag the tragic melancholy night;
Who with their drowsy, slow, and flagging wings
Cleep dead men's graves, and from their misty jaws
Breathe foul contagious darkness in the air.
Therefore bring forth the soldiers of our prize,
For whilst our pinnace anchors in the Downs,
Here shall they make their ransom on the sand,
Or with their blood stain this discolored shore.
Master, this prisoner freely give I thee,
And thou that art his mate, make boot of this;
The other, Walter Whitmore, is thy share.
1. Gent. What is my ransom, master? Let me know.
Mast. A thousand crowns, or else lay down your head.
Mate. And so much shall you give, or off goes yours.
Lieu. What, think you much to pay two thousand crowns,
And bear the name and port of gentlemen?
Cut both the villains' throats; for die you shall.
The lives of those which we have lost in fight
Be counterpois'd with such a petty sum!
1. Gent. I'll give it, sir, and therefore spare my life.
2. Gent. And so will I, and write home for it straight.
Whit. I lost mine eye in laying the prize aboard,
And therefore to revenge it shalt thou die,
[*To Suffolk.*]
And so should these, if I might have my will.
Lieu. Be not so rash, take ransom, let him live.
Suf. Look on my George, I am a gentleman:
Rate me at what thou wilt, thou shalt be paid.
Whit. And so am I; my name is Walter Whitmore.
How now? why starts thou? What, doth death affright?
Suf. Thy name affrights me, in whose sound is death.
A cunning man did calculate my birth
And told me that by water I should die:
Yet let not this make thee be bloody-minded;
Thy name is Gualtier, being rightly sounded.
Whit. Gualtier or Walter, which it is, I care not.
Never yet did base dishonor blur our name
But with our sword we wip'd away the blot;
Therefore, when merchant-like I sell revenge,
Broke be my sword, my arms torn and defac'd,
And I proclaim'd a coward through the world!
Suf. Stay, Whitmore, for thy prisoner is a prince,

The Duke of Suffolk, William de la Pole.
Whit. The Duke of Suffolk muffled up in rags?
Suf. Ay, but these rags are no part of the duke;
[Jove sometime went disguis'd, and why not I?]
Lieu. But Jove was never slain, as thou shalt be.
[*Suf.*] Obscure and lousy swain, King Henry's blood,
The honorable blood of Lancaster,
Must not be shed by such a jaded groom.
Hast thou not kiss'd thy hand and held my stirrup?
Bare-headed plodded by my foot-cloth mule
And thought thee happy when I shook my head?
How often hast thou waited at my cup,
Fed from my trencher, kneel'd down at the board,
When I have feasted with Queen Margaret?
Remember it, and let it make thee crestfall'n,
Ay, and allay this thy abortive pride:
How in our voiding lobby hast thou stood
And duly waited for my coming forth?
This hand of mine hath writ in thy behalf,
And therefore shall it charm thy riotous tongue.
Whit. Speak, captain, shall I stab the forlorn swain?
Lieu. First let my words stab him, as he hath me.
Suf. Base slave, thy words are blunt and so art thou.
Lieu. Convey him hence, and on our longboat's side
Strike off his head.
Suf. Thou dar'st not, for thy own.
[*Lieu.* Yes, Poole.
Suf. Poole?]
Lieu. Poole! Sir Poole! lord!
Ay, kennel, puddle, sink, whose filth and dirt
Troubles the silver spring where England drinks.
Now will I dam up this thy yawning mouth
For swallowing the treasure of the realm.
Thy lips that kiss'd the Queen shall sweep the ground,
And thou that smil'dst at good Duke Humphrey's death
Against the senseless winds shall grin in vain,
Who in contempt shall hiss at thee again;
And wedded be thou to the hags of hell,
For daring to affy a mighty lord
Unto the daughter of a worthless king,
Having neither subject, wealth, nor diadem.
By devilish policy art thou grown great,
And like ambitious Sylla, overgorg'd
With gobbets of thy [mother's] bleeding heart.
By thee Anjou and Maine were sold to France.
The false revolting Normans thorough thee

3. jades: i.e. the dragons that draw the chariot of the night.
6. Cleep: clip, embrace.
8. soldiers . . . prize: i.e. those whom we have captured.
9. pinnace: small sailing vessel. **Downs:** roadstead off the Kentish coast.
11. discolored shore: i.e. shore that will be discolored with their blood.
13. make . . . this: i.e. take your profit from the ransom of this prisoner. **19. port:** demeanor.
25. laying . . . aboard: boarding the captured vessel.
29. George: badge of the Order of the Garter. **30. Rate:** assess.
33. name. *Walter* was pronounced *Water*.
34. A cunning . . . birth: an astrologer cast my horoscope.
35. by . . . die. See I.iv.33. **37. Gualtier:** French form of *Walter*.
41. sell revenge: i.e. for ransom. **42. arms:** coat of arms.

50. lousy swain: louse-infested rustic. **King Henry's blood.** A dubious claim, since Suffolk's connection with the house of Lancaster was at best exceedingly remote. **52. jaded:** ignoble.
54. foot-cloth: ornamental trappings for the mounts of dignitaries, especially in ceremonial processions.
55. shook: nodded (in recognition). **57. trencher:** platter.
60. abortive: monstrous. **61. voiding lobby:** antechamber.
63. writ . . . behalf: i.e. letters of recommendation.
65. forlorn: lost.
71. kennel: gutter. **sink:** cesspool. **74. For:** to prevent.
77. senseless: insensible. **80. affy:** betroth. **83. policy:** cunning.
84. Sylla: Lucius Cornelius Sulla (138–75 B.C.), Roman dictator notorious for his cruelty to his adversaries.
84–85. overgorg'd . . . heart: i.e. stuffed with pieces of raw flesh from the bleeding heart of your mother, England.
87. revolting: disloyal. **thorough:** through.

Disdain to call us lord, and Picardy
Hath slain their governors, surpris'd our forts,
And sent the ragged soldiers wounded home.
The princely Warwick, and the Nevils all,
Whose dreadful swords were never drawn in vain,
As hating thee, [are] rising up in arms;
And now the house of York, thrust from the crown
By shameful murther of a guiltless king
And lofty, proud, encroaching tyranny,
Burns with revenging fire, whose hopeful colors
Advance our half-fac'd sun, striving to shine,
Under the which is writ, "*Invitis nubibus.*"
The commons here in Kent are up in arms,
And to conclude, reproach and beggary
Is crept into the palace of our king,
And all by thee. Away, convey him hence.

Suf. O that I were a god, to shoot forth thunder
Upon these paltry, servile, abject drudges!
Small things make base men proud. This villain here,
Being captain of a pinnace, threatens more
Than Bargulus the strong Illyrian pirate.
Drones suck not eagles' blood, but rob beehives.
It is impossible that I should die
By such a lowly vassal as thyself.
Thy words move rage and not remorse in me.

[*Lieu.* Ay, but my deeds shall stay thy fury soon.]

[*Suf.*] I go of message from the Queen to France;
I charge thee waft me safely cross the Channel.

[*Whit.*] Come, Suffolk, I must waft thee to thy death.

Suf. [*Pene*] *gelidus timor occupat artus:* it is thee I fear.

Whit. Thou shalt have cause to fear before I leave thee.
What, are ye daunted now? Now will ye stoop?

1. Gent. My gracious lord, entreat him, speak him fair.

Suf. Suffolk's imperial tongue is stern and rough,
Us'd to command, untaught to plead for favor.
Far be it we should honor such as these
With humble suit. No, rather let my head
Stoop to the block than these knees bow to any
Save to the God of heaven and to my king;
And sooner dance upon a bloody pole
Than stand uncover'd to the vulgar groom.
True nobility is exempt from fear:
More can I bear than you dare execute.

Lieu. Hale him away, and let him talk no more.

[*Suf.*] Come, soldiers, show what cruelty ye can,
That this my death may never be forgot!
Great men oft die by vild besonians:
A Roman sworder and bandetto slave

95. guiltless king: i.e. Richard II, to whose deposition and murder Shakespeare and the Tudor chroniclers traced the political upheavals of the fifteenth century.
98. Advance: display. **half-fac'd sun.** The sun breaking through the clouds had been the personal badge of Edward III.
99. Invitis nubibus: in spite of clouds.
108. Bargulus: a pirate (Bardulis) alluded to by Cicero (*De Officiis*, II.xi). **109. Drones:** beetles. **114. of message:** as a messenger.
115. waft: convey.
117. Pene . . . artus: cold fear almost overpowers my joints.
131. Hale: haul.
134. vild: vile. **besonians:** scoundrels (from Italian *bisogno*).
135. sworder: gladiator. **bandetto:** bandit.

Murder'd sweet Tully; Brutus' bastard hand
Stabb'd Julius Caesar; savage islanders
Pompey the Great; and Suffolk dies by pirates.

Exit Walter [*Whitmore*] *with Suffolk.*

Lieu. And as for these whose ransom we have set,
It is our pleasure one of them depart;
Therefore come you with us and let him go.

Exeunt Lieutenant and the rest.
Manet the First Gentleman.

Enter WALTER [WHITMORE] *with the body* [*of Suffolk*].

Whit. There let his head and liveless body lie,
Until the Queen his mistress bury it. *Exit Walter.*

1. Gent. O barbarous and bloody spectacle!
His body will I bear unto the King.
If he revenge it not, yet will his friends;
So will the Queen, that living held him dear.

[*Exit with the body.*]

[SCENE II]

Enter [GEORGE] BEVIS *and* JOHN HOLLAND [*with long staves*].

Bevis. Come and get thee a sword, though made of a lath; they have been up these two days.

Holl. They have the more need to sleep now, then.

Bevis. I tell thee, Jack Cade the clothier means to dress the commonwealth, and turn it, and set a new nap upon it.

Holl. So he had need, for 'tis threadbare. Well, I say, it was never merry world in England since gentlemen came up.

Bevis. O miserable age! virtue is not regarded in handicrafts-men.

Holl. The nobility think scorn to go in leather aprons.

Bevis. Nay more, the King's Council are no good workmen.

Holl. True; and yet it is said, labor in thy vocation; which is as much to say as, let the magistrates be laboring men; and therefore should we be magistrates.

Bevis. Thou hast hit it; for there's no better sign of a brave mind than a hard hand.

Holl. I see them, I see them! There's Best's son, the tanner of Wingham—

136. Tully. Marcus Tullius Cicero (106–43 B.C.) was actually hunted down and executed by Mark Antony's soldiers. **Brutus' bastard hand.** Marcus Junius Brutus (78?–42 B.C.), one of the leaders in the conspiracy against Julius Caesar, was erroneously thought to be the illegitimate son of his victim.
138. Pompey the Great. Gnaeus Pompeius (106–48 B.C.) was actually killed by King Ptolemy's soldiers in Egypt, where he had fled following his defeat at the battle of Pharsalia in Thessaly.
142. liveless: lifeless.

IV.ii. Location: Blackheath.
o.s.d. George Bevis, John Holland. Holland was an actor whose name is recorded elsewhere in dramatic documents of the period, and Bevis was no doubt one of his colleagues. Their names here probably derive from a prompter's note.
2. lath: a strip of wood, commonly used as a sword by the Vice in the morality plays. **up:** up in arms. **9. up:** i.e. into fashion.
20. hard: calloused by manual labor.
22. Wingham: village near Canterbury.

Bevis. He shall have the skins of our enemies, to make dog's-leather of.

Holl. And Dick the butcher—

Bevis. Then is sin struck down like an ox, and iniquity's throat cut like a calf.

Holl. And Smith the weaver—

Bevis. Argo, their thread of life is spun.

Holl. Come, come, let's fall in with them.

Drum. Enter CADE, DICK *butcher*, SMITH *the weaver, and a* SAWYER, *with infinite numbers,* [*with long staves*].

Cade. We John Cade, so term'd of our suppos'd father—

Dick. [*Aside.*] Or rather of stealing a cade of herrings.

Cade. For our enemies shall [fall] before us, inspir'd with the spirit of putting down kings and princes—command silence.

Dick. Silence!

Cade. My father was a Mortimer—

Dick. [*Aside.*] He was an honest man, and a good bricklayer.

Cade. My mother a Plantagenet—

Dick. [*Aside.*] I knew her well, she was a midwife.

Cade. My wife descended of the Lacies—

Dick. [*Aside.*] She was indeed a pedlar's daughter, and sold many laces.

Smith. [*Aside.*] But now of late, not able to travel with her furr'd pack, she washes bucks here at home.

Cade. Therefore am I of an honorable house.

Dick. [*Aside.*] Ay, by my faith, the field is honorable, and there was he born, under a hedge; for his father had never a house but the cage.

Cade. Valiant I am.

Smith. [*Aside.*] 'A must needs, for beggary is valiant.

Cade. I am able to endure much.

Dick. [*Aside.*] No question of that; for I have seen him whipt three market-days together.

Cade. I fear neither sword nor fire.

Smith. [*Aside.*] He need not fear the sword, for his coat is of proof.

Dick. [*Aside.*] But methinks he should stand in fear of fire, being burnt i' th' hand for stealing of sheep.

Cade. Be brave then, for your captain is brave, and vows reformation. There shall be in England seven halfpenny loaves sold for a penny; the three-hoop'd pot shall have ten hoops, and I will make it felony to drink small beer. All the realm shall be in common, and in Cheapside shall my palfrey go to grass; and when I am king, as king I will be—

All. God save your Majesty!

Cade. I thank you, good people—there shall be no money; all shall eat and drink on my score, and I will apparel them all in one livery, that they may agree like brothers, and worship me their lord.

Dick. The first thing we do, let's kill all the lawyers.

Cade. Nay, that I mean to do. Is not this a lamentable thing, that of the skin of an innocent lamb should be made parchment? that parchment, being scribbled o'er, should undo a man? Some say the bee stings, but I say, 'tis the bee's wax; for I did but seal once to a thing, and I was never mine own man since. How now? Who's there?

Enter [*one with*] *a* CLERK.

Smith. The clerk of Chartam. He can write and read and cast accompt.

Cade. O monstrous!

Smith. We took him setting of boys' copies.

Cade. Here's a villain!

Smith. H'as a book in his pocket with red letters in't.

Cade. Nay, then he is a conjurer.

Dick. Nay, he can make obligations, and write court-hand.

Cade. I am sorry for't. The man is a proper man, of mine honor; unless I find him guilty, he shall not die. Come hither, sirrah, I must examine thee. What is thy name?

Clerk. Emmanuel.

Dick. They use to write it on the top of letters; 'twill go hard with you.

Cade. Let me alone. Dost thou use to write thy name? or hast thou a mark to thyself, like a honest plain-dealing man?

Clerk. Sir, I thank God, I have been so well brought up that I can write my name.

All. He hath confess'd! away with him! he's a villain and a traitor.

Cade. Away with him, I say! Hang him with his pen and inkhorn about his neck.

Exit one with the Clerk.

Enter MICHAEL.

Mich. Where's our general?

Cade. Here I am, thou particular fellow.

Mich. Fly, fly, fly! Sir Humphrey Stafford and his brother are hard by, with the King's forces.

Cade. Stand, villain, stand, or I'll fell thee down. He shall be encount'red with a man as good as himself. He is but a knight, is 'a?

Mich. No.

24. dog's-leather. Commonly used for making gloves.
29. Argo: i.e. ergo, therefore. **33. cade:** cask.
35. For: because. **fall.** With a play on Latin *cadere*, "to fall."
44. Lacies. Lacy was the family name of the earls of Lincoln.
48. furr'd pack: knapsack of skin with the hair turned outward. **bucks:** soiled clothes. **52. cage:** jail.
54. 'A must needs: he has to be. **58. whipt:** i.e. as a vagabond.
61. of proof: (1) impenetrable; (2) badly worn.
63. burnt . . . hand: i.e. branded with a *T* as a thief.
66. three-hoop'd pot: wooden drinking cup holding a quart.
68. small: weak.
69. Cheapside: the principal commercial street of London.

73. on my score: at my expense.
82. bee's wax: i.e. sealing wax (on legal documents).
82–83. but . . . thing: i.e. put my name only once to a bond.
85. Chartam: Chartham, a town in Kent.
86. cast accompt: i.e. do arithmetic.
88. setting . . . copies: i.e. teaching boys to write.
90. book . . . letters: textbook (probably the primer) with the capital letters in red. **93. make obligations:** draw up bonds.
94. court-hand: type of writing used in legal documents.
99–100. Emmanuel . . . letters. *Emmanuel* ("God with us") was commonly prefixed to documents and letters as a kind of salutation.
112. particular: i.e. private (as opposed to *general*).
118. No: i.e. only a knight.

Cade. To equal him, I will make myself a knight presently. [*Kneels*.] Rise up Sir John Mortimer. [*Rises*.] Now have at him!

Enter SIR HUMPHREY STAFFORD *and his* BROTHER *with Drum and Soldiers*.

Staf. Rebellious hinds, the filth and scum of Kent,
Mark'd for the gallows, lay your weapons down,
Home to your cottages, forsake this groom:
The King is merciful, if you revolt.

Bro. But angry, wrathful, and inclin'd to blood,
If you go forward; therefore yield, or die.

Cade. As for these silken-coated slaves, I pass not,
It is to you, good people, that I speak,
Over whom, in time to come, I hope to reign,
For I am rightful heir unto the crown.

Staf. Villain, thy father was a plasterer,
And thou thyself a shearman, art thou not?

Cade. And Adam was a gardener.

Bro. And what of that?

Cade. Marry, this: Edmund Mortimer, Earl of March,
Married the Duke of Clarence' daughter, did he not?

Staf. Ay, sir.

Cade. By her he had two children at one birth.

Bro. That's false.

Cade. Ay, there's the question; but I say, 'tis true.
The elder of them, being put to nurse,
Was by a beggar-woman stol'n away,
And ignorant of his birth and parentage,
Became a bricklayer when he came to age.
His son am I, deny it if you can.

Dick. Nay, 'tis too true; therefore he shall be king.

Smith. Sir, he made a chimney in my father's house, and the bricks are alive at this day to testify it; therefore deny it not.

Staf. And will you credit this base drudge's words,
That speaks he knows not what?

All. Ay, marry, will we; therefore get ye gone.

Bro. Jack Cade, the Duke of York hath taught you this.

Cade. [*Aside*.] He lies, for I invented it myself.—Go to, sirrah, tell the King from me, that, for his father's sake, Henry the Fift (in whose time boys went to span-counter for French crowns), I am content he shall reign, but I'll be Protector over him.

Dick. And furthermore, we'll have the Lord Say's head for selling the dukedom of Maine.

Cade. And good reason; for thereby is England main'd, and fain to go with a staff, but that my puissance holds it up. Fellow kings, I tell you that that Lord Say hath gelded the commonwealth, and made it an eunuch; and more than that, he can speak French, and therefore he is a traitor.

Staf. O gross and miserable ignorance!

Cade. Nay, answer if you can. The Frenchmen are our enemies. Go to then, I ask but this: can he that speaks with the tongue of an enemy be a good counsellor, or no?

All. No, no, and therefore we'll have his head.

Bro. Well, seeing gentle words will not prevail,
Assail them with the army of the King.

Staf. Herald, away, and throughout every town
Proclaim them traitors that are up with Cade,
That those which fly before the battle ends
May, even in their wives' and children's sight,
Be hang'd up for example at their doors.
And you that be the King's friends, follow me.

Exit [*with his Brother and Men*].

Cade. And you that love the commons, follow me.
Now show yourselves men, 'tis for liberty.
We will not leave one lord, one gentleman;
Spare none but such as go in clouted shoon,
For they are thrifty honest men, and such
As would (but that they dare not) take our parts.

Dick. They are all in order, and march toward us.

Cade. But then are we in order when we are most out of order. Come, march forward. [*Exeunt*.]

120. **presently**: immediately. 122. **hinds**: peasants.
125. **revolt**: turn again (to the King). 128. **pass**: care.
133. **shearman**: one who shears the nap on woollen cloth.
148. **he**: i.e. Cade's father.
158. **span-counter**: game in which the player tosses a coin or counter, trying to land it within a span (nine inches) of another.
163. **main'd**: maimed (with a pun on *Maine*). **fain . . . staff**: forced to walk with a cane.

185. **clouted shoon**: hobnailed shoes.

[SCENE III]

Alarums to the fight, wherein both the STAFFORDS *are slain. Enter* CADE *and the rest*.

Cade. Where's Dick, the butcher of Ashford?

Dick. Here, sir.

Cade. They fell before thee like sheep and oxen, and thou behavedst thyself as if thou hadst been in thine own slaughter-house; therefore thus will I reward thee: the Lent shall be as long again as it is, and thou shalt have a license to kill for a hundred lacking one.

Dick. I desire no more.

Cade. And, to speak truth, thou deserv'st no less. This monument of the victory will I bear [*putting on Stafford's armor*], and the bodies shall be dragg'd at my horse heels till I do come to London, where we will have the Mayor's sword borne before us.

Dick. If we mean to thrive and do good, break open the jails and let out the prisoners.

Cade. Fear not that, I warrant thee. Come, let's march towards London. *Exeunt*.

[SCENE IV]

Enter the KING *with a supplication and the* QUEEN *with Suffolk's head, the* DUKE OF BUCKINGHAM *and the* LORD SAY.

Queen. Oft have I heard that grief softens the mind,
And makes it fearful and degenerate;

IV.iii. **Location**: Scene continues.
6. **Lent**. In Elizabethan England butchers were allowed to kill beasts during Lent only if they had a license to supply those with special needs. 17. **Fear**: doubt.

IV.iv. **Location**: London. The palace.
o.s.d. **supplication**: petition. 2. **fearful**: full of fears.

Think therefore on revenge and cease to weep.
But who can cease to weep and look on this?
Here may his head lie on my throbbing breast;
But where's the body that I should embrace?
Buck. What answer makes your Grace to the rebels' supplication?
King. I'll send some holy bishop to entreat;
For God forbid so many simple souls
Should perish by the sword! And I myself,
Rather than bloody war shall cut them short,
Will parley with Jack Cade their general.
But stay, I'll read it over once again.
Queen. Ah, barbarous villains! hath this lovely face
Rul'd like a wandering planet over me,
And could it not enforce them to relent,
That were unworthy to behold the same?
King. Lord Say, Jack Cade hath sworn to have thy head.
Say. Ay, but I hope your Highness shall have his.
King. How now, madam?
Still lamenting and mourning for Suffolk's death?
I fear me, love, if that I had been dead,
Thou wouldst not have mourn'd so much for me.
Queen. No, my love, I should not mourn, but die for thee.

Enter a Messenger.

King. How now? what news? why com'st thou in such haste?
Mess. The rebels are in Southwark; fly, my lord!
Jack Cade proclaims himself Lord Mortimer,
Descended from the Duke of Clarence' house,
And calls your Grace usurper, openly,
And vows to crown himself in Westminster.
His army is a ragged multitude
Of hinds and peasants, rude and merciless.
Sir Humphrey Stafford and his brother's death
Hath given them heart and courage to proceed.
All scholars, lawyers, courtiers, gentlemen,
They call false caterpillars, and intend their death.
King. O graceless men! they know not what they do.
Buck. My gracious lord, retire to Killingworth,
Until a power be rais'd to put them down.
Queen. Ah, were the Duke of Suffolk now alive,
These Kentish rebels would be soon appeas'd!
King. Lord Say, the traitors hateth thee,
Therefore away with us to Killingworth.
Say. So might your Grace's person be in danger.
The sight of me is odious in their eyes;
And therefore in this city will I stay
And live alone as secret as I may.

Enter another Messenger.

[2.] *Mess.* Jack Cade hath gotten London Bridge:
The citizens fly and forsake their houses;
The rascal people, thirsting after prey,
Join with the traitor, and they jointly swear
To spoil the city and your royal court.
Buck. Then linger not, my lord, away, take horse.
King. Come, Margaret, God, our hope, will succor us.
Queen. My hope is gone, now Suffolk is deceas'd.
King. Farewell, my lord, trust not the Kentish rebels.
Buck. Trust nobody, for fear you [be] betray'd.
Say. The trust I have is in mine innocence,
And therefore am I bold and resolute. *Exeunt.*

[Scene V]

Enter Lord Scales *upon the Tower, walking. Then enters two or three* Citizens *below.*

Scales. How now? is Jack Cade slain?

1. Cit. No, my lord, nor likely to be slain; for they have won the Bridge, killing all those that withstand them. The Lord Mayor craves aid of your honor from the Tower to defend the city from the rebels.

Scales. Such aid as I can spare you shall command,
But I am troubled here with them myself;
The rebels have assay'd to win the Tower.
But get you to Smithfield and gather head,
And thither I will send you Matthew Goffe.
Fight for your king, your country, and your lives,
And so farewell, for I must hence again. *Exeunt.*

[Scene VI]

Enter Jack Cade *and the rest, and strikes his staff on London Stone.*

Cade. Now is Mortimer lord of this city. And here, sitting upon London Stone, I charge and command that, of the city's cost, the pissing-conduit run nothing but claret wine this first year of our reign. And now henceforward it shall be treason for any that calls me other than Lord Mortimer.

Enter a Soldier *running.*

Sold. Jack Cade! Jack Cade!

Cade. Knock him down there. *They kill him.*

[*Smith.*] If this fellow be wise, he'll never call ye Jack Cade more. I think he hath a very fair warning.

Dick. My lord, there's an army gather'd together in Smithfield.

Cade. Come, then, let's go fight with them. But first go and set London Bridge on fire, and if you can, burn down the Tower too. Come, let's away.

Exeunt omnes.

16. planet. Astrologers held that a star in the ascendant controlled the destinies of those born under it.
27. Southwark: section of London on the south bank of the Thames at the end of London Bridge.
39. Killingworth: Kenilworth, a royal castle in Warwickshire.
40. power: army.

53. spoil: loot.

IV.v. Location: London. The Tower.
9. Smithfield: open area outside the city wall, northwest of St. Paul's.
head: a force.

IV.vi. Location: London. Canwick Street (modern Cannon Street).
o.s.d. London Stone: ancient stone in Cannon Street, long famous as a landmark.
3. pissing-conduit: conduit near the junction of Threadneedle Street and Cornhill in the City of London.

[SCENE VII]

Alarums. MATTHEW GOFFE *is slain, and all the rest. Then enter* JACK CADE *with his company.*

Cade. So, sirs. Now go some and pull down the Savoy; others to th' Inns of Court; down with them all.

Dick. I have a suit unto your lordship.

Cade. Be it a lordship, thou shalt have it for that word.

Dick. Only that the laws of England may come out of your mouth.

Holland. [*Aside.*] Mass, 'twill be sore law then, for he was thrust in the mouth with a spear, and 'tis not whole yet.

Smith. [*Aside.*] Nay, John, it will be stinking law, for his breath stinks with eating toasted cheese.

Cade. I have thought upon it, it shall be so. Away, burn all the records of the realm, my mouth shall be the parliament of England.

Holland. [*Aside.*] Then we are like to have biting statutes, unless his teeth be pull'd out.

Cade. And henceforward all things shall be in common.

Enter a MESSENGER.

Mess. My lord, a prize, a prize! Here's the Lord Say, which sold the towns in France; he that made us pay one and twenty fifteens, and one shilling to the pound, the last subsidy.

Enter GEORGE [BEVIS] *with the* LORD SAY.

Cade. Well, he shall be beheaded for it ten times. Ah, thou say, thou serge, nay, thou buckram lord! now art thou within point-blank of our jurisdiction regal. What canst thou answer to my Majesty for giving up of Normandy unto Mounsieur Basimecu, the Dolphin of France? Be it known unto thee by these presence, even the presence of Lord Mortimer, that I am the besom that must sweep the court clean of such filth as thou art. Thou hast most traitorously corrupted the youth of the realm in erecting a grammar school; and whereas, before, our forefathers had no other books but the score and the tally, thou hast caus'd printing to be us'd, and, contrary to the King, his crown, and dignity, thou hast built a paper-mill. It will be prov'd to thy face that thou hast men about thee that usually talk of a noun and a verb, and such abominable words as no Christian ear can endure

IV.vii. Location: London. Smithfield.
2. **Savoy**: London palace, formerly the town seat of the dukes of Lancaster. **Inns of Court**: the legal centre of London.
22–23. **one . . . subsidy.** An exaggerated estimate of the customary tax of one-fifteenth on income from land, frequently levied as a "subsidy" for special purposes.
25. **say, serge, buckram**: kinds of fabric, the first of silk, the second of wool, the third of linen.
28. **Mounsieur Basimecu**: contemptuous term for a Frenchman (*baise mon cul*).
29–30. **these presence**: i.e. these presents, a legal term meaning "the present document." 31. **besom**: broom.
35. **score . . . tally**: primitive device for keeping accounts; one half of a stick notched to record the transactions was held by the debtor and the other by the creditor.
36. **printing.** An anachronism, like the reference to paper-mills in line 37. The first printing press in England was established by William Caxton in 1477, twenty-seven years after Cade's rebellion; the first paper-mill, not until 1588. 39. **usually**: habitually.

to hear. Thou hast appointed justices of peace, to call poor men before them about matters they were not able to answer. Moreover, thou hast put them in prison, and because they could not read, thou hast hang'd them, when, indeed, only for that cause they have been most worthy to live. Thou dost ride in a foot-cloth, dost thou not?

Say. What of that?

Cade. Marry, thou oughtst not to let thy horse wear a cloak, when honester men than thou go in their hose and doublets.

Dick. And work in their shirt too, as myself, for example, that am a butcher.

Say. You men of Kent—

Dick. What say you of Kent?

Say. Nothing but this; 'tis "*bona terra, mala gens.*"

Cade. Away with him, away with him! he speaks Latin.

Say. Hear me but speak, and bear me where you will.
Kent, in the Commentaries Caesar writ,
Is term'd the civill'st place of all this isle:
Sweet is the country, because full of riches,
The people liberal, valiant, active, wealthy,
Which makes me hope you are not void of pity.
I sold not Maine, I lost not Normandy,
Yet to recover them would lose my life.
Justice with favor have I always done;
Pray'rs and tears have mov'd me, gifts could never.
When have I aught exacted at your hands,
[But] to maintain the King, the realm, and you?
Large gifts have I bestow'd on learned clerks,
Because my book preferr'd me to the King;
And seeing ignorance is the curse of God,
Knowledge the wing wherewith we fly to heaven,
Unless you be possess'd with devilish spirits
You cannot but forbear to murther me.
This tongue hath parley'd unto foreign kings
For your behoof—

Cade. Tut, when struck'st thou one blow in the field?

Say. Great men have reaching hands; oft have I struck
Those that I never saw, and struck them dead.

Bevis. O monstrous coward! What, to come behind folks?

Say. These cheeks are pale for watching for your good.

Cade. Give him a box o' th' ear, and that will make 'em red again.

Say. Long sitting to determine poor men's causes
Hath made me full of sickness and diseases.

Cade. Ye shall have a hempen [caudle] then, and the help of hatchet.

Dick. Why dost thou quiver, man?

44. **read**: i.e. claim "benefit of clergy" by demonstrating their literacy.
46. **foot-cloth.** See note to IV.i.54.
51. **hose and doublets**: breeches and coats.
56. **bona . . . gens**: good land, bad people.
69. **exacted**: i.e. as Lord Treasurer. 71. **clerks**: scholars.
72. **book**: i.e. learning.
90–91. **hempen . . . hatchet**: executioner's rope and axe, i.e. hanging and beheading. **caudle**: a warm drink.

Say. The palsy, and not fear, provokes me.

Cade. Nay, he nods at us, as who should say, I'll be even with you. I'll see if his head will stand steadier on a pole, or no. Take him away, and behead him.

Say. Tell me: wherein have I offended most?
Have I affected wealth or honor? Speak.
Are my chests fill'd up with extorted gold?
Is my apparel sumptuous to behold?
Whom have I injur'd that ye seek my death?
These hands are free from guiltless blood-shedding,
This breast from harboring foul deceitful thoughts.
O, let me live!

Cade. [*Aside*.] I feel remorse in myself with his words; but I'll bridle it. He shall die, and it be but for pleading so well for his life.—Away with him, he has a familiar under his tongue, he speaks not a' God's name. Go, take him away I say, and strike off his head presently, and then break into his son-in-law's house, Sir James Cromer, and strike off his head, and bring them both upon two poles hither.

All. It shall be done.

Say. Ah, countrymen! if when you make your pray'rs,
God should be so obdurate as yourselves,
How would it fare with your departed souls?
And therefore yet relent, and save my life.

Cade. Away with him, and do as I command ye. [*Exeunt some with the Lord Say*.] The proudest peer in the realm shall not wear a head on his shoulders, unless he pay me tribute. There shall not a maid be married, but she shall pay to me her maidenhead ere they have it. Men shall hold of me *in capite;* and we charge and command that their wives be as free as heart can wish or tongue can tell.

Dick. My lord, when shall we go to Cheapside and take up commodities upon our bills?

Cade. Marry, presently.

All. O, brave!

Enter one with the heads [*of Say and Cromer upon two poles*].

Cade. But is not this braver? Let them kiss one another, for they lov'd well when they were alive. Now part them again, lest they consult about the giving up of some more towns in France. Soldiers, defer the spoil of the city until night; for with these borne before us, in stead of maces, will we ride through the streets, and at every corner have them kiss. Away!

Exeunt.

[Scene VIII]

Alarum and retreat. Enter again Cade *and all his rabblement*.

98. affected: loved.
102. guiltless blood-shedding: shedding of guiltless blood.
108. familiar: attendant demon. **a':** in.
110. presently: immediately. **123. in capite:** (as tenant) in chief, i.e. by direct grant from the Crown. Note the bilingual pun on "maidenhead" (*capite* is the ablative case of *caput*, "head").
127. take . . . bills: secure merchandise on credit (with a pun on *bills* = weapons). **135. maces:** magistrates' symbols of office.

IV.viii. Location: Southwark.
o.s.d. retreat: signal to recall forces.

Cade. Up Fish Street! down Saint Magnus' Corner! kill and knock down! throw them into Thames! (*Sound a parley*.) What noise is this I hear? Dare any be so bold to sound retreat or parley when I command them kill?

Enter Buckingham *and old* Clifford [*attended*].

Buck. Ay, here they be that dare and will disturb thee.
Know, Cade, we come ambassadors from the King
Unto the commons, whom thou hast misled,
And here pronounce free pardon to them all
That will forsake thee and go home in peace.

Clif. What say ye, countrymen? will ye relent
And yield to mercy whilst 'tis offered you,
Or let a [rebel] lead you to your deaths?
Who loves the King, and will embrace his pardon,
Fling up his cap, and say, "God save his Majesty!"
Who hateth him and honors not his father,
Henry the Fift, that made all France to quake,
Shake he his weapon at us and pass by.

All. God save the King! God save the King!

Cade. What, Buckingham and Clifford, are ye so brave? And you, base peasants, do ye believe him? Will you needs be hang'd with your pardons about your necks? Hath my sword therefore broke through London gates, that you should leave me at the White Hart in Southwark? I thought ye would never have given out these arms till you had recover'd your ancient freedom. But you are all recreants and dastards, and delight to live in slavery to the nobility. Let them break your backs with burthens, take your houses over your heads, ravish your wives and daughters before your faces. For me, I will make shift for one; and so God's curse light upon you all!

All. We'll follow Cade, we'll follow Cade!

Clif. Is Cade the son of Henry the Fift,
That thus you do exclaim you'll go with him?
Will he conduct you through the heart of France,
And make the meanest of you earls and dukes?
Alas, he hath no home, no place to fly to;
Nor knows he how to live but by the spoil,
Unless by robbing of your friends and us.
Were't not a shame that, whilst you live at jar,
The fearful French, whom you late vanquished,
Should make a start o'er seas and vanquish you?
Methinks already in this civil broil
I see them lording it in London streets,
Crying "*Villiago!*" unto all they meet.
Better ten thousand base-born Cades miscarry
Than you should stoop unto a Frenchman's mercy.
To France, to France, and get what you have lost!
Spare England, for it is your native coast.
Henry hath money, you are strong and manly;
God on our side, doubt not of victory.

1–2. Fish Street, Saint Magnus' Corner: places at the north end of London Bridge opposite Southwark.
3. parley: signal to request a conference. **21. brave:** arrogant.
24–25. White Hart: ancient inn in Borough High Street, one of the principal thoroughfares of Southwark. **26. out:** up.
41. at jar: in discord. **42. fearful:** timid.
46. Villiago: rascal (Italian). **47. miscarry:** meet disaster.

All. A Clifford! a Clifford! we'll follow the King and Clifford.

Cade. [*Aside*.] Was ever feather so lightly blown to and fro as this multitude? The name of Henry the Fift hales them to an hundred mischiefs, and makes them leave me desolate. I see them lay their heads together to surprise me. My sword make way for me, for here is no staying.—In despite of the devils and hell, have through the very middest of you! And heavens and honor be witness that no want of resolution in me, but only my followers' base and ignominious treasons, makes me betake me to my heels.

[*He runs through them with his sword and flies away*.] *Exit*.

Buck. What, is he fled? Go some, and follow him,
And he that brings his head unto the King
Shall have a thousand crowns for his reward.

Exeunt some of them.

Follow me, soldiers, we'll devise a mean
To reconcile you all unto the King. *Exeunt omnes*.

[SCENE IX]

Sound trumpets. Enter KING, QUEEN, *and* SOMERSET *on the tarras*.

King. Was ever king that joy'd an earthly throne
And could command no more content than I?
No sooner was I crept out of my cradle
But I was made a king, at nine months old.
Was never subject long'd to be a king
As I do long and wish to be a subject.

Enter BUCKINGHAM *and* [*old*] CLIFFORD.

Buck. Health and glad tidings to your Majesty!

King. Why, Buckingham, is the traitor Cade surpris'd?
Or is he but retir'd to make him strong?

Enter, [*below*,] *multitudes with halters about their necks*.

Clif. He is fled, my lord, and all his powers do yield,
And humbly thus, with halters on their necks,
Expect your Highness' doom, of life or death.

King. Then, heaven, set ope thy everlasting gates
To entertain my vows of thanks and praise!
Soldiers, this day have you redeem'd your lives,
And show'd how well you love your prince and country:
Continue still in this so good a mind,
And Henry, though he be infortunate,
Assure yourselves, will never be unkind.
And so with thanks and pardon to you all,
I do dismiss you to your several countries.

All. God save the King! God save the King!

Enter a MESSENGER.

Mess. Please it your Grace to be advertised
The Duke of York is newly come from Ireland,
And with a puissant and a mighty power
Of gallowglasses and stout kerns
Is marching hitherward in proud array,
And still proclaimeth, as he comes along,
His arms are only to remove from thee
The Duke of Somerset, whom he terms a traitor.

King. Thus stands my state, 'twixt Cade and York distress'd,
Like to a ship that, having scap'd a tempest,
Is straightway [calm'd] and boarded with a pirate.
But now is Cade driven back, his men dispers'd,
And now is York in arms to second him.
I pray thee, Buckingham, go and meet him,
And ask him what's the reason of these arms.
Tell him I'll send Duke Edmund to the Tower;
And, Somerset, we will commit thee thither,
Until his army be dismiss'd from him.

Som. My lord,
I'll yield myself to prison willingly,
Or unto death, to do my country good.

King. In any case, be not too rough in terms,
For he is fierce and cannot brook hard language.

Buck. I will, my lord, and doubt not so to deal
As all things shall redound unto your good.

King. Come, wife, let's in, and learn to govern better,
For yet may England curse my wretched reign.

Flourish. Exeunt.

[SCENE X]

Enter CADE.

Cade. Fie on ambitions! fie on myself, that have a sword, and yet am ready to famish! These five days have I hid me in these woods and durst not peep out, for all the country is laid for me; but now am I so hungry that, if I might have a lease of my life for a thousand years, I could stay no longer. Wherefore, on a brick wall have I climb'd into this garden, to see if I can eat grass, or pick a sallet another while, which is not amiss to cool a man's stomach this hot weather. And I think this word "sallet" was born to do me good; for many a time, but for a sallet, my brain-pan had been cleft with a brown bill; and many a time, when I have been dry and bravely marching, it hath serv'd me instead of a quart pot to drink in; and now the word "sallet" must serve me to feed on.

[*He lies down picking of herbs and eating them*.]

57. hales: draws. **59. surprise:** capture.

IV.ix. Location: Kenilworth Castle.
o.s.d. on the tarras: on the terrace, i.e. on an upper level.
1. joy'd: enjoyed. **12. Expect:** await. **doom:** judgment.
21. countries: localities. **23. advertised:** informed.

26. gallowglasses: heavy-armed Irish foot soldiers. **kerns:** light-armed Irish foot soldiers. **28. still:** continually.
44. terms: language. **45. brook:** endure. **49. yet:** until now.

IV.x. This famous scene is based upon a single sentence in Hall (Bullough, III, 118): "For after a Proclamacion made, that whosoever could apprehende thesaied Jac Cade, should have for his pain, a .M. markes, many sought for hym, but few espied hym, til one Alexander Iden, esquire of Kent found hym in a garden, and there in his defence, manfully slewe the caitife Cade, & brought his ded body to London, whose hed was set on London bridge."
Location: Kent. Iden's garden.
4. laid: set with snares. **6. stay:** wait.
8. sallet: raw vegetable (play in line 11 on the meaning "helmet").
12. brown: bloodstained (?) or varnished to prevent rust (?). **bill:** long weapon with an axe-like head.

Enter IDEN [*followed at a distance by his* SERVANTS].

Iden. Lord, who would live turmoiled in the court
And may enjoy such quiet walks as these?
This small inheritance my father left me
Contenteth me, and worth a monarchy.
I seek not to wax great by others' [waning],
Or gather wealth, I care not with what envy.
Sufficeth that I have maintains my state
And sends the poor well pleased from my gate.

Cade. [*Aside.*] Here's the lord of the soil come to seize me for a stray, for entering his fee-simple without leave.—Ah, villain, thou wilt betray me, and get a thousand crowns of the King by carrying my head to him, but I'll make thee eat iron like an ostridge, and swallow my sword like a great pin, ere thou and I part.

Iden. Why, rude companion, whatsoe'er thou be,
I know thee not, why then should I betray thee?
Is't not enough to break into my garden,
And like a thief to come to rob my grounds,
Climbing my walls in spite of me the owner,
But thou wilt brave me with these saucy terms?

Cade. Brave thee? Ay, by the best blood that ever was broach'd, and beard thee too. Look on me well. I have eat no meat these five days, yet come thou and thy five men, and if I do not leave you all as dead as a doornail, I pray God I may never eat grass more.

Iden. Nay, it shall ne'er be said, while England stands,
That Alexander Iden, an esquire of Kent,
Took odds to combat a poor famish'd man.
Oppose thy steadfast-gazing eyes to mine,
See if thou canst outface me with thy looks.
Set limb to limb, and thou art far the lesser;
Thy hand is but a finger to my fist,
Thy leg a stick compared with this truncheon;
My foot shall fight with all the strength thou hast,
And if mine arm be heaved in the air,
Thy grave is digg'd already in the earth.
As for words, whose greatness answers words,
Let this my sword report what speech forbears.

Cade. By my valor, the most complete champion that ever I heard! Steel, if thou turn the edge, or cut not out the burly-bon'd clown in chines of beef ere thou sleep in thy sheath, I beseech [God] on my knees thou mayst be turn'd to hobnails.

Here they fight [*and Cade falls down*].

O, I am slain! Famine and no other hath slain me. Let ten thousand devils come against me, and give me but the ten meals I have lost, and I'd defy them all. Wither, garden, and be henceforth a burying-place to all that do dwell in this house, because the unconquer'd soul of Cade is fled.

Iden. Is't Cade that I have slain, that monstrous traitor?
Sword, I will hallow thee for this thy deed,
And hang thee o'er my tomb when I am dead.
Ne'er shall this blood be wiped from thy point,
But thou shalt wear it as a herald's coat,
To emblaze the honor that thy master got.

Cade. Iden, farewell, and be proud of thy victory. Tell Kent from me, she hath lost her best man, and exhort all the world to be cowards; for I, that never fear'd any, am vanquish'd by famine, not by valor. *Dies.*

Iden. How much thou wrong'st me, heaven be my judge.
Die, damned wretch, the curse of her that bare thee;
And as I thrust thy body in with my sword,
So wish I, I might thrust thy soul to hell.
Hence will I drag thee headlong by the heels
Unto a dunghill, which shall be thy grave,
And there cut off thy most ungracious head,
Which I will bear in triumph to the King,
Leaving thy trunk for crows to feed upon.

Exit [*dragging out the body, with his Servants*].

[ACT V, SCENE I]

Enter YORK *and his army of Irish with Drum and Colors.*

York. From Ireland thus comes York to claim his right,
And pluck the crown from feeble Henry's head.
Ring bells, aloud, burn bonfires clear and bright
To entertain great England's lawful king!
Ah, *sancta majestas!* who would not buy thee dear?
Let them obey that knows not how to rule;
This hand was made to handle nought but gold.
I cannot give due action to my words,
Except a sword or sceptre balance it.
A sceptre shall it have, have I a soul,
On which I'll toss the flow'r-de-luce of France.

Enter BUCKINGHAM.

Whom have we here? Buckingham, to disturb me?
The King hath sent him sure; I must dissemble.

Buck. York, if thou meanest well, I greet thee well.

York. Humphrey of Buckingham, I accept thy greeting.
Art thou a messenger, or come of pleasure?

Buck. A messenger from Henry, our dread liege,
To know the reason of these arms in peace;
Or why thou, being a subject as I am,
Against thy oath and true allegiance sworn,
Should raise so great a power without his leave,
Or dare to bring thy force so near the court.

York. [*Aside.*] Scarce can I speak, my choler is so great.
O, I could hew up rocks and fight with flint,

16. turmoiled: harried, distraught.
22. Sufficeth . . . state: it suffices that what I have maintains my way of life. **25. stray:** trespasser. **fee-simple:** freehold property.
31. rude companion: base fellow.
36. brave: defy, taunt. **saucy:** insolent.
38. broach'd: shed. **beard:** defy. **39. eat:** eaten.
44. odds: advantage. **49. truncheon:** thick staff (i.e. Iden's leg).
53. answers words: matches your words. **57. chines:** saddles, roasts.

71. emblaze: signify by a heraldic device. **77. bare:** bore.
80. headlong: at full length.

V.i. Location: Fields near St. Albans; the Castle Inn at one side.
o.s.d. Colors: flagbearer.
4. entertain: receive. **5. sancta majestas:** holy majesty.
11. toss: bear aloft. **flow'r-de-luce:** fleur-de-lis, the national emblem of France.

I am so angry at these abject terms;
And now, like Ajax Telamonius,
On sheep or oxen could I spend my fury.
I am far better born than is the King;
More like a king, more kingly in my thoughts;
But I must make fair weather yet a while,
Till Henry be more weak and I more strong.—
Buckingham, I prithee pardon me,
That I have given no answer all this while;
My mind was troubled with deep melancholy.
The cause why I have brought this army hither
Is to remove proud Somerset from the King,
Seditious to his Grace and to the state.

Buck. That is too much presumption on thy part;
But if thy arms be to no other end,
The King hath yielded unto thy demand:
The Duke of Somerset is in the Tower.

York. Upon thine honor, is he prisoner?

Buck. Upon mine honor, he is prisoner.

York. Then, Buckingham, I do dismiss my pow'rs.
Soldiers, I thank you all; disperse yourselves.
Meet me to-morrow in Saint George's Field,
You shall have pay and every thing you wish.
[*Exeunt Soldiers.*]

And let my sovereign, virtuous Henry,
Command my eldest son, nay, all my sons,
As pledges of my fealty and love;
I'll send them all as willing as I live.
Lands, goods, horse, armor, any thing I have
Is his to use, so Somerset may die.

Buck. York, I commend this kind submission;
We twain will go into his Highness' tent.

Enter KING *and* ATTENDANTS.

King. Buckingham, doth York intend no harm to us
That thus he marcheth with thee arm in arm?

York. In all submission and humility
York doth present himself unto your Highness.

King. Then what intends these forces thou dost bring?

York. To heave the traitor Somerset from hence,
And fight against that monstrous rebel Cade,
Who since I heard to be discomfited.

Enter IDEN *with Cade's head.*

Iden. If one so rude and of so mean condition
May pass into the presence of a king,
Lo, I present your Grace a traitor's head,
The head of Cade, whom I in combat slew.

King. The head of Cade! Great God, how just art thou!
O, let me view his visage, being dead,
That living wrought me such exceeding trouble.
Tell me, my friend, art thou the man that slew him?

Iden. I was, an't like your Majesty.

King. How art thou call'd? and what is thy degree?

Iden. Alexander Iden, that's my name,
A poor esquire of Kent, that loves his king.

Buck. So please it you, my lord, 'twere not amiss
He were created knight for his good service.

King. Iden, kneel down. [*He kneels.*] Rise up a knight.
We give thee for reward a thousand marks,
And will that thou henceforth attend on us.

Iden. May Iden live to merit such a bounty,
And never live but true unto his liege! [*Rises.*]

Enter QUEEN *and* SOMERSET.

King. See, Buckingham, Somerset comes with th' Queen.
Go bid her hide him quickly from the Duke.

Queen. For thousand Yorks he shall not hide his head,
But boldly stand and front him to his face.

York. How now? is Somerset at liberty?
Then, York, unloose thy long-imprisoned thoughts,
And let thy tongue be equal with thy heart.
Shall I endure the sight of Somerset?
False king, why hast thou broken faith with me,
Knowing how hardly I can brook abuse?
King did I call thee? No; thou art not king;
Not fit to govern and rule multitudes,
Which dar'st not, no, nor canst not rule a traitor.
That head of thine doth not become a crown:
Thy hand is made to grasp a palmer's staff
And not to grace an aweful princely sceptre.
That gold must round engirt these brows of mine,
Whose smile and frown, like to Achilles' spear,
Is able with the change to kill and cure.
Here is a hand to hold a sceptre up,
And with the same to act controlling laws.
Give place! By heaven, thou shalt rule no more
O'er him whom heaven created for thy ruler.

Som. O monstrous traitor! I arrest thee, York,
Of capital treason 'gainst the King and crown.
Obey, audacious traitor, kneel for grace.

York. Wouldst have me kneel? First let me ask of [these]
If they can brook I bow a knee to man.
Sirrah, call in my [sons] to be my bail.
[*Exit Attendant.*]
I know, ere they will have me go to ward,
They'll pawn their swords [for] my enfranchisement.

Queen. Call hither Clifford, bid him come amain,
To say if that the bastard boys of York
Shall be the surety for their traitor father.
[*Exit Buckingham.*]

York. O blood-bespotted Neapolitan,

25. abject terms: insulting words.
26–27. Ajax . . . fury. According to Homer, Ajax, a Greek warrior driven mad by his jealousy of Ulysses, killed the sheep and oxen which he mistook for his enemies.
30. make fair weather: be pleasant, equivocate.
46. Saint George's Field: open area opposite London on the south bank of the Thames.
49–50. Command . . . As pledges: hold . . . as hostages.
53. so: provided that. **64. rude:** uncultivated.

80. will: command. **86. front:** confront.
92. brook abuse: endure deception. **97. palmer's:** pilgrim's.
99. gold: i.e. golden crown.
100–101. Whose . . . cure. In Greek legend, Telephus, a son of Hercules, was not cured of a wound from Achilles' spear until rust from the weapon was applied to his injury. **103. act:** enact.
111. sons. Actually, York's sons were children at the time (1452), Edward (later Edward IV) being ten and Richard (later Richard III) only a few months old. **112. to ward:** into custody.
114. amain: at full speed.
117. Neapolitan. Margaret's father René (Reignier) was the titular king of Naples.

Outcast of Naples, England's bloody scourge!
The sons of York, thy betters in their birth,
Shall be their father's bail, and bane to those
That for my surety will refuse the boys!

Enter EDWARD *and* RICHARD [PLANTAGENET *with Drum and Soldiers at one door*].

See where they come, I'll warrant they'll make it good.

Enter CLIFFORD [*and his son* YOUNG CLIFFORD *with Drum and Soldiers at the other door*].

Queen. And here comes Clifford to deny their bail.
Clif. Health and all happiness to my lord the King! [*Kneels.*]
York. I thank thee, Clifford. Say, what news with thee?
Nay, do not fright us with an angry look.
We are thy sovereign, Clifford, kneel again;
For thy mistaking so, we pardon thee.
Clif. This is my king, York, I do not mistake,
But thou mistakes me much to think I do.
To Bedlam with him! is the man grown mad?
King. Ay, Clifford, a bedlam and ambitious humor
Makes him oppose himself against his king.
Clif. He is a traitor, let him to the Tower,
And chop away that factious pate of his.
Queen. He is arrested, but will not obey.
His sons, he says, shall give their words for him.
York. Will you not, sons?
Edw. Ay, noble father, if our words will serve.
Rich. And if words will not, then our weapons shall.
Clif. Why, what a brood of traitors have we here!
York. Look in a glass, and call thy image so.
I am thy king, and thou a false-heart traitor.
Call hither to the stake my two brave bears,
That with the very shaking of their chains
They may astonish these fell-lurking curs.
Bid Salisbury and Warwick come to me.

Enter the EARLS OF WARWICK *and* SALISBURY [*with Drum and Soldiers*].

Clif. Are these thy bears? We'll bait thy bears to death,
And manacle the beard in their chains,
If thou dar'st bring them to the baiting-place.
Rich. Oft have I seen a hot o'erweening cur
Run back and bite, because he was withheld,
Who, being suffer'd, with the bear's fell paw
Hath clapp'd his tail between his legs and cried;
And such a piece of service will you do,
If you oppose yourselves to match Lord Warwick.

120. bane: destruction.
131. Bedlam: hospital of St. Mary of Bethlehem, an asylum for lunatics in London.
132. bedlam: mad. **humor:** temperament.
144. two brave bears: i.e. Salisbury and his son Warwick, so called because Warwick's badge was a rampant bear chained to a staff. See note to lines 202–3.
146. astonish: dismay. **fell-lurking:** cruelly waiting.
149. bearard: bear-ward, keeper of bears. Throughout this passage the imagery is derived from the savage Elizabethan sport of bear-baiting. **150. baiting-place:** bear pit.
153. suffer'd: i.e. permitted to attack.
156. oppose yourselves: undertake.

Clif. Hence, heap of wrath, foul indigested lump,
As crooked in thy manners as thy shape!
York. Nay, we shall heat you thoroughly anon.
Clif. Take heed, lest by your heat you burn yourselves.
King. Why, Warwick, hath thy knee forgot to bow?
Old Salisbury, shame to thy silver hair,
Thou mad misleader of thy brain-sick son!
What, wilt thou on thy death-bed play the ruffian,
And seek for sorrow with thy spectacles?
O, where is faith? O, where is loyalty?
If it be banish'd from the frosty head,
Where shall it find a harbor in the earth?
Wilt thou go dig a grave to find out war,
And shame thine honorable age with blood?
Why art thou old, and want'st experience?
Or wherefore dost abuse it if thou hast it?
For shame, in duty bend thy knee to me
That bows unto the grave with mickle age.
Sal. My lord, I have considered with myself
The title of this most renowned duke,
And in my conscience do repute his Grace
The rightful heir to England's royal seat.
King. Hast thou not sworn allegiance unto me?
Sal. I have.
King. Canst thou dispense with heaven for such an oath?
Sal. It is great sin to swear unto a sin,
But greater sin to keep a sinful oath.
Who can be bound by any solemn vow
To do a murd'rous deed, to rob a man,
To force a spotless virgin's chastity,
To reave the orphan of his patrimony,
To wring the widow from her custom'd right,
And have no other reason for this wrong
But that he was bound by a solemn oath?
Queen. A subtle traitor needs no sophister.
King. Call Buckingham, and bid him arm himself.
York. Call Buckingham, and all the friends thou hast,
I am resolv'd for death [or] dignity.
Clif. The first I warrant thee, if dreams prove true.
War. You were best to go to bed and dream again,
To keep thee from the tempest of the field.
Clif. I am resolv'd to bear a greater storm
Than any thou canst conjure up to-day;
And that I'll write upon thy burgonet,
Might I but know thee by thy [household] badge.
War. Now, by my father's badge, old Nevil's crest,
The rampant bear chain'd to the ragged staff,
This day I'll wear aloft my burgonet,
As on a mountain top the cedar shows
That keeps his leaves in spite of any storm,

157. indigested: shapeless, misformed. On Richard's deformity see *Richard III*, I.i.14–27. **165. spectacles:** organs of sight.
171. want'st: lackest. **172. abuse:** disgrace. **174. mickle:** great.
181. dispense with: obtain dispensation from.
187. reave: bereave, rob.
188. custom'd right: i.e. of inheriting part of her husband's estate.
191. sophister: sophist, equivocator. **200. burgonet:** helmet.
202–3. my . . . staff. Actually, the Neville badge was a bull. Warwick's famous badge of a bear chained to a staff was, like his earldom, inherited from his father-in-law Richard Beauchamp.

Even to affright thee with the view thereof.
Clif. And from thy burgonet I'll rend thy bear,
And tread it under foot with all contempt,
Despite the bearard that protects the bear.
Y. Clif. And so to arms, victorious father,
To quell the rebels and their complices.
Rich. Fie! charity, for shame! speak not in spite,
For you shall sup with Jesu Christ to-night.
Y. Clif. Foul stigmatic, that's more than thou canst
tell.
Rich. If not in heaven, you'll surely sup in hell.
Exeunt [*severally*].

[Scene II]

[*Alarums to the battle*.] *Enter* Warwick.

War. Clifford of Cumberland, 'tis Warwick calls!
And if thou dost not hide thee from the bear,
Now when the angry trumpet sounds alarum,
And dead men's cries do fill the empty air,
Clifford, I say, come forth and fight with me.
Proud northern lord, Clifford of Cumberland,
Warwick is hoarse with calling thee to arms.

Enter York.

How now, my noble lord? what, all afoot?
York. The deadly-handed Clifford slew my steed;
But match to match I have encount'red him,
And made a prey for carrion kites and crows
Even of the bonny beast he lov'd so well.

Enter [*old*] Clifford.

War. Of one or both of us the time is come.
York. Hold, Warwick; seek thee out some other
chase,
For I myself must hunt this deer to death.
War. Then nobly, York, 'tis for a crown thou
fight'st.
As I intend, Clifford, to thrive to-day,
It grieves my soul to leave thee unassail'd.
Exit Warwick.
Clif. What seest thou in me, York? Why dost thou
pause?
York. With thy brave bearing should I be in love,
But that thou art so fast mine enemy.
Clif. Nor should thy prowess want praise and
esteem,
But that 'tis shown ignobly and in treason.
York. So let it help me now against thy sword,
As I in justice and true right express it.
Clif. My soul and body on the action both!
York. A dreadful lay! Address thee instantly.
[*They fight, and Clifford falls*.]
Clif. *La fin couronne les* [*œuvres*]. [*Dies*.]

207. thereof: i.e. of the burgonet.
215. stigmatic: literally, a branded person, hence one marked with deformity (i.e. branded by God).

V.ii. Location: Scene continues.
14. chase: game. **21. fast:** unchangeably.
27. lay: wager. **Address thee:** prepare yourself.
28. La fin . . . œuvres: the end crowns the work.

York. Thus war hath given thee peace, for thou art
still.
Peace with his soul, heaven, if it be thy will! [*Exit*.]

Enter Young Clifford.

Y. Clif. Shame and confusion! all is on the rout,
Fear frames disorder, and disorder wounds
Where it should guard. O war, thou son of hell,
Whom angry heavens do make their minister,
Throw in the frozen bosoms of our part
Hot coals of vengeance! Let no soldier fly.
He that is truly dedicate to war
Hath no self-love; nor he that loves himself
Hath not essentially but by circumstance
The name of valor. [*Sees his dead father*.] O, let the
vile world end,
And the premised flames of the last day
Knit earth and heaven together!
Now let the general trumpet blow his blast,
Particularities and petty sounds
To cease! Wast thou ordain'd, dear father,
To lose thy youth in peace, and to achieve
The silver livery of advised age,
And in thy reverence, and thy chair-days, thus
To die in ruffian battle? Even at this sight
My heart is turn'd to stone; and while 'tis mine,
It shall be stony. York not our old men spares;
No more will I their babes. Tears virginal
Shall be to me even as the dew to fire,
And beauty, that the tyrant oft reclaims,
Shall to my flaming wrath be oil and flax.
Henceforth I will not have to do with pity.
Meet I an infant of the house of York,
Into as many gobbets will I cut it
As wild Medea young Absyrtus did;
In cruelty will I seek out my fame.
[*He takes him up on his back*.]
Come, thou new ruin of old Clifford's house:
As did Aeneas old Anchises bear,
So bear I thee upon my manly shoulders;
But then Aeneas bare a living load—
Nothing so heavy as these woes of mine.
[*Exit bearing off his father*.]

Enter Richard *and* Somerset *to fight*. [*Somerset is killed under the sign of the Castle Inn*.]

Rich. So lie thou there;
For underneath an alehouse' paltry sign,
The Castle in Saint Albons, Somerset
Hath made the wizard famous in his death.

32. frames: makes, produces.
35. frozen: i.e. cowardly. **part:** side.
37. dedicate: dedicated. **41. premised:** preordained.
44. Particularities: trifles. **45. ordain'd:** destined.
47. advised: deliberate, wise.
53. dew to fire. Dew was supposed to make fire burn more fiercely.
58. gobbets: pieces.
59. As . . . did. In Greek legend, Medea, before fleeing from Colchos with Jason, hacked her brother Absyrtus into small pieces in order to delay pursuit by her father.
62. As . . . bear. In Virgil's *Aeneid* Aeneas carried his aged father Anchises on his back when he escaped from Troy.
65. Nothing: in no respect.
67–69. underneath . . . death: i.e. by meeting death under the sign of the Castle Inn Somerset has fulfilled the spirit's prophecy (I.iv.35–37).
69. wizard: spirit.

Sword, hold thy temper; heart, be wrathful still:
Priests pray for enemies, but princes kill. [*Exit*.]

Fight. Excursions. Enter KING, QUEEN, *and others.*

Queen. Away, my lord! you are slow, for shame, away!
King. Can we outrun the heavens? Good Margaret, stay.
Queen. What are you made of? You'll nor fight nor fly.
Now is it manhood, wisdom, and defense
To give the enemy way, and to secure us
By what we can, which can no more but fly.
Alarum afar off.
If you be ta'en, we then should see the bottom
Of all our fortunes; but if we haply scape
(As well we may, if not through your neglect),
We shall to London get, where you are lov'd,
And where this breach now in our fortunes made
May readily be stopp'd.

Enter [YOUNG] CLIFFORD.

Y. Clif. But that my heart's on future mischief set,
I would speak blasphemy ere bid you fly.
But fly you must. Uncurable discomfit
Reigns in the hearts of all our present parts.
Away, for your relief! and we will live
To see their day, and them our fortune give.
Away, my lord, away! *Exeunt.*

[SCENE III]

Alarum. Retreat. Enter YORK, RICHARD, [EDWARD,] WARWICK, *and Soldiers with Drum and Colors.*

York. Of Salisbury, who can report of him,

That winter lion, who in rage forgets
Aged contusions and all brush of time;
And like a gallant in the brow of youth,
Repairs him with occasion? This happy day
Is not itself, nor have we won one foot,
If Salisbury be lost.
Rich. My noble father,
Three times to-day I holp him to his horse,
Three times bestrid him; thrice I led him off,
Persuaded him from any further act:
But still, where danger was, still there I met him,
And like rich hangings in a homely house,
So was his will in his old feeble body.
But noble as he is, look where he comes.

Enter SALISBURY.

Sal. Now, by my sword, well hast thou fought to-day;
By th' mass, so did we all. I thank you, Richard.
God knows how long it is I have to live,
And it hath pleas'd him that three times to-day
You have defended me from imminent death.
Well, lords, we have not got that which we have:
'Tis not enough our foes are this time fled,
Being opposites of such repairing nature.
York. I know our safety is to follow them,
For, as I hear, the King is fled to London,
To call a present court of parliament.
Let us pursue him ere the writs go forth.
What says Lord Warwick? shall we after them?
War. After them! Nay, before them, if we can.
Now, by my [faith], lords, 'twas a glorious day.
Saint Albons battle won by famous York
Shall be eterniz'd in all age to come.
Sound drum and trumpets, and to London all,
And more such days as these to us befall! *Exeunt.*

71 s.d. Excursions: sallies, sorties.
73. outrun: escape from. **74. nor . . . nor:** neither . . . nor.
77. what: whatever means. **which:** (we) who.
80. if not: if we don't fail to do so.
86. Uncurable discomfit: irrevocable defeat.
87. present parts: remaining forces.
89. To . . . give: i.e. to see a day of victory like theirs and to give them our misfortune.

V.iii. Location: Scene continues.

2. winter: aged. **3. brush:** attack.
5. Repairs . . . occasion: i.e. restores himself with the opportunity of fresh encounters. **8. holp:** helped.
9. bestrid him: i.e. defended him when he was down.
12. homely: modest.
22. opposites . . . nature: adversaries with such power of recovery.
26. writs: royal summons for a meeting of Parliament.
31. eterniz'd: immortalized.

NOTE ON THE TEXT

There is only one authoritative text of *2 Henry VI*, that in the First Folio (1623); all later texts are derived primarily from that source. There is also, however, a "bad" quarto, or memorially reported version, derived from essentially the same text (with theatrical cuts) as that printed in F1; it was published in 1594 with the title *The First part of the Contention betwixt the two famous Houses of Yorke and Lancaster.* This text (Q1) was reprinted in 1600 (Q2) and 1619 (Q3); Q3, based on Q1, contains some additions and changes which seem to anticipate the F1 text. Although Q1 has no basic authority, it occasionally helps to resolve textual difficulties in F1, and its stage directions (frequently included in the present edition) are especially valuable as giving us some insight into at least one Elizabethan production of the play. C. T. Prouty has attempted to revive the old theory that Q1 is an original play upon which Shakespeare based his *2 Henry VI*, but the arguments he advances are not at all convincing.

The exact nature of the printer's copy behind the F1 text is, as is so often the case, open to question, although most critics agree that it was some form of Shakespearean holograph (i.e., "foul papers" [Greg, Montgomery/Taylor, Hattaway], though Hattaway admits the possibility of a scribal copy of "foul papers"). Cairncross, however, extended the possibilities of corruption in the F1 text by arguing that substantial parts of F1 were set up from a copy of Q3 (with oc-

2 *Henry VI*

casional use of Q2) corrected by collation with a manuscript of the kind postulated above, and that only where Q-copy was so hopelessly corrupt or incomplete was recourse had directly to this manuscript by the compositor. Although such basic use of Q-copy is not generally denied, it is agreed that at least IV.v and the first six lines of IV.vi (Montgomery/Taylor identify some four other such passages) were almost certainly set from a slightly corrected copy of Q3. As noted above, Q3 contains a number of readings which to some extent anticipate the readings of F1. On the surface, this seems to present a textual situation similar to that in *Richard III* and *King Lear*: where F1 adopts a reading from a later quarto not found in Q1 (the readings of the later quartos being presumably without manuscript or any other kind of authority), an editor should adopt the reading of Q1. But in *2 Henry VI* (as also in *3 Henry VI*) the status of Q3 is unusual, since it cannot be described as a mere reprint of Q1 and the new readings it affords which link it with F1 may have been introduced by someone familiar with the play as acted. Hence it would be dangerous to apply the textual approach used in *Richard III* and *King Lear*, particularly as a number of the unique links between Q3 and F1 present only similar, not identical, readings. The present edition, therefore, retains the readings of the F1 text (as does Hattaway), but a complete record of the significant links between F1 and Q3 (or Q2) may be found in the Textual Notes (see, for example, I.i.8, 186; I.ii.26–7, 29, 62–7; I.iii.80; II.i.10, 11–2, 14, 26, 50, 81, 108; II.ii.12–52; II.iii.34, 69; III.i.359; III.ii.20; IV.ii.149; IV.iii.6–7; IV.x.42, 83). Where only one or two of the three quartos are cited, agreement of the uncited quarto (or quartos) with the lemma may be assumed.

As in the case of *1 Henry VI*, the question of the authorship of Parts II and III is equally debated. Some critics (Alexander, Chambers, Cairncross, Hattaway) favor the view that both Parts II and III are essentially the work of Shakespeare alone: others (Hart, Wilson, Montgomery/Taylor, and the present editor) argue that Parts II and III are originally collaborative efforts by the same writers who wrote the *Ur-1 Henry VI* (Greene, Nashe, Peele; see "Note on the Text" to *1 Henry VI* and Wilson's scene by scene authorship analysis), written perhaps as early as 1589–90 and revised by Shakespeare (more heavily than *1 Henry VI*, particularly Part III) at the same time (early 1592) that he revised *1 Henry VI*.

The New Oxford editors (Montgomery/Taylor), as in the New Oxford text of *Henry V*, allow the *Contention* and *The true Tragedie of Richard Duke of Yorke* (1595) an invasive textual authority not hitherto accorded them, a practice they defend on the supposition that behind these memorial reconstructions lies, in each case, a somewhat shortened version officially prepared for performance in London by the acting company then in control of the longer texts now represented by the F1 texts of 2 and *3 Henry VI*. Such a supposition is probable enough, but it runs into dangerous waters when it assumes that certain passages in these reported texts preserve Shakespearean revisions of the earlier texts as they are preserved in 2 and *3 Henry VI*. For such an assumption there is really no evidence, and the danger inherent in this particular kind of eclectic approach may be illustrated by two examples in the New Oxford text of *2 Henry VI*.

(1) In I.i, Montgomery/Taylor substitute the following Q1–3 lines for the Queen's opening speech in F1 (lines 24–31):

> Th'excessiue [*emended to* excess of] loue I beare vnto
> your grace,
> Forbids me to be lauish of my tongue,
> Least I should speake more then [*i.e.,* than] beseemes
> a woman:
> Let this suffice, my blisse is in your liking,
> And nothing can make poore *Margaret* miserable,
> Vnlesse the frowne of mightie Englands King.

First, in no significant sense can these lines be considered either poetically or dramatically superior (the fifth line is metrically awkward, since Shakespeare regularly uses "miserable" as trisyllabic). Second, the second line is probably an echo from *1 Henry VI*, II.v.47, "Among which terms he us'd his lavish tongue" ("lavish tongue" is repeated in Q in IV.i.61, a phrase probably given currency by Marlowe, *1 Tamburlaine*, IV.ii.69; there are at least fourteen other echoes of *1 Henry VI* in *Contention* and *True Tragedie*, despite Montgomery/Taylor's assertion that "there is no reason to believe the reporter knew" *1 Henry VI* [*Textual Companion*]). Third, the phrase "more then beseemes a woman" is closely paralleled in Shakespeare only by *1 Henry VI*, III.i.19, "more than well beseems / A man." Fourth, in the Q line preceding the Queen's speech, the word "perplexed" is most probably an echo (as Alexander suggested) of *1 Henry VI*, V.v.95, "I rest perplexed with a thousand cares," and three lines below the Queen's Q speech the phrase "Lordly Peeres" is a recollection of *2 Henry VI*, I.i.11. Fifth, the last line of the Queen's Q speech (see above) is linked with the second line of the King's following Q speech: "Louely Queene *Margaret* sit down by my side," thus jointly echoing *3 Henry VI*, III.iii.1–4, "Fair Queen of England, worthy Margaret, / sit down with us. . . . /*Q. Mar.* No, mighty King of France . . . ." More obviously, however, the last line of the Queen's Q speech echoes *The Troublesome Raigne of Iohn King of England, Part I* (1591), I.i.11: "As is the throne of mightie *Englands* King." Thus the Queen's speech in Q is not only itself surely memorially contaminated, but is sandwiched between two other speeches also most probably memorially contaminated.

(2) In V.iii, the New Oxford text admits six lines found only in Q1–3: (a) four opening lines added to York's initial speech [F1, 1–7], and (b) two lines assigned to Edward, eldest son of York, following Richard's speech [F1, 7–14]). Of (a), Montgomery/Taylor argue, rightly enough, that, dramatically, Edward, who is to become king in *3 Henry VI*, should appear (as in Q3, s.d. only) with York and Richard, York's youngest son, in this final scene—even though, it should be noted, Edward has only one line in Act V (V.i.139), being completely subordinated to Richard, and takes no part in the following battle scene. I have, therefore, revised the opening stage direction to V.iii by adding "Edward" (following Montgomery/Taylor, as does Hattaway, who otherwise follows F1). While one may admit that these opening lines found only in Q1–3, which begin "How now, boyes" (see Textual Notes for the full text), support Edward's presence in Q1–3, it is very doubtful that they, at least in their present state, represent anything more than the reporter's fudging, since they clearly appear to echo bits of 2 and *3 Henry VI*, etc. (Compare Q1–3 "Whilst faint-heart Henry did vsurpe our rights:" with *2 Henry VI*, I.i.244 (York speaking) "Nor shall proud Lancaster [i.e., Henry] usurp my right,") The same hand is surely at work two lines below (Q1–3, 6): "With bloodie mindes did buckle with the foe,"; compare "bloody mind" *Richard III*, I.ii.99 and *Titus Andronicus*, V.i.101; "bloody-minded" *2 Henry VI*, IV.i.36 and *3 Henry VI*, II.vi.33; "buckle with" *1 Henry VI*, I.ii.95, IV.iv.5, V.ii.28 and *Edward III*, III.i.126.

The (b) addition consists of the following two-line speech (Q, 15–16), assigned to Edward, and is unique to Q1–3:

See noble father, where they both do come,
The onely props vnto the house of Yorke.

Their inclusion in the New Oxford text of *2 Henry VI* raises a different question from that posed by memorial contamination. Even if these lines represent an attempt by somebody, possibly the book-keeper or even Shakespeare, to give Edward a small role in this final scene, as would indeed seem to be the case, should such lines be included in an edited text of *2 Henry VI*, when in neither context do they make connected sense? In F1, Warwick, son of the Earl of Salisbury, enters at the beginning of the scene with York and Richard; thus York need show no concern about Warwick, only about the missing Salisbury. In Q1–3, Warwick enters with Salisbury, after Richard's lines (Q, 9–14), again with no earlier reference to Warwick (Q, 1–14); thus Edward's "See noble father, where they both do come," has no referent for "both," since, as in F1, no mention of Warwick has been made prior to his entry with Salisbury at this point. Moreover, in neither F1 nor Q1–3 does Edward receive any notice in Salisbury's following speech, which is largely devoted to praise of Richard (F1, 15–22; Q, 17–21), or in the rest of the scene. In other words, if somebody did, as seems likely, revise F1 V.iii to integrate Edward into the postulated officially revised version of this scene, this revision was so badly botched by the reporter in Q that inclusion of Edward's Q1–3 speech only results in contextual incoherence.

The Textual Notes generally record the variants in Q1–3 only where they figure in a reading cited in connection with the F1 text. The absence of citation of Q1–3 among the sigla in any entry indicates that the reading of the lemma occurs in a passage which in Q1–3 is either omitted or so differently worded that it offers no recognizable equivalent. Some longer sections of Q1–3, where divergence from the F1 text is most noticeable, may be consulted in the Textual Notes at I.iv.22 s.d., 40 s.d.; II.ii.12–52; IV.ii.21–8, 121; IV.vii.56–8, 125; IV.ix.1–22, 23–49; V.ii.1–7, 19–60, 65 s.d.; V.iii.1–26.

For further information, see: H. C. Hart, ed., Arden *2 Henry VI* (London, 1909; rev. 1931) and *3 Henry VI* (London, 1910); Madeleine Doran, *"Henry VI, Parts II and III": Their Relation to the "Contention" and the "True Tragedy,"* University of Iowa Studies (Humanistic), IV (1928); Peter Alexander, *Shakespeare's "Henry VI" and "Richard III"* (Cambridge, 1929); E. K. Chambers, *William Shakespeare: A Study of Facts and Problems,* 2 vols. (Oxford, 1930). Alfred Hart, *Stolen and Surreptitious Copies: A Comparative Study of Shakespeare's Bad Quartos* (Melbourne, Aus., 1942); C. T. Prouty, *"The Contention" and Shakespeare's "2 Henry VI"* (New Haven, 1954) [for criticisms of Prouty's thesis, see: G. B. Evans, *JEGP*, LIII (1954), 628–37, and J. G. McManaway, *"The Contention* and *2 Henry VI," Studies in Language and Literature Presented to Karl Brunner* (1957), pp. 143–54]; W. W. Greg, *The Shakespeare First Folio* (Oxford, 1955); J. D. Wilson, ed., New Shakespeare *1–3 Henry VI* (Cambridge, 1952); A. S. Cairncross, ed., New Arden *2 Henry VI* (London, 1957) and *3 Henry VI* (London, 1964); Stanley Wells, Gary Taylor, John Jowett, and William Montgomery, eds., *Complete Works* (Oxford, 1986) and *William Shakespeare: A Textual Companion* (Oxford, 1987); Michael Hattaway, ed., New Cambridge *2 Henry VI* (Cambridge, 1991) and *3 Henry VI* (Cambridge, 1993); K. O. Irace, *Reforming the Bad Quartos* (Univ. of Delaware Press, 1994).

TEXTUAL NOTES

Title: The Second . . . Sixth] The second Part of Henry the Sixt, with the death of the Good Duke Humfrey. *F1;* The First part of the Contention betwixt the two famous Houses of Yorke and Lancaster, with the death of the good Duke Humphrey: And the banishment and death of the Duke of Suffolke, and the Tragicall end of the proud Cardinall of Winchester, with the notable Rebellion of Iacke Cade: And the Duke of Yorkes first claime vnto the Crowne. *Q1 (title-page)*

Dramatis personae: *subs. as first given in Rowe*

Act-scene division: *none in Q1–3; F1 marks only I.i; other act-scene divisions from Pope and later editors (see first note to each scene); present act-scene arrangement as a whole first established by Steevens*

I.i

Location: *Capell, Theobald*

o.s.d. **Beauford]** Bewford *Q1–3 (throughout, indicating pronunciation); Q1–3 s.d. reads:* Enter at one doore, King Henry the sixt, and Humphrey Duke of Gloster, the Duke of Sommerset, the Duke of Buckingham, Cardinall Bewford, and others. Enter at the other doore, the Duke of Yorke, and the Marquesse of Suffolke, and Queene Margaret, and the Earle of Salisbury and Warwicke.

8 **twenty]** then the *Q1–2*

28 **alder-liefest]** *Pope;* Alder liefest *F1 (in italics)*

34 **wond'ring]** *Theobald;* Wondring, *F1*

37 s.d. **Flourish.]** *placed as in Cairncross; after l. 38, F1;* Sound Trumpets. *Q1–3 (after l. 38)*

43 **Inprimis]** Imprimis *Q1*

50 **It . . . them,]** *Q1–3*

52 **over]** *Q1–3*

52 **father"—]** *Malone (after Q3* fa—); father. *F1;* fa. *Q1–2*

52 s.d. **Duke . . . fall.]** *Q1–3*

57 s.p. **Car.]** *Q1–2;* Win. *F1;* Yorke. *Q3*

57 s.d. **Reads.]** *Capell (subs.)*

58 **duchy]** *Cairncross;* Dutchesse *F1, Q3;* Duches *Q1;* Dutches *Q2*

58 **the county of]** *Cairncross*

74 s.d. **Exeunt]** *F2;* Exit *F1, Q2–3;* Exet *Q1 (Q1 regularly reads* Exet *for Q2–3, F1* Exit; *this variation not hereafter noted)*

74 s.d. **Manent]** *F2;* Manet *F1*

74 s.d. **stayed by Gloucester]** *ed., from Q1–3 s.d.:* and Duke Humphrey staies all the rest.

89 **Council]** *F3;* Counsell *F1*

105 **peroration]** *F2;* preroration *F1*

110 **Anjou,]** *ed.;* Aniou *F1*

132, 139 s.pp. **Glou.]** *Rowe;* Hum. *F1 (occasionally throughout)*

142 **out.]** *Johnson;* out, *F1*

168 **all together]** *Rowe;* altogether *F1*

178 **Protector]** *Q1–3;* Protectors *F1*

179 s.d. **Exeunt]** *Hanmer;* Exit *F1, Q1–3*

186 **o' th']** of *Q1–2;* of the *Q3*

188 **ruffian]** Ruffin *Q1–2*

207 s.d. **aside]** *Alexander (Theobald at beginning of line)*

212 **Main chance]** *Theobald;* Main-chance *F1, Q1–3*

213 s.d. **Exeunt]** *Hanmer;* Exit *F1, Q1–3*

252 **dear-bought]** *hyphen, Theobald*

254 **milk-white rose]** *Q1–3;* Milke-white-Rose *F1*

256 **in]** *Q1–3;* in in *F1*

257 **grapple]** graffle *Q1–2*

I.ii

I.ii] *Capell*

Location: *Theobald*

o.s.d. **Eleanor]** *Rowe;* Elianor *F1 (throughout, except* Elinor *in l. 41 and III.ii.120);* Ellanor *Q1–3*

1 s.p. **Duch.]** *Capell;* Elia. *F1 (or* Elianor. *throughout scene);* Elnor. *Q1–3 (their usual form)*

26–7 **twain . . . Cardinal)]** two *Q1–2;* twaine, by whom I cannot gesse: / But as I thinke by the Cardinall. What it bodes / God knowes; *Q3*

29 **Edmund Duke of Somerset]** the Cardinall of Winchester *Q1–2*

30 **Pole]** Poule *Q1;* Poole *Q2*

60 s.d. **Exit]** *Q1–3 (subs.);* Ex. *F1*

60 s.d. **with Messenger]** *Capell (subs.)*

62–7 **While . . . pageant.]** But ere it be long, Ile go before them all, / Despight of all that seeke to crosse me thus, *Q1–2;* As long as Gloster beares this base and humble mind: / Were I a man, and Protector as he is, / I'de reach to'th Crowne, or make some hop headlesse. / And being but a woman, ile not behinde / For playing of my part, in spite of all that seek to crosse me thus: *Q3*

69 s.d. **Hume]** Hum *Q1–3 (throughout)*

75 **witch]** Witch of Ely *Q1–2 (i.e. of Eie);* witch of Rye *Q3*

I.iii

I.iii] *Capell*

Location: *Hanmer (after Theobald)*

o.s.d. **Peter]** *Theobald*

1 **let's]** let vs *Q1–2;* lets *Q3*

5 s.d. **Enter . . . Queen.]** Enter the Duke of Suffolke with the Queene, and they take him for Duke Humphrey, and giues him their writings. *Q1–3*

13 s.d. **Reading.]** *Rowe*

20 s.d. **Reads.]** *Rowe*

25 s.d. **Giving his petition.]** *Capell*

27 **to]** vnto *Q1–2*

30 **master]** *Warburton;* Mistresse *F1*
31–2 **King . . . usurper.]** *Q1–3 vary this as follows:* King was an vsurer. / *Queene.* An vsurper thou wouldst say. / *Peter.* I forsooth an vsurper.
35 **your matter]** this *Q1–2;* this thing *Q3*
36 s.d. **Servant with Peter]** *Capell* (Servants)
39 s.d. **Tear the supplication.]** He teares the papers. *Q1–3*
41 s.p. **Petitioners]** *ed.*
41 s.d. **Exeunt.]** *Q2;* Exit. *F1;* Exet Petitioners. *Q1, Q3*
50 **Pole]** *Q3;* Poole *F1 (frequently throughout), Q2;* Poull *Q1*
80 **She . . . back,]** *om. Q1–2;* She beares a Dukes whole reuennewes on her backe. *Q3*
100 **helm.]** *Rowe;* Helme. Exit. *F1*
100 s.d. **Sound . . . Gloucester.]** *Q1–3 read:* Enter King Henry, and the Duke of Yorke and the Duke of Somerset on both sides of the King, whispering with him, and enter [Then entereth *Q3*] Duke Humphrey, Dame Elnor, the Duke of Buckingham, the Earle of Salsbury, the Earle of Warwicke, and the Cardinall of Winchester.
100 s.d. **Somerset]** *Hanmer*
108 **that;]** *Theobald;* that, *F1*
137 s.d. **The . . . fan.]** *Johnson (subs., after Q1–3* The Queene lets fall her gloue, . . .)
150 **needs]** can neede *F2*
176 s.d. **Horner . . . guarded]** *Theobald;* Armorer and his Man. *F1,* (the Armourer) *Q1–3*
187 s.p. **Hor.]** *Malone;* Armorer. *F1, Q1–3 (throughout)*
190 s.d. **holding . . . hands]** *Steevens*
210 **doom.]** *following this line Theobald inserts from Q1–3: King.* Then be it so my Lord of *Somerset.* / We make your grace Regent ouer [ore *Q3*] the French,
214 **man]** my man *F2*

I.iv

I.iv] *Capell*
Location: *Capell*
o.s.d. **Bolingbrook]** *ed. (after Holinshed);* Bullingbrooke *F1 (throughout scene);* Bullenbrooke *Q1–3 (generally throughout)*
11 s.d. **She . . . face.]** *Q1–3*
12 s.d. **Hume following]** *Dyce (subs.); Q1–3 s.d. reads:* She goes vp to the Tower.
13 s.p. **Duch.]** *Capell;* Elianor. *F1 (throughout rest of play);* Elnor. *Q1–3*
16 **silent]** silence *Q1–3*
22 s.d. **Here . . . riseth.]** Bullenbrooke makes a Cirkle. *Q1–3 (before l. 16); after l. 16 Q1–3 read (in place of F1 ll. 17–27):* Wherein the Furies maske in hellish troupes, / Send vp I charge you from *Sosetus* lake, / The spirit *Askalon* to come to me, / To pierce the bowels of this Centricke earth, / And hither come in twinkling of an eye, / *Askalon, Assenda, Assenda [Ascenda, Ascenda Q2].* / It thunders and lightens, and then the spirit riseth vp.
23 **Adsum]** *F2;* Ad sum *F1*
24 s.p. **M. Jord.]** *Rowe;* Witch. *F1*
29 s.d. **Reading . . . paper.]** *Capell*
31 s.d. **As . . . answer.]** *Rowe (subs.)*
32 **Tell me]** *Pope (on the basis of l. 64)*
32 **fate awaits]** *Q2–3;* fates await *F1;* fate awayt *Q1*
34 **betide]** *Q1–3;* befall *F1*
40 s.d. **sinking down again]** *Pelican, from Q1–3:* He sinkes downe againe.; *Q1–3 then add (in place of F1 ll. 39–40): Bullen.* Then downe I say, vnto the damned poule. / Where Pluto in his firie Waggon sits. / Ryding amidst the singde and parched smoakes, / The Rode of *Dytas* by the Riuer Stykes, / There howle and burne for euer in those flames, / Rise *Iordaine* rise, and staie thy charming Spels. / Sonnes [Zounds *Q3*], we are betraide.
40 s.d. **Sir . . . Captain]** *ed.*
52 s.d. **Exeunt . . . guarded.]** *Dyce (after Malone);* Exet Elnor aboue. *Q1–3*
54 s.d. **Guard . . . etc.]** *Rowe; Q1–3 s.d. reads:* Exet with them.
62 **te]** *Theobald*
62 **posse]** *F2;* posso *F1 (in italics)*

II.i

II.i] *Pope*
Location: *Pope*
o.s.d. **with . . . fist]** *Q1–3*
10 **hawks do]** Hawke done *Q1;* hawke doe *Q2*
11–2 **They . . . pitch.]** He knows his maister loues to be aloft. *Q1–2;* They know their master sores a Faulcons pitch. *Q3*
13 **'tis]** it is *Q1;* it's *Q3*
14 **That . . . soar.]** That can sore no higher then a Falkons pitch. *Q1–2;* That sores no higher then a bird can sore. *Q3*
26 **do it]** doate *Q1;* dote *Q2;* do't *Q3*
30 **An't like]** And it like *Q1–2;* and t'like *Q3*
37–51 s.dd. **Aside to Cardinal., Aside to Gloucester.]** *Rowe (subs.)*
38 **dar'st]** darest *Q1–2*
47 s.p. **Car.]** *Theobald; line continued to Gloucester, F1; in Q1–3, which om. ll. 46–9, the first mention of* the east side of the grove *comes from Gloucester*
50 **God's Mother]** Faith *Q1–2*
51 **Medice, teipsum—]** *Cambridge (comma, Theobald);* Medice teipsum, *F1*
56 s.d. **"A miracle!"]** A miracle, a miracle. *Q1, Q3*
65 s.d. **with music]** *Q1–3*
65 s.d. **Simpcox's . . . following]** *Rowe*
72 **Good fellow]** *Theobald;* Good-fellow *F1*
81 s.p. **Simp.]** Poore man. *Q1–3 (throughout scene)*
81 **and't . . . Grace]** sir *Q1–2;* please your Maiesty *Q3 (Q3 gives l. 80 to the King)*
85 **good fellow]** *Pope;* good-fellow *F1*
99–101 **Mass . . . life.]** *as verse, Pope; as prose, F1*
106 **Albon]** *F2;* Albones *F1*
108 **Red]** Why red *Q1–2*
125 **mightst]** mightest *Q1*
130 **his]** *Q1–3;* it, *F1*
137 s.d. **one]** *Q1–3*
139 s.d. **A stool brought.]** *Capell (subs.)*
147–8 **I . . . quickly.]** *as prose, Q1 (?), Q2–3; as verse, F1*
156 s.d. **Exeunt . . . etc.]** *Capell;* Exit. *F1;* Exet Mayor. *Q1–3 (after: Mayor.* It shall be done my Lord.)
176 s.d. **Aside to Gloucester]** *Sisson (Rowe after l. 174)*
184 **tainture]** *Rowe;* Taincture *F1*

II.ii

II.ii] *Capell*
Location: *Capell (after Pope)*
11, 18 **Black Prince]** *Q1–3;* Black-Prince *F1*
12–52 **The second . . . king.]** *these genealogical lines appear in a badly confused form in Q1–3, but Q3 makes an attempt, not very successful, to unscramble them and anticipates several details of the F1 version:* The second was Edmund of Langly, / Duke of York. / The third was Lyonell Duke of Clarence. / The fourth was Iohn of Gaunt, / The Duke of Lancaster. / The fifth was Roger Mortemor, Earle of March. / The sixt was sir Thomas of Woodstocke. / William of Winsore was the seuenth and last. / Now, Edward the blacke Prince he died before his father, and left behinde him Richard, that afterwards was King, Crownde by the name of Richard the second, and he died without an heire. Edmund of Langly Duke of Yorke died, and left behind him two daughters, Anne and Elinor. / Lyonell Duke of Clarence died, and left behinde Alice, Anne, and Elinor, that was after married to my father, and by her I claime the Crowne, as the true heire to Lyonell Duke of Clarence, the third sonne to Edward the third. Now sir. In the time of Richards raigne, Henry of Bullingbrooke, sonne and heire to Iohn of Gaunt, the Duke of Lancaster fourth sonne to Edward the third, he claimde the Crowne, deposde the Merthfull King, and as both you [you both *Q2*] know, in Pomphret Castle harmelesse Richard was shamefully murthered, and so by Richards death came the house of Lancaster vnto the Crowne. / *Sals.* Sauing your tale my Lord, as I haue heard, in the raigne of Bullenbrooke, the Duke of Yorke did claime the Crowne, and but for Owin Glendor, had bene King. / *Yorke.* True. But so it fortuned then, by meanes of that mon- / strous rebel Glendor, the noble Duke of York was done to death, and so euer since the heires of Iohn of Gaunt haue possessed the Crowne. But if the issue of the elder should sucseed before the is- / sue of the yonger, then am I lawfull heire vnto the kingdome. *Q1–2;* The second was *William* of *Hatfield,* / Who dyed young. / The third was *Lyonell,* Duke of *Clarence.* / The fourth was *Iohn of Gaunt,* / The Duke of *Lancaster.* / The fift was *Edmund of Langley,* / Duke of Yorke. The sixt was *William of Windsore,* / Who dyed young. / The seauenth and last was Sir *Thomas of Woodstocke,* Duke of / *Yorke.* / Now *Edward* the blacke Prince dyed before his Father, leauing behinde him two sonnes, *Edward* borne at *Angolesme,* who died young, and *Richard* that was after crowned King, by the name of *Richard* the second, who dyed without an heyre. / Lyonell Duke of Clarence dyed, and left him one only daugh- / ter, named *Phillip,* who was married to Edmund Mortimer earle of March and Vlster: and so by her I claime the Crowne, as the true heire to Lyonell Duke of Clarence, third sonne to Edward the third. Now sir, in time of Richards reigne, . . . [*the remaining lines are essentially the same as in Q1–2, except for* putte to / death *for* done to death] *Q3*
21 **Bullingbrook]** *ed.,* Bullingbrooke *F1 (throughout), Q1, Q3;* Bullenbrooke *Q2*
26 **Pomfret]** *Q3*· Pumfret *F1;* Pomphret *Q1–2*
35, 49 **Philippe]** *Hanmer;* Phillip *F1 (so Q3 in l. 35)*
38 **Eleanor]** *Rowe;* Elianor *F1;* Elinor *Q1–2; om. Q3*
41 **Glendower]** *Hanmer;* Glendour *F1, Q3;* Glendor *Q1–2*
46 **son, son.]** *Alexander;* Sonnes Sonne; *F1*

II.iii

II.iii] *Capell*
Location: *Capell*
o.s.d. **the . . . Salisbury]** *Capell*
o.s.d. **Enter . . . Bolingbrook.]** *Theobald (subs.); Q1–3 s.d. reads:* Enter King Henry, and the Queene, Duke Humphrey, the Duke of Suffolke, and the Duke of Buckingham, the Cardinall, and Dame Elnor Cobham, led with the Officers, and then enter to them the Duke of Yorke, and the Earles of Salsbury and Warwicke.
3 **sins]** *Theobald;* sinne *F1*
16 s.d. **Exeunt . . . guarded.]** *Theobald;* Exet some with Elnor. *Q1, Q3,* (exeunt) *Q2*
34 **ere]** erst *Q1–2*
58 s.d. **Horner . . . Peter]** *Malone*
64 **double beer]** *Q1–3;* Double-Beere *F1*
69 **afraid]** affeard *Q1–2*
90] *Following this line Warburton inserts from Q1–3:* as Beuys of South-hampton fell vpon Askapart.
92 s.d. **Alarum.]** *Capell;* Alarmes, *Q1, Q3;* Alarme: *Q2*
92 s.d. **hits . . . and]** *Q1–3*
94 s.d. **He dies.]** *Q1–3*
97 s.d. **He kneels down.]** *Q1–3*

II.iv

II.iv] *Capell*
Location: *Theobald*
16 s.d. **barefoot]** *Q1–3*

16 s.d. **and . . . on,]** *Q1–3*
16 s.d. **Sir John Stanley]** *Theobald*
20 **dost]** doest *Q1–2*
46 **pointing-stock]** *hyphen, Hanmer*
47 **rascal]** rascald *Q1–2*
55 **canst]** can *Q1–2*
69 s.d. **Herald]** Herald of Armes *Q1–3*
73 s.d. **Exit Herald.]** *Q1–3*
86 s.d. **with his Men]** *from Q1–3 s.d.* Exet [exeunt *Q2*] Humphrey and his men.

III.i

III.i] *Pope*
Location: *Steevens (after Theobald, Capell)*
o.s.d. **Enter . . . Then]** *Q1–3 (the Q1–3 s.d. reads:* Enter to the Parlament. Enter two Haralds before, then the Duke of Buckingham and [*Q3 om.* and] the Duke of Suffolke, and then the Duke of Yorke, and the Cardinall of Winchester, and then the King and the [*Q2 om.* the] Queene, and then the Earle of Salisbury, and the Earle of Warwicke.)
46 **life,]** *Pope;* Life *F1*
87 s.d. **Aside.]** *Rowe*
174 **traitors']** *Capell;* Traytors *F1*
182 **But]** I but *Q1;* Yea but *Q2*
194 s.d. **with . . . Men]** *Q1–3*
218 **dimm'd]** *Rowe (subs.);* dimn'd *F1*
218 **eyes]** *Pope;* eyes; *F1*
222 **traitor,]** *Q1, Q3;* Traytor? *F1, Q2*
222 s.d. **Exit]** *om. in some copies of F1*
222 s.d. **with . . . Warwick]** *from Q1–3* King, Salsbury, and Warwicke *(Buckingham added, Pelican after Cambridge)*
266 **Thrice-noble]** *hyphen, Theobald*
282 s.d. **Post]** Messenger *Q1–3*
287 s.d. **Exit.]** *ed.*
328 **I]** I wil *Q1–2;* I'le *Q3*
333–4 **art . . . death;]** *F4 (subs.);* art; . . . death, *F1*
359] *Following this line Q3 inserts:* (For he is like him euery kinde of way), *thus anticipating ll. 372–3 in F1 (lines om. in Q1–3)*
365 **caper]** *F2;* capre *F1*
382 **Humphrey]** *F3;* Humfrey; *F1*

III.ii

III.ii] *Capell*
Location: *Cambridge (after Theobald)*
o.s.d. **Murderers]** *Capell; Q1–3 s.d. reads:* Then the Curtaines being drawne, Duke Humphrey is discouered in his bed, and two men lying on his brest and smothering him in his bed. And then enter the Duke of Suffolke to them.
1 s.p. **1. Mur.]** *Capell;* 1. *F1 (throughout scene);* One. *Q1–3*
3 s.p. **2. Mur.]** *Capell;* 2. *F1*
14 s.d. **Suffolk]** *om. Q1–3; F1 re-enters Suffolk here after the Cardinal; eds. since Theobald have adopted the Q1–3 arrangement, which leaves Suffolk on stage* (Exet [exeunt *Q2*] murtherers.) *after the Murderers exit)*
20 **'gainst]** against *Q1–2*
24 **nobleman]** *Rowe:* Noble man *F1*
26 **Meg]** *Capell;* Nell *F1 (almost certainly Shakespeare's slip; cf. note below on ll. 79, etc.)*
74 **dost]** doest *Q1*
75 **leper]** *F3;* Leaper *F1, Q2–3;* leoper *Q1*
79, 100, 120 **Margaret]** *Rowe;* Elianor (Elinor *l. 120) F1 (as in l. 26, Shakespeare seems to have confused the names of the Queen and Gloucester's wife)*
80 **statuë]** *Keightley;* Statue *F1*
105 **earnest-gaping sight]** *Pope;* earnest-gaping-sight *F1*
116 **witch]** *Theobald;* watch *F1*
121 s.d. **Salisbury]** *Q1, Q3;* Salsbury *Q2*
135 s.d. **Exit . . . Commons.]** *Alexander (after Theobald);* Exet Salbury *Q1;* (Salsbury) *Q2,* (Salisbury) *Q3*
146 s.d. **with . . . Warwick]** *Cambridge (subs., after Rowe); Q1–3 s.d. reads:* Warwicke drawes the curtaines and showes Duke Humphrey in his bed. *(Some eds. suppose that the curtains mentioned here and in the o.s.d. in Q1–3 refer to bed hangings, but the handling of the scene in Q1–3 makes it more likely that the curtains are those of some kind of inner room.)*
174 **Look,]** *Cambridge;* Looke *F1*
183 s.d. **to Cardinal]** *ed.*
189 **fast by]** *Rowe;* fast-by *F1;* hard-by *Q1;* hard by *Q2–3*
196 **his talons]** your talants *Q1–2;* his talents *Q3*
198 **ease]** case *Q1*
202 s.d. **Exeunt . . . others.]** *Capell;* Exet Cardinall. *Q1–3*
223 **born]** *F3;* borne *F1, Q1–3*
231 s.d. **Suffolk and Warwick]** *Hanmer; Q1–3 s.d. reads:* Warwicke puls him out. Exet Warwicke and Suffolke, and then all the Commons within, cries, downe with Suffolke, downe with Suffolke. And then enter againe, the Duke of Suffolke and Warwicke, with their weapons drawne. *(see l. 236 s.d.)*
241 s.d. **Enter Salisbury.]** *Q1–3 s.d. reads:* The Commons againe cries, downe with Suffolke, downe with Suffolke. And then enter from them, the Earle of Salbury [Salisbury *Q2–3*].
242 s.d. **To . . . within.]** *Kittredge (after Johnson)*
278 s.p. **Commons.]** *Capell*
288 s.d. **Exit Salisbury.]** *Q1,* (Salsbury) *Q2–3*
299 s.d. **with Warwick]** *from Q1–3 s.d.* Exet King and Warwicke, Manet Queene and Suffolke.
327 **screech-owls]** scrike-oules *Q1–2;* scritch-owles *Q3*
350 **Adventure]** *F2;* Aduenrure *F1;* Or venture *Q1–2;* Or venter *Q3*
359 **thence;]** *Pope (subs.);* thence, *F1*
366 s.d. **Vaux]** Vawse *Q1–3 (indicating pronunciation)*
379 s.d. **Vaux]** *Pope*
408 s.d. **She kisseth him.]** *Q1–3*
410 **worth.]** *Theobald;* worth, *F1*
412 s.d. **severally]** *Rowe; Q1–3 s.dd. read:* Exet Suffolke. *after* death. *and* Exet Queene. *after* me.

III.iii

III.iii] *Capell*
Location: *Theobald*
o.s.d. **raving . . . mad]** *from Q1–3 s.d.* Enter King and Salsbury, and then the Curtaines be drawne, and the Cardinall is discouered in his bed, rauing and staring as if he were madde. *(note omission of Warwick)*
8 s.p. **Car.]** *Q1–3;* Beau. *F1*
28 s.d. **The Cardinal dies.]** *Q1–2;* Car. dies. *Q3*

IV.i

IV.i] *Pope*
Location: *Pope*
o.s.d. **Alarum . . . sea.]** *ed. (from F1, Q1–3);* Alarum. Fight at Sea. Ordnance goes off. *F1;* Alarmes within, and the chambers be discharged, like as it were a fight at sea. *Q1–3*
o.s.d. **a Shipmaster . . . prisoners]** *based on Q1–3, plus Rowe; Q1–3 s.d. reads:* And then enter the Captaine of the ship and the Maister, and the Maisters Mate, & the Duke of Suffolke disguised, and others with him, and Water Whickmore [Walter Whickemore *Q2*]*.; F1 s.d. reads:* Enter Lieutenant, Suffolke, and others.
3 **loud-howling]** *hyphen, Capell*
14 **Walter Whitmore]** Water Whickmore *Q1, Q3 (throughout scene, except* Walter *in two s.pp. and one non-F1 passage in Q3);* Walter Whickmore *Q2 (throughout rest of scene); Q1, Q3 spelling makes the wordplay in l. 35 clear; F1 has* Water *in s.d. at l. 138, and see l. 115 below*
22 **sum!]** *White;* summe. *F1*
26 s.d. **To Suffolk.]** *Rowe*
32 **why starts thou?]** *Q1–3 give s.d.* He starteth. *after first mention of Whitmore's name in l. 14*
32 **What,]** *Rowe;* What *F1*
37, 38 **Gualtier]** Gaulter *Q1–3*
48 **Jove . . . I?]** *Q1–3*
50 s.p. **Suf.]** *Q1–3; line continued to Lieutenant in F1, with s.p.* Suf. *before l. 51*
70 **Lieu. Yes . . . Poole?]** *Q1–3 (subs., with Q2 spelling* Poole, *as in last half of line in F1; Q1 reads* Poull *and Q3* Pole; *Q1–3 give the first speech to* Cap.; *s.p.* Lieu. *Neilson)*
77 **shall]** shalt *Q1–3, F2*
84 **Sylla, overgorg'd]** *Pope;* Sylla ouer-gorg'd, *F1*
85 **mother's bleeding]** *Rowe;* Mother-bleeding *F1*
93 **are]** *Rowe;* and *F1*
113 **Lieu. Ay . . . soon.]** *Q1–3 (spoken by* Cap.); *first added by Cairncross*
114 s.p. **Suf.]** *Cairncross*
115] *Following this line F1 reads:* Lieu. Water: W. *followed by l. 116; Cairncross suggests that* Lieu. *is the s.p. for the accidentally omitted l. 113 above and that* Water: W. *should be taken as the s.p. for l. 116*
116 s.p. **Whit.]** *Rowe*
117 **Pene]** *Malone;* Pine *F1*
118, 142 s.pp. **Whit.]** *Rowe;* Wal. *F1*
119 **daunted]** *F3;* danted *F1*
132 s.p. **Suf.]** *Hanmer; line continued to Lieutenant, F1, with s.p.* Suf. *before l. 133*
136 **Brutus']** *Q1–3 (subs.);* Brutsn *F1*
138 s.d. **Walter]** *Q2;* Water *F1, Q1, Q3*
141 s.d. **Exeunt]** *Capell;* Exit *F1;* Exet omnes. *Q1, Q3;* exeunt omnes. *Q2*
141 s.d. **of Suffolk]** *Capell*
147 s.d. **Exit . . . body.]** *Capell (after* Exit. *F2)*

IV.ii

IV.ii] *Pope*
Location: *Capell*
o.s.d. **George]** *Capell; Q1–3 s.d. reads:* Enter two of the Rebels with long staues. *(the s.pp. for these two characters being* George. *and* Nicke.; Holland *and* Bevis *are actors' names)*
o.s.d. **with long staves]** *Q1–3*
17 **say as,]** *Capell (subs.);* say, as *F1*
21–8] *Q1–3 offer a larger list of Cade's followers:* Why theres Dicke the Butcher, and Robin the Sadler, and Will that came a wooing to our Nan last Sunday, and Harry and Tom, and Gregory that should haue your Parnill, and a great sort more is come from Rochester, and from Maydstone, and Canterbury, and all the Townes here abouts, and we must all be [be al *Q3*] Lords or squires, assoone as Iacke Cade is King.
30 s.d. **with long staves]** *from Q1–3 s.d.* Enter Iacke Cade, Dicke Butcher, Robin, Will, Tom, Harry and the rest, with long staues.
33 s.p. **Dick.]** *Q1–3;* But. *F1 (throughout scene)*
33–62 s.dd. **Aside.]** *Capell*
35 **fall]** *F4;* faile *F1*
36–7 **princes—command]** *Alexander;* Princes. Command *F1;* Proclaime *Q1–3*
38 s.p. **Dick.]** All. *Q1–3*
40 s.p. **Dick.]** Nicke. *Q1–2*
44 **Laçies]** Brases *Q1–2*
45 s.p. **Dick.]** Will. *Q1–2;* Nicke. *Q3*
47 s.p. **Smith.]** *Steevens;* Weauer. *F1 (throughout scene);* Robin. *Q1–3*
50 s.p. **Dick.]** Harry. *Q1–3*
57 s.p. **Dick.]** George. *Q1–3*
60 s.p. **Smith.]** *Steevens;* Wea. *F1;* Will. *Q1–3*
80 **should . . . parchment]** should parchment be made *Q1–2;* parchment should be made *Q3*
84 s.d. **one with]** *ed. (after F1, Q1–3 s.d. at l. 110); Q1–3 s.d. reads:* Enter Will with the Clarke of Chattam.

85 s.p. **Smith.]** *Steevens;* Weauer. *F1;* Will. *Q1–3*

85 **Chartam]** Chattam *Q1–3*

90 **H'as]** *Rowe;* Ha's *F1;* hee has *Q1–3*

110 **pen and inkhorn]** penny inckehorne *Q2*

110 s.d. **Michael]** Tom *Q1–3 (Michael's speeches given to Tom in Q1–3)*

120 s.d. **Kneels.]** *Collier*

121 s.d. **Rises.]** *Collier*

121 **him!]** *following this word Theobald inserts from Q1–3:* Is there any more of them that be Knights? / *Tom.* I his brother. / He Knights *Dicke Butcher* [him *Q3* (*s.d. after next line*)]. / *Cade.* Then kneele downe Dicke Butcher, / Rise vp sir Dicke Butcher. / Now sound vp the Drumme. (*the final s.d. being part of Cade's speech in Q3*)

136–7 **Marry . . . not?]** *as verse, Capell (Q1–3); as prose, F1*

136 **this:]** *Theobald (subs.);* this *F1*

147–50 **Nay . . . not.]** *Q1–3 give these lines to* Nicke.

149 **testify it]** testifie *Q1–2*

151–2 **And . . . what?]** *as verse, Pope; as prose, F1*

155 s.d. **Aside.]** *Capell*

164 **Fellow kings]** *Capell;* Fellow-Kings *F1*

172 **counsellor]** *Pope;* Councellour *F1*

181 s.d. **with . . . Men]** *ed. (after Steevens) from Q1–3* Stafford and his men

190 s.d. **Exeunt.]** *Q2* (exeunt omnes.); Exet omnes. *Q1, Q3*

IV.iii

IV.iii] *Capell*

Location: *ed. (after Wilson)*

2 s.p. **Dick.]** *Rowe;* But. *F1 (throughout scene)*

6–7 **and thou]** Thou *Q1–2*

11–2 s.d. **putting . . . armor]** *Collier*

IV.iv

IV.iv] *Pope*

Location: *Capell*

s.d. **with a supplication]** reading of a Letter *Q1–3 (Q1–3 s.d. adds* with others. *after* Lord Say)

19 **have]** *Q1–3;* huae *F1*

49 s.p. **2. Mess.]** *Rowe;* Mess. *F1*

58 **be]** *F2*

IV.v

IV.v] *Pope*

Location: *Capell (after Pope)*

o.s.d. **two or three]** three or foure *Q1–3*

2–5 **No . . . rebels.]** *as prose, Pope; as verse, F1, Q1–3*

IV.vi

IV.vi] *Capell*

Location: *ed. (after Theobald)*

s.d. **staff]** sword *Q1–3*

1–6 **Now . . . Mortimer.]** *as prose, Pope; as verse, F1, Q1–3*

9 s.p. **Smith.]** *Rowe* (Weav.); But. *F1*

13–5 **Come . . . away.]** *as prose, Pope; as verse, F1, Q1–3*

IV.vii

IV.vii] *Capell*

Location: *Theobald*

2 **Court]** the Court *Q1–2*

3, 6 s.pp. **Dick.]** *Q1–3 (second speech given earlier to Cade);* Hut. *and* But. *F1*

8, 16 s.pp. **Holland.]** *Cambridge;* Iohn. *F1;* Dicke. *Q1–3 (om. second speech)*

8, 11, 16 s.dd. **Aside.]** *Capell*

11 s.p. **Smith.]** George. *Q1–3*

16–7 **Then . . . out.]** *as prose, Pope; as verse, F1*

19 s.d. **Messenger.]** George. *Q1–3*

23 s.d. **Bevis]** *Steevens*

25 **serge]** *Rowe;* Surge *F1;* George *Q1–3*

40 **abominable]** *Q2;* abhominable *F1, Q1, Q3*

47 **dost]** doest *Q1*

56–8 **Nothing . . . Latin.]** *Q1–3 read:* Nothing but *bona, terra* [*terra bona Q2*]. / *Cade. Bonum terum,* sounds [zwounds *Q3*] whats that? / *Dicke.* He speakes French. / *Will.* No tis Dutch. / *Nicke.* No tis outtalian [Outalian *Q3*], I know it well inough.

59 **where]** *F3;* wher'e *F1*

69–70 **hands . . . you?]** *Johnson conj.;* hands? Kent to maintaine, . . . you, *F1*

90 **caudle]** *F4;* Candle *F1*

105 s.d. **Aside.]** *Capell*

109 **strike off]** chop of *Q1–2* choppe off *Q3*

119 s.d. **Exeunt . . . Say.]** *Hanmer*

125] *Following the speech that ends with this line, Q1–3 have a scene fragment not found in F1:* Enter *Robin.* / *Robin.* O Captaine, London bridge is a fire. / *Cade.* Runne to Billingsgate, and fetche pitch and flaxe and squench [quench *Q3*] it. / Enter *Dicke* and a Sargiant. / *Sargiant.* Iustice, iustice, I pray you sir, let me haue iustice of this fellow here. / *Cade.* Why what has he done? / *Sarg.* Alasse sir he has rauisht my wife. / *Dicke.* Why my Lord he would haue rested me, / And I went and entred my Action in his wiues paper house. / *Cade.* Dicke follow thy sute in her common place, / You horson villaine, you are a Sargiant youle, [sergeant, youle *Q2–3*] / Take any man by the throate for twelue pence, / And rest a man when hees [he is *Q3*] at dinner, / And haue him to prison ere the meate be out of his [on's *Q3*] mouth. / Go Dicke take him hence, cut [and cut *Q3*] out his toong for cogging, / Hough him for running, and to conclude, / Braue him with his owne mace. / Exet with the Sargiant.

126 s.p. **Dick.]** Nicke. *Q1–3*

129 s.d. **of . . . poles]** *from Q1–3 s.d.* Enter two with the Lord Sayes head, and sir Iames Cromers, vpon two poles.

130–6 **But . . . Away!]** *as prose, Theobald (last two-and-a-half lines prose, Q1–3); as verse, F1*

136 s.d. **Exeunt.]** *Rowe;* Exit *F1*

IV.viii

IV.viii] *Capell*

Location: *Theobald*

1 **Magnus']** *Theobald;* Magnes *F1*

3–5 **What . . . kill?]** *as prose, Capell; as verse, F1*

5 s.d. **old Clifford]** Lord Clifford the Earle of Cumberland *Q1–3*

5 s.d. **attended]** *Theobald*

13 **rebel]** *Singer (after Q1–3* Traitor); rabble *F1*

19] *At the equivalent of this point Q1–3 insert s.d.:* They forsake Cade.

24–5 **White Hart]** *F4 (subs.);* White-heart *F1*

33] *At the equivalent of this point Q1–3 insert s.d.:* They runne to Cade againe.

43 **o'er seas]** *F3;* ore-seas *F1*

55 s.d. **Aside.]** *Dyce*

59 **sword]** staffe *Q1–3*

64 s.d. **He . . . away.]** *ed., after Q1–3 s.d.* He runs through them with his staffe, and flies away. (*but cf. IV.vi o.s.d. in F1, Q1–3*)

IV.ix

IV.ix] *Capell*

Location: *Theobald (subs.)*

1–22] *Q1–3 offer an essentially different version of these lines (see below, ll. 23–49, for the remainder of the scene in Q1–3): King.* Lord Somerset, what newes here [heare *Q2–3*] you of the Rebell Cade? / *Som.* This, my gratious Lord, that the Lord Say is don to death, / And the Citie is almost sackt. / *King.* Gods will be done, for as he hath decreede, so must it [it must *Q2*] be: / And be it [it *om. Q3*] as he please, to stop the pride of those rebellious men. / *Queene.* Had the noble Duke of Suffolke bene aliue, / The Rebell Cade had bene supprest ere this, [*cf. IV.iv.41–2*] / And all the rest that do take part with him. / Enter the Duke of *Buckingham* and *Clifford,* with the Rebels, with halters about their necks. / *Cliff.* Long liue King Henry, Englands lawfull King, / Loe here my Lord, these Rebels are subdude, / And offer their liues before your highnesse feete. / *King.* But tell me Clifford, is there [their *Q2–3*] Captaine here. / *Cliff.* No, my gratious Lord, he is fled away, but proclamations are sent forth, that he that can bring his head, shall haue a thou- / sand crownes. But may it please your Maiestie, to pardon these their faults, that by that [these *Q3*] traitors meanes were thus misled. / *King.* Stand vp you simple men, and giue God praise, / For you did take in hand you know not what, / And go in peace obedient to your King, / And liue as subiects, and you shall not want, / Whilst Henry liues, and weares the English Crowne. / *All.* God saue the King, God saue the King.

6 s.d. **old]** *Capell*

9 s.d. **below]** *Capell*

23–49 **Mess. Please . . . reign.]** *Q1–3 omit the announcement of York's return with an army and substitute the following lines: King.* Come let vs hast to London now with speed, / That solemne prosessions may be sung, / In laud and honour of the God of heauen, / And triumphs of this happie victorie.

33 **calm'd]** *F4;* calme *F1*

IV.x

IV.x] *Steevens*

Location: *Capell (after Pope)*

15 s.d. **He . . . them.]** *Q1–3 (see second note below)*

15 s.d. **Iden]** Eyden *Q1–3 (indicates pronunciation)*

15 s.d. **followed . . . Servants]** *ed. (after Steevens); Q1–3 s.d. reads:* Enter Iacke Cade at one doore, and at the other, maister Alexander Eyden and his men, and Iack Cade lies downe picking of hearbes and eating them. (*Q1–3 begin the scene at this point*)

20 **waning]** *Rowe;* warning *F1*

24 s.d. **Aside.]** *Dyce*

26 **Ah]** *F3;* A *F1;* Stand *Q1–3*

40 **and if I]** and I *Q1–2;* if do *Q3*

42 **shall ne'er]** neuer shall *Q1–2;* shall neuer *Q3*

42 **stands]** doth stand *Q1–2*

45 **steadfast-gazing]** *hyphen, Capell*

57 **burly-bon'd]** *hyphen, Q1, Q3*

58 **God]** *Q1–2;* Ioue *F1; om. Q3*

59 s.d. **and . . . down]** *Q1–3*

83 **to the King]** *om. Q1;* with me *Q2*

84 s.d. **dragging . . . Servants]** *Dyce (subs.)*

V.i

V.i] *Pope*

Location: *ed. (after Capell); eds. usually read* Fields between Dartford and Blackheath, *following Malone, which is historically accurate but ignores the obvious continuity between Scenes i and ii*

11 **flow'r-de-luce]** *ed. (after F3);* Fleure-de-Luce *F1*

23 s.d. **Aside.]** *Rowe*

47 s.d. **Exeunt Soldiers.]** *Q2;* Exet souldiers. *Q1, Q3*

55] *Following this line Q1–3 read:* But see, his grace is comming to meete with vs. (*a line which clarifies the stage business here*)

78 s.d. **He kneels.]** *Johnson*

82 s.d. **Rises.]** *Collier MS*

109 **these]** *Theobald;* thee *F1*

111 **sons]** *Q1–3;* sonne *F1*

111 **bail]** *Q1–3;* bale *F1*

111 s.d. **Exit Attendant.]** *Capell*

113 **for]** *F2;* of *F1*

116 s.d. **Exit Buckingham.]** *Capell*

121 s.d. **Plantagenet . . . door]** *from Q1–3 s.d.:* Enter the Duke of Yorkes sonnes,

Edward the Earle of March, and crookbacke Richard, at the one doore, with Drumme and soldiers, and at the other doore, enter Clifford and his sonne, with Drumme and souldiers, and Clifford kneeles to Henry, and speakes.

122 s.d. **and . . . door**] *Q1–3* (*subs.; see preceding note*)

124 s.d. **Kneels.**] *Johnson* (*after Q1–3*)

136 **arrested**] *Q1–3;* atrested *F1*

147 s.d. **with . . . Soldiers**] *from Q1–3 s.d.* Enter at one doore, the Earles [Earle *Q2*] of Salsbury and Warwicke, with Drumme and souldiers. And at the other [other doore *Q3*], the Duke of Buckingham, with Drumme and souldiers.

153 **suffer'd,**] *Vaughan conj.;* suffer'd *F1*

172 **dost**] *F4;* doest *F1*

193] *Following this line Cairncross inserts from Q1–3:* Both thou and they, shall curse this fatall houre.

194 **or**] *Rowe;* and *F1*

195 s.p. **Clif.**] *Malone;* Old Clif. *F1* (*throughout rest of scene*)

201 **household**] *Q1–3;* housed *F1*

207 **to**] *Q1–3;* io *F1;* so *F2*

213 **Fie! charity,**] *Capell;* Fie, Charitie *F1, Q1–3*

216 s.d. **severally**] *Theobald*

V.ii

V.ii] *Steevens*

Location: *ed.* (*after Wilson*)

o.s.d. **Alarums . . . battle.**] *Q1–3* (Alarmes)

1–7 **Clifford . . . arms.**] *Following an almost identical version of these lines, Q1–3 add:* Clifford speakes within. / Warwicke stand still, and view the way that Clifford hewes with / his murthering Curtelaxe, through the fainting troopes to finde / thee out. / Warwicke stand still, and stir not till I come.

8 **How**] *Johnson; War.* How *F1* (*repeated s.p.*)

9 **deadly-handed**] *hyphen, Pope*

12 **lov'd**] *Q1–3;* loued *F1*

12 s.d. **old**] *Dyce*

19–60 **What . . . fame.**] *Q1–3 offer an essentially different version of these lines: Yorke.* Now Clifford, since we are singled here alone, / Be this the day of doome to one of vs, / For now my heart hath sworne immortall hate / To thee and all the house of Lancaster. / *Cliffood.* And here I stand, and pitch my foot to thine, / Vowing neuer to stir, till thou or I be slaine. / For neuer shall my heart be safe at rest, / Till I haue spoyld the hatefull house of Yorke. / Alarmes, and they fight, and *Yorke* kils *Clifford. / Yorke.* Now Lancaster sit sure, thy sinowes [sinewes *Q2–3*] shrinke, / Come fearefull Henry grouelling on thy face, / Yeeld vp thy Crowne vnto the Prince of Yorke. / *Exet Yorke.* / Alarmes, then enter yoong *Clifford* alone. / *Yoong Clifford.* Father of Comberland, / Where may I [I may *Q3*] seeke my aged father forth? / O! [Oh *Q3*] dismall sight, see where he breathlesse lies, / All smeard and weltred in his luke-warme blood, / Ah, aged pillar of all Comberlands true house, / Sweete father, to thy murthred ghoast I sweare, / Immortall hate vnto the house of Yorke, / Nor neuer shall I sleepe secure one night, / Till I haue furiously reuengde thy death, / And left not one of them to breath on earth.

27 s.d. **They . . . falls.**] *Capell; Q1–3 s.d. reads:* Alarmes, and they fight, and Yorke kils Clifford.

28 **œuvres**] *F2;* eumenes *F1*

28 s.d. **Dies.**] *F2*

30 s.d. **Exit.**] *Q1–3*

31 **confusion!**] *Pope* (*after Rowe*)*;* Confusion *F1*

40 s.d. **Sees . . . father.**] *Theobald* (*subs.*)

52 **babes. Tears virginal**] *Pope* (*subs.*)*;* Babes, Teares Virginall, *F1*

59 **Absyrtus**] *Theobald;* Absirtis *F1*

60 s.d. **He . . . back.**] *Q1–3*

65 s.d. **Exit . . . father.**] *Pope* (*after Q1–3 s.d.* Exet yoong Clifford with his father.); *following the equivalent of F1 ll. 61–5, Q1–3 add:* But staie, heres one of them, / To whom my soule hath sworne immortall hate. / Enter *Richard*, and then *Clifford* laies downe his father, / fights with him, and *Richard* flies away againe. / Out crooktbacke [crook'd-backe *Q3*] villaine, get thee from my sight, / But I will after thee, and once againe / When I haue borne my father to his Tent, / Ile trie my fortune better with thee yet [*Q2 om.* yet]. *Exet* yoong *Clifford* with his father. / Alarmes againe, and then enter three or foure, bearing the Duke / of *Buckingham* wounded to his Tent.

65 s.d. **Somerset . . . Inn**] *from Q1–3 s.d.* Alarmes to the battaile, and then enter the Duke of Somerset and Richard fighting, and [*om. Q2*] Richard kils him vnder the signe of the Castle in saint Albones.

66 **there;**] there, and breathe thy last. *Q1–2;* there, and tumble in thy blood, *Q3*

71 s.d. **Exit.**] *Theobald*

83 s.d. **Young**] *Capell*

84 s.p. **Y. Clif.**] *Capell;* Clif. *F1*

V.iii

V.iii] *Steevens*

Location: *ed. (after Wilson)*

o.s.d. **Alarum. . . . Colors.**] Edward (*from Q3*); Alarmes, and then a flourish, and enter the Duke of Yorke and Richard [Yorke, Edward, and Richard *Q3*]. *Q1–3*

1–26] *Q1–3 offer an essentially different version of these lines: Yorke.* How now boys, fortunate this fight hath bene, / I hope to vs and ours, for Englands good, / And our great honour, that so long we lost, / Whilst faint-heart Henry did vsurpe our rights: / But did you see old Salsbury, since we / With bloodie mindes did buckle with the foe, / I would not for the losse of this right hand, / That ought but well betide that good old man. / *Rich.* My Lord, I saw him in the thickest throng, / Charging his Lance with his old weary armes, / And thrise I saw him beaten from his horse, / And thrise this hand did set him vp againe, / And still he fought with courage gainst his foes, / The boldest sprited [spirited *Q3*] man that ere mine eyes beheld. / Enter *Salsbbury* and *Warwicke*. / *Edward.* See noble father, where they both do come, / The onely props vnto the house of Yorke. / *Sals.* Well hast thou fought this day, thou valiant Duke, / And thou braue bud of Yorkes encreasing house, / The small remainder of my weary life, / I hold for thee, for with thy warlike arme, / Three times this day thou hast preseru'd my life. / *Yorke.* What say you Lords, the King is fled to London? / There as I here [heare *Q2*, heere *Q3*] to hold a Parlament [Parliament *Q3*].

1 **Of**] Old *Q1–3*

29 **faith**] *Q1–3;* hand *F1*

33 s.d. **Exeunt.**] Exeunt. / FINIS. *F1;* Exet [exeunt *Q2*] omnes. / FINIS. *Q1–3*

The "fearful porpentine." From Edward Topsell, *The History of Four-footed Beasts* (1607). Although the "sharp-quill'd porpentine" (i.e. porcupine) is mentioned in *2 Henry VI* (III.i.363), Shakespeare's most famous reference to this prickly rodent occurs in *Hamlet* (I.v.17–20): "Make . . . each particular hair to stand an end, / Like quills upon the fearful porpentine." When alarmed ("fearful"), the porpentine erected its quills and, according to the belief of the time, shot them at its enemy. (*By permission of the Harvard College Library*)

The Third Part of Henry the Sixth

[Dramatis Personae

King Henry the Sixth
Edward, *Prince of Wales, his son*
Lewis the Eleventh, *King of France*
Duke of Somerset
Duke of Exeter
Earl of Oxford
Earl of Northumberland
Earl of Westmerland
Lord Clifford
Richard Plantagenet, *Duke of York*
Edward, *Earl of March, afterwards* King Edward IV } *his sons*
Edmund, *Earl of Rutland* } *his sons*
George, *afterwards Duke of Clarence* } *his sons*
Richard, *afterwards Duke of Gloucester* } *his sons*
Duke of Norfolk
Marquess of Montague
Earl of Warwick
Earl of Pembroke
Lord Hastings
Lord Stafford

Sir John Mortimer } *uncles to the Duke of York*
Sir Hugh Mortimer } *uncles to the Duke of York*
Henry, *Earl of Richmond, a youth*
Lord Rivers, *brother to Lady Grey*
Sir William Stanley
Sir John Montgomery
Sir John Somervile
Tutor, *to Rutland*
Mayor of York, Mayor of Coventry
Lieutenant of the Tower
Nobleman
Two Keepers
Huntsman
Son *that has killed his father*
Father *that has killed his son*

Queen Margaret
Lady Grey, *afterwards Queen to Edward IV*
Bona, *sister to the French Queen*

Soldiers, Attendants, Aldermen, Messengers, Watchmen, *etc.*

Scene: *England and France*]

ACT I, Scene I

Alarum. Enter [Richard] Plantagenet [the Duke of York], Edward, Richard, Norfolk, Montague, Warwick, [*with Drum*] *and Soldiers,* [*with white roses in their hats*].

War. I wonder how the King escap'd our hands.
York. While we pursu'd the horsemen of the north,
He slily stole away and left his men;
Whereat the great Lord of Northumberland,
Whose warlike ears could never brook retreat,
Cheer'd up the drooping army, and himself,
Lord Clifford, and Lord Stafford, all abreast,
Charg'd our main battle's front; and breaking in,
Were by the swords of common soldiers slain.
Edw. Lord Stafford's father, Duke of Buckingham,
Is either slain or wounded dangerous;
I cleft his beaver with a downright blow.
That this is true, father, behold his blood.
Mont. And, brother, here's the Earl of Wiltshire's blood,
Whom I encount'red as the battles join'd.
Rich. Speak thou for me and tell them what I did.
[*Showing the Duke of Somerset's head.*]
York. Richard hath best deserv'd of all my sons.
But is your Grace dead, my Lord of Somerset?
Norf. Such hope have all the line of John of Gaunt!
Rich. Thus do I hope to shake King Henry's head.
War. And so do I, victorious prince of York.

Words and passages enclosed in square brackets in the text above are either emendations of the copy-text or additions to it. The Textual Notes immediately following the play cite the earliest authority for every such change or insertion and supply the reading of the copy-text wherever it is emended in this edition.

I.i. Location: London. The Parliament House.
o.s.d. **Alarum**: call to arms. **Drum**: drummer.
1. **I . . . hands.** Actually, Henry VI, slightly wounded, was captured by the Yorkists after the first battle of St. Albans (1455).
5. **brook**: endure. **retreat**: trumpet call for withdrawal of forces.
7–9. **Clifford . . . slain.** In *2 Henry VI* (V.ii) Clifford is killed by York, a fact alluded to several times in the present play.
8. **main battle**: main body of the army.
12. **beaver**: here, helmet. The word usually refers to the face-guard or visor of a helmet.
14. **brother.** Actually, John Neville, Marquis of Montague, was Warwick's brother and York's nephew. He did not secure his title until 1461, several years after the events represented in this scene.
17. **Richard . . . sons.** Actually, Richard was three years old when the first battle of St. Albans was fought in 1455.

Before I see thee seated in that throne
Which now the house of Lancaster usurps,
I vow by heaven these eyes shall never close.
This is the palace of the fearful king,
And this the regal seat. Possess it, York,
For this is thine and not King Henry's heirs'.

York. Assist me then, sweet Warwick, and I will,
For hither we have broken in by force.

Norf. We'll all assist you; he that flies shall die.

York. Thanks, gentle Norfolk. Stay by me, my lords,
And, soldiers, stay and lodge by me this night.

They go up.

War. And when the King comes, offer him no violence,
Unless he seek to thrust you out perforce.

York. The Queen this day here holds her parliament,
But little thinks we shall be of her council.
By words or blows here let us win our right.

Rich. Arm'd as we are, let's stay within this house.

War. The bloody parliament shall this be call'd,
Unless Plantagenet, Duke of York, be king,
And bashful Henry depos'd, whose cowardice
Hath made us by-words to our enemies.

York. Then leave me not, my lords, be resolute,
I mean to take possession of my right.

War. Neither the King, nor he that loves him best,
The proudest he that holds up Lancaster,
Dares stir a wing if Warwick shake his bells.
I'll plant Plantagenet, root him up who dares.
Resolve thee, Richard, claim the English crown.

[*York takes the throne.*]

Flourish. Enter King Henry, Clifford, Northumberland, Westmerland, Exeter, *and the rest,* [*with red roses in their hats*].

K. Hen. My lords, look where the sturdy rebel sits,
Even in the chair of state. Belike he means,
Back'd by the power of Warwick, that false peer,
To aspire unto the crown and reign as king.
Earl of Northumberland, he slew thy father,
And thine, Lord Clifford, and you both have vow'd revenge
On him, his sons, his favorites, and his friends.

North. If I be not, heavens be reveng'd on me!

Clif. The hope thereof makes Clifford mourn in steel.

West. What, shall we suffer this? Let's pluck him down.
My heart for anger burns, I cannot brook it.

K. Hen. Be patient, gentle Earl of Westmerland.

Clif. Patience is for poltroons, such as he.
He durst not sit there, had your father liv'd.

My gracious lord, here in the parliament
Let us assail the family of York.

North. Well hast thou spoken, cousin, be it so.

K. Hen. Ah, know you not the city favors them,
And they have troops of soldiers at their beck?

[*Exe.*] But when the Duke is slain, they'll quickly fly.

K. Hen. Far be the thought of this from Henry's heart,
To make a shambles of the parliament house!
Cousin of Exeter, frowns, words, and threats
Shall be the war that Henry means to use.
Thou factious Duke of York, descend my throne,
And kneel for grace and mercy at my feet:
I am thy sovereign.

York. I am thine.

Exe. For shame, come down. He made thee Duke of York.

York. It was my inheritance, as the earldom was.

Exe. Thy father was a traitor to the crown.

War. Exeter, thou art a traitor to the crown,
In following this usurping Henry.

Clif. Whom should he follow but his natural king?

War. True, Clifford, that's Richard Duke of York.

K. Hen. And shall I stand, and thou sit in my throne?

York. It must and shall be so. Content thyself.

War. Be Duke of Lancaster, let him be King.

West. He is both King and Duke of Lancaster,
And that the Lord of Westmerland shall maintain.

War. And Warwick shall disprove it. You forget
That we are those which chas'd you from the field,
And slew your fathers, and with colors spread
March'd through the city to the palace gates.

North. Yes, Warwick, I remember it to my grief,
And by his soul, thou and thy house shall rue it.

West. Plantagenet, of thee and these thy sons,
Thy kinsmen and thy friends, I'll have more lives
Than drops of blood were in my father's veins.

Clif. Urge it no more, lest that, in stead of words,
I send thee, Warwick, such a messenger
As shall revenge his death before I stir.

War. Poor Clifford, how I scorn his worthless threats!

York. Will you we show our title to the crown?
If not, our swords shall plead it in the field.

K. Hen. What title hast thou, traitor, to the crown?
[Thy] father was, as thou art, Duke of York,
Thy grandfather, Roger Mortimer, Earl of March:
I am the son of Henry the Fift,
Who made the Dolphin and the French to stoop,
And seiz'd upon their towns and provinces.

War. Talk not of France, sith thou hast lost it all.

25. fearful: full of fears.
32 s.d. They go up. The "chair of state" (line 51) is elevated, probably on a platform. **34. perforce:** by force.
42. by-words: objects of derision. **46. holds up:** supports.
47. shake his bells: i.e. like a falcon with bells attached to its legs.
49 s.d. Flourish: trumpet fanfare.
57. be not: i.e. be not revenged.
58. in steel: i.e. armed, instead of in conventional mourning clothes.

67. city: i.e. London, which was sympathetic to the Yorkists.
74. factious: rebellious.
78. earldom: i.e. the earldom of March, which York inherited from his mother and through which he claimed the throne. See *2 Henry VI*, II.ii.9–52.
79. Thy . . . crown. Richard, Earl of Cambridge, was executed for treason by Henry V. See *Henry V*, II.ii. **91. colors:** flags.
105. Thy . . . York. Actually, York inherited the title from his father's elder brother, Edward, second Duke of York, who fell at Agincourt.
108. Dolphin: i.e. the Dauphin Charles, who succeeded his father as King of France in 1422, a few months after Henry V's death.
110. sith: since.

K. Hen. The Lord Protector lost it, and not I;
When I was crown'd I was but nine months old.
Rich. You are old enough now, and yet methinks you lose.
Father, tear the crown from the usurper's head.
Edw. Sweet father, do so, set it on your head.
Mont. Good brother, as thou lov'st and honorest arms,
Let's fight it out, and not stand cavilling thus.
Rich. Sound drums and trumpets, and the King will fly.
York. Sons, peace!
K. Hen. Peace thou! and give King Henry leave to speak.
War. Plantagenet shall speak first. Hear him, lords,
And be you silent and attentive too,
For he that interrupts him shall not live.
K. Hen. Think'st thou that I will leave my kingly throne,
Wherein my grandsire and my father sat?
No; first shall war unpeople this my realm;
Ay, and their colors, often borne in France,
And now in England to our heart's great sorrow,
Shall be my winding-sheet. Why faint you, lords?
My title's good, and better far than his.
War. Prove it, Henry, and thou shalt be King.
K. Henry. Henry the Fourth by conquest got the crown.
York. 'Twas by rebellion against his king.
K. Hen. [*Aside.*] I know not what to say, my title's weak.—
Tell me, may not a king adopt an heir?
York. What then?
K. Hen. And if he may, then am I lawful king;
For Richard, in the view of many lords,
Resign'd the crown to Henry the Fourth,
Whose heir my father was, and I am his.
York. He rose against him, being his sovereign,
And made him to resign his crown perforce.
War. Suppose, my lords, he did it unconstrain'd,
Think you 'twere prejudicial to his crown?
Exe. No; for he could not so resign his crown
But that the next heir should succeed and reign.
K. Hen. Art thou against us, Duke of Exeter?
Exe. His is the right, and therefore pardon me.
York. Why whisper you, my lords, and answer not?
Exe. My conscience tells me he is lawful king.
K. Hen. [*Aside.*] All will revolt from me and turn to him.
North. Plantagenet, for all the claim thou lay'st,
Think not that Henry shall be so depos'd.
War. Depos'd he shall be, in despite of all.
North. Thou art deceiv'd. 'Tis not thy southern power

111. Lord Protector: i.e. Humphrey, Duke of Gloucester, whose downfall is treated in *2 Henry VI*.
129. faint: grow fainthearted. **137. And if:** if.
139. Resign'd the crown. For Shakespeare's account of Richard II's deposition see *Richard II*, IV.i.
141. him, being: i.e. Richard, who was.
144. his crown: i.e. his legal claim to the crown.
154. despite: spite. **155. deceiv'd:** mistaken.

Of Essex, Norfolk, Suffolk, nor of Kent,
Which makes thee thus presumptuous and proud,
Can set the Duke up in despite of me.
Clif. King Henry, be thy title right or wrong,
Lord Clifford vows to fight in thy defense.
May that ground gape, and swallow me alive,
Where I shall kneel to him that slew my father!
K. Hen. O Clifford, how thy words revive my heart!
York. Henry of Lancaster, resign thy crown.
What mutter you, or what conspire you, lords?
War. Do right unto this princely Duke of York,
Or I will fill the house with armed men,
And over the chair of state, where now he sits,
Write up his title with usurping blood.
He stamps with his foot, and the Soldiers show themselves.
K. Hen. My Lord of Warwick, hear but one word:
Let me for this my life-time reign as king.
York. Confirm the crown to me and to mine heirs,
And thou shalt reign in quiet while thou liv'st.
K. Hen. I am content: Richard Plantagenet,
Enjoy the kingdom after my decease.
Clif. What wrong is this unto the Prince your son!
War. What good is this to England and himself!
West. Base, fearful, and despairing Henry!
Clif. How hast thou injur'd both thyself and us!
West. I cannot stay to hear these articles.
North. Nor I.
Clif. Come, cousin, let us tell the Queen these news.
West. Farewell, faint-hearted and degenerate king,
In whose cold blood no spark of honor bides. [*Exit.*]
North. Be thou a prey unto the house of York,
And die in bands for this unmanly deed! [*Exit.*]
Clif. In dreadful war mayst thou be overcome,
Or live in peace abandon'd and despis'd! [*Exit.*]
War. Turn this way, Henry, and regard them not.
Exe. They seek revenge, and therefore will not yield.
K. Hen. Ah, Exeter!
War. Why should you sigh, my lord?
K. Hen. Not for myself, Lord Warwick, but my son,
Whom I unnaturally shall disinherit.
But be it as it may. [*To York.*] I here entail
The crown to thee and to thine heirs for ever,
Conditionally that here thou take an oath
To cease this civil war, and whilst I live
To honor me as thy king and sovereign,
And neither by treason nor hostility
To seek to put me down and reign thyself.
York. This oath I willingly take and will perform.
War. Long live King Henry! Plantagenet, embrace him.
K. Hen. And long live thou, and these thy forward sons!
York. Now York and Lancaster are reconcil'd.

180. articles: terms of agreement. **186. bands:** bonds.
203. forward: precocious.

Exe. Accurs'd be he that seeks to make them foes!
Sennet. Here they come down.
York. Farewell, my gracious lord, I'll to my castle.
[*Exeunt York and his sons with Soldiers.*]
War. And I'll keep London with my soldiers.
[*Exit with Soldiers.*]
Norf. And I to Norfolk with my followers.
[*Exit with Soldiers.*]
Mont. And I unto the sea, from whence I came.
[*Exit with Soldiers.*]
K. Hen. And I with grief and sorrow to the court.

Enter the QUEEN [MARGARET *and* PRINCE EDWARD].

Exe. Here comes the Queen, whose looks bewray her anger.
I'll steal away.
K. Hen. Exeter, so will I.
Q. Mar. Nay, go not from me, I will follow thee.
K. Hen. Be patient, gentle queen, and I will stay.
Q. Mar. Who can be patient in such extremes?
Ah, wretched man, would I had died a maid
And never seen thee, never borne thee son,
Seeing thou hast prov'd so unnatural a father!
Hath he deserv'd to lose his birthright thus?
Hadst thou but lov'd him half so well as I,
Or felt that pain which I did for him once,
Or nourish'd him as I did with my blood,
Thou wouldst have left thy dearest heart-blood there
Rather than have made that savage duke thine heir,
And disinherited thine only son.
Prince. Father, you cannot disinherit me.
If you be king, why should not I succeed?
K. Hen. Pardon me, Margaret, pardon me, sweet son,
The Earl of Warwick and the Duke enforc'd me.
Q. Mar. Enforc'd thee? Art thou king, and wilt be forc'd?
I shame to hear thee speak. Ah, timorous wretch,
Thou hast undone thyself, thy son, and me,
And giv'n unto the house of York such head
As thou shalt reign but by their sufferance.
To entail him and his heirs unto the crown,
What is it, but to make thy sepulchre,
And creep into it far before thy time?
Warwick is chancellor and the lord of Callice,
Stern Falconbridge commands the Narrow Seas,
The Duke is made Protector of the realm,
And yet shalt thou be safe? Such safety finds
The trembling lamb environed with wolves.
Had I been there, which am a silly woman,
The soldiers should have toss'd me on their pikes,
Before I would have granted to that act.
But thou prefer'st thy life before thine honor;

205 s.d. **Sennet:** trumpet notes to signal a procession.
211. **bewray:** reveal.
226–27. **Father . . . succeed.** At the time represented by this scene (1460) Prince Edward was seven years old.
233. **head:** freedom of action (a term from horsemanship).
238. **Callice:** Calais.
239. **Falconbridge:** perhaps Thomas Neville, a bastard son of William Neville, Baron Fauconberg (d. 1463), and thus a kinsman of the Earl of Warwick. **Narrow Seas:** English Channel.
240. **Duke:** i.e. the Duke of York. 243. **silly:** feeble.
244. **pikes:** weapons with axe-like heads.
245. **granted:** submitted.

And seeing thou dost, I here divorce myself
Both from thy table, Henry, and thy bed,
Until that act of parliament be repeal'd
Whereby my son is disinherited.
The northern lords that have forsworn thy colors
Will follow mine, if once they see them spread;
And spread they shall be, to thy foul disgrace,
And utter ruin of the house of York.
Thus do I leave thee. Come, son, let's away.
Our army is ready; come, we'll after them.
K. Hen. Stay, gentle Margaret, and hear me speak.
Q. Mar. Thou hast spoke too much already; get thee gone.
K. Hen. Gentle son Edward, thou wilt stay [with] me?
Q. Mar. Ay, to be murther'd by his enemies.
Prince. When I return with victory [from] the field
I'll see your Grace; till then, I'll follow her.
Q. Mar. Come, son, away, we may not linger thus.
[*Exeunt Queen Margaret and the Prince.*]
K. Hen. Poor queen, how love to me and to her son
Hath made her break out into terms of rage!
Reveng'd may she be on that hateful duke,
Whose haughty spirit, winged with desire,
Will cost my crown, and like an empty eagle
Tire on the flesh of me and of my son!
The loss of those three lords torments my heart;
I'll write unto them and entreat them fair;
Come, cousin, you shall be the messenger.
Exe. And I, I hope, shall reconcile them all.
Flourish. Exeunt.

[SCENE II]

Enter RICHARD, EDWARD, *and* MONTAGUE.

Rich. Brother, though I be youngest, give me leave.
Edw. No, I can better play the orator.
Mont. But I have reasons strong and forcible.

Enter the DUKE OF YORK.

York. Why, how now, sons and brother, at a strife?
What is your quarrel? how began it first?
Edw. No quarrel, but a slight contention.
York. About what?
Rich. About that which concerns your Grace and us:
The crown of England, father, which is yours.
York. Mine, boys? not till King Henry be dead.
Rich. Your right depends not on his life or death.
Edw. Now you are heir, therefore enjoy it now.
By giving the house of Lancaster leave to breathe,
It will outrun you, father, in the end.
York. I took an oath that he should quietly reign.
Edw. But for a kingdom any oath may be broken:
I would break a thousand oaths to reign one year.
Rich. No; God forbid your Grace should be forsworn.

268. **cost:** i.e. rob me of. **empty:** i.e. hungry.
269. **Tire:** feed ravenously. 271. **fair:** courteously.

I.ii. **Location:** Sandal Castle, near Wakefield, in Yorkshire.
13. **breathe:** rest.

York. I shall be, if I claim by open war.
Rich. I'll prove the contrary, if you'll hear me speak.
York. Thou canst not, son; it is impossible.
Rich. An oath is of no moment, being not took
Before a true and lawful magistrate
That hath authority over him that swears.
Henry had none, but did usurp the place.
Then seeing 'twas he that made you to depose,
Your oath, my lord, is vain and frivolous.
Therefore to arms! And, father, do but think
How sweet a thing it is to wear a crown,
Within whose circuit is Elysium
And all that poets feign of bliss and joy.
Why do we linger thus? I cannot rest
Until the white rose that I wear be dy'd
Even in the lukewarm blood of Henry's heart.
York. Richard, enough; I will be king, or die.
Brother, thou shalt to London presently,
And whet on Warwick to this enterprise.
Thou, Richard, shalt to the Duke of Norfolk,
And tell him privily of our intent.
You, Edward, shall unto my Lord Cobham,
With whom the Kentishmen will willingly rise;
In them I trust, for they are soldiers,
Witty, courteous, liberal, full of spirit.
While you are thus employ'd, what resteth more,
But that I seek occasion how to rise,
And yet the King not privy to my drift,
Nor any of the house of Lancaster?

Enter [a Messenger*].*

But stay, what news? Why com'st thou in such post?
[Mess.] The Queen with all the northern earls and lords
Intend here to besiege you in your castle.
She is hard by with twenty thousand men;
And therefore fortify your hold, my lord.
York. Ay, with my sword. What? think'st thou that we fear them?
Edward and Richard, you shall stay with me,
My brother Montague shall post to London.
Let noble Warwick, Cobham, and the rest,
Whom we have left protectors of the King,
With pow'rful policy strengthen themselves,
And trust not simple Henry nor his oaths.
Mont. Brother, I go; I'll win them, fear it not.
And thus most humbly I do take my leave.

Exit Montague.

Enter [Sir John] Mortimer *and his brother* [Sir Hugh Mortimer].

York. Sir John and Sir Hugh Mortimer, mine uncles,
You are come to Sandal in a happy hour;
The army of the Queen mean to besiege us.

22. moment: force.
26. depose: swear an oath. **36. presently:** at once.
44. what resteth more: what else remains.
46. And . . . drift: without the King's discovering what I am up to.
48. post: haste. **52. hold:** castle. **58. policy:** cunning.
62. uncles. They were brothers of his mother Anne.

Sir John. She shall not need, we'll meet her in the field.
York. What, with five thousand men?
Rich. Ay, with five hundred, father, for a need.
A woman's general: what should we fear?

A march afar off.

Edw. I hear their drums. Let's set our men in order,
And issue forth and bid them battle straight.
York. Five men to twenty! Though the odds be great,
I doubt not, uncle, of our victory.
Many a battle have I won in France
When as the enemy hath been ten to one;
Why should I not now have the like success?

Alarum. Exeunt.

[Scene III]

[Alarums.] Enter Rutland *and his* Tutor.

Rut. Ah, whither shall I fly to scape their hands?
Ah, tutor, look where bloody Clifford comes!

Enter Clifford *[and Soldiers].*

Clif. Chaplain, away, thy priesthood saves thy life.
As for the brat of this accursed duke,
Whose father slew my father, he shall die.
Tut. And I, my lord, will bear him company.
Clif. Soldiers, away with him!
Tut. Ah, Clifford, murther not this innocent child,
Lest thou be hated both of God and man.

Exit [dragged off by Soldiers].

Clif. How now? is he dead already? Or is it fear
That makes him close his eyes? I'll open them.
Rut. So looks the pent-up lion o'er the wretch
That trembles under his devouring paws;
And so he walks, insulting o'er his prey,
And so he comes, to rend his limbs asunder.
Ah, gentle Clifford, kill me with thy sword
And not with such a cruel threat'ning look.
Sweet Clifford, hear me speak before I die:
I am too mean a subject for thy wrath,
Be thou reveng'd on men, and let me live.
Clif. In vain thou speak'st, poor boy; my father's blood
Hath stopp'd the passage where thy words should enter.
Rut. Then let my father's blood open it again,
He is a man, and, Clifford, cope with him.
Clif. Had I thy brethren here, their lives and thine
Were not revenge sufficient for me;
No, if I digg'd up thy forefathers' graves
And hung their rotten coffins up in chains,
It could not slake mine ire nor ease my heart.
The sight of any of the house of York
Is as a fury to torment my soul;
And till I root out their accursed line,
And leave not one alive, I live in hell.

67. for a need: if necessary. **70. straight:** at once.
74. When as: when.

I.iii. Location: A field of battle between Sandal Castle and Wakefield.

Therefore—
Rut. O, let me pray before I take my death!
To thee I pray; sweet Clifford, pity me!
Clif. Such pity as my rapier's point affords.
Rut. I never did thee harm; why wilt thou slay me?
Clif. Thy father hath.
Rut. But 'twas ere I was born.
Thou hast one son, for his sake pity me,
Lest in revenge thereof, sith God is just,
He be as miserably slain as I.
Ah, let me live in prison all my days,
And when I give occasion of offense,
Then let me die, for now thou hast no cause.
Clif. No cause?
Thy father slew my father; therefore die.
[*Stabs him.*]
Rut. *Dii faciant laudis summa sit ista tuae!* [*Dies.*]
Clif. Plantagenet, I come, Plantagenet!
And this thy son's blood cleaving to my blade
Shall rust upon my weapon, till thy blood,
Congeal'd with this, do make me wipe off both.
Exit.

[SCENE IV]

Alarum. Enter RICHARD DUKE OF YORK.

York. The army of the Queen hath got the field:
My uncles both are slain in rescuing me;
And all my followers to the eager foe
Turn back and fly, like ships before the wind,
Or lambs pursu'd by hunger-starved wolves.
My sons, God knows what hath bechanced them;
But this I know, they have demean'd themselves
Like men born to renown by life or death.
Three times did Richard make a lane to me,
And thrice cried, "Courage, father! fight it out!"
And full as oft came Edward to my side
With purple falchion, painted to the hilt
In blood of those that had encount'red him.
And when the hardiest warriors did retire,
Richard cried, "Charge! and give no foot of ground!"
And cried, "A crown, or else a glorious tomb!
A sceptre, or an earthly sepulchre!"
With this we charg'd again; but out, alas,
We bodg'd again, as I have seen a swan
With bootless labor swim against the tide,
And spend her strength with overmatching waves.
A short alarum within.
Ah, hark, the fatal followers do pursue,
And I am faint, and cannot fly their fury;
And were I strong, I would not shun their fury.
The sands are numb'red that makes up my life,
Here must I stay, and here my life must end.

39. ere . . . born. Actually, Edmund, Earl of Rutland, York's second son, was twelve years old at the time of the elder Clifford's death in 1455. **41. sith:** since.
48. Dii . . . tuae: "the gods grant that this be the summit of thy glory" (Ovid, *Heroides*, ii.66).

I.iv. Location: Scene continues.
2. uncles: i.e. Sir John and Sir Hugh Mortimer.
4. Turn back: turn their backs. **7. demean'd:** behaved.
12. falchion: curved sword. **19. bodg'd:** budged, gave way.

Enter the QUEEN [MARGARET], CLIFFORD, NORTHUMBERLAND, *the young* PRINCE [EDWARD], *and Soldiers.*

Come, bloody Clifford, rough Northumberland,
I dare your quenchless fury to more rage.
I am your butt, and I abide your shot.
North. Yield to our mercy, proud Plantagenet.
Clif. Ay, to such mercy as his ruthless arm
With downright payment show'd unto my father.
Now Phaëton hath tumbled from his car,
And made an evening at the noontide prick.
York. My ashes, as the phoenix, may bring forth
A bird that will revenge upon you all;
And in that hope I throw mine eyes to heaven,
Scorning what e'er you can afflict me with.
Why come you not? What, multitudes, and fear?
Clif. So cowards fight when they can fly no further,
So doves do peck the falcon's piercing talons,
So desperate thieves, all hopeless of their lives,
Breathe out invectives 'gainst the officers.
York. O Clifford, but bethink thee once again,
And in thy thought o'errun my former time;
And if thou canst for blushing, view this face,
And bite thy tongue, that slanders him with cowardice
Whose frown hath made thee faint and fly ere this!
Clif. I will not bandy with thee word for word,
But buckler with thee blows, twice two for one.
Q. Mar. Hold, valiant Clifford! for a thousand causes
I would prolong a while the traitor's life.
Wrath makes him deaf; speak thou, Northumberland.
North. Hold, Clifford, do not honor him so much
To prick thy finger, though to wound his heart.
What valor were it, when a cur doth grin,
For one to thrust his hand between his teeth,
When he might spurn him with his foot away?
It is war's prize to take all vantages,
And ten to one is no impeach of valor.
[*They lay hands on York, who struggles.*]
Clif. Ay, ay, so strives the woodcock with the gin.
North. So doth the cony struggle in the net.
York. So triumph thieves upon their conquer'd booty,
So true men yield, with robbers so o'ermatch'd.
North. What would your Grace have done unto him now?
Q. Mar. Brave warriors, Clifford and Northumberland,
Come make him stand upon this molehill here
That raught at mountains with outstretched arms,
Yet parted but the shadow with his hand.
What, was it you that would be England's king?
Was't you that revell'd in our parliament,
And made a preachment of your high descent?

29. butt: target.
33. Phaëton: Phaëthon, son of Apollo, the sun-god, who, when he tried to drive his father's chariot (*car*), was thrown from it and killed.
34. noontide prick: point on the sundial marking noon.
35. phoenix: fabulous bird that was reborn from its own ashes.
36. bird: young one. **45. o'errun:** survey, review.
46. for: on account of. **50. buckler:** catch or ward off (blows).
56. grin: show teeth. **60. impeach:** reproach. **61. gin:** snare.
62. cony: rabbit. **64. true:** honest. **68. raught:** reached.
71. revell'd: rioted.

Where are your mess of sons to back you now,
The wanton Edward, and the lusty George?
And where's that valiant crook-back prodigy,
Dicky, your boy, that with his grumbling voice
Was wont to cheer his dad in mutinies?
Or with the rest, where is your darling, Rutland?
Look, York, I stain'd this napkin with the blood
That valiant Clifford with his rapier's point
Made issue from the bosom of the boy;
And if thine eyes can water for his death,
I give thee this to dry thy cheeks withal.
Alas, poor York, but that I hate thee deadly,
I should lament thy miserable state.
I prithee grieve, to make me merry, York.
What, hath thy fiery heart so parch'd thine entrails
That not a tear can fall for Rutland's death?
Why art thou patient, man? Thou shouldst be mad;
And I, to make thee mad, do mock thee thus.
Stamp, rave, and fret, that I may sing and dance.
Thou wouldst be fee'd, I see, to make me sport:
York cannot speak unless he wear a crown.
A crown for York! and, lords, bow low to him;
Hold you his hands whilest I do set it on.
[*Putting a paper crown on his head.*]
Ay, marry, sir, now looks he like a king!
Ay, this is he that took King Henry's chair,
And this is he was his adopted heir.
But how is it that great Plantagenet
Is crown'd so soon, and broke his solemn oath?
As I bethink me, you should not be king
Till our King Henry had shook hands with death.
And will you pale your head in Henry's glory,
And rob his temples of the diadem,
Now in his life, against your holy oath?
O, 'tis a fault too too unpardonable!
Off with the crown; and, with the crown, his head,
And whilest we breathe, take time to do him dead.
Clif. That is my office, for my father's sake.
Q. Mar. Nay, stay, let's hear the orisons he makes.
York. She-wolf of France, but worse than wolves of France,
Whose tongue more poisons than the adder's tooth!
How ill-beseeming is it in thy sex
To triumph like an Amazonian trull
Upon their woes whom fortune captivates!
But that thy face is vizard-like, unchanging,
Made impudent with use of evil deeds,
I would assay, proud queen, to make thee blush.
To tell thee whence thou cam'st, of whom deriv'd,
Were shame enough to shame thee, wert thou not shameless.
Thy father bears the type of King of Naples,
Of both the Sicils and Jerusalem,
Yet not so wealthy as an English yeoman.
Hath that poor monarch taught thee to insult?
It needs not, nor it boots thee not, proud queen,
Unless the adage must be verified,
That beggars mounted run their horse to death.
'Tis beauty that doth oft make women proud,
But God he knows thy share thereof is small.
'Tis virtue that doth make them most admir'd,
The contrary doth make thee wond'red at.
'Tis government that makes them seem divine,
The want thereof makes thee abominable.
Thou art as opposite to every good
As the antipodes are unto us,
Or as the south to the septentrion.
O tiger's heart wrapp'd in a woman's hide!
How couldst thou drain the life-blood of the child,
To bid the father wipe his eyes withal,
And yet be seen to wear a woman's face?
Women are soft, mild, pitiful, and flexible;
Thou stern, obdurate, flinty, rough, remorseless.
Bid'st thou me rage? why, now thou hast thy wish:
Wouldst have me weep? why, now thou hast thy will:
For raging wind blows up incessant showers,
And when the rage allays, the rain begins.
These tears are my sweet Rutland's obsequies,
And every drop cries vengeance for his death
'Gainst thee, fell Clifford, and thee, false French-woman.
North. Beshrew me, but his passions moves me so
That hardly can I check my eyes from tears.
York. That face of his the hungry cannibals
Would not have touch'd, would not have stain'd with blood;
But you are more inhuman, more inexorable,
O, ten times more, than tigers of Hyrcania.
See, ruthless queen, a hapless father's tears!
This cloth thou dipp'dst in blood of my sweet boy,
And I with tears do wash the blood away.
Keep thou the napkin and go boast of this,
And if thou tell'st the heavy story right,
Upon my soul, the hearers will shed tears;
Yea, even my foes will shed fast-falling tears,
And say, "Alas, it was a piteous deed!"
There, take the crown, and with the crown, my curse,
And in thy need such comfort come to thee
As now I reap at thy too cruel hand!
Hard-hearted Clifford, take me from the world,
My soul to heaven, my blood upon your heads!
North. Had he been slaughter-man to all my kin,
I should not for my life but weep with him,
To see how inly sorrow gripes his soul.
Q. Mar. What, weeping-ripe, my Lord Northumberland?
Think but upon the wrong he did us all,

73. mess: set of four.
75. prodigy: monster. **79. napkin:** handkerchief.
92. fee'd: paid.
96. marry: indeed (originally the name of the Virgin Mary used as an oath). **103. pale:** enclose.
108. breathe: rest. **do him dead:** kill him.
110. orisons: prayers.
114. Amazonian: resembling the Amazons, a race of legendary female warriors. **115. captivates:** subdues.
116. vizard-like: masklike. **118. assay:** essay, try.
121. type: title.
122. both the Sicils: the Kingdom of the Two Sicilies, of which Margaret's father René (Reignier) was titular king.
125. boots: profits. **132. government:** discipline, self-control.
135. antipodes: the opposite side of the globe.
136. septentrion: north.
141. pitiful: full of pity, compassionate. **146. allays:** abates.
149. fell: cruel. **150. Beshrew:** curse.
155. Hyrcania: region near the Caspian Sea noted for its tigers.
171. inly: inward.

And that will quickly dry thy melting tears.
Clif. Here's for my oath, here's for my father's death. [*Stabbing him.*]
Q. Mar. And here's to right our gentle-hearted king. [*Stabbing him.*]
York. Open thy gate of mercy, gracious God!
My soul flies through these wounds to seek out thee. [*Dies.*]
Q. Mar. Off with his head, and set it on York gates,
So York may overlook the town of York.
[*Flourish. Exeunt.*]

[ACT II, SCENE I]

A march. Enter EDWARD, RICHARD, *and their power.*

Edw. I wonder how our princely father scap'd;
Or whether he be scap'd away or no
From Clifford's and Northumberland's pursuit.
Had he been ta'en, we should have heard the news;
Had he been slain, we should have heard the news;
Or had he scap'd, methinks we should have heard
The happy tidings of his good escape.
How fares my brother? Why is he so sad?
Rich. I cannot joy, until I be resolv'd
Where our right valiant father is become.
I saw him in the battle range about,
And watch'd him how he singled Clifford forth.
Methought he bore him in the thickest troop
As doth a lion in a herd of neat,
Or as a bear, encompass'd round with dogs,
Who having pinch'd a few and made them cry,
The rest stand all aloof and bark at him.
So far'd our father with his enemies,
So fled his enemies my warlike father;
Methinks 'tis prize enough to be his son.
[*Three suns appear in the air.*]
See how the morning opes her golden gates,
And takes her farewell of the glorious sun!
How well resembles it the prime of youth,
Trimm'd like a younker prancing to his love!
Edw. Dazzle mine eyes, or do I see three suns?
Rich. Three glorious suns, each one a perfect sun,
Not separated with the racking clouds,
But sever'd in a pale clear-shining sky.
See, see, they join, embrace, and seem to kiss,
As if they vow'd some league inviolable.
Now are they but one lamp, one light, one sun.
In this the heaven figures some event.
Edw. 'Tis wondrous strange, the like yet never heard of.
I think it cites us, brother, to the field,
That we, the sons of brave Plantagenet,
Each one already blazing by our meeds,
Should notwithstanding join our lights together,
And over-shine the earth as this the world.
What e'er it bodes, henceforward will I bear
Upon my target three fair shining suns.
Rich. Nay, bear three daughters; by your leave I speak it,
You love the breeder better than the male.

Enter one [*a* MESSENGER] *blowing.*

But what art thou, whose heavy looks foretell
Some dreadful story hanging on thy tongue?
Mess. Ah, one that was a woeful looker-on
When as the noble Duke of York was slain,
Your princely father and my loving lord!
Edw. O, speak no more, for I have heard too much.
Rich. Say how he died, for I will hear it all.
Mess. Environed he was with many foes,
And stood against them, as the hope of Troy
Against the Greeks that would have ent'red Troy.
But Hercules himself must yield to odds;
And many strokes, though with a little axe,
Hews down and fells the hardest-timber'd oak.
By many hands your father was subdu'd,
But only slaught'red by the ireful arm
Of unrelenting Clifford and the Queen;
Who crown'd the gracious Duke in high despite,
Laugh'd in his face; and when with grief he wept,
The ruthless Queen gave him to dry his cheeks
A napkin steeped in the harmless blood
Of sweet young Rutland, by rough Clifford slain.
And after many scorns, many foul taunts,
They took his head, and on the gates of York
They set the same, and there it doth remain,
The saddest spectacle that e'er I view'd.
Edw. Sweet Duke of York, our prop to lean upon,
Now thou art gone we have no staff, no stay.
O Clifford, boist'rous Clifford, thou hast slain
The flow'r of Europe for his chevalry,
And treacherously hast thou vanquish'd him,
For hand to hand he would have vanquish'd thee.
Now my soul's palace is become a prison;
Ah, would she break from hence, that this my body
Might in the ground be closed up in rest!
For never henceforth shall I joy again,
Never, O never, shall I see more joy!
Rich. I cannot weep; for all my body's moisture
Scarce serves to quench my furnace-burning heart;
Nor can my tongue unload my heart's great burthen,
For self-same wind that I should speak withal
Is kindling coals that fires all my breast,
And burns me up with flames that tears would quench.
To weep is to make less the depth of grief:
Tears then for babes; blows and revenge for me.
Richard, I bear thy name, I'll venge thy death,
Or die renowned by attempting it.

II.i. Location: A plain near Mortimer's Cross in Herefordshire.
10. Where . . . become: i.e. what has happened to him.
14. neat: cattle. **24. younker:** stripling.
25. three suns. According to Hall (Bullough, III, 179), when Edward, before the battle of Mortimer's Cross (which Shakespeare does not represent), saw three suns "sodainly joined all together in one," he "toke suche courage, that he fiercely set on his enemies, & them shortly discomfited: for which cause, men imagined, that he gave the sunne in his full brightnes for his cognisaunce or badge."
27. racking: scudding, drifting. **32. figures:** reveals, portends.
34. cites: urges.

36. meeds: deserts, merits.
40. target: targe, shield. **51. hope of Troy:** i.e. Hector.
70. boist'rous: savage. **71. chevalry:** chivalry, knightly qualities.
78. see more joy: see joy again.

Edw. His name that valiant duke hath left with thee;
His dukedom and his chair with me is left.
Rich. Nay, if thou be that princely eagle's bird,
Show thy descent by gazing 'gainst the sun;
For chair and dukedom, throne and kingdom say,
Either that is thine, or else thou wert not his.

March. Enter WARWICK, MARQUESS MONTAGUE, *and their army.*

War. How now, fair lords? What fare? What news abroad?
Rich. Great Lord of Warwick, if we should recompt
Our baleful news, and at each word's deliverance
Stab poniards in our flesh till all were told,
The words would add more anguish than the wounds.
O valiant lord, the Duke of York is slain!
Edw. O Warwick, Warwick, that Plantagenet,
Which held thee dearly as his soul's redemption,
Is by the stern Lord Clifford done to death.
War. Ten days ago I drown'd these news in tears;
And now, to add more measure to your woes,
I come to tell you things sith then befall'n.
After the bloody fray at Wakefield fought,
Where your brave father breath'd his latest gasp,
Tidings, as swiftly as the posts could run,
Were brought me of your loss and his depart.
I, then in London, keeper of the King,
Muster'd my soldiers, gathered flocks of friends,
[And very well appointed, as I thought,]
March'd toward Saint Albons to intercept the Queen,
Bearing the King in my behalf along;
For by my scouts I was advertised
That she was coming with a full intent
To dash our late decree in parliament
Touching King Henry's oath and your succession.
Short tale to make, we at Saint Albons met,
Our battles join'd, and both sides fiercely fought;
But whether 'twas the coldness of the King,
Who look'd full gently on his warlike queen,
That robb'd my soldiers of their heated spleen;
Or whether 'twas report of her success,
Or more than common fear of Clifford's rigor,
Who thunders to his captives blood and death,
I cannot judge: but, to conclude with truth,
Their weapons like to lightning came and went;
Our soldiers', like the night-owl's lazy flight,
Or like [an idle] thresher with a flail,
Fell gently down, as if they struck their friends.
I cheer'd them up with justice of our cause,
With promise of high pay and great rewards;
But all in vain, they had no heart to fight,
And we, in them, no hope to win the day,
So that we fled: the King unto the Queen;
Lord George your brother, Norfolk, and myself,
In haste, post-haste, are come to join with you;
For in the marches here we heard you were,
Making another head to fight again.
Edw. Where is the Duke of Norfolk, gentle Warwick?
And when came George from Burgundy to England?
War. Some six miles off the Duke is with the soldiers,
And for your brother, he was lately sent
From your kind aunt, Duchess of Burgundy,
With aid of soldiers to this needful war.
Rich. 'Twas odds, belike, when valiant Warwick fled:
Oft have I heard his praises in pursuit,
But ne'er till now his scandal of retire.
War. Nor now my scandal, Richard, dost thou hear;
For thou shalt know this strong right hand of mine
Can pluck the diadem from faint Henry's head,
And wring the aweful sceptre from his fist,
Were he as famous and as bold in war
As he is fam'd for mildness, peace, and prayer.
Rich. I know it well, Lord Warwick, blame me not.
'Tis love I bear thy glories make me speak.
But in this troublous time what's to be done?
Shall we go throw away our coats of steel,
And wrap our bodies in black mourning gowns,
Numb'ring our Ave-Maries with our beads?
Or shall we on the helmets of our foes
Tell our devotion with revengeful arms?
If for the last, say ay, and to it, lords.
War. Why, therefore Warwick came to seek you out,
And therefore comes my brother Montague.
Attend me, lords: the proud insulting Queen,
With Clifford and the haught Northumberland,
And of their feather many moe proud birds,
Have wrought the easy-melting King like wax.
He swore consent to your succession,
His oath enrolled in the parliament;
And now to London all the crew are gone
To frustrate both his oath and what beside
May make against the house of Lancaster.
Their power, I think, is thirty thousand strong.
Now, if the help of Norfolk and myself,
With all the friends that thou, brave Earl of March,
Amongst the loving Welshmen canst procure,
Will but amount to five and twenty thousand,
Why, *via!* to London will we march,

90. chair: i.e. the throne that he had claimed.
92. 'gainst the sun. The eagle was supposedly able to look at the sun without blinking. **108. latest:** last. **110. depart:** death.
116. advertised: informed. **118. dash:** overturn.
121. battles: armies. **124. spleen:** spirit.
138. Lord George: i.e. the Duke of Clarence.

140. marches: border country.
141. Making another head: raising another force.
146. Duchess of Burgundy: i.e. Isabel, wife of Philip, Duke of Burgundy, and a granddaughter of John of Gaunt. According to Hall (Bullough, III, 180), York's widow sent George and Richard, her two surviving younger sons, to Philip's court in Utrecht, "and so there thei remayned, till their brother Edwarde had obteyned the Realme, and gotten the regiment [rule]."
148. odds: i.e. heavy odds, very likely.
149–50. Oft . . . retire: i.e. I have often heard him praised for his eagerness in pursuit but never until now condemned for his disgrace in retreat. **162. beads:** rosary.
164. Tell our devotion: count off our prayers.
169. haught: haughty. **170. moe:** more.
171. wrought: worked, manipulated.
179. Earl of March: i.e. Edward. **182. via:** onward.

And once again bestride our foaming steeds,
And once again cry "Charge!" upon our foes,
But never once again turn back and fly.

Rich. Ay, now methinks I hear great Warwick speak.
Ne'er may he live to see a sunshine day
That cries "Retire!" if Warwick bid him stay.

Edw. Lord Warwick, on thy shoulder will I lean,
And when thou fail'st (as God forbid the hour!)
Must Edward fall, which peril heaven forefend!

War. No longer Earl of March, but Duke of York;
The next degree is England's royal throne;
For King of England shalt thou be proclaim'd
In every borough as we pass along,
And he that throws not up his cap for joy
Shall for the fault make forfeit of his head.
King Edward, valiant Richard, Montague,
Stay we no longer, dreaming of renown,
But sound the trumpets, and about our task.

Rich. Then, Clifford, were thy heart as hard as steel,
As thou hast shown it flinty by thy deeds,
I come to pierce it, or to give thee mine.

Edw. Then strike up drums. God and Saint George for us!

Enter a MESSENGER.

War. How now? what news?

Mess. The Duke of Norfolk sends you word by me
The Queen is coming with a puissant host,
And craves your company for speedy counsel.

War. Why then it sorts, brave warriors. Let's away.
Exeunt omnes.

[SCENE II]

Flourish. Enter the KING [HENRY], *the* QUEEN [MARGARET], CLIFFORD, NORTHUMBERLAND, *and young* PRINCE [EDWARD], *with Drum and Trumpets.*

Q. Mar. Welcome, my lord, to this brave town of York.
Yonder's the head of that arch-enemy
That sought to be encompass'd with your crown.
Doth not the object cheer your heart, my lord?

K. Hen. Ay, as the rocks cheer them that fear their wrack:
To see this sight, it irks my very soul.
Withhold revenge, dear God! 'tis not my fault,
Nor wittingly have I infring'd my vow.

Clif. My gracious liege, this too much lenity
And harmful pity must be laid aside.
To whom do lions cast their gentle looks?
Not to the beast that would usurp their den.
Whose hand is that the forest bear doth lick?

191. **forefend**: forfend, forbid. 193. **degree**: step.
209. **sorts**: fits.

II.ii. Location: Before York.
o.s.d. Trumpets: trumpeters.
2. **Yonder**: i.e. on the gate of the city, where Margaret had ordered York's head placed. 5. **wrack**: destruction.
8. **wittingly**: intentionally. 9. **liege**: sovereign.

Not his that spoils her young before her face.
Who scapes the lurking serpent's mortal sting?
Not he that sets his foot upon her back.
The smallest worm will turn, being trodden on,
And doves will peck in safeguard of their brood.
Ambitious York did level at thy crown,
Thou smiling while he knit his angry brows:
He, but a duke, would have his son a king,
And raise his issue like a loving sire;
Thou, being a king, blest with a goodly son,
Didst yield consent to disinherit him,
Which argued thee a most unloving father.
Unreasonable creatures feed their young,
And though man's face be fearful to their eyes,
Yet in protection of their tender ones,
Who hath not seen them, even with those wings
Which sometime they have us'd with fearful flight,
Make war with him that climb'd unto their nest,
Offering their own lives in their young's defense?
For shame, my liege, make them your president!
Were it not pity that this goodly boy
Should lose his birthright by his father's fault,
And long hereafter say unto his child,
"What my great-grandfather and grandsire got,
My careless father fondly gave away"?
Ah, what a shame were this! Look on the boy,
And let his manly face, which promiseth
Successful fortune, steel thy melting heart
To hold thine own and leave thine own with him.

K. Hen. Full well hath Clifford play'd the orator,
Inferring arguments of mighty force.
But, Clifford, tell me, didst thou never hear
That things ill got had ever bad success?
And happy always was it for that son
Whose father for his hoarding went to hell?
I'll leave my son my virtuous deeds behind,
And would my father had left me no more!
For all the rest is held at such a rate
As brings a thousandfold more care to keep
Than in possession any jot of pleasure.
Ah, cousin York, would thy best friends did know
How it doth grieve me that thy head is here!

Q. Mar. My lord, cheer up your spirits, our foes are nigh,
And this soft courage makes your followers faint.
You promis'd knighthood to our forward son,
Unsheathe your sword, and dub him presently.
Edward, kneel down.

K. Hen. Edward Plantagenet, arise a knight,
And learn this lesson: Draw thy sword in right.

Prince. My gracious father, by your kingly leave,
I'll draw it as apparent to the crown,
And in that quarrel use it to the death.

Clif. Why, that is spoken like a toward prince.

14. **spoils**: destroys. 19. **level**: aim.
26. **Unreasonable creatures**: i.e. animals.
33. **president**: precedent, model.
37. **great-grandfather and grandsire**: i.e. Henry IV and Henry V.
38. **fondly**: foolishly. 44. **Inferring**: adducing.
46. **success**: outcome. 57. **faint**: lose heart.
59. **presently**: at once. 64. **apparent**: heir. 66. **toward**: bold.

Enter a MESSENGER.

Mess. Royal commanders, be in readiness,
For with a band of thirty thousand men
Comes Warwick, backing of the Duke of York,
And in the towns, as they do march along,
Proclaims him king, and many fly to him.
Darraign your battle, for they are at hand.

Clif. I would your Highness would depart the field,
The Queen hath best success when you are absent.

Q. Mar. Ay, good my lord, and leave us to our fortune.

K. Hen. Why, that's my fortune too, therefore I'll stay.

North. Be it with resolution then to fight.

Prince. My royal father, cheer these noble lords,
And hearten those that fight in your defense.
Unsheathe your sword, good father; cry "Saint George!"

March. Enter EDWARD, WARWICK, RICHARD, [GEORGE OF] CLARENCE, NORFOLK, MONTAGUE, *and Soldiers.*

Edw. Now, perjur'd Henry, wilt thou kneel for grace,
And set thy diadem upon my head,
Or bide the mortal fortune of the field?

Q. Mar. Go rate thy minions, proud insulting boy!
Becomes it thee to be thus bold in terms
Before thy sovereign and thy lawful king?

Edw. I am his king, and he should bow his knee.
I was adopted heir by his consent.
Since when, his oath is broke; for, as I hear,
You that are king, though he do wear the crown,
Have caus'd him, by new act of parliament,
To blot out me, and put his own son in.

Clif. And reason too:
Who should succeed the father but the son?

Rich. Are you there, butcher? O, I cannot speak!

Clif. Ay, crook-back, here I stand to answer thee,
Or any he the proudest of thy sort.

Rich. 'Twas you that kill'd young Rutland, was it not?

Clif. Ay, and old York, and yet not satisfied.

Rich. For God's sake, lords, give signal to the fight.

War. What say'st thou, Henry, wilt thou yield the crown?

Q. Mar. Why, how now, long-tongu'd Warwick, dare you speak?
When you and I met at Saint Albons last,
Your legs did better service than your hands.

War. Then 'twas my turn to fly, and now 'tis thine.

Clif. You said so much before, and yet you fled.

War. 'Twas not your valor, Clifford, drove me thence.

North. No, nor your manhood that durst make you stay.

Rich. Northumberland, I hold thee reverently.

69. Duke of York: i.e. Edward.
72. Darraign your battle: draw up your army.
84. rate thy minions: scold your favorites.
85. terms: language. **97. sort:** gang.

Break off the parley, for scarce I can refrain
The execution of my big-swoll'n heart
Upon that Clifford, that cruel child-killer.

Clif. I slew thy father, call'st thou him a child?

Rich. Ay, like a dastard and a treacherous coward,
As thou didst kill our tender brother Rutland,
But ere sunset I'll make thee curse the deed.

K. Hen. Have done with words, my lords, and hear me speak.

Q. Mar. Defy them then, or else hold close thy lips.

K. Hen. I prithee give no limits to my tongue,
I am a king, and privileg'd to speak.

Clif. My liege, the wound that bred this meeting here
Cannot be cur'd by words; therefore be still.

Rich. Then, executioner, unsheathe thy sword.
By Him that made us all, I am resolv'd
That Clifford's manhood lies upon his tongue.

Edw. Say, Henry, shall I have my right, or no?
A thousand men have broke their fasts to-day
That ne'er shall dine unless thou yield the crown.

War. If thou deny, their blood upon thy head,
For York in justice puts his armor on.

Prince. If that be right which Warwick says is right,
There is no wrong, but every thing is right.

[*Rich.*] Whoever got thee, there thy mother stands,
For well I wot, thou hast thy mother's tongue.

Q. Mar. But thou art neither like thy sire nor dam,
But like a foul misshapen stigmatic,
Mark'd by the destinies to be avoided,
As venom toads, or lizards' dreadful stings.

Rich. Iron of Naples hid with English gilt,
Whose father bears the title of a king
(As if a channel should be call'd the sea),
Sham'st thou not, knowing whence thou art extraught,
To let thy tongue detect thy base-born heart?

Edw. A wisp of straw were worth a thousand crowns
To make this shameless callet know herself.
Helen of Greece was fairer far than thou,
Although thy husband may be Menelaus;
And ne'er was Agamemnon's brother wrong'd
By that false woman as this king by thee.
His father revell'd in the heart of France,
And tam'd the King and made the Dolphin stoop;
And had he match'd according to his state,
He might have kept that glory to this day.
But when he took a beggar to his bed,
And grac'd thy poor sire with his bridal day,

110. refrain: give up. **111. execution:** exercise (of powers).
124. resolv'd: convinced. **133. got:** begot. **134. wot:** know.
136. stigmatic: one marked with deformity.
138. venom: poisonous. **141. channel:** gutter.
142. extraught: extracted, derived. **143. detect:** expose.
144. wisp of straw. Mark of disgrace for a scold.
145. callet: strumpet.
146–49. Helen . . . thee. The abduction of Helen, wife of Menelaus, king of Sparta, eventuated in the Trojan war, in which the Greeks were led by Menelaus' brother Agamemnon, king of Mycenae.
152. he: i.e. Henry VI. **match'd:** married.
154–55. when . . . day. An allusion to the overgenerous marriage contract that Suffolk had arranged. See *2 Henry VI*, I.i.57–62.

Even then that sunshine brew'd a show'r for him,
That wash'd his father's fortunes forth of France,
And heap'd sedition on his crown at home.
For what hath broach'd this tumult but thy pride?
Hadst thou been meek, our title still had slept,
And we, in pity of the gentle king,
Had slipp'd our claim until another age.

Geo. But when we saw our sunshine made thy spring,
And that thy summer bred us no increase,
We set the axe to thy usurping root;
And though the edge hath something hit ourselves,
Yet know thou, since we have begun to strike,
We'll never leave till we have hewn thee down,
Or bath'd thy growing with our heated bloods.

Edw. And in this resolution, I defy thee,
Not willing any longer conference,
Since thou deniedst the gentle king to speak.
Sound trumpets! Let our bloody colors wave!
And either victory, or else a grave.

Q. Mar. Stay, Edward.

Edw. No, wrangling woman, we'll no longer stay,
These words will cost ten thousand lives this day.
Exeunt omnes.

[Scene III]

Alarum. Excursions. Enter Warwick.

War. Forespent with toil, as runners with a race,
I lay me down a little while to breathe;
For strokes receiv'd and many blows repaid
Have robb'd my strong-knit sinews of their strength,
And spite of spite needs must I rest awhile.

Enter Edward *running.*

Edw. Smile, gentle heaven! or strike, ungentle death!
For this world frowns, and Edward's sun is clouded.

War. How now, my lord, what hap? what hope of good?

Enter [George of] Clarence.

Geo. Our hap is loss, our hope but sad despair,
Our ranks are broke, and ruin follows us.
What counsel give you? Whither shall we fly?

Edw. Bootless is flight, they follow us with wings,
And weak we are and cannot shun pursuit.

Enter Richard [*running*].

Rich. Ah, Warwick, why hast thou withdrawn thyself?
Thy brother's blood the thirsty earth hath drunk,
Broach'd with the steely point of Clifford's lance;
And in the very pangs of death he cried,
Like to a dismal clangor heard from far,
"Warwick, revenge! brother, revenge my death!"
So underneath the belly of their steeds,
That stain'd their fetlocks in his smoking blood,
The noble gentleman gave up the ghost.

War. Then let the earth be drunken with our blood!
I'll kill my horse, because I will not fly.
Why stand we like soft-hearted women here,
Wailing our losses, whiles the foe doth rage,
And look upon, as if the tragedy
Were play'd in jest by counterfeiting actors?
Here on my knee I vow to God above
I'll never pause again, never stand still,
Till either death hath clos'd these eyes of mine
Or fortune given me measure of revenge.

Edw. O Warwick, I do bend my knee with thine,
And in this vow do chain my soul to thine!
And ere my knee rise from the earth's cold face,
I throw my hands, mine eyes, my heart to Thee,
Thou setter-up and plucker-down of kings,
Beseeching thee (if with thy will it stands)
That to my foes this body must be prey,
Yet that thy brazen gates of heaven may ope
And give sweet passage to my sinful soul!
Now, lords, take leave until we meet again,
Where e'er it be, in heaven or in earth.

Rich. Brother, give me thy hand, and gentle Warwick,
Let me embrace thee in my weary arms.
I, that did never weep, now melt with woe
That winter should cut off our spring-time so.

War. Away, away! Once more, sweet lords, farewell.

Geo. Yet let us all together to our troops,
And give them leave to fly that will not stay;
And call them pillars that will stand to us;
And if we thrive, promise them such rewards
As victors wear at the Olympian games.
This may plant courage in their quailing breasts,
For yet is hope of life and victory.
Foreslow no longer, make we hence amain. *Exeunt.*

[Scene IV]

Excursions. Enter Richard [*at one door*] *and* Clifford [*at the other*].

Rich. Now, Clifford, I have singled thee alone:
Suppose this arm is for the Duke of York,
And this for Rutland, both bound to revenge,
Wert thou environ'd with a brazen wall.

159. broach'd: set flowing. **160. title**: legal claim to the throne.
162. slipp'd: let slide, postponed. **164. increase**: harvest.
166. something: somewhat.

II.iii. Location: Scene continues. (Scenes iii–vi represent the so-called battle of Towton, which took place in the area between Towton and Saxton, near York, but Shakespeare does not specify any change of locale or passage of time between Scene ii [*Before York.*] and Scene iii, and clearly thinks of Scene iii as following immediately in the same general area as Scene ii.)
o.s.d. **Excursions**: sallies, sorties. **1. Forespent**: exhausted.
5. spite of spite: i.e. no matter what happens.

15. Thy . . . drunk. Warwick's illegitimate half-brother, the so-called Bastard of Salisbury, was killed in a skirmish at Ferrybridge two days before the battle of Towton (March 29, 1461). Hall (Bullough, III, 181), who describes him as "a valeaunt yong gentelman, and of great audacitie," says that in his rage and grief Warwick was "like a man desperate." **26. whiles**: while.
27. look upon: look on, be spectators. **56. Foreslow**: delay.

II.iv. Location: Scene continues.
1. singled: chosen.

Clif. Now, Richard, I am with thee here alone:
This is the hand that stabb'd thy father York,
And this the hand that slew thy brother Rutland,
And here's the heart that triumphs in their death,
And cheers these hands that slew thy sire and brother
To execute the like upon thyself—
And so have at thee!

[*Alarums.*] *They fight.* WARWICK *comes; Clifford flies.*

Rich. Nay, Warwick, single out some other chase,
For I myself will hunt this wolf to death. *Exeunt.*

[SCENE V]

Alarum. Enter KING HENRY *alone.*

K. Hen. This battle fares like to the morning's war,
When dying clouds contend with growing light,
What time the shepherd, blowing of his nails,
Can neither call it perfect day nor night.
Now sways it this way, like a mighty sea
Forc'd by the tide to combat with the wind;
Now sways it that way, like the self-same sea
Forc'd to retire by fury of the wind.
Sometime the flood prevails, and then the wind;
Now one the better, then another best;
Both tugging to be victors, breast to breast,
Yet neither conqueror nor conquered;
So is the equal poise of this fell war.
Here on this molehill will I sit me down.
To whom God will, there be the victory!
For Margaret my queen, and Clifford too,
Have chid me from the battle; swearing both
They prosper best of all when I am thence.
Would I were dead, if God's good will were so;
For what is in this world but grief and woe?
O God! methinks it were a happy life
To be no better than a homely swain,
To sit upon a hill, as I do now,
To carve out dials quaintly, point by point,
Thereby to see the minutes how they run:
How many makes the hour full complete,
How many hours brings about the day,
How many days will finish up the year,
How many years a mortal man may live.
When this is known, then to divide the times:
So many hours must I tend my flock,
So many hours must I take my rest,
So many hours must I contemplate,
So many hours must I sport myself,
So many days my ewes have been with young,
So many weeks ere the poor fools will ean,
So many years ere I shall shear the fleece:
So minutes, hours, days, months, and years,
Pass'd over to the end they were created,
Would bring white hairs unto a quiet grave.
Ah! what a life were this! how sweet! how lovely!
Gives not the hawthorn bush a sweeter shade
To shepherds looking on their silly sheep
Than doth a rich embroider'd canopy
To kings that fear their subjects' treachery?
O yes, it doth; a thousandfold it doth.
And to conclude, the shepherd's homely curds,
His cold thin drink out of his leather bottle,
His wonted sleep under a fresh tree's shade,
All which secure and sweetly he enjoys,
Is far beyond a prince's delicates—
His viands sparkling in a golden cup,
His body couched in a curious bed,
When care, mistrust, and treason waits on him.

Alarum. Enter a SON *that hath kill'd his father, at one door,* [*dragging in the dead body*].

Son. Ill blows the wind that profits nobody.
This man whom hand to hand I slew in fight
May be possessed with some store of crowns,
And I that, haply, take them from him now,
May yet, ere night, yield both my life and them
To some man else, as this dead man doth me.
Who's this? O God! it is my father's face,
Whom in this conflict I, unwares, have kill'd.
O heavy times, begetting such events!
From London by the King was I press'd forth;
My father, being the Earl of Warwick's man,
Came on the part of York, press'd by his master;
And I, who at his hands receiv'd my life,
Have by my hands of life bereaved him.
Pardon me, God, I knew not what I did!
And pardon, father, for I knew not thee!
My tears shall wipe away these bloody marks;
And no more words till they have flow'd their fill.

K. Hen. O piteous spectacle! O bloody times!
Whiles lions war and battle for their dens,
Poor harmless lambs abide their enmity.
Weep, wretched man; I'll aid thee tear for tear,
And let our hearts and eyes, like civil war,
Be blind with tears, and break o'ercharg'd with grief.

Enter [*a*] FATHER *that hath kill'd his son, at another door, bearing of his son.*

Fath. Thou that so stoutly hath resisted me,
Give me thy gold—if thou hast any gold—
For I have bought it with an hundred blows.
But let me see: is this our foeman's face?
Ah, no, no, no, it is mine only son!
Ah, boy, if any life be left in thee,
Throw up thine eye! See, see what show'rs arise,
Blown with the windy tempest of my heart
Upon thy wounds, that kills mine eye and heart!
O, pity, God, this miserable age!
What stratagems! how fell! how butcherly!
Erroneous, mutinous, and unnatural,

12. chase: game, prey.

II.v. Location: Scene continues.
3. of: on. **13. poise:** balance.
22. homely swain: simple shepherd.
24. dials: sundials. **quaintly:** carefully. **34. sport:** amuse.
36. ean: yean, bring forth.

43. silly: feeble, helpless.
51. delicates: luxuries. **53. curious:** elaborate.
58. haply: perhaps.
64. press'd forth: impressed, conscripted. **66. part:** side.
75. abide: pay the penalty for.
89. stratagems: wicked deeds. **90. Erroneous:** criminal.

This deadly quarrel daily doth beget!
O boy! thy father gave thee life too soon,
And hath bereft thee of thy life too late.

K. Hen. Woe above woe! grief more than common grief!
O that my death would stay these ruthful deeds!
O, pity, pity, gentle heaven, pity!
The red rose and the white are on his face,
The fatal colors of our striving houses;
The one his purple blood right well resembles,
The other his pale cheeks, methinks, presenteth.
Wither one rose, and let the other flourish;
If you contend, a thousand lives must wither.

Son. How will my mother for a father's death
Take on with me, and ne'er be satisfied!

Fath. How will my wife for slaughter of my son
Shed seas of tears, and ne'er be satisfied!

K. Hen. How will the country for these woeful chances
Misthink the King, and not be satisfied!

Son. Was ever son so ru'd a father's death?

Fath. Was ever father so bemoan'd his son?

K. Hen. Was ever king so griev'd for subjects' woe?
Much is your sorrow; mine ten times so much.

Son. I'll bear thee hence, where I may weep my fill.
[*Exit with his father.*]

Fath. These arms of mine shall be thy winding-sheet;
My heart, sweet boy, shall be thy sepulchre,
For from my heart thine image ne'er shall go;
My sighing breast shall be thy funeral bell;
And so obsequious will thy father be,
[E'en] for the loss of thee, having no more,
As Priam was for all his valiant sons.
I'll bear thee hence, and let them fight that will,
For I have murthered where I should not kill.
Exit [*with his son*].

K. Hen. Sad-hearted men, much overgone with care,
Here sits a king more woeful than you are.

Alarums. Excursions. Enter the QUEEN [MARGARET], *the* PRINCE [EDWARD], *and* EXETER.

Prince. Fly, father, fly! for all your friends are fled,
And Warwick rages like a chafed bull.
Away! for death doth hold us in pursuit.

Q. Mar. Mount you, my lord, towards Berwick post amain.
Edward and Richard, like a brace of greyhounds
Having the fearful flying hare in sight,
With fiery eyes sparkling for very wrath,
And bloody steel grasp'd in their ireful hands,
Are at our backs, and therefore hence amain.

Exe. Away! for vengeance comes along with them.
Nay, stay not to expostulate, make speed,
Or else come after. I'll away before.

K. Hen. Nay, take me with thee, good sweet Exeter;
Not that I fear to stay, but love to go
Whither the Queen intends. Forward, away!
Exeunt.

[SCENE VI]

A loud alarum. Enter CLIFFORD *wounded* [*with an arrow in his neck*].

Clif. Here burns my candle out; ay, here it dies,
Which whiles it lasted, gave King Henry light.
O Lancaster! I fear thy overthrow
More than my body's parting with my soul.
My love and fear glu'd many friends to thee,
And now I fall, thy tough commixtures melts,
Impairing Henry, strength'ning misproud York.
[The common people swarm like summer flies,]
And whither fly the gnats but to the sun?
And who shines now but Henry's enemies?
O Phoebus! hadst thou never given consent
That Phaëton should check thy fiery steeds,
Thy burning car never had scorch'd the earth.
And, Henry, hadst thou sway'd as kings should do,
Or as thy father and his father did,
Giving no ground unto the house of York,
They never then had sprung like summer flies;
I and ten thousand in this luckless realm
Had left no mourning widows for our death,
And thou this day hadst kept thy chair in peace.
For what doth cherish weeds but gentle air?
And what makes robbers bold but too much lenity?
Bootless are plaints, and cureless are my wounds;
No way to fly, nor strength to hold out flight.
The foe is merciless, and will not pity;
For at their hands I have deserv'd no pity.
The air hath got into my deadly wounds,
And much effuse of blood doth make me faint.
Come, York and Richard, Warwick and the rest,
I stabb'd your fathers' bosoms, split my breast.
[*He faints.*]

Alarum and retreat. Enter EDWARD, WARWICK, RICHARD, *and Soldiers*, MONTAGUE, *and* [GEORGE OF] CLARENCE.

Edw. Now breathe we, lords, good fortune bids us pause
And smooth the frowns of war with peaceful looks.
Some troops pursue the bloody-minded queen,
That led calm Henry, though he were a king,
As doth a sail, fill'd with a fretting gust,

93. late: recently. **104. satisfied:** comforted.
108. Misthink: think ill of.
118. obsequious: dutiful in showing respect for the dead.
120. Priam: king of Troy whose fifty sons were killed in the war with the Greeks. **123. overgone:** overpowered. **126. chafed:** enraged.
128. Berwick: town and fortress on the Scottish border at the mouth of the River Tweed. **amain:** at full speed.

II.vi. Location: Scene continues.
o.s.d. Clifford. Actually, Clifford was killed in the skirmish at Ferrybridge where Warwick's half-brother fell. According to Hall (Bullough, III, 181–82), he was struck in the neck by an arrow and "incontinent [forthwith] rendered hys spirite."
5. My . . . fear: love and fear of me.
6. commixtures: i.e. the compound of "love and fear."
7. misproud: arrogant.
11–13. O . . . earth. See note to I.iv.33. Phaëthon was so little able to control (*check*) his father's horses that they drew the sun-chariot too close to the earth and scorched it. **14. sway'd:** ruled.
20. chair: throne. **28. effuse:** effusion.
35. fretting: blowing in gusts.

Command an argosy to stem the waves.
But think you, lords, that Clifford fled with them?
War. No, 'tis impossible he should escape;
For (though before his face I speak the words)
Your brother Richard mark'd him for the grave,
And wheresoe'er he is, he's surely dead.
Clifford groans [and then dies].
Rich. Whose soul is that which takes her heavy leave?
A deadly groan, like life and death's departing.
See who it is.
Edw. And, now the battle's ended,
If friend or foe, let him be gently used.
Rich. Revoke that doom of mercy, for 'tis Clifford,
Who, not contented that he lopp'd the branch
In hewing Rutland when his leaves put forth,
But set his murth'ring knife unto the root
From whence that tender spray did sweetly spring,
I mean our princely father, Duke of York.
War. From off the gates of York fetch down the head,
Your father's head, which Clifford placed there;
In stead whereof let this supply the room:
Measure for measure must be answered.
Edw. Bring forth that fatal screech-owl to our house
That nothing sung but death to us and ours.
Now death shall stop his dismal threat'ning sound,
And his ill-boding tongue no more shall speak.
War. I think [his] understanding is bereft.
Speak, Clifford, dost thou know who speaks to thee?
Dark cloudy death o'ershades his beams of life,
And he nor sees nor hears us what we say.
Rich. O would he did! and so, perhaps, he doth;
'Tis but his policy to counterfeit,
Because he would avoid such bitter taunts
Which in the time of death he gave our father.
Geo. If so thou think'st, vex him with eager words.
Rich. Clifford, ask mercy and obtain no grace.
Edw. Clifford, repent in bootless penitence.
War. Clifford, devise excuses for thy faults.
Geo. While we devise fell tortures for thy faults.
Rich. Thou didst love York, and I am son to York.
Edw. Thou pitiedst Rutland, I will pity thee.
Geo. Where's Captain Margaret, to fence you now?
War. They mock thee, Clifford, swear as thou wast wont.
Rich. What, not an oath? Nay, then the world goes hard
When Clifford cannot spare his friends an oath.
I know by that he's dead, and by my soul,
If this right hand would buy two hours' life
That I, in all despite, might rail at him,
This hand should chop it off; and with the issuing blood
Stifle the villain whose unstanched thirst
York and young Rutland could not satisfy.

36. argosy: large merchant ship. **43. departing**: parting.
44–45. And . . . used. Actually, Edward was so implacable against the defeated Lancastrians that he ordered the execution of all captives of rank. **46. doom**: judgment. **60. bereft**: destroyed.
63. nor . . . nor: neither . . . nor. **68. eager**: bitter.
75. fence: protect. **83. unstanched**: insatiable.

War. Ay, but he's dead. Off with the traitor's head,
And rear it in the place your father's stands.
And now to London with triumphant march,
There to be crowned England's royal king;
From whence shall Warwick cut the sea to France,
And ask the Lady Bona for thy queen.
So shalt thou sinow both these lands together,
And having France thy friend, thou shalt not dread
The scatt'red foe that hopes to rise again;
For though they cannot greatly sting to hurt,
Yet look to have them buzz to offend thine ears.
First will I see the coronation,
And then to Brittany I'll cross the sea
To effect this marriage, so it please my lord.
Edw. Even as thou wilt, sweet Warwick, let it be;
For in thy shoulder do I build my seat,
And never will I undertake the thing
Wherein thy counsel and consent is wanting.
Richard, I will create thee Duke of Gloucester,
And George, of Clarence. Warwick, as ourself,
Shall do and undo as him pleaseth best.
Rich. Let me be Duke of Clarence, George of Gloucester,
For Gloucester's dukedom is too ominous.
War. Tut, that's a foolish observation.
Richard, be Duke of Gloucester. Now to London
To see these honors in possession. *Exeunt.*

[ACT III, SCENE I]

Enter [two KEEPERS*] with cross-bows in their hands.*

[1. Keep.] Under this thick-grown brake we'll shroud ourselves,
For through this laund anon the deer will come,
And in this covert will we make our stand,
Culling the principal of all the deer.
[2. Keep.] I'll stay above the hill, so both may shoot.
[1. Keep.] That cannot be, the noise of thy cross-bow
Will scare the herd, and so my shoot is lost.
Here stand we both and aim we at the best;
And for the time shall not seem tedious,
I'll tell thee what befell me on a day
In this self place where now we mean to stand.

90. Lady Bona: daughter of Louis, Duke of Savoy, and sister-in-law of Louis XI of France. **91. sinow**: sinew, tie firmly.
107. Gloucester's . . . ominous. Three earlier dukes of Gloucester—including Richard II's uncle Thomas of Woodstock and Henry VI's uncle Humphrey—had met violent deaths. Shakespeare apparently remembered Hall, who, commenting on Humphrey of Gloucester's murder, remarked (Bullough, III, 108) "that the name and title of Gloucester, hath been unfortunate and unluckie to diverse, whiche for their honor, have been erected by creacion of princes, to that stile and dignitie, as Hugh Spencer, Thomas of Woodstocke, sonne to kyng Edward the third, and this duke Humfrey, which thre persones, by miserable death finished their daies, and after them kynge Richard the .III. also, duke of Gloucester, in civill warre was slain and confounded: so that this name of Gloucester, is taken for an unhappie and unfortunate stile."

III.i. Location: A forest in the north of England.
o.s.d. Keepers: gamekeepers. **1. brake**: thicket.
2. laund: glade. **8. at the best**: as well as we can.
9. for: in order that. **11. self**: same.

[*2. Keep.*] Here comes a man, let's stay till he be past.

Enter the KING [HENRY, *disguised,*] *with a prayer-book.*

K. Hen. From Scotland am I stol'n, even of pure love,
To greet mine own land with my wishful sight.
No, Harry, Harry, 'tis no land of thine;
Thy place is fill'd, thy sceptre wrung from thee,
Thy balm wash'd off wherewith thou was anointed.
No bending knee will call thee Caesar now,
No humble suitors press to speak for right,
No, not a man comes for redress of thee;
For how can I help them and not myself?

[*1. Keep.*] Ay, here's a deer whose skin's a keeper's fee:
This is the quondam king; let's seize upon him.

K. Hen. Let me embrace [thee,] sour [adversities],
For wise men say it is the wisest course.

[*2. Keep.*] Why linger we? Let us lay hands upon him.

[*1. Keep.*] Forbear awhile, we'll hear a little more.

K. Hen. My queen and son are gone to France for aid;
And, as I hear, the great commanding Warwick
[Is] thither gone to crave the French king's sister
To wife for Edward. If this news be true,
Poor queen and son, your labor is but lost;
For Warwick is a subtle orator,
And Lewis a prince soon won with moving words.
By this account then, Margaret may win him,
For she's a woman to be pitied much.
Her sighs will make a batt'ry in his breast,
Her tears will pierce into a marble heart;
The tiger will be mild whiles she doth mourn;
And Nero will be tainted with remorse
To hear and see her plaints, her brinish tears.
Ay, but she's come to beg; Warwick, to give:
She, on his left side, craving aid for Henry;
He, on his right, asking a wife for Edward.
She weeps, and says her Henry is depos'd;
He smiles, and says his Edward is install'd;
That she, poor wretch, for grief can speak no more;
Whiles Warwick tells his title, smooths the wrong,
Inferreth arguments of mighty strength,
And in conclusion wins the King from her
With promise of his sister and what else,
To strengthen and support King Edward's place.
O Margaret, thus 'twill be, and thou, poor soul,
Art then forsaken, as thou went'st forlorn!

[*2. Keep.*] Say, what art thou talk'st of kings and queens?

K. Hen. More than I seem, and less than I was born to;
A man at least, for less I should not be;
And men may talk of kings, and why not I?

[*2. Keep.*] Ay, but thou talk'st as if thou wert a king.

K. Hen. Why, so I am—in mind, and that's enough.

[*2. Keep.*] But if thou be a king, where is thy crown?

K. Hen. My crown is in my heart, not on my head;
Not deck'd with diamonds and Indian stones,
Nor to be seen. My crown is call'd content,
A crown it is that seldom kings enjoy.

[*2. Keep.*] Well, if you be a king crown'd with content,
Your crown content and you must be contented
To go along with us; for, as we think,
You are the king King Edward hath depos'd;
And we his subjects, sworn in all allegiance,
Will apprehend you as his enemy.

K. Hen. But did you never swear and break an oath?

[*2. Keep.*] No, never such an oath, nor will not now.

K. Hen. Where did you dwell when I was King of England?

[*2. Keep.*] Here in this country where we now remain.

K. Hen. I was anointed king at nine months old,
My father and my grandfather were kings;
And you were sworn true subjects unto me;
And tell me then, have you not broke your oaths?

[*1. Keep.*] No,
For we were subjects but while you were king.

K. Hen. Why? Am I dead? Do I not breathe a man?
Ah, simple men, you know not what you swear!
Look, as I blow this feather from my face,
And as the air blows it to me again,
Obeying with my wind when I do blow,
And yielding to another when it blows,
Commanded always by the greater gust,
Such is the lightness of you common men.
But do not break your oaths, for of that sin
My mild entreaty shall not make you guilty.
Go where you will, the King shall be commanded;
And be you kings: command, and I'll obey.

[*1. Keep.*] We are true subjects to the King, King Edward.

K. Hen. So would you be again to Henry,
If he were seated as King Edward is.

[*1. Keep.*] We charge you, in God's name and the King's,
To go with us unto the officers.

K. Hen. In God's name lead; your king's name be obey'd,
And what God will, that let your king perform;
And what he will, I humbly yield unto. *Exeunt.*

[SCENE II]

Enter KING EDWARD, GLOUCESTER, CLARENCE, LADY GREY.

K. Edw. Brother of Gloucester, at Saint Albons field

14. wishful: longing. **19. speak for right:** ask for justice.
20. of: from. **37. batt'ry:** breach, bruise.
40. Nero. A byword for cruelty. **tainted:** touched.
48. his title: i.e. Edward's claim. **49. Inferreth:** adduces.

71. apprehend: arrest. **81. but:** only.

III.ii. Location: London. The palace.

This lady's husband, Sir Richard Grey, was slain,
His land then seiz'd on by the conqueror.
Her suit is now to repossess those lands,
Which we in justice cannot well deny,
Because in quarrel of the house of York
The worthy gentleman did lose his life.

Glou. Your Highness shall do well to grant her suit;
It were dishonor to deny it her.

K. Edw. It were no less, but yet I'll make a pause.

Glou. [*Aside to Clarence.*] Yea, is it so?
I see the lady hath a thing to grant,
Before the King will grant her humble suit.

Clar. [*Aside to Gloucester.*] He knows the game; how true he keeps the wind!

Glou. [*Aside to Clarence.*] Silence!

K. Edw. Widow, we will consider of your suit,
And come some other time to know our mind.

L. Grey. Right gracious lord, I cannot brook delay.
May it please your Highness to resolve me now,
And what your pleasure is shall satisfy me.

Glou. [*Aside to Clarence.*] Ay, widow? Then I'll warrant you all your lands,
And if what pleases him shall pleasure you.
Fight closer or, good faith, you'll catch a blow.

Clar. [*Aside to Gloucester.*] I fear her not, unless she chance to fall.

Glou. [*Aside to Clarence.*] God forbid that, for he'll take vantages.

K. Edw. How many children hast thou, widow? tell me.

Clar. [*Aside to Gloucester.*] I think he means to beg a child of her.

Glou. [*Aside to Clarence.*] Nay then whip me; he'll rather give her two.

L. Grey. Three, my most gracious lord.

Glou. [*Aside to Clarence.*] You shall have four [and] you'll be rul'd by him.

K. Edw. 'Twere pity they should lose their father's lands.

L. Grey. Be pitiful, dread lord, and grant it then.

K. Edw. Lords, give us leave. I'll try this widow's wit.

Glou. [*Aside to Clarence.*] Ay, good leave have you, for you will have leave
Till youth take leave and leave you to the crutch.

[*Gloucester and Clarence retire.*]

K. Edw. Now tell me, madam, do you love your children?

L. Grey. Ay, full as dearly as I love myself.

K. Edw. And would you not do much to do them good?

L. Grey. To do them good I would sustain some harm.

K. Edw. Then get your husband's lands, to do them good.

L. Grey. Therefore I came unto your Majesty.

K. Edw. I'll tell you how these lands are to be got.

L. Grey. So shall you bind me to your Highness' service.

K. Edw. What service wilt thou do me if I give them?

L. Grey. What you command that rests in me to do.

K. Edw. But you will take exceptions to my boon.

L. Grey. No, gracious lord, except I cannot do it.

K. Edw. Ay, but thou canst do what I mean to ask.

L. Grey. Why then I will do what your Grace commands.

Glou. [*Aside to Clarence.*] He plies her hard, and much rain wears the marble.

Clar. [*Aside to Gloucester.*] As red as fire? nay then, her wax must melt.

L. Grey. Why stops my lord? shall I not hear my task?

K. Edw. An easy task, 'tis but to love a king.

L. Grey. That's soon perform'd, because I am a subject.

K. Edw. Why then, thy husband's lands I freely give thee.

L. Grey. I take my leave with many thousand thanks.

Glou. [*Aside to Clarence.*] The match is made, she seals it with a cur'sy.

K. Edw. But stay thee, 'tis the fruits of love I mean.

L. Grey. The fruits of love I mean, my loving liege.

K. Edw. Ay, but I fear me in another sense.
What love, think'st thou, I sue so much to get?

L. Grey. My love till death, my humble thanks, my prayers—
That love which virtue begs and virtue grants.

K. Edw. No, by my troth, I did not mean such love.

L. Grey. Why then you mean not as I thought you did.

K. Edw. But now you partly may perceive my mind.

L. Grey. My mind will never grant what I perceive
Your Highness aims at, if I aim aright.

K. Edw. To tell thee plain, I aim to lie with thee.

L. Grey. To tell you plain, I had rather lie in prison.

K. Edw. Why then thou shalt not have thy husband's lands.

L. Grey. Why then mine honesty shall be my dower,
For by that loss I will not purchase them.

K. Edw. Therein thou wrong'st thy children mightily.

L. Grey. Herein your Highness wrongs both them and me.

2–7. This . . . life. Actually, Sir John—not Richard—Grey lost his life while fighting for Margaret and the Lancastrians at the second battle of St. Albans in 1461. In *Richard III* (I.iii.126–29) the facts are given accurately.
14. keeps the wind: i.e. so that the game will not catch the scent and be alarmed. **21. warrant:** guarantee.
24. fear: i.e. fear for. **25. vantages:** opportunities. **30. and:** if.
33. give us leave: pardon us, i.e. leave us alone.
34. Ay . . . have leave: yes, may you have pardon, for you will take liberties.

46. boon: request for a favor. **47. except:** unless.
57. cur'sy: curtsy. **68. aim:** guess. **72. honesty:** chastity.

But, mighty lord, this merry inclination
Accords not with the sadness of my suit.
Please you dismiss me, either with ay or no.
K. Edw. Ay, if thou wilt say ay to my request;
No, if thou dost say no to my demand.
L. Grey. Then no, my lord. My suit is at an end.
Glou. [*Aside to Clarence.*] The widow likes him not, she knits her brows.
Clar. [*Aside to Gloucester.*] He is the bluntest wooer in Christendom.
K. Edw. [*Aside.*] Her looks doth argue her replete with modesty,
Her words doth show her wit incomparable,
All her perfections challenge sovereignty:
One way or other, she is for a king,
And she shall be my love or else my queen.—
Say that King Edward take thee for his queen?
L. Grey. 'Tis better said than done, my gracious lord.
I am a subject fit to jest withal,
But far unfit to be a sovereign.
K. Edw. Sweet widow, by my state I swear to thee
I speak no more than what my soul intends,
And that is, to enjoy thee for my love.
L. Grey. And that is more than I will yield unto.
I know I am too mean to be your queen,
And yet too good to be your concubine.
K. Edw. You cavil, widow, I did mean my queen.
L. Grey. 'Twill grieve your Grace my sons should call you father.
K. Edw. No more than when my daughters call thee mother.
Thou art a widow, and thou hast some children,
And by God's Mother, I, being but a bachelor,
Have other some. Why, 'tis a happy thing
To be the father unto many sons.
Answer no more, for thou shalt be my queen.
Glou. [*Aside to Clarence.*] The ghostly father now hath done his shrift.
Clar. [*Aside to Gloucester.*] When he was made a shriver, 'twas for shift.
K. Edw. Brothers, you muse what chat we two have had.
Glou. The widow likes it not, for she looks very sad.
K. Edw. You'ld think it strange if I should marry her.
Clar. To who, my lord?
K. Edw. Why, Clarence, to myself.
Glou. That would be ten days' wonder at the least.
Clar. That's a day longer than a wonder lasts.
Glou. By so much is the wonder in extremes.
K. Edw. Well, jest on, brothers. I can tell you both
Her suit is granted for her husband's lands.

77. **sadness:** seriousness. 93. **state:** i.e. royalty.
104. **other some:** some others.
107. **ghostly father:** spiritual father, confessor. **done his shrift:** heard her confession and given absolution.
108. **shift:** trick, shifty purpose. 109. **muse:** wonder.
114. **That's . . . lasts.** A "nine days' wonder" is still proverbial.

Enter a Nobleman.

Nob. My gracious lord, Henry your foe is taken,
And brought your prisoner to your palace gate.
K. Edw. See that he be convey'd unto the Tower;
And go we, brothers, to the man that took him,
To question of his apprehension.
Widow, go you along. Lords, use her [honorably].
Exeunt. Manet Richard [*of Gloucester*].
Glou. Ay, Edward will use women honorably.
Would he were wasted, marrow, bones, and all,
That from his loins no hopeful branch may spring,
To cross me from the golden time I look for!
And yet, between my soul's desire and me—
The lustful Edward's title buried—
Is Clarence, Henry, and his son young Edward,
And all the unlook'd-for issue of their bodies
To take their rooms, ere I can place myself:
A cold premeditation for my purpose!
Why then I do but dream on sovereignty,
Like one that stands upon a promontory
And spies a far-off shore where he would tread,
Wishing his foot were equal with his eye,
And chides the sea that sunders him from thence,
Saying, he'll lade it dry to have his way:
So do I wish the crown, being so far off,
And so I chide the means that keeps me from it,
And so, I say, I'll cut the causes off,
Flattering me with impossibilities.
My eye's too quick, my heart o'erweens too much,
Unless my hand and strength could equal them.
Well, say there is no kingdom then for Richard;
What other pleasure can the world afford?
I'll make my heaven in a lady's lap,
And deck my body in gay ornaments,
And witch sweet ladies with my words and looks.
O miserable thought! and more unlikely
Than to accomplish twenty golden crowns!
Why, love forswore me in my mother's womb;
And for I should not deal in her soft laws,
She did corrupt frail nature with some bribe,
To shrink mine arm up like a wither'd shrub,
To make an envious mountain on my back,
Where sits deformity to mock my body;
To shape my legs of an unequal size,
To disproportion me in every part,
Like to a chaos, or an unlick'd bear-whelp
That carries no impression like the dam.
And am I then a man to be belov'd?
O monstrous fault, to harbor such a thought!
Then since this earth affords no joy to me
But to command, to check, to o'erbear such
As are of better person than myself,
I'll make my heaven to dream upon the crown,
And whiles I live, t' account this world but hell,
Until my misshap'd trunk that bears this head

129. **buried:** i.e. eliminated. 131. **unlook'd for:** unforeseeable.
133. **cold premeditation:** i.e. chilly prospect.
139. **lade:** empty. 141. **means:** obstacles. 143. **me:** myself.
144. **o'erweens:** presumes. 150. **witch:** bewitch.
154. **for . . . not:** lest I. 157. **envious:** hateful.
161. **unlick'd bear-whelp.** Bear cubs were supposedly born as shapeless lumps of flesh and licked into shape by the mother.
166. **check:** control. **o'erbear:** dominate.

Be round impaled with a glorious crown.
And yet I know not how to get the crown,
For many lives stand between me and home;
And I—like one lost in a thorny wood,
That rents the thorns, and is rent with the thorns,
Seeking a way, and straying from the way,
Not knowing how to find the open air,
But toiling desperately to find it out—
Torment myself to catch the English crown;
And from that torment I will free myself,
Or hew my way out with a bloody axe.
Why, I can smile, and murther whiles I smile,
And cry "Content" to that which grieves my heart,
And wet my cheeks with artificial tears,
And frame my face to all occasions.
I'll drown more sailors than the mermaid shall,
I'll slay more gazers than the basilisk,
I'll play the orator as well as Nestor,
Deceive more slily than Ulysses could,
And like a Sinon, take another Troy.
I can add colors to the chameleon,
Change shapes with Proteus for advantages,
And set the murtherous Machevil to school.
Can I do this, and cannot get a crown?
Tut, were it farther off, I'll pluck it down. *Exit.*

[Scene III]

Flourish. Enter Lewis *the French King, his sister* Bona, *his Admiral, call'd* Bourbon, Prince Edward, Queen Margaret, *and the* Earl of Oxford. *Lewis sits, and riseth up again.*

K. Lew. Fair Queen of England, worthy Margaret,
Sit down with us. It ill befits thy state
And birth that thou shouldst stand while Lewis doth sit.
Q. Mar. No, mighty King of France; now Margaret
Must strike her sail and learn a while to serve
Where kings command. I was, I must confess,
Great Albion's queen in former golden days;
But now mischance hath trod my title down,
And with dishonor laid me on the ground,
Where I must take like seat unto my fortune,
And to my humble seat conform myself.
K. Lew. Why, say, fair queen, whence springs this deep despair?
Q. Mar. From such a cause as fills mine eyes with tears
And stops my tongue, while heart is drown'd in cares.
K. Lew. What e'er it be, be thou still like thyself,
And sit thee by our side. (*Seats her by him.*) Yield not thy neck
To fortune's yoke, but let thy dauntless mind
Still ride in triumph over all mischance.
Be plain, Queen Margaret, and tell thy grief;
It shall be eas'd if France can yield relief.
Q. Mar. Those gracious words revive my drooping thoughts
And give my tongue-tied sorrows leave to speak.
Now therefore be it known to noble Lewis,
That Henry, sole possessor of my love,
Is, of a king, become a banish'd man,
And forc'd to live in Scotland a forlorn;
While proud ambitious Edward, Duke of York,
Usurps the regal title and the seat
Of England's true-anointed lawful king.
This is the cause that I, poor Margaret,
With this my son, Prince Edward, Henry's heir,
Am come to crave thy just and lawful aid;
And if thou fail us, all our hope is done.
Scotland hath will to help, but cannot help;
Our people and our peers are both misled,
Our treasure seiz'd, our soldiers put to flight,
And as thou seest, ourselves in heavy plight.
K. Lew. Renowned queen, with patience calm the storm,
While we bethink a means to break it off.
Q. Mar. The more we stay, the stronger grows our foe.
K. Lew. The more I stay, the more I'll succor thee.
Q. Mar. O, but impatience waiteth on true sorrow.
And see where comes the breeder of my sorrow!

Enter Warwick.

K. Lew. What's he approacheth boldly to our presence?
Q. Mar. Our Earl of Warwick, Edward's greatest friend.
K. Lew. Welcome, brave Warwick! What brings thee to France? *He descends. She ariseth.*
Q. Mar. Ay, now begins a second storm to rise,
For this is he that moves both wind and tide.
War. From worthy Edward, King of Albion,
My lord and sovereign and thy vowed friend,
I come, in kindness and unfeigned love,
First, to do greetings to thy royal person,
And then to crave a league of amity,
And lastly, to confirm that amity
With nuptial knot, if thou vouchsafe to grant
That virtuous Lady Bona, thy fair sister,
To England's king in lawful marriage.
Q. Mar. [*Aside.*] If that go forward, Henry's hope is done.
War. And, gracious madam (*speaking to Bona*), in our king's behalf
I am commanded, with your leave and favor,
Humbly to kiss your hand, and with my tongue

171. impaled: enclosed. **173. home:** i.e. his goal.
175. rents: rends. **184. artificial:** feigned.
186. mermaid. Thought to lure mariners to their death.
187. basilisk: fabulous serpent whose look was thought to cause death. **188, 189. Nestor, Ulysses:** Greek leaders in the Trojan war.
190. Sinon: Greek warrior who contrived the ruse of the wooden horse by which Troy was taken.
192. Proteus: the "Old Man of the Sea" who could change his shape when captured.
193. set . . . school: i.e. teach Machiavelli himself about murder. See note to *1 Henry VI*, V.iv.74.

III.iii. Location: France. The King's palace.
2. state: rank. **5. strike her sail:** humble herself.
7. Albion's: England's.

20. France: i.e. the King of France.
25. of a king: from being a king. **26. forlorn:** outcast.
40. stay: delay. **56. sister:** i.e. sister-in-law.

To tell the passion of my sovereign's heart,
Where fame, late ent'ring at his heedful ears,
Hath plac'd thy beauty's image and thy virtue.
Q. Mar. King Lewis and Lady Bona, hear me speak
Before you answer Warwick. His demand
Springs not from Edward's well-meant honest love,
But from deceit bred by necessity;
For how can tyrants safely govern home,
Unless abroad they purchase great alliance?
To prove him tyrant this reason may suffice,
That Henry liveth still; but were he dead,
Yet here Prince Edward stands, King Henry's son.
Look therefore, Lewis, that by this league and marriage
Thou draw not on thy danger and dishonor;
For though usurpers sway the rule a while,
Yet heav'ns are just, and time suppresseth wrongs.
War. Injurious Margaret!
Prince. And why not Queen?
War. Because thy father Henry did usurp,
And thou no more art prince than she is queen.
Oxf. Then Warwick disannuls great John of Gaunt,
Which did subdue the greatest part of Spain;
And after John of Gaunt, Henry the Fourth,
Whose wisdom was a mirror to the wisest;
And after that wise prince, Henry the Fift,
Who by his prowess conquered all France:
From these our Henry lineally descends.
War. Oxford, how haps it in this smooth discourse
You told not how Henry the Sixt hath lost
All that which Henry the Fift had gotten?
Methinks these peers of France should smile at that.
But for the rest: you tell a pedigree
Of threescore and two years—a silly time
To make prescription for a kingdom's worth.
Oxf. Why, Warwick, canst thou speak against thy liege,
Whom thou obey'dst thirty and six years,
And not bewray thy treason with a blush?
War. Can Oxford, that did ever fence the right,
Now buckler falsehood with a pedigree?
For shame, leave Henry, and call Edward king.
Oxf. Call him my king by whose injurious doom
My elder brother, the Lord Aubrey Vere,
Was done to death? and more than so, my father,
Even in the downfall of his mellow'd years,
When nature brought him to the door of death?
No, Warwick, no; while life upholds this arm,
This arm upholds the house of Lancaster.
War. And I the house of York.

78. Injurious: insulting. **81. disannuls:** cancels.
93. Of . . . years: i.e. from the deposition of Richard II by Henry IV (1399). The time represented here is thus 1461, but Warwick's marriage embassy actually took place in 1463.
94. prescription: a claim founded upon *de facto* possession.
96. thirty . . . years: i.e. the time between Henry VI's accession in 1422 and his open break with Warwick in 1458 (?). Warwick, however, was in fact only thirty in the latter year. **98. fence:** defend.
99. buckler: protect.
101–5. Call . . . death. John de Vere, twelfth Earl of Oxford, and his eldest son Aubrey were attainted and executed as Lancastrian agitators in 1462.

K. Lew. Queen Margaret, Prince Edward, and Oxford,
Vouchsafe, at our request, to stand aside,
While I use further conference with Warwick.
They stand aloof.
Q. Mar. Heavens grant that Warwick's words bewitch him not!
K. Lew. Now, Warwick, tell me, even upon thy conscience,
Is Edward your true king? for I were loath
To link with him that were not lawful chosen.
War. Thereon I pawn my credit and mine honor.
K. Lew. But is he gracious in the people's eye?
War. The more that Henry was unfortunate.
K. Lew. Then further: all dissembling set aside,
Tell me for truth the measure of his love
Unto our sister Bona.
War. Such it seems
As may beseem a monarch like himself.
Myself have often heard him say, and swear,
That this his love was an [eternal] plant,
Whereof the root was fix'd in virtue's ground,
The leaves and fruit maintain'd with beauty's sun,
Exempt from envy, but not from disdain,
Unless the Lady Bona quit his pain.
K. Lew. Now, sister, let us hear your firm resolve.
Bona. Your grant, or your denial, shall be mine.
Yet I confess that often ere this day,
Speaks to Warwick.
When I have heard your king's desert recounted,
Mine ear hath tempted judgment to desire.
K. Lew. Then, Warwick, thus: our sister shall be Edward's.
And now forthwith shall articles be drawn
Touching the jointure that your king must make,
Which with her dowry shall be counterpois'd.
Draw near, Queen Margaret, and be a witness
That Bona shall be wife to the English king.
Prince. To Edward, but not to the English king.
Q. Mar. Deceitful Warwick, it was thy device
By this alliance to make void my suit.
Before thy coming, Lewis was Henry's friend.
K. Lew. And still is friend to him and Margaret.
But if your title to the crown be weak,
As may appear by Edward's good success,
Then 'tis but reason that I be releas'd
From giving aid which late I promised.
Yet shall you have all kindness at my hand
That your estate requires and mine can yield.
War. Henry now lives in Scotland at his ease;
Where having nothing, nothing can he lose.
And as for you yourself, our quondam queen,
You have a father able to maintain you,
And better 'twere you troubled him than France.
Q. Mar. Peace, impudent and shameless Warwick,
Proud setter-up and puller-down of kings!
I will not hence, till with my talk and tears
(Both full of truth) I make King Lewis behold

127. envy: malice. **disdain:** contempt.
128. quit his pain: i.e. relieve his passion with her love.
136. jointure: marriage settlement.
137. counterpois'd: balanced.

Thy sly conveyance and thy lord's false love,
For both of you are birds of self-same feather.
Post blowing a horn within.
K. Lew. Warwick, this is some post to us or thee.

Enter the Post.

Post. My lord ambassador, these letters are for you, *Speaks to Warwick.*
Sent from your brother, Marquess Montague.
These from our king unto your Majesty. *To Lewis.*
And, madam, these for you; from whom I know not. *To Margaret.*
They all read their letters.
Oxf. I like it well that our fair queen and mistress
Smiles at her news, while Warwick frowns at his.
Prince. Nay, mark how Lewis stamps as he were nettled.
I hope all's for the best.
K. Lew. Warwick, what are thy news? And yours, fair queen?
Q. Mar. Mine such as fill my heart with unhop'd joys.
War. Mine full of sorrow and heart's discontent.
K. Lew. What? has your king married the Lady Grey?
And now to soothe your forgery and his,
Sends me a paper to persuade me patience?
Is this th' alliance that he seeks with France?
Dare he presume to scorn us in this manner?
Q. Mar. I told your Majesty as much before:
This proveth Edward's love and Warwick's honesty.
War. King Lewis, I here protest in sight of heaven,
And by the hope I have of heavenly bliss,
That I am clear from this misdeed of Edward's;
No more my king, for he dishonors me,
But most himself if he could see his shame.
Did I forget that by the house of York
My father came untimely to his death?
Did I let pass th' abuse done to my niece?
Did I impale him with the regal crown?
Did I put Henry from his native right?
And am I guerdon'd at the last with shame?
Shame on himself! for my desert is honor;
And to repair my honor lost for him,
I here renounce him and return to Henry.
My noble queen, let former grudges pass,
And henceforth I am thy true servitor.
I will revenge his wrong to Lady Bona,
And replant Henry in his former state.
Q. Mar. Warwick, these words have turn'd my hate to love,
And I forgive and quite forget old faults,
And joy that thou becom'st King Henry's friend.
War. So much his friend, ay, his unfeigned friend,
That if King Lewis vouchsafe to furnish us
With some few bands of chosen soldiers,
I'll undertake to land them on our coast,
And force the tyrant from his seat by war.
'Tis not his new-made bride shall succor him,
And as for Clarence, as my letters tell me,
He's very likely now to fall from him,
For matching more for wanton lust than honor,
Or than for strength and safety of our country.
Bona. Dear brother, how shall Bona be reveng'd
But by thy help to this distressed queen?
Q. Mar. Renowned prince, how shall poor Henry live,
Unless thou rescue him from foul despair?
Bona. My quarrel and this English queen's are one.
War. And mine, fair Lady Bona, joins with yours.
K. Lew. And mine with hers, and thine, and Margaret's.
Therefore, at last, I firmly am resolv'd
You shall have aid.
Q. Mar. Let me give humble thanks for all at once.
K. Lew. Then, England's messenger, return in post,
And tell false Edward, thy supposed king,
That Lewis of France is sending over masquers
To revel it with him and his new bride.
Thou seest what's pass'd, go fear thy king withal.
Bona. Tell him, in hope he'll prove a widower shortly,
I wear the willow garland for his sake.
Q. Mar. Tell him, my mourning weeds are laid aside,
And I am ready to put armor on.
War. Tell him from me that he hath done me wrong,
And therefore I'll uncrown him ere't be long.
There's thy reward, be gone. *Exit Post.*
K. Lew. But, Warwick,
Thou and Oxford, with five thousand men,
Shall cross the seas and bid false Edward battle;
And as occasion serves, this noble queen
And prince shall follow with a fresh supply.
Yet ere thou go, but answer me one doubt:
What pledge have we of thy firm loyalty?
War. This shall assure my constant loyalty,
That if our queen and this young prince agree,
I'll join mine eldest daughter, and my joy,
To him forthwith in holy wedlock bands.
Q. Mar. Yes, I agree, and thank you for your motion.
Son Edward, she is fair and virtuous,
Therefore delay not, give thy hand to Warwick,
And with thy hand, thy faith irrevocable

160. conveyance: deceit. **161 s.d. Post:** messenger.
175. soothe your forgery: palliate your deceit.
176. persuade: advise.
186–87. Did . . . death. Actually, Warwick's father—the Earl of Salisbury of *2 Henry VI*—had been captured at the battle of Wakefield (1460) and executed by the victorious Lancastrians.
188. th' abuse . . . niece. According to Hall (Bullough, III, 188), the notoriously lecherous Edward, while a guest in Warwick's house, "woulde have deflowred his doughter or his nece."
189. impale him: encircle his head. **191. guerdon'd:** rewarded.

205–6. I'll . . . war. Another anachronism. Warwick did not seek Henry VI's restoration until 1470. **210. matching:** marrying.
226. fear: frighten. **withal:** with this.
228. willow garland. Token of a forsaken lover.
242. eldest daughter. Warwick's eldest daughter was Isabella, who married George, Duke of Clarence, in 1469. It was Anne (1456–85), Warwick's second daughter, to whom Prince Edward was betrothed the following year, but his capture and murder at the hands of the Yorkists after the battle of Tewkesbury in 1471 (see V.v) occurred before they could be married. In 1474 she married Richard, Duke of Gloucester (later Richard III). **244. motion:** offer.

That only Warwick's daughter shall be thine.
Prince. Yes, I accept her, for she well deserves it,
And here, to pledge my vow, I give my hand.
He gives his hand to Warwick.
K. Lew. Why stay we now? These soldiers shall be levied,
And thou, Lord Bourbon, our High Admiral,
Shall waft them over with our royal fleet.
I long till Edward fall by war's mischance,
For mocking marriage with a dame of France.
Exeunt. Manet Warwick.
War. I came from Edward as ambassador,
But I return his sworn and mortal foe.
Matter of marriage was the charge he gave me,
But dreadful war shall answer his demand.
Had he none else to make a stale but me?
Then none but I shall turn his jest to sorrow.
I was the chief that rais'd him to the crown,
And I'll be chief to bring him down again;
Not that I pity Henry's misery,
But seek revenge on Edward's mockery. *Exit.*

[ACT IV, SCENE I]

Enter RICHARD [OF GLOUCESTER], CLARENCE, SOMERSET, *and* MONTAGUE.

Glou. Now tell me, brother Clarence, what think you
Of this new marriage with the Lady Grey?
Hath not our brother made a worthy choice?
Clar. Alas, you know, 'tis far from hence to France;
How could he stay till Warwick made return?
Som. My lords, forbear this talk; here comes the King.

Flourish. Enter KING EDWARD, *Lady Grey, [now* QUEEN ELIZABETH,] PEMBROKE, STAFFORD, HASTINGS, *[and others]. Four stand on one side and four on the other.*

Glou. And his well-chosen bride.
Clar. I mind to tell him plainly what I think.
K. Edw. Now, brother of Clarence, how like you our choice,
That you stand pensive as half malecontent?
Clar. As well as Lewis of France or the Earl of Warwick,
Which are so weak of courage and in judgment
That they'll take no offense at our abuse.
K. Edw. Suppose they take offense without a cause;
They are but Lewis and Warwick, I am Edward,
Your king and Warwick's, and must have my will.
Glou. And shall have your will, because our king.
Yet hasty marriage seldom proveth well.
K. Edw. Yea, brother Richard, are you offended too?
Glou. Not I.
No; God forbid that I should wish them sever'd
Whom God hath join'd together; ay, and 'twere pity
To sunder them that yoke so well together.
K. Edw. Setting your scorns and your mislike aside,
Tell me some reason why the Lady Grey
Should not become my wife and England's queen.
And you too, Somerset and Montague,
Speak freely what you think.
Clar. Then this is mine opinion: that King Lewis
Becomes your enemy, for mocking him
About the marriage of the Lady Bona.
Glou. And Warwick, doing what you gave in charge,
Is now dishonored by this new marriage.
K. Edw. What if both Lewis and Warwick be appeas'd
By such invention as I can devise?
Mont. Yet, to have join'd with France in such alliance
Would more have strength'ned this our commonwealth
'Gainst foreign storms than any home-bred marriage.
Hast. Why, knows not Montague that of itself
England is safe, if true within itself?
Mont. But the safer when 'tis back'd with France.
Hast. 'Tis better using France than trusting France.
Let us be back'd with God, and with the seas,
Which he hath giv'n for fence impregnable,
And with their helps only defend ourselves:
In them, and in ourselves, our safety lies.
Clar. For this one speech Lord Hastings well deserves
To have the heir of the Lord Hungerford.
K. Edw. Ay, what of that? It was my will and grant,
And for this once my will shall stand for law.
Glou. And yet methinks your Grace hath not done well
To give the heir and daughter of Lord Scales
Unto the brother of your loving bride.
She better would have fitted me or Clarence;
But in your bride you bury brotherhood.
Clar. Or else you would not have bestow'd the heir
Of the Lord Bonville on your new wife's son,
And leave your brothers to go speed elsewhere.
K. Edw. Alas, poor Clarence! is it for a wife
That thou art malecontent? I will provide thee.

253. waft: convey by water. **260. stale:** laughingstock.

IV.i. Location: London. The palace.
10. malecontent: malcontent. **13. abuse:** insult.
16. will: determination (with following play on the sense "lust").

32. gave in charge: commissioned.
35. invention: design, plan.
47–58. For . . . elsewhere. These allusions to the profitable marriages arranged for the Queen's upstart relatives are probably derived from Hall (Bullough, III, 186–87): "Her father also was created erle Ryvers, and made high Constable of Englande: her brother lorde Anthony, was maried to the sole heyre of Thomas lord Scales, & by her he was lord Scales. Syr Thomas Grey, sonne of syr John Grey, the quenes fyrst husband, was created Marques Dorset, and maried to Cicilie, heyre to the lord Bonvile. Albeit this mariage, at the first apparaunce was very pleasaunt to the king, but more joyous to the quene & profitable to her bloud, which were so highly exalted, yea, & so sodainly promoted, that all the nobilitie more marvayled then allowed this sodayne risyng and swift elevacion." **57. wive's:** wife's.
58. speed: achieve success (in seeking wives for themselves).

Clar. In choosing for yourself, you show'd your judgment;
Which being shallow, you shall give me leave
To play the broker in mine own behalf;
And to that end I shortly mind to leave you.
K. Edw. Leave me, or tarry, Edward will be king,
And not be tied unto his brother's will.
Q. Eliz. My lords, before it pleas'd his Majesty
To raise my state to title of a queen,
Do me but right, and you must all confess
That I was not ignoble of descent,
And meaner than myself have had like fortune.
But as this title honors me and mine,
So your dislikes, to whom I would be pleasing,
Doth cloud my joys with danger and with sorrow.
K. Edw. My love, forbear to fawn upon their frowns.
What danger or what sorrow can befall thee
So long as Edward is thy constant friend
And their true sovereign whom they must obey?
Nay, whom they shall obey, and love thee too,
Unless they seek for hatred at my hands;
Which if they do, yet will I keep thee safe,
And they shall feel the vengeance of my wrath.
Glou. [*Aside.*] I hear, yet say not much, but think the more.

Enter a Post.

K. Edw. Now, messenger, what letters or what news
From France?
Post. My sovereign liege, no letters, and few words,
But such as I (without your special pardon)
Dare not relate.
K. Edw. Go to, we pardon thee; therefore, in brief,
Tell me their words as near as thou canst guess them.
What answer makes King Lewis unto our letters?
Post. At my depart, these were his very words:
"Go tell false Edward, the supposed king,
That Lewis of France is sending over masquers
To revel it with him and his new bride."
K. Edw. Is Lewis so brave? belike he thinks me Henry.
But what said Lady Bona to my marriage?
Post. These were her words, utt'red with mild disdain:
"Tell him, in hope he'll prove a widower shortly,
I'll wear the willow garland for his sake."
K. Edw. I blame not her: she could say little less;
She had the wrong. But what said Henry's queen?
For I have heard that she was there in place.
Post. "Tell him," quoth she, "my mourning weeds are done,
And I am ready to put armor on."
K. Edw. Belike she minds to play the Amazon.
But what said Warwick to these injuries?
Post. He, more incens'd against your Majesty
Than all the rest, discharg'd me with these words:
"Tell him from me that he hath done me wrong,
And therefore I'll uncrown him ere't be long."
K. Edw. Ha? durst the traitor breathe out so proud words?
Well, I will arm me, being thus forewarn'd.
They shall have wars, and pay for their presumption.
But say, is Warwick friends with Margaret?
Post. Ay, gracious sovereign, they are so link'd in friendship
That young Prince Edward marries Warwick's daughter.
Clar. Belike the elder; Clarence will have the younger.
Now, brother king, farewell, and sit you fast,
For I will hence to Warwick's other daughter,
That though I want a kingdom, yet in marriage
I may not prove inferior to yourself.
You that love me and Warwick, follow me.
Exit Clarence, and Somerset follows.
Glou. [*Aside.*] Not I;
My thoughts aim at a further matter: I
Stay not for the love of Edward, but the crown.
K. Edw. Clarence and Somerset both gone to Warwick?
Yet am I arm'd against the worst can happen;
And haste is needful in this desp'rate case.
Pembroke and Stafford, you in our behalf
Go levy men, and make prepare for war;
They are already or quickly will be landed.
Myself in person will straight follow you.
Exeunt Pembroke and Stafford.
But ere I go, Hastings and Montague,
Resolve my doubt. You twain, of all the rest,
Are near to Warwick by blood and by alliance:
Tell me if you love Warwick more than me?
If it be so, then both depart to him;
I rather wish you foes than hollow friends.
But if you mind to hold your true obedience,
Give me assurance with some friendly vow,
That I may never have you in suspect.
Mont. So God help Montague as he proves true!
Hast. And Hastings as he favors Edward's cause!
K. Edw. Now, brother Richard, will you stand by us?
Glou. Ay, in despite of all that shall withstand you.
K. Edw. Why, so! then am I sure of victory.
Now therefore let us hence, and lose no hour,
Till we meet Warwick with his foreign pow'r.
Exeunt.

[Scene II]

Enter Warwick *and* Oxford *in England, with French Soldiers.*

War. Trust me, my lord, all hitherto goes well,

63. broker: agent.
70. I . . . descent. Elizabeth, the first commoner to become a queen of England, was the daughter of Sir Richard Woodville (later Lord Rivers) and Jacquetta of Luxemburg, widow of John, Duke of Bedford. **90. guess:** i.e. approximate.
104. done: i.e. no longer needed.

118. Belike . . . younger. See note to III.iii.242. **121. want:** lack.
131. prepare: preparation. **142. suspect:** suspicion.

IV.ii. Location: A plain in Warwickshire.

The common people by numbers swarm to us.

Enter CLARENCE *and* SOMERSET.

But see where Somerset and Clarence comes!
Speak suddenly, my lords, are we all friends?
Clar. Fear not that, my lord.
War. Then, gentle Clarence, welcome unto Warwick,
And welcome, Somerset! I hold it cowardice
To rest mistrustful where a noble heart
Hath pawn'd an open hand in sign of love;
Else might I think that Clarence, Edward's brother,
Were but a feigned friend to our proceedings.
But welcome, sweet Clarence, my daughter shall be thine.
And now what rests but, in night's coverture,
Thy brother being carelessly encamp'd,
His soldiers lurking in the town about,
And but attended by a simple guard,
We may surprise and take him at our pleasure?
Our scouts have found the adventure very easy;
That as Ulysses and stout Diomede
With sleight and manhood stole to Rhesus' tents
And brought from thence the Thracian fatal steeds,
So we, well cover'd with the night's black mantle,
At unawares may beat down Edward's guard,
And seize himself; I say not, slaughter him,
For I intend but only to surprise him.
You that will follow me to this attempt,
Applaud the name of Henry with your leader.

They all cry, "Henry!"

Why then, let's on our way in silent sort.
For Warwick and his friends, God and Saint George!

Exeunt.

[SCENE III]

Enter three WATCHMEN *to guard the King's tent.*

1. Watch. Come on, my masters, each man take his stand,
The King by this is set him down to sleep.
2. Watch. What, will he not to bed?
1. Watch. Why, no; for he hath made a solemn vow
Never to lie and take his natural rest
Till Warwick or himself be quite suppress'd.
2. Watch. To-morrow then belike shall be the day,
If Warwick be so near as men report.
3. Watch. But say, I pray, what nobleman is that
That with the King here resteth in his tent?
1. Watch. 'Tis the Lord Hastings, the King's chiefest friend.
3. Watch. O, is it so? But why commands the King
That his chief followers lodge in towns about him,
While he himself keeps in the cold field?
2. Watch. 'Tis the more honor, because more dangerous.
3. Watch. Ay, but give me worship and quietness,
I like it better than a dangerous honor.
If Warwick knew in what estate he stands,
'Tis to be doubted he would waken him.
1. Watch. Unless our halberds did shut up his passage.
2. Watch. Ay; wherefore else guard we his royal tent
But to defend his person from night-foes?

Enter WARWICK, CLARENCE, OXFORD, SOMERSET, *and French Soldiers, silent all.*

War. This is his tent, and see where stand his guard.
Courage, my masters! honor now or never!
But follow me, and Edward shall be ours.
1. Watch. Who goes there?
2. Watch. Stay, or thou diest!

Warwick and the rest cry all, "Warwick! Warwick!" *and set upon the Guard, who fly, crying,* "Arm! arm!", *Warwick and the rest following them.*

The Drum playing and Trumpet sounding, enter WARWICK, SOMERSET, *and the rest, bringing the* KING [EDWARD] *out in his gown, sitting in a chair.* RICHARD [OF GLOUCESTER] *and* HASTINGS *flies over the stage.*

Som. What are they that fly there?
War. Richard and Hastings. Let them go, here is
The Duke.
K. Edw. The Duke? Why, Warwick, when we parted,
Thou call'dst me King.
War. Ay, but the case is alter'd.
When you disgrac'd me in my embassade,
Then I degraded you from being king,
And come now to create you Duke of York.
Alas, how should you govern any kingdom,
That know not how to use embassadors,
Nor how to be contented with one wife,
Nor how to use your brothers brotherly,
Nor how to study for the people's welfare,
Nor how to shroud yourself from enemies?
K. Edw. Yea, brother of Clarence, art thou here too?
Nay then I see that Edward needs must down.
Yet, Warwick, in despite of all mischance,
Of thee thyself and all thy complices,
Edward will always bear himself as king.
Though Fortune's malice overthrow my state,
My mind exceeds the compass of her wheel.
War. Then for his mind, be Edward England's king, *Takes off his crown.*

4. suddenly: quickly. **9. pawn'd:** pledged.
13. rests: remains. **coverture:** shadow.
15. lurking: lodging. **18. adventure:** venture.
19–21. That . . . steeds. After an oracle had said that Troy was safe so long as the horses of Rhesus, king of Thrace, grazed on the Trojan plain, Ulysses and Diomedes, in a daring raid by night, killed Rhesus and captured his horses. See *Iliad*, Book X.
23. At unawares: suddenly. **25. surprise:** capture.
28. sort: fashion. **29. Saint George:** patron saint of England.

IV.iii. Location: King Edward's camp, near Warwick.

13. lodge: sleep. **16. worship:** ease and dignity.
18. estate: condition. **19. doubted:** feared.
20. halberds: halberdiers, guards bearing long weapons with axe-like heads. **32. embassade:** embassy.

But Henry now shall wear the English crown,
And be true king indeed, thou but the shadow.
My Lord of Somerset, at my request,
See that forthwith Duke Edward be convey'd
Unto my brother, Archbishop of York.
When I have fought with Pembroke and his fellows,
I'll follow you, and tell what answer
Lewis and the Lady Bona send to him.
Now for awhile farewell, good Duke of York.

They lead him out forcibly.

K. Edw. What fates impose, that men must needs abide;
It boots not to resist both wind and tide.

Exit [guarded, with Somerset].

Oxf. What now remains, my lords, for us to do
But march to London with our soldiers?

War. Ay, that's the first thing that we have to do,
To free King Henry from imprisonment,
And see him seated in the regal throne. *Exeunt.*

[SCENE IV]

Enter RIVERS *and Lady Grey, [now* QUEEN ELIZABETH].

Riv. Madam, what makes you in this sudden change?

Q. Eliz. Why, brother Rivers, are you yet to learn
What late misfortune is befall'n King Edward?

Riv. What? loss of some pitch'd battle against Warwick?

Q. Eliz. No, but the loss of his own royal person.

Riv. Then is my sovereign slain?

Q. Eliz. Ay, almost slain, for he is taken prisoner,
Either betray'd by falsehood of his guard
Or by his foe surpris'd at unawares;
And as I further have to understand,
Is new committed to the Bishop of York,
Fell Warwick's brother, and by that our foe.

Riv. These news I must confess are full of grief,
Yet, gracious madam, bear it as you may:
Warwick may lose, that now hath won the day.

Q. Eliz. Till then fair hope must hinder live's decay;
And I the rather wain me from despair
For love of Edward's offspring in my womb.
This is it that makes me bridle passion,
And bear with mildness my misfortune's cross;
Ay, ay, for this I draw in many a tear,
And stop the rising of blood-sucking sighs,
Lest with my sighs or tears I blast or drown
King Edward's fruit, true heir to th' English crown.

Riv. But, madam, where is Warwick then become?

Q. Eliz. I am inform'd that he comes towards London

53. **brother:** i.e. George Neville (1433?–1476), a notable ecclesiastic and politician who was named chancellor of England in 1460 and again in 1470. 59. **boots:** helps.

IV.iv. Location: London. The palace.
16. **live's:** life's. 17. **wain:** wean.
22. **blood-sucking sighs.** Each sigh was thought to draw a drop of blood from the heart.

To set the crown once more on Henry's head.
Guess thou the rest; King Edward's friends must down.
But to prevent the tyrant's violence
(For trust not him that hath once broken faith),
I'll hence forthwith unto the sanctuary,
To save, at least, the heir of Edward's right;
There shall I rest secure from force and fraud.
Come therefore, let us fly while we may fly,
If Warwick take us we are sure to die. *Exeunt.*

[SCENE V]

Enter RICHARD [OF GLOUCESTER], LORD HASTINGS, *and* SIR WILLIAM STANLEY.

Glou. Now, my Lord Hastings and Sir William Stanley,
Leave off to wonder why I drew you hither
Into this chiefest thicket of the park.
Thus [stands] the case: you know our king, my brother,
Is prisoner to the Bishop here, at whose hands
He hath good usage and great liberty,
And often but attended with weak guard,
[Comes] hunting this way to disport himself.
I have advertis'd him by secret means
That if about this hour he make this way,
Under the color of his usual game,
He shall here find his friends with horse and men
To set him free from his captivity.

Enter KING EDWARD, *and a* HUNTSMAN *with him.*

Hunt. This way, my lord, for this way lies the game.

K. Edw. Nay, this way, man, see where the huntsmen stand.
Now, brother of Gloucester, Lord Hastings, and the rest,
Stand you thus close to steal the Bishop's deer?

Glou. Brother, the time and case requireth haste,
Your horse stands ready at the park-corner.

K. Edw. But whither shall we then?

Hast. To Lynn, my lord—
[*To Gloucester.*] And shipp'd from thence to Flanders?

Glou. Well guess'd, believe me, for that was my meaning.

K. Edw. Stanley, I will requite thy forwardness.

Glou. But wherefore stay we? 'tis no time to talk.

K. Edw. Huntsman, what say'st thou? Wilt thou go along?

Hunt. Better do so than tarry and be hang'd.

Glou. Come then away, let's ha' no more ado.

K. Edw. Bishop, farewell! shield thee from Warwick's frown,
And pray that I may repossess the crown. *Exeunt.*

29. **prevent:** forestall. 32. **right:** claim to the throne.

IV.v. Location: A park near Middleham Castle, in Yorkshire.
3. **chiefest thicket:** thickest section.
9. **advertis'd:** informed. 11. **color:** pretext.
17. **close:** hidden. 18. **case:** circumstances.
20. **Lynn:** seaport in Norfolk. 23. **forwardness:** zeal.

[Scene VI]

Flourish. Enter King Henry the Sixt, Clarence, Warwick, Somerset, *young* Henry [Richmond], Oxford, Montague, *and* Lieutenant [of the Tower].

K. Hen. Master Lieutenant, now that God and friends
Have shaken Edward from the regal seat,
And turn'd my captive state to liberty,
My fear to hope, my sorrows unto joys,
At our enlargement what are thy due fees?
Lieu. Subjects may challenge nothing of their sov'reigns,
But if an humble prayer may prevail,
I then crave pardon of your Majesty.
K. Hen. For what, Lieutenant? For well using me?
Nay, be thou sure, I'll well requite thy kindness,
For that it made my imprisonment a pleasure;
Ay, such a pleasure as incaged birds
Conceive, when, after many moody thoughts,
At last by notes of household harmony
They quite forget their loss of liberty.
But, Warwick, after God, thou set'st me free,
And chiefly therefore I thank God and thee.
He was the author, thou the instrument.
Therefore that I may conquer fortune's spite
By living low, where fortune cannot hurt me,
And that the people of this blessed land
May not be punish'd with my thwarting stars,
Warwick, although my head still wear the crown,
I here resign my government to thee,
For thou art fortunate in all thy deeds.
War. Your Grace hath still been fam'd for virtuous,
And now may seem as wise as virtuous
By spying and avoiding fortune's malice,
For few men rightly temper with the stars;
Yet in this one thing let me blame your Grace,
For choosing me when Clarence is in place.
Clar. No, Warwick, thou art worthy of the sway,
To whom the heav'ns in thy nativity
Adjudg'd an olive branch and laurel crown,
As likely to be blest in peace and war;
And therefore I yield thee my free consent.
War. And I choose Clarence only for Protector.
K. Hen. Warwick and Clarence, give me both your hands.
Now join your hands, and with your hands your hearts,
That no dissension hinder government.
I make you both Protectors of this land,
While I myself will lead a private life,
And in devotion spend my latter days,
To sin's rebuke and my Creator's praise.
War. What answers Clarence to his sovereign's will?
Clar. That he consents, if Warwick yield consent,

IV.vi. Location: London. The Tower.
5. enlargement: setting free.
22. thwarting stars: i.e. evil fortune. 26. still: always.
29. rightly . . . stars: adjust themselves to their destiny.
43. latter: last.

For on thy fortune I repose myself.
War. Why then, though loath, yet must I be content.
We'll yoke together like a double shadow
To Henry's body, and supply his place;
I mean, in bearing weight of government,
While he enjoys the honor and his ease.
And, Clarence, now then it is more than needful
Forthwith that Edward be pronounc'd a traitor,
And all his lands and goods confiscate.
Clar. What else? and that succession be determined.
War. Ay, therein Clarence shall not want his part.
K. Hen. But with the first of all your chief affairs,
Let me entreat (for I command no more)
That Margaret your queen and my son Edward
Be sent for, to return from France with speed;
For till I see them here, by doubtful fear
My joy of liberty is half eclips'd.
Clar. It shall be done, my sovereign, with all speed.
K. Hen. My Lord of Somerset, what youth is that
Of whom you seem to have so tender care?
Som. My liege, it is young Henry, Earl of Richmond.
K. Hen. Come hither, England's hope. (*Lays his hand on his head.*) If secret powers
Suggest but truth to my divining thoughts,
This pretty lad will prove our country's bliss.
His looks are full of peaceful majesty,
His head by nature fram'd to wear a crown,
His hand to wield a sceptre, and himself
Likely in time to bless a regal throne.
Make much of him, my lords, for this is he
Must help you more than you are hurt by me.

Enter a Post.

War. What news, my friend?
Post. That Edward is escaped from your brother,
And fled (as he hears since) to Burgundy.
War. Unsavory news! but how made he escape?
Post. He was convey'd by Richard, Duke of Gloucester,
And the Lord Hastings, who attended him
In secret ambush on the forest side,
And from the Bishop's huntsmen rescu'd him;
For hunting was his daily exercise.
War. My brother was too careless of his charge.
But let us hence, my sovereign, to provide
A salve for any sore that may betide.

Exeunt. Manent Somerset, Richmond, and Oxford.

Som. My lord, I like not of this flight of Edward's;
For doubtless Burgundy will yield him help,
And we shall have more wars before't be long.
As Henry's late presaging prophecy
Did glad my heart with hope of this young Richmond,
So doth my heart misgive me, in these conflicts
What may befall him, to his harm and ours.
Therefore, Lord Oxford, to prevent the worst,
Forthwith we'll send him hence to Brittany,

67. Henry . . . Richmond: Henry Tudor (1457–1509), later Henry VII, founder of the Tudor dynasty. See note to *Richard III*, I.iii.20.
82. attended: awaited. 88. betide: occur, come about.

Till storms be past of civil enmity.
Oxf. Ay; for if Edward repossess the crown,
'Tis like that Richmond with the rest shall down.
Som. It shall be so; he shall to Brittany.
Come therefore, let's about it speedily. *Exeunt.*

[SCENE VII]

Flourish. Enter [KING] EDWARD, RICHARD [OF GLOUCESTER], HASTINGS, *and Soldiers* [*a troop of Hollanders*].

K. Edw. Now, brother Richard, Lord Hastings, and the rest,
Yet thus far fortune maketh us amends,
And says that once more I shall interchange
My waned state for Henry's regal crown.
Well have we pass'd and now repass'd the seas,
And brought desired help from Burgundy.
What then remains, we being thus arriv'd
From Ravenspurgh haven before the gates of York,
But that we enter as into our dukedom?
Glou. The gates made fast? Brother, I like not this;
For many men that stumble at the threshold
Are well foretold that danger lurks within.
K. Edw. Tush, man, abodements must not now affright us.
By fair or foul means we must enter in,
For hither will our friends repair to us.
Hast. My liege, I'll knock once more to summon them.

Enter on the walls the MAYOR OF YORK *and his brethren* [*the* ALDERMEN].

May. My lords, we were forewarned of your coming,
And shut the gates for safety of ourselves;
For now we owe allegiance unto Henry.
K. Edw. But, Master Mayor, if Henry be your king,
Yet Edward, at the least, is Duke of York.
May. True, my good lord, I know you for no less.
K. Edw. Why, and I challenge nothing but my dukedom,
As being well content with that alone.
Glou. [*Aside.*] But when the fox hath once got in his nose,
He'll soon find means to make the body follow.
Hast. Why, Master Mayor, why stand you in a doubt?
Open the gates, we are King Henry's friends.
May. Ay, say you so? The gates shall then be opened. *He descends* [*with the Aldermen*].
Glou. A wise stout captain, and soon persuaded!
Hast. The good old man would fain that all were well,
So 'twere not long of him; but being ent'red,
I doubt not, I, but we shall soon persuade
Both him and all his brothers unto reason.

Enter the MAYOR *and two* ALDERMEN [*below*].

K. Edw. So, Master Mayor; these gates must not be shut,
But in the night, or in the time of war.
What, fear not, man, but yield me up the keys, *Takes his keys.*
For Edward will defend the town and thee,
And all those friends that deign to follow me.

March. Enter MONTGOMERY *with Drum and Soldiers.*

Glou. Brother, this is Sir John Montgomery,
Our trusty friend, unless I be deceiv'd.
K. Edw. Welcome, Sir John! but why come you in arms?
Montg. To help King Edward in his time of storm,
As every loyal subject ought to do.
K. Edw. Thanks, good Montgomery; but we now forget
Our title to the crown, and only claim
Our dukedom, till God please to send the rest.
Montg. Then fare you well, for I will hence again,
I came to serve a king and not a duke.
Drummer, strike up, and let us march away.
The Drum begins to march.
K. Edw. Nay, stay, Sir John, a while, and we'll debate
By what safe means the crown may be recover'd.
Montg. What talk you of debating? In few words,
If you'll not here proclaim yourself our king,
I'll leave you to your fortune, and be gone
To keep them back that come to succor you.
Why shall we fight if you pretend no title?
Glou. Why, brother, wherefore stand you on nice points?
K. Edw. When we grow stronger, then we'll make our claim;
Till then, 'tis wisdom to conceal our meaning.
Hast. Away with scrupulous wit! now arms must rule.
Glou. And fearless minds climb soonest unto crowns.
Brother, we will proclaim you out of hand,
The bruit thereof will bring you many friends.
K. Edw. Then be it as you will; for 'tis my right,
And Henry but usurps the diadem.
Montg. Ay, now my sovereign speaketh like himself,
And now will I be Edward's champion.
Hast. Sound trumpet, Edward shall be here proclaim'd.
Come, fellow soldier, make thou proclamation.
[*Gives him a paper.*] *Flourish. Sound.*
Sold. [*Reads.*] "Edward the Fourth, by the grace of God, King of England and France, and Lord of Ireland, etc."

IV.vii. Location: Before York.
8. Ravenspurgh: i.e. Ravenspur, former seaport on the coast of Yorkshire. 13. abodements: evil omens.
23. challenge: claim. 31. fain: be glad.
32. long of him: owing to him, i.e. his responsibility.

39. deign: are willing. 57. pretend: claim.
58. nice: meticulous. 61. scrupulous wit: prudent wisdom.
64. bruit: report.

Montg. And whosoe'er gainsays King Edward's right,
By this I challenge him to single fight.
Throws down his gauntlet.
All. Long live Edward the Fourth!
K. Edw. Thanks, brave Montgomery, and thanks unto you all.
If fortune serve me, I'll requite this kindness.
Now for this night, let's harbor here in York;
And when the morning sun shall raise his car
Above the border of this horizon,
We'll forward towards Warwick and his mates;
For well I wot that Henry is no soldier.
Ah, froward Clarence, how evil it beseems thee
To flatter Henry and forsake thy brother!
Yet as we may, we'll meet both thee and Warwick.
Come on, brave soldiers; doubt not of the day,
And that once gotten, doubt not of large pay.
Exeunt.

[SCENE VIII]

Flourish. Enter the KING [HENRY], WARWICK, MONTAGUE, CLARENCE, OXFORD, *and* [EXETER].

War. What counsel, lords? Edward from Belgia,
With hasty Germans and blunt Hollanders,
Hath pass'd in safety through the Narrow Seas,
And with his troops doth march amain to London,
And many giddy people flock to him.
K. Hen. Let's levy men, and beat him back again.
Clar. A little fire is quickly trodden out,
Which being suffer'd, rivers cannot quench.
War. In Warwickshire I have true-hearted friends,
Not mutinous in peace, yet bold in war;
Those will I muster up; and thou, son Clarence,
Shalt stir up in Suffolk, Norfolk, and in Kent,
The knights and gentlemen to come with thee.
Thou, brother Montague, in Buckingham,
Northampton, and in Leicestershire, shalt find
Men well inclin'd to hear what thou command'st;
And thou, brave Oxford, wondrous well belov'd,
In Oxfordshire shalt muster up thy friends.
My sovereign, with the loving citizens,
Like to his island, girt in with the ocean,
Or modest Dian, circled with her nymphs,
Shall rest in London till we come to him.
Fair lords, take leave and stand not to reply.
Farewell, my sovereign.
K. Hen. Farewell, my Hector, and my Troy's true hope.
Clar. In sign of truth, I kiss your Highness' hand.
K. Hen. Well-minded Clarence, be thou fortunate!
Mont. Comfort, my lord! and so I take my leave.
Oxf. And thus [*kissing Henry's hand*] I seal my truth, and bid adieu.
K. Hen. Sweet Oxford, and my loving Montague,
And all at once, once more a happy farewell. 31

IV.viii. Location: London. The Bishop of London's palace.
1. Belgia: i.e. the Low Countries.
2. hasty: quick-tempered. **blunt:** harsh.
4. amain: with full speed. **11. son:** i.e. son-in-law.
21. Dian: Diana, the moon-goddess.
25. Hector: i.e. protector. **31. at once:** together.

War. Farewell, sweet lords, let's meet at Coventry.
Exeunt [*all but King Henry and Exeter*].
K. Hen. Here at the palace will I rest a while.
Cousin of Exeter, what thinks your lordship?
Methinks the power that Edward hath in field
Should not be able to encounter mine.
Exe. The doubt is that he will seduce the rest.
K. Hen. That's not my fear, my meed hath got me fame:
I have not stopp'd mine ears to their demands,
Nor posted off their suits with slow delays;
My pity hath been balm to heal their wounds,
My mildness hath allay'd their swelling griefs,
My mercy dried their water-flowing tears;
I have not been desirous of their wealth,
Nor much oppress'd them with great subsidies,
Nor forward of revenge, though they much err'd.
Then why should they love Edward more than me?
No, Exeter, these graces challenge grace;
And when the lion fawns upon the lamb,
The lamb will never cease to follow him.
Shout within, "A Lancaster! A Lancaster!"
Exe. Hark, hark, my lord, what shouts are these?

Enter [KING] EDWARD *and his Soldiers* [*with* GLOUCESTER *and others*].

K. Edw. Seize on the shame-fac'd Henry, bear him hence,
And once again proclaim us King of England.
You are the fount that makes small brooks to flow;
Now stops thy spring, my sea shall suck them dry,
And swell so much the higher by their ebb. 56
Hence with him to the Tower, let him not speak.
Exit [*Exeter*] *with King Henry* [*guarded*].
And, lords, towards Coventry bend we our course,
Where peremptory Warwick now remains.
The sun shines hot, and, if we use delay,
Cold biting winter mars our hop'd-for hay.
Glou. Away betimes, before his forces join,
And take the great-grown traitor unawares.
Brave warriors, march amain towards Coventry.
Exeunt.

[ACT V, SCENE I]

Enter WARWICK, *the* MAYOR OF COVENTRY, *two* MESSENGERS, *and others, upon the walls.*

War. Where is the post that came from valiant Oxford?
How far hence is thy lord, mine honest fellow?
1. Mess. By this at Dunsmore, marching hitherward.
War. How far off is our brother Montague?
Where is the post that came from Montague?

37. doubt: fear.
38. my . . . fame: my merits (for dealing justly) have secured my reputation. **40. posted off:** postponed.
45. subsidies: special taxes. **46. forward of:** eager for.
48. challenge grace: claim favor. **52. shame-fac'd:** shy.
59. peremptory: overbearing.

V.i. Location: Coventry.
3. Dunsmore: hamlet in eastern Warwickshire.

2. Mess. By this at Daintry, with a puissant troop.
Enter [SIR JOHN] SOMERVILE.
War. Say, Somervile, what says my loving son?
And, by thy guess, how nigh is Clarence now?
Som. At Southam I did leave him with his forces,
And do expect him here some two hours hence.
[*Drum heard.*]
War. Then Clarence is at hand, I hear his drum.
Som. It is not his, my lord, here Southam lies;
The drum your honor hears marcheth from Warwick.
War. Who should that be? belike unlook'd-for friends.
Som. They are at hand, and you shall quickly know.

March. Flourish. Enter [KING] EDWARD, RICHARD [OF GLOUCESTER], *and Soldiers.*

K. Edw. Go, trumpet, to the walls, and sound a parle.
Glou. See how the surly Warwick mans the wall!
War. O unbid spite, is sportful Edward come?
Where slept our scouts, or how are they seduc'd,
That we could hear no news of his repair?
K. Edw. Now, Warwick, wilt thou ope the city-gates,
Speak gentle words and humbly bend thy knee,
Call Edward king and at his hands beg mercy?
And he shall pardon thee these outrages.
War. Nay rather, wilt thou draw thy forces hence,
Confess who set thee up and pluck'd thee down,
Call Warwick patron, and be penitent?
And thou shalt still remain the Duke of York.
Glou. I thought, at least, he would have said the King,
Or did he make the jest against his will?
War. Is not a dukedom, sir, a goodly gift?
Glou. Ay, by my faith, for a poor earl to give.
I'll do thee service for so good a gift.
War. 'Twas I that gave the kingdom to thy brother.
K. Edw. Why then 'tis mine, if but by Warwick's gift.
War. Thou art no Atlas for so great a weight;
And, weakling, Warwick takes his gift again,
And Henry is my king, Warwick his subject.
K. Edw. But Warwick's king is Edward's prisoner.
And, gallant Warwick, do but answer this:
What is the body when the head is off?
Glou. Alas, that Warwick had no more forecast,
But, whiles he thought to steal the single ten,
The king was slily finger'd from the deck!
You left poor Henry at the Bishop's palace,
And ten to one you'll meet him in the Tower.

6. **Daintry:** i.e. Daventry, a town in Northamptonshire.
9. **Southam:** hamlet in Gloucestershire.
13. **Warwick:** town south of Coventry.
16. **parle:** signal for a parley.
18. **unbid:** uninvited, i.e. unwelcome. **sportful:** lascivious.
20. **repair:** approach.
36. **Atlas:** in classical mythology, the Titan who upheld the heavens with his hands and shoulders.
43. **single ten:** mere ten-card. 44. **finger'd:** stolen.

K. Edw. 'Tis even so, yet you are Warwick still.
Glou. Come, Warwick, take the time, kneel down, kneel down.
Nay, when? strike now, or else the iron cools.
War. I had rather chop this hand off at a blow,
And with the other fling it at thy face,
Than bear so low a sail to strike to thee.
K. Edw. Sail how thou canst, have wind and tide thy friend,
This hand, fast wound about thy coal-black hair,
Shall, whiles thy head is warm and new cut off,
Write in the dust this sentence with thy blood:
"Wind-changing Warwick now can change no more."

Enter OXFORD *with Drum and Colors.*

War. O cheerful colors! see where Oxford comes!
Oxf. Oxford, Oxford, for Lancaster!
[*He and his forces enter the city.*]
Glou. The gates are open, let us enter too.
K. Edw. So other foes may set upon our backs.
Stand we in good array; for they no doubt
Will issue out again and bid us battle.
If not, the city being but of small defense,
We'll quickly rouse the traitors in the same.
War. O, welcome, Oxford, for we want thy help.

Enter MONTAGUE *with Drum and Colors.*

Mont. Montague, Montague, for Lancaster!
[*He and his forces enter the city.*]
Glou. Thou and thy brother both shall buy this treason
Even with the dearest blood your bodies bear.
K. Edw. The harder match'd, the greater victory:
My mind presageth happy gain and conquest.

Enter SOMERSET *with Drum and Colors.*

Som. Somerset, Somerset, for Lancaster!
[*He and his forces enter the city.*]
Glou. Two of thy name, both Dukes of Somerset,
Have sold their lives unto the house of York,
And thou shalt be the third, [and] this sword hold.

Enter CLARENCE *with Drum and Colors.*

War. And lo, where George of Clarence sweeps along,
Of force enough to bid his brother battle;
With whom [an] upright zeal to right prevails
More than the nature of a brother's love!
[*Gloucester and Clarence whisper together.*]
Come, Clarence, come; thou wilt, if Warwick call.
Clar. Father of Warwick, know you what this means?
Look here, I throw my infamy at thee.
[*Clarence takes his red rose out of his hat and throws it at Warwick.*]

48. **take the time:** seize the opportunity.
52. **strike:** lower sail (in token of submission).
57 s.d. **Colors:** flagbearers. 61. **backs:** rear (of army).
65. **rouse . . . in:** drive . . . from.
73–74. **Two . . . York.** Edmund Beaufort, second Duke of Somerset, was killed while fighting for the Lancastrians at the first battle of St. Albans in 1455, and his son and heir Henry was executed by the Yorkists in 1464. 75. **and:** if.

I will not ruinate my father's house,
Who gave his blood to lime the stones together,
And set up Lancaster. Why, trowest thou, Warwick,
That Clarence is so harsh, so blunt, unnatural,
To bend the fatal instruments of war
Against his brother and his lawful king?
Perhaps thou wilt object my holy oath:
To keep that oath were more impiety
Than Jephthah when he sacrific'd his daughter.
I am so sorry for my trespass made
That to deserve well at my brother's hands,
I here proclaim myself thy mortal foe;
With resolution, wheresoe'er I meet thee
(As I will meet thee, if thou stir abroad),
To plague thee for thy foul misleading me.
And so, proud-hearted Warwick, I defy thee,
And to my brother turn my blushing cheeks.
Pardon me, Edward, I will make amends;
And, Richard, do not frown upon my faults,
For I will henceforth be no more unconstant.

K. Edw. Now welcome more, and ten times more belov'd,
Than if thou never hadst deserv'd our hate.

Glou. Welcome, good Clarence, this is brother-like.

War. O passing traitor, perjur'd and unjust!

K. Edw. What, Warwick, wilt thou leave the town, and fight?
Or shall we beat the stones about thine ears?

War. Alas, I am not coop'd here for defense!
I will away towards Barnet presently,
And bid thee battle, Edward, if thou dar'st.

K. Edw. Yes, Warwick, Edward dares, and leads the way.
Lords, to the field! Saint George and victory!

Exeunt [*King Edward and his company*]. *March. Warwick and his company follows.*

[Scene II]

Alarum and excursions. Enter [King] Edward, *bringing forth* Warwick *wounded.*

K. Edw. So, lie thou there. Die thou, and die our fear,
For Warwick was a bug that fear'd us all.
Now, Montague, sit fast, I seek for thee,
That Warwick's bones may keep thine company.
Exit.

War. Ah, who is nigh? Come to me, friend or foe,
And tell me who is victor, York or Warwick?
Why ask I that? My mangled body shows,
My blood, my want of strength, my sick heart shows,
That I must yield my body to the earth,
And by my fall, the conquest to my foe.
Thus yields the cedar to the axe's edge,
Whose arms gave shelter to the princely eagle,
Under whose shade the ramping lion slept,
Whose top-branch overpeer'd Jove's spreading tree,
And kept low shrubs from winter's pow'rful wind.
These eyes, that now are dimm'd with death's black veil,
Have been as piercing as the midday sun
To search the secret treasons of the world.
The wrinkles in my brows, now fill'd with blood,
Were lik'ned oft to kingly sepulchres;
For who liv'd king, but I could dig his grave?
And who durst smile when Warwick bent his brow?
Lo, now my glory smear'd in dust and blood!
My parks, my walks, my manors that I had,
Even now forsake me; and of all my lands
Is nothing left me but my body's length.
Why, what is pomp, rule, reign, but earth and dust?
And live we how we can, yet die we must.

Enter Oxford *and* Somerset.

Som. Ah, Warwick, Warwick, wert thou as we are,
We might recover all our loss again.
The Queen from France hath brought a puissant power;
Even now we heard the news. Ah, couldst thou fly!

War. Why then I would not fly. Ah, Montague,
If thou be there, sweet brother, take my hand,
And with thy lips keep in my soul a while.
Thou lov'st me not; for, brother, if thou didst,
Thy tears would wash this cold congealed blood
That glues my lips and will not let me speak.
Come quickly, Montague, or I am dead.

Som. Ah, Warwick, Montague hath breath'd his last,
And to the latest gasp cried out for Warwick,
And said, "Commend me to my valiant brother."
And more he would have said, and more he spoke,
Which sounded like a cannon in a vault,
That mought not be distinguish'd; but at last
I well might hear, delivered with a groan,
"O, farewell, Warwick!"

War. Sweet rest his soul! Fly, lords, and save yourselves,
For Warwick bids you all farewell, to meet in heaven. [*He dies.*]

Oxf. Away, away, to meet the Queen's great power! *Here they bear away his body. Exeunt.*

[Scene III]

Flourish. Enter King Edward *in triumph, with* Richard [of Gloucester], Clarence, *and the rest.*

K. Edw. Thus far our fortune keeps an upward course,
And we are grac'd with wreaths of victory.
But in the midst of this bright-shining day,

84. lime: cement. **85. trowest:** thinkest. **89. object:** urge.
91. Jephthah: a judge of Israel who sacrificed his daughter to Jehovah in fulfillment of a vow that if victorious in battle he would offer up whoever met him first on his return. See Judges 11:30–40.
106. passing: surpassing.
110. Barnet: town in Hertfordshire. **presently:** immediately.

V.ii. Location: A field of battle near Barnet.
2. bug: bugbear. **fear'd:** frightened.

13. ramping: upreared, rampant.
14. Jove's spreading tree: i.e. the oak. **41. latest:** last.
45. mought: might.

V.iii. Location: Scene continues.

I spy a black, suspicious, threat'ning cloud,
That will encounter with our glorious sun,
Ere he attain his easeful western bed:
I mean, my lords, those powers that the Queen
Hath rais'd in Gallia have arriv'd our coast,
And as we hear, march on to fight with us.
Clar. A little gale will soon disperse that cloud,
And blow it to the source from whence it came;
Thy very beams will dry those vapors up,
For every cloud engenders not a storm.
Glou. The Queen is valued thirty thousand strong,
And Somerset, with Oxford, fled to her;
If she have time to breathe, be well assur'd
Her faction will be full as strong as ours.
K. Edw. We are advertis'd by our loving friends
That they do hold their course toward Tewksbury.
We, having now the best at Barnet field,
Will thither straight, for willingness rids way,
And as we march, our strength will be augmented
In every county as we go along.
Strike up the drum, cry "Courage!" and away.
Exeunt.

[Scene IV]

Flourish. March. Enter the Queen [Margaret], *young* [Prince] Edward, Somerset, Oxford, *and Soldiers.*

Q. Mar. Great lords, wise men ne'er sit and wail their loss,
But cheerly seek how to redress their harms.
What though the mast be now blown overboard,
The cable broke, the holding-anchor lost,
And half our sailors swallow'd in the flood?
Yet lives our pilot still. Is't meet that he
Should leave the helm and, like a fearful lad,
With tearful eyes add water to the sea,
And give more strength to that which hath too much,
Whiles, in his moan, the ship splits on the rock,
Which industry and courage might have sav'd?
Ah, what a shame, ah, what a fault were this!
Say Warwick was our anchor; what of that?
And Montague our topmast; what of him?
Our slaught'red friends the tackles; what of these?
Why, is not Oxford here another anchor?
And Somerset another goodly mast?
The friends of France our shrouds and tacklings?
And though unskillful, why not Ned and I
For once allow'd the skillful pilot's charge?
We will not from the helm to sit and weep,
But keep our course (though the rough wind say no)
From shelves and rocks that threaten us with wrack.
As good to chide the waves as speak them fair.
And what is Edward but a ruthless sea?
What Clarence but a quicksand of deceit?
And Richard but a [ragged] fatal rock?
All these the enemies to our poor bark.
Say you can swim, alas, 'tis but a while;
Tread on the sand, why, there you quickly sink;
Bestride the rock, the tide will wash you off,
Or else you famish—that's a threefold death.
This speak I, lords, to let you understand,
If case some one of you would fly from us,
That there's no hop'd-for mercy with the brothers
More than with ruthless waves, with sands and rocks.
Why, courage then! what cannot be avoided,
'Twere childish weakness to lament or fear.
Prince. Methinks a woman of this valiant spirit
Should, if a coward heard her speak these words,
Infuse his breast with magnanimity,
And make him, naked, foil a man at arms.
I speak not this as doubting any here;
For did I but suspect a fearful man,
He should have leave to go away betimes,
Lest in our need he might infect another,
And make him of like spirit to himself.
If any such be here—as God forbid!—
Let him depart before we need his help.
Oxf. Women and children of so high a courage,
And warriors faint! why, 'twere perpetual shame.
O brave young prince! thy famous grandfather
Doth live again in thee. Long mayst thou live
To bear his image and renew his glories!
Som. And he that will not fight for such a hope
Go home to bed, and like the owl by day,
If he arise, be mock'd and wond'red at.
Q. Mar. Thanks, gentle Somerset, sweet Oxford, thanks.
Prince. And take his thanks that yet hath nothing else.

Enter a Messenger.

Mess. Prepare you, lords, for Edward is at hand,
Ready to fight; therefore be resolute.
Oxf. I thought no less; it is his policy
To haste thus fast, to find us unprovided.
Som. But he's deceiv'd, we are in readiness.
Q. Mar. This cheers my heart, to see your forwardness.
Oxf. Here pitch our battle, hence we will not budge.

Flourish and march. Enter [King] Edward, Richard [of Gloucester], Clarence, *and Soldiers.*

K. Edw. Brave followers, yonder stands the thorny wood,
Which by the heavens' assistance and your strength,
Must by the roots be hewn up yet ere night.
I need not add more fuel to your fire,
For well I wot ye blaze to burn them out.
Give signal to the fight, and to it, lords!
Q. Mar. Lords, knights, and gentlemen, what I should say
My tears gainsay; for every word I speak,
Ye see I drink the water of my eye.

8. Gallia: France. **16. breathe:** i.e. collect her strength.
18. advertis'd: informed.
19. Tewksbury: Tewkesbury, a town at the confluence of the Avon and the Severn in Gloucestershire.
21. rids way: makes for rapid progress.

V.iv. Location: Plains near Tewkesbury.
18. shrouds: sails. **20. charge:** responsibility.
23. shelves: shoals. **wrack:** destruction.

34. If case: in case. **42. foil:** overcome.
54. image: likeness. **63. unprovided:** unprepared.
66. pitch our battle: draw up our forces.

Therefore no more but this: Henry, your sovereign,
Is prisoner to the foe, his state usurp'd,
His realm a slaughter-house, his subjects slain,
His statutes cancell'd, and his treasure spent;
And yonder is the wolf that makes this spoil.
You fight in justice; then in God's name, lords,
Be valiant, and give signal to the fight.

Alarum [to the battle]. Retreat. [King Edward, with his followers, flies]. Excursions; [the chambers be discharged. Then enter King Edward, Clarence, Gloucester, and the rest of the King's followers and make a great shout, and cry, "For York! for York!"; *and then Queen Margaret is taken, and Prince Edward and Oxford and Somerset.] Exeunt.*

[SCENE V]

Flourish. *Enter* [KING] EDWARD, RICHARD [OF GLOUCESTER *with*] QUEEN [MARGARET *prisoner*], CLARENCE, [*and Soldiers with*] OXFORD, SOMERSET [*prisoners*].

K. Edw. Now here a period of tumultuous broils.
Away with Oxford to Hames Castle straight;
For Somerset, off with his guilty head.
Go bear them hence, I will not hear them speak.
Oxf. For my part, I'll not trouble thee with words.
Som. Nor I, but stoop with patience to my fortune.

Exeunt [Oxford and Somerset, guarded].

Q. Mar. So part we sadly in this troublous world,
To meet with joy in sweet Jerusalem.
K. Edw. Is proclamation made, that who finds Edward
Shall have a high reward, and he his life?
Glou. It is, and lo where youthful Edward comes!

Enter [Soldiers with] the PRINCE [EDWARD].

K. Edw. Bring forth the gallant, let us hear him speak.
What? can so young a thorn begin to prick?
Edward, what satisfaction canst thou make
For bearing arms, for stirring up my subjects,
And all the trouble thou hast turn'd me to?
Prince. Speak like a subject, proud ambitious York!
Suppose that I am now my father's mouth:
Resign thy chair, and where I stand kneel thou,
Whilst I propose the self-same words to thee,
Which, traitor, thou wouldst have me answer to.
Q. Mar. Ah, that thy father had been so resolv'd!
Glou. That you might still have worn the petticoat,
And ne'er have stol'n the breech from Lancaster.
Prince. Let Aesop fable in a winter's night,
His currish riddles sorts not with this place.

82 s.d. chambers: short cannon.

V.v. Location: Scene continues.
1. period: end.
2. Hames Castle: i.e. Hanmes, a castle near Calais. Actually, Oxford, who did not fight at Tewkesbury, was not apprehended and imprisoned until 1474, three years after the time represented in this scene.
24. breech: breeches.
25. Aesop: Greek fabulist who (like Gloucester) was deformed.
26. sorts: agree.

Glou. By heaven, brat, I'll plague ye for that word.
Q. Mar. Ay, thou wast born to be a plague to men.
Glou. For God's sake, take away this captive scold.
Prince. Nay, take away this scolding crook-back, rather.
K. Edw. Peace, willful boy, or I will charm your tongue.
Clar. Untutor'd lad, thou art too malapert.
Prince. I know my duty, you are all undutiful.
Lascivious Edward, and thou perjur'd George,
And thou misshapen Dick, I tell ye all
I am your better, traitors as ye are,
And thou usurp'st my father's right and mine.
K. Edw. Take that, the likeness of this railer here.

Stabs him.

Glou. Sprawl'st thou? take that, to end thy agony.

Richard stabs him.

Clar. And there's for twitting me with perjury.

Clarence stabs him.

Q. Mar. O, kill me too!
Glou. Marry, and shall. *Offers to kill her.*
K. Edw. Hold, Richard, hold, for we have done too much.
Glou. Why should she live, to fill the world with words?
K. Edw. What? doth she swoun? Use means for her recovery.
Glou. Clarence, excuse me to the King my brother;
I'll hence to London on a serious matter.
Ere ye come there, be sure to hear some news.
Clar. What? what?
Glou. [The] Tower, the Tower. *Exit.*
Q. Mar. O Ned, sweet Ned, speak to thy mother, boy!
Canst thou not speak? O traitors, murtherers!
They that stabb'd Caesar shed no blood at all,
Did not offend, nor were not worthy blame,
If this foul deed were by to equal it.
He was a man; this, in respect, a child,
And men ne'er spend their fury on a child.
What's worse than murtherer, that I may name it?
No, no, my heart will burst and if I speak,
And I will speak, that so my heart may burst.
Butchers and villains! bloody cannibals!
How sweet a plant have you untimely cropp'd!
You have no children, butchers; if you had,
The thought of them would have stirr'd up remorse,
But if you ever chance to have a child,
Look in his youth to have him so cut off
As, deathsmen, you have rid this sweet young prince!
K. Edw. Away with her, go bear her hence perforce.
Q. Mar. Nay, never bear me hence, dispatch me here;
Here sheathe thy sword, I'll pardon thee my death.
What? wilt thou not? Then, Clarence, do it thou.
Clar. By heaven, I will not do thee so much ease.

31. charm: cast a spell upon, silence.
32. malapert: impudent. 38. this railer: i.e. Margaret.
39. Sprawl'st: i.e. twitching in the agony of death.
45. swoun: swoon. 48. be sure: expect.
56. in respect: by comparison. 67. rid: removed.

Q. Mar. Good Clarence, do; sweet Clarence, do thou do it.

Clar. Didst thou not hear me swear I would not do it?

Q. Mar. Ay, but thou usest to forswear thyself.
'Twas sin before, but now 'tis charity.
What, wilt thou not? Where is that devil's butcher,
Hard-favor'd Richard? Richard, where art thou?
Thou art not here. Murther is thy alms-deed;
Petitioners for blood thou ne'er put'st back.

K. Edw. Away I say, I charge ye bear her hence.

Q. Mar. So come to you, and yours, as to this prince! *Exit Queen [Margaret, led out forcibly].*

K. Edw. Where's Richard gone?

Clar. To London, all in post, and as I guess,
To make a bloody supper in the Tower.

K. Edw. He's sudden, if a thing comes in his head.
Now march we hence. Discharge the common sort
With pay and thanks, and let's away to London
And see our gentle queen how well she fares.
By this, I hope, she hath a son for me. *Exeunt.*

[Scene VI]

Enter Henry the Sixt *and* Richard [of Gloucester] *with the* Lieutenant, *on the walls.*

Glou. Good day, my lord. What, at your book so hard?

K. Hen. Ay, my good lord—my lord, I should say rather.
'Tis sin to flatter, "good" was little better:
"Good Gloucester" and "good devil" were alike,
And both preposterous; therefore, not "good lord."

Glou. Sirrah, leave us to ourselves, we must confer. *[Exit Lieutenant.]*

K. Hen. So flies the reakless shepherd from the wolf;
So first the harmless sheep doth yield his fleece,
And next his throat unto the butcher's knife.
What scene of death hath Roscius now to act?

Glou. Suspicion always haunts the guilty mind;
The thief doth fear each bush an officer.

K. Hen. The bird that hath been limed in a bush,
With trembling wings misdoubteth every bush;
And I, the hapless male to one sweet bird,
Have now the fatal object in my eye
Where my poor young was lim'd, was caught, and kill'd.

Glou. Why, what a peevish fool was that of Crete
That taught his son the office of a fowl!
And yet, for all his wings, the fool was drown'd.

K. Hen. I, Daedalus; my poor boy, Icarus;
Thy father, Minos, that denied our course;
The sun that sear'd the wings of my sweet boy,
Thy brother Edward; and thyself, the sea
Whose envious gulf did swallow up his life.
Ah, kill me with thy weapon, not with words!
My breast can better brook thy dagger's point
Than can my ears that tragic history.
But wherefore dost thou come? Is't for my life?

Glou. Think'st thou I am an executioner?

K. Hen. A persecutor I am sure thou art.
If murthering innocents be executing,
Why then thou art an executioner.

Glou. Thy son I kill'd for his presumption.

K. Hen. Hadst thou been kill'd when first thou didst presume,
Thou hadst not liv'd to kill a son of mine.
And thus I prophesy, that many a thousand
Which now mistrust no parcel of my fear,
And many an old man's sigh and many a widow's,
And many an orphan's water-standing eye—
Men for their sons, wives for their husbands,
Orphans for their parents' timeless death—
Shall rue the hour that ever thou wast born.
The owl shriek'd at thy birth, an evil sign;
The night-crow cried, aboding luckless time;
Dogs howl'd, and hideous tempest shook down trees;
The raven rook'd her on the chimney's top,
And chatt'ring pies in dismal discords sung;
Thy mother felt more than a mother's pain,
And yet brought forth less than a mother's hope,
To wit, an indigested and deformed lump,
Not like the fruit of such a goodly tree.
Teeth hadst thou in thy head when thou wast born,
To signify thou cam'st to bite the world;
And if the rest be true which I have heard,
Thou cam'st—

Glou. I'll hear no more; die, prophet, in thy speech: *Stabs him.*
For this, amongst the rest, was I ordain'd.

K. Hen. Ay, and for much more slaughter after this.
O God forgive my sins, and pardon thee! *Dies.*

Glou. What? will the aspiring blood of Lancaster
Sink in the ground? I thought it would have mounted.
See how my sword weeps for the poor king's death!
O may such purple tears be alway shed
From those that wish the downfall of our house!
If any spark of life be yet remaining,
Down, down to hell, and say I sent thee thither— *Stabs him again.*
I, that have neither pity, love, nor fear.
Indeed 'tis true that Henry told me of;
For I have often heard my mother say
I came into the world with my legs forward.
Had I not reason, think ye, to make haste,
And seek their ruin that usurp'd our right?

75. thou . . . forswear: you make a habit of swearing falsely.
87. common sort: ordinary soldiers.
90. a son. Actually, Edward's son had been born in November 1470, some six months before the battle of Tewkesbury.

V.vi. Location: London. The Tower.
6. Sirrah: customary form of address to an inferior.
7. reakless: reckless, heedless.
10. What . . . act: i.e. what tragic role have you in mind for me. Roscius was a Roman actor much admired by Cicero.
13. limed: snared with birdlime. **15. male . . . bird:** father . . . son.
18–25. Why . . . life. For the myth of Daedalus and Icarus see note to *1 Henry VI*, IV.vi.54–55. **18. peevish:** silly.

38. mistrust . . . fear: i.e. feel none of the apprehension that I feel.
40. water-standing: i.e. tear-flooded. **42. timeless:** untimely.
45. aboding: foreboding.
47. rook'd: rucked, i.e. squatted, crouched.
48. pies: magpies (birds of ill omen).
64. purple tears: i.e. drops of blood.

The midwife wonder'd and the women cried,
"O, Jesus bless us, he is born with teeth!"
And so I was, which plainly signified
That I should snarl, and bite, and play the dog.
Then since the heavens have shap'd my body so,
Let hell make crook'd my mind to answer it.
I have no brother, I am like no brother;
And this word "love," which greybeards call divine,
Be resident in men like one another,
And not in me: I am myself alone.
Clarence, beware! thou [keep'st] me from the light,
But I will sort a pitchy day for thee;
For I will buzz abroad such prophecies
That Edward shall be fearful of his life,
And then to purge his fear, I'll be thy death.
King Henry and the Prince his son are gone;
Clarence, thy turn is next, and then the rest,
Counting myself but bad till I be best.
I'll throw thy body in another room,
And triumph, Henry, in thy day of doom.
Exit [with the body].

[SCENE VII]

Flourish. Enter KING [EDWARD], QUEEN [ELIZABETH], CLARENCE, RICHARD [OF GLOUCESTER], HASTINGS, NURSE [*with the young Prince*], *and* ATTENDANTS.

K. Edw. Once more we sit in England's royal throne,
Repurchas'd with the blood of enemies.
What valiant foemen, like to autumn's corn,
Have we mow'd down in tops of all their pride!
Three Dukes of Somerset, threefold [renown'd]
For hardy and undoubted champions;
Two Cliffords, as the father and the son,
And two Northumberlands—two braver men
Ne'er spurr'd their coursers at the trumpet's sound;
With them, the two brave bears, Warwick and Montague,

79. answer: match. 85. sort: pick. 91. bad: lowly.

V.vii. Location: London. The palace.
3. corn: grain. 4. in tops: at the height.
6. undoubted: fearless. 7. as: namely.
10. bears. An allusion to the rampant bear chained to a staff, the badge of the House of Warwick. See note on *2 Henry VI*, v.i.202–3.

That in their chains fetter'd the kingly lion,
And made the forest tremble when they roar'd.
Thus have we swept suspicion from our seat,
And made our footstool of security.
Come hither, Bess, and let me kiss my boy.
Young Ned, for thee, thine uncles and myself
Have in our armors watch'd the winter's night,
Went all afoot in summer's scalding heat,
That thou mightst repossess the crown in peace,
And of our labors thou shalt reap the gain.
Glou. [*Aside.*] I'll blast his harvest, [and] your head were laid,
For yet I am not look'd on in the world.
This shoulder was ordain'd so thick to heave,
And heave it shall some weight, or break my back:
Work thou the way—and that [shall] execute.
K. Edw. Clarence and Gloucester, love my lovely queen,
And kiss your princely nephew, brothers both.
Clar. The duty that I owe unto your Majesty
I seal upon the lips of this sweet babe.
[*Q. Eliz.*] [Thanks], noble Clarence, worthy brother, thanks.
Glou. And that I love the tree from whence thou sprang'st,
Witness the loving kiss I give the fruit.
[*Aside.*] To say the truth, so Judas kiss'd his master,
And cried "All hail!" when as he meant all harm.
K. Edw. Now am I seated as my soul delights,
Having my country's peace and brothers' loves.
Clar. What will your Grace have done with Margaret?
[Reignier], her father, to the King of France
Hath pawn'd the Sicils and Jerusalem,
And hither have they sent it for her ransom.
K. Edw. Away with her, and waft her hence to France.
And now what rests but that we spend the time
With stately triumphs, mirthful comic shows,
Such as befits the pleasure of the court?
Sound drums and trumpets! Farewell sour annoy!
For here I hope begins our lasting joy. *Exeunt omnes.*

13. suspicion: anxiety. 21. and . . . laid: i.e. if you were dead.
25. thou . . . that: i.e. my head . . . my hand (indicated by gestures).
40. it: i.e. the money thus raised.

NOTE ON THE TEXT

The First Folio (1623) affords the only authoritative text of *3 Henry VI*; all later editions are derived primarily from that source. Again, however, as with *2 Henry VI*, there is a "bad" quarto (actually an octavo). This memorially reported text, which is based on essentially the same text as that printed in F1, was published in 1595 under the title *The true Tragedie of Richard Duke of Yorke* (see Textual Notes for the full descriptive title). This version (called hereafter Q1 for convenience, rather than O1) was reprinted in 1600 (Q2) and 1619 (Q3). Q3, printed from Q1, like Q3 of *2 Henry VI*, makes a number of changes and one addition (see Textual Notes, V.vi.89–90) that appear to anticipate the F1 text.

The problems of the F1 text seem in all essentials to be similar to those outlined for *2 Henry VI* (see "Note on the Text"). For the reason there suggested, the readings in which F1 agrees with Q3 readings (or, in a few cases, Q2) as against the other two quartos have been retained in the present text (see, for example, Textual Notes, I.i.24, 78, 83, 196, I.iv.63, 75, 166, II.i.104, 123, II.ii.46, 101, 107, 116, II.vi.59, III.ii.183, III.iii.243, IV.i.22, 29, 136, V.i.111, V.v.88, V.vi.71, V.vii.21, 38), except at III.ii.30, V.i.75, and

V.vii.21, where Q1–2 *and* has been substituted for F1, Q3 *if*. It is believed that at least one passage (IV.ii.1–18) was set directly from one of the quartos (probably Q3). Where only one or two of the three quartos are cited, agreement of the uncited quarto (or quartos) with the lemma may be assumed.

The Textual Notes generally record the variants in Q1–3 only where they figure in a reading cited in connection with the F1 text. The absence of citation of Q1–3 among the sigla in any entry indicates that the reading of the lemma occurs in a passage which in Q1–3 is either missing or so differently worded that it offers no recognizable equivalent. Some longer sections of Q1–3, where divergence from the F1 text is most noticeable, may be consulted in the Textual Notes at I.iv.1–6, II.iii.7–13, 15–22, III.iii.1–43, IV.iv, V.i.77, V.ii.50, V.iv.1–50, V.vi.89–90.

For further information, see the works cited in the "Note on the Text" to *2 Henry VI*.

TEXTUAL NOTES

Title: The Third . . . Sixth] The third Part of Henry the Sixt, with the death of the Duke of Yorke. *F1;* The true Tragedie of Richard Duke of Yorke, and the death of good King Henrie the Sixt, with the whole contention betweene the two Houses Lancaster and Yorke, as it was sundrie times acted by the Right Honourable the Earle of Pembrooke his seruants. *Q1 (title-page)*

Dramatis personae: *subs. as first given by Rowe*

Act-scene division: *none in Q1–3; F1 marks only I.i; other act-scene divisions from Rowe and later editors (see first note to each scene); present act-scene arrangement as a whole first established by Capell*

I.i

Location: *Theobald, Capell (after Hanmer)*

o.s.d. Montague] *Q1–2;* Mountague *F1 (throughout), Q3 (here only)*

o.s.d. with Drum] *Q1–3 (Q1–3 include* the yong Earle of Rutland *in the entry)*

o.s.d. with white . . . hats] *Q1–3*

2 s.p. York.] *Q1–3;* Pl. *F1 (or* Plant. *through l. 43)*

6 himself,] *Rowe;* himselfe. *F1*

16 s.d. Showing . . . head.] *Hanmer (after Theobald)*

24 heaven] heauens *Q1–2*

27 heirs'] *Warburton;* Heires *F1, Q1–3*

36 council] *Pope;* counsaile *F1*

49 s.d. York . . . throne.] *Collier MS (after Johnson, but following l. 32); placed as in Johnson*

49 s.d. with . . . hats] *Q1–3*

66 cousin,] *Q1–3;* Cousin *F1*

69 s.p. Exe.] *Q1–3;* Westm. *F1*

78 my] mine *Q1–2*

83 that's] and that is *Q1–2;* and that's *Q3, F2*

93 Yes] No *Q1–3*

102 s.p. York.] *Q1–3;* Plant. *F1 (throughout scene)*

105 Thy] *Q1–3;* My *F1*

120 s.p. K. Hen.] Northum. *Q1–3 (better perhaps)*

134, 151 s.dd. Aside.] *Capell*

170 hear . . . word] heare me speake *Q1–3 (some eds. insert* me *after F1* hear*)*

184, 186, 188 s.dd. Exit.] *Q1–3*

186 unmanly] vnkingly *Q1–2;* vnkindly *Q3*

194 s.d. To York.] *Collier MS*

196 an] thine *Q1–2*

206 s.d. Exeunt . . . Soldiers.] *ed. (after Q1–3* Exit Yorke and [with *Q3]* his sonnes.)

207, 208, 209 s.dd. Exit with Soldiers.] *ed. (after Q1–3* Exit.)

210 s.d. and Prince Edward] *from Q1–3 s.d.* (and the Prince)

213 s.p. Q. Mar.] *Malone;* Queene. *F1 (through II.v), Q1–3 (throughout)*

213 I will] I *Q1–2;* Ile *Q3*

251 northern] Northen *Q1–2*

259 with] *Q1–3*

261 from] *Q1–3;* to *F1*

263 s.d. Exeunt . . . Prince.] *Rowe; Q1–3 (omitting l. 263) give them separate exits after ll. 260 and 262*

273 s.d. Flourish.] *placed as in Wilson; part of entry for next scene, F1*

273 s.d. Exeunt.] *Pope;* Exit *F1*

I.ii

I.ii] *Capell*

Location: *Theobald (after Pope)*

47 s.d. a Messenger] *Q1–3;* Gabriel *F1 (probably Gabriel Spencer, who played the role)*

49 s.p. Mess.] *Q1–3;* Gabriel. *F1*

51 twenty] thirtie *Q1–3*

55 brother] cosen *Q1–3*

61 s.d. Enter . . . Mortimer.] *F1, adjusted after Q1–3* Enter sir Iohn and sir Hugh Mortimer.

75 s.d. Exeunt.] *Q2;* Exit. *F1, Q1, Q3*

I.iii

I.iii] *Capell*

Location: *Theobald*

o.s.d. Alarums] *Q1–3* (Alarmes)

2 s.d. and Soldiers] *Theobald*

9 s.d. dragged . . . Soldiers] *Theobald; Q1–3 s.d. reads:* Exit the Chaplein.

14 o'er] ouer *Q1–2*

47 s.d. Stabs him.] *Rowe*

48 s.d. Dies.] *Theobald*

I.iv

I.iv] *Capell*

Location: *ed. (after Pelican)*

1–6 The . . . them;] *Q1–3 give a different version of these lines:* Ah Yorke, post to thy castell, saue thy life, / The goale is lost thou house of *Lancaster*, / Thrise happie chance is it for thee and thine, / That heauen abridgde my daies and cals me hence, / But God knowes what chance hath betide my sonnes:

26 s.d.] *Q1–3 om.* Prince Edward

60 s.d. They . . . struggles.] *Johnson;* Fight and take him. *Q1–3*

63 conquer'd] conquered *Q1–2*

64 yield, with robbers] *F2;* yeeld with Robbers, *F1*

75 where's] where is *Q1–2*

75 crook-back] Crookbackt *Q1–2;* crooktbackt *Q3*

87 What,] What *Q1–2*

95 s.d. Putting . . . head.] *Rowe*

112 tongue more poisons] tongue more poison'd *Q1–2;* tongue's more poison'd *Q3*

112 than] *Q1–2;* then *F1, Q3*

117 deeds,] *F2;* deedes. *F1;* deedes: *Q1–2;* deeds; *Q3*

133 abominable] *F3;* abhominable *F1*

137 tiger's] *Q1–3* (Tygers); Tygres *F1*

153 stain'd] *(Q1–3);* stayn'd the roses just *F2*

154 inhuman] *Rowe;* inhumane *F1, Q3;* inhumaine *Q1–2*

166 too] two *Q1–2*

172 weeping-ripe] *hyphen, Theobald*

175 s.d. Stabbing him.] *Pope*

176 s.d. Stabbing him.] *Rowe*

178 s.d. Dies.] *Rowe*

180 s.d. Exeunt.] *Q1–3* (Exeunt omnes.); Exit. *F1*

II.i

II.i] *Rowe*

Location: *Capell (after Theobald)*

o.s.d. and their power] with drum and Souldiers *Q1–3*

20 s.d. Three . . . air.] *Q1–3*

25 Dazzle] Dasell *Q1–2*

40 target] *Q1–3;* Targuet *F1*

42 s.d. a Messenger] *from Q3 s.d.:* Enter a Messenger.; *s.d. om. Q1–2*

45 looker-on] *hyphen, Capell*

94 s.d. Montague] *Q1–3;* Mountacute *F1*

95 fare] *Q1–3;* faire *F1*

96 recompt] *F2;* tecompt *F1;* recount *F3;* report *Q1, Q3;* but reporte *Q2*

104 news] things *Q1–2*

113 And . . . thought,] *Q1–3*

123 Who] He *Q1, Q3*

127 captives] *Rowe;* Captiues, *F1;* captaines *Q1–3*

130 soldiers'] *Capell;* Souldiers *F1, Q1–3*

131 an idle] *Q1–3;* a lazie *F1 (*lazie *presumably caught from l. 130)*

177 thirty] fifty *Q1–3*

181 five and twenty] 48. *Q1–2;* eight and forty *Q3*

182 march,] march amaine *Q1–3*

184 "Charge!" . . . foes] *Staunton;* Charge vpon our Foes *F1,* (the foe) *Q1–3 (many eds. read* "Charge . . . foes")

190 fail'st] faints *Q1, Q3;* faint'st *Q2*

198 Richard, Montague] *Q1–3;* Richard Mountague *F1*

209 warriors. Let's] *Capell (subs., after Q1–3* Lordes. Lets); Warriors, let's *F1*

II.ii

II.ii] *Capell*

Location: *Capell (after Pope)*

o.s.d. Northumberland] *F2;* Northum- *F1 (Q1–3 give* Northerne Earles *for Clifford and Northumberland)*

o.s.d. Trumpets] Souldiers *Q1–3*

37 great-grandfather] *hyphen, Capell*

46 ill] euill *Q1–2*

48 hell?] *Q1–3;* hell: *F1*

62 lesson:] lesson boy, *Q1–2*

89 Since] *F2 (continuing the speech to Edward); Cla.* Since *F1; George.* Since *Q1–3*

92 out me] our brother out *Q1–3*

100 signal] synald *Q1–2*

101 fly] flee *Q1–2*

107 Clifford,] Clifford, That *Q1–2*

116 sunset] sunne set *Q1–2;* sun-set *Q3*

133 s.p. Rich.] *Q1–3;* War. *F1*

142 Sham'st] Shames *Q1–2*

163 s.p. Geo.] *Q1–3;* Cla. *F1 (or* Clar., Clarence. *throughout)*

II.iii

II.iii] *Capell*

Location: *ed.*

1 Forespent] Sore spent *Q1–3*

7–13 For . . . pursuit.] *Q1–3 give a different version of these lines:* That we maie die vnlesse we gaine the daie: / What fatall starre malignant frownes from heauen / Vpon the harmelesse line of *Yorkes* true house? / Enter *George.* / *George.* Come brother, come, lets to the field againe, / For yet theres hope inough to win the daie: / Then let vs backe to cheere our fainting Troupes, / Lest they retire now we haue left the field. / *War.* How now my lords: what hap, what hope of good?

13 s.d. **running]** *Q1–3*
15–22 **Thy . . . ghost.]** *Q1–3 give a different version of these lines:* Thy noble father in the thickest thronges, / Cride still for *Warwike* his thrise valiant son, / Vntill with thousand swords he was beset, / And manie wounds made in his aged brest, / And as he tottering [tottring *Q3*] sate vpon his steede, / He waft his hand to me and cride aloud: / *Richard*, commend me to my valiant sonne, [*cf.* V.ii.42] / And still he cride *Warwike* reuenge my death, / And with those words he tumbled off his horse, / And so the noble Salsbury gaue vp the ghost.
37 **setter-up and plucker-down]** *hyphens, Dyce*
49 **all together]** *Rowe;* altogether *F1*

II.iv

II.iv] *Capell*
Location: *ed.* (*after Wilson*)
o.s.d. **at one door . . . at the other]** *Q1–3*
1] *Preceding this line, Q1–3 give: Rich.* A *Clifford* a *Clifford*. / *Clif.* A *Richard* a *Richard*.
8 **death]** deathes *Q1–3* (*perhaps a better reading*)
11 s.d. **Alarums.]** *from Q1–3 s.d.:* Alarmes. They fight, and then enters Warwike and rescues Richard, & then exeunt omnes.

II.v

II.v] *Capell*
Location: *ed.* (*after Wilson*)
54 s.d. **dragging . . . body]** *Capell; Q1–3 s.d. reads:* Enter a souldier with a dead man in his armes.
78 s.d. **that . . . door]** *F1* (*from s.d. at l. 54, where F1 anticipates the Father's entry*); *Q1–3 s.d. reads:* Enter an other souldier, with a dead man.
89 **stratagems]** *F3;* Stragems *F1*
90 **Erroneous]** *F2;* Erreoneous *F1;* ironious *Q1–2;* ironous *Q3*
92–3 **soon . . . late]** late . . . sone *Q1–3*
113 s.d. **Exit . . . father.]** *Q1–3*
119 **E'en]** *Collier MS;* Men *F1*
122 s.d. **with his son]** *Q1–3*
123 **Sad-hearted men]** *F3;* Sad-hearted-men *F1*
124 s.d. **Enter . . . Exeter.]** *in Q1–3 the three characters enter separately, each immediately before speaking, the Queen's entry and speech preceding Prince Edward's*

II.vi

II.vi] *Capell*
Location: *ed.* (*after Wilson*)
o.s.d. **with . . . neck]** *Q1–3*
6 **fall, thy]** *Rowe;* fall. Thy *F1;* die, that *Q1–3*
8 **The . . . flies,]** *Q1–3* (*first inserted by Theobald*)
19 **Had]** *Q1–3;* Hed *F1*
19 **death]** deathes *Q1–3* (*perhaps a better reading*)
30 s.d. **He faints.]** *Rowe*
39 **For (though]** *Capell* (*subs.*); (For though *F1;* For though *Q1–3*
41 s.d. **and then dies]** *Q1–3*
44 **See . . . is.]** *given to Edward, Q1–3*
59 **ill-boding]** euill boding *Q1, Q3;* yll boding *Q2*
60 **his]** *Q1–3;* is *F1*
85 **Off]** *Q1–3;* Of *F1*

III.i

III.i] *Rowe*
Location: *Hanmer* (*after Theobald*)
o.s.d. **two Keepers]** *Q1–3;* Sinklo, and Humfrey *F1* (*actors' names;* Humfrey *is probably Humphrey Jeaffes*)
o.s.d. **cross-bows]** bow and arrowes *Q1–3*
1 s.p. **1. Keep.]** *Malone;* Sink. *F1* (*or* Sinklo. *throughout scene*); Keeper. *Q1–3*
1 **thick-grown]** *hyphen, Pope*
5 s.p. **2. Keep.]** *Malone;* Hum. *F1* (*throughout scene*); Keeper. *Q1–3*
7 **scare]** *F3;* scarre *F1*
11 **self place]** *Capell;* selfe-place *F1*
12 s.d. **disguised]** *Q1–3*
24 **thee]** *Dyce conj.;* the *F1*
24 **adversities]** *Pope;* Aduersaries *F1*
30 **Is]** *F2;* I: *F1*
55 **thou talk'st]** thou that talkes *Q1–3*
56 s.p. **K. Hen.]** *Rowe;* King. *F1* (*throughout rest of scene*); Hen. *Q1–3*

III.ii

III.ii] *Pope*
Location: *Hanmer* (*after Theobald*)
8 s.p. **Glou.]** *Q1–3;* Rich. *F1* (*throughout*)
11, 15, 25, 28 s.dd. **Aside to Clarence.]** *Capell*
14, 24, 27 s.dd. **Aside to Gloucester.]** *Capell*
18 s.p. **L. Grey.]** *Rowe;* Wid. *F1* (*throughout scene*)
21, 30, 34, 57 s.dd. **Aside to Clarence.]** *Cambridge*
25 **God forbid]** Marie godsforbot *Q1;* Marie gods-forbot *Q2;* Marry gods-forbot *Q3*
30 **and]** *Q1–2;* if *F1, Q3*
31 **'Twere]** Were it *Q1–2;* Wer't *Q3*
35 s.d. **Gloucester . . . retire.]** *Johnson*
50, 82, 107 s.dd. **Aside to Clarence.]** *Dyce*
51, 83, 108 s.dd. **Aside to Gloucester.]** *Dyce*
84 s.d. **Aside.]** *Johnson*
104 **other some]** *Q1–3;* other-some *F1*
117 s.d. **Nobleman]** *Rowe;* Noble man *F1;* Messenger *Q1–3*
123 **honorably]** *Q1–3;* honourable *F1*
144 **eye's]** *F3;* Eyes *F1*
150 **witch]** *Q1–3;* 'witch *F1*
183 **that which]** that that *Q1;* that, that *Q2*

III.iii

III.iii] *Capell*
Location: *Pope, Cambridge* (*after Capell*)
o.s.d. **Bourbon]** *Q1–3 om. this character, but add* and others *after* Oxford
1–43 **Fair . . . sorrow!]** *Q1–3 give a different and reduced version of these lines:* Welcome *Queene* Margaret to the Court of *France*, / It fits not *Lewis* to sit while thou dost stand. / Sit by my side, and here I vow to thee, / Thou shalt haue aide to repossesse thy right, / And beat proud Edward from his vsurped seat. / And place king *Henry* in his former rule. / *Queen.* I humblie thanke your royall maiestie. / And pray the God of heauen to blesse thy state, / Great king of *France*, that thus regards our wrongs.
29 **true-anointed]** *hyphen, Theobald*
58 s.d. **Aside.]** *Capell*
78 s.p. **Prince.]** *Rowe;* Edw. *F1;* Prince Ed. *Q1–3*
124 **eternal]** *Q1–3;* externall *F1*
156 **Peace, impudent]** *Theobald;* Peace impudent, *F1*
156 **Warwick,]** Warwicke, Peace, *F2*
157 **setter-up and puller-down]** *hyphens, Dyce*
161 s.d. **Post . . . within.]** *placed as in Capell* (*who reads:* Tucket heard.); *after l. 160, F1;* Sound for a post within. *Q1–3* (*after l. 155; Q1–3 here om. ll. 156–61*)
169–70 **Nay . . . best.]** *as verse, Rowe; as prose, F1* (*Q1–3 om. l.170*)
226 **pass'd]** *Wilson;* past *F1*
233 **Exit Post.]** *om. Q1–2;* Exit Mes. *Q3*
243 **wedlock]** wedlockes *Q1–2*

IV.i

IV.i] *Rowe*
Location: *Capell* (*after Pope*)
6 s.d. **now Queen Elizabeth]** *Rowe* (*subs.*); the Queene *Q1–3* (*om.* Lady Grey)
6 s.d. **Pembroke]** *F2* (*subs.*); Penbrooke *F1, Q1–3*
6 s.d. **and others]** *Capell* (*subs.*); *s.d. in Q1–3, which begin the scene here, reads:* Enter king Edward, the Queene and Clarence, and Gloster, and Montague, and Hastings, and Penbrooke, with souldiers. (*Q3 om. the first four* and*'s*)
22 **pitty]** a pittie *Q1–2*
29 **mine]** my *Q1–2*
34 **What]** *Dyce;* What, *F1*
41 **But]** Yes, but *F2*
60 **malecontent]** mal-content *Q1–2*
66 **brother's will]** *Rowe;* Brothers will *F1;* brothers wils *Q1–3*
67 s.p. **Q. Eliz.]** *Q1–3* (Queen.); Lady Grey. *F1*
83 s.d. **Aside.]** *Johnson*
84–5 **Now . . . France?]** *as verse, Capell* (*after Pope*); *as prose, F1* (*Q1–3 give subs. l. 84 and om. ll. 81–3, replacing them with a line by Montague:* My Lord, heere is the messenger returnd from France.)
116 **they are]** theare *Q1*
124 s.d. **Aside.]** *Rowe*
136 **near]** neerest *Q1–2*

IV.ii

IV.ii] *Capell*
Location: *Capell* (*after Theobald*)

IV.iii

IV.iii] *Capell*
Location: *Capell*
9 **nobleman]** *F4;* Noble man *F1* (*Q1–3 om. ll. 1–22*)
29–30 **Richard . . . Duke.]** *as verse, Pope; as prose, F1, Q1–3*
55–6 **I'll . . . him.]** Ile come and tell thee what the ladie *Bona* saies, *Q1–3*
57 s.d. **out]** *F2;* ont *F1*
59 s.d. **Exit . . . Somerset.]** *Cambridge, Capell;* Exeunt. *F1;* Exeunt some with Edward. *Q1–2,* (Exit) *Q3* (*Q1–3 om. ll. 58–9*)
64 s.d. **Exeunt.]** *Q1–3* (Exeunt omnes.); exit. *F1*

IV.iv

IV.iv] *Capell*
Q1–3 reverse the order of Scenes iv and v; cf. the essentially variant version of this scene in Q1–3: Enter the *Queene* and the Lord *Riuers*. / *Riuers.* Tel me good maddam, why is your grace / So passionate of late? / *Queen.* Why brother *Riuers*, heare you [ye *Q3*] not the newes, / Of that successe king *Edward* had of late? / *Riu.* What? losse of some pitcht battaile against *Warwike*, / Tush, feare not faire *Queen*, but cast those cares aside. / King *Edwards* noble mind his honours doth display: / And *Warwike* maie loose, though then he got the day. / *Queen.* If that were all, my griefes were at an end: / But greater troubles will I feare befall. / *Riu.* What, is he taken prisoner by the foe, / To the danger of his royall person then? / *Queen.* I, thears my griefe, king *Edward* is surprisde, / And led awaie, as prisoner [prison *Q2*] vnto *Yorke*. / *Riu.* The newes is passing strange, I must confesse: / Yet comfort your selfe, for *Edward* hath more friends, / Then *Lancaster* at this time must perceiue, / That some will set him in his throne againe. / *Queen.* God grant they maie, but gentle brother come, / And let me leane vpon thine arme a while, / Vntill I come vnto the sanctuarie, / There to preserue the fruit within my wombe, / K. *Edwards* seed true heire to *Englands* crowne. *Exit.*
Location: *Capell, Theobald*
o.s.d. **now Queen Elizabeth]** *Theobald* (*subs.*); the Queene *Q1–3* (*om.* Lady Grey)
2 s.p. **Q. Eliz.]** *Q1–3* (Queen.); Gray. *F1* (*throughout scene*)
4 **What?]** *Q1–3;* What *F1*
20 **misfortune's]** *Pope;* misfortunes *F1*

IV.v

IV.v] *Capell*
Location: *Theobald* (*after Pope*)
4 **stands]** *F2;* stand *F1*
8 **Comes]** *F2;* Come *F1*
20–1 **lord— . . . Flanders?]** *ed.;* Lord, . . . Flanders. *F1*
21 s.d. **To Gloucester.]** *ed.*

IV.vi

IV.vi] *Capell*
Q1–3 reverse the order of Scenes vi and vii and om. ll. 3–37, 48–64, 77–102 of this scene
Location: *Pope, Theobald*
o.s.d. **Enter . . . Tower.]** Enter Warwike and Clarence, with the Crowne, and then enter Henry, and Oxford, and Summerset, and the yong Earle of Richmond. *Q1–3* (*Q3 om. the third and fourth* and'*s*)
o.s.d. **of the Tower]** *Rowe*
88 s.d. **Manent]** *F2;* Manet *F1*

IV.vii

IV.vii] *Capell*
Location: *Capell* (*after Pope*)
o.s.d. **a . . . Hollanders]** *Q1–3*
4 **waned]** *Steevens;* wained *F1*
8 **Ravenspurgh]** *F2;* Rauenspurre *F1;* Raunspur *Q1, Q3;* Rounspur *Q2*
16 s.d. **the Aldermen]** *Dyce* (*subs.*)
25 s.d. **Aside.]** *Rowe*
29 s.d. **He descends]** Exit Maire. *Q1–3*
29 s.d. **with the Aldermen]** *Dyce* (*after Malone*)
34 s.d. **below]** *Capell; Q1–3 s.d. reads:* The Maire opens the dore, and brings the keies in his hand.
70 s.d. **Gives . . . paper.]** *Capell* (*subs.*)
71 s.d. **Reads.]** *Capell*

IV.viii

IV.viii] *Capell*
Location: *Pope, Kittredge* (*from Wright conj.*)
o.s.d. **Exeter]** *Capell;* Somerset *F1; Q1–3 s.d. reads:* Enter one with a letter to Warwike. (*as continuation of IV.vi, which precedes this scene in Q1–3*)
29 s.d. **kissing Henry's hand]** *Johnson*
32 s.d. **all . . . Exeter]** *Capell* (*subs.*)*; Wilson, following P. A. Daniel's suggestion, marks a new scene here; Q1–3 s.d. reads:* Exeunt omnes. (*following All.* Agreed.*, a speech found only in Q1–3*)
51 s.d. **with Gloucester]** *Hanmer* (*subs.*)
51 s.d. **and others]** *ed., from Q1–3 s.d.:* Enter Edward and his traine.
57 s.d. **Exeter]** *ed.* (*after Pelican*)
57 s.d. **guarded]** *ed.* (*after Pelican*)

V.i

V.i] *Pope*
Location: *Theobald* (*subs.*)
o.s.d. **Enter . . . walls.]** Enter Warwike on the walles. *Q1–3*
3 **Dunsmore]** Daintrie *Q1–3*
6 **Daintry]** Donsmore *Q1–3*
6 s.d. **Sir John]** *Capell*
10 s.d. **Drum heard.]** *Capell*
14 **unlook'd-for]** *hyphen, Pope*
24 **outrages.]** *Pope;* Outrages? *F1*
57 s.d. **Colors.]** souldiers & al crie, *Q1; Q2 makes l. 59 part of the s.d. following* all crie: *Q3 om.* & al crie *and restores l. 59 to Oxford* (*the s.d. follows l. 58 in Q1–3*)
59 s.d. **He . . . city.]** *Capell;* Exit. *Q1, Q3;* Exeunt. *Q2*
66, 71, 75 s.dd. **Colors]** souldiers *Q1–3* (*Somerset precedes Montague in Q1–3*)
67, 72 s.dd. **He . . . city.]** *Malone* (*after Capell*)*;* Exit. *Q1, Q3;* Exeunt. *Q2*
75 **and]** *Q1–2;* if *F1, Q3*
77] *After this line, and omitting ll. 78–9, Q1–3 read: Cla.* Clarence, Clarence, for Lancaster. [Exeunt. *Q2*] / *Edw.* [*om. Q2*] Et tu Brute, wilt thou stab Caesar too? / A parlie sirra to George of Clarence.
78 **an]** *F2;* in *F1*
79 s.d. **Gloucester . . . together.]** *Collier, from Q1–3 s.d.:* Sound a Parlie, and Richard and Clarence whispers togither, and then Clarence takes his red Rose out of his hat, and throwes it at Warwike.
82 s.d. **Clarence . . . Warwick.]** *Q1–3* (*see preceding note*)
91 **Jephthah]** *F3* (*subs.*)*;* Iephah *F1*
111 **dar'st]** darest *Q1–2*
113 s.d. **King . . . company]** *Cambridge*

V.ii

V.ii] *Capell*
Location: *Theobald* (*after Pope*)
o.s.d. **King Edward]** *Q1–3 om. the King from this scene*
44 **cannon]** clamor *Q1–3*
49 s.d. **He dies.]** *Q1–3*
50 **Away . . . power!]** *Q1–3 expand Oxford's single line to six:* Come noble *Summerset*, lets take our horse, / And cause retrait [retreate *Q3*] be sounded through the campe, / That all our friends that yet remaine aliue, / Maie be awarn'd [forwarn'd *Q3*] and saue themselues by flight. / That done, with them weele post vnto the *Queene*, / And once more trie our fortune in the field *Ex.* [*Exit Q3*] *ambo.*

V.iii

V.iii] *Capell*
Location: *ed.* (*after Wilson*)
8 **arriv'd]** *Rowe;* arriued *F1*
22–3 **augmented . . . along.]** *pointing based on sense of Q1–3* (And in euerie countie [country *Q3*] as we passe along / Our strengthes shall be augmented.)*;* augmented: . . . along, *F1*

V.iv

V.iv] *Capell*
Location: *Theobald* (*after Pope*)
o.s.d. **and Soldiers]** with drum and souldiers *Q1–3*
1–50 **Great . . . help.]** *Q1–3 give an essentially different and reduced version of these lines:* Welcome to *England* my louing friends of *France*, / And welcome *Summerset*, and *Oxford* too. / Once more haue we spread our sailes abroad, / And though our tackling be almost consumde, / And *Warwike* as our maine mast ouerthrowne, / Yet warlike Lords raise you that sturdie post, / That beares the sailes to bring vs vnto rest, / And *Ned* and *I* as willing Pilots should / For once with carefull mindes guide on the sterne, / To beare vs throngh [through *Q2–3*] that dangerous gulfe / That heretofore hath swallowed vp our friends. / *Prince.* And if there be, as God forbid there should, / Amongst vs a timorous or fearefull man, / Let him depart before the battels ioine, / Least he in time of need intise another, / And so withdraw the souldiers harts from vs. / *I* will not stand aloofe and bid you fight, / But with my sword presse in the thickest thronges, / And single *Edward* from his strongest guard, / And hand to hand enforce him for to yeeld, / Or leaue my bodie as witnesse of my thoughts.
27 **ragged]** *Rowe;* raged *F1*
66 s.d. **Richard of Gloucester]** Glo. Hast. *Q1–3*
82 s.d. **Alarum . . . Somerset.]** *ed.* (*after Pelican*) *from Q1–3 and F1:* Alarmes to the battell, Yorke flies, then the chambers be discharged. Then enter the king, Cla & Glo. & the rest, & make a great shout and crie, for Yorke, for Yorke, and then the Queene is taken, & the prince, & Oxf. & Sum. and then sound and enter all againe. *Q1–3* (*Q3 rephrases slightly*)*;* Alarum, Retreat, Excursions. Exeunt. *F1*

V.v

V.v] *Capell*
Location: *ed.* (*after Wilson*)
o.s.d. **prisoner]** *Pelican*
o.s.d. **and Soldiers with]** *Capell* (*subs.*)
o.s.d. **prisoners]** *Rowe* (*see Q1–3 s.d. at V.iv.82*)
6 s.d. **Oxford . . . guarded]** *Capell; Q1–3 read* Exit Oxford. *after l. 5 and* Exit Sum. *after l. 6*
11 s.d. **Soldiers with]** *Capell*
30 **crook-back]** Crooktbacke *Q1–2*
38 **the likeness]** the litnes *Q1;* the lightnes *Q2;* thou likenesse *Q3*
38 s.d. **Stabs him.]** *om. Q1–2*
50 **The]** *Q1–3*
66 **off,]** *Q1–3;* off. *F1*
77 **butcher,]** *Q1, Q3;* butcher Richard? *F1;* butcher? *Q2*
82 s.d. **Margaret . . . forcibly]** *Capell*
88 **let's]** let vs *Q1–2*
90 s.d. **Exeunt.]** *Q1–3* (Exeunt Omnes.)*;* Exit. *F1*

V.vi

V.vi] *Capell*
Location: *Pope* (*after Q1–3*)
o.s.d. **Enter . . . walls.]** Enter Gloster to king Henry in the Tower. *Q1–3*
6 s.d. **Exit Lieutenant.]** *Rowe*
7 **reakless]** *ed.;* wreaklesse *F1*
10 **Roscius]** *Pope;* Rossius *F1;* Rosius *Q1–3*
22–3 **course; . . . boy,]** *Rowe; pointing follows sense of Q1–3* (course, / Thy brother *Edward*, the sunne that searde his wings,)*;* course, . . . Boy. *F1*
40 **water-standing eye]** *Rowe;* water-standing-eye *F1;* water standing eie *Q1–3*
41 **husbands,]** (*Q1–3*)*;* Husbands fate,/ And *F2*
57 s.d. **Stabs him.]** He stabs him. *Q1–2*
71 **I]** That I *Q1–2*
79] *Following this line Theobald inserts from Q1–3:* I had no father, I am like no father,
80 **have no brother]** have no brothers *Q1, Q3*
81 **"love"]** [Loue] *F1;* Loue *Q1–3* (*in italics*)
84 **keep'st]** *F3;* keept'st *F1;* keptst *Q1–3*
86] *Following this line Q3 adds:* Vnder pretence of outward seeming ill.
89–90 **King . . . rest,]** *Henry* and his sonne are gone, thou *Clarence* next, / And one by one I will dispatch the rest, *Q1–2;* King *Henry*, and the Prince his sonne are gone, / And *Clarence* thou art next must follow them, / So by one and one dispatching all the rest, *Q3*
93 s.d. **with the body]** *Capell*

V.vii

V.vii] *Capell*
Location: *Theobald*
o.s.d. **Elizabeth]** *Q1–3*
o.s.d. **Richard of Gloucester]** *om. Q1–2*
o.s.d. **with . . . Prince]** *Q1–3*
5 **renown'd]** *Q3;* Renowne *F1;* renowmd *Q1–2*
21, 33 s.dd. **Aside.]** *Rowe*
21 **and]** *Q1–2;* if *F1, Q3*
25 **way—]** *Capell;* way, *F1, Q1–3*
25 **that shall]** *F3;* that shalt *F1;* thou shalt *Q1–3*
26 **Clarence . . . queen,]** Brothers of Clarence and of Gloster, / Pray loue my louely Queene, *Q3* (*om.* brothers *in l. 27*)
30 s.p. **Q. Eliz.]** *Q1–3* (Queen.)*;* Cla. *F1*
30 **Thanks]** *Q1–3;* Thanke *F1*
31 **sprang'st,]** *Q1–3;* sprang'st: *F1*
38 **Reignier]** *Rowe;* Reynard *F1, Q3;* Ranard *Q1–2*
46 s.d. **Exeunt omnes.]** Exeunt omnes / FINIS. *F1, Q1–3*

Richard III

THE EARLY SUCCESS OF *Richard III*, one of the perennial favorites of English dramatic literature, is indicated by the history of its publication. Written probably about 1592, and in any event not long after *3 Henry VI* (to which it forms a sequel), the work appeared in print anonymously in 1597 in a version apparently put together as a memorial reconstruction by actors who no longer had their prompt-book to consult. The text of this "bad" quarto was reprinted in 1598 (with "William Shake-speare" on the title-page), 1602, 1605, 1612 ("As it hath beene lately Acted by the Kings Maiesties seruants"), and 1622; and even after its inclusion, in a better version, in the Folio of 1623, the play was reprinted twice more as a quarto, in 1629 and 1634. Only *1 Henry IV* can show a longer list of early reprints.

Since King Richard III had been an object of stylized abuse and of morbid fascination for a hundred years or more, there was a small library that Shakespeare could have drawn upon for sources. The account of the last and most evil of the Yorkist kings in Polydore Vergil's *Historia Anglica* (1534 ff.), a work that Henry VII had commissioned, did much to establish Richard's reputation as a villain; but even more important was Thomas More's *History of King Richard the Third*. This fragment, an authentic masterpiece of biography, was written about 1513 and survives in both an English and a Latin version that differ in details. The Latin, it has been suggested, was perhaps the work of John Morton, a supporter of the Earl of Richmond who, after his master's accession as Henry VII in 1485, became a stalwart Tudor politician (the Ely of the present play), a cardinal, and a patron of young Thomas More. Even if Morton did not compose the life of Richard, he no doubt provided More with much of the vivid, first-hand information that gives the work distinction. The English version, first printed in a sadly mutilated form in Grafton's continuation of Hardyng's *Chronicle* (1543), was followed almost word for word by Hall in his *Union . . . of Lancaster and York* (1548) and thereafter, in the accommodating fashion of the age, by most of his successors. Although the authentic English text was given in William Rastell's 1557 printing of his famous uncle's *Works* and the Latin in the *Omnia Opera* of 1566, Shakespeare seems to have used Hall and (as the detail about the bleeding corpse at I.ii.55–56 shows) either Holinshed or Stow.

Meanwhile Richard had entered the domain of more or less belletristic literature. The first two editions of *A Mirror for Magistrates* (1559 and 1563) contain some eight "tragedies"—among others, those of Henry VI, George Duke of Clarence, Hastings, Buckingham, and Jane Shore—in which Richard comes off very badly. About 1579 Thomas Legge, Master of Caius College, Cambridge, wrote the Latin *Richardus Tertius*, a three-part Senecan tragedy, based largely on Hall, that depicts Richard as a tyrant. The anonymous *True Tragedy of Richard III*, which was probably written three or four years before its publication in 1594, is a crude but not wholly unsuccessful effort to combine the motif of Senecan revenge with the English history play. If Shakespeare knew this work (as is not unlikely, for he later quotes from it in Hamlet's line about the croaking raven that doth bellow for revenge) he may have been impressed by its use of a central, dominating character (in the style of Marlowe's Tamburlaine); moreover, he could have got from it a few details of plot.

It was More, however, who supplied the main outlines as well as most of the details for Shakespeare's portrait of the tyrant-king. Thus *The History of King*

Richard the Third must be accounted one of the most persistent triumphs in English historical literature, for thanks to Shakespeare's use of it—and despite modern efforts to salvage Richard's reputation—it has lasted to this day. "Little of stature, ill-featured of limbs, crook-backed, his left shoulder much higher than his right," says More in devastating and unforgettable detail, Richard was

> hard-favored of visage, and such as is in states [i.e. rulers] called warly [i.e. warlike], in other men otherwise; he was malicious, wrathful, envious, and, from afore his birth, ever froward. It is for truth reported that the duchess, his mother, had so much ado in her travail that she could not be delivered of him uncut, and that he came into the world with the feet forward, as men be borne outward, and (as the fame runneth) also not untoothed . . . . He was close and secret, a deep dissimuler, lowly of countenance, arrogant of heart, outwardly coumpinable [i.e. companionable] where he inwardly hated, not letting to kiss [i.e. abstaining from kissing] whom he thought to kill; dispitious and cruel, not for evil will alway, but ofter for ambition, and either for the surety or increase of his estate. Friend and foe was muchwhat indifferent; where his advantage grew he spared no man's death whose life withstood his purpose.

As the final unit in the first tetralogy, *Richard III* both closes Shakespeare's long survey of England's troubles in the fifteenth century and completes his exposition of the providential theme that he had got from Hall. Here we see the death-throes of the house of York, and here the little Richmond whom Henry VI had hailed as "England's hope" (*3 Henry VI*, IV.vi.78) fulfills his destiny on Bosworth Field, unites the white rose and the red, and inaugurates the Tudor peace. "England hath long been mad and scarr'd herself," he says in formal valediction,

> The brother blindly shed the brother's blood,
> The father rashly slaughter'd his own son,
> The son, compell'd, been butcher to the sire.
> All this divided York and Lancaster,
> Divided in their dire division,
> O now let Richmond and Elizabeth,
> The true succeeders of each royal house,
> By God's fair ordinance conjoin together!
> And let their heirs (God, if thy will be so)
> Enrich the time to come with smooth-fac'd peace,
> With smiling plenty, and fair prosperous days!
> (V.v.23–34)

But if *Richard III* closes on this apocalyptic note, it is more than Shakespeare's final step in his demonstration of a consoling commonplace. He accepts the Tudor party line and the standard view of Richard, but he adapts and deepens them to serve his purpose. Here, the accredited slogans, the politics and history, are used for more than propaganda. They provide the base for Shakespeare's explorations of the fact of evil and the means by which he shows its strength and limitations. With the earlier villains—Queen Margaret and Beaufort, for example, to say nothing of the witch and strumpet Joan—he had been content to slap his primary colors on in strong, clear lines, and consequently these characters are as simple and sometimes as vulgar as cartoons. But the tyrant that he draws in Richard is more than just a villain: sometimes gay and debonair, sometimes coarse and even brutal, he is a man so driven by the lust for power that despite his wit and charm and intellect—which he possesses in abundance—he becomes the agent of his own destruction. "I am myself alone," Richard had declared when young (*3 Henry VI*, V.vi.83), and although he makes the same bizarre assertion as he prepared for Bosworth Field, he knows that "if I die no soul shall pity me" (V.iii.201). Therefore he can sport and frolic with his victims, and except for that one appalling moment at the end he can contemplate his crimes with dreadful satisfaction. The result is melodrama, to be sure, but melodrama that suggests the more subtle splendors of *Macbeth*. In both plays, Shakespeare's hero is a blood-stained tyrant, but, as Hazlitt pointed out, Richard's cruelty is rooted in his nature, Macbeth's in "accidental circumstances" that do not obliterate his claim upon us as a man.

Although a work of real if intermittent power, *Richard III* is very formal in its language and its structure. The balance of such a line as "If you will live, lament; if die, be brief" attests to the relentless artifice that pervades the language of a play where everything is shaped and planned. Richard's opening soliloquy, for instance, reveals a virtuoso wit, but it is made to serve a triple function of characterizing the speaker, disclosing his motives, and announcing the course of action to be followed; and thus its great creative energy is controlled by Senecan conventions. Even in the scenes of private woe, as when the Lady Anne laments the murder of the last Lancastrian king, the style is tailored to a rhetoric:

> O, cursed be the hand that made these holes!
> Cursed the heart that had the heart to do it!
> Cursed the blood that let this blood from hence!
> (I.ii.14–16)

and in the public, choric lamentations the antiphonal exchanges are so stiff and patterned that grief assumes the form of ritual:

> *Q. Elizabeth.* What stay had I but Edward? and he's gone.
> *Children.* What stay had we but Clarence? and he's gone.
> *Duchess.* What stays had I but they? and they are gone.
> *Q. Elizabeth.* Was never widow had so dear a loss.
> *Children.* Were never orphans had so dear a loss.
> *Duchess.* Was never mother had so dear a loss.
> Alas! I am the mother of these griefs:
> Their woes are parcell'd, mine is general.
> She for an Edward weeps, and so do I;

I for a Clarence weep, so doth not she;
These babes for Clarence weep, and so do I;
I for an Edward weep, so do not they.
Alas! you three on me, threefold distress'd,
Pour all your tears. I am your sorrow's nurse,
And I will pamper it with lamentation.
(II.ii.74–88)

The style of Richard's wooing (I.ii) is more brisk, of course, but no less formal in its stichomythic pattern, and that of such set pieces as Clarence's dream is merely formal in a different way—in its symbolic implications and its dazzling use of sound and color:

O Lord, methought what pain it was to drown!
What dreadful noise of waters in my ears!
What sights of ugly death within my eyes!
Methoughts I saw a thousand fearful wracks;
A thousand men that fishes gnaw'd upon;
Wedges of gold, great anchors, heaps of pearl,
Inestimable stones, unvalued jewels,
All scatt'red in the bottom of the sea:
Some lay in dead men's skulls, and in the holes
Where eyes did once inhabit, there were crept
(As 'twere in scorn of eyes) reflecting gems,
That woo'd the slimy bottom of the deep,
And mock'd the dead bones that lay scatt'red by.
(I.iv.21–33)

In certain massive block-like scenes—for instance, the lamentation of the three queens at IV.iv and the stylized procession of the ghosts of Richard's victims at V.iii—almost the only action is provided by the formal movement of the verse. Even the low language of Clarence's murderers (I.iv) and the commonplaces of the prudent citizens (II.iii), which seem to echo living speech, are shaped into a kind of choric comment on the moral climate of the play:

1. Citizen. Come, come, we fear the worst; all will be well.
3. Citizen. When clouds are seen, wise men put on their cloaks;
When great leaves fall, then winter is at hand;
When the sun sets, who doth not look for night?
Untimely storms makes men expect a dearth.
All may be well; but if God sort it so,
'Tis more than we deserve or I expect.
(II.iii.31–37)

Despite such persistent formality of language, the plot, except for scenes like that of Richard's second wooing (IV.iv), moves very fast. Its velocity depends in part upon the precision and economy with which Shakespeare handles his materials. Unlike *3 Henry VI*, with its sprawling, sometimes ill-articulated action, *Richard III* pulses with a beat that quickens as the play proceeds. Even such surcharged moments as Richard's "Off with his head" when he sends Hastings to the block (III.iv) and his "A horse, a horse! my kingdom for a horse!" when he sees death appear (V.iv) are adjusted to the rising movement of the scenes where they occur; and the many *coups de théâtre* with which the play is dotted—like Richard's offer of his dagger to the Lady Anne (I.ii) and his break with Buckingham (IV.iii)—accelerate but do not punctuate the action. As usual in the histories, Shakespeare preserves the linear contour of events; but here the events are notably compressed and rearranged to maintain the rapid tempo of the plot. Propelled by Richard's stunning initial soliloquy, in Act I we sweep from Clarence's arrest (which occurred in 1477) and the report of Edward's final illness (1483), to a scene that conflates Henry VI's funeral (1471) and Richard's wooing of the Lady Anne, to Richard's appointment as Protector (1483), to the reappearance of old Margaret of Anjou (who had died in France in 1482), to Clarence's death by drowning in the malmsey-butt (1478). Such foreshortening and distortion do great violence to the facts, of course, but as A. P. Rossiter said of *Woodstock* (an anonymous play about the early reign of Richard II), the technique is very useful to a writer more concerned with moral meanings than with the recording of events.

Next to Richard's compelling central role it is Shakespeare's presentation of such moral meanings that most surely shapes the play. If its rather old-fashioned Senecan devices and its swift but episodic action mark *Richard III* as one of Shakespeare's early works, so does its debt to the tradition of the morality play, that remnant of an age when the struggle between good and evil for possession of man's soul was the main concern of drama. Although Shakespeare pointed to the debt himself—after all, the role of Richard, that consummate actor, is "the formal Vice, Iniquity" (III.i.82)—he goes far beyond the didactic crudities of such plays as Bale's *King John*. There can be no question of Richard's being saved like Everyman, of course, but he does epitomize the fact of evil, and his downfall, like that of Marlowe's Doctor Faustus, takes the form of retribution. The world he bustles in is one, despite "the grossness of the age," where effect is linked to cause in moral sequence, and where what happens to a man depends upon the kind of man he is. On one level this moral pattern is made to serve the use of Tudor propaganda, but it also, and more significantly, exemplifies the notion of retributive justice—or Nemesis, as R. G. Moulton called it.

As a Machiavel who takes evil for his good, and whose twisted body signifies his moral nihilism, Richard is a freak. He is not a good man who, when tempted, falls, and who, when fallen, hopes to find redemption. He is a "poisonous bunch-back'd toad," a "bottled spider," an "abortive, rooting hog," who sins with such bravado and exhilaration that E. K. Chambers decided Shakespeare really had no interest in the moral implications of his rise and fall. One finds it hard to follow this interpretation. Admittedly, this play does not unfold the cosmic evil that imparts such terror to *King Lear*: there is a sportive streak in Richard, and his crimes reveal a kind of antic cunning that both he and we enjoy. But that they are crimes is clear, and finally we recoil. Despite his string of quick successes, which seem to sweep the kingdom up into a spiral of corruption, the play is built upon a mounting sequence of crime and retribution—Clarence's, the Woodvilles', Hastings', Buckingham's—that finds its climax in the master-villain's death. The rhythm of this sequence not only confers a moral pattern on the action; it also underscores the words that Richmond, that paragon of sanity and order, addresses to his men as they prepare to meet and overcome their foe:

> Truly, gentlemen,
> A bloody tyrant and a homicide;
> One rais'd in blood, and one in blood established;
> One that made means to come by what he hath,
> And slaughtered those that were the means to help him;
> A base foul stone, made precious by the foil
> Of England's chair, where he is falsely set;
> One that hath ever been God's enemy.
> (V.iii.245–52)

In short, there are few if any moral ambiguities in Shakespeare's presentation of this "abortive, rooting hog," and it is not surprising that Colley Cibber's mangled version of the play (1700), which crudely underscored the fact of Richard's evil, terrified and titillated audiences on both sides of the Atlantic for nearly two centuries.

Herschel Baker

Sword and buckler

Sword and square target

From *Di Grassi His True Art of Defence*, trans. I. G. (1594). (*By permission of the Harvard College Library*)

The Tragedy of Richard the Third

[Dramatis Personae

King Edward the Fourth
Edward, *Prince of Wales, afterwards* King Edward V } *sons to the King*
Richard, *Duke of York* } *sons to the King*
George, *Duke of Clarence* } *brothers to the King*
Richard, *Duke of Gloucester, afterwards* King Richard III } *brothers to the King*
Edward Plantagenet, *Earl of Warwick, a young son of Clarence*
Henry, *Earl of Richmond, afterwards* King Henry VII
Cardinal Bourchier, *Archbishop of Canterbury*
Thomas Rotherham, *Archbishop of York*
John Morton, *Bishop of Ely*
Duke of Buckingham
Duke of Norfolk
Earl of Surrey, *his son*
Earl Rivers (*Anthony Woodvile*), *brother to Queen Elizabeth*
Marquess of Dorset } *sons to Queen Elizabeth*
Lord Grey } *sons to Queen Elizabeth*
Earl of Oxford
Lord Hastings
Lord Stanley, *called also* Earl of Derby
Lord Lovel
Sir Thomas Vaughan
Sir Richard Ratcliffe
Sir William Catesby
Sir James Tyrrel
Sir James Blunt
Sir Walter Herbert
Sir Robert Brakenbury, *Lieutenant of the Tower*
Sir William Brandon
Christopher Urswick, *a priest*
Another Priest
Hastings, *a pursuivant*
Tressel *and* Berkeley, *gentlemen attending on the Lady Anne*
Keeper *in the Tower*
Lord Mayor of London
Sheriff of Wiltshire

Elizabeth, *queen to King Edward IV*
Margaret, *widow of King Henry VI*
Duchess of York, *mother to King Edward IV, Clarence, and Gloucester*
Lady Anne, *widow of Edward, Prince of Wales, son to King Henry VI; afterwards married to Richard, Duke of Gloucester*
Margaret Plantagenet, *Countess of Salisbury, a young daughter of Clarence*

Ghosts *of those murdered by Richard III;* Lords, Gentlemen, *and other* Attendants; Page, Scrivener, Citizens, Bishops, Aldermen, Councillors, Murderers, Messengers, Soldiers, *etc.*

Scene: *London and other parts of England*]

ACT I, Scene I

Enter Richard Duke of Gloucester *solus.*

[*Glou.*] Now is the winter of our discontent
Made glorious summer by this son of York;
And all the clouds that low'r'd upon our house
In the deep bosom of the ocean buried.
Now are our brows bound with victorious wreaths,
Our bruised arms hung up for monuments,
Our stern alarums chang'd to merry meetings,
Our dreadful marches to delightful measures.
Grim-visag'd War hath smooth'd his wrinkled front;
And now, in stead of mounting barbed steeds
To fright the souls of fearful adversaries,
He capers nimbly in a lady's chamber
To the lascivious pleasing of a lute.
But I, that am not shap'd for sportive tricks,
Nor made to court an amorous looking-glass;
I, that am rudely stamp'd, and want love's majesty
To strut before a wanton ambling nymph;
I, that am curtail'd of this fair proportion,

Words and passages enclosed in square brackets in the text above are either emendations of the copy-text or additions to it. The Textual Notes immediately following the play cite the earliest authority for every such change or insertion and supply the reading of the copy-text wherever it is emended in this edition.

I.i. Location: London. A street.
o.s.d. **solus:** alone.
2. **son.** With a pun on *sun* (the badge of Edward IV). For the origin of the sun-badge see *3 Henry VI*, II.i.25–40.

6. **arms:** armor. **monuments:** trophies.
7. **alarums:** calls to arms. 8. **measures:** dances.
9. **wrinkled front:** frowning brow. 10. **barbed:** armored.
11. **fearful:** frightened. 18. **proportion:** shape.

Cheated of feature by dissembling nature,
Deform'd, unfinish'd, sent before my time
Into this breathing world, scarce half made up,
And that so lamely and unfashionable
That dogs bark at me as I halt by them—
Why, I, in this weak piping time of peace,
Have no delight to pass away the time,
Unless to see my shadow in the sun
And descant on mine own deformity.
And therefore, since I cannot prove a lover
To entertain these fair well-spoken days,
I am determined to prove a villain
And hate the idle pleasures of these days.
Plots have I laid, inductions dangerous,
By drunken prophecies, libels, and dreams,
To set my brother Clarence and the King
In deadly hate the one against the other;
And if King Edward be as true and just
As I am subtle, false, and treacherous,
This day should Clarence closely be mew'd up
About a prophecy, which says that G
Of Edward's heirs the murtherer shall be.
Dive, thoughts, down to my soul, here Clarence comes!

Enter CLARENCE, *guarded, and* BRAKENBURY, [*Lieutenant of the Tower*].

Brother, good day. What means this armed guard
That waits upon your Grace?
Clar. His Majesty,
Tend'ring my person's safety, hath appointed
This conduct to convey me to the Tower.
Glou. Upon what cause?
Clar. Because my name is George.
Glou. Alack, my lord, that fault is none of yours;
He should for that commit your godfathers.
O, belike his Majesty hath some intent
That you should be new christ'ned in the Tower.
But what's the matter, Clarence, may I know?
Clar. Yea, Richard, when I know; but I protest
As yet I do not. But, as I can learn,
He hearkens after prophecies and dreams,
And from the cross-row plucks the letter G,
And says a wizard told him that by G
His issue disinherited should be;
And for my name of George begins with G,
It follows in his thought that I am he.
These (as I learn) and such-like toys as these
Hath mov'd his Highness to commit me now.
Glou. Why, this it is, when men are rul'd by women:
'Tis not the King that sends you to the Tower;
My Lady Grey his wife, Clarence, 'tis she
That [tempers] him to this extremity.
Was it not she, and that good man of worship,
Anthony Woodvile, her brother there,
That made him send Lord Hastings to the Tower,
From whence this present day he is delivered?
We are not safe, Clarence, we are not safe.
Clar. By heaven, I think there is no man [is] secure
But the Queen's kindred, and night-walking heralds
That trudge betwixt the King and Mistress Shore.
Heard you not what an humble suppliant
Lord Hastings was [to her for his] delivery?
Glou. Humbly complaining to her deity
Got my Lord Chamberlain his liberty.
I'll tell you what, I think it is our way,
If we will keep in favor with the King,
To be her men and wear her livery.
The jealous o'erworn widow and herself,
Since that our brother dubb'd them gentlewomen,
Are mighty gossips in our monarchy.
Brak. I beseech your Graces both to pardon me:
His Majesty hath straitly given in charge
That no man shall have private conference
(Of what degree soever) with your brother.
Glou. Even so? And please your worship, Brakenbury,
You may partake of any thing we say:
We speak no treason, man. We say the King
Is wise and virtuous, and his noble queen
Well strook in years, fair, and not jealious;
We say that Shore's wife hath a pretty foot,
A cherry lip, a bonny eye, a passing pleasing tongue;
And that the Queen's kindred are made gentlefolks.
How say you, sir? Can you deny all this?
Brak. With this, my lord, myself have nought to do.
Glou. Naught to do with Mistress Shore? I tell thee, fellow,
He that doth naught with her (excepting one)
Were best to do it secretly alone.
Brak. What one, my lord?
Glou. Her husband, knave. Wouldst thou betray me?

19. feature: general appearance. **dissembling:** deceiving.
22. unfashionable: badly fashioned. **23. halt:** limp.
27. descant: comment, discourse. **32. inductions:** preparations.
36. true and just: i.e. naively unsuspecting.
38. mew'd up: caged (like a hawk).
39–40. a prophecy . . . be. According to Hall (Bullough, III, 249), "the fame was that the king or the Quene, or bothe [were] sore troubled with a folysh Prophesye, and by reason thereof began to stomacke & grevously to grudge agaynst the duke [of Clarence]. The effect of which was, after king Edward should reigne, one whose first letter of hys name shoulde be a G." **44. Tend'ring:** caring for.
45. conduct: escort. **49. belike:** probably.
55. cross-row: Christ- (or criss-)cross-row, i.e. the alphabet, so called from the figure of the cross usually prefixed to it in primers.
56. wizard: wise man, prophet. **58. for:** because.
60. toys: trifles.

64. Lady Grey. Queen Elizabeth's first husband was Sir John Grey.
65. tempers: moulds.
67. Anthony Woodvile. Woodvil(l)e succeeded his father as Earl Rivers in 1469. Richard sarcastically strips him and his sister, Queen Elizabeth, of their titles.
68. send . . . Tower. The chroniclers record no such imprisonment for William, Baron Hastings (1430?–1483), who had long and loyally served the House of York.
72. night-walking heralds: i.e. secret emissaries.
73. Mistress Shore: Jane Shore, wife of a London goldsmith and mistress of Edward IV. She long survived her early triumphs, not dying until about 1527. In Elizabethan usage *Mistress* was a title of respect for any woman, married or unmarried.
76. her deity: i.e. Jane Shore.
77. Lord Chamberlain: i.e. Lord Hastings, who served Edward IV in this capacity from 1461 to 1483.
81. widow: i.e. Queen Elizabeth, who was a widow when Edward married her. **83. mighty gossips:** powerful busybodies.
85. straitly: strictly.
87. degree: rank. (*Of what degree* modifies *man.*)
92. Well strook: well struck, i.e. advanced. Elizabeth was about forty at the time. **jealious:** jealous. **94. passing:** exceedingly.
97. nought: nothing. **98. Naught:** wickedness.

Brak. I do beseech your Grace to pardon me, and withal
Forbear your conference with the noble Duke.
Clar. We know thy charge, Brakenbury, and will obey.
Glou. We are the Queen's abjects, and must obey.
Brother, farewell, I will unto the King,
And whatsoe'er you will employ me in,
Were it to call King Edward's widow sister,
I will perform it to enfranchise you.
Mean time, this deep disgrace in brotherhood
Touches me deeper than you can imagine.
Clar. I know it pleaseth neither of us well.
Glou. Well, your imprisonment shall not be long,
I will deliver you, or else lie for you.
Mean time, have patience.
Clar. I must perforce. Farewell.
Exit Clarence [with Brakenbury and Guard].
Glou. Go tread the path that thou shalt ne'er return:
Simple plain Clarence, I do love thee so
That I will shortly send thy soul to heaven,
If heaven will take the present at our hands.
But who comes here? the new-delivered Hastings?
Enter LORD HASTINGS.
Hast. Good time of day unto my gracious lord!
Glou. As much unto my good Lord Chamberlain!
Well are you welcome to [the] open air.
How hath your lordship brook'd imprisonment?
Hast. With patience, noble lord, as prisoners must;
But I shall live, my lord, to give them thanks
That were the cause of my imprisonment.
Glou. No doubt, no doubt, and so shall Clarence too,
For they that were your enemies are his,
And have prevail'd as much on him as you.
Hast. More pity that the eagles should be mew'd,
Whiles kites and buzzards [prey] at liberty.
Glou. What news abroad?
Hast. No news so bad abroad as this at home:
The King is sickly, weak, and melancholy,
And his physicians fear him mightily.
Glou. Now by Saint John, that news is bad indeed!
O, he hath kept an evil diet long,
And overmuch consum'd his royal person:
'Tis very grievous to be thought upon.
Where is he? in his bed?
Hast. He is.
Glou. Go you before, and I will follow you.
Exit Hastings.
He cannot live, I hope, and must not die
Till George be pack'd with post-horse up to heaven.
I'll in, to urge his hatred more to Clarence
With lies well steel'd with weighty arguments,
And if I fail not in my deep intent,
Clarence hath not another day to live:
Which done, God take King Edward to his mercy,
And leave the world for me to bustle in!
For then I'll marry Warwick's youngest daughter.
What though I kill'd her husband and her father?
The readiest way to make the wench amends
Is to become her husband and her father:
The which will I, not all so much for love
As for another secret close intent
By marrying her which I must reach unto.
But yet I run before my horse to market:
Clarence still breathes, Edward still lives and reigns;
When they are gone, then must I count my gains.
Exit.

SCENE II

Enter the corse of HENRY THE SIXT, *with Halberds to guard it,* LADY ANNE *being the mourner, [attended by* TRESSEL *and* BERKELEY*].*

Anne. Set down, set down your honorable load,
If honor may be shrouded in a hearse,
Whilst I awhile obsequiously lament
Th' untimely fall of virtuous Lancaster.
Poor key-cold figure of a holy king,
Pale ashes of the house of Lancaster,
Thou bloodless remnant of that royal blood,
Be it lawful that I invocate thy ghost
To hear the lamentations of poor Anne,
Wife to thy Edward, to thy slaught'red son,
Stabb'd by the self-same hand that made these wounds!
Lo, in these windows that let forth thy life
I pour the helpless balm of my poor eyes.
O, cursed be the hand that made these holes!
Cursed the heart that had the heart to do it!
Cursed the blood that let this blood from hence!
More direful hap betide that hated wretch
That makes us wretched by the death of thee
Than I can wish to wolves—to spiders, toads,
Or any creeping venom'd thing that lives!
If ever he have child, abortive be it,
Prodigious, and untimely brought to light,
Whose ugly and unnatural aspect
May fright the hopeful mother at the view,
And that be heir to his unhappiness!
If ever he have wife, let her be made
More miserable by the [life] of him
Than I am made by my young lord and thee!

103. **withal**: at the same time. 106. **abjects**: servile subjects.
110. **enfranchise**: liberate.
115. **lie for you**: i.e. take your place in prison (with a pun on *lie* as "prevaricate"). 125. **brook'd**: endured.
133. **kites**: scavenger birds, a kind of hawk.
137. **fear**: fear for. 139. **diet**: course of life.
146. **with post-horse**: i.e. as quickly as possible.
148. **steel'd**: hardened, strengthened.

153. **Warwick's youngest daughter**: Anne Neville, daughter of the famous "Kingmaker," who had been betrothed (but not married) to Prince Edward, son of Henry VI. Shakespeare assumes throughout that Anne was Prince Edward's widow. 158. **intent**: design.

I.ii. **Location**: London. Another street.
o.s.d. **corse**: corpse. **Sixt**: Sixth. **Halberds**: halberdiers, guards bearing long weapons with axe-like heads.
2. **hearse**: a coffin on a bier.
3. **obsequiously**: mournfully, in a manner appropriate to a funeral.
5. **key-cold**: i.e. cold as a key, a proverbial expression for "cold as death." 13. **helpless**: useless. 17. **hap betide**: fortune befall.
21. **abortive**: unnatural. 22. **Prodigious**: monstrous.
25. **unhappiness**: evil nature.
28. **by . . . thee**: i.e. by the deaths of Prince Edward and Henry VI.

Come now towards Chertsey with your holy load,
Taken from Paul's to be interred there;
And still as you are weary of this weight,
Rest you, whiles I lament King Henry's corse.

Enter Richard Duke of Gloucester.

Glou. Stay, you that bear the corse, and set it down.
Anne. What black magician conjures up this fiend
To stop devoted charitable deeds?
Glou. Villains, set down the corse, or, by Saint Paul,
I'll make a corse of him that disobeys.
Gentleman. My lord, stand back, and let the coffin pass.
Glou. Unmanner'd dog, [stand] thou when I command.
Advance thy halberd higher than my breast,
Or by Saint Paul I'll strike thee to my foot,
And spurn upon thee, beggar, for thy boldness.
Anne. What do you tremble? are you all afraid?
Alas, I blame you not, for you are mortal,
And mortal eyes cannot endure the devil.—
Avaunt, thou dreadful minister of hell!
Thou hadst but power over his mortal body,
His soul thou canst not have. Therefore be gone.
Glou. Sweet saint, for charity, be not so curst.
Anne. Foul devil, for God's sake hence, and trouble us not,
For thou hast made the happy earth thy hell,
Fill'd it with cursing cries and deep exclaims.
If thou delight to view thy heinous deeds,
Behold this pattern of thy butcheries.
O gentlemen, see, see dead Henry's wounds
Open their congeal'd mouths and bleed afresh!
Blush, blush, thou lump of foul deformity;
For 'tis thy presence that exhales this blood
From cold and empty veins where no blood dwells.
Thy deeds inhuman and unnatural
Provokes this deluge most unnatural.
O God! which this blood mad'st, revenge his death!
O earth! which this blood drink'st, revenge his death!
Either heav'n with lightning strike the murth'rer dead;
Or earth gape open wide and eat him quick,
As thou dost swallow up this good king's blood,
Which his hell-govern'd arm hath butchered!
Glou. Lady, you know no rules of charity,
Which renders good for bad, blessings for curses.
Anne. Villain, thou know'st nor law of God nor man:
No beast so fierce but knows some touch of pity.
Glou. But I know none, and therefore am no beast.
Anne. O wonderful, when devils tell the [troth]!
Glou. More wonderful, when angels are so angry.
Vouchsafe, divine perfection of a woman,
Of these supposed crimes, to give me leave
By circumstance but to acquit myself.
Anne. Vouchsafe, defus'd infection of [a] man,
Of these known evils, but to give me leave
By circumstance [t' accuse] thy cursed self.
Glou. Fairer than tongue can name thee, let me have
Some patient leisure to excuse myself.
Anne. Fouler than heart can think thee, thou canst make
No excuse current but to hang thyself.
Glou. By such despair I should accuse myself.
Anne. And by despairing shalt thou stand excused
For doing worthy vengeance on thyself,
That didst unworthy slaughter upon others.
Glou. Say that I slew them not?
Anne. Then say they were not slain.
But dead they are, and, devilish slave, by thee.
Glou. I did not kill your husband.
Anne. Why then he is alive.
Glou. Nay, he is dead, and slain by Edward's hands.
Anne. In thy foul throat thou li'st! Queen Margaret saw
Thy murd'rous falchion smoking in his blood;
The which thou once didst bend against her breast,
But that thy brothers beat aside the point.
Glou. I was provoked by her sland'rous tongue,
That laid their guilt upon my guiltless shoulders.
Anne. Thou wast provoked by thy bloody mind,
That never dream'st on aught but butcheries.
Didst thou not kill this king?
Glou. I grant ye.
Anne. Dost grant me, hedgehog? Then God grant me too
Thou mayst be damned for that wicked deed!
O, he was gentle, mild, and virtuous!
Glou. The better for the King of Heaven that hath him.
Anne. He is in heaven, where thou shalt never come.
Glou. Let him thank me that holp to send him thither;
For he was fitter for that place than earth.
Anne. And thou unfit for any place, but hell.
Glou. Yes, one place else, if you will hear me name it.
Anne. Some dungeon.
Glou. Your bedchamber.
Anne. Ill rest betide the chamber where thou liest!
Glou. So will it, madam, till I lie with you.
Anne. I hope so.
Glou. I know so. But, gentle Lady Anne,

29. Chertsey: monastery near London on the south side of the Thames. Although the main contents of this scene (such as Anne's presence at Henry VI's funeral) are unhistorical, Holinshed (Bullough, III, 249n.) supplies the detail that when Henry's corpse was exposed in St. Paul's "the same in the presence of the beholders did bleed" (cf. lines 55–56).
30. Paul's: St. Paul's Cathedral in London.
31. still as: whenever. **39. stand:** halt.
40. Advance . . . breast: i.e. keep your weapon upright.
42. spurn: trample. **43. What:** why. **46. Avaunt:** be gone.
49. curst: shrewish. **52. exclaims:** exclamations.
54. pattern: example.
55–56. dead . . . afresh. It was popularly believed that a murdered person's wounds would bleed afresh in the presence of the murderer.
58. exhales: draws out. **65. quick:** alive.
70. nor . . . nor: neither . . . nor.

77. circumstance: detailed argument.
78. defus'd: diffused, i.e. misshapen.
84. current: acceptable, i.e. genuine (a term from coinage).
93–98. Queen . . . shoulders. See *3 Henry VI*, V.v.38–43.
94. falchion: curved sword.
102. hedgehog. Perhaps with an allusion to Richard's badge, a wild boar (hog). **107. holp:** helped.

To leave this keen encounter of our wits
And fall something into a slower method:
Is not the causer of the timeless deaths
Of these Plantagenets, Henry and Edward,
As blameful as the executioner?
Anne. Thou wast the cause, and most accurs'd effect.
Glou. Your beauty was the cause of that effect—
Your beauty, that did haunt me in my sleep
To undertake the death of all the world,
So I might live one hour in your sweet bosom.
Anne. If I thought that, I tell thee, homicide,
These nails should rent that beauty from my cheeks.
Glou. These eyes could not endure that beauty's wrack;
You should not blemish it, if I stood by:
As all the world is cheered by the sun,
So I by that; it is my day, my life.
Anne. Black night o'ershade thy day, and death thy life!
Glou. Curse not thyself, fair creature—thou art both.
Anne. I would I were, to be reveng'd on thee.
Glou. It is a quarrel most unnatural,
To be reveng'd on him that loveth thee.
Anne. It is a quarrel just and reasonable,
To be reveng'd on him that kill'd my husband.
Glou. He that bereft thee, lady, of thy husband,
Did it to help thee to a better husband.
Anne. His better doth not breathe upon the earth.
Glou. He lives, that loves thee better than he could.
Anne. Name him.
Glou. Plantagenet.
Anne. Why, that was he.
Glou. The self-same name, but one of better nature.
Anne. Where is he?
Glou. Here. ([*She*] *spits at him*.) Why dost thou spit at me?
Anne. Would it were mortal poison for thy sake!
Glou. Never came poison from so sweet a place.
Anne. Never hung poison on a fouler toad.
Out of my sight, thou dost infect mine eyes!
Glou. Thine eyes, sweet lady, have infected mine.
Anne. Would they were basilisks, to strike thee dead!
Glou. I would they were, that I might die at once;
For now they kill me with a living death.
Those eyes of thine from mine have drawn salt tears,
Sham'd their aspects with store of childish drops:
These eyes, which never shed remorseful tear—
No, when my father York and Edward wept
To hear the piteous moan that Rutland made
When black-fac'd Clifford shook his sword at him;
Nor when thy warlike father, like a child,
Told the sad story of my father's death,
And twenty times made pause to sob and weep,
That all the standers-by had wet their cheeks
Like trees bedash'd with rain—in that sad time
My manly eyes did scorn an humble tear;
And what these sorrows could not thence exhale,
Thy beauty hath, and made them blind with weeping.
I never sued to friend nor enemy;
My tongue could never learn sweet smoothing word;
But now thy beauty is propos'd my fee,
My proud heart sues, and prompts my tongue to speak.
She looks scornfully at him.
Teach not thy lip such scorn; for it was made
For kissing, lady, not for such contempt.
If thy revengeful heart cannot forgive,
Lo here I lend thee this sharp-pointed sword,
Which if thou please to hide in this true breast,
And let the soul forth that adoreth thee,
I lay it naked to the deadly stroke,
And humbly beg the death upon my knee.
He lays his breast open: she offers at [*it*] *with his sword.*
Nay, do not pause: for I did kill King Henry—
But 'twas thy beauty that provoked me.
Nay, now dispatch: 'twas I that stabb'd young Edward—
But 'twas thy heavenly face that set me on.
She falls the sword.
Take up the sword again, or take up me.
Anne. Arise, dissembler! Though I wish thy death,
I will not be thy executioner.
Glou. Then bid me kill myself, and I will do it.
Anne. I have already.
Glou. That was in thy rage.
Speak it again, and even with the word
This hand, which for thy love did kill thy love,
Shall for thy love kill a far truer love;
To both their deaths shalt thou be accessary.
Anne. I would I knew thy heart.
Glou. 'Tis figur'd in my tongue.
Anne. I fear me both are false.
Glou. Then never [was man] true.
Anne. Well, well, put up your sword.
Glou. Say then my peace is made.
Anne. That shalt thou know hereafter.
Glou. But shall I live in hope?
Anne. All men, I hope, live so.
[*Glou*.] Vouchsafe to wear this ring.
[*Anne*. To take is not to give.]
[*Gloucester slips the ring on her finger*.]
Glou. Look how my ring encompasseth thy finger,
Even so thy breast encloseth my poor heart:
Wear both of them, for both of them are thine.
And if thy poor devoted servant may
But beg one favor at thy gracious hand,
Thou dost confirm his happiness for ever.
Anne. What is it?
Glou. That it may please you leave these sad designs

117. timeless: untimely.
120. effect: agent. **121. effect**: result.
125. homicide: murderer. **126. rent**: rend.
127. wrack: destruction.
141. He lives: i.e. there is a man. **he**: i.e. Prince Edward.
150. basilisks: fabulous serpents whose glance was alleged to cause death. **154. aspects**: appearance.
156–58. when . . . him. See *3 Henry VI*, I.iii.
162. That: so that. **168. smoothing**: flattering.
169. propos'd my fee: held forth as my reward.
178 s.d. offers: thrusts. **182 s.d. falls**: lets fall.
191. accessary: accessory. **193. figur'd**: expressed.
201. Vouchsafe: consent. **206. servant**: (1) menial; (2) lover.

To him that hath most cause to be a mourner,
And presently repair to Crosby House;
Where (after I have solemnly interr'd
At Chertsey monast'ry this noble king,
And wet his grave with my repentant tears)
I will with all expedient duty see you.
For divers unknown reasons, I beseech you,
Grant me this boon.
Anne. With all my heart, and much it joys me too,
To see you are become so penitent.
Tressel and Berkeley, go along with me.
Glou. Bid me farewell.
Anne. 'Tis more than you deserve;
But since you teach me how to flatter you,
Imagine I have said farewell already.
Exeunt two, [Tressel and Berkeley,] with Anne.
[*Glou.* Sirs, take up the corse.]
Gent. Towards Chertsey, noble lord?
Glou. No; to White-Friars, there attend my coming. *Exit corse [with Halberds].*
Was ever woman in this humor woo'd?
Was ever woman in this humor won?
I'll have her, but I will not keep her long.
What? I, that kill'd her husband and his father,
To take her in her heart's extremest hate,
With curses in her mouth, tears in her eyes,
The bleeding witness of my hatred by,
Having God, her conscience, and these bars against me,
And I no friends to back my suit [at all]
But the plain devil and dissembling looks?
And yet to win her! All the world to nothing!
Hah!
Hath she forgot already that brave prince,
Edward, her lord, whom I, some three months since,
Stabb'd in my angry mood at Tewksbury?
A sweeter and a lovelier gentleman,
Fram'd in the prodigality of nature—
Young, valiant, wise, and (no doubt) right royal—
The spacious world cannot again afford.
And will she yet abase her eyes on me,
That cropp'd the golden prime of this sweet prince
And made her widow to a woeful bed?
On me, whose all not equals Edward's moi'ty?
On me, that halts and am misshapen thus?
My dukedom to a beggarly denier,
I do mistake my person all this while!
Upon my life, she finds (although I cannot)
Myself to be a marv'llous proper man.
I'll be at charges for a looking-glass,
And entertain a score or two of tailors
To study fashions to adorn my body:
Since I am crept in favor with myself,
I will maintain it with some little cost.

212. presently: immediately. **Crosby House:** one of Richard's London residences. **216. expedient:** speedy.
217. unknown: secret.
226. White-Friars: Carmelite priory in London. **attend:** await.
227–28. Was . . . won. Cf. *Titus Andronicus*, II.i.82–83; *1 Henry VI*, V.iii.78–79.
240. three months since. Henry's funeral occurred on May 23, 1471, some three weeks after Prince Edward's death at Tewksbury.
249. Edward's moi'ty: half of Edward.
251. denier: a small copper coin. **254. proper:** handsome.
255. be . . . for: buy. **256. entertain:** employ.

But first I'll turn yon fellow in his grave,
And then return lamenting to my love.
Shine out, fair sun, till I have bought a glass,
That I may see my shadow as I pass. *Exit.*

Scene III

Enter the Queen Mother [Elizabeth], Lord Rivers, [Marquess of Dorset,] *and* Lord Grey.

Riv. Have patience, madam, there's no doubt his Majesty
Will soon recover his accustom'd health.
Grey. In that you brook it ill, it makes him worse;
Therefore for God's sake entertain good comfort,
And cheer his Grace with quick and merry eyes.
Q. Eliz. If he were dead, what would betide on me?
Grey. No other harm but loss of such a lord.
Q. Eliz. The loss of such a lord includes all harms.
Grey. The heavens have blest you with a goodly son
To be your comforter when he is gone.
Q. Eliz. Ah! he is young; and his minority
Is put unto the trust of Richard Gloucester,
A man that loves not me, nor none of you.
Riv. Is it concluded he shall be Protector?
Q. Eliz. It is determin'd, not concluded yet;
But so it must be, if the King miscarry.

Enter Buckingham *and* [Lord Stanley, *Earl of*] *Derby.*

Grey. Here [come] the [lords] of Buckingham and Derby.
Buck. Good time of day unto your royal Grace!
Stan. God make your Majesty joyful, as you have been!
Q. Eliz. The Countess Richmond, good my Lord of Derby,
To your good prayer will scarcely say amen.
Yet, Derby, notwithstanding she's your wife
And loves not me, be you, good lord, assur'd
I hate not you for her proud arrogance.
Stan. I do beseech you, either not believe
The envious slanders of her false accusers;
Or if she be accus'd on true report,
Bear with her weakness, which I think proceeds
From wayward sickness and no grounded malice.
Q. Eliz. Saw you the King to-day, my Lord of Derby?

260. in: into.

I.iii. Location: London. The palace.
6. betide on: happen to.
14–15. Is . . . yet. Richard was named Protector by the council on May 4, 1483, almost a month after Edward's death.
14. concluded: officially decreed. **16. miscarry:** i.e. die.
20. Countess Richmond: Margaret Beaufort, great-granddaughter of John of Gaunt and daughter of John Beaufort, Duke of Somerset, to whose marriage with Edmund Tudor, Earl of Richmond, was born (1456) the son whom Henry VI called "England's hope" (*3 Henry VI*, IV.vi.68) and who came to the throne in 1485 as Henry VII. Margaret's second husband was Lord Henry Stafford; her third (who appears throughout this play) was Thomas, Lord Stanley (later Earl of Derby). **24. arrogance:** i.e. ambition for her son.
29. wayward: erratic.

Stan. But now the Duke of Buckingham and I
Are come from visiting his Majesty.
Q. Eliz. What likelihood of his amendment, lords?
Buck. Madam, good hope, his Grace speaks cheerfully.
Q. Eliz. God grant him health! Did you confer with him?
Buck. Ay, madam, he desires to make atonement
Between the Duke of Gloucester and your brothers,
And between them and my Lord Chamberlain,
And sent to warn them to his royal presence.
Q. Eliz. Would all were well! but that will never be:
I fear our happiness is at the height.

Enter RICHARD [DUKE OF GLOUCESTER *and* LORD HASTINGS].

Glou. They do me wrong, and I will not endure it!
Who is it that complains unto the King
That I, forsooth, am stern, and love them not?
By holy Paul, they love his Grace but lightly
That fill his ears with such dissentious rumors.
Because I cannot flatter and look fair,
Smile in men's faces, smooth, deceive, and cog,
Duck with French nods and apish courtesy,
I must be held a rancorous enemy.
Cannot a plain man live and think no harm,
But thus his simple truth must be abus'd
With silken, sly, insinuating Jacks?
Grey. To who in all this presence speaks your Grace?
Glou. To thee, that hast nor honesty nor grace:
When have I injur'd thee? When done thee wrong?
Or thee? or thee? or any of your faction?
A plague upon you all! His royal Grace
(Whom God preserve better than you would wish!)
Cannot be quiet scarce a breathing while
But you must trouble him with lewd complaints.
Q. Eliz. Brother of Gloucester, you mistake the matter:
The King, on his own royal disposition
(And not provok'd by any suitor else),
Aiming, belike, at your interior hatred,
That in your outward action shows itself
Against my children, brothers, and myself,
Makes him to send, that he may learn the ground.
Glou. I cannot tell, the world is grown so bad
That wrens make prey where eagles dare not perch.
Since every Jack became a gentleman,
There's many a gentle person made a Jack.
Q. Eliz. Come, come, we know your meaning, brother Gloucester;
You envy my advancement and my friends'
God grant we never may have need of you!
Glou. Mean time, God grants that I have need of you.

36. atonement: reconciliation. **39. warn:** summon.
41. height: i.e. of Fortune's whirling wheel. **48. cog:** cheat.
49. Duck: bow. **53. Jacks:** worthless fellows.
55. grace: sense of duty or propriety.
60. breathing while: i.e. the length of a breath.
61. lewd: base. **63. disposition:** inclination.

Our brother is imprison'd by your means,
Myself disgrac'd, and the nobility
Held in contempt, while great promotions
Are daily given to ennoble those
That scarce some two days since were worth a noble.
Q. Eliz. By Him that rais'd me to this careful height
From that contented hap which I enjoy'd,
I never did incense his Majesty
Against the Duke of Clarence, but have been
An earnest advocate to plead for him.
My lord, you do me shameful injury
Falsely to draw me in these vile suspects.
Glou. You may deny that you were not the mean
Of my Lord Hastings' late imprisonment.
Riv. She may, my lord, for—
Glou. She may, Lord Rivers! Why, who knows not so?
She may do more, sir, than denying that:
She may help you to many fair preferments,
And then deny her aiding hand therein
And lay those honors on your high desert.
What may she not, she may, ay, marry, may she.
Riv. What, marry, may she?
Glou. What, marry, may she? Marry with a king,
A bachelor, and a handsome stripling too:
Iwis your grandam had a worser match.
Q. Eliz. My Lord of Gloucester, I have too long borne
Your blunt upbraidings and your bitter scoffs.
By heaven, I will acquaint his Majesty
Of those gross taunts that oft I have endur'd.
I had rather be a country servant maid
Than a great queen with this condition,
To be so baited, scorn'd, and stormed at.

Enter old QUEEN MARGARET [*behind*].

Small joy have I in being England's queen.
Q. Mar. [*Aside.*] And less'ned be that small, God I beseech him!
Thy honor, state, and seat is due to me.
Glou. What? threat you me with telling of the King?
[Tell him, and spare not. Look what I have said,]
I will avouch't in presence of the King.
I dare adventure to be sent to th' Tow'r.
'Tis time to speak, my pains are quite forgot.
Q. Mar. [*Aside.*] Out, devil! I do remember them too well:
Thou kill'dst my husband Henry in the Tower,
And Edward, my poor son, at Tewksbury.

77. Our brother: i.e. George, Duke of Clarence.
81. noble: (1) a gold coin; (2) nobleman.
82. careful: full of care, uneasy.
88. in: into. **suspects:** suspicions.
97. What . . . she may: what she may (i.e. should) not do, she does. **marry:** indeed (originally the name of the Virgin Mary used as an oath); with following pun on "wed." **101. Iwis:** certainly.
108. baited: harassed. **s.d. Queen Margaret.** The appearance here of Henry VI's widow—the embodiment of the Lancastrians' blasted hopes—is entirely fictitious. Following the battle of Tewkesbury (1471) she was imprisoned in England for five years and then sent to France, where she lived until 1482 as an unwelcome pensioner of Louis XI.
111. state: rank. **seat:** throne. **115. adventure:** venture, risk.

Glou. Ere you were queen, ay, or your husband king,
I was a pack-horse in his great affairs:
A weeder-out of his proud adversaries,
A liberal rewarder of his friends;
To royalize his blood I spent mine own.
Q. Mar. [*Aside.*] Ay, and much better blood than his or thine.
Glou. In all which time you and your husband Grey
Were factious for the house of Lancaster;
And, Rivers, so were you. Was not your husband
In Margaret's battle at Saint Albons slain?
Let me put in your minds, if you forget,
What you have been ere this, and what you are;
Withal, what I have been, and what I am.
Q. Mar. [*Aside.*] A murth'rous villain, and so still thou art.
Glou. Poor Clarence did forsake his father, Warwick,
Ay, and forswore himself—which Jesu pardon!—
Q. Mar. [*Aside.*] Which God revenge!
Glou. To fight on Edward's party for the crown,
And for his meed, poor lord, he is mewed up.
I would to God my heart were flint, like Edward's,
Or Edward's soft and pitiful, like mine:
I am too childish-foolish for this world.
Q. Mar. [*Aside.*] Hie thee to hell for shame, and leave this world,
Thou cacodemon, there thy kingdom is.
Riv. My Lord of Gloucester, in those busy days,
Which here you urge to prove us enemies,
We follow'd then our lord, our sovereign king.
So should we you, if you should be our king.
Glou. If I should be? I had rather be a pedlar:
Far be it from my heart, the thought thereof!
Q. Eliz. As little joy, my lord, as you suppose
You should enjoy, were you this country's king—
As little joy you may suppose in me
That I enjoy, being the queen thereof.
Q. Mar. [*Aside.*] A little joy enjoys the queen thereof,
For I am she, and altogether joyless.
I can no longer hold me patient. [*Comes forward.*]
Hear me, you wrangling pirates, that fall out
In sharing that which you have pill'd from me!
Which of you trembles not that looks on me?
If not, that I am queen, you bow like subjects,
Yet that, by you depos'd, you quake like rebels?
Ah, gentle villain, do not turn away!
Glou. Foul wrinkled witch, what mak'st thou in my sight?
Q. Mar. But repetition of what thou hast marr'd,
That will I make before I let thee go.
Glou. Wert thou not banished on pain of death?
Q. Mar. I was; but I do find more pain in banishment
Than death can yield me here by my abode.
A husband and a son thou ow'st to me—
And thou a kingdom—all of you allegiance.
This sorrow that I have, by right is yours,
And all the pleasures you usurp are mine.
Glou. The curse my noble father laid on thee
When thou didst crown his warlike brows with paper,
And with thy scorns drew'st rivers from his eyes,
And then, to dry them, gav'st the Duke a clout
Steep'd in the faultless blood of pretty Rutland—
His curses then, from bitterness of soul
Denounc'd against thee, are all fall'n upon thee;
And God, not we, hath plagu'd thy bloody deed.
Q. Eliz. So just is God, to right the innocent.
Hast. O, 'twas the foulest deed to slay that babe,
And the most merciless, that e'er was heard of!
Riv. Tyrants themselves wept when it was reported.
Dor. No man but prophesied revenge for it.
Buck. Northumberland, then present, wept to see it.
Q. Mar. What? were you snarling all before I came,
Ready to catch each other by the throat,
And turn you all your hatred now on me?
Did York's dread curse prevail so much with heaven
That Henry's death, my lovely Edward's death,
Their kingdom's loss, my woeful banishment,
Should all but answer for that peevish brat?
Can curses pierce the clouds and enter heaven?
Why then give way, dull clouds, to my quick curses!
Though not by war, by surfeit die your king,
As ours by murther, to make him a king!
Edward thy son, that now is Prince of Wales,
For Edward our son, that was Prince of Wales,
Die in his youth by like untimely violence!
Thyself a queen, for me that was a queen,
Outlive thy glory like my wretched self!
Long mayst thou live to wail thy children's death,
And see another, as I see thee now,
Deck'd in thy rights as thou art stall'd in mine!
Long die thy happy days before thy death,
And after many length'ned hours of grief,
Die neither mother, wife, nor England's queen!
Rivers and Dorset, you were standers-by,
And so wast thou, Lord Hastings, when my son
Was stabb'd with bloody daggers: God, I pray him
That none of you may live his natural age,
But by some unlook'd accident cut off!

121. pack-horse: workhorse, i.e. drudge.
127. factious for: i.e. a party to the agitation of.
134. father: i.e. father-in-law. Clarence had married Warwick's daughter Isabella, sister of the Lady Anne of this play, and for a time supported the Lancastrians, until he "forswore himself" by returning to the Yorkist side. **137. party:** side. **138. meed:** reward.
143. cacodemon: evil spirit. **145. urge:** cite.
152. in: as regards. **158. pill'd:** pillaged.
160–61. If . . . rebels: i.e. even if you do not bow before me as your queen, you quake because you have deposed me. **164. But:** only.
169. thou: i.e. Richard. **170. thou:** i.e. Queen Elizabeth.
173–77. The curse . . . Rutland. See *3 Henry VI*, I.iv.
176. clout: cloth, i.e. handkerchief.
182. babe: i.e. Rutland. **193. but answer for:** merely equal.
195. quick: animated. **196. surfeit:** dissipation.
201. for: in place of. **205. stall'd:** installed.
209–11. Rivers . . . daggers. Although Hall (Bullough, III, 206) names King Edward and his two brothers, Dorset, and Hastings as parties to Prince Edward's murder, Shakespeare includes only the King and his brothers in his version of the crime at Tewkesbury (*3 Henry VI*, V.v). **213. unlook'd:** unexpected.

Glou. Have done thy charm, thou hateful with'red hag.
Q. Mar. And leave out thee? Stay, dog, for thou shalt hear me.
If heaven have any grievous plague in store
Exceeding those that I can wish upon thee,
O, let them keep it till thy sins be ripe,
And then hurl down their indignation
On thee, the troubler of the poor world's peace!
The worm of conscience still begnaw thy soul!
Thy friends suspect for traitors while thou liv'st,
And take deep traitors for thy dearest friends!
No sleep close up that deadly eye of thine,
Unless it be while some tormenting dream
Affrights thee with a hell of ugly devils!
Thou elvish-mark'd, abortive, rooting hog!
Thou that wast seal'd in thy nativity
The slave of nature and the son of hell!
Thou slander of thy heavy mother's womb!
Thou loathed issue of thy father's loins!
Thou rag of honor! thou detested—
Glou. Margaret.
Q. Mar. Richard!
Glou. Ha!
Q. Mar. I call thee not.
Glou. I cry thee mercy then; for I did think
That thou hadst call'd me all these bitter names.
Q. Mar. Why, so I did, but look'd for no reply.
O, let me make the period to my curse!
Glou. 'Tis done by me, and ends in "Margaret."
Q. Eliz. Thus have you breath'd your curse against yourself.
Q. Mar. Poor painted queen, vain flourish of my fortune!
Why strew'st thou sugar on that bottled spider
Whose deadly web ensnareth thee about?
Fool, fool, thou whet'st a knife to kill thyself.
The day will come that thou shalt wish for me
To help thee curse this poisonous bunch-back'd toad.
Hast. False-boding woman, end thy frantic curse,
Lest to thy harm thou move our patience.
Q. Mar. Foul shame upon you, you have all mov'd mine.
Riv. Were you well serv'd, you would be taught your duty.
Q. Mar. To serve me well, you all should do me duty,
Teach me to be your queen, and you my subjects:
O, serve me well, and teach yourselves that duty!
Dor. Dispute not with her, she is lunatic.
Q. Mar. Peace, Master Marquess, you are malapert,
Your fire-new stamp of honor is scarce current.
O that your young nobility could judge
What 'twere to lose it and be miserable!
They that stand high have many blasts to shake them,
And if they fall, they dash themselves to pieces.
Glou. Good counsel, marry! Learn it, learn it, Marquess.
Dor. It touches you, my lord, as much as me.
Glou. Ay, and much more; but I was born so high,
Our aery buildeth in the cedar's top
And dallies with the wind and scorns the sun.
Q. Mar. And turns the sun to shade—alas, alas!
Witness my son, now in the shade of death,
Whose bright out-shining beams thy cloudy wrath
Hath in eternal darkness folded up.
Your aery buildeth in our aery's nest:
O God that seest it, do not suffer it!
As it is won with blood, lost be it so!
Buck. Peace, peace, for shame! if not, for charity.
Q. Mar. Urge neither charity nor shame to me. [*Turning to the others.*]
Uncharitably with me have you dealt,
And shamefully my hopes, by you, are butcher'd.
My charity is outrage, life my shame,
And in that shame still live my sorrow's rage!
Buck. Have done, have done.
Q. Mar. O princely Buckingham, I'll kiss thy hand
In sign of league and amity with thee.
Now fair befall thee and thy noble house!
Thy garments are not spotted with our blood;
Nor thou within the compass of my curse.
Buck. Nor no one here; for curses never pass
The lips of those that breathe them in the air.
Q. Mar. I will not think but they ascend the sky,
And there awake God's gentle-sleeping peace.
O Buckingham, take heed of yonder dog!
Look when he fawns he bites; and when he bites,
His venom tooth will rankle to the death.
Have not to do with him, beware of him;
Sin, death, and hell have set their marks on him,
And all their ministers attend on him.
Glou. What doth she say, my Lord of Buckingham?
Buck. Nothing that I respect, my gracious lord.
Q. Mar. What, dost thou scorn me for my gentle counsel?
And soothe the devil that I warn thee from?
O but remember this another day,
When he shall split thy very heart with sorrow,
And say poor Margaret was a prophetess!
Live each of you the subjects to his hate,
And he to yours, and all of you to God's! *Exit.*
Buck. My hair doth stand an end to hear her curses.
Riv. And so doth mine. I muse why she's at liberty.
Glou. I cannot blame her; by God's holy Mother,

214. charm: incantation, curse.
221. still begnaw: continually gnaw.
227. elvish-mark'd: deformed by elves. **hog.** See note to I.ii.102.
228. seal'd: stamped, confirmed.
229. slave of nature: i.e. because he was congenitally deformed.
230. heavy: sorrowful. **234. cry thee mercy:** beg your pardon.
237. period: conclusion.
240. painted: counterfeit. **vain . . . fortune:** empty ornament of the position that belongs to me.
241. bottled: swollen, big-bellied.
245. bunch-back'd: hunchbacked.
246. False-boding: falsely prophesying. **250. duty:** obeisance.
254. malapert: impudent.

255. Your . . . current: i.e. your title is so recently minted that it is hardly accepted yet as genuine. Actually, Sir Thomas Grey, Queen Elizabeth's eldest son by her first marriage, had been raised to the peerage as the Earl of Dorset in 1475, eight years before the time represented in this scene. **263. aery:** eagle's brood.
281. fair befall: good luck to.
290. venom: venomous. **rankle:** cause a festering wound.
303. an: on. **304. muse:** wonder.

She hath had too much wrong, and I repent
My part thereof that I have done to her.
[*Q. Eliz.*] I never did her any to my knowledge.
Glou. Yet you have all the vantage of her wrong.
I was too hot to do somebody good
That is too cold in thinking of it now.
Marry, as for Clarence, he is well repaid;
He is frank'd up to fatting for his pains—
God pardon them that are the cause thereof!
Riv. A virtuous and a Christian-like conclusion—
To pray for them that have done scathe to us.
Glou. So do I ever—(*speaks to himself*) being well advis'd;
For had I curs'd now, I had curs'd myself.

Enter CATESBY.

Cate. Madam, his Majesty doth call for you,
And for your Grace, and yours, my gracious lord.
Q. Eliz. Catesby, I come. Lords, will you go with me?
Riv. We wait upon your Grace.
Exeunt all but Gloucester.
Glou. I do the wrong, and first begin to brawl.
The secret mischiefs that I set abroach
I lay unto the grievous charge of others.
Clarence, who I indeed have cast in darkness,
I do beweep to many simple gulls—
Namely, to Derby, Hastings, Buckingham—
And tell them 'tis the Queen and her allies
That stir the King against the Duke my brother.
Now they believe it, and withal whet me
To be reveng'd on Rivers, Dorset, Grey.
But then I sigh, and, with a piece of scripture,
Tell them that God bids us do good for evil:
And thus I clothe my naked villainy
With odd old ends stol'n forth of holy writ,
And seem a saint, when most I play the devil.

Enter two MURTHERERS.

But soft, here come my executioners.
How now, my hardy, stout, resolved mates,
Are you now going to dispatch this thing?
[*1. Mur.*] We are, my lord, and come to have the warrant,
That we may be admitted where he is.
Glou. Well thought upon, I have it here about me.
[*Gives the warrant.*]
When you have done, repair to Crosby Place.
But, sirs, be sudden in the execution,
Withal obdurate, do not hear him plead;
For Clarence is well-spoken, and perhaps
May move your hearts to pity if you mark him.
[*1. Mur.*] Tut, tut, my lord, we will not stand to prate;
Talkers are no good doers. Be assur'd;
We go to use our hands, and not our tongues.

309. vantage of: benefits derived from.
313. frank'd up: penned (as in a sty). **316. scathe:** harm.
322. wait upon: attend. **324. set abroach:** set flowing.
327. gulls: credulous fools. **331. whet:** urge.
339. resolved: resolute. **345. sudden:** quick.

Glou. Your eyes drop millstones, when fools' eyes fall tears.
I like you, lads, about your business straight.
Go, go, dispatch.
[*1. Mur.*] We will, my noble lord. [*Exeunt.*]

SCENE IV

Enter CLARENCE *and* KEEPER.

Keep. Why looks your Grace so heavily to-day?
Clar. O, I have pass'd a miserable night,
So full of fearful dreams, of ugly sights,
That, as I am a Christian faithful man,
I would not spend another such a night
Though 'twere to buy a world of happy days—
So full of dismal terror was the time.
Keep. What was your dream, my lord? I pray you tell me.
Clar. Methoughts that I had broken from the Tower
And was embark'd to cross to Burgundy,
And in my company my brother Gloucester,
Who from my cabin tempted me to walk
Upon the hatches. [Thence] we look'd toward England,
And cited up a thousand heavy times,
During the wars of York and Lancaster,
That had befall'n us. As we pac'd along
Upon the giddy footing of the hatches,
Methought that Gloucester stumbled, and in falling
Strook me (that thought to stay him) overboard
Into the tumbling billows of the main.
O Lord, methought what pain it was to drown!
What dreadful noise of [waters] in [my] ears!
What sights of ugly death within [my] eyes!
Methoughts I saw a thousand fearful wracks;
A thousand men that fishes gnaw'd upon;
Wedges of gold, great anchors, heaps of pearl,
Inestimable stones, unvalued jewels,
All scatt'red in the bottom of the sea:
Some lay in dead men's skulls, and in the holes
Where eyes did once inhabit, there were crept
(As 'twere in scorn of eyes) reflecting gems,
That woo'd the slimy bottom of the deep,
And mock'd the dead bones that lay scatt'red by.
Keep. Had you such leisure in the time of death
To gaze upon these secrets of the deep?
Clar. Methought I had, and often did I strive
To yield the ghost; but still the envious flood
Stopp'd in my soul, and would not let it forth
To find the empty, vast, and wand'ring air,
But smother'd it within my panting bulk,
Who almost burst to belch it in the sea.

352. fall: let fall.

I.iv. Location: London. The Tower.
10. Burgundy. Where, following their father's death, he and his brother Richard had been sent for safety.
13. hatches: movable planks forming a deck.
14. cited up: recalled. **19. stay:** steady.
24. Methoughts: it seemed to me. **wracks:** wrecks.
27. Inestimable: invaluable (?) or numberless (?). **unvalued:** priceless. **37. envious:** malicious. **40. bulk:** body.

Keep. Awak'd you not in this sore agony?
Clar. No, no, my dream was lengthen'd after life.
O then began the tempest to my soul!
I pass'd (methought) the melancholy flood,
With that sour ferryman which poets write of,
Unto the kingdom of perpetual night.
The first that there did greet my stranger soul
Was my great father-in-law, renowned Warwick,
Who spake aloud, "What scourge for perjury
Can this dark monarchy afford false Clarence?"
And so he vanish'd. Then came wand'ring by
A shadow like an angel, with bright hair
Dabbled in blood, and he shriek'd out aloud,
"Clarence is come—false, fleeting, perjur'd Clarence,
That stabb'd me in the field by Tewksbury:
Seize on him, Furies, take him unto torment!"
With that ([methoughts]) a legion of foul fiends
Environ'd me, and howled in mine ears
Such hideous cries that with the very noise
I, trembling, wak'd, and for a season after
Could not believe but that I was in hell,
Such terrible impression made my dream.
Keep. No marvel, lord, though it affrighted you;
I am afraid (methinks) to hear you tell it.
Clar. Ah, Keeper, Keeper, I have done these things
(That now give evidence against my soul)
For Edward's sake, and see how he requites me!
O God! if my deep pray'rs cannot appease thee,
But thou wilt be aveng'd on my misdeeds,
Yet execute thy wrath in me alone!
O, spare my guiltless wife and my poor children!
Keeper, I prithee sit by me awhile.
My soul is heavy, and I fain would sleep.
Keep. I will, my lord. God give your Grace good rest! *[Clarence sleeps.]*

Enter BRAKENBURY, *the Lieutenant.*

Brak. Sorrow breaks seasons and reposing hours,
Makes the night morning and the noontide night:
Princes have but their titles for their glories,
An outward honor for an inward toil,
And for unfelt imaginations
They often feel a world of restless cares;
So that between their titles and low name
There's nothing differs but the outward fame.

Enter two MURTHERERS.

1. Mur. Ho, who's here?
Brak. What wouldst thou, fellow? and how cam'st thou hither?
[1.] Mur. I would speak with Clarence, and I came hither on my legs.
Brak. What, so brief?
[2.] Mur. 'Tis better, sir, than to be tedious. Let him see our commission, and talk no more.
[Brakenbury] reads [it].
Brak. I am in this commanded to deliver
The noble Duke of Clarence to your hands.
I will not reason what is meant hereby,
Because I will be guiltless from the meaning.
There lies the Duke asleep, and there the keys.
I'll to the King and signify to him
That thus I have resign'd to you my charge.
1. Mur. You may, sir, 'tis a point of wisdom. Fare you well. *Exit [Brakenbury with Keeper].*
2. Mur. What, shall [I] stab him as he sleeps?
1. Mur. No, he'll say 'twas done cowardly when he wakes.
2. Mur. Why, he shall never wake until the great Judgment Day.
1. Mur. Why, then he'll say we stabb'd him sleeping.
2. Mur. The urging of that word "judgment" hath bred a kind of remorse in me.
1. Mur. What? art thou afraid?
2. Mur. Not to kill him, having a warrant, but to be damn'd for killing him, from the which no warrant can defend me.
1. Mur. I thought thou hadst been resolute.
2. Mur. So I am—to let him live.
1. Mur. I'll back to the Duke of Gloucester and tell him so.
2. Mur. Nay, I prithee stay a little. I hope this passionate humor of mine will change. It was wont to hold me but while one tells twenty.
1. Mur. How dost thou feel thyself now?
2. Mur. [Faith,] some certain dregs of conscience are yet within me.
1. Mur. Remember our reward when the deed's done.
2. Mur. ['Zounds], he dies! I had forgot the reward.
1. Mur. Where's thy conscience now?
2. Mur. O, in the Duke of Gloucester's purse.
1. Mur. When he opens his purse to give us our reward, thy conscience flies out.
2. Mur. 'Tis no matter, let it go. There's few or none will entertain it.
1. Mur. What if it come to thee again?
2. Mur. I'll not meddle with it, it makes a man a coward. A man cannot steal, but it accuseth him; a man cannot swear, but it checks him; a man cannot lie with his neighbor's wife, but it detects him. 'Tis a blushing shame-fac'd spirit that mutinies in a man's bosom. It fills a man full of obstacles. It made me once restore a purse of gold that (by chance) I found. It beggars any man that keeps it. It is turn'd out of towns and cities for a dangerous thing, and every man that means to live well endeavors to trust to himself and live without it.
1. Mur. ['Zounds,] 'tis even now at my elbow, persuading me not to kill the Duke.
2. Mur. Take the devil in thy mind, and believe him not; he would insinuate with thee but to make thee sigh.

45. melancholy flood: the river Styx, across which Charon rowed the spirits of the dead to the underworld.
53. shadow: i.e. Prince Edward, son of Henry VI.
74. fain: gladly.
80. unfelt imaginations: i.e. glories imagined but not experienced.
94. will be: will to be.
118. passionate humor: compassionate mood.
119. tells: counts. 125. 'Zounds: by God's (Christ's) wounds.
147. Take . . . mind: i.e. subdue the promptings of your conscience.
148. him: the devil, i.e. conscience. insinuate: ingratiate himself.

1. Mur. I am strong-fram'd, he cannot prevail with me.

2. Mur. Spoke like a tall man that respects thy reputation. Come, shall we fall to work?

1. Mur. Take him on the costard with the hilts of thy sword, and then throw him into the malmsey-butt in the next room.

2. Mur. O excellent device! and make a sop of him.

1. Mur. Soft, he wakes.

2. Mur. Strike!

1. Mur. No, we'll reason with him.

Clar. Where art thou, Keeper? Give me a cup of wine.

2. Mur. You shall have wine enough, my lord, anon.

Clar. In God's name, what art thou?

1. Mur. A man, as you are.

Clar. But not, as I am, royal.

[2.] *Mur.* Nor you, as we are, loyal.

Clar. Thy voice is thunder, but thy looks are humble.

1. Mur. My voice is now the King's, my looks mine own.

Clar. How darkly and how deadly dost thou speak!
Your eyes do menace me. Why look you pale?
Who sent you hither? Wherefore do you come?

[*Both.*] To, to, to—

Clar. To murther me?

Both. Ay, ay.

Clar. You scarcely have the hearts to tell me so,
And therefore cannot have the hearts to do it.
Wherein, my friends, have I offended you?

1. Mur. Offended us you have not, but the King.

Clar. I shall be reconcil'd to him again.

2. Mur. Never, my lord, therefore prepare to die.

Clar. Are you drawn forth among a world of men
To slay the innocent? What is my offense?
Where is the evidence that doth accuse me?
What lawful quest have given their verdict up
Unto the frowning judge? or who pronounc'd
The bitter sentence of poor Clarence' death?
Before I be convict by course of law,
To threaten me with death is most unlawful.
I charge you, as you hope [to have redemption
By Christ's dear blood shed for our grievous sins,]
That you depart, and lay no hands on me.
The deed you undertake is damnable.

1. Mur. What we will do, we do upon command.

2. Mur. And he that hath commanded is our King.

Clar. Erroneous vassals, the great King of kings
Hath in the table of his law commanded
That thou shalt do no murther. Will you then
Spurn at his edict, and fulfill a man's?
Take heed; for he holds vengeance in his hand,
To hurl upon their heads that break his law.

2. Mur. And that same vengeance doth he hurl on thee
For false forswearing and for murther too.
Thou didst receive the sacrament to fight
In quarrel of the house of Lancaster.

1. Mur. And like a traitor to the name of God
Didst break that vow, and with thy treacherous blade
Unrip'st the bowels of thy sov'reign's son.

2. Mur. Whom thou wast sworn to cherish and defend.

1. Mur. How canst thou urge God's dreadful law to us,
When thou hast broke it in such dear degree?

Clar. Alas! for whose sake did I that ill deed?
For Edward, for my brother, for his sake.
He sends you not to murther me for this,
For in that sin he is as deep as I.
If God will be avenged for the deed,
O, know you yet he doth it publicly.
Take not the quarrel from his pow'rful arm;
He needs no indirect or lawless course
To cut off those that have offended him.

1. Mur. Who made thee then a bloody minister,
When gallant-springing brave Plantagenet,
That princely novice, was struck dead by thee?

Clar. My brother's love, the devil, and my rage.

1. Mur. Thy brother's love, our duty, and thy faults
Provoke us hither now to slaughter thee.

Clar. [O,] if you love my brother, hate not me!
I am his brother and I love him well.
If you are hir'd for meed, go back again,
And I will send you to my brother Gloucester,
Who shall reward you better for my life
Than Edward will for tidings of my death.

2. Mur. You are deceiv'd, your brother Gloucester hates you.

Clar. O no; he loves me and he holds me dear.
Go you to him from me.

1. Mur. Ay, so we will.

Clar. Tell him, when that our princely father York
Blest his three sons with his victorious arm,
[And charg'd us from his soul to love each other,]
He little thought of this divided friendship.
Bid Gloucester think [of] this, and he will weep.

1. Mur. Ay, millstones, as he lesson'd us to weep.

Clar. O, do not slander him, for he is kind.

1. Mur. Right, as snow in harvest. Come, you deceive yourself,
'Tis he that sends us to destroy you here.

Clar. It cannot be, for he bewept my fortune,
And hugg'd me in his arms, and swore with sobs
That he would labor my delivery.

1. Mur. Why, so he doth, when he delivers you
From this earth's thralldom to the joys of heaven.

2. Mur. Make peace with God, for you must die, my lord.

Clar. Have you that holy feeling in your souls
To counsel me to make my peace with God,

152. tall: brave. **154. costard:** kind of apple, i.e. head.
155. malmsey-butt: i.e. wine cask. Malmsey was a sweet, aromatic wine. **157. sop:** cake soaked in wine. **160. reason:** talk.
184. quest: inquest, i.e. jury. **187. convict:** convicted.
195. Erroneous vassals: criminal wretches.

207. Unrip'st: i.e. unrippedst. **210. dear:** grievous.
221. gallant-springing: i.e. gallant and aspiring.
222. novice: youth.
223. My brother's love: i.e. my love for my brother.
240. lesson'd: taught. **246. labor:** work for.

And are you yet to your own souls so blind
That you will war with God by murd'ring me?
O, sirs, consider, they that set you on
To do this deed will hate you for the deed.

2. Mur. What shall we do?

Clar. Relent, and save your souls.
Which of you, if you were a prince's son,
Being pent from liberty, as I am now,
If two such murtherers as yourselves came to you,
Would not entreat for life?

1. Mur. Relent? No: 'tis cowardly and womanish.

Clar. Not to relent is beastly, savage, devilish.
My friend [*to Second Murderer*], I spy some pity in thy looks.
O, if thine eye be not a flatterer,
Come thou on my side, and entreat for me,
As you would beg, were you in my distress.
A begging prince what beggar pities not?

2. Mur. Look behind you, my lord.

1. Mur. Take that! and that! (*Stabs him.*) If all this will not do,
I'll drown you in the malmsey-butt within.

Exit [*with the body*].

2. Mur. A bloody deed, and desperately dispatch'd!
How fain, like Pilate, would I wash my hands
Of this most grievous murther!

Enter First Murtherer.

1. Mur. How now? what mean'st thou, that thou help'st me not?
By [heavens], the Duke shall know how slack you have been!

2. Mur. I would he knew that I had sav'd his brother!
Take thou the fee and tell him what I say,
For I repent me that the Duke is slain. *Exit.*

1. Mur. So do not I. Go, coward as thou art.
Well, I'll go hide the body in some hole
Till that the Duke give order for his burial;
And when I have my meed, I will away,
For this will out, and then I must not stay. *Exit.*

ACT II, Scene I

Flourish. Enter the King [Edward] *sick, the* Queen [Elizabeth], Lord Marquess Dorset, Rivers, Hastings, Catesby, Buckingham, [Grey, *and others*].

K. Edw. Why, so: now have I done a good day's work.
You peers, continue this united league.
I every day expect an embassage
From my Redeemer to redeem me hence;
And more [in] peace my soul shall part to heaven,
Since I have made my friends at peace on earth.
[Hastings] and Rivers, take each other's hand,
Dissemble not your hatred, swear your love.

Riv. By heaven, my soul is purg'd from grudging hate,
And with my hand I seal my true heart's love.

Hast. So thrive I, as I truly swear the like!

K. Edw. Take heed you dally not before your king,
Lest He that is the supreme King of kings
Confound your hidden falsehood and award
Either of you to be the other's end.

Hast. So prosper I, as I swear perfect love!

Riv. And I, as I love Hastings with my heart!

K. Edw. Madam, yourself is not exempt from this;
Nor you, son Dorset; Buckingham, nor you;
You have been factious one against the other.
Wife, love Lord Hastings, let him kiss your hand,
And what you do, do it unfeignedly.

Q. Eliz. There, Hastings, I will never more remember
Our former hatred, so thrive I and mine!

K. Edw. Dorset, embrace him; Hastings, love Lord Marquess.

Dor. This interchange of love, I here protest,
Upon my part shall be inviolable.

Hast. And so swear I. [*They embrace.*]

K. Edw. Now, princely Buckingham, seal thou this league
With thy embracements to my wive's allies,
And make me happy in your unity.

Buck. When ever Buckingham doth turn his hate
Upon your Grace [*to the Queen*], but with all duteous love
Doth cherish you and yours, God punish me
With hate in those where I expect most love!
When I have most need to employ a friend,
And most assured that he is a friend,
Deep, hollow, treacherous, and full of guile
Be he unto me! This do I beg of [God],
When I am cold in love to you or yours.

[*They*] *embrace.*

K. Edw. A pleasing cordial, princely Buckingham,
Is this thy vow unto my sickly heart.
There wanteth now our brother Gloucester here
To make the blessed period of this peace.

Buck. And in good time,
Here comes Sir Richard Ratcliffe and the Duke.

Enter Ratcliffe *and* Gloucester.

Glou. Good morrow to my sovereign king and queen,
And, princely peers, a happy time of day!

K. Edw. Happy indeed, as we have spent the day.
Gloucester, we have done deeds of charity,
Made peace of enmity, fair love of hate,

258. pent: shut up.

II.i. Location: London. The palace.
o.s.d. Flourish: fanfare of trumpets to announce the arrival of an illustrious person.

8. Dissemble: disguise (under the appearance of affection).
12. dally: trifle.
14–15. award . . . end: i.e. cause each of you to be the means by which the other dies. **20. factious:** quarrelsome.
33. but. Apparently a corruption. The sense of the passage requires *nor.* **41. cordial:** restorative. **43. wanteth:** lacks.

Between these swelling wrong-incensed peers.
Glou. A blessed labor, my most sovereign lord.
Among this princely heap, if any here
By false intelligence or wrong surmise
Hold me a foe—
If I [unwittingly], or in my rage,
Have aught committed that is hardly borne
[By] any in this presence, I desire
To reconcile me to his friendly peace.
'Tis death to me to be at enmity;
I hate it, and desire all good men's love.
First, madam, I entreat true peace of you,
Which I will purchase with my duteous service;
Of you, my noble cousin Buckingham,
If ever any grudge were lodg'd between us;
Of you, and you, Lord Rivers, and of Dorset,
That all without desert have frown'd on me;
Dukes, earls, lords, gentlemen—indeed of all.
I do not know that Englishman alive
With whom my soul is any jot at odds
More than the infant that is born to-night.
I thank my God for my humility.
Q. Eliz. A holy day shall this be kept hereafter.
I would to God all strifes were well compounded.
My sovereign lord, I do beseech your Highness
To take our brother Clarence to your grace.
Glou. Why, madam, have I off'red love for this,
To be so flouted in this royal presence?
Who knows not that the gentle Duke is dead?
They all start.
You do him injury to scorn his corse.
K. Edw. Who knows not he is dead? Who knows he is?
Q. Eliz. All-seeing heaven, what a world is this!
Buck. Look I so pale, Lord Dorset, as the rest?
Dor. Ay, my good lord, and no man in the presence
But his red color hath forsook his cheeks.
K. Edw. Is Clarence dead? The order was revers'd.
Glou. But he, poor man, by your first order died,
And that a winged Mercury did bear;
Some tardy cripple bare the countermand,
That came too lag to see him buried.
God grant that some, less noble and less loyal,
Nearer in bloody thoughts, [but] not in blood,
Deserve not worse than wretched Clarence did,
And yet go current from suspicion!

Enter [STANLEY,] *Earl of Derby.*

Stan. A boon, my sovereign, for my service done!
[*Kneels.*]
K. Edw. I prithee peace, my soul is full of sorrow.
Stan. I will not rise, unless your Highness hear me.
K. Edw. Then say at once what is it thou requests.
Stan. The forfeit, sovereign, of my servant's life,
Who slew to-day a riotous gentleman
Lately attendant on the Duke of Norfolk.
K. Edw. Have I a tongue to doom my brother's death,
And shall that tongue give pardon to a slave?
My brother kill'd no man, his fault was thought,
And yet his punishment was bitter death.
Who sued to me for him? Who (in my wrath)
Kneel'd [at] my feet and bid me be advis'd?
Who spoke of brotherhood? Who spoke of love?
Who told me how the poor soul did forsake
The mighty Warwick and did fight for me?
Who told me, in the field at Tewksbury,
When Oxford had me down, he rescued me,
And said, "Dear brother, live, and be a king"?
Who told me, when we both lay in the field
Frozen (almost) to death, how he did lap me
Even in his [own] garments, and did give himself
(All thin and naked) to the numb cold night?
All this from my remembrance brutish wrath
Sinfully pluck'd, and not a man of you
Had so much grace to put it in my mind.
But when your carters or your waiting vassals
Have done a drunken slaughter, and defac'd
The precious image of our dear Redeemer,
You straight are on your knees for pardon, pardon,
And I (unjustly too) must grant it you. [*Stanley rises.*]
But for my brother not a man would speak,
Nor I (ungracious)speak unto myself
For him, poor soul. The proudest of you all
Have been beholding to him in his life;
Yet none of you would once beg for his life.
O God! I fear thy justice will take hold
On me and you, and mine and yours, for this.
Come, Hastings, help me to my closet. Ah, poor Clarence! *Exeunt some with King and Queen.*
Glou. This is the fruits of rashness! Mark'd you not
How that the guilty kindred of the Queen
Look'd pale when they did hear of Clarence' death?
O, they did urge it still unto the King!
God will revenge it. Come, lords, will you go
To comfort Edward with our company.
Buck. We wait upon your Grace. *Exeunt.*

SCENE II

Enter the old DUCHESS OF YORK *with the two children of Clarence* [EDWARD *and* MARGARET PLANTAGENET].

Boy. Good grandam, tell us, is our father dead?
Duch. No, boy.

52. swelling: i.e. with anger. **54. heap:** band.
55. intelligence: information. **58. hardly borne:** resented.
68. all without desert: entirely without my having deserved it.
75. compounded: settled.
81. scorn his corse: i.e. be facetious about the dead.
85. presence: i.e. of the King.
87. Is . . . revers'd. According to Hall (Bullough, III, 252), Clarence was charged with "heinous treason," and so, "were he in faulte or wer he faultelesse, attainted was he by parliament and judged to death, and there upon hastely drowned in a butte of malmesey within the towre of London. Whose death kynge Edwarde (although he commaunded it) when he wiste it was doen piteously he bewayled and sorowfully repented it."
90. bare: bore. **91. lag:** late. **93. blood:** kinship.
95. go current: pass at face value. **from:** i.e. without.

100. forfeit: i.e. remission of the forfeit. **103. doom:** decree.
108. be advis'd: take careful thought.
113. When . . . down. See note to *3 Henry VI*, V.v.2.
122. carters: draymen. **134. closet:** private quarters.

II.ii. Location: London. The palace.

Girl. Why do [you] weep so oft, and beat your breast,
And cry, "O Clarence, my unhappy son!"?
Boy. Why do you look on us, and shake your head,
And call us orphans, wretches, castaways,
If that our noble father were alive?
Duch. My pretty cousins, you mistake me both:
I do lament the sickness of the King,
As loath to lose him, not your father's death;
It were lost sorrow to wail one that's lost.
Boy. Then you conclude, my grandam, he is dead.
The King mine uncle is to blame for it.
God will revenge it, whom I will importune
With earnest prayers all to that effect.
Girl. And so will I.
Duch. Peace, children, peace, the King doth love you well.
Incapable and shallow innocents,
You cannot guess who caus'd your father's death.
Boy. Grandam, we can; for my good uncle Gloucester
Told me the King, provok'd to it by the Queen,
Devis'd impeachments to imprison him;
And when my uncle told me so, he wept,
And pitied me, and kindly kiss'd my cheek;
Bade me rely on him as on my father,
And he would love me dearly as a child.
Duch. Ah! that deceit should steal such gentle shape,
And with a virtuous visor hide deep vice!
He is my son—ay, and therein my shame,
Yet from my dugs he drew not this deceit.
Boy. Think you my uncle did dissemble, grandam?
Duch. Ay, boy.
Boy. I cannot think it. Hark, what noise is this?

Enter the QUEEN [ELIZABETH] *with her hair about her ears;* RIVERS *and* DORSET *after her.*

Q. Eliz. Ah! who shall hinder me to wail and weep,
To chide my fortune, and torment myself?
I'll join with black despair against my soul,
And to myself become an enemy.
Duch. What means this scene of rude impatience?
Q. Eliz. To make an act of tragic violence.
Edward, my lord, thy son, our king, is dead!
Why grow the branches when the root is gone?
Why wither not the leaves that want their sap?
If you will live, lament; if die, be brief,
That our swift-winged souls may catch the King's,
Or like obedient subjects follow him
To his new kingdom of ne'er-changing night.
Duch. Ah, so much interest have [I] in thy sorrow
As I had title in thy noble husband!
I have bewept a worthy husband's death,
And liv'd with looking on his images;
But now two mirrors of his princely semblance
Are crack'd in pieces by malignant death,
And I for comfort have but one false glass,
That grieves me when I see my shame in him.
Thou art a widow; yet thou art a mother,
And hast the comfort of thy children left;
But death hath snatch'd my husband from mine arms,
And pluck'd two crutches from my feeble hands,
Clarence and Edward. O, what cause have I
(Thine being but a moi'ty of my moan)
To overgo thy woes and drown thy cries!
Boy. Ah, aunt! you wept not for our father's death;
How can we aid you with our kindred tears?
Girl. Our fatherless distress was left unmoan'd,
Your widow-dolor likewise be unwept!
Q. Eliz. Give me no help in lamentation,
I am not barren to bring forth complaints.
All springs reduce their currents to mine eyes,
That I being govern'd by the watery moon,
May send forth plenteous tears to drown the world!
Ah for my husband, for my dear Lord Edward!
Chil. Ah for our father, for our dear Lord Clarence!
Duch. Alas for both, both mine, Edward and Clarence!
Q. Eliz. What stay had I but Edward? and he's gone.
Chil. What stay had we but Clarence? and he's gone.
Duch. What stays had I but they? and they are gone.
Q. Eliz. Was never widow had so dear a loss.
Chil. Were never orphans had so dear a loss.
Duch. Was never mother had so dear a loss.
Alas! I am the mother of these griefs:
Their woes are parcell'd, mine is general.
She for an Edward weeps, and so do I;
I for a Clarence [weep], so doth not she;
These babes for Clarence weep, [and so do I;
I for an Edward weep,] so do not they.
Alas! you three on me, threefold distress'd,
Pour all your tears. I am your sorrow's nurse,
And I will pamper it with lamentation.
Dor. Comfort, dear mother, God is much displeas'd
That you take with unthankfulness his doing.
In common worldly things 'tis call'd ungrateful
With dull unwillingness to repay a debt,
Which with a bounteous hand was kindly lent;
Much more to be thus opposite with heaven,
For it requires the royal debt it lent you.
Riv. Madam, bethink you like a careful mother
Of the young Prince your son. Send straight for him,
Let him be crown'd, in him your comfort lives.
Drown desperate sorrow in dead Edward's grave,
And plant your joys in living Edward's throne.

Enter RICHARD [OF GLOUCESTER], BUCKINGHAM, [STANLEY, *Earl of*] *Derby*, HASTINGS, *and* RATCLIFFE.

8. cousins: kinsmen. **18. Incapable:** not able to understand.
22. impeachments: accusations.
27. gentle shape: appearance of gentleness.
28. virtuous visor: mask of pretended virtue.
40. Edward . . . dead. A characteristic telescoping of events. Clarence's death (1478) preceded that of Edward IV by some five years.
48. title: legal right. **50. images:** i.e. sons.
60. moi'ty: part. **61. overgo:** exceed.
63. kindred tears: i.e. tears of kinsmen.
68. All springs reduce: let all springs lead. **77. dear:** grievous.
81. parcell'd: i.e. distributed to each separately. **general:** inclusive.
94. opposite with: in opposition to. **95. For:** because.

Glou. Sister, have comfort. All of us have cause
To wail the dimming of our shining star;
But none can help our harms by wailing them.
Madam, my mother, I do cry you mercy,
I did not see your Grace. Humbly on my knee
I crave your blessing.
Duch. God bless thee, and put meekness in thy breast,
Love, charity, obedience, and true duty!
Glou. Amen!—[*aside*] and make me die a good old man!
That is the butt-end of a mother's blessing.
I marvel that her Grace did leave it out.
Buck. You cloudy princes and heart-sorrowing peers
That bear this heavy mutual load of moan,
Now cheer each other in each other's love.
Though we have spent our harvest of this king,
We are to reap the harvest of his son.
The broken rancor of your high-swoll'n hates,
But lately splinter'd, knit, and join'd together,
Must gently be preserv'd, cherish'd, and kept.
Me seemeth good that, with some little train,
Forthwith from Ludlow the young Prince be fet
Hither to London, to be crown'd our king.
Riv. Why with some little train, my Lord of Buckingham?
Buck. Marry, my lord, lest by a multitude
The new-heal'd wound of malice should break out,
Which would be so much the more dangerous,
By how much the estate is green and yet ungovern'd.
Where every horse bears his commanding rein
And may direct his course as please himself,
As well the fear of harm, as harm apparent,
In my opinion, ought to be prevented.
Glou. I hope the King made peace with all of us,
And the compact is firm and true in me.
Riv. And so in me, and so (I think) in all.
Yet since it is but green, it should be put
To no apparent likelihood of breach,
Which haply by much company might be urg'd;
Therefore I say with noble Buckingham,
That it is meet so few should fetch the Prince.
Hast. And so say I.
Glou. Then be it so, and go we to determine
Who they shall be that straight shall post to [Ludlow].
Madam, and you, my sister, will you go
To give your censures in this business?
[*Q. Eliz., Duch.* With all our hearts.]
Exeunt. Manent Buckingham and Richard.
Buck. My lord, whoever journeys to the Prince,
For God sake let not us two stay at home;
For by the way, I'll sort occasion,
As index to the story we late talk'd of,
To part the Queen's proud kindred from the Prince.
Glou. My other self, my counsel's consistory,
My oracle, my prophet, my dear cousin,
I, as a child, will go by thy direction.
Toward [Ludlow] then, for we'll not stay behind.
Exeunt.

112. **cloudy:** gloomy. 118. **splinter'd:** bound in splints.
120. **Me seemeth:** it seems to me. **little train:** small entourage.
121. **Ludlow:** castle in Shropshire, Prince Edward's seat in his capacity as justiciar of Wales, an office he had held since 1476. **fet:** fetched.
124. **multitude:** i.e. large entourage.
127. **the estate is green:** i.e. the government is newly established.
128. **bears:** controls. 137. **haply:** perhaps. **urg'd:** provoked.
142. **post:** hasten. 144. **censures:** opinions. 148. **sort:** find.
149. **index:** introduction.

Scene III

Enter one Citizen *at one door and another at the other.*

1. Cit. Good morrow, neighbor, whither away so fast?
2. Cit. I promise you, I scarcely know myself.
Hear you the news abroad?
1. Cit. Yes, that the King is dead.
2. Cit. Ill news, by'r lady—seldom comes the better.
I fear, I fear 'twill prove a giddy world.

Enter another Citizen.

3. Cit. Neighbors, God speed!
1. Cit. Give you good morrow, sir.
3. Cit. Doth the news hold of good King Edward's death?
2. Cit. Ay, sir, it is too true, God help the while!
3. Cit. Then, masters, look to see a troublous world.
1. Cit. No, no, by God's good grace his son shall reign.
3. Cit. Woe to that land that's govern'd by a child!
2. Cit. In him there is a hope of government,
Which in his nonage, council under him,
And in his full and ripened years, himself,
No doubt shall then, and till then, govern well.
1. Cit. So stood the state when Henry the Sixt
Was crown'd in Paris but at nine months old.
3. Cit. Stood the state so? No, no, good friends, God wot,
For then this land was famously enrich'd
With politic grave counsel; then the King
Had virtuous uncles to protect his Grace.
1. Cit. Why, so hath this, both by his father and mother.
3. Cit. Better it were they all came by his father,
Or by his father there were none at all;
For emulation who shall now be nearest
Will touch us all too near, if God prevent not.
O, full of danger is the Duke of Gloucester,
And the Queen's sons and brothers haught and proud!
And were they to be rul'd, and not to rule,
This sickly land might solace as before.
1. Cit. Come, come, we fear the worst; all will be well.
3. Cit. When clouds are seen, wise men put on their cloaks;
When great leaves fall, then winter is at hand;
When the sun sets, who doth not look for night?

151. **consistory:** council chamber, i.e. source of wisdom.

II.iii. **Location:** London. A street.
4. **by'r lady:** by Our Lady. 13. **nonage:** minority.
18. **wot:** knows. 20. **politic:** sagacious. 28. **haught:** haughty.
30. **solace:** be happy.

Untimely storms makes men expect a dearth.
All may be well; but if God sort it so,
'Tis more than we deserve or I expect.

2. Cit. Truly, the hearts of men are full of fear.
You cannot reason (almost) with a man
That looks not heavily and full of dread.

3. Cit. Before the days of change, still is it so.
By a divine instinct men's minds mistrust
Ensuing danger; as by proof we see
The water swell before a boist'rous storm.
But leave it all to God. Whither away?

2. Cit. Marry, we were sent for to the justices.

3. Cit. And so was I. I'll bear you company.

Exeunt.

Scene IV

Enter Archbishop [of York, *the*] *young* [Duke of] York, *the* Queen [Elizabeth], *and the* Duchess [of York].

Arch. Last night, I [hear], they lay at Stony-Stratford,
And at Northampton they do rest to-night.
To-morrow, or next day, they will be here.

Duch. I long with all my heart to see the Prince.
I hope he is much grown since last I saw him.

Q. Eliz. But I hear no; they say my son of York
Has almost overta'en him in his growth.

York. Ay, mother, but I would not have it so.

Duch. Why, my good cousin, it is good to grow.

York. Grandam, one night as we did sit at supper,
My uncle Rivers talk'd how I did grow
More than my brother. "Ay," quoth my uncle Gloucester,
"Small herbs have grace, great weeds do grow apace."
And since, methinks I would not grow so fast,
Because sweet flow'rs are slow and weeds make haste.

Duch. Good faith, good faith, the saying did not hold
In him that did object the same to thee:
He was the wretched'st thing when he was young,
So long a-growing and so leisurely
That if his rule were true, he should be gracious.

[*Arch.*] And so no doubt he is, my gracious madam.

Duch. I hope he is, but yet let mothers doubt.

York. Now by my troth, if I had been rememb'red,
I could have given my uncle's Grace a flout,
To touch his growth nearer than he touch'd mine.

Duch. How, my young York? I prithee let me hear it.

36. sort: arrange, dispose.
39. reason: talk. **42. mistrust:** suspect.

II.iv. Location: London. The palace.
1. Stony-Stratford: town in Buckinghamshire.
2. Northampton: town in Northamptonshire.
6–7. But . . . growth. Edward, Prince of Wales, was thirteen and his brother Richard, Duke of York, eleven when their father died.
16. did not hold: was not exemplified.
17. object . . . to: urge . . . against, i.e. apply . . . to.
23. troth: truth, faith. **been remenb'red:** recollected, considered.
24. my uncle's Grace: his Grace, my uncle. **flout:** gibe.
25. touch . . . mine: i.e. taunt him about his growth more tellingly than he taunted me about mine.

York. Marry (they say) my uncle grew so fast
That he could gnaw a crust at two hours old;
'Twas full two years ere I could get a tooth.
Grandam, this would have been a biting jest.

Duch. I prithee, pretty York, who told thee this?

York. Grandam, his nurse.

Duch. His nurse? why, she was dead ere thou wast born.

York. If 'twere not she, I cannot tell who told me.

Q. Eliz. A parlous boy! Go to, you are too shrewd.

Duch. Good madam, be not angry with the child.

Q. Eliz. Pitchers have ears.

Enter a Messenger.

Arch. Here comes a messenger. What news?

Mess. Such news, my lord, as grieves me to report.

Q. Eliz. How doth the Prince?

Mess. Well, madam, and in health.

Duch. What is thy news?

Mess. Lord Rivers and Lord Grey are sent to Pomfret,
And with them Sir Thomas Vaughan, prisoners.

Duch. Who hath committed them?

Mess. The mighty dukes,
Gloucester and Buckingham.

Arch. For what offense?

Mess. The sum of all I can I have disclos'd.
Why, or for what, the nobles were committed
Is all unknown to me, my gracious lord.

Q. Eliz. Ay me! I see the ruin of my house:
The tiger now hath seiz'd the gentle hind;
Insulting tyranny begins to jut
Upon the innocent and aweless throne.
Welcome destruction, blood, and massacre!
I see (as in a map) the end of all.

Duch. Accursed and unquiet wrangling days,
How many of you have mine eyes beheld!
My husband lost his life to get the crown,
And often up and down my sons were toss'd
For me to joy and weep their gain and loss;
And being seated, and domestic broils
Clean overblown, themselves, the conquerors,
Make war upon themselves, brother to brother,
Blood to blood, self against self. O, preposterous
And frantic outrage, end thy damned spleen,
Or let me die, to look on [death] no more!

Q. Eliz. Come, come, my boy, we will to sanctuary.
Madam, farewell.

Duch. Stay, I will go with you.

Q. Eliz. You have no cause.

Arch. [*To the Queen.*] My gracious lady, go,

35. parlous: clever, precocious. **shrewd:** bitter.
42. Pomfret: Pontefract, in Yorkshire, site of the castle in which Richard II met his death in 1400. **46. can:** know.
50. hind: female deer. **51. jut:** encroach.
52. aweless: inspiring no awe (because of its occupant's youth).
54. as . . . map: i.e. graphically epitomized.
60. seated: enthroned. **64. spleen:** malevolence.
66. sanctuary: a place of refuge (generally a church) for those in danger of their lives. According to More (Bullough, III, 257), as soon as Queen Elizabeth heard the "heavy tidynges" of her son and kinsmen "she toke her younger sonne the duke of Yorke and her doughters and went out of the palays of Westminster into the sanctuary, and there lodged in the abbotes place, and she and all her chyldren and compaignie were regestred for sanctuarye persons."

And thither bear your treasure and your goods.
For my part, I'll resign unto your Grace
The seal I keep, and so betide to me
As well I tender you and all of yours!
Go, I'll conduct you to the sanctuary. *Exeunt.*

ACT III, SCENE I

The trumpets sound. Enter young PRINCE [EDWARD], *the* DUKES OF GLOUCESTER *and* BUCKINGHAM, [LORD] CARDINAL [BOURCHIER, CATESBY, *with others*].

Buck. Welcome, sweet Prince, to London, to your chamber.
Glou. Welcome, dear cousin, my thoughts' sovereign,
The weary way hath made you melancholy.
Prince. No, uncle, but our crosses on the way
Have made it tedious, wearisome, and heavy.
I want more uncles here to welcome me.
Glou. Sweet Prince, the untainted virtue of your years
Hath not yet div'd into the world's deceit;
Nor more can you distinguish of a man
Than of his outward show, which, God he knows,
Seldom or never jumpeth with the heart.
Those uncles which you want were dangerous;
Your Grace attended to their sug'red words,
But look'd not on the poison of their hearts.
God keep you from them, and from such false friends!
Prince. God keep me from false friends!—but they were none.
Glou. My lord, the Mayor of London comes to greet you.

Enter LORD MAYOR [*and his* TRAIN].

May. God bless your Grace with health and happy days!
Prince. I thank you, good my lord, and thank you all. [*Mayor and Train stand aside.*]
I thought my mother and my brother York
Would long ere this have met us on the way.
Fie, what a slug is Hastings, that he comes not
To tell us whether they will come or no!

Enter LORD HASTINGS.

Buck. And in good time, here comes the sweating lord.
Prince. Welcome, my lord. What, will our mother come?
Hast. On what occasion, God he knows, not I,
The Queen your mother and your brother York
Have taken sanctuary. The tender Prince
Would fain have come with me to meet your Grace,
But by his mother was perforce withheld.
Buck. Fie, what an indirect and peevish course
Is this of hers! Lord Cardinal, will your Grace
Persuade the Queen to send the Duke of York
Unto his princely brother presently?
If she deny, Lord Hastings, go with him,
And from her jealous arms pluck him perforce.
Card. My Lord of Buckingham, if my weak oratory
Can from his mother win the Duke of York,
Anon expect him here; but if she be obdurate
To mild entreaties, God in heaven forbid
We should infringe the holy privilege
Of blessed sanctuary! Not for all this land
Would I be guilty of so deep a sin.
Buck. You are too senseless-obstinate, my lord,
Too ceremonious and traditional.
Weigh it but with the grossness of this age,
You break not sanctuary in seizing him.
The benefit thereof is always granted
To those whose dealings have deserv'd the place
And those who have the wit to claim the place.
This prince hath neither claim'd it nor deserv'd it,
And therefore, in mine opinion, cannot have it.
Then taking him from thence that is not there,
You break no privilege nor charter there.
Oft have I heard of sanctuary men,
But sanctuary children never till now.
Card. My lord, you shall overrule my mind for once.
Come on, Lord Hastings, will you go with me?
Hast. I go, my lord.
Prince. Good lords, make all the speedy haste you may. [*Exeunt Cardinal and Hastings.*]
Say, uncle Gloucester, if our brother come,
Where shall we sojourn till our coronation?
Glou. Where it seems best unto your royal self.
If I may counsel you, some day or two
Your Highness shall repose you at the Tower;
Then where you please, and shall be thought most fit
For your best health and recreation.
Prince. I do not like the Tower, of any place.
Did Julius Caesar build that place, my lord?
Buck. He did, my gracious lord, begin that place,
Which, since, succeeding ages have re-edified.
Prince. Is it upon record, or else reported
Successively from age to age, he built it?
Buck. Upon record, my gracious lord.
Prince. But say, my lord, it were not regist'red,
Methinks the truth should live from age to age,
As 'twere retail'd to all posterity,
Even to the general all-ending day.
Glou. [*Aside.*] So wise so young, they say do never live long.
Prince. What say you, uncle?
Glou. I say, without characters fame lives long.
[*Aside.*] Thus, like the formal Vice, Iniquity,

III.i. Location: London. A street.
1. chamber. London was known as "the King's Chamber" (*camera regis*). **4. crosses:** unfortunate events, i.e. the arrests.
6. want: (1) lack; (2) desire. **11. jumpeth:** accords.
22. slug: sluggard. **26. On what occasion:** for what reason.
30. perforce: forcibly.
31. indirect and peevish: irregular and perverse.

34. presently: immediately.
45. ceremonious: bound by formalities.
46. grossness: coarseness, lack of (moral) refinement.
68. of any place: of all places.
75. regist'red: written down. **77. retail'd:** handed down.
81. characters: (1) written records; (2) moral qualities.
82. formal Vice: i.e. the stock character called Iniquity, who in sixteenth-century morality plays represented all the vices.

I moralize two meanings in one word.
Prince. That Julius Caesar was a famous man;
With what his valor did enrich his wit,
His wit set down to make his valure live.
Death makes no conquest of this conqueror,
For now he lives in fame though not in life.
I'll tell you what, my cousin Buckingham—
Buck. What, my gracious lord?
Prince. And if I live until I be a man,
I'll win our ancient right in France again,
Or die a soldier as I liv'd a king.
Glou. [*Aside.*] Short summers lightly have a forward spring.

Enter young York, Hastings, Cardinal [Bourchier].

Buck. Now in good time, here comes the Duke of York.
Prince. Richard of York, how fares our loving brother?
York. Well, my dread lord—so must I call you now.
Prince. Ay, brother, to our grief, as it is yours.
Too late he died that might have kept that title,
Which by his death hath lost much majesty.
Glou. How fares our cousin, noble Lord of York?
York. I thank you, gentle uncle. O my lord,
You said that idle weeds are fast in growth:
The Prince my brother hath outgrown me far.
Glou. He hath, my lord.
York. And therefore is he idle?
Glou. O my fair cousin, I must not say so.
York. Then he is more beholding to you than I.
Glou. He may command me as my sovereign,
But you have power in me as in a kinsman.
York. I pray you, uncle, give me this dagger.
Glou. My dagger, little cousin? with all my heart.
Prince. A beggar, brother?
York. Of my kind uncle, that I know will give,
And being but a toy, which is no grief to give.
Glou. A greater gift than that I'll give my cousin.
York. A greater gift? O, that's the sword to it.
Glou. Ay, gentle cousin, were it light enough.
York. O then I see you will part but with light gifts!
In weightier things you'll say a beggar nay.
Glou. It is too heavy for your Grace to wear.
York. I weigh it lightly, were it heavier.
Glou. What, would you have my weapon, little lord?
York. I would, that I might thank you as you call me.
Glou. How?
York. Little.
Prince. My Lord of York will still be cross in talk.

83. **moralize . . . word:** play upon the double meaning of a phrase (i.e. *live long*). 86. **valure:** valor.
92. **right:** i.e. the English sovereign's legal claim to the French throne. See note to *1 Henry VI*, I.i.80.
94. **Short . . . spring:** i.e. those who die young are usually precocious.
97. **dread:** to be held in reverential fear (as king).
99. **late:** recently. 103. **idle:** useless. 114. **toy:** trifle.
116. **to it:** i.e. to match the dagger. 118. **light:** trivial.
121. **lightly:** as a trifle.
126. **cross:** perverse, i.e. twisting words.

Uncle, your Grace knows how to bear with him.
York. You mean, to bear me, not to bear with me.
Uncle, my brother mocks both you and me:
Because that I am little, like an ape,
He thinks that you should bear me on your shoulders.
Buck. [*Aside to Hastings.*] With what a sharp-provided wit he reasons!
To mitigate the scorn he gives his uncle,
He prettily and aptly taunts himself:
So cunning and so young is wonderful.
Glou. My lord, will't please you pass along?
Myself and my good cousin Buckingham
Will to your mother, to entreat of her
To meet you at the Tower and welcome you.
York. What, will you go unto the Tower, my lord?
Prince. My Lord Protector needs will have it so.
York. I shall not sleep in quiet at the Tower.
Glou. Why, what should you fear?
York. Marry, my uncle Clarence' angry ghost.
My grandam told me he was murd'red there.
Prince. I fear no uncles dead.
Glou. Nor none that live, I hope.
Prince. And if they live, I hope I need not fear.
But come, my lord; with a heavy heart,
Thinking on them, go I unto the Tower.

[*A sennet.*] *Exeunt Prince* [*Edward*], *York, Hastings,* [*Cardinal Bourchier, and others*]. *Manent Richard, Buckingham,* [*and Catesby*].

Buck. Think you, my lord, this little prating York
Was not incensed by his subtile mother
To taunt and scorn you thus opprobriously?
Glou. No doubt, no doubt. O, 'tis a perilous boy,
Bold, quick, ingenious, forward, capable:
He is all the mother's, from the top to toe.
Buck. Well, let them rest. Come hither, Catesby.
Thou art sworn as deeply to effect what we intend
As closely to conceal what we impart.
Thou know'st our reasons urg'd upon the way;
What think'st thou? Is it not an easy matter
To make William Lord Hastings of our mind
For the installment of this noble Duke
In the seat royal of this famous isle?
Cate. He for his father's sake so loves the Prince
That he will not be won to aught against him.
Buck. What think'st thou then of Stanley? Will not he?
Cate. He will do all in all as Hastings doth.
Buck. Well then, no more but this: go, gentle Catesby,
And as it were far off, sound thou Lord Hastings
How he doth stand affected to our purpose,
And summon him to-morrow to the Tower
To sit about the coronation.

130–31. **Because . . . shoulders.** Court jesters and bears (at fairs and carnivals) sometimes carried an ape upon their backs. A slur on Richard's hunchback. 132. **sharp-provided:** keenly reasoned.
148. **And if:** if. **they:** i.e. Rivers and Grey, who had been arrested. Actually, Grey was Prince Edward's stepbrother.
150 s.d. **sennet:** trumpet notes to signal the arrival or departure of a procession. 152. **incensed:** incited.
154. **perilous:** (1) clever, precocious (cf. *parlous*, II.iv.35); (2) dangerous. 160. **way:** i.e. from Ludlow Castle.
163. **installment:** installation.
171. **doth stand affected:** is disposed. 173. **sit about:** discuss.

If thou dost find him tractable to us,
Encourage him, and tell him all our reasons;
If he be leaden, icy, cold, unwilling,
Be thou so too, and so break off the talk,
And give us notice of his inclination;
For we to-morrow hold divided Councils,
Wherein thyself shalt highly be employ'd.
Glou. Commend me to Lord William. Tell him, Catesby,
His ancient knot of dangerous adversaries
To-morrow are let blood at Pomfret Castle,
And bid my lord, for joy of this good news,
Give Mistress Shore one gentle kiss the more.
Buck. Good Catesby, go effect this business soundly.
Cate. My good lords both, with all the heed I can.
Glou. Shall we hear from you, Catesby, ere we sleep?
Cate. You shall, my lord.
Glou. At Crosby House, there shall you find us both. *Exit Catesby.*
Buck. Now, my lord, what shall we do if we perceive
Lord Hastings will not yield to our complots?
Glou. Chop off his head! Something we will determine.
And look when I am king, claim thou of me
The earldom of Herford, and all the moveables
Whereof the King my brother was possess'd.
Buck. I'll claim that promise at your Grace's hand.
Glou. And look to have it yielded with all kindness.
Come, let us sup betimes, that afterwards
We may digest our complots in some form. *Exeunt.*

Scene II

Enter a Messenger *to the door of Hastings.*

Mess. My lord! my lord!
Hast. [*Within.*] Who knocks?
Mess. One from the Lord Stanley.
Hast. [*Within.*] What is't a' clock?
Mess. Upon the stroke of four.

Enter Lord Hastings.

Hast. Cannot my Lord Stanley sleep these tedious nights?
Mess. So it appears by that I have to say:
First, he commends him to your noble self.
Hast. What then?
Mess. Then certifies your lordship that this night
He dreamt the boar had rased off his helm.
Besides, he says there are two Councils kept;
And that may be determin'd at the one
Which may make you and him to rue at th' other.
Therefore he sends to know your lordship's pleasure,
If you will presently take horse with him,
And with all speed post with him toward the north,
To shun the danger that his soul divines.
Hast. Go, fellow, go, return unto thy lord,
Bid him not fear the separated Council:
His honor and myself are at the one,
And at the other is my good friend Catesby;
Where nothing can proceed that toucheth us
Whereof I shall not have intelligence.
Tell him his fears are shallow, without instance;
And for his dreams, I wonder he's so simple
To trust the mock'ry of unquiet slumbers.
To fly the boar before the boar pursues
Were to incense the boar to follow us,
And make pursuit where he did mean no chase.
Go, bid thy master rise and come to me,
And we will both together to the Tower,
Where he shall see the boar will use us kindly.
Mess. I'll go, my lord, and tell him what you say. *Exit.*

Enter Catesby.

Cate. Many good morrows to my noble lord!
Hast. Good morrow, Catesby, you are early stirring.
What news, what news, in this our tott'ring state?
Cate. It is a reeling world indeed, my lord,
And I believe will never stand upright
Till Richard wear the garland of the realm.
Hast. How? wear the garland? Dost thou mean the crown?
Cate. Ay, my good lord.
Hast. I'll have this crown of mine cut from my shoulders
Before I'll see the crown so foul misplac'd.
But canst thou guess that he doth aim at it?
Cate. Ay, on my life, and hopes to find you forward
Upon his party for the gain thereof;
And thereupon he sends you this good news,
That this same very day your enemies,
The kindred of the Queen, must die at Pomfret.
Hast. Indeed I am no mourner for that news,
Because they have been still my adversaries;
But that I'll give my voice on Richard's side
To bar my master's heirs in true descent,
God knows I will not do it, to the death!
Cate. God keep your lordship in that gracious mind!
Hast. But I shall laugh at this a twelvemonth hence,
That they which brought me in my master's hate,

179. divided: separate. More (Bullough, III, 262) explained that Richard "caused all the lordes whiche he knewe to bee faithfull to the kyng to assemble at Baynardes castle to commen [confer] of the ordre of the coronacion, whyle he and other of his complices & of his affinitee at Crosbies place contrived the contrary and to make the protectour kyng: to which counsail there were adhibite [admitted] very fewe, and they very secrete."
181. Lord William: i.e. Hastings.
183. are let blood: bleed, i.e. will be executed.
185. Mistress Shore. According to More (Bullough, III, 264), Hastings "from the death of kyng Edward kept Shores wife."
192. complots: conspiracies. **195. moveables:** personal property.
199. betimes: soon.

III.ii. Location: Before Lord Hastings' house.

10. certifies: informs.
11. boar: i.e. Richard (see note to I.ii.102). **rased . . . helm:** torn off his helmet. **25. instance:** grounds. **27. To:** as to.
43. crown: i.e. head.
46–47. forward . . . party: eager to his cause.
56. gracious: righteous.

I live to look upon their tragedy.
Well, Catesby, ere a fortnight make me older,
I'll send some packing that yet think not on't.

Cate. 'Tis a vile thing to die, my gracious lord,
When men are unprepar'd and look not for it.

Hast. O monstrous, monstrous! and so falls it out
With Rivers, Vaughan, Grey; and so 'twill do
With some men else, that think themselves as safe
As thou and I, who (as thou know'st) are dear
To princely Richard and to Buckingham.

Cate. The princes both make high account of you—
[*Aside.*] For they account his head upon the bridge.

Hast. I know they do, and I have well deserv'd it.

Enter Lord Stanley.

Come on, come on, where is your boar-spear, man?
Fear you the boar, and go so unprovided?

Stan. My lord, good morrow, good morrow, Catesby.
You may jest on, but, by the holy rood,
I do not like these several Councils, I.

Hast. My lord,
I hold my life as dear as [you do] yours,
And never in my days, I do protest,
Was it so precious to me as 'tis now.
Think you, but that I know our state secure,
I would be so triumphant as I am?

Stan. The lords at Pomfret, when they rode from London,
Were jocund, and suppos'd their states were sure,
And they indeed had no cause to mistrust;
But yet you see how soon the day o'ercast.
This sudden stab of rancor I misdoubt;
Pray God, I say, I prove a needless coward!
What, shall we toward the Tower? the day is spent.

Hast. Come, come, have with you. Wot you what, my lord?
To-day the lords you [talk'd] of are beheaded.

Stan. They, for their truth, might better wear their heads
Than some that have accus'd them wear their hats.
But come, my lord, let's away.

Enter a Pursuivant [*also named Hastings*].

Hast. Go on before, I'll talk with this good fellow.
Exeunt Lord Stanley and Catesby.
How now, sirrah? how goes the world with thee?

Purs. The better that your lordship please to ask.

Hast. I tell thee, man, 'tis better with me now
Than when thou met'st me last where now we meet.
Then was I going prisoner to the Tower,
By the suggestion of the Queen's allies;
But now I tell thee (keep it to thyself)
This day those enemies are put to death,
And I in better state than e'er I was.

Purs. God hold it, to your honor's good content!

Hast. Gramercy, fellow. There, drink that for me.
Throws him his purse.

Purs. I thank your honor. *Exit Pursuivant.*

Enter a Priest.

Priest. Well met, my lord, I am glad to see your honor.

Hast. I thank thee, good Sir John, with all my heart.
I am in your debt for your last exercise;
Come the next Sabbath, and I will content you.
[*He whispers in his ear.*]

Priest. I'll wait upon your lordship.

Enter Buckingham.

Buck. What, talking with a priest, Lord Chamberlain?
Your friends at Pomfret, they do need the priest,
Your honor hath no shriving work in hand.

Hast. Good faith, and when I met this holy man
The men you talk of came into my mind.
What, go you toward the Tower?

Buck. I do, my lord, but long I cannot stay there.
I shall return before your lordship thence.

Hast. Nay, like enough, for I stay dinner there.

Buck. [*Aside.*] And supper too, although thou know'st it not.—
Come, will you go?

Hast. I'll wait upon your lordship. *Exeunt.*

Scene III

Enter Sir Richard Ratcliffe *with Halberds, carrying the nobles* [Rivers, Grey, *and* Vaughan] *to death at Pomfret.*

[*Rat.* Come, bring forth the prisoners.]

Riv. Sir Richard Ratcliffe, let me tell thee this:
To-day shalt thou behold a subject die
For truth, for duty, and for loyalty.

Grey. God bless the Prince from all the pack of you!
A knot you are of damned blood-suckers.

Vaug. You live that shall cry woe for this hereafter.

Rat. Dispatch, the limit of your lives is out.

Riv. O Pomfret, Pomfret! O thou bloody prison!
Fatal and ominous to noble peers!
Within the guilty closure of thy walls
Richard the Second here was hack'd to death;
And for more slander to thy dismal seat,
We give to thee our guiltless blood to drink.

69. make . . . you: esteem you highly.
70. account: expect. **bridge:** i.e. London Bridge, where the heads of traitors were exhibited. **75. rood:** cross.
76. several: separate. **82. triumphant:** exultant.
86. o'ercast: became overcast. **87. misdoubt:** suspect.
89. spent: i.e. well advanced. The scene had opened at 4 a.m.
90. have with you: I'll accompany you.
94 s.d. Pursuivant: an official, attendant on a herald, empowered to serve warrants.
96. sirrah: customary form of address to an inferior.
101. suggestion: instigation.
105. hold it: i.e. preserve things as they are.
106. Gramercy: thank you.
109. Sir: a common title of respect for clergymen.
110. exercise: sermon.
115. shriving work: confession and absolution, i.e. ministrations for those about to die.

III.iii. Location: Pomfret Castle.
6. knot: group. **11. closure:** enclosure.
13. for . . . seat: i.e. to add to your evil reputation.

Grey. Now Margaret's curse is fall'n upon our heads,
When she exclaim'd on Hastings, you, and I,
For standing by when Richard stabb'd her son.
Riv. Then curs'd she Richard, then curs'd she Buckingham,
Then curs'd she Hastings. O, remember, God,
To hear her prayer for them, as now for us!
And for my sister and her princely sons,
Be satisfied, dear God, with our true blood,
Which, as thou know'st, unjustly must be spilt.
Rat. Make haste, the hour of death is expiate.
Riv. Come, Grey, come, Vaughan, let us here embrace.
Farewell, until we meet again in heaven. *Exeunt*.

Scene IV

Enter Buckingham, [Stanley, *Earl of*] *Derby*, Hastings, Bishop of Ely, Norfolk, Ratcliffe, Lovel, *with others, at a table*.

Hast. Now, noble peers, the cause why we are met
Is to determine of the coronation.
In God's name speak, when is the royal day?
Buck. Is all things ready for the royal time?
Stan. It is, and wants but nomination.
Ely. To-morrow then I judge a happy day.
Buck. Who knows the Lord Protector's mind herein?
Who is most inward with the noble Duke?
Ely. Your Grace, we think, should soonest know his mind.
Buck. We know each other's faces; for our hearts,
He knows no more of mine than I of yours,
Or I of his, my lord, than you of mine.
Lord Hastings, you and he are near in love.
Hast. I thank his Grace, I know he loves me well;
But for his purpose in the coronation,
I have not sounded him, nor he deliver'd
His gracious pleasure any way therein.
But you, my honorable lords, may name the time,
And in the Duke's behalf I'll give my voice,
Which I presume he'll take in gentle part.

Enter Gloucester.

Ely. In happy time, here comes the Duke himself.
Glou. My noble lords and cousins all, good morrow.
I have been long a sleeper; but I trust
My absence doth neglect no great design,
Which by my presence might have been concluded.
Buck. Had you not come upon your cue, my lord,
William Lord Hastings had pronounc'd your part,
I mean your voice for crowning of the King.
Glou. Than my Lord Hastings no man might be bolder,
His lordship knows me well and loves me well.
My Lord of Ely, when I was last in Holborn,
I saw good strawberries in your garden there.
I do beseech you send for some of them.
Ely. Marry, and will, my lord, with all my heart.
Exit Bishop.
Glou. Cousin of Buckingham, a word with you.
[*Drawing him aside*.]
Catesby hath sounded Hastings in our business,
And finds the testy gentleman so hot
That he will lose his head ere give consent
His master's child, as worshipfully he terms it,
Shall lose the royalty of England's throne.
Buck. Withdraw yourself a while, I'll go with you.
Exeunt [*Gloucester and Buckingham*].
Stan. We have not yet set down this day of triumph.
To-morrow, in my judgment, is too sudden,
For I myself am not so well provided
As else I would be, were the day prolong'd.

Enter the Bishop of Ely.

Ely. Where is my lord the Duke of Gloucester?
I have sent for these strawberries.
Hast. His Grace looks cheerfully and smooth this morning;
There's some conceit or other likes him well,
When that he bids good morrow with such spirit.
I think there's never a man in Christendom
Can lesser hide his love or hate than he,
For by his face straight shall you know his heart.
Stan. What of his heart perceive you in his face
By any livelihood he show'd to-day?
Hast. Marry, that with no man here he is offended;
For were he, he had shown it in his looks.
[*Stan*. I pray God he be not, I say.]

Enter Richard [of Gloucester] *and* Buckingham

Glou. I pray you all, tell me what they deserve
That do conspire my death with devilish plots
Of damned witchcraft, and that have prevail'd
Upon my body with their hellish charms?
Hast. The tender love I bear your Grace, my lord,
Makes me most forward in this princely presence
To doom th' offenders, whosoe'er they be:
I say, my lord, they have deserved death.
Glou. Then be your eyes the witness of their evil.
Look how I am bewitch'd; behold, mine arm
Is like a blasted sapling, wither'd up;
And this is Edward's wife, that monstrous witch,
Consorted with that harlot, strumpet Shore,
That by their witchcraft thus have marked me.
Hast. If they have done this deed, my noble lord—
Glou. If? Thou protector of this damned strumpet,
Talk'st thou to me of "ifs"? Thou art a traitor.
Off with his head! Now by Saint Paul I swear

15–18. Now . . . Buckingham. Actually, Margaret had not included Grey and Vaughan in her execrations, and Buckingham had received not her curse but her prophecy of disaster (I.iii).
24. expiate: fully come.

III.iv. Location: London. The Tower.
2. determine of: decide about. **5. nomination:** setting the date.
8. inward: intimate. **10. for:** as for. **19. voice:** vote.
24. neglect . . . design: i.e. cause no important matter to be neglected.

31. Holborn: district in London where the Bishop of Ely had his residence. **40. royalty:** sovereignty. **45. prolong'd:** postponed.
49. conceit: fancy. **likes:** pleases.
53. straight: straightway. **55. livelihood:** animation.
71. Consorted: associated.

I will not dine until I see the same.
Lovel and Ratcliffe, look that it be done:
The rest that love me, rise, and follow me.
Exeunt. Manent Lovel and Ratcliffe with the Lord Hastings.

Hast. Woe, woe for England, not a whit for me!
For I, too fond, might have prevented this.
Stanley did dream the boar did [rase] our helms,
And I did scorn it and disdain to fly.
Three times to-day my foot-cloth horse did stumble,
And started when he look'd upon the Tower,
As loath to bear me to the slaughter-house.
O now I need the priest that spake to me!
I now repent I told the pursuivant,
As too triumphing, how mine enemies
To-day at Pomfret bloodily were butcher'd,
And I myself secure, in grace and favor.
O Margaret, Margaret, now thy heavy curse
Is lighted on poor Hastings' wretched head!
Rat. Come, come, dispatch, the Duke would be at dinner.
Make a short shrift, he longs to see your head.
Hast. O momentary grace of mortal men,
Which we more hunt for than the grace of God!
Who builds his hope in air of your good looks
Lives like a drunken sailor on a mast,
Ready with every nod to tumble down
Into the fatal bowels of the deep.
Lov. Come, come, dispatch, 'tis bootless to exclaim.
Hast. O bloody Richard! Miserable England!
I prophesy the fearfull'st time to thee
That ever wretched age hath look'd upon.
Come, lead me to the block; bear him my head.
They smile at me who shortly shall be dead. *Exeunt.*

[Scene V]

Enter Richard [of Gloucester] *and* Buckingham *in rotten armor, marvellous ill-favored.*

Glou. Come, cousin, canst thou quake and change thy color,
Murther thy breath in middle of a word,
And then again begin, and stop again,
As if thou were distraught and mad with terror?
Buck. Tut, I can counterfeit the deep tragedian,
Speak and look back, and pry on every side,
Tremble and start at wagging of a straw;
Intending deep suspicion, ghastly looks
Are at my service, like enforced smiles;
And both are ready in their offices
At any time to grace my stratagems.
But what, is Catesby gone?
Glou. He is, and see, he brings the Mayor along.

81. **fond:** foolish.
84. **foot-cloth:** wearing ornamental trappings (as the mount of a dignitary). 95. **shrift:** confession.
98. **in . . . looks:** on your favorable external seeming.
102. **bootless:** useless.

III.v. Location: London. The Tower walls.
o.s.d. **rotten:** rusty. **ill-favored:** ugly. 8. **Intending:** pretending.
10. **offices:** functions.

Enter the Mayor *and* Catesby.

Buck. Lord Mayor—
Glou. Look to the drawbridge there!
Buck. Hark, a drum!
Glou. Catesby, o'erlook the walls.
Buck. Lord Mayor, the reason we have sent—
Glou. Look back, defend thee, here are enemies!
Buck. God and our [innocence] defend and guard us!

Enter Lovel *and* Ratcliffe *with Hastings' head.*

Glou. Be patient, they are friends—Ratcliffe and Lovel.
Lov. Here is the head of that ignoble traitor,
The dangerous and unsuspected Hastings.
Glou. So dear I lov'd the man that I must weep.
I took him for the plainest harmless creature
That breath'd upon the earth a Christian;
Made him my book, wherein my soul recorded
The history of all her secret thoughts.
So smooth he daub'd his vice with show of virtue
That, his apparent open guilt omitted—
I mean, his conversation with Shore's wife—
He liv'd from all attainder of suspects.
Buck. Well, well, he was the covert'st shelt'red traitor
That ever liv'd. [Look ye, my Lord Mayor,]
Would you imagine, or almost believe,
Were't not that by great preservation
We live to tell it, that the subtile traitor
This day had plotted, in the Council-house,
To murther me and my good Lord of Gloucester?
May. Had he done so?
Glou. What? think you we are Turks or infidels?
Or that we would, against the form of law,
Proceed thus rashly in the villain's death,
But that the extreme peril of the case,
The peace of England, and our persons' safety,
Enforc'd us to this execution?
May. Now fair befall you! he deserv'd his death,
And your good Graces both have well proceeded,
To warn false traitors from the like attempts.
Buck. I never look'd for better at his hands
After he once fell in with Mistress Shore.
Yet had we not determin'd he should die
Until your lordship came to see his end,
Which now the loving haste of these our friends,
Something against our meanings, have prevented;
Because, my lord, I would have had you heard
The traitor speak, and timorously confess
The manner and the purpose of his treasons,
That you might well have signified the same
Unto the citizens, who haply may
Misconster us in him and wail his death.

17. **o'erlook:** inspect.
25. **harmless:** i.e. most harmless. (Cf., in line 33, *shelt'red* = most concealed.) 30. **apparent:** manifest.
31. **conversation:** intercourse.
32. **from . . . suspects:** free from all taint of suspicion.
48. **proceeded:** done.
55. **Something . . . meanings:** somewhat contrary to our intentions. **prevented:** anticipated.
61. **Misconster . . . him:** i.e. misconstrue our handling of this business.

May. But, my good lord, your Grace's words shall serve
As well as I had seen, and heard him speak;
And do not doubt, right noble princes both,
But I'll acquaint our duteous citizens
With all your just proceedings in this [cause].
Glou. And to that end we wish'd your lordship here,
T' avoid the censures of the carping world.
Buck. Which since you come too late of our intent,
Yet witness what you hear we did intend.
And so, my good Lord Mayor, we bid farewell.
Exit Mayor.
Glou. Go after, after, cousin Buckingham.
The Mayor towards Guildhall hies him in all post.
There, at your meet'st [advantage] of the time,
Infer the bastardy of Edward's children.
Tell them how Edward put to death a citizen
Only for saying he would make his son
Heir to the Crown—meaning indeed his house,
Which by the sign thereof was termed so.
Moreover, urge his hateful luxury
And bestial appetite in change of lust,
Which stretch'd unto their servants, daughters, wives,
Even where his raging eye or savage heart,
Without control, lusted to make a prey.
Nay, for a need, thus far come near my person:
Tell them, when that my mother went with child
Of that insatiate Edward, noble York,
My princely father, then had wars in France,
And by true computation of the time,
Found that the issue was not his begot;
Which well appeared in his lineaments,
Being nothing like the noble Duke my father.
Yet touch this sparingly, as 'twere far off,
Because, my lord, you know my mother lives.
Buck. Doubt not, my lord, I'll play the orator
As if the golden fee for which I plead
Were for myself—and so, my lord, adieu.
Glou. If you thrive well, bring them to Baynard's Castle,
Where you shall find me well accompanied
With reverend fathers and well-learned bishops.
Buck. I go, and towards three or four a' clock
Look for the news that the Guildhall affords.
Exit Buckingham.
Glou. Go, Lovel, with all speed to Doctor Shaw;
[*To Catesby.*] Go thou to Friar [Penker]; bid them both

Meet me within this hour at Baynard's Castle.
Exeunt [*Lovel and Catesby*].
[*To Ratcliffe.*] Now will I go to take some privy order
To draw the brats of Clarence out of sight,
And to give order that no manner person
Have any time recourse unto the Princes. *Exeunt.*

[Scene VI]

Enter a Scrivener [*with a paper in his hand*].

Scriv. Here is the indictment of the good Lord Hastings,
Which in a set hand fairly is engross'd
That it may be to-day read o'er in Paul's.
And mark how well the sequel hangs together:
Eleven hours I have spent to write it over,
For yesternight by Catesby was it sent me;
The precedent was full as long a-doing,
And yet within these five hours Hastings liv'd,
Untainted, unexamin'd, free, at liberty.
Here's a good world the while! Who is so gross
That cannot see this palpable device?
Yet who['s] so bold but says he sees it not?
Bad is the world, and all will come to nought,
When such ill dealing must be seen in thought. *Exit.*

[Scene VII]

Enter Richard [of Gloucester] *and* Buckingham *at several doors.*

Glou. How now, how now, what say the citizens?
Buck. Now, by the holy Mother of our Lord,
The citizens are mum, say not a word.
Glou. Touch'd you the bastardy of Edward's children?
Buck. I did, with his contract with Lady Lucy,
And his contract by deputy in France,
Th' unsatiate greediness of his desire,
And his enforcement of the city wives,

69. of our intent: i.e. for things to proceed as we intended.
70. witness: bear witness to.
73. Guildhall: seat of municipal government in London. **post:** haste.
74. meet'st . . . time: most favorable opportunity.
75. Infer: assert.
76–79. Tell . . . so. According to More (Bullough, III, 273), when a merchant named Burdet, "dwellyng in Chepesyd[e] at the signe of the Croune," told his son that "he would make hym inheritor of the Croune, meanyng his awne house," King Edward, misconstruing the remark, had him promptly "apprehended, judged, drawen and quartered." **80. luxury:** sensuality.
81. change of lust: i.e. fickleness in shifting from one woman to another. **85. for a need:** if necessary.
86–87. went . . . Of: was pregnant with.
96. golden fee: i.e. the crown.
98. Baynard's Castle: one of Richard's London residences.
103, 104. Shaw, Penker. Among Richard's creatures, says More (Bullough, III, 269–70), were "Raffe Shaa [i.e. Shaw] clearke brother to the Mayre, & Freer Pynkie [i.e. Penker] provinciall of the Augustine Freers," one of whom "made a sermonde in prayse of the Protectour before the coronacion" and the other a similar sermon after the ceremony, "bothe so full of tedious flattery, that no good mans eares coulde abyde them."
106. take . . . order: make some private arrangement.
108–9. that . . . Princes: that no person whatever at any time have access to the Princes.

III.vi. Location: London. A street.
2. set hand: style of script used in legal documents.
7. precedent: first draft. **10. gross:** stupid.
14. seen in thought: i.e. perceived but not spoken of.

III.vii. Location: London. Baynard's Castle.
o.s.d. several: different.
4–6. Touch'd . . . France. As Buckingham argues later in the scene (lines 177–91), Edward's alleged betrothal to Elizabeth Lucy (by whom he had had a child) and his offer of marriage to Bona of Savoy invalidated his marriage with Elizabeth Grey, and thus their children—seven of whom survived infancy—were bastards. On the negotiations with Bona of Savoy see *3 Henry VI*, III.iii.
5. contract: betrothal. **7. unsatiate:** insatiable.
8. enforcement: forcible seduction.

His tyranny for trifles, his own bastardy,
As being got, your father then in France,
And his resemblance, being not like the Duke.
Withal I did infer your lineaments,
Being the right idea of your father,
Both in your form and nobleness of mind;
Laid open all your victories in Scotland,
Your discipline in war, wisdom in peace,
Your bounty, virtue, fair humility;
Indeed, left nothing fitting for your purpose
Untouch'd or slightly handled in discourse.
And when [mine] oratory drew [to an] end,
I bid them that did love their country's good
Cry, "God save Richard, England's royal king!"
Glou. And did they so?
Buck. No, so God help me, they spake not a word,
But like dumb statuës, or breathing stones,
Star'd each on other, and look'd deadly pale;
Which when I saw, I reprehended them,
And ask'd the Mayor what meant this willful silence.
His answer was, the people were not used
To be spoke to but by the Recorder.
Then he was urg'd to tell my tale again:
"Thus saith the Duke, thus hath the Duke inferr'd"—
But nothing [spake] in warrant from himself.
When he had done, some followers of mine own,
At lower end of the hall, hurl'd up their caps,
And some ten voices cried, "God save King Richard!"
And thus I took the vantage of those few:
"Thanks, gentle citizens and friends," quoth I,
"This general applause and cheerful shout
Argues your [wisdoms] and your love to Richard"—
And even here brake off, and came away.
Glou. What tongueless blocks were they! Would they not speak?
[*Buck.* No, by my troth, my lord.]
[*Glou.*] Will not the Mayor then and his brethren come?
Buck. The Mayor is here at hand. Intend some fear,
Be not you spoke with but by mighty suit;
And look you get a prayer-book in your hand,
And stand between two churchmen, good my lord—
For on that ground I'll make a holy descant—
And be not easily won to our requests:
Play the maid's part, still answer nay, and take it.
Glou. I go; and if you plead as well for them
As I can say nay to thee for myself,
No doubt we bring it to a happy issue.
Buck. Go, go up to the leads, the Lord Mayor knocks. [*Exit Gloucester.*]

Enter the MAYOR, [ALDERMEN,] *and* CITIZENS.

Welcome, my lord! I dance attendance here;
I think the Duke will not be spoke withal.

Enter CATESBY.

Now, Catesby, what says your lord to my request?
Cate. He doth entreat your Grace, my noble lord,
To visit him to-morrow or next day.
He is within, with two right reverend fathers,
Divinely bent to meditation,
And in no worldly suits would he be mov'd,
To draw him from his holy exercise.
Buck. Return, good Catesby, to the gracious Duke,
Tell him, myself, the Mayor and Aldermen,
In deep designs, in matter of great moment,
No less importing than our general good,
Are come to have some conference with his Grace.
Cate. I'll signify so much unto him straight. *Exit.*
Buck. Ah ha, my lord, this prince is not an Edward!
He is not lulling on a lewd love-bed,
But on his knees at meditation;
Not dallying with a brace of courtezans,
But meditating with two deep divines;
Not sleeping, to engross his idle body,
But praying, to enrich his watchful soul.
Happy were England, would this virtuous prince
Take on his Grace the sovereignty thereof,
But sure I fear we shall not win him to it.
May. Marry, God defend his Grace should say us nay!
Buck. I fear he will. Here Catesby comes again.

Enter CATESBY.

Now, Catesby, what says his Grace?
Cate. [My lord,]
He wonders to what end you have assembled
Such troops of citizens to come to him,
His Grace not being warn'd thereof before:
He fears, my lord, you mean no good to him.
Buck. Sorry I am my noble cousin should
Suspect me that I mean no good to him.
By heaven, we come to him in perfit love,
And so once more return and tell his Grace. *Exit* [*Catesby*].
When holy and devout religious men
Are at their beads, 'tis much to draw them thence,
So sweet is zealous contemplation.

Enter RICHARD [OF GLOUCESTER] *aloft, between two* BISHOPS. [CATESBY *returns.*]

May. See where his Grace stands, 'tween two clergymen!
Buck. Two props of virtue for a Christian prince,
To stay him from the fall of vanity;
And see, a book of prayer in his hand—
True ornaments to know a holy man.
Famous Plantagenet, most gracious prince,

9. tyranny for trifles: harshness toward trifling offenses.
11. resemblance: appearance.
12. infer your lineaments: comment on your features.
13. right idea: very image.
15. victories in Scotland. As leader of an expedition against the Scots in 1482 Richard had advanced as far as Edinburgh.
30. Recorder: a city official. **32. inferr'd:** asserted.
33. in . . . himself: on his own authority. **41. brake:** broke.
45. Intend: pretend. **46. mighty suit:** urgent entreaty.
49. ground: plain-song or bass. **descant:** variation.
55. leads: i.e. roof (so called from the sheets of metal used for covering).

57. spoke withal: spoken with.
68. No less importing: relating to nothing less.
72. lulling: lolling. **76. engross:** fatten. **81. defend:** forbid.
90. perfit: perfect. **93. beads:** prayers.
97. stay: prevent. **of:** caused by.

Lend favorable ear to our requests,
And pardon us the interruption
Of thy devotion and right Christian zeal.
Glou. My lord, there needs no such apology.
I do beseech your Grace to pardon me,
Who, earnest in the service of my God,
Deferr'd the visitation of my friends.
But leaving this, what is your Grace's pleasure?
Buck. Even that (I hope) which pleaseth God above
And all good men of this ungovern'd isle.
Glou. I do suspect I have done some offense
That seems disgracious in the city's eye,
And that you come to reprehend my ignorance.
Buck. You have, my lord. Would it might please your Grace,
On our entreaties, to amend your fault!
Glou. Else wherefore breathe I in a Christian land?
Buck. Know then, it is your fault that you resign
The supreme seat, the throne majestical,
The sceptred office of your ancestors,
Your state of fortune, and your due of birth,
The lineal glory of your royal house,
To the corruption of a blemish'd stock;
Whiles in the mildness of your sleepy thoughts,
Which here we waken to our country's good,
The noble isle doth want [her] proper limbs;
[Her] face defac'd with scars of infamy,
[Her] royal stock graft with ignoble plants,
And almost should'red in the swallowing gulf
Of dark forgetfulness and deep oblivion.
Which to recure, we heartily solicit
Your gracious self to take on you the charge
And kingly government of this your land:
Not as protector, steward, substitute,
Or lowly factor for another's gain;
But as successively, from blood to blood,
Your right of birth, your empery, your own.
For this, consorted with the citizens,
Your very worshipful and loving friends,
And by their vehement instigation,
In this just cause come I to move your Grace.
Glou. I cannot tell if to depart in silence,
Or bitterly to speak in your reproof,
Best fitteth my degree or your condition.
If not to answer, you might haply think
Tongue-tied ambition, not replying, yielded
To bear the golden yoke of sovereignty,
Which fondly you would here impose on me.
If to reprove you for this suit of yours,
So season'd with your faithful love to me,
Then on the other side, I check'd my friends.
Therefore—to speak, and to avoid the first,
And then, in speaking, not to incur the last—
Definitively thus I answer you:
Your love deserves my thanks, but my desert
Unmeritable shuns your high request.
First, if all obstacles were cut away,
And that my path were even to the crown,
As the ripe revenue and due of birth,
Yet so much is my poverty of spirit,
So mighty and so many my defects,
That I would rather hide me from my greatness—
Being a bark to brook no mighty sea—
Than in my greatness covet to be hid
And in the vapor of my glory smother'd.
But God be thank'd, there is no need of me,
And much I need to help you, were there need:
The royal tree hath left us royal fruit,
Which mellow'd by the stealing hours of time,
Will well become the seat of majesty,
And make (no doubt) us happy by his reign.
On him I lay that you would lay on me,
The right and fortune of his happy stars,
Which God defend that I should wring from him!
Buck. My lord, this argues conscience in your Grace,
But the respects thereof are nice and trivial,
All circumstances well considered.
You say that Edward is your brother's son:
So say we too, but not by Edward's wife;
For first was he contract to Lady Lucy—
Your mother lives a witness to his vow—
And afterward by substitute betroth'd
To Bona, sister to the King of France.
These both put off, a poor petitioner,
A care-craz'd mother to a many sons,
A beauty-waning and distressed widow,
Even in the afternoon of her best days,
Made prize and purchase of his wanton eye,
Seduc'd the pitch and height of his degree
To base declension and loath'd bigamy.
By her, in his unlawful bed, he got
This Edward, whom our manners call the Prince.
More bitterly could I expostulate,
Save that for reverence to some alive,
I give a sparing limit to my tongue.
Then, good my lord, take to your royal self
This proffer'd benefit of dignity;
If not to bless us and the land withal,
Yet to draw forth your noble ancestry
From the corruption of abusing times
Unto a lineal true-derived course.

112. disgracious: displeasing.
123. sleepy: i.e. conducive to repose and meditation.
125. want: lack. **proper:** own. **127. graft:** engrafted.
128. should'red in: plunged into. **130. recure:** remedy.
134. factor: agent. **135. successively:** in order of succession.
136. empery: realm to be ruled. **143. condition:** rank.
147. fondly: foolishly. **149. season'd:** i.e. made palatable.
150. check'd: rebuked.

157. even: unimpeded.
158. revenue: possession ready for enjoyment.
163. in . . . hid: i.e. wish to be protected by my greatness.
166. much I need: I am greatly lacking (in ability).
175. respects: the reasons you advance. **nice:** overscrupulous.
180. Your . . . vow. According to Hall (Bullough, III, 271), Edward's mother was so much troubled by his liaison with Elizabeth Lucy "that either the bishoppe durste not, or the kynge would not proceade to the solemnisacion of the mariage [with Elizabeth Grey] til his fame were clerely purged, and the truth well and openly testified."
183-89. a poor . . . bigamy. For the circumstances of Edward's match with Elizabeth Grey see *3 Henry VI*, III.ii.
187. purchase: booty.
188. Seduc'd: debased. **pitch:** height (a term from falconry).
189. declension: decline.
191. our manners: i.e. we, in mere politeness.
192. expostulate: discuss.
195. good my lord: my good lord.
199. of abusing times: caused by the abuses of the times.

May. Do, good my lord, your citizens entreat you.
Buck. Refuse not, mighty lord, this proffer'd love.
Cate. O, make them joyful, grant their lawful suit!
Glou. Alas, why would you heap this care on me?
I am unfit for state and majesty.
I do beseech you take it not amiss,
I cannot nor I will not yield to you.
Buck. If you refuse it—as, in love and zeal,
Loath to depose the child, your brother's son;
As well we know your tenderness of heart
And gentle, kind, effeminate remorse,
Which we have noted in you to your kindred
And egally indeed to all estates—
Yet know, whe'er you accept our suit or no,
Your brother's son shall never reign our king,
But we will plant some other in the throne,
To the disgrace and downfall of your house;
And in this resolution here we leave you.
Come, citizens. ['Zounds, I'll] entreat no more.
[*Glou.* O, do not swear, my Lord of Buckingham.]
Exeunt [*Buckingham, Mayor, Aldermen, and Citizens*].
Cate. Call him again, sweet prince, accept their suit.
If you deny them, all the land will rue it.
Glou. Will you enforce me to a world of cares?
Call them again, I am not made of stones,
But penetrable to your kind entreaties,
Albeit against my conscience and my soul.

Enter BUCKINGHAM *and the rest.*

Cousin of Buckingham, and sage grave men,
Since you will buckle Fortune on my back,
To bear her burthen whe'er I will or no,
I must have patience to endure the load;
But if black scandal or foul-fac'd reproach
Attend the sequel of your imposition,
Your mere enforcement shall acquittance me
From all the impure blots and stains thereof;
For God doth know, and you may partly see,
How far I am from the desire of this.
May. God bless your Grace! we see it and will say it.
Glou. In saying so you shall but say the truth.
Buck. Then I salute you with this royal title—
Long live Richard, England's worthy king!
All. Amen.
Buck. To-morrow may it please you to be crown'd?
Glou. Even when you please, for you will have it so.
Buck. To-morrow then we will attend your Grace,
And so most joyfully we take our leave.
Glou. [*To the Bishops.*] Come, let us to our holy work again.—
Farewell, my [cousin], farewell, gentle friends.
Exeunt.

211. kind, effeminate remorse: natural, tender pity.
213. egally: equally. **estates:** ranks.
232. imposition: charge (of kingship).
233. mere: downright. **acquittance:** acquit.

ACT IV, SCENE I

Enter the QUEEN [ELIZABETH], *the* DUCHESS OF YORK, *and* MARQUESS DORSET [*at one door*]; ANNE DUCHESS OF GLOUCESTER [*leading* LADY MARGARET PLANTAGENET, *Clarence's young daughter, at another door*].

Duch. Who meets us here? My niece Plantagenet,
Led in the hand of her kind aunt of Gloucester?
Now, for my life, she's wand'ring to the Tower,
On pure heart's love, to greet the tender Prince.
Daughter, well met.
Anne. God give your Graces both
A happy and a joyful time of day!
Q. Eliz. As much to you, good sister! Whither away?
Anne. No farther than the Tower, and as I guess,
Upon the like devotion as yourselves,
To gratulate the gentle Princes there.
Q. Eliz. Kind sister, thanks, we'll enter all together.

Enter the Lieutenant [BRAKENBURY].

And in good time, here the Lieutenant comes.
Master Lieutenant, pray you, by your leave,
How doth the Prince and my young son of York?
Brak. Right well, dear madam. By your patience,
I may not suffer you to visit them,
The King hath strictly charg'd the contrary.
Q. Eliz. The King? who's that?
Brak. I mean the Lord Protector.
Q. Eliz. The Lord protect him from that kingly title!
Hath he set bounds between their love and me?
I am their mother, who shall bar me from them?
Duch. I am their father's mother, I will see them.
Anne. Their aunt I am in law, in love their mother;
Then bring me to their sights. I'll bear thy blame,
And take thy office from thee on my peril.
Brak. No, madam, no; I may not leave it so:
I am bound by oath, and therefore pardon me.
Exit Lieutenant.

Enter STANLEY.

Stan. Let me but meet you, ladies, [an] hour hence,
And I'll salute your Grace of York as mother
And reverend looker-on of two fair queens.
[*To Anne.*] Come, madam, you must straight to Westminster,
There to be crowned Richard's royal queen.
Q. Eliz. Ah, cut my lace asunder,
That my pent heart may have some scope to beat,
Or else I swoon with this dead-killing news!
Anne. Despiteful tidings, O unpleasing news!

IV.i. Location: London. Before the Tower.
1. niece: i.e. granddaughter. **4. On:** out of.
5. Daughter: i.e. daughter-in-law.
7. sister: i.e. sister-in-law. **10. gratulate:** greet.
20. bounds: barriers.
25. take . . . peril: i.e. be responsible for relieving you of your duties.
26. it: i.e. his office. **29. mother:** i.e. mother-in-law.
30. queens: i.e. Elizabeth (consort of Edward IV) and Anne (consort of Richard III). **33. cut . . . asunder:** i.e. loosen my bodice.
36. Despiteful: cruel.

Dor. Be of good cheer. Mother, how fares your Grace?
Q. Eliz. O Dorset, speak not to me, get thee gone!
Death and destruction dogs thee at thy heels;
Thy mother's name is ominous to children.
If thou wilt outstrip death, go cross the seas,
And live with Richmond, from the reach of hell.
Go hie thee, hie thee from this slaughter-house,
Lest thou increase the number of the dead,
And make me die the thrall of Margaret's curse,
Nor mother, wife, nor England's counted queen.
Stan. Full of wise care is this your counsel, madam;
Take all the swift advantage of the hours.
You shall have letters from me to my son
In your behalf, to meet you on the way.
Be not ta'en tardy by unwise delay.
Duch. O ill-dispersing wind of misery!
O my accursed womb, the bed of death!
A cockatrice hast thou hatch'd to the world,
Whose unavoided eye is murtherous.
Stan. Come, madam, come, I in all haste was sent.
Anne. And I with all unwillingness will go.
O would to God that the inclusive verge
Of golden metal that must round my brow
Were red-hot steel, to sear me to the brains!
Anointed let me be with deadly venom,
And die ere men can say, "God save the Queen!"
Q. Eliz. Go, go, poor soul, I envy not thy glory,
To feed my humor wish thyself no harm.
Anne. No! why? When he that is my husband now
Came to me as I follow'd Henry's corse,
When scarce the blood was well wash'd from his hands
Which issued from my other angel husband,
And that dear saint which then I weeping follow'd—
O, when, I say, I look'd on Richard's face,
This was my wish: "Be thou," quoth I, "accurs'd
For making me, so young, so old a widow!
And when thou wed'st, let sorrow haunt thy bed;
And be thy wife—if any be so mad—
More miserable by the life of thee
Than thou hast made me by my dear lord's death!"
Lo, ere I can repeat this curse again,
Within so small a time, my woman's heart
Grossly grew captive to his honey words,
And prov'd the subject of mine own soul's curse,
Which hitherto hath held [my] eyes from rest;
For never yet one hour in his bed
Did I enjoy the golden dew of sleep,
But with his timorous dreams was still awak'd.
Besides, he hates me for my father Warwick,
And will, no doubt, shortly be rid of me.
Q. Eliz. Poor heart, adieu, I pity thy complaining.
Anne. No more than with my soul I mourn for yours.
Dor. Farewell, thou woeful welcomer of glory!
Anne. Adieu, poor soul, that tak'st thy leave of it!
Duch. [*To Dorset.*] Go thou to Richmond, and good fortune guide thee!
[*To Anne.*] Go thou to Richard, and good angels tend thee!
[*To Queen Elizabeth.*] Go thou to sanctuary, and good thoughts possess thee!
I to my grave, where peace and rest lie with me!
Eighty odd years of sorrow have I seen,
And each hour's joy wrack'd with a week of teen.
Q. Eliz. Stay, yet look back with me unto the Tower.
Pity, you ancient stones, those tender babes
Whom envy hath immur'd within your walls—
Rough cradle for such little pretty ones!
Rude ragged nurse, old sullen playfellow
For tender princes—use my babies well!
So foolish sorrows bids your stones farewell. *Exeunt.*

Scene II

Sound a sennet. Enter Richard *in pomp,* [*crowned*]; Buckingham, Catesby, Ratcliffe, Lovel, [*a* Page, *and others*].

K. Rich. Stand all apart. Cousin of Buckingham—
Buck. My gracious sovereign?
K. Rich. Give me thy hand.
[*Here he ascendeth the throne.*] *Sound.*
Thus high, by thy advice
And thy assistance, is King Richard seated;
But shall we wear these glories for a day?
Or shall they last, and we rejoice in them?
Buck. Still live they, and for ever let them last!
K. Rich. Ah, Buckingham, now do I play the touch,
To try if thou be current gold indeed.
Young Edward lives: think now what I would speak.
Buck. Say on, my loving lord.
K. Rich. Why, Buckingham, I say I would be king.
Buck. Why, so you are, my thrice-renowned lord.
K. Rich. Ha? am I king? 'Tis so—but Edward lives.
Buck. True, noble prince.
K. Rich. O bitter consequence,
That Edward still should live true noble prince!
Cousin, thou wast not wont to be so dull.
Shall I be plain? I wish the bastards dead,
And I would have it suddenly perform'd.
What say'st thou now? Speak suddenly, be brief.
Buck. Your Grace may do your pleasure.
K. Rich. Tut, tut, thou art all ice, thy kindness freezes.
Say, have I thy consent that they shall die?

42. Richmond. Henry Tudor, Earl of Richmond (later Henry VII), had been a refugee in Brittany during the reign of Edward IV.
46. counted: esteemed. **49. son:** i.e. stepson.
51. ta'en: taken, i.e. caught.
52. ill-dispersing: i.e. scattering misfortune.
54. cockatrice: basilisk (see note to I.ii.150).
58. inclusive verge: enclosing rim (of the crown).
72. so . . . widow: i.e. because she would have so long to live widowed.
79. Grossly: stupidly. **84. timorous:** fearful.
87. complaining: lament.

95. Eighty odd years. Actually the Duchess of York was sixty-eight at Richard's accession in 1483.
96. wrack'd: destroyed. **teen:** sorrow.

IV.ii. Location: London. The palace.
8. play the touch: assume the function of a touchstone (which was used for testing the quality of gold). **9. current:** genuine.
15. consequence: retort (to Richard's assertion, "Edward lives").

Buck. Give me some little breath, some pause, dear lord,
Before I positively speak in this.
I will resolve you herein presently. *Exit Buckingham.*
Cate. [*Aside to a stander-by.*] The King is angry, see, he gnaws his lip.
K. Rich. I will converse with iron-witted fools
And unrespective boys; none are for me
That look into me with considerate eyes.
High-reaching Buckingham grows circumspect.
Boy!
Page. My lord?
K. Rich. Know'st thou not any whom corrupting gold
Will tempt unto a close exploit of death?
Page. I know a discontented gentleman
Whose humble means match not his haughty spirit.
Gold were as good as twenty orators,
And will, no doubt, tempt him to any thing.
K. Rich. What is his name?
Page. His name, my lord, is Tyrrel.
K. Rich. I partly know the man; go call him hither, boy. *Exit* [*Page*].
The deep-revolving witty Buckingham
No more shall be the neighbor to my counsels.
Hath he so long held out with me untir'd,
And stops he now for breath? Well, be it so.

Enter STANLEY.

How now, Lord Stanley, what's the news?
Stan. Know, my loving lord,
The Marquess Dorset, as I hear, is fled
To Richmond, in the parts where he abides.
[*Stands apart.*]
K. Rich. Come hither, Catesby. Rumor it abroad
That Anne, my wife, is very grievous sick;
I will take order for her keeping close.
Inquire me out some mean poor gentleman,
Whom I will marry straight to Clarence' daughter;
The boy is foolish, and I fear not him.
Look how thou dream'st! I say again, give out
That Anne, my queen, is sick and like to die.
About it, for it stands me much upon
To stop all hopes whose growth may damage me.
[*Exit Catesby.*]
I must be married to my brother's daughter,
Or else my kingdom stands on brittle glass.
Murther her brothers and then marry her—
Uncertain way of gain! But I am in
So far in blood that sin will pluck on sin.
Tear-falling pity dwells not in this eye.

Enter [PAGE *with* SIR JAMES] TYRREL.

Is thy name Tyrrel?
Tyr. James Tyrrel, and your most obedient subject.
K. Rich. Art thou indeed?
Tyr. Prove me, my gracious lord.
K. Rich. Dar'st thou resolve to kill a friend of mine?
Tyr. Please you;
But I had rather kill two enemies.
K. Rich. Why, [there] thou hast it; two deep enemies,
Foes to my rest and my sweet sleep's disturbers,
Are they that I would have thee deal upon:
Tyrrel, I mean those bastards in the Tower.
Tyr. Let me have open means to come to them,
And soon I'll rid you from the fear of them.
K. Rich. Thou sing'st sweet music. Hark, come hither, Tyrrel.
Go, by this token. Rise, and lend thine ear. *Whispers.*
There is no more but so; say it is done,
And I will love thee and prefer thee for it.
Tyr. I will dispatch it straight. *Exit.*

Enter BUCKINGHAM.

Buck. My lord, I have consider'd in my mind
The late request that you did sound me in.
K. Rich. Well, let that rest. Dorset is fled to Richmond.
Buck. I hear the news, my lord.
K. Rich. Stanley, he is your wive's son: well, look unto it.
Buck. My lord, I claim the gift, my due by promise,
For which your honor and your faith is pawn'd,
Th' earldom of [Herford], and the moveables,
Which you have promised I shall possess.
K. Rich. Stanley, look to your wife. If she convey
Letters to Richmond, you shall answer it.
Buck. What says your Highness to my just request?
K. Rich. I do remember me, Henry the Sixt
Did prophesy that Richmond should be king,
When Richmond was a little peevish boy.
A king—perhaps—[perhaps—
Buck. My lord—
K. Rich. How chance the prophet could not at that time
Have told me, I being by, that I should kill him?
Buck. My lord, your promise for the earldom—
K. Rich. Richmond! When last I was at Exeter,
The mayor in courtesy show'd me the castle,
And call'd it Rouge-mount, at which name I started,
Because a bard of Ireland told me once
I should not live long after I saw Richmond.
Buck. My lord—

26. resolve: inform. **29. unrespective:** thoughtless.
30. considerate: thoughtful, reflective.
35. close exploit: secret undertaking. **42. witty:** cunning.
52. take: give. **close:** confined, i.e. imprisoned.
55. boy: i.e. Clarence's eldest son Edward, Earl of Warwick (1475–99), whom Henry VII executed, after long imprisonment, on a trumped-up charge of treason.
58. stands . . . upon: is of great concern to me.
60. my brother's daughter: i.e. Edward's daughter Elizabeth (1465–1503), whom Richard sought to marry, said Hall (Bullough, III, 286), "so by that meanes the erle of Richemonde of the affinite of his nece should be utterly defrauded and beguyled." Richard's plan did not succeed, and in 1486 the marriage of Elizabeth and Henry VII finally united the houses of York and Lancaster.

68. Prove: test. **76. open:** unimpeded.
81. prefer: advance. **84. sound me in:** ask me about.
87. he: i.e. Richmond. **wive's:** wife's. **89. pawn'd:** pledged.
93. answer: answer for.
95–97. Henry . . . boy. See *3 Henry VI*, IV.vi.67–76.
103–7. When . . . Richmond. Although the play on *Rougemont* (Red Mountain) and *Richmond* is forced, the incident is historical.
106. bard of Ireland. Irish bards were credited with prophetic powers.

K. Rich. Ay, what's a' clock?
Buck. I am thus bold to put your Grace in mind
Of what you promis'd me.
K. Rich. Well, but what's a' clock?
Buck. Upon the stroke of ten.
K. Rich. Well, let it strike.
Buck. Why let it strike?
K. Rich. Because that like a Jack thou keep'st the stroke
Betwixt thy begging and my meditation.
I am not in the giving vein to-day.]
Buck. May it please you to resolve me in my suit.
K. Rich. Thou troublest me, I am not in the vein.
Exit [with all but Buckingham].
Buck. And is it thus? repays he my deep service
With such contempt? Made I him king for this?
O, let me think on Hastings, and be gone
To Brecknock while my fearful head is on! *Exit.*

[SCENE III]

Enter TYRREL.

Tyr. The tyrannous and bloody act is done,
The most arch deed of piteous massacre
That ever yet this land was guilty of.
Dighton and Forrest, who I did suborn
To do this piece of [ruthless] butchery,
Albeit they were flesh'd villains, bloody dogs,
Melted with tenderness and [kind] compassion,
Wept like [two] children in their deaths' sad story.
"O, thus," quoth Dighton, "lay the gentle babes."
"Thus, thus," quoth Forrest, "girdling one another
Within their alablaster innocent arms.
Their lips were four red roses on a stalk,
[Which] in their summer beauty kiss'd each other.
A book of prayers on their pillow lay,
Which [once]," quoth Forrest, "almost chang'd my mind;
But O! the devil"—there the villain stopp'd;
When Dighton thus told on, "We smothered
The most replenished sweet work of Nature
That from the prime creation e'er she framed."

Hence both are gone with conscience and remorse
They could not speak; and so I left them both,
To bear this tidings to the bloody King.

Enter [KING] RICHARD.

And here he comes. All health, my sovereign lord!
K. Rich. Kind Tyrrel, am I happy in thy news?
Tyr. If to have done the thing you gave in charge
Beget your happiness, be happy then,
For it is done.
K. Rich. But didst thou see them dead?
Tyr. I did, my lord.
K. Rich. And buried, gentle Tyrrel?
Tyr. The chaplain of the Tower hath buried them,
But where (to say the truth) I do not know.
K. Rich. Come to me, Tyrrel, soon, [at] after-supper,
When thou shalt tell the process of their death.
Mean time, but think how I may do thee good,
And be inheritor of thy desire.
Farewell till then.
Tyr. I humbly take my leave. *[Exit.]*
K. Rich. The son of Clarence have I pent up close,
His daughter meanly have I match'd in marriage,
The sons of Edward sleep in Abraham's bosom,
And Anne my wife hath bid this world good night.
Now for I know the Britain Richmond aims
At young Elizabeth, my brother's daughter,
And by that knot looks proudly on the crown,
To her go I, a jolly thriving wooer.

Enter RATCLIFFE.

Rat. My lord—
K. Rich. Good or bad news, that thou com'st in so bluntly?
Rat. Bad news, my lord. Morton is fled to Richmond,
And Buckingham, back'd with the hardy Welshmen,
Is in the field, and still his power increaseth.
K. Rich. Ely with Richmond troubles me more near

109–15. Ay . . . meditation. The general sense is that Buckingham, obviously on the point of making a request but still not making it, is like a Jack (the manikin in old clocks that strikes the bell) poised for action. Thus he interferes with Richard's "meditation."
117. resolve me in: satisfy me about.
119. deep: i.e. full of danger to oneself.
122. Brecknock: mansion house in Wales. **fearful:** full of fears. According to More (Bullough, III, 281), Buckingham was so much appalled by Richard's murder of the princes ("to the whiche," he told John Morton, Bishop of Ely, "God be my judge I never agreed nor condiscended") that he "abhorred the sighte and much more the compaignie of hym" and so retired to Brecknock.

IV.iii. Location: London. The palace.
2. arch: i.e. heinous.
4. Dighton and Forrest. For the murder of the princes, according to More (Bullough, III, 279), Tyrrel "appoincted Myles Forest one of the foure that before kepte them, a felowe fleshe bred in murther before tyme: and to him he joyned one John Dighton his awne horsekeper, a bygge broade square and strong knave."
6. flesh'd: accustomed to slaughter (a term applied to hounds after they had eaten of the first game they had killed).
11. alablaster: alabaster, marble-white.
18. replenished: complete. **19. prime:** first.

20. gone: overwhelmed. **21. speak:** express, utter.
25. gave in charge: commissioned. **31. after-supper:** dessert.
32. process: story. **34. inheritor:** possessor.
36–37. The son . . . marriage. On Clarence's son Edward, Earl of Warwick, see note to IV.ii.55. Perhaps Shakespeare confused the daughter "meanly" matched in marriage with Lady Cicely, one of Edward IV's children, who, according to Hall (Bullough, III, 254), "not so fortunate as faire, firste wedded to the viscounte Welles, after to one Kyne and lived not in greate wealthe."
38. Abraham's bosom: i.e. heaven (see Luke 16:22 ff.).
39. Anne . . . good night. According to Hall (Bullough, III, 287–88), Richard spread the rumor of his wife's death "to thentent that she takyng some conceipte of this straung fame, should fall into some sodayne sicknes or grevous maladye." As a consequence, "either by inward thought and pensyvenes of hearte, or by intoxicacion of poyson (which is affirmed to be most likely) within a few daies after, the quene departed oute of this transitorie lyfe, and was with dewe solempnite buried in the churche of seint Peter at Westminster." She died in March 1485, less than a year after her only son.
40. for: because. **Britain:** Breton. **42. knot:** alliance.
46. Morton. John Morton (1420?–1500), Bishop of Ely, an associate of Buckingham who ultimately escaped to Flanders, was recalled by Henry VII, and thereafter became one of the new king's most trusted advisers. Named Archbishop of Canterbury in 1486 and cardinal in 1493, he was an early patron of Thomas More and perhaps the author of the Latin version of More's hostile biography of Richard III that Hall and Grafton and others incorporated into their chronicles and that Shakespeare followed closely in the writing of this play.

Than Buckingham and his rash-levied strength.
Come, I have learn'd that fearful commenting
Is leaden servitor to dull delay;
Delay [leads] impotent and snail-pac'd beggary.
Then fiery expedition be my wing,
Jove's Mercury, and herald for a king!
Go muster men. My counsel is my shield;
We must be brief when traitors brave the field.
Exeunt.

Scene [IV]

Enter old Queen Margaret.

Q. Mar. So now prosperity begins to mellow
And drop into the rotten mouth of death.
Here in these confines slily have I lurk'd,
To watch the waning of mine enemies.
A dire induction am I witness to,
And will to France, hoping the consequence
Will prove as bitter, black, and tragical.
Withdraw thee, wretched Margaret; who comes here?
[*Retires.*]

Enter Duchess [of York] *and* Queen [Elizabeth].

Q. Eliz. Ah, my poor princes! ah, my tender babes!
My [unblown] flow'rs, new-appearing sweets!
If yet your gentle souls fly in the air
And be not fix'd in doom perpetual,
Hover about me with your aery wings
And hear your mother's lamentation!

Q. Mar. [*Aside.*] Hover about her; say that right for right
Hath dimm'd your infant morn to aged night.

Duch. So many miseries have craz'd my voice
That my woe-wearied tongue is still and mute.
Edward Plantagenet, why art thou dead?

Q. Mar. [*Aside.*] Plantagenet doth quit Plantagenet,
Edward for Edward pays a dying debt.

Q. Eliz. Wilt thou, O God, fly from such gentle lambs,
And throw them in the entrails of the wolf?
When didst thou sleep when such a deed was done?

Q. Mar. [*Aside.*] When holy Harry died, and my sweet son.

Duch. Dead life, blind sight, poor mortal-living ghost,
Woe's scene, world's shame, grave's due by life usurp'd,

50. rash-levied: hastily recruited.
51. fearful commenting: timorous discussion.
53. leads: leads to. **54. expedition:** haste.
55. Mercury: messenger of the gods. **57. brave:** challenge.

IV.iv. Location: London. Before the palace.
5. induction: beginning (as of a play).
6. will to France. Actually, Margaret had left England for the last time in 1476, some nine years before the time represented in this scene. **consequence:** conclusion (as of a play).
10. sweets: flowers. **15. right for right:** i.e. avenging justice.
17. craz'd: cracked. **20. quit:** requite.
21. Edward for Edward: i.e. Edward V for Prince Edward, Margaret's son. **dying debt:** i.e. a debt to be paid with death.
25. holy Harry: i.e. Henry VI.
26. mortal-living ghost: i.e. a ghost doomed to life.
27. grave's . . . usurp'd: i.e. one who by being still alive is depriving the grave of its due.

Brief abstract and record of tedious days,
Rest thy unrest on England's lawful earth,
[*Sitting down.*]
Unlawfully made drunk with innocent blood!

Q. Eliz. Ah, that thou wouldst as soon afford a grave
As thou canst yield a melancholy seat!
Then would I hide my bones, not rest them here.
Ah, who hath any cause to mourn but we?
[*Sitting down by her.*]

Q. Mar. [*Coming forward.*] If ancient sorrow be most reverent,
Give mine the benefit of seniory,
And let my griefs frown on the upper hand.
If sorrow can admit society,
[*Sitting down with them.*]
[Tell over your woes again by viewing mine:]
I had an Edward, till a Richard kill'd him;
I had a [Harry], till a Richard kill'd him:
Thou hadst an Edward, till a Richard kill'd him;
Thou hadst a Richard, till a Richard kill'd him.

Duch. I had a Richard too, and thou didst kill him;
I had a Rutland too, thou [holp'st] to kill him.

Q. Mar. Thou hadst a Clarence too, and Richard kill'd him.
From forth the kennel of thy womb hath crept
A hell-hound that doth hunt us all to death:
That dog, that had his teeth before his eyes
To worry lambs and lap their gentle blood,
That foul defacer of God's handiwork,
That excellent grand tyrant of the earth
That reigns in galled eyes of weeping souls,
Thy womb let loose to chase us to our graves.
O upright, just, and true-disposing God,
How do I thank thee that this carnal cur
Preys on the issue of his mother's body,
And makes her pew-fellow with others' moan!

Duch. O Harry's wife, triumph not in my woes!
God witness with me, I have wept for thine.

Q. Mar. Bear with me; I am hungry for revenge,
And now I cloy me with beholding it.
Thy Edward he is dead, that kill'd my Edward;
[Thy] other Edward dead, to quit my Edward;
Young York he is but boot, because both they
Match'd not the high perfection of my loss.
Thy Clarence he is dead that stabb'd my Edward,
And the beholders of this frantic play,
Th' adulterate Hastings, Rivers, Vaughan, Grey,
Untimely smoth'red in their dusky graves.
Richard yet lives, hell's black intelligencer,
Only reserv'd their factor to buy souls
And send them thither; but at hand, at hand,
Ensues his piteous and unpitied end.
Earth gapes, hell burns, fiends roar, saints pray,

28. abstract: epitome.
36. seniory: seniority. **37. on . . . hand:** in place of precedence.
42, 43. Thou: i.e. Queen Elizabeth.
44. Richard: i.e. her husband. **50. worry:** pull to pieces.
53. galled: sore (with weeping). **56. carnal:** carnivorous.
58. pew-fellow: companion. **63. Thy Edward:** i.e. Edward IV.
64. Thy other Edward: i.e. Edward V. **quit:** pay for (as a penalty).
65. but boot: i.e. merely something given in addition.
69. adulterate: adulterous. **71. intelligencer:** spy, agent.
72. reserv'd their factor: retained as (hell's) agent.

To have him suddenly convey'd from hence.
Cancel his bond of life, dear God, I pray,
That I may live and say, "The dog is dead."

Q. Eliz. O, thou didst prophesy the time would come
That I should wish for thee to help me curse
That bottled spider, that foul bunch-back'd toad!

Q. Mar. I call'd thee then vain flourish of my fortune;
I call'd thee then poor shadow, painted queen,
The presentation of but what I was;
The flattering index of a direful pageant;
One heav'd a-high, to be hurl'd down below;
A mother only mock'd with two fair babes;
A dream of what thou wast, a garish flag
To be the aim of every dangerous shot;
A sign of dignity, a breath, a bubble;
A queen in jest, only to fill the scene.
Where is thy husband now? Where be thy brothers?
Where be thy two sons? Wherein dost thou joy?
Who sues, and kneels, and says, "God save the Queen"?
Where be the bending peers that flattered thee?
Where be the thronging troops that followed thee?
Decline all this, and see what now thou art:
For happy wife, a most distressed widow;
For joyful mother, one that wails the name;
For one being sued to, one that humbly sues;
For queen, a very caitiff crown'd with care;
For she that scorn'd at me, now scorn'd of me;
For she being feared of all, now fearing one;
For she commanding all, obey'd of none.
Thus hath the course of justice whirl'd about,
And left thee but a very prey to time,
Having no more but thought of what thou wast
To torture thee the more, being what thou art.
Thou didst usurp my place, and dost thou not
Usurp the just proportion of my sorrow?
Now thy proud neck bears half my burthen'd yoke,
From which even here I slip my [weary] head,
And leave the burthen of it all on thee.
Farewell, York's wife, and queen of sad mischance,
These English woes shall make me smile in France.

Q. Eliz. O thou well skill'd in curses, stay awhile,
And teach me how to curse mine enemies!

Q. Mar. Forbear to sleep the [nights], and fast the [days];
Compare dead happiness with living woe;
Think that thy babes were sweeter than they were,
And he that slew them fouler than he is.
Bett'ring thy loss makes the bad causer worse;
Revolving this will teach thee how to curse.

Q. Eliz. My words are dull, O, quicken them with thine!

Q. Mar. Thy woes will make them sharp and pierce like mine. *Exit [Queen] Margaret.*

85. index: table of contents prefixed to a book, hence prologue. **88–89. garish . . . shot:** i.e. gaudy or conspicuous standard-bearer who draws the enemy fire. **90. sign:** (mere) token. **97. Decline:** recite in order. **101. caitiff:** pitiful wretch. **102, 103, 104. of:** by. **111. burthen'd:** burdensome. **122. Bett'ring:** magnifying. **124. quicken:** put life into.

Duch. Why should calamity be full of words?

Q. Eliz. Windy attorneys to their client's woes,
Aery succeeders of [intestate] joys,
Poor breathing orators of miseries,
Let them have scope! though what they will impart
Help nothing else, yet do they ease the heart.

Duch. If so then, be not tongue-tied; go with me,
And in the breath of bitter words let's smother
My damned son that thy two sweet sons smother'd.
The trumpet sounds, be copious in exclaims.

Enter King Richard *and his* Train *[marching, with Drums and Trumpets].*

K. Rich. Who intercepts me in my expedition?

Duch. O, she that might have intercepted thee,
By strangling thee in her accursed womb,
From all the slaughters, wretch, that thou hast done!

Q. Eliz. Hid'st thou that forehead with a golden crown
Where should be branded, if that right were right,
The slaughter of the prince that ow'd that crown,
And the dire death of my poor sons and brothers?
Tell me, thou villain-slave, where are my children?

Duch. Thou toad, thou toad, where is thy brother Clarence?
And little Ned Plantagenet, his son?

Q. Eliz. Where is the gentle Rivers, Vaughan, Grey?

Duch. Where is kind Hastings?

K. Rich. A flourish, trumpets! strike alarum, drums!
Let not the heavens hear these tell-tale women
Rail on the Lord's anointed. Strike, I say!
Flourish. Alarums.
Either be patient and entreat me fair,
Or with the clamorous report of war
Thus will I drown your exclamations.

Duch. Art thou my son?

K. Rich. Ay, I thank God, my father, and yourself.

Duch. Then patiently hear my impatience.

K. Rich. Madam, I have a touch of your condition,
That cannot brook the accent of reproof.

Duch. O, let me speak!

K. Rich. Do then, but I'll not hear.

Duch. I will be mild and gentle in my words.

K. Rich. And brief, good mother, for I am in haste.

Duch. Art thou so hasty? I have stay'd for thee,
God knows, in torment and in agony.

K. Rich. And came I not at last to comfort you?

Duch. No, by the holy rood, thou know'st it well,
Thou cam'st on earth to make the earth my hell.
A grievous burthen was thy birth to me,
Tetchy and wayward was thy infancy;
Thy school-days frightful, desp'rate, wild, and furious,
Thy prime of manhood daring, bold, and venturous;

128. intestate: dead without bequeathing anything. **135 s.d. Drums and Trumpets:** drummers and trumpeters. **136. expedition:** (1) haste; (2) march. **142. ow'd:** owned. **146. Ned Plantagenet.** Actually, he was not one of Richard's victims. See note to IV.ii.55. **152. entreat me fair:** treat me courteously. **158. condition:** disposition. **169. Tetchy:** fretful. **170. frightful:** full of fears. **171. prime of:** early.

Thy age confirm'd, proud, subtle, sly, and bloody,
More mild, but yet more harmful—kind in hatred.
What comfortable hour canst thou name
That ever grac'd me with thy company?

K. Rich. Faith, none, but Humphrey Hour, that call'd your Grace
To breakfast once, forth of my company.
If I be so disgracious in your eye,
Let me march on and not offend you, madam.
Strike up the drum.

Duch. I prithee hear me speak.

K. Rich. You speak too bitterly.

Duch. Hear me a word;
For I shall never speak to thee again.

K. Rich. So.

Duch. Either thou wilt die by God's just ordinance
Ere from this war thou turn a conqueror,
Or I with grief and extreme age shall perish
And never more behold thy face again.
Therefore take with thee my most grievous curse,
Which in the day of battle tire thee more
Than all the complete armor that thou wear'st!
My prayers on the adverse party fight,
And there the little souls of Edward's children
Whisper the spirits of thine enemies
And promise them success and victory.
Bloody thou art, bloody will be thy end;
Shame serves thy life and doth thy death attend. *Exit.*

Q. Eliz. Though far more cause, yet much less spirit to curse
Abides in me; I say amen to her.

K. Rich. Stay, madam, I must talk a word with you.

Q. Eliz. I have no moe sons of the royal blood
For thee to slaughter. For my daughters, Richard,
They shall be praying nuns, not weeping queens;
And therefore level not to hit their lives.

K. Rich. You have a daughter call'd Elizabeth,
Virtuous and fair, royal and gracious.

Q. Eliz. And must she die for this? O, let her live!
And I'll corrupt her manners, stain her beauty,
Slander myself as false to Edward's bed,
Throw over her the veil of infamy.
So she may live unscarr'd of bleeding slaughter,
I will confess she was not Edward's daughter.

K. Rich. Wrong not her birth, she is a royal princess.

Q. Eliz. To save her life, I'll say she is not so.

K. Rich. Her life is safest only in her birth.

Q. Eliz. And only in that safety died her brothers.

K. Rich. Lo at their birth good stars were opposite.

Q. Eliz. No, to their lives ill friends were contrary.

K. Rich. All unavoided is the doom of destiny.

Q. Eliz. True—when avoided grace makes destiny:
My babes were destin'd to a fairer death,
If grace had blest thee with a fairer life.

K. Rich. You speak as if that I had slain my cousins!

Q. Eliz. Cousins indeed, and by their uncle cozen'd
Of comfort, kingdom, kindred, freedom, life.
Whose hand soever lanch'd their tender hearts,
Thy head (all indirectly) gave direction.
No doubt the murd'rous knife was dull and blunt
Till it was whetted on thy stone-hard heart
To revel in the entrails of my lambs.
But that still use of grief makes wild grief tame,
My tongue should to thy ears not name my boys
Till that my nails were anchor'd in thine eyes;
And I, in such a desp'rate bay of death,
Like a poor bark of sails and tackling reft,
Rush all to pieces on thy rocky bosom.

K. Rich. Madam, so thrive I in my enterprise
And dangerous success of bloody wars,
As I intend more good to you and yours
Than ever you [or] yours by me were harm'd!

Q. Eliz. What good is cover'd with the face of heaven,
To be discover'd, that can do me good?

K. Rich. Th' advancement of your children, gentle lady.

Q. Eliz. Up to some scaffold, there to lose their heads.

K. Rich. Unto the dignity and height of fortune,
The high imperial type of this earth's glory.

Q. Eliz. Flatter my sorrow with report of it;
Tell me, what state, what dignity, what honor,
Canst thou demise to any child of mine?

K. Rich. Even all I have—ay, and myself and all—
Will I withal endow a child of thine;
So in the Lethe of thy angry soul
Thou drown the sad remembrance of those wrongs
Which thou supposest I have done to thee.

Q. Eliz. Be brief, lest that the process of thy kindness
Last longer telling than thy kindness' date.

K. Rich. Then know that from my soul I love thy daughter.

Q. Eliz. My daughter's mother thinks it with her soul.

K. Rich. What do you think?

Q. Eliz. That thou dost love my daughter from thy soul;
So from thy soul's love didst thou love her brothers,
And from my heart's love I do thank thee for it.

172. **age confirm'd:** settled maturity. Richard died at thirty-three.
173. **kind in hatred:** vindictive under a pretense of kindness.
176. **Humphrey Hour.** An unexplained sarcasm. Proverbially, "to dine with Duke Humphrey" was to go hungry.
178. **disgracious:** displeasing. 191. **party:** side.
196. **serves:** attends. 200. **moe:** more. 203. **level:** aim.
204. **Elizabeth.** See note to IV.ii.60. 207. **manners:** morals.
210. **So:** provided. 216. **opposite:** adverse.
218. **unavoided:** unavoidable.
219. **avoided grace:** one who rejects God's grace, i.e. Richard.
223. **cozen'd:** cheated.
225. **Whose . . . lanch'd:** whatever hand pierced.
226. **all:** although. 230. **But:** except. **still:** continual.
233. **bay:** inlet. 234. **reft:** bereft.
236–39. **so . . . harm'd:** i.e. may the success of my hazardous endeavors be as certain as my determination to do more good to you and your children than I have done harm in the past.
245. **type:** symbol, i.e. the crown. 248. **demise:** transmit.
251. **Lethe:** river of oblivion in the underworld.
254. **process:** story. 256. **from:** with.
259. 260, 261. **from:** apart from.

K. Rich. Be not so hasty to confound my meaning:
I mean that with my soul I love thy daughter,
And do intend to make her Queen of England.
Q. Eliz. Well then, who dost thou mean shall be her king?
K. Rich. Even he that makes her queen. Who [should be else]?
Q. Eliz. What, thou?
K. Rich. Even so. How think you of it?
Q. Eliz. How canst thou woo her?
K. Rich. That [would I] learn of you,
As one being best acquainted with her humor.
Q. Eliz. And wilt thou learn of me?
K. Rich. Madam, with all my heart.
Q. Eliz. Send to her by the man that slew her brothers
A pair of bleeding hearts; thereon engrave
"Edward" and "York"; then haply will she weep.
Therefore present to her—as [sometimes] Margaret
Did to thy father, steep'd in Rutland's blood—
A [handkercher], which, say to her, did drain
The purple sap from her sweet brother's body,
And bid her wipe her weeping eyes withal.
If this inducement move her not to love,
Send her a letter of thy noble deeds:
Tell her thou mad'st away her uncle Clarence,
Her uncle Rivers, ay (and for her sake!),
Mad'st quick conveyance with her good aunt Anne.
K. Rich. You mock me, madam, this [is] not the way
To win your daughter.
Q. Eliz. There is no other way,
Unless thou couldst put on some other shape
And not be Richard that hath done all this.
K. Rich. Say that I did all this for love of her.
Q. Eliz. Nay then indeed she cannot choose but hate thee,
Having bought love with such a bloody spoil.
K. Rich. Look what is done cannot be now amended:
Men shall deal unadvisedly sometimes,
Which after-hours gives leisure to repent.
If I did take the kingdom from your sons,
To make amends I'll give it to your daughter;
If I have kill'd the issue of your womb,
To quicken your increase, I will beget
Mine issue of your blood upon your daughter.
A grandam's name is little less in love
Than is the doting title of a mother;
They are as children but one step below,
Even of your metal, of your very blood;
Of all one pain, save for a night of groans
Endur'd of her, for whom you bid like sorrow.
Your children were vexation to your youth,
But mine shall be a comfort to your age.
The loss you have is but a son being king,
And by that loss your daughter is made queen.
I cannot make you what amends I would,
Therefore accept such kindness as I can.
Dorset your son, that with a fearful soul
Leads discontented steps in foreign soil,
This fair alliance quickly shall call home
To high promotions and great dignity.
The King, that calls your beauteous daughter wife,
Familiarly shall call thy Dorset brother;
Again shall you be mother to a king;
And all the ruins of distressful times
Repair'd with double riches of content.
What? we have many goodly days to see:
The liquid drops of tears that you have shed
Shall come again, transform'd to orient pearl,
Advantaging their love with interest
Of ten times double gain of happiness.
Go then, my mother, to thy daughter go,
Make bold her bashful years with your experience;
Prepare her ears to hear a wooer's tale;
Put in her tender heart th' aspiring flame
Of golden sovereignty; acquaint the Princess
With the sweet silent hours of marriage joys;
And when this arm of mine hath chastised
The petty rebel, dull-brain'd Buckingham,
Bound with triumphant garlands will I come
And lead thy daughter to a conqueror's bed;
To whom I will retail my conquest won,
And she shall be sole victoress, Caesar's Caesar.
Q. Eliz. What were I best to say? Her father's brother
Would be her lord? Or shall I say her uncle?
Or he that slew her brothers and her uncles?
Under what title shall I woo for thee,
That God, the law, my honor, and her love
Can make seem pleasing to her tender years?
K. Rich. Infer fair England's peace by this alliance.
Q. Eliz. Which she shall purchase with still-lasting war.
K. Rich. Tell her the King, that may command, entreats.
Q. Eliz. That at her hands which the King's King forbids.
K. Rich. Say she shall be a high and mighty queen.
Q. Eliz. To vail the title, as her mother doth.
K. Rich. Say I will love her everlastingly.
Q. Eliz. But how long shall that title "ever" last?
K. Rich. Sweetly in force unto her fair live's end.
Q. Eliz. But how long fairly shall her sweet life last?
K. Rich. As long as heaven and nature lengthens it.
Q. Eliz. As long as hell and Richard likes of it.
K. Rich. Say I, her sovereign, am her subject low.

269. humor: mood.
274–275. as . . . blood. See *3 Henry VI*, I.iv.79–83.
283. conveyance with: riddance of.
290. spoil: slaughter (a term from hunting).
297. quicken your increase: i.e. give (new) life to your progeny.
302. metal: substance. **304. of:** by. **bid:** bided, endured.
310. can: i.e. can provide.
311–12. Dorset . . . soil. When, on his mother's urging (IV.i.38–46), Dorset fled from Richard's terror he first went to Yorkshire, then took part in Buckingham's unsuccessful uprising (1483), and thereafter made his way to Brittany, where he joined Richmond. Although Shakespeare places him at the battle of Bosworth Field (V.iii), he did not in fact return to England until recalled by the new king in 1486. **311. fearful:** full of fears. **322. orient:** shining.
323. Advantaging: adding to the value of. **335. retail:** relate.
343. Infer: allege.
348. vail: lower, yield (in token of submission).
351. live's: life's.

Q. Eliz. But she, your subject, loathes such sovereignty.
K. Rich. Be eloquent in my behalf to her.
Q. Eliz. An honest tale speeds best being plainly told.
K. Rich. Then plainly to her tell my loving tale.
Q. Eliz. Plain and not honest is too harsh a style.
K. Rich. Your reasons are too shallow and too quick.
Q. Eliz. O no, my reasons are too deep and dead—
Too deep and dead, poor infants, in their graves.
K. Rich. Harp not on that string, madam, that is past.
[*Q. Eliz.*] Harp on it still shall I till heart-strings break.
[*K. Rich.*] Now by my George, my Garter, and my crown—
Q. Eliz. Profan'd, dishonor'd, and the third usurp'd.
K. Rich. I swear—
Q. Eliz. By nothing, for this is no oath:
Thy George, profan'd, hath lost his lordly honor;
Thy Garter, blemish'd, pawn'd his knightly virtue;
Thy crown, usurp'd, disgrac'd his kingly glory.
If something thou wouldst swear to be believ'd,
Swear then by something that thou hast not wrong'd.
K. Rich. Then by myself—
Q. Eliz. Thyself is self-misus'd.
K. Rich. Now by the world—
Q. Eliz. 'Tis full of thy foul wrongs.
K. Rich. My father's death—
Q. Eliz. Thy life hath it dishonor'd.
K. Rich. Why then, by [God]—
Q. Eliz. [God's] wrong is most of all:
If thou didst fear to break an oath with him,
The unity the King my husband made
Thou hadst not broken, nor my brothers died.
If thou hadst fear'd to break an oath by him,
Th' imperial metal, circling now thy head,
Had grac'd the tender temples of my child,
And both the Princes had been breathing here,
Which now, two tender bedfellows for dust,
Thy broken faith hath made the prey for worms.
What canst thou swear by now?
K. Rich. The time to come.
Q. Eliz. That thou hast wronged in the time o'erpast;
For I myself have many tears to wash
Hereafter time, for time past wrong'd by thee.
The children live whose fathers thou hast slaughter'd,
Ungovern'd youth, to wail it [in] their age;
The parents live whose children thou hast butcher'd,
Old barren plants, to wail it with their age.
Swear not by time to come, for that thou hast
Misus'd ere us'd, by times ill-us'd [o'erpast].
K. Rich. As I intend to prosper and repent,
So thrive I in my dangerous affairs
Of hostile arms! Myself myself confound!
Heaven and fortune bar me happy hours!
Day, yield me not thy light, nor, night, thy rest!
Be opposite all planets of good luck
To my proceeding, if with dear heart's love,
Immaculate devotion, holy thoughts,
I tender not thy beauteous princely daughter!
In her consists my happiness and thine;
Without her, follows to myself and thee,
Herself, the land, and many a Christian soul,
Death, desolation, ruin, and decay.
It cannot be avoided but by this;
It will not be avoided but by this.
Therefore, dear mother—I must call you so—
Be the attorney of my love to her.
Plead what I will be, not what I have been;
Not my deserts, but what I will deserve.
Urge the necessity and state of times,
And be not peevish[-fond] in great designs.
Q. Eliz. Shall I be tempted of the devil thus?
K. Rich. Ay, if the devil tempt you to do good.
Q. Eliz. Shall I forget myself to be myself?
K. Rich. Ay, if yourself's remembrance wrong yourself.
Q. Eliz. Yet thou didst kill my children.
K. Rich. But in your daughter's womb I bury them;
Where in that nest of spicery they will breed
Selves of themselves, to your recomforture.
Q. Eliz. Shall I go win my daughter to thy will?
K. Rich. And be a happy mother by the deed.
Q. Eliz. I go. Write to me very shortly,
And you shall understand from me her mind.
K. Rich. Bear her my true love's kiss; and so farewell. *Exit Queen* [*Elizabeth*].
Relenting fool, and shallow, changing woman!

Enter RATCLIFFE, [CATESBY *following*].

How now? what news?
Rat. Most mighty sovereign, on the western coast
Rideth a puissant navy; to our shores
Throng many doubtful hollow-hearted friends,
Unarm'd, and unresolv'd to beat them back.
'Tis thought that Richmond is their admiral;
And there they hull, expecting but the aid
Of Buckingham to welcome them ashore.
K. Rich. Some light-foot friend post to the Duke of Norfolk;
Ratcliffe, thyself—or Catesby—where is he?
Cate. Here, my good lord.
K. Rich. Catesby, fly to the Duke.
Cate. I will, my lord, with all convenient haste.
K. Rich. [Ratcliffe], come hither. Post to Salisbury;
When thou com'st thither— [*To Catesby.*] Dull unmindful villain,
Why stay'st thou here, and go'st not to the Duke?

358. **speeds:** succeeds. 361. **quick:** hasty.
366. **George:** pendant with figures of St. George and the Dragon, worn by members of the Order of the Garter. **Garter:** the badge of the Order of the Garter, a blue velvet ribbon worn below the left knee. 390. **Hereafter time:** the future.
392. **Ungovern'd:** i.e. without parents to guide them.
405. **tender:** cherish. 417. **peevish-fond:** perversely foolish.
424. **nest of spicery.** A nest of spices was both the funeral pyre and the birthplace of the phoenix, the fabulous bird who, every five hundred years, was consumed by fire and then rose from its own ashes.
425. **recomforture:** consolation. 434. **puissant:** mighty.
438. **hull:** drift. 444. **Salisbury:** a town in Wiltshire.

Cate. First, mighty liege, tell me your Highness' pleasure,
What from your Grace I shall deliver to him.
K. Rich. O, true, good Catesby. Bid him levy straight
The greatest strength and power that he can make,
And meet me suddenly at Salisbury.
Cate. I go. *Exit.*
Rat. What, may it please you, shall I do at Salisbury?
K. Rich. Why, what wouldst thou do there before I go?
Rat. Your Highness told me I should post before.
K. Rich. My mind is chang'd.

Enter LORD STANLEY.

Stanley, what news with you?
Stan. None good, my liege, to please you with the hearing,
Nor none so bad but well may be reported.
K. Rich. Hoy-day, a riddle! neither good nor bad!
What need'st thou run so many miles about,
When thou mayest tell thy tale the nearest way?
Once more, what news?
Stan. Richmond is on the seas.
K. Rich. There let him sink, and be the seas on him!
White-liver'd runagate, what doth he there?
Stan. I know not, mighty sovereign, but by guess.
K. Rich. Well, as you guess?
Stan. Stirr'd up by Dorset, Buckingham, and Morton,
He makes for England, here to claim the crown.
K. Rich. Is the chair empty? is the sword unsway'd?
Is the King dead? the empire unpossess'd?
What heir of York is there alive but we?
And who is England's king but great York's heir?
Then tell me, what makes he upon the seas?
Stan. Unless for that, my liege, I cannot guess.
K. Rich. Unless for that he comes to be your liege,
You cannot guess wherefore the Welshman comes.
Thou wilt revolt and fly to him, I fear.
Stan. No, my good lord, therefore mistrust me not.
K. Rich. Where is thy power then, to beat him back?
Where be thy tenants and thy followers?
Are they not now upon the western shore,
Safe-conducting the rebels from their ships?
Stan. No, my good lord, my friends are in the north.
K. Rich. Cold friends to me! What do they in the north,
When they should serve their sovereign in the west?
Stan. They have not been commanded, mighty King.
Pleaseth your Majesty to give me leave,
I'll muster up my friends and meet your Grace
Where and what time your Majesty shall please.
K. Rich. Ay, thou wouldst be gone to join with Richmond;
But I'll not trust thee.
Stan. Most mighty sovereign,
You have no cause to hold my friendship doubtful.
I never was nor never will be false.
K. Rich. Go then, and muster men; but leave behind
Your son, George Stanley. Look your heart be firm,
Or else his head's assurance is but frail.
Stan. So deal with him as I prove true to you.
Exit Stanley.

Enter a MESSENGER.

[*1.*] *Mess.* My gracious sovereign, now in Devonshire,
As I by friends am well advertised,
Sir Edward Courtney and the haughty prelate,
Bishop of Exeter, his elder brother,
With many moe confederates, are in arms.

Enter another MESSENGER.

[*2.*] *Mess.* In Kent, my liege, the Guilfords are in arms,
And every hour more competitors
Flock to the rebels, and their power grows strong.

Enter another MESSENGER.

[*3.*] *Mess.* My lord, the army of great Buckingham—
K. Rich. Out on [you], owls! nothing but songs of death? *He striketh him.*
There, take thou that, till thou bring better news.
[*3.*] *Mess.* The news I have to tell your Majesty
Is that by sudden floods and fall of waters
Buckingham's army is dispers'd and scatter'd,
And he himself wand'red away alone,
No man knows whither.
K. Rich. I cry thee mercy;
There is my purse to cure that blow of thine.
Hath any well-advised friend proclaim'd
Reward to him that brings the traitor in?
[*3.*] *Mess.* Such proclamation hath been made, my lord.

Enter another MESSENGER.

[*4.*] *Mess.* Sir Thomas Lovel and Lord Marquess Dorset,
'Tis said, my liege, in Yorkshire are in arms.
But this good comfort bring I to your Highness:
The Britain navy is dispers'd by tempest.

447. liege: sovereign. **451. suddenly:** promptly.
459. Hoy-day: an exclamation of impatience.
464. White-liver'd runagate: cowardly fugitive.
470. empire: kingdom. **473. makes he:** is he doing.
476. Welshman. Richmond was the grandson of Owen Tudor, a Welshman to whom Katherine of Valois, widow of Henry V, bore three sons and a daughter. It is uncertain that they were ever married.

496. assurance: safety.
498–538. My . . . me. Shakespeare telescopes Hall's accounts (Bullough, III, 283–85, 288–89) of Richmond's abortive attempt to invade England and join forces with Buckingham and his associates in October 1483 and his successful invasion in August 1485.
499. advertised: informed.
500–502. Sir . . . arms. One of the many details that Shakespeare got from Hall (Bullough, III, 283): "Sir Edward Courtney and Peter his brother bishop of Exsetter, reised another army in devonshire and cornewall." Actually, Sir Edward and Peter Courtney were cousins.
504. competitors: associates. **521. Britain:** Breton.

Richmond in Dorsetshire sent out a boat
Unto the shore, to ask those on the banks
If they were his assistants, yea or no;
Who answer'd him, they came from Buckingham
Upon his party. He, mistrusting them,
Hois'd sail, and made his course again for Britain.
K. Rich. March on, march on, since we are up in arms,
If not to fight with foreign enemies,
Yet to beat down these rebels here at home.

Enter Catesby.

Cate. My liege, the Duke of Buckingham is taken—
That is the best news. That the Earl of Richmond
Is with a mighty power landed at Milford
Is colder [tidings], yet they must be told.
K. Rich. Away towards Salisbury! while we reason here,
A royal battle might be won and lost.
Some one take order Buckingham be brought
To Salisbury, the rest march on with me.
Flourish. Exeunt.

Scene [V]

Enter [Stanley, *Earl of*] *Derby, and* Sir Christopher [Urswick, *a priest*].

Stan. Sir Christopher, tell Richmond this from me:
That in the sty of the most deadly boar
My son George Stanley is frank'd up in hold;
If I revolt, off goes young George's head;
The fear of that holds off my present aid.
So get thee gone; commend me to thy lord.
Withal say that the Queen hath heartily consented
He should espouse Elizabeth her daughter.
But tell me, where is princely Richmond now?
Chris. At Pembroke or at [Ha'rford-]West in Wales.
Stan. What men of name resort to him?
Chris. Sir Walter Herbert, a renowned soldier,
Sir Gilbert Talbot, Sir William Stanley,
Oxford, redoubted Pembroke, Sir James Blunt,
And Rice ap Thomas, with a valiant crew,
And many other of great name and worth;
And towards London do they bend their power,
If by the way they be not fought withal.
Stan. Well, hie thee to thy lord; I kiss his hand.
My letter will resolve him of my mind.
Farewell. *Exeunt.*

527. **Hois'd:** hoisted. **Britain:** Brittany.

IV.v. Location: London. Lord Stanley's house.
o.s.d. **Sir:** courtesy title for a clergyman.
3. **frank'd . . . hold:** penned in custody (as a hostage).
10. **Pembroke:** county in Wales. **Ha'rford-West:** Haverfordwest, a town in Pembrokeshire. 11. **name:** rank.
14. **redoubted:** dreaded. **Pembroke:** i.e. Jasper Tudor, Earl of Pembroke, second son of Owen Tudor and thus Richmond's uncle. He helped his nephew escape to Brittany after the Yorkist victory at Tewkesbury in 1471 and fourteen years later provided great assistance to the invasion that led to Richard's overthrow and Richmond's accession as Henry VII.
20. **resolve . . . mind:** inform him of my intentions.

ACT V, Scene I

Enter Buckingham, *with Halberds* [*and the* Sheriff], *led to execution.*

Buck. Will not King Richard let me speak with him?
Sher. No, my good lord, therefore be patient.
Buck. Hastings, and Edward's children, Grey and Rivers,
Holy King Henry and thy fair son Edward,
Vaughan, and all that have miscarried
By underhand corrupted foul injustice,
If that your moody discontented souls
Do through the clouds behold this present hour,
Even for revenge mock my destruction!
This is All-Souls' day, fellow, is it not?
Sher. It is, [my lord].
Buck. Why then All-Souls' day is my body's doomsday.
This is the day which, in King Edward's time,
I wish'd might fall on me when I was found
False to his children and his wive's allies;
This is the day wherein I wish'd to fall
By the false faith of him whom most I trusted;
This, this All-Souls' day to my fearful soul,
Is the determin'd respite of my wrongs.
That high All-Seer, which I dallied with,
Hath turn'd my feigned prayer on my head,
And given in earnest what I begg'd in jest.
Thus doth he force the swords of wicked men
To turn their own points in their masters' bosoms;
Thus Margaret's curse falls heavy on my neck:
"When he," quoth she, "shall split thy heart with sorrow,
Remember Margaret was a prophetess."
Come lead me, officers, to the block of shame;
Wrong hath but wrong, and blame the due of blame.
Exeunt Buckingham [*and Sheriff*] *with Officers.*

Scene II

Enter Richmond, Oxford, [Sir James] Blunt, [Sir Walter] Herbert, *and others, with Drum and Colors.*

Richm. Fellows in arms, and my most loving friends,
Bruis'd underneath the yoke of tyranny,
Thus far into the bowels of the land

V.i. Location: Salisbury. An open place.
5. **miscarried:** perished.
7. **moody:** angry. **discontented:** i.e. because their deaths were unavenged.
10. **All-Souls' day:** November 2. According to Hall (Bullough, III, 284), when Buckingham, after his capture and transference to Salisbury, "had confessed the whole facte and conspiracye upon Allsoulen day without arreignemente or judgemente he was at Salsburye in the open merket place on a newe skaffolde behedded and put to death."
13–15. **This . . . allies.** See II.i.32–40.
19. **determin'd . . . wrongs:** i.e. the date fixed to answer for my wrongdoing. *Respite* = day to which something is postponed.
20. **dallied:** trifled.
25–27. **Thus . . . prophetess.** See I.iii.296–300.

V.ii. Location: A camp near Tamworth.
o.s.d. **Colors:** flagbearer.

Have we march'd on without impediment;
And here receive we from our father Stanley
Lines of fair comfort and encouragement.
The wretched, bloody, and usurping boar,
That spoil'd your summer fields and fruitful vines,
Swills your warm blood like wash and makes his trough
In your embowell'd bosoms—this foul swine
Is now even in the centry of this isle,
Near to the town of Leicester, as we learn.
From Tamworth thither is but one day's march.
In God's name cheerly on, courageous friends,
To reap the harvest of perpetual peace
By this one bloody trial of sharp war.
Oxf. Every man's conscience is a thousand men,
To fight against this guilty homicide.
Herb. I doubt not but his friends will turn to us.
Blunt. He hath no friends but what are friends for fear,
Which in his dearest need will fly from him.
Richm. All for our vantage. Then in God's name march!
True hope is swift and flies with swallow's wings,
Kings it makes gods, and meaner creatures kings.
Exeunt omnes.

[SCENE III]

Enter [at one door] KING RICHARD, *in arms, with* NORFOLK, RATCLIFFE, *and the* EARL OF SURREY, [*with others*].

K. Rich. Here pitch our tent, even here in Bosworth field.
My Lord of Surrey, why look you so sad?
Sur. My heart is ten times lighter than my looks.
K. Rich. My Lord of Norfolk—
Nor. Here, most gracious liege.
K. Rich. Norfolk, we must have knocks. Ha, must we not?
Nor. We must both give and take, my loving lord.
K. Rich. Up with my tent! Here will I lie to-night—
[*Soldiers begin to set up the King's tent.*]
But where to-morrow? Well, all's one for that.
Who hath descried the number of the traitors?
Nor. Six or seven thousand is their utmost power.
K. Rich. Why, our battalia trebles that account;
Besides, the King's name is a tower of strength,
Which they upon the adverse faction want.
Up with the tent! Come, noble gentlemen,
Let us survey the vantage of the ground.
Call for some men of sound direction:
Let's lack no discipline, make no delay,
For, lords, to-morrow is a busy day. *Exeunt.*

Enter [at the other door] RICHMOND, SIR WILLIAM BRANDON, OXFORD, *and* DORSET, [BLUNT, HERBERT, *and others. Some of the soldiers pitch Richmond's tent*].

Richm. The weary sun hath made a golden set,
And by the bright tract of his fiery car
Gives token of a goodly day to-morrow.
Sir William Brandon, you shall bear my standard.
Give me some ink and paper in my tent;
I'll draw the form and model of our battle,
Limit each leader to his several charge,
And part in just proportion our small power.
My Lord of Oxford—you, Sir William Brandon—
And [you], Sir Walter Herbert—stay with me.
The Earl of Pembroke keeps his regiment;
Good Captain Blunt, bear my good-night to him,
And by the second hour in the morning
Desire the Earl to see me in my tent.
Yet one thing more, good captain, do for me—
Where is Lord Stanley quarter'd, do you know?
Blunt. Unless I have mista'en his colors much
(Which well I am assur'd I have not done),
His regiment lies half a mile at least
South from the mighty power of the King.
Richm. If without peril it be possible,
Sweet Blunt, make some good means to speak with him,
And give him from me this most needful note.
Blunt. Upon my life, my lord, I'll undertake it,
And so God give you quiet rest to-night!
Richm. Good night, good Captain Blunt. [*Exit Blunt.*] Come, gentlemen,
Let us consult upon to-morrow's business.
In to my tent, the dew is raw and cold.
They withdraw into the tent.

Enter [to his tent KING] RICHARD, RATCLIFFE, NORFOLK, *and* CATESBY.

K. Rich. What is't a' clock?
Cate. It's supper-time, my lord,
It's nine a' clock.
K. Rich. I will not sup to-night.
Give me some ink and paper.
What? is my beaver easier than it was?
And all my armor laid into my tent?
Cate. It is, my liege, and all things are in readiness.
K. Rich. Good Norfolk, hie thee to thy charge,
Use careful watch, choose trusty [sentinels].
Nor. I go, my lord.
K. Rich. Stir with the lark to-morrow, gentle Norfolk.
Nor. I warrant you, my lord. [*Exit.*]
K. Rich. Catesby!
[*Cate.*] My lord?
K. Rich. Send out a pursuivant-at-arms

5. father: i.e. stepfather.
8. spoil'd: despoiled. **9. wash:** swill.
10. embowell'd: disembowelled. **11. centry:** centre.
13. Tamworth: town in Staffordshire. **21. dearest:** most crucial.

V.iii. Location: Bosworth Field.
1. Bosworth: Market Bosworth, town in Leicestershire.
11. battalia: forces.
15. vantage: features likely to give superiority.
16. direction: military judgment.

18 s.d. Dorset. See note to IV.iv.311–12. **19. set:** setting.
20. tract: trace, course. **car:** chariot.
24. form and model: military formation and plan.
25. Limit: appoint. **several charge:** separate command.
29. keeps: stays with.
50. beaver: visor or face-guard of a helmet.
59. pursuivant-at-arms: attendant on a herald.

To Stanley's regiment, bid him bring his power
Before sunrising, lest his son George fall
Into the blind cave of eternal night. [*Exit Catesby.*]
Fill me a bowl of wine. Give me a watch.
Saddle white Surrey for the field to-morrow.
Look that my staves be sound, and not too heavy.
Ratcliffe!

Rat. My lord?

K. Rich. Saw'st thou the melancholy Lord Northumberland?

Rat. Thomas the Earl of Surrey and himself,
Much about cock-shut time, from troop to troop
Went through the army, cheering up the soldiers.

K. Rich. So, I am satisfied. Give me a bowl of wine.
I have not that alacrity of spirit
Nor cheer of mind that I was wont to have.
[*Wine brought.*]
Set it down. Is ink and paper ready?

Rat. It is, my lord.

K. Rich. Bid my guard watch; leave me.
Ratcliffe, about the mid of night come to my tent
And help to arm me. Leave me, I say.
Exit Ratcliffe. [*Richard sleeps.*]

Enter [Stanley, *Earl of*] *Derby, to* Richmond *in his tent,* [Lords *and others attending*].

Stan. Fortune and victory sit on thy helm!

Richm. All comfort that the dark night can afford
Be to thy person, noble father-in-law!
Tell me, how fares our loving mother?

Stan. I, by attorney, bless thee from thy mother,
Who prays continually for Richmond's good.
So much for that. The silent hours steal on,
And flaky darkness breaks within the east.
In brief—for so the season bids us be—
Prepare thy battle early in the morning,
And put thy fortune to the arbitrement
Of bloody strokes and mortal-staring war.
I, as I may—that which I would I cannot—
With best advantage will deceive the time,
And aid thee in this doubtful shock of arms;
But on thy side I may not be too forward,
Lest being seen, thy brother, tender George,
Be executed in his father's sight.
Farewell! the leisure and the fearful time
Cuts off the ceremonious vows of love
And ample interchange of sweet discourse
Which so long sund'red friends should dwell upon.
God give us leisure for these rites of love!
Once more, adieu! Be valiant, and speed well!

60. power: forces.
63. watch: watch-light (?) or sentinel (?).
64. Surrey. The chroniclers speak of Richard's great white horse but the name was apparently Shakespeare's own invention.
65. staves: lance-staffs. **70. cock-shut time:** sunset.
81. father-in-law: i.e. stepfather. **83. attorney:** deputy.
86. flaky: streaked with light (?). **88. battle:** army.
89. arbitrement: decision. **90. mortal-staring:** deadly glaring.
91–92. I, as . . . time. The general sense is that Stanley, although unable to fight openly for Richmond, will mislead the enemy as best he can (by pretending loyalty to Richard). **time:** the people around one, i.e. Richard's soldiers. **95. brother:** i.e. stepbrother.
97. leisure: lack of leisure, i.e. urgency. **fearful:** full of fears.
102. speed well: good luck.

Richm. Good lords, conduct him to his regiment.
I'll strive with troubled thoughts to take a nap,
Lest leaden slumber peize me down to-morrow,
When I should mount with wings of victory.
Once more, good night, kind lords and gentlemen.
Exeunt. [*Manet Richmond.*]
O Thou whose captain I account myself,
Look on my forces with a gracious eye;
Put in their hands thy bruising irons of wrath,
That they may crush down with a heavy fall
The usurping helmets of our adversaries;
Make us thy ministers of chastisement,
That we may praise thee in the victory!
To thee I do commend my watchful soul
Ere I let fall the windows of mine eyes:
Sleeping and waking, O, defend me still! [*Sleeps.*]

Enter the Ghost of young Prince Edward, *son* [*to*] *Henry the Sixt, to Richard.*

Ghost. (*To Richard.*) Let me sit heavy on thy soul to-morrow!
Think how thou stab'st me in my prime of youth
At Tewksbury. Despair therefore and die!
(*To Richmond.*) Be cheerful, Richmond, for the wronged souls
Of butchered princes fight in thy behalf.
King Henry's issue, Richmond, comforts thee.

Enter the Ghost of Henry the Sixt.

Ghost. (*To Richard.*) When I was mortal, my anointed body
By thee was punched full of deadly holes.
Think on the Tower and me. Despair and die!
Harry the Sixt bids thee despair and die.
(*To Richmond.*) Virtuous and holy, be thou conqueror!
Harry, that prophesied thou shouldst be king,
Doth comfort thee in thy sleep. Live and flourish!

Enter the Ghost of Clarence.

Ghost. [*To Richard.*] Let me sit heavy in thy soul to-morrow,
I that was wash'd to death with fulsome wine,
Poor Clarence, by thy guile betray'd to death!
To-morrow in the battle think on me,
And fall thy edgeless sword. Despair and die!
(*To Richmond.*) Thou offspring of the house of Lancaster,
The wronged heirs of York do pray for thee.
Good angels guard thy battle! Live and flourish!

Enter the Ghosts of Rivers, Grey, Vaughan.

[*Ghost of R.*] [*To Richard.*] Let me sit heavy in thy soul to-morrow,
Rivers, that died at Pomfret! Despair and die!

[*Ghost of*] *G.* [*To Richard.*] Think upon Grey, and let thy soul despair!

104. with: i.e. despite.
105. peize: weigh. **116. windows:** i.e. eyelids.
119. stab'st: i.e. stabbedst. **124. mortal:** alive.
129. Harry . . . king. See *3 Henry VI*, IV.vi.68–76.
132. fulsome: cloying.

[Ghost of] V. *[To Richard.]* Think upon Vaughan, and with guilty fear
Let fall thy lance. Despair and die!

All. *(To Richmond.)* Awake and think our wrongs in Richard's bosom
[Will] conquer him! Awake and win the day!

Enter the Ghosts of the two young PRINCES.

Ghosts. *(To Richard.)* Dream on thy cousins smothered in the Tower.
Let us be lead within thy bosom, Richard,
And weigh thee down to ruin, shame, and death!
Thy nephews' souls bid thee despair and die!
(To Richmond.) Sleep, Richmond, sleep in peace and wake in joy.
Good angels guard thee from the boar's annoy!
Live and beget a happy race of kings!
Edward's unhappy sons do bid thee flourish.

Enter the Ghost of HASTINGS.

Ghost. *[To Richard.]* Bloody and guilty, guiltily awake,
And in a bloody battle end thy days!
Think on Lord Hastings. Despair and die!
(To Richmond.) Quiet untroubled soul, awake, awake!
Arm, fight, and conquer for fair England's sake!

Enter the Ghost of LADY ANNE, *his wife.*

[Ghost.] *[To Richard.]* Richard, thy wife, that wretched Anne thy wife,
That never slept a quiet hour with thee,
Now fills thy sleep with perturbations.
To-morrow in the battle think on me,
And fall thy edgeless sword. Despair and die!
(To Richmond.) Thou quiet soul, sleep thou a quiet sleep,
Dream of success and happy victory!
Thy adversary's wife doth pray for thee.

Enter the Ghost of BUCKINGHAM.

[Ghost.] *[To Richard.]* The first was I that help'd thee to the crown;
The last was I that felt thy tyranny.
O, in the battle think on Buckingham,
And die in terror of thy guiltiness!
Dream on, dream on, of bloody deeds and death;
Fainting, despair; despairing, yield thy breath!
(To Richmond.) I died for hope ere I could lend thee aid,
But cheer thy heart, and be thou not dismay'd.
God and good angels fight on Richmond's side,
And Richard falls in height of all his pride!

[The Ghosts vanish.] Richard starteth up out of a dream.

K. Rich. Give me another horse! Bind up my wounds!
Have mercy, Jesu! Soft, I did but dream.
O coward conscience, how dost thou afflict me!
The lights burn blue. It is now dead midnight.
Cold fearful drops stand on my trembling flesh.
What do I fear? Myself? There's none else by.
Richard loves Richard, that is, I [am] I.
Is there a murtherer here? No. Yes, I am.
Then fly. What, from myself? Great reason why—
Lest I revenge. What, myself upon myself?
Alack, I love myself. Wherefore? For any good
That I myself have done unto myself?
O no! Alas, I rather hate myself
For hateful deeds committed by myself.
I am a villain; yet I lie, I am not.
Fool, of thyself speak well; fool, do not flatter:
My conscience hath a thousand several tongues,
And every tongue brings in a several tale,
And every tale condemns me for a villain.
Perjury, perjury, in the highest degree;
Murther, stern murther, in the direst degree;
All several sins, all us'd in each degree,
Throng to the bar, crying all, "Guilty! guilty!"
I shall despair; there is no creature loves me,
And if I die no soul will pity me.
And wherefore should they, since that I myself
Find in myself no pity to myself?
Methought the souls of all that I had murther'd
Came to my tent, and every one did threat
To-morrow's vengeance on the head of Richard.

Enter RATCLIFFE.

Rat. My lord!

K. Rich. 'Zounds, who is there?

Rat. Ratcliffe, my lord, 'tis I. The early village cock
Hath twice done salutation to the morn,
Your friends are up and buckle on their armor.

K. Rich. O Ratcliffe, I have dream'd a fearful dream!
What think'st thou—will our friends prove all true?

Rat. No doubt, my lord.

K. Rich. O Ratcliffe, I fear, I fear!

Rat. Nay, good my lord, be not afraid of shadows.

K. Rich. By the apostle Paul, shadows to-night
Have strook more terror to the soul of Richard
Than can the substance of ten thousand soldiers
Armed in proof and led by shallow Richmond.
'Tis not yet near day. Come, go with me,
Under our tents I'll play the ease-dropper,
To see if any mean to shrink from me. *Exeunt.*

Enter the LORDS *to* RICHMOND *[sitting in his tent].*

Lords. Good morrow, Richmond!

Richm. Cry mercy, lords and watchful gentlemen,
That you have ta'en a tardy sluggard here.

Lords. How have you slept, my lord?

Richm. The sweetest sleep and fairest-boding dreams
That ever ent'red in a drowsy head

151. **boar's annoy:** i.e. injury from Richard.
173. **for hope:** hoping I could aid you.

180. **lights burn blue.** A sign that ghosts are present.
198. **us'd:** committed. **degree:** i.e. of infamy (bad, worse, worst).
219. **proof:** impenetrable armor.
221. **ease-dropper:** eavesdropper.
224. **Cry mercy:** I beg your pardon.
227. **fairest-boding:** most happily prophetic.

Have I since your departure had, my lords.
Methought their souls whose bodies Richard murther'd
Came to my tent and cried on victory.
I promise you, my soul is very jocund
In the remembrance of so fair a dream.
How far into the morning is it, lords?

Lords. Upon the stroke of four.

Richm. Why, then 'tis time to arm and give direction.

His oration to his Soldiers.

More than I have said, loving countrymen,
The leisure and enforcement of the time
Forbids to dwell upon, yet remember this:
God and our good cause fight upon our side;
The prayers of holy saints and wronged souls,
Like high-rear'd bulwarks, stand before our faces.
Richard except, those whom we fight against
Had rather have us win than him they follow:
For what is he they follow? Truly, gentlemen,
A bloody tyrant and a homicide;
One rais'd in blood, and one in blood established;
One that made means to come by what he hath,
And slaughtered those that were the means to help him;
A base foul stone, made precious by the foil
Of England's chair, where he is falsely set;
One that hath ever been God's enemy.
Then if you fight against God's enemy,
God will in justice ward you as his soldiers;
If you do sweat to put a tyrant down,
You sleep in peace, the tyrant being slain;
If you do fight against your country's foes,
Your country's fat shall pay your pains the hire;
If you do fight in safeguard of your wives,
Your wives shall welcome home the conquerors;
If you do free your children from the sword,
Your children's children quits it in your age.
Then in the name of God and all these rights,
Advance your standards, draw your willing swords.
For me, the ransom of my bold attempt
Shall be this cold corpse on the earth's cold face;
But if I thrive, the gain of my attempt
The least of you shall share his part thereof.
Sound drums and trumpets boldly and cheerfully.
God and Saint George! Richmond and victory!
[*Exeunt*.]

Enter King Richard, Ratcliffe, [Attendants, *and forces*].

K. Rich. What said Northumberland as touching Richmond?

Rat. That he was never trained up in arms.

K. Rich. He said the truth, and what said Surrey then?

Rat. He smil'd and said, "The better for our purpose."

K. Rich. He was in the right, and so indeed it is.
The clock striketh.
Tell the clock there. Give me a calendar.
Who saw the sun to-day?

Rat. Not I, my lord.

K. Rich. Then he disdains to shine, for by the book
He should have brav'd the east an hour ago.
A black day will it be to somebody.
Ratcliffe!

Rat. My lord?

K. Rich. The sun will not be seen to-day,
The sky doth frown and low'r upon our army.
I would these dewy tears were from the ground.
Not shine to-day? Why, what is that to me
More than to Richmond? for the self-same heaven
That frowns on me looks sadly upon him.

Enter Norfolk.

Nor. Arm, arm, my lord, the foe vaunts in the field.

K. Rich. Come, bustle, bustle! Caparison my horse!
Call up Lord Stanley, bid him bring his power.
I will lead forth my soldiers to the plain,
And thus my battle shall be ordered:
My foreward shall be drawn out all in length,
Consisting equally of horse and foot;
Our archers shall be placed in the midst;
John Duke of Norfolk, Thomas Earl of Surrey,
Shall have the leading of this foot and horse.
They thus directed, we will follow
In the main battle, whose puissance on either side
Shall be well winged with our chiefest horse.
This, and Saint George to [boot]! What think'st thou, Norfolk?

Nor. A good direction, warlike sovereign.
He sheweth him a paper.
This found I on my tent this morning.
[*Reads*.] "Jockey of Norfolk, be not so bold,
For Dickon thy master is bought and sold."

K. Rich. A thing devised by the enemy.
Go, gentlemen, every man unto his charge.
Let not our babbling dreams affright our souls;
Conscience is but a word that cowards use,
Devis'd at first to keep the strong in awe:
Our strong arms be our conscience, swords our law!
March on, join bravely, let us to it pell-mell;
If not to heaven, then hand in hand to hell.

His oration to his Army.

What shall I say more than I have inferr'd?
Remember whom you are to cope withal:
A sort of vagabonds, rascals, and runaways,
A scum of Britains and base lackey peasants,

231. **cried on:** yelped on the scent (a term from hunting); here, urged on to. 243. **except:** excepted.
250. **foil:** thin sheet of metal used to set off a jewel to advantage.
254. **ward:** guard. 258. **fat:** abundance. **hire:** reward.
262. **quits:** requite. 265. **ransom:** penalty (in case of failure).
270. **Saint George:** patron saint of England.

276. **Tell:** count the strokes of. **calendar:** almanac.
279. **brav'd:** made splendid. 283. **low'r:** lour.
289. **Caparison:** cover with trappings. 293. **foreward:** vanguard.
298. **directed:** deployed. 299. **battle:** army.
300. **winged:** flanked.
304–6. **Jockey . . . enemy.** According to Hall (Bullough, III, 297), John, Duke of Norfolk, had been "warned by dyvers to refrayne from the felde, in so much that the nyghte before he shoulde set forwarde towarde the kynge, one wrote on his gate" the doggerel that Shakespeare quotes. (*Jockey* = Jack; *Dickon* = Dick.)
312. **pell-mell:** with vehement onset. 314. **inferr'd:** stated.
316. **sort:** gang. 317. **Britains:** Bretons.

Whom their o'ercloyed country vomits forth
To desperate adventures and assur'd destruction.
You sleeping safe, they bring to you unrest;
You having lands, and blest with beauteous wives,
They would restrain the one, distain the other.
And who doth lead them but a paltry fellow,
Long kept in Britain at our mother's cost?
A milksop, one that never in his life
Felt so much cold as over shoes in snow?
Let's whip these stragglers o'er the seas again;
Lash hence these overweening rags of France,
These famish'd beggars weary of their lives,
Who (but for dreaming on this fond exploit)
For want of means, poor rats, had hang'd themselves.
If we be conquered, let men conquer us,
And not these bastard Britains, whom our fathers
Have in their own land beaten, bobb'd, and thump'd,
And in record left them the heirs of shame.
Shall these enjoy our lands? lie with our wives?
Ravish our daughters? [*Drum afar off.*] Hark, I hear their drum.
Fight, gentlemen of England! fight, bold yeomen!
Draw, archers, draw your arrows to the head!
Spur your proud horses hard, and ride in blood;
Amaze the welkin with your broken staves!

[*Enter a* MESSENGER.]

What says Lord Stanley? Will he bring his power?
Mess. My lord, he doth deny to come.
K. Rich. Off with his son George's head!
Nor. My lord, the enemy is past the marsh,
After the battle let George Stanley die.
K. Rich. A thousand hearts are great within my bosom.
Advance our standards, set upon our foes.
Our ancient word of courage, fair Saint George,
Inspire us with the spleen of fiery dragons!
Upon them! Victory sits on our helms. *Exeunt.*

[SCENE IV]

Alarum. Excursions. Enter [NORFOLK *and forces fighting; to him*] CATESBY.

Cate. Rescue, my Lord of Norfolk, rescue, rescue!
The King enacts more wonders than a man,
Daring an opposite to every danger.
His horse is slain, and all on foot he fights,
Seeking for Richmond in the throat of death.

322. restrain: deprive you of. **distain:** outrage.
324. mother's. In Holinshed's recension of Hall, which Shakespeare followed, there appears this misprint for *brother's*, i.e. Burgundy's. Despite the fact that he was Richard's brother-in-law (the husband of his sister Margaret), Charles, Duke of Burgundy, had long supported Richmond in exile. In Hall (Bullough, III, 293) the passage reads as follows: "And to begyn with the earle of Richmond Captaine of this rebellion, he is a Welsh mylkesoppe, a man of small courage and of lesse experience in marcyall actes and feates of warr, brought up by my brothers meanes and myne like a captive in a close cage in the court of Fraunces duke of Britaine."
334. bobb'd: thrashed. **341. Amaze the welkin:** terrify the sky.
349. word of courage: battle-cry. **350. spleen:** wrath.

V.iv. Location: Scene continues.
o.s.d. Excursions: sallies, sorties.
3. an opposite: i.e. to oppose himself.

Rescue, fair lord, or else the day is lost!

[*Alarums.*] *Enter* [KING] RICHARD.

K. Rich. A horse, a horse! my kingdom for a horse!
Cate. Withdraw, my lord, I'll help you to a horse.
K. Rich. Slave, I have set my life upon a cast,
And I will stand the hazard of the die.
I think there be six Richmonds in the field;
Five have I slain to-day in stead of him.
A horse, a horse! my kingdom for a horse! [*Exeunt.*]

[SCENE V]

Alarum. Enter [KING] RICHARD *and* RICHMOND; *they fight; Richard is slain. Then, retrait being sounded,* [*flourish, and*] *enter* RICHMOND, [STANLEY, *Earl of*] *Derby, bearing the crown, with other* LORDS, *etc.*

Richm. God and your arms be prais'd, victorious friends,
The day is ours, the bloody dog is dead.
Stan. Courageous Richmond, well hast thou acquit thee.
Lo here this long-usurped royalty
From the dead temples of this bloody wretch
Have I pluck'd off to grace thy brows withal.
Wear it, enjoy it, and make much of it.
Richm. Great God of heaven, say amen to all!
But tell me, is young George Stanley living?
Stan. He is, my lord, and safe in Leicester town,
Whither, if it please you, we may now withdraw us.
Richm. What men of name are slain on either side?
[*Stan.*] John Duke of Norfolk, Walter Lord [Ferrers],
Sir Robert Brakenbury, and Sir William Brandon.
Richm. Inter their bodies as become their births.
Proclaim a pardon to the soldiers fled
That in submission will return to us,
And then as we have ta'en the sacrament,
We will unite the White Rose and the Red.
Smile heaven upon this fair conjunction,
That long have frown'd upon their enmity!
What traitor hears me, and says not amen?
England hath long been mad and scarr'd herself:
The brother blindly shed the brother's blood,
The father rashly slaughter'd his own son,
The son, compell'd, been butcher to the sire.
All this divided York and Lancaster,
Divided in their dire division,
O now let Richmond and Elizabeth,
The true succeeders of each royal house,
By God's fair ordinance conjoin together!
And let their heirs (God, if thy will be so)
Enrich the time to come with smooth-fac'd peace,
With smiling plenty, and fair prosperous days!

9. cast: throw of the dice. **10. die.** Singular of *dice.*
11. six Richmonds: i.e. Richmond and five men dressed like him (a common stratagem in battle).

V.v. Location: Scene continues.
o.s.d. retrait: retreat, trumpet call for withdrawal of forces.
20. conjunction: union.

Abate the edge of traitors, gracious Lord,
That would reduce these bloody days again,
And make poor England weep in streams of blood!
Let them not live to taste this land's increase
That would with treason wound this fair land's peace!
Now civil wounds are stopp'd, peace lives again;
That she may long live here, God say amen!
[*Exeunt.*]

35. Abate: blunt.
36. reduce: bring back.

NOTE ON THE TEXT

Richard III presents a difficult textual problem. The play first appeared in quarto (Q1) in 1597, and five more quarto editions, Q2 (1598), Q3 (1602), Q4 (1605), Q5 (1612), Q6 (1622), were printed before the publication of the First Folio (1623) text. Each of the quartos after Q1 was printed from the immediately preceding edition (Q5 from both Q3 and Q4), each new edition compounding the errors of its predecessor and adding new ones of its own. Two later quartos, published in 1629 (Q7) and 1634 (Q8), are textually of no concern here.

Q1, it is now generally agreed, must be considered to fall into the category of "bad" quartos (i.e., reported or memorially contaminated texts), even though it is an unusually "good" bad quarto, probably a reconstruction memorially reported by Shakespeare's company itself, perhaps to replace a badly damaged or lost prompt-book. Its textual authority is, therefore, extremely dubious. F1 offers a similarly ambiguous authority, since it was printed from copies of Q3 and Q6 (Taylor/Wells have recently shown, where possible, at what points either Q3 or Q6 served as basic copy for the printer), which had been corrected and augmented against an independent manuscript, either Shakespeare's "foul papers" or a scribal copy of the "foul papers," but in any case almost certainly not a manuscript, such as a prompt-book, with direct theatrical connections. Two stretches of the F1 text (III.i.1–158 and V.iii.48 to the end of the play), printed from Q3, show no evidence of any correction against such a manuscript. It may thus be readily seen that, except for some 190 lines found only in F1, lines which probably bring us closer to Shakespeare's actual text than any others in the play, the authority of the greater part of the F1 text rests heavily on the accuracy with which the corrector who collated pages of Q3 or Q6 with the manuscript performed his work. That this corrector carried out his task with some degree of intelligence and care seems borne out by the F1 text in general, but that he was not always careful about single substantive and semi-substantive variants between Q3 and Q6 and the manuscript is proved by, for example, some twenty readings in the F1 text that follow, or are influenced by, readings otherwise unique to Q6. This kind of agreement or influence is damaging because such readings are all the result of unauthorized changes introduced into the text during the several reprintings between Q1 and Q6; since the corrector failed to correct Q3 or Q6 at these points, it seems in the highest degree likely that he was similarly guilty at other places in the text where, unfortunately, we have no means of checking his accuracy. Consequently, no reading in those sections of F1 printed from Q3 or Q6 which agrees with Q1 is entirely above suspicion.

The present text uses F1 as copy-text, except in the two sections set directly from an uncorrected copy of Q3. For these sections (III.i.1–158, V.iii.48 to the end of the play) the copy-text must necessarily be Q1, since Q3 is essentially nothing but a twice-removed reprint of Q1 and such slight changes as appear in it can claim no independent manuscript authority. Where F1, as noticed above, follows a reading originating in Q2–6, except for the additional two lines appearing first in Q2 at I.i.101–2 or where such a reading represents an obvious correction of the Q1 text (e.g., I.iii.33), the present text returns to the reading of Q1. Further, twenty-nine lines or part-lines from Q1, generally accepted as Shakespeare's but missing in F1 for one reason or another, notably the famous "clock" episode (IV.ii.98–116), have also been included.

In view of the extremely complicated relationship between the F1 text and the quartos, the Textual Notes, in addition to providing the usual documentation of the present text, record all significant variants in Q1, together with the readings of Q2–6 for these variants.

For further information, see: Peter Alexander, *Shakespeare's "Henry VI" and "Richard III"* (Cambridge, 1929); D. L. Patrick, *The Textual History of "Richard III"* (Stanford, 1936); Alice Walker, *Textual Problems of the First Folio* (Cambridge, 1953); J. D. Wilson, New Shakespeare *Richard III* (Cambridge, 1953); W. W. Greg, *The Shakespeare First Folio* (Oxford, 1955); J. K. Walton, *The Copy for the Folio Text of "Richard III"* (Auckland, 1955), "The Quarto Copy for the Folio *Richard III*," *RES*, n.s. X (1959), 127–40, and *The Quarto Copy for the First Folio of Shakespeare* (Dublin, 1971) [these studies attempt, unsuccessfully, to rule out any use of Q6 in preparing the printer's copy for F1]; A. S. Cairncross, "The Quartos and the Folio Text of *Richard III*," *RES*, n.s. VIII (1957), 225–33 [argues, not successfully on the whole, for inclusion of Q1 as well as Q6 and Q3 among the copy-texts used for F1]; F. T. Bowers, "The Copy for the Folio *Richard III*," *SQ*, X (1959), 541–4; Kristian Smidt, *Iniurious Impostors and "Richard III"* (Oslo, 1964) [an attempt to disprove Patrick's view of Q1 as a "bad" quarto; makes some interesting points but does not alter the status of Q1 in its relation to F1], ed., *The Tragedy of King Richard the Third* (Oslo, 1969) [a Q1–F1 parallel-text, old-spelling edition, with helpful collations of the quartos], and *Memorial Transmission and Quarto Copy in "Richard III": A Reassessment* (Oslo, 1970); K. P. Wentersdorf, "*Richard III* (Q1) and the Pembroke 'Bad' Quartos," *English Language Notes*, XIV (1977), 257–64; Gary Taylor, "Copy-Text and Collation (with special reference to *Richard III*)," *The Library*, III (1981), 33–42, and "'Praestat difficilior lectio': *All's Well that Ends Well* and *Richard III*," *Renaissance Studies*, II (1988), 27–46; Antony Hammond, ed., New Arden *Richard III* (London, 1981); MacD. P. Jackson, "Two Shakespeare Quartos: *Richard III* (1597) and *1 Henry IV* (1598)," *SB*, XXXV (1982), 173–90; Susan Zimmerman, "The Uses of Headlines: Peter Short's Shakespearian Quartos *1 Henry IV* and *Richard III*," *The Library*, 6th ser., VII (1985), 218–55; Steven Urkowitz, "Reconsidering the Relationship of Quarto and Folio Texts of *Richard III*," *English Literary Renaissance*, XVI (1986), 442–62 [another attempt to discredit Patrick's "memorial reconstruction" argument]; Stanley Wells, Gary Taylor, et al., *William Shakespeare: A Textual Companion* (Oxford, 1987).

Title: **The . . . Third]** The Tragedy of Richard the Third: with the Landing of Earle Richmond, and the Battell at Bosworth Field. *F1;* The Tragedy of King Richard the third. Containing, His treacherous Plots against his brother Clarence: the pittiefull murther of his iunocent [*sic*] nephewes: his tyrannicall vsurpation: with the whole course of his detested life, and most deserued death. As it hath beene lately Acted by the Right honourable the Lord Chamberlaine his seruants. *Q1 (title-page)*

Dramatis personae: *subs. as first given by Rowe*

Act-scene division: *none in Q1–6; from F1, with the following exceptions: III.v–vii (no scene divisions in F1); IV.iii (no scene division in F1); IV.iv, v (numbered IV.iii, iv in F1); V.iii–v (no scene divisions in F1); see first note to each scene; present act-scene arrangement as a whole first established by Dyce*

I.i

Location: *Capell*

1 **s.p. Glou.]** *Capell*

7 **alarums]** alarmes *Q1*

13 **lute]** loue *Q1–6*

26 **see]** spie *Q1–6*

32 **inductions]** inductious *Q1–2*

38 **mew'd]** mewed *Q1–3*

38 **up]** *Q1–6* (vp,); vp: *F1*

40 **murtherer]** murtherers *Q1–2*

41 **s.d. Clarence . . . Brakenbury]** *Rowe;* Clarence, and Brakenbury, guarded. *F1;* Clarence with a gard of men. *Q1–6 (after* soul, *l. 41)*

41 **s.d. Lieutenant . . . Tower]** *Wilson*

42 **day]** dayes *Q1–6*

44 **Tend'ring]** tendering *Q1–6*

45 **the]** *Q1–6;* th' *F1 (line very crowded and final period om.)*

46 **s.p. Glou.]** *Q1–6 (throughout);* Rich. *F1 (generally throughout)*

50 **should be]** shalbe *Q1–6*

50 **christ'ned]** christened *Q1, Q6*

52 **but]** for *Q1–6*

61 **Hath]** Haue *Q1–6*

64 **she]** *Q4–6;* shee. *F1;* she, *Q1–3*

65 **tempers . . . this]** *Q1;* tempts him to this harsh *F1;* tempts him to this *Q2–6*

67 **Woodvile]** *Q1–6;* Woodeulle *F1;* Woodville *F2;* Woodvil *F4*

71 **is secure]** *Capell;* secure *F1;* is securde *Q1–3;* securde *Q4–5;* secur'd *Q6*

74 **you]** ye *Q1–6*

75 **was . . . his]** *Q1–6;* was, for her *F1*

83 **our]** this *Q1–6*

84 **s.p. Brak.]** Bro. *Q1–6 (throughout)*

87 **your]** his *Q1–6*

88 **Brakenbury]** Brokenbury *Q1–6 (throughout, except* Brookenbury *at V.v.14 in Q1–2)*

88 **so?]** *Capell;* so, *F1;* so *Q1–6*

92 **jealious]** iealous *Q1–6*

95 **gentlefolks]** *Q1;* gentle Folkes *F1;* gentle folkes *Q2–6*

100 **to]** he *Q1–6*

101–2 **Brak. What . . . me?]** *these lines first appear in Q2; retained in Q3–6, F1*

103 **do]** *om. Q1–6*

108 **whatsoe'er]** whatsoeuer *Q1–6*

115 **else]** *om. Q1–6*

116 **s.d. with . . . Guard]** *Capell*

124 **the]** *Q1–2;* this *F1, Q3–6*

132 **eagles]** Eagle *Q1–6*

133 **Whiles]** While *Q1–6*

133 **buzzards]** bussards *Q1–2;* buzars *Q3–5*

133 **prey]** *Q1–6;* play *F1*

138 **Saint John]** Saint Paul *Q1–6*

138 **that]** this *Q1–6*

142 **Where]** What *Q1–6*

152 **bustle]** *F4;* bussle *F1;* bussell *Q1–6*

I.ii

Location: *Capell (after Theobald)*

o.s.d. **Enter . . . mourner]** Enter Lady Anne with the hearse of Harry the 6. *Q1–6*

o.s.d. **attended . . . Berkeley]** *Alexander*

1 **load,]** lo *Q1;* lord *Q2;* Lord, *Q3–6*

2 **hearse,]** *Q1–6;* hearse; *F1*

4 **Th']** The *Q1–6*

10 **slaught'red]** slaughtered *Q1–2, Q6*

11 **hand]** hands *Q1–6*

11 **wounds]** holes *Q1–6*

12 **these]** those *Q1–6*

14 **O, cursed]** Curst *Q1–6*

14 **these]** these fatall *Q1–2;* the fatall *Q3–6*

15 **Cursed]** Curst be *Q1–6*

16 **Cursed . . . hence!]** *om. Q1–6 (F1 reads* Cnrsed)

19 **wolves—to]** *Kittredge;* Wolues, to *F1;* adders, *Q1–6*

25 **And . . . unhappiness!]** *om. Q1–6*

27 **More]** As *Q1–6*

27 **life]** *Cibber, Blackstone conj.;* death *F1, Q1–6*

28 **Than]** As *Q1–6*

28 **young]** poore *Q1–6*

31 **this]** the *Q1–6*

34 **s.p. Anne.]** La. *(or* Lady) *Q1–6 (throughout scene)*

36 **Villains]** Villaine *Q1–6*

39 **stand]** *Q1–6;* Stand'st *F1*

60 **deeds]** deed *Q1–6*

60 **inhuman]** *Rowe;* inhumane *F1, Q1–5;* inhumaine *Q6*

62 **mad'st]** madest *Q1–3*

64 **heav'n]** heauen *Q1–6*

64 **murth'rer]** murtherer *Q1–6*

66 **dost]** doest *Q1–5 (frequent, not hereafter recorded);* didst *Q6*

70 **know'st]** knowest *Q1–2*

70 **nor]** no *Q1–6*

73 **troth]** *Q1;* truth *F1, Q2–6*

75 **Vouchsafe]** Voutsafe *Q1;* Vouchafe *Q2*

76 **crimes]** euils *Q1–6*

78 **a]** *Q1–6*

79 **Of]** For *Q1–6*

80 **t' accuse]** *ed. (after Spedding conj.* to accuse); to curse *F1, Q1–6*

86 **shalt]** shouldst *Q1–6*

88 **That]** Which *Q1–6*

89 **Then . . . slain]** Why then they are not dead *Q1–6*

92 **hands]** hand *Q1–6*

93 **li'st]** liest *Q1–6*

94 **murd'rous]** bloudy *Q1–2;* bloodly *Q3–6*

97 **sland'rous]** slaunderous *Q1–6*

98 **That]** Which *Q1–6*

99 **wast]** *Q1–6;* was't *F1*

100 **That]** Which *Q1–6*

100 **dream'st]** dreamt *Q1–6*

101 **ye]** yea *Q1–2*

102 **hedgehog?]** *Pope;* Hedge-hogge, *F1;* hedghogge *Q1;* hedgehog, *Q2–6*

103 **mayst]** maiest *Q1–6*

103 **damned]** damnd *Q1–2*

105 **better]** fitter *Q1–6*

116 **something]** somewhat *Q1–6*

116 **method:]** *Q1–6;* method. *F1*

120 **wast]** *F4;* was't *F1;* art *Q1–6*

122 **that]** which *Q1–6*

124 **live]** rest *Q1–6*

126 **rent]** rend *Q1–6*

127 **not . . . that]** neuer indure sweet *Q1–6*

128 **it]** them *Q1–6*

131 **o'ershade]** ouershade *Q1–6*

133 **reveng'd]** reuenged *Q1–2, Q6*

135 **thee]** you *Q1–6*

137 **kill'd]** slew *Q1–6*

138 **thee]** *Q1–6;* the *F1*

141 **He]** Go to, he *Q1–2;* Go too, he *Q3–6*

141 **thee]** you *Q1–6*

144 **s.d. She]** *Q1 (Q1 s.d. follows* he? *l. 144)*

144 **s.d. spits]** spitteth *Q1–6*

148 **dost infect mine]** doest infect my *Q1–6*

153 **drawn]** drawen *Q1*

153] *Following this line F1 has catchword* For, *(first word of next line is* Sham'd *in F1,* Shamd *in Q1,* Shamed *in Q2–6), either picked up from beginning of l. 152 or indicating an omitted line (or lines) in F1, Q1–6*

154 **aspects]** aspect *Q1–6*

155–66 **These . . . weeping.]** *om. Q1–6*

162 **standers-by]** *hyphen, Rowe*

168 **smoothing word]** soothing words *Q1–6*

170 **s.d. She . . . him.]** *om. Q1–6*

171 **lip . . . it was]** lips . . . they were *Q1–6*

175 **breast]** bosome *Q1–6*

178 **s.d. He . . . sword.]** *om. Q1–6*

178 **s.d. it]** *F2*

179 **for . . . Henry]** twas I that kild your husband *Q1–6*

181 **stabb'd young Edward]** kild King Henry *Q1–6*

182 **s.d. She falls]** Here she lets fall *Q1–6*

185 **thy]** the *Q1–6*

187 **That]** Tush that *Q1–6*

189 **This]** That *Q1–6*

195 **was man]** *Q1–2;* Man was *F1, Q3–6*

198 **shalt thou]** shall you *Q1–6*

201 **s.p. Glou.]** *Q1–6; line continued to Anne, F1*

201 **Vouchsafe]** Voutsafe *Q1*

202 **Anne. To . . . give.]** *Q1–6*

202 **s.d. Gloucester . . . finger.]** *Sisson*

203 **my]** this *Q1–6*

206 **servant]** suppliant *Q1–6*

210 **may please you]** would please thee *Q1–6*

211 **most]** more *Q1–6*

212 **House]** place *Q1–6*

214 **monast'ry]** monastery *Q1–6*

216 **you.]** *Q1–6* (you:); you, *F1*

221 **Tressel]** Tressill *Q1–6*

224 **s.d. Exeunt]** *Rowe;* Exit *F1; Q1–6 s.d. reads:* Exit.

224 **s.d. Tressel and Berkeley]** *Steevens (after Capell); Q1–6 s.d. reads:* Exit.

225 **Glou. Sirs . . . corse.]** *Q1–6*

226 **s.d. with Halberds]** *ed.; Q1–6 s.d. reads:* Exeunt. manet Gl.

230 **What? I]** What I *Q1–2, Q4–6;* What I? *Q3*

233 **my]** her *Q1–6*

235 **no friends]** nothing *Q1–6*

235 **at all]** *Q1–2;* withall *F1, Q3–6*

237 **her!]** *Wilson;* her? *F1;* her *Q1–6*

241 **Tewksbury]** *F3;* Tewkesbury *F1 (throughout);* Tewxbery *Q1;* Tewxbury *Q2–6*

246 **abase]** debase *Q1–6*

250 **halts . . . misshapen]** halt . . . vnshapen *Q1–6*

254 **marv'llous]** merueilous *Q1;* maruailous *Q2–6*

256 **a]** some *Q1–6*

I.iii

Location: *Theobald*

o.s.d. **Marquess of Dorset]** *Hanmer*

5 **with]** *om. Q1*

5 **eyes]** words *Q1–6*

6 **s.p. Q. Eliz.]** *Malone;* Qu. *or* Que. *F1, Q1–6 (throughout scene)*

6 **on]** of *Q1–6 (F1 repeats l. 6 at the beginning of the next page, though the catchword* Gray. *is correct following l. 6)*

7 **s.p. Grey.]** Ry. *Q1–6*

8 **harms]** harme *Q1–6*

11 **Ah]** Oh *Q1–6*

17 **come the lords]** *Q1–2;* comes the Lord *F1;* comes the Lords *Q3–6*

19, 25, 31 **s.pp. Stan.]** *Theobald;* Der. *F1;* Dar. *Q1–6*

20 **Derby,]** *Q1–6* (Darby,); Derby. *F1*

21 **prayer]** praiers *Q1–6*

27 **on]** in *Q1–6*

30 **s.p. Q. Eliz.]** Ry. *Q1–6*

32 **Are come]** Came *Q1–6*

33 **What]** With *Q1–2*

36 **Ay, Madam]** Madame we did *Q1–6*

37–8 **Between . . . between]** Betwixt . . . betwixt *Q1–6*

41 height] highest *Q1–6*
41 s.d. Lord Hastings] *Hanmer*
43 is it] are they *Q1–6*
44 That] *Q1–6;* Thar *F1*
47 look] speake *Q1–6*
53 With] By *Q1–6*
54 s.p. Grey.] Ry. *Q1–6*
54 who] whom *Q1–5;* home *Q6*
54 all] *om. Q6*
58 Grace] person *Q1–6*
63 on] of *Q1–6*
66 That . . . action] Which . . . actions *Q1–6*
67 children, brothers] kindred, brother *Q1, Q6;* kinred, brother *Q2–5*
68 he . . . ground.] thereby he may gather / The ground of your ill will and to remoue it. *Q1–5,* (grounds) *Q6*
69 grown] growen *Q1*
70 perch.] pearch, *Q1–6*
71 gentleman,] Gentleman: *Q1–2;* Gentleman *Q6*
74 friends'] *Knight;* friends *F1, Q1–6*
76 I] we *Q1–6*
79 while great] whilst many faire *Q1–6*
89 mean] cause *Q1–6*
91 for—] *om. Q1–6*
96 desert] deserts *Q1–6*
97 ay] yea *Q1–6*
98 she?] she. *Q1*
100 and] *om. Q1–6*
101 Iwis] *Q1–3;* I wis *F1, Q4–6*
105 Of . . . that oft . . . endur'd] With . . . I often . . . endured *Q1–6*
108 so . . . stormed] thus taunted, scorned, and baited *Q1–6*
108 at.] *Q1–3* (at:); at, *F1, Q6;* at *Q4–5*
108 s.d. behind] *Steevens; s.d. placed as in Q1–6; after l. 109, F1*
110, 117, 125, 133, 136, 142, 154 s.dd. Aside.] *Collier*
110 him] thee *Q1–6*
113 Tell . . . said] *Q1–2,* (*om.* have) *Q3–6*
114 avouch't] auouch *Q1–6*
115 I . . . Tow'r.] *om. Q1–6*
117 do] *om. Q1–6*
118 kill'dst] slewest *Q1–6*
120 ay] yea *Q1–6*
122 weeder-out] *hyphen, Capell*
124 spent] spilt *Q1–6*
124 own] *Q1–6;* owue *F1*
125 Ay] Yea *Q1–6*
129 Albons] Albones *Q1*
130 you] yours *Q1–6*
131 this] now *Q1–6*
133 murth'rous] murtherous *Q1–6*
135 Ay] Yea *Q1–6*
141 childish-foolish] *Theobald;* childish foolish *F1, Q3–6;* childish, foolish *Q1–2*
142 Hie] *Q1–6;* High *F1*
142 this] the *Q1–6*
146 sovereign] lawfull *Q1–6*
149 thereof] of it *Q1–6*
152 you may] may you *Q1–6*
156 s.d. Comes forward.] *Capell (subs.)*
158 pill'd] pild *Q1–6*
159 of] *Q1–6;* off *F1*
160 am] being *Q1–6*
161 rebels?] *Theobald;* Rebells. *F1;* rebels: *Q1–6*
162 Ah] O *Q1–6*
166–8 Glou. Wert . . . abode.] *om. Q1–6*
169 ow'st] owest *Q1–6*
171 This] The *Q1–6*
175 scorns] scorne *Q1–6*
179 fall'n] fallen *Q1–6*
183 e'er] euer *Q1–6*
193 Should] Could *Q1–6*
196 Though] If *Q1–6*
198 that] which *Q1–6*
199 our son, that] my sonne which *Q1–6*
203 mayst] maiest *Q1*
203 death] losse *Q1–6*
207 length'ned] lengthened *Q1–6*
209 standers-by] *hyphen, Rowe*
212 his] your *Q1–6*
214 with'red] *Q1;* wither'd *F1;* withered *Q2–6*
215 thee? Stay] the stay *Q1–2*
225 while] whilest *Q1–5;* whilst *Q6*
227 elvish-mark'd] *hyphen, Pope*
230 heavy mother's] mothers heauy *Q1–6*
232 detested—] detested, &c. *Q1–6*
234 I . . . think] Then I crie thee mercy, for I had thought *Q1–6*
244 day] time *Q1–6*
245 this] that *Q1–6*
258 blasts] blast *Q1*
261 touches] toucheth *Q1–6*
262 Ay] Yea *Q1–6*
262 high,] *Q1–6;* High: *F1*
271 is] was *Q1–6*
272 Peace, peace,] Haue done *Q1–6*
273 s.d. Turning . . . others.] *ed.*
275 my . . . you] by you my hopes *Q1–6*
277 that] my *Q1–6*
278 have done] *om. Q1–6*
279 I'll] I will *Q1–6*
281 noble] Princely *Q1–6*
286 I . . . think] Ile not beleeue *Q1–6*
287 gentle-sleeping] *hyphen, Theobald*
288 take heed] beware *Q1–6*
290 rankle] rackle *Q1*
290 to the] thee to *Q1–6*
297 soothe] *Q3, Q5;* sooth *F1, Q1–2, Q4;* soothd *Q6*
300 poor Margaret] *Q1–6;* (poore Margaret) *F1*
301 to] of *Q1–6*
302 yours] your *Q1–2;* you *Q3–6*
303 s.p. Buck.] Hast. *Q1–6*
303 an] on *Q1–6*
304 muse why] wonder *Q1–6*
305 her;] *Collier;* her, *F1;* her *Q1–6*
307 to her] *om. Q1–6*
308 s.p. Q. Eliz.] *Q1–5* (Qu.), *Capell (subs.);* Mar. *F1;* Hast. *Q6;* Der. *F3*
309 Yet . . . her] But . . . this *Q1–6*
312 repaid] *Q1–6;* repayed *F1*
314 thereof] of it *Q1–6*
316 scathe] *Q1–5;* scath *F1, Q6*
317 s.d. speaks to himself] *placed as in Walker conj.; after advis'd; l. 317, F1; om. Q1–6*
318 curs'd now,] curst, now *Q1–3, Q5–6*
318 s.d. Enter Catesby.] *om. Q1–6*
320 Grace] noble Grace *Q3–6*
320 yours, my gracious lord.] (*comma, F4*); you my noble Lo: *Q1–2;* you my noble Lord. *Q3–6*
321 I . . . me] we . . . vs *Q1–6*
322 We wait upon] Madame we will attend *Q1–6*
322 s.d. all but Gloucester] man. Ri. *Q1–2;* ma. Clo. *Q3, Q5–6;* ma. Glo. *Q4*
323 begin] began *Q1–6*
324 abroach] *Q1–6;* abroaeh *F1*
326 who . . . cast] whom . . . laid *Q1–6*
328 Derby, Hastings] Hastings, Darby *Q1–6*
329 tell them 'tis] say it is *Q1–6*
331 it] me *Q1–6*
332 Dorset] Vaughan *Q1–6*
336 odd old] old odde *Q1–6*
336 forth] out *Q1–6*
337 s.d. Enter two Murtherers.] Enter Executioners. *Q1–6 (after l. 338)*
340 thing] deede *Q1–6*
341, 349 s.pp. 1. Mur.] *Capell;* Vil. *F1;* Execu. *Q1–6*
343 Well] It was well *Q1–6*
343 s.d. Gives the warrant.] *Capell*
344 done,] done *Q1*
349 Tut, tut] Tush feare not *Q1–6*
350 doers. Be assur'd] *F4 (subs.);* dooers, be assur'd *F1;* doers be assured *Q1, Q3–6;* doers, be assured *Q2*
351 go] come *Q1–6*
352 fall] drop *Q1–6*
353–4 straight. . . . lord.] *om. Q1–6*
354 s.p. 1. Mur.] *Capell;* Vil. *F1; speech om. Q1–6*
354 s.d. Exeunt.] *Q1–6*

I.iv

Location: *Pope*
o.s.d. Keeper] *Q1–6 give the Keeper's role to Brakenbury*
3 fearful . . . sights] vgly sights, of gastly dreames *Q1–6*
8 my lord] *om. Q1–6*
8 pray . . . me] long to heare you tell it *Q1–6*
9–10 that . . . cross to] I was imbarkt for *Q1–6*
13 Thence] *Q1–5;* There *F1, Q6*
14 heavy] fearefull *Q1–6*
16 pac'd] pact *Q1;* past *Q2–6*
18 falling] stumbling *Q1–6*
19 Strook] Stroke *Q1–4*
21 O Lord] Lord, Lord *Q1–6*
22 waters] *Q1–5;* water *F1, Q6*
22 my] *Q1;* mine *F1, Q2–6*
23 sights of ugly] vgly sights of *Q1–6*
23 my] *Q1;* mine *F1, Q2–6*
24 Methoughts] Me thought *Q1–6*
25 A] Ten *Q1–6*
28 All . . . sea:] *om. Q1–6*
29 dead men's] *Q1–3, Q5–6 (subs.);* dead-mens *F1;* deadmens *Q4*
29 the] those *Q1–6*
32 That] Which *Q1–6*
32 woo'd] woed *Q1–4;* wade *Q5–6*
35 these] the *Q1–6*
36–7 and . . . ghost;] *om. Q1–6*
37 but] for *Q1–6*
38 Stopp'd] Kept *Q1–6*
39 find] seeke *Q1–2;* keepe *Q3–6*
39 wand'ring] wandering *Q1–2*
41 Who] Which *Q1–6*
42 in] with *Q1–6*
43 No] O *Q1–6*
45 I] Who *Q1–6*
46 sour] grim *Q1–6*
48 stranger soul] *Q1–6;* Stranger-soule *F1*
49 renowned] renowmed *Q1–5*
50 spake] cried *Q1–6*
50 perjury] *Q3–6;* Periurie, *F1;* periury. *Q1–2*
53 with] in *Q1–6*
54 Dabbled] *Q1–5* (Dabled); Dabbel'd *F1;* Dadled *Q6*
54 shriek'd] squakt *Q1;* squeakt *Q2–6*
57 unto torment] to your torments *Q1–6*
58 methoughts] *Q1;* me thought *F1, Q2–6*
59 me] me about *Q1–6*
63 my] the *Q1–6*
64 lord] my Lo: *Q1–6*
65 I . . . methinks] I promise you, I am afraid *Q1–6*
66 Ah, Keeper, Keeper] O Brokenbury *Q1–6*
66 these] those *Q1–6*
67 (That) Which *Q1–6*
67 give] beare *Q1–6*
68 requites] *Q1–6;* requits *F1*
69–72 O . . . children!] *om. Q1–6*
73 Keeper . . . awhile] I pray thee gentle keeper stay by me *Q1–6*
75 s.d. Clarence sleeps.] *Johnson*
75 s.d. Enter . . . Lieutenant.] *om. Q1–6 (ll. 76–83 being assigned to Brakenbury)*
76 breaks] breake *Q1*
76 hours,] howers *Q1–6*
80 imaginations] imagination *Q1–6*
82 between] betwixt *Q1–6*
82 name] names *Q1–6*
83 s.d. Enter two Murtherers.] The murtherers enter. *Q1–6*
84 1. Mur. Ho, who's here?] *om. Q1–6*
85 What . . . thou] In Gods name what are you, and how came you *Q1–6*
86 s.p. 1 Mur.] *Capell;* 2. Mur. *F1:* Execu. *Q1–6*
88 What] Yea, are you *Q1–2;* Yea, are ye *Q3–6*
89 s.p. 2. Mur.] *Capell;* 1. *F1 (from here F1 designates the Murderers as simply* 1 *and* 2 *until l. 276);* 2 Exe. *Q1–6*
89–90 'Tis . . . more.] *as prose, Pope; as verse, F1, Q1–6 (Q1–6 print all the Murderers' speeches as rough verse)*
89 'Tis . . . be] O sir, it is better to be briefe then *Q1–6* (to *om. Q3–6*)
89–90 Let . . . and] Shew him our commission, *Q1–6*
90 s.d. Brakenbury reads it.] *Pope (subs.);* Reads *F1;* He readeth it. *Q1–6*
94 from] of *Q1–6*
95 There . . . keys] Here are the keies, there sits the Duke a sleepe *Q1–6*
96 the King . . . him] his Maiesty, and certifie

his Grace *Q1–6*
97 **to . . . charge]** my charge to you *Q1–2;* my place to you *Q3–6*
98–9 **You . . . well.]** *as prose, Pope; as verse, F1, (?) Q1–6 (see below, ll. 98, 99)*
98 **You . . . 'tis]** Doe so, it is *Q1–6*
99 **Fare you well]** *om. Q1–6*
99 s.d. **Exit . . . Keeper.]** *Collier MS;* Exit. *F1 (after l. 97); om. Q1–6*
100 s.p. **2. Mur.]** *from here Q1–6 designate the Murderers as simply* 1 *and* 2
100 **I]** *Q1–2;* we *F1, Q3–6*
101 **he'll]** then he will *Q1–6*
103 **Why . . . great]** When he wakes, / Why foole he shall neuer wake till the *Q1–6*
105 **he'll]** he will *Q1–6*
108 **What?]** What *Q1–6*
110–2 **Not . . . me.]** *as prose, Pope; as verse, F1, Q1–6*
110 **warrant]** warrant for it *Q1–6*
111 **damn'd]** dāmd *Q1;* damd *Q3*
111 **the]** *om. Q1–6*
112 **me]** vs *Q1–6*
113–4 **1. Mur. I . . . live.]** *om. Q1–6*
115 **I'll]** *om. Q1–6*
115 **and]** *om. Q1–6*
117 **Nay . . . little]** I pray thee stay a whiel *Q1–6*
117–9 **Nay . . . twenty.]** *as prose, Pope; as verse, F1, Q1–6*
117–8 **this . . . mine]** my holy humor *Q1–6*
118–9 **It was . . . tells]** twas . . . would tel *Q1–6*
121 **Faith]** *Q1–6*
123 **deed's]** deede is *Q1–6*
125 **'Zounds]** *Q1–6;* Come *F1*
127 **Where's]** Where is *Q1–6*
128 **O]** *om. Q1–6*
129 **When]** So when *Q1–6*
131 **'Tis no matter]** *om. Q1–6*
133 **What]** How *Q1–6*
134 **with it]** with it, it is a dangerous thing, *Q1–6*
136 **a man . . . a man]** he . . . He *Q1–6*
137 **'Tis]** It is *Q1–6*
138 **shame-fac'd]** shamefast *Q1–6*
139 **a man]** one *Q1–6*
140 **by chance]** *om. Q1–6*
141 **turn'd]** turned *Q1*
142 **towns]** all Townes *Q1–6*
143 **trust to]** trust to / To *Q1*
144 **live]** to liue *Q1–6*
145 **'Zounds]** *Q1–6*
145 **'tis]** it is *Q1–6*
146 **Duke]** *Q1–6;* Dkue *F1*
147–9 **Take . . . sigh.]** *as prose, Pope; as verse, F1, Q1–6*
148 **but]** *om. Q1–6*
150 **I]** Tut, I *Q1–6*
150 **strong-fram'd]** *Capell;* strong fram'd *F1;* strong in fraud *Q1–6*
151 **me.]** me, I warrant thee. *Q1–6*
152 **man . . . thy]** fellow . . . his *Q1–6*
153 **fall to work]** to this geere *Q1–6*
154 **on]** ouer *Q1–6*
155 **throw him into]** we wil chop him in *Q1–6*
157 **and]** *om. Q1–6*
158–9 **Soft . . . Strike!]** Harke he stirs, shall I strike. *Q1–6*
160 s.p. **1. Mur.]** 2 *Q1–6*
160 **we'll]** first lets *Q1–6*
160] *Following this line Q3–6 read:* Cla. awaketh.
163 s.p. **2. Mur.]** 1 *Q1–6*
164, 168 s.pp. **1. Mur.]** 2 *Q1–6*
165 **am,]** *Q1–6;* am *F1*
166 s.p. **2. Mur.]** *Q1–4;* 1 *F1, Q5–6*
170 **Your . . . pale?]** *om. Q1–6*
171 **Who . . . come?]** Tell me who are you, wherefore come you hither? *Q1–6*
172 s.p. **Both.]** *from Q1–6* Am. (= Ambo.); 2 *F1*
172 **to—]** to. *Q1–6*
174 s.p. **Both.]** Am. *Q1–6*
174 **Ay, ay]** *F1* (I, I); I *Q1–6*
181 **drawn forth among]** cald foorth from out *Q1–6*
183 **is . . . doth]** are . . . doe *Q1–2;* are . . . to *Q3–6*
186–7 **death? . . . law,]** *F2;* death, . . . Law? *F1, Q1–6*
189–90 **to . . . sins,]** *Q1–6;* for any goodnesse *F1*
194 **our]** the *Q1–6*
195 **vassals]** Vassaile *Q1–6*
196 **table]** tables *Q1–6*
197 **Will you]** and wilt thou *Q1–6*
199 **hand]** hands *Q1–6*
201 **hurl]** throw *Q1–6*
203 **sacrament]** holy sacrament *Q1–6*
207 **sov'reign's]** soueraignes *Q1–6*
208 **wast]** *Rowe;* was't *F1;* wert *Q1–6*
210 **such]** so *Q1–6*
213 **He]** Why sirs, he *Q1–6*
213 **you]** ye *Q1–6*
214 **that]** this *Q1–6*
215 **avenged]** reuenged *Q1–6*
215 **the]** this *Q1–6*
216 **O . . . publicly.]** *om. Q1–6*
218 **or lawless]** nor lawlesse *Q1;* nor lawfull *Q2–6*
221 **gallant-springing]** *hyphen, Pope*
222 **struck]** stroke *Q1;* strooke *Q2–6*
224 **our duty . . . faults]** the diuell . . . fault *Q1–6*
225 **Provoke . . . slaughter]** Haue brought vs hither now to murder *Q1–6*
226 **O . . . my]** *Q1–3;* If you do loue my *F1;* Oh, if you loue *Q4–6*
228 **are]** be *Q1–6*
230 **shall]** will *Q1–6*
234, 240 s.pp. **1. Mur.]** Am. *Q1–6*
237 **And . . . other,]** *Q1–6*
239 **of]** *Q1–5;* on *F1, Q6*
240 **lesson'd]** *Q1–5;* lessoned *F1, Q6*
242 **Come . . . yourself]** thou deceiu'st thy selfe *Q1–6*
243 **that . . . here]** hath sent vs hither now to slaughter thee *Q1*, (murder) *Q2–5*, (murther) *Q6*
244–5 **he . . . And]** when I parted with him, / He *Q1–6*
247, 249 s.pp. **1. Mur. . . . 2. Mur.]** 2 . . . 1 *Q1–6*
247–8 **when . . . you . . . earth's]** now . . . thee . . . worlds *Q1–6*
249 **Make]** Makes *Q1*
250 **Have you . . . your souls]** Hast thou . . . thy soule *Q1–6*
252 **are you . . . your own souls]** art thou . . . thy owne soule *Q1–6*
253 **you will]** thou wilt *Q1–6*
254 **O]** Ah *Q1–6*
254 **they]** he *Q1–6*
255 **the]** this *Q1–6*
257–60 **Which . . . life?]** *om. Q1–6*
261 **No]** *om. Q1–6*
263 s.d. **to Second Murderer]** *Sisson*
264 **thine]** thy *Q1–6*
266 **As . . . distress.]** *line placed as in Tyrwhitt conj.; after l. 260, F1; om. Q1–6*
268 **2. Mur. Look . . . lord.]** *om. Q1–6*
269 **Take . . . do]** I thus, and thus: if this wil not serue *Q1–6*
269 s.d. **Stabs]** He stabs *Q1–6; s.d. after l. 269, F1, Q1–6; placed as in Capell*
270 **drown . . . within.]** chop thee in the malmesey But, in the next roome. *Q1–6*
270 s.d. **with the body]** *Malone (s.d. om. Q1–6)*
271 **dispatch'd]** performd *Q1–6*
272 **hands]** hand *Q1–6*
273 **murther]** guilty murder done *Q1–6*
273 s.d. **Enter First Murtherer.]** *om. Q1–6*
274–5 **How . . . been!]** *as verse, Rowe, Q1–6; as prose, F1*
274 **How . . . not]** Why doest thou not helpe me *Q1–6*
275 **heavens]** *Q1–5;* Heauen *F1, Q6*
275 **you have been]** thou art *Q1–6*
280 **Well . . . the]** Now must I hide his *Q1–6*
281 **Till . . . give]** Vntill . . . take *Q1–6*
282 **will]** must *Q1–6*
283 **then]** here *Q1–6*
283 s.d. **Exit.]** Exeunt. *Q1–6*

II.i

Location: *Capell*
o.s.d. **Flourish.]** *om. Q1–6*
o.s.d. **Rivers]** *F1 also includes* Wooduill *in s.d., simply another name for Rivers; Q1–2 s.d. reads:* Enter King, Queene, Hastings, Ryuers, Dorcet, &c. *(Q3–6 om.* Dorset*)*
o.s.d. **Grey, and others]** *Capell*
1 **Why, so:]** So, *Q1–6*
1 **have I]** I haue *Q1–6*
5 **more]** now *Q1–6*
5 **in]** *Q1–6;* to *F1*
5 **to]** from *Q1 (u), Q2*
6 **made]** set *Q1–6*
7 **Hastings and Rivers]** *Rowe;* Dorset and Riuers *F1;* Riuers and Hastings *Q1–6*
9 **soul]** heart *Q1–6*
18 **from]** in *Q1–6*
19 **you]** your *Q1–6*
23 **There]** Here *Q1–6*
25 **K. Edw. Dorset . . . Marquess.]** *om. Q1–6*
28 **I.]** I my Lord. *Q1–6*
28 s.d. **They embrace.]** *Capell*
33 **Upon your Grace]** On you or yours *Q1–6*
33 s.d. **to the Queen]** *Rowe*
39 **God]** *Q1–6;* heauen *F1*
40 **love]** zeale *Q1–6*
40 s.d. **They]** *Capell (s.d. om. Q1–6)*
44 **blessed]** perfect *Q1–6*
46 **comes . . . the]** comes the noble *Q1–6*
46 s.d. **Enter . . . Gloucester.]** Enter Glocest. *Q1–6 (after l. 44)*
50 **Gloucester]** Brother *Q1–6*
52 **wrong-incensed]** *hyphen, Rowe*
53 **lord]** liege *Q1–6*
54 **Among]** Amongst *Q1–6*
57 **unwittingly]** *Q1–6;* vnwillingly *F1*
59 **By]** *Q1–6;* To *F1*
67 **Of . . . Dorset]** Of you Lo: Riuers, and Lord Gray of you *Q1–4*, (you my Lord Riuers) *Q5–6*
68 **me;]** me: / Of you Lord Wooduill, and Lord Scales of you, *F1 (both names are titles of Rivers, already referred to in l. 67)*
76 **lord]** liege *Q1–6*
79 **so flouted]** thus scorned *Q1–4;* thus scornde *Q5–6*
80 **gentle]** noble *Q1–6*
82 s.p. **K. Edw.]** Ryu. *Q1–6*
85 **man in the]** one in this *Q1–6*
88 **man]** soule *Q1–6*
89 **winged]** wingled *Q1*
90 **bare]** bore *Q1–6*
93 **but]** *Q1–6;* and *F1*
96, 98, 100 s.pp. **Stan.]** *Theobald;* Der. *F1;* Dar. *Q1–6*
96 s.d. **Kneels.]** *Furnivall conj.*
97 **prithee]** pray thee *Q1–6*
98 **hear me]** grant *Q1–6*
99 **say . . . requests]** speake . . . demaundst *Q1–5*, (demaundest) *Q6*
104 **that tongue]** the same *Q1–6*
105 **kill'd]** slew *Q1–6*
106 **bitter]** cruell *Q1–6*
107 **wrath]** rage *Q1–6*
108 **at]** *Q1–6;* and *F1*
108 **bid]** bad *Q1–6*
109 **spoke . . . spoke]** spake . . . who *Q1–6*
112 **at]** by *Q1–6*
113 **me,]** *Q1–6;* me: *F1*
117 **his own garments]** *Q1–5;* his Garments *F1;* his owne armes *Q6*
117 **did give]** gaue *Q1–6*
118 **numb cold]** numbcold *Q1–2*
123 **defac'd]** defaste *Q1–3*
126 s.d. **Stanley rises.]** *Wilson (after Furnivall conj.)*
131 **beg]** pleade *Q1–6*
134 **Ah]** oh *Q1–6*
134 s.d. **Exeunt . . . Queen.]** Exit. *Q1–6 (after l. 133)*
135 **fruits]** fruit *Q1–6*
139 **Come . . . go]** But come lets in *Q1–6*
141 **Buck. We . . . Grace.]** *om. Q1–6*

II.ii

Location: *Capell*
o.s.d. **the two . . . Clarence]** Clarence Children *Q1–6*
o.s.d. **Edward . . . Plantagenet]** *Sisson*

1 s.p. **Boy.]** Q1–6; Edw. *F1*
1 **Good . . . us]** Tell me good Granam *Q1–6* (Granam *throughout Q1–6, except* Grandam *at II.iv.10 in Q1–2*)
3 s.p. **Girl.]** *Neilson;* Daugh. *F1* (*throughout*); Boy. *Q1–6*
3 **Why . . . oft]** Why doe you wring your hands *Q1–6*
3 **you]** *Q1–6*
5 s.p. **Boy.]** Gerl. *Q1–6*
6 **orphans, wretches]** wretches, Orphanes *Q1–6*
7 **were]** be *Q1–6*
8 **both]** much *Q1–6*
11 **sorrow . . . wail]** labour, to weep for *Q1–6*
12 **you . . . grandam]** Granam you conclude that *Q1–6*
13 **mine]** my *Q1–6*
13 **it]** this *Q1–6*
15 **earnest]** daily *Q1–6*
16 **Girl. And so will I.]** *om. Q1–6*
21 **provok'd to it]** prouoked *Q1–6*
23 **my uncle]** he *Q1–6*
24 **pitied me]** hugd me in his arme *Q1–6*
24 **cheek]** checke *Q1;* cheekes *Q6*
25 **Bade]** And bad *Q1–6*
26 **a]** his *Q1–6*
27 **Ah]** Oh *Q1–6*
27 **shape]** shapes *Q1–6*
28 **visor]** visard *Q1–2;* vizard *Q3–6*
28 **deep vice]** foule guile *Q1–6*
29 **ay]** *F1* (I); yea *Q1–6*
33 s.d. **Enter . . . her.]** Enter the Quee. *Q1–6*
34 **Ah]** Oh *Q1–2;* Wh *Q3–4; om. Q5–6*
40 **thy]** your *Q1–6*
41 **when . . . gone]** now . . . witherd *Q1–2,* (withred) *Q3–6*
42 **that . . . sap]** the sap being gone *Q1–6*
46 **ne'er-changing night]** perpetuall rest *Q1–6*
47 **I]** *Q1–6*
50 **with]** by *Q1–6*
54 **That]** Which *Q1–6*
56 **left]** left thee *Q1–6*
57 **husband]** children *Q1–6*
58 **hands]** limmes *Q1–6*
59 **Clarence and Edward]** Edward and Clarence *Q1–6*
60 **Thine]** Then *Q1–6*
60 **a moi'ty]** moity *Q1–5;* motitie *Q6*
60 **moan]** griefe *Q1–5;* selfe *Q6*
61 **woes]** plaints *Q1–6*
62 **Ah]** Good *Q1–6*
63 **kindred]** kindreds *Q1–6*
65 **widow-dolor]** widdowes dolours *Q1–6*
67 **complaints]** laments *Q1–6*
69 **watery moon]** watry moane *Q1–6*
71 **Ah]** Oh *Q1–6*
71 **dear]** eire *Q1;* eyre *Q2;* heire *Q3–6*
72 s.p. **Chil.]** Ambo *or* Am. *Q1–6* (*throughout scene*)
72 **Ah]** Oh *Q1–6*
74, 75 **he's]** he is *Q1–5;* is he *Q6*
78 **Were]** Was *Q1–6*
78, 79 **so dear a]** a dearer *Q1–6*
80 **griefs]** moans *Q1–6*
81 **is]** are *Q1–6*
82 **an]** *om. Q1–6*
83 **weep]** *Q1–6;* weepes *F1*
84–5 **and . . . weep,]** *Q1–6* (weep *om. Q4*)
86 **distress'd,]** *Q1–2, Q4* (distrest,); distrest: *F1;* distrest. *Q3, Q5–6*
87 **Pour]** *Q1;* Proue *Q2;* Powre *Q3–6;* Power *F1*
88 **lamentation]** lamentations *Q1–6*
89–100 **Dor. Comfort . . . throne.]** *om. Q1–6*
100 s.d. **Enter . . . Ratcliffe.]** Enter Glocest. with others. *Q1–6*
101 **Sister]** Madame *Q1–6*
103 **help our]** cure their *Q1–6*
107 **breast]** minde *Q1–6*
109 s.d. **aside]** *Collier*
110 **That is]** Thats *Q1–6*
111 **that]** why *Q1–6*
112 **cloudy princes]** *Q1–6;* clowdy-Princes *F1*
112 **heart-sorrowing peers]** *Q1–6;* hart-sorowing-Peeres *F1*
113 **heavy mutual]** mutuall heauy *Q1–6*
117 **hates]** hearts *Q1–6*
121 **fet]** fetcht *Q1–6*
123–40 **Riv. Why . . . I.]** *om. Q1–6*
142, 154 **Ludlow]** *Q1–6;* London *F1*
143 **sister]** mother *Q1–6*
144 **business]** waighty busines *Q1–6*
145 s.p. **Q. Eliz., Duch.]** *Staunton* (*subs.*); Ans. *Q1–6; om. F1*
145 **With . . . hearts.]** *Q1–6*
145 s.d. **Manent]** *F2;* Manet *F1, Q3–6;* man. *Q1–2*
147 **stay at home]** stay behinde *Q1;* be behinde *Q2–6*
150 **Prince]** King *Q1–6*
153 **as]** like *Q1–6*
154 **we'll]** we will *Q1–6*
154 **Exeunt.]** *om. Q1–2;* Exit. *Q3–6*

II.iii

Location: *Theobald* (*subs.*)
o.s.d. **Enter . . . other.]** Enter two Citizens. *Q1–6*
1 **Good morrow, neighbor]** Neighbour well met *Q1–6*
3 **Hear]** 1 Heare *Q1–6*
3 s.p. **1. Cit.]** 2 *Q1–6* (*beginning with this speech F1 designates the Citizens as* 1., 2., 3.; *so too Q1–6, except for* 3 Cit. *at l. 6*)
3 **Yes]** I *Q1–6*
4, 38 s.pp. **2. Cit.]** 1 *Q1–6*
4 **Ill]** Bad *Q1–6*
5 **giddy]** troublous *Q1;* troublesome *Q2–6*
6 **Neighbors, God speed]** Good morrow neighbours *Q1–6*
6 **1. Cit. Give . . . sir.]** *om. Q1–6*
7 **the]** this *Q1–6*
8 **2. Cit. Ay . . . while!]** 1 It doth. *Q1–6*
13 **Which]** That *Q1–6*
13 **council]** *Johnson;* counsell *F1, Q1–6*
16 **Henry]** Harry *Q1–6*
17 **in]** at *Q1–6*
18 **No . . . wot]** no good my friend not so *Q1–6*
22, 31 s.pp. **1. Cit.]** 2 *Q1–6*
22 **Why]** *om. Q1–6*
22, 23, 24 **his]** the *Q1–6*
25 **who shall now]** now, who shall *Q1–6*
28 **sons . . . haught]** kindred hauty *Q1–6*
31 **will be]** shalbe *Q1–6*
32 **are seen]** appeare *Q1–6*
32 **wise men]** *Q1–6;* wisemen *F1*
33 **then]** the *Q1–6*
35 **makes]** make *Q1–6*
38 **fear]** bread *Q1–2;* dread *Q3–6*
39 **You]** Yee *Q1–6*
39 **reason (almost)]** almost reason *Q1–6*
40 **dread]** feare *Q1–6*
41 **days]** times *Q1–6*
41 **so.]** *Q1–6* (so:); so, *F1*
43 **Ensuing]** *F1* (*catchword*), *Q1–6;* Pursuing *F1*
43 **danger]** dangers *Q1–6*
44 **water]** waters *Q1–6*
46 **Marry, we were]** We are *Q1–6*
46 **justices]** Iustice *Q1–6*

II.iv

Location: *Capell* (*after Theobald*)
o.s.d. **Archbishop]** Cardinall *Q1–6* (*with* Car. *for s.pp.*)
1 **hear]** *Q1–2;* heard *F1, Q3–6*
1 **Stony-Stratford]** Northhampton *Q1–6*
2 **And . . . rest]** At Stonistratford will they be *Q1–6*
6 s.p. **Q. Eliz.]** *Malone;* Qu. *F1, Q1–6* (*throughout scene*)
9 **my good]** my young *Q1–6*
12 **uncle]** Nnckle *Q1*
13 **do]** *om. Q1–6*
20 **his . . . true]** this were a true rule *Q1–2;* this were a rule *Q3–6*
21 s.p. **Arch.]** *Capell;* Yor. *F1;* Car. *Q1–6*
21 **And . . . Madam]** Why Madame, so no doubt he is *Q1–6*
22 **he . . . yet]** so too, but yer *Q1,* (yet) *Q2–6*
25 **To . . . touch'd]** That should haue neerer toucht his growth then he did *Q1–6*
26 **young . . . prithee]** pretty Yorke? I pray thee *Q1–6*
31 **prithee]** pray thee *Q1–6*
31 **this]** so *Q1–6*
33 **wast]** wert *Q1–6*
35 **parlous]** perilous *Q1–6*
36 s.p. **Duch.]** Car. *Q1–6*
37 s.d. **Enter a Messenger.]** Enter Dorset. *Q1–6* (*with Messenger's lines given to Dorset*)
38 **Arch. Here . . . news?]** *Car.* Here comes your sonne, Lo: M. Dorset. / What newes Lo: Marques? *Q1–6*
39 **report]** vnfold *Q1–6*
40 **doth]** fares *Q1–6*
41 **news]** newes then *Q1–6*
43 **And]** *om. Q1–6*
47 **the]** these *Q1–6*
48 **lord]** Lady *Q1–6*
49 **ruin of my]** downfall of our *Q1–6*
51 **jut]** iet *Q1–6*
52 **aweless]** lawlesse *Q1–6*
53 **blood]** death *Q1–6*
60–1 **broils . . . themselves,]** broiles, / Cleane ouerblowne themselues, *Q1*
62 **brother to brother]** *om. Q1–6*
63 **to]** against *Q1–6*
65 **death]** *Q1–6;* earth *F1*
67 **Madam, farewell.]** *om. Q1–6*
67 **Stay . . . go]** Ile go along *Q1–6*
68 s.p. **Arch.]** Car. *Q1–6*
68 s.d. **To the Queen.]** *Malone*
73 **Go]** Come *Q1–6*

III.i

Location: *Pope, Capell*
o.s.d. **Lord]** *F1* (*Q1 is the basic text for ll. 1–158*)
o.s.d. **Catesby]** *Capell*
o.s.d. **with others]** *F1;* &c. *Q1–6*
8 **div'd]** *F1;* diued *Q1–6*
9 **Nor]** No *F1*
17 s.d. **and his train]** *Capell*
19 s.d. **Mayor . . . aside.]** *Capell* (*subs.*)
40 **in heaven]** *om. Q3–6, F1*
43 **deep]** great *Q3–6, F1*
44 **senseless-obstinate]** *hyphen, Theobald*
49 **deserv'd]** deserued *Q2–6*
51 **claim'd . . . deserv'd]** *F1;* claimed . . . deserued *Q1–6*
56 **never]** ne're *F1*
57 **overrule]** o're-rule *F1*
60 s.d. **Exeunt . . . Hastings.]** *Q3–6* (Exit), *F1*
63 **seems]** thinkst *Q3–6, F1*
71 **since,]** *F1;* since *Q1–6*
73 **age,]** *F1;* age *Q1–6*
78 **all-ending]** ending *Q2–6, F1*
79, 94 s.dd. **Aside.]** *Johnson*
82 s.d. **Aside.]** *F2*
82 **Vice, Iniquity]** *F1;* vice iniquity *Q1–4;* vice, iniquitie *Q5–6*
86 **valure]** valour *Q3–6, F1*
87 **this]** his *Q2–6, F1*
96 **loving]** noble *Q3–6, F1*
97 **dread]** deare *Q3–6, F1*
98 **brother,]** *F1;* brother *Q1–6*
104 **outgrown]** *Q2–6, F1;* outgrowen *Q1*
111 **cousin]** *F1;* Coscn *Q1;* Cousen *Q2–6*
111 **with all]** *Q3–6, F1;* withall *Q1–2*
120 **heavy]** weightie *Q2–6, F1*
123 **as]** as as *Q3;* as, as, *F1*
132 s.d. **Aside to Hastings.]** *Capell*
132 **sharp-provided]** *hyphen, Theobald*
132–3 **reasons! . . . uncle,]** *F1* (*subs.*); reasons, . . . Vnckle: *Q1;* reasons . . . Vnckle: *Q2;* reasons, . . . vncle, *Q3–6*
134 **himself:]** *Q3–6, F1;* himselfe, *Q1–2*
136 **will't]** *Pope;* wilt *Q1–6, F1*
141 **needs]** *om. Q2–6, F1*
144 **Marry]** *F1;* Mary *Q1–6*
145 **grandam]** *F1;* Granam *Q1–6*
145 **murd'red]** murther'd *F1*
149 **with]** and with *F1*
150 s.d. **A Sennet.]** *F1*
150 s.d. **Hastings]** *Hanmer;* Hast. Dors. *Q1–6;* Hastings, and Dorset *F1* (*Dorset has not appeared in the scene*)
150 s.d. **Cardinal . . . others]** *Capell* (*subs.*)
150 s.d. **Manent]** *F2;* Manet *Q1–6, F1*
150 s.d. **and Catesby]** *F1*
159] *With this line F1 becomes again the basic text*
167 **think'st]** thinkest *Q1–6*
167 **Will not he]** what will he *Q1–6*
170 **far]** a farre *Q1–6*

171 doth stand] stands *Q1–6*
171 to] vnto *Q1–6*
171–4 purpose . . . us,] purpose, if he be willing, *Q1–6*
175 tell] shew *Q1–6*
177 the] your *Q1–6*
184 lord] friend *Q1–5;* friends *Q6*
186 go] *om. Q1–6*
187 lords] Lo: *Q1–2*
187 can] may *Q1–6*
190 House] place *Q1–6*
190 s.d. Exit Catesby.] *om. Q1–2; after l. 189, Q3–6*
192 Lord] William Lo: *Q1–6*
193 head . . . determine] head man, somewhat we will doe *Q1–6*
195 Herford] *Q3–5;* Hereford *F1, Q1–2;* Hertford *Q6*
195 all] *om. Q1–6*
196 was] stood *Q1–6*
197 hand] hands *Q1–6*
198 kindness] willingnes *Q1–6*

III.ii

Location: *Theobald*
o.s.d. the door of] Lo: *Q1–6*
1 My lord! my lord!] What ho my Lord. *Q1–6*
2, 4 s.dd. Within.] *Theobald (the second* Within. *implied); Q1–6 enter Lord Hastings after l. 3*
2 knocks?] knockes at the dore. *Q1–6*
3 One] A messenger *Q1–6*
4 What is't] Whats *Q1–6*
6 my Lord Stanley] thy Master *Q1–6*
7 appears] should seeme *Q1–6*
8 self] Lordship *Q1–6*
9 What] And *Q1–6*
10–11 Then . . . off] And then he sends you word. / He dreamt to night the beare had raste *Q1,* (word,) *Q2–4, Q5* (caste); And then he sends you word, / He dreamt to night, the Boare had cast *Q6*
12 kept] held *Q1–6*
14 th'] the *Q1–6*
16 you will presently] presently you will *Q1–6*
17 with him toward] into *Q1–6*
20 Council] counsells *Q1–6*
22 good friend] seruant *Q1–6*
26 he's so simple] he is so fond *Q1–6* (so *om. Q4*)
27 mock'ry] mockery *Q1–6*
28 pursues] pursues vs *Q1–2;* pursue vs *Q3–6*
34 I'll . . . and] My gratious Lo: Ile *Q1–6*
34 s.d. Exit.] *om. Q1–2*
37 tott'ring] tottering *Q1–6*
39 will] it will *Q1–2;* twill *Q3–6*
41 How?] *Q1–2;* How *F1;* Who? *Q3–6*
41 Dost] *F3;* Doest *F1, Q1–6*
44 Before I'll] Ere I will *Q1–6*
46 Ay, . . . life] Vpon my life my Lo: *Q1–6*
52 my adversaries] mine enemies *Q1–6*
55 it,] it *Q1–6*
58 which] who *Q1–6*
60 Well . . . older,] I tell thee Catesby. *Cat.* What my Lord? / *Hast.* Ere a fortnight make me elder, *Q1–6*
61 on't] on it *Q1–6*
66 that] who *Q1–6*
67 know'st] knowest *Q1–2*
70 s.d. Aside.] *F4*
72 Come on, come on] What my Lo: *Q1–6*
78 you do] *Q1–6*
79 days] life *Q1–6*
80 so . . . as 'tis] more . . . then it is *Q1–6*
84 were] was *Q1–6*
86 o'ercast] ouercast *Q1–2*
87 stab] scab *Q1–6*
89–91 What . . . lords] But come my Lo: shall we to the tower? / *Hast.* I go: but stay, heare you not the newes, / This day those men *Q1–6*
91 talk'd] *Q1–2;* talke *F1, Q3–6*
94 let's] let vs *Q1–6*
94 s.d. also named Hastings] *ed., from Q1–6 s.d.:* Hastin. a Purssuant.
95 Go . . . fellow.] Go you before, Ile follow presently. *Q1–6*
95 s.d. Exeunt] *Rowe;* Exit *F1, Q3–6 (after l. 94)*
96 How now, sirrah?] Well met Hastings, *Q1–6 (with repeated s.p.)*
97 your . . . ask] it please your Lo: to aske *Q1–2;* it please your good Lordship to ask *Q3–6*
98 man] fellow *Q1–6*
99 thou met'st me] I met thee *Q1–6*
104 e'er] euer *Q1–6*
106 fellow . . . me] Hastings hold spend thou that *Q1,* (Hastings,) *Q2–6*
106 s.d. Throws] He giues *Q1–6*
107 I . . . honor] God saue your Lordship *Q1–6*
107 s.d. Exit Pursuivant.] *om. Q1–2*
108–9 Priest. Well . . , heart.] *Hast.* What Sir Iohn, you are wel met, *Q1–6*
110 in . . . last] beholding to you for your last daies *Q1–6*
111 Sabbath] *Q8;* Sabboth *F1, Q3–6;* sabaoth *Q1–2*
111 s.d. He . . . ear.] *Q1–6*
112 Priest. I'll . . . lordship.] *om. Q1–6*
113 What . . . Chamberlain] How now Lo: Chamberlaine, what talking with a priest *Q1–6*
117 The] Those *Q1–6*
118 toward the Tower] to the tower my Lord *Q1–6*
119 my lord] *om. Q1–6*
119 cannot stay there] shall not stay *Q1–6*
121 Nay] Tis *Q1–6*
122 s.d. Aside.] *Rowe*
122 know'st] knowest *Q1–2;* knowh *Q6*
123 will you go] shall we go along *Q1–6*
123 Hast. I'll . . . lordship.] *om. Q1–6*

III.iii

Location: *Theobald*
o.s.d. Rivers . . . Vaughan] *from Q1–6 s.d.:* Enter Sir Rickard Ratliffe, with the Lo: Riuers, Gray, and Vaughan, prisoners.
1 Rat. Come . . . prisoners.] *Q1–6*
2 Ratcliffe] Ratliffe *Q1–6*
5 bless] keepe *Q1–6*
7–8 Vaug. You . . . out.] *om. Q1–6 (but l. 8 appears as* Come come dispatch, the limit of your linea [lines *Q2;* liues *Q3–6*] is out., *replacing l. 24 of F1)*
13 seat] soule *Q1–6*
14 to thee . . . blood] thee vp . . . blouds *Q1–6*
16 When . . . I,] *om. Q1–6*
18 Richard] Hastings *Q1–6*
19 Hastings] Richard *Q1–6*
20 prayer] praiers *Q1–6*
21 sons] sonne *Q1–6*
22 blood] blouds *Q1–6*
23 know'st] knowest *Q1–6*
24] *See above, ll. 7–8*
25 here] all *Q1–6*
26 Farewell . . . again] And take our leaue vntill we meete *Q1–5,* (leaues) *Q6*

III.iv

Location: *Pope*
o.s.d. Enter . . . table.] Enter the Lords to Councell. *Q1–6*
1 Now, noble peers] My lords at once *Q1–6*
3 speak . . . the] say . . . this *Q1–6*
4 Is . . . ready . . . the] Are . . . fitting . . . that *Q1–6*
5 s.p. Stan.] *Theobald;* Darb. *F1 (throughout scene);* Dar. *Q1–6*
6 s.p. Ely.] Ryu. *Q1;* Riu. *Q2;* Bish. *Q3–6*
6 judge . . . day] guesse . . . time *Q1–6*
9 Your . . . think] Why you my Lo: me thinkes you *Q1–6*
10 We] Who I my Lo? we *Q1–6*
10 for] But for *Q1–6*
12 Or . . . lord] nor I no more of his *Q1–6*
17 gracious] Graces *Q1–6*
18 honorable lords] noble Lo: *Q1–2;* L. *Q3–6*
20 he'll] he will *Q1–6*
20 s.d. Enter Gloucester.] *after l. 21, Q1–6*
21 In happy] Now in good *Q1–6*
22 lords] L. *Q1–6*
23 trust] hope *Q1–6*
24 design] designes *Q1–6*
26 you not] not you *Q1–6*
26 cue] *Q1–6* (kew); Q *F1*
27 had] had now *Q1–6*
31 My . . . when,] *Hast.* I thanke your Grace. / *Glo.* My Lo: of Elie, *Bish.* My Lo: / *Glo.* When *Q1–6*
34 Marry . . . heart.] I go my Lord. *Q1–6*
34 Marry] *F3;* Mary *F1*
34 s.d. Exit Bishop.] *om. Q1–6*
35 of] *om. Q1–6*
35 s.d. Drawing him aside.] *Capell*
38 That] As *Q1–6*
39 child, as worshipfully] sonne as worshipful *Q1–5,* (wotshipfull) *Q6*
41 yourself . . . with] you hence my Lo: Ile follow *Q1–6*
41 s.d. Gloucester and Buckingham] *Pope; Q1–6 s.d. reads:* Ex. Gl.
43 my judgment] mine opinion *Q1–6*
46 lord . . . Gloucester] L. protector *Q1–6*
48 this morning] to day *Q1–6*
50 that he bids . . . such] he doth bid . . . such a *Q1–6*
51 there's] there is *Q1–6*
52 Can] That can *Q1–6*
55 livelihood] likelihood *Q1–6*
56 Marry] *Q6;* Mary *F1, Q1–5*
57 For . . . had] For if he were, he would haue *Q1–6*
57 shown] shewen *Q1–5*
58 Stan. I . . . say.] *Q1–6 (with s.p.* Dar.)
58 s.d. and Buckingham] *om. Q1–6*
59 tell me what] what do *Q1–6*
64 princely] noble *Q1–6*
65 th' offenders, whosoe'er] the offenders whatsoeuer *Q1–6*
67 their evil] this ill *Q1–6*
68 Look] See *Q1–6*
70 And this is] This is that *Q1–6*
73 deed, my noble] thing my gratious *Q1–6*
75 Talk'st thou to] Telst thou *Q1–6*
76 I swear] *om. Q1–6*
77 dine] dine to day I sweare *Q1–6*
78 Lovel . . . done] some see it done *Q1–6*
79 rise] come *Q1–6*
79 s.d. Exeunt.] *placed as in Q1–6; after l. 78, F1*
79 s.d. Manent] *F2;* Manet *F1, Q1–6*
79 s.d. Lovel . . . Hastings] Cat. with Ha. *Q1–6*
82 rase] *Q1–6* (race); rowse *F1*
82 our helms] his helme *Q1–6 (perhaps correctly)*
83 And . . . disdain] But I disdaind it, and did scorne *Q1–6*
84 foot-cloth horse] *Rowe;* Foot-Cloth-Horse *F1;* footecloth horse *Q1–6*
85 started] startled *Q1–6 (perhaps the better reading)*
87 need] want *Q1–6*
89 too . . . how] twere . . . at *Q1–6*
90 To-day] How they *Q1–6*
94 s.p. Rat.] Cat. *Q1–6*
94 Come, come, dispatch] Dispatch my Lo: *Q1–6*
96 grace of mortal] state of worldly *Q1–6*
97 God] heauen *Q1–6*
98 hope . . . good] hopes . . . faire *Q1–6*
102–5 Lov. Come . . . upon.] *om. Q1–6*

III.v

III.v] *Capell*
Location: *Theobald*
o.s.d. Enter . . . ill-favored.] Enter Duke of Glocester and Buckingham in armonr. *Q1,* (armor) *Q2–6*
3 again begin] beginne againe *Q1–6*
4 were] wert *Q1–6*
5 Tut,] Tut feare not me. *Q1–6*
7 Tremble . . . straw;] *om. Q1–6*
11 At any time] *om. Q1–6*
12–4 But . . . Mayor—] *Glo.* Here comes the Maior. / *Buc.* Let me alone to entertaine him. Lo: Maior, *Q1–6*
13 s.d. Enter . . . Catesby.] Enter Maior. *Q1–6 (after l. 11)*
16, 17] *These lines, in reverse order, follow l. 18 in Q1–6*

16 **Hark,]** Harke, I heare *Q1–6*
17 **o'erlook]** ouerlooke *Q1–6*
18 **Lord . . . sent—]** The reason we haue sent for you. *Q1–6*
20 **innocence]** *Q1*; Innocencie *F1, Q2–6*
20 **and guard]** *om. Q1–6*
20 s.d. **Enter . . . head.]** Enter Catesby with Hast. Head. *Q1–6* (*after l. 21, Q3–6*)
21 **Be . . . Lovel.]** O, O, be quiet, it is Catesby. *Q1–6*
22 s.p. **Lov.]** Cat. *Q1–6*
25 **creature]** man *Q1–6*
26 **the]** this *Q1–6*
32 **liv'd . . . suspects]** laid . . . suspect *Q1–6*
34 **Look . . . Mayor,]** *Q1–6* (*after l. 26*); *placed as in Capell*
35 **you imagine]** you haue imagined *Q1–6*
36 **Were't]** *F3*; Wert *F1, Q1–5*; were *Q6*
36 **that]** *om. Q1–6*
37 **it, that the]** it you? The *Q1–6*
38 **This . . . plotted]** Had this day plotted *Q1–6*
39 **murther]** murder *Q1–6*
40 **Had he done]** What, had he *Q1–6*
43 **in]** to *Q1–6*
48 **your good Graces]** you my good Lords *Q1–6*
50–1 **Buck. I . . . Shore.]** *continued to Mayor, Q1–6*
52–61 **Yet . . . death.]** *given to* Dut. *Q1–2* (*perhaps a misreading for* Buc.); *to* Clo. *Q3, Q5*; *to* Glo. *Q4, Q6*
52 **we not determin'd]** not we determined *Q1–6*
53 **end]** death *Q1–6*
54 **loving]** longing *Q1–6*
55 **Something . . . meanings]** Somewhat . . . meaning *Q1–6*
56 **I]** we *Q1–6*
58 **treasons]** treason *Q1–6*
60 **haply]** happily *Q1–6*
62 **Grace's]** *F4*; Graces *F1, Q1–6*
62 **words]** word *Q1–6*
63 **and]** or *Q1–6*
64 **do not doubt]** doubt you not *Q1–6*
65 **our]** your *Q1–6*
66 **cause]** *Q1–5*; case *F1*; ease *Q6*
68 **T' avoid . . . carping]** To auoyde the carping censures of the *Q1–6*
69 **Which . . . intent]** But . . . intents *Q1–6*
70 **you hear]** *om. Q1–6*
71 **my . . . farewell]** my Lord adue *Q1–6*
71 s.d. **Exit Mayor.]** *after l. 72, Q1–6*
72 **Go]** *om. Q1–6*
74 **meet'st advantage]** *Q1–5*; meetest vantage *F1*; meetest aduantage *Q6*
81 **bestial]** *Q1–5*; beastiall *F1, Q6*
82 **stretch'd unto]** stretched to *Q1–6*
83 **raging]** lustfull *Q1–6*
84 **lusted . . . a]** listed . . . his *Q1–6*
85 **need, thus far]** neede thus farre, *Q1–2*; need thus farre *Q3–6*
87 **insatiate]** vnsatiate *Q1–6*
89 **true]** iust *Q1–6*
93 **Yet . . . 'twere]** But . . . it were *Q1–6*
94 **my . . . know]** you know, my Lord, *Q1–6*
95 **Doubt]** Feare *Q1–6*
97 **and . . . adieu.]** *om. Q1–6* (*but see l. 102*)
101–2 **I . . . affords.]** About three or foure a clocke look to heare / What news Guildhall affordeth, and so my Lord farewell. *Q1–6*
103–5 **Go . . . Castle.]** *om. Q1–6*
104 s.d. **To Catesby.]** *Capell*
104 **Penker]** *Capell*; Peuker *F1*
105 s.d. **Exeunt . . . Catesby.]** *ed.*; Exit. *F1*
106 s.d. **To Ratcliffe.]** *ed.* (*eds. make Ratcliffe exit with Lovel and Catesby, but there is nothing to suggest he does so, and F1 has* Exeunt. *at l. 109*; Exit., *however, Q1–6*)
106 **go]** in *Q1–6*
108 **order . . . manner]** notice, . . . maner of *Q1–6*
109 **Have any time]** At any tyme haue *Q1–6*

III.vi

III.vi] *Capell*
Location: *Capell*
o.s.d. **with . . . hand]** *Q1–6*
1 **Here]** This *Q1–6*
3 **to-day]** this day *Q1–6*
3 **o'er]** ouer *Q1–6*
5 **have]** *om. Q1–6*
6 **sent]** brought *Q1–6*
7 **precedent]** president *Q1–6* (*Shakespeare's usual form*)
8 **Hastings liv'd]** liued Lord Hastings *Q1–6*
10 **Who is]** Why whoes *Q1–2*; Why, who's *Q3–6*
11 **cannot see]** sees not *Q1–6*
12 **who's]** *Q1–2*; who *F1, Q3–6*
12 **bold]** blinde *Q1–6*
14 **ill]** bad *Q1–6*

III.vii

III.vii] *Pope*
Location: *Theobald*
o.s.d. **Richard . . . doors]** Glocester at one doore, Buckingham at another *Q1–6*
1 **how now]** my Lord *Q1–6*
3 **say]** and speake *Q1–6*
5–6 **his . . . France,]** *om. Q1–6*
7 **Th' unsatiate]** the insatiate *Q1–6*
7 **desire]** desires *Q1–6*
8 **And . . . wives,]** *om. Q1–6*
11 **And . . . Duke.]** *om. Q1–6*
13 **idea]** Idea *F1* (*in italics*)
18 **your]** the *F1*
20 **mine]** *Q1–2*; my *F1, Q3–6*
20 **drew]** grew *Q1–6*
20 **to an]** *Q1–2, Q4*; toward *F1*; to *Q3, Q5–6*
23 **And]** A and *Q1*; A, and *Q2–6*
24 **they . . . word,]** *om. Q1–6*
25 **statuës]** *Keightley*; Statues *F1, Q1–6*
26 **Star'd]** Gazde *Q1–6*
29 **used]** wont *Q1–6*
33 **spake]** *Q1–5*; spoke *F1*; speake *Q6*
37 **And . . . few:]** *om. Q1–6*
38 **gentle]** louing *Q1–6*
39 **cheerful]** louing *Q1–6*
40 **wisdoms]** *Q1–2*; wisdome *F1, Q3–6*
41 **even here]** so *Q1–6*
43 **Buck. No . . . lord.]** *Q1–6*
44 s.p. **Glou.]** *Q1–6*
46 **you . . . by]** spoken withall, but with *Q1–6*
48 **between]** betwixt *Q1–6*
49 **make]** build *Q1–6*
50 **And be . . . requests]** Be . . . request *Q1–6*
51 **still . . . and]** say no, but *Q1–6*
52 **I . . . plead]** Feare not me, if thou canst plead *Q1–6*
54 **we]** weele *Q1–6*
55–6 **Go . . . lord!]** You shal see what I can do, get you vp to the leads. *Exit.* / Now my L. Maior, *Q1–6*
55 s.d. **Exit Gloucester.]** *Rowe* (*after l. 54; here placed as in Capell*); Exit. *Q1–6* (*after* leads, *l. 55*)
55 s.d. **Aldermen]** *Capell*
58 **Now . . . request?]** Here comes his seruant: how now *Catesby* what saies he. *Q1–6*
59 **He . . . lord]** My Lord, he doth intreat your grace *Q1–6*
63 **suits]** suite *Q1–6*
65 **the gracious Duke]** thy Lord againe *Q1–6*
66 **Aldermen]** Cittizens *Q1–6*
67 **in matter]** and matters *Q1–6*
70 **signify . . . straight]** tell him what you say my Lord *Q1–6*
71 **Ah]** A *Q1–6*
72 **love-bed]** day bed *Q1–6*
78 **virtuous]** gracious *Q1–6*
79 **his Grace . . . thereof]** himselfe . . . thereon *Q1–6*
80 **not]** neuer *Q1–6*
81 **defend]** forbid *Q1–6*
82 **Here . . . again.]** *om. Q1–6*
83 **Now . . . Grace?]** how now Catesby, / What saies your Lord? *Q1–6*
83 **My lord,]** *Q1–6*
85 **come to]** speake with *Q1–6*
87 **He . . . lord]** My Lord, he feares *Q1–6*
90 **we . . . love]** I come in perfect loue to him *Q1–6*
91 s.d. **Catesby]** *Q1–6*
93 **much]** hard *Q1–6*
94 s.d. **aloft . . . Bishops]** with two bishops a loste *Q1*, (aloft) *Q2–6*
94 s.d. **Catesby returns.]** *Theobald*
95 **his . . . 'tween]** he stands between *Q1–6*
98–9 **And . . . man.]** *om. Q1–6*
101 **ear]** eares *Q1–6*
101 **our requests]** our request *Q1*; my request *Q2–6*
105 **do . . . to]** rather do beseech you *Q1–6*
107 **Deferr'd]** Neglect *Q1–6*
110 **ungovern'd]** vngouerned *Q1–4*
112 **eye]** eies *Q1–6*
114 **might]** *om. Q1–6*
115 **On]** At *Q1–6*
115 **your]** that *Q1–6*
117 **Know then]** Then know *Q1–6*
120 **Your . . . birth,]** *om. Q1–6*
123 **Whiles]** Whilst *Q1*; Whilest *Q2–6*
125 **The]** This *Q1–6*
125 **her]** *Q1–2*; his *F1, Q3–6*
126 **Her]** *Q1–6*; His *F1*
127 **Her . . . plants,]** *om. Q1–6*
127 **Her]** *Pope*; His *F1*
129 **dark . . . deep]** blind . . . darke *Q1–6*
131–2 **charge . . . land:]** soueraingtie thereof, *Q1–6*
140 **cause]** suite *Q1–6*
141 **cannot tell if]** know not whether *Q1–4*; know whither *Q5–6*
144–53 **If . . . you:]** *om. Q1–6*
158 **the . . . of]** my . . . by *Q1–6*
161 **That]** As *Q1–6*
161 **would]** had *Q1–6*
165 **thank'd, there is]** thanked there's *Q1–6*
166 **were there need]** if need were *Q1–6*
171 **that]** what *Q1–6*
179 **was he]** he was *Q1–6*
180 **his]** that *Q1–6*
183 **off]** by *Q1–6*
184 **to . . . sons]** of a many children *Q1*; of many children *Q2–6*
187 **prize]** prise *Q1–3, Q5–6*
187 **wanton]** lustfull *Q1–6*
188 **his degree]** al his thoughts *Q1–6*
191 **call]** terme *Q1–6*
195 **good]** *Q1–6*; good, *F1*
198 **forth . . . ancestry]** out your royall stocke *Q1–6*
199 **times]** time *Q1–6*
200 **true-derived]** *hyphen, Theobald*
201 **Do,]** *F4*; Do *F1, Q1–6*
202 **Buck. Refuse . . . love.]** *om. Q1–6*
204 **this care]** these cares *Q1*; those cares *Q2–6*
205 **majesty]** dignitie *Q1–6*
212 **kindred]** kin *Q1–6*
214 **know, whe'er]** *Theobald*; know, where *F1*; whether *Q1–6*
219 **'Zounds, I'll]** *Q1–6*; we will *F1*
220 **Glou. O . . . Buckingham.]** *Q1–6*
220 s.d. **Buckingham . . . Citizens]** *Dyce* (*s.d. om. Q1–6*)
221 **him . . . prince]** them againe, my lord *Q1–6*
222 **If . . . will]** *Ano.* Doe, good my lord, least all the land do *Q1–6*
223 **Will . . . cares]** Would . . . care *Q1–6*
224 **Call]** Well, call *Q1–6*
225 **entreaties]** intreates *Q1–6*
226 s.d. **Enter . . . rest.]** *om. Q1–6*
227 **sage]** you sage *Q1–6*
229 **whe'er]** *Steevens*; where *F1*; whether *Q1–6*
229 **no,]** *Q1–6*; no. *F1*
231 **foul-fac'd]** soule-fac't *Q1–2*; so foule fac't *Q3–6*
235 **doth know]** he knowes *Q1–6*
236 **of this]** thereof *Q1–6*
239 **royal]** kingly *Q1–6*
240 **Richard]** *Q1–2*; King Richard *F1, Q3–6*
240 **worthy]** royall *Q1–6*
241 s.p. **All.]** Mayor. *Q1–6*
242 **may]** will *Q1–6*
243 **please, for]** will, since *Q1–6*
245 **And . . . leave.]** *om. Q1–6*
246 s.d. **To the Bishops.]** *Johnson* (*subs.*)
246 **work]** taske *Q1–6*
247 **my]** good *Q1–6*
247 **cousin]** *Q1–6*; Cousins *F1*

IV.i

Location: *Theobald* (*after Pope*)

o.s.d. at one door . . . at another door] *Q1–6* (*the order of entry is taken from Q1–6 s.d.:* Enter Quee. mother, Duchesse of Yorke, Marques Dorset, at one doore, Duchesse of Glocest. at another doore.; *F1 s.d. reads:* Enter the Queene, Anne Duchesse of Gloucester, the Duchesse of Yorke, and Marquesse Dorset.)
o.s.d. leading . . . daughter] *Johnson*
2–7 Led . . . away?] *Qu.* Sister well met, whether awaie so fast? *Q1–6*
8 s.p. Anne.] Duch. *Q1–2;* Dut. Glo. *Q3–6*
10 gentle] tender *Q1–6*
11 s.d. the Lieutenant] Lieutenant *Q1–2;* the Lieutenant of the Tower *Q3–6*
14 doth . . . York?] fares the Prince? *Q1–6* (*see also l. 16*)
15 s.p. Brak.] *Capell;* Lieu. *F1, Q1–6* (*throughout scene*)
15 Right . . . patience] Wel Madam, and in health, but by your leaue *Q1–6*
16 them] him *Q1–6*
17 strictly] straightlie *Q1–6*
18 King?] King? whie *Q1–6*
18 I mean] I crie you mercie, I meane *Q1–6*
20 between] betwixt *Q1–6*
21 shall bar] should keepe *Q1–6*
24 bring . . . sights] feare not thou *Q1–6*
26 No . . . so] I doe beseech your graces all to pardon me *Q1–6*
27 and . . . me] I may not doe it *Q1–6*
27 s.d. Exit Lieutenant.] *om. Q1–6*
28 an] *Q1–4;* one *F1;* at an *Q5–6*
30 reverend] reuerente *Q1–6*
30 looker-on] *hyphen, Capell*
31 s.d. To Anne.] *Capell*
31 straight] go with me *Q1–6*
33 Ah . . . asunder] O . . . in sunder *Q1–6*
35 swoon] sound *Q1–6*
36 Anne. Despiteful . . . news!] *om. Q1–6*
37 Be . . . Mother] Madam, haue comfort *Q1–6*
38 gone] hence *Q1–6*
39 dogs . . . thy] dogge . . . the *Q1–6*
48 hours] time *Q1–6*
50 In . . . way] To meete you on the way, and welcome you *Q1–6*
52 ill-dispersing] *hyphen, Theobald*
54 hatch'd] hatch *Q1*
56 come] *om. Q1–6* (*Q3–6 add* for *after* sent)
57 s.p. Anne.] Duch. *Q1–6*
57 with] in *Q1–6*
58 O] I *Q1–6*
60 brains] braine *Q1–6*
61 venom] poyson *Q1–6*
63 Go, go] Alas *Q1–6*
65 why] *om. Q1–6*
69 dear] dead *Q1–6*
75 More . . . life] As . . . death *Q1–6*
76 Than] As *Q1–6*
78 Within . . . time] Euen in so short a space *Q1–6*
80 mine] my *Q1–6*
81 hitherto hath held] euer since hath kept *Q1–6*
81 my] *Q1–5;* mine *F1, Q6*
81 rest] sleepe *Q1–6*
83 Did I enjoy] Haue I enioyed *Q1–6*
84 with . . . awak'd] haue bene waked by his timerous dreames *Q1–6*
87 Poor . . . complaining] Alas poore soule, I pittie thy complaints *Q1–6*
88 with] from *Q1–6*
90 that] thou *Q1–6*
91 s.d. To Dorset.] *F2 (subs.)*
92 s.d. To Anne.] *F2 (subs.)*
92 tend] garde *Q1–6*
93 s.d. To Queen Elizabeth.] *F2 (subs.)*
93 and] *om. Q1–6*
97–103 Q. Eliz. Stay . . . farewell.] *om. Q1–6*
103 s.d. Exeunt.] *om. Q1–6*

IV.ii

Location: *Capell (after Pope)*
o.s.d. Sound a sennet.] The Trumpets sound, *Q1–6*
o.s.d. in pomp] *om. Q1–6*
o.s.d. crowned] *Q2–6;* crownd *Q1*
o.s.d. Ratcliffe] *om. Q1–6*
o.s.d. a Page, and others] *Capell;* with other Nobles *Q1–6*
2 Buck. My gracious sovereign?] *om. Q1–6*
3 s.d. Here . . . the throne.] *Q1–2;* Here . . . throne. *Q3;* Here . . . his throne *Q4–6*
3 s.d. Sound.] *om. Q1–6*
5 glories] honours *Q1–6*
7 let them] may they *Q1–6*
8 Ah] O *Q1–6*
10 speak] say *Q1–6*
11 loving lord] gracious soueraigne *Q1–6*
13 lord] liege *Q1–6*
17 wast] wert *Q1–6*
20 now] *om. Q1–6*
22 freezes] freezeth *Q1–6*
24 little breath, some] breath, some little *Q1–6*
24 dear] my *Q1–6*
25 in this] herein *Q1–6*
26 you herein presently] your grace immediatlie *Q1–6*
27 s.d. Aside . . . by.] *Capell (after Hanmer)*
27 gnaws his] bites the *Q1–6*
32 Boy!] *at beginning of l. 31, Q1–6*
33 s.p. Page.] Boy. *Q1–6 (throughout scene)*
35 Will] Would *Q1–6*
36 I] My lord, I *Q1–6*
37 spirit] mind *Q1–6*
41 I . . . man;] *om. Q1–6*
41 boy] presentlie *Q1–6*
41 s.d. Page] *Pope (subs.); s.d. om. Q1–6*
42 deep-revolving] *hyphen, Pope*
43 counsels] counsell *Q1–6*
45 Well, be it so.] *om. Q1–6*
46 Lord . . . news] What neewes with you *Q1–6*
47–8 Know . . . hear] My Lord, I heare the Marques Dorset *Q1–6*
49 the parts] those partes beyond the seas *Q1–6*
49 s.d. Stands apart.] *Cambridge*
50 Come hither, Catesby.] Catesby. *Cat.* My Lord. *Q1–6*
51 very grievous sick] sicke and like to die *Q1–6*
53 poor] borne *Q1–6*
59 s.d. Exit Catesby.] *Capell*
65 s.d. Page, with] *Capell*
65 s.d. Sir James] *Neilson*
68 lord] soueraigne *Q1–6*
70 Please you] I my Lord *Q1–6*
72 there] *Q1–6;* then *F1*
73 disturbers] disturbs *Q1–6*
78 Hark,] *om. Q1–6*
79 this] that *Q1–6*
79 s.d. Whispers.] he wispers in his eare. *Q1,* (whispers) *Q2–6*
80 There is] Tis *Q1–6*
81 for it] too *Q1–6*
82 I . . . straight.] Tis done my gracious lord. / *King* Shal we heare from thee *Tirrel* ere we sleep? *Enter Buc. / Tir.* Ye shall my lord, *Q1–5* (*apparently a memorial slip repeating III.i.188–9; so Q6, except that it reads Tyrrel's second speech as* Yea my good Lord.)
84 request] demand *Q1–6*
85 rest] passe *Q1–6*
86 the] that *Q1–6*
87 wive's] wifes *Q1* (wive's *is Shakespeare's usual form*)
87 son] sonnes *Q1–3*
87 unto it] to it *Q1–6*
88 the] your *Q1–6*
90 Herford] *Q1–3, Q5–6;* Hertford *F1;* Herfort *Q4*
91 Which . . . shall] The which you promised I should *Q1–6*
94 request] demand *Q1–6*
95 I . . . me] As I remember *Q1–6*
98–116 perhaps . . . to-day.] *Q1–6*
105 call'd] *Pope;* called *Q1–6*
117 May . . . suit.] Whie then resolue me whether you wil or no? *Q1–6*
118 Thou] Tut, tut, thou *Q1–6*
118 s.d. with . . . Buckingham] *Cambridge (subs.)*
119 And . . . deep] Is it euen so, rewardst he my true *Q1,* (rewards) *Q2–6*
120 such] such deepe *Q1–6*

IV.iii

IV.iii] *Pope*
Location: *Capell*
o.s.d. Tyrrel] Sir Francis Tirrell *Q1–6*
1 act] deed *Q1–6*
2 arch deed] arch-act *Q1–3, Q5–6;* arch act *Q4*
4 who] whom *Q1–6*
5 piece of ruthless] *Pope;* peece of ruthfull *F1;* ruthles peece of *Q1–2;* ruthfull peece of *Q3–6*
6 Albeit] Although *Q1–6*
7 Melted] Melting *Q1–6*
7 kind] *Q1–5;* milde *F1; om. Q6*
8 two] *Q1–6;* to *F1*
8 deaths'] *Theobald;* deaths *F1, Q1–3, Q5–6;* death *Q4*
8 story] stories *Q1–6*
9 O] Lo *Q1–6*
9 the gentle] those tender *Q1–5;* these tender *Q6*
10 one] on *Q1–2*
11 alablaster innocent] innocent alablaster *Q1–6*
13 Which] *Q1–5;* And *F1;* When *Q6*
15 once] *Q1–6;* one *F1*
16 But . . . there] *Theobald (after Rowe);* But oh the Diuell, there *F1;* But ô the Diuell their *Q1;* But ô the diuel: their *Q2;* But O the diuel: there *Q3–4;* But O the diuel! there *Q5–6*
17 When] Whilst *Q1, Q3–6;* Whilest *Q2*
17 on,] on *Q1–6*
19 e'er she] euer he *Q1–6*
20 Hence] Thus *Q1–2* (*line om. Q3–6*)
20 remorse] *Kittredge;* Remorse, *F1, Q1–2* (*line om. Q3–6*)
22 bear] bring *Q1–6*
23 health] haile *Q1–6*
25 gave] giue *Q1–2*
27 done] done my Lord *Q1–6*
30 where . . . truth)] how or in what place *Q1–6*
31 at] *Q1–6;* and *F1*
32 When] And *Q1–6*
33 thee] *Q1–6;* the *F1*
35 then] soone *Q1–6*
35 Tyr. I . . . leave.] *om. Q1–6*
35 s.d. Exit.] *Q1–6* (Exit Tirrel. *after l. 34; see preceding note*)*; placed as in Pope*
39 this] the *Q1–6*
39 good night] godnight *Q1–2;* goodnight *Q3–6*
42 on] ore *Q1–6*
43 go I] I go *Q1–6*
43 s.d. Enter Ratcliffe.] Enter Catesby. *Q1–6* (*with Ratcliffe's speeches given to Catesby*)
45 or bad news] newes or bad *Q1–6*
46 Morton] *Rowe;* Mourton *F1;* Ely *Q1–6*
50 rash-levied] *hyphen, Pope*
50 strength] armie *Q1–6*
51 learn'd] heard *Q1–6*
53 leads] *Q1–6;* leds *F1*
56 Go] Come *Q1–6*

IV.iv

IV.iv] *Pope;* Scena Tertia. *F1*
Location: *Capell*
o.s.d. Enter . . . Margaret.] Enter Queene Margaret sola. *Q1–6*
4 enemies] aduersaries *Q1–6*
8 s.d. Retires.] *Collier (subs.)*
8 s.d. Enter . . . Elizabeth.] Enter the Qu. and the Duchesse of Yorke. *Q1–6*
9 poor] young *Q1–6*
10 unblown] *Q1–6;* vnblowed *F1*
10 new-appearing] *hyphen, Pope*
15, 20, 25 s.dd. Aside.] *Collier*
17–9 Duch. So . . . dead?] *after l. 34, Q1–6*
18 still and mute] mute and dumbe *Q1–6*
20–1 Q. Mar. Plantagenet . . . debt.] *om. Q1–6*
26 Dead . . . sight] Blind sight, dead life *Q1–6*
26 mortal-living] *hyphen, Vaughan conj.*
27 due by] *Q1–6;* due, by *F1*
28 Brief . . . days,] *om. Q1–6*
29 s.d. Sitting down.] *Capell (subs.)*
30 innocent] innocents *Q1–6*

31 **Ah . . . as soon]** O . . . aswel *Q1–6*
34 **Ah . . . we]** O . . . I *Q1–6*
34 **s.d. Sitting . . . her.]** *Hanmer (subs.)*
35 **s.d. Coming forward.]** *Collier*
36 **seniory]** *Capell;* signeurie *F1;* signorie *Q1–5;* signiorie *Q6*
37 **griefs]** woes *Q1–6*
37–8 **hand. . . . society,]** *Warburton;* hand . . . Society. *F1;* hand, . . . societie, *Q1–6*
38 **s.d. Sitting . . . them.]** *Capell (subs.)*
39 **Tell . . . mine:]** *Q1–6*
41 **Harry]** *Cambridge;* Husband *F1;* Richard *Q1–6*
45 **holp'st]** *Q3–6;* hop'st *F1;* hopst *Q1–2*
48 **doth]** doeth *Q1*
50 **blood]** blouds *Q1–6*
52, 53] *Order as in Capell; lines transposed in F1; om. Q1–6*
59 **wife]** wifes *Q1*
63 **kill'd]** stabd *Q1–6*
64 **Thy]** *Q1–6;* The *F1*
66 **Match'd]** Match *Q1–6*
67 **stabb'd]** kild *Q1–6*
68 **frantic]** tragicke *Q1–6*
69 **Th']** The *Q1–6*
70 **smoth'red]** *Q1–5;* smother'd *F1;* smoothered *Q6*
73 **hand, at hand]** hand at handes *Q1*
74 **Ensues]** *Q1–6;* Insues *F1*
76 **convey'd from hence]** conueied away *Q1–6*
78 **and]** to *Q1–6*
86 **heav'd]** heaued *Q1–2*
86 **a-high]** *hyphen, Dyce*
87 **fair]** sweete *Q1–6*
88 **wast . . . flag]** wert a breath, a bubble *Q1–6*
89, 90] *Lines transposed, Q1–6*
90 **a . . . bubble]** a garish flagge *Q1–6*
93 **be . . . sons]** are thy children *Q1–2;* be thy children *Q3–6* (*we should perhaps read:* are thy two sons)
94 **and . . . says]** to thee, and cries *Q1–6*
100–4] *Q1–6 om. l. 103 and read the others in the order 101, 100, 104, 102*
102, 104 **she]** one *Q1–6*
105 **whirl'd]** whe'eld *Q1;* wheel'd *Q2–6*
107–8 **wast . . . art.]** *F4;* wast. . . . art, *F1;* wert, . . . art, *Q1–2;* art, . . . art. *Q3–6*
112 **weary]** *Q1–5;* wearied *F1, Q6*
112 **head]** necke *Q1–6*
115 **shall]** will *Q1–6*
118 **nights . . . days]** *Q1–2;* night . . . day *F1, Q3–6*
120 **sweeter]** fairer *Q1–6*
125 **s.d. Exit Queen Margaret.]** *after l. 26, Q1–6*
127 **their client's]** *Pope (reading* your); their Clients *F1;* your Client *Q1–3, Q5–6;* your clients *Q4*
128 **intestate]** *Q1–6;* intestine *F1 (possibly the correct reading)*
130 **will]** do *Q1–6*
131 **nothing else]** not at al *Q1–6*
132 **so then,]** so, then *Q1–6*
134 **that]** which *Q1–6*
135 **The trumpet sounds]** I heare his drum *Q1–6*
135 **s.d. marching . . . Trumpets]** *Q1–6*
136 **me in]** *om. Q1–6*
137 **O]** A *Q1–6*
138 **accursed]** *Q1–6;* aceursed *F1*
141 **Where]** *Q1–6;* Where't *F1*
141 **branded]** grauen *Q1–6*
141 **right,]** *Q1–6;* right? *F1*
142 **ow'd]** owed *Q1–2*
143 **poor]** two *Q1–6*
147–8 **Where . . . Hastings?]** Where is kind *Hastings, Riuers, Vaughan, Gray? Q1–6*
149 **alarum,]** *F4;* Alarum *F1, Q1–6*
151 **s.d. Flourish. Alarums.]** The trumpets *Q1;* The trumpets sound. *Q2;* The trumpets sounds. *Q3–6*
159 **That]** Which *Q1–6*
160 **Duch. O . . . hear.]** *om. Q1–6*
161 **words]** speach *Q1–6*
164 **torment and in]** anguish, paine and *Q1–6*
170 **desp'rate]** desperate *Q1–6*
172 **confirm'd]** confirmed *Q1–4*
172 **sly, and bloody]** bloudie, trecherous *Q1–6*
173 **More . . . hatred.]** *om. Q1–6*
175 **with]** in *Q1–6*
177 **breakfast]** breake fast *Q1*
178 **eye]** sight *Q1–6*
179 **you, madam]** your grace *Q1–6*
180–3 **Strike . . . So.]** *Du.* O heare me speake for I shal neuer see thee more. / *King.* Come, come, you art too bitter. *Q1,* (are) *Q2–6*
187 **more behold]** looke vpon *Q1–6*
188 **grievous]** heauy *Q1–6*
198 **her]** all *Q1–6*
199 **talk]** speake *Q1–6*
200 **moe]** *Q1;* more *F1, Q2–6*
201 **slaughter.]** murther *Q1;* murther, *Q2–6*
205 **gracious.]** *Q1–6;* Gracious? *F1*
206 **live!]** *Q1–2;* liue? *Q3–5;* liue, *F1, Q6*
208–9 **bed, . . . infamy.]** *Pope;* bed: . . . Infamy, *F1;* bed . . . infamie, *Q1;* bed, . . . infamie, *Q2–6*
210 **of]** from *Q1–6*
212 **a royal princess]** of roiall bloud *Q1–6*
214 **safest only]** onlie safest *Q1–6*
215 **died]** *Q1–6;* dyed *F1*
216 **birth]** births *Q1–6 (perhaps a preferable reading)*
217 **ill]** bad *Q1–6*
222–35 **K. Rich. You . . . bosom.]** *om. Q1–6*
236–7 **enterprise . . . wars]** dangerous attempt of hostile armes *Q1–6*
239 **or]** *Q1–5;* and *F1, Q6*
239 **by . . . harm'd]** were by me wrongd *Q1–6*
241 **discover'd]** *Q1–5;* discouered *F1, Q6*
242 **Th']** The *Q1–6*
242 **gentle]** mightie *Q1–6*
244 **Unto]** No to *Q1–6*
244 **fortune]** honor *Q1–6*
246 **sorrow]** sorrowes *Q1–6*
249 **ay]** *F1* (I); yea *Q1–6*
255 **kindness' date]** *Capell;* kindnesse date *F1;* kindnes doe *Q1–6*
259 **soul;]** *F4 (subs.);* soule *F1;* soule, *Q1–6*
264 **do intend]** meane *Q1–6*
265 **Well]** Saie *Q1–6*
266 **Who]** how *Q5*
266 **should be else?]** *Q1;* else should bee? *F1;* should else? *Q2–6*
267 **Even . . . it]** I euen I, what thinke you of it Maddame *Q1–6*
268 **would I]** *Q1–2;* I would *F1, Q3–6*
269 **being]** that are *Q1–2;* that were *Q3–6*
273 **haply]** happelie *Q1–2;* happily *Q3–6*
273 **will she]** she wil *Q1–6*
274 **sometimes]** *Q1–2;* sometime *F1, Q3–6*
275 **steep'd]** a handkercher steept *Q1;* a handkercheffe steept *Q2–6*
276 **handkercher]** *Q1;* hand-kercheefe *F1, Q2–6 (see l. 275)*
276–7 **which . . . body,]** *om. Q1–6*
278 **wipe . . . withal]** drie . . . therewith *Q1–6*
279 **move]** force *Q1–6*
280 **letter . . . deeds]** storie . . . acts *Q1–6*
282 **ay]** *F1* (I); yea *Q1–6*
284 **You . . . madam]** Come, come, you mocke me *Q1–2,* (ye) *Q3–6*
284 **is]** *Q1–6*
288–342 **K. Rich. Say . . . years?]** *om. Q1–6*
324 **Of ten times]** *Theobald;* Of ten-times *F1;* Often-times *F2*
345 **Tell her . . . that]** Saie that . . . which *Q1–6*
348 **vail]** waile *Q1–6*
351 **in force]** inforce *Q1–6*
353, 354 **As]** So *Q1–6*
355 **low]** loue *Q1;* lone *Q2–6*
359 **plainly . . . tell]** in plaine termes tell her *Q1–6*
361 **Your]** Madame your *Q1–6*
364 **K. Rich. Harp . . . past.]** *placed as in Q1; after l. 365, F1; om. Q2–6*
364 **on]** one *Q1*
365 **s.p. Q. Eliz.]** *Q1* (Qu.); King. *Q2; continued, with omission of l. 364, to Queen Elizabeth, Q3–6*
366 **s.p. K. Rich.]** *Q1–6* (King)
368 **swear—]** *Collier;* sweare. *F1;* sweare by nothing. *Q1–6*
369, 370, 371 **Thy]** The *Q1–6*
369 **lordly]** holie *Q1–6*
371 **glory]** dignity *Q1–6*
372 **wouldst]** wilt *Q1–6*
374 **K. Rich. Then . . . self-misus'd.]** *after l. 376, Q1–6*
374 **is self-misus'd]** thy selfe misusest *Q1–6*
376 **it]** that *Q1–6*
377 **God . . . God's]** *Q1–6;* Heauen . . . Heauens *F1*
378 **didst fear . . . with]** hadst feard . . . by *Q1–6*
379 **husband]** brother *Q1–6*
380 **Thou . . . died]** Had not bene broken, nor my brother slaine *Q1–6*
382 **Th']** The *Q1–6*
382 **head]** brow *Q1–6*
385 **bedfellows]** plaie-fellows *Q1–6*
386 **the]** a *Q1–6*
387 **What . . . now?]** *om. Q1–6*
387 **The]** By the *Q1–6*
388 **wronged in the]** wrongd in *Q1–6*
390 **time, for . . . thee.]** time, for time, by the past wrongd, *Q1–2;* time for time, by the past wrongd, *Q3–4;* time for time, by thee past wrongd, *Q5–6 (F1 may be only an unauthoritative sophistication of the Q1 reading, if the is understood as thee, under the influence of Q5–6)*
391 **fathers]** parents *Q1–6*
392 **in]** *Q1–4;* with *F1, Q5–6*
394 **barren]** withered *Q1–6*
396 **times ill-us'd]** time misused *Q1–6*
396 **o'erpast]** *Q1–6;* repast *F1*
398 **affairs]** attempt *Q1–6*
400 **Heaven . . . hours!]** *om. Q1–6*
403 **proceeding . . . dear]** proceedings . . . pure *Q1–6*
407–8 **myself . . . land]** this land and me, / To thee her selfe *Q1–6*
409 **Death]** Sad *Q1–6*
411 **by]** *om. Q1*
412 **dear]** good *Q1–6*
415 **my]** by *Q1–6*
417 **peevish-fond]** *Q3–6* (*hyphen, Malone conj.*); peeuish found *F1;* pieuish, fond *Q1–2*
419 **you]** thee *Q1–6*
422 **Yet]** But *Q1–6*
423 **I bury]** I buried *Q1–2;* Ile burie *Q4–6*
424 **will]** shall *Q1–6*
425 **Selves]** Selfes *Q1–6*
425 **recomforture]** recomfiture *Q1–6*
429 **And . . . mind.]** *om. Q1–6*
430 **and so]** *om. Q1–6*
430 **s.d. Exit Queen Elizabeth.]** *placed as in Q1–6* (Exit. *Q1–2;* Exit Qu. *Q3–6*)*; after l. 429, F1* (Exit. Q.)
431 **shallow, changing]** *Theobald;* shallow-changing *F1;* shallow changing *Q1–6*
431 **s.d. Enter Ratcliffe]** *placed as in Q1–6; after l. 432, F1*
431 **s.d. Catesby following]** *Capell*
432 **How . . . news?]** *om. Q1–6*
433 **Most mighty]** My gracious *Q1–6*
434 **our shores]** the shore *Q1–6*
435 **hollow-hearted]** hollow harted *Q1–4*
440 **Norfolk]** Norff. *Q1–5*
442 **good]** *om. Q1–6*
442 **Catesby]** *om. Q1–6*
443–4 **Cate. I . . . hither.]** *om. Q1–6*
444 **Ratcliffe]** *Rowe;* Catesby *F1*
444 **Post]** post thou *Q1–6*
445 **thither]** there *Q1–6*
445 **s.d. To Catesby.]** *Rowe*
446 **stay'st thou here]** standst thou still *Q1–3, Q5–6,* (stands) *Q4*
447 **liege . . . pleasure]** Soueraigne, let me know your minde *Q1–6*
448 **to him]** them *Q1–2;* him *Q3–6*
450 **that]** *om. Q1–6*
451 **suddenly]** presentlie *Q1–6*
452 **Cate. I go.]** *om. Q1–6*
452 **s.d. Exit.]** *om. Q1–6*
453 **may . . . I]** is it your highnes pleasure, I shall *Q1–4;* it is your highnes pleasure I shall *Q5;* is your highnesse pleasure I shall *Q6*
456 **My mind]** My mind is changd sir, my minde *Q1–6*
456 **s.d. Stanley]** Darbie *Q1–6* (*s.d. after*

you? *l. 456*)
456 **Stanley]** How now *Q1–6*
457 **None good,]** *F4;* None, good *F1;* None good *Q1–6*
457 **liege]** Lord *Q1–6*
458 **well . . . reported]** it may well be told *Q1–6*
460 **needst . . . miles]** doest . . . mile *Q1–2;* doost . . . mile *Q3–6*
461 **mayest . . . the nearest]** maist . . . a neerer *Q1–6*
464 **doth]** doeth *Q1*
466 **as you guess]** sir, as you guesse, as you guesse *Q1–6*
467 **Morton]** Elie *Q1–6*
468 **here]** there *Q1–6*
469 **unsway'd]** vnswaied *Q1–2*
473 **makes . . . seas]** doeth . . . sea *Q1–2;* doth . . . sea *Q3–6*
478 **my good lord]** mightie liege *Q1–6*
480 **be]** are *Q1–6*
482 **Safe-conducting]** Safe conducting *Q1–6*
484 **me]** Richard *Q1–6*
486 **King]** soueraigne *Q1–6*
487 **Pleaseth]** Please it *Q1–6*
490 **Ay]** *F1* (I); I, I *Q1–6*
490 **wouldst]** wouldest *Q1*
491 **But . . . thee]** I will not trust you Sir *Q1–6*
494 **Go . . . but]** Well, go muster men, but heare you *Q1–6*
495 **heart]** faith *Q1–6*
497 **s.d. Exit Stanley.]** *om. Q1–2;* Exit Dar. *Q3–5;* Exit. *Q6*
498 **s.p. 1. Mess.]** *Capell;* Mess. *F1, Q1–6*
500 **Edward]** William *Q1–6*
501 **elder brother]** brother there *Q1–6*
503 **s.p. 2. Mess.]** *Capell;* Mess. *F1, Q1–6*
503 **In . . . liege]** My Liege, in Kent *Q1–6*
505 **the . . . strong]** their aide, and still their power increaseth *Q1–6*
506, 509, 517 **s.pp. 3. Mess.]** *Capell;* Mess. *F1, Q1–6*
506 **great]** the Duke of *Q1–6*
507 **you]** *Q1–5;* ye *F1, Q6*
507 **death?]** *Pope;* Death, *F1;* death. *Q1–6*
507 **s.d. He striketh him.]** *after l. 506, Q1–6*
508 **There . . . bring]** Take that vntill thou bring me *Q1–5,* (you) *Q6*
509–10 **The news . . . waters]** Your grace mistakes, the newes I bring is good, / My newes is that by sudden floud, and fall of water, *Q1–6*
511 **Buckingham's]** The Duke of Buckinghams *Q1–6*
512 **wand'red away alone]** fled *Q1–6*
513–4 **I . . . thine.]** O I crie you mercie, I did mistake, / Ratcliffe reward him, for the blow I gaue him, *Q1–6*
515 **well-advised friend proclaim'd]** well aduised friend giuen out *Q1–6*
516 **Reward . . . in]** Rewardes for him that brings in Buckingham *Q1–6*
517 **lord]** liege *Q1–6*
518 **s.p. 4. Mess.]** *Capell;* Mess. *F1, Q1–6*
519 **in Yorkshire are]** are vp *Q1–6*
520 **But . . . Highness]** Yet . . . grace *Q1–6*
521 **by tempest]** *om. Q1–6*
522 **Dorsetshire]** Dorshire *Q1–5*
523 **Unto . . . banks]** to aske them on the shore *Q1–6*
527 **Hois'd . . . his course again]** Hoist . . . away *Q1–6*
534 **tidings,]** *Q1–5;* Newes, but *F1;* newes, *Q6*
538 **s.d. Flourish.]** *om. Q1–6*

IV.v

IV.v] *Capell;* Scena Quarta. *F1*
Location: *Hanmer*
o.s.d. **Urswick, a priest]** *Theobald, ed.*
1 **s.p. Stan.]** *Pope;* Der. *F1* (*throughout scene*); Dar. *Q1–6* (*throughout scene*)
2 **the most deadly]** this most bloudie *Q1–6*
5 **holds off]** with holds *Q1;* withholds *Q2–5;* with-holds *Q6*
6–7 **So . . . say]** Retourne vnto thy Lord, commend me to him, / Tell him *Q1–6*
6–8 **So . . . daughter.]** *in Q1–6 these lines* (*subs.*) *follow l. 18, replacing l. 19 of F1*
8 **should]** shall *Q1–6*
10 **Pembroke]** *Q1–2;* Penbroke *F1;* Pembrooke *Q3–6*
10 **Ha'rford-West]** *Q1* (Harford-west); Hertford West *F1;* Herford-west *Q2, Q5;* Hertford-west *Q3, Q4;* Hertford west *Q6*
15 **And]** *om. Q1–6*
15 **ap]** vp *Q1–5*
16 **And . . . name]** With many moe of noble fame *Q1–6*
17 **do they]** they do *Q1–6*
17 **power]** course *Q1–6*
19 **Well . . . hand.]** *om. Q1–6*
20 **My letter]** These letters *Q1–6*

V.i

Location: *Capell* (*after Pope*)
o.s.d. **with Halberds . . . led]** *om. Q1–6*
o.s.d. **and the Sheriff]** *Rowe* (*subs.*)
2, 11 **s.pp. Sher.]** Rat. *Q1–6* (*throughout scene*)
2 **good]** *om. Q1–6*
3 **Grey and Rivers]** Riuers, Gray *Q1–6*
10 **fellow]** fellowes *Q1–6*
11 **my lord]** *Q1–6*
12 **doomsday.]** *Q1–6* (*subs.*); doomsday *F1*
13 **which]** that *Q1–6*
17 **whom . . . trusted]** I trusted most *Q1–6*
20 **which]** that *Q1–6*
23 **doth]** doeth *Q1–5*
24 **in . . . bosoms]** on . . . bosome *Q1–6*
25 **Thus . . . neck]** Now Margarets curse, is fallen vpon my head *Q1–6*
28 **lead me, officers]** sirs, conuey me *Q1–6*
29 **s.d. and Sheriff]** *Theobald* (*subs.*); *s.d. om. Q1–6*

V.ii

Location: *Hanmer*
o.s.d. **Enter . . . Colors.]** Enter Richmond with drums and trumpets. *Q1–6*
10 **embowell'd]** inboweld *Q1–5;* imboweld *Q6*
11 **Is]** Lies *Q1–6*
11 **centry]** center *Q1–6*
12 **Near]** *Q1–5;* Ne're *F1;* Neere *Q6*
14 **cheerly]** *F4;* cheerely *F1;* cheerelie *Q1;* cheere *Q2–6*
17 **s.p. Oxf.]** 1 Lo. *Q1–6*
17 **men]** swordes *Q1–6*
18 **this guilty]** that bloudie *Q1–6*
19 **s.p. Herb.]** 2 Lo. *Q1–6*
19 **turn]** flie *Q1–6*
20 **s.p. Blunt.]** 3 Lo. *Q1–6*
20 **what]** who *Q1–6*
21 **dearest . . . fly]** greatest . . . shrinke *Q1–6*
24 **s.d. Exeunt omnes.]** Exit. *Q1; om. Q2–6*

V.iii

V.iii] *Pope*
Location: *Pope*
o.s.d. **at one door]** *Sisson*
o.s.d. **in arms]** *om. Q1–6*
o.s.d. **with others]** *Q1–6* (*Q1–6 enter Catesby here in place of Surrey*)
1 **tent]** tentes *Q1–6*
2 **My . . . sad]** Whie, how now Catesbie, whie lookst thou so bad *Q1,* (sad) *Q2–6*
3 **s.p. Sur.]** Cat, *Q1–6*
4 **My . . . liege.]** Norffolke, come hether. *Q1–6*
6 **loving]** gracious *Q1–6*
7 **tent]** tent there *Q1–6*
7 **s.d. Soldiers . . . tent.]** *ed.* (*after Capell*)
8 **all's]** all is *Q1–6*
9 **traitors]** foe *Q1–6*
10 **power]** number *Q1–6*
11 **battalia]** battalion *Q1–6*
13 **faction]** partie *Q1–6*
14 **the . . . noble]** my tent there, valiant *Q1–6*
15 **ground]** field *Q1–6*
17 **lack]** want *Q1–6*
18 **s.d. at . . . door]** *Sisson; Q1–2 s.d. reads:* Enter Richmond with the Lordes, &c.; *Q3–6 om.* &c.
18 **s.d. Blunt . . . tent]** *Capell*
19 **set]** sete *Q1;* seate *Q2–6*
20 **tract]** tracke *Q1–6*
21 **token]** signall *Q1–6*
22 **Sir . . . you]** Where is Sir William Brandon, he *Q1–6*
23–8 **Give . . . me.]** *Q1–6 shift ll. 23–6 to follow* Blunt. *l. 44 and om. ll. 27–8*
26 **power]** strength *Q1–6*
28 **you]** *F2;* your *F1*
29 **keeps]** keepe *Q1–6*
33 **captain . . . me]** Blunt before thou goest *Q1–6*
34 **Stanley . . . you]** Stanlie quarterd, doest thou *Q1–6*
40 **Sweet . . . him]** Good captaine Blunt beare my good night to him *Q1–6* (*cf. l. 30*)
41 **note]** scrowle *Q1–6*
43 **And . . . to-night.]** *om. Q1–6*
44 **Good . . . Blunt.]** Farewell good Blunt. *Q1–6*
44 **s.d. Exit Blunt.]** *Capell*
44 **gentlemen]** *om. Q1–6*
46 **In to]** *Q1–5;* Into *F1, Q6*
46 **my . . . dew]** our . . . aire *Q1–6*
46 **s.d. They . . . tent.]** *om. Q1–6*
46 **s.d. to his tent]** *Capell*
46 **s.d. and Catesby]** Catesbie, &c. *Q1–2*
47 **is't]** is *Q1–6*
47–8 **It's . . . a' clock.]** It is sixe of clocke, full supper time. *Q1–2,* (of the) *Q3–6*
48 **I . . . to-night.]** *beginning at this half-line, the basic text for the remainder of the play is Q1*
54 **sentinels]** *F1;* centinell *Q1–6*
57 **s.d. Exit.]** *F1*
58 **Catesby]** Ratcliffe *F1*
59 **s.p. Cate.]** *Pope;* Rat. *Q1–6, F1*
61 **sunrising]** *Q6, F1* (Sun-rising); sun rising *Q1–5*
62 **s.d. Exit Catesby.]** *Cambridge*
65–6 **heavy. Ratcliffe!]** *F1* (*subs.*); heauy Ratliffe. *Q1–5;* heauy Ratcliffe. *Q6*
68 **thou]** *om. F1*
74 **s.d. Wine brought.]** *Capell*
77 **Ratcliffe]** *Q3, Q5–6, F1;* Ratliffe *Q1–2, Q4*
78 **s.d. Richard sleeps.]** *Neilson*
78 **s.d. Ratcliffe]** *Q6, F1;* Ratliffe *Q1–5*
78 **s.d. Lords . . . attending]** *Cambridge*
79 **s.p. Stan.]** *Pope;* Dar. *Q1* (*throughout scene*); Der. *F1* (*throughout scene*)
79 **sit]** *Q2–6, F1;* set *Q1*
82 **loving]** noble *Q3–6, F1* (*picked up from l.81*)
85 **that.]** *F1;* that *Q1–2;* that: *Q3–6*
89 **the]** th' *F1*
90 **mortal-staring]** *hyphen, Steevens*
95 **brother, tender]** *F1;* brother tender *Q1–5;* tender brother *Q6*
100 **sund'red]** *F1;* sundried *Q1–2;* sundired *Q3–4;* sundered *Q5–6*
101 **rites]** *F1;* rights *Q1–6*
104 **thoughts]** noise *F1*
107 **s.d. Exeunt.]** *Q3–6, F1;* Exunt. *Q1–2*
107 **s.d. Manet Richmond.]** *F1*
112 **The]** Th' *F1*
114 **the]** thy *Q3–5, F1*
117 **s.d. Sleeps.]** *F1*
117 **s.d. young]** *om. Q3–6, F1*
117 **s.d. to]** *Q2–6, F1*
117 **s.d. Henry]** *Q2–6, F1;* Harry *Q1*
117 **s.d. to Richard]** *om. Q3–6, F1*
122 **butchered]** butcher'd *F1;* butchred *Q3–5*
125 **deadly]** *om. Q2–6, F1*
130 **thy]** *om. F1*
131, 139, 141, 142, 154 **s.dd. To Richard.]** *Rowe*
131 **sit]** *Q2–6, F1;* set *Q1*
139 **s.p. Ghost of R.]** *Dyce;* King *Q1;* Riu. *Q2–6, F1*
141, 142 **s.pp. Ghost of]** *Dyce*
145 **Will]** *Q2–6, F1;* Wel *Q1*
145 **s.d., 146–53 Enter . . . flourish.]** *these lines follow l. 158 in Q3–6, F1* (*this gives a chronological order based on the time of death*)
146 **s.p. Ghosts.]** *F1;* Ghost *Q1–2, 6;* Gho. *Q3–5*
147 **lead]** laid *Q2–6, F1*
149 **souls bid]** soule bids *F1*
153 **s.d. Hastings]** Lord Hastings *Q3–6, F1*
158 **s.d. Lady Anne]** Queene Anne *Q3–6;* Anne *F1*

159, 167 s.pp., s.dd. **Ghost. To Richard.]** *F1*
161 **perturbations]** *Q2–6, F1;* preturbations *Q1*
175 **Richmond's]** *Q2–6, F1;* Richmons *Q1*
176 **falls]** fall *F1*
176 s.d. **The Ghosts vanish.]** *Rowe*
176 s.d. **starteth . . . a]** starteth out of a *Q3–6;* starts out of his *F1*
180 **now]** not *Q2–6, F1*
182 **What . . . Myself?]** What do I feare my selfe? *Q2–6;* What? do I feare my Selfe? *F1*
183 **am]** *Q2–6, F1;* and *Q1* (*though Q1* and *makes possible sense, all eds. accept Q2* am)
185 **reason why—]** *Dyce;* reason whie? *Q1–2;* reason why, *Q3–6;* reason: why? *F1*
196 **Perjury, perjury]** Periurie *Q3–6, F1*
196 **highest]** high'st *F1*
197 **direst]** dyr'st *F1*
199 **Throng]** Throng all *Q3–6, F1*
199 **the]** th' *F1*
199 **all,]** *Q2–6, F1;* all *Q1*
201 **will]** shall *Q3–6, F1*
202 **And]** Nay *F1*
208 **'Zounds, who is]** Who's *F1*
212–4 **K. Rich. O . . . lord.]** *om. F1*
217 **strook]** *Q2–6;* stroke *Q1, F1*
221 **ease-dropper]** *F1;* ease dropper *Q1;* ewse dropper *Q2;* ewse-dropper *Q3;* eawse-dropper *Q4;* ewese-dropper *Q5–6*
222 **see]** heare *Q3–6, F1*
222 s.d. **Exeunt.]** Exeunt Richard & Ratliffe. *F1*
222 s.d. **sitting . . . tent]** *F1*
223 s.p. **Lords.]** *Q3–6;* Lo. *Q1;* Lor. *Q2;* Richm. *F1*
226 s.p. **Lords.]** *F1;* Lo. *Q1;* Lor. *Q2–6*
227 **fairest-boding]** *hyphen, Theobald*
229 **departure]** *Q2–6, F1;* depature *Q1*
232 **soul]** Heart *F1*
235 s.p. **Lords.]** *F4;* Lo. *Q1–2;* Lor. *Q3–6, F1*
242 **high-rear'd]** *hyphen, Pope*
243 **Richard except,]** *Q3–6;* Richard, except *Q1–2;* (Richard except) *F1*
247 **established]** establish'd *F1*
249 **slaughtered]** slaugtered *Q3;* slandered *Q4;* slaughter'd *F1*
250 **foil]** soile *Q3–6, F1*
254 **in]** *Q2–6, F1;* ln *Q1*
255 **sweat]** sweare *Q3–6, F1*
270 s.d. **Exeunt.]** *Capell*
270 s.d. **Attendants, and forces]** *Capell;* &c. *Q1–6;* and Catesby *F1*
274 **smil'd]** *F1;* smiled *Q1–6*
275 s.d. **The clock striketh.]** Clocke strikes. *F1*
280–1 **somebody. Ratcliffe!]** *F1;* some bodie Rat. *Q1–6*
283 **doth]** *Q2–6, F1;* doeth *Q1*
290 **Stanley]** *Q2–6, F1;* Standlie *Q1*
292 **ordered]** ordred *F1*
293 **drawn]** *Q2–6, F1;* drawen *Q1*
293 **out all]** *om. Q2–6, F1*
297 **this]** the *Q3–6, F1*
299 **main]** *Q2–6, F1;* matne *Q1*
300 **well winged]** well-winged *F1*
301 **boot]** *Q3–6, F1;* bootes *Q1–2*
302 s.d. **He . . . paper.]** *om. F1*
304 s.d. **Reads.]** *Rowe*
307 **unto]** to *F1*
309 **Conscience is but]** Conscience is *Q3–6;* For Conscience is *F1*
311 **conscience, swords]** *Q2–6, F1;* conscience swords, *Q1*
312 **to it]** too't *F1*
313 s.d. **His . . . Army.]** *om. F1*
320 **to you]** you to *Q2–6, F1*
321 **wives]** *Q2–6, F1;* wifes *Q1*
325 **milksop]** *Q6, F1;* milkesopt *Q1–5*
335 **in]** on *Q3–6, F1*
337 s.d. **Drum afar off.]** *F1*
338 **Fight]** Right *Q3–6, F1*
338 **bold]** boldly *Q2–6, F1*
341 s.d. **Enter a Messenger.]** *F1*
351 **them! Victory]** *Pope;* them victorie *Q1;* them, Victorie *Q2–6, F1*
351 **helms]** helpes *Q3, Q5–6, F1*
351 s.d. **Exeunt.]** *om. Q3–6, F1*

V.iv

V.iv] *Capell*
Location: *ed.* (*after Rowe*)
o.s.d. **Norfolk . . . him]** *Capell*
6 s.d. **Alarums.]** *F1*
13 s.d. **Exeunt.]** *Theobald*

V.v

V.v] *Dyce*
Location: *ed.* (*after Rowe*)
o.s.d. **Then . . . sounded,]** Retreat *F1*
o.s.d. **flourish, and]** *ed.* (*from F1* and Flourish)
o.s.d. **other]** diuers other *F1*
o.s.d. **etc.]** *om. Q3–6, F1*
3, 10 s.pp. **Stan.]** *Pope;* Dar. *Q1–6;* Der. *F1*
4 **Lo . . . royalty]** Loe here this long vsurped royalties *Q2–6;* Loe, / Heere these long vsurped Royalties *F1*
7 **enjoy it]** *om. Q3–6, F1*
11 **it . . . now]** you please) we may *F1*
13 s.p. **Stan.]** *F1* (Der.)
13 **Walter Lord Ferrers]** *Capell* (*after Holinshed*); Water Lord Ferris *Q1–5;* Walter Lord Ferris *Q6, F1*
14 **Brakenbury]** *F4;* Brookenbury *Q1–2;* Brokenbury *Q3–6, F1*
23 **scarr'd]** *F1;* scard *Q1–6*
25 **slaughter'd]** slaughtered *Q2–6, F1*
28 **division,]** *Johnson conj.;* deuision. *Q1;* Diuision. *Q2–6, F1*
32 **their]** thy *Q3–6, F1*
33 **smooth-fac'd]** *F1;* smooth-faste *Q1–3, Q5;* smooth fast *Q4;* smooth-fac't *Q6*
41 **here]** *F1;* heare *Q1–6*
41 s.d. **Exeunt.]** *F1* (Exeunt / FINIS.); FINIS. *Q1–6*

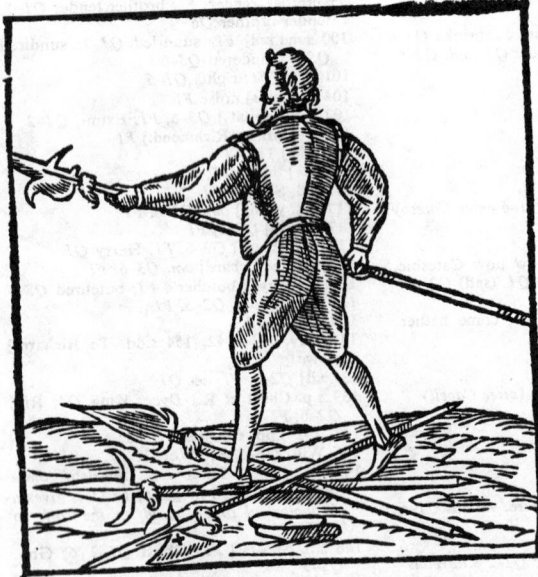

Halberds and bills

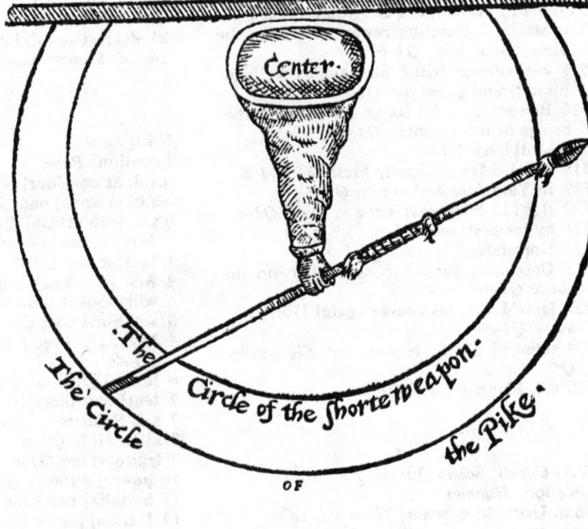

The pike

From *Di Grassi His True Art of Defence*, trans. I. G. (1594). (*By permission of the Harvard College Library*)

King John

THE DATE OF *King John*, a play noted by Francis Meres in 1598 and, so far as we know, first printed in the Folio of 1623, is difficult to fix. Although 1594–95 would seem to be the safest guess, external evidence is altogether lacking and internal evidence is, as usual, oblique and inconclusive. "Basilisco-like" (I.i.244) no doubt derives from the name of a character in *Soliman and Perseda*, a play written between 1589 and 1592 and perhaps subsequently revived. The action of *King John*, about an English monarch who is plagued by a rival with a better claim, by the enmity of Rome, and by a strong invading power, suggests the tangled relationships between Elizabeth, her cousin Mary Stuart, and the King of Spain; but to construe the play as an allegory of the Armada years is to press the case too hard. Moreover, attempts to fix a date from alleged topical allusions to the defeat of the Armada (1588) in the loss of the French fleet, to Henry IV's apostasy (1593) in the vacillation of King Philip and the Dauphin Lewis, and to the death of Shakespeare's son Hamnet (1596) in Constance's laments for Arthur do not impart conviction.

The Troublesome Reign of John, King of England—an anonymous play published in two parts in 1591, ascribed to "W. Sh." on the title-page of the second quarto in 1611, to "W. Shakespeare" in the third quarto in 1622, and subsequently to almost everyone who was writing for the stage in the early 1590's—poses special problems about the source and date of Shakespeare's play and has therefore prompted much conjecture. That *The Troublesome Reign* and *King John* are somehow intimately related is not open to dispute; indeed, the close parallelism of their plots, which, although Shakespeare's play is some three hundred lines shorter than its companion piece, exhibit virtually the same episodes in the same order, makes it clear that one play is based upon the other, unless a common source, now lost, is postulated. This kinship is confirmed by smaller details as well, as when both confusingly identify Widomar, Viscount of Limoges, with Leopold, Archduke of Austria (II.i.5), or deprive Constance of her third husband in order to present her as a strident widow (II.i.32), or show scores of verbal similarities, though only two that extend to as much as a whole line of verse (II.i.528, V.iv.42). *The Troublesome Reign* has long been held a source—in Dover Wilson's opinion, indeed, the only source—of *King John*; but Peter Alexander and E. A. J. Honigmann have separately advanced the theory that *King John* was written first (about 1590–91) and that *The Troublesome Reign* should be regarded as a reported text, or "bad" quarto, of Shakespeare's play. However, the data cited to support this view are at best tangential, and in the absence of more compelling evidence most scholars still prefer to think that Shakespeare wrote *King John*, as E. K. Chambers said, with a copy of *The Troublesome Reign* at hand.

It is most unlikely that Shakespeare knew of John Bale's *King John*, a virulently anti-Catholic play of the 1530's, but he certainly used Holinshed's *Chronicles* and probably Foxe's *Acts and Monuments* for details not included in *The Troublesome Reign*, and he may also have looked at Matthew Paris' *Chronica Majora.* Mr. Honigmann thinks that he got the date of Queen Elinor's death (IV.ii.120)—which was apparently unavailable in any printed source—from the Latin manuscript Wakefield chronicle and that for the great scene (IV.i) between Hubert and Arthur he followed the Latin chronicle of Ralph Coggeshall.

Stylistically, *King John* is marked by tumid rhetoric. It is filled with violent action, but the action often serves as the occasion for debate or disputation, and consequently the play is very verbal. For example, in a wryly comic scene almost at the beginning Faulconbridge and his puny brother contest their patrimony; and the second act presents a sequence of debates—or at any rate of declamations—with John opposed to Philip, Elinor to Constance, the French and English heralds before the city of Angiers, Faulconbridge and Hubert, each advancing his proposal. Elsewhere the action hovers on such forensic exhibitions as Pandulph's equivocating defense of oath-breaking (III.i.253–97), Arthur's moving plea to Hubert for his life (IV.i.253 ff.), and the Dauphin's explanation of his plan to conquer England (V.ii.78–108). Most conspicuous of all are Constance's lamentations, in Acts II and III, for the injuries to her son. "I defy all counsel, all redress," she says when he is captured,

> But that which ends all counsel, true redress:
> Death, death. O amiable lovely death!
> Thou odoriferous stench! sound rottenness!
> Arise forth from the couch of lasting night,
> Thou hate and terror to prosperity,
> And I will kiss thy detestable bones,
> And put my eyeballs in thy vaulty brows,
> And ring these fingers with thy household worms,
> And stop this gap of breath with fulsome dust,
> And be a carrion monster like thyself.
> Come, grin on me, and I will think thou smil'st,
> And buss thee as thy wife. Misery's love,
> O, come to me! (III.iv.23–36)

Philip's comment on this appalling woman's rhetoric (which has endeared the role to many actresses) is one that every reader will endorse: "You are as fond of grief as of your child." On the other hand, such scenes as John's exchange with Hubert (III.iii.64–66) about getting rid of Arthur are so tight and so alive with drama that they mark a new advance in Shakespeare's style:

> *K. John.* Thou art his keeper.
> *Hubert.* And I'll keep him so,
> That he shall not offend your Majesty.
> *K. John.* Death.
> *Hubert.* My lord?
> *K. John.* A grave.
> *Hubert.* He shall not live.
> *K. John.* Enough.

A puzzling and uneven play, *King John* is a daring exploration into the murky depths of *Realpolitik*. In Shakespeare's earlier history plays—the *Henry VI* trilogy and *Richard III*—politics is treated as a branch of morals. The course of events, apparently so jagged and complex, is shown to have a pattern and a direction that reveal a moral purpose coextensive with the will of God. Even if evil seems to triumph over good, as when the tyrant Richard wades through blood to reach the throne, we know that God directs events—the convulsions of dynastic struggle no less than the fall of a sparrow—and that His intentions are benign. This doctrine of providential history, which St. Augustine devised and which most Tudor chroniclers thriftily converted into a tool of party politics, begins to yield to something darker and more subtle in *King John*. Shakespeare is still concerned with politics, of course, but in tracing the link between politics and morals he is less cocksure and doctrinaire. Slogans no longer serve his purpose, nor do the inert, reassuring commonplaces of Hall and Holinshed supply the need for explanation. Instead, the ambiguities of character assert themselves, and history is presented not as a paradigm of moral purpose but as a tangled skein of good and evil, where mixed motives are revealed in indecisive actions, and where even a good man fears to lose his way.

This being a history play, the dynastic situation itself (which Shakespeare, as usual, distorts for his own purpose) exemplifies equivocation. In John, Arthur, and Faulconbridge we are presented, as it were, with three aspects of kingship: a sovereign whose very title is suspect, his youthful rival whose better claim is made the pawn of scheming politicians, and a bastard son of royalty who, finding his identity, is compelled to exercise the awful functions wherein the other two have failed. In other words, the bad, weak man in possession of the throne flouts the helpless rightful heir, brings his kingdom to distraction, and dies as the very "module of confounded royalty" while the Bastard rises to assume the kingly burden that the King himself could not sustain. By juxtaposing these contrapuntal ambiguities Shakespeare does great violence to the notion that might and right are always intertwined, but he makes us look anew at what Edmund Burke called the solemn plausibilities whereby we order our existence.

One such solemn plausibility is the moral authority of kingship, which is scrutinized relentlessly. In this play the eponymous hero is in fact an anti-hero whom we cannot admire and whom we find it easy to detest. Whereas the author of *The Troublesome Reign*, like virtually all the Tudor chroniclers, presents John as a Protestant martyr, a "warlike Christian" who

> set himself against the Man of Rome,
> Until base treason (by a damned wight)
> Did all his former triumphs put to flight,

Shakespeare, subordinating this facile chauvinistic theme, makes him unstable, treacherous, and cruel—an adventurer who has grasped a crown too big for him to wear. He is a king *de facto*, not *de jure*, whose "strong possession," not his "right," is all that he can claim. Even weaker than his title, however, is his conception of what a king should be and do, for he soils everything he touches. At three important junctures of his reign—his accession (which leads to such ignoble consequences), his humiliation and defeat by Rome, and the rebellion of the nobles who were pledged to his protection—he is shown to be a failure; and therefore it remains for his successor

> To set a form upon that indigest
> Which he hath left so shapeless and so rude.

John typifies the world in which he lives, which is a moral swamp and has the "smell of sin." He himself, abetted by his wolfish mother, moves from one betrayal to another; Lady Faulconbridge, accused by her own son of adultery, admits that she has been unfaithful to her husband; Philip of France, adept at power politics, forsakes the helpless Constance to make common cause with John and then betrays his new ally at papal instigation; Salisbury, citing the "infection of the time," deserts his hard-pressed king and then deserts the French when the traitorous Melun reveals their schemes; for all his unctuous piety, Pandulph is a savage papal politician; John, a royal guest, is poisoned by his host. It is therefore not surprising that the Bastard, instructed by his betters, declares that everyone is "mad" and concludes that "tickling commodity," a sly or ruthless sense of self-advantage, is

> the bias of the world—
> The world, who of itself is peized well,
> Made to run even upon even ground,
> Till this advantage, this vile-drawing bias,
> This sway of motion, this commodity,
> Makes it take head from all indifferency,
> From all direction, purpose, course, intent.
> (II.i.574–80)

It is significant, however, that this famous soliloquy (II.i) occurs so early in the play, for it is the start and not the end of the Bastard's hard-bought worldly knowledge. As John, initially so brisk and bold and callous, sinks through moral torpor to defeat, Faulconbridge grows strong in self-awareness. In a world of knaves and fools that is governed by "Commodity" he alone cuts through fraud and privileged error to assert the claims of valor, truth, and loyalty. With neither John's "possession" of the throne nor Arthur's "right" to it, he exemplifies the true regality of character, for in him there shines "the very spirit of Plantagenet."

He is therefore one of Shakespeare's grand creations. In him, as Johnson said, levity and greatness are united. One sign of his distinction is a superb vitality, which has a language all its own. Most of the other characters are insulated, as it were, in a rhetoric appropriate to their rank and function, and therefore it is hard to distinguish, say, Constance from the wailing woman or Pandulph from the papal legate; but Faulconbridge is nothing but himself. Slangy, coarse, and impudent, his language throbs with life; and whether mocking the pretensions of his brother or pointing to the "bare-pick'd bone of majesty" or rousing John to action he speaks in his own voice. As Mark Van Doren has observed, poetry works like yeast in every line he utters. Thus his comment on Hubert's brand of oratory:

> Here's a stay
> That shakes the rotten carcass of old Death
> Out of his rags! Here's a large mouth indeed,
> That spits forth death and mountains, rocks and seas,
> Talks as familiarly of roaring lions
> As maids of thirteen do of puppy-dogs!
> What cannoneer begot this lusty blood?
> He speaks plain cannon-fire, and smoke, and bounce,
> He gives the bastinado with his tongue;
> Our ears are cudgell'd—not a word of his
> But buffets better than a fist of France.
> 'Zounds, I was never so bethump'd with words
> Since I first call'd my brother's father dad.
> (II.i.455–67)

As a stylist, then, Faulconbridge ridicules and undercuts the fustian of the play; as a man of action he provides a contrast to the moral stupefaction of King John and all the others. His own position made uncertain by virtue of his birth, he is in a sense an uncommitted man; he has no dynastic aspirations of his own; and he stands outside the "tug and scamble" of dirty politics. A kind of Machiavel, as J. F. Danby has suggested, he is sometimes witty, saucy, and detached, sometimes blunt and crude, but we cannot resist his candor. As a "beggar," he remarks, he will rail upon the rich, but being rich himself he will "say there is no vice but beggary," for he is an opportunist who, instructed by his betters, is determined to survive at any cost.

> Since kings break faith upon commodity,
> Gain, be my lord, for I will worship thee.
> (II.i.597–98)

And yet Faulconbridge becomes the hero of the play, for he represents a kind of truth that bears the stamp of knowledge. This enables him to root his actions in belief, or at any rate in loyalties that he has tested by experience. He is true to England, which he would save at any cost, and also to his king; and although he does not formulate his politics in systematic terms, his instinct is unerring. Thus the nobles, when they come on Arthur's broken body, vent their wordy grief in rhetoric:

> This is the very top,
> The heighth, the crest, or crest unto the crest,
> Of murther's arms, (IV.iii.45–47)

and then slip into rebellion; but Faulconbridge, no less appalled than they, shows the loyalty and valor that mark him as a special man. Like most people of good will and elemental decency he is lost "among the thorns and dangers of this world," but when action is required, he acts. "Wherefore do you droop?" he asks the spineless, wicked king whom misfortune overwhelms,

> why look you sad?
> Be great in act, as you have been in thought.
> Let not the world see fear and sad distrust
> Govern the motion of a kingly eye.
> Be stirring as the time, be fire with fire,
> Threaten the threat'ner, and outface the brow

Of dragging horror; so shall inferior eyes,
That borrow their behaviors from the great,
Grow great by your example, and put on
The dauntless spirit of resolution.
Away, and glister like the god of war
When he intendeth to become the field.
Show boldness and aspiring confidence.
(V.i.44–56)

Wisely, John gives to Faulconbridge "the ordering of this present time," and Shakespeare gives to him the speech wherein, beneath the clatter of what some have called "Armada rhetoric," lies the final wisdom of the play:

This England never did, nor never shall,
Lie at the proud foot of a conqueror,
But when it first did help to wound itself.
Now these her princes are come home again,
Come the three corners of the world in arms,
And we shall shock them. Nought shall make us rue,
If England to itself do rest but true.

Herschel Baker

THE DESCENDANTS OF HENRY II

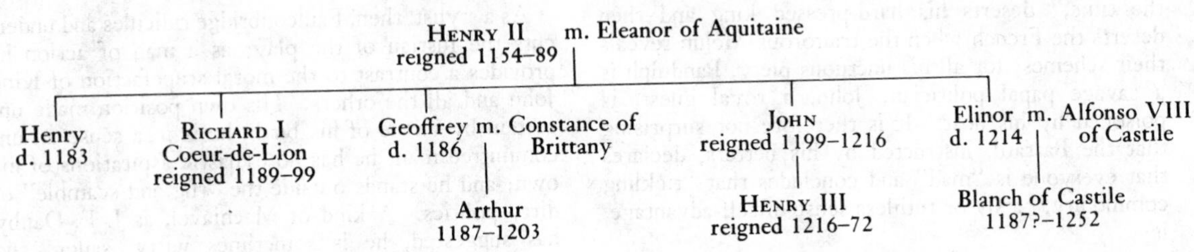

The Life and Death of King John

[Dramatis Personae

King John
Prince Henry, *son to the King*
Arthur, *Duke of Britain, nephew to the King*
Earl of Pembroke
Earl of Essex
Earl of Salisbury
Lord Bigot
Hubert de Burgh
Robert Faulconbridge, *son of Sir Robert Faulconbridge*
Philip the Bastard, *his half-brother (also called* Richard)
James Gurney, *servant to Lady Faulconbridge*
Peter of Pomfret, *a prophet*

Philip, *King of France*
Lewis, *the Dolphin*

Lymoges, *Duke of Austria*
Cardinal Pandulph, *the Pope's legate*
Melune, *a French lord*
Chatillion, *ambassador from France to King John*

Queen Elinor, *widow of Henry II, mother to King John*
Constance, *widow of Geffrey, John's elder brother, mother to Arthur*
Blanch of Spain, *daughter to the King of Castile, niece to King John*
Lady Faulconbridge, *widow of Sir Robert Faulconbridge*

Lords, Citizens *of* Angiers, Sheriff, Heralds, Officers, Soldiers, Executioners, Messengers, *and* Attendants

Scene: *Partly in England, and partly in France*]

ACT I, Scene I

Enter King John, Queen Elinor, Pembroke, Essex, *and* Salisbury, *with the* Chatillion *of France*.

K. John. Now say, Chatillion, what would France with us?
Chat. Thus, after greeting, speaks the King of France
In my behavior to the majesty,
The borrowed majesty, of England here.
El. A strange beginning: "borrowed majesty"!
K. John. Silence, good mother, hear the embassy.
Chat. Philip of France, in right and true behalf
Of thy deceased brother Geffrey's son,
Arthur Plantagenet, lays most lawful claim
To this fair island and the territories,
To Ireland, Poictiers, Anjou, Touraine, Maine,
Desiring thee to lay aside the sword
Which sways usurpingly these several titles,
And put the same into young Arthur's hand,
Thy nephew and right royal sovereign.
K. John. What follows if we disallow of this?
Chat. The proud control of fierce and bloody war,
To enforce these rights so forcibly withheld.
K. John. Here have we war for war and blood for blood,
Controlment for controlment: so answer France.
Chat. Then take my King's defiance from my mouth,
The farthest limit of my embassy.
K. John. Bear mine to him, and so depart in peace.
Be thou as lightning in the eyes of France;
For ere thou canst report, I will be there;
The thunder of my cannon shall be heard.

Words and passages enclosed in square brackets in the text above are either emendations of the copy-text or additions to it. The Textual Notes immediately following the play cite the earliest authority for every such change or insertion and supply the reading of the copy-text wherever it is emended in this edition.

I.i. Location: England. King John's palace.
1. France: King of France.
3. In my behavior: in my words and deeds, i.e. through me.
4. borrowed: stolen, i.e. spurious. **6. embassy:** message.
7–15. Philip . . . sovereign. Just before the death of King Richard I, says Holinshed (Bullough, IV, 25), he had "assigned the crowne of England, and all other his lands and dominions" to his youngest brother John, who was duly crowned in May 1199. On the other hand John's nephew Arthur, posthumous son of Geoffrey of Brittany, inherited from his father the duchies of Anjou, Maine, and Touraine, and was recognized as their "liege and sovereigne lord." There is no evidence for Philip II's bellicose assertion of Arthur's claim to England as Shakespeare represents it here.

9. Plantagenet: family name of members of the royal family. See note to *1 Henry VI*, II.iv o.s.d. **13. titles:** possessions.
14. young Arthur's hand. Depicted in this play as a gentle child of eight or so, Arthur was sixteen when he was murdered, probably at John's instigation, in 1203. Holinshed (Bullough, IV, 26) calls him "but a babe to speake of." **17. control:** compulsion.
26. cannon. An anachronism; gunpowder was not used in western Europe until the fourteenth century.

So hence! Be thou the trumpet of our wrath,
And sullen presage of your own decay.
An honorable conduct let him have.
Pembroke, look to't. Farewell, Chatillion.

Exeunt Chatillion and Pembroke.

El. What now, my son, have I not ever said
How that ambitious Constance would not cease
Till she had kindled France, and all the world,
Upon the right and party of her son?
This might have been prevented and made whole
With very easy arguments of love,
Which now the manage of two kingdoms must
With fearful bloody issue arbitrate.

K. John. Our strong possession and our right for us.

El. Your strong possession much more than your right,
Or else it must go wrong with you and me;
So much my conscience whispers in your ear,
Which none but heaven, and you, and I, shall hear.

Enter a SHERIFF [*and whispers Essex in the ear*].

Essex. My liege, here is the strangest controversy
Come from the country to be judg'd by you
That e'er I heard. Shall I produce the men?

K. John. Let them approach. [*Exit Sheriff.*]
Our abbeys and our priories shall pay
This [expedition's] charge.

Enter ROBERT FAULCONBRIDGE *and* PHILIP [THE BASTARD].

What men are you?

Bast. Your faithful subject I, a gentleman,
Born in Northamptonshire, and eldest son,
As I suppose, to Robert Faulconbridge,
A soldier, by the honor-giving hand
Of Cordelion knighted in the field.

K. John. What art thou?

Rob. The son and heir to that same Faulconbridge.

K. John. Is that the elder, and art thou the heir?
You came not of one mother then, it seems.

Bast. Most certain of one mother, mighty King—
That is well known—and, as I think, one father;
But for the certain knowledge of that truth
I put you o'er to heaven and to my mother.
Of that I doubt, as all men's children may.

El. Out on thee, rude man, thou dost shame thy mother,
And wound her honor with this diffidence.

Bast. I, madam? No, I have no reason for it;
That is my brother's plea and none of mine,
The which if he can prove, 'a pops me out
At least from fair five hundred pound a year.
Heaven guard my mother's honor, and my land!

K. John. A good blunt fellow. Why, being younger born,
Doth he lay claim to thine inheritance?

Bast. I know not why, except to get the land;
But once he slander'd me with bastardy.
But whe'er I be as true begot or no,
That still I lay upon my mother's head,
But that I am as well begot, my liege
(Fair fall the bones that took the pains for me!),
Compare our faces, and be judge yourself.
If old Sir Robert did beget us both,
And were our father, and this son like him,
O old Sir Robert, father, on my knee
I give heaven thanks I was not like to thee!

K. John. Why, what a madcap hath heaven lent us here!

El. He hath a trick of Cordelion's face,
The accent of his tongue affecteth him.
Do you not read some tokens of my son
In the large composition of this man?

K. John. Mine eye hath well examined his parts,
And finds them perfect Richard. Sirrah, speak,
What doth move you to claim your brother's land?

Bast. Because he hath a half-face like my father!
With half that face would he have all my land—
A half-fac'd groat five hundred pound a year!

Rob. My gracious liege, when that my father liv'd,
Your brother did employ my father much—

Bast. Well, sir, by this you cannot get my land;
Your tale must be how he employ'd my mother.

Rob. And once dispatch'd him in an embassy
To Germany, there with the Emperor
To treat of high affairs touching that time.
Th' advantage of his absence took the King,
And in the mean time sojourn'd at my father's;
Where how he did prevail I shame to speak.
But truth is truth. Large lengths of seas and shores
Between my father and my mother lay,
As I have heard my father speak himself,
When this same lusty gentleman was got.
Upon his death-bed he by will bequeath'd
His lands to me, and took it on his death
That this my mother's son was none of his;
And if he were, he came into the world
Full fourteen weeks before the course of time.
Then, good my liege, let me have what is mine,
My father's land, as was my father's will.

K. John. Sirrah, your brother is legitimate,
Your father's wife did after wedlock bear him;
And if she did play false, the fault was hers,
Which fault lies on the hazards of all husbands
That marry wives. Tell me, how if my brother,

28. sullen presage: dismal portent. **decay:** destruction.
34. Upon: in support of. **36. arguments of love:** friendly negotiation.
37. manage: government. **38. issue:** consequence.
44. liege: sovereign.
54. Cordelion: Coeur-de-Lion (Lionheart), i.e. Richard I, who reputedly earned the sobriquet when, pitted against a lion by his captor Leopold, Archduke of Austria, he thrust his hand into the creature's mouth and tore out its heart. **62. put you o'er:** refer you.
64. rude: coarse. **65. diffidence:** mistrust. **68. 'a:** he.

74. once: in short. **75. true:** legitimately.
76. lay . . . head: leave it to my mother to say.
78. Fair fall: may good befall. **81. this son:** i.e. Robert.
85. trick: characteristic expression. **86. affecteth:** resembles.
88. large: general.
90. Sirrah: customary form of address to an inferior.
92. half-face: (1) profile; (2) pinched face.
94. half-fac'd groat: thin silver coin (worth fourpence) bearing the sovereign's head in profile. **96. Your brother:** i.e. King Richard.
108. got: begotten.
110. took . . . death: i.e. took a solemn oath, swore.
113. course: due course. **119. lies on:** is one of.

Who, as you say, took pains to get this son,
Had of your father claim'd this son for his?
In sooth, good friend, your father might have kept
This calf, bred from his cow, from all the world;
In sooth he might; then if he were my brother's,
My brother might not claim him, nor your father,
Being none of his, refuse him. This concludes:
My mother's son did get your father's heir;
Your father's heir must have your father's land.
Rob. Shall then my father's will be of no force
To dispossess that child which is not his?
Bast. Of no more force to dispossess me, sir,
Than was his will to get me, as I think.
El. Whether hadst thou rather be a Faulconbridge,
And like thy brother, to enjoy thy land;
Or the reputed son of Cordelion,
Lord of thy presence and no land beside?
Bast. Madam, and if my brother had my shape
And I had his, Sir Robert's his, like him,
And if my legs were two such riding-rods,
My arms such eel-skins stuff'd, my face so thin
That in mine ear I durst not stick a rose
Lest men should say, "Look where three-farthings goes!"
And to his shape were heir to all this land,
Would I might never stir from off this place,
I would give it every foot to have this face;
It would not be Sir Nob in any case.
El. I like thee well. Wilt thou forsake thy fortune,
Bequeath thy land to him, and follow me?
I am a soldier, and now bound to France.
Bast. Brother, take you my land, I'll take my chance.
Your face hath got five hundred pound a year,
Yet sell your face for five pence and 'tis dear.
Madam, I'll follow you unto the death.
El. Nay, I would have you go before me thither.
Bast. Our country manners give our betters way.
K. John. What is thy name?
Bast. Philip, my liege, so is my name begun,
Philip, good old Sir Robert's wive's eldest son.
K. John. From henceforth bear his name whose form thou bearest:
Kneel thou down Philip, but rise more great,
Arise Sir Richard, and Plantagenet.
Bast. Brother by th' mother's side, give me your hand;
My father gave me honor, yours gave land.
Now blessed be the hour by night or day
When I was got, Sir Robert was away!
El. The very spirit of Plantagenet!
I am thy grandame, Richard, call me so.
Bast. Madam, by chance, but not by truth; what though?
Something about, a little from the right,
In at the window, or else o'er the hatch.
Who dares not stir by day must walk by night,
And have is have, however men do catch.
Near or far off, well won is still well shot,
And I am I, howe'er I was begot.
K. John. Go, Faulconbridge, now hast thou thy desire,
A landless knight makes thee a landed squire.
Come, madam, and come, Richard, we must speed
For France, for France, for it is more than need.
Bast. Brother, adieu, good fortune come to thee!
For thou wast got i' th' way of honesty.
Exeunt all but Bastard.
A foot of honor better than I was,
But many a many foot of land the worse.
Well, now can I make any Joan a lady.
"Good den, Sir Richard!" "God-a-mercy, fellow!"
And if his name be George, I'll call him Peter;
For new-made honor doth forget men's names;
'Tis too respective and too sociable
For your conversion. Now your traveller,
He and his toothpick at my worship's mess,
And when my knightly stomach is suffic'd,
Why then I suck my teeth, and catechize
My picked man of countries. "My dear sir,"
Thus, leaning on mine elbow, I begin,
"I shall beseech you"—that is question now;
And then comes answer like an Absey book:
"O sir," says answer, "at your best command,
At your employment, at your service, sir."
"No, sir," says question, "I, sweet sir, at yours";
And so ere answer knows what question would,
Saving in dialogue of compliment,
And talking of the Alps and Apennines,
The Pyrenean and the river Po,
It draws toward supper in conclusion so.
But this is worshipful society,
And fits the mounting spirit like myself;
For he is but a bastard to the time
That doth not [smack] of observation—
And so am I, whether I smack or no;
And not alone in habit and device,
Exterior form, outward accoutrement,
But from the inward motion to deliver

127. refuse: disclaim. **concludes:** resolves the problem.
137. Lord . . . presence: i.e. your own master (as having royal blood) (?). Cf. II.i.367. **138. and if:** if
139. Sir Robert's his. An archaic double genitive.
140. riding-rods: switches.
143. three-farthings. Certain coins of small value were stamped with a rose behind the Queen's head.
144. to his shape: in addition to inheriting his physique.
147. Nob: nickname for Robert.
156. give . . . way: require that our betters precede us.
159. wive's: wife's.

169. truth: virtue. **170. Something about:** rather indirectly.
171. o'er the hatch: conceived out of wedlock (proverbial). A hatch is the lower half of a door opening in two parts.
182. foot: footing, status.
184. lady: title appropriate for the wife of a knight.
185. Good den: good even. (The Bastard imagines an encounter between himself and a rustic.) **God-a-mercy:** God reward you, i.e. thank you.
188–89. 'Tis . . . conversion: it is showing too much respect and sociability for one just promoted.
190. toothpick. A common affectation with travellers. **my worship's mess:** i.e. my dinner table. A knight was commonly addressed as "your worship." **193. picked:** (1) spruce; (2) with picked teeth.
196. Absey book: ABC book, primer. Such books were often cast in the form of a dialogue between master and pupil.
207. bastard . . . time: no true son of the age, unfashionable.
208. doth . . . observation: is not somewhat given to obsequiousness.
209. so am I: i.e. not a true child of the time.
210. habit: attire. **device:** knightly insignia.
212. from: lacking. **inward motion:** inclination.

Sweet, sweet, sweet poison for the age's tooth,
Which though I will not practice to deceive,
Yet to avoid deceit, I mean to learn;
For it shall strew the footsteps of my rising.
But who comes in such haste in riding-robes?
What woman-post is this? Hath she no husband
That will take pains to blow a horn before her?

Enter LADY FAULCONBRIDGE *and* JAMES GURNEY.

O me, 'tis my mother. How now, good lady,
What brings you here to court so hastily?

Lady F. Where is that slave, thy brother? Where is he,
That holds in chase mine honor up and down?

Bast. My brother Robert, old Sir Robert's son?
Colbrand the giant, that same mighty man?
Is it Sir Robert's son that you seek so?

Lady F. Sir Robert's son! Ay, thou unreverend boy,
Sir Robert's son! Why scorn'st thou at Sir Robert?
He is Sir Robert's son, and so art thou.

Bast. James Gurney, wilt thou give us leave a while?

Gur. Good leave, good Philip.

Bast. Philip? sparrow! James,
There's toys abroad; anon I'll tell thee more.

Exit James [*Gurney*].

Madam, I was not old Sir Robert's son;
Sir Robert might have eat his part in me
Upon Good Friday and ne'er broke his fast.
Sir Robert could do well—marry, to confess—
Could [he] get me. Sir Robert could not do it;
We know his handiwork. Therefore, good mother,
To whom am I beholding for these limbs?
Sir Robert never holp to make this leg.

Lady F. Hast thou conspired with thy brother too,
That for thine own gain shouldst defend mine honor?
What means this scorn, thou most untoward knave?

Bast. Knight, knight, good mother, Basilisco-like.
What, I am dubb'd! I have it on my shoulder.
But, mother, I am not Sir Robert's son,
I have disclaim'd Sir Robert and my land,
Legitimation, name, and all is gone;
Then, good my mother, let me know my father;
Some proper man, I hope. Who was it, mother?

Lady F. Hast thou denied thyself a Faulconbridge?

Bast. As faithfully as I deny the devil.

Lady F. King Richard Cordelion was thy father.
By long and vehement suit I was seduc'd
To make room for him in my husband's bed.
Heaven! lay not my transgression to my charge,
That art the issue of my dear offense,
Which was so strongly urg'd past my defense.

Bast. Now by this light, were I to get again,
Madam, I would not wish a better father.
Some sins do bear their privilege on earth,
And so doth yours: your fault was not your folly;
Needs must you lay your heart at his dispose,
Subjected tribute to commanding love,
Against whose fury and unmatched force
The aweless lion could not wage the fight,
Nor keep his princely heart from Richard's hand.
He that perforce robs lions of their hearts
May easily win a woman's. Ay, my mother,
With all my heart I thank thee for my father!
Who lives and dares but say thou didst not well
When I was got, I'll send his soul to hell.
Come, lady, I will show thee to my kin,
And they shall say, when Richard me begot,
If thou hadst said him nay, it had been sin.
Who says it was, he lies, I say 'twas not. *Exeunt.*

[ACT II,] SCENE [I]

Enter, before Angiers, PHILIP, *King of France,* LEWIS [*the*] *Dolphin,* CONSTANCE, ARTHUR, [*with forces, at one door; at the other,*] AUSTRIA [*with forces*].

[*K. Phi.*] Before Angiers well met, brave Austria.
Arthur, that great forerunner of thy blood,
Richard, that robb'd the lion of his heart,
And fought the holy wars in Palestine,
By this brave duke came early to his grave;
And for amends to his posterity,
At our importance hither is he come
To spread his colors, boy, in thy behalf,
And to rebuke the usurpation
Of thy unnatural uncle, English John.
Embrace him, love him, give him welcome hither.

Arth. God shall forgive you Cordelion's death
The rather that you give his offspring life,
Shadowing their right under your wings of war.
I give you welcome with a powerless hand,

213. poison: i.e. flattery. **tooth:** appetite.
215. deceit: being deceived.
218. woman-post: female messenger.
219. horn. Alluding to the cuckold's horns.
223. holds in chase: pursues.
225. Colbrand: Danish giant overcome by Guy in the popular romance *Guy of Warwick*. **227. unreverend:** disrespectful.
230. give us leave: leave us alone.
231. Philip? sparrow: i.e. use that name for sparrows (which were commonly called Philip), not for me.
232. There's toys abroad. Another jocular hint that interesting things have been happening.
236. do: copulate. **marry:** indeed (originally the name of the Virgin Mary used as an oath). **239. beholding:** beholden, indebted.
240. holp: helped. **243. untoward:** unmannerly.
244. Knight . . . Basilisco-like. An allusion to the contemporary play *Soliman and Perseda*, in which the braggart knight Basilisco is called a knave by his servant.
245. dubb'd: formally created a knight with a sword-tap on the shoulder. **250. proper:** handsome.

256. lay. The implied subject is *thou* (i.e. the Bastard).
257. dear: grievous. **259. get:** be conceived.
261. do . . . privilege: i.e. are venial. **263. dispose:** disposal.

II.i. o.s.d. Angiers: Angers, city in northwestern France, capital of the duchy of Anjou. **Dolphin:** Dauphin, title of the heir apparent of the King of France.
4. fought . . . Palestine. With his allies Philip II of France and Emperor Frederick I (Barbarossa), Richard had been a leader of the Third Crusade (1190–92).
5. By . . . grave. Like the author of *The Troublesome Reign of King John* (Bullough, IV, 83–84), Shakespeare confusingly identifies Widomar, Viscount of Limoges, with Leopold, Archduke of Austria. Richard had been imprisoned briefly by Leopold in 1193–94, and he was fatally wounded while besieging Widomar's castle in 1199.
7. importance: importunity. **8. colors:** flags.
13. offspring: descendants. **14. Shadowing:** protecting.

But with a heart full of unstained love.
Welcome before the gates of Angiers, Duke.
[*K. Phi.*] A noble boy! Who would not do thee right?
Aust. Upon thy cheek lay I this zealous kiss
As seal to this indenture of my love:
That to my home I will no more return
Till Angiers, and the right thou hast in France,
Together with that pale, that white-fac'd shore,
Whose foot spurns back the ocean's roaring tides
And coops from other lands her islanders,
Even till that England, hedg'd in with the main,
That water-walled bulwark, still secure
And confident from foreign purposes,
Even till that utmost corner of the west
Salute thee for her king; till then, fair boy,
Will I not think of home, but follow arms.
Const. O, take his mother's thanks, a widow's thanks,
Till your strong hand shall help to give him strength
To make a more requital to your love!
Aust. The peace of heaven is theirs that lift their swords
In such a just and charitable war.
K. Phi. Well, then to work! Our cannon shall be bent
Against the brows of this resisting town.
Call for our chiefest men of discipline
To cull the plots of best advantages.
We'll lay before this town our royal bones,
Wade to the market-place in Frenchmen's blood,
But we will make it subject to this boy.
Const. Stay for an answer to your embassy,
Lest unadvis'd you stain your swords with blood.
My Lord Chatillion may from England bring
That right in peace which here we urge in war,
And then we shall repent each drop of blood
That hot rash haste so indirectly shed.

Enter CHATILLION.

K. Phi. A wonder, lady! Lo upon thy wish
Our messenger Chatillion is arriv'd!
What England says, say briefly, gentle lord,
We coldly pause for thee; Chatillion, speak.
Chat. Then turn your forces from this paltry siege,
And stir them up against a mightier task.
England, impatient of your just demands,
Hath put himself in arms. The adverse winds,
Whose leisure I have stay'd, have given him time
To land his legions all as soon as I;
His marches are expedient to this town,
His forces strong, his soldiers confident.
With him along is come the mother-queen,
An [Ate,] stirring him to blood and strife;

25. coops: encloses for protection or defense. **27. still**: always.
32. a widow's thanks. Another error copied from *The Troublesome Reign* (Bullough, IV, 95). At the time represented, Constance was married to her third husband, Guy de Thouars. **34. more**: greater.
37. bent: aimed. **39. discipline**: i.e. military science.
40. cull . . . advantages: select the most suitable positions.
43. But: unless. **45. unadvis'd**: unwisely. **49. indirectly**: unjustly.
52. England: the King of England.
53. coldly: calmly, dispassionately. **60. expedient**: speedy.
63. Ate: Greek goddess of discord.

With her her niece, the Lady Blanch of Spain;
With them a bastard of the king's deceas'd,
And all th' unsettled humors of the land,
Rash, inconsiderate, fiery voluntaries,
With ladies' faces and fierce dragons' spleens,
Have sold their fortunes at their native homes,
Bearing their birthrights proudly on their backs,
To make a hazard of new fortunes here.
In brief, a braver choice of dauntless spirits
Than now the English bottoms have waft o'er
Did never float upon the swelling tide
To do offense and scathe in Christendom.
The interruption of their churlish drums
Cuts off more circumstance. They are at hand,
Drum beats.
To parley or to fight, therefore prepare.
K. Phi. How much unlook'd for is this expedition!
Aust. By how much unexpected, by so much
We must awake endeavor for defense,
For courage mounteth with occasion.
Let them be welcome then, we are prepar'd.

Enter [JOHN,] *King of England*, BASTARD, QUEEN [ELINOR], BLANCH, PEMBROKE, *and others.*

K. John. Peace be to France—if France in peace permit
Our just and lineal entrance to our own;
If not, bleed France, and peace ascend to heaven,
Whiles we, God's wrathful agent, do correct
Their proud contempt that beats his peace to heaven.
K. Phi. Peace be to England, if that war return
From France to England, there to live in peace.
England we love, and for that England's sake
With burden of our armor here we sweat.
This toil of ours should be a work of thine;
But thou from loving England art so far
That thou hast under-wrought his lawful king,
Cut off the sequence of posterity,
Outfaced infant state, and done a rape
Upon the maiden virtue of the crown.
Look here upon thy brother Geffrey's face:
These eyes, these brows, were moulded out of his;
This little abstract doth contain that large
Which died in Geffrey; and the hand of time
Shall draw this brief into as huge a volume.
That Geffrey was thy elder brother born,
And this his son; England was Geffrey's right,

64. niece: i.e. granddaughter (a common Elizabethan usage). One of Elinor's daughters by Henry II married King Alfonso of Castile.
65. of . . . deceas'd: of the dead king (a double genitive).
66. unsettled humors: unruly, disaffected men.
67. voluntaries: volunteers.
68. spleens. In Elizabethan psychology the spleen was the seat of passion.
70. Bearing . . . backs: i.e. having squandered everything they possessed on armor. **73. bottoms**: ships. **waft**: wafted.
75. scathe: injury. **76. churlish**: rough.
77. circumstance: detail. **79. expedition**: speed.
82. occasion: emergency. **85. lineal**: due by hereditary right.
91. England's: i.e. Arthur's, for he, as Philip thinks, is the lawful king of England. **95. under-wrought his**: undermined its.
96. posterity: lineal descent.
97. Outfaced infant state: defied the authority of the child-king.
101. little abstract: epitome. **101–2. that large Which**: that which large (=complete, in full).
103. draw this brief: expand this summasy.

And this is Geffrey's in the name of God.
How comes it then that thou art call'd a king,
When living blood doth in these temples beat,
Which owe the crown that thou o'ermasterest?
K. John. From whom hast thou this great commission, France,
To draw my answer from thy articles?
K. Phi. From that supernal judge that stirs good thoughts
In any [breast] of strong authority,
To look into the blots and stains of right.
That judge hath made me guardian to this boy,
Under whose warrant I impeach thy wrong,
And by whose help I mean to chastise it.
K. John. Alack, thou dost usurp authority.
K. Phi. Excuse it is to beat usurping down.
El. Who is it thou dost call usurper, France?
Const. Let me make answer: thy usurping son.
El. Out, insolent, thy bastard shall be king
That thou mayst be a queen, and check the world!
Const. My bed was ever to thy son as true
As thine was to thy husband, and this boy
Liker in feature to his father Geffrey
Than thou and John in manners, being as like
As rain to water, or devil to his dam.
My boy a bastard? By my soul I think
His father never was so true begot—
It cannot be, and if thou wert his mother.
El. There's a good mother, boy, that blots thy father.
Const. There's a good grandame, boy, that would blot thee.
Aust. Peace!
Bast. Hear the crier.
Aust. What the devil art thou?
Bast. One that will play the devil, sir, with you,
And 'a may catch your hide and you alone.
You are the hare of whom the proverb goes,
Whose valor plucks dead lions by the beard;
I'll smoke your skin-coat and I catch you right.
Sirrah, look to't, i' faith I will, i' faith.
Blanch. O, well did he become that lion's robe,
That did disrobe the lion of that robe!
Bast. It lies as sightly on the back of him
As great Alcides' [shows] upon an ass.
But, ass, I'll take that burthen from your back,
Or lay on that shall make your shoulders crack.
Aust. What cracker is this same that deafs our ears
With this abundance of superfluous breath?
King [Philip], determine what we shall do straight.

106. this: i.e. the city of Angers, to which King Philip points (?) Depending on the actor's gesture, it might instead mean Arthur or John's crown. **109. owe:** own. **110. commission:** warrant.
111. articles: items in a formal indictment.
116. impeach: formally accuse.
119. Excuse . . . down: the excuse (for my usurpation of authority) is that I am resisting usurpation. **123. check:** control.
132. blots: slanders.
136. hide: the lion's skin that Austria wears to commemorate his victory over Richard I. **139. smoke:** beat.
140. Sirrah: customary form of address to an inferior (hence an insult here). **143. sightly:** appropriately.
144. Alcides: Hercules, who wore the skin of the Nemean lion that he had slain. **146. that:** that which, i.e. a club.
147. cracker: boaster.

[*K. Phi.*] Women and fools, break off your conference.
King John, this is the very sum of all:
England and Ireland, [Anjou], Touraine, Maine,
In right of Arthur do I claim of thee.
Wilt thou resign them and lay down thy arms?
K. John. My life as soon. I do defy thee, France.
Arthur of Britain, yield thee to my hand,
And out of my dear love I'll give thee more
Than e'er the coward hand of France can win.
Submit thee, boy.
El. Come to thy grandame, child.
Const. Do, child, go to it grandame, child,
Give grandame kingdom, and it grandame will
Give it a plum, a cherry, and a fig.
There's a good grandame.
Arth. Good my mother, peace.
I would that I were low laid in my grave,
I am not worth this coil that's made for me.
El. His mother shames him so, poor boy, he weeps.
Const. Now shame upon you, whe'er she does or no!
His grandame's wrongs, and not his mother's shames,
Draws those heaven-moving pearls from his poor eyes,
Which heaven shall take in nature of a fee;
Ay, with these crystal beads heaven shall be brib'd
To do him justice, and revenge on you.
El. Thou monstrous slanderer of heaven and earth!
Const. Thou monstrous injurer of heaven and earth,
Call not me slanderer! Thou and thine usurp
The dominations, royalties, and rights
Of this oppressed boy. This is thy eldest son's son,
Infortunate in nothing but in thee.
Thy sins are visited in this poor child,
The canon of the law is laid on him,
Being but the second generation
Removed from thy sin-conceiving womb.
K. John. Bedlam, have done.
Const. I have but this to say,
That he is not only plagued for her sin,
But God hath made her sin and her the plague
On this removed issue, plagued for her,
And with her plague, her sin; his injury
Her injury, the beadle to her sin—
All punish'd in the person of this child,
And all for her. A plague upon her!

150. fools: children. **156. Britain:** Brittany.
160–63. Do . . . grandame. Contemptuous baby talk.
165. coil: turmoil.
176. dominations: dominions. **royalties:** royal prerogatives and dignities.
177. eldest son's son: eldest grandson (not "son of your eldest son").
178. Infortunate: unfortunate. **179. visited:** punished.
180. canon . . . law: Exodus 20:5, which asserts that God is jealous, "visiting the iniquity of the fathers upon the children unto the third and fourth generation of them that hate me." **183. Bedlam:** lunatic.
184–90. That . . . upon her. The sense of this obscurely worded passage is clear: Arthur is being chastised for his grandmother's wickedness, and she and John—himself the product of her sin—are sent to punish him unjustly.
184. sin: i.e. in conceiving John out of wedlock (as Constance had implied in lines 129–31). **185. her sin:** i.e. John.
186. removed issue: distant descendant, i.e. Arthur.
187. his injury: i.e. the wrong done to Arthur.
188. Her . . . sin: i.e. the wrong she has done lashes John (*her sin*) on to further wrongs. **beadle:** parish official who administers corporal punishment.

El. Thou unadvised scold, I can produce
A will that bars the title of thy son.
Const. Ay, who doubts that? A will! a wicked will,
A woman's will, a cank'red grandam's will!
K. Phi. Peace, lady, pause, or be more temperate.
It ill beseems this presence to cry aim
To these ill-tuned repetitions.
Some trumpet summon hither to the walls
These men of Angiers; let us hear them speak
Whose title they admit, Arthur's or John's.

Trumpet sounds. Enter [HUBERT *and other* CITIZENS] *upon the walls.*

[*Hub.*] Who is it that hath warn'd us to the walls?
K. Phi. 'Tis France, for England.
K. John. England for itself.
You men of Angiers, and my loving subjects—
K. Phi. You loving men of Angiers, Arthur's subjects,
Our trumpet call'd you to this gentle parle—
K. John. For our advantage—therefore hear us first:
These flags of France, that are advanced here
Before the eye and prospect of your town,
Have hither march'd to your endamagement.
The cannons have their bowels full of wrath,
And ready mounted are they to spit forth
Their iron indignation 'gainst your walls;
All preparation for a bloody siege
And merciless proceeding by these French
[Confronts your] city's eyes, your winking gates;
And but for our approach those sleeping stones,
That as a waist doth girdle you about,
By the compulsion of their ordinance
By this time from their fixed beds of lime
Had been dishabited, and wide havoc made
For bloody power to rush upon your peace.
But on the sight of us, your lawful King,
Who painfully with much expedient march
Have brought a countercheck before your gates,
To save unscratch'd your city's threat'ned cheeks,
Behold, the French amaz'd vouchsafe a parle,
And now instead of bullets wrapp'd in fire,
To make a shaking fever in your walls,
They shoot but calm words folded up in smoke,
To make a faithless error in your ears;
Which trust accordingly, kind citizens,
And let us in—your King, whose labor'd spirits,
Forewearied in this action of swift speed,
Craves harborage within your city walls.
K. Phi. When I have said, make answer to us both.
Lo in this right hand, whose protection
Is most divinely vow'd upon the right
Of him it holds, stands young Plantagenet,
Son to the elder brother of this man,
And king o'er him and all that he enjoys.
For this down-trodden equity, we tread
In warlike march these greens before your town,
Being no further enemy to you
Than the constraint of hospitable zeal
In the relief of this oppressed child
Religiously provokes. Be pleased then
To pay that duty which you truly owe
To him that owes it, namely this young prince,
And then our arms, like to a muzzled bear,
Save in aspect, hath all offense seal'd up;
Our cannons' malice vainly shall be spent
Against th' [invulnerable] clouds of heaven,
And with a blessed and unvex'd retire,
With unhack'd swords, and helmets all unbruis'd,
We will bear home that lusty blood again
Which here we came to spout against your town,
And leave your children, wives, and you in peace.
But if you fondly pass our proffer'd offer,
'Tis not the rounder of your old-fac'd walls
Can hide you from our messengers of war,
Though all these English and their discipline
Were harbor'd in their rude circumference.
Then tell us, shall your city call us lord,
In that behalf which we have challeng'd it?
Or shall we give the signal to our rage,
And stalk in blood to our possession?
[*Hub.*] In brief, we are the King of England's subjects:
For him, and in his right, we hold this town.
K. John. Acknowledge then the King, and let me in.
[*Hub.*] That can we not; but he that proves the King,
To him will we prove loyal. Till that time
Have we ramm'd up our gates against the world.
K. John. Doth not the crown of England prove the King?
And if not that, I bring you witnesses,
Twice fifteen thousand hearts of England's breed—
Bast. Bastards, and else.
K. John. To verify our title with their lives.
K. Phi. As many and as well-born bloods as those—
Bast. Some bastards too.
K. Phi. Stand in his face to contradict his claim.
[*Hub.*] Till you compound whose right is worthiest,
We for the worthiest hold the right from both.
K. John. Then God forgive the sin of all those souls
That to their everlasting residence,
Before the dew of evening fall, shall fleet
In dreadful trial of our kingdom's king!

191. unadvised: rash. **192. A will.** See note to I.i.7–15.
196–97. cry aim To: encourage (a term from archery).
198. trumpet: trumpeter. **205. parle:** parley.
207. advanced: raised. **215. winking:** shut.
218. ordinance: ordnance.
220. dishabited: dislodged. **havoc:** i.e. breach.
223. expedient: speedy. **226. amaz'd:** stunned.
227. bullets: cannon balls. **229. smoke:** i.e. breath.
230. faithless error: disloyal lie. **233. Forewearied in:** exhausted by.
237. divinely: piously. **upon:** i.e. to defend.

241. down-trodden equity: flouted right.
244. constraint: necessity. **248. owes:** owns, has a right to.
250. Save in aspect: except in appearance.
253. unvex'd retire: orderly withdrawal.
258. fondly pass: foolishly reject.
259. rounder: roundure, i.e. circle, circumference.
264. In . . . which: on behalf of him for whom.
270. proves: proves to be. **276. else:** others.
278. bloods: men of spirit and good families.
281. compound: determine. **285. fleet:** leave their bodies.

K. Phi. Amen, amen! Mount, chevaliers! To arms!
Bast. Saint George, that swing'd the dragon, and e'er since
Sits on 's horseback at mine hostess' door,
Teach us some fence! [*To Austria.*] Sirrah, were I at home,
At your den, sirrah, with your lioness,
I would set an ox-head to your lion's hide,
And make a monster of you.
Aust. Peace, no more.
Bast. O, tremble! for you hear the lion roar.
K. John. Up higher to the plain, where we'll set forth
In best appointment all our regiments.
Bast. Speed then to take advantage of the field.
K. Phi. It shall be so, and at the other hill
Command the rest to stand. God and our right!
Exeunt. [*Hubert and Citizens remain above.*]

Here, after excursions, enter the Herald of France *with Trumpets to the gates.*

F. Her. You men of Angiers, open wide your gates,
And let young Arthur Duke of Britain in,
Who by the hand of France this day hath made
Much work for tears in many an English mother,
Whose sons lie scattered on the bleeding ground.
Many a widow's husband grovelling lies,
Coldly embracing the discolored earth,
And victory with little loss doth play
Upon the dancing banners of the French,
Who are at hand, triumphantly displayed,
To enter conquerors, and to proclaim
Arthur of Britain England's King and yours.

Enter English Herald *with Trumpet.*

E. Her. Rejoice, you men of Angiers, ring your bells,
King John, your King and England's, doth approach,
Commander of this hot malicious day.
Their armors, that march'd hence so silver-bright,
Hither return all gilt with Frenchmen's blood.
There stuck no plume in any English crest
That is removed by a staff of France;
Our colors do return in those same hands
That did display them when we first march'd forth;
And like a jolly troop of huntsmen come
Our lusty English, all with purpled hands,
Dy'd in the dying slaughter of their foes.
Open your gates and give the victors way.
Hub. Heralds, from off our tow'rs we might behold,
From first to last, the onset and retire
Of both your armies, whose equality
By our best eyes cannot be censured.
Blood hath bought blood, and blows have answer'd blows;
Strength match'd with strength, and power confronted power:
Both are alike, and both alike we like.
One must prove greatest. While they weigh so even,
We hold our town for neither; yet for both.

Enter the two Kings *with their powers at several doors.*

K. John. France, hast thou yet more blood to cast away?
Say, shall the current of our right roam on?
Whose passage, vex'd with thy impediment,
Shall leave his native channel and o'erswell
With course disturb'd even thy confining shores,
Unless thou let his silver water keep
A peaceful progress to the ocean.
K. Phi. England, thou hast not sav'd one drop of blood
In this hot trial more than we of France,
Rather lost more. And by this hand I swear,
That sways the earth this climate overlooks,
Before we will lay down our just-borne arms
We'll put thee down, 'gainst whom these arms we bear,
Or add a royal number to the dead,
Gracing the scroll that tells of this war's loss
With slaughter coupled to the name of kings.
Bast. Ha, majesty! how high thy glory tow'rs
When the rich blood of kings is set on fire!
O now doth Death line his dead chaps with steel,
The swords of soldiers are his teeth, his fangs,
And now he feasts, mousing the flesh of men,
In undetermin'd differences of kings.
Why stand these royal fronts amazed thus?
Cry "havoc," kings! back to the stained field,
You equal potents, fiery kindled spirits!
Then let confusion of one part confirm
The other's peace. Till then, blows, blood, and death!
K. John. Whose party do the townsmen yet admit?
K. Phi. Speak, citizens, for England. Who's your king?
Hub. The King of England, when we know the King.
K. Phi. Know him in us, that here hold up his right.
K. John. In us, that are our own great deputy,
And bear possession of our person here,
Lord of our presence, Angiers, and of you.
[*Hub.*] A greater pow'r than we denies all this,
And till it be undoubted, we do lock
Our former scruple in our strong-barr'd gates,
Kings of our fear, until our fears, resolv'd,
Be by some certain king purg'd and depos'd.

288–89. Saint George . . . door. The figure of St. George, the patron saint of England, reputed to have slain a dragon, was often represented on inn signs. **swing'd:** thrashed (past tense of *swinge*).
290. fence: swordsmanship. **291. lioness:** i.e. harlot.
292. set an ox-head: i.e. give you horns, make you a cuckold.
299 s.d. excursions: sallies, sorties.
316. gilt. Blood was often called golden. **318. staff:** spear.
323. Dy'd . . . foes: i.e. like hunters who, by custom, celebrated a successful chase by dipping their hands in the blood of the slain deer.
328. censured: impugned, denied (?).
333 s.d. powers: armies. **several:** separate.
338. thy confining shores: i.e. the fealty owed to you (as feudal sovereign of the duchy of Anjou) (?). **344. climate:** part of the sky.
350. glory: vainglory. **352. chaps:** jaws. **354. mousing:** gnawing.
355. undetermin'd differences: unresolved conflicts.
356. fronts: foreheads, i.e. faces.
357. Cry "havoc": proclaim a general slaughter.
358. potents: potentates. **359. confusion:** defeat. **361. yet:** now.
366. bear . . . person: symbolize the rights of sovereignty in our own person. **367. Lord . . . presence.** See note to I.i.137.

Bast. By heaven, these scroyles of Angiers flout you, kings,
And stand securely on their battlements
As in a theatre, whence they gape and point
At your industrious scenes and acts of death.
Your royal presences be rul'd by me:
Do like the mutines of Jerusalem,
Be friends awhile, and both conjointly bend
Your sharpest deeds of malice on this town.
By east and west let France and England mount
Their battering cannon charged to the mouths,
Till their soul-fearing clamors have brawl'd down
The flinty ribs of this contemptuous city.
I'd play incessantly upon these jades,
Even till unfenced desolation
Leave them as naked as the vulgar air.
That done, dissever your united strengths,
And part your mingled colors once again,
Turn face to face and bloody point to point;
Then, in a moment, Fortune shall cull forth
Out of one side her happy minion,
To whom in favor she shall give the day,
And kiss him with a glorious victory.
How like you this wild counsel, mighty states?
Smacks it not something of the policy?
K. John. Now, by the sky that hangs above our heads,
I like it well. France, shall we knit our pow'rs,
And lay this Angiers even with the ground,
Then after fight who shall be king of it?
Bast. And if thou hast the mettle of a king,
Being wrong'd as we are by this peevish town,
Turn thou the mouth of thy artillery,
As we will ours, against these saucy walls,
And when that we have dash'd them to the ground,
Why then defy each other, and pell-mell
Make work upon ourselves, for heaven or hell.
K. Phi. Let it be so. Say, where will you assault?
K. John. We from the west will send destruction
Into this city's bosom.
Aust. I from the north.
K. Phi. Our thunder from the south
Shall rain their drift of bullets on this town.
Bast. [*Aside.*] O prudent discipline! From north to south—
Austria and France shoot in each other's mouth.
I'll stir them to it.—Come, away, away!
Hub. Hear us, great kings! Vouchsafe awhile to stay,
And I shall show you peace and fair-fac'd league;
Win you this city without stroke or wound,
Rescue those breathing lives to die in beds,
That here come sacrifices for the field.
Persever not, but hear me, mighty kings.
K. John. Speak on with favor, we are bent to hear.
Hub. That daughter there of Spain, the Lady Blanch,
Is near to England. Look upon the years
Of Lewis the Dolphin and that lovely maid.
If lusty love should go in quest of beauty,
Where should he find it fairer than in Blanch?
If zealous love should go in search of virtue,
Where should he find it purer than in Blanch?
If love ambitious sought a match of birth,
Whose veins bound richer blood than Lady Blanch?
Such as she is, in beauty, virtue, birth,
Is the young Dolphin every way complete:
If not complete of, say he is not she,
And she again wants nothing, to name want,
If want it be not that she is not he.
He is the half part of a blessed man,
Left to be finished by such as she,
And she a fair divided excellence,
Whose fullness of perfection lies in him.
O, two such silver currents when they join
Do glorify the banks that bound them in;
And two such shores to two such streams made one,
Two such controlling bounds shall you be, kings,
To these two princes, if you marry them.
This union shall do more than battery can
To our fast-closed gates; for at this match,
With swifter spleen than powder can enforce,
The mouth of passage shall we fling wide ope,
And give you entrance; but without this match,
The sea enraged is not half so deaf,
Lions more confident, mountains and rocks
More free from motion, no, not Death himself
In mortal fury half so peremptory,
As we to keep this city.
Bast. Here's a stay
That shakes the rotten carcass of old Death
Out of his rags! Here's a large mouth indeed,
That spits forth death and mountains, rocks and seas,
Talks as familiarly of roaring lions
As maids of thirteen do of puppy-dogs!
What cannoneer begot this lusty blood?
He speaks plain cannon-fire, and smoke, and bounce,
He gives the bastinado with his tongue;
Our ears are cudgell'd—not a word of his
But buffets better than a fist of France.
'Zounds, I was never so bethump'd with words
Since I first call'd my brother's father dad.
El. Son, list to this conjunction, make this match,
Give with our niece a dowry large enough,
For by this knot thou shalt so surely tie
Thy now unsur'd assurance to the crown,

373. **scroyles**: scurvy fellows.
378. **mutines**: mutineers. The reference is to John of Gischala and Simon bar Giora, who combined their factions against the Romans under Titus when Jerusalem was besieged and taken (A.D. 70).
383. **fearing**: frightening.
385. **play . . . upon**: cannonade. **jades**: wretches.
387. **vulgar**: common. 392. **minion**: favorite.
395. **states**: monarchs. 396. **the policy**: i.e. the proper policy.
401. **mettle**: spirit. 402. **peevish**: troublesome.
406. **pell-mell**: headlong. 412. **drift**: shower.

422. **favor**: permission. **bent**: inclined.
424. **near to England**: closely related to the King of England. Blanch was John's niece (see note to II.i.64).
430. **match of birth**: i.e. dynastic marriage. 431. **bound**: contain.
433. **complete**: perfect.
434. **If . . . she**: if he is not perfect it is only because he lacks her. **of**: therein. 435. **wants**: lacks. 446. **battery**: artillery.
447. **match**: (1) marriage; (2) means of firing a charge of gunpowder.
448. **spleen**: eagerness. 454. **peremptory**: determined.
455. **stay**: check (a term from horsemanship). 462. **bounce**: boom.
463. **bastinado**: cudgelling.
466. **'Zounds**: by God's (Christ's) wounds. 468. **list**: listen.

That yon green boy shall have no sun to ripe
The bloom that promiseth a mighty fruit.
I see a yielding in the looks of France;
Mark how they whisper. Urge them while their souls
Are capable of this ambition,
Lest zeal, now melted by the windy breath
Of soft petitions, pity, and remorse,
Cool and congeal again to what it was.

Hub. Why answer not the double majesties
This friendly treaty of our threat'ned town?

K. Phi. Speak England first, that hath been forward first
To speak unto this city: what say you?

K. John. If that the Dolphin there, thy princely son,
Can in this book of beauty read, "I love,"
Her dowry shall weigh equal with a queen;
For [Anjou] and fair Touraine, Maine, Poictiers,
And all that we upon this side the sea
(Except this city now by us besieg'd)
Find liable to our crown and dignity,
Shall gild her bridal bed and make her rich
In titles, honors, and promotions,
As she in beauty, education, blood,
Holds hand with any princess of the world.

K. Phi. What say'st thou, boy? Look in the lady's face.

Lew. I do, my lord, and in her eye I find
A wonder, or a wondrous miracle,
The shadow of myself form'd in her eye,
Which being but the shadow of your son,
Becomes a sun and makes your son a shadow.
I do protest I never lov'd myself
Till now infixed I beheld myself
Drawn in the flattering table of her eye.
Whispers with Blanch.

Bast. [*Aside.*] Drawn in the flattering table of her eye!
Hang'd in the frowning wrinkle of her brow!
And quarter'd in her heart! he doth espy
Himself love's traitor. This is pity now,
That hang'd and drawn and quarter'd there should be
In such a love so vile a lout as he.

Blanch. My uncle's will in this respect is mine.
If he see aught in you that makes him like,
That any thing he sees, which moves his liking,
I can with ease translate it to my will;
Or if you will, to speak more properly,
I will enforce it eas'ly to my love.
Further I will not flatter you, my lord,
That all I see in you is worthy love,

Than this: that nothing do I see in you,
Though churlish thoughts themselves should be your judge,
That I can find should merit any hate.

K. John. What say these young ones? What say you, my niece?

Blanch. That she is bound in honor still to do
What you in wisdom still vouchsafe to say.

K. John. Speak then, Prince Dolphin, can you love this lady?

Lew. Nay, ask me if I can refrain from love,
For I do love her most unfeignedly.

K. John. Then do I give Volquessen, Touraine, Maine,
Poictiers, and Anjou, these five provinces,
With her to thee, and this addition more,
Full thirty thousand marks of English coin.
Philip of France, if thou be pleas'd withal,
Command thy son and daughter to join hands.

K. Phi. It likes us well, young princes; close your hands.

Aust. And your lips too, for I am well assur'd
That I did so when I was first assur'd.

K. Phi. Now, citizens of Angiers, ope your gates,
Let in that amity which you have made,
For at Saint Mary's Chapel presently
The rites of marriage shall be solemniz'd.
Is not the Lady Constance in this troop?
I know she is not, for this match made up
Her presence would have interrupted much.
Where is she and her son? tell me, who knows.

Lew. She is sad and passionate at your Highness' tent.

K. Phi. And by my faith, this league that we have made
Will give her sadness very little cure.
Brother of England, how may we content
This widow lady? In her right we came,
Which we, God knows, have turn'd another way,
To our own vantage.

K. John. We will heal up all,
For we'll create young Arthur Duke of Britain
And Earl of Richmond, and this rich fair town
We make him lord of. Call the Lady Constance;
Some speedy messenger bid her repair
To our solemnity. I trust we shall,
If not fill up the measure of her will,
Yet in some measure satisfy her so
That we shall stop her exclamation.
Go we, as well as haste will suffer us,
To this unlook'd-for, unprepared pomp.
Exeunt [*all but the Bastard*].

Bast. Mad world, mad kings, mad composition!
John, to stop Arthur's title in the whole,
Hath willingly departed with a part,

472. **green**: young. **boy**: i.e. Arthur.
476. **capable of**: susceptible to.
477. **zeal**: i.e. the zeal that Philip has shown in Arthur's cause.
481. **treaty**: proposal. 490. **liable**: subject.
494. **Holds hand with**: equals. 498. **shadow**: reflection.
500. **Becomes a sun**: i.e. because the lady's eyes are so bright.
503. **table**: board or surface on which a picture is painted.
504–9. **Drawn . . . he.** In *The Troublesome Reign* (Bullough, IV, 93) the Bastard says that Elinor had given him "halfe a promise" to Blanch's hand. This fact, although suppressed by Shakespeare, helps us understand these disgruntled comments on a rival.
504–7. **Drawn, Hang'd, quarter'd, traitor.** The Bastard's puns relate to the punishment of traitors, who were hanged, cut down while still alive, disembowelled (*drawn*), and quartered. 509. **love**: lover.
513. **will**: desire. 514. **properly**: precisely.

519. **churlish**: grudging. 522. **still**: always.
530. **thirty thousand marks**: i.e. twenty thousand pounds (since a mark amounted to 13*s.* 4*d.*). 533. **likes**: pleases. **close**: clasp.
535. **assur'd**: betrothed. 538. **presently**: at once.
544. **passionate**: disturbed.
555. **our solemnity**: i.e. the marriage ceremony.
556. **fill . . . will**: gratify her desires completely.
557. **so**: sufficiently. 558. **exclamation**: complaint.
561. **composition**: agreement. 563. **departed**: parted.

And France, whose armor conscience buckled on,
Whom zeal and charity brought to the field
As God's own soldier, rounded in the ear
With that same purpose-changer, that sly devil,
That broker that still breaks the pate of faith,
That daily break-vow, he that wins of all,
Of kings, of beggars, old men, young men, maids,
Who having no external thing to lose
But the word "maid," cheats the poor maid of that,
That smooth-fac'd gentleman, tickling commodity,
Commodity, the bias of the world—
The world, who of itself is peized well,
Made to run even upon even ground,
Till this advantage, this vile-drawing bias,
This sway of motion, this commodity,
Makes it take head from all indifferency,
From all direction, purpose, course, intent—
And this same bias, this commodity,
This bawd, this broker, this all-changing word,
Clapp'd on the outward eye of fickle France,
Hath drawn him from his own determin'd aid,
From a resolv'd and honorable war
To a most base and vile-concluded peace.
And why rail I on this commodity?
But for because he hath not woo'd me yet:
Not that I have the power to clutch my hand
When his fair angels would salute my palm,
But for my hand, as unattempted yet,
Like a poor beggar, raileth on the rich.
Well, whiles I am a beggar, I will rail,
And say there is no sin but to be rich;
And being rich, my virtue then shall be
To say there is no vice but beggary.
Since kings break faith upon commodity,
Gain, be my lord, for I will worship thee. *Exit.*

ACT [III, SCENE I]

Enter CONSTANCE, ARTHUR, *and* SALISBURY.

Const. Gone to be married? Gone to swear a peace?
False blood to false blood join'd! Gone to be friends?
Shall Lewis have Blanch, and Blanch those provinces?
It is not so, thou hast misspoke, misheard;
Be well advis'd, tell o'er thy tale again.
It cannot be, thou dost but say 'tis so.
I trust I may not trust thee, for thy word
Is but the vain breath of a common man.
Believe me, I do not believe thee, man,

566. rounded: whispered. **567. With:** by.
568. broker: agent. **571. Who:** i.e. the maids.
573. tickling: flattering. **commodity:** self-interest, expediency.
574. bias: in the game of bowls, a piece of lead in the side of a bowl, making it take a curved course. **575. peized:** balanced.
577. vile-drawing: attracting to evil. **578. sway:** control.
579. take head: rush away. **indifferency:** evenness, inclining neither to one side nor to the other.
583. Clapp'd on: presented to. **France:** i.e. Philip.
588. But for because: merely because.
589. clutch: close up (in refusal).
590. angels: coins, worth ten shillings, stamped with the figure of an angel. **591. unattempted:** untempted. **597. upon:** on account of.
III.i. Location: France. The French King's pavilion.

I have a king's oath to the contrary.
Thou shalt be punish'd for thus frighting me,
For I am sick and capable of fears,
Oppress'd with wrongs, and therefore full of fears,
A widow, husbandless, subject to fears,
A woman, naturally born to fears;
And though thou now confess thou didst but jest,
With my vex'd spirits I cannot take a truce,
But they will quake and tremble all this day.
What dost thou mean by shaking of thy head?
Why dost thou look so sadly on my son?
What means that hand upon that breast of thine?
Why holds thine eye that lamentable rheum,
Like a proud river peering o'er his bounds?
Be these sad signs confirmers of thy words?
Then speak again, not all thy former tale,
But this one word, whether thy tale be true.
Sal. As true as I believe you think them false
That give you cause to prove my saying true.
Const. O, if thou teach me to believe this sorrow,
Teach thou this sorrow how to make me die,
And let belief and life encounter so
As doth the fury of two desperate men,
Which in the very meeting fall, and die.
Lewis marry Blanch? O boy, then where art thou?
France friend with England, what becomes of me?
Fellow, be gone! I cannot brook thy sight,
This news hath made thee a most ugly man.
Sal. What other harm have I, good lady, done,
But spoke the harm that is by others done?
Const. Which harm within itself so heinous is
As it makes harmful all that speak of it.
Arth. I do beseech you, madam, be content.
Const. If thou that bid'st me be content wert grim,
Ugly, and sland'rous to thy mother's womb,
Full of unpleasing blots and sightless stains,
Lame, foolish, crooked, swart, prodigious,
Patch'd with foul moles and eye-offending marks,
I would not care, I then would be content,
For then I should not love thee; no, nor thou
Become thy great birth nor deserve a crown.
But thou art fair, and at thy birth, dear boy,
Nature and Fortune join'd to make thee great.
Of Nature's gifts thou mayst with lilies boast,
And with the half-blown rose. But Fortune, O,
She is corrupted, chang'd, and won from thee;
Sh' adulterates hourly with thine uncle John,
And with her golden hand hath pluck'd on France
To tread down fair respect of sovereignty,
And made his majesty the bawd to theirs.
France is a bawd to Fortune and King John,
That strumpet Fortune, that usurping John!
Tell me, thou fellow, is not France forsworn?
Envenom him with words, or get thee gone,
And leave those woes alone, which I alone

12. capable of: susceptible to.
16. jest. With a pun on *joust*, leading to the *truce* of line 17.
17. take a truce: make peace.
22. lamentable: sad. **rheum:** moisture, i.e. tears.
27. them: i.e. the French. **42. content:** calm.
44. sland'rous: disgraceful. **45. sightless:** unsightly.
46. swart: swarthy. **prodigious:** monstrous.
54. half-blown: half-opened. **56. adulterates:** commits adultery.
57. pluck'd on: induced. **63. Envenom:** poison.

Am bound to underbear.
Sal. Pardon me, madam,
I may not go without you to the kings.
Const. Thou mayst, thou shalt, I will not go with thee.
I will instruct my sorrows to be proud,
For grief is proud and makes his owner stoop.
To me and to the state of my great grief
Let kings assemble; for my grief's so great
That no supporter but the huge firm earth
Can hold it up. [*Throws herself on the ground.*] Here I and sorrows sit;
Here is my throne, bid kings come bow to it.

Enter King John, [King Philip *of*] *France*, [Lewis *the*] *Dolphin*, Blanch, Elinor, Philip [the Bastard], Austria, [*and* Attendants].

K. Phi. 'Tis true, fair daughter, and this blessed day
Ever in France shall be kept festival.
To solemnize this day the glorious sun
Stays in his course and plays the alchymist,
Turning with splendor of his precious eye
The meagre cloddy earth to glittering gold.
The yearly course that brings this day about
Shall never see it but a holy day.
Const. A wicked day, and not a holy day!
[*Rising.*]
What hath this day deserv'd? what hath it done,
That it in golden letters should be set
Among the high tides in the calendar?
Nay, rather turn this day out of the week,
This day of shame, oppression, perjury.
Or if it must stand still, let wives with child
Pray that their burthens may not fall this day,
Lest that their hopes prodigiously be cross'd;
But on this day let seamen fear no wrack;
No bargains break that are not this day made:
This day all things begun come to ill end,
Yea, faith itself to hollow falsehood change!
K. Phi. By heaven, lady, you shall have no cause
To curse the fair proceedings of this day.
Have I not pawn'd to you my majesty?
Const. You have beguil'd me with a counterfeit
Resembling majesty, which being touch'd and tried,
Proves valueless. You are forsworn, forsworn!
You came in arms to spill mine enemies' blood,
But now in arms you strengthen it with yours.
The grappling vigor and rough frown of war
Is cold in amity and painted peace,
And our oppression hath made up this league.
Arm, arm, you heavens, against these perjur'd kings!
A widow cries; be husband to me, heavens!
Let not the hours of this ungodly day
Wear out the [day] in peace; but ere sunset,

65. **underbear:** endure. 70. **state:** pomp.
86. **high tides:** great festivals.
91. **prodigiously be cross'd:** be thwarted by the birth of a monster (?).
92. **But:** except. **wrack:** shipwreck. 98. **pawn'd:** pledged.
100. **touch'd:** tested (as gold is with a touchstone).
102. **in arms:** armed. 103. **in arms:** embracing.
105. **painted:** i.e. unreal.
106. **our oppression:** i.e. your oppression of us.

Set armed discord 'twixt these perjur'd kings!
Hear me, O, hear me!
Aust. Lady Constance, peace!
Const. War, war, no peace! Peace is to me a war.
O Lymoges, O Austria! thou dost shame
That bloody spoil. Thou slave, thou wretch, thou coward!
Thou little valiant, great in villainy!
Thou ever strong upon the stronger side!
Thou Fortune's champion that dost never fight
But when her humorous ladyship is by
To teach thee safety! thou art perjur'd too,
And sooth'st up greatness. What a fool art thou,
A ramping fool, to brag and stamp and swear
Upon my party! Thou cold-blooded slave,
Hast thou not spoke like thunder on my side?
Been sworn my soldier, bidding me depend
Upon thy stars, thy fortune, and thy strength,
And dost thou now fall over to my foes?
Thou wear a lion's hide! Doff it for shame,
And hang a calve's-skin on those recreant limbs.
Aust. O, that a man should speak those words to me!
Bast. And hang a calve's-skin on those recreant limbs.
Aust. Thou dar'st not say so, villain, for thy life.
Bast. And hang a calve's-skin on those recreant limbs.
K. John. We like not this, thou dost forget thyself.

Enter Pandulph.

K. Phi. Here comes the holy legate of the Pope.
Pand. Hail, you anointed deputies of heaven!
To thee, King John, my holy errand is:
I Pandulph, of fair Milan cardinal,
And from Pope Innocent the legate here,
Do in his name religiously demand
Why thou against the Church, our holy mother,
So willfully dost spurn; and force perforce
Keep Stephen Langton, chosen Archbishop
Of Canterbury, from that holy see?
This, in our foresaid Holy Father's name,
Pope Innocent, I do demand of thee.
K. John. What earthy name to interrogatories
Can taste the free breath of a sacred king?

114. **Lymoges, Austria.** See note to II.i.5.
115. **bloody spoil:** i.e. Richard's lion-skin that Austria wears.
119. **humorous:** whimsical.
121. **sooth'st up greatness:** flatterest powerful men.
123. **Upon my party:** in my support.
129. **calve's-skin.** Often worn by domestic fools and jesters. **recreant:** cowardly.
138–46. **I . . . thee.** John's famous defiance of Rome—which made him a Protestant hero to most Elizabethans—was prompted by Innocent III's consecrating Stephen Langton as Archbishop of Canterbury (1207) after the King and the clergy had been unable to agree upon a candidate. John's rejection of Langton led to a papal interdict against England (1208) and, after prolonged bickering, to a papal bull deposing him (1212). The issue was resolved (1213) only after John had been forced to accept his kingdom as a papal fief (V.i) and to agree to pay an annual tribute to the Pope. In this scene, as elsewhere in the play, chronology is violently distorted. The betrothal of Lewis and Blanch and Pandulph's protest about John's intransigence, which are represented as almost simultaneous events, occurred respectively in 1200 and 1211.
142. **spurn:** kick. **force perforce:** i.e. through violence.
147. **name to interrogatories:** title (or right) to demand answers to interrogations. 148. **taste:** test.

Thou canst not, Cardinal, devise a name
So slight, unworthy, and ridiculous,
To charge me to an answer, as the Pope.
Tell him this tale, and from the mouth of England
Add thus much more, that no Italian priest
Shall tithe or toll in our dominions;
But as we, under [God], are supreme head,
So under Him that great supremacy,
Where we do reign, we will alone uphold
Without th' assistance of a mortal hand.
So tell the Pope, all reverence set apart
To him and his usurp'd authority.

K. Phi. Brother of England, you blaspheme in this.

K. John. Though you and all the kings of Christendom
Are led so grossly by this meddling priest,
Dreading the curse that money may buy out,
And by the merit of vild gold, dross, dust,
Purchase corrupted pardon of a man
Who in that sale sells pardon from himself;
Though you, and all the rest so grossly led,
This juggling witchcraft with revenue cherish,
Yet I alone, alone do me oppose
Against the Pope, and count his friends my foes.

Pand. Then, by the lawful power that I have,
Thou shalt stand curs'd and excommunicate,
And blessed shall he be that doth revolt
From his allegiance to an heretic,
And meritorious shall that hand be call'd,
Canonized and worshipp'd as a saint,
That takes away by any secret course
Thy hateful life.

Const. O, lawful let it be
That I have room with Rome to curse a while!
Good father Cardinal, cry thou amen
To my keen curses; for without my wrong
There is no tongue hath power to curse him right.

Pand. There's law and warrant, lady, for my curse.

Const. And for mine too: when law can do no right,
Let it be lawful that law bar no wrong;
Law cannot give my child his kingdom here,
For he that holds his kingdom holds the law;
Therefore since law itself is perfect wrong,
How can the law forbid my tongue to curse?

Pand. Philip of France, on peril of a curse,
Let go the hand of that arch-heretic,
And raise the power of France upon his head,
Unless he do submit himself to Rome.

El. Look'st thou pale, France? Do not let go thy hand.

Const. Look to that, devil, lest that France repent,
And by disjoining hands hell lose a soul.

Aust. King Philip, listen to the Cardinal.

Bast. And hang a calve's-skin on his recreant limbs.

Aust. Well, ruffian, I must pocket up these wrongs,
Because—

Bast. Your breeches best may carry them.

K. John. Philip, what say'st thou to the Cardinal?

Const. What should he say, but as the Cardinal?

Lew. Bethink you, father, for the difference
Is purchase of a heavy curse from Rome,
Or the light loss of England for a friend.
Forgo the easier.

Blanch. That's the curse of Rome.

Const. O Lewis, stand fast! the devil tempts thee here
In likeness of a new untrimmed bride.

Blanch. The Lady Constance speaks not from her faith,
But from her need.

Const. O, if thou grant my need,
Which only lives but by the death of faith,
That need must needs infer this principle,
That faith would live again by death of need.
O then tread down my need, and faith mounts up;
Keep my need up, and faith is trodden down!

K. John. The King is mov'd, and answers not to this.

Const. O, be remov'd from him, and answer well!

Aust. Do so, King Philip, hang no more in doubt.

Bast. Hang nothing but a calve's-skin, most sweet lout.

K. Phi. I am perplex'd, and know not what to say.

Pand. What canst thou say but will perplex thee more,
If thou stand excommunicate and curs'd?

K. Phi. Good reverend father, make my person yours,
And tell me how you would bestow yourself.
This royal hand and mine are newly knit,
And the conjunction of our inward souls
Married in league, coupled, and link'd together
With all religious strength of sacred vows.
The latest breath that gave the sound of words
Was deep-sworn faith, peace, amity, true love
Between our kingdoms and our royal selves,
And even before this truce, but new before,
No longer than we well could wash our hands
To clap this royal bargain up of peace,
Heaven knows they were besmear'd and over-stain'd
With slaughter's pencil—where revenge did paint
The fearful difference of incensed kings—
And shall these hands, so lately purg'd of blood,
So newly join'd in love, so strong in both,
Unyoke this seizure and this kind regreet?
Play fast and loose with faith? so jest with heaven?
Make such unconstant children of ourselves,

152–60. Tell . . . authority. In Holinshed (Bullough, IV, 35–36) John expresses his defiance in a letter, asserting "that he would never consent that Stephan which had beene brought up & alwaies conversant with his enimies the Frenchmen, should now enjoy the rule of the bishoprike and dioces of Canturburie. Moreover, he declared in the same letters, that he marvelled not a little what the pope ment, in that he did not consider how necessarie the freendship of the king of England was to the see of Rome, sith there came more gains to the Romane church out of that kingdome, than out of any other realme on this side the mountaines. He added hereto, that for the liberties of his crowne he would stand to the death, if the matter so required."
154. tithe: impose tithes. **toll:** collect taxes.
165. vild: vile, base. **167. sells pardon from:** i.e. damns.
180. room with Rome. A homophonic pun for the Elizabethans.
182. without my wrong: i.e. without the motive that the wrong done to me has provided.

209. untrimmed: (1) with flowing locks; (2) unbedded, virgin.
213. infer: imply. **224. make . . . yours:** put yourself in my place.
225. bestow: conduct.
233. even before: just before. **new:** immediately.
238. difference: quarrel. **240. both:** i.e. battle and love.
241. seizure: handclasp. **regreet:** salutation of friendship.

As now again to snatch our palm from palm,
Unswear faith sworn, and on the marriage-bed
Of smiling peace to march a bloody host,
And make a riot on the gentle brow
Of true sincerity? O holy sir,
My reverend father, let it not be so!
Out of your grace devise, ordain, impose
Some gentle order, and then we shall be blest
To do your pleasure and continue friends.
Pand. All form is formless, order orderless,
Save what is opposite to England's love.
Therefore to arms! be champion of our Church,
Or let the Church, our mother, breathe her curse,
A mother's curse, on her revolting son.
France, thou mayst hold a serpent by the tongue,
A cased lion by the mortal paw,
A fasting tiger safer by the tooth,
Than keep in peace that hand which thou dost hold.
K. Phi. I may disjoin my hand, but not my faith.
Pand. So mak'st thou faith an enemy to faith,
And like a civil war set'st oath to oath,
Thy tongue against thy tongue. O, let thy vow
First made to heaven, first be to heaven perform'd,
That is, to be the champion of our Church!
What since thou swor'st is sworn against thyself,
And may not be performed by thyself,
For that which thou hast sworn to do amiss
Is not amiss when it is truly done;
And being not done, where doing tends to ill,
The truth is then most done not doing it.
The better act of purposes mistook
Is to mistake again; though indirect,
Yet indirection thereby grows direct,
And falsehood falsehood cures, as fire cools fire
Within the scorched veins of one new burn'd.
It is religion that doth make vows kept,
But thou hast sworn against religion,
By what thou swear'st against the thing thou swear'st,
And mak'st an oath the surety for thy truth
Against an oath; the truth thou art unsure
To swear, swears only not to be forsworn,
Else what a mockery should it be to swear!
But thou dost swear only to be forsworn,
And most forsworn, to keep what thou dost swear;
Therefore thy later vows, against thy first,
Is in thyself rebellion to thyself;
And better conquest never canst thou make
Than arm thy constant and thy nobler parts
Against these giddy loose suggestions;
Upon which better part our pray'rs come in,
If thou vouchsafe them. But if not, then know
The peril of our curses light on thee
So heavy as thou shalt not shake them off,
But in despair die under their black weight.
Aust. Rebellion, flat rebellion!
Bast. Will't not be?
Will not a calve's-skin stop that mouth of thine?
Lew. Father, to arms!
Blanch. Upon thy wedding-day?

259. **cased:** caged. **mortal:** deadly.
271. **truly:** i.e. as explained by the *truth* of line 273.
292. **suggestions:** temptations. 296. **as:** that.

Against the blood that thou hast married?
What, shall our feast be kept with slaughtered men?
Shall braying trumpets and loud churlish drums,
Clamors of hell, be measures to our pomp?
O husband, hear me! ay, alack, how new
Is "husband" in my mouth! even for that name,
Which till this time my tongue did ne'er pronounce,
Upon my knee I beg, go not to arms
Against mine uncle.
Const. O, upon my knee,
Made hard with kneeling, I do pray to thee,
Thou virtuous Dolphin, alter not the doom
Forethought by heaven!
Blanch. Now shall I see thy love. What motive may
Be stronger with thee than the name of wife?
Const. That which upholdeth him that thee upholds,
His honor. O, thine honor, Lewis, thine honor!
Lew. I muse your Majesty doth seem so cold,
When such profound respects do pull you on.
Pand. I will denounce a curse upon his head.
K. Phi. Thou shalt not need. England, I will fall from thee.
Const. O fair return of banish'd majesty!
El. O foul revolt of French inconstancy!
K. John. France, thou shalt rue this hour within this hour.
Bast. Old Time the clock-setter, that bald sexton Time!
Is it as he will? Well then, France shall rue.
Blanch. The sun's o'ercast with blood; fair day, adieu!
Which is the side that I must go withal?
I am with both, each army hath a hand,
And in their rage, I having hold of both,
They whirl asunder and dismember me.
Husband, I cannot pray that thou mayst win;
Uncle, I needs must pray that thou mayst lose;
Father, I may not wish the fortune thine;
Grandam, I will not wish thy wishes thrive:
Whoever wins, on that side shall I lose;
Assured loss before the match be play'd.
Lew. Lady, with me, with me thy fortune lies.
Blanch. There where my fortune lives, there my life dies.
K. John. Cousin, go draw our puissance together.
[*Exit Bastard.*]
France, I am burn'd up with inflaming wrath,
A rage whose heat hath this condition,
That nothing can allay, nothing but blood,
The blood and dearest-valued blood of France.
K. Phi. Thy rage shall burn thee up, and thou shalt turn
To ashes, ere our blood shall quench that fire.
Look to thyself, thou art in jeopardy.

304. **measures . . . pomp:** music for our wedding.
312. **Forethought:** destined. 317. **muse:** wonder.
318. **respects:** considerations. 319. **denounce:** call down.
333. **Father:** i.e. father-in-law, King Philip.
339. **Cousin:** kinsman. **puissance:** army.
341. **hath this condition:** is such.

K. John. No more than he that threats. To arms let's hie! *Exeunt.*

SCENE II

Alarums, excursions. Enter BASTARD *with Austria's head.*

Bast. Now by my life, this day grows wondrous hot;
Some aery devil hovers in the sky
And pours down mischief. Austria's head lie there,
While Philip breathes.

Enter [KING] JOHN, ARTHUR, HUBERT.

K. John. Hubert, keep this boy. Philip, make up.
My mother is assailed in our tent,
And ta'en, I fear.
Bast. My lord, I rescued her;
Her Highness is in safety, fear you not.
But on, my liege, for very little pains
Will bring this labor to an happy end. *Exeunt.*

[SCENE III]

Alarums, excursions, retreat. Enter [KING] JOHN, ELINOR, ARTHUR, BASTARD, HUBERT, LORDS.

K. John. [*To Elinor.*] So shall it be; your Grace shall stay behind
So strongly guarded. [*To Arthur.*] Cousin, look not sad,
Thy grandame loves thee, and thy uncle will
As dear be to thee as thy father was.
Arth. O, this will make my mother die with grief!
K. John. [*To the Bastard.*] Cousin, away for England! haste before,
And ere our coming see thou shake the bags
Of hoarding abbots, imprisoned angels
Set at liberty. The fat ribs of peace
Must by the hungry now be fed upon.
Use our commission in his utmost force.
Bast. Bell, book, and candle shall not drive me back,
When gold and silver becks me to come on.
I leave your Highness. Grandame, I will pray
(If ever I remember to be holy)
For your fair safety; so I kiss your hand.
El. Farewell, gentle cousin.
K. John. Coz, farewell. [*Exit Bastard.*]
El. Come hither, little kinsman, hark, a word.
[*Takes Arthur aside.*]
K. John. Come hither, Hubert. O my gentle Hubert,
We owe thee much! Within this wall of flesh
There is a soul counts thee her creditor,
And with advantage means to pay thy love;
And, my good friend, thy voluntary oath
Lives in this bosom, dearly cherished.
Give me thy hand. I had a thing to say,
But I will fit it with some better [time].
By heaven, Hubert, I am almost asham'd
To say what good respect I have of thee.
Hub. I am much bounden to your Majesty.
K. John. Good friend, thou hast no cause to say so yet,
But thou shalt have; and creep time ne'er so slow,
Yet it shall come for me to do thee good.
I had a thing to say, but let it go.
The sun is in the heaven, and the proud day,
Attended with the pleasures of the world,
Is all too wanton and too full of gawds
To give me audience. If the midnight bell
Did with his iron tongue and brazen mouth
Sound on into the drowsy race of night;
If this same were a churchyard where we stand,
And thou possessed with a thousand wrongs;
Or if that surly spirit, melancholy,
Had bak'd thy blood and made it heavy, thick,
Which else runs tickling up and down the veins,
Making that idiot, laughter, keep men's eyes
And strain their cheeks to idle merriment—
A passion hateful to my purposes;
Or if that thou couldst see me without eyes,
Hear me without thine ears, and make reply
Without a tongue, using conceit alone,
Without eyes, ears, and harmful sound of words—
Then, in despite of brooded watchful day,
I would into thy bosom pour my thoughts.
But, ah, I will not! yet I love thee well,
And by my troth I think thou lov'st me well.
Hub. So well, that what you bid me undertake,
Though that my death were adjunct to my act,
By heaven, I would do it.
K. John. Do not I know thou wouldst?
Good Hubert, Hubert, Hubert, throw thine eye
On yon young boy. I'll tell thee what, my friend,
He is a very serpent in my way,
And wheresoe'er this foot of mine doth tread,
He lies before me. Dost thou understand me?
Thou art his keeper.
Hub. And I'll keep him so,
That he shall not offend your Majesty.
K. John. Death.
Hub. My lord?
K. John. A grave.
Hub. He shall not live.
K. John. Enough.
I could be merry now. Hubert, I love thee.
Well, I'll not say what I intend for thee.
Remember. Madam, fare you well,
I'll send those powers o'er to your Majesty.

III.ii. Location: France. Plains near Angiers.
o.s.d. Alarums: calls to arms.
2. aery devil. Thought to be the cause of thunderstorms.
4. breathes: catches his breath, rests. **5. make up:** hasten.

III.iii. Location: Scene continues.
o.s.d. retreat: trumpet signal for withdrawal of forces.
11. commission: warrant. **his:** its.
12. Bell . . . candle. Used in the ritual of excommunication.
17. Coz: cousin, i.e. kinsman.
20. We . . . much: i.e. for proposing the match between Lewis and Blanch (?).
22. advantage: interest. **28. respect:** opinion.
36. gawds: toys, gay trifles. **39. race:** course.
44. tickling: tingling. **45. idiot:** jester. **47. passion:** emotion.
50. conceit: thought. **52. brooded:** brooding, i.e. observing (?).
55. troth: truth, faith. **57. adjunct to:** consequent upon.
70. powers: troops.

El. My blessing go with thee!
K. John. For England, cousin, go.
Hubert shall be your man, attend on you
With all true duty. On toward Callice, ho! *Exeunt.*

Scene [IV]

Enter [King Philip *of*] *France,* [Lewis *the*] *Dolphin,* Pandulpho, Attendants.

K. Phi. So by a roaring tempest on the flood,
A whole armado of convicted sail
Is scattered and disjoin'd from fellowship.
Pand. Courage and comfort! all shall yet go well.
K. Phi. What can go well, when we have run so ill?
Are we not beaten? Is not Angiers lost?
Arthur ta'en prisoner? Divers dear friends slain?
And bloody England into England gone,
O'erbearing interruption, spite of France?
Lew. What he hath won, that hath he fortified.
So hot a speed with such advice dispos'd,
Such temperate order in so fierce a cause,
Doth want example. Who hath read or heard
Of any kindred action like to this?
K. Phi. Well could I bear that England had this praise,
So we could find some pattern of our shame.

Enter Constance.

Look who comes here! a grave unto a soul,
Holding th' eternal spirit, against her will,
In the vild prison of afflicted breath.
I prithee, lady, go away with me.
Const. Lo! now! now see the issue of your peace.
K. Phi. Patience, good lady, comfort, gentle Constance!
Const. No, I defy all counsel, all redress,
But that which ends all counsel, true redress:
Death, death. O amiable lovely death!
Thou odoriferous stench! sound rottenness!
Arise forth from the couch of lasting night,
Thou hate and terror to prosperity,
And I will kiss thy detestable bones,
And put my eyeballs in thy vaulty brows,

71. For England. Actually, Arthur was never sent to England. Following the lucky stroke in capturing him at Mirebeau in 1202, John at first tried to woo him from his French allies, says Holinshed (Bullough, IV, 31–32); but when Arthur—by no means the docile boy whom Shakespeare represents—haughtily demanded the English crown as well as "all those other lands and possessions which king Richard had in his hand at the houre of his death," John was so "sore mooved" by his nephew's attitude that he had him "straitlie kept in prison, as first in Falais, and after at Roan within the new castell there." The abortive plan to "put out the yoong gentlemans eies" (IV.i) was hatched while Arthur was incarcerated at Falaise, and his death (IV.iii) occurred at Rouen. **73. Callice:** Calais.

III.iv. Location: France. The French King's pavilion.
2. convicted: doomed (?) or defeated (?).
11. with . . . dispos'd: disciplined by such judgment.
12. cause: quarrel. **13. Doth want example:** lacks precedent.
14. kindred: similar.
16. So: provided. **pattern of:** precedent for. **21. issue:** outcome.
23. defy: renounce. **redress:** relief from trouble.
25. lovely: lovable. **30. vaulty:** arched.

And ring these fingers with thy household worms,
And stop this gap of breath with fulsome dust,
And be a carrion monster like thyself.
Come, grin on me, and I will think thou smil'st,
And buss thee as thy wife. Misery's love,
O, come to me!
K. Phi. O fair affliction, peace!
Const. No, no, I will not, having breath to cry.
O that my tongue were in the thunder's mouth!
Then with a passion would I shake the world,
And rouse from sleep that fell anatomy
Which cannot hear a lady's feeble voice,
Which scorns a modern invocation.
Pand. Lady, you utter madness, and not sorrow.
Const. Thou art [not] holy to belie me so,
I am not mad. This hair I tear is mine,
My name is Constance, I was Geffrey's wife,
Young Arthur is my son, and he is lost.
I am not mad, I would to heaven I were!
For then 'tis like I should forget myself.
O, if I could, what grief should I forget!
Preach some philosophy to make me mad,
And thou shalt be canoniz'd, Cardinal;
For, being not mad, but sensible of grief,
My reasonable part produces reason
How I may be deliver'd of these woes,
And teaches me to kill or hang myself.
If I were mad, I should forget my son,
Or madly think a babe of clouts were he.
I am not mad; too well, too well I feel
The different plague of each calamity.
K. Phi. Bind up those tresses. O, what love I note
In the fair multitude of those her hairs!
Where but by chance a silver drop hath fall'n,
Even to that drop ten thousand wiry [friends]
Do glue themselves in sociable grief,
Like true, inseparable, faithful loves,
Sticking together in calamity.
Const. To England, if you will.
K. Phi. Bind up your hairs.
Const. Yes, that I will; and wherefore will I do it?
I tore them from their bonds, and cried aloud,
"O that these hands could so redeem my son
As they have given these hairs their liberty!"
But now I envy at their liberty,
And will again commit them to their bonds,
Because my poor child is a prisoner.
And, father Cardinal, I have heard you say
That we shall see and know our friends in heaven.
If that be true, I shall see my boy again;
For since the birth of Cain, the first male child,
To him that did but yesterday suspire,
There was not such a gracious creature born.
But now will canker-sorrow eat my bud,

32. fulsome: repulsive. **35. buss:** kiss amorously.
40. fell anatomy: cruel skeleton. **42. modern:** ordinary.
53. sensible: capable.
58. babe of clouts: rag doll (*clout* = cloth).
63. silver drop: i.e. tear. **64. wiry friends:** i.e. hairs.
68. To . . . will. Since this appears to be irelevant it has been cited as proof of revision in this scene, but perhaps it is a delayed response to Philip's invitation in line 20. **80. suspire:** breathe.

And chase the native beauty from his cheek,
And he will look as hollow as a ghost,
As dim and meagre as an ague's fit,
And so he'll die; and rising so again,
When I shall meet him in the court of heaven
I shall not know him: therefore never, never
Must I behold my pretty Arthur more.
Pand. You hold too heinous a respect of grief.
Const. He talks to me that never had a son.
K. Phi. You are as fond of grief as of your child.
Const. Grief fills the room up of my absent child,
Lies in his bed, walks up and down with me,
Puts on his pretty looks, repeats his words,
Remembers me of all his gracious parts,
Stuffs out his vacant garments with his form;
Then, have I reason to be fond of grief?
Fare you well! Had you such a loss as I,
I could give better comfort than you do.
I will not keep this form upon my head
[*Tearing her hair.*]
When there is such disorder in my wit.
O Lord, my boy, my Arthur, my fair son!
My life, my joy, my food, my all the world!
My widow-comfort, and my sorrows' cure! *Exit.*
K. Phi. I fear some outrage, and I'll follow her.
Exit.
Lew. There's nothing in this world can make me joy:
Life is as tedious as a twice-told tale
Vexing the dull ear of a drowsy man;
And bitter shame hath spoil'd the sweet word's taste,
That it yields nought but shame and bitterness.
Pand. Before the curing of a strong disease,
Even in the instant of repair and health,
The fit is strongest; evils that take leave,
On their departure most of all show evil.
What have you lost by losing of this day?
Lew. All days of glory, joy, and happiness.
Pand. If you had won it, certainly you had.
No, no; when Fortune means to men most good,
She looks upon them with a threat'ning eye.
'Tis strange to think how much King John hath lost
In this which he accounts so clearly won.
Are not you griev'd that Arthur is his prisoner?
Lew. As heartily as he is glad he hath him.
Pand. Your mind is all as youthful as your blood.
Now hear me speak with a prophetic spirit;
For even the breath of what I mean to speak
Shall blow each dust, each straw, each little rub,
Out of the path which shall directly lead
Thy foot to England's throne. And therefore mark:
John hath seiz'd Arthur, and it cannot be
That whiles warm life plays in that infant's veins,
The misplac'd John should entertain an hour,
One minute, nay, one quiet breath of rest.

A sceptre snatch'd with an unruly hand
Must be as boisterously maintain'd as gain'd;
And he that stands upon a slipp'ry place
Makes nice of no vild hold to stay him up.
That John may stand, then Arthur needs must fall:
So be it, for it cannot be but so.
Lew. But what shall I gain by young Arthur's fall?
Pand. You, in the right of Lady Blanch your wife,
May then make all the claim that Arthur did.
Lew. And lose it, life and all, as Arthur did.
Pand. How green you are and fresh in this old world!
John lays you plots; the times conspire with you,
For he that steeps his safety in true blood
Shall find but bloody safety, and untrue.
This act so evilly borne shall cool the hearts
Of all his people, and freeze up their zeal,
That none so small advantage shall step forth
To check his reign, but they will cherish it;
No natural exhalation in the sky,
No scope of nature, no distemper'd day,
No common wind, no customed event,
But they will pluck away his natural cause
And call them meteors, prodigies, and signs,
Abortives, presages, and tongues of heaven,
Plainly denouncing vengeance upon John.
Lew. May be he will not touch young Arthur's life,
But hold himself safe in his prisonment.
Pand. O sir, when he shall hear of your approach,
If that young Arthur be not gone already,
Even at that news he dies; and then the hearts
Of all his people shall revolt from him,
And kiss the lips of unacquainted change,
And pick strong matter of revolt and wrath
Out of the bloody fingers' ends of John.
Methinks I see this hurly all on foot;
And O, what better matter breeds for you
Than I have nam'd! The bastard Faulconbridge
Is now in England ransacking the Church,
Offending charity. If but a dozen French
Were there in arms, they would be as a call
To train ten thousand English to their side,
Or as a little snow, tumbled about,
Anon becomes a mountain. O noble Dolphin,
Go with me to the King. 'Tis wonderful
What may be wrought out of their discontent,
Now that their souls are topful of offense.
For England go; I will whet on the King.
Lew. Strong reasons makes strange actions. Let us go;
If you say ay, the King will not say no. *Exeunt.*

90. heinous a respect: terrible a notion. **96. Remembers:** reminds.
101. form: coiffure. **102. wit:** i.e. brain.
110. bitter . . . taste: i.e. the recognition of my failure obliterates even my delight in praise (*sweet word*) for my success (?). Most editors have followed Pope in emending *word's* to *world's*.
128. rub: obstruction. **132. whiles:** while.
133. misplac'd: i.e. usurping.

136. boisterously: violently.
138. Makes nice of: is fastidious about.
146. lays you plots: i.e. lays plots by which you may benefit.
149. borne: executed.
151. none . . . advantage: no opportunity, however small.
153. exhalation: meteor. **154. scope:** freak (?).
156. his: its. **158. Abortives:** abnormalities.
159. denouncing: calling down. **161. hold:** consider.
166. unacquainted: unfamiliar. **169. hurly:** tumult. **on foot:** begun.
174. call: decoy. **175. train:** draw, entice.
180. topful: brimful. **offense:** grievance.

ACT IV, Scene I

Enter Hubert *and* Executioners.

Hub. Heat me these irons hot, and look thou stand
Within the arras. When I strike my foot
Upon the bosom of the ground, rush forth
And bind the boy which you shall find with me
Fast to the chair. Be heedful. Hence, and watch.
[*I.*] *Exec.* I hope your warrant will bear out the deed.
Hub. Uncleanly scruples! fear not you. Look to't.
[*Exeunt Executioners.*]
Young lad, come forth; I have to say with you.

Enter Arthur.

Arth. Good morrow, Hubert.
Hub. Good morrow, little prince.
Arth. As little prince, having so great a title
To be more prince, as may be. You are sad.
Hub. Indeed I have been merrier.
Arth. Mercy on me!
Methinks nobody should be sad but I.
Yet I remember, when I was in France,
Young gentlemen would be as sad as night,
Only for wantonness. By my christendom,
So I were out of prison and kept sheep,
I should be as merry as the day is long;
And so I would be here, but that I doubt
My uncle practices more harm to me.
He is afraid of me and I of him.
Is it my fault that I was Geffrey's son?
No indeed is't not; and I would to heaven
I were your son, so you would love me, Hubert.
Hub. [*Aside.*] If I talk to him, with his innocent prate
He will awake my mercy, which lies dead;
Therefore I will be sudden, and dispatch.
Arth. Are you sick, Hubert? You look pale to-day.
In sooth, I would you were a little sick,
That I might sit all night and watch with you.
I warrant I love you more than you do me.
Hub. [*Aside.*] His words do take possession of my bosom.—
Read here, young Arthur. [*Showing a paper.*]
[*Aside.*] How now, foolish rheum?
Turning dispiteous torture out of door?
I must be brief, lest resolution drop
Out at mine eyes in tender womanish tears.—
Can you not read it? Is it not fair writ?
Arth. Too fairly, Hubert, for so foul effect.
Must you with hot irons burn out both mine eyes?
Hub. Young boy, I must.
Arth. And will you?
Hub. And I will.

Arth. Have you the heart? When your head did but ache,
I knit my handkercher about your brows
(The best I had, a princess wrought it me)
And I did never ask it you again;
And with my hand at midnight held your head;
And like the watchful minutes to the hour,
Still and anon cheer'd up the heavy time,
Saying, "What lack you?" and "Where lies your grief?"
Or "What good love may I perform for you?"
Many a poor man's son would have lien still,
And ne'er have spoke a loving word to you;
But you at your sick service had a prince.
Nay, you may think my love was crafty love,
And call it cunning. Do, and if you will;
If heaven be pleas'd that you must use me ill,
Why then you must. Will you put out mine eyes,
These eyes that never did nor never shall
So much as frown on you?
Hub. I have sworn to do it;
And with hot irons must I burn them out.
Arth. Ah, none but in this iron age would do it!
The iron of itself, though heat red-hot,
Approaching near these eyes, would drink my tears,
And quench [his] fiery indignation
Even in the matter of mine innocence;
Nay, after that, consume away in rust,
But for containing fire to harm mine eye.
Are you more stubborn-hard than hammer'd iron?
And if an angel should have come to me
And told me Hubert should put out mine eyes,
I would not have believ'd him—no tongue but Hubert's.
Hub. Come forth. [*Stamps.*]

[*Enter* Executioners *with a cord, irons, etc.*]

Do as I bid you do.
Arth. O, save me, Hubert, save me! My eyes are out
Even with the fierce looks of these bloody men.
Hub. Give me the iron, I say, and bind him here.
Arth. Alas, what need you be so boist'rous-rough?
I will not struggle, I will stand stone-still.
For heaven sake, Hubert, let me not be bound!
Nay, hear me, Hubert, drive these men away,
And I will sit as quiet as a lamb;
I will not stir, nor winch, nor speak a word,
Nor look upon the iron angerly.
Thrust but these men away, and I'll forgive you,
What ever torment you do put me to.
Hub. Go stand within; let me alone with him.
[*I.*] *Exec.* I am best pleas'd to be from such a deed.
[*Exeunt Executioners.*]
Arth. Alas, I then have chid away my friend!
He hath a stern look, but a gentle heart.

IV.i. Location: England. A castle.
1. me: for me. **2. Within the arras:** behind the wall-hangings.
7. Uncleanly: unbecoming.
10–11. As . . . be: i.e. despite my great title I am as little a prince as it is possible to be.
16. wantonness: affectation. **By my christendom:** as I am a Christian.
17. So: if. **19. doubt:** fear. **20. practices:** plots.
25. prate: prattle. **29. sooth:** truth. **34. dispiteous:** pitiless.
37. fair: legibly. **38. effect:** meaning.

42. knit: bound. **43. wrought:** worked, embroidered.
46. watchful . . . hour: minutes that mark the progress of the hour.
47. Still and anon: continually. **heavy:** dreary.
48. grief: pain. **49. love:** loving service. **50. lien:** lain.
52. your sick service: your service when you were sick.
61. heat: heated. **64. matter . . . innocence:** i.e. my tears.
66. But for containing: only because it contains. **75. what:** why.
80. winch: wince. **85. from:** away from.

Let him come back, that his compassion may
Give life to yours.
Hub. Come, boy, prepare yourself.
Arth. Is there no remedy?
Hub. None, but to lose your eyes.
Arth. O heaven! that there were but a mote in yours,
A grain, a dust, a gnat, a wandering hair,
Any annoyance in that precious sense!
Then feeling what small things are boisterous there,
Your vild intent must needs seem horrible.
Hub. Is this your promise? Go to, hold your tongue.
Arth. Hubert, the utterance of a brace of tongues
Must needs want pleading for a pair of eyes.
Let me not hold my tongue, let me not, Hubert;
Or, Hubert, if you will, cut out my tongue,
So I may keep mine eyes. O, spare mine eyes,
Though to no use but still to look on you!
Lo, by my troth, the instrument is cold,
And would not harm me.
Hub. I can heat it, boy.
Arth. No, in good sooth; the fire is dead with grief,
Being create for comfort, to be us'd
In undeserv'd extremes. See else yourself,
There is no malice in this burning coal;
The breath of heaven hath blown his spirit out,
And strew'd repentant ashes on his head.
Hub. But with my breath I can revive it, boy.
Arth. And if you do, you will but make it blush
And glow with shame of your proceedings, Hubert.
Nay, it perchance will sparkle in your eyes;
And, like a dog that is compell'd to fight,
Snatch at his master that doth tarre him on.
All things that you should use to do me wrong
Deny their office; only you do lack
That mercy which fierce fire and iron extends,
Creatures of note for mercy-lacking uses.
Hub. Well, see to live; I will not touch thine eye
For all the treasure that thine uncle owes.
Yet am I sworn, and I did purpose, boy,
With this same very iron to burn them out.
Arth. O now you look like Hubert! All this while
You were disguis'd.
Hub. Peace; no more. Adieu.
Your uncle must not know but you are dead.
I'll fill these dogged spies with false reports;
And, pretty child, sleep doubtless and secure
That Hubert, for the wealth of all the world,
Will not offend thee.
Arth. O heaven! I thank you, Hubert.
Hub. Silence, no more. Go closely in with me;
Much danger do I undergo for thee. *Exeunt.*

93. **precious sense**: i.e. sight. 94. **boisterous**: painful.
98. **want pleading**: lack pleading, i.e. plead inadequately.
99. **Let me not**: i.e. don't hold me to my promise to.
106. **create**: created.
107. **In undeserv'd extremes**: in (inflicting) undeserved torments.
114. **sparkle**: throw sparks into. 116. **Snatch**: snap. **tarre**: urge.
118. **office**: function, duty.
120. **Creatures of note**: objects notorious. 122. **owes**: owns.
128. **dogged**: fierce. 129. **doubtless**: fearless. **secure**: confident.
131. **offend**: harm. 132. **closely**: secretly.

Scene II

Enter [King] John, Pembroke, Salisbury, *and other* Lords.

K. John. Here once again we sit; once [again] crown'd,
And look'd upon, I hope, with cheerful eyes.
Pem. This "once again" (but that your Highness pleas'd)
Was once superfluous. You were crown'd before,
And that high royalty was ne'er pluck'd off;
The faiths of men ne'er stained with revolt;
Fresh expectation troubled not the land
With any long'd-for change or better state.
Sal. Therefore, to be possess'd with double pomp,
To guard a title that was rich before,
To gild refined gold, to paint the lily,
To throw a perfume on the violet,
To smooth the ice, or add another hue
Unto the rainbow, or with taper-light
To seek the beauteous eye of heaven to garnish,
Is wasteful and ridiculous excess.
Pem. But that your royal pleasure must be done,
This act is as an ancient tale new told,
And, in the last repeating, troublesome,
Being urged at a time unseasonable.
Sal. In this the antique and well-noted face
Of plain old form is much disfigured,
And like a shifted wind unto a sail,
It makes the course of thoughts to fetch about,
Startles and frights consideration,
Makes sound opinion sick, and truth suspected,
For putting on so new a fashion'd robe.
Pem. When workmen strive to do better than well,
They do confound their skill in covetousness,
And oftentimes excusing of a fault
Doth make the fault the worse by th' excuse:
As patches set upon a little breach
Discredit more in hiding of the fault
Than did the fault before it was so patch'd.
Sal. To this effect, before you were new crown'd,
We breath'd our counsel; but it pleas'd your Highness
To overbear it, and we are all well pleas'd,
Since all and every part of what we would
Doth make a stand at what your Highness will.
K. John. Some reasons of this double coronation
I have possess'd you with, and think them strong;
And more, more strong than lesser is my fear,
I shall indue you with. Mean time but ask

IV.ii. Location: England. King John's palace.
1. **once again crown'd.** John had been proclaimed king and was duly crowned at Westminster in May 1199, shortly after Richard's death, but in October 1200, reports Holinshed (Bullough, IV, 31–32), he returned from France to England and "caused himselfe to be crowned againe at Canturburie." In March 1201 he was crowned for the third time. 10. **guard**: adorn.
21. **well-noted**: well-known. 22. **form**: order, customary procedure.
24. **fetch about**: change direction.
25. **frights consideration**: i.e. prompts re-examination of John's title to the throne (?). 29. **confound**: destroy.
32. **breach**: hole. 33. **fault**: defect. 37. **overbear**: ignore.
39. **make a stand**: stop short.
41. **possess'd you with**: informed you of.
42–43. **more . . . with**: i.e. I shall provide you with other reasons which will be strong in proportion as the object of my fear (i.e. Arthur) is lesser.

What you would have reform'd that is not well,
And well shall you perceive how willingly
I will both hear and grant you your requests.

Pem. Then I, as one that am the tongue of these
To sound the purposes of all their hearts,
Both for myself and them—but, chief of all,
Your safety, for the which myself and them
Bend their best studies—heartily request
Th' enfranchisement of Arthur, whose restraint
Doth move the murmuring lips of discontent
To break into this dangerous argument:
If what in rest you have in right you hold,
Why then your fears, which (as they say) attend
The steps of wrong, should move you to mew up
Your tender kinsman, and to choke his days
With barbarous ignorance, and deny his youth
The rich advantage of good exercise.
That the time's enemies may not have this
To grace occasions, let it be our suit
That you have bid us ask his liberty,
Which for our goods we do no further ask
Than whereupon our weal, on you depending,
Counts it your weal he have his liberty.

Enter HUBERT.

K. John. Let it be so; I do commit his youth
To your direction. Hubert, what news with you?
[*Taking him aside.*]

Pem. This is the man should do the bloody deed;
He show'd his warrant to a friend of mine.
The image of a wicked heinous fault
Lives in his eye; that close aspect of his
[Doth] show the mood of a much troubled breast,
And I do fearfully believe 'tis done,
What we so fear'd he had a charge to do.

Sal. The color of the King doth come and go
Between his purpose and his conscience,
Like heralds 'twixt two dreadful battles set:
His passion is so ripe, it needs must break.

Pem. And when it breaks, I fear will issue thence
The foul corruption of a sweet child's death.

K. John. We cannot hold mortality's strong hand.
Good lords, although my will to give is living,
The suit which you demand is gone and dead.
He tells us Arthur is deceas'd to-night.

Sal. Indeed we fear'd his sickness was past cure.

Pem. Indeed we heard how near his death he was
Before the child himself felt he was sick.
This must be answer'd either here or hence.

K. John. Why do you bend such solemn brows on me?
Think you I bear the shears of destiny?
Have I commandement on the pulse of life?

Sal. It is apparent foul play, and 'tis shame
That greatness should so grossly offer it.
So thrive it in your game! and so farewell.

Pem. Stay yet, Lord Salisbury, I'll go with thee,
And find th' inheritance of this poor child,
His little kingdom of a forced grave.
That blood which ow'd the breadth of all this isle,
Three foot of it doth hold; bad world the while!
This must not be thus borne. This will break out
To all our sorrows, and ere long I doubt.
Exeunt [*Lords*].

K. John. They burn in indignation. I repent.

Enter MESSENGER.

There is no sure foundation set on blood;
No certain life achiev'd by others' death.
A fearful eye thou hast. Where is that blood
That I have seen inhabit in those cheeks?
So foul a sky clears not without a storm,
Pour down thy weather. How goes all in France?

Mess. From France to England. Never such a pow'r
For any foreign preparation
Was levied in the body of a land.
The copy of your speed is learn'd by them;
For when you should be told they do prepare,
The tidings comes that they are all arriv'd.

K. John. O, where hath our intelligence been drunk?
Where hath it slept? Where is my mother's care,
That such an army could be drawn in France,
And she not hear of it?

Mess. My liege, her ear
Is stopp'd with dust: the first of April died
Your noble mother; and as I hear, my lord,
The Lady Constance in a frenzy died
Three days before; but this from rumor's tongue
I idly heard—if true or false I know not.

K. John. Withhold thy speed, dreadful occasion!
O, make a league with me, till I have pleas'd
My discontented peers! What? mother dead?
How wildly then walks my estate in France!
Under whose conduct came those pow'rs of France
That thou for truth giv'st out are landed here?

Mess. Under the Dolphin.

Enter BASTARD *and* PETER OF POMFRET.

K. John. Thou hast made me giddy

48. sound: give voice to. **51. studies**: efforts.
55. rest: peace, tranquillity.
56–57. your fears . . . should move: should your fears . . . move.
57. mew up: confine, cage (a term from falconry).
61. the time's enemies: those hostile to the present state of affairs.
62. grace occasions: i.e. justify their disaffection (?).
64. our goods: our own benefit.
65. whereupon: so far as. **weal**: welfare.
72. close: furtive. **75. had a charge**: was commissioned.
78. battles: armies drawn up in readiness for battle.
89. answer'd: answered for, atoned. **hence**: i.e. in heaven.

93. apparent: obvious. **94. grossly offer**: flagrantly attempt.
95. So . . . game: may you have the same ill fortune.
98. forced: (1) involuntary; (2) imposed through violence.
99. ow'd: owned. **106. fearful**: full of fear.
111. preparation: expedition.
113. copy: example. **your speed.** See II.i.56–61.
116. intelligence: information service, spies.
118. drawn: levied.
119–59. My . . . thee. Chronology here, as throughout the play, is freely violated. Whereas the day and month of Elinor's death is, surprisingly, correct, Constance predeceased her mother-in-law by three years (in 1201); and whereas the episode of Peter the Hermit is assigned by Holinshed (Bullough, IV, 41) to 1212, that of the five moons (lines 182–84) must be dated twelve years earlier (Bullough, IV, 29). **124. idly**: by chance. **125. occasion**: course of events.
128. wildly . . . walks: staggers, totters. **estate**: power.
129. conduct: command.

With these ill tidings.—Now! what says the world
To your proceedings? Do not seek to stuff
My head with more ill news, for it is full.
Bast. But if you be afeard to hear the worst,
Then let the worst unheard fall on your head.
K. John. Bear with me, cousin, for I was amaz'd
Under the tide; but now I breathe again
Aloft the flood, and can give audience
To any tongue, speak it of what it will.
Bast. How I have sped among the clergymen
The sums I have collected shall express.
But as I travell'd hither through the land,
I find the people strangely fantasied,
Possess'd with rumors, full of idle dreams,
Not knowing what they fear, but full of fear.
And here's a prophet that I brought with me
From forth the streets of Pomfret, whom I found
With many hundreds treading on his heels;
To whom he sung, in rude harsh-sounding rhymes,
That, ere the next Ascension-day at noon,
Your Highness should deliver up your crown.
K. John. Thou idle dreamer, wherefore didst thou
so?
Peter. Foreknowing that the truth will fall out so.
K. John. Hubert, away with him; imprison him;
And on that day at noon, whereon he says
I shall yield up my crown, let him be hang'd.
Deliver him to safety, and return,
For I must use thee. [*Exit Hubert with Peter*.]
O my gentle cousin,
Hear'st thou the news abroad, who are arriv'd?
Bast. The French, my lord; men's mouths are full
of it.
Besides, I met Lord Bigot and Lord Salisbury,
With eyes as red as new-enkindled fire,
And others more, going to seek the grave
Of Arthur, whom they say is kill'd to-night
On your suggestion.
K. John. Gentle kinsman, go
And thrust thyself into their companies;
I have a way to win their loves again.
Bring them before me.
Bast. I will seek them out.
K. John. Nay, but make haste; the better foot
before.
O, let me have no subject enemies
When adverse foreigners affright my towns
With dreadful pomp of stout invasion!
Be Mercury, set feathers to thy heels,
And fly, like thought, from them to me again.
Bast. The spirit of the time shall teach me speed.
Exit.

133. proceedings: i.e. in looting the monasteries, as John had ordered at III.iii.6–11. **137. amaz'd:** stunned.
141. sped: succeeded.
147–57. And . . . hang'd. Holinshed (Bullough, IV, 41), who identifies Peter as a hermit "dwelling about Yorke," says that when the day that he had predicted as ominous for John passed without "notable damage" he, "togither with his sonne," was hanged.
148. Pomfret: Pontefract, a town in Yorkshire.
151. Ascension-day: the Thursday forty days after Easter.
158. safety: custody. **159. gentle:** noble.
166. suggestion: instigation.
174. Mercury: messenger of the gods, often depicted as wearing winged sandals.

K. John. Spoke like a sprightful noble gentleman.
Go after him; for he perhaps shall need
Some messenger betwixt me and the peers,
And be thou he.
Mess. With all my heart, my liege. [*Exit*.]
K. John. My mother dead!

Enter Hubert.

Hub. My lord, they say five moons were seen
to-night;
Four fixed, and the fift did whirl about
The other four in wondrous motion.
K. John. Five moons?
Hub. Old men and beldames in the streets
Do prophesy upon it dangerously.
Young Arthur's death is common in their mouths,
And when they talk of him, they shake their heads,
And whisper one another in the ear;
And he that speaks doth gripe the hearer's wrist,
Whilst he that hears makes fearful action
With wrinkled brows, with nods, with rolling eyes.
I saw a smith stand with his hammer, thus,
The whilst his iron did on the anvil cool,
With open mouth swallowing a tailor's news,
Who, with his shears and measure in his hand,
Standing on slippers, which his nimble haste
Had falsely thrust upon contrary feet,
Told of a many thousand warlike French
That were embattailed and rank'd in Kent.
Another lean unwash'd artificer
Cuts off his tale and talks of Arthur's death.
K. John. Why seek'st thou to possess me with
these fears?
Why urgest thou so oft young Arthur's death?
Thy hand hath murd'red him. I had a mighty cause
To wish him dead, but thou hadst none to kill him.
Hub. No had, my lord? Why, did you not provoke
me?
K. John. It is the curse of kings to be attended
By slaves that take their humors for a warrant
To break within the bloody house of life,
And on the winking of authority
To understand a law; to know the meaning
Of dangerous majesty, when perchance it frowns
More upon humor than advis'd respect.
Hub. Here is your hand and seal for what I did.
K. John. O, when the last accompt 'twixt heaven
and earth
Is to be made, then shall this hand and seal
Witness against us to damnation!

177. sprightful: high-spirited.
182. five moons. "About the moneth of December [1200]," says Holinshed (Bullough, IV, 29), "there were seene in the province of Yorke five moones, one in the east, the second in the west, the third in the north, the fourth in the south, and the fift as it were set in the middest of the other, having manie stars about it."
185. beldames: old women, crones.
186. prophesy upon it: i.e. expound its significance.
190. gripe: grasp. **191. action:** gestures.
200. embattailed: drawn up in line of battle.
201. artificer: artisan.
207. No had: did I not have. **provoke:** incite.
209. humors: moods. **211. winking:** closing both eyes.
214. upon humor: by caprice. **advis'd respect:** deliberate consideration.

How oft the sight of means to do ill deeds
Make deeds ill done! Hadst not thou been by,
A fellow by the hand of nature mark'd,
Quoted, and sign'd to do a deed of shame,
This murther had not come into my mind;
But taking note of thy abhorr'd aspect,
Finding thee fit for bloody villainy,
Apt, liable to be employ'd in danger,
I faintly broke with thee of Arthur's death;
And thou, to be endeared to a king,
Made it no conscience to destroy a prince.

Hub. My lord—

K. John. Hadst thou but shook thy head or made a pause
When I spake darkly what I purposed,
Or turn'd an eye of doubt upon my face,
As bid me tell my tale in express words,
Deep shame had struck me dumb, made me break off,
And those thy fears might have wrought fears in me.
But thou didst understand me by my signs,
And didst in signs again parley with sin,
Yea, without stop, didst let thy heart consent,
And consequently thy rude hand to act
The deed, which both our tongues held vild to name.
Out of my sight, and never see me more!
My nobles leave me, and my state is braved,
Even at my gates, with ranks of foreign pow'rs;
Nay, in the body of this fleshly land,
This kingdom, this confine of blood and breath,
Hostility and civil tumult reigns
Between my conscience and my cousin's death.

Hub. Arm you against your other enemies,
I'll make a peace between your soul and you.
Young Arthur is alive. This hand of mine
Is yet a maiden and an innocent hand,
Not painted with the crimson spots of blood.
Within this bosom never ent'red yet
The dreadful motion of a murderous thought,
And you have slander'd nature in my form,
Which howsoever rude exteriorly,
Is yet the cover of a fairer mind
Than to be butcher of an innocent child.

K. John. Doth Arthur live? O, haste thee to the peers,
Throw this report on their incensed rage,
And make them tame to their obedience!
Forgive the comment that my passion made
Upon thy feature, for my rage was blind,
And foul imaginary eyes of blood
Presented thee more hideous than thou art.
O, answer not! but to my closet bring
The angry lords with all expedient haste.
I conjure thee but slowly; run more fast. *Exeunt.*

222. **Quoted, and sign'd:** designated and marked.
223. **murther:** murder. 226. **liable:** suitable.
227. **faintly:** hintingly, indirectly. **broke with thee:** broached to you the subject. 229. **Made . . . conscience:** did not scruple.
234. **As:** as if to. **express:** explicit. 240. **act:** perform.
243. **state is braved:** government is challenged.
245. **this fleshly land:** i.e. John's own body.
246. **confine:** (1) region; (2) prison. 255. **motion:** impulse.
256. **nature . . . form:** humanity in my person.
264. **feature:** physical appearance. 265. **imaginary:** imagined.
267. **closet:** chamber. 269. **conjure:** adjure.

Scene III

Enter Arthur *on the walls.*

Arth. The wall is high, and yet will I leap down.
Good ground, be pitiful and hurt me not!
There's few or none do know me; if they did,
This ship-boy's semblance hath disguis'd me quite.
I am afraid, and yet I'll venture it.
If I get down, and do not break my limbs,
I'll find a thousand shifts to get away.
As good to die and go, as die and stay. [*Leaps down.*]
O me, my uncle's spirit is in these stones.
Heaven take my soul, and England keep my bones! *Dies.*

Enter Pembroke, Salisbury, *and* Bigot.

Sal. Lords, I will meet him at Saint Edmundsbury.
It is our safety, and we must embrace
This gentle offer of the perilous time.

Pem. Who brought that letter from the Cardinal?

Sal. The Count Melune, a noble lord of France,
Whose private with me of the Dolphin's love
Is much more general than these lines import.

Big. To-morrow morning let us meet him then.

Sal. Or rather then set forward, for 'twill be
Two long days' journey, lords, or ere we meet.

Enter Bastard.

Bast. Once more to-day well met, distemper'd lords!
The King by me requests your presence straight.

Sal. The King hath dispossess'd himself of us.
We will not line his thin bestained cloak
With our pure honors, nor attend the foot
That leaves the print of blood where e'er it walks.
Return, and tell him so. We know the worst.

Bast. What e'er you think, good words I think were best.

Sal. Our griefs, and not our manners, reason now.

Bast. But there is little reason in your grief;
Therefore 'twere reason you had manners now.

Pem. Sir, sir, impatience hath his privilege.

Bast. 'Tis true—to hurt his master, no [man] else.

Sal. This is the prison. [*Seeing Arthur.*] What is he lies here?

Pem. O death, made proud with pure and princely beauty!
The earth had not a hole to hide this deed.

IV.iii. Location: England. Before the castle.
1–10. The wall . . . bones. Some historians, says Holinshed (Bullough, IV, 33), think that as Arthur "assaied to have escaped out of prison, and prooving to clime over the wals of the castell [of Rouen], he fell into the river of Saine, and so was drowned. Other write, that through verie greefe and languor he pined awaie, and died of naturall sickenesse. But some affirme, that king John secretlie caused him to be murthered and made awaie, so as it is not throughlie agreed upon, in what sort he finished his daies: but verelie king John was had in great suspicion, whether worthilie or not, the lord knoweth." 4. **semblance:** disguise.
7. **shifts:** (1) contrivances; (2) changes of clothing.
11. **him:** i.e. Lewis. **Saint Edmundsbury:** Bury St. Edmunds, ancient town in Suffolk. 16. **private:** private communication.
17. **general:** comprehensive. 20. **or ere:** before.
21. **distemper'd:** disturbed, out of temper.
29. **griefs:** grievances. **reason:** speak.

Sal. Murther, as hating what himself hath done,
Doth lay it open to urge on revenge.
Big. Or when he doom'd this beauty to a grave,
Found it too precious-princely for a grave.
Sal. Sir Richard, what think you? [Have you] beheld,
Or have you read, or heard, or could you think?
Or do you almost think, although you see,
That you do see? Could thought, without this object,
Form such another? This is the very top,
The heighth, the crest, or crest unto the crest,
Of murther's arms. This is the bloodiest shame,
The wildest savagery, the vildest stroke,
That ever wall-ey'd wrath or staring rage
Presented to the tears of soft remorse.
Pem. All murthers past do stand excus'd in this;
And this, so sole and so unmatchable,
Shall give a holiness, a purity,
To the yet unbegotten sin of times;
And prove a deadly bloodshed but a jest,
Exampled by this heinous spectacle.
Bast. It is a damned and a bloody work,
The graceless action of a heavy hand—
If that it be the work of any hand.
Sal. If that it be the work of any hand?
We had a kind of light what would ensue.
It is the shameful work of Hubert's hand,
The practice and the purpose of the King;
From whose obedience I forbid my soul,
Kneeling before this ruin of sweet life,
And breathing to his breathless excellence
The incense of a vow, a holy vow,
Never to taste the pleasures of the world,
Never to be infected with delight,
Nor conversant with ease and idleness,
Till I have set a glory to this hand,
By giving it the worship of revenge.
Pem., Big. Our souls religiously confirm thy words.

Enter HUBERT.

Hub. Lords, I am hot with haste in seeking you.
Arthur doth live, the King hath sent for you.
Sal. O, he is bold, and blushes not at death.
Avaunt, thou hateful villain, get thee gone!
Hub. I am no villain.
Sal. Must I rob the law?
[*Drawing his sword.*]
Bast. Your sword is bright, sir, put it up again.
Sal. Not till I sheathe it in a murtherer's skin.
Hub. Stand back, Lord Salisbury, stand back, I say;
By heaven, I think my sword's as sharp as yours.
I would not have you, lord, forget yourself,
Nor tempt the danger of my true defense,
Lest I, by marking of your rage, forget

41. Sir Richard: i.e. the Bastard. **43. almost:** even.
44. That: that which. **46. heighth:** height.
49. wall-ey'd: i.e. glaring. **50. remorse:** compassion.
54. times: the future. **56. Exampled:** compared with.
58. graceless: impious. **heavy:** wicked.
61. light: premonition. **63. practice:** scheming.
72. worship: honor. **77. Avaunt:** be gone. **84. tempt:** test.

Your worth, your greatness, and nobility.
Big. Out, dunghill! dar'st thou brave a nobleman?
Hub. Not for my life; but yet I dare defend
My innocent life against an emperor.
Sal. Thou art a murtherer.
Hub. Do not prove me so;
Yet I am none. Whose tongue soe'er speaks false,
Not truly speaks; who speaks not truly, lies.
Pem. Cut him to pieces.
Bast. Keep the peace, I say.
Sal. Stand by, or I shall gall you, Faulconbridge.
Bast. Thou wert better gall the devil, Salisbury.
If thou but frown on me, or stir thy foot,
Or teach thy hasty spleen to do me shame,
I'll strike thee dead. Put up thy sword betime,
Or I'll so maul you and your toasting-iron
That you shall think the devil is come from hell.
Big. What wilt thou do, renowned Faulconbridge?
Second a villain and a murtherer?
Hub. Lord Bigot, I am none.
Big. Who kill'd this prince?
Hub. 'Tis not an hour since I left him well.
I honor'd him, I lov'd him, and will weep
My date of life out for his sweet live's loss.
Sal. Trust not those cunning waters of his eyes,
For villainy is not without such rheum,
And he, long traded in it, makes it seem
Like rivers of remorse and innocency.
Away with me, all you whose souls abhor
Th' uncleanly savors of a slaughter-house,
For I am stifled with this smell of sin.
Big. Away toward Bury, to the Dolphin there!
Pem. There, tell the King, he may inquire us out.
Exeunt Lords.
Bast. Here's a good world! Knew you of this fair work?
Beyond the infinite and boundless reach
Of mercy, if thou didst this deed of death,
Art thou damn'd, Hubert.
Hub. Do but hear me, sir.
Bast. Ha? I'll tell thee what;
Thou'rt damn'd as black—nay, nothing is so black—
Thou art more deep damn'd than Prince Lucifer.
There is not yet so ugly a fiend of hell
As thou shalt be, if thou didst kill this child.
Hub. Upon my soul—
Bast. If thou didst but consent
To this most cruel act, do but despair,
And if thou want'st a cord, the smallest thread
That ever spider twisted from her womb
Will serve to strangle thee; a rush will be a beam
To hang thee on; or wouldst thou drown thyself,
Put but a little water in a spoon,
And it shall be as all the ocean,
Enough to stifle such a villain up.
I do suspect thee very grievously.
Hub. If I in act, consent, or sin of thought
Be guilty of the stealing that sweet breath
Which was embounded in this beauteous clay,

90. prove me so: i.e. by forcing me to kill you.
94. gall: injure. **97. spleen:** anger. **106. live's:** life's.
109. traded: experienced. **112. savors:** odors.

Let hell want pains enough to torture me.
I left him well.
Bast. Go, bear him in thine arms.
I am amaz'd, methinks, and lose my way
Among the thorns and dangers of this world.
How easy dost thou take all England up
From forth this morsel of dead royalty!
The life, the right, and truth of all this realm
Is fled to heaven; and England now is left
To tug and scamble, and to part by th' teeth
The unowed interest of proud swelling state.
Now for the bare-pick'd bone of majesty
Doth dogged war bristle his angry crest,
And snarleth in the gentle eyes of peace;
Now powers from home and discontents at home
Meet in one line; and vast confusion waits,
As doth a raven on a sick-fall'n beast,
The imminent decay of wrested pomp.
Now happy he whose cloak and center can
Hold out this tempest. Bear away that child,
And follow me with speed. I'll to the King.
A thousand businesses are brief in hand,
And heaven itself doth frown upon the land. *Exeunt.*

ACT [V], Scene I

Enter King John *and* Pandulph, Attendants.

K. John. Thus have I yielded up into your hand
The circle of my glory. [*Giving the crown.*]
Pand. Take again
From this my hand, as holding of the Pope,
Your sovereign greatness and authority.
K. John. Now keep your holy word, go meet the French,
And from his Holiness use all your power
To stop their marches 'fore we are inflam'd.
Our discontented counties do revolt;
Our people quarrel with obedience,
Swearing allegiance and the love of soul
To stranger blood, to foreign royalty.
This inundation of mistemp'red humor
Rests by you only to be qualified.
Then pause not; for the present time's so sick,
That present med'cine must be minist'red,
Or overthrow incurable ensues.
Pand. It was my breath that blew this tempest up,
Upon your stubborn usage of the Pope;
But since you are a gentle convertite,
My tongue shall hush again this storm of war,
And make fair weather in your blust'ring land.
On this Ascension-day, remember well,
Upon your oath of service to the Pope,
Go I to make the French lay down their arms. *Exit.*
K. John. Is this Ascension-day? Did not the prophet
Say that before Ascension-day at noon
My crown I should give off? Even so I have.
I did suppose it should be on constraint,
But (heav'n be thank'd!) it is but voluntary.

Enter Bastard.

Bast. All Kent hath yielded; nothing there holds out
But Dover castle. London hath receiv'd,
Like a kind host, the Dolphin and his powers.
Your nobles will not hear you, but are gone
To offer service to your enemy;
And wild amazement hurries up and down
The little number of your doubtful friends.
K. John. Would not my lords return to me again
After they heard young Arthur was alive?
Bast. They found him dead and cast into the streets,
An empty casket, where the jewel of life
By some damn'd hand was robb'd and ta'en away.
K. John. That villain Hubert told me he did live.
Bast. So, on my soul, he did, for aught he knew.
But wherefore do you droop? why look you sad?
Be great in act, as you have been in thought.
Let not the world see fear and sad distrust
Govern the motion of a kingly eye.
Be stirring as the time, be fire with fire,
Threaten the threat'ner, and outface the brow
Of bragging horror; so shall inferior eyes,
That borrow their behaviors from the great,
Grow great by your example and put on
The dauntless spirit of resolution.
Away, and glister like the god of war
When he intendeth to become the field.
Show boldness and aspiring confidence.
What, shall they seek the lion in his den,
And fright him there? and make him tremble there?
O, let it not be said! Forage, and run
To meet displeasure farther from the doors,
And grapple with him ere he come so nigh.
K. John. The legate of the Pope hath been with me,
And I have made a happy peace with him,
And he hath promis'd to dismiss the powers
Led by the Dolphin.
Bast. O inglorious league!
Shall we, upon the footing of our land,
Send fair-play orders and make compremise,
Insinuation, parley, and base truce
To arms invasive? Shall a beardless boy,
A cock'red silken wanton, brave our fields,

140. amaz'd: stunned. **146. scamble:** scramble.
147. unowed: of uncertain ownership.
151. powers from home: foreign troops.
154. wrested pomp: usurped authority. **155. center:** cincture, belt.
158. brief in hand: i.e. demanding prompt action.

V.i. Location: England. King John's palace.
1–4. Thus . . . authority. After long defiance of the Pope, says Holinshed (Bullough, IV, 40), John was finally (1213) obliged to come to terms with him. "Wherefore shortlie after (in like manner as pope Innocent had commanded) he tooke the crowne from his owne head, and delivered the same to Pandulph the legat, neither he, nor his heires at anie time thereafter to receive the same, but at the popes hands." **11. stranger:** foreign.
12. mistemp'red: unbalanced (referring to the excess of one of the four bodily humors, a condition that, in Elizabethan physiology, was thought to cause ill health). **13. qualified:** abated.
15. present: immediate. **18. Upon:** following.

36. doubtful: anxious. **55. become:** adorn. **59. Forage:** raven.
66. upon . . . land: standing on our own soil.
67. fair-play: chivalric. **compremise:** compromise.
69. invasive: invading.
70. cock'red: pampered. **brave:** make a splendid show of force in.

And flesh his spirit in a warlike soil,
Mocking the air with colors idlely spread,
And find no check? Let us, my liege, to arms.
Perchance the Cardinal cannot make your peace;
Or if he do, let it at least be said,
They saw we had a purpose of defense.

K. John. Have thou the ordering of this present time.

Bast. Away then with good courage! Yet I know
Our party may well meet a prouder foe. *Exeunt.*

Scene II

Enter, in arms, [Lewis *the*] *Dolphin,* Salisbury, Melune, Pembroke, Bigot, Soldiers.

Lew. My Lord Melune, let this be copied out,
And keep it safe for our remembrance.
Return the president to these lords again,
That having our fair order written down,
Both they and we, perusing o'er these notes,
May know wherefore we took the sacrament,
And keep our faiths firm and inviolable.

Sal. Upon our sides it never shall be broken.
And, noble Dolphin, albeit we swear
A voluntary zeal and an unurg'd faith
To your proceedings, yet believe me, Prince,
I am not glad that such a sore of time
Should seek a plaster by contemn'd revolt,
And heal the inveterate canker of one wound
By making many. O, it grieves my soul,
That I must draw this metal from my side
To be a widow-maker! O, and there
Where honorable rescue and defense
Cries out upon the name of Salisbury!
But such is the infection of the time,
That for the health and physic of our right,
We cannot deal but with the very hand
Of stern injustice and confused wrong.
And is't not pity, O my grieved friends,
That we, the sons and children of this isle,
[Were] born to see so sad an hour as this,
Wherein we step after a stranger, march
Upon her gentle bosom, and fill up
Her enemies' ranks—I must withdraw and weep
Upon the spot of this enforced cause—
To grace the gentry of a land remote,
And follow unacquainted colors here?
What, here? O nation, that thou couldst remove!
That Neptune's arms, who clippeth thee about,
Would bear thee from the knowledge of thyself,
And [gripple] thee unto a pagan shore,
Where these two Christian armies might combine
The blood of malice in a vein of league,
And not to spend it so unneighborly!

Lew. A noble temper dost thou show in this,
And great affections wrastling in thy bosom
Doth make an earthquake of nobility.
O, what a noble combat hast [thou] fought
Between compulsion and a brave respect!
Let me wipe off this honorable dew,
That silverly doth progress on thy cheeks.
My heart hath melted at a lady's tears,
Being an ordinary inundation;
But this effusion of such manly drops,
This show'r, blown up by tempest of the soul,
Startles mine eyes, and makes me more amaz'd
Than had I seen the vaulty top of heaven
Figur'd quite o'er with burning meteors.
Lift up thy brow, renowned Salisbury,
And with a great heart heave away this storm.
Commend these waters to those baby eyes
That never saw the giant world enrag'd,
Nor met with fortune other than at feasts,
Full warm of blood, of mirth, of gossiping.
Come, come; for thou shalt thrust thy hand as deep
Into the purse of rich prosperity
As Lewis himself; so, nobles, shall you all,
That knit your sinews to the strength of mine.

Enter Pandulpho.

And even there, methinks an angel spake.
Look where the holy legate comes apace,
To give us warrant from the hand of heaven,
And on our actions set the name of right
With holy breath.

Pand. Hail, noble Prince of France!
The next is this: King John hath reconcil'd
Himself to Rome, his spirit is come in,
That so stood out against the holy Church,
The great metropolis and see of Rome;
Therefore thy threat'ning colors now wind up,
And tame the savage spirit of wild war,
That like a lion fostered up at hand,
It may lie gently at the foot of peace,
And be no further harmful than in show.

Lew. Your Grace shall pardon me, I will not back.
I am too high-born to be propertied,
To be a secondary at control,
Or useful servingman and instrument
To any sovereign state throughout the world.
Your breath first kindled the dead coal of wars
Between this chastis'd kingdom and myself,
And brought in matter that should feed this fire;

71. flesh: initiate into slaughter. **72. idlely:** idly, carelessly.
76. purpose of defense: intention of defending ourselves.

V.ii. Location: England. The Dolphin's camp at Saint Edmundsbury.
3. president: precedent, i.e. first draft.
4. order: arrangement, proposal.
6. took the sacrament. Holinshed records (Bullough, IV, 42) that in 1214 the disaffected nobles assembled at Bury St. Edmunds and took a "solemne oth" to oppose the King until he restored to them the ancient "liberties" that he had stripped away. This event, a prologue to the signing of Magna Carta in the following year, was historically unrelated to the French invasion in 1216. **16. metal:** i.e. sword.
18–19. Where . . . Salisbury: where those who are honorably defending their country exclaim against Salisbury. **21. physic:** remedy.
27. step after: follow. **stranger:** alien. **30. spot:** stain.
32. unacquainted colors: unfamiliar flags.

36. gripple: grapple.
37–38. combine . . . league: i.e. spend their blood in a united effort (against a common foe).
41. affections: passions. **wrastling:** wrestling.
44. brave respect: gallant regard (for your country).
53. Figur'd: adorned. **70. is come in:** has submitted.
73. wind: furl. **78. back:** go back.
79. propertied: made a chattel of.

And now 'tis far too huge to be blown out
With that same weak wind which enkindled it.
You taught me how to know the face of right,
Acquainted me with interest to this land,
Yea, thrust this enterprise into my heart,
And come ye now to tell me John hath made
His peace with Rome? What is that peace to me?
I, by the honor of my marriage-bed,
After young Arthur, claim this land for mine,
And now it is half conquer'd, must I back
Because that John hath made his peace with Rome?
Am I Rome's slave? What penny hath Rome borne?
What men provided? what munition sent,
To underprop this action? Is't not I
That undergo this charge? Who else but I,
And such as to my claim are liable,
Sweat in this business and maintain this war?
Have I not heard these islanders shout out
"*Vive le roi!*" as I have bank'd their towns?
Have I not here the best cards for the game,
To win this easy match play'd for a crown?
And shall I now give o'er the yielded set?
No, no, on my soul, it never shall be said.

Pand. You look but on the outside of this work.

Lew. Outside or inside, I will not return
Till my attempt so much be glorified
As to my ample hope was promised
Before I drew this gallant head of war,
And cull'd these fiery spirits from the world,
To outlook conquest and to win renown
Even in the jaws of danger and of death.
[*Trumpet sounds*.]
What lusty trumpet thus doth summon us?

Enter BASTARD.

Bast. According to the fair play of the world,
Let me have audience. I am sent to speak:
My holy Lord of Milan, from the King
I come to learn how you have dealt for him;
And, as you answer, I do know the scope
And warrant limited unto my tongue.

Pand. The Dolphin is too willful-opposite,
And will not temporize with my entreaties.
He flatly says he'll not lay down his arms.

Bast. By all the blood that ever fury breath'd,
The youth says well. Now hear our English King,
For thus his royalty doth speak in me:
He is prepar'd, and reason too he should—
This apish and unmannerly approach,
This harness'd masque and unadvised revel,
This [unhair'd] sauciness and boyish troops,
The King doth smile at, and is well prepar'd
To whip this dwarfish war, this pigmy arms,
From out the circle of his territories.
That hand which had the strength, even at your door,
To cudgel you and make you take the hatch,
To dive like buckets in concealed wells,
To crouch in litter of your stable planks,
To lie like pawns lock'd up in chests and trunks,
To hug with swine, to seek sweet safety out
In vaults and prisons, and to thrill and shake
Even at the crying of your nation's crow,
Thinking this voice an armed Englishman;
Shall that victorious hand be feebled here,
That in your chambers gave you chastisement?
No! Know the gallant monarch is in arms,
And like an eagle o'er his aery tow'rs,
To souse annoyance that comes near his nest;
And you degenerate, you ingrate revolts,
You bloody Neroes, ripping up the womb
Of your dear mother England, blush for shame;
For your own ladies and pale-visag'd maids
Like Amazons come tripping after drums,
Their thimbles into armed gauntlets change,
Their needl's to lances, and their gentle hearts
To fierce and bloody inclination.

Lew. There end thy brave, and turn thy face in peace;
We grant thou canst outscold us. Fare thee well!
We hold our time too precious to be spent
With such a brabbler.

Pand. Give me leave to speak.

Bast. No, I will speak.

Lew. We will attend to neither.
Strike up the drums, and let the tongue of war
Plead for our interest and our being here.

Bast. Indeed your drums, being beaten, will cry out;
And so shall you, being beaten. Do but start
An echo with the clamor of thy drum,
And even at hand a drum is ready brac'd
That shall reverberate all as loud as thine.
Sound but another, and another shall
(As loud as thine) rattle the welkin's ear,
And mock the deep-mouth'd thunder; for at hand
(Not trusting to this halting legate here,
Whom he hath us'd rather for sport than need)
Is warlike John; and in his forehead sits
A bare-ribb'd death, whose office is this day
To feast upon whole thousands of the French.

Lew. Strike up our drums, to find this danger out.

Bast. And thou shalt find it, Dolphin, do not doubt.
Exeunt.

89. interest: i.e. my claim. **101. liable:** subject.
104. Vive le roi: long live the king; perhaps alluding also to the name of a playing card (like the king or queen in modern decks), which suggests the figure in the following lines. **bank'd:** sailed past; perhaps with play on another card term, designating the taking of a card.
107. yielded set: game already won. **113. head of war:** army.
115. outlook: outstare, defy.
118. fair play: i.e. chivalric code. **123. limited:** appointed.
124. willful-opposite: stubbornly opposed.
125. temporize: make terms.
132. harness'd masque: masque in armor. **unadvised:** ill-considered.
133. unhair'd: beardless, i.e. youthful.
138. take the hatch: leap over the lower half of the door in haste.
141. pawns: articles in pawnshops. **143. thrill:** shiver.
144. crying . . . crow: i.e. crowing of the cocks (?).
149. aery: nest. **tow'rs:** soars.
150. souse: swoop down on. **151. revolts:** rebels.
152. Neroes: i.e. unfilial wretches (alluding to the Roman emperor Nero, who reputedly murdered and then disembowelled his mother).
155. Amazons: legendary race of female warriors.
157. needl's: needles (monosyllabic, as often).
159. brave: swaggering.
163. attend: listen. **169. brac'd:** tightened.

Scene III

Alarums. Enter [King] John *and* Hubert.

K. John. How goes the day with us? O, tell me, Hubert.
Hub. Badly, I fear. How fares your Majesty?
K. John. This fever, that hath troubled me so long,
Lies heavy on me. O, my heart is sick!

Enter a Messenger.

Mess. My lord, your valiant kinsman, Faulconbridge,
Desires your Majesty to leave the field,
And send him word by me which way you go.
K. John. Tell him toward Swinstead, to the abbey there.
Mess. Be of good comfort; for the great supply,
That was expected by the Dolphin here,
Are wrack'd three nights ago on Goodwin Sands;
This news was brought to Richard but even now.
The French fight coldly, and retire themselves.
K. John. Ay me, this tyrant fever burns me up,
And will not let me welcome this good news.
Set on toward Swinstead. To my litter straight,
Weakness possesseth me, and I am faint. *Exeunt.*

Scene IV

Enter Salisbury, Pembroke, *and* Bigot.

Sal. I did not think the King so stor'd with friends.
Pem. Up once again! Put spirit in the French;
If they miscarry, we miscarry too.
Sal. That misbegotten devil Faulconbridge,
In spite of spite, alone upholds the day.
Pem. They say King John, sore sick, hath left the field.

Enter Melune *wounded.*

Mel. Lead me to the revolts of England here.
Sal. When we were happy we had other names.
Pem. It is the Count Melune.
Sal. Wounded to death.
Mel. Fly, noble English, you are bought and sold!
Unthread the rude eye of rebellion,
And welcome home again discarded faith.
Seek out King John and fall before his feet;
For if the French be lords of this loud day,
He means to recompense the pains you take
By cutting off your heads. Thus hath he sworn,
And I with him, and many moe with me,
Upon the altar at Saint Edmundsbury,
Even on that altar where we swore to you
Dear amity and everlasting love.
Sal. May this be possible? May this be true?
Mel. Have I not hideous death within my view,
Retaining but a quantity of life,
Which bleeds away even as a form of wax
Resolveth from his figure 'gainst the fire?
What in the world should make me now deceive,
Since I must lose the use of all deceit?
Why should I then be false, since it is true
That I must die here and live hence by truth?
I say again, if Lewis do win the day,
He is forsworn if e'er those eyes of yours
Behold another day break in the east;
But even this night, whose black contagious breath
Already smokes about the burning crest
Of the old, feeble, and day-wearied sun,
Even this ill night your breathing shall expire,
Paying the fine of rated treachery
Even with a treacherous fine of all your lives,
If Lewis by your assistance win the day.
Commend me to one Hubert with your king;
The love of him, and this respect besides,
For that my grandsire was an Englishman,
Awakes my conscience to confess all this.
In lieu whereof, I pray you bear me hence
From forth the noise and rumor of the field,
Where I may think the remnant of my thoughts
In peace, and part this body and my soul
With contemplation and devout desires.
Sal. We do believe thee, and beshrew my soul
But I do love the favor and the form
Of this most fair occasion, by the which
We will untread the steps of damned flight,
And like a bated and retired flood,
Leaving our rankness and irregular course,
Stoop low within those bounds we have o'erlook'd,
And calmly run on in obedience
Even to our ocean, to our great King John.
My arm shall give thee help to bear thee hence,
For I do see the cruel pangs of death
Right in thine eye. Away, my friends! New flight,
And happy newness, that intends old right.
Exeunt [*leading off Melune*].

Scene V

Enter [Lewis *the*] *Dolphin and his* Train.

Lew. The sun of heaven, methought, was loath to set,
But stay'd and made the western welkin blush,

V.iii. Location: England. The field of battle.
8. **Swinstead.** Shakespeare's mistake (perhaps derived from Foxe's *Acts and Monuments*) for Swineshead, site of an abbey in Lincolnshire.
9. **supply:** reinforcement.
11. **wrack'd:** shipwrecked. **Goodwin Sands:** dangerous shoal in the English Channel off the coast of Kent.

V.iv. Location: Scene continues.
5. **In spite of spite:** i.e. in spite of everything.
7. **revolts:** rebellious nobles. 10. **bought and sold:** i.e. betrayed.
11. **Unthread . . . rebellion:** i.e. withdraw from rebellion, into which you have been drawn as thread into a needle's eye.
15. **He:** i.e. Lewis. 17. **moe:** more.
23. **quantity:** i.e. small quantity. 25. **Resolveth:** melts. **his:** its.
27. **use:** benefit. 29. **hence:** i.e. to heaven.
34. **smokes:** grows misty. **crest:** helmet.
37. **fine:** penalty. **rated:** correctly estimated. 38. **fine:** end.
41. **respect:** consideration.
44. **In lieu whereof:** i.e. in requital of which information.
45. **rumor:** noise. 49. **beshrew:** curse.
50. **But:** unless. **favor . . . form:** i.e. appearance.
53. **bated:** checked. 54. **rankness:** flooding.
55. **o'erlook'd:** overflowed. 60. **Right:** unmistakable.
61. **intends old right:** has as its goal the restoration of ancient right.

V.v. Location: England. The French camp.

When English measure backward their own ground
In faint retire. O, bravely came we off,
When with a volley of our needless shot,
After such bloody toil, we bid good night,
And wound our tott'ring colors clearly up,
Last in the field, and almost lords of it!

Enter a Messenger.

Mess. Where is my prince, the Dolphin?
Lew. Here: what news?
Mess. The Count Melune is slain; the English lords
By his persuasion are again fall'n off,
And your supply, which you have wish'd so long,
Are cast away, and sunk on Goodwin Sands.
Lew. Ah, foul shrewd news! Beshrew thy very
heart!
I did not think to be so sad to-night
As this hath made me. Who was he that said
King John did fly an hour or two before
The stumbling night did part our weary pow'rs?
Mess. Whoever spoke it, it is true, my lord.
Lew. Well; keep good quarter and good care to-
night;
The day shall not be up so soon as I,
To try the fair adventure of to-morrow. *Exeunt.*

Scene VI

Enter Bastard *and* Hubert *severally.*

Hub. Who's there? Speak ho! speak quickly, or
I shoot.
Bast. A friend. What art thou?
Hub. Of the part of England.
Bast. Whither dost thou go?
Hub. What's that to thee? Why may not I demand
Of thine affairs, as well as thou of mine?
Bast. Hubert, I think.
Hub. Thou hast a perfect thought.
I will upon all hazards well believe
Thou art my friend that know'st my tongue so well.
Who art thou?
Bast. Who thou wilt; and if thou please,
Thou mayst befriend me so much as to think
I come one way of the Plantagenets.
Hub. Unkind remembrance! thou and endless night
Have done me shame. Brave soldier, pardon me
That any accent breaking from thy tongue
Should scape the true acquaintance of mine ear.
Bast. Come, come; sans compliment, what news
abroad?
Hub. Why, here walk I in the black brow of night,
To find you out.
Bast. Brief then; and what's the news?
Hub. O my sweet sir, news fitting to the night,

7. **tott'ring:** flying in tatters. 14. **shrewd:** bad.
18. **stumbling:** i.e. causing to stumble. 20. **quarter:** watch.
22. **adventure:** hazard.

V.vi. **Location:** England. An open place near Swinstead Abbey.
2. **Of the part:** on the side. 6. **perfect:** correct.
12. **Unkind remembrance:** i.e. what a bad memory I have.
14. **accent:** speech.
16. **sans compliment:** without the customary civilities.

Black, fearful, comfortless, and horrible.
Bast. Show me the very wound of this ill news;
I am no woman, I'll not swound at it.
Hub. The King, I fear, is poison'd by a monk.
I left him almost speechless, and broke out
To acquaint you with this evil, that you might
The better arm you to the sudden time
Than if you had at leisure known of this.
Bast. How did he take it? Who did taste to him?
Hub. A monk, I tell you, a resolved villain,
Whose bowels suddenly burst out. The King
Yet speaks, and peradventure may recover.
Bast. Who didst thou leave to tend his Majesty?
Hub. Why, know you not? the lords are all come
back,
And brought Prince Henry in their company,
At whose request the King hath pardon'd them,
And they are all about his Majesty.
Bast. Withhold thine indignation, mighty heaven,
And tempt us not to bear above our power!
I'll tell thee, Hubert, half my power this night,
Passing these flats, are taken by the tide—
These Lincoln Washes have devoured them;
Myself, well mounted, hardly have escap'd.
Away before; conduct me to the King;
I doubt he will be dead or ere I come. *Exeunt.*

Scene VII

Enter Prince Henry, Salisbury, *and* Bigot.

P. Hen. It is too late, the life of all his blood
Is touch'd corruptibly; and his pure brain
(Which some suppose the soul's frail dwelling-house)
Doth by the idle comments that it makes
Foretell the ending of mortality.

22. **swound:** swoon.
23. **poison'd . . . monk.** Pursued by his enemies, says Holinshed (Bullough, IV, 46–47), John ruthlessly ravaged the country as he marched north from Winchester. Disheartened by the loss of "a great part of his armie, with horsses and carriages" while crossing the Welland in Lincolnshire, he "fell into an ague" that grew worse when he gorged himself on raw peaches and cider at Swineshead Abbey, and after being carried on a litter to Newark he died in great agony on October 19, 1216. By Shakespeare's time it was widely thought that he had died of poison, administered perhaps by a monk resentful of his depredations or perhaps by one of his own servants, who, in collusion with a "convert" of Swineshead Abbey, prepared for him a dish of poisoned pears. 26. **sudden time:** emergency.
27. **at leisure:** i.e. later.
28. **it:** i.e. the poison. **taste:** act as the taster (who ate of every dish offered the king, to detect poison).
29–30. **A monk . . . out.** In his *Acts and Monuments* John Foxe, sharing none of Holinshed's reserve, asserts (Bullough, IV, 52–53) that John was "most traiterously poisoned" by a monk named Simon. Having told the abbot of his plan and receiving absolution, Simon prepared the poison from "a most venemous Toad," put it in a cup of wine, "and with a smiling and flattering countenance, he sayde thus to the King: If it shall like your Princely majestie, here is such a cuppe of wine, as yee never dronke a better before in all your life time. I trust this Wassall shal make al England glad. And with that he dranke a great draught thereof, the king pledging him. The Monke anone after went to the farmerye, and there died (his guts gushing out of his belly) and had continually from thencefoorth three Monkes to sing Masse for his soule, confirmed by theyr generall chapter."
34. **Prince Henry:** John's son and heir, the future Henry III (1207–72).
38. **bear . . . power:** suffer beyond our capacity for endurance.
42. **hardly:** with difficulty. 44. **doubt:** fear.

V.vii. **Location:** England. The orchard at Swinstead Abbey.
2. **pure:** i.e. normally clear (?).
4. **idle comments:** i.e. babble. 5. **mortality:** life.

Enter PEMBROKE.

Pem. His Highness yet doth speak, and holds belief
That being brought into the open air,
It would allay the burning quality
Of that fell poison which assaileth him.

P. Hen. Let him be brought into the orchard here.
Doth he still rage? [*Exit Bigot.*]

Pem. He is more patient
Than when you left him; even now he sung.

P. Hen. O vanity of sickness! fierce extremes
In their continuance will not feel themselves.
Death, having prey'd upon the outward parts,
Leaves them invisible, and his siege is now
Against the [mind], the which he pricks and wounds
With many legions of strange fantasies,
Which in their throng and press to that last hold,
Confound themselves. 'Tis strange that death should sing.
I am the [cygnet] to this pale faint swan
Who chaunts a doleful hymn to his own death,
And from the organ-pipe of frailty sings
His soul and body to their lasting rest.

Sal. Be of good comfort, Prince, for you are born
To set a form upon that indigest
Which he hath left so shapeless and so rude.

[KING] JOHN *brought in.*

K. John. Ay, marry, now my soul hath elbow-room,
It would not out at windows nor at doors.
There is so hot a summer in my bosom
That all my bowels crumble up to dust.
I am a scribbled form, drawn with a pen
Upon a parchment, and against this fire
Do I shrink up.

P. Hen. How fares your Majesty?

K. John. Poison'd—ill fare! dead, forsook, cast off,
And none of you will bid the winter come
To thrust his icy fingers in my maw,
Nor let my kingdom's rivers take their course
Through my burn'd bosom, nor entreat the north
To make his bleak winds kiss my parched lips
And comfort me with cold. I do not ask you much,
I beg cold comfort; and you are so strait
And so ingrateful, you deny me that.

P. Hen. O that there were some virtue in my tears,
That might relieve you!

K. John. The salt in them is hot.
Within me is a hell, and there the poison
Is as a fiend confin'd to tyrannize
On unreprievable condemned blood.

Enter BASTARD.

Bast. O, I am scalded with my violent motion
And spleen of speed to see your Majesty!

K. John. O cousin, thou art come to set mine eye.
The tackle of my heart is crack'd and burn'd,

11. **rage**: rave.
16. **invisible**: imperceptibly (?). Some editors emend to *insensible.*
20. **Confound**: destroy. 26. **indigest**: formless confusion.
27. **rude**: crude. 42. **strait**: niggardly. 44. **virtue**: power.
50. **spleen**: eagerness. 51. **set**: close.

And all the shrouds wherewith my life should sail
Are turned to one thread, one little hair.
My heart hath one poor string to stay it by,
Which holds but till thy news be uttered,
And then all this thou seest is but a clod
And module of confounded royalty.

Bast. The Dolphin is preparing hitherward,
Where [God] he knows how we shall answer him;
For in a night the best part of my pow'r,
As I upon advantage did remove,
Were in the Washes all unwarily
Devoured by the unexpected flood. [*The King dies.*]

Sal. You breathe these dead news in as dead an ear.
My liege, my lord! but now a king, now thus.

P. Hen. Even so must I run on, and even so stop.
What surety of the world, what hope, what stay,
When this was now a king, and now is clay?

Bast. Art thou gone so? I do but stay behind
To do the office for thee of revenge,
And then my soul shall wait on thee to heaven,
As it on earth hath been thy servant still.
Now, now, you stars, that move in your right spheres,
Where be your pow'rs? Show now your mended faiths,
And instantly return with me again
To push destruction and perpetual shame
Out of the weak door of our fainting land.
Straight let us seek, or straight we shall be sought;
The Dolphin rages at our very heels.

Sal. It seems you know not then so much as we.
The Cardinal Pandulph is within at rest,
Who half an hour since came from the Dolphin,
And brings from him such offers of our peace
As we with honor and respect may take,
With purpose presently to leave this war.

Bast. He will the rather do it when he sees
Ourselves well sinewed to our defense.

Sal. Nay, 'tis in a manner done already,
For many carriages he hath dispatch'd
To the sea-side, and put his cause and quarrel
To the disposing of the Cardinal,
With whom yourself, myself, and other lords,
If you think meet, this afternoon will post
To consummate this business happily.

Bast. Let it be so, and you, my noble Prince,
With other princes that may best be spar'd,
Shall wait upon your father's funeral.

P. Hen. At Worcester must his body be interr'd,
For so he will'd it.

Bast. Thither shall it then;

53. **shrouds**: ropes. 55. **stay it**: sustain itself.
58. **module**: image. **confounded**: shattered.
59. **preparing**: repairing. 60. **answer**: resist.
62. **upon advantage**: taking advantage of a good opportunity.
65. **dead news**: deadly news. 72. **wait on**: attend.
74. **stars**: i.e. the revolted nobles who had returned to John. **right**: proper. 75. **faiths**: loyalties. 86. **presently**: immediately.
90. **carriages**: baggage vehicles. 94. **post**: hasten.
99. **Worcester**. John's body was taken to Worcester by his "men of warre," says Holinshed (Bullough, IV, 47–48), "each man with his armour on his backe, in warlike order," and there "pompouslie buried in the cathedrall church before the high altar; not for that he had so appointed (as some write) but bicause it was thought to be a place of most suertie for the lords and other of his freends there to assemble, and to take order in their businesse now after his decease."

And happily may your sweet self put on
The lineal state and glory of the land!
To whom with all submission, on my knee,
I do bequeath my faithful services
And true subjection everlastingly.
Sal. And the like tender of our love we make,
To rest without a spot for evermore.
P. Hen. I have a kind soul that would give thanks,
And knows not how to do it but with tears.

101. happily: propitiously. **102. lineal state:** hereditary royalty. **104. bequeath:** give. **106. tender:** offer.

Bast. O, let us pay the time but needful woe,
Since it hath been beforehand with our griefs.
This England never did, nor never shall,
Lie at the proud foot of a conqueror,
But when it first did help to wound itself.
Now these her princes are come home again,
Come the three corners of the world in arms,
And we shall shock them. Nought shall make us rue,
If England to itself do rest but true. *Exeunt.*

116. three . . . world: i.e. all the rest of the world (England being the fourth corner). **117. shock:** meet with force.

NOTE ON THE TEXT

The First Folio (1623) is the only authority for *King John;* all later texts are derived from that source. Opinion is divided over the exact nature of the copy-text underlying F1. Some scholars have argued for a prompt-book provenience; others for a direct use of Shakespeare's "foul papers" (Honigmann). Most recently, however, Jowett/Taylor, Braunmuller, and Beaurline have argued for a scribal transcript (by two scribes) of the "foul papers," the change in scribes occurring between IV.ii.171 and IV.ii.216, and there is nothing in the F1 text which can be said to point unmistakably to the hand of a prompter. The confusion in character names (between King Philip and Lewis the Dolphin, the Citizen and Hubert), the Philip-Richard designation for Faulconbridge, and the inconsistency in certain speech-prefixes (for Lewis and Queen Elinor; see the Textual Notes) are characteristic of "foul papers." On the other hand, these irregularities do not seem serious enough to exclude the possibility that the manuscript underlying F1 had served as a prompt-book, and the difficulty in the F1 act-scene division in what is designated in modern texts (since Theobald) as III.i may perhaps be the result of markings in the manuscript which involved the cutting of the first seventy-four lines. Moreover, the almost complete absence of what may be called Shakespearean spellings in the F1 text (note, however, *moth* for *mote* in IV.i.91) makes it somewhat difficult to believe that the compositors (identified as B and C) were setting directly from Shakespeare's autograph.

Fortunately, it is unnecessary to become too deeply entangled here in the knotty problem of the date of *King John* and its relation to the anonymous two-part play called *The Troublesome Raigne of Iohn King of England (T.R.)* published in 1591, except to notice that comparatively recently there has been some disposition by a few critics (Alexander, Honigmann, and Beaurline) to consider *T.R.* as some kind of imitation based on Shakespeare's *King John,* a view in sharp opposition to the traditional opinion which takes *T.R.* as Shakespeare's principal source (see Ribner, Smallwood, D. Wilson, Greg, Jowett/Taylor, and Braunmuller). The proponents of taking *T.R.* as an awkward imitation of Shakespeare's *King John* are forced, in my view, into arguments that can only be described as special pleading, arguments that attempt, with admitted ingenuity, to explain away a number of important points that militate strongly against any such assumption: (1) the lack of any really significant verbal impact of *King John* on *T.R.* (only one identical line, more than twenty part-lines and phrases, and scattered words often used in different contexts; see Wilson, pp. xxvi–xxxii); (2) the unlikelihood that even Shakespeare could have risen to the commanding quality of Faulconbridge, as character or speaker, in 1590 (nothing really comparable in the *Henry VI* plays, for example); (3) the general agreement of the various verse and language tests on placing *King John* chronologically as falling between *Richard III* and *1 Henry IV* (see *A Textual Companion,* p. 119); (4) the duplication, or near duplication, of five stage directions common to both *King John* and *T.R.,* the direction of borrowing (by Shakespeare from *T.R.*) being virtually determined by the fact that *King John* was not available for consultation (first published, 1623); and (5) the implications of the absence of memorial tags from *King John* in the *Contention* (1594) and *True Tragedy* (1595), the "bad" quartos of 2 and *3 Henry VI,* where, however, tags from *T.R.* do occur. For further arguments supporting the view that *T.R.* is the principal source for *King John,* see Wilson, Ribner, Smallwood, and Braunmuller. Whatever the merits of the "bad" quarto view, *T.R.* itself is of no significant value in dealing with specifically textual problems in the F1 text.

For further information, see: J. D. Wilson, ed., New Shakespeare *King John* (Cambridge, 1936); Peter Alexander, *Shakespeare's Life and Art* (London, 1939); E. A. J. Honigmann, ed., New Arden *King John* (London, 1954); W. W. Greg, *The Shakespeare First Folio* (Oxford, 1955); Geoffrey Bullough, ed., *Narrative and Dramatic Sources of Shakespeare,* IV (London, 1962); Irving Ribner, ed., Pelican *King John* (Baltimore, Maryland, 1969); R. L. Smallwood, ed., New Penguin *King John* (Harmondsworth, Middlesex, 1974); Emrys Jones, *The Origins of Shakespeare* (Oxford, 1977, Appendix D); Stanley Wells, Gary Taylor, John Jowett, and William Montgomery, *William Shakespeare: A Textual Companion* (Oxford, 1987); A. R. Braunmuller, ed., New Oxford *King John* (Oxford, 1989); L. A. Beaurline, ed., New Cambridge *King John* (Cambridge, 1990).

TEXTUAL NOTES

Dramatis personae: *subs. as first given by Rowe*

Act-scene division: *from F1, with the following exceptions: II.i (I.ii in F1); III.i (headed as Act II in F1, which then marks III.i after III.i.74 in the present text); III.iii (no scene division in F1); III.iv (III.iii in F1); V.i (by error numbered IV.i in F1); see first note to each scene; present act-scene arrangement as a whole first established by Dyce*

I.i

Location: *Cambridge*

o.s.d. **Chatillion]** *Rowe (subs.);* Chattylion *F1*

8 **brother]** *F4;* brother, *F1*

11 **Anjou, Touraine]** *Rowe;* Aniowe, Torayne *F1*

30 **s.d. Exeunt]** *Warburton;* Exit *F1*

41 **me;]** *Pope;* me, *F1*

43 **s.d. and . . . ear]** *Capell (after T. R.* & whispers the Earle of *Sals* in the eare.)

47 s.d. **Exit Sheriff.**] *Capell*
49 **expedition's**] *F2 (subs.)*; expeditious *F1*
49 s.d. **Enter . . . Philip**] *placed as in Dyce; after l. 49, F1*
50 s.p. **Bast.**] Philip. *F1 (until l. 138)*
50 **subject I,**] *Capell*; subiect, I *F1*
53 **honor-giving hand**] *Rowe*; Honor-giuing-hand *F1*
79 **yourself.**] *Rowe*; your selfe *F1*
81 **him,**] *Collier*; him: *F1*
122 **his?**] *Theobald*; his, *F1*
139 **his,**] *Rowe*; his *F1*
140 **riding-rods**] *hyphen, Capell*
147 **Sir Nob**] *Capell*; sir nobbe *F1*
170 **about,**] *F4*; about *F1*
182 **A foot**] *Rowe*; *Bast.* A foot *F1 (repeated s.p.)*
189 **conversion.**] *Capell*; conuersion, *F1*
201 **compliment**] *Rowe*; Complement *F1*
203 **Pyrenean**] *Pope*; Perennean *F1*
208 **smack**] *Theobald*; smoake *F1*
218 **woman-post**] *hyphen, F4*
219 s.d. **Enter . . . Gurney.**] *placed as in Capell; after l. 221, F1*
222 s.p. **Lady F.**] *Malone*; Lady. *F1 (throughout scene)*
231 **Philip? sparrow!**] *Upton conj.*; Philip, sparrow, *F1*
236 **well— . . . confess—**] *Vaughan conj.*; well, marrie to confesse *F1*
237 **he**] *Pope*; *om. F1*
237 **me. Sir**] *Vaughan conj.*; me sir *F1*
256 **Heaven!**] *Knight*; Heauen *F1*
269 **Ay**] *Rowe*; aye *F1*

II.i

II.i] *Rowe*; Scaena Secunda. *F1*
o.s.d. **Enter . . . forces.**] *Kittredge (after Capell)*; Enter before Angiers, Philip King of France, Lewis, Daulphin Austria, Constance, Arthur. *F1*
1, 18 s.pp. **K. Phi.**] *Theobald conj.*; Lewis. *F1*
37 s.p. **K. Phi.**] *Rowe*; King. *F1 (until l. 89)*;
37 **work! Our**] *Collier (after Theobald)* worke our *F1*
59 **I;**] *F2 (subs.)*; I *F1*
62 **mother-queen**] *hyphen, F4*
63 **Ate**] *Rowe*; Ace *F1*
89 s.p. **K. Phi.**] *Rowe*; Fran. *F1 (throughout rest of scene)*
113 **breast**] *F2*; beast *F1*
120 s.p. **El.**] *Rowe*; Queen. *F1 (throughout scene, except as noted)*
127 **John in manners,**] *Vaughan conj. (after Capell)*; Iohn, in manners *F1*
144 **shows**] *Theobald*; shooes *F1*
149 **Philip**] *Theobald*; Lewis *F1*
150 s.p. **K. Phi.**] *Theobald*; Lew. *F1*
152 **Anjou**] *Theobald*; Angiers *F1*
166 s.p. **El.**] *Rowe*; Qu. Mo. *F1*
193 **that? A will!**] *Rowe*; that, a Will: *F1*
200 s.d. **Hubert**] *Honigmann (after a suggestion by Wilson)*; a Citizen *F1*
200 s.d. **and other Citizens**] *ed. (after Capell)*
201, 267, 270, 281 s.pp. **Hub.**] *Honigmann*; Cit. *F1*
214 **French**] *Rowe (subs.)*; French. *F1*
215 **Confronts**] *Capell (after Rowe)*; Comfort *F1*
215 **your**] *F3*; yours *F1*
217 **waist**] *F4*; waste *F1*
252 **invulnerable**] *F2*; involuerable *F1*
267 **subjects:**] *Theobald (subs.)*; subiects *F1*
287 **chevaliers! To**] *Capell*; Cheualiers to *F1*
290 s.d. **To Austria.**] *Pope*
299 s.d. **Hubert . . . above.**] *ed.*
306 **earth**] *F2*; earrh *F1*
327 **your**] *F2*; yonr *F1*
335 **on?**] *Pope*; on, *F1*
368 s.p. **Hub.**] *Honigmann*; Fra. *F1*
413 s.d. **Aside.**] *Capell*
468 s.p. **El.**] *Rowe*; Old Qu. *F1*
468 **match,**] *F2*; match *F1*
478 **pity,**] *Theobald*; pittie *F1*
487 **Anjou**] *Pope*; Angiers *F1*
496 s.p. **Lew.**] *Rowe*; Dol. *F1 (throughout scene)*
500 **sun**] *Rowe*; sonne *F1*
504 s.d. **Aside.**] *Dyce*
507 **traitor. . . . now,**] *F4 (subs.)*; traytor, . . . now; *F1*
521 **young ones**] *Rowe*; yong-ones *F1*
536 **Angiers**] *F2*; Angires *F1*
539 **rites**] *F4*; rights *F1*
541 **not,**] *F3*; not *F1*
560 **unlook'd-for**] *hyphen, Warburton*
560 s.d. **all . . . Bastard**] *Rowe*
577 **vile-drawing**] *hyphen, Pope*
582 **all-changing word**] *Pope*; all-changing-word *F1*
588 **woo'd**] *Theobald*; wooed *F1*

III.i

III.i] *Pope*; Actus Secundus *F1*
Location: *Theobald*
3 **Blanch**] *F4*; Blaunch *F1 (throughout scene)*
16–7 **jest, . . . spirits**] *Rowe*; iest . . . spirits, *F1*
63 **Envenom**] *F2*; Euvenom *F1*
73 s.d. **Throws . . . ground.**] *Steevens (after Theobald, Capell; following l. 74)*; *placed as in Kittredge*
74] *Following this line F1 inserts* Actus Tertius, Scaena prima. *(suggests that ll. 1–74 may have been cut in performance); Theobald first continued the scene unbroken*
74 s.d. **Elinor**] *Rowe*; Elianor *F1*
74 s.d. **Austria,**] *Theobald*; Austria, Constance *F1*
83 s.d. **Rising.**] *Theobald*
92 **But . . . day**] *Dyce (after Rowe)*; But (on this day) *F1*
102 **enemies'**] *Capell*; enemies *F1*
107 **kings!**] *Capell (after Rowe)*; Kings, *F1*
108 **cries;**] *Capell*; cries, *F1*
110 **day**] *Theobald*; daies *F1*
144 **see**] *F4*; Sea *F1*
148 **taste**] *F3*; tast *F1*
155 **God**] *Collier MS (after T. R.)*; heauen *F1*
185 **too: . . . right,**] *Rowe (subs.)*; too, . . . right. *F1*
196 **that,**] *Pope*; that *F1*
242 **heaven?**] *ed.*; heauen, *F1*
243 **ourselves**] *F2 (subs.)*; onr selues *F1*
275 **again;**] *Theobald*; again, *F1*
280 **religion,**] *Collier (after Knight)*; religion: *F1*
282–3 **truth . . . oath;**] *Steevens (subs., after Heath conj.)*; truth, . . . oath *F1*
300, 317, 337 s.pp. **Lew.**] *Rowe*; Daul. *or* Dolph. *F1*
324 **clock-setter**] *hyphen, F3*
330 **whirl**] *Rowe*; whurle *F1*
339 s.d. **Exit Bastard.**] *Pope*
347 **let's**] *F3*; le'ts *F1*

III.ii

Location: *Malone*
4 s.d. **Enter . . . Hubert.**] *placed as in Capell; after l. 3, F1 (Pope, omitting l. 4, here inserts from T. R.:* Thus hath K. *Richards* Sonne performde his vowes. / And offred *Austrias* bloud for sacrifice / Unto his fathers euerliuing soule.)
10 s.d. **Exeunt.**] *Rowe*; Exit. *F1*

III.iii

III.iii] *Capell*
Location: *ed. (after Wilson)*
o.s.d. **Elinor**] *Rowe*; Eleanor *F1*
1 s.d. **To Elinor.**] *Hanmer*
2 s.d. **To Arthur.**] *Pope*
6 s.d. **To Bastard.**] *Pope*
17 s.d. **Exit Bastard.**] *Pope*
18 s.d. **Takes Arthur aside.**] *Pope (subs.)*
26 **time**] *Pope*; tune *F1*
66 **lord?**] *Rowe*; Lord. *F1*
67 **now.**] *Rowe*; now, *F1*

III.iv

III.iv] *Capell*; Scena Tertia. *F1*
Location: *Malone (subs.)*
1 s.p. **K. Phi.**] *Rowe*; Fra. *F1 (throughout scene)*
10 s.p. **Lew.**] *Rowe*; Dol. *F1 (throughout scene)*
14 **kindred action**] *Theobald*; kindred-action *F1*
25 **death.**] *Theobald (subs.)*; death, *F1*
35 **Misery's**] *Rowe*; Miseries *F1*
44 **not**] *F4*
64 **friends**] *Rowe*; fiends *F1*
79 **male child**] *Pope*; male-childe *F1*
101 s.d. **Tearing her hair.**] *Collier MS*
105 **sorrows'**] *Capell*; sorrowes *F1*
114–5 **leave, . . . departure**] *Capell*; leaue . . . departure, *F1*
133 **misplac'd John**] *Rowe*; mis-plac'd-Iohn *F1*
180 **offense.**] *Knight*; offence, *F1*

IV.i

Location: *Capell (subs.)*
6, 85 s.pp. **1. Exec.**] *Cambridge (after Capell)*; Exec. *F1*
7 **scruples!**] *Rowe*; scruples *F1*
7 s.d. **Exeunt Executioners.**] *Cambridge (after Capell)*
23 **indeed**] *F2*; in deede *F1*
25, 33 s.dd. **Aside.**] *Rowe*
29 **In sooth**] *Pope*; Insooth *F1*
32 s.d. **Aside.**] *Capell*
33 s.d. **Showing a paper.**] *Rowe*
38 **effect.**] *Rowe*; effect, *F1*
46 **minutes**] *Rowe*; minutes, *F1*
63 **his**] *Capell*; this *F1*
67 **stubborn-hard**] *hyphen, Theobald*
71 s.d. **Stamps.**] *Pope*
71 s.d. **Enter . . . etc.**] *Cambridge (after Pope, Capell)*
75 **boist'rous-rough**] *hyphen, Theobald*
85 s.d. **Exeunt Executioners.**] *Cambridge (after Pope, Capell)*
91 **mote**] *Steevens*; moth *F1*
100 **will,**] *Rowe*; will *F1*
107 **undeserv'd**] *Rowe*; vndeserued *F1*
120 **mercy-lacking**] *Pope*; mercy, lacking *F1*

IV.ii

Location: *Pope, Capell*
1 **again crown'd**] *F3*; against crown'd *F1*
8 **long'd-for change**] *Rowe*; long'd-for-change *F1*
21 **antique**] *Pope*; Anticke *F1*
21 **well-noted**] *hyphen, Pope*
42 **strong**] *Collier*; strong, *F1*
50 **safety,**] *Johnson*; safety: *F1*
51 **studies—**] *Rowe (subs.)*; studies, *F1*
60 **exercise.**] *Rowe*; exercise, *F1*
61 **time's**] *Pope*; times *F1*
65 **Than . . . weal,**] *Pope*; Then, . . . weale *F1*
66 **weal**] *Rowe*; weale: *F1*
68 s.d. **Taking him aside.**] *Capell (subs. after Hanmer)*
73 **Doth**] *Dyce*; Do *F1*
102 s.d. **Lords**] *Capell*
110 **England.**] *Roderick conj.*; England, *F1*
143 **travell'd**] *F4*; trauail'd *F1*
159 s.d. **Exit . . . Peter.**] *Theobald*
180 s.d. **Exit.**] *Rowe*
246 **breath,**] *F4* (breath *F3*); breathe *F1*

IV.iii

Location: *Capell*
8 s.d. **Leaps down.**] *Rowe (T. R. gives the following s.d.:* He leapes, and brusing his bones, after he was from his traunce, speakes thus;)
15 **Melune**] *ed.*; Meloone *F1 (or* Meloon *throughout)*
16 **love**] *Theobald*; loue, *F1*
24 **thin bestained**] *Rowe*; thin-bestained *F1*

33 man] *F2;* mans *F1*
34 s.d. **Seeing Arthur.]** *Pope*
40 **precious-princely]** *hyphen, Capell*
41 **Have you]** *F3;* you haue *F1*
78 s.d. **Drawing his sword.]** *Pope*
115 **There,]** *Theobald;* There *F1*
115 s.d. **Exeunt Lords.]** *Rowe;* Ex. *F1*
159 **Exeunt.]** *Rowe;* Exit. *F1*

V.i

V.i] *Rowe;* Actus Quartus, Scaena prima. *F1*
Location: *Pope, Capell*
2. s.d. **Giving the crown.]** *Pope*
11 **stranger blood]** *Theobald;* stranger-bloud *F1*
67 **fair-play orders]** *Capell;* fayre-play-orders *F1*
67 **compremise]** *ed.;* comprimise *F1*
70 **cock'red silken]** *Fleay (after Pope);* cockred-silken *F1*

V.ii

Location: *Pope, Theobald*
1 s.p. **Lew.]** *Rowe;* Dol. *F1 (throughout scene)*
16 **metal]** *Rowe;* mettle *F1*
26 **Were]** *F2;* Was *F1*
29–32 **ranks— . . . here?]** *Theobald (subs.);* rankes? . . . cause, . . . heere: *F1*
36 **gripple]** *Steevens conj.;* cripple *F1*
43 **thou]** *F4*
56 **baby eyes]** *Capell;* baby-eyes *F1*
57 **giant world]** *Theobald;* giant-world *F1*
72 **see]** *F4;* Sea *F1*
79 **propertied,]** *F4* (propertied *F2*); proportied *F1*
116 s.d. **Trumpet sounds.]** *Rowe*
124 **willful-opposite]** *hyphen, Theobald*
133 **unhair'd]** *Theobald;* vn-heard *F1*
153 **mother England]** *Theobald;* Mother-England *F1*
170 **all]** *Pope;* all, *F1*

V.iii

Location: *Pope*
11 **Sands;]** *Collier (subs.);* sands. *F1*
12 **now.]** *Johnson;* now, *F1*
14 **Ay]** *Rowe;* Aye *F1*

V.iv

Location: *ed. (after Wilson)*
2–3 **French; . . . miscarry,]** *Rowe (subs.);* French, . . . miscarry: *F1*
61 s.d. **leading off Melune]** *Theobald*

V.v

Location: *Hanmer*
7 **wound]** *Rowe;* woon'd *F1*

V.vi

Location: *Theobald*
3 **dost]** *F2;* doest *F1*
16 **compliment]** *Warburton (in italics);* complement *F1*
41 **Lincoln Washes]** *Pope;* Lincolne-Washes *F1*

V.vii

Location: *Theobald*
11 s.d. **Exit Bigot.]** *Capell*
17 **mind]** *Rowe;* winde *F1*
19 **throng]** *F2;* throng, *F1*
21 **cygnet]** *Rowe;* Symet *F1 (possibly a misprint for* Synet, *a variant form of* signet, *in its turn a spelling of* cygnet)
29 **doors.]** *Pope;* doores, *F1*
35 **Poison'd—]** *Capell;* Poyson'd, *F1*
60 **God]** *S. Walker conj.;* heauen *F1 (cf. III.i. 155)*
64 s.d. **The King dies.]** *Rowe*
65 **ear.]** *F4 (subs.);* eare *F1*
88 **sinewed]** *Rowe;* sinew'd *F1*
110 **time]** *Rowe;* time: *F1*

Henry VIII angel

Threepence

Three-farthing piece

Groat

Penny

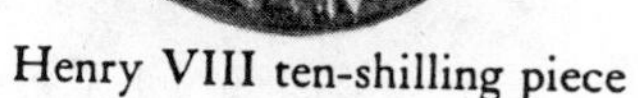

Henry VIII ten-shilling piece

Henry VI noble

Edward IV royal

Milled sixpence

Hammered sixpence

Edward VI shove-groat shilling

From the collection of John Ford Clapp, Jr., Boston; photograph by Mark Silber

Richard II

Unlike Shakespeare's earlier history plays—the Henry VI trilogy, whose authorship and date lie buried under mountains of conjecture; *Richard III*, whose text is such a challenge; and *King John*, whose connection with *The Troublesome Reign* is still a topic of debate—*Richard II* is fairly free of problems. Several pieces of evidence converge to indicate the mid-1590's as the most likely date of composition: the general lyricism of the work, which would put it near the sonnets, *A Midsummer Night's Dream*, and *Romeo and Juliet*; the publication in 1595 of the first installment of Daniel's *Civil Wars*, which most scholars now regard as a source; and an invitation from Sir Edward Hoby to Sir Robert Cecil to what sounds like a private showing of the play at Hoby's house in Canon Row, Westminster, on December 9, 1595 (see Appendix C, Number 15). If the "K. Richard" there presented was indeed Shakespeare's, and if Daniel's poem was indeed a source, *Richard II* can be dated within the limits of a single year, 1595. The piece was entered in the Stationer's Register on August 29, 1597, and published soon thereafter; a string of reprints (see the "Note on the Text" following the play) bear witness to its popularity.

Johnson's flat assertion that the play was "extracted" from Holinshed's *Chronicles* "with very little alteration" has not deterred research, and inevitably the research has complicated what appeared to be a simple problem. Although Shakespeare's debt to the second (1587) edition of Holinshed is clear, not only for the record of the main events of Richard's later reign but sometimes (as in II.iv) for the very language of a scene, several other alleged sources have been put forward. For example, the view of John of Gaunt as a sage and patriotic elder statesman—not a trace of which appears in Holinshed—may reveal a knowledge of Froissart, but A. P. Rossiter has urged the claims of *Woodstock*, an anonymous play about the early reign of Richard II in which the young king's uncle, Thomas of Woodstock, Duke of Gloucester, fills a similar role. If, as seems probable, *Woodstock* is the earlier play, then Gaunt's allusion to "My brother Gloucester, plain well-meaning soul" (II.i.128) and to the old man's murder at Calais (I.ii.3) may be construed as further links, as may many verbal parallels about Richard's misbehavior as a king. *A Mirror for Magistrates* (with its examplary "tragedies" of Woodstock, Mowbray, Northumberland, and Richard II) and Marlowe's *Edward II* (another play about the downfall of a weak and unsuccessful king) do not provide such striking verbal echoes (or perhaps parallels deriving from a common source), but it can hardly be supposed that Shakespeare was uninfluenced by these works. The anonymous *Chronicque de la Traïson et Mort de Richart Deux* and Jean Créton's metrical *Histoire du Roy d'Angleterre Richard*, two anti-Lancastrian accounts of Richard's deposition, were still in manuscript in the later sixteenth century, but they were known to Stow and Holinshed, and Shakespeare may have drawn on them for certain sympathetic touches in his treatment of Richard, especially in the last two acts. His use of Daniel's *Civil Wars*, as Peter Ure and other scholars think, is more direct and therefore more important; also, it helps us date the composition of the play. Such alleged resemblances as those in Carlisle's speech about the horrors of rebellion (IV.i.121–29) may reflect a common Tudor attitude, and others may be merely coincidental; but Richard's entrance into London after he has given up the crown and the parting of the royal lovers (V.i) seems to draw on Daniel's touching treatment of the scene (Book I, Stanzas 66–98), not merely in its language but also in its pathos and intention. In short, Holinshed, whom Johnson took to be the only source, has now been joined by many rivals. Indeed, Dover Wilson, doubting that Shakespeare would have read so many books in preparation for his task, thought that *Richard II* may have had a single source in a now lost play by someone "soaked" in English history.

Shakespeare's eight plays on fifteenth-century history record the rise and fall of the Lancastrian line. In the so-called first tetralogy—the three Henry VI plays and *Richard III*, which were written near the start of his career—he traced its long decline through the crooked course of English politics between the death of Henry V in 1422 and the advent of the Tudors in 1485. In the second sequence—*Richard II*, *1* and *2 Henry IV*, and *Henry V*—he treats its hard-fought rise to power in the early fifteenth century. Here his subject is the Lancastrian Bullingbrook's usurpation of his cousin Richard's throne, his misadventures as a king and his problems as the father of a wayward son, the accession of that son as Henry V and his victory in the foreign wars that brought such glory to his realm and such honor to his line. Whether or not Shakespeare conceived this second series of histories as a unit, these plays are made to serve a quasi-documentary function, for with the customary distortion and rearrangement of events they set forth the main facts of English history between 1398 and 1420. Also, starting as they do with such a dread event as the deposition of a lawful king, passing to its consequences in what Edward Hall in his *Union of . . . Lancaster and York* (1548) termed "the unquiet time" of Henry IV, and ending with "the victorious acts" of Henry V, they define a moral pattern of sin and retribution crowned by expiation and success. On one level, at least, the theme is that which Hall and many other Tudors held so dear: that rebellion is both a crime and a sin, and is bound to lead to trouble until the curse is lifted. Daniel's comment in the preface to his *Civil Wars* (which treats the same materials that Shakespeare treated in the two tetralogies) reflects the widely shared opinion that fifteenth-century history is both appalling and instructive because it shows

> the deformities of civil dissension and the miserable events of rebellions, conspiracies, and bloody revengements which followed (as in a circle) upon that break of the due course of succession by the usurpation of Henry IV; [and because it makes] the blessings of peace and the happiness of an established government (in a direct line) the better to appear.

This motif is very strong in *Richard II*. When urged to seek revenge upon the King for the murder of Gloucester, Gaunt—the very embodiment of political morality and the speaker of the most stirring paean to England ever written (II.i.40–58)—says that he could "never lift / An angry arm" against the Lord's anointed. Later, Gaunt's brother York, though dismayed by Richard's crimes, denounces any show of force as "gross rebellion and detested treason." Inevitably, the weak and foolish king himself, when he confronts disaster, takes comfort in the knowledge that

> Not all the water in the rough rude sea
> Can wash the balm off from an anointed king;
> The breath of worldly men cannot depose
> The deputy elected by the Lord. (III.ii.54–57)

Even after Richard's deposition, Carlisle berates the usurper Bullingbrook for a crime so "heinous, black, obscene," and then he prophesies—what the first tetralogy had already shown—an age of woeful retribution. If Bullingbrook is crowned, he warns,

> The blood of English shall manure the ground,
> And future ages groan for this foul act.
> Peace shall go sleep with Turks and infidels,
> And in this seat of peace tumultuous wars
> Shall kin with kin and kind with kind confound.
> Disorder, horror, fear, and mutiny
> Shall here inhabit, and this land be call'd
> The fields of Golgotha and dead men's skulls.
> (IV.i.137–44)

For his pains, however, Carlisle is promptly (and with flagrant illegality) arrested on a charge of treason, the king whose lost cause he defends is murdered, and Bullingbrook ascends the throne. In short, *Richard II* records with indignation the course and outcome of a successful insurrection.

Also, it records the deposition of a king who shows himself unfit to rule. To regard Richard as sentimentally as he regards himself is to ignore what Shakespeare is at pains to underscore: that whereas rebellion is a crime, kingship is a sacred burden which one must earn the right to bear. An "unstaid youth" burning in a "rash fierce blaze of riot," Richard has nothing but his royal birth and title to justify the misbehavior, and these are not enough to save him from the consequences of his crimes and follies. He acts flippantly toward Bullingbrook and Mowbray, insolently toward his uncles Gaunt and York, and illegally toward his banished cousin. Dissolute and avaricious, and "basely led / By flatterers," he converts his "sceptred isle" into a "pelting farm" and himself into the "landlord" of the realm. Delighting in the ceremonies and symbols of his station but unwilling—or perhaps unable—to assume its obligations, he betrays the trust of greatness. As the head and centre of the state—that delicate equipoise of reciprocal obligations—he should be wise and brave and just; but as the Gardener's servant recognizes, he is in fact the very emblem of disorder:

> Why should we in the compass of a pale
> Keep law and form and due proportion,
> Showing, as in a model, our firm estate,
> When our sea-walled garden, the whole land,
> Is full of weeds, her fairest flowers chok'd up,
> Her fruit-trees all unprun'd, her hedges ruin'd,
> Her knots disordered and her wholesome herbs
> Swarming with caterpillars? (III.iv.40–47)

At last obliged to deal with the realities of his desperate situation, he turns to his own false image of himself—and it shatters like the glass wherein he views his "brittle glory." Therefore Richard's fall, however moving to himself and us as he verbalizes his despair, must be referred as much to his defects of character as to Bullingbrook's ambition.

Since Richard abdicates his royal function before he abdicates the throne, he creates a vacuum that Bullingbrook's ambition enables him to fill. If what he does is criminal, at any rate he saves the state. He is not, like Richard III, a moral monster, and Shakespeare makes it clear that he is not a fool. Lacking his cousin's delicacy of perception and his dazzling skill with words, he also lacks his fatal self-absorption, and in that regard at least he is more fit to be a king. He is verbal when he needs to be (as in the ritual of the lists at Coventry), so adept at politics that he stirs his cousin's envy, angry in a righteous cause, brave and energetic as a leader, and judicious in his use of power. Most important, he is a man of action rather than reflection, and as such the natural foil to Richard, who makes poetry of the fact:

> Here, cousin, seize the crown;
> Here, cousin,
> On this side my hand, and on that side thine.
> Now is this golden crown like a deep well
> That owes two buckets, filling one another,
> The emptier ever dancing in the air,
> The other down, unseen, and full of water:
> That bucket down and full of tears am I,
> Drinking my griefs, whilst you mount up on high.
> (IV.i.181–89)

To which Bullingbrook laconically replies, "I thought you had been willing to resign." This essential difference in their characters not only defines the basic movement of the plot, with Richard's fall producing Bullingbrook's ascent; it also enables Shakespeare to carry on his study of the proper use of power that he had started in the first tetralogy and that would occupy him deeply in the later history plays.

But there is more to *Richard II* than politics and history. Here as in *King John* (which was no doubt close in date of composition) Shakespeare goes beyond the Tudor slogans that had stocked the first tetralogy, and he expands the theme of providential history to such subtle and related questions as the source of political authority and the moral force of one's commitments. Here he uses history not just to prop a dogma or adorn a moral, but to see how men conduct themselves, and why. The Bastard Faulconbridge, almost alone among the swarms of men and women in the earlier history plays, achieves the status of a character, with an identity beyond his dramaturgic and thematic function. Except for moments now and then, we see the others only in their proper roles: Talbot as the man of patriotic valor, Beaufort (or Beauford, in Shakespeare's spelling) as the proud, ambitious prelate, Margaret as the fiend of France, King Henry as the pious weakling, Suffolk as the crafty politician, even Richard of Gloucester (despite his virtuoso skill in acting) as the Yorkist villain. However boldly drawn, they are usually seen in only two dimensions, like the personified abstractions of the old morality plays. Conceived as means instead of ends, they exist to serve a function—to articulate a line of action or represent a type or exemplify a theme—and they wear their function like a badge.

With Richard it is otherwise. He typifies the unsuccessful king, of course, and to that extent instructs us; but it is as a man that he engages and retains our interest. Whereas we learn almost all we need to know about Richard of York from his first soliloquy (*2 Henry VI*, I.i.214–59), we continue to enlarge and modify our view of King Richard as the play proceeds, so that not until the final scene is our response to him complete. As in *King Lear*, this progressive illumination of the regal character is counterpointed with the decline of regal power: from the ceremonial if meretricious splendor of Act I through Richard's brutal treatment of his uncle Gaunt, his ineffectual posturing at Bullingbrook's invasion, and the pathos of his abdication, to the last indignity at Pomfret. Moreover, we can check our progressive recognition of Richard's complicated character by his own assessment of himself. An incorrigible egotist, he contemplates himself with endless fascination, and—poet that he is—he records his findings in poetry so persuasive that we almost think it true. His imperial rhetoric at the start is fitting for his image of himself as king and judge, but on his return from Ireland he assumes the role of king as loving parent, which he plays with ample self-esteem:

> As a long-parted mother with her child
> Plays fondly with her tears and smiles in meeting,
> So weeping, smiling, greet I thee, my earth,
> And do thee favors with my royal hands.
> (III.ii.8–11)

Then, as he learns the facts about his perilous situation, he depicts himself, with subtly modulated irony, as the royal victim of ingratitude:

> throw away respect,
> Tradition, form, and ceremonious duty,
> For you have but mistook me all this while.
> I live with bread like you, feel want,
> Taste grief, need friends: subjected thus,
> How can you say to me I am a king?
> (III.ii.172–77)

He undergoes the same swift change of mood, again expressed in words instead of deeds, when he yields to Bullingbrook at Flint; and in the deposition scene his rhetoric is so adroitly fitted to his fantasies—as when he compares himself to Christ—that the "woeful pageant" of his fall is turned into a play that he himself has staged. He is willing to resign his crown, he says,

> but still my griefs are mine.
> You may my glories and my state depose,
> But not my griefs; still am I king of those.
> (IV.i.191–93)

Even in the tearful parting from his queen he does not cease to dramatize himself, and then to contemplate his own sad image with a certain satisfaction. Finally, in the great aria-like soliloquy at Pomfret, his fantasies take so many shapes, and are expressed in language so complex, that he populates his "little world" with the products of his own "still-breeding thoughts."

It is fitting that a play about a poet-king so much enchanted by the resources, limitations, and ambiguities of language should never stoop to prose. In *Richard II* poetry approaches the condition of music, as Pater noted long ago, and the music lends a heightened function to the style. Limpid, clanging, or sonorous, the intensely musical idiom is so steady through the play—as in Bullingbrook's farewell (I.iii), the famous garden scene (III.iv), and York's account of Richard's entrance into London (V.ii)—that the doggerel in V.iii and V.vi has troubled certain critics. Richard himself is such a virtuoso in the arts of speech that when he fondles words and tropes he seems to listen to himself, tuning his language not merely to the situation but also to his mood, and rejoicing in his skill. Thus he can go from the bold, rhythmically assertive declamation of

> Face to face,
> And frowning brow to brow, ourselves will hear
> The accuser and the accused freely speak
> (I.i.15–17)

to jaunty ease and rancor toward the dying Gaunt, and then, within the compass of a single scene (III.ii), to the soft, caressing music of his salutation to the English earth, the deep-toned splendor of his hymn to royal power, the cacophony of his diatribe on the "three Judases," and finally to his lovely song about the death of kings. Even when he falls into "the mighty hold of Bullingbrook" he is more concerned with style than with emotion as he articulates his grief:

> I'll give my jewels for a set of beads,
> My gorgeous palace for a hermitage,
> My gay apparel for an almsman's gown,
> My figur'd goblets for a dish of wood,
> My sceptre for a palmer's walking-staff,
> My subjects for a pair of carved saints,
> And my large kingdom for a little grave,
> A little little grave, an obscure grave.
> (III.iii.147–54)

The earlier history plays, and notably *Richard III*, are also very formal in their language, but in *Richard II* the verse is more than just a mode of stately utterance: it serves to set the tone and underscore the theme. Richard's tendency to deal in simile and metaphor, for instance, reveals a man who prefers to excogitate and analyze a situation rather than to act, and whose attempts to verbalize his complicated states of mind—as in the deposition scene or in his solitude at Pomfret—engross his whole attention. A born poet, he almost always speaks in tropes (for example, of the sun as symbol of his kingly status, of grief expressed in tears, of England as a blessed plot of earth, of rebellion as a stain), and these tropes state, restate, and amplify the major motifs of the action in ways almost symphonic. Bullingbrook also knows the force of language and bends it to his purpose, but he does not confuse his mental constructs, however deftly verbalized, with hard, unyielding fact; and he does not permit mere words, however sacrosanct and laden with association, to take the place of swift, incisive action.

> O, who can hold a fire in his hand
> By thinking on the frosty Caucasus?
> Or cloy the hungry edge of appetite
> By bare imagination of a feast?
> Or wallow naked in December snow
> By thinking on fantastic summer's heat?
> (I.iii.294–99)

On the other hand, Richard has immense respect for words conceived as symbols; and it is symbols, rather than the things they represent, that govern his behavior. His crown as emblem of the royal power (and as a fertile source of metaphor) is of more concern to him than his duties as a king. His inability to distinguish the external sign or symbol—his royal title, for example, or his sceptre, or a gesture, or the ceremonies of his office—from what the symbol represents is as much a factor in his fall as his abuse of office. "Am I not king?" he says on his return from Ireland (when his cause is clearly hopeless);

> Is not the king's name twenty thousand names?
> Arm, arm, my name! (III.ii.83, 85–86)

The structure of the play is as formal as its language. Its double, complementary plot—the fall of Richard and the rise of Bullingbrook—holds no shock or terror; it is simple, grand, and elemental, like some ancient rite whose progress is prescribed and whose outcome is foreknown. Events are rarely shown directly, with the fresh impact of things as they occur; they come to us not as the realistic imitation of an action but as the ritual presentation of a form or type of action that is framed in ceremony, encased in rhetoric, and draped with rich symbolic implications. Thus we have the protocol of knightly jousts, but not the clash of armed encounter; the circumstances of an armed rebellion, but not the heat and dust of battle; the transaction of an actual deposition, but a deposition that becomes a sacrificial rite. In the light of Rossiter's definition of ritual as "the offering, or the hinting of an offering, of a gesture of regard or respect for something which goes beyond the state-of-affairs or the EVENT," even Richard's death is less a deed of violence than the conclusion of a "woeful pageant" whose subject is the failure of a high ideal.

In addition to the presumed private showing at Sir Edward Hoby's house in 1595, the early theatrical history of *Richard II* is enlivened by the account of a performance at the Globe on February 7, 1601. If this revival, arranged by friends of the Earl of Essex for the very eve of his ill-starred rebellion, was designed as propaganda, it must be regarded as a failure, for it did not lead Londoners to rally to his desperate undertaking. None the less, Elizabeth, a few months later, remarked that she herself was Richard, and she added tartly that the play had been presented forty times "in open streets and houses." Allowing for the Queen's exaggeration, we may infer from her remark and from the play's lively history of quarto publication that the work was widely known, and that the absence of the deposition scene in the earliest printed versions (see the "Note on the Text"), doubtless reflecting a theatrical cut, stemmed from her reluctance to have such lawless doings publicized. That she was not peculiarly sensitive on the subject is indicated by the fact that during the tumults of the late 1670's, when the problem of succession had reached a stage of crisis, Nahum Tate's adaptation of the play was twice suppressed.

Herschel Baker

Rapier and dagger

Rapier and cloak

A "case of rapiers"

The two-hand broadsword

From *Di Grassi His True Art of Defence*, trans. I. G. (1594). (*By permission of the Harvard College Library*)

The Tragedy of King Richard the Second

[Dramatis Personae

King Richard the Second
John of Gaunt, *Duke of Lancaster* } *uncles to the King*
Edmund of Langley, *Duke of York* }
Henry, *surnamed* Bullingbrook, *Duke of Herford, son to John of Gaunt; afterwards* King Henry IV
Duke of Aumerle, *son to the Duke of York*
Thomas Mowbray, *Duke of Norfolk*
Duke of Surrey
Earl of Salisbury
Lord Berkeley
Sir John Bushy }
Sir John Bagot } *favorites to King Richard*
Sir Henry Green }
Earl of Northumberland
Henry Percy, *surnamed* Hotspur, *his son*
Lord Ross
Lord Willoughby

Lord Fitzwater
Bishop of Carlisle
Abbot of Westminster
Lord Marshal
Sir Stephen Scroop
Sir Pierce *of Exton*
Captain *of a band of Welshmen*
Two Gardeners

Queen *to King Richard*
Duchess of York
Duchess of Gloucester, *widow of Thomas of Woodstock, Duke of Gloucester*
Lady *attending on the Queen*

Lords, Heralds, Officers, Soldiers, Keeper, Messenger, Groom, Servingman, *and other* Attendants

Scene: *England and Wales*]

[Act I, Scene I]

Enter King Richard, John of Gaunt, *with other* Nobles *and* Attendants.

K. Rich. Old John of Gaunt, time-honored Lancaster,
Hast thou, according to thy oath and band,
Brought hither Henry Herford thy bold son,
Here to make good the boist'rous late appeal,
Which then our leisure would not let us hear,
Against the Duke of Norfolk, Thomas Mowbray?
Gaunt. I have, my liege.
K. Rich. Tell me, moreover, hast thou sounded him,
If he appeal the Duke on ancient malice,
Or worthily, as a good subject should,
On some known ground of treachery in him?
Gaunt. As near as I could sift him on that argument,
On some apparent danger seen in him
Aim'd at your Highness, no inveterate malice.
K. Rich. Then call them to our presence; face to face,
And frowning brow to brow, ourselves will hear
The accuser and the accused freely speak.
High-stomach'd are they both and full of ire,
In rage, deaf as the sea, hasty as fire.

Words and passages enclosed in square brackets in the text above are either emendations of the copy-text or additions to it. The Textual Notes immediately following the play cite the earliest authority for every such change or insertion and supply the reading of the copy-text wherever it is emended in this edition.

I.i. Location: Windsor. The castle.
1. **Old . . . Gaunt.** Gaunt (so called from his birthplace, Ghent in Flanders) was fifty-eight at the time. 2. **band:** bond.
3. **Herford:** i.e. Hereford; probably pronounced *Harford.* Henry's designation Bullingbrook (derived from the name of his birthplace in Leicestershire) is pronounced without the *g* (and is sometimes spelled so in the early texts). The form *Bolingbroke*, common in modern editions, never occurs in the early texts; it was first employed by Pope in the early eighteenth century. Its adoption by succeeding editors has led to a good deal of uncertainty about the pronunciation.
4. **late appeal:** recent accusation. According to Holinshed (Bullough, III, 387–89), the trouble between Bullingbrook and Mowbray had started at the parliament that met in Shrewsbury in January 1398, when Bullingbrook accused Mowbray of having uttered certain things "sounding highlie to the kings dishonour." Summoned before the council, the two men traded the accusations that are rehearsed later in this scene. After further interrogations the case was adjourned until the following April, when the King would be at Windsor. Other accounts—including those by Hall (Bullough, III, 383), Froissart, and Daniel—have Mowbray begin the altercation by repeating to the King certain complaints about Richard's misrule that Bullingbrook had expressed "more for dolour and lamentacion, then for malice or displeasure." For an authoritative discussion of the quarrel see Charles Oman, *The History of England from the Accession of Richard II to the Death of Richard III* (1910), pp. 141–43.
5. **our, us.** The royal plural (like *ourselves* in line 16). **leisure:** i.e. lack of leisure. 7. **liege:** sovereign. 8. **sounded:** questioned.
9. **appeal:** accuse. **on ancient malice:** because of some old grudge.
12. **sift him:** ascertain his motives through indirect questions. **argument:** topic. 13. **apparent:** manifest.
18. **High-stomach'd:** haughty.

Enter Bullingbrook *and* Mowbray [*with* Attendants].

Bull. Many years of happy days befall
My gracious sovereign, my most loving liege!
Mow. Each day still better other's happiness,
Until the heavens, envying earth's good hap,
Add an immortal title to your crown!
K. Rich. We thank you both, yet one but flatters us,
As well appeareth by the cause you come:
Namely, to appeal each other of high treason.
Cousin of Herford, what dost thou object
Against the Duke of Norfolk, Thomas Mowbray?
Bull. First, heaven be the record to my speech,
In the devotion of a subject's love,
Tend'ring the precious safety of my prince,
And free from other misbegotten hate,
Come I appellant to this princely presence.
Now, Thomas Mowbray, do I turn to thee,
And mark my greeting well; for what I speak
My body shall make good upon this earth,
Or my divine soul answer it in heaven.
Thou art a traitor and a miscreant,
Too good to be so, and too bad to live,
Since the more fair and crystal is the sky,
The uglier seem the clouds that in it fly.
Once more, the more to aggravate the note,
With a foul traitor's name stuff I thy throat,
And wish (so please my sovereign) ere I move,
What my tongue speaks, my right drawn sword may prove.
Mow. Let not my cold words here accuse my zeal.
'Tis not the trial of a woman's war,
The bitter clamor of two eager tongues,
Can arbitrate this cause betwixt us twain;
The blood is hot that must be cool'd for this.
Yet can I not of such tame patience boast
As to be hush'd and nought at all to say.
First, the fair reverence of your Highness curbs me
From giving reins and spurs to my free speech,
Which else would post until it had return'd
These terms of treason doubled down his throat.
Setting aside his high blood's royalty,
And let him be no kinsman to my liege,
I do defy him, and I spit at him,
Call him a slanderous coward, and a villain,
Which to maintain I would allow him odds
And meet him, were I tied to run afoot
Even to the frozen ridges of the Alps,
Or any other ground inhabitable
Where ever Englishman durst set his foot.
Mean time, let this defend my loyalty:
By all my hopes, most falsely doth he lie.
Bull. Pale trembling coward, there I throw my gage,
Disclaiming here the kinred of the King,
And lay aside my high blood's royalty,
Which fear, not reverence, makes thee to except.
If guilty dread have left thee so much strength
As to take up mine honor's pawn, then stoop.
By that, and all the rites of knighthood else,
Will I make good against thee, arm to arm,
What I have spoke, or thou canst worse devise.
Mow. I take it up, and by that sword I swear
Which gently laid my knighthood on my shoulder,
I'll answer thee in any fair degree
Or chivalrous design of knightly trial;
And when I mount, alive may I not light,
If I be traitor or unjustly fight!
K. Rich. What doth our cousin lay to Mowbray's charge?
It must be great that can inherit us
So much as of a thought of ill in him.
Bull. Look what I speak, my life shall prove it true:
That Mowbray hath receiv'd eight thousand nobles
In name of lendings for your Highness' soldiers,
The which he hath detain'd for lewd employments,
Like a false traitor and injurious villain;
Besides I say, and will in battle prove,
Or here or elsewhere to the furthest verge
That ever was surveyed by English eye,
That all the treasons for these eighteen years,
Complotted and contrived in this land,
Fetch from false Mowbray their first head and spring.
Further I say, and further will maintain
Upon his bad life to make all this good,
That he did plot the Duke of Gloucester's death,
Suggest his soon-believing adversaries,
And consequently, like a traitor coward,
Sluic'd out his innocent soul through streams of blood,

23. **hap**: fortune.
24. **Add . . . crown**: i.e. change your earthly crown to a heavenly one.
28. **what . . . object**: on what grounds do you bring the charge (of treason). 32. **Tend'ring**: dutifully regarding.
38. **divine**: immortal. 43. **note**: stigma, i.e. charge of treason.
46. **right**: justly, i.e. in a righteous cause.
47. **accuse my zeal**: impugn my loyalty.
49. **eager**: sharp (French *aigre*). 50. **Can**: that can.
56. **post**: ride at high speed.
58. **his . . . royalty.** Bullingbrook, like Richard, was a grandson of Edward III. 63. **tied**: obliged. 65. **inhabitable**: uninhabitable.

69. **gage**: pledge (here, probably a glove or gauntlet).
70. **kinred**: kinship. 72. **except**: allege as an excuse.
74. **mine honor's pawn**: i.e. the gage flung down.
80–81. **any . . . trial**: any way sanctioned by the laws of chivalry.
85. **inherit us**: put us in possession of. 87. **Look what**: whatever.
88–103. **That . . . blood.** Bullingbrook's charges against Mowbray rake up the scandals of some ten years earlier (1387–88), when the so-called Lords Appellant—a band of conservative peers including the Duke of Gloucester (Thomas of Woodstock), the Earl of Arundel, the Earl of Warwick, Mowbray, and Bullingbrook—brought about the downfall of the young king's favorites and, installed as members of the council, usurped almost all of his executive powers. By 1389 Richard was strong enough to end this humiliating state of affairs and dismiss the Lords Appellant, but it was not until 1397 that he began to pay off his old scores with the arrest, for treason, of Warwick, Arundel, and Gloucester. One of them was banished and another executed, but Gloucester was imprisoned at Calais in the custody of Mowbray and there murdered, almost surely at the King's own instigation (as is implied at I.ii.37–41). These events are treated in the anonymous play *Woodstock*, which some scholars regard as a sort of prologue to *Richard II*.
88. **nobles**: gold coins worth 6*s*. 8*d*.
89. **lendings**: money advanced to soldiers when regular pay is not available. 90. **lewd**: base, improper.
91. **injurious**: malicious. 93. **Or**: either.
95. **these eighteen years.** According to Holinshed (Bullough, III, 390), Bullingbrook told the King that Mowbray "hath beene the occasion of all the treason that hath beene contrived in your realme for the space of these eighteene yeares," that is, since the Peasants' Revolt of 1381. 97. **head**: source.
101. **Suggest**: incite. **soon-believing**: overcredulous.
102. **consequently**: subsequently.

Which blood, like sacrificing Abel's, cries,
Even from the tongueless caverns of the earth,
To me for justice and rough chastisement;
And, by the glorious worth of my descent,
This arm shall do it, or this life be spent.
K. Rich. How high a pitch his resolution soars!
Thomas of Norfolk, what say'st thou to this?
Mow. O, let my sovereign turn away his face,
And bid his ears a little while be deaf,
Till I have told this slander of his blood
How God and good men hate so foul a liar.
K. Rich. Mowbray, impartial are our eyes and ears.
Were he my brother, nay, my kingdom's heir,
As he is but my father's brother's son,
Now by [my] sceptre's awe I make a vow,
Such neighbor nearness to our sacred blood
Should nothing privilege him nor partialize
The unstooping firmness of my upright soul.
He is our subject, Mowbray; so art thou.
Free speech and fearless I to thee allow.
Mow. Then, Bullingbrook, as low as to thy heart
Through the false passage of thy throat thou liest.
Three parts of that receipt I had for Callice
Disburs'd I duly to his Highness' soldiers;
The other part reserv'd I by consent,
For that my sovereign liege was in my debt,
Upon remainder of a dear account,
Since last I went to France to fetch his queen.
Now swallow down that lie. For Gloucester's death,
I slew him not, but to my own disgrace
Neglected my sworn duty in that case.
For you, my noble Lord of Lancaster,
The honorable father to my foe,
Once did I lay an ambush for your life,
A trespass that doth vex my grieved soul;
But ere I last receiv'd the sacrament
I did confess it, and exactly begg'd
Your Grace's pardon, and I hope I had it.
This is my fault. As for the rest appeal'd,
It issues from the rancor of a villain,
A recreant and most degenerate traitor,
Which in myself I boldly will defend,
And interchangeably hurl down my gage
Upon this overweening traitor's foot,
To prove myself a loyal gentleman
Even in the best blood chamber'd in his bosom,

104. **like sacrificing Abel's.** See Genesis 4:4, 8–10.
109. **pitch:** highest point of a falcon's flight.
113. **slander . . . blood:** disgrace to the royal family.
118. **my sceptre's awe:** the reverence due to my sceptre.
120. **nothing:** not at all. **partialize:** render partial.
126. **receipt:** money received. **Callice:** Calais.
129. **For that:** because.
130. **Upon . . . account:** for the balance of a heavy debt.
131. **fetch his queen.** Mowbray had negotiated Richard's second marriage (1396) with Isabella, daughter of Charles VI of France.
135–41. **For . . . it.** "Marie true it is," Holinshed reports Mowbray as confessing (Bullough, III, 391), "that once I laid an ambush to have slaine the duke of Lancaster, that there sitteth: but neverthelesse he hath pardoned me thereof, and there was good peace made betwixt us, for the which I yeeld him hartie thankes."
140. **exactly:** expressly and fully.
142. **appeal'd:** charged against me. 144. **recreant:** faithless.
146. **interchangeably:** in turn.

In haste whereof, most heartily I pray
Your Highness to assign our trial day.
K. Rich. Wrath-kindled [gentlemen], be rul'd by me,
Let's purge this choler without letting blood.
This we prescribe, though no physician;
Deep malice makes too deep incision.
Forget, forgive, conclude and be agreed,
Our doctors say this is no month to bleed.
Good uncle, let this end where it begun;
We'll calm the Duke of Norfolk, you your son.
Gaunt. To be a make-peace shall become my age.
Throw down, my son, the Duke of Norfolk's gage.
K. Rich. And, Norfolk, throw down his.
Gaunt. When, Harry? when?
Obedience bids I should not bid again.
K. Rich. Norfolk, throw down, we bid, there is no boot.
Mow. Myself I throw, dread sovereign, at thy foot,
My life thou shalt command, but not my shame:
The one my duty owes, but my fair name,
Despite of death that lives upon my grave,
To dark dishonor's use thou shalt not have.
I am disgrac'd, impeach'd, and baffled here,
Pierc'd to the soul with slander's venom'd spear,
The which no balm can cure but his heart-blood
Which breath'd this poison.
K. Rich. Rage must be withstood,
Give me his gage. Lions make leopards tame.
Mow. Yea, but not change his spots. Take but my shame,
And I resign my gage. My dear dear lord,
The purest treasure mortal times afford
Is spotless reputation; that away,
Men are but gilded loam or painted clay.
A jewel in a ten-times-barr'd-up chest
Is a bold spirit in a loyal breast.
Mine honor is my life, both grow in one,
Take honor from me, and my life is done.
Then, dear my liege, mine honor let me try;
In that I live, and for that will I die.
K. Rich. Cousin, throw up your gage, do you begin.
Bull. O, God defend my soul from such deep sin!
Shall I seem crestfallen in my father's sight?
Or with pale beggar-fear impeach my height
Before this outdar'd dastard? Ere my tongue

150. **In haste whereof:** to hasten which, i.e. to prove my innocence as soon as possible.
153. **Let's . . . blood:** i.e. let us relieve this wrath (resulting from excess of bile) by a purgative rather than by bleeding the patient.
155. **malice:** enmity. 156. **conclude:** come to terms.
164. **boot:** help for it.
170. **impeach'd:** accused. **baffled:** dishonored (literally, stripped of knighthood). 173. **Which breath'd:** who uttered.
174. **Lions . . . tame.** Lions were the emblem of the English kings; Mowbray's emblem was a leopard.
177. **mortal times:** our earthly lives. 184. **try:** test in combat.
186. **throw . . . gage:** i.e. as a gesture of conciliation throw your gage up to me. The King is probably seated on a high dais. Holinshed records (Bullough, III, 389) that "there was a great scaffold erected within the castell of Windsor for the king to sit with the lords and prelats of his realme."
189. **impeach my height:** discredit my lofty rank.
190. **outdar'd:** cowed.

Shall wound my honor with such feeble wrong,
Or sound so base a parley, my teeth shall tear
The slavish motive of recanting fear,
And spit it bleeding in his high disgrace,
Where shame doth harbor, even in Mowbray's face.
[*Exit Gaunt.*]

K. Rich. We were not born to sue, but to command,
Which since we cannot do to make you friends,
Be ready, as your lives shall answer it,
At Coventry upon Saint Lambert's day.
There shall your swords and lances arbitrate
The swelling difference of your settled hate.
Since we cannot atone you, we shall see
Justice design the victor's chivalry.
Lord Marshal, command our officers-at-arms
Be ready to direct these home alarms. *Exeunt.*

[Scene II]

Enter John of Gaunt *with the* Duchess of Gloucester.

Gaunt. Alas, the part I had in Woodstock's blood
Doth more solicit me than your exclaims
To stir against the butchers of his life!
But since correction lieth in those hands
Which made the fault that we cannot correct,
Put we our quarrel to the will of heaven,
Who, when they see the hour's ripe on earth,
Will rain hot vengeance on offenders' heads.

Duch. Finds brotherhood in thee no sharper spur?
Hath love in thy old blood no living fire?
Edward's seven sons, whereof thyself art one,
Were as seven vials of his sacred blood,
Or seven fair branches springing from one root.
Some of those seven are dried by nature's course,
Some of those branches by the Destinies cut;

191. feeble wrong: false submission.
192. sound . . . parley: i.e. negotiate such a shameful truce. The trumpet signal for a conference was called a parley (or parle).
193. motive: instrument, i.e. tongue. **194. his:** its, i.e. the tongue's.
195 s.d. Exit Gaunt. This exit (from F1) satisfies the stage convention that a character may not leave the stage at the end of one scene and immediately re-enter at the beginning of the next.
199. Saint Lambert's day. "Writers disagree about the daie that was appointed," says Holinshed judiciously (Bullough, III, 391), "for some saie, it was upon a mondaie in August; other upon saint Lamberts daie, being the seventeenth of September, other on the eleventh of September: but true it is, that the king assigned them not onlie the daie, but also appointed them listes and place for the combat, and thereupon great preparation was made, as to such a matter apperteined." **202. atone:** reconcile.
203. design . . . chivalry: determine the victor in a chivalric encounter.
205. home: domestic. **alarms:** calls to arms, i.e. combats.

I.ii.Location: London. The Duke of Lancaster's palace.
1. the part . . . blood: my relationship to Woodstock. John of Gaunt was the fourth and Thomas of Woodstock the sixth of Edward III's seven sons (who are itemized in *2 Henry VI*, II.ii.10–17).
4. those: i.e. Richard's.
14–15. Some . . . cut. Of Edward III's seven sons, two (William of Hatfield and William of Windsor) did not survive their youth; Lionel, Duke of Clarence, died in Italy in 1368; Edward the Black Prince, the heir apparent, predeceased his father by a year in 1376; and Thomas of Woodstock, Duke of Gloucester, was murdered at Calais in 1397. At the time represented in this scene—for which, incidentally, Shakespeare had no source in the chronicles—only John of Gaunt, Duke of Lancaster, and Edmund de Langley, Duke of York, were left, but their lives were nearly done, Gaunt dying in 1399 and York in 1402.

But Thomas, my dear lord, my life, my Gloucester,
One vial full of Edward's sacred blood,
One flourishing branch of his most royal root,
Is crack'd, and all the precious liquor spilt,
Is hack'd down, and his summer leaves all faded,
By envy's hand and murder's bloody axe.
Ah, Gaunt, his blood was thine! That bed, that womb,
That mettle, that self mould, that fashioned thee
Made him a man; and though thou livest and breathest,
Yet art thou slain in him. Thou dost consent
In some large measure to thy father's death,
In that thou seest thy wretched brother die,
Who was the model of thy father's life.
Call it not patience, Gaunt, it is despair.
In suff'ring thus thy brother to be slaught'red,
Thou showest the naked pathway to thy life,
Teaching stern murder how to butcher thee.
That which in mean men we entitle patience
Is pale cold cowardice in noble breasts.
What shall I say? To safeguard thine own life
The best way is to venge my Gloucester's death.

Gaunt. God's is the quarrel, for God's substitute,
His deputy anointed in His sight,
Hath caus'd his death, the which if wrongfully,
Let heaven revenge, for I may never lift
An angry arm against His minister.

Duch. Where then, alas, may I complain myself?

Gaunt. To God, the widow's champion and defense.

Duch. Why then I will. Farewell, old Gaunt!
Thou goest to Coventry, there to behold
Our cousin Herford and fell Mowbray fight.
O, [sit] my husband's wrongs on Herford's spear,
That it may enter butcher Mowbray's breast!
Or if misfortune miss the first career,
Be Mowbray's sins so heavy in his bosom
That they may break his foaming courser's back,
And throw the rider headlong in the lists,
A caitive recreant to my cousin Herford!
Farewell, old Gaunt! thy sometimes brother's wife
With her companion, grief, must end her life.

Gaunt. Sister, farewell, I must to Coventry.
As much good stay with thee as go with me!

Duch. Yet one word more! Grief boundeth where [it] falls,
Not with the empty hollowness, but weight.
I take my leave before I have begun,
For sorrow ends not when it seemeth done.
Commend me to thy brother, Edmund York.
Lo this is all—nay, yet depart not so;
Though this be all, do not so quickly go;
I shall remember more. Bid him—ah, what?—
With all good speed at Plashy visit me.
Alack, and what shall good old York there see

21. envy's: malice's. **23. mettle:** substance. **self:** same.
25–26. consent . . . to: be an accomplice . . . in.
28. model: copy, image. **33. mean:** lowly.
39. his: i.e. Gloucester's. **41. minister:** agent.
46. cousin: kinsman. **fell:** fierce.
49. if . . . career: if disaster for Mowbray does not come at the first charge. **53. caitive:** caitiff, base.
54. thy . . . wife: your brother's former wife (now his widow).
66. Plashy: Pleshey, Gloucester's residence in Essex.

But empty lodgings and unfurnish'd walls,
Unpeopled offices, untrodden stones?
And what hear there for welcome but my groans?
Therefore commend me; let him not come there
To seek out sorrow that dwells every where.
Desolate, desolate, will I hence and die:
The last leave of thee takes my weeping eye. *Exeunt.*

[Scene III]

Enter Lord Marshal *and the* Duke Aumerle.

Mar. My Lord Aumerle, is Harry Herford arm'd?
Aum. Yea, at all points, and longs to enter in.
Mar. The Duke of Norfolk, sprightfully and bold,
Stays but the summons of the appellant's trumpet.
Aum. Why then the champions are prepar'd, and stay
For nothing but his Majesty's approach.

The trumpets sound, and the King *enters with his nobles* [Gaunt, Bushy, Bagot, Green, *and others*]. *When they are set, enter* [Mowbray,] *the Duke of Norfolk, in arms, defendant,* [*with a* Herald].

K. Rich. Marshal, demand of yonder champion
The cause of his arrival here in arms;
Ask him his name, and orderly proceed
To swear him in the justice of his cause.
Mar. In God's name and the King's, say who thou art
And why thou comest thus knightly clad in arms,
Against what man thou com'st, and what thy quarrel.
Speak truly on thy knighthood and thy oath,
As so defend thee heaven and thy valor!
Mow. My name is Thomas Mowbray, Duke of Norfolk,
Who hither come engaged by my oath
(Which God defend a knight should violate!)
Both to defend my loyalty and truth
To God, my king, and my succeeding issue,
Against the Duke of Herford that appeals me,
And by the grace of God, and this mine arm,
To prove him, in defending of myself,
A traitor to my God, my king, and me—
And as I truly fight, defend me heaven!

The trumpets sound. Enter [Bullingbrook,] *Duke of Herford, appellant, in armor,* [*with a* Herald].

K. Rich. Marshal, ask yonder knight in arms,
Both who he is and why he cometh hither
Thus plated in habiliments of war,
And formally, according to our law,
Depose him in the justice of his cause.
Mar. What is thy name? and wherefore com'st thou hither
Before King Richard in his royal lists?
Against whom [com'st] thou? and what's thy quarrel?
Speak like a true knight, so defend thee heaven!
Bull. Harry of Herford, Lancaster, and Derby
Am I, who ready here do stand in arms
To prove by God's grace, and my body's valor,
In lists, on Thomas Mowbray, Duke of Norfolk,
That he is a traitor, foul and dangerous,
To God of heaven, King Richard, and to me—
And as I truly fight, defend me heaven!
Mar. On pain of death, no person be so bold
Or daring-hardy as to touch the lists,
Except the Marshal and such officers
Appointed to direct these fair designs.
Bull. Lord Marshal, let me kiss my sovereign's hand
And bow my knee before his Majesty,
For Mowbray and myself are like two men
That vow a long and weary pilgrimage.
Then let us take a ceremonious leave
And loving farewell of our several friends.
Mar. The appellant in all duty greets your Highness,
And craves to kiss your hand and take his leave.
K. Rich. We will descend and fold him in our arms.
Cousin of Herford, as thy cause is right,
So be thy fortune in this royal fight!
Farewell, my blood, which if to-day thou shed,
Lament we may, but not revenge [thee] dead.
Bull. O, let no noble eye profane a tear
For me, if I be gor'd with Mowbray's spear.
As confident as is the falcon's flight
Against a bird, do I with Mowbray fight.
My loving lord, I take my leave of you;
Of you, my noble cousin, Lord Aumerle;
Not sick, although I have to do with death,
But lusty, young, and cheerly drawing breath.
Lo, as at English feasts, so I regreet
The daintiest last, to make the end most sweet:
O thou, the earthly author of my blood,
Whose youthful spirit, in me regenerate,
Doth with a twofold vigor lift me up
To reach at victory above my head,
Add proof unto mine armor with thy prayers,
And with thy blessings steel my lance's point,
That it may enter Mowbray's waxen coat,
And furbish new the name of John a' Gaunt,
Even in the lusty havior of his son.
Gaunt. God in thy good cause make thee prosperous!
Be swift like lightning in the execution,
And let thy blows, doubly redoubled,
Fall like amazing thunder on the casque
Of thy adverse pernicious enemy.
Rouse up thy youthful blood, be valiant and live.

68. unfurnish'd: bare. **69. offices:** service quarters.

I.iii. Location: The lists at Coventry.
o.s.d. According to Holinshed (Bullough, III, 392), the Duke of Surrey served as high marshal and the Duke of Aumerle as high constable at the lists in Coventry. **2. in:** i.e. into the lists.
3. sprightfully and bold: spiritedly and boldly.
4. Stays: awaits. **18. defend:** forbid. **28. plated:** armored.
30. Depose him: take his sworn deposition.

45. fair designs: orderly proceedings.
59. profane a tear: i.e. weep for one proved to be a traitor.
66. lusty: vigorous, spirited. **young.** Bullingbrook was thirty-one at the time represented in this scene.
67. regreet: salute. **68. The daintiest:** i.e. the best thing.
70. regenerate: reborn. **73. proof:** impenetrability.
75. enter . . . coat: pierce Mowbray's coat of mail as if it were made of wax. **76. a':** of. **77. havior:** conduct.
81. amazing: bewildering, astounding. **casque:** helmet.

Bull. Mine innocence and Saint George to thrive!
Mow. However God or fortune cast my lot,
There lives or dies, true to King Richard's throne,
A loyal, just, and upright gentleman.
Never did captive with a freer heart
Cast off his chains of bondage, and embrace
His golden uncontroll'd enfranchisement,
More than my dancing soul doth celebrate
This feast of battle with mine adversary.
Most mighty liege, and my companion peers,
Take from my mouth the wish of happy years.
As gentle and as jocund as to jest
Go I to fight: truth hath a quiet breast.
K. Rich. Farewell, my lord, securely I espy
Virtue with valor couched in thine eye.
Order the trial, Marshal, and begin.
Mar. Harry of Herford, Lancaster, and Derby,
Receive thy lance, and God defend the right!
Bull. Strong as a tower in hope, I cry amen.
Mar. [*To an Officer*.] Go bear this lance to Thomas Duke of Norfolk.
[*1*.] *Her*. Harry of Herford, Lancaster, and Derby
Stands here for God, his sovereign, and himself,
On pain to be found false and recreant,
To prove the Duke of Norfolk, Thomas Mowbray,
A traitor to his God, his king, and him,
And dares him to set forward to the fight.
2. Her. Here standeth Thomas Mowbray, Duke of Norfolk,
On pain to be found false and recreant,
Both to defend himself and to approve
Henry of Herford, Lancaster, and Derby
To God, his sovereign, and to him disloyal,
Courageously, and with a free desire,
Attending but the signal to begin.
Mar. Sound, trumpets, and set forward, combatants. [*A charge sounded*.]
Stay, the King hath thrown his warder down.
K. Rich. Let them lay by their helmets and their spears,
And both return back to their chairs again.
Withdraw with us, and let the trumpets sound
While we return these dukes what we decree.
[*A long flourish*.]
Draw near,
And list what with our Council we have done:
For that our kingdom's earth should not be soil'd
With that dear blood which it hath fostered;
And for our eyes do hate the dire aspect
Of civil wounds plough'd up with neighbors' sword;
And for we think the eagle-winged pride
Of sky-aspiring and ambitious thoughts,
With rival-hating envy, set on you
To wake our peace, which in our country's cradle
Draws the sweet infant breath of gentle sleep;
Which so rous'd up with boist'rous untun'd drums,
With harsh-resounding trumpets' dreadful bray,
And grating shock of wrathful iron arms,
Might from our quiet confines fright fair peace,
And make us wade even in our kinred's blood:
Therefore we banish you our territories.
You, cousin Herford, upon pain of life,
Till twice five summers have enrich'd our fields
Shall not regreet our fair dominions,
But tread the stranger paths of banishment.
Bull. Your will be done. This must my comfort be,
That sun that warms you here shall shine on me,
And those his golden beams to you here lent
Shall point on me and gild my banishment.
K. Rich. Norfolk, for thee remains a heavier doom,
Which I with some unwillingness pronounce:
The sly, slow hours shall not determinate
The dateless limit of thy dear exile;
The hopeless word of "never to return"
Breathe I against thee, upon pain of life.
Mow. A heavy sentence, my most sovereign liege,
And all unlook'd for from your Highness' mouth.
A dearer merit, not so deep a maim
As to be cast forth in the common air,
Have I deserved at your Highness' hands.
The language I have learnt these forty years,
My native English, now I must forgo,
And now my tongue's use is to me no more
Than an unstringed viol or a harp,
Or like a cunning instrument cas'd up,
Or being open, put into his hands
That knows no touch to tune the harmony.
Within my mouth you have enjail'd my tongue,
Doubly portcullis'd with my teeth and lips,
And dull unfeeling barren ignorance
Is made my jailer to attend on me.
I am too old to fawn upon a nurse,
Too far in years to be a pupil now.
What is thy sentence [then] but speechless death,
Which robs my tongue from breathing native breath?
K. Rich. It boots thee not to be compassionate,
After our sentence plaining comes too late.
Mow. Then thus I turn me from my country's light,
To dwell in solemn shades of endless night.

84. Saint George: patron saint of England.
95. jest: take part in a masque.
97. securely: confidently (modifies *couched* in line 98).
98. couched: expressed. **112. approve**: prove.
116. Attending: awaiting.
118. warder: baton (which Richard held as umpire of the trial by combat).
121. Withdraw with us. Addressed to members of the council.
122. While we return: until we inform. **s.d. A long flourish**: an extended trumpet call (to suggest the passage of time). Holinshed records (Bullough, III, 393) that the combatants waited "two long houres" while Richard and his council discussed the situation.
125. For that: in order that. **127. for**: because.
129–38. And . . . blood. There is some confusion in this passage (in which the *peace* of line 132 frights the *fair peace* of line 137). Kittredge paraphrases it thus: "And this disturbance of the King's peace might drive peace out of the realm."
131. envy: enmity. **set on you**: set you on.
138. kinred's: kindred's. **143. stranger**: alien.
150. determinate: bring to an end.
151. dateless limit: limitless term. **dear**: grievous.
155. unlook'd for. According to Holinshed (Bullough, III, 394), Mowbray hoped "that he shoulde have beene borne out in the matter by the king, which when it fell out otherwise, it greeved him not a little."
156. dearer merit: more valued reward.
163. cunning: skillfully made. **164. open**: uncased.
173. Which: i.e. the sentence.
174. boots: helps. **compassionate**: self-pitying.
175. plaining: complaining.

K. Rich. Return again, and take an oath with thee.
Lay on our royal sword your banish'd hands;
Swear by the duty that y' owe to God
(Our part therein we banish with yourselves)
To keep the oath that we administer:
You never shall, so help you truth and God,
Embrace each other's love in banishment,
Nor never look upon each other's face,
Nor never write, regreet, nor reconcile
This low'ring tempest of your home-bred hate,
Nor never by advised purpose meet
To plot, contrive, or complot any ill
'Gainst us, our state, our subjects, or our land.
Bull. I swear.
Mow. And I, to keep all this.
Bull. Norfolk, so fare as to mine enemy:
By this time, had the King permitted us,
One of our souls had wand'red in the air,
Banish'd this frail sepulchre of our flesh,
As now our flesh is banish'd from this land;
Confess thy treasons ere thou fly the realm;
Since thou hast far to go, bear not along
The clogging burthen of a guilty soul.
Mow. No, Bullingbrook, if ever I were traitor,
My name be blotted from the book of life,
And I from heaven banish'd as from hence!
But what thou art, God, thou, and I do know,
And all too soon, I fear, the King shall rue.
Farewell, my liege, now no way can I stray;
Save back to England, all the world's my way. *Exit.*
K. Rich. Uncle, even in the glasses of thine eyes
I see thy grieved heart. Thy sad aspect
Hath from the number of his banish'd years
Pluck'd four away. [*To Bullingbrook.*] Six frozen winters spent,
Return with welcome home from banishment.
Bull. How long a time lies in one little word!
Four lagging winters and four wanton springs
End in a word: such is the breath of kings.
Gaunt. I thank my liege that in regard of me
He shortens four years of my son's exile,
But little vantage shall I reap thereby;
For ere the six years that he hath to spend
Can change their moons and bring their times about,
My oil-dried lamp and time-bewasted light
Shall be extinct with age and endless [night];
My inch of taper will be burnt and done,
And blindfold Death not let me see my son.
K. Rich. Why, uncle, thou hast many years to live.
Gaunt. But not a minute, King, that thou canst give.
Shorten my days thou canst with sullen sorrow,
And pluck nights from me, but not lend a morrow;
Thou canst help time to furrow me with age,
But stop no wrinkle in his pilgrimage;
Thy word is current with him for my death,
But dead, thy kingdom cannot buy my breath.
K. Rich. Thy son is banish'd upon good advice,
Whereto thy tongue a party-verdict gave.
Why at our justice seem'st thou then to low'r?
Gaunt. Things sweet to taste prove in digestion sour.
You urg'd me as a judge, but I had rather
You would have bid me argue like a father.
O, had't been a stranger, not my child,
To smooth his fault I should have been more mild.
A partial slander sought I to avoid,
And in the sentence my own life destroyed.
Alas, I look'd when some of you should say
I was too strict to make mine own away;
But you gave leave to my unwilling tongue
Against my will to do myself this wrong.
K. Rich. Cousin, farewell; and, uncle, bid him so.
Six years we banish him, and he shall go.
[*Flourish.*] *Exit* [*with his Train*].
Aum. Cousin, farewell! What presence must not know,
From where you do remain let paper show.
Mar. My lord, no leave take I, for I will ride,
As far as land will let me, by your side.
Gaunt. O, to what purpose dost thou hoard thy words,
That thou returnest no greeting to thy friends?
Bull. I have too few to take my leave of you,
When the tongue's office should be prodigal
To breathe the abundant dolor of the heart.
Gaunt. Thy grief is but thy absence for a time.
Bull. Joy absent, grief is present for that time.
Gaunt. What is six winters? they are quickly gone.
Bull. To men in joy, but grief makes one hour ten.
Gaunt. Call it a travel that thou tak'st for pleasure.
Bull. My heart will sigh when I miscall it so,
Which finds it an enforced pilgrimage.
Gaunt. The sullen passage of thy weary steps
Esteem as foil wherein thou art to set
The precious jewel of thy home return.
Bull. Nay rather, every tedious stride I make
Will but remember me what a deal of world
I wander from the jewels that I love.
Must I not serve a long apprenticehood
To foreign passages, and in the end,
Having my freedom, boast of nothing else
But that I was a journeyman to grief?
Gaunt. All places that the eye of heaven visits
Are to a wise man ports and happy havens.

181. **Our part therein**: i.e. your duty to me as king.
193. **as . . . enemy**: as I would wish my enemy to fare.
206. **stray**: take the wrong road. 208. **glasses**: mirrors.
209–11. **Thy . . . away.** According to Holinshed (Bullough, III, 394), Bullingbrook "tooke his leave of the king at Eltham [a castle near London], who there released foure yeares of his banishment." Froissart (Bullough, III, 426) says that the King reduced Bullingbrook's sentence "to please the people withall."
216. **regard**: consideration. 218. **vantage**: profit, advantage.
222. **extinct**: extinguished.
231. **current**: authoritative, decisive.
234. **thy . . . gave**: i.e. you concurred in the verdict of the council.
240. **smooth**: extenuate.
241. **A partial slander**: the reproach of being partial (to my own son).
243. **look'd when**: expected that.
244. **to . . . away**: in making away with my own son.
249. **What . . . know**: i.e. that which I will be unable to learn from personal contact. 256. **office**: duty.
266. **foil**: thin metal leaf set behind a jewel to enhance its brilliance.
269. **remember**: remind.
271–74. **Must . . . grief**: i.e. having served my apprenticeship as an exile and thus earned my privileges (*freedom*), must I remain a journeyman (one who works for daily wages under a master) to grief and know only how to suffer.

Teach thy necessity to reason thus:
There is no virtue like necessity.
Think not the King did banish thee,
But thou the King. Woe doth the heavier sit
Where it perceives it is but faintly borne.
Go, say I sent thee forth to purchase honor,
And not the King exil'd thee; or suppose
Devouring pestilence hangs in our air,
And thou art flying to a fresher clime.
Look what thy soul holds dear, imagine it
To lie that way thou goest, not whence thou com'st.
Suppose the singing birds musicians,
The grass whereon thou tread'st the presence strow'd,
The flowers fair ladies, and thy steps no more
Than a delightful measure or a dance,
For gnarling sorrow hath less power to bite
The man that mocks at it and sets it light.

Bull. O, who can hold a fire in his hand
By thinking on the frosty Caucasus?
Or cloy the hungry edge of appetite
By bare imagination of a feast?
Or wallow naked in December snow
By thinking on fantastic summer's heat?
O no, the apprehension of the good
Gives but the greater feeling to the worse.
Fell Sorrow's tooth doth never rankle more
Than when he bites, but lanceth not the sore.

Gaunt. Come, come, my son, I'll bring thee on thy way;
Had I thy youth and cause, I would not stay.

Bull. Then England's ground, farewell, sweet soil, adieu;
My mother, and my nurse, that bears me yet!
Where e'er I wander, boast of this I can,
Though banish'd, yet a true-born Englishman. *Exeunt.*

[Scene IV]

Enter the King *with* [Green *and* Bagot] *at one door and the* Lord Aumerle *at another.*

K. Rich. We did observe. Cousin Aumerle,
How far brought you high Herford on his way?

Aum. I brought high Herford, if you call him so,
But to the next high way, and there I left him.

K. Rich. And say, what store of parting tears were shed?

Aum. Faith, none for me, except the northeast wind,
Which then blew bitterly against our faces,
Awak'd the sleeping rheum, and so by chance
Did grace our hollow parting with a tear.

281. **faintly:** faintheartedly. 282. **purchase:** acquire.
289. **the presence strow'd:** the royal presence-chamber strewed with rushes. 291. **measure:** stately dance.
292. **gnarling:** snarling. 299. **fantastic:** imaginary.
303. **lanceth:** probes and opens (in order to afford relief).
304. **bring:** escort. 305. **stay:** linger.

I.iv. Location: London. The palace.
1. **We did observe.** As he enters, the King replies to a remark (probably about Bullingbrook's popularity with the "common people": see lines 23 ff.) made by Bagot or Green.
6. **for me:** on my part. 8. **rheum:** moisture, i.e. tears.

K. Rich. What said our cousin when you parted with him?

Aum. "Farewell!"
And for my heart disdained that my tongue
Should so profane the word, that taught me craft
To counterfeit oppression of such grief
That words seem'd buried in my sorrow's grave.
Marry, would the word "farewell" have length'ned hours
And added years to his short banishment,
He should have had a volume of farewells;
But since it would not, he had none of me.

K. Rich. He is our cousin's cousin, but 'tis doubt,
When time shall call him home from banishment,
Whether our kinsman come to see his friends.
Ourself and Bushy, [Bagot here and Green,]
Observ'd his courtship to the common people,
How he did seem to dive into their hearts
With humble and familiar courtesy,
What reverence he did throw away on slaves,
Wooing poor craftsmen with the craft of smiles
And patient underbearing of his fortune,
As 'twere to banish their affects with him.
Off goes his bonnet to an oyster-wench,
A brace of draymen bid God speed him well,
And had the tribute of his supple knee,
With "Thanks, my countrymen, my loving friends,"
As were our England in reversion his,
And he our subjects' next degree in hope.

Green. Well, he is gone, and with him go these thoughts.
Now for the rebels which stand out in Ireland,
Expedient manage must be made, my liege,
Ere further leisure yield them further means
For their advantage and your Highness' loss.

K. Rich. We will ourself in person to this war,
And for our coffers, with too great a court
And liberal largess, are grown somewhat light,
We are enforc'd to farm our royal realm,
The revenue whereof shall furnish us
For our affairs in hand. If that come short,
Our substitutes at home shall have blank charters,
Whereto, when they shall know what men are rich,
They shall subscribe them for large sums of gold,

12. **for:** because. 13. **that:** i.e. my disdain.
16. **Marry:** indeed (originally the name of the Virgin Mary used as an oath).
20. **cousin's cousin.** Richard, Aumerle, and Bullingbrook, the sons of three brothers, were cousins.
23–36. **Ourself . . . hope.** Holinshed (Bullough, III, 394) records of Bullingbrook's departure that "a woonder it was to see what a number of people ran after him in everie towne and street where he came, before he tooke the sea, lamenting and bewailing his departure, as who would saie, that when he departed, the onelie shield, defense, and comfort of the commonwealth was vaded and gone."
29. **underbearing:** endurance. 30. **affects:** affections.
35. **in reversion:** by right of legal succession.
36. **next . . . hope:** i.e. heir presumptive to the throne.
38. **stand out:** rise in insurrection.
39. **Expedient manage:** swift handling (to cope with them).
42. **to:** go to. 45. **farm:** lease the revenues of.
48. **substitutes:** deputies. **charters:** writs authorizing the collection of revenues by agents of the king. These charters, says Holinshed (Bullough, III, 394), produced "great grudge and murmuring" because "the kings officers wrote in the same what liked them [what they pleased], as well for charging the parties with paiment of monie, as otherwise."

And send them after to supply our wants,
For we will make for Ireland presently.

Enter Bushy.

[Bushy, what news?]

Bushy. Old John of Gaunt is grievous sick, my lord,
Suddenly taken, and hath sent post-haste
To entreat your Majesty to visit him.

K. Rich. Where lies he?

Bushy. At Ely House.

K. Rich. Now put it, God, in the physician's mind
To help him to his grave immediately!
The lining of his coffers shall make coats
To deck our soldiers for these Irish wars.
Come, gentlemen, let's all go visit him.
Pray God we may make haste and come too late!

[*All*.] Amen. *Exeunt*.

[ACT II, Scene I]

Enter John of Gaunt, *sick, with the* Duke of York, *etc.*

Gaunt. Will the King come, that I may breathe my last
In wholesome counsel to his unstayed youth?

York. Vex not yourself, nor strive not with your breath,
For all in vain comes counsel to his ear.

Gaunt. O but they say the tongues of dying men
Enforce attention like deep harmony.
Where words are scarce, they are seldom spent in vain,
For they breathe truth that breathe their words in pain.
He that no more must say is listened more
Than they whom youth and ease have taught to glose.
More are men's ends mark'd than their lives before.
The setting sun, and music at the close,
As the last taste of sweets, is sweetest last,
Writ in remembrance more than things long past.
Though Richard my live's counsel would not hear,
My death's sad tale may yet undeaf his ear.

York. No, it is stopp'd with other flattering sounds,
As praises, of whose taste the wise are [fond],
Lascivious metres, to whose venom sound
The open ear of youth doth always listen;
Report of fashions in proud Italy,
Whose manners still our tardy, apish nation
Limps after in base imitation.
Where doth the world thrust forth a vanity—
So it be new, there's no respect how vile—
That is not quickly buzz'd into his ears?
Then all too late comes counsel to be heard,
Where will doth mutiny with wit's regard.
Direct not him whose way himself will choose,
'Tis breath thou lack'st, and that breath wilt thou lose.

Gaunt. Methinks I am a prophet new inspir'd,
And thus expiring do foretell of him:
His rash fierce blaze of riot cannot last,
For violent fires soon burn out themselves;
Small show'rs last long, but sudden storms are short;
He tires betimes that spurs too fast betimes;
With eager feeding food doth choke the feeder;
Light vanity, insatiate cormorant,
Consuming means, soon preys upon itself.
This royal throne of kings, this sceptred isle,
This earth of majesty, this seat of Mars,
This other Eden, demi-paradise,
This fortress built by Nature for herself
Against infection and the hand of war,
This happy breed of men, this little world,
This precious stone set in the silver sea,
Which serves it in the office of a wall,
Or as [a] moat defensive to a house,
Against the envy of less happier lands;
This blessed plot, this earth, this realm, this England,
This nurse, this teeming womb of royal kings,
Fear'd by their breed, and famous by their birth,
Renowned for their deeds as far from home,
For Christian service and true chivalry,
As is the sepulchre in stubborn Jewry
Of the world's ransom, blessed Mary's Son;
This land of such dear souls, this dear dear land,
Dear for her reputation through the world,
Is now leas'd out—I die pronouncing it—
Like to a tenement or pelting farm.
England, bound in with the triumphant sea,
Whose rocky shore beats back the envious siege
Of wat'ry Neptune, is now bound in with shame,
With inky blots and rotten parchment bonds;
That England, that was wont to conquer others,
Hath made a shameful conquest of itself.
Ah, would the scandal vanish with my life,
How happy then were my ensuing death!

Enter King *and* Queen, *etc.* [Aumerle, Bushy, Green, Bagot, Ross, *and* Willoughby].

York. The King is come. Deal mildly with his youth,
For young hot colts being rag'd do rage the more.

Queen. How fares our noble uncle Lancaster?

K. Rich. What comfort, man? how is't with aged Gaunt?

52. presently: immediately.
58. Ely House: the Bishop of Ely's residence in Holborn, a district north of St. Paul's Cathedral.
61. lining of his coffers: i.e. his treasure. **coats:** coats of mail, armor.

II.i. Location: London. Ely House.
2. unstayed: (1) unsupported (by wise counsellors); (2) unchecked.
10. glose: talk glibly, flatter. **12. close:** harmonic close, cadence.
15. my live's counsel: my advice while I lived.
16. My . . . tale: the grave words that I speak while dying. **undeaf.** One of several such negative words in the play. See *unhappied* (III.i.10), *uncurse* (III.ii.137), *unsay* (IV.i.9), *undo* (IV.i.203), *unking* (IV.i.220, V.v.37), *undeck* (IV.i.250), *unkiss* (V.i.74).
21. proud: splendid, lavish.
22. still: always. **apish:** imitative.
25. there's no respect: it makes no difference.
28. will . . . regard: inclination rebels against judgment.
33. riot: dissipation. **36. betimes:** early.
38. Light vanity: heedless extravagance. **cormorant:** voracious bird of prey; here, a glutton. **39. means:** i.e. means of sustaining life.
42. demi-paradise: little paradise.
44. infection: (1) pestilence; (2) moral contamination.
47. office: function.
52. Fear'd . . . breed: i.e. held in awe for their hereditary valor.
55. Jewry: Judea.
60. tenement: property held by a tenant. **pelting:** paltry.
64. bonds: i.e. the "blank charters" of I.iv.47–51.
70. rag'd: enraged through rough treatment (?).

Gaunt. O how that name befits my composition!
Old Gaunt indeed, and gaunt in being old.
Within me grief hath kept a tedious fast;
And who abstains from meat that is not gaunt?
For sleeping England long time have I watch'd,
Watching breeds leanness, leanness is all gaunt.
The pleasure that some fathers feed upon
Is my strict fast—I mean, my children's looks;
And therein fasting, hast thou made me gaunt.
Gaunt am I for the grave, gaunt as a grave,
Whose hollow womb inherits nought but bones.
K. Rich. Can sick men play so nicely with their names?
Gaunt. No, misery makes sport to mock itself:
Since thou dost seek to kill my name in me,
I mock my name, great King, to flatter thee.
K. Rich. Should dying men flatter with those that live?
Gaunt. No, no, men living flatter those that die.
K. Rich. Thou, now a-dying, sayest thou flatterest me.
Gaunt. O no, thou diest, though I the sicker be.
K. Rich. I am in health, I breathe, and see thee ill.
Gaunt. Now He that made me knows I see thee ill,
Ill in myself to see, and in thee, seeing ill.
Thy death-bed is no lesser than thy land,
Wherein thou liest in reputation sick,
And thou, too careless patient as thou art,
Commit'st thy anointed body to the cure
Of those physicians that first wounded thee.
A thousand flatterers sit within thy crown,
Whose compass is no bigger than thy head,
And yet, [incaged] in so small a verge,
The waste is no whit lesser than thy land.
O had thy grandsire with a prophet's eye
Seen how his son's son should destroy his sons,
From forth thy reach he would have laid thy shame,
Deposing thee before thou wert possess'd,
Which art possess'd now to depose thyself.
Why, cousin, wert thou regent of the world,
It were a shame to let this land by lease;
But for thy world enjoying but this land,
Is it not more than shame to shame it so?
Landlord of England art thou now, not king,
Thy state of law is bond-slave to the law,
And thou—
K. Rich. A lunatic lean-witted fool,
Presuming on an ague's privilege,
Darest with thy frozen admonition
Make pale our cheek, chasing the royal blood
With fury from his native residence.

73. **composition**: condition, constitution.
77. **watch'd**: stayed awake. 83. **inherits**: possesses.
84. **nicely**: (1) subtly; (2) trivially.
86. **kill my name**: i.e. by banishing Bullingbrook, my heir.
99. **physicians**: i.e. the King's dissolute favorites.
102. **verge**: (1) rim of the crown; (2) distance of twelve miles from wherever the king happened to be. 104. **grandsire**: i.e. Edward III.
107. **possess'd**: put in possession of the crown.
108. **possess'd**: seized by an evil spirit, therefore mad.
109. **regent**: ruler. 111. **world**: domain.
114. **Thy . . . the law**: i.e. your legal status is no longer that of a ruler by divine right but that of a subject under law.
117. **frozen**: (1) stylistically inept; (2) caused by a chill or ague.

Now by my seat's right royal majesty,
Wert thou not brother to great Edward's son,
This tongue that runs so roundly in thy head
Should run thy head from thy unreverent shoulders.
Gaunt. O, spare me not, my [brother] Edward's son,
For that I was his father Edward's son,
That blood already, like the pelican,
Hast thou tapp'd out and drunkenly carous'd.
My brother Gloucester, plain well-meaning soul,
Whom fair befall in heaven 'mongst happy souls,
May be a president and witness good
That thou respect'st not spilling Edward's blood.
Join with the present sickness that I have,
And thy unkindness be like crooked age,
To crop at once a too long withered flower.
Live in thy shame, but die not shame with thee!
These words hereafter thy tormentors be!
Convey me to my bed, then to my grave;
Love they to live that love and honor have.
Exit [*borne off by his Attendants*].
K. Rich. And let them die that age and sullens have,
For both hast thou, and both become the grave.
York. I do beseech your Majesty, impute his words
To wayward sickliness and age in him.
He loves you, on my life, and holds you dear
As Harry Duke of Herford, were he here.
K. Rich. Right, you say true: as Herford's love, so his,
As theirs, so mine, and all be as it is.

[*Enter* NORTHUMBERLAND.]

North. My liege, old Gaunt commends him to your Majesty.
K. Rich. What says he?
North. Nay, nothing, all is said.
His tongue is now a stringless instrument,
Words, life, and all, old Lancaster hath spent.
York. Be York the next that must be bankrout so!
Though death be poor, it ends a mortal woe.
K. Rich. The ripest fruit first falls, and so doth he;
His time is spent, our pilgrimage must be.
So much for that. Now for our Irish wars:
We must supplant those rough rug-headed kerns,
Which live like venom where no venom else
But only they have privilege to live.
And, for these great affairs do ask some charge,
Towards our assistance we do seize to us
The plate, coin, revenues, and moveables

120. **seat's**: throne's. 122. **roundly**: freely and bluntly.
125. **For that**: because.
126. **pelican**. Popularly thought to feed its young with blood from its own bosom.
127. **tapp'd out**: i.e. in the murder of Gloucester. **carous'd**: drunk in gulps. 129. **Whom fair befall**: to whom good fortune.
130. **president**: precedent, example.
131. **respect'st not**: hast no scruples in.
139. **sullens**: sulks. 140. **become**: are appropriate for.
151. **bankrout**: bankrupt.
156. **supplant**: expel. **kerns**: light-armed Irish foot-soldiers.
157–58. **where . . . live**. An allusion to St. Patrick's allegedly banishing all snakes from Ireland. **venom**: venomous snakes.
159. **for**: because. **do . . . charge**: require some outlay, i.e. are expensive. 161. **moveables**: personal property.

Whereof our uncle Gaunt did stand possess'd.
York. How long shall I be patient? ah, how long
Shall tender duty make me suffer wrong?
Not Gloucester's death, nor Herford's banishment,
Not Gaunt's rebukes, nor England's private wrongs,
Nor the prevention of poor Bullingbrook
About his marriage, nor my own disgrace,
Have ever made me sour my patient cheek,
Or bend one wrinkle on my sovereign's face.
I am the last of noble Edward's sons,
Of whom thy father, Prince of Wales, was first.
In war was never lion rag'd more fierce,
In peace was never gentle lamb more mild,
Than was that young and princely gentleman.
His face thou hast, for even so look'd he,
Accomplish'd with [the] number of thy hours;
But when he frowned it was against the French,
And not against his friends. His noble hand
Did win what he did spend, and spent not that
Which his triumphant father's hand had won.
His hands were guilty of no kinred blood,
But bloody with the enemies of his kin.
O Richard! York is too far gone with grief,
Or else he never would compare between.
K. Rich. Why, uncle, what's the matter?
York. O my liege,
Pardon me, if you please; if not, I, pleas'd
Not to be pardoned, am content withal.
Seek you to seize and gripe into your hands
The royalties and rights of banish'd Herford?
Is not Gaunt dead? and doth not Herford live?
Was not Gaunt just? and is not Harry true?
Did not the one deserve to have an heir?
Is not his heir a well-deserving son?
Take Herford's rights away, and take from Time
His charters and his customary rights;
Let not to-morrow then ensue to-day;
Be not thyself; for how art thou a king
But by fair sequence and succession?
Now afore God—God forbid I say true!—
If you do wrongfully seize Herford's rights,
Call in the letters-patents that he hath
By his attorneys-general to sue
His livery, and deny his off'red homage,
You pluck a thousand dangers on your head,
You lose a thousand well-disposed hearts,
And prick my tender patience to those thoughts
Which honor and allegiance cannot think.
K. Rich. Think what you will, we seize into our hands
His plate, his goods, his money, and his lands.
York. I'll not be by the while. My liege, farewell!
What will ensue hereof, there's none can tell;
But by bad courses may be understood
That their events can never fall out good. *Exit.*
K. Rich. Go, Bushy, to the Earl of Wiltshire straight,
Bid him repair to us to Ely House
To see this business. To-morrow next
We will for Ireland, and 'tis time, I trow.
And we create, in absence of ourself,
Our uncle York lord governor of England;
For he is just and always loved us well.
Come on, our queen, to-morrow must we part.
Be merry, for our time of stay is short.
[*Flourish.*] *Exeunt King and Queen* [*with others*].
Manet Northumberland [*with Willoughby and Ross*].
North. Well, lords, the Duke of Lancaster is dead.
Ross. And living too, for now his son is Duke.
Willo. Barely in title, not in revenues.
North. Richly in both, if justice had her right.
Ross. My heart is great, but it must break with silence,
Ere't be disburdened with a liberal tongue.
North. Nay, speak thy mind, and let him ne'er speak more
That speaks thy words again to do thee harm!
Willo. Tends that thou wouldst speak to the Duke of Herford?
If it be so, out with it boldly, man,
Quick is mine ear to hear of good towards him.
Ross. No good at all that I can do for him,
Unless you call it good to pity him,
Bereft and gelded of his patrimony.
North. Now, afore God, 'tis shame such wrongs are borne
In him, a royal prince, and many moe
Of noble blood in this declining land.
The King is not himself, but basely led
By flatterers, and what they will inform,
Merely in hate, 'gainst any of us all,
That will the King severely prosecute
'Gainst us, our lives, our children, and our heirs.
Ross. The commons hath he pill'd with grievous taxes,
And quite lost their hearts; the nobles hath he fin'd
For ancient quarrels, and quite lost their hearts.
Willo. And daily new exactions are devis'd,

164. tender duty: scrupulous regard (for the King).
166. Gaunt's rebukes: i.e. Richard's rebukes to Gaunt.
167–68. prevention . . . marriage. Richard had blocked Bullingbrook's projected match with the Duc de Berri's daughter, a cousin of Charles VI of France.
170. bend one wrinkle: i.e. frown in the slightest degree.
172. Prince of Wales: Edward the Black Prince, eldest son of Edward III. **173. rag'd more fierce:** more fiercely enraged.
177. Accomplish'd . . . hours: at your age.
182. kinred blood: blood of his kindred.
190. royalties: privileges and perquisites granted by the king (through the "letters-patents" of line 202).
195–96. Take . . . rights: i.e. if you deprive Herford of his inheritance you flout the ancient law of succession, by which "customary rights" descend from father to son. **197. ensue:** follow.
202–4. Call . . . livery: i.e. revoke the royal grant that enables him to bring suit through his attorneys for possession of his hereditary rights.
204. deny . . . homage: i.e. refuse the ceremony of swearing allegiance as required by law for a legatee to secure his inheritance.
205. pluck: pull down.
214. events: results.
215. Earl of Wiltshire: William le Scrope or Scroop, treasurer of the realm and one of the King's notorious favorites. See note to III.ii.122–23.
217. see: see to, superintend. **To-morrow next:** to-morrow.
218. will: will set forth. **trow:** believe. **228. great:** i.e. heavy.
232. Tends . . . speak: does what you want to say concern.
239. moe: more. **243. Merely in hate:** out of pure hatred.
246. pill'd: peeled, stripped bare.

As blanks, benevolences, and I wot not what.
But what a' God's name doth become of this?

North. Wars hath not wasted it, for warr'd he hath not,
But basely yielded upon compromise
That which his noble ancestors achiev'd with blows.
More hath he spent in peace than they in wars.

Ross. The Earl of Wiltshire hath the realm in farm.

Willo. The [King's] grown bankrout, like a broken man.

North. Reproach and dissolution hangeth over him.

Ross. He hath not money for these Irish wars,
His burthenous taxations notwithstanding,
But by the robbing of the banish'd Duke.

North. His noble kinsman—most degenerate king!
But, lords, we hear this fearful tempest sing,
Yet seek no shelter to avoid the storm;
We see the wind sit sore upon our sails,
And yet we strike not, but securely perish.

Ross. We see the very wrack that we must suffer,
And unavoided is the danger now,
For suffering so the causes of our wrack.

North. Not so, even through the hollow eyes of death
I spy life peering, but I dare not say
How near the tidings of our comfort is.

Willo. Nay, let us share thy thoughts, as thou dost ours.

Ross. Be confident to speak, Northumberland:
We three are but thyself, and, speaking so,
Thy words are but as thoughts, therefore be bold.

North. Then thus: I have from Le Port Blanc,
A bay in Britain, receiv'd intelligence
That Harry Duke of Herford, Rainold Lord Cobham,
[Thomas, son and heir to th' Earl of Arundel,]
That late broke from the Duke of Exeter,
His brother, Archbishop late of Canterbury,
Sir Thomas Erpingham, Sir John Ramston,
Sir John Norbery, Sir Robert Waterton, and Francis [Coint]—
All these, well furnished by the Duke of Britain
With eight tall ships, three thousand men of war,
Are making hither with all due expedience,
And shortly mean to touch our northern shore.
Perhaps they had ere this, but that they stay
The first departing of the King for Ireland.
If then we shall shake off our slavish yoke,
Imp out our drooping country's broken wing,
Redeem from broking pawn the blemish'd crown,
Wipe off the dust that hides our sceptre's gilt,
And make high majesty look like itself,
Away with me in post to Ravenspurgh;
But if you faint, as fearing to do so,
Stay, and be secret, and myself will go.

Ross. To horse, to horse! urge doubts to them that fear.

Willo. Hold out my horse, and I will first be there.

Exeunt.

[Scene II]

Enter the Queen, Bushy, Bagot.

Bushy. Madam, your Majesty is too much sad.
You promis'd, when you parted with the King,
To lay aside life-harming heaviness
And entertain a cheerful disposition.

Queen. To please the King I did, to please myself
I cannot do it; yet I know no cause
Why I should welcome such a guest as grief,
Save bidding farewell to so sweet a guest
As my sweet Richard. Yet again methinks
Some unborn sorrow, ripe in fortune's womb,
Is coming towards me, and my inward soul
With nothing trembles; at some thing it grieves,
More than with parting from my lord the King.

Bushy. Each substance of a grief hath twenty shadows,
Which shows like grief itself, but is not so;
For sorrow's eyes, glazed with blinding tears,
Divides one thing entire to many objects,
Like perspectives, which rightly gaz'd upon
Show nothing but confusion; ey'd awry
Distinguish form; so your sweet Majesty,
Looking awry upon your lord's departure,
Find shapes of grief, more than himself, to wail,
Which, look'd on as it is, is nought but shadows
Of what it is not; then, thrice-gracious Queen,
More than your lord's departure weep not—more is not seen,

250. blanks: i.e. the "blank charters" of I.iv.47–51. **benevolences:** forced loans levied with legal authority by the king. This allusion is anachronistic, for they were first employed by Edward IV in 1473. **wot:** know. 251. **a':** in. **this:** i.e. the money illegally collected.
256. **in farm:** on lease.
266. **strike:** (1) lower the sails; (2) strike a blow. **securely:** heedlessly, overconfidently. 268. **unavoided:** unavoidable.
269. **For suffering so:** as a result of permitting.
270. **eyes of death:** eye-sockets of a skull. 278. **Britain:** Brittany.
281. **broke from:** escaped from the custody of.
282. **His:** i.e. the Earl of Arundel's. **late:** until recently.
285–90. **All . . . Ireland.** Holinshed's account of Bullingbrook's expedition (Bullough, III, 397)—which, as the list of names in lines 279–84 indicates, Shakespeare had before him as he wrote—is somewhat less assured. Whereas some sources record that Bullingbrook was supplied by the Duke of Brittany with three thousand men and eight ships, Holinshed points out that "*Froissard* yet speaketh but of three. Moreover, where *Froissard* and also the chronicles of Britaine avouch, that he should land at Plimmouth, by our English writers it seemeth otherwise: for it appeareth by their assured report, that he approching to the shore, did not streight take land, but lay hovering aloofe, and shewed himselfe now in this place, and now in that, to see what countenance was made by the people, whether they meant envioustie to resist him, or freendlie to receive him." Henry actually landed near Ravenspur (the Ravenspurgh of line 296), a village on the Yorkshire coast, in July 1399. 286. **tall:** stately.

287. **expedience:** speed.
292. **Imp out:** graft new feathers on (a term from falconry).
293. **broking pawn:** i.e. pawnbrokers to whom the realm was pledged.
296. **post:** haste. 297. **faint:** are fainthearted.
300. **Hold . . . and:** if my horse holds out.

II.ii. Location: Windsor Castle.
o.s.d. **Queen.** Isabella, daughter of Charles VI of France, had become Richard's second wife in 1396, when she was seven. She was therefore ten at the time represented in this scene.
3. **heaviness:** melancholy. 4. **entertain:** assume. 12. **With:** at.
14. **Each . . . shadows:** i.e. for each real grief there are twenty imaginary griefs.
16–20. **For . . . form.** Bushy somewhat confusingly compares the Queen's tear-glazed eyes first (lines 16–17) to perspective glasses whose multi-faceted lenses multiply a single object into various images, and then (lines 18–20) to perspective pictures or figures that, though seemingly distorted, present a normal appearance (*distinguish form*) when viewed obliquely (*ey'd awry*).

Or if it be, 'tis with false sorrow's eye,
Which for things true weeps things imaginary.
Queen. It may be so; but yet my inward soul
Persuades me it is otherwise. Howe'er it be,
I cannot but be sad; so heavy sad,
As, [though] on thinking on no thought I think,
Makes me with heavy nothing faint and shrink.
Bushy. 'Tis nothing but conceit, my gracious lady.
Queen. 'Tis nothing less: conceit is still deriv'd
From some forefather grief; mine is not so,
For nothing hath begot my something grief,
Or something hath the nothing that I grieve—
'Tis in reversion that I do possess—
But what it is that is not yet known what,
I cannot name; 'tis nameless woe, I wot.

[*Enter* GREEN.]

Green. God save your Majesty! and well met, gentlemen.
I hope the King is not yet shipp'd for Ireland.
Queen. Why hopest thou so? 'Tis better hope he is,
For his designs crave haste, his haste good hope.
Then wherefore dost thou hope he is not shipp'd?
Green. That he, our hope, might have retir'd his power,
And driven into despair an enemy's hope,
Who strongly hath set footing in this land:
The banish'd Bullingbrook repeals himself,
And with uplifted arms is safe arriv'd
At Ravenspurgh.
Queen. Now God in heaven forbid!
Green. Ah, madam! 'tis too true, and that is worse,
The Lord Northumberland, his son young Harry Percy,
The Lords of Ross, Beaumond, and Willoughby,
With all their powerful friends, are fled to him.
Bushy. Why have you not proclaim'd Northumberland
And all the rest revolted faction traitors?
Green. We have, whereupon the Earl of Worcester
Hath broken his staff, resign'd his stewardship,
And all the household servants fled with him
To Bullingbrook.
Queen. So, Green, thou art the midwife to my woe,
And Bullingbrook my sorrow's dismal heir.
Now hath my soul brought forth her prodigy,
And I, a gasping new-deliver'd mother,
Have woe to woe, sorrow to sorrow join'd.
Bushy. Despair not, madam.
Queen. Who shall hinder me?
I will despair, and be at enmity

33. conceit: imagination.
34. 'Tis nothing less: i.e. it is anything but that. **still:** always.
36. something: i.e. real, substantial.
38–40. 'Tis . . . name: i.e. my grief is like my expectation of a legacy, the nature of which is as yet unknown.
38. reversion: legal right of future possession.
46. retir'd his power: drawn back his forces.
49. repeals: recalls (from exile).
50. uplifted arms: brandished weapons. **52. that:** what.
57. rest revolted faction: rest of the rebellious clique.
59. staff: badge of office. **stewardship.** In 1394 Northumberland's brother Thomas Percy, Earl of Worcester, had been appointed steward of the royal household, a post of great honor and importance.
63. dismal heir: ill-omened offspring.
64. prodigy: monstrous birth.

With cozening hope. He is a flatterer,
A parasite, a keeper-back of death,
Who gently would dissolve the bands of life,
Which false hope lingers in extremity.

[*Enter* YORK.]

Green. Here comes the Duke of York.
Queen. With signs of war about his aged neck.
O, full of careful business are his looks!
Uncle, for God's sake speak comfortable words.
York. Should I do so, I should belie my thoughts.
Comfort's in heaven, and we are on the earth,
Where nothing lives but crosses, cares, and grief.
Your husband, he is gone to save far off,
Whilst others come to make him lose at home.
Here am I left to underprop his land,
Who, weak with age, cannot support myself.
Now comes the sick hour that his surfeit made,
Now shall he try his friends that flatter'd him.

[*Enter a* SERVINGMAN.]

Serv. My lord, your son was gone before I came.
York. He was—why, so go all which way it will!
The nobles they are fled, the commons they are cold,
And will, I fear, revolt on Herford's side.
Sirrah, get thee to Plashy, to my sister Gloucester,
Bid her send me presently a thousand pound.
Hold, take my ring.
Serv. My lord, I had forgot to tell your lordship:
To-day, as I came by, I called there—
But I shall grieve you to report the rest.
York. What is't, knave?
Serv. An hour before I came, the Duchess died.
York. God for his mercy, what a tide of woes
Comes rushing on this woeful land at once!
I know not what to do. I would to God
(So my untruth had not provok'd him to it)
The King had cut off my head with my brother's.
What, are there no posts dispatch'd for Ireland?
How shall we do for money for these wars?
Come, sister—cousin, I would say—pray pardon me.
Go, fellow, get thee home, provide some carts,
And bring away the armor that is there.
[*Exit Servingman.*]
Gentlemen, will you go muster men? If I
Know how or which way to order these affairs
Thus disorderly thrust into my hands,
Never believe me. Both are my kinsmen:
T' one is my sovereign, whom both my oath

69. cozening: deceitful. **71. bands:** bonds.
72. Which . . . extremity: i.e. the dissolving of "the bands of life" which false hope postpones, thus delaying the relief that death will bring.
74. signs . . . neck. Perhaps he wears a gorget, a piece of mail covering the throat. **75. careful business:** anxious preoccupation.
76. comfortable: comforting. **79. crosses:** vexations.
84. surfeit: dissipation. **85. try:** test.
86. son: i.e. the Duke of Aumerle.
90. Sirrah: customary form of address to an inferior.
91. presently: immediately.
92. take my ring: i.e. as a sign that you are authorized by me.
96. knave: fellow. **101. untruth:** disloyalty.
102. brother's: i.e. the Duke of Gloucester's.
105. sister—cousin. In his perturbation York momentarily confuses the Queen with the Duchess of Gloucester, who is uppermost in his mind.

And duty bids defend; t' other again
Is my kinsman, whom the King hath wrong'd,
Whom conscience and my kinred bids to right.
Well, somewhat we must do.
Come, cousin, I'll dispose of you.
Gentlemen, go muster up your men,
And meet me presently at Berkeley.
I should to Plashy too,
But time will not permit. All is uneven,
And every thing is left at six and seven.

Exeunt Duke [of York], Queen. Manent Bushy, Green, [Bagot].

Bushy. The wind sits fair for news to go for Ireland,
But none returns. For us to levy power
Proportionable to the enemy
Is all unpossible.

Green. Besides, our nearness to the King in love
Is near the hate of those love not the King.

Bagot. And that is the wavering commons, for their love
Lies in their purses, and whoso empties them
By so much fills their hearts with deadly hate.

Bushy. Wherein the King stands generally condemn'd.

Bagot. If judgment lie in them, then so do we,
Because we ever have been near the King.

Green. Well, I will for refuge straight to Bristow castle:
The Earl of Wiltshire is already there.

Bushy. Thither will I with you, for little office
Will the hateful commons perform for us,
Except like curs to tear us all to pieces.
Will you go along with us?

Bagot. No, I will to Ireland to his Majesty.
Farewell! If heart's presages be not vain,
We three here part that ne'er shall meet again.

Bushy. That's as York thrives to beat back Bullingbrook.

Green. Alas, poor duke, the task he undertakes
Is numb'ring sands and drinking oceans dry;
Where one on his side fights, thousands will fly.
Farewell at once, for once, for all, and ever.

Bushy. Well, we may meet again.

Bagot. I fear me, never. *[Exeunt.]*

[Scene III]

Enter [Bullingbrook, *Duke of*] *Herford*, Northumberland, [*and forces*].

Bull. How far is it, my lord, to Berkeley now?

North. Believe me, noble lord,
I am a stranger here in Gloucestershire.
These high wild hills and rough uneven ways

117. **dispose of:** make arrangements for.
119. **Berkeley:** castle between Bristol and Gloucester, the scene of Edward II's murder in 1327. 124. **power:** forces.
128. **Is near:** involves. **those:** those who.
133. **If . . . we:** if the power to pass judgment is lodged in them, then we too stand condemned. 137. **office:** service.
138. **hateful:** full of hatred, i.e. hostile.

II.iii. Location: Wilds in Gloucestershire.

Draws out our miles and makes them wearisome,
And yet your fair discourse hath been as sugar,
Making the hard way sweet and delectable.
But I bethink me what a weary way
From Ravenspurgh to Cotshall will be found
In Ross and Willoughby, wanting your company,
Which, I protest, hath very much beguil'd
The tediousness and process of my travel.
But theirs is sweet'ned with the hope to have
The present benefit which I possess,
And hope to joy is little less in joy
Than hope enjoyed. By this the weary lords
Shall make their way seem short, as mine hath done
By sight of what I have, your noble company.

Bull. Of much less value is my company
Than your good words. But who comes here?

Enter Harry Percy.

North. It is my son, young Harry Percy,
Sent from my brother Worcester, whencesoever.
Harry, how fares your uncle?

Percy. I had thought, my lord, to have learn'd his health of you.

North. Why, is he not with the Queen?

Percy. No, my good lord, he hath forsook the court,
Broken his staff of office, and dispers'd
The household of the King.

North. What was his reason?
He was not so resolv'd when last we spake together.

Percy. Because your lordship was proclaimed traitor.
But he, my lord, is gone to Ravenspurgh
To offer service to the Duke of Herford,
And sent me over by Berkeley, to discover
What power the Duke of York had levied there,
Then with directions to repair to Ravenspurgh.

North. Have you forgot the Duke of [Herford], boy?

Percy. No, my good lord, for that is not forgot
Which ne'er I did remember. To my knowledge,
I never in my life did look on him.

North. Then learn to know him now, this is the Duke.

Percy. My gracious lord, I tender you my service,
Such as it is, being tender, raw, and young,
Which elder days shall ripen and confirm
To more approved service and desert.

Bull. I thank thee, gentle Percy, and be sure
I count myself in nothing else so happy
As in a soul rememb'ring my good friends,
And as my fortune ripens with thy love,
It shall be still thy true love's recompense.
My heart this covenant makes, my hand thus seals it.

North. How far is it to Berkeley? and what stir
Keeps good old York there with his men of war?

9. **Cotshall:** Cotswold, a range of hills in Gloucestershire.
10. **wanting:** lacking. 12. **tediousness and process:** tedious course.
16. **this:** i.e. the expectation of enjoying Bullingbrook's company.
21. **young Harry Percy.** Actually, young Percy—the Hotspur of *1 Henry IV*—was thirty-five years old at the time. Bullingbrook was thirty-two.
22. **whencesoever:** from somewhere or other (wherever he may be).

Percy. There stands the castle, by yon tuft of trees,
Mann'd with three hundred men, as I have heard,
And in it are the Lords of York, Berkeley, and Seymour,
None else of name and noble estimate.

[*Enter* Ross *and* Willoughby.]

North. Here come the Lords of Ross and Willoughby,
Bloody with spurring, fiery-red with haste.
Bull. Welcome, my lords. I wot your love pursues
A banish'd traitor. All my treasury
Is yet but unfelt thanks, which more enrich'd
Shall be your love and labor's recompense.
Ross. Your presence makes us rich, most noble lord.
Willo. And far surmounts our labor to attain it.
Bull. Evermore thank's the exchequer of the poor,
Which, till my infant fortune comes to years,
Stands for my bounty. But who comes here?
North. It is my Lord of Berkeley, as I guess.

[*Enter* Berkeley.]

Berk. My Lord of Herford, my message is to you.
Bull. My lord, my answer is to Lancaster,
And I am come to seek that name in England,
And I must find that title in your tongue,
Before I make reply to aught you say.
Berk. Mistake me not, my lord, 'tis not my meaning
To rase one title of your honor out.
To you, my lord, I come, what lord you will,
From the most gracious regent of this land,
The Duke of York, to know what pricks you on
To take advantage of the absent time,
And fright our native peace with self-borne arms.

[*Enter* York *attended*.]

Bull. I shall not need transport my words by you,
Here comes his Grace in person. My noble uncle! [*Kneels.*]
York. Show me thy humble heart, and not thy knee,
Whose duty is deceivable and false.
Bull. My gracious uncle—
York. Tut, tut!
Grace me no grace, nor uncle me no uncle.
I am no traitor's uncle, and that word "grace"
In an ungracious mouth is but profane.
Why have those banish'd and forbidden legs
Dar'd once to touch a dust of England's ground?
But then more "why?"—why have they dar'd to march
So many miles upon her peaceful bosom,
Frighting her pale-fac'd villages with war
And ostentation of despised arms?
Com'st thou because the anointed King is hence?
Why, foolish boy, the King is left behind,
And in my loyal bosom lies his power.
Were I but now lord of such hot youth
As when brave Gaunt, thy father, and myself
Rescued the Black Prince, that young Mars of men,
From forth the ranks of many thousand French,
O then how quickly should this arm of mine,
Now prisoner to the palsy, chastise thee,
And minister correction to thy fault!
Bull. My gracious uncle, let me know my fault,
On what condition stands it and wherein?
York. Even in condition of the worst degree,
In gross rebellion and detested treason.
Thou art a banish'd man, and here art come,
Before the expiration of thy time,
In braving arms against thy sovereign.
Bull. As I was banish'd, I was banish'd Herford,
But as I come, I come for Lancaster.
And, noble uncle, I beseech your Grace
Look on my wrongs with an indifferent eye.
You are my father, for methinks in you
I see old Gaunt alive. O then, my father,
Will you permit that I shall stand condemn'd
A wandering vagabond, my rights and royalties
Pluck'd from my arms perforce—and given away
To upstart unthrifts? Wherefore was I born?
If that my cousin king be King in England,
It must be granted I am Duke of Lancaster.
You have a son, Aumerle, my noble cousin,
Had you first died, and he been thus trod down,
He should have found his uncle Gaunt a father
To rouse his wrongs and chase them to the bay.
I am denied to sue my livery here,
And yet my letters-patents give me leave.
My father's goods are all distrain'd and sold,
And these, and all, are all amiss employed.
What would you have me do? I am a subject,
And I challenge law. Attorneys are denied me,
And therefore personally I lay my claim
To my inheritance of free descent.
North. The noble Duke hath been too much abused.
Ross. It stands your Grace upon to do him right.
Willo. Base men by his endowments are made great.

56. estimate: rank.
57 s.d. Ross and Willoughby. According to Holinshed (Bullough, III, 398), Ross and Willoughby had been the first to join Bullingbrook when he came ashore at Ravenspur, and the Percies had thrown their support to him at Doncaster, on his march to Gloucestershire. See note to *1 Henry IV*, V.i.42. **59. wot:** know.
61. unfelt: i.e. expressed by words, not things.
65. Evermore . . . poor: gratitude is always the treasury of the poor (because they can make no other kind of payment in return for favors).
70. my . . . Lancaster: i.e. I answer only to my proper title, which is Duke of Lancaster.
75. rase: erase. **title.** With perhaps a pun on *tittle*.
79. absent time: i.e. time of the King's absence in Ireland.
80. self-borne: borne in one's own selfish interests (rather than in the public good).
84. duty: function (of bowing in allegiance). **deceivable:** deceitful.
95. ostentation: display. **despised:** despicable.
100–102. As . . . French. The incident is unrecorded by the chroniclers. **105. minister:** administer.
107. On . . . wherein: i.e. on what defect of character is it based and in what does it consist. **112. braving:** defiant. **114. for:** as.
116. indifferent: impartial. **120. royalties.** See note to II.i.190.
122. unthrifts: spendthrifts. **born:** i.e. as heir to the Duke of Lancaster. **126. first:** i.e. before Gaunt.
128. rouse: expose; literally, startle from the lair (a term from hunting). **bay:** last stand (a term from hunting).
131. distrain'd: confiscated.
134. challenge law: claim my legal rights.
136. of free descent: through legitimate succession.
138. stands . . . upon: is incumbent upon your Grace.
139. his endowments: i.e. property and revenues that belong to him.

York. My lords of England, let me tell you this:
I have had feeling of my cousin's wrongs,
And labor'd all I could to do him right;
But in this kind to come, in braving arms,
Be his own carver and cut out his way,
To find out right with wrong—it may not be;
And you that do abet him in this kind
Cherish rebellion and are rebels all.

North. The noble Duke hath sworn his coming is
But for his own; and for the right of that
We all have strongly sworn to give him aid;
And let him never see joy that breaks that oath!

York. Well, well, I see the issue of these arms.
I cannot mend it, I must needs confess,
Because my power is weak and all ill left;
But if I could, by Him that gave me life,
I would attach you all, and make you stoop
Unto the sovereign mercy of the King;
But since I cannot, be it known unto you
I do remain as neuter. So fare you well,
Unless you please to enter in the castle,
And there repose you for this night.

Bull. An offer, uncle, that we will accept,
But we must win your Grace to go with us
To Bristow castle, which they say is held
By Bushy, Bagot, and their complices,
The caterpillars of the commonwealth,
Which I have sworn to weed and pluck away.

York. It may be I will go with you, but yet I'll pause,
For I am loath to break our country's laws.
Nor friends, nor foes, to me welcome you are:
Things past redress are now with me past care.
Exeunt.

[SCENE IV]

Enter EARL OF SALISBURY *and a* WELSH CAPTAIN.

Cap. My Lord of Salisbury, we have stay'd ten days,
And hardly kept our countrymen together,
And yet we hear no tidings from the King,
Therefore we will disperse ourselves. Farewell!

Sal. Stay yet another day, thou trusty Welshman.
The King reposeth all his confidence in thee.

Cap. 'Tis thought the King is dead; we will not stay.
The bay-trees in our country are all wither'd,
And meteors fright the fixed stars of heaven,
The pale-fac'd moon looks bloody on the earth,
And lean-look'd prophets whisper fearful change,
Rich men look sad, and ruffians dance and leap,
The one in fear to lose what they enjoy,
The other to enjoy by rage and war.
These signs forerun the death or fall of kings.
Farewell! Our countrymen are gone and fled,
As well assured Richard their king is dead. [*Exit.*]

Sal. Ah, Richard! with the eyes of heavy mind
I see thy glory like a shooting star
Fall to the base earth from the firmament.
Thy sun sets weeping in the lowly west,
Witnessing storms to come, woe, and unrest.
Thy friends are fled to wait upon thy foes,
And crossly to thy good all fortune goes. [*Exit.*]

[ACT III, SCENE I]

Enter [BULLINGBROOK,] *Duke of Herford*, YORK, NORTHUMBERLAND, [ROSS, PERCY, WILLOUGHBY, *with*] BUSHY *and* GREEN *prisoners*.

Bull. Bring forth these men.
Bushy and Green, I will not vex your souls—
Since presently your souls must part your bodies—
With too much urging your pernicious lives,
For 'twere no charity; yet, to wash your blood
From off my hands, here in the view of men
I will unfold some causes of your deaths:
You have misled a prince, a royal king,
A happy gentleman in blood and lineaments,
By you unhappied and disfigured clean;
You have in manner with your sinful hours
Made a divorce betwixt his queen and him,
Broke the possession of a royal bed,
And stain'd the beauty of a fair queen's cheeks
With tears drawn from her eyes by your foul wrongs;
Myself, a prince by fortune of my birth,
Near to the King in blood, and near in love
Till you did make him misinterpret me,
Have stoop'd my neck under your injuries,
And sigh'd my English breath in foreign clouds,
Eating the bitter bread of banishment,
Whilst you have fed upon my signories,
Dispark'd my parks and fell'd my forest woods,

143. kind: manner.
144. Be . . . carver: serve his own portion, i.e. indulge himself.
149. for his own. Bullingbrook had won the Percies' support, says Holinshed (Bullough, III, 398), when he swore to them "that he would demand no more, but the lands that were to him descended by inheritance from his father, and in right of his wife" (Mary Bohun, co-heiress of Hereford). **right:** legality.
152. issue . . . arms: outcome of this resort to force.
154. all ill left: entirely inadequate. **156. attach:** arrest.
159. neuter: neutral. **164. Bristow:** Bristol.
165. complices: accomplices.
170. Nor . . . nor: neither as . . . nor as.

II.iv. Location: A camp in Wales.
2. hardly: with difficulty.
7–9. 'Tis . . . heaven. In this short scene Shakespeare draws on two widely separated passages in Holinshed. In one it is reported (Bullough, III, 400) that Richard, prevented by bad weather from returning to England as soon as he learned of Bullingbrook's invasion, sent the Earl of Salisbury to raise the Welsh in his support. However, the newly mustered troops grew impatient at the King's delay, decided that he was "suerlie dead," and after fourteen (not ten) days "scaled & departed awaie." Earlier, in an account of the general disaffection with Richard's extortions and misrule before he went to Ireland, Holinshed records (Bullough, III, 396) that "throughout all the realme of England, old baie trees withered, and afterwards, contrarie to all mens thinking, grew greene againe, a strange sight, and supposed to import some unknowne event." **22. Witnessing:** signifying.
23. wait upon: offer allegiance to. **24. crossly:** adversely.

III.i. Location: Bristol. Before the castle.
3. presently: immediately. **part:** leave.
4. urging: dwelling on (in order to justify the summary execution).
9. blood: descent.
10. unhappied. See note to II.i.16. **clean:** completely.
11. in manner: so to speak, as it were.
20. foreign clouds: i.e. the air of foreign lands.
22. signories: properties.
23. Dispark'd: i.e. put to uses unrelated to forestry and hunting.

From my own windows torn my household coat,
Ras'd out my imprese, leaving me no sign,
Save men's opinions and my living blood,
To show the world I am a gentleman.
This and much more, much more than twice all this,
Condemns you to the death. See them delivered over
To execution and the hand of death.

Bushy. More welcome is the stroke of death to me
Than Bullingbrook to England. Lords, farewell!

Green. My comfort is, that heaven will take our souls,
And plague injustice with the pains of hell.

Bull. My Lord Northumberland, see them dispatch'd.

[*Exeunt Northumberland and others with the prisoners.*]

Uncle, you say the Queen is at your house,
For God's sake fairly let her be entreated.
Tell her I send to her my kind commends;
Take special care my greetings be delivered.

York. A gentleman of mine I have dispatch'd
With letters of your love to her at large.

Bull. Thanks, gentle uncle. Come, lords, away,
To fight with Glendower and his complices.
A while to work, and after holiday. *Exeunt.*

[Scene II]

[*Drums: flourish and colors.*] *Enter the* King, Aumerle, [*the* Bishop of] Carlisle, *and* [Soldiers].

K. Rich. Barkloughly castle call they this at hand?

Aum. Yea, my lord. How brooks your Grace the air
After your late tossing on the breaking seas?

K. Rich. Needs must I like it well; I weep for joy
To stand upon my kingdom once again.
Dear earth, I do salute thee with my hand,
Though rebels wound thee with their horses' hoofs.
As a long-parted mother with her child
Plays fondly with her tears and smiles in meeting,
So weeping, smiling, greet I thee, my earth,
And do thee favors with my royal hands.
Feed not thy sovereign's foe, my gentle earth,

24. coat: coat of arms.
25. Ras'd: erased. **imprese:** heraldic device consisting of an allegorical picture and a motto (Italian *impresa,* plural *imprese*).
37. entreated: treated. **38. commends:** regards.
41. at large: in full.
43. Glendower. An unhistorical detail. Although Owen Glendower, the fiery Welsh rebel of *1 Henry IV,* resisted Henry IV so strenuously that the newly crowned king launched a campaign against him in 1400, there is no record of a clash between them at the time represented in this scene. This is the only mention of Glendower in the play, unless, as some editors have suggested, he is the "Welsh Captain" of II.iv.

III.ii. Location: The coast of Wales.
o.s.d. flourish and colors: fanfare and (a show of) flags.
1. Barkloughly: Shakespeare's version of Holinshed's *Barclowlie,* itself an error for *Hertlowi,* i.e. Harlech, a castle in northern Wales built by Edward I in 1285. Actually, when Richard returned from Ireland in July 1399 he landed at Milford Haven in southern Wales.
2. brooks: likes.
6. with my hand: i.e. with a gesture of salutation. See line 11.
8. a long-parted mother with: a mother long parted from.
9. fondly: (1) foolishly; (2) dotingly.

Nor with thy sweets comfort his ravenous sense,
But let thy spiders, that suck up thy venom,
And heavy-gaited toads lie in their way,
Doing annoyance to the treacherous feet,
Which with usurping steps do trample thee.
Yield stinging nettles to mine enemies;
And when they from thy bosom pluck a flower,
Guard it, I pray thee, with a lurking adder,
Whose double tongue may with a mortal touch
Throw death upon thy sovereign's enemies.
Mock not my senseless conjuration, lords,
This earth shall have a feeling, and these stones
Prove armed soldiers, ere her native king
Shall falter under foul rebellion's arms.

Car. Fear not, my lord, that Power that made you king
Hath power to keep you king in spite of all.
The means that heavens yield must be embrac'd,
And not neglected; else heaven would,
And we will not. Heaven's offer we refuse,
The proffered means of succors and redress.

Aum. He means, my lord, that we are too remiss,
Whilst Bullingbrook, through our security,
Grows strong and great in substance and in power.

K. Rich. Discomfortable cousin, know'st thou not
That when the searching eye of heaven is hid
Behind the globe, that lights the lower world,
Then thieves and robbers range abroad unseen
In murthers and in outrage [boldly] here,
But when from under this terrestrial ball
He fires the proud tops of the eastern pines
And darts his light through every guilty hole,
Then murthers, treasons, and detested sins,
The cloak of night being pluck'd from off their backs,
Stand bare and naked, trembling at themselves?
So when this thief, this traitor Bullingbrook,
Who all this while hath revell'd in the night,
Whilst we were wand'ring with the antipodes,
Shall see us rising in our throne, the east,
His treasons will sit blushing in his face,
Not able to endure the sight of day,
But self-affrighted tremble at his sin.
Not all the water in the rough rude sea
Can wash the balm off from an anointed king;
The breath of worldly men cannot depose
The deputy elected by the Lord;
For every man that Bullingbrook hath press'd
To lift shrewd steel against our golden crown,
God for his Richard hath in heavenly pay
A glorious angel; then if angels fight,
Weak men must fall, for heaven still guards the right.

13. with . . . sense: gratify his voracious appetite with your bounty.
21. double: forked. **22. Throw:** inflict.
23. senseless conjuration: solemn injunction to things that cannot understand it.
25. native: i.e. legitimate. Richard was born in Bordeaux.
30–31. else . . . not: i.e. otherwise we ignore the will of heaven.
34. security: overconfidence. **35. power:** troops.
36. Discomfortable: discouraging.
38. globe: i.e. the earth. **that:** i.e. the "eye of heaven."
49. antipodes: people on the other side of the earth; here, the Irish.
55. balm: the oil used to anoint a king at his coronation.
56. worldly: earthly. **58. press'd:** conscripted.
59. shrewd: harmful. **62. still:** always.

Enter Salisbury.

Welcome, my lord. How far off lies your power?
Sal. Nor near nor farther off, my gracious lord,
Than this weak arm. Discomfort guides my tongue
And bids me speak of nothing but despair.
One day too late, I fear me, noble lord,
Hath clouded all thy happy days on earth.
O, call back yesterday, bid time return,
And thou shalt have twelve thousand fighting men!
To-day, to-day, unhappy day, too late,
Overthrows thy joys, friends, fortune, and thy state,
For all the Welshmen, hearing thou wert dead,
Are gone to Bullingbrook, dispers'd and fled.
Aum. Comfort, my liege, why looks your Grace so pale?
K. Rich. But now the blood of twenty thousand men
Did triumph in my face, and they are fled;
And till so much blood thither come again,
Have I not reason to look pale and dead?
All souls that will be safe, fly from my side,
For time hath set a blot upon my pride.
Aum. Comfort, my liege, remember who you are.
K. Rich. I had forgot myself, am I not king?
Awake, thou coward majesty! thou sleepest.
Is not the king's name twenty thousand names?
Arm, arm, my name! a puny subject strikes
At thy great glory. Look not to the ground,
Ye favorites of a king, are we not high?
High be our thoughts. I know my uncle York
Hath power enough to serve our turn. But who comes here?

Enter Scroop.

Scroop. More health and happiness betide my liege
Than can my care-tun'd tongue deliver him!
K. Rich. Mine ear is open, and my heart prepar'd,
The worst is worldly loss thou canst unfold.
Say, is my kingdom lost? Why, 'twas my care,
And what loss is it to be rid of care?
Strives Bullingbrook to be as great as we?
Greater he shall not be; if he serve God,
We'll serve Him too, and be his fellow so.
Revolt our subjects? That we cannot mend,
They break their faith to God as well as us.
Cry woe, destruction, ruin, and decay:
The worst is death, and death will have his day.
Scroop. Glad am I that your Highness is so arm'd
To bear the tidings of calamity.
Like an unseasonable stormy day,
Which makes the silver rivers drown their shores,
As if the world were all dissolv'd to tears,
So high above his limits swells the rage
Of Bullingbrook, covering your fearful land
With hard bright steel, and hearts harder than steel.
White-beards have arm'd their thin and hairless scalps
Against thy majesty; boys, with women's voices,
Strive to speak big, and clap their female joints
In stiff unwieldy arms against thy crown;
Thy very beadsmen learn to bend their bows
Of double-fatal yew against thy state;
Yea, distaff-women manage rusty bills
Against thy seat: both young and old rebel,
And all goes worse than I have power to tell.
K. Rich. Too well, too well thou tell'st a tale so ill.
Where is the Earl of Wiltshire? Where is Bagot?
What is become of Bushy? Where is Green?
That they have let the dangerous enemy
Measure our confines with such peaceful steps?
If we prevail, their heads shall pay for it.
I warrant they have made peace with Bullingbrook.
Scroop. Peace have they made with him indeed, my lord.
K. Rich. O villains, vipers, damn'd without redemption!
Dogs, easily won to fawn on any man!
Snakes, in my heart-blood warm'd, that sting my heart!
Three Judases, each one thrice worse than Judas!
Would they make peace? Terrible hell
Make war upon their spotted souls for this!
Scroop. Sweet love, I see, changing his property,
Turns to the sourest and most deadly hate.
Again uncurse their souls, their peace is made
With heads, and not with hands. Those whom you curse
Have felt the worst of death's destroying wound,
And lie full low, grav'd in the hollow ground.
Aum. Is Bushy, Green, and the Earl of Wiltshire dead?
Scroop. Ay, all of them at Bristow lost their heads.
Aum. Where is the Duke my father with his power?
K. Rich. No matter where—of comfort no man speak:
Let's talk of graves, of worms, and epitaphs,
Make dust our paper, and with rainy eyes
Write sorrow on the bosom of the earth.
Let's choose executors and talk of wills;
And yet not so, for what can we bequeath

63 s.d. **Enter Salisbury.** In Holinshed's account (Bullough, III, 400–401), Richard, so "greatlie discomforted" at the news of Bullingbrook's success that he has already discharged his troops, meets Salisbury at Conway after a sorrowful march from "Barclowlie."
64. **near:** nearer. 72. **state:** regal power. 77. **triumph:** shine forth.
91 s.d. **Scroop:** presumably Sir Stephen Scroop (brother of Sir William Scroop, Earl of Wiltshire), whom Holinshed mentions (Bullough, III, 401) as one of Richard's attendants at Conway.
92. **care-tun'd:** tuned to the sounds of sorrow. **deliver:** report to.
109. **his:** its.

112. **thin:** sparsely covered with hair.
114. **female:** i.e. weak (like those of women).
116. **beadsmen:** aged pensioners whose function was to pray for their benefactors.
117. **double-fatal:** i.e. because its foliage is poisonous and its wood was used for making bows.
118–19. **distaff-women . . . seat:** spinning-women wield rusty pikes against your throne.
122–23. **Where . . . Green.** Of the four notorious favorites whom Richard asks about, the Earl of Wiltshire, although reported by Holinshed (Bullough, III, 399), by Scroop in line 142, and by the Gardener in a later scene (III.iv.53) to have been captured and executed with Bushy and Green at Bristol (III.i), does not appear in this play. Bagot, last seen in II.ii, eluded Bullingbrook and reappears in IV.i; but since Richard could not have known of his escape his allusion in line 132 to "three Judases" is puzzling, like Aumerle's omission of Bagot's name in line 141.
125. **Measure our confines:** travel through our realm.
134. **spotted:** i.e. with treason. 135. **his property:** its quality.
137. **uncurse.** See note to II.i.16.

Save our deposed bodies to the ground?
Our lands, our lives, and all are Bullingbrook's,
And nothing can we call our own but death,
And that small model of the barren earth
Which serves as paste and cover to our bones.
For God's sake let us sit upon the ground
And tell sad stories of the death of kings:
How some have been depos'd, some slain in war,
Some haunted by the ghosts they have deposed,
Some poisoned by their wives, some sleeping kill'd,
All murthered—for within the hollow crown
That rounds the mortal temples of a king
Keeps Death his court, and there the antic sits,
Scoffing his state and grinning at his pomp,
Allowing him a breath, a little scene,
To monarchize, be fear'd, and kill with looks,
Infusing him with self and vain conceit,
As if this flesh which walls about our life
Were brass impregnable; and humor'd thus,
Comes at the last and with a little pin
Bores thorough his castle wall, and farewell king!
Cover your heads, and mock not flesh and blood
With solemn reverence, throw away respect,
Tradition, form, and ceremonious duty,
For you have but mistook me all this while.
I live with bread like you, feel want,
Taste grief, need friends: subjected thus,
How can you say to me I am a king?

Car. My lord, wise men ne'er sit and wail their woes,
But presently prevent the ways to wail;
To fear the foe, since fear oppresseth strength,
Gives in your weakness strength unto your foe,
And so your follies fight against yourself.
Fear, and be slain—no worse can come to fight,
And fight and die is death destroying death,
Where fearing dying pays death servile breath.

Aum. My father hath a power, inquire of him,
And learn to make a body of a limb.

K. Rich. Thou chid'st me well. Proud Bullingbrook, I come
To change blows with thee for our day of doom.
This ague fit of fear is overblown,
An easy task it is to win our own.
Say, Scroop, where lies our uncle with his power?
Speak sweetly, man, although thy looks be sour.

Scroop. Men judge by the complexion of the sky
The state and inclination of the day;
So may you by my dull and heavy eye:
My tongue hath but a heavier tale to say.
I play the torturer by small and small
To lengthen out the worst that must be spoken:
Your uncle York is join'd with Bullingbrook,
And all your northern castles yielded up,
And all your southern gentlemen in arms
Upon his party.

K. Rich. Thou hast said enough.
[*To Aumerle.*] Beshrew thee, cousin, which didst lead me forth
Of that sweet way I was in to despair!
What say you now? What comfort have we now?
By heaven, I'll hate him everlastingly
That bids me be of comfort any more.
Go to Flint castle, there I'll pine away—
A king, woe's slave, shall kingly woe obey.
That power I have, discharge, and let them go
To ear the land that hath some hope to grow,
For I have none. Let no man speak again
To alter this, for counsel is but vain.

Aum. My liege, one word.

K. Rich. He does me double wrong
That wounds me with the flatteries of his tongue.
Discharge my followers, let them hence away,
From Richard's night to Bullingbrook's fair day.
[*Exeunt.*]

[SCENE III]

Enter, [with Drum and Colors,] BULLINGBROOK, YORK, NORTHUMBERLAND, [ATTENDANTS, *and forces*].

Bull. So that by this intelligence we learn
The Welshmen are dispers'd, and Salisbury
Is gone to meet the King, who lately landed
With some few private friends upon this coast.

North. The news is very fair and good, my lord:
Richard not far from hence hath hid his head.

York. It would beseem the Lord Northumberland
To say King Richard. Alack the heavy day
When such a sacred king should hide his head!

North. Your Grace mistakes; only to be brief
Left I his title out.

York. The time hath been,
Would you have been so brief with him, he would
Have been so brief [with you] to shorten you,
For taking so the head, your whole head's length.

Bull. Mistake not, uncle, further than you should.

York. Take not, good cousin, further than you should,
Lest you mistake the heavens are over our heads.

153. **model:** mould, shape.
154. **paste:** pie crust. Dr. Johnson remarked that the metaphor is "not of the most sublime kind." 158. **ghosts:** i.e. of kings.
161. **rounds:** encircles.
162–63. **the antic . . . pomp:** the jester sits, mocking the king's regality and grinning at his splendor.
165. **monarchize:** play the monarch.
166. **self . . . conceit:** foolish fancies about himself.
168. **humor'd.** To make Death, rather than the king, subject of the participle would seem to yield the better sense: "having thus amused himself (by his antics with the king), Death comes," etc.
176. **subjected:** (1) liable (to common human needs); (2) made a subject.
179. **presently . . . wail:** immediately block the paths that lead to grief. 183. **to fight:** by fighting.
184–85. **fight . . . breath:** to die fighting is to conquer death by dying, whereas to die in fear is to pay death the tribute of our cowardice.
186. **power:** troop of soldiers.
187. **learn . . . limb:** i.e. augment it by fresh recruits.
189. **for . . . doom:** i.e. to determine which of us will die.

197. **heavier:** more sorrowful.
198. **by small and small:** little by little (like the torturer who prolongs the victim's agony on the rack). 203. **Upon his party:** on his side.
204. **Beshrew:** confound. **forth:** out.
209. **Flint:** fortress near Chester. 212. **ear:** plough.

III.iii. Location: Wales. Before Flint Castle.
o.s.d. **Drum and Colors:** drummer and flagbearer.
1. **intelligence:** information. 13. **to:** as to.
14. **taking so the head:** i.e. being so presumptuous as to omit his title.
17. **mistake:** fail to understand that.

Bull. I know it, uncle, and oppose not myself
Against their will. But who comes here?

Enter [HARRY] PERCY.

Welcome, Harry. What, will not this castle yield?
Percy. The castle royally is mann'd, my lord,
Against thy entrance.
Bull. Royally?
Why, it contains no king.
Percy. Yes, my good lord,
It doth contain a king. King Richard lies
Within the limits of yon lime and stone,
And with him are the Lord Aumerle, Lord Salisbury,
Sir Stephen Scroop, besides a clergyman
Of holy reverence, who, I cannot learn.
North. O, belike it is the Bishop of Carlisle.
Bull. [*To Northumberland.*] Noble [lord],
Go to the rude ribs of that ancient castle;
Through brazen trumpet send the breath of parley
Into his ruin'd ears, and thus deliver:
Henry Bullingbrook
On both his knees doth kiss King Richard's hand,
And sends allegiance and true faith of heart
To his most royal person; hither come
Even at his feet to lay my arms and power,
Provided that my banishment repeal'd
And lands restor'd again be freely granted.
If not, I'll use the advantage of my power,
And lay the summer's dust with show'rs of blood
Rain'd from the wounds of slaughtered Englishmen,
The which, how far off from the mind of Bullingbrook
It is, such crimson tempest should bedrench
The fresh green lap of fair King Richard's land,
My stooping duty tenderly shall show.
Go signify as much, while here we march
Upon the grassy carpet of this plain.
[*Northumberland advances to the castle, with a Trumpet.*]
Let's march without the noise of threat'ning drum,
That from this castle's tottered battlements
Our fair appointments may be well perus'd.
Methinks King Richard and myself should meet
With no less terror than the elements
Of fire and water, when their thund'ring shock
At meeting tears the cloudy cheeks of heaven.
Be he the fire, I'll be the yielding water;
The rage be his, whilst on the earth I rain
My waters—on the earth, and not on him.
March on, and mark King Richard how he looks.

The trumpets sound [*parle without and answer within; then a flourish*]. RICHARD *appeareth on the walls* [*with* CARLISLE, AUMERLE, SCROOP, SALISBURY].

See, see, King Richard doth himself appear,
As doth the blushing discontented sun
From out the fiery portal of the east,
When he perceives the envious clouds are bent
To dim his glory and to stain the track
Of his bright passage to the occident.
York. Yet looks he like a king! Behold, his eye,
As bright as is the eagle's, lightens forth
Controlling majesty. Alack, alack for woe,
That any harm should stain so fair a show!
K. Rich. [*To Northumberland.*] We are amaz'd, and thus long have we stood
To watch the fearful bending of thy knee,
Because we thought ourself thy lawful king;
And if we be, how dare thy joints forget
To pay their aweful duty to our presence?
If we be not, show us the hand of God
That hath dismiss'd us from our stewardship,
For well we know no hand of blood and bone
Can gripe the sacred handle of our sceptre,
Unless he do profane, steal, or usurp.
And though you think that all, as you have done,
Have torn their souls by turning them from us,
And we are barren and bereft of friends,
Yet know, my master, God omnipotent,
Is mustering in his clouds on our behalf
Armies of pestilence, and they shall strike
Your children yet unborn and unbegot,
That lift your vassal hands against my head,
And threat the glory of my precious crown.
Tell Bullingbrook—for yon methinks he stands—
That every stride he makes upon my land
Is dangerous treason. He is come to open
The purple testament of bleeding war;
But ere the crown he looks for live in peace,
Ten thousand bloody crowns of mothers' sons
Shall ill become the flower of England's face,
Change the complexion of her maid-pale peace
To scarlet indignation, and bedew
Her pasters' grass with faithful English blood.
North. The King of heaven forbid our lord the King
Should so with civil and uncivil arms
Be rush'd upon! Thy thrice-noble cousin,
Harry Bullingbrook, doth humbly kiss thy hand,
And by the honorable tomb he swears
That stands upon your royal grandsire's bones,
And by the royalties of both your bloods,
Currents that spring from one most gracious head,
And by the buried hand of warlike Gaunt,
And by the worth and honor of himself,
Comprising all that may be sworn or said,
His coming hither hath no further scope

23–24. Royally . . . king. Actually, Richard, having left Conway in despair, had been ambushed by Northumberland and "constrained" to go to Flint. Hence Bullingbrook's surprise at his presence there is unhistorical. **30. belike:** probably.
34. his ruin'd ears: its (the castle's) ruinous loopholes.
40. repeal'd: revoked. **45. The which:** as to which.
48. stooping duty: i.e. kneeling in submission.
50 s.d. Trumpet: trumpeter.
52. tottered: tattered, i.e. crenellated.
53. appointments: equipment.
61 s.d. parle: trumpet call sounded to request a conference.

63. blushing: i.e. red (like Richard's flushed and angry face). A red sunrise was thought to indicate a stormy day.
65. envious: spiteful. **69. lightens:** flashes.
71. show: appearance. **76. aweful duty:** reverential homage.
77. hand: i.e. written hand, signature. **80. gripe:** seize.
83. torn . . . us: i.e. lacerated their souls through the perjury of transferring their allegiance. **89. vassal:** subject.
94. purple testament: blood-red will. **96. crowns:** heads.
100. pasters': pastures'.
102. civil: employed in civil war. **uncivil:** rude, barbarous.
106. royal grandsire: Edward III, whose "honorable tomb" is in Westminster Abbey. **112. scope:** aim, intention.

Than for his lineal royalties, and to beg
Enfranchisement immediate on his knees,
Which on thy royal party granted once,
His glittering arms he will commend to rust,
His barbed steeds to stables, and his heart
To faithful service of your Majesty.
This swears he, as he is [a prince, is] just,
And as I am a gentleman I credit him.
K. Rich. Northumberland, say thus the King returns:
His noble cousin is right welcome hither,
And all the number of his fair demands
Shall be accomplish'd without contradiction.
With all the gracious utterance thou hast
Speak to his gentle hearing kind commends.
[*Northumberland withdraws to Bullingbrook.*]
[*To Aumerle.*] We do debase ourselves, cousin, do we not,
To look so poorly and to speak so fair?
Shall we call back Northumberland, and send
Defiance to the traitor, and so die?
Aum. No, good my lord, let's fight with gentle words,
Till time lend friends, and friends their helpful swords.
K. Rich. O God, O God, that e'er this tongue of mine
That laid the sentence of dread banishment
On yon proud man should take it off again
With words of sooth! O that I were as great
As is my grief, or lesser than my name!
Or that I could forget what I have been!
Or not remember what I must be now!
Swell'st thou, proud heart? I'll give thee scope to beat,
Since foes have scope to beat both thee and me.
Aum. Northumberland comes back from Bullingbrook.
K. Rich. What must the King do now? Must he submit?
The King shall do it. Must he be depos'd?
The King shall be contented. Must he lose
The name of king? a' God's name let it go.
I'll give my jewels for a set of beads,
My gorgeous palace for a hermitage,
My gay apparel for an almsman's gown,
My figur'd goblets for a dish of wood,
My sceptre for a palmer's walking-staff,
My subjects for a pair of carved saints,
And my large kingdom for a little grave,
A little little grave, an obscure grave—
Or I'll be buried in the king's high way,
Some way of common trade, where subjects' feet
May hourly trample on their sovereign's head;
For on my heart they tread now whilst I live,
And buried once, why not upon my head?
Aumerle, thou weep'st, my tender-hearted cousin!
We'll make foul weather with despised tears;
Our sighs and they shall lodge the summer corn,
And make a dearth in this revolting land.
Or shall we play the wantons with our woes
And make some pretty match with shedding tears?
As thus to drop them still upon one place,
Till they have fretted us a pair of graves
Within the earth, and, therein laid—there lies
Two kinsmen digg'd their graves with weeping eyes.
Would not this ill do well? Well, well, I see
I talk but idlely, and you laugh at me.
Most mighty prince, my Lord Northumberland,
What says King Bullingbrook? Will his Majesty
Give Richard leave to live till Richard die?
You make a leg, and Bullingbrook says ay.
North. My lord, in the base court he doth attend
To speak with you, may it please you to come down.
K. Rich. Down, down I come, like glist'ring Phaëton,
Wanting the manage of unruly jades.
In the base court? Base court, where kings grow base,
To come at traitors' calls and do them grace.
In the base court, come down? Down court! down king!
For night-owls shriek where mounting larks should sing. [*Exeunt above.*]
Bull. What says his Majesty?
North. Sorrow and grief of heart
Makes him speak fondly like a frantic man,
Yet he is come.

[*Enter* KING RICHARD *and his* ATTENDANTS *below.*]

Bull. Stand all apart,
And show fair duty to his Majesty. *He kneels down.*
My gracious lord—
K. Rich. Fair cousin, you debase your princely knee
To make the base earth proud with kissing it.
Me rather had my heart might feel your love
Than my unpleased eye see your courtesy.
Up, cousin, up, your heart is up, I know,
Thus high at least [*touching his crown*], although your knee be low.
Bull. My gracious lord, I come but for mine own.
K. Rich. Your own is yours, and I am yours, and all.

113. lineal royalties: hereditary rights as a member of the royal family.
114. Enfranchisement: freedom (from banishment).
115. party: part. **116. commend:** commit.
117. barbed: armored. **121. returns:** replies.
124. accomplish'd: fulfilled. **126. commends:** regards.
136. sooth: blandishment. **137. name:** title. **146. a':** in.
147. set of beads: rosary.
149. almsman's gown: i.e. the mean garb of one who lives on alms or charity. **150. figur'd:** ornamented.
151. palmer's: pilgrim's. Palmers originally carried palm leaves to show that they had been to Jerusalem. **156. trade:** passage.

162. lodge: beat down. **corn:** wheat.
163. dearth: famine. **revolting:** rebelling.
164. play the wantons: frolic. **165. match:** game.
167. fretted us: eroded for us. **169. digg'd:** who dug.
171. idlely: foolishly. **175. make a leg:** curtsy.
176. base court: lower and outer courtyard of a castle (French *basse cour*).
178. glist'ring: glittering. **Phaëton:** Phaëthon, son of Apollo, the sun-god; he attempted to drive his father's chariot across the sky and was hurled down to his death.
179. Wanting . . . jades: lacking the horsemanship to control unruly nags. *Manage* = manège, the art of horsemanship.
183. night-owls shriek. An omen of disaster.
185. speak fondly: talk nonsense. **frantic:** mad.
187. duty: obeisance. **192. Me rather had:** I had rather.
193. courtesy: (1) civility; (2) curtsy.

Bull. So far be mine, my most redoubted lord,
As my true service shall deserve your love.
K. Rich. Well you deserve; they well deserve to have
That know the strong'st and surest way to get.
Uncle, give me your hands; nay, dry your eyes—
Tears show their love, but want their remedies.
Cousin, I am too young to be your father,
Though you are old enough to be my heir.
What you will have, I'll give, and willing too,
For do we must what force will have us do.
Set on towards London, cousin, is it so?
Bull. Yea, my good lord.
K. Rich. Then I must not say no.
[*Flourish. Exeunt.*]

[Scene IV]

Enter the Queen *with* [*two* Ladies,] *her attendants.*

Queen. What sport shall we devise here in this garden
To drive away the heavy thought of care?
[*1.*] *Lady.* Madam, we'll play at bowls.
Queen. 'Twill make me think the world is full of rubs,
And that my fortune runs against the bias.
[*1.*] *Lady.* Madam, we'll dance.
Queen. My legs can keep no measure in delight,
When my poor heart no measure keeps in grief;
Therefore no dancing, girl, some other sport.
[*1.*] *Lady.* Madam, we'll tell tales.
Queen. Of sorrow or of [joy]?
[*1.*] *Lady.* Of either, madam.
Queen. Of neither, girl;
For if of joy, being altogether wanting,
It doth remember me the more of sorrow;
Or if of grief, being altogether had,
It adds more sorrow to my want of joy;
For what I have I need not to repeat,
And what I want it boots not to complain.
[*1.*] *Lady.* Madam, I'll sing.
Queen. 'Tis well that thou hast cause,
But thou shouldst please me better wouldst thou weep.
[*1.*] *Lady.* I could weep, madam, would it do you good.
Queen. And I could sing, would weeping do me good,
And never borrow any tear of thee.

Enter [*a* Gardener *and two of his* Men].

But stay, here come the gardeners.
Let's step into the shadow of these trees.
My wretchedness unto a row of [pins],
They will talk of state, for every one doth so
Against a change; woe is forerun with woe.
[*Queen and Ladies retire.*]
Gard. Go bind thou up young dangling apricocks,
Which like unruly children make their sire
Stoop with oppression of their prodigal weight;
Give some supportance to the bending twigs.
Go thou, and like an executioner
Cut off the heads of [too] fast growing sprays,
That look too lofty in our commonwealth:
All must be even in our government.
You thus employed, I will go root away
The noisome weeds which without profit suck
The soil's fertility from wholesome flowers.
[*1.*] *Man.* Why should we in the compass of a pale
Keep law and form and due proportion,
Showing as in a model our firm estate,
When our sea-walled garden, the whole land,
Is full of weeds, her fairest flowers chok'd up,
Her fruit-trees all unprun'd, her hedges ruin'd,
Her knots disordered, and her wholesome herbs
Swarming with caterpillars?
Gard. Hold thy peace.
He that hath suffered this disordered spring
Hath now himself met with the fall of leaf.
The weeds which his broad-spreading leaves did shelter,
That seem'd in eating him to hold him up,
Are pluck'd up root and all by Bullingbrook,
I mean the Earl of Wiltshire, Bushy, Green.
[*1.*] *Man.* What, are they dead?
Gard. They are; and Bullingbrook
Hath seiz'd the wasteful King. O, what pity is it
That he had not so trimm'd and dress'd his land
As we this garden! [We] at time of year
Do wound the bark, the skin of our fruit-trees,
Lest being over-proud in sap and blood,
With too much riches it confound itself;
Had he done so to great and growing men,
They might have liv'd to bear and he to taste
Their fruits of duty. Superfluous branches
We lop away, that bearing boughs may live;
Had he done so, himself had borne the crown,
Which waste of idle hours hath quite thrown down.
[*1.*] *Man.* What, think you the King shall be deposed?
Gard. Depress'd he is already, and depos'd
'Tis doubt he will be. Letters came last night
To a dear friend of the good Duke of York's
That tell black tidings.
Queen. O, I am press'd to death through want of speaking!
[*Coming forward.*]

198. redoubted: dreaded.
202. Uncle: i.e. York. **203. want:** lack.
204–5. Cousin . . . heir. Richard and Bullingbrook were in fact both born in 1367.

III.iv. Location: Langley. The Duke of York's garden.
4. rubs: impediments (a term from bowling).
5. against the bias: i.e. unnaturally crooked. In the game of bowls, *bias* = the desirable swerve or curving course of a bowl in motion.
7. measure: stately dance. **8. measure:** moderation.
13. wanting: lacking. **14. remember:** remind.
18. boots not: does no good.

26. My wretchedness unto: i.e. I wager my wretchedness against.
27. state: politics. **28. Against:** in anticipation of.
29. apricocks: apricots. **36. even:** equal.
40. pale: enclosure, i.e. walled garden.
46. knots: flower beds laid out in patterns.
48. suffered: permitted.
57. time of year: i.e. the proper season.
59. over-proud: too luxuriant. **68. Depress'd:** humbled.
69. doubt: fear.
72. press'd to death. Customary penalty in England for refusing to plead guilty or not guilty before a court, i.e. for remaining silent.

Thou old Adam's likeness, set to dress this garden,
How dares thy harsh rude tongue sound this unpleasing news?
What Eve, what serpent, hath suggested thee
To make a second fall of cursed man?
Why dost thou say King Richard is depos'd?
Dar'st thou, thou little better thing than earth,
Divine his downfall? Say, where, when, and how,
[Cam'st] thou by this ill tidings? Speak, thou wretch.

Gard. Pardon me, madam, little joy have I
To breathe this news, yet what I say is true:
King Richard, he is in the mighty hold
Of Bullingbrook; their fortunes both are weigh'd.
In your lord's scale is nothing but himself,
And some few vanities that make him light;
But in the balance of great Bullingbrook,
Besides himself, are all the English peers,
And with that odds he weighs King Richard down.
Post you to London and you will find it so,
I speak no more than every one doth know.

Queen. Nimble mischance, that art so light of foot,
Doth not thy embassage belong to me,
And am I last that knows it? O, thou thinkest
To serve me last that I may longest keep
Thy sorrow in my breast. Come, ladies, go
To meet at London London's king in woe.
What, was I born to this, that my sad look
Should grace the triumph of great Bullingbrook?
Gard'ner, for telling me these news of woe,
Pray God the plants thou graft'st may never grow.

Exit [*with Ladies*].

Gard. Poor queen, so that thy state might be no worse,
I would my skill were subject to thy curse.
Here did she fall a tear, here in this place
I'll set a bank of rue, sour herb of grace.
Rue, even for ruth, here shortly shall be seen,
In the remembrance of a weeping queen. *Exeunt.*

[ACT IV, SCENE I]

Enter BULLINGBROOK *with the Lords* [AUMERLE, NORTHUMBERLAND, PERCY, FITZWATER, SURREY, *the* BISHOP OF CARLISLE, *the* ABBOT OF WESTMINSTER, *and another* LORD] *to parliament;* [HERALD].

Bull. Call forth Bagot.

Enter [OFFICERS *with*] BAGOT.

Now, Bagot, freely speak thy mind,
What thou dost know of noble Gloucester's death,
Who wrought it with the King, and who perform'd
The bloody office of his timeless end.

Bagot. Then set before my face the Lord Aumerle.

Bull. Cousin, stand forth, and look upon that man.

Bagot. My Lord Aumerle, I know your daring tongue
Scorns to unsay what once it hath delivered.
In that dead time when Gloucester's death was plotted,
I heard you say, "Is not my arm of length,
That reacheth from the restful English court
As far as Callice, to mine uncle's head?"
Amongst much other talk, that very time,
I heard you say that you had rather refuse
The offer of an hundred thousand crowns
Than Bullingbrook's return to England,
Adding withal, how blest this land would be
In this your cousin's death.

Aum. Princes and noble lords,
What answer shall I make to this base man?
Shall I so much dishonor my fair stars
On equal terms to give [him] chastisement?
Either I must, or have mine honor soil'd
With the attainder of his slanderous lips.
There is my gage, the manual seal of death,
That marks thee out for hell. I say thou liest,
And will maintain what thou hast said is false
In thy heart-blood, though being all too base
To stain the temper of my knightly sword.

Bull. Bagot, forbear, thou shalt not take it up.

Aum. Excepting one, I would he were the best
In all this presence that hath mov'd me so.

Fitz. If that thy valure stand on sympathy,
There is my gage, Aumerle, in gage to thine.
By that fair sun which shows me where thou stand'st,
I heard thee say, and vauntingly thou spak'st it,
That thou wert cause of noble Gloucester's death.
If thou deniest it twenty times, thou liest,
And I will turn thy falsehood to thy heart,
Where it was forged, with my rapier's point.

Aum. Thou dar'st not, coward, live to see that day.

Fitz. Now by my soul, I would it were this hour.

Aum. Fitzwater, thou art damn'd to hell for this.

Percy. Aumerle, thou liest, his honor is as true
In this appeal as thou art all unjust,

73. old Adam's likeness: i.e. because Adam was the first gardener **dress:** cultivate. **75. suggested:** prompted.
76. cursed: under a curse (like Adam after his fall from grace).
79. Divine: prophesy. **83. hold:** grip, custody.
85. scale: pan of the balance. **90. Post:** hasten.
93. embassage: message, report.
96. Thy sorrow: the sorrow that you report.
102. so that: provided. **104. fall:** drop.
105. sour . . . grace: bitter herb of repentance (which comes through the grace of God).

IV.i. Location: Westminster Hall.

4–5. Who . . . end: i.e. who persuaded the King to order the murder and who did the deed itself.
5. office: service, duty. **timeless:** untimely.
9. unsay. See note to II.i.16. **10. dead:** i.e. dark.
11. of length: long. **12. restful:** i.e. untroubled by Gloucester.
14. that very time. The chronology is confused. Gloucester's murder occurred in 1387, eleven years before Bullingbrook's exile.
16. an hundred thousand crowns. Holinshed, who places Bagot's accusations after Richard's deposition (Bullough, III, 409–10), gives the sum as twenty thousand pounds. A crown was worth five shillings.
17. Than Bullingbrook's return: than have Bullingbrook return.
18. withal: besides. **21. fair stars:** i.e. noble rank.
22. On equal terms: i.e. in formal combat.
24. attainder: foul accusation.
25. gage: pledge (here, a glove, as implied by the following phrase). **manual . . . death:** death warrant sealed by my hand.
31. one: i.e. Bullingbrook.
33. valure: valor. **stand on sympathy:** i.e. requires an opponent of equal rank.
40. rapier's point. An anachronism (as Dr. Johnson noted in disapproval), for rapiers were not in use at the end of the fourteenth century.
45. appeal: accusation. **all unjust:** entirely false.

And that thou art so, there I throw my gage,
To prove it on thee to the extremest point
Of mortal breathing. Seize it, if thou dar'st.
Aum. And if I do not, may my hands rot off,
And never brandish more revengeful steel
Over the glittering helmet of my foe!
Another Lord. I task the earth to the like, forsworn Aumerle,
And spur thee on with full as many lies
As may be hollowed in thy treacherous ear
From [sun] to [sun]. There is my honor's pawn,
Engage it to the trial, if thou darest.
Aum. Who sets me else? By heaven, I'll throw at all!
I have a thousand spirits in one breast,
To answer twenty thousand such as you.
Surrey. My Lord Fitzwater, I do remember well
The very time Aumerle and you did talk.
Fitz. 'Tis very true, you were in presence then,
And you can witness with me this is true.
Surrey. As false, by heaven, as heaven itself is true.
Fitz. Surrey, thou liest.
Surrey. Dishonorable boy!
That lie shall lie so heavy on my sword,
That it shall render vengeance and revenge
Till thou the lie-giver and that lie do lie
In earth as quiet as thy father's skull;
In proof whereof, there is my honor's pawn,
Engage it to the trial, if thou dar'st.
Fitz. How fondly dost thou spur a forward horse!
If I dare eat, or drink, or breathe, or live,
I dare meet Surrey in a wilderness,
And spit upon him whilst I say he lies,
And lies, and lies. There is [my] bond of faith,
To tie thee to my strong correction.
As I intend to thrive in this new world,
Aumerle is guilty of my true appeal;
Besides, I heard the banished Norfolk say
That thou, Aumerle, didst send two of thy men
To execute the noble Duke at Callice.
Aum. Some honest Christian trust me with a gage—
That Norfolk lies, here do I throw down this,
If he may be repeal'd to try his honor.
Bull. These differences shall all rest under gage
Till Norfolk be repeal'd. Repeal'd he shall be,
And though mine enemy, restor'd again
To all his lands and signories. When he is return'd,
Against Aumerle we will enforce his trial.
Car. That honorable day shall never be seen.
Many a time hath banish'd Norfolk fought
For Jesu Christ in glorious Christian field,
Streaming the ensign of the Christian cross
Against black pagans, Turks, and Saracens,
And toil'd with works of war, retir'd himself
To Italy, and there at Venice gave
His body to that pleasant country's earth,
And his pure soul unto his captain Christ,
Under whose colors he had fought so long.
Bull. Why, Bishop, is Norfolk dead?
Car. As surely as I live, my lord.
Bull. Sweet peace conduct his sweet soul to the bosom
Of good old Abraham! Lords appellants,
Your differences shall all rest under gage
Till we assign you to your days of trial.

Enter YORK [*attended*].

York. Great Duke of Lancaster, I come to thee
From plume-pluck'd Richard, who with willing soul
Adopts [thee] heir, and his high sceptre yields
To the possession of thy royal hand.
Ascend his throne, descending now from him,
And long live Henry, fourth of that name!
Bull. In God's name I'll ascend the regal throne.
Car. Marry, God forbid!
Worst in this royal presence may I speak,
Yet best beseeming me to speak the truth.
Would God that any in this noble presence
Were enough noble to be upright judge
Of noble Richard! Then true noblesse would
Learn him forbearance from so foul a wrong.
What subject can give sentence on his king?
And who sits here that is not Richard's subject?
Thieves are not judg'd but they are by to hear,
Although apparent guilt be seen in them,
And shall the figure of God's majesty,
His captain, steward, deputy, elect,
Anointed, crowned, planted many years,
Be judg'd by subject and inferior breath,
And he himself not present? O, forfend it, God,
That in a Christian climate souls refin'd
Should show so heinous, black, obscene a deed!
I speak to subjects, and a subject speaks,
Stirr'd up by God, thus boldly for his king.
My Lord of Herford here, whom you call king,
Is a foul traitor to proud Herford's king,
And if you crown him, let me prophesy,
The blood of English shall manure the ground,
And future ages groan for this foul act.

50. revengeful: avenging.
52. I . . . like: i.e. I too fling my gage upon the ground.
53. lies: accusations of lying.
57. sets: puts up a stake in wager, i.e. challenges (a term from dicing, as is *throw*).
62. in presence: in the king's presence-chamber.
72. fondly: foolishly. **76. bond of faith:** i.e. gage.
78. in . . . world: i.e. under the new king.
85. repeal'd: recalled home.
86. under gage: as standing challenges.
89. signories: properties. **90. trial:** i.e. trial by combat.
94. Streaming: flying.
96. toil'd: exhausted.
103–4. bosom . . . Abraham: i.e. heaven. See Luke 16:22.
104. appellants: accusers.
107–12. Great . . . name. Here as elsewhere in this crowded scene Shakespeare rearranges and compresses the data as given by Holinshed (Bullough, III, 405–12), his principal source. Richard, "committed to safe custodie" in the Tower, "renounced and voluntarilie was deposed from his royall crowne and kinglie dignitie" on September 29, 1399. The next day, Bullingbrook, with the assent of Parliament, ascended the throne as Henry IV, and on October 13 he was duly crowned. Of the other episodes, the challenge to Aumerle and the protest of Thomas Merke, Bishop of Carlisle, occurred within ten days of Henry's coronation, but the Abbot of Westminster's conspiracy was not hatched until December.
115–16. Worst . . . truth: i.e. although in this royal presence I am the least worthy to speak, yet because of my sacred office it best becomes me to speak the truth. **119. noblesse:** nobility.
120. Learn him forbearance: teach him to refrain.
123. judg'd . . . by: condemned except when they are present.
124. apparent: obvious. **126. elect:** chosen one.
129. forfend: forbid.

Peace shall go sleep with Turks and infidels,
And in this seat of peace tumultuous wars
Shall kin with kin and kind with kind confound.
Disorder, horror, fear, and mutiny
Shall here inhabit, and this land be call'd
The field of Golgotha and dead men's skulls.
O, if you raise this house against this house,
It will the woefullest division prove
That ever fell upon this cursed earth.
Prevent it, resist it, let it not be so,
Lest child, child's children, cry against you "woe!"

North. Well have you argued, sir, and, for your pains,
Of capital treason we arrest you here.
My Lord of Westminster, be it your charge
To keep him safely till his day of trial.
[May it please you, lords, to grant the commons' suit?

Bull. Fetch hither Richard, that in common view
He may surrender; so we shall proceed
Without suspicion.

York. I will be his conduct. *Exit.*

Bull. Lords, you that here are under our arrest,
Procure your sureties for your days of answer.
Little are we beholding to your love,
And little look'd for at your helping hands.

Enter RICHARD *and* YORK [*with* OFFICERS *bearing the crown and sceptre*].

K. Rich. Alack, why am I sent for to a king
Before I have shook off the regal thoughts
Wherewith I reign'd? I hardly yet have learn'd
To insinuate, flatter, bow, and bend my knee.
Give sorrow leave a while to tutor me
To this submission. Yet I well remember
The favors of these men. Were they not mine?
Did they not [sometimes] cry "All hail!" to me?
So Judas did to Christ; but He, in twelve,
Found truth in all but one; I, in twelve thousand, none.
God save the King! Will no man say amen?
Am I both priest and clerk? Well then, amen.
God save the King! although I be not he,
And yet amen, if heaven do think him me.
To do what service am I sent for hither?

York. To do that office of thine own good will
Which tired majesty did make thee offer:
The resignation of thy state and crown
To Henry Bullingbrook.

K. Rich. Give me the crown. Here, cousin, seize the crown;
Here, cousin,
On this side my hand, [and] on that side thine.
Now is this golden crown like a deep well
That owes two buckets, filling one another,
The emptier ever dancing in the air,
The other down, unseen, and full of water:
That bucket down and full of tears am I,
Drinking my griefs, whilst you mount up on high.

Bull. I thought you had been willing to resign.

K. Rich. My crown I am, but still my griefs are mine.
You may my glories and my state depose,
But not my griefs; still am I king of those.

Bull. Part of your cares you give me with your crown.

K. Rich. Your cares set up do not pluck my cares down:
My care is loss of care, by old care done,
Your care is gain of care, by new care won;
The cares I give I have, though given away,
They tend the crown, yet still with me they stay.

Bull. Are you contented to resign the crown?

K. Rich. Ay, no, no ay; for I must nothing be;
Therefore no no, for I resign to thee.
Now mark me how I will undo myself:
I give this heavy weight from off my head,
And this unwieldy sceptre from my hand,
The pride of kingly sway from out my heart;
With mine own tears I wash away my balm,
With mine own hands I give away my crown,
With mine own tongue deny my sacred state,
With mine own breath release all duteous oaths;
All pomp and majesty I do forswear;
My manors, rents, revenues I forgo;
My acts, decrees, and statutes I deny;
God pardon all oaths that are broke to me!
God keep all vows unbroke are made to thee!
Make me, that nothing have, with nothing griev'd,
And thou with all pleas'd, that hast all achiev'd!
Long mayst thou live in Richard's seat to sit,
And soon lie Richard in an earthy pit!
God save King Henry, unking'd Richard says,
And send him many years of sunshine days!
What more remains?

North. No more, but that you read [*Presenting a paper.*]
These accusations, and these grievous crimes

141. with: by means of. **confound:** destroy.
145. this house . . . this house: i.e. Lancaster . . . York.
151. Of: on a charge of.
154. the commons' suit. Holinshed reports (Bullough, III, 410–11) that Commons, shortly after Henry's coronation, requested a formal trial for Richard so that "he might have judgment decreed against him" for his crimes against the state. It was then that Thomas Merke, Bishop of Carlisle, "a man both learned, wise, and stout of stomach, boldlie shewed foorth his opinion concerning that demand," and as a consequence was charged with treason. Richard's abdication had occurred almost a month before. **156. surrender:** abdicate.
157. conduct: escort. **160. beholding:** beholden, indebted.
168. favors: (1) countenances; (2) benefits.
179. state: kingship.
181. Give . . . seize the crown. Although Holinshed (Bullough, III, 406–7) has Richard merely sign an instrument of abdication in the presence of commissioners, the more colorful accounts of Froissart, Hall, and Daniel have him hand his crown to Bullingbrook.

185. owes: owns, has.
195–99. Your . . . stay. The elaborate play on *care* as (1) grief and (2) responsibility may be paraphrased as follows: "The fact that you have taken on the cares of state does not relieve my sorrow. I lament the loss of kingly cares, whereas you are concerned about the new responsibilities that you were so eager to assume. I retain the anxieties that I now transfer to you, for although they accompany the crown they none the less remain with me."
201–2. Ay . . . thee. The pun is on *ay* and *I*, which were pronounced alike; moreover, *ay* was often written *I*. Richard says that he cannot answer either "ay" or "no," for with his kingship stripped from him there is no "I," but without an "I" a "no" has no force.
203. undo: i.e. annihilate my royal identity. See note to II.i.16.
209. my sacred state: my status as a ruler by divine right.
213. deny: cancel.
214. oaths: i.e. oaths of allegiance. **215. are:** that are.
218. seat: throne. **220. unking'd.** See note to II.i.16.
221. sunshine: sunny.
223. accusations: i.e. the formal charges brought against Richard at the request of Commons. See note to line 154.

Committed by your person and your followers
Against the state and profit of this land;
That by confessing them, the souls of men
May deem that you are worthily depos'd.
K. Rich. Must I do so? and must I ravel out
My weav'd-up follies? Gentle Northumberland,
If thy offenses were upon record,
Would it not shame thee in so fair a troop
To read a lecture of them? If thou wouldst,
There shouldst thou find one heinous article,
Containing the deposing of a king,
And cracking the strong warrant of an oath,
Mark'd with a blot, damn'd in the book of heaven.
Nay, all of you that stand and look upon me
Whilst that my wretchedness doth bait myself,
Though some of you, with Pilate, wash your hands,
Showing an outward pity, yet you Pilates
Have here deliver'd me to my sour cross,
And water cannot wash away your sin.
North. My lord, dispatch, read o'er these articles.
K. Rich. Mine eyes are full of tears, I cannot see;
And yet salt water blinds them not so much
But they can see a sort of traitors here.
Nay, if I turn mine eyes upon myself,
I find myself a traitor with the rest;
For I have given here my soul's consent
T' undeck the pompous body of a king;
Made glory base, [and] sovereignty a slave;
Proud majesty a subject, state a peasant.
North. My lord—
K. Rich. No lord of thine, thou haught insulting man,
Nor no man's lord. I have no name, no title,
No, not that name was given me at the font,
But 'tis usurp'd. Alack the heavy day,
That I have worn so many winters out
And know not now what name to call myself!
O that I were a mockery king of snow,
Standing before the sun of Bullingbrook,
To melt myself away in water-drops!
Good king, great king, and yet not greatly good,
And if my word be sterling yet in England,
Let it command a mirror hither straight,
That it may show me what a face I have
Since it is bankrout of his majesty.
Bull. Go some of you and fetch a looking-glass.
[*Exit an Attendant.*]
North. Read o'er this paper while the glass doth come.
K. Rich. Fiend, thou torments me ere I come to hell!
Bull. Urge it no more, my Lord Northumberland.
North. The commons will not then be satisfied.
K. Rich. They shall be satisfied. I'll read enough,
When I do see the very book indeed
Where all my sins are writ, and that's myself.
Enter one with a glass.
Give me that glass, and therein will I read.
No deeper wrinkles yet? Hath sorrow struck
So many blows upon this face of mine,
And made no deeper wounds? O flatt'ring glass,
Like to my followers in prosperity,
Thou dost beguile me! Was this face the face
That every day under his household roof
Did keep ten thousand men? Was this the face
That like the sun, did make beholders wink?
Is this the face which fac'd so many follies,
That was at last out-fac'd by Bullingbrook?
A brittle glory shineth in this face,
As brittle as the glory is the face,
[*Dashes the glass against the ground.*]
For there it is, crack'd in an hundred shivers.
Mark, silent king, the moral of this sport,
How soon my sorrow hath destroy'd my face.
Bull. The shadow of your sorrow hath destroy'd
The shadow of your face.
K. Rich. Say that again.
The shadow of my sorrow! Ha, let's see.
'Tis very true, my grief lies all within,
And these external [manners] of laments
Are merely shadows to the unseen grief
That swells with silence in the tortur'd soul.
There lies the substance; and I thank thee, King,
For thy great bounty, that not only giv'st
Me cause to wail, but teachest me the way
How to lament the cause. I'll beg one boon,
And then be gone and trouble you no more.
Shall I obtain it?
Bull. Name it, fair cousin.
K. Rich. "Fair cousin"? I am greater than a king;
For when I was a king my flatterers
Were then but subjects; being now a subject,
I have a king here to my flatterer.
Being so great, I have no need to beg.
Bull. Yet ask.
K. Rich. And shall I have?
Bull. You shall.
K. Rich. Then give me leave to go.
Bull. Whither?
K. Rich. Whither you will, so I were from your sights.
Bull. Go some of you, convey him to the Tower.
K. Rich. O, good! convey! Conveyers are you all,
That rise thus nimbly by a true king's fall.
[*Exeunt Richard, some Lords, and a Guard.*]
Bull. On Wednesday next we solemnly proclaim
Our coronation. Lords, be ready all.
Exeunt. Manent [*Abbot of*] *Westminster, Carlisle, Aumerle.*

225. state and profit: settled prosperity.
226. by confessing: by your confessing. **227. worthily:** justly.
232. read . . . them: i.e. read them out publicly.
233. article: item.
238. Whilst . . . myself: i.e. while I, in my wretchedness, torment myself. **bait:** attack, harass (a term from bearbaiting).
241. sour: bitter. **246. sort:** gang.
250. undeck. See note to II.i.16. **pompous:** splendid.
252. state: royalty. **254. haught:** haughty.
256–57. not . . . usurp'd. Perhaps an allusion to the Lancastrian slander that Richard was illegitimate.
264. sterling: valid (a term from coinage). **269. while:** until.

284. wink: close the eyes. **285. fac'd:** countenanced.
292–93. The shadow . . . face: i.e. the sorrow that overshadows you has destroyed the reflection of your face in the mirror.
296. manners of laments: forms of grief.
300. that: i.e. Bullingbrook. **316. convey:** escort.
317. convey: steal. **Conveyers:** thieves.

Abbot. A woeful pageant have we here beheld.
Car. The woe's to come; the children yet unborn
Shall feel this day as sharp to them as thorn.
Aum. You holy clergymen, is there no plot
To rid the realm of this pernicious blot?
Abbot. My lord,
Before I freely speak my mind herein,
You shall not only take the sacrament
To bury mine intents, but also to effect
What ever I shall happen to devise.
I see your brows are full of discontent,
Your hearts of sorrow, and your eyes of tears.
Come home with me to supper, I'll lay
A plot shall show us all a merry day. *Exeunt.*

[ACT V, SCENE I]

Enter the QUEEN *with her* ATTENDANTS.

Queen. This way the King will come, this is the way
To Julius Caesar's ill-erected tower,
To whose flint bosom my condemned lord
Is doom'd a prisoner by proud Bullingbrook.
Here let us rest, if this rebellious earth
Have any resting for her true king's queen.

Enter RICHARD [*and* GUARD].

But soft, but see, or rather do not see,
My fair rose wither; yet look up, behold,
That you in pity may dissolve to dew
And wash him fresh again with true-love tears.
Ah, thou, the model where old Troy did stand,
Thou map of honor, thou King Richard's tomb,
And not King Richard; thou most beauteous inn,
Why should hard-favor'd grief be lodg'd in thee,
When triumph is become an alehouse guest?
K. Rich. Join not with grief, fair woman, do not so,
To make my end too sudden. Learn, good soul,
To think our former state a happy dream,
From which awak'd, the truth of what we are
Shows us but this. I am sworn brother, sweet,
To grim Necessity, and he and I
Will keep a league till death. Hie thee to France,
And cloister thee in some religious house.
Our holy lives must win a new world's crown,
Which our profane hours here have thrown down.
Queen. What, is my Richard both in shape and mind
Transform'd and weak'ned? Hath Bullingbrook depos'd
Thine intellect? Hath he been in thy heart?

329. To . . . intents: not to reveal my plans.

V.i. Location: London. A street leading to the Tower.
2. Caesar's . . . tower: the Tower of London, popularly believed to have been built by Julius Caesar. **ill-erected:** built with evil consequences (because it had been the scene of so many crimes).
3. flint: flinty. **6. resting:** resting-place.
11. model . . . stand: i.e. pattern of fallen greatness, like the ruins of Troy. **12. map of honor:** mere outline of (former) glory.
13–15. thou . . . guest: i.e. why should grief reside in such a stately mansion (as Richard) when triumph is lodged in such an ugly tavern (as Bullingbrook). **24. new world's:** heavenly.

The lion dying thrusteth forth his paw,
And wounds the earth, if nothing else, with rage
To be o'erpow'r'd, and wilt thou, pupil-like,
Take the correction, mildly kiss the rod,
And fawn on rage with base humility,
Which art a lion and the king of beasts?
K. Rich. A king of beasts indeed—if aught but beasts,
I had been still a happy king of men.
Good sometimes queen, prepare thee hence for France.
Think I am dead, and that even here thou takest,
As from my death-bed, thy last living leave.
In winter's tedious nights sit by the fire
With good old folks and let them tell [thee] tales
Of woeful ages long ago betid;
And ere thou bid good night, to quite their griefs,
Tell thou the lamentable tale of me,
And send the hearers weeping to their beds.
For why, the senseless brands will sympathize
The heavy accent of thy moving tongue,
And in compassion weep the fire out,
And some will mourn in ashes, some coal-black,
For the deposing of a rightful king.

Enter NORTHUMBERLAND [*and others*].

North. My lord, the mind of Bullingbrook is chang'd,
You must to Pomfret, not unto the Tower.
And, madam, there is order ta'en for you,
With all swift speed you must away to France.
K. Rich. Northumberland, thou ladder wherewithal
The mounting Bullingbrook ascends my throne,
The time shall not be many hours of age
More than it is, ere foul sin gathering head
Shall break into corruption. Thou shalt think,
Though he divide the realm and give thee half,
It is too little, helping him to all;
He shall think that thou, which knowest the way
To plant unrightful kings, wilt know again,
Being ne'er so little urg'd, another way
To pluck him headlong from the usurped throne.
The love of wicked men converts to fear,
That fear to hate, and hate turns one or both
To worthy danger and deserved death.
North. My guilt be on my head, and there an end.
Take leave and part, for you must part forthwith.
K. Rich. Doubly divorc'd! Bad men, you violate
A twofold marriage—'twixt my crown and me,
And then betwixt me and my married wife.—
Let me unkiss the oath 'twixt thee and me;
And yet not so, for with a kiss 'twas made.
Part us, Northumberland: I towards the north,

31. To be: at being. **37. sometimes:** sometime, former.
41–42. tales . . . betid: tales of woe that happened long ago.
43. quite their griefs: requite their sad tales.
46. For why: because. **sympathize:** be moved by.
52. Pomfret: Pontefract in Yorkshire, site of a Norman castle.
53. there . . . ta'en: arrangements have been made.
66. converts: changes.
67. one or both: i.e. the "unrightful" king or his sponsor or both.
68. worthy: well-merited.
74. unkiss the oath: i.e. cancel the marriage vow. On *unkiss*, see note to II.i.16.

Where shivering cold and sickness pines the clime;
My wife to France, from whence set forth in pomp
She came adorned hither like sweet May,
Sent back like Hollowmas or short'st of day.

Queen. And must we be divided? must we part?

K. Rich. Ay, hand from hand, my love, and heart from heart.

Queen. Banish us both, and send the King with me.

[*North.*] That were some love, but little policy.

Queen. Then whither he goes, thither let me go.

K. Rich. So two together weeping make one woe.
Weep thou for me in France, I for thee here;
Better far off than, near, be ne'er the near.
Go count thy way with sighs, I mine with groans.

Queen. So longest way shall have the longest moans.

K. Rich. Twice for one step I'll groan, the way being short,
And piece the way out with a heavy heart.
Come, come, in wooing sorrow let's be brief,
Since wedding it, there is such length in grief.
One kiss shall stop our mouths, and dumbly part;
Thus give I mine, and thus take I thy heart.

Queen. Give me mine own again, 'twere no good part
To take on me to keep and kill thy heart.
So now I have mine own again, be gone,
That I may strive to kill it with a groan.

K. Rich. We make woe wanton with this fond delay,
Once more, adieu, the rest let sorrow say. *Exeunt.*

[SCENE II]

Enter DUKE OF YORK *and the* DUCHESS.

Duch. My lord, you told me you would tell the rest,
When weeping made you break the story [off,]
Of our two cousins coming into London.

York. Where did I leave?

Duch. At that sad stop, my lord,
Where rude misgoverned hands from windows' tops
Threw dust and rubbish on King Richard's head.

York. Then, as I said, the Duke, great Bullingbrook,
Mounted upon a hot and fiery steed,
Which his aspiring rider seem'd to know,
With slow but stately pace kept on his course,
Whilst all tongues cried, "God save [thee], Bullingbrook!"
You would have thought the very windows spake,
So many greedy looks of young and old
Through casements darted their desiring eyes
Upon his visage, and that all the walls
With painted imagery had said at once,
"Jesu preserve [thee]! Welcome, Bullingbrook!"
Whilst he, from the one side to the other turning,
Bare-headed, lower than his proud steed's neck,
Bespake them thus: "I thank you, countrymen."
And thus still doing, thus he pass'd along.

Duch. Alack, poor Richard, where rode he the whilst?

York. As in a theatre the eyes of men,
After a well-graced actor leaves the stage,
Are idly bent on him that enters next,
Thinking his prattle to be tedious,
Even so, or with much more contempt, men's eyes
Did scowl on gentle Richard. No man cried "God save him!"
No joyful tongue gave him his welcome home,
But dust was thrown upon his sacred head,
Which with such gentle sorrow he shook off,
His face still combating with tears and smiles,
The badges of his grief and patience,
That had not God, for some strong purpose, steel'd
The hearts of men, they must perforce have melted,
And barbarism itself have pitied him.
But heaven hath a hand in these events,
To whose high will we bound our calm contents.
To Bullingbrook are we sworn subjects now,
Whose state and honor I for aye allow.

Duch. Here comes my son Aumerle.

[*Enter* AUMERLE.]

York. Aumerle that was,
But that is lost for being Richard's friend;
And, madam, you must call him Rutland now.
I am in parliament pledge for his truth
And lasting fealty to the new-made king.

Duch. Welcome, my son! Who are the violets now
That strew the green lap of the new-come spring?

Aum. Madam, I know not, nor I greatly care not,
God knows I had as lief be none as one.

York. Well, bear you well in this new spring of time,
Lest you be cropp'd before you come to prime.
What news from Oxford? Do these justs and triumphs hold?

Aum. For aught I know, my lord, they do.

York. You will be there, I know.

Aum. If God prevent not, I purpose so.

77. **pines the clime**: afflicts the region.
80. **Hollowmas**: Hallowmas, All Saints' Day (November 1).
84. **policy**: astuteness.
88. **Better . . . the near**: i.e. it is better to be widely separated than, though close together, to be never nearer.
101. **make woe wanton**: make a sport of grief. **fond**: (1) affectionate; (2) foolish.

V.ii. Location: London. The Duke of York's palace.
4. **leave**: leave off. 5. **windows' tops**: high windows.
15–16. **walls . . . imagery**: i.e. walls so thick with people that they looked like the painted hangings or tapestries commonly used for pageants and processions. 20. **Bespake**: addressed.
25. **idly**: indifferently. 33. **badges**: signs. 38. **bound**: limit.
40. **allow**: accept.
41–43. **Aumerle . . . now.** As a result of his alleged complicity in the murder of Gloucester (IV.i) Aumerle had lost his ducal status, although he retained the title Earl of Rutland.
46. **violets**: i.e. the new king's favorites.
52. **Do . . . hold**: i.e. are these jousts and pageants going forward as planned. According to Holinshed (Bullough, III, 411–12), the Abbot of Westminster and his accomplices planned to invite the new king to attend a joust at Oxford, where "when he should be most busilie marking the martiall pastime, he suddenlie should be slaine and destroied, and so by that means king Richard, who as yet lived, might be restored to libertie, and have his former estate & dignitie."

York. What seal is that, that hangs without thy bosom?
Yea, look'st thou pale? Let me see the writing.
Aum. My lord, 'tis nothing.
York. No matter then who see it.
I will be satisfied, let me see the writing.
Aum. I do beseech your Grace to pardon me.
It is a matter of small consequence,
Which for some reasons I would not have seen.
York. Which for some reasons, sir, I mean to see.
I fear, I fear—
Duch. What should you fear?
'Tis nothing but some band that he is ent'red into
For gay apparel 'gainst the triumph day.
York. Bound to himself! What doth he with a bond
That he is bound to? Wife, thou art a fool.
Boy, let me see the writing.
Aum. I do beseech you pardon me, I may not show it.
York. I will be satisfied, let me see it, I say.
He plucks it out of his bosom and reads it.
Treason, foul treason! Villain, traitor, slave!
Duch. What is the matter, my lord?
York. Ho, who is within there?

[*Enter a* SERVANT.]

Saddle my horse.
God for his mercy! what treachery is here!
Duch. Why, what is it, my lord?
York. Give me my boots, I say, saddle my horse.
[*Exit Servant.*]
Now by mine honor, by my life, by my troth,
I will appeach the villain.
Duch. What is the matter?
York. Peace, foolish woman.
Duch. I will not peace. What is the matter, Aumerle?
Aum. Good mother, be content, it is no more
Than my poor life must answer.
Duch. Thy life answer?
York. Bring me my boots, I will unto the King.

His MAN *enters with his boots.*

Duch. Strike him, Aumerle. Poor boy, thou art amaz'd.
—Hence, villain! never more come in my sight.
York. Give me my boots, I say.
[*His Man helps him on with his boots and exit.*]
Duch. Why, York, what wilt thou do?
Wilt thou not hide the trespass of thine own?
Have we more sons? or are we like to have?
Is not my teeming date drunk up with time?
And wilt thou pluck my fair son from mine age,
And rob me of a happy mother's name?

56. seal . . . bosom. Instead of being placed directly on a document, a seal was often affixed to a strip of parchment hanging from the border of the document. **65. band:** bond.
66. 'gainst: in anticipation of. **75. God:** i.e. I pray God.
79. appeach: publicly accuse. **83. answer:** answer for.
85. him: i.e. the servant. **amaz'd:** stupefied.
86. villain: i.e. the servant.
90–93. Have . . . name. Actually, Aumerle (who had a brother and a sister) was the Duchess' stepson. All of York's children were by his first wife, Isabel of Castile, who died in 1393.
91. teeming date: time of childbearing.

Is he not like thee? is he not thine own?
York. Thou fond mad woman,
Wilt thou conceal this dark conspiracy?
A dozen of them here have ta'en the sacrament,
And interchangeably set down their hands,
To kill the King at Oxford.
Duch. He shall be none,
We'll keep him here, then what is that to him?
York. Away, fond woman, were he twenty times my son,
I would appeach him.
Duch. Hadst thou groan'd for him
As I have done, thou wouldst be more pitiful.
But now I know thy mind, thou dost suspect
That I have been disloyal to thy bed,
And that he is a bastard, not thy son.
Sweet York, sweet husband, be not of that mind,
He is as like thee as a man may be,
Not like to me, or any of my kin,
And yet I love him.
York. Make way, unruly woman! *Exit.*
Duch. After, Aumerle! mount thee upon his horse,
Spur post, and get before him to the King,
And beg thy pardon ere he do accuse thee.
I'll not be long behind; though I be old,
I doubt not but to ride as fast as York.
An' never will I rise up from the ground
Till Bullingbrook have pardoned thee. Away, be gone!
[*Exeunt.*]

[SCENE III]

Enter the KING [HENRY] *with his nobles* [PERCY *and other* LORDS].

K. Hen. Can no man tell me of my unthrifty son?
'Tis full three months since I did see him last.
If any plague hang over us, 'tis he.
I would to God, my lords, he might be found.
Inquire at London, 'mongst the taverns there,
For there, they say, he daily doth frequent,
With unrestrained loose companions,
Even such, they say, as stand in narrow lanes
And beat our watch and rob our passengers,
Which he, young wanton and effeminate boy,
Takes on the point of honor to support
So dissolute a crew.
Percy. My lord, some two days since I saw the Prince,
And told him of those triumphs held at Oxford.
K. Hen. And what said the gallant?

95. fond: foolish.
97–99. A dozen . . . Oxford. According to Holinshed (Bullough, III, 412), the conspirators headed by the Abbot of Westminster had "an indenture sextipartite made, sealed with their seales, and signed with their hands, in the which each stood bound to other, to do their whole indevour for the accomplishing of their purposed exploit."
100. that: i.e. the plot against the King.
111. his horse: one of his horses.
112. post: posthaste, i.e. as fast as possible. **116. An':** and.

V.iii. Location: Windsor Castle.
1. unthrifty: profligate. **6. frequent:** resort.
9. watch: watchmen. **passengers:** wayfarers.
10. Which. A loose connective here. **young . . . boy:** undisciplined and self-indulgent boy. **14. held:** planned.

Percy. His answer was, he would unto the stews,
And from the common'st creature pluck a glove
And wear it as a favor, and with that
He would unhorse the lustiest challenger.
K. Hen. As dissolute as desperate, yet through both
I see some sparks of better hope, which elder years
May happily bring forth. But who comes here?

Enter AUMERLE *amazed.*

Aum. Where is the King?
K. Hen. What means our cousin, that he stares and looks
So wildly?
Aum. God save your Grace! I do beseech your Majesty,
To have some conference with your Grace alone.
K. Hen. Withdraw yourselves, and leave us here alone. [*Exeunt Percy and Lords.*]
What is the matter with our cousin now?
Aum. For ever may my knees grow to the earth, [*Kneels.*]
My tongue cleave to my roof within my mouth,
Unless a pardon ere I rise or speak.
K. Hen. Intended, or committed, was this fault?
If on the first, how heinous e'er it be,
To win thy after-love I pardon thee.
Aum. Then give me leave that [I] may turn the key,
That no man enter till my tale be done.
K. Hen. Have thy desire.

[*Aumerle locks the door.*] *The Duke of York knocks at the door and crieth.*

York. [*Within.*] My liege, beware! Look to thyself,
Thou hast a traitor in thy presence there.
K. Hen. Villain, I'll make thee safe. [*Draws.*]
Aum. Stay thy revengeful hand, thou hast no cause to fear.
York. [*Within.*] Open the door, secure foolhardy King!
Shall I for love speak treason to thy face?
Open the door, or I will break it open.
[*King Henry unlocks the door.*]

[*Enter* YORK.]

K. Hen. What is the matter, uncle? Speak,
Recover breath, tell us how near is danger
That we may arm us to encounter it.
York. Peruse this writing here, and thou shalt know
The treason that my haste forbids me show.
Aum. Remember, as thou read'st, thy promise pass'd.
I do repent me, read not my name there,
My heart is not confederate with my hand.

16. **stews:** brothels. 23 s.d. **amazed:** distraught.
41. **safe:** harmless. 42. **revengeful:** avenging.
43. **secure:** heedless, unsuspecting.
44. **speak . . . face:** i.e. use such disrespectful language.
50. **my . . . show:** my breathlessness prevents my relating in detail.
51. **pass'd:** already given.

York. It was, villain, ere thy hand did set it down.
I tore it from the traitor's bosom, King;
Fear, and not love, begets his penitence.
Forget to pity him, lest thy pity prove
A serpent that will sting thee to the heart.
K. Hen. O heinous, strong, and bold conspiracy!
O loyal father of a treacherous son!
Thou sheer, immaculate, and silver fountain,
From whence this stream through muddy passages
Hath held his current and defil'd himself!
Thy overflow of good converts to bad,
And thy abundant goodness shall excuse
This deadly blot in thy digressing son.
York. So shall my virtue be his vice's bawd,
An' he shall spend mine honor with his shame,
As thriftless sons their scraping fathers' gold.
Mine honor lives when his dishonor dies,
Or my sham'd life in his dishonor lies:
Thou kill'st me in his life; giving him breath,
The traitor lives, the true man's put to death.
Duch. [*Within.*] What ho, my liege! for God's sake let me in.
K. Hen. What shrill[-voic'd] suppliant makes this eager cry?
Duch. [*Within.*] A woman, and thy aunt, great King, 'tis I.
Speak with me, pity me, open the door!
A beggar begs that never begg'd before.
K. Hen. Our scene is alt'red from a serious thing,
And now chang'd to "The Beggar and the King."
My dangerous cousin, let your mother in,
I know she is come to pray for your foul sin.
York. If thou do pardon, whosoever pray,
More sins for this forgiveness prosper may.
This fest'red joint cut off, the rest rest sound,
This let alone will all the rest confound.

[*Enter* DUCHESS.]

Duch. O King, believe not this hard-hearted man!
Love loving not itself, none other can.
York. Thou frantic woman, what dost thou make here?
Shall thy old dugs once more a traitor rear?
Duch. Sweet York, be patient. Hear me, gentle liege. [*Kneels.*]
K. Hen. Rise up, good aunt.
Duch. Not yet, I thee beseech.
For ever will I walk upon my knees,
And never see day that the happy sees,
Till thou give joy, until thou bid me joy
By pardoning Rutland, my transgressing boy.
Aum. Unto my mother's prayers I bend my knee. [*Kneels.*]

61. **sheer:** pure. **fountain:** spring.
64. **converts:** changes. 66. **digressing:** wayward.
70. **lives:** comes to life, revives.
79–80. **Our . . . King:** i.e. we have now moved from a serious play to a comedy that could be called "The Beggar and the King" (perhaps with an allusion to "King Cophetua and the Beggar Maid," a ballad to which Shakespeare refers several times).
88. **Love . . . can:** i.e. he who does not love his own children can love no one, not even his king. 89. **make:** do.

York. Against them both my true joints bended be. [*Kneels.*]
Ill mayst thou thrive if thou grant any grace!
Duch. Pleads he in earnest? Look upon his face:
His eyes do drop no tears, his prayers are in jest,
His words come from his mouth, ours from our breast;
He prays but faintly, and would be denied,
We pray with heart and soul, and all beside;
His weary joints would gladly rise, I know,
Our knees still kneel till to the ground they grow;
His prayers are full of false hypocrisy,
Ours of true zeal and deep integrity;
Our prayers do outpray his, then let them have
That mercy which true prayer ought to have.
[*K. Hen.*] Good aunt, stand up.
Duch. Nay, do not say "stand up";
Say "pardon" first, and afterwards "stand up."
And if I were thy nurse, thy tongue to teach,
"Pardon" should be the first word of thy speech.
I never long'd to hear a word till now,
Say "pardon," King, let pity teach thee how.
The word is short, but not so short as sweet,
No word like "pardon" for kings' mouths so meet.
York. Speak it in French, King, say "*pardonne moy.*"
Duch. Dost thou teach pardon pardon to destroy?
Ah, my sour husband, my hard-hearted lord,
That sets the word itself against the word!
Speak "pardon" as 'tis current in our land,
The chopping French we do not understand.
Thine eye begins to speak, set thy tongue there;
Or in thy piteous heart plant thou thine ear,
That hearing how our plaints and prayers do pierce,
Pity may move thee "pardon" to rehearse.
K. Hen. Good aunt, stand up.
Duch. I do not sue to stand;
Pardon is all the suit I have in hand.
K. Hen. I pardon him as God shall pardon me.
Duch. O happy vantage of a kneeling knee!
Yet am I sick for fear, speak it again,
Twice saying "pardon" doth not pardon twain,
But makes one pardon strong.
K. Hen. With all my heart
I pardon him.
Duch. A god on earth thou art.
K. Hen. But for our trusty brother-in-law and the abbot,
With all the rest of that consorted crew,
Destruction straight shall dog them at the heels.
Good uncle, help to order several powers
To Oxford, or where e'er these traitors are.
They shall not live within this world, I swear,

106. still: will continue to.
119. pardonne moy: excuse me (a courteous refusal).
124. chopping: shifting in meaning. **125. speak:** i.e. express pity.
137–39. But . . . heels. The King's "trusty brother-in-law" was his sister Elizabeth's husband John Holland, Duke of Exeter and Earl of Huntington, who, like Aumerle, had been degraded from his dukedom for his alleged part in Gloucester's murder. Despite the disclosure of their plot, he and his accomplices (including his nephew Thomas, Duke of Surrey and Earl of Kent) made an abortive effort to kill Henry at Windsor, but as they fled before the King they were trapped at Cirencester, and virtually all of the "consorted crew" were hunted down and executed. See V.vi. **140. powers:** forces.

But I will have them if I once know where.
Uncle, farewell, and, cousin, adieu!
Your mother well hath pray'd, and prove you true.
Duch. Come, my old son, I pray God make thee new. *Exeunt.*

[Scene IV]

[*Enter*] Sir Pierce Exton [*and* Servants].

Exton. Didst thou not mark the King, what words he spake?
"Have I no friend will rid me of this living fear?"
Was it not so?
[*1.*] *Man.* These were his very words.
Exton. "Have I no friend?" quoth he. He spake it twice,
And urg'd it twice together, did he not?
[*1.*] *Man.* He did.
Exton. And speaking it, he wishtly look'd on me
As who should say, "I would thou wert the man
That would divorce this terror from my heart"—
Meaning the king at Pomfret. Come let's go.
I am the King's friend, and will rid his foe. [*Exeunt.*]

[Scene V]

Enter Richard *alone.*

K. Rich. I have been studying how I may compare
This prison where I live unto the world;
And for because the world is populous,
And here is not a creature but myself,
I cannot do it; yet I'll hammer it out.
My brain I'll prove the female to my soul,
My soul the father, and these two beget
A generation of still-breeding thoughts;
And these same thoughts people this little world,
In humors like the people of this world:
For no thought is contented. The better sort,
As thoughts of things divine, are intermix'd
With scruples and do set the word itself
Against the word,
As thus: "Come, little ones," and then again,
"It is as hard to come as for a camel
To thread the postern of a small needle's eye."
Thoughts tending to ambition, they do plot
Unlikely wonders: how these vain weak nails
May tear a passage thorough the flinty ribs
Of this hard world, my ragged prison walls;
And for they cannot, die in their own pride.

V.iv. Location: Windsor Castle.
7. wishtly: intently. **11. rid:** rid him of.

V.v. Location: Pomfret Castle. A dungeon.
3. for because: because. **8. still:** continually.
10. humors: temperaments. **13. scruples:** doubts.
13–14. do . . . word: i.e. oppose Scriptural passages that seem to contradict each other.
15–17. Come . . . eye. See Matthew 19:14, 24.
17. postern: small gate. **needle.** A monosyllable (pronounced *neeld* or *neele*). **21. ragged:** rugged, rough.
22. for: because. **pride:** prime.

Thoughts tending to content flatter themselves
That they are not the first of fortune's slaves,
Nor shall not be the last—like seely beggars
Who sitting in the stocks refuge their shame,
That many have and others must [sit] there;
And in this thought they find a kind of ease,
Bearing their own misfortunes on the back
Of such as have before endur'd the like.
Thus play I in one person many people,
And none contented. Sometimes am I king;
Then treasons make me wish myself a beggar,
And so I am. Then crushing penury
Persuades me I was better when a king;
Then am I king'd again, and by and by
Think that I am unking'd by Bullingbrook,
And straight am nothing. But what e'er I be,
Nor I, nor any man that but man is,
With nothing shall be pleas'd, till he be eas'd
With being nothing. (*The music plays.*) Music do I hear?
Ha, ha, keep time! How sour sweet music is
When time is broke, and no proportion kept!
So is it in the music of men's lives.
And here have I the daintiness of ear
To check time broke in a disordered string;
But for the concord of my state and time
Had not an ear to hear my true time broke.
I wasted time, and now doth time waste me;
For now hath time made me his numb'ring clock:
My thoughts are minutes, and with sighs they jar
Their watches on unto mine eyes, the outward watch,
Whereto my finger, like a dial's point,
Is pointing still, in cleansing them from tears.
Now, sir, the sound that tells what hour it is
Are clamorous groans, which strike upon my heart,
Which is the bell. So sighs, and tears, and groans
Show minutes, times, and hours; but my time
Runs posting on in Bullingbrook's proud joy,
While I stand fooling here, his Jack of the clock.
This music mads me, let it sound no more,
For though it have holp mad men to their wits,
In me it seems it will make wise men mad.
Yet blessing on his heart that gives it me!
For 'tis a sign of love; and love to Richard
Is a strange brooch in this all-hating world.

Enter a GROOM OF THE STABLE.

Groom. Hail, royal prince!
K. Rich. Thanks, noble peer!
The cheapest of us is ten groats too dear.
What art thou? and how comest thou hither,
Where no man never comes, but that sad dog
That brings me food to make misfortune live?

Groom. I was a poor groom of thy stable, King,
When thou wert king; who, travelling towards York,
With much ado (at length) have gotten leave
To look upon my sometimes royal master's face.
O how it ern'd my heart when I beheld
In London streets, that coronation-day,
When Bullingbrook rode on roan Barbary,
That horse that thou so often hast bestrid,
That horse that I so carefully have dress'd!

K. Rich. Rode he on Barbary? Tell me, gentle friend,
How went he under him?

Groom. So proudly as if he disdain'd the ground.

K. Rich. So proud that Bullingbrook was on his back!
That jade hath eat bread from my royal hand,
This hand hath made him proud with clapping him.
Would he not stumble? Would he not fall down,
Since pride must have a fall, and break the neck
Of that proud man that did usurp his back?
Forgiveness, horse! why do I rail on thee,
Since thou, created to be aw'd by man,
Wast born to bear? I was not made a horse,
And yet I bear a burthen like an ass,
Spurr'd, gall'd, and tir'd by jauncing Bullingbrook.

Enter one [*the* KEEPER] *to Richard with meat.*

Keep. Fellow, give place, here is no longer stay.

K. Rich. If thou love me, 'tis time thou wert away.

Groom. What my tongue dares not, that my heart shall say. *Exit Groom.*

Keep. My lord, will't please you to fall to?

K. Rich. Taste of it first, as thou art wont to do.

Keep. My lord, I dare not. Sir Pierce of Exton, who
Lately came from the King, commands the contrary.

K. Rich. The devil take Henry of Lancaster and thee!
Patience is stale, and I am weary of it.
[*Beats the Keeper.*]

Keep. Help, help, help!

The murderers [EXTON *and* SERVANTS] *rush in* [*armed*].

K. Rich. How now, what means death in this rude assault?
Villain, thy own hand yields thy death's instrument,
[*Snatches an axe from a Servant and kills him.*]
Go thou and fill another room in hell.
[*Kills another.*] *Here Exton strikes him down.*
That hand shall burn in never-quenching fire
That staggers thus my person. Exton, thy fierce hand

25. seely: silly, i.e. simple.
26. refuge their shame: seek refuge for their disgrace.
37. unking'd. See note to II.i.16.
46. check: rebuke, i.e. be offended by.
51–54. My . . . tears: i.e. my (sad) thoughts are minutes, and my sighs, like the ticking of a clock, record or tick off (*jar*) their periods (*watches*) in my eyes—the clock face at which my finger, like the minute hand (*dial's point*), is always pointing as it wipes away my tears.
59. posting: with speed.
60. Jack . . . clock: manikin in old clocks that struck the bell.
61. mads: maddens. **62. holp**: helped. **63. wise**: sane.
66. strange brooch: rare ornament. **this all-hating world**: this world in which all hate Richard.
67–68. Hail . . . dear. An elaborate play on coinage. The difference between a *royal* (worth 10*s.*) and a *noble* (worth 6*s.* 8*d.*) was ten groats (40 pence), and since Richard says that the "cheapest of us" (i.e. himself, a prisoner) is "ten groats too dear," he estimates his value no higher than the groom's. **75. sometimes**: former.
76. ern'd: grieved. **85. eat**: eatĕn.
86. with clapping: by patting.
94. jauncing: making the horse prance.
99. Taste: i.e. to see that it was not poisoned.
107. room: place. **108. never-quenching**: never-quenched.

Hath with the King's blood stain'd the King's own land.
Mount, mount, my soul! thy seat is up on high,
Whilst my gross flesh sinks downward, here to die. [*Dies.*]

Exton. As full of valure as of royal blood!
Both have I spill'd; O would the deed were good!
For now the devil that told me I did well
Says that this deed is chronicled in hell.
This dead king to the living king I'll bear;
Take hence the rest, and give them burial here. [*Exeunt.*]

[Scene VI]

[*Flourish.*] *Enter Bullingbrook,* [*now* King Henry,] *with the* Duke of York [*with other* Lords *and* Attendants].

K. Hen. Kind uncle York, the latest news we hear
Is that the rebels have consum'd with fire
Our town of Ciceter in Gloucestershire,
But whether they be ta'en or slain we hear not.

Enter Northumberland.

Welcome, my lord, what is the news?

North. First, to thy sacred state wish I all happiness.
The next news is, I have to London sent
The heads of Salisbury, [Spencer], Blunt, and Kent.
The manner of their taking may appear
At large discoursed in this paper here.

K. Hen. We thank thee, gentle Percy, for thy pains,
And to thy worth will add right worthy gains.

Enter Lord Fitzwater.

Fitz. My lord, I have from Oxford sent to London
The heads of Brocas and Sir Bennet Seely,
Two of the dangerous consorted traitors
That sought at Oxford thy dire overthrow.

K. Hen. Thy pains, Fitzwater, shall not be forgot,
Right noble is thy merit, well I wot.

Enter Harry Percy [*and the* Bishop of Carlisle].

Percy. The grand conspirator, Abbot of Westminster,
With clog of conscience and sour melancholy
Hath yielded up his body to the grave;
But here is Carlisle living, to abide
Thy kingly doom and sentence of his pride.

K. Hen. Carlisle, this is your doom:
Choose out some secret place, some reverent room,
More than thou hast, and with it joy thy life.
So as thou liv'st in peace, die free from strife,
For though mine enemy thou hast ever been,
High sparks of honor in thee have I seen.

Enter Exton *with* [Attendants *bearing*] *the coffin.*

Exton. Great King, within this coffin I present
Thy buried fear. Herein all breathless lies
The mightiest of thy greatest enemies,
Richard of Burdeaux, by me hither brought.

K. Hen. Exton, I thank thee not, for thou hast wrought
A deed of slander with thy fatal hand
Upon my head and all this famous land.

Exton. From your own mouth, my lord, did I this deed.

K. Hen. They love not poison that do poison need,
Nor do I thee. Though I did wish him dead,
I hate the murtherer, love him murthered.
The guilt of conscience take thou for thy labor,
But neither my good word nor princely favor.
With Cain go wander thorough shades of night,
And never show thy head by day nor light.
Lords, I protest my soul is full of woe
That blood should sprinkle me to make me grow.
Come mourn with me for what I do lament,
And put on sullen black incontinent.
I'll make a voyage to the Holy Land,
To wash this blood off from my guilty hand.
March sadly after, grace my mournings here,
In weeping after this untimely bier. [*Exeunt.*]

113. valure: valor.

V.vi. Location: Windsor Castle.
3. Ciceter: Cirencester. **6. state:** royalty.
9. taking: capture. **12. worth:** (1) assets; (2) deserts.

20. clog: burden. **23. doom:** judgment.
25. secret: retired. **reverent room:** i.e. spot appropriate for a religious life. **26. joy:** enjoy. **31. fear:** object of fear.
33. Burdeaux: Bordeaux (Richard's birthplace).
35. of slander: i.e. grave enough to bring disgrace.
43. thorough: through. **48. incontinent:** immediately.
51. grace: dignify.

NOTE ON THE TEXT

Richard II was first published in quarto in 1597 (Q1); two other quarto editions appeared in 1598 (Q2, Q3), and two more (Q4, Q5) in 1608 and 1615 respectively, each reprinted from the quarto immediately preceding. The play was, of course, included in the First Folio (1623), and a sixth quarto (Q6) was issued in 1634, its text derived from the Second Folio (1632).

It is generally believed that Q1, which here serves as copy-text (except for IV.i.154–318; see below), was set up directly from Shakespeare's "foul papers," a view supported by Hinman and Jowett/Taylor, though a transcript (scribal?) of the "foul papers" cannot be entirely ruled out. Such a view would at least help to explain why Q1 shows so few of the usual stigmata of "foul papers" and why so few characteristic Shakespearean spellings find their way into the Q1 text.

Q1 does not contain the so-called "deposition scene" (IV.i.154–318). This part of the scene first appeared in Q4, but in a version which strongly suggests a memorially contaminated text. F1 gives an obviously superior text and has therefore been used as the basic text for these lines, although the lighter punctuation of Q4, as more in keeping with that of Q1, has been followed wherever possible. All Q4 substantive variants for the passage are recorded in the Textual Notes.

Aside from its importance for the "deposition scene," the F1 text requires some respectful notice. It was printed, according to R. E. Hasker (following a suggestion of A. W. Pollard's), from a composite copy made up from Q3 (for I.i.1–V.v.18, except for IV.i.154–318) and Q5 (for IV.1.154–318, V.v.19–V.vi.52), both sporadically corrected at some stage against an official prompt-book. Jowett/Taylor, however, in an important study of the interrelations between Q3, Q5, and F1, argue persuasively that manuscript copy, without reference to Q5, lies behind Fl's text of the "deposition scene" (IV.i.154–318) and that not Q5, but a transcript from Q5, made to replace the last leaf of the prompt-book, somehow either badly damaged or lost, served as the manuscript copy against which Q3 was collated, thus explaining the intrusion of Q5 readings in the last fifty-three lines of the F1 text. A prompt-book provenience for the manuscript against which, at a number of points (see Jowett/Taylor), Q3 was collated in preparing copy for F1 is supported by the substantial number of necessary stage directions added in F1, the omission of some Q1 passages, and, perhaps, the consistency with which, in accordance with the 1606 Act against profanity, *God* is softened to *heaven*. The postulated use, even if somewhat hit or miss, of the official prompt-book in the preparation of copy for F1 suggests that at least some of the substantive readings that appear for the first time in F1 deserve consideration as possible Shakespearean second thoughts, a view thoughtfully argued for by Jowett/Taylor, who admit forty more F1 readings into their New Oxford text than any other editors in the last seventy-five years (the most important of such F1 substitutions may be found in the Textual Notes below at I.i.157, 186; I.iii.227; I.iv.7; III.ii.35, 55, 84, 85, 102, 178, 203; III.iii.171; IV.i.112; V.i.25, 44, 66, 78; V.ii.52; V.iii.1, 21; V.v.13–14, 58). Nevertheless, since we cannot be sure that such new readings are not due to other hands (the prompter's, the actors', the compositor's, or even the hypothetical collator's), very few F1 readings which do not correct obvious errors have been admitted in the present text. All significant readings and omissions originating in F1 are, however, recorded in the Textual Notes.

For further information, see: A. W. Pollard, *"King Richard II": A New Quarto* (London, 1916); J. D. Wilson, ed., New Shakespeare *Richard II* (Cambridge, 1951); R. E. Hasker, "The Copy for the First Folio *Richard II*," *SB*, V (1952–53), 53–72; W. W. Greg, *The Shakespeare First Folio* (Oxford, 1955); M. W. Black, ed., New Variorum *Richard II* (Philadelphia, 1955); Peter Ure, ed., New Arden *Richard II* (London, 1956); Charlton Hinman (and W. W. Greg), eds., *Richard the Second (1597)*, facsimile of Q1 (Oxford, 1966); Andrew Gurr, ed., New Cambridge *Richard II* (Cambridge, 1984); John Jowett and Gary Taylor, "Sprinklings of Authority: The Folio Text of *Richard II*," *SB*, XXXVIII (1985), 151–200; Stanley Wells, Gary Taylor, John Jowett, and William Montgomery, *William Shakespeare: A Textual Companion* (Oxford, 1987).

TEXTUAL NOTES

Title: The . . . Second] The Tragedie of King Richard the second. As it hath beene publikely acted by the right Honourable the Lorde Chamberlaine his Seruants. *Q1 (title-page)*; The life and death of King Richard the Second. *F1*

Act-scene division: *none in Q1–5; from F1, with the following exceptions: V.iv (no scene division in F1); V.v, vi (numbered V.iv, v in F1); see first note to each scene; present act-scene arrangement as a whole first established by Steevens*

I.i

I.i] *F1*
Location: *Wilson*
3 Herford] *see note on I.ii.46*
15 presence;] *Pope;* presence *Q1–5, F1*
19 s.d. with Attendants] *Collier (after Capell)*
46 drawn] *Q2–5, F1;* drawen *Q1*
53 hush'd] *Q2–5, F1;* huisht *Q1*
57 doubled] doubly *F1*
96 land,] *Q3–5, F1;* land: *Q1–2*
101 soon-believing] *hyphen, Pope*
102 traitor] *Q2–5, F1;* taitour *Q1*
104 Abel's,] *Q4–5 (subs.);* Abels *Q1–3, F1*
118 my] *F1*
122 Mowbray;] *Collier;* Mowbray *Q1;* Mowbray, *Q2–5;* (Mowbray) *F1*
129–30 debt, . . . account,] *Q2–5, F1;* debt. / . . . account: *Q1*
133 not,] *Q2–5;* not *Q1;* not; *F1*
139 But] *so two copies of Q1; the other two extant copies read* Ah but *(it is not certain which reading represents the corrected state);* Ah but *Q2–3;* Ah, but *Q4–5*
152 Wrath-kindled] *hyphen, Capell*
152 gentlemen] *F1;* gentleman *Q1–5*
152 rul'd] *F1;* ruled *Q1–5*
157 month] time *F1*
162 when?] *Q2–5, F1;* when *Q1*
163 Obedience bids] obedience bids, / Obedience bids *Q1–5, F1; Pope first om. the repetition, but reads* bids, *(followed by later eds. until White)*
170 baffled] *Rowe;* baffuld *Q1–5;* baffel'd *F1*
172 heart-blood] *hyphen, Pope*
176 gage.] *F1;* gage, *Q1, Q4–5;* gage *Q2–3*
177-8 afford . . . reputation;] *F1 (subs.);* afford, / . . . Reputation *Q1;* afoord, / . . . reputation, *Q2–5*
180 ten-times-barr'd-up] *hyphens, Capell*
186 up] downe *F1*
187 God] heauen *F1*
192 parley] *ed.;* parlee *Q1–5;* parle *F1*
195 s.d. Exit Gaunt.] *F1*
201 hate.] *Q4–5, F1 (subs.);* hate, *Q1–3*
204 officers-at-arms] *hyphens, Delius*
205 s.d. Exeunt.] *F1;* Exit. *Q1–5*

I.ii

I.ii] *F1*
Location: *Theobald*
1 Woodstock's] Glousters *F1*
7 hour's] *Q4–5* (hower's); houres *Q1–3, F1*
12, 17 vials . . . vial] *F2;* viols . . . violl *Q1–5, F1*
23 mettle] *F1;* mettall *Q1–5*
37 God's . . . God's] Heauens . . . heauens] *F1*
37 quarrel,] *Q3–5;* quarrell *Q1–2;* quarrell: *F1*
43 God] heauen *F1*
43 and] to *F1*
46 Herford] *Q2–5, F1;* Hereford *Q1 (Q1 uses both spellings,* Hereford *more frequently, but since a disyllable seems generally called for,* Herford *has been adopted throughout)*
47 sit] *F1;* set *Q1–5*
49 career] *F1* (carreere); carier *Q1–2;* carriere *Q3;* carrier *Q4–5*
58 it] *Q2–5, F1;* is *Q1*
60 begun] *Q2–5, F1;* begone *Q1*
70 hear] cheere *Q1 (u)*

I.iii

I.iii] *F1*
Location: *Pope*
6 s.d. Gaunt . . . others] *F1*
6 s.d. with a Herald] *from F1* and Harrold
15 thee] *Q2–5, F1;* the *Q1*
18 God] heauen *F1*
20 and my] and his *F1*
25 s.d. with a Herald] *from F1* and Harold
28 plated] placed *F1*
33 com'st] *F1;* comes *Q1–4;* comest *Q5*
37 God's] heauens *F1*
43 daring-hardy] *Theobald;* daring, hardy *Q1–5;* daring hardie *F1*
44, 46, 99 Marshal] *Q5, F1;* Martiall *Q1–4*
55 right] iust *F1*
58 thee] *Q3–5, F1;* the *Q1–2*
66 cheerly] *F3;* cheerely *Q1–5, F1*
69 earthly] earthy *F1*
71 vigor] rigor *F1*
76 furbish] furnish *F1*
78, 85, 101 God] Heauen *or* heauen *F1*
82 adverse] amaz'd *F1*
102 hope, I cry] *F1;* hope I cry, *Q1–5*
103 s.d. To an Officer.] *Capell*
104 s.p. 1. Her.] *F1 (subs.);* Herald *Q1–5*
117 s.d. A charge sounded.] *F1 (after l. 116); placed as in Malone*
118 thrown] *Q2–5, F1;* throwen *Q1*
122 s.d. A long flourish.] *F1*
124 Council] *F1;* counsell *Q1–5*
128 civil] cruell *Q1 (u)*
128 neighbors'] *Hanmer;* neighbours *Q1–5, F1*
128 sword] swords *F1*
129–33 And . . . sleep;] *om. F1*
133 sleep;] *Pope;* sleepe *Q1;* sleepe, *Q2–5*
135 harsh-resounding] *hyphen, Theobald*
140 life] death *F1*
172 then] *F1*
180 y' owe] you owe *F1*
180, 183, 204 God] heauen *or* Heauen *F1*
206 stray;] *Roderick conj.;* stray, *Q1–5, F1*
211 s.d. To Bullingbrook.] *Steevens (subs., after Capell)*

221 **time-bewasted]** *hyphen, F1*

222 **extinct]** *Q2–5, F1*; extint *Q1*

222 **night]** *Q4–5, F1*; nightes *Q1–3*

223 **inch]** *Q3–5, F1*; intch *Q1–2*

227 **sullen]** sudden *F1*

233 **advice]** *F1*; aduise *Q1–5*

234 **party-verdict]** *hyphen, F1*

239–42 **O . . . destroyed.]** *om. F1*

248 s.d. **Flourish.]** *F1 (after F1* Exit.*); placed as in Pope*

248 s.d. **with his Train]** *Capell (subs.)*

253 **dost]** *Q5, F1*; doest *Q1–4*

262 **travel]** *F1*; trauaile *Q1–5*

266 **as foil]** a foyle *Q2*; a soyle *Q3–5, F1*

268–93 **Bull. Nay . . . light.]** *om. F1*

269 **world]** *Q2 (c), Q3–5*; world: *Q1, Q2 (u)*

276 **wise man]** *Q3–5*; wiseman *Q1–2*

307 **that]** which *F1*

309 **true-born]** *F1* (true-borne); true borne *Q1–5*

309 **Englishman]** *Q2–5, F1*; English man *Q1*

I.iv

I.iv] *F1*

Location: *Sisson (after Theobald)*

o.s.d. **Green and Bagot]** *F1*; Bushie, &c *Q1–5* *(Q1–5 later enter Bushy at l. 52)*

7 **blew]** grew *F1*

13 **word, . . . craft]** *F1*; word . . . craft, *Q1–5*

15 **words]** word *F1*

20 **cousin's cousin]** *Wilson*; Coosens Coosin *Q1–5*; Cosin (Cosin) *F1*

23 **Bagot . . . Green,]** *Q6*; heere Bagot and Greene *F1*; *om. Q1–5*

24 **Observ'd]** *F1*; Obserued *Q1–5*

28 **smiles]** soules *F1*

30 **him.]** *F1*; him, *Q1–5*

44 **grown]** *Q2–5, F1*; growen *Q1*

47 **hand.]** *F1 (subs.)*; hand *Q1–5*

52 s.d. **Enter Bushy.]** *F1*; Enter Bushie with newes. *Q1–5*

53 **Bushy, what news?]** *F1 (note Q1–5 s.d. at l. 52)*

54 **grievous]** verie *F1*

59, 64 **God]** heauen *F1*

64–5 **late! All. Amen.]** *Staunton*; late, / Amen *Q1*; late, / Amen. *Q2–3*; late: / Amen. *Q4–5*; late. *F1*

65 s.d. **Exeunt.]** Exit. *F1*

II.i

II.i] *F1*

Location: *Theobald*

12 **at]** is *F1*

18 **whose . . . wise]** whose state the wise *Q2*; of his state: then there *Q3–5, F1*

18 **fond]** *Collier conj.*; found *Q1–5*; sound *F1*

27 **Then]** That *F1*

33 **last,]** *F1*; last: *Q1–5*

36 **betimes;]** *F1*; betimes *Q1*; betimes, *Q2*; betimes. *Q3–5*

48 **a]** *Q4–5, F1*

68 s.d. **Aumerle . . . Willoughby]** *F1 (s.d. after l. 70)*

85 **No,]** *Q3–5, F1*; No *Q1–2*

102 **incaged]** *F1*; inraged *Q1–5*

113 **now, not]** *Theobald*; now not, not *Q1–4*; now not, nor *Q5*; and not *F1*

115 **And thou— K. Rich. A]** *Capell*; And thou / *King.* A *Q1*; And thou. / *King.* A *Q2*; And thou. / *King.* Ah *Q3–5*; And— / *Rich.* And thou, a *F1*

118 **chasing]** chafing *F1*

124 **brother]** *Q2–5*; brothers *Q1, F1*

138 s.d. **borne . . . Attendants]** *Capell*

146 s.d. **Enter Northumberland.]** *F1*

172 **first.]** *Q2–5*; first *Q1*; first, *F1*

177 **the]** *F1*; a *Q1–5*

188 **withal]** *Q2, Q5*; with all *Q1, Q3–4, F1*

203 **attorneys-general]** *hyphen, Rowe*

209 **seize]** *Q3–5*; cease *Q1*; ceaze *Q2*; seise *F1*

218 **trow.]** *Q3–5, F1 (subs.)*; trow, *Q1–2*

223 s.d. **Flourish.]** *F1*

223 s.d. **with others]** *Rowe (&c.)*; *F1 om. the whole exeunt part of the s.d.*

223 s.d. **with . . . Ross]** *F1 (subs.)*

229 **Ere't]** *Rowe*; Eart *Q1*; Ert *Q2*; Er't *Q3–5, F1*

238 **God]** heauen *F1*

254 **noble]** *om. F1*

254 **achiev'd]** *F1*; atchiued *Q1*; atchiude *Q2–4*; atchieud *Q5*

257 **King's]** *Q3–5*; King *Q1–2*; Kings *F1*

257 **grown]** *Q2–5, F1*; growen *Q1*

262 **kinsman—]** *Rowe*; kinsman *Q1–5*; Kinsman, *F1*

277 **Le Port Blanc]** *Cambridge (after Holinshed and Pope)*; le Port Blan *Q1–5*; Port le Blan *F1*

280 **Thomas . . . Arundel,]** *ed. (after Hudson; based on Holinshed).*

283 **Ramston]** Rainston *F1*

284 **Coint]** *Halliwell (after Holinshed)*; Coines *F1*; Quoint *F1*

294 **gilt]** *F1*; guilt *Q1–5*

II.ii

II.ii] *F1*

Location: *Clarendon eds.*

3 **life-harming]** life harming *Q2*; halfeharming *Q3–5*; selfe-harming *F1*

11–2 **soul . . . trembles;]** *Rowe*; soule, . . . trembles, *Q1–5*; soule . . . trembles, *F1*

12 **some thing]** *Q2–5*; something *Q1, F1*

16 **eyes]** eye *F1*

24 **thrice-gracious Queen]** *F1*; thrice (gracious Queene) *Q1–5*

25 **more is]** more's *F1*

31 **though]** *Q2–5, F1*; thought *Q1*

37–8 **grieve— . . . possess—]** *Wilson (after Theobald)*; grieue, . . . possesse, *Q1–3, F1*; grieue, . . . possesse: *Q4–5*

39 **known what,]** *Q1* (knowen what,); knowne, what *Q2–5, F1*

40 s.d. **Enter Green.]** *F1*

41 **God]** Heauen *F1*

52 **Ah]** O *F1*

52 **worse,]** *F1*; worse; *Q1–5*

53 **son young Harry]** *ed. (after Q1* son yong H.); yong sonne H. *Q2–5*; yong sonne Henrie *F1*

70 **keeper-back]** *hyphen, Capell*

72 s.d. **Enter York.]** *F1*

76 **God's]** heauens *F1*

77 **Should . . . thoughts.]** *om. F1*

85 s.d. **Enter a Servingman.]** *Kittredge (after F1* Enter a seruant.); *Q1–5 s.pp. are* Seruingman

87 **was—]** *Johnson*; was; *Q1*; was, *Q2–5*; was: *F1*

98, 100 **God]** Heau'n *and* heauen *F1*

103 **no]** two *Q2–5*; *om. F1*

107 s.d. **Exit Servingman.]** *Kittredge (after Capell)*

108 **go]** *om. F1*

119 **Berkeley]** *Theobald (subs.)*; Barkly *Q1–2*; Barckly *Q3–5*; Barkley Castle *F1*

122 s.d. **Exeunt . . . Bagot.]** *ed (from Q1–5* Exeunt Duke, Qu. man. Bush, Green.); Exit *F1*

123 **for]** to *F1*

127 **Besides,]** *Q4–5*; Besides *Q1–3, F1*

129 **that is]** that's *F1*

130 **whoso]** *Q6*; who so *Q1–5, F1*

135 **Bristow]** *Kittredge*; Brist. *Q1–5*; Bristoll *F1*

142 **Farewell! If]** *Rowe (subs.)*; Farewell if *Q1–2*; Farewell, if *Q3–5, F1*

149 s.d. **Exeunt.]** *Rowe*; Exit. *F1*

II.iii

II.iii] *F1*

Location: *Theobald (subs.)*

o.s.d. **and forces]** *Capell (subs.)*

6 **your]** our *F1*

24 **learn'd]** *F1*; learned *Q1–5*

25 **Why,]** *F1*; Why *Q1–2*; Why? *Q3–5*

30 **lordship]** *Q2–5, F1*; Lo: *Q1*

36 **Herford, boy?]** *Q4–5*; Herefords boy? *Q1–2*: **Hereford, boy?** *Q3*; **Hereford** (Boy.) *F1*

55 **Seymour]** *F3*; Seymer *Q1*; Seymor *Q2–5, F1*

56 s.d. **Enter . . . Willoughby.]** *F1*

58 **fiery-red]** *hyphen, Theobald*

65 **thank's]** thankes, *Q5, F1*

68 s.d. **Enter Berkeley.]** *F1* (Barkely; *after l. 67); placed as in Dyce*

75 **rase]** *Valpy*; raze *Q1–5, F1*

80 s.d. **Enter York attended.]** *F1* (Enter Yorke.) *and Capell*

82 **person.]** *F1*; person, *Q1*; person: *Q2–5*

82 s.d. **Kneels.]** *Rowe*

87 **no uncle]** *om. F1*

92 **"why?"]** *quotes, Cambridge*

101 **men,]** *Q3–5, F1*; men. *Q1–2*

125 **cousin]** Kinsman *F1*

134 **I]** *om. F1*

145 **wrong—]** *Capell*; wrong *Q1*; wrong, *Q2, Q4–5*; wrong; *Q3*; Wrongs, *F1*

158 **known unto]** *Collier*; knowen vnto *Q1*; knowne to *Q2–5, F1*

170 **foes,]** *Q2–5, F1*; foes *Q1*

II.iv

II.iv] *F1*

Location: *Capell (after Theobald)*

1, 7 s.pp. **Cap.]** *F1*; Welch. *Q1–5*

1 **stay'd]** *Q3–5, F1*; stayed *Q1–2*

17 s.d. **Exit.]** *F1*

24 s.d. **Exit.]** *F1*

III.i

III.i] *F1*

Location: *Theobald, Capell*

o.s.d. **Ross . . . with]** *F1*

3 **bodies—]** *F1 (subs.)*; bodies *Q1*; bodyes, *Q2–5*

15 **drawn]** *Q2–5, F1*; drawen *Q1*

22 **signories]** *Capell*; segniories *Q1–5*; Seignories *F1*

25 **Ras'd]** Capell *(sub.)*; Rac't *Q1–5*; Raz'd *F1*

25 **imprese]** *Q5, F1*; impreese *Q1–4*

35 s.d. **Exeunt . . . prisoners.]** *Capell*

37 **God's]** Heauens *F1*

43 **Glendower]** *Rowe*; Glendor *Q1–5*; Glendoure *F1*

III.ii

III.ii] *F1*

Location: *Capell (after Pope)*

o.s.d. **Drums . . . Colors.]** *F1*

o.s.d. **and Soldiers]** *F1*; &c. *Q1–5*

29–32 **The . . . redress.]** *om. F1*

30 **neglected;]** *Pope (subs.)*; neglected. *Q1–5*

31 **not.]** *Sisson*; not, *Q1–2*; not; *Q3–5*

35 **power]** friends *F1*

37–8 **hid . . . globe,]** *F1*; hid, . . . globe *Q1*; hid . . . globe *Q2–5*

40 **boldly]** *Collier conj.*; bouldy *Q1 (possibly a form of* boldly); bloudy *Q2–5, F1*

49 **Whilst . . . antipodes,]** *om. F1*

55 **off]** *om. F1*

60 **God]** Heauen *F1*

63 **Welcome]** *F1*; *King* Welcome *Q1–5 (repeated s.p.)*

72 **Overthrows]** Orethrowes *F1*

84 **coward]** sluggard *F1*

85 **twenty]** fortie *F1*

92 **care-tun'd]** *hyphen, F1*

98 **be;]** *Q3–5, F1 (subs.)*; be, *Q1–2*

102 **and]** Losse *F1*

105 **calamity.]** *F1*; calamity, *Q1–5*

112 **White-beards]** *hyphen, Reed*

115 **crown;]** *Rowe*; crowne, *Q1–5*; Crowne *F1*

117 **double-fatal]** *hyphen, Warburton*

117 **yew]** *Hanmer*; ewe *Q1–2*; wo *Q3–5*; Eugh *F1*

118 **distaff-women]** *hyphen, F1*

130 **won]** *Q3–5*; woon *Q1, F1*; woonne *Q2*

131 **heart-blood]** *hyphen, F3*

134 **this!]** this Offence. *F1*

139 **wound]** hand *F1*

155 **God's]** Heauens *F1*

162 **antic]** *Pope*; antique *Q1–5, F1*

178 **wise men]** F1; wisemen Q1–5
178 **sit . . . their]** waile their present F1
182 **And . . . yourself.]** *om.* F1
188 **well.]** Q4–5, F1 *(subs.)*; well, Q1–3
197 **say.]** F1 *(subs.)*; say, Q1–5
203 **party]** Faction F1
204 **s.d. To Aumerle.]** *Theobald*
218 **s.d. Exeunt.]** F1

III.iii

III.iii] F1
Location: *Capell (after Theobald)*
o.s.d. with . . . Colors] F1
o.s.d. Attendants] F1
o.s.d. and forces] *Capell*
13 **with you]** F1
23 **Royally?]** F1; Royally, Q1–5
24 **king.]** King? F1
31 **lord]** F1; Lords Q1–5
31 **s.d. To Northumberland.]** *Rowe*
36 **On both]** vpon F1
41 **restor'd]** F1; restored Q1–5
44 **Englishmen]** Q2–5, F1; English men Q1
50 **s.d. Northumberland . . . Trumpet.]** *Malone (after Capell)*
59 **rain]** F1; raigne. Q1–2; raigne Q3–5
60 **waters—]** *Kittredge (after Rowe)*; water's Q1–5; Waters F1
61 **s.d. parle . . . flourish]** F1
61 **s.d. Richard . . . walls]** Enter on the Walls, Richard F1
61 **s.d. with . . . Salisbury]** F1 *(except for* with*)*
62 **See]** F1; *Bull.* See Q1–5 *(repeated s.p.)*
72 **s.d. To Northumberland.]** *Rowe (after l. 73); placed as in Hudson*
91 **stands]** is F1
100 **pasters']** *ed.*; pastors Q1–5, F1 *(a form representing Shakespeare's pronunciation; cf.* Timon of Athens, *IV.iii.12)*
101 **forbid]** F1; forbid: Q1–3; forbid, Q4–5
119 **a prince, is]** F1; princesse Q1–2; a Prince Q3–5
121 **thus . . . returns:]** *Rowe*; thus, . . . returnes, Q1; thus . . . returnes, Q2; thus: . . . returnes, Q3–4, F1; thus: . . . returnes Q5
126 **s.d. Northumberland . . . Bullingbrook.]** *Collier (subs.)*
127 **s.d. To Aumerle.]** *Rowe*
127 **We]** Q4–5, F1; *King* We Q1–3 *(repeated s.p.)*
171 **laugh]** mock F1
180 **court?]** F1; court, Q1–5
183 **s.d. Exeunt above.]** *Capell (subs.)*
186 **s.d. Enter . . . below.]** *Capell*
195 **s.d. touching his crown]** *Hudson (after Johnson)*
202 **hands]** Hand F1
206 **too]** Q4–5; to Q1–3, F1
209 **s.d. Flourish.]** F1
209 **s.d. Exeunt.]** Q4–5, F1

III.iv

III.iv] F1
Location: *Capell*
o.s.d. two Ladies] F1
3, 6, etc. **s.pp. 1. Lady.]** *Capell*; Lady Q1–5, F1
11 **joy]** *Rowe*; griefe Q1–5, F1
21 **weep, . . . good.]** F1; weepe; . . . good? Q1; weepe . . . good. Q2–5
23 **s.d. a Gardener . . . Men]** *ed. (from* F1 a Gardiner, and two Seruants); Gardeners Q1–5
26 **pins]** F1; pines Q1–5
28 **change;]** F1; change Q1–5
28 **s.d. Queen . . . retire.]** *Pope*
29 **young]** yon Q2–5; yond F1
29 **apricocks]** Q3–5, F1; Aphricokes Q1–2
34 **too]** F1; two Q1–5
40, 54, 67 **s.pp. 1. Man.]** *ed. (after Capell)*; Man. Q1–5; Ser. F1
48 **hath]** Q2–5, F1; htah Q1
50 **broad-spreading]** *hyphen,* F1
55 **seiz'd]** Q3–5, F1; ceasde Q1–2
57 **garden! We]** *Capell*; garden Q1–5; Garden, F1
59 **over-proud]** *hyphen,* Q2–5, F1
63 **duty]** Q2–3, F1; duety Q1, Q4–5; dutie. All F2
72 **s.d. Coming forward.]** *Capell (subs.)*
80 **Cam'st . . . tidings?]** Q2–5, F1; Canst . tidings Q1
84 **weigh'd.]** Q3–5 (weyde.); weyde Q1–2; weigh'd: F1
85 **lord's]** F1; Lo. Q1–5
101 **Pray God]** I would F1
101 **s.d. with Ladies]** *Pope (subs.)*

IV.i

IV.i] F1
Location: *Pope, Malone*
o.s.d. Aumerle . . . Westminster] F1; Aumerle and others Q4–5
o.s.d. and another Lord] *Capell*
o.s.d. to] as to the F1
o.s.d. Herald] *from* F1 Herauld, Officers, and Bagot
1 **s.d. Officers with]** *Halliwell (from* F1 *o.s.d.)*
3 **dost]** Q3–5; doest Q1–2; do'st F1
22 **him]** Q3–5, F1; them Q1; my Q2
28 **heart-blood]** *hyphen, Theobald*
40 **forged,]** Q4–5; forged Q1–3, F1
43 **Fitzwater]** F1; Fitzwaters Q1–5
48 **Seize]** Q3–5; ceaze Q1–2
52–9 **Another Lord. I . . . you.]** *om.* F1
54 **As]** *Johnson*; As it Q1–5
55 **sun to sun]** *Capell*; sinne to sinne Q1–5
61 **Aumerle]** Q2–5, F1; (Aumerle) Q1
62 **'Tis]** My Lord, / 'Tis F1
72 **dost]** Q2–5; doest Q1; do'st F1
76 **my]** Q3–5, F1; *om.* Q1; the Q2
83–4 **gage— . . . lies,]** *Collier (subs.)*; gage, . . . lies, Q1–5; Gage, . . . lyes: F1
101 **Bishop]** Q3–5, F1; B. Q1–2
106 **s.d. attended]** *Capell*
109 **thee]** Q2–5, F1; the Q1
112 **fourth . . . name]** of that Name the Fourth F1
114 **Marry]** F3; Mary Q1–5, F1
114 **God]** Heauen F1
115 **speak,]** F1; speake. Q1–2; speake: Q3–5
126 **deputy,]** Deputie F1
127 **planted many years,]** Q3–5, F1; planted. many yeares Q1; planted many yeares Q2
129 **forfend]** forbid F1
133 **God]** Heauen F1
145 **you]** Q2–5, F1; yon Q1
145 **raise]** reare F1
154–318 **May . . . fall.]** *om.* Q1–Q3 *(the copy-text for these lines is* F1; Q4–5 *present an inferior, probably reported, text)*
154 **commons']** common Q4–5
155 **s.p. Bull.]** *speech continued to Northumberland,* Q4–5
158 **here]** are heere. Q4–5
161 **look'd]** looke Q4–5
161 **s.d. Richard and York]** king Richard Q4–5
161 **s.d. with . . . sceptre]** *Capell (subs.)*
165 **knee.]** limbes? Q4–5
166 **tutor]** Q4–5; tuture F1
169 **sometimes]** Q4–5; sometime F1
180, 220 **Henry]** Harry Q4–5
181 **Give . . . cousin,]** *om.* Q4–5
183 **and]** Q4–5
183 **thine]** yours Q4–5
189 **griefs]** griefe Q4–5
199 **tend]** Q4–5; 'tend F1
201 **Ay, no, no ay;]** *ed.* (Ay . . . ay *Theobald*); I, no; no, I: F1; I, no no I; Q4–5
202 **no no]** Q4–5; no, no F1
210 **duteous oaths]** duties rites Q4–5
212 **manors]** Manners Q4; Mannors Q5
215 **are made]** that sweare Q4–5
222 **s.d. Presenting a paper.]** *Capell*
229 **follies? Gentle Northumberland,]** Folly, gentle Northumberland? Q4–5
237 **all . . . me]** *these two words om.* Q4–5
238 **bait]** bate Q4–5
241 **deliver'd]** deliuer Q4; deliuered Q5
245 **salt water]** Q4–5; salt-Water F1
250 **T' undeck]** To vndecke Q4–5
251 **and]** Q4–5; a F1
254 **haught insulting]** Q4–5; haught-insulting F1
255 **Nor no]** Q4–5; No, nor F1
260 **mockery]** Q4–5; Mockerie, F1
264 **word]** name Q4–5
267 **bankrout]** Q4–5; Bankrupt F1
268 **s.d. Exit an Attendant.]** *Capell*
276 **that]** the Q4–5
276 **and . . . read.]** *om.* Q4–5
277 **struck]** stroke Q4–5
281 **Thou . . . me!]** *om.* Q4–5
281 **this face]** this Q4–5
283–4 **Was . . . wink?]** *om.* Q4–5
285 **Is . . . which]** Was . . . that Q4–5
286 **That]** And Q4–5
288 **s.d. Dashes . . . ground.]** *Theobald*
289 **an]** a Q4–5
296 **manners]** Q4–5; manner F1
299 **There . . . substance;]** *om.* Q4–5
300 **For . . . bounty,]** *om.* Q4–5
304 **Shall . . . it?]** *om.* Q4–5
305 **cousin"?]** Coose, why? Q4–5
311 **have?]** haue it? Q4–5
313 **Then]** Why then Q4–5
318 **s.d. Exeunt . . . Guard.]** *Capell (subs.)*
319 **On Wednesday]** Q4–5, F1; Let it be so, and loe on wednesday Q1–3
320 **s.d. Carlisle]** Q2–5; Caleil Q1; F1 *om.* Manent . . . Aumerle.
326 **My lord]** *om.* Q3–5, F1

V.i

V.i] F1
Location: *Pope, Capell*
2 **ill-erected]** *hyphen,* F1
3 **whose]** Q2–5, F1; wohse Q1
6 **s.d. and Guard]** F1
10 **true-love]** *hyphen,* F1
14 **lodg'd]** F1; lodged Q1–5
17 **sudden.]** F1 *(subs.)*; sudden, Q1–5
25 **thrown]** stricken F1
41 **thee]** Q2–5, F1; the Q1 *(possibly the correct reading)*
43 **night,]** Q3–4, F1; night Q1–2; *om.* Q5
43 **quite]** quit F1
44 **tale]** fall F1
50 **s.d. and others]** *Capell*
64 **urg'd,]** F2; vrgde Q1–5, F1
64 **way]** *Pope*; way, Q1–5, F1
66 **men]** friends F1
72 **marriage—]** *Dyce (after* F1 Marriage;); marriage Q1; marriage, Q2–5
78 **wife]** Queene F1
84 **s.p. North.]** F1; King Q1–5
88 **than, near,]** *Ure*; than neere Q1; then neere Q2–5; then neere, F1

V.ii

V.ii] F1
Location: *Pope*
2 **off,]** F1; of Q1; *om.* Q2–5
11 **thee]** F1; the Q1–5
17 **thee! Welcome,]** *Theobald (from* F1 thee, welcom): the welcome Q1–5
18 **the one]** one F1
22 **Alack]** Q2–5; Alac Q1; Alas F1
28 **gentle]** *om.* F1
28 **Richard]** Q2–5, F1; Ric. Q1
30 **thrown]** Q2–5, F1; throwen Q1
41 **s.d. Enter Aumerle.]** Q4–5, F1 *(after l. 40,* F1*)*
52 **do . . . hold?]** Hold those lusts & Triumphs? F1
71 **s.d. He . . . it.]** Snatches it F1
72 **Treason]** Q4–5, F1; *Yorke* Treason Q1–3 *(repeated s.p.)*
74 **s.d. Enter a Servant.]** *Malone (after Capell)*
75 **God]** Heauen F1
77 **s.d. Exit Servant.]** *Capell*
81 **Aumerle]** Sonne F1
87 **s.d. His . . . exit.]** *ed. (after Wilson and Kittredge)*
94 **thee]** Q2–5, F1; the Q1
104 **thy]** Q2–5, F1; rhy Q1
104 **dost]** Q2–5; doest Q1; do'st F1
112 **Spur]** F1; Spur. Q1–5
116 **An']** *ed.*; An Q1; And Q2–5, F1
117 **s.d. Exeunt.]** *Rowe*; Exit F1

V.iii

V.iii] F1
Location: Theobald
o.s.d. the King] Bullingbrooke F1
o.s.d. Percy . . . Lords] F1
1 s.p. K. Hen.] Bul. F1 (throughout rest of play)
1 me] om. F1
4 God] heauen F1
21 years] dayes F1
28 s.d. Exeunt . . . Lords.] Capell (after Hanmer)
30 s.d. Kneels.] Rowe
35 after-love] hyphen, F2
36 I] Q2–5, F1
38 s.d. Aumerle . . . door.] Capell (subs.)
39 s.d. Within.] F1
41 s.d. Draws.] Johnson (subs.)
43 s.d. Within.] Capell
43 foolhardy] F1 (foole-hardy); foole, hardie Q1–5
45 s.d. King . . . door.] Johnson (subs.)
45 s.d. Enter York.] F1
50 treason] reason F1
51 pass'd] Dyce; past Q1–5, F1
68 An'] ed.; An Q1; And Q2–5, F1
72 life;] Theobald; life Q1–5; life, F1
74 s.d. Within.] F1
74 God's] heauens F1
75 shrill-voic'd] Q3–5, F1 (hyphen, F1); shril voice Q1–2
76 s.d. Within.] Capell
83 pardon,] F1; pardon Q1–5
86 s.d. Enter Duchess.] F1
91, 97, 98 s.dd. Kneels.] Rowe
93 walk] kneele F1
99 Ill . . . grace!] om. F1
102 mouth] Q2–5, F1; month Q1
106 still] shall F1
111 s.p. K. Hen.] Q2–5, F1 (subs.); yorke Q1
112 Say] But F1
119 King, say] F1 (subs.); King say, Q1–5
119 pardonne] Pardon'ne F1
131 God] heauen F1
135–6 With . . . him.] Pope; I pardon him with al my heart. Q1–5, F1
139 heels.] Q3; heeles, Q1–2, Q4–5; heeles: F1
144 cousin] Cosin too Q6
145 pray'd] F1; prayed Q1–5
146 God] heauen F1

V.iv

V.iv] Steevens
Location: Capell (after Theobald)
o.s.d. Enter . . . Servants.] F1 (subs.); Manet sir Pierce Exton, &c. Q1–5 (no scene break in Q1–5, F1)
3, 6 s.pp. 1. Man.] ed.; Man Q1–5; Ser. F1
7 wishtly] wistly Q3–5, F1
11 s.d. Exeunt.] Q4–5; Exit. F1

V.v

V.v.] Steevens; Scaena Quarta. F1
Location: Pope (subs.)
3 for because] Q2, Q4–5, F1; forbecause Q1, Q3
13–4 word . . . word] Faith . . . Faith F1
17 small] om. F1
18 ambition, . . . plot] F1; ambition . . . plot, Q1; ambition . . . plot Q2–5
22 cannot, . . . pride.] F1; cannot . . . pride, Q1–5
25 last—] Theobald (subs.); last Q1–2; last, Q3–5; last. F1
27 sit] Q3–5, F1; set Q1–2
38 be] am F1
41 s.d. The music plays.] placed as in Buell, Yale Shakespeare; after hear? l. 41, Q1–5; Musick F1 (after l. 38)
41 hear?] F1; heare. Q1–3; heare: Q4–5
46 check] heare F1
56 which] that F1
58 times and hours] Houres, and Times F1
73 travelling] Q3–5, F1; trauailling Q1–2
79 bestrid] F1; bestride Q1–5
83 he] he had F1
89 proud] Q2–5, F1; prond Q1
90 horse!] F1 (horse:); horse Q1–2; horse, Q3–5
91 aw'd] Q3–5, F1; awed Q1–2
94 Spurr'd, gall'd] Spur-gall'd F1
94 s.d. Enter . . . meat.] Enter Keeper with a Dish. F1
103 s.d. Beats the Keeper.] Rowe
104 s.d. Exton and Servants] F1
104 s.d. armed] Capell
106 s.d. Snatches . . . him.] Capell (subs., after Pope, Hanmer)
107 s.d. Kills another.] Pope
108 That] F1; Rich. That Q1–5 (repeated s.p.)
112 downward,] F1; downeward Q1–5
112 s.d. Dies.] Rowe
118 s.d. Exeunt.] Rowe; Exit. F1

V.vi

V.vi] Steevens; Scaena Quinta. F1
Location: Theobald (subs.)
o.s.d. Flourish.] F1
o.s.d. now King Henry] ed. (after Dyce)
o.s.d. with . . . Attendants] F1
2 consum'd] F1; consumed Q1–5
8 Salisbury, Spencer] F1 (Salsbury); Oxford, Salisbury Q1–5
12 s.d. Fitzwater] Q6; Fitzwaters Q1–5, F1
17 Fitzwater] Q6; Fitz. Q1–5; Fitzwaters F1
18 s.d. Harry Percy] ed., H. Percie. Q1–2; Henry Percy. Q3–5; Percy F1
18 s.d. and . . . Carlisle] F1 (and Carlisle)
29 s.d. Attendants bearing] Malone (after Capell)
43 thorough shades] Cambridge; through shades Q1; through the shade Q2–5, F1
47 what] that F1
51 mournings] mourning F1
52 s.d. Exeunt.] F1 (Exeunt / FINIS.); FINIS. Q1–6

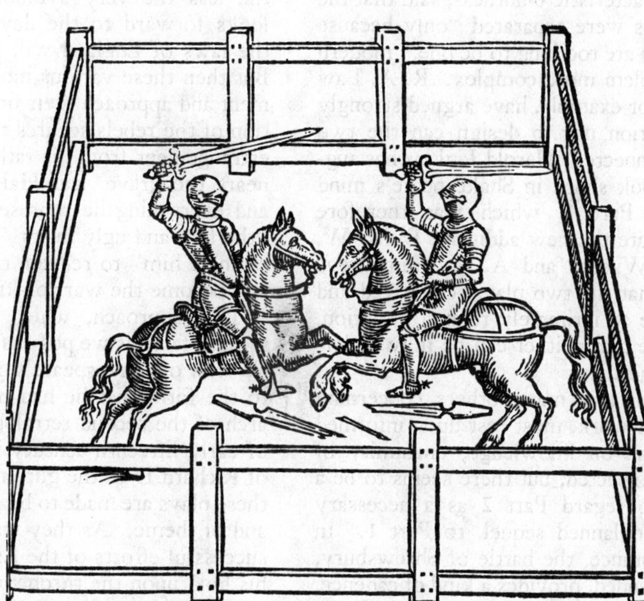

Knightly combat in the lists. From William Segar, *The Book of Honor and Arms* (1590), sig. M3. Two horsed knights in full armor here attack each other with broadswords. As the pair of shattered lances indicates, they have already run a-tilt, as the order of this kind of knightly combat dictated. A similar order of combat would have been followed in the abortive challenge scene in *Richard II*, I.iii. Mounted combat was, of course, impossible within the confines of an Elizabethan stage. Such combat is reported while in progress off-stage in *Pericles*, II.ii, and *The Two Noble Kinsmen*, V.iii. (*By permission of the Huntington Library, San Marino, California*)

Henry IV, Parts 1 and 2

The precise connection between the two parts of *Henry IV* has long been and is likely to remain a matter of dispute. Although Johnson, with characteristic bluntness, said that the plays were separated "only because they are too long to be one," modern scholars find the problem more complex. R. A. Law and M. A. Shaaber, for example, have argued strongly that neither in intention nor in design can the two parts be said to be connected; Harold Jenkins has suggested that Part 2 took shape in Shakespeare's mind while he composed Part 1, which was therefore altered to accommodate the new addition; E. M. W. Tillyard, J. Dover Wilson, and A. R. Humphreys have tried to show that the two plays, conceived and written as a unit, are so intimately related in action, characters, and theme that neither can be fully understood without the other.

Since this question, like many others concerning Shakespeare's life and work, must rest upon informed conjecture rather than on knowledge, unanimity of opinion is not to be expected, but there seems to be a growing tendency to regard Part 2 as a necessary conclusion, not an unplanned sequel, to Part 1. In terms of plot, for instance, the battle of Shrewsbury, with which Part 1 is ended, provides a kind of cadence, but it by no means tidies up the action. King Henry has checked but not destroyed his adversaries, and Hal has won his spurs; but with Northumberland and Archbishop Scroop at large there remains the danger of rebellion, and the Prince, despite his unexpected show of valor, has not resolved his father's doubts or achieved the "reformation" that he promised in Act I. Conversely, Part 2 picks up from its predecessor with no break in time or action: the scattered rebels gather force and make a new assault; the Prince, "exceeding weary" and lethargic after his exertions, continues to concern his ailing father; and Falstaff, laden with the spurious honors he had gained at Shrewsbury but none the less the very symbol of disorder and misrule, looks forward to the day of Hal's accession, when the laws of England will be at his "commandment." But then these various motifs begin to fall into alignment and approach their final resolution. The destruction of the rebels secures the long-sought peace, Hal's estrangement from his father is ended as the old king nears the grave, and Hal himself, rejecting Falstaff and everything he represents, at last breaks through "the foul and ugly mists / Of vapors that did seem to strangle him" to redeem the time as he had promised and become the warrior-king.

This approach, which does no violence to such meagre facts as we possess, enables us to take a synoptic view of Shakespeare's most impressive contribution to the form that he had made his own. In the long arch of the second tetralogy—that serial presentation of early fifteenth-century history from the deposition of Richard II to the glittering triumphs of Henry V—these plays are made to bear the central thrust of action and of theme. As they trace the slow and ultimately successful efforts of the Lancastrian usurper to secure his hold upon the throne, they also trace the preparation of his son for the duties he must learn to bear, and these two lines of plot converge to underscore the massive central theme: the sources, uses, and responsibilities of power.

As the history of their publication shows, Part 1 was by far the more successful. Entered in the Stationers' Register on February 25, 1598, it was printed anonymously as *The History of Henry the Fourth* in two editions (the first surviving as a fragment) before the year was out; and there were five more reprints before it appeared in the Folio of 1623 as *The First Part of Henry the Fourth*. This play was presumably the "Henry the 4." that Francis Meres, in 1598, had cited in his list of Shakespeare's tragedies. Part 2 has no such record of popularity. Following its entry in the Stationers' Register on August 23, 1600, and its quarto publication soon thereafter, *The Second Part of Henry the Fourth* was not reprinted until the Folio of 1623. Whether the notion of a sequel was suggested by the immediate success of the first play or had been conceived earlier, Parts 1 and 2 were no doubt close in composition, and they are generally assigned to 1596–97 and 1598 respectively.

Evidence of one species of revision may be discerned in Hal's allusion (Part 1, I.ii.41) to "my old lad of the castle" and in the speech-prefix "*Old*." (Part 2, I.ii.120), which show that Falstaff was originally called Oldcastle after the corresponding character in *The Famous Victories of Henry the Fifth*, an old play that was one of Shakespeare's sources. In what seems to be an addition to the epilogue of Part 2 (lines 26–34) Shakespeare is careful to dissociate the historical Sir John Oldcastle, Lord Cobham—a notorious Lollard who had been executed for heresy in 1417 and had come to be regarded as a martyr—from the fat knight of the play. Already, however, Shakespeare's distortion of the real Lord Cobham's character had been alluded to with disapproval in the prologue to *Sir John Oldcastle*, a collaboration by Drayton, Munday, Wilson, and Hathaway that was acted in 1599 and printed in 1600. "It is no pampered glutton we present," the authors of this rival play explained,

Nor aged counsellor to youthful sin,
But one whose virtue shone above the rest,
A valiant martyr and a virtuous peer.

It is likely that Shakespeare made the change from Oldcastle to Falstaff in deference to the powerful Sir William Brooke, seventh Baron Cobham, and that he changed the names Harvey and Russell (preserved in the quartos at Part 1, I.ii.162, and Part 2, II.ii o.s.d.) to Peto and Bardolph for a similar reason. The suggestion, made by A. E. Morgan and endorsed by Dover Wilson, that the Oldcastle scenes were originally written in verse has not gained wide support.

For the Henry IV plays Shakespeare supplemented Holinshed, his basic source, with certain collateral materials that he treated very freely. From the second (1587) edition of the *Chronicles* he got not only most of the details of Henry's troubled reign but also several errors (cited in the notes below) that show how closely he relied on Holinshed. As in his other history plays, however, the so-called facts were artfully or ruthlessly deployed to tighten up the action and reinforce the theme. An example is afforded by his treatment of the four main crises punctuating Henry's reign (1399–1413): the Abbot's conspiracy in 1399, the Percies' revolt in 1403, Archbishop Scroop's rebellion in 1405, and Northumberland's uprising in 1408. The first of these was used in *Richard II* (Act V) to show how the new king, unlike his predecessor, exemplified the regal use of power; and the other three, which provide the spine of plot for the two Henry IV plays, are so tightly squeezed together that they appear not widely spaced events but phases of a continuous and accelerating action. Historically, the battle of Shrewsbury, which forms the climax of Part 1, followed Henry's accession by four years and preceded his demise by ten, but in Shakespeare's rearrangement the King, remorseful over Richard's deposition, is found preparing for this battle when he had been but "twelve month" on the throne; the battle itself occurs a few months later; and Scroop's rebellion, with which Part 2 begins, is made to follow very soon, although in fact its date was 1405, eight years before the events with which Part 2 is closed. As for Northumberland's incursion of 1408, it is merely reported as a kind of epilogue to Scroop's abortive undertaking (Part 2, IV.iv.94–101).

As in Daniel's *Civil Wars* (1595 ff.), which Shakespeare almost surely knew and drew upon, these telescopings and distortions give shape and speed and moral meaning to Holinshed's inept narration; and just as they lead us to view Henry's reign as one of urgent and successive perils and as a drawn-out act of penance for the crime of usurpation, so Shakespeare's juggling with the ages and the motives of his characters serves the other, cognate theme of Prince Hal's preparation for the awful burden of the crown. King Henry, who is shown at the beginning as so "shaken" and so "wan with care" that his fatal illness in Part 2 occasions no surprise, was actually only thirty-six when he overcame his foes at Shrewsbury and ten years older when he died. Similarly, his "unthrifty son"—a lad of sixteen at Shrewsbury—is made coeval with Hotspur, who, though depicted as a splendid youth, was actually thirty-nine in 1403 and thus a generation older than the wayward prince to whom he stands, "amongst a grove the very straightest plant," as foil and rival. Among the many other readjustments of motive, circumstance, and chronology are the valor of Prince John at Shrewsbury, the remorseful Henry's hope of leading a crusade to the Holy Land to ease his guilty soul, and the brief but brilliant portraits of the uxorious Mortimer and his lovesick wife, the incisive Lady Percy, and the "extraordinary" Glendower, all of whom were worked up from the merest hints in Holinshed.

For the transformation of the madcap prince into a wise and splendid king, the favorite Elizabethan version of the Prodigal Son story, Shakespeare tapped a very old tradition. Launched shortly after Henry V's death in Tito Livio's quasi-official *Vita Henrici Quinti* (which was translated with additions in the early sixteenth century) and thereafter expanded and embellished, by Shakespeare's time the legend had worked its way into the chronicles and had perhaps inspired some now lost plays. Shakespeare's most important source for this material was *The Famous Victories of Henry the Fifth*, a crude comedy-history in rough-hewn prose which, though acted at least as early as 1588 and licensed six years later, survives only in an edition of 1598 that seems to be a corrupt reported version of a more substantial two-part play. This knockabout farce presents the basic plot and almost all the episodes that Shakespeare reconstructed for his vastly different purposes: the wild young prince who, in consort with a pack of low companions named Sir John Oldcastle, Tom, and Ned, commits a robbery at Gadshill, frequents an Eastcheap dive, and runs afoul the Lord Chief Justice before he is reconciled with his dying father, rejects his former cronies, and emerges as the valiant king who conquers France and takes its princess as his bride.

Shakespeare's use of this material in a work ostensibly devoted to the politics of Henry IV's reign was a stunning innovation, for by the introduction of a low-life comic element he achieved a counterpoint in action, style, and theme that is the glory of these plays. We move back and forth from court to tavern, from the cares of state to bawds and leaping-houses, from the urgency of great events that cut "athwart" the plans of kings and would-be kings to the sloth and heedless self-indulgence of Falstaff and his sleazy crew, from the gravity of a careworn ruler to the irreverent wit of Hal and his fat friend, from bold exploits and valor to chicanery and crime, from verse to prose, from honor to disgrace. This continual oscillation is the most conspicuous feature of these plays. Not all the earlier histories are so gravely uniform as *Richard II*, which contains no prose at all, but they are pitched upon a high and stately plane, and even when they do descend to common men—as in Horner's fight with Peter and in the Jack Cade scenes of *2 Henry VI*—the talk is anything but gay. In the Henry IV plays, however, the double theme of Henry's hard-fought rise to uncontested power and Hal's probation for the throne requires a universe of action that Shakespeare had not touched before. A single style or mood or plot could no longer serve his purpose. Here the brassy declamation and the facile patriotism of *Henry VI*, the dark, pervasive evil of *Richard III*, the rhetorical excesses of *King John*, and the univocal lyricism of *Richard II* yield to life itself, and as a result *Henry IV*, in its vitality and variety, is unmatched by any other history play. It is the triumph of the form.

For all their throbbing sense of life, their profusion of episode and character, and the pressures generated by their complex double plot, where each scene pushes hard upon the next, these plays are built with great precision. A persistent duality is the basic principle of organization. In structure this reveals itself most clearly through the artful alternation of politics and folly, the first centred in the King and the court, the second in the Prince and the tavern. Shuttling from scenes of state and grave affairs to scenes of bawdy wit and dissipation, Shakespeare weaves a rich design where each detail is set against its complementary and contrasting opposite so that they may sharpen one another. In the grouping of the characters the same device is seen. The King and Falstaff are aligned, for instance, through their relationship to Hal, the father standing for convention, duty, and control and his surrogate for disorder, crime, and license. Similarly, Hal and Hotspur form another pair of corresponding but contrasting types, and so do Hal and Henry (as representing youth and age), Falstaff and the Lord Chief Justice (who stand for "riot" and law), Hotspur and Falstaff (who show excess of "honor" and total lack of it).

Also, the comic and the serious elements, contrived not merely to provide relief or to effect changes in pace and style, bear upon and reinforce each other in many subtle ways. They are sometimes parallel, as when King Henry's scheme to meet the troubles in the north (Part 1, I.i) is matched by Hal's and Falstaff's preparations for the Gadshill escapade (Part 1, I.ii); sometimes antithetical, as when the Prince's lethargy and indecision (Part 1, I.ii) are set against the fiery Hotspur's zeal "to pluck bright Honor from the pale-fac'd moon" (Part 1, I.iii); sometimes in parodic contrast, as when Falstaff, with a joint-stool for a throne, a leaden dagger for a sceptre, and a pillow for his crown, plays the part of Prince Hal's father and chides the erring youth (Part 1, II.iv) just as King Henry, though in a very different style, reproves him later in a pair of crucial scenes (Part 1, III.ii; Part 2, IV.v). Sometimes the contrasting elements are almost juxtaposed, sometimes widely spaced. Within fifty lines of Vernon's stirring news about King Henry's forces as they advance upon the foe

All furnish'd, all in arms;
All plum'd like estridges that with the wind
Bated, like eagles having lately bath'd;
Glittering in golden coats, like images;
As full of spirit as the month of May
And gorgeous as the sun at midsummer;
Wanton as youthful goats, wild as young bulls,
(Part 1, IV.i.97–103)

we hear Falstaff describe his ragged troop as "a commodity of warm slaves" so disreputable that he cannot bring himself to march with them. The ceremonial parley before Shrewsbury (Part 1, V.i), where Hal, "to save the blood on either side," proposes a chivalric encounter between Hotspur and himself, is ended with Falstaff left alone upon the stage to jeer at honor as a "mere scutcheon"; and the heroic feats in battle, capped by the Prince's valediction to the "great heart" he has slain, yield to the sight of Falstaff stabbing Hotspur's corpse and claiming credit for the crime. A much greater interval lies between the rebels' high-flown quarrel about the booty they expect to share when the kingdom is divided (Part 1, II.i) and Falstaff's fracas with the Hostess over unpaid bills (Part 2, II.i), or Hotspur's farewell to his lively Kate (Part 1, II.i) and Falstaff's to his drunken Doll (Part 2, II.iv) as they go off to war; but even such widely separated complementary scenes, reverberating one against the other, contribute to the polyphonic structure.

These various techniques of juxtaposition, inversion, and antithesis enable us to watch the action from many points of view. As we first see Henry in Act I, for instance, he is every inch a king. When he talks about his hope

To chase these pagans in those holy fields,
Over whose acres walk'd those blessed feet
Which fourteen hundred years ago were nail'd
For our advantage on the bitter cross, (I.i.24–27)

he speaks in the splendid, spacious verse appropriate to his station; and he maintains but subtly modulates this style in discussing with his "gentle cousin Westmerland" and with Sir Walter Blunt, "a dear, a true industrious friend," the "heavy news" from Wales. But he will not tolerate "the moody frontier of a servant brow," and he checks young Hotspur's insubordination in words so clipped that they admit of no reply:

But, sirrah, henceforth
Let me not hear you speak of Mortimer.
Send me your prisoners with the speediest means,
Or you shall hear in such a kind from me
As will displease you. My Lord Northumberland:
We license your departure with your son.
Send us your prisoners, or you will hear of it.
(I.iii.118–24)

Viewed from Eastcheap, however, Henry is a different man: the querulous, demanding father, the formalist, and the very emblem of an ethic based on duty, honor, and convention that Hal and Falstaff flout. To enlarge our vision further, Hotspur sees him as "this thorn, this canker," and "this vile politician" whose destruction is a point of honor, whereas the King himself, sleepless with the cares of state, soliloquizes on his office as a burden he can scarcely bear (Part 2, III.i). All these partial truths converge when Henry, with the candor of a dying man, assesses his career (Part 2, IV.v), and so our knowledge of this able, ambitious, remorseful, careworn ruler is finally brought into focus.

Hal and Hotspur are subjected to the same incessant contrapuntal presentation. To his father, Hal is the "hot vengeance, and the rod of heaven," sent to punish his "mistreadings"; to Falstaff, the "sweet wag" who, as king, will not let "resolution" be "fubb'd as it is with the rusty curb of old father antic the law"; to Hotspur, a "sword-and-buckler Prince of Wales" whom he would like to poison with a pot of ale; and to himself, a man resolved to "pay the debt I never promised" by shaking off his "loose behavior" and "redeeming time when men think least I will." Opposed to him—in valor and esteem—stands Hotspur, and he provides a gauge whereby to test the shabby prince. Hotspur is introduced (in Henry's words) as "the theme of honor's tongue," and he goes far to justify the appellation. One of Shakespeare's most engaging characters, he is generous, brave, and witty, and so superbly vocal—as when he explains his conduct to the King (Part 1, I.iii) or twits Glendower's pretensions (Part 1, III.i)—that, like Mercutio in *Romeo and Juliet*, he dominates each scene that he is in. But as the play proceeds, we, instructed by his own behavior no less than by what others say of him, begin to modify our view. A willing victim of his own emotions, he is, as his own father says, "a wasp-stung and impatient fool." So much incensed at Henry that his anger turns to rage and his vaunted honor to gesticulation, he is as willing to carve up the realm as to cavil on the ninth part of a hair. Hal, as always, understands the situation, and so, as he assures the anxious King, the day will come

That this same child of honor and renown,
This gallant Hotspur, this all-praised knight,
And your unthought-of Harry chance to meet.
For every honor sitting on his helm,
Would they were multitudes, and on my head
My shames redoubled! For the time will come
That I shall make this northren youth exchange
His glorious deeds for my indignities.
(Part 1, III.ii.139–46)

The fact is, of course, that Hotspur, for all his bravado, wit, and charm, reveals a lack of mental poise. He is a danger to the state and to the heir apparent, and therefore his destruction at the hands of Hal—the seeming wastrel whose temperance, courage, and icy self-control will fit him for the crown that he was born to wear—is more than just a turn of plot: it is a judgment on two basic types of men. Hotspur is so dazzling and bewitching that we endorse Hal's tribute to his fallen foe (Part 1, V.iv) and Kate's assessment of her "wondrous him" (Part 2, II.iii), but we realize, to our sorrow, that the safety of the realm required his death and that he was vanquished by a better man.

As for Falstaff, that authentic triumph of the literary imagination, Hazlitt may have thought of him when he remarked, "If we wish to see the force of human genius, we should read Shakespeare. If we wish to see the insignificance of human learning, we may study his commentators." Falstaff is so various, so equivocal, and so overwhelming that he would seem to baffle judgment, but since the eighteenth century he has probably prompted more discussion than anyone but Hamlet—and, like Hamlet's, his mystery is secure. An amalgam of the Vice of the morality play, the braggart soldier of Roman comedy, the witty parasite, and the Fool as liberator from convention and restraint, he has a complex genealogy, but he transcends the jargon and the categories of the literary historian as easily as he gulls poor Justice Shallow. Although he is a sluggard, liar, glutton, lecher, knave, and cheat, he is so superbly funny—"not only witty in myself, but the cause that wit is in other men" (Part 2, I.ii.9–10)—that as he lumbers through these plays with his tatterdemalion crew of ruffians, whores, and sycophants he seems to shed a flood of light.

One ingredient of his charm is his dazzling intellect. A virtuoso in the arts of language, he can hardly speak a line that does not, like all great literature, sharpen our response and jolt us into new perceptions. He throws us from our stance and makes us look at things afresh. When he trades indecent puns with Hal, parodies the bombast circumstance of old-fashioned drama, makes complicated fun of Bardolph's nose, cites Scripture for his purpose, or mocks the bumbling style of Justice Shallow he shows that language is a tool of intellect which he uses with complete control. He never muffles his own tone of voice or blunts the cutting edge of wit, and even at his most outrageous he continues to instruct, astonish, and delight us by the thrust and vigor of his mind and by his uncanny way with words.

However, he is more than merely witty. His verbal skill is but a function of his complex comic vision, and this vision, if it can be defined at all, may perhaps be said to rest upon a tonic or corrosive disrespect not only for the slogans and the solemn plausibilities to which most men yield assent but also for the values—moral, social, and political—whereby most men organize experience and whereon the social structure rests. Therein lie his fascination and his peril. If Falstaff, incapable of intellectual torpor and indifferent to the curbs that shackle most of us, represents the lawless ease and freedom that every man desires and most men never find, he also represents destruction. An example of the way that Shakespeare forces us to trade our routine, clear-cut misconceptions for the interlocking ambiguities of knowledge, he is both wholesome and malign: he amuses and instructs us by exposing fraud and folly, but he appalls us by annihilating all sense of order. He flouts not merely the civilities, but man's most rooted need—that responsible commitment to his own ideals which gives shape and purpose to existence.

Like Hotspur, then, for a very different reason, Falstaff is a threat that Hal must meet and overcome before he earns the right to power, and therefore his rejection, so necessary and painful, is the moral climax of these plays. When the dying Henry, just before his final reconciliation with his son, foretold what kind of king he feared the Prince would be if Falstaff were his guide, he underscored the central fact:

> Harry the Fift is crown'd! Up, vanity!
> Down, royal state! All you sage counsellors,
> hence! . . .
> For the fift Harry from curb'd license plucks
> The muzzle of restraint, and the wild dog
> Shall flesh his tooth on every innocent.
> O my poor kingdom, sick with civil blows!
> When that my care could not withhold thy riots,
> What wilt thou do when riot is thy care?
> O, thou wilt be a wilderness again,
> Peopled with wolves, thy old inhabitants!
> (Part 2, IV.v.119–20, 130–37)

Hal, of course, had seen the danger too. His "reformation" would perhaps have greater force if he himself had not foretold it from the start (Part 1, I.ii.195–217), but even though we know that Falstaff, "the tutor and the feeder of my riots," is just one aspect of the Prince's test and preparation for the crown, his rejection wrings our heart. It is the price that greatness pays for power.

Herschel Baker

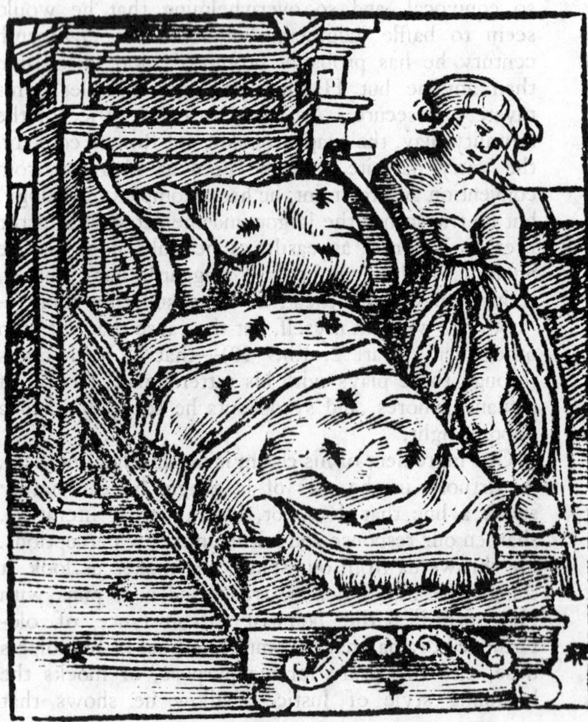

A bed full of fleas. From *Hortus Sanitatis* (1563). In an age when personal cleanliness was not stressed (in fact bathing was considered dangerous to health), travellers were often confronted with the situation in which the good woman in this picture finds herself. As the Second Carrier complains in *1 Henry IV*, after a night in the inn at Rochester, it is "the most villainous house in all London road for fleas," and the First Carrier agrees that "ne'er a king christen could be better bit than I have been since the first cock" (II.i.14–18). *(The Folger Shakespeare Library)*

The First Part of Henry the Fourth

[DRAMATIS PERSONAE

KING HENRY THE FOURTH
HENRY, PRINCE OF WALES } *sons to the King*
PRINCE JOHN OF LANCASTER } *sons to the King*
EARL OF WESTMERLAND
SIR WALTER BLUNT
THOMAS PERCY, *Earl of Worcester*
HENRY PERCY, *Earl of Northumberland*
HENRY PERCY, *surnamed* HOTSPUR, *his son*
EDMUND MORTIMER, *Earl of March*
RICHARD SCROOP, *Archbishop of York*
ARCHIBALD, *Earl of Douglas*
OWEN GLENDOWER
SIR RICHARD VERNON
SIR JOHN FALSTAFF
SIR MICHAEL, *of the household of the Archbishop of York*
EDWARD POINS, *gentleman-in-waiting to Prince Henry*
GADSHILL
PETO
BARDOLPH

LADY PERCY, *wife to Hotspur, and sister to Mortimer*
LADY MORTIMER, *daughter to Glendower, and wife to Mortimer*
MISTRESS QUICKLY, *hostess of the Boar's Head Tavern in Eastcheap*
LORDS, OFFICERS, SHERIFF, VINTNER, CHAMBERLAIN, OSTLER, DRAWERS, *two* CARRIERS, TRAVELLERS, *and* ATTENDANTS

SCENE: *England and Wales*]

[ACT I, SCENE I]

Enter the KING [HENRY], LORD JOHN OF LANCASTER, EARL OF WESTMERLAND, [SIR WALTER BLUNT,] *with others.*

King. So shaken as we are, so wan with care,
Find we a time for frighted peace to pant
And breathe short-winded accents of new broils
To be commenc'd in stronds afar remote.
No more the thirsty entrance of this soil
Shall daub her lips with her own children's blood,
No more shall trenching war channel her fields,
Nor bruise her flow'rets with the armed hoofs
Of hostile paces. Those opposed eyes,
Which, like the meteors of a troubled heaven,
All of one nature, of one substance bred,
Did lately meet in the intestine shock
And furious close of civil butchery,
Shall now, in mutual well-beseeming ranks,
March all one way and be no more oppos'd
Against acquaintance, kindred, and allies.
The edge of war, like an ill-sheathed knife,
No more shall cut his master. Therefore, friends,
As far as to the sepulchre of Christ—
Whose soldier now, under whose blessed cross
We are impressed and engag'd to fight—
Forthwith a power of English shall we levy,
Whose arms were moulded in their mother's womb,
To chase these pagans in those holy fields,
Over whose acres walk'd those blessed feet
Which fourteen hundred years ago were nail'd
For our advantage on the bitter cross.
But this our purpose now is twelve month old,
And bootless 'tis to tell you we will go;
Therefore we meet not now. Then let me hear
Of you, my gentle cousin Westmerland,
What yesternight our Council did decree
In forwarding this dear expedience.

West. My liege, this haste was hot in question.

Words and passages enclosed in square brackets in the text above are either emendations of the copy-text or additions to it. The Textual Notes immediately following the play cite the earliest authority for every such change or insertion and supply the reading of the copy-text wherever it is emended in this edition.

I.i. Location: London. The palace.
2. Find we: let us find. **3. accents:** words.
3–4. new . . . remote. At the close of *Richard II* (V.vi.49–50) the newly crowned Henry IV, remorseful for the death of Richard, had promised to "make a voyage to the Holy Land / To wash this blood off from my guilty hand." **4. stronds:** strands, shores.
5. thirsty entrance: parched mouth. **7. trenching:** cutting.
8–9. armed . . . paces: tread of armed horses in combat.
12. intestine: internal. **13. close:** hand-to-hand combat.
14. mutual: united for a common purpose. **18. his:** its.
21. impressed: conscripted. **engag'd:** pledged.
22. power: force, army.
28. twelve month old. Actually, two years separated Richard II's death (1400) and the battle of Homildon (Shakespeare's Holmedon), news of which reaches the King at lines 52 ff.
29. bootless: useless.
30. Therefore . . . now: it is not for this purpose that we meet now.
31. gentle cousin: noble kinsman.
33. dear expedience: urgent undertaking.
34. liege: sovereign. **hot in question:** under urgent discussion.

And many limits of the charge set down
But yesternight, when all athwart there came
A post from Wales loaden with heavy news,
Whose worst was that the noble Mortimer,
Leading the men of [Herfordshire] to fight
Against the irregular and wild Glendower,
Was by the rude hands of that Welshman taken,
A thousand of his people butchered,
Upon whose dead corpse' there was such misuse,
Such beastly shameless transformation,
By those Welshwomen done as may not be
Without much shame retold or spoken of.
  King. It seems then that the tidings of this broil
Brake off our business for the Holy Land.
  West. This match'd with other did, my gracious lord,
For more uneven and unwelcome news
Came from the north, and thus it did import:
On Holy-rood day, the gallant Hotspur there,
Young Harry Percy, and brave Archibald,
That ever-valiant and approved Scot,
At Holmedon met,
Where they did spend a sad and bloody hour,
As by discharge of their artillery
And shape of likelihood the news was told;
For he that brought them, in the very heat
And pride of their contention did take horse,
Uncertain of the issue any way.
  King. Here is [a] dear, a true industrious friend,
Sir Walter Blunt, new lighted from his horse,
Stain'd with the variation of each soil
Betwixt that Holmedon and this seat of ours;
And he hath brought us smooth and welcome news.
The Earl of Douglas is discomfited:
Ten thousand bold Scots, two and twenty knights,
Balk'd in their own blood, did Sir Walter see
On Holmedon's plains. Of prisoners, Hotspur took
Mordake Earl of Fife and eldest son
To beaten Douglas, and the Earl of Athol,
Of Murray, Angus, and Menteith.
And is not this an honorable spoil?
A gallant prize? Ha, cousin, is it not?
  West. In faith,
It is a conquest for a prince to boast of.
  King. Yea, there thou mak'st me sad, and mak'st me sin
In envy that my Lord Northumberland
Should be the father to so blest a son—
A son who is the theme of honor's tongue,
Amongst a grove the very straightest plant,
Who is sweet Fortune's minion and her pride,
Whilst I, by looking on the praise of him,
See riot and dishonor stain the brow
Of my young Harry. O that it could be prov'd
That some night-tripping fairy had exchang'd
In cradle-clothes our children where they lay,
And call'd mine Percy, his Plantagenet!
Then would I have his Harry and he mine.
But let him from my thoughts. What think you, coz,
Of this young Percy's pride? The prisoners
Which he in this adventure hath surpris'd
To his own use he keeps, and sends me word
I shall have none but Mordake Earl of Fife.
  West. This is his uncle's teaching; this is Worcester,
Malevolent to you in all aspects,
Which makes him prune himself, and bristle up
The crest of youth against your dignity.
  King. But I have sent for him to answer this;
And for this cause a while we must neglect
Our holy purpose to Jerusalem.
Cousin, on Wednesday next our Council we
Will hold at Windsor, so inform the lords.
But come yourself with speed to us again,
For more is to be said and to be done
Than out of anger can be uttered.
  West. I will, my liege. *Exeunt.*

35. **limits . . . down:** specific military responsibilities assigned.
36. **athwart:** across (the plans).
37. **post:** messenger. **heavy:** sad, depressing.
38. **Mortimer.** Shakespeare, like Holinshed, had trouble keeping the Mortimers straight. By marrying (1368) Philippa, daughter of Lionel, Duke of Clarence, third son of Edward III, Edmund Mortimer, third Earl of March, raised his family to a place of great importance. In 1385 his son Roger, fourth Earl of March, was recognized by Richard II as heir presumptive to the throne. In the present scene Shakespeare confuses Glendower's captive Sir Edmund Mortimer (1376–?1409), Roger's younger brother, with Roger's son Edmund (1391–1425), fifth and last Earl of March, who had been named heir presumptive by Richard II in 1398 after the death of the fourth earl. See the genealogical table, pp. 630–31.
40. **irregular:** i.e. because he resorted to guerrilla warfare.
43. **corpse':** corpses.
44. **transformation:** mutilation. According to Holinshed (Bullough, IV, 182), "the shamefull villanie used by the Welsh-women towards the dead carcasses [of the English], was such, as honest eares would be ashamed to heare, and continent toongs to speake thereof."
48. **Brake:** broke.
49. **other:** i.e. other tidings. Actually, the battle at Homildon (or Humbleton) Hill in Northumberland (September 1402) occurred three months after Mortimer's capture by Glendower.
50. **uneven:** disturbing.
52. **Holy-rood day:** September 14.
53. **Young Harry Percy.** Although here and elsewhere (for example, III.ii.103) Shakespeare implies that Sir Henry Percy, eldest son of the first Earl of Northumberland, was a high-spirited youth, he was in fact thirty-eight years old in 1402, twenty-three years the senior of Prince Hal, his rival and presumed contemporary in this play. **brave Archibald:** Archibald Douglas (1369?–1424), fourth Earl of Douglas and first Duke of Touraine, a Scot noted for his valor.
58. **shape of likelihood:** apparent probability.
59. **them:** i.e. the news. 60. **pride:** height.
62. **true industrious:** truly devoted.
69. **Balk'd:** heaped up in balks or ridges.
71. **Mordake.** Murdac Stewart, son of Robert Stewart, first Earl of Albany and "governor" of Scotland. Shakespeare's erroneously calling him the son of Archibald Douglas results from the faulty punctuation in Holinshed (Bullough, IV, 183): "of prisoners among other were these, Mordacke earle of Fife, son to the governour Archembald earle Dowglas, which in the fight lost one of his eies, Thomas erle of Murrey, Robert earle of Angus (and as some writers have) the earles of Atholl & Menteith, with five hundred other of meaner degrees." 82. **plant:** tree. 83. **minion:** darling.
87. **Some . . . fairy.** It was popularly believed that defective children were "changelings" left by fairies in exchange for babies whom they had abducted.
89. **Plantagenet:** family name of the English royal family. See note to *1 Henry VI*, II.iv o.s.d.
91. **from:** go from. **coz:** cousin, i.e. kinsman.
93. **surpris'd:** captured.
94. **To . . . use:** i.e. for purpose of ransom.
95. **none but Mordake.** Although Hotspur could legitimately hold the other prisoners he had taken, the law of arms required that Murdac, being of royal blood, be surrendered to the King.
97. **Malevolent . . . aspects:** i.e. habitually hostile (a metaphor from astrology).
98. **Which:** i.e. Worcester's "teaching." **prune:** preen, trim (a term from falconry). 101. **neglect:** put aside.
107. **uttered:** said in public.

[Scene II]

Enter Prince of Wales *and* Sir John Falstaff.

Fal. Now, Hal, what time of day is it, lad?

Prince. Thou art so fat-witted with drinking of old sack, and unbuttoning thee after supper, and sleeping upon benches after noon, that thou hast forgotten to demand that truly which thou wouldest truly know. What a devil hast thou to do with the time of the day? unless hours were cups of sack, and minutes capons, and clocks the tongues of bawds, and dials the signs of leaping-houses, and the blessed sun himself a fair hot wench in flame-color'd taffata; I see no reason why thou shouldst be so superfluous to demand the time of the day.

Fal. Indeed you come near me now, Hal, for we that take purses go by the moon and the seven stars, and not by Phoebus, he, "that wand'ring knight so fair." And I prithee, sweet wag, when thou art a king, as, God save thy Grace—Majesty I should say, for grace thou wilt have none—

Prince. What, none?

Fal. No, by my troth, not so much as will serve to be prologue to an egg and butter.

Prince. Well, how then? Come, roundly, roundly.

Fal. Marry, then, sweet wag, when thou art king, let not us that are squires of the night's body be call'd thieves of the day's beauty. Let us be Diana's foresters, gentlemen of the shade, minions of the moon, and let men say we be men of good government, being govern'd, as the sea is, by our noble and chaste mistress the moon, under whose countenance we steal.

Prince. Thou sayest well, and it holds well too, for the fortune of us that are the moon's men doth ebb and flow like the sea, being govern'd, as the sea is, by the moon. As, for proof, now: a purse of gold most resolutely snatch'd on Monday night and most dissolutely spent on Tuesday morning; got with swearing "Lay by," and spent with crying "Bring in"; now in as low an ebb as the foot of the ladder, and by and by in as high a flow as the ridge of the gallows.

Fal. By the Lord, thou say'st true, lad. And is not my hostess of the tavern a most sweet wench?

Prince. As the honey of Hybla, my old lad of the castle. And is not a buff jerkin a most sweet robe of durance?

Fal. How now, how now, mad wag? What, in thy quips and thy quiddities? What a plague have I to do with a buff jerkin?

Prince. Why, what a pox have I to do with my hostess of the tavern?

Fal. Well, thou hast call'd her to a reckoning many a time and oft.

Prince. Did I ever call for thee to pay thy part?

Fal. No, I'll give thee thy due, thou hast paid all there.

Prince. Yea, and elsewhere, so far as my coin would stretch, and where it would not, I have us'd my credit.

Fal. Yea, and so us'd it that, were it not here apparent that thou art heir apparent—But I prithee, sweet wag, shall there be gallows standing in England when thou art king? and resolution thus fubb'd as it is with the rusty curb of old father antic the law? Do not thou, when thou art king, hang a thief.

Prince. No, thou shalt.

Fal. Shall I? O rare! By the Lord, I'll be a brave judge.

Prince. Thou judgest false already. I mean thou shalt have the hanging of the thieves, and so become a rare hangman.

Fal. Well, Hal, well, and in some sort it jumps with my humor as well as waiting in the court, I can tell you.

Prince. For obtaining of suits?

Fal. Yea, for obtaining of suits, whereof the hangman hath no lean wardrobe. 'Sblood, I am as melancholy as a gib cat or a lugg'd bear.

Prince. Or an old lion, or a lover's lute.

Fal. Yea, or the drone of a Lincolnshire bagpipe.

Prince. What sayest thou to a hare, or the melancholy of Moor-ditch?

Fal. Thou hast the most unsavory [similes] and art indeed the most comparative, rascalliest, sweet young prince. But, Hal, I prithee trouble me no more with vanity; I would to God thou and I knew where a commodity of good names were to be bought. An old lord of the Council rated me the other day in the street about you, sir, but I mark'd him not, and yet he talk'd very wisely, but I regarded him not, and yet he talk'd wisely, and in the street too.

Prince. Thou didst well, for wisdom cries out in the streets, and no man regards it.

I.ii. Location: London. Prince Henry's house.
3. sack: dry Spanish wine. **8. dials:** clocks.
9. leaping-houses: brothels.
10. taffata: taffeta (often worn by prostitutes).
14. seven stars: constellation of the Pleiades.
15–16. Phoebus . . . fair. Falstaff identifies Phoebus, the sun-god or knight of the sun, with the knight errant ("wand'ring knight") of a popular romance. **16. wag:** rogue.
18. grace: virtue, sense of propriety. **20. troth:** faith.
21. prologue . . . butter: i.e. a short grace before a skimpy meal.
22. roundly: directly.
23. Marry: indeed (originally the name of the Virgin Mary used as an oath).
25–26. Diana's foresters: i.e. thieves (Diana being the moon-goddess).
26. minions: darlings. **27. government:** behavior.
29. countenance: (1) face; (2) protection, patronage.
30. holds well: is apt. **36. Lay by:** hands up.
37. ladder: i.e. to the gallows.
41. Hybla: region of Sicily noted for its honey.
41–42. old . . . castle: (1) cant phrase for roisterer; (2) an allusion to Sir John Oldcastle, the name that Shakespeare originally intended for Falstaff (see the introduction).
42. buff jerkin: leather jacket (often worn by jailers).
42–43. of durance: (1) durable, serviceable; (2) of imprisonment.
45. quiddities: subtle jests. **49. reckoning:** settling of the bill.
60. resolution: i.e. the valor of thieves. **fubb'd:** fobbed, thwarted.
61. antic: clown, buffoon. **64. brave:** fine.
69–70. in . . . humor: in some ways it suits my temperament.
71. suits: petitions (but Falstaff plays on another sense: the clothing of an executed person that was claimed by the hangman).
73. 'Sblood: by God's (Christ's) blood.
74. gib cat: tomcat. **lugg'd:** led (as with a chain).
77. hare: i.e. because of its melancholy appearance.
78. Moor-ditch: open sewer or drainage ditch outside the walls of London.
80. comparative: i.e. given to (unflattering) comparisons.
83. commodity: supply. **84. rated:** berated.
88–89. wisdom . . . it. An echo of Proverbs 1:23, 24.

Fal. O, thou hast damnable iteration, and art indeed able to corrupt a saint. Thou hast done much harm upon me, Hal, God forgive thee for it! Before I knew thee, Hal, I knew nothing, and now am I, if a man should speak truly, little better than one of the wicked. I must give over this life, and I will give it over. By the Lord, and I do not, I am a villain, I'll be damn'd for never a king's son in Christendom.

Prince. Where shall we take a purse to-morrow, Jack?

Fal. 'Zounds, where thou wilt, lad, I'll make one, an' I do not, call me villain and baffle me.

Prince. I see a good amendment of life in thee, from praying to purse-taking.

Fal. Why, Hal, 'tis my vocation, Hal, 'tis no sin for a man to labor in his vocation.

Enter Poins.

Poins! Now shall we know if Gadshill have set a match. O, if men were to be sav'd by merit, what hole in hell were hot enough for him? This is the most omnipotent villain that ever cried "Stand!" to a true man.

Prince. Good morrow, Ned.

Poins. Good morrow, sweet Hal. What says Monsieur Remorse? What says Sir John Sack and Sugar? Jack, how agrees the devil and thee about thy soul that thou soldest him on Good Friday last, for a cup of Madeira and a cold capon's leg?

Prince. Sir John stands to his word, the devil shall have his bargain, for he was never yet a breaker of proverbs. He will give the devil his due.

Poins. Then art thou damn'd for keeping thy word with the devil.

Prince. Else he had been damn'd for cozening the devil.

Poins. But, my lads, my lads, to-morrow morning by four a' clock early, at Gadshill, there are pilgrims going to Canterbury with rich offerings, and traders riding to London with fat purses. I have vizards for you all; you have horses for yourselves. Gadshill lies to-night in Rochester. I have bespoke supper to-morrow night in Eastcheap. We may do it as secure as sleep. If you will go, I will stuff your purses full of crowns; if you will not, tarry at home and be hang'd.

Fal. Hear ye, Yedward, if I tarry at home and go not, I'll hang you for going.

Poins. You will, chops?

Fal. Hal, wilt thou make one?

Prince. Who, I rob? I a thief? Not I, by my faith.

Fal. There's neither honesty, manhood, nor good fellowship in thee, nor thou cam'st not of the blood royal, if thou darest not stand for ten shillings.

Prince. Well then, once in my days I'll be a madcap.

Fal. Why, that's well said.

Prince. Well, come what will, I'll tarry at home.

Fal. By the Lord, I'll be a traitor then, when thou art king.

Prince. I care not.

Poins. Sir John, I prithee leave the Prince and me alone, I will lay him down such reasons for this adventure that he shall go.

Fal. Well, God give thee the spirit of persuasion and him the ears of profiting, that what thou speakest may move and what he hears may be believ'd, that the true prince may (for recreation sake) prove a false thief, for the poor abuses of the time want countenance. Farewell, you shall find me in Eastcheap.

Prince. Farewell, the latter spring! Farewell, All-hallown summer! [*Exit Falstaff.*]

Poins. Now, my good sweet honey lord, ride with us to-morrow. I have a jest to execute that I cannot manage alone. Falstaff, [Bardolph, Peto], and Gadshill shall rob those men that we have already waylaid; yourself and I will not be there; and when they have the booty, if you and I do not rob them, cut this head off from my shoulders.

Prince. How shall we part with them in setting forth?

Poins. Why, we will set forth before or after them and appoint them a place of meeting, wherein it is at our pleasure to fail; and then will they adventure upon the exploit themselves, which they shall have no sooner achiev'd but we'll set upon them.

Prince. Yea, but 'tis like that they will know us by our horses, by our habits, and by every other appointment to be ourselves.

Poins. Tut, our horses they shall not see—I'll tie them in the wood; our vizards we will change after we leave them; and, sirrah, I have cases of buckrom for the nonce, to immask our noted outward garments.

Prince. Yea, but I doubt they will be too hard for us.

Poins. Well, for two of them, I know them to be as true-bred cowards as ever turn'd back; and for the third, if he fight longer than he sees reason, I'll forswear arms. The virtue of this jest will be the incomprehensible lies that this same fat rogue will tell

90. iteration: i.e. trick of repeating Biblical texts (with a satirical twist). **96. and:** if.
100. 'Zounds: by God's (Christ's) wounds. **make one:** be one of the party.
101. an': and, i.e. if. **baffle:** disgrace (literally, deprive a perjured knight of his rank).
106. Gadshill: the name of one of the thieves.
106–7. set a match: planned a robbery. **109. true:** honest.
115. Good Friday: i.e. the most solemn of fast days.
117. stands to: keeps. **119. his due:** i.e. Falstaff's soul.
122. cozening: cheating.
125. Gadshill: hill near Rochester on the road from London to Canterbury, notorious for its robberies.
128. vizards: masks. **129. lies:** lodges.
130. Eastcheap: thoroughfare in London, site of the tavern of line 40.
136. chops: fat-face.
141. royal. With a pun on *royal* = a gold coin worth ten shillings. **stand for:** (1) make a fight for; (2) be worth.
156. want countenance: lack encouragement (from men of rank like the Prince).
158. latter spring: i.e. old man with youthful impulses.
158–59. All-hallown summer: i.e. Indian summer. All-hallows (or All Saints') Day is November 1.
163–64. waylaid: set an ambush for. **175. habits:** clothes.
175–76. appointment: accoutrement.
179. sirrah: customarily a form of address to an inferior; here, a term of comradeship.
179–80. cases . . . nonce: garments of buckram (stiff, coarse cloth) suitable for the occasion. **180. noted:** well-known.
181. doubt: fear. **too hard:** i.e. too many.

us when we meet at supper, how thirty at least he fought with, what wards, what blows, what extremities he endur'd, and in the reproof of this lives the jest.

Prince. Well, I'll go with thee. Provide us all things necessary, and meet me to-morrow night in Eastcheap, there I'll sup. Farewell.

Poins. Farewell, my lord. *Exit Poins.*

Prince. I know you all, and will a while uphold
The unyok'd humor of your idleness,
Yet herein will I imitate the sun,
Who doth permit the base contagious clouds
To smother up his beauty from the world,
That when he please again to be himself,
Being wanted, he may be more wond'red at
By breaking through the foul and ugly mists
Of vapors that did seem to strangle him.
If all the year were playing holidays,
To sport would be as tedious as to work;
But when they seldom come, they wish'd for come,
And nothing pleaseth but rare accidents.
So when this loose behavior I throw off
And pay the debt I never promised,
By how much better than my word I am,
By so much shall I falsify men's hopes,
And like bright metal on a sullen ground,
My reformation, glitt'ring o'er my fault,
Shall show more goodly and attract more eyes
Than that which hath no foil to set it off.
I'll so offend, to make offense a skill,
Redeeming time when men think least I will. *Exit.*

[Scene III]

Enter the King, Northumberland, Worcester, Hotspur, Sir Walter Blunt, *with others.*

King. My blood hath been too cold and temperate,
Unapt to stir at these indignities,
And you have found me, for accordingly
You tread upon my patience; but be sure
I will from henceforth rather be myself,
Mighty and to be fear'd, than my condition,
Which hath been smooth as oil, soft as young down,
And therefore lost that title of respect
Which the proud soul ne'er pays but to the proud.

Wor. Our house, my sovereign liege, little deserves
The scourge of greatness to be us'd on it,
And that same greatness too which our own hands

189. **wards**: postures of defense, parries. 190. **reproof**: disproof.
196. **unyok'd . . . idleness**: undisciplined tendency of your frivolity.
198. **contagious**: noxious (because fogs were thought to breed pestilence). 200. **That**: so that. 201. **wanted**: missed.
207. **rare accidents**: exceptional events.
211. **hopes**: expectations.
212. **sullen ground**: dark background.
215. **foil**: thin sheet of metal set behind a jewel to enhance its brilliance. 216. **to**: as to. **skill**: i.e. something good and clever.
217. **Redeeming time**: making up for misspent time.

I.iii. Location: London. The palace.
2. **Unapt**: slow. 3. **found me**: i.e. found me so mild.
5. **myself**: i.e. my kingly self.
6. **my condition**: my (naturally mild) disposition.
10. **Our house**: i.e. the Percy family, which had thrown its powerful support to Bullingbrook on his return from exile. Worcester was Northumberland's brother and thus Hotspur's uncle.

Have holp to make so portly.

North. My lord—

King. Worcester, get thee gone, for I do see
Danger and disobedience in thine eye.
O, sir, your presence is too bold and peremptory,
And majesty might never yet endure
The moody frontier of a servant brow.
You have good leave to leave us. When we need
Your use and counsel, we shall send for you.
Exit Worcester.
You were about to speak.

North. Yea, my good lord.
Those prisoners in your Highness' name demanded,
Which Harry Percy here at Holmedon took,
Were, as he says, not with such strength denied
As is delivered to your Majesty.
Either envy, therefore, or misprision
Is guilty of this fault, and not my son.

Hot. My liege, I did deny no prisoners,
But I remember, when the fight was done,
When I was dry with rage and extreme toil,
Breathless and faint, leaning upon my sword,
Came there a certain lord, neat, and trimly dress'd,
Fresh as a bridegroom, and his chin new reap'd
Show'd like a stubble-land at harvest-home.
He was perfumed like a milliner,
And 'twixt his finger and his thumb he held
A pouncet-box, which ever and anon
He gave his nose and took't away again,
Who therewith angry, when it next came there,
Took it in snuff—and still he smil'd and talk'd:
And as the soldiers bore dead bodies by,
He call'd them untaught knaves, unmannerly,
To bring a slovenly unhandsome corse
Betwixt the wind and his nobility.
With many holiday and lady terms
He questioned me, amongst the rest demanded
My prisoners in your Majesty's behalf.
I then, all smarting with my wounds being cold,
To be so pest'red with a popingay,
Out of my grief and my impatience
Answer'd neglectingly, I know not what—
He should, or he should not—for he made me mad
To see him shine so brisk and smell so sweet,
And talk so like a waiting-gentlewoman
Of guns, and drums, and wounds, God save the mark!
And telling me the sovereignest thing on earth
Was parmaciti for an inward bruise,

13. **holp**: helped. **portly**: stately. 16. **Danger**: defiance.
17. **peremptory**: imperious.
19. **moody frontier**: i.e. frowning forehead.
25. **strength**: vehemence. 26. **delivered**: reported.
27. **envy**: malice. **misprision**: misunderstanding.
34. **chin new reap'd**: i.e. beard freshly clipped.
35. **Show'd**: looked. 38. **pouncet-box**: pomander, perfume box.
40. **Who**: which (i.e. his nose).
41. **Took . . . snuff**: (1) snuffed it up; (2) was offended. **still**: continually. 44. **corse**: corpse.
46. **many . . . terms**: much dainty and effeminate language.
47. **questioned**: prattled to. **the rest**: other things.
50. **popingay**: popinjay, parrot. 51. **grief**: pain.
52. **neglectingly**: without considering.
56. **God . . . mark**: God forbid.
57. **sovereignest thing**: most efficacious remedy.
58. **parmaciti**: ointment made of spermaceti or whale sperm.

And that it was great pity, so it was,
This villainous saltpetre should be digg'd
Out of the bowels of the harmless earth,
Which many a good tall fellow had destroyed
So cowardly, and but for these vile guns
He would himself have been a soldier.
This bald unjointed chat of his, my lord,
I answered indirectly, as I said,
And I beseech you, let not his report
Come current for an accusation
Betwixt my love and your high Majesty.
Blunt. The circumstance considered, good my lord,
What e'er Lord Harry Percy then had said
To such a person, and in such a place,
At such a time, with all the rest retold,
May reasonably die, and never rise
To do him wrong, or any way impeach
What then he said, so he unsay it now.
King. Why, yet he doth deny his prisoners,
But with proviso and exception,
That we at our own charge shall ransom straight
His brother-in-law, the foolish Mortimer,
Who, on my soul, hath willfully betray'd
The lives of those that he did lead to fight
Against that great magician, damn'd Glendower,
Whose daughter, as we hear, that Earl of March
Hath lately married. Shall our coffers then
Be emptied to redeem a traitor home?
Shall we buy treason? and indent with fears,
When they have lost and forfeited themselves?
No, on the barren mountains let him starve;
For I shall never hold that man my friend
Whose tongue shall ask me for one penny cost
To ransom home revolted Mortimer.
Hot. Revolted Mortimer!
He never did fall off, my sovereign liege,
But by the chance of war; to prove that true
Needs no more but one tongue for all those wounds,
Those mouthed wounds, which valiantly he took,
When on the gentle Severn's sedgy bank,
In single opposition hand to hand,
He did confound the best part of an hour
In changing hardiment with great Glendower.

62. tall: brave. **63. but**: except. **65. bald**: trivial.
68. Come current: be accepted as valid. **71. had**: may have.
75. impeach: discredit. **76. so**: provided that.
78. But . . . exception: unless on the condition.
79. charge: expense. **straight**: immediately.
80. brother-in-law. Hotspur's wife Elizabeth (called Kate in this play) was the sister of Roger, fourth Earl of March, and of Sir Edmund Mortimer (who married Glendower's daughter).
83. magician. Following Mortimer's capture, reports Holinshed (Bullough, IV, 182–83), Henry himself led an expedition to take Glendower, but the Welshman "conveied himself out of the waie, into his knowen lurking places, and (as was thought) through art magike, he caused such foule weather of winds, tempest, raine, snow, and haile to be raised, for the annoiance of the kings armie, that the like had not been heard of."
84–85. Whose . . . married. Once Mortimer had been captured, says Holinshed (Bullough, IV, 184), he, "whether for irkesomnesse of cruell captivitie, or feare of death, or for what other cause, it is uncerteine, agreed to take part with Owen [Glendower], against the king of England, and tooke to wife the daughter of the said Owen."
87. indent with fears: i.e. come to terms with persons who have given us cause to fear them. **92. revolted**: rebellious.
97. mouthed: gaping. **100. confound**: consume.
101. changing hardiment: matching valor.

Three times they breath'd and three times did they
drink,
Upon agreement, of swift Severn's flood,
Who then affrighted with their bloody looks,
Ran fearfully among the trembling reeds,
And hid his crisp head in the hollow bank,
Blood-stained with these valiant combatants.
Never did bare and rotten policy
Color her working with such deadly wounds,
Nor never could the noble Mortimer
Receive so many, and all willingly.
Then let not him be slandered with revolt.
King. Thou dost belie him, Percy, thou dost belie
him;
He never did encounter with Glendower.
I tell thee,
He durst as well have met the devil alone
As Owen Glendower for an enemy.
Art thou not asham'd? But, sirrah, henceforth
Let me not hear you speak of Mortimer.
Send me your prisoners with the speediest means,
Or you shall hear in such a kind from me
As will displease you. My Lord Northumberland:
We license your departure with your son.
Send us your prisoners, or you will hear of it.
Exit King [with Blunt and Train].
Hot. And if the devil come and roar for them,
I will not send them. I will after straight
And tell him so, for I will ease my heart,
Albeit I make a hazard of my head.
North. What? drunk with choler? Stay, and pause
a while.
Here comes your uncle.

Enter WORCESTER.

Hot. Speak of Mortimer!
'Zounds, I will speak of him, and let my soul
Want mercy if I do not join with him.
Yea, on his part I'll empty all these veins,
And shed my dear blood drop by drop in the dust,
But I will lift the down-trod Mortimer
As high in the air as this unthankful king,
As this ingrate and cank'red Bullingbrook.
North. Brother, the King hath made your nephew
mad.
Wor. Who strook this heat up after I was gone?
Hot. He will, forsooth, have all my prisoners,
And when I urg'd the ransom once again
Of my wive's brother, then his cheek look'd pale,
And on my face he turn'd an eye of death,
Trembling even at the name of Mortimer.
Wor. I cannot blame him: was not he proclaim'd
By Richard, that dead is, the next of blood?

102. breath'd: stopped to get their breath.
106. crisp head: curled head, i.e. rippled surface.
108. policy: cunning, trickery.
112. revolt: i.e. accusation of rebellion.
113. belie: not tell the truth about.
126. after straight: go after him at once.
129. choler: anger. **132. Want**: lack.
133. on his part: in his behalf. **137. cank'red**: malignant.
140. forsooth: indeed. **142. wive's**: wife's.

North. He was, I heard the proclamation.
And then it was when the unhappy king
(Whose wrongs in us God pardon!) did set forth
Upon his Irish expedition;
From whence he intercepted did return
To be depos'd, and shortly murdered.
Wor. And for whose death we in the world's wide mouth
Live scandaliz'd and foully spoken of.
Hot. But soft, I pray you, did King Richard then
Proclaim my brother Edmund Mortimer
Heir to the crown?
North. He did, myself did hear it.
Hot. Nay, then I cannot blame his cousin king,
That wish'd him on the barren mountains starve.
But shall it be that you, that set the crown
Upon the head of this forgetful man,
And for his sake wear the detested blot
Of murtherous subornation—shall it be
That you a world of curses undergo,
Being the agents or base second means,
The cords, the ladder, or the hangman rather?
O, pardon me that I descend so low
To show the line and the predicament
Wherein you range under this subtile king!
Shall it for shame be spoken in these days,
Or fill up chronicles in time to come,
That men of your nobility and power
Did gage them both in an unjust behalf
(As both of you—God pardon it!—have done)
To put down Richard, that sweet lovely rose,
And plant this thorn, this canker, Bullingbrook?
And shall it in more shame be further spoken,
That you are fool'd, discarded, and shook off
By him for whom these shames ye underwent?
No, yet time serves wherein you may redeem
Your banish'd honors and restore yourselves
Into the good thoughts of the world again;
Revenge the jeering and disdain'd contempt
Of this proud king, who studies day and night
To answer all the debt he owes to you
Even with the bloody payment of your deaths.
Therefore I say—
Wor. Peace, cousin, say no more.
And now I will unclasp a secret book,
And to your quick-conceiving discontents
I'll read you matter deep and dangerous,
As full of peril and adventerous spirit
As to o'erwalk a current roaring loud
On the unsteadfast footing of a spear.
Hot. If he fall in, good night, or sink or swim.
Send danger from the east unto the west,
So honor cross it from the north to south,
And let them grapple. O, the blood more stirs
To rouse a lion than to start a hare!
North. Imagination of some great exploit
Drives him beyond the bounds of patience.
[*Hot.*] By heaven, methinks it were an easy leap,
To pluck bright honor from the pale-fac'd moon,
Or dive into the bottom of the deep,
Where fadom-line could never touch the ground,
And pluck up drowned honor by the locks,
So he that doth redeem her thence might wear
Without corrival all her dignities;
But out upon this half-fac'd fellowship!
Wor. He apprehends a world of figures here,
But not the form of what he should attend.
Good cousin, give me audience for a while.
Hot. I cry you mercy.
Wor. Those same noble Scots
That are your prisoners—
Hot. I'll keep them all!
By God, he shall not have a Scot of them,
No, if a Scot would save his soul, he shall not!
I'll keep them, by this hand.
Wor. You start away,
And lend no ear unto my purposes.
Those prisoners you shall keep.
Hot. Nay, I will; that's flat.
He said he would not ransom Mortimer,
Forbade my tongue to speak of Mortimer,
But I will find him when he lies asleep,
And in his ear I'll hollow "Mortimer!"
Nay,
I'll have a starling shall be taught to speak
Nothing but "Mortimer," and give it him
To keep his anger still in motion.
Wor. Hear you, cousin, a word.
Hot. All studies here I solemnly defy,
Save how to gall and pinch this Bullingbrook,
And that same sword-and-buckler Prince of Wales,
But that I think his father loves him not
And would be glad he met with some mischance,
I would have him poisoned with a pot of ale.
Wor. Farewell, kinsman! I'll talk to you
When you are better temper'd to attend.
North. Why, what a wasp-stung and impatient fool
Art thou to break into this woman's mood,
Tying thine ear to no tongue but thine own!
Hot. Why, look you, I am [whipt] and scourg'd with rods,
Nettled and stung with pismires, when I hear
Of this vile politician, Bullingbrook.

147–50. I . . . expedition. Shakespeare again confuses the Mortimers; see note to I.i.38.
149. Whose . . . us: i.e. the wrongs that we did to him (by supporting Bullingbrook).
151. intercepted: interrupted (by Bullingbrook's return from exile).
154. scandaliz'd: defamed. **162. detested:** detestable.
163. murtherous subornation: inciting to murder.
168. predicament: category. **169. range:** i.e. are classified.
173. gage: pledge. **them both:** i.e. nobility and power.
176. canker: (1) wild rose; (2) ulcer.
183. disdain'd: disdainful. **185. answer:** discharge.
189. to . . . discontents: i.e. to you, who in your disaffection will be quick to understand me. **191. adventerous:** adventurous.
194. he: i.e. the man attempting such a crossing. **good . . swim:** i.e. he's done for, whether he sinks or stays afloat (for a time).
196. So: provided that. **200. patience:** self-control.
206. redeem: rescue. **207. corrival:** partner.
208. half-fac'd: thin, meagre. **fellowship:** i.e. sharing of honors.
209. apprehends: seizes on. **figures:** figures of speech (an allusion to Hotspur's highly figurative language).
210. attend: be intent upon.
212. cry you mercy: beg your pardon.
228. studies: concerns, pursuits. **defy:** renounce.
230. sword-and-buckler. Like the vulgar "pot of ale" in line 233, an allusion to the Prince's disreputable associates, for in Shakespeare's time swords and bucklers were used only by the lowest class of soldiers. **240. pismires:** ants.
241. vile politician: contemptible schemer.

In Richard's time—what do you call the place?—
A plague upon it, it is in Gloucestershire—
'Twas where the madcap duke his uncle kept—
His uncle York—where I first bow'd my knee
Unto this king of smiles, this Bullingbrook—
'Sblood!
When you and he came back from Ravenspurgh—
North. At Berkeley castle.
Hot. You say true.
Why, what a candy deal of courtesy
This fawning greyhound then did proffer me!
"Look when his infant fortune came to age"
And "gentle Harry Percy" and "kind cousin"—
O, the devil take such cozeners!—God forgive me!
Good uncle, tell your tale—I have done.
Wor. Nay, if you have not, to it again,
We will stay your leisure.
Hot. I have done, i' faith.
Wor. Then once more to your Scottish prisoners:
Deliver them up without their ransom straight,
And make the Douglas' son your only mean
For powers in Scotland, which, for divers reasons
Which I shall send you written, be assur'd
Will easily be granted. [*To Northumberland.*] You, my lord,
Your son in Scotland being thus employed,
Shall secretly into the bosom creep
Of that same noble prelate well belov'd,
The Archbishop.
Hot. Of York, is it not?
Wor. True, who bears hard
His brother's death at Bristow, the Lord Scroop.
I speak not this in estimation,
As what I think might be, but what I know
Is ruminated, plotted, and set down,
And only stays but to behold the face
Of that occasion that shall bring it on.
Hot. I smell it. Upon my life, it will do well.
North. Before the game is afoot thou still let'st slip.
Hot. Why, it cannot choose but be a noble plot.
And then the power of Scotland, and of York,
To join with Mortimer, ha?
Wor. And so they shall.
Hot. In faith, it is exceedingly well aim'd.
Wor. And 'tis no little reason bids us speed,
To save our heads by raising of a head,
For bear ourselves as even as we can,
The King will always think him in our debt,
And think we think ourselves unsatisfied,
Till he hath found a time to pay us home.
And see already how he doth begin
To make us strangers to his looks of love.
Hot. He does, he does, we'll be reveng'd on him.
Wor. Cousin, farewell! No further go in this
Than I by letters shall direct your course.
When time is ripe, which will be suddenly,
I'll steal to Glendower and Lord Mortimer,
Where you and Douglas and our powers at once,
As I will fashion it, shall happily meet
To bear our fortunes in our own strong arms,
Which now we hold at much uncertainty.
North. Farewell, good brother, we shall thrive, I trust.
Hot. Uncle, adieu! O, let the hours be short,
Till fields, and blows, and groans applaud our sport!
Exeunt.

[ACT II, SCENE I]

Enter a CARRIER *with a lantern in his hand.*

1. Car. Heigh-ho! an' it be not four by the day, I'll be hang'd. Charles' wain is over the new chimney, and yet our horse not pack'd. What, ostler!

Ost. [*Within.*] Anon, anon.

1. Car. I prithee, Tom, beat Cut's saddle, put a few flocks in the point. Poor jade is wrung in the withers, out of all cess.

Enter another CARRIER.

2. Car. Peas and beans are as dank here as a dog, and that is the next way to give poor jades the bots. This house is turn'd upside down since Robin ostler died.

1. Car. Poor fellow never joy'd since the price of oats rose, it was the death of him.

2. Car. I think this be the most villainous house in all London road for fleas. I am stung like a tench.

1. Car. Like a tench? by the mass, there is ne'er a king christen could be better bit than I have been since the first cock.

2. Car. Why, they will allow us ne'er a jordan, and then we leak in your chimney, and your chamber-lye

244. kept: resided.
245–46. where . . . Bullingbrook. See *Richard II*, II.iii.
248. Ravenspurgh: Ravenspur, at the mouth of the Humber in Yorkshire, where Henry landed on his return from exile.
251. candy deal: sugary lot.
253–54. Look . . . cousin. See *Richard II*, II.iii.45–49.
255. cozeners: cheats (with obvious pun).
258. stay your leisure: wait until you have time to listen.
260. Deliver them up: liberate them. **straight:** at once.
261. the Douglas' son: i.e. Murdac Stewart. See note to I.i.71. Then as now the head of a prominent Scottish family was designated by his surname preceded by the definite article.
261–62. mean For powers: agent for raising troops.
268. The Archbishop: Richard le Scrope or Scroop (1350?–1405), one of the most prominent of the Percies' allies in their insurrection. In line 271 Shakespeare repeats Holinshed's error in calling him the brother, instead of the cousin, of William Scroop, Earl of Wiltshire (on whom see the notes to *Richard II*, II.i.215, III.ii.122–23).
270. bears hard: greatly resents. **271. Bristow:** Bristol.
272. estimation: (mere) conjecture. **276. occasion:** opportunity.
278. thou . . . slip: you always loose the dogs.
282. aim'd: planned.

284. head: army.
285. even: prudently, carefully. **286. him:** himself.
288. home: fully. **294. suddenly:** soon.
296. powers at once: united forces. **302. fields:** battlefields.

II.i. Location: Rochester. An innyard.
1. by the day: in the morning.
2. Charles' wain: Charlemagne's wagon, i.e. the constellation of the Great Bear (*Ursa Major*). **3. horse:** horses.
4. Anon: at once, i.e. coming.
6. flocks . . . point: tufts of wool in the pommel (to make it more comfortable for the horse).
6. Poor . . . withers: the nag is chafed (by the saddle) along the ridge between its shoulders. **cess:** measure.
9. next: nearest, i.e. quickest.
10. bots: intestinal worms. **14. house:** inn.
16. tench: spotted fish. **17. king christen:** Christian king.
18. first cock: i.e. midnight. **19. jordan:** chamber pot.
20. chamber-lye: urine.

breeds fleas like a loach.

1. Car. What, ostler! come away and be hang'd! come away.

2. Car. I have a gammon of bacon and two razes of ginger, to be deliver'd as far as Charing-cross.

1. Car. God's body, the turkeys in my pannier are quite starv'd. What, ostler! A plague on thee! hast thou never an eye in thy head? Canst not hear? And 'twere not as good deed as drink to break the pate on thee, I am a very villain. Come, and be hang'd! hast no faith in thee?

Enter GADSHILL.

Gads. Good morrow, carriers, what's a' clock?

[1.] Car. I think it be two a' clock.

Gads. I prithee lend me thy lantern, to see my gelding in the stable.

1. Car. Nay, by God, soft, I know a trick worth two of that, i' faith.

Gads. I pray thee lend me thine.

2. Car. Ay, when, canst tell? Lend me thy lantern, quoth he! Marry, I'll see thee hang'd first.

Gads. Sirrah carrier, what time do you mean to come to London?

2. Car. Time enough to go to bed with a candle, I warrant thee. Come, neighbor Mugs, we'll call up the gentlemen. They will along with company, for they have great charge. *Exeunt [Carriers].*

Gads. What ho! chamberlain!

Enter CHAMBERLAIN.

Cham. At hand, quoth pick-purse.

Gads. That's even as fair as—at hand, quoth the chamberlain; for thou variest no more from picking of purses than giving direction doth from laboring: thou layest the plot how.

Cham. Good morrow, Master Gadshill. It holds current that I told you yesternight: there's a franklin in the Wild of Kent hath brought three hundred marks with him in gold. I heard him tell it to one of his company last night at supper, a kind of auditor, one that hath abundance of charge too—God knows what. They are up already, and call for eggs and butter. They will away presently.

Gads. Sirrah, if they meet not with Saint Nicholas' clerks, I'll give thee this neck.

21. like a loach: i.e. as fast as a loach (a kind of fish) spawns loaches.
22. come away: come along, hurry up.
24. gammon of bacon: ham. **razes:** roots.
25. Charing-cross: village between London and Westminster.
28–30. And . . . thee: if it were not as good to clout you on the head as to take a drink. **39. Ay . . . tell:** i.e. never.
45–46. They . . . charge: they will want to travel in a group because of the valuables they are carrying.
47. chamberlain: servant who tended the rooms of an inn.
48. At . . . pick-purse: here I am right beside you, as the pickpocket said. **49. fair:** apt. Inn servants were notoriously dishonest.
50–52. thou . . . how: i.e. you stand in the same relation to pickpockets as a foreman does to workmen, for you make the plans that others carry out. **53–54. holds current:** proves to be true.
54. that: what.
55. franklin: small landowner. **Wild:** Weald (forest).
55–56. three hundred marks: two hundred pounds.
57. auditor: accountant. **60. presently:** at once.
61–62. Saint Nicholas' clerks: highwaymen. In Elizabethan slang St. Nicholas was regarded as the patron of thieves.

Cham. No, I'll none of it, I pray thee keep that for the hangman, for I know thou worshippest Saint Nicholas as truly as a man of falsehood may.

Gads. What talkest thou to me of the hangman? If I hang, I'll make a fat pair of gallows; for if I hang, old Sir John hangs with me, and thou knowest he is no starveling. Tut, there are other Troyans that thou dream'st not of, the which for sport sake are content to do the profession some grace, that would (if matters should be look'd into) for their own credit sake make all whole. I am join'd with no foot land-rakers, no long-staff sixpenny strikers, none of these mad mustachio purple-hu'd malt-worms, but with nobility and tranquility, burgomasters and great oney'rs, such as can hold in, such as will strike sooner than speak, and speak sooner than drink, and drink sooner than pray; and yet, 'zounds, I lie, for they pray continually to their saint, the commonwealth, or rather, not pray to her, but prey on her, for they ride up and down on her, and make her their boots.

Cham. What, the commonwealth their boots? Will she hold out water in foul way?

Gads. She will, she will, justice hath liquor'd her. We steal as in a castle, cock-sure; we have the receipt of fern-seed, we walk invisible.

Cham. Nay, by my faith, I think you are more beholding to the night than to fern-seed for your walking invisible.

Gads. Give me thy hand. Thou shalt have a share in our purchase, as I am a true man.

Cham. Nay, rather let me have it as you are a false thief.

Gads. Go to, *homo* is a common name to all men. Bid the ostler bring my gelding out of the stable. Farewell, you muddy knave. *[Exeunt.]*

[SCENE II]

Enter PRINCE, PETO, *and* [BARDOLPH, *with*] POINS [*following just behind*].

Poins. Come, shelter, shelter! I have remov'd Falstaff's horse, and he frets like a gumm'd velvet.

Prince. Stand close. *[They retire.]*

63. I'll . . . it: i.e. I don't want your neck.
69. Troyans: Trojans, i.e. roisterers.
71. profession: i.e. robbery.
73. join'd: associated. **foot land-rakers:** footpads.
74. long-staff sixpenny strikers: those who, armed only with cudgels, will rob a man of sixpence; i.e. petty thieves.
74–75. mad . . . malt-worms: topers whose mustaches are stained with ale. **76. oney'rs:** ones (?). **77. hold in:** retain secrets.
82. boots: booty.
84. hold . . . way: keep one dryshod in muddy roads, i.e. protect one.
85. liquor'd: (1) greased; (2) bribed.
86. as . . . castle: i.e. in security (with an allusion to Sir John Oldcastle, the name originally given to Falstaff in this play).
87. receipt of fern-seed: procedure for finding fern-seed, which, almost invisible itself, was thought to confer invisibility on whoever carried it. **89. beholding:** beholden, indebted.
92. purchase: booty. **true:** honest.
95. homo: man. Gadshill implies that a generic term, without such adjectives as *true* or *false*, will suffice. **97. muddy:** stupid.

II.ii. Location: The highway near Gadshill.
2. frets: (1) complains; (2) frays. **gumm'd:** stiffened with gum.
3. close: concealed.

Enter Falstaff.

Fal. Poins! Poins, and be hang'd! Poins!

Prince. [*Coming forward.*] Peace, ye fat-kidney'd rascal! what a brawling dost thou keep!

Fal. Where's Poins, Hal?

Prince. He is walk'd up to the top of the hill, I'll go seek him. [*Retires.*]

Fal. I am accurs'd to rob in that thieve's company. The rascal hath remov'd my horse, and tied him I know not where. If I travel but four foot by the squier further afoot, I shall break my wind. Well, I doubt not but to die a fair death for all this, if I scape hanging for killing that rogue. I have forsworn his company hourly any time this two and twenty years, and yet I am bewitch'd with the rogue's company. If the rascal have not given me medicines to make me love him, I'll be hang'd. It could not be else, I have drunk medicines. Poins! Hal! a plague upon you both! Bardolph! Peto! I'll starve ere I'll rob a foot further. And 'twere not as good a deed as drink to turn true man and to leave these rogues, I am the veriest varlet that ever chew'd with a tooth. Eight yards of uneven ground is threescore and ten miles afoot with me, and the stony-hearted villains know it well enough. A plague upon it when thieves cannot be true one to another! (*They whistle.*) Whew! a plague upon you all! Give me my horse, you rogues, give me my horse, and be hang'd!

Prince. [*Coming forward.*] Peace, ye fat-guts, lie down. Lay thine ear close to the ground, and list if thou canst hear the tread of travellers.

Fal. Have you any levers to lift me up again, being down? 'Sblood, I'll not bear my own flesh so far afoot again for all the coin in thy father's exchequer. What a plague mean ye to colt me thus?

Prince. Thou liest, thou art not colted, thou art uncolted.

Fal. I prithee, good prince—Hal!—help me to my horse, good king's son.

Prince. Out, ye rogue! shall I be your ostler?

Fal. Hang thyself in thine own heir-apparent garters! If I be ta'en, I'll peach for this. And I have not ballads made on you all and sung to filthy tunes, let a cup of sack be my poison. When a jest is so forward, and afoot too! I hate it.

Enter Gadshill.

Gads. Stand.

Fal. So I do, against my will.

Poins. [*Coming forward with Bardolph and Peto.*] O, 'tis our setter, I know his voice.

[*Bard.*] What news?

[*Gads.*] Case ye, case ye, on with your vizards. There's money of the King's coming down the hill, 'tis going to the King's exchequer.

6. **keep:** keep up.
10. **thieve's:** thief's. 12. **squier:** square, foot rule.
14. **for:** despite. 18. **medicines:** potions. 37. **colt:** trick.
39. **uncolted:** i.e. deprived of your horse.
43–44. **heir-apparent garters.** An allusion to the Order of the Garter, in which the Prince, as heir apparent, had been installed as a knight.
44. **peach:** turn informer. 46–47. **is so forward:** goes so far.
51. **setter.** See note to I.ii.106–7. 53. **Case ye:** mask yourselves.

Fal. You lie, ye rogue, 'tis going to the King's tavern.

Gads. There's enough to make us all.

Fal. To be hang'd.

Prince. Sirs, you four shall front them in the narrow lane; Ned Poins and I will walk lower. If they scape from your encounter, then they light on us.

Peto. How many be there of them?

Gads. Some eight or ten.

Fal. 'Zounds, will they not rob us?

Prince. What, a coward, Sir John Paunch?

Fal. Indeed I am not John of Gaunt, your grandfather, but yet no coward, Hal.

Prince. Well, we leave that to the proof.

Poins. Sirrah Jack, thy horse stands behind the hedge; when thou need'st him, there thou shalt find him. Farewell, and stand fast.

Fal. Now cannot I strike him, if I should be hang'd.

Prince. [*Aside.*] Ned, where are our disguises?

Poins. [*Aside.*] Here, hard by. Stand close.

[*Exeunt Prince and Poins.*]

Fal. Now, my masters, happy man be his dole, say I, every man to his business.

Enter the Travellers.

[*1.*] *Trav.* Come, neighbor, the boy shall lead our horses down the hill. We'll walk afoot a while, and ease our legs.

Thieves. Stand!

Travellers. Jesus bless us!

Fal. Strike! down with them! cut the villains' throats! Ah, whoreson caterpillars! bacon-fed knaves! they hate us youth. Down with them! fleece them!

[*1.*] *Trav.* O, we are undone, both we and ours for ever!

Fal. Hang ye, gorbellied knaves, are ye undone? No, ye fat chuffs, I would your store were here! On, bacons, on! What, ye knaves, young men must live! You are grandjurors, are ye? We'll jure ye, faith. *Here they rob them and bind them. Exeunt.*

Enter the Prince *and* Poins [*in buckram*].

Prince. The thieves have bound the true men. Now could thou and I rob the thieves and go merrily to London, it would be argument for a week, laughter for a month, and a good jest for ever.

Poins. Stand close, I hear them coming.

Enter the Thieves *again.*

Fal. Come, my masters, let us share, and then to horse before day. And the Prince and Poins be not two arrant cowards, there's no equity stirring.

58. **make us all:** i.e. make our fortunes.
67. **John of Gaunt.** A punning allusion to Hal's thinness (on which see II.iv.244–48). John of Gaunt was so called from his birthplace, Ghent in Flanders. 69. **proof:** test.
76. **happy . . . dole:** i.e. may each man be fortunate; good luck to you. *Dole* = that which is dealt (by fate).
84. **caterpillars:** parasites. 88. **gorbellied:** potbellied.
89. **chuffs:** misers. **your store:** all your possessions.
90. **bacons:** fat men.
91. **grandjurors:** i.e. affluent citizens (eligible for jury duty).
93. **true:** honest. 95. **argument:** topic of conversation.
100. **equity:** judgment, discrimination.

There's no more valor in that Poins than in a wild duck.

As they are sharing, the Prince and Poins set upon them; they all run away, and Falstaff, after a blow or two, runs away too, leaving the booty behind them.

Prince. Your money!
Poins. Villains!

Prince. Got with much ease. Now merrily to horse.
The thieves are all scattered, and possess'd with fear
So strongly that they dare not meet each other;
Each takes his fellow for an officer.
Away, good Ned. Falstaff sweats to death,
And lards the lean earth as he walks along.
Were't not for laughing, I should pity him.
Poins. How the fat rogue roar'd! *Exeunt.*

[Scene III]

Enter Hotspur *solus, reading a letter.*

[*Hot.*] "But, for mine own part, my lord, I could be well contented to be there, in respect of the love I bear your house." He could be contented: why is he not then? In the respect of the love he bears our house: he shows in this, he loves his own barn better than he loves our house. Let me see some more. "The purpose you undertake is dangerous"—why, that's certain. 'Tis dangerous to take a cold, to sleep, to drink, but I tell you, my lord fool, out of this nettle, danger, we pluck this flower, safety. "The purpose you undertake is dangerous, the friends you have nam'd uncertain, the time itself unsorted, and your whole plot too light for the counterpoise of so great an opposition." Say you so, say you so? I say unto you again, you are a shallow, cowardly hind, and you lie. What a lack-brain is this! By the Lord, our plot is a good plot as ever was laid, our friends true and constant: a good plot, good friends, and full of expectation; an excellent plot, very good friends. What a frosty-spirited rogue is this! Why, my Lord of York commends the plot and the general course of the action. 'Zounds, and I were now by this rascal, I could brain him with his lady's fan. Is there not my father, my uncle, and myself? Lord Edmund Mortimer, my Lord of York, and Owen Glendower? is there not besides the Douglas? have I not all their letters to meet me in arms by the ninth of the next month? and are they not some of them set forward already? What a pagan rascal is this! an infidel! Ha, you shall see now in very sincerity of fear and cold heart will he to the King, and lay open all our proceedings. O, I could divide myself and go to buffets, for moving such a dish of skim-milk with so honorable an action! Hang him! let him tell the King: we are prepar'd. I will set forward to-night.

Enter his Lady.

How now, Kate? I must leave you within these two hours.
Lady. O my good lord, why are you thus alone?
For what offense have I this fortnight been
A banish'd woman from my Harry's bed?
Tell me, sweet lord, what is't that takes from thee
Thy stomach, pleasure, and thy golden sleep?
Why dost thou bend thine eyes upon the earth,
And start so often when thou sit'st alone?
Why hast thou lost the fresh blood in thy cheeks,
And given my treasures and my rights of thee
To thick-ey'd musing and curst melancholy?
In thy faint slumbers I by thee have watch'd,
And heard thee murmur tales of iron wars,
Speak terms of manage to thy bounding steed,
Cry "Courage! to the field!" And thou hast talk'd
Of sallies and retires, of trenches, tents,
Of palisadoes, frontiers, parapets,
Of basilisks, of cannon, culverin,
Of prisoners' ransom, and of soldiers slain,
And all the currents of a heady fight;
Thy spirit within thee hath been so at war,
And thus hath so bestirr'd thee in thy sleep,
That beads of sweat have stood upon thy brow,
Like bubbles in a late-disturbed stream,
And in thy face strange motions have appear'd,
Such as we see when men restrain their breath
On some great sudden hest. O, what portents are these?
Some heavy business hath my lord in hand,
And I must know it, else he loves me not.
Hot. What ho!

[*Enter* Servant.]

Is Gilliams with the packet gone?
Serv. He is, my lord, an hour ago.
Hot. Hath Butler brought those horses from the sheriff?
Serv. One horse, my lord, he brought even now.
Hot. What horse? Roan? a crop-ear, is it not?
Serv. It is, my lord.
Hot. That roan shall be my throne.
Well, I will back him straight. O *Esperance!*
Bid Butler lead him forth into the park.

[*Exit Servant.*]

Lady. But hear you, my lord.
Hot. What say'st thou, my lady?
Lady. What is it carries you away?
Hot. Why, my horse, my love, my horse.
Lady. Out, you mad-headed ape!
A weasel hath not such a deal of spleen

109. lards: bastes.

II.iii. Location: Warkworth Castle (stronghold of the Percies in Northumberland). **o.s.d. solus:** alone.
3. house: family. **He.** The writer of the letter is never identified.
12. unsorted: unsuitable.
21. Lord of York: i.e. Archbishop Scroop.
29. pagan: unbelieving. **30. very:** veritable.
32. divide . . . buffets: split in two and have a boxing-match with myself (cf. "I could kick myself").

41. stomach: appetite.
47. faint: light. **49. manage:** manège, horsemanship.
52. palisadoes: stakes set for defense. **frontiers:** ramparts.
53. basilisks: heavy ordnance. **culverin:** light ordnance.
55. heady: headlong. **62. hest:** behest, command.
63. heavy: (1) weighty; (2) sorrowful.
71. Esperance: Hope (the motto of the house of Percy).
78. spleen: nervous energy, impulsiveness.

As you are toss'd with. In faith,
I'll know your business, Harry, that I will.
I fear my brother Mortimer doth stir
About his title, and hath sent for you
To line his enterprise, but if you go—

Hot. So far afoot, I shall be weary, love.

Lady. Come, come, you paraquito, answer me
Directly unto this question that I ask.
In faith, I'll break thy little finger, Harry,
And if thou wilt not tell me all things true.

Hot. Away,
Away, you trifler! Love, I love thee not,
I care not for thee, Kate. This is no world
To play with mammets and to tilt with lips.
We must have bloody noses and crack'd crowns,
And pass them current too. God's me, my horse!
What say'st thou, Kate? What wouldst thou have with me?

Lady. Do you not love me? do you not indeed?
Well, do not then, for since you love me not,
I will not love myself. Do you not love me?
Nay, tell me if you speak in jest or no.

Hot. Come, wilt thou see me ride?
And when I am a' horseback, I will swear
I love thee infinitely. But hark you, Kate,
I must not have you henceforth question me
Whither I go, nor reason whereabout.
Whither I must, I must, and to conclude,
This evening must I leave you, gentle Kate.
I know you wise, but yet no farther wise
Than Harry Percy's wife; constant you are,
But yet a woman, and for secrecy,
No lady closer, for I well believe
Thou wilt not utter what thou dost not know,
And so far will I trust thee, gentle Kate.

Lady. How! so far?

Hot. Not an inch further. But hark you, Kate,
Whither I go, thither shall you go too;
To-day will I set forth, to-morrow you.
Will this content you, Kate?

Lady. It must of force. *Exeunt.*

[SCENE IV]

Enter PRINCE *and* POINS.

Prince. Ned, prithee come out of that fat room, and lend me thy hand to laugh a little.

Poins. Where hast been, Hal?

Prince. With three or four loggerheads amongst three or four score hogsheads. I have sounded the very base-string of humility. Sirrah, I am sworn brother to a leash of drawers, and can call them all by their christen names, as Tom, Dick, and Francis. They take it already upon their salvation, that though I be but Prince of Wales, yet I am the king of courtesy, and tell me flatly I am no proud Jack like Falstaff, but a Corinthian, a lad of mettle, a good boy (by the Lord, so they call me!), and when I am King of England I shall command all the good lads in Eastcheap. They call drinking deep, dyeing scarlet, and when you breathe in your watering, they cry "hem!" and bid you play it off. To conclude, I am so good a proficient in one quarter of an hour, that I can drink with any tinker in his own language during my life. I tell thee, Ned, thou hast lost much honor that thou wert not with me in this action. But, sweet Ned—to sweeten which name of Ned, I give thee this pennyworth of sugar, clapp'd even now into my hand by an under-skinker, one that never spake other English in his life than "Eight shillings and sixpence," and "You are welcome," with this shrill addition, "Anon, anon, sir! Score a pint of bastard in the Half-moon," or so. But, Ned, to drive away the time till Falstaff come, I prithee do thou stand in some by-room, while I question my puny drawer to what end he gave me the sugar, and do thou never leave calling "Francis," that his tale to me may be nothing but "Anon." Step aside, and I'll show thee a [president].

[*Exit Poins.*]

Poins. [*Within.*] Francis!

Prince. Thou art perfect.

[*Poins.*] [*Within.*] Francis!

Enter Drawer [FRANCIS].

Fran. Anon, anon, sir. Look down into the Pomgarnet, Ralph.

Prince. Come hither, Francis.

Fran. My lord?

Prince. How long hast thou to serve, Francis?

Fran. Forsooth, five years, and as much as to—

Poins. [*Within.*] Francis!

Fran. Anon, anon, sir.

Prince. Five year! by'r lady, a long lease for the clinking of pewter. But, Francis, darest thou be so valiant as to play the coward with thy indenture, and show it a fair pair of heels and run from it?

Fran. O Lord, sir, I'll be sworn upon all the books in England, I could find in my heart—

Poins. [*Within.*] Francis!

Fran. Anon, sir.

Prince. How old art thou, Francis?

Fran. Let me see—about Michaelmas next I shall be—

82. title: claim to the throne. **83. line:** support.
92. mammets: dolls (like you).
94. pass them current: cause them to circulate as legal tender, i.e. give them in exchange. Hotspur is playing on two senses of *crowns:* (1) heads; (2) coins worth five shillings. Cracked coins were not normally accepted as currency. **God's me:** God save me. **101. a':** on.
104. whereabout: about what. **109. for:** as for.
117. of force: of necessity.

II.iv. Location: London. The Boar's Head Tavern in Eastcheap.
1. fat: vat (?) or stuffy (?). **4. loggerheads:** blockheads.
7. leash: set of three. **drawers:** tapsters (who sometimes invited favored guests to have their drinks in the cellar).

11. Jack: fellow. **12. Corinthian:** gay blade.
15. dyeing scarlet. Perhaps an allusion to the complexion of hard drinkers. **16. breathe . . . watering:** stop for breath while drinking.
17. play: drink.
23. sugar. Used to sweeten certain wines, especially sack.
24. under-skinker: waiter's assistant.
27. Anon: at once, coming. **Score:** i.e. chalk up, charge. **bastard:** sweet Spanish wine.
27–28. Half-moon. Rooms in inns were often given special names.
30. puny: inexperienced. **33. president:** precedent, example.
38. Pomgarnet: Pomegranate, another room in the tavern.
45. by'r lady: by Our Lady (i.e. the Virgin).
47. indenture: apprentice's contract (which was normally for seven years). **49. books:** i.e. Bibles. **54. Michaelmas:** September 29.

Poins. [*Within.*] Francis!

Fran. Anon, sir. Pray stay a little, my lord.

Prince. Nay, but hark you, Francis: for the sugar thou gavest me, 'twas a pennyworth, was't not?

Fran. O Lord, I would it had been two!

Prince. I will give thee for it a thousand pound. Ask me when thou wilt, and thou shalt have it.

Poins. [*Within.*] Francis!

Fran. Anon, anon.

Prince. Anon, Francis? No, Francis; but to-morrow, Francis; or, Francis, a' Thursday; or indeed, Francis, when thou wilt. But, Francis!

Fran. My lord?

Prince. Wilt thou rob this leathern-jerkin, crystal-button, not-pated, agate-ring, puke-stocking, caddis-garter, smooth-tongue, Spanish-pouch—

Fran. O Lord, sir, who do you mean?

Prince. Why then your brown bastard is your only drink! for look you, Francis, your white canvas doublet will sully. In Barbary, sir, it cannot come to so much.

Fran. What, sir?

Poins. [*Within.*] Francis!

Prince. Away, you rogue, dost thou not hear them call?

Here they both call him; the drawer stands amazed, not knowing which way to go.

Enter Vintner.

Vint. What, stand'st thou still, and hear'st such a calling? Look to the guests within. [*Exit Francis.*] My lord, old Sir John with half a dozen more are at the door, shall I let them in?

Prince. Let them alone awhile, and then open the door. [*Exit Vintner.*] Poins!

Poins. [*Within.*] Anon, anon, sir.

Enter Poins.

Prince. Sirrah, Falstaff and the rest of the thieves are at the door; shall we be merry?

Poins. As merry as crickets, my lad. But hark ye, what cunning match have you made with this jest of the drawer? Come, what's the issue?

Prince. I am now of all humors that have show'd themselves humors since the old days of goodman Adam to the pupil age of this present twelve a' clock at midnight.

[*Enter* Francis *hurrying across the stage with wine.*]

What's a' clock, Francis?

Fran. Anon, anon, sir. [*Exit.*]

Prince. That ever this fellow should have fewer words than a parrot, and yet the son of a woman! His industry is up stairs and down stairs, his eloquence the parcel of a reckoning. I am not yet of Percy's mind, the Hotspur of the north, he that kills me some six or seven dozen of Scots at a breakfast, washes his hands, and says to his wife, "Fie upon this quiet life! I want work." "O my sweet Harry," says she, "how many hast thou kill'd to-day?" "Give my roan horse a drench," says he, and answers, "Some fourteen," an hour after; "a trifle, a trifle." I prithee call in Falstaff. I'll play Percy, and that damn'd brawn shall play Dame Mortimer his wife. "*Rivo!*" says the drunkard. Call in ribs, call in tallow.

Enter Falstaff, [Gadshill, Bardolph, *and* Peto, Francis *following with wine*].

Poins. Welcome, Jack, where hast thou been?

Fal. A plague of all cowards, I say, and a vengeance too! marry and amen! Give me a cup of sack, boy. Ere I lead this life long, I'll sew nether-stocks, and mend them and foot them too. A plague of all cowards! Give me a cup of sack, rogue. Is there no virtue extant? *He drinketh.*

Prince. Didst thou never see Titan kiss a dish of butter, pitiful-hearted Titan, that melted at the sweet tale of the sun's? If thou didst, then behold that compound.

Fal. You rogue, here's lime in this sack too. There is nothing but roguery to be found in villainous man, yet a coward is worse than a cup of sack with lime in it. A villainous coward! Go thy ways, old Jack, die when thou wilt; if manhood, good manhood, be not forgot upon the face of the earth, then am I a shotten herring. There lives not three good men unhang'd in England, and one of them is fat and grows old, God help the while! a bad world, I say. I would I were a weaver, I could sing psalms, or any thing. A plague of all cowards, I say still.

Prince. How now, wool-sack, what mutter you?

Fal. A king's son! If I do not beat thee out of thy kingdom with a dagger of lath, and drive all thy subjects afore thee like a flock of wild geese, I'll never wear hair on my face more. You, Prince of Wales!

Prince. Why, you whoreson round man, what's the matter?

Fal. Are not you a coward? Answer me to that; and Poins there?

Poins. 'Zounds, ye fat paunch, and ye call me coward, by the Lord, I'll stab thee.

69–71. Wilt . . . pouch. The Prince describes Francis' master, the vintner.
70. not-pated: close-cropped. **puke:** dark woollen. **caddis:** worsted.
71. Spanish: of Spanish leather.
74–75. your . . . sully: your costume (as an apprentice) will get dirty (in Barbary), i.e. you'd better stay here. **75. it:** i.e. sugar.
79 s.d. amazed: thoroughly confused.
90–91. what . . . issue: i.e. what's the point of your teasing the servant.
92–95. I . . . midnight: i.e. as a consequence of my foolery with the servant I am now in the mood for anything.
93. goodman: occupational title for a farmer or yeoman.
94. pupil: youthful.

101. parcel . . . reckoning: items of a bill.
107. drench: medicinal drink. **110. brawn:** pig.
111. Rivo: reveller's exclamation (of uncertain origin and meaning).
114. of: on. **116. nether-stocks:** stockings.
119. virtue: manliness. **120. Titan:** the sun.
121. that: i.e. the butter.
123. compound: melting butter, i.e. Falstaff.
124. lime. Sometimes used as an additive to wine to increase its sparkle.
130. shotten herring: (as thin as) a herring that has spawned.
132. the while: in these (bad) times.
133. sing psalms. Elizabethan weavers, many of whom were immigrants from the Low Countries and dissenters, were notorious for psalm-singing.
137. dagger of lath: wooden stick (commonly used by the Vice, the mischievously comic stock character in morality plays).

Fal. I call thee coward! I'll see thee damn'd ere I call thee coward, but I would give a thousand pound I could run as fast as thou canst. You are straight enough in the shoulders, you care not who sees your back. Call you that backing of your friends? A plague upon such backing! give me them that will face me. Give me a cup of sack. I am a rogue if I drunk to-day.

Prince. O villain, thy lips are scarce wip'd since thou drunk'st last.

Fal. All is one for that. (*He drinketh*.) A plague of all cowards, still say I.

Prince. What's the matter?

Fal. What's the matter! There be four of us here have ta'en a thousand pound this day morning.

Prince. Where is it, Jack? where is it?

Fal. Where is it? taken from us it is: a hundred upon poor four of us.

Prince. What, a hundred, man?

Fal. I am a rogue if I were not at half-sword with a dozen of them two hours together. I have scap'd by miracle. I am eight times thrust through the doublet, four through the hose, my buckler cut through and through, my sword hack'd like a hand-saw— *ecce signum!* I never dealt better since I was a man; all would not do. A plague of all cowards! Let them speak; if they speak more or less than truth, they are villains and the sons of darkness.

[*Prince*.] Speak, sirs, how was it?

[*Gads*.] We four set upon some dozen—

Fal. Sixteen at least, my lord.

[*Gads*.] And bound them.

Peto. No, no, they were not bound.

Fal. You rogue, they were bound, every man of them, or I am a Jew else, an Ebrew Jew.

[*Gads*.] As we were sharing, some six or seven fresh men set upon us—

Fal. And unbound the rest, and then come in the other.

Prince. What, fought you with them all?

Fal. All? I know not what you call all, but if I fought not with fifty of them, I am a bunch of radish. If there were not two or three and fifty upon poor old Jack, then am I no two-legg'd creature.

Prince. Pray God you have not murd'red some of them.

Fal. Nay, that's past praying for, I have pepper'd two of them. Two I am sure I have paid, two rogues in buckrom suits. I tell thee what, Hal, if I tell thee a lie, spit in my face, call me horse. Thou knowest my old ward: here I lay, and thus I bore my point. Four rogues in buckrom let drive at me—

Prince. What, four? Thou saidst but two even now.

Fal. Four, Hal, I told thee four.

Poins. Ay, ay, he said four.

Fal. These four came all afront, and mainly thrust at me. I made me no more ado but took all their seven points in my target, thus.

Prince. Seven? why, there were but four even now.

Fal. In buckrom?

Poins. Ay, four, in buckrom suits.

Fal. Seven, by these hilts, or I am a villain else.

Prince. Prithee let him alone, we shall have more anon.

Fal. Dost thou hear me, Hal?

Prince. Ay, and mark thee too, Jack.

Fal. Do so, for it is worth the list'ning to. These nine in buckrom that I told thee of—

Prince. So, two more already.

Fal. Their points being broken—

Poins. Down fell their hose.

Fal. Began to give me ground; but I follow'd me close, came in, foot and hand, and with a thought seven of the eleven I paid.

Prince. O monstrous! eleven buckrom men grown out of two.

Fal. But, as the devil would have it, three misbegotten knaves in Kendal green came at my back and let drive at me, for it was so dark, Hal, that thou couldest not see thy hand.

Prince. These lies are like their father that begets them, gross as a mountain, open, palpable. Why, thou clay-brain'd guts, thou knotty-pated fool, thou whoreson, obscene, greasy tallow-catch—

Fal. What, art thou mad? art thou mad? is not the truth the truth?

Prince. Why, how couldst thou know these men in Kendal green when it was so dark thou couldst not see thy hand? Come, tell us your reason; what sayest thou to this?

Poins. Come, your reason, Jack, your reason.

Fal. What, upon compulsion? 'Zounds, and I were at the strappado, or all the racks in the world, I would not tell you on compulsion. Give you a reason on compulsion? if reasons were as plentiful as blackberries, I would give no man a reason upon compulsion, I.

Prince. I'll be no longer guilty of this sin. This sanguine coward, this bed-presser, this horse-back-breaker, this huge hill of flesh—

Fal. 'Sblood, you starveling, you [eel-]skin, you dried neat's tongue, you bull's pizzle, you stock-fish! O for breath to utter what is like thee! you tailor's yard, you sheath, you bowcase, you vile standing tuck—

Prince. Well, breathe a while, and then to it again, and when thou hast tir'd thyself in base comparisons, hear me speak but this—

Poins. Mark, Jack.

155. All . . . that: i.e. no matter.
164. at half-sword: i.e. at close quarters.
167. hose: breeches. **buckler**: shield.
169. ecce signum: behold the proof. **dealt**: i.e. fought.
179. Ebrew: Hebrew. **183. other**: others.
192. paid: i.e. killed. **194. horse**: i.e. a stupid animal.
195. ward: parry. **lay**: stood.
200. afront: abreast. **mainly**: powerfully.
202. target: shield.
206. these hilts: i.e. the pommel, haft, etc. of a sword (a common oath). **villain**: i.e. no gentleman.
214. points: sword points (but Poins takes the word in a second sense: tagged laces for holding garments together).
217. with a thought: as quick as thought.
222. Kendal: town in Westmorland noted for its textiles.
226. gross: obvious. **227. knotty-pated**: thick-headed.
228. tallow-catch: tallow-tub.
237. strappado: a form of torture.
239. reasons. Pronounced *raisins* (hence the pun with *blackberries*).
242. sanguine: ruddy. **245. neat's**: ox's.
245. stock-fish: dried cod. **248. tuck**: rapier.

Prince. We two saw you four set on four and bound them, and were masters of their wealth. Mark now how a plain tale shall put you down. Then did we two set on you four, and with a word, outfac'd you from your prize, and have it, yea, and can show it you here in the house; and, Falstaff, you carried your guts away as nimbly, with as quick dexterity, and roar'd for mercy, and still run and roar'd, as ever I heard bull-calf. What a slave art thou to hack thy sword as thou hast done, and then say it was in fight! What trick? what device? what starting-hole? canst thou now find out to hide thee from this open and apparent shame?

Poins. Come, let's hear, Jack, what trick hast thou now?

Fal. By the Lord, I knew ye as well as he that made ye. Why, hear you, my masters, was it for me to kill the heir-apparent? Should I turn upon the true prince? Why, thou knowest I am as valiant as Hercules; but beware instinct—the lion will not touch the true prince. Instinct is a great matter; I was now a coward on instinct. I shall think the better of myself, and thee, during my life; I for a valiant lion, and thou for a true prince. But by the Lord, lads, I am glad you have the money. Hostess, clap to the doors! Watch to-night, pray to-morrow. Gallants, lads, boys, hearts of gold, all the titles of good fellowship come to you! What, shall we be merry, shall we have a play extempore?

Prince. Content, and the argument shall be thy running away.

Fal. Ah, no more of that, Hal, and thou lovest me!

Enter HOSTESS.

Host. O Jesu, my lord the Prince!

Prince. How now, my lady the hostess! what say'st thou to me?

Host. Marry, my lord, there is a nobleman of the court at door would speak with you. He says he comes from your father.

Prince. Give him as much as will make him a royal man, and send him back again to my mother.

Fal. What manner of man is he?

Host. An old man.

Fal. What doth gravity out of his bed at midnight? Shall I give him his answer?

Prince. Prithee do, Jack.

Fal. Faith, and I'll send him packing. *Exit.*

Prince. Now, sirs, by'r lady, you fought fair, so did you, Peto, so did you, Bardolph. You are lions too, you ran away upon instinct, you will not touch the true prince, no, fie!

Bard. Faith, I ran when I saw others run.

Prince. Faith, tell me now in earnest, how came Falstaff's sword so hack'd?

Peto. Why, he hack'd it with his dagger, and said he would swear truth out of England but he would make you believe it was done in fight, and persuaded us to do the like.

Bard. Yea, and to tickle our noses with speargrass to make them bleed, and then to beslubber our garments with it and swear it was the blood of true men. I did that I did not this seven year before, I blush'd to hear his monstrous devices.

Prince. O villain, thou stolest a cup of sack eighteen years ago, and wert taken with the manner, and ever since thou hast blush'd extempore. Thou hadst fire and sword on thy side, and yet thou ran'st away; what instinct hadst thou for it?

Bard. My lord, do you see these meteors? do you behold these exhalations? [*Pointing to his own face.*]

Prince. I do.

Bard. What think you they portend?

Prince. Hot livers and cold purses.

Bard. Choler, my lord, if rightly taken.

Enter FALSTAFF.

Prince. No, if rightly taken, halter. Here comes lean Jack, here comes bare-bone. How now, my sweet creature of bumbast, how long is't ago, Jack, since thou sawest thine own knee?

Fal. My own knee? When I was about thy years, Hal, I was not an eagle's talent in the waist, I could have crept into any alderman's thumb-ring. A plague of sighing and grief, it blows a man up like a bladder. There's villainous news abroad. Here was Sir John Bracy from your father; you must to the court in the morning. That same mad fellow of the north, Percy, and he of Wales that gave Amamon the bastinado and made Lucifer cuckold and swore the devil his true liegeman upon the cross of a Welsh hook—what a plague call you him?

Poins. O, Glendower.

Fal. Owen, Owen, the same; and his son-in-law Mortimer, and old Northumberland, and that sprightly Scot of Scots, Douglas, that runs a' horseback up a hill perpendicular—

Prince. He that rides at high speed and with his pistol kills a sparrow flying.

256. with a word: to be brief. **outfac'd:** frightened, bluffed.
263. starting-hole: refuge, loophole; i.e. excuse.
264. apparent: obvious. **281. argument:** subject.
290–91. as much . . . man: i.e. 3*s*. 4*d*., the difference between a noble (6*s*. 8*d*.) and a royal (10*s*.).
291. send . . . mother: i.e. get rid of him permanently. The Prince's mother, Mary de Bohun, had died in 1394. **298. fair:** well.

306. swear . . . England: i.e. vanquish truth by the force of his lies. **but he would:** if he did not.
312. that . . . not: what I hadn't done.
315. taken . . . manner: caught in the act.
317. fire. An allusion to Bardolph's ruddy complexion, the subject of the jests and pun that follow.
319, 320. meteors, exhalations: i.e. the red blotches and carbuncles on Bardolph's face.
322. portend: threaten, presage (continuing the astronomical imagery of *meteors* and *exhalations*).
323. Hot . . . purses: i.e. livers inflamed by liquor and purses emptied to pay for it.
324. Choler . . . taken: i.e. my fiery complexion, if properly understood, indicates a choleric temperament (which makes me quick to anger and dangerous).
325. No . . . halter: i.e. no, if you're arrested as you deserve, you'll get the hangman's noose. Behind *halter* lies a pun on *choler* and *collar*.
327. bumbast: bombast, cotton padding. **330. talent:** talon.
334. Sir John Bracy. Apparently unhistorical.
336. Amamon: the name of a fiend.
337. bastinado: beating on the soles of the feet. **made Lucifer cuckold:** i.e. gave Lucifer his horns (the sign of a cuckold).
338. liegeman: subject.
338–39. Welsh hook: pike with a curved blade.

Fal. You have hit it.

Prince. So did he never the sparrow.

Fal. Well, that rascal hath good mettle in him, he will not run.

Prince. Why, what a rascal art thou then, to praise him so for running!

Fal. A' horseback, ye cuckoo, but afoot he will not budge a foot.

Prince. Yes, Jack, upon instinct.

Fal. I grant ye, upon instinct. Well, he is there too, and one Mordake, and a thousand blue-caps more. Worcester is stol'n away to-night. Thy father's beard is turn'd white with the news. You may buy land now as cheap as stinking mack'rel.

Prince. Why then, it is like, if there come a hot June and this civil buffeting hold, we shall buy maidenheads as they buy hobnails, by the hundreds.

Fal. By the mass, lad, thou sayest true, it is like we shall have good trading that way. But tell me, Hal, art not thou horrible afeard? Thou being heir-apparent, could the world pick thee out three such enemies again as that fiend Douglas, that spirit Percy, and that devil Glendower? Art thou not horribly afraid? Doth not thy blood thrill at it?

Prince. Not a whit, i' faith, I lack some of thy instinct.

Fal. Well, thou wilt be horribly chid to-morrow when thou comest to thy father. If thou love me, practice an answer.

Prince. Do thou stand for my father and examine me upon the particulars of my life.

Fal. Shall I? Content. This chair shall be my state, this dagger my sceptre, and this cushion my crown.

Prince. Thy state is taken for a join'd-stool, thy golden sceptre for a leaden dagger, and thy precious rich crown for a pitiful bald crown!

Fal. Well, and the fire of grace be not quite out of thee, now shalt thou be mov'd. Give me a cup of sack to make my eyes look red, that it may be thought I have wept, for I must speak in passion, and I will do it in King Cambyses' vein.

Prince. Well, here is my leg.

Fal. And here is my speech. Stand aside, nobility.

Host. O Jesu, this is excellent sport, i' faith!

Fal. Weep not, sweet queen, for trickling tears are vain.

Host. O, the father, how he holds his countenance!

Fal. For God's sake, lords, convey my [tristful] queen,
For tears do stop the flood-gates of her eyes.

Host. O Jesu, he doth it as like one of these harlotry players as ever I see!

Fal. Peace, good pint-pot, peace, good ticklebrain. Harry, I do not only marvel where thou spendest thy time, but also how thou art accompanied; for though the camomile, the more it is trodden on, the faster it grows, [yet] youth, the more it is wasted, the sooner it wears. That thou art my son I have partly thy mother's word, partly my own opinion, but chiefly a villainous trick of thine eye, and a foolish hanging of thy nether lip, that doth warrant me. If then thou be son to me, here lies the point: why being son to me, art thou so pointed at? Shall the blessed sun of heaven prove a micher and eat blackberries? a question not to be ask'd. Shall the son of England prove a thief and take purses? a question to be ask'd. There is a thing, Harry, which thou hast often heard of, and it is known to many in our land by the name of pitch. This pitch (as ancient writers do report) doth defile, so doth the company thou keepest; for, Harry, now I do not speak to thee in drink, but in tears; not in pleasure, but in passion; not in words only, but in woes also. And yet there is a virtuous man whom I have often noted in thy company, but I know not his name.

Prince. What manner of man, and it like your Majesty?

Fal. A goodly portly man, i' faith, and a corpulent, of a cheerful look, a pleasing eye, and a most noble carriage, and as I think, his age some fifty, or, by'r lady, inclining to threescore; and now I remember me, his name is Falstaff. If that man should be lewdly given, he deceiveth me; for, Harry, I see virtue in his looks. If then the tree may be known by the fruit, as the fruit by the tree, then peremptorily I speak it, there is virtue in that Falstaff; him keep with, the rest banish. And tell me now, thou naughty varlet, tell me, where hast thou been this month?

Prince. Dost thou speak like a king? Do thou stand for me, and I'll play my father.

Fal. Depose me? If thou dost it half so gravely, so majestically, both in word and matter, hang me up by the heels for a rabbit-sucker or a poulter's hare.

Prince. Well, here I am set.

Fal. And here I stand. Judge, my masters.

Prince. Now, Harry, whence come you?

Fal. My noble lord, from Eastcheap.

Prince. The complaints I hear of thee are grievous.

Fal. 'Sblood, my lord, they are false.—Nay, I'll tickle ye for a young prince, i' faith.

Prince. Swearest thou, ungracious boy? henceforth ne'er look on me. Thou art violently carried away from grace, there is a devil haunts thee in the likeness of an old fat man, a tun of man is thy companion. Why

357. blue-caps: blue bonnets, i.e. Scots. **362. hold:** continue.
370. thrill: run cold. **378. state:** chair of state, i.e. throne.
380. join'd-stool: stool of joiner's work.
382. bald crown: bald pate. **386. in passion:** with deep emotion.
387. in . . . vein: i.e. in a style of ludicrous and old-fashioned rant (like that of Thomas Preston's *Cambyses*, an early Elizabethan play).
388. leg: elaborate bow.
392. holds his countenance: keeps a straight face.
393. convey: escort hence. **tristful:** sorrowful.
395–96. harlotry: knavish. **397. ticklebrain:** strong drink.

400. camomile: plant of the aster family. **405. warrant:** assure.
407. pointed at: i.e. in derision and disapproval.
408. micher: truant. **409. England:** i.e. the King of England.
413. ancient writers. For one, the writer of the Apocryphal book Ecclesiasticus (13:1). **416. passion:** sorrow.
422. portly: stately, imposing. **corpulent:** full-fleshed.
427. lewdly given: wickedly inclined.
428–29. If . . . by the fruit. See Matthew 12:33.
429. peremptorily: decisively.
431–32. naughty varlet: ill-behaved boy.
437. rabbit-sucker: unweaned rabbit. **poulter's:** poulterer's.
438. set: seated (i.e. on the "throne").
443–44. I'll . . . prince: I'll play the role of a young prince so as to delight you. **445. ungracious:** graceless.

dost thou converse with that trunk of humors, that bolting-hutch of beastliness, that swoll'n parcel of dropsies, that huge bombard of sack, that stuff'd cloak-bag of guts, that roasted Manningtree ox with the pudding in his belly, that reverent Vice, that grey Iniquity, that father ruffian, that vanity in years? Wherein is he good, but to taste sack and drink it? wherein neat and cleanly, but to carve a capon and eat it? wherein cunning, but in craft? wherein crafty, but in villainy? wherein villainous, but in all things? wherein worthy, but in nothing?

Fal. I would your Grace would take me with you. Whom means your Grace?

Prince. That villainous abominable misleader of youth, Falstaff, that old white-bearded Sathan.

Fal. My lord, the man I know.

Prince. I know thou dost.

Fal. But to say I know more harm in him than in myself, were to say more than I know. That he is old, the more the pity, his white hairs do witness it, but that he is, saving your reverence, a whoremaster, that I utterly deny. If sack and sugar be a fault, God help the wicked! If to be old and merry be a sin, then many an old host that I know is damn'd. If to be fat be to be hated, then Pharaoh's [lean] kine are to be lov'd. No, my good lord, banish Peto, banish Bardolph, banish Poins, but for sweet Jack Falstaff, kind Jack Falstaff, true Jack Falstaff, valiant Jack Falstaff, and therefore more valiant, being as he is old Jack Falstaff, banish not him thy Harry's company, banish not him thy Harry's company—banish plump Jack, and banish all the world.

Prince. I do, I will.

[*A knocking heard. Exeunt Hostess, Francis, and Bardolph.*]

Enter Bardolph *running.*

Bard. O my lord, my lord, the sheriff with a most monstrous watch is at the door.

Fal. Out, ye rogue, play out the play, I have much to say in the behalf of that Falstaff.

Enter the Hostess.

Host. O Jesu, my lord, my lord!

Prince. Heigh, heigh! the devil rides upon a fiddlestick. What's the matter?

Host. The sheriff and all the watch are at the door, they are come to search the house. Shall I let them in?

Fal. Dost thou hear, Hal? Never call a true piece of gold a counterfeit. Thou art essentially made, without seeming so.

Prince. And thou a natural coward, without instinct.

Fal. I deny your major. If you will deny the sheriff, so, if not, let him enter. If I become not a cart as well as another man, a plague on my bringing up! I hope I shall as soon be strangled with a halter as another.

Prince. Go hide thee behind the arras, the rest walk up above. Now, my masters, for a true face and good conscience.

Fal. Both which I have had, but their date is out, and therefore I'll hide me. [*Exit.*]

Prince. Call in the sheriff.

[*Exeunt all except the Prince and Peto.*]

Enter Sheriff *and the* Carrier.

Now, Master Sheriff, what is your will with me?

Sher. First, pardon me, my lord. A hue and cry
Hath followed certain men unto this house.

Prince. What men?

Sher. One of them is well known, my gracious lord,
A gross fat man.

Car. As fat as butter.

Prince. The man I do assure you is not here,
For I myself at this time have employ'd him.
And, sheriff, I will engage my word to thee
That I will by to-morrow dinner-time
Send him to answer thee, or any man,
For any thing he shall be charg'd withal,
And so let me entreat you leave the house.

Sher. I will, my lord. There are two gentlemen
Have in this robbery lost three hundred marks.

Prince. It may be so. If he have robb'd these men,
He shall be answerable, and so farewell.

Sher. Good night, my noble lord.

Prince. I think it is good morrow, is it not?

Sher. Indeed, my lord, I think it be two a' clock.

Exit [*with Carrier*].

Prince. This oily rascal is known as well as Paul's.
Go call him forth.

Peto. Falstaff!—Fast asleep behind the arras, and snorting like a horse.

Prince. Hark how hard he fetches breath. Search his pockets. (*He searcheth his pocket, and findeth certain papers.*) What hast thou found?

Peto. Nothing but papers, my lord.

Prince. Let's see what they be. Read them.

[*Peto.*] [*Reads.*]

Item, a capon	2s. 2d.
Item, sauce	4d.
Item, sack, two gallons . .	5s. 8d.
Item, anchoves and sack after supper .	2s. 6d.
Item, bread	ob.

449. converse: associate. **humors:** secretions in the body, diseases.
450. bolting-hutch: miller's bin.
451. bombard: large leathern vessel.
452. Manningtree: town in Essex, a region noted for fat oxen.
453. pudding: stuffing. **Vice:** mischievously comic stock character in morality plays who served chiefly as a "misleader of youth" (lines 462–63). *Iniquity* (line 454) is another name for him.
456. cleanly: adroit, dextrous. **457. cunning:** skillful.
460. take . . . you: i.e. go more slowly (so I can keep up with you).
469. saving your reverence: i.e. excuse me for using an offensive term.
473. Pharaoh's lean kine. See Genesis 41:1–4.
483. watch: body of constables.
487–88. the devil . . . fiddlestick: i.e. the Hostess is going to report some astounding event.
491–93. Never . . . so. A much disputed passage. Perhaps Falstaff means that the Prince should not turn him—a true piece of gold—over to the law as a counterfeit coin, for Hal himself, despite misleading appearances, is a true prince (*essentially made*).
495. major: major premise.
495–96. deny the sheriff: i.e. refuse to admit him.
496. cart: i.e. hangman's cart.
500. arras: tapestry wall-hangings. **501. true:** honest.
514. engage: pledge. **517. withal:** with.
524. good morrow: i.e. past midnight.
526. Paul's: St. Paul's Cathedral. **538. anchoves:** anchovies.
539. ob.: obolus; here, halfpenny.

[*Prince.*] O monstrous! but one half-pennyworth of bread to this intolerable deal of sack! What there is else, keep close, we'll read it at more advantage. There let him sleep till day. I'll to the court in the morning. We must all to the wars, and thy place shall be honorable. I'll procure this fat rogue a charge of foot, and I know his death will be a march of twelve score. The money shall be paid back again with advantage. Be with me betimes in the morning, and so good morrow, Peto.

Peto. Good morrow, good my lord. *Exeunt.*

[ACT III, SCENE I]

Enter HOTSPUR, WORCESTER, LORD MORTIMER, OWEN GLENDOWER.

Mort. These promises are fair, the parties sure,
And our induction full of prosperous hope.
Hot. Lord Mortimer, and cousin Glendower,
Will you sit down?
And uncle Worcester—a plague upon it!
I have forgot the map.
Glend. No, here it is.
Sit, cousin Percy, sit, good cousin Hotspur,
For by that name as oft as Lancaster
Doth speak of you, his cheek looks pale, and with
A rising sigh he wisheth you in heaven.
Hot. And you in hell, as oft as he hears
Owen Glendower spoke of.
Glend. I cannot blame him. At my nativity
The front of heaven was full of fiery shapes
Of burning cressets, and at my birth
The frame and huge foundation of the earth
Shak'd like a coward.
Hot. Why, so it would have done
At the same season if your mother's cat had
But kitten'd, though yourself had never been born.
Glend. I say the earth did shake when I was born.
Hot. And I say the earth was not of my mind,
If you suppose as fearing you it shook.
Glend. The heavens were all on fire, the earth did tremble.
Hot. O then the earth shook to see the heavens on fire,
And not in fear of your nativity.
Diseased nature oftentimes breaks forth
In strange eruptions; oft the teeming earth
Is with a kind of colic pinch'd and vex'd
By the imprisoning of unruly wind
Within her womb, which, for enlargement striving,
Shakes the old beldame earth, and topples down
Steeples and moss-grown towers. At your birth
Our grandam earth, having this distemp'rature,
In passion shook.
Glend. Cousin, of many men
I do not bear these crossings. Give me leave
To tell you once again that at my birth
The front of heaven was full of fiery shapes,
The goats ran from the mountains, and the herds
Were strangely clamorous to the frighted fields.
These signs have mark'd me extraordinary,
And all the courses of my life do show
I am not in the roll of common men.
Where is he living, clipt in with the sea
That chides the banks of England, Scotland, Wales,
Which calls me pupil or hath read to me?
And bring him out that is but woman's son
Can trace me in the tedious ways of art,
And hold me pace in deep experiments.
Hot. I think there's no man speaks better Welsh.
I'll to dinner.
Mort. Peace, cousin Percy, you will make him mad.
Glend. I can call spirits from the vasty deep.
Hot. Why, so can I, or so can any man,
But will they come when you do call for them?
Glend. Why, I can teach you, cousin, to command
The devil.
Hot. And I can teach thee, coz, to shame the devil
By telling truth: tell truth and shame the devil.
If thou have power to raise him, bring him hither,
And I'll be sworn I have power to shame him hence.
O, while you live, tell truth and shame the devil!
Mort. Come, come, no more of this unprofitable chat.
Glend. Three times hath Henry Bullingbrook made head
Against my power; thrice from the banks of Wye
And sandy-bottom'd Severn have I sent him
Bootless home and weather-beaten back.
Hot. Home without boots, and in foul weather too!
How scapes he agues, in the devil's name?
Glend. Come, here is the map. Shall we divide our right
According to our threefold order ta'en?
Mort. The Archdeacon hath divided it
Into three limits very equally:
England, from Trent and Severn hitherto,
By south and east is to my part assign'd;

542. close: secret. **542–43. more advantage:** a more opportune time.
546. charge of foot: command of a troop of infantry.
546–47. death . . . score: i.e. a march of 240 yards will kill him.
548. advantage: interest.

III.i. Location: Wales. Glendower's castle. (Holinshed places the events of this scene in the house of the Archdeacon of Bangor [see the note to lines 71–78], but the Archdeacon is not present in the scene and Glendower acts throughout as host.)
2. induction: beginning. **prosperous hope:** hope of prospering.
8. Lancaster: i.e. King Henry. **14. front:** forehead.
15. cressets: fire-baskets mounted on poles; here, meteors.
30. enlargement: release.
31. beldame: grandmother, aged woman.
34. passion: pain. **35. crossings:** contradictions.
43. clipt in with: enclosed by. **45. read to:** i.e. taught.
47. trace . . . art: follow me in the laborious ways of magic.
48. hold me pace: keep up with me. **deep:** occult.
49. better Welsh: i.e. more boastfully and incomprehensibly.
52. vasty deep: lower world. **63. made head:** raised a force.
64. power: armed followers.
66. Bootless: without advantage, i.e. unsuccessful.
69. right: rightful possessions.
71–78. The Archdeacon . . . Trent. According to Holinshed (Bullough, IV, 185), the rebels "by their deputies in the house of the archdeacon of Bangor, divided the realme amongst them, causing a tripartite indenture to be made and sealed with their seales, by the covenants whereof, all England from Severne and Trent, south and eastward, was assigned to the earle of March: all Wales, & the lands beyond Severne westward, were appointed to Owen Glendouer: and all the remnant from Trent northward, to the lord Persie."
72. limits: regions defined by a boundary.
73. hitherto: to this point.

All westward, Wales beyond the Severn shore,
And all the fertile land within that bound,
To Owen Glendower; and, dear coz, to you
The remnant northward lying off from Trent.
And our indentures tripartite are drawn,
Which being sealed interchangeably
(A business that this night may execute),
To-morrow, cousin Percy, you and I
And my good Lord of Worcester will set forth
To meet your father and the Scottish power,
As is appointed us, at Shrewsbury.
My father Glendower is not ready yet,
Nor shall we need his help these fourteen days.
Within that space you may have drawn together
Your tenants, friends, and neighboring gentlemen.
Glend. A shorter time shall send me to you, lords,
And in my conduct shall your ladies come,
From whom you now must steal and take no leave,
For there will be a world of water shed
Upon the parting of your wives and you.
Hot. Methinks my moi'ty, north from Burton here,
In quantity equals not one of yours.
See how this river comes me cranking in,
And cuts me from the best of all my land
A huge half-moon, a monstrous [cantle] out.
I'll have the current in this place damm'd up,
And here the smug and silver Trent shall run
In a new channel fair and evenly.
It shall not wind with such a deep indent,
To rob me of so rich a bottom here.
Glend. Not wind? It shall, it must, you see it doth.
Mort. Yea, but
Mark how he bears his course, and runs me up
With like advantage on the other side,
Gelding the opposed continent as much
As on the other side it takes from you.
Wor. Yea, but a little charge will trench him here,
And on this north side win this cape of land,
And then he runs straight and even.
Hot. I'll have it so, a little charge will do it.
Glend. I'll not have it alt'red.
Hot. Will not you?
Glend. No, nor you shall not.
Hot. Who shall say me nay?
Glend. Why, that will I.
Hot. Let me not understand you then,
Speak it in Welsh.
Glend. I can speak English, lord, as well as you,
For I was train'd up in the English court,

79. our . . . drawn: our agreement is now drawn up in triplicate.
86. father: i.e. father-in-law. **91. conduct:** escort.
95. moi'ty: share. **97. cranking:** winding.
99. cantle: piece, segment. **101. smug:** smooth.
102. fair and evenly: i.e. in a straight course.
104. bottom: valley.
109. Gelding . . . continent: cutting off from the opposite bank.
111. charge: expense.
120. For . . . court. According to Holinshed (Bullough, IV, 180), Glendower "was first set to studie the lawes of the realme, and became an utter barrester, or an apprentise of the law (as they terme him) and served king Richard at Flint castell, when he was taken by Henrie duke of Lancaster, though other have written that he served this king Henry the fourth, before he came to atteine the crowne, in roome of an esquier."

Where being but young I framed to the harp
Many an English ditty lovely well,
And gave the tongue a helpful ornament,
A virtue that was never seen in you.
Hot. Marry,
And I am glad of it with all my heart.
I had rather be a kitten and cry mew
Than one of these same metre ballet-mongers.
I had rather hear a brazen canstick turn'd,
Or a dry wheel grate on the axle-tree,
And that would set my teeth nothing an edge,
Nothing so much as mincing poetry.
'Tis like the forc'd gait of a shuffling nag.
Glend. Come, you shall have Trent turn'd.
Hot. I do not care. I'll give thrice so much land
To any well-deserving friend;
But in the way of bargain, mark ye me,
I'll cavil on the ninth part of a hair.
Are the indentures drawn? Shall we be gone?
Glend. The moon shines fair, you may away by night.
I'll haste the writer, and withal
Break with your wives of your departure hence.
I am afraid my daughter will run mad,
So much she doteth on her Mortimer. *Exit.*
Mort. Fie, cousin Percy, how you cross my father!
Hot. I cannot choose. Sometime he angers me
With telling me of the moldwarp and the ant,
Of the dreamer Merlin and his prophecies,
And of a dragon and a finless fish,
A clip-wing'd griffin and a moulten raven,
A couching lion and a ramping cat,
And such a deal of skimble-skamble stuff
As puts me from my faith. I tell you what:
He held me last night at least nine hours
In reckoning up the several devils' names
That were his lackeys. I cried "hum," and "well, go to,"
But mark'd him not a word. O, he is as tedious
As a tired horse, a railing wife,
Worse than a smoky house. I had rather live
With cheese and garlic in a windmill, far,
Than feed on cates and have him talk to me
In any summer house in Christendom.
Mort. In faith, he is a worthy gentleman,

123. gave . . . ornament: i.e. not only adorned the words with music but also enriched the language with poetry.
124. virtue: accomplishment. **128. ballet:** ballad.
129. canstick turn'd: candlestick turned on a lathe.
133. shuffling: hobbled. **141. withal:** also.
142. Break with: inform.
146–53. Sometimes . . . faith. According to Holinshed (Bullough, IV, 185), the rebels laid their plans "through a foolish credit given to a vaine prophesie, as though king Henrie was the moldwarpe, cursed of Gods owne mouth, and they three were the dragon, the lion, and the woolfe, which should divide this realme betweene them. Such is the deviation (saith *Hall*) and not divination of those blind and fantasticall dreames of the Welsh prophesiers."
147. moldwarp: mole.
148. Merlin: famous prophet and magician of Arthurian legend.
150. griffin: fabulous beast, half lion and half eagle.
151. couching, ramping: parodies of the heraldic terms *couchant* (lying down with the head raised) and *rampant* (rearing).
152. skimble-skamble: nonsensical.
153. puts . . . faith: i.e. kills my confidence (in Glendower).
155. several: various. **161. cates:** delicacies.

Exceedingly well read, and profited
In strange concealments, valiant as a lion,
And wondrous affable, and as bountiful
As mines of India. Shall I tell you, cousin?
He holds your temper in a high respect,
And curbs himself even of his natural scope
When you come 'cross his humor, faith, he does.
I warrant you, that man is not alive
Might so have tempted him as you have done,
Without the taste of danger and reproof.
But do not use it oft, let me entreat you.
Wor. In faith, my lord, you are too willful-blame,
And since your coming hither have done enough
To put him quite besides his patience.
You must needs learn, lord, to amend this fault;
Though sometimes it show greatness, courage, blood—
And that's the dearest grace it renders you—
Yet oftentimes it doth present harsh rage,
Defect of manners, want of government,
Pride, haughtiness, opinion, and disdain,
The least of which haunting a nobleman
Loseth men's hearts and leaves behind a stain
Upon the beauty of all parts besides,
Beguiling them of commendation.
Hot. Well, I am school'd: good manners be your speed!
Here come our wives, and let us take our leave.

Enter GLENDOWER *with the* LADIES.

Mort. This is the deadly spite that angers me:
My wife can speak no English, I no Welsh.
Glend. My daughter weeps, she'll not part with you,
She'll be a soldier too, she'll to the wars.
Mort. Good father, tell her that she and my aunt Percy
Shall follow in your conduct speedily.
Glendower speaks to her in Welsh, and she answers him in the same.
Glend. She is desperate here, a peevish self-will'd harlotry,
One that no persuasion can do good upon.
The lady speaks in Welsh.
Mort. I understand thy looks. That pretty Welsh
Which thou pourest down from these swelling heavens
I am too perfect in, and but for shame,
In such a parley should I answer thee.
The lady again in Welsh.
I understand thy kisses, and thou mine,
And that's a feeling disputation,
But I will never be a truant, love,
Till I have learn'd thy language, for thy tongue
Makes Welsh as sweet as ditties highly penn'd,
Sung by a fair queen in a summer's bow'r,
With ravishing division, to her lute.
Glend. Nay, if you melt, then will she run mad.
The lady speaks again in Welsh.
Mort. O, I am ignorance itself in this!
Glend. She bids you on the wanton rushes lay you down,
And rest your gentle head upon her lap,
And she will sing the song that pleaseth you,
And on your eyelids crown the god of sleep,
Charming your blood with pleasing heaviness,
Making such difference 'twixt wake and sleep
As is the difference betwixt day and night
The hour before the heavenly-harness'd team
Begins his golden progress in the east.
Mort. With all my heart I'll sit and hear her sing.
By that time will our book, I think, be drawn.
Glend. Do so,
And those musicians that shall play to you
Hang in the air a thousand leagues from hence,
And straight they shall be here. Sit and attend.
Hot. Come, Kate, thou art perfect in lying down.
Come, quick, quick, that I may lay my head in thy lap.
Lady P. Go, ye giddy goose. *The music plays.*
Hot. Now I perceive the devil understands Welsh,
And 'tis no marvel he is so humorous.
By'r lady, he is a good musician.
Lady P. Then should you be nothing but musical, for you are altogether govern'd by humors. Lie still, ye thief, and hear the lady sing in Welsh.
Hot. I had rather hear Lady, my brach, howl in Irish.
Lady P. Wouldst thou have thy head broken?
Hot. No.
Lady P. Then be still.
Hot. Neither, 'tis a woman's fault.
Lady P. Now God help thee!
Hot. To the Welsh lady's bed.
Lady P. What's that?
Hot. Peace, she sings.
Here the lady sings a Welsh song.
Hot. Come, Kate, I'll have your song too.
Lady P. Not mine, in good sooth.
Hot. Not yours, in good sooth! Heart, you swear like a comfit-maker's wife: "Not you, in good sooth," and "as true as I live," and "as God shall mend me," and "as sure as day";
And givest such sarcenet surety for thy oaths

164. profited: proficient. **165. concealments:** occult arts.
169. scope: freedom of speech. **172. tempted:** irritated.
175. willful-blame: willfully to blame. **179. blood:** spirit.
180. dearest grace: main distinction. **181. present:** indicate.
182. government: self-control. **183. opinion:** self-conceit.
186. all parts besides: all other (good) qualities.
187. Beguiling: depriving. **188. be your speed:** give you success.
190. spite: vexation. **193. she'll to:** she wants to go to.
194. my aunt Percy: i.e. Hotspur's wife, who was actually the sister, not the aunt, of Glendower's son-in-law. See notes to I.i.38, I.iii.80.
196. She . . . harlotry: she is hopeless on this point, a willful hussy.
198. That pretty Welsh: your language, i.e. your tears.
200. perfect in: well acquainted with.
201. In . . . parley: i.e. by weeping.
203. a feeling disputation: i.e. an exchange of sentiments, not of language.
208. division: embellishment.
211. wanton: luxurious, comfortable. **215. heaviness:** drowsiness.
221. book: i.e. the "indentures tripartite" of line 79.
229–30. Now . . . humorous: i.e. since the devil understands Welsh (which is incomprehensible), it's no wonder that he's so whimsical (*humorous*). **233. humors:** whims. **235. brach:** bitch.
240. Neither . . . fault: I won't be silent either, for that's a woman's trait (and I'm a man). **246. sooth:** truth.
247. Heart: by God's (Christ's) heart.
248. comfit-maker's: confectioner's.
251. sarcenet: i.e. flimsy, insubstantial (from the name of a very fine, soft material made of silk).

As if thou never walk'st further than Finsbury.
Swear me, Kate, like a lady as thou art,
A good mouth-filling oath, and leave "in sooth,"
And such protest of pepper-gingerbread,
To velvet-guards and Sunday-citizens.
Come sing.

Lady P. I will not sing.

Hot. 'Tis the next way to turn tailor, or be redbreast teacher. And the indentures be drawn, I'll away within these two hours, and so come in when ye will. *Exit.*

Glend. Come, come, Lord Mortimer, you are as slow
As hot Lord Percy is on fire to go.
By this our book is drawn, we'll but seal,
And then to horse immediately.

Mort. With all my heart. *Exeunt.*

[SCENE II]

Enter the KING, PRINCE OF WALES, *and others.*

King. Lords, give us leave, the Prince of Wales and I
Must have some private conference, but be near at hand,
For we shall presently have need of you.
Exeunt Lords.
I know not whether God will have it so
For some displeasing service I have done,
That in his secret doom, out of my blood
He'll breed revengement and a scourge for me;
But thou dost in thy passages of life
Make me believe that thou art only mark'd
For the hot vengeance, and the rod of heaven,
To punish my mistreadings. Tell me else,
Could such inordinate and low desires,
Such poor, such bare, such lewd, such mean attempts,
Such barren pleasures, rude society,
As thou art match'd withal and grafted to,
Accompany the greatness of thy blood,
And hold their level with thy princely heart?

Prince. So please your Majesty, I would I could
Quit all offenses with as clear excuse
As well as I am doubtless I can purge
Myself of many I am charg'd withal;
Yet such extenuation let me beg
As in reproof of many tales devis'd,
Which oft the ear of greatness needs must hear

252. **Finsbury:** district much frequented by London citizens and their families. Hotspur implies that his wife's genteel and colorless language makes her sound like a burgher's wife.
255. **such . . . pepper-gingerbread:** i.e. such namby-pamby protestations.
256. **velvet-guards:** velvet trimmings such as citizens' wives wore on their Sunday finery.
259. **next:** quickest. **tailor.** A trade noted for singing.

III.ii. Location: London. The palace.
6. **doom:** judgment. 8. **passages:** actions.
12. **inordinate:** unsuitable (for one of your rank).
13. **lewd:** base, vulgar. 15. **withal:** with.
17. **hold their level:** i.e. maintain their appeal and force.
19. **Quit:** clear myself of. 20. **doubtless:** certain.
23. **reproof:** disproof.

By smiling pick-thanks and base newsmongers,
I may for some things true, wherein my youth
Hath faulty wand'red and irregular,
Find pardon on my true submission.

King. God pardon thee! yet let me wonder, Harry,
At thy affections, which do hold a wing
Quite from the flight of all thy ancestors.
Thy place in Council thou hast rudely lost,
Which by thy younger brother is supplied,
And art almost an alien to the hearts
Of all the court and princes of my blood;
The hope and expectation of thy time
Is ruin'd, and the soul of every man
Prophetically do forethink thy fall.
Had I so lavish of my presence been,
So common-hackney'd in the eyes of men,
So stale and cheap to vulgar company,
Opinion, that did help me to the crown,
Had still kept loyal to possession,
And left me in reputeless banishment,
A fellow of no mark nor likelihood.
By being seldom seen, I could not stir
But like a comet I was wond'red at,
That men would tell their children, "This is he";
Others would say, "Where, which is Bullingbrook?"
And then I stole all courtesy from heaven,
And dress'd myself in such humility
That I did pluck allegiance from men's hearts,
Loud shouts and salutations from their mouths,
Even in the presence of the crowned King.
Thus did I keep my person fresh and new,
My presence, like a robe pontifical,
Ne'er seen but wond'red at, and so my state,
Seldom but sumptuous, show'd like a feast,
And wan by rareness such solemnity.
The skipping King, he ambled up and down,
With shallow jesters, and rash bavin wits,
Soon kindled and soon burnt, carded his state,
Mingled his royalty with cap'ring fools,

25. **pick-thanks:** busybodies, flatterers. Shakespeare may have got the word from Holinshed (Bullough, IV, 195), who, incidentally, dates the King's reproof of and reconciliation with his wayward son after the battle of Shrewsbury: "Thus were the father and the sonne reconciled, betwixt whom the said pickthanks had sowne division, insomuch that the sonne upon a vehement conceit of unkindnesse sproong in the father, was in the waie to be worne out of favour. Which was the more likelie to come to passe, by their informations that privilie charged him with riot and other uncivill demeanor unseemelie for a prince." **newsmongers:** talebearers.
28. **submission:** confession.
30. **affections:** inclinations. **hold a wing:** pursue a course.
32–33. **Thy . . . supplied.** An allusion to the apocryphal story—apparently first told by Sir Thomas Elyot in *The Governor* (1531)—of one of the Prince's most flamboyant escapades. In Holinshed's account (Bullough, IV, 280), "to hie offense of the king his father, he had with his fist striken the cheefe justice [Sir William Gascoigne] for sending one of his minions (upon desert) to prison, when the justice stoutlie commanded himselfe also streict to ward, & he (then prince) obeied. The king after expelled him out of his privie councell, banisht him the court, and made the duke of Clarence (his younger brother) president of councell in his steed." Shakespeare treats the escapade more fully in *2 Henry IV*, V.ii. **rudely:** by violence.
36. **time:** time of life, i.e. youth.
40. **common-hackney'd:** cheapened, vulgarized. A hackney is a horse kept for hire. 42. **Opinion:** i.e. public opinion.
43. **Had:** would have. **possession:** the possessor, i.e. Richard II.
57. **state:** i.e. appearance on state occasions. 59. **wan:** won.
61. **bavin:** brushwood, kindling.
62. **carded:** mixed (and so adulterated), a term from cloth-making. **state:** royal status.

Had his great name profaned with their scorns,
And gave his countenance, against his name,
To laugh at gibing boys, and stand the push
Of every beardless vain comparative,
Grew a companion to the common streets,
Enfeoff'd himself to popularity,
That, being daily swallowed by men's eyes,
They surfeited with honey and began
To loathe the taste of sweetness, whereof a little
More than a little is by much too much.
So when he had occasion to be seen,
He was but as the cuckoo is in June,
Heard, not regarded; seen, but with such eyes
As, sick and blunted with community,
Afford no extraordinary gaze,
Such as is bent on sunlike majesty
When it shines seldom in admiring eyes;
But rather drows'd and hung their eyelids down,
Slept in his face and rend'red such aspect
As cloudy men use to their adversaries,
Being with his presence glutted, [gorg'd], and full.
And in that very line, Harry, standest thou,
For thou hast lost thy princely privilege
With vile participation. Not an eye
But is a-weary of thy common sight,
Save mine, which hath desir'd to see thee more,
Which now doth that I would not have it do,
Make blind itself with foolish tenderness.
Prince. I shall hereafter, my thrice-gracious lord,
Be more myself.
King. For all the world
As thou art to this hour was Richard then
When I from France set foot at Ravenspurgh,
And even as I was then is Percy now.
Now by my sceptre, and my soul to boot,
He hath more worthy interest to the state
Than thou the shadow of succession.
For of no right, nor color like to right,
He doth fill fields with harness in the realm,
Turns head against the lion's armed jaws,
And being no more in debt to years than thou,
Leads ancient lords and reverend bishops on
To bloody battles and to bruising arms.
What never-dying honor hath he got
Against renowmed Douglas! whose high deeds,
Whose hot incursions and great name in arms,
Holds from all soldiers chief majority
And military title capital
Through all the kingdoms that acknowledge Christ.
Thrice hath this Hotspur, Mars in swathling clothes,
This infant warrior, in his enterprises
Discomfited great Douglas, ta'en him once,
Enlarg'd him and made a friend of him,
To fill the mouth of deep defiance up,
And shake the peace and safety of our throne.
And what say you to this? Percy, Northumberland,
The Archbishop's grace of York, Douglas, Mortimer,
Capitulate against us, and are up.
But wherefore do I tell these news to thee?
Why, Harry, do I tell thee of my foes,
Which art my nearest and dearest enemy?
Thou that art like enough, through vassal fear,
Base inclination, and the start of spleen,
To fight against me under Percy's pay,
To dog his heels and curtsy at his frowns,
To show how much thou art degenerate.
Prince. Do not think so, you shall not find it so,
And God forgive them that so much have sway'd
Your Majesty's good thoughts away from me!
I will redeem all this on Percy's head,
And in the closing of some glorious day
Be bold to tell you that I am your son,
When I will wear a garment all of blood,
And stain my favors in a bloody mask,
Which wash'd away shall scour my shame with it.
And that shall be the day, when e'er it lights,
That this same child of honor and renown,
This gallant Hotspur, this all-praised knight,
And your unthought-of Harry chance to meet.
For every honor sitting on his helm,
Would they were multitudes, and on my head
My shames redoubled! For the time will come
That I shall make this northren youth exchange
His glorious deeds for my indignities.
Percy is but my factor, good my lord,
To engross up glorious deeds on my behalf;
And I will call him to so strict account
That he shall render every glory up,
Yea, even the slightest worship of his time,
Or I will tear the reckoning from his heart.
This in the name of God I promise here,
The which if he be pleas'd I shall perform,
I do beseech your Majesty may salve
The long-grown wounds of my intemperance.
If not, the end of life cancels all bands,
And I will die a hundred thousand deaths
Ere break the smallest parcel of this vow.
King. A hundred thousand rebels die in this.
Thou shalt have charge and sovereign trust herein.

Enter BLUNT.

How now, good Blunt? thy looks are full of speed.
Blunt. So hath the business that I come to speak of.

65. gave . . . name: lent his authority, to the jeopardy of his kingly title.
66–67. stand . . . comparative: tolerate the impertinent witticisms of every beardless youth. **69. Enfeoff'd:** sold, surrendered.
70. That: so that. **77. community:** familiarity.
82. aspect: look. **83. cloudy:** sullen.
87. participation: fellowship. **90. that:** that which.
91. foolish tenderness: i.e. tears.
98. more . . . state: a better claim to the throne.
99. shadow: i.e. because your intrinsic merits are so slight.
100. color: pretext. **101. harness:** (men in) armor.
102. Turns head: leads an army.
103. being . . . thou. See note to I.i.53.
107. renowmed: renowned. **109. majority:** supremacy.
110. capital: pre-eminent. **112. swathling:** swaddling.

115. Enlarg'd: freed.
120. Capitulate: combine. **up:** i.e. in arms.
123. dearest: (1) best beloved; (2) direst.
124. like: likely. **vassal:** slavish.
125. start of spleen: fit of caprice and ill temper.
136. favors: features. **138. lights:** dawns.
145. northren: northern. **147. factor:** agent.
148. engross: gather, amass.
151. worship: honor. **time:** time of life, i.e. youth.
156. intemperance: dissolute behavior.
157. bands: bonds, debts. **159. parcel:** part.
161. charge: command of troops, i.e. a commission.

Lord Mortimer of Scotland hath sent word
That Douglas and the English rebels met
The eleventh of this month at Shrewsbury.
A mighty and a fearful head they are,
If promises be kept on every hand,
As ever off'red foul play in a state.
King. The Earl of Westmerland set forth to-day,
With him my son, Lord John of Lancaster,
For this advertisement is five days old.
On Wednesday next, Harry, you shall set forward,
On Thursday we ourselves will march. Our meeting
Is Bridgenorth. And, Harry, you shall march
Through Gloucestershire; by which account,
Our business valued, some twelve days hence
Our general forces at Bridgenorth shall meet.
Our hands are full of business, let's away,
Advantage feeds him fat while men delay. *Exeunt.*

[SCENE III]

Enter FALSTAFF *and* BARDOLPH.

Fal. Bardolph, am I not fall'n away vilely since this last action? do I not bate? do I not dwindle? Why, my skin hangs about me like an old lady's loose gown; I am wither'd like an old apple-john. Well, I'll repent, and that suddenly, while I am in some liking. I shall be out of heart shortly, and then I shall have no strength to repent. And I have not forgotten what the inside of a church is made of, I am a pepper-corn, a brewer's horse. The inside of a church! Company, villainous company, hath been the spoil of me.

Bard. Sir John, you are so fretful you cannot live long.

Fal. Why, there is it. Come sing me a bawdy song, make me merry. I was as virtuously given as a gentleman need to be, virtuous enough: swore little, dic'd not above seven times—a week, went to a bawdy-house not above once in a quarter—of an hour, paid money that I borrow'd—three or four times, liv'd well and in good compass, and now I live out of all order, out of all compass.

Bard. Why, you are so fat, Sir John, that you must needs be out of all compass, out of all reasonable compass, Sir John.

Fal. Do thou amend thy face, and I'll amend my life. Thou art our admiral, thou bearest the lantern in the poop, but 'tis in the nose of thee. Thou art the Knight of the Burning Lamp.

Bard. Why, Sir John, my face does you no harm.

Fal. No, I'll be sworn, I make as good use of it as many a man doth of a death's-head or a *memento mori*. I never see thy face but I think upon hell-fire and Dives that liv'd in purple; for there he is in his robes, burning, burning. If thou wert any way given to virtue, I would swear by thy face; my oath should be "By this fire, that['s] God's angel." But thou art altogether given over, and wert indeed, but for the light in thy face, the son of utter darkness. When thou ran'st up Gadshill in the night to catch my horse, if I did not think thou hadst been an *ignis fatuus* or a ball of wildfire, there's no purchase in money. O, thou art a perpetual triumph, an everlasting bonfire light! Thou hast sav'd me a thousand marks in links and torches, walking with thee in the night betwixt tavern and tavern; but the sack that thou hast drunk me would have bought me lights as good cheap at the dearest chandler's in Europe. I have maintain'd that salamander of yours with fire any time this two and thirty years, God reward me for it!

Bard. 'Sblood, I would my face were in your belly!

Fal. God-a-mercy, so should I be sure to be heart-burnt.

Enter HOSTESS.

How now, Dame Partlet the hen? have you inquir'd yet who pick'd my pocket?

Host. Why, Sir John, what do you think, Sir John? Do you think I keep thieves in my house? I have search'd, I have inquir'd, so has my husband, man by man, boy by boy, servant by servant. The [tithe] of a hair was never lost in my house before.

Fal. Ye lie, hostess, Bardolph was shav'd, and lost many a hair, and I'll be sworn my pocket was pick'd. Go to, you are a woman, go.

Host. Who, I? No, I defy thee. God's light, I was never call'd so in mine own house before.

Fal. Go to, I know you well enough.

Host. No, Sir John, you do not know me, Sir John. I know you, Sir John, you owe me money, Sir John, and now you pick a quarrel to beguile me of it. I bought you a dozen of shirts to your back.

Fal. Dowlas, filthy dowlas. I have given them away to bakers' wives, they have made bolters of them.

Host. Now as I am a true woman, holland of eight shillings an ell. You owe money here besides, Sir John,

164. Mortimer of Scotland: i.e. George Dunbar, the Scottish Earl of the "March," or border, whom Shakespeare confuses with Edmund, Earl of March. **167. head:** army.
171. John of Lancaster: Prince John, third son of Henry IV.
172. advertisement: information.
174. meeting: meeting place, rendezvous.
175. Bridgenorth: town on the Severn River southeast of Shrewsbury.
177. Our business valued: the time necessary for our business being considered.
180. Advantage . . . fat: i.e. opportunity grows lazy. **him:** himself.

III.iii. Location: The Boar's Head Tavern.
1. fall'n away: shrunk.
2. this last action: i.e. the robbery at Gadshill. **bate:** grow thin.
4. apple-john: kind of apple that could be kept a long time and was eaten after its skin had become shrivelled. **5. suddenly:** at once.
5–6. in some liking: (1) in good condition; (2) in the mood.
9. a brewer's horse: i.e. decrepit. **14. given:** inclined.
19. compass: moderation. **22. compass:** circumference, expanse.
25. admiral: flagship.

30–31. memento mori: reminder of death (e.g. a skull engraved on a seal ring).
32. Dives: in Jesus' parable about the beggar Lazarus, "a certain rich man" who went to hell. See Luke 16:19–31.
35. By . . . angel. Perhaps an echo of Exodus 3:2.
36. given over: i.e. to wickedness.
39. ignis fatuus: will-o'-the-wisp. **40. wildfire:** fireworks.
41. triumph: torchlight procession. **42. links:** torches.
45. as good cheap: as cheap.
47. salamander: fabulous lizard believed to live in fire.
52. Dame Partlet: traditional name for a hen. Falstaff alludes to the Hostess' agitation and flutter. **57. tithe:** tenth part.
69. Dowlas: kind of coarse linen.
70. bolters: cloths for sifting flour. **71. holland:** fine linen.
72. ell: a measurement of 45 inches.

for your diet and by-drinkings, and money lent you, four and twenty pound.

Fal. He had his part of it, let him pay.

Host. He? alas, he is poor, he hath nothing.

Fal. How? poor? Look upon his face; what call you rich? Let them coin his nose, let them coin his cheeks. I'll not pay a denier. What, will you make a younker of me? Shall I not take mine ease in mine inn but I shall have my pocket pick'd? I have lost a seal-ring of my grandfather's worth forty mark.

Host. O Jesu, I have heard the Prince tell him, I know not how oft, that that ring was copper!

Fal. How? the Prince is a Jack, a sneak-up. 'Sblood, and he were here, I would cudgel him like a dog if he would say so.

Enter the PRINCE *marching,* [*with* PETO,] *and Falstaff meets him playing upon his truncheon like a fife.*

How now, lad? is the wind in that door, i' faith? must we all march?

Bard. Yea, two and two, Newgate fashion.

Host. My lord, I pray you hear me.

Prince. What say'st thou, Mistress Quickly? How doth thy husband? I love him well, he is an honest man.

Host. Good my lord, hear me.

Fal. Prithee let her alone, and list to me.

Prince. What say'st thou, Jack?

Fal. The other night I fell asleep here behind the arras and had my pocket pick'd. This house is turn'd bawdy-house, they pick pockets.

Prince. What didst thou lose, Jack?

Fal. Wilt thou believe me, Hal, three or four bonds of forty pound a-piece, and a seal-ring of my grandfather's.

Prince. A trifle, some eight-penny matter.

Host. So I told him, my lord, and I said I heard your Grace say so; and, my lord, he speaks most vilely of you, like a foul-mouth'd man as he is, and said he would cudgel you.

Prince. What, he did not?

Host. There's neither faith, truth, nor womanhood in me else.

Fal. There's no more faith in thee than in a stew'd prune, nor no more truth in thee than in a drawn fox, and for womanhood, Maid Marian may be the deputy's wife of the ward to thee. Go, you thing, go.

Host. Say, what thing? what thing?

Fal. What thing? why, a thing to thank God on.

Host. I am no thing to thank God on, I would thou shouldst know it. I am an honest man's wife, and setting thy knighthood aside, thou art a knave to call me so.

73. by-drinkings: drinks between meals.
79. denier: French copper coin of little value.
80. younker: novice, greenhorn.
85. Jack: rascal. **sneak-up:** sneak.
90. Newgate: a London prison.
112–13. stew'd prune: i.e. bawd. Stewed prunes were commonly associated with brothels.
113. drawn: i.e. out of its hole (and seeking to trick its pursuers).
114–15. Maid . . . thee: i.e. compared to you, Maid Marian—a disreputable character in Robin Hood ballads and May-games—was a model of propriety.
120. setting . . . aside: disregarding your rank.

Fal. Setting thy womanhood aside, thou art a beast to say otherwise.

Host. Say, what beast, thou knave, thou?

Fal. What beast? why, an otter.

Prince. An otter, Sir John, why an otter?

Fal. Why? she's neither fish nor flesh, a man knows not where to have her.

Host. Thou art an unjust man in saying so. Thou or any man knows where to have me, thou knave, thou!

Prince. Thou say'st true, hostess, and he slanders thee most grossly.

Host. So he doth you, my lord, and said this other day you ought him a thousand pound.

Prince. Sirrah, do I owe you a thousand pound?

Fal. A thousand pound, Hal? a million, thy love is worth a million; thou owest me thy love.

Host. Nay, my lord, he call'd you Jack, and said he would cudgel you.

Fal. Did I, Bardolph?

Bard. Indeed, Sir John, you said so.

Fal. Yea, if he said my ring was copper.

Prince. I say 'tis copper. Darest thou be as good as thy word now?

Fal. Why, Hal! thou knowest, as thou art but man, I dare, but as thou art Prince, I fear thee as I fear the roaring of the lion's whelp.

Prince. And why not as the lion?

Fal. The King himself is to be fear'd as the lion. Dost thou think I'll fear thee as I fear thy father? Nay, and I do, I pray God my girdle break.

Prince. O, if it should, how would thy guts fall about thy knees! But, sirrah, there's no room for faith, truth, nor honesty in this bosom of thine; it is all fill'd up with guts and midriff. Charge an honest woman with picking thy pocket! Why, thou whoreson, impudent, emboss'd rascal, if there were any thing in thy pocket but tavern-reckonings, memorandums of bawdy-houses, and one poor pennyworth of sugar-candy to make thee long-winded—if thy pocket were enrich'd with any other injuries but these, I am a villain. And yet you will stand to it, you will not pocket up wrong. Art thou not asham'd?

Fal. Dost thou hear, Hal? Thou knowest in the state of innocency Adam fell, and what should poor Jack Falstaff do in the days of villainy? Thou seest I have more flesh than another man, and therefore more frailty. You confess then you pick'd my pocket?

Prince. It appears so by the story.

Fal. Hostess, I forgive thee. Go make ready breakfast; love thy husband, look to thy servants, cherish thy guesse. Thou shalt find me tractable to any honest reason; thou seest I am pacified still. Nay, prithee be gone. (*Exit Hostess.*) Now, Hal, to the news at court for the robbery, lad, how is that answer'd?

128. where . . . her: i.e. how to take her. In lines 129–30 the Hostess, repeating the phrase, stumbles on an unflattering double-entendre.
134. ought: owed.
157. emboss'd: swollen. **rascal:** lean, inferior deer.
161. injuries: things whose loss would be an injury to you (with a play on the phrase *pocket up injuries* = swallow insults).
172. guesse: guests. **173. still:** always. **176. answer'd:** settled.

Prince. O, my sweet beef, I must still be good angel to thee. The money is paid back again.

Fal. O, I do not like that paying back, 'tis a double labor.

Prince. I am good friends with my father and may do any thing.

Fal. Rob me the exchequer the first thing thou doest, and do it with unwash'd hands too.

Bard. Do, my lord.

Prince. I have procur'd thee, Jack, a charge of foot.

Fal. I would it had been of horse. Where shall I find one that can steal well? O for a fine thief, of the age of two and twenty or thereabouts! I am heinously unprovided. Well, God be thank'd for these rebels, they offend none but the virtuous. I laud them, I praise them.

Prince. Bardolph!

Bard. My lord?

Prince. Go bear this letter to Lord John of Lancaster,
To my brother John; this to my Lord of Westmerland.
[*Exit Bardolph*.]
Go, Peto, to horse, to horse, for thou and I
Have thirty miles to ride yet ere dinner-time.
[*Exit Peto*.]
Jack, meet me to-morrow in the Temple Hall
At two [a'] clock in the afternoon;
There shalt thou know thy charge, and there receive
Money and order for their furniture.
The land is burning, Percy stands on high,
And either we or they must lower lie. [*Exit*.]

Fal. Rare words! brave world! Hostess, my breakfast, come!
O, I could wish this tavern were my drum! [*Exit*.]

[ACT IV, SCENE I]

[*Enter* HOTSPUR, WORCESTER, *and* DOUGLAS.]

Hot. Well said, my noble Scot! If speaking truth
In this fine age were not thought flattery,
Such attribution should the Douglas have
As not a soldier of this season's stamp
Should go so general current through the world.
By God, I cannot flatter, I do defy
The tongues of soothers, but a braver place
In my heart's love hath no man than yourself.
Nay, task me to my word, approve me, lord.

Doug. Thou art the king of honor.
No man so potent breathes upon the ground
But I will beard him.

184. with unwash'd hands: i.e. hastily.
186. charge of foot: command of a company of infantry.
190. unprovided: ill equipped (for the campaign).
199. Temple Hall: hall of the Inner Temple, one of the Inns of Court that housed the legal societies of London.
202. furniture: equipment.
206. I . . . drum. A disputed passage. Perhaps Falstaff means merely that he would rather continue to take his ease at the inn than go to the wars.

IV.i. Location: The rebel camp near Shrewsbury.
3. attribution: tribute. **4. stamp:** coinage.
7. soothers: flatterers. **9. task:** challenge. **approve:** test.
12. But . . . him: but that I will defy him.

Enter one [*a* MESSENGER] *with letters*.

Hot. Do so, and 'tis well.—
What letters hast thou there?—I can but thank you.

Mess. These letters come from your father.

Hot. Letters from him! Why comes he not himself?

Mess. He cannot come, my lord, he is grievous sick.

Hot. 'Zounds! how has he the leisure to be sick
In such a justling time? Who leads his power?
Under whose government come they along?

Mess. His letters bears his mind, not I, my [lord].

Wor. I prithee tell me, doth he keep his bed?

Mess. He did, my lord, four days ere I set forth,
And at the time of my departure thence
He was much fear'd by his physicians.

Wor. I would the state of time had first been whole
Ere he by sickness had been visited,
His health was never better worth than now.

Hot. Sick now? droop now? This sickness doth infect
The very life-blood of our enterprise,
'Tis catching hither, even to our camp.
He writes me here, that inward sickness—
And that his friends by deputation could not
So soon be drawn, nor did he think it meet
To lay so dangerous and dear a trust
On any soul remov'd, but on his own.
Yet doth he give us bold advertisement
That with our small conjunction we should on,
To see how fortune is dispos'd to us,
For, as he writes, there is no quailing now,
Because the King is certainly possess'd
Of all our purposes. What say you to it?

Wor. Your father's sickness is a maim to us.

Hot. A perilous gash, a very limb lopp'd off—
And yet, in faith, it is not; his present want
Seems more than we shall find it. Were it good
To set the exact wealth of all our states
All at one cast? to set so rich a main
On the nice hazard of one doubtful hour?
It were not good, for therein should we read
The very bottom and the soul of hope,
The very list, the very utmost bound
Of all our fortunes.

Doug. Faith, and so we should,
Where now remains a sweet reversion,
We may boldly spend upon the hope of what
[Is] to come in.
A comfort of retirement lives in this.

Hot. A rendezvous, a home to fly unto,

18. justling: turbulent. **power:** troops.
19. government: command. **24. fear'd:** feared for.
25. state of time: times. **whole:** sound, healthy.
27. better worth: more important.
30. catching hither: contagious as far away as this.
32. by deputation: through deputies. **33. drawn:** mustered.
34. dear: significant. **35. remov'd:** i.e. less intimately involved.
36. advertisement: advice. **37. conjunction:** allied force.
40. possess'd: informed. **44. want:** absence.
46. set . . . states: i.e. stake the whole of our resources.
47. main: stake. **48. nice:** delicate. **51. list:** limit.
53. reversion: future prospects, expectation.
56. comfort of retirement: refuge to fall back on.

If that the devil and mischance look big
Upon the maidenhead of our affairs.

Wor. But yet I would your father had been here.
The quality and hair of our attempt
Brooks no division. It will be thought
By some that know not why he is away
That wisdom, loyalty, and mere dislike
Of our proceedings kept the Earl from hence,
And think how such an apprehension
May turn the tide of fearful faction,
And breed a kind of question in our cause.
For well you know we of the off'ring side
Must keep aloof from strict arbitrement,
And stop all sight-holes, every loop from whence
The eye of reason may pry in upon us.
This absence of your father's draws a curtain
That shows the ignorant a kind of fear
Before not dreamt of.

Hot. You strain too far.
I rather of his absence make this use:
It lends a lustre and more great opinion,
A larger dare to our great enterprise,
Than if the Earl were here, for men must think,
If we without his help can make a head
To push against a kingdom, with his help
We shall o'erturn it topsy-turvy down.
Yet all goes well, yet all our joints are whole.

Doug. As heart can think. There is not such a word
Spoke of in Scotland as this term of fear.

Enter SIR RICHARD VERNON.

Hot. My cousin Vernon, welcome, by my soul!

Ver. Pray God my news be worth a welcome, lord.
The Earl of Westmerland, seven thousand strong,
Is marching hitherwards, with him Prince John.

Hot. No harm. What more?

Ver. And further, I have learn'd,
The King himself in person is set forth,
Or hitherwards intended speedily,
With strong and mighty preparation.

Hot. He shall be welcome too. Where is his son,
The nimble-footed madcap Prince of Wales,
And his comrades, that daff'd the world aside
And bid it pass?

Ver. All furnish'd, all in arms;
All plum'd like estridges, that with the wind
Bated like eagles having lately bath'd,
Glittering in golden coats like images,
As full of spirit as the month of May,
And gorgeous as the sun at midsummer;
Wanton as youthful goats, wild as young bulls.

58. **big**: threatening. 59. **maidenhead**: i.e. early phase.
61. **hair**: fiber, nature. 62. **Brooks**: permits.
64. **mere**: outright. 67. **fearful faction**: timorous support.
69. **off'ring**: attacking.
70. **strict arbitrement**: scrupulous inspection.
71. **loop**: loophole. 73. **draws**: draws aside.
77. **opinion**: renown. 80. **make a head**: raise an army.
83. **joints**: limbs. 92. **intended**: i.e. intended to come.
96. **daff'd**: thrust. 97. **furnish'd**: equipped.
98. **estridges**: ostriches.
99. **Bated**: beat their wings (a term from falconry).
103. **Wanton**: frolicsome.

I saw young Harry with his beaver on,
His cushes on his thighs, gallantly arm'd,
Rise from the ground like feathered Mercury,
And vaulted with such ease into his seat
As if an angel [dropp'd] down from the clouds
To turn and wind a fiery Pegasus,
And witch the world with noble horsemanship.

Hot. No more, no more! worse than the sun in March,
This praise doth nourish agues. Let them come!
They come like sacrifices in their trim,
And to the fire-ey'd maid of smoky war
All hot and bleeding will we offer them.
The mailed Mars shall on his [altar] sit
Up to the ears in blood. I am on fire
To hear this rich reprisal is so nigh,
And yet not ours. Come let me taste my horse,
Who is to bear me like a thunderbolt
Against the bosom of the Prince of Wales.
Harry to Harry shall, hot horse to horse,
Meet and ne'er part till one drop down a corse.
O that Glendower were come!

Ver. There is more news:
I learn'd in Worcester, as I rode along,
He [cannot] draw his power this fourteen days.

Doug. That's the worst tidings that I hear of [yet].

Wor. Ay, by my faith, that bears a frosty sound.

Hot. What may the King's whole battle reach unto?

Ver. To thirty thousand.

Hot. Forty let it be!
My father and Glendower being both away,
The powers of us may serve so great a day.
Come let us take a muster speedily.
Doomsday is near, die all, die merrily.

Doug. Talk not of dying, I am out of fear
Of death or death's hand for this one half year.

Exeunt.

[SCENE II]

Enter FALSTAFF, BARDOLPH.

Fal. Bardolph, get thee before to Coventry; fill me a bottle of sack. Our soldiers shall march through; we'll to Sutton Co'fil' to-night.

Bard. Will you give me money, captain?

Fal. Lay out, lay out.

Bard. This bottle makes an angel.

Fal. And if it do, take it for thy labor, and if it

104. **beaver**: helmet.
105. **cushes**: cuisses, armor for the thighs. 107. **seat**: saddle.
109. **wind**: wheel. **Pegasus**: winged horse of ancient myth.
112. **agues**: fevers (thought to result from vapors drawn by the sun).
113. **trim**: finery. 114. **fire-ey'd maid**: i.e. Bellona, goddess of war.
116. **mailed**: armored. 118. **reprisal**: prize.
119. **taste**: test. 123. **corse**: corpse.
125. **Worcester**: cathedral city on the Severn River south of Shrewsbury. 126. **draw his power**: assemble his troops.
129. **battle**: army. 135. **out of**: free from.

IV.ii. Location: A public road near Coventry.
3. **Sutton Co'fil'**: Sutton Coldfield, a town in Warwickshire.
5. **Lay out**: i.e. pay for it yourself.
6. **makes an angel**: i.e. brings your debt to ten shillings. An angel was a gold coin stamped with the figure of the archangel Michael.

make twenty, take them all, I'll answer the coinage. Bid my lieutenant Peto meet me at town's end.

Bard. I will, captain, farewell. *Exit.*

Fal. If I be not asham'd of my soldiers, I am a sous'd gurnet. I have misus'd the King's press damnably. I have got, in exchange of a hundred and fifty soldiers, three hundred and odd pounds. I press me none but good householders, [yeomen's] sons, inquire me out contracted bachelors, such as had been ask'd twice on the banes, such a commodity of warm slaves, as had as lieve hear the devil as a drum, such as fear the report of a caliver worse than a struck fowl or a hurt wild duck. I press'd me none but such toasts-and-butter, with hearts in their bellies no bigger than pins' heads, and they have bought out their services; and now my whole charge consists of ancients, corporals, lieutenants, gentlemen of companies—slaves as ragged as Lazarus in the painted cloth, where the glutton's dogs lick'd his sores, and such as indeed were never soldiers, but discarded unjust servingmen, younger sons to younger brothers, revolted tapsters, and ostlers trade-fall'n, the cankers of a calm world and a long peace, ten times more dishonorable ragged than an old feaz'd ancient: and such have I, to fill up the rooms of them as have bought out their services, that you would think that I had a hundred and fifty totter'd prodigals lately come from swine-keeping, from eating draff and husks. A mad fellow met me on the way and told me I had unloaded all the gibbets and press'd the dead bodies. No eye hath seen such scarecrows. I'll not march through Coventry with them, that's flat. Nay, and the villains march wide betwixt the legs, as if they had gyves on, for indeed I had the most of them out of prison. There's not a shirt and a half in all my company, and the half shirt is two napkins tack'd together and thrown over the shoulders like a herald's coat without sleeves; and the shirt, to say the truth, stol'n from my host at Saint Albons, or the red-nose innkeeper of Daventry. But that's all one, they'll find linen enough on every hedge.

Enter the PRINCE, LORD OF WESTMERLAND.

Prince. How now, blown Jack? how now, quilt?

Fal. What, Hal? how now, mad wag? What a devil dost thou in Warwickshire? My good Lord of Westmerland, I cry you mercy! I thought your honor had already been at Shrewsbury.

West. Faith, Sir John, 'tis more than time that I were there, and you too, but my powers are there already. The King, I can tell you, looks for us all, we must away all night.

Fal. Tut, never fear me, I am as vigilant as a cat to steal cream.

Prince. I think, to steal cream indeed, for thy theft hath already made thee butter. But tell me, Jack, whose fellows are these that come after?

Fal. Mine, Hal, mine.

Prince. I did never see such pitiful rascals.

Fal. Tut, tut, good enough to toss, food for powder, food for powder; they'll fill a pit as well as better. Tush, man, mortal men, mortal men.

West. Ay, but, Sir John, methinks they are exceeding poor and bare, too beggarly.

Fal. Faith, for their poverty, I know not where they had that, and for their bareness, I am sure they never learn'd that of me.

Prince. No, I'll be sworn, unless you call three fingers in the ribs bare. But, sirrah, make haste, Percy is already in the field. *Exit.*

Fal. What, is the King encamp'd?

West. He is, Sir John. I fear we shall stay too long.

Fal. Well,
To the latter end of a fray and the beginning of a feast
Fits a dull fighter and a keen guest. *Exeunt.*

[SCENE III]

Enter HOTSPUR, WORCESTER, DOUGLAS, VERNON.

Hot. We'll fight with him to-night.
Wor. It may not be.
Doug. You give him then advantage.
Ver. Not a whit.
Hot. Why say you so? Looks he not for supply?
Ver. So do we.
Hot. His is certain, ours is doubtful.
Wor. Good cousin, be advis'd, stir not to-night.
Ver. Do not, my lord.
Doug. You do not counsel well,
You speak it out of fear and cold heart.
Ver. Do me no slander, Douglas. By my life,
And I dare well maintain it with my life,
If well-respected honor bid me on,
I hold as little counsel with weak fear
As you, my lord, or any Scot that this day lives.
Let it be seen to-morrow in the battle
Which of us fears.

8. answer the coinage: i.e. be responsible for whatever money the purchases "make."
12. sous'd gurnet: pickled fish. **press:** warrant for conscripting.
14. press: conscript.
16. contracted: engaged to be married.
17. banes: banns, i.e. public announcements, repeated on three successive Sundays, of a projected marriage.
17–18. commodity . . . slaves: lot of comfort-loving fellows.
18. lieve: lief. **19. caliver:** musket. **struck:** wounded.
22–23. bought . . . services: i.e. bribed me to let them off.
23. charge: troop.
24. ancients: ensigns, i.e. standard-bearers.
24–25. gentlemen of companies: gentlemen—but not officers—who had volunteered for military service.
25. Lazarus. See note to III.iii.32.
25–26. painted cloth: cheap wall-hangings. **28. unjust:** dishonest.
29. revolted: runaway. **trade-fall'n:** unemployed.
31. feaz'd ancient: tattered flag.
34. totter'd: tattered. **prodigals.** See Luke 15:11 ff.
35. draff: swill. **41. gyves:** fetters, leg-irons.
46. Saint Albons: St. Albans, town north of London.
47. Daventry: town in Northamptonshire. **that's all one:** i.e. no matter. **48. hedge.** Where linen was spread to dry.
49. blown: swollen.

55. powers: troops.
57. must away: must march. **58. fear:** worry about.
65. toss: i.e. on a pike.
73–74. three fingers: i.e. several layers of fat. A finger, used as a measurement, was three-fourths of an inch.

IV.iii. Location: The rebel camp near Shrewsbury.
3. supply: reinforcements.
10. well-respected: well-considered (in contrast to Hotspur's bravado).

Doug. Yea, or to-night.
Ver. Content.
Hot. To-night, say I.
Ver. Come, come, it may not be. I wonder much,
Being men of such great leading as you are,
That you foresee not what impediments
Drag back our expedition. Certain horse
Of my cousin Vernon's are not yet come up.
Your uncle Worcester's horses came but to-day,
And now their pride and mettle is asleep,
Their courage with hard labor tame and dull,
That not a horse is half the half of himself.
Hot. So are the horses of the enemy
In general journey-bated and brought low.
The better part of ours are full of rest.
Wor. The number of the King exceedeth our.
For God's sake, cousin, stay till all come in.
The trumpet sounds a parley.

Enter Sir Walter Blunt.

Blunt. I come with gracious offers from the King,
If you vouchsafe me hearing and respect.
Hot. Welcome, Sir Walter Blunt; and would to God
You were of our determination!
Some of us love you well, and even those some
Envy your great deservings and good name,
Because you are not of our quality,
But stand against us like an enemy.
Blunt. And God defend but still I should stand so,
So long as out of limit and true rule
You stand against anointed majesty.
But to my charge. The King hath sent to know
The nature of your griefs, and whereupon
You conjure from the breast of civil peace
Such bold hostility, teaching his duteous land
Audacious cruelty. If that the King
Have any way your good deserts forgot,
Which he confesseth to be manifold,
He bids you name your griefs, and with all speed
You shall have your desires with interest
And pardon absolute for yourself and these
Herein misled by your suggestion.
Hot. The King is kind, and well we know the King
Knows at what time to promise, when to pay.
My father and my uncle and myself
Did give him that same royalty he wears,
And when he was not six and twenty strong,
Sick in the world's regard, wretched and low,
A poor unminded outlaw sneaking home,
My father gave him welcome to the shore;
And when he heard him swear and vow to God
He came but to be Duke of Lancaster,
To sue his livery and beg his peace,
With tears of innocency and terms of zeal,
My father, in kind heart and pity mov'd,
Swore him assistance, and perform'd it too.
Now when the lords and barons of the realm
Perceiv'd Northumberland did lean to him,
The more and less came in with cap and knee,
Met him in boroughs, cities, villages,
Attended him on bridges, stood in lanes,
Laid gifts before him, proffer'd him their oaths,
Gave him their heirs as pages, followed him
Even at the heels in golden multitudes.
He presently, as greatness knows itself,
Steps me a little higher than his vow
Made to my father, while his blood was poor,
Upon the naked shore at Ravenspurgh,
And now forsooth takes on him to reform
Some certain edicts and some strait decrees
That lie too heavy on the commonwealth,
Cries out upon abuses, seems to weep
Over his [country's] wrongs, and by this face,
This seeming brow of justice, did he win
The hearts of all that he did angle for;
Proceeded further—cut me off the heads
Of all the favorites that the absent King
In deputation left behind him here,
When he was personal in the Irish war.
Blunt. Tut, I came not to hear this.
Hot. Then to the point.
In short time after, he depos'd the King,
Soon after that, depriv'd him of his life,
And in the neck of that, task'd the whole state;
To make that worse, suff'red his kinsman March
(Who is, if every owner were well plac'd,
Indeed his king) to be engag'd in Wales,
There without ransom to lie forfeited;
Disgrac'd me in my happy victories,
Sought to entrap me by intelligence,
Rated mine uncle from the Council-board,
In rage dismiss'd my father from the court,
Broke oath on oath, committed wrong on wrong,
And in conclusion drove us to seek out
This head of safety, and withal to pry
Into his title, the which we find
Too indirect for long continuance.
Blunt. Shall I return this answer to the King?
Hot. Not so, Sir Walter; we'll withdraw a while.
Go to the King, and let there be impawn'd
Some surety for a safe return again,
And in the morning early shall mine uncle
Bring him our purposes. And so farewell.

17. leading: leadership.
19. expedition: (speedy) progress. **horse**: cavalry.
26. journey-bated: weary from travel. **28. our**: our number.
29. s.d. parley: trumpet call sounded to request a conference.
33. of our determination: i.e. on our side. **35. Envy**: begrudge.
36. quality: party. **38. defend**: forbid.
39. limit . . . rule: i.e. the bounds of honest conduct.
51. suggestion: (evil) prompting.
62. sue his livery: claim his inheritance. **beg his peace**: i.e. from King Richard.
63. terms of zeal: i.e. declarations of loyalty.
65. perform'd it: i.e. fulfilled his oath.
68. with . . . knee: with cap in hand and on bended knee, i.e. deferentially. **70. lanes**: rows. **73. golden**: resplendent.
74. knows itself: comes to recognize its power.
76. blood: spirit. **79. strait**: strict. **82. face**: pretense.
88. personal: personally engaged.
92. in . . . that: immediately thereafter. **task'd**: taxed.
94. if . . . plac'd: i.e. if everyone occupied his proper station.
95. engag'd: held as hostage.
96. forfeited: unclaimed, unredeemed.
97. happy: fortunate. **98. intelligence**: espionage.
99. Rated: scolded.
103. head of safety: army for security. **withal**: moreover.
104. title: i.e. to the throne. **108. impawn'd**: pledged.

Blunt. I would you would accept of grace and love.
Hot. And may be so we shall.
Blunt. Pray God you do. [*Exeunt.*]

[Scene IV]

Enter Archbishop of York, Sir Michael.

Arch. Hie, good Sir Michael, bear this sealed brief
With winged haste to the Lord Marshal,
This to my cousin Scroop, and all the rest
To whom they are directed. If you knew
How much they do import, you would make haste.
Sir M. My good lord,
I guess their tenor.
Arch. Like enough you do.
To-morrow, good Sir Michael, is a day
Wherein the fortune of ten thousand men
Must bide the touch; for, sir, at Shrewsbury,
As I am truly given to understand,
The King with mighty and quick-raised power
Meets with Lord Harry; and I fear, Sir Michael,
What with the sickness of Northumberland,
Whose power was in the first proportion,
And what with Owen Glendower's absence thence,
Who with them was a rated sinew too,
And comes not in, overrul'd by prophecies,
I fear the power of Percy is too weak
To wage an instant trial with the King.
Sir M. Why, my good lord, you need not fear,
There is Douglas and Lord Mortimer.
Arch. No, Mortimer is not there.
Sir M. But there is Mordake, Vernon, Lord Harry Percy,
And there is my Lord of Worcester, and a head
Of gallant warriors, noble gentlemen.
Arch. And so there is; but yet the King hath drawn
The special head of all the land together:
The Prince of Wales, Lord John of Lancaster,
The noble Westmerland, and warlike Blunt,
And many moe corrivals and dear men
Of estimation and command in arms.
Sir M. Doubt not, my lord, they shall be well oppos'd.
Arch. I hope no less, yet needful 'tis to fear,
And to prevent the worst, Sir Michael, speed;
For if Lord Percy thrive not, ere the King
Dismiss his power he means to visit us,
For he hath heard of our confederacy,

IV.iv. Location: York. The Archbishop's palace.
o.s.d. Sir Michael. Apparently unhistorical.
1. **brief**: letter.
2. **Lord Marshal**: i.e. Thomas Mowbray, third Duke of Nottingham, son of the Thomas Mowbray of *Richard II* whose quarrel with Bullingbrook led to the exile of both men. He would of course be hostile to the House of Lancaster.
3. **my cousin Scroop**: perhaps the Scroop (presumably Sir Stephen) of *Richard II*, III.ii.91 ff.
10. **bide the touch**: withstand the test (as when gold is tested by the touchstone).
15. **in . . . proportion**: i.e. larger than that of his associates.
17. **rated sinew**: i.e. a force on which they thought they could rely.
20. **wage**: risk. **instant**: immediate. 25. **head**: troop.
31. **moe corrivals**: more associates. **dear**: valued.
35. **prevent**: forestall. 37. **visit**: i.e. attack.

And 'tis but wisdom to make strong against him.
Therefore make haste. I must go write again
To other friends, and so farewell, Sir Michael.
Exeunt.

[ACT V, Scene I]

Enter the King, Prince of Wales, Lord John of Lancaster, Sir Walter Blunt, Falstaff.

King. How bloodily the sun begins to peer
Above yon bulky hill! the day looks pale
At his distemp'rature.
Prince. The southren wind
Doth play the trumpet to his purposes,
And by his hollow whistling in the leaves
Foretells a tempest and a blust'ring day.
King. Then with the losers let it sympathize,
For nothing can seem foul to those that win.
The trumpet sounds.

Enter Worcester [*and* Sir Richard Vernon].

How now, my Lord of Worcester? 'tis not well
That you and I should meet upon such terms
As now we meet. You have deceiv'd our trust,
And made us doff our easy robes of peace,
To crush our old limbs in ungentle steel.
This is not well, my lord, this is not well.
What say you to it? Will you again unknit
This churlish knot of all-abhorred war?
And move in that obedient orb again
Where you did give a fair and natural light,
And be no more an exhal'd meteor,
A prodigy of fear, and a portent
Of broached mischief to the unborn times?
Wor. Hear me, my liege.
For mine own part, I could be well content
To entertain the lag end of my life
With quiet hours; for I protest
I have not sought the day of this dislike.
King. You have not sought it, how comes it then?
Fal. Rebellion lay in his way, and he found it.
Prince. Peace, chewet, peace!
Wor. It pleas'd your Majesty to turn your looks
Of favor from myself and all our house,
And yet I must remember you, my lord,
We were the first and dearest of your friends.
For you my staff of office did I break
In Richard's time, and posted day and night
To meet you on the way, and kiss your hand,
When yet you were in place and in account
Nothing so strong and fortunate as I.
It was myself, my brother, and his son,
That brought you home, and boldly did outdare

V.i. Location: The King's camp near Shrewsbury.
3. **his distemp'rature**: i.e. the sun's abnormal appearance. **southren**: southern. 4. **trumpet**: trumpeter. 7. **sympathize**: accord.
17. **obedient orb**: (customary) sphere of obedience.
19. **exhal'd meteor.** It was believed that meteors were formed of vapors drawn up from the earth (*exhal'd*) by the sun.
20. **prodigy of fear**: terrifying omen. 21. **broached**: set going.
24. **entertain**: pass. 29. **chewet**: jackdaw, i.e. chatterer.
32. **remember**: remind.
34–35. **For . . . time.** See *Richard II*, II.iii.26–28.
38. **Nothing**: by no means.

The dangers of the time. You swore to us,
And you did swear that oath at Doncaster,
That you did nothing purpose 'gainst the state,
Nor claim no further than your new-fall'n right,
The seat of Gaunt, dukedom of Lancaster.
To this we swore our aid. But in short space
It rain'd down fortune show'ring on your head,
And such a flood of greatness fell on you,
What with our help, what with the absent King,
What with the injuries of a wanton time,
The seeming sufferances that you had borne,
And the contrarious winds that held the King
So long in his unlucky Irish wars
That all in England did repute him dead;
And from this swarm of fair advantages
You took occasion to be quickly wooed
To gripe the general sway into your hand,
Forgot your oath to us at Doncaster,
And being fed by us you us'd us so
As that ungentle gull, the cuckoo's bird,
Useth the sparrow; did oppress our nest,
Grew by our feeding to so great a bulk
That even our love durst not come near your sight
For fear of swallowing; but with nimble wing
We were enforc'd for safety sake to fly
Out of your sight and raise this present head,
Whereby we stand opposed by such means
As you yourself have forg'd against yourself
By unkind usage, dangerous countenance,
And violation of all faith and troth
Sworn to us in your younger enterprise.

King. These things indeed you have articulate,
Proclaim'd at market-crosses, read in churches,
To face the garment of rebellion
With some fine color that may please the eye
Of fickle changelings and poor discontents,
Which gape and rub the elbow at the news
Of hurly-burly innovation;
And never yet did insurrection want
Such water-colors to impaint his cause,
Nor moody beggars, starving for a time
Of pell-mell havoc and confusion.

Prince. In both your armies there is many a soul
Shall pay full dearly for this encounter,
If once they join in trial. Tell your nephew
The Prince of Wales doth join with all the world
In praise of Henry Percy. By my hopes,
This present enterprise set off his head,
I do not think a braver gentleman,
More active, valiant, or more valiant, young,
More daring or more bold, is now alive
To grace this latter age with noble deeds.
For my part, I may speak it to my shame,
I have a truant been to chivalry,
And so I hear he doth account me too;
Yet this before my father's Majesty:
I am content that he shall take the odds
Of his great name and estimation,
And will, to save the blood on either side,
Try fortune with him in a single fight.

King. And, Prince of Wales, so dare we venture thee,
Albeit considerations infinite
Do make against it. No, good Worcester, no,
We love our people well, even those we love
That are misled upon your cousin's part,
And, will they take the offer of our grace,
Both he and they and you, yea, every man
Shall be my friend again, and I'll be his.
So tell your cousin, and bring me word
What he will do. But if he will not yield,
Rebuke and dread correction wait on us,
And they shall do their office. So be gone;
We will not now be troubled with reply.
We offer fair, take it advisedly.

Exit Worcester [with Vernon].

Prince. It will not be accepted, on my life.
The Douglas and the Hotspur both together
Are confident against the world in arms.

King. Hence therefore, every leader to his charge,
For on their answer will we set on them,
And God befriend us as our cause is just!

Exeunt. Manent Prince, Falstaff.

Fal. Hal, if thou see me down in the battle and bestride me, so; 'tis a point of friendship.

Prince. Nothing but a Colossus can do thee that friendship. Say thy prayers, and farewell.

Fal. I would 'twere bed-time, Hal, and all well.

Prince. Why, thou owest God a death. [*Exit.*]

Fal. 'Tis not due yet, I would be loath to pay him before his day. What need I be so forward with him that calls not on me? Well, 'tis no matter, honor pricks me on. Yea, but how if honor prick me off when I come on? how then? Can honor set to a leg? No. Or an arm? No. Or take away the grief of a wound? No. Honor hath no skill in surgery then? No. What is honor? A word. What is in that word honor? What is that honor? Air. A trim reckoning! Who hath it? He that died a' Wednesday. Doth he feel it? No. Doth he hear it? No. 'Tis insensible

42. Doncaster: town in Yorkshire. According to Holinshed (Bullough, III, 398), when Bullingbrook reached Doncaster, on his march from Ravenspur, "the earle of Northumberland, and his sonne, sir Henrie Persie, wardens of the marches against Scotland, with the earle of Westmerland, came unto him, where he sware unto those lords that he would demand no more, but the lands that were to him descended by inheritance from his father, and in right of his wife."
44. new-fall'n: recently inherited. **50. injuries:** abuses.
51. sufferances: sufferings. **57. gripe:** seize.
60. ungentle gull: rude nestling.
63. our love: we who loved you.
64. swallowing: i.e. being swallowed.
69. unkind usage: unnatural treatment. **dangerous:** threatening.
70. troth: truth. **72. articulate:** stated in articles.
74. face: trim.
76. changelings: turncoats. **discontents:** malcontents.
77. rub the elbow: i.e. hug themselves with pleasure.
78. innovation: rebellion.
80. water-colors: i.e. thin excuses.
81. moody: sullen, disaffected.
83. both: i.e. the King's and the rebels'.

88. This . . . head: not counting his part in this rebellion.
89. braver: nobler. **98. estimation:** renown.
100. single fight. The Prince's challenge was apparently Shakespeare's own invention. **102. Albeit:** although. **122. so:** good.
126. death: with a homophonic pun on *debt*. **132. grief:** pain.
135. trim reckoning: neat total.
137. insensible: imperceptible to the senses.

then? Yea, to the dead. But will['t] not live with the living? No. Why? Detraction will not suffer it. Therefore I'll none of it, honor is a mere scutcheon. And so ends my catechism. *Exit.*

[Scene II]

Enter Worcester, Sir Richard Vernon.

Wor. O no, my nephew must not know, Sir Richard,
The liberal and kind offer of the King.
Ver. 'Twere best he did.
Wor. Then are we all [undone];
It is not possible, it cannot be,
The King should keep his word in loving us.
He will suspect us still, and find a time
To punish this offense in other faults.
Supposition all our lives shall be stuck full of eyes,
For treason is but trusted like the fox,
Who never so tame, so cherish'd and lock'd up,
Will have a wild trick of his ancestors.
Look how we can, or sad or merrily,
Interpretation will misquote our looks,
And we shall feed like oxen at a stall,
The better cherish'd, still the nearer death.
My nephew's trespass may be well forgot,
It hath the excuse of youth and heat of blood,
And an adopted name of privilege,
A hare-brain'd Hotspur, govern'd by a spleen.
All his offenses live upon my head
And on his father's. We did train him on,
And his corruption being ta'en from us,
We as the spring of all shall pay for all.
Therefore, good cousin, let not Harry know,
In any case, the offer of the King.
Ver. Deliver what you will, I'll say 'tis so.
Here comes your cousin.

Enter Percy [Hotspur *and* Douglas].

Hot. My uncle is return'd,
Deliver up my Lord of Westmerland.
Uncle, what news?
Wor. The King will bid you battle presently.
Doug. Defy him by the Lord of Westmerland.
Hot. Lord Douglas, go you and tell him so.
Doug. Marry, and shall, and very willingly.
Exit Douglas.
Wor. There is no seeming mercy in the King.
Hot. Did you beg any? God forbid!
Wor. I told him gently of our grievances,
Of his oath-breaking, which he mended thus,
By now forswearing that he is forsworn.
He calls us rebels, traitors, and will scourge
With haughty arms this hateful name in us.

Enter Douglas.

Doug. Arm, gentlemen, to arms! for I have thrown
A brave defiance in King Henry's teeth,
And Westmerland, that was engag'd, did bear it,
Which cannot choose but bring him quickly on.
Wor. The Prince of Wales stepp'd forth before the King,
And, nephew, challeng'd you to single fight.
Hot. O would the quarrel lay upon our heads,
And that no man might draw short breath to-day
But I and Harry Monmouth! Tell me, tell me,
How show'd his tasking? seem'd it in contempt?
Ver. No, by my soul, I never in my life
Did hear a challenge urg'd more modestly,
Unless a brother should a brother dare
To gentle exercise and proof of arms.
He gave you all the duties of a man,
Trimm'd up your praises with a princely tongue,
Spoke your deservings like a chronicle,
Making you ever better than his praise
By still dispraising praise valued with you,
And which became him like a prince indeed,
He made a blushing cital of himself,
And chid his truant youth with such a grace
As if he mast'red there a double spirit
Of teaching and of learning instantly.
There did he pause, but let me tell the world,
If he outlive the envy of this day,
England did never owe so sweet a hope,
So much misconstrued in his wantonness.
Hot. Cousin, I think thou art enamored
On his follies. Never did I hear
Of any prince so wild a liberty.
But be he as he will, yet once ere night
I will embrace him with a soldier's arm
That he shall shrink under my courtesy.
Arm, arm with speed! and, fellows, soldiers, friends,
Better consider what you have to do
Than I, that have not well the gift of tongue,
Can lift your blood up with persuasion.

Enter a Messenger.

Mess. My lord, here are letters for you.
Hot. I cannot read them now.
O gentlemen, the time of life is short!
To spend that shortness basely were too long
If life did ride upon a dial's point,
Still ending at the arrival of an hour.
And if we live, we live to tread on kings,
If die, brave death, when princes die with us!

140. scutcheon: heraldic device exhibited at funerals, on coaches, etc.

V.ii. Location: A plain near the rebel camp.
6. still: always. **8. Supposition:** suspicion.
10. never so: however.
11. wild trick: i.e. trace of the characteristic wildness.
18. adopted . . . privilege: i.e. a nickname (Hotspur) that sanctions rash behavior. **19. spleen:** irrational impulse.
21. train: lure (into rebellion). **23. spring:** source.
26. Deliver: report.
28. Deliver up: release. **Westmerland.** The hostage mentioned at IV.iii.108–9. **30. presently:** at once.

42. brave: haughty.
43. engag'd: held as hostage. **50. tasking:** challenge.
52. urg'd: presented. **54. proof:** test. **55. duties:** due merits.
59. dispraising: disparaging, discounting. **valued:** compared.
61. cital: impeachment. **64. instantly:** simultaneously.
66. envy: malice. **67. owe:** own.
71. so . . . liberty: such reckless dissipation.
83. dial's point: clock's hand.
84. Still . . . hour: i.e. lasting only for an hour.

Now for our consciences, the arms are fair
When the intent of bearing them is just.

Enter another [MESSENGER].

[2.] *Mess.* My lord, prepare, the King comes on apace.

Hot. I thank him that he cuts me from my tale,
For I profess not talking; only this—
Let each man do his best, and here draw I
A sword, whose temper I intend to stain
With the best blood that I can meet withal
In the adventure of this perilous day.
Now *Esperance! Percy!* and set on.
Sound all the lofty instruments of war,
And by that music let us all embrace,
For, heaven to earth, some of us never shall
A second time do such a courtesy.

Here they embrace [*and exeunt*].

[SCENE III]

The trumpets sound. The KING *enters with his power* [*and passes over*]. *Alarm to the battle. Then enter* DOUGLAS *and* SIR WALTER BLUNT.

Blunt. What is thy name, that in battle thus
Thou crossest me? What honor dost thou seek
Upon my head?

Doug. Know then, my name is Douglas,
And I do haunt thee in the battle thus
Because some tell me that thou art a king.

Blunt. They tell thee true.

Doug. The Lord of Stafford dear to-day hath bought
Thy likeness, for in stead of thee, King Harry,
This sword hath ended him. So shall it thee,
Unless thou yield thee as my prisoner.

Blunt. I was not born a yielder, thou proud Scot,
And thou shalt find a king that will revenge
Lord Stafford's death.

They fight. Douglas kills Blunt.

Then enter HOTSPUR.

Hot. O Douglas, hadst thou fought at Holmedon thus,
I never had triumph'd upon a Scot.

Doug. All's done, all's won, here breathless lies the King.

Hot. Where?

Doug. Here.

Hot. This, Douglas? No, I know this face full well.
A gallant knight he was, his name was Blunt,
Semblably furnish'd like the King himself.

Doug. [A] fool go with thy soul, whither it goes!
A borrowed title hast thou bought too dear.
Why didst thou tell me that thou wert a king?

Hot. The King hath many marching in his coats.

Doug. Now by my sword, I will kill all his coats;
I'll murder all his wardrop, piece by piece,
Until I meet the King.

Hot. Up and away!
Our soldiers stand full fairly for the day. [*Exeunt.*]

Alarm. Enter FALSTAFF *solus.*

Fal. Though I could scape shot-free at London, I fear the shot here, here's no scoring but upon the pate. Soft, who are you? Sir Walter Blunt. There's honor for you! Here's no vanity! I am as hot as molten lead, and as heavy too. God keep lead out of me! I need no more weight than mine own bowels. I have led my ragamuffins where they are pepper'd; there's not three of my hundred and fifty left alive, and they are for the town's end, to beg during life. But who comes here?

Enter the PRINCE.

Prince. What, stands thou idle here? Lend me thy sword.
Many a nobleman lies stark and stiff
Under the hoofs of vaunting enemies,
Whose deaths are yet unreveng'd. I prithee lend me thy sword.

Fal. O Hal, I prithee give me leave to breathe a while. Turk Gregory never did such deeds in arms as I have done this day. I have paid Percy, I have made him sure.

Prince. He is indeed, and living to kill thee. I prithee lend me thy sword.

Fal. Nay, before God, Hal, if Percy be alive, thou gets not my sword, but take my pistol, if thou wilt.

Prince. Give it me. What? is it in the case?

Fal. Ay, Hal, 'tis hot, 'tis hot. There's that will sack a city.

The Prince draws it out, and finds it to be a bottle of sack.

Prince. What, is it a time to jest and dally now?

He throws the bottle at him. Exit.

Fal. Well, if Percy be alive, I'll pierce him. If he do come in my way, so; if he do not, if I come in his

87. for: as for. **fair:** just.
99. heaven to earth: heaven wagered against earth.

V.iii. Location: Scene continues.
o.s.d. power: army. **Alarm:** trumpet signal to advance.
10. yield thee: surrender yourself.
13. Lord Stafford's death. According to Holinshed (Bullough, IV, 190–91), Hotspur and Douglas, intent on killing the King, "gave such a violent onset upon them that stood about the kings standard, that slaieng his standard-bearer sir Walter Blunt, and overthrowing the standard, they made slaughter of all those that stood about it, as the earle of Stafford, that daie made by the king constable of the realme, and diverse other."

21. Semblably furnish'd: similarly armed and dressed (to serve as a decoy).
22. A fool . . . goes: i.e. may the opprobrious epithet "fool" be attached to you, wherever you're going.
25. The King . . . coats. A common stratagem.
27. wardrop: wardrobe.
29. stand . . . day: i.e. seem to be upon the point of victory.
30. shot-free: i.e. without paying the shot, or tavern bill.
31. scoring: cutting (with a pun on scoring one's bill by making notches on a stick). **33. vanity:** trifling.
38. town's end: i.e. the city gate (where beggars congregated).
45. Turk: stock title for a merciless person. **Gregory:** perhaps Pope Gregory VII, who was famous for his valor.
46. paid: settled with, i.e. killed.
47. made him sure: made sure of him.
48. He is: i.e. he is sure (to be alive and dangerous).
56. pierce. Pronounced *perse*.

willingly, let him make a carbonado of me. I like not such grinning honor as Sir Walter hath. Give me life, which if I can save, so; if not, honor comes unlook'd for, and there's an end. [*Exit.*]

[Scene IV]

Alarm. Excursions. Enter the King, *the* Prince [*wounded*], Lord John of Lancaster, Earl of Westmerland.

King. I prithee,
Harry, withdraw thyself, thou bleedest too much.
Lord John of Lancaster, go you with him.
Lan. Not I, my lord, unless I did bleed too.
Prince. I beseech your Majesty make up,
Lest your retirement do amaze your friends.
King. I will do so.
My Lord of Westmerland, lead him to his tent.
West. Come, my lord, I'll lead you to your tent.
Prince. Lead me, my lord? I do not need your help,
And God forbid a shallow scratch should drive
The Prince of Wales from such a field as this,
Where stain'd nobility lies trodden on,
And rebels' arms triumph in massacres!
Lan. We breathe too long. Come, cousin Westmerland,
Our duty this way lies; for God's sake come.
[*Exeunt Prince John and Westmerland.*]
Prince. By God, thou hast deceiv'd me, Lancaster,
I did not think thee lord of such a spirit.
Before, I lov'd thee as a brother, John,
But now I do respect thee as my soul.
King. I saw him hold Lord Percy at the point,
With lustier maintenance than I did look for
Of such an ungrown warrior.
Prince. O, this boy
Lends mettle to us all! *Exit.*

[*Enter* Douglas.]

Doug. Another king? they grow like Hydra's heads.
I am the Douglas, fatal to all those
That wear those colors on them. What art thou
That counterfeit'st the person of a king?
King. The King himself, who, Douglas, grieves at heart
So many of his shadows thou hast met
And not the very King. I have two boys
Seek Percy and thyself about the field,
But seeing thou fall'st on me so luckily,
I will assay thee, and defend thyself.
Doug. I fear thou art another counterfeit,
And yet in faith thou bearest thee like a king.
But mine I am sure thou art, whoe'er thou be,
And thus I win thee.

They fight; the King being in danger, enter Prince of Wales.

Prince. Hold up thy head, vile Scot, or thou art like
Never to hold it up again! The spirits
Of valiant Shirley, Stafford, Blunt are in my arms.
It is the Prince of Wales that threatens thee,
Who never promiseth but he means to pay.
They fight: Douglas flieth.
Cheerly, my lord, how fares your Grace?
Sir Nicholas Gawsey hath for succor sent,
And so hath Clifton. I'll to Clifton straight.
King. Stay and breathe a while.
Thou hast redeem'd thy lost opinion,
And show'd thou mak'st some tender of my life
In this fair rescue thou hast brought to me.
Prince. O God, they did me too much injury
That ever said I heark'ned for your death.
If it were so, I might have let alone
The insulting hand of Douglas over you,
Which would have been as speedy in your end
As all the poisonous potions in the world,
And sav'd the treacherous labor of your son.
King. Make up to Clifton, I'll to Sir Nicholas Gawsey. *Exit King.*

Enter Hotspur.

Hot. If I mistake not, thou art Harry Monmouth.
Prince. Thou speak'st as if I would deny my name.
Hot. My name is Harry Percy.
Prince. Why then I see
A very valiant rebel of the name.
I am the Prince of Wales, and think not, Percy,
To share with me in glory any more.
Two stars keep not their motion in one sphere,
Nor can one England brook a double reign
Of Harry Percy and the Prince of Wales.
Hot. [Nor] shall it, Harry, for the hour is come
To end the one of us, and would to God
Thy name in arms were now as great as mine!
Prince. I'll make it greater ere I part from thee,
And all the budding honors on thy crest
I'll crop to make a garland for my head.
Hot. I can no longer brook thy vanities.
They fight.

58. carbonado: meat slashed for broiling.

V.iv. Location: Scene continues.
o.s.d. Excursions: sallies, sorties. **5. make up:** advance.
6. amaze: dismay.
13. stain'd: (1) soiled with battle; (2) disgraced.
15. breathe: pause for breath.
22. lustier maintenance: more valiant endurance.
25. Hydra: in Greek mythology, a many-headed monster that grew two new heads for each one struck off. Holinshed (Bullough, IV, 191) reports that Douglas "slue sir Walter Blunt, and three other, apparelled in the kings sute and clothing, saieng: I marvell to see so many kings thus suddenlie arise one in the necke of an other."
27. those colors: i.e. the colors of the King's coat of arms.
30. shadows: likenesses.

31. the very King: the King himself. **32. Seek:** who seek.
34. assay: challenge.
41, 45, 46. Shirley, Gawsey, Clifton. Holinshed (Bullough, IV, 191) mentions "sir Hugh Shorlie," "sir Nicholas Gausell," and "sir John Clifton" as notable casualties of the battle of Shrewsbury.
44 s.d. They . . . flieth. Holinshed (Bullough, IV, 191) records the tradition that the King was struck down by Douglas but does not assign his rescue to the Prince, saying only that the King "was raised."
48. opinion: reputation. **49. mak'st . . . of:** hast some regard for.
54. insulting: exulting. **66. brook:** endure.

Enter FALSTAFF.

Fal. Well said, Hal! to it, Hal! Nay, you shall find no boy's play here, I can tell you.

Enter DOUGLAS; *he fighteth with Falstaff. He* [*Falstaff*] *falls down as if he were dead* [*and exit Douglas*]. *The Prince killeth Percy.*

Hot. O Harry, thou hast robb'd me of my youth!
I better brook the loss of brittle life
Than those proud titles thou hast won of me.
They wound my thoughts worse than thy sword my flesh.
But thoughts, the slaves of life, and life, time's fool,
And time, that takes survey of all the world,
Must have a stop. O, I could prophesy,
But that the earthy and cold hand of death
Lies on my tongue. No, Percy, thou art dust,
And food for— [*Dies.*]

Prince. For worms, brave Percy. Fare thee well, great heart!
Ill-weav'd ambition, how much art thou shrunk!
When that this body did contain a spirit,
A kingdom for it was too small a bound,
But now two paces of the vilest earth
Is room enough. This earth that bears [thee] dead
Bears not alive so stout a gentleman.
If thou wert sensible of courtesy,
I should not make so dear a show of zeal;
But let my favors hide thy mangled face,
And even in thy behalf I'll thank myself
For doing these fair rites of tenderness.
Adieu, and take thy praise with thee to heaven!
Thy ignominy sleep with thee in the grave,
But not remember'd in thy epitaph!

He spieth Falstaff on the ground.

What, old acquaintance! could not all this flesh
Keep in a little life? Poor Jack, farewell!
I could have better spar'd a better man.
O, I should have a heavy miss of thee
If I were much in love with vanity!
Death hath not strook so fat a deer to-day,
Though many dearer, in this bloody fray.
Embowell'd will I see thee by and by,
Till then in blood by noble Percy lie.

Exit. Falstaff riseth up.

Fal. Embowell'd! if thou embowel me to-day, I'll give you leave to powder me and eat me too to-morrow. 'Sblood, 'twas time to counterfeit, or that hot termagant Scot had paid me scot and lot too. Counterfeit? I lie, I am no counterfeit. To die is to be a counterfeit, for he is but the counterfeit of a man who hath not the life of a man; but to counterfeit dying, when a man thereby liveth, is to be no counterfeit, but the true and perfect image of life indeed. The better part of valor is discretion, in the which better part I have sav'd my life. 'Zounds, I am afraid of this gunpowder Percy though he be dead. How if he should counterfeit too and rise? By my faith, I am afraid he would prove the better counterfeit. Therefore I'll make him sure, yea, and I'll swear I kill'd him. Why may not he rise as well as I? Nothing confutes me but eyes, and nobody sees me. Therefore, sirrah [*stabbing him*], with a new wound in your thigh, come you along with me. *He takes up Hotspur on his back.*

Enter PRINCE [*and*] JOHN OF LANCASTER.

Prince. Come, brother John, full bravely hast thou flesh'd
Thy maiden sword.

Lan. But soft, whom have we here?
Did you not tell me this fat man was dead?

Prince. I did, I saw him dead,
Breathless and bleeding on the ground. Art thou alive?
Or is it fantasy that plays upon our eyesight?
I prithee speak, we will not trust our eyes
Without our ears: thou art not what thou seem'st.

Fal. No, that's certain, I am not a double man; but if I be not Jack Falstaff, then am I a Jack. There is Percy [*throwing the body down*]. If your father will do me any honor, so; if not, let him kill the next Percy himself. I look to be either earl or duke, I can assure you.

Prince. Why, Percy I kill'd myself, and saw thee dead.

Fal. Didst thou? Lord, Lord, how this world is given to lying! I grant you I was down and out of breath, and so was he, but we rose both at an instant and fought a long hour by Shrewsbury clock. If I may be believ'd, so; if not, let them that should reward valor bear the sin upon their own heads. I'll take it upon my death, I gave him this wound in the thigh. If the man were alive and would deny it, 'zounds, I would make him eat a piece of my sword.

Lan. This is the strangest tale that ever I heard.

Prince. This is the strangest fellow, brother John.
Come bring your luggage nobly on your back.
For my part, if a lie may do thee grace,
I'll gild it with the happiest terms I have.

A retrait is sounded.

The trumpet sounds retrait, the day is our.
Come, brother, let us to the highest of the field,
To see what friends are living, who are dead.

Exeunt [*Prince and Lancaster*].

Fal. I'll follow, as they say, for reward. He that rewards me, God reward him! If I do grow great, I'll grow less, for I'll purge and leave sack, and live cleanly as a nobleman should do. *Exit.*

83. I could prophesy. Dying men were thought to have the gift of prophecy.
86 s.d. Dies. Holinshed (Bullough, IV, 191) does not credit the Prince with Hotspur's death, saying merely that those loyal to the King, "incouraged by his doings, fought valiantlie, and slue the lord Persie, called sir Henrie Hotspurre." **93. stout:** brave.
95. make . . . zeal: i.e. express my admiration so freely.
96. favors: scarves, gloves, plumes, or the like (with which the Prince covers Hotspur's "mangled face"). **106. vanity:** frivolity.
109. Embowell'd: disembowelled (for embalming).
112. powder: salt. **114. termagant:** violent.
114. scot and lot: completely.
120. part: quality.
130. flesh'd: initiated (with the first taste of blood).
138. double man: (1) spectre; (2) two men. **139. Jack:** rascal.
157. grace: credit.
158 s.d. retrait: retreat, trumpet signal to withdraw.
159. our: ours. **160. highest:** highest point.
164. purge: (1) take laxatives (to reduce); (2) purge my sins, i.e. repent.

[Scene V]

The trumpets sound. Enter the King, Prince of Wales, Lord John of Lancaster, Earl of Westmerland, *with* Worcester *and* Vernon *prisoners.*

King. Thus ever did rebellion find rebuke.
Ill-spirited Worcester, did not we send grace,
Pardon, and terms of love to all of you?
And wouldst thou turn our offers contrary?
Misuse the tenor of thy kinsman's trust?
Three knights upon our party slain to-day,
A noble earl, and many a creature else
Had been alive this hour,
If like a Christian thou hadst truly borne
Betwixt our armies true intelligence.
Wor. What I have done my safety urg'd me to;
And I embrace this fortune patiently,
Since not to be avoided it falls on me.
King. Bear Worcester to the death and Vernon too.
Other offenders we will pause upon.
[*Exeunt Worcester and Vernon guarded.*]
How goes the field?
Prince. The noble Scot, Lord Douglas, when he saw
The fortune of the day quite turn'd from him,
The noble Percy slain, and all his men
Upon the foot of fear, fled with the rest,
And falling from a hill, he was so bruis'd
That the pursuers took him. At my tent
The Douglas is; and I beseech your Grace
I may dispose of him.
King. With all my heart.
Prince. Then, brother John of Lancaster, to you
This honorable bounty shall belong.
Go to the Douglas, and deliver him
Up to his pleasure, ransomless and free.
His valors shown upon our crests to-day
Have taught us how to cherish such high deeds
Even in the bosom of our adversaries.
Lan. I thank your Grace for this high courtesy,
Which I shall give away immediately.
King. Then this remains, that we divide our power.
You, son John, and my cousin Westmerland
Towards York shall bend you with your dearest speed,
To meet Northumberland and the prelate Scroop,
Who, as we hear, are busily in arms.
Myself and you, son Harry, will towards Wales,
To fight with Glendower and the Earl of March.
Rebellion in this land shall lose his sway,
Meeting the check of such another day,
And since this business so fair is done,
Let us not leave till all our own be won. *Exeunt.*

V.v. Location: The command post of the King.
2. grace: assurance of favor.
3. terms of love: expressions of friendship.
5. Misuse . . . trust: i.e. abuse Hotspur's confidence in you (as emissaries). **10. intelligence:** information.
12. patiently: tranquilly. **15. pause upon:** reflect about.
20. Upon . . . fear: fleeing in terror.
21–22. falling . . . him. According to Holinshed (Bullough, IV, 191), "the earle of Dowglas, for hast, falling from the crag of an hie mounteine, brake one of his cullions [testicles], and was taken, and for his valiantnesse, of the king frankelie and freelie delivered."
24. dispose of him: decide what to do with him.
26. honorable bounty: gracious assignment. **27. deliver:** release.
33. give away: i.e. inform Douglas of. **34. power:** army.
36. dearest: most zealous. **43. fair:** successfully.

NOTE ON THE TEXT

The First Part of Henry the Fourth was first published in quarto in 1598. Of this edition (here referred to as Q0) only a single sheet (C) now exists. A second edition, printed in the same year from a copy of Q0, is now generally known as the First Quarto (Q1) and is here used as copy-text, except for I.iii.201–II.ii.111, where Q0 serves as copy-text. Judging by the section of text common to Q0 and Q1, Q1 appears, despite three substantive variants (one, at least, a correction), to be a careful reprint of Q0. Later quartos, each printed from the one immediately preceding, appeared in 1599 (Q2), 1604 (Q3), 1608 (Q4), 1613 (Q5), and 1622 (Q6). After the play had appeared in the First Folio (1623), printed from an edited copy of Q5, two more quarto editions were published, 1632 (Q7) and 1639 (Q8).

The nature of the copy underlying Q0 (and hence at one remove Q1) is open to argument: (a) "foul papers" (Wilson); (b) revised "foul papers" (Humphreys, Bevington); (c) scribal transcript of "foul papers" (Bowers, Jackson, Jowett/Taylor). Q0–Q1's rather pedantic use of uncontracted and generally less colloquial forms, particularly in the prose comic scenes, and the relative scarcity of characteristic Shakespearean spellings would appear to favor the use of a scribal transcript. For the political pressures motivating the change of names from Sir John Oldcastle to Sir John Falstaff, as well as the change from Harvey and Russell (Rossill Q) to Peto and Bardolph, see the Introduction, p. 885, I.ii.41–2, and Textual Notes I.ii.162 and *2 Henry IV*, I.ii.120, II.ii o.s.d.

Aside from the errors inherited from its copy-text (Q5), the F1 text offers a number of slight textual variations, especially in the careful deletion or softening of oaths, but it is not generally believed that these changes have any dependence on prompt-book authority. They suggest rather either the hand of a "literary" editor or, perhaps, the result of a sporadic consultation of, or collation against, some kind of sophisticated transcript, similar, it has been suggested, to the sort of manuscript that served as copy for the F1 text of *2 Henry IV*. Because the particular agency behind the F1 variants is so uncertain, the present text adopts such variants only when they clearly correct the Q0–Q1 text. All significant variants in F1, and all its additions and omissions, have been recorded in the Textual Notes.

In addition to the early printed texts there exists a manuscript version (called the Dering MS, now in the Folger Shakespeare Library) which telescopes the two parts of *Henry IV* into a single play of roughly 3,390 lines. Precisely when the transcript was made (from a copy of Q5 for *1 Henry IV* and of Q [1600] for *2 Henry IV*) is uncertain, but the most likely date is about 1622. Although it has no independent authority, the textual variants stemming presumably from Sir Edward Dering himself, the manuscript affords occasional helpful stage directions and readings, and a few references to it will be found in the Textual Notes. Absence of citation for the Dering MS must not be interpreted as implying agreement with the lemma.

For further information, see: S. B. Hemingway, ed., New Variorum *1 Henry IV* (Philadelphia, 1936), and G. B. Evans, ed., Supplement to New Variorum *1 Henry IV* (Shakespeare Association of America, 1956); J. D. Wilson, ed., New Shakespeare *1 Henry IV* (Cambridge, 1946); Alice Walker, "The Folio Text of *1 Henry IV*," *SB*, VI (1954), 45–59; W. W. Greg, *The Shakespeare First Folio* (Oxford, 1955); G. B. Evans, "The 'Dering MS' of Shakespeare's *Henry IV* and Sir Edward Dering," *JEGP*, LIV (1955), 498–503; A. R. Humphreys, ed., New Arden *1 Henry IV* (London, 1960); Charlton Hinman (and W. W. Greg), eds., *Henry IV, Part I (1598)*, facsimile of Q1 (Oxford, 1966); P. H. Davison, ed., Penguin *1 Henry IV* (Harmondsworth, Middlesex, 1968); J. K. Walton, *The Quarto Copy for the First Folio of Shakespeare* (Dublin, 1971); G. W. Williams and G. B. Evans, eds., *"The History of King Henry the Fourth," As Revised by Sir Edward Dering, Bart.* (Folger Facsimiles, 1974); F. T. Bowers, "Establishing Shakespeare's Text: Poins and Peto in *1 Henry IV*," *SB*, XXXIV (1981), 189–98; MacD. P. Jackson, "Two Shakespeare Quartos: *Richard III* (1597) and *1 Henry IV* (1598)," *SB*, XXXV (1982), 173–90, and "The Manuscript Copy for the Quarto (1598) of Shakespeare's *1 Henry IV*," *N & Q*, n.s. XXXIII (1986), 353–4; Susan Zimmerman, "The Uses of Headlines: Peter Short's Shakespearian Quartos *1 Henry IV* and *Richard III*," *The Library*, 6th. ser., VII (1985), 218–55; David Bevington, ed., New Oxford *1 Henry IV* (Oxford, 1987); Stanley Wells, Gary Taylor, John Jowett, and William Montgomery, *William Shakespeare: A Textual Companion* (Oxford, 1987).

TEXTUAL NOTES

Title: The First . . . Fourth] The History of Henrie the Fourth; With the battell at Shrewsburie, betweene the King and Lord Henry Percy, surnamed Henrie Hotspur of the North. With the humorous conceits of Sir Iohn Falstalffe. *Q1 (title-page);* The First Part of Henry the Fourth, with the Life and Death of Henry Sirnamed Hot-Spurre *F1*

Dramatis personae: *subs. as first given by Rowe*

Act-scene division: *none in Q0, Q1–6; from F1, with the following exceptions: V.iii (no scene division in F1); V.iv, v (numbered V.iii, iv in F1); see first note to each scene; present act-scene arrangement as a whole first established by Capell*

I.i

I.i] *F1*

Location: *Capell (after Pope, Theobald)*

o.s.d. **Sir Walter Blunt]** *Capell*

8 **flow'rets]** *F1* (Flowrets); flourets *Q1–5;* flowers *Q6*

17 **ill-sheathed]** *hyphen, F2*

22 **levy]** *Q2–6, F1;* leauy *Q1*

32 **Council]** *F1;* counsell *Q1–6*

39 **Herfordshire]** *Q7;* Herdforshire *Q1–3;* Herdfordshire *Q4–5;* Herefordshire *Q6, F1*

42 **A]** And a *F1*

43 **corpse']** *W. S. Walker conj.;* corpes *Q1, F1;* corps *Q2–6*

52 **Holy-rood]** *Q2–6, F1 (subs.);* holly rode *Q1*

53 **Archibald]** *Q5–6, F1;* Archibold *Q1–4*

62 **a dear]** *Q5–6, F1;* deere *Q1–4*

69 **blood,]** *Q7;* bloud. *Q1–4;* blood *Q5–6, F1*

70 **plains.]** *F1;* plaines, *Q1–4;* plaines: *Q5;* plaine: *Q6*

73 **Murray]** *Capell;* Murrey *Q1–6;* Murry *F1*

76–7 **West. In . . . of.]** *as in Steevens (after Pope); Q1–6, F1 continue* In . . . is. *to King Henry and begin Westmerland's speech with* A conquest *(in Q1 there is enough space between* not? *and* In *to admit the s.p.* West. *as it appears in the next line)*

87 **night-tripping]** *hyphen, Q2–6, F1*

94 **use he keeps,]** *Q3–6, F1;* vse, he keepes *Q1–2*

104 **so]** and so *F1*

I.ii

I.ii] *F1*

Location: *Sisson (after Theobald)*

4 **after noon]** in the afternoone *F1*

15–6 **"that . . . fair."]** *quotes, Capell*

20 **by my troth]** *om. F1 (oaths are generally om. or softened in F1)*

22 **Come,]** *Theobald;* come *Q1–6, F1*

33 **moon.]** *Q5–6, F1 (subs.);* moone, *Q1–4*

33 **proof, now:]** *Rowe;* proofe. Now *Q1–6, F1*

39 **By the Lord]** *om. F1*

41 **As]** As is *F1*

58 **apparent—]** *Rowe,* apparant. *Q1–6, F1*

61 **law?]** *F1;* law, *Q1–2;* law: *Q3–6*

64 **By the Lord]** *om. F1*

69 **Hal]** *Q2–5, F1;* Hall *Q1, Q6 (this form appears sporadically throughout the Qq; not hereafter recorded)*

73 **'Sblood]** *om. F1*

79 **similes]** *Q5;* smiles *Q1–4, Q6, F1*

82 **to God]** *om. F1*

88–9 **wisdom . . . and]** *om. F1*

100 **'Zounds]** *om. F1*

106 **Poins! Now]** *Theobald (subs.);* Poynes now *Q1;* Poynes, now *Q2–3; Poines.* Now *Q4–6, F1 (taking* Poines. *as s.p.)*

107 **match]** Watch *F1*

113–4 **Sack . . . Jack,]** *Rowe* (Jack, *from Capell);* Sacke, and Sugar Iacke? *Q1–4;* Sacke and Sugar, Iacke? *Q5–6;* Sacke and Sugar: Iacke? *F1*

130 **night]** *om. F1*

131 **sleep.]** *Q2–6, F1 (subs.);* sleepe, *Q1*

136 **chops?]** *Q7;* chops. *Q1–6, F1*

138 **Who, I rob?]** *Q2–6, F1;* Who I rob, *Q1*

138 **by my faith]** *om. F1*

146 **By the Lord]** *om. F1*

152–3 **God give thee . . . him]** maist thou haue . . . he *F1*

159 **s.d. Exit Falstaff.]** *F2*

162 **Falstaff]** *Q6, F1;* Falstalffe *Q1–5 (the most frequent form throughout; not hereafter recorded)*

162 **Bardolph, Peto]** *Theobald;* Haruey, Rossill *Q1–6, F1 (Dering MS substitutes* Peto *for* Rossill *and, in l. 163,* Bardolph *for* Gadshill)

190 **lives]** lyes *Q2–6, F1*

204 **holidays]** *F1;* holly-dayes *Q1–3;* holy daies *Q4–6*

I.iii] *F1*

Location: *Theobald*

23 **name]** *om. F1*

26, 28 **is]** was *F1*

27 **Either envy, therefore]** Who either through enuy *F1*

42 **bore]** bare *F1*

46 **holiday]** *Q5, F1;* holly-day *Q1;* holy-day *Q2–3;* holy day *Q6*

52 **what—]** *Kittredge;* what *Q1;* what, *Q2–6, F1*

60 **This]** That *F1*

66 **I answered]** Made me to answer *F1*

95 **war;]** *Q2–6, F1 (subs.);* war, *Q1*

96 **tongue]** *Hanmer;* tongue: *Q1–6;* tongue, *F1*

98 **sedgy]** *F4;* siedgie *Q1–6, F1*

106 **crisp head]** *Johnson;* crispe-head *Q1–6, F1;* Crise-pe head *Dering MS*

108 **bare]** base *F1*

124 **s.d. with . . . Train]** *Capell (subs.)*

128 **Albeit . . . a]** Although it be with *F1*

129 **drunk]** *Q2–6, F1;* dronk *Q1*

131 **'Zounds]** Yes *F1*

133 **Yea . . . part]** In his behalfe *F1*

135 **down-trod]** downfall *F1*

145 **not he]** he not *F1*

159 **starve]** staru'd *F1*

162 **wear]** wore *F1*

194 **good night]** *Q4–6, F1;* god-night *Q1;* good-night *Q2–3*

194 **swim.]** *F1 (subs.);* swim, *Q1–3;* swime, *Q4;* swimd, *Q5–6*

201] *Beginning with this line and continuing through II.ii.111, the copy-text is Q0 (see "Note on the Text")*

201 **s.p. Hot.]** *Q5–6, F1; lines continued to Northumberland, Q0, Q1–4*

204 **fadom-line]** *hyphen, Q5–6, F1*

208 **half-fac'd]** *hyphen, F1*

211 **a while.]** a-while, / And list to me. *F1*

214 **God]** heauen *F1*

230 **sword-and-buckler]** *hyphens, Pope*

233 **him poisoned]** poyson'd him *F1*

236 **wasp-stung]** waspe-tongue *Q2–6;* Waspe-tongu'd *F1*

239 **whipt]** *Q1–6, F1;* whip *Q0*

244 **kept—]** *Rowe;* kept *Q0, Q1–2;* kept, *Q3–6, F1*

245 **bow'd]** *F1;* bowed *Q0, Q1–6*

247 **'Sblood!]** *om. F1*

256 **I]** for I *F1*

258 **i' faith]** insooth *F1*

264 **granted. You]** *Thirlby conj.;* granted you *Q0, Q1, Q4;* granted you, *Q2–3, Q5–6, F1*

264 **s.d. To Northumberland.]** *Thirlby conj.*

281 **ha?]** *Capell;* ha. *Q0, Q1–6, F1*

293 **course.]** *Rowe (subs.);* course *Q0, Q1–6, F1*

II.i] *F1*

Location: *Capell (after Theobald)*

4 **s.d. Within.]** *Theobald*

6 **Poor]** the poore *F1*

6 **wrung]** *Q2–6, F1;* wroong *Q0, Q1*

9 **that]** this *F1*

10 **ostler]** the Ostler *F1*

14 **be]** to be *Q5–6;* is *F1*

16 **by the mass]** *om. F1*

17 **christen]** in Christendome *F1*

26 **God's body]** *om. F1*

33 **s.p. 1. Car.]** *Hanmer;* Car: *Q0, Q1–6, F1*

36 **by God, soft]** *Q7;* by God soft *Q0, Q1–6;* soft I pray ye *F1*
37 **i' faith]** *om. F1*
39 **when,]** *Q2–6, F1;* when *Q0, Q1*
40 **quoth he!]** *Cowl;* (quoth he) *Q0, Q1–6;* (quoth-a) *F1*
44 **thee.]** *Q2–6, F1;* thee, *Q0, Q1*
46 **s.d. Carriers]** *Rowe*
47 **s.d. Enter Chamberlain.]** *placed as in Kittredge; after l. 46, Q0, Q1–6, F1*
49 **as—]** *Capell;* as *Q0, Q1–6, F1*
55 **franklin]** *Q5–6, F1;* Frankelin *Q0, Q1–4*
64 **Saint]** *Q1–6;* Saine *Q0;* S. *F1*
73 **foot land-rakers]** *Hanmer;* footland rakers *Q0, Q1–3;* foot-landrakers *Q4;* foot-land rakers *Q5–6;* Foot-land-Rakers *F1*
76 **oney'rs]** *M. Spevack (privately);* Oneyres *Q0, Q1;* Oneyers *Q2–6, F1*
79 **'zounds]** *om. F1*
80 **to]** vnto *F1*
81 **not]** not to *F1*
81 **prey]** *Q5–6, F1;* pray *Q0, Q1–4*
88 **by my faith]** *om. F1*
88 **think]** thinke rather *F1*
89 **than to]** then to the *F1*
92 **purchase]** purpose *F1*
96 **my]** the *F1*
97 **s.d. Exeunt.]** *F1*

II.ii

II.ii] *F1*
Location: *Cambridge (after Pope)*
o.s.d. **Enter . . . behind.]** *Wilson (subs.);* Enter Prince, Poines, and Peto, &c. *Q0, Q1–6, (om. &c.) F1*
3 **s.d. They retire.]** *Dyce*
4 **hang'd! Poins!]** *Capell;* hangd Poynes. *Q0, Q1–6, F1*
5 **s.d. Coming forward.]** *Dyce*
9 **s.d. Retires.]** *Dyce*
11 **The]** that *F1*
12 **squier]** *Cambridge;* squire *Q0, Q1–6, F1*
13 **afoot]** *Q2;* a foote *Q0, Q1, Q3–6, F1 (not hereafter recorded unless ambiguous)*
16 **two and twenty]** *Dering MS, F1;* xxii: *Q0, Q1–4;* 22. *Q5–6*
21 **Bardolph]** *Dering MS, F1;* Bardol *Q0;* Bardoll *Q1–6 (throughout)*
21 **I'll rob]** I rob *F1*
22 **as drink]** as to drinke *F1*
23 **true man]** *Q3–6;* true-man *Q0, Q1–2, F1*
26 **stony-hearted]** *hyphen, Dering MS, F1*
29 **upon]** light vpon *F1*
29 **me]** *om. F1*
31 **s.d. Coming forward.]** *Dyce*
31 **fat-guts]** *hyphen, Capell*
35 **'Sblood]** *om. F1*
35 **my]** mine *Q1–6, F1*
40 **prince—Hal!—]** *ed.;* prince, Hall, *Q0;* prince, Hal, *Q1–2;* prince Hal, *Q3–6, F1*
46 **poison.]** *Q2–6, F1 (subs.);* poyson, *Q0, Q1*
50 **s.d. Coming . . . Peto.]** *Dyce*
52 **Bard. What news?]** *Johnson conj.;* Bardoll, what newes. *Q0, Q1–6;* Bardolfe, what newes? *F1 (continued to Poins, Q0, Q1–6, F1)*
53 **s.p. Gads.]** *Johnson;* Bar. *Q0, Q1–6, F1*
61 **Poins]** *om. F1*
63 **be there]** be they *Q2–6;* be *F1*
65 **'Zounds]** *om. F1*
67,73 **s.p. Fal.]** *Q1–6 (subs.), F1;* Fast. *Q0*
69 **Well]** *om. F1*
74 **s.d. Aside.]** *Collier*
75 **s.d. Aside.]** *Dyce*
75 **s.d. Exeunt . . . Poins.]** *Malone (after Capell)*
78, 86 **s.pp. 1. Trav.]** *Capell;* Trauel. *and* Tra. *Q0, Q1–6, F1*
82 **s.p. Travellers.]** *Dyce;* Trauel. *Q0, Q1–6, F1*
84 **Ah]** *Rowe;* a *Q0, Q1–6, F1*
92 **s.d. in buckram]** *Dyce*
101 **s.d. As . . . them.]** *after l. 103, F1 (om. and Falstaff . . . too,)*
104–10 **Got . . . him.]** *as verse, Pope; as prose, Q0, Q1–6, F1*
110 **Were't]** *Q2–3, F1;* wert *Q0, Q1, Q4–6*
111 **fat]** *om. Q1–6, F1; the fragment of Q0 ends with this line*

II.iii

II.iii] *F1*
Location: *Capell*
14 **so?]** *Rowe;* so, *Q1, Q5–6;* so. *Q2–4;* so: *F1*
16 **lack-brain]** *hyphen, Q2–6, F1*
16 **By the Lord]** I protest *F1*
17 **a good]** as good a *F1*
20 **frosty-spirited]** *hyphen, F1*
22 **'Zounds]** By this hand *F1*
22 **and]** if *F1*
33 **skim-milk]** skim'd Milk *F1*
34 **King:]** *Hanmer;* king, *Q1–6;* King *F1*
48 **thee murmur]** *Q2–6, F1;* the murmur, *Q1*
50 **"Courage! . . . field!"]** *Rowe (subs.);* courage to the field. *Q1–6, F1*
51 **retires,]** *Q3–6;* retyres *Q1–2;* Retires; *F1*
51 **of trenches,]** *Q2–3;* of trenches *Q1;* trenches *Q4–6, F1*
59 **late-disturbed]** *hyphen, F1*
65 **s.d. Enter Servant.]** *Dering MS, Rowe*
66 **ago]** agone *F1*
69 **horse?]** *Q3–6, F1;* horse, *Q1–2*
69 **Roan?]** a roane? *Q3–5, F1;* roane, *Q6*
70–2 **That . . . park.]** *as verse, Pope; as prose, Q1–6, F1*
71 **O Esperance!]** *Pope;* O Esperance, *Q1–4;* Esperance, *Q5–6, F1 (all three in italics)*
72 **s.d. Exit Servant.]** *Dering MS, Hanmer*
77–83 **Out . . . go—]** *as verse, Pope; as prose, Q1–6, F1*
79 **faith]** sooth *F1*
85–8 **Come . . . true.]** *as verse, Pope; as prose, Q1–6, F1*
87 **In faith]** Indeede *F1*
88 **And]** *om. F1*
88 **all things]** *om. F1*
90 **trifler! Love,]** *ed. (after F1* trifler: Loue,); trifler, loue, *Q1–3;* trifler, loue; *Q4–6*
113 **How!]** *Theobald;* How, *Q1–6;* How *F1*
113 **far?]** *Q2–6, F1;* far. *Q1*

II.iv

II.iv] *F1*
Location: *Theobald (after Pope)*
4 **amongst]** *Q2, Q4–6;* amongest *Q1, Q3*
6 **base-string]** *hyphen, Dering MS, Dyce*
7 **all]** *om. F1*
9 **salvation]** confidence *F1*
11 **and tell]** telling *F1*
12 **mettle]** *F1;* metall *Q1–6*
13 **(by . . . me!)]** *om. F1*
16 **they]** then they *F1*
33 **president]** *F1;* present *Q1–6*
33 **s.d. Exit Poins.]** *Dyce (after Theobald)*
34, 36 **s.dd. Within.]** *Dyce*
36 **s.p. Poins.]** *Q4–6, F1;* Prin. *Q1–3*
43, 51, 56, 63, 77 **s.dd. Within.]** *Capell*
52 **Anon]** Anon, anon *F1*
60 **Lord]** Lord sir *F1*
69 **leathern-jerkin]** *hyphen, Pope*
69–70 **crystal-button]** *hyphen, Pope*
70 **agate-ring]** *hyphen, Dering MS, Rowe*
70 **puke-stocking]** *hyphen, Dering MS, Rowe*
70–1 **caddis-garter]** *hyphen, Dering MS, Rowe*
71 **smooth-tongue]** *hyphen, Theobald*
71 **Spanish-pouch—]** *Capell (hyphen, Pope);* spanish pouch? *Q1–6;* Spanish pouch. *F1*
78 **not]** *om. F1*
81 **s.d. Exit Francis.]** *Johnson (subs.)*
85 **s.d. Exit Vintner.]** *Dering MS, Theobald*
86 **s.d. Within.]** *Neilson*
93 **goodman]** *Q2–5, F1;* good man *Q1, Q6*
95 **s.d. Enter . . . wine.]** *Malone (subs., after Capell); Dering MS has Francis speak from within*
97 **s.d. Exit.]** *Collier*
112 **s.d. Gadshill . . . wine]** *Dyce (Gadshill, Bardolph, and Peto added by Theobald)*
117 **and foot them]** *om. F1*
122 **sun's?]** *Cambridge;* sonnes, *Q1;* sonnes? *Q2;* sunne? *Q3–6, F1*
132 **while!]** *Theobald;* while, *Q1–6, F1*
133–4 **psalms . . . thing]** all manner of songs *F1*
139 **more.]** *F1;* more, *Q1–6*
139 **You,]** *Wilson;* you *Q1–6, F1*
139 **Wales!]** *T. Johnson (in Variorum);* Wales. *Q1–6;* Wales? *F1*
140 **round man]** *Q4–6, F1;* round-man *Q1–3*
144 **'Zounds]** *om. F1*
145 **by the Lord]** *om. F1*
173 **s.p. Prince.]** *F1;* Gad *Q1–6*
174, 176, 180 **s.pp. Gads.]** *F1;* Ross. *Q1–6 (see note on I.ii.162)*
189 **God]** Heauen *F1*
194 **face,]** *F1;* face; *Q1–6*
194 **horse.]** *Q2–6, F1* (horse:); horse, *Q1*
197 **What,]** *Q2–6, F1;* What *Q1*
200 **afront]** *Q2–4;* a front *Q1, Q5–6;* a-front *F1*
204 **buckrom?]** *Capell;* Buckrom. *Q1–6, F1*
209 **Dost]** *Rowe;* Doest *Q1–6, F1 (so several times, especially in Falstaff's speeches; not hereafter recorded)*
210 **too, Jack]** *Q2–6, F1;* to iacke *Q1*
236 **'Zounds . . . were]** No: were I *F1*
244 **'Sblood]** Away *F1*
244 **eel-skin]** *Hanmer;* elsskin *Q1–2;* elfskin *Q3–6, F1*
257 **here]** *om. F1*
260 **run]** ranne *F1*
263 **starting-hole]** *hyphen, Hanmer*
267 **By the Lord]** *om. F1*
272 **prince.]** *F1 (subs.);* prince, *Q1–6*
275 **by the Lord]** *om. F1*
278 **titles of good]** good Titles of *F1*
283 **Ah]** *Rowe;* A *Q1–6, F1*
284 **O Jesu]** *om. F1*
287 **nobleman]** *Q2–3 (subs.);* noble man *Q1, Q4–6, F1*
303 **Faith]** *om. F1*
320 **s.d. Pointing . . . face.]** *White*
326 **bare-bone]** *hyphen, Q3–6, F1*
329 **knee?]** *Q2–6, F1;* knee, *Q1*
340 **O,]** *Q2–5;* O *Q6, F1;* Owen *Dering MS*
349 **mettle]** *Pope;* mettall *Q1–6, F1*
353 **afoot]** *Q2–3;* a foote *Q1, Q4–5, F1;* on foote *Q6*
371 **i' faith]** *om. F1*
390 **O Jesu]** *om. F1*
393 **tristful]** *Dering's emendation in Dering MS, Rowe;* trustfull *Q1–6, F1*
395 **Jesu]** rare *F1*
401 **yet]** *Q3–6, F1;* so *Q1–2*
435 **me?]** *Theobald;* me, *Q1–2, Q5–6;* me; *Q3–4;* me: *F1*
443 **'Sblood]** Yfaith *F1*
444 **i' faith]** *om. F1*
446 **me.]** *F1 (subs.);* me, *Q1–6*
462 **abominable]** *Q2;* abhominable *Q3–6, F1*
470 **God]** Heauen *F1*
473 **lean]** *Q2–6, F1;* lane *Q1*
481 **s.d. A . . . Bardolph.]** *Malone (after Theobald)*
482 **most]** most most *F1*
486 **Jesu]** *om. F1*
492 **made]** mad *F3*
504 **s.d. Exit.]** *F1*
505 **s.d. Exeunt . . . Peto.]** *Collier*
507–8 **First . . . house.]** *as verse, Pope; as prose, Q1–6, F1*
510–1 **One . . . man.]** *as verse, Pope; as prose, Q1–6, F1*
523 **Good]** *Q3–6, F1;* God *Q1–2*
524 **good]** *Q4–6, F1;* god *Q1–3*
525 **s.d. with Carrier]** *Hanmer (subs.)*
526–7 **This . . . forth.]** *as verse, Pope; as prose, Q1–6, F1*
526 **Paul's]** *F4;* Poules *Q1–6, F1*
532 **What]** *Hanmer;* Pr. What *Q1–6, F1 (repeated s.p.)*
535 **s.p. Peto.]** *F1*
535 **s.d. Reads.]** *Capell*
538 **anchoves]** *Q5–6, F1;* anchaues *Q1–4*
540 **s.p. Prince.]** *F1*

III.i

III.i] *F1*
Location: *Alexander (after Wilson)*
3–10 **Lord . . . heaven.]** *as verse, F1; as prose, Q1–6*

9 **cheek looks]** Cheekes looke *F1*
11–2 **And . . . of.]** *as verse, Pope; as prose, Q1–6, F1*
17 **Shak'd]** *Q5–6, F1;* Shaked *Q1–4*
17–9 **Why . . . born.]** *as verse, Pope; as prose, Q1–6, F1*
31 **topples]** toples *Q5–6;* tombles *F1*
55–6 **Why . . . devil.]** *as verse, Capell; as prose, Q1–6, F1*
73 **England,]** *F1;* England *Q1–6*
73 **Trent]** *Capell;* Trent, *Q1–6, F1*
99 **cantle]** *F1;* scantle *Q1–6*
100 **damm'd]** *Rowe;* damnd *Q1–6, F1*
105 **wind?]** *Q2–6; F1;* wind *Q1*
106–10 **Yea . . . you.]** *as verse, F1; as prose, Q1–6*
128 **metre]** *F1* (Meeter); miter *Q1–6*
128 **ballet-mongers]** *hyphen, Q2–6, F1 (F1 reads* Ballad-mongers)
129 **canstick]** Candlestick *F1*
130 **axle-tree]** *Q2–6, F1;* exle tree *Q1*
132 **mincing]** *F1;* minsing *Q1–6*
140 **night.]** *Q2–6, F1* (night:); night *Q1*
142 **your]** *Q2–6, F1;* your, *Q1*
150 **moulten]** *Q2–6, F1;* molten *Q1*
151 **lion]** *Q2–6, F1;* Leon *Q1*
152 **skimble-skamble]** *hyphen, F1*
160 **windmill,]** *Theobald;* Windmil *Q1–6, F1*
170 **come]** doe *F1*
175 **willful-blame]** *Theobald;* wilfullblame *Q1 (?);* wilfull blame *Q2–6, F1*
178 **fault;]** *F1* (fault:); fault, *Q1–6*
184 **haunting]** *Q5–6, F1;* hanting *Q1–4*
184 **nobleman]** *Q5–6, F1;* noble man *Q1–4*
188 **school'd: good]** *F1;* schoold good *Q1;* schoold, good *Q2–4;* schoold, Good *Q5–6*
195 s.d. **Glendower]** *Q2–6, F1;* Glondower *Q1*
196–7 **She . . . upon.]** *as verse, F1; subs. as prose, Q1–6*
196 **self-will'd]** *Q6, F1;* selfewild *Q1 (?);* selfe wilde *Q2–4;* selfe-wild *Q5*
202 **I]** *Theobald; Mor.* I *Q1–6, F1 (repeated s.p.)*
204 **truant,]** *F1;* truant *Q1–6*
218 **heavenly-harness'd]** *hyphen, Pope*
228 s.p. **Lady P.]** *Malone;* La. *Q1–6, F1 (throughout scene)*
230 **humorous.]** *F1* (humorous:); humorous, *Q1–6*
232–4 **Then . . . Welsh.]** *as prose, Pope; as verse, Q1–6, F1*
235 **hear Lady, my brach,]** *Q4 (subs.; second comma, Pope after Rowe i);* heare lady my brache *Q1;* hear, lady, my brache *Q2–3;* hear *Lady*, my brach *Q5;* hear Lady, my breech *Q6;* heare (Lady) my Brach *F1*
247 **sooth!]** *Rowe;* sooth. *Q1;* sooth? *Q2–6, F1*
247 **Heart]** *om. F1*
255 **pepper-gingerbread]** *F2 (subs.);* pepper ginger bread *Q1–4;* pepper ginger-bread *Q5–6, F1*
256 **velvet-guards]** *hyphen, F2*
256 **Sunday-citizens]** *hyphen, F1*
264 **hot]** *F1;* Hot. *Q1–3;* Hot, *Q4; Hot Q5–6*

III.ii

III.ii] *F1*
Location: *Capell*
4, 29 **God]** Heauen *F1*
32 **Council]** *F1;* counsell *Q1–6*
40 **common-hackney'd]** *hyphen, Pope*
58 **Seldom]** *F1;* Seldome, *Q1–6*
58 **sumptuous,]** *Q2–6, F1;* sumptuous *Q1*
59 **wan]** wonne *F1*
63 **cap'ring]** Carping *F1*
78 **gaze,]** *F1;* gaze. *Q1–6*
84 **gorg'd]** *Q3, F1;* gordge *Q1;* gorgde *Q2, Q4–6*
89 **desir'd]** *F1;* desired *Q1–6*
106 **never-dying]** *hyphen, F2*
110 **capital]** *Q2–3;* capitall. *Q1, Q5–6, F1;* capitall, *Q4*
112 **Hotspur,]** *Warburton;* Hotspur *Q1–6, F1*
130 **God]** Heauen *F1*
141 **unthought-of]** *hyphen, F2*
141 **meet.]** *F1 (subs.);* meet, *Q1–6*
153 **God]** Heauen *F1*
154 **perform,]** *Capell;* performe: *Q1–3;* performe *Q4–6; F1 reads the line:* The which, if I performe, and doe suruiue,
156 **intemperance]** intemperature *F1*
161 s.d. **Enter Blunt.]** *placed as in F1; after l. 162, Q1–6*
162 **Blunt?]** *Q2–6, F1;* blunt *Q1*
176 **Gloucestershire;]** *F1 (subs.);* Glocestershire, *Q1–6*
177 **valued,]** *F4;* valued *Q1–6, F1*

III.iii

III.iii] *F1*
Location: *Theobald (after Pope)*
16 **times—]** *Staunton;* times *Q1–6, F1*
17 **quarter—]** *Hanmer;* quarter *Q1–6, F1*
18 **borrow'd—]** *Hanmer* (borrowed—); borrowed *Q1–6;* borrowed, *F1*
35 **that's God's angel]** *Q3–6;* that Gods Angell *Q1–2; om. F1*
41–2 **bonfire light]** *Q2* (bon-fire light); bonefire light *Q1, Q3;* bone-fire light *Q4;* Bone-fire-light *Q5–6, F1*
46 **chandler's]** *Pope;* Chandlers *Q1–6, F1*
48 **God]** Heauen *F1*
49 **'Sblood]** *om. F1*
50 **God-a-mercy]** *om. F1*
51 s.d. **Enter Hostess.]** *placed as in F1; after inquir'd l. 52, Q1–2; after l. 53, Q3–6*
57 **tithe]** *Theobald;* tight *Q1–6, F1*
62 **God's light]** *om. F1*
65 **John.]** *Q2–6, F1 (subs.);* John, *Q1*
70 **they]** and they *F1*
74 **four and twenty]** *Dering MS, F1;* xxiiii. *Q1–6*
76 **He?]** *Q2–6, F1;* He, *Q1*
83 **O Jesu]** *om. F1*
85 **sneak-up]** *Vaughan conj.;* sneakeup *Q1–2;* sneak-cup *Q3–6, F1*
86 **'Sblood]** *om. F1*
86 **and]** and if *F1*
87 s.d. **with Peto]** *Theobald (subs.)*
88 **How]** *Dyce; Falst.* How *Q1–6, F1 (repeated s.p.)*
88 **i' faith]** *om. F1*
92 **Quickly]** *F1 (in italics);* quickly *Q1–4;* quickly *Q5–6 (in italics)*
94 **me.]** *Q2–6, F1;* me? *Q1*
107 **foul-mouth'd]** *hyphen, F1*
109 **What,]** *F4;* What *Q1–6, F1*
114 **womanhood]** *Q2–6, F1;* womandood *Q1*
114 **Maid Marian]** *Q5–6* (Mayd-marian), *F1* (Maid-marian); maid marion *Q1–4*
115 **thing]** nothing *F1*
117, 118 **God]** heauen *F1*
118 **no thing]** *Q5–6, F1;* nothing *Q1–4*
129 **an]** *om. F1*
146 **Prince]** a Prince *F1*
151 **and]** if *F1*
151 **I pray God]** let *F1*
155 **fill'd]** *Q3, F1;* fild *Q1;* fil'd *Q2;* fillde *Q4;* filde *Q5–6*
160 **long-winded]** *hyphen, Q5–6, F1*
161–2 **these, . . . villain.]** *Q2–6, F1 (subs.);* these; . . . villain, *Q1*
172 **cherish]** and cherish *F1*
172 **guesse]** *ed.;* ghesse *Q1;* ghests *Q2–6;* Guests *F1*
177 **beef]** *Q5–6, F1;* beoffe *Q1–4*
188–9 **the age of]** *om. F1*
189 **two and twenty]** *Dering MS, F1;* xxii. *Q1–6*
196 s.d. **Exit Bardolph.]** *Dyce*
198 s.d. **Exit Peto.]** *Cambridge (after Dyce)*
200 **a']** *Q2–6, F1;* of *Q1*
204 s.d. **Exit.]** *Dyce*
205 **world!]** *Q2–6, F1 (subs.);* world *Q1*
206 s.d. **Exit.]** *Capell;* Exeunt. *Q2–6;* Exeunt omnes. *F1*

IV.i

IV.i] *F1*
Location: *Capell (after Pope)*
o.s.d. **Enter . . . Douglas.]** *Q2–6, F1* (Harrie Hotspurre)
1 s.p. **Hot.]** *Q2–6, F1;* Per. *Q1 (through l. 90)*
5 **world.]** *F1;* world *Q1;* world: *Q2–3, Q5–6;* world, *Q4*
6 **God]** heauen *F1*
12 s.d. **a Messenger]** *F1*
17 **'Zounds]** *om. F1*
17 **sick]** sicke now *F1*
20 **my]** his *Q3–6, F1*
20 **lord]** *Capell;* mind *Q1–6, F1*
29 **life-blood]** *hyphen, Q2–6, F1*
31 **sickness—]** *Rowe;* sicknesse, *Q1–6, F1*
55 **Is]** *F1;* tis *Q1–6*
61 **hair]** heaire *Q4;* heire *Q5–6, F1*
98 **estridges,]** *Q2–6, F1;* Estridges *Q1*
99 **Bated]** *Heath conj.;* Baited *Q1–6, F1*
103 **bulls.]** *F1;* buls, *Q1;* buls: *Q2–6*
108 **dropp'd]** *Q2–6, F1;* drop *Q1*
116 **altar]** *Q4–6, F1;* altars *Q1–3*
122 **shall, hot]** *Johnson;* shal hot *Q1–2;* shall not *Q3–6, F1*
123 **ne'er]** *Q2–6, F1;* neare *Q1*
124 **news:]** *F1;* newes, *Q1–6*
126 **cannot]** *Q5–6, F1;* can *Q1–4*
127 **yet]** *Q5–6, F1;* it *Q1–4*
134 **merrily]** *Q2–6, F1;* merely *Q1*

IV.ii

IV.ii] *F1*
Location: *Theobald*
3 **Co'fil']** *Cambridge;* cop- / hill *Q1, Q3–4;* cophill *Q2;* -cop- / hill *Q5–6;* -cop-hill *F1*
9 **at]** at the *F1*
15 **yeomen's]** *Q2–6, F1;* Yeomans *Q1*
19 **fowl]** *Rowe;* foule *Q1–3;* foole *Q4–6, F1*
21 **toasts-and-butter]** *hyphens, Dyce*
29 **ostlers]** *Q2–6, F1;* Ostlers, *Q1*
31 **old feaz'd]** *Vaughan conj.;* olde fazd *Q1–4;* old faczde *Q5;* old fac'd *Q6;* old-fac'd *F1*
32 **as]** that *F1*
46 **Albons]** *ed.;* Albones *Q1–6, F1*
57 **night]** to Night *F1*
63 **Mine,]** *Q2–4, F1;* Mine *Q1, Q5–6*
65 **enough]** *Q2–6, F1;* inongh *Q1*
78–80 **Well . . . guest.]** *as verse, Pope; as prose, Q1–6, F1*

IV.iii

IV.iii] *F1*
Location: *Pope, Capell (subs.)*
8 **Douglas.]** *F1 (subs.);* Douglas, *Q1–6*
10 **well-respected]** *hyphen, F1*
22 **mettle]** *F3;* mettall *Q1–6, F1*
26 **journey-bated]** *hyphen, F3*
38 **God]** Heauen *F1*
62 **peace,]** *Q5–6, F1;* peace *Q1–3;* peace. *Q4*
72 **heirs as pages,]** *Singer (after Malone);* heires, as Pages *Q1–6, F1*
82 **country's]** *Q5–6, F1;* Countrey *Q1–4*
90 **after,]** *Q2–6, F1;* after *Q1*
92 **state;]** *Q2–6* (state:); state, *Q1;* State. *F1*
99 **Council-board]** *F1;* counsell boord *Q1–6*
113 **God]** Heauen *F1*
113 s.d. **Exeunt.]** *F1*

IV.iv

IV.iv] *F1*
Location: *Theobald*
o.s.d. **Michael]** *Q7;* Mighell *Q1–4 (throughout scene);* Michell *Q5–6, F1 (throughout scene)*
13 **Harry; and]** *Q2–6, F1 (subs.);* Harry And *Q1*
18 **in,]** *F1;* in *Q1–6*
31 **corrivals]** *F1;* coriuals *Q1–6*
36 **not,]** *Q2–3, F1;* not *Q1, Q4–6*

V.i

V.i] *F1*
Location: *Capell (after Theobald)*
o.s.d. **Lancaster]** *Dering MS, Hanmer;* Lancaster, Earle of Westmerland *Q1–6, F1*
2 **bulky]** *the* l *in Q1's* bulky *is unclear;* busky *Q2–6, F1*
8 s.d. **and . . . Vernon]** *Theobald*
9 **How]** *Capell; King.* How *Q1–6, F1 (repeated s.p.)*
25 **I]** I do *F1*
37 **place]** *Q2–3;* place, *Q1, Q4–6, F1*

42 **swear]** *Q2–6, F1;* sware *Q1*
42, 58 **Doncaster]** *F1* (*Q6, l.58*); Dancaster *Q1–6*
44 **new-fall'n]** *hyphen, Dering MS, F1*
71 **your]** *om. F1*
72 **articulate]** articulated *F1*
80 **water-colors]** *hyphen, F1*
81 **time]** *F1;* time, *Q1–6*
83 **your]** our *F1*
85 **trial.]** *F1;* trial, *Q1–6*
88 **off]** *F1;* of *Q1–6*
90 **valiant,]** *ed.;* valiant *Q1–6, F1*
111 **wait]** *Q2–6, F1;* waight *Q1*
114 **s.d. with Vernon]** *Theobald (subs.)*
121–4 **Hal . . . farewell.]** *as prose, Pope; as verse, Q1–6, F1*
122 **so;]** *F1;* so, *Q1–6*
126 **God]** heauen *F1*
126 **s.d. Exit.]** *Hanmer*
130 **Yea]** *om. F1*
131 **then?]** *Q2–3, F1;* then *Q1, Q4–6*
131, 132 **No.]** *Q2–3, F1 (subs.);* no, *Q1, Q4–6*
133 **No. . . . No.]** *F1;* no, . . . no, *Q1;* No: . . . no: *Q2–3;* no, . . . no: *Q4–6*
135 **Air.]** *Q2–6, F1 (subs.);* aire, *Q1*
137 **No. . . . No.]** *F1;* no, . . . no, *Q1;* no: . . . no: *Q2–6*
137 **'Tis]** Is it *F1*
138 **will't]** *ed.;* wil *Q1;* will it *Q2–6, F1*
139 **No.]** *F1;* no, *Q1;* no: *Q2–6*

V.ii

V.ii] *F1*
Location: *Wilson (after Theobald)*
3 **are we]** we are *F1*
3 **undone]** *Q5–6, F1;* vnder one *Q1–4*
12 **merrily]** *Q2–6, F1;* merely *Q1*
15 **cherish'd,]** *Q2–6, F1;* cherisht *Q1*
19 **hare-brain'd]** *F2;* hair-braind *Q1–6, F1*
19 **spleen.]** *Q3, F1 (subs.);* spleene, *Q1–2, Q4–6*
27 **s.d. Hotspur]** *Q2–6, F1*
27 **s.d. and Douglas]** *Rowe; s.d. after l. 25, Q1–6; placed as in F1*
50 **show'd]** *Q3–6, F1;* shewed *Q1–2*
50 **tasking]** talking *Q2–6, F1*
71 **a]** at *Q5–6, F1*
88 **s.d. Messenger]** *F1*
89 **s.p. 2. Mess.]** *Capell;* Mes. *Q1–6, F1*
89 **apace]** *Q2–5, F1;* a pace *Q1, Q6*
91 **talking;]** *F1 (subs.);* talking *Q1;* talking, *Q2–6*
92 **draw I]** I draw *F1*
93 **temper]** worthy temper *F1*
94 **withal]** *Capell;* withall. *Q1;* withall, *Q2–6, F1*
96 **Esperance!]** *Pope;* esperance *Q1–6;* Esperance *F1*
96 **Percy!]** *Theobald;* Percy *Q1–6, F1 (in italics, Q5–6, F1)*
100 **s.d. and exeunt]** *Rowe (subs.)*

V.iii

V.iii] *Capell*
Location: *ed.*
o.s.d. and passes over] *White*
16 **won,]** *Q4–6, F1;* won *Q1;* won: *Q2–3*
19 **This,]** *Q2–5;* This *Q1, Q6, F1*
22 **A fool]** *Capell;* Ah foole, *Q1–6;* Ah foole: *F1*
29 **s.d. Exeunt.]** *F1*
34 **God]** heauen *F1*
36 **ragamuffins]** *Capell;* rag of Muffins *Q1–5, F1;* rag of Muffians *Q6*
37 **hundred and fifty]** *Dering MS, Rowe;* 150. *Q1–6, F1*
37 **are]** *om. F1*
41 **nobleman]** *F1;* noble man *Q1–6*
43 **yet]** *om. F1*
48–9 **He . . . sword.]** *as prose, Cambridge; as verse, Q1–6, F1*
50 **before God]** *om. F1*
55 **What,]** *Q2, Q5–6, F1;* What *Q1;* What? *Q3–4*
57 **way,]** *Q5–6, F1;* way *Q1;* way: *Q2–4*
61 **s.d. Exit.]** *F1*

V.iv

V.iv] *Capell;* Scena Tertia. *F1*
Location: *ed.*
o.s.d. wounded] *Neilson*
11, 17 **God]** heauen *F1*
16 **God's]** heauens *F1*
16 **s.d. Exeunt . . . Westmerland.]** *Capell*
24 **mettle]** *F3;* mettall *Q1–6, F1*
24 **s.d. Enter Douglas.]** *F1*
25 **king?]** *F1;* king *Q1–6*
34 **and]** so *F1*
48 **redeem'd]** *Q5–6, F1;* redeemed *Q1–4*
51, 69 **God]** heauen *F1*
68 **Nor]** *F1;* Now *Q1–6*
76 **s.d. He]** who *F1*
76 **s.d. and exit Douglas]** *Capell*
81 **thoughts,]** *Neilson-Hill;* thoughts *Q1;* thought's *Q2–6, F1*
81 **and life,]** *F1;* and life *Q1–6*
84 **earthy and]** earth and *Q2–6;* Earth, and the *F1*
86 **for—]** *F1;* for. *Q1–6*
87 **Fare thee well]** Farewell *F1*
88 **shrunk!]** *Q2* (shrunke:); shrunke, *Q1;* shruncke? *Q3–6, F1*
86 **s.d. Dies.]** *Rowe*
87 **heart!]** *F1* (heart:); hart *Q1;* heart, *Q2–6*
88 **Ill-weav'd]** *hyphen, F1*
92 **thee]** *Q7;* the *Q1–6, F1*
95 **dear]** great *Q2–6, F1*
95 **zeal;]** *Q2–6 (subs.);* zeale, *Q1;* Zeale. *F1*
98 **rites]** *Q2–6, F1;* rights *Q1*
109, 111 **Embowell'd]** *Q4–6* (Imbowelde *or* Imboweld), *F1* (Imbowell'd); Inboweld *Q1;* Inbowel'd *Q2–3*
111 **embowel]** *Q4–6, F1* (imbowell); inbowel *Q1–3*
113 **'Sblood]** *om. F1*
121 **'Zounds]** *om. F1*
123 **By my faith]** *om. F1*
127 **nobody]** *F1* (no-bodie); no body *Q1–6*
128 **s.d. stabbing him]** *Capell (subs.)*
128 **with]** *om. F1*
129 **s.d. and]** *Q2–6, F1*
140 **s.d. throwing . . . down]** *Capell (subs.)*
144 **Why, Percy]** *Q2–3, F1;* Why Percy, *Q1, Q6;* Why Percy *Q4–5*
150–1 **take it upon]** take't on *F1*
152 **'zounds]** *om. F1*
159 **The]** *F1; Prin.* The *Q1–6 (repeated s.p.)*
159 **our]** ours *Q2–6, F1*
161 **s.d. Prince and Lancaster]** *Capell (subs.)*
163 **God]** heauen *F1*
163 **great]** great again *F1*
165 **nobleman]** *Q4–6, F1;* noble man *Q1–3*

V.v

V.v] *Capell;* Scaena Quarta. *F1*
Location: *Pelican*
1 **rebuke.]** *Q2–3, F1;* rebuke, *Q1, Q4–6*
2 **Ill-spirited]** *hyphen, F1*
2 **not we]** we not *F1*
14 **the]** *om. F1*
15 **s.d. Exeunt . . . Vernon]** *F1*
15 **s.d. guarded]** *Theobald*
32–3 **I . . . immediately.]** *om. Q5–6, F1*
36 **bend]** *Q4–6, F1;* bend, *Q1–3*
41 **lose]** *Q2–3, F1;* loose *Q1, Q4–6*
44 **s.d. Exeunt.]** Exeunt / FINIS. *Q1–6, F1*

The Second Part of Henry the Fourth

[THE ACTORS' NAMES

RUMOR, *the Presenter*

KING HENRY THE FOURTH
PRINCE HENRY, *afterwards crowned* KING HENRY THE FIFTH

PRINCE JOHN OF LANCASTER
HUMPHREY [DUKE] OF GLOUCESTER
THOMAS [DUKE] OF CLARENCE
} *sons to Henry the Fourth and brethren to Henry V*

[EARL OF] NORTHUMBERLAND
[SCROOP,] *the Archbishop of York*
[LORD] MOWBRAY
[LORD] HASTINGS
LORD BARDOLPH
TRAVERS
MORTON
} *retainers of Northumberland* (Travers, Morton)
[SIR JOHN] COLEVILE
} *opposites against King Henry the Fourth*

[EARL OF] WARWICK
[EARL OF] WESTMERLAND
[EARL OF] SURREY
[SIR JOHN BLUNT]
GOWER
HARCOURT
LORD CHIEF JUSTICE
} *of the King's party*

POINS
[SIR JOHN] FALSTAFF
BARDOLPH
PISTOL
PETO
[*Falstaff's*] PAGE
} *irregular humorists*

SHALLOW
SILENCE
} *both country justices*

DAVY, *servant to Shallow*
FANG *and* SNARE, *two sergeants*

MOULDY
SHADOW
WART
FEEBLE
BULLCALF
} *country soldiers*

[FRANCIS, *a drawer*]

NORTHUMBERLAND'S WIFE
[LADY PERCY,] *Percy's widow*
HOSTESS QUICKLY [*of the Boar's Head Tavern, Eastcheap*]
DOLL TEARSHEET

EPILOGUE

[LORDS *and* ATTENDANTS; PORTER,] DRAWERS, BEADLE, [OFFICERS, STREWERS, SERVANTS, *etc.*]

[SCENE: *England*]]

[INDUCTION]

Enter RUMOR, *painted full of tongues.*

[*Rum.*] Open your ears; for which of you will stop
The vent of hearing when loud Rumor speaks?
I, from the orient to the drooping west
(Making the wind my post-horse), still unfold
The acts commenced on this ball of earth.
Upon my tongues continual slanders ride,
The which in every language I pronounce,
Stuffing the ears of men with false reports.
I speak of peace, while covert enmity
Under the smile of safety wounds the world;
And who but Rumor, who but only I,
Make fearful musters and prepar'd defense,
Whiles the big year, swoll'n with some other grief,
Is thought with child by the stern tyrant war,
And no such matter? Rumor is a pipe
Blown by surmises, jealousies, conjectures,
And of so easy and so plain a stop
That the blunt monster with uncounted heads,
The still-discordant wav'ring multitude,
Can play upon it. But what need I thus
My well-known body to anatomize

Words and passages enclosed in square brackets in the text above are either emendations of the copy-text or additions to it. The Textual Notes immediately following the play cite the earliest authority for every such change or insertion and supply the reading of the copy-text wherever it is emended in this edition.

Ind. o.s.d. **Rumor . . . tongues.** This, like many medieval and Renaissance depictions of Rumor, echoes Virgil's account of *Fama* as a monster covered with eyes, ears, and tongues (*Aeneid*, iv.181–83).
4. **still**: continually.

13. **Whiles**: while.
16. **jealousies**: suspicions. 17. **stop**: i.e. fingering.
18. **blunt**: dull, stupid. 20. **what**: why.
21. **anatomize**: dissect, analyze.

Among my household? Why is Rumor here?
I run before King Harry's victory,
Who in a bloody field by Shrewsbury
Hath beaten down young Hotspur and his troops,
Quenching the flame of bold rebellion
Even with the rebels' blood. But what mean I
To speak so true at first? My office is
To noise abroad that Harry Monmouth fell
Under the wrath of noble Hotspur's sword,
And that the King before the Douglas' rage
Stoop'd his anointed head as low as death.
This have I rumor'd through the peasant towns
Between that royal field of Shrewsbury
And this worm-eaten [hold] of ragged stone,
[Where] Hotspur's father, old Northumberland,
Lies crafty-sick. The posts come tiring on,
And not a man of them brings other news
Than they have learnt of me. From Rumor's tongues
They bring smooth comforts false, worse than true wrongs. *Exit Rumor.*

[ACT I, SCENE I]

Enter the LORD BARDOLPH *at one door.*

L. Bard. Who keeps the gate here ho?
[*Enter* PORTER.]
Where is the Earl?
Port. What shall I say you are?
L. Bard. Tell thou the Earl
That the Lord Bardolph doth attend him here.
Port. His lordship is walk'd forth into the orchard.
Please it your honor knock but at the gate,
And he himself will answer.

Enter the EARL NORTHUMBERLAND [*in a night-cap and supporting himself with a staff*].

L. Bard. Here comes the Earl. [*Exit Porter.*]
North. What news, Lord Bardolph? Every minute now
Should be the father of some stratagem.
The times are wild, contention, like a horse
Full of high feeding, madly hath broke loose,
And bears down all before him.
L. Bard. Noble Earl,
I bring you certain news from Shrewsbury.
North. Good, and God will!
L. Bard. As good as heart can wish:
The King is almost wounded to the death,
And in the fortune of my lord your son,
Prince Harry slain outright, and both the Blunts
Kill'd by the hand of Douglas, young Prince John
And Westmerland and Stafford fled the field,
And Harry Monmouth's brawn, the hulk Sir John,
Is prisoner to your son. O, such a day!
So fought, so followed, and so fairly won,
Came not till now to dignify the times,
Since Caesar's fortunes.
North. How is this deriv'd?
Saw you the field? came you from Shrewsbury?
L. Bard. I spake with one, my lord, that came from thence,
A gentleman well bred and of good name,
That freely rend'red me these news for true.
North. Here comes my servant Travers, who I sent
On Tuesday last to listen after news.

Enter TRAVERS.

L. Bard. My lord, I overrode him on the way,
And he is furnish'd with no certainties
More than he haply may retail from me.
North. Now, Travers, what good tidings comes with you?
Tra. My lord, Sir John Umfrevile turn'd me back
With joyful tidings, and being better hors'd,
Outrode me. After him came spurring hard
A gentleman, almost forespent with speed,
That stopp'd by me to breathe his bloodied horse.
He ask'd the way to Chester, and of him
I did demand what news from Shrewsbury.
He told me that rebellion had bad luck,
And that young Harry Percy's spur was cold.
With that he gave his able horse the head,
And bending forward strook his armed heels
Against the panting sides of his poor jade
Up to the rowel-head, and starting so
He seem'd in running to devour the way,
Staying no longer question.
North. Ha? Again.
Said he young Harry Percy's spur was cold?
Of Hotspur, Coldspur? that rebellion
Had met ill luck?
L. Bard. My lord, I'll tell you what:
If my young lord your son have not the day,
Upon mine honor, for a silken point
I'll give my barony. Never talk of it.
North. Why should that gentleman that rode by Travers
Give then such instances of loss?

22. household: i.e. the audience in the theatre.
24. Shrewsbury: town in Shropshire, scene of the battle (July 21, 1403) depicted at the end of *1 Henry IV* in which Sir Henry Percy ("young Hotspur") was killed and the rebellion that he—together with his uncle, the Earl of Worcester, and the Earl of Douglas—had led was crushed. **29. Harry Monmouth:** Prince Henry.
33. peasant towns: country villages (whose rustic inhabitants were particularly susceptible to rumor).
35. hold: fortress. **ragged:** rough.
37. crafty-sick: feigning illness. **The posts . . . on:** the messengers, exhausted by their speed, push on.

I.i. Location: Warkworth. Before Northumberland's castle.
3. attend: await. **10. high feeding:** rich food. **13. and:** if.

16. both the Blunts. Only one Blunt—Sir Walter—is killed by the Earl of Douglas in *1 Henry IV* (V.iii).
19. brawn: fatted swine. **hulk:** large cargo ship.
20. day: day of battle, i.e. combat.
21. followed: carried through.
23. fortunes: successes. **How . . . deriv'd:** i.e. what's the source of your information. **30. overrode:** overtook.
34. Sir John Umfrevile. Apparently not a historical character. Shakespeare perhaps remembered the Sir Robert Umfrevile whom Holinshed mentions (Bullough, IV, 271) as one loyal to the King.
37. forespent: utterly exhausted.
39. Chester: important town north of Shrewsbury.
43. able: powerful.
46. Up . . . rowel-head: i.e. the full depth of the spur.
48. Staying . . . question: awaiting no more talk.
53. point: lace for tying garments, i.e. a thing of no value.

L. Bard. Who, he?
He was some hilding fellow that had stol'n
The horse he rode on, and, upon my life,
Spoke at a venter. Look, here comes more news.

Enter MORTON.

North. Yea, this man's brow, like to a title-leaf,
Foretells the nature of a tragic volume.
So looks the strond whereon the imperious flood
Hath left a witness'd usurpation.
Say, Morton, didst thou come from Shrewsbury?
Mor. I ran from Shrewsbury, my noble lord,
Where hateful death put on his ugliest mask
To fright our party.
North. How doth my son and brother?
Thou tremblest, and the whiteness in thy cheek
Is apter than thy tongue to tell thy arrand.
Even such a man, so faint, so spiritless,
So dull, so dead in look, so woe-begone,
Drew Priam's curtain in the dead of night,
And would have told him half his Troy was burnt;
But Priam found the fire ere he his tongue,
And I my Percy's death ere thou report'st it.
This thou wouldst say, "Your son did thus and thus;
Your brother thus; so fought the noble Douglas"—
Stopping my greedy ear with their bold deeds,
But in the end, to stop my ear indeed,
Thou hast a sigh to blow away this praise,
Ending with "Brother, son, and all are dead."
Mor. Douglas is living, and your brother yet,
But for my lord your son—
North. Why, he is dead.
See what a ready tongue suspicion hath!
He that but fears the thing he would not know
Hath by instinct knowledge from others' eyes
That what he fear'd is chanced. Yet speak, Morton,
Tell thou an earl his divination lies,
And I will take it as a sweet disgrace
And make thee rich for doing me such wrong.
Mor. You are too great to be by me gainsaid,
Your spirit is too true, your fears too certain.
North. Yet for all this, say not that Percy's dead.
I see a strange confession in thine eye.
Thou shak'st thy head, and hold'st it fear or sin
To speak a truth. If he be slain, [say so;]
The tongue offends not that reports his death,
And he doth sin that doth belie the dead,
Not he which says the dead is not alive.
Yet the first bringer of unwelcome news
Hath but a losing office, and his tongue
Sounds ever after as a sullen bell,
Rememb'red tolling a departing friend.
L. Bard. I cannot think, my lord, your son is dead.
Mor. I am sorry I should force you to believe
That which I would to God I had not seen,
But these mine eyes saw him in bloody state,
Rend'ring faint quittance, wearied and outbreath'd,
To Harry Monmouth, whose swift wrath beat down
The never-daunted Percy to the earth,
From whence with life he never more sprung up.
In few, his death, whose spirit lent a fire
Even to the dullest peasant in his camp,
Being bruited once, took fire and heat away
From the best-temper'd courage in his troops,
For from his metal was his party steeled,
Which once in him abated, all the rest
Turn'd on themselves, like dull and heavy lead.
And as the thing that's heavy in itself
Upon enforcement flies with greatest speed,
So did our men, heavy in Hotspur's loss,
Lend to this weight such lightness with their fear
That arrows fled not swifter toward their aim
Than did our soldiers, aiming at their safety,
Fly from the field. Then was that noble Worcester
So soon ta'en prisoner, and that furious Scot,
The bloody Douglas, whose well-laboring sword
Had three times slain th' appearance of the King,
Gan vail his stomach and did grace the shame
Of those that turn'd their backs, and in his flight,
Stumbling in fear, was took. The sum of all
Is that the King hath won, and hath sent out
A speedy power to encounter you, my lord,
Under the conduct of young Lancaster
And Westmerland. This is the news at full.
North. For this I shall have time enough to mourn;
In poison there is physic, and these news,
Having been well, that would have made me sick,
Being sick, have (in some measure) made me well.
And as the wretch whose fever-weak'ned joints,
Like strengthless hinges, buckle under life,
Impatient of his fit, breaks like a fire
Out of his keeper's arms, even so my limbs,
Weak'ned with grief, being now enrag'd with grief,
Are thrice themselves. Hence therefore, thou nice crutch!
A scaly gauntlet now with joints of steel
Must glove this hand; and hence, thou sickly coif!
That art a guard too wanton for the head
Which princes, flesh'd with conquest, aim to hit.
Now bind my brows with iron, and approach
The ragged'st hour that time and spite dare bring
To frown upon th' enrag'd Northumberland!
Let heaven kiss earth! now let not Nature's hand
Keep the wild flood confin'd! let order die!
And let this world no longer be a stage

57. hilding: worthless. **59. venter**: venture.
60. title-leaf: title-page. **62. strond**: strand, shore.
63. a witness'd usurpation: i.e. obvious signs of ravage.
72. Priam: king of Troy who witnessed the destruction of his city by the Greeks. **78. Stopping**: filling. **87. is chanced**: has happened.
95. fear: something to be feared. **98. belie**: lie about.
101. losing office: duty that results in loss or disadvantage.

108. quittance: return of blows. **outbreath'd**: out of breath.
112. In few: in short. **114. bruited**: rumored.
115. best-temper'd: i.e. like fine steel. The metaphor is expanded in the next three lines. **117. abated**: dulled, blunted.
120. Upon enforcement: i.e. forced into motion.
123. aim: mark, goal.
127–28. The bloody . . . King. See *1 Henry IV*, V.iv.25–38, with the note to line 25.
129. Gan . . . stomach: began to lose his courage. **grace**: sanction (by his own example).
131. Stumbling . . . took. See note to *1 Henry IV*, V.v.21–22.
133. power: armed force. **134. conduct**: command.
141. life: i.e. the burden of living. **143. keeper's**: nurse's.
144. grief . . . grief: suffering . . . sorrow.
145. nice: effeminate, delicate. **146. scaly**: mailed.
147. sickly coif: invalid's cap. **148. wanton**: luxurious.
149. flesh'd: made fierce. **151. ragged'st**: roughest.

To feed contention in a ling'ring act;
But let one spirit of the first-born Cain
Reign in all bosoms, that each heart being set
On bloody courses, the rude scene may end,
And darkness be the burier of the dead!
[*L. Bard.*] This strained passion doth you wrong, my lord.
[*Mor.*] Sweet Earl, divorce not wisdom from your honor,
The lives of all your loving complices
[Lean] on [your] health, the which, if you give o'er
To stormy passion, must perforce decay.
[You cast th' event of war, my noble lord,
And summ'd the accompt of chance before you said,
"Let us make head." It was your presurmise
That in the dole of blows your son might drop.
You knew he walk'd o'er perils, on an edge,
More likely to fall in than to get o'er;
You were advis'd his flesh was capable
Of wounds and scars; and that his forward spirit
Would lift him where most trade of danger rang'd;
Yet did you say, "Go forth!" and none of this
(Though strongly apprehended) could restrain
The stiff-borne action. What hath then befall'n?
Or what [doth] this bold enterprise bring forth
More than that being which was like to be?]
L. Bard. We all that are engaged to this loss
Knew that we ventured on such dangerous seas
That if we wrought out life 'twas ten to one,
And yet we ventur'd for the gain propos'd,
Chok'd the respect of likely peril fear'd,
And since we are o'erset, venture again.
Come, we will all put forth, body and goods.
Mor. 'Tis more than time, and, my most noble lord,
I hear for certain and dare speak the truth,
[The gentle Archbishop of York is up
With well-appointed pow'rs. He is a man
Who with a double surety binds his followers.
My lord your son had only but the corpse',
But shadows and the shows of men, to fight;
For that same word, rebellion, did divide
The action of their bodies from their souls,
And they did fight with queasiness, constrain'd
As men drink potions, that their weapons only
Seem'd on our side; but for their spirits and souls,
This word, rebellion, it had froze them up,
As fish are in a pond. But now the Bishop
Turns insurrection to religion.
Suppos'd sincere and holy in his thoughts,
He's follow'd both with body and with mind;
And doth enlarge his rising with the blood
Of fair King Richard, scrap'd from Pomfret stones;
Derives from heaven his quarrel and his cause;
Tells them he doth bestride a bleeding land,
Gasping for life under great Bullingbrook,
And more and less do flock to follow him.]
North. I knew of this before, but to speak truth,
This present grief had wip'd it from my mind.
Go in with me, and counsel every man
The aptest way for safety and revenge.
Get posts and letters, and make friends with speed—
Never so few, and never yet more need. *Exeunt.*

[SCENE II]

Enter SIR JOHN [FALSTAFF] *alone, with his* PAGE [*following behind*] *bearing his sword and buckler.*

Fal. Sirrah, you giant, what says the doctor to my water?

Page. He said, sir, the water itself was a good healthy water, but for the party that ow'd it, he might have moe diseases than he knew for.

Fal. Men of all sorts take a pride to gird at me. The brain of this foolish-compounded clay, man, is not able to invent any thing that intends to laughter more than I invent or is invented on me: I am not only witty in myself, but the cause that wit is in other men. I do here walk before thee like a sow that hath overwhelm'd all her litter but one. If the Prince put thee into my service for any other reason than to set me off, why then I have no judgment. Thou whoreson mandrake, thou art fitter to be worn in my cap than to wait at my heels. I was never mann'd with an agot till now, but I will inset you neither in gold nor silver, but in vile apparel, and send you back again to your master for a jewel—the juvenal, the Prince your master, whose chin is not yet fledge. I will sooner have a beard grow in the palm of my hand than he shall get one [of] his cheek, and yet he will not stick to say his face is a face royal. God may finish it when he will, 'tis not a hair amiss yet. He may keep it still at a face royal, for a barber shall never earn sixpence out

156. **act:** i.e. act of a play.
157. **spirit . . . Cain:** i.e. spirit of murder.
166. **cast th' event:** calculated the outcome.
167. **accompt:** account. 168. **make head:** raise an army.
169. **dole:** distribution. 172. **advis'd:** aware.
172–73. **capable Of:** susceptible to.
174. **most trade:** the greatest resort.
177. **stiff-borne:** obstinately pursued.
180. **engaged to:** involved in.
182. **if . . . one:** it was ten to one against our coming out of it alive.
184. **Chok'd the respect:** checked consideration.
186. **put forth:** venture.
189–90. **The gentle . . . pow'rs.** Actually Archbishop Scroop's rebellion did not occur until nearly two years after the battle of Shrewsbury. According to Holinshed (Bullough, IV, 269–70), the Earl of Northumberland, after a few bellicose feints on learning of Hotspur's death, consented to a friendly meeting with the King, who "gave him faire words, and suffered him (as saith *Hall*) to depart home, although by other it should seeme, that he was committed for a time to safe custodie."
190. **well-appointed pow'rs:** well-equipped troops.
192. **corpse':** corpses, i.e. bodies without souls.
204. **enlarge his rising:** extend his rebellion.
205. **Pomfret:** Pontefract Castle, Yorkshire, the scene of Richard II's murder. 208. **Bullingbrook:** Henry IV.
209. **more and less:** i.e. people of all ranks.
212. **counsel every man:** let every man consider.

I.ii. Location: London. A street.
o.s.d. **buckler:** shield.
1. **Sirrah:** customary form of address to an inferior. **to my water:** about my urine. 4. **ow'd:** owned.
5. **moe:** more. **knew for:** was aware of.
6. **to gird:** in jeering. 8. **intends:** inclines, tends.
14–15. **mandrake:** plant with a forked root thought to resemble a man.
16. **mann'd:** provided (with a servant). **agot:** agate, i.e. little figure carved on an agate stone, cameo. 19. **juvenal:** youth.
20. **fledge:** fledged, i.e. covered with down. 22. **of:** on.
23. **royal.** With a pun on *royal* = a coin stamped with the king's head. 24. **at:** at the value of.

of it; and yet he'll be crowing as if he had writ man ever since his father was a bachelor. He may keep his own grace, but he's almost out of mine, I can assure him. What said Master Dommelton about the satin for my short cloak and my slops?

Page. He said, sir, you should procure him better assurance than Bardolph. He would not take his band and yours, he lik'd not the security.

Fal. Let him be damn'd like the glutton! Pray God his tongue be hotter! A whoreson Achitophel! a [rascally] yea-forsooth knave, to bear a gentleman in hand, and then stand upon security! The whoreson smoothy-pates do now wear nothing but high shoes, and bunches of keys at their girdles, and if a man is through with them in honest taking up, then they must stand upon security. I had as live they would put ratsbane in my mouth as offer to stop it with security. I look'd 'a should have sent me two and twenty yards of satin (as I am a true knight), and he sends me security! Well, he may sleep in security, for he hath the horn of abundance, and the lightness of his wife shines through it; and yet cannot he see, though he have his own lanthorn to light him. Where's Bardolph?

Page. He's gone [into] Smithfield to buy your worship a horse.

Fal. I bought him in Paul's, and he'll buy me a horse in Smithfield; and I could get me but a wife in the stews, I were mann'd, hors'd, and wiv'd.

Enter Lord Chief Justice [*and* Servant].

Page. Sir, here comes the nobleman that committed the Prince for striking him about Bardolph.

Fal. Wait close, I will not see him.

Ch. Just. What's he that goes there?

Serv. Falstaff, and't please your lordship.

Ch. Just. He that was in question for the robb'ry?

Serv. He, my lord, but he hath since done good service at Shrewsbury, and (as I hear) is now going with some charge to the Lord John of Lancaster.

Ch. Just. What, to York? Call him back again.

26. writ man: attained manhood.
28. grace: (1) title appropriate for a prince; (2) favor.
30. slops: baggy breeches.
32. Bardolph: a disreputable friend of Falstaff's, not the Lord Bardolph of I.i. **band**: bond.
34. the glutton: i.e. Dives, the rich man in the parable of Lazarus (Luke 16:19–31).
35. hotter: i.e. than the tongue of Dives, who, in hell, begged that Lazarus would "dip the tip of his finger in water, and cool my tongue." **Achitophel**: Absalom's counsellor (2 Samuel 15–17).
36. yea-forsooth: obsequious, flattering (by agreeing emphatically with whatever is said). **36–37. bear . . . in hand**: lead . . . on.
40. through: straightforward. **taking up**: ordering on credit.
41. live: lief. **43. look'd 'a**: expected that he.
46–48. horn . . . lanthorn. A play on *horn* as (1) cornucopia, (2) the sign of the cuckold, and (3) the window of a lantern.
50. Smithfield: district north of St. Paul's Cathedral noted for its livestock market.
52. in Paul's. Men in search of work congregated in the nave of St. Paul's.
54. stews: brothels. **I . . . wiv'd.** Echoing the proverb that a man who gets a horse at Smithfield, a servant in St. Paul's, and a wife in a brothel is in each instance defrauded.
55–56. here . . . Bardolph. Alluding to the Prince's altercation with Sir William Gascoigne; see note to *1 Henry IV*, III.ii.32–33.
55. committed: imprisoned. **57. close**: near.
60. in question for: examined in connection with.
63. charge: military command.

Serv. Sir John Falstaff!

Fal. Boy, tell him I am deaf.

Page. You must speak louder, my master is deaf.

Ch. Just. I am sure he is, to the hearing of any thing good. Go pluck him by the elbow, I must speak with him.

Serv. Sir John!

Fal. What? a young knave, and begging? is there not wars? is there not employment? doth not the King lack subjects? do not the rebels need soldiers? Though it be a shame to be on any side but one, it is worse shame to beg than to be on the worst side, were it worse than the name of rebellion can tell how to make it.

Serv. You mistake me, sir.

Fal. Why, sir, did I say you were an honest man? Setting my knighthood and my soldiership aside, I had lied in my throat if I had said so.

Serv. I pray you, sir, then set your knighthood and your soldiership aside, and give me leave to tell you you lie in your throat if you say I am any other than an honest man.

Fal. I give thee leave to tell me so? I lay aside that which grows to me? If thou get'st any leave of me, hang me; if thou tak'st leave, thou wert better be hang'd. You hunt counter, hence, avaunt!

Serv. Sir, my lord would speak with you.

Ch. Just. Sir John Falstaff, a word with you.

Fal. My good lord! God give your lordship good time of day. I am glad to see your lordship abroad. I heard say your lordship was sick, I hope your lordship goes abroad by advice. Your lordship, though not clean past your youth, have yet some smack of an ague in you, some relish of the saltness of time in you, and I most humbly beseech your lordship to have a reverend care of your health.

Ch. Just. Sir John, I sent for you before your expedition to Shrewsbury.

Fal. And't please your lordship, I hear his Majesty is return'd with some discomfort from Wales.

Ch. Just. I talk not of his Majesty. You would not come when I sent for you.

Fal. And I hear, moreover, his Highness is fall'n into this same whoreson apoplexy.

Ch. Just. Well, God mend him! I pray you let me speak with you.

Fal. This apoplexy, as I take it, is a kind of lethargy, and't please your lordship, a kind of sleeping in the blood, a whoreson tingling.

Ch. Just. What tell you me of it? Be it as it is.

Fal. It hath it original from much grief, from study, and perturbation of the brain. I have read the cause of his effects in Galen, it is a kind of deafness.

Ch. Just. I think you are fall'n into the disease, for you hear not what I say to you.

78. make: regard, consider.
90. counter: in the wrong direction (perhaps with a pun on *Counter* as the name of two ancient London prisons). **avaunt**: begone.
96. by advice: i.e. with your doctor's approval.
103–4. I . . . Wales. Falstaff perhaps refers—anachronistically—to an unsuccessful expedition that Henry IV led against Glendower in 1405. **114. What**: why. **115. it original**: its origin.
117. Galen: Greek medical authority of the second century A.D.

[*Fal.*] Very well, my lord, very well. Rather, and't please you, it is the disease of not list'ning, the malady of not marking, that I am troubled withal.

Ch. Just. To punish you by the heels would amend the attention of your ears, and I care not if I do become your physician.

Fal. I am as poor as Job, my lord, but not so patient. Your lordship may minister the potion of imprisonment to me in respect of poverty, but how I should be your patient to follow your prescriptions, the wise may make some dram of a scruple, or indeed a scruple itself.

Ch. Just. I sent for you, when there were matters against you for your life, to come speak with me.

Fal. As I was then advis'd by my learned counsel in the laws of this land-service, I did not come.

Ch. Just. Well, the truth is, Sir John, you live in great infamy.

Fal. He that buckles himself in my belt cannot live in less.

Ch. Just. Your means are very slender, and your waste is great.

Fal. I would it were otherwise, I would my means were greater and my waist [slenderer].

Ch. Just. You have misled the youthful prince.

Fal. The young prince hath misled me. I am the fellow with the great belly, and he my dog.

Ch. Just. Well, I am loath to gall a new-heal'd wound. Your day's service at Shrewsbury hath a little gilded over your night's exploit on Gadshill. You may thank th' unquiet time for your quiet o'erposting that action.

Fal. My lord?

Ch. Just. But since all is well, keep it so, wake not a sleeping wolf.

Fal. To wake a wolf is as bad as smell a fox.

Ch. Just. What, you are as a candle, the better part burnt out.

Fal. A wassail candle, my lord, all tallow; if I did say of wax, my growth would approve the truth.

Ch. Just. There is not a white hair in your face but should have his effect of gravity.

Fal. His effect of gravy, gravy, gravy.

Ch. Just. You follow the young prince up and down, like his ill angel.

Fal. Not so, my lord. Your ill angel is light, but I hope he that looks upon me will take me without weighing, and yet in some respects I grant I cannot go. I cannot tell. Virtue is of so little regard in these costermongers' times that true valor is turn'd berrord; pregnancy is made a tapster, and his quick wit wasted in giving reckonings; all the other gifts appertinent to man, as the malice of [this] age shapes [them, are] not worth a gooseberry. You that are old consider not the capacities of us that are young, you do measure the heat of our livers with the bitterness of your galls; and we that are in the vaward of our youth, I must confess, are wags too.

Ch. Just. Do you set down your name in the scroll of youth, that are written down old with all the characters of age? Have you not a moist eye, a dry hand, a yellow cheek, a white beard, a decreasing leg, an increasing belly? Is not your voice broken, your wind short, your chin double, your wit single, and every part about you blasted with antiquity? and will you yet call yourself young? Fie, fie, fie, Sir John!

Fal. My lord, I was born about three of the clock in the afternoon, with a white head and something a round belly. For my voice, I have lost it with hallowing and singing of anthems. To approve my youth further, I will not. The truth is, I am only old in judgment and understanding; and he that will caper with me for a thousand marks, let him lend me the money, and have at him! For the box of the year that the Prince gave you, he gave it like a rude prince, and you took it like a sensible lord. I have check'd him for it, and the young lion repents, [*aside*] marry, not in ashes and sackcloth, but in new silk and old sack.

Ch. Just. Well, God send the Prince a better companion!

Fal. God send the companion a better prince! I cannot rid my hands of him.

Ch. Just. Well, the King hath sever'd you. I hear you are going with Lord John of Lancaster against the Archbishop and the Earl of Northumberland.

Fal. Yea, I thank your pretty sweet wit for it. But look you pray, all you that kiss my Lady Peace at home, that our armies join not in a hot day! for, by the Lord, I take but two shirts out with me, and I mean not to sweat extraordinarily. If it be a hot day, and I brandish any thing but a bottle, I would I might never spit white again. There is not a dangerous action can peep out his head but I am thrust upon it. Well, I cannot last ever, but it was alway yet the trick of our English nation, if they have a good thing, to make it

122. withal: with.
123. punish . . . heels: put you in the stocks (?).
128. in . . . poverty: i.e. because I'm too poor to pay a fine.
130. make . . . scruple: be reluctant to believe. *Scruple* suggests the use of *dram*, since both words designate small weights used by apothecaries. **132. matters:** complaints.
133. for your life: i.e. of capital offenses.
135. land-service: military service.
145–46. I . . . dog. Not satisfactorily explained.
147. gall: irritate. **149. your . . . Gadshill.** See *1 Henry IV*, II.ii.
150. o'erposting: escaping the consequences of.
155. smell a fox: be suspicious.
158. wassail candle: large candle for use at feasts.
159. wax: (1) beeswax; (2) grow. **approve:** confirm.
161. effect: sign, appearance.
165. Your . . . light: i.e. a clipped coin is underweight. An angel was a gold coin bearing the figure of the archangel Michael.

168. go: pass (as genuine).
169. costermongers' times: i.e. commercial days. A costermonger is a dealer in fruits and vegetables. **berrord:** bear-ward, keeper of bears. **170. pregnancy:** intellectual capacity.
175–76. the heat . . . galls: the strength of our passions with the bitterness of your bile (rancor).
176. vaward: vanguard, advance. Falstaff concedes that he is on the verge of middle age.
180. characters: (1) letters; (2) characteristics.
183. single: small, trivial. **188–89. something a:** a somewhat.
190. hallowing: shouting to hounds. **approve:** prove.
193. caper: dance. **mark:** a sum of 13*s.* 4*d.* **194. year:** ear.
196. check'd: rebuked.
197. marry: indeed (originally the name of the Virgin Mary used as an oath). **198. sack:** Spanish wine.
212. spit white. Not satisfactorily explained. Perhaps Falstaff associates white spittle with deep drinking. **action:** i.e. military action.
214. alway: always.

too common. If ye will needs say I am an old man, you should give me rest. I would to God my name were not so terrible to the enemy as it is. I were better to be eaten to death with a rust than to be scour'd to nothing with perpetual motion.

Ch. Just. Well, be honest, be honest, and God bless your expedition!

Fal. Will your lordship lend me a thousand pound to furnish me forth?

Ch. Just. Not a penny, not a penny, you are too impatient to bear crosses. Fare you well! Commend me to my cousin Westmerland.

[*Exeunt Chief Justice and Servant.*]

Fal. If I do, fillip me with a three-man beetle. A man can no more separate age and covetousness than 'a can part young limbs and lechery; but the gout galls the one, and the pox pinches the other, and so both the degrees prevent my curses. Boy!

Page. Sir?

Fal. What money is in my purse?

Page. Seven groats and two pence.

Fal. I can get no remedy against this consumption of the purse; borrowing only lingers and lingers it out, but the disease is incurable. Go bear this letter to my Lord of Lancaster, this to the Prince, this to the Earl of Westmerland, and this to old Mistress Ursula, whom I have weekly sworn to marry since I perceiv'd the first white hair of my chin. About it, you know where to find me. [*Exit Page.*] A pox of this gout! or a gout of this pox! for the one or the other plays the rogue with my great toe. 'Tis no matter if I do halt, I have the wars for my color, and my pension shall seem the more reasonable. A good wit will make use of any thing. I will turn diseases to commodity.

[*Exit.*]

[Scene III]

Enter th' Archbishop [of York], Thomas Mowbray (*Earl Marshal*), *the* Lord Hastings, *and* [Lord] Bardolph.

Arch. Thus have you heard our cause and known our means,
And, my most noble friends, I pray you all
Speak plainly your opinions of our hopes.
And first, Lord Marshal, what say you to it?

Mowb. I well allow the occasion of our arms,
But gladly would be better satisfied
How in our means we should advance ourselves
To look with forehead bold and big enough
Upon the power and puissance of the King.

Hast. Our present musters grow upon the file
To five and twenty thousand men of choice,
And our supplies live largely in the hope
Of great Northumberland, whose bosom burns
With an incensed fire of injuries.

L. Bard. The question then, Lord Hastings, standeth thus:
Whether our present five and twenty thousand
May hold up head without Northumberland?

Hast. With him, we may.

L. Bard. Yea, marry, there's the point!
But if without him we be thought too feeble,
My judgment is we should not step too far
[Till we had his assistance by the hand.
For in a theme so bloody-fac'd as this,
Conjecture, expectation, and surmise
Of aids incertain should not be admitted.]

Arch. 'Tis very true, Lord Bardolph, for indeed
It was young Hotspur's cause at Shrewsbury.

L. Bard. It was, my lord, who lin'd himself with hope,
Eating the air, and promise of supply,
Flatt'ring himself in project of a power
Much smaller than the smallest of his thoughts,
And so with great imagination,
Proper to madmen, led his powers to death,
And winking, leapt into destruction.

Hast. But by your leave, it never yet did hurt
To lay down likelihoods and forms of hope.

L. Bard. [Yes, if this present quality of war—
Indeed the instant action, a cause on foot—
Lives so in hope, as in an early spring
We see th' appearing buds, which to prove fruit
Hope gives not so much warrant, as despair
That frosts will bite them. When we mean to build,
We first survey the plot, then draw the model,
And when we see the figure of the house,
Then must we rate the cost of the erection,
Which if we find outweighs ability,
What do we then but draw anew the model
In fewer offices, or at least desist
To build at all? Much more, in this great work
(Which is, almost, to pluck a kingdom down
And set another up), should we survey
The plot of situation and the model,
Consent upon a sure foundation,
Question surveyors, know our own estate,
How able such a work to undergo,

221. honest: well behaved.
226. crosses: (1) adversities; (2) silver coins stamped with a cross.
228. fillip: strike. **three-man beetle:** heavy sledge or rammer, requiring three men to lift it, for setting paving stones.
231. pinches: torments.
232. degrees: kinds (of disease). **prevent:** anticipate.
235. groats: coins worth fourpence. **245. halt:** limp.
246. color: excuse, pretext. **248. commodity:** profit.

I.iii. Location: York. The Archbishop's palace.
4. Lord Marshal. See note to *1 Henry IV*, IV.iv.2.
5. allow . . . arms: concede that war is justified. **7. in:** with.

10. file: list. **11. of choice:** i.e. exceptionally well qualified.
12. supplies: reinforcements. **largely:** bountifully.
17. hold up head: i.e. succeed. **22. theme:** matter.
26. cause: situation. **27. lin'd:** fortified.
28. Eating the air: i.e. living on (false) hope.
29. project: expectation. **power:** armed force.
33. winking: closing his eyes.
36–41. Yes . . . them. This difficult passage, which has baffled satisfactory explanation, might be roughly paraphrased as follows: "Yes, if the present state of affairs—with war not a theme for speculation but a cruel reality—depended merely on hope, then your optimism would be justified. But beware of overconfidence, as when the buds of early spring lead us to ignore the possibility of killing frosts."
42. plot: site. **model:** plan. **43. figure:** design.
44. rate: calculate. **45. ability:** i.e. our resources.
47. In fewer offices: i.e. more modestly. *Offices* = service quarters. **at least:** at worst. **52. Consent:** agree.
53. surveyors: architects. **estate:** resources.

To weigh against his opposite; or else]
We fortify in paper and in figures,
Using the names of men in stead of men,
Like [one] that draws the model of an house
Beyond his power to build it, who, half thorough,
Gives o'er, and leaves his part-created cost
A naked subject to the weeping clouds
And waste for churlish winter's tyranny.

Hast. Grant that our hopes (yet likely of fair birth)
Should be still-born, and that we now possess'd
The utmost man of expectation,
I think we are so [a] body strong enough,
Even as we are, to equal with the King.

L. Bard. What, is the King but five and twenty thousand?

Hast. To us no more, nay, not so much, Lord Bardolph,
For his divisions, as the times do brawl,
[Are] in three heads: one power against the French,
And one against Glendower; perforce a third
Must take up us. So is the unfirm King
In three divided, and his coffers sound
With hollow poverty and emptiness.

Arch. That he should draw his several strengths together,
And come against us in full puissance,
Need not to be dreaded.

Hast. If he should do so,
[To] French and Welsh he leaves his back unarm'd,
They baying him at the heels. Never fear that.

L. Bard. Who is it like should lead his forces hither?

Hast. The Duke of Lancaster and Westmerland;
Against the Welsh, himself and Harry Monmouth;
But who is substituted against the French,
I have no certain notice.

[*Arch.* Let us on!
And publish the occasion of our arms.
The commonwealth is sick of their own choice,
Their over-greedy love hath surfeited.
An habitation giddy and unsure
Hath he that buildeth on the vulgar heart.
O thou fond many, with what loud applause
Didst thou beat heaven with blessing Bullingbrook
Before he was what thou wouldst have him be!
And being now trimm'd in thine own desires,
Thou, beastly feeder, art so full of him,
That thou provok'st thyself to cast him up.
So, so, thou common dog, didst thou disgorge
Thy glutton bosom of the royal Richard,
And now thou wouldst eat thy dead vomit up,
And howl'st to find it. What trust is in these times?
They that, when Richard liv'd, would have him die,
Are now become enamor'd on his grave.
Thou, that threw'st dust upon his goodly head
When through proud London he came sighing on
After th' admired heels of Bullingbrook,
Cri'st now, "O earth, yield us that king again,
And take thou this!" O thoughts of men accurs'd!
Past and to come seems best; things present worst.]

[*Mowb.*] Shall we go draw our numbers and set on?

Hast. We are time's subjects, and time bids be gone. *Exeunt.*

[ACT II, SCENE I]

Enter HOSTESS [QUICKLY] *of the Tavern and an officer or two* [FANG *and* SNARE, *Snare lagging behind*].

Host. Master Fang, have you ent'red the action?

Fang. It is ent'red.

Host. Where's your yeoman? Is't a lusty yeoman? Will 'a stand to't?

Fang. Sirrah! Where's Snare?

Host. O Lord, ay! good Master Snare.

Snare. Here, here.

Fang. Snare, we must arrest Sir John Falstaff.

Host. Yea, good Master Snare, I have ent'red him and all.

Snare. It may chance cost some of us our lives, for he will stab.

Host. Alas the day, take heed of him! He stabb'd me in mine own house, most beastly, in good faith. 'A cares not what mischief he does, if his weapon be out. He will foin like any devil, he will spare neither man, woman, nor child.

Fang. If I can close with him, I care not for his thrust.

Host. No, nor I neither, I'll be at your elbow.

Fang. And I but fist him once, and 'a come but within my [vice]—

Host. I am undone by his going, I warrant you, he's an infinitive thing upon my score. Good Master Fang, hold him sure. Good Master Snare, let him not scape. 'A comes [continuantly] to Pie-corner (saving your manhoods) to buy a saddle, and he is

55. his opposite: its adversary.
60. part-created cost: expensive half-built house.
62. churlish: rough.
65. The utmost . . . expectation: i.e. as many men as we could reasonably expect to have.
70. as . . . brawl: i.e. made necessary by the disturbed state of affairs.
71. the French. Following the battle of Shrewsbury the French began harassing English shipping in the Channel and English garrisons in France.
72. Glendower. According to Holinshed (Bullough, IV, 270), in the summer of 1403 "the king was minded to have gone into Wales, against the Welsh rebels, that under their cheefteine Owen Glandouer ceassed not to doo much mischeefe still against the English subjects."
74. sound: resound. **76. several:** separate.
81. Who . . . should: who is likely to.
84. substituted: delegated. **90. vulgar:** plebeian.
91. fond many: foolish multitude.
109. draw our numbers: assemble our forces.
110. time: present state of affairs.

II.i. Location: London. A street.
1. ent'red the action: begun the lawsuit.
3. yeoman: assistant. **4. Will . . . to't:** will he fight bravely.
5. Sirrah: customarily a term of address to an inferior, but also used between equals of low status.
9. ent'red: brought suit against. **11. chance:** perchance.
16. foin: thrust (with an indecent equivoque).
18. close: grapple. **21. fist:** grip. **22. vice:** vise, grasp.
24. infinitive: i.e. infinite (one of the Hostess' many malapropisms). **score:** books, accounts.
26. continuantly: continually. **Pie-corner:** intersection in London, so called from its many cooks' shops.
27. saving: i.e. no offense intended to. The Hostess apologizes for mentioning a place so unsavory.

indited to dinner to the Lubber's Head in Lumbert street, to Master Smooth's the silk-man. I pray you, since my exion is ent'red and my case so openly known to the world, let him be brought in to his answer. A hundred mark is a long one for a poor lone woman to bear, and I have borne, and borne, and borne, and have been fubb'd off, and fubb'd off, and fubb'd off, from this day to that day, that it is a shame to be thought on. There is no honesty in such dealing, unless a woman should be made an ass and a beast, to bear every knave's wrong.

Enter Sir John [Falstaff] *and* Bardolph *and the Boy* [Page].

Yonder he comes, and that arrant malmsey-nose knave, Bardolph, with him. Do your offices, do your offices, Master Fang and Master Snare, do me, do me, do me your offices.

Fal. How now, whose mare's dead? what's the matter?

Fang. I arrest you at the suit of Mistress Quickly.

Fal. Away, varlets! Draw, Bardolph, cut me off the villain's head, throw the quean in the channel.

Host. Throw me in the channel? I'll throw thee in the channel. Wilt thou? wilt thou? thou bastardly rogue! Murder, murder! Ah, thou honeysuckle villain! wilt thou kill God's officers and the King's? Ah, thou honeyseed rogue! thou art a honeyseed, a man-queller, and a woman-queller.

Fal. Keep them off, Bardolph.

Officers. A rescue! a rescue!

Host. Good people, bring a rescue or two. [*The Page attacks her.*] Thou wo't, wo't thou? thou wo't, wo't ta? Do, do, thou rogue! do, thou hempseed!

Page. Away, you scullion! you rampallian! you fustilarian! I'll tickle your catastrophe.

Enter Lord Chief Justice *and his* Men.

Ch. Just. What is the matter? Keep the peace here, ho!

Host. Good my lord, be good to me; I beseech you stand to me.

Ch. Just. How now, Sir John? what are you brawling here?
Doth this become your place, your time, and business?
You should have been well on your way to York.
Stand from him, fellow, wherefore hang'st thou upon him?

Host. O my most worshipful lord, and't please your Grace, I am a poor widow of Eastcheap, and he is arrested at my suit.

Ch. Just. For what sum?

Host. It is more than for some, my lord, it is for all I have. He hath eaten me out of house and home, he hath put all my substance into that fat belly of his, but I will have some of it out again, or I will ride thee a' nights like the mare.

Fal. I think I am as like to ride the mare, if I have any vantage of ground to get up.

Ch. Just. How comes this, Sir John? What man of good temper would endure this tempest of exclamation? Are you not asham'd to enforce a poor widow to so rough a course to come by her own?

Fal. What is the gross sum that I owe thee?

Host. Marry, if thou wert an honest man, thyself and the money too. Thou didst swear to me upon a parcel-gilt goblet, sitting in my Dolphin chamber, at the round table by a sea-coal fire, upon Wednesday in Wheeson week, when the Prince broke thy head for liking his father to a singing-man of Windsor, thou didst swear to me then, as I was washing thy wound, to marry me and make me my lady thy wife. Canst thou deny it? Did not goodwife Keech, the butcher's wife, come in then and call me gossip Quickly? coming in to borrow a mess of vinegar, telling us she had a good dish of prawns, whereby thou didst desire to eat some, whereby I told thee they were ill for a green wound? And didst thou not, when she was gone down stairs, desire me to be no more so familiarity with such poor people, saying that ere long they should call me madam? And didst thou not kiss me, and bid me fetch thee thirty shillings? I put thee now to thy book-oath. Deny it if thou canst.

Fal. My lord, this is a poor [mad] soul, and she says up and down the town that her eldest son is like you. She hath been in good case, and the truth is, poverty hath distracted her. But for these foolish officers, I beseech you I may have redress against them.

Ch. Just. Sir John, Sir John, I am well acquainted with your manner of wrenching the true cause the false way. It is not a confident brow, nor the throng of words that come with such more than impudent sauciness from you, can thrust me from a level consideration. You have, as it appears to me, practic'd upon the easy-yielding spirit of this woman, and made her serve your uses both in purse and in person.

Host. Yea, in truth, my lord.

Ch. Just. Pray thee peace. Pay her the debt you owe her, and unpay the villainy you have done with her. The one you may do with sterling money, and the other with current repentance.

28. **indited**: i.e. invited. **Lubber's Head**: an inn.
28–29. **Lumbert street**: Lombard Street, a principal thoroughfare in London. 30. **exion**: i.e. action.
32. **mark**. See note to I.ii.193. 34. **fubb'd**: put.
39. **arrant malmsey-nose**: notorious red-nose. *Malmsey* = a sweet red wine. 40. **offices**: duties.
43. **whose mare's dead**: i.e. what's the commotion.
47. **quean**: slut. **channel**: gutter.
50. **honeysuckle**: blunder for *homicidal.*
52. **honeyseed**: blunder for *homicide.* 53. **man-queller**: man-killer.
58. **hempseed**: gallows-bird.
59. **scullion**: kitchen menial. **rampallian**: ruffian.
60. **fustilarian**: frowsy slut. **catastrophe**: backside.
63. **stand to**: support. 65. **what**: why, for what.

77. **a' nights**: by night. **mare**: nightmare.
79. **get up**: mount (a steed). 84. **gross**: total.
87. **parcel-gilt**: i.e. gilded on the inside (*parcel* = partial). **Dolphin chamber**: a room in the Hostess' tavern.
88. **sea-coal**: mineral coal (as distinguished from charcoal), brought to London by sea. 89. **Wheeson**: Whitsun (Pentecost).
90. **liking**: comparing.
94. **gossip**: familiar term of address for a female friend.
95. **mess**: quantity.
96. **prawns**: shrimps. **whereby**: whereupon. 98. **green**: raw.
101. **call me madam**: i.e. as the wife of a knight.
103. **book-oath**: oath on the Bible.
106. **in good case**: prosperous.
107. **distracted her**: driven her insane. 113. **level**: just.
119. **unpay**: make good. 121. **current**: genuine.

Fal. My lord, I will not undergo this sneap without reply. You call honorable boldness impudent sauciness; if a man will make curtsy and say nothing, he is virtuous. No, my lord, my humble duty rememb'red, I will not be your suitor. I say to you, I do desire deliverance from these officers, being upon hasty employment in the King's affairs.

Ch. Just. You speak as having power to do wrong, but answer in th' effect of your reputation, and satisfy the poor woman.

Fal. Come hither, hostess.

Enter a messenger [MASTER GOWER].

Ch. Just. Now, Master Gower, what news?

Gow. The King, my lord, and Harry Prince of Wales
Are near at hand. The rest the paper tells.

Fal. As I am a gentleman!

Host. Faith, you said so before.

Fal. As I am a gentleman! Come, no more words of it.

Host. By this heav'nly ground I tread on, I must be fain to pawn both my plate and the tapestry of my dining-chambers.

Fal. Glasses, glasses, is the only drinking, and for thy walls, a pretty slight drollery, or the story of the Prodigal, or the German hunting in waterwork, is worth a thousand of these bed-hangers and these fly-bitten [tapestries]. Let it be ten pound, if thou canst. Come, and 'twere not for thy humors, there's not a better wench in England. Go wash thy face, and draw the action. Come, thou must not be in this humor with me, dost not know me? Come, come, I know thou wast set on to this.

Host. Pray thee, Sir John, let it be but twenty nobles. I' faith, I am loath to pawn my plate, so God save me law!

Fal. Let it alone, I'll make other shift. You'll be a fool still.

Host. Well, you shall have it, though I pawn my gown. I hope you'll come to supper. You'll pay me all together?

Fal. Will I live? [*To Bardolph.*] Go, with her, with her, hook on, hook on.

Host. Will you have Doll Tearsheet meet you at supper?

Fal. No more words, let's have her.

Exeunt Hostess and Sergeant [*Fang, Snare, and Bardolph*].

Ch. Just. I have heard better news.

Fal. What's the news, my lord?

Ch. Just. Where lay the King to-night?

Gow. At [Basingstoke], my lord.

Fal. I hope, my lord, all's well. What is the news, my lord?

Ch. Just. Come all his forces back?

Gow. No, fifteen hundred foot, five hundred horse,
Are march'd up to my Lord of Lancaster,
Against Northumberland and the Archbishop.

Fal. Comes the King back from Wales, my noble lord?

Ch. Just. You shall have letters of me presently.
Come, go along with me, good Master Gower.

Fal. My lord!

Ch. Just. What's the matter?

Fal. Master Gower, shall I entreat you with me to dinner?

Gow. I must wait upon my good lord here, I thank you, good Sir John.

Ch. Just. Sir John, you loiter here too long, being you are to take soldiers up in counties as you go.

Fal. Will you sup with me, Master Gower?

Ch. Just. What foolish master taught you these manners, Sir John?

Fal. Master Gower, if they become me not, he was a fool that taught them me. This is the right fencing grace, my lord, tap for tap, and so part fair.

Ch. Just. Now the Lord lighten thee! thou art a great fool. [*Exeunt.*]

[SCENE II]

Enter the PRINCE [HENRY], POINS, *with other.*

Prince. Before God, I am exceeding weary.

Poins. Is't come to that? I had thought weariness durst not have attach'd one of so high blood.

Prince. Faith, it does me, though it discolors the complexion of my greatness to acknowledge it. Doth it not show vildly in me to desire small beer?

Poins. Why, a prince should not be so loosely studied as to remember so weak a composition.

Prince. Belike then my appetite was not princely got, for, by my troth, I do now remember the poor creature, small beer. But indeed these humble considerations make me out of love with my greatness. What a disgrace is it to me to remember thy name, or to know thy face to-morrow, or to take note how many pair of silk stockings thou hast, [*viz.*,] these, and those that were thy peach-color'd once, or to bear the inventory of thy shirts, as one for superfluity,

122. sneap: rebuke.
125. duty: respect (for one of your position).
130. in . . . reputation: suitably to your position.
141. fain: content.
143. Glasses: i.e. in place of old-fashioned metal tankards.
144. pretty slight drollery: comic scene.
145. hunting in waterwork: hunting scene in water color.
148. humors: whims, moods.
149–50. draw the action: withdraw the lawsuit.
154. nobles: gold coins worth 6*s.* 8*d.*
155. law: la (an emphatic interjection).
156. shift: i.e. arrangements. **157. still:** always.
162. hook on: i.e. stick close to her (so she won't change her mind about the loan).

169. Basingstoke: market town west of London.
178. presently: at once. **186. being:** seeing.
187. take . . . up: recruit.
193. grace: style. **fair:** i.e. on good terms.
194. lighten: (1) illuminate; (2) diminish in weight.

II.ii. Location: London. Prince Henry's house.
o.s.d. **other** i.e. others.
3. attach'd: seized on. **4–5. discolors . . . of:** makes blush.
6. vildly: vilely, disreputably. **small:** weak.
8. studied: disposed. **10. got:** begotten.
17. for superfluity: as a spare.

and another for use! But that the tennis-court-keeper knows better than I, for it is a low ebb of linen with thee when thou keepest not racket there; as thou hast not done a great while, because the rest of the low countries have [made a shift to] eat up thy holland. And God knows whether those that [bawl] out the ruins of thy linen shall inherit his kingdom: but the midwives say the children are not in the fault, whereupon the world increases, and kinreds are mightily strengthen'd.

Poins. How ill it follows, after you have labor'd so hard, you should talk so idlely! Tell me how many good young princes would do so, their fathers being so sick as yours at this time is.

Prince. Shall I tell thee one thing, Poins?

Poins. Yes, faith, and let it be an excellent good thing.

Prince. It shall serve among wits of no higher breeding than thine.

Poins. Go to, I stand the push of your one thing that you will tell.

Prince. Marry, I tell thee it is not meet that I should be sad, now my father is sick, albeit I could tell to thee—as to one it pleases me, for fault of a better, to call my friend—I could be sad, and sad indeed too.

Poins. Very hardly, upon such a subject.

Prince. By this hand, thou thinkest me as far in the devil's book as thou and Falstaff, for obduracy and persistency. Let the end try the man. But I tell thee, my heart bleeds inwardly that my father is so sick, and keeping such vile company as thou art hath in reason taken from me all ostentation of sorrow.

Poins. The reason?

Prince. What wouldst thou think of me if I should weep?

Poins. I would think thee a most princely hypocrite.

Prince. It would be every man's thought, and thou art a blessed fellow to think as every man thinks. Never a man's thought in the world keeps the road-way better than thine: every man would think me an hypocrite indeed. And what accites your most worshipful thought to think so?

Poins. Why, because you have been so lewd and so much engraff'd to Falstaff.

Prince. And to thee.

Poins. By this light, I am well spoke on, I can hear it with mine own ears. The worst that they can say of me is that I am a second brother, and that I am a proper fellow of my hands, and those two things I confess I cannot help. By the mass, here comes Bardolph.

Enter BARDOLPH *and Boy* [PAGE].

Prince. And the boy that I gave Falstaff. 'A had him from me Christian, and look if the fat villain have not transform'd him ape.

Bard. God save your Grace!

Prince. And yours, most noble Bardolph!

Poins. Come, you virtuous ass, you bashful fool, must you be blushing? Wherefore blush you now? What a maidenly man-at-arms are you become! Is't such a matter to get a pottle-pot's maidenhead?

Page. 'A calls me [e'en now], my lord, through a red lattice, and I could discern no part of his face from the window. At last I spied his eyes, and methought he had made two holes in the ale-wive's petticoat and so peep'd through.

Prince. Has not the boy profited?

Bard. Away, you whoreson upright [rabbit], away!

Page. Away, you rascally Althaea's dream, away!

Prince. Instruct us, boy, what dream, boy?

Page. Marry, my lord, Althaea dreamt she was deliver'd of a fire-brand, and therefore I call him her dream.

Prince. A crown's worth of good interpretation. There 'tis, boy.

Poins. O that this blossom could be kept from cankers! Well, there is sixpence to preserve thee.

Bard. And you do not make him hang'd among you, the gallows shall have wrong.

Prince. And how doth thy master, Bardolph?

Bard. Well, my lord. He heard of your Grace's coming to town. There's a letter for you.

Poins. Deliver'd with good respect. And how doth the martlemas, your master?

Bard. In bodily health, sir.

Poins. Marry, the immortal part needs a physician, but that moves not him; though that be sick, it dies not.

Prince. I do allow this wen to be as familiar with me as my dog, and he holds his place, for look you how he writes. [*Showing the letter to Poins.*]

Poins. [*Reads the superscription.*] "John Falstaff, knight"—Every man must know that, as oft as he has occasion to name himself; even like those that are kin to the King, for they never prick their finger but they say, "There's some of the King's blood spilt." "How comes that?" says he, that takes upon him not to conceive. The answer is as ready as a [borrower's] cap, "I am the King's poor cousin, sir."

Prince. Nay, they will be kin to us, or they will fetch it from Japhet. But the letter: "Sir John Falstaff, knight, to the son of the King

18–21. But . . . while: i.e. Poins has not played tennis recently because he has no spare shirt to change to after exercising.
21–22. the low . . . holland: i.e. the brothels have contrived to strip you naked. *Shift* = contrivance (with pun on the meaning "shirt"); *holland* = fine linen (with pun on *Holland,* suggested by *low countries*).
23–24. those . . . linen: i.e. Poins's bastards, who wear his cast-off shirts. **26. kinreds:** kindreds. **29. idlely:** idly.
44. Very hardly: with difficulty. **46. obduracy:** persistence in evil.
50. ostentation: display. **60. accites:** prompts. **62. lewd:** base.
63. engraff'd: attached.
67. second: younger (and therefore without inheritance).
67–68. proper . . . hands: good fighter.

78. pottle-pot: two-quart tankard. **80. discern:** distinguish.
89–90. Althaea . . . fire-brand. The page confuses Althaea with Hecuba, who, when pregnant with Paris, dreamed that she would bear a firebrand that would destroy Troy. On Althaea's firebrand see note to *2 Henry VI,* I.i.234–35.
92. crown: coin worth five shillings.
95. cankers: cankerworms, caterpillars.
101. with good respect: in proper form.
102. martlemas: fatted ox killed at Martinmas (November 11).
106. wen: tumor.
114–15. takes . . . conceive: pretends not to understand.
118. fetch . . . Japhet: i.e. trace their ancestry back to Japhet, one of Noah's sons.

Both black and white magic were considered "of the devil," and their practitioners were declared to be magicians, wizards, and witches and were liable to the severest penalties. The woodcut at the top, from the frontispiece to Matthew Hopkins' *Discovery of Witches* (1647), shows the notorious "witch finder," who in one year (1645–46) sent some sixty-eight "witches" to the gallows. Before him are two "witches," accompanied by their several "familiars" (imps or demons) in the forms of more or less domestic animals. Below (left) is an early woodcut from Ulrich Molitor's *De Lamiis* (German ed., 1493), depicting two witches raising a hailstorm by concocting a brew apparently very similar to that prepared by the Weird Sisters in *Macbeth* (IV.i). Beside it is a representation of a magician's circle from Reginald Scot's *Discovery of Witchcraft* (1584), a book that sought to debunk witchcraft and magic. So long as the magician remained within the chalked circle, protected on all sides by the sacred names and symbols, he was supposedly safe from any evil spirit he might summon by conjuration. In the conjuring scene (I.iv) in *2 Henry VI*, however, it is the raised spirit which is said to be made "fast within a hallow'd verge" (line 22).

The Folger Shakespeare Library

Cornell University Libraries

By permission of the Harvard College Library

This is the circle for the maister to sit in, and his fellowe or fellowes, at the first calling, sit backe to backe, when he calleth the spirit ; and for the fairies make this circle with chalke on the ground, as is said before. This spirit Bealphares being once called and found, shall never haue power to hurt thee. Call him in the houre of ♃ or ♀ the ☽ increasing.

All the pictures on these two pages are related by their common use of the concept of the Ptolemaic world picture. Below is a typical sixteenth-century diagram of the Ptolemaic universe (from Andrew Borde's *The First Book of the Introduction to Knowledge*, 1542). It shows the Earth, combined with the second of the four elements, Water, as the centre; above it are the spheres of the other two elements, Air and Fire, and beyond, in ascending order, the spheres of the seven planets, Moon, Mercury, Venus, Sun, Mars, Jupiter, and Saturn, each labelled with its characteristic and associated metal ("The Moone colde and moyste benevolent silver"). Above the planets come, first, the Circle of the Fixed Stars (marked with the signs of the zodiac); second, the Crystalline Sphere; third, the "First Moveable" or Primum Mobile, which imparts motion to all the spheres within it; and fourth, the Empyrean or highest heaven, here described as "The Abitation of the Blessed."

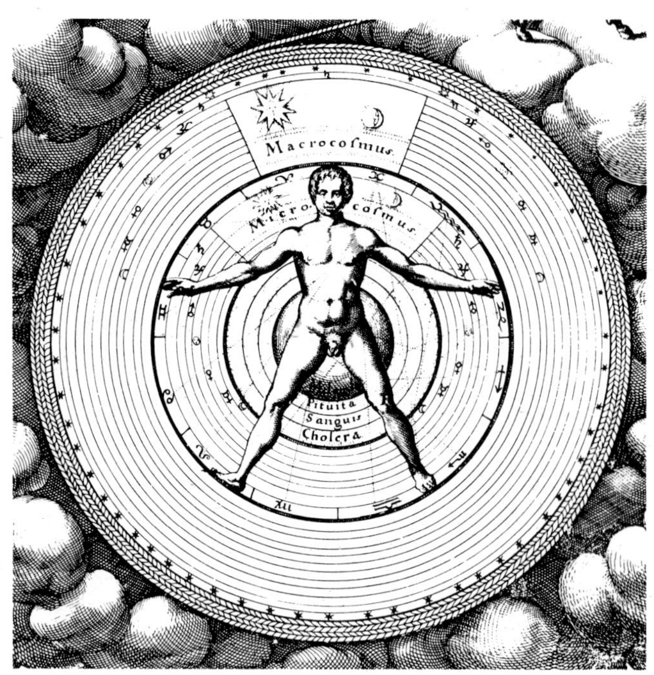

By permission of the Harvard College Library

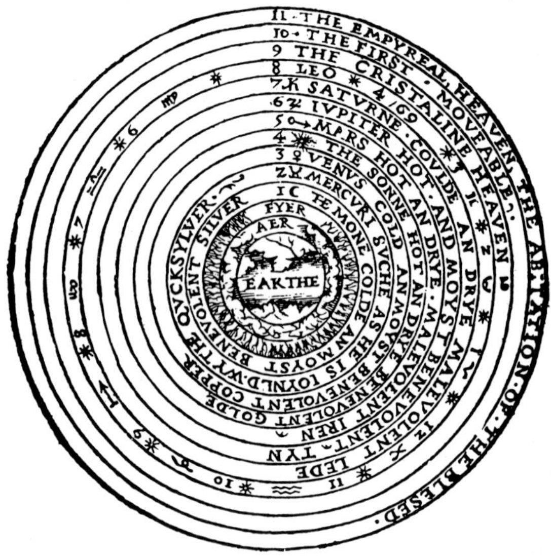

At upper right is a diagram (from Fludd's *Historia*) of "Man as microcosm" in his relation to the universe (the macrocosm). Man is shown as in a real sense the centre of the centre (the Earth), spanning the universe as far as the Circle of the Fixed Stars. Man's four humors (melancholy, blood, phlegm, and choler) are associated with the spheres of the four elements (earth, water, air, fire), and dotted lines indicate the relation of the parts of his body to the signs of the zodiac. At lower right is an adaptation of the Ptolemaic universe to the State of England (from John Case's *Sphaera Civitatis*, 1588). Around "immovable Justice" at the centre revolve Copiousness of Material Things, Eloquence, Clemency, Religion, Fortitude, Prudence, and Majesty; beyond, in the Circle of the Fixed Stars, are the Nobles, Heroes, and Councillors; while above all, more or less in the position of the Primum Mobile and as God's substitute in the affairs of Man, looms the all-embracing figure of the Queen.

By permission of the Harvard College Library

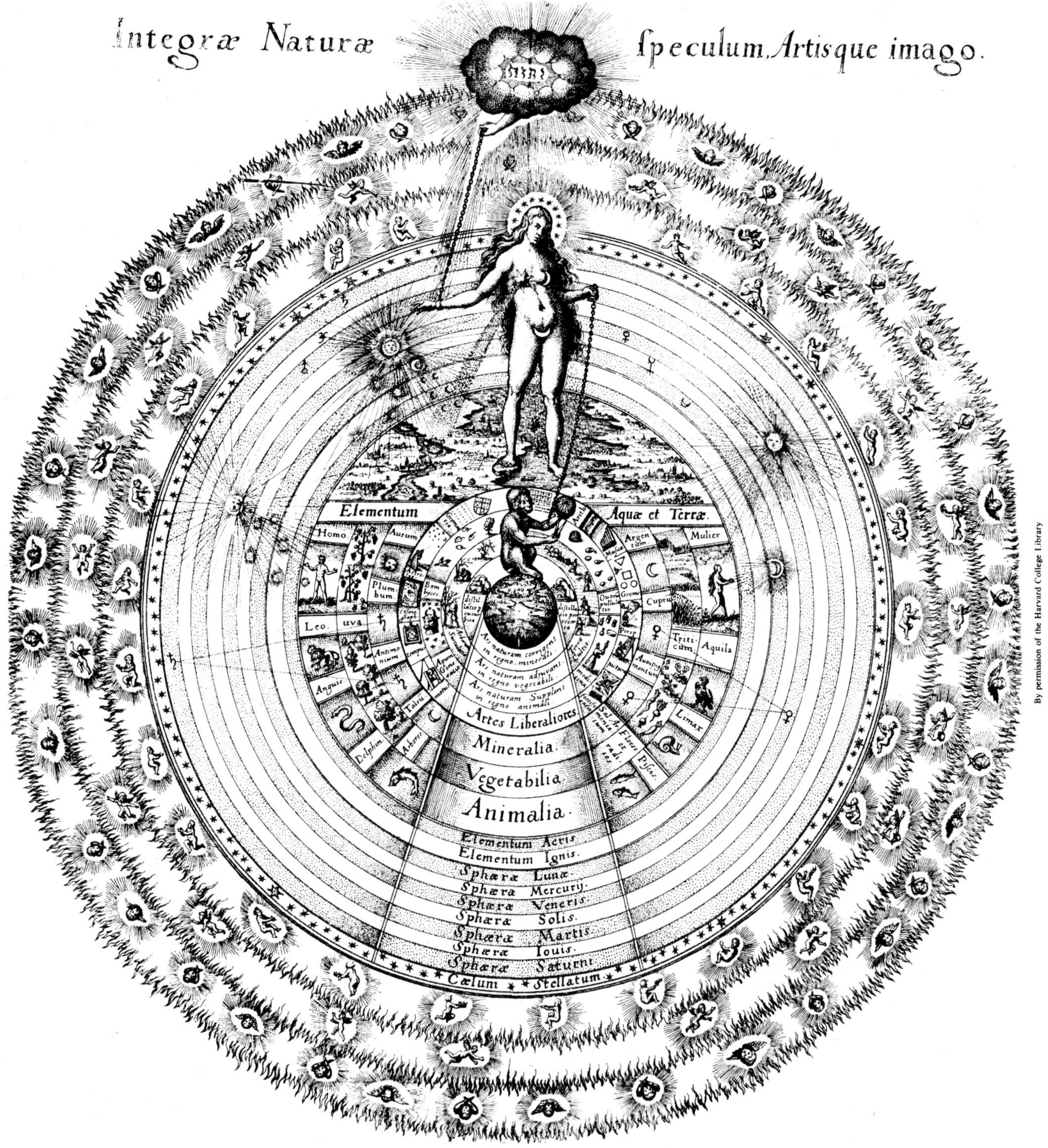

This handsome engraving, from Robert Fludd's *Utriusque Cosmi Historia* (1617–19), depicts the total integration of man, Nature, and God in terms of the cosmos. A chain held by God's hand is attached to Nature, who stands upon the mineral, vegetable, and animal kingdoms (man shown as part of the third); a second chain, held by Nature, is attached to a monkey representing man as "the ape of Nature," who, perched on the planet Earth, applies compasses to a globe (the Earth again) in a symbolic image already introduced in Plate 16. For the Ptolemaic basis of the scheme, see Plate 18.

The Caſtle of Knowledge.
The Sphere of Deſtinye.
Sphæra Fati
whoſe go uernour
is Know ledge.
The wheele
of Fortune.
Sphæra Fortunæ.
QVI MODO SCANDIT, CORRVET STATIM.
whoſe ruler is
Igno raunce.
To KNOWLEDG is this Trophy ſet,
All learninges friendes will it ſupport.
So ſhall their name great honour get,
And gaine great fame with good report
Though ſpitefull Fortune turned her wheele
To ſtaye the Sphere of Vranye,
Yet dooth this Sphere reſiſt that wheele,
And fleeyth all fortunes villanye.
Though earthe do honour Fortunes balle,
And bytells blynde hyr wheele aduaunce,
The heauens to fortune are not thralle,
Theſe Spheres ſurmount al fortunes chance.

The title-page above is from Robert Record's *The Castle of Knowledge* (1556). On either side of the Castle are shown (left) Urania (or Heavenly Wisdom), holding in her hands a pair of compasses (rational means of knowledge) and "The Sphere of Destiny" (i.e. of God's Providence), standing firmly on a solid square block, while the Sun, the governor among the planets, symbolizing reason, shines overhead; and (right) the blind Goddess Fortuna, balanced uneasily on a ball, pulling a cord tied to "The Wheel of Fortune," while the Moon, the symbol of changeableness and irrationality, "lights" her blindness. Compare *Henry V*, III.vi.30–38.

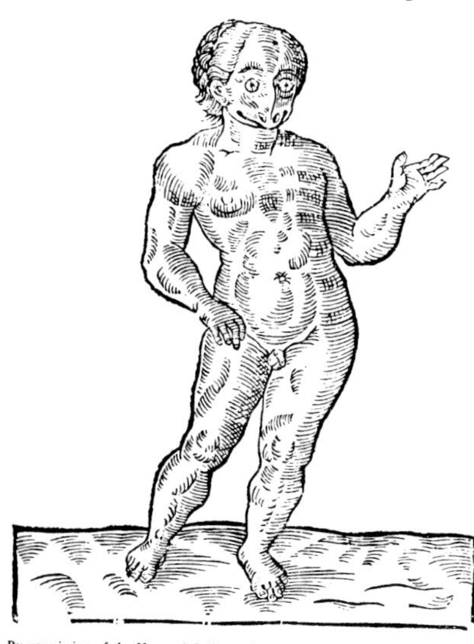

The figure of an infant with a face like a Frog.

Anno Dom. 1517. in the parish of Kings-wood, in the forrest *Biera*, in the way to *Fontain-Bleau*, there was a monster borne, with the face of a Frog, being seen by *John Bellanger*, Chirurgian to the Kings Engineers, before the Justices of the towne of *Harmoy*, principally *John Bribon* the Kings procurator in that place. The fathers name was *Amadæus* the *Little*, his mothers, *Magdalene Sarbucata*, who troubled with a feaver, by a womans perswasion, held a quicke frogge in her hand untill it died, she came thus to bed with her husband and conceived; *Bellanger*, a man of an acute wit, thought this was the cause of the monstrous deformity of the childe.

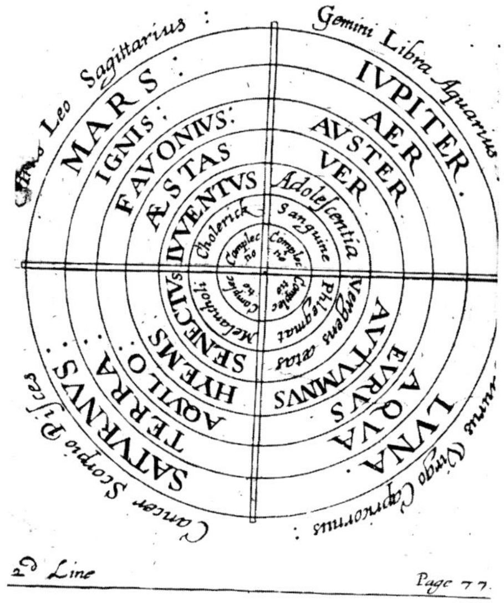

Monstrous births were frequently reported and were often regarded as the work of the devil. The one shown above (left), from Ambroise Paré's *Works* (trans. Thomas Johnson, 1634), is given a more mundane (if scarcely a more scientific) explanation. From the same work comes the illustration (below) of a method of resetting a dislocated shoulder. The diagram at upper right, from T. Walkington's *The Optic Glass* (1639), sets forth the interrelations of the four humors with the associated signs of the zodiac and planets, the four elements, the four winds, the four seasons, and the four principal ages of man—man the microcosm.

By permission of the Harvard College Library

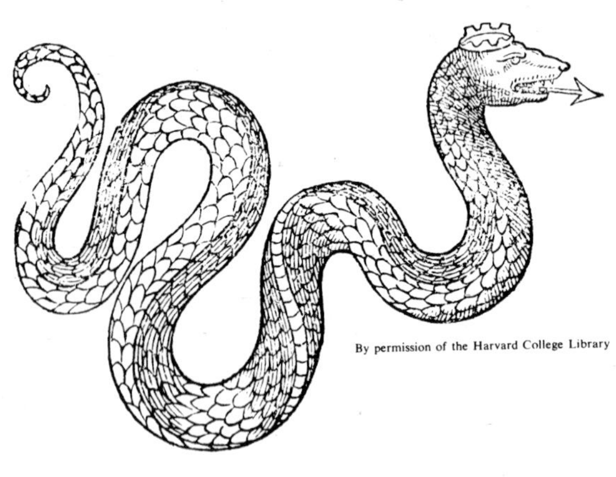

By permission of the Harvard College Library

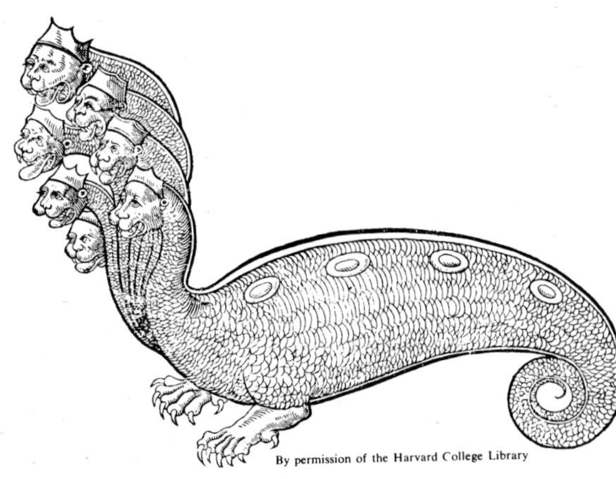

By permission of the Harvard College Library

On this page are shown three fabulous monsters from Edward Topsell's *The History of Serpents* (1608). The picture above, of a ship being devoured by a gigantic sea-serpent, makes up in imaginative verve what it may lack in verisimilitude; many Elizabethans, however, would have thought it credible enough. To the left is a basilisk, so called from the Greek word for "king," and here shown with its mythical regal coronet. It was also called a cockatrice, because it was supposedly hatched by a serpent from a cock's egg. Both the eye and the breath of the basilisk were thought to be mortal to man, but Shakespeare refers only to its death-dealing glance, as when Posthumus cries out, "It is a basilisk unto mine eye, / Kills me to look on't" (*Cymbeline*, II.iv.107–8), or the Duchess of York says in self-accusation, "A cockatrice hast thou hatch'd to the world, / Whose unavoided eye is murtherous" (*Richard III*, IV.i.54–55). The Hydra (below) was fabled to be practically indestructible because as fast as one head was lopped off, another (or two more) grew in its place. In *Coriolanus* Shakespeare equates it with the "many-headed multitude" (II.iii.16–17, III.i.92–93).

(Opposite, top) Shakespeare refers to the "arm'd rhinoceros" in *Macbeth* (III.iv.100). This vigorous rendering, from Topsell's *The History of Four-footed Beasts* (1607), brings home the aptness of the adjective "arm'd," which in Shakespeare's day meant not only "furnished with weapons" but "covered with armor." (Below, left) Since the elephant was popularly believed to have no knee joints, it supposedly slept leaning against a tree. This illustration, from Geffrey Whitney's *A Choice of Emblems* (1586), shows how to catch an elephant by undermining the tree in advance. (Below, right) This is another emblem from Whitney, who comments: "The Pellican, for to revive her younge, / Doth peirce her brest, and geve them of her blood." His expression of this ancient belief seems to be echoed in *Hamlet* (IV.v.147–48): "And like the kind life-rend'ring pelican, / Repast them with my blood."

By permission of the Harvard College Library

PLATE 22

Bodleian Library, University of Oxford

The funeral procession shown above, from a print of about 1625–30, is a satirical attack not only on the extravagance of the fashionable gallant's wardrobe but also on the various tradesmen and servants who have grown fat on his profligacy. Like Shakespeare's Timon of Athens, another large spender, he has his flattering Poet and Painter, as well as his Goldsmith (or Jeweller). Below (from F. Bertelli, *Omnium Fere Gentium Habitus*, 1563) is shown a Venetian lady of fashion wearing chopines, a kind of shoe with a high cork sole. In England, chopines seem to have been associated chiefly with actors. As Hamlet says to the boy actor in the troupe visiting Elsinore: "What, my young lady and mistress! by' lady, your ladyship is nearer to heaven than when I saw you last, by the altitude of a chopine" (*Hamlet*, II.ii.424–27). If we may judge by this picture, the boy may have grown as much as five or six inches!

Print Collection, Miriam and Ira D. Wallach Division of Art, Prints and Photographs. The New York Public Library. Astor, Lenox and Tilden Foundations

nearest his father, Harry Prince of Wales, greeting."

Poins. Why, this is a certificate.

Prince. Peace!
"I will imitate the honorable Romans in brevity."

Poins. He sure means brevity in breath, short-winded.

[*Prince.*] "I commend me to thee, I commend thee, and I leave thee. Be not too familiar with Poins, for he misuses thy favors so much that he swears thou art to marry his sister Nell. Repent at idle times as thou mayst, and so farewell.

Thine, by yea and no, which is as much as to say, as thou usest him, Jack Falstaff with my [familiars], John with my brothers and sisters, and Sir John with all Europe."

Poins. My lord, I'll steep this letter in sack and make him eat it.

Prince. That's to make him eat twenty of his words. But do you use me thus, Ned? Must I marry your sister?

Poins. God send the wench no worse fortune! but I never said so.

Prince. Well, thus we play the fools with the time, and the spirits of the wise sit in the clouds and mock us. Is your master here in London?

Bard. Yea, my lord.

Prince. Where sups he? Doth the old boar feed in the old frank?

Bard. At the old place, my lord, in Eastcheap.

Prince. What company?

Page. Ephesians, my lord, of the old church.

Prince. Sup any women with him?

Page. None, my lord, but old Mistress Quickly and Mistress Doll Tearsheet.

Prince. What pagan may that be?

Page. A proper gentlewoman, sir, and a kinswoman of my master's.

Prince. Even such kin as the parish heckfers are to the town bull. Shall we steal upon them, Ned, at supper?

Poins. I am your shadow, my lord, I'll follow you.

Prince. Sirrah, you boy, and Bardolph, no word to your master that I am yet come to town. There's for your silence.

Bard. I have no tongue, sir.

Page. And for mine, sir, I will govern it.

Prince. Fare you well; go. [*Exeunt Bardolph and Page.*] This Doll Tearsheet should be some road.

Poins. I warrant you, as common as the way between Saint Albons and London.

Prince. How might we see Falstaff bestow himself to-night in his true colors, and not ourselves be seen?

Poins. Put on two leathern jerkins and aprons, and wait upon him at his table as drawers.

Prince. From a God to a bull? a heavy descension! it was Jove's case. From a prince to a prentice? a low transformation! that shall be mine, for in every thing the purpose must weigh with the folly. Follow me, Ned. *Exeunt.*

[Scene III]

Enter Northumberland, *his wife* [Lady Northumberland], *and* [Lady Percy,] *the wife to Harry Percy.*

North. I pray thee, loving wife, and gentle daughter,
Give even way unto my rough affairs;
Put not you on the visage of the times,
And be like them to Percy troublesome.

Lady N. I have given over, I will speak no more;
Do what you will, your wisdom be your guide.

North. Alas, sweet wife, my honor is at pawn,
And but my going, nothing can redeem it.

Lady P. O yet for God's sake, go not to these wars!
The time was, father, that you broke your word
When you were more [endear'd] to it than now,
When your own Percy, when my heart's dear Harry,
Threw many a northward look to see his father
Bring up his powers; but he did long in vain.
Who then persuaded you to stay at home?
There were two honors lost, yours and your son's:
For yours, the God of heaven brighten it!
For his, it stuck upon him as the sun
In the grey vault of heaven, and by his light
Did all the chevalry of England move
To do brave acts. He was indeed the glass
Wherein the noble youth did dress themselves:
[He had no legs that practic'd not his gait;
And speaking thick (which nature made his blemish)
Became the accents of the valiant;
For those that could speak low and tardily
Would turn their own perfection to abuse
To seem like him; so that in speech, in gait,
In diet, in affections of delight,
In military rules, humors of blood,
He was the mark and glass, copy and book,
That fashion'd others. And him, O wondrous him!
O miracle of men! him did you leave,
Second to none, unseconded by you,
To look upon the hideous god of war
In disadvantage, to abide a field

121. a certificate: i.e. couched in legal style.
131. by . . . no. A common oath with Puritans (Matthew 5:37).
137. twenty: i.e. a large number. **147. frank:** sty.
150. Ephesians . . . church: i.e. boon companions of the usual (disreputable) sort. **154. pagan:** harlot. **157. heckfers:** heifers.
166. road: strumpet.
168. Saint Albons: St. Albans, some twenty miles north of London, on the heavily travelled Great North Road.
169. bestow: behave. **171. jerkins:** jackets.
172. drawers: tapsters.

174. Jove's case. To gain Europa's love, Jove transformed himself into a bull. **176. weigh with:** balance, be equal to.

II.iii. Location: Warkworth. Before Northumberland's castle.
1. daughter: i.e. daughter-in-law.
2. Give even way: allow free scope. **8. but:** except for.
10–14. The time . . . vain. On Northumberland's failure to come to Hotspur's aid at the battle of Shrewsbury see *1 Henry IV*, IV.i.13–85.
11. endear'd: bound. **20. chevalry:** chivalry.
21. glass: mirror. **24. thick:** hurriedly.
29. affections of delight: favorite occupations.
30. humors of blood: temperament.
31. mark: pattern. **copy:** example.
36. In disadvantage: i.e. against heavy odds. **abide a field:** sustain a battle.

Where nothing but the sound of Hotspur's name
Did seem defensible: so you left him.
Never, O never, do his ghost the wrong
To hold your honor more precise and nice
With others than with him! Let them alone.
The Marshal and the Archbishop are strong.
Had my sweet Harry had but half their numbers,
To-day might I, hanging on Hotspur's neck,
Have talk'd of Monmouth's grave.]

North. Beshrew your heart,
Fair daughter, you do draw my spirits from me
With new lamenting ancient oversights,
But I must go and meet with danger there,
Or it will seek me in another place,
And find me worse provided.

Lady N. O, fly to Scotland,
Till that the nobles and the armed commons
Have of their puissance made a little taste.

Lady P. If they get ground and vantage of the King,
Then join you with them, like a rib of steel,
To make strength stronger; but, for all our loves,
First let them try themselves. So did your son,
He was so suff'red; so came I a widow,
And never shall have length of life enough
To rain upon remembrance with mine eyes,
That it may grow and sprout as high as heaven,
For recordation to my noble husband.

North. Come, come, go in with me. 'Tis with my mind
As with the tide swell'd up unto his height,
That makes a still-stand, running neither way.
Fain would I go to meet the Archbishop,
But many thousand reasons hold me back.
I will resolve for Scotland; there am I,
Till time and vantage crave my company. *Exeunt.*

[Scene IV]

Enter a Drawer or two [Francis *and a second* Drawer].

Fran. What the devil hast thou brought there? apple-johns? Thou knowest Sir John cannot endure an apple-john.

[2.] *Draw.* Mass, thou say'st true. The Prince once set a dish of apple-johns before him, and told him there were five more Sir Johns, and putting off his hat, said, "I will now take my leave of these six dry, round, old, wither'd knights." It ang'red him to the heart, but he hath forgot that.

Fran. Why then cover and set them down, and see if thou canst find out Sneak's noise. Mistress Tearsheet would fain hear some music.

Enter Will [*a third* Drawer].

[3.] *Draw.* Dispatch. The room where they supp'd is too hot, they'll come in straight.

Fran. Sirrah, here will be the Prince and Master Poins anon, and they will put on two of our jerkins and aprons, and Sir John must not know of it. Bardolph hath brought word.

[3.] *Draw.* By the mass, here will be old utis, it will be an excellent stratagem.

[2. *Draw.*] I'll see if I can find out Sneak.

Exit [*with Third Drawer*].

Enter Mistress Quickly [*the* Hostess] *and* Doll Tearsheet.

Host. I' faith, sweet heart, methinks now you are in an excellent good temperality. Your pulsidge beats as extraordinarily as heart would desire, and your color, I warrant you, is as red as any rose, in good truth law! But, i' faith, you have drunk too much canaries, and that's a marvellous searching wine, and it perfumes the blood ere one can say, "What's this?" How do you now?

Doll. Better than I was. Hem!

Host. Why, that's well said; a good heart's worth gold. Lo here comes Sir John.

Enter Sir John [Falstaff].

Fal. [*Singing.*] "When Arthur first in court"—Empty the jordan. [*Exit Francis.*]—[*Singing.*] "And was a worthy king." How now, Mistress Doll?

Host. Sick of a calm, yea, good faith.

Fal. So is all her sect; and they be once in a calm, they are sick.

Doll. A pox damn you, you muddy rascal, is that all the comfort you give me?

Fal. You make fat rascals, Mistress Doll.

Doll. I make them? Gluttony and diseases make, I make them not.

Fal. If the cook help to make the gluttony, you help to make the diseases, Doll. We catch of you, Doll, we catch of you. Grant that, my poor virtue, grant that.

Doll. Yea, joy, our chains and our jewels.

Fal. "Your brooches, pearls, and ouches." For to serve bravely is to come halting off, you know; to come off the breach with his pike bent bravely, and to surgery bravely; to venture upon the charg'd chambers bravely—

38. defensible: capable of making defense.
40. nice: punctilious.
57. so suff'red: i.e. permitted to try his own strength.
61. recordation: memorial. **65. Fain:** gladly.
67. I . . . Scotland. Actually, as Holinshed makes clear (Bullough, IV, 274), Northumberland—who gave no effective aid to Archbishop Scroop—fled to Scotland *after* the rebels had been seized and executed.

II.iv. Location: London. The Boar's Head Tavern in Eastcheap.
2. apple-johns: wrinkled winter apples. **4. Mass:** by the Mass.
10. cover: i.e. spread the cloth. **11. noise:** band of musicians.

19. old utis: great sport (?).
23. temperality: i.e. temper. **pulsidge:** i.e. pulse.
24. extraordinarily: i.e. ordinarily.
26. canaries: canary, a sweet wine. **27. searching:** strong.
31. heart: disposition.
33. When . . . court: fragment of the ballad "Sir Launcelot du Lake."
34. jordan: chamber pot. **36. calm:** blunder for *qualm.*
37. sect: sex. **39. muddy:** dirty.
41. You . . . rascals. Using *rascal* in the sense of "lean, inferior deer," Falstaff implies that the term is inappropriate for him.
42. diseases: i.e. venereal diseases.
45. catch of: become infected by.
46. poor virtue: sweet virtuous one.
47. Yea . . . jewels. Taking up Falstaff's word *catch,* Doll implies that he has wheedled (or stolen) her trinkets from her.
48. ouches: jewels.
48–52. For . . . bravely. Like almost all the speeches in this scene, Falstaff's military metaphor is filled with indecent double meanings.

Doll. Hang yourself, you muddy cunger, hang yourself!

Host. By my troth, this is the old fashion, you two never meet but you fall to some discord. You are both, i' good truth, as rheumatic as two dry toasts, you cannot one bear with another's confirmities. What the good-year! one must bear, and that must be you, you are the weaker vessel, as they say, the emptier vessel.

Doll. Can a weak empty vessel bear such a huge full hogshead? There's a whole merchant's venture of Burdeaux stuff in him, you have not seen a hulk better stuff'd in the hold. Come, I'll be friends with thee, Jack. Thou art going to the wars, and whether I shall ever see thee again or no, there is nobody cares.

Enter Drawer [Francis].

[*Fran.*] Sir, Ancient Pistol's below, and would speak with you.

Doll. Hang him, swaggering rascal! let him not come hither. It is the foul-mouth'd'st rogue in England.

Host. If he swagger, let him not come here. No, by my faith, I must live among my neighbors; I'll no swaggerers, I am in good name and fame with the very best. Shut the door, there comes no swaggerers here; I have not liv'd all this while to have swaggering now. Shut the door, I pray you.

Fal. Dost thou hear, hostess?

Host. Pray ye pacify yourself, Sir John. There comes no swaggerers here.

Fal. Dost thou hear? It is mine ancient.

Host. Tilly-fally, Sir John, ne'er tell me; and your ancient [swagger, 'a] comes not in my doors. I was before Master Tisick, the debuty, t' other day, and, as he said to me—'twas no longer ago than Wed'sday last, i' good faith—"Neighbor Quickly," says he—Master Dumbe, our minister, was by then—"Neighbor Quickly," says he, "receive those that are civil, for," said he, "you are in an ill name." Now 'a said so, I can tell whereupon. "For," says he, "you are an honest woman, and well thought on, therefore take heed what guests you receive. Receive," says he, "no swaggering companions." There comes none here. You would bless you to hear what he said. No, I'll no swagg'rers.

Fal. He's no swagg'rer, hostess, a tame cheater, i' faith, you may stroke him as gently as a puppy greyhound. He'll not swagger with a Barbary hen, if her feathers turn back in any show of resistance. Call him up, drawer. [*Exit Francis.*]

Host. Cheater, call you him? I will bar no honest man my house, nor no cheater, but I do not love swaggering, by my troth. I am the worse when one says swagger. Feel, masters, how I shake, look you, I warrant you.

Doll. So you do, hostess.

Host. Do I? yea, in very truth, do I, and 'twere an aspen leaf. I cannot abide swagg'rers.

Enter Ancient Pistol *and* [Bardolph *and*] *Boy* [Page].

Pist. God save you, Sir John!

Fal. Welcome, Ancient Pistol. Here, Pistol, I charge you with a cup of sack, do you discharge upon mine hostess.

Pist. I will discharge upon her, Sir John, with two bullets.

Fal. She is pistol-proof, sir; you shall not hardly offend her.

Host. Come, I'll drink no proofs nor no bullets. I'll drink no more than will do me good, for no man's pleasure, I.

Pist. Then to you, Mistress Dorothy, I will charge you.

Doll. Charge me? I scorn you, scurvy companion. What, you poor, base, rascally, cheating, lack-linen mate! Away, you mouldy rogue, away! I am meat for your master.

Pist. I know you, Mistress Dorothy.

Doll. Away, you cutpurse rascal! you filthy bung, away! By this wine, I'll thrust my knife in your mouldy chaps, and you play the saucy cuttle with me. Away, you bottle-ale rascal! you basket-hilt stale juggler, you! Since when, I pray you, sir? God's light, with two points on your shoulder? Much!

Pist. God let me not live, but I will murther your ruff for this.

Fal. No more, Pistol, I would not have you go off here. Discharge yourself of our company, Pistol.

Host. No, good Captain Pistol, not here, sweet captain.

Doll. Captain? thou abominable damn'd cheater, art thou not asham'd to be call'd captain? And captains were of my mind, they would truncheon you out for taking their names upon you before you have earn'd them. You a captain! you slave, for what? for tearing a poor whore's ruff in a bawdy-house? He a captain! hang him, rogue! he lives upon mouldy stew'd pruins and dried cakes. A captain! God's light, these villains will make the word as odious as the word "occupy," which was an excellent good word before it was ill sorted; therefore captains had need look to't.

Bard. Pray thee go down, good ancient.

Fal. Hark thee hither, Mistress Doll.

53. cunger: conger eel. **57. rheumatic:** blunder for *splenetic* (?).
58. confirmities: blunder for *infirmities*.
58–59. What the good-year: a common expletive, roughly equivalent to "deuce take it." **59. you:** i.e. Doll.
63–64. venture . . . stuff: consignment of Bordeaux wine.
64. hulk: cargo ship. **82. ancient:** ensign, lieutenant.
83. Tilly-fally: fiddlesticks. **85. debuty:** deputy.
94. companions: reprobates.
95. bless you: count yourself lucky. **97. cheater:** swindler.
99. Barbary hen: guinea hen.
102. Cheater. The Hostess perhaps takes the word (to mean "escheator," i.e. fiscal officer for the king.

108. and: as if.
112. charge: salute. **discharge upon:** toast.
117. offend: wound. **125. mate:** fellow.
128. bung: pickpocket.
130. chaps: cheeks. **cuttle:** cutpurse (?) or cutthroat (?).
131. bottle: i.e. foamy (?).
131–32. you . . . juggler: you sword-bearing impostor (?). *Basket-hilt* = curved hand-guard on a sword.
133. points: laces for tying a cuirass to the shoulders.
142. truncheon: cudgel.
146–47. stew'd pruins. Stewed prunes were commonly associated with brothels. **149. occupy:** fornicate. **150. ill sorted:** corrupted.

Pist. Not I. I tell thee what, Corporal Bardolph, I could tear her. I'll be reveng'd of her.

Page. Pray thee go down.

Pist. I'll see her damn'd first, to Pluto's damned lake, by this hand, to th' infernal deep, with Erebus and tortures vile also. Hold hook and line, say I. Down, down, dogs! down, faitors! have we not Hiren here? [*Draws his sword.*]

Host. Good Captain Peesel, be quiet, 'tis very late, i' faith. I beseek you now, aggravate your choler.

Pist. These be good humors indeed! Shall pack-horses
And hollow pamper'd jades of Asia,
Which cannot go but thirty mile a day,
Compare with Caesars and with Cannibals
And Troiant Greeks? Nay, rather damn them with
King Cerberus, and let the welkin roar.
Shall we fall foul for toys?

Host. By my troth, captain, these are very bitter words.

Bard. Be gone, good ancient. This will grow to a brawl anon.

Pist. [Die] men like dogs! give crowns like pins! have we not Hiren here?

Host. A' my word, captain, there's none such here. What the good-year, do you think I would deny her? For God's sake be quiet.

Pist. Then feed and be fat, my fair Calipolis.
Come give 's some sack.
"*Si fortune me tormente, sperato me contento.*"
Fear we broadsides? no, let the fiend give fire.
Give me some sack, and, sweet heart, lie thou there.
[*Laying down his sword.*]
Come we to full points here? and are etceteras no things?

Fal. Pistol, I would be quiet.

Pist. Sweet knight, I kiss thy neaf. What! we have seen the seven stars.

Doll. For God's sake thrust him down stairs. I cannot endure such a fustian rascal.

Pist. Thrust him down stairs! Know we not Galloway nags?

Fal. Quoit him down, Bardolph, like a shove-groat shilling. Nay, and 'a do nothing but speak nothing, 'a shall be nothing here.

Bard. Come, get you down stairs.

Pist. What? shall we have incision? shall we imbrue? [*Snatching up his sword.*]
Then death rock me asleep, abridge my doleful days!
Why then let grievous, ghastly, gaping wounds
Untwind the Sisters Three! Come, Atropos, I say!

Host. Here's goodly stuff toward!

Fal. Give me my rapier, boy.

Doll. I pray thee, Jack, I pray thee do not draw.

Fal. Get you down stairs.
[*Drawing, and driving Pistol out.*]

Host. Here's a goodly tumult! I'll forswear keeping house afore I'll be in these tirrits and frights. So! murder, I warrant now. Alas, alas, put up your naked weapons, put up your naked weapons.
[*Exeunt Pistol and Bardolph.*]

Doll. I pray thee, Jack, be quiet, the rascal's gone. Ah, you whoreson little valiant villain, you!

Host. Are you not hurt i' th' groin? Methought 'a made a shrewd thrust at your belly.

[*Enter* Bardolph.]

Fal. Have you turn'd him out a' doors?

Bard. Yea, sir. The rascal's drunk; you have hurt him, sir, i' th' shoulder.

Fal. A rascal! to brave me?

Doll. Ah, you sweet little rogue, you! Alas, poor ape, how thou sweat'st! Come let me wipe thy face. Come on, you whoreson chops. Ah, rogue! i' faith, I love thee. Thou art as valorous as Hector of Troy, worth five of Agamemnon, and ten times better than the Nine Worthies. Ah, villain!

Fal. Ah, rascally slave! I will toss the rogue in a blanket.

Doll. Do, and thou dar'st for thy heart. And thou dost, I'll canvass thee between a pair of sheets.

Enter Music.

Page. The music is come, sir.

Fal. Let them play. Play, sirs. Sit on my knee, Doll. A rascal bragging slave! The rogue fled from me like quicksilver.

Doll. I' faith, and thou follow'dst him like a church. Thou whoreson little tidy Bartholomew boar-pig, when wilt thou leave fighting a' days and foining a' nights, and begin to patch up thine old body for heaven?

156–60. **I'll . . . here.** Pistol's bombast, here and later in the scene, contains echoes of and allusions to various contemporary plays, some of which are identified in the notes that follow.
156. **Pluto:** god of the underworld.
157. **Erebus:** the underworld.
159. **faitors:** swindlers. **Hiren:** the name that Pistol, following the practice of the heroes of romance, gives to his sword (perhaps with a pun on *iron*). Possibly there is also an allusion to *The Turkish Mahomet and Hiren the Fair Greek*, a lost play by George Peele.
162. **aggravate:** blunder for *moderate*.
163–67. **Shall . . . Greeks:** a mangled quotation from Christopher Marlowe's *Tamburlaine*, Part II, lines 3980–81.
166. **Cannibals:** blunder for *Hannibals* (referring to the famous Carthaginian general). 167. **Troiant:** Trojan.
168. **Cerberus:** three-headed dog at the entrance of the underworld.
169. **fall . . . toys:** fight over trifles.
179. **Then . . . Calipolis:** a garbled quotation from *The Battle of Alcazar* by George Peele.
181. **Si . . . contento:** if fortune torments me, hope contents me. (Pistol's ignorant farrago of Spanish and Italian is perhaps a motto engraved on his sword blade.) 182. **give fire:** shoot.
184. **full points:** stops. 186. **neaf:** fist.
187. **the seven stars:** constellation of the Pleiades.
189. **fustian:** worthless.
191. **Galloway nags:** inferior Irish horses.

192. **Quoit:** throw. **shove-groat:** game in which coins were aimed at a mark. 196. **imbrue:** shed blood.
199. **Untwind:** untwine. **Atropos:** one of the Fates ("the Sisters Three"). 200. **toward:** forthcoming. 205. **tirrits:** temper tantrums.
211. **shrewd:** sharp. 215. **brave:** defy. 218. **chops:** fat face.
219–20. **Hector, Agamemnon:** leaders of the Trojans and the Greeks respectively in the Trojan war.
221. **the Nine Worthies:** a group of renowned champions (Hector, Alexander, Caesar, et al.).
222–23. **toss . . . blanket.** A punishment for cowards. In the next speech Doll varies the phrase with a different implication.
226 s.d. **Music:** musicians.
231. **Bartholomew boar-pig.** Roast pig was the chief delicacy at the annual fair on St. Bartholomew's Day (August 24) in Smithfield.
232. **foining:** thrusting.

Enter, [*behind*,] PRINCE [HENRY] *and* POINS, [*disguised*].

Fal. Peace, good Doll, do not speak like a death's-head, do not bid me remember mine end.

Doll. Sirrah, what humor's the Prince of?

Fal. A good shallow young fellow. 'A would have made a good pantler, 'a would 'a' chipp'd bread well.

Doll. They say Poins has a good wit.

Fal. He a good wit? Hang him, baboon! his wit's as thick as Tewksbury mustard, there's no more conceit in him than is in a mallet.

Doll. Why does the Prince love him so then?

Fal. Because their legs are both of a bigness, and 'a plays at quoits well, and eats cunger and fennel, and drinks off candles' ends for flap-dragons, and rides the wild-mare with the boys, and jumps upon join'd-stools, and swears with a good grace, and wears his boots very smooth, like unto the sign of the Leg, and breeds no bate with telling of discreet stories; and such other gambol faculties 'a has, that show a weak mind and an able body, for the which the Prince admits him. For the Prince himself is such another, the weight of a hair will turn scales between their haberdepois.

Prince. Would not this nave of a wheel have his ears cut off?

Poins. Let's beat him before his whore.

Prince. Look whe'er the wither'd elder hath not his pole claw'd like a parrot.

Poins. Is it not strange that desire should so many years outlive performance?

Fal. Kiss me, Doll.

Prince. Saturn and Venus this year in conjunction! What says th' almanac to that?

Poins. And look whether the fiery Trigon, his man, be not lisping to his [master's] old tables, his note-book, his counsel-keeper.

Fal. Thou dost give me flattering busses.

Doll. By my troth, I kiss thee with a most constant heart.

Fal. I am old, I am old.

Doll. I love thee better than I love e'er a scurvy young boy of them all.

Fal. What stuff wilt have a kirtle of? I shall receive money a' Thursday, shalt have a cap to-morrow. A merry song! Come, it grows late, we'll to bed. Thou't forget me when I am gone.

Doll. By my troth, thou't set me a-weeping and thou say'st so. Prove that ever I dress myself handsome till thy return—well, hearken a' th' end.

Fal. Some sack, Francis.

Prince, Poins. Anon, anon, sir. [*Coming forward*.]

Fal. Ha? a bastard son of the King's? And art not thou Poins his brother?

Prince. Why, thou globe of sinful continents, what a life dost thou lead?

Fal. A better than thou: I am a gentleman, thou art a drawer.

Prince. Very true, sir, and I come to draw you out by the ears.

Host. O, the Lord preserve thy Grace! By my troth, welcome to London. Now, the Lord bless that sweet face of thine! O Jesu, are you come from Wales?

Fal. Thou whoreson mad compound of majesty, by this light flesh and corrupt blood, thou art welcome.

Doll. How? you fat fool, I scorn you.

Poins. My lord, he will drive you out of your revenge and turn all to a merriment, if you take not the heat.

Prince. You whoreson candle-mine, you, how vildly did you speak of me [even] now before this honest, virtuous, civil gentlewoman!

Host. God's blessing of your good heart! and so she is, by my troth.

Fal. Didst thou hear me?

Prince. Yea, and you knew me, as you did when you ran away by Gadshill. You knew I was at your back, and spoke it on purpose to try my patience.

Fal. No, no, no, not so, I did not think thou wast within hearing.

Prince. I shall drive you then to confess the willful abuse, and then I know how to handle you.

Fal. No abuse, Hal, a' mine honor, no abuse.

Prince. Not to dispraise me, and call me pantler and bread-chipper, and I know not what?

Fal. No abuse, Hal.

Poins. No abuse?

Fal. No abuse, Ned, i' th' world, honest Ned, none. I disprais'd him before the wicked, that the wicked [*turns to the Prince*] might not fall in love with thee; in which doing, I have done the part of a careful friend and a true subject, and thy father is to give me thanks for it. No abuse, Hal; none, Ned, none; no, faith, boys, none.

Prince. See now whether pure fear and entire cowardice doth not make thee wrong this virtuous gentlewoman to close with us. Is she of the wicked? is thine hostess here of the wicked? or is thy boy of the

236. humor: disposition.
238. pantler: servant in the pantry. **chipp'd:** cut the crusts from.
241. Tewksbury: Tewkesbury, town in Gloucestershire noted for its mustard balls. **241–42. conceit:** wit.
245. cunger and fennel: conger eels seasoned with the herb fennel.
246. drinks . . . flap-dragons: i.e. drinks liquor in which lighted candles are floated.
247. wild-mare: seesaw. **join'd-stools:** stools expertly made by a joiner or carpenter.
248–49. wears . . . Leg: i.e. wears well-fitting boots, like those on the sign over a bootmaker's shop. **250. bate:** discord.
251. gambol: sportive. **252. admits him:** tolerates him (as a friend).
254. haberdepois: avoirdupois.
255. nave: hub (with a pun on *knave*).
255–56. have . . . off. The punishment for slandering royalty.
259. his . . . parrot. Doll is scratching Falstaff's head (*pole* = poll).
263. Saturn and Venus: planets with strong influence on the aged and on lovers respectively. Their conjunction is astronomically impossible.
265. the fiery Trigon. The zodiac was divided into four "trigons" of three signs, characterized as fiery, airy, watery, and earthy. The "fiery Trigon" (Aries, Leo, and Sagittarius) is in allusion to Bardolph's complexion.
266–67. lisping . . . counsel-keeper: i.e. courting the Hostess. **tables:** account book. **268. busses:** kisses. **274. kirtle:** skirt.

280. hearken . . . end: i.e. you'll see that I am faithful to you.
283. bastard. With punning reference to his assumed role as drawer; *bastard* = a sweet Spanish wine.
285. globe . . . continents: (1) terrestrial globe . . . land masses; (2) sphere . . . contents. **285–86. what a:** what kind of.
295. this . . . blood: i.e. Doll.
298–99. take . . . heat: i.e. strike . . . when the iron is hot.
300. candle-mine: i.e. store of tallow. **301. vildly:** basely.
306–7. you . . . Gadshill. See *1 Henry IV*, II.iv.
325. entire: pure. **327. close with:** pacify.

wicked? or honest Bardolph, whose zeal burns in his nose, of the wicked?

Poins. Answer, thou dead elm, answer.

Fal. The fiend hath prick'd down Bardolph irrecoverable, and his face is Lucifer's privy-kitchen, where he doth nothing but roast malt-worms. For the boy, there is a good angel about him, but the devil blinds him too.

Prince. For the women?

Fal. For one of them, she's in hell already, and burns poor souls; for th' other, I owe her money, and whether she be damn'd for that, I know not.

Host. No, I warrant you.

Fal. No, I think thou art not, I think thou art quit for that. Marry, there is another indictment upon thee, for suffering flesh to be eaten in thy house, contrary to the law, for the which I think thou wilt howl.

Host. All vict'lers do so. What's a joint of mutton or two in a whole Lent?

Prince. You, gentlewoman—

Doll. What says your Grace?

Fal. His grace says that which his flesh rebels against. *Peto knocks at door.*

Host. Who knocks so loud at door? Look to th' door there, Francis.

[*Enter* PETO.]

Prince. Peto, how now, what news?

Peto. The King your father is at Westminster,
And there are twenty weak and wearied posts
Come from the north, and as I came along
I met and overtook a dozen captains,
Bare-headed, sweating, knocking at the taverns,
And asking every one for Sir John Falstaff.

Prince. By heaven, Poins, I feel me much to blame
So idly to profane the precious time,
When tempest of commotion, like the south
Borne with black vapor, doth begin to melt
And drop upon our bare unarmed heads.
Give me my sword and cloak. Falstaff, good night.

Exeunt Prince and Poins, [*Peto and Bardolph*].

Fal. Now comes in the sweetest morsel of the night, and we must hence and leave it unpick'd. [*Knocking within*.] More knocking at the door!

[*Enter* BARDOLPH.]

How now, what's the matter?

Bard. You must away to court, sir, presently,
A dozen captains stay at door for you.

Fal. [*To the Page*.] Pay the musicians, sirrah. Farewell, hostess, farewell, Doll. You see, my good wenches, how men of merit are sought after. The undeserver may sleep when the man of action is call'd on. Farewell, good wenches, if I be not sent away post, I will see you again ere I go.

Doll. I cannot speak. If my heart be not ready to burst—well, sweet Jack, have a care of thyself.

Fal. Farewell, farewell.

Exit [*with Bardolph and Page*].

Host. Well, fare thee well. I have known thee these twenty-nine years, come peascod-time, but an honester and truer-hearted man—well, fare thee well.

Bard. [*Within*.] Mistress Tearsheet!

Host. What's the matter?

Bard. [*Within*.] Bid Mistress Tearsheet come to my master.

Host. O, run, Doll, run, run, good Doll. Come. [*To Bardolph*.] She comes blubber'd.—Yea! will you come, Doll? *Exeunt*.

[ACT III, SCENE I]

Enter the KING *in his night-gown, alone*, [*followed by a* PAGE].

King. Go call the Earls of Surrey and of Warwick;
But, ere they come, bid them o'er-read these letters
And well consider of them. Make good speed.

[*Exit Page*.]

How many thousand of my poorest subjects
Are at this hour asleep! O sleep! O gentle sleep!
Nature's soft nurse, how have I frighted thee,
That thou no more wilt weigh my eyelids down,
And steep my senses in forgetfulness?
Why rather, sleep, liest thou in smoky cribs,
Upon uneasy pallets stretching thee,
And hush'd with buzzing night-flies to thy slumber,
Than in the perfum'd chambers of the great,
Under the canopies of costly state,
And lull'd with sound of sweetest melody?
O thou dull god, why li'st thou with the vile
In loathsome beds, and leavest the kingly couch
A watch-case or a common 'larum-bell?
Wilt thou upon the high and giddy [mast]
Seal up the ship-boy's eyes, and rock his brains
In cradle of the rude imperious surge,
And in the visitation of the winds,
Who take the ruffian [billows] by the top,
Curling their monstrous heads and hanging them
With deafing clamor in the slippery clouds,
That with the hurly death itself awakes?
Canst thou, O partial sleep, give [then] repose
To the wet [sea-boy] in an hour so rude,
And in the calmest and most stillest night,
With all appliances and means to boot,
Deny it to a king? Then (happy) low, lie down!
Uneasy lies the head that wears a crown.

332. prick'd down: marked.
334. malt-worms: beer tipplers.
339. burns: i.e. infects with venereal diseases.
342. quit: (1) paid; (2) saved.
344. for . . . house: i.e. for serving meat during Lent.
346. vict'lers: victuallers, purveyors of food.
350–51. says . . . against: i.e. in addressing the Hostess and Doll as "gentlewomen."
363. commotion: sedition, insurrection. **south:** south wind.
364. Borne: laden. **371. presently:** immediately.
372. stay: wait.

378. post: in haste.
383. peascod-time: i.e. early summer (when peas are in pod).

III.i. Location: Westminster. The palace.
o.s.d. night-gown: dressing gown. **9. cribs:** hovels.
13. state: magnificence. **15. vile:** low in rank.
17. watch-case: sentry-box. **'larum-bell:** alarm bell.
25. That: so that. **hurly:** tumult.
29. appliances and means: comforts and inducements (to sleep).
30. low: lowly ones.

Enter WARWICK, SURREY, *and* SIR JOHN BLUNT.

War. Many good morrows to your Majesty!
King. Is it good morrow, lords?
War. 'Tis one a' clock, and past.
King. Why then good morrow to you all, my lords.
Have you read o'er the [letters] that I sent you?
War. We have, my liege.
King. Then you perceive the body of our kingdom
How foul it is, what rank diseases grow,
And with what danger, near the heart of it.
War. It is but as a body yet distempered,
Which to his former strength may be restored
With good advice and little medicine.
My Lord Northumberland will soon be cool'd.
King. O God, that one might read the book of fate,
And see the revolution of the times
Make mountains level, and the continent,
Weary of solid firmness, melt itself
Into the sea, and other times to see
The beachy girdle of the ocean
Too wide for Neptune's hips; how chance's mocks
And changes fill the cup of alteration
With divers liquors! O, if this were seen,
The happiest youth, viewing his progress through,
What perils past, what crosses to ensue,
Would shut the book, and sit him down and die.
'Tis not ten years gone
Since Richard and Northumberland, great friends,
Did feast together, and in two year after
Were they at wars. It is but eight years since
This Percy was the man nearest my soul,
Who like a brother toil'd in my affairs,
And laid his love and life under my foot,
Yea, for my sake, even to the eyes of Richard
Gave him defiance. But which of you was by—
[*To Warwick.*] You, cousin Nevil, as I may remember—
When Richard, with his eye brimful of tears,
Then check'd and rated by Northumberland,
Did speak these words, now prov'd a prophecy?
"Northumberland, thou ladder by the which
My cousin Bullingbrook ascends my throne"
(Though then, God knows, I had no such intent,
But that necessity so bow'd the state
That I and greatness were compell'd to kiss),
"The time shall come," thus did he follow it,
"The time will come, that foul sin, gathering head,
Shall break into corruption": so went on,
Foretelling this same time's condition
And the division of our amity.
War. There is a history in all men's lives,
Figuring the natures of the times deceas'd,
The which observ'd, a man may prophesy,
With a near aim, of the main chance of things
As yet not come to life, who in their seeds
And weak beginning lie intreasured.
Such things become the hatch and brood of time,
And by the necessary form of this
King Richard might create a perfect guess
That great Northumberland, then false to him,
Would of that seed grow to a greater falseness,
Which should not find a ground to root upon
Unless on you.
King. Are these things then necessities?
Then let us meet them like necessities;
And that same word even now cries out on us.
They say the Bishop and Northumberland
Are fifty thousand strong.
War. It cannot be, my lord.
Rumor doth double, like the voice and echo,
The numbers of the feared. Please it your Grace
To go to bed. Upon my soul, my lord,
The powers that you already have sent forth
Shall bring this prize in very easily.
To comfort you the more, I have received
A certain instance that Glendower is dead.
Your Majesty hath been this fortnight ill,
And these unseasoned hours perforce must add
Unto your sickness.
King. I will take your counsel,
And were these inward wars once out of hand,
We would, dear lords, unto the Holy Land. *Exeunt.*

[SCENE II]

Enter JUSTICE SHALLOW *and* JUSTICE SILENCE, [*meeting;* MOULDY, SHADOW, WART, FEEBLE, BULLCALF, *and* SERVANTS *behind*].

Shal. Come on, come on, come on, give me your hand, sir, give me your hand, sir. An early stirrer, by the rood! And how doth my good cousin Silence?

Sil. Good morrow, good cousin Shallow.

Shal. And how doth my cousin, your bedfellow? and your fairest daughter and mine, my goddaughter Ellen?

33. **Is . . . morrow:** i.e. is it already past midnight.
37. **liege:** sovereign. 39. **rank:** festering.
41. **distempered:** diseased. 47. **continent:** dry land.
50. **beachy:** pebbly.
51. **Too . . . hips.** Because the sea, when it recedes, leaves a widened beach. 55. **crosses:** adversities. 57. **gone:** ago.
63. **under my foot:** i.e. at my absolute disposal. 64. **to:** before.
66. **Nevil.** An error. The only Neville to hold the title Earl of Warwick was Richard (1428–71), the famous "Kingmaker" of the reign of Henry VI. He gained the title through his wife, Anne Beauchamp, daughter of the Earl of Warwick in the present play.
68. **check'd and rated:** rebuked and chided.
70–77. **Northumberland . . . corruption.** See *Richard II*, V.i.55–59.
72. **then . . . intent.** Actually, Bullingbrook had already ascended Richard's throne at the time he imperfectly recalls.

81. **Figuring:** showing. **deceas'd:** departed.
83. **aim:** probability. **main chance:** general probability (a term from the game of hazard).
87. **this:** i.e. the principle just enunciated.
94. **cries out on:** exclaims against.
103. **instance:** proof. **Glendower is dead.** In 1409, reports Holinshed (Bullough, IV, 276), the hard-pressed Glendower "fled into desert places and solitarie caves, where being destitute of all releefe and succour, dreading to shew his face to anie creature, and finallie lacking meat to susteine nature, for meere hunger and lacke of food, miserablie pined awaie and died." Modern historians place his death several years later, after the accession of Henry V.
105. **unseasoned:** unseasonable.
107. **inward:** civil. **out of hand:** concluded.
108. **We . . . Land.** See *Richard II*, V.vi.49–50; *1 Henry IV*, I.i.18–30.

III.ii. Location: Gloucestershire. Before Justice Shallow's house.
3. **rood:** cross. 5. **bedfellow:** i.e. wife.

Sil. Alas, a black woosel, cousin Shallow!

Shal. By yea and no, sir. I dare say my cousin William is become a good scholar. He is at Oxford still, is he not?

Sil. Indeed, sir, to my cost.

Shal. 'A must then to the Inns a' Court shortly. I was once of Clement's Inn, where I think they will talk of mad Shallow yet.

Sil. You were call'd lusty Shallow then, cousin.

Shal. By the mass, I was call'd any thing, and I would have done any thing indeed too, and roundly too. There was I, and little John Doit of Staffordshire, and black George Barnes, and Francis Pickbone, and Will Squele, a Cotsole man. You had not four such swingebucklers in all the Inns a' Court again; and I may say to you, we knew where the bona [robas] were and had the best of them all at commandement. Then was Jack Falstaff, now Sir John, a boy, and page to Thomas Mowbray, Duke of Norfolk.

Sil. This Sir John, cousin, that comes hither anon about soldiers?

Shal. The same Sir John, the very same. I see him break Scoggin's head at the court-gate, when 'a was a crack not thus high; and the very same day did I fight with one Samson Stockfish, a fruiterer, behind Gray's Inn. Jesu, Jesu, the mad days that I have spent! And to see how many of my old acquaintance are dead!

Sil. We shall all follow, cousin.

Shal. Certain, 'tis certain, very sure, very sure. Death, as the Psalmist saith, is certain to all, all shall die. How a good yoke of bullocks at [Stamford] fair?

Sil. By my troth, I was not there.

Shal. Death is certain. Is old Double of your town living yet?

Sil. Dead, sir.

Shal. Jesu, Jesu, dead! 'A drew a good bow, and dead! 'A shot a fine shoot. John a' Gaunt lov'd him well, and betted much money on his head. Dead! 'a would have clapp'd i' th' clout at twelvescore, and carried you a forehand shaft a fourteen and fourteen and a half, that it would have done a man's heart good to see. How a score of ewes now?

Sil. Thereafter as they be, a score of good ewes may be worth ten pounds.

Shal. And is old Double dead?

Sil. Here come two of Sir John Falstaff's men, as I think.

Enter BARDOLPH *and one with him.*

[*Shal.*] Good morrow, honest gentlemen.

Bard. I beseech you, which is Justice Shallow?

Shal. I am Robert Shallow, sir, a poor esquire of this county, and one of the King's justices of the peace. What is your good pleasure with me?

Bard. My captain, sir, commends him to you, my captain, Sir John Falstaff, a tall gentleman, by heaven, and a most gallant leader.

Shal. He greets me well, sir. I knew him a good backsword man. How doth the good knight? May I ask how my lady his wife doth?

Bard. Sir, pardon, a soldier is better [accommodated] than with a wife.

Shal. It is well said, in faith, sir, and it is well said indeed too. Better accommodated! it is good, yea indeed is it. Good phrases are surely, and ever were, very commendable. Accommodated! it comes of *accommodo*, very good, a good phrase.

Bard. Pardon, sir, I have heard the word. Phrase call you it? By this day, I know not the phrase, but I will maintain the word with my sword to be a soldier-like word, and a word of exceeding good command, by heaven. Accommodated: that is, when a man is, as they say, accommodated, or when a man is being whereby 'a may be thought to be accommodated—which is an excellent thing.

Enter FALSTAFF.

Shal. It is very just. Look, here comes good Sir John. Give me your good hand, give me your worship's good hand. By my troth, you like well and bear your years very well. Welcome, good Sir John.

Fal. I am glad to see you well, good Master Robert Shallow. Master [Surecard], as I think?

Shal. No, Sir John, it is my cousin Silence, in commission with me.

Fal. Good Master Silence, it well befits you should be of the peace.

Sil. Your good worship is welcome.

Fal. Fie, this is hot weather, gentlemen. Have you provided me here half a dozen sufficient men?

Shal. Marry, have we, sir. Will you sit?

Fal. Let me see them, I beseech you.

Shal. Where's the roll? where's the roll? where's the roll? Let me see, let me see, let me see. So, so, so, so, so, so, so; yea, marry, sir. Rafe Mouldy! Let them appear as I call; let them do so, let them do so. Let me see, where is Mouldy?

Moul. Here, and't please you.

Shal. What think you, Sir John? A good-limb'd fellow, young, strong, and of good friends.

Fal. Is thy name Mouldy?

8. woosel: ousel, blackbird.
13. Inns a' Court: legal societies of London.
14. Clement's Inn: one of the Inns of Chancery, formerly a centre of legal studies preparatory to the Inns of Court.
18. roundly: thoroughly.
21. Cotsole: Cotswold, referring to a range of hills in Gloucestershire. **22. swingebucklers:** swashbucklers.
23. bona robas: harlots.
24. at commandement: at our disposal.
30. Scoggin. Shakespeare was perhaps thinking of John Scogan, court jester to Edward IV and hero of a jestbook popular in the later sixteenth century. **31. crack:** frolicsome boy.
33. Gray's Inn: one of the Inns of Court.
38. How: i.e. what was the price fetched by. **Stamford:** ancient market town in Lincolnshire.
44. shoot: shot (in archery). **John a' Gaunt:** father of Henry IV.
46. clapp'd . . . twelvescore: hit the target at 240 yards.
47. forehand shaft: arrow designed for straightforward shooting (rather than for a curved trajectory).
50. Thereafter . . . be: depending on their quality.

61. tall: brave.
64. backsword: stick with a basket-hilt used in fencing practice.
66–67. accommodated: furnished.
68–72. It . . . phrase. The word *accommodated* was somewhat affected in Shakespeare's time. **70. phrases:** expressions.
76. of . . . command: i.e. appropriate to a commander.
81. just: true.
83. troth: truth. **like well:** are in good condition.
87–88. in . . . me: i.e. a justice of the peace like me.
93. sufficient: fit for service.
103. of good friends: well connected.

Moul. Yea, and't please you.

Fal. 'Tis the more time thou wert us'd.

Shal. Ha, ha, ha! most excellent, i' faith! Things that are mouldy lack use. Very singular good, in faith, well said, Sir John, very well said.

[*Fal.* Prick him.]

Moul. I was prick'd well enough before, and you could have let me alone. My old dame will be undone now for one to do her husbandry and her drudgery. You need not to have prick'd me, there are other men fitter to go out than I.

Fal. Go to, peace, Mouldy, you shall go. Mouldy, it is time you were spent.

Moul. Spent?

Shal. Peace, fellow, peace, stand aside, know you where you are? For th' other, Sir John, let me see: Simon Shadow!

Fal. Yea, marry, let me have him to sit under, he's like to be a cold soldier.

Shal. Where's Shadow?

Shad. Here, sir.

Fal. Shadow, whose son art thou?

Shad. My mother's son, sir.

Fal. Thy mother's son! like enough, and thy father's shadow. So the son of the female is the shadow of the male. It is often so indeed, but much of the father's substance!

Shal. Do you like him, Sir John?

Fal. Shadow will serve for summer, prick him, [*aside*] for we have a number of shadows fill up the muster-book.

Shal. Thomas Wart!

Fal. Where's he?

Wart. Here, sir.

Fal. Is thy name Wart?

Wart. Yea, sir.

Fal. Thou art a very ragged wart.

Shal. Shall I prick him, Sir John?

Fal. It were superfluous, for ['s] apparel is built upon his back, and the whole frame stands upon pins. Prick him no more.

Shal. Ha, ha, ha! you can do it, sir, you can do it, I commend you well. Francis Feeble!

Fee. Here, sir.

Shal. What trade art thou, Feeble?

Fee. A woman's tailor, sir.

Shal. Shall I prick him, sir?

Fal. You may, but if he had been a man's tailor, he'd 'a' prick'd you. Wilt thou make as many holes in an enemy's battle as thou hast done in a woman's petticoat?

Fee. I will do my good will, sir, you can have no more.

Fal. Well said, good woman's tailor! well said, courageous Feeble! Thou wilt be as valiant as the wrathful dove or most magnanimous mouse. Prick the woman's tailor. Well, Master Shallow, deep, Master Shallow.

Fee. I would Wart might have gone, sir.

Fal. I would thou wert a man's tailor, that thou mightst mend him and make him fit to go. I cannot put him to a private soldier that is the leader of so many thousands. Let that suffice, most forcible Feeble.

Fee. It shall suffice, sir.

Fal. I am bound to thee, reverend Feeble. Who is next?

Shal. Peter Bullcalf o' th' green!

Fal. Yea, marry, let's see Bullcalf.

Bull. Here, sir.

Fal. 'Fore God, a likely fellow! Come prick Bullcalf till he roar again.

Bull. O Lord, good my lord captain—

Fal. What, dost thou roar before thou art prick'd?

Bull. O Lord, sir, I am a diseas'd man.

Fal. What disease hast thou?

Bull. A whoreson cold, sir, a cough, sir, which I caught with ringing in the King's affairs upon his coronation-day, sir.

Fal. Come, thou shalt go to the wars in a gown. We will have away thy cold, and I will take such order that thy friends shall ring for thee. Is here all?

Shal. Here is two more call'd than your number, you must have but four here, sir. And so I pray you go in with me to dinner.

Fal. Come, I will go drink with you, but I cannot tarry dinner. I am glad to see you, by my troth, Master Shallow.

Shal. O Sir John, do you remember since we lay all night in the Windmill in Saint George's Field?

Fal. No more of that, Master Shallow, [no more of that].

Shal. Ha, 'twas a merry night. And is Jane Nightwork alive?

Fal. She lives, Master Shallow.

Shal. She never could away with me.

Fal. Never, never, she would always say she could not abide Master Shallow.

Shal. By the mass, I could anger her to th' heart. She was then a bona roba. Doth she hold her own well?

Fal. Old, old, Master Shallow.

Shal. Nay, she must be old, she cannot choose but be old, certain she's old, and had Robin Nightwork by old Nightwork before I came to Clement's Inn.

Sil. That's fifty-five year ago.

108. singular: singularly. **110. Prick:** choose.
111. prick'd: goaded, i.e. nagged. **112. old dame:** mother.
113. husbandry: farm chores. **117. spent:** consumed.
120. other: others.
123. cold: cool (like a shadow), i.e. cowardly.
128–31. Thy . . . substance. The wordplay is on *sun* as opposed to *shadow* (image, likeness).
134. shadows: i.e. names of fictitious recruits whose pay is pocketed by the officer.
144. his . . . pins: i.e. he's held together by pins.
153. prick'd: attired. **154. battle:** line of battle.
167. thousands: i.e. of lice.
182. ringing . . . affairs: i.e. ringing the church bells in honor of the King. **184. gown:** dressing gown. **185. have away:** get rid of.
185–86. take such order: make arrangements.
192. tarry: stay for.
195. Windmill: a brothel. **Saint George's Field:** open area and place of resort on the south bank of the Thames.
201. away with: tolerate.

Shal. Ha, cousin Silence, that thou hadst seen that that this knight and I have seen! Ha, Sir John, said I well?

Fal. We have heard the chimes at midnight, Master Shallow.

Shal. That we have, that we have, that we have, in faith, Sir John, we have. Our watch-word was "Hem, boys!" Come let's to dinner, come let's to dinner. Jesus, the days that we have seen! come, come.

Exeunt [Falstaff and the Justices].

Bull. Good Master Corporate Bardolph, stand my friend, and here's four Harry ten shillings in French crowns for you. In very truth, sir, I had as live be hang'd, sir, as go, and yet for mine own part, sir, I do not care, but rather, because I am unwilling, and for mine own part, have a desire to stay with my friends, else, sir, I did not care for mine own part so much.

Bard. Go to, stand aside.

Moul. And, good Master Corporal Captain, for my old dame's sake stand my friend. She has nobody to do any thing about her when I am gone, and she is old, and cannot help herself. You shall have forty, sir.

Bard. Go to, stand aside.

Fee. By my troth I care not; a man can die but once, we owe God a death. I'll ne'er bear a base mind. And't be my dest'ny, so; and't be not, so. No man's too good to serve 's prince, and let it go which way it will, he that dies this year is quit for the next.

Bard. Well said, th' art a good fellow.

Fee. Faith, I'll bear no base mind.

Enter FALSTAFF *and the* JUSTICES.

Fal. Come, sir, which men shall I have?

Shal. Four of which you please.

Bard. [*To Falstaff.*] Sir, a word with you. [*Aside.*] I have three pound to free Mouldy and Bullcalf.

Fal. Go to, well.

Shal. Come, Sir John, which four will you have?

Fal. Do you choose for me.

Shal. Marry, then, Mouldy, Bullcalf, Feeble, and Shadow.

Fal. Mouldy and Bullcalf! for you, Mouldy, stay at home till you are past service; and for your part, Bullcalf, grow till you come unto it. I will none of you.

Shal. Sir John, Sir John, do not yourself wrong. They are your likeliest men, and I would have you serv'd with the best.

Fal. Will you tell me, Master Shallow, how to choose a man? Care I for the limb, the thews, the stature, bulk, and big assemblance of a man? Give me the spirit, Master Shallow. Here's Wart, you see what a ragged appearance it is. 'A shall charge you and discharge you with the motion of a pewterer's hammer, come off and on swifter than he that gibbets on the brewer's bucket. And this same half-fac'd fellow, Shadow, give me this man. He presents no mark to the enemy, the foeman may with as great aim level at the edge of a penknife. And for a retrait, how swiftly will this Feeble the woman's tailor run off! O, give me the spare men, and spare me the great ones. Put me a caliver into Wart's hand, Bardolph.

Bard. Hold, Wart, traverse! thas, thas, thas.

Fal. Come manage me your caliver. So—very well, go to, very good, exceeding good. O, give me always a little, lean, old, chopp'd, bald shot. Well said, i' faith, Wart, th' art a good scab. Hold, there's a tester for thee.

Shal. He is not his craft's master, he doth not do it right. I remember at Mile-end Green, when I lay at Clement's Inn—I was then Sir Dagonet in Arthur's show—there was a little quiver fellow, and 'a would manage you his piece thus, and 'a would about and about, and come you in and come you in. "Rah, tah, tah," would 'a say, "bounce," would 'a say, and away again would 'a go, and again would 'a come. I shall ne'er see such a fellow.

Fal. These fellows woll do well, Master Shallow. God keep you, Master Silence, I will not use many words with you. Fare you well, gentlemen both, I thank you. I must a dozen mile to-night. Bardolph, give the soldiers coats.

Shal. Sir John, the Lord bless you! God prosper your affairs! God send us peace! At your return visit our house, let our old acquaintance be renew'd. Peradventure I will with ye to the court.

Fal. 'Fore God, would you would.

Shal. Go to, I have spoke at a word. God keep you!

Fal. Fare you well, gentle gentlemen. (*Exeunt* [*Justices*].) On, Bardolph, lead the men away. [*Exeunt Bardolph, recruits, etc.*] As I return, I will fetch off these justices. I do see the bottom of Justice Shallow. Lord, Lord, how subject we old men are to this vice of lying! This same starv'd justice hath done nothing but prate to me of the wildness of his youth, and the feats he hath done about Turnbull Street, and every third word a lie, duer paid to the hearer than the

220. **Corporate**: blunder for *Corporal*.
221. **Harry ten shillings**: coins first minted in the reign of Henry VII (and therefore an anachronism here) that were worth five shillings in Shakespeare's time.
221–22. **French crowns**: coins worth four shillings.
222. **live**: lief. 232. **forty**: i.e. forty shillings.
235. **bear**: harbor, reveal. 238. **quit**: free, clear.
250. **for**: as for.
252. **come unto it**: i.e. attain maturity (with a piay on *calf*).
258. **thews**: strength. 259. **assemblance**: appearance (?).
261–62. **charge . . . you**: load and fire his musket.
262–63. **with . . . hammer**: i.e. with a steady rhythm.
264. **gibbets**: hangs (pails of brew). **bucket**: yoke or beam on a carrier's shoulders. 264–65. **half-fac'd**: thin, meagre.
267. **level**: aim. **retrait**: retreat. 270. **caliver**: musket.
272. **traverse**: march (?) or take aim (?). **thas**: thus.
275. **chopp'd**: chapped. 276. **scab**: i.e. wart.
277. **tester**: sixpence.
279. **Mile-end Green**: open area and drill-ground to the east of London. **lay**: lived.
280–81. **Arthur's show**: annual exhibition at Mile-end Green by a company of London archers (each taking the name of one of King Arthur's knights), in which Sir Dagonet was the fool.
281. **quiver**: nimble.
283. **come you in**: i.e. make a pass or home thrust (a term from fencing). 287. **woll**: will. 290. **must**: must go.
297. **at a word**: in haste, without deliberation.
301. **fetch off**: fleece. 304. **starv'd**: lean, emaciated.
306. **Turnbull Street**: disreputable street in Clerkenwell, one of the lowest districts in London. 307. **duer**: more punctually (?).

Turk's tribute. I do remember him at Clement's Inn, like a man made after supper of a cheese-paring. When 'a was naked, he was for all the world like a fork'd redish, with a head fantastically carv'd upon it with a knife. 'A was so forlorn, that his dimensions to any thick sight were [invisible]. 'A was the very genius of famine, yet lecherous as a monkey, and the whores call'd him mandrake. 'A came [ever] in the rearward of the fashion, and sung those tunes to the overscutch'd huswives that he heard the carmen whistle, and sware they were his fancies or his good-nights. And now is this Vice's dagger become a squire, and talks as familiarly of John a' Gaunt as if he had been sworn brother to him, and I'll be sworn 'a ne'er saw him but once in the Tilt-yard, and then he burst his head for crowding among the marshal's men. I saw it, and told John a' Gaunt he beat his own name, for you might have thrust him and all his apparel into an eel-skin. The case of a treble hoboy was a mansion for him, a court, and now has he land and beefs! Well, I'll be acquainted with him if I return, and't shall go hard but I'll make him a philosopher's two stones to me. If the young dace be a bait for the old pike, I see no reason in the law of nature but I may snap at him: let time shape, and there an end. [*Exit.*]

[ACT IV, SCENE I]

Enter the ARCHBISHOP [OF YORK], MOWBRAY, [LORD] BARDOLPH, HASTINGS, [*and others,*] *within the forest of Gaultree.*

Arch. What is this forest call'd?
Hast. 'Tis Gaultree forest, and't shall please your Grace.
Arch. Here stand, my lords, and send discoverers forth
To know the numbers of our enemies.
Hast. We have sent forth already.
Arch. 'Tis well done.
My friends and brethren in these great affairs,
I must acquaint you that I have receiv'd
New-dated letters from Northumberland,
Their cold intent, tenure, and substance thus:
Here doth he wish his person, with such powers
As might hold sortance with his quality,
The which he could not levy; whereupon
He is retir'd, to ripe his growing fortunes,
To Scotland, and concludes in hearty prayers
That your attempts may overlive the hazard
And fearful meeting of their opposite.
Mowb. Thus do the hopes we have in him touch ground
And dash themselves to pieces.

Enter MESSENGER.

Hast. Now, what news?
Mess. West of this forest, scarcely off a mile,
In goodly form comes on the enemy,
And by the ground they hide, I judge their number
Upon or near the rate of thirty thousand.
Mowb. The just proportion that we gave them out.
Let us sway on and face them in the field.
Arch. What well-appointed leader fronts us here?

Enter WESTMERLAND.

Mowb. I think it is my Lord of Westmerland.
West. Health and fair greeting from our general,
The Prince, Lord John and Duke of Lancaster.
Arch. Say on, my Lord of Westmerland, in peace,
What doth concern your coming.
West. Then, my lord,
Unto your Grace do I in chief address
The substance of my speech. If that rebellion
Came like itself, in base and abject routs,
Led on by bloody youth, guarded with rage,
And countenanc'd by boys and beggary—
I say, if damn'd commotion so [appear'd]
In his true, native, and most proper shape,
You, reverend father, and these noble lords
Had not been here to dress the ugly form
Of base and bloody insurrection
With your fair honors. You, Lord Archbishop,
Whose see is by a civil peace maintain'd,
Whose beard the silver hand of peace hath touch'd,
Whose learning and good letters peace hath tutor'd,
Whose white investments figure innocence,
The dove, and very blessed spirit of peace,
Wherefore do you so ill translate yourself
Out of the speech of peace that bears such grace,
Into the harsh and boist'rous tongue of war?
Turning your books to graves, your ink to blood,
Your pens to lances, and your tongue divine
To a loud trumpet and a point of war?

308. Turk's tribute: annual exaction collected from merchants by the sultan. **311. redish:** radish. **314. genius:** embodiment.
315. mandrake: plant whose roots were thought to resemble a man.
317. overscutch'd: battered. **huswives:** hussies, strumpets. **carmen:** wagoners. **318. sware:** swore.
318–19. fancies, good-nights: types of songs.
319. Vice's dagger: dagger of lath carried by the mischievous comic character in morality plays.
322. Tilt-yard: tournament ground at Westminster.
324–25. his own name: i.e. a gaunt person. **326. hoboy:** oboe.
329–30. a philosopher's two stones: i.e. as valuable as two philosopher's stones, which were supposed to change base metals to gold.
330. dace: small fish used for live bait.

IV.i. Location: Yorkshire. Before the forest of Gaultree (or Galtres, a royal forest of some 100,000 acres north of York). Holinshed (Bullough, IV, 271) sets the scene on "a plaine [i.e. Shipton Moor] within the forrest of Galtree." The date was May 29, 1405.
2. and: if. **3. discoverers:** scouts. **8. New-dated:** i.e. recent.
9. tenure: tenor. **10. powers:** forces.

11. hold . . . quality: be appropriate to his rank.
13. ripe: make ripe.
15–16. overlive . . . opposite: survive the fearful hazard of meeting the adversaries. **22. rate:** estimated total.
23. just . . . out: very number that we estimated.
24. sway on: advance. **25. fronts:** confronts.
28. Duke of Lancaster. Actually, Prince Henry, John's elder brother, was Duke of Lancaster at the time.
30. doth concern: i.e. is the purpose of.
33. routs: disorderly crowds. **34. guarded:** trimmed, adorned.
35. countenanc'd: maintained. **beggary:** beggars.
36. commotion: insurrection.
42. civil peace: i.e. established government.
44. good letters: scholarship (*literae humaniores*).
45. investments figure: vestments symbolize.
47. translate: transform. **52. point:** notes of a trumpet.

Arch. Wherefore do I this? so the question stands.
Briefly, to this end: we are all diseas'd,
[And with our surfeiting and wanton hours
Have brought ourselves into a burning fever,
And we must bleed for it; of which disease
Our late King Richard (being infected) died.
But, my most noble Lord of Westmerland,
I take not on me here as a physician,
Nor do I as an enemy to peace
Troop in the throngs of military men;
But rather show a while like fearful war
To diet rank minds sick of happiness,
And purge th' obstructions which begin to stop
Our very veins of life. Hear me more plainly.
I have in equal balance justly weigh'd
What wrongs our arms may do, what wrongs we suffer,
And find our griefs heavier than our offenses.
We see which way the stream of time doth run,
And are enforc'd from our most quiet there
By the rough torrent of occasion,
And have the summary of all our griefs
(When time shall serve) to show in articles;
Which long ere this we offer'd to the King,
And might by no suit gain our audience.
When we are wrong'd and would unfold our griefs,
We are denied access unto his person
Even by those men that most have done us wrong.]
The dangers of the days but newly gone,
Whose memory is written on the earth
With yet appearing blood, and the examples
Of every minute's instance (present now)
Hath put us in these ill-beseeming arms,
Not to break peace, or any branch of it,
But to establish here a peace indeed,
Concurring both in name and quality.
West. When ever yet was your appeal denied?
Wherein have you been galled by the King?
What peer hath been suborn'd to grate on you?
That you should seal this lawless bloody book
Of forg'd rebellion with a seal divine.
Arch. My brother general, the commonwealth,
I make my quarrel in particular.
West. There is no need of any such redress,
Or if there were, it not belongs to you.
Mowb. Why not to him in part, and to us all
That feel the bruises of the days before,
And suffer the condition of these times
To lay a heavy and unequal hand
Upon our honors?
West. [O, my good Lord Mowbray,
Construe the times to their necessities,
And you shall say, indeed, it is the time,
And not the King, that doth you injuries.
Yet, for your part, it not appears to me,
Either from the King or in the present time,
That you should have an inch of any ground
To build a grief on. Were you not restor'd
To all the Duke of Norfolk's signories,
Your noble and right well-rememb'red father's?
Mowb. What thing, in honor, had my father lost,
That need to be reviv'd and breath'd in me?
The King that lov'd him, as the state stood then,
Was [force] perforce compell'd to banish him;
And then that Henry Bullingbrook and he,
Being mounted and both roused in their seats,
Their neighing coursers daring of the spur,
Their armed staves in charge, their beavers down,
Their eyes of fire sparkling through sights of steel,
And the loud trumpet blowing them together;
Then, then, when there was nothing could have stay'd
My father from the breast of Bullingbrook,
O, when the King did throw his warder down
(His own life hung upon the staff he threw),
Then threw he down himself and all their lives
That by indictment and by dint of sword
Have since miscarried under Bullingbrook.
West. You speak, Lord Mowbray, now you know not what.
The Earl of Herford was reputed then
In England the most valiant gentleman.
Who knows on whom fortune would then have smil'd?
But if your father had been victor there,
He ne'er had borne it out of Coventry;
For all the country in a general voice
Cried hate upon him; and all their prayers and love
Were set on Herford, whom they doted on
And bless'd and grac'd and did, more than the King—]
But this is mere digression from my purpose.
Here come I from our princely general
To know your griefs, to tell you from his Grace
That he will give you audience, and wherein
It shall appear that your demands are just,
You shall enjoy them, every thing set off
That might so much as think you enemies.
Mowb. But he hath forc'd us to compel this offer,

53–87. Wherefore . . . quality. According to Holinshed (Bullough, IV, 272), the Archbishop told Westmorland's emissaries "that he tooke nothing in hand against the kings peace, but that whatsoever he did, tended rather to advance the peace and quiet of the commonwealth, than otherwise; and where he and his companie were in armes, it was for feare of the king, to whom he could have no free accesse, by reason of such a multitude of flatterers as were about him; and therefore he mainteined that his purpose to be good & profitable, as well for the king himselfe, as for the realme, if men were willing to understand a truth: & herewith he shewed foorth a scroll, in which the articles were written." **55. wanton:** self-indulgent.
57. bleed: be bled (as a medical treatment).
60. take . . . as: do not assume the role of. **63. show:** appear.
64. rank: swollen, surfeited. **69. griefs:** grievances.
71. enforc'd . . . there: i.e. forced from our greatest quiet in the "stream of time." **72. occasion:** events.
74. in articles: i.e. systematically set forth.
83. Of . . . instance: presented every minute.
90. suborn'd . . . on: instigated to annoy.
93. My brother general: i.e. the people of England (whose grievance he makes his own because they are his brothers).

100. unequal: unfair. **102. to:** according to.
106. Either . . . time: i.e. whether you blame the King or the disordered times for your supposed grievances. **109. signories:** estates.
112. breath'd: have life breathed into it.
113–27. The King . . . Bullingbrook. See *Richard II*, I.i.iii.
114. force perforce: against his will. **116. roused:** lifted.
118. armed . . . charge: lances in position. **beavers:** visors.
123. warder: staff, mace (which he held as umpire of the trial by combat). **126. dint:** force. **127. miscarried:** perished.
129. Earl of Herford: Bullingbrook.
133. it: i.e. the victor's prize. **Coventry:** site of the abortive encounter between Bullingbrook and Mowbray.
134. in . . . voice: i.e. unanimously. **137. did:** did for (?).
143. set off: disregarded (?) or removed (?).
144. think you: suggest that you are.

And it proceeds from policy, not love.
West. Mowbray, you overween to take it so;
This offer comes from mercy, not from fear.
For lo, within a ken our army lies:
Upon mine honor, all too confident
To give admittance to a thought of fear.
Our battle is more full of names than yours,
Our men more perfect in the use of arms,
Our armor all as strong, our cause the best;
Then reason will our hearts should be as good.
Say you not then our offer is compell'd.
Mowb. Well, by my will we shall admit no parley.
West. That argues but the shame of your offense:
A rotten case abides no handling.
Hast. Hath the Prince John a full commission,
In very ample virtue of his father,
To hear and absolutely to determine
Of what conditions we shall stand upon?
West. That is intended in the general's name.
I muse you make so slight a question.
Arch. Then take, my Lord of Westmerland, this schedule,
For this contains our general grievances:
Each several article herein redress'd,
All members of our cause, both here and hence,
That are ensinewed to this action
Acquitted by a true substantial form
And present execution of our wills—
To us and [to] our purposes confin'd
We come within our aweful banks again,
And knit our powers to the arm of peace.
West. This will I show the general. Please you, lords,
In sight of both our battles we may meet,
[And] either end in peace, which God so frame!
Or to the place of diff'rence call the swords
Which must decide it.
Arch. My lord, we will do so.
Exit Westmerland.
Mowb. There is a thing within my bosom tells me
That no conditions of our peace can stand.
Hast. Fear you not that; if we can make our peace
Upon such large terms and so absolute
As our conditions shall consist upon,
Our peace shall stand as firm as rocky mountains.
Mowb. Yea, but our valuation shall be such
That every slight and false-derived cause,
Yea, every idle, nice, and wanton reason,
Shall to the King taste of this action,

147. overween: presume too much. **149. ken:** sight.
152. Our . . . names: i.e. our army has more illustrious leaders.
155. reason will: i.e. it is reasonable that.
157. by my will: with my consent.
159. rotten case: weak box. **abides:** permits of.
161. In . . . virtue of: with fully delegated power from.
163. what: whatever. **stand:** insist.
164. intended . . . name: i.e. indicated by his title.
165. muse: am astonished. **166. schedule:** document.
168. several: separate. **170. ensinewed to:** i.e. involved in.
171. true substantial form: formal agreement.
172–73. present . . . confin'd: i.e. the immediate satisfaction of our wishes as regards ourselves and our plans.
174. aweful banks: bounds of reverence. **177. battles:** armies.
178. frame: bring to pass. **184. large:** liberal.
185. consist: insist. **187. valuation:** i.e. reputation with the King.
189. idle: foolish. **nice:** petty. **wanton:** trivial.

That were our royal faiths martyrs in love,
We shall be winnow'd with so rough a wind
That even our corn shall seem as light as chaff,
And good from bad find no partition.
Arch. No, no, my lord, note this: the King is weary
Of dainty and such picking grievances,
For he hath found to end one doubt by death
Revives two greater in the heirs of life;
And therefore will he wipe his tables clean
And keep no tell-tale to his memory
That may repeat and history his loss
To new remembrance; for full well he knows
He cannot so precisely weed this land
As his misdoubts present occasion.
His foes are so enrooted with his friends
That, plucking to unfix an enemy,
He doth unfasten so and shake a friend,
So that this land, like an offensive wife
That hath enrag'd him on to offer strokes,
As he is striking, holds his infant up
And hangs resolv'd correction in the arm
That was uprear'd to execution.
Hast. Besides, the King hath wasted all his rods
On late offenders, that he now doth lack
The very instruments of chastisement,
So that his power, like to a fangless lion,
May offer, but not hold.
Arch. 'Tis very true,
And therefore be assur'd, my good Lord Marshal,
If we do now make our atonement well,
Our peace will, like a broken limb united,
Grow stronger for the breaking.
Mowb. Be it so.
Here is return'd my Lord of Westmerland.

Enter WESTMERLAND.

West. The Prince is here at hand. Pleaseth your lordship
To meet his Grace just distance 'tween our armies.
Mowb. Your Grace of York, in God's name then set forward.
Arch. Before, and greet his Grace.—My lord, we come.
[*They march about the stage and then move forward to meet Prince John.*]

[SCENE II]

Enter PRINCE JOHN [OF LANCASTER] *and his army.*

P. John. You are well encount'red here, my cousin Mowbray,

191. were . . . love: i.e. though our fidelity to the King were as intense as the faith of martyrs. **194. partition:** distinction.
196. dainty: minute. **picking:** trifling.
199. tables: tablets, books. **201. history:** record.
203. precisely: entirely. **204. misdoubts:** suspicions, anxieties.
211. hangs resolv'd correction: checks intended punishment.
213. wasted: used up. **217. hold:** grip.
219. atonement: reconciliation.
224. just distance: i.e. halfway. **226. Before:** i.e. go first.

IV.ii. Location: Scene continues.
1. cousin: here, a title of respect.

Good day to you, gentle Lord Archbishop,
And so to you, Lord Hastings, and to all.
My Lord of York, it better show'd with you
When that your flock, assembled by the bell,
Encircled you to hear with reverence
Your exposition on the holy text
[Than] now to see you here an iron man, talking,
Cheering a rout of rebels with your drum,
Turning the word to sword and life to death.
That man that sits within a monarch's heart
And ripens in the sunshine of his favor,
Would he abuse the countenance of the King,
Alack, what mischiefs might he set abroach
In shadow of such greatness? With you, Lord Bishop,
It is even so. Who hath not heard it spoken
How deep you were within the books of God?
To us the speaker in his parliament,
To us th' [imagin'd] voice of God himself,
The very opener and intelligencer
Between the grace, the sanctities of heaven,
And our dull workings? O, who shall believe
But you misuse the reverence of your place,
[Employ] the countenance and grace of heav'n,
As a false favorite doth his prince's name,
In deeds dishonorable? You have ta'en up,
Under the counterfeited zeal of God,
The subjects of his substitute, my father,
And both against the peace of heaven and him
Have here upswarm'd them.
Arch. Good my Lord of Lancaster,
I am not here against your father's peace,
But as I told my Lord of Westmerland,
The time misord'red doth, in common sense,
Crowd us and crush us to this monstrous form
To hold our safety up. I sent your Grace
The parcels and particulars of our grief,
The which hath been with scorn shov'd from the court,
Whereon this Hydra son of war is born,
Whose dangerous eyes may well be charm'd asleep
With grant of our most just and right desires,
And true obedience, of this madness cured,
Stoop tamely to the foot of majesty.
Mowb. If not, we ready are to try our fortunes
To the last man.
Hast. And though we here fall down,
We have supplies to second our attempt;
If they miscarry, theirs shall second them,
And so success of mischief shall be born,
And heir from heir shall hold his quarrel up
Whiles England shall have generation.
P. John. You are too shallow, Hastings, much too shallow,
To sound the bottom of the after-times.
West. Pleaseth your Grace to answer them directly
How far forth you do like their articles.
P. John. I like them all, and do allow them well,
And swear here, by the honor of my blood,
My father's purposes have been mistook,
And some about him have too lavishly
Wrested his meaning and authority.
My lord, these griefs shall be with speed redress'd,
Upon my soul they shall. If this may please you,
Discharge your powers unto their several counties,
As we will ours, and here between the armies
Let's drink together friendly and embrace,
That all their eyes may bear those tokens home
Of our restored love and amity.
Arch. I take your princely word for these redresses.
[*P. John.*] I give it you, and will maintain my word,
And thereupon I drink unto your Grace.
[*Hast.*] Go, captain, and deliver to the army
This news of peace. Let them have pay, and part.
I know it will well please them. Hie thee, captain.
[*Exit Officer.*]
Arch. To you, my noble Lord of Westmerland.
West. I pledge your Grace, and if you knew what pains
I have bestowed to breed this present peace,
You would drink freely. But my love to ye
Shall show itself more openly hereafter.
Arch. I do not doubt you.
West. I am glad of it.
Health to my lord, and gentle cousin, Mowbray.
Mowb. You wish me health in very happy season,
For I am on the sudden something ill.
Arch. Against ill chances men are ever merry,
But heaviness foreruns the good event.
West. Therefore be merry, coz, since sudden sorrow
Serves to say thus, some good thing comes to-morrow.
Arch. Believe me, I am passing light in spirit.
Mowb. So much the worse, if your own rule be true. *Shout* [*within*].
P. John. The word of peace is rend'red. Hark how they shout!
Mowb. This had been cheerful after victory.
Arch. A peace is of the nature of a conquest,
For then both parties nobly are subdued,
And neither party loser.
P. John. Go, my lord,
And let our army be discharged too.
[*Exit Westmerland.*]
And, good my lord, so please you, let our trains
March by us, that we may peruse the men
We should have cop'd withal.
Arch. Go, good Lord Hastings,
And ere they be dismiss'd, let them march by.
[*Exit Hastings.*]

4. it . . . you: i.e. you appeared to more advantage.
8. an iron man. Holinshed reports (Bullough, IV, 271) that the Archbishop appeared before his followers "clad in armor."
9. rout: gang. **10. word:** i.e. the Scripture.
14. set abroach: start flowing.
20. opener and intelligencer: interpreter and intermediary.
22. workings: mental operations.
24. countenance and grace: gracious countenance.
26. ta'en up: enlisted. **28. substitute:** deputy, i.e. the king.
33. common sense: ordinary perception.
36. parcels: details. **grief:** grievance.
38. Hydra: i.e. many-headed (referring to a monstrous snake destroyed by Hercules). **45. supplies:** reinforcements.
47. success: succession.
49. Whiles . . . generation: i.e. so long as Englishmen are born.
57. lavishly: arbitrarily, carelessly. **58. Wrested:** strained.
81. Against: in anticipation of. **85. passing:** exceedingly.
95. cop'd withal: fought with.

Enter WESTMERLAND.

P. John. I trust, lords, we shall lie to-night together.
Now, cousin, wherefore stands our army still?

West. The leaders, having charge from you to stand,
Will not go off until they hear you speak.

P. John. They know their duties.

Enter HASTINGS.

Hast. My lord, our army is dispers'd already:
Like youthful steers unyok'd, they take their courses
East, west, north, south, or, like a school broke up,
Each hurries toward his home and sporting-place.

West. Good tidings, my Lord Hastings! for the which
I do arrest thee, traitor, of high treason,
And you, Lord Archbishop, and you, Lord Mowbray,
Of capital treason I attach you both.

Mowb. Is this proceeding just and honorable?

West. Is your assembly so?

Arch. Will you thus break your faith?

P. John. I pawn'd thee none.
I promis'd you redress of these same grievances
Whereof you did complain, which, by mine honor,
I will perform with a most Christian care.
But for you rebels, look to taste the due
Meet for rebellion [and such acts as yours].
Most shallowly did you these arms commence,
Fondly brought here and foolishly sent hence.
Strike up our drums, pursue the scatt'red stray;
God, and not we, hath safely fought to-day.
Some guard [these traitors] to the block of death,
Treason's true bed and yielder-up of breath. [*Exeunt.*]

[SCENE III]

Alarum. Excursions. Enter FALSTAFF [*and* COLEVILE, *meeting*].

Fal. What's your name, sir? Of what condition are you, and of what place?

Col. I am a knight, sir, and my name is Colevile of the Dale.

Fal. Well then, Colevile is your name, a knight is your degree, and your place the Dale. Colevile shall be still your name, a traitor your degree, and the dungeon your place, a place deep enough; so shall you be still Colevile of the Dale.

Col. Are not you Sir John Falstaff?

Fal. As good a man as he, sir, whoe'er I am. Do ye yield, sir? or shall I sweat for you? If I do sweat, they are the drops of thy lovers, and they weep for thy

105. **sporting-place:** playground.
109. **attach:** arrest. 112. **pawn'd:** pledged.
118. **shallowly:** i.e. without deliberation.
119. **Fondly:** foolishly. 120. **stray:** stragglers.

IV.iii. Location: Scene continues.
o.s.d. **Alarum:** trumpet call to advance. **Excursions:** sallies, sorties. **Colevile.** Holinshed lists (Bullough, IV, 274) "sir John Collevill of the Dale" among those executed by Henry IV as he marched through Durham in pursuit of the scattered rebels.
1. **condition:** rank. 13. **lovers:** friends.

death; therefore rouse up fear and trembling, and do observance to my mercy.

Col. I think you are Sir John Falstaff, and in that thought yield me.

Fal. I have a whole school of tongues in this belly of mine, and not a tongue of them all speaks any other word but my name. And I had but a belly of any indifferency, I were simply the most active fellow in Europe. My womb, my womb, my womb undoes me. Here comes our general.

Enter [PRINCE] JOHN [OF LANCASTER], WESTMERLAND, [BLUNT,] *and the rest.*

P. John. The heat is past, follow no further now;
Call in the powers, good cousin Westmerland.
[*Exit Westmerland.*] *Retrait.*
Now, Falstaff, where have you been all this while?
When every thing is ended, then you come.
These tardy tricks of yours will, on my life,
One time or other break some gallows' back.

Fal. I would be sorry, my lord, but it should be thus. I never knew yet but rebuke and check was the reward of valor. Do you think me a swallow, an arrow, or a bullet? Have I, in my poor and old motion, the expedition of thought? I have speeded hither with the very extremest inch of possibility; I have found'red ninescore and odd posts, and here, travel-tainted as I am, have, in my pure and immaculate valor, taken Sir John Colevile of the Dale, a most furious knight and valorous enemy. But what of that? He saw me, and yielded, that I may justly say, with the hook-nos'd fellow of Rome, "There, cousin, I came, saw, and overcame."

P. John. It was more of his courtesy than your deserving.

Fal. I know not: here he is, and here I yield him, and I beseech your Grace let it be book'd with the rest of this day's deeds, or by the Lord, I will have it in a particular ballad else, with mine own picture on the top on't (Colevile kissing my foot), to the which course if I be enforc'd, if you do not all show like gilt twopences to me, and I in the clear sky of fame o'ershine you as much as the full moon doth the cinders of the element (which show like pins' heads to her), believe not the word of the noble. Therefore let me have right, and let desert mount.

P. John. Thine's too heavy to mount.

Fal. Let it shine then.

P. John. Thine's too thick to shine.

Fal. Let it do something, my good lord, that may do me good, and call it what you will.

18. **school:** crowd.
21. **indifferency:** i.e. moderate size. 22. **womb:** belly.
24. **heat:** urgency (of pursuit).
25 s.d. **Retrait:** retreat, signal for the withdrawal of forces.
31. **check:** reprimand.
34–35. **with . . . possibility:** i.e. as fast as possible.
36. **found'red:** lamed. **posts:** post-horses.
37. **tainted:** stained.
41. **with . . . Rome:** i.e. like Julius Caesar.
42. **I . . . overcame:** "*Veni, vidi, vici,*" Caesar's laconic report about one of his campaigns.
48. **a particular ballad:** i.e. a broadside ballad celebrating this feat.
50. **show:** appear. 51. **to:** compared to.
52–53. **cinders . . . element:** i.e. stars in the sky.

P. John. Is thy name Colevile?
Col. It is, my lord.
P. John. A famous rebel art thou, Colevile.
Fal. And a famous true subject took him.
Col. I am, my lord, but as my betters are
That led me hither. Had they been rul'd by me,
You should have won them dearer than you have.

Fal. I know not how they sold themselves, but thou like a kind fellow gavest thyself away gratis, and I thank thee for thee.

Enter WESTMERLAND.

P. John. Now, have you left pursuit?
West. Retrait is made and execution stay'd.
P. John. Send Colevile with his confederates
To York, to present execution.
Blunt, lead him hence, and see you guard him sure.
[*Exeunt Blunt and others with Colevile.*]
And now dispatch we toward the court, my lords,
I hear the King my father is sore sick.
Our news shall go before us to his Majesty,
Which, cousin, you shall bear to comfort him,
And we with sober speed will follow you.

Fal. My lord, I beseech you give me leave to go through Gloucestershire, and when you come to court stand my good lord in your good report.

P. John. Fare you well, Falstaff. I, in my condition,
Shall better speak of you than you deserve.
[*Exeunt all but Falstaff.*]

Fal. I would you had the wit, 'twere better than your dukedom. Good faith, this same young sober-blooded boy doth not love me, nor a man cannot make him laugh, but that's no marvel, he drinks no wine. There's never none of these demure boys come to any proof, for thin drink doth so over-cool their blood, and making many fish-meals, that they fall into a kind of male green-sickness, and then when they marry, they get wenches. They are generally fools and cowards, which some of us should be too, but for inflammation. A good sherris-sack hath a twofold operation in it. It ascends me into the brain, dries me there all the foolish and dull and crudy vapors which environ it, makes it apprehensive, quick, forgetive, full of nimble, fiery, and delectable shapes, which deliver'd o'er to the voice, the tongue, which is the birth, becomes excellent wit. The second property of your excellent sherris is the warming of the blood, which before (cold and settled) left the liver white and pale, which is the badge of pusillanimity and cowardice; but the sherris warms it, and makes it course from the inwards to the parts' extremes. It illumineth the face, which as a beacon gives warning to all the rest of this little kingdom, man, to arm, and then the vital commoners and inland petty spirits muster me all to their captain, the heart, who great and puff'd up with this retinue, doth any deed of courage; and this valor comes of sherris. So that skill in the weapon is nothing without sack (for that sets it a-work) and learning a mere hoard of gold kept by a devil, till sack commences it and sets it in act and use. Hereof comes it that Prince Harry is valiant, for the cold blood he did naturally inherit of his father, he hath, like lean, sterile, and bare land, manur'd, husbanded, and till'd with excellent endeavor of drinking good and good store of fertile sherris, that he is become very hot and valiant. If I had a thousand sons, the first humane principle I would teach them should be, to forswear thin potations and to addict themselves to sack.

Enter BARDOLPH.

How now, Bardolph?

Bard. The army is discharged all and gone.

Fal. Let them go. I'll through Gloucestershire, and there will I visit Master Robert Shallow, esquire. I have him already temp'ring between my finger and my thumb, and shortly will I seal with him. Come away. [*Exeunt.*]

[SCENE IV]

Enter the KING [*carried in a chair*], WARWICK, THOMAS DUKE OF CLARENCE, HUMPHREY OF GLOUCESTER, [*and others*].

King. Now, lords, if God doth give successful end
To this debate that bleedeth at our doors,
We will our youth lead on to higher fields,
And draw no swords but what are sanctified.
Our navy is address'd, our power collected,
Our substitutes in absence well invested,
And every thing lies level to our wish.
Only, we want a little personal strength;
And pause us till these rebels, now afoot,
Come underneath the yoke of government.
War. Both which we doubt not but your Majesty
Shall soon enjoy.
King. Humphrey, my son of Gloucester,
Where is the Prince your brother?
Glou. I think he's gone to hunt, my lord, at Windsor.

72. **stay'd**: stopped.
74. **present**: immediate. 76. **dispatch we**: let us hurry.
83. **stand . . . lord**: i.e. act as my patron.
84. **condition**: official capacity.
90–91. **come . . . proof**: i.e. stand the test.
91. **thin drink**: i.e. beer.
93. **green-sickness**: an anemic condition, supposed to affect unmarried girls. 94. **get wenches**: beget girls.
96. **inflammation**: i.e. through drinking. **sherris-sack**: sherry.
98. **crudy**: curded.
99. **apprehensive**: perceptive. **forgetive**: inventive.
102. **wit**: mental capacity.
104. **liver**: i.e. the seat of courage.

116. **commences it**: enables it to use its powers.
123. **humane**: human. 130. **temp'ring**: softening.
131. **seal with**: i.e. make use of.

IV.iv. Location: Westminster. The Jerusalem Chamber. (This hall adjacent to Westminster Abbey was so called from its inscriptions concerning Jerusalem.)
2. **debate**: quarrel. 3. **higher fields**: i.e. Palestine.
5–7. **Our . . . wish.** "With sufficient treasure, soldiers, capteins, vittels, munitions, tall ships, strong gallies, and all things necessarie for such a royall journie as he pretended [intended] to take into the holie land," says Holinshed (Bullough, IV, 277), Henry had completed preparations for his long-postponed crusade just before his final illness. 5. **address'd**: prepared.
7. **level to**: in accordance with. 8. **want**: lack.

King. And how accompanied?
Glou. I do not know, my lord.
King. Is not his brother Thomas of Clarence with him?
Glou. No, my good lord, he is in presence here.
Clar. What would my lord and father?
King. Nothing but well to thee, Thomas of Clarence.
How chance thou art not with the Prince thy brother?
He loves thee, and thou dost neglect him, Thomas.
Thou hast a better place in his affection
Than all thy brothers. Cherish it, my boy;
And noble offices thou mayst effect
Of mediation, after I am dead,
Between his greatness and thy other brethren.
Therefore omit him not, blunt not his love,
Nor lose the good advantage of his grace
By seeming cold or careless of his will,
For he is gracious if he be observ'd,
He hath a tear for pity, and a hand
Open as day for [meting] charity;
Yet notwithstanding, being incens'd, he is flint,
As humorous as winter, and as sudden
As flaws congealed in the spring of day.
His temper therefore must be well observ'd.
Chide him for faults, and do it reverently,
When you perceive his blood inclin'd to mirth;
But, being moody, give him time and scope,
Till that his passions, like a whale on ground,
Confound themselves with working. Learn this, Thomas,
And thou shalt prove a shelter to thy friends,
A hoop of gold to bind thy brothers in,
That the united vessel of their blood,
Mingled with venom of suggestion
(As, force perforce, the age will pour it in),
Shall never leak, though it do work as strong
As aconitum or rash gunpowder.
Clar. I shall observe him with all care and love.
King. Why art thou not at Windsor with him, Thomas?
Clar. He is not there to-day, he dines in London.
King. And how accompanied? [Canst thou tell that?]
Clar. With Poins, and other his continual followers.
King. Most subject is the fattest soil to weeds,
And he, the noble image of my youth,
Is overspread with them; therefore my grief
Stretches itself beyond the hour of death.
The blood weeps from my heart when I do shape,
In forms imaginary, th' unguided days
And rotten times that you shall look upon,
When I am sleeping with my ancestors.
For when his headstrong riot hath no curb,

17. in presence: present at court. **27. omit:** neglect.
28. grace: favor. **30. observ'd:** shown respectful attention.
32. meting: dealing out. **34. humorous:** subject to shifting moods.
35. flaws congealed: snowflakes. **38. blood:** disposition.
41. Confound: spend, exhaust. **working:** struggling.
45. venom of suggestion: i.e. poisonous gossip (of those stirring up discord). **46. force perforce:** inevitably.
48. aconitum: poison extracted from monkshood. **rash:** operating quickly. **54. fattest:** richest.
58. shape: conceive, imagine.

When rage and hot blood are his counsellors,
When means and lavish manners meet together,
O, with what wings shall his affections fly
Towards fronting peril and oppos'd decay!
War. My gracious lord, you look beyond him quite:
The Prince but studies his companions
Like a strange tongue, wherein, to gain the language,
'Tis needful that the most immodest word
Be look'd upon and learnt, which once attain'd,
Your Highness knows, comes to no further use
But to be known and hated. So, like gross terms,
The Prince will in the perfectness of time
Cast off his followers, and their memory
Shall as a pattern or a measure live,
By which his Grace must mete the lives of other,
Turning past evils to advantages.
King. 'Tis seldom when the bee doth leave her comb
In the dead carrion.

Enter WESTMERLAND.

Who's here? Westmerland?
West. Health to my sovereign, and new happiness
Added to that that I am to deliver!
Prince John your son doth kiss your Grace's hand.
Mowbray, the Bishop Scroop, Hastings, and all,
Are brought to the correction of your law.
There is not now a rebel's sword unsheath'd,
But Peace puts forth her olive every where.
The manner how this action hath been borne
Here at more leisure may your Highness read,
With every course in his particular.
King. O Westmerland, thou art a summer bird,
Which ever in the haunch of winter sings
The lifting up of day.

Enter HARCOURT.

Look here's more news.
Har. From enemies heavens keep your Majesty,
And, when they stand against you, may they fall
As those that I am come to tell you of!
The Earl Northumberland and the Lord Bardolph,
With a great power of English and of Scots,
Are by the shrieve of Yorkshire overthrown.
The manner and true order of the fight
This packet, please it you, contains at large.
King. And wherefore should these good news make me sick?
Will Fortune never come with both hands full,

64. lavish: unrestrained.
66. oppos'd decay: the ruin facing him.
67. look beyond: misconstrue.
73. gross terms: coarse language.
77. mete: appraise. **other:** others.
79–80. 'Tis . . . carrion: i.e. having placed her comb in a carcass the bee seldom leaves her honey.
84–87. Mowbray . . . every where. Actually, Henry himself supervised the execution of the Archbishop and his co-conspirators at York and then marched north against Northumberland, whose defeat (reported as already accomplished in lines 97–99) took place three years after the events in Gaultree forest, and five years before the King's death.
90. With . . . particular: i.e. with the details fully set forth.
92. haunch: latter end.
99. shrieve: sheriff. He was Sir Thomas Rokeby.

But [write] her fair words still in foulest terms?
She either gives a stomach and no food—
Such are the poor, in health; or else a feast
And takes away the stomach—such are the rich,
That have abundance and enjoy it not.
I should rejoice now at this happy news,
And now my sight fails, and my brain is giddy.
O me! come near me, now I am much ill.
Glou. Comfort, your Majesty!
Clar. O my royal father!
West. My sovereign lord, cheer up yourself, look up.
War. Be patient, Princes, you do know these fits
Are with his Highness very ordinary.
Stand from him, give him air, he'll straight be well.
Clar. No, no, he cannot long hold out these pangs.
Th' incessant care and labor of his mind
Hath wrought the mure that should confine it in
So thin that life looks through [and will break out].
Glou. The people fear me, for they do observe
Unfather'd heirs and loathly births of nature.
The seasons change their manners, as the year
Had found some months asleep and leapt them over.
Clar. The river hath thrice flowed, no ebb between,
And the old folk (time's doting chronicles)
Say it did so a little time before
That our great-grandsire, Edward, sick'd and died.
War. Speak lower, Princes, for the King recovers.
Glou. This apoplexy will certain be his end.
King. I pray you take me up, and bear me hence
Into some other chamber. [Softly, pray.]
[*The King is carried to one side of the stage and placed on a bed.*]

[SCENE V]

[*King.*] Let there be no noise made, my gentle friends,
Unless some dull and favorable hand
Will whisper music to my weary spirit.
War. Call for the music in the other room.
King. Set me the crown upon my pillow here.
Clar. His eye is hollow, and he changes much.
War. Less noise, less noise!

Enter [PRINCE] HARRY.

Prince. Who saw the Duke of Clarence?
Clar. I am here, brother, full of heaviness.

114–15. **these . . . ordinary.** According to Holinshed (Bullough, IV, 277), Henry's ailment "was not a leprosie, striken by the hand of God . . . as foolish friers imagined; but a verie apoplexie, of the which he languished till his appointed houre."
117. **hold out:** endure.
119. **wrought the mure:** made the wall. 121. **fear:** frighten.
122. **Unfather'd heirs:** i.e. persons thought to be miraculously conceived. **loathly births:** loathsome or misshapen offspring.
123. **as:** as if.
125. **The river . . . between.** On October 12, 1411, says Holinshed (Bullough, IV, 276), there "were three flouds in the Thames, the one following upon the other, and no ebbing betweene: which thing no man then living could remember the like to be seene."
128. **Edward:** Edward III. **sick'd:** sickened.

IV.v. Location: Scene continues.
2. **dull:** i.e. making drowsy. **favorable:** kindly.
6. **changes:** i.e. in complexion.

Prince. How now, rain within doors, and none abroad?
How doth the King?
Glou. Exceeding ill.
Prince. Heard he the good news yet?
Tell it him.
Glou. He alt'red much upon the hearing it.
Prince. If he be sick with joy, he'll recover without physic.
War. Not so much noise, my lords. Sweet Prince, speak low,
The King your father is dispos'd to sleep.
Clar. Let us withdraw into the other room.
War. Will't please your Grace to go along with us?
Prince. No, I will sit and watch here by the King.
[*Exeunt all but the Prince.*]
Why doth the crown lie there upon his pillow,
Being so troublesome a bedfellow?
O polish'd perturbation! golden care!
That keep'st the ports of slumber open wide
To many a watchful night, sleep with it now!
Yet not so sound, and half so deeply sweet,
As he whose brow with homely biggen bound
Snores out the watch of night. O majesty!
When thou dost pinch thy bearer, thou dost sit
Like a rich armor worn in heat of day,
That scald'st with safety. By his gates of breath
There lies a downy feather which stirs not.
Did he suspire, that light and weightless down
Perforce must move. My gracious lord! my father!
This sleep is sound indeed, this is a sleep
That from this golden rigol hath divorc'd
So many English kings. Thy due from me
Is tears and heavy sorrows of the blood,
Which nature, love, and filial tenderness
Shall, O dear father, pay thee plenteously.
My due from thee is this imperial crown,
Which as immediate from thy place and blood,
Derives itself to me. [*Puts on the crown.*] Lo where it sits,
Which God shall guard; and put the world's whole strength
Into one giant arm, it shall not force
This lineal honor from me. This from thee
Will I to mine leave, as 'tis left to me. *Exit.*
King. Warwick! Gloucester! Clarence!

Enter WARWICK, GLOUCESTER, CLARENCE, [*and the rest*].

Clar. Doth the King call?

9. **rain:** i.e. tears.
17. **The King . . . sleep.** According to Holinshed (Bullough, IV, 277) Henry's seizure was so profound that "he laie as though all his vitall spirits had beene from him departed. Such as were about him, thinking verelie that he had been departed, covered his face with a linnen cloth." 23. **perturbation:** cause of perturbation.
24. **ports:** gates.
25. **watchful:** sleepless. **sleep with it:** i.e. may you (i.e. the King) sleep well with it beside you.
26. **Yet not:** i.e. yet even so your sleep will not be.
27. **biggen:** nightcap. 29. **pinch:** torment.
31. **scald'st with safety:** i.e. both protects and burns.
33. **suspire:** breathe.
36. **rigol:** circle, i.e. the crown. 38. **blood:** i.e. heart.
42. **immediate from:** nearest to. 43. **Derives itself:** descends.
46. **lineal:** hereditary.

War. What would your Majesty? [How fares your Grace?]
King. Why did you leave me here alone, my lords?
Clar. We left the Prince my brother here, my liege,
Who undertook to sit and watch by you.
King. The Prince of Wales, where is he? Let me see him.
He is not here.
War. This door is open, he is gone this way.
Glou. He came not through the chamber where we stay'd.
King. Where is the crown? who took it from my pillow?
War. When we withdrew, my liege, we left it here.
King. The Prince hath ta'en it hence. Go seek him out.
Is he so hasty that he doth suppose
My sleep my death?
Find him, my Lord of Warwick, chide him hither.
[*Exit Warwick.*]
This part of his conjoins with my disease,
And helps to end me. See, sons, what things you are!
How quickly nature falls into revolt
When gold becomes her object!
For this the foolish over-careful fathers
Have broke their sleep with thoughts, their brains with care,
Their bones with industry;
For this they have engrossed and pil'd up
The cank'red heaps of strange-achieved gold;
For this they have been thoughtful to invest
Their sons with arts and martial exercises;
When like the bee tolling from every flower
[The virtuous sweets],
Our [thighs] pack'd with wax, our mouths with honey,
We bring it to the hive, and like the bees,
Are murd'red for our pains. This bitter taste
Yields his engrossments to the ending father.

Enter WARWICK.

Now, where is he that will not stay so long
Till his friend sickness [have] determin'd me?
War. My lord, I found the Prince in the next room,
Washing with kindly tears his gentle cheeks,
With such a deep demeanor in great sorrow
That tyranny, which never quaff'd but blood,
Would, by beholding him, have wash'd his knife
With gentle eye-drops. He is coming hither.
King. But wherefore did he take away the crown?

Enter [PRINCE] HARRY.

Lo where he comes. Come hither to me, Harry.
Depart the chamber, leave us here alone.
Exeunt [*Warwick and the rest*].

Prince. I never thought to hear you speak again.
King. Thy wish was father, Harry, to that thought:
I stay too long by thee, I weary thee.
Dost thou so hunger for mine empty chair
That thou wilt needs invest thee with my honors
Before thy hour be ripe? O foolish youth,
Thou seek'st the greatness that will overwhelm thee.
Stay but a little, for my cloud of dignity
Is held from falling with so weak a wind
That it will quickly drop; my day is dim.
Thou hast stol'n that which after some few hours
Were thine without offense, and at my death
Thou hast seal'd up my expectation.
Thy life did manifest thou lov'dst me not,
And thou wilt have me die assur'd of it.
Thou hid'st a thousand daggers in thy thoughts,
Whom thou hast whetted on thy stony heart
To stab at half an hour of my life.
What, canst thou not forbear me half an hour?
Then get thee gone, and dig my grave thyself,
And bid the merry bells ring to thine ear
That thou art crowned, not that I am dead.
Let all the tears that should bedew my hearse
Be drops of balm to sanctify thy head;
Only compound me with forgotten dust;
Give that which gave thee life unto the worms,
Pluck down my officers, break my decrees,
For now a time is come to mock at form.
Harry the Fift is crown'd! Up, vanity!
Down, royal state! All you sage counsellors, hence!
And to the English court assemble now,
From every region, apes of idleness!
Now, neighbor confines, purge you of your scum!
Have you a ruffin that will swear, drink, dance,
Revel the night, rob, murder, and commit
The oldest sins the newest kind of ways?
Be happy, he will trouble you no more.
England shall double gild his treble guilt,
England shall give him office, honor, might;
For the fift Harry from curb'd license plucks
The muzzle of restraint, and the wild dog
Shall flesh his tooth on every innocent.
O my poor kingdom, sick with civil blows!
When that my care could not withhold thy riots,
What wilt thou do when riot is thy care?
O, thou wilt be a wilderness again,
Peopled with wolves, thy old inhabitants!
Prince. O, pardon me, my liege! but for my tears,
The moist impediments unto my speech,
I had forestall'd this dear and deep rebuke
Ere you with grief had spoke and I had heard
The course of it so far. There is your crown;
And He that wears the crown immortally
Long guard it yours! If I affect it more

63. part: deed.
68. thoughts: anxieties. **70. engrossed:** accumulated.
71. cank'red: tarnished. **strange-achieved:** acquired by crooked means (?) or by extraordinary exertions (?) or in foreign lands (?).
72. thoughtful: careful. **74. tolling:** gathering.
75. virtuous: essential.
78–79. This . . . father: i.e. his accumulations yield the dying father this bitter taste. **81. determin'd:** ended.
83. kindly: natural. **84. deep:** heartfelt, intense.
94. chair: throne. **103. seal'd up:** confirmed.
113. hearse: coffin on a bier.
114. balm: oil with which a king is anointed at his coronation.
115. compound: mix. **118. form:** ceremony, decorum.
119. vanity: folly. **120. state:** pomp.
122. idleness: frivolity. **123. confines:** regions.
124. ruffin: ruffian.
132. flesh . . . on: plunge his teeth into the flesh of.
134. care: i.e. careful discipline. **140. dear:** grievous.
144. affect: love.

Than as your honor and as your renown,
Let me no more from this obedience rise, [*Kneels.*]
Which my most inward true and duteous spirit
Teacheth this prostrate and exterior bending.
God witness with me, when I here came in,
And found no course of breath within your Majesty,
How cold it strook my heart! If I do feign,
O, let me in my present wildness die,
And never live to show th' incredulous world
The noble change that I have purposed!
Coming to look on you, thinking you dead,
And dead almost, my liege, to think you were,
I spake unto this crown as having sense,
And thus upbraided it: "The care on thee depending
Hath fed upon the body of my father;
Therefore thou best of gold art [worst of] gold.
Other, less fine in carat, [is] more precious,
Preserving life in med'cine potable;
But thou, most fine, most honor'd, most renown'd,
Hast eat thy bearer up." Thus, my most royal liege,
Accusing it, I put it on my head,
To try with it, as with an enemy
That had before my face murdered my father,
The quarrel of a true inheritor.
But if it did infect my blood with joy,
Or swell my thoughts to any strain of pride,
If any rebel or vain spirit of mine
Did with the least affection of a welcome
Give entertainment to the might of it,
Let God for ever keep it from my head,
And make me as the poorest vassal is
That doth with awe and terror kneel to it!

King. [O my son,]
God put [it] in thy mind to take it hence,
That thou mightst win the more thy father's love,
Pleading so wisely in excuse of it!
Come hither, Harry, sit thou by my bed,
And hear (I think) the very latest counsel
That ever I shall breathe. God knows, my son,
By what by-paths and indirect crook'd ways
I met this crown, and I myself know well
How troublesome it sate upon my head.
To thee it shall descend with better quiet,
Better opinion, better confirmation,
For all the soil of the achievement goes
With me into the earth. It seem'd in me
But as an honor snatch'd with boist'rous hand,
And I had many living to upbraid
My gain of it by their assistances,
Which daily grew to quarrel and to bloodshed,
Wounding supposed peace. All these bold fears
Thou seest with peril I have answered;
For all my reign hath been but as a scene
Acting that argument. And now my death
Changes the mood, for what in me was purchas'd
Falls upon thee in a more fairer sort;
So thou the garland wear'st successively.
Yet though thou stand'st more sure than I could do,
Thou art not firm enough, since griefs are green,
And all [my] friends, which thou must make thy friends,
Have but their stings and teeth newly ta'en out;
By whose fell working I was first advanc'd,
And by whose power I well might lodge a fear
To be again displac'd; which to avoid,
I cut them off, and had a purpose now
To lead out many to the Holy Land,
Lest rest and lying still might make them look
Too near unto my state. Therefore, my Harry,
Be it thy course to busy giddy minds
With foreign quarrels, that action, hence borne out,
May waste the memory of the former days.
More would I, but my lungs are wasted so
That strength of speech is utterly denied me.
How I came by the crown, O God forgive,
And grant it may with thee in true peace live!

Prince. [My gracious liege,]
You won it, wore it, kept it, gave it me;
Then plain and right must my possession be,
Which I with more than with a common pain
'Gainst all the world will rightfully maintain.

Enter [PRINCE JOHN OF] LANCASTER.

King. Look, look, here comes my John of Lancaster.

P. John. Health, peace, and happiness to my royal father!

King. Thou bring'st me happiness and peace, son John,
But health, alack, with youthful wings is flown
From this bare wither'd trunk. Upon thy sight
My worldly business makes a period.
Where is my Lord of Warwick?

Prince. My Lord of Warwick!

[*Enter* WARWICK.]

King. Doth any name particular belong
Unto the lodging where I first did swound?

War. 'Tis call'd Jerusalem, my noble lord.

King. Laud be to God! even there my life must end.

146. obedience: obeisance.
147. true: loyal. **150. course:** current.
158. on thee depending: connected with you. **161. carat:** value.
162. potable: drinkable. Gold in solution (*aurum potabile*) was valued as a medicine. **166. try:** ascertain by testing.
170. strain: feeling. **172. affection:** inclination.
182. latest: last.
183–85. God . . . crown. As Holinshed reports (Bullough, IV, 277–78), "Well faire sonne (said the king with a great sigh) what right I had to it [i.e. the crown], God knoweth. Well (said the prince) if you die king, I will have the garland, and trust to keepe it with the sword against all mine enimies, as you have doone."
186. sate: sat. **188. opinion:** i.e. support of public opinion.
189. soil: moral stain.
198. argument: theme.
199. mood: mode, i.e. tonality. **purchas'd:** acquired by exertion.
201. successively: by inheritance.
203. griefs: grievances. **green:** fresh.
206. fell working: violent exertion. **207. lodge:** harbor.
211–12. look . . . state: inspect my (questionable) regality too closely.
214. action . . . out: campaigns conducted abroad.
215. waste: consume. **223. pain:** effort.
229. Upon thy sight: seeing you. **230. period:** end.
233. swound: swoon.
235–40. Laud . . . die. "Then said the king," reports Holinshed (Bullough, IV, 278), "Lauds be given to the father of heaven, for now I know that I shall die heere in this chamber, according to the prophesie of me declared, that I should depart this life in Jerusalem."

It hath been prophesied to me many years,
I should not die but in Jerusalem,
Which vainly I suppos'd the Holy Land.
But bear me to that chamber, there I'll lie,
In that Jerusalem shall Harry die. [*Exeunt.*]

[ACT V, SCENE I]

Enter SHALLOW, FALSTAFF, *and* BARDOLPH, [*with* PAGE].

Shal. By cock and pie, sir, you shall not away to-night. What, Davy, I say!

Fal. You must excuse me, Master Robert Shallow.

Shal. I will not excuse you, you shall not be excus'd, excuses shall not be admitted, there is no excuse shall serve, you shall not be excus'd. Why, Davy!

[*Enter* DAVY.]

Davy. Here, sir.

Shal. Davy, Davy, Davy, Davy, let me see, Davy, let me see, Davy, let me see. Yea, marry, William cook, bid him come hither. Sir John, you shall not be excus'd.

Davy. Marry, sir, thus; those precepts cannot be serv'd; and again, sir, shall we sow the hade land with wheat?

Shal. With red wheat, Davy. But for William cook—are there no young pigeons?

Davy. Yes, sir. Here is now the smith's note for shoeing and plough-irons.

Shal. Let it be cast and paid. Sir John, you shall not be excus'd.

Davy. Now, sir, a new link to the bucket must needs be had; and, sir, do you mean to stop any of William's wages, about the sack he lost at [Hinckley] fair?

Shal. 'A shall answer it. Some pigeons, Davy, a couple of short-legg'd hens, a joint of mutton, and any pretty little tiny kickshaws, tell William cook.

Davy. Doth the man of war stay all night, sir?

Shal. Yea, Davy, I will use him well. A friend i' th' court is better than a penny in purse. Use his men well, Davy, for they are arrant knaves, and will backbite.

Davy. No worse than they are backbitten, sir, for they have marvail's foul linen.

Shal. Well conceited, Davy. About thy business, Davy.

Davy. I beseech you, sir, to countenance William Visor of Woncote against Clement Perkes a' th' Hill.

Shal. There is many complaints, Davy, against that Visor. That Visor is an arrant knave, on my knowledge.

Davy. I grant your worship that he is a knave, sir; but yet God forbid, sir, but a knave should have some countenance at his friend's request. An honest man, sir, is able to speak for himself, when a knave is not. I have serv'd your worship truly, sir, this eight years; and I cannot once or twice in a quarter bear out a knave against an honest man, I have little credit with your worship. The knave is mine honest friend, sir, therefore I beseech you let him be countenanc'd.

Shal. Go to, I say, he shall have no wrong. Look about, Davy. [*Exit Davy.*] Where are you, Sir John? Come, come, come, off with your boots. Give me your hand, Master Bardolph.

Bard. I am glad to see your worship.

Shal. I thank thee with my heart, kind Master Bardolph, and welcome, my tall fellow [*to the Page*]. Come, Sir John.

Fal. I'll follow you, good Master Robert Shallow. [*Exit Shallow.*] Bardolph, look to our horses. [*Exeunt Bardolph and Page.*] If I were saw'd into quantities, I should make four dozen of such bearded hermits' staves as Master Shallow. It is a wonderful thing to see the semblable coherence of his men's spirits and his. They, by observing him, do bear themselves like foolish justices; he, by conversing with them, is turn'd into a justice-like servingman. Their spirits are so married in conjunction with the participation of society that they flock together in consent, like so many wild geese. If I had a suit to Master Shallow, I would humor his men with the imputation of being near their master; if to his men, I would curry with Master Shallow that no man could better command his servants. It is certain that either wise bearing or ignorant carriage is caught, as men take diseases, one of another; therefore let men take heed of their company. I will devise matter enough out of this Shallow to keep Prince Harry in continual laughter the wearing out of six fashions, which is four terms, or two actions, and 'a shall laugh without intervallums. O, it is much that a lie with a slight oath and a jest with a sad brow will do with a fellow that never had the ache in his shoulders! O, you shall see him laugh till his face be like a wet cloak ill laid up.

Shal. [*Within.*] Sir John!

Fal. I come, Master Shallow, I come, Master Shallow. [*Exit.*]

238. vainly: foolishly.

V.i. Location: Gloucestershire. Shallow's house.
1. By . . . pie: a mild oath of uncertain origin.
13. precepts: summonses (that Shallow had issued as a justice of the peace). **14. hade land:** unploughed strip of land.
18. note: bill. **20. cast:** reckoned, i.e. verified.
24. Hinckley: market town in Leicestershire.
26. answer: make restitution for.
28. kickshaws: fancy dish (French *quelque chose*).
34. backbitten: i.e. by lice. **35. marvail's:** marvellous.
36. Well conceited: wittily said.

38. countenance: favor, support.
39. Woncote: Woodmancote, a town in Gloucestershire.
48. bear out: support. **49. credit:** influence.
62. quantities: pieces. **65. semblable coherence:** similarity.
69–70. with . . . society: i.e. through close association.
70. consent: agreement. **73. curry with:** flatter.
80. four terms: i.e. twelve months (there being four terms of court in the legal year). **actions:** lawsuits.
81. intervallums: intervals between terms of court.
82. sad: serious.
85. ill laid up: carelessly packed away (and hence very wrinkled).

[Scene II]

Enter Warwick, Lord Chief Justice, [*meeting*].

War. How now, my Lord Chief Justice, whither away?
Ch. Just. How doth the King?
War. Exceeding well, his cares are now all ended.
Ch. Just. I hope, not dead.
War. He's walk'd the way of nature,
And to our purposes he lives no more.
Ch. Just. I would his Majesty had call'd me with him;
The service that I truly did his life
Hath left me open to all injuries.
War. Indeed I think the young King loves you not.
Ch. Just. I know he doth not, and do arm myself
To welcome the condition of the time,
Which cannot look more hideously upon me
Than I have drawn it in my fantasy.

Enter [Prince] John [of Lancaster], Thomas [of Clarence], *and* Humphrey [of Gloucester], Westmerland, [*and others*].

War. Here come the heavy issue of dead Harry.
O that the living Harry had the temper
Of he, the worst of these three gentlemen!
How many nobles then should hold their places,
That must strike sail to spirits of vile sort!
Ch. Just. O God, I fear all will be overturn'd!
P. John. Good morrow, cousin Warwick, good morrow.
Princes [*Glou., Clar.*] *ambo.* Good morrow, cousin.
P. John. We meet like men that had forgot to speak.
War. We do remember, but our argument
Is all too heavy to admit much talk.
P. John. Well, peace be with him that hath made us heavy!
Ch. Just. Peace be with us, lest we be heavier!
Glou. O, good my lord, you have lost a friend indeed,
And I dare swear you borrow not that face
Of seeming sorrow, it is sure your own.
P. John. Though no man be assur'd what grace to find,
You stand in coldest expectation.
I am the sorrier, would 'twere otherwise!
Clar. Well, you must now speak Sir John Falstaff fair,
Which swims against your stream of quality.
Ch. Just. Sweet Princes, what I did, I did in honor,
Led by th' impartial conduct of my soul;
And never shall you see that I will beg
A ragged and forestall'd remission.
If truth and upright innocency fail me,
I'll to the King my master that is dead,
And tell him who hath sent me after him.
War. Here comes the Prince.

Enter the Prince *and* Blunt.

Ch. Just. Good morrow, and God save your Majesty!
Prince. This new and gorgeous garment, majesty,
Sits not so easy on me as you think.
Brothers, you [mix] your sadness with some fear:
This is the English, not the Turkish court,
Not Amurath an Amurath succeeds,
But Harry Harry. Yet be sad, good brothers,
For by my faith it very well becomes you.
Sorrow so royally in you appears
That I will deeply put the fashion on
And wear it in my heart. Why then be sad,
But entertain no more of it, good brothers,
Than a joint burden laid upon us all.
For me, by heaven (I bid you be assur'd),
I'll be your father and your brother too.
Let me but bear your love, I'll bear your cares.
Yet weep that Harry's dead, and so will I,
But Harry lives, that shall convert those tears
By number into hours of happiness.
Princes. We hope no otherwise from your Majesty.
Prince. You all look strangely on me, and you most.
You are, I think, assur'd I love you not.
Ch. Just. I am assur'd, if I be measur'd rightly,
Your Majesty hath no just cause to hate me.
Prince. No?
How might a prince of my great hopes forget
So great indignities you laid upon me?
What, rate, rebuke, and roughly send to prison
Th' immediate heir of England! Was this easy?
May this be wash'd in Lethe and forgotten?
Ch. Just. I then did use the person of your father,
The image of his power lay then in me,
And in th' administration of his law,
Whiles I was busy for the commonwealth,
Your Highness pleased to forget my place,
The majesty and power of law and justice,
The image of the King whom I presented,
And strook me in my very seat of judgment;
Whereon (as an offender to your father)
I gave bold way to my authority,
And did commit you. If the deed were ill,
Be you contented, wearing now the garland,
To have a son set your decrees at nought?

V.ii. Location: Westminster. The palace.
7. truly: loyally. 13. fantasy: imagination.
14. heavy issue: sorrowful offspring.
16. he, the worst: the worst one.
18. strike sail: i.e. be submissive. 21. s.p. ambo: both.
23. argument: subject.
30. what . . . find: what favor he will find (with the new king).
33. speak . . . fair: address . . . courteously.
34. stream of quality: i.e. natural inclination.
35. what I did. On the grounds for the Chief Justice's apprehension see the note to *1 Henry IV*, III.ii.32–33.
37–38. I . . . remission: i.e. like a beggar I will ask a pardon sure to be refused.
48. Amurath: Murad III, Turkish sultan who, on his accession (1574), strangled his five brothers.
63. strangely: coldly, suspiciously. 70. rate: upbraid.
71. easy: insignificant.
72. Lethe: in Greek mythology, the river of oblivion.
73. use . . . of: i.e. represent. 74. image: symbol.
79. presented: represented. 83. commit: i.e. to prison.

To pluck down justice from your aweful bench?
To trip the course of law and blunt the sword
That guards the peace and safety of your person?
Nay more, to spurn at your most royal image,
And mock your workings in a second body?
Question your royal thoughts, make the case yours:
Be now the father and propose a son,
Hear your own dignity so much profan'd,
See your most dreadful laws so loosely slighted,
Behold yourself so by a son disdained;
And then imagine me taking your part,
And in your power soft silencing your son.
After this cold considerance, sentence me,
And as you are a king, speak in your state
What I have done that misbecame my place,
My person, or my liege's sovereignty.

Prince. You are right justice, and you weigh this well,
Therefore still bear the balance and the sword,
And I do wish your honors may increase,
Till you do live to see a son of mine
Offend you and obey you, as I did.
So shall I live to speak my father's words:
"Happy am I, that have a man so bold,
That dares do justice on my proper son;
And not less happy, having such a son
That would deliver up his greatness so
Into the hands of justice." You did commit me;
For which I do commit into your hand
Th' unstained sword that you have us'd to bear,
With this remembrance, that you use the same
With the like bold, just, and impartial spirit
As you have done 'gainst me. There is my hand.
You shall be as a father to my youth,
My voice shall sound as you do prompt mine ear,
And I will stoop and humble my intents
To your well-practic'd wise directions.
And, princes all, believe me, I beseech you,
My father is gone wild into his grave;
For in his tomb lie my affections,
And with his spirits sadly I survive,
To mock the expectation of the world,
To frustrate prophecies, and to rase out
Rotten opinion, who hath writ me down
After my seeming. The tide of blood in me

86. aweful: awesome. **89. spurn:** kick.
90. your . . . body: the actions of your deputy.
92. propose: imagine. **97. soft:** gently.
98. considerance: consideration. **99. state:** royal capacity.
103. balance: i.e. scales (symbolizing ideal justice).
109. proper: own. **115. remembrance:** reminder.
122–45. And . . . day. "This king even at first appointing with himselfe," says Holinshed (Bullough, IV, 280), "to shew that in his person princelie honors should change publike manners, he determined to put on him the shape of a new man. For whereas aforetime he had made himselfe a companion unto misrulie mates of dissolute order and life, he now banished them all from his presence (but not unrewarded, or else unpreferred) inhibiting them upon a great paine, not once to approch, lodge, or sojourne within ten miles of his court or presence: and in their places he chose men of gravitie, wit, and high policie, by whose wise counsell he might at all times rule to his honour and dignitie."
123. My . . . grave: i.e. my wildness has been buried with my father.
124. affections: (unruly) inclinations. **125. sadly:** soberly.
127. rase: erase, blot.
128–29. who . . . seeming: which has delineated me as I appeared to be. **129. blood:** passion.

Hath proudly flow'd in vanity till now;
Now doth it turn and ebb back to the sea,
Where it shall mingle with the state of floods,
And flow henceforth in formal majesty.
Now call we our high court of parliament,
And let us choose such limbs of noble counsel
That the great body of our state may go
In equal rank with the best govern'd nation,
That war, or peace, or both at once, may be
As things acquainted and familiar to us,
In which you, father, shall have foremost hand.
Our coronation done, we will accite
(As I before rememb'red) all our state,
And (God consigning to my good intents)
No prince nor peer shall have just cause to say,
God shorten Harry's happy life one day! *Exeunt*.

[Scene III]

Enter Sir John [Falstaff], Shallow, Silence, Davy, Bardolph, Page.

Shal. Nay, you shall see my orchard, where, in an arbor, we will eat a last year's pippin of mine own graffing, with a dish of caraways, and so forth. Come, cousin Silence—and then to bed.

Fal. 'Fore God, you have here goodly dwelling and rich.

Shal. Barren, barren, barren, beggars all, beggars all, Sir John! Marry, good air. Spread, Davy, spread, Davy. Well said, Davy.

Fal. This Davy serves you for good uses, he is your servingman and your husband.

Shal. A good varlet, a good varlet, a very good varlet, Sir John. By the mass, I have drunk too much sack at supper. A good varlet. Now sit down, now sit down. Come, cousin.

Sil. Ah, sirrah, quoth 'a, we shall
[*Singing*.]
"Do nothing but eat, and make good cheer,
And praise God for the merry year,
When flesh is cheap and females dear,
And lusty lads roam here and there
So merrily,
And ever among so merrily."

Fal. There's a merry heart! Good Master Silence, I'll give you a health for that anon.

Shal. Give Master Bardolph some wine, Davy.

Davy. Sweet sir, sit, I'll be with you anon, most sweet sir, sit. Master page, good master page, sit. Proface! What you want in meat, we'll have in drink, but you must bear, the heart's all. [*Exit*.]

130. vanity: folly. **132. state of floods:** majesty of the sea.
140. father: i.e. the Chief Justice. **141. accite:** summon.
142. rememb'red: mentioned. **state:** dignitaries and peers.
143. consigning: assenting.

V.iii. Location: Gloucestershire. Shallow's orchard.
2. pippin: kind of apple.
3. graffing: grafting. **caraways.** Caraway seeds were often eaten with apples. **8. Spread:** lay the cloth.
11. husband: steward. **12. varlet:** servant. **16. quoth 'a:** said he.
28. Proface: a term of welcome or good wishes to a guest. **meat:** food.

Shal. Be merry, Master Bardolph, and, my little soldier there, be merry.

Sil. [*Singing.*]

"Be merry, be merry, my wife has all,
For women are shrows, both short and tall;
'Tis merry in hall when beards wags all,
And welcome merry Shrove-tide.
Be merry, be merry."

Fal. I did not think Master Silence had been a man of this mettle.

Sil. Who, I? I have been merry twice and once ere now.

Enter Davy.

Davy. [*To Bardolph.*] There's a dish of leather-coats for you.

Shal. Davy!

Davy. Your worship! I'll be with you straight. A cup of wine, sir?

Sil. [*Singing.*]

"A cup of wine that's brisk and fine,
And drink unto [thee,] leman mine,
And a merry heart lives long-a."

Fal. Well said, Master Silence.

Sil. And we shall be merry, now comes in the sweet a' th' night.

Fal. Health and long life to you, Master Silence.

Sil. [*Singing.*]

"Fill the cup, and let it come,
I'll pledge you a mile to th' bottom."

Shal. Honest Bardolph, welcome. If thou want'st any thing, and wilt not call, beshrew thy heart. Welcome, my little tiny thief [*to the Page*], and welcome indeed too. I'll drink to Master Bardolph, and to all the cabileros about London.

Davy. I hope to see London once ere I die.

Bard. And I might see you there, Davy!

Shal. By the mass, you'll crack a quart together, ha, will you not, Master Bardolph?

Bard. Yea, sir, in a pottle-pot.

Shal. By God's liggens, I thank thee. The knave will stick by thee, I can assure thee that 'a will not out, 'a. 'Tis true bred!

Bard. And I'll stick by him, sir.

Shal. Why, there spoke a king. Lack nothing, be merry! (*One knocks at door.*) Look who's at door there ho! Who knocks? [*Exit Davy.*]

Fal. [*To Silence, seeing him take off a bumper.*] Why, now you have done me right.

Sil. [*Singing.*] "Do me right,
And dub me knight,
Samingo."

Is't not so?

Fal. 'Tis so.

Sil. Is't so? Why then say an old man can do somewhat.

[*Enter* Davy.]

Davy. And't please your worship, there's one Pistol come from the court with news.

Fal. From the court? Let him come in.

Enter Pistol.

How now, Pistol?

Pist. Sir John, God save you!

Fal. What wind blew you hither, Pistol?

Pist. Not the ill wind which blows no man to good. Sweet knight, thou art now one of the greatest men in this realm.

Sil. By'r lady, I think 'a be, but goodman Puff of Barson.

Pist. Puff?
Puff i' thy teeth, most recreant coward base!
Sir John, I am thy Pistol and thy friend,
And helter-skelter have I rode to thee,
And tidings do I bring, and lucky joys,
And golden times, and happy news of price.

Fal. I pray thee now deliver them like a man of this world.

Pist. A foutre for the world and worldlings base!
I speak of Africa and golden joys.

Fal. O base Assyrian knight, what is thy news?
Let King Cophetua know the truth thereof.

Sil. [*Singing.*] "And Robin Hood, Scarlet, and John."

Pist. Shall dunghill curs confront the Helicons?
And shall good news be baffled?
Then, Pistol, lay thy head in Furies' lap.

Shal. Honest gentleman, I know not your breeding.

Pist. Why then lament therefore.

Shal. Give me pardon, sir. If, sir, you come with news from the court, I take it there's but two ways, either to utter them, or conceal them. I am, sir, under the King, in some authority.

Pist. Under which king, besonian? Speak, or die.

Shal. Under King Harry.

Pist. Harry the Fourth, or Fift?

Shal. Harry the Fourth.

Pist. A foutre for thine office!
Sir John, thy tender lambkin now is king;
Harry the Fift's the man. I speak the truth.
When Pistol lies, do this, and fig me like
The bragging Spaniard.

Fal. What, is the old king dead?

Pist. As nail in door. The things I speak are just.

33. shrows: shrews.
35. Shrove-tide: season of merrymaking before Lent.
39. merry: tipsy. **41–42. leather-coats:** kind of apples.
47. leman: sweetheart. **53. let it come:** i.e. pass the cup.
54. a mile . . . bottom: to the bottom even if it were a mile.
56. beshrew: curse. **59. cabileros:** gallants.
62. crack: drink. **64. pottle-pot:** two-quart tankard.
65. liggens. Unexplained.
66. 'a . . . out: i.e. he will not drop out of the drinking (?).
72. done me right: matched me (in drinking).
75. Samingo: name (perhaps corrupted from *San Domingo*) of a character in a popular song.
89. but: except. Silence takes Pistol's *greatest* to mean "fattest."
91. Puff. Interpreted by Pistol as a term of contempt.
96. price: great value. **99. foutre:** coarse term of contempt.
102. King Cophetua. An allusion to the ballad "King Cophetua and the Beggar Maid." **104. Helicons:** i.e. poets.
105. baffled: disgraced.
107. I . . breeding: i.e. don't know who you are.
108. therefore: therefor.
113. besonian: scoundrel (Italian *bisogno*).
118. fig: insult by thrusting the thumb between the fingers.
121. just: true.

Fal. Away, Bardolph! saddle my horse. Master Robert Shallow, choose what office thou wilt in the land, 'tis thine. Pistol, I will double-charge thee with dignities.

Bard. O joyful day! I would not take a [knighthood] for my fortune.

Pist. What? I do bring good news?

Fal. Carry Master Silence to bed. Master Shallow, my Lord Shallow—be what thou wilt, I am Fortune's steward—get on thy boots. We'll ride all night. O sweet Pistol! Away, Bardolph! [*Exit Bardolph.*] Come, Pistol, utter more to me, and withal devise something to do thyself good. Boot, boot, Master Shallow! I know the young king is sick for me. Let us take any man's horses, the laws of England are at my commandement. Blessed are they that have been my friends, and woe to my Lord Chief Justice!

Pist. Let vultures vile seize on his lungs also!
"Where is the life that late I led?" say they.
Why, here it is, welcome these pleasant days! *Exeunt.*

[Scene IV]

Enter [Beadle] *and three or four* Officers [*with* Hostess Quickly *and* Doll Tearsheet].

Host. No, thou arrant knave, I would to God that I might die, that I might have thee hang'd. Thou hast drawn my shoulder out of joint.

[*Bead.*] The constables have deliver'd her over to me, and she shall have whipping cheer, I warrant her. There hath been a man or two kill'd about her.

Doll. Nuthook, nuthook, you lie. Come on! I'll tell thee what, thou damn'd tripe-visag'd rascal, and the child I go with do miscarry, thou wert better thou hadst strook thy mother, thou paper-fac'd villain!

Host. O the Lord, that Sir John were come! I would make this a bloody day to somebody. But I pray God the fruit of her womb miscarry.

[*Bead.*] If it do, you shall have a dozen of cushions again; you have but eleven now. Come, I charge you both go with me, for the man is dead that you and Pistol beat amongst you.

Doll. I'll tell you what, you thin man in a censer, I will have you as soundly swing'd for this—you blue-bottle rogue, you filthy famish'd correctioner, if you be not swing'd, I'll forswear half-kirtles.

[*Bead.*] Come, come, you she knight-arrant, come.

Host. O God, that right should thus overcome might! Well, of sufferance comes ease.

Doll. Come, you rogue, come bring me to a justice.

Host. Ay, come, you starv'd bloodhound.

Doll. Goodman Death, goodman Bones!

Host. Thou atomy, thou!

Doll. Come, you thin thing, come, you rascal.

[*Bead.*] Very well. [*Exeunt.*]

[Scene V]

Enter Strewers of rushes.

1. Strewer. More rushes, more rushes.

2. Strewer. The trumpets have sounded twice.

3. Strewer. 'Twill be two a' clock ere they come from the coronation. Dispatch, dispatch. [*Exeunt.*]

Trumpets sound, and the King *and his* Train *pass over the stage. After them enter* Falstaff, Shallow, Pistol, Bardolph, *and the Boy* [Page].

Fal. Stand here by me, Master Shallow, I will make the King do you grace. I will leer upon him as 'a comes by, and do but mark the countenance that he will give me.

Pist. God bless thy lungs, good knight.

Fal. Come here, Pistol, stand behind me.—O, if I had had time to have made new liveries, I would have bestow'd the thousand pound I borrow'd of you. But 'tis no matter, this poor show doth better, this doth infer the zeal I had to see him.

[*Shal.*] It doth so.

Fal. It shows my earnestness of affection—

[*Shal.*] It doth so.

Fal. My devotion—

[*Shal.*] It doth, it doth, it doth.

Fal. As it were, to ride day and night, and not to deliberate, not to remember, not to have patience to shift me—

Shal. It is best, certain.

[*Fal.*] But to stand stain'd with travel, and sweating with desire to see him, thinking of nothing else, putting all affairs else in oblivion, as if there were nothing else to be done but to see him.

Pist. 'Tis "*semper idem*," for "*obsque hoc nihil est.*" 'Tis [all] in every part.

Shal. 'Tis so indeed.

Pist. My knight, I will inflame thy noble liver,
And make thee rage.
Thy Doll, and Helen of thy noble thoughts,
Is in base durance and contagious prison,
Hal'd thither
By most mechanical and dirty hand.
Rouse up revenge from ebon den with fell Alecto's
snake,

124. double-charge. With a pun on Pistol's name.

V.iv. Location: London. A street.
5. whipping cheer: i.e. whipping for her supper.
7. Nuthook: slang term for an arresting officer; literally, a hooked stick used in nutting. **8. tripe-visag'd:** flabby-faced.
10. paper-fac'd: white-faced.
14–15. If . . . now. He accuses Doll of using a pillow to make herself look pregnant. **17. amongst you:** together.
18. thin . . . censer: figure in low relief embossed on the lid of an incense burner. **19. swing'd:** thrashed (past participle of *swinge*).
19–20. blue-bottle. Alluding to the customary blue coats worn by beadles. **21. half-kirtles:** short skirts. **25. sufferance:** suffering.

29. atomy: the Hostess' confusion of *atom* and *anatomy*, i.e. skeleton.
30. rascal: lean, inferior deer.

V.v. Location: Westminster. Near the Abbey.
6. grace: honor. **leer:** glance sideways.
12. bestow'd: spent. **you:** i.e. Shallow. **14. infer:** imply.
22. shift me: change my clothes.
28–29. 'Tis . . . part: i.e. it's "always the same," for "without this there is nothing." Integrity is everything. (Pistol paraphrases the Latin tags to express his approval of Falstaff's constancy.)
34. contagious: noxious. **36. mechanical:** menial.
37. ebon: black. **Alecto:** one of the Furies.

For Doll is in. Pistol speaks nought but truth.
Fal. I will deliver her.
[*Shouts within. The trumpets sound.*]
Pist. There roar'd the sea, and trumpet-clangor sounds.

Enter the KING *and his* TRAIN, [*the* LORD CHIEF JUSTICE *among them*].

Fal. God save thy Grace, King Hal! my royal Hal!
Pist. The heavens thee guard and keep, most royal imp of fame!
Fal. God save thee, my sweet boy!
King. My Lord Chief Justice, speak to that vain man.
Ch. Just. Have you your wits? know you what 'tis you speak?
Fal. My King, my Jove! I speak to thee, my heart!
King. I know thee not, old man, fall to thy prayers.
How ill white hairs becomes a fool and jester!
I have long dreamt of such a kind of man,
So surfeit-swell'd, so old, and so profane;
But being awak'd, I do despise my dream.
Make less thy body (hence) and more thy grace,
Leave gormandizing, know the grave doth gape
For thee thrice wider than for other men.
Reply not to me with a fool-born jest,
Presume not that I am the thing I was,
For God doth know, so shall the world perceive,
That I have turn'd away my former self;
So will I those that kept me company.
When thou dost hear I am as I have been,
Approach me, and thou shalt be as thou wast,
The tutor and the feeder of my riots.
Till then I banish thee, on pain of death,
As I have done the rest of my misleaders,
Not to come near our person by ten mile.
For competence of life I will allow you,
That lack of means enforce you not to evils,
And as we hear you do reform yourselves,
We will, according to your strengths and qualities,
Give you advancement. Be it your charge, my lord,
To see perform'd the tenure of my word.
Set on. [*Exeunt King and his Train.*]

Fal. Master Shallow, I owe you a thousand pound.

Shal. Yea, marry, Sir John, which I beseech you to let me have home with me.

Fal. That can hardly be, Master Shallow. Do not you grieve at this, I shall be sent for in private to him. Look you, he must seem thus to the world. Fear not your advancements, I will be the man yet that shall make you great.

Shal. I cannot perceive how, unless you give me your doublet and stuff me out with straw. I beseech you, good Sir John, let me have five hundred of my thousand.

Fal. Sir, I will be as good as my word. This that you heard was but a color.

Shal. A color that I fear you will die in, Sir John.

Fal. Fear no colors, go with me to dinner. Come, Lieutenant Pistol, come, Bardolph. I shall be sent for soon at night.

Enter [*the* LORD CHIEF] JUSTICE *and* PRINCE JOHN; [OFFICERS *with them*].

Ch. Just. Go carry Sir John Falstaff to the Fleet.
Take all his company along with him.
Fal. My lord, my lord—
Ch. Just. I cannot now speak, I will hear you soon.
Take them away.
Pist. *Si fortuna me tormenta, spero contenta.*
Exeunt. [*Manent Prince John and the Chief Justice.*]
P. John. I like this fair proceeding of the King's.
He hath intent his wonted followers
Shall all be very well provided for,
But all are banish'd till their conversations
Appear more wise and modest to the world.
Ch. Just. And so they are.
P. John. The King hath call'd his parliament, my lord.
Ch. Just. He hath.
P. John. I will lay odds that ere this year expire,
We bear our civil swords and native fire
As far as France. I heard a bird so sing,
Whose music, to my thinking, pleas'd the King.
Come, will you hence? [*Exeunt.*]

EPILOGUE

First my fear, then my cur'sy, last my speech. My fear, is your displeasure, my cur'sy, my duty, and my speech, to beg your pardons. If you look for a good speech now, you undo me, for what I have to say is of mine own making, and what indeed (I should say) will (I doubt) prove mine own marring. But to the purpose, and so to the venture. Be it known to you, as it is very well, I was lately here in the end of a displeasing play, to pray your patience for it and to promise you a better. I meant indeed to pay you with this, which if like an ill venture it come unluckily home, I break, and you, my gentle creditors, lose. Here I promis'd you I would be, and here I commit my body to your mercies. Bate me some, and I will pay you some, and (as most debtors do) promise you infinitely; and so I kneel down before you—but, indeed, to pray for the Queen.

If my tongue cannot entreat you to acquit me, will you command me to use my legs? And yet that were but light payment, to dance out of your debt. But a

42. **imp:** scion.
44. **vain:** foolish. 50. **surfeit-swell'd:** swollen through gluttony.
52. **hence:** hereafter. **grace:** virtue.
66. **competence of life:** i.e. modest allowance.
69. **qualities:** attainments. 71. **tenure:** tenor.
86. **color:** pretense.

87. **color:** i.e. *collar*, hangman's noose.
88. **colors:** (enemy) flags. 90. **soon at night:** early this evening.
91. **Fleet:** London prison.
96. **Si . . . contenta.** See note to II.iv.181.
100. **conversations:** behavior.
106. **civil . . . fire.** Alluding to the civil broils just ended.

Epi. 1. **cur'sy:** curtsy, bow. 6. **doubt:** fear.
8–9. **a displeasing play.** Not identified.
11. **ill venture:** unsuccessful commercial speculation.
12. **break:** am bankrupt.
14. **Bate me some:** abate me something.

good conscience will make any possible satisfaction, and so would I. All the gentlewomen here have forgiven me; if the gentlemen will not, then the gentlemen do not agree with the gentlewomen, which was never seen in such an assembly.

One word more, I beseech you. If you be not too much cloy'd with fat meat, our humble author will continue the story, with Sir John in it, and make you merry with fair Katherine of France, where (for any thing I know) Falstaff shall die of a sweat, unless already 'a be kill'd with your hard opinions; for Oldcastle died [a] martyr, and this is not the man. My tongue is weary, when my legs are too, I will bid you good night.

27–28. our . . . story. Referring to the sequel of this play, *Henry V.*

32. Oldcastle. On Shakespeare's use of this name for Falstaff in the original form of the Henry IV plays, see the introduction.

NOTE ON THE TEXT

The Second Part of Henry the Fourth was first published in quarto in 1600 (Q). So far as we know, this was the only printing of the play until its inclusion in the First Folio (1623); nor was there any later seventeenth-century separate edition. Q occurs in two distinct issues. In the first issue, the scene which in F1 (and in the present text) is numbered III.i is lacking and was not added until a substantial number had been sold. Sigs. E3 and E4 were then cancelled and replaced by four new leaves which incorporated the missing scene. These two issues are distinguished in the Textual Notes as Qa (first issue) and Qb (second issue); for further discussion, see below.

Q was almost certainly printed from Shakespeare's "foul papers" and here serves—as in all major editions from at least the Old Arden (ed. R. P. Cowl, 1923) until the New Oxford, which prefers F1 (see below)—as the basic text, except for 171 lines first printed in F1 (eight passages: A, I.i.166–69; B, I.i.189–209; C, I.iii.21–4; D, I.iii.36–55; E, I.iii.85–108; F, II.iii.23–45; G, IV.i.55–79; H, IV.i.101–37). For III.i, Qb is of necessity the basic copy; for that portion of the text contained in the two cancelled leaves of Qa (II.iv.241–91, III.ii.1–103, ending with the word *young*), the basic text is of course Qa, but all significant variants in the reset version in Qb are recorded in the Textual Notes.

The evidence for believing that Q was set up from Shakespeare's "foul papers" is very strong. There is considerable inconsistency in the use of speech-prefixes, the most extreme instance being those for Doll Tearsheet, who appears as *Dol.*, *Dorothy*, *Teresh.*, and *Whoore*; a number of the stage directions are authorial in their indefiniteness (see, for example, the Textual Notes at II.i o.s.d., II.iv o.s.d., III.ii.54); the Beadle in V.iv is designated by the actor's name (Sincklo); stage directions list characters who have no part in the play (see I.iii o.s.d., II.ii o.s.d., IV.iv o.s.d.) or in the scene for which they are entered (see III.i.31, IV.i o.s.d.); at I.i.161 Sir John Umfrevile is assigned a speech, but no such character appears in the scene as it now stands; Falstaff appears once with the speech-prefix *Old.* for Oldcastle (I.ii.120); two lines probably marked for deletion by Shakespeare are to be found in the uncorrected state of Q at IV.i.92, 93; and several characteristic Shakespearean spellings have survived the compositor, notably *Scilens, on* (for *one*), and *mas*. Although the various confusions in Q make it certain that the manuscript from which it was printed could never itself have served as a prompt-book, some connection with the theatre may be suggested by the fact that the eight passages first printed in F1 are almost certainly originally part of the "foul papers" (*pace* Jowett/Taylor) and that their absence from Q may best be explained on the supposition that the compositor (Q was set by a single compositor [Ferguson]) found them marked as cuts in the manuscript.

As usual, critical opinions differ on the date of composition of both III.i and the eight passages (see above) first appearing in F1. The omission of III.i from Qa has usually been explained as follows. Since half of the 105 lines of III.i may be taken as roughly equivalent to the average of 49 lines per page in the 147-line scene (Addition II) in *Sir Thomas More,* widely accepted as being in Shakespeare's handwriting, critics, postulating this average as, more or less, a Shakespearean norm, have generally agreed that these lines would about fill two sides (recto and verso) of a single foolscap leaf, which, because it was a complete unit in itself, could have been misplaced in the "foul papers" somewhere after the present equivalent of III.ii. When the leaf containing III.i was eventually discovered, sig. E would have already been printed off and insertion of the scene in the middle of sig. E would have been a costly undertaking requiring the resetting of four pages of sig. E (two leaves) and the addition of another four pages (i.e., III.i). Who later, after the remainder of the play had been set, printed off, and at least in part distributed, forced a reversal of the decision not to include III.i (a decision probably made before June 1603 [McManaway]), will, of course, never be known—conceivably Shakespeare himself, but more likely either Wise and Aspley, the publishers of Q, or Shakespeare's company, the Lord Chamberlain's Men. This explanation assumes that III.i was initially a part of the "foul paper" copy given to the printer, but recently two different answers to the problem of the absence of III.i in Qa have been advanced: (a) that III.i was retrieved too late for inclusion in the "foul papers" from the Ur-version of the play as originally acted (c. 1596) before it underwent a revision forced on Shakespeare's company by Henry Brooke, Lord Cobham, who was outraged by the character, now known as Sir John Falstaff, which then went under the name Sir John Oldcastle, a Protestant martyr and an ancestor of Cobham's, but that the eight passages first printed in F1 *were* part of the printer's copy (Melchiori); (b) that III.i and all but two (B and G; see below) of the passages first printed in F1 were authorial afterthoughts, an explanation that favors one of the Oxford editors' theses that Shakespeare was very much given to revision (Jowett/Taylor). Thus Melchiori and Jowett/Taylor argue for III.i as an addition, which arrived too late to be included in the "foul papers" from which Qa was printed, but differ on when III.i was actually written and on whether the eight passages first printed in F1 were originally an integral part of the "foul papers," but marked for deletion and hence omitted in Q, or that all but two (B and G; Q offers evidence that proves they were originally part of the printer's copy, probably censored for political reasons) were, like III.i, somewhat later authorial additions. None of the explanations for the problems presented by the Q text is capable of anything like proof, and it is difficult, given the evidence, to argue that one is more nearly correct than the others, but Jowett/Taylor's attempt to show that six of the passages first appearing in F1 are examples of Shakespeare's revising hand is seriously open to question, and is effectively countered by Melchiori.

The exact provenience of the F1 text is also open to question. Alice Walker, as W. J. Rolfe had much earlier suggested, argues that F1 was set from a copy of Q which had been augmented from and corrected against a "fair copy" of Shakespeare's "foul papers" (not against the prompt-book, as W. W. Greg argues), a "fair copy" made by a scribe unfriendly to colloquialisms and contracted or elided forms. The use of corrected Q-copy is now, however, generally discounted (Walton). M. A. Shaaber argues vigorously that F1 was set from a transcript of the official prompt-book, a transcript which omitted certain prompt-book notations (such as directions for stage noises), ironed out colloquialisms, and expanded elided forms. A. R. Humphreys, after carefully weighing the arguments on both sides, declares in favor of a transcript which was either a sophisticated copy made from a theatre manuscript by a scribe who kept one eye on Q, or (as Bowers had suggested) a scribal copy prepared from a copy of Q considerably augmented, changed, and sophisticated in the process of collation with a theatre manuscript. Of these alternatives, Humphreys prefers the first, a choice substantially endorsed by Jowett/Taylor and Melchiori.

F1, apart from the 171 additional lines already noticed, generally tidies up the inconsistencies in Q, adds a number of necessary stage directions, occasionally omits but more often bowdlerizes (e.g., "heaven" for "God") oaths in compliance with the 1606 Act "To Restrain Abuses of Players," and offers a sizable number of other verbal variants. The Textual Notes record all significant variants, and all additions and omissions, in F1. For the Dering MS, to which occasional reference is made, see the "Note on the Text" to *1 Henry IV*.

For further information, see: W. J. Rolfe, ed., *2 Henry IV* (New York, 1880); Alfred Hart, *Shakespeare and the Homilies* (Melbourne, 1934), pp. 154–218; M. A. Shaaber, ed., New Variorum *2 Henry IV* (Philadelphia, 1940) and "The Folio Text of *2 Henry IV*," *SQ*, VI (1955), 135–44; James G. McManaway, "The Cancel in the Quarto of *2 Henry IV*," *Studies in Honor of A. H. R. Fairchild* (Univ. of Missouri Press, 1946), pp. 67–80; J. D. Wilson, ed., New Shakespeare *2 Henry IV* (Cambridge, 1946); Alice Walker, *Textual Problems of the First Folio* (Cambridge, 1953); F. T. Bowers, "A Definitive Text of Shakespeare," *Studies in Shakespeare* (Univ. of Miami Press, 1953); W. W. Greg, *The Shakespeare First Folio* (Oxford, 1955); W. C. Ferguson, "The Compositors of *Henry IV, Part 2*, *Much Ado about Nothing*, *The Shoemakers' Holiday*, and *The First Part of the Contention*," *SB*, XIII (1960), 19–29; John H. Smith, "The Cancel in the Quarto of *2 Henry IV* Revisited," *SQ*, XV (1964), 173–6; A. R. Humphreys, ed., New Arden *2 Henry IV* (London, 1966); J. K. Walton, *The Quarto Copy for the First Folio of Shakespeare* (Dublin, 1971); G. W. Williams, "The Text of *2 Henry IV*: Facts and Problems," *Shakespeare Studies*, IX (1976), 173–82; P. H. Davison, "The Printing of the Folio Edition of *2 Henry IV*," *The Library*, XXXII (1977), 256–61; Alan Craven, "The Reliability of Simmes's Compositor A," *SB*, XXXII (1979), 186–9; Eleanor Prosser, *Shakespeare's Anonymous Editors: Scribe and Compositor in the Folio Text of "2 Henry IV"* (Stanford, 1980); G. W. Williams and T. L. Berger, "Variants in the Quarto of Shakespeare's *2 Henry IV*," *The Library*, 6th. ser., III (1981), 109–18; John Jowett and Gary Taylor, "The Three Texts of *2 Henry IV*," *SB*, XL (1987), 31–50; Stanley Wells, Gary Taylor, et al., *William Shakespeare:* A *Textual Companion* (Oxford, 1987); Giorgio Melchiori, ed., New Cambridge *2 Henry IV* (Cambridge, 1989).

TEXTUAL NOTES

Title: The Second . . . Fourth] The Second part of Henrie the fourth, continuing to his death, and coronation of Henrie the fift. With the humours of sir Iohn Falstaffe, and swaggering Pistoll. As it hath been sundrie times publikely acted by the right honourable, the Lord Chamberlaine his seruants. Written by William Shakespeare. *Q (title-page)*; The Second Part of Henry the Fourth, Containing his Death: and the Coronation of King Henry the Fift. *F1*

Dramatis personae: *as in F1; material in square brackets added by Rowe and later eds.*

Strewers] *Wilson;* Groomes *F1*

Act-scene division: *none in Q; from F1, with the following exceptions: I.i–iii (numbered I.ii–iv in F1, which marks the Induction as I.i); IV.ii, iii (no scene divisions in F1); IV.iv (numbered IV.ii in F1); IV.v (no scene division in F1); see first note to each scene; present act-scene arrangement as a whole first established by Cambridge*

Induction

Induction] *F1 (in which this heading is preceded by* Actus Primus. Scoena Prima.)

o.s.d. **painted . . . tongues]** *om. F1*

1 s.p. **Rum.]** *Capell*

6 **tongues]** Tongue *F1*

8 **men]** them *F1*

8 **reports.]** *F1* (Reports:); reports, *Q*

13 **grief]** griefes *F1*

14–5 **war, . . . matter?]** *F1;* Warre? . . . matter. *Q*

16 **jealousies,]** *F1;* Iealousies *Q*

21 **My well-known body]** *F1;* (My wel knowne body) *Q*

21 **anatomize]** *F4;* anothomize *Q;* Anathomize *F1*

27 **rebels']** *Theobald;* rebels *Q, F1*

34 **that]** the *F1*

35 **hold]** *Theobald;* hole *Q, F1*

36 **Where]** *F1;* When *Q*

37 **crafty-sick]** *hyphen, Pope*

40 s.d. **Exit Rumor.]** *Pelican;* exit Rumours. *Q;* Exit. *F1*

I.i

I.i] *Warburton;* Scena Secunda. *F1*

Location: *Capell (subs.)*

o.s.d. **Bardolph]** *Rowe;* Bardolfe *Q, F1 (throughout)*

1 s.d. **Enter Porter.]** *Dyce*

6 s.d. **in . . . staff]** *ed. (after Dering MS:* Enter Northumberland: alone in his garden and Night-Cappe: *and l. 145 below)*

6 s.d. **Exit Porter.]** *Dyce*

7 s.p. **North.]** *F1;* Earle. *Q (throughout scene)*

13 **God]** heauen *F1*

23 **fortunes]** *F1;* fortuncs *Q*

28 **who]** whom *F1*

29 s.d. **Enter Travers.]** *F1; after l. 25, Q*

36 **hard]** head *F1*

41 **bad]** ill *Dering MS, F1*

44 **armed]** able *F1*

48 **Again.]** *F1* (Againe:); againe, *Q*

53 **honor, . . . point]** *F1;* honor . . . point, *Q*

55 **should that]** should the *F1*

59 **Spoke . . . venter]** Speake at aduenture *F1*

64 **Morton]** *F1;* Mourton *Q (and s.p.* Mour, *throughout rest of scene)*

71 **woe-begone]** *hyphen, F1*

79 **my]** mine *F1*

83 **dead.]** *F1;* dead? *Q*

86 **others']** *Capell;* others *Q, F1*

88 **an]** thy *F1*

96 **say so;]** *F1*

97 **tongue]** *F1;* tongne *Q*

103 **tolling]** knolling *F1*

106 **God]** heauen *F1*

109 **Harry]** Henrie *F1*

126 **So]** Too *F1*

127 **well-laboring]** *hyphen, F1*

137 **these]** this *F1*

143 **keeper's]** *Rowe;* keepers *Q, F1*

144 **Weak'ned]** *F1;* Weakened *Q*

155 **this]** the *F1*

161 s.p. **L. Bard.]** *Pope;* Vmfr. *Q; line om. F1; a Sir John Umfrevile is mentioned in l. 34, but he is not present in the scene as we now have it, though possibly Shakespeare included him in an earlier draft.(see Shaaber, New Variorum)*

162 s.p. **Mor.]** *Daniel conj.;* Bard. *Q;* L. Bar. *F1*

163 **The]** *Daniel conj.; Mour.* The *Q; Mor.* The *F1*

164 **Lean on]** *F3 (after F1* Leane-on); Leaue on *Q*

164 **your]** *F1;* you *Q*

164 **which,]** *Theobald;* which *Q, F1*

164–5 **o'er . . . passion,]** *F1;* ore, . . . passion *Q*

166–79 **You . . . be?]** *F1*

170 **edge,]** *Capell;* edge *F1*

178 **doth]** *ed.;* hath *F1*

182 **'twas]** was *F1*

186 **forth,]** *Dyce;* forth *Q;* forth; *F1*

188 **dare]** do *F1*

189–209 **The gentle . . . him.]** *F1*

192 **corpse']** *Dyce;* Corpes *F1*

201–2 **religion. . . . thoughts,]** *Rowe (subs.);* Religion, . . . Thoughts: *F1*
208 **Bullingbrook]** *ed.;* Bullingbrooke *F1 (throughout)*
215 **and]** nor *F1*

I.ii

I.ii] *Steevens;* Scena Tertia. *F1*
Location: *Pope*
o.s.d. **Sir . . . with]** Falstaffe, and *F1*
o.s.d. **following behind]** *ed. (suggested by Q* Enter sir Iohn alone)
1 s.p. **Fal.]** *F1;* Iohn *Q (or* sir Iohn *through l. 66)*
7 **foolish-compounded clay, man,]** *Pope (subs.);* foolish compounded clay-man *Q, F1*
14 **judgment.]** *F1;* iudgement *Q*
16 **heels.]** *F1;* heels *Q*
17 **inset]** *Cambridge;* in-set *Q;* sette *F1*
19 **jewel—]** *Dyce;* iewell, *Q;* Iewell. *F1*
20 **fledge.]** *Vaughan conj. (after Rowe);* fledge, *Q;* fledg'd, *F1*
22 **of]** *Collier conj.;* off *Q;* on *F1*
22 **and]** *om. F1*
23 **God]** Heauen *F1*
24 **'tis]** it is *F1 (F1, as in some other plays, expands contracted forms with considerable frequency, e.g.* he'll *(l. 26),* he's *(l. 28),* Is't *(II.i.3),* to't *(II.i.4),* 'twere *(II.i.148),* there's *(II.i.148), etc.; this type of variant, except in special cases, is not recorded hereafter)*
29 **Dommelton]** Dombledon *F1*
30 **and my]** and *F1*
31 s.p. **Page.]** *F1;* Boy *Q (throughout scene)*
32 **Bardolph]** *F4;* Bardolfe *Q (throughout), F1 (F1 sometimes uses* Bardolph)
34 **Pray God]** may *F1*
36 **rascally . . . knave]** *F1* (Rascally-yea-forsooth-knaue); rascall: yea forsooth knaue *Q;* rascal! yea forsooth—knave! *ed. conj.*
36 **gentleman]** *F1;* gentle man *Q*
38 **smoothy-pates]** smooth-pates *F1*
43 **'a]** hee *F1 (a typical F1 sophistication; not hereafter recorded)*
44 **a]** *om. F1*
45 **Well,]** *F1;* well *Q*
48–9 **Where's Bardolph?]** *placed as in F1; after it; l. 47, Q*
50 **into]** *F1;* in *Q*
53 **and]** If *F1 (a typical F1 sophistication; not hereafter recorded)*
53 **but]** *om. F1*
54 s.d. **and Servant]** *F1*
55 **nobleman]** *F1;* noble man *Q*
58 s.p. **Ch. Just.]** *F1;* Iustice *Q (or* Iust. *through l. 163)*
72 **begging]** beg *F1*
74 **need]** want *F1*
80 s.p. **Fal.]** *F1;* Iohn *Q (through l. 87)*
80–1 **man? Setting]** *F1;* man, setting *Q*
87 **me so?]** *F1;* me, so *Q*
88 **me? If]** *F1;* me, if *Q*
90 **hunt counter]** Hunt-counter *F1*
93 **God]** *om. F1*
94 **of]** of the *F1*
96 **advice.]** *F3;* aduise, *Q;* aduise. *F1*
97 **have]** hath *F1*
98 **an ague]** age *F1*
99 **in you]** *om. F1*
101 **for]** *om. F1*
103 s.p. **Fal.]** *F1;* sir Iohn *Q*
103 **And't]** If it *F1*
103 **lordship]** *F1;* lorship *Q*
109 **God]** heauen *F1*
109 **you]** *om. F1*
111 **as . . . is]** *Neilson;* as I take it? is *Q;* is (as I take it) *F1*
112 **and't . . . of]** a *F1*
113 **in]** of *F1*
120 s.p. **Fal.]** *F1;* Old. *Q (i.e.* Oldcastle, *Falstaff's original name)*
124–5 **do become]** be *F1*
135 **land-service]** *hyphen, F1*
138 **himself]** him *F1*
140 **are]** is *F1*
141 **is]** *om. F1*
143 **waist]** *Hanmer;* waste *Q*
143 **slenderer]** *F1;* slender *Q*
152 **lord?]** *F1;* lord. *Q*
155 **smell]** to smell *F1*
156 **What,]** *F1;* What *Q*
160 **in]** on *F1*
164 **ill]** euill *F1*
168 **tell.]** *F1;* tell, *Q*
169 **costermongers']** *Theobald;* costar-mongers *Q;* Costor-mongers *F1*
169 **times]** *om. F1*
169 **berrord]** *ed. (cf.* Much Ado, *II.i.40);* Berod *Q;* Beare-heard *F1*
170 **and]** and hath *F1*
172 **this]** *F1;* his *Q*
173 **them, are]** *F1;* the one *Q*
174 **do]** *om. F1*
178 s.p. **Ch. Just.]** *F1* (Iust.); Lo. *Q (or* Lord. *throughout rest of scene)*
183 **your chin double,]** *om. F1*
185 **yet]** *om. F1*
187 s.p. **Fal.]** *F1;* Iohn *Q (throughout rest of scene)*
187–8 **about . . . afternoon,]** *om. F1*
194 **him! For]** *F1 (subs.);* him for *Q*
194 **the year]** th' eare *F1*
197 s.d. **aside]** *Wilson*
199, 201 **God]** heauen *and* Heauen *F1*
203 **you.]** you and Prince Harry, *F1*
206 **Yea]** Yes *F1 (a typical F1 sophistication; not hereafter recorded)*
208–9 **by the Lord]** if *F1*
211 **a]** my *F1*
211 **bottle,]** *F1;* bottle. *Q*
211 **I would]** would *F1*
214–20 **but . . . motion.]** *om. F1*
221 **God]** heauen *F1*
227 s.d. **Exeunt . . . Servant.]** *Capell (subs.);* Exit. *F2*
228 **three-man]** *hyphen, F1*
232 **curses. Boy!]** *F1 (subs.);* curses, boy. *Q*
242 **of]** on *F1*
243 s.d. **Exit Page.]** *Capell*
248 s.d. **Exit.]** *Capell;* Exeunt *F1*

I.iii

I.iii] *Steevens;* Scena Quarta. *F1*
Location: *Pope, Theobald*
o.s.d. **Hastings]** *F1;* Hastings, Fauconbridge *Q (the appearance of Fauconbridge here follows Holinshed, but he has nothing to say in the scene and never appears again)*
o.s.d. **Lord]** *F1*
1 s.p. **Arch.]** *F1;* Bishop *Q (or* Bish. *throughout scene)*
1 **cause and known]** causes and kno *F1*
5 s.p. **Mowb.]** *F1;* Marsh. *Q*
18 **Yea]** I *F1 (a typical F1 sophistication; not hereafter recorded)*
21–4 **Till . . . admitted.]** *F1*
26 **cause]** case *F1*
27 **lin'd]** *F1;* lined *Q*
28 **and]** on *F1*
29 **in]** with *F1*
36–55 **Yes . . . else]** *F1*
36–7 **war— . . . foot—]** *Knight (subs.);* warre, / Indeed the instant action: a cause on foot, *F1 (a difficult passage for which many readings have been offered)*
38 **hope,]** *Rowe;* hope: *F1*
55 **opposite;]** *Theobald (subs.);* Opposite? *F1*
56 **We]** *F1;* Bard. We *Q*
58 **one]** *F1;* on *Q*
58 **an]** a *F1*
59 **thorough]** through *F1*
60 **part-created]** *hyphen, F1*
66 **so a]** *Kittredge (after Collier conj.);* so, *Q;* a *F1*
71 **Are]** *F1;* And *Q*
72 **Glendower;]** *F1* (Glendower:); Glendower *Q*
78 **to]** *om. F1*
78–80 **If . . . that.]** *as verse, F1; as prose, Q*
79 **To]** *Capell (who thus adopts the F1 arrangement as verse, but the Q word order); F1 arranges ll. 79–80 as follows:* He leaues his backe vnarm'd, the French, and Welch / Baying him at the heeles: neuer feare that.
80 **heels.]** *F1* (heeles:); heeles, *Q*
84 **against]** 'gainst *F1*
85–108 **Arch. Let . . . worst.]** *F1*
98 **glutton bosom]** *Theobald;* glutton-bosome *F1*
108 **Past . . . worst.]** *in italics, with gnomic quotes, F1*
109 s.p. **Mowb.]** *F1;* Bish. *Q*
110 s.d. **Exeunt.]** *Theobald;* ex. *Q*

II.i

II.i] *F1*
Location: *Pope, Theobald*
o.s.d. **and . . . Snare]** *from Q and F1:* and an Officer or two. *Q;* with two Officers, Fang, and Snare. *F1*
o.s.d. **Snare lagging behind]** *ed. (after Capell)*
1 **Fang]** *F1;* Phang *Q (also in s.pp. throughout scene)*
5 **Sirrah!]** *Shaaber;* Sirra, *Q;* Sirrah, *F1*
6 **O Lord, ay]** *Theobald;* O Lord I *Q;* I, I *F1*
11 **for]** *om. F1*
14 **most . . . 'A]** *Kittredge;* most beastly in good faith, a *Q;* and that most beastly: he *F1*
15 **does]** doth *F1 (common in F1; not hereafter recorded)*
16 **out.]** *F1;* out, *Q*
22 **vice—]** *F1 (dash, Capell);* view. *Q*
23 **by]** with *F1*
23 **going . . . you]** going: I warrant *F1*
24 **score.]** *F1;* score, *Q*
26 **continuantly]** *F1;* continually *Q*
28–9 **Lumbert street]** Lombardstreet *F1*
29 **silk-man]** *Capell;* silk man *Q;* Silkman *F1*
29 **pray you]** pra'ye *F1*
34–5 **and fubb'd off, from]** from *F1*
38 s.d. **Enter . . . Page.]** *placed as F1 s.d.* (Enter Falstaffe and Bardolfe.); *after l. 42, Q*
39 **knave]** *om. F1*
45 **I]** Sir Iohn, I *F1*
48–9 **in the channel]** there *F1*
50, 52 **Ah]** *Cambridge;* a *Q;* O *F1*
53 **man-queller . . . woman-queller]** *hyphens, F1*
55 s.p. **Officers.]** *ed.;* Offic. *Q;* Fang. *F1*
56 **or two]** *om. F1*
56–7 s.d. **The . . . her.]** *Wilson*
57–8 **Thou . . . ta?]** Thou wilt not? thou wilt not? *F1*
59 s.p. **Page.]** *F1;* Boy. *Q*
60 **tickle]** tucke *F1*
61 s.p. **Ch. Just.]** *Rowe (after F1* Iust. *and* Ch. Iust.); Lord *Q (or* Lo. *throughout scene)*
61 **What is]** What's *F1*
68 **thou]** *om. F1*
73 **all]** all: all *F1*
80 **What]** Fy, what a *F1*
85 **Marry]** *F1;* Mary *Q*
87 **parcel-gilt]** *hyphen, F4*
88 **upon]** on *F1*
89 **Wheeson]** Whitson *F1*
90 **liking his father]** lik'ning him *F1*
98 **thou not]** not thou *F1*
99–100 **so familiarity]** familiar *F1*
103 **thou]** *F1;* thou *Q*
104 **mad]** *F1;* made *Q*
114–6 **You . . . person.]** I know you ha' practis'd vpon the easie-yeelding spirit of this woman. *F1*
115 **easy-yielding]** *hyphen, F1*
119 **with]** *om. F1*
124 **make]** *om. F1*
125 **my humble]** your humble *F1*
126 **do]** *om. F1*
132 s.d. **Master Gower]** *F1; s.d. after l. 133, Q; placed as in F1*
134 **Harry]** Henrie *F1*
137 **Faith]** Nay *F1*
138 **gentleman!]** *ed.;* gentleman, *Q;* Gentleman. *F1*
145 **German]** *F1;* Iarman *Q*
146 **bed-hangers]** Bed-hangings *F1*
147 **tapestries]** *F1;* tapestrie *Q*
147 **ten pound]** *F1;* x.*l.* *Q*
150 **the]** thy *F1*
151 **dost . . . Come,]** *om. F1*

154 **nobles.]** *Johnson (subs.)*; nobles, *Q, F1*
154 **I' faith, I am]** I *F1*
154–5 **so . . . me law]** in good earnest la *F1*
158 **though]** although *F1*
159–60 **supper. . . . all together?]** *F1 (subs., reading* altogether); supper, . . . al together. *Q*
161 **s.d. To Bardolph.]** *Capell*
165 **s.d. Exeunt . . . Bardolph.]** *ed. (after Capell;* Exeunt *Pope)*; exit hostesse and sergeant. *Q; om. F1*
166 **better]** bitter *F1*
167 **lord]** good Lord *F1*
168 **to-night]** last night *F1*
169, 173 **s.pp. Gow.]** *Rowe;* Mess. *Q, F1*
169 **Basingstoke]** *F1;* Billingsgate *Q*
186–7 **Sir . . . go.]** *as prose, F1; as verse, Q*
187 **counties]** Countries *F1*
195 **s.d. Exeunt.]** *F1*

II.ii

II.ii] *F1*
Location: *Wilson*
o.s.d. **Enter . . . other.]** *as Rowe;* Enter the Prince, Poynes, sir Iohn Russel, with other. *Q (Russell appears nowhere else in the play and has no lines in this scene; presumably the same as* Rossill *in* 1 Henry IV, *I.ii.162 [see Textual Notes]);* Enter Prince Henry, Pointz, Bardolfe, and Page. *F1 (an example of a so-called "massed entry"; Bardolph and Page actually enter at l. 69)*
1 **Before God]** Trust me *F1*
4 **Faith, it does]** It doth *F1*
10 **by my]** in *F1*
15 **viz.]** *F1;* with *Q*
16 **once]** ones *F1*
18 **another]** one other *F1*
20 **keepest]** kept'st *F1*
20 **there;]** *Theobald;* there, *Q, F1*
21 **the low]** thy Low *F1*
22 **made . . . to]** *F1*
23–7 **And . . . strengthen'd.]** *om. F1*
23 **bawl]** *Pope;* bal *Q*
25 **fault,]** *Pope;* fault *Q*
30 **being]** lying *F1*
31 **at this time]** *om. F1*
33 **faith]** *om. F1*
39 **Marry]** *Collier;* Mary *Q;* Why *F1*
45 **By this hand]** *om. F1*
47 **persistency.]** *F1;* persistancie, *Q*
65 **By this light]** Nay *F1*
65 **spoke on]** spoken of *F1*
66 **ears.]** *F1* (eares:); eares *Q*
69 **By the mass]** Looke, looke *F1*
69 **s.d. and Boy]** *om. F1*
71 **look]** see *F1*
73 **God]** *om. F1*
75 **virtuous]** pernitious *F1*
79, 87, etc. **s.pp. Page.]** *F1;* Boy *Q*
79 **'A calls]** He call'd *F1*
79 **e'en now]** *Cambridge;* enow *Q;* euen now *F1*
82 **petticoat]** new Petticoat *F1*
83 **so]** *om. F1*
84 **Has]** Hath *F1 (common in F1; not hereafter recorded)*
85 **rabbit]** *F1;* rabble *Q*
89, 104 **Marry]** *F1;* Mary *Q*
89 **Althaea]** *F1;* Althear *Q*
94 **blossom]** good Blossome *F1*
96 **him]** him be *F1*
97 **have wrong]** be wrong'd *F1*
99 **lord]** good Lord *F1*
107 **how]** *om. F1*
108 **s.d. Showing . . . Poins.]** *Collier MS (subs.)*
109 **s.d. Reads the superscription.]** *ed. (after Wilson);* Letter. *F1*
114 **that?" says he,]** *F4* (that? (says he . . .); that (saies he) *Q, F1*
115 **conceive. The]** *Rowe (subs., after F4* conceiue) the); conceiue the *Q;* conceiue? the *F1*
115 **borrower's]** *Warburton conj.;* borowed *Q;* borrowed *F1*
117 **or]** but *F1*
118 **But]** But to *F1*
124 **He sure]** Sure he *F1*
126 **s.p. Prince.]** *Theobald; continued to Poins, Q, F1*
133 **familiars]** *F1;* family *Q*
134 **sisters]** Sister *F1*
135 **s.p. Poins.]** *speech continued to Prince, F1*
140 **God . . . wench]** May the Wench haue *F1*
157 **heckfers]** *ed.;* Heicfors *Q;* Heyfors *F1*
161 **come to]** in *F1*
165–6 **s.d. Exeunt . . . Page.]** *Capell*
171 **leathern]** Leather *F1*
172 **as]** like *F1*
173 **bull?]** *F1;* bul, *Q*
173 **descension]** declension *F1*
174 **prince]** *F1;* pince *Q*
174 **prentice?]** *Theobald;* prentise, *Q, F1*
175 **every]** *F1;* enery *Q*

II.iii

II.iii] *F1*
Location: *Capell (subs., after Theobald)*
2 **even]** an euen *F1*
5, 50 **s.pp. Lady N.]** *Rowe;* Wife *Q, F1*
5 **more;]** *F4;* more, *Q, F1*
9, 53 **s.pp. Lady P.]** *Rowe;* Kate *Q;* La. *and* Lady. *F1*
9 **God's]** heauens *F1*
10 **that]** when *F1*
11 **endear'd]** *F1;* endeere *Q*
12 **heart's dear Harry]** heart-deere-Harry *F1*
17 **the . . . heaven]** may heauenly glory *F1*
23–45 **He . . . grave.]** *F1*
32 **wondrous him!]** *Rowe;* wondrous! him, *F1*
64 **still-stand]** *hyphen, F1*

II.iv

II.iv] *F1*
Location: *Theobald (after Pope)*
o.s.d. **Francis . . . Drawer]** *Ridley (subs., after s.pp. in Q); F1 s.d. reads:* Enter two Drawers.
1, 10 **s.pp. Fran.]** 1. Drawer. *F1*
1 **the devil]** *om. F1*
1–2 **there? apple-johns]** *F1;* there apple / Iohns *Q*
4 **s.p. 2. Draw.]** *F1;* Draw. *Q*
4 **Mass]** *Pope;* Mas *Q; om. F1*
12 **hear]** haue *F1*
12 **s.d. Enter . . . Drawer.]** *Alexander (after Ridley conj. and Q s.d.* Enter Will., *following l. 18); om. F1*
13 **s.p. 3. Draw.]** *Alexander (after Ridley conj.);* Dra. *Q*
13–4 **Dispatch . . . straight.]** *om. F1*
15 **s.p. Fran.]** 2. Draw. *F1*
19 **s.p. 3. Draw.]** *Alexander;* Dra. *Q;* 1. Draw. *F1*
19 **By the mass]** *Malone;* By the mas *Q;* Then *F1*
21 **s.p. 2. Draw].** *F1;* Francis *Q*
21 **s.d. with Third Drawer]** *Alexander*
22 **s.p. Host.]** *F1;* Quickly *Q*
22 **I' faith]** *om. F1*
22 **sweet heart]** Sweet-heart *F1*
25–6 **in . . . law]** *om. F1*
26 **i' faith]** *om. F1*
28 **one]** wee *F1*
30, 39, 42 **s.pp. Doll.]** *F1;* Tere. *Q*
31 **that's]** that was *F1*
32 **Lo]** Looke *F1*
33, 34 **s.dd. Singing.]** *Capell (subs.)*
33, 34–5] *given as quotations from F1 italics*
34 **s.d. Exit Francis.]** *Capell (subs.)*
36 **good faith]** good-sooth *F1*
39 **A . . . you,]** *om. F1*
42 **make,]** make them, *F1*
44–5 **help to make]** make *F1*
47 **Yea, joy]** I marry *F1*
48 **"Your . . . ouches."]** *quotes, Capell*
48 **ouches.]** *F1* (Owches:); ouches *Q*
49 **know;]** *Rowe;* know *Q;* know, *F1*
52 **bravely—]** *Rowe;* brauely. *Q, F1*
53–4 **Hang . . . yourself!]** *om. F1*
55 **By my troth]** Why *F1*
57 **i' good truth]** in good troth *F1*
62 **s.p. Doll.]** *F1;* Dorothy *Q (but catchword* Doll.)
68 **s.d. Francis]** *Wilson*
69 **s.p. Fran.]** *Wilson;* Dra. *Q;* Drawer. *F1*
73–4 **No . . . faith]** *om. F1*
74 **among]** amongst *F1*
74 **neighbors;]** *Capell;* neighbours, *Q, F1*
80 **ye]** you *F1*
83 **ne'er]** *Cambridge;* nere *Q;* neuer *F1 (a typical F1 sophistication; not hereafter recorded)*
83 **and]** *om. F1*
84 **swagger, 'a]** *Maxwell (in MLR);* swaggrer *Q;* Swaggerer *F1*
85 **debuty, t' other]** Deputie, the other *F1*
86 **Wed'sday]** Wednesday *F1*
87 **i' good faith— "Neighbor]** *Kittredge;* I good faith neighbor *Q;* Neighbour *F1*
90 **said]** sayth *F1*
97, 102, 103, 140 **cheater]** *F1;* cheter *Q*
97–8 **i' faith]** hee *F1*
101 **s.d. Exit Francis.]** *Wilson (after Capell)*
104 **by my troth]** *om. F1*
107 **s.p. Doll.]** *F1;* Teresh. *Q*
109 **s.d. Bardolph]** *F1*
109 **s.d. and Boy]** *Kittredge;* Bardolfes boy *Q;* his Boy *F1*
110 **God save]** 'Saue *F1*
116 **pistol-proof, sir;]** *Capell;* pistoll proofe: sir, *Q;* Pistoll-proofe (Sir) *F1*
116 **not]** *om. F1*
123, 128, 140 **s.pp. Doll.]** *F1;* Doro. *Q*
131 **bottle-ale . . . basket-hilt]** *hyphens, F1*
132 **God's light]** what *F1*
134 **God . . . but]** *om. F1*
136–7 **Fal. No . . . Pistol.]** *om. F1*
140 **Captain?]** *F1;* Captain, *Q*
140 **abominable]** *F3;* abhominable *Q, F1*
147 **God's light]** *om. F1*
148–50 **as odious . . . sorted;]** Captaine odious: *F1*
154 **of]** on *F1*
155 **s.p. Page.]** *F1;* Boy *Q*
156 **damned]** *Rowe;* damnd *Q;* damn'd *F1*
157 **by this hand]** *om. F1*
157 **with]** where *F1*
159 **faitors]** *Capell;* faters *Q;* Fates *F1*
160 **s.d. Draws his sword.]** *Wilson (after Capell)*
162 **i' faith]** *om. F1*
163–9 **These . . . toys?]** *as verse, Pope; as prose, Q, F1*
165 **mile]** miles *F1*
167 **Troiant]** Troian *F1*
174 **Die]** *F1*
174 **dogs!]** *Dyce;* dogges *Q;* Dogges; *F1*
176 **A']** On *F1 (a typical F1 sophistication; not hereafter recorded)*
178 **For God's sake]** I pray *F1*
179–84 **Then . . . things?]** *as verse, Capell (after Pope); as prose, Q, F1*
180 **give 's]** *Capell;* giues *Q;* giue me *F1*
183 **sweet heart]** Sweet-heart *F1*
183 **s.d. Laying . . . sword.]** *Johnson*
184 **no things]** nothing *F1*
188 **For God's sake]** *om. F1*
192 **Quoit]** *F1;* Quaite *Q*
196–9 **What . . . say!]** *as verse, Capell (after Johnson); as prose, Q*
196 **What?]** *F1;* What *Q*
196 **s.d. Snatching . . . sword.]** *Johnson (after l. 199); placed as in Capell*
198 **grievous]** *F1;* grieuons *Q*
199 **Atropos]** *F1;* Atropose *Q*
200 **goodly]** good *F1*
202 **pray thee . . . pray thee]** prethee . . . prethee *F1*
203 **s.d. Drawing . . . out.]** *Rowe*
205 **afore]** before *F1*
205–6 **frights. So!]** *F1 (subs.);* frights, so, *Q*
207 **s.d. Exeunt . . . Bardolph.]** *Capell*
208 **pray thee]** prethee *F1*
209 **valiant]** *F1;* vliaunt *Q*
211 **s.d. Enter Bardolph.]** *Capell*
212 **a']** of *F1 (a typical F1 sophistication; not hereafter recorded)*
213 **sir.]** *F1* (Sir:); sir, *Q*
215 **rascal!]** *Capell;* rascall *Q, F1*
216, 218, 221 **Ah]** *F1;* A *Q*
218 **i' faith]** *om. F1*

225 **s.d. Enter Music.]** *placed as in F1; after l. 226, Q*
226 **s.p. Page.]** *F1;* Boy *Q*
230 **I' faith]** *om. F1*
230 **church.]** *F1 (subs.);* church *Q*
233 **s.d. behind]** *Dyce*
233 **s.d. disguised]** *F1*
238 **'a']** *Kittredge;* a *Q;* haue *F1*
247 **wild-mare]** *hyphen, F1*
248 **boots]** Boot *F1*
253 **a]** an *F1*
254 **scales]** the Scales *F1*
258 **whe'er]** *Neilson;* where *Q;* if *F1*
259 **pole]** *ed.;* poule *Q;* Poll *F1*
266 **master's]** *F1;* master, *Q*
267 **counsel-keeper]** *hyphen, F1*
269 **By my troth]** Nay truely *F1*
274 **wilt]** wilt thou *F1*
275 **shalt]** thou shalt *F1*
276 **song! Come]** *Humphreys;* song, come *Q;* Song, come: *F1*
277, 278 **Thou't]** Thou wilt *F1*
278 **By my troth]** *om. F1*
280 **return—]** *Rowe;* returne, *Q;* returne: *F1*
280 **a' th']** the *F1*
282 **s.d. Coming forward.]** *Capell*
284 **Poins]** Poines, *F1*
291 **Grace]** good Grace *F1*
291–2 **By my troth]** *om. F1*
292 **the Lord]** Heauen *F1*
293 **O Jesu]** what *F1*
295 **light]** *F1;* light, *Q*
301 **even]** *F1*
303 **God's blessing of]** 'Blessing on *F1*
313 **Hal]** *F3;* Hall *Q (throughout rest of scene);* Hall *F1 (Hal throughout rest of scene)*
315 **bread-chipper]** Bread-chopper *F1*
320 **s.d. turns . . . Prince]** *Sisson*
321 **thee]** him *F1*
324 **faith]** *om. F1*
328 **thy]** the *F1*
336 **blinds]** outbids *F1*
337 **women]** *F1;* weomen *Q*
343 **Marry]** *F1;* mary *Q*
346 **vict'lers]** *Kittredge;* vitlors *Q;* Victuallers *F1*
353 **s.d. Enter Peto.]** *F1*
355 **Westminster]** *Qa, F1;* Weminster *Qb*
366 **s.d. Exeunt . . . Bardolph.]** *Capell;* Exeunt Prince and Poynes. *Q;* Exit. *F1*
369 **s.d. Knocking within.]** *Dyce (after Capell)*
369 **s.d. Enter Bardolph.]** *Capell*
373 **s.d. To the Page.]** *Capell*
381 **s.d. Exit . . . Page.]** *Capell (subs.; Page from Humphreys);* exit. *Qb, F1; om. Qa*
385, 387 **s.dd. Within.]** *Capell*
389 **Doll. Come.]** *Collier;* Doll, come, *Q;* Dol. *F1*
389–91 **Come . . . Doll?]** *om. F1*
390 **s.d. To Bardolph.]** *Alexander (after Collier)*
390 **Yea!]** *Qb;* yea? *Qa*

III.i

III.i] *F1*
This scene does not appear in Qa
Location: *Dyce, Theobald*
o.s.d. followed . . . Page] *ed. (from F1 with a* Page*)*
1 **Warwick;]** *F1 (subs.);* War. *Qb*
3 **s.d. Exit Page.]** *Rowe;* Exit. *F1*
11 **hush'd . . . night-flies]** huisht with bussing Night, flyes *F1*
14 **sound]** sounds *F1*
18 **mast]** *F1;* masse *Qb*
22 **billows]** *F1;* pillowes *Qb*
24 **deafing clamor]** deaff'ning Clamors *F1*
26 **then]** *ed.;* them *Qb;* thy *F1*
27 **sea-boy]** *F1;* season *Qb*
31 **s.d. and . . . Blunt]** *om. F1 (Blunt has no lines in the scene)*
36 **letters]** *F1;* letter *Qb*
43 **advice]** *F1;* aduise *Qb*
43 **medicine.]** *F1 (subs.);* medicine, *Qb*
45 **God]** Heauen *F1*
46 **times]** *F1;* times, *Qb*
51 **chance's mocks]** *Wilson;* chances mockes, *Qb;* Chances mocks *F1*
53–6 **O, if . . . die.]** *om. F1*
59 **year]** yeeres *F1*
66 **s.d. To Warwick.]** *Rowe*
66 **Nevil]** *F1;* Neuel *Q*
67 **eye brimful]** *F1 (subs.);* eye-brimme full *Qb*
71 **Bullingbrook]** *F1* (Bullingbrooke); Bolingbrooke *Qb*
72 **God]** Heauen *F1*
73 **bow'd]** *F1;* bowed *Qb*
78 **Foretelling]** *F1;* Fortelling *Qb*
81 **natures]** nature *F1*
84 **who]** which *F1*
85 **beginning]** beginnings *F1*
97 **voice]** *F4;* voice, *Qb, F1*
99 **soul]** Life *F1*
101 **prize]** *F1;* prise *Qb*

III.ii

III.ii] *F1*
Location: *Cambridge (after Theobald)*
o.s.d meeting] *Capell*
o.s.d. Mouldy . . . Bullcalf] *F1*
o.s.d. and Servants behind] *Malone (after Capell)*
1 **on]** *Qa, F1;* on sir *Qb*
8 **woosel]** Ouzell *F1*
9 **no]** nay *F1*
17 **By the mass]** *om. F1*
20 **Barnes]** Bare *F1*
22 **swingebucklers]** *F1 (subs.);* swinge bucklers *Q*
23 **robas]** *F1;* robes *Q*
27 **This . . . cousin,]** *Qa, F1;* Coosin, this sir Iohn *Qb*
29 **see]** saw *F1*
30 **Scoggin's]** Scoggan's *F1*
33 **Jesu, Jesu]** Oh *F1*
34 **my]** mine *F1*
37 **as . . . saith,]** *om. F1*
38 **Stamford]** *F1;* Samforth *Q*
39 **By my troth]** Truly Cousin *F1*
43 **Jesu, Jesu, dead!]** Dead? See, see: *F1*
47 **a fourteen]** at foureteene *F1*
54 **s.d. one with him]** his Boy *F1*
55 **s.p. Shal.]** *F1;* Bardolfe. *Qa (u); om. Qa (c), Qb*
59 **good]** *om. Qb*
61 **by heaven]** *om. F1*
63 **well, sir.]** *Capell (subs.);* wel, sir, *Q;* well: (Sir) *F1*
66 **accommodated]** *F1;* accommodate *Q*
68 **in faith]** *om. F1*
70–1 **ever were]** euery where *F1*
73 **Pardon]** Pardon me *Qb*
74 **day]** good day *Qb*
76–7 **by heaven]** *om. F1*
78 **is]** is, *Qb, F1*
79 **whereby]** *Qb, F1;* whereby, *Qa*
79 **'a may be]** he *F1*
80 **s.d. Falstaff]** sir Iohn Falstaffe *Qb*
82 **good]** *om. F1*
83 **By my troth]** Trust me *F1*
83 **like]** looke *F1*
86 **Surecard]** *F1;* Soccard *Q*
87, 89 **Silence]** *F1;* Scilens *Qa;* Silens *Qb*
93 **dozen]** dozen of *F1*
97 **Let . . . see.]** *repeated only twice, Qb*
98 **so, so, so;]** *Cambridge (subs.);* so (so, so) *Q; om. F1*
98, 173, 248 **marry]** *F1;* mary *Q*
99 **do so . . . do so]** *Qb, F1;* do, so . . . do, so *Qa*
101 **Here, and't]** *Qa;* Here and it *Qb;* Here, and it *F1*
107 **i' faith]** *om. F1*
108–9 **in faith]** *om. F1*
110 **Fal. Prick him.]** *F1;* Iohn prickes him. *Q (in italics, as s.d., after l. 109)*
116 **go. Mouldy,]** *F1;* go Mouldy *Q*
120 **see:]** *F1;* see *Q*
130 **much]** not *F1*
134 **s.d. aside]** *Wilson*
134 **shadows]** *Ridley;* shadowes, *Q;* shadowes to *F1*
134 **fill]** to fill *F1*
142 **him]** him downe *F1*
143 **for 's]** *ed.;* for *Q;* for his *F1*
153 **he'd 'a']** *Kittredge;* hee'd a *Q;* he would haue *F1*
169 **sir]** *om. F1*
171 **next]** the next *F1*
175 **'Fore God]** Trust me *F1*
175 **prick]** pricke me *F1*
177, 179 **O Lord]** Oh *F1*
188 **Here]** There *F1*
192 **by my]** in good *F1*
195 **Windmill]** *F1* (Winde-mill); windmil *Q*
196 **Master]** good Master *F1*
196–7 **no . . . that.]** *F1*
204 **By the mass]** *om. F1*
204 **could]** *F1;* conld *Q*
210 **year]** yeeres *F1*
211 **Silence]** *F1;* Scilens *Q*
216 **That . . . have,]** *repeated only twice, F1*
218 **Hem, boys]** *Theobald;* Hemboies *Q;* Hem-Boyes *F1*
219 **Jesus]** Oh *F1*
219 **s.d. Falstaff . . . Justices]** *Capell*
234 **By my troth]** *om. F1*
235 **God]** *om. F1*
236 **dest'ny, so;]** *F1 (subs.);* destny: so, *Q*
237 **serve 's]** serue his *F1*
239 **th' art]** thou art *F1 (a typical F1 sophistication; not hereafter recorded)*
240 **Faith, I'll]** Nay, I will *F1*
243 **s.d. To Falstaff.]** *Craig*
243 **s.d. Aside.]** *Capell*
249 **Shadow]** *F1;* Sadow *Q*
260 **Here's]** Where's *F1*
264–5 **half-fac'd]** *hyphen, F1*
272 **traverse]** *F1;* trauers *Q*
272 **thas, thas, thas]** thus, thus, thus *F1*
275 **chopp'd, bald]** *F1 (subs.);* chopt Ballde, *Q*
276 **i' faith]** *om. F1*
279 **Mile-end Green]** *Warburton;* Mile-endgreene *Q;* Mile-end-Greene *F1*
287 **woll]** *ed.;* wooll *Q;* will *F1*
288 **God keep you]** Farewell *F1*
288 **Silence]** *F1;* Scilens *Q*
292–3 **the Lord . . . God . . . God]** Heauen . . . and . . . and *F1*
293 **peace! At your]** *Collier;* peace at your *Q;* Peace. As you *F1*
294 **our]** my *F1*
295 **ye]** you *F1*
296 **'Fore God]** *om. F1*
296 **would you would.]** I would you would, Master Shallow. *F1*
297–8 **God keep you]** Fare you well *F1*
299–300 **s.d. Exeunt Justices.]** *Johnson (subs.);* exit *Q (apparently referring to Falstaff), F1 (after l. 298)*
300 **On]** *F1; Shal.* On *Q (Q thus gives ll. 300–32 to Shallow)*
300–1 **s.d. Exeunt . . . etc.]** *Capell*
303 **Lord, Lord]** *om. F1*
306 **Turnbull Street]** *Cambridge;* Turne-bull street *Q;* Turnball-street *F1*
307 **duer]** *F1;* dewer *Q*
313 **invisible]** *Rowe;* inuincible *Q, F1*
314–5 **yet . . . mandrake.]** *om. F1*
315 **ever]** *F1;* ouer *Q*
316–9 **and . . . good-nights.]** *om. F1*
326 **eel-skin]** *Q (c), F1;* eele-shin *Q (u)*
328 **beefs]** Beeues *F1*
330 **dace]** *F1;* Dase *Q*
332 **him: let]** *Q (u);* him, till *Q (c);* him. Let *F1*
332 **s.d. Exit.]** *Capell;* Exeunt. *F1*

IV.i

IV.i] *F1*
Location: *Pope, Q*
o.s.d. Bardolph] *om. F1 (Lord Bardolph has no lines in the scene)*
o.s.d. Hastings] Hastings, Westmerland, Coleuile. *F1*
o.s.d. and others] *Capell*
o.s.d. within . . . Gaultree] *om. F1*
1 **s.p. Arch.]** *Capell;* Bish. *Q, F1 (or* Bishop *throughout this scene and the next)*
2 **Gaultree]** Gualtree *F1*
6 **in . . . affairs,]** *Pope;* (in . . . affaires) *Q, F1*

29–30 peace, . . . coming.] Dyce; peace, . . . comming? Q; peace: . . . comming? Fl
30 Then, my lord] om. Q (u)
35 beggary—] Fl (subs.); beggary. Q
36 appear'd] Pope; appeare Q, Fl
39 ugly] F3; owgly Q; ougly Fl
42 see] F4; Sea Q, Fl
46 peace,] Capell (subs.); peace. Q, Fl
54 end:] Fl; end Q
55–79 And . . . wrong.] Fl
80 days] Fl; daie's Q
88 denied?] Fl; denied Q
92] Following this line, Q (u) reads: And consecrate commotions bitter edge.; Q (c) and Fl om.
93] Following this line, Q (u) reads: To brother borne an houshold cruelty.; Q (c) and Fl om.
97 Mowb. Why] Fl; Mowbray why Q
101–37 O, my . . . King—] Fl
114 force] Theobald; forc'd, Fl
129 Herford] ed.; Hereford Fl
137 King—] Neilson; King. Fl
138 But] Fl; West. But Q
167–8 grievances: . . . redress'd,] Fl; grieuances, . . . redrest. Q
172–3 wills— . . . confin'd] Humphreys; willes, . . . confinde, Q, Fl
173 to] Fl
176 general.] Fl; Generall, Q
178 And] Thirlby conj.; At Q, Fl
178 God] Heauen Fl
180 s.d. Exit Westmerland.] placed as in Rowe; after it. l. 180, Q; om. Fl
183 not that;] Pope (subs., after F2); not, that Q, Fl
225 God's] heauen's Fl
225 set] om. Fl
226 Grace.—My lord] Johnson (after Theobald); grace (my lord) Q, Fl
226 s.d. They . . . John.] ed.

IV.ii

IV.ii] Capell
Location: ed. (after Ridley)
o.s.d. Enter . . . army.] placed as in Fl s.d. (Enter Prince Iohn.); after IV.i.224, Q
1 s.p. P. John.] Capell; Iohn Q, Fl
4 show'd] Fl; shewed Q
8 Than] Fl; That Q
8 talking] om. Fl
17 God] Heauen Fl
19 imagin'd] Rowe; imagine Q, Fl
19 God himself] Heauen it selfe Fl
24 Employ] Fl; Imply Q (possibly correct, either as a variant spelling of employ or as meaning "hint at")
25–6 name, . . . dishonorable?] Fl; name: . . . dishonorable Q
26 ta'en] taken Fl
27 God] Heauen Fl
28 his] Heauens Fl
37 shov'd] Fl; shoued Q
38 Hydra son] Hanmer; Hidra, sonne Q; Hydra-Sonne Fl
48 his] this Fl
50 s.p. P. John.] Capell; Prince Q (or Prin. throughout rest of scene); Iohn. Fl
51 after-times] hyphen, Fl
60 soul] Life Fl
60 shall.] Fl; shal, Q
67 s.p. P. John.] Fl (Iohn.); speech continued to the Archbishop, Q
69 s.p. Hast.] Fl; Prince Q
71 s.d. Exit Officer.] Capell; Exit. Fl
86 s.d. within] Capell
92 s.d. Exit Westmerland.] Rowe; Exit. Fl (after l. 94)
96 s.d. Exit Hastings.] Rowe; Exit. Fl
102 My lord] om. Fl
102 already] om. Fl
103 take their courses] tooke their course Fl
105 toward] towards Fl
105 sporting-place] hyphen, Pope
116 you rebels,] you (Rebels) Fl
117 and . . . yours.] Fl
121 God . . . hath] Heauen . . . haue Fl
122 these traitors] Fl; this traitour Q
123 yielder-up] hyphen, Dyce
123 s.d. Exeunt.] Fl

IV.iii

IV.iii] Capell
Location: ed. (after Wilson)
o.s.d. Excursions.] placed as in Malone (after Capell); follows Falstaff in Q; om. Fl (together with Alarum.)
o.s.d. and Colevile] Fl (Colleuile)
o.s.d. meeting] Capell
2 place?] place, I pray? Fl
6–7 be still] still be Fl
23 s.d. Blunt] Cambridge
24, 43 s.pp. P. John.] Capell; Iohn Q, Fl
24 further] farther Fl
25 s.d. Exit Westmerland.] Rowe
25 s.d. Retrait.] placed by ed.; after s.d. at l. 23 in Q (see l. 72 in the text); om. Fl
41–2 "There, cousin,] ed.; there cosin, Q (catchword their); om. Fl
47 by the Lord] I sweare Fl
48 else] om. Fl
56 etc. s.pp. P. John.] Capell; Prince Q; Iohn. Fl
69 gratis] om. Fl
71 Now] om. Fl
75 s.d. Exeunt . . . Colevile.] Cambridge; Exit with Colleuile. Fl
83 lord] Lord, 'pray Fl
84–5 Fare . . . deserve.] as verse, Fl; as prose, Q
85 s.d. Exeunt . . . Falstaff.] Capell; Exit. Fl
86 had] had but Fl
90 none] any Fl
92 fish-meals] hyphen, Fl
107 parts'] Wilson; partes Q, Fl
107 illumineth] illuminateth Fl
112 with this] with his Fl
113 sherris.] Fl; sherris, Q
115 hoard] Fl; whoord Q
123 humane] om. Fl
125 s.d. Enter Bardolph.] placed as in Fl; after l. 126, Q
132 s.d. Exeunt.] Fl

IV.iv

IV.iv] Capell; Scena Secunda. Fl
Location: Cambridge (after Theobald)
o.s.d. carried . . . chair] Sisson
o.s.d. Warwick] Fl; Warwike, Kent Q (Kent appears in Holinshed, but nowhere in the play except here)
o.s.d. and others] Capell
1 God] Heauen Fl
12–3 Humphrey . . . brother?] as verse, Pope; as prose, Q, Fl
14, 50 Windsor] Fl; Winsor Q
21 Thomas.] Fl; Thomas, Q
32 meting] ed.; meeting Q; melting Fl
33 notwithstanding,] Fl; notwithstanding Q
39 time] Line, Fl
45–6 Mingled . . . in)] Hanmer; (Mingled . . . in,) Q, Fl (subs.)
51, 53 s.pp. Clar.] Fl; Tho. Q
52 Canst . . . that?] Fl
69 wherein, . . . language,] Fl; wherein . . . language: Q
72 further] farther Fl
77 other] others Fl
78 past evils] Dering MS, F3; past-euils Q, Fl
80 s.d. Enter Westmerland.] placed as in Fl; after Westmerland? l. 80, Q
84 Bishop] Theobald; Bishop, Q
93 s.d. Enter Harcourt.] Fl; enter Harcor. Q (after l. 93)
94 heavens] Heauen Fl
99 shrieve] Sherife Fl
104 write] Fl; wet Q
104 terms] Letters Fl
106 poor,] Fl; poore Q
112, 121, 130 s.pp. Glou.] Dering MS, Fl; Hum. Q
117 out these pangs.] out: these pangs, Fl
120 and . . . out.] Fl
128 great-grandsire] hyphen, Dyce
132 Softly, pray.] Fl
132 s.d. The King . . . bed.] ed. (after Capell)

IV.v

IV.v] Cambridge
Location: ed.
1 s.p. King.] Cambridge; speech continued to the King without any break, Q, Fl
7 s.d. Prince] from Fl Enter Prince Henry.
11, 13, 56 s.pp. Glou.] Fl; Hum. Q
16–7 Not . . . sleep.] as verse, Fl; as prose, Q
19 Will't] Fl; Wilt Q
20 s.d. Exeunt . . . Prince.] Rowe
25 night,] Night: Fl
25 now!] now, Fl
31 safety. By . . . breath] Fl (subs.); safty (by . . . breath) Q
32–3 downy . . . down] F4; dowlny . . . dowlne Q, Fl (subs.)
34 move.] Fl; moue Q
34 lord! my father!] Rowe; lord my father: Q; Lord, my Father, Fl
37 due] Fl; deaw Q
43 s.d. Puts . . . crown.] Capell (subs.)
43 where] here Fl
44 God] Heauen Fl
48 s.d. and the rest] Capell; s.d. after l. 47, Q, Fl; placed as in Capell
49 How . . . Grace?] Fl
51–3 We . . . him.] as verse, Fl; as prose, Q
54 He . . . here.] as verse, Capell; as prose, Q; om. Fl
59 hence. Go] Fl (subs.); hence go Q
62 s.d. Exit Warwick.] Capell
68 sleep] sleepes Fl
70 pil'd] Fl; pilld Q
71 strange-achieved] hyphen, Fl
74 tolling] culling Fl
75 The virtuous sweets,] Fl
76 thighs] Fl; thigh, Q
79 s.d. Enter Warwick.] placed as in Fl; after l. 81, Q
81 have] Ridley; hands Q; hath Fl
87 -drops.] Fl; -drops, Q
88 s.d. Prince] from Fl Enter Prince Henry.; s.d. after l. 87, Q; placed as in Fl
90 s.d. Warwick . . . rest.] Capell
91 s.p. Prince.] Fl (P. Hen.); Harry Q
92 thought:] Fl; thought Q
94 mine] my Fl
107 Whom] Which Fl
111 thine] thy Fl
114 head;] Fl (subs.); head, Q
115 compound] Fl; compouud Q
119 Harry] Henry Fl
124 ruffin] Ruffian Fl
124 will] swill Fl
128 guilt] Fl; gilt Q
131 muzzle] Fl; mussel Q
132 on] in Fl
139 moist] most Fl
146 s.d. Kneels.] White
147 inward true and] true, and inward Fl
148–9 bending. . . . me,] Fl (reading Heauen); bending, . . . me. Q
149 God] Heauen Fl
157 this] the Fl
160 worst of] Fl; worse then Q
161 fine . . . is] Fl (Charract); fine, in karrat Q
164 thy] the Fl
164 most] om. Fl
174, 178, 183 God] heauen or Heauen Fl
177 O my son,] Fl
178 it] Fl
179 win] ioyne Fl
196 answered] Dering MS, Fl; answerd Q
204 my] Tyrwhitt conj.; thy Q, Fl
218 God] heauen Fl
220 My gracious liege,] Fl
224 s.d. Enter . . . Lancaster.] Enter Lord Iohn of Lancaster, and Warwicke. Fl
226 s.p. P. John.] Capell; Lanc. Q; Iohn. Fl
231 s.d. Enter Warwick.] Cambridge (so in MS in Locker-Church-Huntington copy of Q)
235 God] heauen Fl
240 s.d. Exeunt.] Fl

V.i

V.i] Fl
Location: Pope, Theobald

s.d. **with Page**] *from F1 s.d.:* Enter Shallow, Silence, Falstaffe, Bardolfe, Page, and Dauie.; *Q s.d. in right margin opposite IV.v.239–40*
1 **sir**] *om. F1*
8 s.d. **Enter Davy.**] *Theobald (so in MS in the Locker-Church-Huntington copy of Q)*
9 **Davy, Davy, Davy, Davy**] Dauy, Dauy, Dauy *F1*
10 **see . . . see.**] see: *F1*
10 **Yea, marry,**] *Theobald;* yea mary *Q; om. F1*
11, 16, 28 **cook**] *Capell;* Cooke *Q, F1*
14 **hade land**] head-land *F1*
16–7 **cook—are**] *Theobald;* Cooke are *Q;* Cook: are *F1*
20 **paid**] *F1;* payed *Q*
22 **Now**] *om. F1*
24 **lost**] lost the other day, *F1*
24 **Hinckley**] *F1;* Hunkly *Q*
28 **tiny**] tinie *Q;* tine *F1 (perhaps correctly)*
34 **backbitten**] bitten *F1*
35 **marvail's**] *Kittredge;* maruailes *Q;* maruellous *F1*
40 **is**] are *F1*
44 **God**] heauen *F1*
47 **this**] these *F1*
48 **and**] and if *F1*
49 **have**] haue but a very *F1*
51 **you**] your Worship *F1*
52 **to,**] *F1;* to *Q*
53 s.d. **Exit Davy.**] *Capell*
54 **Come, come, come**] Come *F1*
57 **with**] with all *F1*
58 s.d. **to the Page**] *Rowe*
61 s.d. **Exit Shallow.**] *Capell*
61–2 s.d. **Exeunt . . . Page.**] *Capell*
66 **him**] of him *F1*
81 **without**] with *F1*
86 s.d. **Within.**] *Theobald*
87 s.d. **Exit.**] *Theobald;* Exeunt *F1*

V.ii

V.ii] *F1*
Location: *Capell (subs.)*
o.s.d. **Enter . . . Justice**] *F1* (the Earle of Warwicke, and the); Enter Warwike, duke Humphrey, L. chiefe Iustice, Thomas / Clarence, Prince Iohn, Westmerland. *Q (c);* . . . Prince, Iohn Westmerland. *Q (u)*
o.s.d. **meeting**] *Capell*
2 s.p. **Ch. Just.**] *F1;* Iust. *Q (throughout scene)*
4 **hope,**] *F1;* hope *Q*
13 s.d. **Westmerland and others**] *Capell (note that Westmerland is included in Q o.s.d.; om. F1)*
16 **he**] him *F1*
19 **O God**] Alas *F1*
20 s.p. **P. John.**] *Capell;* Iohn *Q, F1 (throughout scene)*
21 s.p. **Glou., Clar.**] *F1*
27 s.p. **Glou.**] *F1;* Humph. *Q*
36 **impartial**] Imperiall *F1*
38–9 **remission. . . . me,**] *F1;* remission, . . . me. *Q*
42 s.d. **and Blunt**] *om. F1; s.d. after l.41, Q; placed as in F1*
43 **God**] heauen *F1*
46 **mix**] *F1;* mixt *Q*
48 **Amurath an Amurath**] Amurah, an Amurah *F1*
50 **by my faith**] to speake truth *F1*
57 **too.**] *F1 (subs.);* too, *Q*
59 **Yet**] But *F1*
62 s.p. **Princes.**] *Staunton;* Bro. *Q;* Iohn, &c. *F1*
62 **otherwise**] other *F1*
72 **Lethe**] *F1;* lethy *Q*
96 **your**] you *F1*
97 **son.**] *F1 (subs.);* sonne, *Q*
106 **you,**] *F1;* you *Q*
110 **not**] no *F1*
112 **justice." You**] *F1 (subs.);* Iustice you *Q*
127 **rase**] *Pope;* race *Q, F1*
140 **foremost**] *Pope;* formost *Q, F1*
143, 145 **God**] heauen *and* Heauen *F1*
145 s.d. **Exeunt.**] *F1;* exit. *Q*

V.iii

V.iii] *F1*
Location: *Pope, Capell*
o.s.d. **Silence**] *F1;* Scilens *Q (throughout scene in text, except* Silens, *l. 23; and in s.pp., except* Silens, *ll. 73, 78, 89)*
1 **my**] mine *F1*
2 **mine**] my *F1*
5 **'Fore God**] *om. F1*
5–6 **goodly . . . rich**] a goodly . . . a rich *F1*
8 **Marry**] *F1;* mary *Q*
13 **By the mass**] *Pope (subs.);* by the mas *Q; om. F1*
16 **Ah**] *F1;* A *Q*
17, 32, 46, 73 s.dd. **Singing.**] *Rowe*
17–22 **"Do . . . merrily."**] *as verse, Malone (after Rowe); as prose, Q, F1*
18 **God**] heauen *F1*
23 s.p. **Fal.**] *F1;* sir Iohn *Q*
23 **heart! . . . Silence,**] *Johnson (subs.);* heart, . . . Silens, *Q, F1* (Silence)
25 **Give Master Bardolph**] Good M. Bardolfe: *F1*
29 **must**] *om. F1*
29 s.d. **Exit.**] *Theobald*
32–6 **"Be . . . merry."**] *as song verse, Capell (after Rowe); as prose, Q; as verse, F1 (but not indicated as a song)*
34 **wags**] wagge *F1*
38 **mettle**] *F1;* mettall *Q*
40 s.d. **Enter Davy.**] *om. F1*
41 s.d. **To Bardolph.**] *Cambridge (after Capell)*
46–8 **"A cup . . . long-a."**] *as song verse, Rowe; as prose, Q, F1*
47 **thee,**] *Wilson;* the *Q, F1*
48 **long-a**] *F1;* long a *Q*
53 s.d. **Singing.**] *Capell*
53–4 **"Fill . . . bottom."**] *as song verse, Capell; as prose, Q, F1*
57 **tiny**] tyne *F1 (perhaps correctly)*
57 s.d. **to the Page**] *Capell*
59 **cabileros**] Cauileroes *F1*
62 **By the mass**] *Malone;* By the mas *Q; om. F1*
65 **By God's liggens**] *om. F1*
66 **that 'a**] that. He *F1*
66–7 **out, 'a. 'Tis**] *Wilson;* out, a tis *Q;* out, he is *F1*
70 s.d. **One . . . door.**] *placed as in Capell; after l. 67, Q; om. F1*
71 s.d. **Exit Davy.**] *Capell*
72 s.d. **To . . . bumper.**] *Capell*
73–5 **"Do . . . Samingo."**] *as song verse, Malone; as prose, Q, F1*
79 s.d. **Enter Davy.**] *Capell*
82 s.d. **Enter Pistol.**] *placed as in F1; after l. 81, Q*
84 **God save you**] 'saue you sir *F1*
86 **no man**] none *F1*
86–7 **good. Sweet knight,**] good, sweet Knight; *F1*
88 **this**] the *F1*
89 **By'r lady**] Indeed *F1*
92–6 **Puff . . . price.**] *as verse, Pope; as prose, Q, F1*
92 **i' thy**] *Neilson;* ith thy *Q;* in thy *F1*
94 **And**] *om. F1*
97 **pray thee**] prethee *F1*
99–102 **A . . . thereof.**] *as verse, F1; as prose, Q*
102 **Cophetua**] *Pope;* Couetua *Q;* Couitha *F1*
103 s.d. **Singing.**] *Johnson*
103 **"And . . . John."**] *quotes, Johnson*
104–6 **Shall . . . lap.**] *as verse, F1; as prose, Q*
106 **Furies'**] *Capell;* Furies *Q, F1*
109 **sir. If**] *F1 (subs.);* sir, if *Q*
111 **or**] or to *F1*
111–2 **sir, . . . King,**] *F1;* sir . . . King *Q*
115–9 **A . . . Spaniard.**] *as verse, F1; as prose, Q*
124 **double-charge**] *hyphen, Capell*
126 **knighthood**] *F1;* Knight *Q*
132 s.d. **Exit Bardolph.**] *Capell*
134 **good.**] *F1;* good, *Q*
137 **Blessed . . . that**] Happie . . . which *F1*
138 **to**] vnto *F1*
139–41 **Let . . . days!**] *as verse, F1; as prose, Q*
140 **"Where . . . led?"**] *quotes, Hanmer*
141 **these**] those *F1*
141 s.d. **Exeunt.**] *F1;* exit. *Q*

V.iv

V.iv] *F1*
Location: *Pope, Theobald*
o.s.d. **Beadle**] *Collier (after Capell);* Sincklo *Q (Sincklo is the name of the actor who played the Beadle); F1 s.d. reads:* Enter Hostesse Quickly, Dol Tearesheete, and Beadles.
o.s.d. **with . . . Tearsheet**] *from F1 (see preceding note)*
1 **to God that**] *om. F1*
4, 14, 22, 31 s.pp. **Bead.**] *Rowe;* Sincklo *or* Sinck. *Q;* Off. *or* Officer. *F1*
5 **cheer**] cheere enough *F1*
6 **two**] two (lately) *F1*
7 s.p. **Doll.**] *F1* (Dol.); Whoore *Q (throughout scene)*
9 **go**] now go *F1*
9 **wert**] had'st *F1*
11 **the Lord**] *om. F1*
11 **I**] hee *F1*
12–3 **pray God**] would *F1*
13 **miscarry**] might miscarry *F1*
17 **amongst**] among *F1*
18 **you . . . you**] thee . . . thou *F1*
18 **censer**] *Theobald;* censor *Q, F1*
19–20 **blue-bottle**] blew-Bottel'd *F1*
22 **she knight-arrant**] *Capell (subs.);* shee-Knight-arrant *Q, F1*
24 **God**] *om. F1*
24 **overcome**] o'recome *F1*
27 **Ay**] *Capell;* I *Q;* Yes *F1*
29 **atomy**] Anatomy *F1*
31 s.d. **Exeunt.**] *F1*

V.v

V.v] *F1*
Location: *Theobald (subs.)*
o.s.d. **Enter . . . rushes.**] Enter two Groomes. *F1*
1, 2, 3 s.pp. **1. Strewer., etc.**] *Wilson;* 1, 2, 3 *Q;* 1. Groo., 2. Groo., 1. Groo. *F1*
3 **a'**] of the *F1*
4 **Dispatch, dispatch.**] *om. F1*
4 s.d. **Exeunt.**] *F3;* Exit Groo. *F1*
4 s.d. **Trumpets . . . them**] *om. F1*
4 s.d. **Page**] *F1*
5 **Shallow**] Robert Shallow *F1*
9 **God**] *om. F1*
15 s.p. **Shal.**] *F1;* Pist. *Q*
16 **of**] in *F1*
16 **affection—**] *Dyce;* affection. *Q, F1*
17, 19 s.pp. **Shal.**] *Hanmer;* Pist. *Q, F1*
18 **devotion—**] *Dyce;* deuotion. *Q, F1*
22 **me—**] *Dyce;* me. *Q, F1*
23 **best,**] *Cambridge;* best *Q;* most *F1*
24 s.p. **Fal.**] *F1; speech continued to Shallow, Q*
24 **travel**] *F3;* trauaile *Q, F1*
26 **else**] *om. F1*
29 **all**] *F1*
31–2 **My . . . rage.**] *as verse, Johnson; as prose, Q, F1*
33–8 **Thy . . . truth.**] *as verse, Capell (after Pope); as prose, Q, F1*
39 s.d. **Shouts within.**] *Steevens*
39 s.d. **The trumpets sound.**] *F1 (after l. 40); placed as in Malone*
40 **roar'd**] *F1;* roared *Q*
40 s.d. **the Lord . . . them**] *Capell; F1 s.d. reads:* Enter King Henrie the Fift, Brothers, Lord Chiefe Iustice.
41 **God**] *om. F1*
41 **Hal . . . Hal**] *Rowe;* Hall . . . Hall *Q, F1*
42 **The . . . fame!**] *as verse, Capell; as prose, Q, F1*
43 **God save**] 'Saue *F1*
45 s.p. **Ch. Just.**] *F1;* Iust *Q (or* Iustice *throughout scene)*
48 **becomes**] become *F1*
51 **awak'd**] awake *F1*
57 **God**] heauen *F1*
67 **evils**] euill *F1*
69 **strengths**] strength *F1*

71 **my]** our *F1*
72 s.d. **Exeunt . . . Train.]** *Capell;* Exit King. *F1*
73 s.p. **Fal.]** *F1;* Iohn *Q* (*throughout rest of scene, except l. 93*)
74 **marry]** *F1;* mary *Q*
79 **advancements]** aduancement *F1*
81 **cannot]** cannot well *F1*
81 **give]** should giue *F1*
87 **color]** *F1;* collor *Q*
87 **that I fear]** I feare, that *F1*
88–90 **Fear . . . night.]** *as prose, Pope; as verse, Q, F1*
90 s.d. **Officers with them]** *Capell; s.d. after* Bardolph. *l. 89, Q; placed as in Pope; om. F1*
94–5 **I . . . away.]** *as verse, F1; as prose, Q*
96 **tormenta . . . contenta]** tormento, spera me contento *F1*
96 s.d. **Exeunt. . . . Justice.]** *F1* (Exit. Manet Lancaster and Chiefe Iustice.); exeunt. *Q* (*after l. 95*)
97, 103, 105 s.pp. **P. John.]** *Capell;* Iohn *Q, F1*
107 **heard]** heare *F1*
109 s.d. **Exeunt.]** *F1* (Exeunt / FINIS.)

Epilogue

5 **indeed . . . say)]** (indeed) I should say, *F1*
10 **meant]** did meane *F1*
16–7 **and so . . . Queen.]** *follows l. 34 in F1*
16 **I]** *om. F1*
22 **would]** will *F1*
25 **seen]** seene before *F1*
29 **Katherine]** *F1;* Katharine *Q*
32 **a]** *F1*
34 **night.]** night. / FINIS. *Q;* night; *F1* (*see above, ll. 16–7*)

A tavern scene. From *Le Centre de l'Amour* (1630?). In Shakespeare's day, as now, music and food were considered proper precursors to amorous dalliance. It is not clear whether the bag of coins on the floor represents recently acquired booty (such as that taken at Gadshill) or is merely symbolic of the wastefulness of riotous living. One sees here the background of the scenes in Mistress Quickly's Boar's Head Tavern in Eastcheap in both *1 Henry IV* (II.iv) and, particularly, *2 Henry IV* (II.iv). In the latter scene "Sneak's noise" (line 11) is called for to assist the festivities. (*By permission of the Harvard College Library*)

A garden repast. From Didymus Mountain [i.e. Thomas Hill], *The Gardener's Labyrinth* (1577). (*The Folger Shakespeare Library*)

Shallow. Nay, you shall see my orchard, where in an arbor we will eat a last year's pippin of my own graffing, with a dish of caraways, and so forth. (*2 Henry IV*, V.iii.1–3)

Henry V

Of Shakespeare's few actual or alleged allusions to contemporary events—for example, Maria's "new map with the augmentation of the Indies" in *Twelfth Night* and Hamlet's "little eyases"—none has seemed more certain than that in the prologue to Act V of *Henry V*, where the Chorus, "by a lower but by loving likelihood," compares the King's triumphal return from France to that in store for "the general of our gracious Empress" when he comes back from Ireland "bringing rebellion broached on his sword." Although generations of scholars have agreed that the apparent reference to the Earl of Essex's Irish expedition of 1599 fixes the date of the first production of the play between March 27 of that year, when the Queen's young favorite left London to the cheers of its enraptured citizens, and September 28, when he slunk back a failure, Warren D. Smith has argued that the prologues (which were first printed in the Folio of 1623) were probably written by another hand for a performance of the play at court and moreover that "the general of our gracious Empress" was Charles Blount, Lord Mountjoy, who was appointed commander-in-chief in 1600, decisively defeated the Irish rebel Tyrone, and returned victorious in April 1603. Whatever the date and circumstances of the prologues, however, certain borrowings from and allusions to *Henry V* in *Sir John Oldcastle* (a play acted in October 1599 and printed the following year) suggest that the traditional assignment of Shakespeare's work to 1599 is valid. It was the last of his eight plays on English history between Richard II's deposition and the advent of the Tudors, and except for *Henry VIII*—which, like *King John*, lies beyond the limits of this great design—his final contribution to the form that he had made his own.

As usual when he dealt with English history, Shakespeare, although he had his Holinshed at hand, did not tie himself to facts. For example, Henry's show of mercy at Harfleur (III.iii) reveals an unrecorded aspect of that bloody monarch's mind, and the telescoping of events between Agincourt and Troyes does such violence to "their huge and proper life" that the Chorus apologizes in the prologue to Act V for the author's license. Sometimes, however, as when Canterbury "justly and religiously" expounds the Salic law (I.ii.33–95) and when Henry upbraids the conspirators (II.ii.166–81), Shakespeare simply versifies Holinshed's *Third Volume of Chronicles* (1587), errors and all; and sometimes he expands the merest hint into such a telling scene as that about the Dauphin's gift of tennis balls (I.ii.259–97).

But if Holinshed—or Edward Hall, whose text in *The Union of the Two Noble and Illustre Families of Lancaster and York* (1548) Holinshed often reproduces with unabashed fidelity—supplied Shakespeare with the fabric of his play, there are signs of other sources too. For more than a century "the victorious acts of King Henry the Fifth," to use Hall's rubric in the *Union*, had been a favorite English theme, and, as noted in the introduction to the Henry IV plays (pp. 884–887), his short but flashy reign has inspired a stream of biography, propaganda, and legend. Widely if not deeply read in English history, Shakespeare could of course have dipped into this Henrician literature, and so there may be traces, as Dover Wilson thinks, of the *Gesta Henrici Quinti* (by one of Henry's chaplains) in such details as Bardolph's "pax of little price" (III.vi.45) or of Tito Livio's *Vita Henrici Quinti* in the Constable's assertion (IV.ii.61) that he "will the banner from a trumpet take." But it is unlikely that Shakespeare could or would have spent time in working through the various fifteenth-century lives of Henry, most of them in manuscript, when Hall and Holinshed—to say nothing of such things as *A Mirror for Magistrates* and Daniel's *Civil Wars*—were so much more accessible. Equally accessible was *The Famous Victories of Henry V*, or at any rate an early version of that work. In its only extant form —a corrupted text of 1598—*The Famous Victories* is a vulgar and dilapidated relic of what may have been a more substantial play (or perhaps a pair of plays) dating from the 1580's. Although it is of course impossible to itemize Shakespeare's debt to this material in writing *1* and *2 Henry IV* and *Henry V*, there are such striking similarities between *The Famous Victories* and Shakespeare's portrait of the wild young prince transformed into the valiant warrior-king that it is easy to infer at least a common source. In the ordonnance of plot, if nothing else, the early play or plays could have served him as a model.

Whatever its appeal to patriotic Englishmen, *Henry V* has not fared well with critics, partly, no doubt, because not even Shakespeare could convert continued triumph into drama, but mainly because of Henry's unattractive character. Johnson hints at this when, having duly noted the scenes of "high dignity" and "easy merriment," he deplores the final act, which deals with Henry's ursine wooing of the French princess, as a blot upon the play. Moving characteristically from literature to politics, the irascible and republican Hazlitt turns his low opinion of "a very favourite monarch with the English nation" into inspired invective, directed not only toward the hero of the play but also toward the man he represents. The real Henry "was fond of war and low company," says Hazlitt, and of very little else. "He was careless, dissolute and ambitious;—idle, or doing mischief. In private, he seemed to have no idea of the common decencies of life, which he subjected to a kind of regal licence; in public affairs, he seemed to have no idea of any rule or right or wrong, but brute force, glossed over with a little religious hypocrisy and archiepiscopal advice." Although Shakespeare's Henry, like his prototype, is the embodiment of irresponsible power and sleazy success, "we like him in the play," says Hazlitt, because we know he is not real.

> There he is a very amiable monster, a very splendid pageant. As we like to gaze at a panther or a young lion in their cages in the Tower, and catch a pleasing horror from their glistening eyes, their velvet paws, and dreadless roar, so we take a very romantic, heroic, patriotic, and poetical delight in the boasts and feats of our younger Harry, as they appear on the stage and are confined to lines of ten syllables; where no blood follows the stroke that wounds our ears, where no harvest bends beneath horses' hoofs, no city flames, no little child is butchered, no dead men's bodies are found piled on heaps and festering the next morning—in the orchestra!

Many later critics have embellished this indictment. Swinburne, usually so idolatrous, concedes not only that Henry cuts a sorry figure as a suitor but that as a ruler he exemplifies the "commodity" or heartless egotism that Shakespeare elsewhere—in *King John*, for instance—shows to be a moral evil. Yeats, noting the conqueror's "gross vices" and "coarse nerves," concludes that Shakespeare measured him correctly and therefore treated his career with tragic irony. Granville-Barker regrets the fatal absence of "some spiritually significant idea" in a play about success. John Masefield calls Henry "the one commonplace man" in the two tetralogies. E. K. Chambers says that sometimes one can recognize in him "the prototype of the blatant modern imperialist, with his insolent talk of 'little England.'" E. M. W. Tillyard thinks that Shakespeare failed to fuse the princely ironist of *Henry IV* with the strutting king of *Henry V*. Mark Van Doren, in a devastating essay, argues that a certain meretricious splendor does not justify the pumped-up language of the play, its "puerile appeal" to sentimental patriotism, its febrile gaiety as a substitute for passion, and its hero in the guise of "mere good fellow, a hearty undergraduate with enormous initials on his chest." Despite J. Dover Wilson's and J. H. Walter's recent efforts to counter these and similar accusations, *Henry V* seems likely to remain a controversial play.

This critical dissatisfaction must be referred to Henry's almost statutory function as the ideal king; and to understand that function we must recall his complex serial presentation through the so-called second tetralogy. This great cycle of history plays, which treats the main events between Richard II's deposition in 1399 through the "unquiet time" of Henry IV to the summit of Lancastrian success at Troyes in 1420, is a continuing dramatic exploration of the massive, unifying theme of power as exemplified in three monarchs: the ineffectual Richard, who superbly vocalizes, but fails to act upon, his sense of injured merit; the "vile politician" and usurper Bullingbrook, whose ambition and efficiency cannot save him from remorse, or from the mounting troubles that dog him to his grave; and the latter's wayward son, whose long, uneasy preparation for the throne is followed by a reign of unexampled triumph.

Through the course of these four plays Hal (like his antithesis in the first tetralogy, the despot Richard III) is subjected to a most extended treatment. Although he does not appear in *Richard II*, his advent is there announced when Henry IV, even while lamenting his "unthrifty son" as a renegade to duty and a disgrace to the royal line, says he sees in him "some sparks of better hope, which elder years / May happily bring forth" (V.iii.21–22). It is the slow fulfillment of this "better hope" on which the two parts of *Henry IV* are built. Here Hal appears not only as the nimble-footed madcap Prince of Wales whose escapades bring sorrow to his father and danger to the realm but also, when he faces his great test at Shrewsbury, as a paragon of princely virtue. Even after his great show of grace and valor on the field, however, he and his disreputable companions so "play the fools with the time," as he himself admits (*2 Henry IV*, II.ii.142), that his dying father prophesies with dread the reign when "the fift Harry from curb'd license plucks / The muzzle of restraint" and turns England to a wilderness again (IV.v.130 ff.). Although Hal, whose way of using people to his own advantage is perhaps the least attractive aspect of his character, had, early in Part 1, soliloquized upon his plan to indulge in systematic "loose behavior" as a means of underscoring his delayed reform, it is not until his troubled father dies that he baffles expectation, rejects the unimitated and inimitable Falstaff, and briskly rises to his royal station. "The tide of blood in me," he thereupon announces,

> Hath proudly flow'd in vanity till now;
> Now doth it turn and ebb back to the sea,
> Where it shall mingle with the state of floods,
> And flow henceforth in formal majesty.
> (*2 Henry IV*, V.ii.129–33)

This paradox of Hal as wastrel and royal heir is the basic fact of *Henry IV*. Shakespeare's complex presentation of the Prince as he advances toward the fearful, splendid burden of the crown generates and unifies the action of these plays, and it brings into alignment all the foils and mighty opposites—Henry IV, Hotspur, the Lord Chief Justice, even Falstaff—as components of the great design whose centre is Prince Hal. Embracing scenes of politics and battle juxtaposed with vivid genre paintings of the London underworld, this design not only gives to *Henry IV* an unmatched sense of life, it enables us to watch the preparation of a king and to gauge the cost of royal power.

It is the product of this preparation that we see in *Henry V*. Here the self-willed prince whose conduct had led his father to believe him marked "For the hot vengeance, and the rod of heaven, / To punish my mistreadings" (*1 Henry IV*, III.ii.10–11) emerges as a Christian king of such astounding merit that were the age of miracles not past, Canterbury would call the change miraculous.

> The breath no sooner left his father's body,
> But that his wildness, mortified in him,
> Seem'd to die too; yea, at that very moment,
> Consideration like an angel came
> And whipt th' offending Adam out of him,
> Leaving his body as a paradise
> T' envelop and contain celestial spirits.
> Never was such a sudden scholar made;
> Never came reformation in a flood
> With such a heady currance, scouring faults;
> Nor never Hydra-headed willfulness
> So soon did lose his seat (and all at once)
> As in this king. (I.i.25–37)

When Ely piously responds, "We are blessed in the change," he might have used the word "conversion."

Whatever the process of this change—and one recent editor is inclined to side with Canterbury in regarding it as supernatural—it is presented as an accomplished fact at the very outset of the play, and so it has a vital bearing on the action. For one thing, it disqualifies the King as hero, at least insofar as the heroic function is exemplified in Shakespeare's other plays. With all his very special prowess—moral, military, political, or other—a hero must exhibit struggle and run the danger of defeat, for through struggle he identifies himself with us and so engages and sustains our interest. Not only must he undergo some sort of trial of which the outcome is in doubt—as when Richard meets with Bullingbrook at Flint or Lear confronts the painful knowledge that he is just a foolish fond old man or Romeo defies the angry stars—but he must share the lot of other men, who, whatever their successes, are bound to lose their last encounter. Despite Henry's own assertion (IV.i.106) that he, as king, "is but a man," he seems to be exempt from the condition of humanity: his important struggle —to establish his credentials for the exercise of regal power—is already won, and here, as in the chronicles, the wild young prince of popular tradition becomes the patriotic emblem of success. Despite the hardships he endures, he is not really imperilled, and as we follow his exploits we have merely to await his predetermined triumph. Therefore when he exposes the conspirators, conquers France against such overwhelming odds, and wins the French princess as his bride we are gratified but not astonished at the ease with which these things are done.

We are not astonished, moreover, at a certain hardness in his character, for successful men, especially those whose talents run to war, are rarely noted for their sweetness and compassion. Perhaps, as some have argued, Henry's dreadful talk before Harfleur (III.iii) and his command to kill the prisoners (IV.vi.37–38) were approved procedures in fifteenth-century war, but his bluff, jocose insensitivity would seem to be his own. Brassy, bold, and self-assertive, he lacks, of course, his cousin Richard's need to contemplate his own emotions, as well as his supple, sensuous way with words, but he also lacks his father's humanizing doubts concerning his own motives and behavior. Despite some twinges of remorse (IV.i.292–305) about the means that Henry IV had used to gain the throne, he shows no burning sense of guilt. He not only exercises royal power with élan but extends it by devices that, however justified by the ecclesiastical politicians of Act I, might well disturb a man of finer moral fibre. Henry IV, mindful not only of his foes but of his ambiguous situation, had unlocked his secret soul when he observed

> how chance's mocks
> And changes fill the cup of alteration
> With divers liquors! O, if this were seen,
> The happiest youth, viewing his progress through,
> What perils past, what crosses to ensue,
> Would shut the book, and sit him down and die.
> (*2 Henry IV*, III.i.51–56)

In a similar situation (*Henry V*, IV.i.230–84), however, his son does not reveal such hard-bought knowledge: he talks not of doubts and ambiguities but of his duties as a king, for it is the royal image that concerns him most and not the promptings of his secret soul. When in II.ii he spreads a net for the conspirators (one of whom had been his special friend) it is as if he took a certain pleasure in the sport, just as he does later in another game with Williams (IV.i.203–21). Although the royal sense of humor, which is very different from the Prince's wit in *Henry IV*, is sometimes flat and coarse (as in V.ii), at other times—when he returns the Dauphin's gift of tennis balls, for instance, or prepares for Agincourt—it shows the pride and gay indifference to mischance essential to a man so self-assured.

Tell the Constable,
We are but warriors for the working-day;
Our gayness and our gilt are all besmirch'd
With rainy marching in the painful field;
There's not a piece of feather in our host—
Good argument I hope we will not fly—
And time hath worn us into slovenry.
But by the mass, our hearts are in the trim;
And my poor soldiers tell me, yet ere night,
They'll be in fresher robes, or they will pluck
The gay new coats o'er the French soldiers' heads,
And turn them out of service. (IV.iii.108–19)

We see Henry at his best, in fact, when he fulfills his patriotic function. Once resolved about the justice of his cause—for I.ii, however dull to modern critics and producers, is a pivot of the play—he shows a jaunty disregard for adversaries, foreign or domestic, that is his most engaging trait. As he conveys to his bedraggled troops something of his own exhilaration he becomes the ideal man of action and the perfect leader of those "very valiant creatures" who, supplied with beef and iron and steel, "eat like wolves and fight like devils." Although the defiant rhetoric of "Once more unto the breach, dear friends" and "We few, we happy few, we band of brothers" does not disclose the workings of a subtle mind, it serves a more important function: these thunderous and inspiriting declamations, written in the decade of the Grand Armada, epitomize the patriotic zeal that is, in fact, the central subject of the play.

Here as elsewhere in Elizabethan literature the patriotism is presented as an aspect of religion. The convenient and consoling notion, assiduously fostered by the Tudors, that God had England in his special care was a crafty misconstruction of the doctrine of providence (see pp. 624–25) that Shakespeare had employed throughout his early history plays and then, it seems, had put aside with other youthful indiscretions. For if *Henry VI* and *Richard III* explain the horrors of the fifteenth century as a divinely sanctioned preparation for the glad event on Bosworth Field, where Henry VII came to power, *Richard II* and *Henry IV*, shunning *post hoc* rationalization, illuminate the interaction of politics and power. Thus in *3 Henry VI* we are invited to believe that the affairs of state reveal a moral pattern preordained by God; in *Richard II* we are shown that Bullingbrook's grasp of political necessities and realities counts for more than Richard's status as the Lord's anointed. In presenting Henry V's career, however, Shakespeare abandons clear-eyed reappraisal for the religio-political slogans of popular tradition. Not only the clergy in Act I but Henry too is much given to asserting his distinction as the leader of a chosen people who, while making England great, effects the will of God. "No tyrant, but a Christian king," as he describes himself, he listens to the insults of the French and then announces his intention: he will conquer France, he says, but his plan to do so

lies all within the will of God,
To whom I do appeal, and in whose name
Tell you the Dolphin I am coming on
To venge me as I may, and to put forth
My rightful hand in a well-hallow'd cause.
(I.ii.289–93)

Henry puts himself at God's disposal on the eve of Agincourt (III.vi.169), and since it is the "God of battles" whom he asks to steel his soldiers' hearts and to forget his father's "fault" (IV.i.289 ff.), he looks upon his victory as a sign of special favor. Exeter, learning the details, exclaims "'Tis wonderful!" but Henry, knowing who arranged the outcome of the battle, organizes a religious celebration and orders death for anyone who fails to give God credit for his part in the affair. If we, like Hazlitt, tend to squirm at Henry's strident patriotic piety, we may prefer to think, with Yeats, that Shakespeare treated it ironically. Perhaps he did, but he none the less preserved the icon of "this star of England" that no Elizabethan audience would wish to see defaced.

If Shakespeare's Henry V was the product of his reputation and thus a special kind of character, he required a special kind of play. Shakespeare's early histories are a string of helter-skelter episodes selected to present the dynastic struggles of the fifteenth century and thus to illustrate the dangers of dissension. Packed with people and events that cover more than sixty years, the three Henry VI plays are crudely stitched together, and despite the presence of a dominating villain in their sequel, *Richard III*, the so-called first tetralogy is mainly rough apprentice work, short on character and construction but long on crime and horror, ghosts and curses, rhetoric and declamation. Although *Richard II*, which inaugurates the second tetralogy, marks a great advance in style and depth of characterization, to say nothing of construction, it partakes almost of ritual in its sombre grace and elevation. With *1* and *2 Henry IV*, however, Shakespeare opens up a new terrain. These are not unwieldy narratives in the style of *Henry VI* or tragic histories in the style of *Richard III* and *Richard II*, but serio-comic treatments of historical events as seen from different levels of perception. Shuttling from verse to prose, from the council-table to the tavern, from Henry's problems as king and father to Hal's as gay young blade and royal heir, they combine a novelistic range of observation with a richly contrapuntal structure that show the full extent of Shakespeare's art.

In writing of a man like Henry V, however, Shakespeare clearly felt the need of something different, for here his subject represents those "king-becoming graces" that Malcolm, in *Macbeth* (IV.iii.92–94), enumerates as

> justice, verity, temp'rance, stableness,
> Bounty, perseverance, mercy, lowliness,
> Devotion, patience, courage, fortitude.

In other words, Shakespeare had in Henry V a hero much too wise and brave and just for real dramatic presentation, and—to make the problem greater—an action almost epic in its scope. He therefore had to try for grandeur—and to settle for the grandiose. The author of the prologues, whether Shakespeare or somebody else, astutely underscores the problem when the Chorus in the prologue to Act I wishes for "a Muse of fire, that would ascend / The brightest heaven of invention" in order to do justice to "so great an object" as Henry's splendid reign. Such choral prologues are employed in Shakespeare's other plays—*Romeo and Juliet* and *2 Henry IV*, for instance—to summarize the action, but here they serve a further function: they proclaim a theme too big for treatment on the stage.

> Can this cockpit hold
> The vasty fields of France? Or may we cram
> Within this wooden O the very casques
> That did affright the air at Agincourt?

This deferential stance is held throughout. The second speech of the Chorus regrets "abuse of distance" in the rapid shifting of the scene; the third suggests we "work" our thoughts to compensate for imperfections in the presentation of a siege; the fourth, which superbly comments on the eve of Agincourt, asks us to "sit and see, / Minding true things by what their mock'ries be"; the fifth, which, as noted earlier, apologizes for the many things omitted from the play, prepares us for the Treaty of Troyes; and the epilogue, in retrospect, concedes that

> with rough and all-unable pen,
> Our bending author hath pursu'd the story,
> In little room confining mighty men,
> Mangling by starts the full course of their glory.

In addition to advancing such apologetic explanations the Chorus also punctuates the action of the play and underscores its structure. *Henry V* reveals no rapid counterpoint like that of *Henry IV*: as befits its hero and its theme it is built of massive, block-like episodes, each with its own curve of action that contributes to the whole. Act I determines Henry's claim to France; Act II brings him through his preparations to his direct challenge to the foe; Act III takes him from Harfleur to Agincourt; Act IV describes his stunning victory; and Act V shows its consequences in the Treaty of Troyes and the union of the royal lovers.

In attempting these effects of size and grandeur Shakespeare has to sacrifice the comic thrust of *Henry IV*. There the comic scenes are contrived not merely to divert us from affairs of state but also to extend the spectrum of the play, for thanks to Falstaff's elemental and protean force they exemplify a mode of action and perception that modifies our own response and endows us with a fresh awareness. We laugh at Falstaff, to be sure, but we also laugh with him, and thus, because we come to share his comic vision, we sharpen and expand our knowledge. In *Henry V*, however, with Falstaff's energizing wit extinguished and with Hal, the subtle ironist, transformed into a pompous king, this comic splendor disappears. What Johnson calls its scenes of "easy merriment" are no longer laced into the fabric of the work, and so they do not cut athwart our stock responses to make us change our stance, nor do they constitute another statement, in a different key, of the "serious" action of the play. Despite his promise in the epilogue to *2 Henry IV* to keep Falstaff alive and let him go to France, Shakespeare really had to kill him off, for Falstaff, with his tonic disrespect and his genius for subversion, would have been a greater threat to Henry V than all the French at Agincourt. Fluellen of course provides a partial compensation; but Nym, Bardolph, and Pistol, deprived of their great chief, are only shabby clowns. Significantly, two of them are hanged and the other slinks away, but in the din of Henry's triumph we hardly hear them go.

Herschel Baker

The Life of Henry the Fifth

[Dramatis Personae

Chorus

King Henry the Fifth
Humphrey Duke of Gloucester } *brothers to the King*
John Duke of Bedford } *brothers to the King*
Duke of Clarence } *brothers to the King*
Duke of Exeter, *uncle to the King*
Duke of York, *cousin to the King*
Earl of Salisbury
Earl of Westmerland
Earl of Warwick
Archbishop of Canterbury
Bishop of Ely
Earl of Cambridge
Lord Scroop
Sir Thomas Grey
Sir Thomas Erpingham } *officers in King Henry's army*
Gower } *officers in King Henry's army*
Fluellen } *officers in King Henry's army*
Macmorris } *officers in King Henry's army*
Jamy } *officers in King Henry's army*
Bates } *soldiers in the same*
Court } *soldiers in the same*
Williams } *soldiers in the same*
Pistol
Nym

Bardolph
Boy
Herald

Charles the Sixth, *King of France*
Lewis, *the Dolphin*
Duke of Burgundy
Duke of Orleance
Duke of Bourbon
Duke of Britain
Duke of Berri
Duke of Beaumont
Constable of France
Rambures } *French lords*
Grandpré } *French lords*
Governor of Harfleur
Montjoy, *a French herald*
Ambassadors *to the King of England*

Isabel, *Queen of France*
Katherine, *daughter to Charles and Isabel*
Alice, *a lady attending on her*
Hostess *of the Boar's Head Tavern in Eastcheap, formerly Mistress Quickly, and now married to Pistol*

Lords, Ladies, Officers, Soldiers, Citizens, Messengers, *and* Attendants

Scene: *England; afterwards France*]

Enter Prologue.

O for a Muse of fire, that would ascend
The brightest heaven of invention!
A kingdom for a stage, princes to act,
And monarchs to behold the swelling scene!
Then should the warlike Harry, like himself,
Assume the port of Mars, and at his heels
(Leash'd in, like hounds) should famine, sword, and fire
Crouch for employment. But pardon, gentles all,
The flat unraised spirits that hath dar'd
On this unworthy scaffold to bring forth
So great an object. Can this cockpit hold
The vasty fields of France? Or may we cram
Within this wooden O the very casques
That did affright the air at Agincourt?
O, pardon! since a crooked figure may
Attest in little place a million,
And let us, ciphers to this great accompt,

Words and passages enclosed in square brackets in the text above are either emendations of the copy-text or additions to it. The Textual Notes immediately following the play cite the earliest authority for every such change or insertion and supply the reading of the copy-text wherever it is emended in this edition.

Pro. 2. invention: poetic power (in rhetorical theory, the "finding" of suitable topics). **4. swelling:** splendid. **6. port:** demeanor. **7. Leash'd in:** led in a group of three.

10. scaffold: stage.
11. cockpit: i.e. circular theatre (the "wooden O" of line 13, referring either to the Curtain in Shoreditch, where Shakespeare's company acted just before moving to the newly completed Globe in the late summer of 1599, or to the Globe itself).
13. the very casques: even the helmets.
14. Agincourt: village in northern France, scene of Henry V's greatest victory on October 25, 1415.
15. crooked figure: i.e. cipher or zero, which, added to a digit, multiplies its value. **16. Attest:** represent.
17. accompt: (1) story (of King Henry V's career); (2) reckoning (continuing the wordplay on "crooked figure" and "wooden O").

On your imaginary forces work.
Suppose within the girdle of these walls
Are now confin'd two mighty monarchies,
Whose high, upreared, and abutting fronts
The perilous narrow ocean parts asunder.
Piece out our imperfections with your thoughts;
Into a thousand parts divide one man,
And make imaginary puissance;
Think, when we talk of horses, that you see them
Printing their proud hoofs i' th' receiving earth;
For 'tis your thoughts that now must deck our kings,
Carry them here and there, jumping o'er times,
Turning th' accomplishment of many years
Into an hour-glass: for the which supply,
Admit me Chorus to this history;
Who, Prologue-like, your humble patience pray,
Gently to hear, kindly to judge, our play. *Exit.*

ACT I, SCENE I

Enter the two Bishops, [*the* ARCHBISHOP] OF CANTERBURY *and* [*the* BISHOP OF] ELY.

Cant. My lord, I'll tell you, that self bill is urg'd
Which in th' eleventh year of the last king's reign
Was like, and had indeed against us pass'd,
But that the scambling and unquiet time
Did push it out of farther question.
Ely. But how, my lord, shall we resist it now?
Cant. It must be thought on. If it pass against us,
We lose the better half of our possession;
For all the temporal lands, which men devout
By testament have given to the Church,
Would they strip from us; being valu'd thus:
As much as would maintain, to the King's honor,
Full fifteen earls and fifteen hundred knights,
Six thousand and two hundred good esquires;
And to relief of lazars, and weak age
Of indigent faint souls past corporal toil,
A hundred almshouses right well supplied;
And to the coffers of the King beside,
A thousand pounds by th' year. Thus runs the bill.

18. your imaginary forces: the power of your imagination.
20. two mighty monarchies: i.e. France and England.
21. fronts: frontiers. **22. narrow ocean:** i.e. English Channel.
25. puissance: troops.
28. deck our kings: equip our actors (as kings).
29. jumping o'er times. The play deals with events between Henry's preparations to invade France in 1414 and the Treaty of Troyes in 1420.
31. for . . . supply: to supply which (i.e. the defects acknowledged).

I.i. Location: London. An antechamber in the King's palace.
1. self: same. **2. in . . . reign:** i.e. in 1410, under Henry IV.
3. like: likely (to pass). **had:** would have.
4. scambling: disorderly. **5. question:** consideration.
7–19. If . . . bill. Here as elsewhere in this act Shakespeare follows Holinshed (Bullough, IV, 377) with extraordinary fidelity: "The effect of which supplication was, that the temporall lands devoutlie given, and disordinatlie spent by religious, and other spirituall persons, should be seized into the kings hands, sith the same might suffice to mainteine, to the honor of the king, and defense of the realme, fifteene earles, fifteene hundred knights, six thousand and two hundred esquiers, and a hundred almesse-houses, for reliefe onelie of the poore, impotent, and needie persons, and the king to have cleerelie to his coffers twentie thousand pounds, with manie other provisions and values of religious houses, which I passe over."
9. temporal lands: i.e. properties not used for strictly religious purposes. **15. lazars:** lepers.

Ely. This would drink deep.
Cant. 'Twould drink the cup and all.
Ely. But what prevention?
Cant. The King is full of grace and fair regard.
Ely. And a true lover of the holy Church.
Cant. The courses of his youth promis'd it not.
The breath no sooner left his father's body,
But that his wildness, mortified in him,
Seem'd to die too; yea, at that very moment,
Consideration like an angel came
And whipt th' offending Adam out of him,
Leaving his body as a paradise
T' envelop and contain celestial spirits.
Never was such a sudden scholar made;
Never came reformation in a flood
With such a heady currance, scouring faults;
Nor never Hydra-headed willfulness
So soon did lose his seat (and all at once)
As in this king.
Ely. We are blessed in the change.
Cant. Hear him but reason in divinity,
And, all-admiring, with an inward wish
You would desire the King were made a prelate;
Hear him debate of commonwealth affairs,
You would say it hath been all in all his study;
List his discourse of war, and you shall hear
A fearful battle rend'red you in music;
Turn him to any cause of policy,
The Gordian knot of it he will unloose,
Familiar as his garter; that, when he speaks,
The air, a charter'd libertine, is still,
And the mute wonder lurketh in men's ears
To steal his sweet and honeyed sentences;
So that the art and practic part of life
Must be the mistress to this theoric;
Which is a wonder how his Grace should glean it,
Since his addiction was to courses vain,
His companies unletter'd, rude, and shallow,
His hours fill'd up with riots, banquets, sports;
And never noted in him any study,
Any retirement, any sequestration
From open haunts and popularity.
Ely. The strawberry grows underneath the nettle,
And wholesome berries thrive and ripen best
Neighbor'd by fruit of baser quality;
And so the Prince obscur'd his contemplation
Under the veil of wildness, which (no doubt)

22. grace . . . regard: favor and kindly interest.
26. mortified: killed. **28. Consideration:** reflection.
29. th' offending Adam: i.e. natural depravity.
34. heady currance: strong current. **scouring:** cleansing.
35. Hydra-headed: i.e. many-headed (from the name of a monstrous snake with many heads, killed by Hercules).
36. seat: i.e. power. **38. divinity:** theology.
41. commonwealth affairs: i.e. politics.
45. cause of policy: question of statecraft.
46. Gordian knot: an intricate knot, devised by King Gordius of Phrygia, that Alexander the Great cut with his sword; i.e. a problem of great complexity. **47. Familiar:** as routinely. **that:** so that.
48. charter'd libertine: licensed freeman.
49–50. the mute . . sentences: i.e. the effects linger in men's memory and keep them silent to hear more.
51. art . . . part: experience and practice.
52. be: have been. **theoric:** theory.
55. companies: companions.
59. open . . . popularity: places of popular resort and common associates.

Grew like the summer grass, fastest by night,
Unseen, yet crescive in his faculty.
Cant. It must be so; for miracles are ceas'd;
And therefore we must needs admit the means
How things are perfected.
Ely. But, my good lord,
How now for mitigation of this bill
Urg'd by the commons? Doth his Majesty
Incline to it, or no?
Cant. He seems indifferent;
Or rather swaying more upon our part
Than cherishing th' exhibiters against us;
For I have made an offer to his Majesty,
Upon our spiritual convocation
And in regard of causes now in hand,
Which I have open'd to his Grace at large,
As touching France, to give a greater sum
Than ever at one time the clergy yet
Did to his predecessors part withal.
Ely. How did this offer seem receiv'd, my lord?
Cant. With good acceptance of his Majesty;
Save that there was not time enough to hear,
As I perceiv'd his Grace would fain have done,
The severals and unhidden passages
Of his true titles to some certain dukedoms,
And generally to the crown and seat of France,
Deriv'd from Edward, his great-grandfather.
Ely. What was th' impediment that broke this off?
Cant. The French embassador upon that instant
Crav'd audience; and the hour, I think, is come
To give him hearing. Is it four a' clock?
Ely. It is.
Cant. Then go we in, to know his embassy;
Which I could with a ready guess declare,
Before the Frenchman speak a word of it.
Ely. I'll wait upon you, and I long to hear it.
Exeunt.

[SCENE II]

Enter the KING, HUMPHREY [DUKE OF GLOUCESTER], BEDFORD, CLARENCE, WARWICK, WESTMERLAND, *and* EXETER, [*and other* ATTENDANTS].

K. Hen. Where is my gracious Lord of Canterbury?
Exe. Not here in presence.
K. Hen. Send for him, good uncle.
West. Shall we call in th' ambassador, my liege?
K. Hen. Not yet, my cousin. We would be resolv'd,
Before we hear him, of some things of weight

66. **crescive . . . faculty:** growing in its natural power.
68. **means:** i.e. natural causes. 72. **indifferent:** i.e. uncommitted.
74. **exhibiters:** sponsors.
76. **Upon . . . convocation:** on behalf of the assembly of clergy.
78. **open'd:** explained. 81. **withal:** with. 85. **fain:** gladly.
86. **severals . . . passages:** details and obvious derivation.
87. **titles:** claims. 88. **seat:** throne.
89. **Edward, his great-grandfather:** i.e. Edward III, whose maternal grandfather was Philip IV of France.
91. **embassador:** ambassador. **upon that instant:** just then.

I.ii. Location: London. The presence-chamber of the palace.
3. **liege:** sovereign. 4. **cousin:** kinsman.
4–5. **resolv'd . . . of:** clear in our mind . . . about.

That task our thoughts, concerning us and France.

Enter two Bishops, [*the* ARCHBISHOP OF CANTERBURY *and the* BISHOP OF ELY].

Cant. God and his angels guard your sacred throne,
And make you long become it!
K. Hen. Sure we thank you.
My learned lord, we pray you to proceed,
And justly and religiously unfold
Why the law Salique, that they have in France,
Or should, or should not, bar us in our claim;
And God forbid, my dear and faithful lord,
That you should fashion, wrest, or bow your reading,
Or nicely charge your understanding soul
With opening titles miscreate, whose right
Suits not in native colors with the truth;
For God doth know how many now in health
Shall drop their blood in approbation
Of what your reverence shall incite us to.
Therefore take heed how you impawn our person,
How you awake our sleeping sword of war—
We charge you, in the name of God, take heed;
For never two such kingdoms did contend
Without much fall of blood, whose guiltless drops
Are every one a woe, a sore complaint,
'Gainst him whose wrongs gives edge unto the swords
That makes such waste in brief mortality.
Under this conjuration speak, my lord;
For we will hear, note, and believe in heart,
That what you speak is in your conscience wash'd
As pure as sin with baptism.
Cant. Then hear me, gracious sovereign, and you peers,
That owe yourselves, your lives, and services
To this imperial throne. There is no bar
To make against your Highness' claim to France
But this, which they produce from Pharamond:
"*In terram Salicam mulieres ne* [*succedant*],"
"No woman shall succeed in Salique land";
Which Salique land the French unjustly gloze
To be the realm of France, and Pharamond
The founder of this law and female bar.
Yet their own authors faithfully affirm
That the land Salique is in Germany,
Between the floods of Sala and of [Elbe];
Where Charles the Great, having subdu'd the Saxons,
There left behind and settled certain French;
Who holding in disdain the German women
For some dishonest manners of their life,
Establish'd then this law: to wit, no female
Should be inheritrix in Salique land;
Which Salique, as I said, 'twixt [Elbe] and Sala,

11. **law Salique.** Explained in lines 35 ff.
12. **Or:** either. **claim:** i.e. to the French throne.
14. **reading:** interpretation.
15. **nicely charge:** foolishly burden.
16. **opening titles miscreate:** expounding spurious claims.
17. **Suits . . . colors:** is naturally incompatible.
19. **approbation:** proof, support. 21. **impawn:** commit.
26. **woe:** grievance. 28. **brief mortality:** i.e. short-lived mortal men.
29. **conjuration:** injunction.
37. **Pharamond:** legendary Frankish king.
39. **Salique:** Salic, Salian, referring to a Frankish tribe that lived on the river Sala, the ancient name for one of the mouths of the Rhine.
40. **gloze:** interpret. 49. **dishonest:** unchaste.

Is at this day in Germany call'd Meisen.
Then doth it well appear the Salique law
Was not devised for the realm of France;
Nor did the French possess the Salique land
Until four hundred one and twenty years
After defunction of King Pharamond,
Idly suppos'd the founder of this law,
Who died within the year of our redemption
Four hundred twenty-six; and Charles the Great
Subdu'd the Saxons, and did seat the French
Beyond the river Sala, in the year
Eight hundred five. Besides, their writers say,
King Pepin, which deposed Childeric,
Did, as heir general, being descended
Of Blithild, which was daughter to King Clothair,
Make claim and title to the crown of France.
Hugh Capet also, who usurp'd the crown
Of Charles the Duke of Lorraine, sole heir male
Of the true line and stock of Charles the Great,
To [fine] his title with some shows of truth,
Though in pure truth it was corrupt and naught,
Convey'd himself as th' heir to th' Lady Lingare,
Daughter to Charlemain, who was the son
To Lewis the Emperor, and Lewis the son
Of Charles the Great. Also King Lewis the Tenth,
Who was sole heir to the usurper Capet,
Could not keep quiet in his conscience,
Wearing the crown of France, till satisfied
That fair Queen Isabel, his grandmother,
Was lineal of the Lady Ermengare,
Daughter to Charles, the foresaid Duke of Lorraine;
By the which marriage the line of Charles the Great
Was re-united to the crown of France.
So that, as clear as is the summer's sun,
King Pepin's title and Hugh Capet's claim,
King Lewis his satisfaction, all appear
To hold in right and title of the female;
So do the kings of France unto this day.
Howbeit, they would hold up this Salique law
To bar your Highness claiming from the female,
And rather choose to hide them in a net
Than amply to imbar their crooked titles
Usurp'd from you and your progenitors.
K. Hen. May I with right and conscience make this claim?
Cant. The sin upon my head, dread sovereign!
For in the book of Numbers is it writ,
When the man dies, let the inheritance
Descend unto the daughter. Gracious lord,
Stand for your own, unwind your bloody flag,
Look back into your mighty ancestors;
Go, my dread lord, to your great-grandsire's tomb,
From whom you claim; invoke his warlike spirit,
And your great-uncle's, Edward the Black Prince,
Who on the French ground play'd a tragedy,
Making defeat on the full power of France,
Whiles his most mighty father on a hill
Stood smiling to behold his lion's whelp
Forage in blood of French nobility.
O noble English, that could entertain
With half their forces the full pride of France,
And let another half stand laughing by,
All out of work and cold for action!
Ely. Awake remembrance of these valiant dead,
And with your puissant arm renew their feats.
You are their heir, you sit upon their throne;
The blood and courage that renowned them
Runs in your veins; and my thrice-puissant liege
Is in the very May-morn of his youth,
Ripe for exploits and mighty enterprises.
Exe. Your brother kings and monarchs of the earth
Do all expect that you should rouse yourself,
As did the former lions of your blood.
West. They know your Grace hath cause, and means, and might;
So hath your Highness. Never King of England
Had nobles richer and more loyal subjects,
Whose hearts have left their bodies here in England,
And lie pavilion'd in the fields of France.
Cant. O, let their bodies follow, my dear liege,
With [blood] and sword and fire, to win your right;
In aid whereof we of the spiritualty
Will raise your Highness such a mighty sum
As never did the clergy at one time
Bring in to any of your ancestors.
K. Hen. We must not only arm t' invade the French,
But lay down our proportions to defend
Against the Scot, who will make road upon us
With all advantages.
Cant. They of those marches, gracious sovereign,
Shall be a wall sufficient to defend
Our inland from the pilfering borderers.
K. Hen. We do not mean the coursing snatchers only,
But fear the main intendment of the Scot,
Who hath been still a giddy neighbor to us;
For you shall read that my great-grandfather
Never went with his forces into France
But that the Scot on his unfurnish'd kingdom
Came pouring like the tide into a breach,
With ample and brim fullness of his force,
Galling the gleaned land with hot assays,

57. **four . . . twenty**: actually, 379 years, i.e. four hundred less one and twenty. The source of the error—as of many details and even phrases in this speech—is Holinshed (Bullough, IV, 378–79).
58. **defunction**: death. 59. **Idly**: foolishly. 62. **seat**: establish.
66. **heir general**: i.e. one who inherits through either the male or female parent. 72. **fine**: embellish.
74. **Convey'd**: misrepresented.
75. **Charlemain**: actually, Charles II ("the Bald"). Here and again in line 77, where Louis IX is confused with Louis X, Shakespeare copies Holinshed's mistakes. 82. **lineal of**: descended from.
93. **hide . . . net**: i.e. rely on a tangle of transparent contradictions.
94. **amply to imbar**: frankly to rule out. **crooked**: fraudulent.
98. **Numbers**. The reference is to 27:8.

106. **tragedy**: i.e. the battle of Crécy (1346), a disaster for the French.
110. **Forage in**: prey on. 111. **entertain**: meet (and overcome).
114. **for**: i.e. for lack of. 118. **renowned**: brought renown to.
120. **youth**. Henry was twenty-seven at the time.
129. **pavilion'd**: tented. 132. **spiritualty**: clergy.
137. **lay . . . proportions**: allocate our forces. 138. **road**: inroad.
139. **With all advantages**: i.e. whenever he sees a good chance.
140. **marches**: border regions.
143. **coursing snatchers**: guerrilla raiders.
144. **intendment**: (hostile) intention.
145. **still**: always. **giddy**: untrustworthy.
148. **unfurnish'd**: unprotected.
151. **Galling . . . assays**: harassing the land depleted of soldiers with strong assaults.

Girding with grievous siege castles and towns;
That England being empty of defense,
Hath shook and trembled at th' ill neighborhood.
Cant. She hath been then more fear'd than harm'd,
my liege;
For hear her but exampled by herself:
When all her chevalry hath been in France,
And she a mourning widow of her nobles,
She hath herself not only well defended
But taken and impounded as a stray
The King of Scots; whom she did send to France
To fill King Edward's fame with prisoner kings,
And make [her] chronicle as rich with praise
As is the ooze and bottom of the sea
With sunken wrack and sumless treasuries.
Ely. But there's a saying very old and true,
"If that you will France win,
Then with Scotland first begin."
For once the eagle (England) being in prey,
To her unguarded nest the weasel (Scot)
Comes sneaking, and so sucks her princely eggs,
Playing the mouse in absence of the cat,
To 'tame and havoc more than she can eat.
Exe. It follows then the cat must stay at home,
Yet that is but a crush'd necessity,
Since we have locks to safeguard necessaries,
And pretty traps to catch the petty thieves.
While that the armed hand doth fight abroad,
Th' advised head defends itself at home;
For government, though high, and low, and lower,
Put into parts, doth keep in one consent,
Congreeing in a full and natural close,
Like music.
Cant. Therefore doth heaven divide
The state of man in divers functions,
Setting endeavor in continual motion;
To which is fixed, as an aim or butt,
Obedience; for so work the honey-bees,
Creatures that by a rule in nature teach
The act of order to a peopled kingdom.
They have a king, and officers of sorts,
Where some, like magistrates, correct at home;
Others, like merchants, venter trade abroad;
Others, like soldiers, armed in their stings,
Make boot upon the summer's velvet buds,
Which pillage they with merry march bring home
To the tent-royal of their emperor;
Who busied in his [majesty] surveys
The singing masons building roofs of gold,
The civil citizens kneading up the honey,
The poor mechanic porters crowding in
Their heavy burthens at his narrow gate,
The sad-ey'd justice, with his surly hum,
Delivering o'er to executors pale
The lazy yawning drone. I this infer,
That many things, having full reference
To one consent, may work contrariously,
As many arrows loosed several ways
Come to one mark; as many ways meet in one town;
As many fresh streams meet in one salt sea;
As many lines close in the dial's centre;
So may a thousand actions, once afoot,
[End] in one purpose, and be all well borne
Without defeat. Therefore to France, my liege!
Divide your happy England into four,
Whereof take you one quarter into France,
And you withal shall make all Gallia shake.
If we, with thrice such powers left at home,
Cannot defend our own doors from the dog,
Let us be worried, and our nation lose
The name of hardiness and policy.
K. Hen. Call in the messengers sent from the
Dolphin. [*Exeunt some Attendants.*]
Now are we well resolv'd, and by God's help
And yours, the noble sinews of our power,
France being ours, we'll bend it to our awe,
Or break it all to pieces. Or there we'll sit,
Ruling in large and ample empery
O'er France and all her (almost) kingly dukedoms,
Or lay these bones in an unworthy urn,
Tombless, with no remembrance over them.
Either our history shall with full mouth
Speak freely of our acts, or else our grave,
Like Turkish mute, shall have a tongueless mouth,
Not worshipp'd with a waxen epitaph.

Enter AMBASSADORS *of France [attended].*

Now are we well prepar'd to know the pleasure
Of our fair cousin Dolphin; for we hear
Your greeting is from him, not from the King.
[*1.*] *Amb.* May't please your Majesty to give us
leave
Freely to render what we have in charge?
Or shall we sparingly show you far off
The Dolphin's meaning and our embassy?

154. neighborhood: neighborliness. **155. fear'd:** frightened.
156. exampled by herself: i.e. instructed by her own example.
157. chevalry: chivalry.
159–62. She . . . kings. In 1346, when Edward III was waging war in France, David II of Scotland was captured by the English. He was not actually taken to France. **165. sumless:** incalculable.
169. in prey: in search of prey.
173. 'tame: attame, i.e. pierce, injure. **havoc:** ravage.
175. crush'd necessity: strained conclusion (in view of what follows).
179. advised: judicious. **181. consent:** harmony.
182. Congreeing: agreeing. **close:** cadence.
186. aim or butt: i.e. target. **189. act of order:** orderly action.
190. sorts: different kinds. **191. correct:** dispense justice.
192. venter: venture. **194. boot:** booty.
197. majesty: royal office.
200. mechanic: menial. **201. burthens:** burdens.
202. sad-ey'd: serious-eyed, grave. **203. executors:** executioners.
205–6. having . . . consent: i.e. united in a common goal.
207. loosed several ways: shot from different directions.
208. mark: target. **ways:** roads.
210. close: converge. **dial's:** sundial's. **212. borne:** conducted.
216. withal: therewith. **Gallia:** France.
219. worried: torn to pieces.
220. name . . . policy: reputation for valor and statesmanship.
221. Dolphin: Dauphin, title of the heir apparent of the French king.
222. Now . . . resolv'd. As Holinshed reports (Bullough, IV, 380), "the duke of Excester used such earnest and pithie persuasions, to induce the king and the whole assemblie of the parlement to credit his words, that immediatlie after he had made an end, all the companie began to crie; Warre, warre; France, France. Hereby the bill for dissolving of religious houses was cleerlie set aside, and nothing was thought on but onelie the recovering of France, according as the archbishop had mooved." **224. our awe:** submission to us.
226. empery: imperial power.
229. Tombless: i.e. without a monument. **remembrance:** epitaph.
233. worshipp'd: honored. **with . . . epitaph:** i.e. even with an epitaph written on wax. **238. render:** report.
239. sparingly . . . off: i.e. tactfully suggest.

K. Hen. We are no tyrant, but a Christian king,
Unto whose grace our passion is as subject
As is our wretches fett'red in our prisons;
Therefore with frank and with uncurbed plainness
Tell us the Dolphin's mind.
[1.] Amb. Thus then in few:
Your Highness, lately sending into France,
Did claim some certain dukedoms, in the right
Of your great predecessor, King Edward the Third.
In answer of which claim, the prince our master
Says that you savor too much of your youth,
And bids you be advis'd: there's nought in France
That can be with a nimble galliard won;
You cannot revel into dukedoms there.
He therefore sends you, meeter for your spirit,
This tun of treasure; and, in lieu of this,
Desires you let the dukedoms that you claim
Hear no more of you. This the Dolphin speaks.
K. Hen. What treasure, uncle?
Exe. Tennis-balls, my liege.
K. Hen. We are glad the Dolphin is so pleasant with us,
His present and your pains we thank you for.
When we have match'd our rackets to these balls,
We will in France, by God's grace, play a set
Shall strike his father's crown into the hazard.
Tell him he hath made a match with such a wrangler
That all the courts of France will be disturb'd
With chaces. And we understand him well,
How he comes o'er us with our wilder days,
Not measuring what use we made of them.
We never valu'd this poor seat of England,
And therefore, living hence, did give ourself
To barbarous license; as 'tis ever common
That men are merriest when they are from home.
But tell the Dolphin I will keep my state,
Be like a king, and show my sail of greatness
When I do rouse me in my throne of France.
For that I have laid by my majesty,
And plodded like a man for working-days;
But I will rise there with so full a glory
That I will dazzle all the eyes of France,
Yea, strike the Dolphin blind to look on us.
And tell the pleasant prince this mock of his
Hath turn'd his balls to gun-stones, and his soul
Shall stand sore charged for the wasteful vengeance
That shall fly with them; for many a thousand widows
Shall this his mock mock out of their dear husbands;
Mock mothers from their sons, mock castles down;
And some are yet ungotten and unborn
That shall have cause to curse the Dolphin's scorn.
But this lies all within the will of God,
To whom I do appeal, and in whose name
Tell you the Dolphin I am coming on
To venge me as I may, and to put forth
My rightful hand in a well-hallow'd cause.
So get you hence in peace; and tell the Dolphin
His jest will savor but of shallow wit,
When thousands weep more than did laugh at it.—
Convey them with safe conduct.—Fare you well.
Exeunt Ambassadors.
Exe. This was a merry message.
K. Hen. We hope to make the sender blush at it.
Therefore, my lords, omit no happy hour
That may give furth'rance to our expedition;
For we have now no thought in us but France,
Save those to God, that run before our business.
Therefore let our proportions for these wars
Be soon collected, and all things thought upon
That may with reasonable swiftness add
More feathers to our wings; for, God before,
We'll chide this Dolphin at his father's door.
Therefore let every man now task his thought,
That this fair action may on foot be brought. *Exeunt.*

[ACT II]

Flourish. Enter CHORUS.

Now all the youth of England are on fire,
And silken dalliance in the wardrobe lies;
Now thrive the armorers, and honor's thought
Reigns solely in the breast of every man.
They sell the pasture now to buy the horse,
Following the mirror of all Christian kings,
With winged heels, as English Mercuries.
For now sits Expectation in the air,
And hides a sword, from hilts unto the point,
With crowns imperial, crowns and coronets,
Promis'd to Harry and his followers.
The French, advis'd by good intelligence
Of this most dreadful preparation,
Shake in their fear, and with pale policy
Seek to divert the English purposes.
O England! model to thy inward greatness,
Like little body with a mighty heart,
What mightst thou do, that honor would thee do,
Were all thy children kind and natural!
But see, thy fault France hath in thee found out,

245. **few:** i.e. few words.
246–58. **Your . . . liege.** There is apparently no historical foundation for this famous episode of the tennis balls.
252. **galliard:** frisky dance. 255. **tun:** barrel.
259. **pleasant:** merry.
263–66. **hazard, wrangler, courts, chaces:** terms of court tennis used punningly. For example, *hazard* means (1) holes or galleries in the walls of a tennis court and (2) jeopardy; **chaces** means (1) missed returns and (2) pursuits.
263. **crown:** (1) coin (staked in a game of chance); (2) the sovereign power of France. 267. **comes o'er:** taunts. 269. **seat:** throne.
272. **from:** away from.
273. **keep my state:** i.e. maintain my royal status.
275. **rouse me in:** mount to. 282. **gun-stones:** cannon balls.
283. **charged:** burdened with the responsibility. **wasteful:** ruinous.
292. **venge:** avenge. **may:** can. 297. **Convey:** escort.
300. **omit . . . hour:** neglect no favorable opportunity.
304. **proportions:** levies. 307. **God before:** i.e. with God's help.
309. **task:** tax.

II.Cho. o.s.d. **Flourish:** trumpet fanfare.
2. **silken . . . lies:** i.e. gay apparel and frivolous pursuits are laid aside.
7. **Mercuries.** In classical mythology, Mercury was the messenger of the gods. 9. **hilts:** i.e. the pommel, haft, etc. of a sword.
10. **With . . . coronets:** i.e. with crowns appropriate for emperors, kings, and nobles respectively.
12. **advis'd:** informed. **intelligence:** espionage.
14. **pale policy:** frightened intrigue.
16. **model to:** small replica of. 18. **would:** would have.
19. **kind and natural:** i.e. naturally affectionate and loyal.
20. **France:** the King of France.

A nest of hollow bosoms, which he fills
With treacherous crowns; and three corrupted men,
One, Richard Earl of Cambridge, and the second,
Henry Lord Scroop of Masham, and the third,
Sir Thomas Grey, knight, of Northumberland,
Have for the gilt of France (O guilt indeed!)
Confirm'd conspiracy with fearful France,
And by their hands this grace of kings must die,
If hell and treason hold their promises,
Ere he take ship for France; and in Southampton.
Linger your patience on, and we'll digest
Th' abuse of distance; force a play:
The sum is paid, the traitors are agreed,
The King is set from London, and the scene
Is now transported, gentles, to Southampton;
There is the playhouse now, there must you sit,
And thence to France shall we convey you safe,
And bring you back, charming the Narrow Seas
To give you gentle pass; for if we may,
We'll not offend one stomach with our play.
But till the King come forth, and not till then,
Unto Southampton do we shift our scene. *Exit.*

[Scene I]

Enter Corporal Nym *and* Lieutenant Bardolph.

Bard. Well met, Corporal Nym.

Nym. Good morrow, Lieutenant Bardolph.

Bard. What, are Ancient Pistol and you friends yet?

Nym. For my part, I care not; I say little; but when time shall serve, there shall be smiles—but that shall be as it may. I dare not fight, but I will wink and hold out mine iron. It is a simple one, but what though? It will toast cheese, and it will endure cold as another man's sword will; and there's an end.

Bard. I will bestow a breakfast to make you friends, and we'll be all three sworn brothers to France. Let't be so, good Corporal Nym.

Nym. Faith, I will live so long as I may, that's the certain of it; and when I cannot live any longer, I will do as I may: that is my rest, that is the rendezvous of it.

Bard. It is certain, corporal, that he is married to Nell Quickly, and certainly she did you wrong, for you were troth-plight to her.

Nym. I cannot tell; things must be as they may. Men may sleep, and they may have their throats about them at that time, and some say knives have edges. It must be as it may; though patience be a tir'd [mare], yet she will plod—there must be conclusions—well, I cannot tell.

Enter Pistol *and* [Hostess] Quickly.

Bard. Here comes Ancient Pistol and his wife. Good corporal, be patient here.

[*Nym.*] How now, mine host Pistol?

Pist. Base tike, call'st thou me host?
Now by [Gadslugs] I swear I scorn the term;
Nor shall my Nell keep lodgers.

Host. No, by my troth, not long; for we cannot lodge and board a dozen or fourteen gentlewomen that live honestly by the prick of their needles but it will be thought we keep a bawdy-house straight. [*Nym and Pistol draw.*] O welliday, Lady, if he be not hewn now, we shall see willful adultery and murther committed.

Bard. Good lieutenant! good corporal! offer nothing here.

Nym. Pish!

Pist. Pish for thee, Iceland dog! thou prick-ear'd cur of Iceland!

Host. Good Corporal Nym, show thy valor, and put up your sword.

Nym. Will you shog off? I would have you solus.

Pist. "Solus," egregious dog? O viper vile!
The "solus" in thy most mervailous face,
The "solus" in thy teeth, and in thy throat,
And in thy hateful lungs, yea, in thy maw, perdy;
And which is worse, within thy nasty mouth!
I do retort the "solus" in thy bowels,
For I can take, and Pistol's cock is up,
And flashing fire will follow.

Nym. I am not Barbason, you cannot conjure me. I have an humor to knock you indifferently well. If you grow foul with me, Pistol, I will scour you with my rapier, as I may, in fair terms. If you would walk off, I would prick your guts a little in good terms, as I may, and that's the humor of it.

Pist. O braggard vile and damned furious wight!
The grave doth gape, and doting death is near,
Therefore exhale.

Bard. Hear me, hear me what I say. He that strikes the first stroke, I'll run him up to the hilts, as I am a soldier. [*Draws.*]

Pist. An oath of mickle might, and fury shall abate.

22. **treacherous crowns:** i.e. bribes. 26. **gilt:** gold.
27. **fearful:** timid. 28. **grace of kings:** honor to kingship.
30. **Southampton:** seaport in southern England.
31–32. **digest . . . distance:** i.e. take care of the violation of the unity of place. 32. **force:** stuff (with incidents). 34. **set:** set forth.
35. **gentles:** ladies and gentlemen.
38. **Narrow Seas:** English Channel.
39. **gentle pass:** smooth voyage.
40. **offend one stomach:** (1) give offense to any spectator; (2) make anyone seasick.

II.i. Location: London. A street.
o.s.d. **Nym, Bardolph.** The fiery-faced Bardolph, together with the blustering Pistol and his new wife the Hostess, were among Falstaff's disreputable companions in *1* and *2 Henry IV*, but Corporal Nym is a new addition to the gang.
3. **Ancient:** ensign, standard-bearer.
7. **wink:** close both eyes. 8. **iron:** weapon.
12. **sworn brothers:** i.e. band of thieves.
16. **rest:** last stake (a term from gaming). **rendezvous.** By this word Nym may mean something like "last word on the subject," but many of his and Pistol's expressions defy explanation.

19. **troth-plight:** betrothed. 29. **tike:** cur.
30. **Gadslugs:** corrupt or meaningless oath (?).
36. **Lady:** (by Our) Lady, a mild oath.
37. **adultery.** Possibly the Hostess here perpetrates a double blunder, intending *assaultery*, her own version of *assault and battery*. **murther:** murder. 39–40. **offer nothing:** i.e. don't fight.
42. **Iceland dog:** kind of terrier with long hair and pointed ears.
45. **shog:** jog, move along. **solus:** (1) alone; (2) unmarried.
47. **mervailous:** marvellous.
49. **maw:** stomach. **perdy:** assuredly. 52. **take:** strike.
54. **Barbason:** name of a fiend (?). **conjure:** i.e. frighten by conjurations and big words.
55. **I . . . humor:** I'm in the mood. 56. **foul:** i.e. from firing.
62. **exhale:** i.e. draw your sword. 66. **mickle:** great.

Give me thy fist, thy fore-foot to me give.
Thy spirits are most tall.

Nym. I will cut thy throat one time or other in fair terms, that is the humor of it.

Pist. *Couple a gorge!*
That is the word. I [thee defy] again.
O hound of Crete, think'st thou my spouse to get?
No, to the spittle go,
And from the powd'ring-tub of infamy
Fetch forth the lazar kite of Cressid's kind,
Doll Tearsheet she by name, and her espouse.
I have, and I will hold, the quondam Quickly
For the only she; and—*pauca*, there's enough too!
Go to.

Enter the Boy.

Boy. Mine host Pistol, you must come to my master, and your hostess. He is very sick, and would to bed. Good Bardolph, put thy face between his sheets, and do the office of a warming-pan. Faith, he's very ill.

Bard. Away, you rogue!

Host. By my troth, he'll yield the crow a pudding one of these days. The King has kill'd his heart. Good husband, come home presently. *Exit [with Boy].*

Bard. Come, shall I make you two friends? We must to France together; why the devil should we keep knives to cut one another's throats?

Pist. Let floods o'erswell, and fiends for food howl on!

Nym. You'll pay me the eight shillings I won of you at betting?

Pist. Base is the slave that pays.

Nym. That now I will have: that's the humor of it.

Pist. As manhood shall compound. Push home.
[They] draw.

Bard. By this sword, he that makes the first thrust, I'll kill him; by this sword, I will. *[Draws.]*

Pist. Sword is an oath, and oaths must have their course.

Bard. Corporal Nym, and thou wilt be friends, be friends; and thou wilt not, why then be enemies with me too. Prithee put up.

[*Nym.* I shall have my eight shillings I won of you at betting?]

Pist. A noble shalt thou have, and present pay,
And liquor likewise will I give to thee,
And friendship shall combine, and brotherhood.
I'll live by Nym, and Nym shall live by me.
Is not this just? For I shall sutler be
Unto the camp, and profits will accrue.
Give me thy hand.

Nym. I shall have my noble?

Pist. In cash, most justly paid.

Nym. Well, then that['s] the humor of't.

Enter Hostess.

Host. As ever you come of women, come in quickly to Sir John. Ah, poor heart! he is so shak'd of a burning quotidian tertian, that it is most lamentable to behold. Sweet men, come to him.

Nym. The King hath run bad humors on the knight, that's the even of it.

Pist. Nym, thou hast spoke the right.
His heart is fracted and corroborate.

Nym. The King is a good king, but it must be as it may; he passes some humors and careers.

Pist. Let us condole the knight, for, lambkins, we will live. *[Exeunt.]*

[Scene II]

Enter Exeter, Bedford, *and* Westmerland.

Bed. 'Fore God, his Grace is bold to trust these traitors.

Exe. They shall be apprehended by and by.

West. How smooth and even they do bear themselves!
As if allegiance in their bosoms sate
Crowned with faith and constant loyalty.

Bed. The King hath note of all that they intend,
By interception which they dream not of.

Exe. Nay, but the man that was his bedfellow,
Whom he hath dull'd and cloy'd with gracious favors—
That he should, for a foreign purse, so sell
His sovereign's life to death and treachery.

Sound trumpets. Enter the King, Scroop, Cambridge, *and* Grey, *[with* Attendants*].*

K. Hen. Now sits the wind fair, and we will aboard.
My Lord of Cambridge, and my kind Lord of Masham,
And you, my gentle knight, give me your thoughts.
Think you not that the pow'rs we bear with us

67. **fist:** hand. 68. **tall:** valiant.
71. **Couple a gorge:** i.e. *couper la gorge,* cut a throat.
74. **spittle:** hospital.
75. **powd'ring-tub:** sort of steam-bath used in treating venereal disease.
76. **lazar . . . kind:** diseased whore like Cressida (the pattern of a depraved woman as depicted in Robert Henryson's *Testament of Cresseid*).
77. **Doll Tearsheet:** another of Falstaff's friends. At the end of *2 Henry IV* (V.iv) she was sent to prison. 79. **pauca:** few (words).
80 s.d. **Boy:** i.e. the page that Prince Hal had given to Falstaff (*2Henry IV,* I.ii).
84. **warming-pan.** Alluding to Bardolph's complexion.
87. **he'll . . . pudding:** i.e. crows will peck the page's flesh (when he's hanging on the gallows).
88. **his:** i.e. Falstaff's alluding to the new king's rejection of his former friend (*2 Henry IV,* V.v) 89. **presently:** immediately.
98. **As . . . compound:** as valor shall determine, i.e. we'll settle it by fighting. 102. **and:** if.
107. **noble:** coin worth 6*s.* 8*d.*, which is less than Pistol owes but is acceptable because it is in ready cash (*present pay*).
111. **sutler:** seller of provisions.
119. **quotidian tertian:** Either the Hostess' characteristic confusion of medical terms for two kinds of fever, one occurring daily (*quotidian*) and the other on alternate days (*tertian*), or a Galenic phrase for a binary fever (semitertian).
121. **run . . . on:** shown ill will toward. 122. **even:** truth.
124. **fracted:** broken. **corroborate:** blunder for *corrupted* (?).
126. **passes . . . careers:** i.e. behaves oddly at times. *Passes* = lets pass; *careers* = gallops (a term from horsemanship).

II.ii. Location: Southampton. A council-chamber.
2. **apprehended by and by:** arrested shortly. 6. **note:** knowledge.
8. **the man . . . bedfellow.** Of the three traitors, one—Lord Scroop—"was in such favour with the king," says Holinshed (Bullough, IV, 384), "that he admitted him sometime to be his bedfellow, in whose fidelitie the king reposed such trust, that when anie privat or publike councell was in hand, this lord had much in the determination of it."
9. **dull'd:** tired.
10. **foreign purse:** For a more important reason for the conspiracy see note to lines 155–57. 15. **pow'rs:** forces.

Will cut their passage through the force of France,
Doing the execution and the act
For which we have in head assembled them?
Scroop. No doubt, my liege, if each man do his best.
K. Hen. I doubt not that, since we are well persuaded
We carry not a heart with us from hence
That grows not in a fair consent with ours;
Nor leave not one behind that doth not wish
Success and conquest to attend on us.
Cam. Never was monarch better fear'd and lov'd
Than is your Majesty. There's not, I think, a subject
That sits in heart-grief and uneasiness
Under the sweet shade of your government.
Grey. True; those that were your father's enemies
Have steep'd their galls in honey, and do serve you
With hearts create of duty and of zeal.
K. Hen. We therefore have great cause of thankfulness,
And shall forget the office of our hand
Sooner than quittance of desert and merit,
According to the weight and worthiness.
Scroop. So service shall with steeled sinews toil,
And labor shall refresh itself with hope
To do your Grace incessant services.
K. Hen. We judge no less. Uncle of Exeter,
Enlarge the man committed yesterday,
That rail'd against our person. We consider
It was excess of wine that set him on,
And on his more advice we pardon him.
Scroop. That's mercy, but too much security.
Let him be punish'd, sovereign, lest example
Breed, by his sufferance, more of such a kind.
K. Hen. O, let us yet be merciful.
Cam. So may your Highness, and yet punish too.
Grey. Sir,
You show great mercy if you give him life
After the taste of much correction.
K. Hen. Alas, your too much love and care of me
Are heavy orisons 'gainst this poor wretch!
If little faults, proceeding on distemper,
Shall not be wink'd at, how shall we stretch our eye
When capital crimes, chew'd, swallow'd, and digested,
Appear before us? We'll yet enlarge that man,
Though Cambridge, Scroop, and Grey, in their dear care
And tender preservation of our person,
Would have him punish'd. And now to our French causes.
Who are the late commissioners?
Cam. I one, my lord.
Your Highness bade me ask for it to-day.

18. **head:** aggressive posture.
22. **grows . . . consent:** is not harmonious.
30. **galls:** bitterness, hostility. 31. **create:** composed.
33. **office:** use, function. 34. **quittance:** reward.
39. **Uncle.** Thomas Beaufort, Duke of Exeter, was the youngest son of John of Gaunt by Katherine Swynford.
40. **Enlarge:** set free. **committed:** imprisoned.
43. **more advice:** thinking better of it. 44. **security:** overconfidence.
46. **his sufferance:** pardoning him. 53. **heavy orisons:** weighty pleas.
54. **proceeding on distemper:** i.e. resulting from drunkenness.
57. **yet:** none the less. 58. **dear:** intense.
61. **late:** recently appointed (to serve during the King's absence).
63. **it:** i.e. document certifying his appointment as commissioner.

Scroop. So did you me, my liege.
Grey. And I, my royal sovereign.
K. Hen. Then, Richard Earl of Cambridge, there is yours;
There yours, Lord Scroop of Masham; and, sir knight,
Grey of Northumberland, this same is yours:
Read them, and know I know your worthiness.
My Lord of Westmerland, and uncle Exeter,
We will aboard to-night.—Why, how now, gentlemen?
What see you in those papers that you lose
So much complexion?—Look ye how they change!
Their cheeks are paper.—Why, what read you there
That have so cowarded and chas'd your blood
Out of appearance?
Cam. I do confess my fault,
And do submit me to your Highness' mercy.
Grey, Scroop. To which we all appeal.
K. Hen. The mercy that was quick in us but late,
By your own counsel is suppress'd and kill'd.
You must not dare (for shame) to talk of mercy,
For your own reasons turn into your bosoms,
As dogs upon their masters, worrying you.
See you, my princes and my noble peers,
These English monsters! My Lord of Cambridge here,
You know how apt our love was to accord
To furnish [him] with all appertinents
Belonging to his honor; and this man
Hath, for a few light crowns, lightly conspir'd
And sworn unto the practices of France
To kill us here in Hampton. To the which
This knight, no less for bounty bound to us
Than Cambridge is, hath likewise sworn. But O,
What shall I say to thee, Lord Scroop, thou cruel,
Ingrateful, savage, and inhuman creature?
Thou that didst bear the key of all my counsels,
That knew'st the very bottom of my soul,
That (almost) mightst have coin'd me into gold,
Wouldst thou have practic'd on me, for thy use?
May it be possible that foreign hire
Could out of thee extract one spark of evil
That might annoy my finger? 'Tis so strange,
That, though the truth of it stands off as gross
As black and white, my eye will scarcely see it.
Treason and murther ever kept together,
As two yoke-devils sworn to either's purpose,
Working so grossly in [a] natural cause
That admiration did not hoop at them;
But thou ('gainst all proportion) didst bring in
Wonder to wait on treason and on murther;
And whatsoever cunning fiend it was
That wrought upon thee so preposterously
Hath got the voice in hell for excellence;
And other devils that suggest by treasons

76. **appearance:** sight. 79. **quick:** alive. 83. **worrying:** tearing.
86. **accord:** consent. 87. **appertinents:** appurtenances.
90. **practices:** plots. 91. **Hampton:** Southampton.
92. **This knight:** i.e. Grey.
99. **practic'd:** i.e. used your wiles. **use:** profit.
103. **stands . . . gross:** shows as clear. 107. **grossly:** obviously.
108. **admiration . . . hoop:** astonishment did not whoop, i.e. no cry of astonishment was raised. 109. **proportion:** natural order.
110. **wait on:** consort with. 112. **preposterously:** contrary to nature.
113. **voice:** vote. 114. **suggest:** seduce.

Do botch and bungle up damnation
With patches, colors, and with forms being fetch'd
From glist'ring semblances of piety;
But he that temper'd thee, bade thee stand up,
Gave thee no instance why thou shouldst do treason,
Unless to dub thee with the name of traitor.
If that same demon that hath gull'd thee thus
Should with his lion gait walk the whole world,
He might return to vasty Tartar back,
And tell the legions, "I can never win
A soul so easy as that Englishman's."
O, how hast thou with jealousy infected
The sweetness of affiance! Show men dutiful?
Why, so didst thou. Seem they grave and learned?
Why, so didst thou. Come they of noble family?
Why, so didst thou. Seem they religious?
Why, so didst thou. Or are they spare in diet,
Free from gross passion, or of mirth or anger,
Constant in spirit, not swerving with the blood,
Garnish'd and deck'd in modest complement,
Not working with the eye without the ear,
And but in purged judgment trusting neither?
Such and so finely bolted didst thou seem.
And thus thy fall hath left a kind of blot
To [mark the] full-fraught man and best indued
With some suspicion. I will weep for thee;
For this revolt of thine, methinks, is like
Another fall of man. Their faults are open,
Arrest them to the answer of the law,
And God acquit them of their practices!

Exe. I arrest thee of high treason, by the name of Richard Earl of Cambridge.

I arrest thee of high treason, by the name of [Henry] Lord Scroop of Masham.

I arrest thee of high treason, by the name of Thomas Grey, knight, of Northumberland.

Scroop. Our purposes God justly hath discover'd,
And I repent my fault more than my death,
Which I beseech your Highness to forgive,
Although my body pay the price of it.

Cam. For me, the gold of France did not seduce,
Although I did admit it as a motive
The sooner to effect what I intended.
But God be thanked for prevention,
Which [I] in sufferance heartily will rejoice,
Beseeching God, and you, to pardon me.

Grey. Never did faithful subject more rejoice
At the discovery of most dangerous treason
Than I do at this hour joy o'er myself,
Prevented from a damned enterprise.
My fault, but not my body, pardon, sovereign.

K. Hen. God quit you in his mercy! Hear your sentence.
You have conspir'd against our royal person,
Join'd with an enemy proclaim'd, and from his coffers
Receiv'd the golden earnest of our death;
Wherein you would have sold your king to slaughter,
His princes and his peers to servitude,
His subjects to oppression and contempt,
And his whole kingdom into desolation.
Touching our person seek we no revenge,
But we our kingdom's safety must so tender,
Whose ruin you [have] sought, that to her laws
We do deliver you. Get you therefore hence,
Poor miserable wretches, to your death;
The taste whereof God of his mercy give
You patience to endure, and true repentance
Of all your dear offenses! Bear them hence.

Exeunt [Cambridge, Scroop, and Grey, guarded].

Now, lords, for France; the enterprise whereof
Shall be to you as us, like glorious.
We doubt not of a fair and lucky war,
Since God so graciously hath brought to light
This dangerous treason lurking in our way
To hinder our beginnings. We doubt not now
But every rub is smoothed on our way.
Then forth, dear countrymen! Let us deliver
Our puissance into the hand of God,
Putting it straight in expedition.
Cheerly to sea! The signs of war advance!
No king of England, if not king of France!

Flourish. [Exeunt.]

[SCENE III]

Enter PISTOL, NYM, BARDOLPH, BOY, *and* HOSTESS.

Host. Prithee, honey-sweet husband, let me bring thee to Staines.

Pist. No; for my manly heart doth ern.
Bardolph, be blithe; Nym, rouse thy vaunting veins;
Boy, bristle thy courage up; for Falstaff he is dead,
And we must ern therefore.

115–17. botch . . . piety: i.e. clumsily conceal the sin of treason by adorning it with pious motives.
116. colors: pretexts. **fetch'd:** derived.
118. temper'd: moulded. **119. instance:** reason.
122. lion gait. See 1 Peter 5:8: "your adversary the devil, as a roaring lion, walketh about, seeking whom he may devour."
123. Tartar: Tartarus, in classical mythology the place of torment; i.e. hell. **126. jealousy:** suspicion. **127. affiance:** trust.
133. blood: passion. **134. complement:** appearance.
135. Not . . . ear: i.e. relying on the evidence of neither eye nor ear alone. **136. purged:** i.e. impartial. **137. bolted:** sifted.
139. full-fraught: i.e. loaded (with good qualities).
142. open: obvious.
155–57. For . . . intended. These lines, hinting at the start of the long struggle between the houses of York and Lancaster for the English throne, are Shakespeare's strangely cryptic introduction to one of the major subjects of his history plays. As a member of the House of York the Earl of Cambridge was eager to replace King Henry with his own brother-in-law Edmund Mortimer, fifth Earl of March, because, as Holinshed points out (Bullough, IV, 386), "after the death of which earle of March, for diverse secret impediments, not able to have issue, the earle of Cambridge was sure that the crowne should come to him by his wife [who was Edmund's sister], and to his children, of hir begotten." On the Mortimers, whose powerful claim to the throne as descendants of Edward III's third son, Lionel, Duke of Clarence, had been recognized by Richard II, see note to *1 Henry IV*, I.i.38. The Earl of Cambridge was himself the son of Edward III's fifth son, Edmund, Duke of York.

159. in sufferance: though suffering punishment.
166. quit: absolve. **169. earnest:** payment to bind a bargain.
175. tender: regard. **181. dear:** grievous. **183. like:** equally.
188. But: but that. **rub:** obstacle (a bowling term).
191. straight in expedition: at once in action.

II.iii. Location: London. Before the Boar's Head Tavern in Eastcheap.
1. bring: escort.
2. Staines: town west of London on the road to Southampton.
3. ern: mourn.

Bard. Would I were with him, wheresome'er he is, either in heaven or in hell!

Host. Nay sure, he's not in hell; he's in Arthur's bosom, if ever man went to Arthur's bosom. 'A made a finer end, and went away and it had been any christom child. 'A parted ev'n just between twelve and one, ev'n at the turning o' th' tide; for after I saw him fumble with the sheets, and play with flowers, and smile upon his finger's end, I knew there was but one way; for his nose was as sharp as a pen, and 'a [babbl'd] of green fields. "How now, Sir John?" quoth I, "what, man? be a' good cheer." So 'a cried out, "God, God, God!" three or four times. Now I, to comfort him, bid him 'a should not think of God; I hop'd there was no need to trouble himself with any such thoughts yet. So 'a bade me lay more clothes on his feet. I put my hand into the bed and felt them, and they were as cold as any stone; then I felt to his knees, and so up'ard and up'ard, and all was as cold as any stone.

Nym. They say he cried out of sack.

Host. Ay, that 'a did.

Bard. And of women.

Host. Nay, that 'a did not.

Boy. Yes, that 'a did, and said they were dev'ls incarnate.

Host. 'A could never abide carnation—'twas a color he never lik'd.

Boy. 'A said once, the dev'l would have him about women.

Host. 'A did in some sort, indeed, handle women; but then he was rheumatic, and talk'd of the whore of Babylon.

Boy. Do you not remember, 'a saw a flea stick upon Bardolph's nose, and 'a said it was a black soul burning in hell?

Bard. Well, the fuel is gone that maintain'd that fire. That's all the riches I got in his service.

Nym. Shall we shog? the King will be gone from Southampton.

Pist. Come, let's away. My love, give me thy lips.
Look to my chattels and my moveables.
Let senses rule; the [word] is "Pitch and pay";
Trust none;
For oaths are straws, men's faiths are wafer-cakes,
And Hold-fast is the only dog, my duck;
Therefore *Caveto* be thy counsellor.
Go, clear thy crystals. Yoke-fellows in arms,
Let us to France, like horse-leeches, my boys,
To suck, to suck, the very blood to suck!

Boy. And that's but unwholesome food, they say.

Pist. Touch her soft mouth, and march.

Bard. Farewell, hostess. [*Kissing her*.]

Nym. I cannot kiss, that is the humor of it; but adieu.

Pist. Let huswifery appear. Keep close, I thee command.

Host. Farewell; adieu. *Exeunt*.

[SCENE IV]

Flourish. Enter the FRENCH KING, *the* DOLPHIN, *the* DUKES OF BERRI *and* BRITAIN, [*the* CONSTABLE, *and others*].

Fr. King. Thus comes the English with full power upon us,
And more than carefully it us concerns
To answer royally in our defenses.
Therefore the Dukes of Berri and of Britain,
Of Brabant and of Orleance, shall make forth,
And you, Prince Dolphin, with all swift dispatch,
To line and new repair our towns of war
With men of courage and with means defendant;
For England his approaches makes as fierce
As waters to the sucking of a gulf.
It fits us then to be as provident
As fear may teach us out of late examples
Left by the fatal and neglected English
Upon our fields.

Dol. My most redoubted father,
It is most meet we arm us 'gainst the foe;
For peace itself should not so dull a kingdom
(Though war nor no known quarrel were in question)
But that defenses, musters, preparations,
Should be maintain'd, assembled, and collected,
As were a war in expectation.
Therefore, I say, 'tis meet we all go forth
To view the sick and feeble parts of France;
And let us do it with no show of fear,
No, with no more than if we heard that England
Were busied with a Whitsun morris-dance;
For, my good liege, she is so idly king'd,
Her sceptre so fantastically borne,
By a vain, giddy, shallow, humorous youth,
That fear attends her not.

Con. O, peace, Prince Dolphin,
You are too much mistaken in this king.
Question your Grace the late embassadors,

9–10. Arthur's bosom. The Hostess confuses Arthur and Abraham. For Abraham's bosom (i.e. heaven) see Luke 16:22 ff.
12. christom: chrisom, i.e. newly christened.
14. play with flowers: i.e. pick at the bedclothes.
27. of sack: against sack, a Spanish wine of which Falstaff had been very fond. **37. handle:** talk of.
38. rheumatic: blunder for *lunatic*, i.e. delirious (?); perhaps with a pun on *rheum-* and *Rome*, then pronounced similarly (see the following note).
38–39. whore of Babylon: common Protestant name for the Roman Catholic Church, regarded as the scarlet woman of Revelation 17:3–6.
49. Let . . . pay: i.e. be prudent; your motto (as hostess of a tavern) should be "cash down, no credit." **51. wafer-cakes:** i.e. fragile.
52. Hold-fast . . . dog. Alluding to the proverb "Brag is a good dog, but Holdfast is a better." **53. Caveto:** beware.
54. clear thy crystals: i.e. dry your eyes.

62. Let . . . close: i.e. be thrifty and do not run around.

II.iv. Location: France. The King's palace.
1. power: forces.
3. answer . . . defenses: i.e. prepare adequate defenses.
4. Britain: Brittany. **5. Orleance:** Orleans.
7. line: reinforce, garrison. **towns of war:** i.e. fortified towns.
8. means defendant: i.e. weapons of defense.
9. England: the King of England. **10. gulf:** whirlpool.
12. late: recent.
13. fatal and neglected: fatally underestimated. The King recalls French defeats at Crécy (1346) and Poitiers (1356) at the hands of Edward III and his son, Edward the Black Prince. **20. As:** as if.
25. Whitsun morris-dance: folk dance celebrating Whitsuntide, a religious festival held in early summer. **26. idly:** worthlessly.
28. humorous: capricious.

With what great state he heard their embassy,
How well supplied with noble counsellors,
How modest in exception, and withal
How terrible in constant resolution,
And you shall find his vanities forespent
Were but the outside of the Roman Brutus,
Covering discretion with a coat of folly,
As gardeners do with ordure hide those roots
That shall first spring and be most delicate.

Dol. Well, 'tis not so, my Lord High Constable;
But though we think it so, it is no matter.
In cases of defense 'tis best to weigh
The enemy more mighty than he seems,
So the proportions of defense are fill'd;
Which, of a weak and niggardly projection,
Doth like a miser spoil his coat with scanting
A little cloth.

Fr. King. Think we King Harry strong;
And, princes, look you strongly arm to meet him.
The kindred of him hath been flesh'd upon us;
And he is bred out of that bloody strain
That haunted us in our familiar paths.
Witness our too much memorable shame
When Cressy battle fatally was struck,
And all our princes captiv'd by the hand
Of that black name, Edward, Black Prince of Wales;
Whiles that his mountain sire, on mountain standing,
Up in the air, crown'd with the golden sun,
Saw his heroical seed, and smil'd to see him,
Mangle the work of nature, and deface
The patterns that by God and by French fathers
Had twenty years been made. This is a stem
Of that victorious stock; and let us fear
The native mightiness and fate of him.

Enter a Messenger.

Mess. Embassadors from Harry King of England
Do crave admittance to your Majesty.

Fr. King. We'll give them present audience. Go,
and bring them.
[*Exeunt Messenger and certain Lords.*]
You see this chase is hotly followed, friends.

Dol. Turn head, and stop pursuit; for coward dogs
Most spend their mouths when what they seem to
threaten
Runs far before them. Good my sovereign,
Take up the English short, and let them know
Of what a monarchy you are the head.
Self-love, my liege, is not so vile a sin
As self-neglecting.

Enter [Lords *with*] Exeter [*and* Train].

Fr. King. From our brother of England?

Exe. From him, and thus he greets your Majesty:
He wills you, in the name of God Almighty,
That you divest yourself, and lay apart
The borrowed glories that by gift of heaven,
By law of nature and of nations, 'longs
To him and to his heirs, namely, the crown,
And all wide-stretched honors that pertain
By custom, and the ordinance of times,
Unto the crown of France. That you may know
'Tis no sinister nor no awkward claim,
Pick'd from the worm-holes of long-vanish'd days,
Nor from the dust of old oblivion rak'd,
He sends you this most memorable line,
In every branch truly demonstrative;
[*Giving a paper.*]
Willing you overlook this pedigree;
And when you find him evenly deriv'd
From his most fam'd of famous ancestors,
Edward the Third, he bids you then resign
Your crown and kingdom, indirectly held
From him, the native and true challenger.

Fr. King. Or else what follows?

Exe. Bloody constraint; for if you hide the crown
Even in your hearts, there will he rake for it.
Therefore in fierce tempest is he coming,
In thunder and in earthquake, like a Jove,
That if requiring fail he will compel;
And bids you, in the bowels of the Lord,
Deliver up the crown, and to take mercy
On the poor souls for whom this hungry war
Opens his vasty jaws; and on your head
Turning the widows' tears, the orphans' cries,
The dead men's blood, the privy maidens' groans,
For husbands, fathers, and betrothed lovers,
That shall be swallowed in this controversy.
This is his claim, his threat'ning, and my message;
Unless the Dolphin be in presence here,
To whom expressly I bring greeting too.

Fr. King. For us, we will consider of this further.
To-morrow shall you bear our full intent
Back to our brother of England.

Dol. For the Dolphin,
I stand here for him. What to him from England?

Exe. Scorn and defiance, slight regard, contempt,
And any thing that may not misbecome
The mighty sender, doth he prize you at.
Thus says my King: and if your father's Highness
Do not, in grant of all demands at large,
Sweeten the bitter mock you sent his Majesty,
He'll call you to so hot an answer of it
That caves and womby vaultages of France

34. exception: raising objections.
36. vanities forespent: former follies.
37. Roman Brutus: Lucius Junius Brutus, early Roman consul who pretended to be stupid (*brutus*) in order to disarm the suspicions of his uncle, the tyrannical King Tarquin.
45. So . . . fill'd: i.e. in order to provide a full defense.
46. Which: i.e. defense. **of:** i.e. if it be of. **projection:** scale.
50. flesh'd upon us: made fierce by feeding on our flesh.
54. Cressy: Crécy; see note to line 13. **struck:** fought.
57. mountain sire: imposing father.
64. native: hereditary. **fate:** i.e. fortunate lot.
69. Turn head: make a stand (a term from hunting). **stop:** put an end to. **70. Most . . . mouths:** bay the loudest.

78. lay apart: set aside, renounce. **80. 'longs:** belongs.
83. ordinance of times: ancient law.
85. sinister: irregular, illegitimate. **awkward:** indirect.
88. line: genealogical table, pedigree. **89. demonstrative:** decisive.
90. Willing you overlook: desiring that you examine.
91. evenly deriv'd: truly descended.
94. indirectly: unjustly, illegally. **95. challenger:** claimant.
97. constraint: display of force. **101. requiring:** requests.
102. bowels: i.e. compassion.
107. privy maidens' groans: maidens' secret laments.
119. prize: assess. **121. grant:** concession.
124. womby vaultages: hollow caverns.

Shall chide your trespass and return your mock
In second accent of his ordinance.

Dol. Say: if my father render fair return,
It is against my will; for I desire
Nothing but odds with England. To that end,
As matching to his youth and vanity,
I did present him with the Paris balls.

Exe. He'll make your Paris Louvre shake for it,
Were it the mistress court of mighty Europe;
And, be assur'd, you'll find a difference,
As we his subjects have in wonder found,
Between the promise of his greener days
And these he masters now. Now he weighs time
Even to the utmost grain; that you shall read
In your own losses, if he stay in France.

Fr. King. To-morrow shall you know our mind at full. *Flourish.*

Exe. Dispatch us with all speed, lest that our King
Come here himself to question our delay;
For he is footed in this land already.

Fr. King. You shall be soon dispatch'd, with fair conditions.
A night is but small breath, and little pause,
To answer matters of this consequence. *Exeunt.*

ACT [III]

Flourish. Enter CHORUS.

Thus with imagin'd wing our swift scene flies
In motion of no less celerity
Than that of thought. Suppose that you have seen
The well-appointed king at [Hampton] pier
Embark his royalty; and his brave fleet
With silken streamers the young Phoebus [fanning].
Play with your fancies: and in them behold
Upon the hempen tackle ship-boys climbing;
Hear the shrill whistle which doth order give
To sounds confus'd; behold the threaden sails,
Borne with th' invisible and creeping wind,
Draw the huge bottoms through the furrowed sea,
Breasting the lofty surge. O, do but think
You stand upon the rivage and behold
A city on th' inconstant billows dancing;
For so appears this fleet majestical,
Holding due course to Harflew. Follow, follow!
Grapple your minds to sternage of this navy,
And leave your England as dead midnight, still,
Guarded with grandsires, babies, and old women,
Either past or not arriv'd to pith and puissance;
For who is he, whose chin is but enrich'd
With one appearing hair, that will not follow
These cull'd and choice-drawn cavaliers to France?
Work, work your thoughts, and therein see a siege;
Behold the ordinance on their carriages,
With fatal mouths gaping on girded Harflew.
Suppose th' embassador from the French comes back,
Tells Harry that the King doth offer him
Katherine his daughter, and with her, to dowry,
Some petty and unprofitable dukedoms.
The offer likes not; and the nimble gunner
With linstock now the devilish cannon touches,
Alarum, and chambers go off.
And down goes all before them. Still be kind,
And eche out our performance with your mind. *Exit.*

[SCENE I]

Enter the KING, EXETER, BEDFORD, *and* GLOUCESTER.
Alarum. [Enter Soldiers with] scaling-ladders at Harflew.

K. Hen. Once more unto the breach, dear friends, once more;
Or close the wall up with our English dead.
In peace there's nothing so becomes a man
As modest stillness and humility;
But when the blast of war blows in our ears,
Then imitate the action of the tiger;
Stiffen the sinews, [conjure] up the blood,
Disguise fair nature with hard-favor'd rage;
Then lend the eye a terrible aspect;
Let it pry through the portage of the head
Like the brass cannon; let the brow o'erwhelm it
As fearfully as doth a galled rock
O'erhang and jutty his confounded base,
Swill'd with the wild and wasteful ocean.
Now set the teeth and stretch the nostril wide,
Hold hard the breath, and bend up every spirit
To his full height. On, on, you [noblest] English,
Whose blood is fet from fathers of war-proof!
Fathers that, like so many Alexanders,

126. second accent: echo. **ordinance:** ordnance, artillery.
127. fair return: conciliatory response.
129. odds with England: i.e. hostility for the English king.
130. vanity: frivolity. **131. Paris balls:** tennis balls.
132. Louvre: palace of the French kings.
133. mistress: principal (a term from tennis), perhaps with pun on *lover*, the approximate pronunciation of *Louvre*.
136. greener: younger.
138. grain: the smallest unit of weight.
143. footed: landed. Actually, Henry's invasion of France (August 1415) followed Exeter's embassy by six months.
145. small breath: i.e. short time.

III.Cho.1. imagin'd wing: wing of imagination.
4. well-appointed: well-equipped. **5. brave:** gallant.
6. the young Phoebus fanning: fluttering against the rising sun. Phoebus is the sun-god of Greek mythology.
7. fancies: imaginations. **9. shrill whistle:** i.e. of the ship-master.
10. threaden: woven of thread. **12. bottoms:** ships.
14. rivage: shore.
16. fleet majestical. Holinshed (Bullough, IV, 386) records "a thousand ships" in Henry's flotilla.
17. Harflew: Harfleur, French port near the mouth of the Seine. Actually, Henry put ashore at Caux, a nearby town.
18. sternage: the sterns. **21. pith:** strength.
26. ordinance: ordnance. **27. girded:** encircled, besieged.
30. Katherine: Katherine of Valois (1401–37), who married Henry V in 1420 and gave birth to the future Henry VI a year later. Following her husband's death (1422) she may have married Owen Tudor, to whom she bore Edmund Tudor (later Earl of Richmond), father of Henry VII. **to:** as. **32. likes:** pleases.
33. linstock: stick to hold the gunner's match. **touches:** fires. **s.d. Alarum:** call to arms. **chambers:** small cannon. **35. eche:** eke.

III.i. Location: France. Before Harfleur.
10. portage: portholes, i.e. eyes. **11. o'erwhelm:** overhang.
12. galled: worn. **13. jutty:** jut over. **confounded:** ruined.
14. Swill'd: washed. **wasteful:** destructive.
18. fet: derived. **of war-proof:** proved in battle.
19. Alexanders. Alexander the Great lamented that there were no more worlds for him to conquer.

Have in these parts from morn till even fought,
And sheath'd their swords for lack of argument.
Dishonor not your mothers; now attest
That those whom you call'd fathers did beget you.
Be copy now to [men] of grosser blood,
And teach them how to war. And you, good yeomen,
Whose limbs were made in England, show us here
The mettle of your pasture; let us swear
That you are worth your breeding, which I doubt not;
For there is none of you so mean and base
That hath not noble lustre in your eyes.
I see you stand like greyhounds in the slips,
[Straining] upon the start. The game's afoot!
Follow your spirit; and upon this charge
Cry, "God for Harry, England, and Saint George!"

[*Exeunt.*] *Alarum, and chambers go off.*

[Scene II]

Enter Nym, Bardolph, Pistol, *and* Boy.

Bard. On, on, on, on, on! To the breach, to the breach!

Nym. Pray thee, corporal, stay. The knocks are too hot; and for mine own part, I have not a case of lives. The humor of it is too hot, that is the very plain-song of it.

Pist. The plain-song is most just; for humors do abound:
"Knocks go and come; God's vassals drop and die;
And sword and shield,
In bloody field,
Doth win immortal fame."

Boy. Would I were in an alehouse in London, I would give all my fame for a pot of ale and safety.

Pist. And I:
"If wishes would prevail with me,
My purpose should not fail with me,
But thither would I hie."

Boy. "As duly, but not as truly,
As bird doth sing on bough."

Enter Fluellen.

Flu. Up to the breach, you dogs! Avaunt, you cullions! [*Driving them forward.*]

Pist. Be merciful, great duke, to men of mould.
Abate thy rage, abate thy manly rage,
Abate thy rage, great duke!
Good bawcock, bate thy rage; use lenity, sweet chuck!

Nym. These be good humors! your honor wins bad humors.

Exit [*with Bardolph and Pistol; Fluellen steps aside*].

Boy. As young as I am, I have observ'd these three swashers. I am boy to them all three, but all they three, though they would serve me, could not be man to me; for indeed three such antics do not amount to a man. For Bardolph, he is white-liver'd and red-fac'd; by the means whereof 'a faces it out, but fights not. For Pistol, he hath a killing tongue and a quiet sword; by the means whereof 'a breaks words, and keeps whole weapons. For Nym, he hath heard that men of few words are the best men, and therefore he scorns to say his prayers, lest 'a should be thought a coward; but his few bad words are match'd with as few good deeds; for 'a never broke any man's head but his own, and that was against a post when he was drunk. They will steal any thing, and call it purchase. Bardolph stole a lute-case, bore it twelve leagues, and sold it for three half-pence. Nym and Bardolph are sworn brothers in filching, and in Callice they stole a fire-shovel. I knew by that piece of service the men would carry coals. They would have me as familiar with men's pockets as their gloves or their handkerchers; which makes much against my manhood, if I should take from another's pocket to put into mine; for it is plain pocketing up of wrongs. I must leave them, and seek some better service. Their villainy goes against my weak stomach, and therefore I must cast it up. *Exit.*

Enter Gower. [*Fluellen comes forward.*]

Gow. Captain Fluellen, you must come presently to the mines; the Duke of Gloucester would speak with you.

Flu. To the mines? Tell you the Duke, it is not so good to come to the mines; for look you, the mines is not according to the disciplines of the war; the concavities of it is not sufficient. For look you, th' athversary—you may discuss unto the Duke, look you—is digt himself four yard under the countermines. By Cheshu, I think 'a will plow up all, if there is not better directions.

Gow. The Duke of Gloucester, to whom the order of the siege is given, is altogether directed by an Irishman, a very valiant gentleman, i' faith.

Flu. It is Captain Macmorris, is it not?

Gow. I think it be.

Flu. By Cheshu, he is an ass, as in the world; I will verify as much in his beard. He has no more directions in the true disciplines of the wars, look you, of the Roman disciplines, than is a puppy-dog.

21. argument: i.e. something to fight about, adversaries.
24. copy: example. **grosser:** less noble. **27. mettle:** quality.
31. slips: leash. **32. upon the start:** i.e. to start.
34. Saint George: patron saint of England.

III.ii. Location: Scene continues.
4. case: set.
5–6. very plain-song: i.e. simple truth. **20. Avaunt:** be off.
21. cullions: wretches (Italian *coglioni*, testicles).
22. men of mould: men of earth, i.e. mere mortals.
25. bawcock: fine fellow (French *beau coq*).
29. swashers: swaggerers. **31. antics:** buffoons.
32. white-liver'd: cowardly.
45. Callice: Calais, seaport in France.
46–47. carry coals: (1) tolerate affronts; (2) do dirty work.
49. makes: i.e. offends.
51. pocketing . . . wrongs: (1) submitting to insults; (2) receiving stolen goods. **55. mines:** excavations near a besieged fortress.
59. disciplines . . . war: military science, tactics.
59–60. concavities: i.e. slope, incline.
61. discuss unto: inform. **62. digt:** digged. **63. plow:** blow.
65–66. The Duke . . . given. Holinshed records (Bullough, IV, 387) that at Harfleur "the duke of Glocecester, to whom the order of the siege was committed, made three mines under the ground, and approching to the wals with his engins and ordinance, would not suffer them within to take anie rest."
71. verify . . . beard: tell him so to his face.
73. Roman disciplines: i.e. traditional tactics. Fluellen apparently has small respect for such innovations as gunpowder.

Enter MACMORRIS *and* CAPTAIN JAMY.

Gow. Here 'a comes, and the Scots captain, Captain Jamy, with him.

Flu. Captain Jamy is a marvellous falorous gentleman, that is certain, and of great expedition and knowledge in th' aunchiant wars, upon my particular knowledge of his directions. By Cheshu, he will maintain his argument as well as any military man in the world, in the disciplines of the pristine wars of the Romans.

Jamy. I say gud day, Captain Fluellen.

Flu. God-den to your worship, good Captain James.

Gow. How now, Captain Macmorris, have you quit the mines? Have the pioners given o'er?

Mac. By Chrish law, 'tish ill done! The work ish give over, the trompet sound the retreat. By my hand I swear, and my father's soul, the work ish ill done; it ish give over. I would have blowed up the town, so Chrish save me law, in an hour! O, 'tish ill done, 'tish ill done; by my hand 'tish ill done!

Flu. Captain Macmorris, I beseech you now, will you voutsafe me, look you, a few disputations with you, as partly touching or concerning the disciplines of the war, the Roman wars, in the way of argument, look you, and friendly communication; partly to satisfy my opinion, and partly for the satisfaction, look you, of my mind: as touching the direction of the military discipline, that is the point.

Jamy. It sall be vary gud, gud feith, gud captens bath, and I sall quit you with gud leve, as I may pick occasion; that sall I, mary.

Mac. It is no time to discourse, so Chrish save me. The day is hot, and the weather, and the wars, and the King, and the Dukes; it is no time to discourse. The town is beseech'd, and the trumpet call us to the breach, and we talk, and be Chrish, do nothing. 'Tis shame for us all. So God sa' me, 'tis shame to stand still, it is shame, by my hand; and there is throats to be cut, and works to be done, and there ish nothing done, so Christ sa' me law!

Jamy. By the mess, ere theise eyes of mine take themselves to slomber, ay'll de gud service, or I'll lig i' th' grund for it; ay, or go to death; and I'll pay't as valorously as I may, that sall I suerly do, that is the breff and the long. Mary, I wad full fain heard some question 'tween you tway.

Flu. Captain Macmorris, I think, look you, under your correction, there is not many of your nation—

Mac. Of my nation? What ish my nation? Ish a villain, and a basterd, and a knave, and a rascal. What ish my nation? Who talks of my nation?

Flu. Look you, if you take the matter otherwise than is meant, Captain Macmorris, peradventure I shall think you do not use me with that affability as in discretion you ought to use me, look you, being as good a man as yourself, both in the disciplines of war, and in the derivation of my birth, and in other particularities.

Mac. I do not know you so good a man as myself. So Chrish save me, I will cut off your head.

Gow. Gentlemen both, you will mistake each other.

Jamy. A! that's a foul fault. *A parley* [*sounded*].

Gow. The town sounds a parley.

Flu. Captain Macmorris, when there is more better opportunity to be required, look you, I will be so bold as to tell you I know the disciplines of war; and there is an end. *Exeunt.*

77. **expedition.** Perhaps Fluellen confuses *experience* and *erudition.*
84. **God-den:** good e'en, i.e. afternoon.
87. **pioners given o'er:** sappers and miners stopped working.
88. **law:** la (an emphatic interjection).
89. **retreat:** signal to withdraw forces. 103. **quit:** requite, answer.
104. **mary:** marry, indeed (originally the name of the Virgin Mary used as an oath). 114. **mess:** Mass. 115. **lig:** lie.

[SCENE III]

[*Enter some* CITIZENS *on the walls.*] *Enter the* KING *and all his* TRAIN *before the gates.*

K. Hen. How yet resolves the governor of the town?
This is the latest parle we will admit;
Therefore to our best mercy give yourselves,
Or like to men proud of destruction,
Defy us to our worst; for as I am a soldier,
A name that in my thoughts becomes me best,
If I begin the batt'ry once again,
I will not leave the half-achieved Harflew
Till in her ashes she lies buried.
The gates of mercy shall be all shut up,
And the flesh'd soldier, rough and hard of heart,
In liberty of bloody hand, shall range,
With conscience wide as hell, mowing like grass
Your fresh fair virgins and your flow'ring infants.
What is it then to me, if impious War,
Arrayed in flames like to the prince of fiends,
Do with his smirch'd complexion all fell feats
Enlink'd to waste and desolation?
What is't to me, when you yourselves are cause,
If your pure maidens fall into the hand
Of hot and forcing violation?
What rein can hold licentious wickedness
When down the hill he holds his fierce career?
We may as bootless spend our vain command
Upon th' enraged soldiers in their spoil,
As send precepts to the leviathan
To come ashore. Therefore, you men of Harflew,
Take pity of your town and of your people,
Whiles yet my soldiers are in my command,
Whiles yet the cool and temperate wind of grace
O'erblows the filthy and contagious clouds
Of headly murther, spoil, and villainy.

136 s.d. **parley:** trumpet signal for negotiations.
139. **required:** found.

III.iii. **Location:** Before the gates of Harfleur.
2. **latest parle:** last discussion.
4. **proud of destruction:** glorying in their own destruction.
7. **batt'ry:** cannonade.
11. **flesh'd:** enraged. See note to II.iv.50. 12. **liberty:** license.
17. **fell:** cruel. 18. **waste:** destruction.
23. **career:** gallop (a term from horsemanship).
24. **bootless:** unprofitably.
26. **precepts:** written instructions.
31. **O'erblows:** blows away, disperses. 32. **headly:** deadly.

If not—why, in a moment look to see
The blind and bloody soldier with foul hand
[Defile] the locks of your shrill-shriking daughters;
Your fathers taken by the silver beards,
And their most reverend heads dash'd to the walls;
Your naked infants spitted upon pikes,
Whiles the mad mothers with their howls confus'd
Do break the clouds, as did the wives of Jewry
At Herod's bloody-hunting slaughter-men.
What say you? Will you yield, and this avoid?
Or guilty in defense, be thus destroy'd?

Enter GOVERNOR [*to the Citizens*].

Gov. Our expectation hath this day an end.
The Dolphin, whom of succors we entreated,
Returns us that his powers are yet not ready
To raise so great a siege. Therefore, great King,
We yield our town and lives to thy soft mercy.
Enter our gates, dispose of us and ours,
For we no longer are defensible.

K. Hen. Open your gates. Come, uncle Exeter,
Go you and enter Harflew; there remain,
And fortify it strongly 'gainst the French.
Use mercy to them all for us, dear uncle.
The winter coming on, and sickness growing
Upon our soldiers, we will retire to Callice.
To-night in Harflew will we be your guest;
To-morrow for the march are we address'd.

Flourish, and enter the town.

[SCENE IV]

Enter KATHERINE *and* [ALICE,] *an old gentlewoman.*

Kath. Alice, tu as été en Angleterre, et tu bien parles le langage.

Alice. Un peu, madame.

Kath. Je te prie, m'enseignez; il faut que j'apprenne à parler. Comment appelez-vous la main en Anglois?

Alice. La main? Elle est appelée de hand.

Kath. De hand. Et les doigts?

[*Alice.*] Les doigts? Ma foi, j'oublie les doigts, mais je me souviendrai. Les doigts? Je pense qu'ils sont appelés de fingres, oui, de fingres.

[*Kath.*] La main, de hand; les doigts, de fingres. Je pense que je suis le bon écolier; j'ai gagné deux mots d'Anglois vitement. Comment appelez-vous les ongles?

Alice. Les ongles? [Nous] les appelons de nailès.

Kath. De nailès. Écoutez, dites-moi si je parle bien: de hand, de fingres, et de nailès.

Alice. C'est bien dit, madame, il est fort bon Anglois.

Kath. Dites-moi l'Anglois pour le bras.

Alice. De arma, madame.

Kath. Et le coude?

Alice. D' elbow.

Kath. D' elbow. Je m'en fais la répétition de tous les mots que vous m'avez appris dès à présent.

Alice. Il est trop difficile, madame, comme je pense.

Kath. Excusez-moi, Alice; écoutez: d' hand, de fingre, de nailès, d' arma, de bilbow.

Alice. D' elbow, madame.

Kath. O Seigneur Dieu, je m'en oublie d' elbow. Comment appelez-vous le col?

Alice. De nick, madame.

Kath. De nick. Et le menton?

Alice. De chin.

Kath. De sin. Le col, de nick; le menton, de sin.

Alice. Oui. Sauf votre honneur, en vérité, vous prononcez les mots aussi droit que les natifs d'Angleterre.

Kath. Je ne doute point d'apprendre, par la grâce de Dieu, et en peu de temps.

Alice. N'avez vous déjà oublié ce que je vous ai enseigné?

Kath. Non, je réciterai à vous promptement: d' hand, de fingre, de mailès—

Alice. De nailès, madame.

Kath. De nailès, de arma, de ilbow.

Alice. Sauf votre honneur, d' elbow.

Kath. Ainsi dis-je; d' elbow, de nick, et de sin. Comment appelez-vous le pied et la robe?

Alice. Le foot, madame, et le count.

34. blind: i.e. with lust. **35. shriking:** shrieking.
40. Jewry: Judea.
41. Herod's . . . slaughter-men. See Matthew 2:16–18.
43. defense: i.e. not surrendering.
46. Returns us: replies. **50. defensible:** capable of defense.
55–56. The winter . . . Callice. Following the fall of Harfleur, says Holinshed (Bullough, IV, 389), King Henry "determined to have proceeded further in the winning of other townes and fortresses: but bicause the dead time of the winter approched, it was determined by advice of his councell, that he should in all convenient speed set forward, and march through the countrie towards Calis by land, least his returne as then homewards should of slanderous toongs be named a running awaie: and yet that journie was adjudged perillous, by reason that the number of his people was much minished by the flix and other fevers, which sore vexed and brought to death above [illegible]ne hundred persons of the armie." **58. address'd:** prepared.

III.iv. Location: Rouen. The French King's palace.
1–62 *Kath.* Alice, you have been in England, and you know the language well. *Alice.* A little, madam. *Kath.* I pray you, teach me; I must learn to speak it. How do you say *la main* in English? *Alice. La main?* It is called de hand. *Kath.* De hand. And *les doigts?* *Alice. Les doigts?* Dear me, I forget *les doigts*, but it will come to me. *Les doigts.* I think they are called de fingres, yes, de fingres. *Kath. La main*, de hand; *les doigts*, de fingres. I think I am a good pupil; I have learned two English words quickly. What do you call *les ongles? Alice. Les ongles?* We call them de nailès. *Kath.* De nailès. Listen, tell me whether I speak correctly: de hand, de fingres, and de nailès. *Alice.* That is quite correct, madam; it is very good English. *Kath.* Tell me the English for *le bras*. *Alice.* De arma, madam. *Kath.* And *le coude? Alice.* D' elbow. *Kath.* D' elbow. I am going to repeat all the words you have taught me so far. *Alice.* That is too hard, madam, I'm afraid. *Kath.* Excuse me, Alice; listen: d' hand, de fingre, de nailès, d' arma, de bilbow. *Alice.* D' elbow, madam. *Kath.* O Lord, I'm forgetting d' elbow. How do you say *le col? Alice.* De nick, madam. *Kath.* De nick. And *le menton? Alice.* De chin. *Kath.* De sin. *Le col*, de nick; *le menton*, de sin. *Alice.* Yes. If I may say so, truly, you pronounce the words as well as the native English. *Kath.* I'm sure I can learn, by God's grace, and very quickly. *Alice.* Haven't you already forgotten what I've taught you? *Kath.* No, I shall recite for you at once: d' hand, de fingre, de mailès— *Alice.* De nailès, madam. *Kath.* De nailès, de arma, de ilbow. *Alice.* Pardon me, d' elbow. *Kath.* That's what I said; d' elbow, de nick, and de sin. What do you call *le pied* and *la robe? Alice.* Le foot, madam, and le count. *Kath.* Le foot and le count! [She mistakes them for indecent French words.] O Lord, those are bad words, wicked, coarse, and immodest, and not proper for well-bred ladies to use. I wouldn't utter those words before French gentlemen for all the world. Foh! le foot and le count! Nevertheless, I shall recite my whole lesson once more: d' hand, de fingre, de nailès, d' arma, d' elbow, de nick, de sin, de foot, le count. *Alice.* Excellent, madam. *Kath.* That's enough for one time; let's go to dinner.

Kath. Le foot et le count! O Seigneur Dieu! ils sont les mots de son mauvais, corruptible, gros, et impudique, et non pour les dames de honneur d'user. Je ne voudrais prononcer ces mots devant les seigneurs de France pour tout le monde. Foh! le foot et le count! Néanmoins, je réciterai une autre fois ma leçon ensemble: d' hand, de fingre, de nailès, d' arma, d' elbow, de nick, de sin, de foot, le count.

Alice. Excellent, madame!

Kath. C'est assez pour une fois: allons-nous à dîner. *Exeunt.*

[Scene V]

Enter the King of France, *the* Dolphin, [*the* Duke of Britain,] *the* Constable of France, *and others.*

Fr. King. 'Tis certain he hath pass'd the river Somme.
Con. And if he be not fought withal, my lord,
Let us not live in France; let us quit all,
And give our vineyards to a barbarous people.
Dol. *O Dieu vivant!* shall a few sprays of us,
The emptying of our fathers' luxury,
Our scions, put in wild and savage stock,
Spirt up so suddenly into the clouds
And overlook their grafters?
Brit. Normans, but bastard Normans, Norman bastards!
Mort [*Dieu,*] *ma vie!* if they march along
Unfought withal, but I will sell my dukedom,
To buy a slobb'ry and a dirty farm
In that nook-shotten isle of Albion.
Con. *Dieu de batailles!* where have they this mettle?
Is not their climate foggy, raw, and dull,
On whom, as in despite, the sun looks pale,
Killing their fruit with frowns? Can sodden water,
A drench for sur-rein'd jades, their barley-broth,
Decoct their cold blood to such valiant heat?
And shall our quick blood, spirited with wine,
Seem frosty? O, for honor of our land,
Let us not hang like roping icicles
Upon our houses' thatch, whiles a more frosty people
Sweat drops of gallant youth in our rich fields!
Poor we call them in their native lords!
Dol. By faith and honor,
Our madams mock at us, and plainly say
Our mettle is bred out, and they will give
Their bodies to the lust of English youth
To new-store France with bastard warriors.
Brit. They bid us to the English dancing-schools,
And teach lavoltas high and swift corantos,
Saying our grace is only in our heels,
And that we are most lofty runaways.
Fr. King. Where is Montjoy the herald? Speed him hence,
Let him greet England with our sharp defiance.
Up, princes, and, with spirit of honor edged
More sharper than your swords, hie to the field!
Charles Delabreth, High Constable of France,
You Dukes of Orleance, Bourbon, and of Berri,
Alanson, Brabant, Bar, and Burgundy,
Jacques Chatillion, Rambures, Vaudemont,
Beaumont, Grandpré, Roussi, and Faulconbridge,
[Foix], Lestrake, Bouciqualt, and Charolois;
High dukes, great princes, barons, lords, and [knights],
For your great seats now quit you of great shames.
Bar Harry England, that sweeps through our land
With pennons painted in the blood of Harflew.
Rush on his host, as doth the melted snow
Upon the valleys whose low vassal seat
The Alps doth spit and void his rheum upon.
Go down upon him, you have power enough,
And in a captive chariot into Roan
Bring him our prisoner.
Con. This becomes the great.
Sorry am I his numbers are so few,
His soldiers sick and famish'd in their march;
For I am sure, when he shall see our army,
He'll drop his heart into the sink of fear,
And for achievement offer us his ransom.
Fr. King. Therefore, Lord Constable, haste on Montjoy,
And let him say to England that we send
To know what willing ransom he will give.
Prince Dolphin, you shall stay with us in Roan.
Dol. Not so, I do beseech your Majesty.
Fr. King. Be patient, for you shall remain with us.
Now forth, Lord Constable and princes all,
And quickly bring us word of England's fall. *Exeunt.*

[Scene VI]

Enter Captains, English and Welsh, Gower *and* Fluellen.

Gow. How now, Captain Fluellen, come you from the bridge?

Flu. I assure you, there is very excellent services committed at the bridge.

Gow. Is the Duke of Exeter safe?

III.v. Location. Rouen. The French King's palace.
1. he . . . Somme: i.e. in retreating to winter quarters at Calais.
2. withal: with.
5. Dieu vivant: living God. sprays: bastards.
6. fathers' luxury: ancestors' lust.
7. scions: slips for grafting. put in: grafted upon.
8. Spirt: shoot. 9. overlook: overtop.
11. Mort . . . vie: death of God! my life. 13. slobb'ry: slovenly.
14. nook-shotten: full of nooks, indented. Albion: England.
15. Dieu de batailles: god of battles.
18. sodden water: boiled water, i.e. ale.
19. drench . . . jades: drink for overworked horses.
20. Decoct: warm. 21. quick: lively.
23. roping: i.e. hanging in rope-like lengths. 32. bid us: bid us go.
33. lavoltas, corantos: kinds of dances.
35. lofty runaways: stylish cowards.
36. Montjoy: title of the chief French herald.
47. seats: fiefs, estates (which were held under the king). quit you: redeem yourselves. 51. vassal: base. 52. rheum: i.e. waters.
54. Roan: Rouen, capital city of Normandy.
59. sink: cesspool. 60. for achievement: in place of victory.

III.vi. Location: The English camp in Picardy.
2. bridge. Trying to secure a vital bridge on the road to Calais, Henry's advance forces found French troops on the point of demolishing it, whereupon, says Holinshed (Bullough, IV, 390), they "assailed them so vigorouslie, that they discomfited them, and tooke and slue them; and so the bridge was preserved till the king came, and passed the river by the same with his whole armie."

Flu. The Duke of Exeter is as magnanimous as Agamemnon, and a man that I love and honor with my soul, and my heart, and my duty, and my live, and my living, and my uttermost power. He is not—God be praised and blessed!—any hurt in the world, but keeps the bridge most valiantly, with excellent discipline. There is an aunchient lieutenant there at the pridge, I think in my very conscience he is as valiant a man as Mark Antony, and he is a man of no estimation in the world, but I did see him do as gallant service.

Gow. What do you call him?

Flu. He is call'd Aunchient Pistol.

Gow. I know him not.

Enter PISTOL.

Flu. Here is the man.

Pist. Captain, I thee beseech to do me favors.
The Duke of Exeter doth love thee well.

Flu. Ay, I praise God, and I have merited some love at his hands.

Pist. Bardolph, a soldier firm and sound of heart,
And of buxom valor, hath by cruel fate,
And giddy Fortune's furious fickle wheel,
That goddess blind,
That stands upon the rolling restless stone—

Flu. By your patience, Aunchient Pistol: Fortune is painted blind, with a muffler afore his eyes, to signify to you that Fortune is blind; and she is painted also with a wheel, to signify to you, which is the moral of it, that she is turning, and inconstant, and mutability, and variation; and her foot, look you, is fixed upon a spherical stone, which rolls, and rolls, and rolls. In good truth, the poet makes a most excellent description of it. Fortune is an excellent moral.

Pist. Fortune is Bardolph's foe, and frowns on him;
For he hath stol'n a pax, and hanged must 'a be—
A damned death!
Let gallows gape for dog, let man go free,
And let not hemp his windpipe suffocate.
But Exeter hath given the doom of death
For pax of little price.
Therefore go speak, the Duke will hear thy voice;
And let not Bardolph's vital thread be cut
With edge of penny cord and vile reproach.
Speak, captain, for his life, and I will thee requite.

Flu. Aunchient Pistol, I do partly understand your meaning.

Pist. Why then rejoice therefore.

Flu. Certainly, aunchient, it is not a thing to rejoice at; for if, look you, he were my brother, I would desire the Duke to use his good pleasure, and put him to execution; for discipline ought to be used.

Pist. Die and be damn'd! and *figo* for thy friendship!

Flu. It is well.

Pist. The fig of Spain. *Exit.*

Flu. Very good.

Gow. Why, this is an arrant counterfeit rascal, I remember him now; a bawd, a cutpurse.

Flu. I'll assure you, 'a utt'red as prave words at the pridge as you shall see in a summer's day. But it is very well; what he has spoke to me, that is well, I warrant you, when time is serve.

Gow. Why, 'tis a gull, a fool, a rogue, that now and then goes to the wars, to grace himself at his return into London under the form of a soldier. And such fellows are perfit in the great commanders' names, and they will learn you by rote where services were done—at such and such a sconce, at such a breach, at such a convoy; who came off bravely, who was shot, who disgrac'd, what terms the enemy stood on; and this they con perfitly in the phrase of war, which they trick up with new-tun'd oaths; and what a beard of the general's cut and a horrid suit of the camp will do among foaming bottles and ale-wash'd wits, is wonderful to be thought on. But you must learn to know such slanders of the age, or else you may be marvellously mistook.

Flu. I tell you what, Captain Gower: I do perceive he is not the man that he would gladly make show to the world he is. If I find a hole in his coat, I will tell him my mind. [*Drum heard.*] Hark you, the King is coming, and I must speak with him from the pridge.

Drum and Colors. Enter the KING *and his poor Soldiers* [*and* GLOUCESTER].

God pless your Majesty!

K. Hen. How now, Fluellen, cam'st thou from the bridge?

Flu. Ay, so please your Majesty. The Duke of Exeter has very gallantly maintain'd the pridge. The French is gone off, look you, and there is gallant and most prave passages. Marry, th' athversary was have possession of the pridge, but he is enforced to retire, and the Duke of Exeter is master of the pridge. I can tell your Majesty, the Duke is a prave man.

K. Hen. What men have you lost, Fluellen?

Flu. The perdition of th' athversary hath been very great, reasonable great. Marry, for my part, I think the Duke hath lost never a man, but one that is like to be executed for robbing a church, one Bardolph, if your Majesty know the man. His face is all bubukles, and whelks, and knobs, and flames a' fire, and his lips blows at his nose, and it is like a coal of fire, sometimes plue and sometimes red, but his nose is executed, and

7. Agamemnon: Grecian leader in the Trojan war.
12. aunchient lieutenant: sub-lieutenant (?). *Ancient* = ensign, standard-bearer. **14. Mark Antony**: famous Roman general.
14–15. estimation: fame. **26. buxom**: brisk.
33. moral: significance. **38. moral**: symbolic figure, emblem.
40. pax: piece of metal with a crucifix stamped on it. Perhaps a mistake for the *pyx* (a box containing the sacramental wafer) that Holinshed reports (Bullough, IV, 389) was stolen by an English soldier who was duly "strangled" for the crime. On landing in France, says Holinshed (Bullough, IV, 386–87), Henry had forbidden "on paine of deathe" any soldier's stealing from churches, molesting priests or other unarmed persons, and brawling.

57. figo: contemptuous gesture made by thrusting the thumb between the next two fingers, or between the teeth.
59. fig of Spain. Presumably an even greater insult than the *figo* of line 57. **67. gull**: simpleton. **70. perfit**: perfect.
72. sconce: part of a fortification. **75. con**: memorize.
77. horrid . . . camp: terrifying soldier's garb.
80. slanders . . . age: i.e. those who are a scandal of the time.
84. a hole . . . coat: i.e. grounds for exposing him.
86 s.d. Drum and Colors: drummer and flagbearer.
98. perdition: losses. **102. bubukles**: carbuncles.
103. whelks: pimples.
105. executed: i.e. slit preparatory to his death on the gallows.

his fire's out.

K. Hen. We would have all such offenders so cut off; and we give express charge that in our marches through the country there be nothing compell'd from the villages; nothing taken but paid for; none of the French upbraided or abus'd in disdainful language; for when [lenity] and cruelty play for a kingdom, the gentler gamester is the soonest winner.

Tucket. Enter MONTJOY.

Mont. You know me by my habit.

K. Hen. Well then, I know thee. What shall I know of thee?

Mont. My master's mind.

K. Hen. Unfold it.

Mont. Thus says my King: Say thou to Harry of England, Though we seem'd dead, we did but sleep; advantage is a better soldier than rashness. Tell him we could have rebuk'd him at Harflew, but that we thought not good to bruise an injury till it were full ripe. Now we speak upon our cue, and our voice is imperial: England shall repent his folly, see his weakness, and admire our sufferance. Bid him therefore consider of his ransom, which must proportion the losses we have borne, the subjects we have lost, the disgrace we have digested; which in weight to re-answer, his pettiness would bow under. For our losses, his exchequer is too poor; for th' effusion of our blood, the muster of his kingdom too faint a number; and for our disgrace, his own person kneeling at our feet but a weak and worthless satisfaction. To this add defiance; and tell him, for conclusion, he hath betray'd his followers, whose condemnation is pronounc'd. So far my King and master; so much my office.

K. Hen. What is thy name? I know thy quality.

Mont. Montjoy.

K. Hen. Thou dost thy office fairly. Turn thee back,
And tell thy King I do not seek him now,
But could be willing to march on to Callice
Without impeachment; for to say the sooth,
Though 'tis no wisdom to confess so much
Unto an enemy of craft and vantage,
My people are with sickness much enfeebled,
My numbers lessen'd; and those few I have
Almost no better than so many French;
Who when they were in health, I tell thee, herald,
I thought upon one pair of English legs
Did march three Frenchmen. Yet forgive me, God,
That I do brag thus! This your air of France
Hath blown that vice in me. I must repent.
Go therefore tell thy master here I am;
My ransom is this frail and worthless trunk;
My army but a weak and sickly guard;
Yet, God before, tell him we will come on,
Though France himself and such another neighbor
Stand in our way. There's for thy labor, Montjoy.
Go bid thy master well advise himself.
If we may pass, we will; if we be hind'red,
We shall your tawny ground with your red blood
Discolor; and so, Montjoy, fare you well.
The sum of all our answer is but this:
We would not seek a battle as we are,
Nor, as we are, we say we will not shun it.
So tell your master.

Mont. I shall deliver so. Thanks to your Highness. [*Exit.*]

Glou. I hope they will not come upon us now.

K. Hen. We are in God's hand, brother, not in theirs.
March to the bridge, it now draws toward night;
Beyond the river we'll encamp ourselves,
And on to-morrow bid them march away. *Exeunt.*

[SCENE VII]

Enter the CONSTABLE OF FRANCE, *the* LORD RAMBURES, ORLEANCE, DOLPHIN, *with others.*

Con. Tut, I have the best armor of the world. Would it were day!

Orl. You have an excellent armor; but let my horse have his due.

Con. It is the best horse of Europe.

Orl. Will it never be morning?

Dol. My Lord of Orleance, and my Lord High Constable, you talk of horse and armor?

Orl. You are as well provided of both as any prince in the world.

Dol. What a long night is this! I will not change my horse with any that treads but on four [pasterns]. *Ça*, ha! he bounds from the earth, as if his entrails were hairs; *le cheval volant*, the Pegasus, *chez les narines de feu!* When I bestride him, I soar, I am a hawk; he trots the air; the earth sings when he touches it; the basest horn of his hoof is more musical than the pipe of Hermes.

Orl. He's of the color of the nutmeg.

106. **his:** its. 113 s.d. **Tucket:** trumpet call.
114. **habit:** i.e. herald's costume. 120. **advantage:** circumspection.
122. **bruise an injury:** squeeze a pimple.
123. **upon our cue:** i.e. at the appropriate time.
125. **admire our sufferance:** be astonished at our patience.
126. **proportion:** be proportionate to. 128. **digested:** endured.
128–29. **which . . . under:** i.e. for which he is too puny to make adequate restitution.
131. **muster:** total population. **faint:** small.
137. **quality:** status and calling. 139. **fairly:** admirably.
142. **impeachment:** impediment.
144. **vantage:** i.e. superior resources.
152. **blown:** brought to bloom.

154. **trunk:** i.e. his own body. 156. **God before:** i.e. God leading us.
159–65. **Go . . . it.** "Mine intent is to doo as it pleaseth God," Holinshed reports Henry as replying to Montjoy (Bullough, IV, 390); "I will not seeke your maister at this time; but if he or his seeke me, I will meet with them God willing. If anie of your nation attempt once to stop me in my journie now towards Calis, at their jeopardie be it: and yet wish I not anie of you so unadvised, as to be the occasion that I die your tawnie ground with your red bloud."
159. **well advise himself:** take careful thought.
172. **bid . . . away:** i.e. order the army to proceed toward Calais.

III.vii. Location: The French camp near Agincourt.
12. **pasterns:** hoofs.
13–14. **as . . . hairs:** i.e. like a tennis ball (which was stuffed with hair). 13. **Ça:** that one.
14. **le cheval volant:** the flying horse. **Pegasus:** in Greek mythology, the winged horse ridden by Perseus.
14–15. **chez . . . feu:** with fiery nostrils.
17. **basest horn:** (1) lowest part of the hoof; (2) noise made by the hoofs striking the earth.
18. **Hermes:** in Greek mythology, the messenger of the gods. Ovid tells how with the music of his pipe he lulled to sleep Argus, a monster with a hundred eyes.

Dol. And of the heat of the ginger. It is a beast for Perseus. He is pure air and fire; and the dull elements of earth and water never appear in him, but only in patient stillness while his rider mounts him. He is indeed a horse, and all other jades you may call beasts.

Con. Indeed, my lord, it is a most absolute and excellent horse.

Dol. It is the prince of palfreys: his neigh is like the bidding of a monarch, and his countenance enforces homage.

Orl. No more, cousin.

Dol. Nay, the man hath no wit that cannot, from the rising of the lark to the lodging of the lamb, vary deserv'd praise on my palfrey. It is a theme as fluent as the sea; turn the sands into eloquent tongues, and my horse is argument for them all. 'Tis a subject for a sovereign to reason on, and for a sovereign's sovereign to ride on; and for the world, familiar to us and unknown, to lay apart their particular functions and wonder at him. I once writ a sonnet in his praise and began thus: "Wonder of nature"—

Orl. I have heard a sonnet begin so to one's mistress.

Dol. Then did they imitate that which I compos'd to my courser, for my horse is my mistress.

Orl. Your mistress bears well.

Dol. Me well, which is the prescript praise and perfection of a good and particular mistress.

Con. Nay, for methought yesterday your mistress shrewdly shook your back.

Dol. So perhaps did yours.

Con. Mine was not bridled.

Dol. O then belike she was old and gentle, and you rode like a kern of Ireland, your French hose off, and in your strait strossers.

Con. You have good judgment in horsemanship.

Dol. Be warn'd by me then: they that ride so, and ride not warily, fall into foul bogs. I had rather have my horse to my mistress.

Con. I had as live have my mistress a jade.

Dol. I tell thee, Constable, my mistress wears his own hair.

Con. I could make as true a boast as that, if I had a sow to my mistress.

Dol. "*Le chien est retourné à son propre vomissement, et la* [*truie*] *lavée au bourbier*." Thou mak'st use of any thing.

Con. Yet do I not use my horse for my mistress, or any such proverb so little kin to the purpose.

Ram. My Lord Constable, the armor that I saw in your tent to-night, are those stars or suns upon it?

Con. Stars, my lord.

Dol. Some of them will fall to-morrow, I hope.

Con. And yet my sky shall not want.

Dol. That may be, for you bear a many superfluously, and 'twere more honor some were away.

Con. Ev'n as your horse bears your praises, who would trot as well, were some of your brags dismounted.

Dol. Would I were able to load him with his desert! Will it never be day? I will trot to-morrow a mile, and my way shall be pav'd with English faces.

Con. I will not say so, for fear I should be fac'd out of my way. But I would it were morning, for I would fain be about the ears of the English.

Ram. Who will go to hazard with me for twenty prisoners?

Con. You must first go yourself to hazard, ere you have them.

Dol. 'Tis midnight, I'll go arm myself. *Exit.*

Orl. The Dolphin longs for morning.

Ram. He longs to eat the English.

Con. I think he will eat all he kills.

Orl. By the white hand of my lady, he's a gallant prince.

Con. Swear by her foot, that she may tread out the oath.

Orl. He is simply the most active gentleman of France.

Con. Doing is activity, and he will still be doing.

Orl. He never did harm, that I heard of.

Con. Nor will do none to-morrow. He will keep that good name still.

Orl. I know him to be valiant.

Con. I was told that by one that knows him better than you.

Orl. What's he?

Con. Marry, he told me so himself, and he said he car'd not who knew it.

Orl. He needs not, it is no hidden virtue in him.

Con. By my faith, sir, but it is; never anybody saw it but his lackey. 'Tis a hooded valor, and when it appears, it will bate.

Orl. "Ill will never said well."

Con. I will cap that proverb with "There is flattery in friendship."

Orl. And I will take up that with "Give the devil his due."

Con. Well plac'd. There stands your friend for the devil; have at the very eye of that proverb with "A pox of the devil."

Orl. You are the better at proverbs, by how much "A fool's bolt is soon shot."

Con. You have shot over.

Orl. 'Tis not the first time you were overshot.

24. jades: nags.
25. absolute: perfect. **27. palfreys:** saddle horses.
32. lodging: lying down. **35. argument:** subject.
36. reason: discourse.
38. lay apart: i.e. combine. **particular:** separate.
46. prescript: prescribed.
47. particular: belonging to only one. **49. shrewdly:** painfully.
53. kern: light-armed Irish soldier. **French hose:** wide breeches.
54. strait strossers: tight trousers. **58. to:** as.
59. live: lief. **jade:** (1) nag; (2) loose woman.
64–65. Le chien . . . bourbier: "The dog is turned to his own vomit again; and the sow that was washed, to his wallowing in the mire" (2 Peter 2:22).
73. sky: i.e. honor. **want:** lack (stars, i.e. honors).
82–83. fac'd . . . way: turned aside. **84. fain:** gladly.
85. go to hazard: wager. The French were so certain of success on the eve of Agincourt, says Holinshed (Bullough, IV, 394), that they "made great triumph, for the capteins had determined before, how to divide the spoile, and the soldiers the night before had plaid [i.e. played for] the Englishman at dice." **99. still:** always.
110–11. never . . . lackey: i.e. he is brave only in beating his servant.
111. hooded. A hawk was masked or hooded until the prey was sighted. **112. bate:** (1) flap the wings; (2) be downcast.
123. shot over: i.e. missed the mark.
124. overshot: i.e. defeated.

Enter a MESSENGER.

Mess. My Lord High Constable, the English lie within fifteen hundred paces of your tents.

Con. Who hath measur'd the ground?

Mess. The Lord Grandpré.

Con. A valiant and most expert gentleman. Would it were day! Alas, poor Harry of England! he longs not for the dawning as we do.

Orl. What a wretched and peevish fellow is this King of England, to mope with his fat-brain'd followers so far out of his knowledge!

Con. If the English had any apprehension, they would run away.

Orl. That they lack; for if their heads had any intellectual armor, they could never wear such heavy head-pieces.

Ram. That island of England breeds very valiant creatures; their mastiffs are of unmatchable courage.

Orl. Foolish curs, that run winking into the mouth of a Russian bear and have their heads crush'd like rotten apples! You may as well say, that's a valiant flea that dare eat his breakfast on the lip of a lion.

Con. Just, just; and the men do sympathize with the mastiffs in robustious and rough coming on, leaving their wits with their wives; and then give them great meals of beef and iron and steel, they will eat like wolves and fight like devils.

Orl. Ay, but these English are shrowdly out of beef.

Con. Then shall we find to-morrow they have only stomachs to eat and none to fight. Now is it time to arm. Come, shall we about it?

Orl. It is now two a' clock; but let me see, by ten
We shall have each a hundred Englishmen. *Exeunt.*

ACT [IV]

[*Enter*] CHORUS.

Now entertain conjecture of a time
When creeping murmur and the poring dark
Fills the wide vessel of the universe.
From camp to camp, through the foul womb of night,
The hum of either army stilly sounds,
That the fix'd sentinels almost receive
The secret whispers of each other's watch.
Fire answers fire, and through their paly flames
Each battle sees the other's umber'd face.
Steed threatens steed, in high and boastful neighs
Piercing the night's dull ear; and from the tents
The armorers, accomplishing the knights,
With busy hammers closing rivets up,
Give dreadful note of preparation.
The country cocks do crow, the clocks do toll,
And the third hour of drowsy morning [name].
Proud of their numbers and secure in soul,
The confident and overlusty French
Do the low-rated English play at dice;
And chide the cripple tardy-gaited night,
Who like a foul and ugly witch doth limp
So tediously away. The poor condemned English,
Like sacrifices, by their watchful fires
Sit patiently and inly ruminate
The morning's danger; and their gesture sad,
Investing lank-lean cheeks and war-worn coats,
Presented them unto the gazing moon
So many horrid ghosts. O now, who will behold
The royal captain of this ruin'd band
Walking from watch to watch, from tent to tent,
Let him cry, "Praise and glory on his head!"
For forth he goes, and visits all his host,
Bids them good morrow with a modest smile,
And calls them brothers, friends, and countrymen.
Upon his royal face there is no note
How dread an army hath enrounded him;
Nor doth he dedicate one jot of color
Unto the weary and all-watched night;
But freshly looks, and overbears attaint
With cheerful semblance and sweet majesty;
That every wretch, pining and pale before,
Beholding him, plucks comfort from his looks.
A largess universal, like the sun,
His liberal eye doth give to every one,
Thawing cold fear, that mean and gentle all
Behold, as may unworthiness define,
A little touch of Harry in the night.
And so our scene must to the battle fly;
Where—O for pity!—we shall much disgrace
With four or five most vile and ragged foils
(Right ill dispos'd, in brawl ridiculous)
The name of Agincourt. Yet sit and see,
Minding true things by what their mock'ries be.
Exit.

[SCENE I]

Enter the KING, BEDFORD, *and* GLOUCESTER.

K. Hen. Gloucester, 'tis true that we are in great danger,
The greater therefore should our courage be.
Good morrow, brother Bedford. God Almighty!
There is some soul of goodness in things evil,
Would men observingly distill it out;

132. peevish: silly. **133. mope:** wander in a daze.
134. out . . . knowledge: beyond his capacity.
135. apprehension: common sense.
143. winking: with closed eyes.
147. Just: true. **sympathize:** resemble.
152. shrowdly out of: devilishly short of (*shrowdly* is a variant form of *shrewdly*).

IV.Cho.1. entertain conjecture of: i.e. imagine.
2. poring dark: i.e. dark in which one must strain to see.
6. That: so that. **8. paly:** pale.
9. battle: army. **umber'd:** dusky.
12. accomplishing: equipping.
17. secure: overconfident.
19. low-rated: underrated. **play at dice.** See note to III.vii.85.
24. inly: inwardly. **25. gesture sad:** serious bearing.
26. Investing: accompanying. **35. note:** indication.
36. enrounded: encircled.
37–38. Nor . . . night: i.e. he has not grown pale from wakefulness.
39. overbears attaint: suppresses all indications of fatigue.
45. mean and gentle: i.e. both commoners and nobles.
46. as . . . define: i.e. as well as their limitations permit.
53. Minding . . . be: representing to yourself the truth of what we imitate so badly.

IV.i. Location: The English camp at Agincourt.

For our bad neighbor makes us early stirrers,
Which is both healthful and good husbandry.
Besides, they are our outward consciences
And preachers to us all, admonishing
That we should dress us fairly for our end.
Thus may we gather honey from the weed,
And make a moral of the devil himself.

Enter Erpingham.

Good morrow, old Sir Thomas Erpingham.
A good soft pillow for that good white head
Were better than a churlish turf of France.

Erp. Not so, my liege, this lodging likes me better,
Since I may say, "Now lie I like a king."

K. Hen. 'Tis good for men to love their present pains
Upon example; so the spirit is eased;
And when the mind is quick'ned, out of doubt,
The organs, though defunct and dead before,
Break up their drowsy grave, and newly move
With casted slough and fresh legerity.
Lend me thy cloak, Sir Thomas. Brothers both,
Commend me to the princes in our camp;
Do my good morrow to them, and anon
Desire them all to my pavilion.

Glou. We shall, my liege.

Erp. Shall I attend your Grace?

K. Hen. No, my good knight;
Go with my brothers to my lords of England.
I and my bosom must debate a while,
And then I would no other company.

Erp. The Lord in heaven bless thee, noble Harry!
Exeunt [*all but the King*].

K. Hen. God-a-mercy, old heart, thou speak'st cheerfully.

Enter Pistol.

Pist. *Qui vous là?*

K. Hen. A friend.

Pist. Discuss unto me, art thou officer,
Or art thou base, common, and popular?

K. Hen. I am a gentleman of a company.

Pist. Trail'st thou the puissant pike?

K. Hen. Even so. What are you?

Pist. As good a gentleman as the Emperor.

K. Hen. Then you are a better than the King.

Pist. The King's a bawcock, and a heart of gold,
A lad of life, an imp of fame,
Of parents good, of fist most valiant.
I kiss his dirty shoe, and from heart-string
I love the lovely bully. What is thy name?

K. Hen. Harry le Roy.

Pist. Le Roy? a Cornish name. Art thou of Cornish crew?

K. Hen. No, I am a Welshman.

Pist. Know'st thou Fluellen?

K. Hen. Yes.

Pist. Tell him I'll knock his leek about his pate
Upon Saint Davy's day.

K. Hen. Do not you wear your dagger in your cap that day, lest he knock that about yours.

Pist. Art thou his friend?

K. Hen. And his kinsman too.

Pist. The *figo* for thee then!

K. Hen. I thank you. God be with you!

Pist. My name is Pistol call'd. *Exit.*

K. Hen. It sorts well with your fierceness.
Manet King [*to one side*].

Enter Fluellen *and* Gower.

Gow. Captain Fluellen!

Flu. So! in the name of Jesu Christ, speak fewer. It is the greatest admiration in the universal world, when the true and aunchient prerogatifes and laws of the wars is not kept. If you would take the pains but to examine the wars of Pompey the Great, you shall find, I warrant you, that there is no tiddle taddle nor pibble babble in Pompey's camp. I warrant you, you shall find the ceremonies of the wars, and the cares of it, and the forms of it, and the sobriety of it, and the modesty of it, to be otherwise.

Gow. Why, the enemy is loud, you hear him all night.

Flu. If the enemy is an ass and a fool, and a prating coxcomb, is it meet, think you, that we should also, look you, be an ass and a fool, and a prating coxcomb, in your own conscience now?

Gow. I will speak lower.

Flu. I pray you, and beseech you, that you will.
Exit [*with Gower*].

K. Hen. Though it appear a little out of fashion,
There is much care and valor in this Welshman.

Enter three soldiers, John Bates, Alexander Court, *and* Michael Williams.

Court. Brother John Bates, is not that the morning which breaks yonder?

Bates. I think it be; but we have no great cause to desire the approach of day.

Will. We see yonder the beginning of the day, but I think we shall never see the end of it. Who goes there?

K. Hen. A friend.

Will. Under what captain serve you?

K. Hen. Under Sir [Thomas] Erpingham.

Will. A good old commander and a most kind gen-

7. good husbandry: i.e. thrifty.
10. dress us fairly: i.e. make proper preparation.
15. churlish: i.e. sparse. **16. likes**: suits.
19. Upon example: as an example, i.e. in exemplary fashion.
23. With casted slough: i.e. like a snake having shed its old skin. **legerity**: nimbleness.
24. Brothers both: i.e. Gloucester and Bedford.
25. Commend me: present my compliments.
26. Do . . . morrow: say good morning for me. **27. Desire**: invite.
34. God-a-mercy: gramercy, i.e. many thanks.
35. Qui vous là: who are you there. **37. Discuss unto**: tell.
38. base . . . popular: i.e. a common soldier.
39. gentleman of a company: i.e. inferior officer.
40. Trail'st . . . pike: i.e. do you serve in the infantry.
44. bawcock. See note to III.ii.25.
45. imp of fame: scion of noble stock.

54–55. I'll . . . day. On October 1 the Welsh wore leeks in their caps to commemorate a victory over the Saxons, as ordered by their patron saint, David. **60. figo.** See note to III.vi.57.
63. sorts well with: befits. **66. admiration**: wonder.
69. Pompey the Great: Roman general.
83. out of fashion: eccentric. **84. care**: carefulness.

tleman. I pray you, what thinks he of our estate?

K. Hen. Even as men wrack'd upon a sand, that look to be wash'd off the next tide.

Bates. He hath not told his thought to the King?

K. Hen. No; nor it is not meet he should. For though I speak it to you, I think the King is but a man, as I am. The violet smells to him as it doth to me; the element shows to him as it doth to me; all his senses have but human conditions. His ceremonies laid by, in his nakedness he appears but a man; and though his affections are higher mounted than ours, yet when they stoop, they stoop with the like wing. Therefore, when he sees reason of fears, as we do, his fears, out of doubt, be of the same relish as ours are; yet in reason, no man should possess him with any appearance of fear, lest he, by showing it, should dishearten his army.

Bates. He may show what outward courage he will; but I believe, as cold a night as 'tis, he could wish himself in Thames up to the neck; and so I would he were, and I by him, at all adventures, so we were quit here.

K. Hen. By my troth, I will speak my conscience of the King: I think he would not wish himself any where but where he is.

Bates. Then I would he were here alone; so should he be sure to be ransom'd, and a many poor men's lives sav'd.

K. Hen. I dare say you love him not so ill to wish him here alone, howsoever you speak this to feel other men's minds. Methinks I could not die any where so contented as in the King's company, his cause being just and his quarrel honorable.

Will. That's more than we know.

Bates. Ay, or more than we should seek after; for we know enough, if we know we are the King's subjects. If his cause be wrong, our obedience to the King wipes the crime of it out of us.

Will. But if the cause be not good, the King himself hath a heavy reckoning to make, when all those legs, and arms, and heads, chopp'd off in a battle, shall join together at the latter day and cry all, "We died at such a place"—some swearing, some crying for a surgeon, some upon their wives left poor behind them, some upon the debts they owe, some upon their children rawly left. I am afeard there are few die well that die in a battle; for how can they charitably dispose of any thing, when blood is their argument? Now, if these men do not die well, it will be a black matter for the King that led them to it; who to disobey were against all proportion of subjection.

K. Hen. So, if a son that is by his father sent about merchandise do sinfully miscarry upon the sea, the imputation of his wickedness, by your rule, should be impos'd upon his father that sent him; or if a servant, under his master's command transporting a sum of money, be assail'd by robbers and die in many irreconcil'd iniquities, you may call the business of the master the author of the servant's damnation. But this is not so. The King is not bound to answer the particular endings of his soldiers, the father of his son, nor the master of his servant; for they purpose not their death when they purpose their services. Besides, there is no king, be his cause never so spotless, if it come to the arbitrement of swords, can try it out with all unspotted soldiers. Some, peradventure, have on them the guilt of premeditated and contriv'd murther; some, of beguiling virgins with the broken seals of perjury; some, making the wars their bulwark, that have before gor'd the gentle bosom of peace with pillage and robbery. Now, if these men have defeated the law and outrun native punishment, though they can outstrip men, they have no wings to fly from God. War is his beadle, war is his vengeance; so that here men are punish'd for before-breach of the King's laws in now the King's quarrel. Where they fear'd the death, they have borne life away; and where they would be safe, they perish. Then if they die unprovided, no more is the King guilty of their damnation than he was before guilty of those impieties for the which they are now visited. Every subject's duty is the King's, but every subject's soul is his own. Therefore should every soldier in the wars do as every sick man in his bed, wash every mote out of his conscience; and dying so, death is to him advantage; or not dying, the time was blessedly lost wherein such preparation was gain'd; and in him that escapes, it were not sin to think that making God so free an offer, He let him outlive that day to see His greatness and to teach others how they should prepare.

Will. 'Tis certain, every man that dies ill, the ill upon his own head, the King is not to answer it.

Bates. I do not desire he should answer for me, and yet I determine to fight lustily for him.

K. Hen. I myself heard the King say he would not be ransom'd.

Will. Ay, he said so, to make us fight cheerfully; but when our throats are cut, he may be ransom'd, and we ne'er the wiser.

K. Hen. If I live to see it, I will never trust his word after.

Will. You pay him then. That's a perilous shot out of an elder-gun, that a poor and a private displeasure can do against a monarch! You may as well go about to turn the sun to ice with fanning in his face with a peacock's feather. You'll never trust his word after! come, 'tis a foolish saying.

96. **estate:** condition. 103. **element shows:** sky appears.
104. **conditions:** qualities, i.e. limitations. **ceremonies:** robes of state. 106. **affections . . . mounted:** desires mount higher.
107. **stoop:** descend (a term from falconry). **with . . . wing:** similarly. 109. **relish:** taste, i.e. kind.
116. **at all adventures:** whatever the risk.
116–17. **quit here:** i.e. out of this.
118. **conscience:** honest opinion.
141. **rawly left:** i.e. unprovided for.
142. **well:** i.e. as Christians. 143. **argument:** i.e. main concern.
145. **who:** whom.
146. **proportion of subjection:** proper relation of subject to sovereign.

152–53. **in . . . iniquities:** i.e. with his sins upon his head.
160. **arbitrement of:** settlement by. **try it out:** i.e. test its merits.
161. **all unspotted:** completely unblemished.
164. **making . . . bulwark:** i.e. taking advantage of military service to escape punishment. 167. **native:** at home.
169. **beadle:** officer who inflicts punishment.
173–74. **unprovided:** unprepared. 176. **visited:** punished.
186. **dies ill:** dies in sin.
198. **elder-gun:** pop-gun, made by removing the pith from a piece of elder.

K. Hen. Your reproof is something too round, I should be angry with you, if the time were convenient.

Will. Let it be a quarrel between us, if you live.

K. Hen. I embrace it.

Will. How shall I know thee again?

K. Hen. Give me any gage of thine, and I will wear it in my bonnet; then if ever thou dar'st acknowledge it, I will make it my quarrel.

Will. Here's my glove; give me another of thine.

K. Hen. There.

Will. This will I also wear in my cap. If ever thou come to me and say, after to-morrow, "This is my glove," by this hand I will take thee a box on the ear.

K. Hen. If ever I live to see it, I will challenge it.

Will. Thou dar'st as well be hang'd.

K. Hen. Well, I will do it, though I take thee in the King's company.

Will. Keep thy word; fare thee well.

Bates. Be friends, you English fools, be friends, we have French quarrels enow, if you could tell how to reckon.

K. Hen. Indeed the French may lay twenty French crowns to one they will beat us, for they bear them on their shoulders; but it is no English treason to cut French crowns, and to-morrow the King himself will be a clipper. *Exeunt Soldiers.*

Upon the King! let us our lives, our souls,
Our debts, our careful wives,
Our children, and our sins lay on the King!
We must bear all. O hard condition,
Twin-born with greatness, subject to the breath
Of every fool whose sense no more can feel
But his own wringing! What infinite heart's ease
Must kings neglect, that private men enjoy!
And what have kings, that privates have not too,
Save ceremony, save general ceremony?
And what art thou, thou idol Ceremony?
What kind of god art thou, that suffer'st more
Of mortal griefs than do thy worshippers?
What are thy rents? what are thy comings-in?
O Ceremony, show me but thy worth!
What is thy soul of [adoration]?
Art thou aught else but place, degree, and form,
Creating awe and fear in other men?
Wherein thou art less happy, being fear'd,
Than they in fearing.
What drink'st thou oft, in stead of homage sweet,
But poison'd flattery? O, be sick, great greatness,
And bid thy ceremony give thee cure!
Thinks thou the fiery fever will go out
With titles blown from adulation?
Will it give place to flexure and low bending?
Canst thou, when thou command'st the beggar's knee,
Command the health of it? No, thou proud dream,
That play'st so subtilly with a king's repose.
I am a king that find thee; and I know
'Tis not the balm, the sceptre, and the ball,
The sword, the mace, the crown imperial,
The intertissued robe of gold and pearl,
The farced title running 'fore the king,
The throne he sits on, nor the tide of pomp
That beats upon the high shore of this world—
No, not all these, thrice-gorgeous ceremony,
Not all these, laid in bed majestical,
Can sleep so soundly as the wretched slave;
Who, with a body fill'd and vacant mind,
Gets him to rest, cramm'd with distressful bread,
Never sees horrid night, the child of hell;
But like a lackey, from the rise to set,
Sweats in the eye of Phoebus, and all night
Sleeps in Elysium; next day after dawn,
Doth rise and help Hyperion to his horse,
And follows so the ever-running year
With profitable labor to his grave:
And, but for ceremony, such a wretch,
Winding up days with toil, and nights with sleep,
Had the forehand and vantage of a king.
The slave, a member of the country's peace,
Enjoys it; but in gross brain little wots
What watch the King keeps to maintain the peace,
Whose hours the peasant best advantages.

Enter ERPINGHAM.

Erp. My lord, your nobles, jealous of your absence,
Seek through your camp to find you.

K. Hen. Good old knight,
Collect them all together at my tent.
I'll be before thee.

Erp. I shall do't, my lord. *Exit.*

K. Hen. O God of battles, steel my soldiers' hearts,
Possess them not with fear! Take from them now
The sense of reck'ning, [if] th' opposed numbers
Pluck their hearts from them. Not to-day, O Lord,
O, not to-day, think not upon the fault
My father made in compassing the crown!
I Richard's body have interred new,
And on it have bestowed more contrite tears,

203. **round**: blunt. 208. **gage**: pledge, token.
215. **take**: give. 223. **enow**: enough.
226. **crowns**: (1) coins; (2) heads.
227. **English treason.** Clipping coins was punished as treason under English law.
228. **cut French crowns**: (1) clip coins; (2) kill Frenchmen.
231. **careful**: burdened by care. 236. **wringing**: stomach ache.
238. **privates**: private men. 243. **rents**: revenues.
245. **thy . . . adoration**: the secret of the admiration paid to you.
246. **place**: rank. 254. **from adulation**: i.e. by flatterers.
255. **flexure**: bowing.

259. **find thee**: discover the truth about you, expose you.
260. **balm**: consecrating oil. **ball**: globe, a symbol of sovereignty.
263. **farced**: stuffed, inflated. 270. **distressful**: hard-earned.
274. **Elysium**: in Greek mythology, the abode of the blest.
275. **Hyperion**: charioteer of the sun. (In Greek mythology it was his son Helios who was the driver.) 279. **Winding up**: filling.
280. **Had**: would have. **forehand**: advantage.
281. **a member of**: i.e. one who shares the benefits of.
282. **wots**: knows. 283. **watch**: wakeful guard.
284. **Whose . . . advantages**: (the King) from whose watchful hours the peasant most benefits. 285. **jealous of**: concerned about.
291. **sense of reck'ning**: ability to count.
293–94. **fault . . . crown**: i.e. the murder of Richard II.
294. **compassing**: obtaining.
295. **I . . . new.** Following his coronation, says Holinshed (Bullough, IV, 281), Henry "caused the bodie of king Richard to be removed with all funerall dignitie convenient for his estate, from Langlie to Westminster, where he was honorablie interred with queene Anne his first wife, in a solemn toome erected and set up at the charges of this king."

Than from it issued forced drops of blood.
Five hundred poor I have in yearly pay,
Who twice a day their wither'd hands hold up
Toward heaven, to pardon blood; and I have built
Two chauntries, where the sad and solemn priests
Sing still for Richard's soul. More will I do;
Though all that I can do is nothing worth,
Since that my penitence comes after all,
Imploring pardon.

Enter GLOUCESTER.

Glou. My liege!
K. Hen. My brother Gloucester's voice? Ay;
I know thy errand, I will go with thee.
The day, my [friends], and all things stay for me.
Exeunt.

[SCENE II]

Enter the DOLPHIN, ORLEANCE, RAMBURES, *and* BEAUMONT.

Orl. The sun doth gild our armor, up, my lords!
Dol. *Montez* [*à*] *cheval!* My horse, varlot lackey! Ha!
Orl. O brave spirit!
Dol. *Via! les eaux et terre.*
Orl. *Rien puis? l'air et feu?*
Dol. [*Cieux*]! cousin Orleance.

Enter CONSTABLE.

Now, my Lord Constable?
Con. Hark how our steeds for present service neigh!
Dol. Mount them, and make incision in their hides,
That their hot blood may spin in English eyes,
And dout them with superfluous courage, ha!
Ram. What, will you have them weep our horses' blood?
How shall we then behold their natural tears?

Enter MESSENGER.

Mess. The English are embattled, you French peers.
Con. To horse, you gallant princes! straight to horse!
Do but behold yond poor and starved band,
And your fair show shall suck away their souls,
Leaving them but the shales and husks of men.
There is not work enough for all our hands,
Scarce blood enough in all their sickly veins
To give each naked curtle-axe a stain,
That our French gallants shall to-day draw out,
And sheathe for lack of sport. Let us but blow on them,
The vapor of our valor will o'erturn them.
'Tis positive against all exceptions, lords,
That our superfluous lackeys and our peasants,
Who in unnecessary action swarm
About our squares of battle, were enow
To purge this field of such a hilding foe;
Though we upon this mountain's basis by
Took stand for idle speculation—
But that our honors must not. What's to say?
A very little little let us do,
And all is done. Then let the trumpets sound
The tucket sonance and the note to mount;
For our approach shall so much dare the field,
That England shall couch down in fear, and yield.

Enter GRANDPRÉ.

Grand. Why do you stay so long, my lords of France?
Yond island carrions, desperate of their bones,
Ill-favoredly become the morning field.
Their ragged curtains poorly are let loose,
And our air shakes them passing scornfully.
Big Mars seems bankrout in their beggar'd host,
And faintly through a rusty beaver peeps.
The horsemen sit like fixed candlesticks,
With torch-staves in their hand; and their poor jades
Lob down their heads, dropping the hides and hips,
The gum down-roping from their pale-dead eyes,
And in their pale dull mouths the [gimmal'd] bit
Lies foul with chaw'd-grass, still and motionless;
And their executors, the knavish crows,
Fly o'er them all, impatient for their hour.
Description cannot suit itself in words
To demonstrate the life of such a battle,
In life so liveless as it shows itself.
Con. They have said their prayers, and they stay for death.
Dol. Shall we go send them dinners and fresh suits,
And give their fasting horses provender,
And after fight with them?
Con. I stay but for my [guidon]; to the field!
I will the banner from a trumpet take,
And use it for my haste. Come, come away!
The sun is high, and we outwear the day. *Exeunt.*

301. chauntries: chantries, chapels where masses for the dead were performed. **sad:** grave. **302. still:** continuously.

IV.ii. Location: The French camp.
2. Montez à cheval: to horse. **varlot:** varlet, valet.
4. Via . . . terre: away, waters and earth. (The Dauphin imagines his horse soaring above streams and solid earth—see III.vii.13–18.)
5–6. Rien . . . Cieux. Orleans asks whether the horse will not also soar above the two other elements, air and fire, and the Dolphin asserts that he will arise to the heavens (*Cieux*) themselves.
8. present: immediate.
11. dout: put out. **superfluous courage:** i.e. blood the horses can spare. **14. embattled:** drawn up in line of battle.
17. fair show: splendid appearance. **18. shales:** shells.
21. curtle-axe: cutlass.
25. positive . . . exceptions: i.e. indisputably true.
29. hilding: worthless. **30. basis:** foot.
31. speculation: looking-on. **35. tucket sonance:** trumpet signal.
36. dare the field: daze the enemy.
39. desperate of: in despair of saving. **41. curtains:** flags, banners.
43. Mars: god of war. **bankrout:** bankrupt.
44. beaver: visor. **47. Lob:** droop. **49. gimmal'd:** jointed.
51. executors: executioners (?) or executors who will dispose of what the dead leave behind (i.e. merely their carcasses) (?).
54. demonstrate . . . of: i.e. depict realistically. **battle:** line of battle.
55. liveless: lifeless. **56. stay:** wait.
60–62. I . . . haste. The French were so eager for battle, says Holinshed (Bullough, IV, 395), that "some of them would not once staie for their standards: as amongst other the duke of Brabant, when his standard was not come, caused a baner to be taken from a trumpet and fastened to a speare, the which he commanded to be borne before him in steed of his standard." **60. guidon:** pennon, standard.
61. trumpet: trumpeter. **63. outwear:** waste.

[Scene III]

Enter Gloucester, Bedford, Exeter, Erpingham *with all his host;* Salisbury *and* Westmerland.

Glou. Where is the King?
Bed. The King himself is rode to view their battle.
West. Of fighting men they have full threescore thousand.
Exe. There's five to one; besides, they all are fresh.
Sal. God's arm strike with us! 'tis a fearful odds.
God buy you, princes all; I'll to my charge.
If we no more meet till we meet in heaven,
Then joyfully, my noble Lord of Bedford,
My dear Lord Gloucester, and my good Lord Exeter,
And my kind kinsman, warriors all, adieu!
Bed. Farewell, good Salisbury, and good luck go with thee!
Exe. Farewell, kind lord; fight valiantly to-day!
And yet I do thee wrong to mind thee of it,
For thou art fram'd of the firm truth of valor.
[*Exit Salisbury.*]
Bed. He is as full of valor as of kindness,
Princely in both.

Enter the King.

West. O that we now had here
But one ten thousand of those men in England
That do no work to-day!
K. Hen. What's he that wishes so?
My cousin Westmerland? No, my fair cousin.
If we are mark'd to die, we are enow
To do our country loss; and if to live,
The fewer men, the greater share of honor.
God's will, I pray thee wish not one man more.
By Jove, I am not covetous for gold,
Nor care I who doth feed upon my cost;
It yearns me not if men my garments wear;
Such outward things dwell not in my desires.
But if it be a sin to covet honor,
I am the most offending soul alive.
No, faith, my coz, wish not a man from England.
God's peace, I would not lose so great an honor
As one man more methinks would share from me,
For the best hope I have. O, do not wish one more!
Rather proclaim it, Westmerland, through my host,
That he which hath no stomach to this fight,
Let him depart, his passport shall be made,
And crowns for convoy put into his purse.
We would not die in that man's company
That fears his fellowship to die with us.
This day is call'd the feast of Crispian:
He that outlives this day, and comes safe home,
Will stand a' tiptoe when this day is named,
And rouse him at the name of Crispian.
He that shall see this day, and live old age,
Will yearly on the vigil feast his neighbors,
And say, "To-morrow is Saint Crispian."
Then will he strip his sleeve and show his scars,
[And say, "These wounds I had on Crispin's day."]
Old men forget; yet all shall be forgot,
But he'll remember with advantages
What feats he did that day. Then shall our names,
Familiar in his mouth as household words,
Harry the King, Bedford and Exeter,
Warwick and Talbot, Salisbury and Gloucester,
Be in their flowing cups freshly rememb'red.
This story shall the good man teach his son;
And Crispin Crispian shall ne'er go by,
From this day to the ending of the world,
But we in it shall be remembered—
We few, we happy few, we band of brothers;
For he to-day that sheds his blood with me
Shall be my brother; be he ne'er so vile,
This day shall gentle his condition;
And gentlemen in England, now a-bed,
Shall think themselves accurs'd they were not here;
And hold their manhoods cheap whiles any speaks
That fought with us upon Saint Crispin's day.

Enter Salisbury.

Sal. My sovereign lord, bestow yourself with speed.
The French are bravely in their battles set,
And will with all expedience charge on us.
K. Hen. All things are ready, if our minds be so.
West. Perish the man whose mind is backward now!
K. Hen. Thou dost not wish more help from England, coz?
West. God's will, my liege, would you and I alone,
Without more help, could fight this royal battle!
K. Hen. Why, now thou hast unwish'd five thousand men;
Which likes me better than to wish us one.
You know your places. God be with you all!

Tucket. Enter Montjoy.

Mont. Once more I come to know of thee, King Harry,

IV.iii. Location: The English camp.
6. buy: be with. **charge:** command post.
10. kinsman: i.e. Westmorland, whose son had married Salisbury's daughter. **14. fram'd:** built.
16–67. O . . . day. Holinshed reports (Bullough, IV, 394) that when Henry "heard one of the host utter his wish to another thus: I would to God there were with us now so manie good soldiers as are at this houre within England! the king answered: I would not wish a man more here than I have, we are indeed in comparison to the enimies but a few, but if God of his clemencie doo favour us, and our just cause (as I trust he will) we shall speed well inough."
25. upon my cost: at my expense. **26. yearns:** grieves.
30. coz: cousin, i.e. kinsman **32. share from me:** deprive me of.
39. fears . . . us: i.e. is unwilling to meet death with me.
40. feast of Crispian: i.e. St. Crispin's Day, October 25. Crispin and Crispinian, the patron saints of shoemakers, were early Christian martyrs. **44. live:** live to see.
45. vigil: i.e. the eve of St. Crispin's Day.
50. advantages: embellishments. **62. vile:** lowly.
63. gentle his condition: raise him to the rank of gentleman.
68. bestow yourself: take your position.
69. bravely . . . set: handsomely drawn up.
70. expedience: speed. **77. likes:** pleases.
79–125. Once . . . Constable. In their "jolitie" the French, says Holinshed (Bullough, IV, 395), sent a herald to King Henry "to inquire what ransome he would offer. Whereunto he answered, that within two or three houres he hoped it would so happen, that the Frenchmen should be glad to common [confer] rather with the Englishmen for their ransoms, than the English to take thought for their deliverance, promising for his owne part, that his dead carcasse should rather be a prize to the Frenchmen, than that his living bodie should paie anie ransome."

If for thy ransom thou wilt now compound,
Before thy most assured overthrow;
For certainly thou art so near the gulf,
Thou needs must be englutted. Besides, in mercy,
The Constable desires thee thou wilt mind
Thy followers of repentance; that their souls
May make a peaceful and a sweet retire
From off these fields, where (wretches!) their poor bodies
Must lie and fester.

K. Hen. Who hath sent thee now?

Mont. The Constable of France.

K. Hen. I pray thee bear my former answer back:
Bid them achieve me, and then sell my bones.
Good God, why should they mock poor fellows thus?
The man that once did sell the lion's skin
While the beast liv'd, was kill'd with hunting him.
A many of our bodies shall no doubt
Find native graves; upon the which, I trust,
Shall witness live in brass of this day's work.
And those that leave their valiant bones in France,
Dying like men, though buried in your dunghills,
They shall be fam'd; for there the sun shall greet them,
And draw their honors reeking up to heaven,
Leaving their earthly parts to choke your clime,
The smell whereof shall breed a plague in France.
Mark then abounding valor in our English:
That being dead, like to the bullet's crasing,
Break out into a second course of mischief,
Killing in relapse of mortality.
Let me speak proudly: tell the Constable
We are but warriors for the working-day;
Our gayness and our gilt are all besmirch'd
With rainy marching in the painful field;
There's not a piece of feather in our host—
Good argument (I hope) we will not fly—
And time hath worn us into slovenry.
But, by the mass, our hearts are in the trim;
And my poor soldiers tell me, yet ere night,
They'll be in fresher robes, or they will pluck
The gay new coats o'er the French soldiers' heads
And turn them out of service. If they do this—
As, if God please, they shall—my ransom then
Will soon be levied. Herald, save thou thy labor.
Come thou no more for ransom, gentle herald,
They shall have none, I swear, but these my joints;
Which if they have as I will leave 'um them,
Shall yield them little, tell the Constable.

Mont. I shall, King Harry. And so fare thee well;
Thou never shalt hear herald any more. *Exit.*

K. Hen. I fear thou wilt once more come again for a ransom.

Enter York.

York. My lord, most humbly on my knee I beg
The leading of the vaward.

K. Hen. Take it, brave York. Now, soldiers, march away,
And how thou pleasest, God, dispose the day!
Exeunt.

[Scene IV]

Alarum. Excursions. Enter Pistol, French Soldier, Boy.

Pist. Yield, cur!

Fr. Sol. *Je pense que vous êtes le gentilhomme de bonne qualité.*

Pist. Qualtitie! [*Calen o*] *custure me!* Art thou a gentleman? What is thy name? Discuss.

Fr. Sol. *O Seigneur Dieu!*

Pist. O Signieur Dew should be a gentleman.
Perpend my words, O Signieur Dew, and mark:
O Signieur Dew, thou diest on point of fox,
Except, O signieur, thou do give to me
Egregious ransom.

Fr. Sol. *O, prenez miséricorde! ayez pitié de moi!*

Pist. Moy shall not serve, I will have forty moys,
[Or] I will fetch thy rim out at thy throat
In drops of crimson blood.

Fr. Sol. *Est-il impossible d'échapper la force de ton bras?*

Pist. Brass, cur?
Thou damned and luxurious mountain goat,
Offer'st me brass?

Fr. Sol. *O, pardonnez moi!*

Pist. Say'st thou me so? Is that a ton of moys?
Come hither, boy, ask me this slave in French
What is his name.

Boy. *Écoutez: comment êtes-vous appelé?*

Fr. Sol. *Monsieur le Fer.*

Boy. He says his name is Master Fer.

Pist. Master Fer! I'll fer him, and firk him, and ferret him. Discuss the same in French unto him.

Boy. I do not know the French for fer, and ferret, and firk.

Pist. Bid him prepare, for I will cut his throat.

Fr. Sol. *Que dit-il, monsieur?*

Boy. *Il me commande à vous dire que vous faites vous prêt; car ce soldat ici est disposé tout* [*à cette heure*] *de couper votre gorge.*

Pist. *Owy, cuppele gorge, permafoy,*

80. compound: make terms.
82. gulf: whirlpool. **83. englutted:** swallowed.
84. mind: remind. **91. achieve:** capture.
93–94. The man . . . him. A somewhat altered version of one of Aesop's fables. **96. native:** at home.
101. reeking: breathing. **105. crasing:** fatal rebound (?).
109. We . . . working-day: i.e. we are here to work.
115. in the trim: (1) sprucely attired; (2) in fine condition.
117. fresher: i.e. heavenly. **124. 'um:** 'em, i.e. them.

131. vaward: vanguard.

IV.iv. Location: The field of battle.
o.s.d. Excursions: sallies, sorties.
2–3. Je . . . qualité: I think you are a gentleman of good family.
4. Qualtitie . . . me. Probably mere nonsense. **5. Discuss:** declare.
6. O Seigneur Dieu: O Lord God. **8. Perpend:** ponder.
9. fox: sword. **12. O . . . moi:** O have mercy, take pity on me.
13. Moy. Pistol takes *moi* (line 12) for the name of a coin. Cf. line 22, and also line 18, where he makes a similar mistake about *bras.*
14. rim: diaphragm.
16–17. Est-il . . . bras: is it impossible to escape the strength of your arm. **19. luxurious:** lascivious.
25. Écoutez . . . appelé: listen: what is your name. **28. firk:** beat.
29. ferret: worry (like a ferret).
33. Que dit-il: what does he say.
34–36. Il . . . gorge: he orders me to tell you to prepare; for this soldier is disposed to cut your throat at once.
37. Owy: Pistol's version of *oui,* "yes." **permafoy:** by my faith.

Peasant, unless thou give me crowns, brave crowns;
Or mangled shalt thou be by this my sword.

Fr. Sol. *O, je vous supplie, pour l'amour de Dieu, me pardonner! Je suis le gentilhomme de bonne maison; gardez ma vie, et je vous donnerai deux cents écus.*

Pist. What are his words?

Boy. He prays you to save his life. He is a gentleman of a good house, and for his ransom he will give you two hundred crowns.

Pist. Tell him my fury shall abate, and I
The crowns will take.

Fr. Sol. *Petit monsieur, que dit-il?*

Boy. *Encore qu'il est contre son jurement de pardonner aucun prisonnier; néanmoins, pour les écus que vous* [*lui*] *promettez, il est content à vous donner la liberté, le franchisement.*

Fr. Sol. *Sur mes genoux* [*je*] *vous donne mille* [*remercîments*]; *et je m'estime heureux que je tombe entre les mains d'un chevalier, je pense, le plus brave, vaillant, et très* [*distingué*] *seigneur d'Angleterre.*

Pist. Expound unto me, boy.

Boy. He gives you, upon his knees, a thousand thanks, and he esteems himself happy that he hath fall'n into the hands of one (as he thinks) the most brave, valorous, and thrice-worthy seigneur of England.

Pist. As I suck blood, I will some mercy show.
Follow me!

Boy. *Suivez-vous le grand capitaine.* [*Exeunt Pistol and French Soldier.*] I did never know so full a voice issue from so empty a heart; but the saying is true, "The empty vessel makes the greatest sound." Bardolph and Nym had ten times more valor than this roaring devil i' th' old play, that every one may pare his nails with a wooden dagger, and they are both hang'd, and so would this be, if he durst steal any thing adventurously. I must stay with the lackeys with the luggage of our camp. The French might have a good prey of us, if he knew of it, for there is none to guard it but boys. *Exit.*

[Scene V]

Enter Constable, Orleance, Bourbon, Dolphin, *and* Rambures.

Con. *O diable!*

Orl. *O Seigneur! le jour est perdu, tout est perdu!*

Dol. *Mort Dieu, ma vie!* all is confounded, all!
Reproach and everlasting shame
Sits mocking in our plumes. *A short alarum.*
O méchante fortune!
Do not run away.

Con. Why, all our ranks are broke.

Dol. O perdurable shame! let's stab ourselves.
Be these the wretches that we play'd at dice for?

Orl. Is this the king we sent to for his ransom?

Bour. Shame and eternal shame, nothing but shame!
Let us die! In once more! back again!
And he that will not follow Bourbon now,
Let him go hence, and with his cap in hand
Like a base pander hold the chamber-door
Whilst [by a] slave, no gentler than my dog,
His fairest daughter is contaminated.

Con. Disorder, that hath spoil'd us, friend us now!
Let us on heaps go offer up our lives.

Orl. We are enow yet living in the field
To smother up the English in our throngs,
If any order might be thought upon.

Bour. The devil take order now! I'll to the throng:
Let life be short, else shame will be too long.
Exeunt.

[Scene VI]

Alarum. Enter the King *and his* Train *with prisoners;* [Exeter *and others*].

K. Hen. Well have we done, thrice-valiant countrymen,
But all's not done—yet keep the French the field.

Exe. The Duke of York commends him to your Majesty.

K. Hen. Lives he, good uncle? Thrice within this hour
I saw him down; thrice up again, and fighting;
From helmet to the spur all blood he was.

Exe. In which array (brave soldier!) doth he lie,
Larding the plain; and by his bloody side
(Yoke-fellow to his honor-owing wounds)
The noble Earl of Suffolk also lies.
Suffolk first died, and York, all haggled over,
Comes to him where in gore he lay insteeped,
And takes him by the beard, kisses the gashes
That bloodily did yawn upon his face.
He cries aloud, "Tarry, my cousin Suffolk!
My soul shall thine keep company to heaven;
Tarry, sweet soul, for mine, then fly abreast,
As in this glorious and well-foughten field
We kept together in our chivalry!"
Upon these words I came and cheer'd him up.
He smil'd me in the face, raught me his hand,
And with a feeble gripe, says, "Dear my lord,
Commend my service to my sovereign."

40–42. O . . . écus: O, I beg you to pardon me, for the love of God. I am a gentleman of good family; preserve my life, and I will give you two hundred crowns. **45. house:** family.
49. Petit . . . dit-il: little sir, what does he say.
50–53. Encore . . . franchisement: once more, that it is contrary to his oath to pardon any prisoner; nevertheless, for the crowns that you promise him, he is willing to give you liberty, freedom.
54–57. Sur . . . d'Angleterre. These lines are translated almost literally in the Boy's next speech.
64. suck blood. Cf. Pistol's words at II.iii.55–56.
66. Suivez-vous . . . capitaine: follow the great captain.
71–72. roaring . . . dagger. The stock character of the Devil in the morality plays was often taunted by the mischievous Vice with an offer to trim his nails with his dagger, made of lath. See the Fool's song in *Twelfth Night*, IV.ii.120–31.

IV.v. Location: Scene continues.
1. O diable: O the devil.
2. O . . . perdu: O Lord, the day is lost, all is lost.

3. Mort . . . vie: death of God! my life. **confounded:** lost.
5. O méchante fortune: O malicious fate. **7. perdurable:** lasting.
18. on: in.

IV.vi. Location: Scene continues.
8. Larding: enriching.
9. honor-owing: honor-owning, i.e. honorable.
11. haggled over: mangled. **20. cheer'd him up:** encouraged him.
21. raught: reached. **22. gripe:** grasp. **23. Commend:** present.

So did he turn and over Suffolk's neck
He threw his wounded arm, and kiss'd his lips,
And so espous'd to death, with blood he seal'd
A testament of noble-ending love.
The pretty and sweet manner of it forc'd
Those waters from me which I would have stopp'd,
But I had not so much of man in me,
And all my mother came into mine eyes
And gave me up to tears.

K. Hen. I blame you not,
For hearing this, I must perforce compound
With [mistful] eyes, or they will issue too. *Alarum.*
But hark, what new alarum is this same?
The French have reinforc'd their scatter'd men.
Then every soldier kill his prisoners,
Give the word through. *Exeunt.*

[Scene VII]

Enter Fluellen *and* Gower.

Flu. Kill the poys and the luggage! 'Tis expressly against the law of arms. 'Tis as arrant a piece of knavery, mark you now, as can be offert; in your conscience, now, is it not?

Gow. 'Tis certain there's not a boy left alive, and the cowardly rascals that ran from the battle ha' done this slaughter. Besides, they have burn'd and carried away all that was in the King's tent; wherefore the King, most worthily, hath caus'd every soldier to cut his prisoner's throat. O, 'tis a gallant king!

Flu. Ay, he was porn at Monmouth, Captain Gower. What call you the town's name where Alexander the Pig was born?

Gow. Alexander the Great.

Flu. Why, I pray you, is not "pig" great? The pig, or the great, or the mighty, or the huge, or the magnanimous, are all one reckonings, save the phrase is a little variations.

Gow. I think Alexander the Great was born in Macedon. His father was called Philip of Macedon, as I take it.

Flu. I think it is in Macedon where Alexander is porn. I tell you, captain, if you look in the maps of the orld, I warrant you sall find, in the comparisons between Macedon and Monmouth, that the situations, look you, is both alike. There is a river in Macedon, and there is also moreover a river at Monmouth. It is call'd Wye at Monmouth; but it is out of my prains what is the name of the other river; but 'tis all one, 'tis alike as my fingers is to my fingers, and there is salmons in both. If you mark Alexander's life well, Harry of Monmouth's life is come after it indifferent well, for there is figures in all things. Alexander, God knows, and you know, in his rages, and his furies, and his wraths, and his cholers, and his moods, and his displeasures, and his indignations, and also being a little intoxicates in his prains, did, in his ales and his angers, look you, kill his best friend, Clytus.

Gow. Our King is not like him in that; he never kill'd any of his friends.

Flu. It is not well done, mark you now, to take the tales out of my mouth, ere it is made and finished. I speak but in the figures and comparisons of it: as Alexander kill'd his friend Clytus, being in his ales and his cups; so also Harry Monmouth, being in his right wits and his good judgments, turn'd away the fat knight with the great belly doublet. He was full of jests, and gipes, and knaveries, and mocks—I have forgot his name.

Gow. Sir John Falstaff.

Flu. That is he. I'll tell you there is good men porn at Monmouth.

Gow. Here comes his Majesty. *[Exit.]*

Alarum. Enter King Harry *and* Bourbon *with [other] prisoners;* [Warwick, Gloucester, Exeter, Heralds, *and others*]. *Flourish.*

K. Hen. I was not angry since I came to France
Until this instant. Take a trumpet, herald,
Ride thou unto the horsemen on yond hill.
If they will fight with us, bid them come down,
Or void the field; they do offend our sight.
If they'll do neither, we will come to them,
And make them skirr away, as swift as stones
Enforced from the old Assyrian slings;
Besides, we'll cut the throats of those we have,
And not a man of them that we shall take
Shall taste our mercy. Go and tell them so.
[Exit a Herald.]

Enter Montjoy.

Exe. Here comes the herald of the French, my liege.

Glou. His eyes are humbler than they us'd to be.

28. pretty: lovely. **33. perforce compound:** necessarily make terms.
34. issue: i.e. weep.
35–38. But . . . through. Holinshed reports (Bullough, IV, 397) that some of the fleeing French cavalry, "either upon a covetous meaning to gaine by the spoile, or upon a desire to be revenged," circled back upon King Henry's camp "and there spoiled the hails [shelters], robbed the tents, brake up chests, and caried awaie caskets, and slue such servants as they found to make anie resistance." When informed of this, Henry, fearing that the enemy would regroup their forces and launch a new attack, "contrarie to his accustomed gentlenes, commanded by sound of trumpet, that everie man (upon paine of death) should incontinentlie slaie his prisoner. When this dolorous decree, and pitifull proclamation was pronounced, pitie it was to see how some Frenchmen were suddenlie sticked with daggers, some were brained with pollaxes, some slaine with malls, other had their throats cut, and some their bellies panched, so that in effect, having respect to the great number, few prisoners were saved."

IV.vii. Location: Scene continues.
1. luggage: i.e. lackeys left to guard the luggage.
11. Monmouth: castle in eastern Monmouthshire. **24. orld:** world.

32. is come after: resembles.
33. indifferent: fairly. **figures:** figurative comparisons, similes.
39. Clytus: Cleitus, close friend and associate whom Alexander killed during a drinking bout.
55–65. I . . . mercy. Holinshed reports (Bullough, IV, 397–98) that to the scattering French Henry sent a herald "commanding them either to depart out of his sight, or else to come forward at once, and give battell: promising herewith, that if they did offer to fight again, not onelie those prisoners which his people alreadie had taken; but also so manie of them as in this new conflict, which they thus attempted should fall into his hands, should die the death without redemption." Appalled by "so terrible a decree," the French "without further delaie parted out of the field."
56. trumpet: trumpeter. **59. void:** abandon.
61. skirr: scurry.

K. Hen. How now, what means this, herald?
Know'st thou not
That I have fin'd these bones of mine for ransom?
Com'st thou again for ransom?
Mont. No, great King;
I come to thee for charitable license,
That we may wander o'er this bloody field
To book our dead, and then to bury them;
To sort our nobles from our common men.
For many of our princes (woe the while!)
Lie drown'd and soak'd in mercenary blood;
So do our vulgar drench their peasant limbs
In blood of princes, and [their] wounded steeds
Fret fetlock deep in gore, and with wild rage
Yerk out their armed heels at their dead masters,
Killing them twice. O, give us leave, great King,
To view the field in safety, and dispose
Of their dead bodies!
K. Hen. I tell thee truly, herald,
I know not if the day be ours or no,
For yet a many of your horsemen peer
And gallop o'er the field.
Mont. The day is yours.
K. Hen. Praised be God, and not our strength, for it!
What is this castle call'd that stands hard by?
Mont. They call it Agincourt.
K. Hen. Then call we this the field of Agincourt,
Fought on the day of Crispin Crispianus.

Flu. Your grandfather of famous memory, an't please your Majesty, and your great-uncle Edward the Plack Prince of Wales, as I have read in the chronicles, fought a most prave pattle here in France.

K. Hen. They did, Fluellen.

Flu. Your Majesty says very true. If your Majesties is rememb'red of it, the Welshmen did good service in a garden where leeks did grow, wearing leeks in their Monmouth caps, which, your Majesty know, to this hour is an honorable badge of the service; and I do believe your Majesty takes no scorn to wear the leek upon Saint Tavy's day.

K. Hen. I wear it for a memorable honor;
For I am Welsh, you know, good countryman.

Flu. All the water in Wye cannot wash your Majesty's Welsh plood out of your pody, I can tell you that. God pless it, and preserve it, as long as it pleases his Grace, and his Majesty too!

K. Hen. Thanks, good my [countryman].

Flu. By Jeshu, I am your Majesty's countryman, I care not who know it. I will confess it to all the orld. I need not to be ashamed of your Majesty, praised be God, so long as your Majesty is an honest man.

K. Hen. [God] keep me so!

69. **fin'd:** staked.
71. **license:** permission. 73. **book:** list.
76. **mercenary blood:** i.e. blood of common soldiers, who, unlike the nobles, fought for pay. 77. **vulgar:** common people.
80. **Yerk:** kick. **armed:** spiked. 85. **peer:** appear.
92. **grandfather:** i.e. great-grandfather, Edward III.
95. **pattle:** i.e. Crécy.
100. **Monmouth caps:** high-crowned, brimless hats.

Enter WILLIAMS.

Our heralds go with him;
Bring me just notice of the numbers dead
On both our parts. Call yonder fellow hither.
[*Exeunt Heralds with Montjoy.*]

Exe. Soldier, you must come to the King.

K. Hen. Soldier, why wear'st thou that glove in thy cap?

Will. And't please your Majesty, 'tis the gage of one that I should fight withal, if he be alive.

K. Hen. An Englishman?

Will. And't please your Majesty, a rascal that swagger'd with me last night; who if alive and ever dare to challenge this glove, I have sworn to take him a box a' th' ear; or if I can see my glove in his cap, which he swore, as he was a soldier, he would wear if alive, I will strike it out soundly.

K. Hen. What think you, Captain Fluellen? is it fit this soldier keep his oath?

Flu. He is a craven and a villain else, and't please your Majesty, in my conscience.

K. Hen. It may be his enemy is a gentleman of great sort, quite from the answer of his degree.

Flu. Though he be as good a gentleman as the devil is, as Lucifer and Belzebub himself, it is necessary, look your Grace, that he keep his vow and his oath. If he be perjur'd, see you now, his reputation is as arrant a villain and a Jack sauce, as ever his black shoe trod upon God's ground and His earth, in my conscience law!

K. Hen. Then keep thy vow, sirrah, when thou meet'st the fellow.

Will. So I will, my liege, as I live.

K. Hen. Who serv'st thou under?

Will. Under Captain Gower, my liege.

Flu. Gower is a good captain, and is good knowledge and literatured in the wars.

K. Hen. Call him hither to me, soldier.

Will. I will, my liege. *Exit.*

K. Hen. Here, Fluellen, wear thou this favor for me and stick it in thy cap. When Alanson and myself were down together, I pluck'd this glove from his helm. If any man challenge this, he is a friend to Alanson, and an enemy to our person. If thou encounter any such, apprehend him, and thou dost me love.

Flu. Your Grace doo's me as great honors as can be desir'd in the hearts of his subjects. I would fain see the man, that has but two legs, that shall find himself aggrief'd at this glove; that is all. But I would fain see it once, and please God of his grace that I might see.

K. Hen. Know'st thou Gower?

Flu. He is my dear friend, and please you.

K. Hen. Pray thee go seek him, and bring him to my tent.

117. **just notice:** precise record. 122. **And:** if. 123. **withal:** with.
136. **quite . . . degree:** i.e. too exalted in rank to accept a challenge from a commoner like Williams.
141. **Jack sauce:** impudent fellow.
144. **sirrah:** form of address to inferiors.
154. **Alanson:** the Duke of Alençon. 158. **apprehend:** arrest.

Flu. I will fetch him. *Exit.*

K. Hen. My Lord of Warwick, and my brother Gloucester,
Follow Fluellen closely at the heels.
The glove which I have given him for a favor
May haply purchase him a box a' th' ear.
It is the soldier's; I by bargain should
Wear it myself. Follow, good cousin Warwick.
If that the soldier strike him, as I judge
By his blunt bearing he will keep his word,
Some sudden mischief may arise of it;
For I do know Fluellen valiant
And touch'd with choler, hot as gunpowder,
And quickly will return an injury.
Follow, and see there be no harm between them.
Go you with me, uncle of Exeter. *Exeunt.*

[SCENE VIII]

Enter GOWER *and* WILLIAMS.

Will. I warrant it is to knight you, captain.

Enter FLUELLEN.

Flu. God's will, and his pleasure, captain, I beseech you now, come apace to the King. There is more good toward you peradventure than is in your knowledge to dream of.

Will. Sir, know you this glove?

Flu. Know the glove? I know the glove is a glove.

Will. I know this, and thus I challenge it. *Strikes him.*

Flu. 'Sblud, an arrant traitor as any's in the universal world, or in France, or in England!

Gow. How now, sir? you villain!

Will. Do you think I'll be forsworn?

Flu. Stand away, Captain Gower, I will give treason his payment into plows, I warrant you.

Will. I am no traitor.

Flu. That's a lie in thy throat. I charge you in his Majesty's name, apprehend him, he's a friend of the Duke Alanson's.

Enter WARWICK *and* GLOUCESTER.

War. How now, how now, what's the matter?

Flu. My Lord of Warwick, here is—praised be God for it!—a most contagious treason come to light, look you, as you shall desire in a summer's day. Here is his Majesty.

Enter KING *and* EXETER.

K. Hen. How now, what's the matter?

Flu. My liege, here is a villain and a traitor, that, look your Grace, has strook the glove which your Majesty is take out of the helmet of Alanson.

Will. My liege, this was my glove, here is the fellow of it; and he that I gave it to in change promis'd to wear it in his cap. I promis'd to strike him, if he did. I met this man with my glove in his cap, and I have been as good as my word.

Flu. Your Majesty hear now, saving your Majesty's manhood, what an arrant, rascally, beggarly, lousy knave it is. I hope your Majesty is pear me testimony and witness, and will avouchment, that this is the glove of Alanson that your Majesty is give me, in your conscience now.

K. Hen. Give me thy glove, soldier. Look, here is the fellow of it.
'Twas I indeed thou promisedst to strike,
And thou hast given me most bitter terms.

Flu. And please your Majesty, let his neck answer for it, if there is any martial law in the world.

K. Hen. How canst thou make me satisfaction?

Will. All offenses, my lord, come from the heart. Never came any from mine that might offend your Majesty.

K. Hen. It was ourself thou didst abuse.

Will. Your Majesty came not like yourself. You appear'd to me but as a common man; witness the night, your garments, your lowliness; and what your Highness suffer'd under that shape, I beseech you take it for your own fault and not mine; for had you been as I took you for, I made no offense; therefore I beseech your Highness pardon me.

K. Hen. Here, uncle Exeter, fill this glove with crowns,
And give it to this fellow. Keep it, fellow,
And wear it for an honor in thy cap
Till I do challenge it. Give him the crowns;
And, captain, you must needs be friends with him.

Flu. By this day and this light, the fellow has mettle enough in his belly. Hold, there is twelvepence for you, and I pray you to serve God, and keep you out of prawls and prabbles, and quarrels and dissensions, and I warrant you it is the better for you.

Will. I will none of your money.

Flu. It is with a good will; I can tell you it will serve you to mend your shoes. Come, wherefore should you be so pashful? your shoes is not so good. 'Tis a good silling, I warrant you, or I will change it.

Enter [*an* ENGLISH] HERALD.

K. Hen. Now, herald, are the dead numb'red?

Her. Here is the number of the slaught'red French. [*Gives a paper.*]

K. Hen. What prisoners of good sort are taken, uncle?

Exe. Charles Duke of Orleance, nephew to the King,
John Duke of Bourbon, and Lord Bouciqualt:

181. injury: insult.

IV.viii. Location: Before King Henry's pavilion.
9. 'Sblud: by God's (Christ's) blood (a strong oath).
29. change: exchange.

35. is pear: will bear.
36. avouchment: i.e. testify. **42. terms:** words.
75. good sort: high rank.
76–106. Charles . . . twenty. These names and statistics are drawn with great precision from Holinshed (Bullough, IV, 399), whose figures should be received with caution. He estimates the English before Agincourt as "onelie two thousand horssemen and thirteene thousand archers, bilmen, and of all sorts of other footmen" (IV, 389) and the French as "threescore thousand horssemen, besides footmen, wagoners and other" (IV, 391). Modern historians set the French losses as perhaps 7,000 and the English as between 400 and 500.

Of other lords and barons, knights and squires,
Full fifteen hundred, besides common men.

K. Hen. This note doth tell me of ten thousand French
That in the field lie slain; of princes, in this number,
And nobles bearing banners, there lie dead
One hundred twenty-six; added to these,
Of knights, esquires, and gallant gentlemen,
Eight thousand and four hundred; of the which,
Five hundred were but yesterday dubb'd knights.
So that, in these ten thousand they have lost,
There are but sixteen hundred mercenaries;
The rest are princes, barons, lords, knights, squires,
And gentlemen of blood and quality.
The names of those their nobles that lie dead:
Charles Delabreth, High Constable of France,
Jacques of Chatillion, Admiral of France,
The master of the cross-bows, Lord Rambures,
Great Master of France, the brave Sir Guichard Dolphin,
John Duke of Alanson, Anthony Duke of Brabant,
The brother to the Duke of Burgundy,
And Edward Duke of Bar; of lusty earls,
Grandpré and Roussi, Faulconbridge and Foix,
Beaumont and Marle, Vaudemont and Lestrake.
Here was a royal fellowship of death!
Where is the number of our English dead?
[*Herald shows him another paper*.]
Edward the Duke of York, the Earl of Suffolk,
Sir Richard Ketly, Davy Gam, esquire;
None else of name; and of all other men
But five and twenty. O God, thy arm was here;
And not to us, but to thy arm alone,
Ascribe we all! When, without stratagem,
But in plain shock and even play of battle,
Was ever known so great and little loss,
On one part and on th' other? Take it, God,
For it is none but thine!

Exe. 'Tis wonderful!

K. Hen. Come, go [we] in procession to the village;
And be it death proclaimed through our host
To boast of this, or take that praise from God
Which is his only.

Flu. Is it not lawful, and please your Majesty, to tell how many is kill'd?

K. Hen. Yes, captain; but with this acknowledgment,
That God fought for us.

Flu. Yes, my conscience, he did us great good.

K. Hen. Do we all holy rites:
Let there be sung *Non nobis* and *Te Deum*,
The dead with charity enclos'd in clay;
And then to Callice, and to England then,
Where ne'er from France arriv'd more happy men.
Exeunt.

80. **note:** list. 82. **banners:** coats of arms.
88. **mercenaries:** common soldiers.
123. **Non nobis:** Psalm 115, beginning "Not unto us, O Lord, not unto us, but unto thy name give glory." **Te Deum:** a hymn of thanksgiving beginning "We praise thee, O God."

ACT V

Enter Chorus.

Vouchsafe to those that have not read the story,
That I may prompt them; and of such as have,
I humbly pray them to admit th' excuse
Of time, of numbers, and due course of things,
Which cannot in their huge and proper life
Be here presented. Now we bear the King
Toward Callice; grant him there; there seen,
Heave him away upon your winged thoughts
Athwart the sea. Behold, the English beach
Pales in the flood with men, wives, and boys,
Whose shouts and claps out-voice the deep-mouth'd sea,
Which like a mighty whiffler 'fore the King
Seems to prepare his way. So let him land,
And solemnly see him set on to London.
So swift a pace hath thought that even now
You may imagine him upon Blackheath;
Where that his lords desire him to have borne
His bruised helmet and his bended sword
Before him through the city. He forbids it,
Being free from vainness and self-glorious pride;
Giving full trophy, signal, and ostent
Quite from himself to God. But now behold,
In the quick forge and working-house of thought,
How London doth pour out her citizens!
The Mayor and all his brethren in best sort,
Like to the senators of th' antique Rome,
With the plebeians swarming at their heels,
Go forth and fetch their conqu'ring Caesar in;
As by a lower but by loving likelihood,
Were now the general of our gracious Empress,
As in good time he may, from Ireland coming,
Bringing rebellion broached on his sword,
How many would the peaceful city quit,
To welcome him! Much more, and much more cause,
Did they this Harry. Now in London place him—
As yet the lamentation of the French
Invites the King of England's stay at home;
The Emperor's coming in behalf of France,
To order peace between them—and omit
All the occurrences, what ever chanc'd,
Till Harry's back-return again to France.
There must we bring him; and myself have play'd
The interim, by rememb'ring you 'tis past.
Then brook abridgment, and your eyes advance,
After your thoughts, straight back again to France.
Exit.

V.Cho.10. **Pales:** fences.
12. **whiffler:** one who clears the way for a procession.
16. **Blackheath:** open space southeast of London.
21. **trophy . . . ostent:** i.e. signs and shows of victory.
25. **sort:** attire.
29. **loving likelihood:** affectionately anticipated possibility.
30. **the general . . . Empress.** On this topical allusion see the introduction. 32. **broached:** spitted.
38–39. **The Emperor . . . them.** Sigismund, the Holy Roman Emperor, arrived in England with a retinue of 800 knights on May 1, 1416, in a futile effort to negotiate a peace between France and England.
41. **Harry's . . . France.** Henry returned to France for a second campaign in August 1417, and as Act V opens he has just made a third invasion—the "back-return" that led to the Treaty of Troyes in 1420, with which the play concludes. 43. **remem'bring:** reminding.
44. **brook abridgment:** tolerate omissions.

[Scene I]

Enter Fluellen *and* Gower.

Gow. Nay, that's right; but why wear you your leek to-day? Saint Davy's day is past.

Flu. There is occasions and causes why and wherefore in all things. I will tell you asse my friend, Captain Gower: the rascally, scald, beggarly, lousy, pragging knave, Pistol, which you and yourself, and all the world, know to be no petter than a fellow, look you now, of no merits, he is come to me, and prings me pread and salt yesterday, look you, and bid me eat my leek. It was in a place where I could not breed no contention with him; but I will be so bold as to wear it in my cap till I see him once again, and then I will tell him a little piece of my desires.

Enter Pistol.

Gow. Why, here he comes, swelling like a turkey-cock.

Flu. 'Tis no matter for his swellings nor his turkey-cocks. God pless you, Aunchient Pistol! you scurvy, lousy knave, God pless you!

Pist. Ha, art thou bedlam? Dost thou thirst, base Troyan,
To have me fold up Parca's fatal web?
Hence! I am qualmish at the smell of leek.

Flu. I peseech you heartily, scurvy, lousy knave, at my desires, and my requests, and my petitions, to eat, look you, this leek; because, look you, you do not love it, nor your affections, and your appetites and your disgestions doo's not agree with it, I would desire you to eat it.

Pist. Not for Cadwallader and all his goats.

Flu. There is one goat for you. (*Strikes him.*) Will you be so good, scald knave, as eat it?

Pist. Base Troyan, thou shalt die.

Flu. You say very true, scald knave, when God's will is. I will desire you to live in the mean time, and eat your victuals. Come, there is sauce for it. [*Strikes him.*] You call'd me yesterday mountain-squire, but I will make you to-day a squire of low degree. I pray you fall to; if you can mock a leek, you can eat a leek.

Gow. Enough, captain, you have astonish'd him.

Flu. I say, I will make him eat some part of my leek, or I will peat his pate four days. Bite, I pray you, it is good for your green wound and your ploody coxcomb.

Pist. Must I bite?

Flu. Yes, certainly, and out of doubt and out of question too, and ambiguities.

Pist. By this leek, I will most horribly revenge—I eat and eat—I swear—

V.i. Location: France. The English camp.
5. scald: scabby. **9. yesterday:** i.e. St. David's Day (March 1).
19. bedlam: mad. **Troyan:** rascal.
20. Parca. In Roman mythology, the Parcae were the Three Fates who spun and drew out and cut the thread of destiny.
25. affections: desires.
28. Cadwallader: last of the Welsh kings.
35. mountain-squire: i.e. lord of worthless land.
36. squire . . . degree. Alluding to the title of a popular romance.
39. astonish'd: stunned. **42. green:** fresh.

Flu. Eat, I pray you. Will you have some more sauce to your leek? There is not enough leek to swear by.

Pist. Quiet thy cudgel, thou dost see I eat.

Flu. Much good do you, scald knave, heartily. Nay, pray you throw none away, the skin is good for your broken coxcomb. When you take occasions to see leeks hereafter, I pray you mock at 'em, that is all.

Pist. Good.

Flu. Ay, leeks is good. Hold you, there is a groat to heal your pate.

Pist. Me a groat?

Flu. Yes, verily, and in truth you shall take it, or I have another leek in my pocket, which you shall eat.

Pist. I take thy groat in earnest of revenge.

Flu. If I owe you any thing, I will pay you in cudgels; you shall be a woodmonger, and buy nothing of me but cudgels. God buy you, and keep you, and heal your pate. *Exit.*

Pist. All hell shall stir for this.

Gow. Go, go, you are a counterfeit cowardly knave. Will you mock at an ancient tradition, [begun] upon an honorable respect, and worn as a memorable trophy of predeceas'd valor, and dare not avouch in your deeds any of your words? I have seen you gleeking and galling at this gentleman twice or thrice. You thought, because he could not speak English in the native garb, he could not therefore handle an English cudgel. You find it otherwise, and henceforth let a Welsh correction teach you a good English condition. Fare ye well. *Exit.*

Pist. Doth Fortune play the huswife with me now?
News have I that my Doll is dead i' th' spittle
Of a malady of France,
And there my rendezvous is quite cut off.
Old I do wax, and from my weary limbs
Honor is cudgell'd. Well, bawd I'll turn,
And something lean to cutpurse of quick hand.
To England will I steal, and there I'll steal;
And patches will I get unto these cudgell'd scars,
And [swear] I got them in the Gallia wars. *Exit.*

[Scene II]

Enter, at one door, King Henry, Exeter, Bedford, [Gloucester,] Warwick, [Westmerland,] *and other* Lords; *at another,* Queen Isabel, *the* King [of France], *the* Duke of Burgundy, [Katherine, Alice,] *and other French.*

K. Hen. Peace to this meeting, wherefore we are met!
Unto our brother France, and to our sister,

58. groat: fourpence.
63. earnest: payment to bind a transaction.
74. gleeking and galling: sneering and scoffing.
80. huswife: hussy, i.e. fickle betrayer.
81. my Doll. On this name, in place of the expected Nell (II.i. 18, 31), see the "Note on the Text." **82. malady of France:** venereal disease.
83. rendezvous: i.e. refuge. **86. something:** somewhat.
89. Gallia: French.

V.ii. Location: France. A royal palace.
1. wherefore: for which (i.e. to make peace).
2. brother . . . sister: i.e. Charles VI and his queen.

Health and fair time of day; joy and good wishes
To our most fair and princely cousin Katherine;
And as a branch and member of this royalty,
By whom this great assembly is contriv'd,
We do salute you, Duke of Burgundy,
And, princes French, and peers, health to you all!

Fr. King. Right joyous are we to behold your face,
Most worthy brother England, fairly met!
So are you, princes English, every one.

Q. Isa. So happy be the issue, brother [England],
Of this good day and of this gracious meeting,
As we are now glad to behold your eyes—
Your eyes, which hitherto have borne in them
Against the French that met them in their bent
The fatal balls of murthering basilisks.
The venom of such looks we fairly hope
Have lost their quality, and that this day
Shall change all griefs and quarrels into love.

K. Hen. To cry amen to that, thus we appear.

Q. Isa. You English princes all, I do salute you.

Bur. My duty to you both, on equal love.
Great Kings of France and England: that I have labor'd
With all my wits, my pains, and strong endeavors
To bring your most imperial Majesties
Unto this bar and royal interview,
Your mightiness on both parts best can witness.
Since then my office hath so far prevail'd,
That face to face, and royal eye to eye,
You have congreeted, let it not disgrace me,
If I demand, before this royal view,
What rub or what impediment there is,
Why that the naked, poor, and mangled Peace,
Dear nurse of arts, plenties, and joyful births,
Should not in this best garden of the world,
Our fertile France, put up her lovely visage?
Alas, she hath from France too long been chas'd,
And all her husbandry doth lie on heaps,
Corrupting in it own fertility.
Her vine, the merry cheerer of the heart,
Unpruned dies; her hedges even-pleach'd,
Like prisoners wildly overgrown with hair,
Put forth disorder'd twigs; her fallow leas
The darnel, hemlock, and rank femetary
Doth root upon, while that the coulter rusts
That should deracinate such savagery;
The even mead, that erst brought sweetly forth
The freckled cowslip, burnet, and green clover,
Wanting the scythe withal, uncorrected, rank,
Conceives by idleness, and nothing teems
But hateful docks, rough thistles, kecksies, burs,
Losing both beauty and utility;
And all our vineyards, fallows, meads, and hedges,
Defective in their natures, grow to wildness.
Even so our houses, and ourselves, and children,
Have lost, or do not learn for want of time,
The sciences that should become our country,
But grow like savages—as soldiers will
That nothing do but meditate on blood—
To swearing and stern looks, defus'd attire,
And every thing that seems unnatural.
Which to reduce into our former favor
You are assembled; and my speech entreats
That I may know the let why gentle Peace
Should not expel these inconveniences,
And bless us with her former qualities.

K. Hen. If, Duke of Burgundy, you would the peace,
Whose want gives growth to th' imperfections
Which you have cited, you must buy that peace
With full accord to all our just demands,
Whose tenures and particular effects
You have enschedul'd briefly in your hands.

Bur. The King hath heard them; to the which, as yet
There is no answer made.

K. Hen. Well then: the peace,
Which you before so urg'd, lies in his answer.

Fr. King. I have but with a [cursitory] eye
O'erglanc'd the articles. Pleaseth your Grace
To appoint some of your Council presently
To sit with us once more, with better heed
To re-survey them, we will suddenly
Pass our accept and peremptory answer.

K. Hen. Brother, we shall. Go, uncle Exeter,
And brother Clarence, and you, brother Gloucester,
Warwick, and Huntington, go with the King,
And take with you free power to ratify,
Augment, or alter, as your wisdoms best
Shall see advantageable for our dignity,
Any thing in or out of our demands,
And we'll consign thereto. Will you, fair sister,
Go with the princes, or stay here with us?

Q. Isa. Our gracious brother, I will go with them.
Happily a woman's voice may do some good,
When articles too nicely urg'd be stood on.

K. Hen. Yet leave our cousin Katherine here with us:
She is our capital demand, compris'd
Within the fore-rank of our articles.

Q. Isa. She hath good leave.

Exeunt omnes. Manent King [Henry] and Katherine [with the gentlewoman Alice].

K. Hen. Fair Katherine, and most fair,

5. royalty: royal family. **12. issue:** outcome.
16. bent: (1) glance; (2) line of fire.
17. fatal balls: (1) eyeballs; (2) cannon balls. **basilisks:** (1) fabulous creatures whose glance was thought to cause death; (2) large cannon. **19. quality:** (deadly) nature. **23. on:** deriving from.
24–27. I . . . interview. Since 1417 Burgundy had actively supported the various abortive attempts to negotiate a peace between France and England. **27. bar:** court. **31. congreeted:** met amicably.
33. rub: obstacle. **40. it:** its.
42. even-pleach'd: smoothly interwoven, plaited.
44. fallow leas: unplanted fields.
45. darnel: a weedy grass. **femetary:** fumitory, another weed.
46. coulter: blade.
47. deracinate such savagery: uproot such wildness.
48. erst: formerly. **50. Wanting:** lacking.
51. Conceives: i.e. produces weeds.

55. Defective . . . natures: i.e. perverted from their natural function, unnatural. **61. defus'd:** disordered.
63. reduce . . . favor: return to our former appearance.
65. let: hindrance. **68. would:** desire.
72. tenures: tenors, general principles.
77. cursitory: cursory. **78. Pleaseth:** if it please.
79. presently: immediately.
81–82. suddenly . . . answer: promptly return our adopted and decisive reply. **93. Happily:** haply, perhaps.
94. nicely: punctiliously. **96. capital:** chief.

Will you vouchsafe to teach a soldier terms,
Such as will enter at a lady's ear,
And plead his love-suit to her gentle heart?

Kath. Your Majesty shall mock at me, I cannot speak your England.

K. Hen. O fair Katherine, if you will love me soundly with your French heart, I will be glad to hear you confess it brokenly with your English tongue. Do you like me, Kate?

Kath. *Pardonnez-moi*, I cannot tell wat is "like me."

K. Hen. An angel is like you, Kate, and you are like an angel.

Kath. *Que dit-il? Que je suis semblable à les anges?*

Alice. *Oui, vraiment, sauf votre grâce, ainsi dit-il.*

K. Hen. I said so, dear Katherine, and I must not blush to affirm it.

Kath. *O bon Dieu! les langues des hommes sont pleines de tromperies.*

K. Hen. What says she, fair one? That the tongues of men are full of deceits?

Alice. *Oui*, dat de tongeus of de mans is be full of deceits: dat is de Princess.

K. Hen. The Princess is the better Englishwoman. I' faith, Kate, my wooing is fit for thy understanding. I am glad thou canst speak no better English, for if thou couldst, thou wouldst find me such a plain king that thou wouldst think I had sold my farm to buy my crown. I know no ways to mince it in love, but directly to say "I love you"; then if you urge me farther than to say "Do you in faith?" I wear out my suit. Give me your answer, i' faith, do, and so clap hands and a bargain. How say you, lady?

Kath. *Sauf votre honneur*, me understand well.

K. Hen. Marry, if you would put me to verses, or to dance for your sake, Kate, why, you undid me: for the one, I have neither words nor measure; and for the other, I have no strength in measure, yet a reasonable measure in strength. If I could win a lady at leap-frog, or by vauting into my saddle with my armor on my back, under the correction of bragging be it spoken, I should quickly leap into a wife. Or if I might buffet for my love, or bound my horse for her favors, I could lay on like a butcher, and sit like a jack-an-apes, never off. But, before God, Kate, I cannot look greenly, nor gasp out my eloquence, nor I have no cunning in protestation; only downright oaths, which I never use till urg'd, nor never break for urging. If thou canst love a fellow of this temper, Kate, whose face is not worth sunburning, that never looks in his glass for love of any thing he sees there, let thine eye be thy cook. I speak to thee plain soldier. If thou canst love me for this, take me! if not, to say to thee that I shall die, is true; but for thy love, by the Lord, no; yet I love thee too. And while thou liv'st, dear Kate, take a fellow of plain and uncoin'd constancy, for he perforce must do thee right, because he hath not the gift to woo in other places; for these fellows of infinite tongue, that can rhyme themselves into ladies' favors, they do always reason themselves out again. What? a speaker is but a prater, a rhyme is but a ballad; a good leg will fall, a straight back will stoop, a black beard will turn white, a curl'd pate will grow bald, a fair face will wither, a full eye will wax hollow; but a good heart, Kate, is the sun and the moon, or rather the sun and not the moon; for it shines bright and never changes, but keeps his course truly. If thou would have such a one, take me! and take me, take a soldier; take a soldier, take a king. And what say'st thou then to my love? Speak, my fair, and fairly, I pray thee.

Kath. Is it possible dat I sould love de ennemie of France?

K. Hen. No, it is not possible you should love the enemy of France, Kate; but in loving me, you should love the friend of France; for I love France so well that I will not part with a village of it; I will have it all mine. And, Kate, when France is mine and I am yours, then yours is France and you are mine.

Kath. I cannot tell wat is dat.

K. Hen. No, Kate? I will tell thee in French, which I am sure will hang upon my tongue like a new-married wife about her husband's neck, hardly to be shook off. *Je quand sur le possession de France, et quand vous avez le possession de moi*—let me see, what then? Saint Denis be my speed!—*donc votre est France et vous êtes mienne.* It is as easy for me, Kate, to conquer the kingdom as to speak so much more French. I shall never move thee in French, unless it be to laugh at me.

Kath. *Sauf votre honneur, le François que vous parlez, il est [meilleur] que l'Anglois lequel je parle.*

K. Hen. No, faith, is't not, Kate; but thy speaking of my tongue, and I thine, most truly falsely, must needs be granted to be much at one. But, Kate, dost thou understand thus much English? Canst thou love me?

Kath. I cannot tell.

K. Hen. Can any of your neighbors tell, Kate? I'll ask them. Come, I know thou lovest me; and at night, when you come into your closet, you'll question this gentlewoman about me; and I know, Kate, you will to her dispraise those parts in me that you love with your heart. But, good Kate, mock me mercifully, the rather, gentle Princess, because I love thee cruelly. If ever thou beest mine, Kate, as I have a saving faith within me tells me thou shalt, I get thee with scambling, and thou must therefore needs prove a good soldier-breeder. Shall not thou and I, between Saint Denis and Saint George, compound a

99. **terms**: words.
111–12. **Que . . . dit-il**: What does he say? That I am like the angels? *Alice.* Yes, truly, save your grace, so he says.
129. **clap**: clasp.
134, 135, 136. **measure**: (1) metre; (2) dancing; (3) amount.
137. **vauting**: vaulting. 140. **buffet**: box.
142. **jack-an-apes**: monkey. 143. **greenly**: bashful.
147. **not worth sunburning**: i.e. because it is already so weather-beaten. 149. **be thy cook**: i.e. add the garnishing.
153. **uncoin'd**: i.e. like unminted metal, not in common use.
159. **fall**: lose its shape.
181–84. **Je . . . mienne.** A halting translation of the last sentence of Henry's preceding speech.
183. **Saint Denis**: patron saint of France. **be my speed**: aid me.
188–89. **Sauf . . . parle**: save your honor, the French you speak is better than the English I speak.
192. **at one**: (1) alike; (2) united. 198. **closet**: chamber.
200. **parts**: qualities. 205. **scambling**: fighting.

boy, half French, half English, that shall go to Constantinople and take the Turk by the beard? Shall we not? What say'st thou, my fair flower-de-luce?

Kath. I do not know dat.

K. Hen. No; 'tis hereafter to know, but now to promise. Do but now promise, Kate, you will endeavor for your French part of such a boy; and for my English moi'ty, take the word of a king and a bachelor. How answer you, *la plus belle Katherine du monde, mon très cher et devin déesse?*

Kath. Your Majestee ave fausse French enough to deceive de most sage demoiselle dat is en France.

K. Hen. Now fie upon my false French! By mine honor, in true English, I love thee, Kate; by which honor I dare not swear thou lovest me, yet my blood begins to flatter me that thou dost—notwithstanding the poor and untempering effect of my visage. Now beshrew my father's ambition! he was thinking of civil wars when he got me; therefore was I created with a stubborn outside, with an aspect of iron, that when I come to woo ladies, I fright them. But in faith, Kate, the elder I wax, the better I shall appear. My comfort is, that old age, that ill layer-up of beauty, can do no more spoil upon my face. Thou hast me, if thou hast me, at the worst; and thou shalt wear me, if thou wear me, better and better; and therefore tell me, most fair Katherine, will you have me? Put off your maiden blushes, avouch the thoughts of your heart with the looks of an empress, take me by the hand, and say, "Harry of England, I am thine"; which word thou shalt no sooner bless mine ear withal, but I will tell thee aloud, "England is thine, Ireland is thine, France is thine, and Henry Plantagenet is thine"; who, though I speak it before his face, if he be not fellow with the best king, thou shalt find the best king of good fellows. Come, your answer in broken music; for thy voice is music and thy English broken; therefore, queen of all, Katherine, break thy mind to me in broken English—wilt thou have me?

Kath. Dat is as it shall please de *roi mon père.*

K. Hen. Nay, it will please him well, Kate; it shall please him, Kate.

Kath. Den it sall also content me.

K. Hen. Upon that I kiss your hand, and I call you my queen.

Kath. Laissez, mon seigneur, laissez, laissez! Ma foi, je ne veux point que vous abaissez votre [*grandeur*] *en baisant la main d'une (Notre Seigneur!) indigne serviteur. Excusez-moi, je vous supplie, mon très puissant seigneur.*

K. Hen. Then I will kiss your lips, Kate.

Kath. Les dames et demoiselles pour être baisées devant leur noces, il n'est pas la coutume de France.

K. Hen. Madam my interpreter, what says she?

210. **flower-de-luce:** fleur-de-lis, the national emblem of France.
215. **moi'ty:** part. 216. **bachelor:** young knight.
216–17. **la plus . . . déesse:** the most beautiful Katherine in the world, my very dear and divine goddess. 222. **blood:** instinct.
224. **untempering:** uningratiating. 229. **wax:** grow.
230. **layer-up:** preserver. 242. **fellow with:** equal to.
243. **broken music:** music in parts. 245. **break:** open, reveal.
247. **de roi mon père:** the king my father.
253–56. **Laissez . . . seigneur:** Don't, my lord, don't, don't. My faith, I don't want you to lower your dignity by kissing the hand of an (Our Lord!) unworthy servant. Excuse me, I beg you, my most mighty lord.

Alice. Dat it is not be de fashon pour les ladies of France—I cannot tell wat is [*baiser*] en Anglish.

K. Hen. To kiss.

Alice. Your Majestee *entendre* bettre *que moi.*

K. Hen. It is not a fashion for the maids in France to kiss before they are married, would she say?

Alice. Oui, vraiment.

K. Hen. O Kate, nice customs cur'sy to great kings. Dear Kate, you and I cannot be confin'd within the weak list of a country's fashion. We are the makers of manners, Kate; and the liberty that follows our places stops the mouth of all find-faults, as I will do yours, for upholding the nice fashion of your country in denying me a kiss; therefore patiently and yielding. [*Kissing her.*] You have witchcraft in your lips, Kate; there is more eloquence in a sugar touch of them than in the tongues of the French council; and they should sooner persuade Harry of England than a general petition of monarchs. Here comes your father.

Enter the French Power *and the* English Lords.

Bur. God save your Majesty! My royal cousin, teach you our princess English?

K. Hen. I would have her learn, my fair cousin, how perfectly I love her, and that is good English.

Bur. Is she not apt?

K. Hen. Our tongue is rough, coz, and my condition is not smooth; so that having neither the voice nor the heart of flattery about me, I cannot so conjure up the spirit of love in her, that he will appear in his true likeness.

Bur. Pardon the frankness of my mirth, if I answer you for that. If you would conjure in her, you must make a circle; if conjure up Love in her in his true likeness, he must appear naked and blind. Can you blame her then, being a maid yet ros'd over with the virgin crimson of modesty, if she deny the appearance of a naked blind boy in her naked seeing self? It were, my lord, a hard condition for a maid to consign to.

K. Hen. Yet they do wink and yield, as love is blind and enforces.

Bur. They are then excus'd, my lord, when they see not what they do.

K. Hen. Then, good my lord, teach your cousin to consent winking.

Bur. I will wink on her to consent, my lord, if you will teach her to know my meaning; for maids, well summer'd and warm kept, are like flies at Bartholomew-tide, blind, though they have their eyes, and then they will endure handling, which before would not abide looking on.

K. Hen. This moral ties me over to time and a hot summer; and so I shall catch the fly, your cousin, in the latter end, and she must be blind too.

Bur. As love is, my lord, before it loves.

K. Hen. It is so; and you may, some of you, thank

264. **entendre . . . moi:** understands better than I.
268. **nice:** overrefined. **cur'sy:** curtsy, i.e. defer, yield.
270. **list:** barrier. 271–72. **follows our places:** befits our rank.
286–87. **condition:** disposition. 300. **wink:** close both eyes.
308. **summer'd:** nurtured. 308–9. **Bartholomew-tide:** August 24.

love for my blindness, who cannot see many a fair French city for one fair French maid that stands in my way.

Fr. King. Yes, my lord, you see them perspectively: the cities turn'd into a maid; for they are all girdled with maiden walls that war hath [never] ent'red.

K. Hen. Shall Kate be my wife?

Fr. King. So please you.

K. Hen. I am content, so the maiden cities you talk of may wait on her; so the maid that stood in the way for my wish shall show me the way to my will.

Fr. King. We have consented to all terms of reason.

K. Hen. Is't so, my lords of England?

West. The King hath granted every article:
His daughter first; and in sequel, all,
According to their firm proposed natures.

Exe. Only he hath not yet subscribed this: Where your Majesty demands that the King of France, having any occasion to write for matter of grant, shall name your Highness in this form, and with this addition, in French, *Notre très cher fils Henri, Roi d'Angleterre, Héritier de France;* and thus in Latin, *Praeclarissimus filius noster Henricus, Rex Angliae, et Heres Franciae.*

Fr. King. Nor this I have not, brother, so denied,
But your request shall make me let it pass.

K. Hen. I pray you then, in love and dear alliance,
Let that one article rank with the rest,
And thereupon give me your daughter.

Fr. King. Take her, fair son, and from her blood raise up
Issue to me, that the contending kingdoms
Of France and England, whose very shores look pale
With envy of each other's happiness,
May cease their hatred; and this dear conjunction
Plant neighborhood and Christian-like accord
In their sweet bosoms, that never war advance
His bleeding sword 'twixt England and fair France.

Lords. Amen!

K. Hen. Now welcome, Kate; and bear me witness all,
That here I kiss her as my sovereign queen. *Flourish.*

Q. Isa. God, the best maker of all marriages,
Combine your hearts in one, your realms in one!
As man and wife, being two, are one in love,
So be there 'twixt your kingdoms such a spousal,
That never may ill office, or fell jealousy,
Which troubles oft the bed of blessed marriage,
Thrust in between the [paction] of these kingdoms,
To make divorce of their incorporate league;
That English may as French, French Englishmen,
Receive each other. God speak this Amen!

All. Amen!

K. Hen. Prepare we for our marriage; on which day,
My Lord of Burgundy, we'll take your oath,
And all the peers', for surety of our leagues.
Then shall I swear to Kate, and you to me,
And may our oaths well kept and prosp'rous be!

Sennet. Exeunt.

Enter CHORUS *[as Epilogue].*

Thus far, with rough and all-unable pen,
Our bending author hath pursu'd the story,
In little room confining mighty men,
Mangling by starts the full course of their glory.
Small time; but in that small most greatly lived
This star of England. Fortune made his sword;
By which the world's best garden he achieved,
And of it left his son imperial lord.
Henry the Sixt, in infant bands crown'd King
Of France and England, did this king succeed;
Whose state so many had the managing,
That they lost France, and made his England bleed;
Which oft our stage hath shown; and for their sake,
In your fair minds let this acceptance take. *[Exit.]*

320–21. perspectively: i.e. as through an optical glass that produces illusions. **322. maiden:** i.e. unconquered.
337–38. for . . . grant: i.e. in formal documents.
339. addition: title.
339–42. Notre . . . Franciae: our dear son Henry, King of England and Heir of France. **343. so:** i.e. so firmly.
352. dear conjunction: solemn union.

363. ill office: graceless act. **fell:** cruel.
365. paction: agreement.
370–74. Prepare . . . be. The royal wedding, which was solemnized with great pomp on June 2, 1420, did not bring the peace predicted here, for the Dauphin, indignant at the concessions that Henry had exacted from his father, continued his resistance. Consequently Henry's last two years of life were spent in an unsuccessful effort to consolidate his gains in France. When he died in 1422, leaving the throne to his infant son, affairs were in the disordered state described at the opening of *1 Henry VI.*

Epi. 1–14. These lines form a Shakespearean sonnet.
2. bending: bowing (?) or stooped with the labor of composition (?).
13. Which . . . shown. Alluding to the great popularity of the Henry VI plays. **14. this acceptance take:** this play find favor.

NOTE ON THE TEXT

The First Folio (1623) offers us our only authoritative text of *Henry the Fifth*; all later texts are basically derived from that source. There is also, however, a "bad" quarto, published in 1600 (Q1), about half the length of the F1 text (containing fifty-five lines unique to Q1), a memorially reconstructed version of the play reported by the actors who played Essex, Pistol, and Gower and who probably doubled as Nym and Scroop and perhaps as York and the Governor of Harfleur (see Irace). Two more quartos, each printed from Q1, were issued in 1602 (Q2) and 1619 (Q3; fraudulently dated 1608). Q3 contains a number of slight variants, some of which anticipate the F1 text (see below). As the Textual Notes show, Q1 is useful for occasional stage directions and for correcting a few errors in the F1 text, but, as a reported version, it has nothing more than what might be called "hearsay" authority.

There is general agreement that Shakespeare's "foul papers," probably slightly edited (e.g., to soften oaths), served as printer's copy for the Fl text. The stigmata of "foul papers" are clearly visible: some inconsistency in speech-prefixes; occasional indefinite stage directions and omission of stage directions; the appearance of a ghost character, Beaumont (in IV.ii o.s.d.); and a few characteristic Shakespearean spellings (see Textual Notes, II.iii.31, 35, IV.i.179, IV.ii.11, V.ii.137; and *mervailous*, II.i.47). A. S. Cairncross's argument (1956) that the Fl text was set up from printer's copy composed of pages of Q2 and Q3 corrected and augmented by reference to the "foul papers" is now generally discounted, because, as J. H. Walter points out, printer's copy such as that postulated by Cairncross would have been very cumbersome and hard to follow—even more so, one would suppose, than Shakespeare's "foul papers." But that there is some kind of bibliographical link between F1 and Q3 seems inescapable, and the problems here involved suggest an analogy with the textual situation in *2* and *3 Henry VI*, including the possible contamination of the F1 text by a later quarto copy-text, as in *Richard III* (see particularly the "Note on the Text" to *2 Henry VI*). In the case of *Henry V*, however, there is a difference, since the Q3(Q2)–F1 links are almost entirely limited to single, usually unimportant, words or contractions as compared with the more significant links (in some instances passages) in the two *Henry VI* plays, and this makes it more difficult to accept Greg's suggestion that they arise from someone connected with the printing of Q3 who had heard a recent performance of the play. In 1979, however, Gary Taylor summarily dismissed any suggestion of Q3 influence on F1, a dismissal he later recanted (1987), proposing that a copy of Q3 was occasionally consulted by the F1 compositors when they found Shakespeare's "foul papers" unclear or illegible. On the other hand, Andrew Gurr denies any Q3 contamination in F1, arguing that the compositor(s) of Q3 consulted at these points (i.e., Q3/F1 agreements against Q1–2) the same manuscript (Shakespeare's "foul papers") from which the F1 text was later derived, a view for which he offers little evidence. Given such opposing views, and, particularly, the very uncertain authority of Q as a memorially reconstructed text, the present text retains the F1 reading where it may appear that F1 has been contaminated by Q3 and where another editor might prefer the reading of Q1, as Taylor does in some cases (see his excellent analysis of the Q3/F1 agreements in *A Textual Companion*). The reader, however, may consult the most significant Q3/F1 links in the Textual Notes; see II.i.33, II.ii.177, II.iii.31, 42 (an especially tempting reading in Q1–2), II.iv.75, III.ii.44, III.vi.158, III.vii.20, IV.i.284 s.d., IV.vi.2, 30, IV.vii.5, 91, 111, 154–5, IV.viii.24, 51, 65, 71, V.i.14, 25, 33, 64, V.ii.171, 340, 341–2. Where only one or two of the three quartos are cited, agreement of the uncited quarto (or quartos) with the lemma may be assumed.

The play as it appears in F1 shows some evidence of revision. It seems likely, for example, that Shakespeare originally intended to include Falstaff among Henry's followers in the French wars and that the scenes connected with his death (II.i, iii) were later additions, a conclusion supported by the feeble extra couplet with which the second Chorus ends. It is even possible that much of Pistol's "business" once belonged to Falstaff, a view that would help to explain the curious reference to Doll Tearsheet (V.i.81), which properly should be to Mistress Quickly, Pistol's wife. Probably, also, the discussion in III.ii between Fluellen, Gower, Macmorris, and Jamy was an afterthought (see the Textual Notes for Fluellen's change of speech-prefix at III.ii.68); neither Macmorris nor Jamy appears again, nor is this part of the scene or these two characters found in Q1–3, where, however, the omission may have been the result of cutting to reduce the number of characters needed for provincial touring. Other evidences of revision have also been noted.

Recently, something like "deconstruction" has overtaken the text of *Henry V*. Because (in both F1 and Q), the French King forbids the Dolphin to participate in the coming battle with the English forces, Taylor (1982), followed by Gurr (1992), despite the latter's repeated caveats about the unreliability of Q1, adopts Q's substitution of the Duke of Bourbon for the Dolphin in III.vii, a scene which takes place on the eve of the battle of Agincourt, arguing that this role change represents Shakespeare's revision to bring III.vii in line with III.v, or, at least, preserves this and later scenes (where Bourbon also replaces the Dolphin in Q) as they were acted on the London stage. Neither assumption can be shown to be much more than a possibility, and the second assumption, even if true, perhaps forced on the company by political pressure from the French ambassador, would not in itself justify such radical textual manipulation; at best, however, both remain unproved assumptions that raise as many problems as they are supposed to solve. Q's substitution of Bourbon for the Dolphin in III.vii sacrifices the climactic balance of the play—the Dolphin as a foil for Henry—a function of the scene, obviously carefully plotted by Shakespeare, contrasting Henry, himself not long ago an "heir apparent" (a point Shakespeare underlines in I.ii by the Dolphin's gift of tennis balls), as, on the eve of battle, he moves disguised through the English camp heartening his soldiers with "a little touch of Harry in the night," while the Dolphin is shown bragging fatuously about his horse and armor and how many English he will kill tomorrow. Replacing the Dolphin in III.vii with Bourbon, a hitherto faceless character, who, in F1, speaks for the first time in IV.v (two speeches, in all nine lines), drastically reduces the thematic impact of the scene and makes it more than difficult to believe that Shakespeare himself could have perpetrated such a dramatic blunder. And why, if not actually forced by external pressures, perhaps, as already noted, political, would anyone, least of all Shakespeare, not solve the apparent contradiction between III.v and III.vii simply by deleting the French King's order (even though it appears in Holinshed) refusing to allow the Dolphin to take part in the coming hostilities (III.v.64–6)?

Having decided to follow Q in the Bourbon substitution change in III.vii, Taylor and Gurr are forced to drop the Dolphin in IV.ii (a scene omitted in Q except for a line-and-a-half tacked on to the end of Q's equivalent of III.vii) and in IV.v, in the second case with unfortunate results. In IV.v, both Bourbon and the Dolphin, for the first time in the F1 text, appear together and (as Irace notes) the rousingly assertive character of Bourbon as here presented by Shakespeare is strongly at odds with the princox showoff character he is assigned when substituted for the Dolphin in III.v. Apparently in order to accommodate the Dolphin/Bourbon shift, Taylor (but not Gurr) adopts Q throughout the scene (the only occasion he does so), omitting four lines (4–7) and two half-lines (6 "Why . . . broke."; 11 "Let us die! In"). The overall patchwork effect is further emphasized by the dropping, throughout, of the Dukes of Bedford and Britain, whose lines, as in Q, are transferred to either the Duke of Clarence or the Duke of Bourbon (Gurr drops only Britain). Such extreme confidence in Q1 (admittedly a "bad quarto") thus substitutes a conflated and suppositious text for a text (F1) that is universally accepted as having been printed from Shakespeare's "foul papers." Thus we are presented with a text based on an unprovable assumption (Shakespeare's supposed responsibility for whatever text lies behind the memorially reported Q) in place of a text that we know to be essentially Shakespeare's.

For the treatment of Shakespeare's French in the present text, see the note at the beginning of III.iv below. The editor is indebted to Professor Charles Knudson for advice on sixteenth-century French forms. From Rowe onward there has been much editorial tinkering with Fluellen's "English"; the present text reproduces his speech as it appears in F1.

The Textual Notes generally record the variants in Q1–3 only where they figure in a reading cited in connection with the F1 text. The absence of citation of Q1–3 among the sigla in any entry indicates that the reading of the lemma occurs in a passage which in Q1–3 is either omitted or so differently worded that it offers no recognizable equivalent.

For further information, see: H. T. Price, *The Text of "Henry V"* (Newcastle-under-Lyme, 1920); J. H. Walter, "'With Sir John in It,'" *MLR*, XLVI (1946), 237–45, and ed., New Arden *King Henry V* (London, 1954; rev. ed., 1960): J. D. Wilson, ed., New Shakespeare *King Henry V* (Cambridge, 1947); W. W. Greg, *The Shakespeare First Folio* (Oxford, 1955); A. S. Cairncross, "Quarto Copy for Folio *Henry V*," *SB*, VIII (1956), 67–93; Alice Walker, "Some Editorial Principles, with Special Reference to *Henry V*," *SB*, VIII (1956), 95–111; G. I. Duthie, "The Quarto of Shakespeare's *Henry V*," *Papers Mainly Shakespearian*, ed. G. I. Duthie (1964), pp. 106–30; Jonathan H. Spinner, "The Composition and Presswork of *Henry V* Q1," *The Library*, XXXII (1977), 37–44 [response by G. W. Williams, *The Library*, XXXIII (1978), 170–1]; Gary Taylor (with Stanley Wells), *Modernizing Shakespeare's Spelling, with Three Studies in the Text of "Henry V"* (Oxford, 1979), ed., New Oxford *Henry V* (Oxford, 1982), and (with Stanley Wells, et al.) *William Shakespeare: A Textual Companion* (Oxford, 1987); Thomas L. Berger, "The Printing of *Henry V*, Q1," *The Library*, 6th ser., I (1979), 114–25, Kathleen Irace, "Reconstruction and Adaptation in Q *Henry V*," *SB*, XLIV (1991), 228–53, and *Reforming the "Bad Quartos"* (Univ. of Delaware Press, 1994); Andrew Gurr, ed., New Cambridge *Henry V* (1992); T. W. Craik, ed., Arden (3rd. ser.) *Henry V* (London, 1995).

TEXTUAL NOTES

Title: The . . . Fifth] The . . . Fift. *F1;* The Cronicle History of Henry the fift, With his battell fought at Agin Court in France. Togither with Auntient Pistoll. As it hath bene sundry times playd by the Right honorable the Lord Chamberlaine his seruants. *Q1 (title-page)*
Dramatis personae▸ *subs. as first given in Rowe*
Act-scene division: *none in Q1–3; F1 marks I.i and thereafter acts only, as follows: Acts II and III at the beginning of Acts III and IV, respectively, of the present numbering, Act IV at the present IV.vii, and Act V as in the present text; other act-scene divisions from Pope and later editors (see first note to each scene); present act-scene arrangement as a whole first established by Capell*

Prologue

Prologue and choruses om. Q1–3

I.i

Scene om. Q1–3
Location: *Malone (after Pope, Theobald)*
1 s.p. Cant.] *Rowe;* Bish. Cant. *F1; (or* B. Cant. *throughout scene)*
6 s.p. Ely.] *Rowe;* Bish. Ely. *F1 (or* B. Ely. *throughout scene)*
11 thus:] *Capell (subs.);* thus, *F1*
36 seat . . . once)] *ed.;* Seat; . . . once; *F1*
66 crescive] *F4;* cressiue *F1*
89 great-grandfather] *hyphen, Dyce*

I.ii

I.ii] *Pope*
Location: *Theobald (subs.)*
o.s.d. and other Attendants] *from Q1–3 s.d.:* Enter King Henry, Exeter, 2. Bishops, Clarence, and other Attendants.
6 s.d. the Archbishop . . . Ely] *Rowe*
38 succedant] *F2;* succedaul *F1*
45, 52 Elbe] *Capell (after Holinshed);* Elue *F1;* Elme *Q1–3 (om. l. 52)*
53 call'd] called *Q1–2*
59 suppos'd] supposed *Q1–2*
72 fine] *Q1–3;* find *F1*
76 Lewis] *Rowe;* Lewes *F1 (throughout; so Holinshed)*
103 great-grandsire's] *hyphen, Dyce*
105 great-uncle's] *hyphen, Dyce*
115 s.p. Ely.] *F3 (subs.);* Bish. *F1 (Q1–3 om. ll. 115–135)*
131 blood] *F3;* Bloods *F1*
138 Against] for *Q1, Q3*
146 great-grandfather] *hyphen, Dyce*
155 fear'd] feared *Q1–2*
156 herself:] *Theobald (subs.);* her selfe, *F1, Q1–3*
163 her] *Johnson conj.;* their *F1;* your *Q1–3*
166 s.p. Ely.] Bish. Ely. *F1;* Lord. *Q1–3 (Holinshed assigns the speech to Westmerland; so also Capell and many later eds.)*
168 begin] *Q1–3;* begia *F1*
173 'tame] *Wilson (after Greg);* tame *F1;* spoyle *Q1–3*
174 then] *Q1–3;* theu *F1*
196 tent-royal] tent royall *Q1–2*
197 majesty] *Q1–3;* Maiesties *F1*
202 sad-ey'd] sad eyde *Q1–2*
208 many] many seuerall *Q1–3*
211 afoot] *Rowe;* a foote *F1, Q1–3*
212 End] *Q1–3;* And *F1*
221 s.d. Exeunt some Attendants.] *Capell*
233 s.d. attended] *Hudson (after Capell)*
234 prepar'd] prepared *Q1–2*
237, 245 s.pp. 1. Amb.] *Dyce;* Amb. *F1, Q1–3*
240 meaning] *F2;* meauing *F1;* pleasure *Q1–3*
269 valu'd] valued *Q1–2*
270 therefore,] *Theobald;* therefore *F1 (cf. Q1–3's reading of ll. 269–70:* We neuer valued [valew'd *Q3*] this poore seate of England. / And therefore gaue our selues to barbarous licence:)
276 that I have] this haue we *Q1–2;* this we haue *Q3*
277 working-days] *hyphen, Capell*

II.Cho.

Act II] *Johnson*
22 crowns; . . . men,] *Theobald;* Crownes, . . . men: *F1*
25 knight,] *Knight;* Knight *F1*
28 die,] *F2;* dye. *F1*

II.i

II.i] *Hanmer*
Location: *Capell*
o.s.d. Bardolph] *F4;* Bardolfe *F1, Q1–3 (throughout scene)*
2 Good morrow] Godmorrow *Q1;* God morrow *Q2*
22 time,] time, and there is [there's *Q3*] the humor of it. *Q1–3*
23 mare] *Q1–3;* name *F1*
28 s.p. Nym.] *Q1–3; speech continued to Bardolph, F1*
29–31 Base . . . lodgers.] *as verse, Q1–3; as prose, F1*
30 Gadslugs] *ed. (from Q1, Q3* gads lugges); this hand *F1;* gads lugge *Q2*
33 gentlewomen] honest gentlewomen *Q1–2*
35–6 s.d. Nym . . . draw.] *Capell (subs.)*
42 Iceland . . . Iceland] *Johnson conj.;* Island . . . Island *F1; Q1–3 read the line:* What dost thou push, thou prickeard cur of Iseland
46–53 "Solus," . . . follow.] *as irregular verse, Q1–3; as prose, F1*
65 s.d. Draws.] *Malone;* They drawe. *Q1–3 (after l. 62)*
67–8 Give . . . tall.] *as verse, Pope; as prose, F1*
71–80 "Couple . . . to.] *as irregular verse, Q1–3; as prosc, F1*
72 thee defy] *Q1–3;* defie thee *F1*
79 and—pauca] *Capell;* and Pauca *F1;* and Paco *Q1–3*
79–80 enough . . . to.] *ed.;* enough to go to. *F1;* inough. *Q1–2;* enough. *Q3*
89 s.d. with Boy] *Capell (subs.)*
95 betting] beating *Q1–2*
98 s.d. They draw.] *Q1–3;* Draw *F1*
100 s.d. Draws.] *Delius*
102 Corporal] *F3;* Coporall *F1*
105–6 Nym. I . . . betting?] *Q1–3* (beating *Q1–2*)
107–12 A . . . accrue.] *as verse, Q1–3; as prose, F1*
116 that's] *F2;* that *F1;* theres *Q1–3*
118 Ah] *Pope;* A *F1*
123–4 Nym . . . corroborate.] *as verse, Capell; as prose, F1*
127 Let . . . live.] *as verse, Capell; as prose, F1 (as single line, Q1–3)*
127 s.d. Exeunt.] *Q1–3* (Exeunt omnes.)

II.ii

II.ii] *Pope*
Location: *Pope, Malone (after Capell)*
11 s.d. with Attendants] *Theobald (subs.)*
19 s.p. Scroop.] Masha. *or* Mash. *Q1–3 (throughout scene)*
29 s.p. Grey.] *Q1–3* (Gray.); Kni. *F1*
56 digested] disgested *Q1–2*
67–8 Masham; . . . knight, Grey] *Q1–3* (Masham. And Sir Thomas Gray [Grey *Q3*] knight); Masham, . . . Knight: Gray *F1*
75 have] hath *Q1–3*
87 him] *Q1–3 (in the phrase* to grace him); *F2*
89, 167 conspir'd] conspired *Q1, Q3*
95 inhuman] *Rowe;* inhumane *F1, Q1–3*
98 have] a *Q1*
99 have] a *Q1–2*
107 a] *F2;* an *F1*
122 lion gait] *Capell;* Lyon-gate *F1*

139 **mark the]** *Theobald;* make thee *F1*
140 **suspicion. . . . thee;]** *Capell (after Pope);* suspition, . . . thee. *F1*
147 **Henry]** *Q1–3;* Thomas *F1*
148 **Masham]** *Q1–3;* Marsham *F1*
150 **knight,]** *Dyce;* Knight *F1, Q1–3*
159 **I]** *F2*
175 **must]** *Q1–3;* uuust *F1*
176 **have]** *Q1–3;* three *F2*
177 **you]** ye *Q1–2*
181 **s.d. Exeunt . . . guarded.]** *Capell (subs.);* Exit. *F1;* Exit three Lords. *Q1–3*
192 **Cheerly]** *Q1–3;* Chearely *F1*
193 **s.d. Exeunt.]** *Q1–3* (Exit omnes.)

II.iii

II.iii] *Pope*
Location: *Theobald (subs.)*
1 **honey-sweet]** *hyphen, Theobald*
3–6 **No . . . therefore.]** *as verse, Pope; as prose, F1 (Q1–3 reduce the lines to:* No fur, no fur.)
16–7 **'a babbl'd]** *Theobald (after anon. conj.* a' talked): a Table *F1*
22 **on]** at *Q1–2; om. Q3*
24 **knees,]** knees, and they were as cold as any stone. *Q1–3*
25 **up'ard and up'ard]** *Wilson;* vp-peer'd, and vpward *F1;* vpward, and vpward *Q1–3*
31 **said]** he sed *Q1–2*
31 **dev'ls]** *ed.;* Deules *F1;* diuels *Q1–3*
33 **s.p. Host.]** *Q1–3;* Woman. *F1*
35 **dev'l]** *ed.;* Deule *F1 (Q1–3 version of speech assigned to* Nim.)
42 **hell]** hell fire *Q1–2*
47–56 **Come . . . suck!]** *as irregular verse, Q1–3; as prose, F1*
49 **word]** *Q1, Q3;* world *F1, Q2*
52 **dog, my duck;]** *pointing from Q1–3* (dog my deare.); Dogge: My Ducke, *F1*
59 **s.d. Kissing her.]** *Capell*
62 **Let . . . command.]** *Q1–3 read:* Keepe fast thy buggle boe.

II.iv

II.iv] *Pope*
Location: *Pope, Theobald*
o.s.d. **the Constable]** *Rowe*
o.s.d. **and others]** *Q1–3*
1 **s.p. Fr. King.]** *Rowe;* King. *F1, Q1–3 (throughout scene)*
33 **counsellors]** *Q1–3;* Councellors *F1*
67 **s.d. Exeunt . . . Lords.]** *Capell*
74–5 **Self-love . . . self-neglecting]** Selfeloue . . . selfe neglecting *Q1–2* (thing *for* sin)
75 **s.d. Enter . . . Train.]** *Capell (subs.);* Enter Exeter. *F1, Q1–3*
75 **of]** *om. Q1–2*
89 **s.d. Giving a paper.]** *Theobald (subs.)*
107 **dead men's]** *Q1–3* (mens); dead-mens *F1*
107 **privy]** pining *Q1–3*
112 **too]** *Q1–3;* to *F1*
131 **Paris balls]** *Q1–3;* Paris-Balls *F1*
132 **Louvre]** *Pope;* Louer *F1, Q1–3;* Loover *F2 (indicates pronunciation)*
134 **difference]** *Q1–3;* diff'rence *F1*

III.Cho.

Act III] *Pope;* Actus Secundus. *F1*
4 **Hampton]** *Theobald;* Douer *F1*
6 **fanning]** *Rowe;* fayning *F1*

III.i

III.i] *Hanmer*
Scene om. Q1–3
Location: *Theobald (after F1 o.s.d.)*
o.s.d. **Enter Soldiers with]** *ed. (after Theobald)*
7 **conjure]** *Walter;* commune *F1*
15 **nostril]** *Rowe;* Nosthrill *F1*
17 **noblest]** *F2;* Noblish *F1*
24 **men]** *F4;* me *F1*
32 **Straining]** *Rowe;* Straying *F1*
34 **s.d. Exeunt.]** *Theobald (subs.)*

III.ii

III.ii] *Hanmer*
Location: *ed. (after Theobald)*
8–11 **"Knocks . . . fame."]** *as verse, Capell (after Pope; as fragmentary verse, Q1–3); as prose, F1*
15–9 **"If . . . bough."]** *as verse, Capell (after Pope; as fragmentary verse, Q1–3); as prose, F1*
17 **hie]** *Q1–3;* high *F1*
21 **s.d. Driving them forward.]** *Capell (subs., after Q1–3* Enter Flewellen and beates them in.)
22–5 **Be . . . chuck!]** *as verse, Pope (omitting l. 25); as prose, F1*
27 **s.d. with . . . Pistol]** *Q1–2 (subs., including the Boy and following his soliloquy)*
27 **s.d. Fluellen steps aside.]** *ed.*
31 **antics]** *Theobald;* Antiques *F1*
43 **lute-case]** Lute case *Q1–2*
44 **half-pence]** hapence *Q1–2*
45 **fire-shovel]** fier shouell *Q1–2*
53 **s.d. Fluellen comes forward.]** *ed.*
63 **Cheshu]** Iesus *Q1–2;* Ieshu *Q3*
66 **Irishman]** *Capell;* Irish man *F1*
68 **s.p. Flu.]** *Rowe;* Welch. *F1 (throughout scene; note that change of s.p. comes with the introduction of Macmorris and Jamy and that the rest of the scene, after l. 64, is om. in Q1–3)*
68 **Macmorris]** *Pope (subs.);* Makmorrice *F1 (throughout scene)*
83 **s.p. Jamy.]** *Rowe;* Scot. *F1 (throughout scene)*
88 **s.p. Mac.]** *Rowe;* Irish. *F1 (throughout scene)*
121 **nation—]** *Pope;* Nation. *F1*
136 **A!]** *Cambridge;* A, *F1*
136 **s.d. sounded]** *Rowe*
141 **s.d. Exeunt.]** *Rowe;* Exit. *F1*

III.iii

III.iii] *Hanmer*
Location: *Theobald*
o.s.d. **Enter . . . walls.]** *Walter (after Capell)*
o.s.d. **Enter . . . gates.]** Enter the King and his Lords alarum. *Q1–2, (om.* alarum) *Q3*
23 **career]** *F3;* Carriere *F1 (Q1–3 om. ll. 11–41)*
32 **headly]** headdy *F2*
35 **Defile]** *Rowe;* Desire *F1*
43 **s.d. to the Citizens]** *ed.*

III.iv

III.iv] *Capell (scene in italics throughout, F1)*
The French in this and later scenes raises many problems for the editor. The F1 text is very corrupt, and Q1–3 are small help. Editors from Rowe on have done much to make these passages recognizable as French, but that they represent sixteenth-century French has sometimes been forgotten. The present text employs modern spelling forms, but only where they do not represent any significant change in sixteenth-century pronunciation. Useful for III.iv is a contemporary listing in French "Of all the members of a mans bodie" in Claudius Holyband's The French Littleton *(1609 edition, ed. M. St. Clare Byrne, 1953). Only the more important emendations are recorded in the notes below.*
Location: *Capell (subs., after Theobald)*
o.s.d. **Alice]** *Q3;* Allice *Q1–2*
1–7] *Something of the quality of the French text in the early editions may be judged by comparing the opening lines as they appear in F1 and Q1–3 with the present text. F1:* Kathe. Alice, tu as este en Angleterre, & tu bien parlas le Language. / *Alice.* En peu Madame. / *Kath.* Ie te prie m'ensigniez, it faut que ie apprend a parlen: Comient appelle vous le main en Anglois? / *Alice.* Le main il & appelle de Hand. *Q1–3: Kate.* Allice venecia, vous aues cates en, / Vou parte fort bon Angloys englatara, / Coman sae palla vou la main en francoy. / *Allice.* La main madam de han.
1 **Alice]** Allice *Q1–2 (throughout scene)*
8 **Et les]** *Capell; Alice.* E le *F1*
9 **s.p. Alice.]** *Theobald;* Kat. *F1*
9 **les doigts]** *Capell (after F2* le doyt); e doyt *F1*
12 **s.p. Kath.]** *Theobald;* Alice. *F1*
13 **écolier; j'ai]** *Theobald (subs.);* escholier. / *Kath.* I'ay *F1*
16 **Nous]** *Cambridge*
16 **nailès]** *Duthie (in Wilson);* Nayles *F1 (throughout scene); Q1–3 do not mention* the nails
22, 47, 58 **arma]** *ed. (from Q1–3, in which this form, indicating stage pronunciation, is used throughout; it occurs also in F1 at l. 29);* Arme *F1*
26 **appris]** *Steevens;* apprins *F1*
42 **vous déjà]** *ed.* (déjà *Theobald);* y desia *F1*
52–3 **ils . . . mots]** *Walter (after Wilson);* il sont le mots *F1*
52 **foot]** fot *Q1–2*
62 **s.d. Exeunt.]** *F2;* Exit. *F1;* Exit omnes. *Q1–3*

III.v

III.v] *Capell*
Location: *Capell (subs., after Theobald)*
o.s.d. **the Duke of Britain]** *Wilson;* Burbon *Q1–2;* Bourbon *Q3*
5 **O Dieu vivant]** Mordeu ma via *Q1–3 (cf. l. 11)*
5 **sprays]** spranes *Q1–3*
7 **scions]** *Malone;* Syens *F1*
11 **Dieu,]** *Alexander (after Wilson and Greg);* du *F1 (Q1–3 support* Dieu *by giving the whole phrase as* mor du)
26 **we]** we may *F2*
33 **corantos]** *Johnson;* Carranto's *F1*
39 **hie]** *F4;* high *F1*
42 **Burgundy]** *F3;* Burgonie *F1*
43 **Vaudemont]** *F2;* Vandemont *F1*
45 **Foix]** *Capell;* Loys *F1*
45 **Lestrake]** *Wilson;* Lestrale *F1*
45 **Bouciqualt]** *Theobald;* Bouciquall *F1*
45 **Charolois]** *Capell;* Charaloyes *F1*
46 **knights]** *Theobald conj.;* Kings *F1*

III.vi

III.vi] *Capell*
Location: *Capell (after Theobald)*
14 **Antony]** *Pope;* Anthony *F1, Q3;* Anthonie *Q1–2*
21–2 **Captain . . . well.]** *as verse, Q1–3; as prose, F1*
25–9 **Bardolph . . . stone—]** *as irregular verse, Q1–3; as prose, F1*
31, 32 **blind]** Plind *Q1–3*
31 **his]** her *Q1–3*
39–49 **Fortune . . . requite.]** *as irregular verse, Q1–3; as prose, F1*
48 **penny cord]** *Q1–3;* Penny-Cord *F1*
60 **Very good.]** *following Fluellen's speech, Q1–3 add: Pist.* I say the fig within thy bowels and thy durty maw. *(having already added:* within thy Iawe. *to the end of l. 59)*
85 **s.d. Drum heard.]** *Capell*
86 **s.d. and . . . Soldiers]** and others *Q1–3*
86 **s.d. Gloucester]** *Malone;* Clarence, Gloster *Q1–3*
87 **God]** *Capell (subs.); Flu.* God *F1 (repeated s.p.)*
99 **my part,]** our own parts, like you now, *Q1–2;* our owne parts *Q3*
111 **upbraided]** abraided *Q1–2*
112 **lenity]** *Q1–3;* Leuitie *F1*
113 **s.d. Montjoy]** *Capell (after Holinshed; so also Q1–3 later in the scene);* Mountioy *F1 (throughout scene)*
123 **cue]** *Q1–3* (kue); Q. *F1*
151 **air]** heire *Q1–2*
158 **There's]** there is *Q1–2*
167 **s.d. Exit.]** *Rowe*

III.vii

III.vii] *Hanmer*
Location: *Theobald*
o.s.d. **Dolphin]** *In Q1–3 the Dolphin does not appear in this scene or in IV.v (they omit IV.ii); this accords with the French King's order (III.v.64–6) that the Dolphin remain*

with him in Rouen. Q1–3's characters in this scene (in IV.v described as the foure French Lords) *are:* Burbon, Constable, Orleance, Gebon.
12 **pasterns]** *F2;* postures *F1*
13 **Ça, ha!]** *Theobald;* ch' ha: *F1*
14 **chez]** *Theobald;* ches *F1*
20 **of the ginger]** a the Ginger *Q1–2*
39 **him.]** *F2;* him, *F1*
62 **had]** had had *Q1*
64 **vomissement]** *F3;* vemissement *F1*
65 **et]** *Rowe;* est *F1*
65 **truie]** *Rowe;* leuye *F1*
89 **s.d. Exit.]** *om. Q1–2*
120 **pox]** Iogge *Q1–3*
157 **Englishmen]** *F4;* English men *F1*

IV.Cho.

Act IV] *Pope;* Actus Tertius. *F1*
o.s.d. Enter] *Rowe*
15-6 **toll, . . . name.]** *Tyrwhitt conj.;* towle: . . . nam'd, *F1*
20 **cripple tardy-gaited]** *Theobald (subs.);* creeple-tardy-gated *F1*
46 **define,]** *F2;* define. *F1*
47 **night.]** *Rowe;* night, *F1*

IV.i

IV.i] *Hanmer*
Location: *Theobald*
3 **Good]** *F3;* God *F1*
18–9 **pains Upon example;]** *Pope (reading* pain); paines, / Vpon example, *F1*
33 **s.d. all . . . King]** *Cambridge*
35 **Qui]** *Rowe;* Che *F1;* Ke *Q1–3*
35 **vous]** ve *Q1–3*
37–8 **Discuss . . . popular?]** *as verse, Q1–3; as prose, F1*
44–8 **The . . . name?]** *as verse, Q1–3; as prose, F1*
54–5 **Tell . . . day.]** *as verse, Pope; as prose, F1*
63 **s.d. to one side]** *ed.*
65 **So!]** *Capell;* 'So, *F1*
65 **fewer]** lewer *Q1–2;* lower *Q3*
82 **s.d. with Gower]** *from Q1–3* Exit Gower, and Flewellen.
84 **s.d. three . . . Williams]** three Souldiers *Q1–3 (unnamed, designated as* 1. Soul., 2. Soul., *and* 3. Soul.)
94 **Thomas]** *Theobald;* Iohn *F1*
104 **human]** *Rowe;* humane *F1*
125 **alone,]** *Collier;* alone: *F1*
126 **minds.]** *Rowe;* minds, *F1*
157 **servant]** seruants *Q1–2*
170 **before-breach]** *hyphen, Capell*
179 **mote]** *Malone;* Moth *F1, Q3;* moath *Q1–2*
197 **You]** Mas youle *Q1–3*
211 **Here's]** Here is *Q1–2*
229 **s.d. Exeunt]** *F2;* Exit *F1, Q1–3; F1 s.d. after l. 224; placed as in Q1–3*
236 **heart's ease]** *Steevens;* hearts-ease *F1*
243 **comings-in]** *hyphen, Pope*
245 **What]** *Knight;* What? *F1*
245 **adoration]** *F2;* Odoration *F1*
275 **Hyperion]** *F2;* Hiperio *F1*
284 **s.d. Enter Erpingham.]** Enter the King [to the King *Q3*], Gloster, Epingam, and Attendants. *Q1–3 (Q3 thus continues the scene as in F1)*
291 **reck'ning, if . . . numbers]** *Tyrwhitt conj.;* reckning of . . . numbers: *F1 (cf. Q1–3:* rekconing [reckoning *Q3*], / That the apposed [opposed *Q2*] multitudes which stand before them, / May not appall their courage.)
309 **friends]** *Q1–3;* friend *F1*

IV.ii

IV.ii] *Capell*
Scene om. Q1–3
Location: *Theobald*
1 **armor,]** *F2 (subs.);* Armour *F1*
2 **à]** *Steevens*
2 **varlot lackey!]** *ed. (after Dyce);* Verlot Lacquay: *F1*
4 **eaux]** *Theobald;* ewes *F1*
5 **l'air]** *Theobald;* le air *F1*
6 **Cieux]** *Wilson conj.;* Cein *F1*
11 **dout]** *Rowe;* doubt *F1*
35 **tucket sonance]** *Johnson;* Tucket Sonuance *F1*
48 **down-roping]** *hyphen, Theobald*
49 **gimmal'd]** *Delius;* Iymold *F1*
60 **guidon;]** *Rann;* Guard: on *F1*

IV.iii

IV.iii] *Capell*
Location: *Theobald*
o.s.d.] *Q1–3 om. Bedford, Erpingham, and Westmerland, and add Clarence*
4 **There's]** There is *Q1–2*
13–4 **And . . . valor.]** *placed as in Q1–3 (a version of these lines spoken by Clarence); after l. 11 as part of Bedford's speech, F1 (transposition suggested by Thirlby)*
14 **s.d. Exit Salisbury.]** *Rowe*
19 **Westmerland?]** *Rowe;* Westmerland. *F1;* Warwick? *Q1–3 (Warwick replaces Westmerland in Q1–3 in this scene although he is not included in the o.s.d.)*
48 **And . . . day.]** *Q1–3* (Crispines *Q1–2;* Crispins *Q3*)
49 **forgot,]** *Steevens;* forgot: *F1*
53–4 **Harry . . . Gloucester]** *Q1–3 om. Talbot and Salisbury and add Clarence and York*
59 **remembered]** *Rowe;* remembred *F1, Q1–3*
65–6 **they . . . speaks]** And hold their manhood cheape, / While any speake *Q1–2;* They were not there, when any speakes *Q3*
105 **crasing]** *F1, Q1–3;* grasing *F2*
109 **working-day]** *hyphen, Capell*
124 **'um]** am *Q1–2*
133 **pleasest,]** *F3;* pleasest *F1, Q1–3*

IV.iv

IV.iv] *Capell*
Q1–3 reverse the order of Scenes iv and v
Location: *Theobald*
2 **s.p. Fr. Sol.]** *Rowe;* French. *F1, Q1–3 (throughout scene)*
4 **Calen o]** *Malone conj.;* calmie *F1*
7–11 **O . . . ransom.]** *as verse, Pope; as prose, F1 (Pistol's lines as prose throughout scene in F1; arranged as verse largely by Johnson; whole scene as irregular verse, Q1–3)*
12 **pitié]** *F2 (subs.);* pitez *F1;* petie *Q1–3*
14 **Or]** *Theobald conj.;* for *F1*
35 **à cette heure]** *Theobald;* asture *F1*
38–9 **Peasant . . . sword.]** Vnlesse thou giue to me egregions raunsome, dye. / One point of a foxe. *Q1–3*
46 **two hundred]** 500. *Q1–3*
52 **lui]** *F2* (luy); layt a *F1*
52 **promettez]** *F2* (promettoz); promets *F1*
54 **je]** *Rowe;* se *F1*
55 **remercîments]** *Rowe (subs.);* remercious *F1*
56 **tombe]** *ed.;* intombe *F1;* ne tombe *F2*
56 **pense]** *F2;* peuse *F1*
57 **distingué]** *Capell;* distinie *F1*
66 **Suivez-vous]** *Rowe (om.* vous); Saaue vous *F1*
66 **capitaine.]** *Rowe;* Capitaine? *F1;* Capitain! *F3*
66–7 **s.d. Exeunt . . . Soldier.]** *Pope*

IV.v

IV.v] *Capell*
Location: *ed. (after Wilson)*
o.s.d. Bourbon] *Rowe;* Burbon *F1, Q1–3 (throughout scene)*
2 **est perdu . . . est perdu!]** *Rowe;* et perdia . . . et perdie. *F1*
3 **Mort Dieu,]** *F2 (comma, Alexander);* Mor Dieu *F1;* Mor du *Q1, Q3;* Mordu *Q2*
11 **die! In . . . again!]** *ed.;* dye in once more backe againe, *F1*
15 **by a]** *Q1–3* (least by a); a base *F1* (base *repeated from l. 14*)
19 **enow]** inough *Q1–2*
23 **s.d. Exeunt.]** *Rowe;* Exit. *F1;* Exit omnes. *Q1–3*

IV.vi

IV.vi] *Capell*
Location: *ed. (after Wilson)*
o.s.d. Exeter and others] *Capell*
2 **all's]** all is *Q1–2*
9 **Yoke-fellow]** Yoake fellow *Q1–2*
9 **honor-owing wounds]** *F4;* honour-owing-wounds *F1;* honour dying wounds *Q1–2;* honour-dying wounds *Q3*
15 **He cries]** And cryde *Q1–3*
18 **well-foughten]** well foughten *Q1–2*
26 **espous'd]** espoused *Q1–2*
27 **noble-ending love]** *Rowe;* Noble-ending-loue *F1;* neuer ending loue *Q1–2;* neuer-ending loue *Q3*
30 **had not]** not *Q1–2*
34 **mistful]** *Warburton conj.;* mixtfull *F1*
38] *Following this line Q1–3 add:* Pist. Couple gorge. *(Pistol is included in Q1–3 o.s.d.; cf. IV.iv.37)*
38 **s.d. Exeunt]** *Rowe;* Exit *F1;* Exit omnes. *Q1–3*

IV.vii

IV.vii] *Capell;* Actus Quartus. *F1*
Location: *ed. (after Wilson)*
1 **Kill]** Godes plud kil *Q1–3*
3 **offert;]** *pointing from Capell* (offer'd;); offert *F1;* desired, *Q1–2;* desired *Q3*
5 **there's]** there is *Q1–2*
11 **Monmouth]** Monmorth *Q1–2*
15 **not]** nat *Q1–2*
16 **great]** *Q1–3;* grear *F1*
54 **s.d. Exit.]** *Sisson*
54 **s.d. other]** *Theobald*
54 **s.d. Warwick, Gloucester, Exeter]** *Capell*
54 **s.d. Heralds]** *Sisson*
54 **s.d. and others]** *Capell*
65 **s.d. Exit a Herald.]** *Capell (subs.)*
68 **this, herald?]** *Steevens;* this Herald? *F1;* this? *Q1–3*
70 **s.p. Mont.]** *Rowe;* Her. *F1, Q1–3 (throughout scene)*
78 **their]** *Malone;* with *F1*
91 **Crispin Crispianus]** Cryspin, Cryspin *Q1–2;* Crispin, Crispianus *Q3*
93 **great-uncle]** *hyphen, Capell*
110 **countryman]** *Q1–3;* Countrymen *F1*
111 **Jeshu]** Iesus *Q1–2;* Iesu *Q3*
116 **God]** *Q1–3;* Good *F1*
118 **s.d. Exeunt . . . Montjoy.]** *Theobald;* Exit Heralds. *Q1, Q3;* Exit Herald. *Q2*
137 **gentleman]** *Q1–3;* Ientleman *F1*
143 **law!]** *F2* (law.); law *F1*
154 **Alanson]** Alonson *Q1–2 (throughout)*
154–5 **myself were]** I was *Q1–2;* I were *Q3*
155 **from his]** off from his *Q1–2;* from's *Q3*
156 **any man]** any do *Q1–2;* any *Q3*

IV.viii

IV.viii] *Capell*
Location: *Theobald*
9 **any's]** *F4;* anyes *F1*
13 **Stand away,]** Gode plut, and his. *Q1–2;* Gods plut, and his *Q3*
24 **what's]** what is *Q1–2*
27 **Majesty]** maiesty in person *Q3*
44 **martial]** *Pope;* Marshall *F1*
51 **but as]** as *Q1–2*
55 **I . . . for]** you seemed *Q1–2;* you seemed then to mee *Q3*
55 **offense]** offence, my gracious Lord *Q3*
65 **prabbles]** brables *Q1–2*
71 **silling]** shilling *Q1–2*
72 **s.d. an English]** *Malone*
74 **s.d. Gives a paper.]** *Capell (subs.)*
77 **Bouciqualt]** *Capell;* Bouchiquald *F1;* Bowchquall *Q1;* Bouchquall *Q2–3*
80 **s.p. K. Hen.]** *lines continued to Essex in Q1–3; in Q2–3 given to Henry at l. 101, returned to Essex at l. 103, and given to Henry again beginning* O God *in l. 106*
94 **Rambures]** Ranbieres *Q1–2;* Rambieres *Q3*
99 **Foix]** *Capell;* Foyes *F1;* Foy *Q1–3*
100 **Vaudemont]** *F2;* Vandemont *F1;* Vandemant *Q1–3*
100 **Lestrake]** *Wilson;* Lestrale *F1;* Lestra *Q1–3*
102 **s.d. Herald . . . paper.]** *Capell*
110–1 **loss, . . . other?]** *Pope (subs.);* losse?

. . . other, *F1;* losse, on one part and an other. *Q1–2,* (another?) *Q3*
113 go we] *F2;* goe me *F1;* let vs go *Q1–3*
122 rites] *Pope;* Rights *F1*

V.Cho.

10 flood] *Pope;* flood; *F1*
10 wives] with Wives *F2*
35–9 him— . . . them—] *Theobald;* him. . . . them: *F1*
41 back-return] *hyphen, Capell*

V.i

V.i] *Hanmer*
Location: *Theobald*
14 he] a *Q1–2*
14–5 turkey-cock] Turkecocke *Q1–2*
19–21 Ha . . . leek.] *as irregular verse, Q1–3; as prose, F1*
19 Dost] *Q1–3;* doest *F1*
25 appetites] appetite *Q1–2*
28 Cadwallader] Cadwalleder *Q1–2*
29–30 There . . . it?] *as prose, Capell; as verse, F1*
33 in the mean] meane *Q1–2;* But in the meane *Q3*
34–5 s.d. Strikes him.] *Pope*
39 him.] him, it is enough. *Q3*
46] *Following this line Q3 inserts s.d.:* He makes Ancient Pistoll bite of the Leeke.
47–8 revenge— . . . swear—] *ed. (after Alexander);* reuenge I eate and eate I sweare. *F1*
58 Hold you, there] There *Q1–2;* Look you now, there *Q3*
64 I will] ile *Q1–2*
66 God buy you] And so God be with you *Q3*
71 begun] *Capell;* began *F1*
80–7 Doth . . . steal;] *as irregular verse, Q1–3; as prose, F1*
80 Doth] *Q1–3;* Doeth *F1*
80 huswife] huswye *Q1–2*
81 dead] sicke *Q1–3*
83–5 And . . . cudgell'd.] *om. Q1–3, which substitute:* The warres affordeth nought, home will I trug.
89 swear] *Q1–3;* swore *F1*

V.ii

V.ii] *Hanmer*
Location: *Capell (subs.)*
o.s.d. **Gloucester]** *Malone*
o.s.d. **Westmerland]** *Capell*
o.s.d. **of France]** *Q1–3*
o.s.d. **Burgundy]** *Rowe;* Bourgongne *F1;* Burbon *Q1–3*
o.s.d. **Katherine]** *Theobald;* Queene Katherine *Q1–3 (possibly an error for* Queene, Katherine)
o.s.d. **Alice]** *Capell*
1 s.p. K. Hen.] *Rowe;* King. *F1;* Harry. *Q1–3 (throughout scene)*
7 Burgundy] *Q3;* **Burgogne** *F1;* **Burgondie** *Q1–2*
9 s.p. Fr. King.] *Rowe;* **Fra.** *F1 (or* **France.** *throughout scene, except l. 320);* Fran. *Q1–3 (or* France. *throughout scene)*
11 princes English,] *Rowe;* Princes (English) *F1;* Princes English *Q1–3*
12 England] *F2;* Ireland *F1*
21 s.p. K. Hen.] *Rowe;* Eng. *F1 (or* England. *throughout rest of scene, except ll. 98–316, where* King. *is used)*
42 even-pleach'd] *hyphen, Hanmer*
50 scythe withal,] *ed.;* Sythe, withall *F1;* Sythe, all *Rowe*
68 Burgundy] *Q3;* **Burgonie** *F1;* **Burgondy** *Q1–2*
77 cursitory] *Wilson;* curselarie *F1;* cursenary *Q1–2;* cursorary *Q3 (the reading adopted by most eds. before Wilson; a nonce-word)*
98 s.d. Exeunt omnes.] Exit King and the Lords. *Q1–2;* Exit French King and the Lords. *Q3*
98 s.d. Manent] *Rowe;* Manet *F1, Q1–3*
98 s.d. with . . . Alice] *from Q1–3 s.d.* and the Gentlewoman
98–168] *Q1–3 reduce these lines to:* Hate. [*Kate. Q2; Har. Q3*] Now *Kate,* you haue a blunt wooer here / Left with you. / If I could win thee at leapfrog, / Or with vawting with my armour on my back, / Into my saddle, / Without brag be it spoken, / Ide make compare with any. / But leauing that *Kate,* / If thou takest me now, / Thou shalt haue me at the worst: / And in wearing, thou shalt haue me better and better, [*cf. ll. 231–3*] / Thou shalt haue a face that is not worth sun-burning. / But doost thou thinke, that thou and I, / Betweene Saint *Denis,* / And Saint *George,* shall get a boy, / That shall goe to *Constantinople,* / And take the great Turke by the beard, ha *Kate?* [*cf. ll. 206–10*]
112 s.p. Alice.] *Capell;* Lady. *F1 (throughout scene); Q1–3, which om. ll. 98–136* (Fair . . . strength.), *264, have* Lady. *at ll. 261, 267*
116 pleines] *Pope;* plein *F1*
137 vauting] *ed.;* vawting *F1*
171 it is] tis *Q1–2*
178 tell thee] tell it you *Q1–2;* tell you *Q3*
189 meilleur] *Hanmer (after Rowe);* melieus *F1*
192–3 But . . . English?] But *Kate,* / In plaine termes, *Q1–2;* But Kate prethee tell me in plaine tearmes, *Q3*
193 Canst thou] do you *Q1–2;* Dost thou *Q3*
243 good fellows] *Pope;* Good-fellowes *F1*
247 de roi] the King *Q1–2;* de king *Q3*
253 Laissez . . . laissez, laissez] *Rowe;* laisse . . . laisse, laisse *F1*
253 laissez! Ma foi,] *Theobald (subs.);* Laisse, may foy: *F1*
254 grandeur] *F2;* grandeus *F1*
255 (Notre Seigneur!)] *ed. (from Knudson);* nostre Seigneur *F1*
255–6 serviteur. Excusez-moi,] *Theobald (subs.);* seruiteur excuse moy. *F1*
259 noces] *Dyce;* nopcese *F1*
261 les] *Theobald;* le *F1*
262 baiser] *Hanmer (after Theobald);* buisse *F1;* bassie *Q1–3*
275 s.d. Kissing her.] *Rowe*
281 Majesty! My] *Pope;* Maiestie, my *F1*
322 never] *Rowe*
333 and in] and then in *F2*
340 d'Angleterre] D'anglaterre *Q1–2*
341–2 Angliae . . . Franciae] Anglie . . . Francie *Q1–2*
365 paction] *Theobald;* Pation *F1*
372 peers'] *Capell;* Peeres *F1*
374 s.d. Sennet. Exeunt.] FINIS. *Q1–3*

Epi.

o.s.d. **as Epilogue]** *Collier MS*
14 s.d. Exit.] *Capell;* FINIS. *F1*

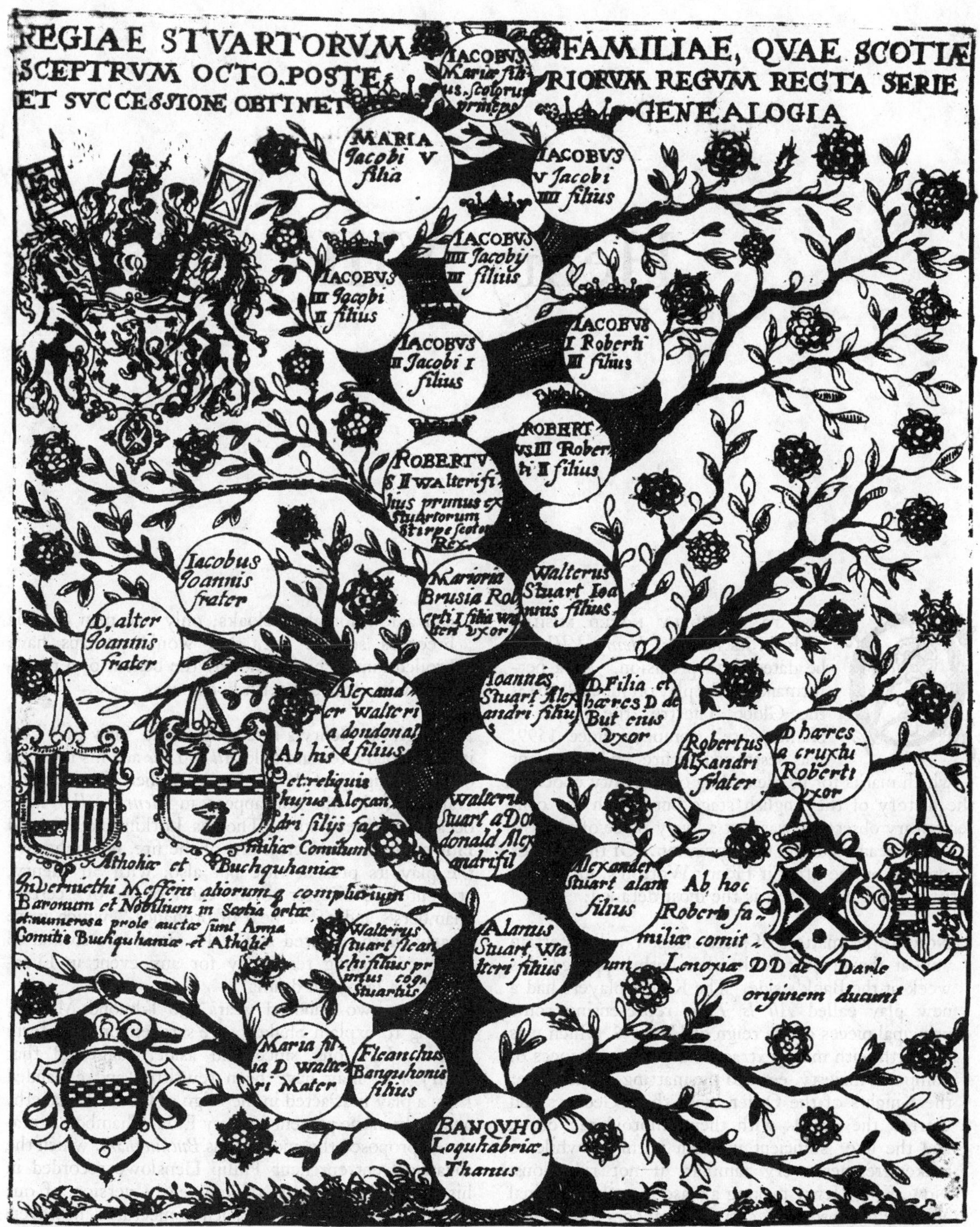

Banquo's royal line and James I. From a broadside in the Sutherland Collection, Ashmolean Museum, Oxford. On the family tree above is shown the derivation of James I (James VI of Scotland) from a mythical Banquo's mythical son Fleance, whose son Walter, we are told, was the first of the line to bear the name Stuart. Another Walter, six generations farther up the trunk, married Marjorie, daughter of Robert I (the Bruce), through whom the right to the throne passed to the Stuarts. Eight Stuart monarchs are shown, from Robert II to Mary, with Prince James (not yet James VI when the pedigree was constructed) at the top. This accords precisely with the Show of Kings in *Macbeth* (IV.i), where Macbeth views eight kings, the last with a mirror revealing "many more," while Banquo "points at them for his." It is not hard to see why Shakespeare altered Holinshed, his principal source for *Macbeth*, in order to draw for King James a Banquo wholly sympathetic.

Henry VIII

OWING TO A WIDELY NOTED MISHAP early in its history, *Henry VIII* can be dated with precision. At a performance of the play on June 29, 1613, the Globe Theatre, the home of Shakespeare's company since 1599, was destroyed by fire, and this event —which marks for us the ending of a mighty epoch in the history of the English stage but which for contemporary observers was just a lively piece of news— at once became a topic for discussion. Of the various comments on the fire, Sir Henry Wotton's, in a letter written three days later, is the most detailed:

> Now, to let matters of state sleep, I will entertain you at the present with what hath happened this week at the Bank's side. The King's players had a new play called *All Is True*, representing some principal pieces of the reign of Henry 8, which was set forth with many extraordinary circumstances of pomp and majesty, even to the matting of the stage; the Knights of the Order, with their Georges and Garter, the guards with their embroidered coats, and the like: sufficient in truth within a while to make greatness very familiar, if not ridiculous. Now, King Henry making a masque at the Cardinal Wolsey's house, and certain chambers [i.e. short cannon] being shot off at his entry, some of the paper, or other stuff wherewith one of them was stopped, did light on the thatch, where being thought at first but an idle smoke, and their eyes more attentive to the show, it kindled inwardly, and ran round like a train, consuming within less than an hour the whole house to the very grounds.
>
> This was the fatal period of that virtuous fabric; wherein yet nothing did perish but wood and straw, and a few forsaken cloaks; only one man had his breeches set on fire, that would perhaps have broiled him, if he had not by the benefit of a provident wit put it out with bottle ale.

Although Sir Henry's reference to the "new play" by its presumed alternate title *All Is True* and his mention of "the Knights of the Order, with their Georges and Garter" (who do not appear in *Henry VIII*) have occasioned speculation, Thomas Lorkin and Edmund Howes, in their descriptions of the fire, not only give the play its present title but also, with Sir Henry, attribute the disaster to the careless use of "certain chambers" and of "a peal of ordnance," which were clearly those required at I.iv.49. It is rare to find so much converging testimony for any event in Elizabethan or Jacobean drama.

Almost two hundred years ago Edmond Malone, seeking to explain Shakespeare's reversion to a form that he had long since laid aside, suggested that *Henry VIII* may have been rewritten and expanded from a play first acted in the reign of Queen Elizabeth; and early in the present century E. K. Chambers tentatively proposed the anonymous *Buckingham*, which the theatrical entrepreneur Philip Henslowe recorded in his *Diary* in 1593, as a likely early version of our work. Lacking proof for such conjectures, however, most scholars now accept the internal evidence of language, prosody, and theme as decisive for a later date. This evidence is reinforced by the strong possibility that the play was somehow related to the wedding of King James's daughter Elizabeth to the Elector Palatine, a leader of the continental Protestants, which was celebrated with great splendor on February 14, 1613. Although not listed among the "fowerteene severall playes" (six of them by Shakespeare) with which the King's Company had entertained the bridal couple before they left for Germany on April 10, it was perhaps not really "new" the following June, as Sir Henry Wotton called it, for its pageantry and its assertive Protestantism would seem to link it to the many masques and entertainments that were written to adorn the royal nuptials. Whether or not it was the unnamed "stage play" scheduled for a court performance on February 16 and then abruptly cancelled because "greater pleasures were preparing," *Henry VIII* was most likely prompted by, if not commissioned for, the sumptuous wedding celebrations, and therefore it may be plausibly assigned to the early months of 1613. Thus it is the latest of Shakespeare's plays to be included in the Folio of 1623, and, except for his possible contributions to *The Two Noble Kinsmen* and the lost *Cardenio*, his valediction to the stage.

For his final history play, as for almost all the others, Shakespeare—or Shakespeare and a putative collaborator—found his basic source in Holinshed (or in Holinshed's reports of Hall), which he eked out here and there with other things. The details of Cranmer's testing in Act V derive from that bottomless reservoir of Protestant propaganda, Foxe's *Acts and Monuments* (1563 ff.), and there may be traces of John Speed's *History of Great Britain* (1611) in certain lines of Wolsey's farewell speeches (such as the one about the "little wanton boys that swim on bladders" at III.ii.359). Although the alleged debt to Samuel Rowley's *When You See Me You Know Me* (1605, reprinted 1613) is less apparent, Henry's frequent use of the ejaculation "Ha!" may reflect a verbal mannerism of the bluff King Harry in that untidy, boisterous play. Since there is no evidence that Shakespeare had access to George Cavendish's life of Wolsey, any echoes from that splendid biography may be traced through Holinshed to John Stow, who had drawn upon the still unpublished work for his *Summary of English Chronicles* (1565 ff.).

If Shakespeare's forays on the 1587 edition of Holinshed are incessant and direct—ranging from single words like "arrogancy" at II.iv.110 and the guest list at the Princess' christening in V.v to extended passages like Katherine's speech at II.iv.13 ff.—he handles this material with a freedom, or a license, that makes the prologue, with its asseverations of the "truth" to be disclosed, seem something less than candid. In *Henry VIII* as elsewhere in the history plays the authorial distortions are most apparent in chronology. Although the action covers twenty years or more—from the Field of the Cloth of Gold (1520) to Cranmer's deadly peril from Bishop Gardiner (1544?)—events are so depicted that not only time but even sequence is destroyed. Whereas Shakespeare's manipulation of chronology in the other history plays involves little more than telescoping and juxtaposing widely spaced events—for instance, the arrest of Clarence and the death of Edward IV in *Richard III*, or the Battle of Agincourt and the Treaty of Troyes in *Henry V*—his procedure here is one of drastic transposition. Thus Buckingham's arrest and execution (1521) follow hard upon the monarchs' meeting in the Vale of Andren and coincide with the rebellion of the weavers (1525), Henry's lustful stirrings toward the Lady Anne (1527?), and the arrival of Campeius to look into the "business" of the King's divorce (1530). In similar confusion the royal wedding (1532) precedes Wolsey's fall (1529), and the birth and christening of the Princess Elizabeth (1533) serve to ease the strain of Katherine's death (1536) and Cranmer's close escape (1544?). There is distortion of a different kind in linking Wolsey's fall to a device—the discovery of a secret inventory (III.ii.120 ff.)—that, according to Holinshed, he himself had used to ruin the Bishop of Durham some twenty years before.

Despite the assumption, in what was said above, of Shakespeare's authorship of *Henry VIII*, his part in its production has long been and is likely to remain a matter of dispute. As early as 1758 one Richard Roderick commented on the remarkable stylistic and prosodic variations in the play, and Johnson thought it possible that Ben Jonson had supplied the prologue and epilogue; but apart from Malone's suggestion, in 1778, that the play had been constructed on an earlier work there was no serious attack on the integrity of the text until 1850, when James Spedding published "Who Wrote Shakespeare's *Henry VIII*?" This famous article, first printed in the *Gentleman's Magazine* and reissued, with a different title, in the 1874 *Transactions* of the New Shakspere Society, posed a question for which a hundred years of scholarship has found no certain answer.

Spedding, whose long exertions on behalf of Francis Bacon had certified his learning, begins by appealing to "the individual consciousness of each reader" to testify whether "the effect of this play *as a whole*" is not so "weak and disappointing" that it appears to be an inept collaboration. As dramaturgic evidence he cites, among other things, the slackened tension of Act V (which leaves us "among persons whom we scarcely know, and events for which we do not care"), the questionable morality of King Henry's behavior (which insures "the ultimate triumph of wrong"), and the disjointed, repetitious structure of the work throughout. As more strictly literary evidence—which "a man of first-rate judgment," later identified as Tennyson, had proposed to him—he cites the presence of two styles in *Henry VIII*: one marked by the complex imagery and the "careless felicities" of Shakespeare's later work, and the other, much simpler and more fluent, marked by an inordinate number of run-on lines and of lines with an unaccented eleventh syllable, as in the plays of Fletcher. The cumulative weight of all this evidence led him to the "clear conviction" that two and possibly three hands are evident in the play, but after Samuel Hickson, working independently, had suggested minor changes, he assigned to Shakespeare I.i–ii, II.iii–iv, III.ii.1–203, and V.i, and all the rest he gave to Fletcher. Spedding's inference from this distribution of the scenes was that Shakespeare, having conceived "the idea of a great historical drama on the subject of Henry VIII" which would comprise the divorce of Katherine, the fall of

Wolsey, the rise of Cranmer, the coronation of Anne Boleyn, and "the final separation of the English from the Romish Church," had got as far, perhaps, as the third act when something more appropriate for the royal wedding was required, whereupon he gave his manuscript to Fletcher, whose alterations and additions resulted in the work we have.

Although a few traditionalists, refusing to concede that anyone but Shakespeare could have written Wolsey's great farewell and Katherine's death-scene, protested Spedding's "bold conjecture," for fifty years or so his theory won such wide acceptance that research on *Henry VIII* was directed mainly toward refining his and Hickson's attributions. Thus whereas W. A. Wright (1891) and D. Nichol Smith (1893) and C. K. Pooler (1915), among others, endorsed the claims of Fletcher, A. H. Thorndike (1901) presented new internal evidence (based upon the use of *'em* and *ye* instead of *them* and *you*) in an effort to confirm the attribution. Going even further, Robert Boyle (1885) and H. D. Sykes (1919) rejected Shakespeare altogether and unwisely gave to Massinger all the non-Fletcherian scenes. Despite a more recent swing away from these and similar theories of disintegration, and toward a neo-orthodox defense of Shakespeare's single authorship, the question is by no means settled. Although Peter Alexander (1930) and G. Wilson Knight (1947), arguing from very different grounds, strongly countered any conjecture of dual composition, A. C. Partridge (1949) just as strongly reasserted Fletcher's presence in the work. More recently, R. A. Foakes (1955) and J. C. Maxwell (1962) have toiled through all the evidence only to emerge with conflicting points of view, Foakes regarding Shakespeare as the only author of a play whose theme and language link it firmly to the late romances, and Maxwell—with J. Dover Wilson's warm endorsement—holding that "the case for joint authorship is as fully established as such a case ever can be on purely internal evidence." If these erudite, opposed opinions may be regarded as prophetic, it seems likely that Spedding's question, like the poor, will be with us forever.

Those who think that Shakespeare wrote all, or nearly all, of *Henry VIII* rely on various kinds of evidence. They point to its inclusion in the Folio of 1623, which permits if it does not compel the inference that Heminge and Condell accepted it as genuine, whereas they rejected not only *The Two Noble Kinsmen* (in which Shakespeare's hand is generally conceded) but also such things as *Locrine* and *Cromwell* (which were once ascribed to Shakespeare but are now universally held to be apocryphal). They deny or minimize the significance of allegedly Fletcherian traits of style and metrics—feminine endings, run-on lines, frequent parenthetical constructions, forms like *'em* and *ye*, and all the rest—on the ground that they not only appear increasingly in Shakespeare's later plays but are common in the period. They hold that despite the unusual structure of the work its use of sources and its imagery suggest, in Foakes's words, "a single mind at work." And finally they point to its thematic correspondence with such plays as *The Winter's Tale* and *The Tempest*, where motifs of suffering, restoration, and compassion are serenely fused into the "vision" of romance. Indeed, G. Wilson Knight, noting its progression "from normality and order, through violent conflict to spiritualized music, and thence to concluding ritual," sees *Henry VIII* as the paradigm of Shakespeare's whole career and thus his culminating work.

But such opinions, however strongly held and eloquently expounded, are not to be confused with facts, and since we do not know the facts of Shakespeare's part in *Henry VIII*, those aspects of the play that prompted Spedding's bold conjecture continue to exacerbate the question of its authorship. Even after all the tests are made and all the data are assembled and applied (on one side or the other), it is entirely possible to concede that Shakespeare, with his enormous power of language, could have moved from the virile, packed ellipses of Norfolk's "clinquant" talk or Buckingham's colloquial rage at Wolsey (I.i) to the gently cadenced verse of Katherine's soft laments (III.i) or Wolsey's stately valediction (III.ii). On the other hand it is surely easier to believe that Shakespeare had assistance in the composition of the play than that he, at the summit of his art, would swing awkwardly between widely different styles, or present muddy motives—notably the King's—in a work so "full of state and woe," or skirt the most compelling issues in a play about the English Reformation, or so botch the themes of reconciliation and compassion that they appear as resignation and caprice. Pending the unlikely discovery of some firm external evidence, it would seem that Spedding's main contention, if not his specific attributions, will remain to challenge speculation.

Considered in the light of Shakespeare's other plays on English history—the last of which predated it by fourteen years or so—*Henry VIII* presents some puzzling features. Although there are echoes here and there from the earlier works, in general this play owes little to its predecessors. Even though its episodic structure overleaps the quasi-epic traits of *Henry V*, the polyphonic splendors of *Henry IV*, and the univocal lyricism of *Richard II* to the crude apprentice work of *Henry VI*, it is episodic with a difference; for whereas a younger Shakespeare had made loosely jointed episodes serve at least the purpose of narration, here events are so distorted that the work of exposition must be entrusted to the handy choral gentlemen (II.i, IV.i) who tell us what we need to know. Another curious aspect of the structure is the use of incremental repetition in the depiction of a string of falls. The ancient *de casibus* tradition, which had inspired that perennial best-seller *A Mirror for Magistrates* (1559 ff.) and thereby filtered into many plays, makes an unexpected reappearance here; moreover, its treatment is unusual in that *Henry VIII*, instead of centring on one imposing figure, exhibits three—and almost four—lugubrious *exempla* of fickle Fortune's power. Consequently the play is not only episodic but also repetitious. *Richard III* reveals the same sequential structure, to be sure, but there each sequence, gathering force with repetition, whirls us toward the master-villain's fall; here each sequence, spinning on a single point, tends to block the forward movement of the play.

Some advocates of Shakespeare's single authorship of *Henry VIII* have made a good deal of the fact that Buckingham, Katherine, and Wolsey, who show the uses of adversity seriatim, exemplify the aging Shakespeare's ripest wisdom on the therapeutic role of tribulation. As he goes to his destruction, Buckingham, already "half in heaven," reveals a new (and wholly unexpected) resignation; in a work of ostentatious Protestantism Katherine is more ennobled by her ancient faith than by all the titles she has lost; and Wolsey—the butt of Holinshed's relentless denigration—achieves a moral grandeur in disgrace that almost cancels out his crimes. But although these three great victims of misfortune have the best-loved speeches in the play, their rhetoric serves to sentimentalize and decorate, rather than illuminate, the action. None of them acquires real status as a character, because we are not shown the process of the change they undergo. Drama becomes morally significant only insofar as it explores the necessary connection between what happens to a man and the kind of man he is or grows to be, and this connection is not clear in *Henry VIII*. Buckingham himself, the haughty duke, commends the "justice" of his ruin, and Wolsey's faults are shown to be so gross that he appears a moral monster; but Katherine, a paragon of wifely virtue and "the queen of earthly queens," is put upon a par with them, and since all three suffer similar degradation their suffering makes no sense. To say, as has been said, that they reveal the healing strength of patience, with its balm of reconciliation, is to ignore the fact that they are ruined by a power that neither they nor we can comprehend.

This power is centred in the King, to whom, as God's vice-regent, we are invited to refer the judgments on the Queen, the Cardinal, and the Duke as well as Cranmer's *deus ex machina* salvation. Henry, however, cannot support the thrust of all these moral obligations. Although some critics have described him as a kind of Prospero who beneficently orders all events, and others as the agent of that providence whose workings, Cranmer says, secure the glory of the realm, his conduct does not warrant such interpretations. Now hearty and jocose, now petulant, now regal and assured, but never anything for very long, he is shifty rather than complex. He equivocates so much about the crucial question of divorce, on which the large dynastic implications of the play depend, that his "conscience" is a topic of derision (II.ii.17–19, IV.i.47), and on this—as on other matters—his position is so morally ambiguous that his judgments seem to be the dictates of his will. Therefore he not only fails to exercise the God-like functions that were arrogated to the Tudor kings, he even fails to comprehend a justice commensurate with his power. Remembering Shakespeare's strenuous efforts to define a monarch's rights and obligations in the earlier history plays, one sees Henry as conclusive proof that these efforts now were ended.

However weak in characterization, *Henry VIII* is very strong in pomp and pageantry, and therefore what Johnson called the "splendour" of its spectacle has always been its main attraction. It starts and ends upon a note of triumph, and between the Field of the Cloth of Gold and Cranmer's apocalyptic vision of the bliss in store for England the interpolation of so many big set scenes makes the drama yield often to lavish exhibition. Some of these elaborate display pieces—notably the coronation and the christening—are so frankly theatrical that they do not require the spoken word, but only sights and sounds; and others, even where the focus is dramatic, are so formal in their presentation that they have the weight and texture of tableaux. Consequently the movement of the work suggests a long procession: from the King surrounded by his council (I.ii) to Wolsey's sumptuous ball (I.iv) to Buckingham's farewell (II.i) to Katherine's trial at Blackfriars (II.v) to the fallen cardinal's valediction (III.ii) to the new queen's coronation (IV.i) to the masque-like scene of Katherine's death (IV.ii) to Cranmer's confrontation with his foes (V.iii) to the christening with which the play concludes. From that regrettable performance on June 29, 1613—which in a sense was defeated by its own pretensions—to the present day, it has apparently always been accorded sumptuous presentations.

Herschel Baker

The Famous History of The Life of King Henry the Eighth

[DRAMATIS PERSONAE

KING HENRY THE EIGHTH
CARDINAL WOLSEY
CARDINAL CAMPEIUS
CAPUCHIUS, *ambassador from the Emperor Charles V*
CRANMER, *Archbishop of Canterbury*
DUKE OF NORFOLK
DUKE OF BUCKINGHAM
DUKE OF SUFFOLK
EARL OF SURREY
LORD CHAMBERLAIN
LORD CHANCELLOR
GARDINER, *secretary to the King, afterwards Bishop of Winchester*
BISHOP OF LINCOLN
LORD ABURGAVENNY
LORD SANDS (*called also* SIR WALTER SANDS)
SIR HENRY GUILFORD
SIR THOMAS LOVELL
SIR ANTHONY DENNY
SIR NICHOLAS VAUX
CROMWELL, *servant to Wolsey*
SECRETARIES *to Wolsey*

GRIFFITH, *gentleman usher to Queen Katherine*
Three GENTLEMEN
DOCTOR BUTTS, *physician to the King*
GARTER KING-AT-ARMS
SURVEYOR *to the Duke of Buckingham*
BRANDON, *and a* SERGEANT-AT-ARMS
DOORKEEPER *of the Council-chamber*
PORTER, *and his* MAN
PAGE *to Gardiner*
CRIER

QUEEN KATHERINE, *wife to King Henry, afterwards divorced*
ANNE BULLEN, *her Maid of Honor, afterwards Queen*
OLD LADY, *friend to Anne Bullen*
PATIENCE, *woman to Queen Katherine*

SPIRITS

Several BISHOPS; LORDS *and* LADIES *in the dumb shows;* WOMEN *attending upon the Queen;* SCRIBES, OFFICERS, GUARDS, *and other* ATTENDANTS

SCENE: *London; Westminster; Kimbolton*]

THE PROLOGUE

I come no more to make you laugh; things now
That bear a weighty and a serious brow,
Sad, high, and working, full of state and woe:
Such noble scenes as draw the eye to flow,
We now present. Those that can pity, here
May (if they think it well) let fall a tear;
The subject will deserve it. Such as give
Their money out of hope they may believe,
May here find truth too. Those that come to see
Only a show or two, and so agree
The play may pass, if they be still and willing,
I'll undertake may see away their shilling
Richly in two short hours. Only they
That come to hear a merry, bawdy play,
A noise of targets, or to see a fellow
In a long motley coat guarded with yellow,
Will be deceiv'd. For, gentle hearers, know,
To rank our chosen truth with such a show
As fool and fight is, beside forfeiting
Our own brains and the opinion that we bring
To make that only true we now intend,
Will leave us never an understanding friend.
Therefore, for goodness sake, and as you are known
The first and happiest hearers of the town,

Words and passages enclosed in square brackets in the text above are either emendations of the copy-text or additions to it. The Textual Notes immediately following the play cite the earliest authority for every such change or insertion and supply the reading of the copy-text wherever it is emended in this edition.

Pro. 3. Sad . . . working: serious, elevated, and moving. **state:** dignity. **10. show:** spectacle.

13. two short hours. Cf. *Romeo and Juliet*, Prologue, line 12: "the two hours' traffic of our stage."
15. noise of targets: clashing of shields.
16. motley . . . yellow. The customary garment of a clown. **guarded:** trimmed.
20–21. the opinion . . . intend: i.e. our intention of presenting a veracious account. Here and elsewhere in the Prologue (lines 9, 25 ff.) the emphasis on truth supports the conjecture that when Sir Henry Wotton, in 1613, called the play *All Is True* he was using its subtitle.
24. happiest: most discriminating.

Be sad, as we would make ye. Think ye see
The very persons of our noble story
As they were living. Think you see them great,
And follow'd with the general throng and sweat
Of thousand friends; then, in a moment, see
How soon this mightiness meets misery;
And if you can be merry then, I'll say
A man may weep upon his wedding-day.

ACT I, Scene I

Enter the Duke of Norfolk *at one door; at the other, the* Duke of Buckingham *and the* Lord Aburgavenny.

Buck. Good morrow, and well met. How have ye done
Since last we saw in France?
Nor. I thank your Grace:
Healthful, and ever since a fresh admirer
Of what I saw there.
Buck. An untimely ague
Stay'd me a prisoner in my chamber when
Those suns of glory, those two lights of men,
Met in the vale of Andren.
Nor. 'Twixt Guynes and Arde—
I was then present, saw them salute on horseback,
Beheld them when they lighted, how they clung
In their embracement, as they grew together,
Which had they, what four thron'd ones could have weigh'd
Such a compounded one?
Buck. All the whole time
I was my chamber's prisoner.
Nor. Then you lost
The view of earthly glory. Men might say
Till this time pomp was single, but now married
To one above itself. Each following day
Became the next day's master, till the last
Made former wonders its. To-day the French,
All clinquant, all in gold, like heathen gods,
Shone down the English; and, to-morrow, they
Made Britain India: every man that stood
Show'd like a mine. Their dwarfish pages were
As cherubins, all gilt; the madams too,
Not us'd to toil, did almost sweat to bear
The pride upon them, that their very labor
Was to them as a painting. Now this masque
Was cried incomparable; and th' ensuing night
Made it a fool and beggar. The two kings,
Equal in lustre, were now best, now worst,
As presence did present them: him in eye
Still him in praise, and being present both,
'Twas said they saw but one, and no discerner
Durst wag his tongue in censure. When these suns
(For so they phrase 'em) by their heralds challeng'd
The noble spirits to arms, they did perform
Beyond thought's compass, that former fabulous story,
Being now seen possible enough, got credit,
That Bevis was believ'd.
Buck. O, you go far.
Nor. As I belong to worship and affect
In honor honesty, the tract of ev'ry thing
Would by a good discourser lose some life,
Which action's self was tongue to. All was royal;
To the disposing of it nought rebell'd,
Order gave each thing view; the office did
Distinctly his full function.
[*Buck.*] Who did guide—
I mean, who set the body and the limbs
Of this great sport together, as you guess?
Nor. One, certes, that promises no element
In such a business.
Buck. I pray you, who, my lord?
Nor. All this was ord'red by the good discretion
Of the right reverend Cardinal of York.
Buck. The devil speed him! no man's pie is freed
From his ambitious finger. What had he
To do in these fierce vanities? I wonder
That such a keech can with his very bulk
Take up the rays o' th' beneficial sun,
And keep it from the earth.
Nor. Surely, sir,
There's in him stuff that puts him to these ends;
For being not propp'd by ancestry, whose grace
Chalks successors their way, nor call'd upon
For high feats done to th' crown, neither allied
To eminent assistants, but spider-like
Out of his self-drawing web, ['a] gives us note
The force of his own merit makes his way—
A gift that heaven gives for him, which buys
A place next to the King.
Abur. I cannot tell

25. **sad**: serious.

I.i. **Location**: London. The palace.
2. **saw in France**: i.e. met at the Field of the Cloth of Gold, scene of a glittering state visit between Henry VIII and Francis I in June 1520. 3. **fresh**: untired. 6. **suns of glory**: i.e. the two monarchs.
7. **vale . . . Arde**. The Vale of Andren, in Picardy, lay between the towns of Guynes and Ardres, which were held respectively by the English and the French.
8–10. **salute . . . together**. "The two kings meeting in the field," reports Holinshed (Bullough, IV, 457), "either saluted other in most loving wise, first on horsebacke, and after alighting on foot eftsoones imbraced with courteous words, to the great rejoising of the beholders." 10. **as**: as if.
11. **Which had they**: i.e. if they had grown together. **weigh'd**: i.e. weighed as much as. 19. **clinquant**: glittering.
20. **they**: i.e. the English.
21. **Made Britain India**: i.e. made Britain seem as rich as India (the symbol of wealth to the Elizabethans).
23. **cherubins, all gilt**: carved and gilded figures of cherubim in churches (?). 25. **pride**: finery.

25–26. **that . . . painting**: i.e. so that they were flushed, as if with rouge, from their exertion. 30. **presence**: public appearance.
30–31. **him . . . praise**: i.e. whichever one of them was visible was most admired.
33. **censure**: judgment, i.e. in distinguishing the more splendid of the two.
38. **Bevis**: Bevis of Hampton (i.e. Southampton), the hero of a popular romance. 39. **worship**: the nobility. **affect**: love.
40. **tract**: description.
41–42. **lose . . . to**: i.e. be less impressive than the thing itself.
43–45. **To . . . function**: i.e. there was nothing inappropriate; things were so arranged that everyone could see; each official did his job perfectly.
48. **certes**: surely. **promises no element**: i.e. would seem to be unsuitable (?). 52. **speed**: prosper.
54. **fierce vanities**: extravagant follies.
55. **keech**: lump of suet (an allusion to Wolsey's being the son of a butcher). 56. **sun**: i.e. King Henry.
58. **stuff . . . ends**: traits that make him do these things.
60. **Chalks . . . way**: marks the path for descendants.
63. **self-drawing**: spun out of his own substance. **'a . . . note**: he reveals to us.

What heaven hath given him—let some graver eye
Pierce into that—but I can see his pride
Peep through each part of him. Whence has he that?
If not from hell, the devil is a niggard,
Or has given all before, and he begins
A new hell in himself.

Buck. Why the devil,
Upon this French going out, took he upon him
(Without the privity o' th' King) t' appoint
Who should attend on him? He makes up the file
Of all the gentry; for the most part such
To whom as great a charge as little honor
He meant to lay upon; and his own letter,
The honorable Board of Council out,
Must fetch him in he papers.

Abur. I do know
Kinsmen of mine, three at the least, that have
By this so sicken'd their estates, that never
They shall abound as formerly.

Buck. O, many
Have broke their backs with laying manors on 'em
For this great journey. What did this vanity
But minister communication of
A most poor issue?

Nor. Grievingly I think
The peace between the French and us not values
The cost that did conclude it.

Buck. Every man,
After the hideous storm that follow'd, was
A thing inspir'd, and, not consulting, broke
Into a general prophecy: that this tempest,
Dashing the garment of this peace, aboded
The sudden breach on't.

Nor. Which is budded out,
For France hath flaw'd the league, and hath attach'd
Our merchants' goods at Burdeaux.

Abur. Is it therefore
Th' ambassador is silenc'd?

Nor. Marry, is't.

Abur. A proper title of a peace, and purchas'd
At a superfluous rate!

Buck. Why, all this business
Our reverend Cardinal carried.

Nor. Like it your Grace,
The state takes notice of the private difference
Betwixt you and the Cardinal. I advise you
(And take it from a heart that wishes towards you
Honor and plenteous safety) that you read
The Cardinal's malice and his potency
Together; to consider further, that
What his high hatred would effect wants not
A minister in his power. You know his nature,
That he's revengeful; and I know his sword
Hath a sharp edge; it's long, and't may be said
It reaches far, and where 'twill not extend,
Thither he darts it. Bosom up my counsel,
You'll find it wholesome. Lo, where comes that rock
That I advise your shunning.

Enter CARDINAL WOLSEY, *the purse borne before him, certain of the* GUARD, *and two* SECRETARIES *with papers. The Cardinal in his passage fixeth his eye on Buckingham, and Buckingham on him, both full of disdain.*

Wol. The Duke of Buckingham's surveyor? ha?
Where's his examination?

[1.] Secr. Here, so please you.

Wol. Is he in person ready?

[1.] Secr. Ay, please your Grace.

Wol. Well, we shall then know more, and Buckingham
Shall lessen this big look.

Exeunt Cardinal and his Train.

Buck. This butcher's cur is venom'd-mouth'd, and I
Have not the power to muzzle him, therefore best
Not wake him in his slumber. A beggar's book
Outworths a noble's blood.

Nor. What, are you chaf'd?
Ask God for temp'rance, that's th' appliance only
Which your disease requires.

Buck. I read in 's looks
Matter against me, and his eye revil'd
Me as his abject object; at this instant
He bores me with some trick. He's gone to th' King;
I'll follow and outstare him.

Nor. Stay, my lord,
And let your reason with your choler question
What 'tis you go about: to climb steep hills
Requires slow pace at first. Anger is like
A full hot horse, who being allow'd his way,

73. going out: excursion.
74. privity: knowledge (of something private).
75. file: list. **77. charge:** expense.
78–80. his . . . papers: i.e. his summons alone—the council not consulted—is enough to force the attendance of whomever he lists (*papers*). "The peeres of the realme receiving letters to prepare themselves to attend the king in this journie," says Holinshed (Bullough, IV, 455), "and no apparant necessarie cause expressed, why nor wherefore; seemed to grudge, that such a costlie journie should be taken in hand to their importunate charges and expenses, without consent of the whole boord of the councell."
82. sicken'd: depleted. **83. abound:** be wealthy.
84. broke . . . 'em: i.e. ruined themselves by spending their estates on costly clothing. **85. What . . . vanity:** what good did this folly do.
86. minister communication: promote a conference.
87. poor issue: inconclusive outcome (with perhaps a pun on the sense "impoverished offspring"). **88. not values:** is not worth.
90. hideous storm. Holinshed (Bullough, IV, 458) records such "an hideous storm of wind and weather" on June 18, 1520, "that manie conjectured it did prognosticate trouble and hatred shortlie after to follow betweene princes." **91. not consulting:** independently.
92. general: common, unanimous. **93. aboded:** foretold.
94. on't: of it (the peace).
95. flaw'd the league: violated the treaty. **attach'd:** seized.
96. Burdeaux: Bordeaux. **therefore:** for this reason.
97. Marry: indeed (a weakened oath, "By the Virgin Mary").
98–99. A proper . . . rate: i.e. what a peace, and achieved at such prodigal expense.

100. carried: managed. **Like it:** if it please. **104. read:** consider.
107–8. What . . . power: i.e. he does not lack the means of doing what his hatred drives him to. **112. Bosom up:** take to heart.
114 s.d. purse: bag containing the Great Seal, one of Wolsey's insignia as chancellor.
115. surveyor: overseer of estates. Although Holinshed (Bullough, IV, 458) names Charles Knevet, who was Buckingham's cousin as well as his "surveyor," as the agent of the Duke's downfall, it was probably his chancellor, Robert Gilbert, who betrayed him.
116. examination: deposition, testimony given under oath.
120. butcher's cur. See note to line 55.
122. book: literary attainments, erudition.
123. blood: high descent. **chaf'd:** angry.
124. appliance: remedy. **127. abject:** castoff.
128. bores: cheats. **130. question:** discuss, determine.

Self-mettle tires him. Not a man in England
Can advise me like you; be to yourself
As you would to your friend.
Buck. I'll to the King,
And from a mouth of honor quite cry down
This Ipswich fellow's insolence; or proclaim
There's difference in no persons.
Nor. Be advis'd;
Heat not a furnace for your foe so hot
That it do singe yourself. We may outrun
By violent swiftness that which we run at,
And lose by overrunning. Know you not
The fire that mounts the liquor till't run o'er
In seeming to augment it wastes it? Be advis'd;
I say again, there is no English soul
More stronger to direct you than yourself,
If with the sap of reason you would quench,
Or but allay, the fire of passion.
Buck. Sir,
I am thankful to you, and I'll go along
By your prescription; but this top-proud fellow,
Whom from the flow of gall I name not, but
From sincere motions, by intelligence,
And proofs as clear as founts in July when
We see each grain of gravel, I do know
To be corrupt and treasonous.
Nor. Say not treasonous.
Buck. To th' King I'll say't, and make my vouch as strong
As shore of rock. Attend. This holy fox,
Or wolf, or both (for he is equal rav'nous
As he is subtile, and as prone to mischief
As able to perform't), his mind and place
Infecting one another, yea, reciprocally,
Only to show his pomp as well in France
As here at home, suggests the King our master
To this last costly treaty—th' interview
That swallowed so much treasure, and like a glass
Did break i' th' wrenching.
Nor. Faith, and so it did.
Buck. Pray give me favor, sir: this cunning Cardinal
The articles o' th' combination drew
As himself pleas'd; and they were ratified
As he cried, "Thus let be!" to as much end
As give a crutch to th' dead. But our count-cardinal
Has done this, and 'tis well; for worthy Wolsey
(Who cannot err), he did it. Now this follows
(Which, as I take it, is a kind of puppy
To th' old dam, treason), Charles the Emperor,

134. Self-mettle: his own high spirit.
138. Ipswich: seaport in Suffolk, Wolsey's birthplace.
139. difference: distinction of rank. **advis'd:** cautious.
144. mounts: causes to rise (by boiling).
151. top-proud: superlatively proud.
152–53. Whom . . . motions: i.e. whom I mention not from spite but from sincere motives. **153. intelligence:** secret information.
157. vouch: evidence, proof. **161. place:** (high) office.
164. suggests: prompts.
165. last: recent. **interview:** i.e. the Field of the Cloth of Gold.
168. give me favor: listen to me. **169. combination:** treaty.
172. count-cardinal: i.e. an ecclesiastic who assumes unwarranted political functions (?).
176–93. Charles . . . advantage. As Emperor of the Holy Roman Empire, King of Spain, and nephew to Queen Katherine, Charles had everything to fear from a close alliance between England and

Under pretense to see the Queen his aunt
(For 'twas indeed his color, but he came
To whisper Wolsey), here makes visitation—
His fears were that the interview betwixt
England and France might through their amity
Breed him some prejudice; for from this league
Peep'd harms that menac'd him—privily
Deals with our Cardinal, and, as I trow—
Which I do well, for I am sure the Emperor
Paid ere he promis'd, whereby his suit was granted
Ere it was ask'd—but when the way was made
And pav'd with gold, the Emperor thus desir'd,
That he would please to alter the King's course,
And break the foresaid peace. Let the King know
(As soon he shall by me) that thus the Cardinal
Does buy and sell his honor as he pleases,
And for his own advantage.
Nor. I am sorry
To hear this of him; and could wish he were
Something mistaken in't.
Buck. No, not a syllable:
I do pronounce him in that very shape
He shall appear in proof.

Enter BRANDON, *a* SERGEANT-AT-ARMS *before him, and two or three of the* GUARD.

Bran. Your office, sergeant; execute it.
Serg. Sir,
My lord the Duke of Buckingham and Earl
Of [Herford], Stafford, and Northampton, I
Arrest thee of high treason, in the name
Of our most sovereign King.
Buck. Lo you, my lord,
The net has fall'n upon me! I shall perish
Under device and practice.
Bran. I am sorry
To see you ta'en from liberty, to look on
The business present. 'Tis his Highness' pleasure
You shall to th' Tower.
Buck. It will help me nothing
To plead mine innocence; for that dye is on me
Which makes my whit'st part black. The will of heav'n
Be done in this and all things! I obey.
O my Lord Aburga'ny, fare you well!
Bran. Nay, he must bear you company. [*To Aburgavenny.*] The King

France. Having come to England, says Holinshed (Bullough, IV, 456–57), to warn against a French alliance but finding Henry already "forward on his journie," he resolved to work through Wolsey. "And forsomuch as he knew the lord cardinall to be woone with rewards, as a fish with a bait: he bestowed on him great gifts, and promised him much more, so that hee would be his friend, and helpe to bring his purpose to passe. The cardinall not able to susteine the least assault by force of such rewards as he presentlie received, and of such large promises as on the emperours behalfe were made to him, promised to the emperour, that he would so use the matter, as his purpose should be sped." **178. color:** pretext. **184. trow:** believe.
189. he: i.e. Wolsey.
195. Something mistaken: somewhat misjudged.
197 s.d. Brandon. According to Holinshed (Bullough, IV, 459) it was Sir Henry Marny, captain of the king's guard, who arrested Buckingham. The event occurred in April 1521, almost a year after the meeting of the two kings at the Field of the Cloth of Gold.
204. device and practice: schemes and plots.
205. look on: witness (?) or (referring to Buckingham, not Brandon) face (?).

Is pleas'd you shall to th' Tower, till you know
How he determines further.
Abur. As the Duke said,
The will of heaven be done, and the King's pleasure
By me obey'd!
Bran. Here is a warrant from
The King t' attach Lord Montacute, and the bodies
Of the Duke's confessor, John de la Car,
One Gilbert [Perk], his [chancellor]—
Buck. So, so;
These are the limbs o' th' plot. No more, I hope?
Bran. A monk o' th' Chartreux.
Buck. O, [Nicholas] Hopkins?
Bran. He.
Buck. My surveyor is false; the o'er-great Cardinal
Hath show'd him gold; my life is spann'd already.
I am the shadow of poor Buckingham,
Whose figure even this instant cloud puts on
By dark'ning my clear sun. My [lord], farewell.
Exeunt.

SCENE II

Cornets. Enter KING HENRY, *leaning on the* CARDINAL'S *shoulder, the* NOBLES, *and* SIR THOMAS LOVELL; *the Cardinal places himself under the King's feet on his right side,* [*his* SECRETARY *in attendance*].

King. My life itself, and the best heart of it,
Thanks you for this great care. I stood i' th' level
Of a full-charg'd confederacy, and give thanks
To you that chok'd it. Let be call'd before us
That gentleman of Buckingham's; in person
I'll hear him his confessions justify,
And point by point the treasons of his master
He shall again relate.

A noise within, crying, "Room for the Queen!" [*who is*] *usher'd by the Duke of Norfolk. Enter the* QUEEN [KATHERINE], NORFOLK, *and* SUFFOLK; *she kneels.* [*The*] *King riseth from his state, takes her up, kisses, and placeth her by him.*

Q. Kath. Nay, we must longer kneel; I am a suitor.
King. Arise, and take place by us. Half your suit
Never name to us; you have half our power.
The other moi'ty ere you ask is given;
Repeat your will and take it.
Q. Kath. Thank your Majesty.
That you would love yourself, and in that love
Not unconsidered leave your honor nor
The dignity of your office, is the point
Of my petition.
King. Lady mine, proceed.
Q. Kath. I am solicited, not by a few,
And those of true condition, that your subjects
Are in great grievance: there have been commissions
Sent down among 'em, which hath flaw'd the heart
Of all their loyalties; wherein, although,
My good Lord Cardinal, they vent reproaches
Most bitterly on you as putter-on
Of these exactions, yet the King our master—
Whose honor heaven shield from soil!—even he escapes not
Language unmannerly; yea, such which breaks
The sides of loyalty, and almost appears
In loud rebellion.
Nor. Not almost appears,
It doth appear; for, upon these taxations,
The clothiers all, not able to maintain
The many to them 'longing, have put off
The spinsters, carders, fullers, weavers, who,
Unfit for other life, compell'd by hunger
And lack of other means, in desperate manner
Daring th' event to th' teeth, are all in uproar,
And danger serves among them.
King. Taxation?
Wherein? and what taxation? My Lord Cardinal,
You that are blam'd for it alike with us,
Know you of this taxation?
Wol. Please you, sir,
I know but of a single part in aught
Pertains to th' state; and front but in that file
Where others tell steps with me.
Q. Kath. No, my lord?
You know no more than others? But you frame
Things that are known alike, which are not wholesome

216–21. Here . . . He. Holinshed (Bullough, IV, 458–59) supplies the names of Buckingham's alleged accomplices. In addition to his son-in-law George Neville, third Baron of Bergavenny, they included "the lord Montacute," "Nicholas Hopkins, a monke of an house of the Chartreux order beside Bristow, called Henton, sometime his [i.e. Buckingham's] confessor," "maister John de la Car *alias* de la Court, the dukes confessor, and sir Gilbert Perke priest, the dukes chancellor." In this play Hopkins is sometimes called by his true name (I. 221 and II.i.22), sometimes Henton (I.ii.147, 148).
217. attach: arrest. **221. Chartreux:** Carthusian order.
223. spann'd: measured out.

I.ii. Location: London. The Council-chamber.
o.s.d. Cornets: horns (not the modern brass instruments). **places . . . feet:** i.e. stands below the dais on which the throne is set.
2. level: aim.
3. full-charg'd confederacy: heavily loaded conspiracy.
6. justify: confirm. **8 s.d. state:** raised throne with a canopy.
12. moi'ty: half. **13. Repeat your will:** state your desire.

18. solicited: informed. **19. true condition:** i.e. loyalty.
20–29. there . . . rebellion. Although Holinshed's account of the rebellion of the weavers (Bullough, IV, 464–65)—which occurred in 1525, four years after the fall of Buckingham—makes no mention of Queen Katherine's intercession, it supplies most of the other details for this scene. "The king being determined thus to make wars in France, & to passe the sea himselfe in person, his councell considered that above all things great treasure and plentie of monie must needes be provided. Wherfore, by the cardinall there was devised strange commissions, and sent in the end of March into everie shire, and commissioners appointed, and privie instructions sent to them how they should proceed in their sittings, and order the people to bring them to their purpose: which was, that the sixt part of everie mans substance should be paid in monie or plate to the king without delaie, for the furniture of his war. Hereof followed such cursing, weeping, and exclamation against both king & cardinall, that pitie it was to heare."
20. commissions: i.e. (tax) agents with writs of authority.
21. flaw'd: cracked. **24. putter-on:** instigator.
32. The many . . . 'longing: i.e. their employees. **put off:** discharged.
33. The spinsters . . . weavers. Holinshed records (Bullough, IV, 464) how the "rich clothiers . . . went about to discharge and put from them their spinners, carders, fullers, weavers, and other artificers, which they kept in worke afore time." **spinsters:** spinners. **carders:** men who clean and disentangle wool by combing. **fullers:** men who clean and thicken cloth.
36. event: outcome. **to th' teeth:** defiantly.
37. danger serves: mischief is rife.
42. front . . . file: merely march in the front rank.
43. tell steps: keep step, i.e. march.
45. alike: to all. **wholesome:** i.e. endorsed as beneficial.

To those which would not know them, and yet must
Perforce be their acquaintance. These exactions
(Whereof my sovereign would have note), they are
Most pestilent to th' hearing, and, to bear 'em,
The back is sacrifice to th' load. They say
They are devis'd by you, or else you suffer
Too hard an exclamation.
King. Still exaction!
The nature of it? in what kind, let's know,
Is this exaction?
Q. Kath. I am much too venturous
In tempting of your patience; but am bold'ned
Under your promis'd pardon. The subject's grief
Comes through commissions, which compels from each
The sixt part of his substance, to be levied
Without delay; and the pretense for this
Is nam'd, your wars in France. This makes bold mouths,
Tongues spit their duties out, and cold hearts freeze
Allegiance in them; their curses now
Live where their prayers did; and it's come to pass
This tractable obedience is a slave
To each incensed will. I would your Highness
Would give it quick consideration, for
There is no primer baseness.
King. By my life,
This is against our pleasure.
Wol. And for me,
I have no further gone in this than by
A single voice, and that not pass'd me but
By learned approbation of the judges. If I am
Traduc'd by ignorant tongues, which neither know
My faculties nor person, yet will be
The chronicles of my doing, let me say
'Tis but the fate of place, and the rough brake
That virtue must go through. We must not stint
Our necessary actions in the fear
To cope malicious censurers, which ever,
As rav'nous fishes, do a vessel follow
That is new trimm'd, but benefit no further
Than vainly longing. What we oft do best,
By sick interpreters (once weak ones) is
Not ours, or not allow'd; what worst, as oft,
Hitting a grosser quality, is cried up
For our best act. If we shall stand still,
In fear our motion will be mock'd or carp'd at,
We should take root here where we sit, or sit
State-statues only.
King. Things done well

And with a care exempt themselves from fear;
Things done without example, in their issue
Are to be fear'd. Have you a president
Of this commission? I believe, not any.
We must not rend our subjects from our laws,
And stick them in our will. Sixt part of each?
A trembling contribution! Why, we take
From every tree, lop, bark, and part o' th' timber;
And, though we leave it with a root, thus hack'd,
The air will drink the sap. To every county
Where this is question'd send our letters, with
Free pardon to each man that has denied
The force of this commission. Pray look to't;
I put it to your care.
Wol. [*Aside to the Secretary.*] A word with you.
Let there be letters writ to every shire,
Of the King's grace and pardon. The grieved commons
Hardly conceive of me; let it be nois'd
That through our intercession this revokement
And pardon comes. I shall anon advise you
Further in the proceeding. *Exit Secretary.*

Enter SURVEYOR.

Q. Kath. I am sorry that the Duke of Buckingham
Is run in your displeasure.
King. It grieves many.
The gentleman is learn'd, and a most rare speaker,
To nature none more bound; his training such
That he may furnish and instruct great teachers
And never seek for aid out of himself. Yet see,
When these so noble benefits shall prove
Not well dispos'd, the mind growing once corrupt,
They turn to vicious forms, ten times more ugly
Than ever they were fair. This man so complete,
Who was enroll'd 'mongst wonders, and when we,
Almost with ravish'd list'ning, could not find
His hour of speech a minute—he, my lady,
Hath into monstrous habits put the graces
That once were his, and is become as black
As if besmear'd in hell. Sit by us, you shall hear
(This was his gentleman in trust) of him
Things to strike honor sad. Bid him recount
The fore-recited practices, whereof
We cannot feel too little, hear too much.
Wol. Stand forth, and with bold spirit relate what you,

46. those: i.e. members of the council.
47. their acquaintance: i.e. known to them.
48. note: knowledge. **50. is sacrifice to:** i.e. bows under.
52. exclamation: reproach.
56. subject's. *Subject* was frequently used in the collective sense "subjects of the realm." **grief:** grievance.
64. a slave: i.e. subordinate.
67. primer baseness: mischief requiring more urgent attention.
69–70. by . . . voice: by . . . vote, i.e. as one among many (who concurred in the decision). **73. faculties:** qualities.
75. brake: thicket. **78. To cope:** of encountering.
80. new trimm'd: newly fitted out, seaworthy.
82. sick interpreters: envious critics. **once weak:** in short, unqualified.
83. Not . . . allow'd: not credited to us, or else denounced.
84. Hitting . . . quality: appealing to coarser natures (?).
90. example: precedent. **issue:** outcome.
91–92. president Of: precedent for.
94. stick . . . will: subject them to our caprice.
95. trembling: accompanied by trembling. **96. lop:** branches.
98–108. To . . . proceeding. Dismayed by rebellion of the weavers, the King, says Holinshed (Bullough, IV, 465), "caused letters to be sent into all shires, that the matter should no further be talked of: & he pardoned all them that had denied the demand openlie or secretlie. The cardinall, to deliver himself of the evill will of the commons, purchased by procuring & advancing of this demand, affirmed, and caused it to be bruted abrode, that through his intercession the king had pardoned and released all things." **101. force:** validity.
104. grace: mercy. **grieved:** aggrieved.
105. Hardly conceive: think harshly.
112. bound: obligated (for natural ability).
114. out of: beyond. **116. dispos'd:** used.
118. complete: accomplished. **120. ravish'd:** enchanted.
122. habits: (1) garments; (2) moral qualities.
125. gentleman in trust: confidential agent.
127. practices: contrivances.

Most like a careful subject, have collected
Out of the Duke of Buckingham.
King. Speak freely.
Surv. First, it was usual with him—every day
It would infect his speech—that if the King
Should without issue die, he'll carry it so
To make the sceptre his. These very words
I've heard him utter to his son-in-law,
Lord Aburga'ny, to whom by oath he menac'd
Revenge upon the Cardinal.
Wol. Please your Highness note
This dangerous conception in this point,
Not friended by his wish, to your high person;
His will is most malignant, and it stretches
Beyond you to your friends.
Q. Kath. My learn'd Lord Cardinal,
Deliver all with charity.
King. Speak on.
How grounded he his title to the crown
Upon our fail? To this point hast thou heard him
At any time speak aught?
Surv. He was brought to this
By a vain prophecy of Nicholas Henton.
King. What was that Henton?
Surv. Sir, a Chartreux friar,
His confessor, who fed him every minute
With words of sovereignty.
King. How know'st thou this?
Surv. Not long before your Highness sped to France,
The Duke being at the Rose, within the parish
Saint Lawrence Poultney, did of me demand
What was the speech among the Londoners
Concerning the French journey. I replied,
Men fear the French would prove perfidious,
To the King's danger. Presently the Duke
Said, 'twas the fear indeed, and that he doubted
'Twould prove the verity of certain words
Spoke by a holy monk "that oft," says he,
"Hath sent to me, wishing me to permit
John de la Car, my chaplain, a choice hour
To hear from him a matter of some moment;
Whom after under the [confession's] seal
He solemnly had sworn that what he spoke
My chaplain to no creature living but
To me should utter, with demure confidence
This pausingly ensu'd: 'Neither the King nor 's heirs
(Tell you the Duke) shall prosper. Bid him strive
To the love o' th' commonalty; the Duke
Shall govern England.' "
Q. Kath. If I know you well,

You were the Duke's surveyor, and lost your office
On the complaint o' th' tenants. Take good heed
You charge not in your spleen a noble person
And spoil your nobler soul; I say, take heed;
Yes, heartily beseech you.
King. Let him on.
Go forward.
Surv. On my soul, I'll speak but truth.
I told my lord the Duke, by th' devil's illusions
The monk might be deceiv'd, and that 'twas dangerous for [him]
To ruminate on this so far, until
It forg'd him some design, which being believ'd,
It was much like to do. He answer'd, "Tush,
It can do me no damage"; adding further
That had the King in his last sickness fail'd,
The Cardinal's and Sir Thomas Lovell's heads
Should have gone off.
King. Ha? what, so rank? Ah ha,
There's mischief in this man. Canst thou say further?
Surv. I can, my liege.
King. Proceed.
Surv. Being at Greenwich,
After your Highness had reprov'd the Duke
About Sir William [Bulmer]—
King. I remember
Of such a time, being my sworn servant,
The Duke retain'd him his. But on; what hence?
Surv. "If," quoth he, "I for this had been committed
As to the Tower, I thought—I would have play'd
The part my father meant to act upon
Th' usurper Richard, who, being at Salisbury,
Made suit to come in 's presence; which if granted,
As he made semblance of his duty would
Have put his knife into him."
King. A giant traitor!
Wol. Now, madam, may his Highness live in freedom,
And this man out of prison?
Q. Kath. God mend all!
King. There's something more would out of thee; what say'st?

130–31. collected Out: gathered from the behavior.
132–209. First . . . purpose. The surveyor's evidence against Buckingham is based on Holinshed, much of it being merely versified from the chronicler's prose (Bullough, IV, 459–60).
132. it . . . him: i.e. he habitually said. **134. carry it so:** contrive.
140. Not . . . wish: i.e. disappointed in his hope that you would die without issue. **143. Deliver:** relate.
145. fail: failure (to have children).
150. of sovereignty: i.e. about his prospects for succeeding to the crown. **152. the Rose:** manor house in Buckingham's possession.
157. Presently: promptly. **158. doubted:** feared.
162. choice hour: appropriate time. **167. demure:** solemn.
170. commonalty: common people.

172–73. You . . . tenants. Before accompanying the King to the Field of the Cloth of Gold, Buckingham, says Holinshed (Bullough, IV, 456), had received "greevous complaints" from "his farmars and tenants against Charles Knevet his surveiour, for such bribing as he had used there [in Kent] amongest them. Whereupon the duke tooke such displeasure against him, that he deprived him of his office, not knowing how that in so dooing he procured his owne destruction."
174. spleen: spite.
175. spoil: destroy. **nobler:** i.e. than the "noble person" (because the soul is of more importance than the body).
184. fail'd: succumbed.
186. Ha. This exclamation, frequently used by the King, no doubt derives from Samuel Rowley's *When You See Me You Know Me* (1605), a history play about Henry VIII in which the term is heavily employed. See III.ii.63. **rank:** arrogant (?) or seditious (?).
188. liege: sovereign. **Greenwich:** royal residence on the lower Thames.
190. Sir William Bulmer: a functionary who, according to Holinshed (Bullough, IV, 454, 459), left the King's service for Buckingham's and thus brought down Henry's wrath on both of them.
195. my father: i.e. Henry Stafford (1454?–1483), second Duke of Buckingham, an adherent of Richard III who turned against his master and was executed after his abortive insurrection failed. He plays a conspicuous part in *Richard III*.
198. made . . . duty: i.e. made as if to kneel. **200. may:** can.

Surv. After "the Duke his father," with the "knife,"
He stretch'd him, and with one hand on his dagger,
Another spread on 's breast, mounting his eyes,
He did discharge a horrible oath, whose tenor
Was, were he evil us'd, he would outgo
His father by as much as a performance
Does an irresolute purpose.
King. There's his period,
To sheathe his knife in us. He is attach'd,
Call him to present trial. If he may
Find mercy in the law, 'tis his; if none,
Let him not seek't of us. By day and night,
He's traitor to th' height. *Exeunt.*

Scene III

Enter Lord Chamberlain *and* Lord Sands.

Cham. Is't possible the spells of France should juggle
Men into such strange mysteries?
San. New customs,
Though they be never so ridiculous
(Nay, let 'em be unmanly), yet are follow'd.
Cham. As far as I see, all the good our English
Have got by the late voyage is but merely
A fit or two o' th' face—but they are shrewd ones,
For when they hold 'em, you would swear directly
Their very noses had been councillors
To Pepin or Clotharius, they keep state so.
San. They have all new legs, and lame ones. One would take it,
That never see 'em pace before, the spavin
[And] springhalt reign'd among 'em.
Cham. Death, my lord,
Their clothes are after such a pagan cut to't,
That sure th' have worn out Christendom.

Enter Sir Thomas Lovell.

How now?
What news, Sir Thomas Lovell?
Lov. Faith, my lord,

203. with: i.e. with mention of.
204. stretch'd him: i.e. rose to his full height.
205. mounting: lifting up. **209. period:** end, aim.
210. attach'd: arrested. **211. present:** immediate.
214. to th' height: in the highest degree.

I.iii. Location: London. The palace.
o.s.d. Lord Chamberlain and Lord Sands. These names present problems. Although this and the following scene—the first perhaps suggested by Holinshed's comments (Bullough, IV, 453) on French fashions at the English court—obviously precede the death of Buckingham in May 1521, the banquet and masque of I.iv occurred, says Holinshed, on January 3, 1527. By that time, Sands (or Sandys)—who, incidentally, was not elevated to the peerage until 1523—was himself Lord Chamberlain. At II.i.53 s.d. he is called a knight.
2. strange mysteries: queer behavior. **4. unmanly:** i.e. effeminate.
6. the late voyage: i.e. to the Field of the Cloth of Gold.
7. A fit . . . face: a grimace or two.
10. Pepin, Clotharius: Frankish kings of the sixth and seventh centuries.
11. legs: i.e. ways of walking (perhaps with second sense "bows"). **lame ones:** i.e. because of an affected gait.
12. see: saw (archaic form).
12, 13. spavin, springhalt: diseases of animals causing lameness.
14. to't: besides.
15. worn out Christendom: i.e. run through all the Christian fashions.

I hear of none but the new proclamation
That's clapp'd upon the court gate.
Cham. What is't for?
Lov. The reformation of our travell'd gallants,
That fill the court with quarrels, talk, and tailors.
Cham. I'm glad 'tis there. Now I would pray our monsieurs
To think an English courtier may be wise
And never see the Louvre.
Lov. They must either
(For so run the conditions) leave those remnants
Of fool and feather that they got in France,
With all their honorable points of ignorance
Pertaining thereunto, as fights and fireworks,
Abusing better men than they can be
Out of a foreign wisdom, renouncing clean
The faith they have in tennis and tall stockings,
Short blist'red breeches, and those types of travel,
And understand again like honest men,
Or pack to their old playfellows. There, I take it,
They may, *cum privilegio*, ["*oui*"] away
The lag end of their lewdness and be laugh'd at.
San. 'Tis time to give 'em physic, their diseases
Are grown so catching.
Cham. What a loss our ladies
Will have of these trim vanities!
Lov. Ay, marry,
There will be woe indeed, lords; the sly whoresons
Have got a speeding trick to lay down ladies.
A French song and a fiddle has no fellow.
San. The devil fiddle 'em! I am glad they are going,
For sure there's no converting of 'em. Now
An honest country lord, as I am, beaten
A long time out of play, may bring his plain-song
And have an hour of hearing, and, by'r lady,
Held current music too.
Cham. Well said, Lord Sands,
Your colt's tooth is not cast yet?
San. No, my lord,
Nor shall not while I have a stump.
Cham. Sir Thomas,
Whither were you a-going?
Lov. To the Cardinal's.
Your lordship is a guest too.
Cham. O, 'tis true;
This night he makes a supper, and a great one,
To many lords and ladies; there will be
The beauty of this kingdom, I'll assure you.
Lov. That churchman bears a bounteous mind indeed,
A hand as fruitful as the land that feeds us;
His dews fall every where.

27. fireworks: i.e. whores.
31. blist'red: puffed. **types:** signs. **33. pack:** go.
34. cum privilegio: with immunity.
34–35. "oui" . . . lewdness: i.e. indulge their lechery in aping the French. *Oui* is the French word for "yes." **36. physic:** medicine.
38. trim vanities: finely dressed fools.
40. speeding: effective. **lay down:** i.e. seduce.
43. converting: reforming.
45. play: i.e. the game of love. **plain-song:** simple tune.
47. current: acceptable.
48. colt's tooth: i.e. wanton impulses (especially in old men). **cast:** lost. **56. fruitful:** generous.

Cham. No doubt he's noble;
He had a black mouth that said other of him.
San. He may, my lord, h'as wherewithal: in him
Sparing would show a worse sin than ill doctrine.
Men of his way should be most liberal,
They are set here for examples.
Cham. True, they are so;
But few now give so great ones. My barge stays;
Your lordship shall along. Come, good Sir Thomas,
We shall be late else, which I would not be,
For I was spoke to, with Sir Henry Guilford
This night to be comptrollers.
San. I am your lordship's. *Exeunt.*

Scene IV

Hoboys. A small table under a state for the Cardinal, a longer table for the guests. Then enter Anne Bullen *and divers other* Ladies *and* Gentlemen *as guests, at one door; at another door, enter* Sir Henry Guilford.

Guil. Ladies, a general welcome from his Grace
Salutes ye all; this night he dedicates
To fair content and you. None here, he hopes,
In all this noble bevy, has brought with her
One care abroad. He would have all as merry
As, first, good company, good wine, good welcome,
Can make good people.

Enter Lord Chamberlain, Lord Sands, *and* Lovell.

O my lord, y' are tardy;
The very thought of this fair company
Clapp'd wings to me.
Cham. You are young, Sir Harry Guilford.
San. Sir Thomas Lovell, had the Cardinal
But half my lay-thoughts in him, some of these
Should find a running banket, ere they rested,
I think would better please 'em. By my life,
They are a sweet society of fair ones.
Lov. O that your lordship were but now confessor
To one or two of these!
San. I would I were,
They should find easy penance.
Lov. Faith, how easy?
San. As easy as a down-bed would afford it.
Cham. Sweet ladies, will it please you sit? Sir Harry,
Place you that side, I'll take the charge of this.
His Grace is ent'ring. Nay, you must not freeze,
Two women plac'd together makes cold weather.
My Lord Sands, you are one will keep 'em waking;
Pray sit between these ladies.
San. By my faith,
And thank your lordship. By your leave, sweet ladies.

59. h'as: he has. **60. Sparing:** frugality. **ill doctrine:** i.e. heresy.
61. way: i.e. way of life. **63. stays:** awaits.
66. spoke to: requested. **67. comptrollers:** masters of ceremonies.

I.iv. Location: Westminster. The presence-chamber in York Place.
o.s.d. **Hoboys:** oboes. **state:** canopy. **4. bevy:** company.
11. lay: i.e. secular (with perhaps a sexual pun).
12. running banket: running banquet, i.e. hurried repast (with a bawdy double meaning). **20. Place you:** i.e. seat the guests on.
23. waking: lively.

If I chance to talk a little wild, forgive me;
I had it from my father.
Anne. Was he mad, sir?
San. O, very mad, exceeding mad, in love too;
But he would bite none. Just as I do now,
He would kiss you twenty with a breath.
[*Kisses her.*]
Cham. Well said, my lord.
So now y' are fairly seated. Gentlemen,
The penance lies on you, if these fair ladies
Pass away frowning.
San. For my little cure,
Let me alone.

Hoboys. Enter Cardinal Wolsey *and takes his state.*

Wol. Y' are welcome, my fair guests. That noble lady
Or gentleman that is not freely merry
Is not my friend. This, to confirm my welcome,
And to you all good health. [*Drinks.*]
San. Your Grace is noble.
Let me have such a bowl may hold my thanks,
And save me so much talking.
Wol. My Lord Sands,
I am beholding to you; cheer your neighbors.
Ladies, you are not merry. Gentlemen,
Whose fault is this?
San. The red wine first must rise
In their fair cheeks, my lord, then we shall have 'em
Talk us to silence.
Anne. You are a merry gamester,
My Lord Sands.
San. Yes, if I make my play.
Here's to your ladyship, and pledge it, madam,
For 'tis to such a thing—
Anne. You cannot show me.
San. I told your Grace they would talk anon.
Drum and trumpet; chambers discharg'd.
Wol. What's that?
Cham. Look out there, some of ye.
[*Exit a Servant.*]
Wol. What warlike voice,
And to what end is this? Nay, ladies, fear not;
By all the laws of war y' are privileg'd.

30. twenty . . . breath: i.e. twenty times without drawing breath.
33. cure: (1) charge, parish (carrying on the figure in line 15); (2) remedy. **34 s.d. state:** chair of state.
41. beholding: beholden, indebted.
46. make my play: i.e. win my game (with an implication of amorous play).
49 s.d. chambers: short cannon. It was probably the firing of these that caused the destruction of the Globe playhouse in 1613.
50–108. Holinshed's account (Bullough, III, 478) of this episode (to which the play is much indebted) opens thus: "On a time the king came suddenlie thither [i.e. to Wolsey's palace] in a maske with a dozen maskers all in garments like sheepheards, made of fine cloth of gold, and crimosin sattin paned, & caps of the same, with visards of good physnomie, their haires & beards either of fine goldwire silke, or blacke silke, having sixteene torch-bearers, besides their drums and other persons with visards, all clothed in sattin of the same color. And before his entring into the hall, he came by water to the water gate without anie noise, where were laid diverse chambers and guns charged with shot, and at his landing they were shot off, which made such a rumble in the aire, that it was like thunder: it made all the noblemen, gentlemen, ladies, and gentlewomen, to muse what it should meane, comming so suddenlie, they sitting quiet at a solemne banket, after this sort."

Enter a SERVANT.

Cham. How now, what is't?
Serv. A noble troop of strangers,
For so they seem. Th' have left their barge and landed,
And hither make, as great embassadors
From foreign princes.
Wol. Good Lord Chamberlain,
Go, give 'em welcome: you can speak the French tongue;
And pray receive 'em nobly and conduct 'em
Into our presence, where this heaven of beauty
Shall shine at full upon them. Some attend him.
[*Exit Chamberlain attended.*] *All rise, and tables remov'd.*
You have now a broken banket, but we'll mend it.
A good digestion to you all; and once more
I show'r a welcome on ye. Welcome all!

Hoboys. Enter KING *and others as Maskers, habited like shepherds, usher'd by the* LORD CHAMBERLAIN. *They pass directly before the Cardinal and gracefully salute him.*

A noble company! What are their pleasures?
Cham. Because they speak no English, thus they pray'd
To tell your Grace, that having heard by fame
Of this so noble and so fair assembly
This night to meet here, they could do no less
(Out of the great respect they bear to beauty)
But leave their flocks, and under your fair conduct
Crave leave to view these ladies, and entreat
An hour of revels with 'em.
Wol. Say, Lord Chamberlain,
They have done my poor house grace; for which I pay 'em
A thousand thanks, and pray 'em take their pleasures.
Choose ladies; King and Anne Bullen.
King. The fairest hand I ever touch'd! O Beauty,
Till now I never knew thee! *Music. Dance.*
Wol. My lord!
Cham. Your Grace?
Wol. Pray tell 'em thus much from me:
There should be one amongst 'em, by his person
More worthy this place than myself, to whom
(If I but knew him) with my love and duty
I would surrender it.
Cham. I will, my lord.
Whisper [*with the Maskers*].
Wol. What say they?
Cham. Such a one, they all confess,
There is indeed, which they would have your Grace
Find out, and he will take it.
Wol. Let me see then,
By all your good leaves, gentlemen; here I'll make
My royal choice.

53. strangers: foreigners. 55. embassadors: ambassadors.
61. broken: interrupted. 70. conduct: permission.
74 s.d. Anne Bullen. Henry's meeting Anne Bullen at Wolsey's banquet is not in Holinshed. 79. this place: i.e. the chair of state.
84. it: i.e. Wolsey's "place."

King. Ye have found him, Cardinal.
[*Unmasking.*]
You hold a fair assembly; you do well, lord.
You are a churchman, or I'll tell you, Cardinal,
I should judge now unhappily.
Wol. I am glad
Your Grace is grown so pleasant.
King. My Lord Chamberlain,
Prithee come hither. What fair lady's that?
Cham. An't please your Grace, Sir Thomas Bullen's daughter—
The Viscount Rochford—one of her Highness' women.
King. By heaven, she is a dainty one. Sweet heart,
I were unmannerly to take you out
And not to kiss you. A health, gentlemen!
Let it go round.
Wol. Sir Thomas Lovell, is the banket ready
I' th' privy chamber?
Lov. Yes, my lord.
Wol. Your Grace,
I fear, with dancing is a little heated.
King. I fear, too much.
Wol. There's fresher air, my lord,
In the next chamber.
King. Lead in your ladies, ev'ry one. Sweet partner,
I must not yet forsake you. Let's be merry,
Good my Lord Cardinal: I have half a dozen healths
To drink to these fair ladies, and a measure
To lead 'em once again, and then let's dream
Who's best in favor. Let the music knock it.
Exeunt with Trumpets.

ACT II, SCENE I

Enter two GENTLEMEN *at several doors.*

1. Gent. Whither away so fast?
2. Gent. O, God save ye!
Ev'n to the hall, to hear what shall become
Of the great Duke of Buckingham.
1. Gent. I'll save you
That labor, sir. All's now done but the ceremony
Of bringing back the prisoner.
2. Gent. Were you there?
1. Gent. Yes indeed was I.
2. Gent. Pray speak what has happen'd.
1. Gent. You may guess quickly what.
2. Gent. Is he found guilty?
1. Gent. Yes, truly is he, and condemn'd upon't.

86. Ye . . . him. According to Holinshed (Bullough, IV, 480), Wolsey first offered his place to Sir Edward Neville, whereupon "the king perceiving the cardinall so deceived, could not forbeare laughing, but pulled down his visar and master Nevels also, and dashed out such a pleasant countenance and cheere, that all the noble estates there assembled, perceiving the king to be there among them, rejoised verie much." 89. unhappily: unfavorably. 90. pleasant: merry.
93. her Highness' women: i.e. Queen Katherine's women in waiting.
95. take you out: i.e. into the dance.
106. measure: stately dance.
108. best in favor: handsomest. knock it: strike up. s.d. Trumpets: trumpeters.
II.i. Location: Westminster. A street.
o.s.d. several: different. 2. hall: Westminster Hall.

2. Gent. I am sorry for't.
1. Gent. So are a number more.
2. Gent. But pray how pass'd it?
1. Gent. I'll tell you in a little. The great Duke
Came to the bar; where to his accusations
He pleaded still not guilty, and alleged
Many sharp reasons to defeat the law.
The King's attorney on the contrary
Urg'd on the examinations, proofs, confessions
Of divers witnesses, which the Duke desir'd
To him brought *vivâ voce* to his face;
At which appear'd against him his surveyor,
Sir Gilbert [Perk] his chancellor, and John Car,
Confessor to him, with that devil monk,
Hopkins, that made this mischief.
2. Gent. That was he
That fed him with his prophecies?
1. Gent. The same;
All these accus'd him strongly, which he fain
Would have flung from him; but indeed he could not.
And so his peers upon this evidence
Have found him guilty of high treason. Much
He spoke, and learnedly, for life; but all
Was either pitied in him or forgotten.
2. Gent. After all this, how did he bear himself?
1. Gent. When he was brought again to th' bar, to hear
His knell rung out, his judgment, he was stirr'd
With such an agony he sweat extremely,
And something spoke in choler, ill, and hasty.
But he fell to himself again, and sweetly
In all the rest show'd a most noble patience.
2. Gent. I do not think he fears death.
1. Gent. Sure he does not,
He never was so womanish. The cause
He may a little grieve at.
2. Gent. Certainly
The Cardinal is the end of this.
1. Gent. 'Tis likely,
By all conjectures: first, Kildare's attendure,
Then deputy of Ireland, who remov'd,
Earl Surrey was sent thither, and in haste too,
Lest he should help his father.
2. Gent. That trick of state
Was a deep envious one.
1. Gent. At his return
No doubt he will requite it. This is noted,
And generally, whoever the King favors,
The Card'nal instantly will find employment,
And far enough from court too.
2. Gent. All the commons
Hate him perniciously, and, o' my conscience,
Wish him ten fadom deep. This duke as much
They love and dote on; call him bounteous Buckingham,
The mirror of all courtesy—

Enter Buckingham *from his arraignment, Tipstaves before him, the axe with the edge towards him, Halberds on each side; accompanied with* Sir Thomas Lovell, Sir Nicholas Vaux, Sir Walter Sands, *and common people, etc.*

1. Gent. Stay there, sir,
And see the noble ruin'd man you speak of.
2. Gent. Let's stand close and behold him.
Buck. All good people,
You that thus far have come to pity me,
Hear what I say, and then go home and lose me.
I have this day receiv'd a traitor's judgment,
And by that name must die; yet, heaven bear witness,
And if I have a conscience, let it sink me,
Even as the axe falls, if I be not faithful!
The law I bear no malice for my death;
'T has done, upon the premises, but justice;
But those that sought it I could wish more Christians.
Be what they will, I heartily forgive 'em;
Yet let 'em look they glory not in mischief,
Nor build their evils on the graves of great men,
For then my guiltless blood must cry against 'em.
For further life in this world I ne'er hope,
Nor will I sue, although the King have mercies
More than I dare make faults. You few that lov'd me
And dare be bold to weep for Buckingham,
His noble friends and fellows, whom to leave
Is only bitter to him, only dying,
Go with me like good angels to my end,
And as the long divorce of steel falls on me,
Make of your prayers one sweet sacrifice,
And lift my soul to heaven. Lead on a' God's name.
Lov. I do beseech your Grace, for charity,
If ever any malice in your heart
Were hid against me, now to forgive me frankly.
Buck. Sir Thomas Lovell, I as free forgive you
As I would be forgiven. I forgive all.
There cannot be those numberless offenses

10. how pass'd it: i.e. what happened at the trial.
11. in a little: in few words.
11–22. The great . . . mischief. These lines follow closely Holinshed's account (Bullough, IV, 461), which begins: "When the lords had taken their place, the duke was brought to the barre, and uppon his arreignement pleaded not guiltie, and put himselfe upon his peeres. Then was his indictment read, which the duke denied to be true, and (as he was an eloquent man) alledged reasons to falsifie the indictment; pleading the matter for his owne justification verie pithilie and earnestlie. The kings attourneie against the dukes reasons alledged the examinations, confessions, and proofes of witnesses."
13–14. alleged . . . defeat: advanced many cogent arguments to overturn. **16. Urg'd . . . examinations:** dwelt on the depositions.
24. which: i.e. which accusations. **fain:** gladly.
28–29. all . . . forgotten: i.e. everything he said was either pitied (rather than believed) or ignored. **34. choler:** anger.
35. fell to: recovered. **40. end:** ultimate cause.
41–44. Kildare's . . . father. According to Holinshed (Bullough, IV, 456), Wolsey had Gerald Fitzgerald, Earl of Kildare and Lord Lieutenant of Ireland, arrested for maladministration and replaced him with Thomas Howard, Earl of Surrey, "there to remaine rather as an exile, than as lieutenant to the king, even at the cardinals pleasure, as he himself well perceived." **41. attendure:** attainder.
44. father: i.e. father-in-law. Surrey was married to Buckingham's oldest daughter.

44. trick of state: political stratagem.
45. envious: malicious. **47. generally:** by everyone.
50. perniciously: so as to desire his death. **51. fadom:** fathom.
53. mirror: i.e. paragon. **s.d. Tipstaves:** bailiffs. **the edge towards him.** Indicating the sentence of death. **Halberds:** halberdiers, soldiers bearing spears with axe-like heads. **57. lose:** forget.
60. sink: ruin. **62. malice:** resentment.
63. premises: evidence (?).
67. evils: hovels (?). **great men:** noblemen. **70. sue:** beg.
73–74. whom . . . dying: i.e. dying is bitter only because it means parting from his friends. **77. sacrifice:** offering.
78. a': in.

'Gainst me, that I cannot take peace with; no black envy
Shall make my grave. Commend me to his Grace;
And if he speak of Buckingham, pray tell him
You met him half in heaven. My vows and prayers
Yet are the King's; and, till my soul forsake,
Shall cry for blessings on him. May he live
Longer than I have time to tell his years;
Ever belov'd and loving may his rule be;
And when old Time shall lead him to his end,
Goodness and he fill up one monument!

Lov. To th' water side I must conduct your Grace;
Then give my charge up to Sir Nicholas Vaux,
Who undertakes you to your end.

Vaux. Prepare there,
The Duke is coming. See the barge be ready;
And fit it with such furniture as suits
The greatness of his person.

Buck. Nay, Sir Nicholas,
Let it alone; my state now will but mock me.
When I came hither, I was Lord High Constable
And Duke of Buckingham; now, poor Edward Bohun.
Yet I am richer than my base accusers,
That never knew what truth meant. I now seal it;
And with that blood will make 'em one day groan for't.
My noble father, Henry of Buckingham,
Who first rais'd head against usurping Richard,
Flying for succor to his servant Banister,
Being distress'd, was by that wretch betray'd,
And without trial fell; God's peace be with him!
Henry the Seventh succeeding, truly pitying
My father's loss, like a most royal prince
Restor'd me to my honors; and out of ruins
Made my name once more noble. Now his son,
Henry the Eight, life, honor, name, and all
That made me happy, at one stroke has taken
For ever from the world. I had my trial,
And must needs say a noble one; which makes me
A little happier than my wretched father.
Yet thus far we are one in fortunes: both
Fell by our servants, by those men we lov'd most;
A most unnatural and faithless service.
Heaven has an end in all; yet, you that hear me,
This from a dying man receive as certain:
Where you are liberal of your loves and counsels,
Be sure you be not loose; for those you make friends
And give your hearts to, when they once perceive
The least rub in your fortunes, fall away
Like water from ye, never found again
But where they mean to sink ye. All good people,
Pray for me! I must now forsake ye. The last hour
Of my long weary life is come upon me.
Farewell!
And when you would say something that is sad,
Speak how I fell. I have done; and God forgive me!
Exeunt Duke and Train.

1. Gent. O, this is full of pity! Sir, it calls,
I fear, too many curses on their heads
That were the authors.

2. Gent. If the Duke be guiltless,
'Tis full of woe; yet I can give you inkling
Of an ensuing evil, if it fall,
Greater than this.

1. Gent. Good angels keep it from us!
What may it be? You do not doubt my faith, sir?

2. Gent. This secret is so weighty, 'twill require
A strong faith to conceal it.

1. Gent. Let me have it;
I do not talk much.

2. Gent. I am confident;
You shall, sir. Did you not of late days hear
A buzzing of a separation
Between the King and Katherine?

1. Gent. Yes, but it held not;
For when the King once heard it, out of anger
He sent command to the Lord Mayor straight
To stop the rumor, and allay those tongues
That durst disperse it.

2. Gent. But that slander, sir,
Is found a truth now; for it grows again
Fresher than e'er it was, and held for certain
The King will venture at it. Either the Cardinal,
Or some about him near, have out of malice
To the good Queen possess'd him with a scruple
That will undo her. To confirm this too,
Cardinal Campeius is arriv'd, and lately,
As all think, for this business.

1. Gent. 'Tis the Cardinal;
And merely to revenge him on the Emperor
For not bestowing on him at his asking
The archbishopric of Toledo, this is purpos'd.

2. Gent. I think you have hit the mark; but is't not cruel
That she should feel the smart of this? The Cardinal
Will have his will, and she must fall.

1. Gent. 'Tis woeful.
We are too open here to argue this;
Let's think in private more. *Exeunt.*

85. envy: malice.
89. forsake: i.e. leave my body. **91. tell**: count.
94. monument: tomb. **97. undertakes**: conducts.
99. furniture: equipment. **101. state**: rank.
103. Bohun. A mistake, copied from Holinshed (Bullough, IV, 462), for Stafford, which was the Duke's family name.
105. seal it: i.e. attest to truth.
107–11. My . . . fell. See *Richard III*, V.i.
108. rais'd head: gathered a military force. **122. by**: through.
124. end: purpose. **127. loose**: careless. **129. rub**: check.
133. long weary life. Buckingham died at forty-three.

146. confident: i.e. of your discretion. **148. buzzing**: rumor.
149. held not: stopped.
150–53. For . . . disperse it. Rumors of Henry's divorce and of his projected marriage with Francis I's sister so much offended the King, says Holinshed (Bullough, IV, 465), that he "sent for sir Thomas Seimor mayor of the citie of London, secretlie charging him to see that the people ceassed from such talke." **152. allay**: silence.
158. possess'd . . . scruple: put into his mind a doubt. Katherine and Prince Arthur (eldest son and heir of Henry VII) had been married in 1501, when both were in their early teens. Arthur died the following year, and after prolonged negotiation—including the securing of a papal dispensation—Katherine married her brother-in-law, the newly crowned Henry VIII, in 1509. It was not until 1527, says Holinshed (Bullough, IV, 468–69), that Henry's conscience became "accombred, vexed, and disquieted" by fear that he had sinned through marriage with his brother's widow.
160. Cardinal . . . lately. Cardinal Campeggio (or Campeius) reached London in 1528, seven years after Buckingham's execution. See note to II.ii.86–96.
162. Emperor: i.e. Charles V, nephew of Queen Katherine.
168. open: public.

Scene II

Enter Lord Chamberlain *reading this letter.*

[*Cham.*] "My lord, the horses your lordship sent for, with all the care I had, I saw well chosen, ridden, and furnish'd. They were young and handsome, and of the best breed in the north. When they were ready to set out for London, a man of my Lord Cardinal's, by commission and main power, took 'em from me, with this reason: his master would be serv'd before a subject, if not before the King, which stopp'd our mouths, sir."

I fear he will indeed. Well, let him have them:
He will have all, I think.

Enter to the Lord Chamberlain the Dukes of Norfolk *and* Suffolk.

Nor. Well met, my Lord Chamberlain.
Cham. Good day to both your Graces.
Suf. How is the King employ'd?
Cham. I left him private,
Full of sad thoughts and troubles.
Nor. What's the cause?
Cham. It seems the marriage with his brother's wife
Has crept too near his conscience.
Suf. [*Aside.*] No, his conscience
Has crept too near another lady.
Nor. 'Tis so;
This is the Cardinal's doing. The king-cardinal,
That blind priest, like the eldest son of Fortune,
Turns what he list. The King will know him one day.
Suf. Pray God he do, he'll never know himself else.
Nor. How holily he works in all his business!
And with what zeal! for now he has crack'd the league
Between us and the Emperor (the Queen's great nephew),
He dives into the King's soul, and there scatters
Dangers, doubts, wringing of the conscience,
Fears, and despairs, and all these for his marriage.
And out of all these to restore the King,
He counsels a divorce, a loss of her
That, like a jewel, has hung twenty years
About his neck, yet never lost her lustre;
Of her that loves him with that excellence
That angels love good men with; even of her
That when the greatest stroke of fortune falls
Will bless the King. And is not this course pious?
Cham. Heaven keep me from such counsel! 'Tis most true
These news are every where; every tongue speaks 'em,
And every true heart weeps for't. All that dare
Look into these affairs see this main end,
The French king's sister. Heaven will one day open
The King's eyes, that so long have slept upon
This bold bad man.
Suf. And free us from his slavery.
Nor. We had need pray,
And heartily, for our deliverance,
Or this imperious man will work us all
From princes into pages. All men's honors
Lie like one lump before him, to be fashion'd
Into what pitch he please.
Suf. For me, my lords,
I love him not, nor fear him; there's my creed.
As I am made without him, so I'll stand,
If the King please; his curses and his blessings
Touch me alike; th' are breath I not believe in.
I knew him, and I know him; so I leave him
To him that made him proud, the Pope.
Nor. Let's in;
And with some other business put the King
From these sad thoughts that work too much upon him.
My lord, you'll bear us company?
Cham. Excuse me,
The King has sent me otherwhere. Besides,
You'll find a most unfit time to disturb him.
Health to your lordships.
Nor. Thanks, my good Lord Chamberlain.

Exit Lord Chamberlain; and the King draws the curtain and sits reading pensively.

Suf. How sad he looks! Sure he is much afflicted.
King. Who's there? ha?
Nor. Pray God he be not angry.
King. Who's there, I say? How dare you thrust yourselves
Into my private meditations?
Who am I? ha?
Nor. A gracious king that pardons all offenses
Malice ne'er meant. Our breach of duty this way
Is business of estate; in which we come
To know your royal pleasure.
King. Ye are too bold.
Go to; I'll make ye know your times of business.
Is this an hour for temporal affairs? ha?

Enter Wolsey *and* Campeius *with a commission.*

Who's there? My good Lord Cardinal? O my Wolsey,
The quiet of my wounded conscience,
Thou art a cure fit for a king. [*To Campeius.*] You're welcome,
Most learned reverend sir, into our kingdom,
Use us and it. [*To Wolsey.*] My good lord, have great care
I be not found a talker.
Wol. Sir, you cannot.

II.ii. Location: London. The palace.
2. ridden: broken in. **3. furnish'd:** equipped.
6. commission: warrant. **14. private:** alone. **15. sad:** serious.
20–21. blind . . . list. Alluding to Fortune's blindness and her wheel. See *Henry V*, III.vi.30–38.
24–28. he . . . marriage. "The cardinall verelie was put in most blame for this scruple now cast into the kings conscience," Holinshed reports (Bullough, IV, 466), "for the hate he bare to the emperor, bicause he would not grant to him the archbishoprike of Toledo, for the which he was a suter. And therefore he did not onlie procure the king of England to joine in freendship with the French king, but also sought a divorce betwixt the king and the queene, that the king might have had in marriage the duchesse of Alanson, sister unto the French king." **35. greatest stroke:** i.e. worst blow.

42. slept upon: been blind to.
49. pitch: height (a term from falconry), i.e. degree of dignity. The figure suggested by *lump* and *fashion'd* (line 48) is not completed.
61 s.d. draws the curtain. Presumably at the back of the stage.
68. this way: in this respect. **69. estate:** state.
78. I . . . talker: i.e. that you translate my hospitable words into action.

I would your Grace would give us but an hour
Of private conference.

King. [*To Norfolk and Suffolk.*] We are busy; go.

Nor. [*Aside to Suffolk.*] This priest has no pride in him?

Suf. [*Aside to Norfolk.*] Not to speak of.
I would not be so sick though for his place.
But this cannot continue.

Nor. [*Aside to Suffolk.*] If it do,
I'll venture one; have at him!

Suf. [*Aside to Norfolk.*] I another.

Exeunt Norfolk and Suffolk.

Wol. Your Grace has given a president of wisdom
Above all princes, in committing freely
Your scruple to the voice of Christendom.
Who can be angry now? What envy reach you?
The Spaniard, tied by blood and favor to her,
Must now confess, if they have any goodness,
The trial just and noble. All the clerks
(I mean the learned ones in Christian kingdoms)
Have their free voices. Rome, the nurse of judgment,
Invited by your noble self, hath sent
One general tongue unto us: this good man,
This just and learned priest, Card'nal Campeius,
Whom once more I present unto your Highness.

King. And once more in mine arms I bid him welcome,
And thank the holy conclave for their loves;
They have sent me such a man I would have wish'd for.

Cam. Your Grace must needs deserve all strangers' loves,
You are so noble. To your Highness' hand
I tender my commission; by whose virtue,
The court of Rome commanding, you, my Lord
Cardinal of York, are join'd with me their servant
In the unpartial judging of this business.

King. Two equal men. The Queen shall be acquainted
Forthwith for what you come. Where's Gardiner?

Wol. I know your Majesty has always lov'd her
So dear in heart not to deny her that
A woman of less place might ask by law:
Scholars allow'd freely to argue for her.

King. Ay, and the best she shall have; and my favor
To him that does best, God forbid else. Cardinal,
Prithee call Gardiner to me, my new secretary.
I find him a fit fellow. [*Exit Wolsey.*]

Enter [WOLSEY *with*] GARDINER.

Wol. [*Aside to Gardiner.*] Give me your hand.
Much joy and favor to you;
You are the King's now.

Gard. [*Aside to Wolsey.*] But to be commanded
For ever by your Grace, whose hand has rais'd me.

King. Come hither, Gardiner.

Walks and whispers.

Cam. My Lord of York, was not one Doctor Pace
In this man's place before him?

Wol. Yes, he was.

Cam. Was he not held a learned man?

Wol. Yes, surely.

Cam. Believe me, there's an ill opinion spread then,
Even of yourself, Lord Cardinal.

Wol. How? of me?

Cam. They will not stick to say you envied him,
And fearing he would rise (he was so virtuous),
Kept him a foreign man still, which so griev'd him,
That he ran mad, and died.

Wol. Heav'n's peace be with him!
That's Christian care enough. For living murmurers
There's places of rebuke. He was a fool—
For he would needs be virtuous. That good fellow,
If I command him, follows my appointment;
I will have none so near else. Learn this, brother,
We live not to be grip'd by meaner persons.

King. Deliver this with modesty to th' Queen.

Exit Gardiner.

The most convenient place that I can think of
For such receipt of learning is Black-Friars;
There ye shall meet about this weighty business.
My Wolsey, see it furnish'd. O my lord,
Would it not grieve an able man to leave
So sweet a bedfellow? But conscience, conscience!
O, 'tis a tender place, and I must leave her. *Exeunt.*

SCENE III

Enter ANNE BULLEN *and an* OLD LADY.

Anne. Not for that neither; here's the pang that pinches:
His Highness having liv'd so long with her, and she

81. This priest: i.e. Wolsey.
82. be . . . place: i.e. have his place at the cost of being so sick with pride.
84. one: i.e. thrust (at Wolsey). **have at him:** A conventional warning that the speaker is about to attack.
85. president: precedent, i.e. example.
86–96. in . . . Campeius. Failing to resolve his doubts about his marriage, Henry, says Holinshed (IV, 466), "sent to all the universities in Italie and France, and to the great clearkes of all christendome, to know their opinions, and desired the court of Rome to send into his realme a legat, which should be indifferent, and of a great and profound judgement, to heare the cause debated. At whose request the whole consistorie of the college of Rome sent thither Laurence Campeius, a preest cardinall, a man of great wit and experience." It was Thomas Cranmer's suggesting this canvass of continental scholars that apparently first brought him to Henry's attention.
87. voice: vote. **89. The Spaniard:** i.e. the Emperor Charles.
91. clerks: clerics.
95. One general tongue: i.e. a spokesman for the whole Roman Church. **99. conclave:** i.e. the College of Cardinals.
101. strangers': foreigners'.
107. equal: impartial. **acquainted:** informed.
110. that: i.e. that which. **111. less place:** lower rank.

115. my new secretary. Stephen Gardiner, who had been secretary to Wolsey, was promoted to the service of the King in July 1529. His diligence about the divorce proceedings earned for him the bishopric of Winchester in 1531.
121. Doctor Pace: Richard Pace (1482?–1536), frequently employed by Wolsey in diplomatic missions to the Continent.
126. stick: hesitate.
128. Kept . . . still: continually sent him abroad on official business.
132. fellow: i.e. Gardiner. **133. appointment:** instructions.
134. none . . . else: i.e. no one not under my control so near the King.
135. grip'd: grasped (?). **136. Deliver:** repeat.
138. such . . . learning: i.e. the reception of such learned men. **Black-Friars:** Dominican convent in London. **141. able:** vigorous.

II.iii. London. The Queen's apartments in the palace.

So good a lady that no tongue could ever
Pronounce dishonor of her—by my life,
She never knew harm-doing—O, now after
So many courses of the sun enthroned,
Still growing in a majesty and pomp, the which
To leave a thousandfold more bitter than
'Tis sweet at first t' acquire—after this process,
To give her the avaunt, it is a pity
Would move a monster.
Old L. Hearts of most hard temper
Melt and lament for her.
Anne. O, God's will, much better
She ne'er had known pomp! Though't be temporal,
Yet if that quarrel, fortune, do divorce
It from the bearer, 'tis a sufferance panging
As soul and body's severing.
Old L. Alas, poor lady!
She's a stranger now again.
Anne. So much the more
Must pity drop upon her. Verily,
I swear, 'tis better to be lowly born,
And range with humble livers in content,
Than to be perk'd up in a glist'ring grief
And wear a golden sorrow.
Old L. Our content
Is our best having.
Anne. By my troth and maidenhead,
I would not be a queen.
Old L. Beshrew me, I would,
And venture maidenhead for't, and so would you
For all this spice of your hypocrisy.
You, that have so fair parts of woman on you,
Have, too, a woman's heart, which ever yet
Affected eminence, wealth, sovereignty;
Which, to say sooth, are blessings; and which gifts
(Saving your mincing) the capacity
Of your soft cheveril conscience would receive
If you might please to stretch it.
Anne. Nay, good troth.
Old L. Yes, troth, and troth. You would not be a queen?
Anne. No, not for all the riches under heaven.
Old L. 'Tis strange. A threepence bow'd would hire me,
Old as I am, to queen it. But I pray you,
What think you of a duchess? Have you limbs
To bear that load of title?
Anne. No, in truth.
Old L. Then you are weakly made; pluck off a little,
I would not be a young count in your way
For more than blushing comes to. If your back
Cannot vouchsafe this burthen, 'tis too weak
Ever to get a boy.
Anne. How you do talk!
I swear again, I would not be a queen
For all the world.
Old L. In faith, for little England
You'ld venture an emballing. I myself
Would for Carnarvonshire, although there 'long'd
No more to th' crown but that. Lo, who comes here?

Enter LORD CHAMBERLAIN.

Cham. Good morrow, ladies. What were't worth to know
The secret of your conference?
Anne. My good lord,
Not your demand; it values not your asking.
Our mistress' sorrows we were pitying.
Cham. It was a gentle business, and becoming
The action of good women. There is hope
All will be well.
Anne. Now I pray God, amen!
Cham. You bear a gentle mind, and heav'nly blessings
Follow such creatures. That you may, fair lady,
Perceive I speak sincerely, and high note's
Ta'en of your many virtues, the King's Majesty
Commends his good opinion of you to you, and
Does purpose honor to you no less flowing
Than Marchioness of Pembroke; to which title
A thousand pound a year, annual support,
Out of his grace he adds.
Anne. I do not know
What kind of my obedience I should tender.
More than my all is nothing: nor my prayers
Are not words duly hallowed, nor my wishes
More worth than empty vanities; yet prayers and wishes
Are all I can return. Beseech your lordship,
Vouchsafe to speak my thanks and my obedience,
As from a blushing handmaid, to his Highness;
Whose health and royalty I pray for.
Cham. Lady,
I shall not fail t' approve the fair conceit
The King hath of you. [*Aside.*] I have perus'd her well;
Beauty and honor in her are so mingled
That they have caught the King; and who knows yet
But from this lady may proceed a gem
To lighten all this isle?—I'll to the King,

4. Pronounce: declare. **7. Still:** always.
9. process: succession of events.
10. give . . . avaunt: bid her be gone.
13. temporal: worldly (as opposed to heavenly).
14. quarrel: quarreller. **15. sufferance panging:** suffering painful.
17. stranger: foreigner. **20. range:** rank. **livers:** persons.
21. perk'd up: decked out.
23. having: possession. **troth:** truth, faith.
27. parts: qualities. **29. Affected:** loved. **30. sooth:** truth.
31. Saving your mincing: i.e. your affectations notwithstanding.
32. cheveril: kid-leather, i.e. elastic, supple. **36. bow'd:** bent.
37. queen. With a pun on *quean*, "strumpet."
40. pluck . . . little: i.e. come down a step.
41. count: i.e. earl (a rank lower than duke).
43. vouchsafe this burthen: (condescendingly) accept this burden.
47. emballing: investiture with the ball or orb, the symbol of sovereignty.
48. Carnarvonshire: notoriously poor Welsh county. **'long'd:** belonged. **51. conference:** conversation.
52. values not: is not worth.
58–65. That . . . adds. Holinshed records (Bullough, IV, 481) that "on the first of September [1532] being Sundaie, the K. being come to Windsor, created the ladie Anne Bullongne marchionesse of Penbroke, and gave to hir one thousand pounds land by the yeare."
61. Commends . . . of you: i.e. presents his compliments.
65. grace: favor. **71. Vouchsafe:** be good enough.
74. approve . . . conceit: confirm the good opinion.
79. lighten: illuminate.

And say I spoke with you.
Anne. My honor'd lord.
Exit Lord Chamberlain.
Old L. Why, this it is! see, see,
I have been begging sixteen years in court
(Am yet a courtier beggarly) nor could
Come pat betwixt too early and too late
For any suit of pounds; and you, O fate!
A very fresh fish here—fie, fie, fie upon
This compell'd fortune!—have your mouth fill'd up
Before you open it.
Anne. This is strange to me.
Old L. How tastes it? Is it bitter? Forty pence, no.
There was a lady once ('tis an old story)
That would not be a queen, that would she not,
For all the mud in Egypt. Have you heard it?
Anne. Come, you are pleasant.
Old L. With your theme, I could
O'ermount the lark. The Marchioness of Pembroke?
A thousand pounds a year for pure respect?
No other obligation? By my life,
That promises moe thousands; honor's train
Is longer than his foreskirt. By this time
I know your back will bear a duchess. Say,
Are you not stronger than you were?
Anne. Good lady,
Make yourself mirth with your particular fancy,
And leave me out on't. Would I had no being
If this salute my blood a jot; it faints me
To think what follows.
The Queen is comfortless, and we forgetful
In our long absence. Pray do not deliver
What here y' have heard to her.
Old L. What do you think me? *Exeunt.*

Scene IV

Trumpets, sennet, and cornets. Enter two Vergers, *with short silver wands; next them, two* Scribes, *in the habit of doctors; after them, the* [Arch]bishop of Canterbury *alone; after him, the* Bishops of Lincoln, Ely, Rochester, *and* Saint Asaph; *next them, with some small distance, follows a* Gentleman *bearing the purse, with the great seal, and a cardinal's hat; then two* Priests *bearing each a silver cross; then a* Gentleman Usher *bare-headed, accompanied with a* Sergeant-at-Arms *bearing a silver mace; then two* Gentlemen *bearing two great silver pillars; after them, side by side, the two* Cardinals; *two* Noblemen *with the sword and mace. The* King *takes place under the cloth of state; the two Cardinals sit under him as judges. The* Queen *takes place some distance from the King. The Bishops place themselves on each side the court, in manner of a consistory; below them, the Scribes. The Lords sit next the Bishops. The rest of the Attendants stand in convenient order about the stage.*

83. **beggarly:** i.e. needy and importunate.
85. **suit of pounds:** petition for money.
87. **compell'd:** i.e. thrust upon you.
89. **Forty pence, no:** i.e. I'll wager forty pence (a trivial sum) that it isn't bitter.
93. **pleasant:** facetious. **With your theme:** i.e. if I had your good fortune. 95. **pure:** mere. 97. **moe:** more.
101. **your particular fancy:** your own daydream.
103. **salute:** stir. **faints me:** makes me faint.

II.iv. Location: London. A hall in Blackfriars.
o.s.d. Some of the details of this elaborate stage direction derive from Holinshed's account (Bullough, IV, 477–78) of Wolsey's love of pomp and luxury; others closely follow Holinshed's description (Bullough, IV, 466–67) of the divorce proceedings at Blackfriars on June 18, 1529. **sennet:** fanfare announcing a procession. **habit of doctors:** i.e. furred gowns and black caps worn by doctors of law. **cloth of state:** canopy. 4. **allow'd:** conceded.

Wol. Whilst our commission from Rome is read,
Let silence be commanded.
King. What's the need?
It hath already publicly been read,
And on all sides th' authority allow'd;
You may then spare that time.
Wol. Be't so; proceed.
Scribe. Say, Henry King of England, come into the court.
Crier. Henry King of England, etc.
King. Here.
Scribe. Say, Katherine Queen of England, come into the court.
Crier. Katherine Queen of England, etc.
The Queen makes no answer, rises out of her chair, goes about the court, comes to the King, and kneels at his feet; then speaks.
[*Q. Kath.*] Sir, I desire you do me right and justice,
And to bestow your pity on me; for
I am a most poor woman, and a stranger,
Born out of your dominions; having here
No judge indifferent, nor no more assurance
Of equal friendship and proceeding. Alas, sir!
In what have I offended you? What cause
Hath my behavior given to your displeasure,
That thus you should proceed to put me off,
And take your good grace from me? Heaven witness,
I have been to you a true and humble wife,
At all times to your will conformable;
Ever in fear to kindle your dislike,
Yea, subject to your countenance—glad, or sorry,
As I saw it inclin'd. When was the hour
I ever contradicted your desire?
Or made it not mine too? Or which of your friends
Have I not strove to love, although I knew
He were mine enemy? What friend of mine
That had to him deriv'd your anger did I
Continue in my liking? nay, gave notice
He was from thence discharg'd? Sir, call to mind
That I have been your wife in this obedience
Upward of twenty years, and have been blest
With many children by you. If, in the course
And process of this time, you can report,
And prove it too, against mine honor aught—
My bond to wedlock or my love and duty,
Against your sacred person—in God's name
Turn me away; and let the foul'st contempt

13–57. **Sir . . . fulfill'd.** Here as elsewhere in this scene Shakespeare follows Holinshed (Bullough, IV, 467–68) so closely that he often merely versifies the chronicler's prose. 17. **indifferent:** impartial.
18. **equal:** fair. **proceeding:** legal process.
21. **put me off:** reject me. 25. **dislike:** displeasure.
32. **deriv'd:** drawn.

Shut door upon me, and so give me up
To the sharp'st kind of justice. Please you, sir,
The King your father was reputed for
A prince most prudent, of an excellent
And unmatch'd wit and judgment; Ferdinand,
My father, King of Spain, was reckon'd one
The wisest prince that there had reign'd by many
A year before. It is not to be question'd
That they had gather'd a wise council to them
Of every realm, that did debate this business,
Who deem'd our marriage lawful; wherefore I humbly
Beseech you, sir, to spare me, till I may
Be by my friends in Spain advis'd, whose counsel
I will implore. If not, i' th' name of God,
Your pleasure be fulfill'd!

Wol. You have here, lady
(And of your choice), these reverend fathers, men
Of singular integrity and learning,
Yea, the elect o' th' land, who are assembled
To plead your cause. It shall be therefore bootless
That longer you desire the court, as well
For your own quiet, as to rectify
What is unsettled in the King.

Cam. His Grace
Hath spoken well and justly; therefore, madam,
It's fit this royal session do proceed,
And that, without delay, their arguments
Be now produc'd and heard.

Q. Kath. Lord Cardinal,
To you I speak.

Wol. Your pleasure, madam?

Q. Kath. Sir,
I am about to weep; but thinking that
We are a queen (or long have dream'd so), certain
The daughter of a king, my drops of tears
I'll turn to sparks of fire.

Wol. Be patient yet.

Q. Kath. I will, when you are humble; nay, before,
Or God will punish me. I do believe
(Induc'd by potent circumstances) that
You are mine enemy, and make my challenge
You shall not be my judge; for it is you
Have blown this coal betwixt my lord and me—
Which God's dew quench! Therefore I say again,
I utterly abhor, yea, from my soul
Refuse you for my judge, whom, yet once more,
I hold my most malicious foe, and think not
At all a friend to truth.

Wol. I do profess
You speak not like yourself, who ever yet
Have stood to charity, and display'd th' effects

47. wit: intelligence. **61. bootless:** profitless.
62. desire the court: i.e. to delay its proceedings.
63–64. rectify . . . King: i.e. resolve Henry's doubts about his marriage. **74. before:** i.e. because you never will be humble.
75–121. I . . . by him. According to Holinshed (Bullough, IV, 469–70), "the queene in presence of the whole court most greevouslie accused the cardinall of untruth, deceit, wickednesse, & malice, which had sowne dissention betwixt hir and the king hir husband; and therefore openlie protested, that she did utterlie abhorre, refuse, and forsake such a judge, as was not onelie a most malicious enimie to hir, but also a manifest adversarie to all right and justice, and there with did she appeale unto the pope, committing hir whole cause to be judged of him." **77. challenge:** formal objection.
81. abhor: protest (a legal term). **86. stood to:** supported.

Of disposition gentle, and of wisdom
O'ertopping woman's pow'r. Madam, you do me wrong,
I have no spleen against you, nor injustice
For you or any. How far I have proceeded,
Or how far further shall, is warranted
By a commission from the consistory,
Yea, the whole consistory of Rome. You charge me
That I have blown this coal. I do deny it.
The King is present: if it be known to him
That I gainsay my deed, how may he wound,
And worthily, my falsehood! yea, as much
As you have done my truth. If he know
That I am free of your report, he knows
I am not of your wrong. Therefore in him
It lies to cure me, and the cure is to
Remove these thoughts from you; the which before
His Highness shall speak in, I do beseech
You, gracious madam, to unthink your speaking
And to say so no more.

Q. Kath. My lord, my lord,
I am a simple woman, much too weak
T' oppose your cunning. Y' are meek and humble-mouth'd,
You sign your place and calling, in full seeming,
With meekness and humility; but your heart
Is cramm'd with arrogancy, spleen, and pride.
You have, by fortune and his Highness' favors,
Gone slightly o'er low steps and now are mounted
Where pow'rs are your retainers, and your words
(Domestics to you) serve your will as't please
Yourself pronounce their office. I must tell you,
You tender more your person's honor than
Your high profession spiritual; that again
I do refuse you for my judge, and here,
Before you all, appeal unto the Pope,
To bring my whole cause 'fore his Holiness,
And to be judg'd by him.

She curtsies to the King and offers to depart.

Cam. The Queen is obstinate,
Stubborn to justice, apt to accuse it, and
Disdainful to be tried by't: 'tis not well.
She's going away.

King. Call her again.

Crier. Katherine Queen of England, come into the court.

Gent. Ush. Madam, you are call'd back.

Q. Kath. What need you note it? pray you keep your way;
When you are call'd, return. Now the Lord help!
They vex me past my patience. Pray you pass on.
I will not tarry; no, nor ever more
Upon this business my appearance make

89. spleen: malice.
96. gainsay my deed: i.e. deny what I have done.
97. worthily: properly.
99. free . . . report: innocent of what you charge me with.
100. am . . . wrong: have done no wrong to you. **103. in:** about.
108. sign: signalize. **in full seeming:** i.e. to all appearances.
112. slightly: easily. **113. pow'rs:** influential persons.
113–15. your words . . . office: i.e. words, like menial servants, are made to serve any function that you choose to give them (?).
116. tender more: care more for. **120. cause:** case.
122. Stubborn: stiff. **129. What:** why.

In any of their courts.
Exeunt Queen and her Attendants.
King. Go thy ways, Kate.
That man i' th' world who shall report he has
A better wife, let him in nought be trusted
For speaking false in that. Thou art alone
(If thy rare qualities, sweet gentleness,
Thy meekness saint-like, wife-like government,
Obeying in commanding, and thy parts
Sovereign and pious else, could speak thee out)
The queen of earthly queens. She's noble born;
And like her true nobility she has
Carried herself towards me.
Wol. Most gracious sir,
In humblest manner I require your Highness
That it shall please you to declare, in hearing
Of all these ears (for, where I am robb'd and bound,
There must I be unloos'd, although not there
At once and fully satisfied), whether ever I
Did broach this business to your Highness, or
Laid any scruple in your way which might
Induce you to the question on't? or ever
Have to you, but with thanks to God for such
A royal lady, spake one the least word that might
Be to the prejudice of her present state,
Or touch of her good person?
King. My Lord Cardinal,
I do excuse you; yea, upon mine honor,
I free you from't. You are not to be taught
That you have many enemies, that know not
Why they are so, but, like to village curs,
Bark when their fellows do: by some of these
The Queen is put in anger. Y' are excus'd;
But will you be more justified? You ever
Have wish'd the sleeping of this business, never desir'd
It to be stirr'd; but oft have hind'red, oft,
The passages made toward it. On my honor,
I speak my good Lord Card'nal to this point,
And thus far clear him. Now, what mov'd me to't,
I will be bold with time and your attention:
Then mark th' inducement. Thus it came; give heed
to't:
My conscience first receiv'd a tenderness,
Scruple, and prick, on certain speeches utter'd
By th' Bishop of Bayonne, then French embassador,
Who had been hither sent on the debating
[A] marriage 'twixt the Duke of Orleance and
Our daughter Mary. I' th' progress of this business,
Ere a determinate resolution, he
(I mean the Bishop) did require a respite,
Wherein he might the King his lord advertise
Whether our daughter were legitimate,
Respecting this our marriage with the dowager,
Sometimes our brother's wife. This respite shook
The bosom of my conscience, enter'd me,
Yea, with a spitting power, and made to tremble
The region of my breast, which forc'd such way,
That many maz'd considerings did throng
And press'd in with this caution. First, methought
I stood not in the smile of heaven, who had
Commanded nature, that my lady's womb,
If it conceiv'd a male-child by me, should
Do no more offices of life to't than
The grave does to th' dead; for her male issue
Or died where they were made, or shortly after
This world had air'd them. Hence I took a thought
This was a judgment on me, that my kingdom
(Well worthy the best heir o' th' world) should not
Be gladded in't by me. Then follows, that
I weigh'd the danger which my realms stood in
By this my issue's fail, and that gave to me
Many a groaning throe. Thus hulling in
The wild sea of my conscience, I did steer
Toward this remedy, whereupon we are
Now present here together: that's to say,
I meant to rectify my conscience—which
I then did feel full sick, and yet not well—
By all the reverend fathers of the land
And doctors learn'd. First I began in private
With you, my Lord of Lincoln. You remember
How under my oppression I did reek
When I first mov'd you.
Lin. Very well, my liege.
King. I have spoke long, be pleas'd yourself to say
How far you satisfied me.
Lin. So please your Highness,
The question did at first so stagger me,
Bearing a state of mighty moment in't
And consequence of dread, that I committed
The daring'st counsel which I had to doubt,
And did entreat your Highness to this course
Which you are running here.
King. I then mov'd you,
My Lord of Canterbury, and got your leave
To make this present summons. Unsolicited
I left no reverend person in this court;
But by particular consent proceeded
Under your hands and seals. Therefore go on,
For no dislike i' th' world against the person
Of the good Queen, but the sharp thorny points
Of my alleged reasons, drives this forward.
Prove but our marriage lawful, by my life
And kingly dignity, we are contented
To wear our mortal state to come with her,
Katherine our queen, before the primest creature

139. government: behavior.
140. Obeying: i.e. observing your own moral code (?). **parts:** qualities. **141. speak thee out:** describe you fully.
144. Carried: behaved. **149. satisfied:** repaid.
155. prejudice: impairment.
156. touch . . . person: taint of her good reputation.
157. excuse: exonerate. **166. passages:** proceedings.
167. I . . . point: i.e. I speak about the Cardinal's attitude in this matter.
175. Duke of Orleance: son (1519–59) of Francis I; later Henry II, King of France. **177. determinate resolution:** final decision.
178. require: request. **179. advertise:** take counsel with.
181. dowager: widow. **182. Sometimes:** formerly.
184. spitting: transfixing. **186. maz'd:** perplexed.
187. caution: warning. **193. Or:** either.
197. gladded in't: i.e. made happy with an heir.
200. hulling: drifting to and fro. **204. rectify:** set right.
209. How . . . reek: how I sweated in distress.
210. mov'd: applied to.
214–15. Bearing . . . dread: concerning a matter of great importance and terrifying consequences.
215–16. committed . . . doubt: i.e. doubted my own advice.
230. primest: most excellent.

That's paragon'd o' th' world.

Cam. So please your Highness,
The Queen being absent, 'tis a needful fitness
That we adjourn this court till further day.
Mean while must be an earnest motion
Made to the Queen to call back her appeal
She intends unto his Holiness.

King. [*Aside.*] I may perceive
These Cardinals trifle with me; I abhor
This dilatory sloth and tricks of Rome.
My learn'd and well-beloved servant, Cranmer,
Prithee return; with thy approach, I know,
My comfort comes along.—Break up the court!
I say, set on. *Exeunt in manner as they enter'd.*

ACT III, Scene I

Enter Queen *and her* Women *as at work.*

Q. Kath. Take thy lute, wench, my soul grows sad with troubles.
Sing, and disperse 'em if thou canst. Leave working.

Song

Orpheus with his lute made trees,
And the mountain tops that freeze,
Bow themselves when he did sing.
To his music plants and flowers
Ever sprung, as sun and showers
There had made a lasting spring.

Every thing that heard him play,
Even the billows of the sea,
Hung their heads, and then lay by.
In sweet music is such art,
Killing care and grief of heart
Fall asleep, or hearing, die.

Enter a Gentleman.

Q. Kath. How now?

Gent. And't please your Grace, the two great Cardinals
Wait in the presence.

Q. Kath. Would they speak with me?

Gent. They will'd me say so, madam.

Q. Kath. Pray their Graces
To come near. [*Exit Gentleman.*] What can be their business
With me, a poor weak woman, fall'n from favor?
I do not like their coming. Now I think on't,
They should be good men, their affairs as righteous.
But all hoods make not monks.

Enter the two Cardinals, Wolsey *and* Campeius.

Wol. Peace to your Highness!

Q. Kath. Your Graces find me here part of a huswife
(I would be all) against the worst may happen.
What are your pleasures with me, reverent lords?

Wol. May it please you, noble madam, to withdraw
Into your private chamber, we shall give you
The full cause of our coming.

Q. Kath. Speak it here;
There's nothing I have done yet, o' my conscience,
Deserves a corner. Would all other women
Could speak this with as free a soul as I do!
My lords, I care not (so much I am happy
Above a number) if my actions
Were tried by ev'ry tongue, ev'ry eye saw 'em,
Envy and base opinion set against 'em,
I know my life so even. If your business
Seek me out, and that way I am wife in,
Out with it boldly: truth loves open dealing.

Wol. *Tanta est erga te mentis integritas, regina serenissima*—

Q. Kath. O, good my lord, no Latin;
I am not such a truant since my coming,
As not to know the language I have liv'd in.
A strange tongue makes my cause more strange, suspicious;
Pray speak in English. Here are some will thank you,
If you speak truth, for their poor mistress' sake;
Believe me, she has had much wrong. Lord Cardinal,
The willing'st sin I ever yet committed
May be absolv'd in English.

Wol. Noble lady,
I am sorry my integrity should breed
(And service to his Majesty and you)
So deep suspicion, where all faith was meant.
We come not by the way of accusation
To taint that honor every good tongue blesses,
Nor to betray you any way to sorrow—
You have too much, good lady; but to know
How you stand minded in the weighty difference
Between the King and you, and to deliver
(Like free and honest men) our just opinions
And comforts to [your] cause.

Cam. Most honor'd madam,
My Lord of York, out of his noble nature,
Zeal and obedience he still bore your Grace,
Forgetting (like a good man) your late censure
Both of his truth and him (which was too far),
Offers, as I do, in a sign of peace,
His service and his counsel.

Q. Kath. [*Aside.*] To betray me.—
My lords, I thank you both for your good wills,
Ye speak like honest men (pray God ye prove so!),
But how to make ye suddenly an answer
In such a point of weight, so near mine honor
(More near my life, I fear), with my weak wit,
And to such men of gravity and learning,

231. paragon'd: regarded as a paragon. **234. motion:** request.

III.i. Location: London. The Queen's apartments.
3. Orpheus: in Greek mythology, a musician of legendary renown.
7. as: as if. **11. lay by:** rested.
17. presence: presence-chamber.

25. all: i.e. entirely given up (to the role of housewife). **against:** in anticipation that. **31. corner:** i.e. to hide in.
32. free: innocent. **36. Envy:** malice. **37. even:** consistent.
38. Seek . . . in: i.e. concerns me in my capacity as a wife.
41. Tanta . . . serenissima: so great is (my) integrity of mind toward you, most serene queen. **45. suspicious:** i.e. even suspicious.
49. willing'st: most deliberate. **59. deliver:** declare.
60. free: frank. **honest:** honorable. **just:** true.
65. far: severe. **66. in a sign:** as a token.
70. suddenly: extempore. **72. wit:** understanding.

In truth I know not. I was set at work
Among my maids, full little, God knows, looking
Either for such men or such business.
For her sake that I have been—for I feel
The last fit of my greatness—good your Graces,
Let me have time and counsel for my cause.
Alas, I am a woman, friendless, hopeless!
Wol. Madam, you wrong the King's love with these fears,
Your hopes and friends are infinite.
Q. Kath. In England
But little for my profit; can you think, lords,
That any Englishman dare give me counsel?
Or be a known friend, 'gainst his Highness' pleasure
(Though he be grown so desperate to be honest),
And live a subject? Nay forsooth, my friends,
They that must weigh out my afflictions,
They that my trust must grow to, live not here.
They are (as all my other comforts) far hence
In mine own country, lords.
Cam. I would your Grace
Would leave your griefs, and take my counsel.
Q. Kath. How, sir?
Cam. Put your main cause into the King's protection,
He's loving and most gracious. 'Twill be much
Both for your honor better and your cause;
For if the trial of the law o'ertake ye,
You'll part away disgrac'd.
Wol. He tells you rightly.
Q. Kath. Ye tell me what ye wish for both—my ruin.
Is this your Christian counsel? Out upon ye!
Heaven is above all yet; there sits a judge
That no king can corrupt.
Cam. Your rage mistakes us.
Q. Kath. The more shame for ye! Holy men I thought ye,
Upon my soul, two reverend cardinal virtues;
But cardinal sins and hollow hearts I fear ye.
Mend 'em for shame, my lords! Is this your comfort?
The cordial that ye bring a wretched lady,
A woman lost among ye, laugh'd at, scorn'd?
I will not wish ye half my miseries,
I have more charity. But say I warn'd ye;
Take heed, for heaven's sake take heed, lest at once
The burthen of my sorrows fall upon ye.
Wol. Madam, this is a mere distraction,
You turn the good we offer into envy.
Q. Kath. Ye turn me into nothing! Woe upon ye
And all such false professors! Would you have me
(If you have any justice, any pity,
If ye be any thing but churchmen's habits)
Put my sick cause into his hands that hates me?
Alas, h'as banish'd me his bed already,
His love, too long ago! I am old, my lords,
And all the fellowship I hold now with him
Is only my obedience. What can happen
To me above this wretchedness? All your studies
Make me a curse like this!
Cam. Your fears are worse.
Q. Kath. Have I liv'd thus long (let me speak myself,
Since virtue finds no friends) a wife, a true one?
A woman (I dare say without vainglory)
Never yet branded with suspicion?
Have I with all my full affections
Still met the King? lov'd him next heav'n? obey'd him?
Been, out of fondness, superstitious to him?
Almost forgot my pray'rs to content him?
And am I thus rewarded? 'Tis not well, lords.
Bring me a constant woman to her husband,
One that ne'er dream'd a joy beyond his pleasure;
And to that woman (when she has done most)
Yet will I add an honor—a great patience.
Wol. Madam, you wander from the good we aim at.
Q. Kath. My lord, I dare not make myself so guilty
To give up willingly that noble title
Your master wed me to. Nothing but death
Shall e'er divorce my dignities.
Wol. Pray hear me.
Q. Kath. Would I had never trod this English earth,
Or felt the flatteries that grow upon it!
Ye have angels' faces, but heaven knows your hearts.
What will become of me now, wretched lady?
I am the most unhappy woman living.
Alas, poor wenches, where are now your fortunes?
Shipwrack'd upon a kingdom, where no pity,
No friends, no hope, no kindred weep for me,
Almost no grave allow'd me. Like the lily,
That once was mistress of the field, and flourish'd,
I'll hang my head and perish.
Wol. If your Grace
Could but be brought to know our ends are honest,
You'ld feel more comfort. Why should we, good lady,
Upon what cause, wrong you? Alas, our places,
The way of our profession is against it;
We are to cure such sorrows, not to sow 'em.
For goodness sake, consider what you do,

74. set: seated. **78. fit:** phase (of a disease).
82–91. In . . . lords. "I need counsell to this case which toucheth me so neere," Holinshed reports Katherine as saying (Bullough, IV, 471), "& for anie counsell or freendship that I can find in England, they are not for my profit. What thinke you my lords, will anie Englishman counsell me, or be freend to me against the K. pleasure that is his subject? Naie foresooth. And as for my counsell in whom I will put my trust, they be not here, they be in Spaine in my owne countrie."
83. profit: advantage.
86. so desperate: i.e. sufficiently reckless.
88. weigh out: counterbalance. **97. part away:** depart.
101. mistakes: misjudges.
103. cardinal virtues: i.e. justice, prudence, temperance, and fortitude. These with the three theological virtues of faith, hope, and charity constitute the seven virtues corresponding to the seven deadly sins to which Katherine alludes in the next line.
106. cordial: restorative. **110. at once:** all at once.
111. burthen: burden.

112. mere distraction: absolute frenzy.
115. professors: i.e. those who profess religion.
117. habits: robes. **119. h'as:** he has.
120. old. Katherine was forty-three, six years older than her husband.
121. fellowship: intercourse.
123–24. All . . . Make: i.e. I defy all your exertions to make.
125. speak: speak for. **131. superstitious:** idolatrous.
148. wenches: i.e. women in waiting on Queen Katherine.
154. ends are honest: purposes are honorable.
156. places: offices.

How you may hurt yourself—ay, utterly
Grow from the King's acquaintance, by this carriage.
The hearts of princes kiss obedience,
So much they love it; but to stubborn spirits
They swell and grow, as terrible as storms.
I know you have a gentle, noble temper,
A soul as even as a calm; pray think us
Those we profess, peacemakers, friends, and servants.
Cam. Madam, you'll find it so. You wrong your virtues
With these weak women's fears. A noble spirit
As yours was put into you, ever casts
Such doubts, as false coin, from it. The King loves you,
Beware you lose it not. For us (if you please
To trust us in your business), we are ready
To use our utmost studies in your service.
Q. Kath. Do what ye will, my lords; and pray forgive me;
If I have us'd myself unmannerly,
You know I am a woman, lacking wit
To make a seemly answer to such persons.
Pray do my service to his Majesty;
He has my heart yet and shall have my prayers
While I shall have my life. Come, reverend fathers,
Bestow your counsels on me. She now begs
That little thought, when she set footing here,
She should have bought her dignities so dear. *Exeunt.*

Scene II

Enter the Duke of Norfolk, Duke of Suffolk, Lord Surrey, *and* Lord Chamberlain.

Nor. If you will now unite in your complaints,
And force them with a constancy, the Cardinal
Cannot stand under them. If you omit
The offer of this time, I cannot promise
But that you shall sustain moe new disgraces
With these you bear already.
Sur. I am joyful
To meet the least occasion that may give me
Remembrance of my father-in-law, the Duke,
To be reveng'd on him.
Suf. Which of the peers
Have uncontemn'd gone by him, or at least
Strangely neglected? When did he regard
The stamp of nobleness in any person
Out of himself?
Cham. My lords, you speak your pleasures.
What he deserves of you and me I know;
What we can do to him (though now the time
Gives way to us) I much fear. If you cannot
Bar his access to th' King, never attempt
Any thing on him; for he hath a witchcraft
Over the King in 's tongue.
Nor. O, fear him not,
His spell in that is out. The King hath found
Matter against him that for ever mars
The honey of his language. No, he's settled
(Not to come off) in his displeasure.
Sur. Sir,
I should be glad to hear such news as this
Once every hour.
Nor. Believe it, this is true.
In the divorce his contrary proceedings
Are all unfolded; wherein he appears
As I would wish mine enemy.
Sur. How came
His practices to light?
Suf. Most strangely.
Sur. O how? how?
Suf. The Cardinal's letters to the Pope miscarried,
And came to th' eye o' th' King, wherein was read
How that the Cardinal did entreat his Holiness
To stay the judgment o' th' divorce; for if
It did take place, "I do," quoth he, "perceive
My king is tangled in affection to
A creature of the Queen's, Lady Anne Bullen."
Sur. Has the King this?
Suf. Believe it.
Sur. Will this work?
Cham. The King in this perceives him, how he coasts
And hedges his own way. But in this point
All his tricks founder, and he brings his physic
After his patient's death. The King already
Hath married the fair lady.
Sur. Would he had!
Suf. May you be happy in your wish, my lord,
For I profess you have it.
Sur. Now all my joy
Trace the conjunction!
Suf. My amen to't!
Nor. All men's!
Suf. There's order given for her coronation.
Marry, this is yet but young, and may be left

161. from: away from. **carriage:** behavior.
176. us'd myself: behaved.
179. do my service: convey my respects.

III.ii. Location: London. The palace.
o.s.d. Lord Surrey. Actually, Thomas Howard, the Earl of Surrey whom Wolsey had sent to Ireland to prevent his aid to his father-n-law Buckingham (see II.i.4–44 and lines 6–9 below), had succeeded his father as Duke of Norfolk in 1524.
2. force: urge. **3–4. omit . . . time:** neglect this opportunity.
11. Strangely neglected: i.e. not strangely neglected (by extension of the negative sense of *uncontemn'd*).
13. Out of: besides.

16. Gives way to: favors.
17–18. attempt . . . him: attack him in any way.
20. spell: magic. **out:** exhausted. **23. come off:** escape.
26. contrary: contradictory, inconsistent. **29. practices:** plots.
30–33. The Cardinal's . . . divorce. Determined to block the King's marriage with Anne Bullen, Wolsey, says Holinshed (Bullough, IV, 472), "began with all diligence to disappoint that match, which by reason of the misliking that he had to the woman, he judged ought to be avoided more than present death. While the matter stood in this state, and that the cause of the queene was to be heard and judged at Rome, by reason of the appeale which by hir was put in: the cardinall required the pope by letters and secret messengers, that in anie wise he should defer the judgement of the divorse, till he might frame the kings mind to his purpose."
33. stay the judgment: delay the proceedings.
38–39. coasts And hedges: i.e. follows indirect courses, as by coasts and hedgerows.
41–42. The King . . . lady. Although Shakespeare thus places Henry's second marriage before Wolsey's fall (which occurred in 1529), the secret wedding was actually performed in January 1533, three years after Wolsey's death.
45. Trace the conjunction: follow the union. **47. young:** recent.

To some ears unrecounted. But, my lords,
She is a gallant creature, and complete
In mind and feature. I persuade me, from her
Will fall some blessing to this land, which shall
In it be memoriz'd.
Sur. But will the King
Digest this letter of the Cardinal's?
The Lord forbid!
Nor. Marry, amen!
Suf. No, no;
There be moe wasps that buzz about his nose
Will make this sting the sooner. Cardinal Campeius
Is stol'n away to Rome, hath ta'en no leave,
Has left the cause o' th' King unhandled, and
Is posted, as the agent of our Cardinal,
To second all his plot. I do assure you
The King cried "Ha!" at this.
Cham. Now God incense him,
And let him cry "Ha!" louder!
Nor. But, my lord,
When returns Cranmer?
Suf. He is return'd in his opinions, which
Have satisfied the King for his divorce,
Together with all famous colleges
Almost in Christendom. Shortly, I believe,
His second marriage shall be publish'd, and
Her coronation. Katherine no more
Shall be call'd Queen, but Princess Dowager
And widow to Prince Arthur.
Nor. This same Cranmer's
A worthy fellow, and hath ta'en much pain
In the King's business.
Suf. He has, and we shall see him
For it an archbishop.
Nor. So I hear.
Suf. 'Tis so.

Enter WOLSEY *and* CROMWELL.

The Cardinal!
Nor. Observe, observe, he's moody.
Wol. The packet, Cromwell, gave't you the King?
Crom. To his own hand, in 's bedchamber.
Wol. Look'd he
O' th' inside of the paper?
Crom. Presently
He did unseal them, and the first he view'd,
He did it with a serious mind; a heed
Was in his countenance. You he bade
Attend him here this morning.
Wol. Is he ready
To come abroad?
Crom. I think by this he is.
Wol. Leave me a while. *Exit Cromwell.*
[*Aside.*] It shall be to the Duchess of Alanson,
The French king's sister; he shall marry her.
Anne Bullen? No; I'll no Anne Bullens for him,
There's more in't than fair visage. Bullen?
No, we'll no Bullens. Speedily I wish
To hear from Rome. The Marchioness of Pembroke?
Nor. He's discontented.
Suf. May be he hears the King
Does whet his anger to him.
Sur. Sharp enough,
Lord, for thy justice!
Wol. [*Aside.*] The late Queen's gentlewoman? a knight's daughter,
To be her mistress' mistress? the Queen's queen?
This candle burns not clear, 'tis I must snuff it,
Then out it goes. What though I know her virtuous
And well deserving? yet I know her for
A spleeny Lutheran, and not wholesome to
Our cause, that she should lie i' th' bosom of
Our hard-rul'd king. Again, there is sprung up
An heretic, an arch-one, Cranmer; one
Hath crawl'd into the favor of the King,
And is his oracle.
Nor. He's vex'd at something.

Enter KING, *reading of a schedule,* [*and* LOVELL].

Sur. I would 'twere something that would fret the string,
The master-cord on 's heart!
Suf. The King, the King!
King. What piles of wealth hath he accumulated
To his own portion! and what expense by th' hour
Seems to flow from him! How, i' th' name of thrift,
Does he rake this together? Now, my lords,
Saw you the Cardinal?
Nor. My lord, we have
Stood here observing him. Some strange commotion
Is in his brain; he bites his lip, and starts,
Stops on a sudden, looks upon the ground,
Then lays his finger on his temple; straight
Springs out into fast gait, then stops again,
Strikes his breast hard, and anon he casts
His eye against the moon. In most strange postures
We have seen him set himself.
King. It may well be,
There is a mutiny in 's mind. This morning
Papers of state he sent me to peruse,
As I requir'd; and wot you what I found

49. **complete:** perfect. 52. **memoriz'd:** made memorable.
53. **Digest:** put up with, "swallow."
56–57. **Cardinal . . . leave.** On the contrary, Holinshed reports (Bullough, IV, 471) that after the divorce proceedings had dragged on for several months Campeius "tooke his leave of the king and nobilitie, and returned towards Rome." 58. **unhandled:** i.e. unresolved.
59. **Is posted:** has hastened.
61–62. **The King . . . louder.** See note to I.ii.186.
64. **He . . . opinions:** he has sent his opinions in advance. In January 1530 Cranmer had been sent abroad with the Earl of Wiltshire, ambassador to the court of Charles V. On Henry's canvass of continental scholars, which Cranmer had proposed in 1529, see note to II.ii.86–96.
68. **publish'd:** proclaimed. The marriage "was kept so secret," says Holinshed (Bullough, IV, 482), "that verie few knew it till Easter next insuing [1533], when it was perceived that she was with child."
72. **pain:** pains.
74. **archbishop.** Cranmer succeeded William Warham as Archbishop of Canterbury in March 1533.
78. **paper:** i.e. wrapper. **Presently:** at once.

83. **this:** now.
85–86. **It . . . her.** An anachronism; this scheme of Wolsey's is assigned by Holinshed (see note to II.ii.24–28) to 1527, shortly before Margaret, Duchess of Alençon, married King Henry of Navarre.
90. **Marchioness of Pembroke.** See II.iii.63.
94. **late:** recent, former. 99. **spleeny:** ardent.
101. **hard-rul'd:** i.e. difficult to guide. 103. **Hath:** who has.
104 s.d. **schedule:** scroll of paper. 105. **fret:** gnaw through.
106. **on 's:** of his. 115. **straight:** at once.
122. **wot:** know.

There (on my conscience, put unwittingly)?
Forsooth, an inventory, thus importing
The several parcels of his plate, his treasure,
Rich stuffs, and ornaments of household, which
I find at such proud rate, that it outspeaks
Possession of a subject.
Nor. It's heaven's will!
Some spirit put this paper in the packet,
To bless your eye withal.
King. If we did think
His contemplation were above the earth,
And fix'd on spiritual object, he should still
Dwell in his musings, but I am afraid
His thinkings are below the moon, not worth
His serious considering.

King takes his seat; whispers Lovell, who goes to the Cardinal.

Wol. Heaven forgive me!
Ever God bless your Highness!
King. Good my lord,
You are full of heavenly stuff, and bear the inventory
Of your best graces in your mind; the which
You were now running o'er. You have scarce time
To steal from spiritual leisure a brief span
To keep your earthly audit; sure in that
I deem you an ill husband, and am [glad]
To have you therein my companion.
Wol. Sir,
For holy offices I have a time; a time
To think upon the part of business which
I bear i' th' state; and Nature does require
Her times of preservation, which perforce
I, her frail son, amongst my brethren mortal,
Must give my tendance to.
King. You have said well.
Wol. And ever may your Highness yoke together
(As I will lend you cause) my doing well
With my well saying!
King. 'Tis well said again,
And 'tis a kind of good deed to say well,
And yet words are no deeds. My father lov'd you,
He said he did, and with his deed did crown
His word upon you. Since I had my office,
I have kept you next my heart, have not alone
Employ'd you where high profits might come home,
But par'd my present havings, to bestow
My bounties upon you.
Wol. [*Aside.*] What should this mean?
Sur. [*Aside.*] The Lord increase this business!
King. Have I not made you
The prime man of the state? I pray you tell me,
If what I now pronounce you have found true;
And if you may confess it, say withal

If you are bound to us, or no. What say you?
Wol. My sovereign, I confess your royal graces
Show'r'd on me daily have been more than could
My studied purposes requite, which went
Beyond all man's endeavors. My endeavors
Have ever come too short of my desires,
Yet fill'd with my abilities. Mine own ends
Have been mine so, that evermore they pointed
To th' good of your most sacred person and
The profit of the state. For your great graces
Heap'd upon me, poor undeserver, I
Can nothing render but allegiant thanks,
My pray'rs to heaven for you, my loyalty,
Which ever has and ever shall be growing,
Till death, that winter, kill it.
King. Fairly answer'd.
A loyal and obedient subject is
Therein illustrated; the honor of it
Does pay the act of it, as i' th' contrary
The foulness is the punishment. I presume
That, as my hand has open'd bounty to you,
My heart dropp'd love, my pow'r rain'd honor, more
On you than any, so your hand and heart,
Your brain, and every function of your power,
Should, notwithstanding that your bond of duty,
As 'twere in love's particular, be more
To me, your friend, than any.
Wol. I do profess
That for your Highness' good I ever labor'd
More than mine own; that am, have, and will be
(Though all the world should crack their duty to you
And throw it from their soul, though perils did
Abound, as thick as thought could make 'em, and
Appear in forms more horrid), yet my duty,
As doth a rock against the chiding flood,
Should the approach of this wild river break,
And stand unshaken yours.
King. 'Tis nobly spoken.
Take notice, lords, he has a loyal breast,
For you have seen him open't. Read o'er this,
[*Giving him papers.*]
And after, this, and then to breakfast with
What appetite you have.

Exit King, frowning upon the Cardinal; the Nobles throng after him, smiling and whispering.

Wol. What should this mean?
What sudden anger's this? How have I reap'd it?
He parted frowning from me, as if ruin
Leap'd from his eyes. So looks the chafed lion
Upon the daring huntsman that has gall'd him;
Then makes him nothing. I must read this paper;
I fear, the story of his anger. 'Tis so!

124. importing: signifying.
125. several parcels: various items. **126. stuffs:** fabrics.
127. proud: high. **outspeaks:** exceeds (?).
134. below the moon: i.e. worldly.
140. spiritual leisure: i.e. religious concerns.
142. ill husband: bad manager. **149. tendance:** attention.
154–56. My . . . you. In 1507 Henry VII had appointed young Wolsey his chaplain and two years later named him Dean of Lincoln.
155. crown: complete. **159. havings:** possessions.
162. prime: first.
166. graces: favors.
171. fill'd with: filled out to the capacity of. Most editors emend to *fil'd with* = kept pace with.
172. so: to this extent. **176. allegiant:** loyal.
181. it: i.e. being loyal to one's sovereign. **182. pay:** repay.
183. foulness: i.e. the moral taint of disloyalty.
188. that . . . duty: i.e. your priestly vows.
189. in love's particular: in the special case of a person you loved.
192. have: have been. **193. crack:** violate.
198. break: stem, check. **206. chafed:** infuriated.
207. gall'd: wounded.

This paper has undone me. 'Tis th' accompt
Of all that world of wealth I have drawn together
For mine own ends (indeed to gain the popedom
And fee my friends in Rome). O negligence!
Fit for a fool to fall by. What cross devil
Made me put this main secret in the packet
I sent the King? Is there no way to cure this?
No new device to beat this from his brains?
I know 'twill stir him strongly; yet I know
A way, if it take right, in spite of fortune
Will bring me off again. What's this? "To th' Pope"?
The letter, as I live, with all the business
I writ to 's Holiness. Nay then, farewell!
I have touch'd the highest point of all my greatness,
And, from that full meridian of my glory,
I haste now to my setting. I shall fall
Like a bright exhalation in the evening,
And no man see me more.

Enter to Wolsey the Dukes of Norfolk *and* Suffolk, *the* Earl of Surrey, *and the* Lord Chamberlain.

Nor. Hear the King's pleasure, Cardinal, who commands you
To render up the great seal presently
Into our hands, and to confine yourself
To Asher-house, my Lord of Winchester's,
Till you hear further from his Highness.
Wol. Stay!
Where's your commission, lords? Words cannot carry
Authority so weighty.
Suf. Who dare cross 'em,
Bearing the King's will from his mouth expressly?
Wol. Till I find more than will or words to do it
(I mean your malice), know, officious lords,
I dare and must deny it. Now I feel
Of what coarse metal ye are moulded, envy,
How eagerly ye follow my disgraces
As if it fed ye, and how sleek and wanton
Ye appear in every thing may bring my ruin!
Follow your envious courses, men of malice!

210–13. 'Tis . . . Rome. One of the charges brought against Wolsey, says Holinshed (Bullough, IV, 474), was "that he had sent innumerable substance to Rome, for the obteining of his dignities, to the great impoverishment of the realme." **210. accompt:** account.
213. fee: pay, bribe. **214. cross:** perverse.
215. main: extremely important. **219. take right:** succeed.
224. meridian: highest point. **226. exhalation:** meteor.
228–50. Hear . . . it. This altercation between Wolsey and the nobles closely follows Holinshed (Bullough, IV, 473): "the seventeenth of November the king sent the two dukes of Norffolke and Suffolke to the cardinals place at Westminster, who went as they were commanded, and finding the cardinall there, they declared that the kings pleasure was that he should surrender up the great seale into their hands, and to depart simplie unto Asher, which was an house situat nigh unto Hampton court, belonging to the bishoprike of Winchester. The cardinall demanded of them their commission that gave them such authoritie, who answered againe, that they were sufficient commissioners, and had authoritie to doo no lesse by the kings mouth. Notwithstanding, he would in no wise agree in that behalfe, without further knowledge of their authoritie, saieng; that the great seale was delivered him by the kings person, to injoy the ministration thereof, with the roome of the chancellor for the terme of his life, whereof for his suertie he had the kings letters patents."
229. presently: at once.
231. Asher-house: Esher, the Bishop of Winchester's residence near Hampton Court. At the time of his fall Wolsey himself—the most insatiable pluralist of the age—was Bishop of Winchester.
233. commission: warrant. **234. cross:** resist.
236. do it: i.e. carry authority. **241. wanton:** loose, impetuous.

You have Christian warrant for 'em, and no doubt
In time will find their fit rewards. That seal
You ask with such a violence, the King
(Mine and your master) with his own hand gave me;
Bade me enjoy it, with the place and honors,
During my life; and, to confirm his goodness,
Tied it by letters-patents. Now, who'll take it?
Sur. The King, that gave it.
Wol. It must be himself then.
Sur. Thou art a proud traitor, priest.
Wol. Proud lord, thou liest!
Within these forty hours Surrey durst better
Have burnt that tongue than said so.
Sur. Thy ambition,
Thou scarlet sin, robb'd this bewailing land
Of noble Buckingham, my father-in-law;
The heads of all thy brother cardinals
(With thee and all thy best parts bound together)
Weigh'd not a hair of his. Plague of your policy!
You sent me deputy for Ireland,
Far from his succor, from the King, from all
That might have mercy on the fault thou gav'st him;
Whilst your great goodness, out of holy pity,
Absolv'd him with an axe.
Wol. This, and all else
This talking lord can lay upon my credit,
I answer is most false. The Duke by law
Found his deserts. How innocent I was
From any private malice in his end,
His noble jury and foul cause can witness.
If I lov'd many words, lord, I should tell you
You have as little honesty as honor,
That in the way of loyalty and truth
Toward the King, my ever royal master,
Dare mate a sounder man than Surrey can be,
And all that love his follies.
Sur. By my soul,
Your long coat, priest, protects you, thou shouldst feel
My sword i' th' life-blood of thee else. My lords,
Can ye endure to hear this arrogance?
And from this fellow? If we live thus tamely,
To be thus jaded by a piece of scarlet,
Farewell nobility! Let his Grace go forward,
And dare us with his cap, like larks.
Wol. All goodness
Is poison to thy stomach.
Sur. Yes, that goodness
Of gleaning all the land's wealth into one,
Into your own hands, Card'nal, by extortion;
The goodness of your intercepted packets
You writ to th' Pope against the King. Your goodness,
Since you provoke me, shall be most notorious.
My Lord of Norfolk, as you are truly noble,
As you respect the common good, the state

244. Christian warrant: i.e. an example in the behavior of other (bad) Christians.
250. letters-patents: documents openly conferring a right or power.
258. parts: qualities. **259. Weigh'd:** i.e. were worth.
262. fault . . . him: offense you charged him with.
265. lay . . . credit: i.e. blame me for. **272. in the way:** as regards.
274. mate: match. **280. jaded:** ridden.
282. dare . . . larks: daze us with his cardinal's hat, as larks are netted with the help of a piece of red cloth.

Of our despis'd nobility, our issues
(Whom, if he live, will scarce be gentlemen),
Produce the grand sum of his sins, the articles
Collected from his life. I'll startle you
Worse than the sacring bell, when the brown wench
Lay kissing in your arms, Lord Cardinal.
Wol. How much, methinks, I could despise this man,
But that I am bound in charity against it!
Nor. Those articles, my lord, are in the King's hand:
But thus much, they are foul ones.
Wol. So much fairer
And spotless shall mine innocence arise
When the King knows my truth.
Sur. This cannot save you.
I thank my memory, I yet remember
Some of these articles, and out they shall.
Now, if you can blush, and cry "Guilty," Cardinal,
You'll show a little honesty.
Wol. Speak on, sir,
I dare your worst objections. If I blush,
It is to see a nobleman want manners.
Sur. I had rather want those than my head. Have at you!
First, that without the King's assent or knowledge,
You wrought to be a legate, by which power
You maim'd the jurisdiction of all bishops.
Nor. Then, that in all you writ to Rome, or else
To foreign princes, "*Ego et Rex meus*"
Was still inscrib'd; in which you brought the King
To be your servant.
Suf. Then, that without the knowledge
Either of King or Council, when you went
Ambassador to the Emperor, you made bold
To carry into Flanders the great seal.
Sur. *Item*, you sent a large commission
To Gregory de Cassado, to conclude,
Without the King's will or the state's allowance,
A league between his Highness and Ferrara.
Suf. That out of mere ambition, you have caus'd
Your holy hat to be stamp'd on the King's coin.
Sur. Then, that you have sent innumerable substance
(By what means got, I leave to your own conscience)
To furnish Rome, and to prepare the ways
You have for dignities, to the mere undoing
Of all the kingdom. Many more there are,
Which since they are of you, and odious,

291. issues: sons. **293. articles:** list of charges.
295. sacring bell: bell rung at the most solemn moment of the Mass.
299. hand: i.e. possession.
300. thus much: i.e. this much I can say.
302. truth: loyalty. **304. shall:** i.e. shall come.
307. objections: accusations. **308. want:** lack.
310–32. First . . . with. These seven charges against Wolsey are drawn from a list of nine that Holinshed records (Bullough, IV, 474).
311. wrought: worked. **legate:** papal representative.
314. Ego et Rex meus: my king and I.
315. still inscrib'd: i.e. always prominently displayed.
320. Item: further, also. **large:** having full power to act.
322. allowance: assent. **324. mere:** pure.
325. holy hat: i.e. cardinal's hat.
326. innumerable substance: measureless wealth. See note to lines 210–13. **329. mere:** utter.

I will not taint my mouth with.
Cham. O my lord,
Press not a falling man too far! 'tis virtue.
His faults lie open to the laws, let them,
Not you, correct him. My heart weeps to see him
So little of his great self.
Sur. I forgive him.
Suf. Lord Cardinal, the King's further pleasure is—
Because all those things you have done of late
By your power legative within this kingdom
Fall into th' compass of a *praemunire*—
That therefore such a writ be sued against you,
To forfeit all your goods, lands, tenements,
[Chattels], and whatsoever, and to be
Out of the King's protection. This is my charge.
Nor. And so we'll leave you to your meditations
How to live better. For your stubborn answer
About the giving back the great seal to us,
The King shall know it, and, no doubt, shall thank you.
So fare you well, my little good Lord Cardinal.
Exeunt all but Wolsey.
Wol. So farewell—to the little good you bear me.
Farewell? a long farewell to all my greatness!
This is the state of man: to-day he puts forth
The tender leaves of hopes, to-morrow blossoms,
And bears his blushing honors thick upon him;
The third day comes a frost, a killing frost,
And when he thinks, good easy man, full surely
His greatness is a-ripening, nips his root,
And then he falls as I do. I have ventur'd,
Like little wanton boys that swim on bladders,
This many summers in a sea of glory,
But far beyond my depth. My high-blown pride
At length broke under me, and now has left me,
Weary and old with service, to the mercy
Of a rude stream that must for ever hide me.
Vain pomp and glory of this world, I hate ye!
I feel my heart new open'd. O how wretched
Is that poor man that hangs on princes' favors!
There is, betwixt that smile we would aspire to,
That sweet aspect of princes, and their ruin,
More pangs and fears than wars or women have;
And when he falls, he falls like Lucifer,
Never to hope again.

Enter CROMWELL, *standing amazed.*

Why, how now, Cromwell?
Crom. I have no power to speak, sir.
Wol. What, amaz'd
At my misfortunes? Can thy spirit wonder
A great man should decline? Nay, and you weep
I am fall'n indeed.
Crom. How does your Grace?
Wol. Why, well;

339. legative: pertaining to a legate.
340. Fall . . . praemunire: constitute violations of the statute of *praemunire* (which made it illegal to submit to a foreign court—for example, the Roman *curia*—matters pertaining to the king's court).
341. sued: issued. **354. blushing:** glowing.
356. easy: easygoing. **359. wanton:** playful.
364. rude: rough. **368. aspire:** rise.
369. their ruin: i.e. the ruin they cause.
372 s.d. amazed: astounded. **375. and:** if.

Never so truly happy, my good Cromwell;
I know myself now, and I feel within me
A peace above all earthly dignities,
A still and quiet conscience. The King has cur'd me,
I humbly thank his Grace; and from these shoulders,
These ruin'd pillars, out of pity taken
A load would sink a navy—too much honor.
O, 'tis a burden, Cromwell, 'tis a burden
Too heavy for a man that hopes for heaven!
Crom. I am glad your Grace has made that right use of it.
Wol. I hope I have. I am able now, methinks
(Out of a fortitude of soul I feel),
To endure more miseries and greater far
Than my weak-hearted enemies dare offer.
What news abroad?
Crom. The heaviest and the worst
Is your displeasure with the King.
Wol. God bless him!
Crom. The next is, that Sir Thomas More is chosen
Lord Chancellor in your place.
Wol. That's somewhat sudden;
But he's a learned man. May he continue
Long in his Highness' favor, and do justice
For truth's sake and his conscience, that his bones,
When he has run his course and sleeps in blessings,
May have a tomb of orphants' tears wept on him!
What more?
Crom. That Cranmer is return'd with welcome,
Install'd Lord Archbishop of Canterbury.
Wol. That's news indeed.
Crom. Last, that the Lady Anne,
Whom the King hath in secrecy long married,
This day was view'd in open as his queen,
Going to chapel; and the voice is now
Only about her coronation.
Wol. There was the weight that pull'd me down. O Cromwell,
The King has gone beyond me! All my glories
In that one woman I have lost for ever.
No sun shall ever usher forth mine honors,
Or gild again the noble troops that waited
Upon my smiles. Go get thee from me, Cromwell!
I am a poor fall'n man, unworthy now
To be thy lord and master. Seek the King!
That sun, I pray, may never set! I have told him
What, and how true, thou art; he will advance thee.
Some little memory of me will stir him
(I know his noble nature) not to let
Thy hopeful service perish too. Good Cromwell,
Neglect him not; make use now, and provide
For thine own future safety.
Crom. O my lord,
Must I then leave you? Must I needs forgo
So good, so noble, and so true a master?
Bear witness, all that have not hearts of iron,
With what a sorrow Cromwell leaves his lord.
The King shall have my service; but my pray'rs
For ever and for ever shall be yours.
Wol. Cromwell, I did not think to shed a tear
In all my miseries; but thou hast forc'd me
(Out of thy honest truth) to play the woman.
Let's dry our eyes; and thus far hear me, Cromwell,
And when I am forgotten, as I shall be,
And sleep in dull cold marble where no mention
Of me more must be heard of, say I taught thee;
Say Wolsey, that once trod the ways of glory,
And sounded all the depths and shoals of honor,
Found thee a way, out of his wrack, to rise in;
A sure and safe one, though thy master miss'd it.
Mark but my fall, and that that ruin'd me:
Cromwell, I charge thee, fling away ambition!
By that sin fell the angels; how can man then
(The image of his Maker) hope to win by it?
Love thyself last, cherish those hearts that hate thee;
Corruption wins not more than honesty.
Still in thy right hand carry gentle peace
To silence envious tongues. Be just, and fear not;
Let all the ends thou aim'st at be thy country's,
Thy God's, and truth's; then if thou fall'st, O Cromwell,
Thou fall'st a blessed martyr!
Serve the King, and—prithee lead me in.
There take an inventory of all I have,
To the last penny, 'tis the King's. My robe,
And my integrity to heaven, is all
I dare now call mine own. O Cromwell, Cromwell,
Had I but serv'd my God with half the zeal
I serv'd my king, He would not in mine age
Have left me naked to mine enemies.
Crom. Good sir, have patience.
Wol. So I have. Farewell
The hopes of court! my hopes in heaven do dwell.
Exeunt.

ACT IV, SCENE I

Enter two GENTLEMEN, *meeting one another.*

1. Gent. Y' are well met once again.
2. Gent. So are you.
1. Gent. You come to take your stand here, and behold
The Lady Anne pass from her coronation?
2. Gent. 'Tis all my business. At our last encounter,
The Duke of Buckingham came from his trial.
1. Gent. 'Tis very true; but that time offer'd sorrow,
This, general joy.
2. Gent. 'Tis well. The citizens

392. displeasure: disgrace.
393–406. The next . . . coronation. Of the events here listed as virtually simultaneous, Wolsey's fall and Sir Thomas More's appointment as chancellor occurred in 1529, Cranmer's consecration as Archbishop of Canterbury and the King's second marriage in 1533.
399. orphants' tears. As chancellor, More would be legally responsible for orphans in their minority. 405. voice: talk.
408. gone beyond: overreached.
420. make use: seize the opportunity.

436. sounded: fathomed.
455–57. Had . . . enemies. According to Holinshed (Bullough, IV, 476), Wolsey said as he lay dying, "if I had served God as diligentlie as I have doone the king, he would not have given me over in my greie haires."

IV.i. Location: Westminster. A street.

I am sure have shown at full their royal minds—
As, let 'em have their rights, they are ever forward
In celebration of this day with shows,
Pageants, and sights of honor.

1. Gent. Never greater,
Nor, I'll assure you, better taken, sir.

2. Gent. May I be bold to ask what that contains,
That paper in your hand?

1. Gent. Yes, 'tis the list
Of those that claim their offices this day
By custom of the coronation.
The Duke of Suffolk is the first, and claims
To be High Steward; next, the Duke of Norfolk,
He to be Earl Marshal. You may read the rest.

[*2. Gent.*] I thank you, sir; had I not known those customs
I should have been beholding to your paper.
But I beseech you, what's become of Katherine,
The Princess Dowager? How goes her business?

1. Gent. That I can tell you too. The Archbishop
Of Canterbury, accompanied with other
Learned and reverend fathers of his order,
Held a late court at Dunstable—six miles off
From Ampthill, where the Princess lay—to which
She was often cited by them, but appear'd not;
And, to be short, for not appearance and
The King's late scruple, by the main assent
Of all these learned men she was divorc'd,
And the late marriage made of none effect;
Since which she was remov'd to Kimmalton,
Where she remains now sick.

2. Gent. Alas, good lady! [*Trumpets.*]
The trumpets sound; stand close, the Queen is coming. *Hoboys.*

THE ORDER OF THE CORONATION

1. *A lively flourish of trumpets.*
2. *Then, two* JUDGES.
3. LORD CHANCELLOR, *with purse and mace before him.*
4. QUIRISTERS, *singing.* *Music.*
5. MAYOR OF LONDON, *bearing the mace. Then* GARTER, *in his coat of arms, and on his head he wore a gilt copper crown.*
6. MARQUESS DORSET, *bearing a sceptre of gold, on his head a demi-coronal of gold. With him, the* EARL OF SURREY, *bearing the rod of silver with the dove, crowned with an earl's coronet. Collars of Esses.*
7. DUKE OF SUFFOLK, *in his robe of estate, his coronet on his head, bearing a long white wand, as High Steward. With him, the* DUKE OF NORFOLK, *with the rod of marshalship, a coronet on his head. Collars of Esses.*
8. *A canopy borne by four of the* CINQUE-PORTS; *under it, the* QUEEN *in her robe, in her hair, richly adorned with pearl, crowned. On each side her, the* BISHOPS OF LONDON *and* WINCHESTER.
9. *The old* DUCHESS OF NORFOLK, *in a coronal of gold, wrought with flowers, bearing the Queen's train.*
10. *Certain* LADIES *or* COUNTESSES, *with plain circlets of gold without flowers.*

Exeunt, first passing over the stage in order and state, and then a great flourish of trumpets.

2. Gent. A royal train, believe me. These I know.
Who's that that bears the sceptre?

1. Gent. Marquess Dorset,
And that the Earl of Surrey, with the rod.

2. Gent. A bold brave gentleman. That should be
The Duke of Suffolk.

1. Gent. 'Tis the same: High Steward.

2. Gent. And that my Lord of Norfolk?

1. Gent. Yes.

2. Gent. Heaven bless thee!
[*Looking on the Queen.*]
Thou hast the sweetest face I ever look'd on.
Sir, as I have a soul, she is an angel;
Our king has all the Indies in his arms,
And more and richer, when he strains that lady.
I cannot blame his conscience.

1. Gent. They that bear
The cloth of honor over her, are four barons
Of the Cinque-Ports.

2. Gent. Those men are happy, and so are all are near her.
I take it, she that carries up the train
Is that old noble lady, Duchess of Norfolk.

1. Gent. It is, and all the rest are countesses.

2. Gent. Their coronets say so. These are stars indeed.

[*1. Gent.*] And sometimes falling ones.

2. Gent. No more of that.
[*Exit the last of the procession; flourish of trumpets.*]

Enter a third GENTLEMAN.

1. Gent. God save you, sir! Where have you been broiling?

3. Gent. Among the crowd i' th' Abbey, where a finger

8. royal minds: royalist sympathies.
9. let . . . rights: i.e. to do them justice. **forward:** eager.
12. taken: received.
24–35. The Archbishop . . . sick. Holinshed records (Bullough, IV, 482–83) that in the spring of 1533, with Katherine still adamant in her appeal to Rome, Cranmer convened an ecclesiastical court at Dunstable, "which is six miles from Ampthill, where the princesse Dowager laie, and there by one doctor Lee she was cited to appeare before the said archbishop in cause of matrimonie in the said towne of Dunstable, and at the daie of appearance she appeared not, but made default, and so she was called peremptorie everie daie fifteene daies togither, and at the last, for lacke of appearance, by the assent of all the learned men there present, she was divorsed from the king, and the marriage declared to be void and of none effect."
27. late: recent. **Dunstable:** town in Bedfordshire.
28. Ampthill: royal residence assigned to Katherine. **lay:** lodged.
29. cited: summoned. **31. main assent:** i.e. consensus.
34. Kimmalton: Kimbolton, a castle in Huntingtonshire.
36. close: aside.
The Order of the Coronation. This elaborate stage direction is compiled from Holinshed (Bullough, IV, 483). **flourish:** fanfare. **Quiristers:** choristers. **Garter:** i.e. Garter King-at-Arms, one of the principal functionaries under the Earl Marshal. **Esses:** S-shaped links. **Cinque-Ports:** wardens of five seaports (Hastings, Dover, Sandwich, Romney, Hythe) that, with several adjacent towns, were formerly entrusted with the defense of the southeast coast of England. **in her hair:** i.e. with flowing locks. **each side her:** each side of her.

37. train: procession. **46. strains:** embraces.
48. cloth of honor: canopy. **50. all:** all who.
55. falling. With a sexual quibble.

Could not be wedg'd in more. I am stifled
With the mere rankness of their joy.
2. Gent. You saw
The ceremony?
3. Gent. That I did.
1. Gent. How was it?
3. Gent. Well worth the seeing.
2. Gent. Good sir, speak it to us.
3. Gent. As well as I am able. The rich stream
Of lords and ladies, having brought the Queen
To a prepar'd place in the choir, fell off
A distance from her; while her Grace sate down
To rest a while, some half an hour or so,
In a rich chair of state, opposing freely
The beauty of her person to the people.
Believe me, sir, she is the goodliest woman
That ever lay by man—which when the people
Had the full view of, such a noise arose
As the shrouds make at sea in a stiff tempest,
As loud and to as many tunes. Hats, cloaks
(Doublets, I think) flew up, and had their faces
Been loose, this day they had been lost. Such joy
I never saw before. Great-bellied women,
That had not half a week to go, like rams
In the old time of war, would shake the press
And make 'em reel before 'em. No man living
Could say, "This is my wife" there, all were woven
So strangely in one piece.
2. Gent. But what follow'd?
3. Gent. At length her Grace rose, and with modest paces
Came to the altar, where she kneel'd, and saint-like
Cast her fair eyes to heaven, and pray'd devoutly;
Then rose again and bow'd her to the people;
When by the Archbishop of Canterbury
She had all the royal makings of a queen,
As holy oil, Edward Confessor's crown,
The rod, and bird of peace, and all such emblems
Laid nobly on her; which perform'd, the choir,
With all the choicest music of the kingdom,
Together sung *Te Deum*. So she parted,
And with the same full state pac'd back again
To York-place, where the feast is held.
1. Gent. Sir,
You must no more call it York-place, that's past;
For since the Cardinal fell that title's lost.
'Tis now the King's, and call'd Whitehall.
3. Gent. I know it;
But 'tis so lately alter'd that the old name
Is fresh about me.
2. Gent. What two reverend bishops
Were those that went on each side of the Queen?
3. Gent. [Stokesly] and Gardiner, the one of Winchester,
Newly preferr'd from the King's secretary,
The other, London.
2. Gent. He of Winchester
Is held no great good lover of the Archbishop's,
The virtuous Cranmer.
3. Gent. All the land knows that.
However, yet there is no great breach; when it comes,
Cranmer will find a friend will not shrink from him.
2. Gent. Who may that be, I pray you?
3. Gent. Thomas Cromwell,
A man in much esteem with th' King, and truly
A worthy friend. The King has made him Master
O' th' Jewel House,
And one, already, of the Privy Council.
2. Gent. He will deserve more.
3. Gent. Yes, without all doubt.
Come, gentlemen, ye shall go my way, which
Is to th' court, and there ye shall be my guests;
Something I can command. As I walk thither,
I'll tell ye more.
Both. You may command us, sir. *Exeunt.*

Scene II

Enter Katherine, *Dowager, sick, led between* Griffith, *her gentleman usher, and* Patience, *her woman.*

Grif. How does your Grace?
Kath. O Griffith, sick to death!
My legs like loaden branches bow to th' earth,
Willing to leave their burthen. Reach a chair.
So; now, methinks, I feel a little ease.
Didst thou not tell me, Griffith, as thou ledst me,
That the great child of honor, Cardinal Wolsey,
Was dead?
Grif. Yes, madam; but I [think] your Grace,
Out of the pain you suffer'd, gave no ear to't.
Kath. Prithee, good Griffith, tell me how he died.
If well, he stepp'd before me happily
For my example.
Grif. Well, the voice goes, madam:
For after the stout Earl Northumberland
Arrested him at York, and brought him forward,
As a man sorely tainted, to his answer,
He fell sick suddenly and grew so ill
He could not sit his mule.
Kath. Alas, poor man!
Grif. At last, with easy roads, he came to Leicester,
Lodg'd in the abbey; where the reverend abbot

59. **mere rankness:** very exuberance. 61. **speak:** describe.
62–94. **The rich . . . held.** This description of the coronation closely follows Holinshed (Bullough, IV, 483–84).
64. **fell off:** withdrew. 67. **opposing:** exhibiting.
72. **shrouds:** ropes. 77. **rams:** battering-rams.
78. **press:** throng.
87. **had . . . queen:** i.e. was invested with the regalia of sovereignty.
91. **choicest music:** best musicians.
92. **Te Deum:** hymn of thanksgiving beginning "We praise thee, O God." **parted:** departed. 93. **state:** pomp.
94. **York-place:** Wolsey's former palace in Westminster.

101. **Stokesly:** John Stokesley, who, as Bishop of London (1530–39), was vigorous in persecuting supposed heretics and Lutherans.

IV.ii. Location: Kimbolton. The Queen's apartments.
10. **happily:** haply, perhaps. 11. **voice:** talk.
12–30. **For . . . peace.** In November 1529 Wolsey was indicted on the charges itemized at III.ii.310–32 but was pardoned by the King. A year later, however, after he retired to Yorkshire, he was arrested on a charge of high treason, and he died at Leicester in November 1530 as he was being brought to London to stand trial. Shakespeare's account of his last days is drawn from Holinshed (Bullough, IV, 475–77). 14. **tainted:** discredited. **answer:** i.e. trial.
17. **roads:** stages.

With all his covent honorably receiv'd him;
To whom he gave these words: "O Father Abbot,
An old man, broken with the storms of state,
Is come to lay his weary bones among ye;
Give him a little earth for charity!"
So went to bed; where eagerly his sickness
Pursu'd him still, and three nights after this,
About the hour of eight, which he himself
Foretold should be his last, full of repentance,
Continual meditations, tears, and sorrows,
He gave his honors to the world again,
His blessed part to heaven, and slept in peace.
Kath. So may he rest, his faults lie gently on him!
Yet thus far, Griffith, give me leave to speak him,
And yet with charity. He was a man
Of an unbounded stomach, ever ranking
Himself with princes; one that by suggestion
Tied all the kingdom. Simony was fair play;
His own opinion was his law. I' th' presence
He would say untruths, and be ever double
Both in his words and meaning. He was never
(But where he meant to ruin) pitiful.
His promises were, as he then was, mighty;
But his performance, as he is now, nothing.
Of his own body he was ill, and gave
The clergy ill example.
Grif. Noble madam,
Men's evil manners live in brass, their virtues
We write in water. May it please your Highness
To hear me speak his good now?
Kath. Yes, good Griffith,
I were malicious else.
Grif. This Cardinal,
Though from an humble stock, undoubtedly
Was fashion'd to much honor. From his cradle
He was a scholar, and a ripe and good one;
Exceeding wise, fair-spoken, and persuading;
Lofty and sour to them that lov'd him not,
But to those men that sought him, sweet as summer.
And though he were unsatisfied in getting
(Which was a sin), yet in bestowing, madam,
He was most princely: ever witness for him
Those twins of learning that he rais'd in you,
Ipswich and Oxford! one of which fell with him,
Unwilling to outlive the good that did it;
The other (though unfinish'd) yet so famous,
So excellent in art, and still so rising,
That Christendom shall ever speak his virtue.
His overthrow heap'd happiness upon him;
For then, and not till then, he felt himself,
And found the blessedness of being little;
And to add greater honors to his age
Than man could give him, he died fearing God.
Kath. After my death I wish no other herald,
No other speaker of my living actions
To keep mine honor from corruption,
But such an honest chronicler as Griffith.
Whom I most hated living, thou hast made me,
With thy religious truth and modesty,
Now in his ashes honor. Peace be with him!
Patience, be near me still, and set me lower;
I have not long to trouble thee. Good Griffith,
Cause the musicians play me that sad note
I nam'd my knell, whilst I sit meditating
On that celestial harmony I go to.
Sad and solemn music.
Grif. She is asleep. Good wench, let's sit down quiet
For fear we wake her; softly, gentle Patience.

THE VISION

Enter, solemnly tripping one after another, six personages, clad in white robes, wearing on their heads garlands of bays, and golden vizards on their faces, branches of bays or palm in their hands. They first congee unto her, then dance; and, at certain changes, the first two hold a spare garland over her head, at which the other four make reverend curtsies. Then the two that held the garland deliver the same to the other next two, who observe the same order in their changes, and holding the garland over her head; which done, they deliver the same garland to the last two, who likewise observe the same order; at which (as it were by inspiration) she makes (in her sleep) signs of rejoicing, and holdeth up her hands to heaven: and so in their dancing vanish, carrying the garland with them. The music continues.

Kath. Spirits of peace, where are ye? Are ye all gone?
And leave me here in wretchedness behind ye?
Grif. Madam, we are here.
Kath. It is not you I call for;
Saw ye none enter since I slept?
Grif. None, madam.
Kath. No? Saw you not even now a blessed troop
Invite me to a banquet, whose bright faces
Cast thousand beams upon me, like the sun?
They promis'd me eternal happiness,
And brought me garlands, Griffith, which I feel
I am not worthy yet to wear. I shall, assuredly.
Grif. I am most joyful, madam, such good dreams
Possess your fancy.
Kath. Bid the music leave,
They are harsh and heavy to me. *Music ceases.*
Pat. Do you note
How much her Grace is alter'd on the sudden?
How long her face is drawn! How pale she looks,
And of an earthy cold! Mark her eyes!
Grif. She is going, wench. Pray, pray.
Pat. Heaven comfort her!

19. covent: convent, i.e. company of religious associates.
28. sorrows: lamentations. **32. speak:** describe.
34. stomach: pride, ambition.
35. suggestion: i.e. underhand methods.
36. Tied: controlled. **37. presence:** i.e. of the King.
43. Of . . . ill: i.e. he was sexually depraved.
47. good: good qualities. **53. Lofty:** haughty.
55. getting: i.e. acquisitions.
59. Ipswich and Oxford. The college that Wolsey founded at his native Ipswich did not survive his fall; Cardinal College, Oxford, of which the King subsequently became the patron, is now Christ Church.
60. good . . . it: good man who founded it.
62. art: learning. **65. felt:** i.e. knew.

70. living actions: i.e. actions while alive.
74. modesty: moderation.
The Vision. bays: bay leaves. **congee:** bow. **changes:** figures in a dance. **94. music leave:** musicians cease playing.
95. heavy: tedious.

Enter a MESSENGER.

Mess. And't like your Grace—
Kath. You are a saucy fellow,
Deserve we no more reverence?
Grif. You are to blame,
Knowing she will not lose her wonted greatness,
To use so rude behavior. Go to, kneel.
Mess. I humbly do entreat your Highness' pardon,
My haste made me unmannerly. There is staying
A gentleman, sent from the King, to see you.
Kath. Admit him entrance, Griffith; but this fellow
Let me ne'er see again. *Exit Messenger.*

Enter LORD CAPUCHIUS.

If my sight fail not,
You should be lord ambassador from the Emperor,
My royal nephew, and your name Capuchius.
Cap. Madam, the same; your servant.
Kath. O my lord,
The times and titles now are alter'd strangely
With me since first you knew me. But I pray you,
What is your pleasure with me?
Cap. Noble lady,
First, mine own service to your Grace, the next,
The King's request that I would visit you,
Who grieves much for your weakness, and by me
Sends you his princely commendations,
And heartily entreats you take good comfort.
Kath. O my good lord, that comfort comes too late,
'Tis like a pardon after execution.
That gentle physic given in time had cur'd me;
But now I am past all comforts here but prayers.
How does his Highness?
Cap. Madam, in good health.
Kath. So may he ever do, and ever flourish,
When I shall dwell with worms, and my poor name
Banish'd the kingdom! Patience, is that letter
I caus'd you write yet sent away?
Pat. No, madam. [*Giving it to Katherine.*]
Kath. Sir, I most humbly pray you to deliver
This to my lord the King.
Cap. Most willing, madam.
Kath. In which I have commended to his goodness
The model of our chaste loves, his young daughter—
The dews of heaven fall thick in blessings on her!—
Beseeching him to give her virtuous breeding—

100. **And't like:** if it please.
102. **lose . . . greatness:** give up her customary regality.
105. **staying:** waiting.
108–58. **If . . . right.** When Katherine "fell into her last sicknesse," says Holinshed (Bullough, IV, 484–85), the King sent "the Emperors ambassador that was legier here with him named Eustacius Caputius, to go to visit hir, and to doo his commendations to hir, and will hir to be of good comfort. The ambassador with all diligence did his duetie therein, comforting hir the best he might: but she within six daies after, perceiving hir selfe to wax verie weake and feeble, and to feele death approching at hand, caused one of hir gentlewomen to write a letter to the king, commending to him hir daughter and his [i.e. Princess Mary], beseeching him to stand good father unto hir: and further desired him to have some consideration of hir gentlewomen that had served hir, and to see them bestowed in marriage. Further, that it would please him to appoint that hir servants might have their due wages, and a yeeres wages beside."
118. **princely commendations:** royal complements.
122. **physic:** remedy. **had:** would have. 132. **model:** image.
134. **virtuous breeding:** good upbringing.

She is young, and of a noble modest nature,
I hope she will deserve well—and a little
To love her for her mother's sake that lov'd him
Heaven knows how dearly. My next poor petition
Is, that his noble Grace would have some pity
Upon my wretched women, that so long
Have follow'd both my fortunes faithfully,
Of which there is not one, I dare avow
(And now I should not lie), but will deserve,
For virtue and true beauty of the soul,
For honesty and decent carriage,
A right good husband (let him be a noble),
And sure those men are happy that shall have 'em.
The last is for my men (they are the poorest,
But poverty could never draw 'em from me),
That they may have their wages duly paid 'em,
And something over to remember me by.
If heaven had pleas'd to have given me longer life
And able means, we had not parted thus.
These are the whole contents, and, good my lord,
By that you love the dearest in this world,
As you wish Christian peace to souls departed,
Stand these poor people's friend, and urge the King
To do me this last right.
Cap. By heaven, I will,
Or let me lose the fashion of a man!
Kath. I thank you, honest lord. Remember me
In all humility unto his Highness.
Say his long trouble now is passing
Out of this world; tell him in death I blest him
(For so I will). Mine eyes grow dim. Farewell,
My lord. Griffith, farewell. Nay, Patience,
You must not leave me yet. I must to bed,
Call in more women. When I am dead, good wench,
Let me be us'd with honor; strew me over
With maiden flowers, that all the world may know
I was a chaste wife to my grave. Embalm me,
Then lay me forth. Although unqueen'd, yet like
A queen, and daughter to a king, inter me.
I can no more. *Exeunt, leading Katherine.*

ACT V, SCENE I

Enter GARDINER, *Bishop of Winchester, a* PAGE *with a torch before him, met by* SIR THOMAS LOVELL.

Gard. It's one a' clock, boy, is't not?
Page. It hath strook.
Gard. These should be hours for necessities,
Not for delights; times to repair our nature
With comforting repose, and not for us
To waste these times. Good hour of night, Sir Thomas!
Whither so late?
Lov. Came you from the King, my lord?
Gard. I did, Sir Thomas, and left him at primero

141. **both:** i.e. good and bad.
145. **honesty . . . carriage:** chastity and good behavior.
151. **over:** in addition. 153. **able:** adequate.
159. **fashion:** nature. 171. **forth:** out (for burial).

V.i. Location: London. A gallery in the palace.
7. **primero:** a card game.

With the Duke of Suffolk.
Lov. I must to him too,
Before he go to bed. I'll take my leave.
Gard. Not yet, Sir Thomas Lovell. What's the matter?
It seems you are in haste. And if there be
No great offense belongs to't, give your friend
Some touch of your late business. Affairs that walk
(As they say spirits do) at midnight, have
In them a wilder nature than the business
That seeks dispatch by day.
Lov. My lord, I love you;
And durst commend a secret to your ear
Much weightier than this work. The Queen's in labor,
They say in great extremity, and fear'd
She'll with the labor end.
Gard. The fruit she goes with
I pray for heartily, that it may find
Good time, and live; but for the stock, Sir Thomas,
I wish it grubb'd up now.
Lov. Methinks I could
Cry the amen, and yet my conscience says
She's a good creature, and, sweet lady, does
Deserve our better wishes.
Gard. But, sir, sir,
Hear me, Sir Thomas, y' are a gentleman
Of mine own way; I know you wise, religious,
And, let me tell you, it will ne'er be well—
'Twill not, Sir Thomas Lovell, take't of me—
Till Cranmer, Cromwell, her two hands, and she
Sleep in their graves.
Lov. Now, sir, you speak of two
The most remark'd i' th' kingdom. As for Cromwell,
Beside that of the Jewel House, is made Master
O' th' Rolls, and the King's secretary; further, sir,
Stands in the gap and trade of moe preferments,
With which the [time] will load him. Th' Archbishop
Is the King's hand and tongue, and who dare speak
One syllable against him?
Gard. Yes, yes, Sir Thomas,
There are that dare, and I myself have ventur'd
To speak my mind of him; and indeed this day,
Sir (I may tell it you), I think I have
Incens'd the lords o' th' Council that he is
(For so I know he is, they know he is)
A most arch-heretic, a pestilence
That does infect the land; with which they moved
Have broken with the King, who hath so far
Given ear to our complaint, of his great grace
And princely care foreseeing those fell mischiefs
Our reasons laid before him, 'hath commanded
To-morrow morning to the Council-board
He be convented. He's a rank weed, Sir Thomas,
And we must root him out. From your affairs
I hinder you too long. Good night, Sir Thomas.
Lov. Many good-nights, my lord! I rest your servant. *Exeunt Gardiner and Page.*

Enter King *and* Suffolk.

King. Charles, I will play no more to-night,
My mind's not on't, you are too hard for me.
Suf. Sir, I did never win of you before.
King. But little, Charles,
Nor shall not, when my fancy's on my play.
Now, Lovell, from the Queen what is the news?
Lov. I could not personally deliver to her
What you commanded me, but by her woman
I sent your message, who return'd her thanks
In the great'st humbleness, and desir'd your Highness
Most heartily to pray for her.
King. What say'st thou? Ha?
To pray for her? What, is she crying out?
Lov. So said her woman, and that her suff'rance made
Almost each pang a death.
King. Alas, good lady!
Suf. God safely quit her of her burthen, and
With gentle travail, to the gladding of
Your Highness with an heir!
King. 'Tis midnight, Charles,
Prithee to bed, and in thy pray'rs remember
Th' estate of my poor queen. Leave me alone,
For I must think of that which company
Would not be friendly to.
Suf. I wish your Highness
A quiet night, and my good mistress will
Remember in my prayers.
King. Charles, good night. *Exit Suffolk.*

Enter Sir Anthony Denny.

Well, sir, what follows?
Den. Sir, I have brought my lord the Archbishop,
As you commanded me.
King. Ha? Canterbury?
Den. Ay, my good lord.
King. 'Tis true; where is he, Denny?
Den. He attends your Highness' pleasure.
King. Bring him to us. [*Exit Denny.*]
Lov. [*Aside.*] This is about that which the Bishop spake.
I am happily come hither.

Enter Cranmer *and* Denny.

King. Avoid the gallery. (*Lovell seems to stay.*) Ha?
I have said. Be gone.
What? *Exeunt Lovell and Denny.*
Cran. [*Aside.*] I am fearful; wherefore frowns he thus?
'Tis his aspect of terror. All's not well.
King. How now, my lord? you do desire to know
Wherefore I sent for you.
Cran. [*Kneeling.*] It is my duty

11. And if: if. **13. touch:** inkling. **17. commend:** entrust.
18. this work: i.e. the matter at hand.
19. fear'd: i.e. it is feared that. **22. time:** fortune.
23. grubb'd: rooted. **24. Cry the amen:** i.e. concur.
28. way: religious persuasion. **33. remark'd:** noted.
36. gap and trade: i.e. open road. **moe:** more.
37. time: course of events. **40. that:** those that.
43. Incens'd: led to believe. **46. moved:** aroused (by anger).
47. broken: communicated. **49. fell:** cruel.
50. 'hath: he hath. **52. convented:** summoned.

68. suff'rance: suffering.
74. estate: condition. **86. Avoid:** leave.

T' attend your Highness' pleasure.
King. Pray you arise,
My good and gracious Lord of Canterbury.
Come, you and I must walk a turn together;
I have news to tell you. Come, come, give me your hand.
Ah, my good lord, I grieve at what I speak,
And am right sorry to repeat what follows.
I have, and most unwillingly, of late
Heard many grievous—I do say, my lord,
Grievous—complaints of you; which, being consider'd,
Have mov'd us and our Council, that you shall
This morning come before us, where I know
You cannot with such freedom purge yourself,
But that till further trial, in those charges
Which will require your answer, you must take
Your patience to you, and be well contented
To make your house our Tow'r. You, a brother of us
It fits we thus proceed, or else no witness
Would come against you.
Cran. [*Kneeling*.] I humbly thank your Highness,
And am right glad to catch this good occasion
Most throughly to be winnowed, where my chaff
And corn shall fly asunder; for I know
There's none stands under more calumnious tongues
Than I myself, poor man.
King. Stand up, good Canterbury!
Thy truth and thy integrity is rooted
In us, thy friend. Give me thy hand, stand up;
Prithee let's walk. Now, by my holidame,
What manner of man are you? My lord, I look'd
You would have given me your petition, that
I should have ta'en some pains to bring together
Yourself and your accusers, and to have heard you
Without indurance further.
Cran. Most dread liege,
The good I stand on is my truth and honesty.
If they shall fail, I, with mine enemies,
Will triumph o'er my person, which I weigh not,
Being of those virtues vacant. I fear nothing
What can be said against me.
King. Know you not
How your state stands i' th' world, with the whole world?
Your enemies are many, and not small; their practices
Must bear the same proportion, and not ever
The justice and the truth o' th' question carries
The due o' th' verdict with it. At what ease
Might corrupt minds procure knaves as corrupt

98. grievous: grave. **100. mov'd**: induced.
102. freedom: i.e. completeness. **purge**: exonerate.
106. brother of us: i.e. a member of the council.
107. fits: is fitting. **110. throughly**: thoroughly.
112. stands under: is liable to.
116. by my holidame: i.e. by Our Lady (by popular etymology from *halidom* = holiness). **121. indurance**: imprisonment.
124–25. which . . . vacant: i.e. which does not interest me if it is devoid of truth and honesty. **125. nothing**: not at all.
128. small: i.e. weak. **practices**: intrigues.
129. bear . . . proportion: i.e. be correspondingly numerous and strong. **ever**: always.
131. due . . . verdict: just verdict. **At what ease**: how easily.

To swear against you? Such things have been done.
You are potently oppos'd, and with a malice
Of as great size. Ween you of better luck,
I mean in perjur'd witness, than your Master,
Whose minister you are, whiles here he liv'd
Upon this naughty earth? Go to, go to!
You take a precipit for no leap of danger,
And woo your own destruction.
Cran. God and your Majesty
Protect mine innocence, or I fall into
The trap is laid for me!
King. Be of good cheer,
They shall no more prevail than we give way to.
Keep comfort to you, and this morning see
You do appear before them. If they shall chance,
In charging you with matters, to commit you,
The best persuasions to the contrary
Fail not to use, and with what vehemency
Th' occasion shall instruct you. If entreaties
Will render you no remedy, this ring
Deliver them, and your appeal to us
There make before them. Look, the good man weeps!
He's honest, on mine honor. God's blest Mother!
I swear he is true-hearted, and a soul
None better in my kingdom. Get you gone,
And do as I have bid you. (*Exit Cranmer*.) He has strangled
His language in his tears.

Enter Old Lady.

Gentleman. (*Within*.) Come back! What mean you?
Old L. I'll not come back, the tidings that I bring
Will make my boldness manners. Now good angels
Fly o'er thy royal head, and shade thy person
Under their blessed wings!
King. Now by thy looks
I guess thy message. Is the Queen deliver'd?
Say ay, and of a boy.
Old L. Ay, ay, my liege,
And of a lovely boy. The God of heaven
Both now and ever bless her! 'tis a girl
Promises boys hereafter. Sir, your queen
Desires your visitation, and to be
Acquainted with this stranger. 'Tis as like you
As cherry is to cherry.
King. Lovell!

135–57. Ween . . . tears. The source for this whole episode of Cranmer's difficulties with the council is John Foxe's *Acts and Monuments* (1583), which is followed very closely. Thus lines 135–57 are matched by this passage in Foxe (Bullough, IV, 486–87): "Thinke you to have better lucke that way, then your maister Christ had," the King asks Cranmer. "I see by it, you will run hedlong to your undoyng, if I would suffer you. Your enemies shall not so prevayle against you, for I have otherwyse devised with my selfe to keepe you out of their handes. Yet notwithstanding to morrow when the Counsaile shal sit, and send for you, resort unto them, and if in chargyng you with this matter, they do commit you to the Tower, require of them, because you are one of them, a Counsailor, that you may have your accusers brought before them without any further indurance [cf. line 121], and use for your selfe as good perswasions that way as you may devise, and if no intreatie or reasonable request will serve, then deliver unto them this my ring." **135. Ween you of**: do you expect.
136. Master: i.e. Christ. **138. naughty**: wicked.
139. precipit: precipice. **142. is**: that is.
143. give way to: permit. **146. commit**: imprison.

[*Enter* Lovell.]

Lov. Sir?
King. Give her an hundred marks. I'll to the Queen. *Exit King.*
Old L. An hundred marks? By this light, I'll ha' more.
An ordinary groom is for such payment.
I will have more or scold it out of him.
Said I for this, the girl was like to him?
I'll have more, or else unsay't; and now,
While 'tis hot, I'll put it to the issue.
Exit Lady [*with Lovell*].

Scene II

[Pursuivants, Pages, *etc., attending.*] *Enter* Cranmer, *Archbishop of Canterbury.*

Cran. I hope I am not too late, and yet the gentleman
That was sent to me from the Council pray'd me
To make great haste. All fast? What means this? Ho!
Who waits there? Sure you know me?

Enter Keeper.

Keep. Yes, my lord;
But yet I cannot help you.
Cran. Why?
Keep. Your Grace must wait till you be call'd for.

Enter Doctor Butts.

Cran. So.
Butts. [*Aside.*] This is a [piece] of malice. I am glad
I came this way so happily; the King
Shall understand it presently. *Exit Butts.*
Cran. [*Aside.*] 'Tis Butts,
The King's physician. As he pass'd along,
How earnestly he cast his eyes upon me!
Pray heaven he sound not my disgrace! for certain
This is of purpose laid by some that hate me
(God turn their hearts! I never sought their malice)
To quench mine honor; they would shame to make me
Wait else at door, a fellow Councillor,
'Mong boys, grooms, and lackeys. But their pleasures
Must be fulfill'd, and I attend with patience.

Enter the King *and* Butts *at a window above.*

Butts. I'll show your Grace the strangest sight—
King. What's that, Butts?
Butts. I think your Highness saw this many a day.
King. Body a' me, where is it?
Butts. There, my lord:
The high promotion of his Grace of Canterbury,
Who holds his state at door 'mongst pursuivants,
Pages, and footboys.

170. an hundred marks: about £65. **172. for:** entitled to.

V.ii. Location: London. Anteroom and Council-chamber.
o.s.d. Pursuivants: messengers, attendants. **3. fast:** shut.
10. presently: at once. **13. sound:** proclaim.
14. laid: contrived. **16. quench mine honor:** destroy my reputation.
18. pleasures: desires. **24. holds his state:** maintains his pomp.

King. Ha? 'tis he indeed.
Is this the honor they do one another?
'Tis well there's one above 'em yet. I had thought
They had parted so much honesty among 'em—
At least good manners—as not thus to suffer
A man of his place, and so near our favor,
To dance attendance on their lordships' pleasures,
And at the door too, like a post with packets.
By holy Mary, Butts, there's knavery.
Let 'em alone, and draw the curtain close;
We shall hear more anon.
[*Curtain, above, partially drawn, but the King and Butts remain listening.*]

A council-table brought in with chairs and stools, and placed under the state. Enter Lord Chancellor; *places himself at the upper end of the table on the left hand; a seat being left void above him, as for Canterbury's seat.* Duke of Suffolk, Duke of Norfolk, Surrey, Lord Chamberlain, Gardiner *seat themselves in order on each side.* Cromwell *at lower end, as secretary.*

Chan. Speak to the business, Master Secretary.
Why are we met in Council?
Crom. Please your honors,
The chief cause concerns his Grace of Canterbury.
Gard. Has he had knowledge of it?
Crom. Yes.
Nor. Who waits there?
Keep. Without, my noble lords?
Gard. Yes.
Keep. My Lord Archbishop;
And has done half an hour, to know your pleasures.
Chan. Let him come in.
Keep. Your Grace may enter now.

Cranmer *approaches the council-table.*

Chan. My good Lord Archbishop, I'm very sorry
To sit here at this present, and behold
That chair stand empty; but we all are men,
In our own natures frail, and capable
Of our flesh; few are angels; out of which frailty
And want of wisdom, you, that best should teach us,
Have misdemean'd yourself, and not a little:
Toward the King first, then his laws, in filling
The whole realm by your teaching and your chaplains'
(For so we are inform'd) with new opinions,
Divers and dangerous; which are heresies,
And, not reform'd, may prove pernicious.
Gard. Which reformation must be sudden too,
My noble lords; for those that tame wild horses
Pace 'em not in their hands to make 'em gentle,

28. parted: shared. **honesty:** decency. **30. place:** rank.
31. dance attendance: stand waiting.
32. post with packets: messenger with letters.
35 s.d. state: canopy. **Lord Chancellor.** Although Sir Thomas More's appointment as chancellor was announced at III.ii.383–94, he is presumably not the officer who appears in this scene. Coming as it does in this play between the birth and christening of Princess Elizabeth (September 1533), Cranmer's citation by the council is anachronistic, for the event actually occurred about 1544.
44. present: present time.
46. capable: i.e. susceptible to weaknesses.
57. Pace . . . hands: i.e. do not train them by leading them.

But stop their mouths with stubborn bits and spur 'em
Till they obey the manage. If we suffer,
Out of our easiness and childish pity
To one man's honor, this contagious sickness,
Farewell all physic! And what follows then?
Commotions, uproars, with a general taint
Of the whole state; as of late days our neighbors,
The upper Germany, can dearly witness,
Yet freshly pitied in our memories.
Cran. My good lords: hitherto, in all the progress
Both of my life and office, I have labor'd,
And with no little study, that my teaching
And the strong course of my authority
Might go one way, and safely; and the end
Was ever to do well; nor is there living
(I speak it with a single heart, my lords)
A man that more detests, more stirs against,
Both in his private conscience and his place,
Defacers of a public peace than I do.
Pray heaven the King may never find a heart
With less allegiance in it! Men that make
Envy and crooked malice nourishment
Dare bite the best. I do beseech your lordships,
That, in this case of justice, my accusers,
Be what they will, may stand forth face to face,
And freely urge against me.
Suf. Nay, my lord,
That cannot be; you are a Councillor,
And by that virtue no man dare accuse you.
Gard. My lord, because we have business of more moment,
We will be short with you. 'Tis his Highness' pleasure
And our consent, for better trial of you,
From hence you be committed to the Tower,
Where being but a private man again,
You shall know many dare accuse you boldly,
More than (I fear) you are provided for.
Cran. Ah, my good Lord of Winchester—I thank you,
You are always my good friend; if your will pass,
I shall both find your lordship judge and juror,
You are so merciful. I see your end,
'Tis my undoing. Love and meekness, lord,
Become a churchman better than ambition;
Win straying souls with modesty again,
Cast none away. That I shall clear myself,
Lay all the weight ye can upon my patience,
I make as little doubt as you do conscience
In doing daily wrongs. I could say more,
But reverence to your calling makes me modest.
Gard. My lord, my lord, you are a sectary,
That's the plain truth. Your painted gloss discovers,

To men that understand you, words and weakness.
Crom. My Lord of Winchester, y' are a little,
By your good favor, too sharp; men so noble,
However faulty, yet should find respect
For what they have been. 'Tis a cruelty
To load a falling man.
Gard. Good Master Secretary,
I cry your honor mercy; you may worst
Of all this table say so.
Crom. Why, my lord?
Gard. Do not I know you for a favorer
Of this new sect? Ye are not sound.
Crom. Not sound?
Gard. Not sound, I say.
Crom. Would you were half so honest!
Men's prayers then would seek you, not their fears.
Gard. I shall remember this bold language.
Crom. Do.
Remember your bold life too.
[*Chan.*] This is too much.
Forbear for shame, my lords.
Gard. I have done.
Crom. And I.
[*Chan.*] Then thus for you, my lord, it stands agreed,
I take it, by all voices: that forthwith
You be convey'd to th' Tower a prisoner;
There to remain till the King's further pleasure
Be known unto us. Are you all agreed, lords?
All. We are.
Cran. Is there no other way of mercy
But I must needs to th' Tower, my lords?
Gard. What other
Would you expect? You are strangely troublesome.
Let some o' th' guard be ready there.

Enter the GUARD.

Cran. For me?
Must I go like a traitor thither?
Gard. Receive him,
And see him safe i' th' Tower.
Cran. Stay, good my lords,
I have a little yet to say. Look there, my lords;
By virtue of that ring, I take my cause
Out of the gripes of cruel men, and give it
To a most noble judge, the King my master.
Cham. This is the King's ring.
Sur. 'Tis no counterfeit.
Suf. 'Tis the right ring, by heav'n! I told ye all,
When we first put this dangerous stone a-rolling,
'Twould fall upon ourselves.
Nor. Do you think, my lords,
The King will suffer but the little finger
Of this man to be vex'd?

59. manage: manège, training (a term from horsemanship). **suffer:** tolerate. **60. easiness:** indifference. **62. physic:** remedy.
63. Commotions: insurrections.
73. with . . . heart: i.e. without duplicity or equivocation.
74. more stirs: is more active.
75. place: office (as archbishop). **83. urge against:** accuse.
85. by that virtue: by virtue of that. **88. trial:** examination.
94. will pass: i.e. desires are followed.
97. undoing: destruction. **99. modesty:** moderation.
102–3. do conscience In: have scruples against.
105. sectary: schismatic.
106. painted gloss discovers: disingenuous speech reveals.

107. words: i.e. mere words.
109. By . . . favor: i.e. begging your pardon.
113. cry . . . mercy: beg your Honor's pardon. **worst:** i.e. least appropriately. **116. sound:** orthodox. **135. gripes:** grasps.
140–42. Do . . . vex'd. After Cranmer had shown the council Henry's ring, says Foxe (Bullough, IV, 488), "the whole Counsaile being thereat somewhat amazed, the Earle of Bedford with a loude voyce confirmyng his wordes with a solemne othe, sayde: when you first began the matter my Lordes, I told you what would come of it. Do you thinke that the King will suffer this mans finger to ake?"

Cham. 'Tis now too certain.
How much more is his life in value with him!
[*Exeunt King and Butts above.*]
Would I were fairly out on't!
Crom. My mind gave me,
In seeking tales and informations
Against this man, whose honesty the devil
And his disciples only envy at,
Ye blew the fire that burns ye. Now have at ye!

Enter King *frowning on them; takes his seat.*

Gard. Dread sovereign, how much are we bound to heaven
In daily thanks, that gave us such a prince,
Not only good and wise but most religious;
One that, in all obedience, makes the Church
The chief aim of his honor, and to strengthen
That holy duty, out of dear respect,
His royal self in judgment comes to hear
The cause betwixt her and this great offender.
King. You were ever good at sudden commendations,
Bishop of Winchester. But know I come not
To hear such flattery now, and in my presence
They are too thin and base to hide offenses.
To me you cannot reach you play the spaniel,
And think with wagging of your tongue to win me;
But whatsoe'er thou tak'st me for, I'm sure
Thou hast a cruel nature and a bloody.
[*To Cranmer.*] Good man, sit down. Now let me see the proudest
He, that dares most, but wag his finger at thee.
By all that's holy, he had better starve
Than but once think his place becomes thee not.
Sur. May it please your Grace—
King. No, sir, it does not please me.
I had thought I had had men of some understanding
And wisdom of my Council; but I find none.
Was it discretion, lords, to let this man,
This good man (few of you deserve that title),
This honest man, wait like a lousy footboy
At chamber-door? and one as great as you are?
Why, what a shame was this? Did my commission
Bid ye so far forget yourselves? I gave ye
Power as he was a Councillor to try him,
Not as a groom. There's some of ye, I see,
More out of malice than integrity,
Would try him to the utmost had ye mean,
Which ye shall never have while I live.
Chan. Thus far,
My most dread sovereign, may it like your Grace
To let my tongue excuse all. What was purpos'd
Concerning his imprisonment was rather
(If there be faith in men) meant for his trial
And fair purgation to the world than malice,
I'm sure, in me.
King. Well, well, my lords, respect him,
Take him, and use him well; he's worthy of it.
I will say thus much for him, if a prince
May be beholding to a subject, I
Am for his love and service so to him.
Make me no more ado, but all embrace him.
Be friends, for shame, my lords! My Lord of Canterbury,
I have a suit which you must not deny me:
That is, a fair young maid that yet wants baptism,
You must be godfather, and answer for her.
Cran. The greatest monarch now alive may glory
In such an honor; how may I deserve it,
That am a poor and humble subject to you?
King. Come, come, my lord, you'd spare your spoons. You shall have
Two noble partners with you, the old Duchess of Norfolk
And Lady Marquess Dorset. Will these please you?
Once more, my Lord of Winchester, I charge you,
Embrace and love this man.
Gard. With a true heart
And brother-love I do it.
Cran. And let heaven
Witness how dear I hold this confirmation.
King. Good man, those joyful tears show thy true [heart].
The common voice, I see, is verified
Of thee, which says thus, "Do my Lord of Canterbury
A shrewd turn, and he's your friend for ever."
Come, lords, we trifle time away; I long
To have this young one made a Christian.
As I have made ye one, lords, one remain:
So I grow stronger, you more honor gain. *Exeunt.*

Scene III

Noise and tumult within. Enter Porter *and his* Man.

Port. You'll leave your noise anon, ye rascals; do you take the court for Parish Garden? Ye rude slaves, leave your gaping.

(*Within.*) Good Master Porter, I belong to th' larder.

Port. Belong to th' gallows, and be hang'd, ye rogue! Is this a place to roar in? Fetch me a dozen crab-tree staves, and strong ones; these are but

143. in value with: valued by. **144. gave:** told.
147. envy at: resent.
152–53. makes . . . honor: i.e. is mainly concerned about the prestige and safety of the Church. **154. dear respect:** intense piety.
161. me: me whom. **166. He:** man. **167. starve:** die.
168. place: i.e. on the council. **174. lousy:** louse-infested.
176. commission: warrant of commission. **181. mean:** means.
183. like: please.

187. purgation: clearing of himself. Seeking to justify their action, some members of the council, according to Foxe (Bullough, IV, 488), "declared, that in requesting his [Cranmer's] indurance, it was rather ment for hys triall, and his purgation agaynst the common fame, and slaunder of the world, then for any malyce conceyved agaynst hym."
201. spoons: christening spoons presented by the sponsor, usually in sets of twelve with a figure of one of the Apostles on each of them.
209. voice: report. **211. shrewd:** ill.
214. one: i.e. united in amity.

V.iii. Location: London. The palace yard.
1. leave: stop. **anon:** right away.
2. Parish Garden: i.e. Paris Garden, a bear- and bull-baiting park in Southwark. **rude:** barbarous. **3. gaping:** bawling.
4. belong to: am employed in.

switches to 'em. I'll scratch your heads; you must be seeing christenings? Do you look for ale and cakes here, you rude rascals?

Man. Pray, sir, be patient; 'tis as much impossible,
Unless we sweep 'em from the door with cannons,
To scatter 'em, as 'tis to make 'em sleep
On May-day morning, which will never be.
We may as well push against Powle's as stir 'em.

Port. How got they in, and be hang'd?

Man. Alas, I know not, how gets the tide in?
As much as one sound cudgel of four foot
(You see the poor remainder) could distribute,
I made no spare, sir.

Port. You did nothing, sir.

Man. I am not Sampson, nor Sir Guy, nor Colbrand,
To mow 'em down before me; but if I spar'd any
That had a head to hit, either young or old,
He or she, cuckold or cuckold-maker,
Let me ne'er hope to see a chine again,
And that I would not for a cow, God save her!

(*Within.*) Do you hear, Master Porter?

Port. I shall be with you presently, good Master Puppy.—Keep the door close, sirrah.

Man. What would you have me do?

Port. What should you do, but knock 'em down by th' dozens? Is this Moorfields to muster in? Or have we some strange Indian with the great tool come to court, the women so besiege us? Bless me, what a fry of fornication is at door! On my Christian conscience, this one christening will beget a thousand, here will be father, godfather, and all together.

Man. The spoons will be the bigger, sir. There is a fellow somewhat near the door, he should be a brazier by his face, for, o' my conscience, twenty of the dog-days now reign in 's nose; all that stand about him are under the line, they need no other penance: that fire-drake did I hit three times on the head, and three times was his nose discharg'd against me; he stands there like a mortar-piece to blow us. There was a haberdasher's wife of small wit near him, that rail'd upon me till her pink'd porringer fell off her head, for kindling such a combustion in the state. I miss'd the meteor once, and hit that woman, who cried out "Clubs!", when I might see from far some forty truncheoners draw to her succor, which were the hope o' th' Strond, where she was quarter'd. They fell on, I made good my place; at length they came to th' broom-staff to me, I defied 'em still, when suddenly a file of boys behind 'em, loose shot, deliver'd such a show'r of pibbles, that I was fain to draw mine honor in, and let 'em win the work. The devil was amongst 'em, I think, surely.

Port. These are the youths that thunder at a playhouse and fight for bitten apples, that no audience but the tribulation of Tower-hill or the limbs of Limehouse, their dear brothers, are able to endure. I have some of 'em in *Limbo Patrum*, and there they are like to dance these three days; besides the running banquet of two beadles that is to come.

Enter Lord Chamberlain.

Cham. Mercy o' me, what a multitude are here!
They grow still too; from all parts they are coming,
As if we kept a fair here! Where are these porters?
These lazy knaves? Y' have made a fine hand, fellows!
There's a trim rabble let in. Are all these
Your faithful friends o' th' suburbs? We shall have
Great store of room, no doubt, left for the ladies,
When they pass back from the christening.

Port. And't please your honor,
We are but men; and what so many may do,
Not being torn a-pieces, we have done.
An army cannot rule 'em.

Cham. As I live,
If the King blame me for't, I'll lay ye all
By th' heels, and suddenly; and on your heads
Clap round fines for neglect. Y' are lazy knaves,
And here ye lie baiting of bombards, when
Ye should do service. Hark, the trumpets sound;
Th' are come already from the christening.
Go break among the press, and find a way out
To let the troop pass fairly; or I'll find
A Marshalsea shall hold ye play these two months.

Port. Make way there for the Princess.

Man. You great fellow,
Stand close up, or I'll make your head ache.

Port. You i' th' chamblet, get up o' th' rail,
I'll peck you o'er the pales else. *Exeunt.*

9. to 'em: i.e. in comparison with cudgels of crab-apple wood (?) or to those who receive the blows (?).
16. Powle's: St. Paul's Cathedral.
22. Sampson: Samson (famed for strength). **Sir Guy, Colbrand.** In the popular English romance *Guy of Warwick* the hero overcomes the Danish giant Colbrand.
26. see a chine: i.e. eat meat (*chine* = backbone).
27. would . . . cow: i.e. would not have happen for anything (proverbial). **30. sirrah:** here, form of address between menials.
33. Moorfields: open space on the outskirts of London, a favorite resort for citizens on Sundays and holidays.
34. tool: sexual organ. **36. fry of fornication:** swarm of bastards.
39. spoons. See note to V.ii.201. **41. brazier:** worker in brass.
42. dog-days: i.e. the hot days of summer, so called because they precede the rise of Sirius the Dog Star in mid-August.
43. under the line: on the equator.
44. fire-drake: fiery dragon (here, perhaps a kind of firework so named), i.e. the man with the red face.
46. mortar-piece: cannon. **blow us:** blow us up.
48. pink'd porringer: round cap ornamented with small holes.
49. combustion: tumult. **51. Clubs:** rallying cry for apprentices.
52. truncheoners: i.e. apprentices wielding clubs.
52–53. hope . . . Strond: young hopefuls of the Strand (a street of substantial houses and shops along the Thames).
53. fell on: attacked. **54. made . . . place:** i.e. held my ground.
54–55. th' broom-staff: i.e. close quarters.
56. loose shot: throwers at random.
57. pibbles: pebbles. **fain:** obliged. **58. work:** fortress.
62. tribulation: i.e. gang of rowdies.
62–63. Limehouse: disreputable dock district below the Tower.
64. Limbo Patrum: abode of the souls of virtuous men who had died before Christ came to earth and were therefore barred from heaven; hence place of confinement, prison. **65. dance:** kick their heels.
65–66. running . . . beadles: i.e. public whipping.
72. suburbs. Outside the limits of city government and hence frequented by low types. **73. store:** plenty. **77. rule:** control.
78–79. lay . . . heels: put you all in the stocks.
80. round: heavy.
81. baiting of bombards: drinking from leather bottles (?) or harassing drunkards (?).
86. Marshalsea: prison in Southwark. **hold ye play:** keep you engaged. **89. chamblet:** camlet, a rough cloth. **rail:** railing.
90. peck . . . pales: pitch you over the palings.

Scene IV

Enter Trumpets, sounding; then two Aldermen, Lord Mayor, Garter, Cranmer, Duke of Norfolk *with his marshal's staff,* Duke of Suffolk, *two* Noblemen *bearing great standing-bowls for the christening gifts; then four* Noblemen *bearing a canopy, under which the* Duchess of Norfolk, *godmother, bearing the child richly habited in a mantle, etc., train borne by a* Lady; *then follows the* Marchioness Dorset, *the other godmother, and* Ladies. *The troop pass once about the stage, and Garter speaks.*

Gart. Heaven, from thy endless goodness send prosperous life, long, and ever happy, to the high and mighty Princess of England, Elizabeth!

Flourish. Enter King *and* Guard.

Cran. [*Kneeling.*] And to your royal Grace and the good Queen,
My noble partners and myself thus pray
All comfort, joy, in this most gracious lady
Heaven ever laid up to make parents happy
May hourly fall upon ye!
King. Thank you, good Lord Archbishop.
What is her name?
Cran. Elizabeth.
King. Stand up, lord.
[*The King kisses the child.*]
With this kiss take my blessing: God protect thee!
Into whose hand I give thy life.
Cran. Amen.
King. My noble gossips, y' have been too prodigal.
I thank ye heartily; so shall this lady,
When she has so much English.
Cran. Let me speak, sir,
For heaven now bids me; and the words I utter
Let none think flattery, for they'll find 'em truth.
This royal infant—heaven still move about her!—
Though in her cradle, yet now promises
Upon this land a thousand thousand blessings,
Which time shall bring to ripeness. She shall be
(But few now living can behold that goodness)
A pattern to all princes living with her,
And all that shall succeed. Saba was never
More covetous of wisdom and fair virtue
Than this pure soul shall be. All princely graces
That mould up such a mighty piece as this is,
With all the virtues that attend the good,
Shall still be doubled on her. Truth shall nurse her,
Holy and heavenly thoughts still counsel her.
She shall be lov'd and fear'd: her own shall bless her;
Her foes shake like a field of beaten corn,
And hang their heads with sorrow. Good grows with her;
In her days every man shall eat in safety
Under his own vine what he plants, and sing
The merry songs of peace to all his neighbors.
God shall be truly known, and those about her
From her shall read the perfect [ways] of honor,
And by those claim their greatness, not by blood.
Nor shall this peace sleep with her; but as when
The bird of wonder dies, the maiden phoenix,
Her ashes new create another heir
As great in admiration as herself,
So shall she leave her blessedness to one
(When heaven shall call her from this cloud of darkness)
Who from the sacred ashes of her honor
Shall star-like rise as great in fame as she was,
And so stand fix'd. Peace, plenty, love, truth, terror,
That were the servants to this chosen infant,
Shall then be his, and like a vine grow to him.
Where ever the bright sun of heaven shall shine,
His honor and the greatness of his name
Shall be, and make new nations. He shall flourish,
And like a mountain cedar reach his branches
To all the plains about him. Our children's children
Shall see this, and bless heaven.
King. Thou speakest wonders.
Cran. She shall be, to the happiness of England,
An aged princess; many days shall see her,
And yet no day without a deed to crown it.
Would I had known no more! but she must die,
She must, the saints must have her; yet a virgin,
A most unspotted lily shall she pass
To th' ground, and all the world shall mourn her.
King. O Lord Archbishop,
Thou hast made me now a man! never, before
This happy child, did I get any thing.
This oracle of comfort has so pleas'd me
That when I am in heaven I shall desire
To see what this child does, and praise my Maker.
I thank ye all. To you, my good Lord Mayor,
And you, good brethren, I am much beholding;
I have receiv'd much honor by your presence,
And ye shall find me thankful. Lead the way, lords,
Ye must all see the Queen, and she must thank ye,
She will be sick else. This day, no man think
H'as business at his house; for all shall stay:
This little one shall make it Holy-day. *Exeunt.*

THE EPILOGUE

'Tis ten to one this play can never please
All that are here. Some come to take their ease,
And sleep an act or two; but those, we fear,
W' have frighted with our trumpets; so 'tis clear,

V.iv. Location: London. The palace.
o.s.d. standing-bowls: heavy bowls resting on legs or bases.
12. gossips: godparents. **prodigal:** i.e. in your gifts. According to Holinshed (Bullough, IV, 484), "the archbishop of Canterburie gave to the princesse a standing cup of gold: the dutches of Norffolke gave to hir a standing cup of gold, fretted with pearle: the marchionesse of Dorset gave three gilt bolles, pounced with a cover: and the marchionesse of Excester gave three standing bolles graven, all gilt with a cover." **17. still:** always.
23. Saba: the Queen of Sheba, who made a long journey to visit Solomon because of his reputation for wisdom (1 Kings 10).
26. piece: personage. **31. beaten corn:** wind-beaten grain.

37. read: learn. **38. greatness:** nobility. **39. sleep:** i.e. die.
40. phoenix: fabulous bird said to live five hundred years and then die and rise again from its own ashes.
42. great in admiration: great an object of wonder.
43. one: i.e. James I of England. **58. deed:** i.e. notable deed.
74. sick: unhappy.
75. H'as: (that) he has. **stay:** i.e. cease work.

They'll say 'tis naught; others, to hear the city
Abus'd extremely, and to cry, "That's witty!"
Which we have not done neither: that I fear
All the expected good w' are like to hear
For this play at this time, is only in
The merciful construction of good women,
For such a one we show'd 'em. If they smile,
And say 'twill do, I know within a while
All the best men are ours; for 'tis ill hap
If they hold when their ladies bid 'em clap.

Epi. 5. **naught:** worthless.
7. **that:** so that. 8. **expected good:** anticipated applause.
10. **construction:** interpretation. 13. **hap:** luck.
14. **hold:** refrain.

NOTE ON THE TEXT

The First Folio (1623) is the only authority for *Henry VIII;* all later texts are derived from that source. It is generally agreed that F1 was printed from a scribal copy of the authors' (or, less probably, author's) manuscript. Whether that manuscript was the "foul papers" or itself a "fair copy" is not certain, though probability seems to favor "foul papers." There is no real evidence that the copy used for F1 had ever served as a prompt-book, but the inconsistencies (presumably authorial) in a few speech-prefixes (for the most part connected with Wolsey) are too slight to exclude the possibility that it had.

No light on the much-debated problem of authorship seems to be afforded by a study of the bibliographical characteristics of the F1 text. It is a clean one and offers comparatively few problems. The pertinent question of authorship—Does *Henry VIII* represent a collaboration between Shakespeare and John Fletcher or is it Shakespeare's unaided work?—is dealt with in some detail in the Introduction. Briefly, the arguments advanced for Shakespeare's sole authorship (see, particularly, Alexander and Foakes) have failed to convince the large majority of critics, who argue, essentially unequivocally, for the Shakespeare/ Fletcher collaboration (see Spedding, Partridge, Greg, Law, Mincoff, Maxwell, Hoy, Montgomery/Wells, Bowers): Spedding's division (1850) of the play, which assigns to Shakespeare I.i–ii, II.iii–iv, III.ii.1–203 (at the King's exit), and V.i, has stood the test of time (supported by a variety of metrical and linguistic tests [see Wells et al., A *Textual Companion,* pp. 133–4]) and has been recently endorsed by Bowers, though Hoy, it should be noted, would give a good deal more of the play to Shakespeare (II.i–ii, touched up by Fletcher; III.ii.204–459, touched up by Fletcher; IV.i–ii, touched up by Fletcher).

For further information, see: James Spedding, "Who Wrote Shakespeare's *Henry VIII," The Gentleman's Magazine,* n.s. XXXIV (August 1850), 115–23; Peter Alexander, "Conjectural History, or Shakespeare's *Henry VIII," Essays and Studies of the English Association,* XVI (1930); A. C. Partridge, *The Problem of "Henry VIII" Re-Opened* (Cambridge, 1949); W. W. Greg, *The Shakespeare First Folio* (Oxford, 1955); R. A. Foakes, ed., New Arden *King Henry VIII* (London, 1957), and "On the First Folio Text of *Henry VIII, SB,* XI (1958), 55–60; R. A. Law, "The Double Authorship of *Henry VIII," SP,* LVI (1959), 471–88; Marco Mincoff, *"Henry VIII* and Fletcher," *SQ,* XII (1961), 239–60; J. C. Maxwell, ed., New Shakespeare *Henry VIII* (Cambridge, 1962); Cyrus Hoy, "The Shares of Fletcher and His Collaborators in the Beaumont and Fletcher Canon (VII)," *SB,* XV (1962), 71–90; A. R. Humphreys, ed., New Penguin *Henry VIII* (Harmondsworth, Middlesex, 1971); Stanley Wells, Gary Taylor, John Jowett, and William Montgomery, *William Shakespeare: A Textual Companion* (Oxford, 1987); F. T. Bowers, ed., *Henry VIII* in *The Dramatic Works in the Beaumont and Fletcher Canon,* VII (Cambridge, 1989); John Margeson, ed., New Cambridge *Henry VIII* (Cambridge, 1990).

TEXTUAL NOTES

Title: **Eighth]** Eight. *Fl*
Dramatis personae: *subs. as first given by* Rowe
Act-scene division: *from Fl*

Prologue

10 agree] *F2;* a gree *Fl*
11 pass, if] *Johnson (after Pope);* passe: If *Fl*

I.i

Location: *Theobald (subs.)*
33 censure.] *Rowe;* censure, *Fl*
42–5 All . . . function.] *continued to Norfolk, Theobald; given to Buckingham, Fl*
45 s.p. Buck.] *Theobald*
47 as you guess?] *F4; Fl makes* As you guesse: *the opening words of Norfolk's next speech*
63 web, 'a] *Capell conj.;* Web. O *Fl*
64 way—] *Theobald (subs.);* way *Fl*
69–70 that? . . . hell,] *Theobald;* that, . . . Hell? *Fl*
78–9 letter, . . . out,] *Pope (subs.);* Letter . . . Councell, out *Fl*
79 in him] *Pope (reading* him in); in, him *Fl*
96 Burdeaux] *F2;* Burdeux *Fl*
114 advise] *F2;* aduice *Fl*
114 s.d. on Buckingham] *F2;* on Buck- / ham *Fl*
115 s.p. Wol.] *Rowe;* Car. *Fl (or* Card. *throughout first act)*
116, 117 s.pp. 1. Secr.] *Capell;* Secr. *Fl*
123 chaf'd] *F3;* chaff'd *Fl*
154 July] *F2;* Inly *Fl (in italics)*
171 "Thus let be!"] *Capell (subs.);* thus let be, *Fl*
183 him—privily] *Alexander;* him. Priuily *Fl*
184–7 trow— . . . ask'd—] *Capell;* troa . . . ask'd. *Fl*
188 gold,] *Capell;* gold: *Fl*
200 Herford] *Vaughan conj.;* Hertford *Fl*
211 Aburga'ny] *ed. (after Theobald);* Abur-gany *Fl*
212 s.d. To Aburgavenny.] *Johnson (subs.)*
219 Perk] *Foakes (from Holinshed);* Pecke *Fl*
219 chancellor] *Theobald (from Holinshed);* Councellour *Fl*
221 Nicholas] *Theobald (from Holinshed);* Michaell *Fl*
226 lord] *Rowe;* Lords *Fl*

I.ii

Location: *Theobald*
o.s.d. **his . . . attendance]** *ed. (after Foakes)*
5 Buckingham's;] *Johnson;* Buckinghams, *Fl*
8 s.d. who is] *Foakes*
13 Majesty.] *F4;* Majesty *Fl*
51 or] *F2;* er *Fl*
53 it?] *Johnson;* it, *Fl*
56 subject's] *Maxwell;* Subiects *Fl*
83 oft,] *Capell;* oft *Fl*
97 root,] *Theobald;* roote *Fl*
102 s.d. Aside . . . Secretary.] Rowe *(Aside added Dyce; after l. 102, Rowe); placed as in Cambridge*
137 Aburga'ny] *ed. (after Theobald);* Abur-gany *Fl*
145 fail? To] *Rowe;* faile; to *Fl*
147, 148 Henton] *Theobald corrects to* Hopkins *from Holinshed, but Shakespeare undoubtedly wrote* Henton *(the name of the priory) because of Holinshed's misleading phrasing*
164 confession's] *Theobald (from Holinshed);* Commissions *Fl*
170 To] To gain *F4*
170 commonalty;] *Theobald;* Commonalty, *Fl*
179 him] *Rowe;* this *Fl*
190 Bulmer] *Clarendon ed. (from Holinshed);* Blumer *Fl*
198 As . . . duty] *ed.;* (As . . . duty) *Fl*
203 "the . . . father,"] *quotes, Capell*
203 "knife,"] *quotes, Capell (who includes* the)

I.iii

Location: *Theobald (subs.)*
o.s.d. **Sands]** *Rowe;* Sandys *Fl (here only)*
7 face— . . . ones,] *Foakes;* face, (but . . . ones) *Fl*
13 And] *Pope;* A *Fl*
13 reign'd] *F2;* rain'd *Fl*
15 s.d. Enter . . . Lovell.] *placed as in Dyce; after* Lovell? *l. 16, Fl*
34 "oui"] *anon. conj. (in Cambridge);* wee *Fl;* weare *F2*
50 a-going] *hyphen, Rowe*

59 **h'as]** *Rowe;* Ha's *F1*

59 **wherewithal: in him]** *Thirlby conj.;* wherewithall in him; *F1*

I.iv

Location: *Kittredge (after Theobald)*

5 **merry]** *Johnson (after F4);* merry: *F1*

25 **ladies.]** *Pope (subs.);* Ladies, *F1*

29 **none.]** *Pope (subs.);* none, *F1*

30 **s.d. Kisses her.]** *Steevens (after Capell)*

38 **s.d. Drinks.]** *Theobald*

48 **thing—]** *Rowe;* thing. *F1*

49 **s.d. Drum . . . discharg'd.]** *placed as in Pope; after l. 48, F1*

50 **s.d. Exit a Servant.]** *Steevens (after Capell)*

60 **s.d. Exit Chamberlain attended.]** *Capell*

81 **s.d. Whisper . . . Maskers.]** *Capell (subs.);* Whisper. *F1 (after it. l. 81)*

86 **s.d. Unmasking.]** *Capell*

II.i

Location: *Globe (after Theobald)*

1 **s.pp. 1. Gent. . . . 2. Gent.]** *Rowe;* 1. . . . 2. *F1 (throughout scene)*

20 **Perk]** *Foakes (from Holinshed);* Pecke *F1*

22 **Hopkins]** *note that this is the same person called* Henton *in I.ii.147, 148 (see note to those lines); I.ii is usually assigned to Shakespeare; the present scene to Fletcher*

53 **s.d. Walter Sands]** *Theobald reads* William Sands, *following Holinshed*

126 **counsels]** *F2;* Councels *F1*

II.ii

Location: *Theobald (subs.)*

1 **s.p. Cham.]** *Capell*

10–1 **I . . . think.]** *as verse, Theobald; as prose, F1*

17 **s.d. Aside.]** *Vaughan conj.*

37 **counsel]** *F2;* councel *F1*

75 **s.d. To Campeius.]** *Theobald*

77 **s.d. To Wolsey.]** *Johnson*

80 **s.d. To . . . Suffolk.]** *Theobald*

81, 83 **s.dd. Aside to Suffolk.]** *Capell (subs.)*

82, 84 **s.dd. Aside to Norfolk.]** *Capell (subs.)*

104 **commanding,]** *F4;* commanding. *F1*

116 **s.d. Exit Wolsey.]** *Johnson*

116 **s.d. Wolsey with]** *Capell (after Johnson)*

117 **s.d. Aside to Gardiner.]** *Capell (subs.)*

118 **s.d. Aside to Wolsey.]** *Capell (subs.)*

140 **furnish'd.]** *F2;* furnish'd, *F1*

II.iii

Location: *Theobald (subs.)*

9 **acquire— . . . process,]** *Steevens (after Capell; comma from F2);* acquire. After this Processe. *F1*

14 **quarrel,]** *F2;* quarrell. *F1*

32 **cheveril]** *Theobald;* Chiuerell *F1*

48 **'long'd]** *Capell;* long'd *F1*

59 **note's]** *Theobald;* notes *F1*

75 **s.d. Aside.]** *Pope*

80 **s.d. Exit Lord Chamberlain.]** *placed as in Capell; after* you. *l. 80, F1*

87 **fill'd]** *F3;* fild *F1*

II.iv

Location: *Capell (after Theobald)*

o.s.d. **Archbishop]** *Johnson;* Bishop *F1*

1, 5 **s.pp. Wol.]** *Rowe;* Car. *F1*

13 **s.p. Q. Kath.]** *Warburton*

39–41 **aught— . . . person—]** *ed.;* aught; . . . Person; *F1*

40 **duty,]** *Malone;* Dutie *F1*

77 **challenge]** *Dyce;* Challenge, *F1*

88 **wrong,]** *F3;* wrong *F1*

91 **shall,]** *Rowe;* (Shall) *F1*

107 **cunning]** *F2;* eunning *F1*

107 **humble-mouth'd,]** *F2;* humble-mouth'd *F1 (line crowded)*

134 **s.d. Exeunt]** *Rowe;* Exit *F1*

147 **robb'd]** *F3;* rob'd *F1*

165 **oft,]** *F4;* oft *F1*

173 **Bayonne]** *Capell;* Bayon *F1*

175 **A]** *Rowe;* And *F1*

191 **to't than]** *F3 (subs.);* too't; then *F1*

200 **throe]** *Pope;* throw *F1*

220 **summons. Unsolicited]** *Theobald;* Summons vnsolicited. *F1*

236 **s.d. Aside.]** *Capell*

240 **return; . . . approach,]** *F4;* returne, . . . approch: *F1*

III.i

Location: *Theobald*

13 **heart]** *Theobald;* heart, *F1*

19 **s.d. Exit Gentleman.]** *Capell*

23 **s.d. Campeius]** *Rowe;* Campian *F1*

24 **huswife]** *ed.;* Houswife *F1*

28 **chamber,]** *Capell;* Chamber; *F1*

40 **s.p. Wol.]** *Rowe;* Card. *F1 (or* Car. *throughout scene except at ll. 81, 97)*

51 **should]** *F2;* shoul *F1*

61 **your]** *F2;* our *F1*

67 **s.d. Aside.]** *Capell*

79 **counsel]** *Capell;* Councell *F1*

82 **England]** *Johnson;* England, *F1*

83 **profit;]** *F2 (subs.);* profit *F1*

84 **Englishman]** *F3;* English man *F1*

84, 99 **counsel]** *F3;* Councell *F1*

100 **judge]** *Knight;* Iudge. *F1;* Iudge, *F2*

119 **h'as]** *Rowe;* has *F1*

150–1 **me, . . . me.]** *Capell (subs.);* me? . . . me? *F1*

155 **You'ld]** *F2;* Youl'd *F1*

170 **was]** *Pope;* was, *F1*

182 **counsels]** *F3;* Councels *F1*

III.ii

Location: *Alexander*

76 **s.p. Wol.]** *Rowe;* Car. *F1 (or* Card. *through l. 252)*

85, 94 **s.d. Aside.]** *Rowe*

90 **Pembroke]** *Pope;* Penbroke *F1*

101 **hard-rul'd]** *hyphen, F4*

104 **s.d. schedule]** *F3;* Scedule *F1*

104 **s.d. and Lovell]** *Theobald*

142 **glad]** *F2;* gald *F1*

160, 161 **s.dd. Aside.]** *Rowe*

201 **s.d. Giving him papers.]** *Pope*

202 **after,]** *Theobald;* after *F1*

209 **fear,]** *Rowe;* feare *F1*

233 **commission, lords?]** *Rowe;* Commission? Lords, *F1*

239 **coarse]** *Pope;* course *F1*

239 **metal]** *F3;* Mettle *F1*

251 **King,]** *Theobald;* King *F1*

277 **life-blood]** *hyphen, Theobald*

300 **But,]** *Capell;* But *F1*

305 **"Guilty,"]** *F4 (subs.);* guiltie *F1*

325 **holy hat]** *Theobald;* holy-Hat *F1*

337–40 **is— . . . praemunire—]** *Pope (subs.);* is, . . . Premunire; *F1*

343 **Chattels]** *Theobald;* Castles *F1*

350 **farewell—]** *Sisson;* farewell, *F1*

357 **a-ripening]** *hyphen, Dyce*

359 **bladders,]** *Rowe;* bladders: *F1*

373 **s.p. Wol.]** *Rowe;* Car. *F1 (or* Card. *throughout rest of scene)*

377 **Cromwell;]** *Pope (subs.);* Cromwell, *F1*

397 **truth's sake]** *Pope;* Truths-sake *F1*

399 **orphants']** *Warburton* (orphans'); Orphants *F1*

450 **King, and—]** *ed. (after Johnson);* King: And *F1*

IV.i

Location: *Theobald*

1 **s.pp. 1. Gent. . . . 2. Gent.]** *Rowe;* 1 . . . 2 *F1 (throughout scene)*

3 **coronation?]** *Capell;* Corronation. *F1*

8 **minds—]** *Capell (subs.);* minds, *F1*

20 **s.p. 2. Gent.]** *F4 (subs.);* 1 *F1*

35 **s.d. Trumpets.]** *Capell*

42 **s.d. Looking . . . Queen.]** *Johnson*

46 **lady.]** *Rowe (subs.);* Lady, *F1*

55 **s.p. 1. Gent.]** *Walker conj.; speech continued to 2. Gent., F1 (with comma after* indeed *l. 53)*

55 **s.d. Exit . . . trumpets.]** *Capell (subs.)*

61 **us.]** *F3;* vs? *F1*

64, 90 **choir]** *Pope;* Quire *F1*

78 **press]** *F4;* prease *F1*

80 **"This . . . wife"]** *quotes, Hanmer*

96 **title's]** *F3;* Titles *F1*

101 **Stokesly]** *F4;* Stokeley *F1*

IV.ii

Location: *Theobald, Pelican*

4 **So;]** *Rowe (subs.),* So *F1*

5 **ledst]** *Rowe (subs.);* lead'st *F1*

7 **think]** *F2;* thanke *F1*

17 **roads]** *F3;* Rodes *F1*

41 **promises were,]** *F4;* Promises, were *F1*

75 **Now . . . ashes]** *Pope;* (Now . . . Ashes) *F1*

82 **s.d. congee]** *F3;* Conge *F1*

128 **s.d. Giving . . . Katherine.]** *Malone (after Capell)*

164 **will). Mine]** *F3 (subs.);* will) mine *F1*

171 **forth. Although unqueen'd,]** *Pope (subs.);* forth (although vnqueen'd) *F1*

V.i

Location: *Capell*

25 **sweet lady]** *F3;* sweet-Ladie *F1*

37 **time]** *F4;* Lime *F1*

50 **'hath]** *Collier;* hath *F1*

55 **s.d. Exeunt]** *Rowe;* Exit *F1; s.d. placed as in Capell; after l. 54, F1, Rowe*

60 **fancy's]** *F3 (subs.);* Fancies *F1*

78 **s.d. Enter . . . Denny.]** *placed as in Johnson; after l. 79, F1*

83 **s.d. Exit Denny.]** *Rowe*

84 **s.d. Aside.]** *Rowe*

87 **s.d. Aside.]** *Capell*

90, 108 **s.dd. Kneeling.]** *Johnson*

97 **unwillingly,]** *F4;* vnwillingly *F1*

98–9 **grievous— . . . Grievous—]** *Alexander (after Kittredge);* greeuous. . . . Greeuous *F1*

131 **due]** *F3;* dew *F1*

139 **precipit]** Precipice *F2*

140 **woo]** *F2;* woe *F1*

152 **good man]** *F3;* goodman *F1*

158 **s.p. Old L.]** *Capell;* Lady. *F1 (throughout scene)*

169 **s.d. Enter Lovell.]** *Steevens*

169 **Sir?]** *Dyce;* Sir. *F1*

176 **s.d. with Lovell]** *ed. (after Capell)*

V.ii

Location: *Foakes (after Theobald)*

o.s.d. **Pursuivants . . . attending.]** *Globe (after Capell)*

7 **s.d. Butts]** *F3;* Buts *F1 (through l. 20)*

8 **s.d. Aside.]** *Dyce*

8 **piece]** *F2;* Peere *F1*

10 **s.d. Aside.]** *Johnson*

10 **Butts,]** *F3;* Buts. *F1*

20 **sight—]** *Rowe;* sight. *F1*

35 **s.d. Curtain . . . listening.]** *ed.*

47 **flesh;]** *Capell;* flesh, *F1*

51 **chaplains']** *Capell;* Chaplaines *F1*

84 **Councillor]** *Rowe;* Counsellor *F1*

110 **faulty]** *F2;* faultly *F1*

120 **s.p. Chan.]** *Capell;* Cham. *F1*

122 **s.p. Chan.]** *Theobald conj.;* Cham. *F1*

143 **s.d. Exeunt . . . above.]** *ed. (after Sisson)*

160 **offenses.]** *Rowe;* offences, *F1*

161 **reach you]** *Rann (after Johnson, but reading* one for me); reach. You *F1*

165 **s.d. To Cranmer.]** *Rowe*

178 **Councillor]** *Cambridge;* Counsellour *F1*

194 **friends,]** *Capell;* friends *F1*

201–3 **Come . . . you?]** *as verse, Capell; as prose, F1*

206 **brother-love]** *Malone;* Brother; loue *F1*

208 **heart]** *F2;* hearts *F1*

V.iii

Location: *Theobald*

54–5 **broom-staff]** *hyphen, F3*

72 **friends]** *F2;* ftiends *F1*

76 **a-pieces]** *hyphen, Dyce*

84 **press]** *F4;* preasse *F1*

84 **a way]** *F2;* away *F1*

V.iv

Location: *Theobald*

1–3 **Heaven . . . Elizabeth!]** *as prose, Capell; as verse, F1*

4 **s.d. Kneeling.]** *Johnson*

6 **joy,]** *Pope;* ioy *F1*

9 **s.d. The . . . child.]** *Johnson*

37 **ways]** *F4;* way *F1*

75 **H'as]** *Rowe;* 'Has *F1*

76 **little one]** *F4;* Little-One *F1*

Epilogue

4 **trumpets]** *F2;* Tumpets *F1*

14 **clap.]** clap. / FINIS. *F1*

Titus Andronicus

TITUS ANDRONICUS, long acknowledged to be the earliest of Shakespeare's tragedies, seems to have been popular during Shakespeare's lifetime, for it appeared in three editions between 1594 and 1611, and was still worth a mention, albeit derogatory, in Ben Jonson's *Bartholomew Fair* (1614). Before the end of the seventeenth century, however, it fell into disfavor; and although Edward Ravenscroft, who adapted it in 1687, had a personal interest in denigrating his original, his description of the play as "a heap of rubbish" seemed on the whole to satisfy the eighteenth-century critics, who inclined to agree with him that Shakespeare could have had little or no part in such a work.

An unwillingness to attribute the play to Shakespeare, testifying as it does to a poor opinion of its merits, has persisted to the present day. But there has been a reaction against the fashion, prevalent in the early years of this century, for "disintegrating" the Shakespeare canon, and some distinguished scholars—H. T. Price and Peter Alexander are instances—now attribute the play wholly to Shakespeare. And at the same time there has been a modest attempt to improve the standing of the play. Price calls it "an excellent piece of stage-craft" and illustrates its careful rhetorical planning; Alexander reminds us that Shakespeare "was a beginner at the beginning of English tragedy, and he had to make what he could of it." Many critics would now accept Irving Ribner's statement that "*Titus Andronicus*, in poetry and characterization, is superior to any play written before it," though this is not intended to be a very high claim. E. M. W. Tillyard more warmly defends its positive merits—the precision of the plotting, the fine lyric passages, the "magnificent comic villain Aaron," and "the high political theme." Howard Baker's *Induction to Tragedy* gives us a more intelligent way of looking at the element of horror, and Eugene Waith has shown that Shakespeare had at least an intelligent purpose in using apparently incongruous imagery. It is not suggested that the race of critics who simply find the play repulsive and unworthy of Shakespeare has died out. But although nobody has called *Titus* anything but the least of Shakespeare's tragedies, there is a growing belief that the play has been unjustly despised.

Philip Henslowe, theatre-owner, referring in his diary to a performance of "Titus & Ondronicus" on January 23, 1594, prefixed to the entry the word "ne" (new). On February 6 the title "A Noble Roman Historye of Tytus Andronicus" was entered in the Stationers' Register; and this almost certainly refers to the quarto of the play published later in the same year with the title *The most Lamentable Romaine Tragedie of Titus Andronicus: As it was Plaide by the Right Honourable the Earle of Darbie, Earle of Pembrooke, and the Earl of Sussex their Seruants*. A copy of this long-lost book, found in Sweden in 1904, and now in the Folger Shakespeare Library, is the basis of modern editions, except for III.ii, which was first added to the printed text in the Folio of 1623. Despite certain small puzzles relating to speech-headings and the unusual re-entry of characters who have just left the stage, this "fly-killing scene" is probably by Shakespeare. Whether it formed part of the original play or was a later addition has not been determined.

The "Longleat Manuscript," which consists of a drawing (reproduced elsewhere in this book) by "Henricus Peacham" showing Tamora begging Titus to spare her sons, over whose heads Aaron holds a sword, dates from 1595, though the textual extracts which accompany it—a mixture of passages from I.i and V.i—seem to have been added later. They do not fit the picture, which in any case does not represent a scene in the play; and the manuscript has no importance.

It is now generally believed that the play could not have been literally "new" in 1594 (and that Henslowe's designation probably means either that it was then new to the repertory of Sussex's Men—a conjecture strengthened by the mention of the Q1 title-page of performances by three different acting groups—or that it had been revised). In 1614 Jonson sneered at people who thought "*Andronicus*" and *The Spanish Tragedy* good plays, saying their judgments had "stood still, these five and twenty, or thirty years." This could push the date of *Titus* back to the mid-eighties, where some are content to have it. But there may be a certain extravagance in Jonson's satirical language. That the play is at least as early as 1592 is suggested by two facts: first, an entry in Henslowe's diary for April 11 of a "new" play called *Titus and Vespasian* ("Tittus & Vespacia"), and second, an apparent allusion to *Titus Andronicus* in an anonymous play, recorded by Henslowe as "new" on June 10: King Edgar is said to be as welcome

As Titus was unto the Roman senators
When he had made a conquest on the Goths.

As to the first of these, the possibility that the play was *Titus Andronicus* in some form may be slightly increased by the existence of the German *Tragoedia von Tito Andronico*, which seems in part to derive from *Titus Andronicus*, and in which Lucius is called "Vespasian." But Vespasian (Emperor, A.D. 69–79) and Titus, who succeeded him, were celebrated in Imperial history and well known from Suetonius; it is probable that the lost play had to do with them, and that the German renaming of Lucius was somehow caused by the mutual attraction of the two names. This piece of evidence is probably worthless. The possible allusion to *Titus* in *A Knack to Know a Knave* creates some presumption that *Titus* existed by 1592, though the reference could well be to the chapbook version mentioned below. J. C. Maxwell has recently suggested that in *The Troublesome Reign of King John* (published 1591) there are two echoes of *Titus*, arguing from the context and from the reputation for plagiarism already earned by the author of that chronicle-play that *Titus* came first.

None of these arguments is strong enough to convince those who point to *Titus*' very strong links with *The Rape of Lucrece* and lesser ones with *Venus and Adonis*, both of which were written during the long closure of the theatres due to the plague in 1592–93; the hypothesis that Shakespeare also wrote *Titus* during this lull and had it acted a few weeks after the theatres reopened temporarily (December 1593) has the merit of simplicity. On the other hand, it may be thought that the occasional ineptitude of *Titus* makes a date so near to that of the virtuoso *Love's Labor's Lost* incredible, at any rate if one assumes Shakespeare's authorship.

The problem of date is involved with that of authorship, and there has grown up a great snarl of argument around one key word, *palliament* (I.i.182). This word, deriving from the Latin *pallium*, occurs in only one other place, George Peele's *The Honor of the Garter*, 1593. *Pallium* was an accepted term for the Garter cloak, and Peele coined the word *palliament* from it. It follows either that Peele wrote the passage in *Titus*, or that, if Shakespeare did so, it is later than *The Honor of the Garter*. And in *Titus* the *palliament* is said to be white, a mistake Peele is unlikely to have made. But *palliament*, though closely examined, has prevented nobody from sticking to his preconceived idea. H. T. Price defends Shakespeare's authorship and the late date; T. W. Baldwin believes in a non-Shakespearean "first *Titus*" written about 1588 or 1589 and revised by Peele and Shakespeare in 1594; Dover Wilson thinks that the original play dates from the summer of 1593, when Peele wrote it for Lord Strange's (the Earl of Derby's) Men, and that for revision at the end of the year Peele and Shakespeare divided up the play, Shakespeare, broadly speaking, revising all save the first act. J. C. Maxwell favors the date 1589–90 and Peele's authorship of Act I.

The argument for Peele's part in the play does not, of course, depend entirely upon his coinage *palliament*. It is primarily an argument from style, the appearance, especially in Act I, of tricks of repetition and syntax paralleled in Peele's poems but rare in Shakespeare. Such arguments are always hard to maintain against learned scepticism. And the earlier the date one accepts for *Titus*, the more probable it becomes that the young Shakespeare would consciously or unconsciously imitate Peele, an established dramatist, or operate in the rhetorical range of the drama of the 1580's. Most scholars would agree that *Titus* is structurally much superior to any extant play of Peele's.

These difficulties seem indeterminable. The main possibilities are (1) sole Shakespearean authorship and an early date; (2) sole Shakespearean authorship, 1593–94; (3) collaboration between Shakespeare and Peele, 1593–94; (4) early composition by Peele, revision in 1593–94 by Shakespeare, or by Peele and Shakespeare. The fourth, or some slight variant upon it, is the most probable in the present state of the evidence; but it should be added that the knowledgeable Francis Meres in *Palladis Tamia* (1598) attributed the play to Shakespeare, and that Heminge and Condell included it in the First Folio.

The nearest thing to a source for *Titus Andronicus* is an eighteenth-century chapbook, now in the Folger Shakespeare Library, called *The History of Titus Andronicus, The Renowned Roman General . . . Newly Translated from the Italian Copy printed at Rome*. It is generally agreed that an ancestor of this chapbook was the source, or a version of the source, of *Titus Andronicus* (or, as Baldwin holds, of the original *Titus*).

The story is set in the fourth century A.D. It tells of Titus saving Rome from the Goths and the loss of twenty-two of his sons and of the marriage of the Emperor to the captive Queen of the Goths against

Titus' advice. The Queen seeks revenge on him, and uses her lover, a Moor, by whom she has a blackamoor child, to procure it. Lavinia is betrothed to a son of the Emperor Theodosius by a former marriage; and Tamora makes a plan to achieve both dynastic security and personal revenge. The Moor and the Queen's sons murder the Emperor's son and throw him into a pit; the sons of Titus are tricked, as in the play, and accused of the murder; and Titus forfeits his hand. The Queen's sons rape Lavinia, who is able to inform on them. Titus feigns madness, and there is an arrow-shooting incident. He traps the Queen's sons and arranges a bloody banquet. He has the Emperor and the Queen killed, himself kills Lavinia, and takes his own life.

The chapbook has nothing corresponding to the election scene at the beginning of *Titus Andronicus*; it lacks the sacrifice of Alarbus, which gives Tamora a stronger motive to persecute Titus and makes the hero in part responsible for the evils which are to beset him. There is no Lucius to lead the invading Gothic army; Aaron is a mere tool of the Queen, and the chapbook knows nothing of his love for the child or of his defiance at the end. The chapbook is more interested in Gothic-Roman relations than is Shakespeare, but less concerned with such political matters as the restoration of a strong government after civil strife (a characteristic Shakespeare preoccupation). The changes, of which the foregoing are the most striking, do not exceed what might be expected of a dramatist who has both to concentrate his story and fit it to the stage, as well as to his own interests.

Other minor sources have been found, especially for the names of the characters; and there are analogues in Renaissance literature. But the most important sources after the story outlined above are Ovid, Seneca, and—to be deliberately vague—Roman history. Ovid, always the most important of the classical poets to Shakespeare, provided the story of Philomela's rape by Tereus and the revenge of Progne, who served Tereus a meal consisting of his son. This story echoes through *Titus*; and Shakespeare also uses Ovid in IV.iii, where Titus remembers the departure of Astraea, which signified the end of the Golden Age on earth. Seneca is an important name in Elizabethan drama. It is possible to believe, with Howard Baker, that the Senecan element in early English tragedy has been exaggerated, even with respect to *The Spanish Tragedy* and *Titus*; certainly we should remember that Elizabethan stoicism is not quite the stoicism of Seneca, and that such works as *A Mirror for Magistrates* provide examples, non-dramatic but easily accessible, of the tragedy-ghost, descriptions of the horrors attending the revenges and deaths of great men, and those moral tags or sentences which can be traced back to Seneca. And just as certainly it should be recalled that the structure of such a tragedy as *Titus*, though it has some superficial Senecan qualities, is characteristic of the native tradition. Nevertheless, Seneca had much prestige at this time, his influence being in part direct, in part mediated by the neo-Senecanism of the Italian theorist and dramatist Cinthio. Certainly the famous banquet of the two sons served by Atreus to their father Thyestes in Seneca's drama of that name can scarcely have been out of Shakespeare's thoughts.

Finally, we may sometimes think of *Titus* as a Roman play. Some years later, Shakespeare was to develop an intense interest in Roman politics of the period when Republic was giving way to Empire; in his late tragedy *Coriolanus* he reverted to an early republican theme of which he is already aware in *Titus* (IV.iv.68); and in 1593 he was already writing Roman history or legend in *The Rape of Lucrece*. From the major Roman plays most of us first learned Roman history, but no one's view of imperial Rome is much affected by *Titus*. It offers, on the face of it, a very confused representation, with features drawn from different periods. There are anachronisms: human sacrifice and panther-hunting were not practiced in Rome, and holy water was not used in marriage. Yet we should remember that it does contain that political interest which distinguishes the later Roman tragedies; it is, as T. J. B. Spencer has argued, "*intended* to be a faithful picture of Roman civilisation"; and, in view of the nature of Elizabethan interest in the subject (which would, for example, distort by magnification the element of hereditary monarchy), it is just to add with Spencer that this "quintessence of impressions derived from . . . eager reading" would strike a sixteenth-century audience as "typical Roman history."

There is small point in denying that an exhibition of horror—rape, murder, severed hands—of the kind usually conveyed by the word "Senecan" is a prime motive of *Titus Andronicus*. But we have also to remember that here, as in *The Rape of Lucrece*, there is a distancing of horror, which is treated with a kind of formality, or embodied in imagery which may strike a modern eye as indecorous (see for example II.iv.16 ff.) but is intended, as Eugene Waith has argued, to reinforce the feeling of strangeness and unreality, to make Lavinia's suffering "an object of contemplation." There is a refined pathos about the fly-killing exemplum which reminds one less of *The Spanish Tragedy* (to which *Titus* is so closely related) than of the sophisticated additions to it which were printed in 1602.

Behind such sophistication lies a long tradition: the great man's—or woman's—complaint against Fortune. But the immediate literary context of *Titus* is theatrical. It belongs to the *genre* of Elizabethan Revenge play. Before it came Kyd's *Spanish Tragedy* (a favorite over many years) and the first *Hamlet*, which Shakespeare himself was to replace in 1600 or 1601. Shakespeare built into the *Titus* story themes associated with this genre, and devised for it a dramatic pattern close to that sketched by earlier Revenge plays. Titus as revenger must, on the official view that vengeance properly belongs to God alone, become something of a villain; and in his insistence on the sacrifice of Alarbus, his doctrinaire stubbornness over the election of Saturninus, and the rash killing of his own son, he forfeits sympathy. The role of Marcus, who insists on the wickedness of vengeful killing, is created to strengthen this impression. But Shakespeare is aware of the possibilities of divided sympathy here, and there is no doubt that when, in the scene of arrows, he gives the grief of Titus a special poignancy, a philosophical quality, or when he allows him the best of the argument in the fly-killing scene, or loads him with sorrows wantonly inflicted by Tamora and her party, he is working to procure such a division. In the same way he uses the boy Lucius to restore sympathy to Titus.

Other features of the Revenge play are: the pretended madness or "feigned ecstasy" of the revenger, which, as Fredson Bowers points out, is better motivated than that of Hamlet (from which, in all probability, it ultimately springs); and the delay in his revenge. The chapbook does not delay Lavinia's revelation of the identity of her attackers as the play does; Titus knows his enemies from the beginning of Act IV, and then waits until the supersubtle plotting of Tamora gives him the chance to serve her with the Thyestean banquet.

Although, in the manner of Revenge tragedy, the design of *Titus* is founded on a blood-feud, the scope is broadened to include dynastic preoccupations. (There is a curious partial parallel between Tamora's attempt to divert Lucius from his purpose and that of Volumnia when Coriolanus arrives at the gates of Rome with the Volscians.) The conduct of the multiple action is skillful enough; and the complaint that the play is episodic probably derives from the careful and somewhat rigid rhetoric by which each part of the action is moulded, so that there is an appearance of static exposition and spasmodic advance.

There have been attempts to show that the whole play is intended as burlesque. These do not succeed; but there are moments when the farcical possibilities inherent in Grand Guignol seem to be deliberately invoked, as when Titus appears as a chef, or when Aaron defies his captors and expresses his soldierly love for the bastard child. It is perfectly easy to underestimate the flexibility of the early Elizabethan theatre, still associated in many ways with all manner of shows and entertainments, still close to the mood of those miracle plays in which Herod is not only a terror but a joke. When T. S. Eliot called *The Jew of Malta* a farce rather than a "tragedy of blood" he was not making an empty paradox; in a way it is both. And Aaron, the most memorable character in *Titus*, has a good deal in him of Marlowe's Barabas. Even now it is his brazen vitality that endears him. His terrific self-sufficiency, an acceptance of the Machiavellian *homo homini lupus*, makes him at once a matter of wonder and a dangerous joke; he rages round a society ostensibly governed by law and custom, a black among the whites. Even Tamora, herself a monster of lust and cruelty, seems in the end to belong to the tamer white world.

There are tracts of verse in *Titus Andronicus* that must be called archaic, rigid. But the play itself, though certainly the least of the tragedies, illustrates the fantastic range of possibilities that were to be explored later. More immediately, it points the way from Kyd and Marlowe to *Hamlet*.

Frank Kermode

The illustration above is from the Folger Library copy of a broadside ballad (printed between 1655 and 1665) entitled "The Lamentable and Tragicall History of Titus Andronicus, with the fall of his five and twenty sons in the wars of [t]he Goaths, with the ravishment of his daughter Lavinia by the Empresse two sons, through the means of a bloody Moor, taken by the sword of Titus in the war, with his revenge upon them for their cruell an[d] inhumane act. To the tune of Fortune my Foe." The woodcut is a composite presentation of several of the principal incidents in the play and ballad.

The Tragedy of Titus Andronicus

[DRAMATIS PERSONAE

SATURNINUS, *son to the late Emperor of Rome, afterwards Emperor*
BASSIANUS, *brother to Saturninus*
TITUS ANDRONICUS, *a noble Roman, general against the Goths*
MARCUS ANDRONICUS, *tribune of the people, brother to Titus*
LUCIUS, QUINTUS, MARTIUS, MUTIUS } *sons to Titus Andronicus*
YOUNG LUCIUS, *a boy, son to Lucius*
AEMILIUS, *a noble Roman*
PUBLIUS, *son to Marcus Andronicus*
SEMPRONIUS, CAIUS, VALENTINE } *kinsmen to Titus*

ALARBUS, DEMETRIUS, CHIRON } *sons to Tamora*
AARON, *a Moor, beloved by Tamora*
CAPTAIN
MESSENGER
TRIBUNE
CLOWN

TAMORA, *Queen of the Goths*
LAVINIA, *daughter to Titus Andronicus*
NURSE, *and a black* CHILD

ROMANS *and* GOTHS, SENATORS, TRIBUNES, OFFICERS, SOLDIERS, *and* ATTENDANTS

SCENE: *Rome, and the country near it*]

[ACT I, SCENE I]

Enter the TRIBUNES, [*among them* MARCUS ANDRONICUS,] *and* SENATORS *aloft, and then enter,* [*below,*] SATURNINUS *and his followers at one door, and* BASSIANUS *and his followers* [*at the other*], *with Drums and Trumpets.*

Sat. Noble patricians, patrons of my right,
Defend the justice of my cause with arms;
And, countrymen, my loving followers,
Plead my successive title with your swords.
I am his first-born son, that was the last
That ware the imperial diadem of Rome,
Then let my father's honors live in me,
Nor wrong mine age with this indignity.
Bas. Romans, friends, followers, favorers of my right,
If ever Bassianus, Caesar's son,
Were gracious in the eyes of royal Rome,
Keep then this passage to the Capitol,
And suffer not dishonor to approach
The imperial seat, to virtue consecrate,
To justice, continence, and nobility;
But let desert in pure election shine,
And, Romans, fight for freedom in your choice.
Marc. [*Holding the crown.*] Princes, that strive by factions and by friends
Ambitiously for rule and empery,
Know that the people of Rome, for whom we stand
A special party, have by common voice,
In election for the Roman empery,
Chosen Andronicus, surnamed Pius
For many good and great deserts to Rome.
A nobler man, a braver warrior,
Lives not this day within the city walls.
He by the Senate is accited home
From weary wars against the barbarous Goths,

Words and passages enclosed in square brackets in the text above are either emendations of the copy-text or additions to it. The Textual Notes immediately following the play cite the earliest authority for every such change or insertion and supply the reading of the copy-text wherever it is emended in this edition.

I.i. Location: Rome. Before the Senate-house. The tomb of the Andronici appearing.
1. patrons: protectors, supporters.
4. successive title: right of succession. **6. ware:** wore.
8. age: seniority (as the elder son).

11. gracious: acceptable. **12. Keep:** guard.
14. consecrate: consecrated.
16. pure election: free choice, i.e. made without regard to primogeniture.
19. empery: status of emperor.
20. people: common people, plebs.
21. A special party: representatives for a particular purpose. **voice:** vote, approval. **23. Chosen:** i.e. nominated.
27. accited: summoned.

That with his sons, a terror to our foes,
Hath yok'd a nation strong, train'd up in arms.
Ten years are spent since first he undertook
This cause of Rome, and chastised with arms
Our enemies' pride; five times he hath return'd
Bleeding to Rome, bearing his valiant sons
In coffins from the field,
And now at last, laden with honor's spoils,
Returns the good Andronicus to Rome,
Renowned Titus, flourishing in arms.
Let us entreat by honor of his name,
Whom worthily you would have now succeed,
And in the Capitol and Senate's right,
Whom you pretend to honor and adore,
That you withdraw you, and abate your strength,
Dismiss your followers, and, as suitors should,
Plead your deserts in peace and humbleness.

Sat. How fair the tribune speaks to calm my thoughts!

Bas. Marcus Andronicus, so I do affy
In thy uprightness and integrity,
And so I love and honor thee and thine,
Thy noble brother Titus and his sons,
And her to whom my thoughts are humbled all,
Gracious Lavinia, Rome's rich ornament,
That I will here dismiss my loving friends;
And to my fortunes and the people's favor
Commit my cause in balance to be weigh'd.

Exeunt Soldiers [of Bassianus].

Sat. Friends, that have been thus forward in my right,
I thank you all and here dismiss you all,
And to the love and favor of my country
Commit myself, my person, and the cause.

[Exeunt Soldiers of Saturninus.]

Rome, be as just and gracious unto me
As I am confident and kind to thee.
Open the gates and let me in.

Bas. Tribunes, and me, a poor competitor.

[Flourish.] They go up into the Senate-house.

Enter a CAPTAIN.

[*Cap.*] Romans, make way! The good Andronicus,
Patron of virtue, Rome's best champion,
Successful in the battles that he fights,
With honor and with fortune is return'd.
From where he circumscribed with his sword,
And brought to yoke, the enemies of Rome.

Sound drums and trumpets, and then enter two of Titus' sons [MARTIUS *and* MUTIUS]; *and then two* MEN *bearing a coffin covered with black; then two other sons* [LUCIUS *and* QUINTUS]. *Then* TITUS ANDRONICUS; *and then* TAMORA, *the Queen of Goths, and her [three] sons* [ALARBUS,] CHIRON, *and* DEMETRIUS; *with* AARON *the Moor, and others as many as can be. Then set down the coffin, and Titus speaks.*

Tit. Hail, Rome, victorious in thy mourning weeds!
Lo, as the bark that hath discharg'd his fraught
Returns with precious lading to the bay
From whence at first she weigh'd her anchorage,
Cometh Andronicus, bound with laurel boughs,
To re-salute his country with his tears,
Tears of true joy for his return to Rome.
Thou great defender of this Capitol,
Stand gracious to the rites that we intend!
Romans, of five and twenty valiant sons,
Half of the number that King Priam had,
Behold the poor remains, alive and dead!
These that survive let Rome reward with love;
These that I bring unto their latest home,
With burial amongst their ancestors.
Here Goths have given me leave to sheathe my sword.
Titus, unkind and careless of thine own,
Why suffer'st thou thy sons, unburied yet,
To hover on the dreadful shore of Styx?
Make way to lay them by their bretheren.

They open the tomb.

There greet in silence, as the dead are wont,
And sleep in peace, slain in your country's wars!
O sacred receptacle of my joys,
Sweet cell of virtue and nobility,
How many sons hast thou of mine in store,
That thou wilt never render to me more!

Luc. Give us the proudest prisoner of the Goths,
That we may hew his limbs and on a pile
Ad [manes] fratrum sacrifice his flesh
Before this earthy prison of their bones,
That so the shadows be not unappeas'd,
Nor we disturb'd with prodigies on earth.

Tit. I give him you, the noblest that survives,
The eldest son of this distressed queen.

Tam. Stay, Roman brethren! Gracious conqueror,
Victorious Titus, rue the tears I shed,
A mother's tears in passion for her son;
And if thy sons were ever dear to thee,
O, think my son to be as dear to me!
Sufficeth not that we are brought to Rome
To beautify thy triumphs, and return
Captive to thee and to thy Roman yoke;
But must my sons be slaughtered in the streets
For valiant doings in their country's cause?
O, if to fight for king and commonweal

30. **yok'd**: tamed, subdued.
35. On this short line see the Textual Notes.
40. **succeed.** Probably a contraction of the past participle *succeeded*: "(the late emperor) whom you want to be followed by a worthy successor."
41. **in . . . right**: in deference to the authority of Capitol and senate.
42. **pretend**: claim. 47. **affy**: trust.
61. **confident**: confiding, trusting. **kind**: attached by natural affection. 63 s.d. **Flourish**: fanfare of trumpets.
68. **circumscribed**: restrained.
71. **his**: its (but often emended to *her* to accord with line 73). **fraught**: freight.
73. **anchorage**: equipment for anchoring, i.e. anchors.
77. **defender**: Jupiter Capitolinus.
80. **Priam**: king of Troy at the time of the Trojan war, and father of fifty sons. 83. **latest**: last.
86. **unkind**: lacking in natural feeling.
88. **Styx**: river boundary of Hades, which the soul could not cross until the body had received proper burial.
98. **Ad manes fratrum**: to the shades of our brothers.
100. **shadows**: shades, ghosts. 101. **prodigies**: events of ill omen.
106. **passion**: grief.
110. **return**: i.e. accompany you on your return. Many editors omit the comma after *triumphs* and construe *return* as a noun.

Were piety in thine, it is in these.
Andronicus, stain not thy tomb with blood!
Wilt thou draw near the nature of the gods?
Draw near them then in being merciful:
Sweet mercy is nobility's true badge.
Thrice-noble Titus, spare my first-born son!
  Tit. Patient yourself, madam, and pardon me.
These are their brethren, whom your Goths beheld
Alive and dead, and for their brethren slain
Religiously they ask a sacrifice:
To this your son is mark'd, and die he must,
T' appease their groaning shadows that are gone.
  Luc. Away with him, and make a fire straight,
And with our swords, upon a pile of wood,
Let's hew his limbs till they be clean consum'd.

Exeunt Titus' sons with Alarbus.

  Tam. O cruel, irreligious piety!
  Chi. Was never Scythia half so barbarous.
  Dem. Oppose not Scythia to ambitious Rome;
Alarbus goes to rest, and we survive
To tremble under Titus' threat'ning look.
Then, madam, stand resolv'd, but hope withal
The self-same gods that arm'd the Queen of Troy
With opportunity of sharp revenge
Upon the Thracian tyrant in his tent
May favor Tamora, the Queen of Goths
(When Goths were Goths and Tamora was queen),
To quit the bloody wrongs upon her foes.

Enter the sons of Andronicus [LUCIUS, QUINTUS, MARTIUS, *and* MUTIUS] *again* [*with their swords bloody*].

  Luc. See, lord and father, how we have perform'd
Our Roman rites. Alarbus' limbs are lopp'd,
And entrails feed the sacrificing fire,
Whose smoke like incense doth perfume the sky.
Remaineth nought but to inter our brethren,
And with loud 'larums welcome them to Rome.
  Tit. Let it be so, and let Andronicus
Make this his latest farewell to their souls.

Sound trumpets, and lay the coffin in the tomb.

In peace and honor rest you here, my sons,
Rome's readiest champions, repose you here in rest,
Secure from worldly chances and mishaps!
Here lurks no treason, here no envy swells,
Here grow no damned drugs, here are no storms,
No noise, but silence and eternal sleep.
In peace and honor rest you here, my sons!

Enter LAVINIA.

  [*Lav.*] In peace and honor live Lord Titus long!
My noble lord and father, live in fame!
Lo at this tomb my tributary tears
I render for my brethren's obsequies;
And at thy feet I kneel, with tears of joy
Shed on this earth for thy return to Rome.
O, bless me here with thy victorious hand,
Whose fortunes Rome's best citizens applaud!
  Tit. Kind Rome, that hast thus lovingly reserv'd
The cordial of mine age to glad my heart!
Lavinia, live, outlive thy father's days,
And fame's eternal date, for virtue's praise!

[*Marcus Andronicus, attended by the other Tribunes, with Saturninus and Bassianus, speaks from above.*]

  Marc. Long live Lord Titus, my beloved brother,
Gracious triumpher in the eyes of Rome!
  Tit. Thanks, gentle tribune, noble brother Marcus.
  Marc. And welcome, nephews, from successful wars,
You that survive, and you that sleep in fame!
Fair lords, your fortunes are alike in all,
That in your country's service drew your swords,
But safer triumph is this funeral pomp,
That hath aspir'd to Solon's happiness,
And triumphs over chance in honor's bed.
Titus Andronicus, the people of Rome,
Whose friend in justice thou hast ever been,
Send thee by me, their tribune and their trust,
This palliament of white and spotless hue,
And name thee in election for the empire,
With these our late-deceased emperor's sons.
Be *candidatus* then and put it on,
And help to set a head on headless Rome.
  Tit. A better head her glorious body fits
Than his that shakes for age and feebleness.
What should I don this robe and trouble you?
Be chosen with proclamations to-day,
To-morrow yield up rule, resign my life,
And set abroad new business for you all?
Rome, I have been thy soldier forty years,
And led my country's strength successfully,
And buried one and twenty valiant sons,
Knighted in field, slain manfully in arms,
In right and service of their noble country.
Give me a staff of honor for mine age,
But not a sceptre to control the world.
Upright he held it, lords, that held it last.
  Marc. Titus, thou shalt obtain and ask the empery.
  Sat. Proud and ambitious tribune, canst thou tell?
  Tit. Patience, Prince Saturninus.
  Sat. Romans, do me right.
Patricians, draw your swords, and sheathe them not
Till Saturninus be Rome's emperor.
Andronicus, would thou were shipp'd to hell,
Rather than rob me of the people's hearts!
  Luc. Proud Saturnine, interrupter of the good
That noble-minded Titus means to thee!

121. Patient yourself: school yourself to patience.
127. straight: straightway.
131. Scythia: region north of the Black Sea, notorious for the barbarity of its inhabitants. **132. Oppose:** compare.
136. Queen of Troy: Hecuba, Priam's queen, who avenged her son Polydorus by killing the sons of his murderer Polymnestor, king of Thrace. **141. quit:** requite, avenge. **147. 'larums:** trumpet calls.
154. drugs: plants which produce poisons.
159. tributary: of tribute.
166. **cordial:** comfort.
177. **aspir'd:** risen. **Solon's happiness.** This philosopher advised, "Call no man happy until he is dead."
182. **palliament:** cloak (from Latin *pallium*). See the introduction, p. 1066.
185. **candidatus:** literally, clad in a white robe (the dress donned by candidates for office).
189. **What:** why. 192. **set abroad:** set on foot.
201. **obtain and ask:** obtain by merely asking.
202. **canst thou tell:** i.e. that's what you think.

Tit. Content thee, Prince, I will restore to thee
The people's hearts, and wean them from themselves.
Bas. Andronicus, I do not flatter thee,
But honor thee, and will do till I die.
My faction if thou strengthen with thy friends,
I will most thankful be, and thanks to men
Of noble minds is honorable meed.
Tit. People of Rome, and people's tribunes here,
I ask your voices and your suffrages:
Will ye bestow them friendly on Andronicus?
Tribunes. To gratify the good Andronicus,
And gratulate his safe return to Rome,
The people will accept whom he admits.
Tit. Tribunes, I thank you, and this suit I make,
That you create our emperor's eldest son,
Lord Saturnine, whose virtues will, I hope,
Reflect on Rome as [Titan's] rays on earth,
And ripen justice in this commonweal.
Then if you will elect by my advice,
Crown him and say, "Long live our emperor!"
Marc. With voices and applause of every sort,
Patricians and plebeians, we create
Lord Saturninus Rome's great emperor,
And say, "Long live our Emperor Saturnine!"
[*A long flourish till they come down.*]
Sat. Titus Andronicus, for thy favors done
To us in our election this day,
I give thee thanks in part of thy deserts,
And will with deeds requite thy gentleness;
And for an onset, Titus, to advance
Thy name and honorable family,
Lavinia will I make my emperess,
Rome's royal mistress, mistress of my heart,
And in the sacred [Pantheon] her espouse.
Tell me, Andronicus, doth this motion please thee?
Tit. It doth, my worthy lord, and in this match
I hold me highly honored of your Grace,
And here in sight of Rome to Saturnine,
King and commander of our commonweal,
The wide world's emperor, do I consecrate
My sword, my chariot, and my prisoners,
Presents well worthy Rome's imperious lord:
Receive them then, the tribute that I owe,
Mine honor's ensigns humbled at thy feet.
Sat. Thanks, noble Titus, father of my life!
How proud I am of thee and of thy gifts
Rome shall record, and when I do forget
The least of these unspeakable deserts,
Romans, forget your fealty to me.
Tit. [*To Tamora.*] Now, madam, are you prisoner to an emperor;
To him that, for your honor and your state,
Will use you nobly and your followers.
Sat. [*Aside.*] A goodly lady, trust me, of the hue
That I would choose were I to choose anew.—
Clear up, fair queen, that cloudy countenance;
Though [chance] of war hath wrought this change of cheer,
Thou com'st not to be made a scorn in Rome;
Princely shall be thy usage every way.
Rest on my word, and let not discontent
Daunt all your hopes. Madam, he comforts you
Can make you greater than the Queen of Goths.
Lavinia, you are not displeas'd with this?
Lav. Not I, my lord, sith true nobility
Warrants these words in princely courtesy.
Sat. Thanks, sweet Lavinia. Romans, let us go;
Ransomless here we set our prisoners free.
Proclaim our honors, lords, with trump and drum.
[*Flourish. Saturninus courts Tamora in dumb show.*]
Bas. Lord Titus, by your leave, this maid is mine.
[*Seizing Lavinia.*]
Tit. How, sir? are you in earnest then, my lord?
Bas. Ay, noble Titus, and resolv'd withal
To do myself this reason and this right.
Marc. *Suum* [*cuique*] is our Roman justice:
This prince in justice seizeth but his own.
Luc. And that he will, and shall, if Lucius live.
Tit. Traitors, avaunt! Where is the Emperor's guard?
Treason, my lord! Lavinia is surpris'd!
Sat. Surpris'd? by whom?
Bas. By him that justly may
Bear his betroth'd from all the world away.
[*Exeunt Bassianus and Marcus with Lavinia.*]
Mut. Brothers, help to convey her hence away,
And with my sword I'll keep this door safe.
[*Exeunt Lucius, Quintus, and Martius.*]
Tit. Follow, my lord, and I'll soon bring her back.
Mut. My lord, you pass not here.
Tit. What, villain boy,
Barr'st me my way in Rome?
Mut. Help, Lucius, help! [*Titus kills him.*]
[*During the fray, exeunt Saturninus, Tamora, Demetrius, Chiron, and Aaron.*]

[*Enter* Lucius.]

Luc. My lord, you are unjust, and more than so,
In wrongful quarrel you have slain your son.
Tit. Nor thou, nor he, are any sons of mine,
My sons would never so dishonor me.

Enter aloft the Emperor *with* Tamora *and her two sons* [Demetrius *and* Chiron] *and* Aaron *the Moor.*

Traitor, restore Lavinia to the Emperor.
Luc. Dead, if you will, but not to be his wife,
That is another's lawful promis'd love. [*Exit.*]
Sat. No, Titus, no, the Emperor needs her not,
Nor her, nor thee, nor any of thy stock.
I'll trust by leisure him that mocks me once,
Thee never, nor thy traitorous haughty sons,
Confederates all thus to dishonor me.
Was none in Rome to make a stale

216. **meed:** reward. 218. **suffrages:** votes.
221. **gratulate:** give thanks for. 224. **create:** elect.
226. **Titan's:** the sun-god's.
236. **in . . . deserts:** as part-payment of the reward you deserve.
237. **gentleness:** nobility, noble action. 238. **onset:** start.
242. **Pantheon:** temple dedicated to all the gods.
243. **motion:** proposal. 250. **imperious:** imperial.
252. **ensigns:** outward signs, tokens.
256. **unspeakable:** inexpressible.

264. **cheer:** countenance. 269. **Can:** who can. 271. **sith:** since.
272. **Warrants:** justifies. 280. **Suum cuique:** to each his own.
284. **surpris'd:** taken. 300. **Nor:** neither.
301. **by leisure:** not in a hurry, i.e. not at all.
304. **stale:** laughingstock.

But Saturnine? Full well, Andronicus,
Agree these deeds with that proud brag of thine,
That saidst I begg'd the empire at thy hands.

Tit. O monstrous! what reproachful words are these?

Sat. But go thy ways, go give that changing piece
To him that flourish'd for her with his sword.
A valiant son-in-law thou shalt enjoy,
One fit to bandy with thy lawless sons,
To ruffle in the commonwealth of Rome.

Tit. These words are razors to my wounded heart.

Sat. And therefore, lovely Tamora, Queen of Goths,
That like the stately [Phoebe] 'mongst her nymphs
Dost overshine the gallant'st dames of Rome,
If thou be pleas'd with this my sudden choice,
Behold, I choose thee, Tamora, for my bride,
And will create thee Emperess of Rome.
Speak, Queen of Goths, dost thou applaud my choice?
And here I swear by all the Roman gods,
Sith priest and holy water are so near,
And tapers burn so bright, and every thing
In readiness for Hymenaeus stand,
I will not re-salute the streets of Rome,
Or climb my palace, till from forth this place
I lead espous'd my bride along with me.

Tam. And here in sight of heaven to Rome I swear,
If Saturnine advance the Queen of Goths,
She will a handmaid be to his desires,
A loving nurse, a mother to his youth.

Sat. Ascend, fair queen, Pantheon. Lords, accompany
Your noble emperor and his lovely bride,
Sent by the heavens for Prince Saturnine,
Whose wisdom hath her fortune conquered.
There shall we consummate our spousal rites.

Exeunt omnes [except Titus].

Tit. I am not bid to wait upon this bride.
Titus, when wert thou wont to walk alone,
Dishonored thus and challenged of wrongs?

Enter Marcus *and Titus' sons* [Lucius, Quintus, *and* Martius].

Marc. O Titus, see! O, see what thou hast done!
In a bad quarrel slain a virtuous son.

Tit. No, foolish tribune, no; no son of mine,
Nor thou, nor these, confederates in the deed
That hath dishonored all our family:
Unworthy brother, and unworthy sons!

Luc. But let us give him burial as becomes,
Give Mutius burial with our bretheren.

Tit. Traitors, away, he rests not in this tomb.
This monument five hundreth years hath stood,
Which I have sumptuously re-edified.
Here none but soldiers and Rome's servitors

309. **piece:** wench.
310. **flourish'd . . . sword:** drew his sword to get her.
312. **bandy:** brawl. 313. **ruffle:** swagger. 316. **Phoebe:** Diana.
325. **Hymenaeus:** god of marriage. 338. **bid:** invited.
340. **challenged:** accused. 347. **becomes:** is fitting.
350. **hundreth:** hundred.

Repose in fame; none basely slain in brawls.
Bury him where you can, he comes not here.

Marc. My lord, this is impiety in you.
My nephew Mutius' deeds do plead for him,
He must be buried with his bretheren.

[*Mart.*] And shall, or him we will accompany.

Tit. "And shall"? What villain was it spake that word?

[*Mart.*] He that would vouch it in any place but here.

Tit. What, would you bury him in my despite?

Marc. No, noble Titus, but entreat of thee
To pardon Mutius and to bury him.

Tit. Marcus! even thou hast strook upon my crest,
And with these boys mine honor thou hast wounded.
My foes I do repute you every one,
So trouble me no more, but get you gone.

[*Quin.*] He is not with himself, let us withdraw.

[*Mart.*] Not I, till Mutius' bones be buried.

The brother and the sons kneel.

Marc. Brother, for in that name doth nature plead—

[*Mart.*] Father, and in that name doth nature speak—

Tit. Speak thou no more, if all the rest will speed.

Marc. Renowmed Titus, more than half my soul—

Luc. Dear father, soul and substance of us all—

Marc. Suffer thy brother Marcus to inter
His noble nephew here in virtue's nest,
That died in honor and Lavinia's cause.
Thou art a Roman, be not barbarous:
The Greeks upon advice did bury Ajax
That slew himself; and wise Laertes' son
Did graciously plead for his funerals;
Let not young Mutius then, that was thy joy,
Be barr'd his entrance here.

Tit. Rise, Marcus, rise.
The dismall'st day is this that e'er I saw,
To be dishonored by my sons in Rome!
Well, bury him, and bury me the next.

They put him in the tomb.

Luc. There lie thy bones, sweet Mutius, with thy friends,
Till we with trophies do adorn thy tomb.

They all kneel and say: No man shed tears for noble Mutius,
He lives in fame, that died in virtue's cause.

All but Marcus and Titus [stand aside].

Marc. My lord, to step out of these dreary dumps,
How comes it that the subtile Queen of Goths
Is of a sudden thus advanc'd in Rome?

360. **vouch:** maintain. 364. **strook:** struck.
368. **not with:** beside.
372. **if . . . speed.** Obscure; perhaps "if my remaining sons are to survive my wrath (as Mutius did not)."
373. **Renowmed:** renowned.
379. **advice:** deliberation. **Ajax:** one of the Greek heroes in the Trojan war. Maddened by resentment when Achilles' arms were granted to Odysseus instead of to him, he slew a flock of sheep under the delusion that they were Greeks, and later committed suicide in shame. The Greeks at first refused him burial as an enemy to Greece but were persuaded by Odysseus (*Laertes' son,* line 380) to give him an honorable funeral.
388. **trophies:** memorials. 391. **dumps:** melancholy fits.

Tit. I know not, Marcus, but I know it is
(Whether by device or no, the heavens can tell).
Is she not then beholding to the man
That brought her for this high good turn so far?
[Yes, and will nobly him remunerate.]

[*Flourish.*] *Enter the* EMPEROR, TAMORA *and her two sons* [DEMETRIUS *and* CHIRON], *with the Moor* [AARON], *at one door; enter, at the other door,* BASSIANUS *and* LAVINIA *with others.*

Sat. So, Bassianus, you have play'd your prize.
God give you joy, sir, of your gallant bride!
Bas. And you of yours, my lord! I say no more,
Nor wish no less, and so I take my leave.
Sat. Traitor, if Rome have law, or we have power,
Thou and thy faction shall repent this rape.
Bas. Rape call you it, my lord, to seize my own,
My true betrothed love, and now my wife?
But let the laws of Rome determine all,
Mean while am I possess'd of that is mine.
Sat. 'Tis good, sir, you are very short with us;
But if we live we'll be as sharp with you.
Bas. My lord, what I have done, as best I may,
Answer I must, and shall do with my life;
Only thus much I give your Grace to know:
By all the duties that I owe to Rome,
This noble gentleman, Lord Titus here,
Is in opinion and in honor wrong'd,
That in the rescue of Lavinia
With his own hand did slay his youngest son,
In zeal to you, and highly mov'd to wrath
To be controll'd in that he frankly gave.
Receive him then to favor, Saturnine,
That hath express'd himself in all his deeds
A father and a friend to thee and Rome.
Tit. Prince Bassianus, leave to plead my deeds,
'Tis thou, and those, that have dishonored me.
Rome and the righteous heavens be my judge,
How I have lov'd and honored Saturnine!
Tam. My worthy lord, if ever Tamora
Were gracious in those princely eyes of thine,
Then hear me speak indifferently for all;
And at my suit, sweet, pardon what is past.
Sat. What, madam, be dishonored openly,
And basely put it up without revenge?
Tam. Not so, my lord, the gods of Rome forfend
I should be author to dishonor you!
But on mine honor dare I undertake
For good Lord Titus' innocence in all,
Whose fury not dissembled speaks his griefs.
Then at my suit look graciously on him;
Lose not so noble a friend on vain suppose,
Nor with sour looks afflict his gentle heart.
[*Aside to Saturnine.*] My lord, be rul'd by me, be won at last,

395. **device**: scheming. 396. **beholding**: beholden, indebted.
399. **play'd your prize**: won your bout. 408. **that**: that which.
416. **opinion**: reputation.
420. **To be controll'd**: at being restrained. **frankly**: unreservedly.
424. **leave**: cease. 430. **indifferently**: impartially.
433. **put it up**: submit to it. 434. **forfend**: forbid.
436. **undertake**: vouch.
440. **vain suppose**: empty or false supposition.

Dissemble all your griefs and discontents.
You are but newly planted in your throne;
Lest then the people, and patricians too,
Upon a just survey take Titus' part,
And so supplant you for ingratitude,
Which Rome reputes to be a heinous sin,
Yield at entreats; and then let me alone,
I'll find a day to massacre them all,
And rase their faction and their family,
The cruel father and his traitorous sons,
To whom I sued for my dear son's life;
And make them know what 'tis to let a queen
Kneel in the streets and beg for grace in vain.—
Come, come, sweet emperor—come, Andronicus—
Take up this good old man, and cheer the heart
That dies in tempest of thy angry frown.
Sat. Rise, Titus, rise, my empress hath prevail'd.
Tit. I thank your Majesty, and her, my lord.
These words, these looks, infuse new life in me.
Tam. Titus, I am incorporate in Rome,
A Roman now adopted happily,
And must advise the Emperor for his good.
This day all quarrels die, Andronicus.
And let it be mine honor, good my lord,
That I have reconcil'd your friends and you.
For you, Prince Bassianus, I have pass'd
My word and promise to the Emperor
That you will be more mild and tractable.
And fear not, lords, and you, Lavinia;
By my advice, all humbled on your knees,
You shall ask pardon of his Majesty.
[*Marcus, Lavinia, and Titus' sons kneel.*]
[*Luc.*] We do, and vow to heaven and to his Highness
That what we did was mildly as we might,
Tend'ring our sister's honor and our own.
Marc. That, on mine honor, here do I protest.
Sat. Away, and talk not, trouble us no more.
Tam. Nay, nay, sweet emperor, we must all be friends.
The tribune and his nephews kneel for grace,
I will not be denied. Sweet heart, look back.
Sat. Marcus, for thy sake and thy brother's here,
And at my lovely Tamora's entreats,
I do remit these young men's heinous faults.
Stand up. [*Marcus and the others rise.*]
Lavinia, though you left me like a churl,
I found a friend, and sure as death I swore
I would not part a bachelor from the priest.
Come, if the Emperor's court can feast two brides,
You are my guest, Lavinia, and your friends.
This day shall be a love-day, Tamora.
Tit. To-morrow, and it please your Majesty
To hunt the panther and the hart with me,
With horn and hound we'll give your Grace *bon jour.*
Sat. Be it so, Titus, and gramercy too.
Exeunt. Sound trumpets. Manet Moor [*Aaron*].

449. **at entreats**: to entreaty. **let me alone**: leave it to me.
457. **Take up**: raise to his feet. 476. **Tend'ring**: having regard for.
486. **like a churl**: rudely, boorishly.
488. **part a bachelor**: depart unmarried.
491. **love-day**: day appointed for friendly settlement of disputes.
492. **and**: if. 495. **gramercy**: many thanks.

[ACT II, SCENE I]

Aar. Now climbeth Tamora Olympus' top,
Safe out of fortune's shot, and sits aloft,
Secure of thunder's crack or lightning flash,
Advanc'd above pale envy's threat'ning reach.
As when the golden sun salutes the morn,
And, having gilt the ocean with his beams,
Gallops the zodiac in his glistering coach,
And overlooks the highest-peering hills:
So Tamora.
Upon her wit doth earthly honor wait,
And virtue stoops and trembles at her frown;
Then, Aaron, arm thy heart, and fit thy thoughts,
To mount aloft with thy imperial mistress,
And mount her pitch, whom thou in triumph long
Hast prisoner held, fett'red in amorous chains,
And faster bound to Aaron's charming eyes
Than is Prometheus tied to Caucasus.
Away with slavish weeds and servile thoughts!
I will be bright, and shine in pearl and gold,
To wait upon this new-made emperess.
To wait, said I? to wanton with this queen,
This goddess, this Semiramis, this nymph,
This siren that will charm Rome's Saturnine,
And see his shipwrack and his commonweal's.
Hollo, what storm is this?

Enter CHIRON *and* DEMETRIUS *braving.*

Dem. Chiron, thy years wants wit, thy wits wants edge,
And manners, to intrude where I am grac'd,
And may, for aught thou knowest, affected be.
Chi. Demetrius, thou dost overween in all,
And so in this, to bear me down with braves.
'Tis not the difference of a year or two
Makes me less gracious, or thee more fortunate;
I am as able and as fit as thou
To serve, and to deserve my mistress' grace,
And that my sword upon thee shall approve,
And plead my passions for Lavinia's love.
Aar. [*Aside.*] Clubs, clubs! these lovers will not keep the peace.
Dem. Why, boy, although our mother, unadvis'd,
Gave you a dancing-rapier by your side,
Are you so desperate grown to threat your friends?
Go to; have your lath glued within your sheath,
Till you know better how to handle it.
Chi. Mean while, sir, with the little skill I have,
Full well shalt thou perceive how much I dare.
Dem. Ay, boy, grow ye so brave? *They draw.*
Aar. [*Coming forward.*] Why, how now, lords?
So near the Emperor's palace dare ye draw,
And maintain such a quarrel openly?
Full well I wot the ground of all this grudge.
I would not for a million of gold
The cause were known to them it most concerns,
Nor would your noble mother for much more
Be so dishonored in the court of Rome.
For shame, put up.
Dem. Not I, till I have sheath'd
My rapier in his bosom, and withal
Thrust those reproachful speeches down his throat,
That he hath breath'd in my dishonor here.
Chi. For that I am prepar'd and full resolv'd,
Foul-spoken coward, that thund'rest with thy tongue,
And with thy weapon nothing dar'st perform!
Aar. Away, I say!
Now, by the gods that warlike Goths adore,
This petty brabble will undo us all.
Why, lords, and think you not how dangerous
It is to jet upon a prince's right?
What, is Lavinia then become so loose,
Or Bassianus so degenerate,
That for her love such quarrels may be broach'd,
Without controlment, justice, or revenge?
Young lords, beware! and should the Empress know
This discord's ground, the music would not please.
Chi. I care not, I, knew she and all the world,
I love Lavinia more than all the world.
Dem. Youngling, learn thou to make some meaner choice,
Lavinia is thine elder brother's hope.
Aar. Why, are ye mad? or know ye not, in Rome
How furious and impatient they be,
And cannot brook competitors in love?
I tell you, lords, you do but plot your deaths
By this device.
Chi. Aaron, a thousand deaths
Would I propose to achieve her whom I love.
Aar. To achieve her how?
Dem. Why makes thou it so strange?
She is a woman, therefore may be woo'd,
She is a woman, therefore may be won,
She is Lavinia, therefore must be lov'd.
What, man, more water glideth by the mill
Than wots the miller of, and easy it is
Of a cut loaf to steal a shive, we know.
Though Bassianus be the Emperor's brother,
Better than he have worn Vulcan's badge.
Aar. [*Aside.*] Ay, and as good as Saturninus may.
Dem. Then why should he despair that knows to court it,
With words, fair looks, and liberality?
What, hast not thou full often strook a doe,

II.i. Location: Scene continues.
4. envy's: malice's. **7. Gallops:** gallops through.
14. her pitch: high point of her flight (a term from falconry).
17. Prometheus . . . Caucasus. Prometheus was chained by the vengeful Zeus to a peak in the Caucasus mountains.
18. weeds: garments. **22. Semiramis:** a voluptuous Assyrian queen.
25 s.d. braving: defying each other. **27. grac'd:** favored.
28. affected: loved. **29. overween:** act presumptuously.
30. braves: defiant threats. **35. approve:** prove.
37. Clubs: i.e. here's a brawl (from the cry summoning London apprentices armed with clubs to join a riot or to quell one).
38. unadvis'd: unwisely.
39. dancing-rapier: purely ornamental sword worn in dances.
41. lath: property sword.
48. wot: know.
53. put up: sheathe your swords. **62. brabble:** quarrel.
64. jet: encroach. **68. controlment:** check, restraint.
70. ground: foundation (with play on the musical sense "bass on which a melody or air is raised").
73. make . . . choice: choose someone of lower rank.
80. propose: face. **87. shive:** slice.
89. worn Vulcan's badge: been made cuckold, as Vulcan was by Venus.
91. knows: knows how. **court it:** carry on a courtship (cf. *trip it*, "dance").

And borne her cleanly by the keeper's nose?
Aar. Why then it seems some certain snatch or so
Would serve your turns.
Chi. Ay, so the turn were served.
Dem. Aaron, thou hast hit it.
Aar. Would you had hit it too!
Then should not we be tir'd with this ado.
Why, hark ye, hark ye, and are you such fools
To square for this? Would it offend you then
That both should speed?
Chi. Faith, not me.
Dem. Nor me, so I were one.
Aar. For shame, be friends, and join for that you jar.
'Tis policy and stratagem must do
That you affect, and so must you resolve,
That what you cannot as you would achieve,
You must perforce accomplish as you may.
Take this of me: Lucrece was not more chaste
Than this Lavinia, Bassianus' love.
A speedier course [than] ling'ring languishment
Must we pursue, and I have found the path:
My lords, a solemn hunting is in hand,
There will the lovely Roman ladies troop;
The forest walks are wide and spacious,
And many unfrequented plots there are,
Fitted by kind for rape and villainy.
Single you thither then this dainty doe,
And strike her home by force, if not by words;
This way, or not at all, stand you in hope.
Come, come, our empress, with her sacred wit
To villainy and vengeance consecrate,
Will we acquaint withal what we intend,
And she shall file our engines with advice,
That will not suffer you to square yourselves,
But to your wishes' height advance you both.
The Emperor's court is like the house of Fame,
The palace full of tongues, of eyes, and ears;
The woods are ruthless, dreadful, deaf, and dull.
There speak, and strike, brave boys, and take your turns,
There serve your lust, shadowed from heaven's eye,
And revel in Lavinia's treasury.
Chi. Thy counsel, lad, smells of no cowardice.
Dem. *Sit fas aut nefas*, till I find the stream
To cool this heat, a charm to calm these fits,
Per Stygia, per manes vehor. *Exeunt.*

94. cleanly: deftly, without detection.
95. snatch: snack (with a sexual innuendo, as also in Chiron's reply).
100. square: quarrel. **101. speed:** succeed.
102. so: so long as.
103. join . . . jar: join forces to win the prize you're quarrelling over.
104. policy: cunning, craftiness. **105. affect:** aim at.
108. Lucrece. The story of her rape by Tarquin is told in Shakespeare's *The Rape of Lucrece*, a poem related in various ways to this play.
112. solemn: ceremonial, magnificent. **116. kind:** nature.
117. Single: single out (as huntsmen select one beast of the herd for pursuit).
118. home: effectually, to the desired point.
120. sacred: devoted. **121. consecrate:** dedicated.
123. file our engines: sharpen our contrivances.
124. square yourselves: fight with or thwart each other.
126. Fame: Rumor.
133. Sit . . . nefas: be it right or wrong.
135. Per . . . vehor: "I am borne through the Stygian regions, through the shades" (adapted from Seneca's *Hippolytus*, and here meaning "I am in hell").

[Scene II]

Enter Titus Andronicus *and his three sons* [Lucius, Quintus, *and* Martius], *making a noise with hounds and horns*, [*and* Marcus].

Tit. The hunt is up, the [morn] is bright and grey,
The fields are fragrant and the woods are green.
Uncouple here and let us make a bay,
And wake the Emperor and his lovely bride,
And rouse the Prince, and ring a hunter's peal,
That all the court may echo with the noise.
Sons, let it be your charge, as it is ours,
To attend the Emperor's person carefully.
I have been troubled in my sleep this night,
But dawning day new comfort hath inspir'd.

Here a cry of hounds, and wind horns in a peal. Then enter Saturninus, Tamora, Bassianus, Lavinia, Chiron, Demetrius, *and their* Attendants.

Many good morrows to your Majesty;
Madam, to you as many and as good.
I promised your Grace a hunter's peal.
Sat. And you have rung it lustily, my lords—
Somewhat too early for new-married ladies.
Bas. Lavinia, how say you?
Lav. I say, no;
I have been broad awake two hours and more.
Sat. Come on then, horse and chariots let us have,
And to our sport. [*To Tamora.*] Madam, now shall ye see
Our Roman hunting.
Marc. I have dogs, my lord,
Will rouse the proudest panther in the chase,
And climb the highest promontory top.
Tit. And I have horse will follow where the game
Makes way, and runs like swallows o'er the plain.
Dem. Chiron, we hunt not, we, with horse nor hound,
But hope to pluck a dainty doe to ground. *Exeunt.*

[Scene III]

Enter Aaron *alone* [*with a bag of gold*].

Aar. He that had wit would think that I had none,
To bury so much gold under a tree,
And never after to inherit it.
Let him that thinks of me so abjectly
Know that this gold must coin a stratagem,
Which cunningly effected will beget
A very excellent piece of villainy.
And so repose, sweet gold, for their unrest,
[*Hides the gold.*]
That have their alms out of the Empress' chest.

II.ii. Location: Rome. Before the Emperor's palace.
1. grey. Used of early daylight, before sunrise.
3. Uncouple: unleash the hounds. **bay:** deep barking.
5. ring: blow. **10 s.d. wind:** blow. **18. horse.** Plural.
21. chase: hunting ground.

II.iii. Location: A forest near Rome.
3. inherit: have possession of.
9. That . . . chest: i.e. who get possession of this gold (which comes from Tamora's treasury).

Enter TAMORA *alone to the Moor.*

Tam. My lovely Aaron, wherefore look'st thou sad,
When every thing doth make a gleeful boast?
The birds chaunt melody on every bush,
The [snake] lies rolled in the cheerful sun,
The green leaves quiver with the cooling wind
And make a checker'd shadow on the ground.
Under their sweet shade, Aaron, let us sit,
And whilst the babbling echo mocks the hounds,
Replying shrilly to the well-tun'd horns,
As if a double hunt were heard at once,
Let us sit down and mark their yellowing noise;
And after conflict such as was suppos'd
The wand'ring prince and Dido once enjoyed,
When with a happy storm they were surpris'd,
And curtain'd with a counsel-keeping cave,
We may, each wreathed in the other's arms
(Our pastimes done), possess a golden slumber,
Whiles hounds and horns and sweet melodious birds
Be unto us as is a nurse's song
Of lullaby to bring her babe asleep.

Aar. Madam, though Venus govern your desires,
Saturn is dominator over mine:
What signifies my deadly-standing eye,
My silence, an' my cloudy melancholy,
My fleece of woolly hair that now uncurls,
Even as an adder when she doth unroll
To do some fatal execution?
No, madam, these are no venereal signs.
Vengeance is in my heart, death in my hand,
Blood and revenge are hammering in my head.
Hark, Tamora, the empress of my soul,
Which never hopes more heaven than rests in thee,
This is the day of doom for Bassianus:
His Philomel must lose her tongue to-day,
Thy sons make pillage of her chastity,
And wash their hands in Bassianus' blood.
Seest thou this letter? take it up, I pray thee,
And give the King this fatal-plotted scroll.
Now question me no more, we are espied.
Here comes a parcel of our hopeful booty,
Which dreads not yet their lives' destruction.

Enter BASSIANUS *and* LAVINIA.

Tam. Ah, my sweet Moor, sweeter to me than life!

Aar. No more, great Empress, Bassianus comes.
Be cross with him, and I'll go fetch thy sons
To back thy quarrels, whatsoe'er they be. [*Exit.*]

Bas. Who have we here? Rome's royal Empress,
Unfurnish'd of her well-beseeming troop?

11. **boast**: display. 20. **yellowing**: loudly baying.
22. **prince**: Aeneas; sheltering from a storm during a hunt, he made love to Dido in a cave. 23. **happy**: lucky.
30, 31. **Venus, Saturn.** Domination by the planet Venus was supposed to produce an amorous temperament; by Saturn, a cold and morose one.
32. **deadly-standing**: fixed in a murderous stare.
37. **venereal**: amorous, erotic (appertaining to Venus).
43. **Philomel**: Athenian princess raped by her brother-in-law Tereus, who cut out her tongue to keep her from exposing him.
49. **parcel**: part. **hopeful**: hoped-for, prospective.
53. **Be cross**: pick a quarrel.
56. **Unfurnish'd . . . troop**: unprovided with her appropriate guard.

Or is it Dian habited like her,
Who hath abandoned her holy groves
To see the general hunting in this forest?

Tam. Saucy controller of my private steps!
Had I the pow'r that some say Dian had,
Thy temples should be planted presently
With horns, as was Actaeon's, and the hounds
Should drive upon thy new-transformed limbs,
Unmannerly intruder as thou art!

Lav. Under your patience, gentle Empress,
'Tis thought you have a goodly gift in horning,
And to be doubted that your Moor and you
Are singled forth to try thy experiments.
Jove shield your husband from his hounds to-day!
'Tis pity they should take him for a stag.

Bas. Believe me, Queen, your [swart] Cimmerian
Doth make your honor of his body's hue,
Spotted, detested, and abominable.
Why are you sequest'red from all your train,
Dismounted from your snow-white goodly steed,
And wand'red hither to an obscure plot,
Accompanied but with a barbarous Moor,
If foul desire had not conducted you?

Lav. And, being intercepted in your sport,
Great reason that my noble lord be rated
For sauciness. I pray you let us hence,
And let her joy her raven-colored love;
This valley fits the purpose passing well.

Bas. The King my brother shall have notice of this.

Lav. Ay, for these slips have made him noted long,
Good king, to be so mightily abused.

Tam. Why, I have patience to endure all this.

Enter CHIRON *and* DEMETRIUS.

Dem. How now, dear sovereign and our gracious mother?
Why doth your Highness look so pale and wan?

Tam. Have I not reason, think you, to look pale?
These two have 'ticed me hither to this place:
A barren detested vale you see it is;
The trees, though summer, yet forlorn and lean,
Overcome with moss and baleful mistletoe;
Here never shines the sun, here nothing breeds,
Unless the nightly owl or fatal raven;
And when they show'd me this abhorred pit,
They told me, here, at dead time of the night,
A thousand fiends, a thousand hissing snakes,
Ten thousand swelling toads, as many urchins,
Would make such fearful and confused cries,

57. **habited**: dressed. 59. **general**: i.e. mortals.
60. **controller**: censurer, would-be restrainer.
62. **presently**: immediately.
63. **Actaeon's.** Actaeon, having by accident seen Diana bathing, was turned into a stag and killed by his own hounds.
64. **drive**: rush.
66. **Under your patience**: if you will allow me to say so.
67. **horning**: cuckolding your husband.
68. **doubted**: suspected.
72. **swart**: swarthy. **Cimmerian**: i.e. black man. According to Homer, the Cimmerians lived in a land of darkness.
74. **Spotted**: infected. 81. **rated**: berated. 83. **joy**: enjoy.
86. **slips**: offenses. **noted**: notorious. 87. **abused**: deceived.
95. **Overcome**: overgrown. 97. **fatal**: ominous.
101. **urchins**: hedgehogs.

As any mortal body hearing it
Should straight fall mad, or else die suddenly.
No sooner had they told this hellish tale,
But straight they told me they would bind me here
Unto the body of a dismal yew,
And leave me to this miserable death.
And then they call'd me foul adulteress,
[Lascivious] Goth, and all the bitterest terms
That ever ear did hear to such effect;
And had you not by wondrous fortune come,
This vengeance on me had they executed:
Revenge it, as you love your mother's life,
Or be ye not henceforth call'd my children.
Dem. This is a witness that I am thy son. *Stab him.*
Chi. And this for me, struck home to show my strength. [*Also stabs Bassianus, who dies.*]
Lav. Ay, come, Semiramis, nay, barbarous Tamora,
For no name fits thy nature but thy own!
Tam. Give me the poniard; you shall know, my boys,
Your mother's hand shall right your mother's wrong.
Dem. Stay, madam, here is more belongs to her:
First thrash the corn, then after burn the straw.
This minion stood upon her chastity,
Upon her nuptial vow, her loyalty,
And with that painted hope braves your mightiness;
And shall she carry this unto her grave?
Chi. And if she do, I would I were an eunuch.
Drag hence her husband to some secret hole,
And make his dead trunk pillow to our lust.
Tam. But when ye have the honey we desire,
Let not this wasp outlive, us both to sting.
Chi. I warrant you, madam, we will make that sure.
Come, mistress, now perforce we will enjoy
That nice-preserved honesty of yours.
Lav. O Tamora, thou bearest a woman's face—
Tam. I will not hear her speak, away with her!
Lav. Sweet lords, entreat her hear me but a word.
Dem. Listen, fair madam, let it be your glory
To see her tears, but be your heart to them
As unrelenting flint to drops of rain.
Lav. When did the tiger's young ones teach the dam?
O, do not learn her wrath—she taught it thee;
The milk thou suck'st from her did turn to marble,
Even at thy teat thou hadst thy tyranny;
Yet every mother breeds not sons alike—
[*To Chiron.*] Do thou entreat her show a woman's pity.
Chi. What, wouldst thou have me prove myself a bastard?
Lav. 'Tis true, the raven doth not hatch a lark,
Yet have I heard—O, could I find it now!—
The lion, mov'd with pity, did endure
To have his princely paws par'd all away.
Some say that ravens foster forlorn children
The whilst their own birds famish in their nests;
O, be to me, though thy hard heart say no,
Nothing so kind, but something pitiful!
Tam. I know not what it means, away with her!
Lav. O, let me teach thee! For my father's sake,
That gave thee life when well he might have slain thee,
Be not obdurate, open thy deaf years.
Tam. Hadst thou in person ne'er offended me,
Even for his sake am I pitiless.
Remember, boys, I pour'd forth tears in vain
To save your brother from the sacrifice,
But fierce Andronicus would not relent.
Therefore away with her, and use her as you will;
The worse to her, the better lov'd of me.
Lav. O Tamora, be call'd a gentle queen,
And with thine own hands kill me in this place!
For 'tis not life that I have begg'd so long,
Poor I was slain when Bassianus died.
Tam. What beg'st thou then? Fond woman, let me go.
Lav. 'Tis present death I beg, and one thing more
That womanhood denies my tongue to tell.
O, keep me from their worse than killing lust,
And tumble me into some loathsome pit,
Where never man's eye may behold my body:
Do this, and be a charitable murderer.
Tam. So should I rob my sweet sons of their fee.
No, let them satisfice their lust on thee.
Dem. Away, for thou hast stay'd us here too long.
Lav. No grace? no womanhood? ah, beastly creature,
The blot and enemy to our general name!
Confusion fall—
Chi. Nay then I'll stop your mouth. Bring thou her husband;
This is the hole where Aaron bid us hide him.
[*Demetrius throws the body of Bassianus into the pit; then exeunt Demetrius and Chiron dragging off Lavinia.*]
Tam. Farewell, my sons, see that you make her sure.
Ne'er let my heart know merry cheer indeed
Till all the Andronici be made away.
Now will I hence to seek my lovely Moor,
And let my spleenful sons this trull deflow'r. [*Exit.*]

Enter Aaron *with two of Titus' sons* [Quintus *and* Martius].

[*Aar.*] Come on, my lords, the better foot before.
Straight will I bring you to the loathsome pit
Where I espied the panther fast asleep.
Quin. My sight is very dull, what e'er it bodes.

110. Lascivious Goth. With a homophonic pun on *Goth/goat;* goats were proverbially lascivious.
124. minion: wench. **stood:** prided herself.
126. painted: unreal, false. The line may be corrupt.
128. And if: if.
132. outlive . . . sting: survive and be dangerous to us.
135. nice-preserved honesty: fastidiously guarded chastity.
143. learn: teach.
152. paws: claws.
153. forlorn children: the abandoned young of other birds.
154. birds: young ones. **156. something:** to some degree.
157. it: i.e. pity. **160. years:** ears (phonetic spelling)
172. Fond: foolish. **173. present:** immediate.
174. denies: forbids. **180. satisfice:** sate.
183. our general name: the reputation of womankind.
184. Confusion: destruction.
187. make her sure: render her incapable of revenge.
189. made away: killed.
191. spleenful: passionate, lustful. **trull:** slut, whore.

Mart. And mine, I promise you; were it not for shame,
Well could I leave our sport to sleep a while.
[*Falls into the pit.*]
Quin. What, art thou fallen? What subtile hole is this,
Whose mouth is covered with rude-growing briers,
Upon whose leaves are drops of new-shed blood
As fresh as morning dew distill'd on flowers?
A very fatal place it seems to me.
Speak, brother, hast thou hurt thee with the fall?
Mart. O brother, with the dismall'st object hurt
That ever eye with sight made heart lament!
Aar. [*Aside.*] Now will I fetch the King to find them here,
That he thereby may have a likely guess,
How these were they that made away his brother.
Exit.
Mart. Why dost not comfort me and help me out
From this [unhallow'd] and blood-stained hole?
Quin. I am surprised with an uncouth fear,
A chilling sweat o'erruns my trembling joints,
My heart suspects more than mine eye can see.
Mart. To prove thou hast a true-divining heart,
Aaron and thou look down into this den,
And see a fearful sight of blood and death.
Quin. Aaron is gone, and my compassionate heart
Will not permit mine eyes once to behold
The thing whereat it trembles by surmise.
O, tell me who it is, for ne'er till now
Was I a child to fear I know not what.
Mart. Lord Bassianus lies [beray'd] in blood,
All on a heap, like to a slaughtered lamb,
In this detested, dark, blood-drinking pit.
Quin. If it be dark, how dost thou know 'tis he?
Mart. Upon his bloody finger he doth wear
A precious ring that lightens all this hole,
Which, like a taper in some monument,
Doth shine upon the dead man's earthy cheeks,
And shows the ragged entrails of this pit:
So pale did shine the moon on [Pyramus]
When he by night lay bath'd in maiden blood.
O brother, help me with thy fainting hand—
If fear hath made thee faint, as me it hath—
Out of this fell devouring receptacle,
As hateful as [Cocytus'] misty mouth.
Quin. Reach me thy hand, that I may help thee out,
Or wanting strength to do thee so much good,
I may be pluck'd into the swallowing womb
Of this deep pit, poor Bassianus' grave.
I have no strength to pluck thee to the brink.
Mart. Nor I no strength to climb without thy help.

202. fatal: ill-omened. **204. object:** sight.
211. surprised: overcome. **uncouth:** unfamiliar, strange.
219. by surmise: even to imagine.
222. beray'd in: made filthy by.
227. ring. Perhaps set with a carbuncle, once believed to shine in the dark. **228. monument:** tomb.
229. earthy: pallid. **230. ragged entrails:** rough interior.
231. Pyramus: lover of Thisbe, who killed himself when he supposed her dead. See *A Midsummer Night's Dream*, III.i.50 ff.
235. fell: dreadful.
236. Cocytus: one of the rivers of Hades; here, hell (hell-mouth, equipped to emit smoke, was a standard stage-property).
238. wanting: lacking. **239. pluck'd:** drawn.

Quin. Thy hand once more; I will not loose again,
Till thou art here aloft or I below.
Thou canst not come to me—I come to thee.
[*Falls in.*]
Enter the EMPEROR *and* AARON *the Moor.*
Sat. Along with me! I'll see what hole is here,
And what he is that now is leapt into it.
Say who art thou that lately didst descend
Into this gaping hollow of the earth?
Mart. The unhappy sons of old Andronicus,
Brought hither in a most unlucky hour,
To find thy brother Bassianus dead.
Sat. My brother dead! I know thou dost but jest.
He and his lady both are at the lodge,
Upon the north side of this pleasant chase;
'Tis not an hour since I left them there.
Mart. We know not where you left them all alive,
But out alas, here have we found him dead.
Enter TAMORA [*with* ATTENDANTS, TITUS] ANDRONICUS, *and* LUCIUS.
Tam. Where is my lord the King?
Sat. Here, Tamora, though griev'd with killing grief.
Tam. Where is thy brother Bassianus?
Sat. Now to the bottom dost thou search my wound;
Poor Bassianus here lies murthered.
Tam. Then all too late I bring this fatal writ,
The complot of this timeless tragedy,
And wonder greatly that man's face can fold
In pleasing smiles such murderous tyranny.
She giveth Saturnine a letter.
Sat. (*Reads the letter.*) "And if we miss to meet him handsomely,
Sweet huntsman—Bassianus 'tis we mean—
Do thou so much as dig the grave for him:
Thou know'st our meaning. Look for thy reward
Among the nettles at the elder-tree,
Which overshades the mouth of that same pit
Where we decreed to bury Bassianus.
Do this and purchase us thy lasting friends."
O Tamora, was ever heard the like?
This is the pit, and this the elder-tree.
Look, sirs, if you can find the huntsman out,
That should have murthered Bassianus here.
Aar. My gracious lord, here is the bag of gold.
Sat. [*To Titus.*] Two of thy whelps, fell curs of bloody kind,
Have here bereft my brother of his life.—
Sirs, drag them from the pit unto the prison,
There let them bide until we have devis'd
Some never-heard-of tortering pain for them.
Tam. What, are they in this pit? O wondrous thing!
How easily murder is discovered!

255. chase: hunting ground. **262. search:** probe.
265. complot: plot (perhaps with a reference to the document called the plot which hung in the tiring-house of the theatre and provided an outline of the play's action). **timeless:** untimely.
268. handsomely: conveniently. **279. should have:** was to have.
281. kind: nature, disposition. **285. tortering:** torturing.
287. discovered: uncovered, brought to light.

Tit. High Emperor, upon my feeble knee
I beg this boon, with tears not lightly shed,
That this fell fault of my accursed sons—
Accursed, if the [fault] be prov'd in them—
Sat. If it be prov'd! you see it is apparent.
Who found this letter? Tamora, was it you?
Tam. Andronicus himself did take it up.
Tit. I did, my lord, yet let me be their bail,
For by my fathers' reverent tomb I vow
They shall be ready at your Highness' will,
To answer their suspicion with their lives.
Sat. Thou shalt not bail them, see thou follow me.
Some bring the murthered body, some the murtherers.
Let them not speak a word, the guilt is plain,
For by my soul, were there worse end than death,
That end upon them should be executed.
Tam. Andronicus, I will entreat the King.
Fear not thy sons, they shall do well enough.
Tit. Come, Lucius, come, stay not to talk with them. *[Exeunt.]*

[Scene IV]

Enter the Empress' sons [Demetrius *and* Chiron] *with* Lavinia, *her hands cut off, and her tongue cut out, and ravish'd.*

Dem. So now go tell, and if thy tongue can speak,
Who 'twas that cut thy tongue and ravish'd thee.
Chi. Write down thy mind, bewray thy meaning so,
And if thy stumps will let thee play the scribe.
Dem. See how with signs and tokens she can scrowl.
Chi. Go home, call for sweet water, wash thy hands.
Dem. She hath no tongue to call, nor hands to wash,
And so let's leave her to her silent walks.
Chi. And 'twere my cause, I should go hang myself.
Dem. If thou hadst hands to help thee knit the cord.
Exeunt [Demetrius and Chiron].

[Wind horns.] *Enter* Marcus *from hunting.*

Marc. Who is this? my niece, that flies away so fast?
Cousin, a word; where is your husband?
If I do dream, would all my wealth would wake me!
If I do wake, some planet strike me down,
That I may slumber an eternal sleep!
Speak, gentle niece: what stern ungentle hands
Hath lopp'd and hew'd, and made thy body bare
Of her two branches, those sweet ornaments
Whose circling shadows kings have sought to sleep in,
And might not gain so great a happiness

292. apparent: obvious.
296. fathers': forefathers'. **reverent:** reverend.
298. their suspicion: the suspicion in which they are held.
305. Fear not: fear not for.

II.iv. Location: Scene continues.
3. bewray: reveal. **5. scrowl:** scrawl. **6. sweet:** perfumed.
9. cause: case. **12. Cousin:** kinswoman.

As half thy love? Why dost not speak to me?
Alas, a crimson river of warm blood,
Like to a bubbling fountain stirr'd with wind,
Doth rise and fall between thy rosed lips,
Coming and going with thy honey breath.
But sure some Tereus hath deflow'red thee,
And lest thou shouldst detect [him], cut thy tongue.
Ah, now thou turn'st away thy face for shame!
And notwithstanding all this loss of blood,
As from a conduit with [three] issuing spouts,
Yet do thy cheeks look red as Titan's face
Blushing to be encount'red with a cloud.
Shall I speak for thee? shall I say 'tis so?
O that I knew thy heart, and knew the beast,
That I might rail at him to ease my mind!
Sorrow concealed, like an oven stopp'd,
Doth burn the heart to cinders where it is.
Fair Philomela, why, she but lost her tongue,
And in a tedious sampler sew'd her mind;
But, lovely niece, that mean is cut from thee.
A craftier Tereus, cousin, hast thou met,
And he hath cut those pretty fingers off
That could have better sew'd than Philomel.
O, had the monster seen those lily hands
Tremble like aspen leaves upon a lute,
And make the silken strings delight to kiss them,
He would not then have touch'd them for his life!
Or had he heard the heavenly harmony
Which that sweet tongue hath made,
He would have dropp'd his knife, and fell asleep,
As Cerberus at the Thracian poet's feet.
Come let us go, and make thy father blind,
For such a sight will blind a father's eye.
One hour's storm will drown the fragrant meads,
What will whole months of tears thy father's eyes?
Do not draw back, for we will mourn with thee.
O, could our mourning ease thy misery! *Exeunt.*

[Act III, Scene I]

Enter the Judges *and* Senators [*and* Tribunes], *with* Titus' *two sons* [Martius *and* Quintus] *bound, passing on the stage to the place of execution, and* Titus *going before, pleading.*

Tit. Hear me, grave fathers! noble tribunes, stay!
For pity of mine age, whose youth was spent
In dangerous wars whilst you securely slept;
For all my blood in Rome's great quarrel shed,
For all the frosty nights that I have watch'd,
And for these bitter tears which now you see
Filling the aged wrinkles in my cheeks,
Be pitiful to my condemned sons,
Whose souls is not corrupted as 'tis thought.

26. Tereus: Philomel's ravisher (see note to II.iii.43).
27. detect: expose. **34. thy heart:** what is in your mind.
39. tedious: laborious. **sampler.** Philomel revealed her story and her ravisher by means of embroidery on a sampler.
40. mean: means.
51. As . . . feet. Orpheus, descending into Hades to recover Eurydice, quieted the three-headed watchdog Cerberus with the music of his lyre.

III.i. Location: Rome. A street.

For two and twenty sons I never wept,
Because they died in honor's lofty bed.
Andronicus lieth down, and the Judges [etc.] pass by him [and exeunt with the prisoners].
For these, tribunes, in the dust I write
My heart's deep languor, and my soul's sad tears:
Let my tears staunch the earth's dry appetite,
My sons' sweet blood will make it shame and blush.
O earth, I will befriend thee more with rain,
That shall distill from these two ancient [urns],
Than youthful April shall with all his show'rs.
In summer's drought I'll drop upon thee still,
In winter with warm tears I'll melt the snow,
And keep eternal spring-time [on thy] face,
So thou refuse to drink my dear sons' blood.

Enter Lucius *with his weapon drawn.*

O reverent tribunes! O gentle, aged men!
Unbind my sons, reverse the doom of death,
And let me say (that never wept before)
My tears are now prevailing orators.
Luc. O noble father, you lament in vain:
The tribunes hear you not, no man is by,
And you recount your sorrows to a stone.
Tit. Ah, Lucius, for thy brothers let me plead.
Grave tribunes, once more I entreat of you—
Luc. My gracious lord, no tribune hears you speak.
Tit. Why, 'tis no matter, man: if they did hear,
They would not mark me; if they did mark,
They would not pity me; yet plead I must,
And bootless unto them.
Therefore I tell my sorrows to the stones,
Who, though they cannot answer my distress,
Yet in some sort they are better than the tribunes,
For that they will not intercept my tale.
When I do weep, they humbly at my feet
Receive my tears, and seem to weep with me,
And were they but attired in grave weeds,
Rome could afford no tribunes like to these.
A stone is soft as wax, tribunes more hard than stones;
A stone is silent, and offendeth not,
And tribunes with their tongues doom men to death.
[*Rises.*]
But wherefore stand'st thou with thy weapon drawn?
Luc. To rescue my two brothers from their death,
For which attempt the judges have pronounc'd
My everlasting doom of banishment.
Tit. O happy man, they have befriended thee!
Why, foolish Lucius, dost thou not perceive
That Rome is but a wilderness of tigers?
Tigers must prey, and Rome affords no prey
But me and mine. How happy art thou then,
From these devourers to be banished!
But who comes with our brother Marcus here?

Enter Marcus *with* Lavinia.

Marc. Titus, prepare thy aged eyes to weep,
Or if not so, thy noble heart to break:
I bring consuming sorrow to thine age.
Tit. Will it consume me? Let me see it then.
Marc. This was thy daughter.
Tit. Why, Marcus, so she is.
Luc. Ay me, this object kills me!
Tit. Faint-hearted boy, arise and look upon her.
Speak, Lavinia, what accursed hand
Hath made thee handless in thy father's sight?
What fool hath added water to the sea?
Or brought a faggot to bright-burning Troy?
My grief was at the height before thou cam'st,
And now like Nilus it disdaineth bounds.
Give me a sword, I'll chop off my hands too,
For they have fought for Rome, and all in vain;
And they have nurs'd this woe, in feeding life;
In bootless prayer have they been held up,
And they have serv'd me to effectless use.
Now all the service I require of them
Is that the one will help to cut the other.
'Tis well, Lavinia, that thou hast no hands,
For hands to do Rome service is but vain.
Luc. Speak, gentle sister, who hath mart'red thee?
Marc. O, that delightful engine of her thoughts,
That blabb'd them with such pleasing eloquence,
Is torn from forth that pretty hollow cage,
Where like a sweet melodious bird it sung
Sweet varied notes, enchanting every ear!
Luc. O, say thou for her, who hath done this deed?
Marc. O, thus I found her straying in the park,
Seeking to hide herself, as doth the deer
That hath receiv'd some unrecuring wound.
Tit. It was my dear, and he that wounded her
Hath hurt me more than had he kill'd me dead:
For now I stand as one upon a rock,
Environ'd with a wilderness of sea,
Who marks the waxing tide grow wave by wave,
Expecting ever when some envious surge
Will in his brinish bowels swallow him.
This way to death my wretched sons are gone,
Here stands my other son, a banish'd man,
And here my brother, weeping at my woes;
But that which gives my soul the greatest spurn
Is dear Lavinia, dearer than my soul.
Had I but seen thy picture in this plight,
It would have madded me; what shall I do
Now I behold thy lively body so?
Thou hast no hands to wipe away thy tears,
Nor tongue to tell me who hath mart'red thee.
Thy husband he is dead, and for his death
Thy brothers are condemn'd, and dead by this.
Look, Marcus! ah, son Lucius, look on her!
When I did name her brothers, then fresh tears
Stood on her cheeks, as doth the honey-dew
Upon a gath'red lily almost withered.

10. two and twenty. Titus is now apparently willing to include Mutius in the number of his sons who have died honorably.
13. languor: grief. **14. staunch:** satisfy.
15. shame: be ashamed. **19. still:** continually.
22. So: provided that. **36. bootless:** without effect.
40. intercept: interrupt. **43. grave weeds:** sober garments.
44. afford: provide.

64. object: sight. **71. Nilus:** the river Nile.
81. mart'red: mutilated. **82. engine:** instrument.
83. blabb'd: uttered. **90. unrecuring:** incurable.
96. Expecting . . . when: awaiting . . . the time when. **envious:** malicious. **97. his:** its.
101. spurn: blow, contemptuous thrust. **105. lively:** living.
109. by this: by this time.

Marc. Perchance she weeps because they kill'd her husband,
Perchance because she knows them innocent.
Tit. If they did kill thy husband, then be joyful,
Because the law hath ta'en revenge on them.
No, no, they would not do so foul a deed;
Witness the sorrow that their sister makes.
Gentle Lavinia, let me kiss thy lips,
Or make some sign how I may do thee ease.
Shall thy good uncle, and thy brother Lucius,
And thou, and I, sit round about some fountain,
Looking all downwards to behold our cheeks,
How they are stain'd like meadows yet not dry,
With miry slime left on them by a flood?
And in the fountain shall we gaze so long
Till the fresh taste be taken from that clearness,
And made a brine-pit with our bitter tears?
Or shall we cut away our hands like thine?
Or shall we bite our tongues, and in dumb shows
Pass the remainder of our hateful days?
What shall we do? Let us that have our tongues
Plot some device of further misery,
To make us wonder'd at in time to come.
Luc. Sweet father, cease your tears, for at your grief
See how my wretched sister sobs and weeps.
Marc. Patience, dear niece. Good Titus, dry thine eyes.
Tit. Ah, Marcus, Marcus! brother, well I wot,
Thy napkin cannot drink a tear of mine,
For thou, poor man, hast drown'd it with thine own.
Luc. Ah, my Lavinia, I will wipe thy cheeks.
Tit. Mark, Marcus, mark! I understand her signs.
Had she a tongue to speak, now would she say
That to her brother which I said to thee:
His napkin, with [his] true tears all bewet,
Can do no service on her sorrowful cheeks.
O, what a sympathy of woe is this,
As far from help as limbo is from bliss!

Enter AARON *the Moor alone.*

Aar. Titus Andronicus, my lord the Emperor
Sends thee this word—that, if thou love thy sons,
Let Marcus, Lucius, or thyself, old Titus,
Or any one of you, chop off your hand
And send it to the King; he for the same
Will send thee hither both thy sons alive,
And that shall be the ransom for their fault.
Tit. O gracious Emperor! O gentle Aaron!
Did ever raven sing so like a lark
That gives sweet tidings of the sun's uprise?
With all my heart I'll send the Emperor my hand.
Good Aaron, wilt thou help to chop it off?
Luc. Stay, father, for that noble hand of thine,
That hath thrown down so many enemies,
Shall not be sent. My hand will serve the turn.
My youth can better spare my blood than you,
And therefore mine shall save my brothers' lives.

140. **napkin**: handkerchief. 141. **drown'd**: soaked.
148. **sympathy**: sharing.
149. **limbo**: abode of those who die unbaptized; loosely (as here), hell.

Marc. Which of your hands hath not defended Rome,
And rear'd aloft the bloody battle-axe,
Writing destruction on the enemy's castle?
O, none of both but are of high desert.
My hand hath been but idle, let it serve
To ransom my two nephews from their death;
Then have I kept it to a worthy end.
Aar. Nay, come, agree whose hand shall go along,
For fear they die before their pardon come.
Marc. My hand shall go.
Luc. By heaven, it shall not go!
Tit. Sirs, strive no more: such with'red herbs as these
Are meet for plucking up, and therefore mine.
Luc. Sweet father, if I shall be thought thy son,
Let me redeem my brothers both from death.
Marc. And for our father's sake, and mother's care,
Now let me show a brother's love to thee.
Tit. Agree between you, I will spare my hand.
Luc. Then I'll go fetch an axe.
Marc. But I will use the axe.
Exeunt [*Lucius and Marcus*].
Tit. Come hither, Aaron. I'll deceive them both;
Lend me thy hand, and I will give thee mine.
Aar. [*Aside.*] If that be call'd deceit, I will be honest,
And never whilst I live deceive men so;
But I'll deceive you in another sort,
And that you'll say ere half an hour pass.
He cuts off Titus' hand.

Enter LUCIUS *and* MARCUS *again.*

Tit. Now stay your strife, what shall be is dispatch'd.
Good Aaron, give his Majesty my hand.
Tell him it was a hand that warded him
From thousand dangers, bid him bury it:
More hath it merited, that let it have.
As for my sons, say I account of them
As jewels purchas'd at an easy price,
And yet dear too, because I bought mine own.
Aar. I go, Andronicus, and for thy hand
Look by and by to have thy sons with thee.
[*Aside.*] Their heads, I mean. O how this villainy
Doth fat me with the very thoughts of it!
Let fools do good, and fair men call for grace,
Aaron will have his soul black like his face. *Exit.*
Tit. O, here I lift this one hand up to heaven,
And bow this feeble ruin to the earth;
If any power pities wretched tears,
To that I call! [*To Lavinia.*] What, wouldst thou kneel with me?
Do then, dear heart, for heaven shall hear our prayers,
Or with our sighs we'll breathe the welkin dim,
And stain the sun with fog, as sometime clouds
When they do hug him in their melting bosoms.

179. **shall**: am to. 194. **warded**: guarded.
199. **dear**: expensive. 201. **Look**: expect.
203. **fat**: feed, i.e. delight.
211. **breathe . . . dim**: make the heavens misty.

Marc. O brother, speak with possibility,
And do not break into these deep extremes.
Tit. Is not my sorrow deep, having no bottom?
Then be my passions bottomless with them!
Marc. But yet let reason govern thy lament.
Tit. If there were reason for these miseries,
Then into limits could I bind my woes:
When heaven doth weep, doth not the earth o'erflow?
If the winds rage, doth not the sea wax mad,
Threat'ning the welkin with his big-swoll'n face?
And wilt thou have a reason for this coil?
I am the sea; hark how her sighs doth [blow]!
She is the weeping welkin, I the earth:
Then must my sea be moved with her sighs;
Then must my earth with her continual tears
Become a deluge, overflow'd and drown'd:
For why my bowels cannot hide her woes,
But like a drunkard must I vomit them.
Then give me leave, for losers will have leave
To ease their stomachs with their bitter tongues.

Enter a MESSENGER, *with two heads and a hand.*

Mess. Worthy Andronicus, ill art thou repaid
For that good hand thou sent'st the Emperor.
Here are the heads of thy two noble sons,
And here's thy hand, in scorn to thee sent back—
Thy grief their sports! thy resolution mock'd!
That woe is me to think upon thy woes,
More than remembrance of my father's death. [*Exit.*]
Marc. Now let hot Aetna cool in Sicily,
And be my heart an ever-burning hell!
These miseries are more than may be borne.
To weep with them that weep doth ease some deal,
But sorrow flouted at is double death.
Luc. Ah, that this sight should make so deep a wound,
And yet detested life not shrink thereat!
That ever death should let life bear his name,
Where life hath no more interest but to breathe!
[*Lavinia kisses Titus.*]
Marc. Alas, poor heart, that kiss is comfortless
As frozen water to a starved snake.
Tit. When will this fearful slumber have an end?
Marc. Now farewell, flatt'ry; die, Andronicus.
Thou dost not slumber; see thy two sons' heads,
Thy warlike hand, thy mangled daughter here,
Thy other banish'd son with this dear sight
Struck pale and bloodless, and thy brother, I,
Even like a stony image, cold and numb.
Ah, now no more will I control thy griefs.
Rent off thy silver hair, thy other hand
Gnawing with thy teeth, and be this dismal sight
The closing up of our most wretched eyes.
Now is a time to storm, why art thou still?
Tit. Ha, ha, ha!

214. **with:** within the bounds of.
217. **passions:** expressions of sorrow. 224. **coil:** disturbance, ado.
230. **For why:** because. 233. **stomachs:** resentments.
239. **That:** so that. 244. **some deal:** somewhat.
248. **bear his name:** i.e. be called life.
251. **starved:** numb with cold. 252. **slumber:** i.e. dream.
256. **dear:** grievous. 259. **control:** attempt to restrain.

Marc. Why dost thou laugh? It fits not with this hour.
Tit. Why, I have not another tear to shed.
Besides, this sorrow is an enemy,
And would usurp upon my wat'ry eyes,
And make them blind with tributary tears;
Then which way shall I find Revenge's cave?
For these two heads do seem to speak to me,
And threat me I shall never come to bliss
Till all these mischiefs be return'd again,
Even in their throats that hath committed them.
Come let me see what task I have to do.
You heavy people, circle me about,
That I may turn me to each one of you,
And swear unto my soul to right your wrongs.
The vow is made. Come, brother, take a head,
And in this hand the other will I bear;
And, Lavinia, thou shalt be employ'd;
Bear thou my hand, sweet wench, between thy teeth.
As for thee, boy, go get thee from my sight;
Thou art an exile, and thou must not stay.
Hie to the Goths and raise an army there,
And if ye love me, as I think you do,
Let's kiss and part, for we have much to do.
Exeunt. [*Manet Lucius.*]
Luc. Farewell, Andronicus, my noble father,
The woefull'st man that ever liv'd in Rome.
Farewell, proud Rome, till Lucius come again;
He loves his pledges dearer than his life.
Farewell, Lavinia, my noble sister,
O would thou wert as thou tofore hast been!
But now nor Lucius nor Lavinia lives
But in oblivion and hateful griefs.
If Lucius live, he will requite your wrongs,
And make proud Saturnine and his emperess
Beg at the gates, like Tarquin and his queen.
Now will I to the Goths and raise a pow'r,
To be reveng'd on Rome and Saturnine. *Exit Lucius.*

[[SCENE II]]

A banket [*set out*]. *Enter* [TITUS] ANDRONICUS, MARCUS, LAVINIA, *and the boy* [*young* LUCIUS].

Tit. So, so, now sit, and look you eat no more
Than will preserve just so much strength in us
As will revenge these bitter woes of ours.
Marcus, unknit that sorrow-wreathen knot;
Thy niece and I, poor creatures, want our hands
And cannot passionate our tenfold grief
With folded arms. This poor right hand of mine

269. **tributary:** paying tribute (to the usurping enemy, sorrow).
276. **heavy:** sorrowful. 281. On this line see the Textual Notes.
291. **He . . . life:** to fulfill his vows is dearer to him than his life. (Some editors, following Rowe, emend *loves* to *leaves.*)
293. **tofore:** hitherto.
298. **Tarquin . . . queen.** After the rape of Lucrece the royal family of the Tarquins was expelled from Rome. 299. **pow'r:** army.

III.ii. Location: Rome. Titus' house.
o.s.d. **banket:** banquet, i.e. light repast.
4. **unknit . . . knot:** unfold your arms. Folded arms were a sign of grief or melancholy.
5. **want:** lack. 6. **passionate:** passionately express.

Is left to tyrannize upon my breast,
Who, when my heart, all mad with misery,
Beats in this hollow prison of my flesh,
Then thus I thump it down.
[*To Lavinia.*] Thou map of woe, that thus dost talk in signs!
When thy poor heart beats with outrageous beating,
Thou canst not strike it thus to make it still.
Wound it with sighing, girl, kill it with groans;
Or get some little knife between thy teeth,
And just against thy heart make thou a hole,
That all the tears that thy poor eyes let fall
May run into that sink, and soaking in,
Drown the lamenting fool in sea-salt tears.

Marc. Fie, brother, fie, teach her not thus to lay
Such violent hands upon her tender life.

Tit. How now! has sorrow made thee dote already?
Why, Marcus, no man should be mad but I.
What violent hands can she lay on her life?
Ah, wherefore dost thou urge the name of hands,
To bid Aeneas tell the tale twice o'er
How Troy was burnt and he made miserable?
O, handle not the theme, to talk of hands,
Lest we remember still that we have none.
Fie, fie, how franticly I square my talk,
As if we should forget we had no hands,
If Marcus did not name the word of hands!
Come, let's fall to, and, gentle girl, eat this.
Here is no drink! Hark, Marcus, what she says;
I can interpret all her martyr'd signs:
She says, she drinks no other drink but tears,
Brew'd with her sorrow, mesh'd upon her cheeks.
Speechless [complainant], I will learn thy thought;
In thy dumb action will I be as perfect
As begging hermits in their holy prayers.
Thou shalt not sigh, nor hold thy stumps to heaven,
Nor wink, nor nod, nor kneel, nor make a sign,
But I, of these, will wrest an alphabet,
And by still practice learn to know thy meaning.

Boy. Good grandsire, leave these bitter deep laments,
Make my aunt merry with some pleasing tale.

Marc. Alas, the tender boy, in passion mov'd,
Doth weep to see his grandsire's heaviness.

Tit. Peace, tender sapling, thou art made of tears,
And tears will quickly melt thy life away.

Marcus strikes the dish with a knife.

What dost thou strike at, Marcus, with [thy] knife?

Marc. At that that I have kill'd, my lord—a fly.

Tit. Out on [thee], murderer! thou kill'st my heart!
Mine eyes [are] cloy'd with view of tyranny.
A deed of death done on the innocent
Becomes not Titus' brother. Get thee gone,
I see thou art not for my company.

Marc. Alas, my lord, I have but kill'd a fly.

Tit. "But"? How if that fly had a father and mother?
How would he hang his slender gilded wings
And buzz lamenting doings in the air!
Poor harmless fly,
That, with his pretty buzzing melody,
Came here to make us merry! and thou hast kill'd him.

Marc. Pardon me, sir, it was a black ill-favor'd fly,
Like to the Empress' Moor, therefore I kill'd him.

Tit. O, O, O,
Then pardon me for reprehending thee,
For thou hast done a charitable deed.
Give me thy knife, I will insult on him,
Flattering myself as if it were the Moor
Come hither purposely to poison me.—
There's for thyself, and that's for Tamora.
Ah, sirrah!
Yet I think we are not brought so low,
But that between us we can kill a fly
That comes in likeness of a coal-black Moor.

Marc. Alas, poor man, grief has so wrought on him,
He takes false shadows for true substances.

Tit. Come, take away. Lavinia, go with me.
I'll to thy closet, and go read with thee
Sad stories chanced in the times of old.
Come, boy, and go with me, thy sight is young,
And thou shalt read when mine begin to dazzle.

Exeunt.]

[ACT IV, SCENE I]

Enter LUCIUS' SON, *and* LAVINIA *running after him, and the boy flies from her, with his books under his arm. Enter* TITUS *and* MARCUS.

Boy. Help, grandsire, help! my aunt Lavinia
Follows me every where, I know not why.
Good uncle Marcus, see how swift she comes.
Alas, sweet aunt, I know not what you mean.

Marc. Stand by me, Lucius, do not fear thine aunt.

Tit. She loves thee, boy, too well to do thee harm.

Boy. Ay, when my father was in Rome she did.

Marc. What means my niece Lavinia by these signs?

Tit. Fear her not, Lucius, somewhat doth she mean.

[*Marc.*] See, Lucius, see, how much she makes of thee;
Somewhither would she have thee go with her.
Ah, boy, Cornelia never with more care
Read to her sons than she hath read to thee

8. tyrannize: i.e. by beating his breast. **9. Who:** which.
12. map: picture, image.
15. Wound . . . sighing. It was believed that every sigh drew a drop of blood from the heart.
19. sink: receptacle. **20. fool.** Often used affectionately.
30. still: continually. **31. square:** frame, regulate.
38. mesh'd: mashed (a term from brewing; in Northern England one "mashes" tea).
40. action: gesture. **perfect.** Cf. *word-perfect.*
43. wink: close your eyes. **44. of:** from. **45. still:** constant.
48. passion: sorrow.
62. lamenting doings: lamentable tales.
71. insult on: triumph over.
72. Flattering . . . if: deceiving myself with the pretense that.
75. sirrah: term of address used to an inferior.
81. take away: clear the table. **82. closet:** private room.
85. mine: i.e. my eyes. **dazzle:** be dazzled, become blurred.

IV.i. Location: Rome. Titus' garden.
12. Cornelia: mother of the Gracchi, Roman political reformers, whose education she had carefully supervised.
13. Read: gave lessons.

Sweet poetry and Tully's Orator.
Canst thou not guess wherefore she plies thee thus?
Boy. My lord, I know not, I, nor can I guess,
Unless some fit or frenzy do possess her;
For I have heard my grandsire say full oft,
Extremity of griefs would make men mad;
And I have read that Hecuba of Troy
Ran mad for sorrow. That made me to fear,
Although, my lord, I know my noble aunt
Loves me as dear as e'er my mother did,
And would not, but in fury, fright my youth,
Which made me down to throw my books, and fly—
Causeless, perhaps. But pardon me, sweet aunt,
And, madam, if my uncle Marcus go,
I will most willingly attend your ladyship.
Marc. Lucius, I will.
[*Lavinia turns over with her stumps the books which Lucius has let fall.*]
Tit. How now, Lavinia? Marcus, what means this?
Some book there is that she desires to see.
Which is it, girl, of these?—Open them, boy.—
But thou art deeper read, and better skill'd;
Come and take choice of all my library,
And so beguile thy sorrow, till the heavens
Reveal the damn'd contriver of this deed.
Why lifts she up her arms in sequence thus?
Marc. I think she means that there were more than one
Confederate in the fact; ay, more there was;
Or else to heaven she heaves them for revenge.
Tit. Lucius, what book is that she tosseth so?
Boy. Grandsire, 'tis Ovid's Metamorphosis,
My mother gave it me.
Marc. For love of her that's gone,
Perhaps, she cull'd it from among the rest.
Tit. Soft, so busily she turns the leaves! Help her.
What would she find? Lavinia, shall I read?
This is the tragic tale of Philomel,
And treats of Tereus' treason and his rape—
And rape, I fear, was root of thy annoy.
Marc. See, brother, see, note how she cotes the leaves.
Tit. Lavinia, wert thou thus surpris'd, sweet girl?
Ravish'd and wrong'd as Philomela was,
Forc'd in the ruthless, vast, and gloomy woods?
See, see!
Ay, such a place there is where we did hunt
(O had we never, never hunted there!),
Pattern'd by that the poet here describes,
By nature made for murthers and for rapes.
Marc. O why should nature build so foul a den,
Unless the gods delight in tragedies?
Tit. Give signs, sweet girl, for here are none but friends,
What Roman lord it was durst do the deed;
Or slunk not Saturnine, as Tarquin erst,
That left the camp to sin in Lucrece' bed?
Marc. Sit down, sweet niece; brother, sit down by me.
Apollo, Pallas, Jove, or Mercury,
Inspire me, that I may this treason find!
My lord, look here; look here, Lavinia.
He writes his name with his staff, and guides it with feet and mouth.
This sandy plot is plain; guide, if thou canst,
This after me. I have writ my name,
Without the help of any hand at all.
Curs'd be that heart that forc'd us to this shift!
Write thou, good niece, and here display at last
What God will have discovered for revenge.
Heaven guide thy pen to print thy sorrows plain,
That we may know the traitors and the truth!
She takes the staff in her mouth, and guides it with her stumps, and writes.
O, do ye read, my lord, what she hath writ?
[*Tit.*] "*Stuprum*—Chiron—Demetrius."
Marc. What, what, the lustful sons of Tamora
Performers of this heinous, bloody deed?
Tit. *Magni Dominator poli,*
Tam lentus audis scelera? tam lentus vides?
Marc. O, calm thee, gentle lord, although I know
There is enough written upon this earth
To stir a mutiny in the mildest thoughts,
And arm the minds of infants to exclaims.
My lord, kneel down with me, Lavinia, kneel,
And kneel, sweet boy, the Roman Hector's hope,
And swear with me, as with the woeful fere
And father of that chaste dishonored dame,
Lord Junius Brutus sware for Lucrece' rape,
That we will prosecute by good advice
Mortal revenge upon these traitorous Goths,
And see their blood or die with this reproach.
Tit. 'Tis sure enough, and you knew how,
But if you hunt these bear-whelps, then beware,
The dam will wake and if she wind ye once,
She's with the lion deeply still in league,
And lulls him whilst she playeth on her back,
And when he sleeps will she do what she list.
You are a young huntsman, Marcus, let alone;
And come, I will go get a leaf of brass,
And with a gad of steel will write these words,
And lay it by. The angry northen wind
Will blow these sands like Sibyl's leaves abroad,
And where's our lesson then? Boy, what say you?
Boy. I say, my lord, that if I were a man,

14. Tully's Orator: Cicero's *De Oratore.* **15. plies:** importunes.
24. but in fury: except in a fit of madness.
33. deeper read: i.e. than a schoolboy. **39. fact:** deed, crime.
41. tosseth: turns the pages of. **49. annoy:** injury.
50. cotes: examines. **53. vast:** waste, desolate.
57. Pattern'd by: on the pattern of.

69. plain: flat. **70. after me:** as I have done.
72. shift: expedient. **78. Stuprum:** rape.
81–82. Magni . . . vides: "Ruler of the great heaven, art thou so slow to hear and see crimes?" (Seneca, *Hippolytus*, lines 671–72).
86. exclaims: exclamations, protests.
88. the Roman Hector: i.e. Lucius, now the champion of Rome as Hector was of Troy.
89–91. as . . . rape. See *The Rape of Lucrece*, lines 1807 ff.
89. fere: mate, husband. **92. good advice:** careful planning.
94. reproach: dishonor. **97. wind:** scent.
98. still: always. **100. list:** likes.
101. young: inexperienced. **let alone:** let it alone.
102. leaf: sheet. **103. gad:** spike. **104. northen:** north.
105. Sibyl's leaves: the leaves on which the Cumaean Sibyl wrote her prophecies. They sometimes blew away before they could be read.

Their mother's bedchamber should not be safe
For these base bondmen to the yoke of Rome.
Marc. Ay, that's my boy! Thy father hath full oft
For his ungrateful country done the like.
Boy. And, uncle, so will I, and if I live.
Tit. Come go with me into mine armory;
Lucius, I'll fit thee, and withal my boy
Shall carry from me to the Empress' sons
Presents that I intend to send them both.
Come, come, thou'lt do my message, wilt thou not?
Boy. Ay, with my dagger in their bosoms, grandsire.
Tit. No, boy, not so, I'll teach thee another course.
Lavinia, come. Marcus, look to my house,
Lucius and I'll go brave it at the court.
Ay, marry, will we, sir, and we'll be waited on.
Exeunt [Titus, Lavinia, and Boy].
Marc. O heavens, can you hear a good man groan
And not relent, or not compassion him?
Marcus, attend him in his ecstasy,
That hath more scars of sorrow in his heart
Than foemen's marks upon his batt'red shield,
But yet so just that he will not revenge.
Revenge the heavens for old Andronicus! *Exit.*

[Scene II]

Enter Aaron, Chiron, *and* Demetrius *at one door; and at the other door young* Lucius *and another with a bundle of weapons, and verses writ upon them.*

Chi. Demetrius, here's the son of Lucius,
He hath some message to deliver us.
Aar. Ay, some mad message from his mad grandfather.
Boy. My lords, with all the humbleness I may,
I greet your honors from Andronicus—
[*Aside.*] And pray the Roman gods confound you both!
Dem. Gramercy, lovely Lucius. What's the news?
Boy. [*Aside.*] That you are both decipher'd, that's the news,
For villains mark'd with rape.—May it please you,
My grandsire, well advis'd, hath sent by me
The goodliest weapons of his armory
To gratify your honorable youth,
The hope of Rome, for so he bid me say;
And so I do, and with his gifts present
Your lordships, [that,] when ever you have need,
You may be armed and appointed well:
And so I leave you both—[*aside*] like bloody villains.
Exit [with Attendant].
Dem. What's here? a scroll, and written round about.
Let's see:
[*Reads.*] "*Integer vitae, scelerisque purus,*
Non eget Mauri jaculis, nec arcu."
Chi. O, 'tis a verse in Horace, I know it well,
I read it in the grammar long ago.
Aar. Ay, just—a verse in Horace, right, you have it.
[*Aside.*] Now, what a thing it is to be an ass!
Here's no sound jest! The old man hath found their guilt,
And sends them weapons wrapp'd about with lines
That wound beyond their feeling to the quick.
But were our witty Empress well afoot,
She would applaud Andronicus' conceit,
But let her rest in her unrest a while.—
And now, young lords, was't not a happy star
Led us to Rome, strangers, and more than so,
Captives, to be advanced to this height?
It did me good, before the palace gate
To brave the tribune in his brother's hearing.
Dem. But me more good to see so great a lord
Basely insinuate and send us gifts.
Aar. Had he not reason, Lord Demetrius?
Did you not use his daughter very friendly?
Dem. I would we had a thousand Roman dames
At such a bay, by turn to serve our lust.
Chi. A charitable wish, and full of love.
Aar. Here lacks but your mother for to say amen.
Chi. And that would she for twenty thousand more.
Dem. Come let us go and pray to all the gods
For our beloved mother in her pains.
Aar. [*Aside.*] Pray to the devils, the gods have given us over. *Trumpets sound [within].*
Dem. Why do the Emperor's trumpets flourish thus?
Chi. Belike for joy the Emperor hath a son.
Dem. Soft, who comes here?

Enter Nurse *with a blackamoor child.*

Nur. Good morrow, lords.
O, tell me, did you see Aaron the Moor?
Aar. Well, more or less, or ne'er a whit at all,
Here Aaron is, and what with Aaron now?
Nur. O gentle Aaron, we are all undone!
Now help, or woe betide thee evermore!
Aar. Why, what a caterwauling dost thou keep!
What dost thou wrap and fumble in thy arms?

114. fit thee: provide you with what you need.
121. brave it: play the bravo, cut a figure (cf. *court it,* II.i.91).
122. marry: indeed (originally, the name of the Virgin Mary used as an oath). **waited on:** given proper attention.
124. compassion: take pity on. **125. ecstasy:** madness, frenzy.
129. Revenge the heavens: may the heavens take vengeance.

IV.ii. Location: Rome. The Emperor's palace.
6. confound: destroy. **7. Gramercy:** many thanks.
8. decipher'd: detected.
10. well advis'd: upon reflection. **12. gratify:** grace.
16. appointed: equipped.

18. round about: all round.
20–21. Integer . . . arcu: "The man who is of pure life and free from crime needs not the arrows or the bow of the Moor" (Horace, *Odes,* I.xxii.1–2).
23. grammar: i.e. Latin grammar. (William Lily's, widely used in Shakespeare's time, quotes these lines.)
24. just: precisely. **26. sound:** wholesome.
28. That . . . quick: that pierce them deeply, though they aren't sensitive enough to feel it.
29. witty: clever. **afoot:** up and about. (Tamora, as soon transpires, is in childbed.)
30. conceit: idea, stratagem. **36. brave:** taunt, defy.
38. insinuate: flatter.
42. At . . . bay: so brought to bay or cornered.
47. pains: labor pains. **50. Belike:** probably.
53. more. Punning on *Moor* in the preceding line.

Nur. O, that which I would hide from heaven's eye,
Our Empress' shame, and stately Rome's disgrace!
She is delivered, lords, she is delivered.
Aar. To whom?
Nur. I mean she is brought a-bed.
Aar. Well, God give her good rest! what hath he sent her?
Nur. A devil.
Aar. Why, then she is the devil's dam: a joyful issue.
Nur. A joyless, dismal, black, and sorrowful issue!
Here is the babe, as loathsome as a toad
Amongst the fair-fac'd breeders of our clime.
The Empress sends it thee, thy stamp, thy seal,
And bids thee christen it with thy dagger's point.
Aar. 'Zounds, ye whore, is black so base a hue?
Sweet blowse, you are a beauteous blossom sure.
Dem. Villain, what hast thou done?
Aar. That which thou canst not undo.
Chi. Thou hast undone our mother.
Aar. Villain, I have done thy mother.
Dem. And therein, hellish dog, thou hast undone her.
Woe to her chance, and damn'd her loathed choice!
Accurs'd the offspring of so foul a fiend!
Chi. It shall not live.
Aar. It shall not die.
Nur. Aaron, it must, the mother wills it so.
Aar. What, must it, nurse? then let no man but I
Do execution on my flesh and blood.
Dem. I'll broach the tadpole on my rapier's point.
Nurse, give it me, my sword shall soon dispatch it.
Aar. Sooner this sword shall plough thy bowels up.
[*Takes the child from the Nurse, and draws.*]
Stay, murtherous villains, will you kill your brother?
Now, by the burning tapers of the sky,
That shone so brightly when this boy was got,
He dies upon my scimitar's sharp point,
That touches this my first-born son and heir!
I tell you, younglings, not Enceladus,
With all his threat'ning band of Typhon's brood,
Nor great Alcides, nor the god of war,
Shall seize this prey out of his father's hands.
What, what, ye sanguine, shallow-hearted boys!
Ye white-lim'd walls! ye alehouse painted signs!
Coal-black is better than another hue,
In that it scorns to bear another hue;
For all the water in the ocean
Can never turn the swan's black legs to white,
Although she lave them hourly in the flood.
Tell the Empress from me, I am of age
To keep mine own, excuse it how she can.
Dem. Wilt thou betray thy noble mistress thus?
Aar. My mistress is my mistress, this myself,
The vigor and the picture of my youth:
This before all the world do I prefer,
This maugre all the world will I keep safe,
Or some of you shall smoke for it in Rome.
Dem. By this our mother is for ever sham'd.
Chi. Rome will despise her for this foul escape.
Nur. The Emperor in his rage will doom her death.
Chi. I blush to think upon this ignomy.
Aar. Why, there's the privilege your beauty bears.
Fie, treacherous hue, that will betray with blushing
The close enacts and counsels of thy heart!
Here's a young lad fram'd of another leer:
Look how the black slave smiles upon the father,
As who should say, "Old lad, I am thine own."
He is your brother, lords, sensibly fed
Of that self blood that first gave life to you,
And from your womb where you imprisoned were
He is enfranchised and come to light.
Nay, he is your brother by the surer side,
Although my seal be stamped in his face.
Nur. Aaron, what shall I say unto the Empress?
Dem. Advise thee, Aaron, what is to be done,
And we will all subscribe to thy advice:
Save thou the child, so we may all be safe.
Aar. Then sit we down and let us all consult.
My son and I will have the wind of you;
Keep there. Now talk at pleasure of your safety.
[*They sit.*]
Dem. How many women saw this child of his?
Aar. Why, so, brave lords, when we join in league
I am a lamb, but if you brave the Moor,
The chafed boar, the mountain lioness,
The ocean swells not so as Aaron storms.
But say again, how many saw the child?
Nur. Cornelia the midwife, and myself,
And no one else but the delivered Empress.
Aar. The Emperess, the midwife, and yourself.
Two may keep counsel when the third's away:
Go to the Empress, tell her this I said. *He kills her.*
Weeke, weeke!—so cries a pig prepared to the spit.
Dem. What mean'st thou, Aaron? wherefore didst thou this?
Aar. O Lord, sir, 'tis a deed of policy.
Shall she live to betray this guilt of ours,
A long-tongu'd babbling gossip? No, lords, no.
And now be it known to you my full intent.
Not far, one Muliteus my countryman
His wife but yesternight was brought to bed;

65. issue: outcome. **66. issue:** child, offspring.
71. 'Zounds: by God's (Christ's) wounds.
72. blowse: "a ruddy, fat-faced wench" (Johnson); used jokingly by Aaron. **76. done:** had sexual intercourse with.
78. chance: fortune. **85. broach:** spit, impale.
90. got: begotten.
93. Enceladus: one of the Titans, primeval Greek deities who fought against the Olympian gods.
94. Typhon: a gigantic monster who also warred with the gods.
95. Alcides: Hercules, descended from Alcaeus.
97. sanguine: ruddy-complexioned (as opposed to black).
98. white-lim'd: whitewashed. **alehouse . . . signs:** signs done cheaply in crude color.

110. maugre: in spite of. **111. smoke:** suffer.
113. escape: sinful adventure. **115. ignomy:** ignominy, shame.
118. enacts: workings, purposes.
119. leer: complexion, countenance. **122. sensibly:** manifestly.
123. self: same. **126. the surer side:** i.e. the mother's.
129. Advise thee: consider. **130. subscribe to:** agree to follow.
131. so: so long as.
133. have . . . you: keep upwind of you (as a hunter does when stalking game). **138. chafed:** enraged.
148. policy: prudent or sagacious course of action.
152–53. one . . . wife: the wife of one Muliteus, my countryman.

His child is like to her, fair as you are.
Go pack with him, and give the mother gold,
And tell them both the circumstance of all,
And how by this their child shall be advanc'd,
And be received for the Emperor's heir,
And substituted in the place of mine,
To calm this tempest whirling in the court;
And let the Emperor dandle him for his own.
Hark ye, lords, you see I have given her physic,
[*Pointing to the Nurse.*]
And you must needs bestow her funeral;
The fields are near, and you are gallant grooms.
This done, see that you take no longer days,
But send the midwife presently to me.
The midwife and the nurse well made away,
Then let the ladies tattle what they please.

Chi. Aaron, I see thou wilt not trust the air
With secrets.

Dem. For this care of Tamora,
Herself and hers are highly bound to thee.

Exeunt [*Demetrius and Chiron, bearing off the Nurse's body*].

Aar. Now to the Goths, as swift as swallow flies,
There to dispose this treasure in mine arms,
And secretly to greet the Empress' friends.
Come on, you thick-lipp'd slave, I'll bear you hence,
For it is you that puts us to our shifts.
I'll make you feed on berries and on roots,
And feed on curds and whey, and suck the goat,
And cabin in a cave, and bring you up
To be a warrior and command a camp. *Exit.*

[Scene III]

Enter Titus, *old* Marcus, *young* Lucius, *and other gentlemen* [Publius, Sempronius, Caius] *with bows; and Titus bears the arrows with letters on the ends of them.*

Tit. Come, Marcus, come; kinsmen, this is the way.
Sir boy, let me see your archery.
Look ye draw home enough, and 'tis there straight.
Terras Astraea reliquit;
Be you remember'd, Marcus, she's gone, she's fled.
Sirs, take you to your tools. You, cousins, shall
Go sound the ocean, and cast your nets;
Happily you may catch her in the sea;
Yet there's as little justice as at land.
No, Publius and Sempronius, you must do it,
'Tis you must dig with mattock and with spade,
And pierce the inmost centre of the earth;
Then when you come to Pluto's region,
I pray you deliver him this petition.
Tell him it is for justice and for aid,
And that it comes from old Andronicus,
Shaken with sorrows in ungrateful Rome.
Ah, Rome! well, well, I made thee miserable
What time I threw the people's suffrages
On him that thus doth tyrannize o'er me.
Go get you gone, and pray be careful all,
And leave you not a man-of-war unsearch'd.
This wicked emperor may have shipp'd her hence,
And, kinsmen, then we may go pipe for justice.

Marc. O Publius, is not this a heavy case,
To see thy noble uncle thus distract?

Pub. Therefore, my lords, it highly us concerns
By day and night t' attend him carefully,
And feed his humor kindly as we may,
Till time beget some careful remedy.

Marc. Kinsmen, his sorrows are past remedy,
But [. . .]
Join with the Goths, and with revengeful war
Take wreak on Rome for this ingratitude,
And vengeance on the traitor Saturnine.

Tit. Publius, how now? how now, my masters?
What, have you met with her?

Pub. No, my good lord, but Pluto sends you word,
If you will have Revenge from hell, you shall.
Marry, for Justice, she is so employ'd,
He thinks, with Jove in heaven, or some where else,
So that perforce you must needs stay a time.

Tit. He doth me wrong to feed me with delays.
I'll dive into the burning lake below,
And pull her out of Acheron by the heels.
Marcus, we are but shrubs, no cedars we,
No big-bon'd men fram'd of the Cyclops' size,
But metal, Marcus, steel to the very back,
Yet wrung with wrongs more than our backs can bear.
And sith there's no justice in earth nor hell,
We will solicit heaven and move the gods
To send down Justice for to wreak our wrongs.
Come, to this gear. You are a good archer, Marcus;
He gives them the arrows.
"*Ad Jovem*," that's for you; here, "*Ad Apollinem*";
"*Ad Martem*," that's for myself;
Here, boy, "*To Pallas*"; here, "*To Mercury*";
"*To* [*Saturn*]," Caius, not to Saturnine:
You were as good to shoot against the wind.
To it, boy! Marcus, loose when I bid.
Of my word, I have written to effect,
There's not a god left unsolicited.

155. pack: conspire. **156. circumstance of all**: all the particulars.
163. bestow: furnish. **164. grooms**: lads, fellows.
165. days: time. **166. presently**: immediately.
173. dispose: dispose of.
175. thick-lipp'd slave. Spoken jocosely.
176. shifts: expedients. **179. cabin**: lodge.

IV.iii. Location: Rome. A public place.
3. home: to the full extent.
4. Terras . . . reliquit: "Astraea, goddess of Justice, has left the earth" (Ovid, *Metamorphoses*, I.150).
5. Be you rememb'red: remember. **8. Happily**: haply, perhaps.

13. Pluto: god of the underworld. **19. What time**: when.
24. pipe: whistle, i.e. look in vain. **25. heavy**: sad.
26. distract: distracted, mad. **29. feed his humor**: humor him.
30. careful: laborious. **32.** On this line see the Textual Notes.
34. wreak: vengeance. **40. for**: as for.
42. stay a time: wait awhile.
44. burning lake: Phlegethon, the burning river of Hades.
45. Acheron: another river in Hades.
47. Cyclops: the one-eyed giants of the *Odyssey*.
50. sith: since. **53. gear**: business.
54. Ad Jovem: to Jupiter. **Ad Apollinem**: to Apollo.
55. Ad Martem: to Mars. **56. Pallas**: Minerva.
58. You . . . wind: you would do as much good by shooting against the wind (as by appealing to Saturninus for justice).
59. loose: shoot.

Marc. Kinsmen, shoot all your shafts into the court,
We will afflict the Emperor in his pride.
Tit. Now, masters, draw. [*They shoot.*] O, well said, Lucius!
Good boy, in Virgo's lap; give it Pallas.
Marc. My lord, I [aim'd] a mile beyond the moon,
Your letter is with Jupiter by this.
Tit. Ha, ha!
Publius, Publius, what hast thou done?
See, see, thou hast shot off one of Taurus' horns.
Marc. This was the sport, my lord. When Publius shot,
The Bull, being gall'd, gave Aries such a knock
That down fell both the Ram's horns in the court,
And who should find them but the Empress' villain?
She laugh'd, and told the Moor he should not choose
But give them to his master for a present.
Tit. Why, there it goes, God give his lordship joy!

Enter the CLOWN *with a basket, and two pigeons in it.*

News, news from heaven! Marcus, the post is come.
Sirrah, what tidings? have you any letters?
Shall I have justice? what says Jupiter?

Clo. Ho, the gibbet-maker? he says that he hath taken them down again, for the man must not be hang'd till the next week.

Tit. But what says Jupiter, I ask thee?

Clo. Alas, sir, I know not Jubiter, I never drank with him in all my life.

Tit. Why, villain, art not thou the carrier?

Clo. Ay, of my pigeons, sir, nothing else.

Tit. Why, didst thou not come from heaven?

Clo. From heaven! alas, sir, I never came there. God forbid I should be so bold to press to heaven in my young days. Why, I am going with my pigeons to the tribunal plebs, to take up a matter of brawl betwixt my uncle and one of the Emperal's men.

Marc. Why, sir, that is as fit as can be to serve for your oration, and let him deliver the pigeons to the Emperor from you.

Tit. Tell me, can you deliver an oration to the Emperor with a grace?

Clo. Nay, truly, sir, I could never say grace in all my life.

Tit. Sirrah, come hither, make no more ado,
But give your pigeons to the Emperor.
By me thou shalt have justice at his hands.
Hold, hold; mean while here's money for thy charges.
Give me pen and ink. Sirrah, can you with a grace deliver up a supplication?

Clo. Ay, sir.

Tit. Then here is a supplication for you; and when you come to him, at the first approach you must kneel, then kiss his foot, then deliver up your pigeons, and then look for your reward. I'll be at hand, sir, see you do it bravely.

Clo. I warrant you, sir, let me alone.

Tit. Sirrah, hast thou a knife? Come let me see it.
Here, Marcus, fold it in the oration,
For [then] hast made it like an humble suppliant.
And when thou hast given it to the Emperor,
Knock at my door, and tell me what he says.
Clo. God be with you, sir, I will. *Exit.*
Tit. Come, Marcus, let us go. Publius, follow me.
Exeunt.

[SCENE IV]

Enter EMPEROR *and* EMPRESS *and her two sons* [DEMETRIUS *and* CHIRON, LORDS, *and others*]; *the Emperor brings the arrows in his hand that Titus shot at him.*

Sat. Why, lords, what wrongs are these! was ever seen
An emperor in Rome thus overborne,
Troubled, confronted thus, and, for the extent
Of egall justice, us'd in such contempt?
My lords, you know, [as know] the mightful gods,
However these disturbers of our peace
Buzz in the people's ears, there nought hath pass'd,
But even with law, against the willful sons
Of old Andronicus. And what and if
His sorrows have so overwhelm'd his wits?
Shall we be thus afflicted in his wreaks,
His fits, his frenzy, and his bitterness?
And now he writes to heaven for his redress.
See, here's to Jove, and this to Mercury,
This to Apollo, this to the god of war:
Sweet scrolls to fly about the streets of Rome!
What's this but libelling against the Senate,
And blazoning our unjustice every where?
A goodly humor, is it not, my lords?
As who would say, in Rome no justice were.
But if I live, his feigned ecstasies
Shall be no shelter to these outrages,
But he and his shall know that justice lives
In Saturninus' health, whom, if he sleep,
He'll so awake as he in fury shall
Cut off the proud'st conspirator that lives.
Tam. My gracious lord, my lovely Saturnine,
Lord of my life, commander of my thoughts,
Calm thee, and bear the faults of Titus' age,
Th' effects of sorrow for his valiant sons,
Whose loss hath pierc'd him deep and scarr'd his heart,

64. said: done.
65. Virgo: a constellation and zodiacal sign (Astraea after her flight from earth).
66. a mile . . . moon. Marcus equivocates, since in addition to the literal meaning this expression was used to suggest wild, extravagant talk. Marcus is humoring Titus but thinks all this a mad game.
70, 72. Taurus, Aries: the Bull and the Ram, two zodiacal signs.
72. gall'd: grazed. **73. horns.** The badge of the cuckold.
74. villain: servant (but the modern sense is also present).
75–76. should . . . But: must.
77. there it goes: a hunting cry. **s.d. Clown:** rustic.
87. carrier: deliverer of letters, etc.
93. tribunal plebs: blunder for *tribunus plebis* (tribune of the plebs). **take up:** achieve a friendly settlement of.
94. Emperal: blunder for *Emperor*. **105. charges:** expenses.

113. bravely: in fine style. **114. let me alone:** leave it to me.
117. hast . . . suppliant: thou hast dressed it up to look like a harmless petitioner (?). Meaning and relevance are obscure.

IV.iv. Location: Rome. Before the Emperor's palace.
3. extent: exercise. **4. egall:** equal. **8. even:** in accord.
9. what and if: what if, supposing that.
11. wreaks: vindictive acts. **17. libelling:** circulating libels.
19. humor: caprice. **21. ecstasies:** fits of madness.

And rather comfort his distressed plight
Than prosecute the meanest or the best
For these contempts. [*Aside.*] Why, thus it shall become
High-witted Tamora to gloze with all;
But, Titus, I have touch'd thee to the quick;
Thy life-blood out, if Aaron now be wise,
Then is all safe, the anchor in the port.

Enter Clown.

How now, good fellow, wouldst thou speak with us?

Clo. Yea forsooth, and your mistriship be emperial.

Tam. Empress I am, but yonder sits the Emperor.

Clo. 'Tis he. God and Saint Steven give you godden. I have brought you a letter and a couple of pigeons here. *He* [*Saturninus*] *reads the letter.*

Sat. Go take him away and hang him presently.

Clo. How much money must I have?

Tam. Come, sirrah, you must be hang'd.

Clo. Hang'd! by' lady, then I have brought up a neck to a fair end. *Exit* [*guarded*].

Sat. Despiteful and intolerable wrongs!
Shall I endure this monstrous villainy?
I know from whence this same device proceeds.
May this be borne as if his traitorous sons,
That died by law for murther of our brother,
Have by my means been butchered wrongfully?
Go drag the villain hither by the hair,
Nor age nor honor shall shape privilege;
For this proud mock I'll be thy slaughter-man,
Sly frantic wretch, that holp'st to make me great,
In hope thyself should govern Rome and me.

Enter Nuntius Aemilius.

What news with thee, Aemilius?

Aemil. Arm, my lords! Rome never had more cause.
The Goths have gathered head, and with a power
Of high-resolved men, bent to the spoil,
They hither march amain, under conduct
Of Lucius, son to old Andronicus,
Who threats, in course of this revenge, to do
As much as ever Coriolanus did.

Sat. Is warlike Lucius general of the Goths?
These tidings nip me, and I hang the head
As flowers with frost, or grass beat down with storms.
Ay, now begins our sorrows to approach.
'Tis he the common people love so much;
Myself hath often heard them say,
When I have walked like a private man,
That Lucius' banishment was wrongfully,
And they have wish'd that Lucius were their emperor.

Tam. Why should you fear? is not your city strong?

35. **High-witted:** clever, cunning. **gloze:** talk smoothly.
43. **godden:** good evening. 45. **presently:** immediately.
46. **must I have:** am I to get. 48. **by' lady:** by Our Lady.
57. **shape privilege:** afford immunity. 59. **holp'st:** helped.
60 s.d. **Nuntius:** messenger.
63. **gathered head:** raised an army. **power:** armed force.
65. **amain:** with speed.
68. **Coriolanus:** Roman general who was banished from Rome, and in revenge allied himself with his former enemies the Volscians and marched against Rome. See Shakespeare's *Coriolanus*.

Sat. Ay, but the citizens favor Lucius,
And will revolt from me to succor him.

Tam. King, be thy thoughts imperious, like thy name.
Is the sun dimm'd, that gnats do fly in it?
The eagle suffers little birds to sing,
And is not careful what they mean thereby,
Knowing that with the shadow of his wings
He can at pleasure stint their melody;
Even so mayest thou the giddy men of Rome.
Then cheer thy spirit, for know thou, Emperor,
I will enchant the old Andronicus
With words more sweet, and yet more dangerous,
Than baits to fish, or honey-stalks to sheep,
When as the one is wounded with the bait,
The other rotted with delicious [feed].

Sat. But he will not entreat his son for us.

Tam. If Tamora entreat him, then he will,
For I can smooth and fill his aged ears
With golden promises, that, were his heart
Almost impregnable, his old years deaf,
Yet should both ear and heart obey my tongue.
[*To Aemilius.*] Go thou before, to be our ambassador.
Say that the Emperor requests a parley
Of warlike Lucius, and appoint the meeting
Even at his father's house, the old Andronicus.

Sat. Aemilius, do this message honorably,
And if he stand [on] hostage for his safety,
Bid him demand what pledge will please him best.

Aemil. Your bidding shall I do effectually. *Exit.*

Tam. Now will I to that old Andronicus,
And temper him with all the art I have,
To pluck proud Lucius from the warlike Goths.
And now, sweet emperor, be blithe again,
And bury all thy fear in my devices.

Sat. Then go successantly, and plead to him.

Exeunt.

[ACT V, Scene I]

[*Flourish.*] *Enter* Lucius *with an army of* Goths, *with Drums and Soldiers.*

Luc. Approved warriors, and my faithful friends,
I have received letters from great Rome
Which signifies what hate they bear their emperor,
And how desirous of our sight they are.
Therefore, great lords, be as your titles witness,
Imperious, and impatient of your wrongs,
And wherein Rome hath done you any scath,
Let him make treble satisfaction.

[*1.*] *Goth.* Brave slip, sprung from the great Andronicus,
Whose name was once our terror, now our comfort,
Whose high exploits and honorable deeds
Ingrateful Rome requites with foul contempt,
Be bold in us, we'll follow where thou lead'st,

84. **careful:** anxious about. 86. **stint:** stop.
87. **giddy:** fickle in allegiance. 91. **honey-stalks:** clover.
92. **When as:** when. 96. **smooth:** flatter. 98. **years:** ears.
105. **stand:** insist. 109. **temper:** work on.
113. **successantly:** immediately.

V.i. Location: Plains near Rome.
1. **Approved:** tested, proven. 7. **scath:** harm. 9. **slip:** scion.
13. **bold:** confident.

Like stinging bees in hottest summer's day,
Led by their master to the flow'red fields,
And be adveng'd on cursed Tamora.
[*Other Goths.*] And as he saith, so say we all with him.
Luc. I humbly thank him, and I thank you all.
But who comes here, led by a lusty Goth?

Enter a Goth *leading of* Aaron *with his child in his arms.*

[2.] *Goth.* Renowmed Lucius, from our troops I stray'd
To gaze upon a ruinous monastery,
And as I earnestly did fix mine eye
Upon the wasted building, suddenly
I heard a child cry underneath a wall.
I made unto the noise, when soon I heard
The crying babe controll'd with this discourse:
"Peace, tawny slave, half me and half thy dame.
Did not thy hue bewray whose brat thou art,
Had nature lent thee but thy mother's look,
Villain, thou mightst have been an emperor.
But where the bull and cow are both milk-white,
They never do beget a coal-black calf.
Peace, villain, peace!"—even thus he rates the babe—
"For I must bear thee to a trusty Goth,
Who, when he knows thou art the Empress' babe,
Will hold thee dearly for thy mother's sake."
With this, my weapon drawn, I rush'd upon him,
Surpris'd him suddenly, and brought him hither
To use as you think needful of the man.
Luc. O worthy Goth, this is the incarnate devil
That robb'd Andronicus of his good hand;
This is the pearl that pleas'd your empress' eye,
And here's the base fruit of her burning lust.
Say, wall-ey'd slave, whither wouldst thou convey
This growing image of thy fiend-like face?
Why dost not speak? What, deaf? not a word?
A halter, soldiers! hang him on this tree,
And by his side his fruit of bastardy.
Aar. Touch not the boy, he is of royal blood.
Luc. Too like the sire for ever being good.
First hang the child, that he may see it sprawl—
A sight to vex the father's soul withal.
Get me a ladder.
[*A ladder brought, which Aaron is made to ascend.*]
Aar. Lucius, save the child
And bear it from me to the Emperess.
If thou do this, I'll show thee wondrous things,
That highly may advantage thee to hear.
If thou wilt not, befall what may befall,
I'll speak no more but "Vengeance rot you all!"
Luc. Say on, and if it please me which thou speak'st,
Thy child shall live, and I will see it nourish'd.
Aar. And if it please thee? Why, assure thee, Lucius,

15. **master.** It was thought that the leader of the hive was a male, the king bee. 16. **adveng'd:** aveng'd.
20. **Renowmed:** renowned. 26. **controll'd:** calmed, soothed.
27. **slave.** Used playfully (like *villain* in lines 30, 33 below).
28. **bewray:** reveal. **brat:** child (not necessarily abusive).
33. **rates:** scolds. 39. **use . . . of:** deal . . . with.
44. **wall-ey'd:** with glaring eyes. 50. **for ever being:** ever to be.

'Twill vex thy soul to hear what I shall speak:
For I must talk of murthers, rapes, and massacres,
Acts of black night, abominable deeds,
Complots of mischief, treason, villainies,
Ruthful to hear, yet piteously perform'd.
And this shall all be buried in my death,
Unless thou swear to me my child shall live.
Luc. Tell on thy mind, I say thy child shall live.
Aar. Swear that he shall, and then I will begin.
Luc. Who should I swear by? thou believest no god:
That granted, how canst thou believe an oath?
Aar. What if I do not? as indeed I do not,
Yet for I know thou art religious,
And hast a thing within thee called conscience,
With twenty popish tricks and ceremonies,
Which I have seen thee careful to observe,
Therefore I urge thy oath; for that I know
An idiot holds his bauble for a god,
And keeps the oath which by that god he swears,
To that I'll urge him: therefore thou shalt vow
By that same god, what god soe'er it be
That thou adorest and hast in reverence,
To save my boy, to nourish and bring him up,
Or else I will discover nought to thee.
Luc. Even by my God I swear to thee I will.
Aar. First know thou, I begot him on the Empress.
Luc. O most insatiate and luxurious woman!
Aar. Tut, Lucius, this was but a deed of charity
To that which thou shalt hear of me anon.
'Twas her two sons that murdered Bassianus;
They cut thy sister's tongue, and ravish'd her,
And cut her hands, and trimm'd her as thou sawest.
Luc. O detestable villain, call'st thou that trimming?
Aar. Why, she was wash'd, and cut, and trimm'd, and 'twas
Trim sport for them which had the doing of it.
Luc. O barbarous, beastly villains like thyself!
Aar. Indeed I was their tutor to instruct them.
That codding spirit had they from their mother,
As sure a card as ever won the set;
That bloody mind I think they learn'd of me,
As true a dog as ever fought at head.
Well, let my deeds be witness of my worth:
I train'd thy brethren to that guileful hole,
Where the dead corpse of Bassianus lay;
I wrote the letter that thy father found,
And hid the gold within that letter mentioned,
Confederate with the Queen and her two sons;
And what not done, that thou hast cause to rue,
Wherein I had no stroke of mischief in it?
I play'd the cheater for thy father's hand,

66. **Ruthful:** lamentable. **piteously:** so as to excite pity.
74. **for:** because. 78. **urge:** insist upon. **for that:** because.
79. **bauble:** fool's stick and emblem.
88. **luxurious:** lecherous. 90. **To:** compared with.
99. **codding:** lecherous; or cheating, deceitful.
100. **set:** trick, game.
102. **at head.** A good bulldog attacked the bull's head directly.
104. **train'd:** lured.
111. **cheater:** swindler, but with play (as Dover Wilson points out) on "officer appointed to look after property forfeited to the Crown (escheats)."

And when I had it, drew myself apart,
And almost broke my heart with extreme laughter.
I pried me through the crevice of a wall,
When, for his hand, he had his two sons' heads,
Beheld his tears, and laugh'd so heartily
That both mine eyes were rainy like to his;
And when I told the Empress of this sport,
She sounded almost at my pleasing tale,
And for my tidings gave me twenty kisses.

[*1.*] *Goth.* What, canst thou say all this and never blush?

Aar. Ay, like a black dog, as the saying is.

Luc. Art thou not sorry for these heinous deeds?

Aar. Ay, that I had not done a thousand more.
Even now I curse the day—and yet I think
Few come within the compass of my curse—
Wherein I did not some notorious ill:
As kill a man, or else devise his death,
Ravish a maid, or plot the way to do it,
Accuse some innocent, and forswear myself,
Set deadly enmity between two friends,
Make poor men's cattle break their necks,
Set fire on barns and haystalks in the night,
And bid the owners quench them with their tears.
Oft have I digg'd up dead men from their graves,
And set them upright at their dear friends' door,
Even when their sorrows almost was forgot,
And on their skins, as on the bark of trees,
Have with my knife carved in Roman letters,
"Let not your sorrow die, though I am dead."
But I have done a thousand dreadful things,
As willingly as one would kill a fly,
And nothing grieves me heartily indeed,
But that I cannot do ten thousand more.

Luc. Bring down the devil, for he must not die
So sweet a death as hanging presently.

Aar. If there be devils, would I were a devil,
To live and burn in everlasting fire,
So I might have your company in hell,
But to torment you with my bitter tongue!

Luc. Sirs, stop his mouth, and let him speak no more.

Enter AEMILIUS.

Goth. My lord, there is a messenger from Rome
Desires to be admitted to your presence.

Luc. Let him come near.
Welcome, Aemilius, what's the news from Rome?

Aemil. Lord Lucius, and you princes of the Goths,
The Roman Emperor greets you all by me,
And for he understands you are in arms,
He craves a parley at your father's house,
Willing you to demand your hostages,
And they shall be immediately delivered.

[*1.*] *Goth.* What says our general?

Luc. Aemilius, let the Emperor give his pledges
Unto my father and my uncle Marcus,
And we will come. March away. [*Flourish. Exeunt.*]

[SCENE II]

Enter TAMORA *and her two sons* [DEMETRIUS *and* CHIRON], *disguised.*

Tam. Thus, in this strange and sad habiliment,
I will encounter with Andronicus,
And say I am Revenge, sent from below
To join with him and right his heinous wrongs.
Knock at his study, where they say he keeps
To ruminate strange plots of dire revenge;
Tell him Revenge is come to join with him,
And work confusion on his enemies.

They knock, and TITUS [*above*] *opens his study door.*

Tit. Who doth molest my contemplation?
Is it your trick to make me ope the door
That so my sad decrees may fly away,
And all my study be to no effect?
You are deceiv'd, for what I mean to do
See here in bloody lines I have set down:
And what is written shall be executed.

Tam. Titus, I am come to talk with thee.

Tit. No, not a word, how can I grace my talk,
Wanting a hand to give['t] that accord?
Thou hast the odds of me, therefore no more.

Tam. If thou didst know me, thou wouldst talk with me.

Tit. I am not mad, I know thee well enough.
Witness this wretched stump, witness these crimson lines,
Witness these trenches made by grief and care,
Witness the tiring day and heavy night,
Witness all sorrow, that I know thee well
For our proud Empress, mighty Tamora.
Is not thy coming for my other hand?

Tam. Know, thou sad man, I am not Tamora;
She is thy enemy, and I thy friend.
I am Revenge, sent from th' infernal kingdom
To ease the gnawing vulture of thy mind,
By working wreakful vengeance on thy foes.
Come down and welcome me to this world's light;
Confer with me of murder and of death.
There's not a hollow cave or lurking-place,
No vast obscurity or misty vale,
Where bloody murther or detested rape
Can couch for fear, but I will find them out,
And in their ears tell them my dreadful name,
Revenge, which makes the foul offender quake.

Tit. Art thou Revenge? and art thou sent to me,
To be a torment to mine enemies?

Tam. I am, therefore come down and welcome me.

113. broke my heart: died. **114. pried me:** peered, spied.
119. sounded: fainted.
122. like . . . dog. Referring to an old proverb.
133. haystalks: haystacks.
141. But: i.e. but why continue the list. Many editors read *Tut* with Q2. **146. presently:** immediately. **158. for:** since.

V.ii. Location: Rome. Court of Titus' house.
1. sad habiliment: dismal costume. **5. keeps:** stays, dwells.
11. sad decrees: sober resolutions.
18. that accord: that agreement, i.e. the proper support. In place of *give it that accord* F1 has *give it action*, an attractive reading: "adorn it with the appropriate gestures."
19. odds of me: advantage over me, i.e. two hands to my one.
23. trenches: wrinkles. **36. vast obscurity:** remote waste.
38. couch: lie hidden.

Tit. Do me some service ere I come to thee.
Lo by thy side where Rape and Murder stands;
Now give some surance that thou art Revenge—
Stab them, or tear them on thy chariot-wheels,
And then I'll come and be thy waggoner,
And whirl along with thee about the globes.
Provide thee two proper palfreys, black as jet,
To hale thy vengeful waggon swift away,
And find out [murderers] in their guilty [caves];
And when thy car is loaden with their heads,
I will dismount, and by thy waggon-wheel
Trot like a servile footman all day long,
Even from [Hyperion's] rising in the east,
Until his very downfall in the sea;
And day by day I'll do this heavy task,
So thou destroy Rapine and Murder there.
Tam. These are my ministers, and come with me.
Tit. Are [they] thy ministers? What are they call'd?
Tam. Rape and Murder, therefore called so
'Cause they take vengeance of such kind of men.
Tit. Good Lord, how like the Empress' sons they are!
And you, the Empress! but we wordly men
Have miserable, mad, mistaking eyes.
O sweet Revenge, now do I come to thee,
And if one arm's embracement will content thee,
I will embrace thee in it by and by. *[Exit above.]*
Tam. This closing with him fits his lunacy.
What e'er I forge to feed his brain-sick humors,
Do you uphold and maintain in your speeches,
For now he firmly takes me for Revenge,
And being credulous in this mad thought,
I'll make him send for Lucius his son;
And whilst I at a banket hold him sure,
I'll find some cunning practice out of hand,
To scatter and disperse the giddy Goths,
Or at the least make them his enemies.
See here he comes, and I must ply my theme.

[Enter Titus *below.]*

Tit. Long have I been forlorn, and all for thee.
Welcome, dread Fury, to my woeful house;
Rapine and Murther, you are welcome too.
How like the Empress and her sons you are!
Well are you fitted, had you but a Moor.
Could not all hell afford you such a devil?
For well I wot the Empress never wags
But in her company there is a Moor;
And would you represent our queen aright,
It were convenient you had such a devil.
But welcome as you are: what shall we do?
Tam. What wouldst thou have us do, Andronicus?
Dem. Show me a murtherer, I'll deal with him.
Chi. Show me a villain that hath done a rape,
And I am sent to be reveng'd on him.
Tam. Show me a thousand that hath done thee wrong,
And I will be revenged on them all.
Tit. Look round about the wicked streets of Rome,
And when thou find'st a man that's like thyself,
Good Murther, stab him, he's a murtherer.
Go thou with him, and when it is thy hap
To find another that is like to thee,
Good Rapine, stab him, he is a ravisher.
Go thou with them, and in the Emperor's court
There is a queen, attended by a Moor;
Well shalt thou know her by thine own proportion,
For up and down she doth resemble thee.
I pray thee do on them some violent death,
They have been violent to me and mine.
Tam. Well hast thou lesson'd us, this shall we do.
But would it please thee, good Andronicus,
To send for Lucius, thy thrice-valiant son,
Who leads towards Rome a band of warlike Goths,
And bid him come and banquet at thy house,
When he is here, even at thy solemn feast,
I will bring in the Empress and her sons,
The Emperor himself and all thy foes,
And at thy mercy shall they stoop and kneel,
And on them shalt thou ease thy angry heart.
What says Andronicus to this device?
Tit. Marcus, my brother! 'tis sad Titus calls.

Enter Marcus.

Go, gentle Marcus, to thy nephew Lucius;
Thou shalt inquire him out among the Goths:
Bid him repair to me, and bring with him
Some of the chiefest princes of the Goths.
Bid him encamp his soldiers where they are.
Tell him the Emperor and the Empress too
Feast at my house, and he shall feast with them.
This do thou for my love, and so let him,
As he regards his aged father's life.
Marc. This will I do, and soon return again. *[Exit.]*
Tam. Now will I hence about thy business,
And take my ministers along with me.
Tit. Nay, nay, let Rape and Murder stay with me,
Or else I'll call my brother back again,
And cleave to no revenge but Lucius.
Tam. *[Aside to her sons.]* What say you, boys, will you abide with him,
Whiles I go tell my lord the Emperor
How I have govern'd our determin'd jest?
Yield to his humor, smooth and speak him fair,
And tarry with him till I turn again.
Tit. *[Aside.]* I knew them all though they suppos'd me mad,
And will o'erreach them in their own devices,
A pair of cursed hell-hounds and their dame.
Dem. Madam, depart at pleasure, leave us here.

50. proper: fine, handsome. **51. hale:** pull, drag.
53. car: chariot. **56. Hyperion:** the sun-god.
63. of . . . men: on those who commit rape and murder.
65. wordly: worldly (variant form).
70. closing: agreeing. **71. forge:** invent. **humors:** whims.
77. practice: plot. **out of hand:** on the spur of the moment.
87. wags: goes about. **90. convenient:** fitting.

101. hap: chance. **107. up and down:** exactly.
115. solemn: stately, ceremonious.
139. govern'd: arranged, managed. **our determin'd jest:** the jest we planned.
140. smooth: flatter. **speak him fair:** humor him.
141. turn: return.

Tam. Farewell, Andronicus, Revenge now goes
To lay a complot to betray thy foes.
Tit. I know thou dost, and, sweet Revenge, farewell. *[Exit Tamora.]*
Chi. Tell us, old man, how shall we be employ'd?
Tit. Tut, I have work enough for you to do.
Publius, come hither! Caius and Valentine!

[*Enter* Publius, Caius, *and* Valentine.]

Pub. What is your will?
Tit. Know you these two?
Pub. The Empress' sons I take them, Chiron, Demetrius.
Tit. Fie, Publius, fie, thou art too much deceiv'd.
The one is Murder, and Rape is the other's name,
And therefore bind them, gentle Publius.
Caius and Valentine, lay hands on them.
Oft have you heard me wish for such an hour,
And now I find it, therefore bind them sure,
And stop their mouths if they begin to cry.
[*Exit Titus. Publius, etc., lay hold on Chiron and Demetrius.*]
Chi. Villains, forbear, we are the Empress' sons.
Pub. And therefore do we what we are commanded.
Stop close their mouths, let them not speak a word.
Is he sure bound? Look that you bind them fast.

Enter Titus Andronicus *with a knife and* Lavinia *with a basin.*

Tit. Come, come, Lavinia, look, thy foes are bound.
Sirs, stop their mouths, let them not speak to me,
But let them hear what fearful words I utter.
O villains, Chiron and Demetrius!
Here stands the spring whom you have stain'd with mud,
This goodly summer with your winter mix'd.
You kill'd her husband, and for that vild fault
Two of her brothers were condemn'd to death,
My hand cut off and made a merry jest;
Both her sweet hands, her tongue, and that more dear
Than hands or tongue, her spotless chastity,
Inhuman traitors, you constrain'd and forc'd.
What would you say if I should let you speak?
Villains, for shame you could not beg for grace.
Hark, wretches, how I mean to martyr you.
This one hand yet is left to cut your throats,
Whiles that Lavinia 'tween her stumps doth hold
The basin that receives your guilty blood.
You know your mother means to feast with me,
And calls herself Revenge, and thinks me mad.
Hark, villains, I will grind your bones to dust,
And with your blood and it I'll make a paste,
And of the paste a coffin I will rear,
And make two pasties of your shameful heads,
And bid that strumpet, your unhallowed dam,
Like to the earth swallow her own increase.
This is the feast that I have bid her to,
And this the banket she shall surfeit on,

163. therefore: for that very reason. **172. vild fault:** vile offense.
188. coffin: pie crust; perhaps with an allusion to the other sense.
191. increase: offspring.

For worse than Philomel you us'd my daughter,
And worse than Progne I will be reveng'd.
And now prepare your throats. Lavinia, come,
Receive the blood, and when that they are dead,
Let me go grind their bones to powder small,
And with this hateful liquor temper it,
And in that paste let their vile heads be bak'd.
Come, come, be every one officious
To make this banket, which I wish may prove
More stern and bloody than the Centaurs' feast.
He cuts their throats.
So now bring them in, for I'll play the cook,
And see them ready against their mother comes.
Exeunt [*bearing the dead bodies*].

[Scene III]

Enter Lucius, Marcus, *and the* Goths [*with* Aaron *prisoner, and his child in the arms of an* Attendant].

Luc. Uncle Marcus, since 'tis my father's mind
That I repair to Rome, I am content.
[*1.*] *Goth.* And ours with thine, befall what fortune will.
Luc. Good uncle, take you in this barbarous Moor,
This ravenous tiger, this accursed devil;
Let him receive no sust'nance; fetter him,
Till he be brought unto the Empress' face
For testimony of her foul proceedings.
And see the ambush of our friends be strong,
I fear the Emperor means no good to us.
Aar. Some devil whisper curses in my ear,
And prompt me that my tongue may utter forth
The venomous malice of my swelling heart!
Luc. Away, inhuman dog, unhallowed slave!
Sirs, help our uncle to convey him in.
[*Exeunt Goths with Aaron.*] *Sound trumpets* [*within*].
The trumpets show the Emperor is at hand.

Enter Emperor *and* Empress *with* [Aemilius,] Tribunes, [Senators,] *and others.*

Sat. What, hath the firmament moe suns than one?
Luc. What boots it thee to call thyself a sun?
Marc. Rome's emperor, and nephew, break the parle,
These quarrels must be quietly debated.
The feast is ready which the careful Titus
Hath ordain'd to an honorable end,
For peace, for love, for league, and good to Rome.
Please you, therefore, draw nigh and take your places.

195. Progne: sister of Philomel and wife of Tereus. In revenge for Tereus' rape she served him a meal consisting of his sons' flesh.
199. temper: mix. **201. officious:** busy, zealous.
203. Centaurs' feast: the wedding feast of Hippodamia and Pirithous, at which the Centaurs attempted to carry off the women, and thus precipitated a bloody battle with the Lapithae.
204. So. Frequently used as an expression of satisfaction.
205. against: by the time that.

V.iii. Location: Rome. Court of Titus' house.
3. ours with thine: our minds accord with yours, i.e. we also are satisfied. **17. moe:** more.
19. break the parle: stop the dispute; or, just possibly, begin the negotiations. **21. careful:** burdened by care.

Sat. Marcus, we will.
[*A table brought in. The company sit down.*]

Trumpets sounding, enter TITUS *like a cook, placing the dishes, and* LAVINIA *with a veil over her face,* [*young* LUCIUS, *and others*].

Tit. Welcome, my lord; welcome, dread queen;
Welcome, ye warlike Goths; welcome, Lucius;
And welcome, all. Although the cheer be poor,
'Twill fill your stomachs, please you eat of it.
Sat. Why art thou thus attir'd, Andronicus?
Tit. Because I would be sure to have all well,
To entertain your Highness and your empress.
Tam. We are beholding to you, good Andronicus.
Tit. And if your Highness knew my heart, you were.
My Lord the Emperor, resolve me this:
Was it well done of rash Virginius
To slay his daughter with his own right hand,
Because she was enforc'd, stain'd, and deflow'r'd?
Sat. It was, Andronicus.
Tit. Your reason, mighty lord?
Sat. Because the girl should not survive her shame,
And by her presence still renew his sorrows.
Tit. A reason mighty, strong, and effectual,
A pattern, president, and lively warrant
For me, most wretched, to perform the like.
Die, die, Lavinia, and thy shame with thee,
And with thy shame thy father's sorrow die!
[*He kills her.*]
Sat. What hast thou done, unnatural and unkind?
Tit. Kill'd her for whom my tears have made me blind.
I am as woeful as Virginius was,
And have a thousand times more cause than he
To do this outrage, and it now is done.
Sat. What, was she ravish'd? Tell who did the deed.
Tit. Will't please you eat? will't please your Highness feed?
Tam. Why hast thou slain thine only daughter thus?
Tit. Not I, 'twas Chiron and Demetrius:
They ravish'd her, and cut away her tongue,
And they, 'twas they, that did her all this wrong.
Sat. Go fetch them hither to us presently.
Tit. Why, there they are, both baked in this pie;
Whereof their mother daintily hath fed,
Eating the flesh that she herself hath bred.
'Tis true, 'tis true, witness my knive's sharp point.
He stabs the Empress.
Sat. Die, frantic wretch, for this accursed deed!
[*Kills Titus.*]
Luc. Can the son's eye behold his father bleed?
There's meed for meed, death for a deadly deed!

28. cheer: food, fare.
36. Virginius. This Roman centurion killed his daughter to *prevent* her rape. Either the dramatist has got the story wrong or he is failing to convey the idea that Titus has a better case for killing Lavinia than Virginius had for killing his daughter.
41. Because: so that. **44. president:** precedent. **lively:** striking.
48. unkind: unnatural. **59. presently:** at once.
63. knive's: knife's. **66. meed for meed:** measure for measure.

[*Kills Saturninus. A great tumult. Exeunt Lucius, Marcus, Aemilius, and others and enter above.*]
Marc. You sad-fac'd men, people and sons of Rome,
By uproars sever'd, as a flight of fowl
Scatter'd by winds and high tempestuous gusts,
O, let me teach you how to knit again
This scattered corn into one mutual sheaf,
These broken limbs again into one body.
[*Aemil.*] Let Rome herself be bane unto herself,
And she whom mighty kingdoms cur'sy to,
Like a forlorn and desperate castaway,
Do shameful execution on herself,
But if my frosty signs and chaps of age,
Grave witnesses of true experience,
Cannot induce you to attend my words.
[*To Lucius.*] Speak, Rome's dear friend, as erst our ancestor,
When with his solemn tongue he did discourse
To love-sick Dido's sad attending ear
The story of that baleful burning night,
When subtile Greeks surpris'd King Priam's Troy.
Tell us what Sinon hath bewitch'd our ears,
Or who hath brought the fatal engine in
That gives our Troy, our Rome, the civil wound.
My heart is not compact of flint nor steel,
Nor can I utter all our bitter grief,
But floods of tears will drown my oratory,
And break my utt'rance, even in the time
When it should move ye to attend me most,
And force you to commiseration.
Here's Rome's young captain, let him tell the tale,
While I stand by and weep to hear him speak.
Luc. Then, gracious auditory, be it known to you
That Chiron and the damn'd Demetrius
Were they that murd'red our Emperor's brother,
And they it were that ravished our sister.
For their fell faults our brothers were beheaded,
Our father's tears despis'd, and basely cozen'd
Of that true hand that fought Rome's quarrel out,
And sent her enemies unto the grave.
Lastly, myself unkindly banished,
The gates shut on me, and turn'd weeping out
To beg relief among Rome's enemies,
Who drown'd their enmity in my true tears,
And op'd their arms to embrace me as a friend.
I am the turned forth, be it known to you,
That have preserv'd her welfare in my blood,
And from her bosom took the enemy's point,
Sheathing the steel in my advent'rous body.
Alas, you know I am no vaunter, I;
My scars can witness, dumb although they are,
That my report is just and full of truth.

71. corn: grain. **mutual:** unified.
73. bane: poison, destroyer.
77. But if: if. **frosty signs:** white hair. **chaps:** wrinkles.
79. attend: listen to.
80. erst: once, formerly. **our ancestor:** i.e. Aeneas.
85. Sinon: the Greek who persuaded the Trojans to admit the wooden horse.
86. fatal engine: deadly contrivance (the wooden horse).
87. civil wound: damage inflicted in civil war.
88. compact: composed. **100. fell:** cruel.
101. cozen'd: cheated.

But soft, methinks I do digress too much,
Citing my worthless praise. O, pardon me,
For when no friends are by, men praise themselves.
Marc. Now is my turn to speak. Behold the child:
[*Pointing to Aaron's child in the arms of an Attendant.*]
Of this was Tamora delivered,
The issue of an irreligious Moor,
Chief architect and plotter of these woes.
The villain is alive in Titus' house,
And as he is to witness, this is true.
Now judge what [cause] had Titus to revenge
These wrongs unspeakable, past patience,
Or more than any living man could bear.
Now have you heard the truth, what say you, Romans?
Have we done aught amiss, show us wherein,
And, from the place where you behold us pleading,
The poor remainder of Andronici
Will hand in hand all headlong hurl ourselves,
And on the ragged stones beat forth our souls,
And make a mutual closure of our house.
Speak, Romans, speak, and if you say we shall,
Lo hand in hand Lucius and I will fall.
Aemil. Come, come, thou reverent man of Rome,
And bring our Emperor gently in thy hand,
Lucius our Emperor, for well I know
The common voice do cry it shall be so.
[*All.*] Lucius, all hail, Rome's royal Emperor!
Marc. [*To Attendants.*] Go, go into old Titus' sorrowful house,
And hither hale that misbelieving Moor
To be [adjudg'd] some direful slaught'ring death,
As punishment for his most wicked life.
[*Exeunt Attendants. Lucius, Marcus, Aemilius, and the others descend.*]
[*All.*] Lucius, all hail, Rome's gracious governor!
Luc. Thanks, gentle Romans, may I govern so,
To heal Rome's harms, and wipe away her woe!
But, gentle people, give me aim a while,
For nature puts me to a heavy task.
Stand all aloof, but, uncle, draw you near
To shed obsequious tears upon this trunk.
O, take this warm kiss on thy pale cold lips,
[*Kisses Titus.*]
These sorrowful drops upon thy blood[-stain'd] face,
The last true duties of thy noble son!
Marc. Tear for tear, and loving kiss for kiss,
Thy brother Marcus tenders on thy lips.
O, were the sum of these that I should pay
Countless and infinite, yet would I pay them!
Luc. Come hither, boy, come, come, and learn of us
To melt in showers; thy grandsire lov'd thee well.
Many a time he danc'd thee on his knee,
Sung thee asleep, his loving breast thy pillow;
Many a story hath he told to thee,
And bid thee bear his pretty tales in mind,
And talk of them when he was dead and gone.
Marc. How many thousand times hath these poor lips,
When they were living, warm'd themselves on thine!
O now, sweet boy, give them their latest kiss!
Bid him farewell, commit him to the grave,
Do them that kindness, and take leave of them.
Boy. O grandsire, grandsire, ev'n with all my heart
Would I were dead, so you did live again!
O Lord, I cannot speak to him for weeping,
My tears will choke me if I ope my mouth.

[*Enter* ATTENDANTS *with* AARON.]

[*Aemil.*] You sad Andronici, have done with woes.
Give sentence on this execrable wretch
That hath been breeder of these dire events.
Luc. Set him breast-deep in earth and famish him,
There let him stand and rave and cry for food.
If any one relieves or pities him,
For the offense he dies. This is our doom.
Some stay to see him fast'ned in the earth.
Aar. Ah, why should wrath be mute and fury dumb?
I am no baby, I, that with base prayers
I should repent the evils I have done.
Ten thousand worse than ever yet I did
Would I perform if I might have my will.
If one good deed in all my life I did,
I do repent it from my very soul.
Luc. Some loving friends convey the Emperor hence,
And give him burial in his fathers' grave.
My father and Lavinia shall forthwith
Be closed in our household's monument.
As for that ravenous tiger Tamora,
No funeral rite, nor man in mourning weed,
No mournful bell shall ring her burial,
But throw her forth to beasts and birds to prey:
Her life was beastly and devoid of pity,
And being dead, let birds on her take pity.
Exeunt.

126. patience: endurance. **133. ragged:** rugged.
134. mutual closure: common end.
149. give me aim: encourage me. **150. puts me to:** sets me.
152. obsequious: such as are appropriate to obsequies (not the modern derogatory sense).
182. doom: judgment. **198. prey:** prey upon.
200. See the Textual Notes for four concluding non-Shakespearean lines first added in Q2.

NOTE ON THE TEXT

Titus Andronicus was first published in quarto in 1594 (Q1). Two other quarto editions, each printed from the preceding quarto, appeared in 1600 (Q2) and 1611 (Q3), and the play was next printed in the First Folio (1623).

There is general agreement that Q1, here used as the basic text except for III.ii (see below), was printed from Shakespeare's "foul papers." All the evidence—the style of the stage directions, some confusions in the text, and a few slight inconsistencies in speech-prefixes—supports the use of author's manuscript, and there is nothing in the Q1 text to suggest any direct connection with the stage.

Q2 presents a sobering situation for those concerned with the authenticity of Shakespeare's text. Until 1904, when the single surviving copy of Q1, now in the Folger Library, was discovered in Sweden, the text of the play had depended essentially on Q2. After the recovery of Q1, however, it was quickly discovered that substantial differences exist between the two texts in the last scene of Act V, and bibliographical investigation has since shown conclusively that these differences were created not by correction from an authoritative source but by accident and consequent unauthorized fudging (Bolton). It is now clear that V.iii in Q2 was printed from a copy of Q1 in which the last three leaves of sig. K had been damaged at the foot in such a way as to affect the text (see Textual Notes, V.iii.25 s.d., 26, 94–7, 132, 133, 164–9, 200). There was also, as Maxwell has pointed out, some slight damage at the top of sig. I4 (see Textual Notes, V.ii.71, 106). Instead of obtaining another copy of Q1, somebody (almost certainly in the printing house) "restored" the missing words or lines as best he could by guesswork. On the last page (sig. K4^v) he outdid himself. Misled by the fact that the text as he found it did not fill out the page and by the chance that the Q1 compositor had placed the final *Exeunt* (now missing because of the damage to the leaf) two lines below the last line of the play, he invented four new and feeble lines relating to Aaron and the disposing of the state (here relegated to the Textual Notes).

The text of F1 was printed from a copy of Q3, which may itself have served as a prompt-book (Greg) or been sporadically collated with a manuscript prompt-book (Waith, Wells/Taylor). It contains a number of additional stage directions, particularly indications of stage sounds, but with one notable exception it shows no certain evidence of correction against an independent manuscript authority. The exception is the second scene of Act III, which appears in F1 for the first time and must therefore have had a manuscript source. The F1 text of this scene, set up very inaccurately by Compositor E, who was usually not allowed to compose from manuscript copy, necessarily serves as copy-text here. F1 also adds a probably authentic line (I.i.398); otherwise, with the possible exception of one reading (see Textual Notes, V.ii.18), it has no more textual authority than Q2 or Q3.

The unresolved (and probably unresolvable) problems surrounding the date of composition and authorship are discussed in the Introduction, but they deserve brief comment here. Despite the best efforts of critics who argue that *Titus Andronicus* is wholly Shakespeare's (Sampley, Price, Waith, Bate), the ghost of George Peele haunts the play, particularly Act I, and stoutly refuses to be exorcised (Wilson, Maxwell, Wells/Taylor), suggesting either Shakespeare's thorough reworking, except for Act I (1593–4), of an earlier version of the play (c. 1589) by Peele and perhaps others. Signs of what are probably second thoughts or revisions have been detected: (a) the addition of the sacrifice of Alarbus (I.i.96–149), shown to be an addition by the presence of three-and-a-half lines following "field." in I.i.35 in Q1, but omitted in Q2–3 and F1 (see Textual Notes), which declare Alarbus to be already sacrificed, thus contradicting his later off-stage death; (b) the addition (though less certain) of the slaying (by Titus) and burial of Mutius (I.i.287–98, 341–90) [some critics see Shakespeare's informing hand in these two additions (Waith, Tobin)]; (c) duplication of speeches (IV.iii.95–101, and 102–106); Wilson, Wells/Taylor and Bate take 102–106 to be a reworking of 95–101; Maxwell takes 98–101 as a first thought; Waith, however, omits 106 (". . .ink.")–114 as a first thought. As Dover Wilson points out in each of the above cases, the lines involved can be omitted without breaking the continuity of the dialogue.

For further information, see E. K. Chambers, "The First Illustration to 'Shakespeare,'" *The Library*, V (1925), 326–30 [discusses a manuscript fragment, dated ?1595, which purports to show a scene from the play]; J. S. G. Bolton, "The Authentic Text of *Titus Andronicus*," *PMLA*, XLIV (1929), 765–88; J. Q. Adams, ed., facsimile of First Quarto of *Titus Andronicus* (New York, 1936); A. M. Sampley, "Plot Structure in Peele's Plays and Poems as a Test of Authorship," *PMLA*, LI (1936), 689–701; H. T. Price, "The Authorship of *Titus Andronicus*," *JEGP*, XLII (1943), 55–81; J. D. Wilson, ed., New Shakespeare *Titus Andronicus* (Cambridge, 1948); J. C. Maxwell, ed., New Arden *Titus Andronicus* (London, 1953; rev. ed., 1963); W. W. Greg, *The Shakespeare First Folio* (Oxford, 1955); Charlton Hinman, *The Printing and Proof-Reading of the First Folio of Shakespeare*, 2 vols. (Oxford, 1963); J. K. Walton, *The Quarto Copy for the First Folio of Shakespeare* (Dublin, 1971); MacD. P. Jackson, *Studies in Attribution: Middleton and Shakespeare* (Salzburg, 1979); J. J. M. Tobin, "Nomenclature and the Dating of *Titus Andronicus*," *N & Q*, CCXXIX (1984), 186–7; E. M. Waith, ed., New Oxford *Titus Andronicus* (Oxford, 1984); Stanley Wells, Gary Taylor, et al., *William Shakespeare: A Shakespeare Companion* (Oxford, 1987); Jonathan Bate, ed., Arden (3rd ser.) *Titus Andronicus* (London, 1995).

TEXTUAL NOTES

Title: The . . . Andronicus] The Most Lamentable Romaine Tragedie of Titus Andronicus: As it was Plaide by the Right Honourable the Earle of Darbie, Earle of Pembrooke, and Earle of Sussex their Seruants. *Q1 (title-page);* The Lamentable Tragedy of Titus Andronicus. *F1*

Dramatis personae: *subs. as first given by Rowe*

Act-scene division: *none in Q1–3; F1 marks acts only, except I.i; other scene divisions by Rowe and later editors (see first note to each scene); present act-scene arrangement as a whole first established by Dyce*

I.i

I.i] *F1*

Location: *Theobald, Capell*

o.s.d. **among . . . Andronicus]** *ed.*

o.s.d. **below]** *Capell (subs.)*

o.s.d. **at the other]** *F1*

o.s.d. **Drums and Trumpets]** Drum and Trumpets *Q2–3;* Drum & Colours *F1*

14 **seat, . . . consecrate,]** *Rowe;* seate to vertue, consecrate *Q1–3;* Seate to Vertue: consecrate *F1*

18 s.p., s.d. **Marc. Holding the crown.]** *Bolton conj. (in Maxwell);* Marcus Andronicus with the Crowne. *Q1–3;* Enter Marcus Andronicus aloft with the Crowne. *F1 (the F1 s.d. arises from the centered s.p. for Marcus in Q1–3)*

23–4 **Pius . . . Rome.]** *Q2–3, F1 (subs.);* Pius: . . . Rome, *Q1*

35] *Following* field, *Q1 gives three-and-a-half lines which Q2–3, F1 deleted because of*

their inconsistency with the Alarbus episode (ll. 96–149): and at this day, / To the Monument of that *Andronicy* / Done sacrifice of expiation, / And slaine the Noblest prisoner of the *Gothes*.
41 **Capitol]** *Q3, F1;* Capitall *Q1–2*
55 **s.d. Exeunt . . . Bassianus.]** *Capell (subs.);* Exit Soldiers. *Q1–3, F1*
56 **right,]** *Q3, F1;* right. *Q1–2*
59 **s.d. Exeunt . . . Saturninus.]** *Capell (subs.)*
63 **s.d. Flourish.]** *F1*
64 **s.p. Cap.]** *F1*
69 **s.d. Martius and Mutius . . . Lucius and Quintus]** *Rowe*
69 **s.d. three sons, Alarbus]** *Rowe (subs.);* two sonnes *Q1–3, F1*
69 **s.d. Aaron]** *F1;* Aron *Q1–3 (throughout)*
74 **boughs]** *F4;* bowes *Q1–3, F1*
76 **Rome.]** *Rowe;* Rome, *Q1–3, F1*
78 **rites]** *Q3, F1;* rights *Q1–2*
85 **sword.]** *F1 (subs.);* sword, *Q1–3*
89 **bretheren]** *Q3, F1;* brethren *Q1–2*
98 **manes]** *F3;* manus *Q1–3, F1*
129 **s.d. Exeunt]** *Rowe;* Exit *Q1–3, F1*
141 **s.d. with . . . bloody]** *Capell*
143 **rites]** *F2;* rights *Q1–3, F1*
144 **entrails]** *Rowe (subs.);* intrals *Q1–3, F1*
151 **Rome's]** *Q2–3, F1;* Roomes *Q1 (occasionally throughout; a spelling reflecting the pronunciation)*
157 **s.p. Lav.]** *Q3, F1*
168 **s.d. Marcus . . . above.]** *ed.*
218 **suffrages:]** *Hanmer (subs.);* suffrages, *Q1–3, F1*
223 **suit]** *Rowe;* sute *Q1–3;* sure *F1*
226 **Titan's]** *Q2–3, F1;* Tytus *Q1*
228 **advice]** *Rowe;* aduise *Q1–3, F1*
230 **s.p. Marc.]** *Rowe;* Marcus An. *Q1–3, F1*
233 **s.d. A . . . down.]** *F1*
240 **emperess]** *F4;* Empresse *Q1–3, F1*
242 **Pantheon]** *F2* (Panthaeon); Pathan *Q1–3, F1*
258 **s.d. To Tamora.]** *Johnson*
261 **s.d. Aside.]** *Capell*
262 **anew]** *Rowe* (a-new); a new *Q1–3, F1*
264 **chance]** *Q2–3, F1;* change *Q1*
266 **way.]** *Q2–3, F1;* waie *Q1*
270 **this?]** *F1;* this. *Q1–3*
275 **s.d. Flourish.]** *Capell*
275 **s.d. Saturninus . . . show.]** *Rowe (subs.)*
276 **s.d. Seizing Lavinia.]** *Rowe*
278 **s.p. Bas.]** Bascianus. *Q1 (frequently throughout)*
280 **cuique]** *F2;* cuiqum *Q1–2;* cuiquam *Q3, F1*
286 **s.d. Exeunt . . . Lavinia.]** *Malone (subs., after Rowe)*
288 **s.d. Exeunt . . . Martius.]** *Malone (after Capell)*
291 **s.d. Titus kills him.]** *Q3, F1* (He)
291 **s.d. During . . . Aaron.]** *Globe*
291 **s.d. Enter Lucius.]** *Capell*
295 **s.d. Enter . . . Moor.]** *placed as in Kittredge; after l. 298, Q1–3, F1*
298 **s.d. Exit.]** *Capell*
299 **s.p. Sat.]** *Rowe;* Emperour. *Q1–3, F1*
304 **Was none in]** Was there none els in *F2*
316 **Phoebe]** *F2;* Thebe *Q1–3, F1*
317 **gallant'st]** *Q2–3, F1;* gallanst *Q1*
327 **climb]** *F2;* clime *Q1–3, F1 (usual spelling)*
333 **queen, Pantheon. Lords,]** *Pope (subs.;* Pantheon *F4);* Queene: Panthean Lords *Q1–2;* Queene, Panthean Lords, *Q3, F1*
337 **s.d. except Titus]** *Theobald (subs.)*
341 **done!]** *Q3, F1;* done *Q1–2*
348 **Mutius]** *Q3, F1;* Mucius *Q1–2*
357 **bretheren]** *Q3, F1;* brethren *Q1–2*
358 **s.p. Mart.]** *Bolton conj. (in Maxwell);* Titus two sonnes speakes. *Q1–3, F1*
360 **s.p. Mart.]** *Capell;* Titus sonne speakes. *Q1–3, F1*
362 **thee]** *Q3, F1* (thee,); thee. *Q1–2*
364 **strook]** *Capell;* stroke *Q1–3, F1*
368 **s.p. Quin.]** *Capell;* 3. Sonne. *Q1–3;* 1. Sonne. *F1*
369, 371 **s.pp. Mart.]** *Capell;* 2. Sonne. *Q1–3, F1*
379 **advice]** *F4;* aduise *Q1–3, F1*
390 **s.d. All . . . aside.]** *Kittredge;* Exit all but Marcus and Titus. *Q1–3;* Exit. *F1*
391 **dreary]** *Pope;* dririe *Q1–3;* sudden *F1*
395 **device]** *Rowe;* deuise *Q1–3, F1*
398 **Yes . . . remunerate.]** *F1*
398 **s.d. Flourish.]** *F1*
405 **seize]** *F2* (seise); ceaze *Q1–3;* cease *F1*
411 **done,]** *F3;* done *Q1–3, F1*
411 **may,]** *Q3, F1;* may. *Q1–2*
442 **s.d. Aside to Saturnine.]** *Rowe (subs.)*
448 **sin,]** *Rowe;* sinne. *Q1–3, F1*
467 **reconcil'd]** *Q3, F1;* reconciled *Q1–2*
472 **advice]** *Rowe;* aduise *Q1–3, F1*
473 **s.d. Marcus . . . kneel.]** *Witherspoon (after Collier)*
474 **s.p. Luc.]** *Rowe; om. Q1–2:* All. *Q3;* Son. *F1*
481 **denied.]** *Theobald (subs.);* denied, *Q1–3, F1*
485 **s.d. Marcus . . . rise.]** *Chambers (subs.)*
495 **s.d. Sound . . . Moor]** *om. F1*

II.i

II.i] *Rowe;* Actus Secunda. *F1 (as the Q1–3 s.d. at the end of I.i makes clear, there is no act or scene break here, Aaron remaining on stage)*
Location: *ed. (after Wilson)*
1] *Preceding this line F1 reads:* Flourish. Enter Aaron alone.
8 **highest-peering]** *hyphen, Theobald*
22 **Semiramis]** *F3;* Semerimis *Q1–3, F1*
37 **s.p. Aar.]** *F1;* Moore. *Q1–3 (throughout scene, except at ll. 81, 103)*
37 **s.d. Aside.]** *Dyce*
39 **dancing-rapier]** *hyphen, Steevens*
45 **s.d. Coming forward.]** *Dyce (subs., after Capell)*
75 **Why,]** *Theobald;* Why *Q1–3, F1*
75 **not, in Rome]** *Theobald;* not in Rome, *Q1–3, F1*
79 **device]** *Theobald;* deuise *Q1–3, F1*
90 **s.d. Aside.]** *Theobald*
93 **What,]** *Pope;* What *Q1–3, F1*
93 **strook]** *Q2;* stroke *Q1, F1;* strucke *Q3, F1*
110 **than]** *Rowe;* this *Q1–3, F1*
123 **advice]** *F4;* aduise *Q1–3, F1*

II.ii

II.ii] *Rowe*
Location: *ed. (after Pelican)*
o.s.d. and Marcus] *F1*
1 **morn]** *Q3, F1;* Moone *Q1–2*
11 **Many]** *Capell;* Titus. Many *Q1–3, F1 (repeated s.p.)*
15 **new-married]** *hyphen, Pope*
19 **s.d. To Tamora.]** *Johnson*

II.iii

II.iii] *Capell*
Location: *Pelican (after Theobald)*
o.s.d. with . . . gold] *Capell*
1, 30, 52 **s.pp. Aar.]** *F1;* Moore. *Q1–3*
8 **s.d. Hides the gold.]** *Malone*
11 **doth]** *Q2–3, F1;* dorh *Q1*
13 **snake]** *Q3, F1;* snakes *Q1–2*
32 **deadly-standing]** *hyphen, Theobald*
47 **fatal-plotted]** *hyphen, Theobald*
48 **more,]** *F1;* more *Q1–3*
50 **lives']** *Warburton;* liues *Q1–3, F1*
54 **s.d. Exit.]** *Rowe*
55, 66 **Emperess]** *Rowe;* Empresse *Q1–3, F1*
69 **thy]** *om. Q2–3, F1*
69 **experiments]** *Q2–3, F1;* experimens *Q1*
72 **swart]** *Capell;* swartie *Q1–2;* swarty *Q3;* swarth *F1 (the Q1–3 form, though acceptable in itself, is metrically very awkward)*
72 **Cimmerian]** *Theobald;* Cymerion *Q1–3, F1*
74 **abominable]** *F3;* abhominable *Q1–3, F1*
86 **s.p. Lav.]** *Q2–3, F1;* Lauinia *Q1 (not clearly intended as s.p.)*
88 **Why,]** *Alexander;* Why *Q1–3, F1*
106 **But]** *Q2–3, F1;* Bu *Q1*
107 **yew]** *F1;* Ewghe *Q1;* Ewgh *Q2;* Ewe *Q3*
110 **Lascivious]** *Q3, F1;* Lauicious *Q1–2*
117 **me, . . . home]** *F1;* me . . . home, *Q1;* me . . . home *Q2–3*
117 **struck]** *Q1–2;* strook *Q3, F1*
117 **s.d. Also . . . dies.]** *Dyce (after Theobald)*
118 **Ay,]** *Hanmer;* I *Q1–3, F1*
118 **Semiramis]** *F2;* Semeranis *Q1;* Semeramis *Q2–3, F1*
126 **hope]** *Malone;* hope, *Q1–3, F1;* hope she *F2*
126 **mightiness]** *Q2–3, F1;* mightenes *Q1*
128 **eunuch]** *F1;* Euenuke *Q1–3*
131 **we]** ye *F2*
132 **outlive,]** *Theobald;* out liue *Q1;* out-liue *Q2–3, F1*
135 **nice-preserved]** *hyphen, F1*
137 **speak,]** *Q2–3, F1;* speake *Q1*
139 **madam,]** *Q2–3, F1;* Maddame *Q1*
140 **them]** *Q2–3;* them: *Q1;* them, *F1*
147 **s.d. To Chiron.]** *Warburton*
150 **heard]** *Q2–3, F1;* hard *Q1*
151 **mov'd]** *F1;* moued *Q1–3*
151 **pity, did endure]** *Q3, F1;* pittie did indure, *Q1–2*
153 **Some]** *Q2–3, F1;* So me *Q1*
158 **thee! For]** *Theobald* (thee:); thee for *Q1–3, F1*
160 **years]** eares *Q3, F1*
164 **brother]** *Q2–3, F1;* brothet *Q1*
172 **then? Fond]** *Q3, F1;* then fond *Q1–2*
180 **satisfice]** *Maxwell;* satisfiee *or, possibly,* satisfice *Q1;* satisfie *Q2–3, F1*
186 **s.d. Demetrius . . . Lavinia.]** *Capell (after Pope);* Exeunt. *F2*
189 **Andronici]** *F1;* Adronicie *Q1–3*
191 **s.d. Exit.]** *F1*
192 **s.p. Aar.]** *F1*
197 **s.d. Falls . . . pit.]** *Rowe*
198 **What,]** *F4;* What *Q1–3, F1*
198 **fallen? What]** *Q3, F1;* fallen what *Q1;* fallen, what *Q2*
199 **rude-growing]** *hyphen, Pope*
200 **new-shed blood]** *Q3* (newshed); new shed blood *Q1–2;* new-shed-blood *F1*
206 **s.d. Aside.]** *Johnson*
208 **s.d. Exit.]** *placed as in Q2–3, F1; after l. 207, Q1;* Exit Aaron. *F1*
210 **unhallow'd]** *F1;* vnhollow *Q1–3*
214 **true-divining]** *hyphen, Theobald*
222 **beray'd in blood]** *Wilson;* bereaud in blood *Q1 (an early MS correction in Q1 reads:* heere reav'd of lyfe); embrewed heere *Q2–3, F1*
224 **blood-drinking]** *hyphen, F1*
230 **entrails]** *Theobald;* intrals *Q1;* intrailes *Q2–3, F1*
231 **Pyramus]** *Q2–3, F1;* Priamus *Q1*
236 **Cocytus']** *F2 (subs.);* Ocitus *Q1–3, F1*
243 **more;]** *Theobald;* more, *Q1–3, F1*
245 **s.d. Falls in.]** *Pope;* Boths fall in. *F1*
246 **me!]** *Wilson (after Theobald);* me, *Q1–3, F1*
258 **s.d. with Attendants]** *Theobald*
260 **s.p. Sat.]** *F2;* King. *Q1–3, F1 (throughout scene)*
269 **huntsman— . . . mean—]** *Kittredge;* huntsman, . . . meane, *Q1, F1;* huntsman . . . meane *Q2–3*
271 **meaning.]** *Pope (subs.);* meaning *Q1;* meaning, *Q2–3, F1*
276 **O]** *Theobald;* King. Oh *Q1–3, F1 (repeated s.p.)*
281 **s.d. To Titus.]** *Rowe*
285 **never-heard-of]** *Pope;* neuer hard of *Q1;* neuer heard of *Q2;* neuer heard-of *Q3, F1*
291 **fault]** *Theobald;* faults *Q1–3, F1*
296 **fathers']** *Delius;* Fathers *Q1–3, F1*
306 **s.d. Exeunt.]** *F1*

II.iv

II.iv] *Dyce*
Location: *ed. (after Rowe)*
10 **s.p. Dem.]** *Q2–3, F1;* Dmet. *Q1*
10 **s.d. Demetrius and Chiron]** *Theobald*
10 **s.d. Wind horns.]** *F1*
10 **s.d. hunting]** hunting, to Lauinia *F1*
27 **him]** *Rowe;* them *Q1–3, F1*
30 **three]** *Hanmer;* their *Q1–3, F1*
39, 43 **sew'd]** *Pope;* sowed *Q1–3, F1*

III.i

III.i] *Rowe;* Actus Tertius. *F1*

Location: Theobald
o.s.d. and Tribunes] Capell (subs.)
11 s.d. etc.] Capell
11 s.d. and . . . prisoners] Capell
17 urns] Hanmer; ruines Q1–3, F1
21 on thy] Q2–3, F1; out hy Q1
34 if] or if Q2–3; oh F1
47 s.d. Rises.] Dyce (after Capell, who places it following man: l. 33)
65 Faint-hearted boy] Q3, F1; Faint-harted-boy Q1–2
66 Lavinia] Q2–3, F1; Lauinea Q1
67 handless] Q2–3, F1; handles Q1
69 bright-burning] hyphen, F3
89 deer] F3; Deare Q1–3, F1
112 honey-dew] hyphen, Knight
134 device] Theobald; deuise Q1–3, F1
146 napkin] Q2–3, F1; napking Q1 (possibly represents Shakespeare's pronunciation)
146 his] F4; her Q1–3, F1
150 s.p. Aar.] Rowe; Moore. Q1–3, F1 (throughout scene)
169 Writing] F1; wrighting Q1–3
169 enemy's] Capell conj.; enemies Q1–3, F1
185 s.d. Lucius and Marcus] Theobald
188, 202 s.dd. Aside.] Rowe
209 s.d. To Lavinia.] Johnson
225 blow] F2; flow Q1–3, F1
229 overflow'd] F1; ouerflowed Q1–3
230 why] Dyce; why, Q1–3, F1
240 s.d. Exit.] Q2–3, F1
241 Sicily] F3; Cycilie Q1–3, F1
249 s.d. Lavinia kisses Titus.] Johnson
275 do.] F3 (subs.); doe, Q1–3, F1
276 about,] Q3, F1; about. Q1–2
281 employ'd;] Munro (subs., after Cambridge conj.); imployde in these Armes, Q1–3; employd in these things: F1 (a difficult passage; the F1 reading is an obvious and wild guess; if, as has been suggested by Cambridge, Armes was intended as someone's softened alternative for teeth in the next line, and if in these was a compositor's attempt to attach Armes, written in above teeth, to l. 281, then clearly the whole phrase should be omitted; it is also possible that in these Armes was some kind of alternative for in this hand in l. 280; see a different explanation in Munro)
287 s.d. Manet Lucius.] F1
293 tofore] Pope; to fore Q1–3, F1

III.ii

III.ii] Capell
Scene om. Q1–3; the copy-text is F1
Location: Theobald (subs.)
o.s.d. A banket set out.] Capell (subs.); A Bnaket, F1
1 s.p. Tit.] Rowe; An. F1 (throughout scene)
8 breast,] F4; breast. F1
12 s.d. To Lavinia.] Johnson
13 with outrageous] F2; without ragious F1
20 sea-salt] hyphen, F2
32 hands,] F4; hands: F1
38 Brew'd] F2; Breu'd F1
38 sorrow,] F4 (sorrows,); sorrow: F1
38 cheeks.] F3; cheekes, F1
39 complainant] Collier MS; complaynet F1 (c); complayne F1(u); complaint, O F2
52 dost] F3; doest F1
52 thy] F2
53 fly] F2; Flys F1
54 thee] F3; the F1
55 are] F2
57 brother] F2; broher F1
60 How] F2; How: F1
72 myself] F2; my selfes F1
74 Tamora] F2; Tamira F1

IV.i

IV.i] Rowe; Actus Quartus. F1
Location: Globe
1 s.p. Boy.] F1; Puer. Q1–3 (throughout scene)
10 Marc.] S. Walker conj.; Q1–3, F1 continue the line to Titus, reading meane, in l. 9; l. 9 is the last line on sig. $F3^v$ of Q1 and the catchword is See
11 Somewhither] Capell; Some whither Q1; Some whether Q2–3, F1
12 Ah] Q3, F1; A Q1–2
19 griefs] Q3, F1; greeues Q1–2
21 sorrow.] Pope (subs.); sorrow, Q1–3, F1
26 perhaps.] Rowe (subs.); perhaps, Q1–3, F1
29 s.d. Lavinia . . . fall.] Malone (subs., after Capell)
36] Following this line F1 inserts, as a separate line: What booke? (note that Titus speaks these same words as part of l. 41)
45 Soft,] Q2–3, F1; Soft Q1
52 Philomela] Q2–3, F1; Phlomela Q1
53 Forc'd] Q2–3, F1; Frocd Q1
59 den,] Q2–3, F1; den. Q1
63 slunk] F1; slonke Q1–3
78 s.p. Tit.] Maxwell; line continued to Marcus, Q1–2; Q3, F1 assign ll. 77–8 to Titus
78 Demetrius] Q2–3, F1; Dmetrius Q1
88 hope] Q2–3, F1; hop or l op Q1 (the type has slipped, leaving a noticeable space after Hectors)
89 me,] Q3, F1; me Q1–2
89 fere] Dyce; feere, Q1–3, F1
91 sware] F3; sweare Q1–3, F1
97 ye] you Q2–3, F1
99 back,] F1; backe. Q1–3
122 s.d. Titus . . . Boy.] Capell
123 good man] Q2–3, F1; goodman Q1

IV.ii

IV.ii] Pope
Location: Theobald
4, 8 s.pp. Boy.] F1; Puer. Q1–3
6, 8, 17 s.dd. Aside.] Capell (as Maxwell notes, the aside in l. 17 seems to be indicated in Q1 by a colon and double spacing after both and a capital L in Like)
8 Boy. That . . . news,] om. F1 (continuing the speech to Demetrius)
15 that,] Pope
17 s.d. with Attendant] Capell (subs.)
20 s.d. Reads.] Capell
24 s.p. Aar.] Q2; Moore. Q1, Q3, F1
25, 48 s.dd. Aside.] Johnson
29 afoot] Rowe (subs.); a foote Q1–3, F1
32 was't] F1 (wa's t); wast Q1–3
48 s.d. within] Capell; F1 s.d. reads: Flourish.
51 Good] Q3, F1; God Q1–2
68 fair-fac'd] Wilson (following O.E.D.); fairefast Q1–2; fairest Q3, F1
71 'Zounds] Out F1
87 s.d. Takes . . . draws.] Capell (subs.)
91 scimitar's] Rowe (subs.); Semitars Q1–3, F1
92 first-born] F3; first borne Q1–3, F1
95 Alcides] Q2–3, F1; Alciades Q1
96 seize] F3; ceaze Q1–3, F1
98 white-lim'd] F3; whitelimde Q1; white-limbde Q2–3; white-limb'd F1
130 advice] F4; aduise Q1–3, F1
134 s.d. They sit.] Rowe (subs.)
143 Emperess] Capell; Empresse Q1–3, F1
161 Emperor] Q2–3, F1; Lmperour Q1
162 s.d. Pointing . . . Nurse.] Johnson
171 s.d. Demetrius . . . body.] Capell (subs.)
175 thick-lipp'd slave] Rowe; thicke-lipt-slaue Q1–3, F1

IV.iii

IV.iii] Capell
Location: Capell (after Theobald)
o.s.d. Publius, Sempronius, Caius] Globe
1 come; kinsmen] Theobald; come, kinsemen Q1–2; come, kinsmen Q3, F1
4 Astraea] F2; Astreá Q1; Astreà Q2; Astrea Q3, F1
32 But . . . .] arranged as in Maxwell; at least one line seems to have dropped out here (in Q1 the catchword on sig. $G4^v$ is But, the first line on sig. H1 beginning Ioine)
40 Marry,] Theobald; Marrie Q1–3, F1
45 Acheron] F2; Acaron Q1–3, F1
47 big-bon'd men] Rowe; big-boand-men Q1; big-bond-men Q2–3; big-bon'd-men F1
53 Come,] Theobald; Come Q1–3, F1
54 Apollinem] Rowe; Apollonem Q1–3; Appollonem F1
57 Saturn,] Capell; Saturnine, to Q1–3, F1
64 s.d. They shoot.] Rowe
65 boy,] Theobald; boy Q1–3, F1
66 aim'd] Hudson; aime Q1–3, F1
67, 80, 84 Jupiter] Q2–3, F1 (F1 also in l. 85); Iubiter Q1
71 lord.] Theobald (subs.); Lord, Q1–3, F1
78 News] Rowe (after Q2–3, F1, which repeat the s.p. Titus.); Clowne, Newes Q1 (Q1 assigns ll. 79–80 to Titus)
81 gibbet-maker] Gibbetmaker Q1; Iiebbet-maker Q2 (probably an attempt to make the pun obvious); Iibbetmaker Q3, F1
85–6 Alas . . . life.] as prose, Capell; as verse, Q1–3, F1
89 Why,] Q2–3, F1; Why Q1
90 From . . . there.] as prose, Pope; as verse, Q1–3, F1
117 then] ed.; thou Q1–3, F1
118 to] om. Q3, F1

IV.iv

IV.iv] Capell
Location: Capell (after Theobald)
o.s.d. Lords, and others] Malone
5 as know] Globe
12 frenzy] Q2–3, F1; frencie Q1
30 Th' effects] Q2–3, F1; The'ffects Q1
34 s.d. Aside.] F1 (after l. 35); placed as in Capell
35 High-witted] hyphen, Pope
35 gloze] Capell; glose Q1–3, F1
36 touch'd] F1; touched Q1–3
36–7 quick; . . . out,] Neilson; quicke, . . . out: Q1–3, F1
37 life-blood] hyphen, F4
43 s.d. Saturninus] Johnson (subs.)
47 hang'd] F1; hanged Q1–3
48 by'] Maxwell; be Q1–3; ber F1
49 s.d. guarded] Capell
52 device] F4; deuise Q1–3, F1
60 s.d. Nuntius] Q2–3, F1; Nutius Q1
60 s.d. Aemilius] F4; Emillius Q1–3, F1 (throughout)
61 What] Capell; Satur. What Q1–3, F1 (repeated s.p.)
69 s.p. Sat.] F2; King. Q1–3, F1 (throughout rest of scene)
81 Tam. King, be] Q2–3, F1 (subs.); Tamora. King Be Q1
88 thou,] Alexander; thou Q1–3, F1
93 feed] Q3; seede Q1–2; foede F1
98 years] eares F1
100 s.d. To Aemilius.] Rowe
103 Even . . . Andronicus] om. Q3, F1
105 on] F4; in Q1–3, F1
112 devices] F3; deuises Q1–3, F1
113 successantly] Q2–3, F1; sucessantly Q1

V.i

V.i] Rowe; Actus Quintus. F1
Location: Capell (after Theobald)
o.s.d. Flourish.] F1 (possibly this should precede the Exeunt. at end of IV.iv)
9, 121, 162, s.pp. 1. Goth.] Capell; Goth. Q1–3, F1
13 us,] Q3, F1; vs Q1–2
16 adveng'd] auengd Q3, F1
17 s.p. Other Goths.] Wilson (after F2 Omn.)
20 s.p. 2. Goth.] Capell; Goth. Q1–3, F1
23 building, suddenly] Q3, F1; building suddainely, Q1–2
37 drawn] Q2–3, F1; drawen Q1
43 here's] Q2–3, F1; her's Q1
46 deaf?] F1; deafe, Q1–3
51 sprawl] Pope; sprall Q1–3, F1
53 Get . . . ladder.] continued to Lucius, Theobald; assigned to Aaron, Q1–3, F1
53 s.d. A . . . ascend.] Capell (subs.)
54 Emperess] F3; Empresse Q1–3, F1
58 more] Q3; more, Q1–2; more: F1
58 "Vengeance . . . all!"] quotes, Globe (after Dyce)
64 abominable] F4; abhominable Q1–3, F1

78 **oath;]** *Theobald;* oath, *Q1–3, F1*
81 **him:]** *Q2–3, F1;* him, *Q1*
97 **barbarous]** *F1;* barberous *Q1–3 (a pun on* barber *has been suggested, but the same spelling appears at V.iii.4)*
112 **apart]** *Q3, F1;* a part *Q1–2*
141 **But]** Tut *Q2–3, F1*
165 **s.d. Flourish.]** *F1*
165 **s.d. Exeunt.]** *Q3, F1*

V.ii

V.ii] *Rowe*
Location: *Capell*
1 **habiliment]** *F3* (Habiliments); habilliament *Q1, Q3, F1;* habillament *Q2*
8 **s.d. above]** *Rowe*
18 **give't that accord]** *ed. (after Pope, who reads* give it); giue that accord *Q1–3;* giue it action *F1*
28 **Know,]** *Capell;* Know *Q1–3, F1*
35 **lurking-place]** *hyphen, Steevens*
52 **murderers]** *Capell;* murder *Q1–3, F1*
52 **caves]** *F2;* cares *Q1–3, F1*
56 **Hyperion's]** *F2 (subs.);* Epeons *Q1–3;* Eptons *F1*
61 **they]** *F2;* them *Q1–3, F1*
63 **'Cause]** *Pope;* Cause *Q1–3, F1*
65 **wordly]** worldly *Q2–3, F1*
66 **miserable, mad,]** *Capell;* miserable mad *Q1–3, F1*
69 **s.d. Exit above.]** *Rowe*
71 **humors]** fits *Q2–3, F1*
80 **s.d. Enter Titus below.]** *Collier MS (after Rowe)*
91 **are:]** *Pope;* are, *Q1–3, F1*
106 **shalt]** maist *Q2–3, F1*
120 **device]** *Pope;* deuise *Q1–3, F1*
121 **s.d. Enter Marcus.]** *placed as in Theobald; after l. 120, Q1–3, F1*
131 **s.d. Exit.]** *F2*
133 **along]** *Q2–3, F1;* a long *Q1*
137 **s.d. Aside . . . sons.]** *Johnson (after Hanmer)*
142 **s.d. Aside.]** *Rowe*
143 **devices]** *Rowe;* deuises *Q1–3, F1*
148 **s.d. Exit Tamora.]** *Rowe (after l. 147); placed as in Capell*
151 **s.d. Enter . . . Valentine.]** *Chambers (after Rowe)*
160 **it,]** *Q2–3, F1;* it *Q1*
161 **s.d. Exit . . . Demetrius.]** *Capell (subs., after Rowe)*
165 **fast.]** fast. Exeunt. *F1*
177 **Inhuman]** *Rowe;* Inhumane *Q1;* Inhumaine *Q2–3, F1*
204 **So,]** *Rowe;* So *Q1–3, F1*
205 **s.d. bearing . . . bodies]** *Capell (subs.)*

V.iii

V.iii] *Capell*
Location: *Globe (after Capell)*
o.s.d. with Aaron prisoner] *Rowe*
o.s.d. and his . . . Attendant] *Kittredge*
3 **s.p. 1. Goth.]** *Capell;* Got. *Q1–3, F1*
11 **s.p. Aar.]** *F1;* Moore. *Q1–3*
13 **venomous]** *Rowe;* venemous *Q1–3, F1*
14 **inhuman]** *Rowe;* inhumane *Q1–3;* Inhumaine *F1*
15 **s.d. Exeunt . . . Aaron.]** *Rowe (after l. 14); placed as in Capell*
15 **s.d. Sound trumpets]** *placed as in Wilson; after l. 16, Q1–3, F1; F1 here adds* Flourish.
15 **s.d. within]** *Capell*
16 **s.d. Aemilius]** *Dyce*
16 **s.d. Senators]** *Capell*
17 **s.p. Sat.]** *F1 (or* Satur., Satu. *throughout scene);* King. *Q1 (throughout scene, except* Emperour. *at l. 64), Q2 (throughout scene, except* Empe. *at ll. 25, 64), Q3 (throughout scene, except* Saturn, *or* Satur. *at ll. 25, 30, 39, 41, 48, and* Empe. *at l. 64)*
25 **s.d. A . . . in.]** *F1 (F1 places* Hoboyes. *before this s.d. but om.* Sound trumpets *of Q2–3 below)*
25 **s.d. The . . . down.]** *Capell (subs.)*
25 **s.d. Trumpets sounding]** Sound trumpets *Q2–3; om. F1*
25 **s.d. dishes]** meat on the Table *Q2–3, F1*
25 **s.d. young . . . others]** *Malone*
26 **lord]** gracious Lord *Q2–3, F1*
28 **all. Although]** *F1 (subs.);* all although *Q1–2;* all, although *Q3*
30 **attir'd]** *F1;* attired *Q1–3*
36 **Virginius]** *Q2–3, F1;* Viginius *Q1*
46 **with]** *Q2–3, F1;* wirh *Q1*
47 **s.d. He kills her.]** *Q3, F1*
54 **Will't . . . will't]** *F4;* Wilt . . . wilt *Q1–3, F1*
60 **are, both]** *Z. Grey (in Maxwell);* are both *Q1;* are both, *Q2–3, F1*
64 **s.d. Kills Titus.]** *Rowe (subs.)*
66 **s.d. Kills Saturninus.]** *Rowe (subs.)*
66 **s.d. A . . . above.]** *ed. (after Globe)*
73 **s.p. Aemil.]** *Sisson;* Romane Lord. *Q1–3;* Goth. *F1*
75 **castaway]** *F1;* cast away *Q1–3*
76 **herself,]** *Sisson;* her selfe. *Q1–3, F1*
79 **words.]** *Sisson;* words, *Q1–3, F1*
80 **s.d. To Lucius.]** *Rowe*
94–7 **Here's . . . Demetrius]** *Q2–3, F1 produce these lines as:* Heere is a Captaine, let him tell the tale, / Your harts will throb and weepe to heare him speake. / *Lucius.* Then [This *F1*] noble auditory be it knowne to you, / That cursed *Chiron* and *Demetrius*
119 **s.d. Pointing . . . Attendant.]** *Capell (subs.)*
124 **witness,]** *Maxwell;* witnes *Q1–3, F1*
124 **true.]** *F1;* true, *Q1–3*
125 **cause]** *F4;* course *Q1–3, F1*
125 **revenge]** *F1;* reuenge. *Q1–2;* reuenge, *Q3*
131, 176 **Andronici]** *F1;* Andronicie *Q1–3*
132 **hurl ourselves]** cast vs downe *Q2–3, F1*
133 **souls]** braines *Q2–3, F1*
141, 146 **s.pp. All.]** *Globe; Q1–3, F1 assign ll. 141–6 to Marcus*
142 **s.d. To Attendants.]** *Capell*
144 **adjudg'd]** *Q3, F1;* adiudge *Q1–2*
145 **s.d. Exeunt Attendants.]** *Globe*
145 **s.d. Lucius . . . descend.]** *Capell (subs.)*
153 **s.d. Kisses Titus.]** *Johnson*
154 **blood-stain'd]** *F3;* blood slaine *Q1–2;* bloud-slaine *Q3, F1*
163 **Sung]** *Q2–3, F1;* Song *Q1*
164–9 **Many . . . kiss!]** *Q2–3, F1 produce these lines as:* Many a matter hath he told to thee, / Meete and agreeing with thine infancie, / In that respect then, like a louing child. [child, *Q3, F1*] / Shed yet some small drops from thy tender spring, / Because kind nature doth require it so, / Friends should associate friends in griefe and woe.
172 **s.p. Boy.]** *F1;* Puer. *Q1–3*
175 **s.d. Enter . . . Aaron.]** *Dyce (after Rowe)*
176 **s.p. Aemil.]** *Sisson;* Romane. *Q1;* Romaine. *Q2–3;* Romans. *F1*
179 **breast-deep]** *hyphen, Rowe*
192 **fathers']** *anon. conj. (in Cambridge);* fathers *Q1–3, F1*
195 **ravenous]** hainous *Q2–3, F1*
196 **rite]** *Q3, F1;* right *Q1–2*
198 **prey]** *Q3, F1;* pray *Q1–2*
200 **dead . . . take]** so, shall haue like want of *Q2–3, F1*
200] *Following this line Q2–3, F1 add four lines:* See iustice done on *Aron* that damn'd Moore, / By [From *F1*] whom our heauie haps had their beginning: / Than [Then *Q3, F1*] afterwards to order well the state, / That like euents may nere it ruinate.
200 **s.d. Exeunt.]** Exeunt. / Finis the Tragedie of Titus Andronicus. *Q1;* FINIS. *Q2–3;* Exeunt omnes. / FINIS. *F1*

Romeo and Juliet

ROMEO AND JULIET, though it has always enjoyed popular esteem, has not often been ranked by professional critics with the tragic masterpieces which followed it. A certain unease about the dramatist's intention, some suspicion that, in the early moments of the play at any rate, he lacks that rhetorical control which marks his great period, and—above all—a conviction that he offends against his own criteria for tragedy by allowing mere chance to determine the destiny of the hero and heroine—all these have conspired to limit the critical prestige of *Romeo and Juliet.* It has been admired for its pathetic rather than for its tragic power; and many would agree with Johnson that in this instance anyway Shakespeare's "pathetic strains are . . . polluted with some unexpected depravations."

More recently, however, there has been a tendency to examine the novelty and stress the magnitude of Shakespeare's achievement in this play. For it is experimental; and it belongs to a period when Shakespeare, though the boldness and strength of *Lear* were still some years off, had found ways of realizing much of his power. Few will argue that it equals its great successors; but it may stand as a great play in its own right, proclaiming from its first scene the characteristic skill and intellect of its author.

Although the Nurse's reference to an earthquake eleven years past (I.iii.23) has by some been held to mean that Shakespeare wrote *Romeo and Juliet* that number of years after the London tremor of 1580, most now date it about 1595; it is to be thought of as roughly contemporary with *Richard II* and *A Midsummer Night's Dream.* The story it tells was well known. The use of a sleeping potion as a way out of an unwelcome marriage goes back to the *Ephesiaca* of the Greek novelist Xenophon in the fourth century A.D. Masuccio of Salerno uses it, together with a tale of star-crossed lovers, in *Il Novellino* (1476). Retelling the story in his *Istoria . . . di due nobili Amanti* (c. 1530), Luigi da Porto lays the scene in Verona and names the feuding families the Montecchi and the Cappellati (names he may have got from Dante's *Purgatorio,* vi.105: *Vieni a veder Montecchi e Cappelletti*). His Romeo goes to a Cappellati ball to see a girl whom he loves but who scorns him, and falls in love with Giulietta, as she with him. After a longer courtship than Shakespeare allows, conducted mostly on the girl's balcony, they marry, with the aid of the Franciscan Lorenzo, who hopes that the families will thus be brought together; but Fortune, "enemy of every earthly joy," prevents this outcome by starting up the feud again. The rest of the story is substantially as in Shakespeare. There was a French adaptation by Adrian Sevin in 1542; an Italian poem by Clízia (1553) and a play by Groto (1578) repeat and adapt the story. As a prose *novella* it is told in a novel by Bandello (1554) and again, in French, by Boiastuau in 1559. This last version Painter translated in his *Palace of Pleasure* (1567), a work known to Shakespeare.

Shakespeare's direct source was, however, none of these, but a poem by Arthur Brooke, based on Boiastuau and published in 1562. *The Tragical History of Romeus and Juliet,* 3,000 lines of verse in poulter's measure, is a very dull work. But it had some popularity and was reprinted in 1587. Shakespeare adapts Brooke freely, but he obviously had the poem on his desk or in his head. Brooke takes a very moral tone about the lovers, especially in his *Address to the Reader* (he is kinder to them in the poem itself), and some of this attitude comes through in the play, largely as part of the admonitions of the Friar. Brooke insists, as some of his predecessors had done, on the important part played by Fate in the story; this is another element employed by Shakespeare in his more complex design. Whenever Shakespeare is working largely from a single text, as here and in *The Winter's Tale* and *As You Like It*, in *Othello* and *Antony and Cleopatra*, one observes his readiness to accept and transform a conventional morality, and to find an appropriately limited place in his play for what had struck the author of his source as being the whole moral bearing of the story.

One also recognizes in these cases the essentially theatrical cast of Shakespeare's mind; he thought in terms of plays. To read Brooke with the play in mind is to be struck repeatedly by the easy skill with which Shakespeare has transformed the tale into a dramatic action, altering and compressing to make a sharp theatrical point, telescoping events, expanding such characters as the Nurse and Mercutio, cutting material and inventing new episodes. The effect is not merely to make the story fit "the two hours' traffic of our stage" and to procure significant juxtapositions of event (for Shakespeare obviously enjoyed the possibilities of antithetical love and hate, youth and age, in the tale) but to display in it qualities of passion and intellectual subtlety hidden under the surface of other versions. There are echoes of word and image, and the run of the story is the same; Brooke must have his due. Yet the play, considered in relation to its source, is one of the dramatist's most brilliant transformations.

That mastery of the opening scene which is the hallmark of the mature Shakespeare is as evident here as in *A Midsummer Night's Dream* and *Richard II*. First the formal prologue telling of the feud and—because this is a tragedy, hung in black, with no surprise survivals—announcing the lovers' fate. This choric sonnet Shakespeare owed in part to Brooke, who began in similar fashion; but he makes it mean more than Brooke could. The sonnet form will recur in the play as a hint that love has its formalities as well as death, and that they are in their way tragic. (*Romeo and Juliet* is the kind of tragedy *A Midsummer Night's Dream* hints at when it mentions the possibility that crazy young love is potentially tragic as well as potentially comic; *A Midsummer Night's Dream* chooses comedy, but Shakespeare states the theme in a tragic minor mode at the outset—"So quick bright things come to confusion" (I.i.149)—and repeats it in a farcical major with the Pyramus play at the happy end.)

We pass direct from the sonnet to the idiotic feuding of the Montague and Capulet servants; Tybalt and Benvolio raise it to a more serious level; and, to show that the continuance of this quarrel is the work of the young, the infirm heads of the families display themselves as no longer capable of fight. Only then do we meet Romeo, spinning his melancholy fancies; and in no sense are we led to think that this young man is worth our sympathy, for his first speeches (I.i.171 ff.) are full of remote self-regarding conceits and affectation. We pass on to the Capulet feast, and Romeo's mind undergoes sudden translation from notional to real love; but not before Mercutio has been amusingly indecent on the subject. Youth in this play is a separate nation; its customs are not understood by the old. For the hot blood which makes love at once a matter of rapture and low jokes is the same that keeps warm the obsolete Montague–Capulet feud. The same passions work towards both ends; and Shakespeare remembers this in the masterly moment when Tybalt—mere "goodman boy" to his uncle Capulet—overhears Romeo's first praise of Juliet's beauty:

> This, by his voice, should be a Montague.
> Fetch me my rapier, boy. (I.v.54–55)

The inability of age to prevent this flow of passion is signified by the unruled nature of Tybalt and Romeo's failure to pacify him, as surely as it is in those other skillful juxtapositions where old Capulet lays his plans with Paris for a sane, cold marriage, while Romeo and Juliet make love in the same house, or when Juliet rapturously invokes the coming night as Tybalt lies dead in the street. One could multiply these instances. From the firm beginning and throughout the main structural design—the use of foreboding dreams, the timing of Romeo's return, not to speak of the skill and plenitude with which difficult moments are turned into richly memorable or psychologically plausible crises (Romeo with the apothecary, Juliet terrified with the potion)—acute dramatic intelligence and imagination develop the plot and explore its potentialities of meaning.

Romeo and Juliet was an experiment in more ways than one. As H. B. Charlton has shown, the Italian dramatist Cinthio was the first to seek new tragic themes appropriate to the modern theatre, to call for stories drawn not from ancient history but from the life of the times. The playwright, he thought, should look for his plots to the novelist (as Shakespeare was later to look to Cinthio's own *novella* about a Moor of Venice). Shakespeare had already written historical tragedies; now he turned to fictional lovers, young aristocrats but not royal—"to choose such folk as these for tragic heroes," observes Charlton, "was aesthetically well-nigh an anarchist's gesture." Little remains of Seneca, save perhaps for the emphasis on Fate, working either through human passion or through the public feud over which the lovers have no control.

More remarkable than the choice of subject are the flexibility and fullness with which Shakespeare developed this apparently narrow tragic theme. It has been objected that the play lacks tragic necessity—that the story becomes tragic only by a trick. Bradley answered this long ago when he called it a rule, from which he did not except *Romeo and Juliet*, that in Shakespearean tragedy "almost all the prominent accidents occur when the action is well advanced and the impression of the causal sequence is too firmly fixed to be impaired." This is true of *Romeo and Juliet*. The completeness and self-surrender of the love between Romeo and Juliet is beautifully rendered; but there is hardly a moment when we are allowed to think that permanence or happiness is part of its nature. The sentences of the Friar are chilled by a sort of benevolent inhumanity—he is not himself familiar with this kind of thing and we are; but nevertheless they sound persistently before the wedding, and the overtones should not be neglected.

> These violent delights have violent ends,
> And in their triumph die. (II.vi.9–10)

It is the wisdom glanced at by Hermia and Lysander in the opening scene of *A Midsummer Night's Dream.* Before the marriage can be consummated, Tybalt is dead, and the quick bright thing has come to confusion. There is the further point, that Romeo is in distress unmanned: "I thought thy disposition better temper'd," says the Friar (III.iii.115). Shakespeare is using Brooke's unqualified moralism: "to this end . . . is this tragical matter written, to describe unto thee a couple of unfortunate lovers, thralling themselves to unhonest desire, neglecting the authority and advice of parents and friends . . . !" But he is not using it crudely. The love he describes is of itself beautiful and valuable; but just as it is in its very nature the business of the young, with passions hardly controlled, so is it in its very nature associated with disaster and death. Portents, whether of the stars or of dreams, will foretell it. Out of this truth one can make a partial morality; but in this play Shakespeare offers a complex pattern of suffering from which a moral man might as well decide for love as against it. Caught in that tragic swirl of events, Romeo and Juliet say more than Brooke's sermon can. Romeo fluctuates from melancholy to high spirits, from unmanly despair to calm, and moves from a recognition that it is "e'en so" to a kind of adult fatalism. Juliet more strikingly changes from a girl too young to have thoughts of marriage into a mature and suffering woman.

It is in this sense that we should understand the emphasis on Fate. It is represented in the law of the world, which neither the dateless passion of the lovers nor the expedients of Friar Lawrence can alter. Fortune throws the characters into attitudes which ironically belie their fine words; the Friar says "Wisely and slow" but acts in haste, stumbles, leaves Juliet to her unnecessary fate; the lovers who have found the real right thing share but one brief night together; Romeo, seeking to end the feud, is forced to kill Tybalt. These are some of the ways in which Shakespeare manipulates a narrative to show more than two dimensions.

There are others. One curious fact emerges from the labor of writing notes to *Romeo and Juliet.* The language is much more difficult, the thought expressed in more rhetorical and conceited ways, in the early parts of the work. Shakespeare was a master of rhetoric not only in the sense of the textbook, the elaboration of figures appropriate to meaning and mood, but in the wider sense that he understood the mixture of rhetorical levels, the clash of styles, which a complex theme requires. He is like Chaucer, perhaps, making his effects from the contrast between a formal rhetoric based on the book, and a kind of anti-rhetoric, a plainness in itself perhaps as artificial as the ornateness against which it is played off. There is a sudden clearing of the verse, a move from the formality befitting the conventional nature of Romeo's love for Rosaline (as much a convention as the feud itself) to an apparent denial of formality by plainness; it is summed up by Juliet's words at her window:

> Fain would I dwell on form, fain, fain deny
> What I have spoke, but farewell compliment!
> (II.ii.88–89)

From the formality of the masque, of the sonnet in which they first speak together, the lovers move to a direct monosyllabic plainness, as if their minds were too much occupied with living to have time for mere fantastic speech:

> *Juliet.* I would not for the world they saw thee here.
> *Romeo.* I have night's cloak to hide me from their eyes,
> And but thou love me, let them find me here.
> (II.ii.74–76)

It is only when Juliet is untrue to her faith, upbraiding Romeo for the murder of Tybalt, that she slips back into the formal rhetoric: "Beautiful tyrant! fiend angelical!" (III.ii.75 ff.). When all seems and indeed is over, Romeo is hardly allowing himself a flourish when he says, "Then I defy you, stars!"; but the true mood of this love is fully established with his "Well, Juliet, I will lie with thee to-night." The reality of the love relationship is even, by a touch of genius, contrasted with the relative falsity even of the grief of parents and Nurse and official lover in the extraordinary passage (IV.v) where the Capulets vie with Paris' conventional outcries and the absurd lamentation of the Nurse over Juliet's body: "O woe, O woeful, woeful, woeful day! / Most lamentable day, most woeful day," etc. There are few more daring rhetorical adventures in all the tragedies.

In view of this we should beware of supposing that Shakespeare's sympathies lay strongly in this or that direction; that he was on the Friar's side when he uttered the conventional condemnation of the lovers in a story which must always have thrived on their attractiveness; or, on the other hand, that he was committed to this surreptitious but virtuous passion as in itself of the highest value. For all the necessary heat of the verse and the pathos of the theme, Shakespeare maintains a remarkable reserve. That *Romeo and Juliet* has a strong thematic interest is clear; but Shakespeare has now passed the stage when one could say, without too much injury to the work, precisely what that interest may have been. *Romeo and Juliet* is not a simple play; to suppose that it is would be the most elementary mistake one could make concerning it.

Frank Kermode

The Tragedy of Romeo and Juliet

[DRAMATIS PERSONAE

CHORUS

ESCALUS, *Prince of Verona*
PARIS, *a young nobleman, kinsman to the Prince*
MONTAGUE } *heads of two houses at variance*
CAPULET } *with each other*
An OLD MAN, *of the Capulet family*
ROMEO, *son to Montague*
MERCUTIO, *kinsman to the Prince, and friend to Romeo*
BENVOLIO, *nephew to Montague, and friend to Romeo*
TYBALT, *nephew to Lady Capulet*
PETRUCHIO, *a (mute) follower of Tybalt*
FRIAR LAWRENCE } *Franciscans*
FRIAR JOHN }
BALTHASAR, *servant to Romeo*
ABRAM, *servant to Montague*

SAMPSON } *servants to Capulet*
GREGORY }
CLOWN
PETER, *servant to Juliet's nurse*
PAGE *to Paris*
APOTHECARY
Three MUSICIANS

LADY MONTAGUE, *wife to Montague*
LADY CAPULET, *wife to Capulet*
JULIET, *daughter to Capulet*
NURSE *to Juliet*
CITIZENS *of Verona; several* GENTLEMEN *and* GENTLEWOMEN *of both houses;* MASKERS, TORCH-BEARERS, PAGES, GUARDS, WATCHMEN, SERVANTS, *and* ATTENDANTS

SCENE: *Verona; Mantua*]

THE PROLOGUE

[*Enter*] CHORUS.

Two households, both alike in dignity,
In fair Verona, where we lay our scene,
From ancient grudge break to new mutiny,
Where civil blood makes civil hands unclean.
From forth the fatal loins of these two foes
A pair of star-cross'd lovers take their life;
Whose misadventur'd piteous overthrows
Doth with their death bury their parents' strife.
The fearful passage of their death-mark'd love,
And the continuance of their parents' rage,
Which, but their children's end, nought could remove,
Is now the two hours' traffic of our stage;
The which if you with patient ears attend,
What here shall miss, our toil shall strive to mend.
[*Exit.*]

Words and passages enclosed in square brackets in the text above are either emendations of the copy-text or additions to it. The Textual Notes immediately following the play cite the earliest authority for every such change or insertion and supply the reading of the copy-text wherever it is emended in this edition.

Pro. 1. dignity: rank.
3. mutiny: strife.
4. civil blood: the blood of civil strife. **civil hands:** citizens' hands.
6. star-cross'd: thwarted by the stars.
12. traffic: business.
14. miss: prove defective (in our performance). **mend:** i.e. mend in future (as the result of knowing your judgment).

[ACT I, SCENE I]

Enter SAMPSON *and* GREGORY, *with swords and bucklers, of the house of Capulet.*

Sam. Gregory, on my word, we'll not carry coals.

Gre. No, for then we should be colliers.

Sam. I mean, and we be in choler, we'll draw.

Gre. Ay, while you live, draw your neck out of collar.

Sam. I strike quickly, being mov'd.

Gre. But thou art not quickly mov'd to strike.

Sam. A dog of the house of Montague moves me.

Gre. To move is to stir, and to be valiant is to stand; therefore, if thou art mov'd, thou run'st away.

Sam. A dog of that house shall move me to stand! I will take the wall of any man or maid of Montague's.

Gre. That shows thee a weak slave, for the weakest goes to the wall.

I.i. Location: Verona. A public place.
1. carry coals: do menial work; figuratively, put up with insults, "eat dirt."
3. and: if. **choler:** anger. **draw:** draw our swords.
4–5. draw . . . collar: avoid hanging.
7. mov'd: angered (with obvious punning in the following lines).
10. stand: make a stand, offer resistance.
12. take the wall. The inner part of the sidewalk being cleaner, it was yielded out of courtesy to superiors; to take it implied a claim to superiority.
13–14. the weakest . . . wall: the weakest must give way (proverbial).

Sam. 'Tis true, and therefore women, being the weaker vessels, are ever thrust to the wall; therefore I will push Montague's men from the wall, and thrust his maids to the wall.

Gre. The quarrel is between our masters, and us their men.

Sam. 'Tis all one; I will show myself a tyrant: when I have fought with the men, I will be civil with the maids; I will cut off their heads.

Gre. The heads of the maids?

Sam. Ay, the heads of the maids, or their maidenheads, take it in what sense thou wilt.

Gre. They must take it [in] sense that feel it.

Sam. Me they shall feel while I am able to stand, and 'tis known I am a pretty piece of flesh.

Gre. 'Tis well thou art not fish; if thou hadst, thou hadst been poor-John. Draw thy tool, here comes [two] of the house of Montagues.

Enter two other servingmen [ABRAM *and* BALTHASAR].

Sam. My naked weapon is out. Quarrel, I will back thee.

Gre. How, turn thy back and run?

Sam. Fear me not.

Gre. No, marry, I fear thee!

Sam. Let us take the law of our sides, let them begin.

Gre. I will frown as I pass by, and let them take it as they list.

Sam. Nay, as they dare. I will bite my thumb at them, which is disgrace to them if they bear it.

Abr. Do you bite your thumb at us, sir?

Sam. I do bite my thumb, sir.

Abr. Do you bite your thumb at us, sir?

Sam. [*Aside to Gregory.*] Is the law of our side if I say ay?

Gre. [*Aside to Sampson.*] No.

Sam. No, sir, I do not bite my thumb at you, sir, but I bite my thumb, sir.

Gre. Do you quarrel, sir?

Abr. Quarrel, sir? No, sir.

Sam. But if you do, sir, I am for you. I serve as good a man as you.

Abr. No better?

Sam. Well, sir.

Enter BENVOLIO.

Gre. Say "better," here comes one of my master's kinsmen.

Sam. Yes, better, sir.

Abr. You lie.

Sam. Draw, if you be men. Gregory, remember thy washing blow. *They fight.*

Ben. Part, fools!
Put up your swords, you know not what you do.
[*Beats down their swords.*]

Enter TYBALT.

Tyb. What, art thou drawn among these heartless hinds?
Turn thee, Benvolio, look upon thy death.

Ben. I do but keep the peace. Put up thy sword,
Or manage it to part these men with me.

Tyb. What, drawn and talk of peace? I hate the word
As I hate hell, all Montagues, and thee.
Have at thee, coward! [*They fight.*]

Enter three or four CITIZENS *with clubs or partisans.*

[*Citizens.*] Clubs, bills, and partisans! Strike! Beat them down!
Down with the Capulets! Down with the Montagues!

Enter old CAPULET *in his gown, and his wife* [LADY CAPULET].

Cap. What noise is this? Give me my long sword ho!

La. Cap. A crutch, a crutch! why call you for a sword?

Cap. My sword, I say! Old Montague is come,
And flourishes his blade in spite of me.

Enter old MONTAGUE *and his wife* [LADY MONTAGUE].

Mon. Thou villain Capulet!—Hold me not, let me go.

La. Mon. Thou shalt not stir one foot to seek a foe.

Enter PRINCE ESCALUS *with his* TRAIN.

Prin. Rebellious subjects, enemies to peace,
Profaners of this neighbor-stained steel—
Will they not hear?—What ho, you men, you beasts!
That quench the fire of your pernicious rage
With purple fountains issuing from your veins—
On pain of torture, from those bloody hands
Throw your mistempered weapons to the ground,
And hear the sentence of your moved prince.
Three civil brawls, bred of an airy word,
By thee, old Capulet, and Montague,
Have thrice disturb'd the quiet of our streets,
And made Verona's ancient citizens
Cast by their grave beseeming ornaments
To wield old partisans, in hands as old,

16. weaker vessels. See 1 Peter 3:7.
19–20. between . . . men: i.e. not with the maids.
27. They . . . feel it: the ones who must take it in sense (= physical sensation) are those who feel it, i.e. the maids.
28. stand. With bawdy pun.
30. fish. With play on the slang sense "female."
31. poor-John: dried hake (a cheap fish). **tool:** weapon (with slang sexual reference that Sampson continues in *naked weapon*, line 33).
36. Fear me not: have no fears about me (deliberately misinterpreted by Gregory).
37. marry: indeed (originally, the name of the Virgin Mary used as an oath). **38. take the law of:** have the law on. **41. list:** like.
42. bite my thumb. Considered an act of insolence or defiance.

63. washing: swashing, slashing.
66. heartless hinds: cowardly servants; with punning sense "female deer without a stag [*hartless*]."
72. Have at thee: here I come at you (formula for announcing attack).
s.d. partisans: broad-headed spears.
73. Clubs: familiar London cry, calling apprentices armed with clubs to riot or to suppress riot. **bills:** hooked blades on long shafts.
78. spite: defiance. **79. villain:** base, ignoble.
82. Profaners . . . steel: profaning your weapons by staining them with your neighbors' blood.
87. mistempered: (1) angry; (2) tempered for use in a bad cause.
89. airy: light, insignificant.
93. Cast . . . ornaments: throw aside appurtenances (like staffs) suitable for dignified age.

Cank'red with peace, to part your cank'red hate;
If ever you disturb our streets again
Your lives shall pay the forfeit of the peace.
For this time all the rest depart away.
You, Capulet, shall go along with me,
And, Montague, come you this afternoon,
To know our farther pleasure in this case,
To old Free-town, our common judgment-place.
Once more, on pain of death, all men depart.

Exeunt [all but Montague, Lady Montague, and Benvolio].

Mon. Who set this ancient quarrel new abroach?
Speak, nephew, were you by when it began?

Ben. Here were the servants of your adversary,
And yours, close fighting ere I did approach.
I drew to part them. In the instant came
The fiery Tybalt, with his sword prepar'd,
Which, as he breath'd defiance to my ears,
He swung about his head and cut the winds,
Who, nothing hurt withal, hiss'd him in scorn.
While we were interchanging thrusts and blows,
Came more and more, and fought on part and part,
Till the Prince came, who parted either part.

La. Mon. O, where is Romeo? Saw you him to-day?
Right glad I am he was not at this fray.

Ben. Madam, an hour before the worshipp'd sun
Peer'd forth the golden window of the east,
A troubled mind drive me to walk abroad,
Where, underneath the grove of sycamore
That westward rooteth from this city side,
So early walking did I see your son.
Towards him I made, but he was ware of me,
And stole into the covert of the wood.
I, measuring his affections by my own,
Which then most sought where most might not be found,
Being one too many by my weary self,
Pursued my humor not pursuing his,
And gladly shunn'd who gladly fled from me.

Mon. Many a morning hath he there been seen,
With tears augmenting the fresh morning's dew,
Adding to clouds more clouds with his deep sighs,
But all so soon as the all-cheering sun
Should in the farthest east begin to draw
The shady curtains from Aurora's bed,
Away from light steals home my heavy son,
And private in his chamber pens himself,
Shuts up his windows, locks fair daylight out,
And makes himself an artificial night.
Black and portendous must this humor prove,
Unless good counsel may the cause remove.

Ben. My noble uncle, do you know the cause?

Mon. I neither know it, nor can learn of him.

Ben. Have you importun'd him by any means?

Mon. Both by myself and many other friends,
But he, [his] own affections' counsellor,
Is to himself (I will not say how true)
But to himself so secret and so close,
So far from sounding and discovery,
As is the bud bit with an envious worm,
Ere he can spread his sweet leaves to the air
Or dedicate his beauty to the [sun].
Could we but learn from whence his sorrows grow,
We would as willingly give cure as know.

Enter Romeo.

Ben. See where he comes. So please you step aside,
I'll know his grievance, or be much denied.

Mon. I would thou wert so happy by thy stay
To hear true shrift. Come, madam, let's away.

Exeunt [Montague and Lady].

Ben. Good morrow, cousin.

Rom. Is the day so young?

Ben. But new strook nine.

Rom. Ay me, sad hours seem long.
Was that my father that went hence so fast?

Ben. It was. What sadness lengthens Romeo's hours?

Rom. Not having that which, having, makes them short.

Ben. In love?

Rom. Out—

Ben. Of love?

Rom. Out of her favor where I am in love.

Ben. Alas that love, so gentle in his view,
Should be so tyrannous and rough in proof!

Rom. Alas that love, whose view is muffled still,
Should, without eyes, see pathways to his will!
Where shall we dine? O me! what fray was here?
Yet tell me not, for I have heard it all:
Here's much to do with hate, but more with love.
Why then, O brawling love! O loving hate!
O any thing, of nothing first [create]!
O heavy lightness, serious vanity,
Misshapen chaos of well[-seeming] forms,
Feather of lead, bright smoke, cold fire, sick health,

95. Cank'red . . . cank'red: rusted . . . malignant.
102. Free-town . . . Brooke's translation of *Villa franca*, the name of Capulet's residence in the Italian story. **common:** public.
104. abroach: open, flowing (as of a barrel of liquor).
112. nothing: not at all. **withal:** therewith.
114. part and part: one side or the other.
115. either part: both sides.
120. drive: drove (an archaic form, pronounced *driv*).
122. this city side: the side of this city.
124. ware: (1) aware; (2) wary. **126. affections:** inclinations.
127. most sought . . . found: wanted most to find somewhere to be solitary.
129. Pursued . . . his: indulged my own mood by not following his moody self. **130. who:** him who. **134. all so:** just as.
136. Aurora: goddess of dawn. **137. heavy:** sad.
139. windows: shutters.
141. Black and portendous: portentous of some dire event. **humor:** capricious or moody behavior.
147. counsellor: confidential adviser, sharer of secrets.
148. true: trustworthy, i.e. wise in his advice.
150. sounding: being fathomed. **151. envious:** malicious.
156. So please you: if you will be so good as to.
158. would . . . happy: hope that you will be fortunate enough.
159. shrift: confession.
160. cousin: kinsman. Romeo and Benvolio are cousins in the modern sense, but the word was applied to any collateral relative more distant than a brother or sister. **161. strook:** struck.
169. his view: its appearance. **170. in proof:** being experienced.
171. view . . . still: eyes are always blindfolded.
172. see . . . will: find his way to get what he wants.
175. to do: ado, tumult.
177. create: created. Romeo ironically justifies this string of paradoxes by recalling the greatest of paradoxes—God's creation of everything *ex nihilo*, from nothing.
178. serious vanity: heavy emptiness.
179. chaos . . . forms. Chaos, technically, is all matter and no form.

Still-waking sleep, that is not what it is!
This love feel I, that feel no love in this.
Dost thou not laugh?

Ben. No, coz, I rather weep.

Rom. Good heart, at what?

Ben. At thy good heart's oppression.

Rom. Why, such is love's transgression.
Griefs of mine own lie heavy in my breast,
Which thou wilt propagate to have it press'd
With more of thine. This love that thou hast shown
Doth add more grief to too much of mine own.
Love is a smoke made with the fume of sighs,
Being purg'd, a fire sparkling in lovers' eyes,
Being vex'd, a sea nourish'd with loving tears.
What is it else? a madness most discreet,
A choking gall, and a preserving sweet.
Farewell, my coz.

Ben. Soft, I will go along;
And if you leave me so, you do me wrong.

Rom. Tut, I have lost myself, I am not here:
This is not Romeo, he's some other where.

Ben. Tell me in sadness, who is that you love?

Rom. What, shall I groan and tell thee?

Ben. Groan? why, no;
But sadly tell me, who?

Rom. [Bid] a sick man in sadness [make] his will—
A word ill urg'd to one that is so ill!
In sadness, cousin, I do love a woman.

Ben. I aim'd so near when I suppos'd you lov'd.

Rom. A right good mark-man! And she's fair I love.

Ben. A right fair mark, fair coz, is soonest hit.

Rom. Well, in that hit you miss: she'll not be hit
With Cupid's arrow, she hath Dian's wit;
And in strong proof of chastity well arm'd,
From Love's weak childish bow she lives uncharm'd.
She will not stay the siege of loving terms,
Nor bide th' encounter of assailing eyes,
Nor ope her lap to saint-seducing gold.
O, she is rich in beauty, only poor
That, when she dies, with beauty dies her store.

Ben. Then she hath sworn that she will still live chaste?

Rom. She hath, and in that sparing [makes] huge waste;
For beauty starv'd with her severity
Cuts beauty off from all posterity.
She is too fair, too wise, wisely too fair,

181. Still-waking: constantly awake.
183. coz: cousin, i.e. kinsman.
185. transgression: overstepping of limit.
187. propagate: increase. **to have:** by having. **press'd:** oppressed (with secondary sense "weighted down by a lover," suggested by *propagate*). **191. purg'd:** i.e. cleared of smoke.
195. Soft: not so fast. **196. And if:** if.
199. sadness: seriousness.
209. Dian's wit: i.e. the good sense to shun love. Diana was the goddess of chastity.
210. proof: armor of tested strength.
211. From . . . uncharm'd. *Uncharmed from* = exempt from the spell of. **212. stay:** abide.
214. ope . . . gold. Like Danaë, whom Jove visited in a shower of gold.
216. store: capital (of beauty, which she should have perpetuated through offspring). **217. still:** always. **218. sparing:** frugality.

To merit bliss by making me despair.
She hath forsworn to love, and in that vow
Do I live dead that live to tell it now.

Ben. Be rul'd by me, forget to think of her.

Rom. O, teach me how I should forget to think.

Ben. By giving liberty unto thine eyes:
Examine other beauties.

Rom. 'Tis the way
To call hers (exquisite) in question more.
These happy masks that kiss fair ladies' brows,
Being black, puts us in mind they hide the fair.
He that is strooken blind cannot forget
The precious treasure of his eyesight lost.
Show me a mistress that is passing fair,
What doth her beauty serve but as a note
Where I may read who pass'd that passing fair?
Farewell, thou canst not teach me to forget.

Ben. I'll pay that doctrine, or else die in debt.
Exeunt.

[Scene II]

Enter Capulet, County Paris, *and the Clown*, [*Capulet's* Servant].

Cap. But Montague is bound as well as I,
In penalty alike, and 'tis not hard, I think,
For men so old as we to keep the peace.

Par. Of honorable reckoning are you both,
And pity 'tis you liv'd at odds so long.
But now, my lord, what say you to my suit?

Cap. But saying o'er what I have said before:
My child is yet a stranger in the world,
She hath not seen the change of fourteen years;
Let two more summers wither in their pride,
Ere we may think her ripe to be a bride.

Par. Younger than she are happy mothers made.

Cap. And too soon marr'd are those so early made.
Earth hath swallowed all my hopes but she;
She's the hopeful lady of my earth.
But woo her, gentle Paris, get her heart,
My will to her consent is but a part;
And she agreed, within her scope of choice
Lies my consent and fair according voice.
This night I hold an old accustom'd feast,
Whereto I have invited many a guest,
Such as I love, and you, among the store
One more, most welcome, makes my number more.
At my poor house look to behold this night
Earth-treading stars that make dark heaven light.
Such comfort as do lusty young men feel
When well-apparell'd April on the heel
Of limping winter treads, even such delight

222. To . . . despair: in earning salvation by chastity which drives me to the dangerous sin of despair.
229. in question more: all the more acutely into consideration.
234. passing: surpassingly.
238. I'll . . . debt: I'll teach you that lesson or feel that I haven't fulfilled a friend's obligation.

I.ii. Location: Verona. A street.
o.s.d. County: count. **4. reckoning:** repute.
8. stranger: newcomer.
15. the hopeful . . . earth: (1) the hope round which my world revolves; (2) the heiress of my wealth.
18. agreed: consenting. **19. according:** agreeing.

Among fresh fennel buds shall you this night
Inherit at my house; hear all, all see;
And like her most whose merit most shall be;
Which [on] more view of many, mine, being one,
May stand in number, though in reck'ning none.
Come go with me. [*To Servant.*] Go, sirrah, trudge about
Through fair Verona, find those persons out
Whose names are written there, and to them say,
My house and welcome on their pleasure stay.
Exit [*with Paris*].

Serv. Find them out whose names are written here! It is written that the shoemaker should meddle with his yard and the tailor with his last, the fisher with his pencil and the painter with his nets; but I am sent to find those persons whose names are here writ, and can never find what names the writing person hath here writ. I must to the learned. In good time!

Enter BENVOLIO *and* ROMEO.

Ben. Tut, man, one fire burns out another's burning,
[One] pain is less'ned by another's anguish;
Turn giddy, and be holp by backward turning;
One desperate grief cures with another's languish:
Take thou some new infection to thy eye,
And the rank poison of the old will die.
Rom. Your plantan leaf is excellent for that.
Ben. For what, I pray thee?
Rom. For your broken shin.
Ben. Why, Romeo, art thou mad?
Rom. Not mad, but bound more than a madman is;
Shut up in prison, kept without my food,
Whipt and tormented, and—God-den, good fellow.
Serv. God gi' god-den. I pray, sir, can you read?
Rom. Ay, mine own fortune in my misery.
Serv. Perhaps you have learn'd it without book.
But I pray, can you read any thing you see?
Rom. Ay, if I know the letters and the language.
Serv. Ye say honestly, rest you merry!
Rom. Stay, fellow, I can read.

(*He reads the letter.*) "Signior Martino and his wife and daughters; County Anselme and his beauteous sisters; the lady widow of [Vitruvio]; Signior Placentio and his lovely nieces; Mercutio and his brother Valentine; mine uncle Capulet, his wife, and daughters; my fair niece Rosaline, [and] Livia; Signior Valentio and his cousin Tybalt; Lucio and the lively Helena."

A fair assembly. Whither should they come?
Serv. Up.
Rom. Whither? to supper?
Serv. To our house.
Rom. Whose house?
Serv. My master's.
Rom. Indeed I should have ask'd [thee] that before.

Serv. Now I'll tell you without asking. My master is the great rich Capulet, and if you be not of the house of Montagues, I pray come and crush a cup of wine. Rest you merry! [*Exit.*]

Ben. At this same ancient feast of Capulet's
Sups the fair Rosaline whom thou so loves,
With all the admired beauties of Verona.
Go thither, and with unattainted eye
Compare her face with some that I shall show,
And I will make thee think thy swan a crow.
Rom. When the devout religion of mine eye
Maintains such falsehood, then turn tears to [fires];
And these, who, often drown'd, could never die,
Transparent heretics, be burnt for liars!
One fairer than my love! The all-seeing sun
Ne'er saw her match since first the world begun.
Ben. Tut, you saw her fair, none else being by,
Herself pois'd with herself in either eye;
But in that crystal scales let there be weigh'd
Your lady's love against some other maid
That I will show you shining at this feast,
And she shall scant show well that now seems best.
Rom. I'll go along no such sight to be shown,
But to rejoice in splendor of mine own. [*Exeunt.*]

[SCENE III]

Enter CAPULET'S WIFE, *and* NURSE.

La. Cap. Nurse, where's my daughter? Call her forth to me.
Nurse. Now by my maidenhead at twelve year old,
I bade her come. What, lamb! What, ladybird!
God forbid! Where's this girl? What, Juliet!

Enter JULIET.

Jul. How now, who calls?
Nurse. Your mother.
Jul. Madam, I am here,
What is your will?
La. Cap. This is the matter. Nurse, give leave a while,
We must talk in secret. Nurse, come back again,
I have rememb'red me, thou s' hear our counsel.
Thou knowest my daughter's of a pretty age.
Nurse. Faith, I can tell her age unto an hour.
La. Cap. She's not fourteen.
Nurse. I'll lay fourteen of my teeth—

29. **fennel:** a fragrant flowering plant.
30. **Inherit:** possess, experience.
32–33. **Which . . . none.** This obscure passage seems to mean: "When you have seen all of them, my daughter, though one of the group, may no longer have a place in your estimation [*reckoning*]." There is punning on *reckoning* in the sense "arithmetical calculation" and on the proverbial saying "One is no number."
34. **sirrah:** customary term of address to an inferior.
46. **another's anguish:** the anguish of another pain.
47. **holp:** helped, i.e. cured. **backward:** in reverse.
48. **cures . . . languish:** is cured by the distress of another grief.
51. **plantan:** plantain, the leaf of which was applied to minor wounds.
52. **broken shin:** broken skin on the shin.
54–56. **bound . . . tormented.** The usual treatment of the insane.
56. **God-den:** good evening (used after noon).
57. **gi':** give you. 59. **without book:** by heart.
62. **rest you merry:** conventional phrase of farewell.

80. **crush:** drink. 83. **loves:** lovest.
85. **unattainted:** uninfected, unprejudiced. 90. **these:** i.e. my eyes.
91. **Transparent:** (1) bright, clear; (2) manifest.
95. **pois'd:** balanced.

I.iii. **Location:** Verona. Capulet's house.
4. **God forbid:** God forbid there should be anything amiss (?) or God forbid I should call her "ladybird" (cant term for a prostitute).
9. **thou s':** thou shalt.

And yet, to my teen be it spoken, I have but four—
She's not fourteen. How long is it now
To Lammas-tide?

La. Cap. A fortnight and odd days.

Nurse. Even or odd, of all days in the year,
Come Lammas-eve at night shall she be fourteen.
Susan and she—God rest all Christian souls!—
Were of an age. Well, Susan is with God,
She was too good for me. But as I said,
On Lammas-eve at night shall she be fourteen,
That shall she, marry, I remember it well.
'Tis since the earthquake now aleven years,
And she was wean'd—I never shall forget it—
Of all the days of the year, upon that day;
For I had then laid wormwood to my dug,
Sitting in the sun under the dove-house wall.
My lord and you were then at Mantua—
Nay, I do bear a brain—but as I said,
When it did taste the wormwood on the nipple
Of my dug and felt it bitter, pretty fool,
To see it teachy and fall out wi' th' dug!
Shake, quoth the dove-house; 'twas no need, I trow,
To bid me trudge.
And since that time it is aleven years,
For then she could stand high-lone; nay, by th' rood,
She could have run and waddled all about;
For even the day before, she broke her brow,
And then my husband—God be with his soul!
'A was a merry man—took up the child.
"Yea," quoth he, "dost thou fall upon thy face?
Thou wilt fall backward when thou hast more wit,
Wilt thou not, Jule?" and by my holidam,
The pretty wretch left crying and said, "Ay."
To see now how a jest shall come about!
I warrant, and I should live a thousand years,
I never should forget it: "Wilt thou not, Jule?" quoth he;
And, pretty fool, it stinted and said, "Ay."

La Cap. Enough of this, I pray thee hold thy peace.

Nurse. Yes, madam, yet I cannot choose but laugh
To think it should leave crying and say, "Ay."
And yet I warrant it had upon it brow
A bump as big as a young cock'rel's stone—
A perilous knock—and it cried bitterly.
"Yea," quoth my husband, "fall'st upon thy face?
Thou wilt fall backward when thou comest to age,
Wilt thou not, Jule?" It stinted and said, "Ay."

Jul. And stint thou too, I pray thee, nurse, say I.

Nurse. Peace, I have done. God mark thee to his grace!

Thou wast the prettiest babe that e'er I nurs'd.
And I might live to see thee married once,
I have my wish.

La. Cap. Marry, that "marry" is the very theme
I came to talk of. Tell me, daughter Juliet,
How stands your dispositions to be married?

Jul. It is an [honor] that I dream not of.

Nurse. An [honor]! were not I thine only nurse,
I would say thou hadst suck'd wisdom from thy teat.

La. Cap. Well, think of marriage now; younger than you,
Here in Verona, ladies of esteem,
Are made already mothers. By my count,
I was your mother much upon these years
That you are now a maid. Thus then in brief:
The valiant Paris seeks you for his love.

Nurse. A man, young lady! Lady, such a man
As all the world—why, he's a man of wax.

La. Cap. Verona's summer hath not such a flower.

Nurse. Nay, he's a flower, in faith, a very flower.

La. Cap. What say you? can you love the gentleman?
This night you shall behold him at our feast;
Read o'er the volume of young Paris' face,
And find delight writ there with beauty's pen;
Examine every married lineament,
And see how one another lends content;
And what obscur'd in this fair volume lies
Find written in the margent of his eyes.
This precious book of love, this unbound lover,
To beautify him, only lacks a cover.
The fish lives in the sea, and 'tis much pride
For fair without the fair within to hide.
That book in many's eyes doth share the glory,
That in gold clasps locks in the golden story;
So shall you share all that he doth possess,
By having him, making yourself no less.

Nurse. No less! nay, bigger: women grow by men.

La. Cap. Speak briefly, can you like of Paris' love?

Jul. I'll look to like, if looking liking move;
But no more deep will I endart mine eye
Than your consent gives strength to make [it] fly.

Enter SERVINGMAN.

Serv. Madam, the guests are come, supper serv'd up, you call'd, my young lady ask'd for, the nurse curs'd in the pantry, and every thing in extremity. I must hence to wait; I beseech you follow straight. [*Exit.*]

La. Cap. We follow thee. Juliet, the County stays.

13. teen: sorrow (*teen* and *four* echo *fourteen*).
15. Lammas-tide: August 1. **23. aleven:** eleven.
29. bear a brain: have a great memory.
31. fool: here, a term of endearment, like *wretch* in line 44.
32. teachy: tetchy, fretful.
33. Shake . . . dove-house: i.e. the dovecot, shaking, suggested it was time she should be off. **trow:** think, assure you.
36. stand high-lone: stand upright alone. **rood:** cross.
38. broke her brow: (fell and) cut her forehead. **40. 'A:** he.
43. holidam: halidom, holiness; but, as the spelling shows, the word was sometimes understood as referring to the Virgin Mary.
45. how . . . about: how something spoken in jest comes true.
48. stinted: ceased (crying). **52. it brow:** its brow.
53. stone: testicle.
68. thy teat: the teat you sucked.
72. much . . . years: at much the same age.
76. man of wax: i.e. handsome as a wax figure.
83. married: harmonious.
86. margent: margin (which in early books frequently contained commentary on the adjacent text).
87. unbound. Referring both to the book and the unmarried man.
88. cover: binding; but, as Dover Wilson suggests, perhaps with quibble on the legal expression *femme couvert*, "married woman."
89. The fish . . . sea: i.e. the fish knows its proper habitat. The sense seems to be that Juliet would give Paris an equally suitable "outside."
95. grow: i.e. become pregnant.
97. look: expect (with obvious pun). **98. endart:** shoot like a dart.
102. curs'd . . . pantry: i.e. for not being on hand to help.
103. straight: straightway. **104. stays:** waits.

Nurse. Go, girl, seek happy nights to happy days.
Exeunt.

[SCENE IV]

Enter ROMEO, MERCUTIO, BENVOLIO, *with five or six other* MASKERS; TORCH-BEARERS.

Rom. What, shall this speech be spoke for our excuse?
Or shall we on without apology?
Ben. The date is out of such prolixity:
We'll have no Cupid hoodwink'd with a scarf,
Bearing a Tartar's painted bow of lath,
Scaring the ladies like a crow-keeper,
[Nor no without-book prologue, faintly spoke
After the prompter, for our entrance;]
But let them measure us by what they will,
We'll measure them a measure and be gone.
Rom. Give me a torch, I am not for this ambling;
Being but heavy, I will bear the light.
Mer. Nay, gentle Romeo, we must have you dance.
Rom. Not I, believe me. You have dancing shoes
With nimble soles, I have a soul of lead
So stakes me to the ground I cannot move.
Mer. You are a lover, borrow Cupid's wings,
And soar with them above a common bound.
Rom. I am too sore enpierced with his shaft
To soar with his light feathers, and so bound
I cannot bound a pitch above dull woe;
Under love's heavy burthen do I sink.
[*Mer.*] And, to sink in it, should you burthen love—
Too great oppression for a tender thing.
Rom. Is love a tender thing? It is too rough,
Too rude, too boist'rous, and it pricks like thorn.
Mer. If love be rough with you, be rough with love;
Prick love for pricking, and you beat love down.
Give me a case to put my visage in, [*Puts on a mask.*]
A visor for a visor! what care I
What curious eye doth cote deformities?
Here are the beetle brows shall blush for me.
Ben. Come knock and enter, and no sooner in,
But every man betake him to his legs.
Rom. A torch for me. Let wantons light of heart
Tickle the senseless rushes with their heels.
For I am proverb'd with a grandsire phrase,
I'll be a candle-holder and look on:
The game was ne'er so fair, and I am [done].
Mer. Tut, dun's the mouse, the constable's own word.
If thou art Dun, we'll draw thee from the mire
[Of this sir-]reverence love, wherein thou stickest
Up to the ears. Come, we burn daylight, ho!
Rom. Nay, that's not so.
Mer. I mean, sir, in delay
We waste our lights in vain, [like] lights by day!
Take our good meaning, for our judgment sits
Five times in that ere once in our [five] wits.
Rom. And we mean well in going to this mask,
But 'tis no wit to go.
Mer. Why, may one ask?
Rom. I dreamt a dream to-night.
Mer. And so did I.
Rom. Well, what was yours?
Mer. That dreamers often lie.
Rom. In bed asleep, while they do dream things true.
Mer. O then I see Queen Mab hath been with you.
She is the fairies' midwife, and she comes
In shape no bigger than an agot-stone
On the forefinger of an alderman,
Drawn with a team of little atomi
Over men's noses as they lie asleep.
Her chariot is an empty hazel-nut,
Made by the joiner squirrel or old grub,
Time out a' mind the fairies' coachmakers.
Her waggon-spokes made of long spinners' legs,
The cover of the wings of grasshoppers,
Her traces of the smallest spider web,
Her collars of the moonshine's wat'ry beams,
Her whip of cricket's bone, the lash of film,
Her waggoner a small grey-coated gnat,
Not half so big as a round little worm
Prick'd from the lazy finger of a [maid].

I.iv. Location: Verona. Before Capulet's house.
1. **speech.** Maskers, arriving thus to pay a complimentary visit at some festivity, would usually preface their masked dance with a speech by the "presenter."
3. **The date . . . prolixity:** such long-winded preliminaries are out of fashion.
4. **Cupid.** The presenter, often a boy, might well be dressed as Cupid. **hoodwink'd:** blindfolded (as part of the role).
5. **Tartar's painted bow.** The mounted Tartar archer presumably used a bow shorter and more curved than the English longbow, and hence closer in form to Cupid's lip-shaped bow.
6. **crow-keeper:** scarecrow.
7. **without-book:** memorized.
10. **measure them a measure:** deal them out a dance.
11. **torch.** As a torch-bearer, he would be disqualified from participation in the masking. 12. **heavy:** low-spirited.
18. **common bound:** ordinary leap (in dancing).
21. **pitch:** height (technical term in falconry).
23. **should . . . love:** i.e. you would have to make yourself a weight on the loved one. 26. **rude:** rough.
28. **Prick . . . pricking:** i.e. ease sexual desire by satisfying it.
29. **case:** mask. 30. **visor . . . visor:** mask . . . ugly face.
31. **cote:** quote, note. 34. **betake . . . legs:** join the dancing.
36. **senseless:** without feeling. **rushes.** Used for floor-covering.
37. **grandsire phrase:** old proverb ("A good candle-holder [i.e. onlooker] proves a good gamester").
39. **The game . . . done.** Alluding to another proverb, "He is wise who gives over when the game is fairest," i.e. when he is winning; but Romeo puns on *game* in the sense "quarry."
40. **dun's the mouse.** A proverb (arising as a quibble on Romeo's *done*) meaning "be silent and unseen"; hence the association with constables.
41. **Dun . . . mire.** In the Christmas game "Dun is in the mire" a log representing a horse stuck in the mud was hauled out by the players.
42. **sir-reverence.** There is a pun on a euphemism for dung; but Mercutio's main point is to apply the notion of "Dun is in the mire" to Romeo's confessed immersion in love.
43. **burn daylight:** waste time. Romeo pretends to take the phrase literally; hence Mercutio's injunction to him to take his "good meaning" (line 46), but Romeo continues his quibbling by taking this in the sense "meaning well."
46–47. **our . . . wits:** i.e. there is five times as much sense in what I mean as in what you hear me say (*five wits* = five senses).
49. **wit:** wisdom. 53. **Queen Mab.** Probably an invention of Shakespeare's, with play on *quean,* "slut." *Mab* was a stock name for a slut. 54. **midwife.** In the sense that she delivers men's dreams. 55. **agot-stone:** agate (often incised with figures and set in rings). 57. **atomi:** tiny creatures. 62. **spinners':** spiders' or (Cairncross) daddy-longlegs'.
68–69. **worm . . . maid.** An old wives' tale maintained that worms grew in the fingers of lazy girls.

And in this state she gallops night by night
Through lovers' brains, and then they dream of love;
[O'er] courtiers' knees, that dream on cur'sies straight;
O'er lawyers' fingers, who straight dream on fees;
O'er ladies' lips, who straight on kisses dream,
Which oft the angry Mab with blisters plagues,
Because their breath with sweetmeats tainted are.
Sometime she gallops o'er a courtier's nose,
And then dreams he of smelling out a suit;
And sometime comes she with a tithe-pig's tail
Tickling a parson's nose as 'a lies asleep,
Then he dreams of another benefice.
Sometime she driveth o'er a soldier's neck,
And then dreams he of cutting foreign throats,
Of breaches, ambuscadoes, Spanish blades,
Of healths five fadom deep; and then anon
Drums in his ear, at which he starts and wakes,
And being thus frighted, swears a prayer or two,
And sleeps again. This is that very Mab
That plats the manes of horses in the night,
And bakes the [elf-]locks in foul sluttish hairs,
Which, once untangled, much misfortune bodes.
This is the hag, when maids lie on their backs,
That presses them and learns them first to bear,
Making them women of good carriage.
This is she—

Rom. Peace, peace, Mercutio, peace!
Thou talk'st of nothing.

Mer. True, I talk of dreams,
Which are the children of an idle brain,
Begot of nothing but vain fantasy,
Which is as thin of substance as the air,
And more inconstant than the wind, who woos
Even now the frozen bosom of the north,
And, being anger'd, puffs away from thence,
Turning his side to the dew-dropping south.

Ben. This wind you talk of blows us from ourselves:
Supper is done, and we shall come too late.

Rom. I fear, too early, for my mind misgives
Some consequence yet hanging in the stars
Shall bitterly begin his fearful date
With this night's revels, and expire the term
Of a despised life clos'd in my breast
By some vile forfeit of untimely death.
But He that hath the steerage of my course
Direct my [sail]! On, lusty gentlemen!

Ben. Strike, drum.

They march about the stage [and stand to one side].

70. state: magnificence.
72. on: of. **cur'sies:** curtsies, i.e. bows.
78. smelling . . . suit: discovering a petitioner whose cause he can further at court in reward for a fee.
79. tithe-pig: pig paid as part of parish dues.
84. breaches: breaching fortifications. **ambuscadoes:** ambushes. **Spanish blades.** The best swords came from Toledo.
85. healths: toasts. **fadom:** fathoms.
90. elf-locks. The matted hair of slovenly people was thought to be the work of elves, who would take revenge if it were untangled.
93. learns: teaches.
94. carriage: (1) deportment; (2) supporting a lover's weight.
102. anger'd: i.e. by his lack of success with the cold north.
108. date: appointed time.
109. expire the term: terminate the duration.
111. untimely: premature.

[SCENE V]

And SERVINGMEN *come forth with napkins.*

[*1.*] *Serv.* Where's Potpan, that he helps not to take away? He shift a trencher? he scrape a trencher?

[*2.*] *Serv.* When good manners shall lie all in one or two men's hands, and they unwash'd too, 'tis a foul thing.

[*1.*] *Serv.* Away with the join-stools, remove the court-cubbert, look to the plate. Good thou, save me a piece of marchpane, and, as thou loves me, let the porter let in Susan Grindstone and Nell. [*Exit Second Servant.*] Anthony and Potpan!

[*Enter* ANTHONY *and* POTPAN.]

[*Ant.*] Ay, boy, ready.

[*1.*] *Serv.* You are look'd for and call'd for, ask'd for and sought for, in the great chamber.

[*Pot.*] We cannot be here and there too. Cheerly, boys, be brisk a while, and the longer liver take all.

Exeunt.

Enter [CAPULET, LADY CAPULET, JULIET, TYBALT, NURSE, SERVINGMEN, *and*] *all the* GUESTS *and* GENTLEWOMEN *to the Maskers.*

Cap. Welcome, gentlemen! Ladies that have their toes
Unplagu'd with corns will walk [a bout] with you.
Ah, my mistresses, which of you all
Will now deny to dance? She that makes dainty,
She I'll swear hath corns. Am I come near ye now?
Welcome, gentlemen! I have seen the day
That I have worn a visor and could tell
A whispering tale in a fair lady's ear,
Such as would please; 'tis gone, 'tis gone, 'tis gone.
You are welcome, gentlemen! Come, musicians, play.

Music plays, and they dance.

A hall, a hall! give room! and foot it, girls.
More light, you knaves, and turn the tables up;
And quench the fire, the room is grown too hot.
Ah, sirrah, this unlook'd-for sport comes well.
Nay, sit, nay, sit, good cousin Capulet,
For you and I are past our dancing days.
How long is't now since last yourself and I
Were in a mask?

2. Cap. By'r lady, thirty years.

Cap. What, man? 'tis not so much, 'tis not so much:
'Tis since the nuptial of Lucentio,
Come Pentecost as quickly as it will,
Some five and twenty years, and then we mask'd.

2. Cap. 'Tis more, 'tis more. His son is elder, sir;
His son is thirty.

Cap. Will you tell me that?

I.v. Location: Scene continues, now as a hall in Capulet's house.
2. trencher: wooden platter.
6. join-stools: joint-stools, stools expertly made by joiners.
7. court-cubbert: (variant of *cupboard*) sideboard. **plate:** silverware.
8. marchpane: marzipan.
15. the longer . . . all: the survivor takes all (proverbial), i.e. live merrily, enjoy life while it lasts. **17. walk a bout:** dance a turn.
19. makes dainty: behaves coyly (by refusing to dance).
20. come near ye: hitting close to the mark.
26. A hall: make room, clear the floor.

His son was but a ward two years ago.
Rom. [*To a Servingman.*] What lady's that which doth enrich the hand
Of yonder knight?
Serv. I know not, sir.
Rom. O, she doth teach the torches to burn bright!
It seems she hangs upon the cheek of night
As a rich jewel in an Ethiop's ear—
Beauty too rich for use, for earth too dear!
So shows a snowy dove trooping with crows,
As yonder lady o'er her fellows shows.
The measure done, I'll watch her place of stand,
And touching hers, make blessed my rude hand.
Did my heart love till now? Forswear it, sight!
For I ne'er saw true beauty till this night.
Tyb. This, by his voice, should be a Montague.
Fetch me my rapier, boy. What dares the slave
Come hither, cover'd with an antic face,
To fleer and scorn at our solemnity?
Now, by the stock and honor of my kin,
To strike him dead I hold it not a sin.
Cap. Why, how now, kinsman, wherefore storm you so?
Tyb. Uncle, this is a Montague, our foe;
A villain that is hither come in spite
To scorn at our solemnity this night.
Cap. Young Romeo is it?
Tyb. 'Tis he, that villain Romeo.
Cap. Content thee, gentle coz, let him alone,
'A bears him like a portly gentleman;
And to say truth, Verona brags of him
To be a virtuous and well-govern'd youth.
I would not for the wealth of all this town
Here in my house do him disparagement;
Therefore be patient, take no note of him;
It is my will, the which if thou respect,
Show a fair presence and put off these frowns,
An ill-beseeming semblance for a feast.
Tyb. It fits when such a villain is a guest.
I'll not endure him.
Cap. He shall be endured.
What, goodman boy? I say he shall, go to!
Am I the master here, or you? go to!
You'll not endure him! God shall mend my soul,
You'll make a mutiny among my guests!
You will set cock-a-hoop! you'll be the man!
Tyb. Why, uncle, 'tis a shame.
Cap. Go to, go to,
You are a saucy boy. Is't so indeed?
This trick may chance to scath you, I know what.
You must contrary me! Marry, 'tis time.—
Well said, my hearts!—You are a princox, go,
Be quiet, or—More light, more light!—For shame,
I'll make you quiet, what!—Cheerly, my hearts!
Tyb. Patience perforce with willful choler meeting
Makes my flesh tremble in their different greeting.
I will withdraw, but this intrusion shall,
Now seeming sweet, convert to bitt'rest gall. *Exit.*
Rom. [*To Juliet.*] If I profane with my unworthiest hand
This holy shrine, the gentle sin is this,
My lips, two blushing pilgrims, ready stand
To smooth that rough touch with a tender kiss.
Jul. Good pilgrim, you do wrong your hand too much,
Which mannerly devotion shows in this:
For saints have hands that pilgrims' hands do touch,
And palm to palm is holy palmers' kiss.
Rom. Have not saints lips, and holy palmers too?
Jul. Ay, pilgrim, lips that they must use in pray'r.
Rom. O then, dear saint, let lips do what hands do,
They pray—grant thou, lest faith turn to despair.
Jul. Saints do not move, though grant for prayers' sake.
Rom. Then move not while my prayer's effect I take. [*Kissing her.*]
Thus from my lips, by thine, my sin is purg'd.
Jul. Then have my lips the sin that they have took.
Rom. Sin from my lips? O trespass sweetly urg'd!
Give me my sin again. [*Kissing her again.*]
Jul. You kiss by th' book.
Nurse. Madam, your mother craves a word with you.
Rom. What is her mother?
Nurse. Marry, bachelor,
Her mother is the lady of the house,
And a good lady, and a wise and virtuous.
I nurs'd her daughter that you talk'd withal;
I tell you, he that can lay hold of her
Shall have the chinks.
Rom. Is she a Capulet?
O dear account! my life is my foe's debt.
Ben. Away, be gone, the sport is at the best.
Rom. Ay, so I fear, the more is my unrest.

40. a ward: under guardianship, not of age. **51. rude:** rough.
55. What: i.e. how. **56. antic face:** grotesque mask.
57. fleer: mock. **solemnity:** festivity. **64. villain:** base fellow.
66. 'A bears him: he conducts himself. **portly:** well-mannered.
77. goodman: title accorded a yeoman, i.e. one below the rank of a gentleman. Hence *goodman boy* is a double-barrelled insult to Tybalt.
80. mutiny: disturbance.
81. set cock-a-hoop: cast off restraint (?). The phrase is explained as referring originally to unrestrained drinking, with the cock or tap removed from the barrel or turned on full. But possibly the notion of a cock crowing (whooping) to proclaim his dominance is also present. **be the man:** play at being a man.
82. shame: insult.
84. trick: foolish behavior. **scath:** scathe, harm (probably a personal threat, "damage your expectations from me"). **I know what:** i.e. I know what I'll do to make you feel my displeasure (?).
85. contrary me: go against my will. **'tis time:** i.e. to teach you a lesson.
86. Well said: bravo (said to the dancers). **princox:** insolent boy.
89. Patience perforce: enforced forbearance.
90. their different greeting: the confrontation of these opposed states of mind.
93–106. These lines make a sonnet in the Shakespearean form.
94. shrine: image. **the gentle sin:** i.e. the sin gentlemen must commit in wooing ladies (?). Most editors emend *sin* to *fine* or *pain* (= penalty).
97. you . . . much: i.e. your touch was not rough (and hence no kiss is called for). **98. mannerly devotion:** proper devoutness.
100. palmers': pilgrims'.
105. move: institute an action. **grant:** they grant.
106. move not: remain still. **110. by th' book:** methodically.
112. What: who. **bachelor:** young man. **115. withal:** with.
117. chinks: money (probably, as Clifford Leech suggests in *TLS*, December 25, 1970, with an indecent pun).
118. dear account: heavy reckoning. **my foe's debt:** in the power of my enemy.
119. Away . . . best. He reminds Romeo of his earlier remark (I.iv.39).

Cap. Nay, gentlemen, prepare not to be gone,
We have a trifling foolish banquet towards.
[*They whisper in his ear.*]
Is it e'en so? Why then I thank you all.
I thank you, honest gentlemen, good night.
More torches here! Come on, then let's to bed.
[*To Second Capulet.*] Ah, sirrah, by my fay, it waxes late,
I'll to my rest. [*Exeunt all but Juliet and Nurse.*]
Jul. Come hither, nurse. What is yond gentleman?
Nurse. The son and heir of old Tiberio.
Jul. What's he that now is going out of door?
Nurse. Marry, that, I think, be young Petruchio.
Jul. What's he that follows here, that would not dance?
Nurse. I know not.
Jul. Go ask his name.—If he be married,
My grave is like to be my wedding-bed.
Nurse. His name is Romeo, and a Montague,
The only son of your great enemy.
Jul. My only love sprung from my only hate!
Too early seen unknown, and known too late!
Prodigious birth of love it is to me
That I must love a loathed enemy.
Nurse. What's tis? what's tis?
Jul. A rhyme I learnt even now
Of one I danc'd withal. *One calls within,* "Juliet!"
Nurse. Anon, anon!
Come let's away, the strangers all are gone. *Exeunt.*

[ACT II]

[*Enter*] Chorus.

Now old desire doth in his death-bed lie,
And young affection gapes to be his heir;
That fair for which love groan'd for and would die,
With tender Juliet [match'd] is now not fair.
Now Romeo is belov'd and loves again,
Alike bewitched by the charm of looks;
But to his foe suppos'd he must complain,
And she steal love's sweet bait from fearful hooks.
Being held a foe, he may not have access
To breathe such vows as lovers use to swear,
And she as much in love, her means much less
To meet her new-beloved any where.
But passion lends them power, time means, to meet,
Temp'ring extremities with extreme sweet. [*Exit.*]

[Scene I]

Enter Romeo *alone.*

Rom. Can I go forward when my heart is here?

122. **banquet:** refreshments (wine, fruit, etc.). **towards:** on the way
124. **honest:** worthy. 126. **fay:** faith.
140. **Prodigious:** ominous. 142. **tis:** i.e. this.
143. **Anon:** right away, coming.

II.Cho.2. **gapes:** longs. 3. **fair:** beautiful woman.
4. **match'd:** compared. 5. **again:** in return.
5. **Alike:** both lovers equally. 7. **complain:** i.e. of his love pains.
8. **fearful:** causing fear, dangerous. 10. **use:** are accustomed.
14. **Temp'ring:** moderating. **extremities:** i.e. their plight.

II.i. Location: Verona. Capulet's orchard.

Turn back, dull earth, and find thy centre out.

Enter Benvolio *with* Mercutio. [*Romeo withdraws.*]

Ben. Romeo! my cousin Romeo! Romeo!
Mer. He is wise,
And, on my life, hath stol'n him home to bed.
Ben. He ran this way and leapt this orchard wall.
Call, good Mercutio.
[*Mer.*] Nay, I'll conjure too.
Romeo! humors! madman! passion! lover!
Appear thou in the likeness of a sigh!
Speak but one rhyme, and I am satisfied;
Cry but "Ay me!", [pronounce] but "love" and ["dove"],
Speak to my gossip Venus one fair word,
One nickname for her purblind son and [heir],
Young Abraham Cupid, he that shot so [trim],
When King Cophetua lov'd the beggar-maid!
He heareth not, he stirreth not, he moveth not,
The ape is dead, and I must conjure him.
I conjure thee by Rosaline's bright eyes,
By her high forehead and her scarlet lip,
By her fine foot, straight leg, and quivering thigh,
And the demesnes that there adjacent lie,
That in thy likeness thou appear to us!
Ben. And if he hear thee, thou wilt anger him.
Mer. This cannot anger him; 'twould anger him
To raise a spirit in his mistress' circle,
Of some strange nature, letting it there stand
Till she had laid it and conjur'd it down.
That were some spite. My invocation
Is fair and honest; in his mistress' name
I conjure only but to raise up him.
Ben. Come, he hath hid himself among these trees
To be consorted with the humorous night.
Blind is his love and best befits the dark.
Mer. If love be blind, love cannot hit the mark.
Now will he sit under a medlar tree,
And wish his mistress were that kind of fruit
As maids call medlars, when they laugh alone.
O, Romeo, that she were, O that she were
An open[-arse], thou a pop'rin pear!
Romeo, good night, I'll to my truckle-bed,
This field-bed is too cold for me to sleep.
Come, shall we go?
Ben. Go then, for 'tis in vain
To seek him here that means not to be found.
Exit [*with Mercutio*].

2. **dull earth:** i.e. his body. **centre.** Juliet is the core of his being, and he will move toward her as things on earth fall toward its centre.
5. **orchard:** garden. 6. **conjure:** call up a spirit (Romeo's).
11. **gossip:** crony (very familiar, suggesting that Venus is a garrulous old woman). 12. **purblind:** dim-sighted.
13. **Abraham:** i.e. beggarly, thieving (alluding to the so-called "Abraham man," a beggar who wandered through the countryside half naked, picking up what he could). **trim:** adeptly, accurately. In the ballad of "King Cophetua and the Beggar Maid" Cupid is called "the blinded boy that shoots so trim."
16. **ape.** Often used playfully or as a term of endearment.
20. **demesnes:** estates. 22. **And if:** if.
24. **spirit.** With pun on the sense "semen," following a pun on *raise;* the double-entendre continues in *circle* and in the next two lines.
27. **spite:** vexation. 31. **humorous:** (1) damp; (2) moody.
34. **medlar:** apple-like fruit.
38. **open-arse:** another name for the medlar, with allusion to female pudenda. **pop'rin pear:** Flemish pear of phallic shape.
39. **truckle-bed:** low bed, made to fit under a larger.

[SCENE II]

[ROMEO *advances.*]

Rom. He jests at scars that never felt a wound.

[*Enter* JULIET *above at her window.*]

But soft, what light through yonder window breaks?
It is the east, and Juliet is the sun.
Arise, fair sun, and kill the envious moon,
Who is already sick and pale with grief
That thou, her maid, art far more fair than she.
Be not her maid, since she is envious;
Her vestal livery is but sick and green,
And none but fools do wear it; cast it off.
It is my lady, O, it is my love!
O that she knew she were!
She speaks, yet she says nothing; what of that?
Her eye discourses, I will answer it.
I am too bold, 'tis not to me she speaks.
Two of the fairest stars in all the heaven,
Having some business, [do] entreat her eyes
To twinkle in their spheres till they return.
What if her eyes were there, they in her head?
The brightness of her cheek would shame those stars,
As daylight doth a lamp; her [eyes] in heaven
Would through the airy region stream so bright
That birds would sing and think it were not night.
See how she leans her cheek upon her hand!
O that I were a glove upon that hand,
That I might touch that cheek!

Jul. Ay me!

Rom. She speaks!
O, speak again, bright angel, for thou art
As glorious to this night, being o'er my head,
As is a winged messenger of heaven
Unto the white-upturned wond'ring eyes
Of mortals that fall back to gaze on him,
When he bestrides the lazy puffing clouds,
And sails upon the bosom of the air.

Jul. O Romeo, Romeo, wherefore art thou Romeo?
Deny thy father and refuse thy name;
Or, if thou wilt not, be but sworn my love,
And I'll no longer be a Capulet.

Rom. [*Aside.*] Shall I hear more, or shall I speak at this?

Jul. 'Tis but thy name that is my enemy;
Thou art thyself, though not a Montague.
What's Montague? It is nor hand nor foot,
Nor arm nor face, [nor any other part]
Belonging to a man. O, be some other name!
What's in a name? That which we call a rose
By any other word would smell as sweet;
So Romeo would, were he not Romeo call'd,
Retain that dear perfection which he owes
Without that title. Romeo, doff thy name,
And for thy name, which is no part of thee,
Take all myself.

Rom. I take thee at thy word.
Call me but love, and I'll be new baptiz'd;
Henceforth I never will be Romeo.

Jul. What man art thou that thus bescreen'd in night
So stumblest on my counsel?

Rom. By a name
I know not how to tell thee who I am.
My name, dear saint, is hateful to myself,
Because it is an enemy to thee;
Had I it written, I would tear the word.

Jul. My ears have yet not drunk a hundred words
Of thy tongue's uttering, yet I know the sound.
Art thou not Romeo, and a Montague?

Rom. Neither, fair maid, if either thee dislike.

Jul. How camest thou hither, tell me, and wherefore?
The orchard walls are high and hard to climb,
And the place death, considering who thou art,
If any of my kinsmen find thee here.

Rom. With love's light wings did I o'erperch these walls,
For stony limits cannot hold love out,
And what love can do, that dares love attempt;
Therefore thy kinsmen are no stop to me.

Jul. If they do see thee, they will murther thee.

Rom. Alack, there lies more peril in thine eye
Than twenty of their swords! Look thou but sweet,
And I am proof against their enmity.

Jul. I would not for the world they saw thee here.

Rom. I have night's cloak to hide me from their eyes,
And but thou love me, let them find me here;
My life were better ended by their hate,
Than death prorogued, wanting of thy love.

Jul. By whose direction foundst thou out this place?

Rom. By love, that first did prompt me to inquire;
He lent me counsel, and I lent him eyes.
I am no pilot, yet, wert thou as far
As that vast shore [wash'd] with the farthest sea,
I should adventure for such merchandise.

Jul. Thou knowest the mask of night is on my face,
Else would a maiden blush bepaint my cheek
For that which thou hast heard me speak to-night.
Fain would I dwell on form, fain, fain deny
What I have spoke, but farewell compliment!
Dost thou love me? I know thou wilt say, "Ay,"
And I will take thy word; yet, if thou swear'st,
Thou mayest prove false: at lovers' perjuries

II.ii. Location: Scene continues.
7. maid: devotee (of the moon-goddess Diana, patroness of virgins).
8. sick and green. Alluding to a kind of anemia called "the green-sickness," supposed to be found in unmarried girls.
17. spheres. According to the Ptolemaic astronomy, the heavenly bodies were fixed in concentric transparent spheres that revolved around the earth. **21. stream:** shine.
29. white-upturned: turned upward so that the whites are visible below the irises.
39. Thou . . . Montague: i.e. you won't change yourself if you change your name.

46. owes: possesses. **48. for:** in exchange for.
53. counsel: private thoughts. **61. dislike:** displease.
66. o'erperch: fly over. **73. proof:** armored. **76. but:** unless.
78. prorogued: put off. **wanting of:** lacking.
83. vast: desolate. **84. adventure:** risk the voyage.
88. Fain: gladly. **dwell on form:** maintain formal behavior.
89. compliment: social conventions.

They say Jove laughs. O gentle Romeo,
If thou dost love, pronounce it faithfully;
Or if thou thinkest I am too quickly won,
I'll frown and be perverse, and say thee nay,
So thou wilt woo, but else not for the world.
In truth, fair Montague, I am too fond,
And therefore thou mayest think my behavior light,
But trust me, gentleman, I'll prove more true
Than those that have [more] coying to be strange.
I should have been more strange, I must confess,
But that thou overheardst, ere I was ware,
My true-love passion; therefore pardon me,
And not impute this yielding to light love,
Which the dark night hath so discovered.

Rom. Lady, by yonder blessed moon I vow,
That tips with silver all these fruit-tree tops—

Jul. O, swear not by the moon, th' inconstant moon,
That monthly changes in her [circled] orb,
Lest that thy love prove likewise variable.

Rom. What shall I swear by?

Jul. Do not swear at all;
Or if thou wilt, swear by thy gracious self,
Which is the god of my idolatry,
And I'll believe thee.

Rom. If my heart's dear love—

Jul. Well, do not swear. Although I joy in thee,
I have no joy of this contract to-night,
It is too rash, too unadvis'd, too sudden,
Too like the lightning, which doth cease to be
Ere one can say it lightens. Sweet, good night!
This bud of love, by summer's ripening breath,
May prove a beauteous flow'r when next we meet.
Good night, good night! as sweet repose and rest
Come to thy heart as that within my breast!

Rom. O, wilt thou leave me so unsatisfied?

Jul. What satisfaction canst thou have to-night?

Rom. Th' exchange of thy love's faithful vow for mine.

Jul. I gave thee mine before thou didst request it;
And yet I would it were to give again.

Rom. Wouldst thou withdraw it? for what purpose, love?

Jul. But to be frank and give it thee again,
And yet I wish but for the thing I have.
My bounty is as boundless as the sea,
My love as deep; the more I give to thee,
The more I have, for both are infinite.
[*Nurse calls within.*]
I hear some noise within; dear love, adieu!
Anon, good nurse! Sweet Montague, be true.
Stay but a little, I will come again. [*Exit above.*]

Rom. O blessed, blessed night! I am afeard,
Being in night, all this is but a dream,
Too flattering-sweet to be substantial.

[*Enter* JULIET *above.*]

Jul. Three words, dear Romeo, and good night indeed.
If that thy bent of love be honorable,
Thy purpose marriage, send me word to-morrow,
By one that I'll procure to come to thee,
Where and what time thou wilt perform the rite,
And all my fortunes at thy foot I'll lay,
And follow thee my lord throughout the world.

[*Nurse. Within.*] Madam!

Jul. I come, anon.—But if thou meanest not well,
I do beseech thee—

[*Nurse. Within.*] Madam!

Jul. By and by, I come—
To cease thy strife, and leave me to my grief.
To-morrow will I send.

Rom. So thrive my soul—

Jul. A thousand times good night! [*Exit above.*]

Rom. A thousand times the worse, to want thy light.
Love goes toward love as schoolboys from their books,
But love from love, toward school with heavy looks.
[*Retiring.*]

Enter JULIET *again* [*above*].

Jul. Hist, Romeo, hist! O, for a falc'ner's voice,
To lure this tassel-gentle back again!
Bondage is hoarse, and may not speak aloud,
Else would I tear the cave where Echo lies,
And make her airy tongue more hoarse than [mine],
With repetition of my [Romeo's name.] Romeo!

Rom. It is my soul that calls upon my name.
How silver-sweet sound lovers' tongues by night,
Like softest music to attending ears!

Jul. Romeo!

Rom. My [niesse]?

Jul. What a' clock to-morrow
Shall I send to thee?

Rom. By the hour of nine.

Jul. I will not fail, 'tis twenty year till then.
I have forgot why I did call thee back.

Rom. Let me stand here till thou remember it.

Jul. I shall forget, to have thee still stand there,
Rememb'ring how I love thy company.

Rom. And I'll still stay, to have thee still forget,
Forgetting any other home but this.

Jul. 'Tis almost morning, I would have thee gone—
And yet no farther than a wanton's bird,
That lets it hop a little from his hand,
Like a poor prisoner in his twisted gyves,
And with a silken thread plucks it back again,
So loving-jealous of his liberty.

Rom. I would I were thy bird.

Jul. Sweet, so would I,
Yet I should kill thee with much cherishing.

97. So thou wilt: i.e. in order to have you.
101. coying: skill at coquetry. **strange:** aloof, standoffish.
106. discovered: revealed.
110. circled orb: sphere (see note on line 17).
113. gracious: endowed with all graces of mind and body.
117. contract: exchange of promises.
118. rash: hasty. **unadvis'd:** ill-considered.
131. frank: generous. **137. Anon:** at once.

143. thy . . . love: the intention of your love.
151. By and by: immediately. **152. strife:** striving, endeavor.
158. Hist. She calls him as a falconer calls his hawk.
159. tassel-gentle: tercel-gentle, male falcon of a type reserved to princes. **167. niesse:** nestling hawk (disyllabic).
172. to: in order to. **still:** always.
177. wanton's: spoiled child's. **179. gyves:** fetters. **181. his:** its.

Good night, good night! Parting is such sweet sorrow,
That I shall say good night till it be morrow.
[*Exit above.*]

[*Rom.*] Sleep dwell upon thine eyes, peace in thy breast!
Would I were sleep and peace, so sweet to rest!
Hence will I to my ghostly [sire's] close cell,
His help to crave, and my dear hap to tell. *Exit.*

[Scene III]

Enter Friar [Lawrence] *alone, with a basket.*

Fri. L. The grey-ey'd morn smiles on the frowning night,
Check'ring the eastern clouds with streaks of light,
And fleckled darkness like a drunkard reels
From forth day's path and Titan's [fiery] wheels.
Now ere the sun advance his burning eye,
The day to cheer and night's dank dew to dry,
I must up-fill this osier cage of ours
With baleful weeds and precious-juiced flowers.
The earth that's nature's mother is her tomb;
What is her burying grave, that is her womb;
And from her womb children of divers kind
We sucking on her natural bosom find:
Many for many virtues excellent,
None but for some, and yet all different.
O, mickle is the powerful grace that lies
In plants, herbs, stones, and their true qualities;
For nought so vile that on the earth doth live
But to the earth some special good doth give;
Nor aught so good but, strain'd from that fair use,
Revolts from true birth, stumbling on abuse.
Virtue itself turns vice, being misapplied,
And vice sometime by action dignified.

Enter Romeo.

Within the infant rind of this weak flower
Poison hath residence and medicine power;
For this, being smelt, with that part cheers each part,
Being tasted, stays all senses with the heart.
Two such opposed kings encamp them still
In man as well as herbs, grace and rude will;
And where the worser is predominant,
Full soon the canker death eats up that plant.

Rom. Good morrow, father.

Fri. L. *Benedicite!*
What early tongue so sweet saluteth me?
Young son, it argues a distempered head
So soon to bid good morrow to thy bed.
Care keeps his watch in every old man's eye,
And where care lodges, sleep will never lie;
But where unbruised youth with unstuff'd brain
Doth couch his limbs, there golden sleep doth reign.
Therefore thy earliness doth me assure
Thou art up-rous'd with some distemp'rature;
Or if not so, then here I hit it right—
Our Romeo hath not been in bed to-night.

Rom. That last is true—the sweeter rest was mine.

Fri. L. God pardon sin! Wast thou with Rosaline?

Rom. With Rosaline? my ghostly father, no;
I have forgot that name, and that name's woe.

Fri. L. That's my good son, but where hast thou been then?

Rom. I'll tell thee ere thou ask it me again.
I have been feasting with mine enemy,
Where on a sudden one hath wounded me
That's by me wounded; both our remedies
Within thy help and holy physic lies.
I bear no hatred, blessed man, for lo
My intercession likewise steads my foe.

Fri. L. Be plain, good son, and homely in thy drift,
Riddling confession finds but riddling shrift.

Rom. Then plainly know my heart's dear love is set
On the fair daughter of rich Capulet.
As mine on hers, so hers is set on mine,
And all combin'd, save what thou must combine
By holy marriage. When and where and how
We met, we woo'd, and made exchange of vow,
I'll tell thee as we pass, but this I pray,
That thou consent to marry us to-day.

Fri. L. Holy Saint Francis, what a change is here!
Is Rosaline, that thou didst love so dear,
So soon forsaken? Young men's love then lies
Not truly in their hearts, but in their eyes.
Jesu Maria, what a deal of brine
Hath wash'd thy sallow cheeks for Rosaline!
How much salt water thrown away in waste,
To season love, that of it doth not taste!
The sun not yet thy sighs from heaven clears,
Thy old groans yet ringing in mine ancient ears;
Lo here upon thy cheek the stain doth sit
Of an old tear that is not wash'd off yet.
If e'er thou wast thyself and these woes thine,
Thou and these woes were all for Rosaline.
And art thou chang'd? Pronounce this sentence then:
Women may fall, when there's no strength in men.

Rom. Thou chidst me oft for loving Rosaline.

Fri. L. For doting, not for loving, pupil mine.

Rom. And badst me bury love.

Fri. L. Not in a grave,

188. ghostly sire: spiritual father, confessor. **close:** secluded (?) or narrow (?). **189. dear hap:** good fortune.

II.iii. Location: Verona. Friar Lawrence's cell.
3. fleckled: dappled.
4. From forth: out of the way of. **Titan's fiery wheels:** the sun-god's chariot wheels.
7. osier cage: willow basket. **13. virtues:** properties, powers.
14. None . . . some: none without some (virtue).
15. mickle: great. **powerful grace:** gracious (i.e. healing) power.
16. true: inherent. **20. true birth:** innate goodness.
21. turns: turns into.
22. by action dignified: may in special circumstances have the quality of a virtue.
25. that part: i.e. the odor. **each part:** i.e. of the body.
26. stays: brings to a halt. **30. canker:** plant-destroying worm.
31. Benedicite: bless you.

33. distempered: disordered, disturbed.
37. unbruised: i.e. not yet injured by life. **unstuff'd:** unburdened, carefree.
52. physic: power to heal (by performing the marriage rite).
54. intercession: petition. **steads:** helps. **55. homely:** plain.
56. shrift: absolution. **63. pass:** go along, proceed.
72. season: preserve (with following play on the sense "flavor").
73. sighs. Thought of as producing mist.
79. sentence: moral saying.

To lay one in, another out to have.
Rom. I pray thee chide me not. Her I love now
Doth grace for grace and love for love allow;
The other did not so.
Fri. L. O, she knew well
Thy love did read by rote that could not spell.
But come, young waverer, come go with me,
In one respect I'll thy assistant be;
For this alliance may so happy prove
To turn your households' rancor to pure love.
Rom. O, let us hence, I stand on sudden haste.
Fri. L. Wisely and slow, they stumble that run fast. *Exeunt.*

[Scene IV]

Enter Benvolio *and* Mercutio.

Mer. Where the dev'l should this Romeo be?
Came he not home to-night?
Ben. Not to his father's, I spoke with his man.
Mer. Why, that same pale hard-hearted wench, that Rosaline,
Torments him so, that he will sure run mad.
Ben. Tybalt, the kinsman to old Capulet,
Hath sent a letter to his father's house.
Mer. A challenge, on my life.
Ben. Romeo will answer it.

Mer. Any man that can write may answer a letter.

Ben. Nay, he will answer the letter's master, how he dares, being dar'd.

Mer. Alas, poor Romeo, he is already dead, stabb'd with a white wench's black eye, run through the ear with a love-song, the very pin of his heart cleft with the blind bow-boy's butt-shaft; and is he a man to encounter Tybalt?

[*Ben.*] Why, what is Tybalt?

Mer. More than Prince of Cats. O, he's the courageous captain of compliments. He fights as you sing prick-song, keeps time, distance, and proportion; he rests his minim rests, one, two, and the third in your bosom: the very butcher of a silk button, a duellist, a duellist; a gentleman of the very first house, of the first and second cause. Ah, the immortal *passado*, the *punto reverso*, the *hay!*

Ben. The what?

Mer. The pox of such antic, lisping, affecting [phantasimes], these new tuners of accent! "By Jesu, a very good blade! a very tall man! a very good whore!" Why, is not this a lamentable thing, grandsire, that we should be thus afflicted with these strange flies, these fashion-mongers, these [pardon-]me's, who stand so much on the new form, that they cannot sit at ease on the old bench? O, their bones, their bones!

Enter Romeo.

Ben. Here comes Romeo, here comes Romeo.

Mer. Without his roe, like a dried herring: O flesh, flesh, how art thou fishified! Now is he for the numbers that Petrarch flow'd in. Laura to his lady was a kitchen wench (marry, she had a better love to berhyme her), Dido a dowdy, Cleopatra a gipsy, Helen and Hero hildings and harlots, Thisby a grey eye or so, but not to the purpose. Signior Romeo, *bon jour!* there's a French salutation to your French slop. You gave us the counterfeit fairly last night.

Rom. Good morrow to you both. What counterfeit did I give you?

Mer. The slip, sir, the slip, can you not conceive?

Rom. Pardon, good Mercutio, my business was great, and in such a case as mine a man may strain courtesy.

Mer. That's as much as to say, such a case as yours constrains a man to bow in the hams.

Rom. Meaning to cur'sy.

Mer. Thou hast most kindly hit it.

Rom. A most courteous exposition.

Mer. Nay, I am the very pink of courtesy.

Rom. Pink for flower.

Mer. Right.

Rom. Why then is my pump well flower'd.

Mer. Sure wit! Follow me this jest now, till thou hast worn out thy pump, that when the single sole of it is worn, the jest may remain, after the wearing, soly singular.

86. **grace:** favor.
88. **did . . . spell:** not being able to read, pretended to do so by reciting what it had learned by heart; i.e. Romeo had only imitated true love. 90. **In one respect:** for one good reason.
92. **To:** as to. 93. **stand:** insist.

II.iv. Location: Verona. A street.
2. **to-night:** last night. 9. **answer it:** accept the challenge.
11. **how:** as. 15. **pin:** peg in the centre of an archery target.
16. **butt-shaft:** blunt arrow for practice, often assigned to Cupid, presumably because he was represented as a child.
19. **Prince of Cats.** In *Reynard the Fox* the Prince of Cats is named Tibalt.
20. **captain of compliments:** master of duelling punctilio.
21. **prick-song:** printed music. Tybalt fights with studied accuracy, like singers who perform from printed music in contrast to those who sing by ear.
22. **proportion:** rhythm. **minim rests:** the shortest rests in music.
23. **butcher . . . button.** An expert could strike any designated button on his opponent's clothing.
24. **duellist.** A word newly introduced into English.
24–25. **first house:** best school of fencing.
25. **first . . . cause.** These were occasions upon which a gentleman ought to take offense and require satisfaction.
26. **passado:** forward thrust. **punto reverso:** backhanded thrust. **hay:** home thrust (apparently a new term to Benvolio).
28–29. **affecting phantasimes:** affected coxcombs.
29. **new . . . accent:** utterers of newfangled phrases.
30. **tall:** brave.
31–32. **grandsire.** He addresses Benvolio, pretending they are old men complaining of the follies of the young.
33. **pardon-me's:** fellows of affected manners.
34. **form:** fashion (with following play on the sense "bench").
35. **bones.** With pun on French *bons*, "good" (plural).
37. **Without his roe:** i.e. looking very thin (lovers were expected to have poor appetites); with play on the first syllable of *Romeo*.
38–39. **numbers:** verses.
39. **Laura:** beloved of Petrarch. All the ladies named in this passage were heroines of famous love stories. **to:** in comparison with.
42. **hildings:** good-for-nothings.
43. **to the purpose:** worth mentioning.
44–45. **French slop:** loose breeches.
48. **The slip.** Counterfeit coins were called *slips*. **can . . . conceive:** i.e. what's the matter with your brain.
50–51. **strain courtesy:** transgress good manners. But Mercutio jocularly interprets Romeo's apology as a description of a man with a venereal infection.
55. **kindly:** naturally, truly. 57. **pink:** flower, i.e. acme.
60. **pump:** shoe. **flower'd:** i.e. pinked, perforated in a decorative pattern. 62. **single:** i.e. thin.
63–64. **soly singular:** quite alone (*soly* is a variant of *solely*).

Rom. O single-sol'd jest, soly singular for the singleness!

Mer. Come between us, good Benvolio, my wits faints.

Rom. Swits and spurs, swits and spurs, or I'll cry a match.

Mer. Nay, if our wits run the wild-goose chase, I am done; for thou hast more of the wild goose in one of thy wits than, I am sure, I have in my whole five. Was I with you there for the goose?

Rom. Thou wast never with me for any thing when thou wast not there for the goose.

Mer. I will bite thee by the ear for that jest.

Rom. Nay, good goose, bite not.

Mer. Thy wit is a very bitter sweeting, it is a most sharp sauce.

Rom. And is it not then well serv'd in to a sweet goose?

Mer. O, here's a wit of cheverel, that stretches from an inch narrow to an ell broad!

Rom. I stretch it out for that word "broad," which, added to the goose, proves thee far and wide a broad goose.

Mer. Why, is not this better now than groaning for love? Now art thou sociable, now art thou Romeo; now art thou what thou art, by art as well as by nature, for this drivelling love is like a great natural that runs lolling up and down to hide his bable in a hole.

Ben. Stop there, stop there.

Mer. Thou desirest me to stop in my tale against the hair.

Ben. Thou wouldst else have made thy tale large.

Mer. O, thou art deceiv'd; I would have made it short, for I was come to the whole depth of my tale, and meant indeed to occupy the argument no longer.

Rom. Here's goodly gear!

Enter NURSE *and her man* [PETER].

A sail, a sail!

Mer. Two, two: a shirt and a smock.

Nurse. Peter!

Pet. Anon!

Nurse. My fan, Peter.

Mer. Good Peter, to hide her face, for her fan's the fairer face.

Nurse. God ye good morrow, gentlemen.

Mer. God ye good den, fair gentlewoman.

Nurse. Is it good den?

Mer. 'Tis no less, I tell ye, for the bawdy hand of the dial is now upon the prick of noon.

Nurse. Out upon you, what a man are you?

Rom. One, gentlewoman, that God hath made, himself to mar.

Nurse. By my troth, it is well said; "for himself to mar," quoth 'a! Gentlemen, can any of you tell me where I may find the young Romeo?

Rom. I can tell you, but young Romeo will be older when you have found him than he was when you sought him. I am the youngest of that name, for fault of a worse.

Nurse. You say well.

Mer. Yea, is the worst well? Very well took, i' faith, wisely, wisely.

Nurse. If you be he, sir, I desire some confidence with you.

Ben. She will indite him to some supper.

Mer. A bawd, a bawd, a bawd! So ho!

Rom. What hast thou found?

Mer. No hare, sir, unless a hare, sir, in a lenten pie, that is something stale and hoar ere it be spent.

[*He walks by them and sings.*]

An old hare hoar,
And an old hare hoar,
Is very good meat in Lent;
But a hare that is hoar
Is too much for a score,
When it hoars ere it be spent.

Romeo, will you come to your father's? We'll to dinner thither.

Rom. I will follow you.

Mer. Farewell, ancient lady, farewell, [*singing*] "lady, lady, lady." *Exeunt* [*Mercutio and Benvolio*].

Nurse. I pray you, sir, what saucy merchant was this, that was so full of his ropery?

Rom. A gentleman, nurse, that loves to hear himself talk, and will speak more in a minute than he will stand to in a month.

Nurse. And 'a speak any thing against me, I'll take him down, and 'a were lustier than he is, and twenty such Jacks; and if I cannot, I'll find those that shall. Scurvy knave, I am none of his flirt-gills, I am none of his skains-mates. [*She turns to Peter, her man.*] And thou must stand by too and suffer every knave to use me at his pleasure!

65. single-sol'd: i.e. feeble.
65–66. soly . . . singleness: in a class by itself for silliness.
69. Swits and spurs: switch and spurs, i.e. keep up the rapid pace.
69–70. cry a match: claim the victory.
71. wild-goose chase: mounted follow-the-leader.
72. done: done for.
74. Was . . . goose: did I score off you with that word *goose*.
76. for the goose: (1) behaving like a goose; (2) looking for a prostitute (slang sense of *goose*). **79. sweeting:** kind of apple.
83. cheverel: kid leather, easily stretched. **84. ell:** 45 inches.
87. broad: large, i.e. obvious; perhaps with a pun on the sense "indecent" (cf. *large* in line 97, which has this sense for one of its meanings).
92. natural: idiot. **lolling:** with his tongue hanging out.
93. bable: bauble, stick carried by a court jester or "natural," with secondary meaning "penis," as also in *tale* (lines 95, 97) and *gear* (line 101). *Occupy* (line 100) is included in the wordplay.
95–96. against the hair: against my wish (with sexual innuendo).
103. shirt . . . smock: man . . . woman.
111. Is . . . den: i.e. is it already past noon.
113. prick: mark on a sundial or clock (with another bawdy pun).
114. what a man: what kind of man. **117. troth:** faith.
127. confidence: i.e. conference (malapropism).
129. indite: i.e. invite (intentional malapropism).
130. So ho: hunter's cry when sighting a hare. (*Bawd* is a dialect word for "hare," and *hare*, like *stale* in line 133 and *meat* in line 137, is slang for "prostitute."
132. lenten pie. This should contain no meat; perhaps one might put in it an old poached hare from the black market. (Mercutio is insulting the Nurse.)
133. hoar: mouldy (with pun on *whore*). **spent:** eaten up.
138. too . . . score: not worth paying for (*score* = reckoning, bill).
144. lady, lady, lady: a ballad refrain.
145. merchant: fellow. **146. ropery:** knavery.
150–51. take him down: humble him (with unintended bawdy second meaning).
152. Jacks: saucy fellows. **153. flirt-gills:** loose women.
154. skains-mates: derogatory term not occurring elsewhere.

Pet. I saw no man use you at his pleasure; if I had, my weapon should quickly have been out. I warrant you, I dare draw as soon as another man, if I see occasion in a good quarrel, and the law on my side.

Nurse. Now, afore God, I am so vex'd that every part about me quivers. Scurvy knave! Pray you, sir, a word: and as I told you, my young lady bid me inquire you out; what she bid me say, I will keep to myself. But first let me tell ye, if ye should lead her in a fool's paradise, as they say, it were a very gross kind of behavior, as they say; for the gentlewoman is young; and therefore, if you should deal double with her, truly it were an ill thing to be off'red to any gentlewoman, and very weak dealing.

Rom. Nurse, commend me to thy lady and mistress. I protest unto thee—

Nurse. Good heart, and, i' faith, I will tell her as much. Lord, Lord, she will be a joyful woman.

Rom. What wilt thou tell her, nurse? Thou dost not mark me.

Nurse. I will tell her, sir, that you do protest, which, as I take it, is a gentleman-like offer.

Rom. Bid her devise
Some means to come to shrift this afternoon,
And there she shall at Friar Lawrence' cell
Be shriv'd and married. Here is for thy pains.

Nurse. No, truly, sir, not a penny.

Rom. Go to, I say you shall.

Nurse. This afternoon, sir? Well, she shall be there.

Rom. And stay, good nurse—behind the abbey wall
Within this hour my man shall be with thee,
And bring thee cords made like a tackled stair,
Which to the high top-gallant of my joy
Must be my convoy in the secret night.
Farewell, be trusty, and I'll quit thy pains.
Farewell, commend me to thy mistress.

Nurse. Now God in heaven bless thee! Hark you, sir.

Rom. What say'st thou, my dear nurse?

Nurse. Is your man secret? Did you ne'er hear say,
"Two may keep counsel, putting one away"?

Rom. 'Warrant thee, my man's as true as steel.

Nurse. Well, sir, my mistress is the sweetest lady—Lord, Lord! when 'twas a little prating thing—O, there is a nobleman in town, one Paris, that would fain lay knife aboard; but she, good soul, had as lieve see a toad, a very toad, as see him. I anger her sometimes and tell her that Paris is the properer man, but I'll warrant you, when I say so, she looks as pale as any clout in the versal world. Doth not rosemary and Romeo begin both with a letter?

Rom. Ay, nurse, what of that? Both with an R.

Nurse. Ah, mocker, that's the [dog's] name. R is for the—no, I know it begins with some other letter—and she hath the prettiest sententious of it, of you and rosemary, that it would do you good to hear it.

Rom. Commend me to thy lady.

Nurse. Ay, a thousand times. [*Exit Romeo.*] Peter!

Pet. Anon!

Nurse. [*Handing him her fan.*] Before, and apace.

Exit [*after Peter*].

[Scene V]

Enter Juliet.

Jul. The clock strook nine when I did send the nurse;
In half an hour she promised to return.
Perchance she cannot meet him—that's not so.
O, she is lame! Love's heralds should be thoughts,
Which ten times faster glides than the sun's beams,
Driving back shadows over low'ring hills;
Therefore do nimble-pinion'd doves draw Love,
And therefore hath the wind-swift Cupid wings.
Now is the sun upon the highmost hill
Of this day's journey, and from nine till twelve
Is [three] long hours, yet she is not come.
Had she affections and warm youthful blood,
She would be as swift in motion as a ball;
My words would bandy her to my sweet love,
And his to me.
But old folks—many feign as they were dead,
Unwieldy, slow, heavy, and pale as lead.

Enter Nurse [*and* Peter].

O God, she comes! O honey nurse, what news?
Hast thou met with him? Send thy man away.

Nurse. Peter, stay at the gate. [*Exit Peter.*]

Jul. Now, good sweet nurse—O Lord, why lookest thou sad?
Though news be sad, yet tell them merrily;
If good, thou shamest the music of sweet news
By playing it to me with so sour a face.

Nurse. I am a-weary, give me leave a while.
Fie, how my bones ache! What a jaunce have I!

Jul. I would thou hadst my bones, and I thy news.
Nay, come, I pray thee speak, good, good nurse, speak.

Nurse. Jesu, what haste! Can you not stay a while?
Do you not see that I am out of breath?

Jul. How art thou out of breath, when thou hast breath

157–58. I . . . out. Peter joins in the indecent quibbling.
170. weak: poor, mean. **171. commend me:** give my regards.
172. protest: solemnly affirm. **176. mark:** pay attention to.
189. tackled stair: rope ladder.
190. top-gallant: highest mast of a ship.
191. convoy: means of passage (continuing the nautical figure).
192. quit: reward.
196. secret: to be trusted with confidential information.
197. keep counsel: keep a secret. **putting one away:** if one of them is away. Cf. the more optimistic variant of this proverb in *Titus Andronicus*, IV.iii.144: "Two may keep counsel when the third's away." **202. lay knife aboard:** i.e. press his claim.
203. lieve: lief, willingly. **204. properer:** handsomer.

206. clout: (white) cloth. **versal:** i.e. universal, entire.
207. a letter: the same letter.
209. dog's name. The letter *r* was called *littera canina*, "the dog's letter," because its sound was thought to resemble a dog's growl.
211. sententious: i.e. sentences, sayings.

II.v. Location: Verona. Capulet's orchard.
7. draw Love: pull Venus (in her chariot). **14. bandy:** toss.
26. jaunce: jouncing, i.e. tiring journey. **29. stay:** wait.

To say to me that thou art out of breath?
The excuse that thou dost make in this delay
Is longer than the tale thou dost excuse.
Is thy news good or bad? Answer to that.
Say either, and I'll stay the circumstance.
Let me be satisfied, is't good or bad?

Nurse. Well, you have made a simple choice, you know not how to choose a man. Romeo! no, not he. Though his face be better than any man's, yet his leg excels all men's, and for a hand and a foot and a body, though they be not to be talk'd on, yet they are past compare. He is not the flower of courtesy, but I'll warrant him, as gentle as a lamb. Go thy ways, wench, serve God. What, have you din'd at home?

Jul. No, no! But all this did I know before.
What says he of our marriage? what of that?

Nurse. Lord, how my head aches! What a head have I!
It beats as it would fall in twenty pieces.
My back a' t' other side—ah, my back, my back!
Beshrew your heart for sending me about
To catch my death with jauncing up and down!

Jul. I' faith, I am sorry that thou art not well.
Sweet, sweet, sweet nurse, tell me, what says my love?

Nurse. Your love says, like an honest gentleman,
An' a courteous, and a kind, and a handsome,
And, I warrant, a virtuous—Where is your mother?

Jul. Where is my mother! why, she is within,
Where should she be? How oddly thou repliest!
"Your love says, like an honest gentleman,
'Where is your mother?' "

Nurse. O God's lady dear!
Are you so hot? Marry, come up, I trow;
Is this the poultice for my aching bones?
Henceforward do your messages yourself.

Jul. Here's such a coil! Come, what says Romeo?

Nurse. Have you got leave to go to shrift to-day?

Jul. I have.

Nurse. Then hie you hence to Friar Lawrence' cell,
There stays a husband to make you a wife.
Now comes the wanton blood up in your cheeks,
They'll be in scarlet straight at any news.
Hie you to church, I must another way,
To fetch a ladder, by the which your love
Must climb a bird's nest soon when it is dark.
I am the drudge, and toil in your delight;
But you shall bear the burthen soon at night.
Go, I'll to dinner, hie you to the cell.

Jul. Hie to high fortune! Honest nurse, farewell.
Exeunt.

[Scene VI]

Enter Friar [Lawrence] *and* Romeo.

Fri. L. So smile the heavens upon this holy act,
That after-hours with sorrow chide us not!

Rom. Amen, amen! but come what sorrow can,
It cannot countervail the exchange of joy
That one short minute gives me in her sight.
Do thou but close our hands with holy words,
Then love-devouring death do what he dare,
It is enough I may but call her mine.

Fri. L. These violent delights have violent ends,
And in their triumph die, like fire and powder,
Which as they kiss consume. The sweetest honey
Is loathsome in his own deliciousness,
And in the taste confounds the appetite.
Therefore love moderately: long love doth so;
Too swift arrives as tardy as too slow.

Enter Juliet.

Here comes the lady. O, so light a foot
Will ne'er wear out the everlasting flint;
A lover may bestride the gossamers
That idles in the wanton summer air,
And yet not fall; so light is vanity.

Jul. Good even to my ghostly confessor.

Fri. L. Romeo shall thank thee, daughter, for us both.

Jul. As much to him, else is his thanks too much.

Rom. Ah, Juliet, if the measure of thy joy
Be heap'd like mine, and that thy skill be more
To blazon it, then sweeten with thy breath
This neighbor air, and let rich [music's] tongue
Unfold the imagin'd happiness that both
Receive in either by this dear encounter.

Jul. Conceit, more rich in matter than in words,
Brags of his substance, not of ornament;
They are but beggars that can count their worth,
But my true love is grown to such excess
I cannot sum up sum of half my wealth.

Fri. L. Come, come with me, and we will make short work,
For by your leaves, you shall not stay alone
Till Holy Church incorporate two in one. [*Exeunt.*]

[ACT III, Scene I]

Enter Mercutio, Benvolio, [Page,] *and* Men.

Ben. I pray thee, good Mercutio, let's retire.
The day is hot, the Capels [are] abroad,
And if we meet we shall not scape a brawl,
For now, these hot days, is the mad blood stirring.

Mer. Thou art like one of these fellows that, when he enters the confines of a tavern, claps me his sword upon the table, and says, "God send me no need of

36. stay the circumstance: wait for the details. **38. simple:** foolish.
42. be not . . . on: are nothing to talk about. **50. a' t':** on the.
51. Beshrew your heart: a mild imprecation (literally, *beshrew* = a curse on). **55. honest:** honorable.
62. hot: impatient. **Marry, come up:** an expression of reproof, implying that Juliet is getting above herself. **65. coil:** fuss.
68. hie: hasten. **70. wanton:** undisciplined, impetuous.
71. They'll . . . news: i.e. you've always blushed easily.
II.vi. Location: Verona. Friar Lawrence's cell.

4. countervail: equal. **13. confounds:** destroys.
18. gossamers: threads spun by spiders. **19. wanton:** sportive.
20. vanity: transitory earthly joy.
23. As much: the same greeting. She returns Romeo's kiss.
24–25. if . . . that: if . . . if.
26. blazon: describe, proclaim.
28. imagin'd: felt within (but not expressed).
30. Conceit: understanding. **31. Brags of:** takes pride in.
34. sum up sum: calculate the total.

III.i. Location: Verona. A public place.
6. claps me: claps (a colloquialism).

thee!" and by the operation of the second cup draws him on the drawer, when indeed there is no need.

Ben. Am I like such a fellow?

Mer. Come, come, thou art as hot a Jack in thy mood as any in Italy, and as soon mov'd to be moody, and as soon moody to be mov'd.

Ben. And what to?

Mer. Nay, and there were two such, we should have none shortly, for one would kill the other. Thou? why, thou wilt quarrel with a man that hath a hair more or a hair less in his beard than thou hast. Thou wilt quarrel with a man for cracking nuts, having no other reason but because thou hast hazel eyes. What eye but such an eye would spy out such a quarrel? Thy head is as full of quarrels as an egg is full of meat, and yet thy head hath been beaten as addle as an egg for quarrelling. Thou hast quarrell'd with a man for coughing in the street, because he hath waken'd thy dog that hath lain asleep in the sun. Didst thou not fall out with a tailor for wearing his new doublet before Easter? with another for tying his new shoes with old riband? and yet thou wilt tutor me from quarrelling!

Ben. And I were so apt to quarrel as thou art, any man should buy the fee-simple of my life for an hour and a quarter.

Mer. The fee-simple! O simple!

Enter TYBALT, PETRUCHIO, *and others.*

Ben. By my head, here comes the Capulets.
Mer. By my heel, I care not.
Tyb. Follow me close, for I will speak to them.
Gentlemen, good den, a word with one of you.

Mer. And but one word with one of us? Couple it with something, make it a word and a blow.

Tyb. You shall find me apt enough to that, sir, and you will give me occasion.

Mer. Could you not take some occasion without giving?

Tyb. Mercutio, thou consortest with Romeo—

Mer. Consort! what, dost thou make us minstrels? And thou make minstrels of us, look to hear nothing but discords. Here's my fiddlestick, here's that shall make you dance. 'Zounds, consort!

Ben. We talk here in the public haunt of men.
Either withdraw unto some private place,
Or reason coldly of your grievances,
Or else depart; here all eyes gaze on us.
Mer. Men's eyes were made to look, and let them gaze;
I will not budge for no man's pleasure, I.

Enter ROMEO.

Tyb. Well, peace be with you, sir, here comes my man.
Mer. But I'll be hang'd, sir, if he wear your livery.
Marry, go before to field, he'll be your follower;
Your worship in that sense may call him man.
Tyb. Romeo, the love I bear thee can afford
No better term than this: thou art a villain.
Rom. Tybalt, the reason that I have to love thee
Doth much excuse the appertaining rage
To such a greeting. Villain am I none;
Therefore farewell, I see thou knowest me not.
Tyb. Boy, this shall not excuse the injuries
That thou hast done me, therefore turn and draw.
Rom. I do protest I never injuried thee,
But love thee better than thou canst devise,
Till thou shalt know the reason of my love,
And so, good Capulet—which name I tender
As dearly as mine own—be satisfied.
Mer. O calm, dishonorable, vile submission!
Alla stoccato carries it away. [*Draws.*]
Tybalt, you rat-catcher, will you walk?
Tyb. What wouldst thou have with me?

Mer. Good King of Cats, nothing but one of your nine lives; that I mean to make bold withal, and as you shall use me hereafter, dry-beat the rest of the eight. Will you pluck your sword out of his pilcher by the ears? Make haste, lest mine be about your ears ere it be out.

Tyb. I am for you. [*Drawing.*]
Rom. Gentle Mercutio, put thy rapier up.
Mer. Come, sir, your *passado*. [*They fight.*]
Rom. Draw, Benvolio, beat down their weapons.
Gentlemen, for shame, forbear this outrage!
Tybalt, Mercutio, the Prince expressly hath
Forbid this bandying in Verona streets.
[*Romeo steps between them.*]
Hold, Tybalt! Good Mercutio!
[*Tybalt under Romeo's arm thrusts Mercutio in.*]
Away Tybalt [*with his followers*].
Mer. I am hurt.
A plague a' both houses! I am sped.
Is he gone and hath nothing?
Ben. What, art thou hurt?
Mer. Ay, ay, a scratch, a scratch, marry, 'tis enough.

8–9. **draws . . . drawer:** draws his sword against the tapster.
12. **moody:** angry. 15. **two:** A quibble on Benvolio's *to.*
23. **meat:** i.e. edible matter.
24. **addle:** addled, i.e. muddled (with reference to brains), rotten (with reference to eggs).
28. **doublet:** jacket.
29. **riband:** ribbon. **tutor me from:** instruct me against.
32. **fee-simple:** absolute ownership.
46. **Consort.** Mercutio takes the word in the sense "play music with." A group of musicians was called a consort. **minstrels.** A disparaging term; cf. IV.v.115.
48. **fiddlestick:** i.e. rapier.
49. **'Zounds:** by God's (Christ's) wounds.
52. **reason coldly of:** discuss calmly. 53. **depart:** part company.
57. **livery.** Mercutio pretends to interpret *my man* as "my servant." Similarly, *follower* (line 58) plays on the sense "attendant."
58. **field:** duelling-place.
59. **man:** i.e. one worthy to be called a man.
63. **excuse . . . rage:** abate the angry reaction appropriate.
68. **protest:** affirm. **injuried:** injured.
69. **devise:** understand. 71. **tender:** value.
74. **Alla stoccato:** literally, at the thrust (fencing term). Mercutio means that Tybalt's onslaught has apparently unarmed Romeo.
75. **rat-catcher.** Alluding to his name; see note on II.iv.19. **walk:** i.e. come outside.
78–79. **as . . . hereafter:** according to your behavior to me in future.
79. **dry-beat:** thrash (without drawing blood).
80. **his pilcher:** its scabbard.
80–81. **by the ears.** Implying that the sword is reluctant to leave the scabbard.
85. **passado:** lunge.
89. **bandying:** exchanging blows.
91. **sped:** dispatched.
93. **a scratch.** Another allusion to Tybalt's name.

Where is my page? Go, villain, fetch a surgeon.
[*Exit Page.*]

Rom. Courage, man, the hurt cannot be much.

Mer. No, 'tis not so deep as a well, nor so wide as a church-door, but 'tis enough, 'twill serve. Ask for me to-morrow, and you shall find me a grave man. I am pepper'd, I warrant, for this world. A plague a' both your houses! 'Zounds, a dog, a rat, a mouse, a cat, to scratch a man to death! a braggart, a rogue, a villain, that fights by the book of arithmetic! Why the dev'l came you between us? I was hurt under your arm.

Rom. I thought all for the best.

Mer. Help me into some house, Benvolio,
Or I shall faint. A plague a' both your houses!
They have made worms' meat of me. I have it,
And soundly too. Your houses!
Exeunt [*Mercutio and Benvolio*].

Rom. This gentleman, the Prince's near ally,
My very friend, hath got this mortal hurt
In my behalf; my reputation stain'd
With Tybalt's slander—Tybalt, that an hour
Hath been my cousin! O sweet Juliet,
Thy beauty hath made me effeminate,
And in my temper soft'ned valor's steel!

Enter Benvolio.

Ben. O Romeo, Romeo, brave Mercutio is dead!
That gallant spirit hath aspir'd the clouds,
Which too untimely here did scorn the earth.

Rom. This day's black fate on moe days doth depend,
This but begins the woe others must end.

[*Enter* Tybalt.]

Ben. Here comes the furious Tybalt back again.

Rom. He [gone] in triumph, and Mercutio slain!
Away to heaven, respective lenity,
And fire[-ey'd] fury be my conduct now!
Now, Tybalt, take the "villain" back again
That late thou gavest me, for Mercutio's soul
Is but a little way above our heads,
Staying for thine to keep him company.
Either thou or I, or both, must go with him.

Tyb. Thou wretched boy, that didst consort him here,
Shalt with him hence.

Rom. This shall determine that.
They fight; Tybalt falls.

Ben. Romeo, away, be gone!
The citizens are up, and Tybalt slain.
Stand not amazed, the Prince will doom thee death
If thou art taken. Hence be gone, away!

Rom. O, I am fortune's fool!

Ben. Why dost thou stay? *Exit Romeo.*

94. villain: fellow (not derogatory here).
99. for this world: as far as this world is concerned.
109. ally: kinsman. **110. very:** true.
115. temper: composition, nature (with pun on the tempering of steel). **117. aspir'd:** mounted to.
119. on . . . depend: hangs over more days than to-day.
123. respective: considerate. **124. conduct:** guide.
133. up: in arms. **134. amazed:** stupefied.
136. fool: plaything, dupe.

Enter Citizens.

[*1.*] *Cit.* Which way ran he that kill'd Mercutio?
Tybalt, that murtherer, which way ran he?

Ben. There lies that Tybalt.

[*1.*] *Cit.* Up, sir, go with me;
I charge thee in the Prince's name, obey.

Enter Prince, *old* Montague, Capulet, *their* Wives, *and all.*

Prin. Where are the vile beginners of this fray?

Ben. O noble Prince, I can discover all
The unlucky manage of this fatal brawl:
There lies the man, slain by young Romeo,
That slew thy kinsman, brave Mercutio.

La. Cap. Tybalt, my cousin! O my brother's child!
O Prince! O husband! O, the blood is spill'd
Of my dear kinsman! Prince, as thou art true,
For blood of ours, shed blood of Montague.
O cousin, cousin!

Prin. Benvolio, who began this bloody fray?

Ben. Tybalt, here slain, whom Romeo's hand did slay!
Romeo that spoke him fair, bid him bethink
How nice the quarrel was, and urg'd withal
Your high displeasure; all this, uttered
With gentle breath, calm look, knees humbly bowed,
Could not take truce with the unruly spleen
Of Tybalt deaf to peace, but that he tilts
With piercing steel at bold Mercutio's breast,
Who, all as hot, turns deadly point to point,
And, with a martial scorn, with one hand beats
Cold death aside, and with the other sends
It back to Tybalt, whose dexterity
Retorts it. Romeo he cries aloud,
"Hold, friends! friends, part!" and swifter than his tongue,
His [agile] arm beats down their fatal points,
And 'twixt them rushes; underneath whose arm
An envious thrust from Tybalt hit the life
Of stout Mercutio, and then Tybalt fled;
But by and by comes back to Romeo,
Who had but newly entertain'd revenge,
And to't they go like lightning, for, ere I
Could draw to part them, was stout Tybalt slain;
And as he fell, did Romeo turn and fly.
This is the truth, or let Benvolio die.

La. Cap. He is a kinsman to the Montague,
Affection makes him false, he speaks not true.
Some twenty of them fought in this black strife,
And all those twenty could but kill one life.
I beg for justice, which thou, Prince, must give:
Romeo slew Tybalt, Romeo must not live.

Prin. Romeo slew him, he slew Mercutio;
Who now the price of his dear blood doth owe?

[*Mon.*] Not Romeo, Prince, he was Mercutio's friend;
His fault concludes but what the law should end,
The life of Tybalt.

142. discover: reveal.
143. manage: conduct. **154. nice:** trivial.
168. envious: malicious. **169. stout:** valorous.
171. entertain'd: admitted the thought of.

Prin. And for that offense
Immediately we do exile him hence.
I have an interest in your hearts' proceeding;
My blood for your rude brawls doth lie a-bleeding;
But I'll amerce you with so strong a fine
That you shall all repent the loss of mine.
[I] will be deaf to pleading and excuses,
Nor tears nor prayers shall purchase out abuses;
Therefore use none. Let Romeo hence in haste,
Else, when he is found, that hour is his last.
Bear hence this body and attend our will;
Mercy but murders, pardoning those that kill.
Exeunt.

[Scene II]

Enter Juliet *alone.*

[*Jul.*] Gallop apace, you fiery-footed steeds,
Towards Phoebus' lodging; such a waggoner
As Phaëton would whip you to the west,
And bring in cloudy night immediately.
Spread thy close curtain, love-performing night,
That [th'] runaway's eyes may wink, and Romeo
Leap to these arms untalk'd of and unseen!
Lovers can see to do their amorous rites
By their own beauties, or, if love be blind,
It best agrees with night. Come, civil night,
Thou sober-suited matron all in black,
And learn me how to lose a winning match,
Play'd for a pair of stainless maidenhoods.
Hood my unmann'd blood, bating in my cheeks,
With thy black mantle, till strange love grow bold,
Think true love acted simple modesty.
Come, night, come, Romeo, come, thou day in night,
For thou wilt lie upon the wings of night,
Whiter than new snow upon a raven's back.
Come, gentle night, come, loving, black-brow'd night,
Give me my Romeo, and, when I shall die,
Take him and cut him out in little stars,
And he will make the face of heaven so fine
That all the world will be in love with night,
And pay no worship to the garish sun.
O, I have bought the mansion of a love,

188. interest: participation, personal concern.
189. My blood. Mercutio is his kinsman.
190. amerce: punish by fine. **193. purchase out:** redeem.
196. attend our will: come to hear my further judgment.
197. murders: i.e. invites other murders by condoning them in advance.

III.ii. Location: Verona. Capulet's house.
1. steeds: the horses drawing the chariot of the sun-god (here identified with Phoebus Apollo, not with the Titan Helios as at II.iii.4).
2. lodging: i.e. below the western horizon.
3. Phaëton: Phaëthon, the sun-god's son; when he drove the sun-chariot he could not keep control and had to be killed by Zeus.
5. close: concealing.
6. runaway's. Unexplained; perhaps corrupt. Night must blind some thing or person that would comment harshly on their love. **wink:** be unable to see (?) or close, because night has come (?).
10. civil: grave.
14. Hood: cover. **unmann'd:** untamed (with obvious pun). **bating:** fluttering. Like *Hood* and *unmann'd*, this term is borrowed from falconry; a hawk "bates" when it attempts to escape from the falconer's wrist. It is controlled by means of a hood placed over its head.
15. strange: reserved, diffident. **grow.** Some editors read *grown;* without this emendation, *And* must be understood at the beginning of line 16. **16. modesty:** chastity.

But not possess'd it, and though I am sold,
Not yet enjoy'd. So tedious is this day
As is the night before some festival
To an impatient child that hath new robes
And may not wear them. O, here comes my nurse,

Enter Nurse [*wringing her hands*], *with* [*the ladder of*] *cords* [*in her lap*].

And she brings news; and every tongue that speaks
But Romeo's name speaks heavenly eloquence.
Now, nurse, what news? What hast thou there? the cords
That Romeo bid thee fetch?
Nurse. Ay, ay, the cords.
[*Throws them down.*]
Jul. Ay me, what news? Why dost thou wring thy hands?
Nurse. Ah, weraday, he's dead, he's dead, he's dead!
We are undone, lady, we are undone!
Alack the day, he's gone, he's kill'd, he's dead!
Jul. Can heaven be so envious?
Nurse. Romeo can,
Though heaven cannot. O Romeo, Romeo!
Who ever would have thought it? Romeo!
Jul. What devil art thou that dost torment me thus?
This torture should be roar'd in dismal hell.
Hath Romeo slain himself? Say thou but ay,
And that bare vowel *I* shall poison more
Than the death[-darting] eye of cockatrice.
I am not I, if there be such an ay,
Or those eyes [shut], that makes thee answer ay.
If he be slain, say ay, or if not, no.
Brief sounds determine my weal or woe.
Nurse. I saw the wound, I saw it with mine eyes—
God save the mark!—here on his manly breast.
A piteous corse, a bloody piteous corse,
Pale, pale as ashes, all bedaub'd in blood,
All in gore blood; I sounded at the sight.
Jul. O, break, my heart, poor bankrout, break at once!
To prison, eyes, ne'er look on liberty!
Vile earth, to earth resign, end motion here,
And thou and Romeo press [one] heavy bier!
Nurse. O Tybalt, Tybalt, the best friend I had!
O courteous Tybalt, honest gentleman,
That ever I should live to see thee dead!
Jul. What storm is this that blows so contrary?
Is Romeo slaught'red? and is Tybalt dead?
My dearest cousin, and my dearer lord?
Then, dreadful trumpet, sound the general doom,
For who is living, if those two are gone?
Nurse. Tybalt is gone, and Romeo banished,

37. weraday: alas. **40. envious:** malicious.
47. cockatrice: basilisk, fabulous creature which killed by its glance.
49. Or . . . shut: or if those eyes (Romeo's) are shut in death.
51. determine: put an end to (?) or decide, settle (?).
53. God . . . mark: expression used to avert ill omen.
54. corse: corpse. **56. sounded:** swooned.
57. bankrout: bankrupt (with play on *break* = go bankrupt).
59. Vile earth: i.e. body. **resign:** surrender.
67. trumpet: the "last trump," signalling the Day of Judgment.

Romeo that kill'd him, he is banished.
Jul. O God, did Romeo's hand shed Tybalt's blood?
[*Nurse.*] It did, it did, alas the day, it did!
[*Jul.*] O serpent heart, hid with a flow'ring face!
Did ever dragon keep so fair a cave?
Beautiful tyrant! fiend angelical!
Dove-feather'd raven! wolvish ravening lamb!
Despised substance of divinest show!
Just opposite to what thou justly seem'st,
A [damned] saint, an honorable villain!
O nature, what hadst thou to do in hell
When thou didst bower the spirit of a fiend
In mortal paradise of such sweet flesh?
Was ever book containing such vile matter
So fairly bound? O that deceit should dwell
In such a gorgeous palace!
Nurse. There's no trust,
No faith, no honesty in men, all perjur'd,
All forsworn, all naught, all dissemblers.
Ah, where's my man? Give me some aqua-vitae;
These griefs, these woes, these sorrows make me old.
Shame come to Romeo!
Jul. Blister'd be thy tongue
For such a wish! he was not born to shame:
Upon his brow shame is asham'd to sit;
For 'tis a throne where honor may be crown'd
Sole monarch of the universal earth.
O, what a beast was I to chide at him!
Nurse. Will you speak well of him that kill'd your cousin?
Jul. Shall I speak ill of him that is my husband?
Ah, poor my lord, what tongue shall smooth thy name,
When I, thy three-hours wife, have mangled it?
But wherefore, villain, didst thou kill my cousin?
That villain cousin would have kill'd my husband.
Back, foolish tears, back to your native spring,
Your tributary drops belong to woe,
Which you, mistaking, offer up to joy.
My husband lives that Tybalt would have slain,
And Tybalt's dead that would have slain my husband.
All this is comfort, wherefore weep I then?
Some word there was, worser than Tybalt's death,
That murd'red me; I would forget it fain,
But O, it presses to my memory
Like damned guilty deeds to sinners' minds:
"Tybalt is dead, and Romeo banished."
That "banished," that one word "banished,"
Hath slain ten thousand Tybalts. Tybalt's death
Was woe enough if it had ended there;
Or if sour woe delights in fellowship,
And needly will be rank'd with other griefs,
Why followed not, when she said, "Tybalt's dead,"
Thy father or thy mother, nay, or both,
Which modern lamentation might have moved?
But with a rearward following Tybalt's death,
"Romeo is banished": to speak that word,
Is father, mother, Tybalt, Romeo, Juliet,
All slain, all dead: "Romeo is banished"!
There is no end, no limit, measure, bound,
In that word's death, no words can that woe sound.
Where is my father and my mother, nurse?
Nurse. Weeping and wailing over Tybalt's corse.
Will you go to them? I will bring you thither.
Jul. Wash they his wounds with tears? Mine shall be spent,
When theirs are dry, for Romeo's banishment.
Take up those cords. Poor ropes, you are beguil'd,
Both you and I, for Romeo is exil'd.
He made you for a highway to my bed,
But I, a maid, die maiden-widowed.
Come, cords, come, nurse, I'll to my wedding-bed,
And death, not Romeo, take my maidenhead!
Nurse. Hie to your chamber. I'll find Romeo
To comfort you, I wot well where he is.
Hark ye, your Romeo will be here at night.
I'll to him, he is hid at Lawrence' cell.
Jul. O, find him! Give this ring to my true knight,
And bid him come to take his last farewell. *Exeunt.*

[Scene III]

Enter Friar [Lawrence].

Fri. L. Romeo, come forth, come forth, thou fearful man:
Affliction is enamor'd of thy parts,
And thou art wedded to calamity.

[*Enter*] Romeo.

Rom. Father, what news? What is the Prince's doom?
What sorrow craves acquaintance at my hand,
That I yet know not?
Fri. L. Too familiar
Is my dear son with such sour company!
I bring thee tidings of the Prince's doom.
Rom. What less than dooms-day is the Prince's doom?
Fri. L. A gentler judgment vanish'd from his lips—
Not body's death, but body's banishment.
Rom. Ha, banishment? Be merciful, say "death";
For exile hath more terror in his look,
Much more than death. Do not say "banishment"!
Fri. L. Here from Verona art thou banished.
Be patient, for the world is broad and wide.
Rom. There is no world without Verona walls,
But purgatory, torture, hell itself.

73. flow'ring: i.e. youthful and fair (?) or perhaps alluding to representations of the serpent in Eden with a human face encircled with flowers. **74. keep:** dwell in.
77. Despised: despicable. **substance . . . show:** reality . . . appearance.
78. Just: exactly. **what . . . seem'st:** your semblance of truth.
81. bower: lodge. **87. naught:** wicked.
88. aqua-vitae: strong alcoholic spirits.
103. Your . . . woe: your tears should be a tribute to woeful events.
104. joy: i.e. the joyful event of Romeo's survival.
117. needly: necessarily. **rank'd:** included in a series.

120. modern: ordinary. **121. rearward:** rearguard.
126. sound: (1) express; (2) fathom.
132. beguil'd: tricked, cheated. **139. wot:** know.

III.iii. Location: Verona. Friar Lawrence's cell.
1. fearful: full of fear (but lines 2–3 suggest that the sense "evoking fear" may also be present). **2. parts:** qualities.
4. doom: judgment, sentence. **9. dooms-day:** i.e. death.
10. vanish'd: issued without possibility of recall (?).
16. Be patient: compose yourself. **17. without:** outside.

Hence "banished" is banish'd from the world,
And world's exile is death; then "banished"
Is death misterm'd. Calling death "banished,"
Thou cut'st my head off with a golden axe,
And smilest upon the stroke that murders me.

Fri. L. O deadly sin! O rude unthankfulness!
Thy fault our law calls death, but the kind Prince,
Taking thy part, hath rush'd aside the law,
And turn'd that black word "death" to "banishment."
This is dear mercy, and thou seest it not.

Rom. 'Tis torture, and not mercy. Heaven is here
Where Juliet lives, and every cat and dog
And little mouse, every unworthy thing,
Live here in heaven and may look on her,
But Romeo may not. More validity,
More honorable state, more courtship lives
In carrion flies than Romeo; they may seize
On the white wonder of dear Juliet's hand,
And steal immortal blessing from her lips,
Who, even in pure and vestal modesty,
Still blush, as thinking their own kisses sin;
But Romeo may not, he is banished.
Flies may do this, but I from this must fly;
They are free men, but I am banished:
And sayest thou yet that exile is not death?
Hadst thou no poison mix'd, no sharp-ground knife,
No sudden mean of death, though ne'er so mean,
But "banished" to kill me? "Banished"?
O friar, the damned use that word in hell;
Howling attends it. How hast thou the heart,
Being a divine, a ghostly confessor,
A sin-absolver, and my friend profess'd,
To mangle me with that word "banished"?

Fri. L. [Thou] fond mad man, hear me a little speak.

Rom. O, thou wilt speak again of banishment.

Fri. L. I'll give thee armor to keep off that word:
Adversity's sweet milk, philosophy,
To comfort thee though thou art banished.

Rom. Yet "banished"? Hang up philosophy!
Unless philosophy can make a Juliet,
Displant a town, reverse a prince's doom,
It helps not, it prevails not. Talk no more.

Fri. L. O then I see that [madmen] have no ears.

Rom. How should they when that wise men have no eyes?

Fri. L. Let me dispute with thee of thy estate.

Rom. Thou canst not speak of that thou dost not feel.
Wert thou as young as I, Juliet thy love,
An hour but married, Tybalt murdered,
Doting like me, and like me banished,
Then mightst thou speak, then mightst thou tear thy hair,
And fall upon the ground, as I do now,

Taking the measure of an unmade grave.

Enter Nurse [within] and knock.

Fri. L. Arise, one knocks. Good Romeo, hide thyself.

Rom. Not I, unless the breath of heart-sick groans
Mist-like infold me from the search of eyes. *Knock.*

Fri. L. Hark how they knock!—Who's there?—Romeo, arise,
Thou wilt be taken.—Stay a while!—Stand up;

[Loud] knock.

Run to my study.—By and by!—God's will,
What simpleness is this?—I come, I come! *Knock.*
Who knocks so hard? Whence come you? What's your will?

Nurse. [*Within.*] Let me come in, and you shall know my errant.
I come from Lady Juliet.

Fri. L. Welcome then. [*Unlocks the door.*]

Enter NURSE.

Nurse. O holy friar, O, tell me, holy friar,
Where's my lady's lord? where's Romeo?

Fri. L. There on the ground, with his own tears made drunk.

Nurse. O, he is even in my mistress' case,
Just in her case. O woeful sympathy!
Piteous predicament! Even so lies she,
Blubb'ring and weeping, weeping and blubb'ring.
Stand up, stand up, stand, and you be a man.
For Juliet's sake, for her sake, rise and stand;
Why should you fall into so deep an O?

Rom. Nurse! [*He rises.*]

Nurse. Ah sir, ah sir, death's the end of all.

Rom. Spakest thou of Juliet? How is it with her?
Doth not she think me an old murtherer,
Now I have stain'd the childhood of our joy
With blood removed but little from her own?
Where is she? and how doth she? and what says
My conceal'd lady to our cancell'd love?

Nurse. O, she says nothing, sir, but weeps and weeps,
And now falls on her bed, and then starts up,
And Tybalt calls, and then on Romeo cries,
And then down falls again.

Rom. As if that name,
Shot from the deadly level of a gun,
Did murther her, as that name's cursed hand
Murder'd her kinsman. O, tell me, friar, tell me,
In what vile part of this anatomy
Doth my name lodge? Tell me, that I may sack
The hateful mansion.

[*He offers to stab himself, and Nurse snatches the dagger away.*]

Fri. L. Hold thy desperate hand!
Art thou a man? Thy form cries out thou art;
Thy tears are womanish, thy wild acts [denote]
The unreasonable fury of a beast.

Romeo and Juliet III.iii

20. world's exile: exile from the world.
25. death: i.e. a capital offense. **26. rush'd:** pushed.
28. dear: precious, rare. **33. validity:** worth, dignity.
34. courtship: courtly state (with play on "opportunity for wooing").
39. kisses: i.e. contact with each other.
45. mean . . . mean: means . . . base. **52. fond:** foolish.
59. Displant: transplant. **60. prevails not:** is of no effect.
63. dispute: discuss. **estate:** situation.

75. Stay a while: wait a moment. **77. simpleness:** foolishness.
79. errant: errand. **85. sympathy:** similarity of suffering.
90. O: fit of groaning. **94. old:** inveterate, hardened.
98. conceal'd lady: secret wife. **103. level:** aim.
111. unreasonable: unreasoning.

Unseemly woman in a seeming man,
And ill-beseeming beast in seeming both,
Thou hast amaz'd me! By my holy order,
I thought thy disposition better temper'd.
Hast thou slain Tybalt? Wilt thou slay thyself,
And slay thy lady that in thy life [lives],
By doing damned hate upon thyself?
Why railest thou on thy birth? the heaven and earth?
Since birth, and heaven, and earth, all three do meet
In thee at once, which thou at once wouldst lose.
Fie, fie, thou shamest thy shape, thy love, thy wit,
Which like a usurer abound'st in all,
And usest none in that true use indeed
Which should bedeck thy shape, thy love, thy wit.
Thy noble shape is but a form of wax,
Digressing from the valor of a man;
Thy dear love sworn but hollow perjury,
Killing that love which thou hast vow'd to cherish;
Thy wit, that ornament to shape and love,
Misshapen in the conduct of them both,
Like powder in a skilless soldier's flask,
Is set afire by thine own ignorance,
And thou dismemb'red with thine own defense.
What, rouse thee, man! thy Juliet is alive,
For whose dear sake thou wast but lately dead:
There art thou happy. Tybalt would kill thee,
But thou slewest Tybalt: there art thou happy.
The law that threat'ned death becomes thy friend,
And turns it to exile: there art thou happy.
A pack of blessings light upon thy back,
Happiness courts thee in her best array,
But like a mishaved and sullen wench,
Thou [pouts upon] thy fortune and thy love.
Take heed, take heed, for such die miserable.
Go get thee to thy love as was decreed,
Ascend her chamber, hence and comfort her.
But look thou stay not till the watch be set,
For then thou canst not pass to Mantua,
Where thou shalt live till we can find a time
To blaze your marriage, reconcile your friends,
Beg pardon of the Prince, and call thee back
With twenty hundred thousand times more joy
Than thou went'st forth in lamentation.
Go before, nurse; commend me to thy lady,
And bid her hasten all the house to bed,
Which heavy sorrow makes them apt unto.
Romeo is coming.

Nurse. O Lord, I could have stay'd here all the night
To hear good counsel. O, what learning is!
My lord, I'll tell my lady you will come.

Rom. Do so, and bid my sweet prepare to chide.

[*Nurse offers to go in, and turns again.*]

Nurse. Here, sir, a ring she bid me give you, sir.
Hie you, make haste, for it grows very late.

Rom. How well my comfort is reviv'd by this!

[*Exit Nurse.*]

Fri. L. Go hence, good night; and here stands all your state:
Either be gone before the watch be set,
Or by the break of day [disguis'd] from hence.
Sojourn in Mantua. I'll find out your man,
And he shall signify from time to time
Every good hap to you that chances here.
Give me thy hand. 'Tis late; farewell, good night.

Rom. But that a joy past joy calls out on me,
It were a grief, so brief to part with thee.
Farewell. *Exeunt.*

[Scene IV]

Enter old Capulet, *his* Wife, *and* Paris.

Cap. Things have fall'n out, sir, so unluckily
That we have had no time to move our daughter.
Look you, she lov'd her kinsman Tybalt dearly,
And so did I. Well, we were born to die.
'Tis very late, she'll not come down to-night.
I promise you, but for your company,
I would have been a-bed an hour ago.

Par. These times of woe afford no times to woo.
Madam, good night, commend me to your daughter.

La. Cap. I will, and know her mind early to-morrow;
To-night she's mewed up to her heaviness.

[*Paris offers to go in, and Capulet calls him again.*]

Cap. Sir Paris, I will make a desperate tender
Of my child's love. I think she will [be] rul'd
In all respects by me; nay more, I doubt it not.
Wife, go you to her ere you go to bed,
Acquaint her here of my son Paris' love,
And bid her—mark you me?—on We'n'sday next—
But soft, what day is this?

Par. Monday, my lord.

Cap. Monday! ha, ha! Well, We'n'sday is too soon,
A' Thursday let it be—a' Thursday, tell her,
She shall be married to this noble earl.
Will you be ready? do you like this haste?
We'll keep no great ado—a friend or two,
For hark you, Tybalt being slain so late,
It may be thought we held him carelessly,
Being our kinsman, if we revel much:
Therefore we'll have some half a dozen friends,
And there an end. But what say you to Thursday?

112. Unseemly woman. The Friar suggests that Romeo is behaving not simply like a woman but like a woman who offends good taste. Similarly *Ill-beseeming beast* in line 113 suggests that he is acting in a way unbecoming even for a normal animal—that he is a sort of hybrid monster. **115. temper'd:** compounded.
120. heaven, and earth: i.e. soul and body. **122. wit:** intellect.
123. Which: (you) who. **usurer:** i.e. one who does not put his possessions to the proper use; a Shylock, not an Antonio who "ventures" in the world.
126. form of wax: waxwork figure.
131. Misshapen: deformed. **conduct:** guidance.
132. flask: powder horn. **134. defense:** means of defense.
137. happy: fortunate. **143. mishaved:** misbehaved.
146. decreed: appointed.
148. watch be set: guard be posted. The city gates would be closed at the same time. **151. blaze:** make known. **friends:** relations.

166. here . . . state: your situation depends on this.
174. brief: hastily.

III.iv. Location: Verona. Capulet's house.
6. promise: assure.
11. mew'd up to: shut up with (a term from falconry). **heaviness:** sorrow. **12. desperate tender:** bold offer.
19. ha, ha. Representing the sound he utters as he considers the matter. **20. A':** on.

Par. My lord, I would that Thursday were tomorrow.
Cap. Well, get you gone, a' Thursday be it then.—
Go you to Juliet ere you go to bed,
Prepare her, wife, against this wedding-day.
Farewell, my lord. Light to my chamber ho!
Afore me, it is so very late that we
May call it early by and by. Good night. *Exeunt.*

[SCENE V]

Enter ROMEO *and* JULIET *aloft* [*at the window*].

Jul. Wilt thou be gone? it is not yet near day.
It was the nightingale, and not the lark,
That pierc'd the fearful hollow of thine ear;
Nightly she sings on yond pomegranate tree.
Believe me, love, it was the nightingale.
Rom. It was the lark, the herald of the morn,
No nightingale. Look, love, what envious streaks
Do lace the severing clouds in yonder east.
Night's candles are burnt out, and jocund day
Stands tiptoe on the misty mountain tops.
I must be gone and live, or stay and die.
Jul. Yond light is not day-light, I know it, I;
It is some meteor that the sun [exhal'd]
To be to thee this night a torch-bearer
And light thee on thy way to Mantua.
Therefore stay yet, thou need'st not to be gone.
Rom. Let me be ta'en, let me be put to death,
I am content, so thou wilt have it so.
I'll say yon grey is not the morning's eye,
'Tis but the pale reflex of Cynthia's brow;
Nor that is not the lark whose notes do beat
The vaulty heaven so high above our heads.
I have more care to stay than will to go.
Come, death, and welcome! Juliet wills it so.
How is't, my soul? Let's talk, it is not day.
Jul. It is, it is! Hie hence, be gone, away!
It is the lark that sings so out of tune,
Straining harsh discords and unpleasing sharps.
Some say the lark makes sweet division;
This doth not so, for she divideth us.
Some say the lark and loathed toad change eyes;
O now I would they had chang'd voices too,
Since arm from arm that voice doth us affray,
Hunting thee hence with hunt's-up to the day.
O now be gone, more light and light it grows.
Rom. More light and light, more dark and dark our woes!

Enter NURSE [*hastily*].

Nurse. Madam!
Jul. Nurse?
Nurse. Your lady mother is coming to your chamber.
The day is broke, be wary, look about. [*Exit.*]
Jul. Then, window, let day in, and let life out.
Rom. Farewell, farewell! One kiss, and I'll descend. [*He goeth down.*]
Jul. Art thou gone so, love, lord, ay, husband, friend!
I must hear from thee every day in the hour,
For in a minute there are many days.
O, by this count I shall be much in years
Ere I again behold my Romeo!
Rom. [*From below.*] Farewell!
I will omit no opportunity
That may convey my greetings, love, to thee.
Jul. O, think'st thou we shall ever meet again?
Rom. I doubt it not, and all these woes shall serve
For sweet discourses in our times to come.
Jul. O God, I have an ill-divining soul!
Methinks I see thee now, thou art so low,
As one dead in the bottom of a tomb.
Either my eyesight fails, or thou lookest pale.
Rom. And trust me, love, in my eye so do you;
Dry sorrow drinks our blood. Adieu, adieu! *Exit.*
Jul. O Fortune, Fortune, all men call thee fickle;
If thou art fickle, what dost thou with him
That is renowm'd for faith? Be fickle, Fortune:
For then I hope thou wilt not keep him long,
But send him back.
La. Cap. [*Within.*] Ho, daughter, are you up?
Jul. Who is't that calls? It is my lady mother.
Is she not down so late, or up so early?
What unaccustom'd cause procures her hither?
[*She goeth down from the window.*]

Enter Mother [LADY CAPULET].

La. Cap. Why, how now, Juliet?
Jul. Madam, I am not well.
La. Cap. Evermore weeping for your cousin's death?
What, wilt thou wash him from his grave with tears?
And if thou couldst, thou couldst not make him live;
Therefore have done. Some grief shows much of love,
But much of grief shows still some want of wit.
Jul. Yet let me weep for such a feeling loss.
La. Cap. So shall you feel the loss, but not the friend
Which you weep for.
Jul. Feeling so the loss,
I cannot choose but ever weep the friend.
La. Cap. Well, girl, thou weep'st not so much for his death,
As that the villain lives which slaughter'd him.

32. **against:** in anticipation of. 34. **Afore me:** a mild oath.

III.v. Location: Verona. Capulet's orchard.
13. **exhal'd.** Meteors were thought to be vapors which had risen from the earth and been ignited by the sun's heat.
20. **reflex:** reflection. **Cynthia's:** the moon's.
23. **care:** concern, desire. 28. **sharps:** high notes.
29. **division:** florid variation on a melody. 31. **change:** exchange.
33. **arm from arm:** out of each other's arms. **affray:** frighten.
34. **hunt's-up:** a song to waken hunters (with possible reference to the custom of singing and horn-playing outside the bridal chamber the morning after the wedding).

43. **friend:** i.e. lover.
46. **much in years:** old. 54. **ill-divining:** premonitory of evil.
59. **Dry . . . blood.** It was thought that sorrow gradually exhausted the blood. *Dry* = thirsty.
61. **what dost thou:** what business have you.
62. **renowm'd:** renowned. 66. **not down:** not yet gone to bed.
67 s.d. **She . . . window.** Apparently she goes out above and re-enters below, the main stage ceasing to be the garden into which Romeo has descended and becoming a room in the house.
74. **feeling:** affecting.

Jul. What villain, madam?
La. Cap. That same villain Romeo.
Jul. [*Aside.*] Villain and he be many miles asunder.—
God pardon [him]! I do with all my heart;
And yet no man like he doth grieve my heart.
La. Cap. That is because the traitor murderer lives.
Jul. Ay, madam, from the reach of these my hands.
Would none but I might venge my cousin's death!
La. Cap. We will have vengeance for it, fear thou not.
Then weep no more. I'll send to one in Mantua,
Where that same banish'd runagate doth live,
Shall give him such an unaccustom'd dram
That he shall soon keep Tybalt company;
And then I hope thou wilt be satisfied.
Jul. Indeed I never shall be satisfied
With Romeo, till I behold him—dead—
Is my poor heart, so for a kinsman vex'd.
Madam, if you could find out but a man
To bear a poison, I would temper it,
That Romeo should, upon receipt thereof,
Soon sleep in quiet. O how my heart abhors
To hear him nam'd, and cannot come to him
To wreak the love I bore my cousin
Upon his body that hath slaughter'd him!
La. Cap. Find thou the means, and I'll find such a man.
But now I'll tell thee joyful tidings, girl.
Jul. And joy comes well in such a needy time.
What are they, beseech your ladyship?
La. Cap. Well, well, thou hast a careful father, child,
One who, to put thee from thy heaviness,
Hath sorted out a sudden day of joy,
That thou expects not, nor I look'd not for.
Jul. Madam, in happy time, what day is that?
La. Cap. Marry, my child, early next Thursday morn,
The gallant, young, and noble gentleman,
The County Paris, at Saint Peter's Church,
Shall happily make thee there a joyful bride.
Jul. Now, by Saint Peter's Church and Peter too,
He shall not make me there a joyful bride.
I wonder at this haste, that I must wed
Ere he that should be husband comes to woo.
I pray you tell my lord and father, madam,
I will not marry yet, and when I do, I swear
It shall be Romeo, whom you know I hate,
Rather than Paris. These are news indeed!
La. Cap. Here comes your father, tell him so yourself;
And see how he will take it at your hands.

Enter CAPULET *and* NURSE.

Cap. When the sun sets, the earth doth drizzle dew,
But for the sunset of my brother's son

83. like: so much as. **89. runagate:** renegade.
97. temper: mix (including the sense "moderate, dilute").
102. his body that: the body of him who.
107. careful: i.e. concerned for your welfare.
109. sudden: soon to come.

It rains downright.
How now, a conduit, girl? What, still in tears?
Evermore show'ring? In one little body
Thou counterfeits a bark, a sea, a wind:
For still thy eyes, which I may call the sea,
Do ebb and flow with tears; the bark thy body is,
Sailing in this salt flood; the winds, thy sighs,
Who, raging with thy tears, and they with them,
Without a sudden calm, will overset
Thy tempest-tossed body. How now, wife?
Have you delivered to her our decree?
La. Cap. Ay, sir, but she will none, she [gives] you thanks.
I would the fool were married to her grave!
Cap. Soft, take me with you, take me with you, wife.
How, will she none? Doth she not give us thanks?
Is she not proud? Doth she not count her blest,
Unworthy as she is, that we have wrought
So worthy a gentleman to be her bride?
Jul. Not proud you have, but thankful that you have.
Proud can I never be of what I hate,
But thankful even for hate that is meant love.
Cap. How how, how how, chopp'd logic! What is this?
"Proud," and "I thank you," and "I thank you not,"
And yet "not proud," mistress minion you?
Thank me no thankings, nor proud me no prouds,
But fettle your fine joints 'gainst Thursday next,
To go with Paris to Saint Peter's Church,
Or I will drag thee on a hurdle thither.
Out, you green-sickness carrion! Out, you baggage!
You tallow-face!
La. Cap. Fie, fie, what, are you mad?
Jul. Good father, I beseech you on my knees,
Hear me with patience but to speak a word.
[*She kneels down.*]
Cap. Hang thee, young baggage! disobedient wretch!
I tell thee what: get thee to church a' Thursday,
Or never after look me in the face.
Speak not, reply not, do not answer me!
My fingers itch. Wife, we scarce thought us blest
That God had lent us but this only child,
But now I see this one is one too much,
And that we have a curse in having her.
Out on her, hilding!

129. conduit: fountain.
136. Without . . . calm: unless they abate very soon.
139. but . . . thanks: but she says "No, thank you." In line 142 *Doth . . . thanks?* = isn't she grateful?
141. take . . . you: let me understand what you mean.
143. proud: elated. **144. wrought:** secured.
145. bride: bridegroom (a sense already rare in Shakespeare's day).
146. thankful: i.e. properly grateful for your solicitude.
149. chopp'd logic: idle sophistry, or idle sophist.
151. minion: spoiled child.
153. fettle: prepare (normally a term of the stable).
155. hurdle: conveyance for dragging criminals to execution.
156. Out: an exclamation of indignant reproach. **green-sickness.** Alluding to Juliet's paleness (as is shown by *carrion*, implying that she is as pale as a corpse), but also to her reluctance to marry, since "the green-sickness" was a disease of unmarried girls. **baggage:** good-for-nothing.
157. Fie . . . mad. Addressed to Capulet.

Nurse. God in heaven bless her!
You are to blame, my lord, to rate her so.
Cap. And why, my Lady Wisdom? Hold your tongue,
Good Prudence, smatter with your gossips, go.
Nurse. I speak no treason.
Cap. O, God-i-goden!
[*Nurse.*] May not one speak?
Cap. Peace, you mumbling fool!
Utter your gravity o'er a gossip's bowl,
For here we need it not.
La. Cap. You are too hot.
Cap. God's bread, it makes me mad! Day, night, work, play,
Alone, in company, still my care hath been
To have her match'd; and having now provided
A gentleman of noble parentage,
Of fair demesnes, youthful and nobly [lien'd],
Stuff'd, as they say, with honorable parts,
Proportion'd as one's thought would wish a man,
And then to have a wretched puling fool,
A whining mammet, in her fortune's tender,
To answer, "I'll not wed, I cannot love;
I am too young, I pray you pardon me."
But and you will not wed, I'll pardon you.
Graze where you will, you shall not house with me.
Look to't, think on't, I do not use to jest.
Thursday is near, lay hand on heart, advise.
And you be mine, I'll give you to my friend;
And you be not, hang, beg, starve, die in the streets,
For, by my soul, I'll ne'er acknowledge thee,
Nor what is mine shall never do thee good.
Trust to't, bethink you, I'll not be forsworn. *Exit.*
Jul. Is there no pity sitting in the clouds,
That sees into the bottom of my grief?
O sweet my mother, cast me not away!
Delay this marriage for a month, a week,
Or if you do not, make the bridal bed
In that dim monument where Tybalt lies.
La. Cap. Talk not to me, for I'll not speak a word.
Do as thou wilt, for I have done with thee. *Exit.*
Jul. O God!—O nurse, how shall this be prevented?
My husband is on earth, my faith in heaven;
How shall that faith return again to earth,
Unless that husband send it me from heaven
By leaving earth? Comfort me, counsel me!
Alack, alack, that heaven should practice stratagems
Upon so soft a subject as myself!
What say'st thou? Hast thou not a word of joy?
Some comfort, nurse.
Nurse. Faith, here it is.
Romeo is banished, and all the world to nothing
That he dares ne'er come back to challenge you;
Or if he do, it needs must be by stealth.
Then, since the case so stands as now it doth,
I think it best you married with the County.
O he's a lovely gentleman!
Romeo's a dishclout to him. An eagle, madam,
Hath not so green, so quick, so fair an eye
As Paris hath. Beshrow my very heart,
I think you are happy in this second match,
For it excels your first; or if it did not,
Your first is dead, or 'twere as good he were
As living here and you no use of him.
Jul. Speak'st thou from thy heart?
Nurse. And from my soul too, else beshrew them both.
Jul. Amen!
Nurse. What?
Jul. Well, thou hast comforted me marvellous much.
Go in, and tell my lady I am gone,
Having displeas'd my father, to Lawrence' cell,
To make confession and to be absolv'd.
Nurse. Marry, I will, and this is wisely done. [*Exit.*]
Jul. [*She looks after Nurse.*] Ancient damnation! O most wicked fiend!
Is it more sin to wish me thus forsworn,
Or to dispraise my lord with that same tongue
Which she hath prais'd him with above compare
So many thousand times? Go, counsellor,
Thou and my bosom henceforth shall be twain.
I'll to the friar to know his remedy;
If all else fail, myself have power to die. *Exit.*

[ACT IV, SCENE I]

Enter FRIAR [LAWRENCE] *and* COUNTY PARIS.

Fri. L. On Thursday, sir? The time is very short.
Par. My father Capulet will have it so,
And I am nothing slow to slack his haste.
Fri. L. You say you do not know the lady's mind?
Uneven is the course, I like it not.
Par. Immoderately she weeps for Tybalt's death,
And therefore have I little [talk'd] of love,
For Venus smiles not in a house of tears.
Now, sir, her father counts it dangerous
That she do give her sorrow so much sway;
And in his wisdom hastes our marriage,
To stop the inundation of her tears,
Which, too much minded by herself alone,
May be put from her by society.
Now do you know the reason of this haste.

169. **rate**: berate. 171. **smatter**: chatter.
172. **God-i-goden**: here, an impatient exclamation equivalent to "for God's sake."
180. **demesnes**: estates. **nobly lien'd**: well connected.
184. **mammet**: doll. **in . . . tender**: when good fortune is offered her. 189. **do not use**: am not accustomed.
190. **advise**: consider well.
205. **my . . . heaven**: i.e. my marriage vow sworn before God.
206–8. **How . . . earth**: i.e. how can I marry again unless Romeo dies.
209. **practice**: devise.
213. **all . . . nothing**: i.e. it is a perfectly safe bet.
214. **challenge**: claim. 219. **to**: in comparison with.
221. **Beshrow**: beshrew (see note on II.v.51).
225. **here**: i.e. on earth.
228. **Amen**: i.e. may they be cursed indeed. The Nurse, who has used *beshrew* in the usual weakened sense, does not follow.
235. **Ancient damnation**: damned old woman.
240. **bosom**: private thoughts. **twain**: separated.

IV.i. Location: Verona. Friar Lawrence's cell.
3. **am nothing slow**: have no reluctance of mind.
5. **Uneven**: irregular.
13. **minded . . . alone**: thought about by her in her solitude.

Fri. L. [*Aside.*] I would I knew not why it should be slowed.—
Look, sir, here comes the lady toward my cell.

Enter JULIET.

Par. Happily met, my lady and my wife!
Jul. That may be, sir, when I may be a wife.
Par. That may be must be, love, on Thursday next.
Jul. What must be shall be.
Fri. L. That's a certain text.
Par. Come you to make confession to this father?
Jul. To answer that, I should confess to you.
Par. Do not deny to him that you love me.
Jul. I will confess to you that I love him.
Par. So will ye, I am sure, that you love me.
Jul. If I do so, it will be of more price,
Being spoke behind your back, than to your face.
Par. Poor soul, thy face is much abus'd with tears.
Jul. The tears have got small victory by that,
For it was bad enough before their spite.
Par. Thou wrong'st it more than tears with that report.
Jul. That is no slander, sir, which is a truth,
And what I spake, I spake it to my face.
Par. Thy face is mine, and thou hast sland'red it.
Jul. It may be so, for it is not mine own.
Are you at leisure, holy father, now,
Or shall I come to you at evening mass?
Fri. L. My leisure serves me, pensive daughter, now.
My lord, we must entreat the time alone.
Par. God shield I should disturb devotion!
Juliet, on Thursday early will I rouse ye;
Till then adieu, and keep this holy kiss. *Exit.*
Jul. O, shut the door, and when thou hast done so,
Come weep with me, past hope, past [cure], past help!
Fri. L. O Juliet, I already know thy grief,
It strains me past the compass of my wits.
I hear thou must, and nothing may prorogue it,
On Thursday next be married to this County.
Jul. Tell me not, friar, that thou hearest of this,
Unless thou tell me how I may prevent it.
If in thy wisdom thou canst give no help,
Do thou but call my resolution wise,
And with this knife I'll help it presently.
God join'd my heart and Romeo's, thou our hands,
And ere this hand, by thee to Romeo's seal'd,
Shall be the label to another deed,
Or my true heart with treacherous revolt
Turn to another, this shall slay them both.
Therefore, out of thy long-experienc'd time,
Give me some present counsel, or, behold,
'Twixt my extremes and me this bloody knife
Shall play the umpeer, arbitrating that
Which the commission of thy years and art
Could to no issue of true honor bring.
Be not so long to speak, I long to die,
If what thou speak'st speak not of remedy.
Fri. L. Hold, daughter! I do spy a kind of hope,
Which craves as desperate an execution
As that is desperate which we would prevent.
If rather than to marry County Paris,
Thou hast the strength of will to [slay] thyself,
Then is it likely thou wilt undertake
A thing like death to chide away this shame,
That cop'st with Death himself to scape from it;
And if thou darest, I'll give thee remedy.
Jul. O, bid me leap, rather than marry Paris,
From off the battlements of any tower,
Or walk in thievish ways, or bid me lurk
Where serpents are; chain me with roaring bears,
Or hide me nightly in a charnel-house,
O'ercover'd quite with dead men's rattling bones,
With reeky shanks and yellow [chapless] skulls;
Or bid me go into a new-made grave,
And hide me with a dead man in his [shroud]—
Things that, to hear them told, have made me tremble—
And I will do it without fear or doubt,
To live an unstain'd wife to my sweet love.
Fri. L. Hold then. Go home, be merry, give consent
To marry Paris. We'n'sday is to-morrow;
To-morrow night look that thou lie alone,
Let not the nurse lie with thee in thy chamber.
Take thou this vial, being then in bed,
And this distilling liquor drink thou off,
When presently through all thy veins shall run
A cold and drowsy humor; for no pulse
Shall keep his native progress, but surcease;
No warmth, no [breath] shall testify thou livest;
The roses in thy lips and cheeks shall fade
To [wanny] ashes, thy eyes' windows fall,
Like death when he shuts up the day of life;
Each part, depriv'd of supple government,
Shall, stiff and stark and cold, appear like death,
And in this borrowed likeness of shrunk death
Thou shalt continue two and forty hours,
And then awake as from a pleasant sleep.
Now when the bridegroom in the morning comes
To rouse thee from thy bed, there art thou dead.
Then, as the manner of our country is,
[In] thy best robes, uncovered on the bier,
Thou shall be borne to that same ancient vault
Where all the kindred of the Capulets lie.
In the mean time, against thou shalt awake,
Shall Romeo by my letters know our drift,
And hither shall he come, an' he and I
Will watch thy [waking], and that very night
Shall Romeo bear thee hence to Mantua.

34. to my face: (1) openly; (2) concerning my face.
39. pensive: sad. **41. shield:** prevent, forbid.
46. thy grief: the cause of your grief.
47. strains: forces. **compass:** boundary, limits.
54. presently: at once.
57. label: i.e. seal (literally, a strip of material attached to a document to carry the seal). **62. extremes:** desperate plight.
63. umpeer: umpire. **64. commission:** authority. **art:** skill.
75. That cop'st with: (you) who would encounter.
79. thievish: infested with thieves.
83. reeky: emitting foul vapor. **chapless:** without lower jaws.
94. distilling: having the power to permeate the body.
96. humor: fluid.
97. keep . . . progress: maintain its natural progression. **surcease:** cease. **100. wanny:** pale. **windows:** shutters, i.e. lids.
102. supple government: control of movement.
113. against: in preparation for the time when. **114. drift:** intent.

And this shall free thee from this present shame,
If no inconstant toy, nor womanish fear,
Abate thy valor in the acting it.

Jul. Give me, give me! O, tell not me of fear!

Fri. L. Hold, get you gone. Be strong and prosperous
In this resolve. I'll send a friar with speed
To Mantua, with my letters to thy lord.

Jul. Love give me strength! and strength shall help afford.
Farewell, dear father! *Exeunt.*

[SCENE II]

Enter FATHER CAPULET, *Mother* [LADY CAPULET], NURSE, *and* SERVINGMEN, *two or three.*

Cap. So many guests invite as here are writ. [*Exit First Servant.*]
Sirrah, go hire me twenty cunning cooks.

[2.] *Serv.* You shall have none ill, sir, for I'll try if they can lick their fingers.

Cap. How canst thou try them so?

[2.] *Serv.* Marry, sir, 'tis an ill cook that cannot lick his own fingers; therefore he that cannot lick his fingers goes not with me.

Cap. Go, be gone. [*Exit Second Servant.*]
We shall be much unfurnish'd for this time.
What, is my daughter gone to Friar Lawrence?

Nurse. Ay forsooth.

Cap. Well, he may chance to do some good on her.
A peevish self[-will'd] harlotry it is.

Enter JULIET.

Nurse. See where she comes from shrift with merry look.

Cap. How now, my headstrong, where have you been gadding?

Jul. Where I have learnt me to repent the sin
Of disobedient opposition
To you and your behests, and am enjoin'd
By holy Lawrence to fall prostrate here
To beg your pardon. [*She kneels down.*] Pardon, I beseech you!
Henceforward I am ever rul'd by you.

Cap. Send for the County, go tell him of this.
I'll have this knot knit up to-morrow morning.

Jul. I met the youthful lord at Lawrence' cell,
And gave him what becomed love I might,
Not stepping o'er the bounds of modesty.

Cap. Why, I am glad on't, this is well, stand up.
This is as't should be. Let me see the County;
Ay, marry, go, I say, and fetch him hither.
Now, afore God, this reverend holy friar,
All our whole city is much bound to him.

119. **inconstant toy:** capricious change of mind.
122. **prosperous:** fortunate.

IV.ii. Location: Verona. Capulet's house.
5. **try them so:** i.e. tell by that test whether they are good cooks.
7. **lick . . . fingers:** i.e. to show his confidence in his own cooking.
10. **unfurnish'd:** unprepared. 14. **harlotry:** wench.
26. **becomed:** befitting.

Jul. Nurse, will you go with me into my closet
To help me sort such needful ornaments
As you think fit to furnish me to-morrow?

La. Cap. No, not till Thursday, there is time enough.

Cap. Go, nurse, go with her, we'll to church to-morrow. *Exeunt* [*Juliet and Nurse*].

La. Cap. We shall be short in our provision,
'Tis now near night.

Cap. Tush, I will stir about,
And all things shall be well, I warrant thee, wife;
Go thou to Juliet, help to deck up her.
I'll not to bed to-night; let me alone,
I'll play the huswife for this once. What ho!
They are all forth. Well, I will walk myself
To County Paris, to prepare up him
Against to-morrow. My heart is wondrous light,
Since this same wayward girl is so reclaim'd. *Exeunt.*

[SCENE III]

Enter JULIET *and* NURSE.

Jul. Ay, those attires are best, but, gentle nurse,
I pray thee leave me to myself to-night,
For I have need of many orisons
To move the heavens to smile upon my state,
Which, well thou knowest, is cross and full of sin.

Enter Mother [LADY CAPULET].

La. Cap. What, are you busy, ho? Need you my help?

Jul. No, madam, we have cull'd such necessaries
As are behoofeful for our state to-morrow.
So please you, let me now be left alone,
And let the nurse this night sit up with you,
For I am sure you have your hands full all,
In this so sudden business.

La. Cap. Good night.
Get thee to bed and rest, for thou hast need.
Exeunt [*Lady Capulet and Nurse*].

Jul. Farewell! God knows when we shall meet again.
I have a faint cold fear thrills through my veins,
That almost freezes up the heat of life.
I'll call them back again to comfort me.
Nurse!—What should she do here?
My dismal scene I needs must act alone.
Come, vial.
What if this mixture do not work at all?
Shall I be married then to-morrow morning?
No, no, this shall forbid it. Lie thou there.
[*Laying down her dagger.*]
What if it be a poison which the friar
Subtilly hath minist'red to have me dead,
Lest in this marriage he should be dishonor'd

33. **closet:** private room.
34. **sort:** select. 42. **let me alone:** leave everything to me.

IV.iii. Location: Verona. Capulet's house.
5. **cross:** perverse. 8. **behoofeful:** needful. **state:** ceremony.
15. **faint cold:** producing faintness and coldness. **thrills:** that pierces.
19. **dismal:** dreadful, fateful.

Because he married me before to Romeo?
I fear it is, and yet methinks it should not,
For he hath still been tried a holy man.
How if, when I am laid into the tomb,
I wake before the time that Romeo
Come to redeem me? there's a fearful point!
Shall I not then be stifled in the vault,
To whose foul mouth no healthsome air breathes in,
And there die strangled ere my Romeo comes?
Or if I live, is it not very like
The horrible conceit of death and night,
Together with the terror of the place—
As in a vault, an ancient receptacle,
Where for this many hundred years the bones
Of all my buried ancestors are pack'd,
Where bloody Tybalt, yet but green in earth,
Lies fest'ring in his shroud, where, as they say,
At some hours in the night spirits resort—
Alack, alack, is it not like that I,
So early waking—what with loathsome smells,
And shrikes like mandrakes' torn out of the earth,
That living mortals, hearing them, run mad—
O, if I [wake], shall I not be distraught,
Environed with all these hideous fears,
And madly play with my forefathers' joints,
And pluck the mangled Tybalt from his shroud,
And in this rage, with some great kinsman's bone,
As with a club, dash out my desp'rate brains?
O, look! methinks I see my cousin's ghost
Seeking out Romeo, that did spit his body
Upon a rapier's point. Stay, Tybalt, stay!
Romeo, Romeo, Romeo! Here's drink—I drink to thee.

[She falls upon her bed, within the curtains.]

[Scene IV]

Enter lady of the house [Lady Capulet] *and* Nurse *[with herbs].*

La. Cap. Hold, take these keys and fetch more spices, nurse.

Nurse. They call for dates and quinces in the pastry.

Enter old Capulet.

Cap. Come, stir, stir, stir! the second cock hath crowed,
The curfew-bell hath rung, 'tis three a' clock.
Look to the bak'd meats, good Angelica,
Spare not for cost.

Nurse. Go, you cot-quean, go,
Get you to bed. Faith, you'll be sick to-morrow
For this night's watching.

Cap. No, not a whit. What, I have watch'd ere now
All night for lesser cause, and ne'er been sick.

La. Cap. Ay, you have been a mouse-hunt in your time,
But I will watch you from such watching now.

Exeunt Lady [Capulet] and Nurse.

Cap. A jealous hood, a jealous hood!

Enter three or four [Servingmen] *with spits and logs and baskets.*

Now, fellow, what is there?

[1. Serv.] Things for the cook, sir, but I know not what.

Cap. Make haste, make haste. *[Exit First Servant.]*
Sirrah, fetch drier logs.
Call Peter, he will show thee where they are.

[2. Serv.] I have a head, sir, that will find out logs,
And never trouble Peter for the matter.

Cap. Mass, and well said, a merry whoreson, ha!
Thou shalt be logger-head. *[Exit Second Servant.]*
Good [faith], 'tis day.
The County will be here with music straight,
For so he said he would. *(Play music [within].)* I hear him near.
Nurse! Wife! What ho! What, nurse, I say!

Enter Nurse.

Go waken Juliet, go and trim her up,
I'll go and chat with Paris. Hie, make haste,
Make haste, the bridegroom he is come already,
Make haste, I say. *[Exit.]*

[Scene V]

Nurse. Mistress! what, mistress! Juliet!—Fast, I warrant her, she.—
Why, lamb! why, lady! fie, you slug-a-bed!
Why, love, I say! madam! sweet heart! why, bride!
What, not a word? You take your pennyworths now;
Sleep for a week, for the next night, I warrant,
The County Paris hath set up his rest
That you shall rest but little. God forgive me!
Marry and amen! How sound is she asleep!
I needs must wake her. Madam, madam, madam!
Ay, let the County take you in your bed,
He'll fright you up, i' faith. Will it not be?

[Draws back the curtains.]

What, dress'd, and in your clothes, and down again?
I must needs wake you. Lady, lady, lady!
Alas, alas! Help, help! my lady's dead!
O, weraday, that ever I was born!
Some aqua-vitae ho! My lord! my lady!

29. still: always. **tried:** proved (by testing). **37. conceit:** idea.
42. green in earth: newly buried.
47. shrikes: shrieks. **mandrakes'.** The mandrake, a plant with a fleshy forked root, was thought to resemble a man. When pulled from the earth it supposedly uttered a shriek that caused anyone who heard it to run mad or die.
53. rage: insane fit. **great:** earlier by one or more generations, as in *great-grandfather*. **57. Stay:** stop.

IV.iv. Location: Scene continues.
2. pastry: pastry-room. **5. Angelica:** i.e. the Nurse.
6. cot-quean: man who plays housewife.

8. watching: staying awake.
11. mouse-hunt: mouse-hunter, i.e. woman-chaser.
13. jealous hood: jealous person (cf. *madcap, bad hat*).
21. logger-head: blockhead.

IV.v. Location: Scene continues.
1. Fast: fast asleep. **4. pennyworths:** small quantities.
6. set . . . rest: firmly resolved (a term from the card game primero).

[*Enter Mother*, Lady Capulet.]

La. Cap. What noise is here?
Nurse. O lamentable day!
La. Cap. What is the matter?
Nurse. Look, look! O heavy day!
La. Cap. O me, O me, my child, my only life!
Revive, look up, or I will die with thee!
Help, help! Call help.

Enter Father [Capulet].

Cap. For shame, bring Juliet forth, her lord is come.
Nurse. She's dead, deceas'd, she's dead, alack the day!
La. Cap. Alack the day, she's dead, she's dead, she's dead!
Cap. Hah, let me see her. Out alas, she's cold,
Her blood is settled, and her joints are stiff;
Life and these lips have long been separated.
Death lies on her like an untimely frost
Upon the sweetest flower of all the field.
Nurse. O lamentable day!
La. Cap. O woeful time!
Cap. Death, that hath ta'en her hence to make me wail,
Ties up my tongue and will not let me speak.

Enter Friar [Lawrence] *and the* County [Paris *with the* Musicians].

Fri. L. Come, is the bride ready to go to church?
Cap. Ready to go, but never to return.—
O son, the night before thy wedding-day
Hath Death lain with thy wife. There she lies,
Flower as she was, deflowered by him.
Death is my son-in-law, Death is my heir,
My daughter he hath wedded. I will die,
And leave him all; life, living, all is Death's.
Par. Have I thought [long] to see this morning's face,
And doth it give me such a sight as this?
La. Cap. Accurs'd, unhappy, wretched, hateful day!
Most miserable hour that e'er time saw
In lasting labor of his pilgrimage!
But one, poor one, one poor and loving child,
But one thing to rejoice and solace in,
And cruel Death hath catch'd it from my sight!
Nurse. O woe! O woeful, woeful, woeful day!
Most lamentable day, most woeful day
That ever, ever, I did yet behold!
O day, O day, O day, O hateful day!
Never was seen so black a day as this.
O woeful day, O woeful day!
Par. Beguil'd, divorced, wronged, spited, slain!
Most detestable Death, by thee beguil'd,
By cruel cruel thee quite overthrown!
O love, O life! not life, but love in death!
Cap. Despis'd, distressed, hated, martyr'd, kill'd!
Uncomfortable time, why cam'st thou now

40. **living:** property. 41. **thought long:** been impatient.
45. **lasting:** ceaseless. 48. **catch'd:** snatched.
60. **Uncomfortable:** comfortless.

To murther, murther our solemnity?
O child, O child! my soul, and not my child!
Dead art thou! Alack, my child is dead,
And with my child my joys are buried.
Fri. L. Peace ho, for shame! Confusion's [cure] lives not
In these confusions. Heaven and yourself
Had part in this fair maid, now heaven hath all,
And all the better is it for the maid.
Your part in her you could not keep from death,
But heaven keeps his part in eternal life.
The most you sought was her promotion,
For 'twas your heaven she should be advanc'd,
And weep ye now, seeing she is advanc'd
Above the clouds, as high as heaven itself?
O, in this love, you love your child so ill
That you run mad, seeing that she is well.
She's not well married that lives married long,
But she's best married that dies married young.
Dry up your tears, and stick your rosemary
On this fair corse, and as the custom is,
And in her best array, bear her to church;
For though [fond] nature bids us all lament,
Yet nature's tears are reason's merriment.
Cap. All things that we ordained festival,
Turn from their office to black funeral:
Our instruments to melancholy bells,
Our wedding cheer to a sad burial feast;
Our solemn hymns to sullen dirges change;
Our bridal flowers serve for a buried corse;
And all things change them to the contrary.
Fri. L. Sir, go you in, and, madam, go with him;
And go, Sir Paris. Every one prepare
To follow this fair corse unto her grave.
The heavens do low'r upon you for some ill;
Move them no more by crossing their high will.

[*They all, but the Nurse and the Musicians, go forth, casting rosemary on her, and shutting the curtains.*]

[*1.*] *Mus.* Faith, we may put up our pipes and be gone.

Nurse. Honest good fellows, ah, put up, put up,
For well you know this is a pitiful case. [*Exit.*]

[*1. Mus.*] Ay, [by] my troth, the case may be amended.

Enter [Peter].

Pet. Musicians, O musicians, "Heart's ease," "Heart's ease"! O, and you will have me live, play "Heart's ease."

[*1. Mus.*] Why "Heart's ease"?

Pet. O musicians, because my heart itself plays

61. **solemnity:** festivity. 65. **Confusion's:** ruin's, loss's.
66. **confusions:** disorderly outcries. 71. **promotion:** advancement.
75. **in this love:** i.e. by lamenting her death.
79. **rosemary:** herb signifying remembrance.
83. **nature's . . . merriment:** that which makes human nature mourn is cause for joy to the reason. 85. **office:** function.
87. **cheer:** banquet. 88. **sullen:** mournful. 95. **Move:** anger.
100–101. **the case . . . amended:** (1) things could be better than they are; (2) the instrument case could well be repaired.
102. **"Heart's ease":** a ballad tune; "My heart is full [of woe]" (line 107) is another.

"My heart is full." O, play me some merry dump to comfort me.

[*1. Mus.*] Not a dump we, 'tis no time to play now.

Pet. You will not then?

[*1. Mus.*] No.

Pet. I will then give it you soundly.

[*1. Mus.*] What will you give us?

Pet. No money, on my faith, but the gleek; I will give you the minstrel.

[*1. Mus.*] Then will I give you the serving-creature.

Pet. Then will I lay the serving-creature's dagger on your pate. I will carry no crotchets, I'll *re* you, I'll *fa* you. Do you note me?

[*1. Mus.*] And you *re* us and *fa* us, you note us.

2. Mus. Pray you put up your dagger, and put out your wit.

[*Pet.*] Then have at you with my wit! I will dry-beat you with an iron wit, and put up my iron dagger. Answer me like men:

"When griping griefs the heart doth wound,
[And doleful dumps the mind oppress,]
Then music with her silver sound"—

why "silver sound"? Why "music with her silver sound"? What say you, Simon Catling?

[*1. Mus.*] Marry, sir, because silver hath a sweet sound.

Pet. [Pretty!] What say you, Hugh Rebeck?

2. Mus. I say, "silver sound," because musicians sound for silver.

Pet. [Pretty] too! What say you, James Soundpost?

3. Mus. Faith, I know not what to say.

Pet. O, I cry you mercy, you are the singer; I will say for you; it is "music with her silver sound," because musicians have no gold for sounding:

"Then music with her silver sound
With speedy help doth lend redress." *Exit.*

[*1. Mus.*] What a pestilent knave is this same!

2. Mus. Hang him, Jack! Come, we'll in here, tarry for the mourners, and stay dinner. *Exeunt.*

[ACT V, SCENE I]

Enter ROMEO.

Rom. If I may trust the flattering truth of sleep,
My dreams presage some joyful news at hand.
My bosom's lord sits lightly in his throne,
And all this day an unaccustom'd spirit
Lifts me above the ground with cheerful thoughts.
I dreamt my lady came and found me dead—
Strange dream, that gives a dead man leave to think!—
And breath'd such life with kisses in my lips
That I reviv'd and was an emperor.
Ah me, how sweet is love itself possess'd,
When but love's shadows are so rich in joy!

Enter Romeo's man [BALTHASAR, *booted*].

News from Verona! How now, Balthasar?
Dost thou not bring me letters from the friar?
How doth my lady? Is my father well?
How doth my Juliet? That I ask again,
For nothing can be ill if she be well.

Bal. Then she is well and nothing can be ill:
Her body sleeps in Capel's monument,
And her immortal part with angels lives.
I saw her laid low in her kindred's vault,
And presently took post to tell it you.
O, pardon me for bringing these ill news,
Since you did leave it for my office, sir.

Rom. Is it [e'en] so? Then I [defy] you, stars!
Thou knowest my lodging, get me ink and paper,
And hire post-horses; I will hence to-night.

Bal. I do beseech you, sir, have patience.
Your looks are pale and wild, and do import
Some misadventure.

Rom. Tush, thou art deceiv'd.
Leave me, and do the thing I bid thee do.
Hast thou no letters to me from the friar?

Bal. No, my good lord.

Rom. No matter, get thee gone,
And hire those horses; I'll be with thee straight.
Exit [*Balthasar*].

Well, Juliet, I will lie with thee to-night.
Let's see for means. O mischief, thou art swift
To enter in the thoughts of desperate men!
I do remember an apothecary—
And hereabouts 'a dwells—which late I noted
In tatt'red weeds, with overwhelming brows,
Culling of simples; meagre were his looks,
Sharp misery had worn him to the bones;
And in his needy shop a tortoise hung,
An alligator stuff'd, and other skins
Of ill-shap'd fishes, and about his shelves
A beggarly account of empty boxes,
Green earthen pots, bladders, and musty seeds,
Remnants of packthread, and old cakes of roses
Were thinly scattered, to make up a show.
Noting this penury, to myself I said,
"An' if a man did need a poison now,
Whose sale is present death in Mantua,

107. dump: mournful tune.
114. gleek: gibe. **115. give . . . minstrel:** call you rogues.
118. carry: (1) endure; (2) sing. **crotchets:** (1) whims; (2) quarter-notes.
118, 119. re, fa: notes of the scale (perhaps with puns on *ray*, "befoul," and *fay*, "clean up").
119–20. note . . . note: heed . . . set to music.
121. put out: display. **124. iron wit:** i.e. merciless wit.
126–28, 142–43. These lines are from Richard Edwards' "In Commendation of Music."
130. Catling: name taken from that of a lute-string.
133. Rebeck: name based on that of a three-stringed violin.
135. sound: play or sing.
136–37. Soundpost: name based on that of the internal structural support of such instruments as the violin.
139. cry you mercy: beg your pardon. **singer.** Implying that he can sing but not speak.
141. have . . . sounding: (1) do not receive gold for playing; (2) possess no gold for jingling in their pockets. **146. stay:** wait for.

V.i. Location: Mantua. A street.
1. flattering: favorable, gratifying.

3. My bosom's lord: i.e. love. **his throne:** i.e. my heart.
21. presently: immediately. **took post:** hired post-horses.
23. office: duty. **35. see for means:** think how to do it.
39. weeds: clothes. **overwhelming:** jutting, overhanging.
40. simples: medicinal herbs. **45. beggarly account:** paltry lot.
47. cakes of roses: rose petals pressed into cake form, for the perfume.
50. An' if: if.
51. present death: punishable by immediate execution.

Here lives a caitiff wretch would sell it him."
O, this same thought did but forerun my need,
And this same needy man must sell it me.
As I remember, this should be the house.
Being holiday, the beggar's shop is shut.
What ho, apothecary!

[*Enter* Apothecary.]

Ap. Who calls so loud?
Rom. Come hither, man. I see that thou art poor.
Hold, there is forty ducats; let me have
A dram of poison, such soon-speeding gear
As will disperse itself through all the veins
That the life-weary taker may fall dead,
And that the trunk may be discharg'd of breath
As violently as hasty powder fir'd
Doth hurry from the fatal cannon's womb.
Ap. Such mortal drugs I have, but Mantua's law
Is death to any he that utters them.
Rom. Art thou so bare and full of wretchedness,
And fearest to die? Famine is in thy cheeks,
Need and oppression starveth in thy eyes,
Contempt and beggary hangs upon thy back;
The world is not thy friend, nor the world's law,
The world affords no law to make thee rich;
Then be not poor, but break it, and take this.
Ap. My poverty, but not my will, consents.
Rom. I [pay] thy poverty, and not thy will.
Ap. Put this in any liquid thing you will
And drink it off, and if you had the strength
Of twenty men, it would dispatch you straight.
Rom. There is thy gold, worse poison to men's souls,
Doing more murther in this loathsome world,
Than these poor compounds that thou mayest not sell.
I sell thee poison, thou hast sold me none.
Farewell! Buy food, and get thyself in flesh.
[*Exit Apothecary.*]
Come, cordial and not poison, go with me
To Juliet's grave, for there must I use thee. *Exit.*

[Scene II]

Enter Friar John.

Fri. J. Holy Franciscan friar! brother, ho!

Enter [Friar] Lawrence.

Fri. L. This same should be the voice of Friar John.
Welcome from Mantua! What says Romeo?
Or, if his mind be writ, give me his letter.
Fri. J. Going to find a barefoot brother out,
One of our order, to associate me,
Here in this city visiting the sick,
And finding him, the searchers of the town,
Suspecting that we both were in a house
Where the infectious pestilence did reign,
Seal'd up the doors and would not let us forth,
So that my speed to Mantua there was stay'd.
Fri. L. Who bare my letter then to Romeo?
Fri. J. I could not send it—here it is again—
Nor get a messenger to bring it thee,
So fearful were they of infection.
Fri. L. Unhappy fortune! By my brotherhood,
The letter was not nice but full of charge,
Of dear import, and the neglecting it
May do much danger. Friar John, go hence,
Get me an iron crow, and bring it straight
Unto my cell.
Fri. J. Brother, I'll go and bring it thee. *Exit.*
Fri. L. Now must I to the monument alone,
Within this three hours will fair Juliet wake.
She will beshrew me much that Romeo
Hath had no notice of these accidents;
But I will write again to Mantua,
And keep her at my cell till Romeo come—
Poor living corse, clos'd in a dead man's tomb! *Exit.*

[Scene III]

Enter Paris *and his* Page [*with flowers and sweet water and a torch*].

Par. Give me thy torch, boy. Hence, and stand aloof.
Yet put it out, for I would not be seen.
Under yond [yew] trees lay thee all along,
Holding thy ear close to the hollow ground,
So shall no foot upon the churchyard tread,
Being loose, unfirm, with digging up of graves,
But thou shalt hear it. Whistle then to me
As signal that thou hearest something approach.
Give me those flowers. Do as I bid thee, go.
Page. [*Aside.*] I am almost afraid to stand alone
Here in the churchyard, yet I will adventure.
[*Retires. Paris strews the tomb with flowers.*]
Par. Sweet flower, with flowers thy bridal bed I strew—
O woe, thy canopy is dust and stones!—
Which with sweet water nightly I will dew,
Or wanting that, with tears distill'd by moans.
The obsequies that I for thee will keep
Nightly shall be to strew thy grave and weep.
Whistle Boy.
The boy gives warning, something doth approach.
What cursed foot wanders this way to-night,

59. ducats: gold coins.
60. soon-speeding gear: quick-working stuff.
67. any he: any man. **utters:** issues, sells.
70. Need and oppression: i.e. oppressive need.
71. Contempt and beggary: i.e. beggary that renders you contemptible.
74. it: i.e. the law. **84. get . . . flesh:** grow fat.
85. cordial: healing medicine, restorative.

V.ii. Location: Verona. Friar Lawrence's cell.
6. associate: travel with. Franciscans journeyed in twos.

8. searchers: health officers.
18. nice: trivial. **charge:** weighty matter.
19. dear: significant, urgent. **21. crow:** crowbar.
26. beshrew: censure. **27. accidents:** events.

V.iii. Location: Verona. A churchyard; in it a tomb belonging to the Capulets.
o.s.d. sweet: perfumed. **1. aloof:** at a distance.
3. all along: flat. **6. Being:** i.e. since the soil is.
10. stand: stay. **16. obsequies:** rites for the dead.

To cross my obsequies and true love's rite?
What, with a torch? Muffle me, night, a while. [*Retires.*]

Enter ROMEO *and* [BALTHASAR *with a torch, a mattock, and a crow of iron*].

Rom. Give me that mattock and the wrenching iron.
Hold, take this letter; early in the morning
See thou deliver it to my lord and father.
Give me the light. Upon thy life I charge thee,
What e'er thou hearest or seest, stand all aloof,
And do not interrupt me in my course.
Why I descend into this bed of death
Is partly to behold my lady's face,
But chiefly to take thence from her dead finger
A precious ring—a ring that I must use
In dear employment—therefore hence be gone.
But if thou, jealous, dost return to pry
In what I farther shall intend to do,
By heaven, I will tear thee joint by joint,
And strew this hungry churchyard with thy limbs.
The time and my intents are savage-wild,
More fierce and more inexorable far
Than empty tigers or the roaring sea.

[*Bal.*] I will be gone, sir, and not trouble ye.

Rom. So shalt thou show me friendship. Take thou that;
Live and be prosperous, and farewell, good fellow.

[*Bal.*] [*Aside.*] For all this same, I'll hide me hereabout,
His looks I fear, and his intents I doubt. [*Retires.*]

Rom. Thou detestable maw, thou womb of death,
Gorg'd with the dearest morsel of the earth,
Thus I enforce thy rotten jaws to open,
And in despite I'll cram thee with more food.
[*Romeo begins to open the tomb.*]

Par. This is that banish'd haughty Montague,
That murd'red my love's cousin, with which grief
It is supposed the fair creature died,
And here is come to do some villainous shame
To the dead bodies. I will apprehend him.
[*Steps forth.*]
Stop thy unhallowed toil, vile Montague!
Can vengeance be pursued further than death?
Condemned villain, I do apprehend thee.
Obey and go with me, for thou must die.

Rom. I must indeed, and therefore came I hither.
Good gentle youth, tempt not a desp'rate man.
Fly hence and leave me, think upon these gone,
Let them affright thee. I beseech thee, youth,
Put not another sin upon my head,
By urging me to fury: O, be gone!
By heaven, I love thee better than myself,
For I come hither arm'd against myself.
Stay not, be gone; live, and hereafter say
A madman's mercy bid thee run away.

Par. I do defy thy [conjuration],

20. cross: interfere with. **33. jealous:** suspicious.
44. fear: am anxious about. **doubt:** suspect.
45. womb: belly. **53. apprehend:** arrest.
68. conjuration: appeal.

And apprehend thee for a felon here.

Rom. Wilt thou provoke me? Then have at thee, boy! [*They fight.*]

[*Page.*] O Lord, they fight! I will go call the watch. [*Exit.*]

Par. O, I am slain! [*Falls.*] If thou be merciful,
Open the tomb, lay me with Juliet. [*Dies.*]

Rom. In faith, I will. Let me peruse this face.
Mercutio's kinsman, noble County Paris!
What said my man, when my betossed soul
Did not attend him as we rode? I think
He told me Paris should have married Juliet.
Said he not so? or did I dream it so?
Or am I mad, hearing him talk of Juliet,
To think it was so? O, give me thy hand,
One writ with me in sour misfortune's book!
I'll bury thee in a triumphant grave.
A grave? O no, a lanthorn, slaught'red youth;
For here lies Juliet, and her beauty makes
This vault a feasting presence full of light.
Death, lie thou there, by a dead man interr'd.
[*Laying Paris in the tomb.*]
How oft when men are at the point of death
Have they been merry, which their keepers call
A lightning before death! O how may I
Call this a lightning? O my love, my wife,
Death, that hath suck'd the honey of thy breath,
Hath had no power yet upon thy beauty:
Thou art not conquer'd, beauty's ensign yet
Is crimson in thy lips and in thy cheeks,
And death's pale flag is not advanced there.
Tybalt, liest thou there in thy bloody sheet?
O, what more favor can I do to thee,
Than with that hand that cut thy youth in twain
To sunder his that was thine enemy?
Forgive me, cousin! Ah, dear Juliet,
Why art thou yet so fair? Shall I believe
That unsubstantial Death is amorous,
And that the lean abhorred monster keeps
Thee here in dark to be his paramour?
For fear of that, I still will stay with thee,
And never from this [palace] of dim night
Depart again. Here, here will I remain
With worms that are thy chambermaids; O, here
Will I set up my everlasting rest,
And shake the yoke of inauspicious stars
From this world-wearied flesh. Eyes, look your last!
Arms, take your last embrace! and, lips, O you
The doors of breath, seal with a righteous kiss
A dateless bargain to engrossing death!
Come, bitter conduct, come, unsavory guide!
Thou desperate pilot, now at once run on
The dashing rocks thy sea-sick weary bark!

78. should have: was to have. **83. triumphant:** magnificent.
84. lanthorn: lantern (variant spelling), i.e. a tower room glassed on all sides. **86. feasting presence:** festival presence chamber.
89. keepers: jailers, or nurses. **96. advanced:** raised.
100. his: i.e. Romeo's. **106. still:** forever.
110. set . . . rest: make my firm resolution to repose for ever (a telescoping of the literal sense of the words and the special use seen in IV.v.6).
115. dateless bargain: contract with no expiration date. **engrossing:** monopolizing (perhaps with pun on the sense "drawing up documents"). **116. conduct:** guide. **118. sea-sick:** weary of voyaging.

Here's to my love! [*Drinks.*] O true apothecary!
Thy drugs are quick. Thus with a kiss I die.
[*Dies.*]

Enter FRIAR [LAWRENCE] *with lanthorn, crow, and spade.*

Fri. L. Saint Francis be my speed! how oft to-night
Have my old feet stumbled at graves! Who's there?
Bal. Here's one, a friend, and one that knows you well.
Fri. L. Bliss be upon you! Tell me, good my friend,
What torch is yond, that vainly lends his light
To grubs and eyeless skulls? As I discern,
It burneth in the Capels' monument.
Bal. It doth so, holy sir, and there's my master,
One that you love.
Fri. L. Who is it?
Bal. Romeo.
Fri. L. How long hath he been there?
Bal. Full half an hour.
Fri. L. Go with me to the vault.
Bal. I dare not, sir.
My master knows not but I am gone hence,
And fearfully did menace me with death
If I did stay to look on his intents.
Fri. L. Stay then, I'll go alone. Fear comes upon me.
O, much I fear some ill unthrifty thing.
Bal. As I did sleep under this [yew] tree here,
I dreamt my master and another fought,
And that my master slew him.
Fri. L. Romeo!
[*Friar stoops and looks on the blood and weapons.*]
Alack, alack, what blood is this, which stains
The stony entrance of this sepulchre?
What mean these masterless and gory swords
To lie discolor'd by this place of peace?
[*Enters the tomb.*]
Romeo, O, pale! Who else? What, Paris too?
And steep'd in blood? Ah, what an unkind hour
Is guilty of this lamentable chance!
The lady stirs. [*Juliet rises.*]
Jul. O comfortable friar! where is my lord?
I do remember well where I should be,
And there I am. Where is my Romeo?
[*Noise within.*]
Fri. L. I hear some noise, lady. Come from that nest
Of death, contagion, and unnatural sleep.
A greater power than we can contradict
Hath thwarted our intents. Come, come away.
Thy husband in thy bosom there lies dead;
And Paris too. Come, I'll dispose of thee
Among a sisterhood of holy nuns.
Stay not to question, for the watch is coming.
Come go, good Juliet [*noise again*], I dare no longer stay.
Exit.

121. speed: aid. **136. unthrifty:** unlucky.
145. unkind: unnatural, cruel.
148. comfortable: providing comfort.

Jul. Go get thee hence, for I will not away.
What's here? A cup clos'd in my true love's hand?
Poison, I see, hath been his timeless end.
O churl, drunk all, and left no friendly drop
To help me after? I will kiss thy lips,
Haply some poison yet doth hang on them,
To make me die with a restorative.
Thy lips are warm.
[*1.*] *Watch.* [*Within.*] Lead, boy, which way?
Jul. Yea, noise? Then I'll be brief. O happy dagger,
[*Taking Romeo's dagger.*]
This is thy sheath [*stabs herself*]; there rust, and let me die.
[*Falls on Romeo's body and dies.*]

Enter [*Paris'*] BOY *and* WATCH.

Page. This is the place, there where the torch doth burn.
[*1.*] *Watch.* The ground is bloody, search about the churchyard.
Go, some of you, whoe'er you find attach.
[*Exeunt some.*]
Pitiful sight! here lies the County slain,
And Juliet bleeding, warm, and newly dead,
Who here hath lain this two days buried.
Go tell the Prince, run to the Capulets,
Raise up the Montagues; some others search.
[*Exeunt others.*]
We see the ground whereon these woes do lie,
But the true ground of all these piteous woes
We cannot without circumstance descry.

Enter [*some of the* WATCH *with*] *Romeo's man* [BALTHASAR].

[*2.*] *Watch.* Here's Romeo's man, we found him in the churchyard.
[*1*]. *Watch.* Hold him in safety till the Prince come hither.

Enter FRIAR [LAWRENCE] *and another* WATCHMAN.

3. Watch. Here is a friar, that trembles, sighs, and weeps.
We took this mattock and this spade from him,
As he was coming from this churchyard's side.
[*1.*] *Watch.* A great suspicion. Stay the friar too.

Enter the PRINCE [*and* ATTENDANTS].

Prince. What misadventure is so early up,
That calls our person from our morning rest?

Enter Capels [CAPULET, LADY CAPULET, *and others*].

Cap. What should it be that is so [shrik'd] abroad?
La. Cap. O, the people in the street cry "Romeo,"
Some "Juliet," and some "Paris," and all run
With open outcry toward our monument.

162. timeless: untimely. **163. churl:** niggard.
164. after: come after, follow.
166. with: by means of. **a restorative.** Because it will restore her to him. Cf. Romeo's "cordial and not poison," V.i.85.
169. happy: opportune. **170. This:** i.e. her breast.
173. attach: arrest.
179. ground . . . woes: earth . . . woeful creatures.
180. ground . . . woes: basis . . . woeful events.
181. circumstance: details. **183. in safety:** securely.

Prince. What fear is this which startles in your ears?
[*1.*] *Watch*. Sovereign, here lies the County Paris slain,
And Romeo dead, and Juliet, dead before,
Warm and new kill'd.
Prince. Search, seek, and know how this foul murder comes.
[*1.*] *Watch*. Here is a friar, and [slaughter'd] Romeo's man,
With instruments upon them, fit to open
These dead men's tombs.
Cap. O heavens! O wife, look how our daughter bleeds!
This dagger hath mista'en, for lo his house
Is empty on the back of Montague,
And it mis-sheathed in my daughter's bosom!
La. Cap. O me, this sight of death is as a bell
That warns my old age to a sepulchre.

Enter MONTAGUE [*and others*].

Prin. Come, Montague, for thou art early up
To see thy son and heir now [early] down.
Mon. Alas, my liege, my wife is dead to-night;
Grief of my son's exile hath stopp'd her breath.
What further woe conspires against mine age?
Prin. Look and thou shalt see.
Mon. O thou untaught! what manners is in this,
To press before thy father to a grave?
Prin. Seal up the mouth of outrage for a while,
Till we can clear these ambiguities,
And know their spring, their head, their true descent,
And then will I be general of your woes,
And lead you even to death. Mean time forbear,
And let mischance be slave to patience.
Bring forth the parties of suspicion.
Fri. L. I am the greatest, able to do least,
Yet most suspected, as the time and place
Doth make against me, of this direful murther;
And here I stand both to impeach and purge
Myself condemned and myself excus'd.
Prin. Then say at once what thou dost know in this.
Fri. L. I will be brief, for my short date of breath
Is not so long as is a tedious tale.
Romeo, there dead, was husband to that Juliet,
And she, there dead, [that] Romeo's faithful wife.
I married them, and their stol'n marriage-day
Was Tybalt's dooms-day, whose untimely death
Banish'd the new-made bridegroom from this city,
For whom, and not for Tybalt, Juliet pin'd.
You, to remove that siege of grief from her,
Betroth'd and would have married her perforce
To County Paris. Then comes she to me,
And with wild looks bid me devise some mean
To rid her from this second marriage,
Or in my cell there would she kill herself.
Then gave I her (so tutor'd by my art)
A sleeping potion, which so took effect
As I intended, for it wrought on her
The form of death. Mean time I writ to Romeo,
That he should hither come as this dire night
To help to take her from her borrowed grave,
Being the time the potion's force should cease.
But he which bore my letter, Friar John,
Was stayed by accident, and yesternight
Return'd my letter back. Then all alone,
At the prefixed hour of her waking,
Came I to take her from her kindred's vault,
Meaning to keep her closely at my cell,
Till I conveniently could send to Romeo.
But when I came, some minute ere the time
Of her awakening, here untimely lay
The noble Paris and true Romeo dead.
She wakes, and I entreated her come forth
And bear this work of heaven with patience.
But then a noise did scare me from the tomb,
And she, too desperate, would not go with me,
But as it seems, did violence on herself.
All this I know, and to the marriage
Her nurse is privy; and if aught in this
Miscarried by my fault, let my old life
Be sacrific'd some hour before his time,
Unto the rigor of severest law.
Prin. We still have known thee for a holy man.
Where's Romeo's man? what can he say to this?
Bal. I brought my master news of Juliet's death,
And then in post he came from Mantua
To this same place, to this same monument.
This letter he early bid me give his father,
And threat'ned me with death, going in the vault,
If I departed not and left him there.
Prin. Give me the letter, I will look on it.
Where is the County's page that rais'd the watch?
Sirrah, what made your master in this place?
Page. He came with flowers to strew his lady's grave,
And bid me stand aloof, and so I did.
Anon comes one with light to ope the tomb,
And by and by my master drew on him,
And then I ran away to call the watch.
Prin. This letter doth make good the friar's words,
Their course of love, the tidings of her death;
And here he writes that he did buy a poison
Of a poor pothecary, and therewithal
Came to this vault, to die and lie with Juliet.
Where be these enemies? Capulet! Montague!
See what a scourge is laid upon your hate,
That heaven finds means to kill your joys with love.
And I for winking at your discords too
Have lost a brace of kinsmen. All are punish'd.

203. house: i.e. scabbard. **210. liege:** sovereign.
216. outrage: impassioned grief.
218. spring: source (of a stream); ***head*** is a synonym.
219. be general: take command.
220. death: i.e. the death of the guilty.
222. of suspicion: suspected.
226–27. both . . . excus'd: both to accuse myself and be found guilty, and to exonerate myself and be excused.
229. my . . . breath: the brief time I have left to live.
247. as this: this very. **255. closely:** secretly.
270. still: always. **280. made:** did.
293. kill your joys: (1) turn your joys to sorrows; (2) kill your children. **with:** by means of.
294. winking at: shutting my eyes to.
295. brace: pair (Mercutio and Paris).

Cap. O brother Montague, give me thy hand.
This is my daughter's jointure, for no more
Can I demand.
Mon. But I can give thee more,
For I will [raise] her statue in pure gold,
That whiles Verona by that name is known,
There shall no figure at such rate be set
As that of true and faithful Juliet.
Cap. As rich shall Romeo's by his lady's lie,
Poor sacrifices of our enmity!
Prin. A glooming peace this morning with it brings,
The sun, for sorrow, will not show his head.
Go hence to have more talk of these sad things;
Some shall be pardon'd, and some punished:
For never was a story of more woe
Than this of Juliet and her Romeo. [*Exeunt omnes.*]

297. jointure: marriage portion. **301. rate:** value.

304. Poor sacrifices of: (1) pitiful victims of; (2) inadequate atonement for. **305. glooming:** cloudy.

NOTE ON THE TEXT

Romeo and Juliet presents a complicated textual problem. The play was first published in a "bad" quarto version (Q1) in 1597. A "good" quarto (Q2), "Newly corrected, augmented, and amended," appeared two years later in 1599. Three other quarto editions were printed, each set up from the immediately preceding edition: Q3 (1609), Q4 (undated, but probably c. 1622), Q5 (1637). The First Folio text (1623) was set directly from a copy of Q3, with almost no attempt at correction apart from the addition of a few obvious stage directions.

Since it is generally agreed that Q1 is a memorially reconstructed text and therefore without any direct authority and that F1 is essentially a reprint of Q3, the weight of textual authority rests with Q2. The Q2 text shows many of the usual signs associated with derivation from Shakespeare's "foul papers": considerable inconsistency and vagueness in the use of speech-prefixes (see, for example, Textual Notes, III.v); permissive stage directions (see, for example, I.i.72 s.d., III.i.34 s.d., IV.ii o.s.d., IV.iv.13 s.d.); the preservation of what seem to be rejected trial wordings of several passages (see Textual Notes, III.iii.40–3, III.v.176, IV.i.110, V.iii.102, 108); and a few Shakespearean spellings (see text or Notes, I.iii.35, II.iv.l, III.i.103, V.i.24). The ultimate authority of Q2, however, is also ambiguous. It is clear, for example, that at least one section of Q2 (I.ii.46–I.iii.34) was set up (with almost no correction) directly from a copy of Q1, and G. I. Duthie, following a theory first suggested by Greta Hjort, believed that a copy of Q1 which had been corrected and expanded from Shakespeare's "foul papers" actually served as the copy-text for Q2. However, it is now generally agreed (Thomas, Greg, Hosley, Williams, Gibbons, Evans, Jowett/Wells) that, although I.ii.46–I.iii.34 was indeed set from an essentially uncorrected copy of Q1, the bulk of Q2 was set up directly from the "foul papers" with consultation of Q1 at points where the manuscript was difficult to read. The present text, based, of course, on Q2, follows the second view, but either position, it must be recognized, leaves an uncomfortable uncertainty about the final authority of the Q2 text in those passages which it shares more or less in common with Q1.

The printer's copy for Q2 obviously offered very real problems for the compositor, and Q2 contains a substantial number of misreadings. As a result, it has been necessary in some sixty cases, not including the correction of mere typographical errors, to adopt the reading of Q1, or of later quartos or F1 supported by Q1, since, "bad" quarto or not, it is the only other text which may be said to derive independently, however indirectly, from some form of Shakespeare's manuscript. Q1 also supplies lines or part-lines at I.iv.7–8, II.ii.41, 163, and IV.v.127, as well as a number of valuable descriptive stage directions.

The undated Q4, although it is clearly based on Q3, makes a number of intelligent emendations, several of which, as the Textual Notes show, support the readings of Q1. Unfortunately, there is no reason to allow the readings of Q4 any independent manuscript authority; they would appear to be the work of someone in the printing-house who was interested in making sense of difficult passages and generally tidying up the text.

The absence of Q1 from the sigla cited in a textual note indicates that the reading of the lemma occurs in a passage which in Q1 is either omitted or so differently worded that it offers no recognizable equivalent. "*(Q1)*" following other sigla indicates agreement of Q1 with the other editions cited. Longer examples of the Q1 text may be consulted in the Textual Notes at II.vi, III.i.100–8, IV.iii.1–5, IV.v.41–64, V.iii.12, 223–69.

For further information, see: Robert Gericke, "*Romeo and Juliet* nach Shakespeares Manuscript," *Shakespeare Jahrbuch*, XIV (1879), 270–2; Greta Hjort, "The Good and Bad Quartos of *Romeo and Juliet* and *Love's Labour's Lost*," *MLR*, XXI (1926), 140–6; H. R. Hoppe, *The Bad Quarto of "Romeo and Juliet": A Bibliographical and Textual Study* (Ithaca, 1948); Sidney Thomas, "The Bibliographical Links between the First Two Quartos of *Romeo and Juliet*," *RES*, XXV (1949), 110–14, and "Henry Chettle and the First Quarto of *Romeo and Juliet*," *RES*, n.s. I (1950), 8–16; G. I. Duthie, "The Text of Shakespeare's *Romeo and Juliet*," *SB*, IV (1951–52), 3–29, and ed. (with J. D. Wilson), New Shakespeare *Romeo and Juliet* (Cambridge, 1955); Richard Hosley, "The Corrupting Influence of the Bad Quarto on the Received Text of *Romeo and Juliet*," *SQ*, IV (1953), 11–33, ed., New Yale *Romeo and Juliet* (New Haven, 1954), and "Quarto Copy for Q2 *Romeo and Juliet*," *SB*, IX (1957), 129–41; W. W. Greg, *The Shakespeare First Folio* (Oxford, 1955); P. L. Cantrell and G. W. Williams, "The Printing of the Second Quarto of *Romeo and Juliet* (1599)," *SB*, IX (1957), 107–28; F. T. Bowers, *Textual and Literary Criticism* (Cambridge, 1959); G. W. Williams, ed., *Romeo and Juliet* (Durham, N.C., 1964); G. B. Evans, "The Douai Manuscript—Six Shakespearean Transcripts (1694–95)," *PQ*, XLI (1962), 158–72, and ed., New Cambridge *Romeo and Juliet* (Cambridge, 1984); J. K. Walton, *The Quarto Copy for the First Folio of Shakespeare* (Dublin, 1971); Brian Gibbons, ed., New Arden *Romeo and Juliet* (London, 1980); S. W. Reid, "The Editing of Folio *Romeo and Juliet*," *SB*, XXXV (1982), 43–66; Stanley Wells, Gary Taylor, John Jowett, and William Montgomery, *William Shakespeare: A Textual Companion* (Oxford 1987); Y. S. Bains, "The Bad Quarto of Shakespeare's *Romeo and Juliet* and the Theory of Memorial Reconstruction," *Shakespeare Jahrbuch*, CLXXVI (1990), 164–73 [another attempt to discredit the "memorial reconstruction" theory].

TEXTUAL NOTES

Title: **The . . . Juliet]** *F1;* The Most Excellent and lamentable Tragedie, of Romeo and Iuliet. Newly corrected, augmented, and amended: As it hath bene sundry times publiquely acted, by the right Honourable the Lord Chamberlaine his Seruants. *Q2 (title-page);* An Excellent conceited Tragedie of Romeo and Iuliet, As it hath been often (with great applause) plaid publiquely, by the right Honourable the L. of Hunsdon his Seruants. *Q1 (title-page)*

Dramatis personae: *subs. as first given in Douai MS and Rowe*

Act-scene division: *none in Q2–4; Q1, beginning with III.v, marks most of what are now considered act-scene divisions by a row of printer's ornaments placed between scenes (noted below following the name of the editor responsible for the act or scene division); F1 marks I.i only; other act-scene divisions from Rowe and later editors (see first note to each scene); present act-scene arrangement as a whole first established by Steevens*

Prologue

Om. F1

o.s.d. **Enter Chorus.]** *Capell;* Corus *Q2;* Chorus *Q3–4*

14 s.d. **Exit.]** *Capell*

I.i

I.i] *F1*

Location: *Capell (after Rowe)*

5 **collar]** *F1 (Q1);* choller *Q2–3;* Coller *Q4*

8 **Montague]** *Theobald;* Mountague *Q2–4, F1 (throughout, except* Montague *at II.ii.98 in Q2);* the Mountagues *(Q1)*

9–12 **To . . . Montague's.]** *as prose, Q1, Pope; as verse, Q2–4, F1*

22 **civil]** cruell *Q4*

23 **I will]** and *F1*

27 **in]** *Q4 (Q1)*

32 **two]** *Q1*

32 s.d. **Abram and Balthasar]** *Rowe*

47 s.d. **Aside to Gregory.]** *Capell*

49 s.d. **Aside to Sampson.]** *Capell*

53 **sir?]** *F1;* sir, *Q2–4*

63 **washing]** swashing *Q4*

64–5 **Part . . . do.]** *as verse, Capell; as prose, Q2–4, F1*

65 s.d. **Beats . . . swords.]** *Capell (subs.)*

72 s.d. **They fight.]** Fight. *F1; Q1, omitting ll. 60–80, adds s.d.:* They draw, to them enters Tybalt, they fight, to them the Prince, old Mountague, and his wife, old Capulet and his wife, and other Citizens and part them.

73 s.p. **Citizens.]** *Cowden Clarke;* Offi. *Q2–4, F1*

73 **partisans]** *Q5;* Partisons *Q2–4, F1*

76 s.p. **La. Cap.]** *Rowe;* Wife. *Q2–4, F1*

76 **crutch, a crutch]** *F1;* crowch, a crowch *Q2–4*

79 **Capulet!—Hold]** *Rowe (subs., after F1);* Capulet, hold *Q2–4*

80 s.p. **La. Mon.]** *Rowe;* M. Wife. 2. *Q2–4;* 2. Wife. *F1*

80 s.d. **Escalus]** *Cambridge (after Arthur Brooke);* Eskales *Q2–4, F1;* the Prince *Q1*

86 **torture, . . . hands]** *F1 (Q1);* torture . . . hands. *Q2–3;* torture. . . . hands. *Q4*

92 **Verona's]** *Q3–4, F1;* Neronas *Q2*

101 **case,]** *Q5 (Q1);* case: *Q2–4, F1*

103 s.d. **all . . . Benvolio]** *Hudson*

104 s.p. **Mon.]** M: wife. *Q1*

111 **swung]** *Pope;* swoong *Q2;* swong *Q3–4, F1*

116 s.p. **La. Mon.]** *Rowe;* Wife. *Q2–4, F1 (Q1)*

120 **drive . . . abroad]** draue . . . abroad *Q3–4, F1;* drew me from companie *Q1*

121 **sycamore]** *F1 (Q1);* Syramour *Q2–4*

130 **shunn'd]** *F1;* shunned *Q2–4*

134 **all-cheering]** *F1;* alcheering *Q2;* all cheering *Q3–4*

147 **his]** *Q3–4, F1;* is *Q2*

153 **sun]** *Theobald conj.;* same *Q2–4, F1*

159 s.d. **Montague and Lady]** *Capell*

177 **create]** *Q1;* created *Q2–4, F1*

179 **well-seeming]** *Q4 (hyphen, F3);* welseeing *Q2–3, F1;* best seeming *Q1*

181 **Still-waking]** *hyphen, F2*

183 **Dost]** *Q5;* Doest *Q2–4, F1 (Q1)*

187 **propagate]** *Q3–4, F1 (Q1);* propogate *Q2 (a possible, if erroneous, form; cf.* Pericles, *I.ii.73)*

189 **to too]** *Q3–4, F1 (Q1);* too too *Q2*

190 **made]** raisde *Q1*

192 **loving]** louers *Q1*

202 **Bid a . . . make]** *Q4 (Q1);* A . . . makes *Q2–3, F1*

203 **A]** Ah *Q1*

206 **mark-man]** *hyphen, Q1*

211 **uncharm'd]** vnharm'd *Q1*

213 **eyes,]** *Q5;* eies. *Q2–4, F1*

214 **saint-seducing]** *hyphen, F1*

218 **makes]** *Q4;* make *Q2–3, F1*

I.ii

I.ii] *Capell*

Location: *Capell*

o.s.d. **Capulet's servant]** *Duthie-Wilson*

21 **guest,]** *Q3–4, F1 (Q1);* guest: *Q2*

29 **fennel]** female *Q1 (usually adopted by eds.)*

32 **Which . . . view]** *Q4;* Which one more view, *Q2–3, F1;* Such amongst view *Q1*

32 **mine,]** *Theobald;* mine *Q2–4, F1 (Q1)*

34 s.d. **To Servant.]** *Staunton*

37 s.d. **with Paris]** *Rowe; Q1 s.d. reads:* Exeunt.

38 **written here!]** *Q1* (here.); written. Here *Q2–4, F1*

44 **writ. I . . . learned. In]** *Pope (subs.);* writ (I . . . learned) in *Q2–4, F1;* I . . . learned. *Q1 (om. rest of speech from nets; l. 41)*

45 **out another's]** *Q3–4, F1 (Q1);* out, an others *Q2*

46–I.iii.34] *These lines in Q2 appear to have been set directly from Q1, with only very slight correction*

46 **One]** *Q3–4, F1 (Q1);* On *Q2*

54 **madman]** *Warburton;* mad man *Q2–4, F1 (Q1)*

59–60 **Perhaps . . . see?]** *as prose, Pope (Q1); as verse, Q2–4, F1*

66 **Vitruvio]** *F3;* Vtruuio *Q2–4, F1*

69 **and Livia]** *Q1;* Liuia *Q2–4, F1*

73 **Whither?]** *F1;* Whither *Q2–4;* Whether *Q1*

77 **thee]** *Q1;* you *Q2–4, F1*

81 s.d. **Exit.]** *F1*

89 **fires]** *Pope;* fier *Q2–4, F1 (Q1)*

92 **love! The]** *F2;* love, the *Q2–4, F1 (Q1)*

92 **all-seeing]** *hyphen, F1*

97 **maid]** *F1 (Q1);* maide: *Q2;* maid, *Q3–4*

101 s.d. **Exeunt.]** *Pope*

I.iii

I.iii] *Capell*

Location: *Rowe*

1–62 **Nurse . . . wish.]** *as verse, Capell (ll. 1, 59–62, Pope; ll. 2–4, Johnson); as prose, Q2–4, F1 (Q1)*

1, 7, 12, 15 s.pp. **La. Cap.]** *Rowe;* Wife. *Q2–4, F1 (Q1)*

2 **maidenhead . . . old,]** *Pope (subs.);* maidenhead, . . . old *Q2–4, F1;* maiden head . . . old *Q1 (in Q2–4 (Q1) the Nurse's speeches are in italics through l. 78)*

9 **thou s']** *ed.;* thou'se *Q2–4, F1 (Q1)*

11 **an]** a *Q1*

17 **shall]** *Q3–4, F1 (Q1);* stal *Q2*

22 **she,]** *F4;* she *Q2–4, F1 (Q1)*

23 **aleven]** *ed.;* eleuen *Q2–4, F1;* e- / leauen *Q1 (cf. l. 35, below)*

24 **wean'd— . . . it—]** *Capell;* weand . . . it, *Q2–4, F1 (Q1)*

32 **teachy]** *ed.;* teachie *Q2–4, F1 (Q1)*

32 **wi' th']** *ed. (after Q1* with); with the *Q2–4, F1*

35 **aleven]** *ed.;* a leuen *Q2–4;* a leauen *Q1;* a eleuen *F1 (cf.* Two Noble Kinsmen, *I.iii.54)*

36 **high-lone]** *Q1 (hyphen, Cambridge);* hylone *Q2;* a lone *Q3;* alone *Q4, F1*

38 **before,]** *Steevens;* before *Q2–4, F1 (Q1)*

38 **broke]** brake *Q1*

41 **dost]** *Q1;* doest *Q2–4, F1*

49, 63, 69, 77, 79, 96 s.pp. **La. Cap.]** *Rowe;* Old La. *Q2–4, F1;* Wife: *Q1 (om. speech at l. 49)*

66, 67 **honor]** *Q1;* houre *Q2–4, F1*

71 **mothers.]** *F1;* mothers *Q2–4*

76 **world—]** *F4;* world. *Q2–4, F1;* world, *Q1*

90 **fair]** *Q3–4, F1;* faire, *Q2*

95 **bigger:]** *F1;* bigger *Q2–4*

99 **it]** *Q4 (Q1)*

99 s.d. **Servingman]** *F1;* Seruing. *Q2–4;* Clowne *Q1*

103 s.d. **Exit.]** *F1*

104 s.p. **La. Cap.]** *Rowe;* Mo. *Q2–4, F1*

I.iv

I.iv] *Steevens*

Location: *ed. (after Duthie-Wilson)*

4 **hoodwink'd]** *Q4 (with hyphen);* hudwinckt *Q2 (Q1);* hud winckt *Q3;* hood winkt *F1*

7–8 **Nor . . . entrance;]** *Q1*

23 s.p. **Mer.]** *Q4;* Horatio. *Q2–3;* Hora. *F1*

29 s.d. **Puts on a mask.]** *Johnson (subs.)*

39 **done]** *F1 (Q1);* dum *Q2;* dun *Q3–4*

42 **Of this sir-reverence]** *Q1;* Or saue you reuerence *Q2–4;* Or saue your reuerence *F1*

45 **like lights]** *Johnson;* lights lights *Q2–4;* lights, lights, *F1; Q1 reads the line:* We burne our lights by night, like Lampes by day,

46 **judgment]** *Q3, F1 (Q1);* indgement *Q2;* Iudgements *Q4*

47 **five]** *Malone;* fine *Q2–4, F1;* right *Q1*

52 **asleep,]** *Capell (after Rowe);* asleep *Q2;* a sleepe *Q3–4, F1 (Q1)*

53] *Q1 follows this line with:* Ben: Queene Mab whats she?

54–91 **She . . . bodes.]** *as verse, Pope (after the irregular verse of Q1); as prose, Q2–4, F1*

57 **atomi]** *Q1;* ottamie *Q2;* atomies *Q3–4, F1*

59–61 **Her . . . coachmakers.]** *placed as in Lettsom conj.; after l. 69, Q2–4, F1; om. Q1*

66 **film]** *F2;* Philome *Q2–4, F1;* filmes *Q1*

69 **maid]** *Q1;* man *Q2–4, F1*

72 **O'er]** *Q1;* On *Q2–4, F1*

72–3 **straight; O'er]** *F1 (subs.);* strait, ore *Q2–4;* dreame / O're *Q1*

74 **on]** *Q3–4, F1 (Q1);* one *Q2*

80 **parson's]** *Q3–4, F1 (Q1) (subs.);* Persons *Q2*

81 **he dreams]** dreames he *Q1*

90 **elf-locks]** *Q4 (Q1);* Elklocks *Q2–3, F1*

95 **she—]** *F2;* she. *Q2–4, F1*

103 **dew-dropping]** *hyphen, Q1*

111 **forfeit]** *Q3–4, F1 (Q1);* fofreit *Q2*

113 **sail]** *Q1;* sute *Q2–4, F1*

114 s.d. **and . . . side]** *Williams*

I.v

I.v] *Steevens (no real scene division is implied here; with the entry of the servants the whole stage, at the side of which the Maskers are already standing, becomes the interior of Capulet's house)*

Location: *ed. (after Pope)*

o.s.d. **napkins.]** *F1;* Napkins. / Enter Romeo. *Q2–4*

1, 6, 12 s.pp. **1. Serv.]** *Rowe;* Ser. *Q2–4, F1*

1–5 **Where's . . . thing.]** *as prose, Pope (ll. 1–2), Q3–4, F1 (ll. 3–5); as verse, Q2*

3 s.p. **2. Serv.]** *Rowe;* 1. *Q2–4, F1*

9 **Nell.]** *Theobald;* Nell, *Q2–4, F1*

9–10 s.d. **Exit Second Servant.]** *Sisson*

10 s.d. **Enter . . . Potpan.]** *Sisson (after Cowden Clarke)*
11 s.p. **Ant.]** *Sisson;* 2. *Q2–4; F1*
14 s.p. **Pot.]** *Sisson;* 3. *Q2–4;* 1 *F1*
14–5 **We . . . all.]** *as prose, Pope; as verse, Q2–4, F1*
14 **Cheerly]** *F1;* chearely *Q2–4*
15 s.d. **Capulet . . . and]** *ed. (after Capell); Q1 s.d. reads:* Enter old Capulet with the Ladies. (*Q1 begins scene here*)
16, 34 s.pp. **Cap.]** *Q1;* 1. Capu. *Q2–4, F1*
17 **Unplagu'd]** *F1 (Q1);* Vnplagued *Q2–4*
17 **a bout]** *Pope;* about *Q2–4, F1 (Q1)*
18 **Ah]** ah ha *Q1*
18 **mistresses]** *Q3–4, F1 (Q1);* mistesses *Q2*
25 **gentlemen! Come]** *Rowe (subs.);* gentlemen come, *Q2;* gentlemen, come *Q3–4, F1*
29 **unlook'd-for]** *hyphen, Pope*
33, 38 s.pp. **2. Cap.]** Cos. *Q1*
33 **By'r lady]** *F4;* **Berlady** *Q2–4, F1;* **By Ladie** *Q1*
35 **Lucentio,]** *F1 (Q1);* **Lucientio:** *Q2;* Lucientio, *Q3–4*
39 s.p. **Cap.]** *Q1;* 1. Capu. *Q2–4;* 3. Cap. *F1*
41 s.d. **To a Servingman.]** *Capell (subs.)*
52 **now? Forswear]** *Q1;* now, forsweare *Q2–4, F1 (possibly correct)*
56 **antic]** *Q1* (Anticke); anticque *Q2;* antique *Q3–4, F1*
84 **you,]** *F1;* you *Q2–4;* you one day *Q1* (*reading* will *for* may chance to)
84 **what,]** *Q1;* what, *Q2–4, F1*
88 **Cheerly]** *F3;* chearely *Q2–4, F1*
93 s.d. **To Juliet.]** *Douai MS, Rowe*
95 **ready]** *Q1;* did readie *Q2–4, F1*
104 **pray—grant thou,]** *Hanmer (subs.);* pray [pray, *Q4*] (grant thou) *Q2–4, F1,* pray, yeeld thou, *Q1*
105 **prayers']** *Warburton;* praiers *Q2–4, F1; Q1 reads the line:* Saints doe not mooue though: grant nor praier forsake.
106 **prayer's]** *Capell;* praiers *Q2–4, F1 (Q1)*
106 s.d. **Kissing her.]** *Rowe*
110 s.d. **Kissing her again.]** *Capell*
119 **be gone]** *Q3–4, F1;* begon *Q2*
122 s.d. **They . . . ear.]** *Q1*
126 s.d. **To Second Capulet.]** *Capell (subs.)*
127 s.d. **Exeunt . . . Nurse.]** *Malone;* Exeunt. *Q1*
134 **name.]** *F1 (subs.);* name, *Q2–4 (Q1)*
139 **seen]** *Q5 (Q1);* seene, *Q2–4, F1*

II.Cho.

Act II] *Rowe*
Chorus om. Q1
o.s.d. **Enter]** *Theobald*
4 **match'd]** *Q3–4, F1;* match *Q2*
5 **belov'd]** *Rowe;* beloued *Q2–4, F1*
12 **new-beloved]** *hyphen, Theobald*
14 s.d. **Exit.]** *Theobald*

II.i

II.i] *Hanmer*
Location: *Duthie-Wilson*
2 s.d. **Romeo withdraws.]** *ed.*
6 s.p. **Mer.]** *Q4 (Q1); speech continued to Benvolio, Q2–3, F1*
7 **passion! lover!]** *Pope;* passion louer, *Q2–3;* passion, louer, *Q4, F1;* passion, liuer, *Q1*
9 **one]** *Q3–4, F1 (Q1);* on *Q2*
10 **pronounce]** *Q4 (Q1);* prouaunt, *Q2–3;* Prouant, *F1*
10 **dove]** *Q1;* day *Q2–3, F1;* die *Q4*
11 **gossip]** *Q4 (Q1);* goship *Q2–3, F1*
12 **heir]** *Q4 (Q1);* her *Q2–3, F1*
13 **Abraham]** *Q4, F1;* Abraham: *Q2–3 (Q1)*
13 **trim]** *Q1;* true *Q2–4, F1*
26 **conjur'd]** *Q1;* coniured *Q2–4, F1*
33 s.p. **Mer.]** *Q3–4, F1 (Q1);* Mar. *Q2*
38 **open-arse]** *ed. (after Hosley);* open, or *Q2–3, F1;* open & catera, and *Q4;* open Et caetera *O1*
42 s.d. **with Mercutio]** *Neilson (subs.); Q4, F1 s.d. reads:* Exeunt.

II.ii

II.ii] *Hanmer*
Location: *ed.*
o.s.d. **Romeo advances.]** *Neilson (subs.)*
1 s.d. **Enter . . . window.]** *Rowe (subs.)*
16 **do]** *Q3–4, F1 (Q1);* to *Q2*
20 **eyes]** *Q1;* eye *Q2–4, F1*
29 **white-upturned]** *hyphen, Theobald*
31 **lazy puffing]** lasie pacing *Q1*
37 s.d. **Aside.]** *Rowe*
41 **nor any . . . part]** *Q1; Malone's arrangement of ll. 41–2*
42 **O . . . name!]** *precedes* Belonging to a man. *in Q2–4, F1; Q1 om. whole line*
44 **word]** name *Q1*
45 **were]** *Q3–4, F1 (Q1);* wene *Q2*
47 **title. Romeo]** *Q5 (subs.);* tytle, Romeo *Q2–4;* title Romeo, *F1;* title Romeo *Q1*
52 **bescreen'd]** *Q3–4, F1;* beschreend *Q2;* beskrind *Q1*
65 **kinsmen]** *Q3–4, F1 (Q1);* kismen *Q2*
80 **prompt]** *Q1;* promp *Q2–4, F1*
82 **pilot]** *Q3–4, F1 (Q1);* Pylat *Q2*
83 **wash'd]** *Q4 (Q1);* washeth *Q2;* washet *Q3;* -washet *F1*
89 **compliment]** *Pope;* complement *Q2–4, F1;* complements *Q1*
90 **Dost]** *F3;* Doest *Q2–4, F1 (Q1)*
92 **false: . . . perjuries]** *F1 (Q1);* false . . . periuries. *Q2;* false, . . . periuries *Q3–4*
93 **laughs.]** *Rowe (subs.);* laughes, *Q2–4;* laught, *F1;* smiles *Q1*
99 **behavior]** hauiour *Q1*
101 **more]** *Q4 (Q1)*
101 **coying]** cunning *Q1*
110 **circled]** *Q3–4, F1 (Q1);* circle *Q2*
116 **swear. . . . thee,]** *Rowe (subs.);* sweare, . . . thee: *Q2–4, F1; Q1 reads the line:* Sweare not at al, though I doo ioy in thee,
120 **Sweet,]** *F4;* sweete *Q2–4, F1*
135 s.d. **Nurse calls within.]** *Rowe (from F1* Cals within.)
138 s.d. **Exit above.]** *Dyce (after Rowe)*
141 **flattering-sweet]** *hyphen, Theobald*
141 s.d. **Enter Juliet above.]** *Rowe*
146 **rite]** *F3;* right *Q2–3, F1 (Q1);* rights *Q4*
149, 151 s.pp. **Nurse.]** *Capell*
149, 151 s.dd. **Within.]** *F1*
149 **Madam!]** *in margin, after* world. *l. 148, Q2–4*
151 **Madam!]** *in margin, after* come— *l. 151, Q2–4*
152 **strife]** sute *Q4 (cf. Brooke's* To cease your sute)
154 s.d. **Exit above.]** *Dyce;* Exit. *F1*
157 s.d. **Retiring.]** *Capell (subs., after l. 156); placed as in Malone*
157 s.d. **above]** *Capell*
159 **tassel-gentle]** *hyphen, Hanmer*
162 **than mine,]** *Q5 (after Q4* then myne); then *Q2–3, F1;* as mine, *Q1*
163 **Romeo's name. Romeo!]** *Q1;* Romeo. *Q2–4, F1*
165 **silver-sweet]** *hyphen, F4*
167 **My niesse]** *Duthie-Wilson;* My Neece *Q2–3, F1;* My Deere *Q4;* My sweete *F2;* Madame *Q1*
167 **What]** At what *Q1*
172 **forget,]** *Q3–4, F1;* forget *Q2*
179 **his]** her *Q1*
181 **loving-jealous]** *hyphen, Theobald*
185 s.d. **Exit above.]** *Dyce (after Pope)*
186 s.p. **Rom.]** *Q4 (Q1);* Iu. *Q2 (ll. 184–5* Parting . . . morrow. *are given to Romeo in Q3, F1)*
187] *Following this line Q2–3, F1 insert four lines which are repeated, with some variations, as the opening lines of II.iii; see notes to II.iii.1–4 below*
188 **sire's]** *Delius conj. (after Brooke);* Friers *Q2–4;* Fries *F1;* fathers *Q1*

II.iii

II.iii] *Hanmer*
Location: *Malone*
1 **grey-ey'd]** *Q3–4, F1 (Q1) (all without hyphen);* grey-eyed *Q2; in the first version of ll. 1–4, which occurs only in Q2–3, F1 (see above, II.ii.187), all read* grey eyde *(subs.)*
2 **Check'ring]** *Q3–4, F1 (Q1) (all reading* Checkring); Checking *Q2; the reading of the first version is* Checkring
3 **fleckled darkness]** *F1;* fleckeld darknesse *Q2–4;* flecked darkenes *Q1; the first version reads:* darkenes fleckted *Q2,* darknesse fleckeld *Q3,* darknesse fleckel'd *F1*
4 **path and]** path, and *Q2–4, F1 (Q1); for these words the first version reads* pathway, made by
4 **fiery]** *Q1;* burning *Q2–4, F1 (apparently picked up by the compositor from l. 5); om. first version (l. 4 as it appears in the first version may most charitably be taken as Shakespeare's first thoughts)*
8 **precious-juiced]** *hyphen, Pope*
13 **many virtues]** *Q3, F1;* many, vertues *Q2;* many vertures *Q4*
22 **sometime]** sometimes *Q1*
25 **smelt,]** *F1;* smelt *Q2–4;* smelt too, *Q1*
45 **Rosaline?]** *Duthie-Wilson;* Rosaline, *Q2–4, F1;* Rosaline *Q1*
50–1 **me . . . wounded; both]** *F1 (subs.);* me: . . . wounded both, *Q2;* me: . . . wounded, both *Q3–4;* me . . . wounded, both *Q1*
62 **woo'd]** *Q5 (Q1);* wooed *Q2–4, F1*
74 **ringing]** ring *Q4 (Q1)*
79 **chang'd? Pronounce]** *Q3–4, F1;* chang'd, pronounce *Q2 (Q1)*
84 **in, another]** *Q3–4, F1;* in an other *Q2;* in another *Q1*
85 **chide . . . Her]** chide not, she whom *Q1*
85 **now]** *Q3–4, F1 (Q1);* now. *Q2*

II.iv

II.iv] *Hanmer*
Location: *Rowe*
o.s.d. **Enter]** *Q3–4, F1 (Q1);* Bnter *Q2*
1–2 **Where . . . to-night?]** *as verse, Capell (Q1); as prose, Q2–4, F1*
6–7 **Tybalt . . . house.]** *as verse, Theobald (Q1); as prose, Q2–4, F1*
6 **kinsman]** *Q3–4, F1 (Q1);* kisman *Q2*
18 s.p. **Ben.]** *F1 (Q1);* Ro. *Q2–4*
19 **Cats.]** cattes I can tell you. *Q1*
20 **compliments]** *Rowe;* Complements *Q2–4, F1 (Q1)*
22 **he rests . . . rests]** *Q3–4;* he rests, his minum rests *Q2;* he rests his minum *F1;* rests me his minum rest *Q1*
25 **house.]** *Q5;* house *Q2–4, F1 (Q1)*
28 **antic]** *Pope;* antique *Q2–4, F1 (Q1)*
29 **phantasimes]** *Crow conj.;* phantacies *Q2–4, F1;* fantasticoes *Q1*
31 **grandsire]** *F1;* graundsir *Q2–4 (Q1)*
33 **pardon-me's]** *F1;* pardons mees *Q2;* pardon mees *Q3;* pardona-mees *Q4;* pardonmees *Q1*
39 **Petrarch]** *Q3–4, F1 (Q1);* Petrach *Q2*
61 **Sure wit!]** *Neilson;* Sure wit *Q2;* Sure wit, *Q3–4, F1;* Well said, *Q1*
61 **this jest now,]** *Capell (after Rowe);* this ieast, now *Q2–4, F1;* nowe that iest *Q1*
65 **single-sol'd]** *hyphen, F4*
101 s.d. **Enter . . . man]** *after l. 100, F1*
102 **A . . . sail!]** *Mer.* A saile, a saile, a saile. *Q1*
103 s.p. **Mer.]** Ben. *Q1*
115 **One, gentlewoman]** *F4;* One gentlewoman *Q2–4, F1;* A Gentleman Nurse *Q1*
133 s.d. **He . . . sings.]** *Q1*
143 s.d. **singing]** *Farmer conj.*
144 s.d. **Mercutio and Benvolio]** *F1*
154 **skains-mates]** *hyphen, F4*
154 s.d. **She . . . man.]** *Q1*
162 **quivers. Scurvy]** *Q1 (subs.);* quiuers, skuruie *Q2–4, F1*
172 **thee—]** *F2;* thee. *Q2–4, F1*
175 **dost]** *F3;* dooest *Q2;* doest *Q3–4, F1*
182 **shriv'd]** *F1;* shrieued *Q2–4*
185 **sir?]** *F1;* sir. *Q2–4*
187 **nurse—]** *Grant White (subs.);* Nurse *Q2–4, F1 (Q1)*
196–7 **Is . . . away"?]** *as verse, Rowe; as prose, Q2–4, F1*
196 **hear]** *F1;* here *Q2–4*
198 **'Warrant]** *ed.;* Warrant *Q2–4, F1;* I warrant *F2*
201 **nobleman]** *Q4;* Noble man *Q2–3, F1*

209 **Ah, mocker,**] *Rowe* (*subs.*); A mocker *Q2–4, F1*
209 **dog's**] *Q3–4, F1;* dog, *Q2*
209 **name. R**] *Q3–4, F1;* name R. *Q2*
210 **the—**] *Ritson conj.;* the *Q2–4, F1*
214–5 **times. Peter!**] *F1* (*Peter?*); times *Peter. Q2;* times *Peter? Q3–4*
214 s.d. **Exit Romeo.**] *from Q1* (Exit)
217 s.d. **Handing . . . fan.**] *ed., based on Q1:* Peter, take my fanne, and goe before.
217 s.d. **after Peter**] *ed.* (*see preceding note*); and Peter *F1; Q1 s.d. reads:* Ex. omnes.

II.v

II.v] *Hanmer*
Location: *Globe* (*after Capell*)
7 **nimble-pinion'd**] *hyphen, Pope*
8 **wind-swift**] *hyphen, Q3, F1*
11 **Is three**] *Q3–4;* Is there *Q2;* I three *F1*
15–9 **And . . . away.**] *continued to Juliet, Q4, F1; headed with s.p.* M. *in Q2–3*
17 s.d. **and Peter**] *Theobald*
20 s.d. **Exit Peter.**] *Theobald*
25 **a-weary**] *Capell* (aweary); a wearie *Q2–4, F1;* wearie *Q1*
26 **I!**] I had? *Q3–4, F1* (*Q1*)
33–4 **dost . . . dost**] *Q3–4, F1;* doest . . . doest *Q2*
39 **he.**] *Theobald* (*subs.*); he *Q2–3, F1;* he, *Q4*
42 **body**] baudie *Q1;* bawdy *F2;* Baw-dy *Rowe*
47 **marriage?**] *F1* (*Q1*); marriage, *Q2–4*
50 **ah**] *Q5;* a *Q2–4;* o *F1*
56 **An'**] *ed.;* An *Q2;* And *Q3–4, F1*

II.vi

II.vi] *Hanmer*
Location: *Capell* (*after Rowe*)
This scene appears in Q1 in an almost totally different form: Enter Romeo, Frier. / Rom: Now Father *Laurence,* in thy holy grant / Consists the good of me and *Iuliet. / Fr:* Without more words I will doo all I may, / To make you happie if in me it lye. / *Rom:* This morning here she pointed we should meet, / And consumate those neuer parting bands, / Witnes of our harts loue by ioyning hands, / And come she will. / *Fr:* I gesse she will indeed, / Youths loue is quicke, swifter than swiftest speed. / *Enter Iuliet somewhat fast, and embraceth Romeo.* / See where she comes. / So light of foote nere hurts the troden flower: / Of loue and ioy, see see the soueraigne power. / *Iul: Romeo.* / *Rom:* My *Iuliet* welcome. As doo waking eyes / (Cloasd in Nights mysts) attend the frolicke Day, / So *Romeo* hath expected *Iuliet,* / And thou art come. / *Iul:* I am (if I be Day) / Come to my Sunne: shine forth, and make me faire. / *Rom:* All beauteous fairnes dwelleth in thine eyes. / *Iul: Romeo* from thine all brightnes doth arise. / *Fr:* Come wantons, come, the stealing houres do passe / Defer imbracements till some fitrer time, / Part for a while, you shall not be alone, / Till holy Church haue ioynd ye both in one. / *Rom:* Lead holy Father, all delay seemes long. / *Iul:* Make hast, make hast, this lingring doth vs wrong. / *Fr:* O, soft and faire makes sweetest worke they say. / Hast is a common hindrer in crosse way. *Exeunt omnes.*
2 **after-hours**] *hyphen, Pope*
27 **music's**] *Q4, F1;* musicke *Q2–3*
37 s.d. **Exeunt.**] *F2;* Exeunt omnes. *Q1*

III.i

III.i] *Rowe*
Location: *Capell* (*after Rowe*)
o.s.d. **Page**] *Capell*
2 **Capels are**] *Q1;* Capels *Q2–3;* Capulets *Q4, F1*
3–4 **And . . . stirring.**] *as verse, Rowe; as prose, Q2–4, F1*
46 **dost**] *Q3–4, F1;* doest *Q2*
52–3 **grievances, . . . depart;**] *F4* (*comma, Q5*); greeuances: . . . depart, *Q2–4, F1*
68 **injuried**] iniured *Q3–4* (*Q1*); iniur'd *F1*
69 **thou**] *Q3–4, F1* (*Q1*); thon *Q2*
69 **devise,**] *Q5* (*Q1*); deuise: *Q2–3, F1;* deuise. *Q4*
74 **Alla stoccato**] *ed.* (*after Knight*): Alla stucatho *Q2–4, F1;* Allastockado *Q1*
74 s.d. **Draws.**] *Capell*
83 s.d. **Drawing.**] *Rowe*
85 s.d. **They fight.**] *Rowe* (*subs.*)
87 **shame,**] *Theobald;* shame *Q2–4, F1*
89 s.d. **Romeo . . . them.**] *Douai MS*
90 s.d. **Tybalt . . . in.**] *from Q1:* Tibalt vnder Romeos arme thrusts Mercutio, in and flyes. *Q1*
90 s.d. **Away Tybalt**] Exit Tybalt. *F1* (*see above for Q1*)
90 s.d. **with his followers**] *Globe* (*after Malone*)
91 **both houses**] both the Houses *F1;* your houses *Q1*
94] *Following this line Q1 adds: Boy:* I goe my Lord.
94 s.d. **Exit Page.**] *Capell* (*from suggestion of Q1; see preceding note*)
100–8 **'Zounds . . . houses!**] *for these lines Q1 substitutes:* I shall be fairely mounted vpon foure mens shoulders: For your house of the *Mountegues* and the *Capolets:* and then some peasantly rogue, some Sexton, some base slaue shall write my Epitapth, that *Tybalt* came and broke the Princes Lawes, and *Mercutio* was slaine for the first and second cause. Wher's the Surgeon? / *Boy.* Hee's come sir. / *Mer.* Now heele keepe a mumbling in my guts on the otherside, come *Benuolio,* lend me thy hand: a poxe of your houses.
100 **'Zounds**] *Q5;* sounds *Q2–4;* What *F1*
108 **soundly too.**] *F3* (*subs.*); soundly, to *Q2;* soundly to *Q3–4, F1*
108 s.d. **Exeunt**] *Q1;* Exit. *Q2–4, F1*
108 s.d. **Mercutio and Benvolio**] *Rowe*
117 **gallant**] *Q3–4, F1* (*Q1*); gallanr *Q2*
120 **begins**] *Q5;* begins, *Q2–4, F1*
120 s.d. **Enter Tybalt.**] *F1* (*Q1*)
122 **He gone**] *Q3–4, F1* (gon); He gan *Q2;* A liue *Q1*
124 **fire-ey'd**] *Q1* (fier eyed; *hyphen, Pope*); fier end *Q2;* fier and *Q3–4, F1*
135 **gone,**] *Q4, F1;* gone *Q2–3*
137, 139 s.pp. **1. Cit.**] *Malone;* Citti. *and* Cit. *Q2–4;* Watch. *Q1*
138 **murtherer**] *Q3–4, F1;* mutherer *Q2;* villaine *Q1*
140 s.d. **Enter . . . all.**] Enter Prince, Capolets wife. *Q1*
142 **all**] *F1* (*Q1*); all: *Q2–4*
145, 148 **kinsman**] *Q3–4, F1* (*Q1*); kisman *Q2*
146, 176 s.p. **La. Cap.**] *Rowe;* Capu. Wi. *and* Ca. Wi. *Q2–4, F1;* M: *and* Mo: *Q1*
147 **O husband**] *Capell* (*withdrawn*), *Dyce;* O Cozen, husband *Q2–4, F1*
149 **shed**] *F1* (*Q1*); shead *Q2–4* (*possibly representing Shakespeare's pronunciation; cf.* Lucrece, *l. 1549, and Sonnet 34:13*)
155 **displeasure;**] *F1* (*subs.*); displeasure *Q2–4*
155 **this, uttered**] *Capell* (*subs., after Pope*); this vttered, *Q2–4, F1*
166 **agile**] *Q4* (*Q1*); aged *Q2–3, F1*
176 **kinsman**] *Q3–4, F1;* kisman *Q2*
183 **owe?**] *Theobald;* owe. *Q2–4, F1*
184 s.p. **Mon.**] *Q4:* Capu. *Q2–3, F1*
188 **hearts'**] *Johnson;* hearts *Q2–4, F1;* hates *Q1*
192 **I**] *Q4* (*Q1*); It *Q2–3, F1*
197 s.d. **Exeunt.**] *F1;* Exit. *Q2–4;* Exeunt omnes. *Q1*

III.ii

III.ii] *Rowe*
Location: *Rowe*
1 s.p. **Jul.**] *F1* (*Q1*)
1 **fiery-footed**] *hyphen, Rowe*
3 **Phaëton**] *Q3–4, F1* (*Q1*); Phaetan *Q2*
6 **th' runaway's**] *Warburton;* runnawayes *Q2–3;* run-awaves *Q4, F1*
8 **rites**] *F4;* rights *Q2–4, F1*
9 **By**] *Q4;* And by *Q2–3, F1*
11 **sober-suited**] *hyphen, F4*
20 **black-brow'd**] *hyphen, Q4;* black browd *Q2;* blackbrowd *Q3;* blackebrow'd *F1*
21 **I**] he *Q4*
28 **enjoy'd.**] *Rowe* (*subs.*); enioyd, *Q2–4, F1*
32 s.d. **wringing . . . lap**] *Q1;* with cords. *Q2–4, F1*
35 s.d. **Throws them down.**] *Capell* (*subs.*)
37 **Ah**] *Pope;* A *Q2–4, F1*
37 **weraday**] welady *Q3, F1;* weladay *Q4;* Alack the day *Q1*
42 **it? Romeo!**] *Capell;* it Romeo? *Q2;* it Romeo. *Q3–4, F1*
44 **roar'd**] *F1* (*Q1*); rored *Q2–4*
45 **ay**] *Rowe;* I *Q2–4, F1*
47 **death-darting**] *Q3–4, F1;* death arting *Q2*
48 **ay,**] *Rowe* (*comma, Q5*); I. *Q2–4, F1*
49, 50 **ay**] *Rowe;* I *Q2–4, F1*
49 **shut**] *Capell;* shot *Q2–4, F1*
51 **Brief sounds**] *F4;* Briefe, sounds, *Q2–4, F1*
51 **my**] of my *F1*
60 **one**] *Q4;* on *Q2–3, F1*
72 s.p. **Nurse.**] *Q1; line continued to Juliet, Q2–4, F1*
73 s.p. **Jul.**] *Q1; Q2–4, F1 give line to Nurse and begin Juliet's speech with l. 74*
76 **Dove-feather'd**] *Theobald* (*hyphen, F1*); Rauenous douefeatherd *Q2–3* (*probably represents Shakespeare's first draft of the line*): Rauenous doue, feathred *Q4;* Rauenous Doue-feather'd *F1*
79 **damned**] *Q4;* dimme *Q2–3;* dimne *F1*
99 **three-hours**] *hyphen, Theobald*
128 **corse**] *Q4;* course *Q2–3;* Coarse *F1* (*Q1*)
133 **I,**] *Q5;* I *Q2–4, F1*
135 **maiden-widowed**] *hyphen, Rowe*
143 s.d. **Exeunt.**] *Q1;* Exit. *Q2–4, F1*

III.iii

III.iii] *Rowe*
Location: *Capell* (*after Rowe*)
o.s.d. **Enter Friar Lawrence.**] *Capell;* Enter Frier and Romeo. *Q2–4, F1* (*see l. 3 s.d.*); Enter Frier. *Q1*
3 s.d. **Enter Romeo.**] *Q1*
15 **Here**] Hence *Q1*
19 **banish'd**] *Q3–4, F1* (*Q1*); blanisht *Q2*
21 **misterm'd.**] *Q5* (*subs.*); mistermd, *Q2–4, F1; Q1 om.* then . . . misterm'd
40–3 **But . . . death?**] *Globe arrangement; Q2–4 read:* This may flyes do, when I from this must flie, / And sayest thou yet, that exile is not death? / But *Romeo* may not, he is banished. / Flies may do this, but I from this must flie: / They are freemen, but I am banished. (*apparently Shakespeare first wrote* This . . . death?; *then inserted a three-line revision of the first line; but when the text was set in type, the revised version was mistakenly placed after the second line instead of before it, and the rejected first line was included in error*): *F1 om. l. 42; Q1 om. ll. 42–3*
42 **free men**] *Q5;* freemen *Q2–4*
50 **sin-absolver**] *F1* (*hyphen*) (*Q1*); sin obsoluer *Q2–4*
52 **Thou**] *Q4* (*Q1*); Then *Q2–3, F1*
61 **madmen**] *Q1;* mad man *Q2;* mad men *Q3–4, F1*
68 **mightst thou speak**] *Q1;* mightest thou speake *Q2–4, F1*
70 s.d. **within**] *Rowe*
70 s.d. **knock**] knockes *Q3, F1; Q4* (*Q1*) *s.d. reads:* Nurse knockes.
73 s.d. **Knock.**] *Q4, F1:* They knocke. *Q2–3*
75 **taken.— . . . while!—**] *Rowe* (*subs.*); taken, . . . while, *Q2–3, F1;* taken (stay a while) *Q4*
75 s.d. **Loud knock.**] *anon. conj.* (*in Cambridge*); Slud knock. *Q2–3;* Knocke againe. *Q4;* Knocke. *F1;* Shee knockes againe. *Q1*
76 **study.— . . . by!—**] *Rowe* (*subs.*); studie by and by, *Q2–3;* studie (by and by) *Q4;* study: by and by, *F1; Q1 here reads: Nur:* Hoe Fryer open the doore, / *Fr:* By and

by I come. Who is there?
79 s.d. **Within.**] *Rowe*
80 s.d. **Unlocks the door.**] *ed.*
80 s.d. **Enter Nurse.**] *placed as in Rowe; after l. 78, Q2–4, F1*
88 **man.**] Q1; man, Q2–4, F1
91 s.d. **He rises.**] Q1
108 s.d. **He . . . away.**] Q1 (*Q1 gives Nurse an* Ah? *following s.d.*)
110 **denote**] Q4, F1 (Q1); deuote Q2–3
117 **lives**] Q1; lies Q2–4, F1
130 **ornament**] Q5; ornament, Q2–4, F1
133 **afire**] *Collier;* a fier Q2–4, F1
138 **happy**] happy too Q1
143 **mishaved**] misbehaude Q1
144 **pouts upon**] Q4; puts vp Q2–3; puttest vp F1; frownst vpon Q1
162 s.d. **Nurse . . . again.**] Q1
163 **sir**] is Q1
165 s.d. **Exit Nurse.**] Q1
168 **disguis'd**] Q3–4, F1; disguise Q2

III.iv

III.iv] *Rowe*
Location: *Rowe*
2 **daughter.**] Q1; daughter, Q2–4; Daughter: F1
10 s.p. **La. Cap.**] *Rowe;* La. Q2–4; Lady. F1
11 s.d. **Paris . . . again.**] Q1
13 **be**] Q3–4, F1 (Q1); me Q2
23 **We'll**] Q3–4, F1 (Q1); Well, Q2
34 **very**] very very Q1

III.v

III.v] *Rowe*, Q1
Location: *Globe (after Rowe)*
o.s.d. **at the window**] Q1
9 **jocund**] F4; iocand Q2; iocond Q3–4, F1 (Q1)
13 **exhal'd**] *Hosley;* exhale Q2; exhales Q3–4, F1 (Q1)
19 **the**] Q3–4, F1 (Q1); the the Q2
25 **talk, it is**] Q4, F1; talke it is Q2–3; talke, tis Q1
26 **gone,**] F4; gone Q2–4, F1; gone, flye hence Q1
36 s.d. **Enter Nurse hastily.**] Q1; Enter Madame and Nurse. Q2–4, F1
40 s.d. **Exit.**] *Theobald*
42 s.d. **He goeth down.**] Q1
43 **love . . . friend**] my Lord, my Loue, my Frend Q1
48 s.d. **From below.**] *Neilson*
54 s.p. **Jul.**] Q4, F1 (Q1); Ro. Q2–3 (*but* Iu. *as catchword*)
54 **ill-divining**] *hyphen, Pope*
64 s.p. **La. Cap.**] *Rowe;* La. Q2–4, F1 (*until l. 103*); Moth: Q1 (*or* Mo: *throughout scene*)
64 s.d. **Within.**] *Capell*
67 s.d. **She . . . window.**] Q1 (*Q1, following this s.d., here indicates a break*)
67 s.d. **Enter Mother**] *placed as in Capell; after* back. *l. 64, Q2–4, F1;* Enter Iuliets Mother, Nurse. Q1 (*also before* Ho, *l. 64*)
81 s.d. **Aside.**] *Hanmer*
82 **pardon**] Q3–4, F1; padon Q2
82 **him**] Q4
94 **him—dead—**] *Pope (after Rowe);* him. Dead Q2–4, F1; him, dead Q1
97 **it,**] Q5; it: Q2–4; it; F1
103 s.p. **La. Cap.**] *Rowe;* Mo. *or* M. Q2–4, F1 (*until l. 139*); *see l. 64 s.p. for* Q1
126 s.d. **Enter . . . Nurse.**] Enter olde Capolet. Q1
129 **tears?**] F1; tears Q2–3; teares. Q4
130 **show'ring?**] Q1; showring Q2–3, F1; showring: Q4
130 **body**] Q1; body? Q2–4, F1
131 **counterfeits a**] F1; countefaits. A Q2; counterfaits. A Q3; counterfaits, a Q4; resemblest a Q1
133–4 **is, . . . flood;**] *Pope (subs.);* is: . . . floud, Q2–4; is . . . floud, F1
139 s.p. **La. Cap.**] *Rowe;* La. Q2–4 (*until l. 175*); Lady. F1 (*until l. 175*); Moth. Q1
139 **gives**] Q3–4, F1; giue Q2; thankes Q1
142 **How,**] F1; How Q2–4; What Q1
149 **chopp'd logic**] chop logicke Q1
156 **green-sickness**] *hyphen, F4*
157 **tallow-face**] *hyphen, F4*
159 s.d. **She kneels down.**] Q1
160 s.p. **Cap.**] Q1; Fa. Q2–4, F1 (*throughout rest of scene*)
171 **Prudence, smatter**] Q3–4, F1; Prudence smatter, Q2; prudence smatter Q1
172 s.p. **Cap.**] Q1, Q4 (Fa.); Q2–3, F1 *read* Father, *in roman as if it were part of the Nurse's speech*
172 **God-i-goden**] F1 (*subs.*); Godigeden Q2–4; goddegodden Q1
173 s.p. **Nurse.**] Q4
174 **gossip's**] Q3–4, F1 (Q1); Goships Q2
175 s.p. **La. Cap.**] *Rowe;* Wi. Q2–4; La. F1; Mo. Q1
176 **Day . . . play,**] *Hoppe's arrangement;* Day, night, houre, tide [ride F1], time, worke, play, Q2–4, F1 (*the words* houre, tide, time *are thus considered to be Shakespeare's trial thoughts for* Day, night); Day, night, early, late, at home, abroad, Q1
177 **Alone,**] Q4 (Q1); Alone Q2–3, F1
180 **lien'd**] *Crow conj.;* liand Q2; allied Q3–4, F1; trainde Q1
184 **fortune's**] *Theobald;* fortunes Q2–4, F1 (Q1)
202 s.p. **La. Cap.**] *Rowe;* Mo. Q2–4, F1 (Q1)
221 **hath.**] *Rowe (subs.);* hath, Q2–4, F1
233 **absolv'd**] Q3–4, F1 (Q1); obsolu'd Q2
234 s.d. **Exit.**] Q4
235 s.d. **She . . . Nurse.**] Q1

IV.i

IV.i] *Rowe*, Q1
Location: *Capell (after Rowe)*
7 **talk'd**] Q1; talke Q2–4, F1
12 **tears,**] F1; teares. Q2–4 (Q1)
16 s.d. **Aside.**] *Theobald*
45 **cure**] Q5 (Q1); care Q2–4, F1 (*cf. IV.v.65*)
46 **O**] Ah Q1
56 **seal'd,**] Q5; seald: Q2–4, F1
60 **long-experienc'd**] *hyphen, Pope*
72 **slay**] Q4 (Q1); stay Q2–3, F1 (*cf. Midsummer Night's Dream, II.i.190*)
75 **Death himself**] Q3–4, F1 (*subs.*); death, himselfe Q2; death it selfe Q1
78 **off**] Q5 (Q1); of Q2–4, F1
83 **yellow**] Q4, F1; yealow Q2–3; yeolow Q1
83 **chapless**] Q4 (Q1); chapels Q2–3, F1
85 **shroud**] Q4; graue F1; Q1 *combines ll. 84–5 as:* Or lay me in tombe with one new dead:
98 **breath**] Q3–4, F1 (Q1); breast Q2
99 **fade**] Q3–4, F1; fade: Q2
100 **To**] F1; Too Q2–4
100 **wanny**] *Kellner conj.;* many Q2–3, F1; paly Q4
110 **In**] Q3–4, F1; Is Q2
110] *Following this line Q2–4, F1 read:* Be borne to buriall in thy kindreds graue: (*this line repeats the essentials of the next two lines and appears to be a cancelled first draft of them*)
115–6 **an' . . . waking,**] *om.* F1
115 **an'**] *ed.;* an Q2; and Q3–4
116 **waking**] Q3–4; walking Q2
126 s.d. **Exeunt.**] Q4 (Q1); Exit. Q2–3, F1

IV.ii

IV.ii] *Rowe*, Q1
Location: *Rowe*
o.s.d. **Enter . . . three.**] Enter olde Capolet, his Wife, Nurse, and Seruingman. Q1
1 s.d. **Exit First Servant.**] *Malone (subs.), after Capell*
3, 6 s.pp. **2. Serv.**] *Malone;* Ser. Q2–4, F1 (Q1)
9 s.d. **Exit Second Servant.**] *Malone (subs.):* Exit Seruingman. Q1
14 **self-will'd**] Q4; selfe wield Q2; selfe willde Q3; selfe-wild F1; selfewild Q1
21 s.d. **She kneels down.**] Q1
26 **becomed**] Q4, F1; bec
36, 38 s.pp. **La. Cap.**] *Ro*
Moth: Q1
37, 39 s.pp. **Cap.**] Q1 (Ca
37 s.d. **Juliet and Nurse**] Q
47 s.d. **Exeunt.**] Q4 (Q
Exeunt Father and Moth

IV.iii

IV.iii] *Rowe*, Q1
Location: *ed. (Scenes iii, iv, tinuous and are here so however, that Q1 indicates IV.iii)*
1–5 **Jul. Ay . . . sin.**] *Q1 her* Come, come, what need yo else? / *Iul:* Nothing good leaue me to my selfe: / For to lye alone to night. / *Nur:* cleane smocke vnder your pil good night. *Exit.*
6, 12 s.pp. **La. Cap.**] *Rowe;* Mo. Moth: Q1
13 s.d. **Lady . . . Nurse**] *Capell*
18 **Nurse!—**] *Hanmer (after Rowe* Q2–4, F1
20 **vial**] Q3–4, F1; Violl Q2
23 s.d. **Laying . . . dagger.**] *Johns Rowe); Douai MS gives:* Lyes penknife.
47 **mandrakes'**] *Capell;* mandrakes Q
49 **wake**] Q4; walke Q2–3, F1
58 **Romeo . . . thee.**] *Romeo* I com doe I drinke to thee. Q1
58 s.d. **She . . . curtains.**] Q1

IV.iv

IV.iv] *Rowe*, Q1
Location: *ed.*
o.s.d. **with herbs**] Q1
2 s.d. **old Capulet**] Oldeman Q1
4 **rung**] F1 (Q1); roong Q2; roung Q3–4
12 s.d. **Exeunt**] *Hanmer;* Exit Q2–4, F1
13 s.d. **Servingmen**] *Capell (subs.); s. follows l. 14, Q2–4, F1; s.d. in Q1 (afte l. 12) reads:* Enter Seruingman with Log & Coales.
15 s.p. **1. Serv.**] *Capell;* Fel. Q2–4, F1; Ser. Q1
16 **haste. Sirrah**] Q5 (*subs.*); haste sirra Q2–4; hast, sirrah F1
16 s.d. **Exit First Servant.**] *Capell (subs.)*
18 s.p. **2. Serv.**] *Capell;* Fel. Q2–4, F1; Ser. Q1
21 **Thou**] Q3–4, F1 (Q1); Twou Q2
21 s.d. **Exit Second Servant.**] *Capell (subs.)*
21 **faith**] Q4; father Q2–3, F1
23 s.d. **within**] *Capell; s.d. follows l. 21,* Q2–4, F1
28 s.d. **Exit.**] *Rowe*

IV.v

IV.v] *Pope*
Location: *ed. (after Rowe)*
7 **little. God**] *Capell (after Rowe);* little, God Q2–4, F1; little. What Q1
11 s.d. **Draws . . . curtains.**] *Capell (subs.)*
16 s.d. **Enter Mother**] F1 (Q1)
17 s.p. **La. Cap.**] *Rowe;* Mo. *or* M. Q2–4, F1 (*throughout scene*); Moth: Q1 (*throughout scene, beginning l. 18*)
22 s.p. **Cap.**] Q1; Fa. Q2–4, F1 (*throughout scene*)
32 s.d. **with the Musicians**] Q4
37 **deflowered**] *Steevens;* deflowred Q2–4, F1; Deflowerd Q1
40 **all; life,**] *Collier (after Capell);* all life Q2–3, F1; all, life Q4
41–64 **Have . . . buried.**] *the following quite different version of these lines appears in Q1:* *Par:* Haue I thought long to see this mornings face, / And doth it now present such prodegies? / Accurst, vnhappy, miserable man, / Forlorne, forsaken, destitute I am: / Borne to the world to be a slaue in it. / Distrest, remediles, and vnfortunate. / O heauens, O nature,

the
from
...xeunt
...unt *F1*
Musi.

Q2–4; Mu.

...ny *Q2*
; Enter Will
the actor who
is preceded by
...xeunt omnes.);

...dler. *Q2–4;* Mu.

...*oughout scene*)

...); Minstrels. *Q2–4;*

...pp **1. Mus.**] *Q1* (1.);
or Min. *Q2–4;* Mu. *F1*
...**el.**] *as prose, Theobald*
...*rse, Q2–4, F1*
...*apell;* Minstrel. *Q2;* Min.

...me?] *as prose, Q4, F1; as*

... Mus.] 2. M. *Q2–4, F1;*
only)
Q4; Q2–3, F1 continue the
. Mus. and begin Peter's speech
, l. 123
. oppress,] *Q1*
...] *Q5;* Mary *Q2–4, F1*
...retty] *Q1;* Prates *Q2;* Pratest
; Pratee *Q4*
...eck] *Rowe;* Rebick *Q2–4, F1*
3. Mus.] 3 M. *Q2–4, F1;* 3. *Q1*
O . . . sounding:] *as prose, Pope* (*Q1*);
erse, Q2–4, F1
...p. **1. Mus.**] *Capell;* Min. *Q2–4;* Mu. *F1*
s.p. **2. Mus.**] M. 2. *Q2–4, F1;* 1. *Q1*
s.d. **Exeunt.**] *Q4* (*Q1*); Exit. *Q2–3, F1*

V.i

V.i] *Rowe, Q1*
Location: *Rowe, Capell*
2 **hand.**] *F1* (*subs.*); hand, *Q2–4*
3 **throne,**] *Q1;* throne: *Q2–4, F1*
7 **dead man**] *Q3–4, F1* (*Q1*); deadman *Q2*
11 s.d. **booted**] *from Q1 s.d.:* Enter Balthasar his man booted.
12 **Balthasar**] *Q1;* Balthazer *Q2–4, F1*

...; doth my Lady *Q2–4, F1;*
...; Man. *Q2–4, F1* (*through-*
...*r;* in *Q2;* euen *Q3–4, F1* (*Q1*)
...denie *Q2–4, F1*
...*Q1*
...Balthasar.] *Q1;* Exit. *Q2–4, F1*
...*d. l. 32*)
...uts] *F3;* here abouts *Q2–4, F1*
...**d.**; An *Q2–4, F1;* And *Q5* (*Q1*)
...nter Apothecary.] *F1* (*Q1*)
...Rom.] *Q3–4, F1* (*Q1*); Kom. *Q2*
...-speeding] *hyphen, F4*
...-weary taker] *Q5;* life-wearie-taker
...*-4, F1;* wearie takers life *Q1*
...5, 77 s.pp. **Ap.**] *F1* (*Q1*); Poti. *Q2–4*
...pay] *Q4* (*Q1*); pray *Q2–3, F1*
s.d. **Exit Apothecary.**] *Duthie-Wilson* (*subs.*)
... s.d. **Exit.**] *Duthie-Wilson* (*subs.*); Exeunt. *Q2–4, F1* (*Q1*)

V.ii

V.ii] *Rowe, Q1*
Location: *Capell* (*after Rowe*)
o.s.d. **Enter Friar John.**] *Q1* (*om., however, any entry for Friar Laurence*); Enter Frier Iohn to Frier Lawrence. *Q2–4, F1*

V.iii

V.iii] *Rowe, Q1*
Location: *Rowe* (*subs.*)
o.s.d. **with . . . water**] *Q1*
o.s.d. **and a torch**] *Rowe* (*subs.*)
3 **yew**] *Q1;* young *Q2–4, F1*
3 **trees**] tree *Q1*
8 **something**] *Q4;* some thing *Q2–3, F1*
10 s.d. **Aside.**] *Capell*
11 s.d. **Retires.**] *Capell*
11 s.d. **Paris . . . flowers.**] *Q1*
12 **Sweet . . . strew—**] *after this line Q1 substitutes the following for ll. 13–17:* Sweete Tombe that in thy circuite dost containe, / The perfect modell of eternitie: / Faire *Iuliet* that with Angells dost remaine, / Accept this latest fauour at my hands, / That liuing honourd thee, and being dead / With funerall praises doo adorne thy Tombe. (*Pope substituted these for Q2's lines and was followed by Theobald, Hanmer, Warburton, and Johnson*)
12–3 **strew— . . . stones!—**] *Staunton* (*subs.*); strew . . . stones, *Q2;* strew, . . . stones, *Q3–4;* strew: . . . stones, *F1*
13 **canopy**] *F1;* Canapie *Q2–4*
15 **moans.**] *Q3–4, F1* (*subs.*); mones, *Q2*
16 **keep**] *Capell;* keepe: *Q2;* keepe, *Q3–4, F1*
17 s.d. **Whistle Boy.**] Boy whistles and calls. My Lord. *Q1*
20 **rite**] *Pope;* right *Q2–4, F1;* rites *Q1*
21 s.d. **Retires.**] *Capell* (Steps aside. *Douai MS*)
21 s.d. **Balthasar . . . iron**] *Q1;* Peter *Q2–3, F1;* Balthazer his man *Q4*
25 **light.**] *Q3–4, F1* (*subs.*); light *Q2*
37 **savage-wild**] *hyphen, Steevens*
40, 43 s.pp. **Bal.**] *Q4* (*Q1*); Pet. *Q2–3, F1*
41 **friendship**] *Q3–4, F1;* friendshid *Q2*
43 s.d. **Aside.**] *Capell*
43 **hereabout**] *Q5;* here about *Q2–4, F1*
44 s.d. **Retires.**] *Hanmer*
48 s.d. **Romeo . . . tomb.**] *Duthie-Wilson, from Q1 s.d.* Romeo opens the tomb.
53 s.d. **Steps forth.**] *Douai MS*
66 **be gone**] *Q3–4, F1;* begone *Q2*
67 **madman's**] *Theobald;* mad mans *Q2–4, F1*
68 **conjuration**] *Capell* (*after Q1* coniuration); commiration *Q2;* commisseration *Q3–4, F1*
70 s.d. **They fight.**] *Q1*
71 s.p. **Page.**] *Q4; line in italics and unassigned, Q2–3;* Pet. *F1;* Boy: *Q1*
71 s.d. **Exit.**] *Capell*
72 s.d. **Falls.**] *Capell*
73 s.d. **Dies.**] *Theobald*
87 s.d. **Laying . . . tomb.**] *Theobald*
102 **Shall I believe**] *in Q2–4, F1 these words are preceded by* I will beleeue, (*clearly a first-draft form*); O I beleeue *Q1*
107 **palace**] *Q3–4, F1;* pallat *Q2*
107 **night**] *Q3–4, F1;* night. *Q2*
108 **Depart again. Here**] *Q2* (*and Q3, F1 subs.*) *read:* Depart againe, come lye thou in my arme, / Heer's to thy health, where ere thou tumblest in. / O true Apothecarie! / Thy drugs are quicke. Thus with a kisse I die. / Depart againe, here (*these lines must represent an earlier version of ll. 119–20; the present arrangement follows Q4* (*Q1*))
119 s.d. **Drinks.**] *Douai MS, Theobald*
120 s.d. **Dies.**] *Douai MS, Theobald;* Falls. *Q1*
120 s.d. **Enter**] *Q3–4, F1* (*Q1*); Entrer *Q2*
120 s.d. **crow, and spade**] *om. Q1* (*Q1 indicates a break before Friar Lawrence's entry*)
121 **Francis**] *Q3–4, F1;* Frances *Q2*
122] *Following this line Steevens inserts from Q1:* Who is it that consorts so late the dead,
123 s.p. **Bal.**] *Q4;* Man. *Q2–3, F1* (*Q1*) (*throughout scene, except* Balth. *Q2–4* (*Q1*) *and* Boy. *F1 in l. 272*)
134 **intents**] *Q5;* entents *Q2–4, F1*
137 **yew**] *Pope;* yong *Q2–4, F1*
139 s.d. **Friar . . . weapons.**] *Q1*
143 s.d. **Enters the tomb.**] *Douai MS, Capell* (*subs.*)
147 s.d. **Juliet rises.**] *Q1*
150 s.d. **Noise within.**] *Capell*
151 **noise, lady.**] *Hoppe;* noise Lady, *Q2–4, F1*
159 s.d. **noise again**] *Capell*
168 s.p. **1. Watch.**] *Capell;* Watch. *Q2–4, F1* (*Q1*)
168 s.d. **Within.**] *Capell* (*Q1 has* Enter Watch. *before its equivalent of l. 168 and repeats* Enter watch. *after s.d. and a marked break at l. 170, indicating that l. 168 was spoken within*)
169 s.d. **Taking Romeo's dagger.**] *Douai MS, Capell*
170 s.d. **stabs herself**] *Capell, from Q1 s.d.:* She stabs herselfe and falles.; Kils herselfe. *F1* (*after* die. *l. 170*); *Q1 here indicates a break*
170 s.d. **Falls . . . dies.**] *Malone; cf. Q1 above*
170 s.d. **Paris'**] *Kittredge; s.d. placed as in Capell from Q1's second* Enter watch. (*see l. 168 s.d. above*)*; s.d. after l. 167, Q2–4, F1*
171 s.p. **Page.**] *Capell;* Watch boy. *Q2–3;* Boy. *Q4, F1* (*the Q2–3 s.p. probably indicates the actual entry of the Watch and Page at this point*)
171 **place,**] *Q3–4, F1;* place *Q2*
172 s.p. **1. Watch.**] *Capell;* Watch. *Q2–4, F1;* Cap: *Q1*
173 s.d. **Exeunt some.**] *Hanmer* (*subs.*)
178 s.d. **Exeunt others.**] *Capell*
181 s.d. **some . . . with**] *Theobald* (*after Rowe*)*; Q1 s.d. reads:* Enter one with Romets Man. (*after l. 187*)
182 s.p. **2. Watch.**] *Rowe;* Watch. *Q2–4, F1;* 1. *Q1*
183, 187 s.pp. **1. Watch.**] *Rowe;* Chief. watch. *Q2–4;* Con. *F1;* Cap: *and* Capt: *Q1*
183 s.d. **Enter . . . Watchman.**] Enter one with the Fryer. *Q1* (*after l. 181*)
184 s.p. **3. Watch.**] 1. *Q1*
187 **too.**] *F1;* too too. *Q2;* too, too. *Q3–4*
187 s.d. **and Attendants**] *Rowe;* with others *Q1*
189 s.d. **Capulet . . . others**] *Capell* (*subs.*); Capulet and his Wife. *Q4, F1;* olde Capolet and his Wife. *Q1*
190 **is so shrik'd**] *Daniel;* is so shrike *Q2;* they so shrike *Q3–4, F1*
191, 206 s.pp. **La. Cap.**] *Rowe;* Wife. *Q2–4, F1;* Moth: *Q1* (*l. 191 only*)
195 s.p. **1. Watch.**] *Capell;* Watch. *Q2–4;* Wat. *F1;* Capt: *Q1*
199 s.p. **1. Watch.**] *Capell;* Watch. *Q2–4;* Wat. *F1*
199 **slaughter'd**] *Q3, F1;* Slaughter *Q2;* slaughtred *Q4*

201] *Following this line Q2–3 read:* Enter Capulet and his wife. (*see above, l. 189*)
205 **it]** is *Q3–4, F1;* it is *Q1*
205 **mis-sheathed]** *F4* (*from F1* misheathed); missheathd *Q2;* misheath'd *Q3–4;* sheathed *Q1*
207 s.d. **and others]** *Capell*
209 **now]** more *Q1*
209 **early]** *Q3–4, F1* (*Q1*); earling *Q2*
210] *Following this line Q1 adds:* And yong *Benuolio* is deceased too:
223–69 **I . . . law.]** *cf. the following version of these lines in Q1:* I am the greatest able to doo least. / Most worthie Prince, heare me but speake the truth. / And Ile informe you how these things fell out. / *Iuliet* here slaine was married to that *Romeo,* / Without her Fathers or her Mothers grant: / The Nurse was priuie to the marriage. / The balefull day of this vnhappie marriage, / Was *Tybalts* doomesday: for which *Romeo* / Was banished from hence to *Mantua.* / He gone, her Father sought by foule constraint / To marrie her to *Paris:* But her Soule / (Loathing a second Contract) did refuse / To giue consent; and therefore did she vrge me / Either to finde a meanes she might auoyd / What so her Father sought to force her too: / Or els all desperately she threatned / Euen in my presence to dispatch her selfe. / Then did I giue her, (tutord by mine arte) / A potion that should make her seeme as dead: / And told her that I would with all post speed / Send hence to *Mantua* for her *Romeo,* / That he might come and take her from the Toombe. / But he that had my Letters (Frier *Iohn*) / Seeking a Brother to associate him, / Whereas the sicke infection remaind, / Was stayed by the Searchers of the Towne. / But *Romeo* vnderstanding by his man, / That *Iuliet* was deceasde, returnde in post / Vnto *Verona* for to see his loue. / What after happened touching *Paris* death, / Or *Romeos* is to me vnknowne at all. / But when I came to take the Lady hence, / I found them dead, and she awakt from sleep: / Whom faine I would haue taken from the tombe, / Which she refused seeing *Romeo* dead. / Anone I heard the watch and then I fled, / What afterhappened I am ignorant of. / And if in this ought haue miscaried. / By me, or by my meanes let my old life / Be sacrificd some houre before his time. / To the most strickest rigor of the Law.
228 **this.]** *Q5;* this? *Q2–4, F1*
232 **that]** *Q4* (*Q1*); thats *Q2–3;* that's *F1*
272 s.p. **Bal.]** Boy. *F1*
274 **place, . . . monument.]** *F1;* place. . . . monument *Q2–4*
281 s.p. **Page.]** *F1;* Boy. *Q2–4* (*Q1*)
290 **vault, to die]** Vault to dye, *F1*
292 **hate,]** *F1;* hate? *Q2–4*
299 **raise]** *Q4, F1;* raie *Q2–3;* erect *Q1*
308 **pardon'd]** *F1;* pardoned *Q2–4* (*Q1*)
310 s.d. **Exeunt omnes.]** *F1* (Exeunt omnes / FINIS.); FINIS. *Q2–4* (*Q1*)

On the way to a masking. From *Le Centre de l'Amour* (1630?). This picture suggests the street scene in *Romeo and Juliet* (I.iv) where Romeo, Mercutio, and Benvolio, accompanied by "five or six other Maskers" and "Torch-bearers," enter on their way to the Capulet party or masking. In Shakespeare, however, their only musical accompaniment appears to be a drum (line 114), and, of course, there is no lady in the company. (*By permission of the Harvard College Library*)

Julius Caesar

JULIUS CAESAR was probably one of the first of Shakespeare's plays to be presented at the Globe Theatre after the Lord Chamberlain's Men transferred their activities to the South Bank of the Thames in 1599. There are clear signs of its popularity then, and it has remained a favorite with scholars and audiences. The relative simplicity of its language, and the skill with which it renders a clash of ideals in terms of plausibly Roman characters, partly account for its success, and there are people who, knowing little of the rest of Shakespeare, remember the dignity of Portia and recall with warm affection the quarrel scene between Brutus and Cassius.

During the present century *Julius Caesar*, like most of the rest of the canon, has yielded some new insights to critics. It is true that certain topics, for example Shakespeare's use of Plutarch in the play, have been so thoroughly studied in the past that the modern investigator might be thought to have no hope of doing much more than refine received opinion. Yet there are problems—first adumbrated by Coleridge—upon which a good deal of modern criticism tends to pause. Briefly, these are political, and concern the interpretation of Shakespeare's motives in presenting the events before and after Caesar's death (including even the theory that he intended to be ambiguous). It has long been commonplace that Brutus is a kind of sketch for Hamlet; but now it is almost equally commonplace that Shakespeare, who had just finished a long series of political studies in English history, could hardly have brought to his play about the great crisis of Roman history and institutions a mind void of political interests. One consequence of this trend is that *Julius Caesar*, so lucid at first reading, has recently, and more than once, been called one of the most difficult of Shakespeare's plays to assess and interpret.

There is no contemporary quarto of *Julius Caesar*, and the play was first printed in the Folio of 1623. The Folio text is exceptionally clean, and was probably set up from a scribal transcript of the playhouse prompt-book. The shortness of the play (except for *Titus Andronicus* and *Timon of Athens*—itself a special case—only *Macbeth* among the tragedies is shorter) has sometimes led scholars to seek evidence of abridgment, though with small success. There is, however, some reason to think that Shakespeare revised the play. IV.iii as it stands imputes to Brutus an almost incredible lie; he tells Messala (182 ff.) that he has not had news of Portia's death, although he had himself informed Cassius of it only forty lines earlier. Shakespeare almost certainly meant one or the other passage to be cancelled. It has also been suggested that II.i.86 ff. was revised, and that Shakespeare had originally intended to write a scene (hinted at in I.iii) which would have been set on the first rather than the Ides of March; but that he abandoned this plan, and instead used parts of the proposed material in II.i (where F1 reads, in line 40, *first*, and editors emend to *Ides*). Ben Jonson, in his *Timber, or Discoveries* (published 1640) accused Shakespeare of writing a nonsensical line, "Caesar did never wrong, but with just cause," and some critics think this means that III.i.47 has been revised; but it seems at least as likely that Jonson is remembering a joking parody of the line as we now have it. The most certain of these revisions is that in IV.iii; perhaps one of the discussions of Portia's death was written into the prompt-copy and the other marked for cancellation, but not so clearly that the scribe could not overlook the note.

The date of *Julius Caesar* can be established with unusual certainty. On September 21, 1599, the Swiss traveller Thomas Platter "crossed the river" to see what was obviously Shakespeare's play at a theatre obviously the Globe. Jonson, in *Every Man Out of His Humor*, a play produced by Shakespeare's company in 1599, makes fun of III.ii.104–5 ("Reason long since is fled to animals, you know" [III.iv.33]). In the same play (V.vi.79) he also uses *Et tu Brute?* (but this appears to have been a not uncommon tag), and in 1600 he probably remembered the famous words of Antony at the end of the play when he wrote Mercury's description of Crites (*Cynthia's Revels*, II.iii.123 ff.). There are other contemporary allusions. Positive evidence that the play was not written earlier than 1599 is wanting; but Meres, needing to mention six tragedies in his panegyric of Shakespeare in *Palladis Tamia* (1598), does not name *Julius Caesar*. Assignment of it to 1599 is a conjecture unlikely to be shaken.

Shakespeare drew most of his material from Plutarch's *Lives* of Brutus, Caesar, and Antony. The student who consults these sources would do well to remember that Shakespeare also read the parallel lives, especially perhaps that of Dion, parallel to Brutus; and he was almost certainly familiar with parts of the *Moralia* also. A further point to remember is that he used North's translation of Amyot's French version of a Latin translation of Plutarch, and so looked at his material through several slightly distorting windows. Plutarch has a predisposition towards the early republican institutions of Rome which it was hard for a sixteenth-century English mind to share, though the example of sixteenth-century Venice, together with Plutarch's own prestige, made it possible for Shakespeare's contemporaries to have a notion at any rate of the merits of a republic; and an exceptional figure such as Montaigne might express admiration for the republican ideal. But the stock reaction to this issue of political theory was that monarchy was obviously the best form of government.

Nevertheless, North renders vividly the Plutarchan biographies, and Shakespeare continually adapts his very words, notably in the interview between Brutus and Portia in II.i, Cassius' speech to Messala before Philippi (V.i.70 ff.), and Lucilius' testimony to Brutus (V.iv.20–25), but also in many other places. Shakespeare adds Lucius and entirely remodels Casca, and his brilliant sketch of Octavius owes more to his own Bullingbrook than to Plutarch; but otherwise all the characters are in Plutarch. The leanness of Cassius, the sleekness of Antony, Brutus' bookishness, Caesar's self-infatuation and illness, the prophecy regarding the Ides of March, the punishment of the tribunes, the offer of a crown, the letters thrown in at Brutus' window, the refusal of an oath, the rejection of Cicero, the decision not to kill Antony and Brutus' mistake in allowing him to speak at the funeral, the courage of the sick Ligarius, the prodigies, Calphurnia's dream, the trick of Decius Brutus, Portia's anxiety, the murder of Cinna the poet (though in Plutarch he is not killed for his bad verses), the apparition of Caesar's ghost (in Plutarch merely Brutus' "evil spirit"), the discussion on suicide, the imprudence of Brutus as general at Philippi (though Shakespeare transfers to Octavius his refusal to comply with his colleague's battle-order), the suicides of Cassius and Brutus, and Antony's eulogy of Brutus: all this and much else is directly from Plutarch. Naturally there are changes, some theatrical, some in the interests of a new presentation of character and politics. There are understandable compressions of time: a period of three years is got into five separate days; there were two battles at Philippi, twenty days apart. Historically, the events of the opening two scenes were separated by months (October to March). Octavius did not reach Rome until six weeks after the death of Caesar, and eighteen months then passed before he allied himself with Antony and Lepidus in the triumvirate.

This free handling of historical material will remind the student of Shakespeare's method in the English history plays, where his object is also the double one of dramatizing an extensive historical narrative and achieving a sharper focus on the relevant political issues and personalities. The effort he clearly made to represent his characters plausibly as antique Romans should not conceal the truth that, as in the English histories, matters of politics tend to take a strong sixteenth-century coloring.

Shakespeare accordingly did not scruple to improve upon mere hints, to invent, or to omit. He does not say that the coolness between Cassius and Brutus at the beginning arose from Caesar's having preferred Brutus over his brother-in-law, nor that the "pale lean" men Caesar mistrusted were Brutus and Cassius, not merely Cassius. He does not tell us that Brutus wounded Caesar "in the privities." He wants to strip Brutus of any suspicion of mercenary envy. Plutarch, however, also insists that Cassius was motivated by private malice, Brutus by hatred of tyranny. Caesar did not have a fit of the falling sickness at the point described by Casca in the play, and the reason why he did not read the memorial of Artemidorus was simply that he could not get at it, though he tried. The stylistic contrast between the two funeral orations is built on a single phrase of Plutarch's about the laconic epistolary style of Brutus. The touching of Calphurnia by the runners seems to be Shakespeare's invention. In brief, to study Plutarch—and there is no substitute for that—is to gain a valuable insight into the operation of Shakespeare's dramatic intelligence; he chooses with inspiration, sometimes a trifle from the text, sometimes even a marginal note which is not Plutarch at all (as when he takes North's hint about the "two capital errors of Brutus concerning Antony"). He emerges with a Brutus and a Caesar based upon those of Plutarch, yet strangely altered. That this intelligence was essentially dramatic may be deduced from the boldness of the opening scene, which risks using characters not to be seen again (indeed, they are "put to silence") in order to sketch Caesar's war with Pompey and the means by which he achieved his present power; and even more so by magnificent economies of the second scene, where, after Caesar's brief appearance, Cassius makes his first proposals to Brutus while flourishes and shouts offstage report Caesar's refusal of the diadem. When the "chidden train" has once more crossed the stage, Casca enters to provide a sour account of the proceedings. The scene ends with Cassius' self-revelatory soliloquy and his somewhat less than noble design on Brutus. It plays for no more than twenty minutes, but without doing violence to Plutarch's Roman context it lays down with masterly firmness the bases of the main issues and characters: Caesar's self-infatuation and dynastic longings; the disgust of Cassius that a weak mortal should so aspire (and his willingness to corrupt Brutus in order to prevent it happening); the conscience and philosophic seriousness of Brutus. It is fair, despite the deep-lying differences, to say that Shakespeare's treatment of his principal source evinces not only remarkable skill and dramatic opportunism, but also fidelity.

There had been a good many plays about Caesar before Shakespeare's. Latin, French, and English analogues are known, and have occasionally been held to have affected Shakespeare's play. Among them are Pescetti's *Cesare* of 1594, and the earlier Senecan works of Muret (1553) and Grévin (1561). A *Caesar Interfectus* was acted at Oxford in 1582, and Henslowe's diary records a two-part Caesar play in 1594. Kyd's *Cornelia*, translated from Robert Garnier's *Cornélie*, was published in 1594, and Shakespeare may have read it. The anonymous *Caesar's Revenge*, which has lately been called a source second in importance only to Plutarch, and which converts the "evil spirit" of Plutarch into Caesar's ghost, was published in 1607; it may have been acted, academically, some years earlier, but there is no strong indication of Shakespeare's having read it—indeed, had Sir William Alexander's *Tragedy of Julius Caesar* (1607) been published a few years earlier, a much better case could be made out for Shakespeare's interest in it. All these plays, except for the unknown pieces named by Henslowe, are academic; and it is hardly surprising that academic dramatists should have cultivated this great moment in history, or that they should have found the mighty but hubristic Julius convenient to their Senecan purposes.

There remain for consideration under this head the historians and political commentators influential in Shakespeare's own time. They had behind them an almost unbroken tradition of commentary stretching back to the Roman historians themselves; but there was also a confusion of opinion reflected by the divergent opinions of Dante, who put Brutus and Cassius with Judas in the deepest part of hell, in the very mouth of Satan, and, say, Michelangelo, who idealized Brutus in a famous bust, or the humanists who revived a sentimental republicanism not unlike that of Plutarch. No Elizabethan attempted a serious history of Rome, but Appian's *Civil Wars* was translated in 1578, and it seems likely that Shakespeare knew this work, and took from it some considerable part of his character of Antony. As Ernest Schanzer has said, Plutarch's Antony, though "gamesome," is a "plain blunt man," whereas Appian's is "an emotional machiavel with great histrionic powers, a blend of boldness and dissimulation." It would be as well also to take the hint of the translator's title-page, which neatly emphasizes the importance to the Christian world of these events in Roman history: "Foure Acts of that prophane Tragedie, whereof flowed our diuine Comoedie."

Appian, unlike Plutarch, does not attempt to contrast Brutus and Cassius, and although he seems to think them good men, he does not profess to know their motives precisely. But he castigates ambition and "the greedy desire of kingdom." The English translator, flattering the Queen, claims that Appian's narrative proves the necessity of monarchy, and thinks it proper that the conspirators should have met a violent death. William Fulbecke, bridging the gap between Livy and Tacitus in his *Historical Collection of the Continual Factions, Tumults, and Massacres of the Romans* (1601, but written in 1586), makes the same point. The fact that the reign of Augustus was preceded by over a century of civil war was much in the Elizabethan mind, and surely in Shakespeare's, since he had recently written so many plays about the similar factions and tumults preceding the advent of the Tudors. Of all Plutarch's observations on the period, his declared conviction that Caesar, however tyrannical, was the strong hand Rome needed to preserve her liberties must have most impressed Shakespeare's contemporaries. Fulbecke treats the matter on those lines. Long before, he says, the first Brutus, in expelling the kings, made Rome "change gold for brass"; yet he cannot deny that the city flourished under the Republic. The last hundred and twenty years before Caesar were, however, "troublesome and ugly, bloody and detestable"; there was too much luxury, men died as often by the banquet as by the blade. Caesar, however, expunged this terrible record and was getting the state back into order when the disaster happened. Fulbecke has a particular dislike of Antony, and seems surprised that Octavius should have turned into Augustus. His brisk book may well have provided Shakespeare with one or two hints, especially in the study of Brutus and in the soliloquy in II.i. So may Thomas Smith's *De Republica Anglorum* (written 1565, published 1583). Smith proposes a cyclical movement of history; the rule of the mob gives place to tyranny, as it did with Caesar; the most pernicious tyranny in Rome was that of the triumvirate of Caesar, Crassus, and Pompey, and then of Octavius, Antony, and Lepidus. Distinguishing between kings and tyrants, he seems to think Julius Caesar not a tyrant, since he achieved power by a plebiscite, whereas Octavius entered upon his power tyrannically, though he thenceforth behaved like a king. Smith has the Elizabethan conviction that to change the status quo usually means to be worse off, and quotes in support the case of Brutus and Cassius. This is merely a sample of the considerable amount of discussion given to the subject in Shakespeare's time. One might also refer to passages in Elyot's *Governor*, to Lucan, whom Marlowe translated, to

Greville, who discussed Caesar as a tyrant in his didactic poem *Of Monarchy*, and to Sidney, who spoke of "rebel Caesar"—thinking, no doubt, as Alexander did, of the Senate as King.

All this additional material merely tends to show that the death of Caesar gave an Elizabethan with a concern for politics plenty to think about. It does not affect the status of Plutarch as incomparably the most important source.

We should remember that in his Comparison between Brutus and Dion, Plutarch insists that the Romans had not the same case for disposing of Caesar as the Syracusans had for getting rid of Dionysius. On the other hand he says that Brutus, unlike Dion, had no private grievance against the tyrant, but "ventured to kill him only to set his country again at liberty" and "to restore the Empire of Rome again to her former state and government."

This leads us directly to the ideological crux of the play, Brutus' soliloquy at the beginning of the second act. It has often been accused of illogic or evasion, most memorably by Coleridge:

> surely nothing can seem more discordant with our historical preconceptions of Brutus, or more *lowering* to the intellect of this Stoico-Platonic tyrannicide, than the tenets here attributed to him, to *him*, the stern Roman republican; viz., that he would have no objection to a king, or to Caesar, a monarch in Rome, would Caesar be as good a monarch as he is now disposed to be. How too could Brutus say he finds no personal cause; *i.e.* none in Caesar's past conduct as a man? Had he not passed the Rubicon? Entered Rome as a conqueror? Placed his Gauls in the Senate? Shakespeare (it may be said) has not brought these things forward. True! and this is just the ground of my perplexity. What character does Shakespeare mean *his* Brutus to be?

Coleridge, and those who have echoed him, prejudge the politics of Brutus, and also fail to observe that one of the sources of the soliloquy is in Plutarch's Comparison. Brutus is objecting to the *crowning* of Caesar; he is a man who attaches much importance to ceremony, even attempting to make a savage murder into a sort of ritual. But Caesar also thinks that crowning is a significant ceremony. The question is of an alteration of Caesar's status. For Plutarch, Caesar is already virtually a king, and Brutus' an act of deposition; it is not so for Shakespeare, who, in the English tradition, attached great importance to coronation. What alarms Brutus is not the present loss of republican freedom, but the coronation, which will put Caesar beyond reprisal: it is as if Caesar were aspiring to the English throne, and as if Brutus were an Elizabethan supporter of the doctrine of non-resistance. Coleridge does not allow for the presence of anachronistic assumptions below the historical surface.

Even so, the history is less inadequate than he supposes. Shakespeare distinguishes Brutus from Cassius, who wants to kill Caesar for what he *is*; and when he makes Brutus say that he "knows no personal cause to spurn at" Caesar, and that the quarrel "will bear no color for the thing he is" (II.i.11, 29), he is not forgetting the Pompeian wars and their outrages; he gave them prominent mention in the first scene. He is remembering Plutarch, who says expressly that

> Caesar's power and government when it came to be established, did indeed much hurt at his first entry and beginning unto those that did resist him; but afterwards, unto them that being overcome had received his government, it had seemed he rather had the name and opinion onely of a tyrante, than otherwise that he was so indeed. For there never followed any tyrannical nor cruel act, but contrarily, it seemed that he was a merciful physician, whom God had ordained of special grace to be Governor of the Empire of Rome, and to set all things again at a quiet stay, the which required the counsel and authority of an absolute Prince. . . .

On the other hand, he says in the *Life* of Caesar that Caesar's passion for the crown was the "chiefest cause that made him mortally hated," and that he did not show a proper respect for the Senate. At the moment of Brutus' speaking, there is nothing to be feared of Caesar except what he may become if crowned (and so given an immunity admittedly anachronistic). The brief appearance of Caesar at the beginning of I.ii, together with his concern at Calphurnia's barrenness, might seem to provide evidence not only of his delusions of royal grandeur, but of dynastic ambitions, and Brutus has some genuine cause for worry. He says nothing more in the soliloquy, which makes perfectly good sense if one thinks of him as a killer of tyrants only, as it were, in the egg, and remembers what Plutarch—strongly echoed, incidentally, by Fulbecke—says of his blameless behavior since he achieved power.

In fact, Brutus' motives are very accurately rendered by Pompey in *Antony and Cleopatra*:

> what
> Made all-honor'd, honest, Roman Brutus,
> With the arm'd rest, courtiers of beauteous freedom,
> To drench the Capitol, but that they would
> Have one man but a man? (II.vi.15–19)

Caesar was beginning to forget his mortality and to believe solely in what theorists of kingship would have called his Dignity. Cassius can think of nothing but his mortality (and to enable him to do so, Shakespeare converts Plutarchan evidence of Caesar's courage into evidence of physical weakness). We are reminded of his infirmities, his slightly ridiculous denials that he is subject to ordinary mortal failings. The problem of Brutus is precisely that to crown Caesar would give him encouragement in this, confer validity upon his assumed Dignity; then, mortality forgotten, he might disjoin remorse from power and cease to be the temperate ruler he remains at this stage.

It is important to remember what Appian's English translator so casually mentioned: Caesar's tragedy is the Christian's comedy. All these events led to the rule of Augustus, under which occurred the birth of

Christ, and ultimately to the Christianization of the Empire under Constantine, whom Elizabeth could think of as a type and predecessor. St. Augustine, whose view of history this reflects, believed that Caesar "used his victory with mercy," but thought the whole matter of importance only to the extent that it was part of such a providential plan.

Now, Shakespeare holds his Romans at arm's length; the historical event itself he could see in some perspective, and his Romans do not behave as his other men do, being much given to philosophical declarations and a kind of histrionic *gravitas*. But this does not mean that he did not see the issues of his play as acutely alive. In Shakespeare's day there was a growth of interest in the problem of defining royal status. Later this became a matter of a contest between genuine Divine Right theory and active republicanism with its insistence on the right of tyrannicide; to Hobbes, for instance, tyrannicide was only a long word for regicide—and incidentally he wanted to forbid the study of Republican Rome—while to Milton Brutus was a noble exemplar. To Shakespeare, before the issues grew so urgent, the question was more delicate. Caesar was a kind of king; his name implied it, Plutarch said it outright; and if not a king he was by common consent the supreme magistrate. Only some important ceremonies were lacking; but without them even a master of orthodoxy like Jewel had—in defense of Elizabeth's church—argued that some right of resistance remained. Some such speculations lie behind the soliloquy of Brutus. On the other hand, the chaos that followed the decision of Brutus seemed sufficient proof of the soundness of the Homily against Willful Rebellion. Furthermore, Brutus had the disadvantage of not knowing the Christian future of the Empire. He is, in short, a Roman considering with pagan conscience a problem to which he cannot know the answer; but he thinks about it in terms not unfamiliar to the Elizabethan student of politics, which is why the offer of a crown seemed more important to him than the crossing of the Rubicon. Shakespeare treats him with delicate sympathy, but cannot have thought his act a right one, however much he may prefer him to Cassius, Octavius, and Antony. What he does make clear is that, quite apart from his tactical mistakes in trusting Cassius and Antony, Brutus faced a real problem, of exactly the kind an Englishman might have to face—did have to face—when a king, some time in the future, might set himself above Parliament and confuse his mortal body with his Dignity. Ironically, Caesar's body dies; but his spirit does not, because it is the dignity of Empire, and its survival was essential to our "divine comedy." The portents, which Cassius, like Edmund in *Lear*, ignores, are a sign of this.

I have spoken of the fine contrivance of the opening scenes. The play is throughout beautifully built, as in the fast-moving, variously lit passage from II.ii to III.i—the decision of Caesar to go to the Senate, Portia's anxiety, the tense minutes before the assassination, the arrival, large and menacing, of Antony, and finally of Octavius' messenger: five hundred lines tightly written, describing one great dramatic curve; and followed instantly by the next movement: funeral orations, riot, war. Bradley castigated the quarrel scene, thinking it irrelevant to the main action. In fact it is a needed relaxation of the historical tempo, and a well-contrived antithesis to the mounting excitement of the conversation between the two men in I.ii. Cassius is never more likable, Brutus never more admirable, than after the quarrel. But nobody could any longer suppose that these men will win their battle; the tone is already of honorable defeat, elegiac. When defeat and suicide come, in the still economical final scenes, it is by a series of chances that have the look of providence, working through the wild Antony and the cold Octavius.

Julius Caesar is a finely made, extremely self-conscious play. One gets that feeling also from the deliberately restricted range of the verse: a sense of control, of dramatic poetry used as a means to indicate, and at the same time to play down, the largeness of the Roman attitudes. It has often been related to the contemporary play of Revenge, a form which Shakespeare was shortly to exploit fully in *Hamlet*. This relation exists; but on the broadest view, the revenger is history, conceived as God-ordained. Its victim Brutus, clearly seen in the perspective of time, was deserving of punishment only because, for all his knowledge, he did not know enough. None of them did, and that may account for the deliberately hollow tone of some of the things they say.

Frank Kermode

The Tragedy of Julius Caesar

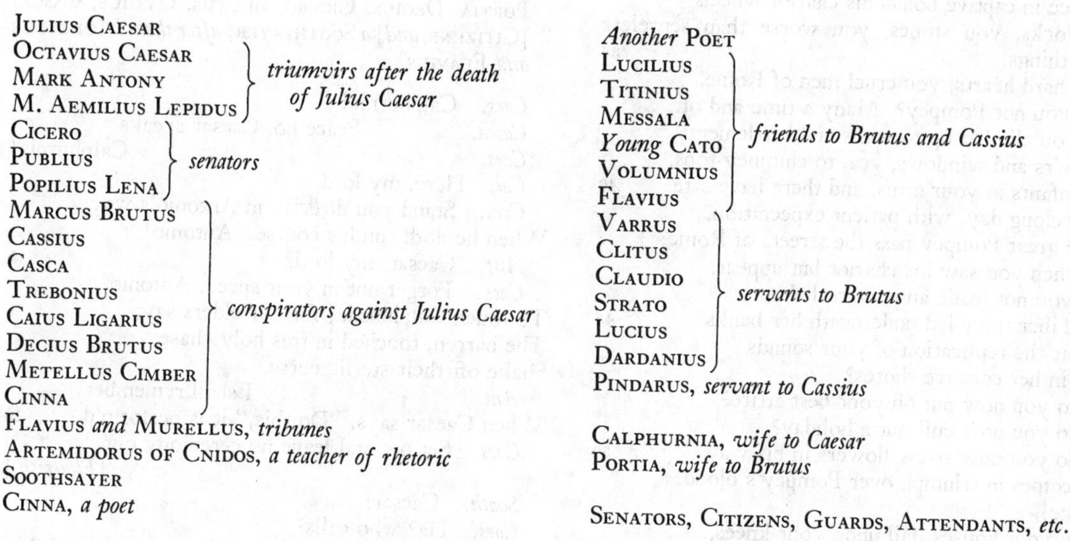

[DRAMATIS PERSONAE

JULIUS CAESAR
OCTAVIUS CAESAR, MARK ANTONY, M. AEMILIUS LEPIDUS — *triumvirs after the death of Julius Caesar*
CICERO, PUBLIUS, POPILIUS LENA — *senators*
MARCUS BRUTUS, CASSIUS, CASCA, TREBONIUS, CAIUS LIGARIUS, DECIUS BRUTUS, METELLUS CIMBER, CINNA — *conspirators against Julius Caesar*
FLAVIUS *and* MURELLUS, *tribunes*
ARTEMIDORUS OF CNIDOS, *a teacher of rhetoric*
SOOTHSAYER
CINNA, *a poet*
Another POET
LUCILIUS, TITINIUS, MESSALA, *Young* CATO, VOLUMNIUS — *friends to Brutus and Cassius*
FLAVIUS, VARRUS, CLITUS, CLAUDIO, STRATO, LUCIUS, DARDANIUS — *servants to Brutus*
PINDARUS, *servant to Cassius*

CALPHURNIA, *wife to Caesar*
PORTIA, *wife to Brutus*

SENATORS, CITIZENS, GUARDS, ATTENDANTS, *etc.*

SCENE: *Rome; near Sardis; near Philippi*]

ACT I, SCENE I

Enter FLAVIUS, MURELLUS, *and certain* COMMONERS *over the stage.*

Flav. Hence! home, you idle creatures, get you home!
Is this a holiday? What, know you not,
Being mechanical, you ought not walk
Upon a laboring day without the sign
Of your profession? Speak, what trade art thou?

Car. Why, sir, a carpenter.

Mur. Where is thy leather apron and thy rule?
What dost thou with thy best apparel on?
You, sir, what trade are you?

Cob. Truly, sir, in respect of a fine workman, I am but, as you would say, a cobbler.

Mur. But what trade art thou? Answer me directly.

Cob. A trade, sir, that I hope I may use with a safe conscience, which is indeed, sir, a mender of bad soles.

Flav. What trade, thou knave? thou naughty knave, what trade?

Cob. Nay, I beseech you, sir, be not out with me; yet if you be out, sir, I can mend you.

Mur. What mean'st thou by that? Mend me, thou saucy fellow?

Cob. Why, sir, cobble you.

Flav. Thou art a cobbler, art thou?

Cob. Truly, sir, all that I live by is with the awl: I meddle with no tradesman's matters, nor women's matters; but withal I am indeed, sir, a surgeon to old shoes; when they are in great danger, I recover them.

Words and passages enclosed in square brackets in the text above are either emendations of the copy-text or additions to it. The Textual Notes immediately following the play cite the earliest authority for every such change or insertion and supply the reading of the copy-text wherever it is emended in this edition.

I.i. Location: Rome. A street.
3. mechanical: of the artisan class.
4–5. sign . . . profession: e.g. tools, aprons, etc.
10. in . . . workman: (1) as far as skilled workmanship is concerned; (2) compared with a skilled workman.
11. cobbler: (1) mender of shoes; (2) botcher (the sense understood by Murellus). **12. directly:** in plain language.
14. soles. With obvious quibble on *souls.*
15. naughty: good-for-nothing. **16. out:** angry.
17. if . . . you: i.e. if your shoes have holes, I can repair them (but Murellus understands "if you are subject to anger, I can reform you").
23. withal: yet (with pun on "with awl").
24. recover: resole (with pun on the sense "cure").

As proper men as ever trod upon neat's-leather have gone upon my handiwork.

Flav. But wherefore art not in thy shop to-day?
Why dost thou lead these men about the streets?

Cob. Truly, sir, to wear out their shoes, to get myself into more work. But indeed, sir, we make holiday to see Caesar, and to rejoice in his triumph.

Mur. Wherefore rejoice? What conquest brings he home?
What tributaries follow him to Rome,
To grace in captive bonds his chariot-wheels?
You blocks, you stones, you worse than senseless things!
O you hard hearts, you cruel men of Rome,
Knew you not Pompey? Many a time and oft
Have you climb'd up to walls and battlements,
To tow'rs and windows, yea, to chimney-tops,
Your infants in your arms, and there have sate
The livelong day, with patient expectation,
To see great Pompey pass the streets of Rome;
And when you saw his chariot but appear,
Have you not made an universal shout,
That Tiber trembled underneath her banks
To hear the replication of your sounds
Made in her concave shores?
And do you now put on your best attire?
And do you now cull out a holiday?
And do you now strew flowers in his way,
That comes in triumph over Pompey's blood?
Be gone!
Run to your houses, fall upon your knees,
Pray to the gods to intermit the plague
That needs must light on this ingratitude.

Flav. Go, go, good countrymen, and for this fault
Assemble all the poor men of your sort;
Draw them to Tiber banks, and weep your tears
Into the channel, till the lowest stream
Do kiss the most exalted shores of all.

Exeunt all the Commoners.

See whe'er their basest metal be not mov'd;
They vanish tongue-tied in their guiltiness.
Go you down that way towards the Capitol,
This way will I. Disrobe the images,
If you do find them deck'd with ceremonies.

Mur. May we do so?
You know it is the feast of Lupercal.

Flav. It is no matter, let no images
Be hung with Caesar's trophies. I'll about,
And drive away the vulgar from the streets;
So do you too, where you perceive them thick.
These growing feathers pluck'd from Caesar's wing
Will make him fly an ordinary pitch,
Who else would soar above the view of men,
And keep us all in servile fearfulness. *Exeunt.*

25. As . . . leather: as handsome men as ever wore shoes (proverbial). **neat's-leather:** cowhide. **26. gone:** walked.
31. triumph: triumphal procession.
33. tributaries: captive princes who will pay tribute.
37. Pompey: former triumvir with Caesar and Crassus, defeated by Caesar at Pharsalia in 48 B.C. and subsequently murdered.
40. sate: sat. **46. replication:** reverberation.
49. cull out: pick this as.
51. blood: offspring. Caesar had defeated Pompey's sons at Munda in Spain in 45 B.C. Murellus is making Plutarch's point that Romans should not celebrate triumphs over Romans, as well as complaining of the crowd's forgetfulness of Pompey. **54. intermit:** withhold.
61. See . . . mov'd: note how even their base natures are affected.
64. Disrobe the images. Caesar's supporters had set up statues of him wearing royal crowns. **65. ceremonies:** symbols of state.
67. feast of Lupercal: the Lupercalia, a Roman festival celebrated on February 15. (Caesar's triumph was actually held in October.)
69. Caesar's trophies: ornaments in honor of Caesar.

70. vulgar: common people, plebs.
72–73. These . . . pitch. A figure from falconry; *pitch* = the highest point of a hawk's flight, from which it swoops down on its prey.

[Scene II]

Enter Caesar, Antony *for the course,* Calphurnia, Portia, Decius, Cicero, Brutus, Cassius, Casca, [Citizens, *and*] *a* Soothsayer; *after them* Murellus *and* Flavius.

Caes. Calphurnia!
Casca. Peace ho, Caesar speaks.
Caes. Calphurnia!
Cal. Here, my lord.
Caes. Stand you directly in Antonio's way
When he doth run his course. Antonio!
Ant. Caesar, my lord?
Caes. Forget not in your speed, Antonio,
To touch Calphurnia; for our elders say,
The barren, touched in this holy chase,
Shake off their sterile curse.
Ant. I shall remember:
When Caesar says, "Do this," it is perform'd.
Caes. Set on, and leave no ceremony out.

[*Flourish.*]

Sooth. Caesar!
Caes. Ha? who calls?
Casca. Bid every noise be still; peace yet again!
Caes. Who is it in the press that calls on me?
I hear a tongue shriller than all the music
Cry "Caesar!" Speak, Caesar is turn'd to hear.
Sooth. Beware the ides of March.
Caes. What man is that?
Bru. A soothsayer bids you beware the ides of March.
Caes. Set him before me, let me see his face.
Cas. Fellow, come from the throng, look upon Caesar.
Caes. What say'st thou to me now? Speak once again.
Sooth. Beware the ides of March.
Caes. He is a dreamer, let us leave him. Pass.

Sennet. Exeunt. Manent Brutus and Cassius.

Cas. Will you go see the order of the course?
Bru. Not I.
Cas. I pray you do.
Bru. I am not gamesome; I do lack some part
Of that quick spirit that is in Antony.

I.ii. Location: Rome. A public place.
o.s.d. for the course: stripped for the race. On the Lupercalia two Romans ran a ceremonial course through the city, carrying goatskin thongs with which they struck those they encountered.
11 s.d. Flourish: trumpet fanfare. **15. press:** throng.
18. ides of March: March 15.
24 s.d. Sennet: trumpet call signalling the entry or exit of an important personage or a procession.
25. the order . . . course: how the race goes.

Let me not hinder, Cassius, your desires;
I'll leave you.
Cas. Brutus, I do observe you now of late;
I have not from your eyes that gentleness
And show of love as I was wont to have.
You bear too stubborn and too strange a hand
Over your friend that loves you.
Bru. Cassius,
Be not deceiv'd. If I have veil'd my look,
I turn the trouble of my countenance
Merely upon myself. Vexed I am
Of late with passions of some difference,
Conceptions only proper to myself,
Which give some soil, perhaps, to my behaviors;
But let not therefore my good friends be griev'd
(Among which number, Cassius, be you one),
Nor construe any further my neglect,
Than that poor Brutus, with himself at war,
Forgets the shows of love to other men.
Cas. Then, Brutus, I have much mistook your passion,
By means whereof this breast of mine hath buried
Thoughts of great value, worthy cogitations.
Tell me, good Brutus, can you see your face?
Bru. No, Cassius; for the eye sees not itself
But by reflection, by some other things.
Cas. 'Tis just,
And it is very much lamented, Brutus,
That you have no such mirrors as will turn
Your hidden worthiness into your eye,
That you might see your shadow. I have heard
Where many of the best respect in Rome
(Except immortal Caesar), speaking of Brutus
And groaning underneath this age's yoke,
Have wish'd that noble Brutus had his eyes.
Bru. Into what dangers would you lead me, Cassius,
That you would have me seek into myself
For that which is not in me?
Cas. Therefore, good Brutus, be prepar'd to hear;
And since you know you cannot see yourself
So well as by reflection, I, your glass,
Will modestly discover to yourself
That of yourself which you yet know not of.
And be not jealous on me, gentle Brutus:
Were I a common laughter, or did use
To stale with ordinary oaths my love
To every new protester; if you know
That I do fawn on men and hug them hard,
And after scandal them; or if you know
That I profess myself in banqueting
To all the rout, then hold me dangerous.
Flourish and shout.

37–39. If . . . myself: if I have turned away from you, it has been in order to turn my disquiet entirely upon myself.
40. passions . . . difference: conflicting emotions. **42. soil:** stain.
49. By means whereof: as a result of which (mistake).
54. just: true. **58. shadow:** reflection. **59. respect:** repute.
66. Therefore: as to that. **69. modestly:** without exaggeration.
71. jealous on: suspicious of.
72. laughter: source of laughter, i.e. frivolous or unserious man.
73. stale: make common. **ordinary:** common, occurring regularly.
74. protester: one who professes friendship. **76. scandal:** defame.
77. profess myself: profess friendship. **78. rout:** mob.

Bru. What means this shouting? I do fear the people
Choose Caesar for their king.
Cas. Ay, do you fear it?
Then must I think you would not have it so.
Bru. I would not, Cassius, yet I love him well.
But wherefore do you hold me here so long?
What is it that you would impart to me?
If it be aught toward the general good,
Set honor in one eye and death i' th' other,
And I will look on both indifferently;
For let the gods so speed me as I love
The name of honor more than I fear death.
Cas. I know that virtue to be in you, Brutus,
As well as I do know your outward favor.
Well, honor is the subject of my story:
I cannot tell what you and other men
Think of this life; but, for my single self,
I had as lief not be as live to be
In awe of such a thing as I myself.
I was born free as Caesar, so were you;
We both have fed as well, and we can both
Endure the winter's cold as well as he;
For once, upon a raw and gusty day,
The troubled Tiber chafing with her shores,
Caesar said to me, "Dar'st thou, Cassius, now
Leap in with me into this angry flood,
And swim to yonder point?" Upon the word,
Accoutred as I was, I plunged in,
And bade him follow; so indeed he did.
The torrent roar'd, and we did buffet it
With lusty sinews, throwing it aside
And stemming it with hearts of controversy;
But ere we could arrive the point propos'd,
Caesar cried, "Help me, Cassius, or I sink!"
I, as Aeneas, our great ancestor,
Did from the flames of Troy upon his shoulder
The old Anchises bear, so from the waves of Tiber
Did I the tired Caesar. And this man
Is now become a god, and Cassius is
A wretched creature, and must bend his body
If Caesar carelessly but nod on him.
He had a fever when he was in Spain,
And when the fit was on him, I did mark
How he did shake—'tis true, this god did shake;
His coward lips did from their color fly,
And that same eye whose bend doth awe the world
Did lose his lustre; I did hear him groan;
Ay, and that tongue of his that bade the Romans
Mark him, and write his speeches in their books,
Alas, it cried, "Give me some drink, Titinius,"
As a sick girl. Ye gods, it doth amaze me
A man of such a feeble temper should
So get the start of the majestic world
And bear the palm alone. *Shout. Flourish.*
Bru. Another general shout!

87. indifferently: impartially. **88. speed me:** cause me to prosper.
91. favor: appearance. **109. of controversy:** excited by the contest.
112. Aeneas: mythical founder of Rome, who carried his father Anchises from the burning ruins of Troy after its fall.
122. His . . . fly. The inversion makes clearer the pun on *color* as (1) hue, (2) flag. **123. bend:** glance. **124. his:** its.
130. get the start of: outstrip.

I do believe that these applauses are
For some new honors that are heap'd on Caesar.

Cas. Why, man, he doth bestride the narrow world
Like a Colossus, and we petty men
Walk under his huge legs, and peep about
To find ourselves dishonorable graves.
Men at some time are masters of their fates;
The fault, dear Brutus, is not in our stars,
But in ourselves, that we are underlings.
Brutus and Caesar: what should be in that "Caesar"?
Why should that name be sounded more than yours?
Write them together, yours is as fair a name;
Sound them, it doth become the mouth as well;
Weigh them, it is as heavy; conjure with 'em,
"Brutus" will start a spirit as soon as "Caesar."
Now in the names of all the gods at once,
Upon what meat doth this our Caesar feed
That he is grown so great? Age, thou art sham'd!
Rome, thou hast lost the breed of noble bloods!
When went there by an age since the great flood
But it was fam'd with more than with one man?
When could they say, till now, that talk'd of Rome,
That her wide walks encompass'd but one man?
Now is it Rome indeed and room enough,
When there is in it but one only man.
O! you and I have heard our fathers say
There was a Brutus once that would have brook'd
Th' eternal devil to keep his state in Rome
As easily as a king.

Bru. That you do love me, I am nothing jealous;
What you would work me to, I have some aim.
How I have thought of this, and of these times,
I shall recount hereafter. For this present,
I would not (so with love I might entreat you)
Be any further mov'd. What you have said
I will consider; what you have to say
I will with patience hear, and find a time
Both meet to hear and answer such high things.
Till then, my noble friend, chew upon this:
Brutus had rather be a villager
Than to repute himself a son of Rome
Under these hard conditions as this time
Is like to lay upon us.

Cas. I am glad that my weak words
Have struck but thus much show of fire from Brutus.

Enter CAESAR *and his* TRAIN.

Bru. The games are done, and Caesar is returning.

Cas. As they pass by, pluck Casca by the sleeve,
And he will (after his sour fashion) tell you
What hath proceeded worthy note to-day.

Bru. I will do so. But look you, Cassius,
The angry spot doth glow on Caesar's brow,
And all the rest look like a chidden train:
Calphurnia's cheek is pale, and Cicero
Looks with such ferret and such fiery eyes
As we have seen him in the Capitol,
Being cross'd in conference by some senators.

Cas. Casca will tell us what the matter is.

Caes. Antonio!

Ant. Caesar?

Caes. Let me have men about me that are fat,
Sleek-headed men and such as sleep a-nights.
Yond Cassius has a lean and hungry look,
He thinks too much; such men are dangerous.

Ant. Fear him not, Caesar, he's not dangerous,
He is a noble Roman, and well given.

Caes. Would he were fatter! but I fear him not.
Yet if my name were liable to fear,
I do not know the man I should avoid
So soon as that spare Cassius. He reads much,
He is a great observer, and he looks
Quite through the deeds of men. He loves no plays,
As thou dost, Antony; he hears no music;
Seldom he smiles, and smiles in such a sort
As if he mock'd himself, and scorn'd his spirit
That could be mov'd to smile at any thing.
Such men as he be never at heart's ease
Whiles they behold a greater than themselves,
And therefore are they very dangerous.
I rather tell thee what is to be fear'd
Than what I fear; for always I am Caesar.
Come on my right hand, for this ear is deaf,
And tell me truly what thou think'st of him.

Sennet. Exeunt Caesar and his Train. [*Casca stays.*]

Casca. You pull'd me by the cloak, would you speak with me?

Bru. Ay, Casca, tell us what hath chanc'd to-day
That Caesar looks so sad.

Casca. Why, you were with him, were you not?

Bru. I should not then ask Casca what had chanc'd.

Casca. Why, there was a crown offer'd him; and being offer'd him, he put it by with the back of his hand thus, and then the people fell a-shouting.

Bru. What was the second noise for?

Casca. Why, for that too.

Cas. They shouted thrice; what was the last cry for?

Casca. Why, for that too.

Bru. Was the crown offer'd him thrice?

Casca. Ay, marry, was't, and he put it by thrice, every time gentler than other; and at every putting-by mine honest neighbors shouted.

Cas. Who offer'd him the crown?

Casca. Why, Antony.

Bru. Tell us the manner of it, gentle Casca.

Casca. I can as well be hang'd as tell the manner of it: it was mere foolery, I did not mark it. I saw Mark

136. Colossus: a gigantic statue, like that of Apollo at Rhodes, believed by some to have bestridden the harbor.
146. conjure: call up spirits. **147. start:** raise.
152. flood: in classical mythology, the inundation which drowned everyone save Deucalion and his wife Pyrrha.
156. Rome, room. Pronounced alike.
159. a Brutus once: Lucius Junius Brutus, a leader in the expulsion of the Tarquins and the establishment of the Roman republic. He figures in Shakespeare's *Rape of Lucrece*. Marcus Brutus thought him an ancestor. **brook'd:** tolerated.
160. keep his state: maintain his court.
162. nothing jealous: not at all doubtful. **163. aim:** guess.
177 s.d. Train: retinue.

186. ferret: i.e. red, angry (like a ferret's).
188. cross'd in conference: opposed in debate.
197. given: disposed. **199. my name:** i.e. I myself.
202–3. looks . . . men: i.e. penetrates to their secret motives.
218. sad: serious.
229. marry: indeed (originally, the name of the Virgin Mary used as an oath). **234. gentle:** noble.

Antony offer him a crown—yet 'twas not a crown neither, 'twas one of these coronets—and as I told you, he put it by once; but for all that, to my thinking, he would fain have had it. Then he offer'd it to him again; then he put it by again; but, to my thinking, he was very loath to lay his fingers off it. And then he offer'd it the third time; he put it the third time by; and still as he refus'd it, the rabblement howted, and clapp'd their chopp'd hands, and threw up their sweaty night-caps, and utter'd such a deal of stinking breath because Caesar refus'd the crown, that it had, almost, chok'd Caesar, for he swounded, and fell down at it; and for mine own part, I durst not laugh, for fear of opening my lips and receiving the bad air.

Cas. But soft I pray you; what, did Caesar swound?

Casca. He fell down in the market-place, and foam'd at mouth, and was speechless.

Bru. 'Tis very like, he hath the falling sickness.

Cas. No, Caesar hath it not; but you, and I,
And honest Casca, we have the falling sickness.

Casca. I know not what you mean by that, but I am sure Caesar fell down. If the tag-rag people did not clap him and hiss him, according as he pleas'd and displeas'd them, as they use to do the players in the theatre, I am no true man.

Bru. What said he when he came unto himself?

Casca. Marry, before he fell down, when he perceiv'd the common herd was glad he refus'd the crown, he pluck'd me ope his doublet, and offer'd them his throat to cut. And I had been a man of any occupation, if I would not have taken him at a word, I would I might go to hell among the rogues. And so he fell. When he came to himself again, he said, if he had done or said any thing amiss, he desir'd their worships to think it was his infirmity. Three or four wenches, where I stood, cried, "Alas, good soul!" and forgave him with all their hearts. But there's no heed to be taken of them; if Caesar had stabb'd their mothers, they would have done no less.

Bru. And after that, he came thus sad away?

Casca. Ay.

Cas. Did Cicero say any thing?

Casca. Ay, he spoke Greek.

Cas. To what effect?

Casca. Nay, and I tell you that, I'll ne'er look you i' th' face again. But those that understood him smil'd at one another, and shook their heads; but, for mine own part, it was Greek to me. I could tell you more news too. Murellus and Flavius, for pulling scarfs off Caesar's images, are put to silence. Fare you well. There was more foolery yet, if I could remember it.

Cas. Will you sup with me to-night, Casca?

Casca. No, I am promis'd forth.

Cas. Will you dine with me to-morrow?

240. **fain:** willingly.
244. **still:** always, each time. **howted:** hooted, cheered.
245. **chopp'd:** chapped, reddened. 248. **swounded:** swooned.
254. **falling sickness:** epilepsy. 261. **true:** honest.
265. **pluck'd me:** plucked (a colloquialism). **doublet:** jacket.
266. **And:** if. 266–67. **man . . . occupation:** working man.
267. **at a word:** at his word. 285. **scarfs:** decorations.

Casca. Ay, if I be alive, and your mind hold, and your dinner worth the eating.

Cas. Good, I will expect you.

Casca. Do so. Farewell both. *Exit.*

Bru. What a blunt fellow is this grown to be!
He was quick mettle when he went to school.

Cas. So is he now in execution
Of any bold or noble enterprise,
However he puts on this tardy form.
This rudeness is a sauce to his good wit,
Which gives men stomach to disgest his words
With better appetite.

Bru. And so it is. For this time I will leave you;
To-morrow, if you please to speak with me,
I will come home to you; or, if you will,
Come home to me, and I will wait for you.

Cas. I will do so; till then, think of the world.
Exit Brutus.
Well, Brutus, thou art noble; yet I see
Thy honorable mettle may be wrought
From that it is dispos'd; therefore it is meet
That noble minds keep ever with their likes;
For who so firm that cannot be seduc'd?
Caesar doth bear me hard, but he loves Brutus.
If I were Brutus now and he were Cassius,
He should not humor me. I will this night,
In several hands, in at his windows throw,
As if they came from several citizens,
Writings, all tending to the great opinion
That Rome holds of his name; wherein obscurely
Caesar's ambition shall be glanced at.
And after this let Caesar seat him sure,
For we will shake him, or worse days endure. *Exit.*

[Scene III]

Thunder and lightning. Enter [from opposite sides] Casca *[with his sword drawn] and* Cicero.

Cic. Good even, Casca; brought you Caesar home?
Why are you breathless, and why stare you so?

Casca. Are not you mov'd, when all the sway of earth
Shakes like a thing unfirm? O Cicero,
I have seen tempests when the scolding winds
Have riv'd the knotty oaks, and I have seen
Th' ambitious ocean swell, and rage, and foam,
To be exalted with the threat'ning clouds;
But never till to-night, never till now,
Did I go through a tempest dropping fire.
Either there is a civil strife in heaven,
Or else the world, too saucy with the gods,
Incenses them to send destruction.

296. **quick mettle:** lively, spirited.
299. **tardy form:** sluggish manner. 300. **wit:** intellect.
301. **disgest:** digest. 307. **the world:** the state of affairs.
310. **that . . . dispos'd:** i.e. his natural temper.
313. **doth . . . hard:** has a grudge against me.
315. **He:** i.e. Brutus. **humor:** persuade, cajole.
316. **several hands:** different handwritings.
318. **tending:** relating.

I.iii. Location: Rome. A street.
1. **brought:** attended, escorted. 3. **sway:** rule, order.
6. **riv'd:** split. 12. **saucy:** insolent.

Cic. Why, saw you any thing more wonderful?
Casca. A common slave—you know him well by sight—
Held up his left hand, which did flame and burn
Like twenty torches join'd; and yet his hand,
Not sensible of fire, remain'd unscorch'd.
Besides—I ha' not since put up my sword—
Against the Capitol I met a lion,
Who glaz'd upon me, and went surly by,
Without annoying me. And there were drawn
Upon a heap a hundred ghastly women,
Transformed with their fear, who swore they saw
Men, all in fire, walk up and down the streets.
And yesterday the bird of night did sit
Even at noon-day upon the market-place,
Howting and shrieking. When these prodigies
Do so conjointly meet, let not men say,
"These are their reasons, they are natural";
For I believe they are portentous things
Unto the climate that they point upon.
Cic. Indeed, it is a strange-disposed time;
But men may construe things after their fashion,
Clean from the purpose of the things themselves.
Comes Caesar to the Capitol to-morrow?
Casca. He doth; for he did bid Antonio
Send word to you he would be there to-morrow.
Cic. Good night then, Casca; this disturbed sky
Is not to walk in.
Casca. Farewell, Cicero. *Exit Cicero.*

Enter Cassius.

Cas. Who's there?
Casca. A Roman.
Cas. Casca, by your voice.
Casca. Your ear is good. Cassius, what night is this!
Cas. A very pleasing night to honest men.
Casca. Who ever knew the heavens menace so?
Cas. Those that have known the earth so full of faults.
For my part, I have walk'd about the streets,
Submitting me unto the perilous night;
And thus unbraced, Casca, as you see,
Have bar'd my bosom to the thunder-stone;
And when the cross blue lightning seem'd to open
The breast of heaven, I did present myself
Even in the aim and very flash of it.
Casca. But wherefore did you so much tempt the heavens?
It is the part of men to fear and tremble
When the most mighty gods by tokens send
Such dreadful heralds to astonish us.
Cas. You are dull, Casca; and those sparks of life
That should be in a Roman you do want,
Or else you use not. You look pale, and gaze,

18. sensible of: feeling. **20. Against:** opposite.
21. glaz'd: stared. **22. annoying:** harming.
22–23. drawn . . . heap: huddled together.
23. ghastly: white-faced. **26. bird of night:** screech-owl.
28. Howting: hooting. **30. These:** such and such.
31–32. portentous . . . climate: things of ill omen to the region.
35. Clean . . . purpose: quite contrary to the actual significance.
48. unbraced: with doublet unfastened. **50. cross:** zigzag.
54. part: proper role. **56. astonish:** stun. **58. want:** lack.

And put on fear, and cast yourself in wonder,
To see the strange impatience of the heavens;
But if you would consider the true cause
Why all these fires, why all these gliding ghosts,
Why birds and beasts from quality and kind,
Why old men, fools, and children calculate,
Why all these things change from their ordinance,
Their natures, and preformed faculties,
To monstrous quality—why, you shall find
That heaven hath infus'd them with these spirits,
To make them instruments of fear and warning
Unto some monstrous state.
Now could I, Casca, name to thee a man
Most like this dreadful night,
That thunders, lightens, opens graves, and roars
As doth the lion in the Capitol—
A man no mightier than thyself, or me,
In personal action, yet prodigious grown,
And fearful, as these strange eruptions are.
Casca. 'Tis Caesar that you mean; is it not, Cassius?
Cas. Let it be who it is; for Romans now
Have thews and limbs like to their ancestors;
But woe the while, our fathers' minds are dead,
And we are govern'd with our mothers' spirits;
Our yoke and sufferance show us womanish.
Casca. Indeed, they say, the senators to-morrow
Mean to establish Caesar as a king;
And he shall wear his crown by sea and land,
In every place, save here in Italy.
Cas. I know where I will wear this dagger then;
Cassius from bondage will deliver Cassius.
Therein, ye gods, you make the weak most strong;
Therein, ye gods, you tyrants do defeat;
Nor stony tower, nor walls of beaten brass,
Nor airless dungeon, nor strong links of iron,
Can be retentive to the strength of spirit;
But life, being weary of these worldly bars,
Never lacks power to dismiss itself.
If I know this, know all the world besides,
That part of tyranny that I do bear
I can shake off at pleasure. *Thunder still.*
Casca. So can I;
So every bondman in his own hand bears
The power to cancel his captivity.
Cas. And why should Caesar be a tyrant then?
Poor man, I know he would not be a wolf,
But that he sees the Romans are but sheep;
He were no lion, were not Romans hinds.
Those that with haste will make a mighty fire
Begin it with weak straws. What trash is Rome?
What rubbish and what offal? when it serves

64. from . . . kind: behaving in a fashion contrary to their true nature.
65. calculate: forecast, prophesy. **66. ordinance:** established order.
67. preformed: original, innate.
68. monstrous: unnatural, abnormal.
71. monstrous state: deformed commonwealth.
77. prodigious: ominous. **81. thews:** sinews.
82. woe the while: woe to the age.
84. Our . . . sufferance: the tyranny we are willing to endure.
93. Nor: neither. **95. be . . . spirit:** hold back a determined spirit.
106. were not: would not be a. **hinds:** female deer (perhaps with quibble on the sense "servants").
108. trash: small pieces of waste wood.
109. offal: chips, shavings.

For the base matter to illuminate
So vile a thing as Caesar! But, O grief,
Where hast thou led me? I, perhaps, speak this
Before a willing bondman; then I know
My answer must be made. But I am arm'd,
And dangers are to me indifferent.
Casca. You speak to Casca, and to such a man
That is no fleering tell-tale. Hold, my hand.
Be factious for redress of all these griefs,
And I will set this foot of mine as far
As who goes farthest.
Cas. There's a bargain made.
Now know you, Casca, I have mov'd already
Some certain of the noblest-minded Romans
To undergo with me an enterprise
Of honorable-dangerous consequence;
And I do know, by this they stay for me
In Pompey's Porch; for now, this fearful night,
There is no stir or walking in the streets;
And the complexion of the element
[In] favor's like the work we have in hand,
Most bloody, fiery, and most terrible.

Enter CINNA.

Casca. Stand close a while, for here comes one in haste.
Cas. 'Tis Cinna, I do know him by his gait,
He is a friend. Cinna, where haste you so?
Cin. To find out you. Who's that? Metellus Cimber?
Cas. No, it is Casca, one incorporate
To our attempts. Am I not stay'd for, Cinna?
Cin. I am glad on't. What a fearful night is this!
There's two or three of us have seen strange sights.
Cas. Am I not stay'd for? tell me.
Cin. Yes, you are.
O Cassius, if you could
But win the noble Brutus to our party—
Cas. Be you content. Good Cinna, take this paper,
And look you lay it in the praetor's chair,
Where Brutus may but find it; and throw this
In at his window; set this up with wax
Upon old Brutus' statue. All this done,
Repair to Pompey's Porch, where you shall find us.
Is Decius Brutus and Trebonius there?
Cin. All but Metellus Cimber, and he's gone
To seek you at your house. Well, I will hie,
And so bestow these papers as you bade me.
Cas. That done, repair to Pompey's theatre.
Exit Cinna.
Come, Casca, you and I will yet, ere day,
See Brutus at his house. Three parts of him

111. vile: worthless. **115. indifferent:** a matter of indifference.
117. fleering: sneering, mocking. **118. Be factious:** form a party.
125. by . . . stay: by now they are waiting.
126. Pompey's Porch: the portico of a theatre built in 55 B.C. by Pompey. **128. element:** sky. **129. favor:** appearance.
131. close: concealed. **135. incorporate:** a party to.
137. on't: of it.
143. praetor's. The praetors were the chief judges, of whom Brutus was at the time first in rank.
144. Where . . . it: where only Brutus may find it.
150. hie: make haste.

Is ours already, and the man entire
Upon the next encounter yields him ours.
Casca. O, he sits high in all the people's hearts;
And that which would appear offense in us,
His countenance, like richest alchymy,
Will change to virtue and to worthiness.
Cas. Him and his worth, and our great need of him,
You have right well conceited. Let us go,
For it is after midnight, and ere day
We will awake him and be sure of him. *Exeunt.*

ACT II, [SCENE I]

Enter BRUTUS *in his orchard.*

Bru. What, Lucius, ho!
I cannot by the progress of the stars
Give guess how near to day. Lucius, I say!
I would it were my fault to sleep so soundly.
When, Lucius, when? Awake, I say! What, Lucius!

Enter LUCIUS.

Luc. Call'd you, my lord?
Bru. Get me a taper in my study, Lucius.
When it is lighted, come and call me here.
Luc. I will, my lord. *Exit.*
Bru. It must be by his death; and for my part,
I know no personal cause to spurn at him,
But for the general. He would be crown'd:
How that might change his nature, there's the question.
It is the bright day that brings forth the adder,
And that craves wary walking. Crown him that,
And then I grant we put a sting in him
That at his will he may do danger with.
Th' abuse of greatness is when it disjoins
Remorse from power; and to speak truth of Caesar,
I have not known when his affections sway'd
More than his reason. But 'tis a common proof
That lowliness is young ambition's ladder,
Whereto the climber-upward turns his face;
But when he once attains the upmost round,
He then unto the ladder turns his back,
Looks in the clouds, scorning the base degrees
By which he did ascend. So Caesar may;
Then lest he may, prevent. And since the quarrel
Will bear no color for the thing he is,
Fashion it thus: that what he is, augmented,
Would run to these and these extremities;
And therefore think him as a serpent's egg,
Which, hatch'd, would as his kind grow mischievous,
And kill him in the shell.

159. countenance: approval, support. **alchymy:** alchemy, which sought methods for transmuting base metals into gold.
162. conceited: understood.

II.i. Location: Rome. Brutus' garden.
o.s.d. orchard: garden. **11. spurn:** kick.
12. general: public good.
15. craves: demands. **that:** i.e. emperor.
19. Remorse: conscience, compassion. **20. affections:** passions.
21. proof: experience. **22. lowliness:** (pretended) humility.
26. degrees: steps, rungs of the ladder.
29. Will . . . is: cannot be persuasively based on his conduct so far.
33. as his kind: according to his nature.

Enter LUCIUS.

Luc. The taper burneth in your closet, sir.
Searching the window for a flint, I found
This paper, thus seal'd up, and I am sure
It did not lie there when I went to bed.
Gives him the letter.

Bru. Get you to bed again, it is not day.
Is not to-morrow, boy, the [ides] of March?

Luc. I know not, sir.

Bru. Look in the calendar, and bring me word.

Luc. I will, sir. *Exit.*

Bru. The exhalations whizzing in the air
Give so much light that I may read by them.
Opens the letter and reads.

"Brutus, thou sleep'st; awake, and see thyself!
Shall Rome, etc. Speak, strike, redress!"
"Brutus, thou sleep'st; awake!"
Such instigations have been often dropp'd
Where I have took them up.
"Shall Rome, etc." Thus must I piece it out:
Shall Rome stand under one man's awe? What, Rome?
My ancestors did from the streets of Rome
The Tarquin drive when he was call'd a king.
"Speak, strike, redress!" Am I entreated
To speak and strike? O Rome, I make thee promise,
If the redress will follow, thou receivest
Thy full petition at the hand of Brutus!

Enter LUCIUS.

Luc. Sir, March is wasted fifteen days.
Knock within.

Bru. 'Tis good. Go to the gate, somebody knocks.
[*Exit Lucius*].
Since Cassius first did whet me against Caesar,
I have not slept.
Between the acting of a dreadful thing
And the first motion, all the interim is
Like a phantasma or a hideous dream.
The Genius and the mortal instruments
Are then in council; and the state of a man,
Like to a little kingdom, suffers then
The nature of an insurrection.

Enter LUCIUS.

Luc. Sir, 'tis your brother Cassius at the door,
Who doth desire to see you.

Bru. Is he alone?

Luc. No, sir, there are moe with him.

Bru. Do you know them?

Luc. No, sir, their hats are pluck'd about their ears,
And half their faces buried in their cloaks,
That by no means I may discover them
By any mark of favor.

Bru. Let 'em enter. [*Exit Lucius.*]
They are the faction. O Conspiracy,
Sham'st thou to show thy dang'rous brow by night,
When evils are most free? O then, by day
Where wilt thou find a cavern dark enough
To mask thy monstrous visage? Seek none, Conspiracy!
Hide it in smiles and affability;
For if thou path, thy native semblance on,
Not Erebus itself were dim enough
To hide thee from prevention.

Enter the conspirators, CASSIUS, CASCA, DECIUS, CINNA, METELLUS, *and* TREBONIUS.

Cas. I think we are too bold upon your rest.
Good morrow, Brutus, do we trouble you?

Bru. I have been up this hour, awake all night.
Know I these men that come along with you?

Cas. Yes, every man of them; and no man here
But honors you; and every one doth wish
You had but that opinion of yourself
Which every noble Roman bears of you.
This is Trebonius.

Bru. He is welcome hither.

Cas. This, Decius Brutus.

Bru. He is welcome too.

Cas. This, Casca; this, Cinna; and this, Metellus Cimber.

Bru. They are all welcome.
What watchful cares do interpose themselves
Betwixt your eyes and night?

Cas. Shall I entreat a word? *They whisper.*

Dec. Here lies the east; doth not the day break here?

Casca. No.

Cin. O, pardon, sir, it doth; and yon grey lines
That fret the clouds are messengers of day.

Casca. You shall confess that you are both deceiv'd.
Here, as I point my sword, the sun arises,
Which is a great way growing on the south,
Weighing the youthful season of the year.
Some two months hence, up higher toward the north
He first presents his fire, and the high east
Stands, as the Capitol, directly here.

Bru. Give me your hands all over, one by one.

Cas. And let us swear our resolution.

Bru. No, not an oath! If not the face of men,
The sufferance of our souls, the time's abuse—
If these be motives weak, break off betimes,
And every man hence to his idle bed;
So let high-sighted tyranny range on,
Till each man drop by lottery. But if these
(As I am sure they do) bear fire enough
To kindle cowards, and to steel with valor
The melting spirits of women, then, countrymen,
What need we any spur but our own cause
To prick us to redress? what other bond

35. closet: private room, study. **44. exhalations:** meteors.
64. motion: proposal. **65. phantasma:** evil vision, hallucination.
66–67. The Genius . . . council: i.e. the reasonable soul takes counsel with its lower powers (called "mortal" because they animate the body). **70. brother.** Cassius had married a sister of Brutus.
72. moe: more. **75. discover:** identify.

83. if . . . on: if you go about wearing your natural expression.
84. Erebus: underworld realm of darkness.
85. prevention: being (recognized and) forestalled.
86. upon: i.e. in breaking in upon, in assaulting.
98. watchful: wakeful, preventing sleep. **104. fret:** interlace.
107. growing: encroaching. **108. Weighing:** considering.
110. high: due. **117. idle:** unused.
118. high-sighted: looking down from a height (like a hawk), haughty.
119. by lottery: i.e. as the tyrant's eye chances to fall on him.

Than secret Romans, that have spoke the word
And will not palter? and what other oath
Than honesty to honesty engag'd
That this shall be, or we will fall for it?
Swear priests and cowards, and men cautelous,
Old feeble carrions, and such suffering souls
That welcome wrongs; unto bad causes swear
Such creatures as men doubt; but do not stain
The even virtue of our enterprise,
Nor th' insuppressive mettle of our spirits,
To think that or our cause or our performance
Did need an oath; when every drop of blood
That every Roman bears, and nobly bears,
Is guilty of a several bastardy,
If he do break the smallest particle
Of any promise that hath pass'd from him.
Cas. But what of Cicero? Shall we sound him?
I think he will stand very strong with us.
Casca. Let us not leave him out.
Cin. No, by no means.
Met. O, let us have him, for his silver hairs
Will purchase us a good opinion,
And buy men's voices to commend our deeds.
It shall be said his judgment rul'd our hands;
Our youths and wildness shall no whit appear,
But all be buried in his gravity.
Bru. O, name him not; let us not break with him,
For he will never follow any thing
That other men begin.
Cas. Then leave him out.
Casca. Indeed he is not fit.
Dec. Shall no man else be touch'd but only Caesar?
Cas. Decius, well urg'd. I think it is not meet,
Mark Antony, so well belov'd of Caesar,
Should outlive Caesar. We shall find of him
A shrewd contriver; and you know, his means,
If he improve them, may well stretch so far
As to annoy us all; which to prevent,
Let Antony and Caesar fall together.
Bru. Our course will seem too bloody, Caius Cassius,
To cut the head off and then hack the limbs—
Like wrath in death and envy afterwards;
For Antony is but a limb of Caesar.
Let's be sacrificers, but not butchers, Caius.
We all stand up against the spirit of Caesar,
And in the spirit of men there is no blood;
O that we then could come by Caesar's spirit,
And not dismember Caesar! But, alas,
Caesar must bleed for it! And, gentle friends,
Let's kill him boldly, but not wrathfully;
Let's carve him as a dish fit for the gods,
Not hew him as a carcass fit for hounds;
And let our hearts, as subtle masters do,
Stir up their servants to an act of rage,
And after seem to chide 'em. This shall make

126. palter: deceive, equivocate. **127. honesty:** personal honor.
129. cautelous: deceitful. **130. carrions:** corpse-like men.
133. even: steadfast. **134. insuppressive:** irrepressible.
135. or . . . or: either . . . or. **138. several:** individual.
150. break with: reveal our secret to. **157. of:** in.
159. improve: make the most of. **160. annoy:** injure.
164. envy: malice. **176. their servants:** i.e. our passions.

Our purpose necessary, and not envious;
Which so appearing to the common eyes,
We shall be call'd purgers, not murderers.
And for Mark Antony, think not of him;
For he can do no more than Caesar's arm
When Caesar's head is off.
Cas. Yet I fear him,
For in the ingrafted love he bears to Caesar—
Bru. Alas, good Cassius, do not think of him.
If he love Caesar, all that he can do
Is to himself—take thought and die for Caesar;
And that were much he should, for he is given
To sports, to wildness, and much company.
Treb. There is no fear in him; let him not die,
For he will live, and laugh at this hereafter.
Clock strikes.
Bru. Peace, count the clock.
Cas. The clock hath stricken three.
Treb. 'Tis time to part.
Cas. But it is doubtful yet
Whether Caesar will come forth to-day or no;
For he is superstitious grown of late,
Quite from the main opinion he held once
Of fantasy, of dreams, and ceremonies.
It may be these apparent prodigies,
The unaccustom'd terror of this night,
And the persuasion of his augurers
May hold him from the Capitol to-day.
Dec. Never fear that. If he be so resolv'd,
I can o'ersway him; for he loves to hear
That unicorns may be betray'd with trees,
And bears with glasses, elephants with holes,
Lions with toils, and men with flatterers;
But when I tell him he hates flatterers
He says he does, being then most flattered.
Let me work;
For I can give his humor the true bent,
And I will bring him to the Capitol.
Cas. Nay, we will all of us be there to fetch him.
Bru. By the eight hour; is that the uttermost?
Cin. Be that the uttermost, and fail not then.
Met. Caius Ligarius doth bear Caesar hard,
Who rated him for speaking well of Pompey;
I wonder none of you have thought of him.
Bru. Now, good Metellus, go along by him.
He loves me well, and I have given him reasons;
Send him but hither, and I'll fashion him.
Cas. The morning comes upon 's. We'll leave you, Brutus,

180. purgers: i.e. physicians who have purged the body politic.
184. ingrafted: deep-rooted.
188. that . . . should: that would be a good deal for him to do, i.e. it isn't likely that he will. **190. no fear:** nothing to fear.
196. from: away from, contrary to. **main:** strong.
197. ceremonies: rites of divination, or the portents they disclose.
198. apparent: that now appear.
204. unicorns . . . trees. Supposedly a hunter bagged a unicorn by standing in front of a tree and inciting the animal to charge, then stepping aside at the last moment so that it buried its horn in the trunk and was caught fast.
205. glasses: mirrors. Bears were reputedly vain. **holes:** pitfalls.
206. toils: nets.
210. humor: inclination, disposition. **bent:** direction.
213. eight: eighth. **216. rated:** upbraided.
218. by him: to his house.

And, friends, disperse yourselves; but all remember
What you have said, and show yourselves true Romans.
Bru. Good gentlemen, look fresh and merrily;
Let not our looks put on our purposes,
But bear it as our Roman actors do,
With untir'd spirits and formal constancy.
And so good morrow to you every one.
Exeunt. Manet Brutus.
Boy! Lucius! Fast asleep? It is no matter,
Enjoy the honey-heavy dew of slumber.
Thou hast no figures nor no fantasies,
Which busy care draws in the brains of men;
Therefore thou sleep'st so sound.

Enter PORTIA.

Por. Brutus, my lord!
Bru. Portia! What mean you? wherefore rise you now?
It is not for your health thus to commit
Your weak condition to the raw cold morning.
Por. Nor for yours neither. Y' have ungently, Brutus,
Stole from my bed; and yesternight at supper
You suddenly arose and walk'd about,
Musing and sighing, with your arms across;
And when I ask'd you what the matter was,
You star'd upon me with ungentle looks.
I urg'd you further; then you scratch'd your head,
And too impatiently stamp'd with your foot.
Yet I insisted, yet you answer'd not,
But with an angry wafter of your hand
Gave sign for me to leave you. So I did,
Fearing to strengthen that impatience
Which seem'd too much enkindled; and withal
Hoping it was but an effect of humor,
Which sometime hath his hour with every man.
It will not let you eat, nor talk, nor sleep;
And could it work so much upon your shape
As it hath much prevail'd on your condition,
I should not know you Brutus. Dear my lord,
Make me acquainted with your cause of grief.
Bru. I am not well in health, and that is all.
Por. Brutus is wise, and were he not in health,
He would embrace the means to come by it.
Bru. Why, so I do. Good Portia, go to bed.
Por. Is Brutus sick? and is it physical
To walk unbraced and suck up the humors
Of the dank morning? What, is Brutus sick?
And will he steal out of his wholesome bed
To dare the vile contagion of the night,
And tempt the rheumy and unpurged air
To add unto his sickness? No, my Brutus,
You have some sick offense within your mind,
Which, by the right and virtue of my place,
I ought to know of; and upon my knees
I charm you, by my once commended beauty,
By all your vows of love, and that great vow
Which did incorporate and make us one,
That you unfold to me, yourself, your half,
Why you are heavy, and what men to-night
Have had resort to you; for here have been
Some six or seven, who did hide their faces
Even from darkness.
Bru. Kneel not, gentle Portia.
Por. I should not need, if you were gentle Brutus.
Within the bond of marriage, tell me, Brutus,
Is it excepted I should know no secrets
That appertain to you? Am I yourself
But, as it were, in sort or limitation.
To keep with you at meals, comfort your bed,
And talk to you sometimes? Dwell I but in the suburbs
Of your good pleasure? If it be no more,
Portia is Brutus' harlot, not his wife.
Bru. You are my true and honorable wife,
As dear to me as are the ruddy drops
That visit my sad heart.
Por. If this were true, then should I know this secret.
I grant I am a woman; but withal
A woman that Lord Brutus took to wife.
I grant I am a woman; but withal
A woman well reputed, Cato's daughter.
Think you I am no stronger than my sex,
Being so father'd and so husbanded?
Tell me your counsels, I will not disclose 'em.
I have made strong proof of my constancy,
Giving myself a voluntary wound
Here, in the thigh; can I bear that with patience,
And not my husband's secrets?
Bru. O ye gods!
Render me worthy of this noble wife! *Knock.*
Hark, hark, one knocks! Portia, go in a while,
And by and by thy bosom shall partake
The secrets of my heart.
All my engagements I will construe to thee,
All the charactery of my sad brows.
Leave me with haste. *Exit Portia.*
Lucius, who's that knocks?

Enter LUCIUS *and* [CAIUS] LIGARIUS.

Luc. Here is a sick man that would speak with you.
Bru. Caius Ligarius, that Metellus spake of.
Boy, stand aside. [*Exit Lucius.*] Caius Ligarius, how?
Lig. Vouchsafe good morrow from a feeble tongue.

225. **put on:** reveal.
227. **formal constancy:** "consistent decorum" (Dover Wilson).
231. **figures:** imaginings. 236. **condition:** state of health.
237. **ungently:** discourteously.
240. **across:** folded across your chest (a conventional sign of melancholy). 246. **wafter:** wafture, waving.
250. **humor:** ill-humor. 254. **condition:** state of mind, disposition.
261. **physical:** healthful. 262. **humors:** damps.
266. **tempt:** risk. **rheumy:** dank. **unpurged:** not yet purified by the sun. 268. **sick offense:** troublesome illness.
271. **charm:** conjure. 275. **heavy:** depressed.
281. **excepted:** stated as a condition in the contract.
283. **in . . . limitation:** in a limited manner only.
285. **suburbs.** This word suggests the *harlot* of line 287; the suburbs were associated with brothels.
295. **Cato:** Cato of Utica, famed for high principles and integrity of conduct. 298. **counsels:** secrets.
299. **constancy:** firmness of mind.
307. **engagements:** commitments.
308. **charactery:** import (literally, handwriting).
313. **Vouchsafe:** deign to accept.

Bru. O, what a time have you chose out, brave Caius,
To wear a kerchief! Would you were not sick!
Lig. I am not sick, if Brutus have in hand
Any exploit worthy the name of honor.
Bru. Such an exploit have I in hand, Ligarius,
Had you a healthful ear to hear of it.
Lig. By all the gods that Romans bow before,
I here discard my sickness! Soul of Rome!
Brave son, deriv'd from honorable loins!
Thou, like an exorcist, hast conjur'd up
My mortified spirit. Now bid me run,
And I will strive with things impossible,
Yea, get the better of them. What's to do?
Bru. A piece of work that will make sick men whole.
Lig. But are not some whole that we must make sick?
Bru. That must we also. What it is, my Caius,
I shall unfold to thee, as we are going,
To whom it must be done.
Lig. Set on your foot,
And with a heart new-fir'd I follow you,
To do I know not what; but it sufficeth
That Brutus leads me on. *Thunder.*
Bru. Follow me then. *Exeunt.*

[Scene II]

Thunder and lightning. Enter Julius Caesar *in his night-gown.*

Caes. Nor heaven nor earth have been at peace to-night.
Thrice hath Calphurnia in her sleep cried out,
"Help, ho! they murther Caesar!" Who's within?

Enter a Servant.

Serv. My lord?
Caes. Go bid the priests do present sacrifice,
And bring me their opinions of success.
Serv. I will, my lord. *Exit.*

Enter Calphurnia.

Cal. What mean you, Caesar? Think you to walk forth?
You shall not stir out of your house to-day.
Caes. Caesar shall forth; the things that threaten'd me
Ne'er look'd but on my back; when they shall see
The face of Caesar, they are vanished.
Cal. Caesar, I never stood on ceremonies,
Yet now they fright me. There is one within,
Besides the things that we have heard and seen,
Recounts most horrid sights seen by the watch.
A lioness hath whelped in the streets,
And graves have yawn'd and yielded up their dead;
Fierce fiery warriors fight upon the clouds
In ranks and squadrons and right form of war,
Which drizzled blood upon the Capitol;
The noise of battle hurtled in the air;
Horses [did] neigh, and dying men did groan,
And ghosts did shriek and squeal about the streets.
O Caesar, these things are beyond all use,
And I do fear them.
Caes. What can be avoided
Whose end is purpos'd by the mighty gods?
Yet Caesar shall go forth; for these predictions
Are to the world in general as to Caesar.
Cal. When beggars die there are no comets seen;
The heavens themselves blaze forth the death of princes.
Caes. Cowards die many times before their deaths,
The valiant never taste of death but once.
Of all the wonders that I yet have heard,
It seems to me most strange that men should fear,
Seeing that death, a necessary end,
Will come when it will come.

Enter a Servant.

What say the augurers?
Serv. They would not have you to stir forth to-day.
Plucking the entrails of an offering forth,
They could not find a heart within the beast.
Caes. The gods do this in shame of cowardice;
Caesar should be a beast without a heart
If he should stay at home to-day for fear.
No, Caesar shall not; Danger knows full well
That Caesar is more dangerous than he.
We [are] two lions litter'd in one day,
And I the elder and more terrible;
And Caesar shall go forth.
Cal. Alas, my lord,
Your wisdom is consum'd in confidence.
Do not go forth to-day; call it my fear
That keeps you in the house, and not your own.
We'll send Mark Antony to the Senate-house,
And he shall say you are not well to-day.
Let me, upon my knee, prevail in this.
Caes. Mark Antony shall say I am not well,
And for thy humor I will stay at home.

Enter Decius.

Here's Decius Brutus, he shall tell them so.
Dec. Caesar, all hail! good morrow, worthy Caesar,
I come to fetch you to the Senate-house.
Caes. And you are come in very happy time
To bear my greeting to the senators,
And tell them that I will not come to-day.
Cannot, is false; and that I dare not, falser:
I will not come to-day. Tell them so, Decius.
Cal. Say he is sick.

315. wear a kerchief: i.e. be ill. **323. exorcist:** raiser of spirits.
324. mortified: deadened.

II.ii. Location: Rome. Caesar's house.
o.s.d. night-gown: dressing gown. **5. present:** immediate.
6. success: the outcome (whether good or bad).
13. stood on ceremonies: heeded omens.

20. right form: regular formation. **25. use:** ordinary experience.
49. confidence: overconfidence. **56. humor:** whim.
60. happy: opportune.

Caes. Shall Caesar send a lie?
Have I in conquest stretch'd mine arm so far,
To be afeard to tell greybeards the truth?
Decius, go tell them Caesar will not come.
Dec. Most mighty Caesar, let me know some cause,
Lest I be laugh'd at when I tell them so.
Caes. The cause is in my will, I will not come:
That is enough to satisfy the Senate.
But for your private satisfaction,
Because I love you, I will let you know.
Calphurnia here, my wife, stays me at home:
She dreamt to-night she saw my statue,
Which, like a fountain with an hundred spouts,
Did run pure blood; and many lusty Romans
Came smiling and did bathe their hands in it.
And these does she apply for warnings and portents
And evils imminent, and on her knee
Hath begg'd that I will stay at home to-day.
Dec. This dream is all amiss interpreted,
It was a vision fair and fortunate.
Your statue spouting blood in many pipes,
In which so many smiling Romans bath'd,
Signifies that from you great Rome shall suck
Reviving blood, and that great men shall press
For tinctures, stains, relics, and cognizance.
This by Calphurnia's dream is signified.
Caes. And this way have you well expounded it.
Dec. I have, when you have heard what I can say;
And know it now: the Senate have concluded
To give this day a crown to mighty Caesar.
If you shall send them word you will not come,
Their minds may change. Besides, it were a mock
Apt to be render'd, for some one to say,
"Break up the Senate till another time,
When Caesar's wife shall meet with better dreams."
If Caesar hide himself, shall they not whisper,
"Lo Caesar is afraid"?
Pardon me, Caesar, for my dear dear love
To your proceeding bids me tell you this;
And reason to my love is liable.
Caes. How foolish do your fears seem now, Calphurnia!
I am ashamed I did yield to them.
Give me my robe, for I will go.

Enter Brutus, Ligarius, Metellus, Casca, Trebonius, Cinna, *and* Publius.

And look where Publius is come to fetch me.
Pub. Good morrow, Caesar.
Caes. Welcome, Publius.
What, Brutus, are you stirr'd so early too?
Good morrow, Casca. Caius Ligarius,
Caesar was ne'er so much your enemy
As that same ague which hath made you lean.
What is't a' clock?
Bru. Caesar, 'tis strucken eight.

75. **stays**: detains. 76. **to-night**: last night.
89. **For . . . cognizance**: "for tinctures, stains, relics—in a word, for a sign that they are devoted to Caesar" (Kittredge).
96–97. **a mock . . . render'd**: a sarcastic answer likely to be made.
103. **proceeding**: advancement, welfare.
104. **liable**: subservient; i.e. he dares, out of love, to tell Caesar what reason suggests will be an unwelcome opinion.

Caes. I thank you for your pains and courtesy.

Enter Antony.

See, Antony, that revels long a-nights,
Is notwithstanding up. Good morrow, Antony.
Ant. So to most noble Caesar.
Caes. Bid them prepare within;
I am to blame to be thus waited for.
Now, Cinna; now, Metellus; what, Trebonius:
I have an hour's talk in store for you;
Remember that you call on me to-day;
Be near me, that I may remember you.
Treb. Caesar, I will; [*aside*] and so near will I be,
That your best friends shall wish I had been further.
Caes. Good friends, go in, and taste some wine with me,
And we, like friends, will straightway go together.
Bru. [*Aside.*] That every like is not the same, O Caesar,
The heart of Brutus earns to think upon! *Exeunt.*

[Scene III]

Enter Artemidorus [*reading a paper*].

[*Art.*] "Caesar, beware of Brutus; take heed of Cassius; come not near Casca; have an eye to Cinna; trust not Trebonius; mark well Metellus Cimber; Decius Brutus loves thee not; thou hast wrong'd Caius Ligarius. There is but one mind in all these men, and it is bent against Caesar. If thou beest not immortal, look about you; security gives way to conspiracy. The mighty gods defend thee!
Thy lover,
Artemidorus."
Here will I stand till Caesar pass along,
And as a suitor will I give him this.
My heart laments that virtue cannot live
Out of the teeth of emulation.
If thou read this, O Caesar, thou mayest live;
If not, the Fates with traitors do contrive. *Exit.*

[Scene IV]

Enter Portia *and* Lucius.

Por. I prithee, boy, run to the Senate-house;
Stay not to answer me, but get thee gone.
Why dost thou stay?
Luc. To know my errand, madam.
Por. I would have had thee there and here again
Ere I can tell thee what thou shouldst do there.—
O constancy, be strong upon my side,

128. **every . . . same.** Referring to the saying *Omne simile non est idem*, and meaning here "Not every professed friend is a friend in fact." 129. **earns**: grieves.

II.iii. Location: Rome. A street near the Capitol.
7. **security**: overconfidence. **gives way**: opens the door.
9. **lover**: friend, well-wisher.
14. **Out . . . emulation**: beyond the reach of envious rivalry.
16. **contrive**: conspire, plot.

II.iv. Location: Rome. Before Brutus' house.

Set a huge mountain 'tween my heart and tongue!
I have a man's mind, but a woman's might.
How hard it is for women to keep counsel!—
Art thou here yet?
Luc. Madam, what should I do?
Run to the Capitol, and nothing else?
And so return to you, and nothing else?
Por. Yes, bring me word, boy, if thy lord look well,
For he went sickly forth; and take good note
What Caesar doth, what suitors press to him.
Hark, boy, what noise is that?
Luc. I hear none, madam.
Por. Prithee listen well;
I heard a bustling rumor, like a fray,
And the wind brings it from the Capitol.
Luc. Sooth, madam, I hear nothing.

Enter the SOOTHSAYER.

Por. Come hither, fellow; which way hast thou been?
Sooth. At mine own house, good lady.
Por. What is't a' clock?
Sooth. About the ninth hour, lady.
Por. Is Caesar yet gone to the Capitol?
Sooth. Madam, not yet; I go to take my stand,
To see him pass on to the Capitol.
Por. Thou hast some suit to Caesar, hast thou not?
Sooth. That I have, lady, if it will please Caesar
To be so good to Caesar as to hear me:
I shall beseech him to befriend himself.
Por. Why, know'st thou any harm's intended towards him?
Sooth. None that I know will be, much that I fear may chance.
Good morrow to you. Here the street is narrow;
The throng that follows Caesar at the heels,
Of senators, of praetors, common suitors,
Will crowd a feeble man almost to death.
I'll get me to a place more void, and there
Speak to great Caesar as he comes along. *Exit.*
Por. I must go in. Ay me! How weak a thing
The heart of woman is! O Brutus,
The heavens speed thee in thine enterprise!
Sure the boy heard me.—Brutus hath a suit
That Caesar will not grant.—O, I grow faint.—
Run, Lucius, and commend me to my lord,
Say I am merry. Come to me again,
And bring me word what he doth say to thee.
Exeunt [severally].

ACT III, [SCENE I]

Flourish. Enter CAESAR, BRUTUS, CASSIUS, CASCA, DECIUS, METELLUS, TREBONIUS, CINNA, ANTONY, LEPIDUS, ARTEMIDORUS, PUBLIUS, [POPILIUS,] *and the* SOOTHSAYER.

Caes. The ides of March are come.

9. counsel: a secret. **18. bustling:** tumultuous. **20. Sooth:** truly. **37. more void:** less crowded. **45. merry:** in good spirits.

III.i. Location: Rome. Before the Capitol.

Sooth. Ay, Caesar, but not gone.
Art. Hail, Caesar! read this schedule.
Dec. Trebonius doth desire you to o'er-read
(At your best leisure) this his humble suit.
Art. O Caesar, read mine first; for mine's a suit
That touches Caesar nearer. Read it, great Caesar.
Caes. What touches us ourself shall be last serv'd.
Art. Delay not, Caesar, read it instantly.
Caes. What, is the fellow mad?
Pub. Sirrah, give place.
Cas. What, urge you your petitions in the street?
Come to the Capitol.
[*Caesar enters the Capitol, the rest following.*]
Pop. I wish your enterprise to-day may thrive.
Cas. What enterprise, Popilius?
Pop. Fare you well.
[*Leaves him and joins Caesar.*]
Bru. What said Popilius Lena?
Cas. He wish'd to-day our enterprise might thrive.
I fear our purpose is discovered.
Bru. Look how he makes to Caesar; mark him.
Cas. Casca, be sudden, for we fear prevention.
Brutus, what shall be done? If this be known,
Cassius or Caesar never shall turn back,
For I will slay myself.
Bru. Cassius, be constant;
Popilius Lena speaks not of our purposes,
For look he smiles, and Caesar doth not change.
Cas. Trebonius knows his time; for look you, Brutus,
He draws Mark Antony out of the way.
[*Exeunt Antony and Trebonius.*]
Dec. Where is Metellus Cimber? Let him go
And presently prefer his suit to Caesar.
Bru. He is address'd; press near and second him.
Cin. Casca, you are the first that rears your hand.
Caes. Are we all ready? What is now amiss
That Caesar and his Senate must redress?
Met. Most high, most mighty, and most puissant Caesar,
Metellus Cimber throws before thy seat
An humble heart. [*Kneeling.*]
Caes. I must prevent thee, Cimber.
These couchings and these lowly courtesies
Might fire the blood of ordinary men,
And turn preordinance and first decree
Into the [law] of children. Be not fond
To think that Caesar bears such rebel blood
That will be thaw'd from the true quality
With that which melteth fools—I mean sweet words,
Low-crooked curtsies, and base spaniel fawning.
Thy brother by decree is banished;
If thou dost bend, and pray, and fawn for him,
I spurn thee like a cur out of my way.

3. schedule: document. **10. give place:** make way.
18. makes to: walks toward. **19. prevention:** being forestalled.
28. presently prefer: immediately present. **29. address'd:** ready.
36. couchings: bowings. **lowly courtesies:** low bows.
38. preordinance and first decree: decisions formerly settled upon.
39. law of children: i.e. something that can be changed at a whim, like the rules of a children's game.
39–40. fond To: so foolish as to.
40. rebel: ready to turn against the law.
41. true quality: i.e. stability, firmness.

Know, Caesar doth not wrong, nor without cause
Will he be satisfied.
Met. Is there no voice more worthy than my own,
To sound more sweetly in great Caesar's ear
For the repealing of my banish'd brother?
Bru. I kiss thy hand, but not in flattery, Caesar;
Desiring thee that Publius Cimber may
Have an immediate freedom of repeal.
Caes. What, Brutus?
Cas. Pardon, Caesar! Caesar, pardon!
As low as to thy foot doth Cassius fall,
To beg enfranchisement for Publius Cimber.
Caes. I could be well mov'd, if I were as you;
If I could pray to move, prayers would move me;
But I am constant as the northern star,
Of whose true-fix'd and resting quality
There is no fellow in the firmament.
The skies are painted with unnumb'red sparks,
They are all fire, and every one doth shine;
But there's but one in all doth hold his place.
So in the world: 'tis furnish'd well with men,
And men are flesh and blood, and apprehensive;
Yet in the number I do know but one
That unassailable holds on his rank,
Unshak'd of motion; and that I am he,
Let me a little show it, even in this—
That I was constant Cimber should be banish'd,
And constant do remain to keep him so.
Cin. O Caesar—
Caes. Hence! wilt thou lift up Olympus?
Dec. Great Caesar—
Caes. Doth not Brutus bootless kneel?
Casca. Speak hands for me! *They stab Caesar.*
Caes. *Et tu, Brute?*—Then fall Caesar! *Dies.*
Cin. Liberty! Freedom! Tyranny is dead!
Run hence, proclaim, cry it about the streets.
Cas. Some to the common pulpits, and cry out,
"Liberty, freedom, and enfranchisement!"
Bru. People and senators, be not affrighted;
Fly not, stand still; ambition's debt is paid.
Casca. Go to the pulpit, Brutus.
Dec. And Cassius too.
Bru. Where's Publius?
Cin. Here, quite confounded with this mutiny.
Met. Stand fast together, lest some friend of Caesar's
Should chance—
Bru. Talk not of standing. Publius, good cheer,
There is no harm intended to your person,
Nor to no Roman else. So tell them, Publius.
Cas. And leave us, Publius, lest that the people,
Rushing on us, should do your age some mischief.
Bru. Do so, and let no man abide this deed,
But we the doers. [*Exeunt all but the Conspirators.*]

51. **repealing:** recall. 54. **freedom of:** permission for.
59. **pray to move:** beg favors of a superior (as you do).
61. **resting:** stable, unmoving. 62. **fellow:** equal.
67. **apprehensive:** intelligent.
69. **holds . . . rank:** maintains his position.
74. **Olympus:** mountain in Greece on which the gods dwelt.
75. **bootless:** in vain. 77. **Et tu, Brute:** and thou, Brutus.
80. **common pulpits:** public platforms.
83. **ambition's debt:** what was due to Caesar for being ambitious.
86. **mutiny:** uproar. 94. **abide:** take the consequences of.

Enter TREBONIUS.

Cas. Where is Antony?
Treb. Fled to his house amaz'd.
Men, wives, and children stare, cry out, and run,
As it were doomsday.
Bru. Fates, we will know your pleasures.
That we shall die, we know, 'tis but the time,
And drawing days out, that men stand upon.
Casca. Why, he that cuts off twenty years of life
Cuts off so many years of fearing death.
Bru. Grant that, and then is death a benefit;
So are we Caesar's friends, that have abridg'd
His time of fearing death. Stoop, Romans, stoop,
And let us bathe our hands in Caesar's blood
Up to the elbows, and besmear our swords;
Then walk we forth, even to the market-place,
And waving our red weapons o'er our heads,
Let's all cry, "Peace, freedom, and liberty!"
Cas. Stoop then, and wash. How many ages hence
Shall this our lofty scene be acted over
In [states] unborn and accents yet unknown!
Bru. How many times shall Caesar bleed in sport,
That now on Pompey's basis [lies] along
No worthier than the dust!
Cas. So oft as that shall be,
So often shall the knot of us be call'd
The men that gave their country liberty.
Dec. What, shall we forth?
Cas. Ay, every man away.
Brutus shall lead, and we will grace his heels
With the most boldest and best hearts of Rome.

Enter a SERVANT.

Bru. Soft, who comes here? A friend of Antony's.
Serv. Thus, Brutus, did my master bid me kneel;
Thus did Mark Antony bid me fall down;
And being prostrate, thus he bade me say:
Brutus is noble, wise, valiant, and honest;
Caesar was mighty, bold, royal, and loving.
Say, I love Brutus, and I honor him;
Say, I fear'd Caesar, honor'd him, and lov'd him.
If Brutus will vouchsafe that Antony
May safely come to him, and be resolv'd
How Caesar hath deserv'd to lie in death,
Mark Antony shall not love Caesar dead
So well as Brutus living; but will follow
The fortunes and affairs of noble Brutus
Thorough the hazards of this untrod state
With all true faith. So says my master Antony.
Bru. Thy master is a wise and valiant Roman,
I never thought him worse.
Tell him, so please him come unto this place,
He shall be satisfied; and, by my honor,
Depart untouch'd.
Serv. I'll fetch him presently. *Exit Servant.*
Bru. I know that we shall have him well to friend.

100. **stand upon:** regard as important.
115. **basis:** pedestal. **along:** prostrate. 126. **honest:** honorable.
131. **be resolv'd:** have explained to him.
136. **Thorough:** through. **untrod state:** unknown state of affairs.
142. **presently:** at once.

Cas. I wish we may; but yet have I a mind
That fears him much; and my misgiving still
Falls shrewdly to the purpose.

Enter ANTONY.

Bru. But here comes Antony. Welcome, Mark Antony!
Ant. O mighty Caesar! dost thou lie so low?
Are all thy conquests, glories, triumphs, spoils,
Shrunk to this little measure? Fare thee well!
I know not, gentlemen, what you intend,
Who else must be let blood, who else is rank;
If I myself, there is no hour so fit
As Caesar's death's hour, nor no instrument
Of half that worth as those your swords, made rich
With the most noble blood of all this world.
I do beseech ye, if you bear me hard,
Now, whilst your purpled hands do reek and smoke,
Fulfill your pleasure. Live a thousand years,
I shall not find myself so apt to die;
No place will please me so, no mean of death,
As here by Caesar, and by you cut off,
The choice and master spirits of this age.
Bru. O Antony! beg not your death of us.
Though now we must appear bloody and cruel,
As by our hands and this our present act
You see we do, yet see you but our hands,
And this the bleeding business they have done.
Our hearts you see not, they are pitiful;
And pity to the general wrong of Rome—
As fire drives out fire, so pity pity—
Hath done this deed on Caesar. For your part,
To you our swords have leaden points, Mark Antony;
Our arms in strength of malice, and our hearts
Of brothers' temper, do receive you in
With all kind love, good thoughts, and reverence.
Cas. Your voice shall be as strong as any man's
In the disposing of new dignities.
Bru. Only be patient till we have appeas'd
The multitude, beside themselves with fear,
And then we will deliver you the cause
Why I, that did love Caesar when I strook him,
Have thus proceeded.
Ant. I doubt not of your wisdom.
Let each man render me his bloody hand.
First, Marcus Brutus, will I shake with you;
Next, Caius Cassius, do I take your hand;
Now, Decius Brutus, yours; now yours, Metellus;
Yours, Cinna; and, my valiant Casca, yours;
Though last, not least in love, yours, good Trebonius.
Gentlemen all—alas, what shall I say?
My credit now stands on such slippery ground
That one of two bad ways you must conceit me,
Either a coward or a flatterer.
That I did love thee, Caesar, O, 'tis true;
If then thy spirit look upon us now,
Shall it not grieve thee dearer than thy death,
To see thy Antony making his peace,
Shaking the bloody fingers of thy foes,
Most noble! in the presence of thy corse?
Had I as many eyes as thou hast wounds,
Weeping as fast as they stream forth thy blood,
It would become me better than to close
In terms of friendship with thine enemies.
Pardon me, Julius! Here wast thou bay'd, brave hart,
Here didst thou fall, and here thy hunters stand,
Sign'd in thy spoil, and crimson'd in thy lethe.
O world! thou wast the forest to this hart,
And this indeed, O world, the heart of thee.
How like a deer, strooken by many princes,
Dost thou here lie!
Cas. Mark Antony—
Ant. Pardon me, Caius Cassius!
The enemies of Caesar shall say this:
Then, in a friend, it is cold modesty.
Cas. I blame you not for praising Caesar so,
But what compact mean you to have with us?
Will you be prick'd in number of our friends,
Or shall we on, and not depend on you?
Ant. Therefore I took your hands, but was indeed
Sway'd from the point, by looking down on Caesar.
Friends am I with you all, and love you all,
Upon this hope, that you shall give me reasons
Why, and wherein, Caesar was dangerous.
Bru. Or else were this a savage spectacle.
Our reasons are so full of good regard
That were you, Antony, the son of Caesar,
You should be satisfied.
Ant. That's all I seek,
And am, moreover, suitor that I may
Produce his body to the market-place,
And in the pulpit, as becomes a friend,
Speak in the order of his funeral.
Bru. You shall, Mark Antony.
Cas. Brutus, a word with you.
[*Aside to Brutus.*] You know not what you do. Do not consent
That Antony speak in his funeral.
Know you how much the people may be mov'd
By that which he will utter?
Bru. By your pardon—
I will myself into the pulpit first,
And show the reason of our Caesar's death.
What Antony shall speak, I will protest
He speaks by leave and by permission;
And that we are contented Caesar shall
Have all true rites and lawful ceremonies.
It shall advantage more than do us wrong.

145. fears: distrusts.
145–46. my . . . purpose: I'm not often wide of the mark when I have doubts of this kind.
152. rank: overripe, ready to be cut down.
157. bear me hard: have a grudge against me. **159. Live:** if I live.
160. apt: ready. **161. mean:** means, manner.
169. pitiful: full of pity.
171. pity pity: i.e. pity for Rome's plight drove out pity for Caesar.
174. in . . . malice: with the same strength as they showed when their object was to hurt. **182. strook:** struck.
192. conceit: conceive, judge.

196. dearer: more keenly. **202. close:** be reconciled.
204. bay'd: brought to bay (like a stag). **hart.** With play on *heart.*
206. Sign'd . . . spoil: marked with the tokens of your death (as, for example, children are "blooded" at a hunt). **lethe:** stream of death, i.e. Caesar's life-blood. **213. modesty:** moderation.
216. prick'd in number: marked on the list.
224. full . . . regard: sound, acceptable. **230. order:** ceremony.
238. protest: proclaim. **241. true:** rightful.

Cas. I know not what may fall, I like it not.
Bru. Mark Antony, here take you Caesar's body.
You shall not in your funeral speech blame us,
But speak all good you can devise of Caesar,
And say you do't by our permission;
Else shall you not have any hand at all
About his funeral. And you shall speak
In the same pulpit whereto I am going,
After my speech is ended.
Ant. Be it so;
I do desire no more.
Bru. Prepare the body then, and follow us.
Exeunt. Manet Antony.
[*Ant.*] O, pardon me, thou bleeding piece of earth,
That I am meek and gentle with these butchers!
Thou art the ruins of the noblest man
That ever lived in the tide of times.
Woe to the hand that shed this costly blood!
Over thy wounds now do I prophesy
(Which like dumb mouths do ope their ruby lips
To beg the voice and utterance of my tongue)
A curse shall light upon the limbs of men;
Domestic fury and fierce civil strife
Shall cumber all the parts of Italy;
Blood and destruction shall be so in use,
And dreadful objects so familiar,
That mothers shall but smile when they behold
Their infants quartered with the hands of war;
All pity chok'd with custom of fell deeds;
And Caesar's spirit, ranging for revenge,
With Ate by his side come hot from hell,
Shall in these confines with a monarch's voice
Cry "Havoc!" and let slip the dogs of war,
That this foul deed shall smell above the earth
With carrion men, groaning for burial.

Enter Octavio's SERVANT.

You serve Octavius Caesar, do you not?
Serv. I do, Mark Antony.
Ant. Caesar did write for him to come to Rome.
Serv. He did receive his letters, and is coming,
And bid me say to you by word of mouth—
O Caesar!— [*Seeing the body.*]
Ant. Thy heart is big; get thee apart and weep.
Passion, I see, is catching, [for] mine eyes,
Seeing those beads of sorrow stand in thine,
Began to water. Is thy master coming?
Serv. He lies to-night within seven leagues of Rome.
Ant. Post back with speed, and tell him what hath chanc'd.
Here is a mourning Rome, a dangerous Rome,
No Rome of safety for Octavius yet;
Hie hence, and tell him so. Yet stay awhile,
Thou shalt not back till I have borne this corse
Into the market-place. There shall I try,

243. **fall:** happen. 257. **tide of times:** course of history.
258. **costly:** precious. 265. **in use:** common.
266. **objects:** sights.
269. **custom . . . deeds:** cruel deeds, grown familiar.
271. **Ate:** goddess of discord. 272. **confines:** regions.
273. **Havoc:** no quarter (a war-cry). **let slip:** unleash.
283. **Passion:** grief. 292. **try:** test.

In my oration, how the people take
The cruel issue of these bloody men,
According to the which thou shalt discourse
To young Octavius of the state of things.
Lend me your hand. *Exeunt* [*with Caesar's body*].

[SCENE II]

Enter BRUTUS *and* CASSIUS *with the* PLEBEIANS.

Plebeians. We will be satisfied! Let us be satisfied!
Bru. Then follow me, and give me audience, friends.
Cassius, go you into the other street,
And part the numbers.
Those that will hear me speak, let 'em stay here;
Those that will follow Cassius, go with him;
And public reasons shall be rendered
Of Caesar's death.
1. Pleb. I will hear Brutus speak.
2. Pleb. I will hear Cassius, and compare their reasons,
When severally we hear them rendered.
[*Exit Cassius with some of the Plebeians. Brutus*] *goes into the pulpit.*
3. Pleb. The noble Brutus is ascended; silence!
Bru. Be patient till the last.

Romans, countrymen, and lovers, hear me for my cause, and be silent, that you may hear. Believe me for mine honor, and have respect to mine honor, that you may believe. Censure me in your wisdom, and awake your senses, that you may the better judge. If there be any in this assembly, any dear friend of Caesar's, to him I say, that Brutus' love to Caesar was no less than his. If then that friend demand why Brutus rose against Caesar, this is my answer: Not that I lov'd Caesar less, but that I lov'd Rome more. Had you rather Caesar were living, and die all slaves, than that Caesar were dead, to live all freemen? As Caesar lov'd me, I weep for him; as he was fortunate, I rejoice at it; as he was valiant, I honor him; but, as he was ambitious, I slew him. There is tears for his love; joy for his fortune; honor for his valor; and death for his ambition. Who is here so base that would be a bondman? If any, speak, for him have I offended. Who is here so rude that would not be a Roman? If any, speak, for him have I offended. Who is here so vile that will not love his country? If any, speak, for him have I offended. I pause for a reply.

All. None, Brutus, none.

Bru. Then none have I offended. I have done no more to Caesar than you shall do to Brutus. The question of his death is enroll'd in the Capitol: his glory not extenuated, wherein he was worthy; nor his offenses enforc'd, for which he suffer'd death.

294. **issue:** deed. 295. **the which:** i.e. the outcome of the test.

III.ii. Location: Rome. The Forum.
1. **be satisfied:** have affairs explained to our satisfaction.
13. **lovers:** friends. 15. **have respect to:** bear in mind.
16. **Censure:** judge. 31. **rude:** barbarous.
38. **question . . . enroll'd:** justification for his death is on record.
39. **extenuated:** diminished. 40. **enforc'd:** unduly stressed.

Enter MARK ANTONY [*and others*] *with Caesar's body.*

Here comes his body, mourn'd by Mark Antony, who, though he had no hand in his death, shall receive the benefit of his dying, a place in the commonwealth, as which of you shall not? With this I depart, that, as I slew my best lover for the good of Rome, I have the same dagger for myself, when it shall please my country to need my death.

All. Live, Brutus, live, live!
1. Pleb. Bring him with triumph home unto his house.
2. Pleb. Give him a statue with his ancestors.
3. Pleb. Let him be Caesar.
4. Pleb. Caesar's better parts
Shall be crown'd in Brutus.
1. Pleb. We'll bring him to his house
With shouts and clamors.
Bru. My countrymen—
2. Pleb. Peace, silence! Brutus speaks.
1. Pleb. Peace ho!
Bru. Good countrymen, let me depart alone,
And, for my sake, stay here with Antony.
Do grace to Caesar's corpse, and grace his speech
Tending to Caesar's glories, which Mark Antony
(By our permission) is allow'd to make.
I do entreat you, not a man depart,
Save I alone, till Antony have spoke. *Exit.*
1. Pleb. Stay ho, and let us hear Mark Antony.
3. Pleb. Let him go up into the public chair,
We'll hear him. Noble Antony, go up.
Ant. For Brutus' sake, I am beholding to you.
[*Goes into the pulpit.*]
4. Pleb. What does he say of Brutus?
3. Pleb. He says, for Brutus' sake
He finds himself beholding to us all.
4. Pleb. 'Twere best he speak no harm of Brutus here!
1. Pleb. This Caesar was a tyrant.
3. Pleb. Nay, that's certain:
We are blest that Rome is rid of him.
2. Pleb. Peace, let us hear what Antony can say.
Ant. You gentle Romans—
All. Peace ho, let us hear him.
Ant. Friends, Romans, countrymen, lend me your ears!
I come to bury Caesar, not to praise him.
The evil that men do lives after them,
The good is oft interred with their bones;
So let it be with Caesar. The noble Brutus
Hath told you Caesar was ambitious;
If it were so, it was a grievous fault,
And grievously hath Caesar answer'd it.
Here, under leave of Brutus and the rest
(For Brutus is an honorable man,
So are they all, all honorable men),
Come I to speak in Caesar's funeral.
He was my friend, faithful and just to me;
But Brutus says he was ambitious,
And Brutus is an honorable man.
He hath brought many captives home to Rome,
Whose ransoms did the general coffers fill;
Did this in Caesar seem ambitious?
When that the poor have cried, Caesar hath wept;
Ambition should be made of sterner stuff:
Yet Brutus says he was ambitious,
And Brutus is an honorable man.
You all did see that on the Lupercal
I thrice presented him a kingly crown,
Which he did thrice refuse. Was this ambition?
Yet Brutus says he was ambitious,
And sure he is an honorable man.
I speak not to disprove what Brutus spoke,
But here I am to speak what I do know.
You all did love him once, not without cause;
What cause withholds you then to mourn for him?
O judgment! thou [art] fled to brutish beasts,
And men have lost their reason. Bear with me,
My heart is in the coffin there with Caesar,
And I must pause till it come back to me.
1. Pleb. Methinks there is much reason in his sayings.
2. Pleb. If thou consider rightly of the matter,
Caesar has had great wrong.
3. Pleb. Has he, masters?
I fear there will a worse come in his place.
4. Pleb. Mark'd ye his words? He would not take the crown,
Therefore 'tis certain he was not ambitious.
1. Pleb. If it be found so, some will dear abide it.
2. Pleb. Poor soul, his eyes are red as fire with weeping.
3. Pleb. There's not a nobler man in Rome than Antony.
4. Pleb. Now mark him, he begins again to speak.
Ant. But yesterday the word of Caesar might
Have stood against the world; now lies he there,
And none so poor to do him reverence.
O masters! if I were dispos'd to stir
Your hearts and minds to mutiny and rage,
I should do Brutus wrong, and Cassius wrong,
Who (you all know) are honorable men.
I will not do them wrong; I rather choose
To wrong the dead, to wrong myself and you,
Than I will wrong such honorable men.
But here's a parchment with the seal of Caesar,
I found it in his closet, 'tis his will.
Let but the commons hear this testament—
Which, pardon me, I do not mean to read—
And they would go and kiss dead Caesar's wounds,
And dip their napkins in his sacred blood;
Yea, beg a hair of him for memory,
And dying, mention it within their wills,
Bequeathing it as a rich legacy
Unto their issue.
4. Pleb. We'll hear the will. Read it, Mark Antony.

51. parts: qualities.
57. Do grace: pay respect. **grace his speech:** give his speech a courteous hearing. **65. beholding:** beholden, indebted.
80. answer'd: paid for.

114. dear abide it: pay dearly for it.
120. none . . . reverence: no one is so lowly as to be subservient to Caesar. **122. mutiny:** disorder, turbulence.
129. closet: private room, study. **130. commons:** common people.
133. napkins: handkerchiefs.

All. The will, the will! we will hear Caesar's will.
Ant. Have patience, gentle friends, I must not read it.
It is not meet you know how Caesar lov'd you:
You are not wood, you are not stones, but men;
And, being men, hearing the will of Caesar,
It will inflame you, it will make you mad.
'Tis good you know not that you are his heirs,
For if you should, O, what would come of it?
4. Pleb. Read the will, we'll hear it, Antony.
You shall read us the will, Caesar's will.
Ant. Will you be patient? Will you stay awhile?
I have o'ershot myself to tell you of it.
I fear I wrong the honorable men
Whose daggers have stabb'd Caesar; I do fear it.
4. Pleb. They were traitors; honorable men!
All. The will! the testament!
2. Pleb. They were villains, murderers. The will, read the will!
Ant. You will compel me then to read the will?
Then make a ring about the corpse of Caesar,
And let me show you him that made the will.
Shall I descend? and will you give me leave?
All. Come down.
2. Pleb. Descend.
3. Pleb. You shall have leave.
[*Antony comes down from the pulpit.*]
4. Pleb. A ring, stand round.
1. Pleb. Stand from the hearse, stand from the body.
2. Pleb. Room for Antony, most noble Antony.
Ant. Nay, press not so upon me, stand far off.
All. Stand back; room, bear back!
Ant. If you have tears, prepare to shed them now.
You all do know this mantle. I remember
The first time ever Caesar put it on;
'Twas on a summer's evening, in his tent,
That day he overcame the Nervii.
Look, in this place ran Cassius' dagger through;
See what a rent the envious Casca made;
Through this the well-beloved Brutus stabb'd,
And as he pluck'd his cursed steel away,
Mark how the blood of Caesar followed it,
As rushing out of doors to be resolv'd
If Brutus so unkindly knock'd or no;
For Brutus, as you know, was Caesar's angel.
Judge, O you gods, how dearly Caesar lov'd him!
This was the most unkindest cut of all;
For when the noble Caesar saw him stab,
Ingratitude, more strong than traitors' arms,
Quite vanquish'd him. Then burst his mighty heart,
And in his mantle muffling up his face,
Even at the base of Pompey's statuë
(Which all the while ran blood) great Caesar fell.
O, what a fall was there, my countrymen!
Then I, and you, and all of us fell down,
Whilst bloody treason flourish'd over us.
O now you weep, and I perceive you feel

165. **hearse:** bier.
173. **Nervii:** a Belgian tribe defeated by Caesar in 57 B.C.
175. **envious:** malicious. 179. **be resolv'd:** make certain.
180. **unkindly:** cruelly and unnaturally.
192. **flourish'd:** triumphed arrogantly.

The dint of pity. These are gracious drops.
Kind souls, what weep you when you but behold
Our Caesar's vesture wounded? Look you here,
[*Lifting Caesar's mantle.*]
Here is himself, marr'd as you see with traitors.
1. Pleb. O piteous spectacle!
2. Pleb. O noble Caesar!
3. Pleb. O woeful day!
4. Pleb. O traitors, villains!
1. Pleb. O most bloody sight!
2. Pleb. We will be reveng'd!
[*All.*] Revenge! About! Seek! Burn! Fire! Kill!
Slay! Let not a traitor live!
Ant. Stay, countrymen.
1. Pleb. Peace there, hear the noble Antony.
2. Pleb. We'll hear him, we'll follow him, we'll die with him.
Ant. Good friends, sweet friends, let me not stir you up
To such a sudden flood of mutiny.
They that have done this deed are honorable.
What private griefs they have, alas, I know not,
That made them do it. They are wise and honorable,
And will no doubt with reasons answer you.
I come not, friends, to steal away your hearts.
I am no orator, as Brutus is;
But (as you know me all) a plain blunt man
That love my friend, and that they know full well
That gave me public leave to speak of him.
For I have neither [wit], nor words, nor worth,
Action, nor utterance, nor the power of speech
To stir men's blood; I only speak right on.
I tell you that which you yourselves do know,
Show you sweet Caesar's wounds, poor, poor, dumb mouths,
And bid them speak for me. But were I Brutus,
And Brutus Antony, there were an Antony
Would ruffle up your spirits, and put a tongue
In every wound of Caesar, that should move
The stones of Rome to rise and mutiny.
All. We'll mutiny.
1. Pleb. We'll burn the house of Brutus.
3. Pleb. Away then, come, seek the conspirators.
Ant. Yet hear me, countrymen, yet hear me speak.
All. Peace ho, hear Antony, most noble Antony!
Ant. Why, friends, you go to do you know not what.
Wherein hath Caesar thus deserv'd your loves?
Alas you know not! I must tell you then:
You have forgot the will I told you of.
All. Most true. The will! Let's stay and hear the will.
Ant. Here is the will, and under Caesar's seal:
To every Roman citizen he gives,
To every several man, seventy-five drachmaes.

194. **dint:** impression. **gracious:** full of grace, doing you honor.
213. **griefs:** grievances.
221. **wit:** intellectual power. **words:** facility with words, fluency. **worth:** position (to give authority to my words).
222. **Action:** effective gestures. **utterance:** good delivery.
228. **ruffle up:** rouse to anger. 230. **mutiny:** run riot.
242. **several:** individual.

2. Pleb. Most noble Caesar! we'll revenge his death.
3. Pleb. O royal Caesar!
Ant. Hear me with patience.
All. Peace ho!
Ant. Moreover, he hath left you all his walks,
His private arbors and new-planted orchards,
On this side Tiber; he hath left them you,
And to your heirs for ever—common pleasures,
To walk abroad and recreate yourselves.
Here was a Caesar! when comes such another?
1. Pleb. Never, never! Come, away, away!
We'll burn his body in the holy place,
And with the brands fire the traitors' houses.
Take up the body.
2. Pleb. Go fetch fire.
3. Pleb. Pluck down benches.
4. Pleb. Pluck down forms, windows, any thing.
Exeunt Plebeians [with the body].
Ant. Now let it work. Mischief, thou art afoot,
Take thou what course thou wilt!

Enter SERVANT.

How now, fellow?
Serv. Sir, Octavius is already come to Rome.
Ant. Where is he?
Serv. He and Lepidus are at Caesar's house.
Ant. And thither will I straight to visit him;
He comes upon a wish. Fortune is merry,
And in this mood will give us any thing.
Serv. I heard him say, Brutus and Cassius
Are rid like madmen through the gates of Rome.
Ant. Belike they had some notice of the people,
How I had mov'd them. Bring me to Octavius.
Exeunt.

[SCENE III]

Enter CINNA *the poet, and after him the* PLEBEIANS.

Cin. I dreamt to-night that I did feast with Caesar,
And things unluckily charge my fantasy.
I have no will to wander forth of doors,
Yet something leads me forth.
1. Pleb. What is your name?
2. Pleb. Whither are you going?
3. Pleb. Where do you dwell?
4. Pleb. Are you a married man or a bachelor?
2. Pleb. Answer every man directly.
1. Pleb. Ay, and briefly.
4. Pleb. Ay, and wisely.
3. Pleb. Ay, and truly, you were best.
Cin. What is my name? Whither am I going? Where do I dwell? Am I a married man or a bachelor? Then to answer every man directly and briefly, wisely and truly: wisely, I say, I am a bachelor.

250. **common pleasures:** public pleasure-grounds.
259. **forms:** benches. **windows:** shutters. 265. **straight:** at once.
266. **upon a wish:** just as I was wishing it. **is merry:** i.e. smiles upon me. 269. **Are rid:** have ridden. 270. **Belike:** probably.

III.iii. Location: Rome. A street.
1. **to-night:** last night.
2. **unluckily . . . fantasy:** fill my imagination with dark forebodings.

2. Pleb. That's as much as to say, they are fools that marry. You'll bear me a bang for that, I fear. Proceed directly.
Cin. Directly, I am going to Caesar's funeral.
1. Pleb. As a friend or an enemy?
Cin. As a friend.
2. Pleb. That matter is answer'd directly.
4. Pleb. For your dwelling—briefly.
Cin. Briefly, I dwell by the Capitol.
3. Pleb. Your name, sir, truly.
Cin. Truly, my name is Cinna.
1. Pleb. Tear him to pieces, he's a conspirator.
Cin. I am Cinna the poet, I am Cinna the poet.
4. Pleb. Tear him for his bad verses, tear him for his bad verses.
Cin. I am not Cinna the conspirator.
4. Pleb. It is no matter, his name's Cinna. Pluck but his name out of his heart, and turn him going.
3. Pleb. Tear him, tear him! Come, brands ho, fire-brands! To Brutus', to Cassius'; burn all! Some to Decius' house, and some to Casca's; some to Ligarius'. Away, go!
Exeunt all the Plebeians [dragging off Cinna].

ACT IV, [SCENE I]

Enter ANTONY, OCTAVIUS, *and* LEPIDUS.

Ant. These many then shall die, their names are prick'd.
Oct. Your brother too must die; consent you, Lepidus?
Lep. I do consent—
Oct. Prick him down, Antony.
Lep. Upon condition Publius shall not live,
Who is your sister's son, Mark Antony.
Ant. He shall not live; look, with a spot I damn him.
But, Lepidus, go you to Caesar's house;
Fetch the will hither, and we shall determine
How to cut off some charge in legacies.
Lep. What? shall I find you here?
Oct. Or here or at the Capitol. *Exit Lepidus.*
Ant. This is a slight unmeritable man,
Meet to be sent on errands; is it fit,
The threefold world divided, he should stand
One of the three to share it?
Oct. So you thought him,
And took his voice who should be prick'd to die
In our black sentence and proscription.
Ant. Octavius, I have seen more days than you,
And though we lay these honors on this man
To ease ourselves of divers sland'rous loads,

18. **bear . . . bang:** get a blow from me.
34. **turn him going:** send him off, dispatch him.

IV.i. Location: Rome. Antony's house.
1. **prick'd:** checked on a list. 6. **spot:** mark (on the list).
12. **unmeritable:** not deserving (respect or honor).
14. **threefold world divided.** Octavius, Antony, and Lepidus constituted themselves *triumviri* in 43 B.C. and divided the responsibilities of the Empire among themselves.
16. **took his voice:** accepted his vote.
20. **sland'rous loads:** burdens of slander.

He shall but bear them as the ass bears gold,
To groan and sweat under the business,
Either led or driven, as we point the way;
And having brought our treasure where we will,
Then take we down his load, and turn him off
(Like to the empty ass) to shake his ears
And graze in commons.

Oct. You may do your will;
But he's a tried and valiant soldier.

Ant. So is my horse, Octavius, and for that
I do appoint him store of provender.
It is a creature that I teach to fight,
To wind, to stop, to run directly on,
His corporal motion govern'd by my spirit;
And in some taste is Lepidus but so:
He must be taught, and train'd, and bid go forth;
A barren-spirited fellow; one that feeds
On objects, arts, and imitations,
Which, out of use and stal'd by other men,
Begin his fashion. Do not talk of him
But as a property. And now, Octavius,
Listen great things. Brutus and Cassius
Are levying powers; we must straight make head;
Therefore let our alliance be combin'd,
Our best friends made, our means stretch'd,
And let us presently go sit in council,
How covert matters may be best disclos'd,
And open perils surest answered.

Oct. Let us do so; for we are at the stake,
And bay'd about with many enemies,
And some that smile have in their hearts, I fear,
Millions of mischiefs. *Exeunt.*

[Scene II]

Drum. Enter Brutus, Lucilius, [Lucius,] *and the army.* Titinius *and* Pindarus *meet them.*

Bru. Stand ho!

Lucil. Give the word ho! and stand.

Bru. What now, Lucilius, is Cassius near?

Lucil. He is at hand, and Pindarus is come
To do you salutation from his master.

Bru. He greets me well. Your master, Pindarus,
In his own change, or by ill officers,
Hath given me some worthy cause to wish
Things done undone; but if he be at hand
I shall be satisfied.

Pin. I do not doubt
But that my noble master will appear
Such as he is, full of regard and honor.

Bru. He is not doubted. A word, Lucilius,
How he receiv'd you; let me be resolv'd.

Lucil. With courtesy and with respect enough,
But not with such familiar instances,
Nor with such free and friendly conference,
As he hath us'd of old.

Bru. Thou hast describ'd
A hot friend cooling. Ever note, Lucilius,
When love begins to sicken and decay
It useth an enforced ceremony.
There are no tricks in plain and simple faith;
But hollow men, like horses hot at hand,
Make gallant show and promise of their mettle;
Low march within.
But when they should endure the bloody spur,
They fall their crests, and like deceitful jades
Sink in the trial. Comes his army on?

Lucil. They mean this night in Sardis to be quarter'd.
The greater part, the horse in general,
Are come with Cassius.

Enter Cassius *and his powers.*

Bru. Hark, he is arriv'd.
March gently on to meet him.

Cas. Stand ho!

Bru. Stand ho! Speak the word along.

[*1. Sol.*] Stand!

[*2. Sol.*] Stand!

[*3. Sol.*] Stand!

Cas. Most noble brother, you have done me wrong.

Bru. Judge me, you gods! wrong I mine enemies?
And if not so, how should I wrong a brother?

Cas. Brutus, this sober form of yours hides wrongs,
And when you do them—

Bru. Cassius, be content,
Speak your griefs softly; I do know you well.
Before the eyes of both our armies here
(Which should perceive nothing but love from us)
Let us not wrangle. Bid them move away;
Then in my tent, Cassius, enlarge your griefs,
And I will give you audience.

Cas. Pindarus,
Bid our commanders lead their charges off
A little from this ground.

Bru. [Lucius], do you the like, and let no man
Come to our tent till we have done our conference.
Let [Lucilius] and Titinius guard our door.

Exeunt. Manent Brutus and Cassius, [who withdraw into Brutus' tent, while Lucilius and Titinius mount guard without].

26. empty: relieved of his load. **32. wind:** turn.
34. taste: degree.
37. objects . . . imitations. Whether or not this list is of essentially trivial interests (as has been argued), Antony's main charge is that Lipidus takes them up at second hand.
39. Begin his fashion: he then picks up as his own usage.
40. property: tool. **42. make head:** raise an army.
43. combin'd: augmented, strengthened.
44. made: brought in. **stretch'd:** fully extended.
45. presently: at once.
46. How . . . disclos'd: (to make plans) how hidden dangers may best be uncovered. **47. surest answered:** most safely met.
48. at the stake: like a bear fastened to a post with the dogs loosed to attack it (a favorite Elizabethan sport).
49. bay'd about: surrounded as by baying dogs.

IV.ii. Location: Camp near Sardis. Before Brutus' tent.
6. greets me well: sends a good man to greet me. **8. worthy:** just.
10. be satisfied: have affairs explained to my satisfaction.

12. regard and honor: i.e. a care for your joint affairs which is consistent with his integrity. **14. resolv'd:** informed.
16. familiar instances: tokens of intimacy.
17. conference: conversation.
23. hollow; insincere. **hot at hand:** lively at the start.
26. fall: let fall. **jades:** inferior horses, nags. **27. Sink:** fail.
29. horse in general: all the cavalry. **31. gently:** slowly.
41. content: calm. **42. griefs:** grievances.
46. enlarge: express fully. **47. give you audience:** hear you out.

[Scene III]

Cas. That you have wrong'd me doth appear in this:
You have condemn'd and noted Lucius Pella
For taking bribes here of the Sardians;
Wherein my letters, praying on his side,
Because I knew the man, was slighted off.
Bru. You wrong'd yourself to write in such a case.
Cas. In such a time as this it is not meet
That every nice offense should bear his comment.
Bru. Let me tell you, Cassius, you yourself
Are much condemn'd to have an itching palm,
To sell and mart your offices for gold
To undeservers.
Cas. I, an itching palm?
You know that you are Brutus that speaks this,
Or, by the gods, this speech were else your last.
Bru. The name of Cassius honors this corruption,
And chastisement doth therefore hide his head.
Cas. Chastisement?
Bru. Remember March, the ides of March remember:
Did not great Julius bleed for justice' sake?
What villain touch'd his body, that did stab
And not for justice? What? shall one of us,
That struck the foremost man of all this world
But for supporting robbers, shall we now
Contaminate our fingers with base bribes?
And sell the mighty space of our large honors
For so much trash as may be grasped thus?
I had rather be a dog, and bay the moon,
Than such a Roman.
Cas. Brutus, bait not me,
I'll not endure it. You forget yourself
To hedge me in. I am a soldier, I,
Older in practice, abler than yourself
To make conditions.
Bru. Go to; you are not, Cassius.
Cas. I am.
Bru. I say you are not.
Cas. Urge me no more, I shall forget myself;
Have mind upon your health; tempt me no farther.
Bru. Away, slight man!
Cas. Is't possible?
Bru. Hear me, for I will speak.
Must I give way and room to your rash choler?
Shall I be frighted when a madman stares?
Cas. O ye gods, ye gods, must I endure all this?
Bru. All this? ay, more. Fret till your proud heart break;
Go show your slaves how choleric you are,
And make your bondmen tremble. Must I bouge?

IV.iii. Location: Scene continues in Brutus' tent.
2. noted: branded with disgrace.
4. letters: letter (paralleling Latin *litterae*, plural in form but singular in meaning). **5. slighted off:** contemptuously disregarded.
8. nice: trivial. **bear his comment:** be subjected to critical scrutiny.
10. to have: for having. **11. mart:** traffic in.
15. honors: causes to seem honorable.
25. the mighty . . . honors: the greatness of our reputations.
28. bait: harass. **30. hedge me in:** place restrictions on me.
32. make conditions: decide how affairs shall be managed.
35. Urge: push. **36. tempt:** try, provoke.
39. rash choler: anger that flares up suddenly. **40. stares:** glares.
44. bouge: budge, flinch.

Must I observe you? Must I stand and crouch
Under your testy humor? By the gods,
You shall digest the venom of your spleen
Though it do split you; for, from this day forth,
I'll use you for my mirth, yea, for my laughter,
When you are waspish.
Cas. Is it come to this?
Bru. You say you are a better soldier:
Let it appear so; make your vaunting true,
And it shall please me well. For mine own part,
I shall be glad to learn of noble men.
Cas. You wrong me every way; you wrong me, Brutus:
I said an elder soldier, not a better.
Did I say "better"?
Bru. If you did, I care not.
Cas. When Caesar liv'd, he durst not thus have mov'd me.
Bru. Peace, peace, you durst not so have tempted him.
Cas. I durst not?
Bru. No.
Cas. What? durst not tempt him?
Bru. For your life you durst not.
Cas. Do not presume too much upon my love,
I may do that I shall be sorry for.
Bru. You have done that you should be sorry for.
There is no terror, Cassius, in your threats;
For I am arm'd so strong in honesty
That they pass by me as the idle wind,
Which I respect not. I did send to you
For certain sums of gold, which you denied me;
For I can raise no money by vile means.
By heaven, I had rather coin my heart
And drop my blood for drachmaes than to wring
From the hard hands of peasants their vile trash
By any indirection. I did send
To you for gold to pay my legions,
Which you denied me. Was that done like Cassius?
Should I have answer'd Caius Cassius so?
When Marcus Brutus grows so covetous
To lock such rascal counters from his friends,
Be ready, gods, with all your thunderbolts,
Dash him to pieces!
Cas. I denied you not.
Bru. You did.
Cas. I did not. He was but a fool that brought
My answer back. Brutus hath riv'd my heart.
A friend should bear his friend's infirmities;
But Brutus makes mine greater than they are.
Bru. I do not, till you practice them on me.
Cas. You love me not.
Bru. I do not like your faults.
Cas. A friendly eye could never see such faults.
Bru. A flatterer's would not, though they do appear
As huge as high Olympus.
Cas. Come, Antony, and young Octavius, come,

45. observe: defer to.
47. digest: swallow (rather than vent). **spleen:** irascible temper.
58. mov'd: angered. **67. honesty:** honor, integrity.
69. respect not: pay no attention to.
75. indirection: dishonest means.
80. rascal counters: worthless discs.

Revenge yourselves alone on Cassius,
For Cassius is a-weary of the world;
Hated by one he loves, brav'd by his brother,
Check'd like a bondman, all his faults observ'd,
Set in a note-book, learn'd, and conn'd by rote,
To cast into my teeth. O, I could weep
My spirit from mine eyes! There is my dagger,
And here my naked breast; within, a heart
Dearer than Pluto's mine, richer than gold:
If that thou be'st a Roman, take it forth.
I, that denied thee gold, will give my heart:
Strike as thou didst at Caesar; for I know,
When thou didst hate him worst, thou lovedst him better
Than ever thou lovedst Cassius.

Bru. Sheathe your dagger.
Be angry when you will, it shall have scope;
Do what you will, dishonor shall be humor.
O Cassius, you are yoked with a lamb
That carries anger as the flint bears fire,
Who, much enforced, shows a hasty spark,
And straight is cold again.

Cas. Hath Cassius liv'd
To be but mirth and laughter to his Brutus,
When grief and blood ill-temper'd vexeth him?

Bru. When I spoke that, I was ill-temper'd too.

Cas. Do you confess so much? Give me your hand.

Bru. And my heart too.

Cas. O Brutus!

Bru. What's the matter?

Cas. Have not you love enough to bear with me,
When that rash humor which my mother gave me
Makes me forgetful?

Bru. Yes, Cassius, and from henceforth,
When you are over-earnest with your Brutus,
He'll think your mother chides, and leave you so.

Enter a Poet [*to Lucilius and Titinius as they stand on guard*].

Poet. Let me go in to see the generals.
There is some grudge between 'em; 'tis not meet
They be alone.

Lucil. You shall not come to them.

Poet. Nothing but death shall stay me.

[*Brutus and Cassius step out of the tent.*]

Cas. How now? what's the matter?

Poet. For shame, you generals! what do you mean?
Love, and be friends, as two such men should be,
For I have seen more years, I'm sure, than ye.

Cas. Ha, ha! how vildly doth this cynic rhyme!

Bru. Get you hence, sirrah; saucy fellow, hence!

Cas. Bear with him, Brutus, 'tis his fashion.

Bru. I'll know his humor, when he knows his time.

94. alone on Cassius: on Cassius alone. **96. brav'd:** defied.
97. Check'd: reproved.
102. Pluto: god of the underworld, here confused, as commonly, with Plutus, god of wealth. **108. scope:** free play.
109. dishonor . . . humor: I shall interpret your insults as effects of your quick temper. **110. lamb:** i.e. Brutus.
115. blood ill-temper'd: bad humor.
120. rash humor: irritable temper. **123. leave you so:** stop at that.
133. vildly: vilely. **cynic:** rude philosopher.
136. I'll . . . time: I'll indulge his odd behavior when he chooses an appropriate time to exhibit it.

What should the wars do with these jigging fools?
Companion, hence!

Cas. Away, away, be gone! *Exit Poet.*

Bru. Lucilius and Titinius, bid the commanders
Prepare to lodge their companies to-night.

Cas. And come yourselves, and bring Messala with you
Immediately to us. [*Exeunt Lucilius and Titinius.*]

Bru. [*To Lucius within.*] Lucius, a bowl of wine! [*Brutus and Cassius return into the tent.*]

Cas. I did not think you could have been so angry.

Bru. O Cassius, I am sick of many griefs.

Cas. Of your philosophy you make no use,
If you give place to accidental evils.

Bru. No man bears sorrow better. Portia is dead.

Cas. Ha? Portia?

Bru. She is dead.

Cas. How scap'd I killing when I cross'd you so?
O insupportable and touching loss!
Upon what sickness?

Bru. Impatient of my absence,
And grief that young Octavius with Mark Antony
Have made themselves so strong—for with her death
That tidings came. With this she fell distract,
And (her attendants absent) swallow'd fire.

Cas. And died so?

Bru. Even so.

Cas. O ye immortal gods!

Enter Boy [Lucius] *with wine and tapers.*

Bru. Speak no more of her. Give me a bowl of wine.
In this I bury all unkindness, Cassius. *Drinks.*

Cas. My heart is thirsty for that noble pledge.
Fill, Lucius, till the wine o'erswell the cup;
I cannot drink too much of Brutus' love.
[*Drinks. Exit Lucius.*]

Enter Titinius *and* Messala.

Bru. Come in, Titinius. Welcome, good Messala.
Now sit we close about this taper here,
And call in question our necessities.

Cas. Portia, art thou gone?

Bru. No more, I pray you.
Messala, I have here received letters
That young Octavius and Mark Antony
Come down upon us with a mighty power,
Bending their expedition toward Philippi.

Mes. Myself have letters of the self-same tenure.

Bru. With what addition?

Mes. That by proscription and bills of outlawry
Octavius, Antony, and Lepidus
Have put to death an hundred senators.

Bru. Therein our letters do not well agree;
Mine speak of seventy senators that died

138. Companion: fellow.
145. philosophy. Brutus professed Stoicism.
146. give place to: yield to, allow yourself to be affected by. **accidental evils:** evils caused by chance (to which Stoics professed immunity). **154. her death:** i.e. news of her death.
156. fire. According to Plutarch, burning coals.
165. call in question: discuss. **169. power:** army.
170. expedition: speedy course. **171. tenure:** tenor, import.

By their proscriptions, Cicero being one.
Cas. Cicero one?
Mes. Cicero is dead,
And by that order of proscription.
Had you your letters from your wife, my lord?
Bru. No, Messala.
Mes. Nor nothing in your letters writ of her?
Bru. Nothing, Messala.
Mes. That, methinks, is strange.
Bru. Why ask you? Hear you aught of her in yours?
Mes. No, my lord.
Bru. Now as you are a Roman tell me true.
Mes. Then like a Roman bear the truth I tell:
For certain she is dead, and by strange manner.
Bru. Why, farewell, Portia. We must die, Messala.
With meditating that she must die once,
I have the patience to endure it now.
Mes. Even so great men great losses should endure.
Cas. I have as much of this in art as you,
But yet my nature could not bear it so.
Bru. Well, to our work alive. What do you think
Of marching to Philippi presently?
Cas. I do not think it good.
Bru. Your reason?
Cas. This it is:
'Tis better that the enemy seek us;
So shall he waste his means, weary his soldiers,
Doing himself offense, whilst we, lying still,
Are full of rest, defense, and nimbleness.
Bru. Good reasons must of force give place to better:
The people 'twixt Philippi and this ground
Do stand but in a forc'd affection,
For they have grudg'd us contribution.
The enemy, marching along by them,
By them shall make a fuller number up,
Come on refresh'd, new-added, and encourag'd;
From which advantage shall we cut him off
If at Philippi we do face him there,
These people at our back.
Cas. Hear me, good brother.
Bru. Under your pardon. You must note beside
That we have tried the utmost of our friends,
Our legions are brimful, our cause is ripe:
The enemy increaseth every day;
We, at the height, are ready to decline.
There is a tide in the affairs of men,
Which taken at the flood, leads on to fortune;
Omitted, all the voyage of their life
Is bound in shallows and in miseries.
On such a full sea are we now afloat,
And we must take the current when it serves,
Or lose our ventures.

184. Nothing, Messala. This anomaly is discussed in the introduction to the play. **191. once:** at some time. **192. patience:** fortitude.
194. art: philosophic theory. **196. alive:** of present concern.
197. presently: immediately. **209. new-added:** reinforced.
213. Under your pardon: i.e. allow me to finish.
220. Omitted: missed.
224. our ventures: all that we have risked (literally, merchandise risked in trade).

Cas. Then with your will go on;
We'll along ourselves, and meet them at Philippi.
Bru. The deep of night is crept upon our talk,
And nature must obey necessity,
Which we will niggard with a little rest.
There is no more to say?
Cas. No more. Good night.
Early to-morrow will we rise, and hence.
Bru. Lucius!

Enter Lucius.

My gown. [*Exit Lucius.*]
Farewell, good Messala.
Good night, Titinius. Noble, noble Cassius,
Good night, and good repose.
Cas. O my dear brother!
This was an ill beginning of the night.
Never come such division 'tween our souls!
Let it not, Brutus.

Enter Lucius *with the gown.*

Bru. Every thing is well.
Cas. Good night, my lord.
Bru. Good night, good brother.
Tit., Mes. Good night, Lord Brutus.
Bru. Farewell every one.
Exeunt [all but Brutus and Lucius].
Give me the gown. Where is thy instrument?
Luc. Here in the tent.
Bru. What, thou speak'st drowsily?
Poor knave, I blame thee not, thou art o'erwatch'd.
Call Claudio and some other of my men,
I'll have them sleep on cushions in my tent.
Luc. Varrus and Claudio!

Enter Varrus *and* Claudio.

Var. Calls my lord?
Bru. I pray you, sirs, lie in my tent and sleep;
It may be I shall raise you by and by
On business to my brother Cassius.
Var. So please you, we will stand and watch your pleasure.
Bru. I will not have it so. Lie down, good sirs,
It may be I shall otherwise bethink me.
[*Varrus and Claudio lie down.*]
Look, Lucius, here's the book I sought for so;
I put it in the pocket of my gown.
Luc. I was sure your lordship did not give it me.
Bru. Bear with me, good boy, I am much forgetful.
Canst thou hold up thy heavy eyes awhile,
And touch thy instrument a strain or two?
Luc. Ay, my lord, an't please you.
Bru. It does, my boy.
I trouble thee too much, but thou art willing.
Luc. It is my duty, sir.
Bru. I should not urge thy duty past thy might;
I know young bloods look for a time of rest.

224. with your will: as you wish.
228. niggard: put off with a scant allowance.
241. knave: boy. **o'erwatch'd:** worn out from lack of sleep.
249. watch your pleasure: keep awake and wait for your commands.
251. otherwise . . . me: change my mind. **261. might:** strength.
262. young bloods: youthful constitutions.

Luc. I have slept, my lord, already.
Bru. It was well done, and thou shalt sleep again;
I will not hold thee long. If I do live,
I will be good to thee. *Music, and a song.*
This is a sleepy tune. O murd'rous slumber!
Layest thou thy leaden mace upon my boy,
That plays thee music? Gentle knave, good night;
I will not do thee so much wrong to wake thee.
If thou dost nod, thou break'st thy instrument,
I'll take it from thee; and, good boy, good night.
Let me see, let me see; is not the leaf turn'd down
Where I left reading? Here it is, I think.

Enter the Ghost of Caesar.

How ill this taper burns! Ha! who comes here?
I think it is the weakness of mine eyes
That shapes this monstrous apparition.
It comes upon me. Art thou any thing?
Art thou some god, some angel, or some devil,
That mak'st my blood cold, and my hair to stare?
Speak to me what thou art.
Ghost. Thy evil spirit, Brutus.
Bru. Why com'st thou?
Ghost. To tell thee thou shalt see me at Philippi.
Bru. Well; then I shall see thee again?
Ghost. Ay, at Philippi.
Bru. Why, I will see thee at Philippi then.
[*Exit Ghost.*]
Now I have taken heart thou vanishest.
Ill spirit, I would hold more talk with thee.
Boy, Lucius! Varrus! Claudio! Sirs, awake!
Claudio!
Luc. The strings, my lord, are false.
Bru. He thinks he still is at his instrument.
Lucius, awake!
Luc. My lord?
Bru. Didst thou dream, Lucius, that thou so criedst out?
Luc. My lord, I do not know that I did cry.
Bru. Yes, that thou didst. Didst thou see any thing?
Luc. Nothing, my lord.
Bru. Sleep again, Lucius. Sirrah Claudio!
[*To Varrus.*] Fellow thou, awake!
Var. My lord?
Clau. My lord?
Bru. Why did you so cry out, sirs, in your sleep?
Both [*Var., Clau.*]. Did we, my lord?
Bru. Ay. Saw you any thing?
Var. No, my lord, I saw nothing.
Clau. Nor I, my lord.
Bru. Go and commend me to my brother Cassius;
Bid him set on his pow'rs betimes before,
And we will follow.
Both [*Var., Clau.*]. It shall be done, my lord.
Exeunt.

268. **leaden:** heavy, dulling. **mace:** rod of office, here as used by a sheriff's officer making an arrest.
275. **How . . . burns.** Candles were thought to become dim in the presence of ghosts.
280. **stare:** stand on end. 291. **false:** out of tune.
307. **set . . . before:** advance his troops early in the morning, before me.

ACT V, [Scene I]

Enter Octavius, Antony, *and their army.*

Oct. Now, Antony, our hopes are answered.
You said the enemy would not come down,
But keep the hills and upper regions.
It proves not so: their battles are at hand;
They mean to warn us at Philippi here,
Answering before we do demand of them.
Ant. Tut, I am in their bosoms, and I know
Wherefore they do it. They could be content
To visit other places, and come down
With fearful bravery, thinking by this face
To fasten in our thoughts that they have courage;
But 'tis not so.

Enter a Messenger.

Mess. Prepare you, generals.
The enemy comes on in gallant show;
Their bloody sign of battle is hung out,
And something to be done immediately.
Ant. Octavius, lead your battle softly on
Upon the left hand of the even field.
Oct. Upon the right hand I, keep thou the left.
Ant. Why do you cross me in this exigent?
Oct. I do not cross you; but I will do so. *March.*

Drum. Enter Brutus, Cassius, *and their army;* [Lucilius, Titinius, Messala, *and others*].

Bru. They stand, and would have parley.
Cas. Stand fast, Titinius; we must out and talk.
Oct. Mark Antony, shall we give sign of battle?
Ant. No, Caesar, we will answer on their charge.
Make forth, the generals would have some words.
Oct. Stir not until the signal.
Bru. Words before blows; is it so, countrymen?
Oct. Not that we love words better, as you do.
Bru. Good words are better than bad strokes, Octavius.
Ant. In your bad strokes, Brutus, you give good words;
Witness the hole you made in Caesar's heart,
Crying, "Long live! hail, Caesar!"
Cas. Antony,
The posture of your blows are yet unknown;
But for your words, they rob the Hybla bees,
And leave them honeyless.
Ant. Not stingless too?
Bru. O yes, and soundless too;
For you have stol'n their buzzing, Antony,
And very wisely threat before you sting.
Ant. Villains! you did not so, when your vile daggers
Hack'd one another in the sides of Caesar.

V.i. Location: The plains of Philippi.
4. **battles:** forces. 5. **warn:** challenge.
7. **am . . . bosoms:** know their secrets.
8–9. **could . . . places:** would really prefer to be somewhere else.
10. **fearful bravery:** a fine display to hide their fear. **face:** show of courage. 16. **softly:** slowly. 19. **exigent:** emergency.
24. **answer . . . charge:** retaliate when they attack.
33. **The posture . . . blows:** what kind of blows you can deliver.
34. **Hybla:** a place in Sicily famous for honey.

You show'd your [teeth] like apes, and fawn'd like hounds,
And bow'd like bondmen, kissing Caesar's feet;
Whilst damned Casca, like a cur, behind
Strook Caesar on the neck. O you flatterers!
Cas. Flatterers? Now, Brutus, thank yourself;
This tongue had not offended so to-day,
If Cassius might have rul'd.
Oct. Come, come, the cause. If arguing make us sweat,
The proof of it will turn to redder drops.
Look,
I draw a sword against conspirators;
When think you that the sword goes up again?
Never, till Caesar's three and thirty wounds
Be well aveng'd; or till another Caesar
Have added slaughter to the sword of traitors.
Bru. Caesar, thou canst not die by traitors' hands,
Unless thou bring'st them with thee.
Oct. So I hope;
I was not born to die on Brutus' sword.
Bru. O, if thou wert the noblest of thy strain,
Young man, thou couldst not die more honorable.
Cas. A peevish schoolboy, worthless of such honor,
Join'd with a masker and a reveller!
Ant. Old Cassius still!
Oct. Come, Antony; away!
Defiance, traitors, hurl we in your teeth.
If you dare fight to-day, come to the field;
If not, when you have stomachs.
Exeunt Octavius, Antony, and army.
Cas. Why now blow wind, swell billow, and swim bark!
The storm is up, and all is on the hazard.
Bru. Ho, Lucilius, hark, a word with you.
Lucilius and [then] Messala stand forth.
Lucil. My lord.
[Brutus and Lucilius converse apart.]
Cas. Messala!
Mes. What says my general?
Cas. Messala,
This is my birthday; as this very day
Was Cassius born. Give me thy hand, Messala.
Be thou my witness that against my will
(As Pompey was) am I compell'd to set
Upon one battle all our liberties.
You know that I held Epicurus strong,
And his opinion; now I change my mind,
And partly credit things that do presage.
Coming from Sardis, on our former ensign
Two mighty eagles fell, and there they perch'd,
Gorging and feeding from our soldiers' hands,
Who to Philippi here consorted us.
This morning are they fled away and gone,
And in their steads do ravens, crows, and kites
Fly o'er our heads, and downward look on us
As we were sickly prey. Their shadows seem
A canopy most fatal, under which
Our army lies, ready to give up the ghost.
Mes. Believe not so.
Cas. I but believe it partly,
For I am fresh of spirit, and resolv'd
To meet all perils very constantly.
Bru. Even so, Lucilius.
Cas. Now, most noble Brutus,
The gods to-day stand friendly, that we may,
Lovers in peace, lead on our days to age!
But since the affairs of men rests still incertain,
Let's reason with the worst that may befall.
If we do lose this battle, then is this
The very last time we shall speak together:
What are you then determined to do?
Bru. Even by the rule of that philosophy
By which I did blame Cato for the death
Which he did give himself—I know not how,
But I do find it cowardly and vile,
For fear of what might fall, so to prevent
The time of life—arming myself with patience
To stay the providence of some high powers
That govern us below.
Cas. Then, if we lose this battle,
You are contented to be led in triumph
Thorough the streets of Rome?
Bru. No, Cassius, no. Think not, thou noble Roman,
That ever Brutus will go bound to Rome;
He bears too great a mind. But this same day
Must end that work the ides of March begun.
And whether we shall meet again I know not;
Therefore our everlasting farewell take:
For ever, and for ever, farewell, Cassius!
If we do meet again, why, we shall smile;
If not, why then this parting was well made.
Cas. For ever, and for ever, farewell, Brutus!
If we do meet again, we'll smile indeed;
If not, 'tis true this parting was well made.
Bru. Why then lead on. O that a man might know
The end of this day's business ere it come!
But it sufficeth that the day will end,
And then the end is known. Come ho, away!
Exeunt.

41. show'd your teeth: grinned.
47. rul'd: prevailed (see II.i.155–61).
48. the cause: to the business in hand. **49. proof:** test, trial.
52. goes up: will be sheathed.
55. added slaughter to: been slaughtered by.
59. strain: family line.
62. masker . . . reveller. On Antony's fondness for revelry (which becomes a major element in *Antony and Cleopatra*) see I.ii.28–29, 203–4, II.i.188–89, II.ii.116.
66. stomachs: appetites, i.e. a desire to fight.
68. on the hazard: at stake. **71. as:** as of. **74. set:** stake.
76. Epicurus. Epicureans thought the gods uninterested in men and so had no belief in omens and portents.
79. former ensign: foremost banner. **80. fell:** swooped down.
82. consorted: accompanied.
84. ravens . . . kites. Eaters of carrion, and hence not only regarded as ignoble (in contrast to the kingly eagles) but traditionally believed to forebode death where they appeared.
86. As: as if. **93. The gods . . . stand:** may the gods . . . be.
94. Lovers: close friends. **96. reason with:** consider.
99. are . . . determined: have . . . decided.
100. philosophy: i.e. Stoicism.
101. Cato: Brutus' father-in-law (see note to II.i.295), who fought on Pompey's side and killed himself at Utica when about to be taken by Caesar.
104–5. prevent The time: i.e. cut short the natural duration.
106. stay: wait for.
108. in triumph: i.e. as a captive in a triumphal procession.
111. bound: in fetters.

[Scene II]

Alarum. Enter Brutus *and* Messala.

Bru. Ride, ride, Messala, ride, and give these bills
Unto the legions on the other side. *Loud alarum.*
Let them set on at once; for I perceive
But cold demeanor in Octavio's wing,
And sudden push gives them the overthrow.
Ride, ride, Messala, let them all come down. *Exeunt.*

[Scene III]

Alarums. Enter Cassius *and* Titinius.

Cas. O, look, Titinius, look, the villains fly!
Myself have to mine own turn'd enemy.
This ensign here of mine was turning back;
I slew the coward, and did take it from him.
Tit. O Cassius, Brutus gave the word too early,
Who, having some advantage on Octavius,
Took it too eagerly. His soldiers fell to spoil,
Whilst we by Antony are all enclos'd.

Enter Pindarus.

Pin. Fly further off, my lord, fly further off;
Mark Antony is in your tents, my lord;
Fly therefore, noble Cassius, fly far off.
Cas. This hill is far enough. Look, look, Titinius,
Are those my tents where I perceive the fire?
Tit. They are, my lord.
Cas. Titinius, if thou lovest me,
Mount thou my horse, and hide thy spurs in him
Till he have brought thee up to yonder troops
And here again, that I may rest assur'd
Whether yond troops are friend or enemy.
Tit. I will be here again, even with a thought.
Exit.
Cas. Go, Pindarus, get higher on that hill;
My sight was ever thick; regard Titinius,
And tell me what thou not'st about the field.
[*Pindarus goes up.*]
This day I breathed first: time is come round,
And where I did begin, there shall I end;
My life is run his compass. Sirrah, what news?
Pin. (*Above.*) O my lord!
Cas. What news?
Pin. Titinius is enclosed round about
With horsemen, that make to him on the spur,
Yet he spurs on. Now they are almost on him.
Now, Titinius! Now some light. O, he lights too.
He's ta'en. (*Shout.*) And hark, they shout for joy.
Cas. Come down, behold no more.
O, coward that I am, to live so long,
To see my best friend ta'en before my face!
Pindarus [*descends*].
Come hither, sirrah.
In Parthia did I take thee prisoner,
And then I swore thee, saving of thy life,
That whatsoever I did bid thee do,
Thou shouldst attempt it. Come now, keep thine oath;
Now be a freeman, and with this good sword,
That ran through Caesar's bowels, search this bosom.
Stand not to answer; here, take thou the hilts,
And when my face is cover'd, as 'tis now,
Guide thou the sword. [*Pindarus stabs him.*] Caesar,
thou art reveng'd,
Even with the sword that kill'd thee. [*Dies.*]
Pin. So, I am free; yet would not so have been,
Durst I have done my will. O Cassius,
Far from this country Pindarus shall run,
Where never Roman shall take note of him. [*Exit.*]

Enter Titinius *and* Messala.

Mes. It is but change, Titinius; for Octavius
Is overthrown by noble Brutus' power,
As Cassius' legions are by Antony.
Tit. These tidings will well comfort Cassius.
Mes. Where did you leave him?
Tit. All disconsolate,
With Pindarus his bondman, on this hill.
Mes. Is not that he that lies upon the ground?
Tit. He lies not like the living. O my heart!
Mes. Is not that he?
Tit. No, this was he, Messala,
But Cassius is no more. O setting sun,
As in thy red rays thou dost sink to-night,
So in his red blood Cassius' day is set!
The sun of Rome is set. Our day is gone,
Clouds, dews, and dangers come; our deeds are done!
Mistrust of my success hath done this deed.
Mes. Mistrust of good success hath done this deed.
O hateful error, melancholy's child,
Why dost thou show to the apt thoughts of men
The things that are not? O error, soon conceiv'd,
Thou never com'st unto a happy birth,
But kill'st the mother that engend'red thee!
Tit. What, Pindarus? Where art thou, Pindarus?
Mes. Seek him, Titinius, whilst I go to meet
The noble Brutus, thrusting this report
Into his ears; I may say "thrusting" it;
For piercing steel, and darts envenomed,
Shall be as welcome to the ears of Brutus
As tidings of this sight.
Tit. Hie you, Messala,
And I will seek for Pindarus the while.
[*Exit Messala.*]
Why didst thou send me forth, brave Cassius?
Did I not meet thy friends? and did not they
Put on my brows this wreath of victory,
And bid me give it thee? Didst thou not hear their
shouts?

V.ii. Location: Scene continues. o.s.d. **Alarum:** call to arms.
1. **bills:** written orders. 4. **cold demeanor:** lack of spirit.

V.iii. Location: Scene continues.
3. **ensign:** standard-bearer. 4. **it:** i.e. the standard.
7. **spoil:** looting. 19. **with a thought:** as quick as thought.
21. **thick:** dim, short. **regard:** observe.
29. **make . . . spur:** ride rapidly toward him. 31. **light:** alight.
38. **swore thee:** made you swear. **saving of:** when I spared.
42. **search:** penetrate. 51. **change:** exchange (of advantage).
64. **dews.** Damps and dew were thought to favor infection and illness.
65. **Mistrust . . . success:** fears as to the outcome of my mission.
67. **melancholy's child.** Because sufferers from melancholy imagine non-existent evils. 68. **apt:** only too ready (to be deceived).
71. **the mother:** here, the deluded melancholic, i.e. Cassius.

Alas, thou hast misconstrued every thing.
But hold thee, take this garland on thy brow;
Thy Brutus bid me give it thee, and I
Will do his bidding. Brutus, come apace,
And see how I regarded Caius Cassius.
By your leave, gods!—this is a Roman's part.
Come, Cassius' sword, and find Titinius' heart. *Dies.*

Alarum. Enter BRUTUS, MESSALA, *young* CATO, STRATO, VOLUMNIUS, *and* LUCILIUS.

Bru. Where, where, Messala, doth his body lie?
Mes. Lo yonder, and Titinius mourning it.
Bru. Titinius' face is upward.
Cato. He is slain.
Bru. O Julius Caesar, thou art mighty yet!
Thy spirit walks abroad, and turns our swords
In our own proper entrails. *Low alarums.*
Cato. Brave Titinius!
Look whe'er he have not crown'd dead Cassius!
Bru. Are yet two Romans living such as these?
The last of all the Romans, fare thee well!
It is impossible that ever Rome
Should breed thy fellow. Friends, I owe moe tears
To this dead man than you shall see me pay.
I shall find time, Cassius; I shall find time.
Come therefore, and to [Thasos] send his body;
His funerals shall not be in our camp,
Lest it discomfort us. Lucilius, come,
And come, young Cato, let us to the field,
Labio and Flavio set our battles on.
'Tis three a' clock, and, Romans, yet ere night
We shall try fortune in a second fight. *Exeunt.*

[SCENE IV]

Alarum. Enter BRUTUS, MESSALA, [*young*] CATO, LUCILIUS, *and* FLAVIUS.

Bru. Yet, countrymen! O yet, hold up your heads! [*Exit.*]
Cato. What bastard doth not? Who will go with me?
I will proclaim my name about the field.
I am the son of Marcus Cato, ho!
A foe to tyrants, and my country's friend.
I am the son of Marcus Cato, ho!

Enter SOLDIERS *and fight.*

[*Lucil.*] And I am Brutus, Marcus Brutus, I,
Brutus, my country's friend; know me for Brutus!
[*Young Cato is slain.*]
O young and noble Cato, art thou down?
Why, now thou diest as bravely as Titinius,
And mayst be honor'd, being Cato's son.
[*1.*] *Sold.* Yield, or thou diest.
Lucil. Only I yield to die;
There is so much that thou wilt kill me straight:
Kill Brutus, and be honor'd in his death.
[*1.*] *Sold.* We must not. A noble prisoner!

Enter ANTONY.

2. Sold. Room ho! Tell Antony, Brutus is ta'en.
1. Sold. I'll tell [the] news. Here comes the general.
Brutus is ta'en, Brutus is ta'en, my lord!
Ant. Where is he?
Lucil. Safe, Antony, Brutus is safe enough.
I dare assure thee that no enemy
Shall ever take alive the noble Brutus;
The gods defend him from so great a shame!
When you do find him, or alive or dead,
He will be found like Brutus, like himself.
Ant. This is not Brutus, friend, but, I assure you,
A prize no less in worth. Keep this man safe,
Give him all kindness; I had rather have
Such men my friends than enemies. Go on,
And see whe'er Brutus be alive or dead,
And bring us word unto Octavius' tent
How every thing is chanc'd. *Exeunt.*

[SCENE V]

Enter BRUTUS, DARDANIUS, CLITUS, STRATO, *and* VOLUMNIUS.

Bru. Come, poor remains of friends, rest on this rock.
Cli. Statilius show'd the torchlight, but, my lord,
He came not back. He is or ta'en or slain.
Bru. Sit thee down, Clitus; slaying is the word,
It is a deed in fashion. Hark thee, Clitus.
[*Whispering.*]
Cli. What, I, my lord? No, not for all the world.
Bru. Peace then, no words.
Cli. I'll rather kill myself.
Bru. Hark thee, Dardanius. [*Whispering.*]
Dar. Shall I do such a deed?
Cli. O Dardanius!
Dar. O Clitus!
Cli. What ill request did Brutus make to thee?
Dar. To kill him, Clitus. Look, he meditates.
Cli. Now is that noble vessel full of grief,
That it runs over even at his eyes.
Bru. Come hither, good Volumnius; list a word.
Vol. What says my lord?
Bru. Why, this, Volumnius:
The ghost of Caesar hath appear'd to me
Two several times by night; at Sardis once,
And this last night, here in Philippi fields.
I know my hour is come.
Vol. Not so, my lord.
Bru. Nay, I am sure it is, Volumnius.
Thou seest the world, Volumnius, how it goes;

96. own proper: own. **97. Look . . . not:** i.e. see how he has.
104. Thasos: an island near Philippi. Plutarch records that Cassius was buried there.

V.iv. Location: Scene continues.
2. What . . . not: who is so base as not to do so.
12. Only . . . die: I yield only in order to die (not to escape death).
13. There . . . straight: here is what will make you kill me at once (i.e. the announcement in the next line that he is Brutus).

V.v. Location: Scene continues.
2. show'd the torchlight: i.e. as a signal.

Our enemies have beat us to the pit. *Low alarums.*
It is more worthy to leap in ourselves
Than tarry till they push us. Good Volumnius,
Thou know'st that we two went to school together;
Even for that our love of old, I prithee
Hold thou my sword-hilts, whilest I run on it.
Vol. That's not an office for a friend, my lord.
Alarum still.
Cli. Fly, fly, my lord, there is no tarrying here.
Bru. Farewell to you, and you, and you, Volumnius.
Strato, thou hast been all this while asleep;
Farewell to thee too, Strato. Countrymen,
My heart doth joy that yet in all my life
I found no man but he was true to me.
I shall have glory by this losing day
More than Octavius and Mark Antony
By this vile conquest shall attain unto.
So fare you well at once, for Brutus' tongue
Hath almost ended his live's history.
Night hangs upon mine eyes, my bones would rest,
That have but labor'd to attain this hour.
Alarum. Cry within, "Fly, fly, fly!"
Cli. Fly, my lord, fly.
Bru. Hence! I will follow.
[*Exeunt Clitus, Dardanius, and Volumnius.*]
I prithee, Strato, stay thou by thy lord.
Thou art a fellow of a good respect;
Thy life hath had some smatch of honor in it.
Hold then my sword, and turn away thy face,
While I do run upon it. Wilt thou, Strato?
Stra. Give me your hand first. Fare you well, my lord.
Bru. Farewell, good Strato. [*Runs on his sword.*]
Caesar, now be still,
I kill'd not thee with half so good a will. *Dies.*

Alarum. Retreat. Enter ANTONY, OCTAVIUS, MESSALA, LUCILIUS, *and the army.*

23. beat: driven. **pit:** (1) hole into which an animal is driven to be captured; (2) grave. **45. respect:** reputation.
46. smatch: smack, taste.

Oct. What man is that?
Mes. My master's man. Strato, where is thy master?
Stra. Free from the bondage you are in, Messala;
The conquerors can but make a fire of him;
For Brutus only overcame himself,
And no man else hath honor by his death.
Lucil. So Brutus should be found. I thank thee, Brutus,
That thou hast prov'd Lucilius' saying true.
Oct. All that serv'd Brutus, I will entertain them.
Fellow, wilt thou bestow thy time with me?
Stra. Ay, if Messala will prefer me to you.
Oct. Do so, good Messala.
Mes. How died my master, Strato?
Stra. I held the sword, and he did run on it.
Mes. Octavius, then take him to follow thee,
That did the latest service to my master.
Ant. This was the noblest Roman of them all:
All the conspirators, save only he,
Did that they did in envy of great Caesar;
He, only in a general honest thought
And common good to all, made one of them.
His life was gentle, and the elements
So mix'd in him that Nature might stand up
And say to all the world, "This was a man!"
Oct. According to his virtue let us use him,
With all respect and rites of burial.
Within my tent his bones to-night shall lie,
Most like a soldier, ordered honorably.
So call the field to rest, and let's away,
To part the glories of this happy day. *Exeunt omnes.*

56. Brutus . . . himself: i.e. only Brutus conquered Brutus.
59. Lucilius' saying. See V.iv. 21–25.
60. entertain: take into service. **61. bestow:** employ.
62. prefer: recommend. **67. latest:** last.
71–72. He . . . them: he alone joined the conspiracy out of honorable concern for the common weal.
73. gentle: noble. **the elements:** the four bodily fluids, or humors, recognized by the old physiology as determinants of a man's temperament.
74. mix'd: balanced. **76. use:** treat.
79. ordered honorably: treated with respect.
80. field: army. **81. part:** share.

NOTE ON THE TEXT

The First Folio (1623) is the sole authority for *Julius Caesar*; all later editions are derived from that source. Two dated (1684 and 1691) and four undated so-called actors' quartos were published during the Restoration period.

Bowers (1978) proposed that the F1 text was most probably printed from a careful scribal transcript made from Shakespeare's "foul papers," the transcript having then been marked up by the book-keeper or some other theatrical agent in preparation for using it as copy for an official prompt-book; but Dorsch (1953) while also arguing for a transcript from "foul papers," suggested that this transcript itself was used as the official prompt-book and served as copy for the F1 text, a view endorsed by Jowett/Wells (1987), in great part because serious question has been thrown on the widely held theory that the F1 text of *Julius Caesar* shows quite extensive revision (see below). Use of a manuscript in Shakespeare's hand is made most unlikely by the absence of characteristically Shakespearean spellings in the F1 text. Good evidence of theatre provenience may be seen in the unusually careful stage directions, the consistently clear speech-prefixes, and the number of off-stage sounds indicated.

The text as a whole is a good one; in fact, it has been called the best printed play in F1. Even so, the F1 text is not without its problems. Best known, of course, is the twice-told tale of Portia's suicide in IV.iii. In the first account (lines 143–62, plus 166), which occurs as the final part of what has been argued is a larger revision (lines 124–62, plus 166), that begins with the entry of the angry Poet, Brutus confides Portia's death to Cassius, using it as an excuse to explain his ill temper in his argument with Cassius earlier in the scene. In the second account (lines 181–95), Brutus, professing ignorance, is informed of Portia's death by Messala. Brents Stirling argues that this second account is the original version and may be identified as such by its consistent use of the speech-prefix *Cassi.* for Cassius, the form used throughout the F1 text except in lines 124–62, plus 166 (and in II.i; see below), where the speech-prefix suddenly changes to *Cas.* or occasionally, *Cass.* More recently, however, Clayton and Jowett, independently, find the revision theory, at least so far as it is based on these two variant blocks of speech-prefixes in II.i and IV.iii, unacceptable. They demonstrate that the change from *Cassi.* to *Cas.* (or *Cass.*) results from the severe drain on a compositor's stock of the *ssi* ligature, heavily used in both the speech-prefix and the name *Cassius*, which, like other proper names in the F1 text always appears in italics. They very neatly tie up their argument by noting that, aside from the absence of the speech-prefix *Cassi.* in these two passages claimed as revisions, within the text proper the name *Cassius* is also spelled without the *ssi* ligature (i.e., the first italic "long *s*" is followed by an italic "short *s*")—in other words, the compositor, having exhausted his supply of the *ssi* ligature, was forced to use either an italic "short *s*" or a "long *ss*" ligature. This evidence successfully negates the main reason for considering any part of II.i as revised, though it should be noted, perhaps, that Shakespeare does seem to have changed his original intention by introducing a group of six of the principal conspirators at line 85 in place of two (Cassius and Casca) as earlier promised in I.iii.153–4. Dismissal of the speech-prefix evidence leaves the case for revision in IV.iii depending solely on the apparent contradiction between the Brutus/Cassius and the Messala/Brutus accounts of Portia's death. Although perhaps most critics still treat the two accounts as alternative versions that call for the dropping of the Messala/Brutus account, Clayton and Jowett (following W. D. Smith, 1953) strongly argue for the view that there is no necessary revision here (or in II.i.59–222) and that the two accounts are complementary, not alternatives, the first (Brutus/Cassius) allowing us to see into the private Brutus, a man badly shaken and deeply moved by his wife's suicide, and the second (Messala/Brutus) displaying the public Brutus, a general that smothers his true feelings under the cloak of his duty as a responsible leader, even though, like a politician, he must lie and angle for the opportunity to do so, a sacrifice of "truth" that even a Brutus, as a public figure, cannot, either unconsciously or (sadly) consciously, wholly evade.

One other point relating to the F1 text, because it presents us with a unique situation, deserves notice. In *Timber, or Discoveries*, Ben Jonson quotes a line from *Julius Caesar* (see III.i.47–8), which he claims "could not escape laughter." An unspecified character, addressing Caesar, is quoted as saying, "Caesar, thou dost me wrong.", to which Caesar replied, "Caesar did never wrong, but with just cause."—a line (quoted again in the Induction to *The Staple of News*, acted in 1625) that Jonson dubs "ridiculous." Actually, the line only appears on first sight to be ridiculous and can properly be taken to mean in Elizabethan terms, "Caesar never did hurt or injury without a valid reason." In response to Jonson's criticism, Shakespeare (or someone else) is supposed to have altered the offending line, reading "Know, Caesar doth not wrong, nor without cause / Will he be satisfied." We do not know when Jonson made his comment, since *Discoveries*, not published until 1640/41, is a series of more or less unorganized comments "made upon men and [literary] matter," any one of which could have been recorded, most probably, between 1623 (the year in which Jonson's manuscripts perished in a fire) and 1637, the year of Jonson's death, but the fact that he thought the peccant line was worth parodying as late as 1625 (see above) would seem to suggest that it had only recently caught his attention, which in turn suggests that the change in the F1 text was made some years after Shakespeare's death (1616). The statement ("Caesar, thou dost me wrong.") which elicited Caesar's reply does not occur in the F1 text, though Jonson may perhaps have picked it up from Cassius' comment to Brutus in IV.ii.37, "Most noble brother, you have done me wrong." As early as 1778, Thomas Tyrwhitt proposed combining Jonson's line with the F1 text: "Know, Caesar doth not wrong, but with just cause; / Nor without cause will he be satisfied."—an arrangement that neatly completes the dangling half-line (l. 48) in the F1 text. Aside from Hudson (1880/81), no other editor, to my knowledge, has incorporated the additional phrase ("but with just cause") into the text until Jowett/Wells. For a full discussion of the textual and critical history of Jonson's comment, see J. J. Furness, Jr., New Variorum *Julius Caesar* (1913), 136–40, and J. D. Wilson, "Ben Jonson and *Julius Caesar*," *S.Sur.*, II (1949), 36–43.

The present edition has retained the occasional use of Italianate forms of character names, such as *Antonio, Claudio, Flavio, Octavio*, since there is no reason to doubt that they represent what Shakespeare actually wrote. *Antonius*, for example, the form adopted by most editors since Pope, does not occur in the F1 text, and the form *Anthonio* (side by side with *Anthonius*) appears twice in the later *Antony and Cleopatra*, a play believed to have been set from some form of Shakespeare's manuscript. Similarly, *Varrus* has been retained in preference to the usual editorial *Varro*, however superior as a Latin form *Varro* is.

For further information, see: J. D. Wilson, ed., New Shakespeare *Julius Caesar* (Cambridge, 1949); Warren D. Smith, "The Duplicate Revelations of Portia's Death," *SQ* IV (1953), 153–61; W. W. Greg, *The Shakespeare First Folio* (Oxford, 1955); T. S. Dorsch, ed., New Arden *Julius Caesar* (London, 1955); Brents Stirling, "*Julius Caesar* in Revision," *SQ* XIII (1962), 187–205; Maurice Charney, ed., *Julius Caesar* (Indianapolis and New York, 1969); F. T. Bowers, "The Copy for Shakespeare's *Julius Caesar*," *South Atlantic Bulletin*, XLIII (1978), 23–36; J. K. Rogers, "The Folio Composition of *Julius Caesar*," *AEB*, VI (1982), 143–72; Thomas Clayton, "Shall Brutus Never Taste of Portia's Death but Once?: Text and Performance in *Julius Caesar*," *SEL*, XXIII (1983), 247–55; Arthur Humphreys, ed., New Oxford *Julius Caesar* (Oxford, 1984); John Jowett, "Ligature Shortage and Speech-prefix Variation in *Julius Caesar*," *The Library*, 6th ser., VI (1984), 244–53; Stanley Wells, Gary Taylor, John Jowett, William Montgomery, *William Shakespeare: A Textual Companion* (Oxford, 1987); Marvin Spevack, ed., New Cambridge *Julius Caesar* (Cambridge, 1988).

TEXTUAL NOTES

Dramatis personae: ***subs. as given in Rowe (earlier lists in Folger and Douai MSS)***

Act-scene division: ***F1 marks acts only, except I.i; other scene divisions from Rowe and later editors (see first note to each scene); present act-scene arrangement as a whole first established by Capell***

I.i

Location: *Rowe, Theobald*

o.s.d. **Murellus]** *F1 (throughout); eds., following Theobald, usually read* Marullus *(so Plutarch)*

14 soles] *F4* (soals); soules *F1*

30, 49 holiday] *Theobald;* Holy-day *and* Holyday *F1*

37 Pompey? Many . . . oft] *Folger, Douai MSS, Rowe;* Pompey many . . . oft? *F1*

61 whe'er] *Theobald;* where *F1*

61 metal] *Johnson;* mettle *F1*

I.ii

I.ii] *Pope*

Location: *Capell*

o.s.d. Citizens, and] *Sisson*
3 Antonio's] *the F1 form, here and elsewhere, has been retained since it occurs twice in* Antony and Cleopatra *(II.ii.7, II.v.26), a play believed to have been set from Shakespeare's autograph; Pope first introduced the more "Roman" form* Antonius', *which does not occur in the F1 text*
11 s.d. Flourish.] *Globe (after Capell)*
24 s.d. Manent] *F2;* Manet *F1*
139 some time] *F3;* sometime *F1*
143 yours?] *F2;* yours *F1*
166 (so with] *Theobald;* so (with *F1*
214 s.d. Casca stays.] *Capell*
222 a-shouting] *hyphen, Dyce*
254 like,] *Rowe;* like *F1*
268 rogues.] *Rowe (subs.);* Rogues, *F1*
276 away?] *Theobald;* away. *F1*

I.iii

I.iii] *Capell*
Location: *Capell*
o.s.d. from opposite sides] *Capell*
o.s.d. with . . . drawn] *Capell*
10 tempest dropping fire] *Rowe;* Tempest-dropping-fire *F1*
33 strange-disposed] *hyphen, Theobald*
42 this!] *Dyce;* this? *F1*
111 Caesar!] *Knight;* Caesar. *F1*
124 honorable-dangerous] *hyphen, Capell*
125 know, by this] *Rowe;* know by this, *F1*
129 In favor's] *Q(1691);* Is Fauors, *F1*
137 this!] *Rann;* this? *F1*

II.i

II.i] *Rowe*
Location: *Malone (after Theobald)*
23 climber-upward] *hyphen, Warburton*
40 ides] *Theobald-Warburton;* first *F1*
52 What,] *Rowe;* What *F1*
60, 76 s.dd. Exit Lucius.] *Theobald*
83 path,] *F2;* path *F1*
115 time's] *Rowe;* times *F1*
118 high-sighted tyranny] *Rowe;* high-sighted-Tyranny *F1*
122 women,] *Collier;* women. *F1*
129 cautelous,] *F3;* Cautelous *F1*
136 oath;] *Hanmer (subs.);* Oath. *F1*
157 Caesar.] *Rowe (subs.);* Caesar, *F1*
187 Caesar;] *F2 (subs.);* Caesar, *F1*
230 honey-heavy dew] *Theobald;* hony-heauy-Dew *F1*
267 his] *F2;* hit *F1*
274 yourself, your half,] *Pope (after F4);* your selfe; your halfe *F1*
280 the] *F2;* tho *F1*
295 well reputed,] *Capell (subs.);* well reputed: *F1*
309 s.d. Enter . . . Ligarius.] *placed as in Dyce; after s.d.* Exit Portia. *l. 309, F1*
312 s.d. Exit Lucius.] *Capell*
313 s.p. Lig.] *Capell;* Cai. *F1 (throughout)*

II.ii

II.ii] *Rowe*
Location: *Globe (afterRowe)*
23 did] *F2;* do *F1*
46 are] *Upton conj.;* heare *F1 (graphically Theobald's* were *is tempting, but the context seems to demand the present tense)*
76 statuë] *Keightley (after Steevens);* Statue *F1*
89 relics] *Rowe;* Reliques *F1*
93 now:] *Rann (after Capell);* now, *F1*
124 s.d. aside] *Douai MS, Rowe*
128 s.d. Aside.] *Douai MS, Pope*

II.iii

II.iii] *Rowe*
Location: *Capell*
o.s.d. reading a paper] *Rowe*
1 s.p. Art.] *Capell*

II.iv

II.iv] *Capell*
Location: *Capell (subs.)*
3 dost] *F3;* doest *F1*
18 bustling] *Rowe;* bussling *F1*
36 almost] *Rowe;* (almost) *F1*
46 s.d. severally] *Theobald*

III.i

III.i] *Rowe*
Location: *Globe (subs., after Rowe)*
o.s.d. Popilius] *F2 (om.* Publius*)*
3 schedule] *F3;* Scedule *F1*
12 s.d. Caesar . . . following.] *Steevens (after Capell)*
14 s.d. Leaves . . . Caesar.] *Capell*
26 s.d. Exeunt . . . Trebonius.] *Capell*
35 s.d. Kneeling.] *Rowe*
39 law] *Johnson conj.;* lane *F1*
43 Low-crooked curtsies] *Theobald;* Low-crooked-curtsies *F1*
45 dost] *F3;* doest *F1*
61 true-fix'd] *hyphen, Capell*
77 Brute] *F2;* Brutè *F1*
95 s.d. Exeunt . . . Conspirators.] *Capell*
113 states] *F2;* State *F1*
115 lies] *F2;* lye *F1*
170–1 Rome— . . . pity—] *Pope (subs.);* Rome, . . . pitty *F1*
198–9 foes, . . . corse?] *Rowe;* Foes? . . . Coarse, *F1*
206 lethe] *Warburton (after* Lethe *F2);* Lethee *F1*
208 heart] *Theobald;* Hart *F1*
209 strooken] *Capell;* stroken *F1;* stricken *F2*
225 you,] *Theobald;* you *F1*
232 s.d. Aside to Brutus.] *Rowe (subs.)*
254 s.p. Ant.] *Rowe*
269 deeds;] *F4 (subs.);* deeds, *F1*
275 s.d. Octavio's] *so F1 (cf. V.ii.4); eds. since Rowe (except Charney) read* Octavius's *or* Octavius'
281 s.d. Seeing the body.] *Rowe*
283 catching, for] *F2;* catching from *F1*
291 corse] *F3 (*Coarse*);* course *F1*
297 s.d. with Caesar's body] *Rowe*

III.ii

III.ii] *Rowe*
Location: *Rowe*
o.s.d. Brutus] *as Capell;* Brutus and goes into the Pulpit, *F1 (see l. 10 s.d.)*
1 s.p. Plebeians.] *Kittredge (after Dyce);* Ple. *F1*
7, 10 rendered] *Pope;* rendred *F1*
10 s.d. Exit . . . Plebeians.] *Rowe (subs.)*
10 s.d. Brutus . . . pulpit.] *Capell (subs.), from F1 o.s.d.*
40 s.d. and others] *Malone (after Capell)*
65 s.d. Goes . . . pulpit.] *Globe (after Capell)*
92–3 stuff: . . . ambitious,] *F4;* stuffe, . . . Ambitious: *F1*
101 am] *F3;* am, *F1*
104 art] *F2;* are *F1*
131 Which, pardon me,] *Rowe;* (Which pardon me) *F1*
157 will?] *Pope;* Will: *F1*
163 s.d. Antony . . . pulpit.] *Rowe (subs., after l. 161); placed as in Capell*
177 away,] *F4;* away: *F1*
188 statuë] *Keightley (after Malone conj.);* Statue *F1*
196 s.d. Lifting Caesar's mantle.] *Neilson*
204 s.p. All.] *White; lines continued to 2. Pleb., F1*
204–5 Revenge . . . live!] *as prose, Pope; as verse, F1*
221 wit] *F2;* writ *F1*
249 Tiber;] *Theobald;* Tyber, *F1*
250 pleasures,] *Rowe;* pleasures *F1*
259 s.d. Exeunt . . . body.] *Rowe;* Exit Plebeians. *F1*
261 s.d. Enter Servant.] *placed as in Capell; after l. 261, F1*
271 mov'd] *Rowe;* moued *F1*

III.iii

III.iii] *Capell*
Location: *Capell*
36–8 Brutus', to Cassius' . . . Decius' . . . Ligarius'] *Capell;* Brutus, to Cassius . . . Decius . . . Ligarius *F1*
38 s.d. dragging off Cinna] *Dorsch (after Collier)*

IV.i

IV.i] *Rowe*
Location: *Capell (subs.)*
32–3 on, . . . spirit;] *Rowe;* on: . . . Spirit, *F1*
33 motion govern'd] *Pope;* Motion, gouern'd *F1*
36 barren-spirited] *hyphen, Pope*
37 imitations,] *Rowe;* Imitations. *F1*
41 Brutus] *F2;* Brntus *F1*
44 our means stretch'd] and our best meanes stretcht out *F2*
49 bay'd] *Pope;* bayed *F1*

IV.ii

IV.ii] *Rowe*
Location: *Rowe*
o.s.d. Lucius] *Capell*
13 Lucilius,] *F3;* Lucillius *F1*
34–6 s.pp. 1. Sol. . . . 2. Sol. . . . 3. Sol.] *Globe (after Capell)*
50–2 Lucius . . . Lucilius] *Craik;* Lucillius . . . Lucius *F1*
52 s.d. Manent] *F2;* Manet *F1*
52 s.d. who . . . without] *ed.*

IV.iii

IV.iii] *Pope (but the F1 s.d. at the end of IV.ii makes it clear that no scene break is intended here, though the action moves to another part of the stage)*
Location: *Theobald, ed.*
5 man,] *F2 (which also reads* Letter *in l. 4);* man *F1*
19 justice'] *Capell;* Iustice *F1*
22 foremost] *Rowe;* Formost *F1*
32 not,] *Hanmer;* not *F1*
60 not?] *Kittredge (after Rowe);* not. *F1*
116 ill-temper'd] *F2 (hyphen, Rowe);* ill remper'd *F1*
123 s.d. to . . . guard] *ed.*
128 s.d. Brutus . . . tent.] *ed. (based on s.d. following l. 123 in Folger, Douai MSS:* they come forward
142 s.d. Exeunt . . . Titinius.] *Rowe*
142 s.d. To Lucius within.] *ed.*
142 s.d. Brutus . . . tent.] *ed.*
162 s.d. Drinks.] *Capell*
162 s.d. Exit Lucius.] *Globe (after* Titinius. *l. 163); placed as in Kittredge*
173 outlawry] *F4;* Outlarie *F1*
180–1 proscription. Had] *F3;* proscription / Had *F1*
181–95 Had . . . so.] *these lines are generally taken as Shakespeare's first version of the report of Portia's death, his second and final version being represented by ll. 143–58, 166*
209 new-added] *hyphen, Capell*
210 off] *Rowe (subs.);* off. *F1*
229 say?] *Capell;* say. *F1*
231 s.d. Enter Lucius.] *placed as in Globe; after l. 230, F1*
231 s.d. Exit Lucius.] *Hanmer*
238 s.d. all . . . Lucius] *Neilson (after Capell)*
242, 244 Claudio, Varrus] *F1 consistently uses these forms; eds. since Rowe (except Charney) read* Claudius *and* Varro
251 s.d. Varrus . . . down.] *Malone (subs., after Capell)*
267 slumber] *F3;* slumbler *F1*
286 s.d. Exit Ghost.] *Rowe (after l. 285); placed as in Dyce*
294, 301, 302 lord?] *Dyce;* Lord. *F1*
296 Lucius] *F2;* Lucus *F1*
300 s.d. To Varrus.] *Globe (subs., after Warburton conj.)*
304, 308 s.pp. Var., Clau.] *Capell*

V.i

V.i] *Rowe*
Location: *Capell (after Rowe)*
20 s.d. Lucilius . . . others] *Capell*
35 too?] *Delius conj.;* too. *F1*
41 teeth] *F3;* teethes *F1*

60 **Young man]** *Rowe;* Yong-man *F1*
66 s.d. **Exeunt]** *Rowe;* Exit *F1*
69 s.d. **then]** *ed.*
69 s.d. **Brutus . . . apart.]** *Rowe (subs.)*
102 **himself— . . . how,]** *Pope (subs.);* himselfe, . . . how: *F1*
105 **life—]** *Theobald (subs.);* life, *F1*

V.ii

V.ii] *Capell*
Location: *ed. (after Wilson)*
4 **Octavio's]** *so F1 (cf. III.i.275 s.d.); eds. (except Charney) since Pope read* Octavius'

V.iii

V.iii] *Capell*
Location: *ed. (after Wilson)*
22 s.d. **Pindarus goes up.]** *Dyce (after Collier MS)*
35 s.d. **Pindarus descends.]** *Folger, Douai MSS, Dyce;* Enter Pindarus. *F1*
45 s.d. **Pindarus stabs him.]** *Folger, Douai MSS (subs.), Globe;* Kills him. *F2 (after l. 46); F1 indicates the action at this point by a long dash after* sword. *l. 45*
46 s.d. **Dies.]** *Folger, Douai MSS, Capell*
50 s.d. **Exit.]** *Folger, Douai MSS, Rowe*
61 **dost]** *F3;* doest *F1*
79 s.d. **Exit Messala.]** *Folger, Douai MSS, Pope*
97 **whe'er]** *Capell;* where *F1*
97 **not]** *F1 (c); om. F1 (u)*
101 **moe]** *F1 (c);* no *F1 (u)*
104 **Thasos]** *S. Walker conj. (after Theobald, from Plutarch's* Thassos); Tharsus *F1*
108 **Labio]** *so F1 (and Plutarch); eds. since Hanmer (except Charney) read* Labeo
108 **Flavio]** *so F1; eds. (except Charney) adopt F2* Flavius *(so Plutarch)*

V.iv

V.iv] *Capell*
Location: *ed. (after Wilson)*
o.s.d. **young]** *Dyce*
1 s.d. **Exit.]** *Dorsch (after Wilson)*
7 s.p. **Lucil.]** *Macmillan; F1 has no s.p., but assigns the speech beginning at l. 9 to* Luc. *(i.e.* Lucilius)
8 s.d. **Young . . . slain.]** *Capell (subs.)*
12, 15 s.pp. **1. Sold.]** *Capell;* Sold. *F1*
17 **the news]** *Pope;* thee newes *F1*
26 **Brutus,]** *F4;* Brutus *F1*
30 **whe'er]** *Capell;* where *F1*

V.v

V.v] *Capell*
Location: *ed. (after Wilson)*
5 s.d. **Whispering.]** *Douai MS, Rowe*
8 s.d. **Whispering.]** *Douai MS, Capell*
23 s.d. **Low]** *F1 (c);* Loud *F1 (u)*
28 **sword-hilts]** *hyphen, Malone*
33 **thee too]** *Theobald;* thee, to *F1*
33 **Strato. Countrymen,]** *Theobald;* Strato Countrymen: *F1*
43 s.d. **Exeunt . . . Volumnius.]** *Capell*
50 s.d. **Runs . . . sword.]** *Rowe; represented by a long dash, F1*
64 **master, Strato]** *pointing from F3* (Lord, Strato); Master Strato *F1*
77 **With all]** *F3;* Withall *F1*
81 s.d. **Exeunt omnes.]** Exeunt omnes. / FINIS. *F1*

Sledded "Polacks." From Sigmund Herberstein, *Rerum Moscoviticarum Commentarii* (1549). Although the figures here seen "sledded" on the ice may not be strictly Polacks, the picture gives a vivid realization of what the elder Hamlet encountered when "in an angry parle / He smote the sledded Polacks on the ice" (I.i.62–63). (*By permission of the Harvard College Library*)

Hamlet, Prince of Denmark

NO BRIEF INTRODUCTION can take account of centuries of debate and disagreement concerning *Hamlet*, except perhaps to register the belief that the endless commentary—inspired, or dull; shrewd, or absurd—testifies to the fact that this is a play which history, as well as its own extraordinary merit, has given a special place apart, with such works as the *Commedia* and *Faust*. Certainly no play before *Hamlet* could have accommodated so much and so diverse metaphysical and psychological speculation. How Shakespeare came to write it is, of course, a mystery on which it is useless to speculate; but although it is formally related to a popular set of dramatic conventions (which we know from many other surviving examples), *Hamlet* clearly works on a different level from any other play of its kind, and indeed from any preceding play of Shakespeare's. Somehow, as Granville-Barker suggested, he himself became a different man in those early years at the Globe; he found his *daimon*. *Hamlet*, in addition to all its other titles to veneration and notoriety, was the first great tragedy Europe had produced for two thousand years.

T. S. Eliot's well-known judgment that *Hamlet* is "certainly an artistic failure" stems, as much other criticism does, from a not unreasonable conviction that in expanding a simpler Revenge play Shakespeare produced something which is inexplicably confused as drama, something distorted by the pressure of a personal emotion which did not succeed in finding an objective equivalent in so simple and archaic a form. Thus the action of the play gives rise to many problems, for reader and producer alike; and there is—especially in the part of Hamlet himself—an evident charge of passion, a wild contrariety between his language and its occasions, which blur the outline of the work, and have encouraged generations of critics since Coleridge to use it only as a glass in which to see a flatteringly distorted image of themselves.

Coleridge's "I have a smack of Hamlet" may, however, be a tribute to the world's remaking of Everyman in Hamlet's image, and it is something we are all, in a time of obligatory and schematic introspection, entitled in some degree to feel. We are no longer satisfied with simple accounts of motive, and we are ready enough to find metaphysics to explain why our response to any such stimulus as "duty" seems inhibited beyond anything the immediate crude circumstances appear to justify. In the perplexed figure of Hamlet, just because of our sense that his mind lacks definite boundaries, we find ourselves. And no amount of explanation in terms of Elizabethan conventions or Renaissance psychology, useful and interesting as such inquiries have been in deepening the complexities they sought to remove, can abolish our natural and historic right to do so. (By the same token, the conjectures of such psychologists as Ernest Jones have a relevance scholarship should not deny.) It may be that Hamlet's "buffoonery" is "the buffoonery of an emotion which Shakespeare cannot express in art" (save that he must in some sense have expressed it if we know of its existence); it may be that on a possible definition of art such expression is either limited or excessive. Certainly *Hamlet* is problematic, full of doubt concretely as well as discursively projected, unsparing of words, even to the point of habitually using two for one, as it uses two characters and two themes for one. It is of no clear shape, oblique, dubitant, duplicate. What Harry Levin has said of Hamlet himself applies equally to the play as a whole: "it is not so much a perplexing personality as . . . a state of perplexity into which we enter." But its affective power, its "negative capability" or failure to assert any of the possible ethical or metaphysical positions it creates, while at the same time generating its unique atmosphere of anxiety and its genuine hints of charity, made it a model for the new mind of Europe.

The history of the text of *Hamlet* is very complex. Techniques of scholarly inquiry grow more subtle, but as yet they have achieved no certainty on some issues crucial to the task of editing *Hamlet*. The play was entered in the Stationers' Register in 1602, presumably in an attempt to block unauthorized publication; but the First Quarto of 1603 was a piracy, perhaps the work of the actor who played Marcellus and Lucianus, with the part of Voltemand at hand. It is a brief, mutilated text, based on Shakespeare's *Hamlet* at some stage in its history, but evidently also reflecting material not in the later authorized texts. Polonius is called Corambis, the "To be or not to be" soliloquy is placed earlier in the play, and there are other differences. The compilers supplied the defects of their memories from other plays and notably from recollections of an old *Hamlet;* this play, probably by Kyd, is mentioned with some contempt by Nashe as early as 1589, and seems to have been well known in the 'nineties. The lost *Ur-Hamlet*, as it is called, is also reflected in a German play called *Der bestrafte Brudermord* (*Fratricide Punished*), existing in a text of 1710 and possibly the corrupt descendant of a *Hamlet* performed by English actors on a German tour in the early seventeenth century. Here Polonius is called Corambus. Attempts to reconstruct the *Ur-Hamlet* have to rely largely on Q1 and the German play. In any case, Q1 has no textual authority, although, for reasons explained in the "Note on the Text" below, editors cannot ignore it.

The Second Quarto, dated 1604 in some copies and 1605 in others, was authorized, and claimed, correctly, to be "enlarged to almost as much againe as it was." It is a notoriously ill-printed book, but has of course great authority. The First Folio text of 1623 differs from Q2 in hundreds of readings, and has about eighty-five lines missing from Q2 to compensate for over two hundred that it lacks. An account of the complex relationships between the three main texts, and of the principles of the present recension, is given in the "Note on the Text."

Q1, it will be observed, is no longer regarded as representing an earlier Shakespearean version of *Hamlet*. The old *Hamlet*, as Henslowe's diary testifies, was performed in June 1594, but probably belongs to the 'eighties; Nashe in the Epistle to Greene's *Menaphon* (1589) speaks satirically of "whole Hamlets, I should say handfuls of tragical speeches." We may think of it as the archetype of Revenge plays, and as preceding *The Spanish Tragedy* (whether or no Kyd wrote both), since so many recurring features of the theatrical revenge plot belong to the original Hamlet story. It seems likely that a vogue for Revenge plays grew up around 1599, when Marston's *Antonio's Revenge* was played by a boys' company; this would explain the decision of Shakespeare's company to revive *Hamlet* in a modernized form. In 1601 some very sophisticated additions were made to *The Spanish Tragedy*.

Some scholars believe that Shakespeare rehandled *Hamlet* more than once. The facts as we know them suggest, at any rate, that he rewrote the old play in 1600. Gabriel Harvey's observation that Shakespeare's play and *The Rape of Lucrece* "haue it in them, to please the wiser sort" was written in a copy of Speght's *Chaucer* (1598), and in the same context Harvey spoke of the Earl of Essex in the present tense. Essex was executed in February 1601; and on the balance of evidence Harvey's note appears to indicate that Shakespeare's play existed before that date.[1] But the passage in F1 (not in Q2) about the child actors and the War of the Theatres (II.ii.337–62) cannot have been written before the middle of 1601. The allusions to "innovation" and "inhibition" in the same scene (332–33) have often been thought to refer to the rebellion of Essex (February 8, 1601); *innovation* is a word Shakespeare uses of political upheavals, and Shakespeare's company, which was commissioned to act *Richard II* as a curtain-raiser to the insurrection, might in consequence have been "inhibited," that is, officially forbidden to play in the city for a time. But in fact it was not; and the words are more likely to refer to a Privy Council order of 1600 limiting the number of performances by the two major companies —a kind of "inhibition"—and to the new popularity of the boys' companies—taking *innovation* in the sense of *novelty*, a word which the pirates of Q1 used to render *innovation*. Probably Shakespeare wrote *Hamlet* after *Julius Caesar* (1599) and finished it before February 1601, adding the reference to the War of the Theatres late in that year.

The Hamlet story has its origins in Norse legend. The name Amlothi has been explained as signifying "desperate in battle," with a hint of madness attached, or, alternatively, as meaning "simpleton." Perhaps a piece of folklore about a hero who assumed madness or stupidity for purposes of revenge became attached to a semihistorical figure of the same kind as the Brutus of Roman prehistory. In such guise he appears in the *Historia Danica* of Saxo Grammaticus (c. 1200; printed 1514), which contains in its Third Book the story which is the foundation of *Hamlet*. Here Hamlet's father kills the king of Norway in single combat. Saxo's prince is a very clever boy, with method in his madness. His enemies set on a beautiful courtesan (a curious ancestor for Ophelia) to seduce him, but he rapes her. He makes a voyage to England, where his wit wins him the king's daughter; and on his return kills the usurper, having changed swords with him. Saxo has the germs of the fratricide, the incest, the king's love of drink, and much else. The tone of course is very different. Amleth's revenge is extremely brutal; he boils the ancestor of Polonius and feeds him to the pigs. He upbraids his mother in language as strong as Shakespeare's. Despite his vigor he is

[1] For a different possibility see the headnote to the reprint of Harvey's comment in Appendix C, Number 18, below.

also somewhat melancholic, but his revenge is brisk and involves burning down the palace.

When the French writer Belleforest used this story in his collection of *Histoires Tragiques* (1576)[1] he apologized for its primitive ferocity and gave it, what it retained, the setting of a contemporary court. He kept the main features of the story as outlined above, but has some emphases different from Shakespeare. Thus in his story, as in Saxo's but not as in Shakespeare's, it is generally known that Claudius killed Hamlet's father; his defense is that he did so in order to save the life of the Queen. In Belleforest the Queen is clearly an adultress. The young Hamlet (by no means thirty, as he is in Shakespeare's last act) pretends madness in self-protection, a rationalization of the Clever Boy folk-theme that survived into Saxo and in a sense re-emerges in Shakespeare. Claudius tries to prove him sane, first by a trick involving the girl he loves (in Belleforest she is, in fact, his mistress) and then by planting a spy in Gertrude's chamber. Hamlet avoids the first of these traps through a friend's warning, and the second he escapes by pretending to be mad, rushing about the chamber, and discovering the spy, whom he kills. After this scene Gertrude is on Hamlet's side. He then goes to England for a year, procures the death of his companions, and marries the English king's daughter. On his return, still feigning madness, he kills Claudius after an exchange of swords, and burns down the banqueting-hall.

Belleforest must have been the principal source of the *Ur-Hamlet*, which would doubtless have added the Ghost, the dumb Show, and the fencing match. Whether it accepted the motivation of Belleforest's plot, which Shakespeare clearly rejects, and which for the most part keeps Hamlet on the defensive against a powerful opponent, we cannot certainly know. V. K. Whitaker, in the most careful recent reconstruction, suggests that it had a secret murder, a doubtful ghost, and feigned madness used as a way of aggression, not defense. It perhaps made the girl in the story the daughter of the spy, and gave the spy an avenging son, so creating the Polonius family. Thus it established not only the Hamlet/Laertes contrasts, but a contrast between the real insanity of Ophelia and Hamlet's antic disposition. The play within the play was probably not a means to revenge, as in *The Spanish Tragedy*, but a test of the Ghost's veracity; but as yet it was probably only a dumb show, with no text. After the closet scene Gertrude was Hamlet's accomplice. Polonius was called Corambis, as in Q1. The nunnery scene took place immediately after its planning, not, as in Q2 and F1, some time later, with consequent difficulties to the producer and the interpreter.

There is no doubt that on a purely dramaturgical level the changes made by Shakespeare reduce plausibility. If the old play followed Belleforest in stressing Hamlet's difficulty in getting at the King, Shakespeare was not much interested, and located the problems within the hero's own personality. It may have had a much more plausible Horatio, who in Shakespeare's play is a somewhat chameleontic figure—a stranger or an habitué of the court as the need arises. Its Ghost was doubtless a simple affair, raising none of the problems caused by Shakespeare's equipping it with a Christian context and perhaps even inviting some theological controversy. In short, Shakespeare, not for the first or last time, shows less interest in mere probability than in thematic development of a subtler kind. Consequently this play—difficult enough in all conscience to comprehend, a mass of problems indeed—is made even less simple by the presence of certain inconsistencies and anomalies entailed by the drastic rehandling of the sources.

Although Hamlet says that "the story is extant, and writ in very choice Italian," there is no known source of the Gonzago plot, though there are a few hints in Belleforest. Shakespeare seems even to have altered the details of King Hamlet's murder in order to make the play-within-the-play fit, though this may have been done in the earlier play to allow for the introduction of a Ghost, and to make the murder a secret instead of common knowledge. As to minor sources, the handling of Hamlet's mental condition owes something to Timothy Bright's *Treatise of Melancholy* (1586), and there are some much-debated echoes of Montaigne, especially in the soliloquies on suicide. Florio's translation of the *Essays* was published in 1603, but existed for some years before, under circumstances which do not make it improbable that Shakespeare could have read it, even supposing he had not read the original French (published in full in 1588).

Hamlet is a multiple play; Shakespeare not only alters the old plot but expands it at every opportunity. For implicit comment on Hamlet's attitude to his task of revenge, we have the carefully-built-up Laertes; we see how he feels about his family, how he is cherished by the King who fears Hamlet, how he dares damnation and the loss of "both the worlds" for instant and savage revenge, and is willing to use any amount of "policy" to make it possible. And if this is not enough, we have also Fortinbras, contrasted with Hamlet not only in I.ii, before the story is launched, but in IV.iv, where he becomes an "occasion" that expressly "informs" against Hamlet. We have Ophelia's madness as a foil to Hamlet's "antic disposition," and the factitious grief of the player who "acts" without motive when Hamlet, with all the motive in the world—as he tells us—cannot act at all. Polonius dies, and Rosencrantz and Guildenstern "go to it," not so much because they are spies as to show that Hamlet can kill. The Mouse-trap becomes a great excuse for a long lecture on acting, the death of Ophelia for hundreds of melancholic lines on death. And these instances of the apparently leisurely, expansive construction of *Hamlet* could be multiplied. Everything conspires to make the play long: those wild changes of mood from antic to melancholic; those fierce renewals of passion as when he turns

[1] An English translation, *The History of Hamblet* (1608), may have existed in earlier editions no longer extant.

again on his already reeling mother in the closet scene; the game of feeding suspicions with evidence as when he helps Polonius to believe that love is the cause of his distemper, and Rosencrantz and Guildenstern to compile reports on his ambition; all these, and Hamlet's own pale cast of thought, make of *Hamlet* a delaying play at least as surely as Hamlet himself is a delaying revenger.

The unusual obliquity of the opening is worth noting. Shakespeare normally opens with plot and thematic material of the highest importance, shrewdly and economically presented; *Julius Caesar*, the last tragedy before *Hamlet*, is a fine instance. In *Hamlet* all is different; one has almost to assume an audience that knew the story and was willing to be teased by indirection. To be sure, the opening scene is as economical in the creation of atmosphere as that of *Macbeth*. There is the challenge of Barnardo, who nervously steals the sentry's words; the telling "I am sick at heart"; the cold and the fear. "Shakespeare," says T. S. Eliot, "had worked for a long time in the theatre, and written a good many plays before reaching the point at which he could write those twenty-two lines." Out of their varied rhythms, and the beautifully unexpected speech of Marcellus, "It faded on the crowing of the cock," there arises, as Eliot says, "a kind of musical design." But meanwhile the ghost —"this thing"—has appeared. (Horatio as sceptic raises questions as to its status which could have been avoided.) There has been speculation as to its purpose, but one thing seems sure: it has to do with the state of the nation—it "bodes some strange eruption to our state"—and with the armaments drive now in progress under the threat from Norway. That it genuinely has to do with the state of the nation—its spiritual rather than its merely political state—we shall learn; and to give us a "musical" sense that this is so, there is the unexpected speech about Christmas. But so far as plot goes, this might be the opening scene of a play about a Caesar-like Hamlet now dead but still posthumously interested in empire. Young Hamlet is not even mentioned until line 170—after nearly nine minutes' playing time.

The second scene opens with a passage of formal pomp, dwelling on the late King and his successor, and moving on first to the question of the threat of war and then to the departure of Laertes. Only when the ambassadors leave does Hamlet enter the story or the dialogue. The effect is, of course, theatrical and calculated. We have had before us Hamlet's two rivals, Fortinbras and Laertes; we have seen his enemy, the King, formidably in action; we have met the mature and rational Horatio; and then at last, twelve minutes after the start, the black Hamlet. He opens with an antic quibble, and his first sustained speech is a melancholy moralizing on the great gulf between being and seeming. Finally he rejects the proper *consolatio* offered by the King, and—before he commences business as a revenger, be it noted—soliloquizes on his disgust with life in a corrupt world. Only then, in his examination of Horatio and his companions, do we see the Hamlet of sharp practical intelligence and fine charity of manner; and then too, for the first time, we hear mention of specific "foul deeds" about to arise. We await with new interest his encounter with the Ghost; but seven minutes of mutual moral exhortation in the Polonius family intervene. Even as he waits on the battlements, Hamlet is given time to discourse thoughtfully on the dangers of scandal in public life; and Horatio, with his fear of the Ghost as potentially evil, delays the meeting yet again, until Hamlet follows, hears, swears instant revenge, and gives the first of those displays of manic behavior which prove him—lapsed in passion—to be punished with a sore distraction.

This, for all its violent action, is the mood of the play, a play in which an Osric can postpone the imminent catastrophe for over a hundred affected lines, in which even Hamlet's soliloquies seem slightly misplaced; in which the characters busy themselves with rival theories about the nature of Hamlet's unease. For Polonius it is disappointed love, for his mother "His father's death and our o'erhasty marriage"; for Rosencrantz and Guildenstern it is thwarted ambition, and for Ophelia simple lunacy. Nor is this all the theorizing in the play. Hamlet himself theorizes constantly—about the Ghost, about passion, about action; about manners and acting and suicide and custom. If those long delays at the outset are intended to kindle the interest of the audience in this new Hamlet—how will he differ from the old? what kind of hero and revenger will he be?—they will find that there is no simple answer to their questions. *Hamlet* is not what they expected; they must join with the other characters in the great *Hamlet* activity of guessing, theorizing, waiting, testing. Above all, they are kept waiting and kept doubting. Shakespeare will no more than Hamlet sweep to his revenge with wings as swift as meditation or the thoughts of love. For both of them, it seems, the murder of the old Hamlet is simply a particular instance of a general evil. And in the delays which follow—delays which we, fascinated by the uniquely irregular rhythm of the play, might not note for ourselves if Hamlet did not draw our attention to them—we are always conscious that we are being offered not so much a man, but a play, or a world, that delays and doubts; suddenly inventing, for instance, the problem of whether the Ghost is to be believed, questioning not the difficulties of the particular act of murder but the questionable shape of all action.

This is not a complexity entailed by the sources, where, as we have seen, Hamlet's practical difficulties are emphasized, and the Ghost is a Senecan theatrical invention designed primarily to start the revenge action. Nor can we explain the doubts which the Mouse-trap is intended to settle as merely ethical. It is true enough that on Elizabethan views to be a revenger was to be oneself condemned: the scourge of God will be scourged: woe to him by whom the offense cometh. But if we look at Revenge plays where the ethical issues are central—*The Atheist's Tragedy*, say, or *The Revenge of Bussy*—we see at once that *Hamlet* is different. Hamlet, for instance, doubts, or professes to doubt, the truth of the Ghost's word, not the wisdom of complying with his instructions. And since this doubt begets the *dumb show* and the play, it is worth observing also that the arrival of the players creates a problem very remote from simple morality, namely, the question of the nature of action, or rather of motive abstractly considered. Further, Shakespeare makes the Mouse-trap itself ambiguous; it explains as much to the King as it does to Hamlet, and makes the problem of *acting* much more difficult.

Hamlet is an extremely theatrical play. It is part of the story of the development of the Elizabethan theatre that as it grew more and more professional and self-conscious, it more and more distanced its audience. The medieval custom of using direct address for simple exposition, of treating the spectators as part of the show, rapidly disappears; only the soliloquy survives, and we see how far even that is in *Hamlet* from the tradition of direct explanation. *Hamlet* does not pretend the stage is the little world. It reminds us that all this is occurring in a theatre, with the Ghost in the "cellarage" and the stage peopled by actors. The play-within-the-play is introduced by topical gossip about the London theatre. The whole question of being and seeming is considered in terms of the theatre. The purpose of playing is to hold up a mirror to nature, but that is in itself an artificial act, calling for high skill. The actor simulates genuine passion by artificially stiffening the sinews, summoning up the blood. By enacting the appearance of passion he persuades us of its reality. But he is "play-acting," not "acting." Hamlet's problem is a problem of action, but has more than a mere semantic relation to play-acting: hence the great soliloquy "O, what a rogue . . ." and its rapidly following sequel, "To be, or not to be," each of them dealing with a sense of the word *act*. This at least gives one a notion of the urgency and complexity of Shakespeare's intentions. *Hamlet* raises issues as to the validity of its own existence as a play—an appearance which dares to comment on reality—and at the same time tells us to attend not so much to the difficulties its hero experiences in the performance of a specific act, as to his difficulties over action in general, to an irresolution which explains itself in terms of the undoubtedly corrupt society around him.

It has sometimes of late been argued that Hamlet himself shares the corruption, and this may in a sense be so. He is an actor, after all, both in fact and in the play, and sometimes the play makes him a bad one. It is not merely that he cannot act, and, like Fortinbras and his soldiers, make mouths at the invisible event. He also muddles occasions; it is at the very moment when his own enterprise has lost "the name of action" and he is bound for England under guard that he falsely professes to have strength and means and will to kill the King.

The most striking characteristic of Hamlet as play-actor is the "antic disposition." His antic quibbles reinforce the deliberate semantic puzzlement of the play, and are very much a theatrical matter. But his pretense of "idleness" also shows us that a great man, a courtier, a man noted for generosity and acuteness of mind (he has been called the most intelligent figure ever represented in literature) can have the reality of his intellect clouded by assuming the appearance of madness. Hamlet is punished by the sore distraction he assumes; so he tells Laertes in one of those moments of charity. Someone remarked that his madness is the shadow thrown on Hamlet by the evil that surrounds him. To some degree his judgment is clouded; Polonius is not the fool Hamlet takes him for, the King far from the contemptible figure of Hamlet's words to Horatio and his mother. And even Horatio sees that Hamlet needs to control his wild and whirling moods, to beget a temperance in his passion, as an actor should. But there are important respects in which Hamlet judges right, as in his attribution of his suffering not to particular threats but to the seduction of his mother; though even in that marvellous unpacking of his heart with words we are allowed to think he acts intemperately, as if his emotional ruin is enacted at the very moment when he discovers its cause. The treatment of Ophelia in the nunnery scene—whether or no Hamlet is supposed to know of the presence of the King and Polonius—is another instance of the same thing. We are entitled to infer that corruption has shadowed the courtier's and scholar's mind.

The environment has been tainted by that evil, by what H. D. F. Kitto, aptly quoting Aeschylus, calls the *protarchos ate*—the crime that sets crime in motion, the crime of the King. As Wolfgang Clemen says, the "leprous distillment" of the poisoning is shown as corrupting the body politic as well as killing the old King. This crime has a kind of totality resembling that of Eve's: it involves pride, murder, lust, gluttony, and the rest. Given the curious duplicity of the play, we see Claudius as politic in both senses: basely scheming, but effective as a ruler (though Hamlet of course sees him single). We see him anguished by guilt and preparing to incur more guilt. We observe that the imagery of disease which so echoes in the play—the quick of the ulcer, the undivulged disease—is concentrated in Claudius' lines, as he makes his evil plans; but he is tortured by guilt, his own undivulged disease. He is a drunkard; yet twice at least—at the play, and after the Queen has drunk the poisoned liquor—our attention is drawn to his self-control. But Claudius is a tyrant; boundless intemperance was traditionally the habit of tyrants. He is even treated as a usurper, and we are encouraged to build upon hints that Hamlet "the Dane"—a term normally used of the King—will treat him so. The air breathed by tyrants is tainted; you have a court of immoralists like Laertes and rich idiots like Osric. It is a court where espials are lawful (the play is full of spying, of "tricks"—a repeated word; and Hamlet does his share, setting Horatio to watch the King). Power is abused—another repeated word—as in the letter to England (by which Hamlet also benefits). Custom is maintained in bad instances, broken in good. The evil of the tyrant is a contagious blastment for Ophelia. One may infer that the heaven which rejects his prayers will also ensure, as it was held ever to have done, that the tyrant's life is a short one.

And here we do touch the quick of the ulcer. Hamlet calls himself "scourge and minister" (III.iv.175); the two functions are sometimes sharply differentiated, but I do not think they should be. Hamlet is not asking himself whether he is required to be one or the other. It is true that he will not, like Laertes, disregard "both the worlds," and indeed that he explicitly considers them in soliloquy; and it is true that he will not, like Fortinbras, find his quarrel in a straw. He is aware of the moral danger of being a scourge of God. On his departure to England his thoughts, he says, will be bloody. Yet on his return, as everybody notices, his mood is different. As to the deaths of Rosencrantz and Guildenstern, "Why, even in that," he says, "was heaven ordinant" (V.ii.48). What Hamlet has discovered is simply that "there's a divinity that shapes our ends, / Rough-hew them how we will" (V.ii.10–11). He does not have to decide whether or not to be a scourge. Even the death of Ophelia is made merely an aspect of death in general, part of the large arrangements of Providence. Every chance, every evil intention such as the King's wager, is now part of a plan; and Hamlet's part is compliance. "Over and over again in *Hamlet*," says John Holloway, "chance turns into a larger design, randomness becomes retribution." If the "positive" of the play has been the universal encroachment of death, the Hamlet of the last scenes has come to see this, and everything else, as part of an inexplicable and painful plan. He therefore acquiesces. That Chance is a mask of Providence most Elizabethans, at any rate, believed. In the last moments Laertes dies by his own rapier, and Claudius by his own poison, as Polonius has died in a lawful espial. Hamlet dies, having served as scourge but also as minister, as a man who has acted properly under a discipline higher than the Ghost's. Then he is a soldier and, briefly, a king. His last decisive act is to name as his successor a man capable of "enterprises of great pitch and moment."

Hamlet ends with a strong sense of purgation; the *protarchos ate* has been thoroughly purged, at the cost of extinguishing the two families involved. This may, then, be the catharsis. But in rendering account of the pleasures of *Hamlet*, we should recall also much that may seem to be external to this purgation; the pleasures of theatrical hesitation and duplicity, of alienation and illusion; our strong intellectual delight in the calms and furies, the great rhythmical pulse of the play, in its invention of a new mirror to hold up to a changed nature.

Frank Kermode

"Springes to catch woodcocks." From Henry Parrot, *Laquei ridiculosi: or Springes for Woodcocks* (1613). The proverbial phrase just quoted is Polonius' worldly-wise indictment of lovers' vows—"the holy vows of heaven," as Ophelia terms them (*Hamlet*, I.iii.114). The woodcock was considered unusually stupid, even for a bird, and easily snared in traps ("springes"). "Woodcock" was therefore a common term for a gullible fool of either sex. In V.ii.306 the dying Laertes calls himself a woodcock who has been caught in a springe of his own devising. *(By permission of the Harvard College Library)*

The Tragedy of Hamlet, Prince of Denmark

[DRAMATIS PERSONAE

CLAUDIUS, *King of Denmark*
HAMLET, *son to the late King Hamlet, and nephew to the present King*
POLONIUS, *Lord Chamberlain*
HORATIO, *friend to Hamlet*
LAERTES, *son to Polonius*
VOLTEMAND, CORNELIUS, ROSENCRANTZ, GUILDENSTERN, OSRIC, GENTLEMAN — *courtiers*
MARCELLUS, BARNARDO — *officers*
FRANCISCO, *a soldier*
REYNALDO, *servant to Polonius*
FORTINBRAS, *Prince of Norway*
NORWEGIAN CAPTAIN
DOCTOR OF DIVINITY
PLAYERS
Two CLOWNS, *grave-diggers*
ENGLISH AMBASSADORS

GERTRUDE, *Queen of Denmark, and mother to Hamlet*
OPHELIA, *daughter to Polonius*

GHOST *of Hamlet's Father*

LORDS, LADIES, OFFICERS, SOLDIERS, SAILORS, MESSENGERS, *and* ATTENDANTS

SCENE: *Denmark*]

ACT I, SCENE I

Enter BARNARDO *and* FRANCISCO, *two sentinels*, [*meeting*].

Bar. Who's there?
Fran. Nay, answer me. Stand and unfold yourself.
Bar. Long live the King!
Fran. Barnardo.
Bar. He.
Fran. You come most carefully upon your hour.
Bar. 'Tis now strook twelf. Get thee to bed, Francisco.
Fran. For this relief much thanks. 'Tis bitter cold,
And I am sick at heart.
Bar. Have you had quiet guard?
Fran. Not a mouse stirring.
Bar. Well, good night.
If you do meet Horatio and Marcellus,
The rivals of my watch, bid them make haste.

Enter HORATIO *and* MARCELLUS.

Fran. I think I hear them. Stand ho! Who is there?
Hor. Friends to this ground.
Mar. And liegemen to the Dane.
Fran. Give you good night.
Mar. O, farewell, honest [soldier].
Who hath reliev'd you?
Fran. Barnardo hath my place.
Give you good night. *Exit Francisco.*
Mar. Holla, Barnardo!
Bar. Say—
What, is Horatio there?
Hor. A piece of him.
Bar. Welcome, Horatio, welcome, good Marcellus.
Hor. What, has this thing appear'd again to-night?
Bar. I have seen nothing.
Mar. Horatio says 'tis but our fantasy,
And will not let belief take hold of him
Touching this dreaded sight twice seen of us;
Therefore I have entreated him along,
With us to watch the minutes of this night,
That if again this apparition come,
He may approve our eyes and speak to it.
Hor. Tush, tush, 'twill not appear.

Words and passages enclosed in square brackets in the text above are either emendations of the copy-text or additions to it. The Textual Notes immediately following the play cite the earliest authority for every such change or insertion and supply the reading of the copy-text wherever it is emended in this edition.

I.i. Location: Elsinore. A guard-platform of the castle.
2. answer me: i.e. *you* answer *me*. Francisco is on watch; Barnardo has come to relieve him. unfold yourself: make known who you are.
3. Long . . . King. Perhaps a password, perhaps simply an utterance to allow the voice to be recognized.
7. strook twelf: struck twelve.
9. sick at heart: in low spirits. 13. rivals: partners.
15. liegemen . . . Dane: loyal subjects to the King of Denmark.
16. Give: God give. 23. fantasy: imagination.
29. approve: corroborate.

Bar. Sit down a while,
And let us once again assail your ears,
That are so fortified against our story,
What we have two nights seen.
Hor. Well, sit we down,
And let us hear Barnardo speak of this.
Bar. Last night of all,
When yond same star that's westward from the pole
Had made his course t' illume that part of heaven
Where now it burns, Marcellus and myself,
The bell then beating one—

Enter GHOST.

Mar. Peace, break thee off! Look where it comes again!
Bar. In the same figure like the King that's dead.
Mar. Thou art a scholar, speak to it, Horatio.
Bar. Looks 'a not like the King? Mark it, Horatio.
Hor. Most like; it [harrows] me with fear and wonder.
Bar. It would be spoke to.
Mar. Speak to it, Horatio.
Hor. What art thou that usurp'st this time of night,
Together with that fair and warlike form
In which the majesty of buried Denmark
Did sometimes march? By heaven I charge thee speak!
Mar. It is offended.
Bar. See, it stalks away!
Hor. Stay! Speak, speak, I charge thee speak!
Exit Ghost.
Mar. 'Tis gone, and will not answer.
Bar. How now, Horatio? you tremble and look pale.
Is not this something more than fantasy?
What think you on't?
Hor. Before my God, I might not this believe
Without the sensible and true avouch
Of mine own eyes.
Mar. Is it not like the King?
Hor. As thou art to thyself.
Such was the very armor he had on
When he the ambitious Norway combated.
So frown'd he once when in an angry parle
He smote the sledded [Polacks] on the ice.
'Tis strange.
Mar. Thus twice before, and jump at this dead hour,
With martial stalk hath he gone by our watch.
Hor. In what particular thought to work I know not,
But in the gross and scope of mine opinion,
This bodes some strange eruption to our state.
Mar. Good now, sit down, and tell me, he that knows,
Why this same strict and most observant watch
So nightly toils the subject of the land,
And [why] such daily [cast] of brazen cannon,
And foreign mart for implements of war,
Why such impress of shipwrights, whose sore task
Does not divide the Sunday from the week,
What might be toward, that this sweaty haste
Doth make the night joint-laborer with the day:
Who is't that can inform me?
Hor. That can I,
At least the whisper goes so: our last king,
Whose image even but now appear'd to us,
Was, as you know, by Fortinbras of Norway,
Thereto prick'd on by a most emulate pride,
Dar'd to the combat; in which our valiant Hamlet
(For so this side of our known world esteem'd him)
Did slay this Fortinbras, who, by a seal'd compact
Well ratified by law and heraldy,
Did forfeit (with his life) all [those] his lands
Which he stood seiz'd of, to the conqueror;
Against the which a moi'ty competent
Was gaged by our king, which had [return'd]
To the inheritance of Fortinbras,
Had he been vanquisher; as by the same comart
And carriage of the article [design'd],
His fell to Hamlet. Now, sir, young Fortinbras,
Of unimproved mettle hot and full,
Hath in the skirts of Norway here and there
Shark'd up a list of lawless resolutes
For food and diet to some enterprise
That hath a stomach in't, which is no other,
As it doth well appear unto our state,
But to recover of us, by strong hand
And terms compulsatory, those foresaid lands
So by his father lost; and this, I take it,
Is the main motive of our preparations,
The source of this our watch, and the chief head
Of this post-haste and romage in the land.
Bar. I think it be no other but e'en so.
Well may it sort that this portentous figure
Comes armed through our watch so like the King
That was and is the question of these wars.
Hor. A mote it is to trouble the mind's eye.
In the most high and palmy state of Rome,
A little ere the mightiest Julius fell,

36. **pole:** pole star.
37. **his:** its (the commonest form of the neuter possessive singular in Shakespeare's day). 41. **like:** in the likeness of.
42. **a scholar:** i.e. one who knows how best to address it.
43. **'a:** he.
45. **It . . . to.** A ghost had to be spoken to before it could speak.
46. **usurp'st.** The ghost, a supernatural being, has invaded the realm of nature. 48. **majesty . . . Denmark:** late King of Denmark.
49. **sometimes:** formerly.
57. **sensible:** relating to the senses. **avouch:** guarantee.
61. **Norway:** King of Norway. 62. **parle:** parley.
63. **sledded:** using sleds or sledges. **Polacks:** Poles.
65. **jump:** precisely.
67–68. **In . . . opinion:** while I have no precise theory about it, my general feeling is that. *Gross* = wholeness, totality; *scope* = range.
69. **eruption:** upheaval.
72. **toils:** causes to work. **subject:** subjects.
74. **foreign mart:** dealing with foreign markets.
75. **impress:** forced service. 77. **toward:** in preparation.
83. **emulate:** emulous, proceeding from rivalry.
87. **law and heraldy:** heraldic law (governing combat). *Heraldy* is a variant of *heraldry*. 89. **seiz'd of:** possessed of.
90. **moi'ty:** portion. **competent:** adequate, i.e. equivalent.
91. **gaged:** pledged. **had:** would have.
92. **inheritance:** possession. 93. **comart:** bargain.
94. **carriage:** tenor. **design'd:** drawn up.
96. **unimproved:** untried (?) or not directed to any useful end (?).
97. **skirts:** outlying territories.
98. **Shark'd up:** gathered up hastily and indiscriminately.
100. **stomach:** relish of danger (?) or demand for courage (?).
106. **head:** source. 107. **romage:** rummage, bustling activity.
109. **sort:** fit. **portentous:** ominous.

The graves stood [tenantless] and the sheeted dead
Did squeak and gibber in the Roman streets.
As stars with trains of fire, and dews of blood,
Disasters in the sun; and the moist star
Upon whose influence Neptune's empire stands
Was sick almost to doomsday with eclipse.
And even the like precurse of [fear'd] events,
As harbingers preceding still the fates
And prologue to the omen coming on,
Have heaven and earth together demonstrated
Unto our climatures and countrymen.

Enter Ghost.

But soft, behold! lo where it comes again!
It spreads his arms.
I'll cross it though it blast me. Stay, illusion!
If thou hast any sound or use of voice,
Speak to me.
If there be any good thing to be done
That may to thee do ease, and grace to me,
Speak to me.
If thou art privy to thy country's fate,
Which happily foreknowing may avoid,
O speak!
Or if thou hast uphoarded in thy life
Extorted treasure in the womb of earth,
For which, they say, your spirits oft walk in death,
Speak of it, stay and speak! (*The cock crows.*) Stop it,
Marcellus.

Mar. Shall I strike it with my partisan?

Hor. Do, if it will not stand.

Bar. 'Tis here!

Hor. 'Tis here!

Mar. 'Tis gone! [*Exit Ghost.*]
We do it wrong, being so majestical,
To offer it the show of violence,
For it is as the air, invulnerable,
And our vain blows malicious mockery.

Bar. It was about to speak when the cock crew.

Hor. And then it started like a guilty thing
Upon a fearful summons. I have heard
The cock, that is the trumpet to the morn,
Doth with his lofty and shrill-sounding throat
Awake the god of day, and at his warning,
Whether in sea or fire, in earth or air,
Th' extravagant and erring spirit hies
To his confine; and of the truth herein
This present object made probation.

Mar. It faded on the crowing of the cock.
Some say that ever 'gainst that season comes
Wherein our Saviour's birth is celebrated,
This bird of dawning singeth all night long,
And then they say no spirit dare stir abroad,
The nights are wholesome, then no planets strike,
No fairy takes, nor witch hath power to charm,
So hallowed, and so gracious, is that time.

Hor. So have I heard and do in part believe it.
But look, the morn in russet mantle clad
Walks o'er the dew of yon high eastward hill.
Break we our watch up, and by my advice
Let us impart what we have seen to-night
Unto young Hamlet, for, upon my life,
This spirit, dumb to us, will speak to him.
Do you consent we shall acquaint him with it,
As needful in our loves, fitting our duty?

Mar. Let's do't, I pray, and I this morning know
Where we shall find him most convenient.
Exeunt.

[Scene II]

Flourish. Enter Claudius, King of Denmark, Gertrude the Queen; Council: *as* Polonius; *and his son* Laertes, Hamlet, *cum aliis* [*including* Voltemand *and* Cornelius].

King. Though yet of Hamlet our dear brother's death
The memory be green, and that it us befitted
To bear our hearts in grief, and our whole kingdom
To be contracted in one brow of woe,
Yet so far hath discretion fought with nature
That we with wisest sorrow think on him
Together with remembrance of ourselves.
Therefore our sometime sister, now our queen,
Th' imperial jointress to this warlike state,
Have we, as 'twere with a defeated joy,
With an auspicious, and a dropping eye,
With mirth in funeral, and with dirge in marriage,
In equal scale weighing delight and dole,
Taken to wife; nor have we herein barr'd
Your better wisdoms, which have freely gone
With this affair along. For all, our thanks.
Now follows that you know young Fortinbras,
Holding a weak supposal of our worth,
Or thinking by our late dear brother's death
Our state to be disjoint and out of frame,
Co-leagued with this dream of his advantage,

116. One or more lines may have been lost between this line and the next.
118. **Disasters**: ominous signs. **moist star**: moon.
119. **Neptune's empire stands**: the seas are dependent.
120. **sick . . . doomsday**: i.e. almost totally darkened. When the Day of Judgment is imminent, says Matthew 24:29, "the moon shall not give her light." **eclipse**. There were a solar and two total lunar eclipses visible in England in 1598; they caused gloomy speculation.
121. **precurse**: foreshadowing.
122. **harbingers**: advance messengers. **still**: always.
123. **omen**: i.e. the events portended.
125. **climatures**: regions. 126 s.d. **his**: its.
127. **cross it**: cross its path, confront it directly. **blast**: wither (by supernatural means). 134. **happily**: haply, perhaps.
138. **your**: Colloquial and impersonal; cf. I.v.167, IV.iii.21, 23. Most editors adopt *you* from F1. 140. **partisan**: long-handled spear.
146. **malicious mockery**: mockery of malice, i.e. empty pretenses of harming it. 150. **trumpet**: trumpeter.
154. **extravagant**: wandering outside its proper bounds. **erring**: wandering abroad. **hies**: hastens.

156. **object**: sight. **probation**: proof. 158. **'gainst**: just before.
162. **strike**: exert malevolent influence.
163. **takes**: bewitches, charms. 164. **gracious**: blessed.
166. **russet**: coarse greyish-brown cloth.

I.ii. Location: The castle.
o.s.d. **Flourish**: trumpet fanfare. **cum aliis**: with others.
2. **befitted**: would befit.
4. **contracted in**: (1) reduced to; (2) knit or wrinkled in. **brow of woe**: mournful brow. 9. **jointress**: joint holder.
10. **defeated**: impaired.
11. **auspicious . . . dropping**: cheerful . . . weeping.
15. **freely**: fully, without reservation.
17. **know**: be informed, learn.
18. **supposal**: conjecture, estimate. 21. **Co-leagued**: joined.

He hath not fail'd to pester us with message
Importing the surrender of those lands
Lost by his father, with all bands of law,
To our most valiant brother. So much for him.
Now for ourself, and for this time of meeting,
Thus much the business is: we have here writ
To Norway, uncle of young Fortinbras—
Who, impotent and bedred, scarcely hears
Of this his nephew's purpose—to suppress
His further gait herein, in that the levies,
The lists, and full proportions are all made
Out of his subject; and we here dispatch
You, good Cornelius, and you, Voltemand,
For bearers of this greeting to old Norway,
Giving to you no further personal power
To business with the King, more than the scope
Of these delated articles allow. [*Giving a paper.*]
Farewell, and let your haste commend your duty.

Cor., Vol. In that, and all things, will we show our duty.

King. We doubt it nothing; heartily farewell.
[*Exeunt Voltemand and Cornelius.*]
And now, Laertes, what's the news with you?
You told us of some suit, what is't, Laertes?
You cannot speak of reason to the Dane
And lose your voice. What wouldst thou beg, Laertes,
That shall not be my offer, not thy asking?
The head is not more native to the heart,
The hand more instrumental to the mouth,
Than is the throne of Denmark to thy father.
What wouldst thou have, Laertes?

Laer. My dread lord,
Your leave and favor to return to France,
From whence though willingly I came to Denmark
To show my duty in your coronation,
Yet now I must confess, that duty done,
My thoughts and wishes bend again toward France,
And bow them to your gracious leave and pardon.

King. Have you your father's leave? What says Polonius?

Pol. H'ath, my lord, wrung from me my slow leave
By laborsome petition, and at last
Upon his will I seal'd my hard consent.
I do beseech you give him leave to go.

King. Take thy fair hour, Laertes, time be thine,
And thy best graces spend it at thy will!
But now, my cousin Hamlet, and my son—

Ham. [*Aside.*] A little more than kin, and less than kind.

King. How is it that the clouds still hang on you?

Ham. Not so, my lord, I am too much in the sun.

Queen. Good Hamlet, cast thy nighted color off,
And let thine eye look like a friend on Denmark.
Do not for ever with thy vailed lids
Seek for thy noble father in the dust.
Thou know'st 'tis common, all that lives must die,
Passing through nature to eternity.

Ham. Ay, madam, it is common.

Queen. If it be,
Why seems it so particular with thee?

Ham. Seems, madam? nay, it is, I know not "seems."
'Tis not alone my inky cloak, [good] mother,
Nor customary suits of solemn black,
Nor windy suspiration of forc'd breath,
No, nor the fruitful river in the eye,
Nor the dejected havior of the visage,
Together with all forms, moods, [shapes] of grief,
That can [denote] me truly. These indeed seem,
For they are actions that a man might play,
But I have that within which passes show,
These but the trappings and the suits of woe.

King. 'Tis sweet and commendable in your nature, Hamlet,
To give these mourning duties to your father.
But you must know your father lost a father,
That father lost, lost his, and the survivor bound
In filial obligation for some term
To do obsequious sorrow. But to persever
In obstinate condolement is a course
Of impious stubbornness, 'tis unmanly grief,
It shows a will most incorrect to heaven,
A heart unfortified, or mind impatient,
An understanding simple and unschool'd:
For what we know must be, and is as common
As any the most vulgar thing to sense,
Why should we in our peevish opposition
Take it to heart? Fie, 'tis a fault to heaven,
A fault against the dead, a fault to nature,
To reason most absurd, whose common theme
Is death of fathers, and who still hath cried,
From the first corse till he that died to-day,
"This must be so." We pray you throw to earth
This unprevailing woe, and think of us
As of a father, for let the world take note
You are the most immediate to our throne,
And with no less nobility of love
Than that which dearest father bears his son
Do I impart toward you. For your intent
In going back to school in Wittenberg,
It is most retrograde to our desire,
And we beseech you bend you to remain
Here in the cheer and comfort of our eye,

22. pester . . . message: trouble me with persistent messages (the original sense of *pester* is "overcrowd").
23. Importing: having as import. **24. bands**: bonds, binding terms.
29. impotent and bedred: feeble and bedridden.
31. gait: proceeding.
31–33. in . . . subject: since the troops are all drawn from his subjects.
38. delated: extended, detailed (a variant of *dilated*).
41. nothing: not at all. **45. lose**: waste.
47. native: closely related. **48. instrumental**: serviceable.
51. leave and favor: gracious permission.
56. pardon: permission to depart.
58. H'ath: he hath. **60. hard**: reluctant.
64. cousin: kinsman (used in familiar address to any collateral relative more distant than a brother or sister; here to a nephew).
65. A little . . . kind: closer than a nephew, since you are my mother's husband; yet more distant than a son, too (and not well disposed to you).
67. sun. With obvious quibble on *son*.
70. vailed: downcast. **72. common**: general, universal.
75. particular: individual, personal. **80. fruitful**: copious.
92. obsequious: proper to obsequies. **93. condolement**: grief.
95. incorrect: unsubmissive.
99. any . . . sense: what is perceived to be commonest.
101. to: against. **103. absurd**: contrary.
107. unprevailing: unavailing. **111. dearest**: most loving.
112. impart: i.e. impart love.

Our chiefest courtier, cousin, and our son.
Queen. Let not thy mother lose her prayers, Hamlet,
I pray thee stay with us, go not to Wittenberg.
Ham. I shall in all my best obey you, madam.
King. Why, 'tis a loving and a fair reply.
Be as ourself in Denmark. Madam, come.
This gentle and unforc'd accord of Hamlet
Sits smiling to my heart, in grace whereof,
No jocund health that Denmark drinks to-day,
But the great cannon to the clouds shall tell,
And the King's rouse the heaven shall bruit again,
Respeaking earthly thunder. Come away.
Flourish. Exeunt all but Hamlet.
Ham. O that this too too sallied flesh would melt,
Thaw, and resolve itself into a dew!
Or that the Everlasting had not fix'd
His canon 'gainst [self-]slaughter! O God, God,
How [weary], stale, flat, and unprofitable
Seem to me all the uses of this world!
Fie on't, ah fie! 'tis an unweeded garden
That grows to seed, things rank and gross in nature
Possess it merely. That it should come [to this]!
But two months dead, nay, not so much, not two.
So excellent a king, that was to this
Hyperion to a satyr, so loving to my mother
That he might not beteem the winds of heaven
Visit her face too roughly. Heaven and earth,
Must I remember? Why, she should hang on him
As if increase of appetite had grown
By what it fed on, and yet, within a month—
Let me not think on't! Frailty, thy name is woman!—
A little month, or ere those shoes were old
With which she followed my poor father's body,
Like Niobe, all tears—why, she, [even she]—
O God, a beast that wants discourse of reason
Would have mourn'd longer—married with my uncle,
My father's brother, but no more like my father
Than I to Hercules. Within a month,
Ere yet the salt of most unrighteous tears
Had left the flushing in her galled eyes,
She married—O most wicked speed: to post
With such dexterity to incestious sheets,
It is not, nor it cannot come to good,
But break my heart, for I must hold my tongue.

Enter HORATIO, MARCELLUS, *and* BARNARDO.

Hor. Hail to your lordship!
Ham. I am glad to see you well.
Horatio—or I do forget myself.
Hor. The same, my lord, and your poor servant ever.
Ham. Sir, my good friend—I'll change that name with you.
And what make you from Wittenberg, Horatio?
Marcellus.
Mar. My good lord.
Ham. I am very glad to see you. [*To Barnardo.*] Good even, sir.—
But what, in faith, make you from Wittenberg?
Hor. A truant disposition, good my lord.
Ham. I would not hear your enemy say so,
Nor shall you do my ear that violence
To make it truster of your own report
Against yourself. I know you are no truant.
But what is your affair in Elsinore?
We'll teach you to drink [deep] ere you depart.
Hor. My lord, I came to see your father's funeral.
Ham. I prithee do not mock me, fellow studient,
I think it was to [see] my mother's wedding.
Hor. Indeed, my lord, it followed hard upon.
Ham. Thrift, thrift, Horatio, the funeral bak'd-meats
Did coldly furnish forth the marriage tables.
Would I had met my dearest foe in heaven
Or ever I had seen that day, Horatio!
My father—methinks I see my father.
Hor. Where, my lord?
Ham. In my mind's eye, Horatio.
Hor. I saw him once, 'a was a goodly king.
Ham. 'A was a man, take him for all in all,
I shall not look upon his like again.
Hor. My lord, I think I saw him yesternight.
Ham. Saw, who?
Hor. My lord, the King your father.
Ham. The King my father?
Hor. Season your admiration for a while
With an attent ear, till I may deliver,
Upon the witness of these gentlemen,
This marvel to you.
Ham. For God's love let me hear!
Hor. Two nights together had these gentlemen,
Marcellus and Barnardo, on their watch,
In the dead waste and middle of the night,
Been thus encount'red: a figure like your father,
Armed at point exactly, cap-a-pe,
Appears before them, and with solemn march
Goes slow and stately by them; thrice he walk'd
By their oppress'd and fear-surprised eyes
Within his truncheon's length, whilst they, distill'd
Almost to jelly with the act of fear,
Stand dumb and speak not to him. This to me
In dreadful secrecy impart they did,
And I with them the third night kept the watch,
Where, as they had delivered, both in time,

127. **rouse:** bumper, drink. **bruit:** loudly declare.
129. **sallied:** sullied. See the Textual Notes. Many editors prefer the F1 reading, *solid*. 132. **canon:** law. 134. **uses:** customs.
137. **merely:** utterly. 139. **to:** in comparison with.
140. **Hyperion:** the sun-god. 141. **beteem:** allow.
147. **or ere:** before.
149. **Niobe.** She wept endlessly for her children, whom Apollo and Artemis had killed.
150. **wants . . . reason:** lacks the power of reason (which distinguishes men from beasts). 154. **unrighteous:** i.e. hypocritical.
155. **flushing:** redness. **galled:** inflamed.
157. **incestious:** incestuous. The marriage of a man to his brother's widow was so regarded until long after Shakespeare's day.
163. **change:** exchange.
164. **what . . . from:** what are you doing away from.
169. **truant disposition:** inclination to play truant.
177. **studient:** student. 181. **coldly:** when cold.
182. **dearest:** most intensely hated. 183. **Or:** ere, before.
192. **Season:** temper. **admiration:** wonder.
193. **deliver:** report. 198. **waste:** empty expanse.
200. **at point exactly:** in every particular. **cap-a-pe:** from head to foot. 203. **fear-surprised:** overwhelmed by fear.
204. **truncheon:** short staff carried as a symbol of military command.
205. **act:** action, operation.
207. **dreadful:** held in awe, i.e. solemnly sworn.

Form of the thing, each word made true and good,
The apparition comes. I knew your father,
These hands are not more like.
Ham. But where was this?
Mar. My lord, upon the platform where we watch.
Ham. Did you not speak to it?
Hor. My lord, I did,
But answer made it none. Yet once methought
It lifted up it head and did address
Itself to motion like as it would speak;
But even then the morning cock crew loud,
And at the sound it shrunk in haste away
And vanish'd from our sight.
Ham. 'Tis very strange.
Hor. As I do live, my honor'd lord, 'tis true,
And we did think it writ down in our duty
To let you know of it.
Ham. Indeed, [indeed,] sirs. But this troubles me.
Hold you the watch to-night?
[*Mar.*, *Bar.*] We do, my lord.
Ham. Arm'd, say you?
[*Mar.*, *Bar.*] Arm'd, my lord.
Ham. From top to toe?
[*Mar.*, *Bar.*] My lord, from head to foot.
Ham. Then saw you not his face.
Hor. O yes, my lord, he wore his beaver up.
Ham. What, look'd he frowningly?
Hor. A countenance more
In sorrow than in anger.
Ham. Pale, or red?
Hor. Nay, very pale.
Ham. And fix'd his eyes upon you?
Hor. Most constantly.
Ham. I would I had been there.
Hor. It would have much amaz'd you.
Ham. Very like, [very like]. Stay'd it long?
Hor. While one with moderate haste might tell a hundreth.
Both [*Mar.*, *Bar.*]. Longer, longer.
Hor. Not when I saw't.
Ham. His beard was grisl'd, no?
Hor. It was, as I have seen it in his life,
A sable silver'd.
Ham. I will watch to-night,
Perchance 'twill walk again.
Hor. I warr'nt it will.
Ham. If it assume my noble father's person,
I'll speak to it though hell itself should gape
And bid me hold my peace. I pray you all,
If you have hitherto conceal'd this sight,
Let it be tenable in your silence still,
And whatsomever else shall hap to-night,
Give it an understanding but no tongue.
I will requite your loves. So fare you well.
Upon the platform 'twixt aleven and twelf
I'll visit you.
All. Our duty to your honor.

212. are . . . like: i.e. do not resemble each other more closely than the apparition resembled him. **216. it:** its.
216–217. address . . . motion: begin to make a gesture.
230. beaver: visor. **237. tell a hundreth:** count a hundred.
239. grisl'd: grizzled, mixed with grey. **247. tenable:** held close.
251. aleven: eleven.

Ham. Your loves, as mine to you; farewell.
Exeunt [*all but Hamlet*].
My father's spirit—in arms! All is not well,
I doubt some foul play. Would the night were come!
Till then sit still, my soul. [Foul] deeds will rise,
Though all the earth o'erwhelm them, to men's eyes.
Exit.

[Scene III]

Enter Laertes *and* Ophelia, *his sister.*

Laer. My necessaries are inbark'd. Farewell.
And, sister, as the winds give benefit
And convey [is] assistant, do not sleep,
But let me hear from you.
Oph. Do you doubt that?
Laer. For Hamlet, and the trifling of his favor,
Hold it a fashion and a toy in blood,
A violet in the youth of primy nature,
Forward, not permanent, sweet, not lasting,
The perfume and suppliance of a minute—
No more.
Oph. No more but so?
Laer. Think it no more:
For nature crescent does not grow alone
In thews and [bulk], but as this temple waxes,
The inward service of the mind and soul
Grows wide withal. Perhaps he loves you now,
And now no soil nor cautel doth besmirch
The virtue of his will, but you must fear,
His greatness weigh'd, his will is not his own,
[For he himself is subject to his birth:]
He may not, as unvalued persons do,
Carve for himself, for on his choice depends
The safety and health of this whole state,
And therefore must his choice be circumscrib'd
Unto the voice and yielding of that body
Whereof he is the head. Then if he says he loves you,
It fits your wisdom so far to believe it
As he in his particular act and place
May give his saying deed, which is no further
Than the main voice of Denmark goes withal.
Then weigh what loss your honor may sustain
If with too credent ear you list his songs,
Or lose your heart, or your chaste treasure open
To his unmast'red importunity.
Fear it, Ophelia, fear it, my dear sister,
And keep you in the rear of your affection,

255. doubt: suspect.

I.iii. Location: Polonius' quarters in the castle.
1. inbark'd: embarked, abroad.
3. convey is assistant: means of transport is available.
6. a fashion: i.e. standard behavior for a young man. **toy in blood:** idle fancy of youthful passion. **7. primy:** springlike.
8. Forward: early of growth. **9. suppliance:** pastime.
11. crescent: growing, increasing. **12. thews:** muscles, sinews.
12–14. as . . . withal: as the body develops, the powers of mind and spirit grow along with it.
15. soil: stain. **cautel:** deceit. **16. will:** desire.
17. His greatness weigh'd: considering his princely status.
19. unvalued: of low rank.
20. Carve for himself: indulge his own wishes.
23. voice: vote, approval. **yielding:** consent. **that body:** i.e. the state.
26. in . . . place: i.e. acting as he must act in the position he occupies.
28. main: general. **goes withal:** accord with.
30. credent: credulous.

Out of the shot and danger of desire.
The chariest maid is prodigal enough
If she unmask her beauty to the moon.
Virtue itself scapes not calumnious strokes.
The canker galls the infants of the spring
Too oft before their buttons be disclos'd,
And in the morn and liquid dew of youth
Contagious blastments are most imminent.
Be wary then, best safety lies in fear:
Youth to itself rebels, though none else near.

Oph. I shall the effect of this good lesson keep
As watchman to my heart. But, good my brother,
Do not, as some ungracious pastors do,
Show me the steep and thorny way to heaven,
Whiles, [like] a puff'd and reckless libertine,
Himself the primrose path of dalliance treads,
And reaks not his own rede.

Laer. O, fear me not.

Enter POLONIUS.

I stay too long—but here my father comes.
A double blessing is a double grace,
Occasion smiles upon a second leave.

Pol. Yet here, Laertes? Aboard, aboard, for shame!
The wind sits in the shoulder of your sail,
And you are stay'd for. There—[*laying his hand on Laertes' head*] my blessing with thee!
And these few precepts in thy memory
Look thou character. Give thy thoughts no tongue,
Nor any unproportion'd thought his act.
Be thou familiar, but by no means vulgar:
Those friends thou hast, and their adoption tried,
Grapple them unto thy soul with hoops of steel,
But do not dull thy palm with entertainment
Of each new-hatch'd, unfledg'd courage. Beware
Of entrance to a quarrel, but being in,
Bear't that th' opposed may beware of thee.
Give every man thy ear, but few thy voice,
Take each man's censure, but reserve thy judgment.
Costly thy habit as thy purse can buy,
But not express'd in fancy, rich, not gaudy,
For the apparel oft proclaims the man,
And they in France of the best rank and station
[Are] of a most select and generous chief in that.
Neither a borrower nor a lender [be],
For [loan] oft loses both itself and friend,
And borrowing dulleth [th'] edge of husbandry.
This above all: to thine own self be true,
And it must follow, as the night the day,
Thou canst not then be false to any man.
Farewell, my blessing season this in thee!

Laer. Most humbly do I take my leave, my lord.

Pol. The time invests you, go, your servants tend.

Laer. Farewell, Ophelia, and remember well
What I have said to you.

Oph. 'Tis in my memory lock'd,
And you yourself shall keep the key of it.

Laer. Farewell. *Exit Laertes.*

Pol. What is't, Ophelia, he hath said to you?

Oph. So please you, something touching the Lord Hamlet.

Pol. Marry, well bethought.
'Tis told me, he hath very oft of late
Given private time to you, and you yourself
Have of your audience been most free and bounteous.
If it be so—as so 'tis put on me,
And that in way of caution—I must tell you,
You do not understand yourself so clearly
As it behooves my daughter and your honor.
What is between you? Give me up the truth.

Oph. He hath, my lord, of late made many tenders
Of his affection to me.

Pol. Affection, puh! You speak like a green girl,
Unsifted in such perilous circumstance.
Do you believe his tenders, as you call them?

Oph. I do not know, my lord, what I should think.

Pol. Marry, I will teach you: think yourself a baby
That you have ta'en these tenders for true pay,
Which are not sterling. Tender yourself more dearly,
Or (not to crack the wind of the poor phrase,
[Wringing] it thus) you'll tender me a fool.

Oph. My lord, he hath importun'd me with love
In honorable fashion.

Pol. Ay, fashion you may call it. Go to, go to.

Oph. And hath given countenance to his speech, my lord,
With almost all the holy vows of heaven.

Pol. Ay, springes to catch woodcocks. I do know,
When the blood burns, how prodigal the soul
Lends the tongue vows. These blazes, daughter,
Giving more light than heat, extinct in both
Even in their promise, as it is a-making,
You must not take for fire. From this time
Be something scanter of your maiden presence,
Set your entreatments at a higher rate
Than a command to parle. For Lord Hamlet,
Believe so much in him, that he is young,

35. shot: range.
39. canker: canker-worm. **40. buttons:** buds. **disclos'd:** opened.
42. blastments: withering blights. **44. to:** of.
47. ungracious: graceless. **49. puff'd:** bloated.
51. reaks: recks, heeds. **rede:** advice. **fear me not:** don't worry about me.
54. Occasion: opportunity (here personified, as often). **smiles upon:** i.e. graciously bestows. **59. character:** inscribe.
60. unproportion'd: unfitting.
61. familiar: affable, sociable. **vulgar:** friendly with everybody.
62. their adoption tried: their association with you tested and proved.
65. courage: spirited, young blood.
67. Bear't that: manage it in such a way that.
69. Take: listen to. **censure:** opinion.
74. generous: noble. **chief:** eminence (?). But the line is probably corrupt. Perhaps *of a* is intrusive, in which case *chief* = chiefly.
77. husbandry: thrift.

81. season: preserve (?) or ripen, make fruitful (?).
83. invests: besieges. **tend:** wait.
90. Marry: indeed (originally the name of the Virgin Mary used as an oath). **94. put on:** told to.
99. tenders: offers. **102. Unsifted:** untried.
106. tenders. With play on the sense "money offered in payment" (as in *legal tender*). **107. Tender:** hold, value.
109. Wringing: straining, forcing to the limit. **tender . . . fool:** (1) show me that you are a fool; (2) make me look like a fool; (3) present me with a (bastard) grandchild.
112. fashion. See note on line 6. **113. countenance:** authority.
115. springes: snares. **woodcocks.** Proverbially gullible birds.
122–23. Set . . . parle: place a higher value on your favors; do not grant interviews simply because he asks for them. Polonius uses a military figure: *entreatments* = negotiations for surrender; *parle* = parley, discuss terms.
124. so . . . him: no more than this with respect to him.

And with a larger teder may he walk
Than may be given you. In few, Ophelia,
Do not believe his vows, for they are brokers,
Not of that dye which their investments show,
But mere [implorators] of unholy suits,
Breathing like sanctified and pious bonds,
The better to [beguile]. This is for all:
I would not, in plain terms, from this time forth
Have you so slander any moment leisure
As to give words or talk with the Lord Hamlet.
Look to't, I charge you. Come your ways.

Oph. I shall obey, my lord. *Exeunt.*

[Scene IV]

Enter Hamlet, Horatio, *and* Marcellus.

Ham. The air bites shrowdly, it is very cold.

Hor. It is [a] nipping and an eager air.

Ham. What hour now?

Hor. I think it lacks of twelf.

Mar. No, it is strook.

Hor. Indeed? I heard it not. It then draws near the season
Wherein the spirit held his wont to walk.

A flourish of trumpets, and two pieces goes off [within].

What does this mean, my lord?

Ham. The King doth wake to-night and takes his rouse,
Keeps wassail, and the swagg'ring up-spring reels;
And as he drains his draughts of Rhenish down,
The kettle-drum and trumpet thus bray out
The triumph of his pledge.

Hor. Is it a custom?

Ham. Ay, marry, is't,
But to my mind, though I am native here
And to the manner born, it is a custom
More honor'd in the breach than the observance.
This heavy-headed revel east and west
Makes us traduc'd and tax'd of other nations.
They clip us drunkards, and with swinish phrase
Soil our addition, and indeed it takes
From our achievements, though perform'd at height,
The pith and marrow of our attribute.
So, oft it chances in particular men,
That for some vicious mole of nature in them,
As in their birth, wherein they are not guilty
(Since nature cannot choose his origin),
By their o'ergrowth of some complexion
Oft breaking down the pales and forts of reason,
Or by some habit, that too much o'er-leavens
The form of plausive manners—that these men,
Carrying, I say, the stamp of one defect,
Being nature's livery, or fortune's star,
His virtues else, be they as pure as grace,
As infinite as man may undergo,
Shall in the general censure take corruption
From that particular fault: the dram of [ev'l]
Doth all the noble substance of a doubt
To his own scandal.

Enter Ghost.

Hor. Look, my lord, it comes!

Ham. Angels and ministers of grace defend us!
Be thou a spirit of health, or goblin damn'd,
Bring with thee airs from heaven, or blasts from hell,
Be thy intents wicked, or charitable,
Thou com'st in such a questionable shape
That I will speak to thee. I'll call thee Hamlet,
King, father, royal Dane. O, answer me!
Let me not burst in ignorance, but tell
Why thy canoniz'd bones, hearsed in death,
Have burst their cerements; why the sepulchre,
Wherein we saw thee quietly [inurn'd,]
Hath op'd his ponderous and marble jaws
To cast thee up again. What may this mean,
That thou, dead corse, again in complete steel
Revisits thus the glimpses of the moon,
Making night hideous, and we fools of nature
So horridly to shake our disposition
With thoughts beyond the reaches of our souls?
Say why is this? wherefore? what should we do?

[Ghost] beckons [Hamlet].

Hor. It beckons you to go away with it,
As if it some impartment did desire
To you alone.

Mar. Look with what courteous action
It waves you to a more removed ground,
But do not go with it.

Hor. No, by no means.

125. larger teder: longer tether. **127. brokers:** procurers.
128. Not . . . show: not of the color that their garments (*investments*) exhibit, i.e. not what they seem. **129. mere:** out-and-out.
130. bonds: (lover's) vows or assurances. Many editors follow Theobald in reading *bawds*.
133. slander: disgrace. **moment:** momentary.
135. Come your ways: come along.

I.iv. Location: The guard-platform of the castle.
1. shrowdly: shrewdly, wickedly. **2. eager:** sharp.
6 s.d. pieces: cannon.
8. doth . . . rouse: i.e. holds revels far into the night.
9. wassail: carousal. **up-spring:** wild dance.
10. Rhenish: Rhine wine.
12. triumph . . . pledge: accomplishment of his toast (by draining his cup at a single draught). **15. manner:** custom (of carousing).
16. More . . . observance: which it is more honorable to break than to observe. **18. tax'd of:** censured by. **19. clip:** clepe, call.
20. addition: titles of honor. **21. at height:** most excellently.
22. attribute: reputation. **23. particular:** individual.
24. vicious . . . nature: small natural blemish. **26. his:** its.
27. By . . . complexion: by the excess of some one of the humors (which were thought to govern the disposition). **28. pales:** fences.
29. o'er-leavens: makes itself felt throughout (as leaven works in the whole mass of dough). **30. plausive:** pleasing.
32. Being . . . star: i.e. whether they were born with it, or got it by misfortune. *Star* means "blemish."
34. undergo: carry the weight of, sustain.
35. general censure: popular opinion.
36. dram: minute amount. **ev'l:** evil, with a pun on *eale*, "yeast" (cf. *o'er-leavens* in line 29).
37. of a doubt. A famous crux, for which many emendations have been suggested, the most widely accepted being Steevens' *often dout* (i.e. extinguish).
38. To . . . scandal: i.e. so that it all shares in the disgrace.
40. of health: wholesome, good. **43. questionable:** inviting talk.
47. canoniz'd: buried with the prescribed rites.
48. cerements: grave-clothes. **52. complete steel:** full armor.
53. Revisits. The *-s* ending in the second person singular is common.
54. fools of nature: the children (or the dupes) of a purely natural order, baffled by the supernatural. **55. disposition:** nature.
59. impartment: communication.

Ham. It will not speak, then I will follow it.
Hor. Do not, my lord.
Ham. Why, what should be the fear?
I do not set my life at a pin's fee,
And for my soul, what can it do to that,
Being a thing immortal as itself?
It waves me forth again, I'll follow it.
Hor. What if it tempt you toward the flood, my lord,
Or to the dreadful summit of the cliff
That beetles o'er his base into the sea,
And there assume some other horrible form
Which might deprive your sovereignty of reason,
And draw you into madness? Think of it.
The very place puts toys of desperation,
Without more motive, into every brain
That looks so many fadoms to the sea
And hears it roar beneath.
Ham. It waves me still.—
Go on, I'll follow thee.
Mar. You shall not go, my lord.
Ham. Hold off your hands.
Hor. Be rul'd, you shall not go.
Ham. My fate cries out,
And makes each petty artere in this body
As hardy as the Nemean lion's nerve.
Still am I call'd. Unhand me, gentlemen.
By heaven, I'll make a ghost of him that lets me!
I say away!—Go on, I'll follow thee.
Exeunt Ghost and Hamlet.
Hor. He waxes desperate with [imagination].
Mar. Let's follow. 'Tis not fit thus to obey him.
Hor. Have after. To what issue will this come?
Mar. Something is rotten in the state of Denmark.
Hor. Heaven will direct it.
Mar. Nay, let's follow him. *Exeunt.*

[Scene V]

Enter Ghost *and* Hamlet.

Ham. Whither wilt thou lead me? Speak, I'll go no further.
Ghost. Mark me.
Ham. I will.
Ghost. My hour is almost come
When I to sulph'rous and tormenting flames
Must render up myself.
Ham. Alas, poor ghost!
Ghost. Pity me not, but lend thy serious hearing
To what I shall unfold.
Ham. Speak, I am bound to hear.
Ghost. So art thou to revenge, when thou shalt hear.
Ham. What?
Ghost. I am thy father's spirit,
Doom'd for a certain term to walk the night,
And for the day confin'd to fast in fires,
Till the foul crimes done in my days of nature
Are burnt and purg'd away. But that I am forbid
To tell the secrets of my prison-house,
I could a tale unfold whose lightest word
Would harrow up thy soul, freeze thy young blood,
Make thy two eyes like stars start from their spheres,
Thy knotted and combined locks to part,
And each particular hair to stand an end,
Like quills upon the fearful porpentine.
But this eternal blazon must not be
To ears of flesh and blood. List, list, O, list!
If thou didst ever thy dear father love—
Ham. O God!
Ghost. Revenge his foul and most unnatural murther.
Ham. Murther!
Ghost. Murther most foul, as in the best it is,
But this most foul, strange, and unnatural.
Ham. Haste me to know't, that I with wings as swift
As meditation, or the thoughts of love,
May sweep to my revenge.
Ghost. I find thee apt,
And duller shouldst thou be than the fat weed
That roots itself in ease on Lethe wharf,
Wouldst thou not stir in this. Now, Hamlet, hear:
'Tis given out that, sleeping in my orchard,
A serpent stung me, so the whole ear of Denmark
Is by a forged process of my death
Rankly abus'd; but know, thou noble youth,
The serpent that did sting thy father's life
Now wears his crown.
Ham. O my prophetic soul!
My uncle?
Ghost. Ay, that incestuous, that adulterate beast,
With witchcraft of his wits, with traitorous gifts—
O wicked wit and gifts that have the power
So to seduce!—won to his shameful lust
The will of my most seeming virtuous queen.
O Hamlet, what [a] falling-off was there
From me, whose love was of that dignity
That it went hand in hand even with the vow
I made to her in marriage, and to decline
Upon a wretch whose natural gifts were poor
To those of mine!
But virtue, as it never will be moved,
Though lewdness court it in a shape of heaven,
So [lust], though to a radiant angel link'd,
Will [sate] itself in a celestial bed
And prey on garbage.
But soft, methinks I scent the morning air,
Brief let me be. Sleeping within my orchard,

65. fee: worth.
73. deprive . . . reason: unseat reason from the rule of your mind.
75. toys of desperation: fancies of desperate action, i.e. inclinations to jump off. **77. fadoms:** fathoms.
82. artere: variant spelling of *artery;* here, ligament, sinew.
83. Nemean lion. Slain by Hercules as one of his twelve labors. **nerve:** sinew. **85. lets:** hinders. **91. it:** i.e. the issue.

I.v. Location: On the battlements of the castle.

11. fast: do penance. **12. crimes:** sins.
17. spheres: eye-sockets; with allusion to the revolving spheres in which, according to the Ptolemaic astronomy, the stars were fixed.
19. an end: on end. **20. fearful porpentine:** frightened porcupine.
21. eternal blazon: revelation of eternal things.
30. meditation: thought.
33. Lethe: river of Hades, the water of which made the drinker forget the past. **wharf:** bank. **35. orchard:** garden.
37. forged process: false account. **38. abus'd:** deceived.
42. adulterate: adulterous. **54. shape of heaven:** angelic form.

My custom always of the afternoon,
Upon my secure hour thy uncle stole,
With juice of cursed hebona in a vial,
And in the porches of my ears did pour
The leprous distillment, whose effect
Holds such an enmity with blood of man
That swift as quicksilver it courses through
The natural gates and alleys of the body,
And with a sudden vigor it doth [posset]
And curd, like eager droppings into milk,
The thin and wholesome blood. So did it mine,
And a most instant tetter bark'd about,
Most lazar-like, with vile and loathsome crust
All my smooth body.
Thus was I, sleeping, by a brother's hand
Of life, of crown, of queen, at once dispatch'd,
Cut off even in the blossoms of my sin,
Unhous'led, disappointed, unanel'd,
No reck'ning made, but sent to my account
With all my imperfections on my head.
O, horrible, O, horrible, most horrible!
If thou hast nature in thee, bear it not,
Let not the royal bed of Denmark be
A couch for luxury and damned incest.
But howsomever thou pursues this act,
Taint not thy mind, nor let thy soul contrive
Against thy mother aught. Leave her to heaven,
And to those thorns that in her bosom lodge
To prick and sting her. Fare thee well at once!
The glow-worm shows the matin to be near,
And gins to pale his uneffectual fire.
Adieu, adieu, adieu! remember me. [*Exit.*]

Ham. O all you host of heaven! O earth! What else?
And shall I couple hell? O fie, hold, hold, my heart,
And you, my sinows, grow not instant old,
But bear me [stiffly] up. Remember thee!
Ay, thou poor ghost, whiles memory holds a seat
In this distracted globe. Remember thee!
Yea, from the table of my memory
I'll wipe away all trivial fond records,
All saws of books, all forms, all pressures past
That youth and observation copied there,
And thy commandement all alone shall live
Within the book and volume of my brain,
Unmix'd with baser matter. Yes, by heaven!
O most pernicious woman!
O villain, villain, smiling, damned villain!
My tables—meet it is I set it down
That one may smile, and smile, and be a villain!

61. **secure:** carefree.
62. **hebona:** ebony (which Shakespeare, following a literary tradition, and perhaps also associating the word with *henbane*, thought the name of a poison). 68. **posset:** curdle. 69. **eager:** sour.
71. **tetter:** scabby eruption. **bark'd:** formed a hard covering, like bark on a tree. 72. **lazar-like:** leper-like.
75. **at once:** all at the same time. **dispatch'd:** deprived.
77. **Unhous'led:** without the Eucharist. **disappointed:** without (spiritual) preparation. **unanel'd:** unanointed, without extreme unction. 81. **nature:** natural feeling. 83. **luxury:** lust.
89. **matin:** morning. 90. **gins:** begins. 94. **sinows:** sinews.
97. **globe:** head. 98. **table:** writing tablet. 99. **fond:** foolish.
100. **saws:** wise sayings. **forms:** shapes, images. **pressures:** impressions.

At least I am sure it may be so in Denmark. [*He writes.*]
So, uncle, there you are. Now to my word:
It is "Adieu, adieu! remember me."
I have sworn't.

Hor. [*Within.*] My lord, my lord!

Mar. [*Within.*] Lord Hamlet!

Enter HORATIO *and* MARCELLUS.

Hor. Heavens secure him!

Ham. So be it!

Mar. Illo, ho, ho, my lord!

Ham. Hillo, ho, ho, boy! Come, [bird,] come.

Mar. How is't, my noble lord?

Hor. What news, my lord?

Ham. O, wonderful!

Hor. Good my lord, tell it.

Ham. No, you will reveal it.

Hor. Not I, my lord, by heaven.

Mar. Nor I, my lord.

Ham. How say you then, would heart of man once think it?—
But you'll be secret?

Both [*Hor., Mar.*]. Ay, by heaven, [my lord].

Ham. There's never a villain dwelling in all Denmark
But he's an arrant knave.

Hor. There needs no ghost, my lord, come from the grave
To tell us this.

Ham. Why, right, you are in the right,
And so, without more circumstance at all,
I hold it fit that we shake hands and part,
You, as your business and desire shall point you,
For every man hath business and desire,
Such as it is, and for my own poor part,
I will go pray.

Hor. These are but wild and whirling words, my lord.

Ham. I am sorry they offend you, heartily,
Yes, faith, heartily.

Hor. There's no offense, my lord.

Ham. Yes, by Saint Patrick, but there is, Horatio,
And much offense too. Touching this vision here,
It is an honest ghost, that let me tell you.
For your desire to know what is between us,
O'ermaster't as you may. And now, good friends,
As you are friends, scholars, and soldiers,
Give me one poor request.

Hor. What is't, my lord, we will.

Ham. Never make known what you have seen to-night.

Both [*Hor., Mar.*]. My lord, we will not.

Ham. Nay, but swear't.

Hor. In faith,
My lord, not I.

Mar. Nor I, my lord, in faith.

110. **word:** i.e. word of command from the Ghost.
116. **Hillo . . . come.** Hamlet answers Marcellus' halloo with a falconer's cry. 127. **circumstance:** ceremony.
138. **honest:** true, genuine. 143. **What is't:** whatever it is.

Ham. Upon my sword.
Mar. We have sworn, my lord, already.
Ham. Indeed, upon my sword, indeed.
Ghost cries under the stage.
Ghost. Swear.
Ham. Ha, ha, boy, say'st thou so? Art thou there, truepenny?
Come on, you hear this fellow in the cellarage,
Consent to swear.
Hor. Propose the oath, my lord.
Ham. Never to speak of this that you have seen,
Swear by my sword.
Ghost. [*Beneath.*] Swear.
Ham. *Hic et ubique?* Then we'll shift our ground.
Come hither, gentlemen,
And lay your hands again upon my sword.
Swear by my sword
Never to speak of this that you have heard.
Ghost. [*Beneath.*] Swear by his sword.
Ham. Well said, old mole, canst work i' th' earth so fast?
A worthy pioner! Once more remove, good friends.
Hor. O day and night, but this is wondrous strange!
Ham. And therefore as a stranger give it welcome.
There are more things in heaven and earth, Horatio,
Than are dreamt of in your philosophy.
But come—
Here, as before, never, so help you mercy,
How strange or odd some'er I bear myself—
As I perchance hereafter shall think meet
To put an antic disposition on—
That you, at such times seeing me, never shall,
With arms encumb'red thus, or this headshake,
Or by pronouncing of some doubtful phrase,
As "Well, well, we know," or "We could, and if we would,"
Or "If we list to speak," or "There be, and if they might,"
Or such ambiguous giving out, to note
That you know aught of me—this do swear,
So grace and mercy at your most need help you.
Ghost. [*Beneath.*] Swear. [*They swear.*]
Ham. Rest, rest, perturbed spirit! So, gentlemen,
With all my love I do commend me to you,
And what so poor a man as Hamlet is
May do t' express his love and friending to you,
God willing, shall not lack. Let us go in together,
And still your fingers on your lips, I pray.
The time is out of joint—O cursed spite,
That ever I was born to set it right!
Nay, come, let's go together. *Exeunt.*

147. Upon my sword: i.e. on the cross formed by the hilt.
150. truepenny: trusty fellow.
156. Hic et ubique: here and everywhere.
163. pioner: digger, miner (variant of *pioneer*).
165. as . . . welcome: give it the welcome due in courtesy to strangers.
167. your. See note on I.i.138. **philosophy:** i.e. natural philosophy, science.
172. put . . . on: behave in some fantastic manner, act like a madman.
174. encumb'red: folded. **176. and if:** if.
177. list: cared, had a mind. **178. note:** indicate.
187. still: always.
190. Nay . . . together. They are holding back to let him go first.

[ACT II, SCENE I]

Enter old POLONIUS *with his man* [REYNALDO].

Pol. Give him this money and these notes, Reynaldo.
Rey. I will, my lord.
Pol. You shall do marvell's wisely, good Reynaldo,
Before you visit him, to make inquire
Of his behavior.
Rey. My lord, I did intend it.
Pol. Marry, well said, very well said. Look you, sir,
Inquire me first what Danskers are in Paris,
And how, and who, what means, and where they keep,
What company, at what expense; and finding
By this encompassment and drift of question
That they do know my son, come you more nearer
Than your particular demands will touch it.
Take you as 'twere some distant knowledge of him,
As thus, "I know his father and his friends,
And in part him." Do you mark this, Reynaldo?
Rey. Ay, very well, my lord.
Pol. "And in part him—but," you may say, "not well.
But if't be he I mean, he's very wild,
Addicted so and so," and there put on him
What forgeries you please: marry, none so rank
As may dishonor him, take heed of that,
But, sir, such wanton, wild, and usual slips
As are companions noted and most known
To youth and liberty.
Rey. As gaming, my lord.
Pol. Ay, or drinking, fencing, swearing, quarrelling,
Drabbing—you may go so far.
Rey. My lord, that would dishonor him.
Pol. Faith, as you may season it in the charge:
You must not put another scandal on him,
That he is open to incontinency—
That's not my meaning. But breathe his faults so quaintly
That they may seem the taints of liberty,
The flash and outbreak of a fiery mind,
A savageness in unreclaimed blood,
Of general assault.
Rey. But, my good lord—
Pol. Wherefore should you do this?
Rey. Ay, my lord,
I would know that.
Pol. Marry, sir, here's my drift,
And I believe it is a fetch of wit:
You laying these slight sallies on my son,

II.i. Location: Polonius' quarters in the castle.
3. marvell's: marvellous(ly). **7. Danskers:** Danes.
8. keep: lodge.
10. encompassment: circuitousness. **drift of question:** directing of the conversation. **12. particular demands:** direct questions.
20. forgeries: invented charges. **22. wanton:** sportive.
26. Drabbing: whoring.
28. Faith. Most editors read *Faith, no,* following F1; this makes easier sense. **season:** qualify, temper.
30. open to incontinency: habitually profligate.
31. quaintly: artfully. **34. unreclaimed:** untamed.
35. Of general assault: i.e. to which young men are generally subject.
38. fetch of wit: ingenious device. **39. sallies:** sullies, blemishes.

As 'twere a thing a little soil'd [wi' th'] working,
Mark you,
Your party in converse, him you would sound,
Having ever seen in the prenominate crimes
The youth you breathe of guilty, be assur'd
He closes with you in this consequence:
"Good sir," or so, or "friend," or "gentleman,"
According to the phrase or the addition
Of man and country.
Rey. Very good, my lord.
Pol. And then, sir, does 'a this—'a does—what was I about to say?
By the mass, I was about to say something.
Where did I leave?
Rey. At "closes in the consequence."
Pol. At "closes in the consequence," ay, marry.
He closes thus: "I know the gentleman.
I saw him yesterday, or th' other day,
Or then, or then, with such or such, and as you say,
There was 'a gaming, there o'ertook in 's rouse,
There falling out at tennis"; or, perchance,
"I saw him enter such a house of sale,"
Videlicet, a brothel, or so forth. See you now,
Your bait of falsehood take this carp of truth,
And thus do we of wisdom and of reach,
With windlasses and with assays of bias,
By indirections find directions out;
So by my former lecture and advice
Shall you my son. You have me, have you not?
Rey. My lord, I have.
Pol. God buy ye, fare ye well.
Rey. Good my lord.
Pol. Observe his inclination in yourself.
Rey. I shall, my lord.
Pol. And let him ply his music.
Rey. Well, my lord.
Pol. Farewell. *Exit Reynaldo.*

Enter OPHELIA.

How now, Ophelia, what's the matter?
Oph. O my lord, my lord, I have been so affrighted!
Pol. With what, i' th' name of God?
Oph. My lord, as I was sewing in my closet,
Lord Hamlet, with his doublet all unbrac'd,
No hat upon his head, his stockins fouled,
Ungart'red, and down-gyved to his ankle,
Pale as his shirt, his knees knocking each other,
And with a look so piteous in purport
As if he had been loosed out of hell

To speak of horrors—he comes before me.
Pol. Mad for thy love?
Oph. My lord, I do not know,
But truly I do fear it.
Pol. What said he?
Oph. He took me by the wrist, and held me hard,
Then goes he to the length of all his arm,
And with his other hand thus o'er his brow,
He falls to such perusal of my face
As 'a would draw it. Long stay'd he so.
At last, a little shaking of mine arm,
And thrice his head thus waving up and down,
He rais'd a sigh so piteous and profound
As it did seem to shatter all his bulk
And end his being. That done, he lets me go,
And with his head over his shoulder turn'd,
He seem'd to find his way without his eyes,
For out a' doors he went without their helps,
And to the last bended their light on me.
Pol. Come, go with me. I will go seek the King.
This is the very ecstasy of love,
Whose violent property fordoes itself,
And leads the will to desperate undertakings
As oft as any passions under heaven
That does afflict our natures. I am sorry—
What, have you given him any hard words of late?
Oph. No, my good lord, but as you did command
I did repel his letters, and denied
His access to me.
Pol. That hath made him mad.
I am sorry that with better heed and judgment
I had not coted him. I fear'd he did but trifle
And meant to wrack thee, but beshrow my jealousy!
By heaven, it is as proper to our age
To cast beyond ourselves in our opinions,
As it is common for the younger sort
To lack discretion. Come, go we to the King.
This must be known, which, being kept close, might move
More grief to hide, than hate to utter love.
Come. *Exeunt.*

[SCENE II]

Flourish. Enter KING *and* QUEEN, ROSENCRANTZ *and* GUILDENSTERN [*cum aliis*].

King. Welcome, dear Rosencrantz and Guildenstern!
Moreover that we much did long to see you,
The need we have to use you did provoke
Our hasty sending. Something have you heard

40. **soil'd . . . working:** i.e. shopworn.
43. **Having:** if he has. **prenominate crimes:** aforementioned faults.
45. **closes:** falls in. **in this consequence:** as follows.
47. **addition:** style of address.
56. **o'ertook in 's rouse:** overcome by drink.
61. **reach:** capacity, understanding.
62. **windlasses:** roundabout methods. **assays of bias:** indirect attempts (a figure from the game of bowls, in which the player must make allowance for the curving course his bowl will take toward its mark). 63. **directions:** the way things are going.
65. **have me:** understand me.
66. **God buy ye:** good-bye (a contraction of *God be with you*).
68. **in:** by. Polonius asks him to observe Laertes directly, as well as making inquiries. 70. **let him ply:** see that he goes on with.
74. **closet:** private room. 75. **unbrac'd:** unlaced.
76. **stockins fouled:** stockings dirty.
77. **down-gyved:** hanging down like fetters on a prisoner's legs.

92. **bulk:** body. 99. **ecstasy:** madness.
100. **property:** quality. **fordoes:** destroys.
109. **coted:** observed.
110. **beshrow:** beshrew, plague take. **jealousy:** suspicious mind.
111. **proper . . . age:** characteristic of men of my age.
112. **cast beyond ourselves:** overshoot, go too far (by way of caution).
115. **close:** secret.
115–16. **move . . . love:** cause more grievous consequences by its concealment than we shall incur displeasure by making it known.

II.ii. **Location:** The castle.
2. **Moreover . . . you:** besides the fact that we wanted to see you for your own sakes.

Of Hamlet's transformation; so call it,
Sith nor th' exterior nor the inward man
Resembles that it was. What it should be,
More than his father's death, that thus hath put him
So much from th' understanding of himself,
I cannot dream of. I entreat you both
That, being of so young days brought up with him,
And sith so neighbored to his youth and havior,
That you voutsafe your rest here in our court
Some little time, so by your companies
To draw him on to pleasures, and to gather
So much as from occasion you may glean,
Whether aught to us unknown afflicts him thus,
That, open'd, lies within our remedy.

Queen. Good gentlemen, he hath much talk'd of you,
And sure I am two men there is not living
To whom he more adheres. If it will please you
To show us so much gentry and good will
As to expend your time with us a while
For the supply and profit of our hope,
Your visitation shall receive such thanks
As fits a king's remembrance.

Ros. Both your Majesties
Might, by the sovereign power you have of us,
Put your dread pleasures more into command
Than to entreaty.

Guil. But we both obey,
And here give up ourselves, in the full bent,
To lay our service freely at your feet,
To be commanded.

King. Thanks, Rosencrantz and gentle Guildenstern.

Queen. Thanks, Guildenstern and gentle Rosencrantz.
And I beseech you instantly to visit
My too much changed son. Go some of you
And bring these gentlemen where Hamlet is.

Guil. Heavens make our presence and our practices
Pleasant and helpful to him!

Queen. Ay, amen!

Exeunt Rosencrantz and Guildenstern [with some Attendants].

Enter Polonius.

Pol. Th' embassadors from Norway, my good lord,
Are joyfully return'd.

King. Thou still hast been the father of good news.

Pol. Have I, my lord? I assure my good liege
I hold my duty as I hold my soul,
Both to my God and to my gracious king;
And I do think, or else this brain of mine
Hunts not the trail of policy so sure
As it hath us'd to do, that I have found
The very cause of Hamlet's lunacy.

King. O, speak of that, that do I long to hear.

Pol. Give first admittance to th' embassadors;
My news shall be the fruit to that great feast.

King. Thyself do grace to them, and bring them in. [*Exit Polonius*.]
He tells me, my dear Gertrude, he hath found
The head and source of all your son's distemper.

Queen. I doubt it is no other but the main,
His father's death and our [o'erhasty] marriage.

Enter [Polonius *with* Voltemand *and* Cornelius, *the*] *Embassadors*.

King. Well, we shall sift him.—Welcome, my good friends!
Say, Voltemand, what from our brother Norway?

Vol. Most fair return of greetings and desires.
Upon our first, he sent out to suppress
His nephew's levies, which to him appear'd
To be a preparation 'gainst the Polack;
But better look'd into, he truly found
It was against your Highness. Whereat griev'd,
That so his sickness, age, and impotence
Was falsely borne in hand, sends out arrests
On Fortinbras, which he, in brief, obeys,
Receives rebuke from Norway, and in fine,
Makes vow before his uncle never more
To give th' assay of arms against your Majesty.
Whereon old Norway, overcome with joy,
Gives him three thousand crowns in annual fee,
And his commission to employ those soldiers,
So levied, as before, against the Polack,
With an entreaty, herein further shown, [*Giving a paper*.]
That it might please you to give quiet pass
Through your dominions for this enterprise,
On such regards of safety and allowance
As therein are set down.

King. It likes us well,
And at our more considered time we'll read,
Answer, and think upon this business.
Mean time, we thank you for your well-took labor.
Go to your rest, at night we'll feast together.
Most welcome home!

Exeunt Embassadors [and Attendants].

Pol. This business is well ended.
My liege, and madam, to expostulate
What majesty should be, what duty is,
Why day is day, night night, and time is time,
Were nothing but to waste night, day, and time;
Therefore, [since] brevity is the soul of wit,
And tediousness the limbs and outward flourishes,
I will be brief. Your noble son is mad:
Mad call I it, for to define true madness,
What is't but to be nothing else but mad?
But let that go.

6. Sith: since. **11. of**: from.
13. voutsafe your rest: vouchsafe to remain.
21. more adheres: is more attached. **22. gentry**: courtesy.
24. supply and profit: support and advancement.
30. in . . . bent: to our utmost. **40. embassadors**: ambassadors.
42. still: always. **43. liege**: sovereign.
47. policy: statecraft.

52. fruit: dessert.
55. head. Synonymous with *source*. **distemper**: (mental) illness.
56. doubt: suspect. **main**: main cause.
61. Upon our first: at our first representation.
65. griev'd: aggrieved, offended.
67. borne in hand: taken advantage of.
69. in fine: in the end. **71. assay**: trial.
79. On . . . allowance: with such safeguards and provisos.
80. likes: pleases. **81. consider'd**: suitable for consideration.
86. expostulate: expound. **90. wit**: understanding, wisdom.

Queen. More matter with less art.
Pol. Madam, I swear I use no art at all.
That he's mad, 'tis true, 'tis true 'tis pity,
And pity 'tis 'tis true—a foolish figure,
But farewell it, for I will use no art.
Mad let us grant him then, and now remains
That we find out the cause of this effect,
Or rather say, the cause of this defect,
For this effect defective comes by cause:
Thus it remains, and the remainder thus.
Perpend.
I have a daughter—have while she is mine—
Who in her duty and obedience, mark,
Hath given me this. Now gather, and surmise.
[*Reads the salutation of the letter.*]
"To the celestial and my soul's idol, the most beautified Ophelia"—
That's an ill phrase, a vile phrase, "beautified" is a vile phrase. But you shall hear. Thus:
"In her excellent white bosom, these, etc."
Queen. Came this from Hamlet to her?
Pol. Good madam, stay awhile. I will be faithful.
[*Reads the*] *letter.*
"Doubt thou the stars are fire,
Doubt that the sun doth move,
Doubt truth to be a liar,
But never doubt I love.
O dear Ophelia, I am ill at these numbers. I have not art to reckon my groans, but that I love thee best, O most best, believe it. Adieu.
Thine evermore, most dear lady,
whilst this machine is to him, Hamlet."
This in obedience hath my daughter shown me,
And more [above], hath his solicitings,
As they fell out by time, by means, and place,
All given to mine ear.
King. But how hath she
Receiv'd his love?
Pol. What do you think of me?
King. As of a man faithful and honorable.
Pol. I would fain prove so. But what might you think,
When I had seen this hot love on the wing—
As I perceiv'd it (I must tell you that)
Before my daughter told me—what might you,
Or my dear Majesty your queen here, think,
If I had play'd the desk or table-book,
Or given my heart a [winking,] mute and dumb,
Or look'd upon this love with idle sight,
What might you think? No, I went round to work,
And my young mistress thus I did bespeak:
"Lord Hamlet is a prince out of thy star;
This must not be"; and then I prescripts gave her,
That she should lock herself from [his] resort,
Admit no messengers, receive no tokens.
Which done, she took the fruits of my advice;
And he repell'd, a short tale to make,
Fell into a sadness, then into a fast,
Thence to a watch, thence into a weakness,
Thence to [a] lightness, and by this declension,
Into the madness wherein now he raves,
And all we mourn for.
King. Do you think ['tis] this?
Queen. It may be, very like.
Pol. Hath there been such a time—I would fain know that—
That I have positively said, "'Tis so,"
When it prov'd otherwise?
King. Not that I know.
Pol. [*Points to his head and shoulder.*] Take this from this, if this be otherwise.
If circumstances lead me, I will find
Where truth is hid, though it were hid indeed
Within the centre.
King. How may we try it further?
Pol. You know sometimes he walks four hours together
Here in the lobby.
Queen. So he does indeed.
Pol. At such a time I'll loose my daughter to him.
Be you and I behind an arras then,
Mark the encounter: if he love her not,
And be not from his reason fall'n thereon,
Let me be no assistant for a state,
But keep a farm and carters.
King. We will try it.

Enter HAMLET [*reading on a book*].

Queen. But look where sadly the poor wretch comes reading.
Pol. Away, I do beseech you, both away.
I'll board him presently. *Exeunt King and Queen.*
O, give me leave,
How does my good Lord Hamlet?
Ham. Well, God-a-mercy.
Pol. Do you know me, my lord?
Ham. Excellent well, you are a fishmonger.
Pol. Not I, my lord.
Ham. Then I would you were so honest a man.
Pol. Honest, my lord?
Ham. Ay, sir, to be honest, as this world goes, is to be one man pick'd out of ten thousand.
Pol. That's very true, my lord.
Ham. For if the sun breed maggots in a dead dog,

95. **art:** i.e. rhetorical art. 98. **figure:** figure of speech.
103. **For . . . cause:** for this effect (which shows as a defect in Hamlet's reason) is not merely accidental, and has a cause we may trace.
105. **Perpend:** consider.
109–10. **beautified:** beautiful (not an uncommon usage).
118. **Doubt:** suspect.
120. **ill . . . numbers:** bad at versifying.
121. **reckon:** count (with a quibble on *numbers*).
124. **machine:** body. 126. **more above:** furthermore.
131. **fain:** willingly, gladly.
136. **play'd . . . table-book:** i.e. noted the matter secretly.
137. **winking:** closing of the eyes.
138. **idle sight:** noncomprehending eyes.
139. **round:** straightforwardly. 140. **bespeak:** address.
141. **star:** i.e. sphere, lot in life.
145. **took . . . of:** profited by, i.e. carried out.
146. **repell'd:** repulsed. 148. **watch:** sleeplessness.
149. **lightness:** lightheadedness.
159. **centre:** i.e. of the earth (which in the Ptolemaic system is also the centre of the universe).
163. **arras:** hanging tapestry. 165. **thereon:** because of that.
170. **board:** accost. **presently:** at once.
172. **God-a-mercy:** thank you.
174. **fishmonger.** Usually explained as slang for "bawd," but no evidence has been produced for such a usage in Shakespeare's day.

being a good kissing carrion—Have you a daughter?

Pol. I have, my lord.

Ham. Let her not walk i' th' sun. Conception is a blessing, but as your daughter may conceive, friend, look to't.

Pol. [*Aside.*] How say you by that? still harping on my daughter. Yet he knew me not at first, 'a said I was a fishmonger. 'A is far gone. And truly in my youth I suff'red much extremity for love—very near this. I'll speak to him again.—What do you read, my lord?

Ham. Words, words, words.

Pol. What is the matter, my lord?

Ham. Between who?

Pol. I mean, the matter that you read, my lord.

Ham. Slanders, sir; for the satirical rogue says here that old men have grey beards, that their faces are wrinkled, their eyes purging thick amber and plum-tree gum, and that they have a plentiful lack of wit, together with most weak hams; all which, sir, though I most powerfully and potently believe, yet I hold it not honesty to have it thus set down, for yourself, sir, shall grow old as I am, if like a crab you could go backward.

Pol. [*Aside.*] Though this be madness, yet there is method in't.—Will you walk out of the air, my lord?

Ham. Into my grave.

Pol. Indeed that's out of the air. [*Aside.*] How pregnant sometimes his replies are! a happiness that often madness hits on, which reason and [sanity] could not so prosperously be deliver'd of. I will leave him, [and suddenly contrive the means of meeting between him] and my daughter.—My lord, I will take my leave of you.

Ham. You cannot take from me any thing that I will not more willingly part withal—except my life, except my life, except my life.

Pol. Fare you well, my lord.

Ham. These tedious old fools!

Enter GUILDENSTERN *and* ROSENCRANTZ.

Pol. You go to seek the Lord Hamlet, there he is.

Ros. [*To Polonius.*] God save you, sir!

[*Exit Polonius.*]

Guil. My honor'd lord!

Ros. My most dear lord!

Ham. My [excellent] good friends! How dost thou, Guildenstern? Ah, Rosencrantz! Good lads, how do you both?

Ros. As the indifferent children of the earth.

Guil. Happy, in that we are not [over-]happy, on Fortune's [cap] we are not the very button.

Ham. Nor the soles of her shoe?

Ros. Neither, my lord.

Ham. Then you live about her waist, or in the middle of her favors?

Guil. Faith, her privates we.

Ham. In the secret parts of Fortune? O, most true, she is a strumpet. What news?

Ros. None, my lord, but the world's grown honest.

Ham. Then is doomsday near. But your news is not true. [Let me question more in particular. What have you, my good friends, deserv'd at the hands of Fortune, that she sends you to prison hither?

Guil. Prison, my lord?

Ham. Denmark's a prison.

Ros. Then is the world one.

Ham. A goodly one, in which there are many confines, wards, and dungeons, Denmark being one o' th' worst.

Ros. We think not so, my lord.

Ham. Why then 'tis none to you; for there is nothing either good or bad, but thinking makes it so. To me it is a prison.

Ros. Why then your ambition makes it one. 'Tis too narrow for your mind.

Ham. O God, I could be bounded in a nutshell, and count myself a king of infinite space—were it not that I have bad dreams.

Guil. Which dreams indeed are ambition, for the very substance of the ambitious is merely the shadow of a dream.

Ham. A dream itself is but a shadow.

Ros. Truly, and I hold ambition of so airy and light a quality that it is but a shadow's shadow.

Ham. Then are our beggars bodies, and our monarchs and outstretch'd heroes the beggars' shadows. Shall we to th' court? for, by my fay, I cannot reason.

Both [*Ros., Guil.*]. We'll wait upon you.

Ham. No such matter. I will not sort you with the rest of my servants; for to speak to you like an honest man, I am most dreadfully attended.] But in the beaten way of friendship, what make you at Elsinore?

Ros. To visit you, my lord, no other occasion.

Ham. Beggar that I am, I am [even] poor in thanks—but I thank you, and sure, dear friends, my thanks are too dear a halfpenny. Were you not sent for? is it your own inclining? is it a free visitation? Come, come, deal justly with me. Come, come—nay, speak.

Guil. What should we say, my lord?

Ham. Any thing but to th' purpose. You were sent for, and there is a kind of confession in your looks, which your modesties have not craft enough to color. I know the good King and Queen have sent for you.

Ros. To what end, my lord?

182. **good kissing carrion:** flesh good enough for the sun to kiss.
184. **Conception:** understanding (with following play on the sense "conceiving a child").
193. **matter:** subject; but Hamlet replies as if he had understood Polonius to mean "cause for a quarrel."
202. **honesty:** a fitting thing.
206. **method:** orderly arrangement, sequence of ideas. **out . . . air.** Outdoor air was thought to be bad for invalids.
209. **pregnant:** apt. 212. **suddenly:** at once.
227. **indifferent:** average.

234. **privates:** (1) intimate friends; (2) genitalia.
236. **strumpet.** A common epithet for Fortune, because she grants favors to all men. 246. **wards:** cells.
263. **bodies:** i.e. not shadows (since they lack ambition).
264. **outstretch'd:** i.e. with their ambition extended to the utmost (and hence producing stretched-out or elongated shadows).
265. **fay:** faith. 266. **wait upon you:** attend you thither.
267. **sort:** associate. 269. **dreadfully:** execrably.
274. **too . . . halfpenny:** too expensive priced at a halfpenny, i.e. not worth much. 276. **justly:** honestly.
278. **but.** Ordinarily punctuated with a comma preceding, to give the sense "provided that it is"; but Q2 has no comma, and Hamlet may intend, or include, the sense "except."
280. **modesties:** sense of shame.

Ham. That you must teach me. But let me conjure you, by the rights of our fellowship, by the consonancy of our youth, by the obligation of our ever-preserv'd love, and by what more dear a better proposer can charge you withal, be even and direct with me, whether you were sent for or no!

Ros. [*Aside to Guildenstern.*] What say you?

Ham. [*Aside.*] Nay then I have an eye of you!—If you love me, hold not off.

Guil. My lord, we were sent for.

Ham. I will tell you why, so shall my anticipation prevent your discovery, and your secrecy to the King and Queen moult no feather. I have of late—but wherefore I know not—lost all my mirth, forgone all custom of exercises; and indeed it goes so heavily with my disposition, that this goodly frame, the earth, seems to me a sterile promontory; this most excellent canopy, the air, look you, this brave o'erhanging firmament, this majestical roof fretted with golden fire, why, it appeareth nothing to me but a foul and pestilent congregation of vapors. What [a] piece of work is a man, how noble in reason, how infinite in faculties, in form and moving, how express and admirable in action, how like an angel in apprehension, how like a god! the beauty of the world; the paragon of animals; and yet to me what is this quintessence of dust? Man delights not me—nor women neither, though by your smiling you seem to say so.

Ros. My lord, there was no such stuff in my thoughts.

Ham. Why did ye laugh then, when I said, "Man delights not me"?

Ros. To think, my lord, if you delight not in man, what lenten entertainment the players shall receive from you. We coted them on the way, and hither are they coming to offer you service.

Ham. He that plays the king shall be welcome—his Majesty shall have tribute on me, the adventerous knight shall use his foil and target, the lover shall not sigh gratis, the humorous man shall end his part in peace, [the clown shall make those laugh whose lungs are [tickle] a' th' sere,] and the lady shall say her mind freely, or the [blank] verse shall halt for't. What players are they?

Ros. Even those you were wont to take such delight in, the tragedians of the city.

Ham. How chances it they travel? Their residence, both in reputation and profit, was better both ways.

Ros. I think their inhibition comes by the means of the late innovation.

Ham. Do they hold the same estimation they did when I was in the city? Are they so follow'd?

Ros. No indeed are they not.

[*Ham.* How comes it? do they grow rusty?

Ros. Nay, their endeavor keeps in the wonted pace; but there is, sir, an aery of children, little eyases, that cry out on the top of question, and are most tyrannically clapp'd for't. These are now the fashion, and so [berattle] the common stages—so they call them—that many wearing rapiers are afraid of goose-quills and dare scarce come thither.

Ham. What, are they children? Who maintains 'em? How are they escoted? Will they pursue the quality no longer than they can sing? Will they not say afterwards, if they should grow themselves to common players (as it is [most like], if their means are [no] better), their writers do them wrong, to make them exclaim against their own succession?

Ros. Faith, there has been much to do on both sides, and the nation holds it no sin to tarre them to controversy. There was for a while no money bid for argument, unless the poet and the player went to cuffs in the question.

Ham. Is't possible?

Guil. O, there has been much throwing about of brains.

Ham. Do the boys carry it away?

Ros. Ay, that they do, my lord—Hercules and his load too.]

284–85. **consonancy . . . youth**: similarity of our ages.
287. **charge**: urge, adjure. **even**: frank, honest (cf. modern "level with me"). 290. **of**: on.
294. **prevent your discovery**: forestall your disclosure (of what the King and Queen have said to you in confidence).
295. **moult no feather**: not be impaired in the least.
297. **custom of exercises**: my usual athletic activities.
300. **brave**: splendid. 301. **fretted**: ornamented as with fretwork.
303. **piece of work**: masterpiece.
304–7. **how infinite . . . god.** See the Textual Notes for the different punctuation in F1. 305. **express**: exact.
308. **quintessence**: finest and purest extract.
316. **lenten entertainment**: meagre reception.
317. **coted**: outstripped. 320. **on**: of, from.
320–21. **adventerous**: adventurous, i.e. wandering in search of adventure.
321. **foil and target**: light fencing sword and small shield.
322. **gratis**: without reward. **humorous**: dominated by some eccentric trait (like the melancholy Jaques in *As You Like It*).
324. **tickle . . . sere**: i.e. easily made to laugh (literally, describing a gun that goes off easily; *sere* = a catch in the gunlock; *tickle* = easily affected, highly sensitive to stimulus).
325. **halt**: limp, come off lamely (the verse will not scan if she omits indecent words).

332. **inhibition**: hindrance (to playing in the city). The word could be used of an official prohibition. See next note.
333. **innovation.** Shakespeare elsewhere uses this word of a political uprising or revolt, and lines 332–33 are often explained as meaning that the company had been forbidden to play in the city as the result of some disturbance. It is commonly conjectured that the allusion is to the Essex rebellion of 1601, but it is known that Shakespeare's company, though to some extent involved on account of the special performance of *Richard II* they were commissioned to give on the eve of the rising, were not in fact punished by inhibition. A second interpretation explains *innovation* as referring to the new theatrical vogue described in lines 339 ff., and conjectures that *inhibition* may allude to a Privy Council order of 1600 restricting the number of London playhouses to two and the number of performances to two a week.
337–62. **How . . . too.** This passage refers topically to the "War of the Theatres" between the child actors and their poet Jonson on the one side, and on the other the adults, with Dekker, Marston, and possibly Shakespeare as spokesmen, in 1600–1601.
339. **aery**: nest. **eyases**: unfledged hawks.
340. **cry . . . question**: cry shrilly above others in controversy.
341. **tyrannically**: outrageously.
342. **berattle**: cry down, satirize. **common stages**: public theatres (the children played at the Blackfriars, a private theatre).
344. **goose-quills**: pens (of satirical playwrights).
346. **escoted**: supported.
347. **quality**: profession (of acting). **no . . . sing**: i.e. only until their voices change. 351. **succession**: future. 352. **to do**: ado.
353. **tarre**: incite. 355. **argument**: plot of a play.
356. **in the question**: i.e. as part of the script.
360. **carry it away**: win.
361–62. **Hercules . . . too.** Hercules in the course of one of his twelve labors supported the world for Atlas; the children do better, for they carry away the world and Hercules as well. There is an allusion to the Globe playhouse, which reportedly had for its sign the figure of Hercules upholding the world.

Ham. It is not very strange, for my uncle is King of Denmark, and those that would make mouths at him while my father liv'd, give twenty, forty, fifty, a hundred ducats a-piece for his picture in little. 'Sblood, there is something in this more than natural, if philosophy could find it out. *A flourish* [*for the Players*].

Guil. There are the players.

Ham. Gentlemen, you are welcome to Elsinore. Your hands, come then: th' appurtenance of welcome is fashion and ceremony. Let me comply with you in this garb, [lest my] extent to the players, which, I tell you, must show fairly outwards, should more appear like entertainment than yours. You are welcome; but my uncle-father and aunt-mother are deceiv'd.

Guil. In what, my dear lord?

Ham. I am but mad north-north-west. When the wind is southerly I know a hawk from a hand-saw.

Enter POLONIUS.

Pol. Well be with you, gentlemen!

Ham. [*Aside to them.*] Hark you, Guildenstern, and you too—at each ear a hearer—that great baby you see there is not yet out of his swaddling-clouts.

Ros. Happily he is the second time come to them, for they say an old man is twice a child.

Ham. I will prophesy, he comes to tell me of the players, mark it. [*Aloud.*] You say right, sir, a' Monday morning, 'twas then indeed.

Pol. My lord, I have news to tell you.

Ham. My lord, I have news to tell you. When Roscius was an actor in Rome—

Pol. The actors are come hither, my lord.

Ham. Buzz, buzz!

Pol. Upon my honor—

Ham. "Then came each actor on his ass"—

Pol. The best actors in the world, either for tragedy, comedy, history, pastoral, pastoral-comical, historical-pastoral, [tragical-historical, tragical-comical-historical-pastoral,] scene individable, or poem unlimited; Seneca cannot be too heavy, nor Plautus too light, for the law of writ and the liberty: these are the only men.

Ham. O Jephthah, judge of Israel, what a treasure hadst thou!

Pol. What a treasure had he, my lord?

Ham. Why—

"One fair daughter, and no more,
The which he loved passing well."

Pol. [*Aside.*] Still on my daughter.

Ham. Am I not i' th' right, old Jephthah?

Pol. If you call me Jephthah, my lord, I have a daughter that I love passing well.

Ham. Nay, that follows not.

Pol. What follows then, my lord?

Ham. Why—

"As by lot, God wot,"

and then, you know,

"It came to pass, as most like it was"—

the first row of the pious chanson will show you more, for look where my abridgment comes.

Enter the PLAYERS, [*four or five*].

You are welcome, masters, welcome all. I am glad to see thee well. Welcome, good friends. O, old friend! why, thy face is valanc'd since I saw thee last; com'st thou to beard me in Denmark? What, my young lady and mistress! by' lady, your ladyship is nearer to heaven than when I saw you last, by the altitude of a chopine. Pray God your voice, like a piece of uncurrent gold, be not crack'd within the ring. Masters, you are all welcome. We'll e'en to't like [French] falc'ners—fly at any thing we see; we'll have a speech straight. Come give us a taste of your quality, come, a passionate speech.

[*1.*] *Play.* What speech, my good lord?

Ham. I heard thee speak me a speech once, but it was never acted, or if it was, not above once; for the play, I remember, pleas'd not the million, 'twas caviary to the general, but it was—as I receiv'd it, and others, whose judgments in such matters cried in the top of mine—an excellent play, well digested in the scenes, set down with as much modesty as cunning. I remember one said there were no sallets in the lines to make the matter savory, nor no matter in the phrase that might indict the author of affection, but call'd it an honest method, as wholesome as sweet, and by very much more handsome than fine. One speech in't I chiefly lov'd, 'twas Aeneas' [tale] to Dido, and thereabout of it especially when he speaks of Priam's slaughter. If it live in your memory, begin at

364. mouths: derisive faces.
366. 'Sblood: by God's (Christ's) blood.
372. comply: observe the formalities.
373. garb: fashion, manner. **my extent:** i.e. the degree of courtesy I show.
374–75. more . . . yours: seem to be a warmer reception than I have given you.
379. hawk, hand-saw. Both cutting-tools; but also both birds, if *hand-saw* quibbles on *hernshaw*, "heron," a bird preyed upon by the hawk. **383. swaddling-clouts:** swaddling clothes.
384. Happily: haply, perhaps.
385. twice: i.e. for the second time.
391. Roscius: the most famous of Roman actors (died 62 B.C.). News about him would be stale news indeed.
393. Buzz: exclamation of impatience at someone who tells news already known.
399. scene individable: play observing the unity of place.
399–400. poem unlimited: play ignoring rules such as the three unities.
400. Seneca: Roman writer of tragedies. **Plautus:** Roman writer of comedies.
401. for . . . liberty: for strict observance of the rules, or for freedom from them (with possible allusion to the location of playhouses, which were not built in properties under city jurisdiction, but in the "liberties"—land once monastic and now outside the jurisdiction of the city authorities).
402. only: very best (a frequent use).
403. Jephthah . . . Israel: title of a ballad, from which Hamlet goes on to quote. For the story of Jephthah and his daughter, see Judges 11.
419. row: stanza. **chanson:** song, ballad.
420. abridgment: (1) interruption; (2) pastime.
423. valanc'd: fringed, i.e. bearded.
424. beard: confront boldly (with obvious pun).
425. by' lady: by Our Lady. **427. chopine:** thick-soled shoe.
428. crack'd . . . ring: i.e. broken to the point where you can no longer play female roles. A coin with a crack extending far enough in from the edge to cross the circle surrounding the stamp of the sovereign's head was unacceptable in exchange (*uncurrent*).
431. straight: straightway. **432. quality:** professional skill.
437. caviary . . . general: caviare to the common people, i.e. too choice for the multitude.
438–39. cried . . . of: were louder than, i.e. carried more authority than.
441. sallets: salads, i.e. spicy jokes. **442. savory:** zesty.
443. affection: affectation. **445. fine:** showily dressed (in language).
448. Priam's slaughter: the slaying of Priam (at the fall of Troy).

this line—let me see, let me see:
"The rugged Pyrrhus, like th' Hyrcanian beast—"
'Tis not so, it begins with Pyrrhus:
"The rugged Pyrrhus, he whose sable arms,
Black as his purpose, did the night resemble
When he lay couched in th' ominous horse,
Hath now this dread and black complexion smear'd
With heraldy more dismal: head to foot
Now is he total gules, horridly trick'd
With blood of fathers, mothers, daughters, sons,
Bak'd and impasted with the parching streets,
That lend a tyrannous and a damned light
To their lord's murther. Roasted in wrath and fire,
And thus o'er-sized with coagulate gore,
With eyes like carbuncles, the hellish Pyrrhus
Old grandsire Priam seeks."
So proceed you.

Pol. 'Fore God, my lord, well spoken, with good accent and good discretion.

[*1.*] *Play.* "Anon he finds him
Striking too short at Greeks. His antique sword,
Rebellious to his arm, lies where it falls,
Repugnant to command. Unequal match'd,
Pyrrhus at Priam drives, in rage strikes wide,
But with the whiff and wind of his fell sword
Th' unnerved father falls. [Then senseless Ilium,]
Seeming to feel this blow, with flaming top
Stoops to his base, and with a hideous crash
Takes prisoner Pyrrhus' ear; for lo his sword,
Which was declining on the milky head
Of reverent Priam, seem'd i' th' air to stick.
So as a painted tyrant Pyrrhus stood
[And,] like a neutral to his will and matter,
Did nothing.
But as we often see, against some storm,
A silence in the heavens, the rack stand still,
The bold winds speechless, and the orb below
As hush as death, anon the dreadful thunder
Doth rend the region; so after Pyrrhus' pause,
A roused vengeance sets him new a-work,
And never did the Cyclops' hammers fall
On Mars's armor forg'd for proof eterne
With less remorse than Pyrrhus' bleeding sword
Now falls on Priam.
Out, out, thou strumpet Fortune! All you gods,
In general synod take away her power!
Break all the spokes and [fellies] from her wheel,
And bowl the round nave down the hill of heaven
As low as to the fiends!"

Pol. This is too long.

Ham. It shall to the barber's with your beard. Prithee say on, he's for a jig or a tale of bawdry, or he sleeps. Say on, come to Hecuba.

[*1.*] *Play.* "But who, ah woe, had seen the mobled queen"—

Ham. "The mobled queen"?

Pol. That's good, ["[mobled] queen" is good].

[*1.*] *Play.* "Run barefoot up and down, threat'ning the flames
With bisson rheum, a clout upon that head
Where late the diadem stood, and for a robe,
About her lank and all o'er-teemed loins,
A blanket, in the alarm of fear caught up—
Who this had seen, with tongue in venom steep'd,
'Gainst Fortune's state would treason have pronounc'd.
But if the gods themselves did see her then,
When she saw Pyrrhus make malicious sport
In mincing with his sword her [husband's] limbs,
The instant burst of clamor that she made,
Unless things mortal move them not at all,
Would have made milch the burning eyes of heaven,
And passion in the gods."

Pol. Look whe'er he has not turn'd his color and has tears in 's eyes. Prithee no more.

Ham. 'Tis well, I'll have thee speak out the rest of this soon. Good my lord, will you see the players well bestow'd? Do you hear, let them be well us'd, for they are the abstract and brief chronicles of the time. After your death you were better have a bad epitaph than their ill report while you live.

Pol. My lord, I will use them according to their desert.

Ham. God's bodkin, man, much better: use every man after his desert, and who shall scape whipping? Use them after your own honor and dignity—the less they deserve, the more merit is in your bounty. Take them in.

Pol. Come, sirs. [*Exit.*]

Ham. Follow him, friends, we'll hear a play tomorrow. [*Exeunt all the Players but the First.*] Dost thou hear me, old friend? Can you play "The Murther of Gonzago"?

[*1.*] *Play.* Ay, my lord.

Ham. We'll ha't to-morrow night. You could for need study a speech of some dozen or sixteen lines, which I would set down and insert in't, could you not?

[*1.*] *Play.* Ay, my lord.

Ham. Very well. Follow that lord, and look you mock him not. [*Exit First Player.*] My good friends, I'll leave you [till] night. You are welcome to Elsinore.

450. Pyrrhus: another name for Neoptolemus, Achilles' son. **Hyrcanian beast.** Hyrcania in the Caucasus was notorious for its tigers.
452. sable arms. The Greeks within the Trojan horse had blackened their skin so as to be inconspicuous when they emerged at night.
456. heraldy: heraldry. **dismal:** ill-boding.
457. gules: red (heraldic term). **trick'd:** adorned.
459. Bak'd: caked. **impasted:** crusted. **with . . . streets:** i.e. by the heat from the burning streets.
462. o'er-sized: covered over as with a coat of sizing.
463. carbuncles: jewels believed to shine in the dark.
471. Repugnant: resistant, hostile. **473. fell:** cruel.
474. unnerved: drained of strength. **senseless:** insensible. **Ilium:** the citadel of Troy. **479. reverent:** reverend, aged.
481. like . . . matter: i.e. poised midway between intention and performance. **483. against:** just before.
484. rack: cloud-mass. **487. region:** i.e. air.
489. Cyclops: giants who worked in Vulcan's smithy, where armor was made for the gods. **490. proof eterne:** eternal endurance.
491. remorse: pity. **495. fellies:** rims.

496. nave: hub.
500. jig: song-and-dance entertainment performed after the main play. **502. mobled:** muffled.
506. bisson rheum: blinding tears. **clout:** cloth.
508. o'er-teemed: worn out by childbearing.
511. state: rule, government. **517. milch:** moist (literally, milky).
518. passion: grief. **519. Look . . . not:** i.e. note how he has.
523. bestow'd: lodged. **us'd:** treated.
529. God's bodkin: by God's (Christ's) little body.
541. for need: if necessary.

Ros. Good my lord!
Ham. Ay so, God buy to you.
Exeunt [*Rosencrantz and Guildenstern*].
Now I am alone.
O, what a rogue and peasant slave am I!
Is it not monstrous that this player here,
But in a fiction, in a dream of passion,
Could force his soul so to his own conceit
That from her working all the visage wann'd,
Tears in his eyes, distraction in his aspect,
A broken voice, an' his whole function suiting
With forms to his conceit? And all for nothing,
For Hecuba!
What's Hecuba to him, or he to [Hecuba],
That he should weep for her? What would he do
Had he the motive and [the cue] for passion
That I have? He would drown the stage with tears,
And cleave the general ear with horrid speech,
Make mad the guilty, and appall the free,
Confound the ignorant, and amaze indeed
The very faculties of eyes and ears. Yet I,
A dull and muddy-mettled rascal, peak
Like John-a-dreams, unpregnant of my cause,
And can say nothing; no, not for a king,
Upon whose property and most dear life
A damn'd defeat was made. Am I a coward?
Who calls me villain, breaks my pate across,
Plucks off my beard and blows it in my face,
Tweaks me by the nose, gives me the lie i' th' throat
As deep as to the lungs? Who does me this?
Hah, 'swounds, I should take it; for it cannot be
But I am pigeon-liver'd, and lack gall
To make oppression bitter, or ere this
I should 'a' fatted all the region kites
With this slave's offal. Bloody, bawdy villain!
Remorseless, treacherous, lecherous, kindless villain!
Why, what an ass am I! This is most brave,
That I, the son of a dear [father] murthered,
Prompted to my revenge by heaven and hell,
Must like a whore unpack my heart with words,
And fall a-cursing like a very drab,
A stallion. Fie upon't, foh!
About, my brains! Hum—I have heard
That guilty creatures sitting at a play
Have by the very cunning of the scene
Been strook so to the soul, that presently
They have proclaim'd their malefactions:
For murther, though it have no tongue, will speak
With most miraculous organ. I'll have these players
Play something like the murther of my father
Before mine uncle. I'll observe his looks,
I'll tent him to the quick. If 'a do blench,
I know my course. The spirit that I have seen
May be a [dev'l], and the [dev'l] hath power
T' assume a pleasing shape, yea, and perhaps,
Out of my weakness and my melancholy,
As he is very potent with such spirits,
Abuses me to damn me. I'll have grounds
More relative than this—the play's the thing
Wherein I'll catch the conscience of the King. *Exit.*

553. **conceit**: imaginative conception.
556. **his whole function**: the operation of his whole body.
557. **forms**: actions, expressions. 564. **free**: innocent.
565. **amaze**: confound.
567. **muddy-mettled**: dull-spirited. **peak**: mope.
568. **John-a-dreams**: a sleepy fellow. **unpregnant of**: unquickened by. 571. **defeat**: destruction.
574–75. **gives . . . lungs**: calls me a liar in the extremest degree.
576. **'swounds**: by God's (Christ's) wounds. **should**: would certainly.
577. **am . . . gall**: i.e. am constitutionally incapable of resentment. That doves were mild because they had no gall was a popular belief.
579. **region kites**: kites of the air. 580. **offal**: entrails.
581. **kindless**: unnatural.
587. **stallion**: male whore. Most editors adopt the F1 reading *scullion*, "kitchen menial." 588. **About**: to work.
591. **presently**: at once, then and there.
597. **tent**: probe. **blench**: flinch.
602. **spirits**: states of temperament. 603. **Abuses**: deludes.
604. **relative**: closely related (to fact), i.e. conclusive.

[ACT III, SCENE I]

Enter KING, QUEEN, POLONIUS, OPHELIA, ROSENCRANTZ, GUILDENSTERN, LORDS.

King. An' can you by no drift of conference
Get from him why he puts on this confusion,
Grating so harshly all his days of quiet
With turbulent and dangerous lunacy?
Ros. He does confess he feels himself distracted,
But from what cause 'a will by no means speak.
Guil. Nor do we find him forward to be sounded,
But with a crafty madness keeps aloof
When we would bring him on to some confession
Of his true state.
Queen. Did he receive you well?
Ros. Most like a gentleman.
Guil. But with much forcing of his disposition.
Ros. Niggard of question, but of our demands
Most free in his reply.
Queen. Did you assay him
To any pastime?
Ros. Madam, it so fell out that certain players
We o'erraught on the way; of these we told him,
And there did seem in him a kind of joy
To hear of it. They are here about the court,
And as I think, they have already order
This night to play before him.
Pol. 'Tis most true,
And he beseech'd me to entreat your Majesties
To hear and see the matter.
King. With all my heart, and it doth much content me
To hear him so inclin'd.
Good gentlemen, give him a further edge,
And drive his purpose into these delights.
Ros. We shall, my lord.
Exeunt Rosencrantz and Guildenstern.
King. Sweet Gertrude, leave us two,
For we have closely sent for Hamlet hither,

III.i. Location: The castle.
See the Textual Notes for the Q1 version of parts of this scene.
1. **An'**: and. **drift of conference**: leading on of conversation.
7. **forward**: readily willing. **sounded**: plumbed, probed.
8. **crafty madness**: i.e. mad craftiness, the shrewdness that mad people sometimes exhibit. 12. **disposition**: inclination.
13. **question**: conversation. **demands**: questions.
14. **assay**: attempt to win.
17. **o'erraught**: passed (literally, overreached).
26. **edge**: stimulus. 27. **into**: on to. 29. **closely**: privately.

That he, as 'twere by accident, may here
Affront Ophelia. Her father and myself,
We'll so bestow ourselves that, seeing unseen,
We may of their encounter frankly judge,
And gather by him, as he is behav'd,
If't be th' affliction of his love or no
That thus he suffers for.
  Queen. I shall obey you.
And for your part, Ophelia, I do wish
That your good beauties be the happy cause
Of Hamlet's wildness. So shall I hope your virtues
Will bring him to his wonted way again,
To both your honors.
  Oph. Madam, I wish it may. [*Exit Queen.*]
  Pol. Ophelia, walk you here.—Gracious, so please you,
We will bestow ourselves. [*To Ophelia.*] Read on this book,
That show of such an exercise may color
Your [loneliness]. We are oft to blame in this—
'Tis too much prov'd—that with devotion's visage
And pious action we do sugar o'er
The devil himself.
  King. [*Aside.*] O, 'tis too true!
How smart a lash that speech doth give my conscience!
The harlot's cheek, beautied with plast'ring art,
Is not more ugly to the thing that helps it
Than is my deed to my most painted word.
O heavy burthen!
  Pol. I hear him coming. Withdraw, my lord.
[*Exeunt King and Polonius.*]

Enter HAMLET.

  Ham. To be, or not to be, that is the question:
Whether 'tis nobler in the mind to suffer
The slings and arrows of outrageous fortune,
Or to take arms against a sea of troubles,
And by opposing, end them. To die, to sleep—
No more, and by a sleep to say we end
The heart-ache and the thousand natural shocks
That flesh is heir to; 'tis a consummation
Devoutly to be wish'd. To die, to sleep—
To sleep, perchance to dream—ay, there's the rub,
For in that sleep of death what dreams may come,
When we have shuffled off this mortal coil,
Must give us pause; there's the respect
That makes calamity of so long life:
For who would bear the whips and scorns of time,
Th' oppressor's wrong, the proud man's contumely,
The pangs of despis'd love, the law's delay,
The insolence of office, and the spurns
That patient merit of th' unworthy takes,
When he himself might his quietus make
With a bare bodkin; who would fardels bear,
To grunt and sweat under a weary life,
But that the dread of something after death,
The undiscover'd country, from whose bourn
No traveller returns, puzzles the will,
And makes us rather bear those ills we have,
Than fly to others that we know not of?
Thus conscience does make cowards [of us all],
And thus the native hue of resolution
Is sicklied o'er with the pale cast of thought,
And enterprises of great pitch and moment
With this regard their currents turn awry,
And lose the name of action.—Soft you now,
The fair Ophelia. Nymph, in thy orisons
Be all my sins rememb'red.
  Oph. Good my lord,
How does your honor for this many a day?
  Ham. I humbly thank you, well, [well, well].
  Oph. My lord, I have remembrances of yours
That I have longed long to redeliver.
I pray you now receive them.
  Ham. No, not I,
I never gave you aught.
  Oph. My honor'd lord, you know right well you did,
And with them words of so sweet breath compos'd
As made these things more rich. Their perfume lost,
Take these again, for to the noble mind
Rich gifts wax poor when givers prove unkind.
There, my lord.
  Ham. Ha, ha! are you honest?
  Oph. My lord?
  Ham. Are you fair?
  Oph. What means your lordship?
  Ham. That if you be honest and fair, [your honesty] should admit no discourse to your beauty.
  Oph. Could beauty, my lord, have better commerce than with honesty?
  Ham. Ay, truly, for the power of beauty will sooner transform honesty from what it is to a bawd than the force of honesty can translate beauty into his likeness. This was sometime a paradox, but now the time gives it proof. I did love you once.
  Oph. Indeed, my lord, you made me believe so.
  Ham. You should not have believ'd me, for virtue cannot so [inoculate] our old stock but we shall relish of it. I lov'd you not.
  Oph. I was the more deceiv'd.

31. **Affront:** meet. 33. **frankly:** freely.
44. **exercise:** i.e. religious exercise (as the next sentence makes clear).
44–45. **color Your loneliness:** make your solitude seem natural.
46. **too much prov'd:** too often proved true.
47. **action:** demeanor.
51. **to . . . it:** in comparison with the paint that makes it look beautiful.
55–89. See the Textual Notes for the version of this soliloquy in Q1.
56. **suffer:** submit to, endure patiently.
62. **consummation:** completion, end.
64. **rub:** obstacle (a term from the game of bowls).
66. **shuffled off:** freed ourselves from. **this mortal coil:** the turmoil of this mortal life. 67. **respect:** consideration.
68. **of . . . life:** so long-lived. 69. **time:** the world.
74. **his quietus make:** write paid to his account.
75. **bare bodkin:** mere dagger. **fardels:** burdens.
78. **undiscover'd:** not disclosed to knowledge; about which men have no information. **bourn:** boundary, i.e. region.
79. **puzzles:** paralyzes.
82. **conscience:** reflection (but with some of the modern sense, too).
83. **native hue:** natural (ruddy) complexion.
84. **pale cast:** pallor. **thought:** i.e. melancholy thought, brooding.
85. **pitch:** loftiness (a term from falconry, signifying the highest point of a hawk's flight). 88. **orisons:** prayers. 102. **honest:** chaste.
113. **sometime:** formerly. **paradox:** tenet contrary to accepted belief.
116–18. **virtue . . . it:** virtue, engrafted on our old stock (of viciousness), cannot so change the nature of the plant that no trace of the original will remain.

Ham. Get thee [to] a nunn'ry, why wouldst thou be a breeder of sinners? I am myself indifferent honest, but yet I could accuse me of such things that it were better my mother had not borne me: I am very proud, revengeful, ambitious, with more offenses at my beck than I have thoughts to put them in, imagination to give them shape, or time to act them in. What should such fellows as I do crawling between earth and heaven? We are arrant knaves, believe none of us. Go thy ways to a nunn'ry. Where's your father?

Oph. At home, my lord.

Ham. Let the doors be shut upon him, that he may play the fool no where but in 's own house. Farewell.

Oph. O, help him, you sweet heavens!

Ham. If thou dost marry, I'll give thee this plague for thy dowry: be thou as chaste as ice, as pure as snow, thou shalt not escape calumny. Get thee to a nunn'ry, farewell. Or if thou wilt needs marry, marry a fool, for wise men know well enough what monsters you make of them. To a nunn'ry, go, and quickly too. Farewell.

Oph. Heavenly powers, restore him!

Ham. I have heard of your paintings, well enough. God hath given you one face, and you make yourselves another. You jig and amble, and you [lisp,] you nickname God's creatures and make your wantonness [your] ignorance. Go to, I'll no more on't, it hath made me mad. I say we will have no moe marriage. Those that are married already (all but one) shall live, the rest shall keep as they are. To a nunn'ry, go.

Exit.

Oph. O, what a noble mind is here o'erthrown!
The courtier's, soldier's, scholar's, eye, tongue, sword,
Th' expectation and rose of the fair state,
The glass of fashion and the mould of form,
Th' observ'd of all observers, quite, quite down!
And I, of ladies most deject and wretched,
That suck'd the honey of his [music] vows,
Now see [that] noble and most sovereign reason
Like sweet bells jangled out of time, and harsh;
That unmatch'd form and stature of blown youth
Blasted with ecstasy. O, woe is me
T' have seen what I have seen, see what I see!

[*Ophelia withdraws.*]

Enter King *and* Polonius.

King. Love? his affections do not that way tend,
Nor what he spake, though it lack'd form a little,
Was not like madness. There's something in his soul
O'er which his melancholy sits on brood,
And I do doubt the hatch and the disclose
Will be some danger; which for to prevent,
I have in quick determination
Thus set it down: he shall with speed to England
For the demand of our neglected tribute.
Haply the seas, and countries different,
With variable objects, shall expel
This something-settled matter in his heart,
Whereon his brains still beating puts him thus
From fashion of himself. What think you on't?

Pol. It shall do well; but yet do I believe
The origin and commencement of his grief
Sprung from neglected love. [*Ophelia comes forward.*]
How now, Ophelia?
You need not tell us what Lord Hamlet said,
We heard it all. My lord, do as you please,
But if you hold it fit, after the play
Let his queen-mother all alone entreat him
To show his grief. Let her be round with him,
And I'll be plac'd (so please you) in the ear
Of all their conference. If she find him not,
To England send him, or confine him where
Your wisdom best shall think.

King. It shall be so.
Madness in great ones must not [unwatch'd] go.

Exeunt.

[Scene II]

Enter Hamlet *and three of the* Players.

Ham. Speak the speech, I pray you, as I pronounc'd it to you, trippingly on the tongue, but if you mouth it, as many of our players do, I had as live the town-crier spoke my lines. Nor do not saw the air too much with your hand, thus, but use all gently, for in the very torrent, tempest, and, as I may say, whirlwind of your passion, you must acquire and beget a temperance that may give it smoothness. O, it offends me to the soul to hear a robustious periwig-pated fellow tear a passion to totters, to very rags, to spleet the ears of the groundlings, who for the most part are capable of nothing but inexplicable dumb shows and noise. I would have such a fellow whipt for o'erdoing Termagant, it out-Herods Herod, pray you avoid it.

[*1.*] *Play.* I warrant your honor.

Ham. Be not too tame neither, but let your own discretion be your tutor. Suit the action to the word, the word to the action, with this special observance, that you o'erstep not the modesty of nature: for any thing so o'erdone is from the purpose of playing, whose end, both at the first and now, was and is, to hold as 'twere the mirror up to nature: to show virtue

121. indifferent honest: tolerably virtuous.
138. monsters. Alluding to the notion that the husbands of unfaithful wives grew horns. **139. you**: you women.
144–45. You . . . creatures: i.e. you walk and talk affectedly.
145–46. make . . . ignorance: excuse your affectation as ignorance.
147. moe: more.
152. expectation: hope. **rose**: ornament. **fair.** Probably proleptic: "(the kingdom) made fair by his presence."
153. glass: mirror. **mould of form**: pattern of (courtly) behavior.
154. observ'd . . . observers. Shakespeare uses *observe* to mean not only "behold, mark attentively" but also "pay honor to."
159. blown: in full bloom.
160. Blasted: withered. **ecstasy**: madness.
162. affections: inclinations, feelings.
166. doubt: fear. **disclose.** Synonymous with *hatch;* see also V.i.287.

178. neglected: unrequited.
183. his grief: what is troubling him. **round**: blunt, outspoken.
185. find him: learn the truth about him.

III.ii. Location: The castle.
2. mouth: pronounce with exaggerated distinctness or declamatory effect. **3. live**: lief, willingly. **10. totters**: tatters. **spleet**: split.
11. groundlings: those who paid the lowest admission price and stood on the ground in the "yard" or pit of the theatre. **capable of**: able to take in.
13. Termagant: a supposed god of the Saracens, whose role in medieval drama, like that of Herod (line 14), was noisy and violent.
19. modesty: moderation. **20. from**: contrary to.

her feature, scorn her own image, and the very age and body of the time his form and pressure. Now this overdone, or come tardy off, though it makes the unskillful laugh, cannot but make the judicious grieve; the censure of which one must in your allowance o'erweigh a whole theatre of others. O, there be players that I have seen play—and heard others [praise], and that highly—not to speak it profanely, that, neither having th' accent of Christians nor the gait of Christian, pagan, nor man, have so strutted and bellow'd that I have thought some of Nature's journeymen had made men, and not made them well, they imitated humanity so abominably.

[*1.*] *Play.* I hope we have reform'd that indifferently with us, [sir].

Ham. O, reform it altogether. And let those that play your clowns speak no more than is set down for them, for there be of them that will themselves laugh to set on some quantity of barren spectators to laugh too, though in the mean time some necessary question of the play be then to be consider'd. That's villainous, and shows a most pitiful ambition in the fool that uses it. Go make you ready. [*Exeunt Players.*]

Enter Polonius, Guildenstern, *and* Rosencrantz.

How now, my lord? Will the King hear this piece of work?

Pol. And the Queen too, and that presently.

Ham. Bid the players make haste. [*Exit Polonius.*]
Will you two help to hasten them?

Ros. Ay, my lord. *Exeunt they two.*

Ham. What ho, Horatio!

Enter Horatio.

Hor. Here, sweet lord, at your service.

Ham. Horatio, thou art e'en as just a man
As e'er my conversation cop'd withal.

Hor. O my dear lord—

Ham. Nay, do not think I flatter,
For what advancement may I hope from thee
That no revenue hast but thy good spirits
To feed and clothe thee? Why should the poor be flatter'd?
No, let the candied tongue lick absurd pomp,
And crook the pregnant hinges of the knee
Where thrift may follow fawning. Dost thou hear?

23. **scorn:** i.e. that which is worthy of scorn.
24. **pressure:** impression (as of a seal), exact image.
25. **tardy:** inadequately.
27. **censure:** judgment. **which one:** (even) one of whom. **allowance:** estimation. 30. **profanely:** irreverently.
33–35. **some . . . abominably:** i.e. they were so unlike men that it seemed Nature had not made them herself, but had delegated the task to mediocre assistants. 36–37. **indifferently:** pretty well.
40. **of them:** some of them.
45. **fool:** (1) stupid person; (2) actor playing a fool's role. **uses it.** See the Textual Notes for an interesting passage following these words in Q1. 46–47. **piece of work:** masterpiece (said jocularly).
48. **presently:** at once.
54. **thou . . . man:** i.e. you come as close to being what a man should be (*just* = exact, precise).
55. **my . . . withal:** my association with people has brought me into contact with.
60. **candied:** sugared, i.e. flattering. **absurd:** tasteless (Latin sense).
61. **pregnant:** moving readily. 62. **thrift:** thriving, profit.

Since my dear soul was mistress of her choice
And could of men distinguish her election,
Sh' hath seal'd thee for herself, for thou hast been
As one in suff'ring all that suffers nothing,
A man that Fortune's buffets and rewards
Hast ta'en with equal thanks; and blest are those
Whose blood and judgment are so well co-meddled,
That they are not a pipe for Fortune's finger
To sound what stop she please. Give me that man
That is not passion's slave, and I will wear him
In my heart's core, ay, in my heart of heart,
As I do thee. Something too much of this.
There is a play to-night before the King,
One scene of it comes near the circumstance
Which I have told thee of my father's death.
I prithee, when thou seest that act afoot,
Even with the very comment of thy soul
Observe my uncle. If his occulted guilt
Do not itself unkennel in one speech,
It is a damned ghost that we have seen,
And my imaginations are as foul
As Vulcan's stithy. Give him heedful note,
For I mine eyes will rivet to his face,
And after we will both our judgments join
In censure of his seeming.

Hor. Well, my lord.
If 'a steal aught the whilst this play is playing,
And scape [detecting], I will pay the theft.

[*Sound a flourish. Danish march.*] *Enter Trumpets and Kettle-drums,* King, Queen, Polonius, Ophelia, [Rosencrantz, Guildenstern, *and other* Lords *attendant, with his* Guard *carrying torches*].

Ham. They are coming to the play. I must be idle;
Get you a place.

King. How fares our cousin Hamlet?

Ham. Excellent, i' faith, of the chameleon's dish: I eat the air, promise-cramm'd—you cannot feed capons so.

King. I have nothing with this answer, Hamlet, these words are not mine.

Ham. No, nor mine now. [*To Polonius.*] My lord, you play'd once i' th' university, you say?

Pol. That did I, my lord, and was accounted a good actor.

Ham. What did you enact?

Pol. I did enact Julius Caesar. I was kill'd i' th' Capitol; Brutus kill'd me.

Ham. It was a brute part of him to kill so capital a calf there. Be the players ready?

Ros. Ay, my lord, they stay upon your patience.

Queen. Come hither, my dear Hamlet, sit by me.

69. **blood:** passions. **co-meddled:** mixed, blended.
73. **my heart of heart:** the heart of my heart.
79. **very . . . soul:** your most intense critical observation.
80. **occulted:** hidden. 81. **unkennel:** bring into the open.
82. **damned ghost:** evil spirit, devil. 84. **stithy:** forge.
87. **censure . . . seeming:** reaching a verdict on his behavior.
90. **be idle:** act foolish, pretend to be crazy.
92. **fares.** Hamlet takes up this word in another sense.
93. **chameleon's dish.** Chameleons were thought to feed on air. Hamlet says that he subsists on an equally nourishing diet, the promise of succession. There is probably a pun on *air/heir.*
96. **have nothing with:** do not understand.
97. **mine:** i.e. an answer to my question. 105. **part:** action.

Ham. No, good mother, here's metal more attractive. [*Lying down at Ophelia's feet.*]

Pol. [*To the King.*] O ho, do you mark that?

Ham. Lady, shall I lie in your lap?

Oph. No, my lord.

[*Ham.* I mean, my head upon your lap?

Oph. Ay, my lord.]

Ham. Do you think I meant country matters?

Oph. I think nothing, my lord.

Ham. That's a fair thought to lie between maids' legs.

Oph. What is, my lord?

Ham. Nothing.

Oph. You are merry, my lord.

Ham. Who, I?

Oph. Ay, my lord.

Ham. O God, your only jig-maker. What should a man do but be merry, for look you how cheerfully my mother looks, and my father died within 's two hours.

Oph. Nay, 'tis twice two months, my lord.

Ham. So long? Nay then let the dev'l wear black, for I'll have a suit of sables. O heavens, die two months ago, and not forgotten yet? Then there's hope a great man's memory may outlive his life half a year, but, by'r lady, 'a must build churches then, or else shall 'a suffer not thinking on, with the hobby-horse, whose epitaph is, "For O, for O, the hobby-horse is forgot."

The trumpets sounds. Dumb show follows.

Enter a King and a Queen [*very lovingly*], *the Queen embracing him and he her.* [*She kneels and makes show of protestation unto him.*] *He takes her up and declines his head upon her neck. He lies him down upon a bank of flowers. She, seeing him asleep, leaves him. Anon come in another man, takes off his crown, kisses it, pours poison in the sleeper's ears, and leaves him. The Queen returns, finds the King dead, makes passionate action. The pois'ner with some three or four* [*mutes*] *come in again, seem to condole with her. The dead body is carried away. The pois'ner woos the Queen with gifts; she seems harsh* [*and unwilling*] *awhile, but in the end accepts love.* [*Exeunt.*]

Oph. What means this, my lord?

Ham. Marry, this' [miching] mallecho, it means mischief.

Oph. Belike this show imports the argument of the play.

Enter Prologue.

Ham. We shall know by this fellow. The players cannot keep [counsel], they'll tell all.

Oph. Will 'a tell us what this show meant?

Ham. Ay, or any show that you will show him. Be not you asham'd to show, he'll not shame to tell you what it means.

Oph. You are naught, you are naught. I'll mark the play.

Pro. For us, and for our tragedy,
Here stooping to your clemency,
We beg your hearing patiently. [*Exit.*]

Ham. Is this a prologue, or the posy of a ring?

Oph. 'Tis brief, my lord.

Ham. As woman's love.

Enter [*two Players,*] King *and* Queen.

[*P.*] *King.* Full thirty times hath Phoebus' cart gone round
Neptune's salt wash and Tellus' orbed ground,
And thirty dozen moons with borrowed sheen
About the world have times twelve thirties been,
Since love our hearts and Hymen did our hands
Unite comutual in most sacred bands.

[*P.*] *Queen.* So many journeys may the sun and moon
Make us again count o'er ere love be done!
But woe is me, you are so sick of late,
So far from cheer and from [your] former state,
That I distrust you. Yet though I distrust,
Discomfort you, my lord, it nothing must,
[For] women's fear and love hold quantity,
In neither aught, or in extremity.
Now what my [love] is, proof hath made you know,
And as my love is siz'd, my fear is so.
Where love is great, the littlest doubts are fear;
Where little fears grow great, great love grows there.

[*P.*] *King.* Faith, I must leave thee, love, and shortly too;
My operant powers their functions leave to do,
And thou shalt live in this fair world behind,
Honor'd, belov'd, and haply one as kind
For husband shalt thou—

[*P.*] *Queen.* O, confound the rest!
Such love must needs be treason in my breast.
In second husband let me be accurs'd!
None wed the second but who kill'd the first.

Ham. [*Aside.*] That's wormwood!

[*P. Queen.*] The instances that second marriage move
Are base respects of thrift, but none of love.
A second time I kill my husband dead,
When second husband kisses me in bed.

[*P.*] *King.* I do believe you think what now you speak,
But what we do determine, oft we break.

116. country matters: indecency.
125. only: very best. **jig-maker:** one who composed or played in the farcical song-and-dance entertainments that followed plays.
127. 's: this.
129–30. let . . . sables: i.e. to the devil with my garments; after so long a time I am ready for the old man's garb of sables (fine fur).
134. not thinking on: not being thought of, i.e. being forgotten.
135. For . . . forgot: line from a popular ballad lamenting puritanical suppression of such country sports as the May-games, in which the hobby-horse, a character costumed to resemble a horse, traditionally appeared. **137. this' miching mallecho:** this is sneaking mischief.
139. argument: subject, plot. **142. counsel.** secrets.
145. Be not you: if you are not. **147. naught:** wicked.
152. posy . . . ring: verse motto inscribed in a ring (necessarily short).
155–73. See the Textual Notes for the corresponding lines in Q1.
155. Phoebus' cart: the sun-god's chariot.
156. Tellus: goddess of the earth. **159. Hymen:** god of marriage.
160. bands: bonds. **165. distrust:** fear for.
167. hold quantity: are related in direct proportion.
169. proof: experience.
174. operant: active, vital. **leave to do:** cease to perform.
177. confound the rest: may destruction befall what you are about to speak of—a second marriage on my part.
182. instances: motives. **move:** give rise to.
183. respects of thrift: considerations of advantage.

Purpose is but the slave to memory,
Of violent birth, but poor validity,
Which now, the fruit unripe, sticks on the tree,
But fall unshaken when they mellow be.
Most necessary 'tis that we forget
To pay ourselves what to ourselves is debt.
What to ourselves in passion we propose,
The passion ending, doth the purpose lose.
The violence of either grief or joy
Their own enactures with themselves destroy.
Where joy most revels, grief doth most lament;
Grief [joys], joy grieves, on slender accident.
This world is not for aye, nor 'tis not strange
That even our loves should with our fortunes change:
For 'tis a question left us yet to prove,
Whether love lead fortune, or else fortune love.
The great man down, you mark his favorite flies,
The poor advanc'd makes friends of enemies.
And hitherto doth love on fortune tend,
For who not needs shall never lack a friend,
And who in want a hollow friend doth try,
Directly seasons him his enemy.
But orderly to end where I begun,
Our wills and fates do so contrary run
That our devices still are overthrown,
Our thoughts are ours, their ends none of our own:
So think thou wilt no second husband wed,
But die thy thoughts when thy first lord is dead.

[P.] Queen. Nor earth to me give food, nor heaven light,
Sport and repose lock from me day and night,
To desperation turn my trust and hope,
[An] anchor's cheer in prison be my scope!
Each opposite that blanks the face of joy
Meet what I would have well and it destroy!
Both here and hence pursue me lasting strife,
If once a widow, ever I be wife!

Ham. If she should break it now!

[P.] King. 'Tis deeply sworn. Sweet, leave me here a while,
My spirits grow dull, and fain I would beguile
The tedious day with sleep. *[Sleeps.]*

[P.] Queen. Sleep rock thy brain,
And never come mischance between us twain! *Exit.*

Ham. Madam, how like you this play?

Queen. The lady doth protest too much, methinks.

Ham. O but she'll keep her word.

King. Have you heard the argument? is there no offense in't?

Ham. No, no, they do but jest, poison in jest—no offense i' th' world.

King. What do you call the play?

Ham. "The Mouse-trap." Marry, how? tropically: this play is the image of a murther done in Vienna; Gonzago is the duke's name, his wife, Baptista. You shall see anon. 'Tis a knavish piece of work, but what of that? Your Majesty, and we that have free souls, it touches us not. Let the gall'd jade winch, our withers are unwrung.

Enter LUCIANUS.

This is one Lucianus, nephew to the king.

Oph. You are as good as a chorus, my lord.

Ham. I could interpret between you and your love, if I could see the puppets dallying.

Oph. You are keen, my lord, you are keen.

Ham. It would cost you a groaning to take off mine edge.

Oph. Still better, and worse.

Ham. So you mistake your husbands. Begin, murtherer, leave thy damnable faces and begin. Come, the croaking raven doth bellow for revenge.

Luc. Thoughts black, hands apt, drugs fit, and time agreeing,
[Confederate] season, else no creature seeing,
Thou mixture rank, of midnight weeds collected,
With Hecat's ban thrice blasted, thrice [infected],
Thy natural magic and dire property
On wholesome life usurps immediately.
[Pours the poison in his ears.]

Ham. 'A poisons him i' th' garden for his estate. His name's Gonzago, the story is extant, and written in very choice Italian. You shall see anon how the murtherer gets the love of Gonzago's wife.

Oph. The King rises.

[Ham. What, frighted with false fire?]

Queen. How fares my lord?

Pol. Give o'er the play.

King. Give me some light. Away!

Pol. Lights, lights, lights!

Exeunt all but Hamlet and Horatio.

Ham. "Why, let the strooken deer go weep,
The hart ungalled play,
For some must watch while some must sleep,
Thus runs the world away."

189. validity: strength, power to last.
192–93. Most . . . debt: i.e. such resolutions are debts we owe to ourselves, and it would be foolish to pay such debts.
194. passion: violent emotion.
196–97. The violence . . . destroy: i.e. both violent grief and violent joy fail of their intended acts because they destroy themselves by their very violence. **199. slender accident:** slight occasion.
209. seasons: ripens, converts into.
212. devices: devisings, intentions. **still:** always.
219. anchor's cheer: hermit's fare. **my scope:** the extent of my comforts.
220. blanks: blanches, makes pale (a symptom of grief).
233. offense: offensive matter (but Hamlet quibbles on the sense "crime"). **234. jest:** i.e. pretend.

237–38. tropically: figuratively (with play on *trapically*—which is the reading of Q1—and probably with allusion to the children's saying *marry trap*, meaning "now you're caught").
238. image: representation.
242. free souls: clear consciences. **gall'd jade:** chafed horse.
243. winch: wince. **withers:** ridge between a horse's shoulders. **unwrung:** not rubbed sore.
245. chorus: i.e. one who explains the forthcoming action.
246–47. I . . . dallying: I could speak the dialogue between you and your lover like a puppet-master (with an indecent jest).
248. keen: bitter, sharp.
251. better, and worse: i.e. more pointed and less decent.
252. So: i.e. "for better, for worse," in the words of the marriage service. **mistake:** i.e. mis-take, take wrongfully. Their vows, Hamlet suggests, prove false. **253. faces:** facial expressions.
254. the croaking . . . revenge. Misquoted from an old play, *The True Tragedy of Richard III.*
256. Confederate season: the time being my ally.
258. Hecat's ban: the curse of Hecate, goddess of witchcraft.
266. false fire: i.e. a blank cartridge.
271. strooken: struck, i.e. wounded.
272. ungalled: unwounded. **273. watch:** stay awake.

Would not this, sir, and a forest of feathers—if the rest of my fortunes turn Turk with me—with [two] Provincial roses on my raz'd shoes, get me a fellowship in a cry of players?

Hor. Half a share.

Ham. A whole one, I.

"For thou dost know, O Damon dear,
This realm dismantled was
Of Jove himself, and now reigns here
A very, very"—pajock.

Hor. You might have rhym'd.

Ham. O good Horatio, I'll take the ghost's word for a thousand pound. Didst perceive?

Hor. Very well, my lord.

Ham. Upon the talk of the pois'ning?

Hor. I did very well note him.

Ham. Ah, ha! Come, some music! Come, the recorders!

For if the King like not the comedy,
Why then belike he likes it not, perdy.

Come, some music!

Enter Rosencrantz *and* Guildenstern.

Guil. Good my lord, voutsafe me a word with you.

Ham. Sir, a whole history.

Guil. The King, sir—

Ham. Ay, sir, what of him?

Guil. Is in his retirement marvellous distemp'red.

Ham. With drink, sir?

Guil. No, my lord, with choler.

Ham. Your wisdom should show itself more richer to signify this to the doctor, for for me to put him to his purgation would perhaps plunge him into more choler.

Guil. Good my lord, put your discourse into some frame, and [start] not so wildly from my affair.

Ham. I am tame, sir. Pronounce.

Guil. The Queen, your mother, in most great affliction of spirit, hath sent me to you.

Ham. You are welcome.

Guil. Nay, good my lord, this courtesy is not of the right breed. If it shall please you to make me a wholesome answer, I will do your mother's commandement; if not, your pardon and my return shall be the end of [my] business.

Ham. Sir, I cannot.

Ros. What, my lord?

Ham. Make you a wholesome answer—my wit's diseas'd. But, sir, such answer as I can make, you shall command, or rather, as you say, my mother. Therefore no more, but to the matter: my mother, you say—

Ros. Then thus she says: your behavior hath strook her into amazement and admiration.

Ham. O wonderful son, that can so stonish a mother! But is there no sequel at the heels of this mother's admiration? Impart.

Ros. She desires to speak with you in her closet ere you go to bed.

Ham. We shall obey, were she ten times our mother. Have you any further trade with us?

Ros. My lord, you once did love me.

Ham. And do still, by these pickers and stealers.

Ros. Good my lord, what is your cause of distemper? You do surely bar the door upon your own liberty if you deny your griefs to your friend.

Ham. Sir, I lack advancement.

Ros. How can that be, when you have the voice of the King himself for your succession in Denmark?

Ham. Ay, sir, but "While the grass grows"—the proverb is something musty.

Enter the Players *with recorders.*

O, the recorders! Let me see one.—To withdraw with you—why do you go about to recover the wind of me, as if you would drive me into a toil?

Guil. O my lord, if my duty be too bold, my love is too unmannerly.

Ham. I do not well understand that. Will you play upon this pipe?

Guil. My lord, I cannot.

Ham. I pray you.

Guil. Believe me, I cannot.

Ham. I do beseech you.

Guil. I know no touch of it, my lord.

Ham. It is as easy as lying. Govern these ventages with your fingers and [thumbs], give it breath with your mouth, and it will discourse most eloquent music. Look you, these are the stops.

Guil. But these cannot I command to any utt'rance of harmony. I have not the skill.

Ham. Why, look you now, how unworthy a thing you make of me! You would play upon me, you would seem to know my stops, you would pluck out the heart of my mystery, you would sound me from my lowest note to [the top of] my compass; and there is much music, excellent voice, in this little organ, yet cannot you make it speak. 'Sblood, do you think I am easier to be play'd on than a pipe? Call me what instrument you will, though you fret me, [yet] you cannot play upon me.

Enter Polonius.

God bless you, sir.

Pol. My lord, the Queen would speak with you,

275. feathers: the plumes worn by tragic actors.
276. turn Turk: i.e. go to the bad.
276–77. Provincial roses: rosettes designed to look like a variety of French rose.
277. raz'd: with decorating slashing. **fellowship:** partnership.
278. cry: company. **282. dismantled:** divested, deprived.
284. pajock: peacock (substituting for the rhyme-word *ass*). The natural history of the time attributed many vicious qualities to the peacock. **294. perdy:** assuredly (French *pardieu*, "by God").
303. choler: anger (but Hamlet willfully takes up the word in the sense "biliousness").
305–6. put . . . purgation: i.e. prescribe for what's wrong with him.
309. frame: logical structure. **316. wholesome:** sensible, rational.
317. pardon: permission for departure.
327. amazement and admiration: bewilderment and wonder.
328. stonish: astound. **331. closet:** private room.
336. pickers and stealers: hands; which, as the Catechism says, we must keep "from picking and stealing."
344. proverb: i.e. "While the grass grows, the steed starves." **something musty:** somewhat stale.
346. recover the wind: get to windward. **347. toil:** snare.
357. ventages: stops. **368. organ:** instrument.
371. fret: (1) finger (an instrument); (2) vex.

and presently.

Ham. Do you see yonder cloud that's almost in shape of a camel?

Pol. By th' mass and 'tis, like a camel indeed.

Ham. Methinks it is like a weasel.

Pol. It is back'd like a weasel.

Ham. Or like a whale.

Pol. Very like a whale.

Ham. Then I will come to my mother by and by. [*Aside.*] They fool me to the top of my bent.—I will come by and by.

[*Pol.*] I will say so. [*Exit.*]

Ham. "By and by" is easily said. Leave me, friends. [*Exeunt all but Hamlet.*]

'Tis now the very witching time of night,
When churchyards yawn and hell itself [breathes] out
Contagion to this world. Now could I drink hot blood,
And do such [bitter business as the] day
Would quake to look on. Soft, now to my mother.
O heart, lose not thy nature! let not ever
The soul of Nero enter this firm bosom,
Let me be cruel, not unnatural;
I will speak [daggers] to her, but use none.
My tongue and soul in this be hypocrites—
How in my words somever she be shent,
To give them seals never my soul consent! *Exit.*

[SCENE III]

Enter KING, ROSENCRANTZ, *and* GUILDENSTERN.

King. I like him not, nor stands it safe with us
To let his madness range. Therefore prepare you.
I your commission will forthwith dispatch,
And he to England shall along with you.
The terms of our estate may not endure
Hazard so near 's as doth hourly grow
Out of his brows.

Guil. We will ourselves provide.
Most holy and religious fear it is
To keep those many many bodies safe
That live and feed upon your Majesty.

Ros. The single and peculiar life is bound
With all the strength and armor of the mind
To keep itself from noyance, but much more
That spirit upon whose weal depends and rests
The lives of many. The cess of majesty
Dies not alone, but like a gulf doth draw
What's near it with it. Or it is a massy wheel
Fix'd on the summit of the highest mount,
To whose [huge] spokes ten thousand lesser things
Are mortis'd and adjoin'd, which when it falls,
Each small annexment, petty consequence,
Attends the boist'rous [ruin]. Never alone
Did the King sigh, but [with] a general groan.

King. Arm you, I pray you, to this speedy viage,
For we will fetters put about this fear,
Which now goes too free-footed.

Ros. We will haste us.

Exeunt Gentlemen [Rosencrantz and Guildenstern].

Enter POLONIUS.

Pol. My lord, he's going to his mother's closet.
Behind the arras I'll convey myself
To hear the process. I'll warrant she'll tax him home,
And as you said, and wisely was it said,
'Tis meet that some more audience than a mother,
Since nature makes them partial, should o'erhear
The speech, of vantage. Fare you well, my liege,
I'll call upon you ere you go to bed,
And tell you what I know.

King. Thanks, dear my lord.

Exit [Polonius].

O, my offense is rank, it smells to heaven,
It hath the primal eldest curse upon't,
A brother's murther. Pray can I not,
Though inclination be as sharp as will.
My stronger guilt defeats my strong intent,
And, like a man to double business bound,
I stand in pause where I shall first begin,
And both neglect. What if this cursed hand
Were thicker than itself with brother's blood,
Is there not rain enough in the sweet heavens
To wash it white as snow? Whereto serves mercy
But to confront the visage of offense?
And what's in prayer but this twofold force,
To be forestalled ere we come to fall,
Or [pardon'd] being down? then I'll look up.
My fault is past, but, O, what form of prayer
Can serve my turn? "Forgive me my foul murther"?
That cannot be, since I am still possess'd
Of those effects for which I did the murther:
My crown, mine own ambition, and my queen.
May one be pardon'd and retain th' offense?
In the corrupted currents of this world
Offense's gilded hand may [shove] by justice,
And oft 'tis seen the wicked prize itself
Buys out the law, but 'tis not so above:
There is no shuffling, there the action lies

375. presently: at once.
384. They . . . bent: they make me play the fool to the limit of my ability. **385. by and by:** at once.
388. witching: i.e. when the powers of evil are at large.
393. nature: natural affection, filial feeling.
394. Nero. Murderer of his mother. **398. shent:** rebuked.
399. give them seals: confirm them by deeds.

III.iii. Location: The castle.
1. him: i.e. his state of mind, his behavior.
3. dispatch: have drawn up.
5. terms: conditions, nature. **our estate:** my position (as king).
7. his brows: the madness visible in his face (?).
8. fear: concern. **11. single and peculiar:** individual and private.
13. noyance: injury. **15. cess:** cessation, death.
16. gulf: whirlpool.
20. mortis'd: fixed. **22. Attends:** accompanies. **ruin:** fall.
24. Arm: prepare. **viage:** voyage. **25. fear:** object of fear.
29. process: course of the talk. **tax him home:** take him severely to task.
33. of vantage: from an advantageous position (?) or in addition (?).
36–72. See the Textual Notes for the corresponding lines in Q1.
37. primal eldest curse: i.e. God's curse on Cain, who also slew his brother.
39. Though . . . will: though my desire is as strong as my resolve to do so. **41. bound:** committed. **43. neglect:** omit.
46–47. Whereto . . . offense: i.e. what function has mercy except when there has been sin.
56. th' offense: i.e. the "effects" or fruits of the offense.
57. currents: courses. **58. gilded:** i.e. bribing.
59. wicked prize: rewards of vice.
61. shuffling: evasion. **the action lies:** the charge comes for legal consideration.

In his true nature, and we ourselves compell'd,
Even to the teeth and forehead of our faults,
To give in evidence. What then? What rests?
Try what repentance can. What can it not?
Yet what can it, when one can not repent?
O wretched state! O bosom black as death!
O limed soul, that struggling to be free
Art more engag'd! Help, angels! Make assay,
Bow, stubborn knees, and heart, with strings of steel,
Be soft as sinews of the new-born babe!
All may be well. *[He kneels.]*

Enter HAMLET.

Ham. Now might I do it [pat], now 'a is a-praying;
And now I'll do't—and so 'a goes to heaven,
And so am I [reveng'd]. That would be scann'd:
A villain kills my father, and for that
I, his sole son, do this same villain send
To heaven.
Why, this is [hire and salary], not revenge.
'A took my father grossly, full of bread,
With all his crimes broad blown, as flush as May,
And how his audit stands who knows save heaven?
But in our circumstance and course of thought
'Tis heavy with him. And am I then revenged,
To take him in the purging of his soul,
When he is fit and season'd for his passage?
No!
Up, sword, and know thou a more horrid hent:
When he is drunk asleep, or in his rage,
Or in th' incestious pleasure of his bed,
At game a-swearing, or about some act
That has no relish of salvation in't—
Then trip him, that his heels may kick at heaven,
And that his soul may be as damn'd and black
As hell, whereto it goes. My mother stays,
This physic but prolongs thy sickly days. *Exit.*
King. *[Rising.]* My words fly up, my thoughts remain below:
Words without thoughts never to heaven go. *Exit.*

[SCENE IV]

Enter [QUEEN] GERTRUDE *and* POLONIUS.

Pol. 'A will come straight. Look you lay home to him.
Tell him his pranks have been too broad to bear with,
And that your Grace hath screen'd and stood between
Much heat and him. I'll silence me even here;
Pray you be round [with him].
Queen. I'll [warr'nt] you, fear me not. Withdraw,
I hear him coming. *[Polonius hides behind the arras.]*

Enter HAMLET.

Ham. Now, mother, what's the matter?
Queen. Hamlet, thou hast thy father much offended.
Ham. Mother, you have my father much offended.
Queen. Come, come, you answer with an idle tongue.
Ham. Go, go, you question with a wicked tongue.
Queen. Why, how now, Hamlet?
Ham. What's the matter now?
Queen. Have you forgot me?
Ham. No, by the rood, not so:
You are the Queen, your husband's brother's wife,
And would it were not so, you are my mother.
Queen. Nay, then I'll set those to you that can speak.
Ham. Come, come, and sit you down, you shall not boudge;
You go not till I set you up a glass
Where you may see the [inmost] part of you.
Queen. What wilt thou do? Thou wilt not murther me?
Help ho!
Pol. *[Behind.]* What ho, help!
Ham. *[Drawing.]* How now? A rat? Dead, for a ducat, dead! *[Kills Polonius through the arras.]*
Pol. *[Behind.]* O, I am slain.
Queen. O me, what hast thou done?
Ham. Nay, I know not, is it the King?
Queen. O, what a rash and bloody deed is this!
Ham. A bloody deed! almost as bad, good mother,
As kill a king, and marry with his brother.
Queen. As kill a king!
Ham. Ay, lady, it was my word.
[Parts the arras and discovers Polonius.]
Thou wretched, rash, intruding fool, farewell!
I took thee for thy better. Take thy fortune;
Thou find'st to be too busy is some danger.—
Leave wringing of your hands. Peace, sit you down,
And let me wring your heart, for so I shall
If it be made of penetrable stuff,
If damned custom have not brass'd it so
That it be proof and bulwark against sense.
Queen. What have I done, that thou dar'st wag thy tongue
In noise so rude against me?
Ham. Such an act
That blurs the grace and blush of modesty,
Calls virtue hypocrite, takes off the rose
From the fair forehead of an innocent love
And sets a blister there, makes marriage vows
As false as dicers' oaths, O, such a deed

63. Even . . . forehead: i.e. fully recognizing their features, extenuating nothing. **64. rests:** remains.
68. limed: caught (as in birdlime, a sticky substance used for catching birds). **69. engag'd:** entangled.
75. would be scann'd: must be carefully considered.
80. grossly: in a gross state; not spiritually prepared.
81. crimes: sins. **broad blown:** in full bloom. **flush:** lusty, vigorous. **82. audit:** account.
83. in . . . thought: i.e. to the best of our knowledge and belief.
88. Up: into the sheath. **know . . . hent:** be grasped at a more dreadful time. **92. relish:** trace.
96. physic: (attempted) remedy, i.e. prayer.

III.iv. Location: The Queen's closet in the castle.
1. lay . . . him: reprove him severely.
2. broad: unrestrained.
5. round: plain-spoken.
6. fear me not: have no fears about my handling of the situation.
11. idle: foolish. **14. rood:** cross. **18. boudge:** budge.
24. for a ducat: I'll wager a ducat.
33. busy: officious, meddlesome.
37. damned custom: i.e. the habit of ill-doing. **brass'd:** hardened, literally, plated with brass.
38. proof: armor. **sense:** feeling. **44. blister:** brand of shame.

As from the body of contraction plucks
The very soul, and sweet religion makes
A rhapsody of words. Heaven's face does glow
O'er this solidity and compound mass
With heated visage, as against the doom;
Is thought-sick at the act.
Queen. Ay me, what act,
That roars so loud and thunders in the index?
Ham. Look here upon this picture, and on this,
The counterfeit presentment of two brothers.
See what a grace was seated on this brow:
Hyperion's curls, the front of Jove himself,
An eye like Mars, to threaten and command,
A station like the herald Mercury
New lighted on a [heaven-]kissing hill,
A combination and a form indeed,
Where every god did seem to set his seal
To give the world assurance of a man.
This was your husband. Look you now what follows:
Here is your husband, like a mildewed ear,
Blasting his wholesome brother. Have you eyes?
Could you on this fair mountain leave to feed,
And batten on this moor? ha, have you eyes?
You cannot call it love, for at your age
The heyday in the blood is tame, it's humble,
And waits upon the judgment, and what judgment
Would step from this to this? Sense sure you have,
Else could you not have motion, but sure that sense
Is apoplex'd, for madness would not err,
Nor sense to ecstasy was ne'er so thrall'd
But it reserv'd some quantity of choice
To serve in such a difference. What devil was't
That thus hath cozen'd you at hoodman-blind?
Eyes without feeling, feeling without sight,
Ears without hands or eyes, smelling sans all,
Or but a sickly part of one true sense
Could not so mope. O shame, where is thy blush?
Rebellious hell,
If thou canst mutine in a matron's bones,
To flaming youth let virtue be as wax
And melt in her own fire. Proclaim no shame
When the compulsive ardure gives the charge,
Since frost itself as actively doth burn,
And reason [panders] will.
Queen. O Hamlet, speak no more!
Thou turn'st my [eyes into my very] soul,
And there I see such black and [grained] spots
As will [not] leave their tinct.
Ham. Nay, but to live
In the rank sweat of an enseamed bed,
Stew'd in corruption, honeying and making love
Over the nasty sty!
Queen. O, speak to me no more!
These words like daggers enter in my ears.
No more, sweet Hamlet!
Ham. A murtherer and a villain!
A slave that is not twentith part the [tithe]
Of your precedent lord, a Vice of kings,
A cutpurse of the empire and the rule,
That from a shelf the precious diadem stole,
And put it in his pocket—
Queen. No more!

Enter Ghost [*in his night-gown*].

Ham. A king of shreds and patches—
Save me, and hover o'er me with your wings,
You heavenly guards! What would your gracious figure?
Queen. Alas, he's mad!
Ham. Do you not come your tardy son to chide,
That, laps'd in time and passion, lets go by
Th' important acting of your dread command?
O, say!
Ghost. Do not forget! This visitation
Is but to whet thy almost blunted purpose.
But look, amazement on thy mother sits,
O, step between her and her fighting soul.
Conceit in weakest bodies strongest works,
Speak to her, Hamlet.
Ham. How is it with you, lady?
Queen. Alas, how is't with you,
That you do bend your eye on vacancy,
And with th' incorporal air do hold discourse?
Forth at your eyes your spirits wildly peep,
And as the sleeping soldiers in th' alarm,
Your bedded hair, like life in excrements,
Start up and stand an end. O gentle son,
Upon the heat and flame of thy distemper
Sprinkle cool patience. Whereon do you look?
Ham. On him, on him! look you how pale he glares!
His form and cause conjoin'd, preaching to stones,
Would make them capable.—Do not look upon me,
Lest with this piteous action you convert

46. contraction: the making of contracts, i.e. the assuming of solemn obligation. **47. religion:** i.e. sacred vows.
48. rhapsody: miscellaneous collection, jumble. **glow:** i.e. with anger.
49. this . . . mass: i.e. the earth. *Compound* = compounded of the four elements.
50. as . . . doom: as if for Judgment Day.
52. index: i.e. table of contents. The index was formerly placed at the beginning of a book.
54. counterfeit presentment: painted likenesses.
56. Hyperion's: the sun-god's. **front:** forehead.
58. station: bearing. **64. ear:** i.e. of grain.
67. batten: gorge. **69. heyday:** excitement.
71. Sense: sense perception, the five senses.
73. apoplex'd: paralyzed.
73–76. madness . . . difference: i.e. madness itself could not go so far astray, nor were the senses ever so enslaved by lunacy that they did not retain the power to make so obvious a distinction.
77. cozen'd: cheated. **hoodman-blind:** blindman's bluff.
79. sans: without. **81. mope:** be dazed. **83. mutine:** rebel.
85–88. Proclaim . . . will: do not call it sin when the hot blood of youth is responsible for lechery, since here we see people of calmer age on fire for it; and reason acts as procurer for desire, instead of restraining it. *Ardure* = ardor.
90. grained: fast-dyed, indelible.
91. leave their tinct: lose their color.
92. enseamed: greasy. **97. twentith:** twentieth.
98. precedent: former. **Vice:** buffoon (like the Vice of the morality plays). **101 s.d. night-gown:** dressing gown.
102. of . . . patches: clownish (alluding to the motley worn by jesters) (?) or patched-up, beggarly (?).
107. laps'd . . . passion: "having suffered time to slip and passion to cool" (Johnson). **108. important:** urgent.
112. amazement: utter bewilderment. **114. Conceit:** imagination.
120. in th' alarm: when the call to arms is sounded.
121. excrements: outgrowths; here, hair (also used of nails).
122. an end: on end. **124. patience:** self-control.
126. His . . . cause: his appearance and what he has to say.
127. capable: sensitive, receptive. **128. convert:** alter.

My stern effects, then what I have to do
Will want true color—tears perchance for blood.
Queen. To whom do you speak this?
Ham. Do you see nothing there?
Queen. Nothing at all, yet all that is I see.
Ham. Nor did you nothing hear?
Queen. No, nothing but ourselves.
Ham. Why, look you there, look how it steals away!
My father, in his habit as he lived!
Look where he goes, even now, out at the portal!
Exit Ghost.
Queen. This is the very coinage of your brain,
This bodiless creation ecstasy
Is very cunning in.
Ham. [Ecstasy?]
My pulse as yours doth temperately keep time,
And makes as healthful music. It is not madness
That I have utt'red. Bring me to the test,
And [I] the matter will reword, which madness
Would gambol from. Mother, for love of grace,
Lay not that flattering unction to your soul,
That not your trespass but my madness speaks;
It will but skin and film the ulcerous place,
Whiles rank corruption, mining all within,
Infects unseen. Confess yourself to heaven,
Repent what's past, avoid what is to come,
And do not spread the compost on the weeds
To make them ranker. Forgive me this my virtue,
For in the fatness of these pursy times
Virtue itself of vice must pardon beg,
Yea, curb and woo for leave to do him good.
Queen. O Hamlet, thou hast cleft my heart in twain.
Ham. O, throw away the worser part of it,
And [live] the purer with the other half.
Good night, but go not to my uncle's bed—
Assume a virtue, if you have it not.
That monster custom, who all sense doth eat,
Of habits devil, is angel yet in this,
That to the use of actions fair and good
He likewise gives a frock or livery
That aptly is put on. Refrain [to-]night,
And that shall lend a kind of easiness
To the next abstinence, the next more easy;
For use almost can change the stamp of nature,
And either [. . . .] the devil or throw him out
With wondrous potency. Once more good night,
And when you are desirous to be blest,
I'll blessing beg of you. For this same lord,
[*Pointing to Polonius.*]
I do repent; but heaven hath pleas'd it so
To punish me with this, and this with me,
That I must be their scourge and minister.
I will bestow him, and will answer well
The death I gave him. So again good night.
I must be cruel only to be kind.
This bad begins and worse remains behind.
One word more, good lady.
Queen. What shall I do?
Ham. Not this, by no means, that I bid you do:
Let the bloat king tempt you again to bed,
Pinch wanton on your cheek, call you his mouse,
And let him, for a pair of reechy kisses,
Or paddling in your neck with his damn'd fingers,
Make you to ravel all this matter out,
That I essentially am not in madness,
But mad in craft. 'Twere good you let him know,
For who that's but a queen, fair, sober, wise,
Would from a paddock, from a bat, a gib,
Such dear concernings hide? Who would do so?
No, in despite of sense and secrecy,
Unpeg the basket on the house's top,
Let the birds fly, and like the famous ape,
To try conclusions in the basket creep,
And break your own neck down.
Queen. Be thou assur'd, if words be made of breath,
And breath of life, I have no life to breathe
What thou hast said to me.
Ham. I must to England, you know that?
Queen. Alack,
I had forgot. 'Tis so concluded on.
Ham. There's letters seal'd, and my two school-fellows,
Whom I will trust as I will adders fang'd,
They bear the mandate, they must sweep my way
And marshal me to knavery. Let it work,
For 'tis the sport to have the enginer
Hoist with his own petar, an't shall go hard
But I will delve one yard below their mines,
And blow them at the moon. O, 'tis most sweet
When in one line two crafts directly meet.
This man shall set me packing;
I'll lug the guts into the neighbor room.
Mother, good night indeed. This counsellor
Is now most still, most secret, and most grave,
Who was in life a foolish prating knave.

129. effects: (purposed) actions.
130. want true color: lack its proper appearance.
135. habit: dress.
137–216. See the Textual Notes for the conclusion of the scene in Q1.
138. ecstasy: madness. **144. gambol:** start, jerk away.
145. flattering unction: soothing ointment.
151. compost: manure. **153. pursy:** puffy, out of condition.
155. curb and woo: bow and entreat.
161. all . . . eat: wears away all natural feeling.
162. Of habits devil: i.e. though it acts like a devil in establishing bad habits. Most editors read (in lines 161–62) *eat / Of habits evil*, following Theobald.
164–65. frock . . . on: i.e. a "habit" or customary garment, readily put on without need of any decision. **168. use:** habit.
169. A word seems to be wanting after *either;* for conjectures see the Textual Notes. **171. desirous . . . blest:** i.e. repentant.
175. scourge and minister: the agent of heavenly justice against human crime. *Scourge* suggests a permissive cruelty (Tamburlaine was the "scourge of God"), but "woe to him by whom the offense cometh"; the scourge must suffer for the evil it performs.
176. bestow: dispose of. **answer:** answer for.
179. behind: to come. **184. reechy:** filthy.
190. paddock: toad. **gib:** tom-cat.
191. dear concernings: matters of intense concern.
193. Unpeg the basket: open the door of the cage.
194. famous ape. The actual story has been lost.
195. conclusions: experiments (to see whether he too can fly if he enters the cage and then leaps out). **196. down:** by the fall.
205. knavery: some knavish scheme against me.
206. enginer: deviser of military "engines" or contrivances.
207. Hoist with: blown up by. **petar:** petard, bomb.
210. crafts: plots.
211. packing: (1) taking on a load; (2) leaving in a hurry.

Come, sir, to draw toward an end with you.
Good night, mother.

Exeunt [severally, Hamlet tugging in Polonius].

[ACT IV, SCENE I]

Enter KING *and* QUEEN *with* ROSENCRANTZ *and* GUILDENSTERN.

King. There's matter in these sighs, these profound heaves—
You must translate, 'tis fit we understand them.
Where is your son?

Queen. Bestow this place on us a little while.

[Exeunt Rosencrantz and Guildenstern.]

Ah, mine own lord, what have I seen to-night!

King. What, Gertrude? How does Hamlet?

Queen. Mad as the sea and wind when both contend
Which is the mightier. In his lawless fit,
Behind the arras hearing something stir,
Whips out his rapier, cries, "A rat, a rat!"
And in this brainish apprehension kills
The unseen good old man.

King. O heavy deed!
It had been so with us had we been there.
His liberty is full of threats to all,
To you yourself, to us, to every one.
Alas, how shall this bloody deed be answer'd?
It will be laid to us, whose providence
Should have kept short, restrain'd, and out of haunt
This mad young man; but so much was our love,
We would not understand what was most fit,
But like the owner of a foul disease,
To keep it from divulging, let it feed
Even on the pith of life. Where is he gone?

Queen. To draw apart the body he hath kill'd,
O'er whom his very madness, like some ore
Among a mineral of metals base,
Shows itself pure: 'a weeps for what is done.

King. O Gertrude, come away!
The sun no sooner shall the mountains touch,
But we will ship him hence, and this vile deed
We must with all our majesty and skill
Both countenance and excuse. Ho, Guildenstern!

Enter ROSENCRANTZ *and* GUILDENSTERN.

Friends both, go join you with some further aid:
Hamlet in madness hath Polonius slain,
And from his mother's closet hath he dragg'd him.
Go seek him out, speak fair, and bring the body
Into the chapel. I pray you haste in this.

[Exeunt Rosencrantz and Guildenstern.]

Come, Gertrude, we'll call up our wisest friends

216. **draw . . . end:** finish my conversation.

IV.i. Location: The castle.
11. **brainish apprehension:** crazy notion.
16. **answer'd:** i.e. satisfactorily accounted for to the public.
17. **providence:** foresight.
18. **short:** on a short leash. **out of haunt:** away from other people.
22. **divulging:** being revealed.
25. **ore:** vein of gold. 26. **mineral:** mine.

And let them know both what we mean to do
And what's untimely done, [. . .]
Whose whisper o'er the world's diameter,
As level as the cannon to his blank,
Transports his pois'ned shot, may miss our name,
And hit the woundless air. O, come away!
My soul is full of discord and dismay. *Exeunt.*

[SCENE II]

Enter HAMLET.

Ham. Safely stow'd.

[*Gentlemen.* (*Within.*) Hamlet! Lord Hamlet!]

[*Ham.*] But soft, what noise? Who calls on Hamlet? O, here they come.

Enter ROSENCRANTZ *and* [GUILDENSTERN].

Ros. What have you done, my lord, with the dead body?

Ham. [Compounded] it with dust, whereto 'tis kin.

Ros. Tell us where 'tis, that we may take it thence,
And bear it to the chapel.

Ham. Do not believe it.

Ros. Believe what?

Ham. That I can keep your counsel and not mine own. Besides, to be demanded of a spunge, what replication should be made by the son of a king?

Ros. Take you me for a spunge, my lord?

Ham. Ay, sir, that soaks up the King's countenance, his rewards, his authorities. But such officers do the King best service in the end: he keeps them, like [an ape] an apple, in the corner of his jaw, first mouth'd, to be last swallow'd. When he needs what you have glean'd, it is but squeezing you, and, spunge, you shall be dry again.

Ros. I understand you not, my lord.

Ham. I am glad of it, a knavish speech sleeps in a foolish ear.

Ros. My lord, you must tell us where the body is, and go with us to the King.

Ham. The body is with the King, but the King is not with the body. The King is a thing—

Guil. A thing, my lord?

Ham. Of nothing, bring me to him. [Hide fox, and all after.] *Exeunt.*

40. Some words are wanting at the end of the line. Capell's conjecture, *so, haply, slander*, probably indicates the intended sense of the passage.
42. **As level:** with aim as good. **blank:** target.
44. **woundless:** incapable of being hurt.

IV.ii. Location: The castle.
12. **demanded of:** questioned by. **spunge:** sponge.
13. **replication:** reply. 15–16. **countenance:** favor.
23. **sleeps:** is meaningless.
27–28. **The body . . . the body.** Possibly alluding to the legal fiction that the king's dignity is separate from his mortal body.
30. **Of nothing:** of no account. Cf. "Man is like a thing of nought, his time passeth away like a shadow" (Psalm 144:4 in the Prayer Book version). "Hamlet at once insults the King and hints that his days are numbered" (Dover Wilson).
30–31. **Hide . . . after.** Probably a cry in some game resembling hide-and-seek.

[Scene III]

Enter King *and two or three.*

King. I have sent to seek him, and to find the body.
How dangerous is it that this man goes loose!
Yet must not we put the strong law on him.
He's lov'd of the distracted multitude,
Who like not in their judgment, but their eyes,
And where 'tis so, th' offender's scourge is weigh'd,
But never the offense. To bear all smooth and even,
This sudden sending him away must seem
Deliberate pause. Diseases desperate grown
By desperate appliance are reliev'd,
Or not at all.

Enter Rosencrantz.

How now, what hath befall'n?

Ros. Where the dead body is bestow'd, my lord,
We cannot get from him.

King. But where is he?

Ros. Without, my lord, guarded, to know your pleasure.

King. Bring him before us.

Ros. Ho, bring in the lord.

They [Hamlet *and* Guildenstern] *enter.*

King. Now, Hamlet, where's Polonius?

Ham. At supper.

King. At supper? where?

Ham. Not where he eats, but where 'a is eaten; a certain convocation of politic worms are e'en at him. Your worm is your only emperor for diet: we fat all creatures else to fat us, and we fat ourselves for maggots; your fat king and your lean beggar is but variable service, two dishes, but to one table—that's the end.

King. Alas, alas!

Ham. A man may fish with the worm that hath eat of a king, and eat of the fish that hath fed of that worm.

King. What dost thou mean by this?

Ham. Nothing but to show you how a king may go a progress through the guts of a beggar.

King. Where is Polonius?

Ham. In heaven, send thither to see; if your messenger find him not there, seek him i' th' other place yourself. But if indeed you find him not within this month, you shall nose him as you go up the stairs into the lobby.

King. [*To Attendants.*] Go seek him there.

Ham. 'A will stay till you come.

[*Exeunt Attendants.*]

King. Hamlet, this deed, for thine especial safety—
Which we do tender, as we dearly grieve
For that which thou hast done—must send thee hence
[With fiery quickness]; therefore prepare thyself,
The bark is ready, and the wind at help,
Th' associates tend, and every thing is bent
For England.

Ham. For England.

King. Ay, Hamlet.

Ham. Good.

King. So is it, if thou knew'st our purposes.

Ham. I see a cherub that sees them. But come, for England! Farewell, dear mother.

King. Thy loving father, Hamlet.

Ham. My mother: father and mother is man and wife, man and wife is one flesh—so, my mother. Come, for England! *Exit.*

King. Follow him at foot, tempt him with speed aboard.
Delay it not, I'll have him hence to-night.
Away, for every thing is seal'd and done
That else leans on th' affair. Pray you make haste.

[*Exeunt Rosencrantz and Guildenstern.*]

And, England, if my love thou hold'st at aught—
As my great power thereof may give thee sense,
Since yet thy cicatrice looks raw and red
After the Danish sword, and thy free awe
Pays homage to us—thou mayst not coldly set
Our sovereign process, which imports at full,
By letters congruing to that effect,
The present death of Hamlet. Do it, England,
For like the hectic in my blood he rages,
And thou must cure me. Till I know 'tis done,
How e'er my haps, my joys [were] ne'er [begun]. *Exit.*

[Scene IV]

Enter Fortinbras *with his army over the stage.*

Fort. Go, captain, from me greet the Danish king.
Tell him that by his license Fortinbras
Craves the conveyance of a promis'd march
Over his kingdom. You know the rendezvous.
If that his Majesty would aught with us,
We shall express our duty in his eye,
And let him know so.

Cap. I will do't, my lord.

Fort. Go softly on. [*Exeunt all but the Captain.*]

Enter Hamlet, Rosencrantz, [Guildenstern,] *etc.*

Ham. Good sir, whose powers are these?

Cap. They are of Norway, sir.

IV.iii. Location: The castle.
4. **distracted:** unstable. 6. **scourge:** i.e. punishment.
7. **bear:** manage.
8–9. **must . . . pause:** i.e. must be represented as a maturely considered decision.
20. **politic:** crafty, prying; "such worms as might breed in a politician's corpse" (Dowden). **e'en:** even now.
21. **for diet:** with respect to what it eats.
23–24. **variable service:** different courses of a meal.
31. **progress:** royal journey of state.

41. **tender:** regard with tenderness, hold dear. **dearly:** with intense feeling. 44. **at help:** favorable.
45. **Th':** thy. **tend:** await. **bent:** made ready.
48. **I . . . them:** i.e. heaven sees them.
54. **at foot:** at his heels, close behind. 57. **leans on:** relates to.
58. **England:** King of England. 60. **cicatrice:** scar.
61–62. **thy . . . Pays:** your fear makes you pay voluntarily.
62. **coldly set:** undervalue, disregard. 63. **process:** command.
64. **congruing to:** in accord with. 65. **present:** immediate.
66. **hectic:** continuous fever. 68. **haps:** fortunes.

IV.iv. Location: The Danish coast, near the castle.
3. **conveyance of:** escort for. 6. **eye:** presence.
8. **softly:** slowly. 9. **powers:** forces.

Ham. How purpos'd, sir, I pray you?
Cap. Against some part of Poland.
Ham. Who commands them, sir?
Cap. The nephew to old Norway, Fortinbras.
Ham. Goes it against the main of Poland, sir,
Or for some frontier?
Cap. Truly to speak, and with no addition,
We go to gain a little patch of ground
That hath in it no profit but the name.
To pay five ducats, five, I would not farm it;
Nor will it yield to Norway or the Pole
A ranker rate, should it be sold in fee.
Ham. Why then the Polack never will defend it.
Cap. Yes, it is already garrison'd.
Ham. Two thousand souls and twenty thousand ducats
Will not debate the question of this straw.
This is th' imposthume of much wealth and peace,
That inward breaks, and shows no cause without
Why the man dies. I humbly thank you, sir.
Cap. God buy you, sir. [*Exit.*]
Ros. Will't please you go, my lord?
Ham. I'll be with you straight—go a little before.
[*Exeunt all but Hamlet.*]
How all occasions do inform against me,
And spur my dull revenge! What is a man,
If his chief good and market of his time
Be but to sleep and feed? a beast, no more.
Sure He that made us with such large discourse,
Looking before and after, gave us not
That capability and godlike reason
To fust in us unus'd. Now whether it be
Bestial oblivion, or some craven scruple
Of thinking too precisely on th' event—
A thought which quarter'd hath but one part wisdom
And ever three parts coward—I do not know
Why yet I live to say, "This thing's to do,"
Sith I have cause, and will, and strength, and means
To do't. Examples gross as earth exhort me:
Witness this army of such mass and charge,
Led by a delicate and tender prince,
Whose spirit with divine ambition puff'd
Makes mouths at the invisible event,
Exposing what is mortal and unsure
To all that fortune, death, and danger dare,
Even for an egg-shell. Rightly to be great
Is not to stir without great argument,
But greatly to find quarrel in a straw
When honor's at the stake. How stand I then,
That have a father kill'd, a mother stain'd,
Excitements of my reason and my blood,
And let all sleep, while to my shame I see
The imminent death of twenty thousand men,
That for a fantasy and trick of fame
Go to their graves like beds, fight for a plot
Whereon the numbers cannot try the cause,
Which is not tomb enough and continent
To hide the slain? O, from this time forth,
My thoughts be bloody, or be nothing worth! *Exit.*

[SCENE V]

Enter HORATIO, [QUEEN] GERTRUDE, *and a* GENTLEMAN.

Queen. I will not speak with her.
Gent. She is importunate, indeed distract.
Her mood will needs be pitied.
Queen. What would she have?
Gent. She speaks much of her father, says she hears
There's tricks i' th' world, and hems, and beats her heart,
Spurns enviously at straws, speaks things in doubt
That carry but half sense. Her speech is nothing,
Yet the unshaped use of it doth move
The hearers to collection; they yawn at it,
And botch the words up fit to their own thoughts,
Which as her winks and nods and gestures yield them,
Indeed would make one think there might be thought,
Though nothing sure, yet much unhappily.
Hor. 'Twere good she were spoken with, for she may strew
Dangerous conjectures in ill-breeding minds.
[*Queen.*] Let her come in. [*Exit Gentleman.*]
[*Aside.*] To my sick soul, as sin's true nature is,
Each toy seems prologue to some great amiss,
So full of artless jealousy is guilt,
It spills itself in fearing to be spilt.

Enter OPHELIA [*distracted, with her hair down, playing on a lute*].

Oph. Where is the beauteous majesty of Denmark?
Queen. How now, Ophelia?
Oph. "How should I your true-love know *She sings.*
From another one?
By his cockle hat and staff,
And his sandal shoon."

15. **main:** main territory.
20. **To pay:** i.e. for an annual rent of. **farm:** lease.
22. **ranker:** higher. **in fee:** outright.
26. **Will not debate:** i.e. will scarcely be enough to fight out.
27. **imposthume:** abscess. 32. **inform against:** denounce, accuse.
34. **market:** purchase, profit. 36. **discourse:** reasoning power.
39. **fust:** grow mouldy. 40. **oblivion:** forgetfulness.
41. **event:** outcome. 46. **gross:** large, obvious.
47. **mass and charge:** size and expense.
50. **Makes mouths at:** treats scornfully. **invisible:** i.e. unforeseeable. 54. **Is not to:** i.e. is *not* not to. **argument:** cause.
55. **greatly:** nobly. 58. **Excitements of:** urgings by.

61. **fantasy:** caprice. **trick:** trifle.
63. **Whereon . . . cause:** which isn't large enough to let the opposing armies engage upon it. 64. **continent:** container.

IV.v. **Location:** The castle.
1–20. See the Textual Notes for the lines that replace these in Q1.
6. **Spurns . . . straws:** spitefully takes offense at trifles. **in doubt:** obscurely. 7. **Her speech:** what she says.
8. **unshaped use:** distracted manner.
9. **collection:** attempts to gather the meaning. **yawn at:** gape eagerly (as if to swallow). Most editors adopt the F1 reading *aim at.*
10. **botch:** patch. 11. **Which:** i.e. the words.
12. **thought:** inferred, conjectured.
15. **ill-breeding:** conceiving ill thoughts, prone to think the worst.
18. **toy:** trifle. **amiss:** calamity.
19. **artless jealousy:** uncontrolled suspicion. 20. **spills:** destroys.
23–24. These lines resemble a passage in an earlier ballad beginning "As you came from the holy land / Of Walsingham." Probably all the song fragments sung by Ophelia were familiar to the Globe audience, but only one other line (187) is from a ballad still extant.
25. **cockle hat:** hat bearing a cockle shell, the badge of a pilgrim to the shrine of St. James of Compostela in Spain. **staff.** Another mark of a pilgrim.
26. **shoon:** shoes (already an archaic form in Shakespeare's day).

Queen. Alas, sweet lady, what imports this song?
Oph. Say you? Nay, pray you mark.
"He is dead and gone, lady, *Song.*
He is dead and gone,
At his head a grass-green turf,
At his heels a stone."
O ho!
Queen. Nay, but, Ophelia—
Oph. Pray you mark.
[*Sings.*] "White his shroud as the mountain snow"—

Enter KING.

Queen. Alas, look here, my lord.
Oph. "Larded all with sweet flowers, *Song.*
Which bewept to the ground did not go
With true-love showers."
King. How do you, pretty lady?
Oph. Well, God dild you! They say the owl was a baker's daughter. Lord, we know what we are, but know not what we may be. God be at your table!
King. Conceit upon her father.
Oph. Pray let's have no words of this, but when they ask you what it means, say you this:
"To-morrow is Saint Valentine's *Song.*
day,
All in the morning betime,
And I a maid at your window,
To be your Valentine.

"Then up he rose and donn'd his clo'es,
And dupp'd the chamber-door,
Let in the maid, that out a maid
Never departed more."
King. Pretty Ophelia!
Oph. Indeed without an oath I'll make an end on't.
[*Sings.*] "By Gis, and by Saint Charity,
Alack, and fie for shame!
Young men will do't if they come to't,
By Cock, they are to blame.

"Quoth she, 'Before you tumbled me,
You promis'd me to wed.' "
(He answers.)
" 'So would I 'a' done, by yonder sun,
And thou hadst not come to my bed.' "
King. How long hath she been thus?
Oph. I hope all will be well. We must be patient, but I cannot choose but weep to think they would lay him i' th' cold ground. My brother shall know of it, and so I thank you for your good counsel. Come, my coach! Good night, ladies, good night. Sweet ladies, good night, good night. [*Exit.*]
King. Follow her close, give her good watch, I pray you. [*Exit Horatio.*]

O, this is the poison of deep grief, it springs
All from her father's death—and now behold!
O Gertrude, Gertrude,
When sorrows come, they come not single spies,
But in battalions: first, her father slain;
Next, your son gone, and he most violent author
Of his own just remove; the people muddied,
Thick and unwholesome in [their] thoughts and whispers
For good Polonius' death; and we have done but greenly
In hugger-mugger to inter him; poor Ophelia
Divided from herself and her fair judgment,
Without the which we are pictures, or mere beasts;
Last, and as much containing as all these,
Her brother is in secret come from France,
Feeds on this wonder, keeps himself in clouds,
And wants not buzzers to infect his ear
With pestilent speeches of his father's death,
Wherein necessity, of matter beggar'd,
Will nothing stick our person to arraign
In ear and ear. O my dear Gertrude, this,
Like to a murd'ring-piece, in many places
Gives me superfluous death. *A noise within.*
[*Queen.* Alack, what noise is this?]
King. Attend!
Where is my Swissers? Let them guard the door.

Enter a MESSENGER.

What is the matter?
Mess. Save yourself, my lord!
The ocean, overpeering of his list,
Eats not the flats with more impiteous haste
Than young Laertes, in a riotous head,
O'erbears your officers. The rabble call him lord,
And as the world were now but to begin,
Antiquity forgot, custom not known,
The ratifiers and props of every word,
[They] cry, "Choose we, Laertes shall be king!"
Caps, hands, and tongues applaud it to the clouds,
"Laertes shall be king, Laertes king!" *A noise within.*
Queen. How cheerfully on the false trail they cry!
O, this is counter, you false Danish dogs!

Enter LAERTES *with others.*

King. The doors are broke.
Laer. Where is this king? Sirs, stand you all without.
All. No, let 's come in.
Laer. I pray you give me leave.

38. Larded: adorned.
39. not. Contrary to the expected sense, and unmetrical; explained as Ophelia's alteration of the line to accord with the facts of Polonius' burial (see line 84).
42. dild: yield, reward. **owl.** Alluding to the legend of a baker's daughter whom Jesus turned into an owl because she did not respond generously to his request for bread.
45. Conceit: fanciful brooding. **53. dupp'd:** opened.
58. Gis: contraction of *Jesus.* **61. Cock:** corruption of *God.*
66. And: if.

78. spies: i.e. soldiers sent ahead of the main force to reconnoiter, scouts. **81. muddied:** confused. **83. greenly:** unwisely.
84. In hugger-mugger: secretly and hastily.
89. in clouds: i.e. in cloudy surmise and suspicion (rather than the light of fact).
90. wants: lacks. **buzzers:** whispering informers.
92. of matter beggar'd: destitute of facts.
93. nothing . . . arraign: scruple not at all to charge me with the crime.
95. murd'ring-piece: cannon firing a scattering charge.
98. Swissers: Swiss guards.
100. overpeering . . . list: rising higher than its shores.
102. in . . . head: with a rebellious force.
104. as: as if. **106. word:** pledge, promise.
111. counter: on the wrong scent (literally, following the scent backward).

All. We will, we will.
Laer. I thank you, keep the door. [*Exeunt Laertes' followers.*] O thou vile king,
Give me my father!
Queen. Calmly, good Laertes.
Laer. That drop of blood that's calm proclaims me bastard,
Cries cuckold to my father, brands the harlot
Even here between the chaste unsmirched brow
Of my true mother.
King. What is the cause, Laertes,
That thy rebellion looks so giant-like?
Let him go, Gertrude, do not fear our person:
There's such divinity doth hedge a king
That treason can but peep to what it would,
Acts little of his will. Tell me, Laertes,
Why thou art thus incens'd. Let him go, Gertrude.
Speak, man.
Laer. Where is my father?
King. Dead.
Queen. But not by him.
King. Let him demand his fill.
Laer. How came he dead? I'll not be juggled with.
To hell, allegiance! vows, to the blackest devil!
Conscience and grace, to the profoundest pit!
I dare damnation. To this point I stand,
That both the worlds I give to negligence,
Let come what comes, only I'll be reveng'd
Most throughly for my father.
King. Who shall stay you?
Laer. My will, not all the world's:
And for my means, I'll husband them so well,
They shall go far with little.
King. Good Laertes,
If you desire to know the certainty
Of your dear father, is't writ in your revenge
That, swoopstake, you will draw both friend and foe,
Winner and loser?
Laer. None but his enemies.
King. Will you know them then?
Laer. To his good friends thus wide I'll ope my arms,
And like the kind life-rend'ring pelican,
Repast them with my blood.
King. Why, now you speak
Like a good child and a true gentleman.
That I am guiltless of your father's death,
And am most sensibly in grief for it,
It shall as level to your judgment 'pear
As day does to your eye.
A noise within: "Let her come in!"
Laer. How now, what noise is that?

Enter OPHELIA.

O heat, dry up my brains! tears seven times salt
Burn out the sense and virtue of mine eye!
By heaven, thy madness shall be paid with weight
[Till] our scale turn the beam. O rose of May!
Dear maid, kind sister, sweet Ophelia!
O heavens, is't possible a young maid's wits
Should be as mortal as [an old] man's life?
[Nature is fine in love, and where 'tis fine,
It sends some precious instance of itself
After the thing it loves.]
Oph. "They bore him barefac'd on the bier, *Song.*
[Hey non nonny, nonny, hey nonny,]
And in his grave rain'd many a tear"—
Fare you well, my dove!
Laer. Hadst thou thy wits and didst persuade revenge,
It could not move thus.

Oph. You must sing, "A-down, a-down," and you call him a-down-a. O how the wheel becomes it! It is the false steward, that stole his master's daughter.

Laer. This nothing's more than matter.

Oph. There's rosemary, that's for remembrance; pray you, love, remember. And there is pansies, that's for thoughts.

Laer. A document in madness, thoughts and remembrance fitted.

Oph. [*To Claudius.*] There's fennel for you, and columbines. [*To Gertrude.*] There's rue for you, and here's some for me; we may call it herb of grace a' Sundays. You may wear your rue with a difference. There's a daisy. I would give you some violets, but they wither'd all when my father died. They say 'a made a good end—
[*Sings.*] "For bonny sweet Robin is all my joy."

Laer. Thought and afflictions, passion, hell itself,
She turns to favor and to prettiness.
Oph. "And will 'a not come again? *Song.*
And will 'a not come again?
No, no, he is dead,
Go to thy death-bed,
He never will come again.

"His beard was as white as snow,
[All] flaxen was his pole,
He is gone, he is gone,
And we cast away moan,
God 'a' mercy on his soul!"

123. fear: fear for. **125. would:** i.e. would like to do.
135. both . . . negligence: i.e. I don't care what the consequences are in this world or in the next.
137. throughly: thoroughly. **138. world's:** i.e. world's will.
143. swoopstake: sweeping up everything without discrimination (modern *sweepstake*).
147. pelican. The female pelican was believed to draw blood from her own breast to nourish her young.
149. good child: faithful son. **151. sensibly:** feelingly.
152. level: plain.

156. virtue: faculty. **162. fine in:** refined or spiritualized by.
163. instance: proof, token. So delicate is Ophelia's love for her father that her sanity has pursued him into the grave.
169. persuade: argue logically for.
171–72. and . . . a-down-a: "if he indeed agrees that Polonius is 'a-down,' i.e. fallen low" (Dover Wilson).
172. wheel: refrain (?) or spinning-wheel, at which women sang ballads (?). **174. matter:** lucid speech.
178. A document in madness: a lesson contained in mad talk.
180, 181. fennel, columbines. Symbols respectively of flattery and ingratitude. **181. rue.** Symbolic of sorrow and repentance.
183. with a difference: i.e. to represent a different cause of sorrow. *Difference* is a term from heraldry, meaning a variation in a coat of arms made to distinguish different members of a family.
184. daisy, violets. Symbolic respectively of dissembling and faithfulness. It is not clear who are the recipients of these.
188. Thought: melancholy. **189. favor:** grace, charm.
196. flaxen: white. **pole:** poll, head.

And of all Christians' souls, [I pray God]. God buy you. *[Exit.]*
Laer. Do you [see] this, O God?
King. Laertes, I must commune with your grief,
Or you deny me right. Go but apart,
Make choice of whom your wisest friends you will,
And they shall hear and judge 'twixt you and me.
If by direct or by collateral hand
They find us touch'd, we will our kingdom give,
Our crown, our life, and all that we call ours,
To you in satisfaction; but if not,
Be you content to lend your patience to us,
And we shall jointly labor with your soul
To give it due content.
Laer. Let this be so.
His means of death, his obscure funeral—
No trophy, sword, nor hatchment o'er his bones,
No noble rite nor formal ostentation—
Cry to be heard, as 'twere from heaven to earth,
That I must call't in question.
King. So you shall,
And where th' offense is, let the great axe fall.
I pray you go with me. *Exeunt.*

[Scene VI]

Enter Horatio *and others.*

Hor. What are they that would speak with me?

Gentleman. Sea-faring men, sir. They say they have letters for you.

Hor. Let them come in. *[Exit Gentleman.]*
I do not know from what part of the world
I should be greeted, if not from Lord Hamlet.

Enter Sailors.

[1.] Sail. God bless you, sir.

Hor. Let him bless thee too.

[1.] Sail. 'A shall, sir, and['t] please him. There's a letter for you, sir—it came from th' embassador that was bound for England—if your name be Horatio, as I am let to know it is.

Hor. *[Reads.]* "Horatio, when thou shalt have overlook'd this, give these fellows some means to the King, they have letters for him. Ere we were two days old at sea, a pirate of very warlike appointment gave us chase. Finding ourselves too slow of sail, we put on a compell'd valor, and in the grapple I boarded them. On the instant they got clear of our ship, so I alone became their prisoner. They have dealt with me like thieves of mercy, but they knew what they did: I am to do a [good] turn for them. Let the King have the letters I have sent, and repair thou to me with as much speed as thou wouldest fly death. I have words to speak in thine ear will make thee dumb, yet are they much too light for the [bore] of the matter. These good fellows will bring thee where I am. Rosencrantz and Guildenstern hold their course for England, of them I have much to tell thee. Farewell.

[He] that thou knowest thine,
Hamlet."

Come, I will [give] you way for these your letters,
And do't the speedier that you may direct me
To him from whom you brought them. *Exeunt.*

207. **collateral:** i.e. indirect. 208. **touch'd:** guilty.
215. **trophy:** memorial. **hatchment:** heraldic memorial tablet.
216. **formal ostentation:** fitting and customary ceremony.
218. **That:** so that.

IV.vi. Location: The castle.
See the Textual Notes for a scene unique to Q1.
21. **thieves of mercy:** merciful thieves.

[Scene VII]

Enter King *and* Laertes.

King. Now must your conscience my acquittance seal,
And you must put me in your heart for friend,
Sith you have heard, and with a knowing ear,
That he which hath your noble father slain
Pursued my life.
Laer. It well appears. But tell me
Why you [proceeded] not against these feats
So criminal and so capital in nature,
As by your safety, greatness, wisdom, all things else
You mainly were stirr'd up.
King. O, for two special reasons,
Which may to you perhaps seem much unsinow'd,
But yet to me th' are strong. The Queen his mother
Lives almost by his looks, and for myself—
My virtue or my plague, be it either which—
She is so [conjunctive] to my life and soul,
That, as the star moves not but in his sphere,
I could not but by her. The other motive,
Why to a public count I might not go,
Is the great love the general gender bear him,
Who, dipping all his faults in their affection,
Work like the spring that turneth wood to stone,
Convert his gyves to graces, so that my arrows,
Too slightly timber'd for so [loud a wind],
Would have reverted to my bow again,
But not where I have aim'd them.
Laer. And so have I a noble father lost,
A sister driven into desp'rate terms,
Whose worth, if praises may go back again,
Stood challenger on mount of all the age
For her perfections—but my revenge will come.
King. Break not your sleeps for that. You must not think
That we are made of stuff so flat and dull

26. **bore:** calibre, size (gunnery term).

IV.vii. Location: The castle.
1. **my acquittance seal:** ratify my acquittal, i.e. acknowledge my innocence in Polonius' death.
6. **feats:** acts. 8. **safety:** i.e. regard for your own safety.
9. **mainly:** powerfully. 10. **unsinow'd:** unsinewed, i.e. weak.
13. **either which:** one or the other.
14. **conjunctive:** closely joined.
15. **in his sphere:** by the movement of the sphere in which it is fixed (as the Ptolemaic astronomy taught).
17. **count:** reckoning. 18. **the general gender:** everybody.
21. **gyves:** fetters. 26. **terms:** condition.
27. **go back again:** i.e. refer to what she was before she went mad.
28. **on mount:** pre-eminent.
30. **for that:** i.e. for fear of losing your revenge.
31. **flat:** spiritless.

That we can let our beard be shook with danger
And think it pastime. You shortly shall hear more.
I lov'd your father, and we love ourself,
And that, I hope, will teach you to imagine—

Enter a Messenger *with letters.*

[How now? What news?]
Mess. Letters, my lord, from Hamlet:]
These to your Majesty, this to the Queen.
King. From Hamlet? Who brought them?
Mess. Sailors, my lord, they say, I saw them not.
They were given me by Claudio. He receiv'd them
Of him that brought them.
King. Laertes, you shall hear them.
—Leave us. [*Exit Messenger.*]
[*Reads.*] "High and mighty, You shall know I am set naked on your kingdom. To-morrow shall I beg leave to see your kingly eyes, when I shall, first asking you pardon thereunto, recount the occasion of my sudden [and more strange] return.
[Hamlet.]"
What should this mean? Are all the rest come back?
Or is it some abuse, and no such thing?
Laer. Know you the hand?
King. 'Tis Hamlet's character. "Naked"!
And in a postscript here he says "alone."
Can you devise me?
Laer. I am lost in it, my lord. But let him come,
It warms the very sickness in my heart
That I [shall] live and tell him to his teeth,
"Thus didst thou."
King. If it be so, Laertes—
As how should it be so? how otherwise?—
Will you be rul'd by me?
Laer. Ay, my lord,
So you will not o'errule me to a peace.
King. To thine own peace. If he be now returned
As [checking] at his voyage, and that he means
No more to undertake it, I will work him
To an exploit, now ripe in my device,
Under the which he shall not choose but fall;
And for his death no wind of blame shall breathe,
But even his mother shall uncharge the practice,
And call it accident.
Laer. My lord, I will be rul'd,
The rather if you could devise it so
That I might be the organ.
King. It falls right.
You have been talk'd of since your travel much,
And that in Hamlet's hearing, for a quality
Wherein they say you shine. Your sum of parts
Did not together pluck such envy from him
As did that one, and that, in my regard,
Of the unworthiest siege.
Laer. What part is that, my lord?
King. A very riband in the cap of youth,
Yet needful too, for youth no less becomes
The light and careless livery that it wears
Than settled age his sables and his weeds,
Importing health and graveness. Two months since
Here was a gentleman of Normandy:
I have seen myself, and serv'd against, the French,
And they can well on horseback, but this gallant
Had witchcraft in't, he grew unto his seat,
And to such wondrous doing brought his horse,
As had he been incorps'd and demi-natur'd
With the brave beast. So far he topp'd [my] thought,
That I in forgery of shapes and tricks
Come short of what he did.
Laer. A Norman was't?
King. A Norman.
Laer. Upon my life, Lamord.
King. The very same.
Laer. I know him well. He is the brooch indeed
And gem of all the nation.
King. He made confession of you,
And gave you such a masterly report
For art and exercise in your defense,
And for your rapier most especial,
That he cried out 'twould be a sight indeed
If one could match you. The scrimers of their nation
He swore had neither motion, guard, nor eye,
If you oppos'd them. Sir, this report of his
Did Hamlet so envenom with his envy
That he could nothing do but wish and beg
Your sudden coming o'er to play with you.
Now, out of this—
Laer. What out of this, my lord?
King. Laertes, was your father dear to you?
Or are you like the painting of a sorrow,
A face without a heart?
Laer. Why ask you this?
King. Not that I think you did not love your father,
But that I know love is begun by time,
And that I see, in passages of proof,
Time qualifies the spark and fire of it.
There lives within the very flame of love
A kind of week or snuff that will abate it,
And nothing is at a like goodness still,
For goodness, growing to a plurisy,
Dies in his own too much. That we would do,

32. let . . . shook. To ruffle or tweak a man's beard was an act of insolent defiance that he could not disregard without loss of honor. Cf. II.ii.573. **with:** by. **44. naked:** destitute.
46. pardon thereunto: permission to do so. **50. abuse:** deceit.
51. character: handwriting. **53. devise me:** explain it to me.
58. As . . . otherwise: How can he have come back? Yet he obviously has. **60. So:** provided that.
62. checking at: turning from (like a falcon diverted from its quarry by other prey).
67. uncharge the practice: adjudge the plot no plot, i.e. fail to see the plot. **70. organ:** instrument, agent. **72. quality:** skill.
73. Your . . . parts: all your (other) accomplishments put together.
76. unworthiest: i.e. least important (with no implication of unsuitableness). **siege:** status, position.
80. weeds: (characteristic) garb.
81. Importing . . . graveness: signifying prosperity and dignity.
84. can . . . horseback: are excellent riders.
87. incorps'd: made one body. **demi-natur'd:** i.e. become half of a composite animal. **89. forgery:** mere imagining.
93. brooch: ornament (worn in the hat).
95. made . . . you: acknowledged your excellence.
100. scrimers: fencers. **105. sudden:** speedy.
111. time: i.e. a particular set of circumstances.
112. in . . . proof: i.e. by the test of experience, by actual examples.
113. qualifies: moderates. **115. week:** wick.
116. nothing . . . still: nothing remains forever at the same pitch of perfection.
117. plurisy: plethora (a variant spelling of *pleurisy*, which was erroneously related to *plus*, stem *plur-*, "more, overmuch."
118. too much: excess.

We should do when we would; for this "would" changes,
And hath abatements and delays as many
As there are tongues, are hands, are accidents,
And then this "should" is like a spendthrift's sigh,
That hurts by easing. But to the quick of th' ulcer:
Hamlet comes back. What would you undertake
To show yourself indeed your father's son
More than in words?

Laer. To cut his throat i' th' church.

King. No place indeed should murther sanctuarize,
Revenge should have no bounds. But, good Laertes,
Will you do this, keep close within your chamber.
Hamlet return'd shall know you are come home.
We'll put on those shall praise your excellence,
And set a double varnish on the fame
The Frenchman gave you, bring you in fine together,
And wager o'er your heads. He, being remiss,
Most generous, and free from all contriving,
Will not peruse the foils, so that with ease,
Or with a little shuffling, you may choose
A sword unbated, and in a [pass] of practice
Requite him for your father.

Laer. I will do't,
And for [that] purpose I'll anoint my sword.
I bought an unction of a mountebank,
So mortal that, but dip a knife in it,
Where it draws blood, no cataplasm so rare,
Collected from all simples that have virtue
Under the moon, can save the thing from death
That is but scratch'd withal. I'll touch my point
With this contagion, that if I gall him slightly,
It may be death.

King. Let's further think of this,
Weigh what convenience both of time and means
May fit us to our shape. If this should fail,
And that our drift look through our bad performance,
'Twere better not assay'd; therefore this project
Should have a back or second, that might hold
If this did blast in proof. Soft, let me see.
We'll make a solemn wager on your cunnings—
I ha't!
When in your motion you are hot and dry—
As make your bouts more violent to that end—
And that he calls for drink, I'll have preferr'd him
A chalice for the nonce, whereon but sipping,
If he by chance escape your venom'd stuck,
Our purpose may hold there. But stay, what noise?

Enter QUEEN.

Queen. One woe doth tread upon another's heel,
So fast they follow. Your sister's drown'd, Laertes.

Laer. Drown'd! O, where?

Queen. There is a willow grows askaunt the brook,
That shows his hoary leaves in the glassy stream,
Therewith fantastic garlands did she make
Of crow-flowers, nettles, daisies, and long purples
That liberal shepherds give a grosser name,
But our cull-cold maids do dead men's fingers call them.
There on the pendant boughs her crownet weeds
Clamb'ring to hang, an envious sliver broke,
When down her weedy trophies and herself
Fell in the weeping brook. Her clothes spread wide,
And mermaid-like awhile they bore her up,
Which time she chaunted snatches of old lauds,
As one incapable of her own distress,
Or like a creature native and indued
Unto that element. But long it could not be
Till that her garments, heavy with their drink,
Pull'd the poor wretch from her melodious lay
To muddy death.

Laer. Alas, then she is drown'd?

Queen. Drown'd, drown'd.

Laer. Too much of water hast thou, poor Ophelia,
And therefore I forbid my tears; but yet
It is our trick, Nature her custom holds,
Let shame say what it will; when these are gone,
The woman will be out. Adieu, my lord,
I have a speech a' fire that fain would blaze,
But that this folly drowns it. *Exit.*

King. Let's follow, Gertrude.
How much I had to do to calm his rage!
Now fear I this will give it start again,
Therefore let's follow. *Exeunt.*

[ACT V, SCENE I]

Enter two CLOWNS [*with spades and mattocks*].

1. Clo. Is she to be buried in Christian burial when she willfully seeks her own salvation?

2. Clo. I tell thee she is, therefore make her grave straight. The crowner hath sate on her, and finds it Christian burial.

1. Clo. How can that be, unless she drown'd herself in her own defense?

122. spendthrift's sigh. A sigh was supposed to draw blood from the heart.
123. hurts by easing: injures us at the same time that it gives us relief.
127. sanctuarize: offer asylum to.
129. Will . . . this: if you want to undertake this.
131. put on those: incite those who.
132. double varnish: second coat of varnish. **133. in fine:** finally.
134. remiss: careless, overtrustful.
135. generous: noble-minded. **free . . . contriving:** innocent of sharp practices. **136. peruse:** examine.
137. shuffling: cunning exchange.
138. unbated: not blunted. **pass of practice:** tricky thrust.
141. unction: ointment. **mountebank:** travelling quack-doctor.
142. mortal: deadly. **143. cataplasm:** poultice.
144. simples: medicinal herbs. **virtue:** curative power.
147. gall: graze. **150. fit . . . shape:** i.e. suit our purposes best.
151. drift: purpose. **look through:** become visible, be detected.
153. back or second: i.e. a second plot in reserve for emergency.
154. blast in proof: blow up while being tried (an image from gunnery).
158. As: i.e. and you should.
159. preferr'd: offered to. Most editors adopt the F1 reading *prepar'd.*
160. nonce: occasion.

161. stuck: thrust (from *stoccado,* a fencing term).
166. askaunt: sideways over. **167. hoary:** grey-white.
168. Therewith: i.e. with willow branches.
169. long purples: wild orchids.
170. liberal: free-spoken. **171. cull-cold:** chaste.
172. crownet: made into coronets.
173. envious sliver: malicious branch. **177. lauds:** hymns.
178. incapable: insensible. **179. indued:** habituated.
187. It: i.e. weeping. **trick:** natural way.
188. these: these tears.
189. The woman . . . out: my womanish traits will be gone for good.

V.i. Location: A churchyard.
o.s.d. **Clowns:** rustics.
4. straight: immediately. **crowner:** coroner.

2. Clo. Why, 'tis found so.

1. Clo. It must be [*se offendendo*], it cannot be else. For here lies the point: if I drown myself wittingly, it argues an act, and an act hath three branches—it is to act, to do, to perform; [argal], she drown'd herself wittingly.

2. Clo. Nay, but hear you, goodman delver—

1. Clo. Give me leave. Here lies the water; good. Here stands the man; good. If the man go to this water and drown himself, it is, will he, nill he, he goes, mark you that. But if the water come to him and drown him, he drowns not himself; argal, he that is not guilty of his own death shortens not his own life.

2. Clo. But is this law?

1. Clo. Ay, marry, is't—crowner's quest law.

2. Clo. Will you ha' the truth an't? If this had not been a gentlewoman, she should have been buried out a' Christian burial.

1. Clo. Why, there thou say'st, and the more pity that great folk should have count'nance in this world to drown or hang themselves, more than their even-Christen. Come, my spade. There is no ancient gentlemen but gard'ners, ditchers, and grave-makers; they hold up Adam's profession.

2. Clo. Was he a gentleman?

1. Clo. 'A was the first that ever bore arms.

[*2. Clo.* Why, he had none.

1. Clo. What, art a heathen? How dost thou understand the Scripture? The Scripture says Adam digg'd; could he dig without arms?] I'll put another question to thee. If thou answerest me not to the purpose, confess thyself—

2. Clo. Go to.

1. Clo. What is he that builds stronger than either the mason, the shipwright, or the carpenter?

2. Clo. The gallows-maker, for that outlives a thousand tenants.

1. Clo. I like thy wit well, in good faith. The gallows does well; but how does it well? It does well to those that do ill. Now thou dost ill to say the gallows is built stronger than the church; argal, the gallows may do well to thee. To't again, come.

2. Clo. Who builds stronger than a mason, a shipwright, or a carpenter?

1. Clo. Ay, tell me that, and unyoke.

2. Clo. Marry, now I can tell.

1. Clo. To't.

2. Clo. Mass, I cannot tell.

Enter HAMLET *and* HORATIO [*afar off*].

1. Clo. Cudgel thy brains no more about it, for your dull ass will not mend his pace with beating, and when you are ask'd this question next, say "a grave-maker": the houses he makes lasts till doomsday. Go

9. se offendendo: blunder for *se defendendo*, "in self-defense."
12. argal: blunder for *ergo*, "therefore."
15–20. Here . . . life. Alluding to a very famous suicide case, that of Sir James Hales, a judge who drowned himself in 1554; it was long cited in the courts. The clown gives a garbled account of the defense summing-up and the verdict. **17. nill he:** will he not.
22. quest: inquest. **28–29. even-Christen:** fellow-Christians.
34. none: i.e. no coat of arms.
52. unyoke: i.e. cease to labor, call it a day.
55. Mass: by the mass.

get thee in, and fetch me a sup of liquor.

[*Exit Second Clown. First Clown digs.*]

"In youth when I did love, did love, *Song.*
Methought it was very sweet,
To contract—O—the time for—a—my behove,
O, methought there—a—was nothing—a—meet."

Ham. Has this fellow no feeling of his business? 'a sings in grave-making.

Hor. Custom hath made it in him a property of easiness.

Ham. 'Tis e'en so, the hand of little employment hath the daintier sense.

1. Clo. "But age with his stealing steps *Song.*
Hath clawed me in his clutch,
And hath shipped me into the land,
As if I had never been such."

[*Throws up a shovelful of earth with a skull in it.*]

Ham. That skull had a tongue in it, and could sing once. How the knave jowls it to the ground, as if 'twere Cain's jaw-bone, that did the first murder! This might be the pate of a politician, which this ass now o'erreaches, one that would circumvent God, might it not?

Hor. It might, my lord.

Ham. Or of a courtier, which could say, "Good morrow, sweet lord! How dost thou, sweet lord?" This might be my Lord Such-a-one, that prais'd my Lord Such-a-one's horse when 'a [meant] to beg it, might it not?

Hor. Ay, my lord.

Ham. Why, e'en so, and now my Lady Worm's, chopless, and knock'd about the [mazzard] with a sexton's spade. Here's fine revolution, and we had the trick to see't. Did these bones cost no more the breeding, but to play at loggats with them? Mine ache to think on't.

1. Clo. "A pickaxe and a spade, a spade, *Song.*
For and a shrouding sheet:
O, a pit of clay for to be made
For such a guest is meet."

[*Throws up another skull.*]

Ham. There's another. Why may not that be the skull of a lawyer? Where be his quiddities now, his quillities, his cases, his tenures, and his tricks? Why does he suffer this mad knave now to knock him about the sconce with a dirty shovel, and will not tell him of his action of battery? Hum! This fellow might be in 's time a great buyer of land, with his statutes, his

63. contract . . . behove: shorten, i.e. spend agreeably . . . advantage. The song, punctuated by the grunts of the clown as he digs, is a garbled version of a poem by Thomas Lord Vaux, entitled "The Aged Lover Renounceth Love." **67. Custom:** habit.
67–68. a property of easiness: i.e. a thing he can do with complete ease of mind.
70. daintier sense: more delicate sensitivity.
76. jowls: dashes. **78. politician:** schemer, intriguer.
79. o'erreaches: gets the better of (with play on the literal sense). **circumvent God:** bypass God's law.
89. chopless: lacking the lower jaw. **mazzard:** head.
90. revolution: change. **and:** if.
91. trick: knack, ability. **Did . . . cost:** were . . . worth.
92. loggats: a game in which blocks of wood were thrown at a stake.
99. quiddities: subtleties, quibbles.
100. quillities: fine distinctions. **tenures:** titles to real estate.
102. sconce: head.
104, 105. statutes, recognizances: bonds securing debts by attaching land and property.

recognizances, his fines, his double vouchers, his recoveries. [Is this the fine of his fines, and the recovery of his recoveries,] to have his fine pate full of fine dirt? Will [his] vouchers vouch him no more of his purchases, and [double ones too], than the length and breadth of a pair of indentures? The very conveyances of his lands will scarcely lie in this box, and must th' inheritor himself have no more, ha?

Hor. Not a jot more, my lord.

Ham. Is not parchment made of sheep-skins?

Hor. Ay, my lord, and of calves'-skins too.

Ham. They are sheep and calves which seek out assurance in that. I will speak to this fellow. Whose grave's this, sirrah?

1. Clo. Mine, sir.

[*Sings.*] "[O], a pit of clay for to be made
[For such a guest is meet]."

Ham. I think it be thine indeed, for thou liest in't.

1. Clo. You lie out on't, sir, and therefore 'tis not yours; for my part, I do not lie in't, yet it is mine.

Ham. Thou dost lie in't, to be in't and say it is thine. 'Tis for the dead, not for the quick; therefore thou liest.

1. Clo. 'Tis a quick lie, sir, 'twill away again from me to you.

Ham. What man dost thou dig it for?

1. Clo. For no man, sir.

Ham. What woman then?

1. Clo. For none neither.

Ham. Who is to be buried in't?

1. Clo. One that was a woman, sir, but, rest her soul, she's dead.

Ham. How absolute the knave is! we must speak by the card, or equivocation will undo us. By the Lord, Horatio, this three years I have took note of it: the age is grown so pick'd that the toe of the peasant comes so near the heel of the courtier, he galls his kibe. How long hast thou been grave-maker?

1. Clo. Of [all] the days i' th' year, I came to't that day that our last king Hamlet overcame Fortinbras.

Ham. How long is that since?

1. Clo. Cannot you tell that? Every fool can tell that. It was that very day that young Hamlet was born—he that is mad, and sent into England.

Ham. Ay, marry, why was he sent into England?

1. Clo. Why, because 'a was mad. 'A shall recover his wits there, or if 'a do not, 'tis no great matter there.

Ham. Why?

1. Clo. 'Twill not be seen in him there, there the men are as mad as he.

Ham. How came he mad?

1. Clo. Very strangely, they say.

Ham. How strangely?

1. Clo. Faith, e'en with losing his wits.

Ham. Upon what ground?

1. Clo. Why, here in Denmark. I have been sexton here, man and boy, thirty years.

Ham. How long will a man lie i' th' earth ere he rot?

1. Clo. Faith, if 'a be not rotten before 'a die—as we have many pocky corses, that will scarce hold the laying in—'a will last you some eight year or nine year. A tanner will last you nine year.

Ham. Why he more than another?

1. Clo. Why, sir, his hide is so tann'd with his trade that 'a will keep out water a great while, and your water is a sore decayer of your whoreson dead body. Here's a skull now hath lien you i' th' earth three and twenty years.

Ham. Whose was it?

1. Clo. A whoreson mad fellow's it was. Whose do you think it was?

Ham. Nay, I know not.

1. Clo. A pestilence on him for a mad rogue! 'a pour'd a flagon of Rhenish on my head once. This same skull, sir, was, sir, Yorick's skull, the King's jester.

Ham. This? [*Takes the skull.*]

1. Clo. E'en that.

Ham. Alas, poor Yorick! I knew him, Horatio, a fellow of infinite jest, of most excellent fancy. He hath bore me on his back a thousand times, and now how abhorr'd in my imagination it is! my gorge rises at it. Here hung those lips that I have kiss'd I know not how oft. Where be your gibes now, your gambols, your songs, your flashes of merriment, that were wont to set the table on a roar? Not one now to mock your own grinning—quite chop-fall'n. Now get you to my lady's [chamber], and tell her, let her paint an inch thick, to this favor she must come; make her laugh at that. Prithee, Horatio, tell me one thing.

Hor. What's that, my lord?

Ham. Dost thou think Alexander look'd a' this fashion i' th' earth?

Hor. E'en so.

Ham. And smelt so? pah! [*Puts down the skull.*]

Hor. E'en so, my lord.

Ham. To what base uses we may return, Horatio! Why may not imagination trace the noble dust of Alexander, till 'a find it stopping a bunghole?

Hor. 'Twere to consider too curiously, to consider so.

Ham. No, faith, not a jot, but to follow him thither with modesty enough and likelihood to lead it: Alexander died, Alexander was buried, Alexander returneth to dust, the dust is earth, of earth we make loam, and why of that loam whereto he was converted might they not stop a beer-barrel?

105, 106. fines, recoveries: procedures for converting an entailed estate to freehold.
105. double vouchers: documents guaranteeing title to real estate, signed by two persons. **106. fine:** end.
110. pair of indentures: legal document cut into two parts which fitted together on a serrated edge. Perhaps Hamlet thus refers to the two rows of teeth in the skull, or to the bone sutures.
110–11. conveyances: documents relating to transfer of property.
111. this box: i.e. the skull itself. **112. inheritor:** owner.
118. sirrah: term of address to inferiors. **137. absolute:** positive.
138. by the card: by the compass, i.e. punctiliously. **equivocation:** ambiguity. **140. pick'd:** refined.
141. galls his kibe: rubs the courtier's chilblain.

166. pocky: rotten with venereal disease.
166–67. hold . . . in: last out the burial.
192. chop-fall'n: (1) lacking the lower jaw; (2) downcast.
194. favor: appearance. **205. curiously:** closely, minutely.
208. modesty: moderation.
210. loam: a mixture of moistened clay with sand, straw, etc.

Imperious Caesar, dead and turn'd to clay,
Might stop a hole to keep the wind away.
O that that earth which kept the world in awe
Should patch a wall t' expel the [winter's] flaw!
But soft, but soft awhile, here comes the King,

Enter KING, QUEEN, LAERTES, *and* [*a* DOCTOR OF DIVINITY, *following*] *the corse*, [*with* LORDS *attendant*].

The Queen, the courtiers. Who is this they follow?
And with such maimed rites? This doth betoken
The corse they follow did with desp'rate hand
Foredo it own life. 'Twas of some estate.
Couch we a while and mark. [*Retiring with Horatio.*]
Laer. What ceremony else?
Ham. That is Laertes, a very noble youth. Mark.
Laer. What ceremony else?
Doctor. Her obsequies have been as far enlarg'd
As we have warranty. Her death was doubtful,
And but that great command o'ersways the order,
She should in ground unsanctified been lodg'd
Till the last trumpet; for charitable prayers,
[Shards,] flints, and pebbles should be thrown on her.
Yet here she is allow'd her virgin crants,
Her maiden strewments, and the bringing home
Of bell and burial.
Laer. Must there no more be done?
Doctor. No more be done:
We should profane the service of the dead
To sing a requiem and such rest to her
As to peace-parted souls.
Laer. Lay her i' th' earth,
And from her fair and unpolluted flesh
May violets spring! I tell thee, churlish priest,
A minist'ring angel shall my sister be
When thou liest howling.
Ham. What, the fair Ophelia!
Queen. [*Scattering flowers.*] Sweets to the sweet, farewell!
I hop'd thou shouldst have been my Hamlet's wife.
I thought thy bride-bed to have deck'd, sweet maid,
And not have strew'd thy grave.
Laer. O, treble woe
Fall ten times [treble] on that cursed head
Whose wicked deed thy most ingenious sense
Depriv'd thee of! Hold off the earth a while,
Till I have caught her once more in mine arms.
[*Leaps in the grave.*]
Now pile your dust upon the quick and dead,
Till of this flat a mountain you have made
T' o'ertop old Pelion, or the skyish head
Of blue Olympus.

213. **Imperious:** imperial. 216. **flaw:** gust.
219. **maimed rites:** lack of customary ceremony.
221. **Foredo:** fordo, destroy. **it:** its. **estate:** rank.
222. **Couch we:** let us conceal ourselves.
227. **doubtful:** i.e. the subject of an "open verdict."
228. **order:** customary procedure. 229. **should:** would certainly.
230. **for:** instead of. 232. **crants:** garland.
233. **maiden strewments:** flowers scattered on the grave of an unmarried girl.
233–34. **bringing . . . burial:** i.e. burial in consecrated ground, with the bell tolling. 237. **requiem:** dirge.
243. **Sweets:** flowers. 248. **ingenious:** intelligent.
253, 254. **Pelion, Olympus:** mountains in northeastern Greece.

Ham. [*Coming forward.*] What is he whose grief
Bears such an emphasis, whose phrase of sorrow
Conjures the wand'ring stars and makes them stand
Like wonder-wounded hearers? This is I,
Hamlet the Dane! [*Hamlet leaps in after Laertes.*]
Laer. The devil take thy soul!
[*Grappling with him.*]
Ham. Thou pray'st not well.
I prithee take thy fingers from my throat.
For though I am not splenitive [and] rash,
Yet have I in me something dangerous,
Which let thy wisdom fear. Hold off thy hand!
King. Pluck them asunder.
Queen. Hamlet, Hamlet!
All. Gentlemen!
Hor. Good my lord, be quiet.
[*The Attendants part them, and they come out of the grave.*]
Ham. Why, I will fight with him upon this theme
Until my eyelids will no longer wag.
Queen. O my son, what theme?
Ham. I lov'd Ophelia. Forty thousand brothers
Could not with all their quantity of love
Make up my sum. What wilt thou do for her?
King. O, he is mad, Laertes.
Queen. For love of God, forbear him.
Ham. 'Swounds, show me what thou't do.
Woo't weep, woo't fight, woo't fast, woo't tear thyself?
Woo't drink up eisel, eat a crocadile?
I'll do't. Dost [thou] come here to whine?
To outface me with leaping in her grave?
Be buried quick with her, and so will I.
And if thou prate of mountains, let them throw
Millions of acres on us, till our ground,
Singeing his pate against the burning zone,
Make Ossa like a wart! Nay, and thou'lt mouth,
I'll rant as well as thou.
Queen. This is mere madness,
And [thus] a while the fit will work on him;
Anon, as patient as the female dove,
When that her golden couplets are disclosed,
His silence will sit drooping.
Ham. Hear you, sir,
What is the reason that you use me thus?
I lov'd you ever. But it is no matter.
Let Hercules himself do what he may,
The cat will mew, and dog will have his day.
Exit Hamlet.

255. **emphasis, phrase.** Rhetorical terms, here used in disparaging reference to Laertes' inflated language.
256. **Conjures:** puts a spell upon. **wand'ring stars:** planets.
258. **the Dane.** This title normally signifies the King.
261. **splenitive:** impetuous. 274. **thou't:** thou wilt.
275. **Woo't:** wilt thou.
276. **eisel:** vinegar. **crocadile:** crocodile.
280. **if . . . mountains.** Referring to lines 251–54.
282. **burning zone:** sphere of the sun.
283. **Ossa:** another mountain in Greece, near Pelion and Olympus. **mouth:** talk bombast (synonymous with *rant* in the next line).
284. **mere:** utter. 286. **patient:** calm.
287. **golden couplets:** pair of baby birds, covered with yellow down. **disclosed:** hatched.
291–92. **Let . . . day:** i.e. nobody can prevent another from making the scenes he feels he has a right to.

King. I pray thee, good Horatio, wait upon him.
[*Exit*] *Horatio.*
[*To Laertes.*] Strengthen your patience in our last night's speech,
We'll put the matter to the present push.—
Good Gertrude, set some watch over your son.
This grave shall have a living monument.
An hour of quiet [shortly] shall we see,
Till then in patience our proceeding be. *Exeunt.*

[SCENE II]

Enter HAMLET *and* HORATIO.

Ham. So much for this, sir, now shall you see the other—
You do remember all the circumstance?
Hor. Remember it, my lord!
Ham. Sir, in my heart there was a kind of fighting
That would not let me sleep. [Methought] I lay
Worse than the mutines in the [bilboes]. Rashly—
And prais'd be rashness for it—let us know
Our indiscretion sometime serves us well
When our deep plots do pall, and that should learn us
There's a divinity that shapes our ends,
Rough-hew them how we will—
Hor. That is most certain.
Ham. Up from my cabin,
My sea-gown scarf'd about me, in the dark
Grop'd I to find out them, had my desire,
Finger'd their packet, and in fine withdrew
To mine own room again, making so bold,
My fears forgetting manners, to [unseal]
Their grand commission; where I found, Horatio—
Ah, royal knavery!—an exact command,
Larded with many several sorts of reasons,
Importing Denmark's health and England's too,
With, ho, such bugs and goblins in my life,
That, on the supervise, no leisure bated,
No, not to stay the grinding of the axe,
My head should be strook off.
Hor. Is't possible?
Ham. Here's the commission, read it at more leisure.
But wilt thou hear now how I did proceed?
Hor. I beseech you.
Ham. Being thus benetted round with [villainies],
Or I could make a prologue to my brains,
They had begun the play. I sat me down,
Devis'd a new commission, wrote it fair.
I once did hold it, as our statists do,
A baseness to write fair, and labor'd much
How to forget that learning, but, sir, now
It did me yeman's service. Wilt thou know
Th' effect of what I wrote?
Hor. Ay, good my lord.
Ham. An earnest conjuration from the King,
As England was his faithful tributary,
As love between them like the palm might flourish,
As peace should still her wheaten garland wear
And stand a comma 'tween their amities,
And many such-like [as's] of great charge,
That on the view and knowing of these contents,
Without debatement further, more or less,
He should those bearers put to sudden death,
Not shriving time allow'd.
Hor. How was this seal'd?
Ham. Why, even in that was heaven ordinant.
I had my father's signet in my purse,
Which was the model of that Danish seal;
Folded the writ up in the form of th' other,
[Subscrib'd] it, gave't th' impression, plac'd it safely,
The changeling never known. Now the next day
Was our sea-fight, and what to this was sequent
Thou knowest already.
Hor. So Guildenstern and Rosencrantz go to't.
Ham. [Why, man, they did make love to this employment,]
They are not near my conscience. Their defeat
Does by their own insinuation grow.
'Tis dangerous when the baser nature comes
Between the pass and fell incensed points
Of mighty opposites.
Hor. Why, what a king is this!
Ham. Does it not, think thee, stand me now upon—
He that hath kill'd my king and whor'd my mother,
Popp'd in between th' election and my hopes,
Thrown out his angle for my proper life,
And with such coz'nage—is't not perfect conscience
[To quit him with this arm? And is't not to be damn'd,

294–99. See the Textual Notes for the lines that replace these in Q1.
294. in: i.e. by recalling. **295. present push:** immediate test.
297. living: enduring (?) or in the form of a lifelike effigy (?).

V.ii. Location: The castle.
1. see the other: i.e. hear the other news I have to tell you (hinted at in the letter to Horatio, IV.vi.24–25).
6. mutines: mutineers (but the term *mutiny* was in Shakespeare's day used of almost any act of rebellion against authority). **bilboes:** fetters attached to a heavy iron bar. **Rashly:** on impulse.
7. know: recognize, acknowledge.
9. pall: lose force, come to nothing. **learn:** teach.
10. shapes our ends: gives final shape to our designs.
11. Rough-hew them: block them out in initial form.
15. Finger'd: filched, "pinched."
20. Larded: garnished. **21. Importing:** relating to.
22. bugs . . . life: terrifying things in prospect if I were permitted to remain alive. *Bugs* = bugaboos.
23. supervise: perusal. **bated:** deducted (from the stipulated speediness). **24. stay:** wait for.

30. Or: before.
32. fair: i.e. in a beautiful hand (such as a professional scribe would use). **33. statists:** statesmen, public officials.
34. A baseness: i.e. a skill befitting men of low rank.
36. yeman's: yeoman's, i.e. solid, substantial.
37. effect: purport, gist. **42. comma:** connective, link.
43. as's . . . charge: (1) weighty clauses beginning with *as;* (2) asses with heavy loads.
47. shriving time: time for confession and absolution.
48. ordinant: in charge, guiding. **50. model:** small copy.
52. Subscrib'd: signed.
53. changeling: i.e. Hamlet's letter, substituted secretly for the genuine letter, as fairies substituted their children for human children. **never known:** never recognized as a substitution (unlike the fairies' changelings). **56. go to't:** i.e. are going to their death.
58. defeat: ruin, overthrow.
59. insinuation: winding their way into the affair.
60. baser: inferior. **61. pass:** thrust. **fell:** fierce.
63. stand . . . upon: i.e. rest upon me as a duty.
65. election: i.e. as King of Denmark.
66. angle: hook and line. **proper:** very.
67. coz'nage: trickery. **68. quit him:** pay him back.

To let this canker of our nature come
In further evil?

Hor. It must be shortly known to him from England
What is the issue of the business there.

Ham. It will be short; the interim's mine,
And a man's life's no more than to say "one."
But I am very sorry, good Horatio,
That to Laertes I forgot myself,
For by the image of my cause I see
The portraiture of his. I'll [court] his favors.
But sure the bravery of his grief did put me
Into a tow'ring passion.

Hor. Peace, who comes here?]

Enter [young Osric,*] a courtier.*

Osr. Your lordship is right welcome back to Denmark.

Ham. I [humbly] thank you, sir.—Dost know this water-fly?

Hor. No, my good lord.

Ham. Thy state is the more gracious, for 'tis a vice to know him. He hath much land, and fertile; let a beast be lord of beasts, and his crib shall stand at the King's mess. 'Tis a chough, but, as I say, spacious in the possession of dirt.

Osr. Sweet lord, if your lordship were at leisure, I should impart a thing to you from his Majesty.

Ham. I will receive it, sir, with all diligence of spirit. [Put] your bonnet to his right use, 'tis for the head.

Osr. I thank your lordship, it is very hot.

Ham. No, believe me, 'tis very cold, the wind is northerly.

Osr. It is indifferent cold, my lord, indeed.

Ham. But yet methinks it is very [sultry] and hot [for] my complexion.

Osr. Exceedingly, my lord, it is very sultry—as 'twere—I cannot tell how. My lord, his Majesty bade me signify to you that 'a has laid a great wager on your head. Sir, this is the matter—

Ham. I beseech you remember.

[*Hamlet moves him to put on his hat.*]

Osr. Nay, good my lord, for my ease, in good faith. Sir, here is newly come to court Laertes, believe me, an absolute [gentleman], full of most excellent differences, of very soft society, and great showing; indeed, to speak sellingly of him, he is the card or calendar of gentry; for you shall find in him the continent of what part a gentleman would see.

Ham. Sir, his definement suffers no perdition in you, though I know to divide him inventorially would dozy th' arithmetic of memory, and yet but yaw neither in respect of his quick sail; but in the verity of extolment, I take him to be a soul of great article, and his infusion of such dearth and rareness as, to make true diction of him, his semblable is his mirror, and who else would trace him, his umbrage, nothing more.

Osr. Your lordship speaks most infallibly of him.

Ham. The concernancy, sir? Why do we wrap the gentleman in our more rawer breath?

Osr. Sir?

Hor. Is't not possible to understand in another tongue? You will to't, sir, really.

Ham. What imports the nomination of this gentleman?

Osr. Of Laertes?

Hor. His purse is empty already: all 's golden words are spent.

Ham. Of him, sir.

Osr. I know you are not ignorant—

Ham. I would you did, sir, yet, in faith, if you did, it would not much approve me. Well, sir?

Osr. You are not ignorant of what excellence Laertes is—

Ham. I dare not confess that, lest I should compare with him in excellence, but to know a man well were to know himself.

Osr. I mean, sir, for [his] weapon, but in the imputation laid on him by them, in his meed he's unfellow'd.

Ham. What's his weapon?

Osr. Rapier and dagger.

Ham. That's two of his weapons—but well.

Osr. The King, sir, hath wager'd with him six Barbary horses, against the which he has impawn'd, as I take it, six French rapiers and poniards, with their assigns, as girdle, [hangers], and so. Three of the

69. canker: cancerous sore. **69–70. come In:** grow into.
74. a man's . . . more: i.e. to kill a man takes no more time. **say "one."** Perhaps this is equivalent to "deliver one sword thrust"; see line 280 below, where Hamlet says "One" as he makes the first hit.
77. image: likeness.
79. bravery: ostentatious expression.
82. water-fly: i.e. tiny, vainly agitated creature.
84. gracious: virtuous.
85–87. let . . . mess: i.e. if a beast owned as many cattle as Osric, he could feast with the King.
87. chough: jackdaw, a bird that could be taught to speak.
92. bonnet: hat. **97. indifferent:** somewhat.
99. complexion: temperament.
105. for my ease: i.e. I am really more comfortable with my hat off (a polite insistence on maintaining ceremony).
107. absolute: complete, possessing every quality a gentleman should have. **differences:** distinguishing characteristics, personal qualities.
108. soft: agreeable. **great showing:** splendid appearance.
109. sellingly: i.e. like a seller to a prospective buyer; in a fashion to do full justice. Most editors follow Q3 in reading *feelingly* = with exactitude, as he deserves. **card or calendar:** chart or register, i.e. compendious guide. **110. gentry:** gentlemanly behavior.
110–11. the continent . . . part: one who contains every quality.
112. perdition: loss. **114. dozy:** make dizzy.
115. yaw: keep deviating erratically from its course (said of a ship). **neither:** for all that. **in respect of:** compared with.
115–16. in . . . extolment: to praise him truly.
117. article: scope (?) or importance (?). **infusion:** essence, quality. **dearth:** scarceness.
118. make true diction: speak truly. **his semblable:** his only likeness or equal.
119. who . . . him: anyone else who tries to follow him.
119–20. umbrage: shadow. **122. concernancy:** relevance.
123. more rawer breath: i.e. words too crude to describe him properly.
125–26. in another tongue: i.e. when someone else is the speaker.
126. You . . . really: i.e. you can do it if you try.
127. nomination: naming, mention. **135. approve:** commend.
138–39. compare . . . excellence: i.e. seem to claim the same degree of excellence for myself. **139. but.** The sense seems to require *for.*
140. himself: i.e. oneself.
141–42. in . . . them: i.e. in popular estimation.
142. meed: merit. **148. impawn'd:** staked.
150. assigns: appurtenances. **hangers:** straps on which the swords hang from the girdle.

carriages, in faith, are very dear to fancy, very responsive to the hilts, most delicate carriages, and of very liberal conceit.

Ham. What call you the carriages?

Hor. I knew you must be edified by the margent ere you had done.

Osr. The [carriages], sir, are the hangers.

Ham. The phrase would be more germane to the matter if we could carry a cannon by our sides; I would it [might be] hangers till then. But on: six Barb'ry horses against six French swords, their assigns, and three liberal-conceited carriages; that's the French bet against the Danish. Why is this all [impawn'd, as] you call it?

Osr. The King, sir, hath laid, sir, that in a dozen passes between yourself and him, he shall not exceed you three hits; he hath laid on twelve for nine; and it would come to immediate trial, if your lordship would vouchsafe the answer.

Ham. How if I answer no?

Osr. I mean, my lord, the opposition of your person in trial.

Ham. Sir, I will walk here in the hall. If it please his Majesty, it is the breathing time of day with me. Let the foils be brought, the gentleman willing, and the King hold his purpose, I will win for him and I can; if not, I will gain nothing but my shame and the odd hits.

Osr. Shall I deliver you so?

Ham. To this effect, sir—after what flourish your nature will.

Osr. I commend my duty to your lordship.

Ham. Yours. [*Exit Osric.*] ['A] does well to commend it himself, there are no tongues else for 's turn.

Hor. This lapwing runs away with the shell on his head.

Ham. 'A did [comply], sir, with his dug before 'a suck'd it. Thus has he, and many more of the same breed that I know the drossy age dotes on, only got the tune of the time, and out of an habit of encounter, a kind of [yesty] collection, which carries them through and through the most [profound] and [winnow'd] opinions, and do but blow them to their trial, the bubbles are out.

Enter a Lord.

Lord. My lord, his Majesty commended him to you by young Osric, who brings back to him that you attend him in the hall. He sends to know if your pleasure hold to play with Laertes, or that you will take longer time.

Ham. I am constant to my purposes, they follow the King's pleasure. If his fitness speaks, mine is ready; now or whensoever, provided I be so able as now.

Lord. The King and Queen and all are coming down.

Ham. In happy time.

Lord. The Queen desires you to use some gentle entertainment to Laertes before you fall to play.

Ham. She well instructs me. [*Exit Lord.*]

Hor. You will lose, my lord.

Ham. I do not think so; since he went into France I have been in continual practice. I shall win at the odds. Thou wouldst not think how ill all's here about my heart—but it is no matter.

Hor. Nay, good my lord—

Ham. It is but foolery, but it is such a kind of [gain-]giving, as would perhaps trouble a woman.

Hor. If your mind dislike any thing, obey it. I will forestall their repair hither, and say you are not fit.

Ham. Not a whit, we defy augury. There is special providence in the fall of a sparrow. If it be [now], 'tis not to come; if it be not to come, it will be now; if it be not now, yet it [will] come—the readiness is all. Since no man, of aught he leaves, knows what is't to leave betimes, let be.

A table prepar'd, [and flagons of wine on it. Enter] Trumpets, Drums, and Officers with cushions, foils, daggers; King, Queen, Laertes, [Osric,] *and all the State.*

King. Come, Hamlet, come, and take this hand from me.

[*The King puts Laertes' hand into Hamlet's.*]

Ham. Give me your pardon, sir. I have done you wrong,
But pardon't as you are a gentleman.
This presence knows,
And you must needs have heard, how I am punish'd
With a sore distraction. What I have done
That might your nature, honor, and exception
Roughly awake, I here proclaim was madness.
Was't Hamlet wrong'd Laertes? Never Hamlet!
If Hamlet from himself be ta'en away,
And when he's not himself does wrong Laertes,

151. **carriages**: properly, gun-carriages; here used affectedly in place of *hangers*. **fancy**: taste.
151–52. **very responsive to**: matching well.
153. **liberal conceit**: elegant design.
155. **must . . . margent**: would require enlightenment from a marginal note. 165. **laid**: wagered.
166–67. **he . . . hits.** Laertes must win by at least eight to four (if none of the "passes" or bouts are draws), since at seven to five he would be only two up.
167. **he . . . nine.** Not satisfactorily explained despite much discussion. One suggestion is that Laertes has raised the odds against himself by wagering that out of twelve bouts he will win nine.
169. **answer**: encounter (as Hamlet's following quibble forces Osric to explain in his next speech).
174. **breathing . . . me**: my usual hour for exercise.
180. **after what flourish**: with whatever embellishment of language.
182. **commend my duty**: offer my dutiful respects (but Hamlet picks up the phrase in the sense "praise my manner of bowing").
185. **lapwing**: a foolish bird which upon hatching was supposed to run with part of the eggshell still over its head. (Osric has put his hat on at last.)
187. **comply . . . dug**: bow politely to his mother's nipple.
189. **drossy**: i.e. worthless.
190. **tune . . . time**: i.e. fashionable ways of talk. **habit of encounter**: mode of social intercourse.
191. **yesty**: yeasty, frothy. **collection**: i.e. anthology of fine phrases.
192. **winnow'd**: sifted, choice.

193. **opinions**: judgments. **blow . . . trial**: test them by blowing on them, i.e. make even the least demanding trial of them.
194. **out**: blown away (?) or at an end, done for (?).
201. **If . . . ready**: i.e. if this is a good moment for him, it is for me also. 206–7. **gentle entertainment**: courteous greeting.
216. **gain-giving**: misgiving.
219–20. **special . . . sparrow.** See Matthew 10:29.
223. **of aught**: i.e. whatever.
223–24. **knows . . . betimes**: knows what is the best time to leave it.
224 s.d. **State**: nobles. 228. **presence**: assembled court.
229. **punish'd**: afflicted. 231. **exception**: objection.

Then Hamlet does it not, Hamlet denies it.
Who does it then? His madness. If't be so,
Hamlet is of the faction that is wronged,
His madness is poor Hamlet's enemy.
[Sir, in this audience,]
Let my disclaiming from a purpos'd evil
Free me so far in your most generous thoughts,
That I have shot my arrow o'er the house
And hurt my brother.

Laer. I am satisfied in nature,
Whose motive in this case should stir me most
To my revenge, but in my terms of honor
I stand aloof, and will no reconcilement
Till by some elder masters of known honor
I have a voice and president of peace
To [keep] my name ungor'd. But [till] that time
I do receive your offer'd love like love,
And will not wrong it.

Ham. I embrace it freely,
And will this brothers' wager frankly play.
Give us the foils. [Come on.]

Laer. Come, one for me.

Ham. I'll be your foil, Laertes; in mine ignorance
Your skill shall like a star i' th' darkest night
Stick fiery off indeed.

Laer. You mock me, sir.

Ham. No, by this hand.

King. Give them the foils, young Osric. Cousin Hamlet,
You know the wager?

Ham. Very well, my lord.
Your Grace has laid the odds a' th' weaker side.

King. I do not fear it, I have seen you both;
But since he is [better'd], we have therefore odds.

Laer. This is too heavy; let me see another.

Ham. This likes me well. These foils have all a length?
[*Prepare to play*.]

Osr. Ay, my good lord.

King. Set me the stoups of wine upon that table.
If Hamlet give the first or second hit,
Or quit in answer of the third exchange,
Let all the battlements their ord'nance fire.
The King shall drink to Hamlet's better breath,
And in the cup an [union] shall he throw,
Richer than that which four successive kings
In Denmark's crown have worn. Give me the cups,
And let the kettle to the trumpet speak,

241. **my . . . evil:** my declaration that I intended no harm.
242. **Free:** absolve.
244. **in nature:** so far as my personal feelings are concerned.
246. **in . . . honor:** i.e. as a man governed by an established code of honor.
249–50. **have . . . ungor'd:** can secure an opinion backed by precedent that I can make peace with you without injury to my reputation.
253. **brothers':** i.e. amicable, as if between brothers. **frankly:** freely, without constraint.
255. **foil:** thin sheet of metal placed behind a jewel to set it off.
257. **Stick . . . off:** blaze out in contrast.
261. **laid the odds:** i.e. wagered a higher stake (horses to rapiers).
263. **is better'd:** has perfected his skill. **odds:** i.e. the arrangement that Laertes must take more bouts than Hamlet to win.
265. **likes:** pleases. **a length:** the same length.
267. **stoups:** tankards.
269. **quit . . . exchange:** pays back wins by Laertes in the first and second bouts by taking the third.
272. **union:** an especially fine pearl. 275. **kettle:** kettle-drum.

The trumpet to the cannoneer without,
The cannons to the heavens, the heaven to earth,
"Now the King drinks to Hamlet." Come begin;
Trumpets the while.
And you, the judges, bear a wary eye.

Ham. Come on, sir.

Laer. Come, my lord.
[*They play and Hamlet scores a hit.*]

Ham. One.

Laer. No.

Ham. Judgment.

Osr. A hit, a very palpable hit.

Laer. Well, again.

King. Stay, give me drink. Hamlet, this pearl is thine,
Here's to thy health! Give him the cup.
Drum, trumpets [sound] flourish. A piece goes off [within].

Ham. I'll play this bout first, set it by a while.
Come. [*They play again.*] Another hit; what say you?

Laer. [A touch, a touch,] I do confess't.

King. Our son shall win.

Queen. He's fat, and scant of breath.
Here, Hamlet, take my napkin, rub thy brows.
The Queen carouses to thy fortune, Hamlet.

Ham. Good madam!

King. Gertrude, do not drink.

Queen. I will, my lord, I pray you pardon me.

King. [*Aside.*] It is the pois'ned cup, it is too late.

Ham. I dare not drink yet, madam; by and by.

Queen. Come, let me wipe thy face.

Laer. My lord, I'll hit him now.

King. I do not think't.

Laer. [*Aside.*] And yet it is almost against my conscience.

Ham. Come, for the third, Laertes, you do but dally.
I pray you pass with your best violence;
I am sure you make a wanton of me.

Laer. Say you so? Come on. [*They play.*]

Osr. Nothing, neither way.

Laer. Have at you now!
[*Laertes wounds Hamlet; then, in scuffling, they change rapiers.*]

King. Part them, they are incens'd.

Ham. Nay, come again.
[*Hamlet wounds Laertes. The Queen falls.*]

Osr. Look to the Queen there ho!

Hor. They bleed on both sides. How is it, my lord?

Osr. How is't, Laertes?

Laer. Why, as a woodcock to mine own springe, Osric:
I am justly kill'd with mine own treachery.

Ham. How does the Queen?

King. She sounds to see them bleed.

Queen. No, no, the drink, the drink—O my dear Hamlet—
The drink, the drink! I am pois'ned. [*Dies.*]

287. **fat:** sweaty. 289. **carouses:** drinks a toast.
299. **make . . . me:** i.e. are holding back in order to let me win, as one does with a spoiled child (*wanton*).
306. **springe:** snare. 308. **sounds:** swoons.

Ham. O villainy! Ho, let the door be lock'd!
Treachery! Seek it out.
Laer. It is here, Hamlet. [Hamlet,] thou art slain.
No med'cine in the world can do thee good;
In thee there is not half an hour's life.
The treacherous instrument is in [thy] hand,
Unbated and envenom'd. The foul practice
Hath turn'd itself on me. Lo here I lie,
Never to rise again. Thy mother's pois'ned.
I can no more—the King, the King's to blame.
Ham. The point envenom'd too!
Then, venom, to thy work. [*Hurts the King.*]
All. Treason! treason!
King. O, yet defend me, friends, I am but hurt.
Ham. Here, thou incestious, [murd'rous], damned Dane,
Drink [off] this potion! Is [thy union] here?
Follow my mother! [*King dies.*]
Laer. He is justly served,
It is a poison temper'd by himself.
Exchange forgiveness with me, noble Hamlet.
Mine and my father's death come not upon thee,
Nor thine on me! [*Dies.*]
Ham. Heaven make thee free of it! I follow thee.
I am dead, Horatio. Wretched queen, adieu!
You that look pale, and tremble at this chance,
That are but mutes or audience to this act,
Had I but time—as this fell sergeant, Death,
Is strict in his arrest—O, I could tell you—
But let it be. Horatio, I am dead,
Thou livest. Report me and my cause aright
To the unsatisfied.
Hor. Never believe it;
I am more an antique Roman than a Dane.
Here's yet some liquor left.
Ham. As th' art a man,
Give me the cup. Let go! By heaven, I'll ha't!
O God, Horatio, what a wounded name,
Things standing thus unknown, shall I leave behind me!
If thou didst ever hold me in thy heart,
Absent thee from felicity a while,
And in this harsh world draw thy breath in pain
To tell my story. *A march afar off* [*and a shot within*].
What warlike noise is this?
[*Osric goes to the door and returns.*]
Osr. Young Fortinbras, with conquest come from Poland,
To th' embassadors of England gives
This warlike volley.
Ham. O, I die, Horatio,
The potent poison quite o'er-crows my spirit.
I cannot live to hear the news from England,
But I do prophesy th' election lights
On Fortinbras, he has my dying voice.
So tell him, with th' occurrents more and less
Which have solicited—the rest is silence. [*Dies.*]
Hor. Now cracks a noble heart. Good night, sweet prince,
And flights of angels sing thee to thy rest!
[*March within.*]
Why does the drum come hither?

Enter Fortinbras *with the* [English] Embassadors, [*with Drum, Colors, and Attendants*].

Fort. Where is this sight?
Hor. What is it you would see?
If aught of woe or wonder, cease your search.
Fort. This quarry cries on havoc. O proud death,
What feast is toward in thine eternal cell,
That thou so many princes at a shot
So bloodily hast strook?
[*1.*] *Emb.* The sight is dismal,
And our affairs from England come too late.
The ears are senseless that should give us hearing,
To tell him his commandment is fulfill'd,
That Rosencrantz and Guildenstern are dead.
Where should we have our thanks?
Hor. Not from his mouth,
Had it th' ability of life to thank you.
He never gave commandement for their death.
But since so jump upon this bloody question,
You from the Polack wars, and you from England,
Are here arrived, give order that these bodies
High on a stage be placed to the view,
And let me speak to [th'] yet unknowing world
How these things came about. So shall you hear
Of carnal, bloody, and unnatural acts,
Of accidental judgments, casual slaughters,
Of deaths put on by cunning and [forc'd] cause,
And in this upshot, purposes mistook
Fall'n on th' inventors' heads: all this can I
Truly deliver.
Fort. Let us haste to hear it,
And call the noblest to the audience.
For me, with sorrow I embrace my fortune.
I have some rights, of memory in this kingdom,
Which now to claim my vantage doth invite me.
Hor. Of that I shall have also cause to speak,
And from his mouth whose voice will draw [on] more.
But let this same be presently perform'd
Even while men's minds are wild, lest more mischance
On plots and errors happen.
Fort. Let four captains
Bear Hamlet like a soldier to the stage,
For he was likely, had he been put on,

317. Unbated: not blunted. **foul practice:** vile plot.
322 s.d. Hurts: wounds. **328. temper'd:** mixed.
332. make thee free: absolve you.
335. mutes or audience: silent spectators.
336. fell: cruel. **sergeant:** sheriff's officer.
341. antique Roman: i.e. one who will commit suicide on such an occasion.
353. o'er-crows: triumphs over (a term derived from cockfighting). **spirit:** vital energy. **356. voice:** vote.

357. occurrents: occurrences. **358. solicited:** instigated.
364. This . . . havoc: this heap of corpses proclaims a massacre.
365. toward: in preparation. **372. his:** i.e. the King's.
375. jump: precisely, pat. **question:** matter.
378. stage: platform.
382. judgments: retributions. **casual:** happening by chance.
383. put on: instigated. **389. of memory:** unforgotten.
390. my vantage: i.e. my opportune presence at a moment when the throne is empty.
392. his . . . more: the mouth of one (Hamlet) whose vote will induce others to support your claim. **393. presently:** at once.
394. wild: distraught.
397. put on: put to the test (by becoming king).

To have prov'd most royal; and for his passage,
The soldiers' music and the rite of war
Speak loudly for him.
Take up the bodies. Such a sight as this

398. passage: death.

Becomes the field, but here shows much amiss.
Go bid the soldiers shoot.
Exeunt [marching; after the which a peal of ordinance are shot off].

402. Becomes . . . amiss: befits the battlefield, but appears very much out of place here.

NOTE ON THE TEXT

Hamlet offers a textual situation too complicated to permit here more than a sketch of the principal problems involved.

There are three early and significant editions of *Hamlet*: First Quarto (Q1), 1603; Second Quarto (Q2), 1604/5; First Folio (F1), 1623. Three more quartos, stemming from Q2, appeared before the Restoration: Q3 (1611); Q4 (undated); Q5 (1637). The first of several Players' Quartos (Betterton's acting version) was printed in 1676.

Q1, approximately half the length of Q2, is one of the so-called "bad" quartos, i.e., a memorially reconstructed version, in this case, one based most probably on a much shortened text prepared by Shakespeare's company for provincial touring, the principal reporter, it is generally agreed, being the actor who doubled in the roles of Marcellus, Lucianus (the villain in the play-within-the-play who represents Hamlet's uncle, Claudius), and perhaps, Voltemand. Thus, although in one sense a substantive text, Q1 is without any real textual authority, but its stage directions and very occasionally its readings are valuable in supplementing, corroborating, or correcting Q2 and F1. It also contains one scene (see Textual Notes, IV.vi) not found in Q2–4 or F1. Recently, a few critics, whose views have received almost no acceptance, have resurrected the long outmoded theory that Q1 represents Shakespeare's first draft of *Hamlet*.

Since the pioneer work of John Dover Wilson in 1934, the position of Q2 as the basic copy-text for a critical edition has, until very recently (see below), gone unchallenged. Wilson was able to show with near certainty that Q2 was printed from some form of Shakespeare's autograph, most probably the "foul papers," containing among other evidence of authorial origin occasional "first" shots (e.g., II.ii.73, 541; III.ii.166, 168, 223). One qualification of this view, however, is now generally admitted: Act I, as Greg had earlier suggested, was set in good part not from the manuscript but from a copy of Q1 corrected and enlarged by collation with the manuscript. This qualification has important bearings on the relative authority of the Q2 text in Act I where its readings agree with Q1 against those of F1. Another influential theory advanced by Wilson—that Q2 was badly printed because the work was set up by a young and inexperienced compositor—must now be abandoned. Fredson Bowers and J. R. Brown have proved that two compositors set Q2 and that the printing errors and supposed omissions, etc. are pretty evenly distributed between them. Such a view suggests that at least some words and passages found only in F1 were probably not accidentally omitted by Wilson's hypothetical inexperienced compositor but were not present in Shakespeare's manuscript when it served as copy for Q2. This suggestion, if accepted, raises one of several questions about the provenience of the F1 text.

The exact status of the F1 text has become increasingly uncertain in recent years. The theory that F1 was printed from a copy of Q2 which had been brought into some measure of conformity (by verbal substitutions, deletion of some 230 lines, and addition of some 83 lines) with a playhouse manuscript has been generally discounted. Textual critics now agree that F1 was set up, with occasional reference to Q2–4, from some kind of manuscript at one or more removes from Shakespeare's "foul papers," but whether the provenience of such a manuscript was prompt-copy, at one point theatre related, or scribal or authorial "fair copy" remains debatable. Such a theory allows the F1 text an independent authority apart from Q2 and strengthens the authority of readings in which F1 and Q2 agree. F1 also contains a number of substantive readings which reflect early stage usage, as is shown by the quite frequent agreement, against Q2, between F1 and Q1 (e.g., 17 in II.ii). This would appear to suggest a date for the F1 text of sometime shortly before the publication of Q1 in 1603. On the other hand, Q1 also shares a substantial number of readings with Q2, which differ in their turn from F1 readings (e.g., 43 in II.ii). This divergence in Q1 readings suggests, I believe, that a distinction must be drawn between the manuscript underlying the reported Q1 text (as suggested above, probably an official abridgement by Shakespeare's company) and the manuscript that served as printer's copy for the F1 text, which should in all likelihood, though not necessarily, be dated sometime after 1602–3. In other words the manuscript from which F1 was set must have undergone at least one more transcription, thus differing in many readings from the manuscript from which the abridgement underlying Q1's reported text had been derived, in order to account for F1's variant readings in those places where Q1 had agreed with Q2 against F1. Whether such F1 readings (as well as some of the additions in F1) represent possible Shakespearean revision (the major additions, unless, as some have argued, they were accidentally omitted when Q2 was set from Shakespeare's "foul papers," probably do) or actors' or bookholder's changes must in the present state of our knowledge remain uncertain, though Jenkins argues that the F1 text shows definite signs of contamination from actors' adlibbing. The present text has been influenced by Jenkins's suggestion.

It was noted above that, since 1934, Q2 has been accepted (as in the present edition) as the basic copy-text for *Hamlet*. In the last few years, however, there has been a reversion by Taylor/Wells (*Complete Works*, Oxford, 1986) and Hibbard (Oxford, 1987) to F1 as the basic copy-text (for substantive readings) on the unprovable assumption that Shakespeare himself was responsible for all or most of the additions, omissions (see below), and multiple word substitutions which distinguish F1 from Q2, surely a questionable decision considering its extremely uncertain provenience. This reversion to F1 is, of course, the outgrowth of two further assumptions: (a) the recently fashionable view that Shakespeare was an inveterate reviser (see Werstine for a critical analysis of privileging either Q2 or F1); and (b) the dangerous premise that an editor should prefer an acting text (despite the obvious fact that such a text would inevitably change over the years, even from performance to performance) instead of what is described as a "literary" text such as Q2.

A reader who wishes to reconstruct the main outlines of the F1 text as it differs from that of Q2 may do so (a) by noting those passages found only in F1, which in the present text are enclosed in square brackets, and (b) by marking the following F1 omissions (single words and phrases are generally not included; agreement with Q1 omissions is indicated by (*Q1*) following each F1 omission): I.i.108–25 (*Q1*); I.ii.58–60 ("wrung . . . consent."), partly in Q1; I.iv.17–38 (". . . scandal.") (*Q1*), 75–8 (". . . beneath.") (*Q1*); II.ii.17 (*Q1*), 444–5 ("as wholesome . . . fine."), partly in Q1, 465 ("So proceed you."), equivalent in Q1; III.ii.171–2 (*Q1*), 218–9 (*Q1*); III.iv.71–6 ("Sense . . . difference.") (*Q1*), 78–81 (". . . mope.") (*Q1*), 161–5 (". . . on.") (*Q1*), 167–70 ("the next more . . . potency.") (*Q1*), 180 ("One . . . lady.") (*Q1*), 202–10) (*Q1*); IV.i.4 (*Q1*), 41–4 (". . . air.") (*Q1*); IV.iii.26–8 ("*King*. Alas . . . worm."), equivalent in Q1; IV.iv.9–66 (*Q1*, except l. 14); IV.v.76 ("and now behold!") (*Q1*), 97 ("Attend!") (*Q1*); IV.vii.59 ("Ay, my lord.") (*Q1*), 68–81 ("My . . . graveness.") (*Q1*, except for a variant reading of l. 68), 100–02 ("The scrimers . . . them.") (*Q1*), 114–23 (*Q1*); V.i.264 ("Gentlemen!") (*Q1*); V.ii.106 ("Sir . . .")–43, except F1 retains a compacted version of ll. 136–7 and part of l. 141 (all omitted, *Q1*), 155–6 (*Q1*).

Since the textual situation in *Hamlet* is so intricate, the Textual Notes offer as complete a picture of the interrelations between Q2, F1, and Q1 as considerations of space allow. All significant variants between Q2–4 and F1, as well as additions and omissions, are listed, together with a record of Q1's concurrence or disagreement with Q2 and F1 in these and some other readings. (*Q1*) immediately after the square bracket or following other sigla indicates that Q1 here agrees with Q2 or with the other editions listed. The absence of citation of Q1 in any entry indicates that the reading of the lemma occurs in a passage which in Q1 is either omitted or so differently worded that it offers no recognizable equivalent. To help the reader in appreciating the debased nature of the Q1 text, especially where it differs most markedly from Q2–4 and F1, some longer passages (including the Q1 version of "To be, or not to be," III.i.55–89) are given in the Textual Notes (see I.iii.135–6, II.ii.546–8, III.i opening, III.ii.45, 155–73, III.iii.36–72, III.iv.137, IV.v opening and line 96, IV.vi, IV.vii.140, V.i.294–9, V.ii.165–9).

Der bestrafte Brudermord, oder Prinz Hamlet aus Dännemark (Fratricide Punished), referred to occasionally in the Textual Notes, is a German adaptation of *Hamlet* played by visiting English comedians in the early years of the seventeenth century. It shows several interesting points of contact with Q1, but it is ultimately derived from Shakespeare's text as it appears in Q2, or possibly through performance of the officially shortened text which underlies Q1's reported text.

For further information, see: J. D. Wilson, *The Manuscript of Shakespeare's "Hamlet,"* 2 vols. (Cambridge, 1934), and ed., New Shakespeare *Hamlet* (Cambridge, 1934, rev. ed., 1948); T. M. Parrott and Hardin Craig, eds., *The Tragedy of Hamlet* (Madison, Wisc., 1938); G. I. Duthie, *The "Bad" Quarto of "Hamlet," A Critical Study* (Cambridge, 1941); Alice Walker, *Textual Problems of the First Folio* (Cambridge, 1953); W. W. Greg, *The Shakespeare First Folio* (Oxford, 1955); J. R. Brown, "The Compositors of *Hamlet* Q2 and *The Merchant of Venice,*" *SB,* VII (1955), 17–40; F. T. Bowers, "The Printing of *Hamlet*, Q2," *SB* VII (1955) 41–50; Harold Jenkins, "The Relation between the Second Quarto and the Folio Text of *Hamlet,*" *SB,* VII (1955), 69–83, "Playhouse Interpolations in the Folio Text of *Hamlet,*" *SB,* XIII (1960), 31–47, and ed., New Arden *Hamlet* (London, 1982); J. M. Nosworthy, *Shakespeare's Occasional Plays* (London, 1965); J. K. Walton, *The Quarto Copy for the First Folio of Shakespeare* (Dublin, 1971); Gary Taylor, "The Folio Copy for *Hamlet, King Lear,* and *Othello,*" *SQ,* XXXIV (1983), 44–61; Philip Edwards, ed., New Cambridge *Hamlet, Prince of Denmark* (Cambridge, 1985); G. R. Hibbard, ed., New Oxford *Hamlet* (Oxford, 1987); Stanley Wells, Gary Taylor, et al., *William Shakespeare: A Textual Companion* (Oxford, 1987); Paul Werstine, "The Textual Mystery of *Hamlet,*" *SQ,* XXXIX (1988), 1–26; Thomas Clayton, *ed., The "Hamlet" First Published (Q1, 1603): Origins, Form, Intertextualities* (Newark, N.J., 1992).

TEXTUAL NOTES

Title: The . . . Denmark] *F1;* The Tragicall Historie of Hamlet, Prince of Denmarke. By William Shakespeare. Newly imprinted and enlarged to almost as much againe as it was, according to the true and perfect Coppie. *Q2 (title-page);* The Tragicall Historie of Hamlet Prince of Denmarke By William Shake-speare. As it hath beene diuerse times acted by his Highnesse seruants in the Cittie of London: as also in the two Vniuersities of Cambridge and Oxford, and else-where *Q1 (title-page)*
Dramatis personae: *subs. as first given in Q (1676)*
Act-scene division: *none in Q1–4; F1 marks I.i–iii, Act II, II.ii; other act-scene divisions from Q (1676), Rowe, and later editors (see first note to each scene); present act-scene division as a whole first established by Capell*

I.i

I.i] *F1*
Location: *Alexander (after Rowe)*
o.s.d. **meeting]** *ed.; Q1 s.d. reads:* Enter two Centinels. (*with s.pp. distinguishing Barnardo and Francisco only as* 1. *and* 2.)
4 **Barnardo.]** Barnardo? *F1*
7 **twelf]** twelue *Q3–4, F1*
14 **ho! Who is]** who's *F1;* who is *Q1*
16 **soldier]** *F1 (Q1);* souldiers *Q2–4*
17 **hath my]** *(Q1);* ha's my *F1*
21 s.p. **Hor.]** Mar. *F1 (Q1)*
33 **have two nights]** *(Q1);* two Nights haue *F1*
40 **off]** *Q3–4 (Q1);* of *Q2, F1*
41 **figure]** figure, *F1*
43 **'a]** it *F1 (Q1)*
44 **harrows]** *F1;* horrowes *Q2–4;* horrors *Q1*
45 **Speak to]** Question *F1 (Q1)*
51 s.d. **Exit Ghost.]** *placed as in F1; after* offended, *l. 50, Q2–4*
55 **you on't]** *F1 (Q1);* you-ont *Q2;* you of it *Q3–4*
61 **he]** *(Q1); om. F1*
61 **the]** *(Q1);* th' *F1*
63 **smote]** *Q3–4;* smot *Q2, F1 (Q1)*
63 **sledded]** *F1;* sleaded *Q2–4 (Q1)*
63 **Polacks]** *Malone;* pollax *Q2–4, F1 (Q1)*
65 **jump]** *(Q1);* iust *F1*
68 **mine]** my *F1 (Q1)*
73 **why]** *F1 (Q1);* with *Q2–4*
73 **cast]** *F1;* cost *Q2–4 (Q1)*
79 **I,]** *F1 (Q1);* I. *Q2–4*
87 **heraldy]** Heraldrie *F1, Q3–4 (Q1)*
88 **those]** *F1 (Q1);* these *Q2–4*
89 **of]** *(Q1);* on *F1*
91 **return'd]** *F1;* returne *Q2–4*
93 **comart]** Cou'nant *F1*
94 **design'd]** *F2;* desseigne *Q2–4, F1*
98 **lawless]** *(Q1);* Landlesse *F1*
101 **As]** And *F1*
103 **compulsatory]** Compulsatiue *F1*
108–25 **I . . . countrymen.]** *om. F1 (Q1)*
108 **e'en so]** *Collier;* enso *Q2;* euen so *Q3–4*
112 **mote]** *Q4;* moth *Q2–3*
115 **tenantless]** *Q3–4;* tennatlesse *Q2*
116 **streets.]** *Theobald (subs.);* streets *Q2–4*
121 **fear'd]** *Collier conj.;* feare *Q2;* fearce *Q3;* fierce *Q4*
125 s.d. **Ghost]** Ghost againe *F1*
126 **again!]** *F1 (subs.);* againe *Q2–4;* againe, *Q1*
126 s.d. **It . . . arms.]** *om. F1 (Q1)*
138 **your]** you *F1 (Q1)*
139 s.d. **The cock crows.]** *placed as in Cambridge; after l. 138, Q2–4; om. F1 (Q1)*
140 **it]** at ir *F1*
142 s.d. **Exit Ghost.]** *F1 (Q1)*
150 **morn]** day *F1;* morning *Q1*
151 **shrill-sounding]** *hyphen, F1;* shrill crowing *Q1*
158 **say]** *(Q1);* sayes *F1*
160 **This]** The *F1 (Q1)*
161 **dare stir]** can walke *F1;* dare walke *Q1*
163 **takes]** *(Q1);* talkes *F1*
164 **that]** *(Q1);* the *F1*
167 **eastward hill.]** *Q3–4 (subs.);* Eastward hill *Q2;* Easterne Hill, *F1;* mountaine top, *Q1*
168 **advice]** *F1;* aduise *Q2–4 (Q1)*
175 **convenient]** conueniently *F1 (Q1)*

I.ii

I.ii] *F1*
Location: *Capell (subs., after Rowe)*
o.s.d. **Flourish. . . . aliis]** Enter Claudius King of Denmarke, Gertrude the Queene, Hamlet, Polonius, Laertes, and his Sister Ophelia, Lords Attendant. *F1;* Enter King, Queene, Hamlet, Leartes, Corambis, and the two Ambassadors, with Attendants. *Q1* (Leartes *for* Laertes *and* Corambis *for* Polonius *throughout; cf.* Corambus *in* Der bestrafte Brudermord)
o.s.d. **Gertrude]** *F1 (throughout);* Gertrad

Q2–4 (*or* Gertrard *throughout, except* Gertrud *at II.ii.54 in Q3–4*); Gertred *Q1* (*or* Gerterd *throughout*)
o.s.d. **including . . . Cornelius]** *from Q1* (*see above*); *F1 brings in the Ambassadors at l. 25*
8 **sometime]** sometimes *F1*
9 **to]** of *F1*
11 **an . . . a]** one . . . one *F1*
16 **all,]** *Pope;* all *Q2–4, F1*
17 **follows]** follows, *F1*
21 **Co-leagued]** *Capell;* Coleagued *Q2;* Colegued *Q3;* Collegued *Q4;* Colleagued *F1*
21 **this]** the *F1*
22 **pester]** *F1, Q3–4;* pestur *Q2*
24 **bands]** Bonds *F1*
29 **bedred]** *cf.* Love's Labor's Lost, *I.i.138, and* Lucrece, *l. 975*); bedrid *F1;* bed-rid *Q1*
34 **Cornelius]** Cornelia *Q1*
34 **Voltemand]** *F1;* Valtemand *Q2–4;* Voltemar *Q1* (*throughout*)
35 **bearers]** (*Q1*); bearing *F1*
38 **delated]** dilated *F1;* related *Q1*
38 s.d. **Giving a paper.]** *Collier MS* (*subs., after Capell*)
40 s.p. **Cor., Vol.]** Volt. *F1*
41 s.d. **Exeunt . . . Cornelius.]** *F1* (Exit . . .)
50 **My dread]** Dread my *F1;* My gratious *Q1*
55 **toward]** towards *F1;* for *Q1*
58 **H'ath]** *ed.;* Hath *Q2;* He hath *Q3–4, F1*(*Q1*)
58–60 **wrung . . . consent.]** *om. F1;* wrung from me a forced graunt, *Q1*
58 **wrung]** *Q3–4* (*Q1*); wroung *Q2*
65 s.d. **Aside.]** *Theobald*
67 **so]** *F1;* so much *Q2–4*
67 **in the]** i' th' *F1*
67 **sun]** *F1;* sonne *Q2–4*
68 **nighted]** nightly *F1*
72 **common,]** *F1;* common *Q2–4*
77 **good mother]** *F1;* coold mother *Q2;* could smother *Q3–4*
82 **shapes]** *Q3–4;* chapes *Q2;* shewes *F1*
83 **denote]** *F1;* deuote *Q2–3;* deuoute *Q4*
85 **passes]** passeth *F1*
96 **or]** a *F1*
97 **unschool'd:]** *F1;* vnschoold *Q2;* vnschoold, *Q3–4*
105 **corse]** *Capell;* course *Q2–4;* Coarse *F1*
112 **toward]** towards *F1*
112 **you.]** *F1;* you *Q2–4*
114 **retrograde]** *F1;* retrogard *Q2–3;* retrograd *Q4*
119 **pray thee]** prythee *F1*
126 **tell,]** *F1;* tell. *Q2–4;* tell *Q1*
127 **rouse]** *Malone;* rowse *Q2–4* (*Q1*); Rouce *F1*
127 **heaven]** Heauens *F1*
128 s.d. **Flourish]** *om. F1* (*Q1*)
128 s.d. **Exeunt . . . Hamlet.]** (*Q1*); Exeunt Manet Hamlet. *F1*
129 **sallied]** *cf.* sallies *at II.i.39 and* vnsallied *in* Love's Labor's Lost, *V.ii.352;* solid *F1;* grieu'd and sallied *Q1*
132 **self-slaughter]** *F1;* seale slaughter *Q2–4*
132 **God, God,]** God, O God! *F1*
133 **weary]** *F1;* wary *Q2–4*
134 **Seem]** Seemes *F1*
135 **ah fie]** Oh fie, fie *F1*
137 **merely. That]** *F1;* meerely that *Q2–4*
137 **to this]** *F1;* thus *Q2–4*
140 **satyr]** *F4;* satire *Q2–3;* Satyre *F1, Q4*
141 **beteem]** beteene *F1*
143 **Why,]** *Pope;* why *Q2–4, F1*
143 **should]** would *F1* (*Q1*)
147 **month, or]** *F1;* month or *Q2;* month. Or *Q3–4*
149 **even she]** *F1*
150 **God]** (*Q1*); Heauen *F1*
151 **my]** mine *F1* (*Q1*)
155 **in]** (*Q1*); of *F1*
156 **married—O]** *ed.;* married, ô *Q2;* married Oh! *Q3–4;* married. O *F1;* married, well *Q1*
156 **speed:]** *ed.;* speed; *Q2–4;* speed, *F1* (*Q1*)
157 **incestious]** Incestuous *F1* (*Q1*)
158 **good,]** good. *F1;* good: *Q1*
159 s.d. **Barnardo]** *Wilson;* Bernardo *Q2–4;* Barnard *F1; Q1 s.d. om. Barnardo*
167 s.d. **To Barnardo.]** *Cambridge*
170 **hear]** haue *F1*
171 **my]** mine *F1*
174 **Elsinore]** *Malone;* Elsonoure *Q2–4;* Elsenour *F1;* Elsenoure *Q1*
175 **to drink deep]** *F1* (*Q1*); for to drinke *Q2–4*
177 **prithee]** pray thee *F1;* O I pre thee *Q1*
177 **studient]** (*Q1*); Student *F1, Q3–4*
178 **see]** *F1* (*Q1*)
183 **Or . . . had]** Ere I had euer *F1;* Ere euer I had *Q1*
185 **Where]** (*Q1*); Oh where *F1*
186 **'a]** he *F1* (*Q1*) (*the usual F1 form*)
187 **'A]** He *F1* (*Q1*)
191 **lord,]** *F1* (*Q1*); Lord *Q2–4*
195 **God's]** (*Q1*); Heauens *F1*
198 **waste]** *F2;* wast *Q2–3, F1;* vast *Q4* (*Q1*)
200 **Armed at point]** Arm'd at all points *F1;* Armed to poynt *Q1*
200 **point exactly, cap-a-pe]** *F1* (points); poynt, exactly Capapea *Q2* (*Q1*); poynt, exactly Cap apea *Q3–4*
203 **fear-surprised]** *hyphen, F1;* feare opressed *Q1*
204 **distill'd]** bestil'd *F1;* distilled *Q1*
209 **Where, as]** *Q5;* Whereas *Q2–4, F1;* Where as *Q1*
213 **watch]** watcht *F1;* watched *Q1*
224 **indeed]** *F1* (*Q1*)
225, 227, 228 s.pp. **Mar., Bar.]** *Capell* (*after F1* Both.); All. *Q2–4* (*Q1*)
231 **What, look'd]** *F1;* What look't *Q2–4;* How look't *Q1* (*with a comma after* he)
236 **very like]** *F1* (*Q1*)
237 **hundreth]** hundred *F1* (*Q1*)
238 s.p. **Mar., Bar.]** *Capell; F1 s.p.* All.; *Q1 s.p.* Mar.
239 **grisl'd]** *Warburton;* grissl'd *Q2–3;* grisseld *Q4;* grisly *F1;* grisleld *Q1*
241 **I will]** (*Q1*); Ile *F1*
241 **to-night]** *F1, Q3–4* (*Q1*); to nigh *Q2*
242 **warr'nt]** *Kittredge* (*after Wilson*); warn't *Q2–4;* warrant you *F1;* warrant *Q1*
247 **tenable]** treble *F1;* tenible *Q1*
248 **whatsomever]** *Wilson;* what someuer *Q2;* what what soeuer *Q3;* whatsoeuer *F1, Q4* (*Q1*)
250 **fare]** *F1, Q3–4* (*Q1*); farre *Q2*
250 **you]** (*Q1*); ye *F1*
251 **aleven]** *ed.;* a leauen *Q2–3;* eleuen *F1, Q4* (*Q1*)
251 **twelf]** twelue *Q3–4, F1* (*Q1*)
253 **Your loves]** Your loue *F1;* O your loues, your loues *Q1*
253 s.d. **all but Hamlet]** *Cambridge* (*after Capell*); *s.d. after l. 252, Q2–4, F1* (*Q1*); *placed as in Capell*
256 **Foul]** *F1, Q3–4* (*Q1*); fonde *Q2*

I.iii

I.iii] *F1*
Location: *ed.* (*after Pope*)
o.s.d. **Ophelia]** Ofelia *Q1* (*throughout*)
o.s.d. **his sister]** *om. F1* (*Q1*)
1 **inbark'd]** (*Q1*); imbark't *F1, Q4*
3 **convey]** *ed.;* conuay, *Q2–4;* Conuoy *F1*
3 **is]** *F1;* in *Q2–4*
5 **favor]** fauours *F1*
8 **Forward]** Froward *F1*
9 **perfume and]** *om. F1* (*Q1*)
9 **minute—]** *F2* (*subs.*); minute *Q2–4;* minute? *F1*
10 **so?]** *Rowe;* so. *Q2–4, F1*
12 **bulk]** *F1;* bulkes *Q2–4*
12 **this]** his *F1*
16 **will]** feare *F1*
18 **For . . . birth:]** *F1*
21 **safety]** sanctity *F1*
21 **this whole]** the weole *F1;* the whole *F2*
26 **particular . . . place]** peculiar Sect and force *F1*
34 **you in]** within *F1*
36, 38, 39] *Q2–4 mark these lines with gnomic quotes*
37 **moon.]** *Q1;* Moone *Q2–4;* Moone: *F1*
40 **their]** the *F1*
46 **watchman]** watchmen *F1*
49 **Whiles]** Whilst *F1*
49 **like]** *F1* (*Q1*)
51 **reaks]** recks *Q1*
51 s.d. **Enter Polonius.]** *placed as in F1; after* rede. *l. 51, Q2–4;* Enter Corambis. *Q1* (*after l. 54*)
57 **stay'd]** *F1* (*Q1*); stayed *Q2–4*
57 **for. There—]** *Theobald;* for, there *Q2–4* (*Q1*); for there: *F1*
57 s.d. **laying . . . head]** *Theobald*
57 **thee]** (*Q1*); you *F1*
59 **Look]** See *F1*
62 **Those]** (*Q1*); The *F1*
63 **unto thy soul]** to thy Soule *F1;* to thee *Q1*
65 **new-hatch'd]** *hyphen, Pope;* vnhatch't *F1;* new *Q1*
65 **courage]** (*Q1*); Comrade *F1*
68 **thy ear]** thine eare *F1*
74 **Are]** *F1, Q4* (*Q1*); Or *Q2;* Ar *Q3*
74 **generous]** *F1;* generous, *Q2–4;* generall *Q1*
74 **chief]** (*Q1*); cheff *F1*
75 **be]** *F1;* boy *Q2–4*
76 **loan]** *F1* (lone); loue *Q2–4*
77 **dulleth th' edge]** *Q3–4* (*reading* the); dulleth edge *Q2;* duls the edge *F1*
83 **invests]** inuites *F1*
97–8 **honor. What]** *F1;* honor, / What *Q2–4*
98 **you?]** *Q5;* you *Q2–4;* you, *F1*
105 **I will]** Ile *F1*
106 **these]** his *F1*
109 **Wringing]** *Theobald;* Wrong *Q2–4;* Roaming *F1;* tendring *Q1*
114 **almost . . . vows]** all the vowes *F1; Q1 reads the line:* And withall, such earnest vowes.
115 **springes]** *F1, Q3–4* (*Q1*); springs *Q2*
117 **Lends]** (*Q1*); Giues *F1*
120 **fire. From]** *Q3–4* (*subs.*); fire, from *Q2;* fire. For *F1*
120 **time]** time Daughter *F1*
121 **something]** somewhat *F1*
123 **parle]** parley *F1*
125 **teder]** *Q3–4;* tider *Q2;* tether *F1*
128 **that dye]** the eye *F1*
129 **implorators]** *F1, Q3–4;* imploratotors *Q2*
131 **beguile]** *F1, Q3–4;* beguide *Q2*
135–6 **Come . . . lord.]** *Q1 ends the scene with the following lines:* Cor. Ofelia, receiue none of his letters, / "For louers lines are snares to intrap the heart; / "Refuse his tokens, both of them are keyes / To vnlocke Chastitie vnto Desire; / Come in *Ofelia,* such men often proue, / "Great in their wordes, but little in their loue. (*the final couplet seems to be a recollection of* Twelfth Night, *II.iv.117–8*)

I.iv

I.iv] *Capell*
Location: *Alexander* (*after Rowe*)
1 **shrowdly]** shrewdly *F1;* shrewd *Q1*
1 **it . . . cold.]** is it very cold? *F1*
2 **a]** *F1;* An *Q1*
3 **twelf]** twelue *F1, Q3–4* (*Q1*)
5 **It then]** then it *F1*
6 s.d. **off]** *Q3–4;* of *Q2; s.d. om. F1; Q1 gives* Sound Trumpets. *after l. 3*
6 s.d. **within]** *Rowe*
9 **wassail]** (*Q1*); wassels *F1*
14 **But]** And *F1*
17–38 **This . . . scandal.]** *om. F1* (*Q1*)
17 **heavy-headed]** *hyphen, Q3–4*
17 **revel]** *Q3–4;* reueale *Q2*
18 **traduc'd]** *Q3* (tradu'cd) *-4;* **tradust** *Q2*
18 **tax'd]** *Pope;* taxed *Q2–4*
23 **So,]** *Theobald;* So *Q2–4*
36 **ev'l]** *ed.* (*after Keightley*); eale *Q2;* ease *Q3–4*
42 **intents]** euents *F1*
45 **Dane. O]** *F1* (Dane: Oh, oh); Dane, ô *Q2–4*
48 **cerements]** cerments *F1;* ceremonies *Q1*
49 **inurn'd]** *F1* (enurn'd); interr'd *Q2–4* (*Q1*)
56 **the]** (*Q1*); thee; *F1*
57 s.d. **Ghost beckons Hamlet.]** *F1;* Beckins *Q2–4*
61 **waves]** (*Q1*); wafts *F1*
63 **I will]** will I *F1* (*Q1*)
70 **summit]** *Rowe;* somnet *Q2–4;* Sonnet *F1*

70 cliff] *F1;* cleefe *Q2-4*
71 beetles] *F1;* bettles *Q2;* bettels *Q3-4;* beckles *Q1*
72 assume] (*Q1*); assumes *F1*
75-8 The . . . beneath.] *om. F1* (*Q1*)
78 waves] wafts *F1*
80 hands] hand *F1*
82 artere] *Wilson;* arture *Q2;* artyre *Q3;* attire *Q4;* artery *Q5;* Artire *F1;* Artiue *Q1*
83 Nemean] *Q3-4;* Nemeon *Q2* (*Q1*); Nemian *F1*
86 s.d. Exeunt] *F1;* Exit *Q2-4*
87 imagination] *F1, Q3-4* (*Q1*); imagion *Q2*

I.v

I.v] *Capell*
Location: *Alexander*
1 Whither] *Q1;* **Whether** *Q2-4;* **Where** *F1*
3 sulph'rous] *Kittredge* (*after Q3-4* **sulphrous**); **sulphrus** *Q2;* **sulphurous** *F1*
18 knotted] (*Q1*); knotty *F1*
20 fearful] fretfull *F1* (*Q1*)
22 List . . . list!] list *Hamlet,* oh list, *F1;* **Hamlet,** *Q1*
24 God] (*Q1*); Heauen *F1*
29 Haste . . . that I] Hast, hast me to know it / That *F1;* Haste me to knowe it that *Q1*
33 roots] (*Q1*); rots *F1*
35 'Tis] (*Q1*); It's *F1*
35 my] (*Q1*); mine *F1*
38 know,] *F4;* knowe *Q2-4, F1* (*Q1*)
41 My uncle?] mine Vncle? *F1;* my vncle! my vncle! *Q1*
43 with traitorous gifts—] *Pope* (*subs., after Rowe*); with trayterous gifts, *Q2-4;* hath Traitorous guifts. *F1;* with gifts, *Q1*
45 to his] (*Q1*); to to this *F1*
47 a] *F1*
47 falling-off] *hyphen, Capell*
55 lust] *F1* (*Q1*); but *Q2-4*
56 angel] *F1;* Angle *Q2-4* (*Q1*)
56 sate] *F1;* sort *Q2-4;* fate *Q1*
58 morning] Mornings *F1* (*Q1*)
59 my] (*Q1*); mine *F1*
60 of] in *F1* (*Q1*)
62 hebona] (*Q1*); Hebenon *F1*
62 vial] (*Q1*); Violl *F1*
63 my] (*Q1*); mine *F1*
64 leprous] (*Q1*); leaperous *F1*
67 alleys] *Hanmer;* allies *Q2-4, F1*
68 posset] *F1;* possesse *Q2-4*
69 eager] (*Q1*); Aygre *F1*
71 bark'd] bak'd *F1;* barked *Q1*
75 of queen] (*Q1*); and Queene *F1*
77 Unhous'led] *ed.* (*after Theobald*); Vnhuzled *Q2;* Vnnuzled *Q3-4;* Vnhouzzled *F1*
77 unanel'd] *Pope;* vnanueld *Q2;* vn-anueld *Q3-4;* vnnaneld *F1*
79 With all] *F1, Q3-4* (*Q1*); Withall *Q2*
84 howsomever] howsoeuer *F1* (*Q1*)
84 pursues] pursuest *F1*
91 adieu, adieu!] adue, *Hamlet: F1; Q1 reads the line:* Hamlet adue, adue, adue: remember me.
91 s.d. Exit.] *F1*
93 hold,] *om. F1* (*Q1*)
94 sinows] sinnewes *F1*
95 stiffly] *F1;* swiftly *Q2-4*
96 whiles] while *F1*
102 commandement] Commandment *F1*
104 Yes] yes, yes *F1* (*Q1*)
107 My tables—] *Pope;* My tables, *Q2-4;* My Tables, my Tables; *F1;* (My tables) *Q1*
109 I am] (*Q1*); I'm *F1*
109 s.d. He writes.] *Rowe* (*subs.*)
113 s.p. Hor.] Hor. & Mar. *F1*
113 s.dd. Within.] *F1 gives the first, Capell the second*
113 s.d. Enter . . . Marcellus.] *placed by ed.; after l. 112, Q2-4; after* lord! *l. 113, F1; opposite l. 113, Q1*
113 Heavens] (*Q1*); Heauen *F1*
114 s.p. Ham.] Mar. *F1*
115 s.p. Mar.] Hor. *F1* (*Q1*)
116 boy! Come, bird,] *F1* (*subs.*); boy come, and *Q2-4;* so, come boy, *Q1*
119 you will] you'l *F1* (*Q1*)
121 it?] *F1* (*Q1*); it, *Q2-4*
122 secret?] *F1;* secret. *Q2-4* (*Q1*)
122 s.p. Hor., Mar.] *Capell*
122 my lord] *F1* (*Q1*)
123 never] (*Q1*); nere *F1*
126 in the] (*Q1*); i' th' *F1*
129 desire] desires *F1* (*Q1*)
130 hath] (*Q1*); ha's *F1*
131 my] (*Q1*); mine *F1*
132 I will] Looke you, Ile *F1;* ile *Q1*
133 whirling] *Theobald;* whurling *Q2-4;* hurling *F1;* wherling *Q1*
134 I am] (*Q1*); I'm *F1*
136 Horatio] (*Q1*); my Lord *F1*
137 too.] *Q5* (*subs.*); to, *Q2-4;* too, *F1* (*Q1*)
140 O'ermaster't] *F1, Q3-4;* Oremastret *Q2;* Or'emaister it *Q1*
145 s.p. Hor., Mar.] *Capell*
150 Ha] (*Q1*); Ah *F1*
151 on, you hear] one you here *F1;* you here, *Q1*
151 cellarage] *Johnson;* Sellerige *Q2* (*Q1*); selleredge *F1*
155, 161, 181 s.dd. Beneath.] *Capell*
156 ubique?] *F1;* vbique, *Q2-4* (*Q1*)
156 our] (*Q1*); for *F1*
159 Swear . . . sword,] *follows l. 160, F1* (*Q1*)
161 by his sword] *om. F1* (*Q1*)
162 i' th'] *F1;* it'h *Q2-4;* in the *Q1*
162 earth] (*Q1*); ground *F1*
167 your] (*Q1*); our *F1*
170-8 How . . . note] *F1* (*subs.*); (How . . . note) *Q2-4*
170 some'er] *Wilson;* so mere *Q2-4;* so ere *F1;* soere *Q1*
173 times] (*Q1*); time *F1*
174 this] (*Q1*); thus, *F1*
176 Well, well,] (*Q1*); well, *F1*
177 they] (*Q1*); there *F1*
179 do swear,] not to doe: *F1*
180 you.] you: / Sweare. *F1* (*Q1*)
181 s.d. They swear.] *Globe* (*after l. 182*); *placed as in Kittredge*
183 With all] *F1, Q3-4;* Withall *Q2;* In all *Q1*
187 pray.] *Rowe;* pray, *Q2-4, F1* (*Q1*)

II.i

II.i] *Q* (*1676*); Actus Secundus. *F1*
Location: *ed.* (*after Rowe*)
o.s.d. with . . . Reynaldo] *from Q2-4. F1 s.dd.:* with his man or two *Q2-4;* and Reynoldo *F1; Q1 s.d. reads:* Enter Corambis, and Montano.
1 this] his *F1;* this same *Q1*
1 Reynaldo] Reynoldo *F1* (*throughout*); Montano *Q1* (*throughout*)
3 marvell's] *Dyce;* meruiles *Q2;* maruelous *Q3-4;* maruels *F1*
4 to make inquire] you make inquiry *F1;* To inquire *Q1*
6 Marry] *F1, Q4;* Mary *Q2-3*
14 As] (*Q1*); And *F1*
18 if't] *F1;* y'ft *Q2-4*
28 Faith,] Faith no, *F1;* I faith not a whit, no not a whit, *Q1*
34 unreclaimed] *Q4;* vnreclamed *Q2-3;* vnreclaim'd *F1*
38 wit] warrant *F1*
39 sallies] *see I.ii.129;* sullies *Q3-4;* sulleyes *F1*
40 wi' th'] *ed.;* with *Q2-4;* i' th' *F1*
43 seen] seene. *F1*
43 prenominate] *F1, Q4;* prenominat *Q2-3*
47 or] and *F1*
47 addition] *F1, Q3-4;* addistion *Q2*
49 'a . . . 'a] he . . . He *F1*
49 this— . . . does—] *Capell* (*after Rowe*); this, . . . doos, *Q2;* this, . . . doos: *Q3-4;* this? . . . does: *F1*
50 By the mass] *om. F1* (*Q1*)
51 consequence.] consequence: / At friend, or so, and Gentleman. *F1*
53 closes thus:] closes with you thus. *F1;* closeth with him thus, *Q1*
54 th' other] tother *F1* (*Q1*)
55 or such] and such *F1*
56 'a] he *F1*
56 gaming, there o'ertook] *F1;* gaming there, or tooke *Q2-4*
58 sale] saile *F1;* lightnes *Q1*
59 forth.] *F1;* forth, *Q2-4*
60 take] takes *F1*
60 carp] Cape *F1*
64 advice] *F1;* aduise *Q2-4*
66 ye . . . ye] you . . . you *F1*
71 s.d. Exit Reynaldo.] *placed as in Dyce* (*after Singer*); *after l. 70, Q2-4;* Exit. *F1* (*Q1*) (*after l. 70*)
71 s.d. Enter Ophelia.] *placed as in Singer; after l. 70, Q2-4, F1* (*Q1*)
72 O . . . I] Alas, my Lord, I *F1*
73 i' th'] in the *F1*
73 God] Heauen *F1*
74 closet] Chamber *F1*
76 stockins] stockings *F1*
77 down-gyved] *hyphen, F2*
88 'a] he *F1*
92 As] That *F1*
94 shoulder] (*Q1*); shoulders *F1*
96 a' doors] *Q3* (a doores); adoores *Q2;* of doores *Q4* (*Q1*); adores *F1*
96 helps] helpe *F1* (*Q1*)
98 Come] *om. F1* (*Q1*)
102 passions] passion *F1*
103 sorry—] *Capell;* sorry, *Q2-4, F1*
108 heed] speed *F1*
109 coted] quoted *F1*
109 fear'd] feare *F1*
111 By heaven] It seemes *F1;* By heau'n *Q1*
117 Come.] *om. F1* (*Q1*)

II.ii

II.ii] *F1*
Location: *Capell* (*after Rowe*)
o.s.d. Flourish.] *om. F1* (*Q1*)
o.s.d. Rosencrantz] *Malone;* Rosencraus *Q2-4* (*so generally throughout, except* Rosencrans *at II.ii.34*); Rosincrane *F1* (*also* Rosencrance *and* Rosincran *elsewhere*); Rossencraft *Q1*
o.s.d. Guildenstern] Guyldensterne *Q2-4* (*also* Guyldersterne *elsewhere*), *F1;* Gilderstone *Q1*
o.s.d. cum aliis] *F1*
5 so] so I *F1*
6 Sith nor] Since not *F1*
10 dream] deeme *F1*
12 sith] since *F1*
12 neighbored] *Q3-4;* nabored *Q2;* Neighbour'd *F1*
12 havior] humour *F1*
13 voutsafe] vouchsafe *F1, Q4*
16 occasion] Occasions *F1*
17 Whether . . . thus,] *om. F1* (*Q1*)
20 is] are *F1*
29 But] *om. F1* (*Q1*)
31 service] Seruices *F1*
36 you] ye *F1*
37 these] the *F1*
39 Ay] *Capell;* I *Q2-4; om. F1* (*Q1*)
39 s.d. with some Attendants] *Capell; F1 s.d. is* Exit. (*after* him! *l. 39*)
43 I assure] (*Q1*); Assure you, *F1*
45 and] (*Q1*); one *F1*
48 it hath] I haue *F1;* it had *Q1*
50 do I] I do *F1*
52 fruit] Newes *F1*
53 s.d. Exit Polonius.] *Rowe*
54 dear Gertrude] *Q5;* deere Gertrard *Q2;* decree: Gertrud *Q3-4;* sweet Queene, that *F1*
57 o'erhasty] *F1;* hastie *Q2-4*
57 s.d. Polonius . . . the] *F1* (*subs., reading* Voltumand)
58 my] *om. F1* (*Q1*)
63, 75 Polack] (*Q1*); Poleak *F1*
73 three] *F1* (*Q1*); threescore *Q2-4*
76 shown] *F1* (shewne) (*Q1*); shone *Q2-4*
76 s.d. Giving a paper.] *Malone* (*after Capell*)
78 this] his *F1;* that *Q1*
85 s.d. Exeunt Embassadors] (*Q1 subs.*); Exit. Ambass. *F1*
85 s.d. and Attendants] *Alexander*
85 well] very well *F1*
90 since] *F1*
97 he's] he is *F1*
98 'tis 'tis] it is *F1*
104 thus.] *F1;* thus *Q2-4*

106 **while]** (*Q1*); whil'st *F1*
108 s.d. **Reads . . . letter.]** *ed.;* The Letter. *F1*
111 **vile . . . vile]** vilde . . . vilde *F1*
112 **hear. Thus:]** *Jennens* (*subs.*); heare: thus *Q2–4* (*Polonius' comments are given as part of the letter in Q2–4*); heare these *F1*
113 **etc.]** *om. F1* (*Q1*)
115 s.d. **Reads the]** *Rowe*
125 **This]** *F1; Pol.* This *Q2–4* (*repeated s.p.*)
125 **shown]** shew'd *F1*
126 **above]** *F1;* about *Q2–4*
126 **solicitings]** soliciting *F1*
137 **winking,]** *F1;* working *Q2–4*
142 **prescripts]** Precepts *F1*
143 **his]** *F1, Q3–4;* her *Q2*
145 **advice]** *F1;* aduise *Q2–4*
146 **repell'd]** repulsed *F1*
148 **watch]** *F1, Q3–4;* wath *Q2*
149 **a]** *F1*
150 **wherein]** whereon *F1*
151 **mourn]** waile *F1*
151 **'tis]** *F1* (*Q1*)
152 **be,]** *Capell;* be *Q2–4, F1*
152 **like]** likely *F1*
153 **I would]** I'de *F1;* I would very *Q1*
156 s.d. **Points . . . shoulder.]** *Theobald*
161 **does]** ha's *F1*
167 **But]** And *F1*
167 s.d. **reading on a book]** *F1; in Q1 the King describes the entrance of Hamlet* poring vppon a booke; *Q1* (*like* Der bestrafte Brudermord) *inserts at this point its version of III.i.43–175*
169 **you,]** *F1;* you *Q2–4*
170 s.d. **Exeunt]** *Rowe;* Exit *Q2–4, F1; s.d. placed as in F1; after l. 169, Q2–4*
174 **Excellent]** Excellent, excellent *F1;* Yea very *Q1*
174 **you are]** y'are *F1* (*Q1*)
177 **lord?]** *F1;* Lord. *Q2–4*
178–9 **Ay . . . thousand.]** *as prose, F1; as verse, Q2–4* (*Q1*)
179 **ten]** (*Q1*); two *F1*
184–6 **Let . . . to't.]** *as prose, F1; as verse, Q2–4*
185 **but]** but not *F1*
187 s.d. **Aside.]** *Capell*
188 **'a]** he *F1* (*Q1*)
189 **'A]** he *F1*
189 **gone]** gone, farre gone *F1*
195 **that]** *om. F1* (*Q1*)
195 **read]** (*Q1*); meane *F1*
196 **rogue]** slaue *F1;* Satyre *Q1*
198 **and]** or *F1*
199 **lack]** locke *F1*
200 **most]** *om. F1;* pittifull *Q1*
202 **yourself]** (*Q1*); you your selfe *F1*
203 **shall grow]** should be *F1;* shalbe *Q1*
205 s.d. **Aside.]** *Johnson*
208 **that's . . . the]** (*Q1*); that is out o' th' *F1*
208 s.d. **Aside.]** *Capell*
210 **sanity]** *F1;* sanctity *Q2–4*
212–3 **and . . . him]** *F1*
213 **lord . . . take]** (*Q1*); Honourable Lord, I will most humbly / Take *F1*
215 **cannot . . . thing]** cannot Sir . . . thing *F1;* can take nothing from me sir *Q1*
216 **not]** *om. F1* (*Q1*)
216–7 **withal— . . . life.]** withall, except my life, my life. *F1*
219 s.d. **Enter . . . Rosencrantz.]** *placed as in Capell; after l. 217, Q2–4; after l. 220, F1; after l. 214, Q1*
220 **the]** my *F1*
221 s.d. **To Polonius.]** *Malone*
221 s.d. **Exit Polonius.]** *Q1* (exit.)
222 **My]** Mine *F1*
224 **excellent]** *F1, Q4;* extent *Q2;* exelent *Q3*
225 **Ah]** *Q5;* A *Q2–4;* Oh *F1*
226 **you]** ye *F1*
228 **over-happy,]** *F1* (ouer-happy:); euer happy *Q2–4*
229 **cap]** *F1;* lap *Q2–4*
230 **shoe?]** *F1;* shooe. *Q2–4*
233 **favors]** fauour *F1*
236 **What]** What's the *F1*
237 **but]** but that *F1*
239–69 **Let . . . attended.]** *F1*
266 s.p. **Ros., Guil.]** *Capell*
270 **Elsinore]** *Malone;* Elsonoure *Q2–4;* Elsonower *F1;* Elsanoure *Q1*
272 **even]** *F1;* euer *Q2–4*
275 **come]** *om. F1* (*Q1*)
278 **Any thing]** Why any thing. *F1*
279 **of]** (*Q1*); *om. F1*
287 **can]** could *F1*
289 s.d. **Aside to Guildenstern.]** *Globe* (*after Theobald*)
290 s.d. **Aside.]** *Steevens*
294 **and]** of *F1*
297 **exercises]** exercise *F1*
297 **heavily]** heauenly *F1*
301 **firmament]** *om. F1* (*Q1*)
302 **appeareth . . . but]** appeares no other thing to me then *F1*
303 **a]** *F1*
304–7 **how infinite . . . god:]** how infinite in faculty? in forme and mouing how expresse and admirable? in Action, how like an Angel? in apprehension, how like a God? *F1* (*c*) (*the uncorrected state has no pointing after* God)
309 **nor]** no, nor *F1* (*Q1*)
309 **women]** Woman *F1, Q3–4* (*Q1*)
313 **ye]** you *F1* (*Q1*)
313 **then]** (*Q1*); *om. F1*
317 **coted]** coated *F1;* boorded *Q1*
320 **on]** of *F1* (*Q1*)
323–4 **the . . . sere,]** *F1* (*Q1, in part*)
324 **tickle]** *Staunton conj.;* tickled *F1* (*Q1*)
325 **blank]** *F1, Q3–4* (*Q1*); black *Q2*
327 **such]** *om. F1* (*Q1*)
329 **travel]** *Q1;* trauaile *Q2–4, F1*
336 **are they]** they are *F1*
337–62 **Ham. How . . . too.]** *F1*
339 **eyases]** *Theobald;* Yases *F1*
342 **berattle]** *F3* (be-rattle); be-ratled *F1;* be ratle *F2*
349 **most like]** *Pope;* like most *F1*
350 **no]** *Rowe;* not *F1* (*the t is uncertain*), *F2*
363 **very]** *om. F1* (*Q1*)
364 **mouths at him]** mowes at him *F1;* mops and moes / At my vncle *Q1*
365 **fifty]** *om. F1* (*Q1*)
365 **a]** (*Q1*); an *F1*
366 **'Sblood]** *om. F1* (*Q1*)
368 s.d. **for the Players]** *F1; Q1 s.d. reads:* The Trumpets sound,
371 **hands, come then:]** *F1* (*which om.* then); hands come then, *Q2;* hands, Come then *Q3–4*
373 **this]** the *F1*
373 **lest my]** *F1;* let me *Q2;* let my *Q3–4*
374 **outwards]** outward *F1*
379 **hand-saw]** *Q3–4;* hand saw *Q2;* Handsaw *F1*
381 s.d. **Aside to them.]** *Neilson*
383 **swaddling-clouts]** (*Q1*); swathing clouts *F1*
384 **he is]** he's *F1*
387 s.d. **Aloud.]** *Neilson*
387 **a']** (*Q1*); for a *F1*
388 **then]** so *F1* (*Q1*)
391 **was]** (*Q1*); *om. F1*
394 **my]** mine *F1*
395 **"Then . . . ass"]** *quotes, Johnson conj.*
395 **came]** can *F1*
397–8 **pastoral-comical, historical-pastoral]** *hyphens, Q3–4;* Pastoricall-Comicall-Historicall-Pastorall *F1;* Pastorall, Historicall, Historicall, Comicall *Q1*
398–9 **tragical- . . . -pastoral,]** *F1;* Comicall historicall, Pastorall, Tragedy historicall: *Q1*
400 **Seneca]** *F1, Q3–4* (*Q1*); Sceneca *Q2*
403, 410, 411 **Jephthah]** *Hanmer;* Ieptha *Q2–4;* Iephta *F1;* Iepha *Q1* (*om. l. 410*)
407–8 **One . . . well.]** *as verse, F1* (*Q1*); *as prose, Q2–4; quotes, Pope*
409 s.d. **Aside.]** *Capell*
416–8 **"As . . . was"]** *as partly quoted verse, Malone* (*after Pope*); *as prose, Q2–4, F1; as irregular verse, Q1, reading:* Why by lot, or God wot, or as it came to passe, / And so it was,
419 **pious chanson]** Pons Chanson *F1* (*in italics*); godly Ballet *Q1*
420 **abridgment comes]** (*Q1*); Abridgements come *F1*
420 s.d. **four or five]** *F1* (*before* Players)
421 **You]** *F1* (*reading* Y'); *Ham.* You *Q2–4* (*repeated s.p.*); *s.p. and* You are *om. Q1*
422 **old]** my olde *F1* (*Q1*)
423 **why]** *om. F1* (*Q1*)
423 **valanc'd]** *Q3–4;* valanct *Q2;* valiant *F1;* vallanced *Q1*
425 **by' lady]** *ed.;* by lady *Q2–3;* my Ladie *Q4;* Byrlady *F1;* burlady *Q1*
425 **to]** *om. F1* (*Q1*)
429 **e'en to't]** *F1;* ento't *Q2–4;* euen too't *Q1*
430 **French]** *F1* (*Q1*); friendly *Q2–4*
430 **falc'ners]** *Q3–4* (Faukners); Fankners *Q2;* Faulconers *F1* (*Q1*)
433, 468, 502, 505 s.pp. **1. Play.]** *F1;* Player. *or* Play. *Q2–4;* Players *Q1* (*later* Play.)
433 **good]** (*Q1*); *om. F1*
438 **judgments]** (*Q1*); iudgement *F1*
441 **were]** was *F1* (*Q1*)
443 **affection]** affectation *F1*
444–5 **as wholesome . . . fine.]** *om. F1* (*Q1, in part*)
445 **speech]** (*Q1*); cheefe Speech *F1*
446 **tale]** *F1* (*Q1*); talke *Q2–4*
447 **thereabout]** *F1;* there about *Q2–4;* then *Q1* (*om.* of it)
447 **when]** (*Q1*); where *F1*
450 **"The . . . beast"]** *as verse, Q1, Capell; as prose, Q2–4, F1*
450 **Hyrcanian]** *F1;* ircanian *Q2–4;* arganian *Q1*
451 **'Tis]** It is *F1;* No t'is *Q1*
454 **th']** the *F1*
456 **heraldy]** Heraldry *F1* (*Q1*)
456 **dismal:]** *F1;* dismall *Q2–4;* dismall, *Q1*
457 **total gules]** to take Geulles *F1;* totall guise *Q1*
460 **and a]** and *F1*
461 **lord's murther]** (*apostrophe, Steevens*); vilde Murthers *F1*
462 **o'ersized]** *F1;* ore-cised *Q2–4*
465 **So proceed you.]** *om. F1;* So goe on. *Q1*
469 **antique]** *Pope;* anticke *Q2–4, F1* (*Q1*)
471 **match'd]** match *F1*
474 **Then senseless Ilium,]** *F1*
475 **this]** his *F1*
481 **And]** *F1*
488 **a-work]** *F1;* a worke *Q2–4*
490 **Mars's armor]** *Capell;* Marses Armor *Q2–4;* Mars his Armours *F1*
495 **fellies]** *F4;* follies *Q2;* folles *Q3;* fellowes *Q4;* Fallies *F1*
499 **to the]** (*Q1*); to'th *F1*
502 **ah woe]** *Q5;* a woe *Q2–4;* O who *F1* (*Q1*)
502, 503 **mobled]** (*Q1, l. 502; om. l. 503*); inobled *F1*
504 **mobled . . . good]** *F2;* Inobled . . . good *F1; Q1 reads the line:* Mobled Queene is good, faith very good.
505 **flames]** flame *F1*
506 **bisson rheum]** *F1; Bison* rehume *Q2; Bison* rhume *Q3–4*
506 **clout upon]** clout about *F1;* kercher on *Q1*
509 **alarm]** Alarum *F1* (*Q1*)
514 **husband's]** *F1, Q3–4* (*Q1*); husband *Q2*
519 **whe'er]** *Theobald* (*subs.*); where *Q2–4, F1;* if *Q1*
520 **Prithee]** Pray you *F1;* no more good heart *Q1*
522 **of this]** *om. F1* (*Q1*)
523 **you]** ye *F1*
524 **abstract]** Abstracts *F1* (*Q1*)
526 **live]** (*Q1*); liued *F1*
529 **bodkin]** bodykins *F1*
529 **much]** *om. F1;* farre *Q1*
530 **shall]** should *F1* (*Q1*)
534 s.d. **Exit.]** *F1* (*Q1*); *Q2–4 give exit for Polonius and Players after l. 545*
536 s.d. **Exeunt . . . First.]** *Dyce*
539, 544 s.pp. **1. Play.]** *Capell;* Play. *Q2–4, F1;* players *Q1*
540 **ha't]** *F1;* hate *Q2;* hau't *Q3–4*
541 **need]** a need *F1* (*Q1*)
541 **dozen or]** *F1* (*Q1*); dosen lines, or *Q2–4*
543 **you]** ye *F1*
546 s.d. **Exit First Player.]** *Dyce*
546–8 **My . . . lord!]** Gentlemen, for your kindnes I thanke you, / And for a time I

would desire you leaue me. / *Gil.* Our loue and duetie is at your command. *Q1*
547 **till]** *F1, Q3–4;* tell *Q2*
547 **Elsinore]** *Malone;* Elsonoure *Q2–4;* Elsonower *F1*
549 **Ay so,]** *F1* (I so,), *Q3–4;* I so *Q2*
549 **to]** *om. F1 (Q1)*
549 **you.]** *pointing after F1* ('ye:'); you, *Q2–4*
549 s.d. **Rosencrantz and Guildenstern]** *Capell; s.d. placed as in Globe; after l. 548, Q2–4, F1 (Q1)*
553 **own]** whole *F1*
554 **the]** his *F1*
554 **wann'd]** *Steevens (after Warburton);* wand *Q2–4;* warm'd *F1*
555 **in his]** in's *F1*
556 **an']** *ed.;* an *Q2;* and *F1, Q3–4*
559 **Hecuba]** *F1 (Q1);* her *Q2–4*
561 **the cue]** *F1;* that *Q2–4; Q1 reads l. 561 as:* and if he had my losse?
564 **appall]** *Rowe;* appale *Q2;* appeale *Q3–4;* apale *F1*
566 **faculties]** faculty *F1*
567 **muddy-mettled]** *hyphen, F1*
576 **'swounds]** Why *F1;* Sure *Q1*
577 **pigeon-liver'd]** *hyphen, F1*
579 **'a']** *ed.;* a *Q2 (Q1);* haue *F1, Q3–4*
580 **offal. Bloody,]** *Q5 (subs.);* offall, bloody, *Q2–4;* **Offall, bloudy: a** *F1;* **offell, this** *Q1 (substituting* damned villaine *for* bawdy villain)
581 **villain!]** villaine! / Oh Vengeance! *F1*
582 **Why,]** Who? *F1*
582 **This]** I sure, this *F1*
583 **a dear father]** *Q3–4;* a deere *Q2;* the Deere *F1;* my deare father *Q1*
587 **stallion]** Scullion *F1;* scalion *Q1*
588 **About,]** *Theobald;* About *Q2–4, F1 (Q1)*
588 **brains]** *Q2* (*c*), *Q3–4;* braues *Q2* (*u*); Braine *F1 (Q1)*
588 **Hum]** *om. F1 (Q1)*
597 **If 'a do]** If he but *F1;* And if he doe not *Q1*
599 **a dev'l . . . dev'l]** *ed.;* a deale . . . deale *Q2;* a diuell . . . diuell *Q3–4;* the Diuell . . . Diuel *F1;* the Diuell, *Q1*

III.i

III.i] *Q (1676)*
Location: *Capell (subs., after Rowe)*
Cf. the following version of this scene in Q1 (see note at l. 43 s.d. below): Enter the King, Queene, and Lordes. / King Lordes, can you by no meanes finde / The cause of our sonne Hamlets lunacie? / You being so neere in loue, euen from his youth, / Me thinkes should gaine more than a stranger should. / *Gil.* My lord, we haue done all the best we could, / To wring from him the cause of all his griefe, / But still he puts vs off, and by no meanes / Would make an answere to that we exposde. / *Ross.* Yet was he something more inclin'd to mirth / Before we left him, and I take it, / He hath giuen order for a play to night, / At which he craues your highnesse company. / *King* With all our heart, it likes vs very well: / Gentlemen, seeke still to increase his mirth, / Spare for no cost, our coffers shall be open, / And we vnto your selues will still be thankefull. / *Both* In all wee can, be sure you shall command. / *Queene* Thankes gentlemen, and what the Queene of *Denmarke* / May pleasure you, be sure you shall not want. / *Gil.* Weele once againe vnto the noble Prince. / *King* Thanks to you both: Gertred you'l see this play. / *Queene* My lord I will, and it ioyes me at the soule / He is inclin'd to any kinde of mirth. / *Cor.* Madame, I pray be ruled by me: / And my good Soueraigne, giue me leaue to speake, / We cannot yet finde out the very ground / Of his distemperance, therefore / I holde it meete, if so it please you, / Else they shall not meete, and thus it is. / *King* What i'st *Corambis*? / *Cor.* Mary my good lord this, soone when the sports are done, / Madam, send you in haste to speake with him, / And I myselfe will stand behind the Arras, / There question you the cause of all his griefe, / And then in loue and nature vnto you, hee'le tell you all: / My Lord, how thinke you on't? / *King* It likes vs well, Gerterd, what say you? / *Queene* With all my heart, soone will I send for him. / *Cor.* My selfe will be that happy messenger, / Who hopes his griefe will be reueal'd to her. *exeunt omnes*
1 **An']** *ed.;* An *Q2;* And *F1, Q3–4*
1 **conference]** circumstance *F1;* meanes *Q1*
6 **'a]** he *F1*
17 **o'er-raught]** ore-wrought *F1*
19 **here]** *om. F1 (Q1)*
27 **into]** on / To *F1*
28 s.d. **Exeunt . . . Guildenstern.]** Exeunt. *F1*
28 **two]** too *F1*
30 **here]** there *F1*
31–2 **myself, We'll]** my selfe (lawful espials) / Will *F1*
41 s.d. **Exit Queen.]** *Theobald*
42 **please you]** please ye *F1*
43 s.d. **To Ophelia.]** *Johnson; the Q1 version of ll. 43–175 appears in II.ii following l. 167*
45 **loneliness]** *F1;* lowlines *Q2–4*
47 **sugar]** surge *F1*
48 s.d. **Aside.]** *Capell (after Pope, at l. 49)*
48 **too]** *om. F1 (Q1)*
54 **Withdraw]** let's withdraw *F1*
54 s.d. **Exeunt]** *F1*
54 s.d. **King and Polonius]** *Capell*
54 s.d. **Enter Hamlet.]** *placed as in F1; after l. 53, Q2–4*
55–89 **To . . . rememb'red.]** *This soliloquy appears in the following form in Q1:* To be, or not to be, I there's the point, / To Die, to sleepe, is that all? I all: / No, to sleepe, to dreame, I mary there it goes, / For in that dreame of death, when wee awake, / And borne before an euerlasting Iudge, / From whence no passenger euer retur'nd, / The vndiscouered country, at whose sight / The happy smile, and the accursed damn'd. / But for this, the ioyfull hope of this, / Whol'd beare the scornes and flattery of the world, / Scorned by the right rich, the rich cursssed of the poore? / The widow being oppressed, the orphan wrong'd, / The taste of hunger, or a tirants raigne, / And thousand more calamities besides, / To grunt and sweate vnder this weary life, / When that he may his full *Quietus* make, / With a bare bodkin, who would this indure, / But for a hope of something after death? / Which pusles the braine, and doth confound the sence, / Which makes vs rather beare those euilles we haue, / Than flie to others that we know not of. / I that, O this conscience makes cowardes of vs all, / Lady in thy orizons, be all my sinnes remembred. *(Q1 places this soliloquy, and the interview between Hamlet and Ophelia which follows, in II.ii after the equivalent of ll. 169–70;* Der bestrafte Brudermord, *though it omits the soliloquy, also places the Hamlet-Ophelia interview essentially as in Q1)*
59 **them.]** *F1, Q3–4 (subs.);* them, *Q2*
59 **die,]** *F1 (Q1);* die *Q2–4*
59 **sleep—]** *Pope;* sleepe *Q2–4, F1;* sleepe, *Q1*
63 **wish'd.]** *F1;* wisht *Q2–4*
63 **die,]** *Globe (after Pope);* die *Q2–4, F1*
70 **proud]** poore *F1*
71 **despis'd]** dispriz'd *F1*
74 **quietus]** *F1, Q4 (Q1);* quietas *Q2–3*
75 **fardels]** these Fardles *F1*
78 **bourn]** *Capell (after Pope);* **borne** *Q2–4, F1*
82 **of us all]** *F1 (Q1)*
84 **sicklied]** *F1;* sickled *Q2–4*
85 **pitch]** pith *F1*
86 **awry]** away *F1*
91 **well, well]** *F1*
94 **No, not I]** No, no *F1*
96 **you know]** I know *F1*
98 **these]** the *F1*
98 **rich. Their]** *Q3–4 (subs.);* rich, their *Q2;* rich, then *F1*
98 **lost,]** left: *F1*
106–7 **your honesty]** *F1;* you *Q2–4;* Your beauty *Q1*
108–9 **Could . . . honesty?]** *as prose, F1; as verse, Q2–4 (Q1)*
109 **with]** *(Q1);* your *F1*
117 **inoculate]** *F1;* euocutat *Q2;* euacuat *Q3;* euacuate *Q4*
120 **to]** *F1 (Q1)*
127–8 **earth and heaven]** Heauen and Earth *F1 (Q1)*
128 **knaves]** Knaues all *F1 (Q1)*
131–2 **Let . . . Farewell!]** *as prose, F1; as verse, Q2–4 (Q1)*
132 **where]** *(Q1);* way *F1*
137 **nunn'ry,]** Nunnery. Go, *F1 (Q1)*
141 **Heavenly powers]** O heavenly Powers *F1;* Pray God *Q1*
142 **paintings]** pratlings too *F1;* paintings too *Q1*
143 **hath . . . face]** *(Q1);* has . . . pace *F1*
143 **yourselves]** *Q4 (Q1);* your selfes *Q2–3;* your selfe *F1*
144 **jig and]** gidge, you *F1;* fig, and you *Q1*
144 **lisp, you]** *from F1* lispe, and; list you *Q2–4*
146 **your]** *F1 (Q1)*
147 **moe marriage]** more Marriages *F1 (Q1)*
152 **expectation]** expectansie *F1*
155 **And]** Haue *F1*
156 **music]** *F1, Q4;* musickt *Q2–3*
157 **that]** *F1;* what *Q2–4*
158 **time]** tune *F1*
159 **stature]** Feature *F1*
161 s.d. **Ophelia withdraws.]** *ed. (after Wilson);* Exit. *Q2–4 (Q1)*
162 **Love?]** *F1 (Q1);* Loue, *Q2;* Loue: *Q3–4*
167 **for]** *om. F1 (Q1)*
173 **something-settled]** *hyphen, Warburton*
177 **his]** this *F1*
178 s.d. **Ophelia comes forward.]** *Wilson*
183 **grief]** Greefes *F1*
188 **unwatch'd]** *F1;* vnmatcht *Q2–4*

III.ii

III.ii] *Capell*
Location: *Alexander (after Capell)*
o.s.d. **three . . . Players]** two or three of the Players *F1;* the Players *Q1*
1 **pronounc'd]** *F1, Q3–4;* pronoun'd *Q2*
3 **our]** your *F1 (Q1)*
4 **spoke]** had spoke *F1*
4 **with]** *(Q1); om. F1*
6 **torrent,]** *F1;* torrent *Q2–4*
6 **whirlwind of your]** the Whirle-winde of *F1*
9 **hear]** *(Q1);* see *F1*
9 **periwig-pated]** *F1 (subs.);* perwig-pated *Q2–4;* periwig *Q1*
10 **totters]** *(Q1);* tatters *F1*
10 **spleet]** split *F1 (Q1)*
12 **would]** *(Q1);* could *F1*
14 **out-Herods]** *hyphen, F1;* out, Herodes *Q1*
15, 36 s.pp. **1. Play.]** *Capell;* Player. *or* Play. *Q2–4, F1;* players *Q1*
19 **o'erstep]** ore-stop *F1*
20 **o'erdone]** ouer-done *F1*
23 **feature]** owne Feature *F1*
25 **makes]** make *F1*
27 **which]** the which *F1*
29 **praise]** *F1;* praysd *Q2–4*
32 **nor man]** or Norman *F1;* Nor Turke *Q1*
35 **abominably]** *Q3–4;* abhominably *Q2, F1;* abhominable *Q1*
37 **sir]** *F1*
45 **uses it.]** *Following these words Q1 reads:* And then you haue some agen, that keepes one sute / Of ieasts, as a man is knowne by one sute of / Apparell, and Gentlemen quotes his ieasts downe / In their tables, before they come to the play, as thus: / Cannot you stay till I eate my porrige? and, you owe me / A quarters wages: and, my coate wants a cullison: / And, your beere is sowre: and, blabbering with his lips, / And thus keeping in his cinkapase of ieasts, / When, God knows, the warme Clowne cannot make a iest / Vnlesse by chance, as the blinde man catcheth a hare: / Maisters tell him of it.

45 s.d. **Exeunt Players.**] *F1* (Exit) (*Q1*)

45 s.d. **Enter . . . Rosencrantz.**] *placed as in F1; after l. 48, Q2–4*

49 s.d. **Exit Polonius.**] *F1*

51 **Ros. Ay**] *Both.* We will *F1*

51 s.d. **they two**] *om. F1; Q1 om. the entrance of Rosencrantz, Guildenstern, and Polonius at l. 45*

52 **ho**] *F4;* howe *Q2–4;* hoa *F1*

60 **lick**] like *F1*

62 **fawning**] faining *F1*

63 **her**] my *F1*

65 **Sh' hath**] *Wilson;* S'hath *Q2;* S hath *Q3;* Shath *Q4;* Hath *F1*

68 **Hast**] Hath *F1*

69 **co-meddled**] co-mingled *F1*

78 **afoot**] *F1* (*Q1*)*;* a foote *Q2–4*

79 **thy**] my *F1*

80 **my**] mine *F1*

84 **stithy**] Stythe *F1*

84 **heedful**] needfull *F1*

87 **In**] To *F1*

88 **'a**] he *F1*

89 **detecting**] *F1;* detected *Q2–4*

89 s.d. **Sound . . . march.**] *F1* (*at end of s.d.*)

89 s.d. **Rosencrantz . . . torches**] *F1; Q1 s.d. reads:* Enter King, Queene, Corambis, and other Lords.

93–9 **Excellent . . . say?**] *as prose, F1; as verse, Q2–4*

94 **promise-cramm'd**] *hyphen, F1, Q3–4;* Promiscram'd *Q2;* capon cramm'd *Q1*

98 **mine now.**] *Johnson;* mine now *Q2–4;* mine. Now *F1*

98 s.d. **To Polonius.**] *Rowe*

100 **did I**] I did *F1* (*Q1*)

102 **What**] (*Q1*)*;* And what *F1*

103–6 **I . . . ready?**] *as prose, F1* (*Q1, in part*)*; as verse, Q2–4*

108 s.p. **Queen.**] *F1* (*Q1*)*;* Ger. *Q2–4*

108 **dear**] good *F1*

109 **metal**] *Q5;* mettle *Q2–4, F1* (*Q1*)

110 s.d. **Lying . . . feet.**] *Rowe*

111 s.d. **To the King.**] *Capell*

114–5 **Ham. I . . . lord.**] *F1* (*Q1, in part*)

116 **country**] contrary *Q1*

129 **dev'l**] *ed.;* deule *Q2;* diuell *Q3–4;* Diuel *F1*

133 **by'r**] *F1;* ber *Q2–4*

133–4 **'a . . . 'a**] he . . . he *F1* (*Q1*)

135 s.d. **The trumpets sounds.**] Hoboyes play. *F1*

135 s.d. **Dumb show follows.**] The dumbe shew enters. *F1; Q1 s.d. reads:* Enter in a Dumbe Shew, the King and the Queene, he sits downe in an Arbor, she leaues him: Then enters Lucianus with poyson in a Viall, and powres it in his eares, and goes away: Then the Queene commeth and findes him dead: and goes away with the other.

135 s.d. **a Queen**] Queene *F1*

135 s.d. **very lovingly**] *F1*

135 s.d. **and he her**] *om. F1*

135 s.d. **She . . . him.**] *F1*

135 s.d. **he lies**] Layes *F1*

135 s.d. **come**] comes *F1, Q3–4*

135 s.d. **another man**] a Fellow *F1*

135 s.d. **pours**] and powres *F1*

135 s.d. **sleeper's . . . him**] Kings eares, and Exits *F1*

135 s.d. **makes**] and makes *F1*

135 s.d. **pois'ner . . . pois'ner**] poysoner . . . poisoner *F1, Q3–4*

135 s.d. **three or four**] two or three *F1*

135 s.d. **mutes**] *F1*

135 s.d. **come**] comes *F1, Q3–4*

135 s.d. **seem to condole**] seeming to lament *F1*

135 s.d. **harsh**] loath *F1*

135 s.d. **and unwilling**] *F1*

135 s.d. **love**] his loue *F1*

135 s.d. **Exeunt.**] *F1*

137 **this'**] *ed.;* this *Q2;* tis *Q3;* it is *Q4;* this is *F1* (*Q1*)

137 **miching**] *F1* (*Q1*)*;* munching *Q2–4* (miching *is a Middle English variant of* munching)

137 **mallecho**] *Malone;* Mallico *Q2–4* (*Q1*)*;* Malicho *F1*

137 **it**] that *F1* (*Q1*)

140 s.d. **Enter Prologue.**] *placed as in Theobald; after* fellow. *l. 141, Q2–4; after l. 148, F1; after l. 136, Q1*

141–2 **We . . . all.**] *as prose, F1; as verse, Q2–4; Q1 reduces to:* you shall heare anone, this fellow will tell you all.

141 **this fellow**] (*Q1*)*;* these Fellowes *F1*

142 **counsel**] *F1* (*Q1*)

143 **'a**] they *F1;* he *Q1*

144 **you will**] you'l *F1* (*Q1*)

151 s.d. **Exit.**] *Globe*

152 **posy**] Poesie *F1* (*Q1*)

154 s.d. **two Players,**] *Globe; Q1 s.d. reads:* Enter the Duke and Dutchesse.

155 etc. s.pp. **P. King.**] *Steevens;* King. *Q2–4, F1;* Duke *Q1*

155–73] *Cf. the following version of these lines in Q1: Duke* Full fortie yeares are past, their date is gone, / Since happy time ioyn'd both our hearts as one: / And now the blood that fill'd my youthfull veines, / Runnes weakely in their pipes, and all the straines / Of musicke, which whilome pleasde mine eare, / Is now a burthen that Age cannot beare: / And therefore sweete Nature must pay his due, / To heauen must I, and leaue the earth with you. / *Dutchesse* O say not so, lest that you kill my heart, / When death takes you, let life from me depart.

156 **orbed**] *F1;* orb'd the *Q2–4*

161 etc. s.pp. **P. Queen.**] *Steevens;* Quee. *Q2–4;* Bap. *F1* (*except* Qu. *at l. 227*)*;* Dutchesse *Q1*

164 **your**] *F1, Q3–4;* our *Q2*

166] *In Q2–4 this line is followed by what appears to be a first draft of l. 167:* For women feare too much, euen as they loue, (*note the absence of a rhyming line, and see note on l. 168 below*)

167 **For**] *F1;* And *Q2–4*

167 **hold**] holds *F1*

168 **In neither aught**] *an apparent first draft of these words precedes them in Q2–4:* Eyther none, (*cf. l. 166 above*)

168 **aught**] *Malone;* ought *Q2–4, F1*

169 **love**] *F1;* Lord *Q2–4*

170 **siz'd**] *F1;* ciz'd *Q2;* ciz'st *Q3–4*

171–2 **Where . . . there.**] *om. F1* (*Q1*)

174 **their**] my *F1*

181 s.d. **Aside.**] *Capell*

181 **That's wormwood!**] Wormwood, Wormwood. *F1;* O wormewood, wormewood! *Q1*

182 s.p. **P. Queen.**] *Steevens* (*after Rowe*)*; om. Q2–4;* Bapt. *F1*

190 **the fruit**] like Fruite *F1*

196 **either**] other *F1*

197 **enactures**] ennactors *F1*

199 **joys**] *F1;* ioy *Q2–4*

199 **grieves**] *F1;* griefes *Q2–4*

204 **favorite**] fauourites *F1*

212 **devices**] *F1, Q3–4;* deuises *Q2;* demises *Q1*

216 **me give**] giue me *F1*

218–9 **To . . . scope!**] *om. F1* (*Q1*)

219 **An**] *Theobald;* And *Q2–4*

223 **once . . . wife**] *F1* (*Q1*)*;* once I be a widdow, euer I be a wife *Q2–4*

227 s.d. **Sleeps.**] *F1* (*after l. 227*)*; placed as in Rowe*

228 s.d. **Exit.**] *F1;* Exeunt. *Q2–4;* exit Lady *Q1*

230 **doth protest**] protests *F1* (*Q1*)

237 **Marry**] *F1;* mary *Q2–4* (*Q1*)

237–8 **how? tropically:**] *F1;* how tropically, *Q2–4;* how trapically: *Q1*

239 **Vienna**] guyana *Q1*

239 **Gonzago**] Albertus *Q1*

241 **of that**] o'that *F1;* A that *Q1*

243 **unwrung**] *Q3–4;* vnwrong *Q2;* vnrung *F1*

243 s.d. **Enter Lucianus.**] *placed as in F1; after l. 244, Q2–4*

245 **as good as a**] (*Q1*)*;* a good *F1*

246–7 **I . . . dallying.**] *as prose, F1* (*Q1*)*; as verse, Q2–4*

250 **mine**] my *F1*

252 **mistake**] must take *Q1*

252 **your**] (*Q1*)*; om. F1*

253 **leave**] Pox, leaue *F1;* a poxe, leaue *Q1*

256 **Confederate**] *F1* (*Q1*)*;* Considerat *Q2–3;* Considerate *Q4*

258 **ban**] bane *Q1*

258 **infected**] *F1, Q3–4* (*Q1*)*;* inuected *Q2*

260 **usurps**] (*Q1*)*;* vsurpe *F1*

260 s.d. **Pours . . . ears.**] *F1*

261 **'A**] He *F1* (*Q1*)

261 **for his**] (*Q1*)*;* for's *F1*

262 **name's**] *F1;* names *Q2–4*

262–3 **written in very**] writ in *F1*

266 **Ham. What . . . fire?**] *F1* (*Q1, reading* fires)

270 s.p. **Pol.**] All. *F1;* Cor. *Q1* (*thus supporting Q2*)

271 **Why,**] *Theobald;* Why *Q2–4, F1;* Then *Q1*

271 **strooken**] strucken *F1;* stricken *Q1*

274 **Thus**] (*Q1*)*;* So *F1*

276 **two**] *F1*

278 **players?**] Players sir. *F1*

284 **very—**] *Warburton;* very *Q2–4, F1*

291 **Ah**] Oh *F1*

296 **voutsafe**] vouchsafe *F1*

303 **with**] rather with *F1*

305 **the**] his *F1*

306 **more**] farre more *F1*

309 **start**] *F1;* stare *Q2–4*

318 **my**] *F1*

320 s.p. **Ros.**] Guild. *F1*

322 **answer**] answers *F1*

323 **as**] *om. F1* (*Q1, which om. ll. 298–330, 338–350* (You do . . . that.))

328 **stonish**] astonish *F1*

330 **impart.**] *om. F1* (*Q1*)

336 **And**] So I *F1*

338 **surely**] freely *F1*

338 **upon**] of *F1*

343 **sir**] *om. F1* (*Q1*)

344 s.d. **the . . . recorders**] one with a Recorder *F1; s.d. placed as in F1; after l. 342, Q2–4*

345 **recorders**] Recorder *F1*

345 **one.—**] *Capell* (*after Rowe*)*;* one, *Q2–4; om. F1* (*Q1*)

357 **It is**] 'Tis *F1*

358 **fingers**] finger *F1*

358 **thumbs**] *Wilson;* the vmber *Q2;* the thumb *Q3–4;* thumbe *F1*

359 **eloquent**] excellent *F1;* delicate *Q1*

367 **the top of**] *F1*

369 **it speak. 'Sblood**] it. Why *F1;* Zownds *Q1*

369 **think**] (*Q1*)*;* thinke, that *F1*

371 **fret**] can fret *F1* (*Q1*)

371 **yet**] *Q1;* not *Q2–4; om. F1*

372 s.d. **Enter Polonius.**] *placed as in Capell; after l. 373, Q2–4, F1* (*Q1*)

376 **yonder**] (*Q1*)*;* that *F1*

377 **of**] (*Q1*)*;* like *F1*

378 **mass**] Misse *F1*

378 **'tis,**] it's *F1;* T'is *Q1*

383 s.p. **Ham**] *from catchword in Q2; om. in text proper*

383–5 **Then . . . by.**] *as prose, Pope; as verse Q2–4, F1* (*Q1*)

383 **I will**] will I *F1;* i'le *Q1*

384 s.d. **Aside.**] *Staunton*

386 **Pol. I will say so.**] *F1; Q2–4 read* I will, say so. *and continue the line to Hamlet. The Q2 arrangement* (*see also l. 387 below*) *is perhaps what Shakespeare originally intended; l. 386 as pointed in Q2 and spoken by Hamlet means:* "Yes, I will come. Say so." *and should be taken as addressed to Polonius, who has lingered after the others have gone out in obedience to Hamlet's* Leave me, friends. (*immediately preceding l. 386 in Q2*)*. Q1, significantly perhaps, gives Corambis* (*i.e. Polonius*) *no exit line, suggesting that the F1 arrangement may be a later sophistication.*

386 s.d. **Exit.**] *F1;* exit Coram. *Q1* (*after l. 383*)

387 **Leave me, friends.**] *placed as in F1;*

after by and by. *l. 385, Q2–4*
387 s.d. **Exeunt . . . Hamlet.]** *Capell (subs.)*
389 **breathes]** *F1*; breakes *Q2–4*
391 **bitter . . . the]** *F1*; busines as the bitter *Q2–4*
396 **daggers]** *F1 (Q1)*; dagger *Q2–4*
399 s.d. **Exit.]** *(Q1)*; *om. F1*

III.iii

III.iii] *Capell*
Location: *Alexander (after Capell)*
6 **near 's]** dangerous *F1*
7 **brows]** Lunacies *F1*
14 **weal]** spirit *F1*
15 **many. The]** *Q5*; many, the *Q2–4, F1*
15 **cess]** cease *F1*
17 **Or]** *om. F1 (Q1, see ll. 36–72 below)*
18 **summit]** *Rowe*; somnet *Q2–4, F1 (see I.iv.70)*
19 **huge]** *F1, Q4*; hough *Q2*; hugh *Q3*
22 **ruin]** *F1*; raine *Q2–4*
23 **with]** *F1*
24 **viage]** Voyage *F1*
25 **about]** vpon *F1*
26 s.p. **Ros.]** Both. *F1*
26 s.d. **Gentlemen]** *Warburton*; Gent. *Q2–4, F1*
26 s.d. **Rosencrantz and Guildenstern]** *Hanmer*
33 **speech,]** *Theobald*; speech *Q2–4, F1*
35 s.d. **Exit Polonius.]** *Capell*; Exit. *Q2–4 (after* know. *l. 35)*
36–72] *Q1, om. everything before, begins the scene with Claudius' soliloquy, which reads as follows: King* O that this wet that falles vpon my face / Would wash the crime cleere from my conscience! / When I looke vp to heauen, I see my trespasse, / The earth doth still crie out vpon my fact, / Pay me the murder of a brother and a king, / And the adulterous fault I haue committed: / O these are sinnes that are vnpardonable: / Why say thy sinnes were blacker then is ieat, / Yet may contrition make them as white as snowe: / I but still to perseuer in a sinne, / It is an act gainst the vniuersall power, / Most wretched man, stoope, bend thee to thy prayer, / Aske grace of heauen to keepe thee from despaire. / *hee kneeles. enters Hamlet*
39 **will.]** *F1 (subs.)*; will, *Q2–4*
43 **neglect.]** *F1, Q3–4 (subs.)*; neglect, *Q2*
50 **pardon'd]** *F1*; pardon *Q2–4*
58 **shove]** *F1*; showe *Q2–4*
66 **can not]** *Capell*; cannot *Q2–4, F1*
69 **engag'd]** *F1*; ingaged *Q2–4*
69 **angels! Make]** *Theobald (subs.)*; Angels make *Q2*; Angles make *Q3–4*; Angels, make *F1*
72 s.d. **He kneels.]** *Q1*
73 **it pat]** *F1*; it, but *Q2–4*
73 **'a]** he *F1*
73 **a-praying]** praying *F1*
74 **'a]** he *F1*
75 **reveng'd]** *F1*; reuendge *Q2–3*; reuenged *Q4 (Q1)*
77 **sole]** foule *F1*
79 **Why]** Oh *F1*
79 **hire and salary]** *F1*; base and silly *Q2–4*; a benefit *Q1*
80 **'A]** He *F1 (Q1)*
81 **With all]** *F1*; Withall *Q2–4*
81 **flush]** fresh *F1*
89 **drunk asleep]** *F1*; drunke, a sleepe *Q2–4*; drinking drunke *Q1*
90 **incestious]** incestuous *F1 (Q1)*
91 **game a-swearing]** *ed. (after Cambridge)*; game a swearing *Q2*; game, a swearing *Q3–4*; gaming, swearing *F1*; game swaring *Q1*
97 s.d. **Rising.]** *Capell*

III.iv

III.iv] *Capell*
Location: *Steevens*
1 **'A]** He *F1*
4 **I'll . . . here]** I'le shrowde my selfe behinde the Arras. *exit Cor. Q1*
4 **even]** e'ene *F1*
5 **with him]** *F1*
5 **him]** him. / *Ham. within.* Mother, mother, mother. *F1; Q1 reads: Ham.* Mother, mother, O are you here?
6 **warr'nt]** *Wilson (subs.)*; wait *Q2–4*; warrant *F1*
7 s.d. **Polonius . . . arras.]** *Rowe, supported by the Q1 reading quoted at l. 4 above*
7 s.d. **Enter Hamlet.]** *placed as in F1; after* round *l. 5, Q2–4*
12 **wicked]** idle *F1*
16 **And would it]** But would you *F1*
20 **inmost]** *F1*; most *Q2–4*
22 **Help ho]** *Q3–4 (Q1)*; **Helpe how** *Q2*; Helpe, helpe, hoa *F1*
23 s.d. **Behind.]** *Rowe (subs.)*
23 **What ho, help]** *Q3–4 (subs.)*; What how helpe *Q2*; What hoa, helpe, helpe, helpe *F1*; Helpe for the Queene *Q1*
24 s.d. **Drawing.]** *Malone (after* rat?*)*; *placed as in Globe*
24 s.d. **Kills Polonius]** *F1 (after* slain. *l. 25)*; *placed as in Warburton*
24 s.d. **through the arras]** *Capell*
25 s.d. **Behind.]** *Capell*
30 **it was]** 'twas *F1*
30 s.d. **Parts . . . Polonius.]** *Capell (subs., after l. 25)*; *placed as in Dyce*
32 **better]** *(Q1)*; Betters *F1*
37 **brass'd]** braz'd *F1*
38 **be]** is *F1*
42 **off]** *F1*; of *Q2–4*
44 **sets]** makes *F1*
48 **does]** doth *F1*
49 **O'er]** Yea *F1*
50 **heated]** tristfull *F1*
50 **doom;]** *ed.*; doome *Q2–4*; doome, *F1*
51 **thought-sick]** *hyphen, F1, Q3–4*
51 **act.]** *Q3–4, F1*; act *Q2*
52 **That . . . index?]** *continued to Queen, F1; assigned to Hamlet, Q2–4*
55 **this]** his *F1*
57 **and]** or *F1*
59 **heaven-kissing]** *F1*; heaue, a kissing *Q2–4*
65 **brother]** breath *F1*
71–6 **Sense . . . difference.]** *om. F1 (Q1)*
76 **was't]** *F1*; wast *Q2–4*
77 **hoodman-blind]** *F1*; hodman blind *Q2*; hodman-blind *Q3–4*; hob-man blinde *Q1*
78–81 **Eyes . . . mope.]** *om. F1 (Q1)*
88 **And]** As *F1*
88 **panders]** *F1*; pardons *Q2–4*
89 **turn'st my]** turn'st mine *F1*
89 **eyes . . . very]** *F1*; very eyes into my *Q2–4*
90 **grained]** *F1*; greeued *Q2–4*
91 **not leave]** *F1*; leaue there *Q2–4*
92 **enseamed]** *F1*; inseemed *Q2*; incestuous *Q3–4*; *cf. Q1:* To liue in the incestuous pleasure of his bed?
93 **Stew'd]** *F1*; Stewed *Q2–4*
97 **twentith part]** twentieth patt *F1*
97 **tithe]** *F1*; kyth *Q2–4*
101 s.d. **in his nightgown]** *Q1*
104 **your]** you *F1*
117 **you do]** you *F1*; thus you *Q1*
118 **th' incorporal]** their corporall *F1*
131 **whom]** who *F1*
137] *The greatly abridged and variant conclusion of this scene in Q1 begins at the equivalent of this line and is interesting in view of Gertrude's active role in aiding Hamlet against Claudius in the sources and her attitude in the Q1 text of IV.vi (see Textual Notes): Queene* Alas, it is the weakenesse of thy braine, / Which makes thy tongue to blazon thy hearts griefe: / But as I haue a soule, I sweare by heauen, / I neuer knew of this most horride murder: / But Hamlet, this is onely fantasie, / And for my loue forget these idle fits. / *Ham.* Idle, no mother, my pulse doth beate like yours, / It is not madnesse that possesseth Hamlet. / O mother, if euer you did my deare father loue, / Forbeare the adulterous bed to night, / And win your selfe by little as you may, / In time it may be you wil lothe him quite: / And mother, but assist mee in reuenge, / And in his death your infamy shall die. / *Queene Hamlet,* I vow by that maiesty, / That knowes our thoughts, and lookes into our hearts, / I will conceale, consent, and doe my best, / What stratagem soe're thou shalt deuise. [*The last two lines seem to be a recollection of Kyd's* Spanish Tragedy, *IV.i.46–7.*] / *Ham.* It is enough, mother good night: / Come sir, I'le prouide for you a graue, / Who was in life a foolish prating knaue. / *Exit Hamlet with the dead body.*
139 **Ecstasy?]** *F1*
143 **I]** *F1*
145 **that]** a *F1*
148 **Whiles]** Whil'st *F1*
151 **on]** or *F1*
152 **ranker]** ranke *F1*
153 **these]** this *F1*
158 **live]** *F1*; leaue *Q2–4*
160 **Assume]** *F1, Q3–4*; Assune *Q2*
161–5 **That . . . on.]** *om. F1 (Q1)*
161–2 **eat, . . . this,]** *Q5*; eate . . . this *Q2–4*
165 **on. Refrain to-night]** *F1 (om. through* on.; *see above, ll. 161–5)*; on to refraine night *Q2–4*; Forbeare the adulterous bed to night *Q1*
167–70 **the next more . . . potency.]** *om. F1 (Q1)*
169 **either . . . . the devil]** *a word apparently om. Q2; many emendations suggested:* master *(Q3–4),* curb *(Malone),* quell *(Singer),* shame *(Hudson), etc.; C. J. Monro (in Cambridge) suggests reading* entertain *in place of* either, *a reading strongly argued for by A. S. Cairncross in* SQ, *IX (1958)*
170 **wondrous]** *Q4*; wonderous *Q2–3*
172 **you. For]** *F1*; you, for *Q2–4*
172 s.d. **Pointing to Polonius.]** *Rowe*
179 **This]** Thus *F1*
180 **One . . . lady.]** *om. F1 (Q1)*
182 **bloat]** *Warburton*; blowt *Q2–4*; blunt *F1*
186 **ravel]** *F1*; rouell *Q2–4*
188 **mad]** made *F1*
188 **craft. 'Twere]** *F1*; craft, t'were *Q2–4*
190 **paddock]** *F1*; paddack *Q2–4*
200 **that?]** *F1*; that. *Q2*; that, *Q3–4*
202–10 **There's . . . meet.]** *om. F1 (Q1)*
210 **meet.]** *Q5*; meete, *Q2–4*
215 **foolish]** *F1 (Q1)*; most foolish *Q2–4*
217 s.d. **Exeunt . . . Polonius.]** *F1 (Capell adding* severally*)*; Exit. *Q2–4*; Exit Hamlet with the dead body. *Q1*

IV.i

IV.i] *Q (1676); Q2–4, F1, Q1 indicate no scene or act break here, the Queen remaining on stage to meet Claudius (see III.iv. 217 s.d.); Q2–4, however, also re-enter the Queen as for a new scene*
Location: *Alexander (after Rowe)*
o.s.d. **Enter . . . Guildenstern.]** Enter King. *F1*; Enter the King and Lordes. *Q1 (Lordes being Rosencrantz and Guildenstern)*
1 **matter]** matters *F1*
1 **heaves—]** *Rowe (subs.)*; heaues, *Q2–4*; heaues *F1*
4 **Bestow . . . while.]** *om. F1 (Q1)*; *note that Rosencrantz and Guildenstern are absent in F1*
4 s.d. **Exeunt . . . Guildenstern.]** *Capell*
5 **mine own]** my good *F1*
7 **sea]** *(Q1)*; Seas *F1*
8 **mightier.]** *Rowe (subs.)*; mightier, *Q2, F1*; mightier *Q3–4*
9 **something]** *F1*; some thing *Q2–4*
10 **Whips . . . rapier,]** He whips his Rapier out, and *F1*; but whips me / Out his rapier, and *Q1*
11 **this]** his *F1 (Q1)*
22 **let]** let's *F1*
27 **'a]** He *F1*
30 **vile]** vilde *F1*
32 s.d. **Enter . . . Guildenstern.]** *placed as in Dyce; after l. 31, Q2–4; after* excuse. *l. 32, F1*
35 **mother's closet]** Mother Clossets *F1*
35 **dragg'd]** *F1, Q3–4*; dreg'd *Q2*

37 s.d. **Exeunt . . . Guildenstern.]** *Rowe;* Exit Gent. *F1;* Exeunt Lordes. *Q1*

39 **And]** To *F1*

40 **done, ...]** *apparently the last part of this line is missing in Q2–4 (om. F1, Q1 as part of a cut); Capell suggests reading* so, haply, slander,

41–4 **Whose . . . air.]** *om. F1 (Q1)*

IV.ii

IV.ii] *Pope*

Scene om. Q1

Location: *Alexander (after Capell)*

o.s.d. **Enter Hamlet.]** *F1;* Enter Hamlet Rosencraus, and others. *Q2–4*

2 **Gentlemen. (Within.) Hamlet! Lord Hamlet!]** *F1*

3 s.p. **Ham.]** *F1*

3 **But soft]** *om. F1*

4 s.d. **Enter . . . Guildenstern.]** *F1; for Q2–4, see o.s.d. above*

6 **Compounded]** *F1, Q3–4;* Compound *Q2*

18 **like . . . apple]** *Farmer conj.;* like an apple *Q2–4;* like an Ape *F1;* as an Ape doth nuttes *Q1*

28 **thing—]** *F1;* thing. *Q2–4*

30–1 **Hide . . . after.]** *F1*

IV.iii

IV.iii] *Pope*

Location: *Alexander (after Capell)*

o.s.d. **Enter . . . three.]** Enter King. *F1*

6 **weigh'd]** *F1;* wayed *Q2–4*

7 **never]** neerer *F1*

11 s.d. **Enter Rosencrantz.]** *F1* (Rosincrane); Enter Rosencraus and all the rest. *Q2–4;* Enter Hamlet and the Lordes. *Q1*

11 **How]** *F1; King.* How *Q2–4 (repeated s.p.)*

15 **Ho, . . . lord.]** *Q3–4;* How, . . . Lord. *Q2;* Hoa, Guildensterne? Bring in my Lord. *F1*

15 s.d. **Hamlet and Guildenstern]** *F1*

19 **'a]** he *F1 (Q1)*

20 **convocation]** *F1, Q4;* conuacation *Q2–3;* company *Q1*

20 **politic]** *(Q1); om. F1*

22 **ourselves]** our selfe *F1*

24 **two]** *(Q1);* to *F1*

26–8 **King. Alas . . . worm.]** *om. F1;* Looke you, a man may fish with that worme / That hath eaten of a King, / And a Beggar eate that fish, / Which that worme hath caught. *Q1*

29 s.p. **King.]** *F1, Q3–4 (Q1);* King. King. *Q2*

34 **there]** *F1, Q3–4 (Q1);* thrre *Q2*

35 **if indeed]** indeed, if *F1;* if *Q1*

36 **within]** *om. F1 (Q1)*

38 s.d. **To Attendants.]** *Capell (subs.)*

39 **'A will]** He will *F1;* hee'le *Q1*

39 **you]** *(Q1);* ye *F1*

39 s.d. **Exeunt Attendants.]** *Capell*

40 **deed,]** deed of thine, *F1*

43 **With fiery quickness]** *F1*

45 **is]** at *F1*

48–9 **I . . . mother.]** *as prose, F1; as verse, Q2–4*

48 **them]** him *F1*

51–3 **My . . . England!]** *as prose, F1; as verse, Q2–4 (Q1)*

52 **so]** and so *F1 (Q1)*

57 s.d. **Exeunt . . . Guildenstern.]** *Theobald*

64 **congruing]** coniuring *F1*

68 **were ne'er begun]** *F1;* will nere begin *Q2–4*

IV.iv

IV.iv] *Pope*

Location: *ed. (after Pelican)*

o.s.d. **Enter . . . stage.]** Enter Fortenbrasse, Drumme and Souldiers. *Q1*

3 **Craves]** *(Q1);* Claimes *F1*

8 **softly]** safely *F1*

8 s.d. **Exeunt . . . Captain.]** *Kittredge (after Theobald);* Exit. *F1;* Exeunt all. *Q1*

8. s.d. **Guildenstern,]** *Theobald; s.d. om. F1 (Q1)*

9–66 **Ham. Good . . . worth!]** *om. F1 (Q1), except l. 14 in Q1*

19 **name.]** *Pope;* name *Q2–4;* name, *Q5*

30 s.d. **Exit.]** *Capell*

31 s.d. **Exeunt . . . Hamlet.]** *Rowe (subs.)*

IV.v

IV.v] *Pope*

Location: *Alexander (after Rowe)*

o.s.d., 1–20] *For this passage in Q2–4, F1, the following lines are substituted in Q1: enter King and Queene. / King* Hamlet is ship't for England, fare him well, / I hope to heare good newes from thence ere long, / If euery thing fall out to our content, / As I doe make no doubt but so it shall. / *Queene* God grant it may, heau'ns keep my *Hamlet* safe: / But this mischance of olde *Corambis* death, / Hath piersed so the yong *Ofeliaes* heart, / That she, poore maide, is quite bereft her wittes. / *King* Alas deere heart! And on the other side, / We vnderstand her brother's come from *France,* / And he hath halfe the heart of all our Land, / And hardly hee'le forget his fathers death, / Vnlesse by some meanes he be pacified. / *Qu.* O see where the yong *Ofelia* is! *[There are some vague echoes here of ll. 74–94 below.]*

o.s.d. **a Gentleman.]** *om. F1 (which assigns his speeches to Horatio)*

2, 4 s.pp. **Gent.]** Hor. *F1*

9 **yawn]** ayme *F1*

12 **might]** would *F1*

15 **ill-breeding]** *hyphen, Rowe*

15 **minds.]** *F1;* mindes, *Q2–4*

16 s.p. **Queen.]** *from F1 at l. 14 (F1 gives ll. 14–20 to Queen); Q2–4 continue l. 16 to Horatio*

16 s.d. **Exit Gentleman.]** *Hanmer*

17 s.d. **Aside.]** *Capell*

17–20 **To . . . spilt.]** *marked with gnomic quotes, Q2–4*

20 s.d. **distracted . . . lute]** *from F1* (distracted) *and Q1, which reads:* playing on a Lute, and her haire downe singing.; *Q2–4 s.d. follows l. 16; placed as in F1*

23 **true-love]** *hyphen, Capell*

23 s.d. **She sings.]** *om. F1 (see l. 20 s.d. for Q1)*

26 **sandal]** *F1 (Q1);* Sendall *Q2–4*

28 **you?]** *F1;* you, *Q2–4*

29 etc. s.dd. **Song.]** *om. F1 (Q1) (throughout scene; in F1 the songs are in italics)*

33 **O ho!]** *om. F1 (Q1)*

36, 58 s.dd. **Sings.]** *Capell*

36 s.d. **Enter King.]** *after l. 32, F1*

38 **all]** *om. F1 (Q1)*

39 **bewept]** *F1 (Q1);* beweept *Q2–4*

39 **ground]** graue *F1 (Q1)*

40 **true-love]** *F1;* true loue *Q2–4;* true louers *Q1*

41 **do you]** do ye *F1;* i'st with you *Q1*

42 **God]** *F1 (Q1);* good *Q2–4*

46 **Pray]** Pray you *F1 (Q1)*

48–66 **"To-morrow . . . more."]** *Q1 transfers this song so that it follows l. 173 below. It is thus heard by Laertes, on whom its implications might be expected to have an especially powerful effect in arousing him further against Hamlet; Q1 also transfers the song at ll. 190–9, making it follow Ophelia's first song at ll. 23–32.*

52 **clo'es]** *Wilson;* close *Q2–4;* clothes *F1 (Q1)*

57 **Indeed]** Indeed la? *F1*

64 **(He answers.)]** *om. F1 (Q1)*

65 **'a']** *Kittredge;* a *Q2–4 (Q1);* ha *F1*

67 **thus]** this *F1*

69 **would]** should *F1*

72–3 **Good . . . night.]** *pointing from Q2–4, which, however, read* God *and* god *for* Good *and* good; Goodnight Ladies: Goodnight sweet Ladies: Goodnight, goodnight. *F1;* God be with you Ladies, God be with you. *Q1*

73 s.d. **Exit.]** *F1 (Q1)*

74 s.d. **Exit Horatio.]** *Theobald*

76 **and now behold!]** *om. F1 (Q1)*

78 **come,]** comes, *F1*

79 **battalions]** *Q (1676);* battalians *Q2–4;* Battaliaes *F1*

82 **their]** *F1*

89 **Feeds]** Keepes *F1*

89 **this]** his *F1*

92 **Wherein]** Where in *F1*

93 **person]** persons *F1*

96 **Queen. Alack . . . this?]** *F1;* How now, what noyse is that? *Q1 (spoken by the King and preceded by four lines found only in Q1: king* A pretty wretch! this is a change indeede: / O Time, how swiftly runnes our ioyes away? / Content on earth was neuer certaine bred, / To day we laugh and liue, to morrow dead.)

97 **Attend!]** *om. F1 (Q1)*

98 **is]** are *F1*

98 **Swissers]** Switzers *F1*

98 s.d. **Enter a Messenger.]** *placed as in Capell; after* death. *l. 96, Q2–4, F1*

107 **They]** *F1;* The *Q2–4*

109 s.d. **with others]** *om. F1 (Q1); Laertes' followers do not enter in Q1*

113 **this]** the *F1*

116 s.d. **Exeunt Laertes' followers.]** *Kittredge (after Theobald)*

116 **vile]** vilde *F1 (Q1)*

118 **that's calm]** that calmes *F1*

128 **Where is]** Where's *F1 (Q1)*

133–4 **pit! . . . damnation.]** *F1 (subs.);* pit . . . damnation, *Q2–4*

138 **world's]** *Pope;* worlds *Q2–4;* world *F1 (Q1)*

142 **father]** Fathers death *F1*

142 **is't]** *Q5;* i'st *Q2–4;* if *F1*

143 **swoopstake]** *from Q1* Swoop-stake-like; soopstake *Q2;* soope-stake *Q3;* soop-stake *Q4, F1*

144 **loser?]** *Q5;* looser. *Q2–4, F1;* all? *Q1*

147 **pelican]** Politician *F1*

151 **sensibly]** sensible *F1, Q4;* sencible *Q3*

152 **'pear]** *Johnson;* peare *Q2–4;* pierce *F1*

153 s.d. **"Let . . . in!"]** *as F1; given to Laertes, Q2–4*

154 s.d. **Enter Ophelia.]** *placed as in Theobald; before Laertes' speech in Q2–4, F1 (see preceding note)*

157 **paid with]** payed by *F1*

158 **Till]** *F1, Q3–4;* Tell *Q2*

158 **turn]** turnes *F1*

161 **an old]** *F1 (Q1);* a poore *Q2–4*

162–4 **Nature . . . loves.]** *F1*

165 **barefac'd]** *F1, Q3–4;* bare-faste *Q2*

166 **Hey . . . nonny,]** *F1*

167 **in]** on *F1*

167 **rain'd]** raines *F1*

171–3 **You . . . daughter.]** *as prose, F1; as verse, Q2–4 (Q1)*

171–2 **"A-down, a-down," . . . a-down-a.]** *hyphens, F1 (but reading* downe a-downe,); a downe, And you a downe a, *Q1; quotes, Wilson (after Capell)*

176 **you]** *om. F1 (Q1)*

176 **pansies]** *Johnson;* Pancies *Q2–4;* Paconcies *F1;* pansey *Q1*

180 s.d. **To Claudius.]** *Wilson*

181 s.d. **To Gertrude.]** *Wilson*

182 **herb of grace]** Herb-Grace *F1;* hearb a grace *Q1*

183 **You may]** Oh you must *F1;* you must *Q1*

185 **'a]** he *F1*

187 s.d. **Sings.]** *Capell*

188 **afflictions]** *(Q1);* Affliction *F1*

190–1 **'a . . . 'a]** he . . . he *F1 (Q1)*

195 **was]** *om. F1 (Q1)*

196 **All]** *F1 (Q1)*

199 **God 'a' mercy]** *Kittredge;* God a mercy *Q2–4 (Q1);* Gramercy *F1*

200 **Christians']** *ed.;* Christians *Q2–4;* Christian *F1;* christen *Q1*

200 **I pray God]** *F1 (Q1)*

200–1 **buy you]** buy ye *F1;* buy yous *Q3–4;* be with you *Q1*

201 s.d. **Exit.]** *F1 (Q1)*

202 **see]** *F1*

202 **O God]** you Gods *F1;* O God, O God *Q1*

203 **commune]** common *F1*

207 **collateral]** *F1;* colaturall *Q2–4*

214 **funeral]** buriall *F1*

215 **trophy]** *Q5;* Trophee *F1;* trophe *Q2;* trophae *Q3–4*

216 **rite]** *F1;* right *Q2–4*

218 call't] call *F1*

IV.vi

IV.vi] *Capell*

Location: *Alexander (after Capell)*

Scene om. Q1, which at this point contains the following scene not found in Q2–4 or F1: Enter Horatio and the Queene. / Hor. Madame, your sonne is safe arriv'de in *Denmarke,* / This letter I euen now receiv'd of him, / Whereas he writes how he escap't the danger, / And subtle treason that the king had plotted, / Being crossed by the contention of the windes, / He found the Packet sent to the king of *England,* / Wherein he saw himselfe betray'd to death, / As at his next conuersion with your grace, / He will relate the circumstance at full. / *Queene* Then I perceiue there's treason in his lookes / That seem'd to sugar o're his villanie: / But I will soothe and please him for a time, / For murderous mindes are alwayes jealous, / But know not you *Horatio* where he is? / *Hor.* Yes Madame, and he hath appoynted me / To meete him on the east side of the Cittie / To morrow morning. / *Queene* O faile not, good *Horatio,* and withall, commend me / A mothers care to him, bid him a while / Be wary of his presence, lest that he / Faile in that he goes about. / *Hor.* Madam, neuer make doubt of that: / I thinke by this the news be come to court: / He is arriv'de, obserue the king, and you shall / Quickely finde, *Hamlet* being here, / Things fell not to his minde. / *Queene* But what became of *Gilderstone* and *Rossencraft? / Hor.* He being set ashore, they went for *England,* / And in the Packet there writ down that doome / To be perform'd on them poynted for him: / And by great chance he had his fathers Seale, / So all was done without discouerie. / *Queene* Thankes be to heauen for blessing of the prince, / *Horatio* once againe I take my leaue, / With thowsand mothers blessings to my sonne. / *Horat.* Madam adue. *(four of Horatio's lines seem to echo passages in IV.vi and V.ii)*

o.s.d. and others] with an Attendant *F1*

2 Gentleman. Sea-faring men] *Ser.* Saylors *F1*

4 s.d. Exit Gentleman.] *Hanmer*

6 greeted,] *F1;* greeted. *Q2–4*

6 s.d. Sailors] Saylor *F1*

7, 9 s.pp. l. Sail.] *Capell;* Say. *Q2–4, F1*

9 'A] Hee *F1*

9 and't] *F1;* and *Q2–4*

10 came] comes *F1*

11 embassador] Ambassadours *F1*

13 s.d. Reads.] *F1* (Reads the Letter.)

16 warlike] Warlicke *F1*

18 and] *om. F1*

22 good] *F1*

24 speed] hast *F1*

25 thine] your *F1*

26 bore] *F1;* bord *Q2–4*

30 He] *F1;* So *Q2–4*

30 thine,] *F1;* thine *Q2–4*

32 Come] *F1; Hor.* Come *Q2–4 (repeated s.p.)*

32 give] *F1; om. Q2;* make *Q3–4*

IV.vii

IV.vii] *Capell*

Location: *Alexander (after Capell)*

6 proceeded] *F1;* proceede *Q2–4*

7 criminal] crimefull *F1*

8 greatness] *om. F1 (Q1, om. everything down to about l. 50)*

10 unsinow'd] vnsinnowed *F1*

11 But] And *F1*

11 th' are] *Alexander;* tha'r *Q2–4;* they are *F1*

14 She is] She's *F1*

14 conjunctive] *F1;* concliue *Q2–4*

22 loud a wind] *F1;* loued Arm'd *Q2;* loued armes *Q3–4*

24 But . . . have aim'd] And . . . had arm'd *F1*

26 desp'rate] *ed.;* desprat *Q2;* desperate *F1, Q3–4*

27 Whose worth] Who was *F1*

29 perfections—] *Pope;* perfections, *Q2–4;* perfections. *F1*

34 lov'd] *F1, Q3–4;* loued *Q2*

35 imagine—] *F1 (subs.);* imagine. *Q2–4*

35 s.d. with letters] *om. F1 (Q1)*

36 How . . . Hamlet:] *F1*

37 These] This *F1*

40 receiv'd] *F1;* receiued *Q2–4*

41 Of . . . them.] *om. F1 (Q1)*

42 s.d. Exit Messenger.] *F1*

43 s.d. Reads.] *Capell*

46 you] your *F1*

46 pardon thereunto,] *F1 (subs.);* pardon, there-vnto *Q2–4*

46 the occasion] th'Occasions *F1*

47 and more strange] *F1*

48 Hamlet.] *F1*

49 What] *F1; King.* What *Q2–4 (repeated s.p.)*

50 and] Or *F1*

53 devise] aduise *F1*

54 I am] I'm *F1*

56 shall] *F1 (Q1)*

57 didst] diddest *F1*

59 Ay, my lord,] *om. F1 (Q1)*

60 So you will] If so you'l *F1*

62 checking at] *F1;* the King at *Q2–3;* liking not *Q4*

64 device] *F1;* deuise *Q2–4*

68–81 Laer. My . . . graveness.] *om. F1 (Q1, except for a variant version of l. 68)*

71 travel] *Q4;* trauaile *Q2–3*

77 riband] *Q3–4;* ribaud *Q2*

81 Two months since] Some two Monthes hence *F1*

83 I have] I'ue *F1*

83 against,] *Hanmer;* against *Q2–4, F1*

84 can] ran *F1*

85 unto] into *F1*

88 topp'd] past *F1*

88 my] *F1;* me *Q2–4*

90 was't] *F1;* wast *Q2–4*

92 Lamord] Lamound *F1*

94 the] our *F1*

95 made] mad *F1*

98 especial] especially *F1*

100–2 The . . . them.] *om. F1 (Q1)*

100 scrimers] *Q3–4;* Scrimures *Q2*

105 you] him *F1*

106 What out of] Why out of *F1;* And how for *Q1*

114–23 There . . . ulcer:] *om. F1 (Q1)*

121 accidents] *Q4;* accedents *Q2–3*

122 spendthrift's] *Q3–4 (subs.);* spend thirfts *Q2;* spend-thrift *Q5*

125 indeed . . . son] your Fathers sonne indeed *F1*

127 sanctuarize] Sancturize *F1*

129 chamber.] *Steevens;* chamber, *Q2, F1;* chamber *Q3–4*

133 Frenchman] *F1, Q4;* french man *Q2–3*

134 o'er] on *F1*

138 pass] *F1;* pace *Q2–4*

139 Requite] Requit *F1*

140] *In Q1 and* Der bestrafte Brudermord *the suggestion for poisoning Laertes' sword comes from Claudius. In Q1 the King says:* . . . now this being granted, / When you are hot in midst of all your play, / Among the foyles shall a keene rapier lie, / Steeped in a mixture of deadly poyson, / That if it drawes but the least dramme of blood, / In any part of him, he cannot liue: / This being done will free you from suspition, / And not the deerest friend that *Hamlet* lov'de / Will euer haue Leartes in suspect.

140 that] *F1*

142 that, but dip] I but dipt *F1*

149 Weigh] *F1, Q4;* Wey *Q2–3*

150 shape. If . . . fail,] *Rowe;* shape if . . . fayle, *Q2–4;* shape, if . . . faile; *F1;* And lest that all should miss, *Q1*

154 did] should *F1*

155 cunnings] commings *F1*

156 ha't] *F1;* hate *Q2;* hau't *Q3–4*

158 that] the *F1*

159 preferr'd] *Q3–4;* prefard *Q2;* prepar'd *F1*

162 But . . . noise?] how sweet Queene. *F1;* How now Gertred, why looke you heauily? *Q1*

164 they] they'l *F1*

166 askaunt the] aslant a *F1;* by a *Q1*

167 hoary] hore *F1*

168 Therewith . . . make] There with . . . come *F1*

171 cull-cold] cold *F1*

172 crownet] *Wilson;* cronet *Q2;* Coronet *F1, Q3–4*

174 her] the *F1*

177 snatches . . . lauds] snatches of old tunes *F1;* olde sundry tunes *Q1*

181 their] *(Q1);* her *F1*

182 lay] buy *F1*

183 she is] *(Q1);* is she *F1*

190 a'] of *F1*

191 drowns] doubts *F1*

V.i

V.i] *Q (1676)*

Location: *Capell (after Rowe)*

o.s.d. with mattocks] *Q (1676)*

1 s.p. l. Clo.] *Rowe;* Clowne. *Q2–4, F1 (Q1) (throughout)*

1–2 when she] that *F1*

3 s.p. 2. Clo.] *Rowe;* Other. *Q2–4, F1 (throughout);* 2. *Q1*

3 therefore] and therefore *F1*

9 se offendendo] *F1;* so offended *Q2–4*

12 to act] an Act *F1*

12 do] doe and *F1*

12 perform; argal,] *F1 (subs.);* performe, or all; *Q2–4;* Ergo *Q1*

14 goodman] *F1;* good man *Q2–4*

16 good.] *F1 (subs.);* good, *Q2–4*

17 himself] himsele *F1*

18 that. But] *Q5 (subs.);* that, but *Q2–4;* that? But *F1*

23 an't] on't *F1*

25 a'] of *F1*

28 even-Christen] *hyphen, Furness;* euen Christian *F1*

33 'A] He *F1*

34–7 2. Clo. Why . . . arms?] *F1 (s.p.* Other)

39 thyself—] *F1;* thy selfe. *Q2–4*

43 that] *(Q1);* that Frame *F1*

55 s.d. afar off] *F1; s.d. after l. 64, Q2–4 (Q1); placed as in F1*

59 houses] *(Q1);* Houses that *F1*

59 lasts] last *Q4 (Q1)*

60 in, and] to Yaughan *F1*

60 sup] *Kermode conj. (privately);* soope *Q2–4;* stoupe *F1;* stope *Q1*

60 s.d. Exit . . . digs.] *Rowe (subs.)*

61 s.d. Song.] Sings. *F1*

64 a—was nothing—a—meet.] was nothing meete. *F1;* most meete. *Q1*

66 'a . . . grave-making] that he sings at Graue-making *F1;* That is thus merry in making of a graue *Q1*

70 daintier] *F1, Q3–4;* dintier *Q2*

71, 94 s.dd. Song.] sings *F1*

72 clawed] caught *F1*

73 into] intill *F1*

74 s.d. Throws . . . it.] *ed., from Q1 and Capell; Q1 reads:* he throwes vp a shouel.

77 'twere] it were *F1*

78 This] It *F1*

79 now o'erreaches] o're Offices *F1*

79 would] could *F1*

83 sweet] good *F1*

85 'a] he *F1 (Q1)*

85 meant] *F1, Q3–4 (Q1);* went *Q2*

88 Worm's,] *F1 (subs.);* wormes *Q2–4*

89 chopless] *Wilson;* Choples *Q2–4;* Chaplesse *F1*

89 mazzard] *F1;* massene *Q2;* mazer *Q3–4*

90 and] if *F1*

92 them] 'em *F1*

94 pickaxe] *(Q1);* Pickhaxe *F1*

97 s.d. Throws . . . skull.] *Capell*

98 may] might *F1 (Q1)*

99 of] of of *F1*

99 quiddities] Quiddits *F1;* Quirkes *Q1*

100 quillities] *Q3–4;* quillites *Q2;* Quillets *F1*

100 tenures] *F1, Q4;* tenurs *Q2–3*

101 mad] rude *F1*

106–7 **Is . . . recoveries,]** *F1*
108 **his]** *F1*
109 **double ones too]** *F1*; doubles *Q2–4*
111 **scarcely]** hardly *F1*; scarse *Q1*
115 **calves'-skins]** (*Q1*); Calue-skinnes *F1, Q3–4*
116 **which]** that *F1*
118 **sirrah]** Sir *F1*; *Q1 reads the line:* Now my friend, whose graue is this?
120 **s.d. Sings.]** *Capell*
120 **O]** *F1*; or *Q2–4*
121 **For . . . meet.]** *F1*
123 **'tis]** it is *F1*
124 **yet]** and yet *F1*
125 **it is]** 'tis *F1*
139 **this three]** these three *F1*; this seauen *Q1*
139 **I . . . of]** I haue taken note of *F1*; haue I noted *Q1*
141 **heel . . . courtier]** (*Q1*); heeles of our Courtier *F1*
142 **been]** been a *F1*
143 **all]** *F1*
144 **overcame]** o'recame *F1*
147 **that very]** the very *F1*
148 **is]** was *F1*; 's *Q1*
150 **'a]** he *F1*
150–1 **'A . . . 'a]** hee . . . he *F1* (*Q1*)
151 **'tis]** (*Q1*); it's *F1*
154 **him there,]** him, *F1*
161–2 **I . . . thirty years.]** *Q1 om. this passage which makes Hamlet thirty years old; see ll. 173–4 below.*
161 **sexton]** sixeteene *F1*
165 **Faith]** Ifaith *F1* (*Q1*)
165 **'a . . . 'a]** he . . . he *F1* (*Q1*)
166 **corses]** (*Q1*); Coarses now adaies *F1*
167 **'a]** he *F1* (*Q1*)
171 **'a]** he *F1*; it *Q1*
173–4 **hath . . . years.]** *Q2–4* (23. yeeres); this Scul, has laine in the earth three & twenty years. *F1*; hath bin here this dozen yeare, *Q1* (*Q1 thus makes Hamlet a very young man; see ll. 161–2 above*)
179 **pestilence]** pestlence *F1*; plague *Q1*
180–1 **This same skull, sir]** *repeated, F1*
181 **sir, Yorick's]** *Wilson;* sir Yoricks *Q2–4;* Yoricks *F1*; one Yorickes *Q1*
182 **s.d. Takes the skull.]** *Capell*
184 **Alas]** Let me see. Alas *F1*; I prethee let me see it, alas *Q1*
186 **bore]** borne *F1*; caried *Q1*
186 **now]** (*Q1*); *om. F1*
187 **in . . . it]** my Imagination *F1*
191 **Not]** No *F1*
192 **grinning]** Ieering *F1*
193 **chamber]** *F1* (*Q1*); table *Q2–4*
197 **a']** o' *F1*
200 **so? pah]** *Q5*; so pah *Q2*; so: pah *Q3–4*; so? Puh *F1*
200 **s.d. Puts . . . skull.]** *Collier*
204 **'a]** he *F1*
208 **it:]** it; as thus. *F1*; as thus of *Q1*
210 **to]** into *F1*
213 **imperious]** (*Q1*); Imperiall *F1*
216 **winter's]** *F1*; waters *Q2–4*
217 **awhile]** aside *F1*
217 **s.d. Enter . . . attendant.]** *based on Q2–4, F1; Q1 s.dd.:* Enter K. Q. Laertes and the corse. *Q2–4;* Enter King, Queene, Laertes, and a Coffin, with Lords attendant. *F1;* Enter King and Queene, Leartes, and other lordes, with a Priest after the coffin. *Q1* (a Doctor of Divinity *from Wilson;* following *from Q1* after)
220 **desp'rate]** disperate *F1*
221 **of]** *om. F1* (*Q1*)
222 **s.d. Retiring with Horatio.]** *Capell*
226, 235 **s.pp. Doctor.]** *Priest. F1* (*Q1, l. 226*)
227 **warranty]** warrantis *F1*
229 **been]** (*Q1*); haue *F1*
230 **prayers]** praier *F1*
231 **Shards]** *F1*
232 **allow'd]** allowed *F1*
232 **crants]** Rites *F1*
237 **a]** sage *F1*
243 **s.d. Scattering flowers.]** *Johnson*
243 **Sweets . . . sweet,]** (*Q1*); Sweets, . . . sweet *F1*
246 **have]** t'haue *F1*
246 **treble woe]** terrible woer *F1*
247 **treble]** *F1*; double *Q2–4*
249 **Depriv'd]** *F1*; Depriued *Q2–4*
250 **s.d. Leaps . . . grave.]** *F1* (*Q1 subs.*)
254 **s.d. Coming forward.]** *Collier MS* (*subs.*)
254 **grief]** griefes *F1*
256 **Conjures]** (*Q1*); Coniure *F1*
257 **wonder-wounded]** *hyphen, F1*
258 **s.d. Hamlet . . . Laertes.]** *Q1*
259 **s.d. Grappling with him.]** *Rowe*
261 **For]** Sir *F1*
261 **and]** *F1*
262 **in me something]** something in me *F1* (*Q1*)
263 **wisdom]** (*Q1*); wisenesse *F1* (*c*); wisensse *F1* (*u*)
263 **Hold off]** (*Q1*); Away *F1*
264 **All. Gentlemen!]** *om. F1* (*Q1*)
265 **s.p. Hor.]** Gen. *F1*
265 **s.d. The . . . grave.]** *Capell* (*subs.*)
269 **lov'd]** *F1, Q3–4* (*Q1*); loued *Q2*
274 **'Swounds]** Come *F1*
274 **thou't]** *Q5*; th'owt *Q2*; th'out *Q3–4*; thou'lt *F1*; thou wilt *Q1*
275 **woo't fast,]** *om. F1*; wilt fast *Q1*
276 **eisel]** *Theobald;* Esill *Q2–4;* Esile *F1*; vessels *Q1*
276 **crocadile]** (*Q1*); Crocodile *F1* (*c*); Crocadile *F1* (*u*)
277 **thou]** *F1* (*Q1*)
284 **s.p. Queen.]** Kin. *F1*; King. *Q1*
285 **thus]** *F1*; this *Q2–4*
287 **couplets]** Cuplet *F1*
292, 293 **s.dd. Exit Hamlet., Exit Horatio.]** *as in F1 and Pope; Q2–4 combine these in one s.d.* Exit Hamlet / and Horatio. *opposite ll. 292, 293* (*so Q1 after l. 292, om. l. 293*)
293 **thee]** you *F1*
294–9] *Q1 substitutes the following lines: Queene.* Alas, it is his madnes makes him thus, / And not his heart, *Leartes. / King.* My lord, t'is so: but wee'le no longer trifle, / This very day shall *Hamlet* drinke his last, / For presently we meane to send to him, / Therfore *Leartes* be in readynes. / *Lear.* My lord, till then my soule will not bee quiet. / *King.* Come *Gertred,* wee'l haue *Leartes,* and our sonne, / Made friends and Louers, as befittes them both, / Euen as they tender vs, and loue their countrie. / *Queene* God grant they may. *exeunt omnes.*
294 **s.d. To Laertes.]** *Rowe*
294 **your]** you *F1*
298 **shortly]** *F1*; thirtie *Q2* (*u*); thereby *Q2* (*c*), *Q3–4*
298 **see,]** *Q5*; see *Q2–4*; see; *F1*
299 **Till]** *F1*; Tell *Q2–4*

V.ii

V.ii] *Rowe*
Location: *Alexander* (*after Theobald*)
1 **shall you]** let me *F1*; *Q1 om. ll. 1–74*
3 **lord!]** *Capell;* Lord. *Q2–4;* Lord? *F1*
5 **Methought]** *F1, Q3–4;* my thought *Q2*
6 **bilboes]** *F1, Q3–4;* bilbo *Q2*
7 **prais'd]** praise *F1*
8 **sometime]** sometimes *F1, Q4*
9 **deep]** deare *F1*
9 **pall]** *Q2* (*u*); fall *Q2* (*c*), *Q3–4;* paule *F1*
9 **learn]** teach *F1*
11 **Rough-hew]** *hyphen, F1*
13 **me,]** *Q5*; me *Q2–4, F1*
16–7 **bold, . . . manners,]** *F1* (*subs.*); bold . . . manners *Q2–4*
17 **unseal]** *F1*; vnfold *Q2–4*
19 **Ah]** *Delius conj.;* A *Q2–4;* Oh *F1*
20 **reasons]** reason *F1*
22 **ho]** *Pope;* hoe *Q2–4;* hoo *F1*
27 **now]** me *F1*
29 **villainies]** *Capell;* villaines *Q2–4, F1*
30 **Or]** Ere *F1*
36 **yeman's]** *F3;* yemans *Q2–3;* Yeomans *F1, Q4*
37 **Th' effect]** The effects *F1*
40 **like]** as *F1*
40 **might]** should *F1*
43 **as's]** *Rowe;* as sir *Q2–4;* Assis *F1*
44 **knowing]** know *F1*
46 **those]** the *F1*
47 **allow'd]** *Q4;* alow'd *Q2–3;* allowed *F1*
48 **ordinant]** ordinate *F1*
51 **in the]** in *F1*
52 **Subscrib'd]** *F1, Q3–4;* Subscribe *Q2*
54 **sequent]** sement *F1*
55 **knowest]** know'st *F1*
57 **Why . . . employment,]** *F1*
58 **defeat]** debate *F1*
59 **Does]** Doth *F1*
63 **think]** thinkst *F1*
63 **upon—]** *Boswell;* vppon? *Q2–4;* vpon *F1*
67 **coz'nage—]** *Boswell* (*subs.*); cusnage, *Q2;* cosnage, *Q3–4;* coozenage, *F1*
68–80 **To . . . here?]** *F1; ll. 75–78 in substance in Q1*
78 **court]** *Rowe;* count *F1*
80 **s.d. young Osric]** *F1; s.d. in Q1 reads:* Enter a Bragart Gentleman.
81, 89, etc. **s.pp. Osr.]** *F1;* Cour. *Q2–4;* Gent. *Q1*
82 **humbly]** *Q3–4, F1*; humble *Q2*
87 **say]** saw *F1*
89 **lordship]** friendship *F1*
91 **sir]** (*Q1*); *om. F1*
91 **with all]** *F1, Q3–4;* withall *Q2*
92 **Put]** *F1*
94 **it is]** 'tis *F1*
98 **But yet]** *om. F1* (*Q1*)
98 **sultry]** *F1, Q3–4* (soultry); sully *Q2*
99 **for]** *F1*; or *Q2–4*
100 **sultry]** *F1, Q3–4* (soultry); soultery *Q2;* swoltery *Q1*
101 **My]** but my *F1*
102 **'a]** he *F1*
102 **laid]** *F1*; layed *Q2–4*
103 **matter—]** *Rowe;* matter. *Q2–4, F1*
104 **s.d. Hamlet . . . hat.]** *Johnson*
105 **good my lord]** in good faith *F1*
105 **my]** mine *F1*
106–43 **Sir . . . unfellow'd.]** *om. F1, except for:* Sir, you are not ignorant of what excellence *Laertes* is at / his weapon.; *om. Q1*
107 **gentleman]** *Q3–4;* gentlemen *Q2*
109 **sellingly]** *Q2* (*u*); fellingly *Q2* (*c*); feelingly *Q3–4*
114 **dozy]** *Kittredge;* dosie *Q2* (*u*); dazzie *Q2* (*c*); dizzie *Q3–4*
115 **yaw]** *Q2* (*u*); raw *Q2* (*c*), *Q3–4*
122 **sir? Why]** *Capell;* sir, why *Q2–4*
126 **to't]** too't *Q2* (*u*); doo't *Q2* (*c*), *Q3–4*
135 **me. Well, sir?]** *Globe* (*after Theobald*); me, well sir. *Q2–4*
141 **his]** *Q5;* this *Q2–4*
142 **them, . . . meed]** *Steevens;* them . . . meed, *Q2–4*
147 **King, sir]** sir King *F1*; sweete Prince *Q1*
147 **hath wager'd]** ha's wag'd *F1*; hath layd a wager *Q1*
148 **against]** *F1, Q3–4* (*Q1*); againgst *Q2*
148 **has impawn'd]** impon'd *F1*
150 **hangers]** *F1*; hanger *Q2–4*
150 **and]** or *F1*
155–6 **Hor. I . . . done.]** *om. F1* (*Q1*)
157 **carriages]** *F1*; carriage *Q2–4*
158 **germane]** *F1* (Germaine); Ierman *Q2;* German *Q3–4;* cosin german *Q1*
159 **matter]** matter: *F1*; phrase, *Q1*
159 **a]** *om. F1*; the *Q1*
160 **might be]** *F1, Q3–4;* be might *Q2* (*c*); be *Q2* (*u*)
160 **on:]** *Pope;* on, *Q2–4;* on *F1*
161 **Barb'ry]** Barbary *F1*
162 **liberal-conceited]** *hyphen, Pope*
163 **bet]** but *F1*
163–4 **all impawn'd, as]** *Wilson* (*after Malone*); all *Q2–4;* impon'd as *F1*
165–9 **Osr. The . . . answer.]** *Q1 gives two statements on the wager; the first in IV.vii: King.* Mary Leartes thus: I'le lay a wager, / Shalbe on *Hamlets* side, and you shall giue the oddes, / The which will draw him with a more desire, / To try the maistry, that in twelue venies / You gaine not three of him:; *the second, here: Gent.* Mary sir,

that yong Leartes in twelue venies / At Rapier and Dagger do not get three oddes of you, / And on your side the King hath laide, / And desires you to be in readinesse.
165 **laid, sir,**] laid *F1* (*Q1*)
166 **yourself**] you *F1*
167 **laid on**] one *F1*
167 **nine**] mine *F1*
168 **it**] that *F1*
173 **hall.**] *F1* (*subs.*); hall, *Q2–4*
174 **it is**] 'tis *F1*
176 **purpose,**] *Theobald;* purpose; *Q2–4, F1*
176 **him and**] him if *F1*
177 **I will**] Ile *F1*
179 **deliver you**] redeliuer you ee'n *F1; Q1 reads the line:* I shall deliuer your most sweet answer.
183 **Yours.**] *Jennens* (*after Capell*); Yours *Q2–4;* Yours, yours; *F1*
183 s.d. **Exit Osric.**] *Capell;* exit. *Q1*
183 **'A**] *ed.* (*Parrott-Craig conj.*); hee *F1; om. Q2–4*
184 **turn**] tongue *F1*
187 **'A . . . 'a**] He . . . hee *F1*
187 **comply**] *F1; om. Q2* (*u*); so *Q2* (*c*), *Q3–4*
188 **has**] had *F1*
188 **many**] mine *F1*
189 **breed**] Beauy *F1*
190 **out of an**] outward *F1*
191 **yesty**] *F1;* histy *Q2;* misty *Q3–4*
192 **profound**] *Bailey conj.* (*in Cambridge*); prophane *Q2–4;* fond *F1; Warburton conj.* (*in Hanmer*), fann'd
192 **winnow'd**] *F1* (winnowed); trennowed *Q2;* trennowned *Q3–4*
193 **trial**] tryalls *F1*
194 s.d., 195–208 **Enter . . . me.**] *om. F1* (*Q1, except ll. 203–4*)
196 **Osric**] *from the regular F1 form;* Ostricke *Q2–4* (*subs., throughout, except* Osrick *at l. 349 s.d.*)
208 s.d. **Exit Lord.**] *Theobald*
209 **lose**] lose this wager *F1*
212 **Thou wouldst**] but thou wouldest *F1*
212 **ill all's**] all *F1*
216 **gain-giving**] *F1;* gamgiuing *Q2;* game-giuing *Q3–4*
217 **it**] *om. F1* (*Q1*)
218 **forestall**] *F1, Q3–4;* forstal *Q2*
219 **There is**] there's a *F1* (*Q1*)
220 **now**] *F1* (*Q1*)
222 **will**] *F1, Q3–4;* well *Q2*
222 **all.**] *Rowe* (*subs.*); all, *Q2–4, F1*
223–4 **of . . . be.**] ha's ought of what he leaues. What is't to leaue betimes? *F1*
224 s.d. **A . . . state.**] *from Q2–4 and F1 s.dd.:* A table prepard, Trumpets, Drums, and officers with Cushions, King, Queene, and all the state, Foiles, daggars, and Laertes. *Q2–4;* Enter King, Queene, Laertes and Lords, with other Attendants with Foyles, and Gauntlets, a Table and Flagons of Wine on it. *F1; Q1 reads:* Enter King, Queene, Leartes, Lordes.
224 s.d. **Osric**] *Theobald*
225 s.d. **The . . . Hamlet's.**] *Johnson*
226 **I have**] I'ue *F1*
230 **a**] *om. F1* (*Q1*)
230 **distraction. What**] *Q3–4* (*subs.*); distraction, what *Q2;* distraction? What *F1*
231 **nature, honor,**] nature honour *F1*
233 **Was't . . . wrong'd**] *F1;* Wast . . . wronged *Q2–4*
238 **wronged**] wrong'd *F1*
240 **Sir . . . audience,**] *F1*
244 **brother**] (*Q1*); Mother *F1*
250 **keep**] *F1*
250 **ungor'd**] vngorg'd *F1*
250 **till**] *F1;* all *Q2–4*
252–3 **I . . . play.**] *as verse, F1; as prose, Q2–4*
252 **I**] I do *F1*
253 **brothers'**] *M. Edel* (*privately*); brothers *Q2–4, F1*
254 **Come on.**] *F1*
257 **off**] *F1;* of *Q2–4*
261 **has**] hath *F1* (*Q1*)
261 **laid**] *F1, Q3–4* (*Q1*); layed *Q2*
263 **better'd**] *F1;* better *Q2–4*
265 s.d. **Prepare to play.**] *F1*
267 **stoups**] *Johnson;* stoopes *Q2–4;* Stopes *F1*
270 **ord'nance**] Ordinance *F1*
272 **union**] *F1;* Vnice *Q2* (*u*); Onixe *Q2* (*c*), *Q3–4*
275 **trumpet**] **Trumpets** *F1*
278 s.d. **Trumpets the while.**] *om. F1* (*Q1*)
279 s.d. **They . . . hit.**] *from F1 and Q1:* They play. *F1;* a hit. / Heere they play: *Q1* (*although* a hit *is in italics and is separated from Hamlet's concluding words* come on sir:, *it is perhaps part of his speech*)
280 **my lord**] on sir *F1*
283 s.d. **sound flourish**] *ed.* (*after F1 and placed as in F1*); and shot. / Florish, *Q2–4* (*after l. 281*); *F1 s.d. reads:* Trumpets sound, and shot goes off.
283 s.d. **within**] *Capell*
284 **it**] (*Q1*); *om. F1*
285 **Come.**] *F1* (*subs.*); Come, *Q2–4*
285 s.d. **They play again.**] *Q1*
286 **A touch, a touch,**] *F1* (*Q1*)
286 **confess't**] *Q* (*1676*); confest *Q2–4;* confesse *F1;* grant *Q1*
288 **Here . . . my**] (*Q1*); Heere's a *F1*
292, 296 s.dd. **Aside.**] *Rowe*
296 **it . . . against**] 'tis almost 'gainst *F1*
297 **do**] *om. F1* (*Q1*)
299 **sure**] affear'd *F1*
300 s.d. **They play.**] *F1* (Play.)
302 s.d. **Laertes . . . rapiers.**] *Rowe* (*incorporating F1* In scuffling they change Rapiers.); They catch one anothers Rapiers, and both are wounded, Leartes falles downe, the Queene falles downe and dies. *Q1; the s.d. in* Der bestrafte Brudermord *is interesting at this point:* Dieser [i.e. Leonhardus-Laertes] lässt das Rappier fallen, und ergreift den vergifteten Degen welcher parat lieget, und stösst dem Prinzen die Quarte in den Arm. Hamlet pariret auf Leonhardo, dass sie beyde die Gewehre fallen lassen. Sie laufen ein jeder nach dem Rappier. Hamlet bekommt den vergifteten Degen, und sticht Leonhardus todt. [i.e. He lets his foil fall and seizes the poisoned sword, which is lying ready, and deals him a thrust in the left arm. Hamlet parries, so that both drop their weapons. They each run to pick up a foil. Hamlet takes the poisoned sword and kills Leonhardus (*lit.* sticks Leonhardus dead).]
303 **come**] come, *F1*
303 s.d. **Hamlet wounds Laertes.**] *Rowe* (*as end of s.d. at l. 302*); *placed as in Sisson*
303 s.d. **The Queen falls.**] *Capell after Q1* (*see l. 302 s.d.*)
303 **ho**] *Q3–4* (hoe); howe *Q2;* hoa *F1*
304 **is it**] is't *F1*
306 **own**] *om. F1* (*Q1*)
310 **pois'ned**] poyson'd *F1*
310 s.d. **Dies.**] *Rowe after Q1* (*see l. 302 s.d.*)
311 **Ho**] *Q3–4* (hoe); how *Q2;* How? *F1*
313 **Hamlet,**] *F1*
314 **med'cine**] Medicine *F1;* medecine *Q4*
315 **hour's**] *Q* (*1676*); houres *Q2–4;* houre of *F1* (*Q1*)
316 **thy**] *F1* (*Q1*); my *Q2–4*
319 **pois'ned**] (*Q1*); poyson'd *F1*
322 s.d. **Hurts the King.**] *F1*
325 **Here**] *F1, Q3–4;* Heare *Q2*
325 **incestious**] incestuous *F1*
325 **murd'rous**] *F1*
326 **off**] *F1;* of *Q2–4*
326 **thy union**] *F1* (*Q1*); the Onixe *Q2–4*
327 s.d. **King dies.**] *F1* (*Q1* The king dies.)
328 **temper'd**] temp'red *F1*
331 s.d. **Dies.**] *F1* (*Q1* Leartes dies.)
337 **strict**] strick'd *F1*
339 **cause aright**] *Q3–4;* cause a right *Q2;* causes right *F1*
341 **antique**] *Q5;* anticke *Q2;* Antike *F1, Q3–4*
343 **ha't**] *Capell;* hate *Q2–4;* haue't *F1*
344 **God**] good *F1;* fie *Q1*
345 **I leave**] liue *F1;* thou leaue *Q1*
349 s.d. **and . . . within**] *F1* (shout), *Steevens* (shot)
349 s.d. **Osric . . . returns.**] *ed., based on* Enter Osrick. *at this point in Q2–4, F1*
358 **silence.**] silence. O, o, o, o. *F1*
358 s.d. **Dies.**] *F1* (*Q1* Ham. dies.)
359 **cracks**] cracke *F1*
360 s.d. **March within.**] *Capell*
361 s.d. **English**] *F1* (*Q1* from England)
361 s.d. **Embassadors**] (*Q1, subs.*); Ambassador *F1*
361 s.d. **with . . . Attendants**] *F1; Q1 s.d. reads:* Enter Voltemar and the Ambassadors from England. enter Fortenbrasse with his traine.
362 **you**] ye *F1*
364 **This**] His *F1*
364 **proud**] *F1, Q3–4;* prou'd *Q2;* imperious *Q1*
366 **a shot**] a shoote *F1;* one draft *Q1*
367 s.p. **1. Emb.**] *Capell;* Embas. *Q2–4;* Amb. *F1* (*Q1*)
374 **commandement**] command'ment *F1*
376 **Polack**] *F3;* Pollack *Q2;* Pollock *Q3–4;* Polake *F1*
379 **th'**] *F1, Q3–4*
383 **forc'd**] *F1;* for no *Q2–4*
389 **rights,**] Rites *F1;* rights *Q1*
390 **now to**] (*Q1*); are ro *F1*
391 **also**] alwayes *F1*
392 **on**] *F1;* no *Q2–4*
394 **while**] whiles *F1*
395 **plots**] plots, *F1*
398 **prov'd**] *F1* (*Q1*); prooued *Q2–4*
398 **royal**] (*Q1*); royally *F1*
399 **rite**] *Wilson;* right *Q2–4;* rites *F1*
401 **bodies**] body *F1* (*Q1*)
403 s.d. **Exeunt**] Exeunt. / FINIS. *Q2–4;* Exeunt . . . off. / FINIS. *F1* (*see following note*); FINIS. *Q1*
403 s.d. **marching . . . off**] *F1*

Othello, the Moor of Venice

OTHELLO no less than the other great tragedies invents its own idiom. The voice of the Moor has its own orotundity, verging, as some infer, on hollowness; the dialect of Iago is appropriate to the archetypal Shakespearean evildoer. Of Cassio and Desdemona too we may use Jonson's language: "Speak, that I may see thee." Venice, Cyprus, and the sea between, give the work its particular local splendor, as of a great and typical action occurring on the outposts of civilization. For all its relative tautness of structure and simplicity of action, *Othello* enacts its story of a great man's fall into the barbarism of human nature against a scene no less regal than that of the other three masterpieces. Yet it is the uniqueness of the play, its idiosyncratic power, that impresses us most. And it proves in the patient or anxious hands of critics to be capable of a multitude of conflicting interpretations.

Othello presents the editor with an intractable textual problem, as the "Note on the Text" explains. Though publication was delayed until 1622 and 1623, the play cannot be of later date than 1604; an entry in the Revels accounts (once held to be a forgery but now authenticated) records a performance at court on November 1, 1604. It has been argued that verbal echoes of *Othello* are to be found in the "bad" quarto of *Hamlet* (1603); this is uncertain, but there is no objection to the date 1603, though present opinion favors 1604. *Othello* was, then, the next tragedy after *Hamlet*.

The source of *Othello* is a *novella* by Giraldi Cinthio, the seventh of the third decade of his *Hecatommithi*, published in Venice in 1565. There was no English translation available, and some think Shakespeare read the work in a French version by Gabriel Chappuys (Paris, 1584). Such evidence of verbal indebtedness as can be found tends to show that he looked at Cinthio's Italian, and so does his account of the wounding of Cassio. Cinthio had recommended that tragic writers should choose plots from stories of modern life, and Shakespeare takes his advice, choosing a story by the man who had called fiction the mythology of the modern world, more in touch with the values and interests of a contemporary audience than the old Greek myths.

But Shakespeare did not find in the tale the same values as Cinthio. Each, of course, exploits its themes of love, jealousy, and revenge. But to Cinthio the point of the story is, briefly, that Desdemona made an unhappy choice in marrying a man so different from her in every way—unsuitable by reason of race, creed, and education. Shakespeare indeed emphasizes the color difference, but he firmly establishes Othello as a Christian, and—not for the only time in his career[1]—allows the original moral of the story to degenerate into an aspect of the partial or evil interpretations put upon the events by disaffected or incompetent observers: Cinthio's moral is expressed only by Brabantio and Iago.

In Cinthio the principal character is known only as "the Moor." He marries Disdemona[2] against the wishes of her parents, but they live happily together in Venice. When he is appointed to command the garrison at Cyprus, he decides to take the risk of allowing Disdemona to accompany him on a dangerous voyage rather than be parted from her, and they move to Cyprus (in the same ship). There Disdemona's closest friend is the wife of the Moor's ensign. A

[1] See the introduction to *Antony and Cleopatra*.

[2] Cinthio's spelling.

frequent visitor is a captain. The Ensign, a man of hidden wickedness, passionately desires Disdemona. She gives him no encouragement and so he seeks a plan to satisfy what has become his hatred for her. His chance comes when the Captain is degraded for misbehavior. Disdemona pleads for his reinstatement, and the Ensign uses this turn of events to plant in the Moor's mind the idea that she has more than an innocent concern for the Captain's welfare. The Ensign proceeds by suggesting that the Moor's blackness had become displeasing to his wife; when the Moor demands ocular proof of her infidelity, he takes advantage of Disdemona's being in his house, visiting his wife, to steal the handkerchief the Moor had given her. He leaves it in the Captain's bedroom. The Captain tries to return it to Disdemona, but is frightened away from the house by the Moor. After a passage which is the source of the scene in which Iago questions Cassio about Bianca while Othello looks on, the Ensign is able to tell the Moor that the Captain has confessed his adultery with Disdemona and admitted that he had the handkerchief as a present from her. Questioned about the handkerchief, Disdemona is embarrassed and confused, so that the Moor thinks his suspicions confirmed, especially when the Ensign points out to him a woman sitting near a window in the Captain's house and copying the handkerchief. Disdemona concludes from the change in him that Italian ladies should not marry Moors. Meanwhile the Ensign helps the Moor to work out a plot to murder Disdemona; and himself, for a large sum of money, contracts to murder the Captain. He botches the murder, but escapes blame. Disdemona's lamentations over the Captain's injuries anger the Moor, and he and the Ensign go on to carry out her murder. The Ensign beats her to death with a stocking filled with sand, and they then pull down a portion of the ceiling to make her death appear an accident. The Moor, penitent, cashiers the Ensign, who informs on him, whereupon he is tortured, banished, and later assassinated by relatives of Disdemona.

It will be observed that Shakespeare allowed this story to change as it germinated in his mind, so that the resemblances which remain have almost the look of accidents. To discuss the nature of the differences is to discuss the whole structure and themes of the play. It will, however, be useful to note that Shakespeare ennobles the Moor, both in character and in birth, and gives to the love between him and his wife a quality of exaltation and spirituality lacking in Cinthio. At the same time he allows them no quiet married life in Venice; their marriage now begins among the tensions and alarms of a remote and embattled Cyprus. Shakespeare's Iago, though he would seduce her if he could, is so far from being in love with Desdemona that he specifically declares himself contemptuous of the very notion as he observes it in Roderigo. In the play the lovers are reunited, one might almost say married, in Cyprus; in Cinthio they travel safely in the same ship, without alarms. Emilia becomes the waiting-woman of Desdemona, and has no three-year-old child, as in Cinthio (Iago as the father of a tender infant is an improbable consideration). The handkerchief, as the foregoing summary indicates, plays a different part. In Cinthio, Iago is responsible neither for Cassio's drunken indiscretion nor for his use of Desdemona as pleader. Roderigo is an entirely new invention. The end of the story is quite changed.

To read Cinthio's little story gives one a sharpened sense of the scope of Shakespeare's mind, and also of the essentially dramatic character of his imagination. One thinks, for instance, of the development of hints and accidental suggestions into the magnificent III.iii, so audacious, so capable of bearing the weight of this great idea; and one thinks too of the famous problem of "double time" in this play. For good reasons Shakespeare wanted an intense concentration of event —the blissful reunion at Cyprus, the consummation of the marriage, interrupted by the Cassio brawl; and the next day a rapid darkening of the scene: Othello blasted, reduced from a type of magnanimity to a grotesque dupe by unsuspected wickedness and his own ignorance of men. That the events are crushed into brief time Shakespeare frequently forces us to notice. From the landing in Cyprus the whole story unfolds in a space of one and a half days. He gives Iago a much more active part in arranging disasters than Cinthio's Ensign; improviser as Iago is, he makes capital out of anything, sometimes so absurdly that for Othello simply to "send for" or meet Cassio would put an end to his schemes. But there is no time. Othello murders his wife on the second night in Cyprus.

The difficulty, of which Shakespeare was clearly aware, arises from the fact that this leaves no time for her to have had "stol'n hours of lust," certainly not to have enjoyed them repeatedly, as Iago alleges. In such allusions to frequent adultery as III.iii.340–43 and V.ii.211–12, Shakespeare slides over from Short to Long Time very successfully; the audience is not invited to consider that Othello is forgetting that Desdemona was not in the same ship as Cassio, and has had no chance since. We accept it as possible for her to have been unfaithful, though we know she was not. The trick depends upon the conventions of Elizabethan drama in respect of the treatment of time, which is habitually episodic and extensive, more as in a novel than as in a classical play. Although Shakespeare, for his purposes, can remind us that only a short time is elapsing, we shall, in the immediate absence of such reminders, assume that the action has picked out only significant spots of time, in the usual way. Thus he gets the advantages of both systems. It should be remembered that he could have avoided the problem altogether, as Boito does in his libretto for Verdi's opera. But he wanted not only plausibility but also pace and sudden shocking contrasts; he wanted white to be suddenly blackened, not to pass through indeterminate greys of growing suspicion and meanness. In the rapid progress of its plot, and the violence of its thematic oppositions, *Othello* stands in extraordinary contrast with *Hamlet*, its hesitant, deliberately delaying predecessor.

"Double time" is a classical topic of *Othello* criticism; one of its uses is to remind us that the play, more largely considered, is characterized by a kind of imaginative duplicity. Thus one can isolate a plot of monumental and satisfying simplicity without forgetting that the text can be made to support very different interpretations. The richness of the tragedy derives from uncancelled suggestions, from latent subplots operating in terms of imagery as well as character, even from hints of large philosophical and theological contexts which are not fully developed.

In the simplest terms, one could describe the main business of the play thus. Othello is a magnanimous soldier, dedicated to an unquestioned code of conduct which belongs to the field of honor rather than to the city. Considered in relation to this sphere of action, he is a complete man, self-controlled, superbly sure of his powers, and totally honest (to use the word in its broadest sense). His marriage to Desdemona, founded upon her just understanding of his virtue, is a triumph over appearances; it is grounded in reality and independent of such accidents as color or the easy lusts of the flesh; it is more like the love of Adam and Eve before than after the Fall. The archaic grandeur of Othello's diction (as in the long speeches to the Senate in I.iii) and the extreme innocence of Desdemona (as the courtly Cassio celebrates it in II.i) are ways of emphasizing these simple themes; one may see them ideally reflected in the music Verdi wrote for Otello's heroic entry, and the soaring purity of his Desdemona.

Othello has lived for nine months or so (I.iii.84) in the city. It is notable for its wealth, its power, and its justice; but also it is not Eden but a fallen world. The order in which we are allowed to see the events occur is not without its simple importance; and the first thing we see in Venice is baseness—the whining of Roderigo, the envy and the sharp low talk of Iago, and profane shouting outside a senator's house. The climate of Othello's love may be fertile, but it is plagued with flies; and before we learn that he and Desdemona love each other in total honesty, we hear them described as old black ram and white ewe, or the beast with two backs. There is room for another and more worldly view of the honesty of Desdemona's proceedings; Iago and Brabantio express it. Her penetrating to the truth of Othello under an appearance conventionally thought repulsive can seem less a result of her purity of response than of some pagan witchcraft of his. It is precisely because such a union must appear to the disenchanted worldly eye perverse or absurd that Iago can destroy it. He represents a sort of metropolitan knowingness, a pride in being without illusion and a power to impose upon others an illusory valuation of himself. He converts to his own uses all the praise of honesty which properly belongs to Othello and Desdemona. It has often been said that Shakespeare's idea of a truly evil man is one in whom, to quote Bradley, "evil is [seen to be] compatible with, and even appears to ally itself easily with, exceptional powers of will and intellect." Iago is the most striking instance. He is provided with motives for hating Othello—the false suspicion of his adultery with Emilia, and the promotion of Cassio—but the much-maligned formula "motiveless malignity" has something to recommend it. Over the ancient figure of the Vice—a familiar shape for abstract evil—Iago wears the garb of a modern devil. Iago's naturalist ethic, as expounded to Roderigo at the close of Act I, is a wicked man's version of Montaigne, an instance of the way in which men convert to evil the precepts of a common sense supported by no act of faith. The reason which commands the sensuality of an unfallen Adam or an unfallen Othello controls also the carnal stings of an Iago, but for ends which, in the absence of *Aberglaube*, of the love which alone makes society tolerable, become entirely and monstrously selfish.

The storm divides the lovers and reunites them in an absolute content, honorably and courteously celebrated by Cassio; but again their nuptial night is disturbed by a civic brawl, and this time courtesy is permanently dishonored. Cassio, cashiered, thinks he has lost what Othello is soon really to lose, his reputation: "I have lost the immortal part of myself, and what remains is bestial" (II.iii.263–64). (We must think of "reputation" as meaning not merely the good word of others, but that self-respect which is indispensable to social beings, and without which they cannot function well in private or public life. Without it, a man is no more than a beast.) The object of Iago's wit is to make Othello see Desdemona and love as deceitful and bestial; to destroy the harmonies of honor and replace them with more lifelike discords. Dramaturgically, the central problem of the enterprise was to make plausible the corruption of Othello's mind, and Iago's success in persuading him to assess the world not by the old assumptions of honor, but as Thersites might. It is very important to see that Othello's self-estimate—"one not easily jealous, but, being wrought, / Perplexed in the extreme" (V.ii.345–46)—is, as Bradley says, "perfectly just," and perfectly consistent with the release of unsuspected grossness of language and imagery under the shock of discovering infidelity in the loved one. The peculiar pain of sexual jealousy is deeply involved with the excremental aspect of the sexual organs, and the emotion in betrayal in a supremely intimate trust is involved with agonizing associations of filth and animality. This kind of shock has no necessary connection with temperamental jealousy, that is, holding a partner in habitual suspicion. There are similarities, of course—neither the permanently jealous man, nor the man who suffers the single shock of a discovered infidelity can bear the thought that he keeps "a corner in the thing [he loves] / For others' uses" (III.iii.272–73). But Othello's is the case of the man who knows nothing of the infernal power of jealousy till he is suddenly and by evil led into an unsuspected area of human experience, an area where innocence merely increases the pain and shock. And it is worth noting that Shakespeare, who shows with incomparable authenticity the surrender of Othello's mind to these dark experiences, shows him also restored to dignity, though still terribly in error, in the scene of Desdemona's murder (Shakespeare's honorable murderers always behave like priests at a sacrifice) and in the self-recognition of the closing moments.

All these effects, however, depend on the success of the temptation—or corruption—scene, III.iii. There are expert witnesses who read this scene as evidence that Othello succumbs too quickly, that he is a hollow man ironically represented as incapable of dealing with reality except in the narrow selection of it made by conventional men of honor. There may be, in the stream, an eddy or two that can be interpreted thus; but that this reading perverts the main movement of the play there is surely little doubt. The whiteness of Desdemona blackened, we see the white and tranquil mind of Othello darkened by atavistic shock and disgust—"where's that palace whereinto foul things / Sometimes intrude not?" (III.iii.137–38). This must happen quickly, yet not implausibly; there is the basic technical problem, and Shakespeare solves it with intelligence and resource. Iago hints, is disarmed by Desdemona's innocent candor. She pleads, is indulgently heard, and departs:

> *Oth.* Excellent wretch! Perdition catch my soul
> But I do love thee! and when I love thee not,
> Chaos is come again.
> *Iago.* My noble lord—

Iago at once begins again, and within a hundred lines his wit has ensnared Othello. As J. C. Maxwell says, the central speech is Othello's at lines 177–92, and I can do no more than echo his very penetrating remarks on it. Othello's demand for ocular proof to settle the matter of Desdemona's fidelity is logically absurd, since there could be no such proof of *fidelity*; evidence can only be on the other side.

> Once Othello's mind is turned in this direction, Iago can consolidate his position by infecting Othello with his own gross visualizing lust; he can do so in part by insisting on what Othello will *not* be able to see (III.iii.395–409), and he also has in reserve the one tangible and visible token, the handkerchief. It is not introduced until all the ground has been prepared for its transformation. In the world to which the love of Othello and Desdemona belongs, it is a token of unquestioning faith. In the world into which Iago has initiated Othello, it becomes merely divorce-court evidence.[1]

Henceforth Desdemona appears to Othello "a supersubtle Venetian," an inhabiter of the fallen world; he himself, as he later recognizes, becomes for a time "an erring barbarian." He accepts, though with horror, Iago's version of the world; he begins to use Iago's gross vocabulary. There is the singularly horrible opening of Act IV, a crescendo of prurience which ends with Othello's lapse from an unbearable consciousness. Thereafter follows a passage which dreadfully adapts a scene from farce, as Othello eavesdrops on Cassio and Bianca; then the public display of his disgraced condition before the Venetian envoys, and the "brothel" scene.

Out of the confusions of the last act one certainty emerges, and that in the mind of Othello himself. It is no use asking the devil why he ensnares souls; but one can at least see what it is to be fallen, one's occupation gone. Othello's final speech is perhaps not the whole story, but neither is it untruthful. He has behaved like the Turk (used throughout the play as an enemy of civility and grace, a type of cunning and disorder). He has become that person of different "clime, complexion, and degree" whom it was wanton of Desdemona to marry. He has beaten a Venetian and traduced the state. So he punishes himself as he punished the Turk. Apart from Gratiano's "All that is spoke is marr'd," there is no reference to the impropriety of this act in the Christian Othello; this is not to Shakespeare's purpose. Othello is self-recognized as a Turk. He is an enemy of Venice, and the justice he carries out is that of the city, ideally considered.

Thus a simple (and fragmentary) reading of the play, or its main plot. But such a reading can conform to no one's total impression of the play; so much goes on in it that stands in no logical relation to this primary movement. This is proved by the gross evidence of many different readings. Some defend Iago, others develop critical positions which almost impose on the play a sophisticated version of Cinthio's moral. The play can be quoted in favor of a reading so consistently brilliant and perverse as that of W. H. Auden, for instance (Iago as practical joker, "trying to find out what Othello's like"; perhaps Cassio really did have the dream Iago describes; Desdemona cannot cope with Othello's alien sensibility; Othello's early appearance of good nature is merely a compensation for his suspicion and insecurity; the audience is expected to blame his stupidity in failing to spot the absurdity of Iago's story). At the end of that road lie speculations like those on the sex of Hamlet. Nevertheless there are in *Othello* quite strongly developed thematic patterns which modify the simple account of its action given above. R. B. Heilman has given a notable account in his *Magic in the Web* of the ways in which "poetry" modifies "plot." There is the further point that, taut as *Othello* seems in structure, it shares with most of Shakespeare's plays a certain deliberate redundancy of detail and character. Roderigo, for instance, is dispensable; he serves no real purpose except to keep Iago in funds. Yet he provides a valuable parallel instance of gratuitous corruption by Iago ("'tis but a man gone"). The Clown is inessential, but the play is not quite the same without him. There are the passages which tell us about events rather than narrate them: Cassio's conversation with Iago about Desdemona's beauty, Emilia's views on chastity; all this intangibly contributes to theme and atmosphere. Above all there are the recurrent words and images, bringing simultaneity to what, in the simplest mode, unfolds chronologically, and so endlessly complicating the meaning.

[1] "Shakespeare: The Middle Plays," in *The Age of Shakespeare*, ed. Boris Ford (Penguin Books, 1955), page 225.

There is, finally, the figural aspect of the work. Obscurely, it is, no doubt, an enactment of the Fall. There are psychological analogues, so that we can momentarily see the play as a psychomachia, with Iago as the bestial parts of man, and Othello as the higher—as, in a high sense, Reputation. None of this is inconsistent with a sober plain view of the play as a representation of human reality; the truer that representation, the more it suggests conformity to ancient schemes and formulae explaining the human condition. The greatness of *Othello* lies, in the end, there—in the beautiful complexity with which it renders an individual instance of generic Pascalian man, repository of truth, sink of uncertainty and error. "Whence it appears clearly that, by means of grace, man is made like God and participates in his divinity; and that without grace, he resembles the beasts of the field." So Pascal; and somewhere off the margins of the text the meaning of Shakespeare's Reputation touches that of Grace.

Frank Kermode

"Men whose heads / Do grow beneath their shoulders." From *The Voyages and Travels of Sir John Mandeville* (1582). The quotation above from *Othello*, I.iii.144–45, illustrates something of the unnatural natural history that Shakespeare knew how to turn to his purpose to lend an exotic touch to Othello's romantic background. The book from which the woodcut is taken is an Elizabethan reprint of the fabulous journeys ascribed to Sir John Mandeville, first compiled, from various sources, in the fourteenth century. It is full of reports of other wonders equally well authenticated. As Celia says (*As You Like It*, III.ii.191–93), "most wonderful wonderful! and yet again wonderful, and after that, out of all hooping!" (*Curators of the Bodleian Library*)

The Tragedy of Othello, the Moor of Venice

THE NAMES OF THE ACTORS

DUKE OF VENICE
BRABANTIO, [*a senator*,] *father to Desdemona*
[*Other*] SENATORS
GRATIANO, [*brother to Brabantio*] } *two noble*
LODOVICO, [*kinsman to Brabantio*] } *Venetians*
OTHELLO, *the Moor*, [*in the military service of Venice*]
CASSIO, *an honorable lieutenant*
IAGO, [*an ensign*,] *a villain*
RODERIGO, *a gull'd gentleman*

MONTANO, *governor of Cyprus* [*before Othello*]
CLOWN, [*servant to Othello*]

DESDEMONA, [*daughter to Brabantio and*] *wife to Othello*
EMILIA, *wife to Iago*
BIANCA, *a courtezan*

GENTLEMEN *of Cyprus*, SAILORS, [OFFICERS, MESSENGER, HERALD, MUSICIANS, *and* ATTENDANTS]

[SCENE: *Venice; a sea-port in Cyprus*]

ACT I, SCENE I

Enter RODERIGO *and* IAGO.

Rod. [Tush,] never tell me! I take it much unkindly
That thou, Iago, who hast had my purse
As if the strings were thine, shouldst know of this.
Iago. ['Sblood,] but you'll not hear me.
If ever I did dream of such a matter,
Abhor me.
Rod. Thou toldst me thou didst hold him in thy hate.
Iago. Despise me if I do not. Three great ones of the city,
In personal suit to make me his lieutenant,
Off-capp'd to him; and, by the faith of man,
I know my price, I am worth no worse a place.
But he (as loving his own pride and purposes)
Evades them with a bumbast circumstance
Horribly stuff'd with epithites of war,
[And in conclusion,]
Nonsuits my mediators; for, "Certes," says he,
"I have already chose my officer."
And what was he?
Forsooth, a great arithmetician,
One Michael Cassio, a Florentine
(A fellow almost damn'd in a fair wife),
That never set a squadron in the field,
Nor the division of a battle knows
More than a spinster—unless the bookish theoric,
Wherein the [toged] consuls can propose
As masterly as he. Mere prattle, without practice,
Is all his soldiership. But he, sir, had th' election;
And I, of whom his eyes had seen the proof
At Rhodes, at Cyprus, and on [other] grounds
Christen'd and heathen, must be belee'd and calm'd
By debitor and creditor—this counter-caster,
He (in good time!) must his lieutenant be,
And I ([God] bless the mark!) his Moorship's ancient.
Rod. By heaven, I rather would have been his hangman.
Iago. Why, there's no remedy. 'Tis the curse of service;
Preferment goes by letter and affection,
And not by old gradation, where each second

Words and passages enclosed in square brackets in the text above are either emendations of the copy-text or additions to it. The Textual Notes immediately following the play cite the earliest authority for every such change or insertion and supply the reading of the copy-text wherever it is emended in this edition.

I.i. Location: Venice. A street.
3. this: i.e. Othello's marriage to Desdemona.
4. 'Sblood: by God's (Christ's) blood.
13. bumbast: bombast, a cotton material used for padding; here, inflated. The figure is continued in *stuff'd* (line 14). circumstance: circumlocution, rigmarole.
14. epithites of war: military jargon (*epithites*, a variant spelling of *epithets*, = expressions, terms).
16. Nonsuits: refuses. Certes: certainly.
19. arithmetician: i.e. one adept at figures, not at fighting; cf. line 31.
21. almost . . . wife. Unexplained. Perhaps Shakespeare originally intended to follow his source Cinthio in giving Cassio a wife. There is no evidence that Cassio has yet met Bianca.
23. division: arrangement. battle: battalion.
24. spinster: i.e. housewife (one of whose duties was spinning).
25. toged: wearing togas (dressed for the council-chamber, not the battlefield). consuls: senators. propose: talk.
28. his: i.e. Othello's.
30. be . . . calm'd: have the wind taken out of my sails and be left becalmed.
31. debitor and creditor: i.e. bookkeeper. counter-caster: accountant; literally, one who calculates with the aid of metal counters.
32. in good time. Ironic. 33. ancient: ensign, standard-bearer.
34. his hangman: the one to hang him.
36. Preferment: advancement. letter and affection: private recommendation and favoritism.
37. old gradation: seniority, as in the good old days.

Stood heir to th' first. Now, sir, be judge yourself
Whether I in any just term am affin'd
To love the Moor.
Rod. I would not follow him then.
Iago. O, sir, content you;
I follow him to serve my turn upon him.
We cannot all be masters, nor all masters
Cannot be truly follow'd. You shall mark
Many a duteous and knee-crooking knave
That (doting on his own obsequious bondage)
Wears out his time, much like his master's ass,
For nought but provender, and when he's old, cashier'd.
Whip me such honest knaves. Others there are
Who, trimm'd in forms and visages of duty,
Keep yet their hearts attending on themselves,
And throwing but shows of service on their lords,
Do well thrive by them; and when they have lin'd their coats,
Do themselves homage. These fellows have some soul,
And such a one do I profess myself. For, sir,
It is as sure as you are Roderigo,
Were I the Moor, I would not be Iago.
In following him, I follow but myself;
Heaven is my judge, not I for love and duty,
But seeming so, for my peculiar end;
For when my outward action doth demonstrate
The native act and figure of my heart
In complement extern, 'tis not long after
But I will wear my heart upon my sleeve
For daws to peck at: I am not what I am.
Rod. What a [full] fortune does the thick-lips owe
If he can carry't thus!
Iago. Call up her father.
Rouse him, make after him, poison his delight,
Proclaim him in the streets; incense her kinsmen,
And though he in a fertile climate dwell,
Plague him with flies. Though that his joy be joy,
Yet throw such [changes] of vexation on't,
As it may lose some color.
Rod. Here is her father's house, I'll call aloud.
Iago. Do, with like timorous accent and dire yell
As when, by night and negligence, the fire
Is spied in populous cities.
Rod. What ho! Brabantio, Signior Brabantio, ho!
Iago. Awake! what ho, Brabantio! thieves, thieves!
Look to your house, your daughter, and your bags!
Thieves, thieves!

[*Enter* BRABANTIO] *above* [*at a window*].

Bra. What is the reason of this terrible summons?
What is the matter there?
Rod. Signior, is all your family within?
Iago. Are your doors lock'd?
Bra. Why? Wherefore ask you this?
Iago. ['Zounds,] sir, y' are robb'd! For shame, put on your gown;
Your heart is burst, you have lost half your soul;
Even now, now, very now, an old black ram
Is tupping your white ewe. Arise, arise!
Awake the snorting citizens with the bell,
Or else the devil will make a grandsire of you.
Arise, I say!
Bra. What, have you lost your wits?
Rod. Most reverend signior, do you know my voice?
Bra. Not I; what are you?
Rod. My name is Roderigo.
Bra. The worser welcome;
I have charg'd thee not to haunt about my doors.
In honest plainness thou hast heard me say
My daughter is not for thee; and now, in madness
(Being full of supper and distemp'ring draughts),
Upon malicious [bravery] dost thou come
To start my quiet.
Rod. Sir, sir, sir—
Bra. But thou must needs be sure
My spirits and my place have in their power
To make this bitter to thee.
Rod. Patience, good sir.
Bra. What tell'st thou me of robbing? This is Venice;
My house is not a grange.
Rod. Most grave Brabantio,
In simple and pure soul I come to you.

Iago. ['Zounds,] sir, you are one of those that will not serve God, if the devil bid you. Because we come to do you service, and you think we are ruffians, you'll have your daughter cover'd with a Barbary horse, you'll have your nephews neigh to you; you'll have coursers for cousins, and gennets for germans.

Bra. What profane wretch art thou?

Iago. I am one, sir, that comes to tell you your daughter and the Moor are [now] making the beast with two backs.

Bra. Thou art a villain.
Iago. You are a senator.
Bra. This thou shalt answer; I know thee, Roderigo.
Rod. Sir, I will answer any thing. But I beseech you,
If't be your pleasure and most wise consent
(As partly I find it is) that your fair daughter,
At this odd-even and dull watch o' th' night,

39. term: respect. **affin'd:** bound.
41. content you: calm yourself. **48. cashier'd:** dismissed.
50. trimm'd . . . duty: wearing the manners and countenance of humble service.
60. peculiar: private. **62. figure:** shape.
63. complement extern: external show corresponding to these hidden motives. **66. thick-lips:** i.e. Othello. **owe:** own.
67. carry't thus: carry this off.
70. though . . . dwell: i.e. though his general situation is a fortunate one. *Climate* = region, country.
71. flies: i.e. petty annoyances.
72. changes of vexation: vexatious changes.
73. some color: i.e. some of its fresh gloss.
75. timorous: terrifying.
76. by . . . negligence: at night and as the result of negligence.

86. 'Zounds: by God's (Christ's) wounds. **90. snorting:** snoring.
99. distemp'ring: disordering, intoxicating.
100. Upon malicious bravery: with hostile intent to defy me.
101. start: startle. **106. grange:** isolated farmhouse.
107. simple: sincere. **112. nephews:** i.e. grandsons.
113. coursers: horses. **cousins:** kinsmen. **gennets:** Spanish horses. **germans:** close relatives.
118. villain: base fellow. **119. answer:** be held answerable for.
123. odd-even: i.e. about midnight, when there is scarcely any distinction between the end of one day and the beginning of the next.

Transported with no worse nor better guard
But with a knave of common hire, a gundolier,
To the gross clasps of a lascivious Moor—
If this be known to you, and your allowance,
We then have done you bold and saucy wrongs;
But if you know not this, my manners tell me
We have your wrong rebuke. Do not believe
That, from the sense of all civility,
I thus would play and trifle with your reverence.
Your daughter (if you have not given her leave),
I say again, hath made a gross revolt,
Tying her duty, beauty, wit, and fortunes
In an extravagant and wheeling stranger
Of here and every where. Straight satisfy yourself.
If she be in her chamber or your house,
Let loose on me the justice of the state
For thus deluding you.
Bra. Strike on the tinder, ho!
Give me a taper! Call up all my people!
This accident is not unlike my dream,
Belief of it oppresses me already.
Light, I say, light! *Exit [above].*
Iago. Farewell; for I must leave you.
It seems not meet, nor wholesome to my place,
To be producted (as, if I stay, I shall)
Against the Moor; for I do know the state
(How ever this may gall him with some check)
Cannot with safety cast him, for he's embark'd
With such loud reason to the Cyprus wars
(Which even now stands in act) that, for their souls,
Another of his fadom they have none
To lead their business; in which regard,
Though I do hate him as I do hell-pains,
Yet, for necessity of present life,
I must show out a flag and sign of love,
Which is indeed but sign. That you shall surely find him,
Lead to the Sagittary the raised search;
And there will I be with him. So farewell. *Exit.*

Enter [below] BRABANTIO *[in his night-gown] with* SERVANTS *and torches.*

Bra. It is too true an evil; gone she is;
And what's to come of my despised time
Is nought but bitterness. Now, Roderigo,
Where didst thou see her?—O unhappy girl!—
With the Moor, say'st thou?—Who would be a father!—

124. with: by. **125. But:** than. **gundolier:** gondolier.
127. allowance: approval. **128. saucy:** insolent.
131. from . . . civility: contrary to all sense of decency.
136. extravagant: expatriate; literally, wandering beyond his due limits. **wheeling:** roving. **stranger:** foreigner.
137. Straight: straightway. **142. accident:** occurrence.
146. producted: produced, brought forward (to give evidence).
148. gall . . . check: bring on him some irritating rebuke (*gall* = rub sore). **149. cast:** dismiss.
150. loud reason: i.e. evident rightness of choice.
151. stands in act: are under way.
152. fadom: fathom, i.e. capability.
153. in which regard: because of which consideration.
158. Sagittary: an inn (so called because its sign bore the conventional figure of Sagittarius, the Archer—a Centaur shooting an arrow). **raised search:** party of searchers who have been roused from their beds.
159 s.d. night-gown: dressing gown.
161. what's . . . time: the hateful remainder of my life.

How didst thou know 'twas she?—O, she deceives me
Past thought!—What said she to you?—Get moe tapers;
Raise all my kindred.—Are they married, think you?
Rod. Truly, I think they are.
Bra. O heaven! how got she out? O treason of the blood!
Fathers, from hence trust not your daughters' minds
By what you see them act. Is there not charms
By which the property of youth and maidhood
May be abus'd? Have you not read, Roderigo,
Of some such thing?
Rod. Yes, sir, I have indeed.
Bra. Call up my brother.—O would you had had her!—
Some one way, some another.—Do you know
Where we may apprehend her and the Moor?
Rod. I think I can discover him, if you please
To get good guard and go along with me.
Bra. Pray you lead on. At every house I'll call
(I may command at most).—Get weapons, ho!
And raise some special officers of [night].—
On, good Roderigo, I will deserve your pains.
Exeunt.

SCENE II

Enter OTHELLO, IAGO, ATTENDANTS *with torches.*

Iago. Though in the trade of war I have slain men,
Yet do I hold it very stuff o' th' conscience
To do no contriv'd murder. I lack iniquity
Sometime to do me service. Nine or ten times
I had thought t' have yerk'd him here under the ribs.
Oth. 'Tis better as it is.
Iago. Nay, but he prated,
And spoke such scurvy and provoking terms
Against your honor,
That with the little godliness I have
I did full hard forbear him. But I pray you, sir,
Are you fast married? Be assur'd of this,
That the magnifico is much belov'd,
And hath in his effect a voice potential
As double as the Duke's. He will divorce you,
Or put upon you what restraint or grievance
The law (with all his might to enforce it on)
Will give him cable.
Oth. Let him do his spite;
My services which I have done the signiory
Shall out-tongue his complaints. 'Tis yet to know—

166. moe: more. **169. of the blood:** within the family.
171. charms: magic spells. **172. property:** nature.
173. abus'd: deceived.
178. discover: uncover, bring to light.
181. I . . . most: i.e. I can be sure of help from most of them.
183. deserve: i.e. reward.

I.ii. Location: Venice. Another street.
1. trade: i.e. actual business. **2. stuff:** material, substance.
3. contriv'd: premeditated. **5. yerk'd:** stabbed.
10. did . . . him: had a hard time keeping my hands off him.
13. potential: powerful.
14. double: of double strength (like the Duke's voting power in the Senate). **17. cable:** scope (cf. "give one rope enough").
18. signiory: Venetian government.
19. yet to know: not yet public knowledge.

Which, when I know that boasting is an honor,
I shall [provulgate]—I fetch my life and being
From men of royal siege, and my demerits
May speak, unbonneted, to as proud a fortune
As this that I have reach'd; for know, Iago,
But that I love the gentle Desdemona,
I would not my unhoused free condition
Put into circumscription and confine
For the sea's worth. But look, what lights come yond?

Enter Cassio *with* [Officers *and*] *torches*.

Iago. Those are the raised father and his friends.
You were best go in.

Oth. Not I; I must be found.
My parts, my title, and my perfect soul
Shall manifest me rightly. Is it they?

Iago. By Janus, I think no.

Oth. The servants of the [Duke]? and my lieutenant?
The goodness of the night upon you, friends!
What is the news?

Cas. The Duke does greet you, general,
And he requires your haste-post-haste appearance,
Even on the instant.

Oth. What is the matter, think you?

Cas. Something from Cyprus, as I may divine;
It is a business of some heat. The galleys
Have sent a dozen sequent messengers
This very night at one another's heels;
And many of the consuls, rais'd and met,
Are at the Duke's already. You have been hotly call'd for;
When, being not at your lodging to be found,
The Senate hath sent about three several quests
To search you out.

Oth. 'Tis well I am found by you.
I will but spend a word here in the house,
And go with you. [*Exit*.]

Cas. Ancient, what makes he here?

Iago. Faith, he to-night hath boarded a land carract.
If it prove lawful prize, he's made for ever.

Cas. I do not understand.

Iago. He's married.

Cas. To who?

[*Enter* Othello.]

Iago. Marry, to—Come, captain, will you go?

Oth. Have with you.

Cas. Here comes another troop to seek for you.

21. provulgate: make publicly known.
22. siege: seat, i.e. rank. **demerits:** deserts, merits.
23. unbonneted. Explained either as "without taking my hat off, i.e. on equal terms" (the opposite of the word's expected meaning, but in *Coriolanus*, II.ii.27, *bonneted* = took off their caps) or as a parenthetical "I say it in all due modesty."
26. unhoused: unconfined.
28. the sea's worth: all the treasure in the sea.
31. parts: qualities, personal merits. **title:** position. **perfect soul:** clear conscience, conviction that I have done no wrong.
33. Janus: the two-faced god (dear to Iago).
38. matter: business. **41. sequent:** one after another.
49. makes he: is he doing.
50. carract: carrack, large trading ship. **51. prize:** booty.
53. Marry: indeed (originally, the name of the Virgin Mary used as an oath). **Have with you:** a formula equivalent to "yes, let's go."

Enter Brabantio, Roderigo, *with* Officers [*with*] *torches* [*and weapons*].

Iago. It is Brabantio. General, be advis'd,
He comes to bad intent.

Oth. Holla, stand there!

Rod. Signior, it is the Moor.

Bra. Down with him, thief!

[*They draw on both sides*.]

Iago. You, Roderigo! come, sir, I am for you.

Oth. Keep up your bright swords, for the dew will rust them.
Good signior, you shall more command with years
Than with your weapons.

Bra. O thou foul thief, where hast thou stow'd my daughter?
Damn'd as thou art, thou hast enchanted her,
For I'll refer me to all things of sense,
If she in chains of magic were not bound,
Whether a maid so tender, fair, and happy,
So opposite to marriage that she shunn'd
The wealthy curled [darlings] of our nation,
Would ever have, t' incur a general mock,
Run from her guardage to the sooty bosom
Of such a thing as thou—to fear, not to delight!
Judge me the world, if 'tis not gross in sense,
That thou hast practic'd on her with foul charms,
Abus'd her delicate youth with drugs or minerals
That weakens motion. I'll have't disputed on,
'Tis probable, and palpable to thinking.
I therefore apprehend and do attach thee
For an abuser of the world, a practicer
Of arts inhibited and out of warrant.
Lay hold upon him, if he do resist
Subdue him at his peril.

Oth. Hold your hands,
Both you of my inclining, and the rest.
Were it my cue to fight, I should have known it
Without a prompter. Whither will you that I go
To answer this your charge?

Bra. To prison, till fit time
Of law and course of direct session
Call thee to answer.

Oth. What if [I] do obey?
How may the Duke be therewith satisfied,
Whose messengers are here about my side,
Upon some present business of the state,
To bring me to him?

Off. 'Tis true, most worthy signior;
The Duke's in council, and your noble self
I am sure is sent for.

Bra. How? the Duke in council?
In this time of the night? Bring him away;
Mine's not an idle cause. The Duke himself,

55. advis'd: on your guard. **59. Keep up:** sheathe.
63. enchanted: bewitched, cast a spell upon.
64. refer . . . sense: i.e. submit my case to the court of ordinary common sense. **71. fear:** frighten.
72. gross in sense: obvious to perception (synonymous with *palpable to thinking* in line 76). **73. practic'd on:** plotted against.
75. motion: the mental powers. **I'll . . . on:** I'll submit it to experts for judgment. **77. attach:** arrest.
79. inhibited: prohibited. **out of warrant:** unwarrantable, illegal.
82. inclining: party. **86. direct:** regular. **94. away:** right along.
95. idle: trivial.

Or any of my brothers of the state,
Cannot but feel this wrong as 'twere their own;
For if such actions may have passage free,
Bond-slaves and pagans shall our statesmen be.
Exeunt.

Scene III

Enter Duke [*and*] Senators [*set at a table, with lights*] *and* Officers.

Duke. There's no composition in [these] news
That gives them credit.
1. Sen. Indeed, they are disproportioned;
My letters say a hundred and seven galleys.
Duke. And mine, a hundred forty.
2. Sen. And mine, two hundred!
But though they jump not on a just accompt
(As in these cases where the aim reports,
'Tis oft with difference), yet do they all confirm
A Turkish fleet, and bearing up to Cyprus.
Duke. Nay, it is possible enough to judgment.
I do not so secure me in the error
But the main article I do approve
In fearful sense.
Sailor. (*Within.*) What ho, what ho, what ho!

Enter Sailor.

Off. A messenger from the galleys.
Duke. Now? what's the business?
Sail. The Turkish preparation makes for Rhodes,
So was I bid report here to the state
By Signior Angelo. [*Exit Sailor.*]
Duke. How say you by this change?
1. Sen. This cannot be
By no assay of reason; 'tis a pageant
To keep us in false gaze. When we consider
Th' importancy of Cyprus to the Turk,
And let ourselves again but understand
That, as it more concerns the Turk than Rhodes,
So may he with more facile question bear it,
For that it stands not in such warlike brace,
But altogether lacks th' abilities
That Rhodes is dress'd in—if we make thought of this,
We must not think the Turk is so unskillful
To leave that latest which concerns him first,
Neglecting an attempt of ease and gain
To wake and wage a danger profitless.
Duke. Nay, in all confidence, he's not for Rhodes.
Off. Here is more news.

Enter a Messenger.

I.iii. Location: Venice. A council-chamber.
1. composition: consistency.
5. jump: agree. **just:** exact. **accompt:** accounting, number.
6. the aim: i.e. conjecture.
10–11. so . . . approve: take such assurance from the discrepancy that I don't accept the central item. **12. fearful:** alarming.
14. preparation: force prepared for war; here, fleet (so also at line 221 below). **17. by:** about.
18. assay of reason: test of common sense. **pageant:** mere show.
19. in false gaze: looking in the wrong direction.
23. with . . . it: capture it more easily. **24. brace:** readiness.
27. unskillful: unable to weigh the situation, undiscriminating.
28. latest: last.
29. of . . . gain: i.e. that will yield easy success.
30. wage: risk.

Mess. The Ottomites, reverend and gracious,
Steering with due course toward the isle of Rhodes,
Have there injointed them with an after fleet.
1. Sen. Ay, so I thought. How many, as you guess?
Mess. Of thirty sail; and now they do restem
Their backward course, bearing with frank appearance
Their purposes toward Cyprus. Signior Montano,
Your trusty and most valiant servitor,
With his free duty recommends you thus,
And prays you to believe him. [*Exit Messenger.*]
Duke. 'Tis certain then for Cyprus.
Marcus Luccicos, is not he in town?
1. Sen. He's now in Florence.
Duke. Write from us to him, post-post-haste. Dispatch!
1. Sen. Here comes Brabantio and the valiant Moor.

Enter Brabantio, Othello, Cassio, Iago, Roderigo, *and* Officers.

Duke. Valiant Othello, we must straight employ you
Against the general enemy Ottoman.
[*To Brabantio.*] I did not see you; welcome, gentle signior,
We lack'd your counsel and your help to-night.
Bra. So did I yours. Good your Grace, pardon me:
Neither my place, nor aught I heard of business,
Hath rais'd me from my bed, nor doth the general care
Take hold on me; for my particular grief
Is of so flood-gate and o'erbearing nature
That it engluts and swallows other sorrows,
And it is still itself.
Duke. Why? what's the matter?
Bra. My daughter! O, my daughter!
[*All.*] Dead?
Bra. Ay, to me:
She is abus'd, stol'n from me, and corrupted
By spells and medicines bought of mountebanks;
For nature so prepost'rously to err
(Being not deficient, blind, or lame of sense)
Sans witchcraft could not.
Duke. Who e'er he be that in this foul proceeding
Hath thus beguil'd your daughter of herself,
And you of her, the bloody book of law
You shall yourself read in the bitter letter
After your own sense; yea, though our proper son
Stood in your action.
Bra. Humbly I thank your Grace.
Here is the man—this Moor, whom now, it seems,
Your special mandate for the state affairs
Hath hither brought.
All. We are very sorry for't.

38. with frank appearance: openly, without disguising their intention.
41. his free duty: i.e. expressions of unwavering loyalty. **recommends:** informs.
49. general: universal, i.e. of all Christendom.
50. gentle: noble. **55. particular:** private.
56. flood-gate: i.e. overwhelming (like the onrushing water when flood-gates are opened). **57. engluts:** engulfs.
60. abus'd: deceived, deluded. **62. err:** suffer aberration.
63. deficient: defective. **sense:** reason. **64. Sans:** without.
69. After . . . sense: giving it your own interpretation. **proper:** own.
70. Stood . . . action: were the one who faced your charges.

Duke. [*To Othello.*] What, in your own part, can you say to this?
Bra. Nothing, but this is so.
Oth. Most potent, grave, and reverend signiors,
My very noble and approv'd good masters:
That I have ta'en away this old man's daughter,
It is most true; true I have married her;
The very head and front of my offending
Hath this extent, no more. Rude am I in my speech,
And little bless'd with the soft phrase of peace;
For since these arms of mine had seven years' pith,
Till now some nine moons wasted, they have us'd
Their dearest action in the tented field;
And little of this great world can I speak
More than pertains to feats of broils and battle,
And therefore little shall I grace my cause
In speaking for myself. Yet (by your gracious patience)
I will a round unvarnish'd tale deliver
Of my whole course of love—what drugs, what charms,
What conjuration, and what mighty magic
(For such proceeding I am charg'd withal)
I won his daughter.
Bra. A maiden, never bold;
Of spirit so still and quiet that her motion
Blush'd at herself; and she, in spite of nature,
Of years, of country, credit, every thing,
To fall in love with what she fear'd to look on!
It is a judgment main'd, and most imperfect,
That will confess perfection so could err
Against all rules of nature, and must be driven
To find out practices of cunning hell
Why this should be. I therefore vouch again
That with some mixtures pow'rful o'er the blood,
Or with some dram (conjur'd to this effect)
He wrought upon her.
[*Duke.*] To vouch this is no proof,
Without more wider and more [overt] test
Than these thin habits and poor likelihoods
Of modern seeming do prefer against him.
[*1.*] *Sen.* But, Othello, speak.
Did you by indirect and forced courses
Subdue and poison this young maid's affections?
Or came it by request, and such fair question
As soul to soul affordeth?
Oth. I do beseech you,
Send for the lady to the Sagittary,
And let her speak of me before her father.
If you do find me foul in her report,
The trust, the office I do hold of you,
Not only take away, but let your sentence
Even fall upon my life.
Duke. Fetch Desdemona hither.
[*Exeunt two or three.*]
Oth. Ancient, conduct them; you best know the place. [*Exit Iago.*]
And, [till] she come, as truly as to heaven
I do confess the vices of my blood,
So justly to your grave ears I'll present
How I did thrive in this fair lady's love,
And she in mine.
Duke. Say it, Othello.
Oth. Her father lov'd me, oft invited me;
Still question'd me the story of my life
From year to year—the [battles], sieges, [fortunes],
That I have pass'd.
I ran it through, even from my boyish days
To th' very moment that he bade me tell it;
Wherein I spoke of most disastrous chances:
Of moving accidents by flood and field,
Of hair-breadth scapes i' th' imminent deadly breach,
Of being taken by the insolent foe
And sold to slavery, of my redemption thence
And portance in my [travel's] history;
Wherein of antres vast and deserts idle,
Rough quarries, rocks, [and] hills whose [heads] touch heaven,
It was my hint to speak—such was my process—
And of the Cannibals that each [other] eat,
The Anthropophagi, and men whose heads
[Do grow] beneath their shoulders. These things to hear
Would Desdemona seriously incline;
But still the house affairs would draw her [thence],
Which ever as she could with haste dispatch,
She'ld come again, and with a greedy ear
Devour up my discourse. Which I observing,
Took once a pliant hour, and found good means
To draw from her a prayer of earnest heart
That I would all my pilgrimage dilate,
Whereof by parcels she had something heard,
But not [intentively]. I did consent,
And often did beguile her of her tears,
When I did speak of some distressful stroke
That my youth suffer'd. My story being done,
She gave me for my pains a world of [sighs];
She swore, in faith 'twas strange, 'twas passing strange;
'Twas pitiful, 'twas wondrous pitiful.
She wish'd she had not heard it, yet she wish'd
That heaven had made her such a man. She thank'd me,
And bade me, if I had a friend that lov'd her,
I should but teach him how to tell my story,

77. approv'd: proved.
80. The very . . . offending: i.e. my offense at the utmost.
81. Rude: unpolished. **83. pith:** i.e. strength.
90. round: plain. **93. withal:** with.
95–96. her . . . herself: any stirring of her feelings made her blush (as if it were improper). **97. credit:** reputation.
99. main'd: maimed. **100. confess:** aver, declare.
101. must: i.e. the unmaimed judgment must.
102. practices: plots. **103. vouch:** affirm. **104. blood:** passions.
105. conjur'd . . . effect: made thus efficacious by spells.
107. more wider: i.e. fuller.
108. thin habits: thin clothing, i.e. slight appearances.
109. modern: commonplace, insignificant. **seeming:** supposition. **prefer:** present. **113. question:** conversation.

123. vices . . . blood: my human failings.
124. justly: exactly, truthfully. **129. Still:** continually.
135. accidents: events.
136. imminent deadly: threatening death. **breach:** gap made in fortifications. **139. portance:** behavior.
140. antres: caves. **idle:** barren, empty.
141. Rough quarries: rugged stone-masses.
142. hint: occasion. **process:** proceeding (?) or story (?).
144. Anthropophagi: man-eaters.
151. pliant: convenient, favorable. **153. dilate:** relate in detail.
154. by parcels: by snatches, in bits and pieces.
155. intentively: with continuous attention.

And that would woo her. Upon this hint I spake:
She lov'd me for the dangers I had pass'd,
And I lov'd her that she did pity them.
This only is the witchcraft I have us'd.
Here comes the lady; let her witness it.

Enter Desdemona, Iago, Attendants.

Duke. I think this tale would win my daughter too.
Good Brabantio,
Take up this mangled matter at the best;
Men do their broken weapons rather use
Than their bare hands.
Bra. I pray you hear her speak.
If she confess that she was half the wooer,
Destruction on my head if my bad blame
Light on the man! Come hither, gentle mistress.
Do you perceive in all this noble company
Where most you owe obedience?
Des. My noble father,
I do perceive here a divided duty:
To you I am bound for life and education;
My life and education both do learn me
How to respect you; you are the lord of duty;
I am hitherto your daughter. But here's my husband;
And so much duty as my mother show'd
To you, preferring you before her father,
So much I challenge that I may profess
Due to the Moor, my lord.
Bra. God be with you! I have done.
Please it your Grace, on to the state affairs.
I had rather to adopt a child than get it.
Come hither, Moor:
I here do give thee that with all my heart
Which but thou hast already, with all my heart
I would keep from thee. For your sake, jewel,
I am glad at soul I have no other child,
For thy escape would teach me tyranny,
To hang clogs on them. I have done, my lord.
Duke. Let me speak like yourself, and lay a sentence,
Which as a grise or step, may help these lovers
[Into your favor].
When remedies are past, the griefs are ended
By seeing the worst, which late on hopes depended.
To mourn a mischief that is past and gone
Is the next way to draw new mischief on.
What cannot be preserv'd when Fortune takes,
Patience her injury a mock'ry makes.
The robb'd that smiles steals something from the thief;

166. **hint**: opportunity.
173. **Take . . . best**: make the best of this badly damaged situation.
182. **education**: rearing. 183. **learn**: teach.
184. **respect**: regard.
185. **I . . . daughter**: i.e. until now I have owed all my obedience to you as my father. 188. **challenge**: claim.
189. **God . . . you**: good-bye. 191. **get**: beget.
195. **For your sake**: because of what you have done.
197. **escape**: transgression.
198. **clogs**: blocks of wood hung on criminals or animals to prevent their running away.
199. **like yourself**: as you should. **sentence**: maxim, moral saying.
200. **grise**: degree, step. 202. **remedies**: i.e. hopes of remedy.
203. **which**: i.e. the griefs. **hopes**: anticipations.
204. **mischief**: injury. 205. **next**: nearest.
207. **Patience . . . makes**: patient endurance of the loss makes a mockery of Fortune's intended injury.

He robs himself that spends a bootless grief.
Bra. So let the Turk of Cyprus us beguile,
We lose it not, so long as we can smile.
He bears the sentence well that nothing bears
But the free comfort which from thence he hears;
But he bears both the sentence and the sorrow
That, to pay grief, must of poor patience borrow.
These sentences, to sugar or to gall,
Being strong on both sides, are equivocal.
But words are words; I never yet did hear
That the bruis'd heart was pierced through the [ear].
I humbly beseech you proceed to th' affairs of state.

Duke. The Turk with a most mighty preparation makes for Cyprus. Othello, the fortitude of the place is best known to you; and though we have there a substitute of most allow'd sufficiency, yet opinion, a sovereign mistress of effects, throws a more safer voice on you. You must therefore be content to slubber the gloss of your new fortunes with this more stubborn and boist'rous expedition.

Oth. The tyrant custom, most grave senators,
Hath made the flinty and steel [couch] of war
My thrice-driven bed of down. I do agnize
A natural and prompt alacrity
I find in hardness; and do undertake
This present wars against the Ottomites.
Most humbly therefore bending to your state,
I crave fit disposition for my wife,
Due reference of place and exhibition,
With such accommodation and besort
As levels with her breeding.
Duke. [If you please,
Be't] at her father's.
Bra. I will not have it so.
Oth. Nor I.
Des. Nor [I; I would not] there reside,
To put my father in impatient thoughts
By being in his eye. Most gracious Duke,
To my unfolding lend your prosperous ear,
And let me find a charter in your voice
T' assist my simpleness.
Duke. What would you, Desdemona?
Des. That I [did] love the Moor to live with him,
My downright violence, and storm of fortunes,
May trumpet to the world. My heart's subdu'd
Even to the very quality of my lord.

209. **bootless**: unavailing. 213. **free**: i.e. unmixed with sorrow.
215. **poor patience**: i.e., endurance, which hasn't much to lend.
219. **pierced**: i.e. relieved as by a surgeon's lancet. Some editors adopt Warburton's emendation *pieced* = mended.
221. **preparation**: fleet. 222. **fortitude**: military strength.
223–24. **substitute**: representative. 224. **allow'd**: acknowledged.
224–25. **opinion . . . effects**: public opinion, the ultimate arbiter of what is to be done.
225–26. **throws . . . you**: gives you the reputation of being safer.
227. **slubber**: sully. 228. **stubborn**: rough.
231. **thrice-driven**: thrice-winnowed (to obtain the smallest and softest feathers). **agnize**: recognize. 232. **alacrity**: readiness.
233. **hardness**: hardship. 235. **state**: i.e. authority.
236. **fit disposition**: suitable provision.
237. **reference of place**: assignment of residence. **exhibition**: allowance of money. 238. **besort**: suitable company.
244. **prosperous**: favorable. 245. **charter**: authorization, privilege.
249. **downright**: plain, open. **violence**: i.e. boldly aggressive action, breach of customary behavior. **storm of fortunes**: taking my fortune by storm.
250–51. **subdu'd Even to**: brought completely into accord with.
251. **quality**: (1) nature, character; (2) profession, mode of life.

I saw Othello's visage in his mind,
And to his honors and his valiant parts
Did I my soul and fortunes consecrate.
So that, dear lords, if I be left behind,
A moth of peace, and he go to the war,
The rites for why I love him are bereft me,
And I a heavy interim shall support
By his dear absence. Let me go with him.

Oth. Let her have your voice.
Vouch with me, heaven, I therefore beg it not
To please the palate of my appetite,
Nor to comply with heat (the young affects
In [me] defunct) and proper satisfaction;
But to be free and bounteous to her mind.
And heaven defend your good souls, that you think
I will your serious and great business scant
[For] she is with me. No, when light-wing'd toys
Of feather'd Cupid seel with wanton dullness
My speculative and offic'd [instruments],
That my disports corrupt and taint my business,
Let housewives make a skillet of my helm,
And all indign and base adversities
Make head against my estimation!

Duke. Be it as you shall privately determine,
Either for her stay or going; th' affair cries haste,
And speed must answer it.

[*1.*] *Sen.* You must away to-night.

[*Des.* To-night, my lord?

Duke. This night.]

Oth. With all my heart.

Duke. At nine i' th' morning here we'll meet again.
Othello, leave some officer behind,
And he shall our commission bring to you;
And such things else of quality and respect
As doth import you.

Oth. So please your Grace, my ancient;
A man he is of honesty and trust.
To his conveyance I assign my wife,
With what else needful your good Grace shall think
To be sent after me.

Duke. Let it be so.
Good night to every one. [*To Brabantio.*] And, noble signior,
If virtue no delighted beauty lack,
Your son-in-law is far more fair than black.

[*1.*] *Sen.* Adieu, brave Moor, use Desdemona well.

Bra. Look to her, Moor, if thou hast eyes to see;
She has deceiv'd her father, and may thee.

Exeunt [*Duke, Senators, Officers, etc.*].

Oth. My life upon her faith! Honest Iago,
My Desdemona must I leave to thee.
I prithee let thy wife attend on her,
And bring them after in the best advantage.
Come, Desdemona, I have but an hour
Of love, of wordly matter and direction,
To spend with thee. We must obey the time.

Exit [*with Desdemona*].

Rod. Iago—

Iago. What say'st thou, noble heart?

Rod. What will I do, think'st thou?

Iago. Why, go to bed and sleep.

Rod. I will incontinently drown myself.

Iago. If thou dost, I shall never love thee after. Why, thou silly gentleman?

Rod. It is silliness to live, when to live is torment; and then have we a prescription to die, when death is our physician.

Iago. O villainous! I have look'd upon the world for four times seven years, and since I could distinguish betwixt a benefit and an injury, I never found man that knew how to love himself. Ere I would say I would drown myself for the love of a guinea hen, I would change my humanity with a baboon.

Rod. What should I do? I confess it is my shame to be so fond, but it is not in my virtue to amend it.

Iago. Virtue? a fig! 'tis in ourselves that we are thus or thus. Our bodies are our gardens, to the which our wills are gardeners; so that if we will plant nettles or sow lettuce, set hyssop and weed up [tine], supply it with one gender of herbs or distract it with many, either to have it sterile with idleness or manur'd with industry—why, the power and corrigible authority of this lies in our wills. If the [beam] of our lives had not one scale of reason to poise another of sensuality, the blood and baseness of our natures would conduct us to most prepost'rous conclusions. But we have reason to cool our raging motions, our carnal stings, [our] unbitted lusts; whereof I take this that you call love to be a sect or scion.

Rod. It cannot be.

Iago. It is merely a lust of the blood and a permission of the will. Come, be a man! Drown thyself? drown cats and blind puppies! I have profess'd me thy friend, and I confess me knit to thy deserving with cables of perdurable toughness. I could never better stead thee than now. Put money in thy purse; follow thou the wars; defeat thy favor with

253. parts: qualities. **256. moth:** mere idle consumer, parasite.
257. rites. Perhaps to be taken as a variant spelling of *rights*, i.e. all the rights (including love-rites) involved in sharing his life to the full.
259. dear: heartfelt.
263–64. Nor . . . defunct: nor to serve sexual appetite—since the excesses of youthful passion are in me over and done with.
264. proper: personal, private. **266. defend:** forbid.
268. For: because.
269. seel: blind (literally, sew shut the eyelids of a hawk to tame it). **wanton dullness:** dullness produced by sexual indulgence.
270. My . . . instruments: my faculties of perception when they have duties to perform. *Speculative* means literally "having power to see," and the line has been explained by some annotators as referring to the eyes, but it probably refers to the powers of mental perception, the "mind's eye." **271. That:** so that.
273. indign: unworthy, shameful.
274. Make head: raise an armed force. **estimation:** reputation.
282. of . . respect: pertaining to your rank and privilege.
283. import: concern. **284. honesty:** honor.
289. delighted: delightful.

297. in . . . advantage: at . . . opportunity.
299. wordly: worldly (a variant spelling).
305. incontinently: at once.
309. prescription: (1) perfect right; (2) doctor's order.
311. villainous: wretched nonsense. **318. virtue:** nature.
319–20. 'tis . . . thus: it is in our own power to make ourselves what we will.
322. hyssop: a fragrant herb. **tine:** tares, wild grasses.
323. gender: kind. **325. corrigible:** corrective.
326. beam: balance. **327. poise:** counterbalance.
328. blood and baseness: base passions.
330. motions: desires, appetites.
332. sect or scion: cutting or offshoot. **338. perdurable:** lasting.
339. stead: serve, help. **340. defeat thy favor:** alter your appearance.

an usurp'd beard. I say put money in thy purse. It cannot be long that Desdemona should continue her love to the Moor—put money in thy purse—nor he his to her. It was a violent commencement in her, and thou shalt see an answerable sequestration—put but money in thy purse. These Moors are changeable in their wills—fill thy purse with money. The food that to him now is as luscious as locusts, shall be to him shortly as [acerb] as [the] coloquintida. She must change for youth; when she is sated with his body, she will find the [error] of her choice. [She must have change, she must;] therefore put money in thy purse. If thou wilt needs damn thyself, do it a more delicate way than drowning. Make all the money thou canst. If sanctimony and a frail vow betwixt an erring barbarian and [a] super-subtle Venetian be not too hard for my wits and all the tribe of hell, thou shalt enjoy her; therefore make money. A pox of drowning thyself, it is clean out of the way. Seek thou rather to be hang'd in compassing thy joy than to be drown'd and go without her.

Rod. Wilt thou be fast to my hopes, if I depend on the issue?

Iago. Thou art sure of me—go make money. I have told thee often, and I retell thee again and again, I hate the Moor. My cause is hearted; thine hath no less reason. Let us be conjunctive in our revenge against him. If thou canst cuckold him, thou dost thyself a pleasure, me a sport. There are many events in the womb of time which will be deliver'd. Traverse, go, provide thy money. We will have more of this to-morrow. Adieu.

Rod. Where shall we meet i' th' morning?
Iago. At my lodging.
Rod. I'll be with thee betimes.
Iago. Go to, farewell. Do you hear, Roderigo?
[*Rod.* What say you?
Iago. No more of drowning, do you hear?
Rod. I am chang'd.
Iago. Go to, farewell. Put money enough in your purse.]
Rod. I'll sell all my land. *Exit.*
Iago. Thus do I ever make my fool my purse;
For I mine own gain'd knowledge should profane
If I would time expend with such [a] snipe
But for my sport and profit. I hate the Moor,
And it is thought abroad that 'twixt my sheets
[H'as] done my office. I know not if't be true,
But I, for mere suspicion in that kind,
Will do as if for surety. He holds me well,
The better shall my purpose work on him.

341. **usurp'd**: to which you have no right (because you are scarcely old enough to grow it).
345. **answerable sequestration**: correspondingly abrupt ending (or separation). 347. **wills**: lusts.
348. **locusts**: the sweet fruit of the carob tree.
349. **acerb**: bitter. **coloquintida**: colocynth or "bitter apple," used as a purgative. 354. **Make**: raise, get together.
355. **sanctimony**: religious bond or ceremony. **erring**: vagabond.
356. **super-subtle**: highly refined and sensitive. 362. **fast**: true.
366. **hearted**: rooted in my heart, i.e. deeply and passionately felt.
367. **conjunctive**: united. 371. **Traverse**: forward.
376. **Do you hear**: just a minute, one more thing.
385. **snipe**: woodcock; used contemptuously of an insignificant or silly person. 387. **it . . . abroad**: there is gossip.
390. **do . . . surety**: act as if on the basis of proved fact.

Cassio's a proper man. Let me see now:
To get his place and to plume up my will
In double knavery—How? how?—Let's see—
After some time, to abuse Othello's [ear]
That he is too familiar with his wife.
He hath a person and a smooth dispose
To be suspected—fram'd to make women false.
The Moor is of a free and open nature,
That thinks men honest that but seem to be so,
And will as tenderly be led by th' nose
As asses are.
I have't. It is engend'red. Hell and night
Must bring this monstrous birth to the world's light.
[*Exit.*]

ACT II, SCENE I

Enter MONTANO *and two* GENTLEMEN.

Mon. What from the cape can you discern at sea?
1. Gent. Nothing at all, it is a high-wrought flood.
I cannot, 'twixt the heaven and the main,
Descry a sail.
Mon. Methinks the wind hath spoke aloud at land,
A fuller blast ne'er shook our battlements.
If it hath ruffian'd so upon the sea,
What ribs of oak, when mountains melt on them,
Can hold the mortise? What shall we hear of this?
2. Gent. A segregation of the Turkish fleet:
For do but stand upon the foaming shore,
The chidden billow seems to pelt the clouds,
The wind-shak'd surge, with high and monstrous mane,
Seems to cast water on the burning Bear,
And quench the guards of th' ever-fixed Pole;
I never did like molestation view
On the enchafed flood.
Mon. If that the Turkish fleet
Be not enshelter'd and embay'd, they are drown'd;
It is impossible to bear it out.

Enter a [third] GENTLEMAN.

3. Gent. News, lads! our wars are done.
The desperate tempest hath so bang'd the Turks,
That their designment halts. A noble ship of Venice
Hath seen a grievous wrack and sufferance
On most part of their fleet.
Mon. How? is this true?
3. Gent. The ship is here put in,
A Veronesa; Michael Cassio,

392. **proper**: handsome. 393. **plume . . . will**: pamper my ego.
397. **dispose**: bearing. 401. **tenderly**: readily.

II.i. **Location**: A seaport in Cyprus. An open place near the quay.
9. **hold the mortise**: hold their joints together.
10. **segregation**: dispersion.
13. **mane**. Many editors prefer *main* = power. F1 *Maine* and Q1 *mayne* are ambiguous.
15. **guards**: two stars in the Little Bear, in line with the pole star.
22. **designment**: plan. **halts**: is lame. 23. **sufferance**: damage.
26. **Veronesa**. If this word means "Veronese," there is difficulty about applying it either to the ship, which has just been described as "of Venice," or to Cassio, who is called a Florentine at I.i.20. Modern editors usually explain it as designating a ship furnished by Verona for the Venetian service. But the word may not mean "Veronese" at all; some suspect a connection with an Italian word for a particular type of ship.

Lieutenant to the warlike Moor Othello,
Is come on shore; the Moor himself at sea,
And is in full commission here for Cyprus.
Mon. I am glad on't; 'tis a worthy governor.
3. Gent. But this same Cassio, though he speak of
comfort
Touching the Turkish loss, yet he looks sadly,
And [prays] the Moor be safe; for they were parted
With foul and violent tempest.
Mon. Pray [heaven] he be;
For I have serv'd him, and the man commands
Like a full soldier. Let's to the sea-side, ho!
As well to see the vessel that's come in
As to throw out our eyes for brave Othello,
Even till we make the main and th' aerial blue
An indistinct regard.
[3.] Gent. Come, let's do so;
For every minute is expectancy
Of more [arrivance].

Enter Cassio.

Cas. Thanks you, the valiant of [this] warlike isle,
That so approve the Moor! O, let the heavens
Give him defense against the elements,
For I have lost him on a dangerous sea.
Mon. Is he well shipp'd?
Cas. His bark is stoutly timber'd, and his pilot
Of very expert and approv'd allowance;
Therefore my hopes (not surfeited to death)
Stand in bold cure. *Within*, "A sail, a sail, a sail!"

[Enter a Messenger.]

Cas. What noise?
[Mess.] The town is empty; on the brow o' th' sea
Stand ranks of people, and they cry, "A sail!"
Cas. My hopes do shape him for the governor.
[A shot.]
[2.] Gent. They do discharge their shot of courtesy;
Our friends at least.
Cas. I pray you, sir, go forth,
And give us truth who 'tis that is arriv'd.
[2.] Gent. I shall. *Exit.*
Mon. But, good lieutenant, is your general wiv'd?
Cas. Most fortunately: he hath achiev'd a maid
That paragons description and wild fame;
One that excels the quirks of blazoning pens,
And in th' essential vesture of creation
Does tire the [ingener].

Enter [Second] Gentleman.

How now? who has put in?
[2.] Gent. 'Tis one Iago, ancient to the general.
Cas. H'as had most favorable and happy speed:
Tempests themselves, high seas, and howling winds,
The gutter'd rocks and congregated sands,
Traitors ensteep'd to enclog the guiltless keel,
As having sense of beauty, do omit
Their mortal natures, letting go safely by
The divine Desdemona.
Mon. What is she?
Cas. She that I spake of, our great captain's captain,
Left in the conduct of the bold Iago,
Whose footing here anticipates our thoughts
A se'nnight's speed. Great Jove, Othello guard,
And swell his sail with thine own pow'rful breath,
That he may bless this bay with his tall ship,
Make love's quick pants in Desdemona's arms,
Give renew'd fire to our extincted spirits,
[And bring all Cyprus comfort!]

Enter Desdemona, Iago, Roderigo, *and* Emilia, *[with* Attendants].

O, behold,
The riches of the ship is come on shore!
You men of Cyprus, let her have your knees.
Hail to thee, lady! and the grace of heaven,
Before, behind thee, and on every hand,
Enwheel thee round!
Des. I thank you, valiant Cassio.
What tidings can you tell [me] of my lord?
Cas. He is not yet arriv'd, nor know I aught
But that he's well and will be shortly here.
Des. O, but I fear—How lost you company?
Cas. The great contention of [the] sea and skies
Parted our fellowship.
Within, "A sail, a sail!" *[A shot.]*
But hark! a sail.
[2.] Gent. They give [their] greeting to the citadel.
This likewise is a friend.
Cas. See for the news.
[Exit Second Gentleman.]
Good ancient, you are welcome. *[To Emilia.]* Wel-
come, mistress.
Let it not gall your patience, good Iago,
That I extend my manners; 'tis my breeding
That gives me this bold show of courtesy.
[Kissing her.]
Iago. Sir, would she give you so much of her lips
As of her tongue she oft bestows on me,
You would have enough.
Des. Alas! she has no speech.
Iago. In faith, too much;
I find it still, when I have [list] to sleep.
Marry, before your ladyship, I grant,
She puts her tongue a little in her heart,
And chides with thinking.
Emil. You have little cause to say so.
Iago. Come on, come on; you are pictures out
[a' doors],

39. **An indistinct regard:** indistinguishable to the sight.
43. **Thanks you:** thanks to you. 44. **approve:** commend, admire.
49. **expert . . . allowance:** i.e. of acknowledged and proved skill.
50–51. **my . . . cure:** since I have not had to indulge my hopes so long that they are near death, I am confident that they will be fulfilled.
62. **paragons description:** surpasses whatever praise is uttered of her.
63. **quirks:** conceits, flourishes. **blazoning:** listing her beauties.
64–65. **in . . . ingener:** in her native beauty defeats all attempts of the inventive poet to praise her adequately.
69. **gutter'd:** jagged. 70. **ensteep'd:** submerged.
71. **omit:** give up, do not act in accordance with.
72. **mortal:** deadly. 76. **footing:** landing, arrival.
83. **riches.** Singular (from French *richesse*). 98. **extend:** show.
104. **list:** inclination.
107. **with thinking:** i.e. without speaking her thoughts.
109. **pictures:** i.e. painted.

Bells in your parlors, wild-cats in your kitchens,
Saints in your injuries, devils being offended,
Players in your huswifery, and huswives in your beds.

Des. O, fie upon thee, slanderer!

Iago. Nay, it is true, or else I am a Turk:
You rise to play, and go to bed to work.

Emil. You shall not write my praise.

Iago. No, let me not.

Des. What wouldst write of me, if thou shouldst praise me?

Iago. O gentle lady, do not put me to't,
For I am nothing if not critical.

Des. Come on, assay.—There's one gone to the harbor?

Iago. Ay, madam.

Des. I am not merry; but I do beguile
The thing I am by seeming otherwise.—
Come, how wouldst thou praise me?

Iago. I am about it, but indeed my invention
Comes from my pate as birdlime does from frieze,
It plucks out brains and all. But my Muse labors,
And thus she is deliver'd:
If she be fair and wise, fairness and wit,
The one's for use, the other useth it.

Des. Well prais'd! How if she be black and witty?

Iago. If she be black, and thereto have a wit,
She'll find a white that shall her blackness [hit].

Des. Worse and worse.

Emil. How if fair and foolish?

Iago. She never yet was foolish that was fair,
For even her folly help'd her to an heir.

Des. These are old fond paradoxes to make fools laugh i' th' alehouse. What miserable praise hast thou for her that's foul and foolish?

Iago. There's none so foul and foolish thereunto,
But does foul pranks which fair and wise ones do.

Des. O heavy ignorance! thou praisest the worst best. But what praise couldst thou bestow on a deserving woman indeed—one that in the authority of her merit, did justly put on the vouch of very malice itself?

Iago. She that was ever fair, and never proud,
Had tongue at will, and yet was never loud,
Never lack'd gold, and yet went never gay,
Fled from her wish, and yet said, "Now I may";
She that being ang'red, her revenge being nigh,
Bade her wrong stay, and her displeasure fly;
She that in wisdom never was so frail
To change the cod's head for the salmon's tail;
She that could think, and nev'r disclose her mind,
See suitors following, and not look behind:
She was a wight (if ever such [wight] were)—

Des. To do what?

Iago. To suckle fools and chronicle small beer.

Des. O most lame and impotent conclusion! Do not learn of him, Emilia, though he be thy husband. How say you, Cassio? is he not a most profane and liberal counsellor?

Cas. He speaks home, madam. You may relish him more in the soldier than in the scholar.

Iago. [*Aside.*] He takes her by the palm; ay, well said, whisper. With as little a web as this will I ensnare as great a fly as Cassio. Ay, smile upon her, do; I will gyve thee in thine own courtship. You say true, 'tis so indeed. If such tricks as these strip you out of your lieutenantry, it had been better you had not kiss'd your three fingers so oft, which now again you are most apt to play the sir in. Very good; well kiss'd! [an] excellent [courtesy]! 'Tis so indeed. Yet again, your fingers to your lips? Would they were clyster-pipes for your sake! [*Trumpets within.*]—The Moor! I know his trumpet.

Cas. 'Tis truly so.

Des. Let's meet him and receive him.

Cas. Lo, where he comes!

Enter OTHELLO *and* ATTENDANTS.

Oth. O my fair warrior!

Des. My dear Othello!

Oth. It gives me wonder great as my content
To see you here before me. O my soul's joy!
If after every tempest come such calms,
May the winds blow till they have waken'd death!
And let the laboring bark climb hills of seas
Olympus-high, and duck again as low
As hell's from heaven! If it were now to die,
'Twere now to be most happy; for I fear
My soul hath her content so absolute
That not another comfort like to this
Succeeds in unknown fate.

Des. The heavens forbid
But that our loves and comforts should increase
Even as our days do grow!

Oth. Amen to that, sweet powers!
I cannot speak enough of this content,
It stops me here; it is too much of joy.
And this, and this, the greatest discords be [*They kiss.*]
That e'er our hearts shall make!

Iago. [*Aside.*] O, you are well tun'd now!
But I'll set down the pegs that make this music,
As honest as I am.

110. Bells: i.e. with tongues going like bell-clappers.
111. Saints . . . injuries: when you offend, you do it with an air of sanctity.
112. Players: actors, i.e. people making a pretense (?) or perfunctory triflers (?). **huswifery:** household management. **huswives:** hussies, wantons.
119. critical: censorious. **120. assay:** try.
123. The thing I am: my anxious self.
126. birdlime: sticky substance used to catch birds. **frieze:** coarse wool. **131. black:** brunette.
133. white. With a pun on *wight,* "person." **hit:** suit, fit (with sexual quibble). **137. folly.** With second sense "wantonness."
138. fond: foolish. **140. foul:** ugly.
145. in the authority: by virtue.
146. put . . . vouch: compel the favorable testimony.
150. gay: extravagantly dressed.
151. Fled . . . may: i.e. did not indulge herself even though she was free to do so. **153. wrong stay:** sense of injury cease.
155. change . . . tail. Obscure. Perhaps "give up something common but valuable in exchange for something showy but worthless," but more probably a sexual innuendo.
160. suckle . . . beer: tend babies and keep petty household accounts.
164. liberal: free-spoken. **165. home:** bluntly.
166. in: in the character of. **167–68. well said:** well done.
170. gyve: fetter, entangle. **courtship:** display of courtly manners.
174. sir: gentleman, gallant. **175. courtesy:** bow.
177. clyster-pipes: enema tubes.
200. set . . . pegs: i.e. untune the instrument (and so produce discords).

Oth. Come; let us to the castle.
News, friends: our wars are done; the Turks are drown'd.
How does my old acquaintance of this isle?
Honey, you shall be well desir'd in Cyprus,
I have found great love amongst them. O my sweet,
I prattle out of fashion, and I dote
In mine own comforts. I prithee, good Iago,
Go to the bay and disembark my coffers.
Bring thou the master to the citadel;
He is a good one, and his worthiness
Does challenge much respect. Come, Desdemona,
Once more, well met at Cyprus.

Exeunt Othello and Desdemona [with all but Iago and Roderigo].

Iago. [*To an Attendant, as he is going out.*] Do thou meet me presently at the harbor.—Come [hither]. If thou be'st valiant (as they say base men being in love have then a nobility in their natures more than is native to them), list me. The lieutenant to-night watches on the court of guard. First, I must tell thee this: Desdemona is directly in love with him.

Rod. With him? why, 'tis not possible.

Iago. Lay thy finger thus; and let thy soul be instructed. Mark me with what violence she first lov'd the Moor, but for bragging and telling her fantastical lies. To love him still for prating—let not thy discreet heart think it. Her eye must be fed; and what delight shall she have to look on the devil? When the blood is made dull with the act of sport, there should be, [again] to inflame it and to give satiety a fresh appetite, loveliness in favor, sympathy in years, manners, and beauties—all which the Moor is defective in. Now for want of these requir'd conveniences, her delicate tenderness will find itself abus'd, begin to heave the gorge, disrelish and abhor the Moor; very nature will instruct her in it and compel her to some second choice. Now, sir, this granted (as it is a most pregnant and unforc'd position), who stands so eminent in the degree of this fortune as Cassio does? a knave very voluble; no further conscionable than in putting on the mere form of civil and humane seeming, for the better compass of his salt and most hidden loose affection? Why, none, why, none—a slipper and subtle knave, a finder[-out] of occasion; that [has] an eye can stamp and counterfeit advantages, though true advantage never present itself; a devilish knave. Besides, the knave is handsome, young, and hath all those requisites in him that folly and green minds look after; a pestilent complete knave, and the woman hath found him already.

Rod. I cannot believe that in her, she's full of most bless'd condition.

Iago. Bless'd fig's-end! The wine she drinks is made of grapes. If she had been bless'd, she would never have lov'd the Moor. Bless'd pudding! Didst thou not see her paddle with the palm of his hand? Didst not mark that?

Rod. Yes, that I did; but that was but courtesy.

Iago. Lechery, by this hand; an index and obscure prologue to the history of lust and foul thoughts. They met so near with their lips that their breaths embrac'd together. Villainous thoughts, Roderigo! When these [mutualities] so marshal the way, hard at hand comes the master and main exercise, th' incorporate conclusion. Pish! But, sir, be you rul'd by me. I have brought you from Venice. Watch you to-night; for the command, I'll lay't upon you. Cassio knows you not. I'll not be far from you. Do you find some occasion to anger Cassio, either by speaking too loud, or tainting his discipline, or from what other course you please, which the time shall more favorably minister.

Rod. Well.

Iago. Sir, he's rash and very sudden in choler, and happily may strike at you—provoke him that he may; for even out of that will I cause these of Cyprus to mutiny, whose qualification shall come into no true taste again but by the displanting of Cassio. So shall you have a shorter journey to your desires by the means I shall then have to prefer them; and the impediment most profitably remov'd, without the which there were no expectation of our prosperity.

Rod. I will do this, if you can bring it to any opportunity.

Iago. I warrant thee. Meet me by and by at the citadel. I must fetch his necessaries ashore. Farewell.

Rod. Adieu. *Exit.*

Iago. That Cassio loves her, I do well believe't;
That she loves him, 'tis apt and of great credit.
The Moor (howbeit that I endure him not)
Is of a constant, loving, noble nature,
And I dare think he'll prove to Desdemona
A most dear husband. Now I do love her too,
Not out of absolute lust (though peradventure
I stand accomptant for as great a sin),
But partly led to diet my revenge,
For that I do suspect the lusty Moor
Hath leap'd into my seat; the thought whereof
Doth (like a poisonous mineral) gnaw my inwards;
And nothing can or shall content my soul

204. **desir'd:** welcomed, loved.
206. **out of fashion:** irrelevantly (?) or unconventionally (?)
208. **coffers:** baggage. 209. **master:** ship's captain.
211. **challenge:** claim, deserve.
215. **base men:** even men of low birth.
218. **watches . . . guard:** has charge of the watch.
221. **thus:** i.e. on your lips. 224. **still:** always.
226. **the devil.** Traditionally black.
229. **favor:** face, appearance. **sympathy:** similarity, correspondence.
231–32. **conveniences:** compatibilities.
233. **heave the gorge:** feel nauseated. 236. **pregnant:** obvious.
238. **conscionable:** bound by considerations of conscience.
239. **civil and humane:** polite and courteous.
240. **salt:** lewd. 241. **affection:** passion. 242. **slipper:** slippery.
243. **stamp:** coin, manufacture. **advantages:** opportunities.
246. **folly:** wantonness.

247. **green:** youthful, lusty. 248. **found him:** sized him up.
250. **condition:** disposition, character. 253. **pudding:** sausage.
257. **index:** table of contents at the beginning of a book.
261. **mutualities:** exchanges.
261–62. **hard at hand:** very soon after. 263. **incorporate:** carnal.
264. **Watch:** serve as a member of the watch.
265. **lay't upon you:** arrange for your orders.
268. **tainting:** discrediting. 272. **rash:** impetuous.
273. **happily:** haply, perhaps. 275. **mutiny:** riot.
275–76. **whose . . . taste:** whose anger will not be acceptably diluted.
283. **I warrant thee:** I guarantee you'll have opportunity.
287. **apt . . . credit:** likely and credible.
293. **accomptant:** accountable.

Till I am even'd with him, wife for wife;
Or failing so, yet that I put the Moor
At least into a jealousy so strong
That judgment cannot cure. Which thing to do,
If this poor trash of Venice, whom I trace
For his quick hunting, stand the putting on,
I'll have our Michael Cassio on the hip,
Abuse him to the Moor in the [rank] garb
(For I fear Cassio with my night-cap too),
Make the Moor thank me, love me, and reward me,
For making him egregiously an ass,
And practicing upon his peace and quiet
Even to madness. 'Tis here; but yet confus'd,
Knavery's plain face is never seen till us'd. *Exit.*

Scene II

Enter Othello's Herald *with a proclamation;* [*people following*].

Her. It is Othello's pleasure, our noble and valiant general, that upon certain tidings now arriv'd, importing the mere perdition of the Turkish fleet, every man put himself into triumph; some to dance, some to make bonfires, each man to what sport and revels his [addiction] leads him; for besides these beneficial news, it is the celebration of his nuptial. So much was his pleasure should be proclaim'd. All offices are open, and there is full liberty of feasting from this present hour of five till the bell have told eleven. [Heaven] bless the isle of Cyprus and our noble general Othello! *Exeunt.*

[Scene III]

Enter Othello, Desdemona, Cassio, *and* Attendants.

Oth. Good Michael, look you to the guard to-night.
Let's teach ourselves that honorable stop,
Not to outsport discretion.

Cas. Iago hath direction what to do;
But notwithstanding with my personal eye
Will I look to't.

Oth. Iago is most honest.
Michael, good night. To-morrow with your earliest
Let me have speech with you. [*To Desdemona.*] Come, my dear love,
The purchase made, the fruits are to ensue;
That profit's yet to come 'tween me and you.—
Good night. *Exit* [*with Desdemona and Attendants*].

303. **trace.** Obscure. The meaning must be something like "train," or "check to make more eager"; the latter is the sense of Steevens' widely accepted emendation *trash*, meaning to hang weights on a hound to prevent his hunting too fast.
304. **stand . . . on:** perform properly when the moment comes for me to set him on.
305. **on the hip:** in a position where I can throw him (wrestling term).
306. **rank garb:** coarse fashion.
310. **practicing upon:** plotting against.

II.ii. Location: Cyprus. A street.
3. **mere perdition:** utter destruction.
8. **offices:** kitchens, food storerooms, etc.

II.iii. Location: Cyprus. The citadel.
3. **outsport:** carry our sports beyond.

Enter Iago.

Cas. Welcome, Iago; we must to the watch.

Iago. Not this hour, lieutenant; 'tis not yet ten o' th' clock. Our general cast us thus early for the love of his Desdemona; who let us not therefore blame. He hath not yet made wanton the night with her; and she is sport for Jove.

Cas. She's a most exquisite lady.

Iago. And I'll warrant her, full of game.

Cas. Indeed she's a most fresh and delicate creature.

Iago. What an eye she has! Methinks it sounds a parley to provocation.

Cas. An inviting eye; and yet methinks right modest.

Iago. And when she speaks, is it not an alarum to love?

Cas. She is indeed perfection.

Iago. Well—happiness to their sheets! Come, lieutenant, I have a stope of wine, and here without are a brace of Cyprus gallants that would fain have a measure to the health of black Othello.

Cas. Not to-night, good Iago, I have very poor and unhappy brains for drinking. I could well wish courtesy would invent some other custom of entertainment.

Iago. O, they are our friends—but one cup, I'll drink for you.

Cas. I have drunk but one cup to-night—and that was craftily qualified too—and behold what innovation it makes here. I am infortunate in the infirmity, and dare not task my weakness with any more.

Iago. What, man? 'Tis a night of revels, the gallants desire it.

Cas. Where are they?

Iago. Here, at the door; I pray you call them in.

Cas. I'll do't, but it dislikes me. *Exit.*

Iago. If I can fasten but one cup upon him,
With that which he hath drunk to-night already,
He'll be as full of quarrel and offense
As my young mistress' dog. Now, my sick fool Roderigo,
Whom love hath turn'd almost the wrong side out,
To Desdemona hath to-night carous'd
Potations pottle-deep; and he's to watch.
Three else of Cyprus, noble swelling spirits
That hold their honors in a wary distance,
The very elements of this warlike isle,
Have I to-night fluster'd with flowing cups,
And they watch too. Now 'mongst this flock of drunkards

13. **Not this hour:** not for an hour yet. 14. **cast:** dismissed.
23. **parley:** trumpet signal for a conference.
26. **alarum:** trumpet signal to arms.
30. **stope:** stoup, large drinking vessel.
40. **craftily qualified:** cannily diluted.
40–41. **innovation:** insurrection. 41. **here:** i.e. in his head.
47. **it dislikes me:** I don't care for it.
51. **my . . . dog:** a young lady's pet dog (likely to be spoiled).
53. **carous'd:** drunk off.
54. **pottle-deep:** to the bottom of the tankard. A pottle was a two-quart vessel.
55. **else:** others. **swelling:** proud.
56. **hold . . . distance:** i.e. are very touchy about their honor.
57. **very elements:** typical products.

Am I [to put] our Cassio in some action
That may offend the isle. But here they come.

Enter Cassio, Montano, *and* Gentlemen; [Servants *follow with wine*].

If consequence do but approve my dream,
My boat sails freely, both with wind and stream.

Cas. 'Fore [God], they have given me a rouse already.

Mon. Good faith, a little one; not past a pint, as I am a soldier.

Iago. Some wine ho!
[*Sings.*] "And let me the canakin clink, clink;
And let me the canakin clink.
A soldier's a man;
O, man's life's but a span;
Why then let a soldier drink."
Some wine, boys!

Cas. 'Fore [God], an excellent song.

Iago. I learn'd it in England, where indeed they are most potent in potting; your Dane, your German, and your swag-bellied Hollander—Drink ho!—are nothing to your English.

Cas. Is your [Englishman] so exquisite in his drinking?

Iago. Why, he drinks you, with facility, your Dane dead drunk; he sweats not to overthrow your Almain; he gives your Hollander a vomit ere the next pottle can be fill'd.

Cas. To the health of our general!

Mon. I am for it, lieutenant; and I'll do you justice.

Iago. O sweet England!
[*Sings.*]
"King Stephen was and-a worthy peer,
His breeches cost him but a crown;
He held them sixpence all too dear,
With that he call'd the tailor lown;
He was a wight of high renown,
And thou art but of low degree.
'Tis pride that pulls the country down,
[Then] take thy auld cloak about thee."
Some wine ho!

Cas. ['Fore God,] this is a more exquisite song than the other.

Iago. Will you hear't again?

Cas. No; for I hold him to be unworthy of his place that does those things. Well, [God's] above all; and there be souls must be sav'd, and there be souls must not be sav'd.

Iago. It's true, good lieutenant.

Cas. For mine own part—no offense to the general, nor any man of quality—I hope to be sav'd.

Iago. And so do I too, lieutenant.

Cas. Ay; but by your leave, not before me; the lieutenant is to be sav'd before the ancient. Let's have no more of this; let's to our affairs.—[God] forgive us our sins!—Gentlemen, let's look to our business. Do not think, gentlemen, I am drunk: this is my ancient, this is my right hand, and this is my left [hand]. I am not drunk now; I can stand well enough, and I speak well enough.

[*All.*] Excellent well.

Cas. Why, very well then; you must not think then that I am drunk. *Exit.*

Mon. To th' platform, masters, come, let's set the watch. [*The Gentlemen follow Cassio off.*]

Iago. You see this fellow that is gone before:
He's a soldier fit to stand by Caesar
And give direction; and do but see his vice,
'Tis to his virtue a just equinox,
The one as long as th' other. 'Tis pity of him.
I fear the trust Othello puts him in,
On some odd time of his infirmity,
Will shake this island.

Mon. But is he often thus?

Iago. 'Tis evermore [the] prologue to his sleep.
He'll watch the horologe a double set
If drink rock not his cradle.

Mon. It were well
The general were put in mind of it.
Perhaps he sees it not, or his good nature
Prizes the virtue that appears in Cassio,
And looks not on his evils. Is not this true?

Enter Roderigo.

Iago. [*Aside to him.*] How now, Roderigo?
I pray you, after the lieutenant, go. [*Exit Roderigo.*]

Mon. And 'tis great pity that the noble Moor
Should hazard such a place as his own second
With one of an ingraft infirmity;
It were an honest action to say
So to the Moor.

Iago. Not I, for this fair island.
I do love Cassio well; and would do much
To cure him of this evil. [*Cry within:* "Help! help!"]
But hark, what noise?

Enter Cassio *pursuing* Roderigo.

Cas. ['Zounds,] you rogue! you rascal!

Mon. What's the matter, lieutenant?

Cas. A knave teach me my duty? I'll beat the knave into a twiggen bottle.

Rod. Beat me?

Cas. Dost thou prate, rogue? [*Striking Roderigo.*]

Mon. Nay, good lieutenant; I pray you, sir, hold your hand. [*Staying him.*]

Cas. Let me go, sir, or I'll knock you o'er the mazzard.

Mon. Come, come—you're drunk.

Cas. Drunk? [*They fight.*]

Iago. [*Aside to Roderigo.*] Away, I say; go out and cry a mutiny. [*Exit Roderigo.*]

62. If ... dream: if the sequel corresponds to my fond hope.
63. stream: current. **64. rouse:** drink.
69–73. And ... drink. Probably an old drinking song.
72. span: i.e. brief stretch of time. **83. Almain:** German.
87. do you justice: i.e. match you in drinking that toast.
89–96. King ... thee. From an old ballad which is also alluded to in *The Tempest*, IV.i.222. **92. lown:** rascal.
95. pride: ostentation, extravagance.

124. just equinox: exact counterpart (of dark against light).
130. watch ... set: stay awake twice round the clock.
139–40. hazard ... With: take risks with a position as important as that of his own deputy by appointing.
140. ingraft: ingrained, inveterate.
148. twiggen: wicker-covered. **154. mazzard:** head.

Nay, good lieutenant—[God's will], gentlemen—
Help ho!—lieutenant—sir—Montano—[sir]—
Help, masters!—Here's a goodly watch indeed!
[*A bell rung.*]
Who's that which rings the bell? *Diablo*, ho!
The town will rise. [God's will], lieutenant, [hold]!
You'll be asham'd for ever.

Enter OTHELLO *and* [GENTLEMEN *with weapons*].

Oth. What is the matter here?
Mon. ['Zounds,] I bleed still,
I am hurt to th' death. He dies.
[*Assailing Cassio again.*]
Oth. Hold, for your lives!
Iago. Hold ho! Lieutenant—sir—Montano—gentlemen—
Have you forgot all place of sense and duty?
Hold! the general speaks to you; hold, for shame!
Oth. Why, how now ho? from whence ariseth this?
Are we turn'd Turks, and to ourselves do that
Which heaven hath forbid the Ottomites?
For Christian shame, put by this barbarous brawl.
He that stirs next to carve for his own rage
Holds his soul light; he dies upon his motion.
Silence that dreadful bell, it frights the isle
From her propriety. What is the matter, masters?
Honest Iago, that looks dead with grieving,
Speak: who began this? On thy love, I charge thee!
Iago. I do not know. Friends all, but now, even now;
In quarter, and in terms like bride and groom
Devesting them for bed; and then, but now
(As if some planet had unwitted men),
Swords out, and tilting one at other's [breast],
In opposition bloody. I cannot speak
Any beginning to this peevish odds;
And would in action glorious I had lost
Those legs that brought me to a part of it.
Oth. How comes it, Michael, you are thus forgot?
Cas. I pray you pardon me, I cannot speak.
Oth. Worthy Montano, you were wont to be civil;
The gravity and stillness of your youth
The world hath noted, and your name is great
In mouths of wisest censure. What's the matter
That you unlace your reputation thus,
And spend your rich opinion for the name
Of a night-brawler? Give me answer to it.
Mon. Worthy Othello, I am hurt to danger.
Your officer, Iago, can inform you—
While I spare speech, which something now offends me—
Of all that I do know, nor know I aught
By me that's said or done amiss this night,
Unless self-charity be sometimes a vice,

167. **place of sense**: i.e. the ordinary decencies. Some editors adopt Hanmer's emendation *sense of place*.
171. **Which . . . Ottomites**: i.e. by wrecking their fleet.
173. **carve . . . rage**: indulge his own impulse.
174. **light**: of small value.
176. **propriety**: natural temper (of calmness and order).
180. **quarter**: bounds. 185. **peevish odds**: childish quarrel.
188. **are thus forgot**: have forgotten yourself in this way.
193. **censure**: judgment. 194. **unlace**: lay open.
195. **opinion**: reputation. 199. **offends**: pains.

And to defend ourselves it be a sin
When violence assails us.
Oth. Now by heaven,
My blood begins my safer guides to rule,
And passion, having my best judgment collied,
Assays to lead the way. ['Zounds,] if I stir,
Or do but lift this arm, the best of you
Shall sink in my rebuke. Give me to know
How this foul rout began; who set it on;
And he that is approv'd in this offense,
Though he had twinn'd with me, both at a birth,
Shall lose me. What, in a town of war,
Yet wild, the people's hearts brimful of fear,
To manage private and domestic quarrel?
In night, and on the court and guard of safety?
'Tis monstrous. Iago, who began't?
Mon. If partially affin'd, or [leagu'd] in office,
Thou dost deliver more or less than truth,
Thou art no soldier.
Iago. Touch me not so near;
I had rather have this tongue cut from my mouth
Than it should do offense to Michael Cassio;
Yet I persuade myself, to speak the truth
Shall nothing wrong him. [Thus] it is, general:
Montano and myself being in speech,
There comes a fellow crying out for help,
And Cassio following him with determin'd sword
To execute upon him. Sir, this gentleman
Steps in to Cassio and entreats his pause;
Myself the crying fellow did pursue,
Lest by his clamor (as it so fell out)
The town might fall in fright. He, swift of foot,
Outran my purpose; and I return'd [the] rather
For that I heard the clink and fall of swords,
And Cassio high in oath; which till to-night
I ne'er might say before. When I came back
(For this was brief), I found them close together
At blow and thrust, even as again they were
When you yourself did part them.
More of this matter cannot I report.
But men are men; the best sometimes forget.
Though Cassio did some little wrong to him,
As men in rage strike those that wish them best,
Yet surely Cassio, I believe, receiv'd
From him that fled some strange indignity
Which patience could not pass.
Oth. I know, Iago,
Thy honesty and love doth mince this matter,
Making it light to Cassio. Cassio, I love thee,
But never more be officer of mine.

Enter DESDEMONA *attended*.

Look if my gentle love be not rais'd up!
I'll make thee an example.
Des. What is the matter, dear?
Oth. All's well [now], sweeting;

205. **blood**: anger. **safer guides**: i.e. rational controls.
206. **collied**: darkened. 211. **approv'd . . . offense**: found guilty.
215. **manage**: carry on.
216. **on . . . safety**: i.e. at the very headquarters on which the security of the town depends.
218. **partially affin'd**: biased (in Cassio's favor) because of your connection with him. 233. **rather**: sooner, i.e. more speedily.
246. **pass**: pass over. 247. **mince**: cut fine, i.e. try to make light of.

Come away to bed. [*To Montano.*] Sir, for your hurts,
Myself will be your surgeon.—Lead him off.
[*Some lead Montano off.*]
Iago, look with care about the town,
And silence those whom this vild brawl distracted.
Come, Desdemona, 'tis the soldiers' life
To have their balmy slumbers wak'd with strife.
Exit [*with Desdemona, Gentlemen, and Attendants*].

Iago. What, are you hurt, lieutenant?

Cas. Ay, past all surgery..

Iago. Marry, [God] forbid!

Cas. Reputation, reputation, reputation! O, I have lost my reputation! I have lost the immortal part of myself, and what remains is bestial. My reputation, Iago, my reputation!

Iago. As I am an honest man, I had thought you had receiv'd some bodily wound; there is more sense in that than in reputation. Reputation is an idle and most false imposition; oft got without merit, and lost without deserving. You have lost no reputation at all, unless you repute yourself such a loser. What, man, there are more ways to recover the general again. You are but now cast in his mood, a punishment more in policy than in malice, even so as one would beat his offenseless dog to affright an imperious lion. Sue to him again, and he's yours.

Cas. I will rather sue to be despis'd than to deceive so good a commander with so slight, so drunken, and so indiscreet an officer. Drunk? and speak parrot? and squabble? swagger? swear? and discourse fustian with one's own shadow? O thou invisible spirit of wine, if thou hast no name to be known by, let us call thee devil!

Iago. What was he that you follow'd with your sword? What had he done to you?

Cas. I know not.

Iago. Is't possible?

Cas. I remember a mass of things, but nothing distinctly; a quarrel, but nothing wherefore. O [God], that men should put an enemy in their mouths to steal away their brains! that we should, with joy, pleasance, revel, and applause, transform ourselves into beasts!

Iago. Why, but you are now well enough. How came you thus recover'd?

Cas. It hath pleas'd the devil drunkenness to give place to the devil wrath: one unperfectness shows me another, to make me frankly despise myself.

Iago. Come, you are too severe a moraler. As the time, the place, and the condition of this country stands, I could heartily wish this had not befall'n; but since it is as it is, mend it for your own good.

Cas. I will ask him for my place again, he shall tell me I am a drunkard! Had I as many mouths as Hydra, such an answer would stop them all. To be now a sensible man, by and by a fool, and presently a beast! O strange! Every inordinate cup is unbless'd, and the ingredient is a devil.

Iago. Come, come; good wine is a good familiar creature, if it be well us'd; exclaim no more against it. And, good lieutenant, I think you think I love you.

Cas. I have well approv'd it, sir. I drunk!

Iago. You, or any man living, may be drunk at a time, man. [I'll] tell you what you shall do. Our general's wife is now the general—I may say so in this respect, for that he hath devoted and given up himself to the contemplation, mark, and [denotement] of her parts and graces. Confess yourself freely to her; importune her help to put you in your place again. She is of so free, so kind, so apt, so bless'd a disposition, she holds it a vice in her goodness not to do more than she is requested. This broken joint between you and her husband entreat her to splinter; and my fortunes against any lay worth naming, this crack of your love shall grow stronger than it was before.

Cas. You advise me well.

Iago. I protest, in the sincerity of love and honest kindness.

Cas. I think it freely; and betimes in the morning I will beseech the virtuous Desdemona to undertake for me. I am desperate of my fortunes if they check me [here].

Iago. You are in the right. Good night, lieutenant, I must to the watch.

Cas. Good night, honest Iago. *Exit Cassio.*

Iago. And what's he then that says I play the villain,
When this advice is free I give, and honest,
Probal to thinking, and indeed the course
To win the Moor again? For 'tis most easy
Th' inclining Desdemona to subdue
In any honest suit; she's fram'd as fruitful
As the free elements. And then for her
To win the Moor, were['t] to renounce his baptism,
All seals and symbols of redeemed sin,
His soul is so enfetter'd to her love,
That she may make, unmake, do what she list,
Even as her appetite shall play the god
With his weak function. How am I then a villain,
To counsel Cassio to this parallel course,
Directly to his good? Divinity of hell!
When devils will the blackest sins put on,
They do suggest at first with heavenly shows,
As I do now; for whiles this honest fool
Plies Desdemona to repair his fortune,
And she for him pleads strongly to the Moor,

267. sense: physical sensation.
269. imposition: i.e. something laid on from outside; what others say of him, and not the man himself.
272. recover: regain the favor of.
273. cast: dismissed. **mood:** anger.
274. policy: expediency. **malice:** ill will.
274–75. as . . . lion. Proverbial. **278. slight:** worthless.
279. speak parrot: talk nonsense. **280. fustian:** gibberish.
304. Hydra: many-headed snake killed by Hercules as one of his twelve labors.
306. sensible: in possession of one's faculties.
309. familiar: domestic, serviceable.
312. approv'd: tested and found true.
313–14. at a time: at some time, on some occasion.
317. mark: marking, observing. **denotement:** noting.
318. parts: good qualities.
320. free: generous. **apt:** willing. **321. vice:** defect.
323. splinter: bind up with splints. **324. lay:** wager.
327. protest: declare. **337. free:** free from guile.
338. Probal to thinking: something that thought would show to be true. **341. fruitful:** generous. **348. function:** mental faculties.
349. parallel: i.e. conforming with these facts.
350. Divinity: theology. **352. suggest:** tempt.

I'll pour this pestilence into his ear—
That she repeals him for her body's lust,
And by how much she strives to do him good,
She shall undo her credit with the Moor.
So will I turn her virtue into pitch,
And out of her own goodness make the net
That shall enmesh them all.

Enter Roderigo.

How now, Roderigo?

Rod. I do follow here in the chase, not like a hound that hunts, but one that fills up the cry. My money is almost spent; I have been to-night exceedingly well cudgell'd; and I think the issue will be, I shall have so much experience for my pains; and so, with no money at all and a little more wit, return again to Venice.

Iago. How poor are they that have not patience!
What wound did ever heal but by degrees?
Thou know'st we work by wit, and not by witchcraft,
And wit depends on dilatory time.
Does't not go well? Cassio hath beaten thee,
And thou by that small hurt [hast] cashier'd Cassio.
Though other things grow fair against the sun,
Yet fruits that blossom first will first be ripe.
Content thyself a while. [By the mass], 'tis morning;
Pleasure and action make the hours seem short.
Retire thee, go where thou art billeted.
Away, I say, thou shalt know more hereafter.
Nay, get thee gone. (*Exit Roderigo.*) Two things are to be done:
My wife must move for Cassio to her mistress—
I'll set her on—
Myself a while to draw the Moor apart,
And bring him jump when he may Cassio find
Soliciting his wife. Ay, that's the way;
Dull not device by coldness and delay. *Exit.*

ACT III, Scene I

Enter Cassio [*with*] Musicians.

Cas. Masters, play here, I will content your pains;
Something that's brief; and bid "Good morrow, general."

[*They play, and enter the*] Clown.

Clo. Why, masters, have your instruments been in Naples, that they speak i' th' nose thus?

[*1.*] *Mus.* How, sir? how?

Clo. Are these, I pray you, wind instruments?

[*1.*] *Mus.* Ay, marry, are they, sir.

Clo. O, thereby hangs a tail.

[*1.*] *Mus.* Whereby hangs a tale, sir?

Clo. Marry, sir, by many a wind instrument that I know. But, masters, here's money for you; and the general so likes your music, that he desires you for love's sake to make no more noise with it.

[*1.*] *Mus.* Well, sir, we will not.

Clo. If you have any music that may not be heard, to't again; but (as they say) to hear music the general does not greatly care.

[*1.*] *Mus.* We have none such, sir.

Clo. Then put up your pipes in your bag, for I'll away. Go, vanish into air, away! *Exeunt Musicians.*

Cas. Dost thou hear, mine honest friend?

Clo. No, I hear not your honest friend; I hear you.

Cas. Prithee keep up thy quillets. There's a poor piece of gold for thee. If the gentlewoman that attends the [general's wife] be stirring, tell her there's one Cassio entreats her a little favor of speech. Wilt thou do this?

Clo. She is stirring, sir. If she will stir hither, I shall seem to notify unto her.

Cas. [Do, good my friend.] *Exit Clown.*

Enter Iago.

In happy time, Iago.

Iago. You have not been a-bed then?

Cas. Why, no; the day had broke
Before we parted. I have made bold, Iago,
To send in to your wife. My suit to her
Is that she will to virtuous Desdemona
Procure me some access.

Iago. I'll send her to you presently;
And I'll devise a mean to draw the Moor
Out of the way, that your converse and business
May be more free.

Cas. I humbly thank you for't. *Exit* [*Iago*].
I never knew a Florentine more kind and honest.

Enter Emilia.

Emil. Good morrow, good lieutenant. I am sorry
For your displeasure; but all will sure be well.
The general and his wife are talking of it,
And she speaks for you stoutly. The Moor replies
That he you hurt is of great fame in Cyprus,
And great affinity; and that in wholesome wisdom
He might not but refuse you. But he protests he loves you,
And needs no other suitor but his likings
[To take the safest occasion by the front]
To bring you in again.

Cas. Yet I beseech you,
If you think fit, or that it may be done,
Give me advantage of some brief discourse
With Desdemon alone.

Emil. Pray you come in.
I will bestow you where you shall have time
To speak your bosom freely.

Cas. I am much bound to you. [*Exeunt.*]

357. repeals: recalls, i.e. seeks to reinstate. **364. cry:** pack.
386. jump: at the precise moment. **388. device:** plotting.

III.i. Location: The citadel.
1. content: requite.
4. speak . . . thus: i.e. sound like a man whose nose has been affected by syphilis (a disease supposed to have originated in Naples).

15. may not: cannot.
23. keep up: do not bring out. **quillets:** quibbles, puns.
26. a little . . . speech: the favor of a brief conference.
30. In happy time: opportunely met.
40. a Florentine: i.e. even a Florentine, one of my own townsmen.
42. displeasure: loss of favor. **46. affinity:** family connections.
49. occasion: opportunity. **front:** forelock.
55. bosom: most private concerns.

Scene II

Enter Othello, Iago, *and* Gentlemen.

Oth. These letters give, Iago, to the pilot,
And by him do my duties to the Senate.
That done, I will be walking on the works;
Repair there to me.
Iago. Well, my good lord, I'll do't.
Oth. This fortification, gentlemen, shall we see't?
Gentlemen. We'll wait upon your lordship. *Exeunt.*

Scene III

Enter Desdemona, Cassio, *and* Emilia.

Des. Be thou assur'd, good Cassio, I will do
All my abilities in thy behalf.
Emil. Good madam, do. I warrant it grieves my husband
As if the cause were his.
Des. O, that's an honest fellow. Do not doubt, Cassio,
But I will have my lord and you again
As friendly as you were.
Cas. Bounteous madam,
What ever shall become of Michael Cassio,
He's never any thing but your true servant.
Des. I know't; I thank you. You do love my lord;
You have known him long, and be you well assur'd
He shall in strangeness stand no farther off
Than in a politic distance.
Cas. Ay, but, lady,
That policy may either last so long,
Or feed upon such nice and waterish diet,
Or breed itself so out of circumstances,
That I being absent and my place supplied,
My general will forget my love and service.
Des. Do not doubt that; before Emilia here,
I give thee warrant of thy place. Assure thee,
If I do vow a friendship, I'll perform it
To the last article. My lord shall never rest,
I'll watch him tame, and talk him out of patience;
His bed shall seem a school, his board a shrift,
I'll intermingle every thing he does
With Cassio's suit. Therefore be merry, Cassio,
For thy solicitor shall rather die
Than give thy cause away.

Enter Othello *and* Iago.

Emil. Madam, here comes my lord.
Cas. Madam, I'll take my leave.
Des. Why, stay, and hear me speak.
Cas. Madam, not now; I am very ill at ease,
Unfit for mine own purposes.
Des. Well, do your discretion. *Exit Cassio.*
Iago. Hah? I like not that.
Oth. What dost thou say?
Iago. Nothing, my lord; or if—I know not what.
Oth. Was not that Cassio parted from my wife?
Iago. Cassio, my lord? No, sure, I cannot think it,
That he would steal away so guilty-like,
Seeing your coming.
Oth. I do believe 'twas he.
Des. How now, my lord?
I have been talking with a suitor here,
A man that languishes in your displeasure.
Oth. Who is't you mean?
Des. Why, your lieutenant, Cassio. Good my lord,
If I have any grace or power to move you,
His present reconciliation take;
For if he be not one that truly loves you,
That errs in ignorance and not in cunning,
I have no judgment in an honest face.
I prithee call him back.
Oth. Went he hence now?
Des. [Yes, faith]; so humbled
That he hath left part of his grief with me
To suffer with him. Good love, call him back.
Oth. Not now, sweet Desdemon, some other time.
Des. But shall't be shortly?
Oth. The sooner, sweet, for you.
Des. Shall't be to-night at supper?
Oth. No, not to-night.
Des. To-morrow dinner then?
Oth. I shall not dine at home;
I meet the captains at the citadel.
Des. Why then to-morrow night, [or] Tuesday morn;
On Tuesday noon, or night; on We'n'sday morn.
I prithee name the time, but let it not
Exceed three days. In faith, he's penitent;
And yet his trespass, in our common reason
(Save that they say the wars must make example
Out of her best), is not almost a fault
T' incur a private check. When shall he come?
Tell me, Othello. I wonder in my soul
What you would ask me that I should deny,
Or stand so mamm'ring on. What? Michael Cassio,
That came a-wooing with you, and so many a time,
When I have spoke of you dispraisingly,
Hath ta'en your part—to have so much to do
To bring him in! [By'r lady], I could do much—
Oth. Prithee no more; let him come when he will;
I will deny thee nothing.
Des. Why, this is not a boon;
'Tis as I should entreat you wear your gloves,
Or feed on nourishing dishes, or keep you warm,
Or sue to you to do a peculiar profit

III.ii. Location: The citadel.
2. do my duties: send my dutiful respects.
3. works: fortifications.

III.iii. Location: The garden of the citadel.
12. strangeness: aloofness. **13. politic:** dictated by policy.
15. feed . . . diet: i.e. require so little to keep it alive (*nice* = trivial).
16. breed . . . circumstances: be revived by some accident or other.
17. supplied: filled. **19. doubt:** fear. **21. friendship:** friendly act.
23. watch him tame: keep him awake till he capitulates (as in training a hawk). **talk . . . patience:** keep talking until he can't endure it any longer. **24. shrift:** confessional. **28. away:** up.
47. reconciliation: repentance. **49. in cunning:** wittingly.
66. her. *Wars* was frequently construed as a singular. See I.i.150–51, I.iii.234, III.iii.349–50. **not almost:** scarcely.
67. a private check: even a private rebuke.
70. mamm'ring: hesitating. **73. to do:** ado, fuss.
74. bring him in: i.e. restore him to your favor.
79. peculiar profit: personal benefit.

To your own person. Nay, when I have a suit
Wherein I mean to touch your love indeed,
It shall be full of poise and difficult weight,
And fearful to be granted.
Oth. I will deny thee nothing;
Whereon, I do beseech thee, grant me this,
To leave me but a little to myself.
Des. Shall I deny you? No. Farewell, my lord.
Oth. Farewell, my Desdemona, I'll come to thee straight.
Des. Emilia, come.—Be as your fancies teach you;
What e'er you be, I am obedient. *Exit [with Emilia].*
Oth. Excellent wretch! Perdition catch my soul
But I do love thee! and when I love thee not,
Chaos is come again.
Iago. My noble lord—
Oth. What dost thou say, Iago?
Iago. Did Michael Cassio, when [you] woo'd my lady,
Know of your love?
Oth. He did, from first to last. Why dost thou ask?
Iago. But for a satisfaction of my thought,
No further harm.
Oth. Why of thy thought, Iago?
Iago. I did not think he had been acquainted with her.
Oth. O yes, and went between us very oft.
Iago. Indeed!
Oth. Indeed? ay, indeed. Discern'st thou aught in that?
Is he not honest?
Iago. Honest, my lord?
Oth. Honest? ay, honest.
Iago. My lord, for aught I know.
Oth. What dost thou think?
Iago. Think, my lord?
Oth. Think, my lord? [By heaven], thou echo'st me,
As if there were some monster in thy thought
Too hideous to be shown. Thou dost mean something.
I heard thee say even now, thou lik'st not that,
When Cassio left my wife. What didst not like?
And when I told thee he was of my counsel
[In] my whole course of wooing, thou criedst, "Indeed!"
And didst contract and purse thy brow together,
As if thou then hadst shut up in thy brain
Some horrible conceit. If thou dost love me,
Show me thy thought.
Iago. My lord, you know I love you.
Oth. I think thou dost;
And for I know thou'rt full of love and honesty,
And weigh'st thy words before thou giv'st them breath,
Therefore these stops of thine fright me the more;
For such things in a false disloyal knave
Are tricks of custom; but in a man that's just
They're close dilations, working from the heart,

82. poise: weight. **84. Whereon:** in return for which.
91. But I do: if I do not. **111. of my counsel:** in my confidence.
123. close dilations: expressions of secret thought.

That passion cannot rule.
Iago. For Michael Cassio,
I dare be sworn I think that he is honest.
Oth. I think so too.
Iago. Men should be what they seem,
Or those that be not, would they might seem none!
Oth. Certain, men should be what they seem.
Iago. Why then I think Cassio's an honest man.
Oth. Nay, yet there's more in this.
I prithee speak to me as to thy thinkings,
As thou dost ruminate, and give thy worst of thoughts
The worst of words.
Iago. Good my lord, pardon me:
Though I am bound to every act of duty,
I am not bound to that all slaves are free [to].
Utter my thoughts? Why, say they are vild and false,
As where's that palace whereinto foul things
Sometimes intrude not? Who has that breast so pure
[But some] uncleanly apprehensions
Keep leets and law-days and in sessions sit
With meditations lawful?
Oth. Thou dost conspire against thy friend, Iago,
If thou but think'st him wrong'd, and mak'st his ear
A stranger to thy thoughts.
Iago. I do beseech you,
Though I perchance am vicious in my guess
(As I confess it is my nature's plague
To spy into abuses, and [oft] my jealousy
Shapes faults that are not), that your wisdom [then],
From one that so imperfectly [conjects],
Would take no notice, nor build yourself a trouble
Out of his scattering and unsure observance.
It were not for your quiet nor your good,
Nor for my manhood, honesty, and wisdom,
To let you know my thoughts.
Oth. ['Zounds,] what dost thou mean?
Iago. Good name in man and woman, dear my lord,
Is the immediate jewel of their souls.
Who steals my purse steals trash; 'tis something, nothing;
'Twas mine, 'tis his, and has been slave to thousands;
But he that filches from me my good name
Robs me of that which not enriches him,
And makes me poor indeed.
Oth. [By heaven,] I'll know thy thoughts.
Iago. You cannot, if my heart were in your hand,
Nor shall not, whilst 'tis in my custody.
Oth. Ha?
Iago. O, beware, my lord, of jealousy!
It is the green-ey'd monster which doth mock
The meat it feeds on. That cuckold lives in bliss
Who, certain of his fate, loves not his wronger;
But O, what damned minutes tells he o'er
Who dotes, yet doubts; suspects, yet [strongly] loves!
Oth. O misery!

124. passion cannot rule: i.e. the man because of his impassioned state cannot control. **131. as to:** with respect to.
135. that . . . to: that which even a slave is not bound to.
139. apprehensions: thoughts. **140. leets:** sessions of local courts.
141. With meditations lawful: along with innocent thoughts.
147. jealousy: suspicion. **148. then:** on that account.
163. if: even if.
167. meat . . . on: i.e. the heart of the man who suffers it.

Iago. Poor and content is rich, and rich enough,
But riches fineless is as poor as winter
To him that ever fears he shall be poor.
Good [God], the souls of all my tribe defend
From jealousy!
Oth. Why? why is this?
Think'st thou I'ld make a life of jealousy?
To follow still the changes of the moon
With fresh suspicions? No! to be once in doubt
Is [once] to be resolv'd. Exchange me for a goat,
When I shall turn the business of my soul
To such [exsufflicate] and [blown] surmises,
Matching thy inference. 'Tis not to make me jealious
To say my wife is fair, feeds well, loves company,
Is free of speech, sings, plays, and dances [well];
Where virtue is, these are more virtuous.
Nor from mine own weak merits will I draw
The smallest fear or doubt of her revolt,
For she had eyes, and chose me. No, Iago,
I'll see before I doubt; when I doubt, prove;
And on the proof, there is no more but this—
Away at once with love or jealousy!
Iago. I am glad of this, for now I shall have reason
To show the love and duty that I bear you
With franker spirit; therefore (as I am bound)
Receive it from me. I speak not yet of proof.
Look to your wife, observe her well with Cassio,
Wear your eyes thus, not jealious nor secure.
I would not have your free and noble nature,
Out of self-bounty, be abus'd; look to't.
I know our country disposition well:
In Venice they do let [God] see the pranks
They dare not show their husbands; their best conscience
Is not to leave't undone, but keep't unknown.
Oth. Dost thou say so?
Iago. She did deceive her father, marrying you,
And when she seem'd to shake and fear your looks,
She lov'd them most.
Oth. And so she did.
Iago. Why, go to then.
She that so young could give out such a seeming
To seel her father's eyes up, close as oak,
He thought 'twas witchcraft—but I am much to blame;
I humbly do beseech you of your pardon
For too much loving you.
Oth. I am bound to thee for ever.
Iago. I see this hath a little dash'd your spirits.
Oth. Not a jot, not a jot.
Iago. [I' faith], I fear it has.
I hope you will consider what is spoke
Comes from [my] love. But I do see y' are mov'd.
I am to pray you not to strain my speech

To grosser issues nor to larger reach
Than to suspicion.
Oth. I will not.
Iago. Should you do so, my lord,
My speech should fall into such vild success
Which my thoughts aim'd not. Cassio's my worthy friend—
My lord, I see y' are mov'd.
Oth. No, not much mov'd:
I do not think but Desdemona's honest.
Iago. Long live she so! and long live you to think so!
Oth. And yet how nature erring from itself—
Iago. Ay, there's the point; as (to be bold with you)
Not to affect many proposed matches
Of her own clime, complexion, and degree,
Whereto we see in all things nature tends—
Foh, one may smell in such, a will most rank,
Foul disproportions, thoughts unnatural.
But (pardon me) I do not in position
Distinctly speak of her, though I may fear
Her will, recoiling to her better judgment,
May fall to match you with her country forms,
And happily repent.
Oth. Farewell, farewell!
If more thou dost perceive, let me know more;
Set on thy wife to observe. Leave me, Iago.
Iago. [*Going*.] My lord, I take my leave.
Oth. Why did I marry? This honest creature, doubtless,
Sees and knows more, much more, than he unfolds.
Iago. [*Returning*.] My lord, I would I might entreat your honor
To scan this thing no farther; leave it to time.
Although 'tis fit that Cassio have his place—
For sure he fills it up with great ability—
Yet if you please to [hold] him off awhile,
You shall by that perceive him and his means.
Note if your lady strain his entertainment
With any strong or vehement importunity;
Much will be seen in that. In the mean time,
Let me be thought too busy in my fears
(As worthy cause I have to fear I am)
And hold her free, I do beseech your honor.
Oth. Fear not my government.
Iago. I once more take my leave. *Exit.*
Oth. This fellow's of exceeding honesty,
And knows all [qualities], with a learned spirit,
Of human dealings. If I do prove her haggard,
Though that her jesses were my dear heart-strings,

173. **fineless**: boundless. 180. **once**: once for all.
182. **exsufflicate and blown.** Both adjectives may mean "blown-up, inflated," or the phrase may mean "spat-out and fly-blown."
183. **jealious**: jealous, suspicious.
188. **doubt**: suspicion. **revolt**: unfaithfulness.
190. **prove**: test.
198. **secure**: culpably free of anxiety, overconfident.
200. **self-bounty**: inherent goodness.
210. **oak.** A close-grained wood. 213. **bound**: indebted.

219. **issues**: conclusions. **reach**: scope. 222. **success**: effect.
225. **honest**: chaste. 229. **affect**: desire, look with favor on.
230. **clime**: region, country. 232. **will**: desire, appetite.
233. **disproportions**: abnormality.
234. **in position**: i.e. in arguing thus.
235. **Distinctly speak of**: refer specifically to.
236. **recoiling . . . judgment**: reverting to a more natural preference.
237. **match**: compare. **her country forms**: the appearance of her countrymen. 238. **happily**: haply, perchance.
250. **strain his entertainment**: repeatedly urge his reappointment.
255. **free**: guiltless. 256. **government**: conduct, self-control.
259. **qualities**: types, conditions.
260. **haggard**: wild (a term from falconry).
261. **jesses**: leather straps on the hawk's legs, by which it was fastened to the leash held by the falconer.

I'ld whistle her off, and let her down the wind
To prey at fortune. Haply, for I am black,
And have not those soft parts of conversation
That chamberers have, or for I am declin'd
Into the vale of years (yet that's not much),
She's gone. I am abus'd, and my relief
Must be to loathe her. O curse of marriage!
That we can call these delicate creatures ours,
And not their appetites! I had rather be a toad
And live upon the vapor of a dungeon
Than keep a corner in the thing I love
For others' uses. Yet 'tis the plague [of] great ones,
Prerogativ'd are they less than the base;
'Tis destiny unshunnable, like death.
Even then this forked plague is fated to us
When we do quicken. Look where she comes:

Enter DESDEMONA *and* EMILIA.

If she be false, [O then] heaven [mocks] itself!
I'll not believe't.
Des. How now, my dear Othello?
Your dinner, and the generous islanders
By you invited, do attend your presence.
Oth. I am to blame.
Des. Why do you speak so faintly?
Are you not well?
Oth. I have a pain upon my forehead, here.
Des. [Faith], that's with watching, 'twill away again.
Let me but bind it hard, within this hour
It will be well.
Oth. Your napkin is too little;
[*He puts the handkerchief from him, and it drops.*]
Let it alone. Come, I'll go in with you.
Des. I am very sorry that you are not well.
Exit [*with Othello*].
Emil. I am glad I have found this napkin;
This was her first remembrance from the Moor.
My wayward husband hath a hundred times
Woo'd me to steal it; but she so loves the token
(For he conjur'd her she should ever keep it)
That she reserves it evermore about her
To kiss and talk to. I'll have the work ta'en out,
And give't Iago. What he will do with it
Heaven knows, not I;
I nothing but to please his fantasy.

Enter IAGO.

Iago. How now? what do you here alone?
Emil. Do not you chide; I have a thing for you.
Iago. You have a thing for me? It is a common thing—
Emil. Hah?
Iago. To have a foolish wife.
Emil. O, is that all? What will you give me now
For that same handkerchief?
Iago. What handkerchief?
Emil. What handkerchief?
Why, that the Moor first gave to Desdemona,
That which so often you did bid me steal.
Iago. Hast stol'n it from her?
Emil. No, [faith]; she let it drop by negligence,
And to th' advantage, I, being here, took't up.
Look, here 'tis.
Iago. A good wench, give it me.
Emil. What will you do with't, that you have been so earnest
To have me filch it?
Iago. [*Snatching it*]. Why, what is that to you?
Emil. If it be not for some purpose of import,
Give't me again. Poor lady, she'll run mad
When she shall lack it.
Iago. Be not acknown on't; I have use for it.
Go, leave me. *Exit Emilia.*
I will in Cassio's lodging lose this napkin,
And let him find it. Trifles light as air
Are to the jealious confirmations strong
As proofs of holy writ; this may do something.
The Moor already changes with my poison:
Dangerous conceits are in their natures poisons,
Which at the first are scarce found to distaste,
But with a little act upon the blood
Burn like the mines of sulphur.

Enter OTHELLO.

I did say so.
Look where he comes! Not poppy, nor mandragora,
Nor all the drowsy syrups of the world
Shall ever medicine thee to that sweet sleep
Which thou ow'dst yesterday.
Oth. Ha, ha, false to me?
Iago. Why, how now, general? No more of that.
Oth. Avaunt, be gone! thou hast set me on the rack.
I swear 'tis better to be much abus'd
Than but to know't a little.
Iago. How now, my lord?
Oth. What sense had I in her stol'n hours of lust?
I saw't not, thought it not; it harm'd not me.
I slept the next night well, fed well, was free and merry;
I found not Cassio's kisses on her lips.
He that is robb'd, not wanting what is stol'n,
Let him not know't, and he's not robb'd at all.
Iago. I am sorry to hear this.
Oth. I had been happy, if the general camp,
Pioners and all, had tasted her sweet body,
So I had nothing known. O now, for ever
Farewell the tranquil mind! farewell content!
Farewell the plumed troops and the big wars

262. down the wind. To release the hawk downwind was to court its loss. **263. at fortune:** at random. **for:** because.
264. soft . . . conversation: pleasing qualities of social behavior.
265. chamberers: gallants. **274. Prerogativ'd:** privileged.
276. forked plague: curse of cuckold's horns.
277. quicken: begin to live. **280. generous:** noble.
285. with watching: from lack of sleep. **287. napkin:** handkerchief.
288. Let it alone: don't trouble yourself about it.
292. wayward: capricious. **296. work ta'en out:** pattern copied.
299. I nothing but: my only thought is. **fantasy:** fancy, whim.

312. to th' advantage: upon the opportunity.
319. Be . . . on't: pretend not to know of it.
328. with . . . act: after they have acted for a little while.
330. mandragora: an opiate, made of the mandrake.
333. ow'dst: didst own. **338. in:** of.
340. free: carefree. **342. wanting:** missing.
346. Pioners: the lowest rank of soldier, primarily used for manual labor, not fighting. **349. big:** stately.

That makes ambition virtue! O, farewell!
Farewell the neighing steed and the shrill trump,
The spirit-stirring drum, th' ear-piercing fife,
The royal banner, and all quality,
Pride, pomp, and circumstance of glorious war!
And O you mortal engines, whose rude throats
Th' immortal Jove's dread clamors counterfeit,
Farewell! Othello's occupation's gone.

Iago. Is't possible, my lord?

Oth. Villain, be sure thou prove my love a whore;
[*Taking him by the throat.*]
Be sure of it. Give me the ocular proof,
Or by the worth of mine eternal soul,
Thou hadst been better have been born a dog
Than answer my wak'd wrath!

Iago. Is't come to this?

Oth. Make me to see't; or (at the least) so prove it
That the probation bear no hinge nor loop
To hang a doubt on; or woe upon thy life!

Iago. My noble lord—

Oth. If thou dost slander her and torture me,
Never pray more; abandon all remorse;
On horror's head horrors accumulate;
Do deeds to make heaven weep, all earth amaz'd;
For nothing canst thou to damnation add
Greater than that.

Iago. O grace! O heaven forgive me!
Are you a man? Have you a soul? or sense?
God buy you; take mine office. O wretched fool,
That lov'st to make thine honesty a vice!
O monstrous world! Take note, take note, O world,
To be direct and honest is not safe.
I thank you for this profit, and from hence
I'll love no friend, sith love breeds such offense.

Oth. Nay, stay. Thou shouldst be honest.

Iago. I should be wise—for honesty's a fool
And loses that it works for.

Oth. By the world,
I think my wife be honest, and think she is not;
I think that thou art just, and think thou art not.
I'll have some proof. [Her] name, that was as fresh
As Dian's visage, is now begrim'd and black
As mine own face. If there be cords, or knives,
Poison, or fire, or suffocating streams,
I'll not endure it. Would I were satisfied!

Iago. I see, [sir], you are eaten up with passion;
I do repent me that I put it to you.
You would be satisfied?

Oth. Would? nay, and I will.

Iago. And may; but how? How satisfied, my lord?
Would you, the [supervisor], grossly gape on?
Behold her topp'd?

Oth. Death and damnation! O!

Iago. It were a tedious difficulty, I think,
To bring them to that prospect; damn them then,
If ever mortal eyes do see them bolster
More than their own. What then? How then?
What shall I say? Where's satisfaction?
It is impossible you should see this,
Were they as prime as goats, as hot as monkeys,
As salt as wolves in pride, and fools as gross
As ignorance made drunk. But yet, I say,
If imputation and strong circumstances
Which lead directly to the door of truth
Will give you satisfaction, you might have't.

Oth. Give me a living reason she's disloyal.

Iago. I do not like the office;
But sith I am ent'red in this cause so far
(Prick'd to't by foolish honesty and love),
I will go on. I lay with Cassio lately,
And being troubled with a raging tooth,
I could not sleep.
There are a kind of men, so loose of soul,
That in their sleeps will mutter their affairs;
One of this kind is Cassio.
In sleep I heard him say, "Sweet Desdemona,
Let us be wary, let us hide our loves";
And then, sir, would he gripe and wring my hand;
Cry, "O sweet creature!" then kiss me hard,
As if he pluck'd up kisses by the roots
That grew upon my lips; [then] laid his leg
[Over] my thigh, and [sigh'd], and [kiss'd], and then
[Cried], "Cursed fate that gave thee to the Moor!"

Oth. O monstrous! monstrous!

Iago. Nay, this was but his dream.

Oth. But this denoted a foregone conclusion.

[*Iago.*] 'Tis a shrewd doubt, though it be but a dream,
And this may help to thicken other proofs
That do demonstrate thinly.

Oth. I'll tear her all to pieces.

Iago. Nay, yet be wise; yet we see nothing done;
She may be honest yet. Tell me but this,
Have you not sometimes seen a handkerchief
Spotted with strawberries in your wive's hand?

Oth. I gave her such a one; 'twas my first gift.

Iago. I know not that; but such a handkerchief
(I am sure it was your wive's) did I to-day
See Cassio wipe his beard with.

Oth. If it be that—

Iago. If it be that, or any [that] was hers,
It speaks against her with the other proofs.

Oth. O that the slave had forty thousand lives!
One is too poor, too weak for my revenge.
Now do I see 'tis true. Look here, Iago,
All my fond love thus do I blow to heaven.
'Tis gone.
Arise, black vengeance, from the hollow hell!

353. **quality:** character, attributes.
354. **Pride:** proud display. **pomp:** dignity. **circumstance:** ceremonial splendor.
355. **mortal:** deadly. **engines:** instruments of war; here, cannon.
365. **probation:** proof. 369. **remorse:** pity.
371. **amaz'd:** utterly confounded.
375. **God buy you:** God be with you, i.e. goodbye.
376. **vice:** flaw, failing. 379. **profit:** valuable lesson.
380. **sith:** since. **offense:** injury (to the one who loves).
381. **Thou shouldst be:** i.e. all indications point to the fact that you are.
382. **should be:** ought to be. 395. **supervisor:** onlooker, spectator.

398–99. **damn . . . ever:** i.e. to condemn them only if.
399. **bolster:** go to bed together. 400. **More:** other (eyes).
402. **see:** i.e. contrive to be an actual witness of.
403. **prime:** lustful. 404. **salt:** lecherous. **pride:** heat.
421. **gripe:** grip, clasp.
428. **foregone conclusion:** act already performed.
429. **shrewd doubt:** strong reason for suspicion.
430. **thicken:** substantiate. 435. **wive's:** wife's.
442. **the slave:** i.e. Cassio.

Yield up, O love, thy crown and hearted throne
To tyrannous hate! Swell, bosom, with thy fraught,
For 'tis of aspics' tongues!

Iago. Yet be content.

Oth. O blood, blood, blood!

Iago. Patience, I say; your mind [perhaps] may change.

Oth. Never, Iago. Like to the Pontic Sea,
Whose icy current and compulsive course
Nev'r [feels] retiring ebb, but keeps due on
To the Propontic and the Hellespont,
Even so my bloody thoughts, with violent pace,
Shall nev'r look back, nev'r ebb to humble love,
Till that a capable and wide revenge
Swallow them up. [*He kneels.*] Now by yond marble heaven,
In the due reverence of a sacred vow
I here engage my words.

Iago. Do not rise yet. [*Iago kneels.*]
Witness, you ever-burning lights above,
You elements that clip us round about,
Witness that here Iago doth give up
The execution of his wit, hands, heart,
To wrong'd Othello's service! Let him command,
And to obey shall be in me remorse,
What bloody business ever. [*They rise.*]

Oth. I greet thy love,
Not with vain thanks, but with acceptance bounteous,
And will upon the instant put thee to't:
Within these three days let me hear thee say
That Cassio's not alive.

Iago. My friend is dead; 'tis done at your request.
But let her live.

Oth. Damn her, lewd minx! O, damn her, damn her!
Come go with me apart, I will withdraw
To furnish me with some swift means of death
For the fair devil. Now art thou my lieutenant.

Iago. I am your own for ever. *Exeunt.*

SCENE IV

Enter DESDEMONA, EMILIA, *and* CLOWN.

Des. Do you know, sirrah, where Lieutenant Cassio lies?

Clo. I dare not say he lies any where.

Des. Why, man?

Clo. He's a soldier, and for me to say a soldier lies, 'tis stabbing.

Des. Go to! where lodges he?

Clo. To tell you where he lodges, is to tell you where I lie.

448. **hearted:** established in my heart. 449. **fraught:** burden.
450. **aspics':** asps'. 453. **Pontic Sea:** Black Sea.
459. **capable:** capacious, comprehensive.
460. **marble:** shining (?) or enduring, changeless (cf. *marble-constant*, in *Antony and Cleopatra*, V.ii.240) (?).
464. **clip:** embrace. 466. **execution:** action.
468–69. **to . . . ever:** i.e. in Othello's service even the cruellest acts will be as allowable as if they were gentle and prompted by pity (*remorse*). 476. **minx:** wanton.

III.iv. Location: Before the citadel.
1. **sirrah:** term of address to inferiors. 2. **lies:** lodges.

Des. Can any thing be made of this?

Clo. I know not where he lodges, and for me to devise a lodging and say he lies here, or he lies there, were to lie in mine own throat.

Des. Can you inquire him out, and be edified by report?

Clo. I will catechize the world for him, that is, make questions, and by them answer.

Des. Seek him, bid him come hither. Tell him I have mov'd my lord on his behalf, and hope all will be well.

Clo. To do this is within the compass of man's wit, and therefore I will attempt the doing it. *Exit Clown.*

Des. Where should I lose the handkerchief, Emilia?

Emil. I know not, madam.

Des. Believe me, I had rather have lost my purse
Full of crusadoes; and but my noble Moor
Is true of mind, and made of no such baseness
As jealious creatures are, it were enough
To put him to ill thinking.

Emil. Is he not jealious?

Des. Who, he? I think the sun where he was born
Drew all such humors from him.

Emil. Look where he comes.

Enter OTHELLO.

Des. I will not leave him now till Cassio
Be call'd to him.—How is't with you, my lord?

Oth. Well, my good lady. [*Aside.*] O, hardness to dissemble!—
How do you, Desdemona?

Des. Well, my good lord.

Oth. Give me your hand. This hand is moist, my lady.

Des. It [yet] hath felt no age nor known no sorrow.

Oth. This argues fruitfulness and liberal heart;
Hot, hot, and moist. This hand of yours requires
A sequester from liberty: fasting and prayer,
Much castigation, exercise devout,
For here's a young and sweating devil here
That commonly rebels. 'Tis a good hand,
A frank one.

Des. You may, indeed, say so;
For 'twas that hand that gave away my heart.

Oth. A liberal hand. The hearts of old gave hands;
But our new heraldry is hands, not hearts.

Des. I cannot speak of this. Come now, your promise.

Oth. What promise, chuck?

Des. I have sent to bid Cassio come speak with you.

13. **lie . . . throat:** tell a gross and deliberate lie.
19. **mov'd:** urged, made suit to.
23. **should I lose:** could I have lost.
26. **crusadoes:** Portuguese coins stamped with a cross.
31. **humors:** bodily fluids (which were thought to determine temperament). 40. **sequester:** sequestration, separation.
41. **castigation:** corrective discipline, penance.
44. **frank.** Desdemona takes this as meaning "generous," but Othello may have in mind also the meanings "lusty, vigorous" and "open, unable to conceal secrets." So *liberal* in line 46 means both "generous" and "licentious."
47. **our . . . hearts:** under our newfangled heraldry, hands (given in marriage) no longer signify that hearts are given also.
49. **chuck:** a term of endearment, related to *chick*.

Oth. I have a salt and sorry rheum offends me;
Lend me thy handkerchief.
Des. Here, my lord.
Oth. That which I gave you.
Des. I have it not about me.
Oth. Not?
Des. No, [faith], my lord.
Oth. That's a fault. That handkerchief
Did an Egyptian to my mother give;
She was a charmer, and could almost read
The thoughts of people. She told her, while she kept it,
'Twould make her amiable, and subdue my father
Entirely to her love; but if she lost it,
Or made a gift of it, my father's eye
Should hold her loathed, and his spirits should hunt
After new fancies. She, dying, gave it me,
And bid me, when my fate would have me wiv'd,
To give it her. I did so; and take heed on't,
Make it a darling like your precious eye.
To lose't or give't away were such perdition
As nothing else could match.
Des. Is't possible?
Oth. 'Tis true; there's magic in the web of it.
A sibyl, that had numb'red in the world
The sun to course two hundred compasses,
In her prophetic fury sew'd the work;
The worms were hallowed that did breed the silk,
And it was dy'd in mummy which the skillful
Conserv'd of maidens' hearts.
Des. [I' faith]! is't true?
Oth. Most veritable, therefore look to't well.
Des. Then would to [God] that I had never seen't!
Oth. Ha? wherefore?
Des. Why do you speak so startingly and rash?
Oth. Is't lost? Is't gone? Speak, is't out o' th' way?
Des. [Heaven] bless us!
Oth. Say you?
Des. It is not lost; but what and if it were?
Oth. How?
Des. I say, it is not lost.
Oth. Fetch't, let me see't.
Des. Why, so I can, [sir,] but I will not now.
This is a trick to put me from my suit.
Pray you let Cassio be receiv'd again.
Oth. Fetch me the handkerchief, my mind misgives.
Des. Come, come;
You'll never meet a more sufficient man.
Oth. The handkerchief!
[*Des.* I pray talk me of Cassio.
Oth. The handkerchief!]
Des. A man that all his time
Hath founded his good fortunes on your love,
Shar'd dangers with you—
Oth. The handkerchief!
Des. [I' faith], you are to blame.
Oth. ['Zounds!] *Exit Othello.*
Emil. Is not this man jealious?
Des. I nev'r saw this before.
Sure, there's some wonder in this handkerchief;
I am most unhappy in the loss of it.
Emil. 'Tis not a year or two shows us a man:
They are all but stomachs, and we all but food;
They eat us hungerly, and when they are full
They belch us.

Enter Iago *and* Cassio.

Look you, Cassio and my husband!
Iago. There is no other way: 'tis she must do't;
And lo the happiness! Go, and importune her.
Des. How now, good Cassio, what's the news with you?
Cas. Madam, my former suit. I do beseech you
That by your virtuous means I may again
Exist, and be a member of his love
Whom I, with all the office of my heart,
Entirely honor. I would not be delay'd.
If my offense be of such mortal kind
That nor my service past, nor present sorrows,
Nor purpos'd merit in futurity,
Can ransom me into his love again,
But to know so must be my benefit;
So shall I clothe me in a forc'd content,
And shut myself up in some other course,
To fortune's alms.
Des. Alas, thrice-gentle Cassio,
My advocation is not now in tune.
My lord is not my lord; nor should I know him
Were he in favor as in humor alter'd.
So help me every spirit sanctified,
As I have spoken for you all my best,
And stood within the blank of his displeasure
For my free speech! You must awhile be patient.
What I can do, I will; and more I will
Than for myself I dare. Let that suffice you.
Iago. Is my lord angry?
Emil. He went hence but now;
And certainly in strange unquietness.
Iago. Can he be angry? I have seen the cannon
When it hath blown his ranks into the air,
And like the devil from his very arm
Puff'd his own brother—and is he angry?
Something of moment then. I will go meet him.
There's matter in't indeed, if he be angry.
Des. I prithee do so. *Exit* [*Iago*].
Something sure of state,
Either from Venice, or some unhatch'd practice
Made demonstrable here in Cyprus to him,
Hath puddled his clear spirit; and in such cases

51. salt . . . rheum: distressing watering of the eyes.
57. charmer: magician. **59. amiable:** desirable.
65. her: i.e. to my wife. **67. perdition:** loss.
69. web: fabric. **70. sibyl:** prophetess.
72. prophetic fury: the divine frenzy which enabled her to prophesy.
74. mummy: fluid drawn from embalmed bodies.
75. Conserv'd: prepared.
79. startingly and rash: disjointedly and impetuously.
83. and if: if. **91. sufficient:** able, complete.

104. but: nothing but. **108. happiness:** good luck.
111. virtuous: efficacious. **113. office:** devoted service.
115. mortal: fatal.
117. purpos'd . . . futurity: intention to serve well in the future.
119. But: merely.
122. fortune's alms: pittances handed out by Fortune to beggars.
125. favor: appearance.
128. blank: centre of a target, i.e. direct line of aim.
141. unhatch'd practice: plot not yet ready for execution.
143. puddled: muddied.

Men's natures wrangle with inferior things,
Though great ones are their object. 'Tis even so;
For let our finger ache, and it endues
Our other healthful members even to a sense
Of pain. Nay, we must think men are not gods,
Nor of them look for such observancy
As fits the bridal. Beshrew me much, Emilia,
I was (unhandsome warrior as I am)
Arraigning his unkindness with my soul;
But now I find I had suborn'd the witness,
And he's indicted falsely.
Emil. Pray heaven it be state matters, as you think,
And no conception nor no jealious toy
Concerning you.
Des. Alas the day, I never gave him cause.
Emil. But jealious souls will not be answer'd so;
They are not ever jealious for the cause,
But jealious for they're jealious. It is a monster
Begot upon itself, born on itself.
Des. Heaven keep the monster from Othello's mind!
Emil. Lady, amen.
Des. I will go seek him. Cassio, walk hereabout;
If I do find him fit, I'll move your suit
And seek to effect it to my uttermost.
Cas. I humbly thank your ladyship.
Exeunt [Desdemona and Emilia].

Enter BIANCA.

Bian. 'Save you, friend Cassio!
Cas. What make you from home?
How is't with you, my most fair Bianca?
[I'faith], sweet love, I was coming to your house.
Bian. And I was going to your lodging, Cassio.
What? keep a week away? seven days and nights?
Eightscore eight hours? and lovers' absent hours,
More tedious than the dial eightscore times?
O weary reck'ning!
Cas. Pardon me, Bianca.
I have this while with leaden thoughts been press'd,
But I shall in a more continuate time
Strike off this score of absence. Sweet Bianca,
[Giving her Desdemona's handkerchief.]
Take me this work out.
Bian. O Cassio, whence came this?
This is some token from a newer friend;
To the felt absence now I feel a cause.
Is't come to this? Well, well.
Cas. Go to, woman!
Throw your vild guesses in the devil's teeth,
From whence you have them. You are jealious now
That this is from some mistress, some remembrance;
No, [by my faith], Bianca.
Bian. Why, whose is it?

146. **endues:** makes conformable.
149. **observancy:** devoted attention.
150. **Beshrew me.** A very mild imprecation.
151. **unhandsome:** unskillful. 152. **with:** before the bar of.
153. **suborn'd the witness:** caused the witness to lie, i.e. misinterpreted Othello's behavior. 156. **toy:** fancy.
162. **Begot . . . itself:** i.e. spontaneously generated, without cause.
169. **'Save you:** God save you. 178. **continuate:** uninterrupted.
179. **Strike . . . score:** settle this account.

Cas. I know not, neither; I found it in my chamber.
I like the work well; ere it be demanded
(As like enough it will) I would have it copied.
Take it, and do't, and leave me for this time.
Bian. Leave you? Wherefore?
Cas. I do attend here on the general,
And think it no addition, nor my wish,
To have him see me woman'd.
Bian. Why, I pray you?
Cas. Not that I love you not.
Bian. But that you do not love me.
I pray you bring me on the way a little,
And say if I shall see you soon at night.
Cas. 'Tis but a little way that I can bring you,
For I attend here; but I'll see you soon.
Bian. 'Tis very good; I must be circumstanc'd.
Exeunt omnes.

ACT IV, SCENE I

Enter OTHELLO *and* IAGO.

Iago. Will you think so?
Oth. Think so, Iago?
Iago. What,
To kiss in private?
Oth. An unauthoriz'd kiss!
Iago. Or to be naked with her friend in bed
An hour, or more, not meaning any harm?
Oth. Naked in bed, Iago, and not mean harm?
It is hypocrisy against the devil.
They that mean virtuously, and yet do so,
The devil their virtue tempts, and they tempt heaven.
Iago. If they do nothing, 'tis a venial slip;
But if I give my wife a handkerchief—
Oth. What then?
Iago. Why then 'tis hers, my lord, and being hers,
She may, I think, bestow't on any man.
Oth. She is protectress of her honor too;
May she give that?
Iago. Her honor is an essence that's not seen;
They have it very oft that have it not.
But for the handkerchief—
Oth. By heaven, I would most gladly have forgot it.
Thou saidst (O, it comes o'er my memory,
As doth the raven o'er the infectious house,
Boding to all) he had my handkerchief.
Iago. Ay; what of that?
Oth. That's not so good now.
Iago. What
If I had said I had seen him do you wrong?
Or heard him say—as knaves be such abroad,
Who having by their own importunate suit,
Or voluntary dotage of some mistress,
Convinced or supplied them, cannot choose
But they must blab—
Oth. Hath he said any thing?

189. **demanded:** inquired for. 194. **addition:** credit.
201. **be circumstanc'd:** yield to circumstances, accept your conditions.

IV.i. **Location:** Before the citadel.
17. **They . . . oft:** i.e. often individuals are credited with it.
28. **Convinced or supplied:** conquered or satisfied.

Iago. He hath, my lord, but be you well assur'd,
No more than he'll unswear.
Oth. What hath he said?
Iago. [Faith], that he did—I know not what he did.
Oth. What? what?
Iago. Lie—
Oth. With her?
Iago. With her? On her; what you will.
Oth. Lie with her? lie on her? We say lie on her, when they belie her. Lie with her! ['Zounds,] that's fulsome! Handkerchief—confessions—handkerchief! To confess, and be hang'd for his labor—first to be hang'd, and then to confess. I tremble at it. Nature would not invest herself in such shadowing passion without some instruction. It is not words that shakes me thus. Pish! Noses, ears, and lips. Is't possible? Confess? Handkerchief? O devil! *Falls in a trance.*
Iago. Work on,
My medicine, [work]! Thus credulous fools are caught,
And many worthy and chaste dames even thus
(All guiltless) meet reproach.—What ho! my lord!
My lord, I say! Othello!

Enter Cassio.

How now, Cassio?
Cas. What's the matter?
Iago. My lord is fall'n into an epilepsy.
This is his second fit; he had one yesterday.
Cas. Rub him about the temples.
Iago. [No, forbear,]
The lethargy must have his quiet course;
If not, he foams at mouth, and by and by
Breaks out to savage madness. Look, he stirs.
Do you withdraw yourself a little while,
He will recover straight. When he is gone,
I would on great occasion speak with you.
[*Exit Cassio.*]
How is it, general? Have you not hurt your head?
Oth. Dost thou mock me?
Iago. I mock you not, by heaven.
Would you would bear your fortune like a man!
Oth. A horned man's a monster and a beast.
Iago. There's many a beast then in a populous city,
And many a civil monster.
Oth. Did he confess it?
Iago. Good sir, be a man;
Think every bearded fellow that's but yok'd
May draw with you. There's millions now alive
That nightly lie in those unproper beds
Which they dare swear peculiar; your case is better.
O, 'tis the spite of hell, the fiend's arch-mock,
To lip a wanton in a secure couch,
And to suppose her chaste! No, let me know,
And knowing what I am, I know what she shall be.

40. **shadowing**: coming over one like a shadow, i.e. overwhelming suddenly (?) or filling the imagination with shapes and figures (?). **passion**: paroxysm of emotion. 41. **instruction**: prompting, cause.
53. **lethargy**: coma. **his**: its.
59. **hurt your head**. Othello takes this as alluding to the cuckold's horns. 64. **civil**: i.e. among the citizenry, city-dwelling.
66. **yok'd**: married. 67. **draw**: pull (like oxen under the yoke).
68. **unproper**: not their own. 69. **peculiar**: their own.
71. **secure**: free from suspicion.

Oth. O, thou art wise; 'tis certain.
Iago. Stand you a while apart,
Confine yourself but in a patient list.
Whilst you were here o'erwhelmed with your grief
(A passion most [unsuiting] such a man),
Cassio came hither. I shifted him away,
And laid good 'scuses upon your ecstasy;
Bade him anon return and here speak with me,
The which he promis'd. Do but encave yourself,
And mark the fleers, the gibes, and notable scorns
That dwell in every region of his face,
For I will make him tell the tale anew:
Where, how, how oft, how long ago, and when
He hath, and is again to cope your wife.
I say, but mark his gesture. Marry, patience,
Or I shall say y' are all in all in spleen,
And nothing of a man.
Oth. Dost thou hear, Iago,
I will be found most cunning in my patience;
But (dost thou hear) most bloody.
Iago. That's not amiss,
But yet keep time in all. Will you withdraw?
[*Othello withdraws.*]
Now will I question Cassio of Bianca,
A huswife that by selling her desires
Buys herself bread and [clothes]. It is a creature
That dotes on Cassio (as 'tis the strumpet's plague
To beguile many and be beguil'd by one);
He, when he hears of her, cannot restrain
From the excess of laughter. Here he comes.

Enter Cassio.

As he shall smile, Othello shall go mad;
And his unbookish jealousy must [conster]
Poor Cassio's smiles, gestures, and light behaviors
Quite in the wrong. How do you [now], lieutenant?
Cas. The worser that you give me the addition
Whose want even kills me.
Iago. Ply Desdemona well, and you are sure on't.
[*Speaking lower.*] Now, if this suit lay in Bianca's [pow'r],
How quickly should you speed!
Cas. Alas, poor caitiff!
Oth. Look how he laughs already!
Iago. I never knew woman love man so.
Cas. Alas, poor rogue, I think, [i' faith], she loves me.
Oth. Now he denies it faintly, and laughs it out.
Iago. Do you hear, Cassio?
Oth. Now he importunes him
To tell it o'er. Go to, well said, well said.
Iago. She gives it out that you shall marry her.
Do you intend it?
Cas. Ha, ha, ha!
Oth. Do [you] triumph, Roman? do you triumph?

75. **in . . . list**: within the bounds of patience. 79. **ecstasy**: trance.
82. **fleers**: sneers. **notable**: obvious. 86. **cope**: encounter with.
88. **spleen**. Considered the seat of sudden and capricious impulses.
94. **huswife**: hussy.
101. **unbookish**: uninstructed, unpracticed. **conster**: construe, interpret. The figure is of a person trying to translate a language he is ignorant of. 104. **addition**: title. 108. **caitiff**: wretch.
112. **faintly**: not very earnestly.
118. **Roman**: exultant fellow (suggested by *triumph*).

Cas. I marry [her]! What? a customer! Prithee bear some charity to my wit, do not think it so unwholesome. Ha, ha, ha!

Oth. So, so, so, so; they laugh that wins.

Iago. [Faith], the cry goes that you marry her.

Cas. Prithee say true.

Iago. I am a very villain else.

Oth. Have you scor'd me? Well.

Cas. This is the monkey's own giving out. She is persuaded I will marry her, out of her own love and flattery, not out of my promise.

Oth. Iago [beckons] me; now he begins the story.

Cas. She was here even now; she haunts me in every place. I was the other day talking on the sea-bank with certain Venetians, and thither comes the bauble, and [by this hand,] falls me thus about my neck—

Oth. Crying, "O dear Cassio!" as it were; his gesture imports it.

Cas. So hangs, and lolls, and weeps upon me; so [hales] and pulls me. Ha, ha, ha!

Oth. Now he tells how she pluck'd him to my chamber. O, I see that nose of yours, but not that dog I shall throw it to.

Cas. Well, I must leave her company.

Iago. Before me! look where she comes.

Enter Bianca.

Cas. 'Tis such another fitchew! marry, a perfum'd one!—What do you mean by this haunting of me?

Bian. Let the devil and his dam haunt you! What did you mean by that same handkerchief you gave me even now? I was a fine fool to take it. I must take out the work? A likely piece of work, that you should find it in your chamber, and know not who left it there! This is some minx's token, and I must take out the work? There, give it your hobby-horse. Wheresoever you had it, I'll take out no work on't.

Cas. How now, my sweet Bianca? how now? how now?

Oth. By heaven, that should be my handkerchief!

Bian. [An'] you'll come to supper to-night, you may; [an'] you will not, come when you are next prepar'd for. *Exit.*

Iago. After her, after her.

Cas. [Faith,] I must, she'll rail in the streets else.

Iago. Will you sup there?

Cas. [Faith], I intend so.

Iago. Well, I may chance to see you; for I would very fain speak with you.

Cas. Prithee come; will you?

Iago. Go to; say no more. [*Exit Cassio.*]

Oth. [*Advancing.*] How shall I murther him, Iago?

Iago. Did you perceive how he laugh'd at his vice?

Oth. O Iago!

Iago. And did you see the handkerchief?

Oth. Was that mine?

Iago. Yours, by this hand. And to see how he prizes the foolish woman your wife! She gave it him, and he hath giv'n it his whore.

Oth. I would have him nine years a-killing. A fine woman! a fair woman! a sweet woman!

Iago. Nay, you must forget that.

Oth. Ay, let her rot, and perish, and be damn'd to-night, for she shall not live. No, my heart is turn'd to stone; I strike it, and it hurts my hand. O, the world hath not a sweeter creature! she might lie by an emperor's side and command him tasks.

Iago. Nay, that's not your way.

Oth. Hang her, I do but say what she is. So delicate with her needle! an admirable musician! O, she will sing the savageness out of a bear. Of so high and plenteous wit and invention!

Iago. She's the worse for all this.

Oth. O, a thousand, a thousand times. And then of so gentle a condition!

Iago. Ay, too gentle.

Oth. Nay, that's certain. But yet the pity of it, Iago! O Iago, the pity of it, Iago!

Iago. If you are so fond over her iniquity, give her patent to offend, for if it touch not you, it comes near nobody.

Oth. I will chop her into messes. Cuckold me!

Iago. O, 'tis foul in her.

Oth. With mine officer!

Iago. That's fouler.

Oth. Get me some poison, Iago, this night. I'll not expostulate with her, lest her body and beauty unprovide my mind again. This night, Iago.

Iago. Do it not with poison; strangle her in her bed, even the bed she hath contaminated.

Oth. Good, good; the justice of it pleases; very good.

Iago. And for Cassio, let me be his undertaker. You shall hear more by midnight.

Oth. Excellent good. [*A trumpet.*] What trumpet
is that same?

Iago. I warrant, something from Venice.

Enter Lodovico, Desdemona, *and* Attendants.

'Tis Lodovico—
This comes from the Duke. See, your wife's with him.

Lod. [God] save you, worthy general!

Oth. With all my heart, sir.

Lod. The Duke and the senators of Venice greet
you. [*Gives him a letter.*]

Oth. I kiss the instrument of their pleasures.
[*Opens the letter and reads.*]

Des. And what's the news, good cousin Lodovico?

119. **customer:** prostitute.
120–21. **unwholesome:** unsound. 126. **scor'd:** scored off, beaten.
128–29. **own . . . flattery:** self-love and self-satisfaction.
130. **beckons:** signals. 135. **bauble:** plaything.
146. **fitchew:** polecat (thought to be very lecherous as well as strong-smelling). 154. **hobby-horse:** woman of easy virtue.
159. **An':** and, i.e. if.

186. **your way:** your proper course, the direction your mind should take.
193. **of . . condition:** so nobly born and bred.
194. **gentle:** i.e. generous with her favors.
197. **fond:** dotingly foolish. 198. **patent:** license.
200. **messes:** portions of food, i.e. little pieces.
205. **body and beauty:** physical beauty.
211. **be his undertaker:** undertake to dispatch him.
216. **With . . . heart:** i.e. I heartily thank you.

Iago. I am very glad to see you, signior;
Welcome to Cyprus.
Lod. I thank you. How does Lieutenant Cassio?
Iago. Lives, sir.
Des. Cousin, there's fall'n between him and my lord
An unkind breach; but you shall make all well.
Oth. Are you sure of that?
Des. My lord?
Oth. [*Reads.*] "This fail you not to do, as you will—"
Lod. He did not call; he's busy in the paper.
Is there division 'twixt my lord and Cassio?
Des. A most unhappy one. I would do much
T' atone them, for the love I bear to Cassio.
Oth. Fire and brimstone!
Des. My lord?
Oth. Are you wise?
Des. What, is he angry?
Lod. May be th' letter mov'd him;
For as I think, they do command him home,
Deputing Cassio in his government.
Des. [By my troth], I am glad on't.
Oth. Indeed?
Des. My lord?
Oth. I am glad to see you mad.
Des. Why, sweet Othello?
Oth. [*Striking her.*] Devil!
Des. I have not deserv'd this.
Lod. My lord, this would not be believ'd in Venice,
Though I should swear I saw't. 'Tis very much,
Make her amends; she weeps.
Oth. O devil, devil!
If that the earth could teem with woman's tears,
Each drop she falls would prove a crocodile.
Out of my sight!
Des. I will not stay to offend you. [*Going.*]
Lod. Truly, [an] obedient lady:
I do beseech your lordship call her back.
Oth. Mistress!
Des. My lord?
Oth. What would you with her, sir?
Lod. Who, I, my lord?
Oth. Ay, you did wish that I would make her turn.
Sir, she can turn, and turn; and yet go on
And turn again; and she can weep, sir, weep;
And she's obedient, as you say, obedient;
Very obedient.—Proceed you in your tears.—
Concerning this, sir—O well-painted passion!—
I am commanded home.—Get you away;
I'll send for you anon.—Sir, I obey the mandate,
And will return to Venice.—Hence, avaunt!
[*Exit Desdemona.*]
Cassio shall have my place. And, sir, to-night
I do entreat that we may sup together.
You are welcome, sir, to Cyprus.—Goats and monkeys!
Exit.
Lod. Is this the noble Moor whom our full Senate
Call all in all sufficient? Is this the nature

233. **atone:** reconcile. 245. **teem with:** be made pregnant by.
246. **falls:** lets fall. 260. **avaunt:** begone.
263. **Goats and monkeys.** Cf. III.iii.403.

Whom passion could not shake? whose solid virtue
The shot of accident nor dart of chance
Could neither graze nor pierce?
Iago. He is much chang'd.
Lod. Are his wits safe? Is he not light of brain?
Iago. He's that he is; I may not breathe my censure
What he might be. If what he might he is not,
I would to heaven he were!
Lod. What? strike his wife?
Iago. Faith, that was not so well; yet would I knew
That stroke would prove the worst!
Lod. Is it his use?
Or did the letters work upon his blood,
And new-create [this] fault?
Iago. Alas, alas!
It is not honesty in me to speak
What I have seen and known. You shall observe him,
And his own courses will denote him so
That I may save my speech. Do but go after,
And mark how he continues.
Lod. I am sorry that I am deceiv'd in him.
Exeunt.

Scene II

Enter Othello *and* Emilia.

Oth. You have seen nothing then?
Emil. Nor ever heard—nor ever did suspect.
Oth. Yes, you have seen Cassio and she together.
Emil. But then I saw no harm, and then I heard
Each syllable that breath made up between them.
Oth. What? did they never whisper?
Emil. Never, my lord.
Oth. Nor send you out o' th' way?
Emil. Never.
Oth. To fetch her fan, her gloves, her mask, nor nothing?
Emil. Never, my lord.
Oth. That's strange.
Emil. I durst, my lord, to wager she is honest;
Lay down my soul at stake. If you think other,
Remove your thought; it doth abuse your bosom.
If any wretch have put this in your head,
Let heaven requite it with the serpent's curse!
For if she be not honest, chaste, and true,
There's no man happy; the purest of their wives
Is foul as slander.
Oth. Bid her come hither; go. *Exit Emilia.*
She says enough; yet she's a simple bawd
That cannot say as much. This is a subtile whore,
A closet lock and key of villainous secrets;
And yet she'll kneel and pray; I have seen her do't.

269. **safe:** sound.
270–71. **censure . . . be:** i.e. opinion as to whether he is insane.
272. **I . . . were:** i.e. because otherwise his behavior is unpardonable.
274. **use:** habit. 275. **blood:** passions.

IV.ii. Location: The citadel.
16. **the serpent's curse:** the curse laid by God on the serpent that tempted Eve. Emilia implies that the crime of a slanderer of Desdemona, who is as innocent as Eve was before the fall, would be of the same magnitude.
20–21. **she's . . . much:** the bawd who cannot say as much is a stupid one.
22. **closet:** place where private papers could be locked up.

Enter DESDEMONA *and* EMILIA.

Des. My lord, what is your will?
Oth. Pray you, chuck, come hither.
Des. What is your pleasure?
Oth. Let me see your eyes;
Look in my face.
Des. What horrible fancy's this?
Oth. [*To Emilia.*] Some of your function, mistress;
Leave procreants alone, and shut the door;
Cough, or cry "hem," if anybody come.
Your mystery, your mystery; [nay], dispatch.
Exit Emilia.
Des. Upon my knee, what doth your speech import?
I understand a fury in your words,
[But not the words].
Oth. Why? what art thou?
Des. Your wife, my lord; your true
And loyal wife.
Oth. Come swear it, damn thyself,
Lest being like one of heaven, the devils themselves
Should fear to seize thee; therefore be double damn'd:
Swear thou art honest.
Des. Heaven doth truly know it.
Oth. Heaven truly knows that thou art false as hell.
Des. To whom, my lord? With whom? How am I false?
Oth. Ah, Desdemon! Away, away, away!
Des. Alas the heavy day! Why do you weep?
Am I the motive of these tears, my lord?
If happily you my father do suspect
An instrument of this your calling back,
Lay not your blame on me. If you have lost him,
[Why,] I have lost him too.
Oth. Had it pleas'd heaven
To try me with affliction, had they rain'd
All kind of sores and shames on my bare head,
Steep'd me in poverty to the very lips,
Given to captivity me and my utmost hopes,
I should have found in some place of my soul
A drop of patience; but, alas, to make me
The fixed figure for the time of scorn
To point his slow [unmoving] finger at!
Yet could I bear that too, well, very well;
But there, where I have garner'd up my heart,
Where either I must live or bear no life;
The fountain from the which my current runs
Or else dries up: to be discarded thence!
Or keep it as a cestern for foul toads
To knot and gender in! Turn thy complexion there,
Patience, thou young and rose-lipp'd cherubin—
Ay, here look grim as hell!
Des. I hope my noble lord esteems me honest.

Oth. O ay, as summer flies are in the shambles,
That quicken even with blowing. O thou weed!
Who art so lovely fair and smell'st so sweet
That the sense aches at thee, would thou hadst never been born!
Des. Alas, what ignorant sin have I committed?
Oth. Was this fair paper, this most goodly book,
Made to write "whore" upon? What committed?
Committed? O thou public commoner,
I should make very forges of my cheeks,
That would to cinders burn up modesty,
Did I but speak thy deeds. What committed?
Heaven stops the nose at it, and the moon winks;
The bawdy wind, that kisses all it meets,
Is hush'd within the hollow mine of earth
And will not hear't. What committed?
[Impudent strumpet!]
Des. By heaven, you do me wrong.
Oth. Are not you a strumpet?
Des. No, as I am a Christian.
If to preserve this vessel for my lord
From any other foul unlawful touch
Be not to be a strumpet, I am none.
Oth. What, not a whore?
Des. No, as I shall be sav'd.
Oth. Is't possible?
Des. O, heaven forgive us!
Oth. I cry you mercy then.
I took you for that cunning whore of Venice
That married with Othello.—[*Raising his voice.*] You, mistress,

Enter EMILIA.

That have the office opposite to Saint Peter,
And keeps the gate of hell! You, you! ay, you!
We have done our course; there's money for your pains.
I pray you turn the key and keep our counsel. *Exit.*
Emil. Alas, what does this gentleman conceive?
How do you, madam? how do you, my good lady?
Des. Faith, half asleep.
Emil. Good madam, what's the matter with my lord?
Des. With who?
Emil. Why, with my lord, madam.
Des. Who is thy lord?
Emil. He that is yours, sweet lady.
Des. I have none. Do not talk to me, Emilia;
I cannot weep, nor answers have I none
But what should go by water. Prithee to-night
Lay on my bed my wedding-sheets—remember;
And call thy husband hither.
Emil. Here's a change indeed! *Exit.*
Des. 'Tis meet I should be us'd so, very meet.
How have I been behav'd, that he might stick
The small'st opinion on my least misuse?

27. **Some . . . function:** go about your bawd's business (of standing watch outside the door). 30. **mystery:** trade.
43. **motive:** moving force, cause. 48. **they:** i.e. the gods.
54. **time of scorn:** scornful world.
55. **slow unmoving finger.** A troublesome phrase; perhaps the meaning is that the finger points steadily and is slow to alter its aim, or that it rises slowly to its aim and then remains fixed.
59. **fountain:** source, spring. 61. **cestern:** cistern.
62. **Turn:** change. **there:** at that point, when that happens.

67. **quicken . . . blowing:** come to life as soon as the eggs are deposited.
73. **commoner:** prostitute. 77. **winks:** shuts her eyes.
81. **Impudent:** shameless. 88. **cry you mercy:** beg your pardon.
104. **go by water:** be rendered by tears.
109. **opinion:** censure. **my least misuse:** the slightest misconduct on my part.

Enter IAGO *and* EMILIA.

Iago. What is your pleasure, madam? How is't
with you?
Des. I cannot tell. Those that do teach young babes
Do it with gentle means and easy tasks.
He might have chid me so; for in good faith
I am a child to chiding.
Iago. What is the matter, lady?
Emil. Alas, Iago, my lord hath so bewhor'd her,
Thrown such despite and heavy terms upon her,
That true hearts cannot bear it.
Des. Am I that name, Iago?
Iago. What name, fair lady?
Des. Such as she said my lord did say I was.
Emil. He call'd her whore. A beggar in his drink
Could not have laid such terms upon his callet.
Iago. Why did he so?
Des. I do not know; I am sure I am none such.
Iago. Do not weep, do not weep. Alas the day!
Emil. Hath she forsook so many noble matches?
Her father? and her country? and her friends?
To be call'd whore? Would it not make one weep?
Des. It is my wretched fortune.
Iago. Beshrew him for't!
How comes this trick upon him?
Des. Nay, heaven doth know.
Emil. I will be hang'd if some eternal villain,
Some busy and insinuating rogue,
Some cogging, cozening slave, to get some office,
Have not devis'd this slander. I will be hang'd else.
Iago. Fie, there is no such man; it is impossible.
Des. If any such there be, heaven pardon him!
Emil. A halter pardon him! and hell gnaw his
bones!
Why should he call her whore? Who keeps her company?
What place? what time? what form? what likelihood?
The Moor's abus'd by some most villainous knave,
Some base notorious knave, some scurvy fellow.
O [heaven], that such companions thou'dst unfold,
And put in every honest hand a whip
To lash the rascals naked through the world
Even from the east to th' west!
Iago. Speak within door.
Emil. O fie upon them! Some such squire he was
That turn'd your wit the seamy side without,
And made you to suspect me with the Moor.
Iago. You are a fool; go to.
Des. Alas, Iago,
What shall I do to win my lord again?
Good friend, go to him; for by this light of heaven,
I know not how I lost him. Here I kneel:
If e'er my will did trespass 'gainst his love,
Either in discourse of thought or actual deed,

Or that mine eyes, mine ears, or any sense
Delighted them [in] any other form;
Or that I do not yet, and ever did,
And ever will (though he do shake me off
To beggarly divorcement) love him dearly,
Comfort forswear me! Unkindness may do much,
And his unkindness may defeat my life,
But never taint my love. I cannot say "whore."
It does abhor me now I speak the word;
To do the act that might the addition earn,
Not the world's mass of vanity could make me.
Iago. I pray you be content; 'tis but his humor.
The business of the state does him offense,
[And he does chide with you].
Des. If 'twere no other—
Iago. It is but so, I warrant.
[*Trumpets within.*]
Hark how these instruments summon to supper!
The messengers of Venice stays the meat.
Go in, and weep not; all things shall be well.
Exeunt Desdemona and Emilia.

Enter RODERIGO.

How now, Roderigo?
Rod. I do not find that thou deal'st justly with me.
Iago. What in the contrary?
Rod. Every day thou daff'st me with some device, Iago, and rather, as it seems to me now, keep'st from me all conveniency than suppliest me with the least advantage of hope. I will indeed no longer endure it; nor am I yet persuaded to put up in peace what already I have foolishly suff'red.

Iago. Will you hear me, Roderigo?

Rod. [Faith,] I have heard too much; [for] your words and performances are no kin together.

Iago. You charge me most unjustly.

Rod. With nought but truth. I have wasted myself out of my means. The jewels you have had from me to deliver Desdemona would half have corrupted a votarist. You have told me she hath receiv'd them and return'd me expectations and comforts of sudden respect and acquaintance, but I find none.

Iago. Well, go to; very well.

Rod. Very well! go to! I cannot go to, man, nor 'tis not very well. [By this hand,] I think it is scurvy, and begin to find myself fopp'd in it.

Iago. Very well.

Rod. I tell you 'tis not very well. I will make myself known to Desdemona. If she will return me my jewels, I will give over my suit and repent my unlawful solicitation; if not, assure yourself I will seek satisfaction of you.

Iago. You have said now.

Rod. Ay; and said nothing but what I protest intendment of doing.

121. **callet**: whore. 129. **trick**: odd behavior.
130. **eternal**: inveterate.
131. **insinuating**: worming his way into favor.
132. **cogging**: cheating. **cozening**: deceiving.
138. **form**: shape, i.e. specific circumstances.
141. **companions**: fellows. **unfold**: expose.
144. **within door**: i.e. less loudly.
146. **seamy side without**: wrong side out.
153. **discourse of thought**: process of thinking.

160. **defeat**: destroy. 162. **abhor me**: fill me with abhorrence.
163. **addition**: designation. 165. **humor**: mood.
170. **stays the meat**: wait to dine.
175. **daff'st me**: puttest me off.
177. **conveniency**: i.e. opportunity to meet Desdemona.
179. **put up**: tolerate, stomach. 187–88. **votarist**: nun.
189–90. **sudden respect**: immediate consideration.
194. **fopp'd**: made a fool of, duped.

Iago. Why, now I see there's mettle in thee, and even from this instant do build on thee a better opinion than ever before. Give me thy hand, Roderigo. Thou hast taken against me a most just exception; but yet I protest I have dealt most directly in thy affair.

Rod. It hath not appear'd.

Iago. I grant indeed it hath not appear'd; and your suspicion is not without wit and judgment. But, Roderigo, if thou hast that in thee indeed, which I have greater reason to believe now than ever (I mean purpose, courage, and valor), this night show it. If thou the next night following enjoy not Desdemona, take me from this world with treachery and devise engines for my life.

Rod. Well; what is it? Is it within reason and compass?

Iago. Sir, there is especial commission come from Venice to depute Cassio in Othello's place.

Rod. Is that true? Why then Othello and Desdemona return again to Venice.

Iago. O no; he goes into Mauritania and taketh away with him the fair Desdemona, unless his abode be ling'red here by some accident; wherein none can be so determinate as the removing of Cassio.

Rod. How do you mean, removing him?

Iago. Why, by making him uncapable of Othello's place: knocking out his brains.

Rod. And that you would have me to do?

Iago. Ay; if you dare do yourself a profit and a right. He sups to-night with a harlotry, and thither will I go to him—he knows not yet of his honorable fortune. If you will watch his going thence (which I will fashion to fall out between twelve and one), you may take him at your pleasure. I will be near to second your attempt, and he shall fall between us. Come, stand not amaz'd at it, but go along with me; I will show you such a necessity in his death that you shall think yourself bound to put it on him. It is now high supper-time, and the night grows to waste. About it.

Rod. I will hear further reason for this.

Iago. And you shall be satisfied. *Exeunt.*

Scene III

Enter Othello, Lodovico, Desdemona, Emilia, *and* Attendants.

Lod. I do beseech you, sir, trouble yourself no
further.
Oth. O, pardon me; 'twill do me good to walk.
Lod. Madam, good night; I humbly thank your
ladyship.
Des. Your honor is most welcome.
Oth. Will you walk, sir?
O, Desdemona!
Des. My lord?

216–17. **engines for:** plots against.
227. **determinate:** effectual. 233. **harlotry:** slut.
242–43. **grows to waste:** is being wasted.
IV.iii. Location: The citadel.

Oth. Get you to bed on th' instant, I will be return'd forthwith. Dismiss your attendant there. Look't be done.
Des. I will, my lord.
Exeunt [Othello, Lodovico, and Attendants].
Emil. How goes it now? He looks gentler than
he did.
Des. He says he will return incontinent,
And hath commanded me to go to bed,
And bid me to dismiss you.
Emil. Dismiss me?
Des. It was his bidding; therefore, good Emilia,
Give me my nightly wearing, and adieu.
We must not now displease him.
Emil. I would you had never seen him!
Des. So would not I. My love doth so approve him,
That even his stubbornness, his checks, his frowns—
Prithee unpin me—have grace and favor [in them].
Emil. I have laid those sheets you bade me on the
bed.
Des. All's one. Good [faith], how foolish are our
minds!
If I do die before [thee], prithee shroud me
In one of these same sheets.
Emil. Come, come; you talk.
Des. My mother had a maid call'd Barbary;
She was in love, and he she lov'd prov'd mad,
And did forsake her. She had a song of "Willow,"
An old thing 'twas, but it express'd her fortune,
And she died singing it. That song to-night
Will not go from my mind; I have much to do
But to go hang my head all at one side
And sing it like poor Barbary. Prithee dispatch.
Emil. Shall I go fetch your night-gown?
Des. No, unpin me here.
This Lodovico is a proper man.
Emil. A very handsome man.
Des. He speaks well.
Emil. I know a lady in Venice would have walk'd barefoot to Palestine for a touch of his nether lip.
Des. [*Singing.*]
"The poor soul sat [sighing] by a sycamore tree,
Sing all a green willow;
Her hand on her bosom, her head on her knee,
Sing willow, willow, willow.
The fresh streams ran by her, and murmur'd her
moans,
Sing willow, willow, willow;
Her salt tears fell from her, and soft'ned the stones,
Sing willow"—
Lay by these—
[*Singing.*] "—willow, willow"—
Prithee hie thee; he'll come anon—
[*Singing.*]
"Sing all a green willow must be my garland.
Let nobody blame him, his scorn I approve"—
Nay, that's not next. Hark, who is't that knocks?

12. **incontinent:** at once. 20. **stubbornness:** roughness.
21. **favor:** attractiveness. 25. **talk:** i.e. prattle idly.
27. **mad:** wild, i.e. untrue.
28. **Willow.** Symbolic of disappointed love.
31–32. **I . . . to:** it's all I can do not to.
50. **hie thee:** make haste.

Emil. It's the wind.
Des. [*Singing.*]
"I call'd my love false love; but what said he then?
Sing willow, willow, willow;
If I court moe women, you'll couch with moe men."—
So get thee gone, good night. Mine eyes do itch;
Doth that bode weeping?
Emil. 'Tis neither here nor there.
Des. I have heard it said so. O, these men, these men!
Dost thou in conscience think—tell me, Emilia—
That there be women do abuse their husbands
In such gross kind?
Emil. There be some such, no question.
Des. Wouldst thou do such a deed for all the world?
Emil. Why, would not you?
Des. No, by this heavenly light!
Emil. Nor I neither by this heavenly light;
I might do't as well i' th' dark.
Des. Wouldst thou do such a deed for all the world?
Emil. The world's a huge thing; it is a great price
For a small vice.
Des. [Good] troth, I think thou wouldst not.

Emil. [By my] troth, I think I should, and undo't when I had done['t]. Marry, I would not do such a thing for a joint-ring, nor for measures of lawn, nor for gowns, petticoats, nor caps, nor any petty exhibition; but, for all the whole world—['ud's pity], who would not make her husband a cuckold to make him a monarch? I should venture purgatory for't.

Des. Beshrew me, if I would do such a wrong
For the whole world.

Emil. Why, the wrong is but a wrong i' th' world; and having the world for your labor, 'tis a wrong in your own world, and you might quickly make it right.

Des. I do not think there is any such woman.

Emil. Yes, a dozen; and as many to th' vantage as would store the world they play'd for.
But I do think it is their husbands' faults
If wives do fall. Say that they slack their duties,
And pour our treasures into foreign laps;
Or else break out in peevish jealousies,
Throwing restraint upon us; or say they strike us,
Or scant our former having in despite:
Why, we have galls; and though we have some grace,
Yet have we some revenge. Let husbands know
Their wives have sense like them; they see, and smell,
And have their palates both for sweet and sour,
As husbands have. What is it that they do
When they change us for others? Is it sport?
I think it is. And doth affection breed it?
I think it doth. Is't frailty that thus errs?

61. **in conscience:** sincerely, truly.
69. **price:** prize.
73. **joint-ring:** cheap ring made in separable halves. **lawn:** fine linen. 74. **exhibition:** gift.
75. **'ud's:** a corruption of *God's*. 84. **to th' vantage:** in addition.
87. **duties:** marital duties.
88. **foreign laps:** i.e. the laps of other women.
89. **peevish:** silly, childish.
91. **scant:** reduce. **having:** allowance. **despite:** spite.
92. **galls:** tempers, the capacity to resent such treatment.
94. **sense:** bodily senses.

It is so too. And have not we affections,
Desires for sport, and frailty, as men have?
Then let them use us well; else let them know,
The ills we do, their ills instruct us so.
Des. Good night, good night. [God] me such uses send,
Not to pick bad from bad, but by bad mend. *Exeunt.*

ACT V, Scene I

Enter Iago *and* Roderigo.

Iago. Here, stand behind this [bulk], straight will he come.
Wear thy good rapier bare, and put it home.
Quick, quick, fear nothing; I'll be at thy elbow.
It makes us, or it mars us, think on that,
And fix most firm thy resolution.
Rod. Be near at hand, I may miscarry in't.
Iago. Here, at thy hand; be bold, and take thy stand. [*Retires.*]
Rod. I have no great devotion to the deed,
And yet he hath given me satisfying reasons.
'Tis but a man gone. Forth my sword; he dies.
Iago. I have rubb'd this young quat almost to the sense,
And he grows angry. Now, whether he kill Cassio,
Or Cassio him, or each do kill the other,
Every way makes my gain. Live Roderigo,
He calls me to a restitution large
Of gold and jewels that I bobb'd from him
As gifts to Desdemona;
It must not be. If Cassio do remain,
He hath a daily beauty in his life
That makes me ugly; and besides, the Moor
May unfold me to him; there stand I in much peril.
No, he must die. [Be't] so. I [hear] him coming.

Enter Cassio.

Rod. I know his gait, 'tis he.—Villain, thou diest!
[*Makes a pass at Cassio.*]
Cas. That thrust had been mine enemy indeed,
But that my coat is better than thou know'st.
I will make proof of thine.
[*Draws, and wounds Roderigo.*]
Rod. O, I am slain.
[*Iago from behind wounds Cassio in the leg, and exit.*]
Cas. I am maim'd for ever. Help ho! murther, murther! [*Falls.*]

Enter Othello.

Oth. The voice of Cassio! Iago keeps his word.
Rod. O, villain that I am!
Oth. It is even so.

104. **me . . . send:** i.e. enable me to make it my practice.
105. **Not . . . mend:** not to use others' ill conduct as an excuse for behaving likewise, but rather to learn from it how to behave otherwise.

V.i. Location: A street near the citadel.
1. **bulk:** shop-stall protruding into the street.
11. **quat:** pimple, small boil. **sense:** quick.
16. **bobb'd:** swindled.
25. **coat.** Possibly he wears a rapier-proof vest under his outer clothing.

Cas. O, help ho! light! a surgeon!
Oth. 'Tis he!—O brave Iago, honest and just,
That hast such noble sense of thy friend's wrong!
Thou teachest me. Minion, your dear lies dead,
And your unblest fate hies. Strumpet, I come.
[Forth] of my heart those charms, thine eyes, are blotted;
Thy bed, lust-stain'd, shall with lust's blood be spotted.
Exit Othello.

Enter Lodovico *and* Gratiano.

Cas. What ho! no watch? no passage? Murther, murther!
Gra. 'Tis some mischance, the voice is very direful.
Cas. O, help!
Lod. Hark!
Rod. O wretched villain!
Lod. Two or three groan. 'Tis heavy night;
These may be counterfeits; let's think't unsafe
To come in to the cry without more help.
Rod. Nobody come? Then shall I bleed to death.

Enter Iago [*with a light*].

Lod. Hark!
Gra. Here's one comes in his shirt, with light and weapons.
Iago. Who's there? Whose noise is this that cries on murther?
Lod. We do not know.
Iago. [Did] not you hear a cry?
Cas. Here, here! for heaven sake help me!
Iago. What's the matter?
Gra. This is Othello's ancient, as I take it.
Lod. The same indeed, a very valiant fellow.
Iago. What are you here that cry so grievously?
Cas. Iago? O, I am spoil'd, undone by villains!
Give me some help.
Iago. O me, lieutenant! what villains have done this?
Cas. I think that one of them is hereabout,
And cannot make away.
Iago. O treacherous villains!
[*To Lodovico and Gratiano.*] What are you there? Come in, and give some help.
Rod. O, help me there!
Cas. That's one of them.
Iago. O murd'rous slave! O villain!
[*Stabs Roderigo.*]
Rod. O damn'd Iago! O inhuman dog!
Iago. Kill men i' th' dark?—Where be these bloody thieves?—
How silent is this town!—Ho, murther, murther!—
What may you be? Are you of good or evil?
Lod. As you shall prove us, praise us.
Iago. Signior Lodovico?
Lod. He, sir.
Iago. I cry you mercy. Here's Cassio hurt by villains.
Gra. Cassio?
Iago. How is't, brother?
Cas. My leg is cut in two.
Iago. Marry, heaven forbid!
Light, gentlemen! I'll bind it with my shirt.

Enter Bianca.

Bian. What is the matter ho? Who is't that cried?
Iago. Who is't that cried?
Bian. O my dear Cassio, my sweet Cassio!
O Cassio, Cassio, Cassio!
Iago. O notable strumpet! Cassio, may you suspect
Who they should be that have thus mangled you?
Cas. No.
Gra. I am sorry to find you thus; I have been to seek you.
Iago. Lend me a garter. So.—O for a chair
To bear him easily hence!
Bian. Alas, he faints! O Cassio, Cassio, Cassio!
Iago. Gentlemen all, I do suspect this trash
To be a party in this injury.—
Patience awhile, good Cassio.—Come, come;
Lend me a light. Know we this face or no?
Alas, my friend and my dear countryman
Roderigo! No—yes, sure—[O heaven,] Roderigo!
Gra. What, of Venice?
Iago. Even he, sir; did you know him?
Gra. Know him? ay.
Iago. Signior Gratiano? I cry your gentle pardon;
These bloody accidents must excuse my manners
That so neglected you.
Gra. I am glad to see you.
Iago. How do you, Cassio? O, a chair, a chair!
Gra. Roderigo!
Iago. He, he, 'tis he. [*A chair brought in.*] O, that's well said: the chair.
Some good man bear him carefully from hence,
I'll fetch the general's surgeon. [*To Bianca.*] For you, mistress,
Save you your labor.—He that lies slain here, Cassio,
Was my dear friend. What malice was between you?
Cas. None in the world; nor do I know the man.
Iago. [*To Bianca.*] What? look you pale?—O, bear him [out] o' th' air.
[*Cassio and Roderigo are borne off.*]
Stay you, good gentlemen.—Look you pale, mistress?
Do you perceive the gastness of her eye?—
Nay, [an'] you stare, we shall hear more anon.—
Behold her well; I pray you look upon her.
Do you see, gentlemen? Nay, guiltiness will speak,
Though tongues were out of use.

[*Enter* Emilia.]

Emil. Alas, what is the matter? What is the matter, husband?
Iago. Cassio hath here been set on in the dark
By Roderigo and fellows that are scap'd.
He's almost slain, and Roderigo quite dead.

31. brave: excellent, noble. **33. Minion:** hussy.
34. hies: approaches rapidly. **37. passage:** passers-by.
42. heavy: dark. **48. cries on:** cries out. **50. heaven:** heaven's.
54. spoil'd: destroyed.

98. well said: well done. **102. malice:** enmity.
104. out . . . air. Fresh air was considered bad for wounds.
106. gastness: terror.

Emil. Alas, good gentleman! alas, good Cassio!
Iago. This is the fruits of whoring. Prithee, Emilia,
Go know of Cassio where he supp'd to-night.
[*To Bianca.*] What, do you shake at that?
Bian. He supp'd at my house, but I therefore shake not.
Iago. O, did he so? I charge you go with me.
Emil. O fie upon thee, strumpet!
Bian. I am no strumpet, but of life as honest
As you that thus abuse me.
Emil. As I? [Fough,] fie upon thee!
Iago. Kind gentlemen, let's go see poor Cassio dress'd.
Come, mistress, you must tell 's another tale.
Emilia, run you to the citadel,
And tell my lord and lady what hath happ'd.—
Will you go on afore? [*Aside.*] This is the night
That either makes me, or foredoes me quite. *Exeunt.*

Scene II

Enter Othello [*with a light*] *and* Desdemona *in her bed* [*asleep*].

Oth. It is the cause, it is the cause, my soul;
Let me not name it to you, you chaste stars,
It is the cause. Yet I'll not shed her blood,
Nor scar that whiter skin of hers than snow,
And smooth as monumental alablaster.
Yet she must die, else she'll betray more men.
Put out the light, and then put out the light:
If I quench thee, thou flaming minister,
I can again thy former light restore,
Should I repent me; but once put out thy light,
Thou cunning'st pattern of excelling nature,
I know not where is that Promethean heat
That can thy light relume. When I have pluck'd thy rose,
I cannot give it vital growth again,
It needs must wither. I'll smell thee on the tree.
[*Kisses her.*]
O balmy breath, that dost almost persuade
Justice to break her sword! One more, one more.
Be thus when thou art dead, and I will kill thee
And love thee after. One more, and that's the last.
So sweet was ne'er so fatal. I must weep,
But they are cruel tears. This sorrow's heavenly,
It strikes where it doth love. She wakes.
Des. Who's there? Othello?
Oth. Ay, Desdemona.
Des. Will you come to bed, my lord?
Oth. Have you pray'd to-night, Desdemon?
Des. Ay, my lord.

129. **foredoes:** destroys.

V.ii. **Location:** The citadel.
1. **the cause:** the crime (not the criminal). Othello sees himself as an agent of justice, not an avenger of his own honor.
5. **alablaster:** alabaster. 10. **repent me:** change my mind.
12. **Promethean:** i.e. divine (since Prometheus brought down fire from heaven). 13. **relume:** rekindle. 21. **cruel:** unrelenting.
21–22. **This . . . love.** Cf. Hebrews 12:6: "For whom the Lord loveth he chasteneth. . . ."

Oth. If you bethink yourself of any crime
Unreconcil'd as yet to heaven and grace,
Solicit for it straight.
Des. Alack, my lord, what may you mean by that?
Oth. Well, do it, and be brief, I will walk by.
I would not kill thy unprepared spirit,
No, [heaven] forefend! I would not kill thy soul.
Des. Talk you of killing?
Oth. Ay, I do.
Des. Then heaven
Have mercy on me!
Oth. Amen, with all my heart!
Des. If you say [so], I hope you will not kill me.
Oth. Humh!
Des. And yet I fear you; for you're fatal then
When your eyes roll so. Why I should fear I know not,
Since guiltiness I know not; but yet I feel I fear.
Oth. Think on thy sins.
Des. They are loves I bear to you.
Oth. Ay, and for that thou di'st.
Des. That death's unnatural that kills for loving.
Alas, why gnaw you so your nether lip?
Some bloody passion shakes your very frame.
These are portents; but yet I hope, I hope,
They do not point on me.
Oth. Peace, and be still!
Des. I will so. What's the matter?
Oth. That handkerchief which I so lov'd, and gave thee,
Thou gav'st to Cassio.
Des. No, by my life and soul!
Send for the man, and ask him.
Oth. Sweet soul, take heed,
Take heed of perjury, thou art on thy death-bed.
Des. Ay, but not yet to die.
Oth. [Yes,] presently:
Therefore confess thee freely of thy sin;
For to deny each article with oath
Cannot remove nor choke the strong conception
That I do groan withal. Thou art to die.
Des. [Then Lord] have mercy on me!
Oth. I say, amen.
Des. And have you mercy too! I never did
Offend you in my life; never lov'd Cassio
But with such general warranty of heaven
As I might love. I never gave him token.
Oth. By heaven, I saw my handkerchief in 's hand.
O perjur'd woman, thou dost stone my heart,
And [mak'st] me call what I intend to do
A murther, which I thought a sacrifice.
I saw the handkerchief.
Des. He found it then;
I never gave it him. Send for him hither;
Let him confess a truth.
Oth. He hath confess'd.
Des. What, my lord?

26. **crime:** sin.
32. **forefend:** forfend, forbid. 46. **point on:** point to, aim at.
52. **presently:** at once.
55. **conception:** i.e. conviction of your guilt.
59. **Offend:** wrong. 60. **warranty:** approval, allowance.
63. **stone:** turn to stone. 65. **sacrifice:** i.e. offering to justice.

Oth. That he hath us'd thee.
Des. How? unlawfully?
Oth. Ay.
Des. He will not say so.
Oth. No—his mouth is stopp'd;
Honest Iago hath ta'en order for't.
Des. O, my fear interprets. What, is he dead?
Oth. Had all his hairs been lives, my great revenge
Had stomach for them all.
Des. Alas, he is betray'd and I undone!
Oth. Out, strumpet! weep'st thou for him to my face?
Des. O, banish me, my lord, but kill me not!
Oth. Down, strumpet!
Des. Kill me to-morrow, let me live to-night!
Oth. Nay, [an'] you strive—
Des. But half an hour!
Oth. Being done, there is no pause.
Des. But while I say one prayer!
Oth. It is too late. *Smothers her.*
[*Des.* O Lord, Lord, Lord!]
Emil. (*At the door,* [*within*].) My lord, my lord! What ho! my lord, my lord!
Oth. What noise is this? Not dead? not yet quite dead?
I that am cruel am yet merciful,
I would not have thee linger in thy pain.
So, so.
Emil. (*Within.*) What ho! my lord, my lord!
Oth. Who's there?
Emil. [*Within.*] O, good my lord, I would speak a word with you!
Oth. Yes.—'Tis Emilia.—By and by.—She's dead.
'Tis like she comes to speak of Cassio's death;
The noise was high. Hah, no more moving?
Still as the grave. Shall she come in? Were't good?
I think she stirs again. No. What's best to do?
If she come in, she'll sure speak to my wife.
My wife, my wife! what wife? I have no wife.
O insupportable! O heavy hour!
Methinks it should be now a huge eclipse
Of sun and moon, and that th' affrighted globe
Did yawn at alteration.
Emil. [*Within.*] I do beseech you
That I may speak with you. O, good my lord!
Oth. I had forgot thee. O, come in, Emilia.—
Soft, by and by, let me the curtains draw.—
Where art thou? [*Unlocks the door.*]

Enter EMILIA.

What's the matter with thee now?
Emil. O, my good lord, yonder's foul murthers done!
Oth. What? now?
Emil. But now, my lord.

72. ta'en order for't: taken steps to effect it.
81. strive: struggle. **82. Being done:** since all is over.
93. The noise was high: i.e. it caused a great commotion. Many editors, following Q1, read *The noise was here,* referring to the noise in the bed (line 86).
101. yawn. It was commonly believed that eclipses were accompanied by earthquakes. **alteration:** the great change on earth.
104. Soft: wait a moment.

Oth. It is the very error of the moon,
She comes more nearer earth than she was wont,
And makes men mad.
Emil. Cassio, my lord, hath kill'd a young Venetian
Call'd Roderigo.
Oth. Roderigo kill'd?
And Cassio kill'd?
Emil. No, Cassio is not kill'd.
Oth. Not Cassio kill'd? Then murther's out of tune,
And sweet revenge grows harsh.
Des. O, falsely, falsely murder'd!
Emil. [O Lord], what cry is that?
Oth. That? what?
Emil. Out, and alas, that was my lady's voice.
Help, help, ho, help! O lady, speak again!
Sweet Desdemona, O sweet mistress, speak!
Des. A guiltless death I die.
Emil. O, who hath done this deed?
Des. Nobody; I myself. Farewell!
Commend me to my kind lord. O, farewell! [*Dies.*]
Oth. Why, how should she be murd'red?
Emil. Alas! who knows?
Oth. You [heard] her say herself, it was not I.
Emil. She said so; I must needs report the truth.
Oth. She's like a liar gone to burning hell:
'Twas I that kill'd her.
Emil. O, the more angel she,
And you the blacker devil!
Oth. She turn'd to folly, and she was a whore.
Emil. Thou dost belie her, and thou art a devil.
Oth. She was false as water.
Emil. Thou art rash as fire to say
That she was false. O, she was heavenly true!
Oth. Cassio did top her; ask thy husband else.
O, I were damn'd beneath all depth in hell
But that I did proceed upon just grounds
To this extremity. Thy husband knew it all.
Emil. My husband?
Oth. Thy husband.
Emil. That she was false to wedlock?
Oth. Ay, with Cassio. [Nay,] had she been true,
If heaven would make me such another world
Of one entire and perfect chrysolite,
I'ld not have sold her for it.
Emil. My husband?
Oth. Ay, 'twas he that told me on her first.
An honest man he is, and hates the slime
That sticks on filthy deeds.
Emil. My husband?
Oth. What needs this iterance, woman? I say thy husband.
Emil. O mistress, villainy hath made mocks with love!
My husband say she was false?
Oth. He, woman;
I say thy husband; dost understand the word?
My friend, thy husband, honest, honest Iago.

109. error: aberration, deviation from the normal course.
119. Out: exclamation of grief. **134. rash:** impetuous.
145. chrysolite: topaz. **150. iterance:** repetition.
151. with: at.

Emil. If he say so, may his pernicious soul
Rot half a grain a day! He lies to th' heart.
She was too fond of her most filthy bargain.
Oth. Hah?
Emil. Do thy worst!
This deed of thine is no more worthy heaven
Than thou wast worthy her.
Oth. Peace, you were best.
Emil. Thou hast not half that pow'r to do me harm
As I have to be hurt. O gull, O dolt,
As ignorant as dirt! Thou hast done a deed—
I care not for thy sword, I'll make thee known,
Though I lost twenty lives. Help, help, ho, help!
The Moor hath kill'd my mistress! Murther, murther!

Enter MONTANO, GRATIANO, *and* IAGO, [*with others*].

Mon. What is the matter? How now, general?
Emil. O, are you come, Iago? You have done well,
That men must lay their murthers on your neck.
Gra. What is the matter?
Emil. Disprove this villain, if thou be'st a man.
He says thou toldst him that his wife was false.
I know thou didst not; thou'rt not such a villain.
Speak, for my heart is full.
Iago. I told him what I thought, and told no more
Than what he found himself was apt and true.
Emil. But did you ever tell him she was false?
Iago. I did.
Emil. You told a lie, an odious, damned lie;
Upon my soul, a lie, a wicked lie.
She false with Cassio? did you say with Cassio?
Iago. With Cassio, mistress. Go to, charm your tongue.
Emil. I will not charm my tongue; I am bound to speak.
My mistress here lies murthered in her bed—
All. O heavens forefend!
Emil. And your reports have set the murder on.
Oth. Nay, stare not, masters, it is true indeed.
Gra. 'Tis a strange truth.
Mon. O monstrous act!
Emil. Villainy, villainy, villainy!
I think upon't, I think—I smell't—O villainy!
I thought so then—I'll kill myself for grief—
O villainy! villainy!
Iago. What, are you mad? I charge you get you home.
Emil. Good gentlemen, let me have leave to speak.
'Tis proper I obey him; but not now.
Perchance, Iago, I will ne'er go home.
Oth. O, O, O! [*Othello falls on the bed.*]
Emil. Nay, lay thee down and roar;
For thou hast kill'd the sweetest innocent
That e'er did lift up eye.
Oth. [*Rising.*] O, she was foul!
I scarce did know you, uncle; there lies your niece,
Whose breath, indeed, these hands have newly stopp'd.
I know this act shows horrible and grim.

163. **be hurt:** i.e. endure hurt. **gull:** dupe.
177. **apt:** credible.
183. **charm:** i.e. silence, as if with a magic spell.
192. **I . . . then.** See IV.ii.130–33.

Gra. Poor Desdemon! I am glad thy father's dead.
Thy match was mortal to him, and pure grief
Shore his old thread in twain. Did he live now,
This sight would make him do a desperate turn,
Yea, curse his better angel from his side,
And fall to reprobance.
Oth. 'Tis pitiful; but yet Iago knows
That she with Cassio hath the act of shame
A thousand times committed. Cassio confess'd it,
And she did gratify his amorous works
With that recognizance and pledge of love
Which I first gave her. I saw it in his hand;
It was a handkerchief, an antique token
My father gave my mother.
Emil. O [God]! O heavenly [God]!
Iago. ['Zounds], hold your peace.
Emil. 'Twill out, 'twill out! I peace?
No, I will speak as liberal as the north:
Let heaven and men and devils, let them all,
All, all, cry shame against me, yet I'll speak.
Iago. Be wise, and get you home.
Emil. I will not. [*Iago offers to stab Emilia.*]
Gra. Fie,
Your sword upon a woman?
Emil. O thou dull Moor, that handkerchief thou speak'st of
I found by fortune, and did give my husband;
For often, with a solemn earnestness
(More than indeed belong'd to such a trifle),
He begg'd of me to steal't.
Iago. Villainous whore!
Emil. She give it Cassio? No, alas, I found it,
And I did give't my husband.
Iago. Filth, thou liest!
Emil. By heaven, I do not, I do not, gentlemen.
O murd'rous coxcomb, what should such a fool
Do with so good a wife?
Oth. Are there no stones in heaven
But what serves for the thunder?—Precious villain!
[*The Moor runs at Iago; Montano disarms Othello; Iago kills his wife.*]
Gra. The woman falls; sure he hath kill'd his wife.
Emil. Ay, ay! O, lay me by my mistress' side.
[*Exit Iago.*]
Gra. He's gone, but his wife's kill'd.
Mon. 'Tis a notorious villain. Take you this weapon
Which I have [here] recover'd from the Moor.
Come guard the door without; let him not pass,
But kill him rather. I'll after that same villain,
For 'tis a damned slave.
Exit [*with all but Othello and Emilia*].
Oth. I am not valiant neither,
But every puny whipster gets my sword.

206. **Shore:** sheared, cut. **thread:** i.e. thread of life.
207. **turn:** act. 209. **to reprobance:** into damnation.
214. **recognizance:** token.
220. **liberal:** unrestrainedly. **as the north:** as the north wind blows.
228. **belong'd:** was appropriate. 233. **coxcomb:** fool.
235. **for the thunder:** i.e. as thunderbolts.
239. **notorious:** exceptional, egregious.
240. **recover'd:** taken away.
244. **whipster:** insignificant or contemptible person.

But why should honor outlive honesty?
Let it go all.
Emil. What did thy song bode, lady?
Hark, canst thou hear me? I will play the swan,
And die in music. [*Sings.*] "Willow, willow, willow."
Moor, she was chaste; she lov'd thee, cruel Moor;
So come my soul to bliss, as I speak true;
So speaking as I think, alas, I die. [*Dies.*]
Oth. I have another weapon in this chamber;
It was a sword of Spain, the ice-brook's temper—
O, here it is. Uncle, I must come forth.
Gra. [*Within.*] If thou attempt it, it will cost thee dear:
Thou hast no weapon, and perforce must suffer.
Oth. Look in upon me then and speak with me,
Or naked as I am I will assault thee.

[*Enter* GRATIANO.]

Gra. What is the matter?
Oth. Behold, I have a weapon;
A better never did itself sustain
Upon a soldier's thigh. I have seen the day
That with this little arm, and this good sword,
I have made my way through more impediments
Than twenty times your stop. But (O vain boast!)
Who can control his fate? 'tis not so now.
Be not afraid though you do see me weapon'd;
Here is my journey's end, here is my butt
And very sea-mark of my utmost sail.
Do you go back dismay'd? 'Tis a lost fear;
Man but a rush against Othello's breast,
And he retires. Where should Othello go?
Now—how dost thou look now? O ill-starr'd wench,
Pale as thy smock! when we shall meet at compt,
This look of thine will hurl my soul from heaven,
And fiends will snatch at it. Cold, cold, my girl?
Even like thy chastity. O cursed, cursed slave!
Whip me, ye devils,
From the possession of this heavenly sight!
Blow me about in winds! roast me in sulphur!
Wash me in steep-down gulfs of liquid fire!
O Desdemon! dead, Desdemon! dead!
O, O!

Enter LODOVICO, CASSIO [*in a chair*], MONTANO, *and* IAGO [*guarded*], *with* OFFICERS.

Lod. Where is this rash and most unfortunate man?
Oth. That's he that was Othello; here I am.
Lod. Where is that viper? Bring the villain forth.
Oth. I look down towards his feet; but that's a fable.
If that thou be'st a devil, I cannot kill thee.
[*Wounds Iago.*]
Lod. Wrench his sword from him.
Iago. I bleed, sir, but not kill'd.
Oth. I am not sorry neither, I'ld have thee live;
For in my sense, 'tis happiness to die.
Lod. O thou Othello, that was once so good,
Fall'n in the practice of a [damned] slave,
What shall be said to thee?
Oth. Why, any thing:
An honorable murderer, if you will;
For nought I did in hate, but all in honor.
Lod. This wretch hath part confess'd his villainy.
Did you and he consent in Cassio's death?
Oth. Ay.
Cas. Dear general, I never gave you cause.
Oth. I do believe it, and I ask your pardon.
Will you, I pray, demand that demi-devil
Why he hath thus ensnar'd my soul and body?
Iago. Demand me nothing; what you know, you know:
From this time forth I never will speak word.
Lod. What? not to pray?
Gra. Torments will ope your lips.
Oth. Well, thou dost best.
Lod. Sir, you shall understand what hath befall'n,
Which, as I think, you know not. Here is a letter
Found in the pocket of the slain Roderigo,
And here another. The one of them imports
The death of Cassio to be undertook
By Roderigo.
Oth. O villain!
Cas. Most heathenish and most gross!
Lod. Now here's another discontented paper,
Found in his pocket too; and this it seems
Roderigo meant t' have sent this damned villain;
But that, belike, Iago in the [nick]
Came in and satisfied him.
Oth. O thou pernicious caitiff!—
How came you, Cassio, by that handkerchief
That was my wive's?
Cas. I found it in my chamber:
And he himself confess'd it but even now,
That there he dropp'd it for a special purpose
Which wrought to his desire.
Oth. O fool, fool, fool!
Cas. There is besides, in Roderigo's letter,
How he upbraids Iago, that he made him
Brave me upon the watch, whereon it came
That I was cast; and even but now he spake
(After long seeming dead) Iago hurt him,
Iago set him on.
Lod. You must forsake this room and go with us.
Your power and your command is taken off,
And Cassio rules in Cyprus. For this slave,
If there be any cunning cruelty
That can torment him much, and hold him long,
It shall be his. You shall close prisoner rest,
Till that the nature of your fault be known
To the Venetian state. Come, bring away.

245. honor: i.e. personal prowess and courage, and one's reputation for them. **honesty:** inward integrity.
253. the ice-brook's temper: i.e. its steel tempered in icy water.
258. naked: unarmed. **264. stop:** power to stop.
267. butt: goal.
268. sea-mark: beacon or other object marking the entrance to a harbor; hence, destination, end. **269. lost:** idle, unnecessary.
270. Man . . . rush: hold a mere reed.
273. compt: accounting, i.e. Judgment Day. **283. rash:** overhasty.
286. I . . . feet: i.e. to see if they are cloven, as the devil's were thought to be. **that's a fable:** i.e. the fact that your feet aren't cloven doesn't prove that you aren't a devil.
290. in my sense: i.e. to one who feels as I do.
292. practice: plotting. **313. gross:** monstrous.
323. wrought to: worked toward, fitted in with.
326. Brave: defy, behave insolently toward.

Oth. Soft you; a word or two before you go.
I have done the state some service, and they know't—
No more of that. I pray you, in your letters,
When you shall these unlucky deeds relate,
Speak of me as I am; nothing extenuate,
Nor set down aught in malice. Then must you speak
Of one that lov'd not wisely but too well;
Of one not easily jealious, but being wrought,
Perplexed in the extreme; of one whose hand
(Like the base [Indian]) threw a pearl away
Richer than all his tribe; of one whose subdu'd eyes,
Albeit unused to the melting mood,
Drops tears as fast as the Arabian trees
Their medicinable gum. Set you down this;
And say besides, that in Aleppo once,
Where a malignant and a turban'd Turk
Beat a Venetian and traduc'd the state,
I took by th' throat the circumcised dog,

342. extenuate: tone down (literally, make thin).
345. wrought: worked upon.
346. Perplexed: bewildered, distraught.
347. Indian. This, the Q1 reading, relates to the not unfamiliar notion of an Indian ignorant of the value of some precious object he finds. (*Base* = low in the scale of civilization.) A few editors prefer to read *Judean*, after F1; this is taken as an allusion to Judas, or to Herod the Great, who in a fit of jealousy had his beloved wife Mariamne killed.
351. medicinable: medicinal.

And smote him—thus. [*He stabs himself.*]
Lod. O bloody period!
Gra. All that is spoke is marr'd.
Oth. I kiss'd thee ere I kill'd thee. No way but this,
Killing myself, to die upon a kiss.
[*Falls on the bed and*] *dies.*
Cas. This did I fear, but thought he had no weapon;
For he was great of heart.
Lod. [*To Iago.*] O Spartan dog,
More fell than anguish, hunger, or the sea!
Look on the tragic loading of this bed;
This is thy work. The object poisons sight,
Let it be hid. Gratiano, keep the house,
And seize upon the fortunes of the Moor,
For they succeed on you. To you, Lord Governor,
Remains the censure of this hellish villain,
The time, the place, the torture, O, enforce it!
Myself will straight aboard, and to the state
This heavy act with heavy heart relate. *Exeunt.*

357. period: conclusion.
361. Spartan dog: a kind of bloodhound, noted for its silence as well as its skill. **362. fell:** cruel. **364. object:** sight, spectacle.
365. keep: remain in. **366. seize upon:** take legal possession of.
368. censure: judgment, sentence.

NOTE ON THE TEXT

The textual situation in *Othello* is unusually confused. A quarto edition (Q1) was published in 1622 by Thomas Walkley (see his address to the reader at the beginning of the Textual Notes). The play was next printed in the First Folio (1623). A second quarto (Q2) was published in 1630; it is based on Q1, but with additions and corrections from F1. Later quartos, stemming from Q2, appeared in 1655 (Q3), 1681, 1687, and 1695, the last three editions representing the play as performed on the Restoration stage.

The relative textual authority of Q1 and F1 and the exact relation between the two texts have been the subject of much discussion, and none of the various theories advanced is without its own difficulties. For a full treatment of the complicated and often conflicting evidence on which these theories rest, the reader must consult the detailed studies cited below, in particular that of Greg. All that can be attempted here is to suggest some of the problems and indicate the general trend of the several views proposed.

F1 and Q1 differ materially. There are more than a thousand verbal variants between the two texts, aside from about 160 lines found only in F1 and some 13 lines or part-lines unique to Q1. The situation is analogous in some ways to that presented by the quarto-folio texts of *Troilus and Cressida* and *King Lear*.

Although until comparatively recently scholars had generally agreed, as proposed by Walker, that F1 was set from a copy of Q1 that had been corrected and amplified by collation against some kind of authoritative manuscript (an early official prompt-book, Greg; a later official transcript of the then official prompt-book, allowing for the impact of years of stage adaptation and contamination, Ridley; a "fair copy," possibly authorial, but apparently not a prompt-book, Walker), it is now argued that F1 was printed from an independent manuscript (Walton, Taylor, Sanders, MacD. P. Jackson), perhaps a scribal copy of Shakespeare's revised holograph manuscript (Wells/Taylor, Honigmann [1996], who also proposes that the scribe was Ralph Crane).

The printer's source for the copy behind Q1 is equally debatable. Was Q1 printed from (a) a scribal transcript, prepared about 1620, perhaps for a private collector of Shakespeare's "foul papers" (Greg); (b) a memorially contaminated transcript of the prompt-book by the book-keeper, who relied all too frequently on his recollection of the play, particularly as acted (Walker); (c) a transcript, prepared about 1604, from the "foul papers," for use as the official prompt-book (Chambers?, Ridley?, Coghill); (d) a scribal transcript of the "foul papers" (Sanders, Wells/Taylor; Honigmann [1996]; compare Greg)?

After all this, where does an editor of *Othello* stand? Not firmly or happily! In view of the debatable authority of the two main texts, he may (as suggested by Honigmann in 1965) take a high editorial hand, choosing those readings from either text which seem in his judgment to be superior. Although admittedly a somewhat more liberal attitude towards the "sanctity of the copy-text" may be justified in the case of *Othello*, such an approach would leave nobody satisfied, except perhaps the editor. The present edition, therefore, accepts F1 as the basic copy-text, since it is considered by the majority of earlier editors as generally superior, showing, to some indeterminable degree (a large number of the F1/Q1 variant readings are indifferent), evidence of Shakespearean revision of the text as represented by Q1, but it also admits, either from necessity or by editorial choice, roughly 190 readings from Q1. Moreover, because of the ambiguity of the whole textual situation, a record of all significant variants, a few elided forms excepted, between F1 and Q1 is included in the Textual Notes, so that particular editorial decisions may be judged on the basis of all the evidence.

For further information, see: E. K. Chambers, *William Shakespeare*, 2 vols. (Oxford, 1930); Charlton Hinman, "The

'Copy' for the Second Quarto of *Othello* (1630)," *J. Q. Adams Memorial Studies*, ed. J. G. McManaway, et al. (Washington, 1948), 373–89, and *The Printing and Proof-Reading of the First Folio of Shakespeare*, 2 vols. (Oxford, 1963); Alice Walker, *Textual Problems of the First Folio* (Cambridge, 1953) and ed. (with J. D. Wilson), New Shakespeare *Othello* (Cambridge, 1957); W. W. Greg, *The Shakespeare First Folio* (Oxford, 1955); M. R. Ridley, ed., New Arden *Othello* (London, 1958); F. T. Bowers, *Bibliography and Textual Criticism* (Oxford, 1964); Nevill Coghill, *Shakespeare's Professional Skills* (Oxford, 1964); E. A. J. Honigmann, *The Stability of Shakespeare's Text* (London, 1965), "Shakespeare's Revised Plays: *King Lear* and *Othello*," *The Library*, 6th ser., IV (1982), 142–73, and *The Texts of "Othello" and Shakespearian Revision* (London, 1996); J. K. Walton, *The Quarto Copy for the First Folio of Shakespeare* (Dublin, 1971); M. T. Jones, "Press-Variants and Proofreading in the First Quarto of *Othello* (1622)," *SB*, XXVII (1974), 177–87; Gary Taylor, "The Folio Copy for *Hamlet, King Lear*, and *Othello*," *SQ*, XXXIV (1983), 44–61 (see below under Wells); Norman Sanders, ed., New Cambridge *Othello* (Cambridge, 1984); MacD. P. Jackson, "Printer's Copy for the First Folio Text of *Othello*: The Evidence of Misreadings," *The Library*, IX (1987), 262–7; Stanley Wells, Gary Taylor, et al., *William Shakespeare: A Textual Companion* (Oxford, 1987); T. L. Berger, "The Second Quarto of *Othello* and the Question of Textual 'Authority,'" *AEB*, II (1988), 141–59.

TEXTUAL NOTES

Q1 contains the following advertisement by the publisher: The Stationer to the Reader. To set forth a booke without an Epistle, were like to the old English prouerbe, *A blew coat without a badge*, & the Author being dead, I thought good to take that piece of worke vpon mee: To commend it, I will not, for that which is good, I hope euery man will commend, without intreaty: and I am the bolder, because the Authors name is sufficient to vent his worke. Thus leauing euery one to the liberty of iudgement: I haue ventered to print this Play, and leaue it to the generall censure. Yours, Thomas Walkley.

Dramatis personae: *as in F1, following the play, with some descriptive additions and rearrangement by various editors*

Act-scene division: *from F1, except II.iii; Q1 marks II.i, Act IV, and Act V only*

I.i

Location: *Theobald (after Rowe)*
o.s.d. **Roderigo]** *Q1;* Rodorigo *F1 (throughout); Iago and Roderigo named in reverse order in Q1 s.d.*
1 **Tush,]** *Q1*
2 **thou]** you *Q1*
2 **hast]** has *Q1*
4 **'Sblood,]** *Q1*
4 **you'll]** you will *Q1*
8 **great ones]** *Q1;* Great-ones *F1*
10 **Off-capp'd]** Oft capt *Q1*
15 **And in conclusion,]** *Q1*
16 **for, "Certes,"]** *Steevens (in 1773 ed. only);* For certes, *F1;* for certes, *Q1*
17 **chose]** chosen *Q1*
21 **damn'd]** dambd *Q1*
24 **spinster—]** *F2 (subs.);* Spinster. *F1;* Spinster, *Q1*
25 **toged]** *Q1;* Tongued *F1*
27 **th']** the *Q1 (not hereafter recorded)*
29 **Cyprus]** *F2;* Ciprus *F1 (but* Cyprus *elsewhere throughout);* Cipres *Q1 (or* Cypres, Cypresse *throughout)*
29 **other]** *Q1;* others *F1*
30 **Christen'd]** Christian *Q1*
30 **belee'd]** led *Q1*
31 **creditor—this]** *Globe (subs.);* Creditor. This *F1;* Creditor, this *Q1 (with colon after* counter-caster)
33 **God]** *Q1*
33 **Moorship's]** Worships *Q1*
35 **Why]** But *Q1*
37 **And not by]** Not by the *Q1*
39 **affin'd]** assign'd *Q1*
43 **all be]** be all *Q1*
44 **mark]** marke. *Q1*
48 **nought]** *Q1* (noughe); naught *F1*
53 **them]** 'em *Q1*
54 **These]** Those *Q1*
61 **doth]** does *Q1*
65 **daws]** Doues *Q1*
66 **full]** *Q1;* fall *F1*
66 **thick-lips]** *Q1* (thicklips); Thicks-lips *F1*
67 **carry't]** carry'et *Q1*
69 **streets]** streete *Q1*
72 **changes]** *Q1;* chances *F1*
72 **on't]** out *Q1*
75 **timorous]** *F2;* timerous *F1, Q1*
79 **thieves, thieves!]** Theeues, theeues, theeues: *Q1*
80 **your daughter]** you Daughter *Q1*
81 s.d. **Enter]** *Rowe*
81 s.d. **Brabantio . . . window.]** *Q1 (above from F1)*
85 **your doors lock'd]** all doore lockts *Q1*
86 **'Zounds]** *Q1*
86 **y' are]** you are *Q1*
86 **robb'd]** *F2;* rob'd *F1;* robd *Q1*
87 **soul;]** *Q1;* soule *F1*
88 **now, now,]** now, *Q1*
95 **worser]** worse *Q1*
100 **bravery]** *Q1;* knauerie *F1*
103 **spirits]** spirit *Q1*
103 **their]** them *Q1*
108 **'Zounds]** *Q1* (Zouns)
110 **service, and]** seruice, *Q1*
113 **germans]** *Q1* (Iermans); Germaines *F1*
115 **comes]** come *Q1*
116 **now]** *Q1*
121–37 **If't . . . yourself.]** *om. Q1*
123 **odd-even]** *hyphen, Malone*
123 **night,]** *Q2;* night *F1*
140 **thus . . . you]** this delusion *Q1*
144 s.d. **above]** *Hanmer; s.d. om. Q1*
145 **place]** pate *Q1*
146 **producted]** produc'd *Q1*
148 **However]** *F1, Q1 (c);* Now euer *Q1 (u)*
149 **cast him,]** *Q1;* cast-him. *F1*
152 **fadom]** fathome *Q1*
152 **none]** not *Q1*
154 **hell-pains]** *Capell (hyphen, Dyce);* hell apines *F1;* hells paines *Q1*
157 **Which . . . him,]** *Rowe (subs.);* (Which . . . sign) that . . . him *F1;* Which . . . sign, that . . . him: *Q1*
158 **Sagittary]** Sagittar *Q1*
159 s.d. **below]** *Capell*
159 s.d. **in his night-gown]** *Q1*
159 s.d. **with Servants and]** and seruants with *Q1*
162 **nought]** *Q1;* naught *F1*
162 **bitterness.]** bitternesse *Q1*
165 **she deceives]** thou deceiuest *Q1*
166 **moe]** more *Q1*
172 **maidhood]** manhood *Q1*
174 **Yes . . . indeed.]** I haue sir. *Q1*
175 **would]** that *Q1*
176 **you]** yon *Q1*
180 **you lead on.]** leade me on, *Q1*
182 **night]** *Q1;* might *F1*
183 **I will]** Ile *Q1*

I.ii

Location: *Theobald (after Rowe)*
o.s.d. **Iago,]** Iago, and *Q1*
2 **stuff o' th']** stuft of *Q1*
4 **Sometime]** Sometimes *Q1*
5 **t']** to *Q1 (not generally recorded hereafter)*
5 **yerk'd]** ierk'd *Q1*
10 **you]** *om. Q1*
11 **Be assur'd]** For be sure *Q1*
12 **belov'd]** beloued *Q1 (Q1 is erratic in its use of -'d and -ed in verse; later instances not generally recorded)*
15 **or]** and *Q1*
16 **The]** That *Q1*
17 **Will]** Weele *Q1*
20 **Which . . . know]** *om. Q1*
21 **provulgate—]** *Ridley (after Q1 and Dyce);* promulgate. *F1;* provulgate, *Q1*
22 **siege,]** *Globe;* Siege. *F1;* height, *Q1*
28 **sea's]** *Theobald;* Seas *F1, Q1*
28 **yond]** yonder *Q1*
28 s.d. **Officers and]** *Q1; Q1 s.d. reads:* Enter Cassio with lights, Officers, and torches. *(after* worth. *l. 28)*
29 **Those]** These *Q1*
32 **Is it]** it is *Q1*
34 **Duke]** *Q1;* Dukes *F1*
35 **you]** your *Q1*
37 **haste-post-haste]** *Steevens;* haste, Post-haste *F1;* hast, post hast *Q1*
38 **What is]** What's *Q1*
41 **sequent]** frequent *Q1*
46 **hath]** *om. Q1*
46 **about]** aboue *Q1*
48 **I will but]** Ile *Q1*
49 s.d. **Exit.]** *Rowe*
50 **carract]** Carrick *Q1*
52 s.d. **Enter Othello.]** *Rowe*
53 **Have with you.]** Ha, with who? *Q1*
54 s.d. **with Officers]** and others *Q1 (Q1 s.d. after l. 52)*
54 s.d. **with]** *Q1*
54 s.d. **and weapons]** *Q1*
57 s.d. **They . . . sides.]** *Rowe*

58 **Roderigo! come]** *Q1* (Roderigo,); Rodorigoc? Cme *F1* (Rodorigoc *in italics*)
59–61 **Keep . . . weapons.]** *as verse, Q1; as prose, F1*
59 **them]** em *Q1*
63 **Damn'd]** Dambd *Q1*
64 **things]** thing *Q1*
65 **If . . . bound,]** *om. Q1*
68 **darlings]** *Q1;* Deareling *F1*
72–7 **Judge . . . thee]** *om. Q1*
78 **For]** Such *Q1*
83 **cue]** Qu. *Q1*
84 **Whither]** *F2;* Whether *F1;* where *Q1*
85 **To answer]** And answer *Q1*
87 **I]** *Q1*
88 **satisfied]** *Q1;* satisfi'd *F1*
91 **bring]** beare *Q1*
92 **Duke's]** *Q1;* Dukes *F1*
92, 93 **council]** *Q1* (Councell); Counsell *F1*

I.iii

Location: *Capell*
o.s.d. **and]** *Q1*
o.s.d. **set . . . lights]** *Q1*
o.s.d. **Officers]** Attendants *Q1*
1 **There's]** There is *Q1*
1 **these]** *Q1;* this *F1*
4 **hundred]** hundred and *Q1*
5 **accompt]** account *Q1*
6 **the aim]** they aym'd *Q1*
10 **in]** to *Q1*
11 **article]** Articles *Q1*
12 s.p. **Sailor.]** One *Q1*
12 s.d. **Sailor]** a Messenger *Q1* (*Q1 s.d. after sense. l. 12*)
13 s.p. **Off.]** Sailor. *Q1*
13 **galleys]** Galley *Q1*
13 **Now? what's]** Now, *Q1*
15 s.d. **Exit Sailor.]** *ed. (after Capell)*
16 **By Signior Angelo]** *om. Q1*
19–20 **gaze. . . . Turk,]** *Globe;* gaze, . . . Turke; *F1;* gaze: . . . Turke: *Q1*
24–30 **For . . . profitless.]** *om. Q1*
29–30 **ease . . . wake]** *Q2;* ease, and gaine / To wake, *F1*
31 **Nay]** And *Q1*
32 s.d. **Messenger]** 2. Messenger *Q1*
33 **Ottomites]** *Q2;* Ottamites *F1, Q1* (*generally throughout*)
35 **them]** *om. Q1*
36 **1. Sen. Ay . . . guess?]** *om. Q1*
37 **restem]** resterine *Q1;* resterne *Q2*
39 **toward]** towards *Q1*
42 s.d. **Exit Messenger.]** *ed. (after Capell)*
44 **he in town?]** here in Towne. *Q1*
46 **us to him]** *Q2;* vs, / To him, *F1;* vs, wish him *Q1*
46 **post-post-haste. Dispatch!]** *ed.,* (*after Capell; first hyphen, Steevens*); Post, Post-haste, dispatch. *F1;* post, post hast dispatch: *Q1*
47 s.d. **Cassio, Iago, Roderigo]** Roderigo, Iago, Cassio, Desdemona *Q1* (*Q1 s.d. after l. 46*)
50 s.d. **To Brabantio.]** *Theobald*
51 **lack'd]** lacke *Q1*
53 **nor]** *Q1;* hor *F1;* for *F2*
55 **hold on]** any hold of *Q1*
55 **grief]** griefes *Q1*
57 **and]** *Q1;* snd *F1*
59 s.p. **All.]** *Q1;* Sen. *F1*
63 **(Being . . . sense)]** *om. Q1*
64 **Sans]** Saunce *Q1* (*c*); Since *Q1* (*u*)
69 **your]** its *Q1*
69 **yea]** *om. Q1*
74 s.d. **To Othello.]** *Theobald*
74 **your]** *Q1;* yonr *F1*
81 **extent,]** *Q2;* extent; *F1;* extent *Q1*
82 **soft]** set *Q1*
84 **now]** *Q1;* now, *F1*
87 **feats]** feate *Q1*
87 **broils]** broyle *Q1*
90 **tale]** *Q1;* u Tale *F1*
93 **proceeding I am]** proceedings am I *Q1*
94–5 **bold; Of spirit]** bold of spirit, *Q1*
99 **main'd]** maim'd *Q1*
99 **imperfect,]** *Q1;* imperfect. *F1*
100 **could]** would *Q1*
104 **pow'rful]** powerfull *Q1* (*this kind of* re *or* er *variant not generally recorded hereafter*)
106 **wrought upon]** *Q1;* wtought vp on *F1*
106 s.p. **Duke.]** *Q1*
106 **vouch]** youth *Q1*
107 **wider]** certaine *Q1*
107 **overt]** *Q1;* ouer *F1*
108 **Than these]** These are *Q1*
109 **seeming do]** seemings, you *Q1*
110 s.p. **1. Sen.]** *Q1;* Sen. *F1*
115 **Sagittary]** Sagittar *Q1*
118 **The . . . you,]** *om. Q1*
120 s.d. **Exeunt . . . three.]** *Q1* (Exit)
121 s.d. **Exit Iago.]** *Rowe*
122 **till]** *Q1;* tell *F1*
122 **truly]** faithfull *Q1*
123 **I . . . blood,]** *om. Q1*
130 **battles]** *Q1;* Battaile *F1*
130 **fortunes]** *Q1;* Fortune *F1*
133 **bade]** *Q1;* bad *F1*
134 **spoke]** spake *Q1*
135 **accidents by]** accident of *Q1*
138 **slavery,]** *Q1;* slauery. *F1*
138 **of]** and *Q1*
139 **portance in]** with it all *Q1*
139 **travel's]** *Q1* (*apostrophe, Pope*); Trauellours *F1*
140 **antres]** *Q1* (Antrees); Antars *F1*
141 **and]** *Q1*
141 **heads]** *Q1;* head *F1*
142 **hint]** hent *Q1*
142 **my]** the *Q1*
143 **other]** *Q1;* others *F1*
144 **Anthropophagi]** *F2;* Anthropophague *F1;* Anthropophagie *Q1*
145 **Do grow]** *Q1;* Grew *F1*
145 **These things]** This *Q1*
147 **thence]** *Q1;* hence *F1*
148 **Which]** And *Q1*
149 **She'ld]** Shee'd *Q1*
154 **parcels]** parcell *Q1*
155 **intentively]** *Q1;* instinctiuely *F1*
157 **distressful]** distressed *Q1*
159 **sighs]** *Q1;* kisses *F1*
160 **in faith]** Ifaith *Q1*
160–1 **strange, . . . strange; 'Twas pitiful,]** *Q1;* strange: . . . strange, 'Twas pittifull: *F1*
166 **hint]** heate *Q1*
170 s.d. **Attendants]** and the rest *Q1*
171 **too.]** to,—*Q1*
175 **speak.]** *Q1;* speake? *F1*
177 **on my head]** lite on me *Q1*
184 **the lord of]** Lord of all my *Q1*
189 **be with you]** bu'y *Q1*
189 **have]** ha *Q1*
194 **Which . . . heart]** *om. Q1*
196 **soul]** soule. *Q1*
198 **them]** em *Q1*
200 **grise]** greese *Q1*
200 **lovers]** *Q1;* Louers. *F1*
201 **Into your favor]** *Q1*
205 **new]** more *Q1*
206 **preserv'd]** *Q1;* presern'd *F1*
206 **takes,]** *Q1;* takes: *F1*
207 **mock'ry]** mockery *Q1*
208 **robb'd]** *F2;* rob'd *F1, Q1*
218 **words; . . . hear]** *F3* (*subs.*); words, . . . heare: *F1;* words, . . . heare, *Q1*
219 **bruis'd]** *Q1;* bruized *F1*
219 **pierced]** *Q1;* pierc'd *F1*
219 **ear]** *Q1;* eares *F1*
220 **I . . . state.]** Beseech you now, to the affaires of the state. *Q1*
221 **a]** *om. Q1*
225 **sovereign]** *Q1;* more soueraigne *F1*
228 **boist'rous]** boisterous *Q1*
229 **grave]** great *Q1*
230 **couch]** *Pope;* Coach *F1;* Cooch *Q1*
232 **alacrity]** *Q1;* Alacartie *F1*
233 **do]** would *Q1*
237 **reference]** reuerence *Q1*
238 **With such accommodation]** Which such accomodation? *Q1*
239–40 **If . . . Be't]** *Q1;* Why *F1*
240 **I will]** Ile *Q1*
241 **I; I would not]** *Q1;* would I *F1*
243 **gracious]** *Q1;* Grcaious *F1*
244 **your prosperous]** a gracious *Q1*
246 **T' assist]** And if *Q1*
247 **you, Desdemona?]** you—speake. *Q1*
248 **did]** *Q1*
249 **storm]** scorne *Q1*
251 **very quality]** vtmost pleasure *Q1*
257 **why]** which *Q1*
260–1 **Let . . . heaven]** Your voyces Lords: beseech you let her will, / Haue a free way *Q1*
263–4 **(the . . . me defunct)]** *Steevens;* the . . . my defunct, *F1, Q1*
265 **to her]** of her *Q1*
267 **great]** good *Q1*
268 **For]** *Q1;* When *F1*
268 **light-wing'd]** *hyphen, Q1*
269 **Of . . . seel]** And . . . foyles *Q1*
270 **offic'd]** actiue *Q1*
270 **instruments]** *Q1;* Instrument *F1*
272 **housewives]** huswiues *Q1*
274 **against]** *Q1;* againsf *F1*
274 **estimation]** reputation *Q1*
276 **her]** *om. Q1*
276 **affair cries]** affaires cry *Q1*
277 **it]** *om. Q1*
277 s.p. **1. Sen.]** *Smock Alley PB, Dyce,* Sen. *F1; line continued to Duke, Q1*
277 **away]** hence *Q1*
278 **Des. To-night . . . night.]** *Q1*
279 **nine]** ten *Q1*
282 **And . . . and]** With . . . or *Q1*
283 **import]** concerne *Q1*
283 **So]** *om. Q1*
288 s.d. **To Brabantio.]** *Capell*
291 s.p. **1. Sen.]** *Q1;* Sen. *F1*
292 **if . . . eyes]** haue a quicke eye *Q1*
293 **and may]** may doe *Q1*
293 s.d. **Exeunt . . . etc.]** *Malone* (*after Theobald, Capell*); Exit. *F1;* Exeunt. *Q1*
297 **them]** her *Q1*
299 **wordly matter]** worldly matters *Q1*
300 **the time]** *Q1;* the the time *F1*
300 s.d. **with Desdemona]** *from Q1 s.d.:* Exit Moore and Desdemona.
301 **Iago—]** *Johnson;* Iago. *F1, Q1*
302 **say'st]** saiest *Q1*
303 **think'st]** thinkest *Q1*
306 **If]** Well, if *Q1*
306 **dost]** doest *Q1* (*hereafter the regular form in Q1; not further recorded*)
306 **after.]** after it, *Q1*
308 **torment]** a torment *Q1*
309 **have we]** we haue *Q1*
311 **O villainous!]** *om. Q1*
313 **betwixt]** betweene *Q1*
313 **injury,]** *Q1;* Iniurie: *F1*
314 **man]** a man *Q1*
321 **our]** *om. Q1*
322 **hyssop]** *F4;* Hisope *F1;* Isop *Q1*
322 **tine]** *A. Walker;* Time *F1, Q1*
326 **beam]** *Theobald;* braine *F1;* ballance *Q1*
331 **our]** *Q1;* or *F1*
332 **scion]** *Steevens;* Seyen *F1;* syen *Q1*
336 **have profess'd]** professe *Q1*
339 **stead]** *Hanmer;* steed *F1, Q1*
340 **thou the]** these *Q1*
342 **be . . . should]** be, that *Desdemona* should long *Q1*
343 **to]** vnto *Q1*
343 **Moor—put . . . purse—]** *Q1;* Moore. Put . . . purse: *F1*
343 **his]** *om. Q1*
344 **in her]** *om. Q1*
349 **acerb as the]** *Q1;* bitter as *F1*
349–50 **She . . . youth;]** *om. Q1*
351 **error]** *Q1;* errors *F1*
351–2 **She . . . must;]** *Q1*
356 **a]** *Q1*
358 **of]** a *Q1*
358–9 **thyself, it is]** tis *Q1*
362–3 **if . . . issue?]** *om. Q1*
365 **retell]** tell *Q1*
367 **hath]** has *Q1*
367 **conjunctive]** communicatiue *Q1*
369 **me]** and me *Q1*
377–81 **Rod. What . . . purse.]** *Q1* (*eds., except Alexander, usually replace ll. 379–82 with a single speech by Roderigo as in Q2:* I am chang'd, Ile goe sell all my land.)

385 **a snipe**] Q1; Snpe F1
388 **H'as**] Q1 (Ha's); She ha's F1; He ha's F2
389 **But**] Yet Q1
393 **his**] this Q1
393 **plume**] make Q1
394 **In**] A Q1
394 **Let's**] let me Q1
395 **ear**] Q1; eares F1
397 **hath**] has Q1
399 **is . . . nature**] a free and open nature too Q1
400 **seem**] seemes Q1
401 **led**] Q1; lead F1
403 **have't**] ha't Q1
404 s.d. **Exit.**] Q1

II.i

Location: *Globe (after Malone)*
o.s.d. **Montano**] Montanio Q1 *(throughout, except at V.ii.167, 282 s.dd.); Q1 s.d. reads:* Enter Montanio, Governor of Cypres, with two other Gentlemen.
2 **high-wrought**] *hyphen, F4*
3 **heaven**] hauen Q1
5 **hath spoke**] does speake Q1
7 **hath**] ha Q1
8 **mountains . . . them**] the huge mountaine mes lt Q1
9 **mortise?**] *Theobald;* Morties. F1; morties, — Q1
10 s.p. **2. Gent.**] Q1; 2 F1
11 **foaming**] banning Q1
12 **chidden**] chiding Q1
13 **wind-shak'd surge**] F3; winde-shak'd-Surge F1; winde shak'd surge Q1
13 **mane**] *Knight;* Maine F1; mayne Q1
15 **ever-fixed**] euer fired Q1
19 **to**] they Q1
19 s.d. **third**] Q1
20, 25, 31 s.pp. **3. Gent.**] Q1; 3 F1
20 **lads! our**] Lords, your Q1
21 **Turks**] Turke Q1
22 **A noble**] Another Q1
24 **their**] the Q1
25–6 **in, A Veronesa;**] *Theobald;* in: A Verennessa, F1; in: / A Veronessa, Q1
28 **on shore**] ashore Q1
33 **prays**] Q1; praye F1
34 **heaven**] Q1; Heauens F1
38 **throw out**] Q1; throw-out F1
39–40 **Even . . . regard.**] *om.* Q1
39 **th' aerial**] *Pope;* th' Eriall F1; th' Ayre all Q2
40 s.p. **3. Gent.**] Q1; Gent. F1
42 **arrivance**] Q1; Arriuancie F1
43 **you,**] to Q1
43 **this**] Q1; the F1
43 **warlike**] worthy Q1
44 **O**] And Q1
45 **the**] their Q1
48 **pilot**] Pilate Q1
50 **hopes**] F3; hope's F1
51 s.d. **Within, "A**] *Mess.* A Q1
51 s.d. **Enter a Messenger.**] Q1 *(after* cure. *l. 51); placed as in Malone*
53 s.p. **Mess.**] Q1; Gent. F1
54 **Stand**] otand Q1
55 **governor**] guernement Q1
55 s.d. **A shot.**] Q1 *(after* least. *l. 57); placed as in Capell*
56, 59, 66 s.pp. **2. Gent.**] Q1; Gent. F1
56 **their**] the Q1
57 **friends**] friend Q1
63 **quirks of**] *om.* Q1
65 **tire the ingener**] *Steevens conj.;* tyre the Ingeniuer F1; beare all excellency Q1
65 s.d. **Second**] Q1 (2.); Q1 *s.d. after l. 65*
65 **How**] *om.* Q1
67 **H'as**] He has Q1 *(Q1 gives ll. 67–73 to* 2 Gent.)
68 **high**] by Q1
69 **gutter'd rocks**] Q1 *(reading* guttered); gutter'd-Rockes F1
70 **ensteep'd**] enscerped Q1
70 **enclog**] clog Q1
72 **mortal**] common Q1
74 **spake**] spoke Q1
80 **Make . . . in**] And swiftly come to Q1
82 **And . . . comfort!**] Q1
82 s.d. **Emilia**] *from* Q1 Emillia *(generally throughout);* Æmilia F1 *(generally throughout);* Q1 *s.d. after l. 80 (Roderigo and Emilia named in reverse order)*
82 s.d. **with Attendants**] *Malone (subs., after Capell)*
83 **on shore**] ashore Q1
84 **You**] Ye Q1
88 **me**] Q1
92 **the**] Q1
93 **Within, . . . sail!**] *placed as in Collier; after* sail. *l. 93,* F1; *after l. 91,* Q1
93 s.d. **A shot.**] *Johnson (subs.)*
94 s.p. **2. Gent.**] Q1; Gent. F1
94 **their**] Q1; this F1
95 **See . . . news.**] So speakes this voyce: Q1
95 s.d. **Exit Second Gentleman.**] *Capell (subs.)*
96 s.d. **To Emilia.**] *Rowe*
99 s.d. **Kissing her.**] *Johnson (subs.)*
100 **Sir**] For Q1
101 **oft bestows**] has bestowed Q1
102 **You would**] You'd Q1
103 **In faith**] I know Q1
104 **still,**] I; for Q1
104 **have**] ha Q1
104 **list**] Q1; leaue F1
108 **have**] ha Q1
109–12 **Come . . . beds.**] *as verse,* Q1; *as prose,* F1
109 **a' doors**] *Capell* (o' doors); of doore F1; adores Q1
113 s.p. **Des.**] *om.* Q1
114 **true, . . . Turk:**] *Pope (subs.);* true: . . . Turke, F1; true, . . . Turke, Q1
117 **What . . . me?**] *as verse,* Q1; *as prose,* F1
117 **wouldst**] wouldst thou Q1
125–8 **I . . . deliver'd:**] *as verse,* Q1; *as prose,* F1
127 **brains**] braine Q1
129 **wise,**] Q1; wise: F1
130 **useth**] vsing Q1
133 **hit**] Q1; fit F1
137 **an heir**] a haire Q1
138 **fond**] *om.* Q1
142 **wise ones**] Q1; wise-ones F1
143 **thou praisest**] that praises Q1
145 **indeed—**] *Dyce;* indeed? F1, Q1
145 **authority**] Q1; authorithy F1
146 **merit**] merrits Q1
147 **itself?**] Q1; it selfe. F1
155 **cod's head**] F3; Cods-head F1; Codshead Q1
156 **nev'r**] ne're Q1
157 **See . . . behind:**] *om.* Q1
158 **wight**] Q1; wightes F1
158 **were)—**] *Johnson;* were) F1; were. Q1
167 s.d. **Aside.**] *Rowe*
168 **With**] *om.* Q1
168 **I**] *om.* Q1
169 **fly**] Flee Q1
170 **gyve thee**] F2; giue thee F1; catch you Q1
170 **thine own courtship**] your owne courtesies Q1
173 **kiss'd**] rist Q1
174 **Very**] *om.* Q1
175 **an . . . courtesy**] Q1; and . . . Curtsie F1
176 **to**] at Q1
177 **clyster-pipes**] Q1 (Clisterpipes); Clusterpipes F1
177–8 s.d. **Trumpets within.**] Q1 *(after l. 178); placed as in Rowe*
178 **Moor!**] *Collier;* Moore F1; Moore, Q1
185 **calms**] calmenesse Q1
188 **Olympus-high**] *hyphen, Steevens*
190 **fear**] Q1; feare, F1
195 **sweet powers!**] *Rowe;* (sweet Powers) F1; sweete power, Q1
198 **discords**] discord Q1
198 s.d. **They kiss.**] Q1
199 s.d. **Aside.**] *Rowe*
199–201 **O . . . am.**] *as verse,* Q1; *as prose,* F1
203 **does my**] doe our Q1
203 **this**] the Q1
212 s.d. **Exeunt . . . Roderigo.**] *Cambridge (subs., after Capell);* Exit Othello and Desdemona. F1; Exit. Q1
213 s.d. **To . . . out.**] *Kittredge (subs.)*
214 **harbor**] Habor Q1
214 **hither.**] *Steevens;* thither, F1; hither, Q1
217 **list me**] Q1; list-me F1
218 **must**] will Q1
218–9 **thee this:**] thee, this Q1
224 **lies. To**] lies; and will she Q1
224 **thy**] the Q1
225 **it**] so Q1
228 **again**] Q1; a game F1
228 **to give satiety**] giue saciety Q1
229 **appetite, loveliness**] *Theobald;* appetite. Louelinesse F1; appetite. Loue lines Q1
234 **in**] to Q1
237 **eminent**] eminently Q1
239–40 **humane seeming**] hand- / seeming Q1
240 **compass**] compassing Q1
240–1 **most . . . loose**] hidden Q1
241 **affection**] affections Q1
241 **Why . . . none—**] *om.* Q1
242 **slipper and subtle**] subtle slippery Q1
242 **finder-out**] Q1 *(hyphen, Capell);* finder F1
242 **occasion**] occasions Q1
243 **has**] Q1; he's F1
244–5 **true . . . knave.**] the true aduantages neuer present themselues. Q1
248 **hath**] has Q1
253 **Bless'd pudding!**] *om.* Q1
255 **Didst . . . that?**] *om.* Q1
256 **that I did**] *om.* Q1
257 **obscure**] *om.* Q1
260 **Villainous thoughts, Roderigo!**] *om.* Q1
261 **mutualities**] Q1; mutabilities F1
261 **hard**] hand Q1
262 **master and**] *om.* Q1
263 **Pish!**] *om.* Q1
265 **the**] your Q1
269 **course**] cause Q1
272 **he's**] he is Q1
273 **happily**] F2; happely F1; haply Q1
273 **may strike**] with his Trunchen may strike Q1
275 **mutiny,**] Q1; Mutiny. F1
276 **taste again**] trust again't Q1
279 **the**] *om.* Q1
281 **you**] I Q1
286 **believe't**] beleeue it Q1
288 **(howbeit**] howbe't, Q1
289 **loving, noble**] noble, louing Q1
293 **accomptant**] accountant Q1
294 **led**] lead Q1
295 **lusty**] lustfull Q1
298 **or**] nor Q1
299 **even'd**] euen Q1
299 **for wife**] Q1; for wift F1
303 **trace**] crush Q1
306 **rank**] Q1; right F1
307 **night-cap**] Q1; Night-Cape F1

II.ii

Location: *Pope*
o.s.d. **Othello's Herald with**] a Gentleman reading Q1
o.s.d. **people following**] *Malone*
2 **general,**] Q1; Generall. F1
3 **mere**] meete Q1
3 **every**] that euery Q1
4 **to make**] make Q1
5 **bonfires**] bonefires Q1
6 **addiction**] Q2; addition F1; minde Q1
7 **nuptial**] Nuptialls Q1
9 **of feasting**] *om.* Q1
9 **present**] Q1; presenr F1
10 **have**] hath Q1
10 **Heaven**] Q1
12 s.d. **Exeunt.**] *Capell;* Exit. F1; *om.* Q1

II.iii

II.iii] *Capell*
Location: *Alexander (after Theobald)*
o.s.d. **Desdemona . . . Attendants**] Cassio, and Desdemona Q1
2 **that**] the Q1
4 **direction**] directed Q1
8 s.d. **To Desdemona.**] *Johnson*
10 **That profit's . . . 'tween**] The profits . . . twixt Q1
11 s.d. **with . . . Attendants**] *Capell (subs.);* Othello and Desdemona Q1
13–4 **o' th' clock**] aclock Q1
18 **She's**] She is Q1

20 **she's**] she is Q1
22–7 **What . . . love?**] *as prose, Pope (ll. 24–7, Q1); as verse,* F1
23 **to**] of Q1
26 **is it not**] tis Q1
28 **She**] It Q1
32 **of**] of the Q1
39 **have**] ha Q1
41 **infortunate**] vnfortunate Q1
52 **hath**] has Q1
52 **out**] outward Q1
53 **carous'd**] Q1; Carrows'd. F1
55 **else**] lads Q1
56 **honors**] honour Q1
59 **they**] the Q1
60 **Am I**] I am Q1
60 **to put**] Q1; put to F1
61 s.d. **Cassio . . . Gentlemen**] Montanio, Cassio, and others Q1
61 s.d. **Servants . . . wine**] *Dyce (subs.)*
64 **God**] Q1; heauen F1
66 **Good faith**] Q1; Good-faith F1
69, 89 s.dd. **Sings.**] *Rowe*
70 **clink**] clinke, clinke Q1
72 **O, man's**] a Q1
75 **God**] Q1; Heauen F1
80 **Englishman**] Q1; Englishmen F1
80 **exquisite**] expert Q1
87 **I'll**] I will Q1
89 **and-a**] a Q1
91 **them**] 'em Q1
96 **Then**] Q1; And F1
96 **thy**] thine Q1
96 **auld**] Q2; awl'd F1; owd Q1
98 **'Fore God,**] Q1; Why F1
101 **to be**] *om.* Q1
102 **God's**] Q1; heau'ns F1
103 **souls**] soules that Q1
103–4 **and . . . sav'd.**] *om.* Q1
105 **It's**] It is Q1
108 **too**] *om.* Q1
111 **have**] ha Q1
111 **God**] Q1
115 **hand**] Q1
116 **I**] *om.* Q1
117 s.p. **All.**] Q1; Gent. F1
118 **Why**] *om.* Q1
118 **think then**] thinke Q1
120 **platform**] plotforme Q1
120 s.d. **The . . . off.**] *ed. (after Pope)*
122 **He's**] He is Q1
126 **puts**] put Q1
129 **the**] Q1; his F1
132 **were**] wete Q1
134 **Prizes the virtue**] Praises the vertues Q1
135 **looks**] looke Q1
136 s.d. **Aside to him.**] *Capell*
137 s.d. **Exit Roderigo.**] Q1
142 **island.**] Q1 *(subs.)*; Island, F1
144 s.d. **Cry . . . help!"**] *Theobald (after Q1* Helpe, helpe, within *following l. 143)*
144 s.d. **pursuing**] driuing in Q1
145 **'Zounds,**] Q1 (Zouns,)
147 **I'll**] but Ile Q1
148 **twiggen bottle**] F2; Twiggen-Bottle F1; wicker bottle Q1
150 s.d. **Striking Roderigo.**] *Capell (subs.)*
151–4 **Nay . . . mazzard.**] *as prose,* Q1; *as verse,* F1
151 **Nay**] *om.* Q1
151 **I pray you**] pray Q1
152 s.d. **Staying him.**] *Rowe*
155 **you're**] you are Q1
156 s.d. **They fight.**] Q1
157 s.d. **Aside to Roderigo.**] *Capell*
157 s.d. **Exit Roderigo.**] Q2
158 **God's will**] Q1 (godswill); Alas F1
159 **sir—Montano—sir—**] *Capell (after Theobald, but adapting* Q1*)*; Sir Montano: F1; Sir Montanio, sir, Q1
160 s.d. **A bell rung.**] Q1 *(after l. 157); placed as in* Q2
161 **which**] that Q1
162 **God's will**] Q1 (godswill); Fie, fie F1
162 **hold**] Q1
163 **You'll be asham'd**] You will be sham'd Q1
163 s.d. **Gentlemen with weapons**] Q1; Attendants F1
164 **'Zounds,**] Q1 (Zouns,)
165 **hurt**] hurt, Q1; hurt, but not F2
165 **He dies.**] *om.* Q1; he faints. Q2 *(as s.d.)*
165 s.d. **Assailing Cassio again.**] *Capell*
166 **Hold ho!**] Hold, hold Q1
166 **sir—Montano—**] *Rowe;* Sir Montano, F1; sir Montanio, Q1
168 **hold**] hold, hold Q1
169 **ariseth**] arises Q1
171 **hath**] has Q1
173 **for**] forth Q1
176 **What is**] what's Q1
181 **for**] to Q1
183 **breast**] Q1; breastes F1
187 **Those**] These Q1
188 **comes . . . are**] came . . . were Q1
190 **to**] *om.* Q1
192 **noted,**] Q1; noted. F1
193 **mouths**] men Q1
196 **to it**] to't Q1
199 **me—**] *Capell;* me. F1; me, Q1
202 **sometimes**] sometime Q1
206 **collied**] coold Q1
207 **'Zounds, if I**] Q1 (Zouns,); If I once F1
212 **twinn'd**] twin'd Q1
213 **What,**] Q1; What F1
215 **quarrel**] quarrels Q1
217 **began't**] began Q1
218 **partially**] partiality Q1
218 **leagu'd**] *Pope;* league F1, Q1
221 **have**] ha Q1
221 **cut**] out Q1
224 **Thus**] Q1; This F1
235 **the**] Q1; then F1
235 **oath**] oaths Q1
236 **say**] see Q1
240 **cannot I**] can I not Q1
241 **forget.**] Q1 (forget;); forget, F1
249 s.d. **attended**] with others Q1
252 **dear**] *om.* Q1 252 **now**] Q1
253 s.d. **To Montano.**] *Johnson*
254 s.d. **Some . . . off.**] *Capell (subs.)*
256 **vild**] *ed.;* vil'd F1; vile Q1
258 s.d. **with . . . Attendants**] *Capell (subs.), from* Q1 *s.d.* Exit Moore, Desdemona, and attendants. *(after l. 259)*
261 **God**] Q1; Heauen F1
262 **reputation! . . . have**] I ha Q1
263 **have**] ha Q1
263 **part**] part sir Q1
266 **I had**] I Q1
267 **sense**] offence Q1
271 **What,**] *Capell;* What F1, Q1
272 **more**] *om.* Q1
273–4 **a . . . malice,**] Q1 *(subs.)*; (a . . . malice) F1
278 **slight**] light Q1
279 **so**] *om.* Q1
279–81 **Drunk? . . . shadow?**] *om.* Q1
289 **God**] Q1
292 **pleasance, revel**] Reuell, pleasure Q1
294 **Why, but**] Q1; Why? But F1
300 **and**] *om.* Q1
301 **not**] not so Q1
305 **them**] em Q1
307 **O strange!**] *om.* Q1
307 **inordinate**] vnordinate Q1
308 **ingredient**] ingredience Q1
309 **familiar**] Q1; famillar F1
313–4 **a time, man.**] some time: Q1
314 **I'll**] Q1; I F1
316 **hath**] has Q1
317 **mark,**] Q1; mark: F1
317 **denotement**] *Theobald;* deuotement F1, Q1
319 **help**] shee'll helpe Q1
320 **of**] *om.* Q1
321 **she**] that she Q1
322 **broken joint**] braule Q1
325 **stronger**] Q1; stonger F1
325 **it was**] twas Q1
327 **protest,**] *Theobald;* protest F1, Q1
330 **I will**] will I Q1
332 **here**] Q1
335 s.d. **Cassio**] *om.* Q1
343 **were't**] Q1; were F1
344 **sin,**] Q1; sin: F1
351 **the**] their Q1
353 **whiles**] while Q1
354 **fortune**] fortunes Q1
362 **them**] em Q1
362 s.d. **Enter Roderigo.**] *placed as in* Q1; *after l. 362,* F1
365 **have**] ha Q1
366 **and**] *om.* Q1
367–8 **pains; . . . again**] paines, as that comes to, and no money at all, and with that wit returne Q1
370 **have**] ha Q1
372 **know'st**] knowest Q1
374 **Does't**] *Rowe;* Dos't F1; Do'st Q1
374 **hath**] has Q1
375 **hast**] Q1; hath F1
377 **Yet**] But Q1
378 **By the mass**] Q1; Introth F1
382 s.d. **Exit Roderigo.**] *om.* Q1
382 **Two**] Some Q1
384–5 **on—Myself**] *Theobald;* on my selfe F1; on. / My selfe Q1
388 s.d. **Exit.**] Exeunt. Q1

III.i

Location: *Alexander (after Rowe, Theobald)*
o.s.d. **Enter . . . Musicians.**] Q2; Enter Cassio, Musitians, and Clowne. F1; Enter Cassio, with Musitians and the Clowne. Q1
2 s.d. **They . . . Clown.**] Q2
3 **have**] ha Q1
3 **in**] at Q1
5, 7, 9, 14, 18 s.pp. **1. Mus.**] *Capell;* Mus. F1; Boy. Q1
6 **you**] cald Q1
8 **tail**] Q1; tale F1
12–3 **for love's sake**] of all loues Q1
18 **have**] ha Q1
19 **up**] *om.* Q1
20 **into air**] *om.* Q1
20 s.d. **Exeunt Musicians.**] *Theobald;* Exit Mu. F1; *om.* Q1
21 **hear, mine**] *Warburton conj. (in Theobald) from* Q1 heare my; heare me, mine F1
22 **No . . . you.**] *as prose,* Q1; *as verse,* F1
25 **general's wife**] Q1 (Cenerals wife); Generall F1
30 **Do . . . friend.**] Q1
30 s.d. **Exit Clown.**] *om.* Q1
30 s.d. **Enter Iago.**] *after l. 29,* Q1
31, 33 **have**] ha Q1
39 **for't**] for it Q1
39 s.d. **Exit Iago.**] *Capell;* Exit F1, Q1 *(both after free. l. 39)*
42 **sure**] soone Q1
49 **To . . . front**] Q1 (front,)
53 **Desdemon**] Desdemona Q1
55 **Cas. I . . . you.**] *om.* Q1
55 s.d. **Exeunt.**] Q1

III.ii

Location: *Alexander*
o.s.d. **Gentlemen**] other Gentlemen Q1
1 **pilot**] Pilate Q1
2 **Senate**] State Q1
6 s.p. **Gentlemen.**] *A. Walker;* Gent. F1, Q1
6 **We'll**] F3; Well F1; We Q1

III.iii

Location: *Alexander (after Dyce)*
3 **warrant**] know Q1
4 **cause**] case Q1
5 **fellow.**] Q1 (fellow:—); Fellow, F1
5 **doubt,**] F3; doubt F1, Q1
10 **I know't;**] O sir, Q1
12 **strangeness**] strangest Q1
14 **That**] The Q1
16 **circumstances**] circumstance Q1
28 **thy cause**] thee cause: Q1
28 s.d. **Iago**] Iago, and Gentlemen Q1
33 **purposes**] purpose Q1
39 **steal**] sneake Q1
40 **your**] you Q1
45 **lieutenant,**] *Dyce;* Lieutenant F1, Q1
52 **Yes, faith**] Q1; I sooth F1
53 **hath**] has Q1
53 **grief**] griefes Q1
54 **To**] I Q1
55 **Desdemon**] Desdemona Q1
60 **or**] Q1; on F1
61 **noon**] morne Q1

61 **on]** or Q1
63 **In faith]** F4; Infaith F1; Ifaith Q1
65 **example]** examples Q1
69 **would]** could Q1
70 **mamm'ring]** muttering Q1
71 **a-wooing]** *Dyce;* a woing F1; a wooing Q1
71 **with]** Q1; wirh F1
74 **By'r lady]** Q1; Trust me F1
74 **much—]** Q2; much. F1, Q1
82 **difficult weight]** difficulty Q1
88 **Be]** be it Q1
89 **s.d. with Emilia]** *from* Q1 *s.d.* Desd. and Em.
94 **you]** Q1; he F1
97 **thought]** thoughts Q1
100 **oft]** often Q1
102 **ay]** *Rowe;* I F1; *om.* Q1
106 **By heaven]** Q1; Alas F1
106 **thou echo'st]** he ecchoes Q1
107 **thy]** his Q1
108 **dost]** didst Q1
109 **even]** but Q1
112 **In]** Q1; Of F1
115 **conceit]** counsell Q1
118 **thou'rt]** thou art Q1
119 **weigh'st]** weighest Q1
119 **giv'st]** giue Q1
119 **them]** em Q1
120 **fright]** affright Q1
123 **They're]** They are Q1
123 **dilations]** denotements Q1
125 **be sworn]** presume Q1
126 **what]** that Q1
131 **as]** *om.* Q1
132–3 **thy . . . thoughts . . . words]** the . . . thought . . . word Q1
135 **that all]** Q1; that: All F1
135 **to]** Q1
136 **vild]** vile Q1
138 **that]** a Q1
139 **But some]** Q1; Wherein F1
140 **sessions]** Session Q1
143 **think'st]** thinkest Q1
147 **oft]** Q1; of F1
148 **that your wisdom]** I entreat you Q1
148 **then]** Q1
149 **conjects]** Q1; conceits F1
150 **Would]** You'd Q1
151 **his]** my Q1
153 **and]** or Q1
154 **'Zounds,]** Q1 (Zouns.)
154 **what . . . mean?]** *om.* Q1
155 **woman]** woman's Q1
156 **their]** our Q1
162 **By heaven,]** Q1
162 **thoughts]** thought Q1
165 **Oth. Ha?]** *om.* Q1
165 **my lord, of]** *om.* Q1
167 **The]** That Q1
170 **strongly]** Q1; soundly F1
175 **God]** Q1; Heauen F1
177 **jealousy?]** Q1; Iealousie; F1
180 **once]** Q1
182 **exsufflicate]** *Capell;* exufflicate F1, Q1
182 **blown]** Q1; blow'd F1
183 **jealious]** iealous Q1 (*throughout*)
185 **well]** Q1
193 **this]** it Q1
198 **eyes]** eie Q1
202 **God]** Q1; Heauen F1
203 **not]** *om.* Q1
204 **leave't]** leaue Q1
204 **keep't]** Q2; kept F1; keepe Q1
210 **seel]** seale Q1
211 **witchcraft—]** *Rowe;* witchcraft. F1; witchcraft: Q1
215 **I' faith]** Q1; Trust me F1
217 **my]** Q1; your F1
217 **y' are]** you are Q1
220 **vild]** vile Q1
223 **Which . . . not.]** As my thoughts aime not at: Q1
223 **worthy]** trusty Q1
223 **friend—]** *Globe;* Friend: F1, Q1
224 **y' are]** you are Q1
232 **Foh, one]** Fie we Q1
232 **such, a will]** such a will, Q1
233 **disproportions]** disproportion Q1
238 **farewell!]** *om.* Q1
241 s.d. **Going.]** *Rowe*
244 **s.d. Returning.]** *Capell*
244 **My . . . honor]** *continued to Othello,* Q1
245 **farther]** further Q1
246 **Although 'tis]** Tho it be Q1
248 **hold]** Q1; put F2
250 **his]** her Q1
259 **qualities]** Q1; Quantities F1
259 **learned]** Q1; learn'd F1
260 **human]** *Rowe;* humane F1; humaine Q1
260 **dealings]** dealing Q1
262 **I'ld]** I'de Q1
263 **Haply]** Happily Q1
266 **vale]** valt Q1 271 **of]** in Q1
272 **the]** a Q1
273 **of]** Q1; to F1
273 **great ones]** Q1; Great-ones F1
277 **Look where she]** Desdemona Q1
277 **s.d. Enter Desdemona and Emilia.]** *after* believe't. *l.* 279, Q1
278 **O . . . mocks]** Q1; Heauen mock'd F1
279 **believe't]** beleeue it Q1
280 **islanders]** Ilander Q1
282 **Why . . . faintly?]** Why is your speech so faint? Q1
285 **Faith]** Q1; Why F1
286 **it hard]** your head Q1
287 **well]** well againe Q1
287 **s.d. He . . . drops.]** *Capell*
289 **s.d. with Othello]** *from* Q1 *s.d.* Ex. Oth. and Desd. (*after l.* 290); *s.d. after l.* 288, F1; *placed as in Rowe*
296 **talk to]** Q1; talke too F1
296 **have]** ha Q1
297 **he will]** hee'll Q1
299 **but to please]** know, but for Q1
299 **s.d. Enter Iago.]** *after l.* 298, Q1
302 **You have]** *om.* Q1
304 **wife]** thing Q1
306 **handkerchief]** handkercher Q1 (*throughout*)
310 **stol'n]** stole Q1
311 **faith;]** Q1; but F1
313 **'tis]** it is Q1
314–5 **What . . . it?]** *as verse,* Q1; *as prose,* F1
314 **with't]** with it Q1
315 **s.d. Snatching it.]** *Rowe*
315 **what is]** what's Q1
317 **Give't me]** Giue mee't Q1
319 **acknown]** you knowne Q1
325 **The . . . poison:]** *om.* Q1
326 **conceits]** Q1; conceites, F1
327 **distaste,]** *Dyce;* distaste: F1; distast. Q1
328 **act]** art, Q1
328 **blood]** *Cambridge;* blood, F1, Q1
329 **mines]** mindes Q1
329 **s.d. Enter Othello.]** *placed as in Globe; after l.* 329, F1; *after l.* 328, Q1
333 **me]** me, to me Q1
337 **know't]** know Q1
338 **in]** of Q1
340 **fed well]** *om.* Q1
349 **troops]** troope Q1
355 **you]** ye Q1
355 **rude]** wide Q1
356 **dread clamors]** great clamor Q1
356 **dread clamors]** great clamor Q1
359 **thou]** F1, Q1 (c); you Q1 (u)
359 **s.d. Taking . . . throat.]** *Capell* (*after Rowe*)
361 **mine]** mans Q1
367 **lord—]** *Pope;* Lord. F1, Q1
369 **remorse;]** Q1 (remorce.); remorse F1
370 **horror's]** *Hanmer;* Horrors F1, Q1
373 **forgive]** defend Q1
375–6 **mine . . . thine]** F1, Q1 (c); thine . . . mine Q1 (u)
376 **lov'st]** liuest Q1
380 **sith]** since Q1
383–90 **Oth. By . . . satisfied!]** *om.* Q1
386 **Her]** Q2; My F1
391 **sir]** Q1
393 **and]** *om.* Q1
395 **supervisor]** Q1; super-vision F1
398 **them . . . them]** em . . . em Q1
399 **do]** did Q1
408 **might]** may Q1
409 **reason]** reason that Q1
411 **in]** into Q1
420 **wary]** merry Q1
422 **"O . . . creature!"]** out, sweete creature, and Q1
424 **then]** Q1
425 **Over]** Q1; ore F1
425 **sigh'd, and kiss'd]** Q1; sigh, and kisse F1
426 **Cried]** Q1; cry F1
428 **denoted]** deuoted Q1
429 **s.p. Iago.]** Q1; *line continued to Othello,* F1
432 **yet]** but Q1
439 **If it]** If't Q1
440 **that]** *Malone;* it F1, Q1
444 **true]** time Q1
447 **the hollow hell]** thy hollow Cell Q1
450 **Yet]** Pray Q1
451 **blood, blood, blood]** blood, *Iago,* blood Q1
452 **perhaps]** Q1
453–60 **Iago . . . heaven,]** *om.* Q1
455 **Nev'r]** Ne'r Q2
455 **feels]** Q2; keepes F1
458 **nev'r . . . nev'r]** ne're . . . ne're Q2
460 **s.d. He kneels.]** Q1 (*after l.* 450), Q2 (*after* tongues! *l.* 450) (Q1 *om. ll.* 453–60); *placed as in Craig.*
462 **s.d. Iago kneels.]** Q1 (*after l.* 464); *placed as in* Q2
466 **execution]** excellency Q1
466 **hands]** hand Q1
468 **in me]** *om.* Q1
469 **business]** worke so Q1
469 **s.d. They rise.]** *Cambridge* (*after Capell*)
474 **at your]** as you Q1
476 **damn her!]** *om.* Q1

III.iv

Location: *Alexander* (*after Dyce*)
o.s.d. **Clown]** the Clowne Q1
1 **Lieutenant]** the Leiutenant Q1
5 **s.p. Clo.]** *om.* Q1
5 **He's]** He is Q1
5 **me]** one Q1
6 **'tis]** is Q1
8–10 **Clo. To . . . this?]** *om.* Q1
12 **here . . . lies]** *om.* Q1
13 **mine own]** my Q1
19 **on]** in Q1
21 **man's wit]** a man Q1
22 **I will]** I'le Q1
22 **it]** of it Q1
22 **s.d. Clown]** *om.* Q1
23 **the]** that Q1
25 **have lost]** loose Q1
29 **ill thinking]** Q1; ill-thinking F1
32 **now till]** now, / Let Q1
33 **is't]** is it Q1
34 **s.d. Aside.]** *Hanmer*
37 **yet]** Q1
37 **hath]** has Q1
39 **Hot]** Not Q1
40 **prayer]** praying Q1
48 **Come now,]** *Capell;* Come, now F1; come, come, Q1; come now Q2
51 **sorry]** sullen Q1
54 **faith]** Q1; indeed F1
62 **loathed]** lothely Q1
64 **wiv'd]** wiue Q1
67 **lose't]** *Theobald;* loose't F1; loose Q1
71 **course]** make Q1
74 **which]** with Q1
75 **Conserv'd]** Conserues Q1
75 **I' faith]** Q1; Indeed F1
77 **God]** Q1; Heauen F1
77 **seen't]** seene it Q1
79 **rash]** rashly Q1
80 **is't]** is it Q1
81 **Heaven]** Q1
84 **How?]** Ha. Q1
85 **see't]** see it Q1
86 **sir,]** Q1
88 **Pray you]** I pray Q1
89 **the]** that Q1
92–3 **Des. I . . . handkerchief!]** Q1 (handkercher)
95 **you—]** *Steevens* (*after Capell*); you. F1, Q1
97 **I' faith]** Q1; Insooth F1
98 **'Zounds!]** Q1 (Zouns.); Away. F1

98 s.d. **Othello]** *om. Q1*
100 **nev'r]** ne're *Q1*
102 **the]** *F1, Q1* (*c*); this *Q1* (*u*)
102 **of it]** *om. Q1*
113 **office]** duty *Q1*
114 **honor.]** *Rowe;* honour, *F1, Q1*
116 **nor my]** neither *Q1*
121 **shut]** shoote *Q1*
137 **is he]** can he be *Q1*
140 s.d. **Iago]** *Capell; F1 s.d. after l. 140; s.d. om. Q1*
145 **their]** the *Q1*
147 **a]** that *Q1*
149 **observancy]** obseruances *Q1*
161 **they're]** they are *Q1*
161 **It is]** tis *Q1*
162 **born]** *F3;* borne *F1, Q1*
163 **the]** that *Q1*
165 **hereabout]** *F3;* heere about *F1, Q1*
168 s.d. **Exeunt . . . Emilia.]** *Q1* (*after l. 166*); Exit. *F1* (*after l. 167*)*; placed as in Pope*
168 s.d. **Enter Bianca.]** *after* Cassio! *l. 169, Q1*
170 **is't]** is it *Q1*
171 **I'faith]** *Q1;* Indeed *F1*
174 **lovers']** *Theobald;* Louers *F1, Q1*
176 **O]** No *Q1*
177 **leaden]** laden *Q1*
178 **continuate]** conuenient *Q1*
179 s.d. **Giving . . . handkerchief.]** *Rowe*
181–2 **friend; . . . felt absence]** *Theobald;* Friend, / . . . felt-Absence: *F1;* friend, / . . . felt absence, *Q1*
183 **Well, well.]** *om. Q1*
184 **vild]** vile *Q1*
184 **devil's]** *Rowe;* Diuels *F1;* diueils *Q1*
187 **by my faith]** *Q1;* in good troth *F1*
188 **neither]** sweet *Q1*
190 **I would]** I'de *Q1*
195–6 **Bian. Why . . . not.]** *om. Q1*
195 **pray]** *Q2;* ptay *F1*
201 s.d. **omnes]** *om. Q1*

IV.i

Location: *Alexander* (*after Capell*)
o.s.d.] *Q1 reverses order of entry*
3, 5 **in bed]** abed *Q1*
9 **If]** So *Q1*
21 **infectious]** infected *Q1*
27 **Or]** Or by the *Q1*
28 **Convinced]** *F1, Q1* (*c*); coniured *Q1* (*u*)
32 **Faith]** *Q1;* Why *F1*
33 **What?]** But *Q1*
36 **belie her]** *Q1;* be-lye-her *F1*
36 **'Zounds,]** *Q1* (Zouns,)
37 **Handkerchief—confessions—handkerchief!]** handkerchers—Confession, handkerchers. *Q1*
38–43 **To . . . devil!]** *om. Q1*
43 s.d. **Falls . . . trance.]** He fals downe. *Q1* (*c*); *om. Q1* (*u*)
45 **work]** *Q1;* workes *F1*
48 s.d. **Enter Cassio.]** *after* Cassio? *l. 48, Q1*
52 **No, forbear,]** *Q1*
58 s.d. **Exit Cassio.]** *Q2* (*after* me? *l. 61*)*; placed as in Rowe*
60 **you not,]** you? no *Q1*
61 **fortune]** fortunes *Q1*
65 **it]** *om. Q1*
65 **Good]** *F1, Q1* (*c*); God *Q1* (*u*)
68 **lie]** lyes *Q1*
71 **couch]** Coach *Q1*
75 **list.]** *Q1* (*subs.*); List, *F1*
76 **o'erwhelmed]** ere while, mad *Q1*
77 **unsuiting]** *Q1* (*c*); vnfitting *Q1* (*u*); resulting *F1*
79 **'scuses]** scuse *Q1*
80 **Bade . . . return]** Bid . . . retire *Q1*
81 **Do]** *om. Q1*
82 **fleers]** Ieeres *Q1* (*c*); geeres *Q1* (*u*)
86 **hath]** has *Q1*
88 **y' are]** you are *Q1*
92 s.d. **Othello withdraws.]** *Rowe*
95 **clothes]** *Q1;* Cloath *F1*
98 **restrain]** refraine *Q1*
99 s.d. **Enter Cassio.]** *after l. 97, Q1*
101 **conster]** *Q1;* conserue *F1*
102 **behaviors]** behauiour *Q1*
103 **now]** *Q1*
107 s.d. **Speaking lower.]** *Rowe*
107 **pow'r]** *ed.* (*after Q1* power); dowre *F1*
110 **woman]** a woman *Q1*
111 **i' faith]** *Q1;* indeed *F1*
114 **o'er]** on *Q1*
114 **well said, well said]** well said *Q1*
118 **you]** *Q1;* ye *F1*
119–21 **I . . . ha!]** *as prose, Pope; as verse, F1, Q1*
119 **her]** *Q1*
119 **What? a customer!]** *om. Q1*
119 **Prithee]** I prethee *Q1*
122 **they]** *om. Q1*
123 **Faith]** *Q1;* Why *F1*
123 **that you]** you shall *Q1*
126 **Have]** Ha *Q1*
126 **scor'd me?]** stor'd me *Q1*
127–9 **This . . . promise.]** *as prose, Q1; as verse, F1*
130 **beckons]** *Q1;* becomes *F1*
133 **the other]** tother *Q1*
134 **the]** this *Q1*
135 **and]** *om. Q1*
135 **by this hand,]** *Q1*
135 **falls me]** she fals *Q1*
136 **neck—]** *Rowe;* neck, *F1, Q1*
139–40 **So . . . ha!]** *as prose, Q1; as verse, F1*
140 **hales]** *Q1;* shakes *F1*
142 **O]** *om. Q1*
143 **throw it]** throw't *Q1*
145 s.d. **Enter Bianca.]** *after l. 144, Q1*
146 s.p. **Cas.]** *speech continued to Iago, Q1*
146 **fitchew]** ficho *Q1*
151 **the]** the whole *Q1*
152 **know not]** not know *Q1*
154 **your]** the *Q1*
154 **hobby-horse.]** *Q2* (hobby horse;); Hobbey-horse, *F1;* hobby horse, *Q1*
156–7 **How . . . now?]** *as prose, Q1; as verse, F1*
159–60 **An' . . . an']** *Q1;* If . . . if *F1*
163 **Faith,]** *Q1*
163 **in the]** i'the *Q1*
163 **streets]** streete *Q1*
165 **Faith]** *Q1;* Yes *F1*
169 s.d. **Exit Cassio.]** *Q1*
170 s.d. **Advancing.]** *Collier*
175–7 **Yours . . . whore.]** *om. Q1* (*but catchword calls for a speech by Iago*)
178–9 **I . . . woman!]** *as prose, Q1; as verse, F1*
180 **that]** *om. Q1*
181 **Ay]** *Rowe;* I *F1;* And *Q1*
184 **hath]** has *Q1*
192–3 **O . . . condition!]** *as prose, Q1; as verse, F1*
192 **O . . . times]** A thousand thousand times *Q1*
195–6 **Nay . . . Iago!]** *as prose, Q1; as verse, F1*
195 **Nay]** I *Q1*
196 **O . . . Iago!]** the pitty. *Q1*
197 **are]** be *Q1*
198 **touch]** touches *Q1*
204 **night.]** night *Q1*
207–12 **Do . . . midnight.]** *as prose, Q1; as verse, F1*
209 **pleases;]** pleases *Q1*
213 s.d. **A trumpet.]** *Q1* (*after l. 212*)*; placed as in Dyce*
214 **I warrant]** *om. Q1*
214–5 **Venice. . . . comes]** Venice sure, tis Lodouico, / Come *Q1*
214 s.d. **Enter . . . Attendants.]** *placed as in Theobald; after l. 212, F1, Q1*
214–5 **Lodovico—This]** *Alexander;* Lodouico, this, *F1* (*see ll. 214–5 above for Q1*)
215 **See]** and see *Q1*
215 **wife's]** wife is *Q1*
216 **God]** *Q1*
216 **you,]** *F3;* you *F1;* the *Q1*
217 **the]** *om. Q1*
217 s.d. **Gives . . . letter.]** *Rowe*
218 s.d. **Opens . . . reads.]** *Capell* (*subs.*)
228 s.d. **Reads.]** *Theobald*
231 **'twixt my]** betweene thy *Q1*
233 **T' atone]** To attone *Q1*
238 **By my troth]** *Q1;* Trust me *F1*
239 **Why]** How *Q1*
240 s.d. **Striking her.]** *Theobald*
245 **woman's]** womens *Q1*
247 s.d. **Going.]** *Rowe*
248 **an]** *Q1*
252 **Ay]** *Theobald;* I *F1, Q1*
255 **obedient, . . . obedient;]** *Q1;* obedient: . . . obedient. *F1*
258 **home]** here *Q1*
260 s.d. **Exit Desdemona.]** *Rowe*
265 **Is this the]** This the noble *Q1*
270 **censure]** *Jennens;* censure. *F1;* censure, *Q1*
271 **what]** as *Q1*
276 **new-create]** *hyphen, Pope*
276 **this]** *Q1;* his *F1*
279 **denote]** *Q1;* deonte *F1* (*c*); deuote *F1* (*u*)

IV.ii

Location: *Alexander* (*after Malone*)
3 **you]** and you *Q1*
5 **them]** 'em *Q1*
9 **gloves, her mask]** mask, her gloues *Q1*
15 **have]** ha *Q1*
16 **heaven]** heauens *Q1*
16 **requite]** *Q1;* requit *F1*
18 **their wives]** her Sex *Q1*
19 s.d. **Exit Emilia.]** *after* slander. *l. 19, Q1*
22 **closet . . . key]** closet, locke and key, *Q1*
23 **have]** ha *Q1*
24 **you]** *om. Q1*
27 s.d. **To Emilia.]** *Hanmer*
30 **nay]** *Q1;* May *F1*
31 **knee]** knees *Q1*
31 **doth]** does *Q1*
33 **But . . . words.]** *Q1*
35–8 **Come . . . honest.]** *as verse, Q1; as prose, F1*
41 **Ah, Desdemon]** O Desdemona *Q1*
43 **motive of these]** occasion of those *Q1*
44 **happily]** *F4;* happely *F1;* haply *Q1*
46–7 **lost . . . lost]** left . . . left *Q1*
47 **Why,]** *Q1*
48 **they rain'd]** he ram'd *Q1*
49 **kind]** kindes *Q1*
49 **bare head]** *Q1;* bare-head *F1*
51 **utmost]** *om. Q1*
52 **place]** part *Q1*
54 **The]** A *Q1*
55 **unmoving]** *Q1;* and mouing *F1*
55 **finger]** fingers *Q1*
55 **at!]** at—oh, oh, *Q1*
57 **there,]** *Q2;* there *F1;* there: *Q1*
62 **there,]** *Q1;* there: *F1*
63 **thou]** thy *Q1*
64 **Ay,]** *Theobald;* I *F1, Q1*
66 **summer]** summers *Q1*
67 **weed]** blacke weede *Q1*
68 **Who . . . fair]** why . . . faire? *Q1*
68 **and]** Thou *Q1*
69 **never]** ne're *Q1*
71 **paper,]** *Q1;* Paper? *F1*
72 **upon]** on *Q1*
73–6 **Committed . . . committed?]** *om. Q1*
79 **hollow]** hallow *Q1*
81 **Impudent strumpet!]** *Q1*
84 **other]** hated *Q1*
88 **forgive us]** forgiuenesse *Q1*
88 **then]** *om. Q1*
90 s.d. **Raising his voice.]** *Globe*
90 s.d. **Enter Emilia.]** *after l. 86, Q1*
92 **gate of]** gates in *Q1*
92 **You, you! ay,]** *Rowe* (*subs.*); You, you: I *F1;* I, you, you, *Q1*
93 **have]** ha *Q1*
101 **Des. Who . . . lady.]** *om. Q1*
102 **have]** ha *Q1*
103 **answers]** answer *Q1*
104 **But]** *Q1;* Bnt *F1*
105 **my wedding]** our wedding *Q1*
106 **Here's]** Here is *Q1*
107 **meet.]** well; *Q1*
109 **small'st]** smallest *Q1*
109 **least misuse]** greatest abuse *Q1*
113 **have]** ha *Q1*
114 **to]** at *Q1*
117 **That]** As *Q1*
117 **hearts]** heart *F1* (*u*)

117 bear it] beare Q1
119 said] sayes Q1
120 drink] Q1 (drinke,); drinke: F1
125 Hath] Has Q1
126 and] all Q1
128 for't] for it Q1
133 I will] I'le Q1
138 form] for me Q1
139 most villainous] outragious Q1
141 heaven] Q1; Heauens F1
143 rascals] rascall Q1
144 door] dores Q1
145 them] him Q1
146 seamy side] Q1; seamy-side F1
148 Alas] O Good Q1
151–64 Here . . . me.] om. Q1
155 them in] Q2; them: or F1
155 form;] Q2; Forme. F1
167 And . . . you] Q1
168 It is . . . warrant.] Tis . . . warrant you; Q1
168 s.d. Trumpets within.] Rowe
169 summon] summon you Q1
170 The messengers] And the great Messengers Q1
170 stays] stay Q1
170 the meat] om. Q1
171 s.d. Exeunt . . . Emilia.] Exit women. Q1
171 s.d. Enter Roderigo.] after l. 172, Q1
173 I . . . me.] as prose, Q1; as verse, F1
175 daff'st] Collier; dafts F1; doffest Q1
175 device] F2; deuise F1, Q1
176 now, keep'st] thou keepest Q1
182 Faith,] Q1; and F1
182 for] Q1; and F1
183 performances] performance Q1
185 With . . . truth.] om. Q1
186 my] om. Q1
187 deliver] deliuer to Q1
188 hath] has Q1
188 them] em Q1
189 expectations] expectation Q1
190 acquaintance] acquittance Q1
191 well.] good. Q1
192–3 nor 'tis] it is Q1
193 By this hand] Q1; Nay F1
193 think it is] say tis very Q1
196 tell you 'tis] say it is Q1
199 I will] I'le Q1
202 and] and I haue Q1
205 instant] time Q1
207 exception] conception Q1
208 affair] affaires Q1
212 in] within Q1
215 the] Q1; rhe F1
215 enjoy] enioyest Q1
218 what is it?] om. Q1
218 within] Q1; within, F1
220 commission] command Q1
224 taketh] takes Q1
228 removing] remouing of Q1
232 Ay;] Rowe (subs.); I: F1; I, and Q1
232 and a] and Q1
233 harlotry] harlot Q1
235 fortune.] Q1 (fortune:); Fortune, F1
243 waste] F3; wast F1, Q1
245 s.d. Exeunt.] Ex. Iag. and Rod. Q1

IV.iii

Location: Alexander (after Capell)
o.s.d. Lodovico, Desdemona] order reversed, Q1; Q1 s.d. after IV.ii.243
2 'twill] it shall Q1
7 bed . . . instant,] bed, o'the instant Q1
8 Dismiss] dispatch Q1
9 Look't] looke it Q1
10 s.d. Exeunt . . . Attendants.] Capell; Exit. F1; Exeunt. Q1 (both after l. 9)
13 And] He Q1
14 bid] bad Q1
18 I] Q1; I, F1
20 his frowns] and frownes Q1
21 in them] Q1
22 those] these Q1
22 bade] Q1; bad F1
23 faith] Q1; Father F1
24 thee] Q1
25 these] those Q1
28 had] has Q1
31–53 I . . . next.] om. Q1
40 s.d. Singing.] from Desdemona sings. Q2
40 sighing] Q2; singing F1 (c); sining F1 (u)
45, 56 willow, willow, willow;] Q2; Willough, &c. F1
47 willow"—] Capell; Willough, &c. F1
49, 51, 55 s.dd. Singing.] Dyce
53 who is't] who's Q1
54 It's] It is Q1
55–7 "I . . . men."] om. Q1
58 So] Now Q1
59 Doth] does Q1
60–3 I have . . . question.] om. Q1
67 do't] doe it Q1
68 Wouldst] Would Q1
68 deed] thing Q1
69 world's] world is Q1
70 Good] Q1; In F1
71 By my troth] Q1; Introth F1
72 done't] A. Walker; done F1; done it Q1
73 joint-ring] hyphen, Q2
73 nor] or Q1
74 petticoats] or Petticotes Q1
74 petty] such Q1
75 all] om. Q1
75 'ud's pity] Q1 (vds); why F1
76 cuckold] Cuckole Q1
77 for't] for it Q1
86–103 But . . . so.] om. Q1
104 God] Q1; Heauen F1
104 uses] vsage Q1

V.i

Location: Rowe
1 bulk] Q1; Barke F1
4 on] of Q1
7 stand] sword Q1
7 s.d. Retires.] Globe (after Capell)
8 deed] dead Q1
9 hath] has Q1
11 quat] gnat Q1
12 angry. Now] angry now: Q1
14 gain] game Q1
16 Of] For Q1
19 hath] has Q1
21 much] om. Q1
22 Be't . . . hear] Q1; But so, I heard F1
23 s.d. Makes . . . Cassio.] Capell
24 mine] my Q1
25 know'st] think'st Q1
26 s.d. Draws . . . Roderigo.] Capell
26 s.d. Iago . . . exit.] Theobald (subs.)
27 maim'd] maind Q1
27 Help] light Q1
27 s.d. Falls.] Capell (after ever. l. 27); placed as in Malone
29 It is] Hearke tis Q1
34 unblest fate hies] fate hies apace Q1
35 Forth] Q1; For F1
36 s.d. Othello] om. Q1
38 voice] cry Q1
42 groan] grones Q1
42 'Tis] it is a Q1
44 in to] Capell; into F1, Q1
45 come?] Theobald; come: F1; come, Q1
45 s.d. with a light] Q1
47 light] lights Q1
49 We] I Q1
49 Did] Q1; Do F1
50 heaven] heauens Q1
56 me] my Q1
57 that] the Q1
59 s.d. To . . . Gratiano.] Theobald
60 there] here Q1
61 them] em Q1
61 murd'rous] murderous Q1
61 s.d. Stabs Roderigo.] Rowe; Thrusts him in. Q2
62 inhuman] Rowe; inhumane F1; inhumaine Q1
62 dog!] dog,—o, o, o. Q1
63 men] him Q1
63 these] those Q1
71 is't] is it Q1
76 my] O my Q1
77 O . . . Cassio!] Cassio, Cassio, Q1
79 have thus] thus haue Q1
82–3 Iago. Lend . . . hence!] om. Q1
86 be . . . injury.] beare a part in this: Q1
87 Come, come] om. Q1
90 O heaven,] Q1; Yes, 'tis F1
92 ay] Hanmer; I F1, Q1
93 your] you Q1
98 He, he] He Q1
98 s.d. A . . . in.] Capell (subs.)
98 the] a Q1
100, 104 s.dd. To Bianca.] Johnson (the second after Rowe)
102 between] betwixt Q1
103 man.] Q1; man? F1
104 out] Q1
104 s.d. Cassio . . . off.] Capell
105 gentlemen] Gentlewoman Q1
106 gastness] ieastures Q1
107 an'] Q1; if F1
107 stare . . . hear] stirre . . . haue Q1
108 well;] well Q1
110 s.d. Enter Emilia.] Q1
111 Alas] 'Las Q1
111 what is . . . What is] what's . . . what's Q1
112 hath] has Q1
114 quite] om. Q1
116 fruits] fruite Q1
116 Prithee] Pray Q1
118 s.d. To Bianca.] Neilson
121 O fie] Fie, fie Q1
123 Fough,] Q1; now Q2
127 hath] has Q1
128 afore] I pray Q1
128 s.d. Aside.] Steevens
129 makes] markes Q1

V.ii

Location: Alexander
o.s.d. with a light] Q1; Q1 om. and . . . bed
o.s.d. asleep] Rowe
10 thy light] thine Q1
11 cunning'st] cunning Q1
13 relume] Malone; re-Lume F1; returne Q1
13 thy] the Q1
15 needs must] must needes Q1
15 thee] it Q1
15 s.d. Kisses her.] Q2; He kisses her. Q1 (after l. 19)
16 O] A Q1
16 dost] doth Q1
17 Justice] Iustice her selfe Q1
17 sword! . . . more.] sword once more, Q1
19 One] once Q1
19 that's] this Q1
22 where it doth] when it does Q1
23 Ay] Rowe; I F1, Q1
25 Desdemon] Desdemona Q1
29 Alack] Alas Q1
32 heaven] Q1; Heauens F1
35 so] Q1
36 Humh] Hum Q1
37 you're] you are Q1
41 Ay] Rowe; I F1; om. Q1
41 di'st] diest Q1
43 nether lip] Q1 (neather); nether-lip F1
45 I hope, I hope] I hope Q1
47 will so.] will, so, Q1
52 Yes,] Q1
55 conception] conceit Q1
57 Then Lord] Q1; O Heauen F1
62 in 's] in his Q1
63 my] thy Q1
64 mak'st] Q2; makes F1; makest Q1
68 Let] And let Q1
68 hath] has Q1
70 us'd thee] vds death Q1
73 O, . . . interprets.] My feare interprets then,— Q1
75 them] 'em Q1
77 Out] O Q1
77 weep'st] weepest Q1
81 an'] Q1; if F1
82 Oth. Being . . . pause.] om. Q1
83 It is] Tis Q1
83 s.d. Smothers her.] he stifles her. Q1
84 Des. O . . . Lord!] Q1
85 s.d. within] from Q1 s.d. Emillia calls within.
86 noise] voyce Q1

89 s.d. **(Within.)]** *om. Q1*
90, 101 s.dd. **Within.]** *Malone*
90 **I would]** I'de *Q1*
93 **high]** here *Q1*
95 **best to do?]** the best? *Q1*
97 **what]** my *Q1*
97 **have]** ha *Q1*
101 **Did]** Should *Q1*
102 **That]** *om. Q1*
102 **O]** *om. Q1*
105 s.d. **Unlocks the door.]** *Theobald*
105 s.d. **Enter Emilia.]** *placed as in Dyce; after l. 105, F1; after l. 104, Q1*
106 **yonder's]** *Q1;* yonders *F1*
110 **nearer]** neere the *Q1*
112 **hath]** has *Q1*
117 **O Lord,]** *Q1;* Alas! *F1*
119 **that was]** it is *Q1*
123 **hath]** has *Q1*
125 s.d. **Dies.]** *Q1* (she dies.)
127 **heard]** *Q1;* heare *F1*
128 **the]** a *Q1*
134 **art]** as *Q1*
137 **hell]** *Q1* (hell,); hell: *F1*
143 **Nay,]** *Q1*
147 **on her]** *om. Q1*
150 **iterance, woman?]** iteration? woman, *Q1*
151–4 **Emil. O . . . Iago.]** *om. Q1*
152 **say]** say that *Q2*
159 **worst]** *Q1;* wotst *F1*
162 **that]** the *Q1*
164–5 **deed—I . . . sword,]** *Q1;* deed / (I . . . Sword) *F1*
165 **known]** know *Q1*
166 **ho]** *Capell;* hoa *F1;* O *Q1*
167 **hath]** has *Q1*
167 s.d. **with others]** *Q1* (and)
170 **murthers]** murder *Q1*
171 s.p. **Gra.]** All. *Q1*
174 **thou'rt]** thou art *Q1*
185–93 **My . . . villainy!]** *om. Q1*
186 **heavens]** *Q2;* Heauens, *F1*
198 s.d. **Othello . . . bed.]** *Q1*
200 s.d. **Rising.]** *Theobald*
203 **horrible]** terrible *Q1*
204 **Desdemon]** Desdemona *Q1*
206 **in twain]** atwane *Q1*
209 **reprobance]** reprobation *Q1*
214 **that]** the *Q1*
218 **God . . . God]** *Q1;* Heauen . . . Powres *F1*
219 **'Zounds]** *Q1* (Zouns); Come *F1*
219 **'twill out!]** 'twill: *Q1*
219 **I peace?]** I hold my peace sir, *Q1*
220 **I . . . as]** I'le be in speaking *Q1*
220 **north]** ayre *Q1*
221 **them]** em *Q1*
223 s.d. **Iago . . . Emilia.]** *Rowe*
225 **of]** on *Q1*
229 **steal't]** steale it *Q1*
230 **give]** gaue *Q1*
234 **wife]** woman *Q1*
235 s.d. **The . . . wife.]** *Q1 (after* wife? *l. 234); placed as in Capell; Dyce adds (subs.)* Montano disarms Othello
236 **hath]** has *Q1*
237 **Ay, ay]** *Rowe;* I, I *F1, Q1*
237 s.d. **Exit Iago.]** *Q1*
239 **you this]** your *Q1*
240 **here]** *Q1*
243 s.d. **with . . . Emilia]** *Pelican (after Globe);* Mont. and Gratiano. *Q1*
243 **neither,]** *Q1;* neither: *F1*
246–8 **What . . . willow!"]** *om. Q1*
248 s.d. **Sings.]** *Dyce (subs.)*
251 **alas]** I die *Q1*
251 s.d. **Dies.]** *Q1* (she dies.)
253 **was]** is *Q1*
253 **ice-brook's]** *Johnson;* Ice brookes *F1;* Isebrookes *Q1*
255 s.d. **Within.]** *from Q1* Gra. within.
257 **with]** to *Q1*
258 s.d. **Enter Gratiano.]** *Theobald*
264 **your]** you *Q1*
266–72 **Be . . . wench,]** *om. Q1*
273 **compt]** count *Q1*
276 **cursed, cursed]** cursed *Q1*
277 **ye]** you *Q1*
281 **Desdemon! dead, Desdemon!]** Desdemona, Desdemona, *Q1*
282 **O, O!]** O, o, o. *Q1*
282 s.d. **in a chair]** *from Q1 s.d.* Enter Lodouico, Montano, Iago, and Officers Cassio in a Chaire.
282 s.d. **guarded]** *ed. (after Rowe)*
283 **unfortunate]** infortunate *Q1*
285 **that]** this *Q1*
287 **that]** *om. Q1*
287 s.d. **Wounds Iago.]** *Rowe*
287 **be'st]** *Johnson;* bee'st *F1;* beest *Q1*
288 **Wrench]** Wring *Q1*
289 **live]** *F1, Q1 (c);* loue *Q1 (u)*
291 **was]** wert *Q1*
292 **damned]** *Q1;* cursed *F1*
293 **shall]** should *Q1*
295 **I did]** did I *Q1*
299 **never gave]** did neuer giue *Q1*
300 **your]** you *Q1*
301 **I]** *om. Q1*
308 **not.]** *Q1* (not:); not) *F1*
311–2 **undertook By]** vndertooke—by *Q1*
316 **t' have]** to haue *Q1*
317 **nick]** *Q1;* interim *F1*
318 **thou]** the *Q1*
319 **that]** a *Q1*
320 **wive's]** wifes *Q1*
321 **but]** *om. Q1*
337 **bring]** bring him *Q1*
338 **before you go]** *om. Q1*
342 **me . . . am]** them as they are *Q1*
346 **Perplexed]** Perplext *Q1*
347 **Indian]** *Q1;* Iudean *F1*
351 **medicinable]** medicinall *Q1*
353 **turban'd Turk]** *Q1;* Turbond-Turke *F1*
356 s.d. **He stabs himself.]** *Q1*
357 **that is]** that's *Q1*
359 s.d. **Falls . . . and]** *Globe (after Collier MS); Q1 s.d. reads:* He dies.
361 s.d. **To Iago.]** *Theobald*
363 **loading]** lodging *Q1*
367 **on]** to *Q1*
368–9 **villain,]** *Q1;* villaine: *F1*
371 s.d. **Exeunt.]** Exeunt. / FINIS. *F1;* Exeunt omnes. / FINIS. *Q1*

King Lear

BRADLEY began his lectures on *King Lear* by asking why this work, repeatedly described as Shakespeare's greatest, was "the least popular of the famous four"; why for a century and a half it was never played in its original form; and why so many readers have shared with Dr. Johnson a kind of distaste for a work whose greatness seems undeniable. In his answer he concurs with what he takes to be the opinion of the common reader, pronouncing *Lear* "Shakespeare's greatest achievement, but . . . *not* his best play." As a play he finds it inferior to the other three of his quartet; but when he thinks of it not as a play but as "the fullest revelation of Shakespeare's power," it takes its place in his mind with "the *Prometheus Vinctus* and the *Divine Comedy*, and even with the greatest symphonies of Beethoven and the statues in the Medici Chapel." The trouble is that it "is too huge for the stage."

Nowadays few would defend this last opinion. The play acts well; and the status of *Lear*, far from being reduced, is higher than before. The reason may be partly that the modern theatre knows better how to present it; there have been great twentieth-century *Lears*. It is also true that the drama of our own time has, in a sense, caught up with *Lear*: in 1962 an English theatre-critic, commenting on the Stratford production of Peter Brook, noticed that the trial scene, and Gloucester's attempted suicide, seem absolutely modern to playgoers now used to Beckett. But the chief reason must be that, to quote Edmund, "men / Are as the time is"; from our particular point of vantage we perhaps see a *Lear* that Bradley, for all his power, could not apprehend. The case is that of Matthew Arnold who wrote in 1851 that it was "no longer . . . possible that we should feel a deep interest" in the *Antigone* of Sophocles; Antigone's problem suddenly came alive in our century. Now *Lear* is, in part, a play about the end of the world, and twentieth-century critics must owe something to the fact that they know an "image of that horror." They are accordingly less inclined to hesitate over the improbabilities which troubled Bradley as he studied "the most terrible picture that Shakespeare painted of the world." And for most of them *Lear* is beyond question the greatest of all tragedies, a view they do not find consistent with its being an inferior play.

King Lear was entered in the Stationers' Register on November 26, 1607, and the entry mentions that it was performed "uppon S. Stephans night at Christmas last," that is, December 26, 1606. The lower limit is March 1603, when Samuel Harsnett published his *Declaration of Egregious Popish Impostures*, a work from which Shakespeare took the names of Edgar's devils, and which he also remembered at some other points. The gap between these two dates can be narrowed. In Sharpham's play *The Fleer*, registered on May 13, 1606, and probably on the stage early in the year, there is a rather close imitation of the scene in which Lear takes the disguised Kent into his service. This pushes *King Lear* back into 1605. On May 8th of that year there was registered a play called *King Leir*. This was an old piece which had been performed by the Queen's Men before 1594 and, though entered that year in the Stationers' Register, had never before been published. Since this play is the most important single source of *King Lear*, it used to be assumed that Shakespeare could not have written his play until after the publication of *Leir* in 1605. Thus we should have a firm date of late 1605. But most scholars incline to accept the view of Greg that someone (who had access to a good playhouse manuscript) published *King Leir* in order to profit by the current success of Shakespeare's play. The evidence for this is, first, that the Register entry originally referred to the play as a "Tragedie" but this was altered to read "Tragecall historie"; and secondly, that it refers to the play "sundry times lately acted." The first point is that whoever made the original entry must have been thinking of Shakespeare's play, since the old play is not a tragedy but a chronicle; and the second is that such an old-fashioned piece is unlikely to have been "lately acted." This evidence is less strong than has sometimes been thought; we need not perhaps expect pedantically accurate nomenclature from Elizabethan publishers, and various old plays were repeatedly, and against all probability, revived. And there was something of a Jacobean vogue for ancient Britain in the theatre. However, if Greg's argument is accepted, Shakespeare's play had by May 8, 1605, been "sundry times lately acted"; and this could push its date of composition back once more, to early 1605 or late 1604. Some corroborative evidence comes from a sonnet by William Strachey which was published with Jonson's *Sejanus*, a play registered in November 1604; this sonnet has some verbal resemblances, which, if not accidental, are presumably reminiscences of *Lear*. Some, however, still hold that Gloucester's words on "These late eclipses" (I.ii.103) allude to eclipses of the moon and sun on September 17 and October 2, 1605. Professor G. B. Harrison thinks the phenomena referred to are those described in a pamphlet called *Strange News in Croatia*, published in February 1606. However, there were notable eclipses only a few years earlier, in 1601, and it is not necessary to suppose that those referred to by Gloucester had occurred in recent weeks, or indeed that Shakespeare had in mind any specific eclipses whatsoever. 1604–5 seems the best compromise.

If Shakespeare could not have read the printed book of *Leir* or seen a revival before he wrote his play, he must either have remembered its story and somehow recalled ideas and phrases from a performance a dozen years earlier, or read it in manuscript. Kenneth Muir prefers the former explanation, conjecturing that Shakespeare might even have played Perillus, a prototype of Kent. But there is less improbability in the hypothesis of a manuscript available to Shakespeare, for *Leir* could have been among the books which fell to the share of the Lord Chamberlain's Men in 1594.

Leir is a reasonably well-composed play, and some critics, without going as far as Tolstoy, who preferred it to Shakespeare's, have openly admitted that the anonymous author manages the opening scene better than his successor. He begins with the King seeking sons-in-law, being without a male heir, and what he wants from his three daughters is a promise that each will marry the suitor of his choosing. Cordella, as he calls the youngest, evades the issue. Lear had intended to make them equal heirs; but in his anger at Cordella he divides the kingdom equally between Ragan and Gonorill, and abdicates at once (an innovation, since in the traditional story Lear is deposed by rebellion). Shakespeare for whatever good reasons sacrifices this more plausible opening. He also makes Cordelia a much more attractive character. But he borrows largely from the old play, freely adapting it as he goes. His Kent stems from Perillus; he develops the storm from *Leir*; he makes Goneril's husband a good man among villains; he takes over Ragan's messenger and makes him into Oswald; he has Lear kneel before Cordelia. And he repeatedly echoes the language of the old play. It obviously left a deep impression; Mumford in *Leir* is an ancestor of Enobarbus in *Antony and Cleopatra*, and, as I have said, there seem to be anticipations of *Hamlet* and even of *Richard III*. The greatest difference is that Leir and Cordella in the old play survive and live happily.

The basic story was well known. Originally a folk tale in which a daughter tells her father she loves him as much as salt and dissipates his anger by demonstrating that this means he is essential to her, it made its first literary appearance in the twelfth-century *History* of Geoffrey of Monmouth. Sixteenth-century interest in British history gave it wider circulation, and it is told by John Higgins in the 1574 edition of *A Mirror for Magistrates*, by Warner in *Albion's England* (1586), by Holinshed (1577), and by Spenser in *The Faerie Queene*, Bk. II (1590). The probability is that Shakespeare knew all of these. The spelling "Regan" may have come from Holinshed; it is he too who marries her to Cornwall, in *Leir* the husband of Gonorill. Holinshed also makes the marriage of Cordeilla dowerless, and credits her with a successful invasion. His Cordeilla restores her father and succeeds him; but she kills herself with a knife five years later. Shakespeare alone has Cordelia murdered. Spenser's Cordelia (he uses both this form and "Cordeill"), after being deposed and imprisoned by the children of her sisters, hangs herself. *A Mirror for Magistrates* probably gave Shakespeare the hint for the passages describing how Goneril and Regan strip Lear of his hundred servants.

One cannot begin to estimate the dramatist's debt to any one of these sources. He had some sort of access to *Leir*; and from habit he would probably look up the story in Holinshed. Professor Muir has shown that Edgar's description of the imaginary fiend at Dover cliffs is based on a passage in Holinshed two pages earlier than his account of Lear. The other accounts Shakespeare may have looked up, or perhaps only remembered with more or less precision.

The subplot of Gloucester and his sons has no historical connection with the Lear story, and is borrowed from the story of the Paphlagonian King in Sidney's *Arcadia*. There a king is estranged from his legitimate son by the false accusation of his bastard, who deposes his father and blinds him. The good son rescues him, and prevents him committing suicide by leaping from a rock. Sidney emphasizes the tragic character of these "unnaturall dealings" so strongly that it has been suggested that this tale, with possible support from other elements of the *Arcadia*, was the primary inspiration of Shakespeare's play. Sidney seeks in a chaotic situation some "hope that mankind is not grown monstrous," and Shakespeare, grafting this episode on to British history (as later, in *Cymbeline*, he was again to blend romance with a tale of an ancient British king), augments the tragic thought in the greatest of his double plots.

Minor sources of the play are Harsnett's *Declaration*, from which, as Muir by fairly extensive verbal parallels has shown, Shakespeare took more than the names of Poor Tom's devils; and Florio's translation of Montaigne, in which critics have found not only verbal resemblances but similarities of idea. Many of these are sceptical treatments of topics almost commonplace at the time; but it is likely enough that Shakespeare would have read Florio quite recently, and that Montaigne's ideas would be fresh in his mind.

If *King Lear* is what Shelley called it, "the most perfect specimen of dramatic poetry existing in the world," it is so by virtue of being different not in kind but in degree from the other plays of Shakespeare. Like them it is essentially a dramatic exposition of a story—indeed it has an unusually complicated plot—in the course of which the poet devotes his imaginative powers, with perhaps unparalleled intensity, to the illustration or incarnation of themes and images he observes to be implicit in that story, and which in *Lear* helped to reshape the story in his mind. "Never," writes C. J. Sisson, "did Shakespeare take a more deliberate or a more striking decision than to reject version after version of the story" and remodel it as he did, with all Bradley's tabulated implausibilities on its head. Many of these are minute and unnoticeable in the theatre; others have been exaggerated, as Sisson points out when he cites from contemporary lawsuits such stories as that of Sir William Allen, Lord Mayor of London in 1571, who, growing old and frail, shared his estates between three married daughters, and arranged to stay with each in turn. They resented the charge of his upkeep and said he was rude to their servants; he cursed them and died in misery. But this unexpected testimony to the verisimilitude of the first scene does not affect the general issue: Shakespeare removes the anachronistic Christianity of the old play, converts its storm from a signal that divine justice is impending into an image of evil chaos, allows Cordelia to be defeated and murdered, and will not allow Lear to enjoy the restored majesty offered him by Albany as he bends over the dead body of his daughter. Gloucester's suffering, the wickedness of Edmund, the multiple role of Edgar, the brilliant commentary of the Fool, the sexual looseness of Goneril and Regan—all this is new to the Lear story. Changes of such magnitude cannot be studied in isolation; one's view of Shakespeare's object in making them depends upon his view of the whole play.

Lear is not, at the outset of Shakespeare's play, represented as a king with understandable anxieties over the succession. It is often said that a Jacobean audience would instantly observe that his plan to divide the kingdom was liable to breed disaster; many plays had made the point, especially during the previous reign, when the succession was a perennial political worry. This is true enough, but it is to be noted that Lear in his moments of self-knowledge never reproaches himself with *political* error; what he and the good characters, including Kent and the Fool, complain of is his madness in disinheriting Cordelia, and his mistake in supposing that he could remain a king after surrendering the cares of kingship and placing even his human right to shelter in the hands of Goneril and Regan. And his kingly status is only one aspect of Lear at the opening; he assumes a right to love and respect also in his capacity as father, and as an old man.

Rightly seen, these aspects of Lear are inseparable. But what more extreme emblem of impotent mortality than a naked, dying king, denied the love which makes mortality without dignity tolerable? Shakespeare had repeatedly, in the history plays, emphasized the double nature of a king—both "anointed flesh" and "poor, bare, fork'd animal." This contrast is not of course original with Shakespeare; the idea of the King's "two bodies" was part of English legal theory, and at royal funerals an effigy representing the King's Dignity, and dressed in his coronation regalia, was borne above his coffin. "The jurists," says Ernst Kantorowicz, "discovered the immortality of the Dignity; but by this very discovery they made the ephemeral nature of the mortal incumbent all the more tangible." The king has a man's body that God made, subject to all infirmity; only the effigy, man-made, the work of art, is "utterly void of . . . old Age and other defects and Imbecilities." Lear, we may say, is in deep confusion over his two bodies.

He appears in the opening scene as Justice itself, illustrating, as Sisson points out, the two main branches of Justice according to Aristotle: Distributive, as when he portions out his kingdom, and Retributive, as when he punishes Cordelia for her lack of compliance. But as a man he is well aware of old age and its imbecilities. He proceeds to separate the mortal body from the effigy of Dignity, and the play never lets us forget the tragic character of this divorce. Lear sees his actual mortal body as only "Lear's shadow." As a man he has—just, perhaps, because he failed to distinguish not only between love and professions of love but between his mortal nature and his borrowed majesty—"but slenderly known himself." In his mortal capacity neither his age nor his parenthood, unsupported by royal power, can keep the respect of his daughters. And, in a sense, the play of *Lear* is a *danse macabre* in which a decrepit old king is forced to come to terms with his mortality.

What turns a living man into a visible effigy of Dignity is largely a matter of dress: the furred gown of the justice, the gorgeous wear of the princesses. Lear comes to terms with his mortal body when he goes unbonneted in the storm, finds Poor Tom naked under his blanket, and tears at his own clothes: "Off, off, you lendings!" Now he sees Dignity as the appearance, and the frail, impotent body as the reality; and he pities his own mortality in Tom.

The process of stripping Lear has gone on from the first moment, when he gives away his lands; by the end of the second act Goneril and Regan have punished his foolish presumption that as mortal man he possesses native dignity by paring away all his followers and denying him shelter. When Tom appears, the King is ready to face essential mortality, and to see himself as a poor, bare, forked animal. Only at the height of his madness in the great scene with Gloucester (IV.vi) does Lear assume again his lost Dignity, though now his regalia are wild flowers. "No, they cannot touch me for coining, I am the King himself. . . . Nature's above art in that respect," he says, remembering that his natural features have authenticated the artist's effigy on a coin. Now he recalls that his men had respected his Dignity and not his mortal paternity; they said " 'ay' and 'no' to every thing that I said! . . . When the rain came to wet me once, and the wind to make me chatter, when the thunder would not peace at my bidding, there I found 'em, there I smelt 'em out." Gloucester, with no eyes for regalia, recognizes "the trick of that voice" and asks, "Is't not the King?" "Ay, every inch a king!" replies Lear from under his crown of weeds; but when Gloucester would kiss his hand, he remembers that "it smells of mortality." He reminds the Gentleman who comes to fetch him that he is a king. "You are a royal one," says the Gentleman; but Lear runs off: "Come, and you get it, you shall get it by running." He means his royalty, his Dignity, which he knows can be taken away.

Since it is in his Dignity that the King dispenses Justice, what becomes of Justice when Dignity proves perishable? At the outset Justice itself, in Lear's person, behaves selfishly, unjustly. As the play proceeds we more than once observe mock-Justice dispensed. In III.vi Goneril and Regan are arraigned before a court consisting of a Fool and a Bedlam beggar. In the next scene Cornwall perverts justice in order to take his revenge on Gloucester ("Though well we may not pass upon his life / Without the form of justice, yet our power / Shall do a court'sy to our wrath"); and in the final scene Goneril, confronted with the evidence of her own guilt, answers from the Dignity conferred on her by Lear: "Who can arraign me for't?" The royal dignity is above the law it makes, though not, as she will discover, above the law of nature.

Human justice, then, seems a mockery; when we deal with "the thing itself" and not with furred robes and emblems of Dignity, it appears that in nature it has no more validity than the bonds between king and subject or father and child. When Shakespeare came to write the scene of Lear and Gloucester—which, although it is the boldest effort of imagination in Shakespeare, has no *narrative* value—he associated with the theme of mortality and the imbecility of age Lear's great condemnation of Justice. No punishment for fornicators: they understand the thing itself, the common bestial appetites of man. And anyway, who should punish them? The judge is as guilty as the thief or the adulterer: "Through tatter'd clothes small vices do appear; / Robes and furr'd gowns hide all." Shakespeare had dealt recently in *Measure for Measure* with the man "that judgest them which do such things, and doest the same"; but in that play he endorses the rhetorical question with which St. Paul follows his condemnation: "thinkest thou . . . that thou shalt escape the judgment of God?" In *King Lear*, however, Heavenly Justice is equally put to the question.

The image of justice, divine as well as human, is, in *King Lear*, turned this way and that, and subjected to most kinds of comment that suffering men can make about it. Edmund and the wicked sisters rejoice in the apparent absence of justice—atheist naturalists like Iago, who glory in this exaltation of human power and license. Lear urges the stormy heavens to let fall their "horrible pleasure," and accuses them of siding with his "pernicious daughters" against his aged head. Gloucester begins in astrological determinism and progresses through a despairing belief in divine cruelty ("As flies to wanton boys are we to th' gods") to patience, calling these gods "ever-gentle." Kent reduces Providence to mere Fortune. Albany, emerging through the action of the play into a positive, commanding figure, sees divine justice in the death of Cornwall: "This shows you are above, / You justicers"; and he calls the deaths of Goneril and Regan "This judgment of the heavens." Cornwall's servants make their faith in the justice of the gods depend upon the divine punishment meted out to Regan and Cornwall after the blinding of Gloucester; they expect speedy execution on the cruel tyrants. Their expectation is realized; up to this point the action of the play seems to endorse the idea of heavenly retribution, and even Edmund accepts his brother's assurance that "The gods are just." One other note is sounded; Gloucester's "ever-gentle" is supported by Edgar's reference on Dover cliff to "the clearest gods," and Cordelia behaves as if the gods were, as she calls them, "kind," even at a moment when her father imagines himself in hell.

But the gods themselves do not intervene in *King Lear*; if some good is restored, some justice seen to be done, this almost seems to proceed from a self-limiting factor in the nature of evil. The wicked bring destruction upon themselves, and the world somehow restarts with the good survivors, with Albany and Edgar. The play echoes a grim joke of Marlorat, an Elizabethan commentator, speaking of the sufferings of the just and unjust in *Revelation*: "the godly are affected to their own profit: namely that they may be murthered into patience. . . . But the ungodly are consumed."

This presentation of divine justice has naturally invited attention from Shakespeare's critics. Bradley, for example, held that it does "violence not merely to language but to any healthy moral sense" to argue that Lear suffered in the degree that he deserved; and most would agree with that. More recently William Rosen has remarked that "Lear discovers . . . there are no special laws in the universe for man," and suggestively compares the old man's quest for an order of justice with Alyosha's agony, in *The Brothers Karamazov*, at the premature corruption of Zossima's body, which seemed to him an outrage upon natural justice.

L. C. Knights finds that the values of the play are ultimately Christian, but "the play does not take them for granted; it takes nothing for granted but Nature, and natural energies and passions." All these opinions can be true in their different ways; and all may perhaps be reconciled by the reflection, which no one is likely to contest, that the play has a biblical grandeur, and that the Bible also affords great instances of the apparent injustice of the skies.

There are, indeed, as John Holloway suggests, remarkable parallels between *King Lear* and *Job*. In *Job*, Satan, with divine permission, tempts Job to curse God. Job becomes the very type of affliction, and Lear is conscious of this when he undertakes to be "the pattern of all patience." The terrors of God set themselves in array against him. God breaketh him with a tempest. His own kinsfolk forsake him, the servants of his own house take him for a stranger, he calls his servant and he gives him no answer. He sees the wicked grow old and rich; he sees them force the naked to lodge without garment and embrace the rock for want of covering. His comforters tell him he is to blame for his suffering: "Who ever perished being innocent?" they ask. "Doth God pervert justice?" God speaks out of the whirlwind, and Job comes to self-knowledge ("Wherefore I abhor myself . . ."). Finally he is restored. But no merciful power speaks to Lear, except Cordelia; and she is reunited with him only to protract his suffering further. Lear's is Job's trial protracted, and without tangible relief; unlike Job, he does not know that his Redeemer liveth; and only death unbinds him from his wheel of fire.

There can be little doubt that Shakespeare, perhaps taking a hint from the old *Leir*, had Job in mind; and Job prefigured Christian patience. He showed God working his good will by human suffering and resistance to the temptations it brings: despair, a conviction of God's indifference or even malevolence. But Shakespeare does not make Lear quite innocent; and he allows his protractive trial to go on beyond even Job's. In the opening scene Lear, unaware of the implications of his act, makes himself only a man, openly, nakedly mortal; and as a man he must suffer, struggle to achieve patience, suffer more and, when offered his kingship again, reject it and die. As he bends over Cordelia's body, he has no ears for Albany's offer. Dignity is forgotten, mortality alone concerns him. Shakespeare's theme is not a king's political imprudence, but human suffering. "Greater issues are afoot in this play," as Sisson observes, "than the verdicts of justice"; and it is even doubtful whether Lear's hard-earned charity—when, in the depths, he cares for the safety of Poor Tom and the Fool more than for himself—or the redemptive role of Cordelia—"O dear father! / It is thy business that I go about"—are not in the end reduced to nothing by madness and treachery.

For another book of the Bible was in Shakespeare's mind: *Revelation*, and especially its account of the last days before final judgment. In a period which thought of the world's end as imminent, and which interpreted *Revelation* as an exact prediction of historical events, Gloucester's saying "we have seen the best of our time" was a familiar one, and his fears of "these late eclipses" were very much akin to the general concern over *novae* and other unexplained astronomical occurrences which were thought of as presaging that collapse of universal order, that final loosing of the wounded beast, which would herald the "promis'd end" and the Last Judgment, in which Heaven would at last weigh everybody in a scrupulous balance. As Hooker puts it, "Nature is . . . God's instrument . . . in the course whereof Dionysius perceiving some sudden disturbance is said to have cried out, . . . 'either God himself doth suffer impediment, and is by a greater than himself hindered; or if that be impossible, then hath he determined to make a present dissolution of the world; the execution of that law beginning now to stand still, without which the world cannot stand.' " Gloucester cannot accept the explanations of natural philosophy, and fears that chaos, having begun to resume its reign, will spread into the social order which reflects that of the great world. Among the "ruinous disorders" already upon him he notes the treachery of Edgar, the unnatural conduct of the King to Cordelia. It is the base Edmund who glories in a world and a society conceived as purely natural, where man is wolf to man, and the human will in the service of personal appetite rules conduct. The "custom" he hates is law and respect; and when the unchecked will reigns there follow the consequences he predicts: "unnaturalness between the child and the parent, death, dearth, dissolutions of ancient amities; divisions in state. . . ." This is the world of the play, a world in dissolution. True Judgment lies in the future, when the terror is over. But now the powers of heaven are shaken; the great world wears out to nought; humanity preys upon itself like monsters of the deep; "Our flesh and blood . . . is grown so vild / That it doth hate what gets it." Human society decays; Holloway reminds us that of the very great number of animal images and allusions which in this play conspire to emphasize the theme of "man's life is cheap as beast's," there is an especial concentration at the end of the first act, "surrounding the human characters with the subhuman creatures whose appearance they are fast assuming." Immediately afterwards the settled society of men seems to be "transformed into a confusion of people constantly leaving their homes." The upshot is that a king has nowhere to lay his head, and seeks to be free not only of human society but even of the animals who provided his clothing; to be himself, the poor "thing" that is as near to nothing as can be got.

Through all this apocalyptic turmoil runs the word *nothing*, first spoken in the opening dialogue between Lear and Cordelia. Cordelia offers nothing above the natural bond, and in the end what Regan and Goneril offer—a hundred, fifty, ten, one, no horsemen—comes to nothing, and so does the natural bond. God made the world out of nothing (Lear agrees with Aristotle that nothing can come of nothing, but Christian philosophy knew that God created the world *ex nihilo*) and to nothing it seems to be returning, so far as mere nature can accomplish that. From a king to the thing itself, unaccommodated man, from order to chaos, from love to hatred, from custom to nature is the first movement of the play. The evil sisters (who speak a language as artfully and icily involved as that of compliment, however base their meaning) are the people who hope to benefit from the tearing down of all the restraints art could place upon nature, from the return to a riot of natural lust and cruelty. Yet this naturalism is a kind of nihilism; Regan and Goneril behave as women who desire some disastrous end. Nature alone, however, cannot quite provide it; as one adaptation of Aristotle's famous saying expressed it, *de nihilo nihilum, in nihilum nil posse reverti*, nothing can come of nothing nor yet return to it. We seem to be left at the end of the play not only with a mere remnant of the great men and women, just or unjust, who began it, but with a mere remnant of time. Before everything was annihilated, evil destroyed itself, and Edgar has a future to face; but it comes toward him desolate and drained of meaning.

So it is indeed a question whether any "positives" emerge from *King Lear*. There is Kent, who is probably more important as a sign of the loyalty of the old order than as an exponent of Stoicism. There is the Fool, another representative of a more generous way of life, and a part the depth and subtlety of which has best been studied by Enid Welsford in her book *The Court Fool*; there is Edgar attending both the King and his father, teaching him that suicide is the enemy of "ripeness," but learning (in the remarkable opening lines of the fourth act) that no man can even *say* his trials are at an end; and there is Cordelia. This brief part has been most important to those who see in *Lear* a Christian allegory. She is mistaken by Lear for a soul in bliss; she is about her father's business; she "redeems nature from the general curse / That twain have brought her to"; and every description of her contributes to our sense of her inhabiting a realm of grace as her sisters grovel in nature. All this is brought to a head when Lear asks her forgiveness ("No cause, no cause") and plans their happy secluded future life in prison. But Shakespeare snatches it all away at the end.

In much the same way, he leads Lear to charity and compassion, to a kind of peace he can achieve only if he keeps his thoughts off his pelican daughters. He balances between heaven and hell but, with the arrival of Poor Tom, thinks of them again ("Didst thou give all to thy daughters?"), and they become, as Norman MacLean puts it, "his total occupation." So he descends into the pit and the lake of darkness to arraign them. When we see him again, his pity for the world's injustice to its houseless wretches has been lost in mania; he does not know the difference between life and death, or between his mortality and his Dignity, or between heaven, earth, and hell. Gloucester stumbled when he saw, and the loss of his eyes gave him, as it gave Samson, a keener spiritual vision; but he and his son have no time left together, and what he chiefly learns is to wait for death with patience, expecting an end that will be as full of woe as, so Lear reminds us, the beginning is.

"For what takes place in *King Lear*," says L. C. Knights, "we can find no other word than renewal." If that is so, then it is a monstrously difficult birth. But one must finally agree with Knights that "the play's marvellous technique, the particular way in which it enlivens and controls our sympathies and perceptions," give us the sense of an affirmation; "affirmation *in spite of everything*," as he says, yet affirmation of life. We need not see the matter as Lear and Gloucester saw it, nor indeed as Edgar and Albany; we have the play before us, and they had not. And the truth may perhaps be put in the words of J. C. Maxwell: "The fact that Shakespeare can assume in his audience a different religious standpoint from that of any of his characters gives him a peculiar freedom, and makes possible an unusual complexity and richness." Yet, finally, it is in *Lear* that the years of inquiry into the complex relation of mortality and dignity, justice and iniquity, shadow and substance, come to their climax, in a representation of the fate of a man at the world's end.

Frank Kermode

The Tragedy of King Lear

[Dramatis Personae

Lear, *King of Britain*
King of France
Duke of Burgundy
Duke of Cornwall, *husband to Regan*
Duke of Albany, *husband to Goneril*
Earl of Kent
Earl of Gloucester
Edgar, *son to Gloucester*
Edmund, *bastard son to Gloucester*
Curan, *a courtier*
Oswald, *steward to Goneril*
Old Man, *tenant to Gloucester*

Doctor
Fool, *to Lear*
Captain *employed by Edmund*
Gentleman *attendant on Cordelia*
Herald
Servants *to Cornwall*

Goneril, Regan, Cordelia } *daughters to Lear*

Knights *of Lear's train*, Gentlemen, Officers, Messengers, Soldiers, *and* Attendants

Scene: *Britain*]

ACT I, Scene I

Enter Kent, Gloucester, *and* Edmund.

Kent. I thought the King had more affected the Duke of Albany than Cornwall.

Glou. It did always seem so to us; but now in the division of the kingdom, it appears not which of the Dukes he values most, for [equalities] are so weigh'd, that curiosity in neither can make choice of either's moi'ty.

Kent. Is not this your son, my lord?

Glou. His breeding, sir, hath been at my charge. I have so often blush'd to acknowledge him, that now I am braz'd to't.

Kent. I cannot conceive you.

Glou. Sir, this young fellow's mother could; whereupon she grew round-womb'd, and had indeed, sir, a son for her cradle ere she had a husband for her bed. Do you smell a fault?

Kent. I cannot wish the fault undone, the issue of it being so proper.

Glou. But I have a son, sir, by order of law, some year elder than this, who yet is no dearer in my account. Though this knave came something saucily to the world before he was sent for, yet was his mother fair, there was good sport at his making, and the whoreson must be acknowledg'd. Do you know this noble gentleman, Edmund?

Edm. No, my lord.

Glou. My Lord of Kent. Remember him hereafter as my honorable friend.

Edm. My services to your lordship.

Kent. I must love you, and sue to know you better.

Edm. Sir, I shall study deserving.

Glou. He hath been out nine years, and away he shall again. ([*Sound a*] *sennet.*) The King is coming.

Enter [*one bearing a coronet, then*] King Lear, Cornwall, Albany, Goneril, Regan, Cordelia, *and* Attendants.

Lear. Attend the lords of France and Burgundy,
Gloucester.

Glou. I shall, my lord. *Exit* [*with Edmund*].

Lear. Mean time we shall express our darker purpose.
Give me the map there. Know that we have divided
In three our kingdom; and 'tis our fast intent
To shake all cares and business from our age,

Words and passages enclosed in square brackets in the text above are either emendations of the copy-text or additions to it. The Textual Notes immediately following the play cite the earliest authority for every such change or insertion and supply the reading of the copy-text wherever it is emended in this edition.

I.i. Location: Britain. King Lear's palace.
1. affected: liked. 2. Albany: northern Britain.
6. weigh'd: precisely balanced. curiosity: meticulous scrutiny.
7. moi'ty: portion. 9. breeding: rearing. charge: expense.
11. braz'd: brazened, hardened.
12. conceive: understand (with following quibble).
17. issue: (1) outcome; (2) offspring.
18. proper: (1) excellent; (2) handsome.

19. by . . . law: legitimate.
21. account: estimation. knave: young fellow (not derogatory). something: somewhat. 32. out: abroad.
33 s.d. sennet: trumpet call signalling the arrival or departure of a procession. 36. darker: more secret. 38. fast: firm.

Conferring them on younger strengths, while we
Unburthen'd crawl toward death. Our son of Cornwall,
And you, our no less loving son of Albany,
We have this hour a constant will to publish
Our daughters' several dowers, that future strife
May be prevented now. The princes, France and Burgundy,
Great rivals in our youngest daughter's love,
Long in our court have made their amorous sojourn,
And here are to be answer'd. Tell me, my daughters
(Since now we will divest us both of rule,
Interest of territory, cares of state),
Which of you shall we say doth love us most,
That we our largest bounty may extend
Where nature doth with merit challenge? Goneril,
Our eldest-born, speak first.

Gon. Sir, I love you more than [words] can wield the matter,
Dearer than eyesight, space, and liberty,
Beyond what can be valued, rich or rare,
No less than life, with grace, health, beauty, honor;
As much as child e'er lov'd, or father found;
A love that makes breath poor, and speech unable:
Beyond all manner of so much I love you.

Cor. [*Aside.*] What shall Cordelia speak? Love, and be silent.

Lear. Of all these bounds, even from this line to this,
With shadowy forests and with champains rich'd,
With plenteous rivers and wide-skirted meads,
We make thee lady. To thine and Albany's [issue]
Be this perpetual. What says our second daughter,
Our dearest Regan, wife of Cornwall? [Speak.]

Reg. I am made of that self metal as my sister,
And prize me at her worth. In my true heart
I find she names my very deed of love;
Only she comes too short, that I profess
Myself an enemy to all other joys
Which the most precious square of sense [possesses],
And find I am alone felicitate
In your dear Highness' love.

Cor. [*Aside.*] Then poor Cordelia!
And yet not so, since I am sure my love's
More ponderous than my tongue.

Lear. To thee and thine hereditary ever
Remain this ample third of our fair kingdom,
No less in space, validity, and pleasure,
Than that conferr'd on Goneril.—Now, our joy,
Although our last and least, to whose young love
The vines of France and milk of Burgundy
Strive to be interess'd, what can you say to draw
A third more opulent than your sisters'? Speak.

Cor. Nothing, my lord.

Lear. Nothing?

Cor. Nothing.

Lear. Nothing will come of nothing, speak again.

Cor. Unhappy that I am, I cannot heave
My heart into my mouth. I love your Majesty
According to my bond, no more nor less.

Lear. How, how, Cordelia? Mend your speech a little,
Lest you may mar your fortunes.

Cor. Good my lord,
You have begot me, bred me, lov'd me: I
Return those duties back as are right fit,
Obey you, love you, and most honor you.
Why have my sisters husbands, if they say
They love you all? Happily, when I shall wed,
That lord whose hand must take my plight shall carry
Half my love with him, half my care and duty.
Sure I shall never marry like my sisters,
[To love my father all].

Lear. But goes thy heart with this?

Cor. Ay, my good lord.

Lear. So young, and so untender?

Cor. So young, my lord, and true.

Lear. Let it be so: thy truth then be thy dow'r!
For by the sacred radiance of the sun,
The [mysteries] of Hecat and the night;
By all the operation of the orbs,
From whom we do exist and cease to be;
Here I disclaim all my paternal care,
Propinquity and property of blood,
And as a stranger to my heart and me
Hold thee from this for ever. The barbarous Scythian,
Or he that makes his generation messes
To gorge his appetite, shall to my bosom
Be as well neighbor'd, pitied, and reliev'd,
As thou my sometime daughter.

Kent. Good my liege—

Lear. Peace, Kent!
Come not between the dragon and his wrath;
I lov'd her most, and thought to set my rest
On her kind nursery. [*To Cordelia.*] Hence, and avoid my sight!—
So be my grave my peace, as here I give
Her father's heart from her. Call France. Who stirs?

43. publish: announce publicly. **44. several:** individual.
50. Interest: possession.
53. Where . . . challenge: where natural affection in addition to (other) merit claims it. **60. breath:** voice.
64. champains: unwooded plains. **rich'd:** made rich.
65. wide-skirted: extensive.
69. self: same. **metal.** With some of the sense of modern *mettle.*
70. prize . . . worth: esteem myself her equal (in love for you).
71. she . . . love: she exactly describes my love. **72. that:** in that.
74. square. Usually glossed as "region" or "criterion," but more probably *square of sense* is figurative for the human body or human life. See *The Faerie Queene,* II.ix.22, "a quadrate was the base" (the lower part of the soul, which works through sense).
75. felicitate: made happy. **78. ponderous:** weighty.
81. validity: value. **pleasure:** pleasing features.
83. last and least. Cordelia is the youngest child and therefore ranks below her sisters.
84. milk: pasture lands (?).
85. be interess'd: establish a claim. **draw:** win.
90. Nothing . . . nothing. Echoing the famous Aristotelian doctrine *Ex nihilo nihil fit* (denied by Christian philosophers in respect of the Creation). **93. bond:** duty.
97. Return . . . fit: am properly dutiful in return.
100. Happily: haply, perhaps. **101. plight:** marriage pledge.
110. Hecat: Hecate, goddess of witchcraft and of the moon.
111. operation: influence. **orbs:** stars.
112. From whom: by the effect of which.
114. Propinquity: closeness. **property:** identity.
116. from this: from this time forth. **Scythian.** The Scythians' reputation for barbarity extended back to classical times.
117. makes . . . messes: makes meals of his progeny.
120. liege: sovereign. **122. his wrath:** the object of its wrath.
123. set my rest: (1) stake my all (a term from the card game primero); (2) depend for my repose.
124. kind nursery: loving care. **avoid:** leave.

Call Burgundy. Cornwall and Albany,
With my two daughters' dow'rs digest the third;
Let pride, which she calls plainness, marry her.
I do invest you jointly with my power,
Pre-eminence, and all the large effects
That troop with majesty. Ourself, by monthly course,
With reservation of an hundred knights
By you to be sustain'd, shall our abode
Make with you by due turn. Only we shall retain
The name, and all th' addition to a king;
The sway, revenue, execution of the rest,
Beloved sons, be yours, which to confirm,
This coronet part between you.

Kent. Royal Lear,
Whom I have ever honor'd as my king,
Lov'd as my father, as my master follow'd,
As my great patron thought on in my prayers—

Lear. The bow is bent and drawn, make from the shaft.

Kent. Let it fall rather, though the fork invade
The region of my heart; be Kent unmannerly
When Lear is mad. What wouldest thou do, old man?
Think'st thou that duty shall have dread to speak
When power to flattery bows? To plainness honor's bound,
When majesty falls to folly. Reserve thy state,
And in thy best consideration check
This hideous rashness. Answer my life my judgment,
Thy youngest daughter does not love thee least,
Nor are those empty-hearted whose low sounds
Reverb no hollowness.

Lear. Kent, on thy life, no more.

Kent. My life I never held but as [a] pawn
To wage against thine enemies, ne'er [fear'd] to lose it,
Thy safety being motive.

Lear. Out of my sight!

Kent. See better, Lear, and let me still remain
The true blank of thine eye.

Lear. Now, by Apollo—

Kent. Now, by Apollo, King,
Thou swear'st thy gods in vain.

Lear. O vassal! miscreant!
[*Starts to draw his sword.*]

Alb., Corn. Dear sir, forbear.

Kent. Kill thy physician, and [the] fee bestow
Upon the foul disease. Revoke thy gift,
Or whilst I can vent clamor from my throat,
I'll tell thee thou dost evil.

Lear. Hear me, recreant,
On thine allegiance, hear me!
That thou hast sought to make us break our [vow]—
Which we durst never yet—and with strain'd pride
To come betwixt our sentence and our power,
Which nor our nature nor our place can bear,
Our potency made good, take thy reward.
Five days we do allot thee, for provision
To shield thee from disasters of the world,
And on the sixt to turn thy hated back
Upon our kingdom. If, on the tenth day following,
Thy banish'd trunk be found in our dominions,
The moment is thy death. Away! By Jupiter,
This shall not be revok'd.

Kent. Fare thee well, King; sith thus thou wilt appear,
Freedom lives hence, and banishment is here.
[*To Cordelia.*] The gods to their dear shelter take thee, maid,
That justly think'st and hast most rightly said!
[*To Regan and Goneril.*] And your large speeches may your deeds approve,
That good effects may spring from words of love.
Thus Kent, O princes, bids you all adieu,
He'll shape his old course in a country new. *Exit.*

Flourish. Enter GLOUCESTER *with* FRANCE *and* BURGUNDY, ATTENDANTS.

[*Glou.*] Here's France and Burgundy, my noble lord.

Lear. My Lord of Burgundy,
We first address toward you, who with this king
Hath rivall'd for our daughter. What, in the least,
Will you require in present dower with her,
Or cease your quest of love?

Bur. Most royal Majesty,
I crave no more than hath your Highness offer'd,
Nor will you tender less.

Lear. Right noble Burgundy,
When she was dear to us, we did hold her so,
But now her price is fallen. Sir, there she stands:
If aught within that little seeming substance,
Or all of it, with our displeasure piec'd,
And nothing more, may fitly like your Grace,
She's there, and she is yours.

Bur. I know no answer.

Lear. Will you, with those infirmities she owes,
Unfriended, new adopted to our hate,
Dow'r'd with our curse, and stranger'd with our oath,
Take her, or leave her?

Bur. Pardon me, royal sir,
Election makes not up in such conditions.

Lear. Then leave her, sir, for by the pow'r that made me,
I tell you all her wealth. [*To France.*] For you, great King,
I would not from your love make such a stray
To match you where I hate; therefore beseech you

128. digest: assimilate. **136. addition:** honors and prerogatives.
143. make from: get out of range of.
144. fall: strike. **fork:** two-pronged head.
149. Reserve thy state: retain control of your kingdom.
151. Answer . . . judgment: i.e. I'll stake my life on my opinion.
154. Reverb no hollowness: do not reverberate hollowly. *Hollowness* means both "emptiness" and "insincerity." **155. pawn:** stake.
156. wage: wager. **159. blank:** centre of the target.
161. miscreant: villain (literally, misbeliever).
166. recreant: traitor. **168. That:** since.
169. strain'd: excessive.

171. Which . . . place: which neither my temperament nor my dignity as king. **172. Our . . . good:** to prove my authority.
174. disasters: misfortunes. **175. sixt:** sixth. **180. sith:** since.
184. approve: validate. **187. s.d. Flourish:** trumpet fanfare.
195. tender: offer.
198. seeming substance: deceptive appearance of reality; creature who seems substantial but is nothing. **199. piec'd:** joined.
200. like: please. **202. owes:** possesses.
204. stranger'd with: made a stranger by.
206. Election . . . conditions: it is impossible to choose on these terms.
209. make . . . stray: deviate so far. **210. To:** as to.

T' avert your liking a more worthier way
Than on a wretch whom Nature is asham'd
Almost t' acknowledge hers.
France. This is most strange,
That she, whom even but now was your [best] object,
The argument of your praise, balm of your age,
The best, the dearest, should in this trice of time
Commit a thing so monstrous, to dismantle
So many folds of favor. Sure her offense
Must be of such unnatural degree
That monsters it, or your fore-vouch'd affection
Fall into taint; which to believe of her
Must be a faith that reason without miracle
Should never plant in me.
Cor. I yet beseech your Majesty—
If for I want that glib and oily art
To speak and purpose not, since what I [well] intend,
I'll do't before I speak—that you make known
It is no vicious blot, murther, or foulness,
No unchaste action, or dishonored step,
That hath depriv'd me of your grace and favor,
But even for want of that for which I am richer—
A still-soliciting eye, and such a tongue
That I am glad I have not, though not to have it
Hath lost me in your liking.
Lear. Better thou
Hadst not been born than not t' have pleas'd me better.
France. Is it but this—a tardiness in nature
Which often leaves the history unspoke
That it intends to do? My Lord of Burgundy,
What say you to the lady? Love's not love
When it is mingled with regards that stands
Aloof from th' entire point. Will you have her?
She is herself a dowry.
Bur. Royal King,
Give but that portion which yourself propos'd,
And here I take Cordelia by the hand,
Duchess of Burgundy.
Lear. Nothing. I have sworn, I am firm.
Bur. I am sorry then you have so lost a father
That you must lose a husband.
Cor. Peace be with Burgundy!
Since that [respects of fortune] are his love,
I shall not be his wife.
France. Fairest Cordelia, that art most rich being poor,
Most choice forsaken, and most lov'd despis'd,
Thee and thy virtues here I seize upon,
Be it lawful I take up what's cast away.
Gods, gods! 'tis strange that from their cold'st neglect
My love should kindle to inflam'd respect.
Thy dow'rless daughter, King, thrown to my chance,
Is queen of us, of ours, and our fair France.

215. argument: theme. **217. dismantle**: strip off.
218. folds of favor. The image is of Cordelia wrapped in garments signifying the royal favor.
220. That monsters it: as makes it monstrous. **or**: before.
221. Fall into taint: decay. **223. Should**: could.
224. for I want: because I lack.
225. and purpose not: without intending to make good what I say.
228. dishonored: dishonorable.
231. still-soliciting: continually begging.
239–40. regards . . . point: totally irrelevant considerations.
248. respects: considerations.
255. inflam'd respect: impassioned regard.

Not all the dukes of wat'rish Burgundy
Can buy this unpriz'd precious maid of me.
Bid them farewell, Cordelia, though unkind,
Thou losest here, a better where to find.
Lear. Thou hast her, France, let her be thine, for we
Have no such daughter, nor shall ever see
That face of hers again. [*To Cordelia*.] Therefore be gone,
Without our grace, our love, our benison.—
Come, noble Burgundy.
Flourish. *Exeunt* [*all but France*, *Goneril*, *Regan*, *and Cordelia*].
France. Bid farewell to your sisters.
Cor. The jewels of our father, with wash'd eyes
Cordelia leaves you. I know you what you are,
And like a sister am most loath to call
Your faults as they are named. Love well our father;
To your professed bosoms I commit him,
But yet, alas, stood I within his grace,
I would prefer him to a better place.
So farewell to you both.
Reg. Prescribe not us our duty.
Gon. Let your study
Be to content your lord, who hath receiv'd you
At fortune's alms. You have obedience scanted,
And well are worth the want that you have wanted.
Cor. Time shall unfold what plighted cunning hides,
Who covers faults, at last with shame derides.
Well may you prosper!
France. Come, my fair Cordelia.
Exeunt France and Cordelia.

Gon. Sister, it is not little I have to say of what most nearly appertains to us both. I think our father will hence to-night.

Reg. That's most certain, and with you; next month with us.

Gon. You see how full of changes his age is; the observation we have made of it hath [not] been little. He always lov'd our sister most, and with what poor judgment he hath now cast her off appears too grossly.

Reg. 'Tis the infirmity of his age, yet he hath ever but slenderly known himself.

Gon. The best and soundest of his time hath been but rash; then must we look from his age to receive not alone the imperfections of long-ingraff'd condition, but therewithal the unruly waywardness that infirm and choleric years bring with them.

258. wat'rish: (1) well-watered; (2) watery, feeble.
259. unpriz'd: not valued (by Lear).
261. here: this place. **where**: place elsewhere.
265. grace: favor. **benison**: blessing. **268. wash'd**: tear-washed.
271. as . . . named: by their true names.
272. professed: love-professing. **274. prefer**: recommend.
278. At fortune's alms: as a small handout from fortune. **scanted**: come short in.
279. are . . . wanted: deserve to suffer the same lack of affection (from your husband) that you have shown (to your father).
280. what . . . hides: what is concealed under cunning folds (*plighted* = pleated). **281. Who**: i.e. time. **292. grossly**: obviously.
295–96. The best . . . rash: even in the prime of life he was impetuous and irascible. **297. long-ingraff'd**: deep-rooted.
298. therewithal: along with that.

Reg. Such unconstant starts are we like to have from him as this of Kent's banishment.

Gon. There is further compliment of leave-taking between France and him. Pray you let us [hit] together; if our father carry authority with such disposition as he bears, this last surrender of his will but offend us.

Reg. We shall further think of it.

Gon. We must do something, and i' th' heat.

Exeunt.

Scene II

Enter [Edmund *the*] *Bastard* [*with a letter*].

Edm. Thou, Nature, art my goddess, to thy law
My services are bound. Wherefore should I
Stand in the plague of custom, and permit
The curiosity of nations to deprive me,
For that I am some twelve or fourteen moonshines
Lag of a brother? Why bastard? Wherefore base?
When my dimensions are as well compact,
My mind as generous, and my shape as true,
As honest madam's issue? Why brand they us
With base? with baseness? bastardy? base, base?
Who, in the lusty stealth of nature, take
More composition, and fierce quality,
Than doth within a dull, stale, tired bed
Go to th' creating a whole tribe of fops,
Got 'tween asleep and wake? Well then,
Legitimate Edgar, I must have your land.
Our father's love is to the bastard Edmund
As to th' legitimate. Fine word, "legitimate"!
Well, my legitimate, if this letter speed
And my invention thrive, Edmund the base
Shall [top] th' legitimate. I grow, I prosper:
Now, gods, stand up for bastards!

Enter Gloucester.

Glou. Kent banish'd thus? and France in choler parted?
And the King gone to-night? Prescrib'd his pow'r,
Confin'd to exhibition? All this done
Upon the gad? Edmund, how now? what news?

Edm. So please your lordship, none.

[*Putting up the letter.*]

Glou. Why so earnestly seek you to put up that letter?

Edm. I know no news, my lord.

Glou. What paper were you reading?

Edm. Nothing, my lord.

Glou. No? What needed then that terrible dispatch of it into your pocket? The quality of nothing hath not such need to hide itself. Let's see. Come, if it be nothing, I shall not need spectacles.

Edm. I beseech you, sir, pardon me. It is a letter from my brother that I have not all o'er-read; and for so much as I have perus'd, I find it not fit for your o'erlooking.

Glou. Give me the letter, sir.

Edm. I shall offend either to detain or give it: the contents, as in part I understand them, are to blame.

Glou. Let's see, let's see.

Edm. I hope, for my brother's justification, he wrote this but as an essay or taste of my virtue.

Glou. (*Reads.*) "This policy and reverence of age makes the world bitter to the best of our times; keeps our fortunes from us till our oldness cannot relish them. I begin to find an idle and fond bondage in the oppression of aged tyranny, who sways, not as it hath power, but as it is suffer'd. Come to me, that of this I may speak more. If our father would sleep till I wak'd him, you should enjoy half his revenue for ever, and live the belov'd of your brother. Edgar." Hum? conspiracy? "Sleep till I wake him, you should enjoy half his revenue." My son Edgar! had he a hand to write this? a heart and brain to breed it in? —When came you to this? Who brought it?

Edm. It was not brought me, my lord; there's the cunning of it. I found it thrown in at the casement of my closet.

Glou. You know the character to be your brother's?

Edm. If the matter were good, my lord, I durst swear it were his; but in respect of that, I would fain think it were not.

Glou. It is his.

Edm. It is his hand, my lord; but I hope his heart is not in the contents.

Glou. Has he never before sounded you in this business?

Edm. Never, my lord. But I have heard him oft maintain it to be fit that, sons at perfect age and fathers declin'd, the father should be as ward to the son, and the son manage his revenue.

Glou. O villain, villain! his very opinion in the letter. Abhorred villain! unnatural, detested, brutish villain! worse than brutish! Go, sirrah, seek him; I'll apprehend him. Abominable villain! Where is he?

Edm. I do not well know, my lord. If it shall please you to suspend your indignation against my

300. **starts:** ill-considered actions. 302. **compliment:** ceremony.
303–4. **hit together:** agree on our course of action.
305. **last surrender:** latest action of giving up rule.
306. **offend:** injure. 308. **i' th' heat:** while the iron is hot.

I.ii. Location: The Earl of Gloucester's castle.
3. **Stand . . . custom:** undergo the trials imposed by convention (on bastards). Custom is opposed to Nature.
4. **curiosity of nations:** finicking distinctions of society (with reference to the expression "the law of nations"). 5. **For that:** because.
6. **Lag of:** behind, younger than. 7. **compact:** composed, framed.
8. **generous:** befitting one who is well-born. 9. **honest:** chaste.
11. **lusty . . . nature:** stealthy enjoyment of natural sexual appetite.
12. **composition:** strength of constitution. **fierce:** vigorous.
14. **fops:** fools. 15. **Got:** begotten. 19. **speed:** succeed.
20. **invention thrive:** scheme go well. 24. **Prescrib'd:** limited.
25. **exhibition:** an allowance of money.
26. **gad:** spur of the moment.

32. **terrible:** terrified. 39. **o'erlooking:** perusal.
42. **to blame:** blameworthy. 45. **essay or taste:** trial or test.
46. **policy . . . of:** policy of revering. In Elizabethan English *policy* regularly connotes craftiness; here the implication is that deference to age has been imposed upon society by old men.
47. **best . . . times:** best part of our lives (i.e. youth, when fathers are still alive, to the inconvenience of their heirs).
49. **idle and fond:** useless and foolish.
50–51. **who . . . suffer'd:** which rules not by reason of its own power but because we put up with it. 61. **closet:** private room.
62. **character:** handwriting. 64. **fain:** gladly.
72. **perfect age:** full maturity.
76. **Abhorred:** abhorrent. **detested:** destestable.
77. **sirrah:** familiar form of address used by parents to children or by masters to servants.

brother till you can derive from him better testimony of his intent, you should run a certain course; where, if you violently proceed against him, mistaking his purpose, it would make a great gap in your own honor and shake in pieces the heart of his obedience. I dare pawn down my life for him that he hath writ this to feel my affection to your honor, and to no other pretense of danger.

Glou. Think you so?

Edm. If your honor judge it meet, I will place you where you shall hear us confer of this, and by an auricular assurance have your satisfaction, and that without any further delay than this very evening.

Glou. He cannot be such a monster—

[*Edm.* Nor is not, sure.

Glou. To his father, that so tenderly and entirely loves him. Heaven and earth!] Edmund, seek him out; wind me into him, I pray you. Frame the business after your own wisdom. I would unstate myself to be in a due resolution.

Edm. I will seek him, sir, presently; convey the business as I shall find means, and acquaint you withal.

Glou. These late eclipses in the sun and moon portend no good to us. Though the wisdom of nature can reason it thus and thus, yet nature finds itself scourg'd by the sequent effects. Love cools, friendship falls off, brothers divide: in cities, mutinies; in countries, discord; in palaces, treason; and the bond crack'd 'twixt son and father. This villain of mine comes under the prediction; there's son against father: the King falls from bias of nature; there's father against child. We have seen the best of our time. Machinations, hollowness, treachery, and all ruinous disorders follow us disquietly to our graves. Find out this villain, Edmund, it shall lose thee nothing, do it carefully. And the noble and true-hearted Kent banish'd! his offense, honesty! 'Tis strange. *Exit.*

Edm. This is the excellent foppery of the world, that when we are sick in fortune—often the surfeits of our own behavior—we make guilty of our disasters the sun, the moon, and stars, as if we were villains on necessity, fools by heavenly compulsion, knaves, thieves, and treachers by spherical predominance; drunkards, liars, and adulterers by an enforc'd obedience of planetary influence; and all that we are evil in, by a divine thrusting on. An admirable evasion of whoremaster man, to lay his goatish disposition on the charge of a star! My father compounded with my mother under the Dragon's tail, and my nativity was under Ursa Major, so that it follows, I am rough and lecherous. [Fut,] I should have been that I am, had the maidenl'est star in the firmament twinkled on my bastardizing. [Edgar—]

Enter EDGAR.

Pat! he comes like the catastrophe of the old comedy. My cue is villainous melancholy, with a sigh like Tom o' Bedlam.—O, these eclipses do portend these divisions! *fa, sol, la, mi.* [*Humming these notes.*]

Edg. How now, brother Edmund, what serious contemplation are you in?

Edm. I am thinking, brother, of a prediction I read this other day, what should follow these eclipses.

Edg. Do you busy yourself with that?

Edm. I promise you, the effects he writes of succeed unhappily, [as of unnaturalness between the child and the parent, death, dearth, dissolutions of ancient amities, divisions in state, menaces and maledictions against king and nobles, needless diffidences, banishment of friends, dissipation of cohorts, nuptial breaches, and I know not what.

Edg. How long have you been a sectary astronomical?

Edm. Come, come,] when saw you my father last?

Edg. The night gone by.

Edm. Spake you with him?

Edg. Ay, two hours together.

Edm. Parted you in good terms? Found you no displeasure in him by word nor countenance?

Edg. None at all.

Edm. Bethink yourself wherein you may have offended him; and at my entreaty forbear his presence until some little time hath qualified the heat of his displeasure, which at this instant so rageth in him, that with the mischief of your person it would scarcely allay.

Edg. Some villain hath done me wrong.

Edm. That's my fear. I pray you have a continent forbearance till the speed of his rage goes slower; and as I say, retire with me to my lodging, from whence I will fitly bring you to hear my lord speak. Pray ye go, there's my key. If you do stir abroad, go arm'd.

Edg. Arm'd, brother?

Edm. Brother, I advise you to the best; I am no honest man if there be any good meaning toward you. I have told you what I have seen and heard; but faintly, nothing like the image and horror of it. Pray you away.

Edg. Shall I hear from you anon?

82. certain: safe. **where:** whereas. **86. feel:** test, sound out.
87–88. pretense of danger: dangerous intention.
98. wind . . . him: worm your way into his confidence (*me* is the so-called "ethical dative").
99–100. unstate . . . resolution: give all I own to have my uncertainty resolved. **101. presently:** at once. **convey:** manage.
103. late: recent.
104. wisdom of nature: natural philosophy, i.e. science.
105. reason . . . and thus: i.e. give explanations of the occurrence of eclipses. **107. mutinies:** insurrections, riots.
111. falls . . . nature: acts contrary to the natural tendencies of a father. In the game of bowls, *bias* = the curving course of the bowl, which in Shakespeare's day was weighted on one side.
118. foppery: foolishness. **119. surfeits:** diseased effects.
123. treachers: traitors. **spherical predominance:** ascendancy of some one of the planets (each of which was thought to be fixed in a revolving sphere). **126. divine:** supernatural.
127. goatish: lecherous.
129, 130. Dragon, Ursa Major: names of constellations.
131. Fut: contemptuous exclamation (from "God's foot").
134. catastrophe: the event that resolves the plot.
136. Tom o' Bedlam: lunatic beggar, so called from Bethlehem Hospital, the London madhouse. **143. succeed:** follow.
144. unnaturalness: disaffection. **145. dearth:** famine.
147. needless diffidences: groundless suspicions.
148. dissipation of cohorts: dissolution of troops, i.e. large-scale desertion. **150–51. sectary astronomical:** devotee of astrology.
157. countenance: demeanor. **161. qualified:** moderated.
163. mischief: injury. **164. allay:** be abated.
166–67. have . . . forbearance: keep discreetly out of his way (*continent* = self-restrained). **169. fitly:** at the proper moment.
175. image and horror: horrible actuality (*image* = true likeness).

Edm. I do serve you in this business. *Exit* [*Edgar*].
A credulous father and a brother noble,
Whose nature is so far from doing harms
That he suspects none; on whose foolish honesty
My practices ride easy. I see the business.
Let me, if not by birth, have lands by wit:
All with me's meet that I can fashion fit. *Exit.*

Scene III

Enter Goneril *and Steward* [Oswald].

Gon. Did my father strike my gentleman for chiding of his Fool?

Osw. Ay, madam.

Gon. By day and night he wrongs me, every hour
He flashes into one gross crime or other
That sets us all at odds. I'll not endure it.
His knights grow riotous, and himself upbraids us
On every trifle. When he returns from hunting,
I will not speak with him; say I am sick.
If you come slack of former services,
You shall do well; the fault of it I'll answer.
[*Horns within.*]

Osw. He's coming, madam, I hear him.

Gon. Put on what weary negligence you please,
You and your fellows; I'd have it come to question.
If he distaste it, let him to my sister,
Whose mind and mine I know in that are one,
[Not to be overrul'd. Idle old man,
That still would manage those authorities
That he hath given away! Now by my life
Old fools are babes again, and must be us'd
With checks as flatteries, when they are seen abus'd.]
Remember what I have said.

Osw. Well, madam.

Gon. And let his knights have colder looks among you;
What grows of it, no matter. Advise your fellows so.
[I would breed from hence occasions, and I shall,
That I may speak.] I'll write straight to my sister
To hold my [very] course. Prepare for dinner.
Exeunt.

Scene IV

Enter Kent [*disguised as Caius*].

Kent. If but as [well] I other accents borrow,
That can my speech defuse, my good intent
May carry through itself to that full issue
For which I raz'd my likeness. Now, banish'd Kent,
If thou canst serve where thou dost stand condemn'd,
So may it come, thy master, whom thou lov'st,
Shall find thee full of labors.

Horns within. Enter Lear, [Knights,] *and* Attendants [*from hunting*].

Lear. Let me not stay a jot for dinner, go get it ready. [*Exit an Attendant.*] How now, what art thou?

Kent. A man, sir.

Lear. What dost thou profess? What wouldst thou with us?

Kent. I do profess to be no less than I seem, to serve him truly that will put me in trust, to love him that is honest, to converse with him that is wise and says little, to fear judgment, to fight when I cannot choose, and to eat no fish.

Lear. What art thou?

Kent. A very honest-hearted fellow, and as poor as the King.

Lear. If thou be'st as poor for a subject as he's for a king, [th'] art poor enough. What wouldst thou?

Kent. Service.

Lear. Who wouldst thou serve?

Kent. You.

Lear. Dost thou know me, fellow?

Kent. No, sir, but you have that in your countenance which I would fain call master.

Lear. What's that?

Kent. Authority.

Lear. What services canst do?

Kent. I can keep honest counsel, ride, run, mar a curious tale in telling it, and deliver a plain message bluntly. That which ordinary men are fit for, I am qualified in, and the best of me is diligence.

Lear. How old art thou?

Kent. Not so young, sir, to love a woman for singing, nor so old to dote on her for any thing. I have years on my back forty-eight.

Lear. Follow me, thou shalt serve me. If I like thee no worse after dinner, I will not part from thee yet. Dinner, ho, dinner! Where's my knave? my Fool? Go you and call my Fool hither. [*Exit an Attendant.*]

Enter Steward [Oswald].

You, you, sirrah, where's my daughter?

Osw. So please you— *Exit.*

Lear. What says the fellow there? Call the clotpole back. [*Exit a Knight.*] Where's my Fool? Ho! I think the world's asleep.

[*Enter* Knight.]

How now? where's that mungrel?

182. practices: plots.
184. fashion fit: manipulate to serve my purpose.

I.iii. Location: The Duke of Albany's palace.
3. By . . . night. Possibly an oath.
4. crime: offense (milder than in modern usage).
9. come slack: fall short. **13. question:** discussion, issue.
14. distaste: be displeased by. **16. Idle:** foolish.
20. as: for, in place of. **abus'd:** deluded.
25. straight: straightway.

I.iv. Location: Scene continues.
1. as well: i.e. as well as I have disguised my person.
2. defuse: disguise.
4. raz'd my likeness: destroyed my identity.
7. full of labors: excellent in service.
11. What . . . profess: what's your skill.
13. profess: avow myself, claim.
14. put . . . trust: give me his confidence.
15. honest: honorable. **converse:** associate.
16. judgment: i.e. God's judgment.
16–17. cannot choose: have no alternative.
17. eat no fish: be a Protestant (?) or be a hearty fellow, a meat-eater (?). **32. keep honest counsel:** respect confidences.
33. curious: elaborate, intricate.
45. So please you: i.e. sorry, I'm busy.
46. clotpole: clotpoll, blockhead. **49. mungrel:** mongrel.

Knight. He says, my lord, your [daughter] is not well.

Lear. Why came not the slave back to me when I call'd him?

Knight. Sir, he answer'd me in the roundest manner, he would not.

Lear. He would not?

Knight. My lord, I know not what the matter is, but to my judgment your Highness is not entertain'd with that ceremonious affection as you were wont. There's a great abatement of kindness appears as well in the general dependants as in the Duke himself also, and your daughter.

Lear. Ha? say'st thou so?

Knight. I beseech you pardon me, my lord, if I be mistaken, for my duty cannot be silent when I think your Highness wrong'd.

Lear. Thou but rememb'rest me of mine own conception. I have perceiv'd a most faint neglect of late, which I have rather blam'd as mine own jealous curiosity than as a very pretense and purpose of unkindness. I will look further into't. But where's my Fool? I have not seen him this two days.

Knight. Since my young lady's going into France, sir, the Fool hath much pin'd away.

Lear. No more of that, I have noted it well. Go you and tell my daughter I would speak with her. [*Exit an Attendant.*] Go you call hither my Fool.
[*Exit another Attendant.*]

Enter Steward [Oswald].

O, you, sir, you, come you hither, sir. Who am I, sir?

Osw. My lady's father.

Lear. "My lady's father"? My lord's knave! You whoreson dog, you slave, you cur!

Osw. I am none of these, my lord, I beseech your pardon.

Lear. Do you bandy looks with me, you rascal?
[*Striking him.*]

Osw. I'll not be strucken, my lord.

Kent. Nor tripp'd neither, you base football player.
[*Tripping up his heels.*]

Lear. I thank thee, fellow. Thou serv'st me, and I'll love thee.

Kent. Come, sir, arise, away! I'll teach you differences. Away, away! If you will measure your lubber's length again, tarry; but away! Go to, have you wisdom? So. [*Pushes Oswald out.*]

Lear. Now, my friendly knave, I thank thee, there's earnest of thy service. [*Giving Kent money.*]

Enter Fool.

Fool. Let me hire him too, here's my coxcomb.
[*Offering Kent his cap.*]

Lear. How now, my pretty knave, how dost thou?

Fool. Sirrah, you were best take my coxcomb.

[*Kent.*] Why, [Fool]?

Fool. Why? for taking one's part that's out of favor. Nay, and thou canst not smile as the wind sits, thou'lt catch cold shortly. There, take my coxcomb. Why, this fellow has banish'd two on 's daughters, and did the third a blessing against his will; if thou follow him, thou must needs wear my coxcomb.—How now, nuncle? Would I had two coxcombs and two daughters!

Lear. Why, my boy?

Fool. If I gave them all my living, I'ld keep my coxcombs myself. There's mine, beg another of thy daughters.

Lear. Take heed, sirrah—the whip.

Fool. Truth's a dog must to kennel, he must be whipt out, when the Lady Brach may stand by th' fire and stink.

Lear. A pestilent gall to me!

Fool. Sirrah, I'll teach thee a speech.

Lear. Do.

Fool. Mark it, nuncle:
Have more than thou showest,
Speak less than thou knowest,
Lend less than thou owest,
Ride more than thou goest,
Learn more than thou trowest,
Set less than thou throwest;
Leave thy drink and thy whore,
And keep in a' door,
And thou shalt have more
Than two tens to a score.

Kent. This is nothing, Fool.

Fool. Then 'tis like the breath of an unfee'd lawyer, you gave me nothing for't. Can you make no use of nothing, nuncle?

Lear. Why, no, boy, nothing can be made out of nothing.

Fool. [*To Kent.*] Prithee tell him, so much the rent of his land comes to. He will not believe a fool.

Lear. A bitter fool!

Fool. Dost know the difference, my boy, between a bitter fool and a sweet one?

Lear. No, lad, teach me.

Fool. [That lord that counsell'd thee
To give away thy land,
Come place him here by me,
Do thou for him stand.
The sweet and bitter fool
Will presently appear:
The one in motley here,
The other found out there.

54. roundest: bluntest. **67. remember'rest:** remindest. **68. faint:** indolent. **70. very pretense:** deliberate intention. **86. football player.** Football was a lower-class diversion in Shakespeare's day. **90. differences:** distinctions of rank. **94. earnest:** down payment.

100. and: if. **smile . . . sits:** i.e. ingratiate yourself with the party in power. **101. catch cold:** i.e. find yourself out in the cold. **102–3. banish'd . . . blessing.** This reverses the situation as Lear sees it—the more fool he, the Fool implies. **102. on 's:** of his. **105. nuncle:** mine uncle; familiar form of address from Fool to master. **107. living:** property. **107–8. keep my coxcombs:** i.e. to show that I was a double fool. **112. Brach:** hound bitch (here apparently symbolizing flattering falsehood). **114. gall:** source of irritation. **120. owest:** ownest. **121. goest:** walkest. **122. Learn:** i.e. hear. **trowest:** believest. **123. Set . . . throwest:** (presumably) stake less than your all on a throw of the dice. **125. in a' door:** indoors. **126–27. thou . . . score:** i.e. you will grow richer. **136. bitter:** vexatious. **140. That lord:** i.e. Lear himself, as the Fool comes close to saying in line 143. **147. there.** Pointing at Lear, the "bitter fool."

Lear. Dost thou call me fool, boy?

Fool. All thy other titles thou hast given away, that thou wast born with.

Kent. This is not altogether fool, my lord.

Fool. No, faith, lords and great men will not let me; if I had a monopoly out, they would have part an't. And ladies too, they will not let me have all the fool to myself, they'll be snatching.] Nuncle, give me an egg, and I'll give thee two crowns.

Lear. What two crowns shall they be?

Fool. Why, after I have cut the egg i' th' middle and eat up the meat, the two crowns of the egg. When thou clovest thy [crown] i' th' middle and gav'st away both parts, thou bor'st thine ass on thy back o'er the dirt. Thou hadst little wit in thy bald crown when thou gav'st thy golden one away. If I speak like myself in this, let him be whipt that first finds it so.

[*Sings.*] "Fools had ne'er less grace in a year,
For wise men are grown foppish,
And know not how their wits to wear,
Their manners are so apish."

Lear. When were you wont to be so full of songs, sirrah?

Fool. I have us'd it, nuncle, e'er since thou mad'st thy daughters thy mothers, for when thou gav'st them the rod, and put'st down thine own breeches,

[*Sings.*] "Then they for sudden joy did weep,
And I for sorrow sung,
That such a king should play bo-peep,
And go the [fools] among."

Prithee, nuncle, keep a schoolmaster that can teach thy Fool to lie—I would fain learn to lie.

Lear. And you lie, sirrah, we'll have you whipt.

Fool. I marvel what kin thou and thy daughters are. They'll have me whipt for speaking true; thou'lt have me whipt for lying; and sometimes I am whipt for holding my peace. I had rather be any kind o' thing than a Fool, and yet I would not be thee, nuncle: thou hast par'd thy wit o' both sides, and left nothing i' th' middle. Here comes one o' the parings.

Enter GONERIL.

Lear. How now, daughter? what makes that frontlet on? You are too much of late i' th' frown.

Fool. Thou wast a pretty fellow when thou hadst no need to care for her frowning, now thou art an O without a figure. I am better than thou art now, I am a Fool, thou art nothing. [*To Goneril.*] Yes, forsooth, I will hold my tongue; so your face bids me, though you say nothing.

Mum, mum:
He that keeps nor crust [nor] crumb,
Weary of all, shall want some.

[*Pointing to Lear.*] That's a sheal'd peascod.

Gon. Not only, sir, this your all-licens'd Fool,
But other of your insolent retinue
Do hourly carp and quarrel, breaking forth
In rank and not-to-be-endur'd riots. Sir,
I had thought, by making this well known unto you,
To have found a safe redress, but now grow fearful,
By what yourself too late have spoke and done,
That you protect this course and put it on
By your allowance; which if you should, the fault
Would not scape censure, nor the redresses sleep,
Which, in the tender of a wholesome weal,
Might in their working do you that offense,
Which else were shame, that then necessity
Will call discreet proceeding.

Fool. For you know, nuncle,
"The hedge-sparrow fed the cuckoo so long,
That [it] had it head bit off by it young."
So out went the candle, and we were left darkling.

Lear. Are you our daughter?

Gon. I would you would make use of your good wisdom
(Whereof I know you are fraught) and put away
These dispositions which of late transport you
From what you rightly are.

Fool. May not an ass know when the cart draws the horse?
[*Sings.*] "Whoop, Jug! I love thee."

Lear. Does any here know me? This is not Lear.
Does Lear walk thus? speak thus? Where are his eyes?
Either his notion weakens, his discernings
Are lethargied—Ha! waking? 'Tis not so.
Who is it that can tell me who I am?

Fool. Lear's shadow.

[*Lear.* I would learn that, for by the marks of sovereignty,
Knowledge, and reason, I should be false persuaded
I had daughters.

152. No . . . me. The Fool quibbles on Kent's *altogether fool* in the sense "the sum total of folly."
153. monopoly. Both Elizabeth and James granted monopolies in various commodities to favorite courtiers. There was much complaint; Dover Wilson suggests that the satire here may have caused the censor to excise this passage from the manuscript that was the basis of the F1 text. **an't:** on it, i.e. of it.
154–55. ladies . . . snatching. Probably alluding to the Fool's traditional bauble, of phallic shape.
161–62. bor'st . . . dirt: i.e. foolishly reversed the order of nature. The allusion is to one of Aesop's fables.
164. like myself: i.e. like a fool.
165. finds it so: learns from experience that it is true.
166–69. Fools . . . apish. The point is that fools are no longer in demand since wise men now do their work.
166. grace: favor. **in a year:** in any year, i.e. ever.
168. wear: use. **172. us'd it:** made it my practice.
175–78. Then . . . among. These verses parody the "Ballad of John Carelesse." **177. bo-peep:** a children's game.
181. And: if.
189–90. frontlet: band worn on the forehead; here, frown.
192–93. an O . . . figure: a zero without another digit in front of it.
198–99. He . . . some: i.e. he who gives everything away because he's tired of it will later need some part of what he has lost.
198. crumb: the part of the loaf that is not crust; "crust and crumb" = the whole loaf. **200. sheal'd:** shelled, empty. **peascod:** pea pod.
201. all-licens'd: privileged to do and say anything he likes.
207. too late: all too recently. **208. put it on:** encourage it.
209. allowance: permission.
211. tender of: care for. **weal:** commonweal, state.
213. else were: under other circumstances would be.
215. cuckoo. The cuckoo laid its eggs in other birds' nests.
216. it head . . . it young: its head . . . its nestling, i.e. the cuckoo.
217. darkling: in the dark.
220. fraught: freighted, amply provided.
221. dispositions: capricious moods.
225. Whoop . . . thee. Origin unknown; *Jug* is a nickname for *Joan*, and *jug* sometimes means "whore."
228. notion: mental power. **discernings:** senses.
232–33. by . . . reason: i.e. everything—the outward signs that I am king, my memory, my common sense—suggests (falsely) that I am the man who had daughters.

Fool. Which they will make an obedient father.]
Lear. Your name, fair gentlewoman?
Gon. This admiration, sir, is much o' th' savor
Of other your new pranks. I do beseech you
To understand my purposes aright,
As you are old and reverend, should be wise.
Here do you keep a hundred knights and squires,
Men so disorder'd, so debosh'd and bold,
That this our court, infected with their manners,
Shows like a riotous inn. Epicurism and lust
Makes it more like a tavern or a brothel
Than a grac'd palace. The shame itself doth speak
For instant remedy. Be then desir'd
By her, that else will take the thing she begs,
A little to disquantity your train,
And the remainders that shall still depend,
To be such men as may besort your age,
Which know themselves and you.
Lear. Darkness and devils!
Saddle my horses; call my train together!
Degenerate bastard, I'll not trouble thee;
Yet have I left a daughter.
Gon. You strike my people,
And your disorder'd rabble make servants of their betters.

Enter Albany.

Lear. Woe, that too late repents!—[O, sir, are you come?]
Is it your will? Speak, sir.—Prepare my horses.—
Ingratitude! thou marble-hearted fiend,
More hideous when thou show'st thee in a child
Than the sea-monster.
Alb. Pray, sir, be patient.
Lear. [*To Goneril.*] Detested kite, thou liest.
My train are men of choice and rarest parts,
That all particulars of duty know,
And in the most exact regard support
The worships of their name. O most small fault,
How ugly didst thou in Cordelia show!
Which, like an engine, wrench'd my frame of nature
From the fix'd place; drew from my heart all love,
And added to the gall. O Lear, Lear, Lear!
Beat at this gate, that let thy folly in
[*Striking his head.*]
And thy dear judgment out! Go, go, my people.
[*Exeunt Knights and Kent.*]
Alb. My lord, I am guiltless as I am ignorant
Of what hath moved you.
Lear. It may be so, my lord.
Hear, Nature, hear, dear goddess, hear!
Suspend thy purpose, if thou didst intend
To make this creature fruitful.

Into her womb convey sterility,
Dry up in her the organs of increase,
And from her derogate body never spring
A babe to honor her! If she must teem,
Create her child of spleen, that it may live
And be a thwart disnatur'd torment to her.
Let it stamp wrinkles in her brow of youth,
With cadent tears fret channels in her cheeks,
Turn all her mother's pains and benefits
To laughter and contempt, that she may feel
How sharper than a serpent's tooth it is
To have a thankless child!—Away, away! *Exit.*
Alb. Now, gods that we adore, whereof comes this?
Gon. Never afflict yourself to know more of it,
But let his disposition have that scope
As dotage gives it.

Enter Lear.

Lear. What, fifty of my followers at a clap?
Within a fortnight?
Alb. What's the matter, sir?
Lear. I'll tell thee. [*To Goneril.*] Life and death! I am asham'd
That thou hast power to shake my manhood thus,
That these hot tears, which break from me perforce,
Should make thee worth them. Blasts and fogs upon thee!
Th' untented woundings of a father's curse
Pierce every sense about thee! Old fond eyes,
Beweep this cause again, I'll pluck ye out,
And cast you, with the waters that you loose,
To temper clay. [Yea, is't come to this?]
Ha? let it be so: I have another daughter,
Who I am sure is kind and comfortable.
When she shall hear this of thee, with her nails
She'll flea thy wolvish visage. Thou shalt find
That I'll resume the shape which thou dost think
I have cast off for ever. *Exit.*
Gon. Do you mark that?
Alb. I cannot be so partial, Goneril,
To the great love I bear you—
Gon. Pray you, content.—What, Oswald, ho!
[*To the Fool.*] You, sir, more knave than fool, after your master.
Fool. Nuncle Lear, nuncle Lear, tarry, take the Fool with thee.
A fox, when one has caught her,
And such a daughter,
Should sure to the slaughter,
If my cap would buy a halter,
So the Fool follows after. *Exit.*

235. **Which**: whom. 237. **admiration**: i.e. pretended wonderment.
242. **disorder'd**: disorderly. **debosh'd**: debauched.
244. **Epicurism**: sensuality; perhaps specifically "gluttony" in view of *tavern* in line 245. 246. **grac'd**: honored.
249. **disquantity**: reduce the size of.
250. **still depend**: continue to be your dependents.
251. **besort**: befit. 257. **Woe, that**: woe to him who.
261. **patient**: calm. 263. **parts**: qualities, accomplishments.
266. **worships . . . name**: their honorable reputation.
268. **engine**: mechanical device. **frame of nature**: natural frame, normal being. 269. **the fix'd place**: its firm base.
272. **dear**: precious. 274. **moved**: angered.

280. **derogate**: debased. 281. **teem**: breed.
282. **spleen**: malice, spitefulness.
283. **thwart**: perverse. **disnatur'd**: unnatural, unfilial.
285. **cadent**: falling.
286. **mother's**: maternal. **pains and benefits**: beneficent care.
287. **laughter**: mockery. 293. **As**: which.
299. **Blasts**: blights. **fogs**. Supposed to breed infection.
300. **untented**: too deep to be probed, i.e. incurable.
301. **fond**: foolish. 304. **temper**: soften.
306. **comfortable**: ready to offer comfort. 308. **flea**: flay.
315–16. **take . . . thee**: (1) take me with you; (2) take the name "fool" with you, i.e. goodbye, fool (a stock phrase).

Gon. This man hath had good counsel—a hundred knights!
'Tis politic and safe to let him keep
At point a hundred knights; yes, that on every dream,
Each buzz, each fancy, each complaint, dislike,
He may enguard his dotage with their pow'rs,
And hold our lives in mercy.—Oswald, I say!
Alb. Well, you may fear too far.
Gon. Safer than trust too far.
Let me still take away the harms I fear,
Not fear still to be taken. I know his heart.
What he hath utter'd I have writ my sister;
If she sustain him and his hundred knights,
When I have show'd th' unfitness—

Enter Steward [OSWALD].

How now, Oswald?
What, have you writ that letter to my sister?
Osw. Ay, madam.
Gon. Take you some company, and away to horse.
Inform her full of my particular fear,
And thereto add such reasons of your own
As may compact it more. Get you gone,
And hasten your return. [*Exit Oswald.*] No, no, my lord,
This milky gentleness and course of yours
Though I condemn not, yet, under pardon,
[You] are much more [attax'd] for want of wisdom
Than prais'd for harmful mildness.
Alb. How far your eyes may pierce I cannot tell:
Striving to better, oft we mar what's well.
Gon. Nay then—
Alb. Well, well, th' event. *Exeunt.*

SCENE V

Enter LEAR, KENT [*disguised as Caius*], *and* FOOL.

Lear. Go you before to Gloucester with these letters. Acquaint my daughter no further with any thing you know than comes from her demand out of the letter. If your diligence be not speedy, I shall be there afore you.

Kent. I will not sleep, my lord, till I have deliver'd your letter. *Exit.*

Fool. If a man's brains were in 's heels, were't not in danger of kibes?

Lear. Ay, boy.

Fool. Then I prithee be merry, thy wit shall not go slip-shod.

Lear. Ha, ha, ha!

Fool. Shalt see thy other daughter will use thee kindly, for though she's as like this as a crab's like an apple, yet I can tell what I can tell.

Lear. What canst tell, boy?

Fool. She will taste as like this as a crab does to a crab. Thou canst tell why one's nose stands i' th' middle on 's face?

Lear. No.

Fool. Why, to keep one's eyes of either side 's nose, that what a man cannot smell out, he may spy into.

Lear. I did her wrong.

Fool. Canst tell how an oyster makes his shell?

Lear. No.

Fool. Nor I neither; but I can tell why a snail has a house.

Lear. Why?

Fool. Why, to put 's head in, not to give it away to his daughters, and leave his horns without a case.

Lear. I will forget my nature. So kind a father! Be my horses ready?

Fool. Thy asses are gone about 'em. The reason why the seven stars are no moe than seven is a pretty reason.

Lear. Because they are not eight.

Fool. Yes indeed, thou wouldst make a good Fool.

Lear. To take't again perforce! Monster ingratitude!

Fool. If thou wert my Fool, nuncle, I'ld have thee beaten for being old before thy time.

Lear. How's that?

Fool. Thou shouldst not have been old till thou hadst been wise.

Lear. O, let me not be mad, not mad, sweet heaven!
Keep me in temper, I would not be mad!

[*Enter* GENTLEMAN.]

How now, are the horses ready?
Gent. Ready, my lord.
Lear. Come, boy. [*Exeunt Lear and Gentleman.*]
Fool. She that's a maid now, and laughs at my departure,
Shall not be a maid long, unless things be cut shorter.
Exit.

ACT II, SCENE I

Enter Bastard [EDMUND] *and* CURAN *severally.*

Edm. 'Save thee, Curan.

Cur. And [you,] sir. I have been with your father, and given him notice that the Duke of Cornwall and Regan his duchess will be here with him this night.

324. At point: armed. **325. buzz:** rumor.
327. in mercy: at his mercy. **329. still:** always.
330. Not . . . taken: not always be in fear of danger from those harms.
337. particular: own. **339. compact:** confirm.
341. milky . . . course: mildly gentle course of action.
342. under pardon: if you will allow me to say so.
343. attax'd: to be censured.
344. harmful mildness: mildness that may well have harmful consequences. **348. th' event:** we'll see what happens.

I.v. Location: The court before Albany's palace.
1. Gloucester. The city, not the Earl. Some editors prefer to read *Cornwall.* **1–2. these letters:** this letter (Latin *litterae*).
3. demand out of: question arising from. **9. kibes:** chilblains.
11–12. thy . . . slip-shod: your wits won't get chilblains, because they aren't in your heels, i.e. there is no sense in your proposed journey. *Go slip-shod* = wear slippers (because of chilblains).
15. kindly: according to her nature (i.e. just the same as Goneril, but the sense "with natural affection" is ironically present). **crab:** crab apple. **20. on 's:** of his. **22. of:** on.
35. seven stars: Pleiades. **moe:** more. **39. again:** back.
47. temper: mental balance.
51–52. She . . . long: a girl who would laugh at the prospect before Lear and the Fool would be so simple that she couldn't long preserve her virginity.

II.i. Location: Gloucester's castle.
1. 'Save: God save.

Edm. How comes that?
Cur. Nay, I know not. You have heard of the news abroad, I mean the whisper'd ones, for they are yet but ear-[bussing] arguments?
Edm. Not I. Pray you, what are they?
Cur. Have you heard of no likely wars toward, 'twixt the Dukes of Cornwall and Albany?
Edm. Not a word.
Cur. You may do then in time. Fare you well, sir.
Exit.
Edm. The Duke be here to-night? The better! best!
This weaves itself perforce into my business.
My father hath set guard to take my brother,
And I have one thing, of a queasy question,
Which I must act. Briefness and fortune, work!
Brother, a word! Descend. Brother, I say!

Enter EDGAR.

My father watches: O sir, fly this place,
Intelligence is given where you are hid;
You have now the good advantage of the night.
Have you not spoken 'gainst the Duke of Cornwall?
He's coming hither, now i' th' night, i' th' haste,
And Regan with him. Have you nothing said
Upon his party 'gainst the Duke of Albany?
Advise yourself.
Edg. I am sure on't, not a word.
Edm. I hear my father coming. Pardon me:
In cunning I must draw my sword upon you.
Draw, seem to defend yourself; now quit you well.—
Yield! Come before my father. Light ho, here!—
Fly, brother.—Torches, torches!—So farewell.
Exit Edgar.
Some blood drawn on me would beget opinion
[*Wounds his arm.*]
Of my more fierce endeavor. I have seen drunkards
Do more than this in sport.—Father, father!
Stop, stop! No help?

Enter GLOUCESTER, *and* SERVANTS *with torches.*

Glou. Now, Edmund, where's the villain?
Edm. Here stood he in the dark, his sharp sword out,
Mumbling of wicked charms, conjuring the moon
To stand ['s] auspicious mistress.
Glou. But where is he?
Edm. Look, sir, I bleed.
Glou. Where is the villain, Edmund?
Edm. Fled this way, sir, when by no means he could—
Glou. Pursue him, ho! Go after. [*Exeunt some Servants.*] By no means what?
Edm. Persuade me to the murther of your lordship,
But that I told him, the [revengive] gods
'Gainst parricides did all the thunder bend,
Spoke, with how manifold and strong a bond
The child was bound to th' father; sir, in fine,
Seeing how loathly opposite I stood
To his unnatural purpose, in fell motion
With his prepared sword he charges home
My unprovided body, latch'd mine arm;
And when he saw my best alarum'd spirits,
Bold in the quarrel's right, rous'd to th' encounter,
Or whether gasted by the noise I made,
Full suddenly he fled.
Glou. Let him fly far.
Not in this land shall he remain uncaught;
And found—dispatch. The noble Duke my master,
My worthy arch and patron, comes to-night.
By his authority I will proclaim it,
That he which finds him shall deserve our thanks,
Bringing the murderous coward to the stake;
He that conceals him, death.
Edm. When I dissuaded him from his intent,
And found him pight to do it, with curst speech
I threaten'd to discover him; he replied,
"Thou unpossessing bastard, dost thou think,
If I would stand against thee, would the reposal
Of any trust, virtue, or worth in thee
Make thy words faith'd? No. What [I should] deny
(As this I would, [ay,] though thou didst produce
My very character), I'ld turn it all
To thy suggestion, plot, and damned practice;
And thou must make a dullard of the world
If they not thought the profits of my death
Were very pregnant and potential spirits
To make thee seek it."
Glou. O strange and fast'ned villain!
Would he deny his letter, said he? [I never got him.]
Tucket within.
Hark, the Duke's trumpets! I know not [why] he comes.
All ports I'll bar, the villain shall not scape;
The Duke must grant me that. Besides, his picture
I will send far and near, that all the kingdom
May have due note of him, and of my land,
Loyal and natural boy, I'll work the means
To make thee capable.

Enter CORNWALL, REGAN, *and* ATTENDANTS.

Corn. How now, my noble friend? since I came hither

8. ear-bussing: ear-kissing, whispered (with pun on *bussing/buzzing*). **arguments:** topics of conversation. **10. toward:** imminent.
17. of . . . question: needing delicate handling.
18. Briefness . . . work: may expedition and good luck be with me.
26. Upon . . . 'gainst: having to do with his enmity toward.
27. Advise yourself: consider carefully.
30. quit you: acquit yourself.
33–34. beget . . . endeavor: create an impression that I had fought fiercely.
40. stand . . . mistress: shed favorable influence upon him (*'s* = his).
45. that: when. **revengive:** revenging. **48. in fine:** finally.
49. loathly opposite: abhorringly opposed.
50. in fell motion: with a deadly thrust.
52. unprovided: unarmed. **latch'd:** caught. Many editors follow Q1 in reading *lanch'd* = lanced, pierced.
53. alarum'd: called to arms, aroused to action.
54. quarrel's right: justice of the cause. **55. gasted:** scared.
59. arch: chief. **65. pight:** pitched, determined. **curst:** angry.
66. discover: reveal. **70. faith'd:** believed.
72. My very character: i.e. incriminating evidence in my own handwriting. **73. suggestion:** instigation. **practice:** plot.
74. make . . . world: think people very stupid.
76. pregnant and potential: ready and powerful. **spirits:** i.e. tempters (like devils). Many editors adopt the Q1 reading *spurs.*
77. fast'ned: confirmed.
78. got: begot. **s.d. Tucket:** flourish on a trumpet.
85. capable: legally able to inherit.

(Which I can call but now) I have heard [strange news].
Reg. If it be true, all vengeance comes too short
Which can pursue th' offender. How dost, my lord?
Glou. O madam, my old heart is crack'd, it's crack'd!
Reg. What, did my father's godson seek your life?
He whom my father nam'd, your Edgar?
Glou. O lady, lady, shame would have it hid!
Reg. Was he not companion with the riotous knights
That tended upon my father?
Glou. I know not, madam. 'Tis too bad, too bad.
Edm. Yes, madam, he was of that consort.
Reg. No marvel then, though he were ill affected:
'Tis they have put him on the old man's death,
To have th' expense and waste of his revenues.
I have this present evening from my sister
Been well inform'd of them, and with such cautions,
That if they come to sojourn at my house,
I'll not be there.
Corn. Nor I, assure thee, Regan.
Edmund, I hear that you have shown your father
A child-like office.
Edm. It was my duty, sir.
Glou. He did bewray his practice, and receiv'd
This hurt you see, striving to apprehend him.
Corn. Is he pursued?
Glou. Ay, my good lord.
Corn. If he be taken, he shall never more
Be fear'd of doing harm. Make your own purpose,
How in my strength you please. For you, Edmund,
Whose virtue and obedience doth this instant
So much commend itself, you shall be ours.
Natures of such deep trust we shall much need;
You we first seize on.
Edm. I shall serve you, sir,
Truly, however else.
Glou. For him I thank your Grace.
Corn. You know not why we came to visit you?
Reg. Thus out of season, threading dark-ey'd night:
Occasions, noble Gloucester, of some [poise],
Wherein we must have use of your advice.
Our father he hath writ, so hath our sister,
Of differences, which I best [thought] it fit
To answer from our home; the several messengers
From hence attend dispatch. Our good old friend,
Lay comforts to your bosom, and bestow
Your needful counsel to our businesses,
Which craves the instant use.
Glou. I serve you, madam.
Your Graces are right welcome. *Flourish. Exeunt.*

97. **consort:** band, company.
98. **aspir'd . . . affected:** that he became ill-disposed.
99. **put him on:** incited him to plan.
100. **expense . . . of:** power to spend wastefully.
106. **child-like:** filial.
107. **bewray his practice:** reveal his (Edgar's) plot.
111. **of doing:** lest he do. 112. **strength:** authority, power.
115. **trust:** trustworthiness.
117. **however else:** i.e. whether ably or not.
120. **poise:** weight, importance. 124. **from:** away from.
125. **attend dispatch:** are waiting to be sent back.
127. **needful:** needed.
128. **craves . . . use:** require immediate attention.

Scene II

Enter Kent [*disguised as Caius*] *and Steward* [Oswald] *severally.*

Osw. Good dawning to thee, friend. Art of this house?

Kent. Ay.

Osw. Where may we set our horses?

Kent. I' th' mire.

Osw. Prithee, if thou lov'st me, tell me.

Kent. I love thee not.

Osw. Why then I care not for thee.

Kent. If I had thee in Lipsbury pinfold, I would make thee care for me.

Osw. Why dost thou use me thus? I know thee not.

Kent. Fellow, I know thee.

Osw. What dost thou know me for?

Kent. A knave, a rascal, an eater of broken meats; a base, proud, shallow, beggarly, three-suited, hundred-pound, filthy worsted-stocking knave; a lily-liver'd, action-taking, whoreson, glass-gazing, superserviceable, finical rogue; one-trunk-inheriting slave; one that wouldst be a bawd in way of good service, and art nothing but the composition of a knave, beggar, coward, pandar, and the son and heir of a mungril bitch; one whom I will beat into [clamorous] whining, if thou deni'st the least syllable of thy addition.

Osw. Why, what a monstrous fellow art thou, thus to rail on one that is neither known of thee nor knows thee?

Kent. What a brazen-fac'd varlet art thou, to deny thou knowest me? Is it two days since I tripp'd up thy heels, and beat thee before the King? Draw, you rogue, for though it be night, yet the moon shines; [*drawing his sword*] I'll make a sop o' th' moonshine of you, you whoreson cullionly barber-monger, draw!

Osw. Away, I have nothing to do with thee.

Kent. Draw, you rascal! You come with letters

II.ii. Location: Before Gloucester's castle.
6. if . . . me: a conventional phrase equivalent to "of your good will"; but Kent quibbles on the literal sense.
9. If . . . pinfold. A pinfold is a pound for stray animals; Lipsbury is an invented place-name (Lipville) presumably meaning "mouth"; i.e. if I had you between my teeth.
15. broken meats: kitchen scraps.
16. three-suited: having three suits (a servant's annual allowance).
16–17. hundred-pound. Perhaps a sneer at the small amount of wealth underlying Oswald's pretensions.
17. worsted-stocking: wearing woollen stockings (gentlemen wore silk). lily-liver'd: white-livered, i.e. cowardly.
18. action-taking: preferring litigation to fighting. glass-gazing: mirror-gazing, i.e. vain or effeminate.
18–19. superserviceable: officious.
19. finical: foppish. one-trunk-inheriting: owning no more than will fit into a single trunk (*inherit* = possess).
19–20. one . . . service: one willing to regard pandering as part of his duties. 21. composition: combination.
24. thy addition: the titles I have given you.
32–33. make . . . you: pierce your body so that it can soak up moonlight as a sop (a piece of toast floating in a drink) soaks up liquor.
33. cullionly: rascally. barber-monger: frequenter of barber-shops, fop.

against the King, and take Vanity the puppet's part against the royalty of her father. Draw, you rogue, or I'll so carbonado your shanks! Draw, you rascal! Come your ways.

Osw. Help ho! murther, help!

Kent. Strike, you slave! Stand, rogue, stand, you neat slave! Strike! [*Beating him.*]

Osw. Help ho! murther, murther!

Enter Bastard [EDMUND, *with his rapier drawn*].

Edm. How now, what's the matter? Part!

Kent. With you, goodman boy, [and] you please!
Come, I'll flesh ye, come on, young master.

[*Enter*] CORNWALL, REGAN, GLOUCESTER, SERVANTS.

Glou. Weapons? arms? What's the matter here?

Corn. Keep peace, upon your lives!
He dies that strikes again. What is the matter?

Reg. The messengers from our sister and the King.

Corn. What is your difference? speak.

Osw. I am scarce in breath, my lord.

Kent. No marvel, you have so bestirr'd your valor. You cowardly rascal, Nature disclaims in thee: a tailor made thee.

Corn. Thou art a strange fellow. A tailor make a man?

Kent. A tailor, sir; a stone-cutter or a painter could not have made him so ill, though they had been but two years o' th' trade.

Corn. Speak yet, how grew your quarrel?

Osw. This ancient ruffian, sir, whose life I have spar'd at suit of his grey beard—

Kent. Thou whoreson zed, thou unnecessary letter! My lord, if you['ll] give me leave, I will tread this unbolted villain into mortar, and daub the wall of a jakes with him. Spare my grey beard, you wagtail?

Corn. Peace, sirrah!
You beastly knave, know you no reverence?

Kent. Yes, sir, but anger hath a privilege.

Corn. Why art thou angry?

Kent. That such a slave as this should wear a sword,
Who wears no honesty. Such smiling rogues as these,
Like rats, oft bite the holy cords a-twain
Which are t' intrinse t' unloose; smooth every passion
That in the natures of their lords rebel,
Being oil to fire, snow to the colder moods;
[Renege,] affirm, and turn their halcyon beaks
With every [gale] and vary of their masters,
Knowing nought (like dogs) but following.
A plague upon your epileptic visage!
Smile you my speeches, as I were a fool?
Goose, [and] I had you upon Sarum plain,
I'ld drive ye cackling home to Camelot.

Corn. What, art thou mad, old fellow?

Glou. How fell you out? say that.

Kent. No contraries hold more antipathy
Than I and such a knave.

Corn. Why dost thou call him knave? What is his fault?

Kent. His countenance likes me not.

Corn. No more, perchance, does mine, nor his, nor hers.

Kent. Sir, 'tis my occupation to be plain:
I have seen better faces in my time
Than stands on any shoulder that I see
Before me at this instant.

Corn. This is some fellow
Who, having been prais'd for bluntness, doth affect
A saucy roughness, and constrains the garb
Quite from his nature. He cannot flatter, he,
An honest mind and plain, he must speak truth!
And they will take['t], so; if not, he's plain.
These kind of knaves I know, which in this plainness
Harbor more craft and more corrupter ends
Than twenty silly-ducking observants
That stretch their duties nicely.

Kent. Sir, in good faith, in sincere verity,
Under th' allowance of your great aspect,
Whose influence, like the wreath of radiant fire
On [flick'ring] Phoebus' front—

Corn. What mean'st by this?

Kent. To go out of my dialect, which you discommend so much. I know, sir, I am no flatterer. He that beguil'd you in a plain accent was a plain knave, which for my part I will not be, though I should win your displeasure to entreat me to't.

Corn. What was th' offense you gave him?

Osw. I never gave him any.
It pleas'd the King his master very late
To strike at me upon his misconstruction,
When he, compact, and flattering his displeasure,

36. **Vanity the puppet**: i.e. Goneril, abstract Vanity (like a character in a morality puppet-show) opposed to abstract Royalty in Kent's figure. 38. **carbonado**: slash. 39. **Come your ways**: come on.
42. **neat**: foppish.
44. **matter**: cause of the quarrel (so also *difference* in line 51).
45. **goodman boy**: a form of address intended to deflate a presumptuous youth. **and**: if. 46. **flesh**: initiate into fighting.
54. **disclaims in thee**: denies that she had any hand in creating you.
64. **zed**: the letter *z*, unnecessary because its sound could usually be represented by *s*. 66. **unbolted**: unsifted, i.e. coarse.
67. **jakes**: privy. **wagtail.** The image is of a bird waggling or fluttering its tail feathers.
69. **beastly**: beastlike (because he shows no proper respect for rank).
73. **honesty**: honorable character.
74. **holy cords**: i.e. bonds of natural affection.
75. **t' intrinse**: too intricately knotted. **smooth**: humor, flatter.
78. **Renege**: deny. **halcyon**: kingfisher; its body, when hung up, supposedly behaved like a weathervane.
79. **gale and vary**: changing wind. 81. **epileptic**: grimacing.
82. **Smile**: smile at. **as**: as if. 83. **Sarum**: Salisbury.
84. **Camelot**: the site of King Arthur's court, variously identified; perhaps Winchester is intended here. 90. **likes**: pleases.
97. **constrains the garb**: assumes the plain manner.
98. **from . . . nature**: contrary to his own nature, i.e. hypocritically (?) or (if *his* = its) apart from the real nature of plainness (which is courageous speaking of the truth).
100. **And**: if. **so**: well and good.
103. **observants**: obsequious attendants.
104. **nicely**: with excessive concern for every detail.
105. **faith**: truth.
106. **aspect**: (1) countenance; (2) astrological position of a planet.
107. **influence.** Another astrological term; Cornwall is being likened to a heavenly body.
108. **Phoebus' front**: the sun-god's forehead.
109. **dialect**: manner of speech.
111. **He . . . accent**: the plain-speaking man who misled you into your estimate of plain-speakers.
113. **your displeasure.** Ironically analogous with such expressions as "your Grace" (?). Or perhaps, as Sisson suggests, *to entreat me to't* means "if you requested me to be a plain knave, i.e. to flatter you."
116. **very late**: recently.
118. **compact**: leagued (with the King), i.e. taking the King's side.

Tripp'd me behind; being down, insulted, rail'd,
And put upon him such a deal of man
That worthied him, got praises of the King
For him attempting who was self-subdued,
And in the fleshment of this [dread] exploit,
Drew on me here again.

Kent. None of these rogues and cowards
But Ajax is their fool.

Corn. Fetch forth the stocks!
You stubborn ancient knave, you reverent braggart,
We'll teach you.

Kent. Sir, I am too old to learn.
Call not your stocks for me, I serve the King,
On whose employment I was sent to you.
You shall do small respects, show too bold malice
Against the grace and person of my master,
Stocking his messenger.

Corn. Fetch forth the stocks! As I have life and honor,
There shall he sit till noon.

Reg. Till noon? Till night, my lord, and all night too.

Kent. Why, madam, if I were your father's dog,
You should not use me so.

Reg. Sir, being his knave, I will.

Corn. This is a fellow of the self-same color
Our sister speaks of. Come, bring away the stocks!
Stocks brought out.

Glou. Let me beseech your Grace not to do so.
[His fault is much, and the good King his master
Will check him for't. Your purpos'd low correction
Is such as basest and [contemned'st] wretches
For pilf'rings and most common trespasses
Are punish'd with.] The King must take it ill
That he, so slightly valued in his messenger,
Should have him thus restrained.

Corn. I'll answer that.

Reg. My sister may receive it much more worse
To have her gentleman abus'd, assaulted,
[For following her affairs. Put in his legs.]
[*Kent is put in the stocks.*]
Come, my [good] lord, away.
Exit [*with all but Gloucester and Kent*].

Glou. I am sorry for thee, friend, 'tis the Duke['s] pleasure,
Whose disposition, all the world well knows,
Will not be rubb'd nor stopp'd. I'll entreat for thee.

Kent. Pray do not, sir. I have watch'd and travell'd hard:
Some time I shall sleep out, the rest I'll whistle.
A good man's fortune may grow out at heels.
Give you good morrow!

Glou. The Duke's to blame in this, 'twill be ill taken. *Exit.*

Kent. Good King, that must approve the common saw,
Thou out of heaven's benediction com'st
To the warm sun!
Approach, thou beacon to this under globe,
That by thy comfortable beams I may
Peruse this letter. Nothing almost sees miracles
But misery. I know 'tis from Cordelia,
Who hath most fortunately been inform'd
Of my obscured course; [*reads*] "—and shall find time
From this enormous state—seeking to give
Losses their remedies."—All weary and o'erwatch'd,
Take vantage, heavy eyes, not to behold
This shameful lodging.
Fortune, good night; smile once more, turn thy wheel.
[*Sleeps.*]

[Scene III]

Enter Edgar.

Edg. I heard myself proclaim'd,
And by the happy hollow of a tree
Escap'd the hunt. No port is free, no place
That guard and most unusual vigilance
Does not attend my taking. Whiles I may scape
I will preserve myself, and am bethought
To take the basest and most poorest shape
That ever penury, in contempt of man,
Brought near to beast. My face I'll grime with filth,
Blanket my loins, elf all my hairs in knots,
And with presented nakedness outface
The winds and persecutions of the sky.
The country gives me proof and president
Of Bedlam beggars, who, with roaring voices,
Strike in their numb'd and mortified arms
Pins, wooden pricks, nails, sprigs of rosemary;
And with this horrible object, from low farms,
Poor pelting villages, sheep-cotes, and mills,
Sometimes with lunatic bans, sometime with prayers,

120. put . . . man: struck such heroic attitudes.
121. That worthied him: as caused him to be esteemed worthy.
122. For . . . self-subdued: for his courage in taking on a man who offered no resistance.
123. fleshment of: wild excitement engendered by.
124–25. None . . . fool: villains of this kind are always willing to boast that they are braver than Ajax.
126. reverent: reverend, i.e. aged.
130. malice: ill will.
131. grace and person: honor as king and personal honor.
139. away: along. **142. check:** rebuke.
147. answer: answer for.
154. be rubb'd: tolerate any obstacle (a term from the game of bowls).
155. watch'd: gone without sleep.

157. A good . . . heels: i.e. one must not repine at misfortune, since it befalls even good men.
160. approve . . . saw: prove the proverb true.
161–62. out . . . sun: i.e. go from better to worse.
163. beacon . . . globe: i.e. the moon.
164. comfortable: aiding.
165–66. Nothing . . . misery: there's hardly anything like misery for putting one in the way of miracles (since then any change for the better seems miraculous [?]). **168. obscured:** disguised.
169. enormous: abnormal, monstrous. **state:** state of affairs.
170. o'erwatch'd: exhausted from lack of sleep.
171. Take vantage: take advantage (of sleep).
172. shameful lodging: i.e. the stocks.

II.iii. Location: Scene continues. (The sleeping Kent remains on stage.)
2. happy: opportune. **4. That:** in which.
5. attend my taking: wait to take me prisoner.
6. am bethought: have in mind, intend.
10. elf: tangle, as in elf-locks. **11. presented:** exposed.
13. proof: example. **president:** precedent.
14. Bedlam beggars. See note on I.ii.136.
15. mortified: deadened to feeling. **17. object:** sight.
18. pelting: paltry. **19. bans:** curses.

Enforce their charity. Poor Turlygod! poor Tom!
That's something yet: Edgar I nothing am. *Exit.*

[Scene IV]

Enter Lear, Fool, *and* Gentleman. [Kent, *disguised as Caius, in the stocks.*]

Lear. 'Tis strange that they should so depart from home,
And not send back my [messenger].

Gent. As I learn'd,
The night before there was no purpose in them
Of this remove.

Kent. Hail to thee, noble master!

Lear. Ha?
Mak'st thou this shame thy pastime?

Kent. No, my lord.

Fool. Hah, ha, he wears cruel garters. Horses are tied by the heads, dogs and bears by th' neck, monkeys by th' loins, and men by th' legs. When a man['s] overlusty at legs, then he wears wooden nether-stocks.

Lear. What's he that hath so much thy place mistook
To set thee here?

Kent. It is both he and she,
Your son and daughter.

Lear. No.

Kent. Yes.

Lear. No, I say.

Kent. I say yea.

[*Lear.* No, no, they would not.

Kent. Yes, they have.]

Lear. By Jupiter, I swear no.

Kent. By Juno, I swear ay.

Lear. They durst not do't;
They could not, would not do't. 'Tis worse than murther
To do upon respect such violent outrage.
Resolve me with all modest haste which way
Thou mightst deserve, or they impose, this usage,
Coming from us.

Kent. My lord, when at their home
I did commend your Highness' letters to them,
Ere I was risen from the place that showed
My duty kneeling, came there a reeking post,
Stew'd in his haste, half breathless, [panting] forth
From Goneril his mistress salutations;
Deliver'd letters, spite of intermission,
Which presently they read; on those contents
They summon'd up their meiny, straight took horse,
Commanded me to follow, and attend
The leisure of their answer, gave me cold looks:
And meeting here the other messenger,
Whose welcome I perceiv'd had poison'd mine—
Being the very fellow which of late
Display'd so saucily against your Highness—
Having more man than wit about me, drew.
He rais'd the house with loud and coward cries.
Your son and daughter found this trespass worth
The shame which here it suffers.

Fool. Winter's not gone yet, if the wild geese fly that way.

Fathers that wear rags
Do make their children blind,
But fathers that bear bags
Shall see their children kind.
Fortune, that arrant whore,
Ne'er turns the key to th' poor.

But for all this, thou shalt have as many dolors for thy daughters as thou canst tell in a year.

Lear. O how this mother swells up toward my heart!
[*Hysterica*] *passio*, down, thou climbing sorrow,
Thy element's below.—Where is this daughter?

Kent. With the Earl, sir, here within.

Lear. Follow me not,
Stay here. *Exit.*

Gent. Made you no more offense but what you speak of?

Kent. None.
How chance the King comes with so small a number?

Fool. And thou hadst been set i' th' stocks for that question, thou'dst well deserv'd it.

Kent. Why, Fool?

Fool. We'll set thee to school to an ant, to teach thee there's no laboring i' th' winter. All that follow their noses are led by their eyes but blind men, and there's not a nose among twenty but can smell him that's stinking. Let go thy hold when a great wheel runs down a hill, lest it break thy neck with following; but the great one that goes upward, let him draw thee after. When a wise man gives thee better counsel, give me mine again, I would have none but knaves follow it, since a fool gives it.

20. Turlygod. Unexplained. **poor Tom.** Catch phrase of the Bedlam beggars, who became known as "poor Toms."
21. That's . . . am: there's that much left for me; as Edgar I am nothing at all.

II.iv. Location: Scene continues.
6. Mak'st . . . pastime: are you undergoing this humiliation for a joke.
7. cruel garters: i.e. the stocks (with pun on *crewel*, "worsted").
10. 's . . . legs: i.e. has run away from service.
11. nether-stocks: stockings.
12. place: position (as the King's messenger).
24. upon respect: against the respect due to the King in his messenger (?), or against the whole principle of subordination (?).
25. Resolve: inform. **modest:** moderate, reasonable.
28. commend: deliver. **30. reeking:** steaming.
33. spite of intermission: careless of interrupting me.
34. on: in consequence of. **35. meiny:** household servants.
41. Display'd so saucily: showed himself so insolent.
46–47. Winter's . . . way: i.e. this behavior is a sure sign that your troubles aren't over.
49. blind: i.e. blind to their fathers' needs and comforts.
50. bags: i.e. money bags. **53. turns the key:** unlocks the door.
54. dolors: sorrows (with pun on *dollars*). **for:** because of.
55. tell: relate (with quibble on the sense "count").
56. mother: hysteria.
57. Hysterica passio: hysteria, thought to be the result of the ascent of vapors from abdomen to head.
67–68. We'll . . . winter: i.e. the wise ant knows that labor in winter is unprofitable; Lear in his "winter" is bound to be deserted by the shrewd.
68–71. All . . . stinking: i.e. if they couldn't see that he was out of Fortune's favor, they could smell it.
76. knaves. Expressing the Fool's opinion of those who deserted Lear.

That sir which serves and seeks for gain,
And follows but for form,
Will pack when it begins to rain,
And leave thee in the storm.
But I will tarry, the Fool will stay,
And let the wise man fly.
The knave turns fool that runs away,
The Fool no knave, perdie.

Kent. Where learn'd you this, Fool?

Fool. Not i' th' stocks, fool.

Enter LEAR *and* GLOUCESTER.

Lear. Deny to speak with me? They are sick? they are weary?
They have travell'd all the night? Mere fetches,
The images of revolt and flying off.
Fetch me a better answer.

Glou. My dear lord,
You know the fiery quality of the Duke,
How unremovable and fix'd he is
In his own course.

Lear. Vengeance! plague! death! confusion!
Fiery? What quality? Why, Gloucester, Gloucester,
I'ld speak with the Duke of Cornwall and his wife.

Glou. Well, my good lord, I have inform'd them so.

Lear. Inform'd them? Dost thou understand me, man?

Glou. Ay, my good lord.

Lear. The King would speak with Cornwall, the dear father
Would with his daughter speak, commands, tends service.
Are they inform'd of this? My breath and blood!
Fiery? the fiery Duke? Tell the hot Duke that—
No, but not yet, may be he is not well:
Infirmity doth still neglect all office
Whereto our health is bound; we are not ourselves
When nature, being oppress'd, commands the mind
To suffer with the body. I'll forbear,
And am fallen out with my more headier will,
To take the indispos'd and sickly fit
For the sound man. [*Looking on Kent.*] Death on my state! wherefore
Should he sit here? This act persuades me
That this remotion of the Duke and her
Is practice only. Give me my servant forth.
Go tell the Duke, and 's wife, I'ld speak with them—
Now, presently. Bid them come forth and hear me,
Or at their chamber-door I'll beat the drum
Till it cry sleep to death.

Glou. I would have all well betwixt you. *Exit.*

Lear. O me, my heart! my rising heart! But down!

Fool. Cry to it, nuncle, as the cockney did to the eels when she put 'em i' th' paste alive; she knapp'd 'em o' th' coxcombs with a stick, and cried, "Down, wantons, down!" 'Twas her brother that, in pure kindness to his horse, butter'd his hay.

Enter CORNWALL, REGAN, GLOUCESTER, SERVANTS.

Lear. Good morrow to you both.

Corn. Hail to your Grace!

Kent here set at liberty.

Reg. I am glad to see your Highness.

Lear. Regan, I think [you] are; I know what reason
I have to think so. If thou shouldst not be glad,
I would divorce me from thy [mother's] tomb,
Sepulchring an adult'ress. [*To Kent.*] O, are you free?
Some other time for that. [*Exit Kent.*] Beloved Regan,
Thy sister's naught. O Regan, she hath tied
Sharp-tooth'd unkindness, like a vulture, here.
[*Points to his heart.*]
I can scarce speak to thee; thou'lt not believe
With how deprav'd a quality—O Regan!

Reg. I pray you, sir, take patience. I have hope
You less know how to value her desert
Than she to scant her duty.

Lear. Say? How is that?

Reg. I cannot think my sister in the least
Would fail her obligation. If, sir, perchance
She have restrain'd the riots of your followers,
'Tis on such ground and to such wholesome end
As clears her from all blame.

Lear. My curses on her!

Reg. O sir, you are old,
Nature in you stands on the very verge
Of his confine. You should be rul'd and led
By some discretion that discerns your state
Better than you yourself. Therefore I pray you
That to our sister you do make return.
Say you have wrong'd her.

Lear. Ask her forgiveness?
Do you but mark how this becomes the house!
"Dear daughter, I confess that I am old; [*Kneeling.*]
Age is unnecessary. On my knees I beg
That you'll vouchsafe me raiment, bed, and food."

Reg. Good sir, no more; these are unsightly tricks.
Return you to my sister.

Lear. [*Rising.*] Never, Regan:
She hath abated me of half my train;
Look'd black upon me, strook me with her tongue,
Most serpent-like, upon the very heart.
All the stor'd vengeances of heaven fall

80. **pack**: be off.
84. **The knave . . . away.** Again, the Fool's true opinion; those who run away are the actual fools.
85. **perdie**: assuredly (a weakened oath, like French *pardieu*, originally "by God"). 89. **fetches**: deceptive excuses.
90. **images**: signs. **flying off.** Synonymous with *revolt*.
92. **quality**: nature. 95. **confusion**: destruction.
102. **tends**: attends, awaits. 106. **office**: duty.
107. **bound**: obligated.
110. **am . . . will**: chide my impetuous disposition.
111. **To take**: for taking. 112. **state**: royal power.
114. **remotion**: keeping apart, aloofness. 115. **practice**: trickery.
119. **cry . . . death**: make sleep impossible with the din.

122. **it**: i.e. your heart. **cockney**: city woman (ignorant of the ways of eels). 123. **knapp'd**: knocked.
124–25. **Down, wantons**: lie down, you lively creatures. The Fool implies that Lear's cry to his heart will be just as effectual.
132. **Sepulchring**: in the certainty that it sepulchred.
134. **naught**: wicked. 138. **take patience**: control yourself.
140. **scant.** Modern idiom would require *do* or *fulfill*.
148. **his confine**: its extreme limit.
153. **becomes the house**: befits family decorum.
155. **Age is unnecessary**: old people are useless.
160. **strook**: struck.

On her ingrateful top! Strike her young bones,
You taking airs, with lameness!
Corn. Fie, sir, fie!
Lear. You nimble lightnings, dart your blinding flames
Into her scornful eyes! Infect her beauty,
You fen-suck'd fogs, drawn by the pow'rful sun,
To fall and blister!
Reg. O the blest gods! so
Will you wish on me, when the rash mood is on.
Lear. No, Regan, thou shalt never have my curse.
Thy tender-hefted nature shall not give
Thee o'er to harshness. Her eyes are fierce, but thine
Do comfort, and not burn. 'Tis not in thee
To grudge my pleasures, to cut off my train,
To bandy hasty words, to scant my sizes,
And in conclusion to oppose the bolt
Against my coming in. Thou better know'st
The offices of nature, bond of childhood,
Effects of courtesy, dues of gratitude:
Thy half o' th' kingdom hast thou not forgot,
Wherein I thee endow'd.
Reg. Good sir, to th' purpose.
Lear. Who put my man i' th' stocks?
Tucket within.

Enter Steward [OSWALD].

Corn. What trumpet's that?
Reg. I know't, my sister's. This approves her letter,
That she would soon be here. [*To Oswald.*] Is your lady come?
Lear. This is a slave whose easy-borrowed pride
Dwells in the [fickle] grace of her he follows.
Out, varlet, from my sight!
Corn. What means your Grace?

Enter GONERIL.

Lear. Who stock'd my servant? Regan, I have good hope
Thou didst not know on't. Who comes here? O heavens!
If you do love old men, if your sweet sway
Allow obedience, if you yourselves are old,
Make it your cause; send down, and take my part.
[*To Goneril.*] Art not asham'd to look upon this beard?
O Regan, will you take her by the hand?
Gon. Why not by th' hand, sir? How have I offended?
All's not offense that indiscretion finds
And dotage terms so.
Lear. O sides, you are too tough!
Will you yet hold? How came my man i' th' stocks?

Corn. I set him there, sir; but his own disorders
Deserv'd much less advancement.
Lear. You? Did you?
Reg. I pray you, father, being weak, seem so.
If till the expiration of your month
You will return and sojourn with my sister,
Dismissing half your train, come then to me.
I am now from home, and out of that provision
Which shall be needful for your entertainment.
Lear. Return to her? and fifty men dismiss'd?
No, rather I abjure all roofs, and choose
To wage against the enmity o' th' air,
To be a comrade with the wolf and owl—
Necessity's sharp pinch. Return with her?
Why, the hot-bloodied France, that dowerless took
Our youngest born, I could as well be brought
To knee his throne, and squire-like, pension beg
To keep base life afoot. Return with her?
Persuade me rather to be slave and sumpter
To this detested groom. [*Pointing at Oswald.*]
Gon. At your choice, sir.
Lear. I prithee, daughter, do not make me mad.
I will not trouble thee, my child; farewell:
We'll no more meet, no more see one another.
But yet thou art my flesh, my blood, my daughter—
Or rather a disease that's in my flesh,
Which I must needs call mine. Thou art a bile,
A plague-sore, or embossed carbuncle,
In my corrupted blood. But I'll not chide thee,
Let shame come when it will, I do not call it.
I do not bid the thunder-bearer shoot,
Nor tell tales of thee to high-judging Jove.
Mend when thou canst, be better at thy leisure,
I can be patient, I can stay with Regan,
I and my hundred knights.
Reg. Not altogether so,
I look'd not for you yet, nor am provided
For your fit welcome. Give ear, sir, to my sister,
For those that mingle reason with your passion
Must be content to think you old, and so—
But she knows what she does.
Lear. Is this well spoken?
Reg. I dare avouch it, sir. What, fifty followers?
Is it not well? What should you need of more?
Yea, or so many? sith that both charge and danger
Speak 'gainst so great a number? How in one house
Should many people under two commands
Hold amity? 'Tis hard, almost impossible.
Gon. Why might not you, my lord, receive attendance
From those that she calls servants or from mine?
Reg. Why not, my lord? If then they chanc'd to slack ye,

163. top: head. **young bones.** It has been argued that the reference is to an unborn child of Goneril's. **164. taking:** infectious.
168. fall: strike.
171. tender-hefted: moved by a tender nature, lovingly inclined.
175. sizes: allowances. **176. oppose the bolt:** lock the door.
178. offices of nature: natural duties.
179. Effects of courtesy: courteous actions.
183. approves: confirms.
185. easy-borrowed: borrowed from his betters, without charge to himself. **191. Allow:** approve.

200. much less advancement: i.e. far worse treatment.
201. seem so: do not pretend to be otherwise.
209. wage: contend.
212. hot-bloodied: hot-blooded, choleric (cf. I.ii.23).
216. sumpter: pack-horse, drudge. **223. bile:** boil.
224. embossed: swollen, risen to a head. **226. call:** summon.
228. high-judging: judging from on high.
232. look'd not for: did not expect.
234. mingle . . . passion: bring reason to the consideration of your passion. **237. avouch:** vouch for. **239. charge:** expense.
245. slack: be negligent toward.

We could control them. If you will come to me
(For now I spy a danger), I entreat you
To bring but five and twenty; to no more
Will I give place or notice.
Lear. I gave you all—
Reg. And in good time you gave it.
Lear. Made you my guardians, my depositaries,
But kept a reservation to be followed
With such a number. What, must I come to you
With five and twenty? Regan, said you so?
Reg. And speak't again, my lord, no more with me.
Lear. Those wicked creatures yet do look well-favor'd
When others are more wicked; not being the worst
Stands in some rank of praise. [*To Goneril*.] I'll go with thee,
Thy fifty yet doth double five and twenty,
And thou art twice her love.
Gon. Hear me, my lord:
What need you five and twenty? ten? or five?
To follow in a house where twice so many
Have a command to tend you?
Reg. What need one?
Lear. O, reason not the need! our basest beggars
Are in the poorest thing superfluous.
Allow not nature more than nature needs,
Man's life is cheap as beast's. Thou art a lady;
If only to go warm were gorgeous,
Why, nature needs not what thou gorgeous wear'st,
Which scarcely keeps thee warm. But for true need—
You heavens, give me that patience, patience I need!
You see me here, you gods, a poor old man,
As full of grief as age, wretched in both.
If it be you that stirs these daughters' hearts
Against their father, fool me not so much
To bear it tamely; touch me with noble anger,
And let not women's weapons, water-drops,
Stain my man's cheeks! No, you unnatural hags,
I will have such revenges on you both
That all the world shall—I will do such things—
What they are yet I know not, but they shall be
The terrors of the earth! You think I'll weep:
No, I'll not weep.
I have full cause of weeping, but this heart

Storm and tempest.

Shall break into a hundred thousand flaws
Or ere I'll weep. O Fool, I shall go mad!

Exeunt [*Lear, Gloucester, Gentleman, and Fool*].

Corn. Let us withdraw, 'twill be a storm.
Reg. This house is little, the old man and 's people
Cannot be well bestow'd.
Gon. 'Tis his own blame hath put himself from rest,
And must needs taste his folly.

Reg. For his particular, I'll receive him gladly,
But not one follower.
Gon. So am I purpos'd.
Where is my Lord of Gloucester?
Corn. Followed the old man forth.

Enter Gloucester.

He is return'd.
Glou. The King is in high rage.
Corn. Whither is he going?
Glou. He calls to horse, but will I know not whither.
Corn. 'Tis best to give him way, he leads himself.
Gon. My lord, entreat him by no means to stay.
Glou. Alack, the night comes on, and the [bleak] winds
Do sorely ruffle; for many miles about
There's scarce a bush.
Reg. O sir, to willful men,
The injuries that they themselves procure
Must be their schoolmasters. Shut up your doors.
He is attended with a desperate train,
And what they may incense him to, being apt
To have his ear abus'd, wisdom bids fear.
Corn. Shut up your doors, my lord, 'tis a wild night,
My Regan counsels well. Come out o' th' storm.

Exeunt.

ACT III, Scene I

Storm still. Enter Kent [*disguised as Caius*] *and a* Gentleman *severally*.

Kent. Who's there, besides foul weather?
Gent. One minded like the weather, most unquietly.
Kent. I know you. Where's the King?
Gent. Contending with the fretful elements;
Bids the wind blow the earth into the sea,
Or swell the curled waters 'bove the main,
That things might change or cease, [tears his white hair,
Which the impetuous blasts with eyeless rage
Catch in their fury, and make nothing of,
Strives in his little world of man to outscorn
The to-and-fro-conflicting wind and rain.
This night, wherein the cub-drawn bear would couch,
The lion and the belly-pinched wolf
Keep their fur dry, unbonneted he runs,
And bids what will take all.]
Kent. But who is with him?
Gent. None but the Fool, who labors to outjest
His heart-strook injuries.

246. control: correct. **249. notice:** recognition.
251. my guardians, my depositaries: the protectors and trustees of my kingdom. **252. kept a reservation:** reserved the right.
265. Are . . . superfluous: have some wretched things they could manage without. **266. Allow not:** if you don't allow.
271. patience: endurance, fortitude.
275–76. fool . . . To: do not make me such a fool as to.
285. flaws: fragments. **286. Or ere:** before.
289. bestow'd: lodged.

292. For his particular: as far as he himself is concerned.
301. ruffle: bluster. **307. abus'd:** deceived.

III.i. Location: A heath near Gloucester's castle.
6. main: mainland.
9. make nothing of: handle irreverently.
10. little . . . man. Alluding to the idea of man as a microcosm, image of the macrocosm or universe.
12. cub-drawn: sucked dry, therefore hungry. **couch:** remain in her den. **16. outjest:** relieve by his jests.

Kent. Sir, I do know you,
And dare upon the warrant of my note
Commend a dear thing to you. There is division
(Although as yet the face of it is cover'd
With mutual cunning) 'twixt Albany and Cornwall;
Who have—as who have not, that their great stars
Thron'd and set high?—servants, who seem no less,
Which are to France the spies and speculations
Intelligent of our state. What hath been seen,
Either in snuffs and packings of the Dukes,
Or the hard rein which both of them hath borne
Against the old kind King; or something deeper,
Whereof (perchance) these are but furnishings—
[But true it is, from France there comes a power
Into this scattered kingdom, who already
Wise in our negligence, have secret feet
In some of our best ports, and are at point
To show their open banner. Now to you:
If on my credit you dare build so far
To make your speed to Dover, you shall find
Some that will thank you, making just report
Of how unnatural and bemadding sorrow
The King hath cause to plain.
I am a gentleman of blood and breeding,
And from some knowledge and assurance, offer
This office to you.]

Gent. I will talk further with you.

Kent. No, do not.
For confirmation that I am much more
Than my out-wall, open this purse and take
What it contains. If you shall see Cordelia
(As fear not but you shall), show her this ring,
And she will tell you who that fellow is
That yet you do not know. Fie on this storm!
I will go seek the King.

Gent. Give me your hand. Have you no more to say?

Kent. Few words, but to effect, more than all yet:
That when we have found the King—in which your pain
That way, I'll this—he that first lights on him
Holla the other. *Exeunt [severally].*

Scene II

Storm still. Enter Lear *and* Fool.

Lear. Blow, winds, and crack your cheeks! rage, blow!
You cataracts and hurricanoes, spout
Till you have drench'd our steeples, [drown'd] the cocks!
You sulph'rous and thought-executing fires,
Vaunt-couriers of oak-cleaving thunderbolts,
Singe my white head! And thou, all-shaking thunder,
Strike flat the thick rotundity o' th' world!
Crack nature's moulds, all germains spill at once
That makes ingrateful man!

Fool. O nuncle, court holy-water in a dry house is better than this rain-water out o' door. Good nuncle, in, ask thy daughters blessing. Here's a night pities neither wise men nor fools.

Lear. Rumble thy bellyful! Spit, fire! Spout, rain!
Nor rain, wind, thunder, fire are my daughters.
I tax not you, you elements, with unkindness;
I never gave you kingdom, call'd you children;
You owe me no subscription. Then let fall
Your horrible pleasure. Here I stand your slave,
A poor, infirm, weak, and despis'd old man;
But yet I call you servile ministers,
That will with two pernicious daughters join
Your high-engender'd battles 'gainst a head
So old and white as this. O, ho! 'tis foul.

Fool. He that has a house to put 's head in has a good head-piece.

The codpiece that will house
Before the head has any,
The head and he shall louse:
So beggars marry many.
The man that makes his toe
What he his heart should make,
Shall of a corn cry woe,
And turn his sleep to wake.

For there was never yet fair woman but she made mouths in a glass.

Enter Kent *[disguised as Caius].*

Lear. No, I will be the pattern of all patience,
I will say nothing.

Kent. Who's there?

Fool. Marry, here's grace and a codpiece—that's a wise man and a fool.

Kent. Alas, sir, are you here? Things that love night

18. note: observation, i.e. knowledge (of you).
19. Commend: entrust. **dear:** important.
23. no less: no other. **24. speculations:** secret observers.
25. Intelligent of: who furnish intelligence relating to.
26. snuffs: quarrels. **packings:** plots.
29. furnishings: superficial additions, i.e. pretexts.
30. power: army. **31. scattered:** divided.
32. Wise in: profiting by. **33. at point:** ready.
35. credit: trustworthiness. **39. plain:** complain of.
41. knowledge and assurance: assured knowledge.
45. out-wall: exterior. **48. fellow:** companion.
52. to effect: in importance. **53. pain:** effort, i.e. search.

III.ii. Location: The heath.
2. hurricanoes: waterspouts.
3. drench'd: drowned, submerged. **cocks:** weathercocks.
4. thought-executing: acting as quick as thought.
5. Vaunt-couriers: precursors. **oak-cleaving thunderbolts.** The damage caused by lightning was formerly thought to be due to a stone projectile discharged from the clouds during a storm.
8. germains: germens, seeds; the *semina* existing in nature from which all, including man, is created. **spill:** destroy.
10. court holy-water: flattery.
12. ask . . . blessing: ask a blessing of your daughters, i.e. submit to their authority (since the normal procedure would be for them to ask a blessing of him). **18. subscription:** submission, deference.
21. ministers: agents.
23. high-engender'd: bred in the heavens. **battles:** battalions, forces. **26. head-piece:** (1) head-covering; (2) brain.
27–30. The cod-piece . . . many: he who engages in sexual intercourse before he can afford to keep up a house ends in beggary.
31–34. The man . . . wake: he who cherishes his toe as he should cherish his heart (as Lear has favored Goneril and Regan rather than Cordelia) will be caused such suffering by his toe that he will be unable to sleep.
35–36. made . . . glass: practiced facial expressions in front of a mirror.
40. Marry: indeed (originally, the name of the Virgin Mary used as an oath).

Love not such nights as these. The wrathful skies
Gallow the very wanderers of the dark,
And make them keep their caves. Since I was man,
Such sheets of fire, such bursts of horrid thunder,
Such groans of roaring wind and rain, I never
Remember to have heard. Man's nature cannot carry
Th' affliction nor the fear.

Lear. Let the great gods,
That keep this dreadful pudder o'er our heads,
Find out their enemies now. Tremble, thou wretch
That hast within thee undivulged crimes
Unwhipt of justice! Hide thee, thou bloody hand;
Thou perjur'd, and thou simular of virtue
That art incestuous! Caitiff, to pieces shake,
That under covert and convenient seeming
Has practic'd on man's life! Close pent-up guilts,
Rive your concealing continents, and cry
These dreadful summoners grace. I am a man
More sinn'd against than sinning.

Kent. Alack, bare-headed?
Gracious my lord, hard by here is a hovel,
Some friendship will it lend you 'gainst the tempest.
Repose you there, while I to this hard house
(More harder than the stones whereof 'tis rais'd,
Which even but now, demanding after you,
Denied me to come in) return, and force
Their scanted courtesy.

Lear. My wits begin to turn.
Come on, my boy. How dost, my boy? Art cold?
I am cold myself. Where is this straw, my fellow?
The art of our necessities is strange
And can make vild things precious. Come, your hovel.
Poor Fool and knave, I have one part in my heart
That's sorry yet for thee.

Fool. [*Sings.*]
"He that has and a little tine wit—
With heigh-ho, the wind and the rain—
Must make content with his fortunes fit,
Though the rain it raineth every day."

Lear. True, boy. Come bring us to this hovel.
Exit [*with Kent*].

Fool. This is a brave night to cool a courtezan.
I'll speak a prophecy ere I go:
When priests are more in word than matter;
When brewers mar their malt with water;
When nobles are their tailors' tutors;

44. Gallow: terrify. **45. keep:** stay inside.
48. carry: hold out against. **49. affliction:** i.e. physical impact.
50. pudder: pother, turmoil. **54. simular:** dissembler.
55. Caitiff: wretch.
56. covert . . . seeming: i.e. a concealing pretense of virtue.
57. practic'd on: plotted against.
58. Rive: burst. **continents:** containers, bounds.
58–59. cry . . . grace: ask . . . for mercy.
61. hovel: shed for animals or for storing grain or tools.
65. demanding: inquiring (modifies *me* in the next line).
70. art: skill. **71. vild:** vile, worthless.
74. tine: tiny (a variant spelling).
81–94. When . . . feet. Lines 81–86 are "a satirical description of the present manners as future," with "its proper inference or deduction"; lines 87–94 are "a satirical description of future manners, which the corruption of the present would prevent from ever happening," with "its proper inference or deduction" (Warburton). In F1 lines 85–86 follow line 92. The whole is a parody of a pseudo-Chaucerian "Merlin's Prophecy."
83. nobles . . . tutors: i.e. pay so much attention to clothes that they can instruct their tailors.

No heretics burn'd, but wenches' suitors;
Then shall the realm of Albion
Come to great confusion.
When every case in law is right;
No squire in debt, nor no poor knight;
When slanders do not live in tongues;
Nor cutpurses come not to throngs;
When usurers tell their gold i' th' field,
And bawds and whores do churches build;
Then comes the time, who lives to see't,
That going shall be us'd with feet.
This prophecy Merlin shall make, for I live before his time. *Exit.*

Scene III

Enter Gloucester *and* Edmund [*with lights*].

Glou. Alack, alack, Edmund, I like not this unnatural dealing. When I desir'd their leave that I might pity him, they took from me the use of mine own house, charg'd me on pain of perpetual displeasure neither to speak of him, entreat for him, or any way sustain him.

Edm. Most savage and unnatural!

Glou. Go to; say you nothing. There is division between the Dukes, and a worse matter than that. I have receiv'd a letter this night—'tis dangerous to be spoken; I have lock'd the letter in my closet. These injuries the King now bears will be reveng'd home; there is part of a power already footed: we must incline to the King. I will look him and privily relieve him. Go you and maintain talk with the Duke, that my charity be not of him perceiv'd. If he ask for me, I am ill and gone to bed. If I die for['t] (as no less is threat'ned me), the King my old master must be reliev'd. There is strange things toward, Edmund, pray you be careful. *Exit.*

Edm. This courtesy, forbid thee, shall the Duke
Instantly know, and of that letter too.
This seems a fair deserving, and must draw me
That which my father loses: no less than all.
The younger rises when the old doth fall. *Exit.*

Scene IV

Enter Lear, Kent [*disguised as Caius*], *and* Fool.

Kent. Here is the place, my lord; good my lord, enter,
The tyranny of the open night's too rough
For nature to endure. *Storm still.*

Lear. Let me alone.

84. burn'd. The suitors are "burned" by venereal disease.
87. right: just. **91. tell . . . field:** count their money openly.
92. churches build: endow churches (as penance for their sins).
94. going . . . feet: walking will be done on foot.

III.iii. Location: Gloucester's castle.
3. pity: i.e. aid, relieve. **12. home:** fully. **13. footed:** landed.
14. incline to: side with. **look:** seek.
21. forbid: which is forbidden.
23. fair deserving: action to make me deserving of reward.

III.iv. Location: The heath. Before a hovel.

Kent. Good my lord, enter here.
Lear. Wilt break my heart?
Kent. I had rather break mine own. Good my lord, enter.
Lear. Thou think'st 'tis much that this contentious storm
Invades us to the skin; so 'tis to thee;
But where the greater malady is fix'd,
The lesser is scarce felt. Thou'dst shun a bear,
But if [thy] flight lay toward the roaring sea,
Thou'dst meet the bear i' th' mouth. When the mind's free,
The body's delicate; [this] tempest in my mind
Doth from my senses take all feeling else,
Save what beats there—filial ingratitude!
Is it not as this mouth should tear this hand
For lifting food to't? But I will punish home.
No, I will weep no more. In such a night
To shut me out? Pour on, I will endure.
In such a night as this? O Regan, Goneril!
Your old kind father, whose frank heart gave all—
O, that way madness lies, let me shun that!
No more of that.
Kent. Good my lord, enter here.
Lear. Prithee go in thyself, seek thine own ease.
This tempest will not give me leave to ponder
On things would hurt me more. But I'll go in.
[*To the Fool.*] In, boy, go first.—You houseless poverty—
Nay, get thee in; I'll pray, and then I'll sleep.
Exit [*Fool*].
Poor naked wretches, wheresoe'er you are,
That bide the pelting of this pitiless storm,
How shall your houseless heads and unfed sides,
Your [loop'd] and window'd raggedness, defend you
From seasons such as these? O, I have ta'en
Too little care of this! Take physic, pomp,
Expose thyself to feel what wretches feel,
That thou mayst shake the superflux to them,
And show the heavens more just.

Edg. [*Within.*] Fathom and half, fathom and half! Poor Tom!

[*Enter*] *Fool* [*from the hovel*].

Fool. Come not in here, nuncle, here's a spirit. Help me, help me!

Kent. Give me thy hand. Who's there?

Fool. A spirit, a spirit! he says his name's poor Tom.

Kent. What art thou that dost grumble there i' th' straw? Come forth.

Enter EDGAR [*disguised as a madman*].

Edg. Away, the foul fiend follows me! Through the sharp hawthorn blow the [cold] winds. Humh, go to thy bed and warm thee.

Lear. Didst thou give all to thy daughters? And art thou come to this?

Edg. Who gives any thing to poor Tom? whom the foul fiend hath led through fire and through flame, through [ford] and whirlpool, o'er bog and quagmire; that hath laid knives under his pillow, and halters in his pew, set ratsbane by his porridge, made him proud of heart, to ride on a bay trotting-horse over four-inch'd bridges, to course his own shadow for a traitor. Bless thy five wits! Tom's a-cold—O do de, do de, do de. Bless thee from whirlwinds, star-blasting, and taking! Do poor Tom some charity, whom the foul fiend vexes. There could I have him now—and there—and there again—and there. *Storm still.*

Lear. Has his daughters brought him to this pass? Couldst thou save nothing? Wouldst thou give 'em all?

Fool. Nay, he reserv'd a blanket, else we had been all sham'd.

Lear. Now all the plagues that in the pendulous air
Hang fated o'er men's faults light on thy daughters!
Kent. He hath no daughters, sir.
Lear. Death, traitor! nothing could have subdu'd nature
To such a lowness but his unkind daughters.
Is it the fashion, that discarded fathers
Should have thus little mercy on their flesh?
Judicious punishment! 'twas this flesh begot
Those pelican daughters.

Edg. Pillicock sat on Pillicock-Hill, alow! alow, loo, loo!

Fool. This cold night will turn us all to fools and madmen.

Edg. Take heed o' th' foul fiend. Obey thy parents, keep thy word's justice, swear not, commit not with man's sworn spouse, set not thy sweet heart on proud array. Tom's a-cold.

Lear. What hast thou been?

Edg. A servingman! proud in heart and mind; that curl'd my hair; wore gloves in my cap; serv'd the lust of my mistress' heart, and did the act of darkness with her; swore as many oaths as I spake words, and broke them in the sweet face of heaven: one that slept in the contriving of lust, and wak'd to do it. Wine lov'd I [deeply], dice dearly; and in woman out-paramour'd

4. **break my heart:** i.e. by freeing my mind for thought.
8. **fix'd:** entrenched, deep-rooted. 11. **free:** at ease.
12. **delicate:** sensitive. 14. **there:** i.e. in my mind.
15. **as:** as if. 20. **frank:** generous. 29. **bide:** endure.
31. **loop'd:** full of holes (synonymous with *window'd*).
33. **pomp:** i.e. men who live in splendor.
35. **superflux:** superfluity, wealth above one's needs.
37. **Fathom and half.** Sailor's cry. The hovel is shipping water.
46. **Away:** keep away. **follows:** attends (cf. line 140).
46–47. **Through . . . winds.** Possibly a ballad fragment. It reappears in "The Friar of Orders Grey," an eighteenth-century pastiche. **Humh.** Perhaps he imitates the sound of the wind.
54–55. **knives, halters, ratsbane.** Inducements to suicide and so to damnation. 55. **porridge:** soup.
57. **four-inch'd:** i.e. very narrow. Such riding would require diabolic help. **course:** hunt.
59. **star-blasting:** malign astrological influence.
60. **taking:** being bewitched (?) or pestilence (?).
61–62. **There . . . there.** He slaps vermin on his body.
67. **pendulous:** overhanging. 68. **fated:** as agencies of fate.
74. **Judicious:** befitting the offense.
75. **pelican.** The young pelican was believed to feed upon its mother's blood.
76. **Pillicock . . . Pillicock-Hill.** Perhaps from some song or rhyme, but in any case suggested by the phonetic similarity of *pelican* and *Pillicock*, which would commend itself to a madman.
80–83. **Obey . . array.** Apparently poor Tom's recollection of the Ten Commandments. *Justice* = integrity.
86. **gloves.** As favors from his mistress.
91–92. **out-paramour'd the Turk:** had more mistresses than the Sultan.

the Turk. False of heart, light of ear, bloody of hand; hog in sloth, fox in stealth, wolf in greediness, dog in madness, lion in prey. Let not the creaking of shoes nor the rustling of silks betray thy poor heart to woman. Keep thy foot out of brothels, thy hand out of plackets, thy pen from lenders' books, and defy the foul fiend. Still through the hawthorn blows the cold wind: says suum, mun, nonny. Dolphin my boy, boy, sessa! let him trot by. *Storm still.*

Lear. Thou wert better in a grave than to answer with thy uncover'd body this extremity of the skies. Is man no more than this? Consider him well. Thou ow'st the worm no silk, the beast no hide, the sheep no wool, the cat no perfume. Ha? here's three on 's are sophisticated. Thou art the thing itself: unaccommodated man is no more but such a poor, bare, fork'd animal as thou art. Off, off, you lendings! Come, unbutton here. [*Tearing off his clothes.*]

Fool. Prithee, nuncle, be contented, 'tis a naughty night to swim in. Now a little fire in a wild field were like an old lecher's heart, a small spark, all the rest on 's body cold.

Enter GLOUCESTER *with a torch.*

Look, here comes a walking fire.

Edg. This is the foul [fiend] Flibbertigibbet; he begins at curfew, and walks [till the] first cock; he gives the web and the pin, [squinies] the eye, and makes the hare-lip; mildews the white wheat, and hurts the poor creature of earth.

Swithold footed thrice the 'old,
He met the night-mare and her nine-fold;
Bid her alight,
And her troth plight,
And aroint thee, witch, aroint thee!

Kent. How fares your Grace?
Lear. What's he?
Kent. Who's there? What is't you seek?
Glou. What are you there? Your names?

Edg. Poor Tom, that eats the swimming frog, the toad, the todpole, the wall-newt, and the water; that in the fury of his heart, when the foul fiend rages, eats cow-dung for sallets; swallows the old rat and the ditch-dog; drinks the green mantle of the standing pool; who is whipt from tithing to tithing, and [stock-]punish'd and imprison'd; who hath [had] three suits to his back, six shirts to his body—

Horse to ride, and weapon to wear;
But mice and rats, and such small deer,
Have been Tom's food for seven long year.

Beware my follower. Peace, Smulkin, peace, thou fiend!

Glou. What, hath your Grace no better company?

Edg. The prince of darkness is a gentleman. Modo he's call'd, and Mahu.

Glou. Our flesh and blood, my lord, is grown so vild
That it doth hate what gets it.
Edg. Poor Tom's a-cold.
Glou. Go in with me; my duty cannot suffer
T' obey in all your daughters' hard commands.
Though their injunction be to bar my doors,
And let this tyrannous night take hold upon you,
Yet have I ventured to come seek you out,
And bring you where both fire and food is ready.
Lear. First let me talk with this philosopher.
What is the cause of thunder?
Kent. Good my lord, take his offer, go into th' house.
Lear. I'll talk a word with this same learned Theban.
What is your study?
Edg. How to prevent the fiend, and to kill vermin.
Lear. Let me ask you one word in private.
Kent. Importune him once more to go, my lord,
His wits begin t' unsettle.
Glou. Canst thou blame him? *Storm still.*
His daughters seek his death. Ah, that good Kent!
He said it would be thus, poor banish'd man.
Thou sayest the King grows mad, I'll tell thee, friend,
I am almost mad myself. I had a son,
Now outlaw'd from my blood; he sought my life,
But lately, very late. I lov'd him, friend,
No father his son dearer; true to tell thee,
The grief hath craz'd my wits. What a night's this!
I do beseech your Grace—
Lear. O, cry you mercy, sir.
Noble philosopher, your company.
Edg. Tom's a-cold.

92. light of ear: credulous (of evil) (?) or attentive to levity and falsehood (?). **94. prey:** preying.
97. plackets: openings in petticoats. **lenders' books:** money-lenders' account-books (in which borrowers signed statements of their debts).
99. Dolphin my boy, boy. Perhaps another quotation (which possibly should extend to the end of the sentence).
100. sessa. Unexplained; perhaps equivalent to "let it (him, them) go." Cf. III.vi.74, where it follows a reference to dogs running, and *The Taming of the Shrew*, Ind.i.6, where it follows the words "let the world slide." **102. extremity:** extreme violence.
105. cat: civet cat. **on 's:** of us.
106. sophisticated: adulterated.
106–7. unaccommodated: unfurnished, without additions.
108. lendings: i.e. garments, borrowed from animals.
110–11. be . . . swim in: i.e. don't take off your clothes; it's a very bad night to go swimming.
111. wild: uncultivated, barren. **113. on 's:** of his.
115. Flibbertigibbet. A devil's name (from Harsnett).
116. curfew: 9 p.m. **first cock:** midnight.
117. web . . . pin: cataract. **squinies:** causes to squint.
118. white: i.e. ripe.
120. Swithold: St. Withold, who protects suppliants from disaster. **footed:** walked over. **'old:** wold, upland plain.
121. night-mare: demon thought to afflict people while they slept. **nine-fold:** nine offspring (?).
122. alight: i.e. leave the person she was afflicting (?).
123. her troth plight: i.e. promise to do no harm.
124. aroint thee: begone.

130. todpole: tadpole. **water:** i.e. water-newt.
132. sallets: salads, savories.
133. mantle: scum. **standing:** stagnant. **134. tithing:** district.
138. deer: animals. (Lines 137–39 are adapted from the romance *Bevis of Hampton.*)
140. follower: attendant devil. **Smulkin.** The name comes from Harsnett, like *Modo* and *Mahu* in lines 143, 144.
146. gets: begets.
148. my . . . suffer: i.e. as a dutiful subject I cannot endure.
154. philosopher: natural philosopher, scientist. Lear's appropriate question is of the type answered in contemporary encyclopedias.
157. Theban: i.e. scholar.
158. study: special field of knowledge. Edgar quibbles on the sense "preoccupation."
159. prevent the fiend: thwart the devil, i.e. avoid damnation.
171. cry you mercy: I beg your pardon.

Glou. In, fellow, there, into th' hovel; keep thee
warm.

Lear. Come, let's in all.

Kent. This way, my lord.

Lear. With him;
I will keep still with my philosopher.

Kent. Good my lord, soothe him; let him take the
fellow.

Glou. Take him you on.

Kent. Sirrah, come on; go along with us.

Lear. Come, good Athenian.

Glou. No words, no words, hush.

Edg. Child Rowland to the dark tower came,
His word was still, "Fie, foh, and fum,
I smell the blood of a British man."

Exeunt.

Scene V

Enter Cornwall *and* Edmund.

Corn. I will have my revenge ere I depart his house.

Edm. How, my lord, I may be censur'd, that nature thus gives way to loyalty, something fears me to think of.

Corn. I now perceive, it was not altogether your brother's evil disposition made him seek his death; but a provoking merit, set a-work by a reprovable badness in himself.

Edm. How malicious is my fortune, that I must repent to be just! This is the letter which he spoke of, which approves him an intelligent party to the advantages of France. O heavens! that this treason were not; or not I the detector!

Corn. Go with me to the Duchess.

Edm. If the matter of this paper be certain, you have mighty business in hand.

Corn. True or false, it hath made thee Earl of Gloucester. Seek out where thy father is, that he may be ready for our apprehension.

Edm. [*Aside.*] If I find him comforting the King, it will stuff his suspicion more fully.—I will persever in my course of loyalty, though the conflict be sore between that and my blood.

Corn. I will lay trust upon thee; and thou shalt find a [dearer] father in my love. *Exeunt.*

176. will . . . with: refuse to be separated from.
177. soothe: humor. **180. Athenian:** i.e. philosopher.
182. Child . . . came. Perhaps from some lost ballad dealing with Roland, hero of the French *Chanson de Roland*. *Child* means an aspirant to knighthood.
183. word: watchword. **still:** always.
183–84. Fie . . . man. Traditional, with *English* for *British*.

III.v. Location: Gloucester's castle.
2. censur'd: judged.
3. something fears: somewhat frightens.
6. his: i.e. Gloucester's.
7–8. a provoking . . . himself: i.e. a deserving (on Gloucester's part) to be killed, which provoked Edgar to plot his father's death, though he was also moved by an evil propensity in himself which must be condemned.
11. approves: proves. **intelligent . . . to: informed . . . of (?) or supplying information . . . for (?). party:** partisan.
19. ready . . . apprehension: available for arrest.
20. comforting: helping.
21. his suspicion: suspicion of him.

Scene VI

Enter Kent [*disguised as Caius*] *and* Gloucester.

Glou. Here is better than the open air, take it thankfully. I will piece out the comfort with what addition I can. I will not be long from you.

Kent. All the pow'r of his wits have given way to his impatience. The gods reward your kindness!

Exit [*Gloucester*].

Enter Lear, Edgar, *and* Fool.

Edg. Frateretto calls me, and tells me Nero is an angler in the lake of darkness. Pray, innocent, and beware the foul fiend.

Fool. Prithee, nuncle, tell me whether a madman be a gentleman or a yeoman?

Lear. A king, a king!

Fool. No, he's a yeoman that has a gentleman to his son; for he's a mad yeoman that sees his son a gentleman before him.

Lear. To have a thousand with red burning spits
Come hizzing in upon 'em—

[*Edg.* The foul fiend bites my back.

Fool. He's mad that trusts in the tameness of a wolf, a horse's health, a boy's love, or a whore's oath.

Lear. It shall be done, I will arraign them straight.
[*To Edgar.*] Come sit thou here, most learned
[justicer];
[*To the Fool.*] Thou, sapient sir, sit here. [Now], you
she-foxes—

Edg. Look where he stands and glares! Want'st thou eyes at trial, madam? [*Sings.*]
"Come o'er the [bourn], Bessy, to me"—

Fool. [*Sings.*]
Her boat hath a leak,
And she must not speak
Why she dares not come over to thee.

Edg. The foul fiend haunts poor Tom in the voice of a nightingale. Hoppedance cries in Tom's belly for two white herring. Croak not, black angel, I have no food for thee.

Kent. How do you, sir? Stand you not so amaz'd. Will you lie down and rest upon the cushions?

Lear. I'll see their trial first, bring in their evidence.
[*To Edgar.*] Thou robed man of justice, take thy
place,
[*To the Fool.*] And thou, his yoke-fellow of equity,

III.vi. Location: An outbuilding of Gloucester's castle.
2. piece: eke.
5. impatience: inability to endure more.
6. Frateretto. Another Harsnett devil.
6–7. Nero . . . angler. A legend from Chaucer's "Monk's Tale," lines 485–86, suggested by passages in Harsnett immediately following his mention of Frateretto.
7. innocent. He addresses the Fool.
23. he: i.e. the fiend that Edgar pretends to see.
24. eyes at trial: spectators at your trial.
25. Come . . . me. A line from an old song. Lines 26–28 are the Fool's own indecent addition. **bourn:** burn, brook.
30. Hoppedance. Harsnett has *Hoberdidance*. His cries are the rumbling of Tom's empty stomach.
31. white: fresh, unsmoked (with following play on *black* = smoked, i.e. blackened by the smoke of hell). **33. amaz'd:** bewildered.
35. their evidence: the witnesses against them.
36. robed. Referring to Tom's blanket.

Bench by his side. [*To Kent.*] You are o' th' commission,
Sit you too.

Edg. Let us deal justly. [*Sings.*]
Sleepest or wakest thou, jolly shepherd?
Thy sheep be in the corn,
And for one blast of thy minikin mouth,
Thy sheep shall take no harm.
Purr the cat is grey.

Lear. Arraign her first, 'tis Goneril. I here take my oath before this honorable assembly, [she] kick'd the poor king her father.

Fool. Come hither, mistress. Is your name Goneril?

Lear. She cannot deny it.

Fool. Cry you mercy, I took you for a join-stool.

Lear. And here's another, whose warp'd looks proclaim
What store her heart is made an. Stop her there!
Arms, arms, sword, fire! Corruption in the place!
False justicer, why hast thou let her scape?]

Edg. Bless thy five wits!

Kent. O pity! Sir, where is the patience now
That you so oft have boasted to retain?

Edg. [*Aside.*] My tears begin to take his part so much,
They mar my counterfeiting.

Lear. The little dogs and all,
Trey, Blanch, and Sweetheart, see, they bark at me.

Edg. Tom will throw his head at them. Avaunt, you curs!
Be thy mouth or black or white,
Tooth that poisons if it bite;
Mastiff, greyhound, mongril grim,
Hound or spaniel, brach or [lym],
Or bobtail [tike] or trundle-tail,
Tom will make him weep and wail,
For with throwing thus my head,
Dogs leapt the hatch, and all are fled.
Do de, de, de. Sessa! Come, march to wakes and fairs and market towns. Poor Tom, thy horn is dry.

Lear. Then let them anatomize Regan; see what breeds about her heart. Is there any cause in nature that make these hard hearts? [*To Edgar.*] You, sir, I

38. o' th' commission: appointed one of the judges.
41–44. Sleepest . . . harm. If this is a quoted stanza, its source has not been found. **42. corn:** wheatfield.
43–44. And . . . harm: if you call back your sheep we will let them off without putting them in the pound (?) or we will consider a song from you compensation for the damage done by the sheep (?).
43. blast: blowing, strain. **minikin:** dainty.
45. Purr the cat. A devil in Harsnett; witches' familiars often took the form of cats.
52. join-stool: joint-stool, stool expertly made by a joiner. The Fool's words are a jocular formula of apology for overlooking the presence of a person. **54. store:** material. **an:** on (=of)
55. Corruption . . . place: bribery in the court.
64. throw . . . them: stare them down (?).
68. mongril: mongrel. **69. lym:** bloodhound.
70. bobtail tike: short-tailed cur. **trundle-tail:** long-tailed dog.
73. hatch: lower half of a divided or "Dutch" door.
74. wakes: parish merrymakings.
75. thy . . . dry. Beggars carried animal horns to hold drink given as alms. Edgar is repeating a begging formula; perhaps he is also implying that he cannot maintain his impersonation much longer.
76. anatomize: dissect.

entertain for one of my hundred; only I do not like the fashion of your garments. You will say they are Persian, but let them be chang'd.

Kent. Now, good my lord, lie here and rest awhile.

Lear. Make no noise, make no noise, draw the curtains. So, so; we'll go to supper i' th' morning.

Fool. And I'll go to bed at noon.

Enter GLOUCESTER.

Glou. Come hither, friend; where is the King my master?

Kent. Here, sir, but trouble him not—his wits are gone.

Glou. Good friend, I prithee take him in thy arms;
I have o'erheard a plot of death upon him.
There is a litter ready, lay him in't,
And drive toward Dover, friend, where thou shalt meet
Both welcome and protection. Take up thy master;
If thou shouldst dally half an hour, his life,
With thine and all that offer to defend him,
Stand in assured loss. Take up, take up,
And follow me, that will to some provision
Give thee quick conduct.

[*Kent.* Oppressed nature sleeps.
This rest might yet have balm'd thy broken sinews,
Which, if convenience will not allow,
Stand in hard cure. [*To the Fool.*] Come help to bear thy master;
Thou must not stay behind.]

[*Glou.*] Come, come, away.

Exeunt [*all but Edgar*].

[*Edg.* When we our betters see bearing our woes,
We scarcely think our miseries our foes.
Who alone suffers, suffers most i' th' mind,
Leaving free things and happy shows behind,
But then the mind much sufferance doth o'erskip,
When grief hath mates, and bearing fellowship.
How light and portable my pain seems now,
When that which makes me bend makes the King bow:
He childed as I fathered! Tom, away!
Mark the high noises, and thyself bewray
When false opinion, whose wrong thoughts defile thee,
In thy just proof repeals and reconciles thee.
What will hap more to-night, safe scape the King!
Lurk, lurk.] [*Exit.*]

79. entertain: engage.
80–81. You . . . Persian: you will tell me that they are the fashion in Persia (where dress was reputed to be elaborate). Perhaps there is an echo of Horace's famous line, *Odes*, i.38: *Persicos odi, puer, apparatus* (My boy, I detest Persian pomp).
84. curtains: bed-curtains. Lear supposes he is in his usual bed.
85. I'll . . . noon: i.e. I'll play the fool (proverbial).
89. upon: against.
95. Stand . . . loss: will certainly be lost.
98. balm'd: soothed, healed. **sinews:** nerves (serving the brain).
100. Stand . . . cure: will be hard to cure.
102. bearing our woes: suffering woes like ours.
103. We . . . foes: i.e. we almost forget our own misery.
104. suffers . . . mind: has the greatest mental suffering.
105. free: carefree.
107. bearing fellowship: suffering (has) company.
111. high noises: rumors of great events. **bewray:** disclose.
113. In . . . proof: upon your being proved guiltless. **repeals:** recalls. **reconciles thee:** restores you to favor.
114. What: whatever.

Scene VII

Enter Cornwall, Regan, Goneril, *Bastard* [Edmund], *and* Servants.

Corn. [*To Goneril.*] Post speedily to my lord your husband, show him this letter. The army of France is landed.—Seek out the traitor Gloucester.

[*Exeunt some of the Servants.*]

Reg. Hang him instantly.
Gon. Pluck out his eyes.
Corn. Leave him to my displeasure. Edmund, keep you our sister company; the revenges we are bound to take upon your traitorous father are not fit for your beholding. Advise the Duke, where you are going, to a most [festinate] preparation; we are bound to the like. Our posts shall be swift and intelligent betwixt us. Farewell, dear sister, farewell, my Lord of Gloucester.

Enter Steward [Oswald].

How now? where's the King?
Osw. My Lord of Gloucester hath convey'd him hence.
Some five or six and thirty of his knights,
Hot questrists after him, met him at gate,
Who, with some other of the lord's dependants,
Are gone with him toward Dover, where they boast
To have well-armed friends.
Corn. Get horses for your mistress.
Gon. Farewell, sweet lord, and sister.
Corn. Edmund, farewell.

Exeunt [*Goneril, Edmund, and Oswald*].

Go seek the traitor Gloucester,
Pinion him like a thief, bring him before us.

[*Exeunt other Servants.*]

Though well we may not pass upon his life
Without the form of justice, yet our power
Shall do a court'sy to our wrath, which men
May blame, but not control.

Enter Gloucester [*brought in by two or three*] Servants.

Who's there? The traitor?
Reg. Ingrateful fox, 'tis he.
Corn. Bind fast his corky arms.
Glou. What means your Graces? Good my friends, consider
You are my guests. Do me no foul play, friends.
Corn. Bind him, I say. [*Servants bind him.*]
Reg. Hard, hard. O filthy traitor!
Glou. Unmerciful lady as you are, I'm none.
Corn. To this chair bind him. Villain, thou shalt find— [*Regan plucks his beard.*]
Glou. By the kind gods, 'tis most ignobly done
To pluck me by the beard.

Reg. So white, and such a traitor?
Glou. Naughty lady,
These hairs which thou dost ravish from my chin
Will quicken and accuse thee. I am your host,
With robber's hands my hospitable favors
You should not ruffle thus. What will you do?
Corn. Come, sir, what letters had you late from France?
Reg. Be simple-answer'd, for we know the truth.
Corn. And what confederacy have you with the traitors
Late footed in the kingdom?
Reg. To whose hands you have sent the lunatic King—
Speak.
Glou. I have a letter guessingly set down,
Which came from one that's of a neutral heart,
And not from one oppos'd.
Corn. Cunning.
Reg. And false.
Corn. Where hast thou sent the King?
Glou. To Dover.
Reg. Wherefore to Dover? Wast thou not charg'd at peril—
Corn. Wherefore to Dover? Let him answer that.
Glou. I am tied to th' stake, and I must stand the course.
Reg. Wherefore to Dover?
Glou. Because I would not see thy cruel nails
Pluck out his poor old eyes, nor thy fierce sister
In his anointed flesh [rash] boarish fangs.
The sea, with such a storm as his bare head
In hell-black night endur'd, would have buoy'd up
And quench'd the stelled fires;
Yet, poor old heart, he holp the heavens to rain.
If wolves had at thy gate howl'd that [dearn] time,
Thou shouldst have said, "Good porter, turn the key."
All cruels else subscribe; but I shall see
The winged vengeance overtake such children.
Corn. See't shalt thou never. Fellows, hold the chair,
Upon these eyes of thine I'll set my foot.
Glou. He that will think to live till he be old,
Give me some help! O cruel! O you gods!
Reg. One side will mock another; th' other too.
Corn. If you see vengeance—
[*1.*] *Serv.* Hold your hand, my lord!
I have serv'd you ever since I was a child;
But better service have I never done you
Than now to bid you hold.
Reg. How now, you dog?

III.vii. Location: Gloucester's castle.
7. **bound:** required.
10. **festinate:** speedy. **are bound to:** intend (?) or are committed to (?). 11. **be . . . intelligent:** carry information swiftly.
17. **questrists:** seekers. 24. **pass . . . life:** sentence him to death.
26. **do a court'sy:** be indulgent, make a concession.
29. **corky:** withered.
34. s.d. **plucks his beard.** An act of extreme contempt.

37. **Naughty:** wicked. 39. **quicken:** assume life.
40. **hospitable favors:** features of your host.
41. **ruffle:** snatch at roughly. 42. **late:** lately.
43. **Be simple-answer'd:** give straightforward answers.
54. **course:** attack of the dogs (figure from bear-baiting).
58. **anointed:** consecrated with holy oil (as king). **rash:** strike violently, as a boar with his tusks. 60. **buoy'd:** risen up.
61. **stelled fires:** fires of the stars. 62. **holp:** helped.
63. **dearn:** dire, dread.
64. **turn the key:** i.e. open the door and let them in.
65. **All . . . subscribe:** all other cruel beings would yield thus to pity (though you do not).
66. **winged:** (1) swooping down from heaven; (2) swift.
69. **will think:** hopes.

[1.] Serv. If you did wear a beard upon your chin,
I'ld shake it on this quarrel. What do you mean?
Corn. My villain! [*Draw and fight.*]
[1.] Serv. Nay then come on, and take the chance of anger. [*Cornwall is wounded.*]
Reg. Give me thy sword. A peasant stand up thus?
[*She takes a sword and runs at him behind;*] *kills him.*
[1.] Serv. O, I am slain! My lord, you have one eye left
To see some mischief on him. O! [*He dies.*]
Corn. Lest it see more, prevent it. Out, vild jelly!
Where is thy lustre now?
Glou. All dark and comfortless! Where's my son Edmund?
Edmund, enkindle all the sparks of nature,
To quit this horrid act.
Reg. Out, treacherous villain!
Thou call'st on him that hates thee. It was he
That made the overture of thy treasons to us,
Who is too good to pity thee.
Glou. O my follies! then Edgar was abus'd.
Kind gods, forgive me that, and prosper him!
Reg. Go thrust him out at gates, and let him smell
His way to Dover. *Exit [one] with Gloucester.*
How is't, my lord? How look you?
Corn. I have receiv'd a hurt; follow me, lady.—
Turn out that eyeless villain; throw this slave
Upon the dunghill. Regan, I bleed apace,
Untimely comes this hurt. Give me your arm.
Exit [led by Regan].
[[2.] Serv. I'll never care what wickedness I do,
If this man come to good.
[3.] Serv. If she live long,
And in the end meet the old course of death,
Women will all turn monsters.
[2.] Serv. Let's follow the old Earl, and get the Bedlam
To lead him where he would; his roguish madness
Allows itself to any thing.
[3.] Serv. Go thou. I'll fetch some flax and whites of eggs
To apply to his bleeding face. Now heaven help him!
Exeunt [severally].]

ACT IV, Scene I

Enter Edgar.

Edg. Yet better thus, and known to be contemn'd,
Than still contemn'd and flatter'd. To be worst,
The lowest and most dejected thing of fortune,
Stands still in esperance, lives not in fear.
The lamentable change is from the best,
The worst returns to laughter. Welcome then,
Thou unsubstantial air that I embrace:
The wretch that thou hast blown unto the worst
Owes nothing to thy blasts.

Enter Gloucester *[led by] an* Old Man.

But who comes here?
My father, [parti-ey'd]? World, world, O world!
But that thy strange mutations make us hate thee,
Life would not yield to age.
Old Man. O my good lord,
I have been your tenant, and your father's tenant,
These fourscore years.
Glou. Away, get thee away! Good friend, be gone,
Thy comforts can do me no good at all;
Thee they may hurt.
Old Man. You cannot see your way.
Glou. I have no way, and therefore want no eyes;
I stumbled when I saw. Full oft 'tis seen,
Our means secure us, and our mere defects
Prove our commodities. O dear son Edgar,
The food of thy abused father's wrath!
Might I but live to see thee in my touch,
I'ld say I had eyes again.
Old Man. How now? who's there?
Edg. [*Aside.*] O gods! Who is't can say, "I am at the worst"?
I am worse than e'er I was.
Old Man. 'Tis poor mad Tom.
Edg. [*Aside.*] And worse I may be yet: the worst is not
So long as we can say, "This is the worst."
Old Man. Fellow, where goest?
Glou. Is it a beggar-man?
Old Man. Madman and beggar too.
Glou. He has some reason, else he could not beg.
I' th' last night's storm I such a fellow saw,
Which made me think a man a worm. My son
Came then into my mind, and yet my mind
Was then scarce friends with him. I have heard more since.
As flies to wanton boys are we to th' gods,
They kill us for their sport.
Edg. [*Aside.*] How should this be?
Bad is the trade that must play fool to sorrow,
Ang'ring itself and others.—Bless thee, master!
Glou. Is that the naked fellow?

77. on this quarrel: in this cause. **What . . . mean:** how dare you. Many editors give this sentence to Regan. **78. villain:** serf.
82. mischief: injury. **86. nature:** filial feeling.
87. quit: requite. **Out:** an exclamation of anger.
89. overture: disclosure. **91. abus'd:** wronged.
94. How look you: how is it with you.
101. old: usual, natural.
102. Women . . . monsters. Because they will not fear divine punishment for crimes.
104–5. his . . . thing: the fact that he is a madman and a vagabond allows him to do anything with impunity.

IV.i. Location: The heath.
1. known . . . contemn'd: to know that one is despised.
3. most . . . fortune: thing most cast down by fortune.
4. Stands . . . esperance: can always hope.
6. The worst . . . laughter: i.e. any change from the worst must be for the better.
9. Owes nothing: cannot be called on to pay anything more.
10. parti-ey'd: with his eyes "motley" or parti-colored, i.e. bleeding. (On this reading see the Textual Notes. Most editors read *poorly led.*)
11–12. But . . . age: if the strange changes of fortune didn't make us hate life, we should never be reconciled to old age and death.
16. comforts: attempts to help me.
20. Our . . . us: prosperity makes us careless.
20–21. our . . . commodities: our utter disadvantages prove benefits.
22. food of: object fed upon by. **abused:** deceived.
23. in: by means of. **36. wanton:** playful.
39. Ang'ring: distressing.

Old Man. Ay, my lord.
Glou. [Then prithee] get thee away. If for my sake
Thou wilt o'ertake us hence a mile or twain
I' th' way toward Dover, do it for ancient love,
And bring some covering for this naked soul,
Which I'll entreat to lead me.
Old Man. Alack, sir, he is mad.
Glou. 'Tis the time's plague, when madmen lead the blind.
Do as I bid thee, or rather do thy pleasure;
Above the rest, be gone.
Old Man. I'll bring him the best 'parel that I have,
Come on't what will. *Exit.*
Glou. Sirrah, naked fellow—
Edg. Poor Tom's a-cold. [*Aside.*] I cannot daub it further.
Glou. Come hither, fellow.
Edg. [*Aside.*] And yet I must.—Bless thy sweet eyes, they bleed.
Glou. Know'st thou the way to Dover?
Edg. Both stile and gate, horse-way and foot-path. Poor Tom hath been scar'd out of his good wits. Bless thee, good man's son, from the foul fiend! [Five fiends have been in poor Tom at once: of lust, as Obidicut; Hobbididence, prince of dumbness; Mahu, of stealing; Modo, of murder; Flibbertigibbet, of [mopping] and mowing, who since possesses chambermaids and waiting-women. So, bless thee, master!]
Glou. Here, take this purse, thou whom the heav'ns' plagues
Have humbled to all strokes. That I am wretched
Makes thee the happier; heavens, deal so still!
Let the superfluous and lust-dieted man,
That slaves your ordinance, that will not see
Because he does not feel, feel your pow'r quickly;
So distribution should undo excess,
And each man have enough. Dost thou know Dover?
Edg. Ay, master.
Glou. There is a cliff, whose high and bending head
Looks fearfully in the confined deep.
Bring me but to the very brim of it,
And I'll repair the misery thou dost bear
With something rich about me. From that place
I shall no leading need.
Edg. Give me thy arm;
Poor Tom shall lead thee. *Exeunt.*

52. **daub it further:** continue this dissembling.
59–61. **Obidicut . . . Flibbertigibbet.** The names of the five devils are derived, sometimes with changed spelling, from Harsnett.
61–62. **mopping and mowing:** making faces.
66. **happier:** i.e. less wretched.
67. **superfluous:** having too much. **lust-dieted:** having provision for indulging his appetites.
68. **slaves your ordinance:** makes your law subservient to his own desires. 73. **bending:** overhanging.
74. **the confined deep:** the sea held in on both sides (probably the Straits of Dover).

Scene II

Enter Goneril, *Bastard* [Edmund].

Gon. Welcome, my lord. I marvel our mild husband
Not met us on the way.
[*Enter* Oswald, *the Steward.*]
Now, where's your master?
Osw. Madam, within, but never man so chang'd.
I told him of the army that was landed;
He smil'd at it. I told him you were coming;
His answer was, "The worse." Of Gloucester's treachery,
And of the loyal service of his son,
When I inform'd him, then he call'd me sot,
And told me I had turn'd the wrong side out.
What most he should dislike seems pleasant to him;
What like, offensive.
Gon. [*To Edmund.*] Then shall you go no further.
It is the cowish terror of his spirit
That dares not undertake; he'll not feel wrongs
Which tie him to an answer. Our wishes on the way
May prove effects. Back, Edmund, to my brother,
Hasten his musters and conduct his pow'rs.
I must change names at home, and give the distaff
Into my husband's hands. This trusty servant
Shall pass between us. Ere long you are like to hear
(If you dare venture in your own behalf)
A mistress's command. Wear this; spare speech.
Decline your head: this kiss, if it durst speak,
Would stretch thy spirits up into the air.
Conceive, and fare thee well.
Edm. Yours in the ranks of death. *Exit.*
Gon. My most dear Gloucester!
O, the difference of man and man!
To thee a woman's services are due,
[A] fool usurps my [bed].
Osw. Madam, here comes my lord. [*Exit.*]

Enter Albany.

Gon. I have been worth the [whistling].
Alb. O Goneril,
You are not worth the dust which the rude wind
Blows in your face. [I fear your disposition;
That nature which contemns it origin
Cannot be bordered certain in itself.

IV.ii. Location: Before Albany's palace.
8. **sot:** fool.
9. **turn'd . . . out:** reversed things (since the loyal service was Gloucester's and the treachery Edmund's). 12. **cowish:** cowardly.
13–14. **he'll . . . answer:** he'll ignore such insults as require in honor to be answered. 15. **prove effects:** be realized.
16. **musters:** assembling of forces.
17. **change names:** exchange names, i.e. assume the responsibilities that should be my husband's and hand over my wifely duties to him.
22. **Decline your head:** i.e. for a kiss.
24. **Conceive:** (1) take my meaning; (2) let the seed I have planted in your mind quicken and bear fruit.
29. **I . . . whistling:** i.e. there was a time when you would have thought me worth the trouble of coming to meet me (alluding to the proverb "It is a poor dog that is not worth the whistling").
31. **fear your disposition:** have fears concerning your nature.
32. **it:** its. 33. **bordered certain:** kept safely within bounds.

She that herself will sliver and disbranch
From her material sap, perforce must wither,
And come to deadly use.
Gon. No more, the text is foolish.
Alb. Wisdom and goodness to the vild seem vild,
Filths savor but themselves. What have you done?
Tigers, not daughters, what have you perform'd?
A father, and a gracious aged man,
Whose reverence even the head-lugg'd bear would lick,
Most barbarous, most degenerate, have you madded.
Could my good brother suffer you to do it?
A man, a prince, by him so benefited!
If that the heavens do not their visible spirits
Send quickly down to tame [these] vild offenses,
It will come,
Humanity must perforce prey on itself,
Like monsters of the deep.]
Gon. Milk-liver'd man,
That bear'st a cheek for blows, a head for wrongs,
Who hast not in thy brows an eye discerning
Thine honor from thy suffering, [that not know'st
Fools do those villains pity who are punish'd
Ere they have done their mischief, where's thy drum?
France spreads his banners in our noiseless land,
With plumed helm thy state begins [to threat],
Whilst thou, a moral fool, sits still and cries,
"Alack, why does he so?"]
Alb. See thyself, devil!
Proper deformity [shows] not in the fiend
So horrid as in woman.
Gon. O vain fool!
[*Alb.* Thou changed and self-cover'd thing, for shame
Bemonster not thy feature. Were't my fitness
To let these hands obey my blood,
They are apt enough to dislocate and tear
Thy flesh and bones. Howe'er thou art a fiend,
A woman's shape doth shield thee.
Gon. Marry, your manhood mew!]

Enter a MESSENGER.

[*Alb.* What news?]
Mess. O my good lord, the Duke of Cornwall's dead,
Slain by his servant, going to put out
The other eye of Gloucester.

34. sliver and disbranch. Both verbs mean "cut off."
35. material sap: vital sustenance.
36. to deadly use: to destruction (as branches are destroyed by use as firewood).
37. text. She implies that he has been preaching a sermon.
39. Filths . . . themselves: to the filthy everything seems filthy.
42. head-lugg'd: dragged by the head. **46. visible:** in visible form.
50. Milk-liver'd: white-livered, cowardly.
52–53. discerning . . . suffering: able to distinguish what should be borne from what should be resented. **54. Fools:** i.e. only fools.
56. noiseless: not yet aroused; without military preparation.
58. moral: moralizing.
60–61. Proper . . . woman: deformity can show itself more horribly in a woman than in the devil himself, because it is appropriate to him.
62. changed: transformed (into a monster). **self-cover'd:** whose true nature is concealed.
63. feature: (human) appearance. **my fitness:** suitable for me.
64. blood: impulse.
68. mew: mew up, keep under restraint (a term from falconry). Many editors insert a comma or a dash after *manhood* and interpret *mew* as a derisive exclamation.

Alb. Gloucester's eyes?
Mess. A servant that he bred, thrill'd with remorse,
Oppos'd against the act, bending his sword
To his great master, who, [thereat] enraged,
Flew on him, and amongst them fell'd him dead,
But not without that harmful stroke which since
Hath pluck'd him after.
Alb. This shows you are above,
You [justicers], that these our nether crimes
So speedily can venge! But, O poor Gloucester,
Lost he his other eye?
Mess. Both, both, my lord.
This letter, madam, craves a speedy answer;
'Tis from your sister.
Gon. [*Aside.*] One way I like this well,
But being widow, and my Gloucester with her,
May all the building in my fancy pluck
Upon my hateful life. Another way,
The news is not so tart.—I'll read, and answer. [*Exit.*]
Alb. Where was his son when they did take his eyes?
Mess. Come with my lady hither.
Alb. He is not here.
Mess. No, my good lord, I met him back again.
Alb. Knows he the wickedness?
Mess. Ay, my good lord; 'twas he inform'd against him,
And quit the house on purpose that their punishment
Might have the freer course.
Alb. Gloucester, I live
To thank thee for the love thou show'dst the King,
And to revenge thine eyes. Come hither, friend,
Tell me what more thou know'st. *Exeunt.*

[[SCENE III]

Enter KENT *and a* GENTLEMAN.

Kent. Why the King of France is so suddenly gone back, know you no reason?

Gent. Something he left imperfect in the state, which since his coming forth is thought of, which imports to the kingdom so much fear and danger that his personal return was most requir'd and necessary.

Kent. Who hath he left behind him general?

Gent. The Marshal of France, Monsieur La Far.

Kent. Did your letters pierce the Queen to any demonstration of grief?

Gent. Ay, [sir], she took them, read them in my presence,
And now and then an ample tear trill'd down
Her delicate cheek. It seem'd she was a queen
Over her passion, who, most rebel-like,
Sought to be king o'er her.

73. thrill'd: pierced. **remorse:** pity. **74. bending:** directing.
75. To: against. **76. amongst them:** together with the others.
79. nether: i.e. committed on earth.
85. all . . . pluck: pull down all that I have constructed in my imagination.
86. my hateful life: my life, which would then become hateful.
90. back: on his way back.

IV.iii. Location: The French camp near Dover.
12. trill'd: trickled.

Kent. O then it mov'd her.
Gent. Not to a rage, patience and sorrow [strove]
Who should express her goodliest. You have seen
Sunshine and rain at once; her smiles and tears
Were like a better way: those happy smilets
That play'd on her ripe lip [seem'd] not to know
What guests were in her eyes, which, parted thence,
As pearls from diamonds dropp'd. In brief,
Sorrow would be a rarity most beloved,
If all could so become it.
Kent. Made she no verbal question?
Gent. Faith, once or twice she heav'd the name of "father"
Pantingly forth, as if it press'd her heart;
Cried, "Sisters, sisters! Shame of ladies, sisters!
Kent! father! sisters! What, i' th' storm? i' th' night?
Let pity not be believ'd!" There she shook
The holy water from her heavenly eyes,
And, clamor-moistened, then away she started
To deal with grief alone.
Kent. It is the stars,
The stars above us, govern our conditions,
Else one self mate and make could not beget
Such different issues. You spoke not with her since?
Gent. No.
Kent. Was this before the King return'd?
Gent. No, since.
Kent. Well, sir, the poor distressed Lear's i' th' town,
Who sometime, in his better tune, remembers
What we are come about, and by no means
Will yield to see his daughter.
Gent. Why, good sir?
Kent. A sovereign shame so elbows him: his own unkindness,
That stripp'd her from his benediction, turn'd her
To foreign casualties, gave her dear rights
To his dog-hearted daughters—these things sting
His mind so venomously, that burning shame
Detains him from Cordelia.
Gent. Alack, poor gentleman!
Kent. Of Albany's and Cornwall's powers you heard not?
Gent. 'Tis so, they are afoot.
Kent. Well, sir, I'll bring you to our master Lear,
And leave you to attend him. Some dear cause
Will in concealment wrap me up awhile;
When I am known aright, you shall not grieve
Lending me this acquaintance. I pray you go
Along with me. *Exeunt.*]

19. **like . . . way:** similar, but after a better fashion.
23. **rarity:** precious thing.
24. **If . . . it:** if it were as becoming to all as it is to her. **verbal question:** comment in words.
29. **believ'd:** i.e. believed to exist.
31. **clamor-moistened:** "having her emotion calmed by a flood of tears, as the storm is assuaged by a shower of rain" (Craig).
33. **conditions:** characters.
34. **one . . . make:** one and the same husband and wife.
39. **better tune:** saner moments.
41. **yield:** consent.
42. **sovereign:** overruling. **elbows:** pushes away.
44. **foreign casualties:** chances in a foreign land.
51. **dear cause:** important reason.
53. **grieve:** repent.

Scene [IV]

Enter, with Drum and Colors, Cordelia, [Doctor], *and* Soldiers.

Cor. Alack, 'tis he! Why, he was met even now
As mad as the vex'd sea, singing aloud,
Crown'd with rank [femiter] and furrow-weeds,
With hardocks, hemlock, nettles, cuckoo-flow'rs,
Darnel, and all the idle weeds that grow
In our sustaining corn. A [century] send forth;
Search every acre in the high-grown field,
And bring him to our eye. [*Exit an Officer.*] What can man's wisdom
In the restoring his bereaved sense?
He that helps him take all my outward worth.
[*Doct.*] There is means, madam.
Our foster-nurse of nature is repose,
The which he lacks; that to provoke in him
Are many simples operative, whose power
Will close the eye of anguish.
Cor. All blest secrets,
All you unpublish'd virtues of the earth,
Spring with my tears; be aidant and remediate
In the good man's [distress]! Seek, seek for him,
Lest his ungovern'd rage dissolve the life
That wants the means to lead it.

Enter Messenger.

Mess. News, madam!
The British pow'rs are marching hitherward.
Cor. 'Tis known before; our preparation stands
In expectation of them. O dear father,
It is thy business that I go about;
Therefore great France
My mourning and importun'd tears hath pitied.
No blown ambition doth our arms incite,
But love, dear love, and our ag'd father's right.
Soon may I hear and see him! *Exeunt.*

Scene [V]

Enter Regan *and Steward* [Oswald].

Reg. But are my brother's pow'rs set forth?
Osw. Ay, madam.
Reg. Himself in person there?
Osw. Madam, with much ado;
Your sister is the better soldier.

IV.iv. **Location:** The French camp.
3. **rank:** luxuriant. **femiter:** fumitory, an herb.
4. **hardocks:** burdocks, or harlock (wild mustard).
5. **Darnel:** a weedy grass.
6. **sustaining corn:** life-supporting wheat. **A century:** a hundred soldiers.
8. **can man's wisdom:** i.e. can medical knowledge accomplish.
12. **Our . . . nature:** the fostering nurse of our nature.
14. **simples:** medicinal herbs. **operative:** effective.
16. **unpublish'd:** not generally known. **virtues:** i.e. beneficial herbs.
17. **Spring:** grow (as her tears water them). **aidant:** helpful. **remediate:** healing. 19. **rage:** frenzy.
20. **wants:** lacks. **the means:** i.e. his reason.
22. **our preparation:** the troops we have ready.
26. **importun'd:** importunate. 27. **blown:** puffed-up.

IV.v. **Location:** Gloucester's castle.
2. **with much ado:** after much persuasion.

Reg. Lord Edmund spake not with your lord at home?
Osw. No, madam.
Reg. What might import my sister's letter to him?
Osw. I know not, lady.
Reg. Faith, he is posted hence on serious matter.
It was great ignorance, Gloucester's eyes being out,
To let him live; where he arrives he moves
All hearts against us. Edmund, I think, is gone,
In pity of his misery, to dispatch
His nighted life; moreover to descry
The strength o' th' enemy.
Osw. I must needs after him, madam, with my letter.
Reg. Our troops set forth to-morrow, stay with us;
The ways are dangerous.
Osw. I may not, madam;
My lady charg'd my duty in this business.
Reg. Why should she write to Edmund? Might not you
Transport her purposes by word? Belike
Some things—I know not what. I'll love thee much—
Let me unseal the letter.
Osw. Madam, I had rather—
Reg. I know your lady does not love her husband,
I am sure of that; and at her late being here
She gave strange eliads and most speaking looks
To noble Edmund. I know you are of her bosom.
Osw. I, madam?
Reg. I speak in understanding: y' are; I know't.
Therefore I do advise you take this note:
My lord is dead; Edmund and I have talk'd,
And more convenient is he for my hand
Than for your lady's. You may gather more.
If you do find him, pray you give him this;
And when your mistress hears thus much from you,
I pray desire her call her wisdom to her.
So fare you well.
If you do chance to hear of that blind traitor,
Preferment falls on him that cuts him off.
Osw. Would I could meet [him,] madam! I should show
What party I do follow.
Reg. Fare thee well. *Exeunt.*

Scene [VI]

Enter Gloucester *and* Edgar *[dressed like a peasant].*

Glou. When shall I come to th' top of that same hill?
Edg. You do climb up it now. Look how we labor.
Glou. Methinks the ground is even.

9. **ignorance:** folly.
18. **charg'd my duty:** i.e. gave me strict orders to carry out my instructions. 21. **love thee much:** i.e. make it worth your while.
25. **eliads:** oeillades, amorous glances.
26. **of her bosom:** in her confidence.
29. **take this note:** to take note of what I say.
31. **convenient:** fitting.
32. **gather more:** i.e. make your own inferences.

IV.vi. Location: The country near Dover.

Edg. Horrible steep.
Hark, do you hear the sea?
Glou. No, truly.
Edg. Why then your other senses grow imperfect
By your eyes' anguish.
Glou. So may it be indeed.
Methinks thy voice is alter'd, and thou speak'st
In better phrase and matter than thou didst.
Edg. Y' are much deceiv'd. In nothing am I chang'd
But in my garments.
Glou. Methinks y' are better spoken.
Edg. Come on, sir, here's the place; stand still. How fearful
And dizzy 'tis, to cast one's eyes so low!
The crows and choughs that wing the midway air
Show scarce so gross as beetles. Half way down
Hangs one that gathers sampire, dreadful trade!
Methinks he seems no bigger than his head.
The fishermen that [walk] upon the beach
Appear like mice; and yond tall anchoring bark,
Diminish'd to her cock; her cock, a buoy
Almost too small for sight. The murmuring surge,
That on th' unnumb'red idle pebble chafes,
Cannot be heard so high. I'll look no more,
Lest my brain turn, and the deficient sight
Topple down headlong.
Glou. Set me where you stand.
Edg. Give me your hand. You are now within a foot
Of th' extreme verge. For all beneath the moon
Would I not leap upright.
Glou. Let go my hand.
Here, friend, 's another purse; in it a jewel
Well worth a poor man's taking. Fairies and gods
Prosper it with thee! Go thou further off:
Bid me farewell, and let me hear thee going.
Edg. Now fare ye well, good sir.
Glou. With all my heart.
Edg. [*Aside.*] Why I do trifle thus with his despair
Is done to cure it.
Glou. O you mighty gods! [*He kneels.*]
This world I do renounce, and in your sights
Shake patiently my great affliction off.
If I could bear it longer, and not fall
To quarrel with your great opposeless wills,
My snuff and loathed part of nature should
Burn itself out. If Edgar live, O bless him!
Now, fellow, fare thee well. [*He falls.*]
Edg. Gone, sir; farewell!
And yet I know not how conceit may rob
The treasury of life, when life itself
Yields to the theft. Had he been where he thought,

13. **choughs:** jackdaws. 14. **gross:** large.
15. **sampire:** samphire, an aromatic plant eaten pickled.
19. **cock:** cockboat, small ship's boat.
23. **the deficient sight:** i.e. I, my sight failing.
29. **Fairies.** Thought to guard and multiply hidden treasure.
33. **Why . . . trifle:** i.e. what I do, trifling.
38. **To quarrel with:** into rebellion against. **opposeless:** not to be opposed (because opposition is both sinful and futile).
39. **My . . . nature:** the smouldering wick and hateful remnant of my life. 42. **conceit:** imagination. 44. **Yields:** consents.

By this had thought been past. Alive or dead?—
Ho, you, sir! friend! Hear you, sir! speak!—
Thus might he pass indeed; yet he revives.—
What are you, sir?

Glou. Away, and let me die.

Edg. Hadst thou been aught but goss'mer, feathers, air
(So many fathom down precipitating),
Thou'dst shiver'd like an egg: but thou dost breathe,
Hast heavy substance, bleed'st not, speak'st, art sound.
Ten masts at each make not the altitude
Which thou hast perpendicularly fell.
Thy life's a miracle. Speak yet again.

Glou. But have I fall'n, or no?

Edg. From the dread summit of this chalky bourn.
Look up a-height, the shrill-gorg'd lark so far
Cannot be seen or heard. Do but look up.

Glou. Alack, I have no eyes.
Is wretchedness depriv'd that benefit,
To end itself by death? 'Twas yet some comfort,
When misery could beguile the tyrant's rage,
And frustrate his proud will.

Edg. Give me your arm.
Up—so. How is't? Feel you your legs? You stand.

Glou. Too well, too well.

Edg. This is above all strangeness.
Upon the crown o' th' cliff, what thing was that
Which parted from you?

Glou. A poor unfortunate beggar.

Edg. As I stood here below, methought his eyes
Were two full moons; he had a thousand noses,
Horns welk'd and waved like the [enridged] sea.
It was some fiend; therefore, thou happy father,
Think that the clearest gods, who make them honors
Of men's impossibilities, have preserved thee.

Glou. I do remember now. Henceforth I'll bear
Affliction till it do cry out itself
"Enough, enough," and die. That thing you speak of,
I took it for a man; often 'twould say,
"The fiend, the fiend!"—he led me to that place.

Edg. Bear free and patient thoughts.

Enter LEAR [*mad, crowned with weeds and flowers*].

But who comes here?
The safer sense will ne'er accommodate
His master thus.

Lear. No, they cannot touch me for [coining,] I am the King himself.

Edg. O thou side-piercing sight!

Lear. Nature's above art in that respect. There's your press-money. That fellow handles his bow like a crow-keeper; draw me a clothier's yard. Look, look, a mouse! Peace, peace, this piece of toasted cheese will do't. There's my gauntlet, I'll prove it on a giant. Bring up the brown bills. O, well flown, bird! i' th' clout, i' th' clout—hewgh! Give the word.

Edg. Sweet marjorum.

Lear. Pass.

Glou. I know that voice.

Lear. Ha! Goneril with a white beard? They flatter'd me like a dog, and told me I had the white hairs in my beard ere the black ones were there. To say "ay" and "no" to every thing that I said! "Ay," and "no" too, was no good divinity. When the rain came to wet me once, and the wind to make me chatter, when the thunder would not peace at my bidding, there I found 'em, there I smelt 'em out. Go to, they are not men o' their words: they told me I was every thing. 'Tis a lie, I am not ague-proof.

Glou. The trick of that voice I do well remember;
Is't not the King?

Lear. Ay, every inch a king!
When I do stare, see how the subject quakes.
I pardon that man's life. What was thy cause?
Adultery?
Thou shalt not die. Die for adultery? No,
The wren goes to't, and the small gilded fly
Does lecher in my sight.
Let copulation thrive; for Gloucester's bastard son
Was kinder to his father than my daughters
Got 'tween the lawful sheets.
To't, luxury, pell-mell, for I lack soldiers.
Behold yond simp'ring dame,
Whose face between her forks presages snow;
That minces virtue, and does shake the head
To hear of pleasure's name—
The fitchew nor the soiled horse goes to't
With a more riotous appetite.
Down from the waist they are Centaurs,
Though women all above;
But to the girdle do the gods inherit,
Beneath is all the fiends': there's hell, there's darkness,
There is the sulphurous pit, burning, scalding,
Stench, consumption. Fie, fie, fie! pah, pah!

47. pass: die.
49. goss'mer: gossamer, floating thread spun by a spider.
53. at each: end to end.
57. chalky bourn: i.e. chalk cliff bounding the sea.
58. a-height: on high. **shrill-gorg'd:** shrill-throated.
63. beguile: cheat. **71. welk'd:** convoluted. **enridged:** furrowed.
72. happy father: fortunate old man. Edgar's use of *father* here and later does not betray his identity.
73–74. who . . . impossibilities: who acquire our reverence by doing deeds impossible to men. **80. free:** serene.
81. The safer sense: a sane mind.
86. Nature's . . . respect: "a king who coins by divine right standing for Nature and a forger for Art" (Dover Wilson).
87. press-money: money paid to a conscript.
88. crow-keeper: boy hired to drive crows away. **me:** for me. **clothier's yard:** arrow a cloth-yard long.
90. There's my gauntlet. He issues a challenge. **prove it on:** maintain my cause against.
91. brown bills: men carrying pikes painted brown to prevent rusting. **bird:** i.e. arrow.
92. clout: centre of target. **hewgh.** He imitates the sound of an arrow in flight. **word:** password.
93. Sweet marjorum. Offered as password. The herb marjoram was used to treat mental disease. **97. like a dog:** i.e. fawningly.
97–98. had . . . beard: i.e. had wisdom.
99. say . . . said: i.e. contradict me in nothing.
100. no good divinity: bad theology. James 5:12 says, ". . . let your yea be yea; and your nay, nay." **103. found 'em:** found them out.
106. trick: characteristic quality. **108. the subject:** my subjects.
109. cause: offense.
117. luxury: lust. **pell-mell:** promiscuously.
119. Whose . . . snow: who seems icily chaste. **forks:** legs (*between her forks* modifies *snow*). **120. minces:** coyly affects.
121. pleasure's name: the very name of sexual pleasure.
122. The fitchew: (neither) the polecat. **soiled:** high-spirited from feeding on fresh grass in spring.
124. Centaurs: i.e. beasts (like the horse of line 122).
126. inherit: possess.
127. hell. Traditional slang for the female genitals.

Give me an ounce of civet; good apothecary,
Sweeten my imagination. There's money for thee.
Glou. O, let me kiss that hand!
Lear. Let me wipe it first, it smells of mortality.
Glou. O ruin'd piece of nature! This great world
Shall so wear out to nought. Dost thou know me?
Lear. I remember thine eyes well enough. Dost thou squiny at me? No, do thy worst, blind Cupid, I'll not love. Read thou this challenge; mark but the penning of it.
Glou. Were all thy letters suns, I could not see.
Edg. [*Aside.*] I would not take this from report; it is,
And my heart breaks at it.
Lear. Read.
Glou. What, with the case of eyes?
Lear. O ho, are you there with me? No eyes in your head, nor no money in your purse? Your eyes are in a heavy case, your purse in a light, yet you see how this world goes.
Glou. I see it feelingly.
Lear. What, art mad? A man may see how this world goes with no eyes. Look with thine ears; see how yond justice rails upon yond simple thief. Hark in thine ear: change places, and handy-dandy, which is the justice, which is the thief? Thou hast seen a farmer's dog bark at a beggar?
Glou. Ay, sir.
Lear. And the creature run from the cur? There thou mightst behold the great image of authority: a dog's obey'd in office.
Thou rascal beadle, hold thy bloody hand!
Why dost thou lash that whore? Strip thy own back,
Thou hotly lusts to use her in that kind
For which thou whip'st her. The usurer hangs the cozener.
Thorough tatter'd clothes [small] vices do appear;
Robes and furr'd gowns hide all. [Plate sin] with gold,
And the strong lance of justice hurtless breaks;
Arm it in rags, a pigmy's straw does pierce it.
None does offend, none, I say none, I'll able 'em.
Take that of me, my friend, who have the power
To seal th' accuser's lips. Get thee glass eyes,
And like a scurvy politician, seem
To see the things thou dost not. Now, now, now, now.
Pull off my boots; harder, harder—so.

Edg. [*Aside.*] O, matter and impertinency mix'd,
Reason in madness!
Lear. If thou wilt weep my fortunes, take my eyes.
I know thee well enough, thy name is Gloucester.
Thou must be patient; we came crying hither.
Thou know'st, the first time that we smell the air
We wawl and cry. I will preach to thee. Mark.
[*Lear takes off his crown of weeds and flowers.*]
Glou. Alack, alack the day!
Lear. When we are born, we cry that we are come
To this great stage of fools.—This' a good block.
It were a delicate stratagem, to shoe
A troop of horse with felt. I'll put't in proof,
And when I have stol'n upon these son-in-laws,
Then kill, kill, kill, kill, kill, kill!

Enter a GENTLEMAN [*with* ATTENDANTS].

Gent. O, here he is: lay hand upon him.—Sir,
Your most dear daughter—
Lear. No rescue? What, a prisoner? I am even
The natural fool of fortune. Use me well,
You shall have ransom. Let me have surgeons,
I am cut to th' brains.
Gent. You shall have any thing.
Lear. No seconds? All myself?
Why, this would make a man a man of salt
To use his eyes for garden water-pots,
[Ay, and laying autumn's dust.
Gent. Good sir—]
Lear. I will die bravely, like a smug bridegroom. What?
I will be jovial. Come, come, I am a king,
Masters, know you that?
Gent. You are a royal one, and we obey you.
Lear. Then there's life in't. Come, and you get it, you shall get it by running. Sa, sa, sa, sa.
Exit [*running; Attendants follow*].
Gent. A sight most pitiful in the meanest wretch,
Past speaking of in a king! Thou hast [one] daughter
Who redeems nature from the general curse
Which twain have brought her to.
Edg. Hail, gentle sir.
Gent. Sir, speed you: what's your will?
Edg. Do you hear aught, sir, of a battle toward?
Gent. Most sure and vulgar; every one hears that,
Which can distinguish sound.
Edg. But by your favor,
How near's the other army?
Gent. Near and on speedy foot; the main descry
Stands on the hourly thought.
Edg. I thank you, sir, that's all.

130. civet: perfume.
134. piece: masterpiece, i.e. man; the little world.
135. so: in the same way.
137. squiny: squint. **blind.** As Cupid traditionally was; hence he was sometimes used as a brothel-sign.
141. take: believe. **144. case:** sockets.
145. are . . . me: is that the way things are.
147. heavy case: sad condition.
149. feelingly: (1) by means of my sense of touch; (2) with keen emotion.
153. handy-dandy: i.e. take your choice.
157. creature: human being.
160. beadle: parish officer who administered corporal punishment.
162. kind: way.
163. The usurer . . . cozener: the justice guilty of usury sentences the petty cheat to be hanged.
165. Plate . . . gold: clothe sin in gold armor.
166. hurtless: without doing any harm.
168. able 'em: authorize them, i.e. exempt everyone from legal guilt.
171. scurvy: vile. **politician:** trickster.

174. impertinency: irrelevance, incoherence.
183. This': this is. **block:** style of hat (here the weeds and flowers from his hair—which he has taken off to preach his sermon).
185. in proof: to the test. **191. natural:** born. **fool:** plaything.
194. seconds: supporters. **195. salt:** tears.
198. smug: trimly dressed. The simile of the "smug bridegroom" arises from quibbles on the sexual sense of *die* and on *bravely* in the sense "finely attired."
202. there's life in't: the situation isn't hopeless. **and:** if.
203. Sa . . . sa. A hunting cry. **206. general:** universal.
208. gentle: noble. **209. toward:** imminent.
210. vulgar: of common knowledge.
213–14. the main . . . thought: any hour now we expect to catch sight of the main body.

Gent. Though that the Queen on special cause is here,
Her army is mov'd on.
Edg. I thank you, sir. *Exit* [*Gentleman*].
Glou. You ever-gentle gods, take my breath from me,
Let not my worser spirit tempt me again
To die before you please!
Edg. Well pray you, father.
Glou. Now, good sir, what are you?
Edg. A most poor man, made tame to fortune's blows,
Who, by the art of known and feeling sorrows,
Am pregnant to good pity. Give me your hand,
I'll lead you to some biding.
Glou. Hearty thanks;
The bounty and the benison of heaven
To boot, and boot!

Enter Steward [OSWALD].

Osw. A proclaim'd prize! Most happy!
That eyeless head of thine was first fram'd flesh
To raise my fortunes. Thou old unhappy traitor,
Briefly thyself remember; the sword is out
That must destroy thee.
Glou. Now let thy friendly hand
Put strength enough to't. [*Edgar interposes.*]
Osw. Wherefore, bold peasant,
[Durst] thou support a publish'd traitor? Hence,
Lest that th' infection of his fortune take
Like hold on thee. Let go his arm.
Edg. Chill not let go, zir, without vurther [cagion].
Osw. Let go, slave, or thou di'st!
Edg. Good gentleman, go your gait, and let poor voke pass. And chud ha' bin zwagger'd out of my life, 'twould not ha' bin zo long as 'tis by a vortnight. Nay, come not near th' old man; keep out, che vor' ye, or Ice try whither your costard or my ballow be the harder. Chill be plain with you.
Osw. Out, dunghill! [*They fight.*]
Edg. Chill pick your teeth, zir. Come, no matter vor your foins.
Osw. Slave, thou hast slain me. Villain, take my purse:
If ever thou wilt thrive, bury my body,
And give the letters which thou find'st about me
To Edmund Earl of Gloucester; seek him out
Upon the English party. O untimely death!
Death! [*He dies.*]
Edg. I know thee well; a serviceable villain,
As duteous to the vices of thy mistress
As badness would desire.
Glou. What, is he dead?
Edg. Sit you down, father; rest you.
Let's see these pockets; the letters that he speaks of
May be my friends. He's dead; I am only sorry
He had no other deathsman. Let us see.
Leave, gentle wax, and, manners, blame us not:
To know our enemies' minds, we rip their hearts,
Their papers is more lawful.
(*Reads the letter.*) "Let our reciprocal vows be remember'd. You have many opportunities to cut him off; if your will want not, time and place will be fruitfully offer'd. There is nothing done, if he return the conqueror; then am I the prisoner, and his bed my jail; from the loath'd warmth whereof deliver me, and supply the place for your labor.
Your (wife, so I would say) affectionate servant,
Goneril."
O indistinguish'd space of woman's will!
A plot upon her virtuous husband's life,
And the exchange my brother! Here, in the sands,
Thee I'll rake up, the post unsanctified
Of murtherous lechers; and in the mature time
With this ungracious paper strike the sight
Of the death-practic'd Duke. For him 'tis well
That of thy death and business I can tell.
Glou. The King is mad; how stiff is my vild sense
That I stand up, and have ingenious feeling
Of my huge sorrows! Better I were distract,
So should my thoughts be sever'd from my griefs,
And woes by wrong imaginations lose
The knowledge of themselves. *Drum afar off.*
Edg. Give me your hand;
Far off methinks I hear the beaten drum.
Come, father, I'll bestow you with a friend. *Exeunt.*

SCENE VII

Enter CORDELIA, KENT [*still dressed as Caius*], *and* [DOCTOR].

Cor. O thou good Kent, how shall I live and work
To match thy goodness? My life will be too short,
And every measure fail me.
Kent. To be acknowledg'd, madam, is o'erpaid.
All my reports go with the modest truth,
Nor more nor clipt, but so.

215. on special cause: for special reason.
218. worser spirit: evil angel. **221. tame**: submissive.
222. by . . . sorrows: i.e. by virtue of the heartfelt sorrows I have experienced. **223. pregnant**: readily disposed.
224. biding: lodging.
226. To boot: in addition. **A proclaim'd prize**: i.e. a man with a price on his head.
229. thyself remember: i.e. think on your soul's welfare.
232. publish'd: proclaimed.
235. Chill: I will. (Edgar takes the part of a peasant and uses Somerset dialect.) **cagion**: occasion. **237. gait**: way.
238. voke: folk. **And chud**: if I could.
240. che vor' ye: I warrant you.
241. Ice: I shall. **whither**: whether. **costard**: head (from the name of a kind of apple.) **ballow**: cudgel. **245. foins**: thrusts.
250. Upon . . . party: on the English side.
258. deathsman: executioner. **259. Leave**: by your leave.
264. want: be lacking.
265. fruitfully: plentifully. **There . . . done**: i.e. we shall have achieved nothing.
268. for your labor. With obvious double meaning.
269. servant: lover.
271. indistinguish'd space: boundless range. **will**: lust.
274. rake: cover. **post unsanctified**: damnable messenger.
275. in . . . time: when the time is ripe. **276. ungracious**: wicked.
277. death-practic'd: whose death is plotted.
279. stiff: stubborn. **sense**: mental powers.
280. ingenious feeling: keen consciousness. **281. distract**: mad.
283. wrong imaginations: delusions. **286. bestow**: lodge.

IV.vii. Location: A tent in the French camp.
3. measure: i.e. attempt to measure out an adequate recompense.
5. go: accord. **modest**: moderate, i.e. strictly accurate.

Cor. Be better suited,
These weeds are memories of those worser hours;
I prithee put them off.
Kent. Pardon, dear madam,
Yet to be known shortens my made intent.
My boon I make it, that you know me not
Till time and I think meet.
Cor. Then be't so, my good lord. [*To the Doctor.*]
How does the King?
[*Doct.*] Madam, sleeps still.
Cor. O you kind gods!
Cure this great breach in his abused nature,
Th' untun'd and jarring senses, O, wind up
Of this child-changed father!
[*Doct.*] So please your Majesty
That we may wake the King? he hath slept long.
Cor. Be govern'd by your knowledge, and proceed
I' th' sway of your own will. Is he array'd?
Gent. Ay, madam; in the heaviness of sleep
We put fresh garments on him.
[*Doct.*] Be by, good madam, when we do awake him,
I doubt [not] of his temperance.
[*Cor.* Very well.]

Enter LEAR *in a chair carried by* SERVANTS. [GENTLEMAN *in attendance. Soft music.*]

[*Doct.* Please you draw near.—Louder the music there!]
Cor. O my dear father, restoration hang
Thy medicine on my lips, and let this kiss
Repair those violent harms that my two sisters
Have in thy reverence made.
Kent. Kind and dear princess!
Cor. Had you not been their father, these white flakes
Did challenge pity of them. Was this a face
To be oppos'd against the [warring] winds?
[To stand against the deep dread-bolted thunder?
In the most terrible and nimble stroke
Of quick cross lightning? to watch—poor perdu!—
With this thin helm?] Mine enemy's dog,
Though he had bit me, should have stood that night
Against my fire, and wast thou fain, poor father,
To hovel thee with swine and rogues forlorn
In short and musty straw? Alack, alack,
'Tis wonder that thy life and wits at once
Had not concluded all. He wakes, speak to him.
[*Doct.*] Madam, do you, 'tis fittest.

9. Yet . . . intent: to reveal my identity at this point would cause the purpose I have formed to fall short of its mark.
10. My . . . it: I beg it as a special favor.
15. jarring: discordant. **wind up:** tune (figure from stringed instrument). **16. child-changed:** changed by his children.
19. I' th' sway: under the direction.
23. temperance: self-control.
29. Had you: even if you had. **white flakes:** snowy locks.
30. Did challenge: would have demanded.
32. deep: deep-toned. **dread-bolted:** accompanied by the dread thunderbolt.
34. cross: zigzag. **perdu:** sentinel at a dangerous post.
35. thin helm: light helmet, i.e. his hair. **37. fain:** glad, i.e. forced.
38. rogues: vagabonds.
39. short: scanty (?) or broken up by earlier use as bedding (?).
41. all: altogether.

Cor. How does my royal lord? How fares your Majesty?
Lear. You do me wrong to take me out o' th' grave:
Thou art a soul in bliss, but I am bound
Upon a wheel of fire, that mine own tears
Do scald like molten lead.
Cor. Sir, do you know me?
Lear. You are a spirit, I know; [when] did you die?
Cor. Still, still, far wide!
[*Doct.*] He's scarce awake, let him alone a while.
Lear. Where have I been? Where am I? Fair daylight?
I am mightily abus'd; I should ev'n die with pity
To see another thus. I know not what to say.
I will not swear these are my hands. Let's see,
I feel this pin prick. Would I were assur'd
Of my condition!
Cor. O, look upon me, sir,
And hold your hand in benediction o'er me.
[No, sir,] you must not kneel.
Lear. Pray do not mock me.
I am a very foolish fond old man,
Fourscore and upward, not an hour more nor less;
And to deal plainly,
I fear I am not in my perfect mind.
Methinks I should know you, and know this man,
Yet I am doubtful: for I am mainly ignorant
What place this is, and all the skill I have
Remembers not these garments; nor I know not
Where I did lodge last night. Do not laugh at me,
For (as I am a man) I think this lady
To be my child Cordelia.
Cor. And so I am; I am.
Lear. Be your tears wet? Yes, faith. I pray weep not.
If you have poison for me, I will drink it.
I know you do not love me, for your sisters
Have (as I do remember) done me wrong:
You have some cause, they have not.
Cor. No cause, no cause.
Lear. Am I in France?
Kent. In your own kingdom, sir.
Lear. Do not abuse me.
[*Doct.*] Be comforted, good madam, the great rage,
You see, is kill'd in him, [and yet it is danger
To make him even o'er the time he has lost.]
Desire him to go in, trouble him no more
Till further settling.
Cor. Will't please your Highness walk?
Lear. You must bear with me.
Pray you now forget, and forgive; I am old and foolish.
Exeunt. [*Manent Kent and Gentleman.*]
[*Gent.* Holds it true, sir, that the Duke of Cornwall was so slain?
Kent. Most certain, sir.
Gent. Who is conductor of his people?
Kent. As 'tis said, the bastard son of Gloucester.

46. wheel of fire. One of the punishments associated with both hell and purgatory in medieval accounts. **that:** so that.
49. wide: astray. **52. abus'd:** confused.
64. mainly: completely. **76. abuse:** deceive.
79. even o'er: fill in. **87. conductor:** leader.

Gent. They say Edgar, his banish'd son, is with the Earl of Kent in Germany.

Kent. Report is changeable. 'Tis time to look about, the powers of the kingdom approach apace.

Gent. The arbiterment is like to be bloody. Fare you well, sir. [*Exit.*]

Kent. My point and period will be throughly wrought,
Or well or ill, as this day's battle's fought. *Exit.*]

ACT V, SCENE I

Enter, with Drum and Colors, EDMUND, REGAN, GENTLEMEN, *and* SOLDIERS.

Edm. Know of the Duke if his last purpose hold,
Or whether since he is advis'd by aught
To change the course. He's full of alteration
And self-reproving—bring his constant pleasure.
[*To a Gentleman, who goes out.*]
Reg. Our sister's man is certainly miscarried.
Edm. 'Tis to be doubted, madam.
Reg. Now, sweet lord,
You know the goodness I intend upon you:
Tell me but truly, but then speak the truth,
Do you not love my sister?
Edm. In honor'd love.
Reg. But have you never found my brother's way
To the forfended place?
[*Edm.* That thought abuses you.
Reg. I am doubtful that you have been conjunct
And bosom'd with her—as far as we call hers.]
Edm. No, by mine honor, madam.
Reg. I never shall endure her. Dear my lord,
Be not familiar with her.
Edm. Fear [me] not.
She and the Duke her husband!

Enter, with Drum and Colors, ALBANY, GONERIL, SOLDIERS.

[*Gon.* [*Aside.*] I had rather lose the battle than that sister
Should loosen him and me.]
Alb. Our very loving sister, well bemet.
Sir, this I heard: the King is come to his daughter,
With others whom the rigor of our state
Forc'd to cry out. [Where I could not be honest,
I never yet was valiant. For this business,

91–92. **look about:** be on guard.
93. **arbiterment:** decisive encounter.
95–96. **My . . . fought:** this battle will decide for good or ill the outcome of my life.

V.i. **Location:** The British camp near Dover.
2. **advis'd by aught:** persuaded by any consideration.
4. **constant pleasure:** firm decision.
5. **is . . . miscarried:** has met with some accident.
6. **doubted:** feared. 9. **honor'd:** honorable.
11. **forfended:** forbidden. **abuses:** wrongs.
12. **doubtful:** suspicious.
12–13. **conjunct And bosom'd.** Regan uses words that might be used of a traitor—"in league with her and admitted to her private counsel"—but intends them in their primary physical sense, as her following words show.
16. **Fear me not:** have no such fears about me.
22. **rigor . . . state:** harshness of our rule.
23. **honest:** honorable.

It touches us as France invades our land,
Not bolds the King, with others whom, I fear,
Most just and heavy causes make oppose.
Edm. Sir, you speak nobly.]
Reg. Why is this reason'd?
Gon. Combine together 'gainst the enemy;
For these domestic and particular broils
Are not the question here.
Alb. Let's then determine
With th' ancient of war on our proceeding.
[*Edm.* I shall attend you presently at your tent.]
Reg. Sister, you'll go with us?
Gon. No.
Reg. 'Tis most convenient, pray go with us.
Gon. [*Aside.*] O ho, I know the riddle.—I will go.
Exeunt both the armies.

[*As they are going out,*] *enter* EDGAR [*disguised. Albany remains*].

Edg. If e'er your Grace had speech with man so poor,
Hear me one word.
Alb. I'll overtake you.—Speak.
Edg. Before you fight the battle, ope this letter.
If you have victory, let the trumpet sound
For him that brought it. Wretched though I seem,
I can produce a champion that will prove
What is avouched there. If you miscarry,
Your business of the world hath so an end,
And machination ceases. Fortune [love] you!
Alb. Stay till I have read the letter.
Edg. I was forbid it.
When time shall serve, let but the herald cry,
And I'll appear again.
Alb. Why, fare thee well, I will o'erlook thy paper. *Exit* [*Edgar*].

Enter EDMUND.

Edm. The enemy's in view, draw up your powers.
Here is the guess of their true strength and forces,
By diligent discovery, but your haste
Is now urg'd on you.
Alb. We will greet the time. *Exit.*
Edm. To both these sisters have I sworn my love;
Each jealous of the other, as the stung
Are of the adder. Which of them shall I take?
Both? one? or neither? Neither can be enjoy'd
If both remain alive: to take the widow
Exasperates, makes mad her sister Goneril,
And hardly shall I carry out my side,
Her husband being alive. Now then, we'll use
His countenance for the battle, which being done,

25. **touches us as:** concerns us in so far as.
26. **Not bolds:** i.e. not in so far as he supports.
28. **reason'd:** discussed.
30. **domestic and particular:** family and personal.
32. **ancient of war:** experienced officers.
37. **know the riddle:** know why you say so (Regan wants to keep Goneril and Edmund apart). 43. **prove:** i.e. in trial by combat.
44. **avouched:** maintained. 50. **o'erlook:** read over.
53. **discovery:** scouting. 54. **greet the time:** meet the occasion.
56. **jealous:** suspicious.
61. **hardly:** with difficulty. **carry . . . side:** win my game.
63. **His countenance:** the authority of his name.

Let her who would be rid of him devise
His speedy taking off. As for the mercy
Which he intends to Lear and to Cordelia,
The battle done, and they within our power,
Shall never see his pardon; for my state
Stands on me to defend, not to debate. *Exit.*

Scene II

Alarum within. Enter, with Drum and Colors, [*the* Powers *of France*] *over the stage,* Cordelia [*with her* Father *in her hand,*] *and exeunt.*

Enter Edgar *and* Gloucester.

Edg. Here, father, take the shadow of this tree
For your good host; pray that the right may thrive.
If ever I return to you again,
I'll bring you comfort.
Glou. Grace go with you, sir! *Exit* [*Edgar*].

Alarum and retreat within. Enter Edgar.

Edg. Away, old man, give me thy hand, away!
King Lear hath lost, he and his daughter ta'en.
Give me thy hand; come on.
Glou. No further, sir, a man may rot even here.
Edg. What, in ill thoughts again? Men must endure
Their going hence even as their coming hither,
Ripeness is all. Come on.
Glou. And that's true too. *Exeunt.*

Scene III

Enter in conquest, with Drum and Colors, Edmund, Lear *and* Cordelia *as prisoners,* Soldiers, Captain.

Edm. Some officers take them away. Good guard,
Until their greater pleasures first be known
That are to censure them.
Cor. We are not the first
Who with best meaning have incurr'd the worst.
For thee, oppressed king, I am cast down,
Myself could else out-frown false Fortune's frown.
Shall we not see these daughters and these sisters?
Lear. No, no, no, no! Come let's away to prison:
We two alone will sing like birds i' th' cage;
When thou dost ask me blessing, I'll kneel down
And ask of thee forgiveness. So we'll live,
And pray, and sing, and tell old tales, and laugh
At gilded butterflies, and hear poor rogues
Talk of court news; and we'll talk with them too—
Who loses and who wins; who's in, who's out—

68. **Shall:** they shall. 69. **Stands on:** requires.

V.ii. Location: A field between the two camps.
o.s.d. **Alarum:** trumpet signal to advance. 2. **host:** shelterer.
4 s.d. **retreat:** trumpet signal to withdraw.
11. **Ripeness is all:** the only thing that matters with regard to death is to be ready for it when it comes.

V.iii. Location: Scene continues.
2. **their greater pleasures:** the desires of those greater persons.
3. **censure:** pass judgment on.
13. **gilded butterflies:** trivial and ephemeral people.

And take upon 's the mystery of things
As if we were God's spies; and we'll wear out,
In a wall'd prison, packs and sects of great ones,
That ebb and flow by th' moon.
Edm. Take them away.
Lear. Upon such sacrifices, my Cordelia,
The gods themselves throw incense. Have I caught thee?
He that parts us shall bring a brand from heaven,
And fire us hence like foxes. Wipe thine eyes;
The good-years shall devour them, flesh and fell,
Ere they shall make us weep! We'll see 'em starv'd first.
Come. *Exit* [*with Cordelia, guarded*].
Edm. Come hither, captain; hark.
Take thou this note [*giving a paper*]; go follow them to prison.
One step I have advanc'd thee; if thou dost
As this instructs thee, thou dost make thy way
To noble fortunes. Know thou this, that men
Are as the time is: to be tender-minded
Does not become a sword. Thy great employment
Will not bear question; either say thou'lt do't,
Or thrive by other means.
Capt. I'll do't, my lord.
Edm. About it, and write happy when th' hast done.
Mark, I say instantly, and carry it so
As I have set it down.
[*Capt.* I cannot draw a cart, nor eat dried oats,
If it be man's work, I'll do't.] *Exit Captain.*

Flourish. Enter Albany, Goneril, Regan, [*another* Captain,] Soldiers.

Alb. Sir, you have show'd to-day your valiant strain,
And fortune led you well. You have the captives
Who were the opposites of this day's strife;
I do require them of you, so to use them
As we shall find their merits and our safety
May equally determine.
Edm. Sir, I thought it fit
To send the old and miserable King
To some retention [and appointed guard],
Whose age had charms in it, whose title more,
To pluck the common bosom on his side,
And turn our impress'd lances in our eyes
Which do command them. With him I sent the Queen,
My reason all the same, and they are ready
To-morrow, or at further space, t' appear

17. **God's spies:** beings sent from heaven to watch men's doings, i.e. detached observers with special insight. **wear out:** outlast.
18. **packs and sects:** groups of intriguers and partisans.
20. **such sacrifices:** i.e. as Cordelia's for her father (?) or as their giving up the world (?).
22–23. **He . . . foxes:** i.e. it would take a torch from heaven, not an earthly one, to smoke us out of our prison refuge (as foxes were smoked out of their holes). 22. **shall:** must.
24. **good-years.** Obviously referring to some evil force, but not satisfactorily explained. **flesh and fell:** both flesh and skin, i.e. altogether. 33. **question:** discussion.
35. **write happy:** call yourself lucky (because I shall reward you well).
38. **I . . . oats:** I can't do a horse's work.
40. **strain:** lineage. 42. **opposites:** opponents.
47. **retention:** confinement.
49. **common bosom:** sympathy of the multitude.
50–51. **turn . . . Which:** i.e. turn our conscript soldiers against us who.

Where you shall hold your session. [At this time
We sweat and bleed: the friend hath lost his friend,
And the best quarrels, in the heat, are curs'd
By those that feel their sharpness.
The question of Cordelia and her father
Requires a fitter place.]

Alb. Sir, by your patience,
I hold you but a subject of this war,
Not as a brother.

Reg. That's as we list to grace him.
Methinks our pleasure might have been demanded
Ere you had spoke so far. He led our powers,
Bore the commission of my place and person,
The which immediacy may well stand up,
And call itself your brother.

Gon. Not so hot.
In his own grace he doth exalt himself,
More than in your addition.

Reg. In my rights,
By me invested, he compeers the best.

[*Gon.*] That were the most, if he should husband you.

Reg. Jesters do oft prove prophets.

Gon. Holla, holla!
That eye that told you so look'd but a-squint.

Reg. Lady, I am not well, else I should answer
From a full-flowing stomach. General,
Take thou my soldiers, prisoners, patrimony;
Dispose of them, of me; the walls is thine.
Witness the world, that I create thee here
My lord and master.

Gon. Mean you to enjoy him?

Alb. The let-alone lies not in your good will.

Edm. Nor in thine, lord.

Alb. Half-blooded fellow, yes.

Reg. [*To Edmund.*] Let the drum strike, and prove my title thine.

Alb. Stay yet, hear reason. Edmund, I arrest thee
On capital treason, and in thy [attaint],
This gilded serpent [*pointing to Goneril*]. For your claim, fair [sister],
I bar it in the interest of my wife;
'Tis she is sub-contracted to this lord,
And I, her husband, contradict your banes.
If you will marry, make your loves to me,
My lady is bespoke.

Gon. An enterlude!

Alb. Thou art armed, Gloucester, let the trumpet sound.
If none appear to prove upon thy person
Thy heinous, manifest, and many treasons,
There is my pledge [*throwing down a glove*]. I'll make it on thy heart,

56. **quarrels:** causes. 61. **list:** wish, choose.
62. **demanded:** ascertained. 65. **immediacy:** close connection.
67. **grace:** meritorious qualities.
68. **your addition:** the honors you have conferred on him.
69. **compeers:** equals.
70. **That . . . most:** he would be most fully invested in your rights.
74. **stomach:** anger. 76. **the walls:** i.e. the citadel of my heart.
79. **let-alone:** power of preventing it.
80. **Half-blooded fellow:** bastard.
83. **in thy attaint:** as accessory to your treason.
87. **banes:** banns of marriage. 89. **enterlude:** interlude, play.
93. **make:** prove (which is the Q1 reading).

Ere I taste bread, thou art in nothing less
Than I have here proclaim'd thee.

Reg. Sick, O, sick!

Gon. [*Aside.*] If not, I'll ne'er trust medicine.

Edm. There's my exchange [*throwing down a glove*]. What in the world [he is]
That names me traitor, villain-like he lies.
Call by the trumpet; he that dares approach:
On him, on you—who not?—I will maintain
My truth and honor firmly.

Alb. A herald, ho!

[*Edm.* A herald, ho, a herald!]

[*Alb.*] Trust to thy single virtue, for thy soldiers,
All levied in my name, have in my name
Took their discharge.

Reg. My sickness grows upon me.

Alb. She is not well, convey her to my tent.

[*Exit Regan, led.*]

Enter a HERALD.

Come hither, herald. Let the trumpet sound,
And read out this.

[*Capt.* Sound, trumpet!] *A trumpet sounds.*

Her. (*Reads.*) "If any man of quality or degree within the lists of the army will maintain upon Edmund, supposed Earl of Gloucester, that he is a manifold traitor, let him appear by the third sound of the trumpet. He is bold in his defense."

First trumpet.

[*Edm.* Sound!] *Second trumpet.*

Her. Again! *Third trumpet.*

Her. Again! *Trumpet answers within.*

Enter EDGAR [*at the third sound,*] *armed,* [*a Trumpet before him*].

Alb. Ask him his purposes, why he appears
Upon this call o' th' trumpet.

Her. What are you?
Your name, your quality? and why you answer
This present summons?

Edg. Know, my name is lost,
By treason's tooth bare-gnawn and canker-bit,
Yet am I noble as the adversary
I come to cope.

Alb. Which is that adversary?

Edg. What's he that speaks for Edmund Earl of Gloucester?

Edm. Himself; what say'st thou to him?

Edg. Draw thy sword,
That, if my speech offend a noble heart,
Thy arm may do thee justice; here is mine:
Behold, it is my privilege,
The privilege of mine honors,
My oath, and my profession. I protest,
Maugre thy strength, place, youth, and eminence,
[Despite] thy victor-sword and fire-new fortune,

94. **in nothing less:** in no detail of the charge less guilty.
96. **medicine:** i.e. poison. 97. **What:** whoever.
103. **single virtue:** unaided valor. 122. **canker-bit:** worm-eaten.
124. **cope:** encounter.
130. **The privilege . . . honors:** my privilege as a knight.
131. **profession:** i.e. knighthood. **protest:** solemnly declare.
132. **Maugre:** in spite of. 133. **fire-new:** brand-new.

Thy valor, and thy heart, thou art a traitor;
False to thy gods, thy brother, and thy father,
Conspirant 'gainst this high illustrious prince,
And from th' extremest upward of thy head
To the descent and dust below thy foot,
A most toad-spotted traitor. Say thou "No,"
This sword, this arm, and my best spirits are bent
To prove upon thy heart, whereto I speak,
Thou liest.
Edm. In wisdom I should ask thy name,
But since thy outside looks so fair and warlike,
And that thy tongue some say of breeding breathes,
What safe and nicely I might well delay
By rule of knighthood, I disdain and spurn.
Back do I toss these treasons to thy head,
With the hell-hated lie o'erwhelm thy heart,
Which for they yet glance by, and scarcely bruise,
This sword of mine shall give them instant way
Where they shall rest for ever. Trumpets, speak!
Alarums. [*They fight. Edmund falls.*]
Alb. Save him, save him!
Gon. This is practice, Gloucester.
By th' law of war thou wast not bound to answer
An unknown opposite. Thou art not vanquish'd,
But cozen'd and beguil'd.
Alb. Shut your mouth, dame,
Or with this paper shall I [stopple] it. Hold, sir.—
Thou worse than any name, read thine own evil.
No tearing, lady, I perceive you know it.
Gon. Say if I do, the laws are mine, not thine;
Who can arraign me for't?
Alb. Most monstrous! O!
Know'st thou this paper?
[*Gon.*] Ask me not what I know. *Exit.*
Alb. Go after her; she's desperate, govern her.
Edm. What you have charg'd me with, that have I done,
And more, much more, the time will bring it out.
'Tis past, and so am I. But what art thou
That hast this fortune on me? If thou'rt noble,
I do forgive thee.
Edg. Let's exchange charity.
I am no less in blood than thou art, Edmund;
If more, the more th' hast wrong'd me.
My name is Edgar, and thy father's son.
The gods are just, and of our pleasant vices
Make instruments to plague us:
The dark and vicious place where thee he got
Cost him his eyes.
Edm. Th' hast spoken right, 'tis true.
The wheel is come full circle, I am here.
Alb. Methought thy very gait did prophesy

134. heart: courage. **138. descent:** lowest part.
139. toad-spotted: i.e. stained with infamy.
140. bent: prepared, ready for action.
144. that: since. **say:** trace.
145. safe and nicely: cautiously and with technical correctness.
147. treasons: accusations of treason.
148. hell-hated: hated as hell is hated. **149. for:** since.
152. practice: trickery. **156. stopple:** stop up.
162. govern: restrain. **166. fortune on:** victory over.
171. pleasant: pleasurable.
175. wheel: wheel of fortune. **here:** i.e. at the bottom, where I began.

A royal nobleness. I must embrace thee.
Let sorrow split my heart, if ever I
Did hate thee or thy father.
Edg. Worthy prince, I know't.
Alb. Where have you hid yourself?
How have you known the miseries of your father?
Edg. By nursing them, my lord. List a brief tale,
And when 'tis told, O that my heart would burst!
The bloody proclamation to escape,
That follow'd me so near (O, our lives' sweetness!
That we the pain of death would hourly die
Rather than die at once!), taught me to shift
Into a madman's rags, t' assume a semblance
That very dogs disdain'd; and in this habit
Met I my father with his bleeding rings,
Their precious stones new lost; became his guide,
Led him, begg'd for him, sav'd him from despair;
Never (O fault!) reveal'd myself unto him,
Until some half hour past, when I was arm'd.
Not sure, though hoping, of this good success,
I ask'd his blessing, and from first to last
Told him our pilgrimage. But his flaw'd heart
(Alack, too weak the conflict to support!)
'Twixt two extremes of passion, joy and grief,
Burst smilingly.
Edm. This speech of yours hath mov'd me,
And shall perchance do good: but speak you on,
You look as you had something more to say.
Alb. If there be more, more woeful, hold it in,
For I am almost ready to dissolve,
Hearing of this.
[*Edg.* This would have seem'd a period
To such as love not sorrow, but another,
To amplify too much, would make much more,
And top extremity. Whilst I
Was big in clamor, came there in a man,
Who, having seen me in my worst estate,
Shunn'd my abhorr'd society, but then finding
Who 'twas that so endur'd, with his strong arms
He fastened on my neck and bellowed out
As he'd burst heaven, threw [him] on my father,
Told the most piteous tale of Lear and him
That ever ear received, which in recounting,
His grief grew puissant and the strings of life
Began to crack. Twice then the trumpets sounded,
And there I left him tranc'd.
Alb. But who was this?
Edg. Kent, sir, the banish'd Kent, who in disguise
Followed his enemy king, and did him service
Improper for a slave.]

Enter a GENTLEMAN [*with a bloody knife*].

Gent. Help, help! O, help!
Edg. What kind of help?
Alb. Speak, man.

195. success: outcome. **197. flaw'd:** cracked.
206. love not: are not in love with.
206–8. but . . . extremity: one more such circumstance, amplifying what is already too much, would increase it and pass all limits.
209. big in clamor: loud in lamentation.
217. strings of life: heart-strings. **219. tranc'd:** unconscious.
221. enemy: hostile. **222. Improper:** i.e. too menial.

Edg. What means this bloody knife?
Gent. 'Tis hot, it smokes,
It came even from the heart of—O, she's dead!
Alb. Who dead? Speak, man.
Gent. Your lady, sir, your lady; and her sister
By her is poison'd; she confesses it.
Edm. I was contracted to them both; all three
Now marry in an instant.
Edg. Here comes Kent.

Enter KENT.

Alb. Produce the bodies, be they alive or dead.
[*Exit Gentleman.*]
This judgment of the heavens, that makes us tremble,
Touches us not with pity.—O, is this he?
The time will not allow the compliment
Which very manners urges.
Kent. I am come
To bid my king and master aye good night.
Is he not here?
Alb. Great thing of us forgot!
Speak, Edmund, where's the King? and where's Cordelia? *Goneril and Regan's bodies brought out.*
Seest thou this object, Kent?
Kent. Alack, why thus?
Edm. Yet Edmund was belov'd!
The one the other poison'd for my sake,
And after slew herself.
Alb. Even so. Cover their faces.
Edm. I pant for life. Some good I mean to do,
Despite of mine own nature. Quickly send
(Be brief in it) to th' castle, for my writ
Is on the life of Lear and on Cordelia.
Nay, send in time.
Alb. Run, run, O, run!
Edg. To who, my lord? Who has the office? Send
Thy token of reprieve.
Edm. Well thought on. Take my sword. [The captain—]
Give it the captain.
[*Alb.*] Haste thee, for thy life. [*Exit Edgar.*]
Edm. He hath commission from thy wife and me
To hang Cordelia in the prison, and
To lay the blame upon her own despair,
That she fordid herself.
Alb. The gods defend her! Bear him hence awhile.
[*Edmund is borne off.*]

Enter LEAR *with Cordelia in his arms,* [EDGAR *and a* GENTLEMAN *following*].

Lear. Howl, howl, howl! O, [you] are men of stones!
Had I your tongues and eyes, I'ld use them so
That heaven's vault should crack. She's gone for ever!
I know when one is dead, and when one lives;
She's dead as earth. Lend me a looking-glass,
If that her breath will mist or stain the stone,
Why then she lives.
Kent. Is this the promis'd end?
Edg. Or image of that horror?
Alb. Fall, and cease!
Lear. This feather stirs, she lives! If it be so,
It is a chance which does redeem all sorrows
That ever I have felt.
Kent. [*Kneeling.*] O my good master!
Lear. Prithee away.
Edg. 'Tis noble Kent, your friend.
Lear. A plague upon you, murderers, traitors all!
I might have sav'd her, now she's gone for ever!
Cordelia, Cordelia, stay a little. Ha!
What is't thou say'st? Her voice was ever soft,
Gentle, and low, an excellent thing in woman.
I kill'd the slave that was a-hanging thee.
Gent. 'Tis true, my lords, he did.
Lear. Did I not, fellow?
I have seen the day, with my good biting falchion
I would have made [them] skip. I am old now,
And these same crosses spoil me. Who are you?
Mine eyes are not o' th' best; I'll tell you straight.
Kent. If Fortune brag of two she lov'd and hated,
One of them we behold.
Lear. This is a dull sight. Are you not Kent?
Kent. The same:
Your servant Kent. Where is your servant Caius?
Lear. He's a good fellow, I can tell you that;
He'll strike, and quickly too. He's dead and rotten.
Kent. No, my good lord, I am the very man—
Lear. I'll see that straight.
Kent. That from your first of difference and decay,
Have follow'd your sad steps—
Lear. [You] are welcome hither.
Kent. Nor no man else. All's cheerless, dark, and deadly.
Your eldest daughters have foredone themselves,
And desperately are dead.
Lear. Ay, so I think.
Alb. He knows not what he says, and vain is it
That we present us to him.
Edg. Very bootless.

Enter a MESSENGER.

Mess. Edmund is dead, my lord.
Alb. That's but a trifle here.
You lords and noble friends, know our intent.
What comfort to this great decay may come
Shall be applied. For us, we will resign,
During the life of this old majesty,

234. **compliment:** ceremony. 239. **object:** sight.
240. **Yet:** in spite of all. 256. **fordid:** destroyed.
263. **stone:** mirror of polished stone.

264. **promis'd end:** i.e. end of the world.
265. **image:** exact likeness. **Fall, and cease:** i.e. let the earth come to its end. 277. **falchion:** light sword.
279. **crosses:** adversities. **spoil me:** wear me down.
280. **tell you straight:** recognize you in a moment (*straight* = straightway).
281. **two . . . hated:** i.e. the two men who best illustrate her fickleness in raising up and then casting down (?) or the man she loved most and the man she hated most (?).
283. **This . . . sight:** my eyes really are failing. 288. **see:** see to.
289. **first . . . decay:** beginning of the deterioration of your fortunes (*difference and decay* = change and decline, i.e. change for the worse).
291. **Nor . . . else:** no, neither I nor anyone else.
293. **desperately:** out of despair, i.e. by their own hands (true only of Goneril's death). 298. **great decay:** great man fallen into ruin.

To him our absolute power. [*To Edgar and Kent.*]
You, to your rights,
With boot, and such addition as your honors
Have more than merited. All friends shall taste
The wages of their virtue, and all foes
The cup of their deservings. O, see, see!
Lear. And my poor fool is hang'd! No, no, no life!
Why should a dog, a horse, a rat, have life,
And thou no breath at all? Thou'lt come no more,
Never, never, never, never, never.
Pray you undo this button. Thank you, sir.
Do you see this? Look on her! Look her lips,
Look there, look there! *He dies.*
Edg. He faints. My lord, my lord!
Kent. Break, heart, I prithee break!
Edg. Look up, my lord.

302. boot: advantage, augmentation. **addition:** additional marks of distinction.
306. fool. Here, as often, a term of endearment; it refers to Cordelia.

Kent. Vex not his ghost. O, let him pass, he hates him
That would upon the rack of this tough world
Stretch him out longer.
Edg. He is gone indeed.
Kent. The wonder is he hath endur'd so long,
He but usurp'd his life.
Alb. Bear them from hence. Our present business
Is general woe. [*To Kent and Edgar.*] Friends of my soul, you twain
Rule in this realm, and the gor'd state sustain.
Kent. I have a journey, sir, shortly to go:
My master calls me, I must not say no.
Edg. The weight of this sad time we must obey,
Speak what we feel, not what we ought to say:
The oldest hath borne most; we that are young
Shall never see so much, nor live so long.
Exeunt with a dead march.

314. ghost: departing spirit. **321. gor'd:** wounded.

NOTE ON THE TEXT

King Lear presents a number of extremely complicated and confusing textual problems. There are two primary texts, the First Quarto (Q1) (1608) and the First Folio (F1) (1623). A second quarto (Q2), also dated 1608 but actually printed in 1619, is essentially an occasionally corrected reprint of Q1, with one or two slight additions (see Textual Notes, III.vi.47, IV.vi.197); a third quarto (Q3), printed from Q2 and of no textual significance, appeared in 1655.

The exact provenience of the manuscript underlying Q1 has been variously accounted for: (1) a manuscript resulting from dictation by two boy actors (perhaps those who played Goneril and Regan) one of whom, reading from Shakespeare's "foul papers" (i.e., rough draft), allowed his memory of the play to contaminate his reading, the other, only hearing, not seeing, the text, made aural errors and not infrequently reduced verse to prose (Walker, Duthie [1960]; earlier [1949] Duthie had shown the older stenographic theory [Greg, 1940] to be unworkable); (2) a manuscript taken down in long-hand during one or more performances at the Globe, like (1), allowing for actors' aural and verse/prose errors (Stone); (3) a manuscript sharked up by memorial reconstruction by one or more actors, thus showing (as Q1 appears to do) such typical characteristics of a reported text as anticipations, recollections, transpositions, substitutions, paraphrases, improvisations, and so on, although the resulting text is considerably better in most ways than the memorially reconstructed texts in the "bad" quartos of *Romeo and Juliet* (Q1) and *Hamlet* (Q1) (Kirschbaum, Walton); (4) Shakespeare's holograph "foul papers," the corrupt state of the Q1 text being explained by the occasional difficulty of Shakespeare's handwriting (see the Introduction to *Sir Thomas More*) and an unusually untidy and messy manuscript, plagued with a number of revised "first thoughts" made, *currente calamo*, in the heat of composition, and set by two compositors (one at least inexperienced) in a printing shop (Nicholas Oke's), which, having a comparatively limited supply of type, was faced with printing its first play script (Doran [later withdrawn], Urkowitz, Blayney, Taylor, Halio). Although none of the above explanations can be entirely ruled out, and each presents difficulties of one kind or another, the fourth is at present most widely accepted, in part perhaps because it best fits the new "two-*Lear*" theory (see below), even though, as Greg has said (1955, p. 379), it is difficult to believe that "Shakespeare, and that at the height of his powers, could ever have written the clumsy and fumbling lines we find in Q."

Similar problems of provenience plague the F1 text. It is now generally agreed that, in some way, either directly or through a transcription, the copy underlying the F1 text made use of either Q1 or Q2 (or both), the printed quarto involved having been annotated by collation against some kind of playhouse manuscript, perhaps the official prompt-book. However, several different interpretations within this framework have been advanced: (1) Greg, Duthie, and Walton argue for the direct use of a copy of Q1 that had been annotated, by correction, deletion, and expansion, against a playhouse manuscript; (2) Werstine and Taylor argue for similar copy, but using a copy of Q2 instead of Q1; (3) Doran, Howard-Hill, and Blayney propose that F1 copy was based on a transcript of either (a) Shakespeare's holograph manuscript (? "fair copy") revised and used as the prompt-book (Doran); (b) a transcript of the prompt-book eked out where unclear, substantively or in accidentals, by consultation of a copy of Q2 and, but less immediately, a copy of Q1, particularly by the inexperienced Compositor E, who was responsible for setting the greater part of the F1 text (Howard-Hill); (c) a transcript of a copy of Q1 which had been annotated by a reviser against the official prompt-book (or at least some theatre-related manuscript), Compositor E, however, making frequent reference for clarification to a copy of Q2; this manuscript then became the new official prompt-book (Blaney, Halio). It should be noted that, in the case of (b) or (c), the use of manuscript copy for the F1 text (the theory now most widely accepted) opens the way to a fourth source of potential corruption, adding to the other three (collator, compositor, and proof-reader) the scribe responsible for copying out the annotated copy of either Q1 or Q2.

It will, I think, be clear by now that no two edited texts of *Lear*, given the complexity and uncertainty of the whole textual situation, will ever be exactly alike. There are too many points in both the Q1–2 and F1 texts which force an editor to choose between readings on essentially subjective grounds. The present text is based on that of F1, a text that, it is now generally agreed, was significantly influenced whether directly or indirectly by both Q1 and Q2. The F1 text contains about 133 lines and part-lines found in neither Q1 or Q2. In addition, however, roughly 288 lines and part-lines (which include one whole scene, IV.iii) unique to Q1 and Q2 have been incorporated, and more than a hundred individual readings from Q1 (and, rarely, from Q2) have been drawn upon to supplement or correct the F1 text. The reasons for this frequent dependence on Q1 (and occasionally its virtual reprint, Q2) are several. First, as noted above, there are numerous textual errors in F1 for which Q1 offers the most authoritative corrections. Second, when the F1 text is influenced by an uncorrected state of Q1 it is occasionally necessary to restore the corrected state of Q1 (as in III.iv.12; IV.i.10, IV.ii.28, 29, 60, 79). Third, where F1 follows a reading otherwise unique to Q2, such readings being without textual authority, the Q1 reading has been preferred (e.g., I.iv.22, 31, 137; II.i.20), except in a few cases where Q2 (1619) reflects a normalized form (e.g., Q1 "a" *v.* Q2 "he") which would have been altered by the F1 editor(s) (see IV.vi.70; also the practice in other F1 plays) regardless of Q2's reading, or where, for metrical, assonantal, or some other special reason, the Q2/F1 reading seems preferable to that of Q1 (e.g., IV.vi.269–70). Fourth, Q1 occasionally offers readings which, it has been generally agreed, are superior to those in F1 (e.g., II.i.45; III.vii.58, 63), the F1 reading in such cases arising, it is argued, from interference by the book-keeper or actors, who presumably wished to get rid of difficult or esoteric words.

Some few years ago, a group of critics (Warren, Urkowitz, Wells, Taylor, and others, in *The Division of the Kingdoms*, 1983, and elsewhere) proposed that the F1 text represented a version of the play so significantly different from that in Q1–2 in tighter dramatic structure and acting pace, as well as in its treatment of a number of characters (Lear, Albany, the Fool, and Goneril) that it must be considered a separate play in its own right, and that these differences were the result of a careful revision undertaken by Shakespeare himself. No one, of course, would deny that the F1 text differs in several ways from the Q1–2 text; it omits some 288 lines or part-lines, adds some 133 lines or part-lines, differs in a substantial number of substantive readings (single words and phrases; see the Textual Notes), and handles the war theme more diplomatically by getting rid of Q1–2 references to Cordelia's attempt to rescue Lear as a French invasion of England. These are the facts. But the premise on which the proponents of the two-*Lear* theory build their case—that the F1 text represents Shakespeare's own revision of the play as it appears in Q1–2—is, so far as any hard evidence is concerned, grounded on subjective interpretations of the "facts" by critics, who, taking Shakespeare's full involvement as a given, discover exaggerated indications of a planned revision even in the most trifling differences, none of which, except perhaps, but not necessarily, for the lines unique to F1 (a number of which, however, are almost certainly due to omissions by the Q1 compositors), are not beyond the capability of an intelligent, but careless, book-keeper. T. H. Howard-Hill well describes the critical dangers inherent in such an *a priori* approach:

> Despite the confidence with which the contributors to *The Division of the Kingdoms* hold that Q/F variations represent literary revision and are not merely the effects of faulty textual transmission, the trivial or indifferent character of many of the variations which are brought forward to illustrate the revision can allow readers reasonably to suspect that (although textual variations do affect the character of the play in which they appear, and variations as numerous as those in Q and F must have considerable effects) the distinctive literary consequences of the variation are more a measure of the critical sensitivity of the scholars who interpret them than an indication of a purposed, consistent revision of an existing play into another distinct form.

(Howard-Hill is quoted from a review of *The Division of the Kingdoms* in *The Library,* 6th ser., VII (1985), 164; see also similar critiques by Carroll, Edwards, Foakes, Knowles, Muir, Thomas, Trousdale, Honigmann [1990], Kermode, Meyer, and Clare.)

In any case, a reader who wishes to reconstruct the main outlines of the F1 text as it differs from that of Q1–2 may do so by noting those passages found only in Q1–2, which in the present text are enclosed in square brackets; similarly, the main outlines of the Q1–2 text may be reconstructed by marking the following passages omitted from the Q1–2 text (single words or phrases are generally not included): I.i.40–5 ("while . . . now."), 49–50, 84–5 ("The vines . . . interess'd,"), 86 ("Speak."), 88–9 ("*Lear.* Nothing? *Cor.* Nothing."), 162 ("*Alb., Corn.* Dear sir, forbear."), 245 ("I am firm."); I.ii.18 ("Fine word, 'legitimate'!"), 109–14 ("This . . . graves."), 137 ("*fa, sol, la, mi.*"), 166–71 ("I pray . . . brother?"); I.iv.6 ("So . . . come,"), 261 ("*Alb.* Pray . . . patient."), 274 ("Of . . . you."), 305 ("Ha? . . . so."), 322–33 ("This . . . Oswald?"); II.ii.44 ("Part!"); II.iv.6 ("*Kent.* No, my lord."), 22 ("*Kent.* By . . . ay."), 46–55 ("Winter's . . . year."), 98–9 ("*Glou.* Well, . . . man?"), 103 ("Are . . . blood!"), 140–5 ("*Lear.* Say? . . . blame."); III.i.22–9; III.ii.79–96; III.iv.17 ("In . . .")–18, 26–7, 37–8 ("*Edg.* Fathom . . . Tom!"), 58–9 ("O do de . . . do de."); III.vi.12–14 ("*Fool.* No . . . him."), 85 ("*Fool.* And . . . noon."); IV.i.6–9 ("Welcome . . . But"), 54 ("And . . . must."); IV.ii.26 ("O . . . man."); IV.vi.165–70 ("Plate . . . lips."), 185 ("I'll . . . proof,"), 203 ("Sa . . . sa."); V.i.46 ("And machination ceases."); V.ii.11 ("*Glou.* And . . . too."); V.iii.76, 89 ("*Gon.* An enterlude!"), 90 ("let . . . sound."), 145, 156 ("Hold, sir."), 223 ("O, help!"), 225 ("O, she's dead!"), 256 (omitted Q2 only), 283 ("This . . . sight."), 311–12 ("Do . . . there!").

Since the textual situation is so uncertain, it has seemed worthwhile to include in the Textual Notes all variants between F1 and Q1 (a few elided forms not included).

For further information, see: Madeleine Doran, *The Text of "King Lear"* (Stanford, 1931); W. W. Greg, *The Variants in the First Quarto of "King Lear"* (The Bibliographical Society, London, 1940) [a classic study], and *The Shakespeare First Folio* (Oxford, 1955); Leo Kirschbaum, *The True Text of "King Lear"* (Baltimore, 1940); G. I. Duthie, ed., *Shakespeare's "King Lear"* (Oxford, 1949), *Elizabethan Shorthand and the First Quarto of "King Lear"* (Oxford, 1949), and ed., New Shakespeare *King Lear* (Cambridge, 1960); Philip Williams, "Two Problems in the Folio Text of *King Lear,*" *SQ*, IV (1953), 451–60; Alice Walker, *Textual Problems of the First Folio* (Cambridge, 1953); A. S. Cairncross, "The Quartos and the First Folio Text of *King Lear,*" *RES*, n.s. VI (1955), 252–6; Charlton Hinman, "The Prentice Hand in the Tragedies of the Shakespeare First Folio: Compositor E," *SB,* IX (1957), 3–20, and Supplementary Introduction to the Oxford facsimile of Quarto 1 (1964); J. S. G. Bolton, "Wear and Tear as Factors in the Textual History of the Quarto Version of *King Lear,*" *SQ*, XI (1960), 427–38; Kenneth Muir, ed., New Arden *King Lear* (London, rev. ed., 1963) and *Shakespeare: Contrasts and Controversies* (Norman, Oklahoma, 1985), 51–66; E. A. J. Honigmann, *The Stability of Shakespeare's Text* (London, 1965) and "Shakespeare's Revised Plays: *King Lear* and *Oth-*

ello," *The Library*, 6th ser., IV (1982), 142–73; J. K. Walton, *The Quarto Copy for the First Folio of Shakespeare* (Dublin, 1971); Michael Warren, "Quarto and Folio *King Lear* and the Interpretation of Albany and Edgar," in *Shakespeare: Pattern of Excelling Nature*, ed. David Bevington and J. L. Halio (Newark, 1976), 95–107, and ed., *The Complete Lear, 1608–1623* (Berkeley, 1989: reviewed by E. A. J. Honigmann, *New York Review of Books* [25 October 1990], pp. 58–60); Steven Urkowitz, *Shakespeare's Revision of "King Lear"* (Princeton, 1980; see reviews by Richard Knowles, *MP*, LXXIX [1981], 197–200; Phillip Edwards, *MLR*, LXXVII [1982], 694–8); P. W. K. Stone, ed. *The Textual History of "King Lear"* (London, 1980); P. W. M. Blayney, *The Texts of "King Lear": Vol. I, Nicholas Okes and the First Quarto* (Cambridge, 1982); T. H. Howard-Hill, "The Problem of Manuscript Copy for Folio *King Lear*," *The Library*, 6th ser., IV (1982), 1–24 and "Q1 and the Copy for Folio *Lear*," *PBSA*, LXXX (1986), 419–35; Richard Knowles, "The Printing of the Second Quarto (1619) of *King Lear*," *SB*, XXXV (1982), 191–206; Gary Taylor, "The Folio Copy for *Hamlet, King Lear*, and *Othello*," *SQ*, XXXIV (1983), 44–61; Gary Taylor and Michael Warren, eds., *The Division of the Kingdoms: Shakespeare's Two Versions of "King Lear"* (Oxford, 1983); S. W. Reid, *The Text of "King Lear"* (Stanford, 1983); Sidney Thomas, "Shakespeare's Supposed Revision of *King Lear*," *SQ*, XXXV (1984), 506–11; Gary Taylor, "Folio Compositors and Folio Copy: *King Lear* and Its Context," *PBSA*, LXXIX (1985), 17–74, and "The Rhetorics of Reaction," in *Crisis in Editing: Texts of the English Renaissance*, ed. Randall McLeod (New York, 1994), 19–59 [a counterattack against what Taylor terms the "reactionary" criticisms levelled at the two-*Lear* hypothesis and the New Oxford Shakespeare]; R. A. Foakes, "Textual Revision and the Fool in *King Lear*," in *Essays in Honour of Peter Davison: Trivium*, XX (Wales, 1985, 33–47; Marion Trousdale, "A Trip Through the Divided Kingdoms," *SQ*, XXXVII (1986), 218–23; Stanley Wells, Gary Taylor, et al., *William Shakespeare: A Textual Companion* (Oxford, 1987); W. C. Carroll, "New Plays vs. Old Readings: *The Division of the Kingdoms* and Folio Deletions in *King Lear*," *SP*, LXXXV (1988), 225–44; Jay L. Halio, ed., New Cambridge *The Tragedy of King Lear* (Cambridge, 1992) and ed., *The First Quarto of "King Lear"* (Cambridge, 1994); A. R. Meyer, "Shakespeare's Art and the Texts of *King Lear*," *SB*, XLVII (1994), 128–46; Sir Frank Kermode, "Disintegration Once More," *Proceedings of the British Academy*, LXXXIV(1994), 93–111; Robert Clare, "The Theory of Authorial Revision between Quarto and Folio Texts of *King Lear*," *The Library*, 6th ser., XVII (1995), 34–59.

TEXTUAL NOTES

Title: The . . . Lear] M. William Shak-speare: His True Chronicle Historie of the life and death of King Lear and his three Daughters. With the vnfortunate life of Edgar, sonne and heire to the Earle of Gloster, and his sullen and assumed humor of Tom of Bedlam: As it was played before the Kings Maiestie at Whitehall vpon S. Stephans night in Christmas Hollidayes. By his Maiesties seruants playing vsually at the Gloabe on the Bancke-side. *Q1 (title-page)*

Dramatis personae: *subs. as first given in Rowe*

Act-scene division: *none in Q1–2; from F1, with the following exceptions: II.iii, iv (no scene divisions in F1); IV.iii (scene om. F1); IV.iv–vi (numbered IV.iii–v in F1); see first note to each of these scenes; present act-scene arrangement as a whole first established by Steevens*

I.i

Location: *Theobald (after Rowe)*

o.s.d. **Edmund]** Bastard *Q1–2*

4 **kingdom]** kingdomes *Q1–2*

5 **equalities]** *Q1–2;* qualities *F1*

11 **to't]** to it *Q1–2*

19 **a son, sir]** sir a sonne *Q1–2*

20–1 **this, . . . account.]** *Theobald (subs.);* this; . . . account, *F1;* this, . . . account, *Q1–2*

22 **to]** into *Q1–2*

25 **Edmund]** *Q1–2 (throughout, except* Edmond *at V.iii.168 in Q1);* Edmond *F1 (through I.ii and at V.iii.168)*

26 s.p. **Edm.]** Bast. *Q1–2 (subs. throughout)*

27–8 **My . . . friend.]** *as prose, Q1–2; as verse, F1*

33 s.d. **Sound a sennet.]** *Q1–2;* Sennet. *F1 (all after* coming. *l. 33); placed as in Dyce*

33 s.d. **one . . . then]** *Q1–2; Q1–2 s.d. reads:* Enter one bearing a Coronet, then Lear, then the Dukes of Albany, and Cornwell [Cornwall *Q2*], next Gonorill, Regan, Cordelia, with followers.

33 s.d. **Goneril]** Gonorill *Q1–2 (throughout, except* Gonoril *in Q1 at III.vi.36)*

34 **the]** my *Q1–2*

35 **lord]** Leige *Q1–2*

35 s.d. **with Edmund]** *Capell (subs.); s.d. om. Q1–2*

36 **shall]** will *Q1–2*

36 **purpose.]** purposes, *Q1–2*

37 **Give . . . that]** The map there; know *Q1–2*

38 **fast]** first *Q1–2*

39 **from our age]** of our state *Q1–2*

40 **Conferring]** Confirming *Q1–2*

40 **strengths]** yeares *Q1–2*

40–5 **while . . . now.]** *om. Q1–2*

45 **The princes]** The two great Princes *Q1–2*

49–50 **(Since . . . state),]** *om. Q1–2*

53 **nature . . . challenge]** merit doth most challenge it *Q1–2*

55 **I]** I do *Q1–2*

55 **words]** *Q1–2;* word *F1 (line very crowded in F1)*

56 **and]** or *Q1–2*

59 **as . . . lov'd]** a . . . loued *Q1–2*

59 **found]** friend *Q1–2*

62, 76 s.dd. **Aside.]** *Pope*

62 **speak?]** doe, *Q1–2*

64 **shadowy]** shady *Q1–2*

64–5 **and . . . rivers,]** *om. Q1–2*

64 **rich'd,]** *Rowe;* rich'd *F1*

66 **Albany's]** *Rowe;* Albanies *F1, Q2;* Albaines *Q1*

66 **issue]** *Q1–2;* issues *F1*

68 **of Cornwall]** to Cornwell *Q1 (Cornwell throughout scene);* to Cornwall *Q2 (Cornwall throughout scene)*

68 **Speak.]** *Q1–2*

69 **I . . . sister]** Sir I am made of the selfe same mettall that my sister is *Q1,* (selfe-same) *Q2*

69 **self metal]** *Capell;* selfe-mettle *F1; see preceding note for Q1–2*

70 **worth.]** worth *Q1–2*

72 **comes too short]** came short *Q1–2*

74 **possesses]** *Q1–2;* professes *F1*

76 **Cordelia]** Cord. *Q1*

77 **love's]** loues *Q1*

78 **ponderous]** richer *Q1–2*

82 **conferr'd]** confirm'd *Q1–2*

82 **Now]** but now *Q1–2*

83 **Although . . . love]** Although the last, not least in our deere loue, *Q1–2*

84–5 **The . . . interess'd,]** *om. Q1–2*

85 **interess'd]** *Malone;* interest *F1*

85 **draw]** win *Q1–2*

86 **opulent]** *Q1–2;* opilent *F1*

86 **sisters']** *ed.;* Sisters *F1, Q1–2*

86 **Speak.]** *om. Q1–2*

88–9 **Lear. Nothing? Cor. Nothing.]** *om. Q1–2*

90 **Nothing will]** How, nothing can *Q1–2*

93 **no]** nor *Q1–2*

94 **How, how, Cordelia?]** Goe to, goe to, *Q1;* Go too, go too, *Q2*

95 **you]** it *Q1–2*

96 **lov'd]** loued *Q1–2 (the* 'd *and* -ed *variants between F1 and Q1–2 are not hereafter recorded, since Q1–2 seem haphazard in making any distinction)*

100 **Happily]** Happely *Q1;* Haply *Q2*

104 **To . . . all.]** *Q1–2*

105 **thy . . . this]** this with thy heart *Q1–2*

105 **Ay, my good]** I good my *Q1–2*

108 **Let]** Well let *Q1–2*

110 **mysteries]** *F2;* miseries *F1;* mistresse *Q1–2*

110 **Hecat]** *F2;* Heccat *F1, Q1–2*

110 **night]** might *Q1–2*

118 **to my bosom]** *om. Q1–2*

124 s.d. **To Cordelia.]** *Rowe*

127 **Burgundy.]** *Rowe (subs.);* Burgundy, *F1, Q1–2*

128 **dow'rs]** dower *Q1–2*

128 **the]** this *Q1–2*

130 **with]** in *Q1–2*

131 **Pre-eminence]** *Jennens;* Preheminence *F1, Q1–2*

135 **turn]** turnes *Q1–2*

135 **we shall]** we still *Q1–2*

136 **th' addition]** the addicions *Q1–2*

139 **between]** betwixt *Q1–2*

146 **mad]** man *Q1*

146 **wouldest]** wilt *Q1–2*

149 **falls]** stoops *Q1–2*

149 **folly. Reserve]** *Rowe (subs.);* folly, reserue *F1;* folly, / Reuerse *Q1–2*

149 **state]** doome *Q1–2*

151 **rashness. . . . judgment,]** *Rowe (subs.);* rashnesse, . . . iudgement: *F1;* rashnes, . . . iudgement, *Q1–2*

153–4 **sounds Reverb]** sound / Reverbs *Q1–2*

155 **a]** *Q1–2*

156 **thine enemies, ne'er]** thy enemies, nor *Q1–2*

156 **fear'd]** *Furness conj.;* feare *F1, Q1–2*

157 **motive]** the motiue *Q1–2*

160 s.pp. **Lear. . . . Kent.]** *Q1–2;* Kear. . . . Lent. *F1*

160 **Apollo—]** *Q2;* Apollo, *F1;* Appollo, *Q1*

161 **swear'st]** swearest *Q1*

161 **O]** *om. Q1–2*

161 **miscreant]** recreant *Q1–2*

161 s.d. **Starts . . . sword.]** *Rowe (subs.)*

162 Alb., Corn. Dear sir, forbear.] *om. Q1–2; F1 reads s.p. as* Cor.
163 Kill] Doe, kill Q1–2
163 the] Q1–2; thy F1
164 gift] doome Q1–2
166–7 recreant, On thine] on thy Q1–2
168 That] Since Q1–2
168 vow] Q1–2; vowes F1
169 strain'd] straied Q1–2
170 betwixt] betweene Q1–2
170 sentence] F1 (u), Q1–2; sentences F1 (c)
173 Five] Foure Q1
173 thee, for provision] *Capell;* thee for prouision, F1, Q1–2
174 disasters] diseases Q1–2
175 sixt] fift Q1–2
178 death. Away!] *Pope (subs.);* death, away. F1; death, away, Q1–2
180 Fare] Why fare Q1–2
180 King; sith] *Theobald;* King, sith F1; king, since Q1–2
181 Freedom] Friendship Q1–2
182 s.d. To Cordelia.] *Hanmer*
182 dear . . . thee] protection take the Q1–2
183 justly think'st . . . rightly] rightly thinks . . . iustly Q1–2
184 s.d. To . . . Goneril.] *Hanmer*
187 s.d. Flourish.] *om. Q1–2*
187 s.d. Enter . . . Attendants.] Enter France and Burgundie with Gloster. Q1–2
188 s.p. Glou.] Q1–2; Cor. F1 *(possibly correct, if* Cor. *is an abbreviated form of* Cornwall)
190 toward] towards Q1–2
190 this] a Q1–2
193 Most] *om. Q1–2*
194 hath] what Q1–2
195 less.] F4; lesse? F1, Q1–2
197 price] prise Q1
200 more] else Q1–2
202 Will] Sir will Q1; Sir, will Q2
204 Dow'r'd] Couered Q1–2
206 in] On Q1–2
208 s.d. To France.] *Pope*
214 whom] that Q1–2
214 best] Q1–2
216 The best, the] most best, most Q1–2
220 it,] Q1–2; it: F1
220 your fore-vouch'd affection] you for voucht affections Q1–2
221 Fall] Falne Q1–2
221 taint;] *Steevens;* taint, F1, Q1–2
223 Should] Could Q1–2
225 well] Q1–2; will F1
226 make known] may know Q1–2
228 unchaste] vncleane Q1–2
230 richer] rich Q1–2
231 still-soliciting] *hyphen, Warburton*
232 That] As Q1–2
233 Better] Goe to, goe to, better Q1–2
235 but] no more but Q1–2
236 Which] That Q1–2
238 Love's] Loue is Q1–2
239 regards] respects Q1–2
240 point.] *Steevens (after Pope);* point, F1, Q2; point Q1
241 a dowry] and dowre Q1; and dower Q2
241 King] Leir Q1; Lear Q2
245 Nothing.] *Rowe (subs.);* Nothing, F1, Q1–2
245 I am firm.] *om. Q1–2*
248 respects of fortune] Q1–2; respect and Fortunes F1
252 seize] ceaze Q1
256 my] thy Q1–2
258 of] in Q1–2
259 Can] Shall Q1–2
264 s.d. To Cordelia.] *Neilson (after anon. conj. in Cambridge)*
266 s.d. all . . . Cordelia] *Globe (after Capell);* Lear and Burgundie Q1–2
271 Love] vse Q1–2
276 s.p. Reg.] Gonorill. Q1–2
276 duty] duties Q1–2
276 s.p. Gon.] Regan. Q1–2
279 want] worth Q1–2
280 plighted] pleated Q1–2
281 with shame] shame them Q1–2
282 my] *om. Q1–2*
282 s.d. Exeunt] F3; Exit F1, Q1–2
283–5 Sister . . . to-night.] *as prose, Capell; as verse, F1, Q1–2*
283 little] a little Q1–2
289 not] Q1–2
292 grossly] grosse Q1–2
296–7 from . . . long-ingraff'd] to receiue from his age not alone the imperfection of long ingrafted Q1–2
298 the unruly] vnruly Q1–2
302 compliment] *Johnson;* complement F1, Q1–2
303 Pray you] pray Q1–2
303 let us] lets Q1–2
303 hit] Q1–2; sit F1
304 disposition] dispositions Q1–2
307 of it] on't Q1–2

I.ii

Location: *Pope*
o.s.d. with a letter] *Theobald*
1 s.p. Edm.] *Theobald;* Bast. F1 *(through l. 159),* Q1–2 *(throughout)*
4 me,] Q1–2; me? F1
10 baseness?] *Rowe;* basenes F1; base, Q1–2
10 bastardy] Q1–2; Barstadie F1
10 base, base?] *om. Q1–2*
13 dull, stale, tired] stale dull lyed Q1; stale, dull lied Q2
14 a] of a Q1–2
15 asleep] *Capell;* a sleepe F1, Q1; sleepe Q2
15 then] the Q1–2
18 Fine word, "legitimate"!] *om. Q1–2*
21 top] *Edwards conj.;* to' F1; too Q1–2
24 Prescrib'd] subscribd Q1–2
27 s.d. Putting . . . letter.] *Rowe*
32 needed] needes Q1–2
32 terrible] terribe Q1
37 and] *om. Q1–2*
39 o'erlooking] liking Q1–2
41–2 I . . . blame.] *as prose, Q1–2; as verse,* F1
46 s.d. (Reads.)] Q1–2 *describe ll. 46–54 as* A Letter.
46 and reverence] *om. Q1–2*
54 brother.] brother Q1–2
55 Sleep . . . wake] slept . . . wakt Q1–2
58 you to this] this to you Q1–2
64 his; . . . that,] his but in respect, of that Q1; his, but in respect of that, Q2
66 It is his.] It is his? Q1; Is it his? Q2
69 Has] Hath Q1–2
69 before] heretofore Q1–2
71 heard him oft] often heard him Q1–2
72 perfect] perfit Q1–2
73 declin'd, the] declining, his Q1–2
74 his] the Q1–2
77 sirrah] sir Q1–2
77 I'll] I Q1–2
78 Abominable] F4; Abhominable F1, Q1–2
82 his] this Q1–2
86 that . . . writ] he hath wrote Q1–2
87 other] further Q1–2
92 auricular] aurigular Q1–2
95–7 Edm. Nor . . . earth!] Q1–2
98 him, . . . the] him, I pray you frame your Q1–2
101 will] shall Q1–2
102 find] see Q1–2
105 it] *om. Q1–2*
108 discord] discords Q1–2
108 in] *om. Q1–2*
108 and] *om. Q1–2*
109 'twixt] betweene Q1–2
109–14 This . . . graves.] *om. Q1–2*
117 honesty] honest Q1–2
117 'Tis strange.] strange strange! Q1; strange, strange! Q2
117 s.d. Exit.] *om. Q1–2*
119 surfeits] surfeit Q1–2
121 and] and the Q1–2
122 on] by Q1–2
123 treachers] Trecherers Q1–2
123 spherical] spirituall Q1–2
127 whoremaster man] Q1–2; Whore-master-man F1
128 on . . . star] to the charge of Starres Q1–2
131 Fut] Q1–2
132 in] of Q1–2
133 bastardizing.] bastardy Q1; bastardy; Q2
133 Edgar—] Q1 (Edgar;); Edgar, Q2
133 s.d. Enter Edgar.] *in left margin, opposite* Edgar— *l. 133,* Q1
134 Pat] and out Q1–2
135 My cue] mine Q1–2
135 sigh] sith Q1
136 Tom o'] them of Q1–2
137 fa . . . mi] *om. Q1–2*
137 s.d. Humming these notes.] *Hanmer (subs.)*
142 with] about Q1–2
143 writes] writ Q1–2
144–52 as . . . come,] Q1–2
146 amities] armies Q2
153 The] Why, the Q1; Why the Q2
155 Ay] *Rowe;* I F1; *om. Q1–2*
157 nor] or Q1–2
161 until] till Q1–2
163 scarcely] scarce Q1–2
166 fear.] feare brother, Q1–2
166–71 I . . . brother?] *om. Q1–2 (except for* go arm'd *[l. 170], which follows* I advise you to the best; *[l. 172])*
173 toward] towards Q1–2
174 heard;] heard, Q1–2
174 faintly,] Q1–2; faintly. F1
178 s.d. Exit Edgar.] Q1 (Fdgar), Q2; Exit. F1 *(after l. 177)*

I.iii

Location: *Rowe*
o.s.d. Steward Oswald] *Collier;* Steward F1; Gentleman Q1–2
2 s.p. Osw.] *Collier;* Ste. F1 *(throughout);* Gent. Q1–2 *(throughout scene)*
2 Ay] *Rowe;* I F1; Yes Q1–2
3 night] Q1–2; night, F1
6 upbraids] obrayds Q1
6–7 us . . . When] vs, / On euery trifell when Q1, (vs) Q2
10 s.d. Horns within.] *Capell*
13 fellows] fellow seruants Q1; fellow-seruants Q2
13 to] in Q1–2
14 distaste] dislike Q1–2
14 my] our Q1–2
16–20 Not . . . abus'd.] Q1–2 *(as prose; as verse, Theobald)*
21 have said] tell you Q1–2
21 Well] Very well Q1–2
22–3 And . . . so.] *as verse, Capell (after Hanmer); as prose,* F1, Q1–2
24–5 I . . . speak.] Q1–2 *(as prose; as verse, Capell)*
25–6 I'll . . . dinner.] *as verse, Hanmer; as prose,* F1, Q1–2
26 very] Q1–2
26 Prepare] goe prepare Q1–2

I.iv

Location: *ed. (after Pelican)*
o.s.d. disguised as Caius] *Rowe*
1 well] Q1–2; will F1
4 raz'd] Q1; raiz'd F1; raizd Q2
6 So . . . come,] *om. Q1–2*
6 lov'st] louest Q1–2
7 thee] the Q1–2
7 labors] labour Q1–2
7 s.d. Knights] *Rowe;* Q1–2 *s.d. reads:* Enter Lear.
7 s.d. from hunting] *ed.*
9 s.d. Exit an Attendant.] *Malone (after Capell)*
21 be'st] be Q1–2
21 he's] he is Q1–2
22 th' art] Q1; thou art F1, Q2
31 canst] Q1; canst thou F1, Q2
37 sir] *om. Q1–2*
40 me.] *Rowe (subs.);* me, F1, Q1–2
42 Dinner, ho,] *Theobald;* Dinner ho, F1, Q2; dinner, ho Q1
43 s.d. Exit an Attendant.] *Dyce*
43 s.d. Enter Steward Oswald.] *placed as in Capell; after l. 44,* F1, Q1–2

44 you] *om. Q1–2*
45 s.d. Exit.] *om. Q1–2*
46 clotpole] clat-pole *Q1–2*
47 s.d. Exit a Knight.] *Dyce*
47 Ho!] *Rowe;* Ho, *F1, Q2;* ho *Q1*
48 asleep.] *Theobald (subs.);* asleepe, *F1, Q1–2*
48 s.d. Enter Knight.] *Dyce*
50 s.p. Knight.] Kent. *Q1–2*
50 daughter] *Q1–2;* Daughters *F1*
54, 57, 64, 73 s.pp. Knight.] seruant. *Q1–2*
56 He] A *Q1*
60 of kindness] *om. Q1–2*
66 wrong'd] is wrong'd *Q2*
70 purpose] purport *Q1–2*
71 my] this *Q1–2*
75 well] *om. Q1–2*
77 s.d. Exit an Attendant.] *Dyce*
77 s.d. Exit another Attendant.] *Dyce*
77 s.d. Enter Steward Oswald.] *placed as in Johnson; after l. 78, F1; om. Q1–2*
78 you, come] you sir, come *Q1–2*
78 hither, sir] hither *Q1–2*
82–3 I . . . pardon.] *as prose, Q1–2; as verse F1*
82 these] this *Q1–2*
82–3 your pardon] you pardon me *Q1–2*
84 s.d. Striking him.] *Rowe*
85 strucken] struck *Q1–2*
86 s.d. Tripping . . . heels.] *Rowe*
87–8 I . . . thee.] *as prose, Q1–2; as verse, F1*
89 arise, away] *om. Q1–2*
91–2 Go . . . So.] you haue wisedome. *Q1–2*
92 wisdom? So.] *Theobald (subs.);* wisedome, so. *F1;* wisedome. *Q1–2*
92 s.d. Pushes Oswald out.] *Theobald*
93 my] *om. Q1–2*
94 s.d. Giving Kent money.] *Johnson*
95 s.d. Offering . . . cap.] *Capell*
98 Kent. Why, Fool?] *Q1–2; Lear.* Why my Boy? *F1 (anticipating l. 106)*
99 Why?] Why *Q1–2*
99 one's] on's *Q1;* ones *Q2*
101 thou'lt] thou't *Q1–2*
102 has] hath *Q1–2*
103 did] done *Q1–2*
107 all my] any *Q1–2*
111 Truth's a dog] Truth is a dog that *Q1,* (is,) *Q2*
112 the Lady Brach] Ladie oth'e brach *Q1–2*
114 gall] gull *Q1–2*
117 nuncle] vncle *Q1–2*
128 s.p. Kent.] Lear. *Q1–2*
129 'tis] *om. Q1–2*
131 nuncle] vncle *Q1–2*
132–3 Why . . . nothing.] *as prose, Q1–2; as verse, F1*
134 s.d. To Kent.] *Rowe*
137 Dost] *Q1* (Doo'st)*;* Do'st thou *F1;* Dost thou *Q2*
138 one] foole *Q1–2*
140–55 That . . . snatching.] *Q1–2*
153 an't] on't *Q2*
154 ladies] lodes *Q2*
154 the] *om. Q2*
155–6 Nuncle . . . egg] giue me an egge Nuncle *Q1–2*
160 crown] *Q1–2;* Crownes *F1*
161 thine] thy *Q1–2*
161 on thy] at'h *Q1*
166, 175 s.dd. Sings.] *Rowe (subs.)*
166 grace] wit *Q1–2*
167 wise men] *Q1–2;* wisemen *F1*
168 And . . . to] They . . . doe *Q1–2*
172 e'er] euer *Q1–2*
173 mothers] mother *Q1–2*
178 fools] *Q1–2;* Foole *F1*
179 Prithee] *F3 (subs.);* Pry'thy *F1;* prethe *Q1;* prethee *Q2*
181 sirrah] *om. Q1–2*
183 thou'lt] thou wilt *Q1–2*
184 sometimes] sometime *Q1–2*
186 o'] of *Q1–2*
187 o'] a *Q1–2*
188 o'] of *Q1–2*
190 You] Me thinks you *Q1;* Me-thinkes you *Q2*
190 Of late] alate *Q1–2*
192 frowning] frowne *Q1–2*
194 s.d. To Goneril.] *Pope*
198 nor crust] neither crust *Q1–2*
198 nor] *Q1–2;* not *F1*
200 s.d. Pointing to Lear.] *Johnson*
204 and . . . riots. Sir,] *Capell (subs.);* and (not to be endur'd) riots Sir. *F1;* & (not to be indured riots,) Sir *Q1;* and (not to be endured riots) Sir, *Q2*
208 it] *om. Q1–2*
210 redresses] redresse *Q1–2*
213 Which] that *Q1–2*
214 Will] must *Q1–2*
214 proceeding] proceedings *Q1–2*
214 know] trow *Q1–2*
215–6 "The . . . young."] *as verse, Pope; as prose, F1, Q1–2*
216 it had] *Q1–2;* it's had *F1*
216 by it] beit *Q1–2*
219 I] Come sir, I *Q1–2*
219 your] that *Q1–2*
221 which . . . transport] that . . . transforme *Q1–2*
225 s.d. Sings.] *ed.*
225 "Whoop . . . thee."] *quotes, Furness*
226, 227 Does] Doth *Q1–2*
226 This] why this *Q1–2*
228 weakens,] weaknes, or *Q1–2*
229 lethargied . . . 'Tis] *(dash, Rowe);* lethergie, sleeping, or wakeing; ha! sure tis *Q1–2*
231 Lear's shadow.] Lears shadow? *Q1–2 (spoken by Lear)*
232–5 Lear. I . . . father.] *Q1–2* (ll. 232–4 *continued to Lear*)*.*
232–4 I . . . daughters.] *as verse, Kittredge (after Pope); as prose, Q1–2*
237 This admiration, sir,] Come sir, this admiration *Q1–2*
239 To] *om. Q1–2*
239 aright,] *Q1–2;* aright: *F1*
240 should] you should *Q2*
242 debosh'd] deboyst *Q1–2*
245 Makes it] make *Q1–2*
245 a brothel] brothell *Q1–2*
246 grac'd] great *Q1–2*
247 then] thou *Q1–2*
250 remainders] remainder *Q1–2*
252 Which] that *Q1;* and *Q2*
255–6 You . . . betters.] *as verse, Rowe; as prose, F1, Q1–2*
256 s.d. Albany] Duke *Q1–2*
257 Woe . . . repents] We . . . repent's *Q1;* We . . . repent's vs *Q2*
257 O . . . come?] *Q1–2*
258 will? . . . my] will that wee prepare any *Q1–2*
261 Alb. Pray . . . patient.] *om. Q1–2*
262 s.d. To Goneril.] *Rowe*
262 liest.] list *Q1;* lessen *Q2*
263 are] and *Q1–2*
268 Which] that *Q1–2*
270 Lear, Lear!] Lear! *Q1–2*
271 s.d. Striking his head.] *Pope*
272 s.d. Exeunt . . . Kent.] *Alexander*
274 Of . . . you.] *om. Q1–2*
275 Hear] harke *Q1–2*
275 hear!] *om. Q1–2*
277–8 fruitful. . . . convey] fruitful into her wombe, conuey *Q1;* fruitefull, into her wombe conuey *Q2*
283 thwart disnatur'd] thourt disuetur'd *Q1–2*
285 cadent] accent *Q1–2*
287 that . . . feel] *repeated, Q1*
289 Away, away.] goe, goe, my people? *Q1–2*
289 s.d. Exit.] *Lear's exit here and re-entry at l. 293 om. Q1–2*
291 more of it] the cause *Q1–2*
293 As] that *Q1–2*
295 What's] What is *Q1–2*
296 s.d. To Goneril.] *Theobald*
296 death!] *Q1–2;* death, *F1*
298 which] that *Q1–2*
299 thee . . . Blasts] the worst blasts *Q1–2*
299–300 upon thee! Th'] vpon the *Q1–2*
301 thee! Old] the old *Q1–2*
302 ye] you *Q1–2*
303 cast you] you cast *Q1–2*
303 loose] make *Q1–2*
304 Yea . . . this?] *Q1–2*
305 Ha . . . so:] *om. Q1–2*
305–6 I . . . Who] yet haue I left a daughter, whom *Q1–2*
310 ever.] euer, thou shalt I warrant thee. *Q1–2*
310 that?] that my Lord? *Q1–2*
312 you—] *Theobald;* you. *F1, Q2;* you, *Q1*
313–4 Pray . . . more] Come sir no more, you, more *Q1;* Come sir, no more; you, more *Q2*
314 s.d. To the Fool.] *Johnson*
315–6 Nuncle . . . thee.] *as prose, Q1–2; as verse, F1*
315 take] and take *Q1–2*
316–7 with thee. A] with a *Q1–2*
322–33 This . . . unfitness—] *om. Q1–2*
333 unfitness—] *Rowe;* vnfitnesse. *F1*
333 How now, Oswald?] *Gon.* What Oswald, ho. *Oswald.* Here Madam. *Q1–2 (Q1–2 om. Oswald's re-entry)*
334 What,] *Q2 (Gon.* What,)*;* What *F1; Gon.* What *Q1*
334 that] this *Q1–2*
335 Ay] *Rowe;* I *F1;* Yes *Q1–2*
337 fear] feares *Q1–2*
340 s.d. Exit Oswald.] *Rowe*
340 No, no] now *Q1;* —now *Q2*
342 condemn] dislike *Q1–2*
343 You are] *F2;* Your are *F1;* y'are *Q1–2*
343 attax'd] *Greg;* at task *F1;* alapt *Q1 (u), Q2;* attaskt *Q1 (c) (cf. III.ii.16)*
344 prais'd] *F2;* prai'sd *F1;* praise *Q1–2*
346 better, oft] better ought, *Q1–2*
347 then—] then. *Q1*
348 th' event] *Rowe;* the'uent *F1;* the euent *Q1–2*

I.v

Location: *Capell (after Theobald)*
o.s.d. Enter . . . Fool.] *Q2;* Enter Lear, Kent, Gentleman, and Foole. *F1;* Enter Lear. *Q1*
5 afore] before *Q1–2*
8 were] where *Q1*
8 in 's] in his *Q1–2*
8 were't] *Rowe;* wert *F1, Q1–2*
11 not] nere *Q1–2*
15 crab's] crab is *Q1–2*
16 can tell] con, *Q1–2*
17 What . . . tell] Why what canst thou tell my *Q1–2*
18 She will] Sheel *Q1–2*
18 does] doth *Q1–2*
19 Canst] canst not *Q1–2*
19–20 stands . . . on 's] stande in the middle of his *Q1,* (stands) *Q2*
22 one's eyes of] his eyes on *Q1–2*
23 he] a *Q1*
30 put 's] put his *Q1–2*
31 daughters] daughter *Q1–2*
32 nature.] *Pope (subs.);* Nature, *F1, Q1–2*
34 'em] them *Q1–2*
35 moe] more *Q1–2*
38 indeed] *om. Q1–2*
39 Monster] Monster, *Q1–2*
41 I'ld] *Globe;* Il'd *F1;* id'e *Q1–2*
44 till] before *Q1–2*
46–8 O . . . ready?] *as verse, Pope; as prose, F1, Q1–2*
46 not mad,] *om. Q1–2*
46 heaven!] heauen! I would not be mad, *Q1–2*
47 s.d. Enter Gentleman.] *Theobald*
48 How now,] *om. Q1–2*
49 s.p. Gent.] Seruant. *Q1–2*
50 s.d. Exeunt . . . Gentleman.] *Capell;* Exit. *Q1–2*
51 that's a] that is *Q1–2*
52 unless] except *Q1–2*
52 s.d. Exit.] *Q1–2;* Exeunt. *F1*

II.i

Location: *Rowe*
o.s.d. severally] meeting *Q1;* meetes him *Q2*
1 s.p. Edm.] *Theobald;* Bast. *F1, Q1–2 (throughout scene)*
2–4 And . . . night.] *as prose, Q1–2; as verse, F1*

2 **you]** *Q1-2;* your *F1*
4 **Regan]** *om. Q1-2*
4 **this night]** to night *Q1-2*
7 **they]** there *Q1-2*
8 **ear-bussing]** *Q1-2;* ear-kissing *F1*
9 **Not I.]** Not, I *Q1-2*
10-2 **Cur. Have . . . word.]** *om. Q2*
10-1 **Have . . . Albany?]** *as prose, Q1; as verse, F1*
10 **toward]** towards *Q1*
11 **Dukes]** two Dukes *Q1*
13 **You . . . sir.]** *as prose, Q1-2; as verse, F1*
13 **do]** *om. Q1-2*
14 **better! best!]** *Pope;* better best, *F1, Q1-2*
18 **I must act.]** must aske *Q1-2*
18 **fortune, work]** *Capell;* Fortune worke *F1;* fortune helpe *Q1-2*
19 s.d. **Enter Edgar.]** *placed as in Theobald; after l. 18, F1; in left margin opposite l. 15, Q1; after* Which *l. 18, Q2*
20 **sir]** *om. Q1-2*
23 **Cornwall?]** Cornwall ought, *Q1-2*
26 **'gainst]** against *Q1-2*
27 **yourself.]** your— *Q1-2*
28 **coming.]** *Rowe;* comming, *F1, Q1-2*
28-9 **me: In cunning]** me in crauing *Q1-2*
30 **Draw]** *om. Q1-2*
31 **Light ho]** light here *Q1-2*
32 **brother]** brother flie *Q1-2*
33 s.d. **Wounds his arm.]** *Rowe*
36 s.d. **and . . . torches]** *om. Q1-2*
37 **where's]** where is *Q1*
39 **Mumbling]** warbling *Q1-2*
40 **stand 's]** *Q1;* stand *F1;* stand his *Q2*
42 **could—]** *Q1-2;* could. *F1*
43 **ho]** *om. Q1-2*
43 s.d. **Exeunt some Servants.]** *Dyce*
45 **revengive]** *Q1-2;* reuenging *F1*
46 **the thunder]** their thunders *Q1-2*
47 **manifold]** many fould *Q1-2*
48 **in fine]** in a fine *Q1-2*
49 **loathly]** *Q1;* lothly *F1, Q2*
50 **in]** with *Q1-2*
52 **latch'd]** lancht *Q1;* launcht *Q2*
53 **And]** but *Q1-2*
54 **quarrel's right]** *Pope;* quarrels right *F1, Q2;* quarrels, rights *Q1*
56 **Full]** but *Q1-2*
57 **uncaught; . . . dispatch.]** *Steevens (after Johnson);* vncaught / And found; dispatch, *F1, Q2;* vncaught and found, dispatch, *Q1*
62 **coward]** caytife *Q1-2*
68 **would the reposal]** could the reposure *Q1-2*
70 **I should]** *Q1-2;* should I *F1*
71 **ay]** *Capell;* I *Q1-2*
72 **I'ld]** id'e *Q1-2*
73 **practice]** pretence *Q1-2*
76 **spirits]** spurres *Q1-2*
77 **O strange]** Strong *Q1-2*
78 **said he]** *om. Q1-2*
78 **I . . . him.]** *Q1-2*
78 s.d. **Tucket within.]** *placed as in Steevens; after* it." *l. 77, F1; om. Q1-2*
79 **why]** *Q1-2;* wher *F1*
83 **due]** *om. Q1-2*
87 **strange news]** *Q1-2;* strangenesse *F1*
90 **O]** *om. Q1-2*
90 **it's]** is *Q1-2*
92 **nam'd,]** named *Q1-2*
93 **O]** I *Q1-2*
95 **tended]** tends *Q1-2*
97 **of that consort]** *om. Q1-2*
100 **th' expense . . . his]** the wast and spoyle of his *Q1 (c);* these—and wast of this his *Q1 (u), Q2*
105 **hear]** heard *Q1-2*
106 **It was]** Twas *Q1-2*
107 **bewray]** betray *Q1-2*
115-6 **need; You]** need you, *Q1;* need, you *Q2*
116 **sir]** *om. Q1-2*
117 **however]** *Rowe;* how euer *F1, Q1-2*
119 **threading]** threatning *Q1-2*
119 **night:]** *Theobald (subs.);* night, *F1, Q1-2*
120 **poise]** poyse *Q1 (c);* prise *Q1 (u);* prize *F1, Q2*
121 **advice]** *Q2;* aduise *F1, Q1*
123 **best]** *F1, Q1 (u), Q2;* lest *Q1 (c)*
123 **thought]** *Q1-2;* though *F1*
127 **businesses]** busines *Q1;* businesse *Q2*
129 s.d. **Flourish. Exeunt.]** *Cambridge;* Exeunt. Flourish. *F1;* Exeunt. *Q1;* Exit. *Q2 (both after* use. *l. 128)*

II.ii

Location: *Capell*
o.s.d. **and]** *Q1-2;* aad *F1*
1 **dawning]** euen *Q1 (c), Q2;* deuen *Q1 (u)*
1 **this]** the *Q1-2*
6 **lov'st]** loue *Q1-2*
16-7 **three-suited, hundred-pound]** *F2 (subs.);* three-suited-hundred pound *F1;* three shewted hundred pound *Q1 (c), Q2;* three-snyted hundred pound *Q1 (u)*
17 **worsted-stocking]** *Theobald;* woosted-stocking *F1;* worsted-stocken *Q1 (c), Q2;* wosted stocken *Q1 (u)*
18 **action-taking]** action taking knaue, a *Q1-2*
18-9 **superserviceable, finical]** superfinicall *Q1-2*
19 **one-trunk-inheriting]** *F3;* one Trunke-inheriting *F1;* one truncke inheriting *Q1-2*
23 **one]** *om. Q1-2*
23 **clamorous]** *Q1-2;* clamours *F1*
24 **deni'st]** denie *Q1-2*
24 **thy]** the *Q1-2*
25 **Why]** *om. Q1-2*
26 **that is]** that's *Q1-2*
29 **days]** dayes agoe *Q1-2*
29-30 **tripp'd . . . thee]** beat thee, and tript vp thy heeles *Q1-2*
31 **yet]** *om. Q1-2*
32 s.d. **drawing his sword]** *Rowe (after l. 33); placed as in Craig*
32 **of]** a *Q1-2*
33 **you, you]** you, draw you *Q1-2*
33 **cullionly]** *Q1-2;* Cullyenly *F1*
35 **come with]** bring *Q1-2*
42 s.d. **Beating him.]** *Rowe*
43 **murther, murther]** murther, helpe *Q1-2*
43 s.d. **Edmund . . . drawn]** *Q1-2*
44 s.p. **Edm.]** *Theobald;* Bast. *F1, Q1-2*
44 **Part!]** *om. Q1-2*
45 **and]** *Q1-2;* if *F1*
45-6 **please! Come,]** *Kittredge (after Theobald);* please, come, *F1;* please come, *Q1-2*
46 **ye]** you *Q1-2*
46 s.d. **Enter . . . Servants.]** *Staunton; part of Edmund's entry, F1, Q1-2 (om.* Servants)
48-9 **Keep . . . matter?]** *as verse, Capell; as prose F1, Q1-2*
49 **What is]** what's *Q1-2*
50 **King.]** *Q1-2;* King? *F1*
51 **What is]** Whats *Q1;* What's *Q2*
51 **difference? speak.]** *Rowe;* difference, speake? *F1, Q1-2*
53 **valor.]** *Theobald (subs.);* valour, *F1, Q1-2*
58 **A]** I, a *Q1-2*
58 **sir;]** *Q1;* Sir, *F1, Q2*
59 **they]** hee *Q1-2*
60 **years o' th']** houres at the *Q1-2*
61 s.p. **Corn.]** Glost. *Q1-2*
62 **ruffian]** ruffen *Q1 (possibly a Shakespearean form)*
63 **grey beard—]** *F3 (dash, Rowe);* gray-beard. *F1, Q1-2*
65 **you'll]** *Q1;* you will *F1, Q2*
66 **wall]** walles *Q1-2*
67 **jakes]** iaques *Q1;* Iaques *Q2*
67 **grey beard]** *Q1;* gray-beard *F1, Q2*
68 **sirrah]** sir *Q1-2*
69 **know you]** you haue *Q1-2*
70 **hath]** has *Q1-2*
73 **Who]** That *Q1-2*
74 **the . . . a-twain]** those cordes in twaine *Q1-2*
75 **t' intrinse t' unloose;]** to intrench, to inloose *Q1-2*
77 **Being]** Bring *Q1-2*
77 **fire]** stir *Q1-2*
77 **the]** their *Q1-2*
77 **colder moods]** colder-moods *Q1*
78 **Renege]** *Q1-2;* Reuenge *F1*
79 **gale]** *Q1-2;* gall *F1*
80 **dogs)]** dayes *Q1-2*
82 **Smile]** *F4;* Smoile *F1, Q2;* smoyle *Q1 (possibly a dialect form)*
83 **and]** *Q1;* if *F1, Q2*
84 **I'ld drive ye]** Id'e send you *Q1-2*
84 **Camelot]** Camulet *Q1-2*
86 **out? say that.]** out, say that? *Q1-2*
89 **What . . . fault?]** what's his offence. *Q1;* what's his offence? *Q2*
91 **nor his, nor]** or his, or *Q1-2*
94 **Than]** *Q2;* Then *F1;* That *Q1*
95 **some]** a *Q1-2*
97 **roughness]** ruffines *Q1-2*
99 **An . . . and]** he must be *Q1-2*
100 **take't,]** *Q1 (comma, Rowe);* take it *F1, Q2*
105 **faith,]** sooth, or *Q1-2*
106 **great]** graund *Q1;* grand *Q2*
108 **On]** In *Q1-2*
108 **flick'ring]** *ed. (after Pope);* flicking *F1;* flitkering *Q1-2*
108 **front—]** *Rowe;* front. *F1, Q1-2*
108 **mean'st]** mean'st thou *Q1-2*
109 **dialect]** dialogue *Q1-2*
114 **What was th']** What's the *Q1-2*
118 **compact]** coniunct *Q1-2*
121 **That]** that, / That *Q1;* that / That *Q2*
123 **fleshment]** flechuent *Q1-2*
123 **dread]** *Q1-2;* dead *F1*
125 **Ajax]** A'Iax *Q1-2*
125 **their]** *Q1-2;* there *F1*
125 **Fetch . . . stocks!]** Bring . . . stockes ho? *Q1-2*
126 **ancient]** ausrent *Q1 (u);* miscreant *Q1 (c), Q2*
127 **Sir]** *om. Q1-2*
129 **employment]** imployments *Q1-2*
130 **shall]** should *Q1-2*
130 **respects]** respect *Q1-2*
132 **Stocking]** Stopping *Q1 (c), Q2;* Stobing *Q1 (u)*
137 **should]** could *Q1-2*
138 **color]** nature *Q1-2*
139 **speaks]** speake *Q1*
139 s.d. **Stocks brought out.]** *placed as in Dyce; after l. 37, F1; om. Q1-2*
141-5 **His . . . with]** *Q1-2*
143 **contemned'st]** *Capell;* temnest *Q1 (c), Q2;* contaned *Q1 (u)*
145 **The King must]** *Q1-2;* The King his Master, needs must *F1 (the F1 reading represents metrical padding to compensate for the cutting of ll. 141-5)*
146 **he]** hee's *Q1-2*
149 **gentleman]** Gentlemen *Q1*
150 **For . . . legs.]** *Q1-2*
150 s.d. **Kent . . . stocks.]** *Rowe (after l. 147)*
151 **Come . . . away.]** *continued to Regan, Q1-2; assigned to Cornwall, F1*
151 **good]** *Q1; om. F1, Q2*
151 s.d. **with . . . Kent]** *Globe (subs., after Capell); s.d. om. Q1*
152 **Duke's]** *Q1-2;* Duke *F1*
155 **Pray]** Pray you *Q1-2*
155 **travell'd]** *F3;* trauail'd *F1, Q1-2*
156 **Some time . . . out]** Sometime . . . ont *Q1*
159 **Duke's]** Dukes *Q1*
159 **to]** *Q1;* too *F1, Q2*
159 **taken]** tooke *Q1-2*
159 s.d. **Exit.]** *om. Q1*
165 **miracles]** my wracke *Q1 (c), Q2;* my rackles *Q1 (u)*
168 s.d. **reads]** *Jennens (and Jennens' quotes following)*
169 **enormous]** enormious *Q1-2*
170 **o'erwatch'd]** ouerwatch *Q1;* ouerwatcht *Q2*
172 **shameful]** *Q1-2;* shamefnll *F1*
173 **smile once more,]** Smile, once more *Q1-2*
173 s.d. **Sleeps.]** *Q1;* He sleepes. *Q2*

II.iii

II.iii] Steevens
Location: *ed. (after Pelican, from A. Schmidt's ed., 1879)*

1 heard] heare Q1
4 unusual] Q1; vnusall F1, Q2
5 Does] Dost Q1-2
5 taking. Whiles . . . scape] taking while . . . scape, Q1-2
10 elf . . . in] else all my haire with Q1-2
12 winds and persecutions] wind, and persecution Q1-2
15 arms] bare armes Q1-2
16 wooden pricks] Q2; Wodden-prickes F1; wodden prickes Q1
17 farms] seruice Q1-2
18 sheep-cotes] Q1-2; Sheeps-Coates F1
19 Sometimes] Sometime Q1-2

II.iv

II.iv] Steevens
Location: ed. (after Pelican)
o.s.d. Enter . . . Gentleman.] Enter King. Q1; Enter King, and a Knight. Q2
o.s.d. Kent . . . stocks.] Dyce
1 home] hence Q1-2
2 messenger] Q1-2; Messengers F1
2, 61 s.pp. Gent.] Knight. Q1-2
3-4 in . . . this] of his Q1-2
5 Ha?] How, Q1-2
6 thy] Q1-2; ahy F1
6 Kent. No, my lord.] om. Q1-2
7 he] looke he Q1; looke, he Q2
7 cruel] crewell Q1-2
7 garters. Horses] F2 (subs.); Garters Horses F1; garters, / Horses Q1-2
8 heads] heeles Q1-2
10 man's] Q2; man F1; mans Q1
10 wooden] Q1-2; wodden F1
19-20 Lear. No . . . have.] Q1-2
22 Kent. By . . . ay.] om. Q1-2
23 could not, would] would not, could Q1-2
26 mightst . . . impose] may'st . . . purpose Q1-2
31 panting] Q1-2; painting F1
34 those] whose Q1-2
35 meiny] men Q1-2
40 which] that Q1-2
42 wit about me,] wit, about me Q1
45 The] This Q1-2
46-55 Fool. Winter's . . . year.] om. Q1-2
46 Winter's] F3; Winters F1
46 wild] F2; wil'd F1
57 Hysterica] F4; Historica F1, Q1-2
59 With] Q1-2; Wirh F1
59 here] om. Q1-2
60 here.] there? Q1; there. Q2
61 but] then Q1-2
62 None] No Q1-2
63 number] traine Q1-2
65 thou'dst] thou ha'dst Q1; thou hadst Q2
70 twenty] a 100. Q1; a hundred Q2
73 following] following it Q1-2
74 upward] vp the hill Q1-2
75, 83 wise man] Q1-2; wiseman F1
76 have] Q1-2; hause F1
78 which] that Q1-2
78 and seeks] om. Q1-2
80 begins] begin Q1
87 fool] om. Q1-2
87 s.d. Enter . . . Gloucester.] placed as in Q1-2; after l. 85, F1
88 They are . . . they are] th'are . . . th'are Q1-2
88 sick? . . . weary?] Johnson; sicke, . . . weary, F1, Q1-2
89 have . . . fetches] traueled hard to night, meare Iustice Q1-2
89 travell'd] Q1-2; trauail'd F1
90 The] I the Q1-2
95 plague! death!] death, plague, Q1-2
96 Fiery? What quality?] what fierie quality, Q1; what fiery quality; Q2
97 I'ld] id'e Q1; ide Q2
98-9 Glou. Well . . . man?] om. Q1-2
102 commands, tends] Muir; commands. tends, F1; come and tends Q1 (u); commands her Q1 (c), Q2
103 Are . . . blood!] om. Q1-2
104 Fiery? . . . Duke?] Fierie Duke, Q1 (c), Q2; The fierie Duke Q1 (u)
104 that—] that Lear, Q1-2
107 Whereto] where to Q1-2
108 commands] Command Q1
112 s.d. Looking on Kent.] Johnson (after wherefore l. 112); placed as in Cambridge
115 practice only.] practice, only Q1-2
116 Go tell] Tell Q1-2
116 I'ld] F4; Il'd F1; Ile Q1-2
120 s.d. Exit.] om. Q1-2
121 O . . . down!] O my heart, my heart. Q1; O my heart! my heart. Q2
123 put 'em] put vm Q1; put them vp Q2
123-4 knapp'd 'em o' th'] rapt vm ath Q1-2
126 s.d. Gloucester, Servants] om. Q1-2 (see l. 120 above)
129 you] Q1-2; your F1
130 so.] Q2 (so;); so, F1, Q1
131 mother's] Q1-2; Mother F1
132 s.d. To Kent.] Rowe
132 O] yea Q1-2
133 s.d. Exit Kent.] Ringler conj.
134 sister's] F3; Sisters F1; sister is Q1-2
135 here.] Q2; heere, F1; heare, Q1
135 s.d. Points . . . heart.] Pope
136 thou'lt] thout Q1-2
137 With] Of Q1-2
137 deprav'd] depriued Q1 (c), Q2; deptoued Q1 (u)
137 quality—] Rowe; quality. F1; qualitie, Q1-2
138 you] om. Q1-2
140 scant] slacke Q1-2
140-5 Lear. Say . . . blame.] om. Q1-2
143 restrain'd] F3; restrained F1
143 followers] F2; Followres F1
147 in] on Q1-2
148 his] her Q1-2
150 you] om. Q1-2
152 her.] her Sir? Q1; her sir. Q2
153 but] om. Q1-2
154 s.d. Kneeling.] Hanmer (subs.)
158 s.d. Rising.] Collier MS (subs.)
158 Never] No Q1-2
164 sir, fie] fie sir Q1-2
165 s.p. Lear.] om. Q1
168 blister!] blast her pride. Q1-2
169 mood is on.] mood— Q1-2
171 Thy tender-hefted] The tender hested Q1-2
172 Thee] the Q1
177 know'st] knowest Q1-2
182 s.d. Tucket within.] placed as in Collier; after l. 181, F1
183 know't,] know't Q1-2
183 letter] letters Q1-2
184 s.d. To Oswald.] Capell (subs.)
185 easy-borrowed] hyphen, Theobald
186 fickle] Q1-2; fickly F1
186 he] a Q1
188 s.p. Lear.] Gon. Q1-2
188 stock'd] struck Q1-2
189 on't] ant Q1-2
189 Who] Lear. Who Q1-2
190 your] you Q1-2
191 you] om. Q1-2
193 s.d. To Goneril.] Johnson
194 will you] wilt thou Q1-2
210 owl—] Steevens; Owle, F1, Q1-2
212 hot-bloodied] F1 (c); hot-blooded F1 (u); hot bloud in Q1-2
214 beg] bag Q1
215 afoot] Q1-2; a foote F1
217 s.d. Pointing at Oswald.] Dyce
218 I] Now I Q1-2
222 that's in] that lies within Q1-2
224 or] an Q1-2
231 so] so sir Q1-2
232 look'd] looke Q1-2
235 you] you are Q1-2
235 so—] Rowe; so, F1, Q1-2
236 spoken] spoken now Q1-2
237 What,] Rowe; what F1, Q1-2
240 Speak] Speakes Q1-2
240 one] a Q1-2
245 ye] you Q1-2
246 control] Q1 (controwle), Q2; comptroll F1
250 all—] Rowe; all. F1, Q1-2
256 look] seem Q1-2
258 s.d. To Goneril.] Hanmer
263 need] needes Q1-2
264 need] deed Q1-2
266 nature . . . needs,] Q1-2; nature, . . . needs: F1
267 life is] life as Q1; life's as Q2
267 beast's] Capell; Beastes F1, Q1-2
269 wear'st] wearest Q1-2
270 warm.] Rowe (subs.); warme, F1, Q1-2
272 man] fellow Q1-2
275 so] to Q1; too Q2
276 tamely] lamely Q1-2
277 And] O Q1-2
280 shall—] shall, Q1
280 things—] Hanmer; things, F1, Q1-2
281 are yet] Q1; are yet, F1; are, yet Q2
285 into] in Q1-2
285 flaws] flowes Q1-2
286 s.d. Lear . . . Fool] Ringler conj.; Lear, Leister, Kent, and Foole Q1; Lear, Glocester, Kent, and Foole Q2
288 and 's] F2; an'ds F1; and his Q1-2
293 s.p. Gon.] Duke. Q1-2
293 purpos'd] puspos'd Q1
295 s.p. Corn.] Reg. Q1-2
295 s.d. Enter Gloucester.] placed as in Kittredge; after l. 294, F1, Q1-2 (in right margin, Q1)
296-7 rage. . . . whither.] rage, & wil I know not whether. Q1-2
298 s.p. Corn.] Re. Q1-2
298 best] good Q1-2
300 bleak] Q1-2; high F1
301 ruffle] russel Q1-2
302 scarce] not Q1-2
308 wild] Q1-2; wil'd F1
309 Regan] Reg Q1
309 o' th'] at'h Q1; ath Q2

III.i

Location: ed. (after Rowe)
o.s.d. severally] at seuerall doores Q1-2
1 Who's there, besides] Whats here beside Q1, (What's) Q2
4 elements] element Q1-2
7-15 tears . . . all.] Q1-2
11 to-and-fro-conflicting] hyphens, Theobald
13 belly-pinched] hyphen, Pope
18 note] Arte Q1-2
20 is] be Q1-2
22-9 Who . . . furnishings—] om. Q1-2
29 furnishings—] Rowe; furnishings. F1
30-42 But . . . you.] Q1-2
32 feet] fee Q2; see Q3
43 further] farther Q1-2
44 am] om. Q1-2
45 out-wall,] Q1-2; out-wall; F1
48 that] your Q1-2
53-4 in . . . this] Ile this way, you that Q1-2
55 Holla] hollow Q1-2
55 s.d. severally] Theobald

III.ii

Location: ed. (after Sisson)
1 winds] wind Q1-2
1 blow!] Pope; blow F1, Q1-2
2 cataracts] caterickes Q1; cartericks Q2
2 hurricanoes] F2; Hyrricano's F1; Hircanios Q1-2
3 drench'd our steeples,] drencht, / The steeples Q1; drencht / The steeples, Q2
3 drown'd] Q1-2; drown F1
5 Vaunt-couriers of] vaunt-currers to Q1-2
7 Strike] smite Q1-2
8 moulds] Mold Q1-2
9 makes] make Q1-2
11 o' door] a doore Q1-2
12 in] in, and Q1-2
13 neither] nether Q1, neyther Q2
13 wise men] Pope. Wisemen F1; wise man Q1-2
13 fools] foole Q1-2
14 bellyful] Malone; belly full F1, Q1-2
16 tax] taske Q1-2 (cf. I.iv.343)
18 Then] why then Q1-2
22 will . . . join] haue . . . ioin'd Q1-2
23 battles] battel Q1-2
24 O, ho!] O Q1-2

25 **put 's]** put his *Q1–2*
28–9 **head . . . The]** head, has any the *Q1–2*
33 **of]** haue *Q1–2*
40 **codpiece]** codpis *Q1–2*
41 **wise man]** *Pope;* Wiseman *F1, Q1–2*
42 **are]** sit *Q1–2*
44 **Gallow . . . wanderers]** gallow, . . . wanderer *Q1–2*
45 **make]** makes *Q1–2*
47 **never]** ne're *Q1–2*
49 **fear]** force *Q1–2*
50 **pudder]** Powther *Q1;* Thundring *Q2*
54 **of]** man of *Q1–2*
55 **incestuous]** incestious *Q1–2*
55 **to]** in *Q1–2*
57 **Has]** hast *Q1–2*
58 **concealing continents]** concealed centers *Q1–2*
60 **than]** their *Q1–2*
63 **while]** whilst *Q1–2*
64 **harder . . . stones]** hard then is the stone *Q1–2*
65 **you]** me *Q1–2*
67 **wits begin]** wit begins *Q1–2*
71 **And]** that *Q1–2*
71–2 **your hovel. Poor]** you houell poore, *Q1–2*
72 **in]** of *Q1–2*
73 **That's sorry]** That sorrowes *Q1–2*
74 **s.d. Sings.]** *Capell*
74 **has and]** has *Q1–2*
74 **little tine]** *Q1–2;* little-tyne *F1*
77 **Though]** for *Q1–2*
78 **boy]** my good boy *Q1–2*
78 **s.d. with Kent]** *Capell (subs); s.d. om. Q1–2*
79–96 **Fool. This . . . time.]** *om. Q1–2; ll. 79–80 as prose, Malone; as verse, F1*
85–6 **Then . . . confusion.]** *placed as in Duthie; after l. 92 in F1*

III.iii

Location: *Rowe (subs.)*
o.s.d. **with lights]** *Q1–2*
1 **this]** this, *Q1*
3 **from me]** me from me *Q1*
4 **perpetual]** their *Q1–2*
5 **or]** nor *Q1–2*
8 **There is]** ther's a *Q1–2*
9 **between]** betwixt *Q1–2*
13 **there is]** Ther's *Q1–2*
13 **footed]** landed *Q1–2*
14 **look]** seeke *Q1–2*
17 **bed. If]** *Rowe (subs.);* bed, if *F1;* bed, though *Q1–2*
17 **for't]** *Q1;* for it *F1, Q2*
19 **strange things]** Some strange thing *Q1–2*
21 **courtesy,]** curtesie *Q1–2*
24 **loses]** *Q2;* looses *F1, Q1*
25 **The]** Then *Q1–2*
25 **doth]** doe *Q1–2*

III.iv

Location: *Rowe (subs.)*
2 **night's]** nights *Q1*
4 **here]** *om. Q1–2*
6 **contentious]** tempestious *Q1 (c);* crulentious *Q1 (u), Q2*
7 **skin; so]** *Rowe;* skinso: *F1;* skin, so *Q1–2*
10 **thy]** *Q1–2;* they *F1*
12 **body's]** *Rowe;* bodies *F1, Q1–2*
12 **this]** *Q1 (c);* the *F1, Q1 (u), Q2*
14 **there—]** *Singer;* there, *F1;* their *Q1–2*
14 **ingratitude!]** *Rowe;* ingratitude, *F1, Q1–2*
16 **home]** sure *Q1–2*
17–8 **In . . . endure.]** *om. Q1–2*
20 **gave]** gaue you *Q1–2*
20 **all—]** *Rowe;* all, *F1, Q1–2*
22 **here]** *om. Q1–2*
23 **thine own]** thy one *Q1;* thy owne *Q2*
26 **s.d. To the Fool.]** *Johnson*
26–7 **In . . . sleep.]** *om. Q1–2*
26 **poverty—]** *Rowe;* pouertie, *F1*
27 **s.d. Fool]** *Rowe; s.d. follows l. 26 in F1, Rowe; placed as in Hanmer; s.d. om. Q1–2*
29 **storm]** night *Q1–2*
31 **loop'd]** *Q1–2* (loopt); lop'd *F1*
37–8 **Edg. Fathom . . . Tom!]** *om. Q1–2*
37 **s.d. Within.]** *Theobald*
38 **s.d. Enter . . . hovel.]** *from F1* Enter Edgar, and Foole. *(after l. 36) and Theobald (after l. 40); placed as in Capell; om. Q1–2*
42 **A . . . says]** A spirit, he sayes, *Q1,* (sayes) *Q2*
45 **s.d. Enter . . . madman.]** *from F1 (see l. 38 s.d.) and Theobald; om. Q1–2*
46–7 **"Through . . . winds."]** *quotes, Staunton*
46 **Through]** thorough *Q1*
47 **blow]** blowes *Q1–2*
47 **cold]** *Q1–2*
47 **winds]** wind *Q1–2*
47 **Humh!]** *om. Q1–2*
48 **bed]** cold bed *Q1–2*
49 **Didst thou give]** Hast thou giuen *Q1–2*
49 **thy]** thy two *Q1–2*
52 **through fire]** *Q1–2;* though Fire *F1*
52 **through flame]** *om. Q1–2*
53 **ford]** *Q1–2* (foord); Sword *F1*
53 **whirlpool]** whirli-poole *Q1–2*
54 **hath]** has *Q1–2*
55 **porridge]** pottage *Q1–2*
56 **trotting-horse]** *hyphen, Steevens*
57 **four-inch'd]** *hyphen, Capell*
58, 59 **Bless]** *Q1–2,* Blisse *F1*
58 **a-cold]** *Pope;* a cold *F1, Q1–2 (throughout)*
58–9 **O . . . de.]** *om. Q1–2*
59 **star-blasting]** starre-blusting *Q1–2*
62 **and there]** *om. Q1–2*
63 **Has]** What, *Q1–2*
64 **Wouldst . . . 'em]** didst . . . them *Q1–2*
68 **light]** fall *Q1–2*
76 **Pillicock-Hill]** *hyphen, Rowe;* pelicocks hill *Q1–2*
76–7 **alow! alow, loo, loo!]** a lo lo lo. *Q1–2*
80 **o' th']** at'h *Q1;* of the *Q2*
81 **word's justice]** *Knight;* words Iustice *F1;* words iustly *Q1–2*
82 **sweet heart]** *Q1–2;* Sweet-heart *F1*
91 **deeply]** *Q1–2;* deerely *F1*
91 **out-paramour'd]** out paromord *Q1;* out paramord *Q2*
95 **rustling]** ruslngs *Q1;* ruslings *Q2*
96 **woman]** women *Q1–2*
96 **brothels]** brothell *Q1–2*
97 **plackets]** placket *Q1–2*
97 **books]** booke *Q1–2*
99 **says . . . nonny.]** *after Capell;* Sayes . . . nonny, *F1;* hay no on ny, *Q1–2*
99 **boy, boy]** boy, my boy *Q1–2*
100 **sessa!]** *Malone;* Sesey: *F1 (in italics);* caese *Q1;* cease *Q2*
101 **Thou]** Why thou *Q1–2*
101 **a]** thy *Q1–2*
103 **more than this?]** more, but this *Q1;* more but this? *Q2*
105 **Ha?]** *om. Q1–2*
108–9 **Come, unbutton here.]** come on *Q1 (c);* come on bee true. *Q1 (u), Q2*
109 **s.d. Tearing . . . clothes.]** *Rowe*
110 **contented, 'tis]** content, this is *Q1–2*
113 **on 's]** in *Q1–2*
113 **s.d. Enter . . . torch.]** *placed as in Sisson; after l. 109, F1;* Enter Gloster. *Q1–2 (after l. 114)*
115 **fiend]** *Q1–2*
115 **Flibbertigibbet]** fliberdegibek *Q1 (c);* Scriberdegibit *Q1 (u);* Sirberdegibit *Q2*
116 **till the]** *Q1–2;* at *F1*
117 **pin, squinies]** *Greg (after anon. conj.);* Pin, squints *F1;* pin-queues *Q1 (u);* pin, squemes *Q1 (c);* pinqueuer *Q2*
120 **Swithold]** swithald *Q1–2*
120 **'old]** *Cambridge;* old *F1, Q1–2*
122 **alight]** *Rowe;* a-light *F1;* O light *Q1–2*
123 **troth plight]** *Q1–2;* troth-plight *F1*
124 **aroint . . . aroint]** arint thee, witch arint *Q1 (c);* arint thee, with arint *Q1 (u); Q2*
135 **stock-punish'd]** *Q1–2* (-punisht); stockt, punish'd *F1*
135 **had]** *Q1–2*
137 **Horse . . . wear;]** *as part of preceding prose speech in Q1–2*
139 **Have]** Hath *Q1–2*
140 **Smulkin]** snulbug *Q1–2*
144 **Mahu.]** ma hu— *Q1–2*
145–6 **Our . . . it.]** *as verse, Pope; as prose, F1, Q1–2*
145 **my . . . vild]** is growne so vild my Lord *Q1–2*
152 **ventured]** venter'd *Q1–2*
153 **fire and food]** food and fire *Q1–2*
156 **Good my]** My good *Q1–2*
157 **same]** most *Q1–2*
161 **once more]** *om. Q1–2*
163 **Ah]** O *Q1–2*
167 **he]** a *Q1*
168 **lately,]** *Q1–2;* lately: *F1*
169 **true]** truth *Q2*
171 **Grace—]** *Capell;* grace. *F1, Q1–2*
171–2 **mercy, sir. Noble]** mercie noble *Q1–2*
174 **into th']** in't *Q1*
175–6 **him; . . . still]** him I wil keep stil, *Q1–2*
177 **soothe]** *Collier;* sooth *F1, Q1–2*
182 **tower came]** towne come *Q1–2*

III.v

Location: *Rowe*
1 **his]** the *Q1–2*
2 **How,]** *F4;* How *F1, Q1–2*
3 **something]** some thing *Q1;* some-thing *Q2*
10 **which]** *om. Q1–2*
12–3 **this . . . not]** his treason were *Q1–2*
20 **s.d. Aside.]** *Theobald*
21 **persever]** perseuere *Q1–2*
25 **dearer]** *Q1–2;* deere *F1*

III.vi

Location: *Capell (subs.)*
o.s.d. **Enter . . . Gloucester.]** Enter Gloster and Lear, Kent, Foole, and Tom. *Q1, (om. first* and) *Q2*
5 **his]** *om. Q1–2*
5 **reward]** deserue *Q1–2*
5 **s.d. Exit Gloucester.]** *Capell;* Exit. *F1 (after l. 3); s.d. om. Q1–2*
6 **Fraterretto]** *Capell;* Fraterretto *F1;* Freter-eto *Q1–2*
7 **and]** *om. Q1–2*
9 **madman]** mad man *Q1–2*
12–4 **Fool. No . . . him.]** *om. Q1–2*
16 **'em—]** *Theobald;* 'em. *F1;* them. *Q1–2*
17–56 **Edg. The . . . scape?]** *Q1–2*
21, 36 **s.dd. To Edgar.]** *Capell*
21 **justicer]** *Theobald;* Iustice *Q1–2*
22, 37 **s.dd. To the Fool.]** *Capell*
22 **Now]** *Q2;* no *Q1*
23 **Want'st]** *Q2;* wanst *Q1*
24 **eyes at trial]** *Q2;* eyes, at tral *Q1*
24, 26 **s.dd. Sings.]** *Cambridge conj.*
25 **"Come . . . me"—]** *as verse, Capell; as part of preceding prose speech, Q1–2*
25 **bourn]** *Capell (subs.);* broome *Q1–2*
26–7 **"Her . . . speak]** *as two verse lines, Capell; as one verse line, Q1–2*
28 **come]** *Q2;* come, *Q1*
33–4 **How . . . cushions?]** *as verse, Theobald; as prose, Q1–2*
34 **cushions]** *Q2;* cushings *Q1*
35–9 **I'll . . . too.]** *as verse, Pope (subs.); as prose, Q1–2*
36 **robed]** *Pope;* robbed *Q1–2*
38 **s.d. To Kent.]** *Capell*
38 **o' th']** *Q2;* ot'h *Q1*
40 **s.d. Sings.]** *Cambridge conj.*
41–4 **"Sleepest . . . harm."]** *as verse, Theobald; as prose, Q1–2*
47 **she]** *Q2*
52 **join-stool]** ioynt stoole *Q2*
58 **pity!]** *Rowe;* pitty: *F1;* pity *Q1–2*
60 **s.d. Aside.]** *Rowe*
61 **They]** Theile *Q1;* They'l *Q2*
68–9 **mongril grim, Hound]** *Rowe (subs.);* Mongrill, Grim, / Hound *F1;* mungril, grim-hound *Q1;* Mungrel, Grim-hound *Q2*
69 **lym]** *Hanmer;* Hym *F1;* him *Q1;* Him *Q2*
70 **Or]** *om. Q1–2*
70 **tike]** *Q1–2;* tight *F1*
70 **trundle-tail]** *Q1* (trundletaile), *Q2;* Troudle taile *F1*
71 **him]** them *Q1–2*
73 **leapt]** leape *Q1–2*

74–5 Do . . . dry.] *as prose, Capell (after Q1–2); as verse, F1*

74 Do . . . Sessa] *Malone;* Do . . . sese *F1;* loudla doodla *Q1–2*

77 her heart.] her / Hart *Q1;* her, / Hart *Q2*

78 make . . . hearts] *F3;* make these hard-hearts *F1;* makes this hardnes *Q1–2*

78 s.d. To Edgar.] *Capell*

79 for] you for *Q1–2*

80 garments . . . say] garments youle say, *Q1;* garment; you'l say *Q2*

81 Persian] Persian attire *Q1–2*

82 and rest] *om. Q1–2*

84 So, so] so, so, so *Q1–2*

84 morning.] morning, so, so, so, *Q1*, (. . . so.) *Q2*

85 Fool. And . . . noon.] *om. Q1–2*

85 s.d. Enter Gloucester.] *Q1–2; after l. 81, F1*

91 toward] towards *Q1–2*

95 Take . . . up] Take vp the King *Q1 (c);* Take vp to keepe *Q1 (u), Q2*

97–101 Kent. Oppressed . . . behind.] *Q1–2*

98 balm'd] *Theobald;* balmed *Q1–2*

99 allow,] *Q2;* alow *Q1*

100 s.d. To the Fool.] *Theobald*

101 s.p. Glou.] *Q1–2*

101 s.d. all but Edgar] *Globe*

102–15 Edg. When . . . lurk.] *Q1–2*

102–3 When . . . foes.] *as verse, Q2; as prose, Q1*

104 suffers, suffers] *Theobald;* suffers suffers, *Q1;* suffers, *Q2*

104 i' th'] *Q2;* it'h *Q1*

110 fathered] fatherd *Q2*

115 s.d. Exit.] *Theobald*

III.vii

Location: *Rowe*

1 s.d. To Goneril.] *Furness*

2 him] hin *F1 (u) (unrecorded)*

3 traitor] vilaine *Q1–2*

3 s.d. Exeunt . . . Servants.] *Capell*

7 revenges] reuenge *Q1–2*

9 Advise] *Q1–2;* Advice *F1*

10 festinate] *F2;* festiuate *F1;* festuant *Q1–2*

11 posts] post *Q1–2*

11 intelligent] intelligence *Q1–2*

17 questrists] questrits *Q1–2*

18 lord's] *Rowe;* Lords, *F1;* Lords *Q1–2*

19 toward] towards *Q1–2*

22 s.d. Exeunt . . . Oswald.] *Capell (subs., after l. 21; placed as in Dyce);* Exit *F1 (after l. 21);* Exit Gon. and Bast. *Q1–2 (after l. 21)*

23 s.d. Exeunt other Servants.] *Capell*

24 well] *om. Q1–2*

26 court'sy] *Rowe;* curt'sie *F1;* curtesie *Q1–2*

27 control] *Q1–2;* comptroll *F1*

27 s.d. brought . . . three] *Q1–2;* and *F1*

31 guests] *Q2;* Ghests *F1;* gests *Q1*

32 s.d. Servants bind him.] *Rowe (subs.)*

33 lady] *Q1–2;* Lady, *F1*

33 I'm none] I am true *Q1–2*

34 find—] *Q1–2;* finde. *F1*

34 s.d. Regan . . . beard.] *Johnson*

40 robber's] *Pope;* Robbers *F1, Q1–2*

43 simple-answer'd] *hyphen, Hanmer;* simple answerer *Q1–2*

44–5 And . . . kingdom?] *as verse, Rowe; as prose, F1, Q1–2*

46–7 King—Speak.] *ed. (after Duthie);* King: Speake. *F1;* King speake? *Q1;* king, speak? *Q2*

52 Wast] *Q1–2;* Was't *F1*

52 peril—] *Q1–2;* perill. *F1*

53 him] him first *Q1–2*

55 Dover] Douer sir *Q1–2*

58 rash] *Q1–2;* sticke *F1*

59 as his bare] on his lowd *Q1 (c);* of his lou'd *Q1 (u), Q2*

60 hell-black night] *Pope;* Hell-blacke-night *F1;* hell blacke night *Q1–2*

60 buoy'd] bod *Q1 (c);* layd *Q1 (u);* laid *Q2*

62 holp] holpt *Q1–2*

62 rain] rage *Q1–2*

63 howl'd] heard *Q1–2*

63 dearn] *Q1–2;* sterne *F1*

65 subscribe:] subscrib'd *Q1;* subscrib'd, *Q2*

68 these] those *Q1–2*

70 you] ye *Q1–2*

71 th' other too] tother to *Q1–2*

72 vengeance—] *Q1–2;* vengeance. *F1*

72, 76, 79, 81 s.pp. 1. Serv.] *Capell;* Seru. *F1, Q1–2*

73 you] *om. Q1*

77 I'ld] id'e *Q1;* ide *Q2*

78 s.d. Draw and fight.] *Q1–2*

79 Nay] Why *Q1–2*

79 s.d. Cornwall is wounded.] *ed. (after Rowe)*

80 s.d. She . . . behind;] *Q1–2*

80 s.d. kills him] *om. Q1–2*

81 slain!] slaine *Q1–2*

81 you have] yet haue you *Q1–2*

82 s.d. He dies.] *Q2*

86 enkindle] vnbridle *Q1–2*

87 treacherous] *om. Q1–2*

94 s.d. one] *Globe*

97 dunghill. Regan,] dungell Regan, *Q1;* dunghill, Regan *Q2*

98 s.d. Exit . . . Regan.] *Theobald;* Exeunt, *F1;* Exit. *Q1–2*

99–107 2. Serv. I'll . . . him!] *Q1–2*

99 s.p. 2. Serv.] *Capell;* Seruant. *Q1–2*

100 s.p. 3. Serv.] *Capell;* 2 Seruant. *Q1–2*

100–2 If . . . monsters.] *as verse, Theobald; as prose, Q1–2*

103 s.p. 2. Serv.] *Capell;* 1 Ser. *Q1–2*

104 roguish] *om. Q1 (c)*

106 s.p. 3. Serv.] *Capell;* 2 Ser. *Q1–2*

106–7 Go . . . him!] *as verse, Warburton; as prose, Q1–2*

107 s.d. Exeunt severally.] *Theobald;* Exit. *Q1–2*

IV.i

Location: *Capell (after Rowe)*

2 flatter'd. . . . worst,] *Pope;* flatter'd, to be worst: *F1;* flattered to be worst, *Q1–2*

4 esperance] experience *Q1–2*

6–9 Welcome . . . But] *om. Q1–2*

9 s.d. led by] *Q1–2;* and *F1; Q1–2 s.d. after* age. *l. 12*

9 who comes] Who's *Q1–2*

10 parti-ey'd] *ed. (after Davenport conj., from* parti, eyd *Q1 (c));* poorlie, leed *Q1 (u);* poorely led *F1, Q2*

14 These fourscore years.] this forescore— *Q1–2*

17 You] Alack sir, you *Q1–2*

21 O] ah *Q1–2*

24 I'ld] Id'e *Q1;* Ide *Q2*

25, 27, 37, 52, 54 s.dd. Aside.] *Johnson*

26 e'er] *Rowe;* ere *F1, Q1–2*

28 So] As *Q1–2*

31 He] A *Q1*

36 to] are toth' *Q1;* are to'th *Q2*

37 kill] bitt *Q1;* bit *Q2*

38 fool] the foole *Q1–2*

39 Then prithee] *Q1–2*

41 away] gon *Q1;* gone *Q2*

42 hence] here *Q1–2*

45 Which] Who *Q1–2*

46 time's] *Rowe;* times *F1, Q1–2*

51 fellow—] *Capell;* fellow. *F1, Q1–2*

52 daub it further] dance it farther *Q1–2*

54 And . . . must.] *om. Q1–2*

57 scar'd] *Q1–2;* scarr'd *F1*

58 thee . . . son] the good man *Q1–2*

58–63 Five . . . master!] *Q1–2 (as verse; as prose, Pope)*

61 Flibbertigibbet] *Pope;* Stiberdigebit *Q1–2*

61 mopping] *Theobald;* Mobing *Q1–2*

62 mowing] *Theobald (after Pope);* Mohing *Q1–2 (in italics as proper name)*

64 plagues] plagues. *Q1*

66 heavens,] *Capell;* Heauens *F1, Q1–2*

68 slaves] stands *Q1–2*

70 undo] vnder *Q1–2*

74 fearfully] firmely *Q1–2*

IV.ii

Location: *Capell (after Rowe)*

o.s.d. Enter . . . Bastard] *Q1–2;* Enter Gonerill, Bastard, and Steward. *F1*

2 s.d. Enter . . . Steward.] *Theobald (subs.);* Enter Steward. *Q1–2 (after l. 2); see above for F1*

10 most . . . dislike] hee should most desire *Q1–2*

11 s.d. To Edmund.] *Hanmer*

15 Edmund] *Q2;* Edmond *F1;* Edgar *Q1*

17 names] armes *Q1–2*

24 fare thee well] far you well *Q1;* faryewell *Q2*

25 s.d. Exit.] *om. Q1–2*

26 O . . . man!] *om. Q1–2*

28 A] *Q1 (c);* My *F1, Q1 (u), Q2*

28 fool] foote *Q1 (u), Q2*

28 bed] *Q1 (c);* body *F1, Q1 (u);* head *Q2*

28 s.d. Exit.] *Q1–2* (Exit Stew.)

29 whistling] *Q1 (c);* whistle *F1, Q1 (u), Q2*

31–50 I . . . deep.] *Q1–2*

31 disposition;] *Theobald (subs.);* disposition *Q1;* disposition, *Q2*

32 it] ith *Q1 (c);* its *Q3*

42 even] *om. Q2*

42–3 lick, . . . madded.] *Capell;* lick. . . . madded, *Q1;* licke; . . . madded; *Q2*

45 benefited] *Q1 (c);* beneflicted, *Q1 (u), Q2*

47 these] *Heath conj.;* the *Q1 (u), Q2;* this *Q1 (c)*

49 Humanity] Humanly *Q1 (u), Q2*

51 bear'st] bearest *Q1–2*

52 eye discerning] *Rowe;* eye-discerning *F1;* eye deseruing *Q1–2*

53–9 that . . . so?] *Q1–2*

53–4 know'st Fools] *Hanmer;* know'st, fools *Q1 (c);* know'st fools, *Q1 (u), Q2*

54 those] these *Q2*

56 noiseless] noystles *Q1 (u)*

57 state . . . threat] *Jennens;* state begins thereat *Q1 (c);* slayer begin threats *Q1 (u);* slaier begins threats *Q2*

58 Whilst] Whil's *Q1 (u);* Whiles *Q2*

60 shows] *Q1 (c)* (shewes); seemes *F1, Q1 (u), Q2*

62–8 Alb. Thou . . . mew!] *Q1–2*

65 dislocate] *Q3;* dislecate *Q1–2*

66 bones. Howe'er] *Theobald (subs.);* bones, how ere *Q1–2*

68 mew!] *Daniel conj.;* mew— *Q1 (c);* now— *Q1 (u), Q2*

68 s.d. Enter a Messenger.] *placed as Q2 s.d.; after l. 61, F1;* Enter a Gentleman. *Q1 (after l. 69), Q2*

69 Alb. What news?] *Q1–2*

70 s.p. Mess.] Gent. *Q1–2 (throughout scene)*

72 eyes?] *Q1–2;* eyes. *F1*

73 thrill'd] thrald *Q1–2*

75 thereat enraged] *Q1–2;* threat-enrag'd *F1*

79 justicers] *Q1 (c);* Iustices *F1, Q1 (u), Q2*

83 s.d. Aside.] *Johnson*

85 in] on *Q1–2*

87 tart] tooke *Q1–2*

87 s.d. Exit.] *Q1–2*

93 their] there *Q1*

96 thine] thy *Q1–2*

IV.iii

IV.iii] *Pope*

Entire scene from Q1–2; om. F1; first included by Pope

Location: *Capell (subs.)*

2 no] the *Q2*

7 him] *Pope;* him, *Q1–2*

11 Ay, sir] *Johnson;* I say *Q1–2*

13 seem'd] *Q2;* seemed *Q1*

14 Over] ore *Q2*

15 mov'd] *Pope;* moued *Q1–2*

16 strove] *Pope;* streme *Q1–2*

17–8 goodliest. . . . once;] *Pope (subs.);* goodliest . . . once, *Q1*, (goodliest,) *Q2*

18 Sunshine] *Q2;* Sun shine *Q1*

19 way:] *Globe;* way *Q1;* way, *Q2*

20 seem'd] *Pope;* seeme *Q1–2*

21 eyes,] *Q2;* eyes *Q1*

22 dropp'd. In] *Q2 (subs.);* dropt in *Q1*

28 Kent!] *Theobald;* Kent, *Q1;* Kent. *Q2*

28 storm? i' th'] *Theobald;* storme ith *Q1–2*

29 believ'd!] *Capell (subs.);* beleeft *Q1;* beleeu'd, *Q2*

31 **clamor-moistened]** *hyphen first appears in Theobald's notes (later conj. by W. S. Walker);* clamour moystened her *Q1–2 (Theobald first om.* her)
34 **make]** mate *Q2*
35 **since?]** *Q2;* since. *Q1*
39 **sometime]** *Q2;* some time *Q1*
42 **him:]** *Capell;* him *Q1;* him, *Q2*
43–4 **benediction, . . . casualties,]** *Q2;* benediction turnd her, To forraine casualties *Q1*
48 **not?]** *Q2;* not. *Q1*
49 **so,]** *Pope;* so *Q1–2*
49 **afoot]** *Q2;* a foote *Q1*
51 **him.]** *Pope;* him *Q1;* him, *Q2*
52 **awhile]** a while *Q2*
53 **grieve]** *Pope;* greeue, *Q1–2*
55 **s.d. Exeunt.]** *Pope;* Exit. *Q1–2*

IV.iv

IV.iv] *Pope;* Scena Tertia. *F1*
Location: *Capell*
o.s.d. **Doctor]** *Q1–2;* Gentlemen *F1*
o.s.d. **Soldiers]** others *Q1–2*
2 **vex'd]** vent *Q1–2*
3 **femiter]** *Q1–2;* Fenitar *F1*
3 **furrow-weeds]** *hyphen, Dyce*
4 **hardocks]** *F3;* Hardokes *F1;* hor-docks *Q1–2*
4 **cuckoo-flow'rs]** *hyphen, Q2*
6 **sustaining corn.]** sustayning, corne, *Q1–2*
6 **century]** *Q1–2;* Centery *F1*
6 **send]** is sent *Q1–2*
8 **s.d. Exit an Officer.]** *Malone (after Capell)*
8 **wisdom]** wisedome do *Q2 (do may have dropped out of the type line in Q1; the end of the next line shows evidence of type dislocation)*
9 **sense?]** *Q2;* Sense; *F1;* sence, *Q1*
10 **helps]** can helpe *Q1–2*
11 **s.p. Doct.]** *Q1–2;* Gent. *F1*
13 **lacks;]** lackes *Q1;* lackes, *Q2*
18 **good man's distress]** *Q1–2;* Goodmans desires *F1*
26 **importun'd]** important *Q1–2*
27 **incite]** in sight *Q1;* insite *Q2*
28 **right]** *Q1–2;* Rite *F1*

IV.v

IV.v] *Pope;* Scena Quarta. *F1*
Location: *Capell (subs.)*
2 **there]** *om. Q1–2*
4 **lord]** Lady *Q1–2*
6 **letter]** letters *Q1*
11 **Edmund]** and now *Q1–2*
14 **o' th' enemy]** at'h army *Q1;* of the Army *Q2*
15 **madam]** *om. Q1–2*
15 **letter]** letters *Q1–2*
16 **troops set]** troope sets *Q1–2*
21 **Some things—]** *Pope (reading* Something); Some things, *F1;* Some thing, *Q1;* Something, *Q2*
22 **I had]** I'de *Q1;* Ide *Q2*
25 **eliads]** aliads *Q1–2*
27 **madam?]** Madam. *Q1–2*
28 **y' are;]** for I *Q1–2*
32 **more.]** more *Q1;* more, *Q2*
36 **you]** *om. Q1–2*
39 **him]** *Q1–2*
39 **should]** would *Q1–2*
40 **party]** Lady *Q1–2*

IV.vi

IV.vi] *Pope;* Scena Quinta. *F1*
Location: *Theobald (after Rowe)*
o.s.d. **Edgar]** Edmund *Q1–2*
o.s.d. **dressed . . . peasant]** *Theobald (subs.)*
1 **I]** we *Q1–2*
2 **up it now]** it vpnow *Q1;* it vp now *Q2*
6 **eyes']** *Capell;* eyes *F1, Q1–2*
7 **speak'st]** speakest *Q1*
8 **In]** With *Q1–2*
17 **walk]** *Q1–2;* walk'd *F1*
18 **yond]** yon *Q1–2*
21 **chafes]** chaffes *Q1;* chafe *Q2*
22 **heard so high.]** heard, its so hie *Q1;* heard: it is so hie *Q2*
30 **further]** farther *Q1–2*
32 **ye]** you *Q1–2*
33 **s.d. Aside.]** *Capell*
34 **s.d. He kneels.]** *Q1–2*
39 **snuff]** snurff *Q1*
40 **him]** *om. Q1–2*
41 **s.d. He falls.]** *Q1–2*
41 **sir;]** *Knight (subs.);* sir, *F1, Q1–2*
42 **may]** my *Q1*
46 **friend!]** *Rowe;* Friend, *F1; om. Q1–2*
49 **goss'mer]** *Pope;* Gozemore *F1;* gosmore *Q1–2*
50 **fathom]** fadome *Q1–2*
51 **Thou'dst]** Thou hadst *Q1–2*
52 **speak'st]** speakest *Q1*
56 **no?]** no I *Q1*
57 **summit]** *Rowe;* Somnet *F1;* sommons *Q1–2*
57 **bourn.]** *Pope (subs.);* Bourne *F1;* borne, *Q1–2*
58 **a-height]** *hyphen, Warburton*
62 **death?]** death *Q1*
65 **How is't? Feel]** how feele *Q1–2*
67 **cliff,]** *Q2;* cliffe. *F1;* cliffe *Q1*
68 **beggar]** bagger *Q1;* begger *Q2*
69 **methought]** *Q2;* me thought *F1;* me thoughts *Q1*
70 **he]** a *Q1–2*
71 **welk'd]** *ed.;* wealk'd *F1;* welk't *Q1;* welkt *Q2*
71 **enridged]** *Q1–2;* enraged *F1*
73 **make them]** made their *Q1–2*
77 **die.]** die *Q1;* dye: *Q2*
78 **'twould]** would it *Q1;* would he *Q2*
79 **fiend!"—]** *Rowe (subs.);* Fiend, *F1, Q1–2*
80 **s.d. mad . . . flowers]** *ed. (after Duthie-Wilson);* mad *Q1–2 (s.d. after l. 82)*
81 **ne'er]** neare *Q1;* nere *Q2*
83 **coining,]** *Q1–2;* crying. *F1*
86 **Nature's]** Nature is *Q1–2*
89 **piece of]** *om. Q1–2*
91–2 **bird . . . hewgh!]** bird in the ayre, hagh, *Q1;* birde in the ayre. Hagh, *Q2*
93 **marjorum]** Margerum *Q1–2*
96 **Goneril . . . beard?]** Gonorill, ha Regan, *Q1–2*
97 **the]** *om. Q1–2*
99 **every thing that]** euery thing *Q1;* all *Q2*
103 **'em . . . 'em]** them . . . them *Q1–2*
105 **ague-proof]** argue-proofe *Q1–2*
107 **Ay]** *Rowe;* I *F1, Q1–2*
107 **every]** euer *Q1*
107 **king!]** King *Q1;* King: *Q2*
111 **die. . . . adultery?]** die for adulterie, *Q1;* dye for adultery: *Q2*
113 **Does]** doe *Q1–2*
118–31 **Behold . . . thee.]** *as verse, Johnson (subs.); as prose, F1, Q1–2*
118 **yond]** yon *Q1–2*
119 **presages]** presageth *Q1–2*
120 **does]** do *Q1–2*
121 **To]** *om. Q1–2*
122 **The]** to *Q1–2*
124 **they are]** tha're *Q1 (type-line crowded)*
127 **fiends']** *Capell;* Fiends *F1, Q1–2*
128 **There . . . sulphurous]** ther's the sulphury *Q1–2*
129 **consumption]** consumation *Q1–2*
130 **civet;]** Ciuet, *Q1–2*
131 **Sweeten]** to sweeten *Q1–2*
133 **Let me]** Here *Q1–2*
135 **Shall]** should *Q1;* shold *Q2*
135 **Dost thou]** do you *Q1–2*
136 **thine]** thy *Q1–2*
137 **at]** on *Q1–2*
138 **this]** that *Q1–2*
138–9 **but . . . it]** the penning oft *Q1;* the penning on't *Q2*
140 **thy]** the *Q1–2*
140 **see]** see one *Q1–2*
141 **s.d. Aside.]** *Capell*
144 **What,]** *Q2;* What *F1;* What! *Q1*
145–6 **me? . . . purse?]** me, . . . purse, *Q1*
150 **this]** the *Q1–2*
151 **thine]** thy *Q1–2*
152 **yond . . . yond]** yon . . . yon *Q1–2*
153 **thine . . . handy-dandy]** thy eare handy, dandy *Q1;* thy eare, handy dandy *Q2*
154 **justice . . . thief]** theefe . . . Iustice *Q1–2*
157 **cur?]** *Q2;* Cur: *F1;* cur, *Q1*
159 **dog's obey'd]** dogge, so bade *Q1;* dogge, so bad *Q2*
160–3 **Thou . . . cozener.]** *as verse, Pope; as prose, F1, Q1–2*
161 **thy]** thine *Q1–2*
162 **Thou]** thy bloud *Q1–2*
163–4 **cozener. . . . clothes]** cosioner, through tottered raggs, *Q1;* cozener, through tattered ragges *Q2*
164–73 **Thorough . . . so.]** *as verse, Rowe (subs.); as prose, F1, Q1–2*
164 **small]** *Q1–2;* great *F1 (a reading defended by J. C. Maxwell in Duthie-Wilson)*
165 **hide]** hides *Q1–2*
165–70 **Plate . . . lips.]** *om. Q1–2*
165 **Plate sin]** *Theobald (after Pope);* Place sinnes *F1*
170 **glass eyes]** *Q1–2;* glasse-eyes *F1*
172 **Now . . . now.]** no now *Q1;* No, now *Q2*
174 **s.d. Aside.]** *Capell*
174 **impertinency mix'd,]** impertinencie mixt *Q1;* impertinency, mixt *Q2*
176 **fortunes]** fortune *Q1–2*
179 **know'st]** knowest *Q1*
180 **wawl]** wayl *Q1–2*
180 **Mark]** marke me *Q1–2*
180 **s.d. Lear . . . flowers.]** *ed. (after Duthie-Wilson)*
183 **This']** *Singer;* This *F1, Q1–2*
184 **shoe]** shoot *Q1–2*
185 **felt]** fell *Q1–2*
185 **I'll . . . proof,]** *om. Q1–2*
186 **stol'n]** stole *Q1–2*
186 **son-in-laws]** sonnes in law *Q2*
187 **s.d. a Gentleman]** three Gentlemen *Q1–2*
187 **s.d. with Attendants]** *Rowe*
188 **hand]** hands *Q1–2*
188 **him.—Sir,]** *Rowe (subs.);* him, Sir. *F1;* him sirs, *Q1;* him sirs. *Q2 (om.* Your . . . daughter)
189 **daughter]** *om. Q1 (see preceding note for Q2)*
190 **even]** eene *Q1–2*
191 **well,]** well *Q1*
192 **surgeons]** a churgion *Q1;* a Chirurgeon *Q2*
195 **a man a man]** a man *Q1–2*
197 **Ay . . . sir—]** *Q2 (reading* I; Ay *Jennens);* I and laying Autums dust. *Q1*
198 **smug]** *om. Q1–2*
200 **Masters]** my maisters *Q1–2*
202–3 **Then . . . sa.]** *as prose, Q1–2 (om.* Sa . . . sa.); *as verse, F1*
202 **Come]** nay *Q1–2*
203 **by]** with *Q1–2*
203 **Sa . . . sa.]** *om. Q1–2*
203 **s.d. running . . . follow]** *Capell;* King running. *Q1–2*
205 **one]** *Q1–2;* a *F1*
207 **have]** hath *Q1–2*
209 **sir]** *om. Q1–2*
210 **vulgar; . . . that]** vulgar euery one here's that *Q1;* vulgar, euery one heares *Q2*
211 **Which . . . sound]** That . . . sence *Q1–2*
213 **speedy foot;]** speed fort *Q1;* speed for't, *Q2*
213 **descry]** descryes *Q1–2*
214 **Stands]** Standst *Q1*
214 **thought]** thoughts *Q1–2*
216 **s.d. Exit Gentleman.]** *Johnson;* Exit. *F1 (after on. l. 216), Q1–2*
217 **ever-gentle]** *hyphen, Capell*
219 **Well]** Well, *Q1*
221 **tame to]** lame by *Q1–2*
226 **To boot, and boot!]** to boot, to boot. *Q1 (c), Q2;* to saue thee. *Q1 (u)*
226 **happy!]** *Q2* (happy;); happie *F1;* happy, *Q1*
228 **old]** most *Q1–2*
231 **s.d. Edgar interposes.]** *Collier (after Johnson)*
232 **Durst]** *Q1;* Dar'st *F1, Q2*
233 **that th']** the *Q1–2*
235 **zir]** sir *Q1–2*
235 **vurther]** *om. Q1–2*
235 **cagion]** *Q1–2;* 'casion *F1*

237 **and]** *om.* Q1–2
238 **voke]** Q1; volke F1, Q2
238 **ha' bin zwagger'd]** haue beene swaggar'd Q1; haue beene zwaggar'd Q2
239 **'twould . . . 'tis]** it would not haue beene so long Q1; it wold not haue bene zo long Q2
241 **Ice]** ile Q1–2
241 **ballow]** bat Q1 (c), Q2; battero Q1 (u)
242 **Chill]** ile Q1
243 **s.d. They fight.]** Q1–2
244 **zir]** sir Q1
245 **vor]** for Q1–2
250 **English]** Brittish Q1 (c); British Q1 (u), Q2 (*Q1–2's form is historically correct, but* English *must have been in the MS against which copy for F1 was corrected*)
251 **s.d. He dies.]** Q1–2
256 **these]** his Q1–2
256 **the]** These Q1–2
257 **sorry]** sorrow Q1
259 **manners, . . . not:]** *Capell;* manners: . . . not F1; manners . . . not Q1; manners . . . not, Q2
260 **we]** wee'd Q1–2
262 **s.d. Reads the letter.]** A letter. Q1 (c), Q2; *om.* Q1 (u)
262 **our]** your Q1–2
265–6 **done, if . . . conqueror;]** *Pope (subs.);* done. If . . . Conqueror, F1; done, If . . . conquerour, Q1; done: If . . . Conquerour, Q2
269 **say)]** say) your Q1; say) & your Q2
269–70 **servant, Goneril.]** seruant and for you her owne for *Venter, Gonorill.* Q1; seruant, *Gonorill.* Q2
271 **indistinguish'd]** Q1; indinguish'd F1; vndistinguisht Q2
271 **will]** wit Q1–2
273 **brother!]** brother Q1; Brother: Q2
273 **in the]** Q1–2; in rhe F1
282 **sever'd]** fenced Q1–2
284 **s.d. Drum afar off.]** *placed as in Q1–2* (A drum); *after l. 281, F1*

IV.vii

Location: *Capell*
o.s.d. **still . . . Caius]** *ed.*
o.s.d. **Doctor]** Q1–2; Gentleman. F1
8 **Pardon]** Pardon me Q1–2
12 **be't]** beet Q1; be it Q2
12 **so, . . . lord.]** so, . . . Lord Q1; so: my Lord Q2
12 **s.d. To the Doctor.]** *Theobald (subs.)*
13, 16, 42, 50, 77 **s.pp. Doct.]** Q1–2; Gent. *or* Gen. F1
15 **jarring]** hurrying Q1–2
19 **will.]** *Johnson;* will: F1, Q2; will Q1
20 **s.p. Gent.]** Doct. Q1–2
20 **of]** of his Q1–2
22 **s.p. Doct.]** *Capell (subs.); speech continued to Gentleman, F1;* Gent. Q1; Kent. Q2
22 **Be . . . madam]** Good madam be by Q1–2
23 **not]** Q1–2
23 **Cor. Very well.]** Q1–2
23 **s.d. Enter . . . Servants.]** *placed as in Duthie-Wilson; after* array'd *l. 19, F1; om.* Q1–2
23 **s.d. Gentleman in attendance.]** *Neilson*
23 **s.d. Soft music.]** *White*
24 **Doct. Please . . . there!]** Q1–2
30 **Did challenge]** Had challengd Q1–2
31 **oppos'd]** exposd Q1–2
31 **warring]** Q1–2; iarring F1
32–5 **To . . . helm?]** Q1–2
32 **dread-bolted]** *hyphen, Theobald*
34 **lightning?]** *Theobald;* lightning Q1; lightning, Q2
34 **watch—poor perdu!—]** *Capell (subs.);* watch poore *Per du,* Q1–2
35 **helm?]** Q2; helme Q1
35 **enemy's]** iniurious Q1–2
37 **wast]** Q1–2; was't F1
44 **o' th']** ath Q1; a'th Q2
47 **scald]** Q1–2; scal'd, F1
47 **do . . . me?]** know me. Q1; know ye me? Q2
48 **You are]** Yar Q1; Y'are Q2
48 **when]** Q2; where F1, Q1
51 **I? Fair]** I faire Q1
57 **hand]** hands Q1–2
58 **No, sir]** Q1–2
58 **me]** *om.* Q1
60 **not . . . less]** *om.* Q1–2
69 **I am.]** *om.* Q1–2
78 **kill'd] cured** Q1–2
78–9 **and . . . lost.]** Q1–2 *(as prose; as verse, Theobald)*
82 **Will't]** *Rowe;* Wilt F1, Q1–2
83 **you]** *om.* Q1–2
83 **s.d. Manent . . . Gentleman.]** Q1–2 (Manet)
84–96 **Gent. Holds . . . fought. Exit.]** Q1–2
94 **s.d. Exit.]** *Theobald*
96 **battle's]** *Theobald;* battels Q1–2
96 **s.d. Exit.]** *om.* Q2

V.i

Location: *Capell (after Rowe)*
3 **course. He's]** *Rowe (subs.);* course, he's F1, Q1; course, he is Q2
4 **s.d. To . . . out.]** *Globe (after Capell)*
9 **In]** I, Q1; I Q2
11 **forfended]** Q1; fore-fended F1; forefended Q2
11–3 **Edm. That . . . hers.]** Q1–2
12–3 **I . . . hers.]** *as verse,* Q2; *as prose,* Q1
16 **me]** Q1–2
16 **not.]** *Rowe (subs.);* not, F1,Q1–2
17 **husband!]** *Delius;* husband. F1, Q1–2
18–9 **Gon. I . . . me.]** Q1–2 *(as prose,* Q1; *as verse, Theobald, after* Q2)
18 **s.d. Aside.]** *Theobald*
20–1 **bemet. Sir, . . . heard:]** be-met / For . . . heare Q1, (be-met,) Q2
23–8 **Where . . . nobly.]** Q1–2
25 **touches]** toucheth Q2
26 **whom,]** *Theobald;* whome Q1–2
30 **and particular broils]** dore particulars Q1; doore particulars, Q2
31 **the]** to Q1–2
31 **Let's]** Let vs Q1–2
32 **proceeding]** proceedings Q1–2
33 **Edm. I . . . tent.]** Q1–2 *(with s.p.* Bast.)
36 **pray]** pray you Q1–2
37 **s.d. Aside.]** *Capell*
37 **s.d. As . . . out,]** *Theobald*
37 **s.d. disguised]** *Theobald*
37 **s.d. Albany remains.]** *Pope*
46 **And machination ceases.]** *om.* Q1–2
46 **love]** Q1–2; loues F1
50 **thy]** the Q1–2
50 **s.d. Exit Edgar.]** *Dyce;* Exit. F1, Q1–2 *(after l. 49)*
52 **Here]** Hard Q1–2
52 **guess]** quesse Q1
52 **true]** great Q1–2
55 **sisters]** sister Q1
56 **stung]** sting Q1–2
58 **Both? one?]** both one Q1–2
64 **who]** that Q1–2
65 **the]** his Q1–2
66 **intends]** entends Q1; extends Q2

V.ii

Location: *Capell (after Rowe)*
o.s.d. **the Powers . . . hand]** Q1–2; Lear, Cordelia, and Souldiers, ouer the Stage F1
1 **tree]** bush Q1–2
4 **s.d. Edgar]** *Pope*
8 **further]** farther Q1–2
11 **all.]** *Rowe (subs.);* all F1, Q1–2
11 **Glou. And . . . too.]** *om.* Q1–2

V.iii

Location: *ed. (after Ridley)*
2 **first]** best Q1–2
5 **I am]** am I Q1–2
8 **No . . . no!]** No, no, Q1–2
13 **hear poor rogues]** Q1–2; heere (poore Rogues) F1
24 **good-years]** *hyphen, Globe;* good Q1–2
24 **them, flesh]** em, fleach Q1–2
25 **'em starv'd]** vm starue Q1; em starue Q2
26 **Come.]** *om.* Q2
26 **s.d. with Cordelia, guarded]** *Theobald (subs.); s.d. om.* Q1
27 **s.d. giving a paper]** *Malone (after Capell)*
32 **sword.]** *Rowe (subs.);* Sword, F1, Q1–2
33 **thou'lt]** thout Q1–2
35 **th' hast]** thou hast Q1–2
36 **Mark,]** *Rowe;* Marke F1, Q1–2
38–9 **Capt. I . . . do't.]** Q1–2
39 **s.d. another Captain]** *Globe;* Q1–2 *s.d. reads:* Enter Duke [the Duke Q2], the two ladies, and others.
42 **Who]** That Q1–2
43 **I . . . them]** We . . . then Q1–2
43 **you,]** Q1; you F1, Q2
47 **and appointed guard]** Q1 (c), Q2; *om.* Q1 (u)
48 **had]** has Q1–2
49 **on]** of Q1–2
51–2 **Queen, My reason]** *Neilson;* Queen: / My reason F1, Q2; queen / My reason, Q1
54 **session.]** session Q1–2 *(see next note)*
54–9 **At . . . place.]** Q1–2 *(reading* at)
54 **time]** time, Q1; time: Q2
55 **We]** Q1 (c), Q2; mee Q1 (u)
57 **sharpness]** Q1 (c), Q2, sharpes Q1 (u) *(Greg suggests that the uncorrected reading may be that of the MS, in the sense of "sharp edges or points")*
62 **might]** should Q1–2
65 **immediacy]** imediate Q1–2
68 **addition]** aduancement Q1–2
68 **rights]** right Q1–2
70 **s.p. Gon.]** Q1–2; Alb. F1
72 **a-squint]** *Rowe;* a squint F1, Q1–2
76 **Dispose . . . thine.]** *om.* Q1–2
78 **him]** him then Q1–2
79 **let-alone]** *hyphen, Capell*
81 **s.p. Reg.]** Bast. Q1–2
81 **s.d. To Edmund.]** *Hanmer (subs.)*
81 **thine]** good Q1–2
83 **thy]** thine Q1–2
83 **attaint]** Q1–2; arrest F1
84 **s.d. pointing to Goneril]** *Johnson*
84 **sister]** Q1–2; Sisters F1
85 **bar]** *Rowe;* bare F1, Q1–2
87 **your]** the Q1–2
88 **loves]** loue Q1–2
89 **Gon. An enterlude!]** *om.* Q1–2
90 **let . . . sound.]** *om.* Q1–2
90 **trumpet]** F2; Trmpet F1
91 **person]** head Q1–2
93, 97 **s.dd. throwing . . . glove]** *Malone (after Capell)*
93 **make]** proue Q1–2
96 **s.d. Aside.]** *Rowe*
96 **medicine]** poyson Q1–2
97 **he is]** Q1–2; hes F1
99 **the]** thy Q1–2
102 **Edm. A . . . herald!]** Q1–2 *(with s.p.* Bast.)
103 **s.p. Alb.]** Q1–2
105 **My]** This Q1–2
106 **s.d. Exit Regan, led.]** *Theobald*
106 **s.d. Enter a Herald.]** *placed as in Hanmer; after l. 101, F1; om.* Q1–2
107 **trumpet]** Q1–2; Trumper F1
109 **Capt. Sound, trumpet!]** Q1–2
109 **s.d. trumpet]** F2; Tumpet F1; *s.d. om.* Q1–2
111 **within the lists]** in the hoast Q1–2
112 **he is]** he's Q1–2
113 **by]** at Q1–2
115 **Edm. Sound!]** Q1–2 *(with s.p.* Bast.)
115 **s.d. First trumpet.]** *placed as in Capell; after l. 114, F1* (1. Trumpet.)
116 **Her. Again!]** Q1–2 *assign apparently to* Bast. *and om. the repeated* Again! *of l. 117 and the s.dd. in ll. 115–7 (including* Trumpet answers within.)
117 **s.d. at . . . sound]** Q1–2
117 **s.d. a]** Q1; with a Q2
118 **purposes,]** purposes Q1
120 **your quality]** and qualitie Q1–2
121 **Know]** O know Q1–2
121–2 **lost, . . . tooth]** *Theobald* (lost;); lost . . . tooth: F1, Q2; lost . . . tooth. Q1
123–4 **Yet . . . cope]** yet are I mou't / Where is the aduersarie I come to cope with all

Q1 (*Q2 om.* yet . . . mou't)
126 **say'st]** saiest *Q1*
129–30 **my . . . honors]** the priuiledge of my tongue *Q1–2*
132 **place, youth]** youth, place *Q1–2*
133 **Despite]** *Q1–2;* Despise *F1*
133 **victor-sword . . . fortune]** victor, sword and fire new fortun'd *Q1*, (sword,) *Q2*
133 **fire-new]** *hyphen, Rowe*
136 **Conspirant]** Conspicuate *Q1–2*
136 **illustrious]** *Q1–2;* illustrious *F1*
138 **below thy foot]** beneath thy feet *Q1–2*
139 **traitor. . . . "No,"]** traytor say thou no *Q1;* traitor: say thou no, *Q2*
140 **are]** As *Q1;* Is *Q2*
142 **should]** sholud *Q1*
144 **tongue]** being *Q1–2*
144 **some say]** *Q1–2;* (some say) *F1*
145 **What . . . delay]** *om. Q1–2*
146 **rule]** right *Q1–2*
147 **Back . . . these]** Heere . . . those *Q1; line om. Q2*
148 **hell-hated . . . o'erwhelm]** hell hatedly, oreturnd *Q1;* hell hatedly ore-turn'd *Q2*
149 **scarcely]** *Q1–2;* scarely *F1*
151 s.d. **Alarums.]** *placed as in Pope; after l. 152, F1; om. Q1–2*
151 s.d. **They . . . falls.]** *Capell;* Fights. *F1* (*after l. 152*)*; om. Q1–2*
152 **practice]** meere practise *Q1–2*
153 **war thou wast]** armes / Thou art *Q1–2*
155 **Shut]** Stop *Q1–2*
156 **stopple]** *Q1;* stop *F1, Q2*
156 **Hold, sir.—]** *om. Q1–2*
157 **name]** thing *Q1–2*
158 **No]** nay no *Q1;* Nay, no *Q2*
158 **know it]** know't *Q1–2*
160 **can]** shal *Q1–2*
160 **Most monstrous! O!]** Most monstrous *Q1;* Monster, *Q2*
161 s.p. **Gon.]** *Q1–2;* Bast. *F1*
161 s.d. **Exit.]** *placed as in Q1–2* (Exit. Gonorill.)*; after* for't *l. 160, F1*
166 **thou'rt]** thou bee'st *Q1–2*
169 **th' hast]** thou hast *Q1–2*
171 **vices]** vertues. *Q1;* vertues *Q2*
172 **plague]** scourge *Q1–2*
174 **Th' hast]** Thou hast *Q1–2*
174 **right, 'tis true.]** *Capell* (*subs.*)*;* right, 'tis true, *F1;* truth, *Q1–2*
175 **circle]** circled *Q1;* circkled *Q2*
178–9 **ever I Did]** I did euer *Q1–2*
183 **burst!]** *Theobald;* burst. *F1, Q2;* burst *Q1*
186 **we]** with *Q1–2*
191 **Their]** The *Q1–2*
191 **lost;]** lost *Q1*
193 **fault]** Father *Q1–2*
194 **past,]** *Q1;* past *F1, Q2*
197 **our]** my *Q1–2*
205 **Hearing of this.]** *om. Q2*
205–22 **Edg. This . . . slave.]** *Q1–2*
208 **extremity. Whilst]** *Q2;* extreamitie / Whil'st *Q1*
212 **endur'd,]** *Q2;* indur'd *Q1*
214 **him]** *Theobald;* me *Q1–2*
215 **Told the most]** And told the *Q2*
218 **crack. Twice]** *Theobald* (*subs.*)*;* cracke twice, *Q1–2*
222 s.d. **a Gentleman]** one *Q1–2*
222 s.d. **with . . . knife]** *Q1–2*
223 **O, help!]** *om. Q1–2*
223–4 **What . . . knife?]** *assigned to* Alb. *in Q1–2* (*reading* that *for* this *and om.* Alb. Speak, man.)
224 **'Tis]** Its *Q1–2*
225 **O, she's dead!]** *om. Q1–2*
226 **Who . . . man.]** Who man, speake? *Q1;* Who man? speake. *Q2*
228 **poison'd; she confesses]** poysoned, she hath confest *Q1;* poyson'd: she has confest *Q2*
231 **the]** their *Q1–2*
231 s.d. **Exit Gentleman.]** *Malone* (*after Capell; following l. 233*)*; placed as in Cambridge*
232 **judgment]** Iustice *Q1–2*
232 **tremble,]** *Q1–2;* tremble. *F1*
233 **pity.]** pity. *Edg.* Here comes *Kent* sir. *Enter Kent Q1–2* (*cf. l. 230 and s.d. in F1*)
233 **is this he?]** tis he, *Q1–2*
234 **compliment]** *Pope;* complement *F1, Q1–2*
235 **Which]** that *Q1–2*
237 s.p. **Alb.]** Duke. *Q1* (*throughout rest of scene*)*; Q2 agrees with F1 except for* Duke*: at l. 319*
238 s.d. **Goneril . . . out.]** *placed as in Dyce; after l. 231, F1; after l. 239, Q1–2*
241 **poison'd]** poysoned *Q1*
245 **mine]** my *Q1–2*
246 **brief . . . th']** briefe, int toth' *Q1;* briefe, into the *Q2*
246–7 **castle, . . . Is]** castle for my writ, / Is *Q1;* Castle for my / Writ, tis *Q2*
249 **has]** hath *Q1–2*
251 **sword. The captain—]** *ed.* (*after Jennens*) *from Q1* sword the Captaine, (the Captaine *om. F1, Q2*)
252 s.p. **Alb.]** *Q2;* Edg. *F1;* Duke. *Q1*
252 s.d. **Exit Edgar.]** *Malone*
256 **That . . . herself.]** *om. Q2*
257 s.d. **Edmund . . . off.]** *Theobald*
257 s.d. **Enter]** *Q1–2;* Entor *F1*
257 s.d. **Edgar . . . following]** *Neilson* (*after Capell*)
258 **howl!]** howle, howle, *Q1–2*
258 **you]** *Q1–2;* your *F1*
259 **I'ld]** *F3;* Il'd *F1;* I would *Q1–2*
264 **Why]** *om. Q2*
265 **horror?]** *Q2;* horror. *F1, Q1*
268 s.d. **Kneeling.]** *Theobald*
268 **O]** A *Q1–2*
270 **you, murderers,]** your murderous *Q1;* you murdrous *Q2*
274 **woman]** women *Q1–2*
276 s.p. **Gent.]** Cap. *Q1–2*
277 **falchion]** Fauchon *Q1;* Fauchion *Q2*
278 **them]** *Q1–2;* him *F1*
280 **best;]** *Pope* (*subs.*)*;* best, *F1, Q1–2*
281 **brag]** bragd *Q1–2*
281 **and]** or *Q1–2*
283 **This . . . sight.]** *om. Q1–2*
283 **you not]** not you *Q1–2*
285 **you]** *om. Q1–2*
287 **man—]** *Pope;* man. *F1, Q1–2*
289 **first]** life *Q1–2*
290 **You're]** *Q1* (You'r)*;* Your are *F1;* You are *Q2*
292 **foredone]** foredoome *Q1;* fore-doom'd *Q2*
293 **Ay . . . think.]** So thinke I to. *Q1;* So I thinke too. *Q2*
294 **says]** sees *Q1–2*
294 **is it]** it is *Q1–2*
295 s.d. **Enter a Messenger.]** *placed as Q1–2 s.d.* Enter Captaine.*; after* him. *l. 295, F1*
296 s.p. **Mess.]** Capt. *Q1–2*
298 **great]** *om. Q1–2*
301 s.d. **To . . . Kent.]** *Malone* (*after Rowe*)
302 **honors]** honor *Q1*
306 **No, no, no]** no, no *Q1–2*
307 **have]** of *Q1*
308 **Thou'lt]** O thou wilt *Q1–2*
309 **Never . . . never!]** neuer, neuer, neuer, *Q1;* neuer, neuer, neuer: *Q2*
311–2 **Do . . . there!]** O, o, o, o. *Q1;* O, o, o, o. *Q2*
312 s.d. **dies]** *F2;* dis *F1; om. Q1–2*
312 **faints.]** *Theobald* (*subs.*)*;* faints, *F1, Q2;* faints *Q1*
313 s.p. **Kent.]** Lear. *Q1–2*
315 **rack]** *F4;* wracke *F1, Q1–2*
316 **He]** O he *Q1–2*
319 s.p. **Alb.]** Duke. *Q1, Q2*
320 **Is]** Is to *Q1–2*
320 s.d. **To . . . Edgar.]** *Johnson*
321 **realm]** kingdome *Q1–2*
323 **calls me,]** cals, and *Q1–2*
324 s.p. **Edg.]** Duke. *Q1–2*
326 **hath]** haue *Q1–2*
327 s.d. **Exeunt . . . march.]** Exeunt . . . March. / FINIS. *F1;* FINIS. *Q1–2*

Macbeth

MACBETH is the last of the four "great tragedies," and perhaps the darkest. Bradley began his study by pointing out that "almost all the scenes which at once recur to the memory take place either at night or in some dark spot." That peculiar compression, pregnancy, energy, even violence, which distinguishes the verse is a further contribution to the play's preoccupation with the fears and tensions of darkness. On the other hand, as Bradley also observed, it is a play of color too—and if this color is mostly the red of blood, it is also the slow light of dawn. *Macbeth* is a play about the eclipse of civility and manhood, the temporary triumph of evil; when it ends, virtue and justice are restored, the time is free, the "weal" once more made "gentle."

In no other play does Shakespeare show a nation so cruelly occupied by the powers of darkness; and *Macbeth* is, for all its brevity, his most intensive study of evil at work in the individual and in the world at large. Yet it is also the most topical of the tragedies, a play shaped as none of the others seems to be by the interests of the reigning monarch. There is no inconsistency here, though there may be an indication of some of the difficulties *Macbeth* holds for the modern audience. For King James and his contemporaries the Weird Sisters were not mere fantasies, and a man's decision to deal with the forces of evil belonged to life and not to fairy tale. The mirror carried by the last king in the Show of Kings represented the Stuart posterity stretching out "to th' crack of doom" (IV.i.117); thus the overthrow of Macbeth meant not only a general purgation of the country's evil, but the establishment of a line of kings, one of whom sat in Shakespeare's audience hundreds of years later and was almost morbidly aware that the same evils continued to beset great men. It is difficult for us to credit the supernatural manifestations in this play with the right degree of actuality; perhaps a fuller consideration of its topical quality may be an aid to doing so.

Macbeth was first published in the Folio of 1623. Its unusual brevity has prompted many conjectures as to abridgment; but there is also evidence of interpolated scenes. It is never very easy to prove that a play has been abridged; we should probably not suspect cuts in the Folio *Lear* had the 1608 quarto not survived. The evidence consists largely of genuine or imaginary inconsistencies in the play as it stands: for instance, it is argued that Cawdor must have been shown to have a secret league with the King of Norway, unknown to Macbeth, and that Lady Macbeth's "Nor time, nor place, / Did then adhere" (I.vii.51–52) suggests an earlier scene in which Macbeth had originally made his proposal more boldly. Another theory has it that in an earlier version Lady Macbeth was entrusted with the murder, but in a lost scene transferred the duty to her husband. Other suggestions are that there must have been a scene in which Banquo troubled Macbeth's sleep, and another to explain the Third Murderer. Once speculation begins, every allusion by any character to an event not represented in the play becomes evidence of abridgment. The thinness of the evidence offered does not, however, entitle us to dismiss the view that the play was cut. If so, the cutting was well done, and we shall hardly discover the nature of what is lost.

Several critics have maintained that the play was fairly extensively tampered with, arguing not only for cuts but for interpolations. It is well known that Coleridge regarded the Porter scene as an interpolation; others so regard I.i and I.ii. These, and other similar suggestions, may safely be ignored; but there is a large measure of agreement that the whole of III.v and IV.i.39–43, 125–32 are spurious. These passages are usually attributed to Thomas Middleton because the interpolated songs called for in the stage directions at III.v.33 and IV.i.43 are certainly his, but it has recently been argued that Middleton's Hecate in his play *The Witch*, where the songs appear, bears no resemblance to the Hecate of *Macbeth*, and that some other, still anonymous, author must have the credit or blame for the material by which Middleton's songs are foisted into Shakespeare's play.

Although J. Dover Wilson in his New Cambridge edition of the play argues for an Elizabethan version of *Macbeth* (performed in Scotland), it seems obvious that the play celebrates the establishment of the first Stuart king of England, and that it cannot, therefore, be earlier than 1603. Simon Forman, the astrologer, saw it at the Globe in April 1611, but there are fairly clear allusions to the play in 1607. The references to the "equivocation" of Father Garnet during his trial for complicity in the Gunpowder Plot are unlikely to be interpolations, since the play as a whole is so deeply concerned with "equivocation"; and this trial occurred in the spring of 1606. In the summer of the previous year King James had visited Oxford, where an entertainment called *Tres Sibyllae* used these counterparts of the Weird Sisters to congratulate him on his ancestry, and there was also a debate on the question of "whether the imagination can produce real effects." If Shakespeare heard of these entertainments, which is not improbable, it is also possible, as H. N. Paul suggests, that he learned of the King's preference for short plays, which James happened to mention while in Oxford; though as a servant of the King retained for play-making he must surely have known of it already. In any case, the evidence that *Macbeth* belongs to 1606, and probably to the second half of the year, is strong.

Shakespeare's principal source was the *Chronicles* of Holinshed, and the main outline of his story is found in Holinshed's account of the reigns of Duncan and Macbeth (1034–57). He makes many changes, however, and not merely for economy, which explains the conflation of two separate wars, one fought against the rebellious Macdonwald and the other against the Norwegian Sueno. Holinshed does not describe the murder of Duncan, merely saying that with the connivance of certain friends (including Banquo) Macbeth killed the king at Inverness. But he describes in detail the murder of an earlier Scottish king, Duff, by Donwald, and this passage provided Shakespeare with needed material. Donwald was "set on" by his wife; he killed Duff in his castle at Forres; he made the chamberlains drunk. While his assassins were murdering Duff, he himself was with the watch outside, and when the alarm was given he rushed in and killed the chamberlains. From another place in Holinshed Shakespeare took the voice which speaks to the murderer in the night: after King Kenneth has killed his nephew he hears himself reproached and threatened by a mysterious voice, and is deprived of sleep. From the account of Edward the Confessor's reign Shakespeare borrows a few details, notably the King's "touching" for scrofula—a practice revived by James I.

The actual words of Holinshed are sometimes closely followed, notably in IV.ii, but Shakespeare deals freely with his source, making Duncan old and venerable, instead of a young and weak-willed man. This is part of the general blackening of Macbeth's character. Shakespeare also omits to mention that it was wrong for Duncan, an elective monarch, to proclaim Malcolm his heir; and that Macbeth ruled well for ten years. He also, for excellent reasons, makes Banquo honorable, whereas in Holinshed he connives at the murder. There are many other slight deviations, and some episodes which Shakespeare simply invented, like the banquet scene and the appearance of Banquo's ghost. More important than any variation of detail is the change in the whole presentation of Macbeth, who is, in the *Chronicles*, a tough fighting man not given to self-examination or remorse, and, as a king, capable in a conventional way.

Some of these changes, it will be noted, are related to the peculiar circumstances in which Shakespeare's play was written. The glorification of Banquo and of Fleance, founder of the Stuart line, was an essential part of the Stuart political myth, which sought to provide the Stuarts with a proper ancestry, stretching back through Banquo to the first king, Kenneth Macalpine. This is given expression in other books, such as Leslie's *De Origine . . . Scotorum* (1578). However, the idea was doubtless much in people's minds, and the Show of Kings confirms the words of King James himself, who expressed the hope that he and his descendants would "rule over [Britain] to the end of the world."

The interests of James I are reflected in other ways, too. He was a believer in witchcraft, and his *Daemonologie* (1599) was well known. He was a theologian and philosopher, much concerned with the explanation of such evil phenomena as repeatedly occur in the play. Only a year before *Macbeth* the Gunpowder Plot had put him in serious danger of his life, and he must have been as alert as anyone in the audience to the talk of "equivocation," a Jesuit device by which a prisoner under interrogation might pervert the truth in order to avoid self-accusation. The current use of this word, and the circumstances which gave rise to its fame, must be accounted part of the source material of *Macbeth*.

Some part of the theme of *Macbeth* may be expressed in the language of Milton, whose Christ thus accuses Satan:

> That hath been thy craft,
> By mixing somewhat true to vent more lies.
> But what have been thy answers, what but dark,
> Ambiguous, and with double sense deluding?
> (*Paradise Regain'd*, I.432–35)

Macbeth is subjected to a temptation which, like those undergone by Christ, exactly reflects what the powers of evil know to be the desires of the mind. It is not inhuman or even extraordinary to undergo such a temptation, but to succumb to it is precisely to give one's eternal jewel to the common enemy of man. From "th' equivocation of the fiend / That lies like truth" (V.v.42–43) arise not only the central themes of *Macbeth* but also some of the difficulties felt by a modern audience. Not only equivocation, but the reality of the fiend; not only the true character of Macbeth's villainy in succumbing, but his relevance to the human predicament more generally considered: these are problems for the modern reader.

The meanings of "equivocation" current at the time we have already touched on. When Father Garnet and his friends defended the practice, they incurred a charge to which Jesuits were anyway liable, that they had placed themselves on the side of the devil. Furthermore, as no man (the position is traditional) can choose an apparent good in preference to a real one unless his will is corrupted by appearance, evil acts imply the constant presence of equivocating factors in the world of moral choice. In other words, no one does an evil act unless the consequences of it appear to him more desirable than the consequences of not doing it; and since they cannot be so in truth, they clearly present themselves to him, as he deliberates upon the issue, in an equivocal manner. Before we see Macbeth deliberate, as he does at some length in the play, we have also seen evil present itself to him equivocally, under the forms of the Weird Sisters. Later they assist him, by further equivocation, to make progressively easier decisions for self-destructive acts of evil.

The role of the Weird Sisters is, then, to represent that equivocal evil in the nature of things which helps deceive the human will. But they are not mere allegories or the abstractions they might be in a modern play. Whether or no Shakespeare believed in demonic powers, in black and white magic, as King James did, he means the Sisters to be really *there*, visible to whom they wish, and endowed with the powers appropriate to demons. They are not mere witches, though they have some of the powers of witches, for, though produced by nature, they share with angels a freedom from limitation of space and time, a power to perceive the causes of things, and to see some distance into the human mind. They assume bodies of air or mist ("the earth hath bubbles"). They are real—Banquo sees them; and Banquo's ghost is also, for all we can know, real. Shakespeare seems here, and with the apparition of the dagger, to be inviting reflections as to whether the imagination can produce real effects; but dramatically they are undoubtedly real. The evils within and without Macbeth's mind are subtly twinned.

James knew all about this, and he knew also that the Sisters had no direct power over Macbeth's soul (he had told his witch-tormentor Bothwell the same thing years before). The Weird Sisters, knowing of his ambitions, could persuade Macbeth to evil, but they could not compel him to it; by an equivocal representation of a foreseen future they could tempt him to choose an apparent before a real good. Thus they subjected him to the temptations he was least able to withstand, but had no direct power over his free will. It is in this sense that Macbeth is an Everyman; and for him as for all habitual sinners the guilt that is at first a matter of choice becomes, as his will atrophies, a matter of fate. His torments of conscience no longer come between desire and act. He loses his distinctive humanity. The great moment of moral crisis is in the soliloquy "If it were done . . ." (I.vii), which wonderfully enacts the deliberation preceding choice. The fatal dismissal from consideration of "the life to come" disables the case for the real as against the apparent good to such a degree that Lady Macbeth, even less aware of the spiritual issues and penalties, can ignore it altogether a moment later, ridiculing as effeminate the merely human reasons against murder, and showing, as against her husband's view, that the thing is possible. There are many answers to the objection that a man like Macbeth should not speak great poetry, but the best is that he is merely a special case of a universal human problem; before the murder he enacts a characteristically human moral agony, and that is a province of great poetry.

Macbeth's humanity is, therefore, represented as a condition we share. It is, of course, imperfect. He is a brave man, a man of blood, Bellona's bridegroom; but like Coriolanus later he exhibits the defects of these qualities. He has an affinity with blood and darkness, and Shakespeare silently contrasts him with Duncan, who is benign and trusting, but also, as a king should be, properly associated (by the imagery) with order and fertility. Shakespeare makes Macbeth's courage ring hollow, and Duncan's professions of confidence in him are subtly undermined by little dramatic ironies:

> No more that Thane of Cawdor shall deceive
> Our bosom interest. Go pronounce his present death,
> And with his former title greet Macbeth.
> (I.ii.63–65)

And a little later, still thinking of the old Cawdor, he reflects that

> There's no art
> To find the mind's construction in the face:
> He was a gentleman on whom I built
> An absolute trust.
> *Enter* MACBETH . . . .
> O worthiest cousin! (I.iv.11–14)

In such ways we are almost unconsciously prepared for the inadequacy of Macbeth to the temptation which has already begun, and which will unman him. Already in I.iii he is tormented by the "solicitation" of the Weird Sisters, which, he says, "cannot be ill; cannot be good" (131). He knows the terrors of conscience, and imagines an appalling future after the crime; "nothing is / But what is not" (141–42). He has his notion of *virtus*, the quality of being a man, and it serves him well in war; but it does not include the power to deal with the evil growing in his mind.

He dares do all that may become a man, he says; but his unnatural act is, precisely, more than becomes a man, and he sinks below manhood, as his wife, by an evil effort of will, casts off womanhood and so loses her mind in guilt. To live among men they must pretend to be what they are not: "To beguile the time, / Look like the time . . . look like th' innocent flower, / But be the serpent under't" (I.v.63–66); "False face must hide what the false heart doth know" (I.vii.82); "And make our faces vizards to our hearts, / Disguising what they are" (III.ii.34–35). The time will come when the corruption of this seeming has spread, and the sorrows of his subjects are deepest; then a man will need to remind himself that it remains possible to appear good without really being evil:

> Angels are bright still, though the brightest fell.
> Though all things foul would wear the brows of grace,
> Yet grace must still look so. (IV.iii.22–24)

This enslavement to appearance is proper to a man who has himself mistaken supernatural ill for good; but the true unmanning of Macbeth is not only in this, not only in the passionless reception of his wife's death, and his animal courage when the fiends prove to have "paltered." It is also in his self-betrayal to fear and sleeplessness. The voice cried "Sleep no more!" and at the moment when he thought to have entered into the full enjoyment of his kingdom Macbeth must speak of his "restless ecstasy," and of "these terrible dreams / That shake us nightly." He lacks "the season of all natures, sleep." His remedy is murder—first Banquo, then Lady Macduff; but henceforth nothing, not even becoming "old in deed" and making "the very firstlings of [his] heart . . . / the firstlings of [his] hand," can make him anything but the slave of his fantasy, the faculty which now, under the influence of perpetual fear and guilt, takes command from the reason. As husband and wife grow apart in their own torments, Lady Macbeth discovers what it is to invite an "unsexing" which amounts to demonic possession: the slight human compunction which prevents her murdering Duncan grows into a curse upon her unwomaned body, and she finds that "a little water" will not clear her of this deed.

The suffering of the Macbeths may be thought of as caused by the pressure of the world of order slowly resuming its true shape and crushing them. This is the work of time; as usual in Shakespeare, evil, however great, burns itself out, and time is the servant of providence. Nowhere is this clearer than in *Macbeth*. The damnation of the principal characters involves murder and destruction, outrage not only upon the state but upon the whole cosmos; but the balance is restored. Macbeth, who is allowed to say many wise things, observes early that "Time and the hour runs through the roughest day" (I.iii.147). The number of allusions to Time is indeed evidence that Shakespeare was at work in his customary way, hinting at a philosophical pattern, by using the word in a considerable variety of contexts which we may relate as we will. Macbeth, confronted by the Weird Sisters, finds his mind inhabiting a time when the deed is done; his letters transport his wife beyond the "ignorant present" so that she feels "the future in the instant" (I.v.57–58). In the great soliloquy at the beginning of I.vii Macbeth says he would be content to deal in a time and to ignore eternity if he could escape punishment on earth. Lady Macbeth taunts him with the inability to proceed (in time) from desire to act. And they try to "mock the time with fairest show" (81). But Time is not mocked; at the news of Macduff's flight, Macbeth says that Time anticipates his "dread exploits." He hopes to defeat it by abolishing the time between desire and act (IV.i.144 ff.); but it is Malcolm that time will befriend (IV.iii.10), and when Macduff enters with Macbeth's head he can say "The time is free" (V.ix.21). As in Spenser, Time, apparently the destroyer, is the redeemer; yet it is itself redeemed. It seems very characteristic of the deeply allusive intellect of Shakespeare that there should be, in the greatest of the plays about human guilt, these semantic complexities concerning time, the element in which human life succeeds or fails, in which virtue is tested and evil brought to good.

But Macbeth is not only Everyman turned villain. He is also a king, or rather a tyrannical usurper. It has been suggested that this play was in part intended to replace *Richard III* in the repertory, and the two works have something in common. But Macbeth is not a lover of evil, and not a Machiavel; Richard III would not have said, "If chance will have me king, why, chance may crown me" (I.iii.143); and there is a boisterousness in him which Macbeth always lacks. Both have traits of the villain-hero, and both remember their Senecan origins—Macbeth uses some of the most famous Senecan tags. But he comes to murder by means of demonic equivocation; there is no Machiavellian plotting against the succession, but one critical stroke. Like all tyrants, he can expect a violent end; he brings horror to his country, and is overthrown by Malcolm in a role like that of Richmond. But the tyrannical rule of Macbeth is an outward reflection of a tyranny within. The long, rather stilted debate between Macduff and Malcolm in IV.iii deals with the question of tyranny in a somewhat abstract (but deliberately equivocal) way, and the repeated reference to Macbeth as a dwarf wearing the cloak of a giant is an emblem of usurpation and misrule. So is the darkness in which the major scenes take place; so is the ironical collapse of ceremony (order in the state) when Macbeth's fit (disorder in the king) seizes him at the banquet. That he should be a tyrant is a fact used to emphasize, not as in *Richard III* the long terror of civil war, but the mystical relation between the king's two bodies. Macduff explicitly links the inner and the outward tyranny. To the south Edward the Confessor practices good government and good magic, and sends a virtuous expedition against Scotland, to redeem the time. Thus the enactment of Macbeth's fears and his guilt involve the whole state, and indeed, as we see in the unruly night of the murder, the whole creation; the restoration of nature requires his death (suitably motivated by the equivocating fiends) and in stilling his disorder quiets also the disorder of the body politic.

Such remarks would not mean much if one did not also stress the complex magnificence of the structure which bears these meanings, and the power of the poetry in which they are figured. The opening scene is unique in the canon. It is the end of a witches' sabbath—more fully represented in IV.i—and its dozen lines have no mere atmospheric value, but at their close set up an equivocal refrain—"Fair is foul" —which instantly sounds in the speech of Macbeth at his first entry in the third scene. Briefly, between these two scenes, we hear of the Scottish victory, and the part played by the man of blood, Macbeth; then we are rushed forward to hear of the devil speaking true, and the stolen robes with which the hero already, in his imagination, dresses himself. His aside "This supernatural soliciting . . ." (I.iii.130 ff.) is the first instance of that entirely original rhythm devised by Shakespeare for this play, and of the poetic rendering of articulate terror. Another brief scene in which Duncan congratulates and rewards Macbeth, but names Malcolm his successor; and then Lady Macbeth enters with the letter, and speaks another soliloquy characterized by the same diseased excitement, the same "sickening see-saw rhythm," as L. C. Knights calls it:

> Thou wouldst be great,
> Art not without ambition, but without
> The illness should attend it. What thou wouldst highly,
> That wouldst thou holily; wouldst not play false,
> And yet wouldst wrongly win. (I.v.18–22)

In this scene the "unsexed" Lady Macbeth prepares for the corruption of her husband. One more glance of Duncan in the next scene, finding nothing but good in his host's castle; and then the key soliloquy, "If it were done . . ." (I.vii.1 ff.) and the final decision to commit murder. Twenty minutes of stage action, the scene alternating between Duncan and the Macbeths, and the first act ends.

The second, a new movement played continuously, is a night-piece. The opening words establish that; the murder is done to nocturnal noises, owls scream and sleepers stir. The tolling bell and the knocking of the second scene (which becomes the knocking on hell gate in the third) link all together. The Porter, superbly and unconsciously relevant to a story of murder, equivocation, and the pains of hell, is improved from a slight hint in Holinshed's tale of Donwald at the murder of King Duff; here his scene creates a perfectly timed pause, before the murder is discovered, the grooms are murdered, and Malcolm flees. There follows the moment of guilty calm, Macbeth in possession of his borrowed robes at the cost of ineradicable unease; and then the next murders, the apparitions, the growing estrangement of the Macbeths, and the sleepwalking, retribution, and death. Only with the Porter and at the English court does the pace slacken. *Macbeth* is extremely brief, but surely it is hard to feel that it lacks substance. It is dark, but with a variety of color seen against the dark; its poetry is a "statement of evil," certainly, but "hell is energy" and *Macbeth* has extraordinary energy; it represents a fierce engagement between the mind and its guilt, and it brings into play intellectual and imaginative resources nowhere else employed in the tragedies.

Frank Kermode

The Tragedy of Macbeth

[DRAMATIS PERSONAE

DUNCAN, *King of Scotland*
MALCOLM, DONALBAIN } *his sons*
MACBETH, BANQUO } *generals of the King's army*
MACDUFF, LENNOX, ROSSE, MENTETH, ANGUS, CATHNESS } *noblemen of Scotland*
FLEANCE, *son to Banquo*
SIWARD, *Earl of Northumberland, general of the English forces*
YOUNG SIWARD, *his son*
SEYTON, *an officer attending on Macbeth*
BOY, *son to Macduff*

ENGLISH DOCTOR
SCOTS DOCTOR
SERGEANT
PORTER
OLD MAN
Three MURDERERS

LADY MACBETH
LADY MACDUFF
GENTLEWOMAN *attending on Lady Macbeth*

Three WITCHES, *the Weird Sisters*
Three other WITCHES
HECAT
APPARITIONS

LORDS, GENTLEMEN, OFFICERS, SOLDIERS, ATTENDANTS, *and* MESSENGERS

SCENE: *Scotland; England*]

ACT I, SCENE I

Thunder and lightning. Enter three WITCHES.

1. Witch. When shall we three meet again?
In thunder, lightning, or in rain?
2. Witch. When the hurly-burly's done,
When the battle's lost and won.
3. Witch. That will be ere the set of sun.
1. Witch. Where the place?
2. Witch. Upon the heath.
3. Witch. There to meet with Macbeth.
1. Witch. I come, Graymalkin.
[*2. Witch.*] Paddock calls.
[*3. Witch.*] Anon.
All. Fair is foul, and foul is fair,
Hover through the fog and filthy air. *Exeunt.*

Words and passages enclosed in square brackets in the text above are either emendations of the copy-text or additions to it. The Textual Notes immediately following the play cite the earliest authority for every such change or insertion and supply the reading of the copy-text wherever it is emended in this edition.

I.i. Location: An open place.
3. hurly-burly: commotion, uproar, i.e. the battle that is described in the following scene.
8, 9. Graymalkin, Paddock: i.e. grey cat, toad; the names of the familiars or spirits who serve the witches. In IV.i.3 we learn that the familiar of the Third Witch is called Harpier, apparently meaning "harpy." **10. Anon:** right away, coming (spoken to her familiar).

SCENE II

Alarum within. Enter KING [DUNCAN], MALCOLM, DONALBAIN, LENNOX, *with* ATTENDANTS, *meeting a bleeding* [SERGEANT].

Dun. What bloody man is that? He can report,
As seemeth by his plight, of the revolt
The newest state.
Mal. This is the sergeant,
Who like a good and hardy soldier fought
'Gainst my captivity. Hail, brave friend!
Say to the King the knowledge of the broil
As thou didst leave it.
[*Serg.*] Doubtful it stood,
As two spent swimmers that do cling together
And choke their art. The merciless Macdonwald
(Worthy to be a rebel, for to that
The multiplying villainies of nature
Do swarm upon him) from the Western Isles
Of kerns and [gallowglasses] is supplied,
And Fortune, on his damned [quarrel] smiling,
Show'd like a rebel's whore. But all's too weak;

I.ii. Location: Scotland. A camp.
o.s.d. **Alarum:** trumpet call to arms. **6. broil:** battle.
9. art: skill (in swimming). **10. that:** i.e. that end.
12. Western Isles: islands west of Scotland.
13. Of: with. **kerns and gallowglasses:** light- and heavy-armed foot soldiers. **14. quarrel:** cause. **15. Show'd:** appeared.

For brave Macbeth (well he deserves that name),
Disdaining Fortune, with his brandish'd steel,
Which smok'd with bloody execution,
(Like Valor's minion) carv'd out his passage
Till he fac'd the slave;
Which nev'r shook hands, nor bade farewell to him,
Till he unseam'd him from the nave to th' chops,
And fix'd his head upon our battlements.
Dun. O valiant cousin, worthy gentleman!
[*Serg.*] As whence the sun gins his reflection
Shipwracking storms and direful thunders [break],
So from that spring whence comfort seem'd to come
Discomfort swells. Mark, King of Scotland, mark!
No sooner justice had, with valor arm'd,
Compell'd these skipping kerns to trust their heels,
But the Norweyan lord, surveying vantage,
With furbish'd arms and new supplies of men,
Began a fresh assault.
Dun. Dismay'd not this
Our captains, Macbeth and Banquo?
[*Serg.*] Yes,
As sparrows eagles; or the hare the lion.
If I say sooth, I must report they were
As cannons overcharg'd with double cracks, so they
Doubly redoubled strokes upon the foe.
Except they meant to bathe in reeking wounds,
Or memorize another Golgotha,
I cannot tell—
But I am faint, my gashes cry for help.
Dun. So well thy words become thee as thy wounds,
They smack of honor both. Go get him surgeons.
[*Exit Sergeant, attended.*]

Enter Rosse *and* Angus.

Who comes here?
Mal. The worthy Thane of Rosse.
Len. What a haste looks through his eyes! So should he look
That seems to speak things strange.
Rosse. God save the King!
Dun. Whence cam'st thou, worthy thane?
Rosse. From Fife, great King,
Where the Norweyan banners flout the sky
And fan our people cold.
Norway himself, with terrible numbers,
Assisted by that most disloyal traitor,
The Thane of Cawdor, began a dismal conflict,

Till that Bellona's bridegroom, lapp'd in proof,
Confronted him with self-comparisons,
Point against point, rebellious arm 'gainst arm,
Curbing his lavish spirit; and to conclude,
The victory fell on us.
Dun. Great happiness!
Rosse. That now
Sweno, the Norways' king, craves composition;
Nor would we deign him burial of his men
Till he disbursed at Saint Colme's inch
Ten thousand dollars to our general use.
Dun. No more that Thane of Cawdor shall deceive
Our bosom interest. Go pronounce his present death,
And with his former title greet Macbeth.
Rosse. I'll see it done.
Dun. What he hath lost, noble Macbeth hath won.
Exeunt.

Scene III

Thunder. Enter the three Witches.

1. Witch. Where hast thou been, sister?
2. Witch. Killing swine.
3. Witch. Sister, where thou?
1. Witch. A sailor's wife had chestnuts in her lap,
And mounch'd, and mounch'd, and mounch'd. "Give me!" quoth I.
"Aroint thee, witch!" the rump-fed ronyon cries.
Her husband's to Aleppo gone, master o' th' *Tiger*;
But in a sieve I'll thither sail,
And like a rat without a tail,
I'll do, I'll do, and I'll do.
2. Witch. I'll give thee a wind.
1. Witch. Th' art kind.
3. Witch. And I another.
1. Witch. I myself have all the other,
And the very ports they blow,
All the quarters that they know
I' th' shipman's card.
I'll drain him dry as hay:
Sleep shall neither night nor day
Hang upon his penthouse lid;
He shall live a man forbid;
Weary sev'nnights, nine times nine,
Shall he dwindle, peak, and pine;
Though his bark cannot be lost,
Yet it shall be tempest-toss'd.
Look what I have.
2. Witch. Show me, show me.

16. name: i.e. designation "brave." **19. minion:** darling.
21. shook hands: i.e. took leave. **22. nave:** navel. **chops:** jaws.
24. cousin: kinsman (used familiarly of any collateral relative except a brother or sister). Duncan and Macbeth were grandsons of King Malcolm.
25. gins his reflection: begins its turning back (at the vernal equinox).
27. spring: (1) spring season; (2) source. **28. swells:** wells up.
30. skipping: highly mobile (because light-armed, but with implication that they are quick to retreat).
31. surveying vantage: seeing his opportunity.
37. cracks: charges. **so:** in such a way. **39. Except:** unless.
40. memorize another Golgotha: make the field as memorable for slaughter as Golgotha, i.e. Calvary, "the place of skulls."
47. seems to: seems about to.
49–50. flout . . . cold: mock the sky and fan cold fear into our people. It has been suggested that Rosse begins his account in the so-called historic present tense.
51. Norway: the King of Norway. **53. dismal:** ill-boding.

54. Till that: till. **Bellona's bridegroom:** i.e. Macbeth. Bellona was the goddess of war; she was a virgin, but Shakespeare is making a conceit, not a mistake, since *1 Henry IV*, IV.i.114, proves that he knew the facts. **lapp'd in proof:** clad in tested armor.
55. self-comparisons: i.e. deeds as valorous as his own.
57. lavish: unrestrained, wild. **59. composition:** terms of peace.
61. Saint Colme's inch: Inchcolm, a small island in the Firth of Forth.
64. bosom interest: dearest concerns. **present:** immediate.

I.iii. Location: A heath.
6. Aroint: be gone. **rump-fed:** fat-rumped (?). **ronyon:** scabby woman. **9. like:** in the shape of.
11. wind. Witches were believed to sell winds.
15. blow: i.e. blow from; the ships are kept out of port by winds.
17. shipman's card: compass card; or, possibly, chart.
20. penthouse lid: i.e. eyelid (*penthouse* = lean-to with a sloping roof). **21. forbid:** under a curse. **23. peak:** grow emaciated.

1. Witch. Here I have a pilot's thumb,
Wrack'd as homeward he did come. *Drum within.*
3. Witch. A drum, a drum!
Macbeth doth come.
All. The weïrd sisters, hand in hand,
Posters of the sea and land,
Thus do go, about, about,
Thrice to thine, and thrice to mine,
And thrice again, to make up nine.
Peace, the charm's wound up.

Enter MACBETH *and* BANQUO.

Macb. So foul and fair a day I have not seen.
Ban. How far is't call'd to [Forres]? What are these
So wither'd and so wild in their attire,
That look not like th' inhabitants o' th' earth,
And yet are on't? Live you? or are you aught
That man may question? You seem to understand me,
By each at once her choppy finger laying
Upon her skinny lips. You should be women,
And yet your beards forbid me to interpret
That you are so.
Macb. Speak, if you can: what are you?
1. Witch. All hail, Macbeth, hail to thee, Thane of Glamis!
2. Witch. All hail, Macbeth, hail to thee, Thane of Cawdor!
3. Witch. All hail, Macbeth, that shalt be King hereafter!
Ban. Good sir, why do you start, and seem to fear
Things that do sound so fair?—I' th' name of truth,
Are ye fantastical, or that indeed
Which outwardly ye show? My noble partner
You greet with present grace, and great prediction
Of noble having and of royal hope,
That he seems rapt withal; to me you speak not.
If you can look into the seeds of time,
And say which grain will grow, and which will not,
Speak then to me, who neither beg nor fear
Your favors nor your hate.
1. Witch. Hail!
2. Witch. Hail!
3. Witch. Hail!
1. Witch. Lesser than Macbeth, and greater.
2. Witch. Not so happy, yet much happier.
3. Witch. Thou shalt get kings, though thou be none.
So all hail, Macbeth and Banquo!
1. Witch. Banquo and Macbeth, all hail!
Macb. Stay, you imperfect speakers, tell me more:
By Sinel's death I know I am Thane of Glamis,
But how of Cawdor? The Thane of Cawdor lives
A prosperous gentleman; and to be king
Stands not within the prospect of belief,
No more than to be Cawdor. Say from whence
You owe this strange intelligence, or why
Upon this blasted heath you stop our way
With such prophetic greeting? Speak, I charge you.
Witches vanish.
Ban. The earth hath bubbles, as the water has,
And these are of them. Whither are they vanish'd?
Macb. Into the air; and what seem'd corporal melted,
As breath into the wind. Would they had stay'd!
Ban. Were such things here as we do speak about?
Or have we eaten on the insane root
That takes the reason prisoner?
Macb. Your children shall be kings.
Ban. You shall be king.
Macb. And Thane of Cawdor too; went it not so?
Ban. To th' self-same tune and words. Who's here?

Enter ROSSE *and* ANGUS.

Rosse. The King hath happily receiv'd, Macbeth,
The news of thy success; and when he reads
Thy personal venture in the rebels' fight,
His wonders and his praises do contend
Which should be thine or his. Silenc'd with that,
In viewing o'er the rest o' th' self-same day,
He finds thee in the stout Norweyan ranks,
Nothing afeard of what thyself didst make,
Strange images of death. As thick as tale
[Came] post with post, and every one did bear
Thy praises in his kingdom's great defense,
And pour'd them down before him.
Ang. We are sent
To give thee from our royal master thanks,
Only to herald thee into his sight,
Not pay thee.
Rosse. And for an earnest of a greater honor,
He bade me, from him, call thee Thane of Cawdor;
In which addition, hail, most worthy thane,
For it is thine.
Ban. What, can the devil speak true?
Macb. The Thane of Cawdor lives; why do you dress me
In borrowed robes?
Ang. Who was the thane lives yet,
But under heavy judgment bears that life
Which he deserves to lose. Whether he was combin'd
With those of Norway, or did line the rebel
With hidden help and vantage, or that with both
He labor'd in his country's wrack, I know not;

32. weird. Spelled *weyard* or *weyward* in F1; from Old English *wyrd*, "fate." **33. Posters of:** swift travellers over.
37. wound up: i.e. ready for action. **43. question:** converse with.
44. choppy: chapped. **53. fantastical:** imaginary.
54. show: appear to be.
55. with present grace: i.e. by his present title, as Thane of Glamis.
55–56. prediction . . . noble having: i.e. as Thane of Cawdor.
57. rapt: carried out of himself. **withal:** with (by) it.
60–61. beg . . . hate: beg your favors nor fear your hate.
67. get: beget. **70. imperfect:** giving an incomplete account.
71. Sinel: Macbeth's father, according to Holinshed.
76. owe: possess. **intelligence:** information.
77. blasted: blighted, barren.
84. on: of. **insane:** causing insanity. The root has been variously identified.
92–93. His . . . his: i.e. Duncan does not know whether to speak of his astonishment or his admiration.
93. that: i.e. the conflict between his astonishment and his admiration.
96. Nothing: not at all.
97. images: figures, forms. **As . . . tale:** as fast as they could be "told" or counted.
98. post with post: one messenger after another.
104. earnest: token, pledge. **106. addition:** title.
109. Who . . . thane: he who once held that title.
111. combin'd: allied.
112. line: support. **the rebel:** i.e. Macdonwald.

But treasons capital, confess'd and prov'd,
Have overthrown him.
Macb. [*Aside.*] Glamis, and Thane of Cawdor!
The greatest is behind. [*To Rosse and Angus.*] Thanks
for your pains.
[*Aside to Banquo.*] Do you not hope your children shall
be kings,
When those that gave the Thane of Cawdor to me
Promis'd no less to them?
Ban. [*Aside to Macbeth.*] That, trusted home,
Might yet enkindle you unto the crown,
Besides the Thane of Cawdor. But 'tis strange;
And oftentimes, to win us to our harm,
The instruments of darkness tell us truths,
Win us with honest trifles, to betray 's
In deepest consequence.—
Cousins, a word, I pray you.
Macb. [*Aside.*] Two truths are told,
As happy prologues to the swelling act
Of the imperial theme.—I thank you, gentlemen.
[*Aside.*] This supernatural soliciting
Cannot be ill; cannot be good. If ill,
Why hath it given me earnest of success,
Commencing in a truth? I am Thane of Cawdor.
If good, why do I yield to that suggestion
Whose horrid image doth unfix my hair
And make my seated heart knock at my ribs,
Against the use of nature? Present fears
Are less than horrible imaginings:
My thought, whose murther yet is but fantastical,
Shakes so my single state of man that function
Is smother'd in surmise, and nothing is
But what is not.
Ban. Look how our partner's rapt.
Macb. [*Aside.*] If chance will have me king, why,
chance may crown me
Without my stir.
Ban. New honors come upon him,
Like our strange garments, cleave not to their mould
But with the aid of use.
Macb. [*Aside.*] Come what come may,
Time and the hour runs through the roughest day.
Ban. Worthy Macbeth, we stay upon your leisure.
Macb. Give me your favor; my dull brain was
wrought
With things forgotten. Kind gentlemen, your pains
Are regist'red where every day I turn
The leaf to read them. Let us toward the King.
[*Aside to Banquo.*] Think upon what hath chanc'd; and
at more time,

The interim having weigh'd it, let us speak
Our free hearts each to other.
Ban. Very gladly.
Macb. Till then, enough.—Come, friends. *Exeunt.*

Scene IV

Flourish. Enter King [Duncan], Lennox, Malcolm, Donalbain, *and* Attendants.

Dun. Is execution done on Cawdor? [Are] not
Those in commission yet return'd?
Mal. My liege,
They are not yet come back. But I have spoke
With one that saw him die; who did report
That very frankly he confess'd his treasons,
Implor'd your Highness' pardon, and set forth
A deep repentance. Nothing in his life
Became him like the leaving it. He died
As one that had been studied in his death,
To throw away the dearest thing he ow'd,
As 'twere a careless trifle.
Dun. There's no art
To find the mind's construction in the face:
He was a gentleman on whom I built
An absolute trust.

Enter Macbeth, Banquo, Rosse, *and* Angus.

O worthiest cousin!
The sin of my ingratitude even now
Was heavy on me. Thou art so far before,
That swiftest wing of recompense is slow
To overtake thee. Would thou hadst less deserv'd,
That the proportion both of thanks and payment
Might have been mine! Only I have left to say,
More is thy due than more than all can pay.
Macb. The service and the loyalty I owe,
In doing it, pays itself. Your Highness' part
Is to receive our duties; and our duties
Are to your throne and state children and servants;
Which do but what they should, by doing every thing
Safe toward your love and honor.
Dun. Welcome hither!
I have begun to plant thee, and will labor
To make thee full of growing. Noble Banquo,
That hast no less deserv'd, nor must be known
No less to have done so, let me infold thee
And hold thee to my heart.
Ban. There if I grow,
The harvest is your own.
Dun. My plenteous joys,
Wanton in fullness, seek to hide themselves
In drops of sorrow. Sons, kinsmen, thanes,
And you whose places are the nearest, know

117. **behind:** beyond, to come. 120. **home:** completely.
121. **enkindle you unto:** give you cause to hope for.
126. **deepest consequence:** the very important events that follow.
127. **Cousins:** i.e. fellow lords.
128. **swelling act:** grand dramatic action.
130. **soliciting:** incitement, temptation (so also *suggestion* in line 134).
137. **use:** custom. **fears:** objects of fear.
139. **whose:** in which. **fantastical:** imagined.
140. **single . . . man:** weak human constitution. **function:** the normal operation of its powers. 141. **surmise:** imagined action.
141–42. **nothing . . . not:** i.e. nothing has reality for me but what is imaginary. 144. **stir:** exertion, initiative.
145. **strange:** new. **their mould:** i.e. the shape of him who wears them. 149. **favor:** pardon. **wrought:** agitated.
151–52. **regist'red . . . them:** i.e. recorded in my memory.

155. **Our free hearts:** i.e. our thoughts freely.

I.iv. **Location:** Forres. The palace.
2. **in commission:** i.e. delegated to see the execution carried out. **liege:** sovereign. 9. **been studied:** made it his study.
10. **ow'd:** owned. 11. **careless:** uncared-for. 16. **before:** ahead.
19–20. **That . . . mine:** so that I could thank you and reward you as you deserve. 27. **Safe toward:** to secure.
34. **Wanton:** unrestrained.

We will establish our estate upon
Our eldest, Malcolm, whom we name hereafter
The Prince of Cumberland; which honor must
Not unaccompanied invest him only,
But signs of nobleness, like stars, shall shine
On all deservers. From hence to Enverness,
And bind us further to you.

Macb. The rest is labor, which is not us'd for you.
I'll be myself the harbinger, and make joyful
The hearing of my wife with your approach;
So humbly take my leave.

Dun. My worthy Cawdor!

Macb. [*Aside.*] The Prince of Cumberland! that is
a step
On which I must fall down, or else o'erleap,
For in my way it lies. Stars, hide your fires,
Let not light see my black and deep desires;
The eye wink at the hand; yet let that be
Which the eye fears, when it is done, to see. *Exit.*

Dun. True, worthy Banquo! he is full so valiant,
And in his commendations I am fed;
It is a banquet to me. Let's after him,
Whose care is gone before to bid us welcome:
It is a peerless kinsman. *Flourish. Exeunt.*

Scene V

Enter Macbeth's Wife *alone, with a letter.*

Lady M. [*Reads.*] "They met me in the day of success; and I have learn'd by the perfect'st report, they have more in them than mortal knowledge. When I burnt in desire to question them further, they made themselves air, into which they vanish'd. Whiles I stood rapt in the wonder of it, came missives from the King, who all-hail'd me 'Thane of Cawdor,' by which title, before, these weïrd sisters saluted me, and referr'd me to the coming on of time with 'Hail, King that shalt be!' This have I thought good to deliver thee, my dearest partner of greatness, that thou mightst not lose the dues of rejoicing by being ignorant of what greatness is promis'd thee. Lay it to thy heart, and farewell."

Glamis thou art, and Cawdor, and shalt be
What thou art promis'd. Yet do I fear thy nature,
It is too full o' th' milk of human kindness
To catch the nearest way. Thou wouldst be great,
Art not without ambition, but without
The illness should attend it. What thou wouldst
highly,
That wouldst thou holily; wouldst not play false,

37. **establish our estate:** settle the succession.
39. **Prince of Cumberland:** title of the Scottish heir apparent.
42. **Enverness:** Inverness, seat of the Thane of Cawdor.
44. **The rest . . . you:** i.e. leisure which is not spent in your service is wearisome.
45. **harbinger:** one sent ahead to arrange for lodging.
52. **wink . . . hand:** be blind to what the hand does. **be:** come to pass. 54. **full so valiant:** i.e. every bit as valiant as you say.

I.v. Location: Inverness. Macbeth's castle.
2. **perfect'st report:** most reliable information.
6. **missives:** messengers. 10. **deliver:** inform.
16. **fear:** fear for, feel uneasy about. 20. **illness:** wickedness.

And yet wouldst wrongly win. Thou'ldst have, great
Glamis,
That which cries, "Thus thou must do," if thou have it;
And that which rather thou dost fear to do
Than wishest should be undone. Hie thee hither,
That I may pour my spirits in thine ear,
And chastise with the valor of my tongue
All that impedes thee from the golden round,
Which fate and metaphysical aid doth seem
To have thee crown'd withal.

Enter Messenger.

What is your tidings?

Mess. The King comes here to-night.

Lady M. Thou'rt mad to say it!
Is not thy master with him? who, were't so,
Would have inform'd for preparation.

Mess. So please you, it is true; our thane is coming.
One of my fellows had the speed of him,
Who, almost dead for breath, had scarcely more
Than would make up his message.

Lady M. Give him tending,
He brings great news. *Exit Messenger.*
The raven himself is hoarse
That croaks the fatal entrance of Duncan
Under my battlements. Come, you spirits
That tend on mortal thoughts, unsex me here,
And fill me from the crown to the toe topful
Of direst cruelty! Make thick my blood,
Stop up th' access and passage to remorse,
That no compunctious visitings of nature
Shake my fell purpose, nor keep peace between
Th' effect and [it]! Come to my woman's breasts,
And take my milk for gall, you murth'ring ministers,
Wherever in your sightless substances
You wait on nature's mischief! Come, thick night,
And pall thee in the dunnest smoke of hell,
That my keen knife see not the wound it makes,
Nor heaven peep through the blanket of the dark
To cry, "Hold, hold!"

Enter Macbeth.

Great Glamis! worthy Cawdor!
Greater than both, by the all-hail hereafter!
Thy letters have transported me beyond
This ignorant present, and I feel now
The future in the instant.

Macb. My dearest love,
Duncan comes here to-night.

Lady M. And when goes hence?

Macb. To-morrow, as he purposes.

Lady M. O, never
Shall sun that morrow see!

24. **fear to do:** shrink from doing. 25. **Hie:** hasten.
28. **round:** crown. 29. **metaphysical:** supernatural.
30. **withal:** with. 35. **had . . . of:** outdistanced.
41. **mortal:** deadly, murderous. 44. **remorse:** pity.
45. **nature:** natural feeling.
46. **fell:** cruel. **keep peace:** intervene.
47. **Th' effect and it:** i.e. my purpose and its accomplishment.
48. **for:** in exchange for. 49. **sightless:** invisible.
50. **nature's mischief:** evil done to, or within, nature.
51. **pall thee:** wrap yourself. **dunnest:** darkest.
56. **letters:** letter (cf. Latin *litterae*).
57. **ignorant:** i.e. ignorant of what the future will bring.

Your face, my thane, is as a book, where men
May read strange matters. To beguile the time,
Look like the time; bear welcome in your eye,
Your hand, your tongue; look like th' innocent flower,
But be the serpent under't. He that's coming
Must be provided for; and you shall put
This night's great business into my dispatch,
Which shall to all our nights and days to come
Give solely sovereign sway and masterdom.
Macb. We will speak further.
Lady M. Only look up clear:
To alter favor ever is to fear.
Leave all the rest to me. *Exeunt.*

Scene VI

Hoboys and torches. Enter King [Duncan], Malcolm, Donalbain, Banquo, Lennox, Macduff, Rosse, Angus, *and* Attendants.

Dun. This castle hath a pleasant seat, the air
Nimbly and sweetly recommends itself
Unto our gentle senses.
Ban. This guest of summer,
The temple-haunting [marlet], does approve,
By his lov'd [mansionry], that the heaven's breath
Smells wooingly here; no jutty, frieze,
Buttress, nor coign of vantage, but this bird
Hath made his pendant bed and procreant cradle.
Where they [most] breed and haunt, I have observ'd
The air is delicate.

Enter Lady [Macbeth].

Dun. See, see, our honor'd hostess!
The love that follows us sometime is our trouble,
Which still we thank as love. Herein I teach you
How you shall bid God 'ield us for your pains,
And thank us for your trouble.
Lady M. All our service
In every point twice done, and then done double,
Were poor and single business to contend
Against those honors deep and broad wherewith
Your Majesty loads our house. For those of old,
And the late dignities heap'd up to them,
We rest your ermites.
Dun. Where's the Thane of Cawdor?
We cours'd him at the heels, and had a purpose
To be his purveyor; but he rides well,

63. beguile the time: deceive the world.
68. dispatch: management. **71. clear:** serene.
72. favor: expression. **to fear:** i.e. to create fear.

I.vi. Location: Inverness. Before Macbeth's castle.
o.s.d. Hoboys: oboes. **1. seat:** situation.
4. temple-haunting: given to building its nest in churches. **marlet:** martin. **5. mansionry:** i.e. nest-building. **6. jutty:** projection.
7. coign of vantage: convenient corner. **10. delicate:** soft.
12. Which: i.e. the trouble. **thank as love:** are grateful for because it arises from love.
13. God . . . pains: God reward *me* for *your* trouble. Duncan is gently facetious. **16. single:** feeble.
16–17. contend Against: i.e. try to match.
20. We . . . ermites: we are ever your hermits, i.e. we will always gratefully pray for you.
22. be his purveyor: i.e. get here ahead of him and arrange for his welcome (a purveyor being one who goes ahead to secure food and lodging).

And his great love, sharp as his spur, hath holp him
To his home before us. Fair and noble hostess,
We are your guest to-night.
Lady M. Your servants ever
Have theirs, themselves, and what is theirs, in compt,
To make their audit at your Highness' pleasure,
Still to return your own.
Dun. Give me your hand.
Conduct me to mine host, we love him highly,
And shall continue our graces towards him.
By your leave, hostess. *Exeunt.*

Scene VII

Hoboys, torches. Enter a Sewer *and divers* Servants *with dishes and service over the stage. Then enter* Macbeth.

Macb. If it were done, when 'tis done, then 'twere well
It were done quickly. If th' assassination
Could trammel up the consequence, and catch
With his surcease, success; that but this blow
Might be the be-all and the end-all—here,
But here, upon this bank and [shoal] of time,
We'ld jump the life to come. But in these cases
We still have judgment here, that we but teach
Bloody instructions, which, being taught, return
To plague th' inventor. This even-handed justice
Commends th' ingredience of our poison'd chalice
To our own lips. He's here in double trust:
First, as I am his kinsman and his subject,
Strong both against the deed; then, as his host,
Who should against his murtherer shut the door,
Not bear the knife myself. Besides, this Duncan
Hath borne his faculties so meek, hath been
So clear in his great office, that his virtues
Will plead like angels, trumpet-tongu'd, against
The deep damnation of his taking-off;
And pity, like a naked new-born babe,
Striding the blast, or heaven's cherubin, hors'd
Upon the sightless couriers of the air,
Shall blow the horrid deed in every eye,
That tears shall drown the wind. I have no spur
To prick the sides of my intent, but only
Vaulting ambition, which o'erleaps itself,
And falls on th' other—

23. holp: helped. **26. in compt:** in trust; subject to account.
27. audit: accounting. **28. Still:** always.

I.vii. Location: Inverness. Inner court of Macbeth's castle.
o.s.d. Sewer: butler.
3. trammel up: entangle as in a net. **the consequence:** the events arising from it.
4. his surcease: its (the assassination's) conclusion (?) or Duncan's death (?). **5. here:** in this world.
6. shoal. This emendation of Theobald's is generally accepted; but some prefer to read *school* after F1, taking *bank* to mean "bench" and citing lines 8–9 in support. **7. jump:** risk.
8. still: always. **have judgment:** are punished. **that:** in that.
10. even-handed: impartial.
11. Commends: presents. **ingredience:** contents, ingredients.
17. faculties: royal powers. **18. clear:** blameless.
22. Striding: bestriding. **cherubin.** Construed as singular, with plural *cherubins*, everywhere else in Shakespeare; hence many editors emend to *cherubins* here, in view of *couriers* in line 23.
23. sightless couriers: invisible runners, i.e. winds.
25. tears . . . wind. As rain stills the wind. **28. other:** other side.

Enter Lady [Macbeth].

How now? what news?

Lady M. He has almost supp'd. Why have you left the chamber?

Macb. Hath he ask'd for me?

Lady M. Know you not he has?

Macb. We will proceed no further in this business:
He hath honor'd me of late, and I have bought
Golden opinions from all sorts of people,
Which would be worn now in their newest gloss,
Not cast aside so soon.

Lady M. Was the hope drunk
Wherein you dress'd yourself? Hath it slept since?
And wakes it now to look so green and pale
At what it did so freely? From this time
Such I account thy love. Art thou afeard
To be the same in thine own act and valor
As thou art in desire? Wouldst thou have that
Which thou esteem'st the ornament of life,
And live a coward in thine own esteem,
Letting "I dare not" wait upon "I would,"
Like the poor cat i' th' adage?

Macb. Prithee peace!
I dare do all that may become a man;
Who dares [do] more is none.

Lady M. What beast was't then
That made you break this enterprise to me?
When you durst do it, then you were a man;
And to be more than what you were, you would
Be so much more the man. Nor time, nor place,
Did then adhere, and yet you would make both:
They have made themselves, and that their fitness now
Does unmake you. I have given suck, and know
How tender 'tis to love the babe that milks me;
I would, while it was smiling in my face,
Have pluck'd my nipple from his boneless gums,
And dash'd the brains out, had I so sworn as you
Have done to this.

Macb. If we should fail?

Lady M. We fail?
But screw your courage to the sticking place,
And we'll not fail. When Duncan is asleep
(Whereto the rather shall his day's hard journey
Soundly invite him), his two chamberlains
Will I with wine and wassail so convince,
That memory, the warder of the brain,
Shall be a fume, and the receipt of reason
A limbeck only. When in swinish sleep
Their drenched natures lies as in a death,
What cannot you and I perform upon

32. bought: won. **34. would:** want to.
37. green: sickly. **42. the ornament of life:** i.e. the crown.
45. th' adage: i.e. "The cat would eat fish, and would not wet her feet." **47. none:** not a man, i.e. either more than human or less.
48. break: broach.
52. Did then adhere: were then suitable. **would:** wanted to.
53. that their fitness: that fitness of theirs.
60. But: only. **sticking place:** probably, the mark to which a soldier screwed up the cord of a crossbow.
63. chamberlains: personal attendants.
64. wassail: carousing. **convince:** overpower.
66. receipt: receptacle.
67. limbeck: alembic, upper part of a still to which the fumes rise. It was believed that the fumes of wine rose from the stomach to the brain and intoxicated it.

Th' unguarded Duncan? what not put upon
His spungy officers, who shall bear the guilt
Of our great quell?

Macb. Bring forth men-children only!
For thy undaunted mettle should compose
Nothing but males. Will it not be receiv'd,
When we have mark'd with blood those sleepy two
Of his own chamber, and us'd their very daggers,
That they have done't?

Lady M. Who dares receive it other,
As we shall make our griefs and clamor roar
Upon his death?

Macb. I am settled, and bend up
Each corporal agent to this terrible feat.
Away, and mock the time with fairest show:
False face must hide what the false heart doth know.
Exeunt.

ACT II, Scene I

Enter Banquo, *and* Fleance *with a torch before him.*

Ban. How goes the night, boy?

Fle. The moon is down; I have not heard the clock.

Ban. And she goes down at twelve.

Fle. I take't, 'tis later, sir.

Ban. Hold, take my sword. There's husbandry in heaven,
Their candles are all out. Take thee that too.
[*Gives him his belt and dagger.*]
A heavy summons lies like lead upon me,
And yet I would not sleep. Merciful powers,
Restrain in me the cursed thoughts that nature
Gives way to in repose!

Enter Macbeth, *and a* Servant *with a torch.*

Give me my sword.
Who's there?

Macb. A friend.

Ban. What, sir, not yet at rest? the King's a-bed.
He hath been in unusual pleasure, and
Sent forth great largess to your offices.
This diamond he greets your wife withal,
By the name of most kind hostess, and shut up
In measureless content.

Macb. Being unprepar'd,
Our will became the servant to defect,
Which else should free have wrought.

Ban. All's well.
I dreamt last night of the three weïrd sisters:
To you they have show'd some truth.

Macb. I think not of them;

71. spungy: spongy, i.e. soaked with drink.
72. quell: killing, murder.
73. mettle: composition, temperament.
74. receiv'd: believed. **77. other:** otherwise.
78. As: inasmuch as. **79. bend up:** make taut, strain.
81. mock the time: deceive the world.

II.i. Location: Inverness. Inner court of Macbeth's castle.
4. husbandry: economy. **6. heavy summons:** i.e. sleepiness.
7. would not sleep: do not want to go to bed and to sleep.
14. largess: gifts. **offices:** kitchens and other household departments. **16. shut up:** concluded.
17. In: i.e. with an expression of. **18. defect:** deficiency.
19. free: fully, without limitation.

Yet when we can entreat an hour to serve,
We would spend it in some words upon that business,
If you would grant the time.

Ban. At your kind'st leisure.

Macb. If you shall cleave to my consent, when 'tis,
It shall make honor for you.

Ban. So I lose none
In seeking to augment it, but still keep
My bosom franchis'd and allegiance clear,
I shall be counsell'd.

Macb. Good repose the while!

Ban. Thanks, sir; the like to you!

Exit Banquo [with Fleance].

Macb. Go bid thy mistress, when my drink is ready,
She strike upon the bell. Get thee to bed.

Exit [Servant].

Is this a dagger which I see before me,
The handle toward my hand? Come, let me clutch thee:
I have thee not, and yet I see thee still.
Art thou not, fatal vision, sensible
To feeling as to sight? or art thou but
A dagger of the mind, a false creation,
Proceeding from the heat-oppressed brain?
I see thee yet, in form as palpable
As this which now I draw.
Thou marshal'st me the way that I was going,
And such an instrument I was to use.
Mine eyes are made the fools o' th' other senses,
Or else worth all the rest. I see thee still;
And on thy blade and dudgeon gouts of blood,
Which was not so before. There's no such thing:
It is the bloody business which informs
Thus to mine eyes. Now o'er the one half world
Nature seems dead, and wicked dreams abuse
The curtain'd sleep; witchcraft celebrates
Pale Hecat's off'rings; and wither'd Murther,
Alarum'd by his sentinel, the wolf,
Whose howl's his watch, thus with his stealthy pace,
With Tarquin's ravishing [strides], towards his design
Moves like a ghost. Thou [sure] and firm-set earth,
Hear not my steps, which [way they] walk, for fear
The very stones prate of my whereabout,
And take the present horror from the time,
Which now suits with it. Whiles I threat, he lives:
Words to the heat of deeds too cold breath gives.

A bell rings.

I go, and it is done; the bell invites me.
Hear it not, Duncan, for it is a knell,
That summons thee to heaven or to hell. *Exit.*

25. cleave . . . 'tis: support my cause when the time comes.
28. franchis'd: free from guilt. **clear:** unstained.
29. counsell'd: willing to listen. **36. sensible:** perceptible.
39. heat-oppressed: fevered. **46. dudgeon:** handle. **gouts:** drops.
48. informs: creates shapes. **49. half world:** hemisphere.
50. abuse: deceive.
52. Pale Hecat's off'rings: its rites to Hecate (goddess of witchcraft and also of the moon, hence "pale").
53. Alarum'd: given the signal for action.
54. watch: watchword (like the announcement of the hour called out by a watchman).
55. Tarquin: ravisher of Lucrece. **design:** i.e. intended victim.
59. horror: i.e. dreadful silence.

Scene II

Enter Lady [Macbeth].

Lady M. That which hath made them drunk hath made me bold;
What hath quench'd them hath given me fire. Hark! Peace!
It was the owl that shriek'd, the fatal bellman,
Which gives the stern'st good-night. He is about it:
The doors are open; and the surfeited grooms
Do mock their charge with snores. I have drugg'd their possets,
That death and nature do contend about them,
Whether they live or die.

Macb. [*Within.*] Who's there? What ho?

Lady M. Alack, I am afraid they have awak'd,
And 'tis not done; th' attempt, and not the deed,
Confounds us. Hark! I laid their daggers ready,
He could not miss 'em. Had he not resembled
My father as he slept, I had done't.

Enter Macbeth.

My husband!

Macb. I have done the deed. Didst thou not hear a noise?

Lady M. I heard the owl scream and the crickets cry.
Did not you speak?

Macb. When?

Lady M. Now.

Macb. As I descended?

Lady M. Ay.

Macb. Hark! Who lies i' th' second chamber?

Lady M. Donalbain.

Macb. This is a sorry sight.

[*Looking on his hands.*]

Lady M. A foolish thought, to say a sorry sight.

Macb. There's one did laugh in 's sleep, and one cried, "Murther!"
That they did wake each other. I stood and heard them;
But they did say their prayers, and address'd them
Again to sleep.

Lady M. There are two lodg'd together.

Macb. One cried, "God bless us!" and "Amen!" the other,
As they had seen me with these hangman's hands.
List'ning their fear, I could not say "Amen,"
When they did say "God bless us!"

Lady M. Consider it not so deeply.

Macb. But wherefore could not I pronounce "Amen"?
I had most need of blessing, and "Amen"
Stuck in my throat.

II.ii. Location: Scene continues.
3. fatal bellman: night watchman who rang a bell at midnight outside the cell of prisoners scheduled for execution in the morning. The screech owl is often thought to presage death.
5. grooms: servants; here the chamberlains of I.vii.63.
6. mock their charge: make a mockery of their assigned duty. **possets:** drinks made with wine and hot milk.
10. th' attempt . . . deed: the deed unsuccessfully attempted.
11. Confounds: ruins utterly. **22. address'd them:** i.e. settled down.
25. hangman's. His hands would be bloody after quartering his victim.

Lady M. These deeds must not be thought
After these ways; so, it will make us mad.

Macb. Methought I heard a voice cry, "Sleep no more!
Macbeth does murther sleep"—the innocent sleep,
Sleep that knits up the ravell'd sleave of care,
The death of each day's life, sore labor's bath,
Balm of hurt minds, great nature's second course,
Chief nourisher in life's feast.

Lady M. What do you mean?

Macb. Still it cried, "Sleep no more!" to all the house;
"Glamis hath murther'd sleep, and therefore Cawdor
Shall sleep no more—Macbeth shall sleep no more."

Lady M. Who was it that thus cried? Why, worthy thane,
You do unbend your noble strength, to think
So brain-sickly of things. Go get some water,
And wash this filthy witness from your hand.
Why did you bring these daggers from the place?
They must lie there. Go carry them, and smear
The sleepy grooms with blood.

Macb. I'll go no more.
I am afraid to think what I have done;
Look on't again I dare not.

Lady M. Infirm of purpose!
Give me the daggers. The sleeping and the dead
Are but as pictures; 'tis the eye of childhood
That fears a painted devil. If he do bleed,
I'll gild the faces of the grooms withal,
For it must seem their guilt. *Exit. Knock within.*

Macb. Whence is that knocking?
How is't with me, when every noise appalls me?
What hands are here? Hah! they pluck out mine eyes.
Will all great Neptune's ocean wash this blood
Clean from my hand? No; this my hand will rather
The multitudinous seas incarnadine,
Making the green one red.

Enter LADY [MACBETH].

Lady M. My hands are of your color; but I shame
To wear a heart so white. (*Knock.*) I hear a knocking
At the south entry. Retire we to our chamber.
A little water clears us of this deed;
How easy is it then! Your constancy
Hath left you unattended. (*Knock.*) Hark, more knocking.
Get on your night-gown, lest occasion call us
And show us to be watchers. Be not lost
So poorly in your thoughts.

Macb. To know my deed, 'twere best not know myself. *Knock.*
Wake Duncan with thy knocking! I would thou couldst! *Exeunt.*

30. **thought**: thought about.
34. **knits . . . sleave**: straightens out the tangled skein.
42. **unbend**: loosen, let go slack. 44. **witness**: evidence.
53. **gild.** Blood was often called golden. See II.iii.118.
59. **multitudinous seas**: multitudes of seas. **incarnadine**: turn blood-red. 60. **one red**: completely red.
66. **left you unattended**: i.e. deserted you.
67. **night-gown**: dressing gown.
68. **watchers**: people who have stayed up.
70. **To . . . myself**: if I am to come to terms with what I have done, I shall need to avoid self-scrutiny (?) or if not being lost in my thoughts means seeing clearly what I have done, I'd better remain lost in my thoughts (?).

SCENE III

Enter a PORTER. *Knocking within.*

Port. Here's a knocking indeed! If a man were porter of Hell Gate, he should have old turning the key. (*Knock.*) Knock, knock, knock! Who's there, i' th' name of Belzebub? Here's a farmer, that hang'd himself on th' expectation of plenty. Come in time! Have napkins enow about you, here you'll sweat for't. (*Knock.*) Knock, knock! Who's there, in th' other devil's name? Faith, here's an equivocator, that could swear in both the scales against either scale, who committed treason enough for God's sake, yet could not equivocate to heaven. O, come in, equivocator. (*Knock.*) Knock, knock, knock! Who's there? Faith, here's an English tailor come hither for stealing out of a French hose. Come in, tailor, here you may roast your goose. (*Knock.*) Knock, knock! Never at quiet! What are you? But this place is too cold for hell. I'll devil-porter it no further. I had thought to have let in some of all professions that go the primrose way to th' everlasting bonfire. (*Knock.*) Anon, anon! [*Opens the gate.*] I pray you remember the porter.

Enter MACDUFF *and* LENNOX.

Macd. Was it so late, friend, ere you went to bed,
That you do lie so late?

Port. Faith, sir, we were carousing till the second cock; and drink, sir, is a great provoker of three things.

Macd. What three things does drink especially provoke?

Port. Marry, sir, nose-painting, sleep, and urine. Lechery, sir, it provokes, and unprovokes: it provokes the desire, but it takes away the performance. Therefore much drink may be said to be an equivocator with lechery: it makes him, and it mars him; it sets him on, and it takes him off; it persuades him, and disheartens him; makes him stand to, and not stand to; in conclusion, equivocates him in a sleep, and giving him the lie, leaves him.

II.iii. Location: Scene continues.
2. **old**: plenty of.
4–5. **farmer . . . plenty**: i.e. one who had hoarded grain to sell at high prices and foresaw his ruin when the prospect of plentiful crops threatened to bring the prices down.
5. **Come in time**: opportunely arrived. 6. **napkins**: handkerchiefs.
7–8. **other devil's name.** He cannot remember the name of a second devil.
8. **equivocator.** Alluding to Jesuits, and particularly to Father Garnet, who claimed the right to make ambiguous answers when under examination so as not to incriminate himself. The word was current during the investigation that followed the Gunpowder Plot of 1605.
9. **both . . . scale**: either scale against the other.
14. **French hose**: French breeches. There were two kinds, one loose, the other tight. Presumably the tailor stole cloth from the supply brought to him by a customer for making the former. Or perhaps, relying too much on his skill, he tried it on the latter and so was found out. 15. **roast your goose**: heat your iron.
24–25. **the second cock**: i.e. 3 a.m.
28. **Marry**: indeed (originally, the name of the Virgin Mary used as an oath). 35. **equivocates . . . sleep**: deceives him in a dream.
35–36. **giving . . . lie.** The passage puns on at least three senses of *give one the lie*: (1) call one a liar, (2) lay one out flat, (3) cause one to urinate (*lie* = *lye*, slang for "urine").

Macd. I believe drink gave thee the lie last night.

Port. That it did, sir, i' the very throat on me; but I requited him for his lie, and (I think) being too strong for him, though he took up my legs sometime, yet I made a shift to cast him.

Macd. Is thy master stirring?

Enter Macbeth.

Our knocking has awak'd him; here he comes.

Len. Good morrow, noble sir.

Macb. Good morrow, both.

Macd. Is the King stirring, worthy thane?

Macb. Not yet.

Macd. He did command me to call timely on him,
I have almost slipp'd the hour.

Macb. I'll bring you to him.

Macd. I know this is a joyful trouble to you;
But yet 'tis one.

Macb. The labor we delight in physics pain.
This is the door.

Macd. I'll make so bold to call,
For 'tis my limited service. *Exit Macduff.*

Len. Goes the King hence to-day?

Macb. He does; he did appoint so.

Len. The night has been unruly. Where we lay,
Our chimneys were blown down, and (as they say)
Lamentings heard i' th' air; strange screams of death,
And prophesying, with accents terrible,
Of dire combustion and confus'd events
New hatch'd to th' woeful time. The obscure bird
Clamor'd the livelong night. Some say, the earth
Was feverous, and did shake.

Macb. 'Twas a rough night.

Len. My young remembrance cannot parallel
A fellow to it.

Enter Macduff.

Macd. O horror, horror, horror! Tongue nor heart
Cannot conceive nor name thee!

Macb. and Len. What's the matter?

Macd. Confusion now hath made his masterpiece!
Most sacrilegious murther hath broke ope
The Lord's anointed temple, and stole thence
The life o' th' building!

Macb. What is't you say—the life?

Len. Mean you his Majesty?

Macd. Approach the chamber, and destroy your sight
With a new Gorgon. Do not bid me speak;
See, and then speak yourselves.

Exeunt Macbeth and Lennox.

Awake, awake!
Ring the alarum-bell! Murther and treason!
Banquo and Donalbain! Malcolm, awake!
Shake off this downy sleep, death's counterfeit,
And look on death itself! Up, up, and see
The great doom's image! Malcolm! Banquo!
As from your graves rise up, and walk like sprites,
To countenance this horror! Ring the bell.

Bell rings.

Enter Lady [Macbeth].

Lady M. What's the business,
That such a hideous trumpet calls to parley
The sleepers of the house? Speak, speak!

Macd. O gentle lady,
'Tis not for you to hear what I can speak:
The repetition in a woman's ear
Would murther as it fell.

Enter Banquo.

O Banquo, Banquo,
Our royal master's murther'd!

Lady M. Woe, alas!
What, in our house?

Ban. Too cruel any where.
Dear Duff, I prithee contradict thyself,
And say, it is not so.

Enter Macbeth, Lennox, Rosse.

Macb. Had I but died an hour before this chance,
I had liv'd a blessed time; for from this instant
There's nothing serious in mortality:
All is but toys: renown and grace is dead,
The wine of life is drawn, and the mere lees
Is left this vault to brag of.

Enter Malcolm *and* Donalbain.

Don. What is amiss?

Macb. You are, and do not know't.
The spring, the head, the fountain of your blood
Is stopp'd, the very source of it is stopp'd.

Macd. Your royal father's murther'd.

Mal. O, by whom?

Len. Those of his chamber, as it seem'd, had done't.
Their hands and faces were all badg'd with blood;
So were their daggers, which unwip'd we found
Upon their pillows. They star'd and were distracted;
No man's life was to be trusted with them.

Macb. O, yet I do repent me of my fury,
That I did kill them.

Macd. Wherefore did you so?

Macb. Who can be wise, amaz'd, temp'rate, and furious,
Loyal, and neutral, in a moment? No man.
Th' expedition of my violent love

38–41. That . . . him. These lines describe the effects of too much drink in terms of a wrestling match.
41. made a shift: managed. **cast:** (1) throw off; (2) vomit.
46. timely: early.
50. The labor . . . pain: the pleasure we take in labor of some kinds cures it of laboriousness. **52. limited:** appointed.
58. combustion: tumult.
59. obscure bird: bird of darkness, i.e. owl.
61. feverous. Referring to the chills and fever of ague.
66. Confusion: utter ruin.
68. Lord's anointed temple: i.e. body of the King.
72. Gorgon: i.e. Medusa, who turned to stone anyone who looked at her face.
78. great doom's image: exact likeness of Doomsday.
80. countenance: (1) accord with; (2) behold.
85. repetition: report.
93. serious in mortality: worthwhile in human life.
94. toys: trifles.
96. vault: (1) wine vault; (2) world (for which the sky is a vaulted roof). **98. spring, head, fountain.** All three words mean "source."
102. badg'd: marked. **108. amaz'd:** bewildered.
110. expedition: haste.

Outrun the pauser, reason. Here lay Duncan,
His silver skin lac'd with his golden blood,
And his gash'd stabs look'd like a breach in nature
For ruin's wasteful entrance; there, the murtherers,
Steep'd in the colors of their trade, their daggers
Unmannerly breech'd with gore. Who could refrain,
That had a heart to love, and in that heart
Courage to make 's love known?

Lady M. Help me hence, ho!

Macd. Look to the lady.

Mal. [*Aside to Donalbain.*] Why do we
hold our tongues,
That most may claim this argument for ours?

Don. [*Aside to Malcolm.*] What should be spoken
here, where our fate,
Hid in an auger-hole, may rush and seize us?
Let's away,
Our tears are not yet brew'd.

Mal. [*Aside to Donalbain.*] Nor our
strong sorrow
Upon the foot of motion.

Ban. Look to the lady.

[*Lady Macbeth is carried out.*]

And when we have our naked frailties hid,
That suffer in exposure, let us meet
And question this most bloody piece of work,
To know it further. Fears and scruples shake us.
In the great hand of God I stand, and thence
Against the undivulg'd pretense I fight
Of treasonous malice.

Macd. And so do I.

All. So all.

Macb. Let's briefly put on manly readiness,
And meet i' th' hall together.

All. Well contented.

Exeunt [*all but Malcolm and Donalbain*].

Mal. What will you do? Let's not consort with
them;
To show an unfelt sorrow is an office
Which the false man does easy. I'll to England.

Don. To Ireland, I; our separated fortune
Shall keep us both the safer. Where we are,
There's daggers in men's smiles; the near in blood,
The nearer bloody.

Mal. This murtherous shaft that's shot
Hath not yet lighted, and our safest way
Is to avoid the aim. Therefore to horse,
And let us not be dainty of leave-taking,
But shift away. There's warrant in that theft

111. pauser: i.e. more deliberate mover.
113. breach in nature: gap in the defenses of life.
114. wasteful: destructive.
116. breech'd: covered, as if with breeches.
120. argument: subject, topic.
122. Hid . . . auger-hole: concealed in some unsuspected cranny.
124. Our . . . brew'd: i.e. we haven't yet time for weeping.
125. Upon . . . motion: ready to act.
126. frailties hid: bodies clothed. **128. question:** discuss.
129. scruples: doubts, suspicions.
130. In . . . hand: i.e. under . . . protection.
131. undivulg'd pretense: secret design. **132. malice:** enmity.
133. briefly: quickly. **readiness:** i.e. dress.
140. near: nearer (an older comparative form than *nearer*).
141. The nearer bloody: i.e. the greater the danger of murder.
142. lighted: i.e. spent its force. **144. dainty of:** particular about.
145. shift away: quietly disappear. **warrant:** justification.

Which steals itself, when there's no mercy left.

Exeunt.

Scene IV

Enter Rosse *with an* Old Man.

Old Man. Threescore and ten I can remember well,
Within the volume of which time I have seen
Hours dreadful and things strange; but this sore night
Hath trifled former knowings.

Rosse. Ha, good father,
Thou seest the heavens, as troubled with man's act,
Threatens his bloody stage. By th' clock 'tis day,
And yet dark night strangles the travelling lamp.
Is't night's predominance, or the day's shame,
That darkness does the face of earth entomb,
When living light should kiss it?

Old Man. 'Tis unnatural,
Even like the deed that's done. On Tuesday last,
A falcon, tow'ring in her pride of place,
Was by a mousing owl hawk'd at, and kill'd.

Rosse. And Duncan's horses (a thing most strange
and certain),
Beauteous and swift, the minions of their race,
Turn'd wild in nature, broke their stalls, flung out,
Contending 'gainst obedience, as they would make
War with mankind.

Old Man. 'Tis said, they eat each other.

Rosse. They did so—to th' amazement of mine eyes
That look'd upon't.

Enter Macduff.

Here comes the good Macduff.
How goes the world, sir, now?

Macd. Why, see you not?

Rosse. Is't known who did this more than bloody
deed?

Macd. Those that Macbeth hath slain.

Rosse. Alas the day,
What good could they pretend?

Macd. They were suborned.
Malcolm and Donalbain, the King's two sons,
Are stol'n away and fled, which puts upon them
Suspicion of the deed.

Rosse. 'Gainst nature still!
Thriftless ambition, that will ravin up
Thine own live's means! Then 'tis most like
The sovereignty will fall upon Macbeth.

Macd. He is already nam'd, and gone to Scone

146. steals itself: goes away stealthily.

II.iv. Location: Inverness. Outside Macbeth's castle.
3. sore: grievous, dreadful.
4. trifled former knowings: made earlier experiences seem trifling.
5. heavens. With play on the theatrical sense "roof over the stage," beginning a figure continued in *act* and *stage*.
7. lamp: torch, i.e. sun.
12. tow'ring . . . place: circling upward to the highest pitch of her flight.
13. mousing: i.e. whose natural prey is small creatures on the ground.
15. minions: darlings, finest specimens.
18. eat: ate (pronounced *et*).
24. What . . . pretend: i.e. what could they have hoped to gain by it. **suborned:** bribed.
28. ravin: devour ravenously. **29. live's:** life's.
31. nam'd: chosen. **Scone.** Site of the coronation of Scottish kings.

To be invested.
Rosse. Where is Duncan's body?
Macd. Carried to Colmekill,
The sacred store-house of his predecessors
And guardian of their bones.
Rosse. Will you to Scone?
Macd. No, cousin, I'll to Fife.
Rosse. Well, I will thither.
Macd. Well, may you see things well done there: adieu,
Lest our old robes sit easier than our new!
Rosse. Farewell, father.
Old Man. God's benison go with you, and with those
That would make good of bad, and friends of foes!
Exeunt omnes.

ACT III, Scene I

Enter Banquo.

Ban. Thou hast it now: King, Cawdor, Glamis, all,
As the weïrd women promis'd, and I fear
Thou play'dst most foully for't; yet it was said
It should not stand in thy posterity,
But that myself should be the root and father
Of many kings. If there come truth from them—
As upon thee, Macbeth, their speeches shine—
Why, by the verities on thee made good,
May they not be my oracles as well,
And set me up in hope? But hush, no more.

Sennet sounded. Enter Macbeth *as King*, Lady [Macbeth *as Queen*], Lennox, Rosse, Lords, *and* Attendants.

Macb. Here's our chief guest.
Lady M. If he had been forgotten,
It had been as a gap in our great feast,
And all-thing unbecoming.
Macb. To-night we hold a solemn supper, sir,
And I'll request your presence.
Ban. Let your Highness
Command upon me, to the which my duties
Are with a most indissoluble tie
For ever knit.
Macb. Ride you this afternoon?
Ban. Ay, my good lord.
Macb. We should have else desir'd your good advice
(Which still hath been both grave and prosperous)
In this day's council; but we'll take to-morrow.
Is't far you ride?
Ban. As far, my lord, as will fill up the time
'Twixt this and supper. Go not my horse the better,
I must become a borrower of the night
For a dark hour or twain.
Macb. Fail not our feast.
Ban. My lord, I will not.
Macb. We hear our bloody cousins are bestow'd
In England and in Ireland, not confessing
Their cruel parricide, filling their hearers
With strange invention. But of that to-morrow,
When therewithal we shall have cause of state
Craving us jointly. Hie you to horse; adieu,
Till you return at night. Goes Fleance with you?
Ban. Ay, my good lord. Our time does call upon 's.
Macb. I wish your horses swift and sure of foot;
And so I do commend you to their backs.
Farewell. *Exit Banquo.*
Let every man be master of his time
Till seven at night. To make society
The sweeter welcome, we will keep ourself
Till supper-time alone; while then, God be with you!
Exeunt Lords [with Lady Macbeth and others. Manent Macbeth and a Servant].
Sirrah, a word with you. Attend those men
Our pleasure?
Serv. They are, my lord, without the palace gate.
Macb. Bring them before us. *Exit Servant.*
To be thus is nothing,
But to be safely thus. Our fears in Banquo
Stick deep, and in his royalty of nature
Reigns that which would be fear'd. 'Tis much he dares,
And to that dauntless temper of his mind,
He hath a wisdom that doth guide his valor
To act in safety. There is none but he
Whose being I do fear; and under him
My Genius is rebuk'd, as it is said
Mark Antony's was by Caesar. He chid the sisters
When first they put the name of king upon me,
And bade them speak to him; then prophet-like
They hail'd him father to a line of kings.
Upon my head they plac'd a fruitless crown,
And put a barren sceptre in my gripe,
Thence to be wrench'd with an unlineal hand,
No son of mine succeeding. If't be so,
For Banquo's issue have I fil'd my mind,
For them the gracious Duncan have I murther'd,
Put rancors in the vessel of my peace
Only for them, and mine eternal jewel
Given to the common enemy of man,
To make them kings—the seeds of Banquo kings!
Rather than so, come fate into the list,
And champion me to th' utterance! Who's there?

33. Colmekill: Iona, where Scottish kings were then buried.
36. Fife. Macduff is Thane of Fife. **40. benison:** blessing.

III.i. Location: Forres. The palace.
7. As: i.e. as may well be since. **shine:** i.e. are brilliantly fulfilled.
10 s.d. Sennet: trumpet call. **13. all-thing:** wholly.
14. solemn: formal. **16. to the which:** i.e. to which command.
21. still: ever. **grave and prosperous:** weighty and profitable.
25. Go . . . better: if my horse go not faster (than I expect).

29. are bestow'd: have taken up residence.
33–34. cause . . . jointly: official business requiring our joint attention.
38. commend: commit, entrust. **43. while:** until.
44. Sirrah: term of address used to inferiors. **47. thus:** i.e. king.
48. in: concerning. **49. royalty of nature:** natural kingliness.
50. would: must. **51. to:** in addition to.
55. Genius: guardian spirit. **rebuk'd:** daunted.
56. Caesar: Octavius Caesar. See *Antony and Cleopatra*, II.iii.19–38.
61. gripe: grip, grasp.
62. with: by. **unlineal:** from another family line.
64. fil'd: defiled. **65. gracious:** good.
67. eternal jewel: i.e. immortal soul.
68. common . . . man: the devil. **70. list:** lists, arena.
71. champion me: contend with me as an opposing champion. **to th' utterance:** to the end (French *a outrance*), i.e. until I perish or fate is thwarted.

Enter SERVANT *and two* MURTHERERS.

Now go to the door, and stay there till we call.
Exit Servant.
Was it not yesterday we spoke together?
[*Both*] *Mur.* It was, so please your Highness.
Macb. Well then, now
Have you consider'd of my speeches?—know
That it was he in the times past which held you
So under fortune, which you thought had been
Our innocent self? This I made good to you
In our last conference, pass'd in probation with you:
How you were borne in hand, how cross'd, the instruments,
Who wrought with them, and all things else that might
To half a soul and to a notion craz'd
Say, "Thus did Banquo."
1. Mur. You made it known to us.
Macb. I did so; and went further, which is now
Our point of second meeting. Do you find
Your patience so predominant in your nature
That you can let this go? Are you so gospell'd,
To pray for this good man, and for his issue,
Whose heavy hand hath bow'd you to the grave,
And beggar'd yours for ever?
1. Mur. We are men, my liege.
Macb. Ay, in the catalogue ye go for men,
As hounds and greyhounds, mungrels, spaniels, curs,
Shoughs, water-rugs, and demi-wolves are clipt
All by the name of dogs; the valued file
Distinguishes the swift, the slow, the subtle,
The house-keeper, the hunter, every one,
According to the gift which bounteous nature
Hath in him clos'd; whereby he does receive
Particular addition, from the bill
That writes them all alike: and so of men.
Now, if you have a station in the file,
Not i' th' worst rank of manhood, say't,
And I will put that business in your bosoms,
Whose execution takes your enemy off,
Grapples you to the heart and love of us,
Who wear our health but sickly in his life,
Which in his death were perfect.
2. Mur. I am one, my liege,
Whom the vile blows and buffets of the world
Hath so incens'd that I am reckless what
I do to spite the world.
1. Mur. And I another,
So weary with disasters, tugg'd with fortune,
That I would set my life on any chance,
To mend it, or be rid on't.
Macb. Both of you
Know Banquo was your enemy.
[*Both*] *Mur.* True, my lord.
Macb. So is he mine; and in such bloody distance,
That every minute of his being thrusts
Against my near'st of life; and though I could
With barefac'd power sweep him from my sight,
And bid my will avouch it, yet I must not,
For certain friends that are both his and mine,
Whose loves I may not drop, but wail his fall
Who I myself struck down. And thence it is
That I to your assistance do make love,
Masking the business from the common eye
For sundry weighty reasons.
2. Mur. We shall, my lord,
Perform what you command us.
1. Mur. Though our lives—
Macb. Your spirits shine through you. Within this hour, at most,
I will advise you where to plant yourselves,
Acquaint you with the perfect spy o' th' time,
The moment on't, for't must be done to-night,
And something from the palace; always thought
That I require a clearness: and with him—
To leave no rubs nor botches in the work—
Fleance his son, that keeps him company,
Whose absence is no less material to me
Than is his father's, must embrace the fate
Of that dark hour. Resolve yourselves apart,
I'll come to you anon.
[*Both*] *Mur.* We are resolv'd, my lord.
Macb. I'll call upon you straight; abide within.
[*Exeunt Murderers.*]
It is concluded: Banquo, thy soul's flight,
If it find heaven, must find it out to-night. *Exit.*

SCENE II

Enter MACBETH'S LADY *and a* SERVANT.

Lady M. Is Banquo gone from court?
Serv. Ay, madam, but returns again to-night.
Lady M. Say to the King, I would attend his leisure
For a few words.
Serv. Madam, I will. *Exit.*
Lady M. Nought's had, all's spent,
Where our desire is got without content;
'Tis safer to be that which we destroy
Than by destruction dwell in doubtful joy.

77. under: out of favor with.
79. pass'd in probation: reviewed and proved true.
80. borne in hand: deceived. **cross'd:** thwarted.
82. To: even to. **notion:** mind.
87. gospell'd: under the spell of the Gospel.
91. catalogue: comprehensive listing. **go for:** are entered as.
93. Shoughs: shaggy lap-dogs. **water-rugs:** long-haired water-dogs. **demi-wolves:** hybrids bred of dogs and wolves. **clipt:** called.
94. valued file: list which specifies values.
96. house-keeper: watchdog. **98. clos'd:** enclosed.
99. addition: title, description. **from:** in contrast with.
100. writes . . . alike: lists them all together indiscriminately.
106. in his life: while he lives. **111. tugg'd with:** pulled about by.
112. set: stake.

115. distance: enmity (in fencing, the space maintained between combatants). **117. near'st of life:** most vital part, i.e. heart.
119. avouch: justify. **120. For:** on account of.
121. wail: i.e. must wail. **123. to . . . love:** woo your aid.
128. advise: instruct.
129. perfect spy: probably, precise information (*spy* = espial, i.e. intelligence). Some see here a reference to the Third Murderer, who appears in III.iii.
131. something from: some distance away from. **thought:** borne in mind. **132. require a clearness:** must remain free of suspicion.
133. rubs: rough spots, imperfections.
137. Resolve yourselves apart: go off and make up your minds.

III.ii. Location: Forres. The palace.
5. content: happiness, satisfaction. **7. doubtful:** apprehensive.

Enter MACBETH.

How now, my lord, why do you keep alone,
Of sorriest fancies your companions making,
Using those thoughts which should indeed have died
With them they think on? Things without all remedy
Should be without regard: what's done, is done.

Macb. We have scorch'd the snake, not kill'd it;
She'll close and be herself, whilest our poor malice
Remains in danger of her former tooth.
But let the frame of things disjoint, both the worlds
  suffer,
Ere we will eat our meal in fear, and sleep
In the affliction of these terrible dreams
That shake us nightly. Better be with the dead,
Whom we, to gain our peace, have sent to peace,
Than on the torture of the mind to lie
In restless ecstasy. Duncan is in his grave;
After life's fitful fever he sleeps well.
Treason has done his worst; nor steel, nor poison,
Malice domestic, foreign levy, nothing,
Can touch him further.

Lady M. Come on;
Gentle my lord, sleek o'er your rugged looks,
Be bright and jovial among your guests to-night.

Macb. So shall I, love, and so, I pray, be you.
Let your remembrance apply to Banquo,
Present him eminence both with eye and tongue:
Unsafe the while, that we
Must lave our honors in these flattering streams,
And make our faces vizards to our hearts,
Disguising what they are.

Lady M. You must leave this.

Macb. O, full of scorpions is my mind, dear wife!
Thou know'st that Banquo and his Fleance lives.

Lady M. But in them nature's copy's not eterne.

Macb. There's comfort yet, they are assailable.
Then be thou jocund; ere the bat hath flown
His cloister'd flight, ere to black Hecat's summons
The shard-borne beetle with his drowsy hums
Hath rung night's yawning peal, there shall be done
A deed of dreadful note.

Lady M. What's to be done?

Macb. Be innocent of the knowledge, dearest
  chuck,
Till thou applaud the deed. Come, seeling night,
Scarf up the tender eye of pitiful day,
And with thy bloody and invisible hand
Cancel and tear to pieces that great bond
Which keeps me pale! Light thickens, and the crow
Makes wing to th' rooky wood;
Good things of day begin to droop and drowse,
Whiles night's black agents to their preys do rouse.
Thou marvel'st at my words, but hold thee still:
Things bad begun make strong themselves by ill.
So prithee go with me. *Exeunt.*

9. **sorriest:** most wretched. 10. **Using:** entertaining.
11. **without all:** beyond any possible.
12. **without regard:** i.e. not thought about.
13. **scorch'd:** slashed, i.e. merely wounded.
14. **close:** heal. **poor malice:** feeble enmity.
15. **her former tooth:** her poison fang exactly as before.
16. **disjoint:** fall apart. **both . . . suffer:** heaven and earth suffer destruction.
17. **Ere we will:** rather than that we should. 21. **torture:** i.e. rack.
22. **restless ecstasy:** a frenzy of agitation. 23. **fitful:** intermittent.
27. **Gentle my lord:** my noble lord. **sleek:** smooth. **rugged:** rough. 30. **apply:** be given. 31. **eminence:** special favor.
32–33. **Unsafe . . . streams:** for the time we are unsafe, so that we must make our honors look clean by washing them in these streams of flattery. 34. **vizards:** masks.
38. **copy:** (1) copyhold, a lease subject to cancellation; (2) casting (from the mould used by Nature to form men). **eterne:** everlasting.
39. **There's:** i.e. in that thought there is.
41. **cloister'd:** circumscribed, restricted (?) or through cloisters (?).
42. **shard-borne:** carried on scaly wings (?) or a variant spelling of *shard-born*, i.e. dung-bred (?). (In F1 modern *born* is usually spelled *borne*). 45. **chuck:** a term of endearment (from *chick*).
46. **seeling:** blinding. The eyelids of falcons were sewn together (seeled) in order to tame them. 47. **pitiful:** compassionate.
49. **bond:** Banquo's lease on life. 50. **crow:** rook.
51. **rooky:** frequented by rooks.

SCENE III

Enter three MURTHERERS.

1. Mur. But who did bid thee join with us?

3. Mur. Macbeth.

2. Mur. He needs not our mistrust, since he de-
  livers
Our offices, and what we have to do,
To the direction just.

1. Mur. Then stand with us.
The west yet glimmers with some streaks of day;
Now spurs the lated traveller apace
To gain the timely inn, [and] near approaches
The subject of our watch.

3. Mur. Hark, I hear horses.

Ban. (*Within.*) Give us a light there, ho!

2. Mur. Then 'tis he; the rest
That are within the note of expectation
Already are i'th' court.

1. Mur. His horses go about.

3. Mur. Almost a mile; but he does usually,
So all men do, from hence to th' palace gate
Make it their walk.

Enter BANQUO, *and* FLEANCE *with a torch.*

2. Mur. A light, a light!

3. Mur. 'Tis he.

1. Mur. Stand to't.

Ban. It will be rain to-night.

1. Mur. Let it come down.
[*They assault Banquo.*]

Ban. O, treachery! Fly, good Fleance, fly, fly, fly!
Thou mayst revenge. O slave! [*Dies. Fleance escapes.*]

3. Mur. Who did strike out the light?

1. Mur. Was't not the way?

3. Mur. There's but one down; the son is fled.

2. Mur. We have lost
Best half of our affair.

1. Mur. Well, let's away, and say how much is
  done. *Exeunt.*

III.iii. **Location:** Forres. A park near the palace.
2. **He . . . mistrust:** we need feel no suspicion of him (the Third Murderer). 3. **offices:** duties.
4. **To . . . just:** precisely according to Macbeth's instructions.
6. **lated:** belated.
10. **within . . . expectation:** on the list of expected guests.

SCENE IV

Banquet prepar'd. Enter MACBETH, LADY [MACBETH], ROSSE, LENNOX, LORDS, *and* ATTENDANTS.

Macb. You know your own degrees, sit down. At first
And last, the hearty welcome.
Lords. Thanks to your Majesty.
Macb. Ourself will mingle with society,
And play the humble host.
Our hostess keeps her state, but in best time
We will require her welcome.
Lady M. Pronounce it for me, sir, to all our friends,
For my heart speaks they are welcome.

Enter FIRST MURTHERER [*to the door*].

Macb. See, they encounter thee with their hearts' thanks.
Both sides are even; here I'll sit i' th' midst.
Be large in mirth; anon we'll drink a measure
The table round.— [*Goes to the door.*]
There's blood upon thy face.
Mur. 'Tis Banquo's then.
Macb. 'Tis better thee without than he within.
Is he dispatch'd?
Mur. My lord, his throat is cut;
That I did for him.
Macb. Thou art the best o' th' cut-throats,
Yet he's good that did the like for Fleance.
If thou didst it, thou art the nonpareil.
Mur. Most royal sir, Fleance is scap'd.
Macb. Then comes my fit again. I had else been perfect,
Whole as the marble, founded as the rock,
As broad and general as the casing air;
But now I am cabin'd, cribb'd, confin'd, bound in
To saucy doubts and fears. But Banquo's safe?
Mur. Ay, my good lord; safe in a ditch he bides,
With twenty trenched gashes on his head,
The least a death to nature.
Macb. Thanks for that:
There the grown serpent lies; the worm that's fled
Hath nature that in time will venom breed,
No teeth for th' present. Get thee gone; to-morrow
We'll hear ourselves again. *Exit Murderer.*
Lady M. My royal lord,
You do not give the cheer. The feast is sold
That is not often vouch'd, while 'tis a-making,
'Tis given with welcome. To feed were best at home;
From thence, the sauce to meat is ceremony,
Meeting were bare without it.

Enter the GHOST OF BANQUO *and sits in Macbeth's place.*

Macb. Sweet remembrancer!
Now good digestion wait on appetite,
And health on both!
Len. May't please your Highness sit.
Macb. Here had we now our country's honor roof'd,
Were the grac'd person of our Banquo present,
Who may I rather challenge for unkindness
Than pity for mischance.
Rosse. His absence, sir,
Lays blame upon his promise. Please't your Highness
To grace us with your royal company?
Macb. The table's full.
Len. Here is a place reserv'd, sir.
Macb. Where?
Len. Here, my good lord. What is't that moves your Highness?
Macb. Which of you have done this?
Lords. What, my good lord?
Macb. Thou canst not say I did it; never shake
Thy gory locks at me.
Rosse. Gentlemen, rise, his Highness is not well.
Lady M. Sit, worthy friends; my lord is often thus,
And hath been from his youth. Pray you keep seat.
The fit is momentary, upon a thought
He will again be well. If much you note him,
You shall offend him and extend his passion.
Feed, and regard him not.—Are you a man?
Macb. Ay, and a bold one, that dare look on that
Which might appall the devil.
Lady M. O proper stuff!
This is the very painting of your fear;
This is the air-drawn dagger which you said
Led you to Duncan. O, these flaws and starts
(Impostors to true fear) would well become
A woman's story at a winter's fire,
Authoriz'd by her grandam. Shame itself,
Why do you make such faces? When all's done,
You look but on a stool.
Macb. Prithee see there!
Behold! look! lo! how say you?
Why, what care I? if thou canst nod, speak too.
If charnel-houses and our graves must send
Those that we bury back, our monuments
Shall be the maws of kites. [*Exit Ghost.*]
Lady M. What? quite unmann'd in folly?
Macb. If I stand here, I saw him.
Lady M. Fie, for shame!
Macb. Blood hath been shed ere now, i' th' olden time,

III.iv. Location: Forres. The palace.
1. degrees: ranks and hence order of seating.
1–2. At . . . last: once for all. **5. state:** chair of state.
6. require: request. **9. encounter:** respond to.
11. large: free, unrestrained. **measure:** bumper.
14. thee . . . within: i.e. on your face than in his body.
21. founded: immovable.
22. broad and general: free and unconfined. **casing:** enveloping.
24. saucy: importunate. **28. worm:** here, young serpent.
31. hear ourselves: confer.
32. give the cheer: play the convivial host.
32–34. The feast . . . welcome: unless the guests are frequently assured of their welcome, a feast is no better than a meal that one pays for.
34. To feed: i.e. simply to eat. **35. From thence:** away from home.
39. honor: nobility. **roof'd:** under one roof.
41. challenge for: charge with.
54. upon a thought: in a moment.
56. offend him: make him worse. **extend his passion:** prolong his attack. **59. proper:** fine.
61. air-drawn: drawn on the air (a sense supported by *painting* in line 60) or drawn through the air (supported by line 62).
62. flaws: sudden bursts of passion (properly used of gusty winds).
63. to: compared with. **become:** befit.
65. Authoriz'd: told on the authority of.
71–72. our . . . kites: our tombs had better be the stomachs of birds of prey, i.e. there is no point in burying the dead.

Ere humane statute purg'd the gentle weal;
Ay, and since too, murthers have been perform'd
Too terrible for the ear. The [time] has been,
That when the brains were out, the man would die,
And there an end; but now they rise again
With twenty mortal murthers on their crowns,
And push us from our stools. This is more strange
Than such a murther is.
Lady M. My worthy lord,
Your noble friends do lack you.
Macb. I do forget.
Do not muse at me, my most worthy friends,
I have a strange infirmity, which is nothing
To those that know me. Come, love and health to all,
Then I'll sit down. Give me some wine, fill full.

Enter Ghost.

I drink to th' general joy o' th' whole table,
And to our dear friend Banquo, whom we miss;
Would he were here! to all, and him, we thirst,
And all to all.
Lords. Our duties, and the pledge.
Macb. Avaunt, and quit my sight! let the earth hide thee!
Thy bones are marrowless, thy blood is cold;
Thou hast no speculation in those eyes
Which thou dost glare with!
Lady M. Think of this, good peers,
But as a thing of custom. 'Tis no other;
Only it spoils the pleasure of the time.
Macb. What man dare, I dare.
Approach thou like the rugged Russian bear,
The arm'd rhinoceros, or th' Hyrcan tiger,
Take any shape but that, and my firm nerves
Shall never tremble. Or be alive again,
And dare me to the desert with thy sword;
If trembling I inhabit then, protest me
The baby of a girl. Hence, horrible shadow!
Unreal mock'ry, hence! *[Exit Ghost.]*
Why, so; being gone,
I am a man again. Pray you sit still.
Lady M. You have displac'd the mirth, broke the good meeting,
With most admir'd disorder.
Macb. Can such things be,
And overcome us like a summer's cloud,
Without our special wonder? You make me strange
Even to the disposition that I owe,
When now I think you can behold such sights,
And keep the natural ruby of your cheeks,
When mine is blanch'd with fear.
Rosse. What sights, my lord?
Lady M. I pray you speak not. He grows worse and worse,
Question enrages him. At once, good night.
Stand not upon the order of your going,
But go at once.
Len. Good night, and better health
Attend his Majesty!
Lady M. A kind good night to all!
Exeunt Lords [and Attendants].
Macb. It will have blood, they say; blood will have blood.
Stones have been known to move and trees to speak;
Augures and understood relations have
By maggot-pies and choughs and rooks brought forth
The secret'st man of blood. What is the night?
Lady M. Almost at odds with morning, which is which.
Macb. How say'st thou, that Macduff denies his person
At our great bidding?
Lady M. Did you send to him, sir?
Macb. I hear it by the way; but I will send.
There's not a one of them but in his house
I keep a servant fee'd. I will to-morrow
(And betimes I will) to the weïrd sisters.
More shall they speak; for now I am bent to know,
By the worst means, the worst. For mine own good
All causes shall give way. I am in blood
Stepp'd in so far that, should I wade no more,
Returning were as tedious as go o'er.
Strange things I have in head, that will to hand,
Which must be acted ere they may be scann'd.
Lady M. You lack the season of all natures, sleep.
Macb. Come, we'll to sleep. My strange and self-abuse
Is the initiate fear that wants hard use:
We are yet but young in deed. *Exeunt.*

Scene V

Thunder. Enter the three Witches, *meeting* Hecat.

1. Witch. Why, how now, Hecat? you look angerly.

75. humane. Elizabethan spelling did not distinguish between *human* and *humane*; many editors read *human* here, perhaps rightly. **purg'd . . . weal:** cleansed the commonwealth and made it gentle.
80. mortal murthers: deadly wounds. **crowns:** heads.
84. muse: wonder. **90. thirst:** i.e. drink eagerly.
91. all to all: all good to all (?) or let everyone drink to all (?). **the pledge:** i.e. we drink the toast you have proposed.
94. speculation: sight. **99. like:** in the likeness of.
100. arm'd: armored. **Hyrcan:** of Hyrcania, near the Caspian Sea.
101. nerves: sinews.
103. the desert: i.e. some uninhabited place (where nobody would intervene).
104. If . . . inhabit: if the body I inhabit feels fear. **protest:** proclaim.
105. The baby . . . girl: a baby girl. **109. admir'd:** wondered at.
110. overcome: pass over. **like . . . cloud:** i.e. suddenly.
111–12. strange . . . owe: i.e. feel a stranger to the courageous man I supposed myself to be.
117. Question enrages him: talk aggravates his condition. **At once:** to you all. **119. at once:** all together.
123. Augures: auguries, omens. **understood relations:** occult significances and relationships perceived.
124. By: by means of. **maggot-pies and choughs:** magpies and jackdaws (which, like rooks, could be taught to speak) **brought forth:** revealed. **125. man of blood:** murderer.
127. How say'st thou: what do you think of the fact.
129. by the way: indirectly. **132. betimes:** very early.
133. bent: determined. **135. causes:** (other) considerations.
136. should I: even if I were to. **more:** farther.
137. were: would be. **go:** going.
139. ere . . . scann'd: without being properly studied.
140. season: preservative.
141. strange and self-abuse: strange self-delusion.
142. initiate . . . use: fear felt by the beginner who lacks the experience that hardens one. **143. deed:** i.e. crime.

III.v. This scene is probably spurious.
Location: An open place.

Hec. Have I not reason, beldams as you are?
Saucy and overbold, how did you dare
To trade and traffic with Macbeth
In riddles and affairs of death;
And I, the mistress of your charms,
The close contriver of all harms,
Was never call'd to bear my part,
Or show the glory of our art?
And which is worse, all you have done
Hath been but for a wayward son,
Spiteful and wrathful, who (as others do)
Loves for his own ends, not for you.
But make amends now. Get you gone,
And at the pit of Acheron
Meet me i' th' morning; thither he
Will come to know his destiny.
Your vessels and your spells provide,
Your charms and every thing beside.
I am for th' air; this night I'll spend
Unto a dismal and a fatal end.
Great business must be wrought ere noon:
Upon the corner of the moon
There hangs a vap'rous drop profound,
I'll catch it ere it come to ground;
And that, distill'd by magic sleights,
Shall raise such artificial sprites
As by the strength of their illusion
Shall draw him on to his confusion.
He shall spurn fate, scorn death, and bear
His hopes 'bove wisdom, grace, and fear;
And you all know, security
Is mortals' chiefest enemy.

Music, and a song. Sing within: "Come away, come away, etc."

Hark, I am call'd; my little spirit, see,
Sits in a foggy cloud, and stays for me. [*Exit.*]

1. Witch. Come, let's make haste, she'll soon be back again. *Exeunt.*

Scene VI

Enter Lennox *and another* Lord.

Len. My former speeches have but hit your thoughts,
Which can interpret farther; only I say
Things have been strangely borne. The gracious Duncan
Was pitied of Macbeth; marry, he was dead.
And the right valiant Banquo walk'd too late,
Whom you may say (if't please you) Fleance kill'd,
For Fleance fled. Men must not walk too late.
Who cannot want the thought, how monstrous
It was for Malcolm and for Donalbain
To kill their gracious father? Damned fact!
How it did grieve Macbeth! Did he not straight
In pious rage the two delinquents tear,
That were the slaves of drink and thralls of sleep?
Was not that nobly done? Ay, and wisely too;
For 'twould have anger'd any heart alive
To hear the men deny't. So that, I say,
He has borne all things well, and I do think
That had he Duncan's sons under his key
(As, and't please heaven, he shall not), they should find
What 'twere to kill a father; so should Fleance.
But peace! for from broad words, and 'cause he fail'd
His presence at the tyrant's feast, I hear
Macduff lives in disgrace. Sir, can you tell
Where he bestows himself?

Lord. The [son] of Duncan
(From whom this tyrant holds the due of birth)
Lives in the English court, and is receiv'd
Of the most pious Edward with such grace
That the malevolence of fortune nothing
Takes from his high respect. Thither Macduff
Is gone to pray the holy king, upon his aid
To wake Northumberland and warlike Siward,
That by the help of these (with Him above
To ratify the work) we may again
Give to our tables meat, sleep to our nights;
Free from our feasts and banquets bloody knives;
Do faithful homage and receive free honors;
All which we pine for now. And this report
Hath so exasperate [the] King that he
Prepares for some attempt of war.

Len. Sent he to Macduff?

Lord. He did; and with an absolute "Sir, not I,"
The cloudy messenger turns me his back,
And hums, as who should say, "You'll rue the time
That clogs me with this answer."

Len. And that well might
Advise him to a caution, t' hold what distance
His wisdom can provide. Some holy angel
Fly to the court of England, and unfold
His message ere he come, that a swift blessing
May soon return to this our suffering country
Under a hand accurs'd!

Lord. I'll send my prayers with him. *Exeunt.*

2. beldams: hags. **7. close:** secret.
11. wayward son: i.e. a disciple who is untrue to our teaching.
15. Acheron: a river in Hades; here, hell itself.
21. dismal: ill-boding, sinister.
24. profound: low-hanging, i.e. ready to drop off.
27. artificial sprites: spirits produced by magic arts.
29. confusion: ruin. **32. security:** overconfidence.
33. s.d. "Come . . . etc." For this song see the Textual Notes.

III.vi. Location: Somewhere in Scotland.
1. My former speeches: what I have been saying. **hit:** coincided with. **2. interpret farther:** draw further inferences.
3. borne: managed, carried on. **gracious:** good.
4. of: by. **marry . . . dead:** to be sure, that was after he died (not before).
8. cannot . . . thought: i.e. can help thinking.
10. fact: deed, crime. **12. pious:** loyal. **19. and:** if.
21. from broad words: because of his outspokenness.
24. bestows himself: has taken refuge.
25. holds . . . birth: withholds his birthright (the crown).
27. pious: saintly. **Edward:** Edward the Confessor. **grace:** favor.
28–29. That . . . respect: i.e. that he is held in as high respect as if ill fortune had not deprived him of the kingship.
30. upon his aid: on Malcolm's behalf.
34. Give . . . meat: hold our usual feasts.
35. Free from . . . knives: free . . . from knives.
36. faithful: sincere (not pretended, as now). **free:** freely given (not bought by acquiescence in evildoing).
38. the King: i.e. Macbeth.
41. cloudy: scowling. **turns me:** turns (a colloquialism).
42. hums: says humph. **43. clogs:** encumbers.
44–45. Advise . . . provide: warn him to keep as far out of Macbeth's way as he can contrive.
48–49. suffering country Under: country suffering under.

ACT IV, Scene I

Thunder. Enter the three Witches.

1. Witch. Thrice the brinded cat hath mew'd.
2. Witch. Thrice, and once the hedge-pig whin'd.
3. Witch. Harpier cries, "'Tis time, 'tis time."
1. Witch. Round about the cauldron go;
In the poison'd entrails throw;
Toad, that under cold stone
Days and nights has thirty-one
Swelt'red venom sleeping got,
Boil thou first i' th' charmed pot.
All. Double, double, toil and trouble;
Fire burn, and cauldron bubble.
2. Witch. Fillet of a fenny snake,
In the cauldron boil and bake;
Eye of newt and toe of frog,
Wool of bat and tongue of dog,
Adder's fork and blind-worm's sting,
Lizard's leg and howlet's wing,
For a charm of pow'rful trouble,
Like a hell-broth boil and bubble.
All. Double, double, toil and trouble;
Fire burn, and cauldron bubble.
3. Witch. Scale of dragon, tooth of wolf,
Witch's mummy, maw and gulf
Of the ravin'd salt-sea shark,
Root of hemlock digg'd i' th' dark,
Liver of blaspheming Jew,
Gall of goat, and slips of yew
Sliver'd in the moon's eclipse,
Nose of Turk and Tartar's lips,
Finger of birth-strangled babe
Ditch-deliver'd by a drab,
Make the gruel thick and slab.
Add thereto a tiger's chawdron,
For th' ingredience of our cau'dron.
All. Double, double, toil and trouble;
Fire burn, and cauldron bubble.
2. Witch. Cool it with a baboon's blood,
Then the charm is firm and good.

Enter Hecat *and the other three* Witches.

Hec. O, well done! I commend your pains,
And every one shall share i' th' gains.
And now about the cauldron sing,
Like elves and fairies in a ring,
Enchanting all that you put in.
Music and a song: "Black spirits, etc." [*Exit Hecat.*]
2. Witch. By the pricking of my thumbs,
Something wicked this way comes. [*Knocking.*]
Open, locks,
Whoever knocks!

Enter Macbeth.

Macb. How now, you secret, black, and midnight hags?
What is't you do?
All. A deed without a name.
Macb. I conjure you, by that which you profess
(How e'er you come to know it), answer me:
Though you untie the winds, and let them fight
Against the churches; though the yesty waves
Confound and swallow navigation up;
Though bladed corn be lodg'd, and trees blown down;
Though castles topple on their warders' heads;
Though palaces and pyramids do slope
Their heads to their foundations; though the treasure
Of nature's [germains] tumble all together,
Even till destruction sicken; answer me
To what I ask you.
1. Witch. Speak.
2. Witch. Demand.
3. Witch. We'll answer.
1. Witch. Say, if th' hadst rather hear it from our mouths,
Or from our masters'?
Macb. Call 'em; let me see 'em.
1. Witch. Pour in sow's blood, that hath eaten
Her nine farrow; grease that's sweaten
From the murderer's gibbet throw
Into the flame.
All. Come high or low;
Thyself and office deftly show!

Thunder. First Apparition, *an armed Head.*

Macb. Tell me, thou unknown power—
1. Witch. He knows thy thought:
Hear his speech, but say thou nought.
1. App. Macbeth! Macbeth! Macbeth! beware Macduff,
Beware the Thane of Fife. Dismiss me. Enough.
He descends.
Macb. What e'er thou art, for thy good caution, thanks;
Thou hast harp'd my fear aright. But one word more—
1. Witch. He will not be commanded. Here's another,
More potent than the first.

Thunder. Second Apparition, *a bloody Child.*

2. App. Macbeth! Macbeth! Macbeth!
Macb. Had I three ears, I'ld hear thee.
2. App. Be bloody, bold, and resolute: laugh to scorn
The pow'r of man; for none of woman born
Shall harm Macbeth. *Descends.*

IV.i. Location: A cave; in the middle, a boiling cauldron.
1. brinded: brindled, streaked. **3. Harpier.** See note on I.i.9–10.
8. Swelt'red: exuded in sweaty drops.
12. Fillet: slice. **fenny:** inhabiting swamps.
16. fork: forked tongue. **17. howlet's:** owlet's.
23. mummy: medicinal substance made from a mummy. **maw and gulf:** stomach and gullet.
24. ravin'd: glutted with prey (?) or voracious (?).
28. Sliver'd: cut off. **31. drab:** whore. **32. slab:** sticky.
33. chawdron: entrails. **39–43.** Probably spurious.
43 s.d. "Black spirits, etc." For this song see the Textual Notes.
50. that . . . profess: i.e. the demonic arts.
53. yesty: yeasty, foamy.
55. bladed corn: ripe wheat. **lodg'd:** beaten down.
57. slope: bend.
59. germains: germens, seeds; the *semines* existing in nature from which all, including man, is created. **60. sicken:** be satiated.
65. nine farrow: litter of nine.
68 s.d. an armed Head. Perhaps signifying the rebellion of Macduff.
74. harp'd . . . aright: hit upon the tune my fear has been playing.
76 s.d. a bloody Child. Signifying Macduff, "untimely ripped" from his mother's womb (see V.viii.15–16).

Macb. Then live, Macduff; what need I fear of thee?
But yet I'll make assurance double sure,
And take a bond of fate: thou shalt not live,
That I may tell pale-hearted fear it lies,
And sleep in spite of thunder.

Thunder. THIRD APPARITION, *a Child crowned, with a tree in his hand.*

What is this
That rises like the issue of a king,
And wears upon his baby-brow the round
And top of sovereignty?
All. Listen, but speak not to't.
3. App. Be lion-mettled, proud, and take no care
Who chafes, who frets, or where conspirers are:
Macbeth shall never vanquish'd be until
Great Birnan wood to high Dunsinane hill
Shall come against him. *Descend.*
Macb. That will never be.
Who can impress the forest, bid the tree
Unfix his earth-bound root? Sweet bodements! good!
Rebellious dead, rise never till the wood
Of Birnan rise, and our high-plac'd Macbeth
Shall live the lease of nature, pay his breath
To time and mortal custom. Yet my heart
Throbs to know one thing: tell me, if your art
Can tell so much, shall Banquo's issue ever
Reign in this kingdom?
All. Seek to know no more.
Macb. I will be satisfied. Deny me this,
And an eternal curse fall on you! Let me know.
Why sinks that cauldron? and what noise is this? *Hoboys.*
1. Witch. Show!
2. Witch. Show!
3. Witch. Show!
All. Show his eyes, and grieve his heart;
Come like shadows, so depart.

A show of eight KINGS, [*the eighth*] *with a glass in his hand, and* BANQUO *last.*

Macb. Thou art too like the spirit of Banquo; down!
Thy crown does sear mine eyeballs. And thy hair,
Thou other gold-bound brow, is like the first.
A third is like the former. Filthy hags,
Why do you show me this?—A fourth? Start, eyes!
What, will the line stretch out to th' crack of doom?
Another yet? A seventh? I'll see no more.
And yet the eight appears, who bears a glass
Which shows me many more; and some I see
That twofold balls and treble sceptres carry.
Horrible sight! Now I see 'tis true,
For the blood-bolter'd Banquo smiles upon me,
And points at them for his. [*Apparitions vanish.*]
What? is this so?
1. Witch. Ay, sir, all this is so. But why
Stands Macbeth thus amazedly?
Come, sisters, cheer we up his sprites,
And show the best of our delights.
I'll charm the air to give a sound,
While you perform your antic round;
That this great king may kindly say
Our duties did his welcome pay.
Music. The Witches dance and vanish.
Macb. Where are they? Gone? Let this pernicious hour
Stand aye accursed in the calendar!
Come in, without there!

Enter LENNOX.

Len. What's your Grace's will?
Macb. Saw you the weïrd sisters?
Len. No, my lord.
Macb. Came they not by you?
Len. No indeed, my lord.
Macb. Infected be the air whereon they ride,
And damn'd all those that trust them! I did hear
The galloping of horse. Who was't came by?
Len. 'Tis two or three, my lord, that bring you word
Macduff is fled to England.
Macb. Fled to England!
Len. Ay, my good lord.
Macb. [*Aside.*] Time, thou anticipat'st my dread exploits:
The flighty purpose never is o'ertook
Unless the deed go with it. From this moment
The very firstlings of my heart shall be
The firstlings of my hand. And even now,
To crown my thoughts with acts, be it thought and done:
The castle of Macduff I will surprise,
Seize upon Fife, give to th' edge o' th' sword
His wife, his babes, and all unfortunate souls
That trace him in his line. No boasting like a fool;
This deed I'll do before this purpose cool.
But no more sights!—Where are these gentlemen?
Come bring me where they are. *Exeunt.*

84. take . . . fate: i.e. bind Fate to its contract by killing Macduff.
86 s.d. a Child crowned. Signifying Malcolm. **tree.** Foreshadowing the action of Malcolm's soldiers in cutting down and carrying boughs to Dunsinane. **87. like:** in the likeness of.
88–89. round And top: crown. **95. impress:** force into service.
96. bodements: prophecies.
97. Rebellious dead. Referring, presumably, to Banquo. Many editors adopt Theobald's emendation *Rebellious head* or his conjecture *Rebellion's head.*
99. the lease of nature: his full span of life (i.e. he will die a natural death). **100. mortal custom:** i.e. death that comes to everyone.
106. noise: music (a frequent meaning).
111 s.d. glass: mirror (here, a magic one). **119. eight:** eighth.
121. twofold . . . sceptres. James I of England and VI of Scotland was twice crowned, at Scone and Westminster. Thus the orb, part of the regalia, is here called "twofold." The English coronation uses two sceptres, the Scottish, one; hence *treble sceptres,* though this may refer to the title "King of Great Britain, France, and Ireland." Banquo was the legendary founder of the Stuart dynasty: see Introduction.
123. blood-bolter'd: with his hair matted with blood.
125–32. Probably spurious.
126. amazedly: as in a trance. **127. sprites:** spirits.
130. antic round: fantastic circular dance.
132. Our . . . pay: our attentions repaid the welcome he gave us.
140. horse: horses (a common plural) or horsemen.
144. anticipat'st: forestallest.
145. The flighty purpose: i.e. a purpose, always fleeting.
146. Unless . . . it: unless it is performed as soon as conceived.
147–48. The very . . . hand: i.e. intention shall coincide with performance. **firstlings:** first-born.
150. surprise: seize upon. **153. trace:** follow.

Scene II

Enter Macduff's Wife, *her* Son, *and* Rosse.

L. Macd. What had he done, to make him fly the land?
Rosse. You must have patience, madam.
L. Macd. He had none;
His flight was madness. When our actions do not,
Our fears do make us traitors.
Rosse. You know not
Whether it was his wisdom or his fear.
L. Macd. Wisdom? to leave his wife, to leave his babes,
His mansion and his titles, in a place
From whence himself does fly? He loves us not,
He wants the natural touch; for the poor wren,
The most diminutive of birds, will fight,
Her young ones in her nest, against the owl.
All is the fear, and nothing is the love;
As little is the wisdom, where the flight
So runs against all reason.
Rosse. My dearest coz,
I pray you school yourself. But for your husband,
He is noble, wise, judicious, and best knows
The fits o' th' season. I dare not speak much further,
But cruel are the times when we are traitors,
And do not know ourselves; when we hold rumor
From what we fear, yet know not what we fear,
But float upon a wild and violent sea
Each way, and move. I take my leave of you;
'Shall not be long but I'll be here again.
Things at the worst will cease, or else climb upward
To what they were before. My pretty cousin,
Blessing upon you!
L. Macd. Father'd he is, and yet he's fatherless.
Rosse. I am so much a fool, should I stay longer,
It would be my disgrace and your discomfort.
I take my leave at once. *Exit Rosse.*
L. Macd. Sirrah, your father's dead,
And what will you do now? How will you live?
Son. As birds do, mother.
L. Macd. What, with worms and flies?
Son. With what I get, I mean, and so do they.
L. Macd. Poor bird, thou'dst never fear the net nor lime,
The pitfall nor the gin.
Son. Why should I, mother? Poor birds they are not set for.
My father is not dead, for all your saying.
L. Macd. Yes, he is dead. How wilt thou do for a father?
Son. Nay, how will you do for a husband?
L. Macd. Why, I can buy me twenty at any market.
Son. Then you'll buy 'em to sell again.
L. Macd. Thou speak'st with all thy wit, and yet, i' faith,
With wit enough for thee.
Son. Was my father a traitor, mother?
L. Macd. Ay, that he was.
Son. What is a traitor?
L. Macd. Why, one that swears and lies.
Son. And be all traitors that do so?
L. Macd. Every one that does so is a traitor, and must be hang'd.
Son. And must they all be hang'd that swear and lie?
L. Macd. Every one.
Son. Who must hang them?
L. Macd. Why, the honest men.
Son. Then the liars and swearers are fools; for there are liars and swearers enow to beat the honest men and hang up them.
L. Macd. Now God help thee, poor monkey! But how wilt thou do for a father?
Son. If he were dead, you'ld weep for him; if you would not, it were a good sign that I should quickly have a new father.
L. Macd. Poor prattler, how thou talk'st!

Enter a Messenger.

Mess. Bless you, fair dame! I am not to you known,
Though in your state of honor I am perfect.
I doubt some danger does approach you nearly.
If you will take a homely man's advice,
Be not found here; hence with your little ones.
To fright you thus, methinks I am too savage;
To do worse to you were fell cruelty,
Which is too nigh your person. Heaven preserve you!
I dare abide no longer. *Exit Messenger.*
L. Macd. Whither should I fly?
I have done no harm. But I remember now
I am in this earthly world—where to do harm
Is often laudable, to do good sometime
Accounted dangerous folly. Why then, alas,
Do I put up that womanly defense,
To say I have done no harm?

Enter Murtherers.

What are these faces?
[*1.*] *Mur.* Where is your husband?
L. Macd. I hope, in no place so unsanctified

IV.ii. Location: Fife. Macduff's castle.
2. have patience: exercise self-control.
7. titles: title deeds, hence estates.
9. wants: lacks. **natural touch:** i.e. the feeling natural to a husband and father. **14. coz:** cousin, i.e. kinswoman.
15. school: control.
17. fits . . . season: disturbances of the time (another use of the figure of a recurrent fever).
19. know ourselves: recognize ourselves as such. **hold:** credit (?) or interpret (?).
20. From what we fear: because of (or in accordance with) our fears.
22. Each . . . move. Probably corrupt, unless Rosse in his haste breaks off his sentence (some editors read *move—*). Proposed emendations include *And each way move, And move each way, Each way it moves;* most editors adopt Dover Wilson's reading, *Each way and none.*
23. but: before. **29. It . . . discomfort:** i.e. I should weep.
34. lime: birdlime, a sticky substance spread to catch birds.
35. pitfall . . . gin: trap . . . snare.
43. With . . . thee: i.e. you are quite clever enough for a child.
47. swears and lies: swears an oath and breaks it (doubtless with another allusion to the "equivocation" of Father Garnet and others).
51. swear: use profanity (as lines 56–58 make clear).
66. in . . . perfect: I know well your honored position.
67. doubt: fear. **68. homely:** plain.
70. To fright: i.e. even to frighten.
71. To do worse: i.e. to do you actual harm. **fell:** savage.
72. Which: i.e. such cruelty. **78. womanly:** womanish.

Where such as thou mayst find him.
[1.] Mur. He's a traitor.
Son. Thou li'st, thou shag-ear'd villain!
[1.] Mur. What, you egg! *[Stabbing him.]*
Young fry of treachery!
Son. He has kill'd me, mother:
Run away, I pray you! *[Dies.]*
Exit [Lady Macduff] crying "Murther!" *[and pursued by the Murderers].*

Scene III

Enter Malcolm *and* Macduff.

Mal. Let us seek out some desolate shade, and there
Weep our sad bosoms empty.
Macd. Let us rather
Hold fast the mortal sword, and like good men
Bestride our downfall birthdom. Each new morn
New widows howl, new orphans cry, new sorrows
Strike heaven on the face, that it resounds
As if it felt with Scotland, and yell'd out
Like syllable of dolor.
Mal. What I believe, I'll wail,
What know, believe; and what I can redress,
As I shall find the time to friend, I will.
What you have spoke, it may be so perchance.
This tyrant, whose sole name blisters our tongues,
Was once thought honest; you have lov'd him well;
He hath not touch'd you yet. I am young, but something
You may discern of him through me, and wisdom
To offer up a weak, poor, innocent lamb
T' appease an angry god.
Macd. I am not treacherous.
Mal. But Macbeth is.
A good and virtuous nature may recoil
In an imperial charge. But I shall crave your pardon;
That which you are, my thoughts cannot transpose:
Angels are bright still, though the brightest fell.
Though all things foul would wear the brows of grace,
Yet grace must still look so.
Macd. I have lost my hopes.
Mal. Perchance even there where I did find my doubts.
Why in that rawness left you wife and child,
Those precious motives, those strong knots of love,
Without leave-taking? I pray you,
Let not my jealousies be your dishonors,
But mine own safeties. You may be rightly just,
What ever I shall think.
Macd. Bleed, bleed, poor country!
Great tyranny, lay thou thy basis sure,
For goodness dare not check thee; wear thou thy wrongs,
The title is affeer'd! Fare thee well, lord,
I would not be the villain that thou think'st
For the whole space that's in the tyrant's grasp,
And the rich East to boot.
Mal. Be not offended;
I speak not as in absolute fear of you.
I think our country sinks beneath the yoke:
It weeps, it bleeds, and each new day a gash
Is added to her wounds. I think withal
There would be hands uplifted in my right;
And here from gracious England have I offer
Of goodly thousands. But, for all this,
When I shall tread upon the tyrant's head,
Or wear it on my sword, yet my poor country
Shall have more vices than it had before,
More suffer, and more sundry ways than ever,
By him that shall succeed.
Macd. What should he be?
Mal. It is myself I mean; in whom I know
All the particulars of vice so grafted
That, when they shall be open'd, black Macbeth
Will seem as pure as snow, and the poor state
Esteem him as a lamb, being compar'd
With my confineless harms.
Macd. Not in the legions
Of horrid hell can come a devil more damn'd
In evils to top Macbeth.
Mal. I grant him bloody,
Luxurious, avaricious, false, deceitful,
Sudden, malicious, smacking of every sin
That has a name; but there's no bottom, none,
In my voluptuousness. Your wives, your daughters,
Your matrons, and your maids could not fill up
The cestern of my lust, and my desire
All continent impediments would o'erbear
That did oppose my will. Better Macbeth
Than such an one to reign.
Macd. Boundless intemperance
In nature is a tyranny; it hath been
Th' untimely emptying of the happy throne,
And fall of many kings. But fear not yet

83. shag-ear'd: with shaggy hair about your ears. Some editors prefer Steevens' conjecture *shag-hair'd*. **84. fry:** spawn.

IV.iii. Location: England. Before King Edward's palace.
3. mortal: deadly.
4. Bestride: stand over protectively. **downfall:** downfallen. **birthdom:** native land. **8. Like . . . dolor:** a similar cry of pain.
10. to friend: favorable. **12. sole:** mere. **13. honest:** honorable.
14. young: i.e. inexperienced.
14–15. something . . . me: you may see a way of ingratiating yourself with him by betraying me. Most editors follow Theobald in emending *discern* to *deserve*.
15. wisdom: i.e. it would be the way of worldly wisdom.
19. recoil: give way, retrograde.
20. In . . . charge: at a king's command, or under pressure brought by a king. **21. transpose:** change.
23–24. Though . . . so: even if every wickedness assumes the appearance of virtue, virtue must still retain that appearance; i.e. even in these bad times an appearance of virtue must not be taken as a sure sign of villainy. **24. hopes:** i.e. of Malcolm's cooperation.
25. doubts: i.e. of Macduff's loyalty.

26. rawness: unprotected state.
27. motives: persons moving you to love and protect them.
29. jealousies: suspicions.
33. wrongs: wrongful gains, usurped powers.
34. affeer'd: confirmed, authoritatively settled.
37. to boot: in addition. **38. absolute fear:** complete distrust.
39. think: am mindful that. **41. withal:** besides.
43. England: the King of England. **48. and more:** and in more.
51. particulars: varieties. **52. open'd:** disclosed.
57. top: surpass. **58. Luxurious:** lecherous.
59. Sudden: violent. **63. cestern:** cistern.
64. continent: (1) restraining; (2) chaste.
67. nature: i.e. a man's nature. **is a tyranny.** Because its rule is absolute.

To take upon you what is yours. You may
Convey your pleasures in a spacious plenty,
And yet seem cold, the time you may so hoodwink.
We have willing dames enough; there cannot be
That vulture in you to devour so many
As will to greatness dedicate themselves,
Finding it so inclin'd.
Mal. With this, there grows
In my most ill-compos'd affection such
A stanchless avarice that, were I king,
I should cut off the nobles for their lands,
Desire his jewels, and this other's house,
And my more-having would be as a sauce
To make me hunger more, that I should forge
Quarrels unjust against the good and loyal,
Destroying them for wealth.
Macd. This avarice
Sticks deeper, grows with more pernicious root
Than summer-seeming lust; and it hath been
The sword of our slain kings. Yet do not fear,
Scotland hath foisons to fill up your will
Of your mere own. All these are portable,
With other graces weigh'd.
Mal. But I have none. The king-becoming graces,
As justice, verity, temp'rance, stableness,
Bounty, perseverance, mercy, lowliness,
Devotion, patience, courage, fortitude,
I have no relish of them, but abound
In the division of each several crime,
Acting it many ways. Nay, had I pow'r, I should
Pour the sweet milk of concord into hell,
Uproar the universal peace, confound
All unity on earth.
Macd. O Scotland, Scotland!
Mal. If such a one be fit to govern, speak.
I am as I have spoken.
Macd. Fit to govern?
No, not to live. O nation miserable!
With an untitled tyrant bloody-sceptred,
When shalt thou see thy wholesome days again,
Since that the truest issue of thy throne
By his own interdiction stands accus'd,
And does blaspheme his breed? Thy royal father
Was a most sainted king; the queen that bore thee,
Oft'ner upon her knees than on her feet,
Died every day she liv'd. Fare thee well,
These evils thou repeat'st upon thyself
Hath banish'd me from Scotland. O my breast,
Thy hope ends here!
Mal. Macduff, this noble passion,
Child of integrity, hath from my soul
Wip'd the black scruples, reconcil'd my thoughts
To thy good truth and honor. Devilish Macbeth
By many of these trains hath sought to win me
Into his power, and modest wisdom plucks me
From over-credulous haste. But God above
Deal between thee and me! for even now
I put myself to thy direction, and
Unspeak mine own detraction; here abjure
The taints and blames I laid upon myself,
For strangers to my nature. I am yet
Unknown to woman, never was forsworn,
Scarcely have coveted what was mine own,
At no time broke my faith, would not betray
The devil to his fellow, and delight
No less in truth than life. My first false speaking
Was this upon myself. What I am truly
Is thine and my poor country's to command:
Whither indeed, before [thy] here-approach,
Old Siward, with ten thousand warlike men
Already at a point, was setting forth.
Now we'll together, and the chance of goodness
Be like our warranted quarrel! Why are you silent?
Macd. Such welcome and unwelcome things at once
'Tis hard to reconcile.

Enter a Doctor.

Mal. Well, more anon.—Comes the King forth,
I pray you?
Doct. Ay, sir; there are a crew of wretched souls
That stay his cure. Their malady convinces
The great assay of art; but at his touch,
Such sanctity hath heaven given his hand,
They presently amend.
Mal. I thank you, doctor. *Exit [Doctor].*
Macd. What's the disease he means?
Mal. 'Tis call'd the evil:
A most miraculous work in this good king,
Which often, since my here-remain in England,
I have seen him do. How he solicits heaven,
Himself best knows; but strangely-visited people,
All swoll'n and ulcerous, pitiful to the eye,
The mere despair of surgery, he cures,
Hanging a golden stamp about their necks,
Put on with holy prayers, and 'tis spoken,
To the succeeding royalty he leaves
The healing benediction. With this strange virtue,
He hath a heavenly gift of prophecy,
And sundry blessings hang about his throne
That speak him full of grace.

70. what is yours: i.e. the throne.
71. Convey: manage stealthily.
72. cold: chaste. **hoodwink:** blindfold.
77. affection: character. **78. stanchless:** insatiable.
86. summer-seeming: summer-beseeming, i.e. appropriate to one's heyday (and hence tending to lessen with age, unlike avarice).
88. foisons: abundance.
89. Of . . . own: i.e. in royal property alone. **portable:** bearable.
90. With . . . weigh'd: balanced by virtuous qualities.
93. lowliness: humility. **95. relish:** trace.
96. division: subdivisions, various manifestations. **several crime:** separate sin.
99. Uproar . . . peace: change into a tumult the orderliness of the universe. **confound:** utterly destroy.
104. untitled: unrightful, usurping.
105. wholesome: healthful, sound.
107. interdiction: declaration of incompetence (?).
108. blaspheme: defame.
111. Died: i.e. to the world (cf. 1 Corinthians 15:31).
118. trains: stratagems, devices.
119. modest wisdom: wise moderation, prudent caution.
125. For: as. **135. at a point:** completely prepared.
136. goodness: success.
137. like . . . quarrel: as good as our cause is just.
142–43. convinces . . . art: defeats the best medical skill.
145. presently: immediately.
146. evil: scrofula ("the king's evil," supposedly cured by the royal touch).
150. strangely-visited: afflicted in unusual ways. **152. mere:** utter.
153. stamp: coin. **156. virtue:** power. **159. grace:** God's grace.

Enter ROSSE.

Macd. See who comes here.
Mal. My countryman; but yet I know him not.
Macd. My ever gentle cousin, welcome hither.
Mal. I know him now. Good God betimes remove
The means that makes us strangers!
Rosse. Sir, amen.
Macd. Stands Scotland where it did?
Rosse. Alas, poor country,
Almost afraid to know itself! It cannot
Be call'd our mother, but our grave; where nothing,
But who knows nothing, is once seen to smile;
Where sighs, and groans, and shrieks that rent the air
Are made, not mark'd; where violent sorrow seems
A modern ecstasy. The dead man's knell
Is there scarce ask'd for who, and good men's lives
Expire before the flowers in their caps,
Dying or ere they sicken.
Macd. O relation!
Too nice, and yet too true.
Mal. What's the newest grief?
Rosse. That of an hour's age doth hiss the speaker;
Each minute teems a new one.
Macd. How does my wife?
Rosse. Why, well.
Macd. And all my children?
Rosse. Well too.
Macd. The tyrant has not batter'd at their peace?
Rosse. No, they were well at peace when I did leave 'em.
Macd. Be not a niggard of your speech; how goes't?
Rosse. When I came hither to transport the tidings,
Which I have heavily borne, there ran a rumor
Of many worthy fellows that were out,
Which was to my belief witness'd the rather,
For that I saw the tyrant's power afoot.
Now is the time of help; your eye in Scotland
Would create soldiers, make our women fight,
To doff their dire distresses.
Mal. Be't their comfort
We are coming thither. Gracious England hath
Lent us good Siward, and ten thousand men;
An older and a better soldier none
That Christendom gives out.
Rosse. Would I could answer
This comfort with the like! But I have words
That would be howl'd out in the desert air,
Where hearing should not latch them.
Macd. What concern they?
The general cause? or is it a fee-grief
Due to some single breast?
Rosse. No mind that's honest
But in it shares some woe, though the main part
Pertains to you alone.
Macd. If it be mine,
Keep it not from me, quickly let me have it.
Rosse. Let not your ears despise my tongue for ever,
Which shall possess them with the heaviest sound
That ever yet they heard.
Macd. Humh! I guess at it.
Rosse. Your castle is surpris'd; your wife, and babes,
Savagely slaughter'd. To relate the manner,
Were on the quarry of these murther'd deer
To add the death of you.
Mal. Merciful heaven!
What, man, ne'er pull your hat upon your brows;
Give sorrow words. The grief that does not speak
Whispers the o'er-fraught heart, and bids it break.
Macd. My children too?
Rosse. Wife, children, servants, all
That could be found.
Macd. And I must be from thence!
My wife kill'd too?
Rosse. I have said.
Mal. Be comforted.
Let's make us med'cines of our great revenge
To cure this deadly grief.
Macd. He has no children. All my pretty ones?
Did you say all? O hell-kite! All?
What, all my pretty chickens, and their dam,
At one fell swoop?
Mal. Dispute it like a man.
Macd. I shall do so;
But I must also feel it as a man:
I cannot but remember such things were,
That were most precious to me. Did heaven look on,
And would not take their part? Sinful Macduff,
They were all strook for thee! naught that I am,
Not for their own demerits, but for mine,
Fell slaughter on their souls. Heaven rest them now!
Mal. Be this the whetstone of your sword, let grief
Convert to anger; blunt not the heart, enrage it.
Macd. O, I could play the woman with mine eyes,
And braggart with my tongue! But, gentle heavens,
Cut short all intermission. Front to front
Bring thou this fiend of Scotland and myself;
Within my sword's length set him; if he scape,
Heaven forgive him too!
Mal. This [tune] goes manly.
Come go we to the King, our power is ready,
Our lack is nothing but our leave. Macbeth

160. know: recognize. **161. gentle:** noble.
166–67. nothing, But who: no one except him who.
168. rent: rend. **169. mark'd:** noticed.
170. modern ecstasy: commonplace emotion.
173. or ere: before. **relation:** report.
174. nice: precise, accurately detailed.
175. hiss the speaker: cause the speaker to be hissed (for telling stale news). **176. teems:** breeds, brings forth.
182. heavily: sorrowfully. **183. out:** in arms.
184. witness'd the rather: made the more credible.
185. power: forces.
186. time of help: moment to apply the cure.
192. gives out: proclaims (?) or furnishes example of (?).
194. would: demand to. **desert air:** air in some unpopulated spot.
195. latch: catch.
196. fee-grief: private woe (*fee* = absolute ownership).
197. Due to: i.e. the property of.
206. quarry: heap of slaughtered bodies.
210. o'er-fraught: overburdened. **212. must.** Past tense.
219. swoop: i.e. swoop of the hell-kite.
220. Dispute: oppose, fight against.
225. for: on account of. **naught:** wicked.
229. Convert: be changed. **232. Front to front:** face to face.
235. too: i.e. as I must have done, to let him escape.
237. Our . . . leave: we need only take leave of the King.

Is ripe for shaking, and the pow'rs above
Put on their instruments. Receive what cheer you may,
The night is long that never finds the day.

Exeunt.

ACT V, SCENE I

Enter a DOCTOR OF PHYSIC *and a* WAITING-GENTLEWOMAN.

Doct. I have two nights watch'd with you, but can perceive no truth in your report. When was it she last walk'd?

Gent. Since his Majesty went into the field, I have seen her rise from her bed, throw her night-gown upon her, unlock her closet, take forth paper, fold it, write upon't, read it, afterwards seal it, and again return to bed; yet all this while in a most fast sleep.

Doct. A great perturbation in nature, to receive at once the benefit of sleep and do the effects of watching! In this slumb'ry agitation, besides her walking and other actual performances, what, at any time, have you heard her say?

Gent. That, sir, which I will not report after her.

Doct. You may to me, and 'tis most meet you should.

Gent. Neither to you nor any one, having no witness to confirm my speech.

Enter LADY [MACBETH] *with a taper.*

Lo you, here she comes! This is her very guise, and upon my life, fast asleep. Observe her, stand close.

Doct. How came she by that light?

Gent. Why, it stood by her. She has light by her continually, 'tis her command.

Doct. You see her eyes are open.

Gent. Ay, but their sense are shut.

Doct. What is it she does now? Look how she rubs her hands.

Gent. It is an accustom'd action with her, to seem thus washing her hands. I have known her continue in this a quarter of an hour.

Lady M. Yet here's a spot.

Doct. Hark, she speaks. I will set down what comes from her, to satisfy my remembrance the more strongly.

Lady M. Out, damn'd spot! out, I say! One—two—why then 'tis time to do't. Hell is murky. Fie, my lord, fie, a soldier, and afeard? What need we fear who knows it, when none can call our pow'r to accompt? Yet who would have thought the old man to have had so much blood in him?

Doct. Do you mark that?

Lady M. The Thane of Fife had a wife; where is she now? What, will these hands ne'er be clean? No more o' that, my lord, no more o' that; you mar all with this starting.

Doct. Go to, go to; you have known what you should not.

Gent. She has spoke what she should not, I am sure of that; heaven knows what she has known.

Lady M. Here's the smell of the blood still. All the perfumes of Arabia will not sweeten this little hand. O, O, O!

Doct. What a sigh is there! The heart is sorely charg'd.

Gent. I would not have such a heart in my bosom for the dignity of the whole body.

Doct. Well, well, well.

Gent. Pray God it be, sir.

Doct. This disease is beyond my practice; yet I have known those which have walk'd in their sleep who have died holily in their beds.

Lady M. Wash your hands, put on your night-gown, look not so pale. I tell you yet again, Banquo's buried; he cannot come out on 's grave.

Doct. Even so?

Lady M. To bed, to bed; there's knocking at the gate. Come, come, come, come, give me your hand. What's done cannot be undone. To bed, to bed, to bed.

Exit Lady.

Doct. Will she go now to bed?

Gent. Directly.

Doct. Foul whisp'rings are abroad. Unnatural deeds
Do breed unnatural troubles; infected minds
To their deaf pillows will discharge their secrets.
More needs she the divine than the physician.
God, God, forgive us all! Look after her,
Remove from her the means of all annoyance,
And still keep eyes upon her. So good night.
My mind she has mated, and amaz'd my sight.
I think, but dare not speak.

Gent. Good night, good doctor. *Exeunt.*

SCENE II

Drum and Colors. Enter MENTETH, CATHNESS, ANGUS, LENNOX, SOLDIERS.

Ment. The English pow'r is near, led on by Malcolm,
His uncle Siward, and the good Macduff.
Revenges burn in them; for their dear causes
Would to the bleeding and the grim alarm
Excite the mortified man.

Ang. Near Birnan wood
Shall we well meet them; that way are they coming.

239. Put . . . instruments: arm themselves (?) or incite us, their agents (?).

V.i. Location: Dunsinane. Macbeth's castle.
10–11. do . . . watching: perform waking actions.
11. agitation: activity.
19. her very guise: exactly what she has been doing.
20. close: out of sight. **25. sense:** powers of sight.
33. satisfy: confirm. **39. accompt:** account.

45. this starting: these startled movements.
54. charg'd: burdened. **59. practice:** professional skill.
64. on 's: of his. **76. annoyance:** (self-)injury.
77. still: constantly.
78. mated: stupefied. **amaz'd:** bewildered.

V.ii. Location: The country near Dunsinane.
3. dear: heartfelt.
4. bleeding . . . alarm: i.e. bloody and grim battle.
5. mortified: moribund (?) or paralyzed (?).
6. well: no doubt.

Cath. Who knows if Donalbain be with his brother?
Len. For certain, sir, he is not; I have a file
Of all the gentry. There is Siward's son,
And many unrough youths that even now
Protest their first of manhood.
Ment. What does the tyrant?
Cath. Great Dunsinane he strongly fortifies.
Some say he's mad; others that lesser hate him
Do call it valiant fury; but for certain
He cannot buckle his distemper'd cause
Within the belt of rule.
Ang. Now does he feel
His secret murthers sticking on his hands;
Now minutely revolts upbraid his faith-breach;
Those he commands move only in command,
Nothing in love. Now does he feel his title
Hang loose about him, like a giant's robe
Upon a dwarfish thief.
Ment. Who then shall blame
His pester'd senses to recoil and start,
When all that is within him does condemn
Itself for being there?
Cath. Well, march we on
To give obedience where 'tis truly ow'd.
Meet we the med'cine of the sickly weal,
And with him pour we, in our country's purge,
Each drop of us.
Len. Or so much as it needs
To dew the sovereign flower and drown the weeds.
Make we our march towards Birnan.
Exeunt marching.

Scene III

Enter Macbeth, Doctor, *and* Attendants.

Macb. Bring me no more reports, let them fly all.
Till Birnan wood remove to Dunsinane
I cannot taint with fear. What's the boy Malcolm?
Was he not born of woman? The spirits that know
All mortal consequences have pronounc'd me thus:
"Fear not, Macbeth, no man that's born of woman
Shall e'er have power upon thee." Then fly, false thanes,
And mingle with the English epicures!
The mind I sway by, and the heart I bear,
Shall never sag with doubt, nor shake with fear.

Enter Servant.

The devil damn thee black, thou cream-fac'd loon!
Where got'st thou that goose-look?
Serv. There is ten thousand—
Macb. Geese, villain?
Serv. Soldiers, sir.
Macb. Go prick thy face, and over-red thy fear,
Thou lily-liver'd boy. What soldiers, patch?
Death of thy soul! those linen cheeks of thine
Are counsellors to fear. What soldiers, whey-face?
Serv. The English force, so please you.
Macb. Take thy face hence. [*Exit Servant.*] Seyton!
—I am sick at heart
When I behold—Seyton, I say!—This push
Will cheer me ever, or [disseat] me now.
I have liv'd long enough: my way of life
Is fall'n into the sear, the yellow leaf,
And that which should accompany old age,
As honor, love, obedience, troops of friends,
I must not look to have; but in their stead,
Curses, not loud but deep, mouth-honor, breath,
Which the poor heart would fain deny, and dare not.
Seyton!

Enter Seyton.

Sey. What's your gracious pleasure?
Macb. What news more?
Sey. All is confirm'd, my lord, which was reported.
Macb. I'll fight, till from my bones my flesh be hack'd.
Give me my armor.
Sey. 'Tis not needed yet.
Macb. I'll put it on.
Send out moe horses, skirr the country round,
Hang those that talk of fear. Give me mine armor.
How does your patient, doctor?
Doct. Not so sick, my lord,
As she is troubled with thick-coming fancies,
That keep her from her rest.
Macb. Cure [her] of that.
Canst thou not minister to a mind diseas'd,
Pluck from the memory a rooted sorrow,
Raze out the written troubles of the brain,
And with some sweet oblivious antidote
Cleanse the stuff'd bosom of that perilous stuff
Which weighs upon the heart?
Doct. Therein the patient
Must minister to himself.
Macb. Throw physic to the dogs, I'll none of it.
Come, put mine armor on; give me my staff.
Seyton, send out. Doctor, the thanes fly from me.—
Come, sir, dispatch.—If thou couldst, doctor, cast
The water of my land, find her disease,

8. file: list. **10. unrough:** unbearded.
11. Protest . . . manhood: assert their manhood for the first time.
15. distemper'd: swollen with disease.
16. rule: self-control, temperate behavior.
18. minutely revolts: i.e. fresh revolts every minute.
19. in command: because they are ordered to.
23. pester'd senses: tormented faculties. **start:** move fitfully.
27. med'cine: i.e. Malcolm. **weal:** state.
30. sovereign: (1) royal; (2) supreme in curative power.

V.iii. Location: Dunsinane. Macbeth's castle.
1. them: i.e. the thanes (see line 7). **fly:** desert.
3. taint: be infected.
5. mortal consequences: human destinies.
8. epicures: i.e. devotees of soft living.
9. sway: rule myself, control my actions. **11. loon:** rascal.

15. lily-liver'd: i.e. cowardly. **patch:** clown, fool. **16. of:** on.
17. Are . . . fear: will urge others to be fearful. **20. push:** effort.
21. disseat: dethrone. This is Jennens' conjecture for F1 *dis-eate*, and some argue that *cheer* should be *chair* to match it. The later folios read *disease*, i.e. deprive of comfort and peace of mind—a good guess, and appropriate to *cheer*.
22. way: course. (Dr. Johnson's famous conjecture *May* is unnecessary.) **25. As:** such as, namely.
35. moe: more. **skirr:** scour.
42. Raze out: erase. **written troubles of:** troubles written on.
43. oblivious: causing forgetfulness. **48. staff:** lance.
50. dispatch: hurry up.
50–51. cast The water: analyze the urine, i.e. diagnose the disorder.

And purge it to a sound and pristine health,
I would applaud thee to the very echo,
That should applaud again.—Pull't off, I say.—
What rhubarb, cyme, or what purgative drug,
Would scour these English hence? Hear'st thou of them?

Doct. Ay, my good lord; your royal preparation
Makes us hear something.

Macb. Bring it after me.—
I will not be afraid of death and bane,
Till Birnan forest come to Dunsinane.

[*Exeunt all but the Doctor.*]

Doct. Were I from Dunsinane away and clear,
Profit again should hardly draw me here. *Exit.*

SCENE IV

Drum and Colors. Enter MALCOLM, SIWARD, MACDUFF, SIWARD'S SON, MENTETH, CATHNESS, ANGUS, [LENNOX, ROSSE,] *and* SOLDIERS, *marching.*

Mal. Cousins, I hope the days are near at hand
That chambers will be safe.

Ment. We doubt it nothing.

Siw. What wood is this before us?

Ment. The wood of Birnan.

Mal. Let every soldier hew him down a bough,
And bear't before him, thereby shall we shadow
The numbers of our host, and make discovery
Err in report of us.

Soldiers. It shall be done.

Siw. We learn no other but the confident tyrant
Keeps still in Dunsinane, and will endure
Our setting down before't.

Mal. 'Tis his main hope;
For where there is advantage to be given,
Both more and less have given him the revolt,
And none serve with him but constrained things,
Whose hearts are absent too.

Macd. Let our just censures
Attend the true event, and put we on
Industrious soldiership.

Siw. The time approaches
That will with due decision make us know
What we shall say we have, and what we owe.
Thoughts speculative their unsure hopes relate,
But certain issue strokes must arbitrate,
Towards which advance the war. *Exeunt marching.*

52. pristine: i.e. perfect, as formerly.
54. Pull't off. Referring to some part of the armor not properly adjusted. **55. cyme:** possibly another word for *senna.*
56. scour: purge.
62. Profit . . . here: i.e. no fee would be large enough to bring me back.

V.iv. Location: The country near Birnan wood.
2. chambers: bedrooms (such as Duncan's).
6. discovery: reconnaissance. **9. Keeps:** remains.
10. setting down before: laying siege to.
11. advantage: opportunity. **12. more and less:** great and lowly.
14. our just censures: i.e. our judgments, in order that they may be just. **15. Attend . . . event:** await the actual outcome.
18. owe: own.
19–20. Thoughts . . . arbitrate: talking about the event in advance is to deal in mere hopes, uncertain of fulfillment; the real issue must be decided by action.

SCENE V

Enter MACBETH, SEYTON, *and* SOLDIERS, *with Drum and Colors.*

Macb. Hang out our banners on the outward walls,
The cry is still, "They come!" Our castle's strength
Will laugh a siege to scorn; here let them lie
Till famine and the ague eat them up.
Were they not forc'd with those that should be ours,
We might have met them dareful, beard to beard,
And beat them backward home.

A cry within of women.

What is that noise?

Sey. It is the cry of women, my good lord. [*Exit.*]

Macb. I have almost forgot the taste of fears.
The time has been, my senses would have cool'd
To hear a night-shriek, and my fell of hair
Would at a dismal treatise rouse and stir
As life were in't. I have supp'd full with horrors;
Direness, familiar to my slaughterous thoughts,
Cannot once start me.

[*Enter* SEYTON.]

Wherefore was that cry?

Sey. The Queen, my lord, is dead.

Macb. She should have died hereafter;
There would have been a time for such a word.
To-morrow, and to-morrow, and to-morrow,
Creeps in this petty pace from day to day,
To the last syllable of recorded time;
And all our yesterdays have lighted fools
The way to dusty death. Out, out, brief candle!
Life's but a walking shadow, a poor player,
That struts and frets his hour upon the stage,
And then is heard no more. It is a tale
Told by an idiot, full of sound and fury,
Signifying nothing.

Enter a MESSENGER.

Thou com'st to use thy tongue;
Thy story quickly.

Mess. Gracious my lord,
I should report that which I say I saw,
But know not how to do't.

Macb. Well, say, sir.

Mess. As I did stand my watch upon the hill,
I look'd toward Birnan, and anon methought
The wood began to move.

Macb. Liar and slave!

Mess. Let me endure your wrath, if't be not so.
Within this three mile may you see it coming;
I say, a moving grove.

Macb. If thou speak'st false,
Upon the next tree shalt thou hang alive,
Till famine cling thee; if thy speech be sooth,
I care not if thou dost for me as much.

V.v. Location: Dunsinane. Macbeth's castle.
5. forc'd: reinforced. **6. dareful:** boldly.
10. cool'd: been chilled with terror.
11. my . . . hair: the hair on my skin. **12. treatise:** story.
15. once start me: ever make me start.
17. should . . . hereafter: was bound to die later (if not to-day). *Should* = would certainly. **39. cling:** shrivel. **sooth:** truth.

I pull in resolution, and begin
To doubt th' equivocation of the fiend
That lies like truth. "Fear not, till Birnan wood
Do come to Dunsinane," and now a wood
Comes toward Dunsinane. Arm, arm, and out!
If this which he avouches does appear,
There is nor flying hence, nor tarrying here.
I gin to be a-weary of the sun,
And wish th' estate o' th' world were now undone.
Ring the alarum-bell! Blow wind, come wrack,
At least we'll die with harness on our back. *Exeunt.*

Scene VI

Drum and Colors. Enter Malcolm, Siward, Macduff, *and their army, with boughs.*

Mal. Now near enough; your leavy screens throw down,
And show like those you are. You, worthy uncle,
Shall with my cousin, your right noble son,
Lead our first battle. Worthy Macduff and we
Shall take upon 's what else remains to do,
According to our order.
Siw. Fare you well.
Do we but find the tyrant's power to-night,
Let us be beaten, if we cannot fight.
Macd. Make all our trumpets speak, give them all breath,
Those clamorous harbingers of blood and death.
Exeunt. Alarums continued.

Scene VII

Enter Macbeth.

Macb. They have tied me to a stake; I cannot fly,
But bear-like I must fight the course. What's he
That was not born of woman? Such a one
Am I to fear, or none.

Enter Young Siward.

Y. Siw. What is thy name?
Macb. Thou'lt be afraid to hear it.
Y. Siw. No; though thou call'st thyself a hotter name
Than any is in hell.
Macb. My name's Macbeth.
Y. Siw. The devil himself could not pronounce a title
More hateful to mine ear.
Macb. No; nor more fearful.
Y. Siw. Thou liest, abhorred tyrant, with my sword
I'll prove the lie thou speak'st.
Fight, and Young Siward slain.
Macb. Thou wast born of woman.
But swords I smile at, weapons laugh to scorn,
Brandish'd by man that's of a woman born. *Exit.*

Alarums. Enter Macduff.

Macd. That way the noise is. Tyrant, show thy face!
If thou beest slain and with no stroke of mine,
My wife and children's ghosts will haunt me still.
I cannot strike at wretched kerns, whose arms
Are hir'd to bear their staves; either thou, Macbeth,
Or else my sword with an unbattered edge
I sheathe again undeeded. There thou shouldst be;
By this great clatter, one of greatest note
Seems bruited. Let me find him, Fortune!
And more I beg not. *Exit. Alarums.*

Enter Malcolm *and* Siward.

Siw. This way, my lord, the castle's gently rend'red:
The tyrant's people on both sides do fight,
The noble thanes do bravely in the war,
The day almost itself professes yours,
And little is to do.
Mal. We have met with foes
That strike beside us.
Siw. Enter, sir, the castle.
Exeunt. Alarum.

[Scene VIII]

Enter Macbeth.

Macb. Why should I play the Roman fool, and die
On mine own sword? Whiles I see lives, the gashes
Do better upon them.

Enter Macduff.

Macd. Turn, hell-hound, turn!
Macb. Of all men else I have avoided thee.
But get thee back, my soul is too much charg'd
With blood of thine already.
Macd. I have no words,
My voice is in my sword, thou bloodier villain
Than terms can give thee out! *Fight. Alarum.*
Macb. Thou losest labor.
As easy mayst thou the intrenchant air
With thy keen sword impress as make me bleed.
Let fall thy blade on vulnerable crests,
I bear a charmed life, which must not yield
To one of woman born.
Macd. Despair thy charm,

41. pull in: rein in, check. **49. estate:** settled order.
50. wrack: ruin. **51. harness:** armor.

V.vi. Location: Dunsinane. Plain before Macbeth's castle.
2. show . . . are: appear in your own forms.
4. battle: battalion. **6. order:** plan of attack.

V.vii. Location: Scene continues.
2. course: round of bearbaiting.

16. still: always.
18. staves: spears. **20. undeeded:** having no deeds to its credit.
22. bruited: announced.
24. gently rend'red: surrendered without resistance.
29. strike beside us: fight on our side (?) or deliberately avoid hitting us (?).

V.viii. Location: Scene continues.
1. Roman fool: i.e. noble suicide.
8. terms . . . out: words can describe.
9. intrenchant: incapable of being cut. **13. Despair:** despair of.

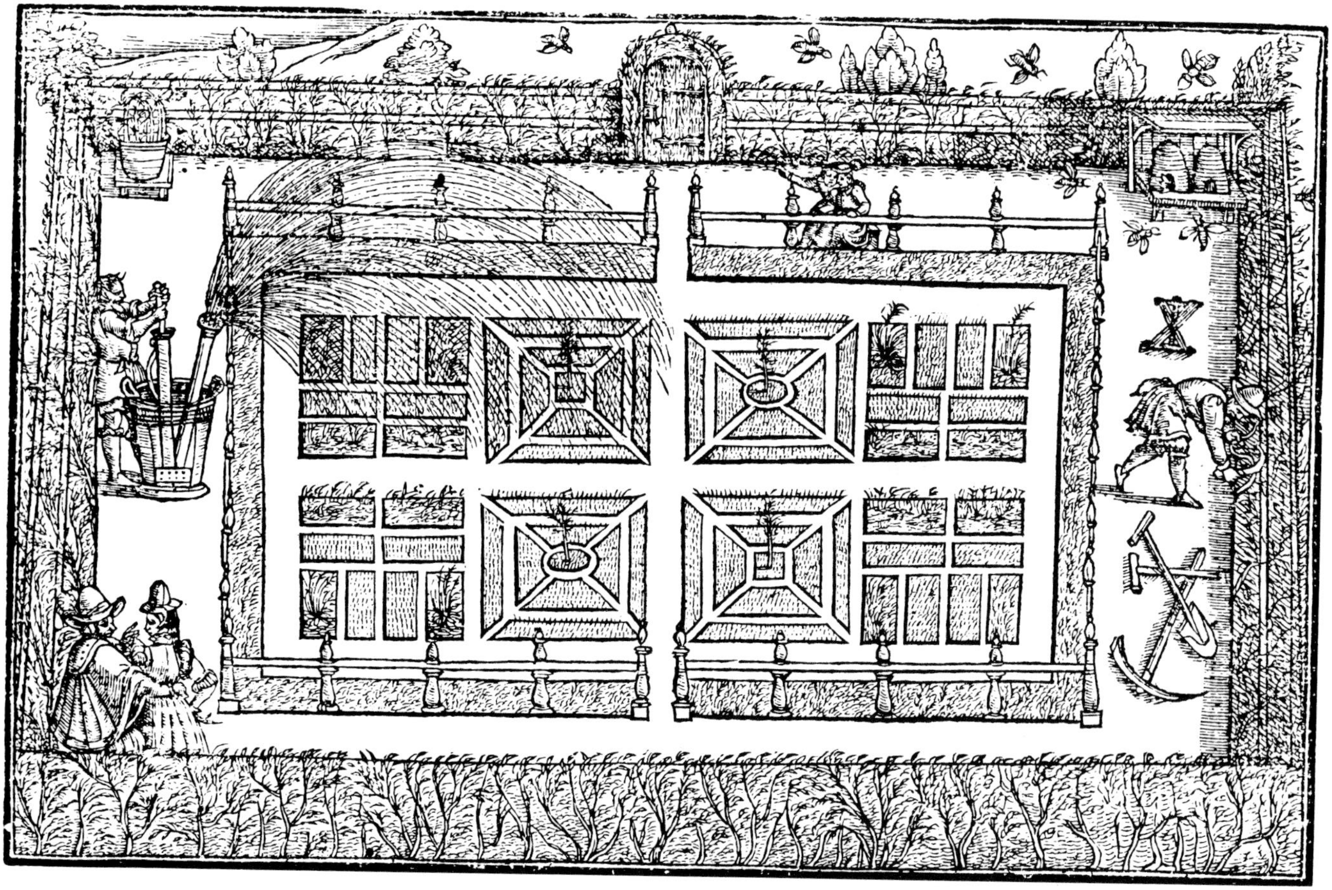

The Englishman's love of his garden is proverbial, and Elizabethan nobility and gentry set great store by a well-planned and well-tended formal garden—or orchard, as it was often called. The design pictured above is generally characteristic. Such a garden was walled for privacy, with a single door ("This other [key] doth command a little door, / Which from the vineyard to the garden leads," *Measure for Measure*, IV.i.32–33), and in addition to the central flower beds and grass plots, geometrically laid out and surrounded by gravel walks, it contained fruit trees trained to grow flat against the inside of the walls. Note the beehives in the upper right corner and the quite sophisticated watering system being operated at left centre. The second picture supplies an element missing in the first: an arbor, complete with table and benches, where the master of the house could entertain his guests with light refreshment, as Master Shallow does in *2 Henry IV* (V.iii). Both woodcuts are from Didymus Mountain [i.e. Thomas Hill], *The Gardener's Labyrinth* (1577).

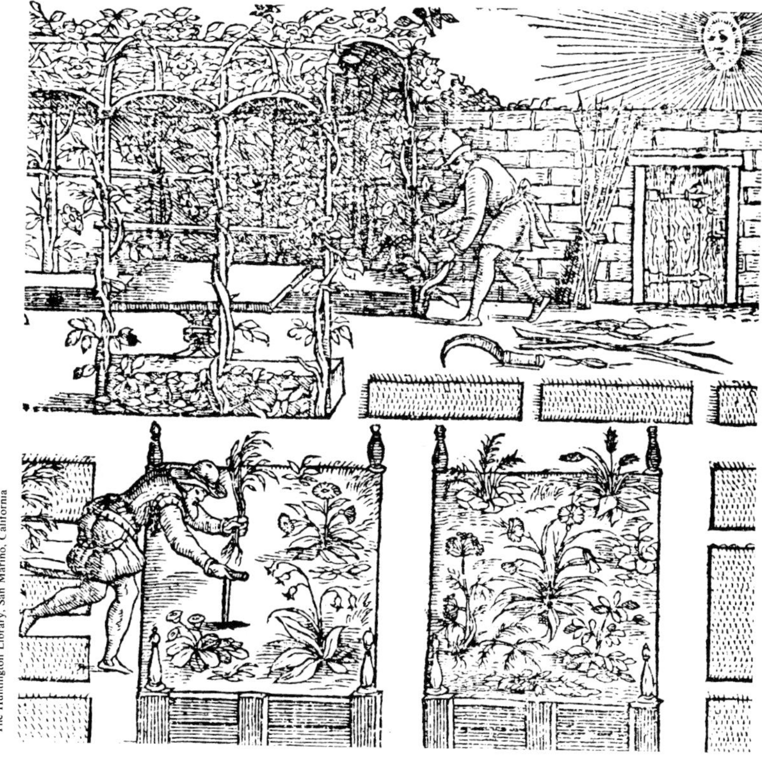

By permission of the Harvard College Library

By permission of the Harvard College Library

Waterworks and fireworks were considered standard parts of special entertainments and often displayed great ingenuity. The woodcuts on this page, from John Bate's *The Mysteries of Nature and Art* (1634), show (above, left) a mechanical trumpeter who rotates and expels a jet of water from his trumpet; (above, right) a wild man or woodwose (a popular character in pageants and processions) who is carrying a large firework; and (below) a fire-drake (i.e. fiery dragon) that runs along a stretched rope as the firework discharges. In *Henry VIII* (V.iii.44) a man with a very red face is called a fire-drake.

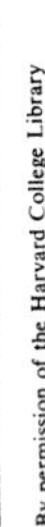

By permission of the Harvard College Library

The handsome engraving facing this page is taken from Famianus Strada's *De Bello Belgico* (Vol. II, 1647). It shows the siege of Neuss by Spanish and Italian forces under Alexander Farnese, Duke of Parma, in 1586, the same year in which Sir Philip Sidney fell at the battle of Zutphen, and illustrates with vivid detail something of the confusion and horror of war that Shakespeare paints in *Henry V* and *1 Henry VI*.

Above (from Robert Ward's *Animadversions of War*, 1639) is a petard, a small war machine with a bell-shaped head charged with gunpowder. This device was fastened against a gate or wall in order to breach it. From the haste with which the man who has just lit the fuse is running away, one may see how, as Hamlet says, the "enginer" might very easily be "Hoist with his own petar" (*Hamlet*, III.iv.206–7). Below is shown an Elizabethan surgeon's chest for use on the battlefield (from William Clowes' *Profitable and Necessary Book of Observations*, 1596). Note the royal arms on the lid. The large peaked tent at the left (like those in the upper right corner of the Strada plate) is of the type called a pavilion (as, for example, in *Troilus and Cressida*, Prologue, line 15).

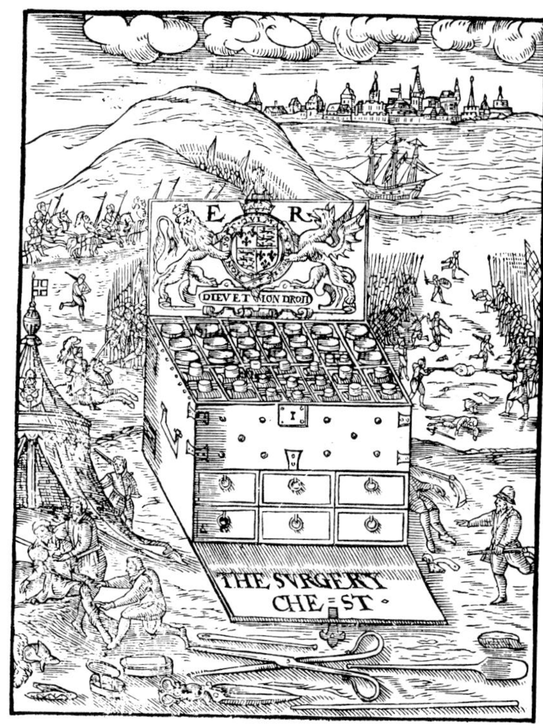

The Folger Shakespeare Library

The Huntington Library, San Marino, California

PLATE 29

The woodcuts on these two pages show Elizabethan gentlemen and huntsmen or foresters (as well as Queen Elizabeth herself) engaged in the pastimes of hawking and hunting. In the upper picture opposite, from the title-page of George Turberville's *The Book of Falconry or Hawking* (1575), one of the three fashionably dressed gentlemen carries on his left fist (gloved for protection) a hooded, belled, and leashed falcon. The dogs are spaniels, used for retrieving the birds "hawk'd at, and kill'd" by the falcon "tow'ring in her pride of place" (*Macbeth*, II.iv.12–13). The lower picture, from Turberville's *The Noble Art of Venery* (1575), represents a stag hunt in progress. Above (from the same book), Queen Elizabeth, at the "kill" of such a hunt, is handed a knife to make assay of "the grease of the deer," i.e. to determine how fat, hence how flavorful, it may be. Prince Hal tells Falstaff, whom he later calls "so fat a deer," that his assay is "three fingers in the ribs" (*1 Henry IV*, IV.ii.73–74, V.iv.107).

from Julian Marshall, *The Annals of Tennis*, 1878. The Boston Public Library

The Huntington Library, San Marino, California

Tennis as practiced in the sixteenth century differed from the modern game principally in being played in a walled and roofed court and in using the walls (end and side) as surfaces from which to ricochet the ball into the opponent's court. Another difference was that points could be scored by driving the ball into one of several artfully placed apertures in the walls. In the court depicted above, note on the left side (the "service side") the window-like opening (the "dedans") below and the small circular hole ("la lune") above the projecting penthouse roof (which likewise figured in the game); on the right (the "hazard side"), the "grille" and another "lune." Shakespeare uses a graphic figure from tennis in *Henry V*. Henry, on hearing of the Dauphin's insulting gift of a tun of tennis balls, answers proudly: "When we have match'd our rackets to these balls, / We will in France, by God's grace, play a set / Shall strike his father's crown into the hazard" (I.ii.261–63). (From *Illustrissimi Wirtembergici Ducalis Novi Collegii Quod Tubingae*, n.d. [c. 1589])

The performing horse Morocco, shown in the woodcut at the left (from John Dando [pseud.], *Maroccus Extaticus, or Banks' Bay Horse in a Trance*, 1594), was famous for the number and variety of his tricks. Shakespeare refers to two of his accomplishments, dancing and arithmetical computation, in *Love's Labor's Lost*: "and how easy it is to put 'years' to the word 'three,' and study three years in two words, the dancing horse will tell you" (I.ii.51–54).

And let the angel whom thou still hast serv'd
Tell thee, Macduff was from his mother's womb
Untimely ripp'd.
Macb. Accursed be that tongue that tells me so,
For it hath cow'd my better part of man!
And be these juggling fiends no more believ'd,
That palter with us in a double sense,
That keep the word of promise to our ear,
And break it to our hope. I'll not fight with thee.
Macd. Then yield thee, coward,
And live to be the show and gaze o' th' time!
We'll have thee, as our rarer monsters are,
Painted upon a pole, and underwrit,
"Here may you see the tyrant."
Macb. I will not yield,
To kiss the ground before young Malcolm's feet,
And to be baited with the rabble's curse.
Though Birnan wood be come to Dunsinane,
And thou oppos'd, being of no woman born,
Yet I will try the last. Before my body
I throw my warlike shield. Lay on, Macduff,
And damn'd be him that first cries, "Hold, enough!"
Exeunt fighting. Alarums.

Enter fighting, and MACBETH *slain.* [MACDUFF *carries off Macbeth's body.*]

[SCENE IX]

Retreat and flourish. Enter, with Drum and Colors, MALCOLM, SIWARD, ROSSE, THANES, *and* SOLDIERS.

Mal. I would the friends we miss were safe arriv'd.
Siw. Some must go off; and yet, by these I see,
So great a day as this is cheaply bought.
Mal. Macduff is missing, and your noble son.
Rosse. Your son, my lord, has paid a soldier's debt.
He only liv'd but till he was a man,
The which no sooner had his prowess confirm'd
In the unshrinking station where he fought,
But like a man he died.
Siw. Then he is dead?
Rosse. Ay, and brought off the field. Your cause of sorrow
Must not be measur'd by his worth, for then
It hath no end.
Siw. Had he his hurts before?
Rosse. Ay, on the front.
Siw. Why then, God's soldier be he!
Had I as many sons as I have hairs,
I would not wish them to a fairer death.
And so his knell is knoll'd.
Mal. He's worth more sorrow,
And that I'll spend for him.
Siw. He's worth no more;
They say he parted well, and paid his score,
And so God be with him! Here comes newer comfort.

Enter MACDUFF *with Macbeth's head.*

Macd. Hail, King! for so thou art. Behold where stands
Th' usurper's cursed head: the time is free.
I see thee compass'd with thy kingdom's pearl,
That speak my salutation in their minds;
Whose voices I desire aloud with mine:
Hail, King of Scotland!
All. Hail, King of Scotland! *Flourish.*
Mal. We shall not spend a large expense of time
Before we reckon with your several loves,
And make us even with you. My thanes and kinsmen,
Henceforth be earls, the first that ever Scotland
In such an honor nam'd. What's more to do,
Which would be planted newly with the time,
As calling home our exil'd friends abroad
That fled the snares of watchful tyranny,
Producing forth the cruel ministers
Of this dead butcher and his fiend-like queen,
Who (as 'tis thought) by self and violent hands
Took off her life; this, and what needful else
That calls upon us, by the grace of Grace,
We will perform in measure, time, and place.
So thanks to all at once and to each one,
Whom we invite to see us crown'd at Scone.
Flourish. Exeunt omnes.

14. angel: bad angel, evil genius. **16. Untimely:** prematurely.
18. better . . . man: i.e. courage. **20. palter:** equivocate.
26. Painted . . . pole: i.e. with your picture carried on a pole.
29. baited: harassed.
32. the last: i.e. his unaided strength and courage.

V.ix. Location: Dunsinane. Macbeth's castle.
2. go off: die. **by:** to judge by.
8. unshrinking . . . fought: station where he fought without shrinking.
16. knoll'd: tolled. **18. parted:** departed.
20. stands. On a pole, according to Holinshed.
22. compass'd . . . pearl: surrounded by the noblest in your realm.
27. reckon: make an accounting.
28. make . . . you: i.e. reward you as you deserve.
31. would . . . time: should be performed as this new era begins.
34. Producing forth: bringing forward for trial.
36. self and violent: her own violent.
39. in . . . place: i.e. with due ceremony at the proper time and place.

NOTE ON THE TEXT

Our only authority for *Macbeth* is the First Folio (1623); all later texts are derived from that source. There is general agreement that the copy behind the F1 text was a prompt-book, probably a scribal transcript based on Shakespeare's "foul papers." A quarto, printed from F1, was published in 1673.

The F1 text is felt to be on the whole a reasonably accurate reproduction of its manuscript copy, but there are a number of reasons for believing that the manuscript itself presented a shortened and somewhat adapted version of the play as Shakespeare originally wrote it. Among the reasons for this view are: the unusual brevity of the F1 text (it is the fifth shortest play in the canon and is at least a thousand lines shorter than any of the other tragedies written after *Julius Caesar* with the exception of *Timon of Athens*, itself a special case); the confusion arising apparently from cutting, possibly even of an entire scene or scenes, and rearrangement (note, for example, the implications of I.vii.46–54 and the raggedness and ambiguity of I.ii); and the intrusion, by a revising hand, most probably Thomas Middleton's, of the Hecate material in the witch scenes (III.v, IV.i.39–43, 125–32). See the Textual Notes for the texts of two songs from Middleton's *The Witch* (date uncertain, but probably c. 1615), which are called for in III.v and IV.i. These exceptional features, and the obviously interpolated compliment to James I in IV.iii.140–59, point to the likelihood that the F1 *Macbeth* may represent a version specially prepared for court performance.

Simon Forman saw a performance of *Macbeth* at the Globe in 1611 (20 April); his account of the performance may be consulted in Appendix C, No. 20. Certain differences between Forman's account and the play as it appeared in F1 suggest that F1's text underwent some (probably, further) revision after 1611; critics have noticed, for example, that Forman makes no mention of Hecate.

For further information, see: J. D. Wilson, ed., New Shakespeare *Macbeth* (Cambridge, 1947); Kenneth Muir, ed., New Arden *Macbeth* (London, 1951); W. W. Greg, *The Shakespeare First Folio* (Oxford, 1955); D. A. Amnéus, "A Missing Scene in *Macbeth,*" *JEGP*, LX (1961), 435–40; Christopher Spencer, *Davenant's "Macbeth" from the Yale Manuscript* (New Haven, 1961) and ed., *Five Restoration Adaptations of Shakespeare* (Urbana, 1965); J. M. Nosworthy, *Shakespeare's Occasional Plays* (London, 1965); G. K. Hunter, ed., New Penguin *Macbeth* (Harmondsworth, Middlesex, 1967); Stanley Wells, Gary Taylor, et al., *William Shakespeare: A Textual Companion* (Oxford, 1987); Nicholas Brooke, ed., New Oxford *Macbeth* (Oxford, 1990); John Jowett and Gary Taylor, "'With New Additions': Theatrical Interpolation in *Measure for Measure* [and *Macbeth*]," in Gary Taylor and John Jowett, *Shakespeare Reshaped, 1606–1623* (Oxford, 1993).

TEXTUAL NOTES

Dramatis personae: *first given in Q (1673); expanded by Rowe and Capell*
Act-scene division: *from F1, with the exception of V.viii, ix, for which F1 indicates no break (see first notes to these scenes); present act-scene arrangement as a whole first established by Wilson*

I.i

Location: *Theobald*
1, 3, 5 s.pp. 1. Witch. . . . 2. Witch. . . . 3. Witch.] *Rowe;* 1 . . . 2 . . . 3 *F1 (throughout)*
9–10 2. Witch. . . . Anon!] *Hunter conj.; All.* Padock calls anon: *F1*

I.ii

Location: *Wilson (after Capell)*
o.s.d. King Duncan, Malcolm] *F2 (subs.);* King Malcome *F1*
o.s.d. Sergeant] *Globe;* Captaine *F1*
1 s.p. Dun.] *Capell;* King. *F1 (throughout)*
7, 25, 34 s.pp. Serg.] *Globe;* Cap. *F1*
13 gallowglasses] *F2 (subs.);* Gallowgrosses *F1*
14 quarrel] *Douai MS, Hanmer;* Quarry *F1*
26 thunders break,] *Pope;* Thunders: *F1;* Thunders breaking *F2*
32 furbish'd] *Rowe;* furbusht *F1*
33–4 Dismay'd . . . Banquo?] *as verse, Douai MS, Pope; as prose, F1*
34 Banquo] *F3;* Banquoh *F1 (the only appearance of this spelling, perhaps Shakespeare's; cf. Holinshed's* Banquho*)*
41 tell—] *Rowe;* tell: *F1*
44 s.d. Exit Sergeant, attended.] *Globe*
59 Norways'] *Steevens;* Norwayes *F1*

I.iii

Location: *Rowe (subs.)*
32 weïrd] *Theobald;* weyward *F1 (F1 varies between* weyward *and* weyard*, the latter probably approximating the pronunciation)*
39 Forres] *Pope* (Foris); Soris *F1*
57 rapt] *Pope;* wrapt *F1*
91 rebels'] *Theobald;* Rebels *F1*
96 make,] *Rowe;* make *F1*
97 death.] *Rowe (subs.);* death, *F1*
98 Came] *Rowe;* Can *F1*
102 herald] *F2;* harrold *F1*
112 did] else did *F2*
116 s.d. Aside.] *Rowe*
117 s.d. To . . . Angus.] *White*
118 s.d. Aside to Banquo.] *Kittredge*
120 s.d. Aside to Macbeth.] *Kittredge*
127, 143 s.dd. Aside.] *Rowe*
130 s.d. Aside.] *Capell*
135 hair] *Rowe;* Heire *F1*
144 him,] *F4;* him *F1*
146 s.d. Aside.] *Hanmer*
153 s.d. Aside to Banquo.] *Kittredge*
154 interim] *Pope;* Interim *F1 (in italics)*

I.iv

Location: *Capell (after Rowe)*
1 Are] *F2;* Or *F1*
25 throne . . . children] *Rowe;* Throne, and State, Children, *F1*
42 Enverness] *ed.;* Envernes *F1;* Enuerns *Holinshed*
45 harbinger] *Rowe;* Herbenger *F1*
48 s.d. Aside.] *Douai MS, Rowe*
53 done,] *Q (1673);* done *F1*

I.v

Location: *Pope (after Rowe)*
1 s.p. Lady M.] *Capell;* Lady. *F1 (throughout)*
1 s.d. Reads.] *Neilson (after Capell)*
8 weïrd] *Theobald;* weyward *F1*
17 human] *Rowe;* humane *F1*
23 "Thus . . . do,"] *quotes, Hunter conj.*
25 Hie] *F4;* High *F1*
28 impedes thee] *Pope;* impeides thee *F1;* thee hinders *F2*
47 it] *F3;* hit *F1*
63 matters. To . . . time,] *Theobald;* matters, to . . . time. *F1*

I.vi

Location: *Theobald*
4 marlet] *Collier MS (after Rowe);* Barlet *F1*
5 lov'd] *Rowe;* loued *F1*
5 mansionry] *Theobald;* Mansonry *F1*
6 jutty,] *Steevens;* Iutty *F1*
8–9 cradle. . . . haunt,] *Rowe;* Cradle, . . . haunt: *F1*
9 most] *Rowe;* must *F1*
13 God 'ield] *Neilson (after Craig);* God-eyld *F1*
26 theirs, in] *Pope;* theirs in *F1*
29 host,] *F3;* Host *F1*

I.vii

Location: *ed. (after Pelican)*
1 well] *Rowe;* well, *F1*
5 be-all . . . end-all] *hyphens, Pope*
5 end-all—here,] *Rowe (subs.);* end all. Heere, *F1*
6 shoal] *Theobald;* Schoole *F1 (probably a variant spelling of* shoal*)*
20 taking-off] *hyphen, Capell*
21 new-born babe] *F4;* New-borne-Babe *F1*
28 other—] *Rowe;* other. *F1*
30 not] *Pope;* not, *F1*
47 do] *Rowe;* no *F1*
55 me;] *Capell (subs., after Rowe);* me, *F1*
68 lies] lye *F2*

II.i

Location: *ed. (after Capell)*
5 s.d. Gives . . . dagger.] *ed. (after Wilson)*
20 weïrd] *Theobald;* weyward *F1*
30 s.d. with Fleance] *Theobald (subs.)*
32 s.d. Servant] *Rowe*
52 Hecat's] *Johnson;* Heccats *F1;* Heccates *F2*
55 strides] *Pope;* sides *F1*
56 sure] *Pope conj.;* sowre *F1*
57 way they] *Rowe;* they may *F1*

II.ii

Location: *ed. (after Wilson)*
4 it:] *Capell (after Rowe);* it, *F1*
8 s.d. Within.] *Steevens*
13 s.d. Enter Macbeth.] *placed as in Globe; after* die. *l. 8, F1*
15 scream] *F4;* schreame *F1*
18 s.d. Looking . . . hands.] *Pope*
32–3 "Sleep . . . sleep"] *quotes, Johnson*
34 sleave] *Seward conj.;* Sleeue *F1*
38 more!"] *Hanmer (subs.);* more *F1*
39–40 "Glamis . . . more."] *quotes, Hanmer*
59 incarnadine] *Rowe;* incarnardine *F1*
60 one red] *Q(1673), F4;* one, Red *F1*
70 s.d. Knock.] *placed as in Capell; after* deed, *l. 70, F1*

II.iii

Location: *ed. (after Wilson)*
5 time!] *Kittredge;* time, *F1*
20 s.d. Opens the gate.] *Malone (after Capell; following l. 21); placed as in Kittredge*
34 to . . . to] *F2;* too . . . too *F1*
42 s.d. Enter Macbeth.] *placed as in Collier; after l. 41, F1*
56 screams] *F4;* Schreemes *F1*
73 s.d. Exeunt . . . Lennox.] *placed as in Dyce; after l. 73, F1*
119, 124 s.dd. Aside to Donalbain.] *Staunton*
121 s.d. Aside to Malcolm.] *Staunton*
125 s.d. Lady . . . out.] *Rowe*
134 s.d. all . . . Donalbain] *Hanmer*

II.iv

Location: *Theobald*
7 travelling] *F3;* trauailing *F1*
16 flung] *F3;* flong *F1*
28 ravin] *Theobald;* rauen *F1*
37 Well,] *Theobald;* Well *F1*

III.i

Location: *Capell, Theobald*
2 **weïrd]** *Theobald;* weyard *F1*
10 s.d. **Lady . . . . Queen, Lennox]** *Capell (after Rowe);* Lady Lenox *F1*
41–2 **night. . . . welcome,]** *Theobald;* Night, . . . welcome: *F1*
43 s.d. **with . . . others]** *ed. (after Rowe, Pelican)*
43 s.d. **Manent . . . Servant.]** *Kittredge*
55 **Genius]** *as Rowe; in italics, F1*
56 **Antony's]** *Douai MS (subs.), Pope;* Anthonies *F1*
74 s.p. **Both Mur.]** *ed.;* Murth. *F1*
75 **speeches?— know]** *Muir;* speeches: Know, *F1*
78 **self?]** *Muir;* selfe. *F1*
105 **heart]** *Pope;* heart; *F1*
114, 138 s.pp. **Both Mur.]** *Dyce;* Murth. *F1*
134 **Fleance]** *F4 (so Holinshed);* Fleans *F1 (throughout rest of play)*
139 s.d. **Exeunt Murderers.]** *Theobald*
141 s.d. **Exit.]** *Theobald;* Exeunt. *F1*

III.ii

Location: *Capell, Theobald (subs.)*
41 **Hecat's]** *F3;* Heccats *F1*
42 **shard-borne]** shard-born *F3*

III.iii

Location: *Rowe (subs.)*
7 **and]** *F2;* end *F1*
16 s.d. **They assault Banquo.]** *Theobald*
18 s.d. **Dies. Fleance escapes.]** *Pope*

III.iv

Location: *Pope (subs.)*
8 s.d. **to the door]** *Capell*
9 **thanks.]** *Pope;* thanks *F1;* thanks, *Q (1673)*
12 s.d. **Goes . . . door.]** *White (subs.)*
33 **a-making,]** *Dyce (comma, Pope);* a making: *F1*
34 **given]** *F3;* giuen, *F1*
69 **I? if]** *Hanmer;* I, if *F1*
72 s.d. **Exit Ghost.]** *F2*
77 **time]** *White;* times *F1*
106 s.d. **Exit Ghost.]** *F2* (Exit.)
120 s.d. **Exeunt]** *F2;* Exit *F1*
120 s.d. **and Attendants]** *Capell*
127 **thou,]** *Rowe;* thou *F1*
128 **bidding?]** *F3;* bidding. *F1*
132 **weïrd]** *Theobald;* weyard *F1*
134 **worst. For]** *Johnson;* worst, for *F1*
143 **in deed]** *Theobald;* indeed *F1*

III.v

Location: *Pelican*
2 **beldams]** *Douai MS* (beldames), *Knight;* (Beldams) *F1*
33 **mortals']** *Theobald;* Mortals *F1*
33 s.d. **Sing . . . etc.]** *placed as in Capell; after l. 35, F1. The song here referred to occurs in Middleton's* The Witch *(written c. 1615), in Davenant's operatic adaptation of* Macbeth *(printed 1674, but produced as early as 1663–4), and in Q (1673). Since it seems highly probable that Davenant derived this song (and the one referred to at IV.i.43; see Textual Notes) from some earlier prompt-book of Shakespeare's* Macbeth *(Middleton's play was not printed until the late eighteenth century), the following text of the song is given from Davenant's version (III.viii).*

Musick and Song.

[*Sing within.*] *Heccate, Heccate, Heccate!* Oh come away:
[*Hec.*] Hark, I am call'd, my little Spirit see,
Sits in a foggy Cloud, and stays for me.
[*Machine descends.*
Sing within. Come away, *Heccate, Heccate!* Oh come away:
Hec. I come, I come, with all the speed I may,
With all the speed I may.
Where's *Stadling?*
2. Here.
Hec. Where's *Puckle?*
3. Here, and *Hopper* too, and *Helway* too.
1. We want but you, we want but you:
Come away make up the Count.
Hec. I will but Noint, and then I mount,
I will but, &c.
1. Here comes down one to fetch his due, a Kiss,
A Cull, a sip of blood.
And why thou staist so long, I muse,
Since th' Air's so sweet and good.
O art thou come; What News?
2. All goes fair for our delight,
Either come, or else refuse,
Now I'm furnish'd for the flight
Now I go, and now I flye,
Malking my sweet Spirit and I.
3. O what a dainty pleasure's this,
To sail i'th' Air while the *Moon* shines fair;
To Sing, to Toy, to Dance and Kiss,
Over Woods, high Rocks and Mountains;
Over Hills, and misty Fountains:
Over Steeples, Towers, and Turrets:
We flye by night 'mongst troops of Spirits.
No Ring of Bells to our Ears sounds,
No howles of Wolves, nor Yelps of Hounds;
No, nor the noise of Waters breach,
Nor Cannons Throats our Height can reach.

The song in The Witch *(III.iii), which actually begins* Come away: Come away: / Heccat: Heccat, Come away *as the s.d. in* Macbeth *suggests, differs in the disposition of the singers (the whole song being divided between Hecate and voices* in the aire, *while* A Spirit like a Cat descends *following* Ther's one comes downe, *etc.) and in a few readings, notably in the lines:* Ouer Seas, our Mistris Fountaines, Ouer Steepe Towres, and Turretts, *(cf.* Over Hills . . . Turrets:*). Q (1673), which also contains two other songs first appearing in Davenant (following II.ii, from Davenant II.v, and II.iii, from Davenant II.v [first 16 lines only]), offers an inferior text of this song, derived almost certainly from Davenant, and the whole song is sung by three Witches only (the line* Over Hills . . . Fountains: *reading* Over misty Hills and Fountains,*).*
35 s.d. **Exit.]** *Capell*

III.vi

Location: *Muir*
21 **'cause]** *Pope;* cause *F1*
24 **son]** *Theobald;* Sonnes *F1*
31 **Siward]** *Theobald (from Holinshed);* Seyward *F1 (throughout)*
38 **the]** *Hanmer;* their *F1*

IV.i

Location: *Rowe (subs.); a "cave scene" was actually used in the Smock Alley (c. 1674–82) production, probably suggested by Davenant's version of the play (1674), and a Cauldorne is called for in the Padua prompt-book (c. 1640)*
5 **throw;]** *Douai MS (subs.), Rowe (subs.);* throw *F1*
7 **thirty-one]** *Capell (subs.);* thirty one: *F1*
23 **Witch's]** *Singer;* Witches *F1*
24 **salt-sea]** *hyphen, Capell*
34 **cau'dron]** *ed.;* Cawdron *F1*
43 s.d. **song: "Black spirits, etc."]** *The song here referred to occurs in Middleton's* The Witch *(c. 1609), V.iii, and in Davenant's adaptation of* Macbeth *(1674), IV.i, but not in Q (1673). The following text of the song, like that printed in the note to III.iv.33 s.d., is taken from Davenant, since it seems probable that he derived it from an earlier prompt-book of Shakespeare's play.*

Musick and Song.

Hec. Black Spirits, and white,
Red Spirits and gray;
Mingle, mingle, mingle,
You that mingle may.
1. *Witch. Tiffin, Tiffin,* keep it stiff in.
2. Fire drake *Puckey,* make it luckey:
Hec. Lyer *Robin,* you must bob in.
Chor. A round, a round, a round, about, about,
All ill come running in, all good keep out.
1. Here's the blood of a Bat!
Hec. O put in that, put in that.
2. Here's Lizards brain.
Hec. Put in a grain.
1. Here's Juice of Toad, here's oyl of Adder
That will make the Charm grow madder.
2. Put in all these, 'twill raise the stanch.
Hec. Nay here's three ownces of a red-hair'd Wench.
Chor. A round, a round, &c.

The text in The Witch *is essentially the same, the most interesting variants being* Libbards Bane *for* Lizards brain, *the* yonker madder *for* the Charm grow madder, *and* rid the Stench *for* raise the stanch.
43 s.d. **Exit Hecat.]** *ed. (after Dyce)*
45 s.d. **Knocking.]** *Collier*
47 **Whoever]** *F3;* who euer *F1*
59 **nature's germains]** *Pope;* Natures Germaine *F1*
59 **all together]** *Pope;* altogether *F1*
63 **masters']** *Capell;* Masters *F1*
65 **grease]** *Pope;* Greaze *F1*
68, 86 s.dd. **Apparition]** Apparation *F1*
69 **power—]** *Rowe;* power. *F1*
73 **thanks;]** *F3 (subs.);* thanks *F1*
74 **more—]** *Rowe;* more. *F1*
83 **assurance]** *Pope;* assurance: *F1*
90 **lion-mettled]** *hyphen, Pope*
93 **Birnan]** *ed.;* Byrnam *F1 (the only occurrence of this form in F1; elsewhere* Byrnan(e) *or* Birnan(e)*; Holinshed has* Bernane *and* Birnane*)*
93 **Dunsinane]** *Rowe;* Dunsmane *F1*
98 **high-plac'd]** *hyphen, F3*
111 s.d. **the eighth]** *Kittredge; F1 s.d. reads:* A shew of eight Kings, and Banquo last, with a glasse in his hand.
114 **gold-bound brow]** *Theobald;* Gold-bound-brow *F1*
124 s.d. **Apparitions vanish.]** *Globe*
130 **antic]** *Theobald;* Antique *F1*
136 **weïrd]** *Theobald;* Weyard *F1*
144 s.d. **Aside.]** *Johnson*

IV.ii

Location: *Theobald (after Rowe)*
1 s.p. **L. Macd.]** *Rowe;* Wife. *F1 (throughout scene)*
10 **diminutive]** *F4;* diminitiue *F1*
23 **'Shall]** *ed.;* Shall *F1*
41 **buy]** *F3;* by *F1*
42 **with all]** *F2;* withall *F1*
49–50 **Every . . . hang'd.]** *as prose, Pope; as verse, F1*
59–60 **Now . . . father?]** *as prose, Pope; as verse, F1*
69–70 **ones. . . . thus,]** *F2 (subs.);* ones . . . thus. *F1*
79 s.d. **Enter Murtherers.]** *placed as in Globe; after l. 79, F1*
80, 82, 83 s.pp. **1. Mur.]** *Capell*
83 s.d. **Stabbing him.]** *Rowe*
85 s.d. **Dies.]** *Capell*
85 s.d. **Lady Macduff . . . and . . . Murderers]** *Theobald (subs.)*

IV.iii

Location: *Dyce (after Rowe)*
4 **birthdom]** *Johnson;* Birthdome *F1*
34 **affeer'd]** *Hanmer;* affear'd *F1*
72 **cold,]** *Theobald;* cold. *F1*
104 **bloody-sceptred]** *hyphen, Pope*

107 **accus'd]** *Wilson;* accust *F1; accurst F2*
109 **sainted king]** *F4;* Sainted-King *F1*
127 **own,]** *F2;* owne. *F1*
133 **thy]** *F2;* they *F1*
133 **here-approach]** *hyphen, Pope*
145 **s.d. Exit Doctor.]** *Capell;* Exit. *F1 (after amend. l. 145)*
148 **here-remain]** *hyphen, Pope*
150 **strangely-visited]** *hyphen, Pope*
170 **dead man's]** *Johnson;* Deadmans *F1*
195–6 **they? . . . cause?]** *Theobald;* they, . . . cause, *F1*
233 **myself;]** *Theobald;* my selfe *F1*
235 **tune]** *Rowe;* time *F1*

V.i

Location: *Capell (subs., after Rowe)*
26–7 **What . . . hands.]** *as prose, Douai MS, Pope; as verse, F1*
37 **fear]** *Rowe;* feare? *F1*
46–7 **Go . . . not.]** *as prose, Douai MS, Pope; as verse, F1*

V.ii

Location: *Capell*
10 **unrough]** *Theobald;* vnruffe *F1*
28 **we,]** *Rowe;* we *F1*

V.iii

Location: *Capell (after Rowe)*
1 **two]** *F2;* too *F1*
19 **s.d. Exit Servant.]** *Dyce*
19–20 **Seyton!— . . . say!—]** *Rowe;* Seyton, I am sick at hart, / When I behold: Seyton, I say, *F1*
21 **disseat]** *Jennens conj.;* dis-eate *F1;* disease *F2*
24 **old age]** *F2;* Old-Age *F1*
39 **her]** *F2*
52 **pristine]** *F2;* pristiue *F1*
60 **s.d. Exeunt . . . Doctor.]** *Dyce (after Steevens)*
62 **s.d. Exit.]** *Steevens;* Exeunt *F1*

V.iv

Location: *Globe (after Pope)*
o.s.d. **Lennox, Rosse]** *Malone*
7 **s.p. Soldiers.]** *Dyce;* Sold. *F1*
14–5 **just censures Attend]** best Censures / Before *F2*

V.v

Location: *Theobald (subs., after Pope)*
7 **s.d. A . . . women.]** *placed as in Dyce; after l. 7, F1*
8 **s.d. Exit.]** *Collier MS*
15 **s.d. Enter Seyton.]** *Collier MS*
37 **false]** *F2;* fhlse *F1*

V.vi

Location: *Capell (after Rowe)*

V.vii

Location: *ed. (after Wilson)*
20 **be;]** *Pope (subs.);* be, *F1*

V.viii

V.viii] *Dyce*
Location: *ed. (after Ridley)*
34 **s.d. Macduff . . body.]** *ed.*

V.ix

V.ix] *Wilson (after Kittredge conj.)*
Location: *ed. (after Wilson)*
41 **s.d. Exeunt omnes.]** Exeunt Omnes. / FINIS. *F1*

The Weird Sisters meet Macbeth and Banquo. From Raphael Holinshed, *The First Volume of the Chronicles of England, Scotland, and Ireland* (1577). This well-known woodcut, from the first edition of Holinshed's *Chronicles*, may or may not have been seen by Shakespeare, who regularly used the second, unillustrated edition (1587). If he knew it, he clearly chose to create his Weird Sisters in a different mould—"so wither'd and so wild in their attire, / That look not like the inhabitants o' th' earth, . . . each at once her choppy finger laying / Upon her skinny lips. You should be women, / And yet your beards forbid me to interpret / That you are so" (*Macbeth*, I.iii.40–47)—namely, in accordance with the contemporary conception of the witch. Holinshed's text describes the figures as "three women in strange and wild apparall, resembling creatures of elder world . . . either the weird sisters, that is (as ye would say) the goddesses of destiny, or else some nymphs or feiries." The woodcut itself depicts figures vaguely resembling the classical ("elder world") Parcae or the Fates, dressed for the most part like Elizabethan ladies of rank. (*By permission of the Harvard College Library*)

Antony and Cleopatra

ANTONY AND CLEOPATRA is Shakespeare's return, after an interval of some eight years, not only to Roman history but to the theme of world empire. From Johnson to Bradley (who called it "the most faultily constructed of all the tragedies"), critics have censured its apparently loose construction —the rapid alternation of short scenes in places remote from one another, which characterizes the third and fourth acts in particular. This has not prevented others from applying Coleridge's famous encomium of the "happy valiancy" of the style to the play as a whole; the bold scene-changes from Rome to Alexandria are now understood as a reflection of a basic thematic opposition. Consequently, and rightly, the play is now quite commonly considered to be among Shakespeare's supreme achievements. An age which has the theatrical conditions necessary to reproduce the rapid flow of scene easily disposes of the objections of Bradley and Johnson. There is now much less to prevent us from sensing, in the theatre or in the study, the sustained interplay of theme and poetry that makes this one of the most highly-wrought of all the tragedies.

The play was first printed in the Folio of 1623. In the Stationers' Register for May 20, 1608, there appears an entry of Edward Blount for "A booke Called Anthony and Cleopatra." This is probably a "blocking entry," i.e. a device to forestall piratical publishers rather than a genuine intention to publish. At any rate, no publication followed. The date of the play is probably somewhat earlier than 1608. In 1607 Daniel brought out a heavily revised version of his *Cleopatra* (originally published in 1594), and his alterations seem to owe something to Shakespeare's play. This suggests late 1606 or early 1607 as the likeliest date for *Antony and Cleopatra*.

Shakespeare may have known the earlier version of Daniel's play, and it has been suggested that he had also looked at the Countess of Pembroke's *Antonius* (1590), a translation of Garnier's *Marc Antoine*. But it has never been denied that his main source was North's version of Plutarch's *Life of Antony*. The debt is indeed great. It is well known that in the famous speech of Enobarbus (II.ii.195) Shakespeare stays remarkably close to North's very words about Cleopatra's barge:

> the poop whereof was of gold, the sails of purple, and the oars of silver, which kept stroke in rowing after the sound of the music of flutes, hautboys, citherns, viols . . . . And now for the person of herself, she was laid under a pavilion of cloth of gold of tissue, apparelled and attired like the goddess Venus commonly drawn in picture; and hard by her, on either hand of her, pretty fair boys apparelled as painters do set forth god Cupid, with little fans in their hands . . .

and so on, for many lines. And this is only the most celebrated of many instances of an unusually intimate relationship with the source. Shakespeare adds little to Plutarch's narrative, nor does he omit much. He even maintains, for the most part, the order in which Plutarch sets down the incidents of the story. Naturally he compresses: the series of events described opened in 40 B.C.; Actium was fought in 31 B.C.; Antony and Cleopatra died in 30 B.C. The play allows one vaguely to suppose that considerable periods of time elapse, but is nowhere specific; and it certainly does not suggest the passage of ten years. Shakespeare runs together events more or less widely separated, such as the news of Fulvia's war, the revolt of Sextus Pompeius, and the advance of the Parthians. He rearranges many minor details, makes only oblique reference to some important political and military events, including the troublesome Parthian campaigns alluded to in I.ii and III.i. He omits to mention Antony's children by Octavia. He ignores the months that elapsed between Actium and the deaths of Antony and Cleopatra, and makes them die on the same day, as they did not. He develops many characters, such as Iras and Charmian, from hints in Plutarch, and Enobarbus is wholly his. Whether he intended to follow a hint of Plutarch's in making the Seleucus scene a deliberate trick Cleopatra plays on Caesar is still disputed. Above all, though he maintains Plutarch's political interest, he greatly changes the main roles. Whatever one's view of the play, it would clearly be inadequate to argue that Shakespeare follows Plutarch in his opinion that the love of Cleopatra was "the last and extremest mischief" that befell Antony. Characters in the play do hold this view; but we remember that the characters in *Othello* who hold Cinthio's views on the lesson to be learned from the story of Desdemona are Iago and Brabantio.

Antony and Cleopatra is a history play, and like the English history plays it embodies certain attitudes towards the events it describes without always making them very explicit. These events are thought of as in some way predetermined, or even as providential; their outcome must be "the time of universal peace" which Caesar prophesies (IV.vi.4), speaking better than he knows. This was "the Augustan peace," during which Christ was born and the pagan Empire—which Virgil called the Empire without end—was established as a divine preparation for the Christian Empire; Octavius, himself a pagan and demanding no veneration, unknowingly prepared a way for the true City, and his struggles affected not merely the state but all human society, the *orbis terrae* of Augustine, the World. Bradley calls the play "the picture of a world catastrophe"; and so it is, for the extinction of the pagan way of life represented by Antony and Cleopatra is a disaster of the same order as the silencing of the oracles, and the death of the god Pan, at the time of Christ's birth. Shakespeare's sense of the world-altering character of the story he tells is conveyed by persistent reminders of the universal authority of Antony and Octavius. Friendship between them would be a "hoop" to hold them "staunch from edge to edge / A' th' world" (II.ii.115–16); by murdering them Pompey can make himself "lord of all the world," owner of "What e'er the ocean pales, or sky inclips" (II.vii.61, 74). Octavia says that war between her husband and her brother would be "As if the world should cleave" (III.iv.31); Antony at Actium loses "half the bulk o' th' world" (III.xi.64); and there are many similar lines—the word *world* occurs some forty-five times in the play. And this world-shaking struggle Octavius had to win for the sake of the future.

Shakespeare divides this world into Rome and Egypt, and under that main division subsumes a series of systematic antitheses: Virtue and Pleasure, empire and self-destruction, firmness and infirmity of purpose, solidity and instability, reason and passion, lucky winner and generous loser, the rising and the falling man; Caesar and Antony, Octavia and Cleopatra. Although Shakespeare somewhat mitigates the adverse opinions on Antony, one could very easily discover in the play a simple moral scheme as expressed by Plutarch, in which Antony neglects his rational responsibilities out of pure sensual indolence and enslavement to a Circe-figure, an enemy of heroic virtue. There is the evidence of the opening lines, usually a strong indication of the moral line to be taken in a Shakespeare play: Antony's Egyptian dotage has subdued his Roman virtue. At the outset he neglects the news from Rome at Cleopatra's command; and the whole of the first scene seems, in isolation, to predict a rich but basically simple study in Antony's falling-off. Later, when he is struck by "a Roman thought," we hear him resolve to break "These strong Egyptian fetters" (I.ii.83, 116), but although he yields to the "strong necessity" (I.iii.42) of the time, his future conduct bears out Caesar's opinion in I.iv; and the defense offered in that scene by Lepidus is one which Hamlet had, before Octavius, pronounced inadequate. Antony's compact with Octavius, his marriage with Octavia, are all forgotten; they may be "strong necessities," but for him Cleopatra is an even stronger one, as Shakespeare suggests by placing immediately after the scene of high Roman politics Enobarbus' description of Cleopatra in her barge. It is a matter of mere minutes of playing time (as against the years that actually passed) till Antony says, "I will to Egypt, . . . I' th' East my pleasure lies" (II.iii.38–40). Returning there after the truce with Pompey, Antony disgusts Octavius with oriental ostentation, forfeits his chance of victory by accepting Cleopatra's military whims and imitating her flight at Actium; emulates her again in an unreasonable maltreatment of a messenger; and, accepting that he, like the "rack," is breaking up, seeks a last affirmation of his Roman *virtus*, manliness and temperate control of passion, as well as courage, in a "Roman" death.

By means of this partial reading, we see that the play can afford a simple and traditional interpretation of the story. A similarly conventional reference may be found in Spenser (*The Faerie Queene*, V.viii.2); and Tasso has it also, using Antony as a warning that sensual indulgence is the enemy of heroic virtue. Shakespeare even bore in mind, and made oblique allusion to, the famous exemplum of Hercules at the Crossroads; this was the tale of the youthful Hercules confronted by Pleasure, with her straight road and easy delights, on the one hand, and Virtue, with her steep path and distant rewards, on the other. Plutarch tells us that Antony claimed descent from Hercules, and sought to confirm this in all his doings; he adds that "there appeared such a manly look in his countenance as is commonly seen in Hercules' pictures." In the comparison of Antony with Demetrius, he relates Antony in the toils of Cleopatra to Hercules made effeminate by Omphale. These and other

Herculean resemblances mentioned by Plutarch are used by Shakespeare; nor is that all, for in order to enhance the Herculean element, the dramatist plays down the Bacchic aspect of Antony, which in Plutarch is of almost equal importance. One of Shakespeare's most striking minor alterations of the source occurs in the beautiful scene (IV.iii) in which the god Hercules deserts Antony; in Plutarch the god is Bacchus. There is no doubt that Shakespeare's presentation of Antony choosing between Roman virtue and the voluptuous banquets of the East contained hints that would enable some of his auditors to relate it to the famous story; and since Voluptas was often given the iconographical attributes of Venus, Cleopatra, so often compared to that goddess, fills the role exactly.

Probably, as Ernst Schanzer has suggested, Shakespeare also wanted us to see the resemblance between his story and another famous account of a conflict between love and the necessities of empire, the desertion of Dido by Aeneas. Had Aeneas not left Dido, there would have been no Rome; had Antony and Egyptian pleasure prevailed, there would have been no Empire. Octavius is the true Aeneas, as Virgil saw; Antony is the Aeneas who stayed with Dido. These moralistic analogues and contrasts strengthen the argument for *Antony and Cleopatra* as basically a play of simple ethical design. Furthermore, there is a current of criticism of Antony's failings throughout; he sees them himself, others comment on them continually; the scene of Ventidius (III.i) and the talk of Antony's injustice over Pompey's house (II.vi.26–29) are inserted to remind us of the ruthlessness and duplicity that go with greatness.

Yet, as Bradley observed, the total effect of the play is as much belied by taking the Roman view of Antony as by taking the Egyptian ("The nobleness of life is to do thus"). The bold rich language of the play, the unforeseen splendor of Cleopatra in the last act, the strange ironies introduced against Caesar, and much else too, conspire to destroy these simple moral paradigms. Under the pressure of historical necessity Voluptas must lose, whether represented by Cleopatra or Falstaff; but the defeat is not the easy and obvious matter of a morality play.

Here we may better understand the defeated by considering the victor. Octavius is a chilly personality, very temperate, efficient, and cunning. Throughout he is a politician (always a bad word in Shakespeare), treacherous when necessary, as to Lepidus and, though overreached, to Cleopatra at the end. He has the Machiavellian *virtù* as well as the Roman *virtus*; and above all he has the luck. Shakespeare spends twenty significant lines on this in II.iii: "The very dice obey him, / And in our sports my better cunning faints / Under his chance." Towards the end the losers remember him and his luck together, almost inseparably: Cleopatra speaks of "the full-fortun'd Caesar" (IV.xv.24) and "The luck of Caesar" (V.ii.286); and, in final defiance, claims that it is "paltry to be Caesar; / Not being Fortune, he's but Fortune's knave, / A minister of her will" (V.ii.2–4). He is "paltry" because he is a mere instrument of Fate, which she intends by dying to command. But, as the word "minister" suggests, Octavius is *fortunatus*, the man of destiny; the future lies with him. And only when, at the moment of death, human empire has come to seem a small matter, can Cleopatra defeat his purposes and deride his quiet conviction that reason and peace lie in his way, not theirs. Yet we are not allowed to think of Cleopatra as merely "cheering herself up"; it was a notable feat of imagination to give Octavius, in the midst of the clinical observations he makes over the dead queen, the most remarkable of all the tributes to "her strong toil of grace": a recognition of a different system of values from those by which he lives, and of the cost of empire in terms of vivid, sensual life. And these values, this life, are also embodied in the play.

For there are other patterns of theme and image which, though they should not stimulate us to uncritical acceptance of the opposite or "Egyptian" view of the whole matter, should certainly not be omitted from any consideration of its total effect. These elements might for convenience be labelled hints of apotheosis and divine fertility. I have mentioned that Antony is insistently associated with Hercules, and Cleopatra with Venus; but it is not less important that they have also associations with Egyptian divinities. Cleopatra appears in the habiliments of the goddess Isis, and accepts (up to the last moment) the affinity with the moon which this identification with its goddess suggests: she is the "terrene moon" reigning over the sphere of Antony's mutability. And Antony plays Osiris to her Isis. The union of these divinities assures the fertility of Egypt; in Plutarch's study of the myth (well known in Shakespeare's time) Osiris is the Nile which floods and makes fertile the land: he is form, the seminal principle, and Isis is matter. From their union are bred not only the crops but animals, such as the serpents of the Nile.[1] Typhon, the crocodile, born of Nile mud, represents for Plutarch the irrational, bestial part of the soul, by which Osiris is deceived and torn to pieces. The presence of this myth in Shakespeare's imagination is suggested by the numerous references to the Nile, its floods, and its serpents. Cleopatra is Antony's "serpent of old Nile" (I.v.25) and she herself speaks twice in II.v of the serpents and "scaled snakes" that breed from the melting of Egypt into Nile. A little later, at the revelry on Pompey's galley, Antony explains the Nile's fertilizing powers (II.vii.17 ff.) and must at once discuss with Lepidus the generation of crocodiles. A Nile serpent is the means of the Queen's death; and the play has many images of earth and water, the elements Cleopatra expressly abandons "to baser life" in her dying speech. In his first extended speech Antony wants Rome to melt in Tiber (as he has melted into Egypt); and the luxury and feasting of the Egyptian court image a natural plenty which is curbed by no Roman temperance. From the

[1] Shakespeare was perhaps remembering Spenser, as he so often did; and especially *The Faerie Queene*, III.viii.8.

Egyptian point of view, Octavius is the Typhon-crocodile—treacherous, powerful creature, destructive of natural beauty yet also an emblem of the sun—who destroys Osiris.

There is obviously in the play a strong sense of the goodness of this fertility, destructive as it must be in its intemperance, and of the godlike status of its agents. Thus when Antony disintegrates in the fourth act, it seems that an age is ending; and the extraordinary lamentation of Cleopatra—

O, wither'd is the garland of the war,
The soldier's pole is fall'n! Young boys and girls
Are level now with men; the odds is gone,
And there is nothing left remarkable
Beneath the visiting moon— (IV.xv.64–68)

leads into the vision of Antony as not merely the ruler of the world, but almost the world itself—as power, fertility, riches—in an age now past. That great speech (V.ii.76 ff.) leaves its effect with the auditor when the gentle remonstrations of Dolabella are forgotten. At the end of the play Caesar looks forward to the imperial future; yet the last hours of Cleopatra seem to assert a divine generosity that makes his pact with Fortune and his worldly happiness seem mean and conventional. Roman values are at this moment not to be applied to the excesses of Egypt, even by Romans.

Much has been written about the characterization of Cleopatra. On the ethical level she is irresponsible in every way—lubricious, cruel, self-regarding; but to disregard the divine attributes of this "triple-turn'd whore" (IV.xii.13) is to ignore the text. The testimony of Enobarbus to the enchantments of "this great fairy" (IV.viii.12) are later echoed by Dolabella and by Caesar himself. Most of all, those lines of Charmian—"O eastern star . . ." (V.ii.308), "It is well done, and fitting for a princess / Descended of so many royal kings" (V.ii.326–27)—are as clear an indication as Shakespeare can give that we are to find this noble (even if it involves self-deception), not only by contrast with her wantonness in earlier scenes, but also by contrast with policied Caesar. Empire is necessary; but it cannot therefore be held that natural fecundity, the banqueting and lovemaking that belong to the state which lacks these supernaturally sanctioned restraints, is not to be regretted. Because she contributes so vitally to the natural values of the Egypt of the play, without ever becoming a mere type of Riot, and at the end moves into her own imperial dignities without any discontinuity, Cleopatra deserves to be called the greatest of Shakespeare's female characterizations. The fluctuations of her moods are reflected in the less volatile Antony; his Roman qualities are dispersed, replaced by an Egyptian fluctuation of temperament, which finally breaks him up like the cloud of which he speaks to Eros (IV.xiv.2 ff.). With him and with the rock-like, stable Octavius one feels again that superbly easy grasp of personality, of thematic and narrative interests fully identified, which are Shakespeare's only. Structurally the use of Octavia, and of Enobarbus, and of many other minor figures, is equally assured; one notes especially the skill with which the defection of Enobarbus is turned into a tribute to Antony's boundless generosity of mind. It is the same power to choose the right, unexpected detail that makes for the greatness of the purely atmospheric scene in which the god Hercules leaves Antony.

The verse of *Antony and Cleopatra* is Shakespeare's late manner at its happiest—muscular, prolific of metaphor, crowded with meaning, yet lacking the occasionally extreme harshness and obscurity that can be found in *Coriolanus*, and even in the Romances. Thus the plot of the play is endlessly modified by the complex figurations of the poetry, to a degree that makes all explication desperately partial. What we may surely say is that Shakespeare's moral is not Plutarch's: "the unreined horse of concupiscence did put out of Antony's head all honest and commendable thoughts." Shakespeare's Antony certainly "would make his will / Lord of his reason" (III.xiii.3–4); but "will" in this sense is the pleasures of the senses, represented not merely as a voluptuary's weakness, the soft beds of the East, but as a divine fertility like that of the Nile; it is the richness of the world of Isis before the death of Osiris and the birth of the Empire under temperate Caesar.

Frank Kermode

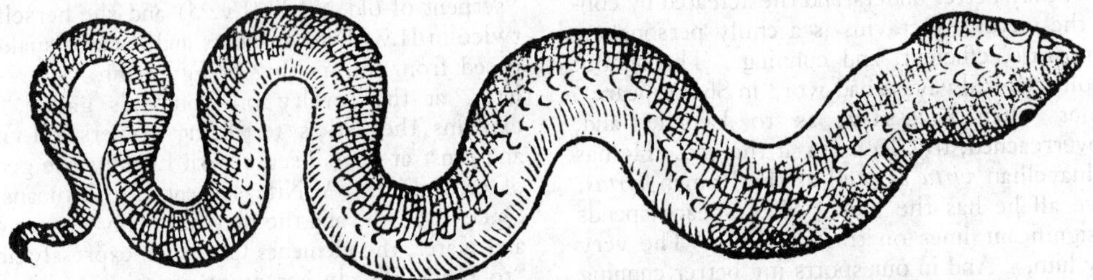

An asp—"the pretty worm of Nilus." From Edward Topsell, *The History of Serpents* (1608). Near the end of *Antony and Cleopatra* (V.ii.245–58) the Clown ("a rural fellow") warns Cleopatra: "I would not be the party that should desire to touch him, for his biting is immortal; those that do die of it do seldom or never recover . . . . the worm's an odd worm." But when he leaves her, sensing how she intends to use the asps he has brought her, he says with a deep human understanding of the situation: "I wish you joy of the worm." (*By permission of the Harvard College Library*)

The Tragedy of Antony and Cleopatra

[Dramatis Personae

MARK ANTONY, OCTAVIUS CAESAR, M. AEMILIUS LEPIDUS — *triumvirs*
SEXTUS POMPEIUS
DOMITIUS ENOBARBUS, VENTIDIUS, EROS, SCARUS, DECRETAS, DEMETRIUS, PHILO — *friends to Antony*
CANIDIUS, *lieutenant-general to Antony*
MAECENAS, AGRIPPA, DOLABELLA, PROCULEIUS, THIDIAS, GALLUS — *friends to Caesar*
TAURUS, *lieutenant-general to Caesar*
MENAS, MENECRATES, VARRIUS — *friends to Pompey*

SILIUS, *an officer in Ventidius' army*
SCHOOLMASTER, *acting as an ambassador from Antony to Caesar*
ALEXAS, MARDIAN, *a eunuch*, SELEUCUS, DIOMEDES — *attendants on Cleopatra*
SOOTHSAYER
LAMPRIUS, RANNIUS, LUCILLIUS, *three Romans appearing as mutes in I.ii*
CLOWN

CLEOPATRA, *Queen of Egypt*
OCTAVIA, *sister to Caesar and wife to Antony*
CHARMIAN, IRAS — *attendants on Cleopatra*

OFFICERS, SOLDIERS, MESSENGERS, *and other* ATTENDANTS

SCENE: *In several parts of the Roman Empire*]

ACT I, SCENE I

Enter DEMETRIUS *and* PHILO.

Phi. Nay, but this dotage of our general's
O'erflows the measure. Those his goodly eyes,
That o'er the files and musters of the war
Have glow'd like plated Mars, now bend, now turn
The office and devotion of their view
Upon a tawny front; his captain's heart,
Which in the scuffles of great fights hath burst
The buckles on his breast, reneges all temper,
And is become the bellows and the fan
To cool a gipsy's lust.

Flourish. Enter ANTONY, CLEOPATRA, *her* LADIES, *the* TRAIN, *with eunuchs fanning her.*

Look where they come!
Take but good note, and you shall see in him
The triple pillar of the world transform'd
Into a strumpet's fool. Behold and see.

Cleo. If it be love indeed, tell me how much.
Ant. There's beggary in the love that can be reckon'd.
Cleo. I'll set a bourn how far to be belov'd.
Ant. Then must thou needs find out new heaven, new earth.

Enter a MESSENGER.

Mess. News, my good lord, from Rome.
Ant. Grates me, the sum.

Words and passages enclosed in square brackets in the text above are either emendations of the copy-text or additions to it. The Textual Notes immediately following the play cite the earliest authority for every such change or insertion and supply the reading of the copy-text wherever it is emended in this edition.

I.i. Location: Alexandria. Cleopatra's palace.
4. plated: in armor. **5. office:** service.
6. tawny front: dark face.
8. reneges: renounces. (The *g* is hard.) **temper:** self-restraint.
10. gipsy: Egyptian (of which *gipsy* is a shortened form). Gipsies were thought to have originated in Egypt. **s.d. Flourish:** trumpet fanfare.
12. triple pillar: i.e. one of the three pillars (triumvirs).
13. fool: dupe, plaything. **16. bourn:** limit.
18. Grates: it irritates. **the sum:** give me the gist.

Cleo. Nay, hear them, Antony.
Fulvia perchance is angry; or who knows
If the scarce-bearded Caesar have not sent
His pow'rful mandate to you: "Do this, or this;
Take in that kingdom, and enfranchise that;
Perform't, or else we damn thee."
Ant. How, my love?
Cleo. Perchance? Nay, and most like.
You must not stay here longer, your dismission
Is come from Caesar, therefore hear it, Antony.
Where's Fulvia's process?—Caesar's, I would say—
both?
Call in the messengers. As I am Egypt's queen,
Thou blushest, Antony, and that blood of thine
Is Caesar's homager; else so thy cheek pays shame
When shrill-tongu'd Fulvia scolds. The messengers!
Ant. Let Rome in Tiber melt, and the wide arch
Of the rang'd empire fall! Here is my space,
Kingdoms are clay; our dungy earth alike
Feeds beast as man; the nobleness of life
Is to do thus [*embracing*]—when such a mutual pair
And such a twain can do't, in which I bind,
[On] pain of punishment, the world to weet
We stand up peerless.
Cleo. Excellent falsehood!
Why did he marry Fulvia, and not love her?
I'll seem the fool I am not. Antony
Will be himself.
Ant. But stirr'd by Cleopatra.
Now for the love of Love, and her soft hours,
Let's not confound the time with conference harsh;
There's not a minute of our lives should stretch
Without some pleasure now. What sport to-night?
Cleo. Hear the ambassadors.
Ant. Fie, wrangling queen!
Whom every thing becomes—to chide, to laugh,
To weep; [whose] every passion fully strives
To make itself (in thee) fair and admir'd!
No messenger but thine, and all alone,
To-night we'll wander through the streets and note
The qualities of people. Come, my queen,
Last night you did desire it. [*To the Messenger.*] Speak
not to us.
Exeunt [*Antony and Cleopatra*] *with the Train,*
[*followed by the Messenger*].
Dem. Is Caesar with Antonius priz'd so slight?
Phi. Sir, sometimes when he is not Antony,
He comes too short of that great property
Which still should go with Antony.
Dem. I am full sorry
That he approves the common liar, who

19. **them:** i.e. the news. 20. **Fulvia:** Antony's wife.
21. **scarce-bearded.** Octavius Caesar was twenty-three at this time (40 B.C.), Antony about twenty years older.
26. **dismission:** order to depart. 28. **process:** summons.
31. **Is Caesar's homager:** does homage to Caesar.
34. **rang'd:** ordered (?) or far-flung (?).
37. **mutual:** i.e. equal in passion. 39. **weet:** know.
42. **the fool . . . not:** i.e. so gullible as to believe him.
43. **stirr'd:** inspired. 45. **confound:** destroy, i.e. waste.
50. **passion:** emotion, mood. 54. **qualities:** characteristics.
56. **with:** by. 58. **property:** distinctive quality.
59. **still:** always.
60. **approves:** confirms. **the common liar:** i.e. general gossip, usually untrue.

Thus speaks of him at Rome; but I will hope
Of better deeds to-morrow. Rest you happy!
Exeunt.

[Scene II]

Enter Enobarbus, Lamprius, *a* Soothsayer, Rannius, Lucillius, Charmian, Iras, Mardian *the Eunuch, and* Alexas.

Char. Lord Alexas, sweet Alexas, most any thing Alexas, almost most absolute Alexas, where's the soothsayer that you prais'd so to th' Queen? O that I knew this husband, which, you say, must change his horns with garlands!
Alex. Soothsayer!
Sooth. Your will?
Char. Is this the man? Is't you, sir, that know things?
Sooth. In nature's infinite book of secrecy
A little I can read.
Alex. Show him your hand.
Eno. [*To Servants within.*] Bring in the banket quickly; wine enough,
Cleopatra's health to drink.
Char. Good sir, give me good fortune.
Sooth. I make not, but foresee.
Char. Pray then, foresee me one.
Sooth. You shall be yet far fairer than you are.
Char. He means in flesh.
Iras. No, you shall paint when you are old.
Char. Wrinkles forbid!
Alex. Vex not his prescience, be attentive.
Char. Hush!
Sooth. You shall be more beloving than beloved.
Char. I had rather heat my liver with drinking.
Alex. Nay, hear him.
Char. Good now, some excellent fortune! Let me be married to three kings in a forenoon, and widow them all. Let me have a child at fifty, to whom Herod of Jewry may do homage. Find me to marry me with Octavius Caesar, and companion me with my mistress.
Sooth. You shall outlive the lady whom you serve.
Char. O, excellent, I love long life better than figs.
Sooth. You have seen and prov'd a fairer former fortune
Than that which is to approach.
Char. Then belike my children shall have no

I.ii. **Location:** Alexandria. Cleopatra's palace.
o.s.d. **Lamprius . . . Lucillius.** Lamprius (unless he is the Soothsayer), Rannius, and Lucillius have no lines in this scene and do not appear again. Mardian, though mute here, is a speaking character in later scenes. 2. **absolute:** perfect.
4. **change:** i.e. dress up. Most editors prefer Warburton's *charge*, "load." In either case the betrayed husband is to have his cuckold's horns decked with flowers, like those of a sacrificial beast happily unaware of his fate.
12. **banket:** banquet, i.e. light repast of wine, fruit, etc.
18. **in flesh.** *Fair in flesh* = plump.
21. **his prescience.** A mock title patterned after such honorifics as *his worship, his reverence.*
24. **with drinking:** i.e. rather than with loving. The liver was regarded as the seat of sexual passion. 26. **Good:** good sir.
28. **Herod:** i.e. even Herod, who had ordered the Slaughter of the Innocents and whom the miracle plays had established as the type of the raging tyrant. 33. **prov'd:** experienced.
35–36. **have no names:** be illegitimate.

names. Prithee, how many boys and wenches must I have?

Sooth. If every of your wishes had a womb,
And [fertile] every wish, a million.

Char. Out, fool, I forgive thee for a witch.

Alex. You think none but your sheets are privy to your wishes.

Char. Nay, come, tell Iras hers.

Alex. We'll know all our fortunes.

Eno. Mine, and most of our fortunes to-night, shall be—drunk to bed.

Iras. There's a palm presages chastity, if nothing else.

Char. E'en as the o'erflowing Nilus presageth famine.

Iras. Go, you wild bedfellow, you cannot soothsay.

Char. Nay, if an oily palm be not a fruitful prognostication, I cannot scratch mine ear. Prithee tell her but a worky-day fortune.

Sooth. Your fortunes are alike.

Iras. But how, but how? give me particulars.

Sooth. I have said.

Iras. Am I not an inch of fortune better than she?

Char. Well, if you were but an inch of fortune better than I, where would you choose it?

Iras. Not in my husband's nose.

Char. Our worser thoughts heavens mend! Alexas—come, his fortune, his fortune! O, let him marry a woman that cannot go, sweet Isis, I beseech thee! and let her die too, and give him a worse! and let worse follow worse, till the worst of all follow him laughing to his grave, fiftyfold a cuckold! Good Isis, hear me this prayer, though thou deny me a matter of more weight; good Isis, I beseech thee!

Iras. Amen. Dear goddess, hear that prayer of the people! for, as it is a heart-breaking to see a handsome man loose-wiv'd, so it is a deadly sorrow to behold a foul knave uncuckolded; therefore, dear Isis, keep decorum, and fortune him accordingly!

Char. Amen.

Alex. Lo now, if it lay in their hands to make me a cuckold, they would make themselves whores but they'ld do't!

Enter CLEOPATRA.

Eno. Hush, here comes Antony.
Char. Not he, the Queen.
Cleo. [Saw] you my lord?
Eno. No, lady.
Cleo. Was he not here?
Char. No, madam.
Cleo. He was dispos'd to mirth, but on the sudden

A Roman thought hath strook him. Enobarbus!
Eno. Madam?
Cleo. Seek him, and bring him hither. Where's Alexas?
Alex. Here, at your service. My lord approaches.

Enter ANTONY *with a* MESSENGER [*and* ATTENDANTS].

Cleo. We will not look upon him. Go with us.
Exeunt [*Cleopatra, Enobarbus, and Train*].

Mess. Fulvia thy wife first came into the field.
Ant. Against my brother Lucius?
Mess. Ay;
But soon that war had end, and the time's state
Made friends of them, jointing their force 'gainst Caesar,
Whose better issue in the war from Italy,
Upon the first encounter, drave them.
Ant. Well, what worst?
Mess. The nature of bad news infects the teller.
Ant. When it concerns the fool or coward. On:
Things that are past are done with me. 'Tis thus:
Who tells me true, though in his tale lie death,
I hear him as he flatter'd.
Mess. Labienus
(This is stiff news) hath with his Parthian force
Extended Asia; from Euphrates
His conquering banner shook, from Syria
To Lydia and to Ionia,
Whilst—
Ant. Antony, thou wouldst say—
Mess. O, my lord!
Ant. Speak to me home, mince not the general tongue;
Name Cleopatra as she is call'd in Rome.
Rail thou in Fulvia's phrase, and taunt my faults
With such full license as both truth and malice
Have power to utter. O then we bring forth weeds
When our quick winds lie still, and our ills told us
Is as our earing. Fare thee well awhile.
Mess. At your noble pleasure. *Exit Messenger.*
Ant. From Sicyon how the news? Speak there!
1. [*Att.*] The man from Sicyon—is there such an one?
2. [*Att.*] He stays upon your will.
Ant. Let him appear.
These strong Egyptian fetters I must break,
Or lose myself in dotage.

Enter another MESSENGER *with a letter.*

What are you?
[2.] *Mess.* Fulvia thy wife is dead.
Ant. Where died she?

36. wenches: girls.
40. Out: an expression of indignation or reproach. **I . . . witch:** I exonerate you from the charge of witchcraft, i.e. I don't think much of your performance as a soothsayer.
52. oily palm: moist palm (considered a sign of licentiousness).
52–53. fruitful prognostication: presager of fertility.
54. worky-day: ordinary, commonplace.
64. cannot go: is an unsatisfactory sexual partner (?). **Isis:** chief goddess of the Egyptians, sometimes identified with the moon-goddess.
66. follow him: i.e. follow his coffin as a presumed mourner.
73. foul: ugly.
73–74. keep decorum: deal appropriately with the case.

92. jointing: uniting. **93. better issue:** success.
99. as: as if. **Labienus:** Quintus Labienus, who had supported Brutus and Cassius against the triumvirate, had secured a force from the king of Parthia and at its head was overrunning the Roman provinces in Asia. **101. Extended:** seized upon.
105. home: i.e. frankly and bluntly. **mince:** cut fine, i.e. reduce, tone down. **general tongue:** common talk. **108. malice:** ill will.
110. quick winds: fertile furrows (dialect *wints*) (?) or fresh breezes (supposedly good for the soil; cf. *3 Henry VI*, II.vi.21, "For what doth cherish weeds but gentle air?") (?). Most editors emend *winds* to *minds*, following Warburton.
111. earing: being ploughed (to destroy the weeds).
113. Sicyon: town in Greece where Antony had left Fulvia.

[2.] *Mess.* In Sicyon:
Her length of sickness, with what else more serious
Importeth thee to know, this bears. [*Gives a letter.*]
Ant. Forbear me. [*Exit Second Messenger.*]
There's a great spirit gone! Thus did I desire it.
What our contempts doth often hurl from us,
We wish it ours again. The present pleasure,
By revolution low'ring, does become
The opposite of itself. She's good, being gone;
The hand could pluck her back that shov'd her on.
I must from this enchanting queen break off;
Ten thousand harms, more than the ills I know,
My idleness doth hatch. How now, Enobarbus?

Enter ENOBARBUS.

Eno. What's your pleasure, sir?

Ant. I must with haste from hence.

Eno. Why then we kill all our women. We see how mortal an unkindness is to them; if they suffer our departure, death's the word.

Ant. I must be gone.

Eno. Under a compelling occasion, let women die. It were pity to cast them away for nothing, though between them and a great cause, they should be esteem'd nothing. Cleopatra, catching but the least noise of this, dies instantly; I have seen her die twenty times upon far poorer moment. I do think there is mettle in death, which commits some loving act upon her, she hath such a celerity in dying.

Ant. She is cunning past man's thought.

Eno. Alack, sir, no, her passions are made of nothing but the finest part of pure love. We cannot call her winds and waters sighs and tears; they are greater storms and tempests than almanacs can report. This cannot be cunning in her; if it be, she makes a show'r of rain as well as Jove.

Ant. Would I had never seen her!

Eno. O, sir, you had then left unseen a wonderful piece of work, which not to have been blest withal would have discredited your travel.

Ant. Fulvia is dead.

Eno. Sir?

Ant. Fulvia is dead.

Eno. Fulvia?

Ant. Dead.

Eno. Why, sir, give the gods a thankful sacrifice. When it pleaseth their deities to take the wife of a man from him, it shows to man the tailors of the earth; comforting therein, that when old robes are worn out, there are members to make new. If there were no more women but Fulvia, then had you indeed a cut, and the case to be lamented. This grief is crown'd with consolation: your old smock brings forth a new petticoat, and indeed the tears live in an onion that should water this sorrow.

Ant. The business she hath broached in the state
Cannot endure my absence.

Eno. And the business you have broach'd here cannot be without you, especially that of Cleopatra's, which wholly depends on your abode.

Ant. No more light answers. Let our officers
Have notice what we purpose. I shall break
The cause of our expedience to the Queen,
And get her [leave] to part. For not alone
The death of Fulvia, with more urgent touches,
Do strongly speak to us; but the letters too
Of many our contriving friends in Rome
Petition us at home. Sextus Pompeius
[Hath] given the dare to Caesar, and commands
The empire of the sea. Our slippery people,
Whose love is never link'd to the deserver
Till his deserts are past, begin to throw
Pompey the Great and all his dignities
Upon his son, who, high in name and power,
Higher than both in blood and life, stands up
For the main soldier; whose quality, going on,
The sides o' th' world may danger. Much is breeding,
Which, like the courser's hair, hath yet but life,
And not a serpent's poison. Say our pleasure,
To such whose places under us require,
Our quick remove from hence.

Eno. I shall do't. [*Exeunt.*]

[SCENE III]

Enter CLEOPATRA, CHARMIAN, ALEXAS, *and* IRAS.

Cleo. Where is he?

Char. I did not see him since.

Cleo. See where he is, who's with him, what he does.
I did not send you. If you find him sad,
Say I am dancing; if in mirth, report
That I am sudden sick. Quick, and return. [*Exit Alexas.*]

Char. Madam, methinks if you did love him dearly,
You do not hold the method to enforce

121. **Forbear:** leave.
125. **By revolution low'ring:** brought downward by the shifting of our feelings (as on a turning wheel).
127. **could:** i.e. would now gladly.
128. **enchanting:** casting a spell. 141. **noise:** rumor.
142. **poorer moment:** slighter cause.
143–44. **there . . . dying:** i.e. death must be a satisfying lover (*mettle* = sexual vigor), so quickly she succumbs to him. Enobarbus plays on *die* in the sense "experience sexual climax."
155. **discredited your travel:** proved you a bad sightseer.
163–65. **it . . . new:** it reveals to a man that there are means of making more women to replace those that are worn-out, as tailors replace old robes. Enobarbus continues his bawdy punning through this speech and the next. 166. **cut:** wound.

171. **broached:** opened up. 175. **abode:** remaining.
176. **our.** Antony shifts to the royal plural.
178. **expedience:** haste. 179. **part:** depart.
180. **urgent touches:** pressing motives.
182. **contriving:** conspiring with us, on our side.
183. **Petition . . . home:** beg for my return to Rome. **Sextus Pompeius:** son of Pompey the Great, who controlled the sea routes by virtue of his possession of Sicily.
185. **slippery people:** fickle populace. 187. **throw:** confer.
190. **blood and life:** courage and vigor.
190–91. **stands up For:** is winning a position as.
191. **main:** leading, chief. **quality:** nature and position. **going on:** i.e. if this development continues.
192. **sides:** frame. **danger:** endanger.
193. **courser's hair.** It was believed that a horse-hair if put into water would come to life as a snake.

I.iii. Location: Alexandria. Cleopatra's palace.
1. **since:** lately. 3. **sad:** serious.
7. **hold the method:** pursue the right course.

The like from him.
Cleo. What should I do, I do not?
Char. In each thing give him way, cross him in nothing.
Cleo. Thou teachest like a fool: the way to lose him.
Char. Tempt him not so too far; I wish, forbear.
In time we hate that which we often fear.

Enter ANTONY.

But here comes Antony.
Cleo. I am sick and sullen.
Ant. I am sorry to give breathing to my purpose—
Cleo. Help me away, dear Charmian, I shall fall.
It cannot be thus long, the sides of nature
Will not sustain it.
Ant. Now, my dearest queen—
Cleo. Pray you stand farther from me.
Ant. What's the matter?
Cleo. I know by that same eye there's some good news.
What, says the married woman you may go?
Would she had never given you leave to come!
Let her not say 'tis I that keep you here,
I have no power upon you; hers you are.
Ant. The gods best know—
Cleo. O, never was there queen
So mightily betrayed! yet at the first
I saw the treasons planted.
Ant. Cleopatra—
Cleo. Why should I think you can be mine, and true
(Though you in swearing shake the throned gods),
Who have been false to Fulvia? Riotous madness,
To be entangled with those mouth-made vows,
Which break themselves in swearing!
Ant. Most sweet queen—
Cleo. Nay, pray you seek no color for your going,
But bid farewell, and go. When you sued staying,
Then was the time for words; no going then;
Eternity was in our lips and eyes,
Bliss in our brows' bent; none our parts so poor
But was a race of heaven. They are so still,
Or thou, the greatest soldier of the world,
Art turn'd the greatest liar.
Ant. How now, lady?
Cleo. I would I had thy inches, thou shouldst know
There were a heart in Egypt.
Ant. Hear me, Queen:
The strong necessity of time commands
Our services awhile; but my full heart
Remains in use with you. Our Italy
Shines o'er with civil swords; Sextus Pompeius
Makes his approaches to the port of Rome;
Equality of two domestic powers
Breed scrupulous faction; the hated, grown to strength,
Are newly grown to love; the condemn'd Pompey,
Rich in his father's honor, creeps apace
Into the hearts of such as have not thrived
Upon the present state, whose numbers threaten,
And quietness, grown sick of rest, would purge
By any desperate change. My more particular,
And that which most with you should safe my going,
Is Fulvia's death.
Cleo. Though age from folly could not give me freedom,
It does from childishness. Can Fulvia die?
Ant. She's dead, my queen.
Look here, and at thy sovereign leisure read
The garboils she awak'd: at the last, best,
See when and where she died.
Cleo. O most false love!
Where be the sacred vials thou shouldst fill
With sorrowful water? Now I see, I see,
In Fulvia's death, how mine receiv'd shall be.
Ant. Quarrel no more, but be prepar'd to know
The purposes I bear; which are, or cease,
As you shall give th' advice. By the fire
That quickens Nilus' slime, I go from hence
Thy soldier, servant, making peace or war
As thou affects.
Cleo. Cut my lace, Charmian, come!
But let it be; I am quickly ill, and well,
So Antony loves.
Ant. My precious queen, forbear,
And give true evidence to his love, which stands
An honorable trial.
Cleo. So Fulvia told me.
I prithee turn aside, and weep for her,
Then bid adieu to me, and say the tears
Belong to Egypt. Good now, play one scene
Of excellent dissembling, and let it look
Like perfect honor.
Ant. You'll heat my blood; no more.
Cleo. You can do better yet; but this is meetly.
Ant. Now, by [my] sword—
Cleo. And target.—Still he mends.
But this is not the best. Look, prithee, Charmian,
How this Herculean Roman does become

11. Tempt: try. **I wish:** I wish you would, i.e. my advice is.
13. sullen: depressed. **14. breathing:** utterance.
16. sides of nature: human frame.
20. the married woman: i.e. Fulvia.
31. break . . . swearing: are broken even while they are being sworn.
32. color: pretext. **33. sued staying:** begged to stay.
35. our. The royal plural. **36. bent:** arch.
37. was . . . heaven: was of divine origin (*race* = root) (?) or tasted of heaven (*race* = flavor) (?).
41. heart: i.e. a capacity for resenting insults. **Egypt:** the Queen of Egypt. **44. in use:** in trust (legal term).
45. civil: of civic factions.
48. scrupulous faction: divisive disagreements over small matters.
50. creeps: worms his way.
52. state: government (of the triumvirate).
53. purge: i.e. seek a cure. It was a common notion that the indulgences of peacetime bred diseases in the body politic that were relieved by the bloodletting of war.
54. particular: personal reason.
55. with . . . going: should reassure you about my departure.
61. garboils: disturbances.
63. sacred vials: small bottles buried with the dead, and supposed to contain tears.
67–68. which . . . advice: which shall go forward or not, as you determine. **68. fire:** i.e. sun.
71. affects: desirest. **lace:** laces (of stays or bodice).
73. So: so long as, provided that (?) or (more probably) in the same way, i.e. with the same sudden changes (?).
74. give true evidence: bear true witness.
78. Belong to Egypt: i.e. are shed for Cleopatra's sake.
81. meetly: pretty good. **82. target:** shield.
84–85. How . . . chafe: how excellently his angry demeanor becomes this Herculean Roman. (Antony claimed descent from Hercules.)

The carriage of his chafe.
Ant. I'll leave you, lady.
Cleo. Courteous lord, one word:
Sir, you and I must part, but that's not it;
Sir, you and I have lov'd, but there's not it;
That you know well. Something it is I would—
O, my oblivion is a very Antony,
And I am all forgotten.
Ant. But that your royalty
Holds idleness your subject, I should take you
For idleness itself.
Cleo. 'Tis sweating labor
To bear such idleness so near the heart
As Cleopatra this. But, sir, forgive me,
Since my becomings kill me when they do not
Eye well to you. Your honor calls you hence,
Therefore be deaf to my unpitied folly,
And all the gods go with you! Upon your sword
Sit laurel victory, and smooth success
Be strew'd before your feet!
Ant. Let us go. Come;
Our separation so abides and flies,
That thou residing here, goes yet with me;
And I hence fleeting, here remain with thee.
Away! *Exeunt.*

[Scene IV]

Enter Octavius [Caesar] *reading a letter,* Lepidus, *and their* Train.

Caes. You may see, Lepidus, and henceforth know,
It is not Caesar's natural vice to hate
[Our] great competitor. From Alexandria
This is the news: he fishes, drinks, and wastes
The lamps of night in revel; is not more manlike
Than Cleopatra; nor the queen of Ptolomy
More womanly than he; hardly gave audience, or
[Vouchsaf'd] to think he had partners. You shall find there
A man who is th' [abstract] of all faults
That all men follow.
Lep. I must not think there are
Evils enow to darken all his goodness:
His faults, in him, seem as the spots of heaven,
More fiery by night's blackness; hereditary,
Rather than purchas'd; what he cannot change,
Than what he chooses.
Caes. You are too indulgent. Let's grant it is not
Amiss to tumble on the bed of Ptolomy,

To give a kingdom for a mirth, to sit
And keep the turn of tippling with a slave,
To reel the streets at noon, and stand the buffet
With knaves that smells of sweat: say this becomes him
(As his composure must be rare indeed
Whom these things cannot blemish), yet must Antony
No way excuse his foils, when we do bear
So great weight in his lightness. If he fill'd
His vacancy with his voluptuousness,
Full surfeits and the dryness of his bones
Call on him for't. But to confound such time
That drums him from his sport and speaks as loud
As his own state and ours, 'tis to be chid—
As we rate boys who, being mature in knowledge,
Pawn their experience to their present pleasure,
And so rebel to judgment.

Enter a Messenger.

Lep. Here's more news.
Mess. Thy biddings have been done, and every hour,
Most noble Caesar, shalt thou have report
How 'tis abroad. Pompey is strong at sea,
And it appears he is belov'd of those
That only have fear'd Caesar; to the ports
The discontents repair, and men's reports
Give him much wrong'd.
Caes. I should have known no less:
It hath been taught us from the primal state
That he which is was wish'd, until he were;
And the ebb'd man, ne'er lov'd till ne'er worth love,
Comes [dear'd] by being lack'd. This common body,
Like to a vagabond flag upon the stream,
Goes to and back, [lackeying] the varying tide,
To rot itself with motion.
Mess. Caesar, I bring thee word
Menecrates and Menas, famous pirates,
Makes the sea serve them, which they ear and wound
With keels of every kind. Many hot inroads
They make in Italy; the borders maritime
Lack blood to think on't, and flush youth revolt.
No vessel can peep forth, but 'tis as soon
Taken as seen; for Pompey's name strikes more
Than could his war resisted.
Caes. Antony,

90. **oblivion**: i.e. unreliable memory.
91. **I . . . forgotten**: (1) I have forgotten what I wanted to say; (2) I am completely forgotten (by Antony).
92. **idleness**: frivolity, absurd behavior.
93. **labor**: i.e. the opposite of idleness.
94. **such idleness**: i.e. what you call frivolity (but what is actually my grief at your departure).
96. **my becomings**: i.e. even my graces. 97. **Eye**: appear.
102. **abides and flies**: consists of both staying and going.

I.iv. Location: Rome. Caesar's house.
2. **vice**: fault. 3. **competitor**: partner.
6. **queen of Ptolomy**. Cleopatra had been nominally married to her younger brother Ptolemy, now dead.
9. **abstract**: epitome. 14. **purchas'd**: acquired.

18. **mirth**: jest. 19. **keep . . . of**: take turns.
20. **stand the buffet**: exchange blows.
22. **As**: i.e. as is highly doubtful since. **his composure**: that man's make-up. 24. **foils**: disgraceful actions.
25. **in his lightness**: because of his levity.
26. **His vacancy**: merely his leisure.
27–28. **Full . . . for't**: i.e. let the physical consequences of his indiscretions be his penalty (with no rebuke from me).
29. **drums**: summons as with a martial drum.
30. **state**: position of authority. 31. **rate**: scold.
33. **to judgment**: against their own common sense.
38. **That . . . Caesar**: i.e. that have followed Caesar out of fear, not love. 40. **Give him**: give him out, represent him as.
41. **primal state**: very first government.
42. **is**: is in power. **were**: came to power.
43. **ebb'd**: declined in power.
44. **Comes dear'd**: becomes endeared, comes to seem more valuable. **common body**: general populace. 45. **flag**: iris.
46. **lackeying**: following like a lackey. 49. **ear**: plough.
52. **Lack blood**: grow pale. **flush**: lusty.
55. **war**: strength in war. **resisted**: if it were resisted.

Leave thy lascivious [wassails]. When thou once
Was beaten from Modena, where thou slew'st
Hirtius and Pansa, consuls, at thy heel
Did famine follow, whom thou fought'st against
(Though daintily brought up) with patience more
Than savages could suffer. Thou didst drink
The stale of horses and the gilded puddle
Which beasts would cough at; thy palate then did deign
The roughest berry on the rudest hedge;
Yea, like the stag, when snow the pasture sheets,
The barks of trees thou brows'd. On the Alps
It is reported thou didst eat strange flesh,
Which some did die to look on; and all this
(It wounds thine honor that I speak it now)
Was borne so like a soldier, that thy cheek
So much as lank'd not.

Lep. 'Tis pity of him.

Caes. Let his shames quickly
Drive him to Rome. 'Tis time we twain
Did show ourselves i' th' field, and to that end
Assemble [we] immediate council. Pompey
Thrives in our idleness.

Lep. To-morrow, Caesar,
I shall be furnish'd to inform you rightly
Both what by sea and land I can be able
To front this present time.

Caes. Till which encounter,
It is my business too. Farewell.

Lep. Farewell, my lord. What you shall know mean time
Of stirs abroad, I shall beseech you, sir,
To let me be partaker.

Caes. Doubt not, sir,
I knew it for my bond. *Exeunt.*

[Scene V]

Enter Cleopatra, Charmian, Iras, *and* Mardian.

Cleo. Charmian!

Char. Madam?

Cleo. Ha, ha!
Give me to drink mandragora.

Char. Why, madam?

Cleo. That I might sleep out this great gap of time
My Antony is away.

Char. You think of him too much.

Cleo. O, 'tis treason!

Char. Madam, I trust not so.

Cleo. Thou, eunuch Mardian!

Mar. What's your Highness' pleasure?

Cleo. Not now to hear thee sing. I take no pleasure
In aught an eunuch has. 'Tis well for thee,
That being unseminar'd, thy freer thoughts

56. wassails: drunken carousings.
62. stale: urine. **gilded:** covered with yellow slime.
71. lank'd: grew thin.
78. what . . . able: what my military resources can be.
84. bond: duty, obligation.

I.v. Location: Alexandria. Cleopatra's palace.
3. Ha, ha. Probably indicating a yawn.
4. mandragora: opiate derived from the mandrake plant.
11. unseminar'd: castrated. **freer:** more lascivious.

May not fly forth of Egypt. Hast thou affections?

Mar. Yes, gracious madam.

Cleo. Indeed?

Mar. Not in deed, madam, for I can do nothing
But what indeed is honest to be done;
Yet have I fierce affections, and think
What Venus did with Mars.

Cleo. O Charmian!
Where think'st thou he is now? Stands he, or sits he?
Or does he walk? Or is he on his horse?
O happy horse, to bear the weight of Antony!
Do bravely, horse, for wot'st thou whom thou mov'st?
The demi-Atlas of this earth, the arm
And burgonet of men. He's speaking now,
Or murmuring, "Where's my serpent of old Nile?"
(For so he calls me). Now I feed myself
With most delicious poison. Think on me,
That am with Phoebus' amorous pinches black,
And wrinkled deep in time? Broad-fronted Caesar,
When thou wast here above the ground, I was
A morsel for a monarch; and great Pompey
Would stand and make his eyes grow in my brow;
There would he anchor his aspect, and die
With looking on his life.

Enter Alexas *from* [*Antony*].

Alex. Sovereign of Egypt, hail!

Cleo. How much unlike art thou Mark Antony!
Yet coming from him, that great med'cine hath
With his tinct gilded thee.
How goes it with my brave Mark Antony?

Alex. Last thing he did, dear Queen,
He kiss'd—the last of many doubled kisses—
This orient pearl. His speech sticks in my heart.

Cleo. Mine ear must pluck it thence.

Alex. "Good friend," quoth he,
"Say the firm Roman to great Egypt sends
This treasure of an oyster; at whose foot,
To mend the petty present, I will piece
Her opulent throne with kingdoms. All the East,
Say thou, shall call her mistress." So he nodded,
And soberly did mount an arm-gaunt steed,
Who neigh'd so high that what I would have spoke
Was beastly [dumb'd] by him.

Cleo. What, was he sad, or merry?

Alex. Like to the time o' th' year between the extremes
Of hot and cold, he was nor sad nor merry.

12. of: from. **affections:** sexual desires.
16. honest: chaste. **22. wot'st:** knowest.
23. demi-Atlas: half-Atlas, because he accomplishes half the task of Atlas, who held up the whole world (?) or quasi-Atlas, because like his ancestor Hercules he also supports the weight of the whole globe (?).
24. burgonet: helmet; thus both in attack (*arm*) and defense (*burgonet*) the greatest man—the champion and protector of all men.
28. Phoebus': the sun-god's. **black:** swarthy.
29. Broad-fronted: with broad forehead. **Caesar:** Julius Caesar.
31. Pompey: Cneius Pompey, son of Pompey the Great.
33. aspect: gaze.
36. great med'cine: i.e. the substance by means of which alchemists hoped to transform base metal into gold.
37. With his tinct: by means of its alchemical power. *Tincture* was another name for the "great medicine."
41. orient: shining, lustrous. **45. piece:** augment.
48. arm-gaunt: lean with much war service.
50. dumb'd: made inaudible.

Cleo. O well-divided disposition! Note him,
Note him, good Charmian, 'tis the man; but note him:
He was not sad, for he would shine on those
That make their looks by his; he was not merry,
Which seem'd to tell them his remembrance lay
In Egypt with his joy; but between both.
O heavenly mingle! Be'st thou sad or merry,
The violence of either thee becomes,
So does it no man's else. Met'st thou my posts?

Alex. Ay, madam, twenty several messengers.
Why do you send so thick?

Cleo. Who's born that day
When I forget to send to Antony,
Shall die a beggar. Ink and paper, Charmian.
Welcome, my good Alexas. Did I, Charmian,
Ever love Caesar so?

Char. O that brave Caesar!

Cleo. Be chok'd with such another emphasis!
Say "the brave Antony."

Char. The valiant Caesar!

Cleo. By Isis, I will give thee bloody teeth,
If thou with Caesar paragon again
My man of men.

Char. By your most gracious pardon,
I sing but after you.

Cleo. My salad days,
When I was green in judgment, cold in blood,
To say as I said then! But come, away,
Get me ink and paper.
He shall have every day a several greeting,
Or I'll unpeople Egypt. *Exeunt.*

[ACT II, SCENE I]

Enter POMPEY, MENECRATES, *and* MENAS, *in warlike manner.*

Pom. If the great gods be just, they shall assist
The deeds of justest men.

[*Menas.*] Know, worthy Pompey,
That what they do delay, they not deny.

Pom. Whiles we are suitors to their throne, decays
The thing we sue for.

Mene. We, ignorant of ourselves,
Beg often our own harms, which the wise pow'rs
Deny us for our good; so find we profit
By losing of our prayers.

Pom. I shall do well:
The people love me, and the sea is mine;
My powers are crescent, and my auguring hope
Says it will come to th' full. Mark Antony
In Egypt sits at dinner, and will make
No wars without-doors. Caesar gets money where
He loses hearts. Lepidus flatters both,
Of both is flatter'd; but he neither loves,
Nor either cares for him.

[*Menas.*] Caesar and Lepidus
Are in the field, a mighty strength they carry.

Pom. Where have you this? 'Tis false.

[*Menas.*] From Silvius, sir.

Pom. He dreams; I know they are in Rome together,
Looking for Antony. But all the charms of love,
Salt Cleopatra, soften thy wan'd lip!
Let witchcraft join with beauty, lust with both,
Tie up the libertine in a field of feasts,
Keep his brain fuming; epicurean cooks
Sharpen with cloyless sauce his appetite,
That sleep and feeding may prorogue his honor,
Even till a Lethe'd dullness—

Enter VARRIUS.

How now, Varrius?

Var. This is most certain that I shall deliver:
Mark Antony is every hour in Rome
Expected. Since he went from Egypt, 'tis
A space for farther travel.

Pom. I could have given less matter
A better ear. Menas, I did not think
This amorous surfeiter would have donn'd his helm
For such a petty war. His soldiership
Is twice the other twain; but let us rear
The higher our opinion, that our stirring
Can from the lap of Egypt's widow pluck
The [ne'er-]lust-wearied Antony.

[*Menas.*] I cannot hope
Caesar and Antony shall well greet together:
His wife that's dead did trespasses to Caesar;
His brother [warr'd] upon him, although I think
Not mov'd by Antony.

Pom. I know not, Menas,
How lesser enmities may give way to greater.
Were't not that we stand up against them all,
'Twere pregnant they should square between themselves,
For they have entertained cause enough
To draw their swords; but how the fear of us
May cement their divisions, and bind up
The petty difference, we yet not know.
Be't as our gods will have't! it only stands
Our lives upon to use our strongest hands.
Come, Menas. *Exeunt.*

53. **disposition:** temperament.
56. **make . . . his:** are obliged to imitate his demeanor.
61. **posts:** messengers. 62. **several:** separate.
67. **brave:** splendid. 71. **paragon:** match.
73. **sing . . . you:** merely repeat your song.
74. **green:** young and inexperienced, "raw."
78. **Or . . . Egypt:** i.e. if he doesn't, it will mean that I have used up the entire population as messengers.

II.i. Location: Messina. Pompey's house.
1. **shall:** will certainly. 10. **crescent:** growing.
11. **come . . . full.** As a crescent moon does.

13. **wars . . . doors:** i.e. military as opposed to amorous wars.
20. **Looking for:** expecting. 21. **Salt:** lascivious. **wan'd:** faded.
23. **Tie . . . feasts:** i.e. keep him in a field whence he will not stray since the feeding is so good there.
24. **Keep . . . fuming.** Fumes of wine were thought to ascend to the brain and cause drunkenness. 26. **prorogue:** suspend.
27. **Lethe'd:** steeped in forgetfulness (from the name of the river Lethe in the underworld whose water caused the drinker to forget the past).
31. **space . . . travel:** interval long enough for an even longer journey. **less:** lesser. 36. **opinion:** i.e. of ourselves.
38. **hope:** expect. 39. **greet:** be friends.
45. **pregnant:** very probable. **square:** quarrel.
50–51. **it . . . hands:** our lives depend on our exerting our maximum strength.

[Scene II]

Enter Enobarbus *and* Lepidus.

Lep. Good Enobarbus, 'tis a worthy deed,
And shall become you well, to entreat your captain
To soft and gentle speech.
Eno. I shall entreat him
To answer like himself. If Caesar move him,
Let Antony look over Caesar's head
And speak as loud as Mars. By Jupiter,
Were I the wearer of Antonio's beard,
I would not shave't to-day.
Lep. 'Tis not a time
For private stomaching.
Eno. Every time
Serves for the matter that is then born in't.
Lep. But small to greater matters must give way.
Eno. Not if the small come first.
Lep. Your speech is passion;
But pray you stir no embers up. Here comes
The noble Antony.

Enter Antony *and* Ventidius.

Eno. And yonder, Caesar.

Enter Caesar, Maecenas, *and* Agrippa.

Ant. If we compose well here, to Parthia.
Hark, Ventidius.
Caes. I do not know,
Maecenas; ask Agrippa.
Lep. Noble friends,
That which combin'd us was most great, and let not
A leaner action rend us. What's amiss,
May it be gently heard. When we debate
Our trivial difference loud, we do commit
Murther in healing wounds. Then, noble partners,
The rather for I earnestly beseech,
Touch you the sourest points with sweetest terms,
Nor curstness grow to th' matter.
Ant. 'Tis spoken well.
Were we before our armies, and to fight,
I should do thus. *Flourish.*
Caes. Welcome to Rome.
Ant. Thank you.
Caes. Sit.
Ant. Sit, sir.
Caes. Nay then.
Ant. I learn you take things ill which are not so—
Or being, concern you not.
Caes. I must be laugh'd at
If, or for nothing or a little, I
Should say myself offended, and with you
Chiefly i' th' world; more laugh'd at, that I should

II.ii. Location: Rome. Lepidus' house.
4. **like himself**: i.e. in a manner that does justice to his own character. **move**: anger.
8. **I . . . shave't**: i.e. I would do Caesar the deliberate discourtesy of coming to the meeting ill-groomed (?) or I would provoke Caesar to pluck it as a challenge (?).
9. **stomaching**: resentment.
15. **compose**: agree. 22. **healing**: i.e. trying to heal.
23. **The rather for**: and all the more because.
25. **Nor . . . grow**: nor let bad temper be added.
30. **being**: i.e. if they are ill. 31. **or . . . or**: either . . . or.

Once name you derogately, when to sound your name
It not concern'd me.
Ant. My being in Egypt, Caesar,
What was't to you?
Caes. No more than my residing here at Rome
Might be to you in Egypt; yet if you there
Did practice on my state, your being in Egypt
Might be my question.
Ant. How intend you, practic'd?
Caes. You may be pleas'd to catch at mine intent
By what did here befall me. Your wife and brother
Made wars upon me, and their contestation
Was theme for you—you were the word of war.
Ant. You do mistake your business, my brother never
Did urge me in his act. I did inquire it,
And have my learning from some true reports
That drew their swords with you. Did he not rather
Discredit my authority with yours,
And make the wars alike against my stomach,
Having alike your cause? Of this my letters
Before did satisfy you. If you'll patch a quarrel,
As matter whole you have to make it with,
It must not be with this.
Caes. You praise yourself
By laying defects of judgment to me; but
You patch'd up your excuses.
Ant. Not so, not so:
I know you could not lack, I am certain on't,
Very necessity of this thought, that I,
Your partner in the cause 'gainst which he fought,
Could not with graceful eyes attend those wars
Which fronted mine own peace. As for my wife,
I would you had her spirit in such another;
The third o' th' world is yours, which with a snaffle
You may pace easy, but not such a wife.
Eno. Would we had all such wives, that the men might go to wars with the women!
Ant. So much uncurbable, her garboils, Caesar,
Made out of her impatience—which not wanted
Shrowdness of policy too—I grieving grant
Did you too much disquiet. For that you must
But say I could not help it.
Caes. I wrote to you,
When rioting in Alexandria you
Did pocket up my letters; and with taunts
Did gibe my missive out of audience.
Ant. Sir,

34. **derogately**: disparagingly.
39. **practice . . . state**: plot against my power.
40. **question**: business.
44. **theme for you**: argued (i.e. carried on) in your behalf (?) or your concern (?). **you were . . . war**: the war was waged in your name (*word* = watchword). 46. **urge me**: use my name.
47. **reports**: reporters, informants. 49. **Discredit**: reject.
50. **stomach**: liking. 51. **Having**: i.e. I having.
52. **satisfy you**: give you a full account. **patch a quarrel**: patch up a cause for quarrelling out of bits and pieces.
53. **As . . . have**: even though you have more substantial material. Many editors, following Rowe, emend *have* to *have not*: "as (you must if you want to quarrel, for) you haven't enough whole material."
60. **graceful**: approving. 61. **fronted**: opposed.
63. **snaffle**: bridle suitable for use with gentle horses.
64. **pace**: train, teach its paces.
67. **uncurbable**: unmanageable even with a curb rein. **garboils**: disturbances. 69. **Shrowdness**: shrewdness.
74. **missive**: messenger.

He fell upon me, ere admitted, then;
Three kings I had newly feasted, and did want
Of what I was i' th' morning; but next day
I told him of myself, which was as much
As to have ask'd him pardon. Let this fellow
Be nothing of our strife; if we contend,
Out of our question wipe him.

Caes. You have broken
The article of your oath, which you shall never
Have tongue to charge me with.

Lep. Soft, Caesar!

Ant. No, Lepidus, let him speak.
The honor is sacred which he talks on now,
Supposing that I lack'd it. But on, Caesar,
The article of my oath.

Caes. To lend me arms and aid when I requir'd them,
The which you both denied.

Ant. Neglected, rather;
And then when poisoned hours had bound me up
From mine own knowledge. As nearly as I may,
I'll play the penitent to you; but mine honesty
Shall not make poor my greatness, nor my power
Work without it. Truth is, that Fulvia,
To have me out of Egypt, made wars here;
For which myself, the ignorant motive, do
So far ask pardon as befits mine honor
To stoop in such a case.

Lep. 'Tis noble spoken.

Maec. If it might please you, to enforce no further
The griefs between ye: to forget them quite
Were to remember that the present need
Speaks to atone you.

Lep. Worthily spoken, Maecenas.

Eno. Or, if you borrow one another's love for the instant, you may, when you hear no more words of Pompey, return it again. You shall have time to wrangle in when you have nothing else to do.

Ant. Thou art a soldier only, speak no more.

Eno. That truth should be silent I had almost forgot.

Ant. You wrong this presence, therefore speak no more.

Eno. Go to then—your considerate stone.

Caes. I do not much dislike the matter, but
The manner of his speech; for't cannot be
We shall remain in friendship, our conditions
So diff'ring in their acts. Yet if I knew
What hoop should hold us staunch from edge to edge
A' th' world, I would pursue it.

Agr. Give me leave, Caesar—

Caes. Speak, Agrippa.

Agr. Thou hast a sister by the mother's side,
Admir'd Octavia. Great Mark Antony

76. **want:** fall short.
78. **told . . . myself:** explained to him what my condition had been.
80. **Be nothing of:** have no place in. 82. **article:** terms.
88. **requir'd:** requested.
92–94. **mine . . . it:** my honorable behavior (in thus admitting a fault) shall not impair my position of power, and by the same token my power shall not exempt me from behaving honorably.
97. **honor:** honorable position, dignity.
100. **griefs:** grievances. 102. **atone:** reconcile.
109. **presence:** dignified company. 110. **considerate:** thinking.
113. **conditions:** dispositions. 116. **A':** of.

Is now a widower.

Caes. Say not [so], Agrippa;
If Cleopatra heard you, your [reproof]
Were well deserv'd of rashness.

Ant. I am not married, Caesar;
Let me hear Agrippa further speak.

Agr. To hold you in perpetual amity,
To make you brothers, and to knit your hearts
With an unslipping knot, take Antony
Octavia to his wife; whose beauty claims
No worse a husband than the best of men;
Whose virtue and whose general graces speak
That which none else can utter. By this marriage,
All little jealousies, which now seem great,
And all great fears, which now import their dangers,
Would then be nothing. Truths would be tales,
Where now half tales be truths. Her love to both
Would each to other and all loves to both
Draw after her. Pardon what I have spoke,
For 'tis a studied, not a present thought,
By duty ruminated.

Ant. Will Caesar speak?

Caes. Not till he hears how Antony is touch'd
With what is spoke already.

Ant. What power is in Agrippa,
If I would say, "Agrippa, be it so,"
To make this good?

Caes. The power of Caesar, and
His power unto Octavia.

Ant. May I never
(To this good purpose, that so fairly shows)
Dream of impediment! Let me have thy hand
Further this act of grace; and from this hour
The heart of brothers govern in our loves,
And sway our great designs!

Caes. There's my hand.
A sister I bequeath you, whom no brother
Did ever love so dearly. Let her live
To join our kingdoms and our hearts, and never
Fly off our loves again!

Lep. Happily, amen!

Ant. I did not think to draw my sword 'gainst Pompey,
For he hath laid strange courtesies and great
Of late upon me. I must thank him only,
Lest my remembrance suffer ill report;
At heel of that, defy him.

Lep. Time calls upon 's.
Of us must Pompey presently be sought,
Or else he seeks out us.

Ant. Where lies he?

Caes. About the Mount Misena.

121–22. **your . . . rashness:** you would receive a well-merited reproof for your overboldness.
131. **jealousies:** suspicions. 132. **import:** carry with them.
133–34. **Truths . . . truths:** even true reports (of a disquieting nature) would then be dismissed as empty rumors; whereas now mere half-truths are taken for gospel.
137. **present:** i.e. just now conceived, hence unconsidered.
152. **Fly off:** be estranged. 154. **strange:** extraordinary.
156. **remembrance:** memory (of benefits received).
157. **At heel of:** immediately after.
158. **Of:** by. **presently:** at once.
160. **Misena:** Misenum, a hilly promontory in southern Italy.

Ant. What is his strength by land?
Caes. Great, and increasing; but by sea
He is an absolute master.
Ant. So is the fame.
Would we had spoke together! Haste we for it,
Yet ere we put ourselves in arms, dispatch we
The business we have talk'd of.
Caes. With most gladness,
And do invite you to my sister's view,
Whither straight I'll lead you.
Ant. Let us, Lepidus,
Not lack your company.
Lep. Noble Antony,
Not sickness should detain me.
Flourish. Exeunt omnes. Manent Enobarbus, Agrippa, Maecenas.
Maec. Welcome from Egypt, sir.
Eno. Half the heart of Caesar, worthy Maecenas!
My honorable friend, Agrippa!
Agr. Good Enobarbus!
Maec. We have cause to be glad that matters are so well disgested. You stay'd well by't in Egypt.
Eno. Ay, sir, we did sleep day out of countenance, and made the night light with drinking.
Maec. Eight wild-boars roasted whole at a breakfast, and but twelve persons there; is this true?
Eno. This was but as a fly by an eagle; we had much more monstrous matter of feast, which worthily deserv'd noting.
Maec. She's a most triumphant lady, if report be square to her.
Eno. When she first met Mark Antony, she purs'd up his heart upon the river of Cydnus.
Agr. There she appear'd indeed; or my reporter devis'd well for her.
Eno. I will tell you.
The barge she sat in, like a burnish'd throne,
Burnt on the water. The poop was beaten gold,
Purple the sails, and so perfumed that
The winds were love-sick with them; the oars were silver,
Which to the tune of flutes kept stroke, and made
The water which they beat to follow faster,
As amorous of their strokes. For her own person,
It beggar'd all description: she did lie
In her pavilion—cloth of gold, of tissue—
O'er-picturing that Venus where we see
The fancy outwork nature. On each side her
Stood pretty dimpled boys, like smiling Cupids,
With divers-color'd fans, whose wind did seem
To [glow] the delicate cheeks which they did cool,
And what they undid did.
Agr. O, rare for Antony!
Eno. Her [gentlewomen], like the Nereides,
So many mermaids, tended her i' th' eyes,
And made their bends adornings. At the helm
A seeming mermaid steers; the silken tackle
Swell with the touches of those flower-soft hands,
That yarely frame the office. From the barge
A strange invisible perfume hits the sense
Of the adjacent wharfs. The city cast
Her people out upon her; and Antony
Enthron'd i' th' market-place, did sit alone,
Whistling to th' air, which, but for vacancy,
Had gone to gaze on Cleopatra too,
And made a gap in nature.
Agr. Rare Egyptian!
Eno. Upon her landing, Antony sent to her,
Invited her to supper. She replied,
It should be better he became her guest;
Which she entreated. Our courteous Antony,
Whom ne'er the word of "No" woman heard speak,
Being barber'd ten times o'er, goes to the feast;
And for his ordinary pays his heart
For what his eyes eat only.
Agr. Royal wench!
She made great Caesar lay his sword to bed;
He ploughed her, and she cropp'd.
Eno. I saw her once
Hop forty paces through the public street;
And having lost her breath, she spoke, and panted,
That she did make defect perfection,
And breathless, pow'r breathe forth.
Maec. Now Antony
Must leave her utterly.
Eno. Never, he will not:
Age cannot wither her, nor custom stale
Her infinite variety. Other women cloy
The appetites they feed, but she makes hungry
Where most she satisfies; for vildest things
Become themselves in her, that the holy priests
Bless her when she is riggish.
Maec. If beauty, wisdom, modesty, can settle
The heart of Antony, Octavia is
A blessed lottery to him.
Agr. Let us go.
Good Enobarbus, make yourself my guest
Whilst you abide here.
Eno. Humbly, sir, I thank you. *Exeunt.*

163. fame: rumor, report.
164. Would . . . together: i.e. would that we had consulted earlier on this danger. **167. do:** I do.
172. Half the heart: dear friend (?) or one of his two dearest friends (the other being Agrippa) (?).
176. digested: digested, i.e. arranged. **stay'd well by't:** kept at it tirelessly, showed great stamina.
177. sleep . . . countenance: abash the day by sleeping through it.
178. light: (1) bright as day; (2) light-headed, tipsy.
184. triumphant: splendid, magnificent. **185. square:** just.
187. purs'd up: pocketed. **189. devis'd:** invented.
199. cloth of gold, of tissue: rich fabric interwoven with gold threads.
200–201. O'er-picturing . . . nature: outdoing the famous picture of Venus (by Apelles) in which the painter's art was said to transcend nature. **202. like:** attired as.
204. glow: cause to glow.
206. Nereides: sea-nymphs, daughters of Nereus.
207. i' th' eyes: i.e. in her sight, not in the background.
208. made . . . adornings: with their graceful bows added to the effect of her beauty.
211. yarely frame: deftly perform.
216. but for vacancy: except that it would have created a vacuum in nature.
225. ordinary: meal. Enobarbus humorously uses the term for a meal at the public table in a tavern.
228. cropp'd: bore fruit (her son Caesarion).
231. That: in such a way that. **232. pow'r:** i.e. charm.
237. vildest: vilest, basest.
238. Become themselves: are becoming. **that:** so that.
239. riggish: wanton.
242. lottery: stroke of fortune, prize.

[SCENE III]

Enter ANTONY, CAESAR, OCTAVIA *between them.*

Ant. The world and my great office will sometimes
Divide me from your bosom.
Oct. All which time
Before the gods my knee shall bow my prayers
To them for you.
Ant. Good night, sir. My Octavia,
Read not my blemishes in the world's report.
I have not kept my square, but that to come
Shall all be done by th' rule. Good night, dear lady.
[*Oct.*] Good night, sir.
Caes. Good night. *Exit [with Octavia].*

Enter SOOTHSAYER.

Ant. Now, sirrah; you do wish yourself in Egypt?
Sooth. Would I had never come from thence, nor you thither.
Ant. If you can, your reason?
Sooth. I see it in my motion, have it not in my tongue;
But yet hie you to Egypt again.
Ant. Say to me, whose fortunes shall rise higher, Caesar's or mine?
Sooth. Caesar's.
Therefore, O Antony, stay not by his side.
Thy daemon, that thy spirit which keeps thee, is
Noble, courageous, high unmatchable,
Where Caesar's is not; but near him, thy angel
Becomes a fear, as being o'erpow'r'd: therefore
Make space enough between you.
Ant. Speak this no more.
Sooth. To none but thee; no more but when to thee.
If thou dost play with him at any game,
Thou art sure to lose; and of that natural luck,
He beats thee 'gainst the odds. Thy lustre thickens
When he shines by. I say again, thy spirit
Is all afraid to govern thee near him;
But he [away,] 'tis noble.
Ant. Get thee gone.
Say to Ventidius I would speak with him.
Exit [Soothsayer].
He shall to Parthia. Be it art or hap,
He hath spoken true. The very dice obey him,
And in our sports my better cunning faints
Under his chance. If we draw lots, he speeds;
His cocks do win the battle still of mine,
When it is all to nought; and his quails ever
Beat mine, inhoop'd, at odds. I will to Egypt;
And though I make this marriage for my peace,
I' th' East my pleasure lies.

Enter VENTIDIUS.

O, come, Ventidius,
You must to Parthia. Your commission's ready;
Follow me, and receive't. *Exeunt.*

II.iii. Location: Rome. Caesar's house.
6. kept my square: regulated my life well, kept to a straight course.
10. sirrah: term of address to inferiors.
14. motion: thoughts, mind. **15. hie:** hasten. **27. of:** by.
28. thickens: grows dim. **29. by:** near.
33. art or hap: skill or luck. **36. chance:** luck. **speeds:** wins.
37. still: always. **38. all to nought:** high odds in my favor.
39. inhoop'd: fighting in an enclosure.

[SCENE IV]

Enter LEPIDUS, MAECENAS, *and* AGRIPPA.

Lep. Trouble yourselves no further; pray you hasten
Your generals after.
Agr. Sir, Mark Antony
Will e'en but kiss Octavia, and we'll follow.
Lep. Till I shall see you in your soldier's dress,
Which will become you both, farewell.
Maec. We shall,
As I conceive the journey, be at [the] Mount
Before you, Lepidus.
Lep. Your way is shorter,
My purposes do draw me much about.
You'll win two days upon me.
Both. Sir, good success!
Lep. Farewell. *Exeunt.*

[SCENE V]

Enter CLEOPATRA, CHARMIAN, IRAS, *and* ALEXAS.

Cleo. Give me some music; music, moody food
Of us that trade in love.
Omnes. The music, ho!

Enter MARDIAN *the Eunuch.*

Cleo. Let it alone, let's to billards. Come, Charmian.
Char. My arm is sore, best play with Mardian.
Cleo. As well a woman with an eunuch play'd
As with a woman. Come, you'll play with me, sir?
Mar. As well as I can, madam.
Cleo. And when good will is show'd, though't come too short,
The actor may plead pardon. I'll none now.
Give me mine angle, we'll to th' river; there,
My music playing far off, I will betray
Tawny[-finn'd] fishes; my bended hook shall pierce
Their slimy jaws; and as I draw them up,
I'll think them every one an Antony,
And say, "Ah, ha! y' are caught."
Char. 'Twas merry when
You wager'd on your angling; when your diver
Did hang a salt-fish on his hook, which he
With fervency drew up.
Cleo. That time? O times!
I laugh'd him out of patience; and that night
I laugh'd him into patience; and next morn,
Ere the ninth hour, I drunk him to his bed;
Then put my tires and mantles on him, whilst
I wore his sword Philippan.

II.iv. Location: Rome. A street.
6. the Mount: Misenum. **8. much about:** by a circuitous route.

II.v. Location: Alexandria. Cleopatra's palace.
3. billards: variant of *billiards.*
10. angle: rod and line. **22. tires:** headdresses.
23. sword Philippan: the sword with which he had defeated Brutus and Cassius at Philippi.

Enter a Messenger.

O, from Italy!
Ram thou thy fruitful tidings in mine ears,
That long time have been barren.
Mess. Madam, madam—
Cleo. Antonio's dead! If thou say so, villain,
Thou kill'st thy mistress; but well and free,
If thou so yield him, there is gold, and here
My bluest veins to kiss—a hand that kings
Have lipp'd, and trembled kissing.
Mess. First, madam, he is well.
Cleo. Why, there's more gold.
But, sirrah, mark, we use
To say the dead are well. Bring it to that,
The gold I give thee will I melt and pour
Down thy ill-uttering throat.
Mess. Good madam, hear me.
Cleo. Well, go to, I will.
But there's no goodness in thy face, if Antony
Be free and healthful—so tart a favor
To trumpet such good tidings! If not well,
Thou shouldst come like a Fury crown'd with snakes,
Not like a formal man.
Mess. Will't please you hear me?
Cleo. I have a mind to strike thee ere thou speak'st;
Yet if thou say Antony lives, 'tis well,
Or friends with Caesar, or not captive to him,
I'll set thee in a shower of gold, and hail
Rich pearls upon thee.
Mess. Madam, he's well.
Cleo. Well said.
Mess. And friends with Caesar.
Cleo. Th' art an honest man.
Mess. Caesar and he are greater friends than ever.
Cleo. Make thee a fortune from me.
Mess. But yet, madam—
Cleo. I do not like "but yet," it does allay
The good precedence; fie upon "but yet"!
"But yet" is as a jailer to bring forth
Some monstrous malefactor. Prithee, friend,
Pour out the pack of matter to mine ear,
The good and bad together: he's friends with Caesar,
In state of health thou say'st, and thou say'st free.
Mess. Free, madam, no; I made no such report.
He's bound unto Octavia.
Cleo. For what good turn?
Mess. For the best turn i' th' bed.
Cleo. I am pale, Charmian.
Mess. Madam, he's married to Octavia.
Cleo. The most infectious pestilence upon thee!
Strikes him down.
Mess. Good madam, patience.
Cleo. What say you? *Strikes him.* Hence,
Horrible villain, or I'll spurn thine eyes

27. **free.** Explained by line 44.
38. **tart a favor:** sour a face. 40. **like:** in the likeness of.
41. **like . . . man:** in normal human form.
50. **allay:** qualify, dilute.
51. **The good precedence:** the good news that went before.
63. **spurn:** kick.

Like balls before me; I'll unhair thy head,
She hales him up and down.
Thou shalt be whipt with wire, and stew'd in brine,
Smarting in ling'ring pickle.
Mess. Gracious madam,
I that do bring the news made not the match.
Cleo. Say 'tis not so, a province I will give thee,
And make thy fortunes proud; the blow thou hadst
Shall make thy peace for moving me to rage,
And I will boot thee with what gift beside
Thy modesty can beg.
Mess. He's married, madam.
Cleo. Rogue, thou hast liv'd too long.
Draw a knife.
Mess. Nay then I'll run.
What mean you, madam? I have made no fault. *Exit.*
Char. Good madam, keep yourself within yourself,
The man is innocent.
Cleo. Some innocents scape not the thunderbolt.
Melt Egypt into Nile! and kindly creatures
Turn all to serpents! Call the slave again,
Though I am mad, I will not bite him. Call!
Char. He is afeard to come.
Cleo. I will not hurt him.
These hands do lack nobility that they strike
A meaner than myself, since I myself
Have given myself the cause. Come hither, sir.

Enter the Messenger *again.*

Though it be honest, it is never good
To bring bad news. Give to a gracious message
An host of tongues, but let ill tidings tell
Themselves when they be felt.
Mess. I have done my duty.
Cleo. Is he married?
I cannot hate thee worser than I do,
If thou again say yes.
Mess. He's married, madam.
Cleo. The gods confound thee, dost thou hold there still?
Mess. Should I lie, madam?
Cleo. O, I would thou didst;
So half my Egypt were submerg'd and made
A cestern for scal'd snakes! Go get thee hence!
Hadst thou Narcissus in thy face, to me
Thou wouldst appear most ugly. He is married?
Mess. I crave your Highness' pardon.
Cleo. He is married?
Mess. Take no offense that I would not offend you;
To punish me for what you make me do
Seems much unequal. He's married to Octavia.
Cleo. O, that his fault should make a knave of thee,
That art not what th' art sure of. Get thee hence;
The merchandise which thou hast brought from Rome

71. **boot thee with:** give you in addition.
72. **modesty:** moderation (implying that anything he can ask will seem moderate to her).
78. **kindly:** having good natural qualities, benign.
92. **confound:** destroy. 94. **So:** even if.
96. **Narcissus:** beautiful youth of Greek myth.
99. **Take . . . you:** i.e. don't be offended with me for hesitating to give an answer that will offend you. 101. **unequal:** unjust.
103. **what . . . of:** i.e. as bad as the news you bear.

Are all too dear for me. Lie they upon thy hand,
And be undone by 'em! [*Exit Messenger.*]
Char. Good your Highness, patience.
Cleo. In praising Antony I have disprais'd Caesar.
Char. Many times, madam.
Cleo. I am paid for't now.
Lead me from hence;
I faint, O Iras, Charmian! 'Tis no matter.
Go to the fellow, good Alexas, bid him
Report the feature of Octavia, her years,
Her inclination; let him not leave out
The color of her hair. Bring me word quickly.
[*Exit Alexas.*]
Let him for ever go—let him not, Charmian—
Though he be painted one way like a Gorgon,
The other way's a Mars. [*To Mardian.*] Bid you Alexas
Bring me word how tall she is. Pity me, Charmian,
But do not speak to me. Lead me to my chamber.
Exeunt.

[SCENE VI]

Flourish. Enter POMPEY, MENAS *at one door, with Drum and Trumpet: at another,* CAESAR, LEPIDUS, ANTONY, ENOBARBUS, MAECENAS, AGRIPPA, *with* SOLDIERS *marching.*

Pom. Your hostages I have, so have you mine;
And we shall talk before we fight.
Caes. Most meet
That first we come to words, and therefore have we
Our written purposes before us sent,
Which if thou hast considered, let us know
If 'twill tie up thy discontented sword,
And carry back to Sicily much tall youth
That else must perish here.
Pom. To you all three,
The senators alone of this great world,
Chief factors for the gods: I do not know
Wherefore my father should revengers want,
Having a son and friends, since Julius Caesar,
Who at Philippi the good Brutus ghosted,
There saw you laboring for him. What was't
That mov'd pale Cassius to conspire? and what
Made all-honor'd, honest, Roman Brutus,
With the arm'd rest, courtiers of beauteous freedom,
To drench the Capitol, but that they would
Have one man but a man? And that is it
Hath made me rig my navy, at whose burthen
The anger'd ocean foams, with which I meant
To scourge th' ingratitude that despiteful Rome
Cast on my noble father.
Caes. Take your time.

105. **Lie . . . hand:** let them remain in your possession unsold.
106. **undone:** ruined, made bankrupt.
112. **feature:** appearance. 113. **inclination:** disposition.
116–17. **Though . . . Mars.** Alluding to trick pictures known as "perspectives," which showed different objects when viewed from different angles. 117. **'s:** he is.

II.vi. Location: Near Misenum.
7. **tall:** valiant. 10. **factors:** agents.
13. **Brutus ghosted:** appeared as a ghost to Brutus.
16. **honest:** honorable.

Ant. Thou canst not fear us, Pompey, with thy sails;
We'll speak with thee at sea. At land, thou know'st
How much we do o'er-count thee.
Pom. At land indeed
Thou dost o'er-count me of my father's house;
But since the cuckoo builds not for himself,
Remain in't as thou mayst.
Lep. Be pleas'd to tell us
(For this is from the present) how you take
The offers we have sent you.
Caes. There's the point.
Ant. Which do not be entreated to, but weigh
What it is worth embrac'd.
Caes. And what may follow,
To try a larger fortune.
Pom. You have made me offer
Of Sicily, Sardinia; and I must
Rid all the sea of pirates; then, to send
Measures of wheat to Rome. This 'greed upon,
To part with unhack'd edges and bear back
Our targes undinted.
Omnes [*Caes., Ant., Lep.*]. That's our offer.
Pom. Know then
I came before you here a man prepar'd
To take this offer; but Mark Antony
Put me to some impatience. Though I lose
The praise of it by telling, you must know,
When Caesar and your brother were at blows,
Your mother came to Sicily and did find
Her welcome friendly.
Ant. I have heard it, Pompey,
And am well studied for a liberal thanks,
Which I do owe you.
Pom. Let me have your hand.
I did not think, sir, to have met you here.
Ant. The beds i' th' East are soft, and thanks to you,
That call'd me timelier than my purpose hither;
For I have gain'd by't.
Caes. Since I saw you last,
There's a change upon you.
Pom. Well, I know not
What counts harsh Fortune casts upon my face,
But in my bosom shall she never come,
To make my heart her vassal.
Lep. Well met here.
Pom. I hope so, Lepidus. Thus we are agreed.
I crave our composition may be written
And seal'd between us.
Caes. That's the next to do.

24. **fear:** frighten.
25. **speak with:** encounter. 26. **o'er-count:** outnumber.
27. **o'er-count:** cheat. According to Plutarch, Antony had bought the elder Pompey's house but refused to pay for it.
30. **from the present:** irrelevant to the present business.
33. **embrac'd:** if you accept it.
33–34. **what . . . fortune:** what the consequences may be if you try for more (by deciding to oppose us).
38. **edges:** swords. 39. **targes:** shields.
47. **well studied:** fully prepared.
51. **timelier . . . purpose:** earlier than I had intended.
54. **What . . . casts:** what accounts harsh Fortune keeps, i.e. what lines she cuts (since accounts were often kept by means of marks on tallies). 58. **composition:** agreement.

Pom. We'll feast each other ere we part, and let's
Draw lots who shall begin.
Ant. That will I, Pompey.
Pom. No, Antony, take the lot; but first
Or last, your fine Egyptian cookery
Shall have the fame. I have heard that Julius Caesar
Grew fat with feasting there.
Ant. You have heard much.
Pom. I have fair [meanings], sir.
Ant. And fair words to them.
Pom. Then so much have I heard;
And I have heard, Apollodorus carried—
Eno. No more [of] that; he did so.
Pom. What, I pray you?
Eno. A certain queen to Caesar in a mattress.
Pom. I know thee now: how far'st thou, soldier?
Eno. Well,
And well am like to do, for I perceive
Four feasts are toward.
Pom. Let me shake thy hand,
I never hated thee. I have seen thee fight,
When I have envied thy behavior.
Eno. Sir,
I never lov'd you much, but I ha' prais'd ye
When you have well deserv'd ten times as much
As I have said you did.
Pom. Enjoy thy plainness,
It nothing ill becomes thee.
Aboard my galley I invite you all.
Will you lead, lords?
All [Caes., Ant., Lep.]. Show 's the way, sir.
Pom. Come.

Exeunt. Manent Enobarbus and Menas.

Men. [*Aside.*] Thy father, Pompey, would ne'er have made this treaty.—You and I have known, sir.

Eno. At sea, I think.

Men. We have, sir.

Eno. You have done well by water.

Men. And you by land.

Eno. I will praise any man that will praise me, though it cannot be denied what I have done by land.

Men. Nor what I have done by water.

Eno. Yes, something you can deny for your own safety: you have been a great thief by sea.

Men. And you by land.

Eno. There I deny my land service. But give me your hand, Menas; if our eyes had authority, here they might take two thieves kissing.

Men. All men's faces are true, whatsome'er their hands are.

Eno. But there is never a fair woman has a true face.

Men. No slander, they steal hearts.

Eno. We came hither to fight with you.

Men. For my part, I am sorry it is turn'd to a drinking. Pompey doth this day laugh away his fortune.

Eno. If he do, sure he cannot weep't back again.

Men. Y' have said, sir. We look'd not for Mark Antony here. Pray you, is he married to Cleopatra?

Eno. Caesar's sister is call'd Octavia.

Men. True, sir, she was the wife of Caius Marcellus.

Eno. But she is now the wife of Marcus Antonius.

Men. Pray ye, sir?

Eno. 'Tis true.

Men. Then is Caesar and he for ever knit together.

Eno. If I were bound to divine of this unity, I would not prophesy so.

Men. I think the policy of that purpose made more in the marriage than the love of the parties.

Eno. I think so too. But you shall find the band that seems to tie their friendship together will be the very strangler of their amity. Octavia is of a holy, cold, and still conversation.

Men. Who would not have his wife so?

Eno. Not he that himself is not so; which is Mark Antony. He will to his Egyptian dish again. Then shall the sighs of Octavia blow the fire up in Caesar, and (as I said before) that which is the strength of their amity shall prove the immediate author of their variance. Antony will use his affection where it is; he married but his occasion here.

Men. And thus it may be. Come, sir, will you aboard? I have a health for you.

Eno. I shall take it, sir; we have us'd our throats in Egypt.

Men. Come, let's away. *Exeunt.*

[Scene VII]

Music plays. Enter two or three Servants *with a banket.*

1. Serv. Here they'll be, man. Some o' their plants are ill rooted already, the least wind i' th' world will blow them down.

2. Serv. Lepidus is high[-color'd].

1. Serv. They have made him drink alms-drink.

2. Serv. As they pinch one another by the disposition, he cries out, "No more"; reconciles them to his entreaty, and himself to th' drink.

1. Serv. But it raises the greater war between him and his discretion.

2. Serv. Why, this it is to have a name in great men's fellowship. I had as live have a reed that will do

68. Apollodorus carried. Alluding to an earlier escapade of Cleopatra's when she became the mistress of Julius Caesar.
73. toward: in preparation.
78. plainness: bluntness, plain speaking. **79. nothing:** not at all.
83. known: been acquainted. **94. There:** with respect to that.
95. authority: i.e. to make an arrest.
96. two thieves kissing: (1) two robbers putting their heads together; (2) two thieving hands clasping.
97. true: honest. Enobarbus' reply quibbles on the sense "without make-up."

116. divine: prophesy. **118. made:** counted for.
123. conversation: deportment. **130. affection:** passion.
131. his occasion: what his situation required.

II.vii. Location: On board Pompey's galley, off Misenum.
5. alms-drink: drink given in charity; here (as explained in the next speech), extra rounds of drinking to mark the restoration of friendliness after each quarrelsome outburst.
6–7. pinch . . . disposition: take the chances of irritating one another that their different temperaments offer.
7. No more: i.e. no more unfriendly talk.
11. a name: i.e. merely a name (without corresponding greatness of nature). **12. as live:** as lief, just as soon.
12–13. a reed . . . service: a useless reed, i.e. no weapon at all.

me no service as a partisan I could not heave.

1. Serv. To be call'd into a huge sphere, and not to be seen to move in't, are the holes where eyes should be, which pitifully disaster the cheeks.

A sennet sounded. Enter CAESAR, ANTONY, POMPEY, LEPIDUS, AGRIPPA, MAECENAS, ENOBARBUS, MENAS, *with other Captains.*

Ant. [*To Caesar.*] Thus do they, sir: they take the flow o' th' Nile
By certain scales i' th' pyramid; they know,
By th' height, the lowness, or the mean, if dearth
Or foison follow. The higher Nilus swells,
The more it promises; as it ebbs, the seedsman
Upon the slime and ooze scatters his grain,
And shortly comes to harvest.

Lep. Y' have strange serpents there?

Ant. Ay, Lepidus.

Lep. Your serpent of Egypt is bred now of your mud by the operation of your sun. So is your crocodile.

Ant. They are so.

Pom. Sit—and some wine! A health to Lepidus!

Lep. I am not so well as I should be; but I'll ne'er out.

Eno. Not till you have slept; I fear me you'll be in till then.

Lep. Nay certainly, I have heard the Ptolomies' pyramises are very goodly things; without contradiction, I have heard that.

Men. [*Aside to Pompey.*] Pompey, a word.

Pom. [*Aside to Menas.*] Say in mine ear, what is't.

Men. (*Whispers in 's ear.*) Forsake thy seat, I do beseech thee, captain,
And hear me speak a word.

Pom. [*Aside to Menas.*] Forbear me till anon.—
This wine for Lepidus!

Lep. What manner o' thing is your crocodile?

Ant. It is shap'd, sir, like itself, and it is as broad as it hath breadth. It is just so high as it is, and moves with it own organs. It lives by that which nourisheth it, and the elements once out of it, it transmigrates.

Lep. What color is it of?

Ant. Of it own color too.

Lep. 'Tis a strange serpent.

Ant. 'Tis so, and the tears of it are wet.

Caes. Will this description satisfy him?

13. **partisan:** long-handled spear with double blade. **heave:** lift.
14–16. **To . . . cheeks:** i.e. to possess an office one can't discharge is like having eyeless sockets, a tragic disfigurement. (The allusion is to a planet which moves within its sphere; *disaster* continues the astrological idea, since its technical reference is to unfavorable planetary influence.)
16 s.d. **sennet:** trumpet call announcing the arrival of an important personage.
17. **take the flow:** measure the height of the flooding.
19–20. **dearth Or foison:** famine or plenty.
26. **Your.** Indefinite in sense; a common colloquialism.
31. **out:** drop out, fail to drink my share. 32. **in:** in drink.
35. **pyramises.** The singular *pyramis* was common, but Lepidus does not know its proper plural, *pyramides* (see V.ii.61). **goodly:** fine, handsome. 44. **it:** its.
45. **elements:** vital forces. **transmigrates.** Alluding to the Pythagorean doctrine, which originated in Egypt, of the transmigration of souls.

Ant. With the health that Pompey gives him, else he is a very epicure. [*Menas whispers again.*]

Pom. [*Aside to Menas.*] Go hang, sir, hang! Tell me of that? Away!
Do as I bid you.—Where's this cup I call'd for?

Men. [*Aside to Pompey.*] If for the sake of merit thou wilt hear me,
Rise from thy stool.

Pom. [*Aside to Menas.*] I think th' art mad. The matter? [*Rises and walks aside.*]

Men. I have ever held my cap off to thy fortunes.

Pom. Thou hast serv'd me with much faith; what's else to say?—
Be jolly, lords.

Ant. These quicksands, Lepidus,
Keep off them, for you sink.

Men. Wilt thou be lord of all the world?

Pom. What say'st thou?

Men. Wilt thou be lord of the whole world? That's twice.

Pom. How should that be?

Men. But entertain it,
And though thou think me poor, I am the man
Will give thee all the world.

Pom. Hast thou drunk well?

Men. No, Pompey, I have kept me from the cup.
Thou art, if thou dar'st be, the earthly Jove.
What e'er the ocean pales, or sky inclips,
Is thine, if thou wilt ha't.

Pom. Show me which way.

Men. These three world-sharers, these competitors,
Are in thy vessel. Let me cut the cable,
And when we are put off, fall to their throats:
All there is thine.

Pom. Ah, this thou shouldst have done,
And not have spoke on't! In me 'tis villainy,
In thee't had been good service. Thou must know,
'Tis not my profit that does lead mine honor;
Mine honor, it. Repent that e'er thy tongue
Hath so betray'd thine act. Being done unknown,
I should have found it afterwards well done,
But must condemn it now. Desist, and drink.

Men. [*Aside.*] For this,
I'll never follow thy pall'd fortunes more.
Who seeks, and will not take when once 'tis offer'd,
Shall never find it more.

Pom. This health to Lepidus!

Ant. Bear him ashore. I'll pledge it for him, Pompey.

Eno Here's to thee, Menas!

Men. Enobarbus, welcome!

Pom. Fill till the cup be hid.

Eno. There's a strong fellow, Menas.
[*Pointing to the Attendant who carries off Lepidus.*]

Men. Why?

52. **epicure:** glutton. (Antony is quibbling on *satisfy.*)
55. **merit:** my merits, i.e. my past services.
57. **held . . . to:** respectfully served. 58. **faith:** faithfulness.
63. **entertain:** receive, accept.
68. **pales:** fences in. **inclips:** embraces.
70. **competitors:** confederates, colleagues.
82. **pall'd:** waned.

Eno. 'A bears the third part of the world, man; seest not?
Men. The third part then is drunk. Would it were all,
That it might go on wheels!
Eno. Drink thou; increase the reels.
Men. Come.
Pom. This is not yet an Alexandrian feast.
Ant. It ripens towards it. Strike the vessels ho!
Here's to Caesar!
Caes. I could well forbear't.
It's monstrous labor when I wash my brain
And it grow fouler.
Ant. Be a child o' th' time.
Caes. Possess it, I'll make answer.
But I had rather fast from all, four days,
Than drink so much in one.
Eno. [*To Antony.*] Ha, my brave emperor!
Shall we dance now the Egyptian bacchanals
And celebrate our drink?
Pom. Let's ha't, good soldier.
Ant. Come, let's all take hands,
Till that the conquering wine hath steep'd our sense
In soft and delicate Lethe.
Eno. All take hands.
Make battery to our ears with the loud music;
The while I'll place you, then the boy shall sing.
The holding every man shall [bear] as loud
As his strong sides can volley.
Music plays. Enobarbus places them hand in hand.

THE SONG

Come, thou monarch of the vine,
Plumpy Bacchus with pink eyne!
In thy fats our cares be drown'd,
With thy grapes our hairs be crown'd!
Cup us till the world go round,
Cup us till the world go round!

Caes. What would you more? Pompey, good night. Good brother,
Let me request you [off,] our graver business
Frowns at this levity. Gentle lords, let's part,
You see we have burnt our cheeks. Strong Enobarb
Is weaker than the wine, and mine own tongue
Spleets what it speaks; the wild disguise hath almost
Antick'd us all. What needs more words? Good night.
Good Antony, your hand.
Pom. I'll try you on the shore.
Ant. And shall, sir, give 's your hand.
Pom. O Antony,
You have my [father's] house—But what, we are friends?
Come down into the boat.

90. **'A:** he. 93. **go on wheels:** run smoothly (proverbial).
97. **Strike the vessels:** open more bottles.
99. **monstrous:** unnatural.
101. **Possess . . . answer:** i.e. drink your toast, and I'll drink in return. 103. **brave:** splendid. 108. **Lethe:** obliviousness.
111. **holding:** refrain. 114. **pink eyne:** half-shut eyes.
115. **fats:** vats. 119. **brother:** i.e. brother-in-law.
120. **request you off:** ask you to come away.
124. **Spleets:** splits, mutilates. **disguise:** drunken revelry.
125. **Antick'd:** made buffoons of.
126. **try you:** test your drinking powers.

Eno. Take heed you fall not.
[*Exeunt all but Enobarbus and Menas.*]
Menas, I'll not on shore.
[*Men.*] No, to my cabin.
These drums, these trumpets, flutes! what!
Let Neptune hear we bid a loud farewell
To these great fellows. Sound and be hang'd, sound out! *Sound a flourish, with drums.*
Eno. Hoo, says 'a. There's my cap.
Men. Ho, noble captain, come. *Exeunt.*

[ACT III, SCENE I]

Enter VENTIDIUS *as it were in triumph* [*with* SILIUS *and other* ROMANS, OFFICERS, *and* SOLDIERS], *the dead body of Pacorus borne before him.*

Ven. Now, darting Parthia, art thou strook, and now
Pleas'd Fortune does of Marcus Crassus' death
Make me revenger. Bear the King's son's body
Before our army. Thy Pacorus, Orodes,
Pays this for Marcus Crassus.
[*Sil.*] Noble Ventidius,
Whilst yet with Parthian blood thy sword is warm,
The fugitive Parthians follow. Spur through Media,
Mesopotamia, and the shelters whither
The routed fly; so thy grand captain, Antony,
Shall set thee on triumphant chariots, and
Put garlands on thy head.
Ven. O Silius, Silius,
I have done enough; a lower place, note well,
May make too great an act. For learn this, Silius:
Better to leave undone, than by our deed
Acquire too high a fame when him we serve's away.
Caesar and Antony have ever won
More in their officer than person. Sossius,
One of my place in Syria, his lieutenant,
For quick accumulation of renown,
Which he achiev'd by th' minute, lost his favor.
Who does i' th' wars more than his captain can
Becomes his captain's captain; and ambition
(The soldier's virtue) rather makes choice of loss
Than gain which darkens him.
I could do more to do Antonius good,
But 'twould offend him; and in his offense
Should my performance perish.
[*Sil.*] Thou hast, Ventidius, that
Without the which a soldier and his sword
Grants scarce distinction. Thou wilt write to Antony?
Ven. I'll humbly signify what in his name,
That magical word of war, we have effected;
How with his banners, and his well-paid ranks,

III.i. Location: A plain in Syria.
1. **darting.** The Parthians were famed bowmen. **strook:** struck.
2. **Crassus' death.** Crassus was a member, with the elder Pompey and Julius Caesar, of the first triumvirate. He was killed by the Parthians after they had defeated him in 53 B.C. under King Orodes.
12. **a lower place:** i.e. a subordinate.
18. **of my place:** of rank equivalent to mine.
20. **by th' minute:** minute by minute, continually.
24. **darkens him:** causes him to lose favor.
27–29. **that . . . distinction:** i.e. discretion, but for which there is very little difference between a soldier and his sword.

The ne'er-yet-beaten horse of Parthia
We have jaded out o' th' field.
[Sil.] Where is he now?
Ven. He purposeth to Athens, whither, with what haste
The weight we must convey with 's will permit,
We shall appear before him. On, there, pass along!
Exeunt.

[SCENE II]

Enter AGRIPPA *at one door*, ENOBARBUS *at another.*

Agr. What, are the brothers parted?
Eno. They have dispatch'd with Pompey, he is gone;
The other three are sealing. Octavia weeps
To part from Rome; Caesar is sad, and Lepidus,
Since Pompey's feast, as Menas says, is troubled
With the green-sickness.
Agr. 'Tis a noble Lepidus.
Eno. A very fine one. O, how he loves Caesar!
Agr. Nay, but how dearly he adores Mark Antony!
Eno. Caesar? Why, he's the Jupiter of men.
[Agr.] What's Antony? The god of Jupiter.
Eno. Spake you of Caesar? How, the nonpareil!
Agr. O Antony! O thou Arabian bird!
Eno. Would you praise Caesar, say "Caesar," go no further.
Agr. Indeed he plied them both with excellent praises.
Eno. But he loves Caesar best, yet he loves Antony.
Hoo, hearts, tongues, [figures], scribes, bards, poets, cannot
Think, speak, cast, write, sing, number, hoo!
His love to Antony. But as for Caesar,
Kneel down, kneel down, and wonder.
Agr. Both he loves.
Eno. They are his shards, and he their beetle, so.
[Trumpet within.]
This is to horse. Adieu, noble Agrippa.
Agr. Good fortune, worthy soldier, and farewell.

Enter CAESAR, ANTONY, LEPIDUS, *and* OCTAVIA.

Ant. No further, sir.
Caes. You take from me a great part of myself;
Use me well in't. Sister, prove such a wife
As my thoughts make thee, and as my farthest band
Shall pass on thy approof. Most noble Antony,
Let not the piece of virtue which is set
Betwixt us, as the cement of our love
To keep it builded, be the ram to batter
The fortress of it; for better might we
Have lov'd without this mean, if on both parts
This be not cherish'd.
Ant. Make me not offended
In your distrust.
Caes. I have said.
Ant. You shall not find,
Though you be therein curious, the least cause
For what you seem to fear. So the gods keep you,
And make the hearts of Romans serve your ends!
We will here part.
Caes. Farewell, my dearest sister, fare thee well,
The elements be kind to thee, and make
Thy spirits all of comfort! Fare thee well.
Oct. My noble brother!
Ant. The April's in her eyes, it is love's spring,
And these the showers to bring it on. Be cheerful.
Oct. Sir, look well to my husband's house; and—
Caes. What,
Octavia?
Oct. I'll tell you in your ear.
Ant. Her tongue will not obey her heart, nor can
Her heart inform her tongue—the swan's down feather,
That stands upon the swell at the full of tide,
And neither way inclines.
Eno. *[Aside to Agrippa.]* Will Caesar weep?
Agr. *[Aside to Enobarbus.]* He has a cloud in 's face.
Eno. *[Aside to Agrippa.]* He were the worse for that were he a horse;
So is he being a man.
Agr. *[Aside to Enobarbus.]* Why, Enobarbus?
When Antony found Julius Caesar dead,
He cried almost to roaring; and he wept
When at Philippi he found Brutus slain.
Eno. *[Aside to Agrippa.]* That year indeed he was troubled with a rheum;
What willingly he did confound he wail'd,
Believe't—till I weep too.
Caes. No, sweet Octavia,
You shall hear from me still; the time shall not
Outgo my thinking on you.
Ant. Come, sir, come,
I'll wrastle with you in my strength of love.
Look, here I have you, thus I let you go,
And give you to the gods.
Caes. Adieu, be happy.
Lep. Let all the number of the stars give light
To thy fair way.
Caes. Farewell, farewell. *Kisses Octavia.*
Ant. Farewell. *Trumpets sound. Exeunt.*

33. **horse**: cavalry.
34. **jaded**: driven like jades (inferior horses that cannot stay the course).

III.ii. Location: Rome. Caesar's house.
3. **sealing**: sealing their agreement, settling final details.
4. **sad**: sober.
6. **green-sickness**: anemia in unmarried girls, here jocularly used of Lepidus' hangover. 12. **Arabian bird**: phoenix (supposed unique).
17. **cast**: calculate, compute. **number**: versify.
20. **shards**: wing-cases. 26. **farthest band**: utmost pledge.
27. **pass . . . approof**: certify that you will prove to be.
28. **piece**: masterpiece.
32. **mean**: means (?) or intermediary (?). 34. **In**: by, at.
35. **therein curious**: minutely inquisitive in looking for it.
40. **The elements**: i.e. external nature as it will affect her journey (?) or the bodily humors that determine her own health and state of mind (?). Perhaps both: "may all things go well with you."
47–50. **Her . . . inclines**: i.e. the forces pulling her in opposite directions act upon her tongue to keep it motionless, like a floating feather at the moment of high tide, when the forces of ebb and flow are equal.
52. **were . . . horse.** A horse with a totally dark face was apparently considered unreliable or vicious; see *The Two Noble Kinsmen*, V.iv.50–53. 57. **rheum**: watering of the eyes.
58. **confound**: destroy. **wail'd**: bewailed.
59. **till . . . too.** "Which he thought would be never" (Capell). Most editors follow Theobald in emending *weep* to *wept*.
60. **still**: regularly and often.

[Scene III]

Enter Cleopatra, Charmian, Iras, *and* Alexas.

Cleo. Where is the fellow?
Alex. Half afeard to come.
Cleo. Go to, go to. Come hither, sir.

Enter the Messenger *as before.*

Alex. Good Majesty!
Herod of Jewry dare not look upon you
But when you are well pleas'd.
Cleo. That Herod's head
I'll have; but how, when Antony is gone,
Through whom I might command it? Come thou near.
Mess. Most gracious Majesty!
Cleo. Didst thou behold Octavia?
Mess. Ay, dread Queen.
Cleo. Where?
Mess. Madam, in Rome;
I look'd her in the face, and saw her led
Between her brother and Mark Antony.
Cleo. Is she as tall as me?
Mess. She is not, madam.
Cleo. Didst hear her speak? Is she shrill-tongu'd or low?
Mess. Madam, I heard her speak; she is low-voic'd.
Cleo. That's not so good. He cannot like her long.
Char. Like her? O Isis! 'tis impossible.
Cleo. I think so, Charmian: dull of tongue, and dwarfish.
What majesty is in her gait? Remember,
If e'er thou look'st on majesty.
Mess. She creeps;
Her motion and her station are as one;
She shows a body rather than a life,
A statue, than a breather.
Cleo. Is this certain?
Mess. Or I have no observance.
Char. Three in Egypt
Cannot make better note.
Cleo. He's very knowing,
I do perceive't. There's nothing in her yet.
The fellow has good judgment.
Char. Excellent.
Cleo. Guess at her years, I prithee.
Mess. Madam,
She was a widow—
Cleo. Widow? Charmian, hark.
Mess. And I do think she's thirty.
Cleo. Bear'st thou her face in mind? Is't long or round?
Mess. Round, even to faultiness.
Cleo. For the most part, too, they are foolish that are so.
Her hair, what color?
Mess. Brown, madam; and her forehead

III.iii. Location: Alexandria. Cleopatra's palace.
3. Herod of Jewry: i.e. even the fiercest tyrant (see note on I.ii.28).
14. good: i.e. favorable for Octavia.
19. motion . . . station: moving . . . standing still.
20. shows: appears to be.

As low as she would wish it.
Cleo. There's gold for thee,
Thou must not take my former sharpness ill.
I will employ thee back again; I find thee
Most fit for business. Go, make thee ready,
Our letters are prepar'd. [*Exit Messenger.*]
Char. A proper man.
Cleo. Indeed he is so; I repent me much
That so I harried him. Why, methinks, by him,
This creature's no such thing.
Char. Nothing, madam.
Cleo. The man hath seen some majesty, and should know.
Char. Hath he seen majesty? Isis else defend!
And serving you so long!
Cleo. I have one thing more to ask him yet, good Charmian—
But 'tis no matter, thou shalt bring him to me
Where I will write. All may be well enough.
Char. I warrant you, madam. *Exeunt.*

[Scene IV]

Enter Antony *and* Octavia.

Ant. Nay, nay, Octavia, not only that—
That were excusable, that, and thousands more
Of semblable import—but he hath wag'd
New wars 'gainst Pompey; made his will, and read it
To public ear;
Spoke scantly of me; when perforce he could not
But pay me terms of honor, cold and sickly
He vented [them,] most narrow measure lent me;
When the best hint was given him, he not [took]'t,
Or did it from his teeth.
Oct. O my good lord,
Believe not all, or if you must believe,
Stomach not all. A more unhappy lady,
If this division chance, ne'er stood between,
Praying for both parts.
The good gods will mock me presently,
When I shall pray, "O, bless my lord and husband!"
Undo that prayer, by crying out as loud,
"O, bless my brother!" Husband win, win brother,
Prays, and destroys the prayer, no midway
'Twixt these extremes at all.
Ant. Gentle Octavia,
Let your best love draw to that point which seeks
Best to preserve it. If I lose mine honor,
I lose myself; better I were not yours
Than [yours] so branchless. But as you requested,
Yourself shall go between 's. The mean time, lady,
I'll raise the preparation of a war

34. As . . . it: so low that she wouldn't wish it any lower, i.e. very low. A high forehead was then the ideal. 38. proper: excellent.
40. by him: by his report. 41. no such thing: nothing much.
43. else defend: forbid that it could possibly be otherwise.

III.iv. Location: Athens. Antony's house.
3. semblable: similar. 9. hint: occasion.
10. from his teeth: i.e. not from his heart.
12. Stomach: resent. 15. presently: at once.
24. branchless: with my honors cut off.
26. the preparation . . . war: i.e. an armed force.

Shall stain your brother. Make your soonest haste;
So your desires are yours.
Oct. Thanks to my lord.
The Jove of power make me most weak, most weak,
[Your] reconciler! Wars 'twixt you twain would be
As if the world should cleave, and that slain men
Should solder up the rift.
Ant. When it appears to you where this begins,
Turn your displeasure that way, for our faults
Can never be so equal that your love
Can equally move with them. Provide your going,
Choose your own company, and command what cost
Your heart [has] mind to. *Exeunt.*

[SCENE V]

Enter ENOBARBUS *and* EROS, [*meeting*].

Eno. How now, friend Eros?
Eros. There's strange news come, sir.
Eno. What, man?
Eros. Caesar and Lepidus have made wars upon Pompey.
Eno. This is old, what is the success?
Eros. Caesar, having made use of him in the wars 'gainst Pompey, presently denied him rivality, would not let him partake in the glory of the action, and not resting here, accuses him of letters he had formerly wrote to Pompey; upon his own appeal, seizes him. So the poor third is up, till death enlarge his confine.
Eno. Then, [world,] thou [hast] a pair of chaps—no more,
And throw between them all the food thou hast,
They'll grind [th'] one] the other. Where's Antony?
Eros. He's walking in the garden—thus, and spurns
The rush that lies before him; cries, "Fool Lepidus!"
And threats the throat of that his officer
That murd'red Pompey.
Eno. Our great navy's rigg'd.
Eros. For Italy and Caesar. More, Domitius,
My lord desires you presently; my news
I might have told hereafter.
Eno. 'Twill be naught,
But let it be. Bring me to Antony.
Eros. Come, sir. *Exeunt.*

[SCENE VI]

Enter AGRIPPA, MAECENAS, *and* CAESAR.

Caes. Contemning Rome, he has done all this and more
In Alexandria. Here's the manner of't:
I' th' market-place, on a tribunal silver'd,
Cleopatra and himself in chairs of gold
Were publicly enthron'd. At the feet sat
Caesarion, whom they call my father's son,
And all the unlawful issue that their lust
Since then hath made between them. Unto her
He gave the stablishment of Egypt, made her
Of lower Syria, Cyprus, Lydia,
Absolute queen.
Maec. This in the public eye?
Caes. I' th' common show-place, where they exercise.
His sons [he there] proclaim'd the [kings] of kings:
Great Media, Parthia, and Armenia
He gave to Alexander; to Ptolomy he assign'd
Syria, Cilicia, and Phoenicia. She
In th' abiliments of the goddess Isis
That day appear'd; and oft before gave audience,
As 'tis reported, so.
Maec. Let Rome be thus
Inform'd.
Agr. Who, queasy with his insolence
Already, will their good thoughts call from him.
Caes. The people knows it, and have now receiv'd
His accusations.
Agr. Who does he accuse?
Caes. Caesar, and that having in Sicily
Sextus Pompeius spoil'd, we had not rated him
His part o' th' isle. Then does he say he lent me
Some shipping unrestor'd. Lastly, he frets
That Lepidus of the triumpherate
Should be depos'd; and being, that we detain
All his revenue.
Agr. Sir, this should be answer'd.
Caes. 'Tis done already, and the messenger gone.
I have told him Lepidus was grown too cruel,
That he his high authority abus'd,
And did deserve his change. For what I have conquer'd,
I grant him part; but then, in his Armenia
And other of his conquer'd kingdoms, I
Demand the like.
Maec. He'll never yield to that.
Caes. Nor must not then be yielded to in this.

Enter OCTAVIA *with her* TRAIN.

Oct. Hail, Caesar, and my lord! hail, most dear Caesar!
Caes. That ever I should call thee castaway!
Oct. You have not call'd me so, nor have you cause.
Caes. Why have you stol'n upon us thus? You come not
Like Caesar's sister. The wife of Antony
Should have an army for an usher, and
The neighs of horse to tell of her approach,

27. Shall . . . brother: which shall make your brother's look small.
33. where this begins: i.e. whether responsibility for this lies with Caesar or with me.

III.v. Location: Scene continues.
6. success: outcome. **8. rivality:** equal rights as a partner.
10. resting here: stopping with this.
11. his own appeal: Caesar's own accusation.
12. up: shut up. **13. chaps:** jaws.
14. throw: even though you throw. **16. spurns:** kicks at.
18. that his officer: that officer of his.
19. That murd'red Pompey. Probably at Antony's command.
22. naught: something foolish or ill-advised.

III.vi. Location: Rome. Caesar's house.
3. tribunal: platform.
6. my father's: i.e. Julius Caesar's. Octavius was his adopted son.
9. stablishment: rule. **17. abiliments:** habiliments, attire.
20. queasy: disgusted, "fed up."
25. spoil'd: plundered. **rated:** allotted.
28. of: from. **triumpherate:** variant of *triumvirate*.
29. being: i.e. being deposed. **45. horse.** Plural.

Long ere she did appear; the trees by th' way
Should have borne men, and expectation fainted,
Longing for what it had not; nay, the dust
Should have ascended to the roof of heaven,
Rais'd by your populous troops. But you are come
A market-maid to Rome, and have prevented
The ostentation of our love, which, left unshown,
Is often left unlov'd. We should have met you
By sea and land, supplying every stage
With an augmented greeting.
Oct. Good my lord,
To come thus was I not constrain'd, but did it
On my free will. My lord, Mark Antony,
Hearing that you prepar'd for war, acquainted
My grieved ear withal; whereon I begg'd
His pardon for return.
Caes. Which soon he granted,
Being an abstract 'tween his lust and him.
Oct. Do not say so, my lord.
Caes. I have eyes upon him,
And his affairs come to me on the wind.
Where is he now?
Oct. My lord, in Athens.
Caes. No, my most wronged sister, Cleopatra
Hath nodded him to her. He hath given his empire
Up to a whore, who now are levying
The kings o' th' earth for war. He hath assembled
Bocchus, the King of Libya; Archelaus
Of Cappadocia; Philadelphos, King
Of Paphlagonia; the Thracian king, Adallas;
King Manchus of Arabia; King of Pont;
Herod of Jewry; Mithridates, King
Of Comagena; Polemon and Amyntas,
The Kings of Mede and Lycaonia,
With a more larger list of sceptres.
Oct. Ay me, most wretched,
That have my heart parted betwixt two friends
That does afflict each other!
Caes. Welcome hither!
Your letters did withhold our breaking forth,
Till we perceiv'd both how you were wrong led
And we in negligent danger. Cheer your heart,
Be you not troubled with the time, which drives
O'er your content these strong necessities,
But let determin'd things to destiny
Hold unbewail'd their way. Welcome to Rome,
Nothing more dear to me. You are abus'd
Beyond the mark of thought; and the high gods,
To do you justice, makes his ministers
Of us and those that love you. Best of comfort,
And ever welcome to us.
Agr. Welcome, lady.

51. prevented: forestalled, come too soon to allow.
52. ostentation: proper display.
53. left unlov'd: thought not to be love at all (?).
60. pardon: permission.
61. Being an abstract: (your departure) being the removal of something intervening. Many editors prefer Theobald's *Being an obstruct*, "(you) being an obstruction." **67. who**: i.e. and they.
79. withhold: restrain.
81. negligent danger: danger through our negligence.
84. destiny: their predestined conclusion. **87. mark**: scope, reach.
88. makes his. Sisson explains the singular forms: "*the high gods* is a collective phrase, the equivalent of *God.*" **ministers**: agents, instruments.

Maec. Welcome, dear madam,
Each heart in Rome does love and pity you;
Only th' adulterous Antony, most large
In his abominations, turns you off,
And gives his potent regiment to a trull
That noises it against us.
Oct. Is it so, sir?
Caes. Most certain. Sister, welcome. Pray you
Be ever known to patience. My dear'st sister!
Exeunt.

[Scene VII]

Enter Cleopatra *and* Enobarbus.

Cleo. I will be even with thee, doubt it not.
Eno. But why, why, why?
Cleo. Thou hast forespoke my being in these wars,
And say'st it is not fit.
Eno. Well; is it, is it?
Cleo. If not denounc'd against us, why should not we
Be there in person?
Eno. [*Aside.*] Well, I could reply:
If we should serve with horse and mares together,
The horse were merely lost; the mares would bear
A soldier and his horse.
Cleo. What is't you say?
Eno. Your presence needs must puzzle Antony,
Take from his heart, take from his brain, from 's time,
What should not then be spar'd. He is already
Traduc'd for levity, and 'tis said in Rome
That Photinus an eunuch and your maids
Manage this war.
Cleo. Sink Rome, and their tongues rot
That speak against us! A charge we bear i' th' war,
And as the president of my kingdom will
Appear there for a man. Speak not against it,
I will not stay behind.

Enter Antony *and* Canidius.

Eno. Nay, I have done,
Here comes the Emperor.
Ant. Is it not strange, Canidius,
That from Tarentum and Brundusium
He could so quickly cut the Ionian Sea,
And take in Toryne? You have heard on't, sweet?
Cleo. Celerity is never more admir'd
Than by the negligent.
Ant. A good rebuke,
Which might have well becom'd the best of men,
To taunt at slackness. Canidius, we
Will fight with him by sea.
Cleo. By sea, what else?
Can. Why will my lord do so?

93. large: unrestrained.
95. regiment: rule, authority. **96. noises it**: is clamorous.

III.vii. Location: Antony's camp near Actium.
3. forespoke: forspoken, spoken against.
5. If . . . us: even if it were not declared against me (?). Many editors, following Rowe, read *Is't . . . us?*
8. were merely: would be utterly.
10. puzzle: bewilder, confound. **16. charge**: responsibility.
23. take in: conquer. **24. admir'd**: wondered at.

Ant. For that he dares us to't.
Eno. So hath my lord dar'd him to single fight.
Can. Ay, and to wage this battle at Pharsalia,
Where Caesar fought with Pompey. But these offers,
Which serve not for his vantage, he shakes off,
And so should you.
Eno. Your ships are not well mann'd,
Your mariners are [muleters], reapers, people
Ingross'd by swift impress. In Caesar's fleet
Are those that often have 'gainst Pompey fought;
Their ships are yare, yours heavy. No disgrace
Shall fall you for refusing him at sea,
Being prepar'd for land.
Ant. By sea, by sea.
Eno. Most worthy sir, you therein throw away
The absolute soldiership you have by land,
Distract your army, which doth most consist
Of war-mark'd footmen, leave unexecuted
Your own renowned knowledge, quite forgo
The way which promises assurance, and
Give up yourself merely to chance and hazard,
From firm security.
Ant. I'll fight at sea.
Cleo. I have sixty sails, Caesar none better.
Ant. Our overplus of shipping will we burn,
And, with the rest full-mann'd, from th' head of [Actium]
Beat th' approaching Caesar. But if we fail,
We then can do't at land.

Enter a MESSENGER.

Thy business?
Mess. The news is true, my lord: he is descried;
Caesar has taken Toryne.
Ant. Can he be there in person? 'Tis impossible
Strange that his power should be. Canidius,
Our nineteen legions thou shalt hold by land,
And our twelve thousand horse. We'll to our ship,
Away, my Thetis!

Enter a SOLDIER.

How now, worthy soldier?
Sold. O noble Emperor, do not fight by sea,
Trust not to rotten planks. Do you misdoubt
This sword, and these my wounds? Let th' Egyptians
And the Phoenicians go a-ducking; we
Have us'd to conquer standing on the earth,
And fighting foot to foot.
Ant. Well, well, away!

Exeunt Antony, Cleopatra, and Enobarbus.

Sold. By Hercules, I think I am i' th' right.
Can. Soldier, thou art; but his whole action grows
Not in the power on't. So our leader's [led],
And we are women's men.
Sold. You keep by land
The legions and the horse whole, do you not?
[*Can.*] Marcus Octavius, Marcus Justeius,
Publicola, and Caelius are for sea;
But we keep whole by land. This speed of Caesar's
Carries beyond belief.
Sold. While he was yet in Rome,
His power went out in such distractions as
Beguil'd all spies.
Can. Who's his lieutenant, hear you?
Sold. They say, one Taurus.
Can. Well I know the man.

Enter a MESSENGER.

Mess. The Emperor calls Canidius.
Can. With news the time's with labor, and throes forth
Each minute some. *Exeunt.*

[SCENE VIII]

Enter CAESAR *with his army* [*and* TAURUS], *marching.*

Caes. Taurus!
Taur. My lord?
Caes. Strike not by land, keep whole, provoke not battle
Till we have done at sea. Do not exceed
The prescript of this scroll. Our fortune lies
Upon this jump. *Exeunt.*

[SCENE IX]

Enter ANTONY *and* ENOBARBUS.

Ant. Set we our squadrons on yond side o' th' hill,
In eye of Caesar's battle, from which place
We may the number of the ships behold,
And so proceed accordingly. *Exeunt.*

[SCENE X]

CANIDIUS *marcheth with his land army one way over the stage, and* TAURUS, *the lieutenant of Caesar, the other way. After their going in, is heard the noise of a sea-fight.*

Alarum. Enter ENOBARBUS.

Eno. Naught, naught, all naught! I can behold no longer.
Th' *Antoniad*, the Egyptian admiral,
With all their sixty, fly and turn the rudder.
To see't mine eyes are blasted.

35. muleters: muleteers, mule drivers.
36. Ingross'd: gathered up wholesale. **impress:** conscription.
38. yare: easily maneuvered. **39. fall:** befall.
43. Distract: divide.
44. leave unexecuted: offer no opportunity for the use of.
57. power: army.
60. Thetis: a sea-goddess, mother of Achilles.
68–69. his . . . on't: i.e. his plan of action is not based on the true source of his strength.

76. distractions: separate groups.
80. throes forth: brings painfully to birth.

III.viii. Location: A plain near Actium.
5. prescript: direction. **6. jump:** hazard.

III.ix. Location: Scene continues.
2. battle: battle line.

III.x. Location: Scene continues.
2. admiral: flagship.

Enter Scarus.

Scar. Gods and goddesses,
All the whole synod of them!
Eno. What's thy passion?
Scar. The greater cantle of the world is lost
With very ignorance, we have kiss'd away
Kingdoms and provinces.
Eno. How appears the fight?
Scar. On our side like the token'd pestilence,
Where death is sure. Yon ribaudred nag of Egypt
(Whom leprosy o'ertake!) i' th' midst o' th' fight,
When vantage like a pair of twins appear'd,
Both as the same, or rather ours the elder—
The breeze upon her, like a cow in [June]—
Hoists sails and flies.
Eno. That I beheld.
Mine eyes did sicken at the sight and could not
Endure a further view.
Scar. She once being loof'd,
The noble ruin of her magic, Antony,
Claps on his sea-wing, and (like a doting mallard),
Leaving the fight in heighth, flies after her.
I never saw an action of such shame;
Experience, manhood, honor, ne'er before
Did violate so itself.
Eno. Alack, alack!

Enter Canidius.

Can. Our fortune on the sea is out of breath,
And sinks most lamentably. Had our general
Been what he knew himself, it had gone well.
O, [he] has given example for our flight,
Most grossly, by his own!
Eno. Ay, are you thereabouts?
Why then good night indeed.
Can. Toward Peloponnesus are they fled.
Scar. 'Tis easy to't, and there I will attend
What further comes.
Can. To Caesar will I render
My legions and my horse: six kings already
Show me the way of yielding.
Eno. I'll yet follow
The wounded chance of Antony, though my reason
Sits in the wind against me. [*Exeunt severally.*]

[Scene XI]

Enter Antony *with* Attendants.

Ant. Hark, the land bids me tread no more upon't,
It is asham'd to bear me. Friends, come hither:
I am so lated in the world, that I
Have lost my way for ever. I have a ship
Laden with gold, take that, divide it; fly,
And make your peace with Caesar.
Omnes. Fly? not we.
Ant. I have fled myself, and have instructed cowards
To run and show their shoulders. Friends, be gone,
I have myself resolv'd upon a course
Which has no need of you. Be gone.
My treasure's in the harbor; take it. O,
I follow'd that I blush to look upon.
My very hairs do mutiny; for the white
Reprove the brown for rashness, and they them
For fear and doting. Friends, be gone, you shall
Have letters from me to some friends that will
Sweep your way for you. Pray you look not sad,
Nor make replies of loathness; take the hint
Which my despair proclaims: let [that] be left
Which leaves itself. To the sea-side straightway;
I will possess you of that ship and treasure.
Leave me, I pray, a little; pray you now,
Nay, do so; for indeed I have lost command,
Therefore I pray you. I'll see you by and by.
Sits down.

Enter Cleopatra *led by* Charmian *and* Eros, [Iras *following*].

Eros. Nay, gentle madam, to him, comfort him.
Iras. Do, most dear Queen.
Char. Do? why, what else?
Cleo. Let me sit down. O Juno!
Ant. No, no, no, no, no.
Eros. See you here, sir?
Ant. O fie, fie, fie!
Char. Madam!
Iras. Madam, O good Empress!
Eros. Sir, sir!
Ant. Yes, my lord, yes; he at Philippi kept
His sword e'en like a dancer, while I strook
The lean and wrinkled Cassius, and 'twas I
That the mad Brutus ended. He alone
Dealt on lieutenantry, and no practice had
In the brave squares of war; yet now—No matter.
Cleo. Ah, stand by.
Eros. The Queen, my lord, the Queen.
Iras. Go to him, madam, speak to him,
He's unqualited with very shame.
Cleo. Well then, sustain me. O!
Eros. Most noble sir, arise, the Queen approaches.
Her head's declin'd, and death will seize her, but
Your comfort makes the rescue.

5. synod: assembly. **6. cantle:** corner, i.e. segment, portion.
7. With very ignorance: by utter folly.
9. token'd pestilence: the plague when the characteristic "tokens" or plague-spots appear.
10. ribaudred: lewd (not found elsewhere, but apparently related to *ribald,* also spelled *ribaud*).
12. When . . . appear'd: i.e. when advantages were evenly balanced.
13. elder: i.e. greater. **14. breeze:** gadfly.
17. loof'd: ready to sail away. **19. mallard:** wild drake.
20. in heighth: at its height.
28. thereabouts: of that mind (referring to Canidius' "our flight").
31. to't: i.e. to get there.
33. legions . . . horse: foot soldiers . . cavalry.
35. chance: fortunes. **36. Sits . . . me:** opposes me.
III.xi. Location: Alexandria. Cleopatra's palace.

3. lated: belated (like a traveller overtaken by night).
8. shoulders: i.e. backs. **12. that:** what. **18. hint:** opportunity.
19. that: i.e. Antony himself. **left:** abandoned.
20. leaves itself: is no longer itself.
23. command: (1) the right to command you to do so; (2) command of my feelings. **35. kept:** i.e. kept in its sheath.
36. like a dancer: i.e. as if he had been wearing it for ornament, not use. **39. Dealt on lieutenantry:** did his fighting by proxy.
40. brave squares: splendid squadrons.
44. unqualited: unqualitied, i.e. without his natural powers, not himself. **47. but:** unless.

Ant. I have offended reputation,
A most unnoble swerving.
Eros. Sir, the Queen.
Ant. O, whither hast thou led me, Egypt? See
How I convey my shame out of thine eyes
By looking back what I have left behind
'Stroy'd in dishonor.
Cleo. O my lord, my lord,
Forgive my fearful sails! I little thought
You would have followed.
Ant. Egypt, thou knew'st too well
My heart was to thy rudder tied by th' strings,
And thou shouldst [tow] me after. O'er my spirit
[Thy] full supremacy thou knew'st, and that
Thy beck might from the bidding of the gods
Command me.
Cleo. O, my pardon!
Ant. Now I must
To the young man send humble treaties, dodge
And palter in the shifts of lowness, who
With half the bulk o' th' world play'd as I pleas'd,
Making and marring fortunes. You did know
How much you were my conqueror, and that
My sword, made weak by my affection, would
Obey it on all cause.
Cleo. Pardon, pardon!
Ant. Fall not a tear, I say, one of them rates
All that is won and lost. Give me a kiss.
Even this repays me. We sent our schoolmaster,
Is 'a come back? Love, I am full of lead.
Some wine, within there, and our viands! Fortune knows
We scorn her most when most she offers blows.
Exeunt.

[SCENE XII]

Enter CAESAR, AGRIPPA, [THIDIAS,] *and* DOLABELLA, *with others.*

Caes. Let him appear that's come from Antony.
Know you him?
Dol. Caesar, 'tis his schoolmaster,
An argument that he is pluck'd, when hither
He sends so poor a pinion of his wing,
Which had superfluous kings for messengers
Not many moons gone by.

Enter AMBASSADOR *from Antony.*

Caes. Approach and speak.
Amb. Such as I am, I come from Antony.
I was of late as petty to his ends
As is the morn-dew on the myrtle leaf
To his grand sea.
Caes. Be't so, declare thine office.
Amb. Lord of his fortunes he salutes thee, and
Requires to live in Egypt, which not granted,
He lessons his requests, and to thee sues
To let him breathe between the heavens and earth,
A private man in Athens: this for him.
Next, Cleopatra does confess thy greatness,
Submits her to thy might, and of thee craves
The circle of the Ptolomies for her heirs,
Now hazarded to thy grace.
Caes. For Antony,
I have no ears to his request. The Queen
Of audience nor desire shall fail, so she
From Egypt drive her all-disgraced friend,
Or take his life there. This if she perform,
She shall not sue unheard. So to them both.
Amb. Fortune pursue thee!
Caes. Bring him through the bands.
[Exit Ambassador.]
[*To Thidias.*] To try thy eloquence, now 'tis time; dispatch.
From Antony win Cleopatra, promise,
And in our name, what she requires; add more,
From thine invention, offers. Women are not
In their best fortunes strong, but want will perjure
The ne'er-touch'd vestal. Try thy cunning, Thidias,
Make thine own edict for thy pains, which we
Will answer as a law.
Thid. Caesar, I go.
Caes. Observe how Antony becomes his flaw,
And what thou think'st his very action speaks
In every power that moves.
Thid. Caesar, I shall. *Exeunt.*

[SCENE XIII]

Enter CLEOPATRA, ENOBARBUS, CHARMIAN, *and* IRAS.

Cleo. What shall we do, Enobarbus?
Eno. Think, and die.
Cleo. Is Antony or we in fault for this?
Eno. Antony only, that would make his will
Lord of his reason. What though you fled
From that great face of war, whose several ranges
Frighted each other? Why should he follow?
The itch of his affection should not then
Have nick'd his captainship, at such a point,
When half to half the world oppos'd, he being
The mered question. 'Twas a shame no less

49. **reputation:** honor.
53. **looking back:** i.e. averting my face as if I were looking back at.
62. **treaties:** proposals.
63. **palter:** shuffle, be crafty in a mean way. **shifts of lowness:** tricks that must be resorted to by one without power.
67. **affection:** passion. 68. **on all cause:** whatever the occasion.
69. **Fall:** let fall. **rates:** is worth.
71. **schoolmaster:** i.e. the tutor of his and Cleopatra's children.

III.xii. Location: Egypt. Caesar's camp.
3. **argument:** piece of evidence. 5. **Which:** who.
8. **petty to:** insignificant in relation to.
10. **his grand sea:** i.e. its source and ultimate destination, the great ocean. 12. **Requires:** requests.
13. **lessons:** subjects to correction, disciplines. 18. **circle:** crown.
19. **hazarded . . . grace:** dependent for its fate on your favor.
21. **so:** provided that. 22. **friend:** lover.
28–29. **more . . . offers:** further offers of your own devising.
30. **In . . . fortunes:** at the best of times.
32. **Make . . . edict:** name . . . reward.
34. **becomes his flaw:** bears his reverse. 35. **speaks:** signifies.
36. **every . . . moves:** i.e. every motion he makes.

III.xiii. Location: Alexandria. Cleopatra's palace.
1. **Think:** grieve. *Thought* often signified "melancholy, grief"; see IV.vi.34–35. 3. **will:** desire. 5. **ranges:** lines of battle.
8. **nick'd:** impaired (?) or won against, got the better of (term from the game of hazard) (?). 10. **mered question:** sole point at issue.

Than was his loss, to course your flying flags,
And leave his navy gazing.
Cleo. Prithee peace.

Enter the AMBASSADOR *with* ANTONY.

Ant. Is that his answer?
Amb. Ay, my lord.
Ant. The Queen shall then have courtesy, so she
Will yield us up.
Amb. He says so.
Ant. Let her know't.
To the boy Caesar send this grizzled head,
And he will fill thy wishes to the brim
With principalities.
Cleo. That head, my lord?
Ant. To him again, tell him he wears the rose
Of youth upon him; from which the world should note
Something particular. His coin, ships, legions,
May be a coward's, whose ministers would prevail
Under the service of a child as soon
As i' th' command of Caesar. I dare him therefore
To lay his gay comparisons apart,
And answer me declin'd, sword against sword,
Ourselves alone. I'll write it. Follow me.
[*Exeunt Antony and Ambassador.*]
Eno. [*Aside.*] Yes, like enough! high-battled Caesar will
Unstate his happiness, and be stag'd to th' show
Against a sworder! I see men's judgments are
A parcel of their fortunes, and things outward
Do draw the inward quality after them,
To suffer all alike. That he should dream,
Knowing all measures, the full Caesar will
Answer his emptiness! Caesar, thou hast subdu'd
His judgment too.

Enter a SERVANT.

Serv. A messenger from Caesar.
Cleo. What, no more ceremony? See, my women,
Against the blown rose may they stop their nose
That kneel'd unto the buds. Admit him, sir.
[*Exit Servant.*]
Eno. [*Aside.*] Mine honesty and I begin to square.
The loyalty well held to fools does make
Our faith mere folly; yet he that can endure
To follow with allegiance a fall'n lord
Does conquer him that did his master conquer,
And earns a place i' th' story.

Enter THIDIAS.

Cleo. Caesar's will?

11. course: pursue.
22. Something particular: some feat personally achieved (such as victory in single combat).
26. comparisons: i.e. advantages in comparison with me.
27. declin'd: (1) advanced in years; (2) fallen in fortune.
29. high-battled: possessing great armies.
30. Unstate his happiness: strip his good fortune of its dignity. **be . . . show:** make a public spectacle of himself.
32. A parcel of: of a piece with. **33. quality:** nature.
34. To . . . alike: so that they all deteriorate at the same rate.
35. Knowing all measures: i.e. being acquainted with every level of fortune. The figure in *measures* is continued in *full* and *emptiness.*
39. blown: i.e. overblown, past its prime.
41. honesty: honor. **43. mere:** utter.

Thid. Hear it apart.
Cleo. None but friends: say boldly.
Thid. So haply are they friends to Antony.
Eno. He needs as many, sir, as Caesar has,
Or needs not us. If Caesar please, our master
Will leap to be his friend; for us, you know
Whose he is we are, and that is Caesar's.
Thid. So.
Thus then, thou most renown'd: Caesar entreats
Not to consider in what case thou stand'st
Further than he is [Caesar].
Cleo. Go on: right royal.
Thid. He knows that you embrace not Antony
As you did love, but as you fear'd him.
Cleo. O!
Thid. The scars upon your honor, therefore, he
Does pity, as constrained blemishes,
Not as deserved.
Cleo. He is a god and knows
What is most right. Mine honor was not yielded,
But conquer'd merely.
Eno. [*Aside.*] To be sure of that,
I will ask Antony. Sir, sir, thou art so leaky
That we must leave thee to thy sinking, for
Thy dearest quit thee. *Exit Enobarbus.*
Thid. Shall I say to Caesar
What you require of him? for he partly begs
To be desir'd to give. It much would please him,
That of his fortunes you should make a staff
To lean upon; but it would warm his spirits
To hear from me you had left Antony,
And put yourself under his shroud,
The universal landlord.
Cleo. What's your name?
Thid. My name is Thidias.
Cleo. Most kind messenger,
Say to great Caesar this in [deputation]:
I kiss his conqu'ring hand. Tell him, I am prompt
To lay my crown at 's feet, and there to kneel.
Tell him, from his all-obeying breath I hear
The doom of Egypt.
Thid. 'Tis your noblest course.
Wisdom and fortune combating together,
If that the former dare but what it can,
No chance may shake it. Give me grace to lay
My duty on your hand.
Cleo. Your Caesar's father oft
(When he hath mus'd of taking kingdoms in)
Bestow'd his lips on that unworthy place,
As it rain'd kisses.

Enter ANTONY *and* ENOBARBUS.

Ant. Favors? By Jove that thunders!
What art thou, fellow?
Thid. One that but performs

50. Or . . . us: i.e. or else might just as well have none.
55. Caesar: i.e. himself, a magnanimous victor.
59. constrained: forced. **61. right:** true.
71. shroud: shelter, protection.
74. in deputation: as my deputy, on my behalf.
77. all-obeying: obeyed by all.
78. doom of Egypt: judgment of the Queen of Egypt.
80. but . . . can: only what lies within its power to do.
85. As: as if.

The bidding of the fullest man, and worthiest
To have command obey'd.
Eno. [*Aside.*] You will be whipt.
Ant. [*Calling for Servants.*] Approach there!—Ah, you kite!—Now gods and devils!
Authority melts from me. Of late, when I cried "Ho!"
Like boys unto a muss, kings would start forth
And cry, "Your will?"—Have you no ears?—I am
Antony yet.

Enter a SERVANT, [*others following*].

Take hence this Jack and whip him.
Eno. [*Aside.*] 'Tis better playing with a lion's whelp
Than with an old one dying.
Ant. Moon and stars!
Whip him. Were't twenty of the greatest tributaries
That do acknowledge Caesar, should I find them
So saucy with the hand of she here—what's her name,
Since she was Cleopatra? Whip him, fellows,
Till like a boy you see him cringe his face,
And whine aloud for mercy. Take him hence.
Thid. Mark Antony—
Ant. Tug him away. Being whipt,
Bring him again; the Jack of Caesar's shall
Bear us an arrant to him.
Exeunt [*Servants*] *with Thidias.*
You were half blasted ere I knew you; ha?
Have I my pillow left unpress'd in Rome,
Forborne the getting of a lawful race,
And by a gem of women, to be abus'd
By one that looks on feeders?
Cleo. Good my lord—
Ant. You have been a boggler ever,
But when we in our viciousness grow hard
(O misery on't!), the wise gods seel our eyes,
In our own filth drop our clear judgments, make us
Adore our errors, laugh at 's while we strut
To our confusion.
Cleo. O, is't come to this?
Ant. I found you as a morsel, cold upon
Dead Caesar's trencher; nay, you were a fragment
Of Cneius Pompey's—besides what hotter hours,
Unregist'red in vulgar fame, you have
Luxuriously pick'd out; for I am sure,
Though you can guess what temperance should be,
You know not what it is.
Cleo. Wherefore is this?
Ant. To let a fellow that will take rewards
And say "God quit you!" be familiar with
My playfellow, your hand, this kingly seal
And plighter of high hearts! O that I were

87. **fullest:** Cf. line 35. 89. **kite:** harlot. 91. **muss:** scramble (as for small objects thrown on the ground). 93. **Jack:** base fellow. 104. **arrant:** errand, message. 108. **abus'd:** deceived. 109. **feeders:** servants. 110. **boggler:** shifty one. 112. **seel:** sew up (as trainers sewed together a hawk's eyelids as a means of taming it). 117. **trencher:** wooden dish. **fragment:** leftover scrap. 119. **vulgar fame:** common gossip. 120. **Luxuriously:** lustfully. 124. **quit:** reward. 126–28. **O . . . herd.** Cf. Psalms 22:12: ". . . fat bulls of Basan close me in on every side." Antony belongs with the bulls because he wears a cuckold's horns.

Upon the hill of Basan, to outroar
The horned herd! for I have savage cause,
And to proclaim it civilly were like
A halter'd neck which does the hangman thank
For being yare about him.

Enter a SERVANT *with* THIDIAS.

Is he whipt?
Serv. Soundly, my lord.
Ant. Cried he? and begg'd 'a pardon?
Serv. He did ask favor.
Ant. If that thy father live, let him repent
Thou wast not made his daughter, and be thou sorry
To follow Caesar in his triumph, since
Thou hast been whipt for following him. Henceforth
The white hand of a lady fever thee,
Shake thou to look on't. Get thee back to Caesar,
Tell him thy entertainment. Look thou say
He makes me angry with him; for he seems
Proud and disdainful, harping on what I am,
Not what he knew I was. He makes me angry,
And at this time most easy 'tis to do't:
When my good stars, that were my former guides,
Have empty left their orbs, and shot their fires
Into th' abysm of hell. If he mislike
My speech and what is done, tell him he has
Hipparchus, my enfranched bondman, whom
He may at pleasure whip, or hang, or torture,
As he shall like, to quit me. Urge it thou:
Hence with thy stripes, be gone! *Exit Thidias.*
Cleo. Have you done yet?
Ant. Alack, our terrene moon
Is now eclips'd, and it portends alone
The fall of Antony!
Cleo. I must stay his time.
Ant. To flatter Caesar, would you mingle eyes
With one that ties his points?
Cleo. Not know me yet?
Ant. Cold-hearted toward me?
Cleo. Ah, dear, if I be so,
From my cold heart let heaven engender hail,
And poison it in the source, and the first stone
Drop in my neck; as it determines, so
Dissolve my life! The next Caesarion [smite],
Till by degrees the memory of my womb,
Together with my brave Egyptians all,
By the [discandying] of this pelleted storm,
Lie graveless, till the flies and gnats of Nile
Have buried them for prey!
Ant. I am satisfied.
Caesar sets down in Alexandria, where
I will oppose his fate. Our force by land
Hath nobly held; our sever'd navy too

128. **savage cause:** reason to run wild. 129. **civilly:** in civilized accents (rather than in a savage roar). 131. **yare:** quick. 140. **thy entertainment:** how you were received. 146. **orbs:** spheres. 149. **enfranched:** enfranchised, freed. 151. **quit me:** pay me back. 153. **terrene:** earthly. 155. **stay his time:** wait until he is ready to hear me. 157. **points:** laces (used to attach hose to doublet). 161. **determines:** comes to an end, melts. 163. **memory:** memorials, i.e. children. 165. **discandying:** melting. 168. **sets down in:** lays siege to. 169. **oppose his fate:** challenge his fortune.

Have knit again, and fleet, threat'ning most sea-like.
Where hast thou been, my heart? Dost thou hear, lady?
If from the field I shall return once more
To kiss these lips, I will appear in blood;
I and my sword will earn our chronicle.
There's hope in't yet.

Cleo. That's my brave lord!

Ant. I will be treble-sinew'd, hearted, breath'd,
And fight maliciously; for when mine hours
Were nice and lucky, men did ransom lives
Of me for jests; but now I'll set my teeth,
And send to darkness all that stop me. Come,
Let's have one other gaudy night. Call to me
All my sad captains, fill our bowls once more;
Let's mock the midnight bell.

Cleo. It is my birthday,
I had thought t' have held it poor; but since my lord
Is Antony again, I will be Cleopatra.

Ant. We will yet do well.

Cleo. Call all his noble captains to my lord.

Ant. Do so, we'll speak to them, and to-night I'll force
The wine peep through their scars. Come on, my queen,
There's sap in't yet. The next time I do fight,
I'll make death love me; for I will contend
Even with his pestilent scythe.

Exeunt [all but Enobarbus].

Eno. Now he'll outstare the lightning: to be furious
Is to be frighted out of fear, and in that mood
The dove will peck the estridge; and I see still
A diminution in our captain's brain
Restores his heart. When valor [preys on] reason,
It eats the sword it fights with. I will seek
Some way to leave him. *Exit.*

[ACT IV, SCENE I]

Enter CAESAR, AGRIPPA, *and* MAECENAS, *with his army; Caesar reading a letter.*

Caes. He calls me boy, and chides as he had power
To beat me out of Egypt. My messenger
He hath whipt with rods, dares me to personal combat,
Caesar to Antony. Let the old ruffian know
I have many other ways to die; mean time
Laugh at his challenge.

Maec. Caesar must think,
When one so great begins to rage, he's hunted

Even to falling. Give him no breath, but now
Make boot of his distraction: never anger
Made good guard for itself.

Caes. Let our best heads
Know that to-morrow the last of many battles
We mean to fight. Within our files there are,
Of those that serv'd Mark Antony but late,
Enough to fetch him in. See it done,
And feast the army; we have store to do't,
And they have earn'd the waste. Poor Antony!

Exeunt.

[SCENE II]

Enter ANTONY, CLEOPATRA, ENOBARBUS, CHARMIAN, IRAS, ALEXAS, *with others.*

Ant. He will not fight with me, Domitius?

Eno. No.

Ant. Why should he not?

Eno. He thinks, being twenty times of better fortune,
He is twenty men to one.

Ant. To-morrow, soldier,
By sea and land I'll fight; or I will live,
Or bathe my dying honor in the blood
Shall make it live again. Woo't thou fight well?

Eno. I'll strike, and cry, "Take all!"

Ant. Well said, come on.
Call forth my household servants, let's to-night
Be bounteous at our meal.

Enter three or four SERVITORS.

Give me thy hand,
Thou hast been rightly honest—so hast thou—
Thou—and thou—and thou. You have serv'd me well,
And kings have been your fellows.

Cleo. [*Aside to Enobarbus.*] What means this?

Eno. [*Aside to Cleopatra.*] 'Tis one of those odd tricks which sorrow shoots
Out of the mind.

Ant. And thou art honest too.
I wish I could be made so many men,
And all of you clapp'd up together in
An Antony, that I might do you service
So good as you have done.

Omnes. The gods forbid!

Ant. Well, my good fellows, wait on me to-night.
Scant not my cups, and make as much of me
As when mine empire was your fellow too,
And suffer'd my command.

Cleo. [*Aside to Enobarbus.*] What does he mean?

Eno. [*Aside to Cleopatra.*] To make his followers weep.

Ant. Tend me to-night;

171. fleet: float. **172. heart:** courage, spirit.
174. blood: full vigor, high mettle.
175. our chronicle: the record of our achievements, our page in history. **176. brave:** noble.
177. hearted, breath'd. The *treble-* of *treble-sinew'd* is understood with both these words also. **178. maliciously:** savagely.
179. nice: capable of chivalrous distinctions (because things went well with him). **182. gaudy:** joyous, festive.
185. held it poor: celebrated it meanly. **191. sap:** i.e. life.
192. contend: compete. **196. estridge:** goshawk.

IV.i. Location: Caesar's camp before Alexandria.
6. Laugh: (tell him) I laugh. **7. rage:** rave.

8. breath: breathing space, time to recover.
9. Make boot of: profit from. **distraction:** frenzy, rage.
10. heads: commanders. **12. files:** ranks.
14. fetch him in: take him captive. **16. waste:** expenditure.

IV.ii. Alexandria. Cleopatra's palace.
5. or: either. **7. Woo't:** wilt. **8. Take all:** i.e. winner take all.
13. been your fellows: i.e. served me too.
16. made . . . men: divided into as many men as you number.
22. fellow: i.e. fellow servant. **23. suffer'd:** submitted to.

May be it is the period of your duty;
Haply you shall not see me more, or if,
A mangled shadow. Perchance to-morrow
You'll serve another master. I look on you
As one that takes his leave. Mine honest friends,
I turn you not away, but like a master
Married to your good service, stay till death.
Tend me to-night two hours, I ask no more,
And the gods yield you for't!

Eno. What mean you, sir,
To give them this discomfort? Look, they weep,
And I, an ass, am onion-ey'd. For shame,
Transform us not to women.

Ant. Ho, ho, ho!
Now the witch take me, if I meant it thus!
Grace grow where those drops fall, my hearty friends!
You take me in too dolorous a sense,
For I spake to you for your comfort, did desire you
To burn this night with torches. Know, my hearts,
I hope well of to-morrow, and will lead you
Where rather I'll expect victorious life
Than death and honor. Let's to supper, come,
And drown consideration. *Exeunt.*

[SCENE III]

Enter a company of SOLDIERS.

1. Sold. Brother, good night; to-morrow is the day.

2. Sold. It will determine one way; fare you well.
Heard you of nothing strange about the streets?

1. Sold. Nothing. What news?

2. Sold. Belike 'tis but a rumor. Good night to you.

1. Sold. Well, sir, good night.

They meet other SOLDIERS.

2. Sold. Soldiers, have careful watch.

[3.] *Sold.* And you. Good night, good night.

They place themselves in every corner of the stage.

2. Sold. Here we. And if to-morrow
Our navy thrive, I have an absolute hope
Our landmen will stand up.

1. Sold. 'Tis a brave army,
And full of purpose.

Music of the hoboys is under the stage.

2. Sold. Peace, what noise?

1. Sold. List, list!

2. Sold. Hark!

1. Sold. Music i' th' air.

3. Sold. Under the earth.

4. Sold. It signs well, does it not?

3. Sold. No.

1. Sold. Peace, I say.
What should this mean?

25. **period:** end. 26. **if:** i.e. if you do. 33. **yield:** reward.
37. **the witch take me:** may I be bewitched.
45. **consideration:** melancholy thoughts.

IV.iii. **Location:** Alexandria. Before Cleopatra's palace.
2. **one way:** i.e. one way or the other. 5. **Belike:** probably.
12 s.d. **hoboys:** oboes. 14. **signs well:** is a good omen.

2. Sold. 'Tis the god Hercules, whom Antony lov'd,
Now leaves him.

1. Sold. Walk; let's see if other watchmen
Do hear what we do.

2. Sold. How now, masters?

Omnes. (*Speak together.*) How now?
How now? Do you hear this?

1. Sold. Ay, is't not strange?

3. Sold. Do you hear, masters? Do you hear?

1. Sold. Follow the noise so far as we have quarter;
Let's see how it will give off.

Omnes. Content. 'Tis strange. *Exeunt.*

[SCENE IV]

Enter ANTONY *and* CLEOPATRA, [CHARMIAN,] *with others.*

Ant. Eros, mine armor, Eros!

Cleo. Sleep a little.

Ant. No, my chuck. Eros, come, mine armor, Eros!

Enter EROS [*with armor*].

Come, good fellow, put thine iron on.
If Fortune be not ours to-day, it is
Because we brave her. Come.

Cleo. Nay, I'll help too.
What's this for?

[*Ant.*] Ah, let be, let be! thou art
The armorer of my heart. False, false; this, this.

[*Cleo.*] Sooth law, I'll help. Thus it must be.

Ant. Well, well,
We shall thrive now. Seest thou, my good fellow?
Go, put on thy defenses.

Eros. Briefly, sir.

Cleo. Is not this buckled well?

Ant. Rarely, rarely:
He that unbuckles this, till we do please
To daff't for our repose, shall hear a storm.
Thou fumblest, Eros, and my queen's a squire
More tight at this than thou; dispatch. O love,
That thou couldst see my wars to-day, and knew'st
The royal occupation, thou shouldst see
A workman in't.

Enter an armed SOLDIER.

Good morrow to thee, welcome.
Thou look'st like him that knows a warlike charge.
To business that we love we rise betime,
And go to't with delight.

Sold. A thousand, sir,

21. **as . . . quarter:** as far as our assigned territory extends.
22. **give off:** end.

IV.iv. **Location:** Alexandria. Cleopatra's palace.
2. **chuck:** term of endearment (related to *chick*).
3. **thine iron:** i.e. the armor you have there for me. 5. **brave:** defy.
7. **of my heart:** i.e. not of my body. **False:** i.e. the wrong piece.
8. **Sooth:** in truth. **law:** la (an exclamation).
10. **Briefly:** in a moment. 13. **daff't:** take it off.
15. **tight:** deft. 18. **workman:** i.e. professional, expert.
19. **charge:** responsibility.

Early though't be, have on their riveted trim,
And at the port expect you.
Shout. Trumpets flourish.

Enter Captains *and* Soldiers.

[*Capt.*] The morn is fair. Good morrow, general.
All. Good morrow, general.
Ant. 'Tis well blown, lads.
This morning, like the spirit of a youth
That means to be of note, begins betimes.
So, so; come give me that: this way—well said.
Fare thee well, dame, what e'er becomes of me.
This is a soldier's kiss; rebukable
And worthy shameful check it were, to stand
On more mechanic compliment. I'll leave thee
Now like a man of steel. You that will fight,
Follow me close, I'll bring you to't. Adieu.
Exeunt [Antony, Eros, Captains, and Soldiers].
Char. Please you retire to your chamber?
Cleo. Lead me.
He goes forth gallantly. That he and Caesar might
Determine this great war in single fight!
Then, Antony—but now—Well, on. *Exeunt.*

[Scene V]

Trumpets sound. Enter Antony *and* Eros, [*a* Soldier *meeting them*].

[*Sold.*] The gods make this a happy day to Antony!
Ant. Would thou and those thy scars had once prevail'd
To make me fight at land!
[*Sold.*] Hadst thou done so,
The kings that have revolted, and the soldier
That has this morning left thee, would have still
Followed thy heels.
Ant. Who's gone this morning?
[*Sold.*] Who?
One ever near thee. Call for Enobarbus,
He shall not hear thee, or from Caesar's camp
Say "I am none of thine."
Ant. What sayest thou?
Sold. Sir,
He is with Caesar.
Eros. Sir, his chests and treasure
He has not with him.
Ant. Is he gone?
Sold. Most certain.
Ant. Go, Eros, send his treasure after; do it,
Detain no jot, I charge thee. Write to him
(I will subscribe) gentle adieus and greetings;
Say that I wish he never find more cause

22. riveted trim: armor. **23. port:** gate.
25. blown: opened (?) or sounded by the trumpeters (?).
28. well said: well done. **31. check:** reproof.
32. mechanic: formal, labored.

IV.v. Location: Antony's camp before Alexandria.
1. happy: fortunate.
2. once: on a former occasion (III.vii.61–62).
14. subscribe: sign.

To change a master. O, my fortunes have
Corrupted honest men! Dispatch. Enobarbus!
Exeunt.

[Scene VI]

Flourish. Enter Agrippa, Caesar, *with* Enobarbus *and* Dolabella.

Caes. Go forth, Agrippa, and begin the fight.
Our will is Antony be took alive;
Make it so known.
Agr. Caesar, I shall. [*Exit.*]
Caes. The time of universal peace is near.
Prove this a prosp'rous day, the three-nook'd world
Shall bear the olive freely.

Enter a Messenger.

Mess. Antony
Is come into the field.
Caes. Go charge Agrippa
Plant those that have revolted in the vant,
That Antony may seem to spend his fury
Upon himself. *Exeunt [all but Enobarbus].*
Eno. Alexas did revolt, and went to Jewry on
Affairs of Antony, there did dissuade
Great Herod to incline himself to Caesar,
And leave his master Antony; for this pains
Caesar hath hang'd him. Canidius and the rest
That fell away have entertainment, but
No honorable trust. I have done ill,
Of which I do accuse myself so sorely
That I will joy no more.

Enter a Soldier *of Caesar's.*

Sold. Enobarbus, Antony
Hath after thee sent all thy treasure, with
His bounty overplus. The messenger
Came on my guard, and at thy tent is now
Unloading of his mules.
Eno. I give it you.
Sold. Mock not, Enobarbus,
I tell you true. Best you saf'd the bringer
Out of the host; I must attend mine office,
Or would have done't myself. Your emperor
Continues still a Jove. *Exit.*
Eno. I am alone the villain of the earth,
And feel I am so most. O Antony,
Thou mine of bounty, how wouldst thou have paid
My better service, when my turpitude
Thou dost so crown with gold! This blows my heart.
If swift thought break it not, a swifter mean
Shall outstrike thought, but thought will do't, I feel.

IV.vi. Location: Caesar's camp.
4. The time . . . peace. Referring to the "Augustan peace" that attended the reign of the speaker.
5. three-nook'd world: three-cornered world (Europe, Asia, Africa).
8. vant: vanguard.
12. dissuade: i.e. from his allegiance to Antony. Some editors adopt Rowe's *persuade*. **16. entertainment:** employment.
22. on my guard: while I was on guard.
25. saf'd: gave safe-conduct to.
29. alone the villain: the only (i.e. the greatest) villain.
30. feel . . . most: am myself the person most painfully aware of the fact. **33. blows:** swells to the bursting point.
34. thought: grief.

I fight against thee? No, I will go seek
Some ditch wherein to die; the foul'st best fits
My latter part of life. *Exit.*

[Scene VII]

Alarum. Drums and Trumpets. Enter Agrippa *[and others].*

Agr. Retire, we have engag'd ourselves too far.
Caesar himself has work, and our oppression
Exceeds what we expected. *Exeunt.*

Alarums. Enter Antony, *and* Scarus *wounded.*

Scar. O my brave Emperor, this is fought indeed!
Had we done so at first, we had droven them home
With clouts about their heads.
Ant. Thou bleed'st apace.
Scar. I had a wound here that was like a T,
But now 'tis made an H. *[Sound retreat] far off.*
Ant. They do retire.
Scar. We'll beat 'em into bench-holes. I have yet
Room for six scotches more.

Enter Eros.

Eros. They are beaten, sir, and our advantage serves
For a fair victory.
Scar. Let us score their backs,
And snatch 'em up, as we take hares, behind:
'Tis sport to maul a runner.
Ant. I will reward thee
Once for thy sprightly comfort, and tenfold
For thy good valor. Come thee on.
Scar. I'll halt after. *Exeunt.*

[Scene VIII]

Alarum. Enter Antony *again, in a march,* Scarus, *with others.*

Ant. We have beat him to his camp. Run one before,
And let the Queen know of our [gests]. To-morrow,
Before the sun shall see 's, we'll spill the blood
That has to-day escap'd. I thank you all,
For doughty-handed are you, and have fought
Not as you serv'd the cause, but as't had been
Each man's like mine; you have shown all Hectors.
Enter the city, clip your wives, your friends,
Tell them your feats, whilst they with joyful tears
Wash the congealment from your wounds, and kiss
The honor'd gashes whole.

IV.vii. Location: A field of battle between the camps.
2. **has work:** has his work cut out for him. **our oppression:** the heavy opposition against us. 5. **droven:** driven.
6. **clouts:** cloths, bandages.
8. **H.** With pun on *ache,* pronounced *aitch.*
9. **into bench-holes:** into holes of privies, i.e. to the point where they will snatch at any refuge. 10. **scotches:** cuts.
15. **sprightly:** spirited, high-hearted. 16. **halt:** limp.

IV.viii. Location: Scene continues.
2. **gests:** deeds. 6. **as:** as if. 8. **clip:** embrace.

Enter Cleopatra *[attended].*

[To Scarus.] Give me thy hand;
To this great fairy I'll commend thy acts,
Make her thanks bless thee. *[To Cleopatra.]* O thou day o' th' world,
Chain mine arm'd neck, leap thou, attire and all,
Through proof of harness to my heart, and there
Ride on the pants triumphing!
Cleo. Lord of lords!
O infinite virtue, com'st thou smiling from
The world's great snare uncaught?
Ant. Mine nightingale,
We have beat them to their beds. What, girl, though grey
Do something mingle with our younger brown, yet ha' we
A brain that nourishes our nerves, and can
Get goal for goal of youth. Behold this man,
Commend unto his lips thy [favoring] hand.
Kiss it, my warrior; he hath fought to-day
As if a god, in hate of mankind, had
Destroyed in such a shape.
Cleo. I'll give thee, friend,
An armor all of gold; it was a king's.
Ant. He has deserv'd it, were it carbuncled
Like holy Phoebus' car. Give me thy hand.
Through Alexandria make a jolly march,
Bear our hack'd targets like the men that owe them.
Had our great palace the capacity
To camp this host, we all would sup together,
And drink carouses to the next day's fate,
Which promises royal peril. Trumpeters,
With brazen din blast you the city's ear,
Make mingle with our rattling taborines,
That heaven and earth may strike their sounds together,
Applauding our approach. *Exeunt.*

[Scene IX]

Enter a Sentry *and his* Company. Enobarbus *follows.*

Sent. If we be not reliev'd within this hour,
We must return to th' court of guard. The night
Is shiny, and they say we shall embattle
By th' second hour i' th' morn.
1. Watch. This last day was
A shrewd one to 's.
Eno. O, bear me witness, night—
2. Watch. What man is this?
1. Watch. Stand close, and list him.

12. **fairy:** enchantress. 15. **proof of harness:** impenetrable armor.
17. **virtue:** valor. 21. **nerves:** sinews.
22. **Get . . . youth:** match youth at this game.
28. **carbuncled:** studded with bright gems. (Carbuncles were thought to shine in the dark.)
29. **Phoebus' car:** the sun-god's chariot.
31. **targets:** shields. **like:** as becomes. **owe:** own.
37. **taborines:** drums.

IV.ix. Location: Caesar's camp.
2. **court of guard:** guardroom.
3. **embattle:** take our battle positions. 5. **shrewd:** cursed.
6. **close:** in concealment. **list:** listen to.

Eno. Be witness to me, O thou blessed moon,
When men revolted shall upon record
Bear hateful memory: poor Enobarbus did
Before thy face repent.
Sent. Enobarbus?
2. Watch. Peace!
Hark further.
Eno. O sovereign mistress of true melancholy,
The poisonous damp of night dispunge upon me,
That life, a very rebel to my will,
May hang no longer on me. Throw my heart
Against the flint and hardness of my fault,
Which being dried with grief will break to powder,
And finish all foul thoughts. O Antony,
Nobler than my revolt is infamous,
Forgive me in thine own particular,
But let the world rank me in register
A master-leaver and a fugitive.
O Antony! O Antony! [*Dies.*]
1. Watch. Let's speak to him.
Sent. Let's hear him, for the things he speaks
May concern Caesar.
2. Watch. Let's do so. But he sleeps.
Sent. Swoonds rather, for so bad a prayer as his
Was never yet for sleep.
1. Watch. Go we to him.
2. Watch. Awake, sir, awake, speak to us.
1. Watch. Hear you, sir?
Sent. The hand of death hath raught him. (*Drums afar off.*) Hark, the drums
Demurely wake the sleepers. Let us bear him
To th' court of guard; he is of note. Our hour
Is fully out.
2. Watch. Come on then, he may recover yet.
Exeunt [*with the body*].

[Scene X]

Enter Antony *and* Scarus *with their army.*

Ant. Their preparation is to-day by sea,
We please them not by land.
Scar. For both, my lord.
Ant. I would they'ld fight i' th' fire or i' th' air;
We'ld fight there too. But this it is: our foot
Upon the hills adjoining to the city
Shall stay with us—order for sea is given,
They have put forth the haven—
Where their appointment we may best discover,
And look on their endeavor. *Exeunt.*

13. poisonous . . . night: Night mists were believed to be noxious. **dispunge:** drop as from a squeezed sponge.
20. in . . . particular: so far as you yourself are concerned.
22. master-leaver: runaway servant. **fugitive:** deserter.
26. Swoonds: swoons.
29. raught: reached, seized.
30. Demurely: with solemn sound.
31. of note: someone of importance.

IV.x. Location: A field of battle between the camps.
3. fire, air. They are already fighting in the other two elements.
4. foot: foot soldiers.
8. appointment: arrangement.

[Scene XI]

Enter Caesar *and his army.*

Caes. But being charg'd, we will be still by land,
Which as I take't we shall, for his best force
Is forth to man his galleys. To the vales,
And hold our best advantage. *Exeunt.*

[Scene XII]

Enter Antony *and* Scarus.

Ant. Yet they are not join'd. Where yond pine does stand
I shall discover all; I'll bring thee word
Straight how 'tis like to go. *Exit.*
Alarum afar off, as at a sea-fight.
Scar. Swallows have built
In Cleopatra's sails their nests. The auguries
Say they know not, they cannot tell, look grimly,
And dare not speak their knowledge. Antony
Is valiant, and dejected, and by starts
His fretted fortunes give him hope and fear
Of what he has, and has not.

Enter Antony.

Ant. All is lost!
This foul Egyptian hath betrayed me.
My fleet hath yielded to the foe, and yonder
They cast their caps up and carouse together
Like friends long lost. Triple-turn'd whore! 'tis thou
Hast sold me to this novice, and my heart
Makes only wars on thee. Bid them all fly;
For when I am reveng'd upon my charm,
I have done all. Bid them all fly, be gone.
[*Exit Scarus.*]
O sun, thy uprise shall I see no more,
Fortune and Antony part here, even here
Do we shake hands. All come to this? The hearts
That [spannell'd] me at heels, to whom I gave
Their wishes, do discandy, melt their sweets
On blossoming Caesar; and this pine is bark'd,
That overtopp'd them all. Betray'd I am.
O this false soul of Egypt! this grave charm,
Whose eye beck'd forth my wars and call'd them home,
Whose bosom was my crownet, my chief end,
Like a right gipsy, hath at fast and loose

IV.xi. Location: Scene continues.
1. But being charg'd: unless we are attacked. **still:** inactive.
4. hold . . . advantage: take the most advantageous position possible.

IV.xii. Location: Scene continues.
1. join'd: joined in battle.
3 s.d. Alarum: signal to advance to battle. **4. auguries:** augurs.
8. fretted: (1) variegated, i.e. shifting; (2) eroded, decayed.
13. Triple-turn'd: thrice faithless (to Julius Caesar, Cneius Pompey, and Antony).
16. charm: i.e. the woman who bewitched me (so also *spell* in line 30).
21. spannell'd: spanieled, followed like a fawning dog.
22. discandy: melt.
23. bark'd: killed by being stripped of its bark.
25. grave: heavy, deadening.
27. crownet: coronet, reward that crowns labor.
28. right: true. **fast and loose:** a cheating game.

Beguil'd me to the very heart of loss.
What, Eros, Eros!

Enter CLEOPATRA.

Ah, thou spell! Avaunt!

Cleo. Why is my lord enrag'd against his love?

Ant. Vanish, or I shall give thee thy deserving,
And blemish Caesar's triumph. Let him take thee
And hoist thee up to the shouting plebeians!
Follow his chariot, like the greatest spot
Of all thy sex; most monster-like, be shown
For poor'st diminutives, for dolts, and let
Patient Octavia plough thy visage up
With her prepared nails. *Exit Cleopatra.*
'Tis well th' art gone,
If it be well to live; but better 'twere
Thou fell'st into my fury, for one death
Might have prevented many. Eros, ho!
The shirt of Nessus is upon me; teach me,
Alcides, thou mine ancestor, thy rage.
Let me lodge Lichas on the horns o' th' moon,
And with those hands, that grasp'd the heaviest club,
Subdue my worthiest self. The witch shall die.
To the young Roman boy she hath sold me, and I fall
Under this plot. She dies for't. Eros, ho! *Exit.*

[SCENE XIII]

Enter CLEOPATRA, CHARMIAN, IRAS, MARDIAN.

Cleo. Help me, my women! O, he's more mad
Than Telamon for his shield; the boar of Thessaly
Was never so emboss'd.

Char. To th' monument!
There lock yourself, and send him word you are dead.
The soul and body rive not more in parting
Than greatness going off.

Cleo. To th' monument!
Mardian, go tell him I have slain myself;
Say that the last I spoke was "Antony,"
And word it, prithee, piteously. Hence, Mardian,
And bring me how he takes my death. To th' monument! *Exeunt.*

35. **spot:** blot, blemish.
37. **diminutives, dolts:** contemptuous terms for the spectators of the triumph. Many editors read *doits*, following Thirlby, and explain both words as designating small coins charged for admission.
39. **prepared:** sharpened, or allowed to grow long, for the purpose.
41. **into:** a victim to.
42. **many:** i.e. mental anguish equal to many deaths (?).
43–45. **shirt . . . Lichas.** The Centaur Nessus, fatally wounded by one of the poisoned arrows of Hercules (*Alcides*), told the latter's wife Dejanira that his blood would act as a love charm. Later she attempted to regain her husband's love by sending him a shirt smeared with the blood, which stuck to his skin and caused him frightful pain. In his death agony he threw his servant Lichas, who had brought the shirt, into the sea.

IV.xiii. Location: Alexandria. Cleopatra's palace.
2. **Telamon:** Ajax Telamon, one of the greatest of the Greeks who fought at Troy; he went mad with resentment when Achilles' armor was awarded to Ulysses instead of to himself. **boar of Thessaly.** Sent by Artemis to lay waste Calydon.
3. **emboss'd:** frenzied, in a fury (like a beast hunted to extremity). **th' monument:** i.e. a tomb that Cleopatra had had erected in preparation for her own death.
5. **rive not more:** do not create a greater cleavage.

[SCENE XIV]

Enter ANTONY *and* EROS.

Ant. Eros, thou yet behold'st me?

Eros. Ay, noble lord.

Ant. Sometime we see a cloud that's dragonish,
A vapor sometime like a bear or lion,
A [tower'd] citadel, a pendant rock,
A forked mountain, or blue promontory
With trees upon't that nod unto the world,
And mock our eyes with air. Thou hast seen these signs,
They are black vesper's pageants.

Eros. Ay, my lord.

Ant. That which is now a horse, even with a thought
The rack dislimns, and makes it indistinct
As water is in water.

Eros. It does, my lord.

Ant. My good knave Eros, now thy captain is
Even such a body. Here I am Antony,
Yet cannot hold this visible shape, my knave.
I made these wars for Egypt, and the Queen,
Whose heart I thought I had, for she had mine—
Which whilst it was mine had annex'd unto't
A million moe (now lost)—she, Eros, has
Pack'd cards with Caesar's, and false-play'd my glory
Unto an enemy's triumph.
Nay, weep not, gentle Eros, there is left us
Ourselves to end ourselves.

Enter MARDIAN.

O, thy vild lady!
She has robb'd me of my sword.

Mar. No, Antony,
My mistress lov'd thee, and her fortunes mingled
With thine entirely.

Ant. Hence, saucy eunuch, peace!
She hath betray'd me, and shall die the death.

Mar. Death of one person can be paid but once,
And that she has discharg'd. What thou wouldst do
Is done unto thy hand; the last she spake
Was "Antony, most noble Antony!"
Then in the midst a tearing groan did break
The name of Antony; it was divided
Between her heart and lips. She rend'red life,
Thy name so buried in her.

Ant. Dead then?

Mar. Dead.

Ant. Unarm, Eros, the long day's task is done,
And we must sleep. [*To Mardian.*] That thou depart'st hence safe

IV.xiv. Location: Alexandria. Cleopatra's palace.
8. **black vesper's pageants:** displays heralding the approach of night.
9. **even . . . thought:** instantly, as quick as thought.
10. **rack:** drifting cloud. **dislimns:** effaces.
12. **knave:** boy. 18. **moe:** more.
19. **Pack'd . . . Caesar's:** stacked the deck in Caesar's favor. Most editors emend *Caesar's* to *Caesar*, following Rowe.
20. **triumph:** (1) victory; (2) trump card. 22. **vild:** vile.
23. **sword:** i.e. martial prowess.
26. **die the death:** be put to death for it (used of judicial execution).
27. **of:** by. 29. **done . . . hand:** already done for you.
32–33. **it . . . lips:** i.e. she pronounced only half of it before dying.
33. **rend'red:** surrendered, yielded.

Does pay thy labor richly; go. *Exit Mardian.*
Off, pluck off,
The sevenfold shield of Ajax cannot keep
The battery from my heart. O, cleave, my sides!
Heart, once be stronger than thy continent,
Crack thy frail case! Apace, Eros, apace.
No more a soldier. Bruised pieces, go,
You have been nobly borne.—From me awhile.
Exit Eros.
I will o'ertake thee, Cleopatra, and
Weep for my pardon. So it must be, for now
All length is torture; since the torch is out,
Lie down and stray no farther. Now all labor
Mars what it does; yea, very force entangles
Itself with strength. Seal then, and all is done.
Eros!—I come, my queen!—Eros!—Stay for me!
Where souls do couch on flowers, we'll hand in hand,
And with our sprightly port make the ghosts gaze.
Dido and her Aeneas shall want troops,
And all the haunt be ours. Come, Eros, Eros!

Enter Eros.

Eros. What would my lord?
Ant. Since Cleopatra died
I have liv'd in such dishonor that the gods
Detest my baseness. I, that with my sword
Quarter'd the world, and o'er green Neptune's back
With ships made cities, condemn myself to lack
The courage of a woman—less noble mind
Than she which by her death our Caesar tells,
"I am conqueror of myself." Thou art sworn, Eros,
That when the exigent should come, which now
Is come indeed, when I should see behind me
Th' inevitable prosecution of
Disgrace and horror, that on my command
Thou then wouldst kill me. Do't, the time is come.
Thou strik'st not me, 'tis Caesar thou defeat'st.
Put color in thy cheek.
Eros. The gods withhold me!
Shall I do that which all the Parthian darts,
Though enemy, lost aim and could not?
Ant. Eros,
Wouldst thou be window'd in great Rome, and see
Thy master thus with pleach'd arms, bending down
His corrigible neck, his face subdu'd
To penetrative shame, whilst the wheel'd seat
Of fortunate Caesar, drawn before him, branded
His baseness that ensued?
Eros. I would not see't.
Ant. Come then; for with a wound I must be cur'd.
Draw that thy honest sword, which thou hast worn
Most useful for thy country.
Eros. O, sir, pardon me!
Ant. When I did make thee free, swor'st thou not then
To do this when I bade thee? Do it at once,
Or thy precedent services are all
But accidents unpurpos'd. Draw, and come.
Eros. Turn from me then that noble countenance,
Wherein the worship of the whole world lies.
Ant. Lo thee! [*Turning from him.*]
Eros. My sword is drawn.
Ant. Then let it do at once
The thing why thou hast drawn it.
Eros. My dear master,
My captain, and my emperor: let me say,
Before I strike this bloody stroke, farewell.
Ant. 'Tis said, man, and farewell.
Eros. Farewell, great chief. Shall I strike now?
Ant. Now, Eros.
Eros. Why, there then. (*Kills himself.*) Thus I do escape the sorrow
Of Antony's death.
Ant. Thrice-nobler than myself!
Thou teachest me, O valiant Eros, what
I should, and thou couldst not. My queen and Eros
Have by their brave instruction got upon me
A nobleness in record; but I will be
A bridegroom in my death, and run into't
As to a lover's bed. Come then; and, Eros,
Thy master dies thy scholar: to do thus
[*Falling on his sword.*]
I learnt of thee. How, not dead? not dead?
The guard, ho! O, dispatch me!

Enter [Decretas *and*] *a* Guard.

1. Guard. What's the noise?
Ant. I have done my work ill, friends. O, make an end
Of what I have begun.
2. Guard. The star is fall'n.
1. Guard. And time is at his period.
All. Alas, and woe!
Ant. Let him that loves me strike me dead.
1. Guard. Not I.
2. Guard. Nor I.
3. Guard. Nor any one. *Exeunt* [*Guard*].
Dec. Thy death and fortunes bid thy followers fly.
This sword but shown to Caesar, with this tidings,
Shall enter me with him.

Enter Diomedes.

Dio. Where's Antony?
Dec. There, Diomed, there.
Dio. Lives he?
Wilt thou not answer, man? [*Exit Decretas.*]
Ant. Art thou there, Diomed? Draw thy sword, and give me

39. **The battery**: i.e. the assault of sorrow and ill-fortune.
40. **thy continent**: that which contains you.
46. **length**: i.e. prolongation of life.
48–49. **force . . . strength**: i.e. natural vigor is an embarrassment to the necessary course of action. 49. **Seal**: conclude (the business).
52. **sprightly**: high-spirited (perhaps with play on the sense "ghostly"). **port**: bearing. 53. **want troops**: lack admiring followers.
54. **all . . . ours**: everyone will flock to gaze at us.
59. **to lack**: for lacking. 63. **exigent**: necessity.
65. **inevitable prosecution**: pursuit from which there is no escape.
68. **defeat'st**: frustratest. 73. **pleach'd**: folded.
74. **corrigible**: submissive. 75. **penetrative**: piercing deeply.
76–77. **branded . . . ensued**: stigmatized the abject status of him who followed. 79. **honest**: honorable.

80. **pardon me**: excuse me from this.
86. **the worship . . . world**: i.e. everything in the world that is worthy of reverence and devotion. 98. **got upon me**: gained over me.
99. **record**: history. 107. **his period**: its end.
113. **enter me with**: win me admission to the service of.

Sufficing strokes for death.
Dio. Most absolute lord,
My mistress Cleopatra sent me to thee.
Ant. When did she send thee?
Dio. Now, my lord.
Ant. Where is she?
Dio. Lock'd in her monument. She had a prophesying fear
Of what hath come to pass; for when she saw
(Which never shall be found) you did suspect
She had dispos'd with Caesar, and that your rage
Would not be purg'd, she sent you word she was dead;
But fearing since how it might work, hath sent
Me to proclaim the truth, and I am come,
I dread, too late.
Ant. Too late, good Diomed. Call my guard, I prithee.
Dio. What ho! the Emperor's guard! The guard, what ho!
Come, your lord calls!

Enter four or five of the GUARD *of Antony.*

Ant. Bear me, good friends, where Cleopatra bides,
'Tis the last service that I shall command you.
1. Guard. Woe, woe are we, sir, you may not live to wear
All your true followers out.
All. Most heavy day!
Ant. Nay, good my fellows, do not please sharp fate
To grace it with your sorrows. Bid that welcome
Which comes to punish us, and we punish it
Seeming to bear it lightly. Take me up.
I have led you oft, carry me now, good friends,
And have my thanks for all. *Exeunt bearing Antony.*

[SCENE XV]

Enter CLEOPATRA *and her maids aloft, with* CHARMIAN *and* IRAS.

Cleo. O Charmian, I will never go from hence.
Char. Be comforted, dear madam.
Cleo. No, I will not.
All strange and terrible events are welcome,
But comforts we despise; our size of sorrow,
Proportion'd to our cause, must be as great
As that which makes it.

Enter DIOMED [*below*].

How now? is he dead?
Dio. His death's upon him, but not dead.
Look out o' th' other side your monument,
His guard have brought him thither.

Enter [*below*] ANTONY, *and the* GUARD [*bearing him*].

Cleo. O sun,
Burn the great sphere thou mov'st in! darkling stand
The varying shore o' th' world! O Antony,
Antony, Antony! Help, Charmian, help, Iras, help;
Help, friends below, let's draw him hither.
Ant. Peace!
Not Caesar's valor hath o'erthrown Antony,
But Antony's hath triumph'd on itself.
Cleo. So it should be, that none but Antony
Should conquer Antony, but woe 'tis so!
Ant. I am dying, Egypt, dying; only
I here importune death awhile, until
Of many thousand kisses the poor last
I lay upon thy lips.
Cleo. I dare not, dear—
Dear my lord, pardon—I dare not,
Lest I be taken. Not th' imperious show
Of the full-fortun'd Caesar ever shall
Be brooch'd with me, if knife, drugs, serpents have
Edge, sting, or operation. I am safe:
Your wife Octavia, with her modest eyes
And still conclusion, shall acquire no honor
Demuring upon me. But come, come, Antony—
Help me, my women—we must draw thee up.
Assist, good friends.
Ant. O, quick, or I am gone.
Cleo. Here's sport indeed! How heavy weighs my lord!
Our strength is all gone into heaviness,
That makes the weight. Had I great Juno's power,
The strong-wing'd Mercury should fetch thee up,
And set thee by Jove's side. Yet come a little—
Wishers were ever fools—O, come, come, come,
They heave Antony aloft to Cleopatra.
And welcome, welcome! Die when thou hast liv'd,
Quicken with kissing. Had my lips that power,
Thus would I wear them out.
All. A heavy sight!
Ant. I am dying, Egypt, dying.
Give me some wine, and let me speak a little.
Cleo. No, let me speak, and let me rail so high,
That the false huswife Fortune break her wheel,
Provok'd by my offense.
Ant. One word, sweet queen:
Of Caesar seek your honor, with your safety. O!
Cleo. They do not go together.
Ant. Gentle, hear me:
None about Caesar trust but Proculeius.
Cleo. My resolution and my hands I'll trust,
None about Caesar.
Ant. The miserable change now at my end
Lament nor sorrow at; but please your thoughts
In feeding them with those my former fortunes
Wherein I liv'd, the greatest prince o' th' world,
The noblest; and do now not basely die,
Not cowardly put off my helmet to

122. found: found true. **123. dispos'd:** made terms.
136. To grace: by honoring.

IV.xv. Location: Alexandria. Cleopatra's monument.
10. darkling: in darkness.

11. varying: i.e. which normally varies between light and dark.
19. importune . . . awhile: beg death to delay for a short time.
21. dare not: i.e. dare not come down from the monument.
23. imperious show: imperial triumph. **25. brooch'd:** adorned.
28. still conclusion: silent judgment.
29. Demuring: looking demurely.
33. heaviness: (1) sorrow; (2) weight.
38. Die . . . liv'd: i.e. live a little longer before you die. Many editors emend *when* to *where*, after Pope. **39. Quicken:** revive.
44. huswife: hussy, harlot. **45. offense:** offensive words.

My countryman—a Roman by a Roman
Valiantly vanquish'd. Now my spirit is going,
I can no more.
Cleo. Noblest of men, woo't die?
Hast thou no care of me? Shall I abide
In this dull world, which in thy absence is
No better than a sty? O, see, my women:
[*Antony dies.*]
The crown o' th' earth doth melt. My lord!
O, wither'd is the garland of the war,
The soldier's pole is fall'n! Young boys and girls
Are level now with men; the odds is gone,
And there is nothing left remarkable
Beneath the visiting moon. [*Faints.*]
Char. O, quietness, lady!
Iras. She's dead too, our sovereign.
Char. Lady!
Iras. Madam!
Char. O madam, madam, madam!
Iras. Royal Egypt!
Empress!
Char. Peace, peace, Iras!
Cleo. No more but [e'en] a woman, and commanded
By such poor passion as the maid that milks
And does the meanest chares. It were for me
To throw my sceptre at the injurious gods,
To tell them that this world did equal theirs
Till they had stol'n our jewel. All's but naught:
Patience is sottish, and impatience does
Become a dog that's mad. Then is it sin
To rush into the secret house of death
Ere death dare come to us? How do you, women?
What, what, good cheer! Why, how now, Charmian?
My noble girls! Ah, women, women! Look
Our lamp is spent, it's out. Good sirs, take heart,
We'll bury him; and then, what's brave, what's noble,
Let's do't after the high Roman fashion,
And make death proud to take us. Come, away,
This case of that huge spirit now is cold.
Ah, women, women! Come, we have no friend
But resolution and the briefest end.
Exeunt, [those above] bearing off Antony's body.

[ACT V, SCENE I]

Enter CAESAR *with his council of war:* AGRIPPA, DOLABELLA, [MAECENAS, GALLUS, PROCULEIUS].

Caes. Go to him, Dolabella, bid him yield;
Being so frustrate, tell him, he mocks
The pauses that he makes.
Dol. Caesar, I shall. [*Exit.*]

59. **woo't:** wilt thou. 64. **garland:** i.e. crowning glory.
65. **pole:** pole star (?) or standard, banner (?) or garlanded pole around which villagers danced, hence symbolic of festivity and joy (?).
66. **odds:** difference, distinction. 73. **a woman:** i.e. not a queen.
75. **chares:** chores. **were:** i.e. would be fitting.
79. **sottish:** appropriate for fools.
85. **sirs.** Addressed to the women. 91. **briefest:** swiftest.

V.i. Location: Caesar's camp.
2. **frustrate:** baffled, defeated.
2–3. **he . . . makes:** his delays are ridiculous.

Enter DECRETAS *with the sword of Antony.*

Caes. Wherefore is that? and what art thou that dar'st
Appear thus to us?
Dec. I am call'd Decretas;
Mark Antony I serv'd, who best was worthy
Best to be serv'd. Whilst he stood up and spoke,
He was my master, and I wore my life
To spend upon his haters. If thou please
To take me to thee, as I was to him
I'll be to Caesar; if thou pleasest not,
I yield thee up my life.
Caes. What is't thou say'st?
Dec. I say, O Caesar, Antony is dead.
Caes. The breaking of so great a thing should make
A greater crack. The round world
Should have shook lions into civil streets,
And citizens to their dens. The death of Antony
Is not a single doom, in the name lay
A moi'ty of the world.
Dec. He is dead, Caesar,
Not by a public minister of justice,
Nor by a hired knife, but that self hand
Which writ his honor in the acts it did
Hath, with the courage which the heart did lend it,
Splitted the heart. This is his sword,
I robb'd his wound of it; behold it stain'd
With his most noble blood.
Caes. Look you sad, friends?
The gods rebuke me, but it is tidings
To wash the eyes of kings.
[*Agr.*] And strange it is
That nature must compel us to lament
Our most persisted deeds.
Maec. His taints and honors
Wag'd equal with him.
[*Agr.*] A rarer spirit never
Did steer humanity; but you gods will give us
Some faults to make us men. Caesar is touch'd.
Maec. When such a spacious mirror's set before him,
He needs must see himself.
Caes. O Antony,
I have followed thee to this; but we do launch
Diseases in our bodies. I must perforce
Have shown to thee such a declining day,
Or look on thine; we could not stall together
In the whole world. But yet let me lament,
With tears as sovereign as the blood of hearts,
That thou, my brother, my competitor
In top of all design, my mate in empire,
Friend and companion in the front of war,
The arm of mine own body, and the heart

5. **thus:** i.e. with a drawn sword.
14. **breaking:** (1) disclosure; (2) destruction.
15. **crack:** (1) loud noise; (2) gap.
16. **civil:** city. 19. **moi'ty:** half. 21. **self:** same.
27. **but it is:** if it is not.
30. **Our . . . deeds:** what we worked for most persistently.
31. **Wag'd equal with:** were evenly matched in.
32. **humanity:** any man.
36. **followed:** pursued. **launch:** lance.
39. **stall:** dwell peaceably. 41. **sovereign:** potent.
42–43. **competitor . . . design:** partner in loftiest enterprise.

Where mine his thoughts did kindle—that our stars,
Unreconciliable, should divide
Our equalness to this. Hear me, good friends—

Enter an EGYPTIAN.

But I will tell you at some meeter season,
The business of this man looks out of him;
We'll hear him what he says.—Whence are you?
Egyp. A poor Egyptian yet; the Queen my mistress,
Confin'd in all she has, her monument,
Of thy intents desires instruction,
That she preparedly may frame herself
To th' way she's forc'd to.
Caes. Bid her have good heart.
She soon shall know of us, by some of ours,
How honorable and how kindly we
Determine for her; for Caesar cannot [live]
To be ungentle.
Egyp. So the gods preserve thee! *Exit.*
Caes. Come hither, Proculeius. Go and say
We purpose her no shame. Give her what comforts
The quality of her passion shall require,
Lest in her greatness, by some mortal stroke
She do defeat us; for her life in Rome
Would be eternal in our triumph. Go,
And with your speediest bring us what she says,
And how you find of her.
Pro. Caesar, I shall. *Exit Proculeius.*
Caes. Gallus, go you along. [*Exit Gallus.*]
Where's Dolabella,
To second Proculeius?
All. Dolabella!
Caes. Let him alone; for I remember now
How he's employ'd; he shall in time be ready.
Go with me to my tent, where you shall see
How hardly I was drawn into this war,
How calm and gentle I proceeded still
In all my writings. Go with me, and see
What I can show in this. *Exeunt.*

[SCENE II]

Enter CLEOPATRA, CHARMIAN, IRAS, *and* MARDIAN.

Cleo. My desolation does begin to make
A better life. 'Tis paltry to be Caesar;
Not being Fortune, he's but Fortune's knave,
A minister of her will: and it is great
To do that thing that ends all other deeds,
Which shackles accidents and bolts up change,
Which sleeps, and never palates more the dung,
The beggar's nurse and Caesar's.

Enter PROCULEIUS.

Pro. Caesar sends greeting to the Queen of Egypt,
And bids thee study on what fair demands
Thou mean'st to have him grant thee.
Cleo. What's thy name?
Pro. My name is Proculeius.
Cleo. Antony
Did tell me of you, bade me trust you, but
I do not greatly care to be deceiv'd,
That have no use for trusting. If your master
Would have a queen his beggar, you must tell him
That majesty, to keep decorum, must
No less beg than a kingdom. If he please
To give me conquer'd Egypt for my son,
He gives me so much of mine own as I
Will kneel to him with thanks.
Pro. Be of good cheer;
Y' are fall'n into a princely hand, fear nothing.
Make your full reference freely to my lord,
Who is so full of grace that it flows over
On all that need. Let me report to him
Your sweet dependancy, and you shall find
A conqueror that will pray in aid for kindness
Where he for grace is kneel'd to.
Cleo. Pray you tell him
I am his fortune's vassal, and I send him
The greatness he has got. I hourly learn
A doctrine of obedience, and would gladly
Look him i' th' face.
Pro. This I'll report, dear lady.
Have comfort, for I know your plight is pitied
Of him that caus'd it.

[*Enter* ROMAN SOLDIERS *behind Cleopatra.*]

You see how easily she may be surpris'd.
Guard her till Caesar come.
Iras. Royal Queen!
Char. O Cleopatra! thou art taken, Queen.
Cleo. Quick, quick, good hands.
[*Drawing a dagger.*]
Pro. Hold, worthy lady, hold!
[*Seizes and disarms her.*]
Do not yourself such wrong, who are in this
Reliev'd, but not betray'd.
Cleo. What, of death too,
That rids our dogs of languish?
Pro. Cleopatra,
Do not abuse my master's bounty by
Th' undoing of yourself. Let the world see

46. his: its.
52. yet: still (though Egypt will soon be absorbed into Rome).
57. ours: my people.
63. quality . . . passion: her condition of passionate grief.
65–66. her . . . triumph: her presence, alive, in my triumphal procession in Rome would cause it to be remembered forever.
74. hardly: reluctantly. **76. writings:** i.e. letters to Antony.

V.ii. Location: Alexandria. The monument.
3. knave: servant.
7–8. never . . . Caesar's: no longer suffers the necessity of using the base food upon which life depends whether one is Caesar or a beggar. Some editors follow Theobald in emending *dung* to *dug*, which, despite the agreement with *nurse*, is much inferior.

8. nurse: nourisher.
10. fair demands: requests for favorable treatment.
14. to be: i.e. whether I am.
17. keep decorum: speak as befits it.
23. Make . . . freely: refer your case without reserve.
26. sweet dependancy: mild submission.
27. pray in aid: ask your assistance (legal term). **for kindness:** i.e. in devising ways to be kind.
29–30. I . . . got: I send him the great thing he has already possessed himself of, i.e. I acknowledge his sovereignty over Egypt and Egypt's queen. **31. doctrine:** lesson. **35. surpris'd:** overcome, captured.
41. Reliev'd: rescued. **of death:** i.e. treacherously cheated (*betray'd*) of death. **42. languish:** lingering misery.

His nobleness well acted, which your death
Will never let come forth.
Cleo. Where art thou, death?
Come hither, come! Come, come, and take a queen
Worth many babes and beggars!
Pro. O, temperance, lady!
Cleo. Sir, I will eat no meat, I'll not drink, sir;
If idle talk will once be necessary,
I'll not sleep neither. This mortal house I'll ruin,
Do Caesar what he can. Know, sir, that I
Will not wait pinion'd at your master's court,
Nor once be chastis'd with the sober eye
Of dull Octavia. Shall they hoist me up,
And show me to the shouting varlotry
Of censuring Rome? Rather a ditch in Egypt
Be gentle grave unto me! rather on Nilus' mud
Lay me stark-nak'd, and let the water-flies
Blow me into abhorring! rather make
My country's high pyramides my gibbet,
And hang me up in chains!
Pro. You do extend
These thoughts of horror further than you shall
Find cause in Caesar.

Enter DOLABELLA.

Dol. Proculeius,
What thou hast done thy master Caesar knows,
And he hath sent for thee. For the Queen,
I'll take her to my guard.
Pro. So, Dolabella,
It shall content me best. Be gentle to her.
[*To Cleopatra.*] To Caesar I will speak what you shall please,
If you'll employ me to him.
Cleo. Say, I would die.
Exit Proculeius [*with Soldiers*].
Dol. Most noble Empress, you have heard of me?
Cleo. I cannot tell.
Dol. Assuredly you know me.
Cleo. No matter, sir, what I have heard or known.
You laugh when boys or women tell their dreams;
Is't not your trick?
Dol. I understand not, madam.
Cleo. I dreamt there was an Emperor Antony.
O, such another sleep, that I might see
But such another man!
Dol. If it might please ye—
Cleo. His face was as the heav'ns, and therein stuck
A sun and moon, which kept their course, and lighted
The little O, th' earth.
Dol. Most sovereign creature—
Cleo. His legs bestrid the ocean, his rear'd arm
Crested the world, his voice was propertied
As all the tuned spheres, and that to friends;
But when he meant to quail and shake the orb,
He was as rattling thunder. For his bounty,
There was no winter in't; an [autumn] it was
That grew the more by reaping. His delights
Were dolphin-like, they show'd his back above
The element they liv'd in. In his livery
Walk'd crowns and crownets; realms and islands were
As plates dropp'd from his pocket.
Dol. Cleopatra!
Cleo. Think you there was or might be such a man
As this I dreamt of?
Dol. Gentle madam, no.
Cleo. You lie up to the hearing of the gods!
But if there be, nor ever were one such,
It's past the size of dreaming. Nature wants stuff
To vie strange forms with fancy; yet t' imagine
An Antony were nature's piece 'gainst fancy,
Condemning shadows quite.
Dol. Hear me, good madam:
Your loss is as yourself, great; and you bear it
As answering to the weight. Would I might never
O'ertake pursu'd success, but I do feel,
By the rebound of yours, a grief that [smites]
My very heart at root.
Cleo. I thank you, sir.
Know you what Caesar means to do with me?
Dol. I am loath to tell you what I would you knew.
Cleo. Nay, pray you, sir.
Dol. Though he be honorable—
Cleo. He'll lead me then in triumph?
Dol. Madam, he will, I know't. *Flourish.*

Enter PROCULEIUS, CAESAR, GALLUS, MAECENAS, *and others of his Train,* [SELEUCUS *following*].

All. Make way there! Caesar!
Caes. Which is the Queen of Egypt?
Dol. It is the Emperor, madam. *Cleopatra kneels.*
Caes. Arise, you shall not kneel.
I pray you rise, rise, Egypt.
Cleo. Sir, the gods
Will have it thus, my master and my lord
I must obey.
Caes. Take to you no hard thoughts.
The record of what injuries you did us,
Though written in our flesh, we shall remember
As things but done by chance.
Cleo. Sole sir o' th' world,
I cannot project mine own cause so well
To make it clear, but do confess I have

45. acted: carried out.
48. babes and beggars. Favorite victims of death.
50. If . . . necessary: even if it means that for once I must merely prattle in order to stay awake.
53. wait: attend, serve. **pinion'd:** like a bird with clipped wings.
56. varlotry: rabble. **57. censuring:** passing judgment.
60. Blow . . . abhorring: lay their eggs in my body and make it abhorrent with maggots. **75. trick:** way, habit.
83. Crested. In heraldry, a raised arm was sometimes mounted on a helmet.
83–84. was . . . spheres: possessed the full harmony attributed to the unheard music of the planets.
85. quail: cause to quail, terrify.
88–90. His . . . in: i.e. in his pleasures he rose above the common as a dolphin rises out of its element, the sea.
90–91. In . . . crownets: i.e. kings and princes wore his livery (were his servants). **92. plates:** silver coins. **93. might:** could.
96. if . . . such: i.e. whether or no there is or ever was such a man.
97. size: capacity. **wants stuff:** lacks material.
98. vie . . . fancy: compete with imagination in the creation of remarkable forms.
99. piece 'gainst: masterpiece in the competition with.
100. shadows: i.e. the imaginary creations of fancy.
103. but I do: if I do not. **121. project:** set forth.
122. clear: blameless.

Been laden with like frailties which before
Have often sham'd our sex.
Caes. Cleopatra, know
We will extenuate rather than enforce.
If you apply yourself to our intents,
Which towards you are most gentle, you shall find
A benefit in this change; but if you seek
To lay on me a cruelty, by taking
Antony's course, you shall bereave yourself
Of my good purposes, and put your children
To that destruction which I'll guard them from
If thereon you rely. I'll take my leave.
Cleo. And may, through all the world; 'tis yours, and we,
Your scutcheons and your signs of conquest, shall
Hang in what place you please. Here, my good lord.
Caes. You shall advise me in all for Cleopatra.
Cleo. [*Giving a scroll.*] This is the brief: of money, plate, and jewels
I am possess'd of; 'tis exactly valued,
Not petty things admitted. Where's Seleucus?
Sel. Here, madam.
Cleo. This is my treasurer, let him speak, my lord,
Upon his peril, that I have reserv'd
To myself nothing. Speak the truth, Seleucus.
Sel. Madam,
I had rather seel my lips than to my peril
Speak that which is not.
Cleo. What have I kept back?
Sel. Enough to purchase what you have made known.
Caes. Nay, blush not, Cleopatra, I approve
Your wisdom in the deed.
Cleo. See, Caesar! O, behold,
How pomp is followed! Mine will now be yours,
And should we shift estates, yours would be mine.
The ingratitude of this Seleucus does
Even make me wild. O slave, of no more trust
Than love that's hir'd! What, goest thou back? Thou shalt
Go back, I warrant thee; but I'll catch thine eyes
Though they had wings. Slave, soulless villain, dog!
O rarely base!
Caes. Good Queen, let us entreat you.
Cleo. O Caesar, what a wounding shame is this,
That thou, vouchsafing here to visit me,
Doing the honor of thy lordliness
To one so meek, that mine own servant should
Parcel the sum of my disgraces by
Addition of his envy! Say, good Caesar,
That I some lady trifles have reserv'd,
Immoment toys, things of such dignity
As we greet modern friends withal, and say
Some nobler token I have kept apart
For Livia and Octavia, to induce
Their mediation, must I be unfolded
With one that I have bred? The gods! it smites me
Beneath the fall I have. [*To Seleucus.*] Prithee go hence,
Or I shall show the cinders of my spirits
Through th' ashes of my chance. Wert thou a man,
Thou wouldst have mercy on me.
Caes. Forbear, Seleucus. [*Exit Seleucus.*]
Cleo. Be it known that we, the greatest, are misthought
For things that others do; and when we fall,
We answer others' merits in our name,
Are therefore to be pitied.
Caes. Cleopatra,
Not what you have reserv'd, nor what acknowledg'd,
Put we i' th' roll of conquest. Still be't yours,
Bestow it at your pleasure, and believe
Caesar's no merchant, to make prize with you
Of things that merchants sold. Therefore be cheer'd,
Make not your thoughts your prisons; no, dear Queen,
For we intend so to dispose you as
Yourself shall give us counsel. Feed, and sleep.
Our care and pity is so much upon you,
That we remain your friend, and so adieu.
Cleo. My master, and my lord!
Caes. Not so. Adieu.
Flourish. Exeunt Caesar and his Train.
Cleo. He words me, girls, he words me, that I should not
Be noble to myself. But hark thee, Charmian.
[*Whispers Charmian.*]
Iras. Finish, good lady, the bright day is done,
And we are for the dark.
Cleo. Hie thee again.
I have spoke already, and it is provided;
Go put it to the haste.
Char. Madam, I will.

Enter DOLABELLA.

Dol. Where's the Queen?
Char. Behold, sir. [*Exit.*]
Cleo. Dolabella!
Dol. Madam, as thereto sworn by your command
(Which my love makes religion to obey),
I tell you this: Caesar through Syria
Intends his journey, and within three days
You with your children will he send before.
Make your best use of this. I have perform'd
Your pleasure and my promise.
Cleo. Dolabella,
I shall remain your debtor.

125. extenuate . . . enforce: minimize . . . emphasize.
126. apply: adapt, conform.
137. You . . . Cleopatra: you shall be consulted as to all that affects you. **138. brief:** summary listing. **146. seel:** sew up.
151. How . . . followed: what faithless servants great persons have (?) or how high place attracts followers (?). **Mine . . . yours:** i.e. my servants are now deserting me and going over to you.
152. should . . . estates: if our fortunes should be reversed (*estates* = states, conditions). **155. hir'd:** paid for.
163. Parcel: add another item to. **164. envy:** malice.
166. Immoment toys: trifles of no value.

167. modern: ordinary. **169. Livia:** Caesar's wife.
170–71. unfolded With: exposed by.
173. cinders: smouldering coals. **174. chance:** (ill) fortune.
175. Forbear: withdraw. **176. misthought:** misjudged.
178. answer . . . name: answer in our own name for the ill-meriting deeds of others. *Merits* = what one deserves (whether good or ill).
183. make prize: haggle.
185. Make . . . prisons: don't be the prisoner of your own thoughts; you are free.

Dol. I your servant.
Adieu, good Queen, I must attend on Caesar.

Cleo. Farewell, and thanks! (*Exit* [*Dolabella*].)
Now, Iras, what think'st thou?
Thou, an Egyptian puppet, shall be shown
In Rome as well as I. Mechanic slaves
With greasy aprons, rules, and hammers shall
Uplift us to the view. In their thick breaths,
Rank of gross diet, shall we be enclouded,
And forc'd to drink their vapor.

Iras. The gods forbid!

Cleo. Nay, 'tis most certain, Iras. Saucy lictors
Will catch at us like strumpets, and scald rhymers
Ballad 's out a' tune. The quick comedians
Extemporally will stage us, and present
Our Alexandrian revels: Antony
Shall be brought drunken forth, and I shall see
Some squeaking Cleopatra boy my greatness
I' th' posture of a whore.

Iras. O the good gods!

Cleo. Nay, that's certain.

Iras. I'll never see't! for I am sure mine nails
Are stronger than mine eyes.

Cleo. Why, that's the way
To fool their preparation, and to conquer
Their most absurd intents.

Enter CHARMIAN.

Now, Charmian!
Show me, my women, like a queen; go fetch
My best attires. I am again for Cydnus
To meet Mark Antony. Sirrah Iras, go.
Now, noble Charmian, we'll dispatch indeed,
And when thou hast done this chare, I'll give thee leave
To play till doomsday. [*To Iras.*] Bring our crown and all. [*Exit Iras.*] *A noise within.*
Wherefore's this noise?

Enter a GUARDSMAN.

Guard. Here is a rural fellow
That will not be denied your Highness' presence.
He brings you figs.

Cleo. Let him come in. *Exit Guardsman.*
What poor an instrument
May do a noble deed! He brings me liberty.
My resolution's plac'd, and I have nothing
Of woman in me; now from head to foot
I am marble-constant; now the fleeting moon
No planet is of mine.

Enter GUARDSMAN *and* CLOWN [*with a basket*].

Guard. This is the man.

Cleo. Avoid, and leave him. *Exit Guardsman.*
Hast thou the pretty worm of Nilus there,
That kills and pains not?

Clown. Truly, I have him; but I would not be the party that should desire you to touch him, for his biting is immortal; those that do die of it do seldom or never recover.

Cleo. Remember'st thou any that have died on't?

Clown. Very many, men and women too. I heard of one of them no longer than yesterday, a very honest woman—but something given to lie, as a woman should not do but in the way of honesty—how she died of the biting of it, what pain she felt. Truly, she makes a very good report o' th' worm; but he that will believe all that they say, shall never be sav'd by half that they do. But this is most falliable, the worm's an odd worm.

Cleo. Get thee hence, farewell.

Clown. I wish you all joy of the worm.
[*Setting down his basket.*]

Cleo. Farewell.

Clown. You must think this, look you, that the worm will do his kind.

Cleo. Ay, ay, farewell.

Clown. Look you, the worm is not to be trusted but in the keeping of wise people; for indeed, there is no goodness in the worm.

Cleo. Take thou no care, it shall be heeded.

Clown. Very good. Give it nothing, I pray you, for it is not worth the feeding.

Cleo. Will it eat me?

Clown. You must not think I am so simple but I know the devil himself will not eat a woman. I know that a woman is a dish for the gods, if the devil dress her not. But truly, these same whoreson devils do the gods great harm in their women; for in every ten that they make, the devils mar five.

Cleo. Well, get thee gone, farewell.

Clown. Yes, forsooth; I wish you joy o' th' worm.
Exit.

[*Enter* IRAS *with a robe, crown, etc.*]

Cleo. Give me my robe, put on my crown, I have
Immortal longings in me. Now no more
The juice of Egypt's grape shall moist this lip.
Yare, yare, good Iras; quick. Methinks I hear
Antony call; I see him rouse himself
To praise my noble act. I hear him mock
The luck of Caesar, which the gods give men
To excuse their after wrath. Husband, I come!
Now to that name my courage prove my title!
I am fire and air; my other elements
I give to baser life. So, have you done?
Come then, and take the last warmth of my lips.
Farewell, kind Charmian, Iras, long farewell.
[*Kisses them. Iras falls and dies.*]

209. **Mechanic slaves**: laborers.
212. **Rank . . . diet**: smelling strongly of coarse food. (The poor ate inferior brown bread that quickly turned musty and many onions because they were cheap.)
213. **drink**: breathe in.
214. **Saucy lictors**: insolent (or lascivious) officers.
215. **scald**: scurvy. 216. **quick**: lively.
220. **boy**. Referring to the playing of female roles by boys on the Elizabethan stage. 221. **posture**: demeanor.
231. **chare**: task. 240. **fleeting**: changeable.
241 s.d. **Clown**: rustic. 242. **Avoid**: depart.

243. **worm**: serpent. 251. **of**: from.
252. **lie**. Quibbling on the sense "lie with a man."
254. **died**. Quibbling on the sense "experienced sexual climax."
255–57. **but . . . do**. The Clown has presumably transposed *all* and *half*. 257. **falliable**: blunder for *infallible*.
263. **do his kind**: act in accordance with its nature.
274. **dress**: prepare (term from cookery).
287. **their**: i.e. the gods'. 288. **title**: right.
289. **other elements**: i.e. earth and water. 290. **baser**: i.e. mortal.

Have I the aspic in my lips? Dost fall?
If thou and nature can so gently part,
The stroke of death is as a lover's pinch,
Which hurts, and is desir'd. Dost thou lie still?
If thus thou vanishest, thou tell'st the world
It is not worth leave-taking.

Char. Dissolve, thick cloud, and rain, that I may say
The gods themselves do weep!

Cleo. This proves me base.
If she first meet the curled Antony,
He'll make demand of her, and spend that kiss
Which is my heaven to have. Come, thou mortal wretch,

[*To an asp, which she applies to her breast.*]

With thy sharp teeth this knot intrinsicate
Of life at once untie. Poor venomous fool,
Be angry, and dispatch. O, couldst thou speak,
That I might hear thee call great Caesar ass
Unpolicied!

Char. O eastern star!

Cleo. Peace, peace!
Dost thou not see my baby at my breast,
That sucks the nurse asleep?

Char. O, break! O, break!

Cleo. As sweet as balm, as soft as air, as gentle—
O Antony!—Nay, I will take thee too:

[*Applying another asp to her arm.*]

What should I stay— *Dies.*

Char. In this [vild] world? So fare thee well!
Now boast thee, death, in thy possession lies
A lass unparallel'd. Downy windows, close,
And golden Phoebus never be beheld
Of eyes again so royal! Your crown's [awry],
I'll mend it, and then play—

Enter the GUARD *rustling in.*

1. Guard. Where's the Queen?

Char. Speak softly, wake her not.

1. Guard. Caesar hath sent—

Char. Too slow a messenger.

[*Applies an asp.*]

O, come apace, dispatch! I partly feel thee.

1. Guard. Approach ho, all's not well; Caesar's beguil'd.

2. Guard. There's Dolabella sent from Caesar; call him.

1. Guard. What work is here, Charmian? Is this well done?

Char. It is well done, and fitting for a princess
Descended of so many royal kings.
Ah, soldier! *Charmian dies.*

Enter DOLABELLA.

Dol. How goes it here?

2. Guard. All dead.

Dol. Caesar, thy thoughts
Touch their effects in this: thyself art coming
To see perform'd the dreaded act which thou
So sought'st to hinder.

Enter CAESAR *and all his* TRAIN, *marching.*

All. A way there, a way for Caesar!

Dol. O, sir, you are too sure an augurer;
That you did fear is done.

Caes. Bravest at the last,
She levell'd at our purposes, and being royal
Took her own way. The manner of their deaths?
I do not see them bleed.

Dol. Who was last with them?

1. Guard. A simple countryman, that brought her figs.
This was his basket.

Caes. Poison'd then.

1. Guard. O Caesar,
This Charmian liv'd but now, she stood and spake.
I found her trimming up the diadem
On her dead mistress; tremblingly she stood,
And on the sudden dropp'd.

Caes. O noble weakness!
If they had swallow'd poison, 'twould appear
By external swelling; but she looks like sleep,
As she would catch another Antony
In her strong toil of grace.

Dol. Here, on her breast,
There is a vent of blood, and something blown;
The like is on her arm.

1. Guard. This is an aspic's trail, and these fig leaves
Have slime upon them, such as th' aspic leaves
Upon the caves of Nile.

Caes. Most probable
That so she died; for her physician tells me
She hath pursu'd conclusions infinite
Of easy ways to die. Take up her bed,
And bear her women from the monument.
She shall be buried by her Antony;
No grave upon the earth shall clip in it
A pair so famous. High events as these
Strike those that make them; and their story is
No less in pity than his glory which
Brought them to be lamented. Our army shall
In solemn show attend this funeral,
And then to Rome. Come, Dolabella, see
High order in this great solemnity. *Exeunt omnes.*

293. aspic: asp. **298. leave-taking:** taking leave of.
302. make . . . her: i.e. ask her for news of me. **spend:** i.e. reward her with. **303. mortal wretch:** deadly creature.
304. intrinsicate: intricate.
308. Unpolicied: outdone in craftiness (in the contest with Cleopatra).
313. What: why. **316. windows:** eyelids. **319 s.d. rustling in:** moving with a rustling sound (of armor).

330. Touch their effects: are realized.
336. levell'd at: aimed truly, i.e. guessed correctly.
349. blown: swollen. **355. conclusions:** experiments.
359. clip: inclose.
361. Strike . . . them: cause sorrow to those whose actions have caused them.

NOTE ON THE TEXT

The only authority for the text of *Antony and Cleopatra* is the First Folio (1623); all later editions are derived from that source. Recent scholarship favors the view that the printer's copy for the F1 text (set by Compositors B and E) was some kind of transcript of Shakespeare's "foul papers," more probably by a scribe than by Shakespeare himself. Although a number of Shakespearean spellings are preserved in the F1 text (see below), Wells/Taylor and Spevack argue that a transcript by someone other than Shakespeare is more likely than direct use of either Shakespeare's "foul papers" (Greg) or "fair copy." They cite as evidence (1) six uses of the speech-prefix *Omnes*, spread over the work of both compositors, instead of *All*, Shakespeare's usual form in texts believed to have been printed from his holograph and in Addition II of *Sir Thomas More*, a scene almost universally accepted as being in Shakespeare's hand (see the introduction to *Sir Thomas More*); and (2) the great prevalence in the F1 text, again found in the work of both compositors, of "Oh" instead of "O", the latter being Shakespeare's very clear preference as shown in texts printed from his holograph.

The well-known textual problem posed by V.ii.34 s.d. has been neatly and persuasively explained by Hinman as arising from the omission of the necessary stage direction by Compositor B in order to make good a miscalculation in casting-off copy. This miscalculation left him with more material than he could fit into the remaining space on sig. zz1[r], the verso being already set up and in process of printing off. There is nothing in the F1 text to suggest that the manuscript copy had been used as a prompt-book.

F1 shows a good many characteristic Shakespearean spelling forms (see the text or the Textual Notes at I.i.39, I.ii.113, I.iii.103, II.iii.32, III.vi.28, III.xi.47, III.xiii.104, IV.xiv.104, IV.xv.73). The forms of certain proper names, where there is reason to suspect authorial carelessness or compositorial misreading, have been emended in conformity with Shakespeare's source in North's translation of Plutarch's Life of Antony, but *Thidias* and *Decretas* have been retained in place of the commonly adopted emendations *Thyreus* (so in North's Plutarch, but *Thyrsus* in Plutarch) and *Decertas* (North, *Dercetaeus*, and F1, only once, *Dercetus*). To avoid confusion, the form *Antony* as found in North and in *Julius Caesar* (where, however, the printer's copy was almost certainly not a Shakespearean autograph) has been adopted in preference to the spelling with *-th-* which appears consistently in F1 (except at IV.xv.11–12, where F1 has a single very crowded line and reads "Antony, Antony, Antony" to fit the printer's measure). The Italianate form *Antonio's* (F1 *Anthonio's* and *Anthonyo's*) has been preserved at II.ii.7 and II.v.26 (see "Note on the Text" to *Julius Caesar*). The spelling *Cleopater* which occurs occasionally (e.g., in II.ii.121, 217, II.v o.s.d.) may be Shakespearean, though it also occurs in the title of the play in the F1 "Catalogue of the seuerall Comedies, Histories, and Tragedies contained in this Volume." All references to Plutarch in the Textual Notes are to North's translation unless otherwise indicated.

For further information, see: J. D. Wilson, ed., New Shakespeare *Antony and Cleopatra* (Cambridge, 1950); M. R. Ridley, ed., New Arden *Antony and Cleopatra* (London, 1954); W. W. Greg, *The Shakespeare First Folio* (Oxford, 1955); P. G. Phialas, ed., New Yale *Antony and Cleopatra* (New Haven, 1955); David Galloway, "'I am dying, Egypt, dying': Folio Repetitions and the Editors," *N & Q*, CCIII (1958), 330–5; Charlton Hinman, *The Printing and Proof-Reading of the First Folio*, 2 vols. (Oxford, 1963); Richard Hosley, "The Staging of the Monument Scenes in *Antony and Cleopatra*," *The Library Chronicle*, XXX (1964), 62–71; Maynard Mack, ed., Pelican *Antony and Cleopatra* (Baltimore, Maryland, 1969); Stanley Wells, Gary Taylor, et al., *William Shakespeare: A Textual Companion* (Oxford, 1987); David Bevington, ed., New Cambridge *Antony and Cleopatra* (Cambridge, 1990); Marvin Spevack, ed., New Variorum *Antony and Cleopatra* (New York, 1990); Michael Neill, ed., New Oxford *Anthony and Cleopatra* (Oxford, 1994); John Wilders, ed., Arden (3rd ser.) *Antony and Cleopatra* (London, 1995).

TEXTUAL NOTES

Title: **Antony]** *Rowe;* Anthonie *F1 (see I.i.10 below)*
Dramatis personae: *subs. as first given by Rowe*
Act-scene division: *F1 marks I.i only; other act-scene divisions from Rowe and later editors (see first note to each scene); present act-scene arrangement as a whole first established by Dyce*

I.i

Location: *Rowe, Theobald (subs.)*
4 **Mars, now]** *F3;* Mars: / Now *F1*
10 s.d. **Antony]** *Rowe (so Plutarch);* Anthony *F1 (or* Anthonie *throughout, except IV.xv.11–2)*
12 **The . . . world]** *F2;* (The . . . world) *F1*
32 **messengers!]** *Collier;* Messengers. *F1*
37 s.d. **embracing]** *Pope*
39 **On]** *F2;* One *F1*
50 **whose]** *F2;* who *F1*
55 s.d. **To the Messenger.]** *Wilson*
55 s.d. **Antony and Cleopatra]** *Capell*
55 s.d. **followed . . . Messenger]** *ed.*
59–62 **I . . . happy!]** *as verse, Johnson (after Pope); as prose, F1*

I.ii

I.ii] *Pope*
Location: *Alexander (after Capell)*
o.s.d. **Lamprius]** *possibly intended as the name of the Soothsayer* (Southsayer *F1)*
1 **Lord]** *Johnson;* L. *F1*
10–1 **In . . . read.]** *as verse, Theobald; as prose, F1*
12 s.d. **To Servants within.]** *Sisson (subs., after Capell)*
26 **now,]** *F4;* now *F1*
33–4 **You . . . approach.]** *as verse, Capell; as prose, F1*
33 **prov'd]** *Capell;* proued *F1*
38–9 **If . . . million.]** *as verse, Rowe; as prose, F1*
39 **fertile]** *Theobald;* fore- / tell *F1*
46 **be—]** *Capell;* be *F1*
54 **worky-day]** *hyphen, Capell*
62–3 **Alexas—come]** *Theobald; Alexas.* Come *F1* (Alexas. *as s.p.)*
70 **Amen.]** *Capell;* Amen, *F1*
74 **decorum]** *as Capell; in italics, F1*
80 **Saw you]** *F2;* Saue you, *F1*
85 **Alexas]** *F2;* Alexias *F1*
86 s.d. **and Attendants]** *Rowe*
87 s.d. **Cleopatra . . . Train]** *Capell (subs.)*
112] *Following this line F1 reads:* Enter another Messenger.; *first om. Rowe*
113, 114, 119 **Sicyon]** *Pope;* Scicion *F1 (probably a Shakespearean spelling)*
114 s.p. **1. Att.]** *Capell;* 1. Mes. *F1*
115 s.p. **2. Att.]** *Capell;* 2. Mes. *F1*
118 s.p. **2. Mess.]** *Rowe;* 3. Mes. *F1*
119 s.p. **2. Mess.]** *Rowe;* Mes. *F1*
121 s.d. **Gives a letter.]** *Johnson*
121 **me.]** *Rowe;* me *F1*
121 s.d. **Exit Second Messenger.]** *Theobald*
130 s.d. **Enter Enobarbus.]** *placed as in Rowe; after* hatch. *l. 130, F1*
134 **them;]** *Theobald;* them, *F1*
137 **occasion]** *Rowe;* an occasion *F1*
155 **travel]** *F3;* Trauaile *F1*
157 **Sir?]** *Capell;* Sir. *F1*
179 **leave]** *Pope;* loue *F1*
184 **Hath]** *F2;* Haue *F1*
191 **quality,]** *Capell;* quality *F1*
193 **hair]** *Rowe;* heire *F1*
195 **us require,]** *Ridley;* vs, require *F1;* us, requires *F2*
197 s.d. **Exeunt.]** *F2*

I.iii

I.iii] *Capell*
Location: *Alexander (after Capell)*
5 s.d. **Exit Alexas.]** *Capell*
11 **wish,]** *Rowe;* wish *F1*
20 **What,]** *Sisson;* What *F1*
25 **first]** *F2;* fitst *F1*
36 **brows']** *Johnson;* browes *F1*
43 **services]** *F2;* Seruicles *F1*
63 **vials]** *Pope;* Violles *F1*
80 **blood;]** *Rowe;* blood *F1*
80 **more.]** *Rowe;* more? *F1*
82 **my]** *F2*

89 **well.]** *Theobald (subs.);* well, *F1*
103 **residing]** *F2;* reciding *F1*

I.iv

I.iv] *Capell*
Location: *Rowe, Capell (after Theobald)*
3 **Our]** *Heath conj.;* One *F1*
8 **Vouchsaf'd]** *Johnson;* vouchsafe *F1*
9 **abstract]** *F2;* abstracts *F1*
10 **are]** *F4;* are, *F1*
44 **dear'd]** *Theobald;* fear'd *F1*
46 **lackeying]** *Theobald;* lacking *F1*
48 **Menecrates]** *F4 (so Plutarch);* Menacrates *F1*
53 **forth,]** *F2;* forth: *F1*
56 **wassails]** *Pope;* Vassailes *F1*
57 **Modena]** *Johnson (so Plutarch);* Medena *F1*
58 **Hirtius]** *F4;* Hirsius *F1 (Plutarch* Hircius)
58 **Pansa]** *F2;* Pausa *F1*
75 **we]** *F2;* me *F1*
75 **council]** *F3* (councel); counsell *F1*

I.v

I.v] *Capell*
Location: *Rowe, Theobald*
2 **Madam?]** *Dyce;* Madam. *F1*
4 **mandragora]** *Johnson;* Mandragoru *F1;* Mandragoras *F2*
5 **time]** *Knight (after Rowe);* time: *F1*
16 **indeed]** *F2;* in deede *F1*
18 **Charmian]** *F2;* Charmion *F1*
23 **demi-Atlas]** *hyphen, Steevens*
24 **burgonet]** *F2;* Burganet *F1*
29 **time?]** *Capell;* time. *F1*
34 **s.d. Antony]** *Collier MS;* Caesar *F1*
40 **kiss'd— . . . kisses—]** *Steevens (after Theobald);* kist . . . kisses *F1*
50 **dumb'd]** *Theobald;* dumbe *F1*
50 **What,]** *Rowe;* What *F1*
61 **man's]** *Sisson;* mans *F1;* man *F2*
63–7 **Who's . . . so?]** *as verse, Rowe; as prose, F1*
71 **again]** *F2;* againe: *F1*
77–8 **He . . . Egypt.]** *as verse, Johnson (after Hanmer); as prose, F1*

II.i

II.i] *Rowe*
Location: *Capell*
2 **s.p. Menas.]** *Capell conj.;* Mene. *F1*
2–5 **Know . . . for.]** *as verse, Rowe; as prose, F1*
13 **without-doors]** *hyphen, Neilson*
16, 18 **s.pp. Menas.]** *Malone;* Mene. *F1*
21 **wan'd]** *Percy conj.;* wand *F1*
27 **Lethe'd]** *Pope;* Lethied *F1*
31 **travel]** *F3;* Trauaile *F1*
38 **ne'er-lust-wearied]** *Theobald;* neere Lust-wearied *F1*
38 **s.p. Menas.]** *Capell;* Mene. *F1*
41 **warr'd]** *F2;* wan'd *F1*
43 **greater.]** *F4;* greater, *F1*
44 **all,]** *Rowe;* all: *F1*
48 **cement]** *F3;* Ciment *F1*
51 **hands.]** *F4 (subs.);* hands *F1;* hands, *F2*

II.ii

II.ii] *Rowe*
Location: *Rowe, Capell*
7 **Antonio's]** *Rowe;* Anthonio's *F1*
9–10 **Every . . . in't.]** *as verse, Pope (after Rowe); as prose, F1*
10 **born]** *F3;* borne *F1*
14 **s.d. Maecenas]** *Cambridge (so Plutarch);* Mecenas *F1 (throughout)*
37 **residing]** *F2;* reciding *F1*
48–51 **you . . . cause?]** *F3;* you, . . . cause. *F1*
54–6 **You . . . excuses.]** *as verse, Pope; as prose, F1*
70 **disquiet.]** *Theobald (subs.);* disquiet, *F1*
70 **must]** *Theobald;* must, *F1*
81–3 **You . . . with.]** *as verse, Rowe; as prose, F1*
86 **on.]** *F3;* on *F1*
88–9 **To . . . denied.]** *as verse, F4; as prose, F1*
91 **knowledge.]** *Rowe (subs.);* knowledge, *F1*
101 **remember]** *F2 (subs.);* remember: *F1*
107 **soldier only,]** *Theobald;* Souldier, onely *F1*
118–20 **Thou . . . widower.]** *as verse, Rowe; as prose, F1*
120–2 **Say . . . rashness.]** *as verse, Theobald (after Pope); as prose, F1*
120 **so]** *Rowe;* say *F1*
121 **Cleopatra]** *F2;* Cleopater *F1*
121 **reproof]** *Warburton conj.;* proofe *F1*
122 **deserv'd]** *Theobald;* deserued *F1*
122–3 **I . . . speak.]** *as verse, ed. (after Rowe); as prose, F1*
160 **Mount Misena]** *Sisson (so Plutarch);* Mount-Mesena *F1*
168–70 **Let . . . me.]** *as verse, Hanmer; as prose, F1*
170 **s.d. Exeunt omnes. Manent]** *F2;* Exit omnes. Manet *F1*
187 **Cydnus]** *F2 (so Plutarch);* Sidnis *F1*
194 **love-sick with them;]** *Pope (subs.);* Loue-sicke. With them *F1*
199 **pavilion— . . . tissue—]** *Capell (subs.);* Pauillion, . . . Tissue, *F1*
200 **Venus]** *F2;* Venns *F1*
203 **divers-color'd]** *hyphen, F4*
204 **glow]** *Rowe;* gloue *F1*
206 **gentlewomen]** *F2;* Gentlewoman *F1*
207 **mermaids,]** *Theobald;* Mer-maides *F1*
208 **helm]** *F3* (Helm,); Helme. *F1*
217 **Cleopatra]** *F2;* Cleopater *F1*
222 **entreated.]** *F4 (subs.);* entreated, *F1*
223 **"No"]** *Pope (subs.);* no *F1*
223 **heard]** *F3;* hard *F1*
232 **breathless,]** *Hanmer;* breathlesse *F1*
232 **breathe]** *F3;* breath *F1*
233 **Never,]** *F3;* Neuer *F1*
242–4 **Let . . . here.]** *as verse, Rowe; as prose, F1*

II.iii

II.iii] *Capell*
Location: *Capell*
2–4 **All . . . you.]** *as verse, Rowe; as prose, F1*
3 **prayers]** *F2;* ptayers *F1*
8 **s.p. Oct.]** *F2; line continued to Antony, F1*
9 **s.d. with Octavia]** *Rowe (subs.)*
19 **side.]** *F3;* side *F1*
23 **fear. . . o'erpow'r'd:]** *Pope (subs.);* feare: . . . or'e-powr'd, *F1*
25 **thee; . . . thee.]** *Theobald;* thee no more but: when to thee, *F1*
31 **away,]** *Pope;* alway *F1*
32 **Ventidius]** *F2;* Ventigius *F1 (throughout scene; this spelling, probably Shakespeare's, occurs also in* Timon of Athens)
32 **s.d. Soothsayer]** *Rowe*
33 **Parthia.]** *Pope (subs.);* Parthia, *F1*
36 **chance.]** *Rowe (subs.);* chance, *F1*
41 **s.d. Enter Ventidius.]** *placed as in Dyce; after l. 41, F1*
42 **commission's]** *F3;* Commissions *F1*

II.iv

II.iv] *Capell*
Location: *Capell*
1–2 **Trouble . . . after.]** *as verse, Rowe; as prose, F1*
2–3 **Sir . . . follow.]** *as verse, Theobald; as prose, F1*
5–9 **We . . . me.]** *as verse, Pope (after Rowe); as prose, F1*
6 **the]** *F2*

II.v

II.v] *Pope*
Location: *Rowe, Theobald*
o.s.d. **Cleopatra]** *F2;* Cleopater *F1*
1–2 **Give . . . love.]** *as verse, Rowe; as prose, F1*
3 **billards]** Billiards *F2*
5–6 **As . . . sir?]** *as verse, Rowe; as prose, F1*
8 **show'd]** *Pope;* shewed *F1*
10 **river; there,]** *Capell (subs.);* riuer there *F1*
11 **off,]** *F4;* off. *F1*
12 **Tawny-finn'd]** *Theobald (hyphen, F3);* Tawny fine *F1*
15–8 **'Twas . . . up.]** *as verse, Pope; as prose, F1*
23 **s.d. Enter a Messenger.]** *placed as in Collier; after l. 23, F1*
26 **Antonio's]** *Neilson;* Anthonyo's *F1;* Anthony's *F2*
28 **him, there]** *Pope;* him. / There *F1*
35 **ill-uttering]** *hyphen, F3*
41 **Will't]** *Rowe;* Wilt *F1*
52 **But]** *F2;* Bur *F1*
96 **face, to me]** *F2;* face to me, *F1*
106 **s.d. Exit Messenger.]** *Rowe*
111 **Alexas,]** *F3;* Alexas *F1*
114 **s.d. Exit Alexas.]** *Capell*
117 **way 's]** *F4;* wayes *F1*
117 **s.d. To Mardian.]** *Capell*

II.vi

II.vi] *Pope*
Location: *Rowe*
o.s.d. **Menas]** *placed as in Rowe; follows* Agrippa *in F1*
7, 35, 45 **Sicily]** *F2;* Cicelie *F1 (Plutarch* Sicile)
10 **gods:]** *Ridley (after Theobald);* Gods. *F1*
19 **man? And]** *Theobald;* man, and *F1*
19 **is]** *F2;* his *F1*
20 **navy,]** *Collier;* Nauie. *F1*
30 **(For . . . take]** *Theobald;* (For . . . present how you take) *F1*
37 **'greed]** *F3;* greed *F1*
39 **s.p. Caes., Ant., Lep.]** *Capell*
43 **telling,]** *Theobald;* telling. *F1*
58 **composition]** *F2;* composion *F1*
62–5 **No . . . there.]** *as verse, Rowe; as prose, F1*
66 **meanings]** *Heath conj.;* meaning *F1*
69 **of]** *F3*
70 **mattress]** *Pope;* Matris *F1*
81 **s.p. Caes., Ant., Lep.]** *Capell*
81 **s.d. Manent]** *F2;* Manet *F1*
82 **s.d. Aside.]** *Johnson*
107 **sir.]** *Rowe (subs.);* Sir, *F1*
113 **sir?]** *Pope;* sir. *F1*

II.vii

II.vii] *Pope*
Location: *Capell (after Rowe)*
1, 4 **s.pp. 1. Serv. . . . 2. Serv.]** *Rowe;* 1 . . . 2 *F1 (throughout scene)*
1 **o' their]** *F2;* o'th'their *F1*
4 **high-color'd]** *F2 (hyphen, F3);* high Conlord *F1*
9 **greater]** *F2;* greatet *F1*
16 **s.d. Menas]** *F2;* Menes *F1*
17 **s.d. To Caesar.]** *Capell*
19 **mean,]** *Rowe;* meane: *F1*
29 **Sit—]** *Capell;* Sit, *F1*
30–1 **I . . . out.]** *as prose, Hanmer; as verse, F1*
35 **pyramises]** *Capell;* Pyramisis *F1*
37, 55 **s.dd. Aside to Pompey.]** *Dyce (after Rowe)*
37, 39 **s.dd. Aside to Menas.]** *Dyce (after Rowe)*
38 **s.d. Whispers in 's ear.]** *placed as in Wilson; after l. 39, F1*
41 **What]** *F2;* Whar *F1*
52 **s.d. Menas whispers again.]** *Wilson*
53, 56 **s.dd. Aside to Menas.]** *Johnson (subs.)*
56 **s.d. Rises . . . aside.]** *Johnson*
58–9 **Thou . . . lords.]** *as verse, Hanmer; as prose, F1*
60 **off them,]** *F2;* off, them *F1*
63–5 **But . . . world.]** *as verse, Pope; as prose, F1*
77 **it. Repent]** *Pope (subs.);* it, Repent *F1;* is, Repent *F2*
81 **s.d. Aside.]** *Capell*
88 **s.d. Pointing . . . Lepidus.]** *Steevens (after Rowe)*
92–3 **The . . . wheels!]** *as verse, Theobald; as prose, F1*
92 **then]** *Rowe;* then he *F1*
98–100 **I . . . fouler.]** *as verse, Pope; as prose, F1*
101–3 **Possess . . . one.]** *as verse, Dyce (after Hanmer); as prose, F1*
103 **s.d. To Antony.]** *Capell*
103–5 **Ha . . . drink?]** *as verse, Johnson (after Hanmer); as prose, F1*

104 Bacchanals] F2 (subs.); Backenals F1
109 music;] Capell (subs.); Musicke, F1
111 bear] Theobald; beate F1
120 off,] ed. (after Rowe); of F1
124 Spleets] F2; Spleet's F1; Splits F4
127 give 's] F3; giues F1
128 father's] F2; Father F1 (possibly a very late example of the uninflected genitive)
128 house—] Capell; house. F1
129–30 not. Menas,] Capell; not Menas: F1
129 s.d. Exeunt . . . Menas.] Capell
130 s.p. Men.] Capell; speech continued to Enobarbus, F1
131 flutes! what!] Rowe; Flutes: what F1
132 hear we] Steevens; heare, we F1 (c); heare a, we F1 (u)
132 a loud] Rowe; aloud F1 (a barely possible reading, retained by Capell)
133 s.d. flourish,] Pope; Flourish F1
134 'a. There's] Rowe (subs.); a there's F1

III.i

III.i] Rowe
Location: Capell (after Theobald)
o.s.d. with . . . Soldiers] Capell (after Theobald)
1 strook] F3; stroke F1
4 army.] Rowe (subs.); Army F1
4 Orodes] Rowe (so Plutarch); Orades F1
5, 27, 34 s.pp Sil.] Theobald; Romaine. or Rom. F1
8 Mesopotamia] Pope (so Plutarch); Mesapotamia F1
15 serve's] F2; serues F1
27–9 Thou . . . Antony?] as verse, Capell (after Rowe); as prose, F1
29 Antony?] Theobald; Anthony. F1
33 ne'er-yet-beaten] Theobald; nere-yet beaten F1
36 permit,] Rowe; permit: F1

III.ii

III.ii] Rowe
Location: Capell (subs., after Rowe)
10 s.p. Agr.] Rowe; Ant. F1
10 Antony? The . . . Jupiter.] Johnson; Anthony, the . . . Iupiter? F1
13 "Caesar,"] F2 (subs.); Caesar F1
16 figures] Hanmer; Figure F1
17 number, hoo!] Theobald (subs.); number: hoo, F1
20 s.d. Trumpet within.] Capell
29 cement] F3; Cyment F1
32 on both] F2; onboth F1 (a proof-sheet of this page, sig. xx6ᵛ, is extant and shows that the proof-reader marked the bad spacing for correction, but his correction was ignored by the corrector)
36 fear.] Rowe (subs.); feare, F1
50, 52, 57 s.dd. Aside to Agrippa.] Capell (subs.)
51, 53 s.dd. Aside to Enobarbus.] Capell (subs.)
52–3 He . . . man.] as verse, Pope; as prose, F1
53 Enobarbus?] Rowe; Enobarbus: F1
59 Believe't—] Alexander; Beleeu't F1

III.iii

III.iii] Rowe
Location: Theobald (after Rowe)
2–6 Good . . . it?] as verse, Pope; as prose, F1
8–10 Madam . . . Antony.] as verse, Capell (after Rowe); as prose, F1
12 shrill-tongu'd] hyphen, Rowe
13 low-voic'd] hyphen, Pope
16 dwarfish.] F3; dwarfish F1
31–2 For . . . color?] as verse, F3; as prose, F1
38 s.d. Exit Messenger.] Hanmer
43–7 Hath . . . enough.] as verse, Rowe; as prose, F1

III.iv

III.iv] Rowe
Location: Capell (subs., after Rowe)
6–7 me; . . . honor,] Rowe; me, . . . Honour: F1
8 them, . . . me;] Rowe (subs.); then most narrow measure: lent me, F1
9 him,] Rowe; him: F1
9 took't] Thirlby conj.; look't F1
24 yours] F2; your F1
25 between 's.] Rowe (subs.); between's, F1
30 Your] F2; You F1
32 solder] Pope; soader F1
38 has] F2; he's F1

III.v

III.v] Capell
Location: ed. (after Pelican)
o.s.d. meeting] Capell
3 What,] Rowe; What F1
13–5 Then . . . Antony?] as verse, Hanmer; as prose, F1
13 world, thou hast] Hanmer (subs.); would thou hadst F1
13 chaps—] Alexander (after Theobald); chaps F1
15 th' one] ed. (after Johnson conj. the one)
16 garden—] Steevens (after Capell); garden F1
19 navy's] F3; Nauies F1
20 Caesar.] Rowe (subs.); Caesar, F1
22–3 'Twill . . . Antony.] as verse, Hanmer; as prose, F1

III.vi

III.vi] Capell
Location: Capell (after Rowe, Theobald)
12 show-place] hyphen, Rowe
13 he there] Johnson; hither F1
13 proclaim'd] F3; proclaimed F1
13 kings of] Rowe (so Plutarch); King of F1
16 Cilicia] Rowe; Silicia F1
16 Phoenicia] F2; Phoenetia F1 (Plutarch Phenecia)
19 reported,] F2; reported F1
24 Sicily] F2; Cicilie F1 (Plutarch Sicile)
28 triumpherate] Triumvirate F2 (the F1 form, presumably Shakespeare's, occurs also in Love's Labor's Lost, IV.iii.53)
29 being, that] Rowe; being that, F1
39 lord] F3; L. F1
43 sister. The] F3 (subs.); Sister, The F1
57 free will] F4; free-will F1
69 Archelaus] Theobald (so Plutarch); Archilaus F1
71 Adallas] Rowe (so Plutarch); Adullas F1
72 Manchus] Dover Wilson (so Plutarch); Mauchus F1
74 Comagena] ed. (so Plutarch); Comageat F1; Rowe and later eds. read Comagene
74 Polemon] Theobald (so Plutarch); Polemen F1
75 Lycaonia] F2 (so Plutarch); Licoania F1
94 abominations] F4; abhominations F1

III.vii

III.vii] Capell
Location: Capell (after Rowe)
4 it is] F2; it it F1
5–9 If . . . horse.] as verse, Hanmer; as prose, F1
5 not] Malone conj.; not, F1
6 s.d. Aside.] Johnson
19 s.d. Canidius] Rowe (so Plutarch); Camidius F1 (throughout, except IV.vi.15)
21 Brundusium] F2 (so Plutarch); Brandusium F1
23 Toryne] F2 (so Plutarch); Troine F1
26 men,] Capell; men F1
29 s.p. Can.] Rowe; Cam. F1 (throughout)
35 muleters] F2 (Muliters); Militers F1
44 war-mark'd footmen] Rowe; Warre-markt-footmen F1
51 full-mann'd] hyphen, F3
51 Actium] F2; Action F1
57 Strange] Pope; Strange, F1
64 a-ducking] hyphen, Dyce
66 s.d. Exeunt] F2; exit F1
69 leader's led] Theobald; Leaders leade F1
70–1 You . . . not?] as verse, Rowe; as prose, F1
72 s.p. Can.] Pope; Ven. F1
72 Justeius] Theobald (so Plutarch); Iusteus F1; Iustius F2
73 Caelius] Theobald (so Plutarch); Celius F1
78 Taurus] Theobald (so Plutarch); Towrus F1 (throughout)
78 Well] Rowe; Well, F1
80 time's] F2; times F1
80 throes] Theobald; throwes F1

III.viii

III.viii] Capell
Location: Malone (after Capell)
o.s.d. and Taurus] Capell
2 lord?] Dyce; Lord. F1
6 s.d. Exeunt.] Pope; exit. F1

III.ix

III.ix] Dyce
Location: ed. (after Wilson)
4 s.d. Exeunt.] Pope; exit. F1

III.x

III.x] Dyce
Location: ed. (after Wilson)
o.s.d Enobarbus] Rowe; Enobarbus and Scarus F1
2 Th' Antoniad] Capell (subs.); Thantoniad F1 (in italics)
14 The . . . her,] Rowe; (The . . . her) F1
14 June] F2; Inne F1
27 he] F2; his F1
28–9 Ay . . . indeed.] as verse, Dyce (after Hanmer); as prose, F1
36 s.d. Exeunt severally.] Theobald

III.xi

III.xi] Dyce
Location: Capell (subs.)
19 that] Capell; them F1
20 straightway] F3; straight way F1
22 pray, a] F3; pray a F1
24 you.] Rowe (subs.); you, F1
24 s.d. Iras following] Wilson (after Pope)
27 Do?] Rowe; Do, F1
47 seize] F2; cease F1 (a Shakespearean spelling)
54 'Stroy'd] Pope; Stroy'd F1
58 tow] Rowe (towe); stowe F1
59 Thy] Theobald; The F1
63 lowness] F3; lownes F1

III.xii

III.xii] Dyce
Location: Rowe (subs.)
o.s.d Thidias] Rowe
13 lessons] Lessens F2
25 s.d. Exit Ambassador.] Rowe
26 s.d. To Thidias.] Rowe
31 Thidias] so F1 throughout, except III.xiii.104 s.d.; Plutarch reads Thyrsus; North's Plutarch, Thyreus (so Theobald and many eds.)

III.xiii

III.xiii] Dyce
Location: Capell (subs., after Rowe)
16–8 Let . . . brim] as verse, Rowe; as prose, F1
28 s.d. Exeunt . . . Ambassador.] Capell (subs., after Rowe)
29 s.d. Aside.] Capell
29 high-battled] hyphen, F2
34 alike.] Rowe; alike, F1
40 s.d. Exit Servant.] Capell (subs.)
41 s.d. Aside.] Capell
41 square.] Rowe (subs.); square, F1
46 will?] Theobald; will. F1
51 us,] Steevens; vs F1
55 Caesar] F2; Caesars F1
55 on:] Theobald (subs.); on, F1
57 fear'd] Theobald; feared F1
58 scars] F2; scarre's F1
62 s.d. Aside.] Hanmer
74 deputation:] Theobald (colon, Ridley); disputation, F1
88, 94 s.dd. Aside.] Capell
89 s.d. Calling for Servants.] B. Everett (in Signet ed.; after Wilson)
90 me. Of late,] Johnson (subs.); me of late. F1
93 s.d. others following] ed.; F1 s.d. after l. 93; placed as in Dyce

104 s.d. **Servants]** *Dyce* (*after Capell*)
104 s.d. **Thidias]** *F2;* Thidius *F1*
110 **boggler]** *Rowe;* boggeler *F1* (*indicating trisyllabic pronunciation*)
112–3 **eyes, . . . filth]** *Warburton* (*subs.*); eyes . . . filth, *F1*
118 **Cneius]** *F2;* Gneius *F1* (*Plutarch* Cneus)
131 s.d. **Enter . . . Thidias.]** *placed as in Collier; after l. 131, F1*
132 **'a]** *Theobald;* a *F1*
137 **whipt . . . him.]** *Rowe* (*subs.*); whipt. For following him, *F1*
155 **time.]** *F3;* time? *F1*
162 **Caesarion]** *Hanmer* (*so Plutarch*); Caesarian *F1*
162 **smite]** *Rowe;* smile *F1*
165 **discandying]** *Thirlby conj.;* discandering *F1*
177 **treble-sinew'd]** *Pope;* trebble-sinewed *F1*
193 s.d. **all but Enobarbus]** *Dyce* (*after Capell*)
198 **preys on]** *Rowe;* prayes in *F1*
200 s.d. **Exit.]** *Rowe;* Exeunt. *F1*

IV.i

IV.i] *Rowe*
Location: *Capell* (*after Rowe*)
3 **combat,]** *Rowe;* Combat. *F1*

IV.ii

IV.ii] *Rowe*
Location: *Theobald* (*after Rowe*)
1 **Domitius]** *Rowe* (*so Plutarch and III.v.20*); Domitian *F1*
1 **No.]** *Theobald;* No? *F1*
10 s.d. **Enter . . . Servitors.]** *placed as in Dyce; after l. 9, F1*
13, 23 s.dd. **Aside to Enobarbus.]** *Capell* (*subs.*)
14 s.d. **Aside to Cleopatra.]** *Johnson* (*subs.*)
24 s.d. **Aside to Cleopatra.]** *Capell* (*subs.*)
38 **fall, . . . friends!]** *Ridley* (*subs.*); fall (my hearty Friends) *F1*

IV.iii

IV.iii] *Hanmer*
Location: *Capell* (*after Theobald*)
8 s.p. **3. Sold.]** *Capell;* 1 *F1* (*the remaining s.pp. for the soldiers follow F1, because none of the suggested reassignments essentially reduces the problems involved; a principal difficulty is that at the beginning of the scene the First and Second Soldiers appear to be parting from each other, but as the scene progresses they seem to be closely linked*)
16 **lov'd]** *Capell;* loued *F1*
18 s.d. **Speak together.]** *placed as in Dyce; after* masters? *l. 18, F1* (*preceding s.p.* Omnes.)

IV.iv

IV.iv] *Capell*
Location: *Pope* (*subs.*)
o.s.d. **Charmian]** *Johnson*
2 s.d. **with armor]** *Capell*
6 s.p. **Ant.]** *Capell; F1 reads* Anthony *after* helpe too, *l. 5, as part of Cleopatra's speech, and gives her all that follows through* must bee. *l. 8*
8 s.p. **Cleo.]** *Hanmer*
8 **Sooth law]** *ed.;* Sooth-law *F1*
13 **daff't]** *Dyce;* daft *F1*
24 s.p. **Capt.]** *Rowe;* Alex. *F1*
28 **that: . . . said]** *Pope* (*subs.*), that, this way, well-sed *F1*
29 **me.]** *Johnson;* me, *F1*
32 **compliment]** *Rowe;* Complement *F1*
32 **thee]** *Theobald* (*after Rowe*); thee. *F1*
33 **steel.]** *Rowe;* Steele, *F1*
34 s.d. **Antony . . . Soldiers]** *Capell*
38 **Antony—but now—]** *Rowe;* Anthony; but now. *F1*

IV.v

IV.v] *Hanmer*
Location: *Capell* (*after Theobald*)
o.s.d. **a . . . them]** *Theobald*

1 s.p. **Sold.]** *Thirlby conj.;* Eros. *F1*
3, 6 s.pp. **Sold.]** *Capell;* Eros. *F1*
17 **Dispatch. Enobarbus!]** *Steevens* (*after Capell*); Dispatch Enobarbus. *F1*
17 s.d. **Exeunt.]** *Rowe;* Exit *F1*

IV.vi

IV.vi] *Hanmer*
Location: *Capell* (*after Rowe*)
3 s.d. **Exit.]** *Capell*
5 **three-nook'd]** *hyphen, F3*
7 **Agrippa]** *Capell;* Agrippa, *F1*
10 s.d. **all but Enobarbus]** *Dyce* (*after Capell*)
11 **Jewry]** *F2;* Iewrij *F1*
15 **Canidius]** *Rowe;* Camindius *F1*
19 **more]** *F2;* mote *F1*
31 **paid]** *Rowe;* payed *F1*
33–4 **heart. . . . not,]** *Rowe* (*subs.*); hart, . . . not: *F1*
35 **do't, I feel.]** *Rowe;* doo't. I feele *F1*

IV.vii

IV.vii] *Hanmer*
Location: *Capell*
o.s.d. **and others]** *Steevens* (*after Capell*)
3 s.d. **Exeunt.]** *Capell;* Exit. *F1*
8 s.d. **Sound retreat]** *Kittredge* (*after Capell*); *F1 s.d. after* heads. *l. 6*
13 **hares,]** *Theobald;* Hares *F1*

IV.viii

IV.viii] *Capell*
Location: *ed.* (*after Wilson*)
2 **gests]** *Theobald* (*after Warburton*); guests *F1*
11 **honor'd gashes]** *F4;* Honour'd-gashes *F1*
11 s.d. **attended]** *Capell*
11 s.d. **To Scarus.]** *Rowe*
13 s.d. **To Cleopatra.]** *Neilson*
23 **favoring]** *Theobald;* sauouring *F1*

IV.ix

IV.ix] *Capell*
Location: *Rowe*
o.s.d. **Sentry]** *Johnson* (*after Theobald*); Centerie *F1*
1, 10, *etc.* s.pp. **Sent.]** *Johnson;* Cent. *F1*
22 **master-leaver]** *hyphen, F4*
23 s.d. **Dies.]** *Rowe*
29 **Hark,]** *Malone* (*after Theobald*); Hearke *F1*
33 s.d. **with the body]** *Capell*

IV.x

IV.x] *Capell*
Location: *Rowe* (*subs.*)
6–7 **us— . . . haven—]** *Knight* (*subs.*); vs. Order . . . Hauen: *F1*

IV.xi

IV.xi] *Dyce*
Location: *ed.* (*after Wilson*)

IV.xii

IV.xii] *Dyce*
Location: *ed.* (*after Wilson*)
3 s.d. **Alarum . . . sea-fight.]** *placed as in Wilson; precedes o.s.d. in F1*
17 s.d. **Exit Scarus.]** *Capell*
21 **spannell'd]** *ed.* (*after Hanmer*); pannelled *F1*
45 **Lichas]** *Theobald;* Licas *F1*

IV.xiii

IV.xiii] *Dyce*
Location: *Capell* (*subs.*)
10 **death. To]** *Pope;* death to' *F1*

IV.xiv

IV.xiv] *Dyce*
Location: *Rowe*
4 **tower'd]** *Rowe;* toward *F1*
10 **dislimns]** *Theobald* (*after Rowe*); dislimes *F1*
14 **shape, my knave.]** *Rowe;* shape (my Knaue) *F1*
19 **Caesar's]** *Collier;* Caesars *F1*
19 **false-play'd]** *hyphen, Capell*
23 **robb'd]** *F3;* rob'd *F1*
35 **Unarm,]** *F3;* Vnarme *F1*
36 s.d. **To Mardian.]** *Globe*
50 **me!]** *Capell* (*subs.*); me, *F1*
87 s.d. **Turning from him.]** *Rowe*
90 **emperor:]** *Ridley;* Emperor. *F1*
94 s.d. **Kills himself.]** *placed as in Rowe; after l. 93, F1*
96 **me,]** *Rowe;* me: *F1*
102 s.d. **Falling . . . sword.]** *Rowe*
104 **ho]** *Theobald;* how *F1* (*a Shakespearean spelling*)
104 s.d. **Decretas and]** *Rowe*
110 s.d. **Guard]** *Pope*
111 s.p. **Dec.]** *Rowe;* Dercetus. *F1* (*this form, although closer to Plutarch's* Dercetaeus, *occurs in F1 only here; elsewhere* Decretas *or* Dec.)
111 **fly.]** *F3;* fly *F1*
115 s.d. **Exit Decretas]** *Capell* (*subs.*)
140 s.d. **Exeunt]** *F2;* Exit *F1*

IV.xv

IV.xv] *Dyce*
Location: *Capell* (*after Rowe*)
6, 9 s.dd. **below]** *Collier*
9 s.d. **bearing him]** *Pelican* (*after Rowe*)
35 **strong-wing'd]** *hyphen, Pope*
54 **liv'd,]** *Steevens;* (*after Theobald*); liued. *F1*
57 **countryman—]** *Theobald* (*subs.*); Countreyman. *F1*
62 s.d. **Antony dies.]** *Rowe* (*after* more. *l. 59*); *placed as in Capell*
65 **soldier's]** *Pope;* Souldiers *F1*
68 s.d. **Faints.]** *Rowe*
73 **e'en]** *Capell;* in *F1* (*a Shakespearean spelling*)
83 **what.]** *Theobald;* what *F1*
91 s.d. **those above]** *Capell*
91 s.d. **off]** *Rowe;* of *F1*

V.i

V.i] *Pope*
Location: *Rowe* (*subs.*)
o.s.d. **Enter . . . Proculeius.]** *arranged by ed.; F1 s.d. reads:* Enter Caesar, Agrippa, Dollabella, Menas, with his Counsell of Warre.
o.s.d. **council]** *Globe;* Counsell *F1*
o.s.d. **Maecenas]** *Thirlby conj.* (Mecaenas); Menas *F1*
o.s.d. **Gallus]** *Theobald*
o.s.d. **Proculeius]** *Capell*
1 **yield;]** *Theobald;* yeeld, *F1*
3 s.d. **Exit.]** *Theobald*
21 **self hand]** *Capell;* selfe-hand *F1*
26 **Look . . . friends?]** *Hanmer;* Looke you sad Friends, *F1*
28, 31 s.pp. **Agr.]** *Theobald;* Dol. *and* Dola. *F1*
48 s.d. **Enter an Egyptian.]** *placed as in Capell; after* says. *l. 51, F1*
52 **yet;]** *Rowe;* yet, *F1*
53 **all . . . monument,]** *Rowe;* all, she has her Monument *F1*
54 **intents desires]** *Pope* (*after Rowe*); intents, desires, *F1*
59 **live]** *Rowe;* leaue *F1*
69–70 **Gallus . . . Proculeius?]** *as verse, Pope; as prose, F1*
69 s.d. **Exit Gallus.]** *Theobald*

V.ii

V.ii] *Pope*
Location: *Capell* (*after Rowe*)
16 **queen]** *F2;* Queece *F1*
17 **decorum]** *as Capell; in italics, F1*
26 **dependancy]** *F2;* dependacie *F1*
32 **report, dear lady.]** *Pope;* report (deere Lady) *F1*
34 s.d. **Enter . . . Cleopatra.]** *Phialas* (*after Harrison*); *eds., following Malone, usually place the following s.d., based on North's Plutarch, after l. 35:* Here Proculeius and two of the Guard ascend the monument by a ladder placed against a window, and come behind Cleopatra. Some of the Guard

unbar and open the gates. (*see "Note on the Text"*)
35 **You]** *Johnson; Pro.* You *F1* (*repeated s.p.*); *Char.* You *F2* (*many eds., since Theobald, assign to Gallus*)
39 s.d. **Drawing a dagger.]** *Theobald* (*from Plutarch*)
39 s.d. **Seizes . . . her.]** *Malone* (*after Theobald and Plutarch*)
42 **languish?]** *F2;* languish *F1*
56 **varlotry]** *F2;* Varlotarie *F1*
57 **Egypt]** *Pope;* Egypt. *F1;* Egypt, *F2*
69 s.d. **To Cleopatra.]** *Hanmer*
70 s.d. **with Soldiers]** *Capell* (*subs.*); *F1 s.d. after* him. *l. 70; placed as in Pope*
71 **me?]** *Capell;* me. *F1*
81 **little O, th']** *Steevens* (*subs.*); little o' th' *F1*
87 **autumn]** *Thirlby conj., Theobald;* Anthony *F1*
99 **piece]** *Johnson* (*after Theobald*); peece, *F1*
102–3 **weight. Would . . . success,]** *Rowe* (*subs.*); waight, would . . . successe: *F1*
104 **smites]** *Capell;* suites *F1*
107 **what]** *Rowe;* what, *F1*
109 **triumph?]** *Pope;* Triumph. *F1*
110 s.d. **Seleucus following]** *ed.* (*after Capell*)
111 **there!]** *Rowe* (*subs.*); there *F1;* there, *F2*
138 s.d. **Giving a scroll.]** *Craig* (*after Collier MS*)
157 **soulless]** *Pope;* Soule-lesse, *F1*
172 s.d. **To Seleucus.]** *Johnson*
175 s.d. **Exit Seleucus.]** *Capell*
178 **merits . . . name,]** *Steevens* (*after Johnson*); merits, . . . name *F1*
192 s.d. **Whispers Charmian.]** *Theobald*
197 s.d. **Exit.]** *Capell*
207 s.d. **Exit Dolabella.]** *Capell;* Exit *F1* (*after l. 206*)
216 **Ballad 's out a']** *ed.;* Ballads vs out a *F1*
220 **Cleopatra boy]** *Pope;* Cleopatra Boy *F1*
228 **Cydnus]** *Rowe* (*subs.*); Cidrus *F1*
230 **Now . . . indeed,]** *Rowe;* (Now . . . indeede,) *F1*
232 s.d. **To Iras.]** *ed.*
232 s.d. **Exit Iras.]** *Capell*
240 **marble-constant]** *hyphen, Capell*
241 s.d. **with a basket]** *Rowe*
260 s.d. **Setting . . . basket.]** *Capell*
279 s.d. **Enter . . . etc.]** *Malone* (*after Capell*)
292 s.d. **Kisses . . . dies.]** *Malone* (*after Hanmer, Capell*)
303 s.d. **To . . . breast.]** *Capell* (*after Pope*)
312 s.d. **Applying . . . arm.]** *Theobald*
314 **vild]** *Steevens conj.* (*after Capell*); wilde *F1*
318 **awry]** *Rowe;* away *F1*
319 s.d. **in.]** *Rowe;* in; and Dolabella. *F1* (*F1 enters Dolabella again at l. 328*)
321 s.d. **Applies an asp.]** *Pope*
337 **deaths?]** *F4;* deaths, *F1*
342 **diadem]** *Pope;* Diadem; *F1;* Diadem, *F3*
343 **mistress;]** *Theobald;* Mistris *F1;* Mistris, *F2*
366 s.d. **Exeunt omnes.]** Exeunt omnes / FINIS. *F1*

Coriolanus

CORIOLANUS is by no means a favorite among Shakespeare's tragedies. It is harsh in its manner, political in its interests, and has a hero who is not—whatever else may be said of him—presented as a sympathetic character. Wyndham Lewis was not alone in finding Coriolanus the least lovable of tragic heroes; he calls the play "an astonishingly close picture of a particularly cheerless . . . snob, such as must have pullulated in the court of Elizabeth"—a schoolboy crazed with notions of privilege, and possessed of a "demented ideal of authority." Lewis uses him to illustrate the theme suggested by his title, *The Lion and the Fox*: Aufidius plays fox to the stupid lion of Coriolanus; what stings the hero to his last fatal outburst of raw anger is a charge of disloyalty, and, significantly, the word "boy." He is an ugly political innocent: "What his breast forges, that his tongue must vent." There is no gap between his crude mind and his violent tongue. And such men are dangerous. Yet the gracelessness of the hero and the harshness of the verse do not in themselves discredit T. S. Eliot's judgment that *Coriolanus* is Shakespeare's finest artistic achievement in tragedy; and when Shaw called it the best of Shakespeare's comedies he was perhaps making much the same point by means of a paradox: this is a tragedy of ideas, schematic, finely controlled.

The style of *Coriolanus* suggests a late date, and this is confirmed by the scanty external evidence. The simile of the "coal of fire upon the ice" (I.i.173) may have been suggested by fires built on the frozen Thames in January 1608; there had been no comparable frost since 1565. In Jonson's *Epicoene* (1609) there is what looks like another of his gibes at Shakespeare in the line "You have lurch'd your friends of the better half of the garland" (compare II.ii.101). More impressively, the play almost certainly contains allusions to serious riots and disturbances in the Midlands in 1607. In any case, *Coriolanus* could not have been written before the publication of Camden's *Remains* in 1605, since the fable of the belly (I.i.96 ff.), though mainly based on Plutarch, derives something from Camden's version of the same tale. On the whole, 1607–8 seems the most likely date.

The source of the play is North's version of Plutarch's *Life of Coriolanus*, and Shakespeare follows it in his usual way—sometimes very closely, with a liberal use of North's language, sometimes altering emphases, and changing the tone and balance by omission and addition. The events are transcribed almost in Plutarch's order, and the occasional closeness of the rendering of North's text may be gauged by a comparison with the source of the speech in which Coriolanus offers his services to Aufidius (IV.v.65 ff.) and that in which Volumnia pleads with her son to spare Rome (V.iii.94 ff.). Most of the characters are substantially taken from Plutarch, though Shakespeare modifies them in many ways.

Coriolanus himself is in Plutarch "churlish and uncivil, and altogether unfit for any man's conversation"; and although Shakespeare has his own view of the significance of this aristocratic loutishness, one cannot ignore the importance to his theme of Plutarch's prefatory observations on the hero's improper education. He represents this obliquely in the scene of the Roman ladies with their talk of the young Martius (I.iii), which has no source in Plutarch; and many of the alterations he makes are calculated to develop the idea that the education and presumptions of an aristocrat can make him unfit for rule in a complex society. Coriolanus has an imperfectly viable conception of *virtus*, of the duty of a man; it takes no account of social obligations, being based on a narrower concept of military courage and honor (see III.i.318–21). Thus he is able and honorable above all others in battle; and his modesty and piety in ordinary circumstances are suited to the role of happy warrior. But the spirit of anger, licensed in war, prevents him from dealing sensibly with the plebs, and such dealing is a necessary part of aristocracy, for which prospective leaders require a proper training. Volumnia, herself harshly embracing such narrow ideals of virtue and honor, could not give him this. Coriolanus' subservience to his mother is a mark of immaturity not only in family relationships but also in elementary politics: he is the ungoverned governor, the ill-educated prince.

Shakespeare therefore makes Volumnia more fierce than she is in Plutarch, and emphasizes the powerlessness of Virgilia's pacific spirit and her inability to affect the course of her husband's life, or even her son's. Menenius is much elaborated from the source, being useful as a commentator and as a link with the tribunes; but Shakespeare characterizes him with considerable exactness in such a way as to show that the strife between his class and the common people is not by any means the sole responsibility of Coriolanus, whose friends all share some responsibility for a situation they are anxious to ameliorate by hypocritical displays of compliance.

On the other side of the political dispute, Shakespeare is also at pains to make the behavior of the people and their tribunes somewhat less responsible and more treacherous than it is in the source. In Plutarch, the plebs have real cause for political action; before the Volscian war they are oppressed by usurers, and after it by famine. Shakespeare pays more attention to the characteristic fickleness of the mob, and to their dangerous demands, than to their needs; he does not deny members of the crowd sense and even generosity, but he will not represent their factiousness as the legitimate protest of a starving populace. He also makes them cowards in war, which in Plutarch they are not. As to the tribunes, Plutarch represents them as politicians exploiting new opportunities of power, but in nothing like the same base degree as Shakespeare. For Shakespeare looked at the story not with the sentimental republicanism of Plutarch but with a predisposition to deplore the attribution of power to the people. Given a state without kings (and *Coriolanus* is set in a Rome which has only recently exiled them), the proper focus of power is in Coriolanus and his friends; but they are tragically inept in its use, and negligent of the love they owe to inferiors.

The analogy of the body politic with the human body, so prominently stated in the opening scene, is vital to an understanding of the political *données* of the play, and much more important in Shakespeare than in Plutarch, though this does not mean that Shakespeare endorses the actions of his aristocrats or of Coriolanus in his double betrayal of Rome and Corioles. Coriolanus is habitually negligent of his inferiors—Shakespeare reminds us of this when he cancels out the hero's impulse of generosity towards a plebeian benefactor, whose name he can't remember at the important moment. In Plutarch this man is a patrician.

That there is a considerable element of political debate in the play is undoubted. Telling a story of early Republican Rome in the England of James I, Shakespeare not only modified certain Plutarchian details and emphases concerning institutions, but remembered the recent agrarian disturbances in the Midlands. Tudors and Stuarts alike feared mobs, and made propaganda against all forms of levelling; and Shakespeare's mobs, from *Henry VI* on, are dangerous beasts, in which upstart passions have taken control of reason. The risings of 1607 were part of a series of ominous events which had caused foreign observers to prophesy revolution; a royal proclamation of 1607 announced that it was "a thing notorious that many of the meanest sort of our people have presumed lately to assemble themselves riotously in multitudes." Various forms of religious communism gave the genuine grievances of some of these insurgents an ideological coloring. And a few years before *Coriolanus* there had been, in the rebellion of Essex, an aristocratic threat to state security. Essex too was an ungoverned governor; and it was said of him at the time that "great natures prove either excellently good or dangerously wicked: it is spoken by Plato but applied by Plutarch unto Coriolanus, a gallant young, but a discontented Roman, who might make a fit parallel for the late Earl, if you read his life."[1] As in *Julius Caesar*, Shakespeare here adapted Plutarch to fit more urgent interests; he is never merely telling an old tale.

We know Shakespeare as a master of the seminal opening scene, and *Coriolanus* provides a fine example. Here begins a clash of interests and prejudices between members of one body, and the result is disease in the body politic. By the time we reach Act III we can see why Shakespeare has allowed Menenius so deliberate an exposition of his parable. In III.i the imagery of the state as a diseased body becomes dominant. Coriolanus calls the people "measles" that "tetter us" (78–79), speaks of the wars they fear as touching "the navel of the state" (123), and refers to the common people as a "bosom" (stomach) (131), so reversing the allegory of Menenius; they are a "multitudinous tongue" (156) licking up a poison that will kill the state. Meanwhile Coriolanus himself appears to the tribunes as "a disease that must be cut away" (293) and as a gangrened foot (305).

Between the opening scene and this crisis, Shakespeare has proceeded economically, even schematically. At the outset Coriolanus calls the citizens "scabs" (I.i.166); but a war intervenes, and produces a situation in which he is the master-man, and they are weak cowards. As a soldier, Coriolanus is a kind of engine of war—we hear of "the thunder-like percussion" of his sounds (I.iv.59); "before him he carries noise, and behind him he leaves tears" (II.i.158–59). But out of his occupation of war, he feels himself reduced to a mere actor, forced to seek

[1] From a sermon preached at Paul's Cross in 1601 by William Barlow.

the suffrage of those who left him to enter the gates of Corioles alone; and it is this one-sidedness of Coriolanus that invites not only the vengeful meditation of Aufidius at the end of Act I but the fox-like stratagems of the tribunes in the next part of the play, which concerns Coriolanus in his role of suitor to the electorate.

As we have seen, the idea of the diseased body politic informs this central section, up to the banishment of Coriolanus. Health depends upon his ability to "temp'rately transport his honors" (II.i.224) from the field to the arena of politics; and the tribunes are right in thinking that he cannot—indeed, this is the theme of the tragedy. It has been intelligently suggested that Shakespeare had consciously in mind the saying of Aristotle—which circulated widely at the time—that a man "incapable of living in a society is either a god or a beast." Coriolanus evidently is thus incapable; and it is as a "lonely dragon" that he eventually is cast out from Rome into the void, though he finds again the medium of his narrow nobility in the Volscian service. Throughout the central section, up to his banishment, Coriolanus is repeatedly examined in relation to the concept of "nobility." If it consists in the licensed rage of war, he is noble enough to be a god; if it is the conduct of a man in civil society, he is a beast. He finds the behavior of the tribunes impossible for a nobleman to bear, and calls the people "foes to nobleness" (III.i.45); Sicinius sneeringly but accurately informs him that he needs "a gentler spirit" to "be so noble as a consul" (55–56). To him the plebs are merely necessary and ignoble "voices"; "his nature is too noble for the world" (254). But by the time Menenius says this, we have heard the words *noble* and *nobility* acquire much irony, and the patrician use of the word sometimes applies best to the behavior of the young Martius as he "mammocks" the butterfly.

The truth about the nobility of Coriolanus is most fully stated in the great speech of Aufidius at the end of the fourth act, where he finds his rival

> not moving
> From th' casque to th' cushion, but commanding peace
> Even with the same austerity and garb
> As he controll'd the war. (IV.vii.42–45)

Nobility requires a proper decorum in war and also in peaceful council (the "cushion" of the Senate). In the first, it may display itself as mere "sovereignty of nature"; in the second it calls for arts of dissimulation such as Machiavelli urges upon princes for the good of their people. There is no question that men of Coriolanus' stamp ought to be obeyed; and that is why they must be properly educated to power. This was a preoccupation shared by the Renaissance with Plutarch; and although Coriolanus brings his troubles upon himself through lack of such education, we are left in no doubt that the health of the Roman body politic suffers from his absence. Rome without Coriolanus is at the mercy of its enemies; the momentary calm, the period when the citizens, unprotected by their lion, worked peacefully in their shops, was merely a dangerous illusion. "You have made good work!"

Leading the Volscians against Rome, Coriolanus, in the final movement of the play, can again behave like a god (IV.vi.90); but the only love or piety he recognizes—that excessive respect for his mother which uses up all the love he needs for good government—finally overthrows him. To put it differently, Volumnia forces him to surrender a position in which it is enough for him to be a soldier, and to plunge himself into complexities with which it is impossible for him to deal. There is no moment in the play when one feels more sympathy for him than when he recognizes the implications of this surrender; he sees that it is dangerous, "if not most mortal" (V.iii.189). The final disaster happens because Aufidius has correctly estimated the temper of Coriolanus; with a burst of his old, narrowly military nobility he combats the most dreaded of insults:

> If you have writ your annals true, 'tis there
> That, like an eagle in a dove-cote, I
> Flutter'd your Volscians in Corioles.
> Alone I did it. (V.vi.113–16)

At the end, when our minds are charged with many ambiguous senses of the word, Aufidius grants him "a *noble* memory" (V.vi.153).

Coriolanus has been called a debate rather than a tragedy; but this is incautious. It has admittedly proved its durability as political comment (there was a famous Paris performance between the wars at which both Communists and Fascists rioted because they construed the play as propaganda against their respective causes). But it is, as is usual in Shakespeare, much more of a vivid dramatic meditation on certain political themes than a dramatized political debate; and at the heart of it is a hero. Deeply flawed, like Timon and Antony, he is also for the most part unsympathetic, harsh, and graceless; but that he is a great man, that his decision before Rome is crucial and painful—and must (as his mother explains) be in any case wrong—involves us in his fate, exactly as the Rome he "banished" was involved in it. Few plays so completely state their own theme. The skill with which Shakespeare relates the behavior of Coriolanus to his imperfect education is one instance; the brilliant invention of the scene at Aufidius' house is another, when the hero, who in departing from Rome seems to have departed from life, materializes suddenly, presenting himself in an enemy household as an inhabitant of "th' city of kites and crows" (IV.v.42) and, dressed in his poor and worn clothes, asserts his *virtus* not merely over the servants but over Aufidius and the senators of Corioles.

The verse of the play has its own absolutely decorous power. There is more to be said of the late verse of Shakespeare, as to what makes it seem "late," than talk of verse paragraphing, of weak and feminine endings, can yield. Here is verse so far from smooth that it is as if deliberately written in the vein of Hotspur's speech in *I Henry IV*. Hotspur would

rather hear a brazen canstick turn'd,
Or a dry wheel grate on the axle-tree,

than have his teeth set on edge by "mincing poetry" (III.i.129–32); and some of the verse of *Coriolanus* has this grating vigor. It has been observed that in this play there is an unusual degree of comment from various characters on the central figure. This is so; but it should also be observed that Shakespeare's turning inward of all the attention upon the hero (before society excludes him altogether) is a movement paralleled by that of the poetry. The verse is whirled about by the anger of Coriolanus; it clanks and thunders and revels in images of physical violence; it denies itself any more gracious aspect. (Virgilia, the tenderest of the characters, is famous for her silence.) Decorum ("which it is the grand masterpiece to observe") was something Shakespeare had continued to learn about. He had known the long, slow pleasures of accurate rhetorical expatiation, and indulged them in *Titus*—even, perhaps, as late as *Richard II*. But with *Coriolanus* we reach an extreme where no indecorous sweetness of language intrudes upon the military violence of the theme. Students come to recognize a certain extraordinary harshness of diction and violence of imagination as characteristics of late Shakespeare. Nowhere is it more exactly reined and controlled than here. The tone is set by the opening words of Coriolanus; then others use it in celebrating his triumph ("[he] struck / Corioles like a planet"). It infects the tribunes, as in Brutus' description of the crowd (II.i.205–21); it is heard finely in the mouth of Aufidius at the end of Act IV. But it is the voice of Coriolanus, the hard tone of nobility understood as military potency. He himself hums like a battery, and so does his play. Against this noise Shakespeare counterpoints the brisk character-writer's patter of Menenius, the elegant conversation of ladies, the lively, unheroic prose of the good fellows in the crowd. But the dominant noise is the exasperated shout of the beast-god Coriolanus. The energy of it is as superb as the control. We never feel that the author allows the hero to come very close to him or to us, but in spite of his keeping Coriolanus at a critical arm's length, Shakespeare can rarely have more fully extended his powers than he does here. There is a sense in which this inhospitable play is one of the supreme tests of a genuine understanding of Shakespeare's achievement.

Frank Kermode

The Great Frost of 1607–8. From the title-page of Thomas Dekker, *The Great Frost: Cold Doings in London* (1608). It was unusual for the Thames to freeze over, and the Londoners here shown disporting themselves on the ice just below London Bridge are obviously making the most of the occasion. Note the man having his head bandaged, the tent tavern, and the figure playing at some form of bowls. The placing of pans of coals on the ice (such as the one shown here in the centre foreground, heating water for the barber-surgeon [?]) is thought to be alluded to in *Coriolanus* (I.i.170–71): "You are no surer, no, / Than is the coal of fire upon the ice, / Or hailstone in the sun." *(By permission of the Harvard College Library)*

The Tragedy of Coriolanus

[DRAMATIS PERSONAE

CAIUS MARTIUS, *afterwards* CAIUS MARTIUS CORIOLANUS
TITUS LARTIUS, COMINIUS } *generals against the Volscians*
MENENIUS AGRIPPA, *friend to Coriolanus*
SICINIUS VELUTUS, JUNIUS BRUTUS } *tribunes of the people*
Young MARTIUS, *son to Coriolanus*
Roman HERALD
NICANOR, *a Roman*
TULLUS AUFIDIUS, *general of the Volscians*
LIEUTENANTS *to Aufidius and Coriolanus*
CONSPIRATORS *with Aufidius*
ADRIAN, *a Volscian*
CITIZEN *of Antium*
Two Volscian GUARDS

VOLUMNIA, *mother to Coriolanus*
VIRGILIA, *wife to Coriolanus*
VALERIA, *friend to Virgilia*
GENTLEWOMAN, *attending on Virgilia*
Roman and Volscian SENATORS, PATRICIANS, AEDILES, LICTORS, SOLDIERS, CITIZENS, MESSENGERS, SERVANTS *to Aufidius, and other* ATTENDANTS

SCENE: *Rome and the neighborhood; Corioles and the neighborhood; Antium*]

ACT I, SCENE I

Enter a company of mutinous CITIZENS *with staves, clubs, and other weapons.*

1. Cit. Before we proceed any further, hear me speak.

All. Speak, speak.

1. Cit. You are all resolv'd rather to die than to famish?

All. Resolv'd, resolv'd.

1. Cit. First, you know Caius Martius is chief enemy to the people.

All. We know't, we know't.

1. Cit. Let us kill him, and we'll have corn at our own price. Is't a verdict?

All. No more talking on't; let it be done. Away, away!

2. Cit. One word, good citizens.

1. Cit. We are accounted poor citizens, the patricians good. What authority surfeits [on] would relieve us. If they would yield us but the superfluity while it were wholesome, we might guess they reliev'd us humanely; but they think we are too dear. The leanness that afflicts us, the object of our misery, is as an inventory to particularize their abundance; our sufferance is a gain to them. Let us revenge this with our pikes, ere we become rakes; for the gods know I speak this in hunger for bread, not in thirst for revenge.

2. Cit. Would you proceed especially against Caius Martius?

[*1. Cit.*] Against him first; he's a very dog to the commonalty.

2. Cit. Consider you what services he has done for his country?

1. Cit. Very well, and could be content to give him good report for't, but that he pays himself with being proud.

[*2. Cit.*] Nay, but speak not maliciously.

1. Cit. I say unto you, what he hath done famously, he did it to that end. Though soft-conscienc'd men can be content to say it was for his country, he did it to please his mother, and to be partly proud, which he is, even to the altitude of his virtue.

2. Cit. What he cannot help in his nature, you account a vice in him. You must in no way say he is covetous.

1. Cit. If I must not, I need not be barren of accusations; he hath faults (with surplus) to tire in

Words and passages enclosed in square brackets in the text above are either emendations of the copy-text or additions to it. The Textual Notes immediately following the play cite the earliest authority for every such change or insertion and supply the reading of the copy-text wherever it is emended in this edition.

I.i. Location: Rome. A street.
10. corn: grain, wheat.
16. good. With a quibble on the meaning "well-to-do."
18. wholesome: (still) fit to eat.
19. dear: (1) expensive; (2) valuable (as he goes on to explain).
20. object: sight. 22. sufferance: suffering.
23. rakes: i.e. thin as rakes.
36. what . . . famously: the deeds by which he has become famous.
37. to that end: i.e. to become famous. soft-conscienc'd: tender-minded. 39. to be partly: partly to be.
40. to . . . virtue: in the same degree as he is valorous.
44. If: i.e. even if.

repetition. (*Shouts within.*) What shouts are these? The other side a' th' city is risen; why stay we prating here? To th' Capitol!

All. Come, come.

1. Cit. Soft, who comes here?

Enter MENENIUS AGRIPPA.

2. Cit. Worthy Menenius Agrippa, one that hath always lov'd the people.

1. Cit. He's one honest enough; would all the rest were so!

Men. What work's, my countrymen, in hand? Where go you
With bats and clubs? The matter? Speak, I pray you.

[1.] Cit. Our business is not unknown to th' Senate; they have had inkling this fortnight what we intend to do, which now we'll show 'em in deeds. They say poor suitors have strong breaths; they shall know we have strong arms too.

Men. Why, masters, my good friends, mine honest neighbors,
Will you undo yourselves?

[1.] Cit. We cannot, sir, we are undone already.

Men. I tell you, friends, most charitable care
Have the patricians of you. For your wants,
Your suffering in this dearth, you may as well
Strike at the heaven with your staves as lift them
Against the Roman state, whose course will on
The way it takes, cracking ten thousand curbs
Of more strong link asunder than can ever
Appear in your impediment. For the dearth,
The gods, not the patricians, make it, and
Your knees to them (not arms) must help. Alack,
You are transported by calamity
Thither where more attends you, and you slander
The helms o' th' state, who care for you like fathers,
When you curse them as enemies.

[1.] Cit. Care for us? True indeed! They ne'er car'd for us yet. Suffer us to famish, and their store-houses cramm'd with grain; make edicts for usury, to support usurers; repeal daily any wholesome act establish'd against the rich, and provide more piercing statutes daily to chain up and restrain the poor. If the wars eat us not up, they will; and there's all the love they bear us.

Men. Either you must
Confess yourselves wondrous malicious,
Or be accus'd of folly. I shall tell you
A pretty tale. It may be you have heard it,
But, since it serves my purpose, I will venture
To [stale]'t a little more.

[1.] Cit. Well, I'll hear it, sir; yet you must not think to fob off our disgrace with a tale. But and't please you, deliver.

46. **repetition:** reporting. 47. **a':** of. **prating:** talking foolishly.
50. **Soft:** not so fast, wait a bit.
56. **bats and clubs.** Familiar weapons in the street brawls of London apprentices.
60. **suitors:** petitioners. **strong breaths:** i.e. because poor men ate many onions. 63. **undo:** ruin. 66. **For:** as for.
67. **dearth:** famine.
71–72. **than . . . impediment:** than your opposition can possibly present. 76. **attends:** waits.
77. **helms:** i.e. helmsmen. 81. **for:** permitting.
92. **stale't . . . more:** make it staler, tell it again.
94. **fob . . . disgrace:** cajole us from our feeling of injury. **and:** if.

Men. There was a time when all the body's members
Rebell'd against the belly; thus accus'd it:
That only like a gulf it did remain
I' th' midst a' th' body, idle and unactive,
Still cupboarding the viand, never bearing
Like labor with the rest, where th' other instruments
Did see and hear, devise, instruct, walk, feel,
And, mutually participate, did minister
Unto the appetite and affection common
Of the whole body. The belly answer'd—

[1.] Cit. Well, sir, what answer made the belly?

Men. Sir, I shall tell you. With a kind of smile,
Which ne'er came from the lungs, but even thus—
For, look you, I may make the belly smile
As well as speak—it [tauntingly] replied
To th' discontented members, the mutinous parts
That envied his receipt; even so most fitly
As you malign our senators for that
They are not such as you.

[1.] Cit. Your belly's answer—what?
The kingly-crowned head, the vigilant eye,
The counsellor heart, the arm our soldier,
Our steed the leg, the tongue our trumpeter,
With other muniments and petty helps
In this our fabric, if that they—

Men. What then?
'Fore me, this fellow speaks! What then? what then?

[1.] Cit. Should by the cormorant belly be restrain'd,
Who is the sink a' th' body—

Men. Well, what then?

[1.] Cit. The former agents, if they did complain,
What could the belly answer?

Men. I will tell you;
If you'll bestow a small (of what you have little)
Patience awhile, you'st hear the belly's answer.

[1.] Cit. Y' are long about it.

Men. Note me this, good friend:
Your most grave belly was deliberate,
Not rash like his accusers, and thus answered:
"True is it, my incorporate friends," quoth he,
"That I receive the general food at first
Which you do live upon; and fit it is,
Because I am the store-house and the shop
Of the whole body. But, if you do remember,
I send it through the rivers of your blood,
Even to the court, the heart, to th' seat o' th' brain,
And, through the cranks and offices of man,

98. **gulf:** deep pit; the "swallowing gulf" of *The Rape of Lucrece,* line 557. 100. **Still:** always.
101. **where:** whereas. **instruments:** organs.
103. **participate:** cooperating.
104. **affection:** inclination, desire.
108. **lungs.** The organ of laughter.
112. **his receipt:** what it received. 113. **for that:** because.
118. **muniments:** means of protection. **petty:** i.e. lesser.
120. **'Fore me:** a mild oath. **speaks:** i.e. can talk.
122. **sink:** sewer. 126. **you'st:** you shall.
128. **Your:** this. **grave:** worthy, reverend (probably with play on "heavy"). 129. **rash:** hasty, impetuous.
130. **incorporate:** united in one body. 133. **shop:** workshop.
136. **th' seat . . . brain:** i.e. the throne, which is the brain.
137. **cranks and offices:** winding passages and remoter rooms.

The strongest nerves and small inferior veins
From me receive that natural competency
Whereby they live. And though that all at once"—
You, my good friends, this says the belly, mark me.
[*1.*] *Cit.* Ay, sir, well, well.
Men. "Though all at once cannot
See what I do deliver out to each,
Yet I can make my audit up, that all
From me do back receive the flour of all,
And leave me but the bran." What say you to't?
[*1.*] *Cit.* It was an answer. How apply you this?
Men. The senators of Rome are this good belly,
And you the mutinous members: for examine
Their counsels and their cares; disgest things rightly
Touching the weal a' th' common, you shall find
No public benefit which you receive
But it proceeds or comes from them to you,
And no way from yourselves. What do you think,
You, the great toe of this assembly?
[*1.*] *Cit.* I the great toe? Why the great toe?
Men. For that, being one o' th' lowest, basest, poorest
Of this most wise rebellion, thou goest foremost;
Thou rascal, that art worst in blood to run,
Lead'st first to win some vantage.
But make you ready your stiff bats and clubs,
Rome and her rats are at the point of battle,
The one side must have bale.

Enter Caius Martius.

Hail, noble Martius!
Mar. Thanks. What's the matter, you dissentious rogues,
That rubbing the poor itch of your opinion
Make yourselves scabs?
[*1.*] *Cit.* We have ever your good word.
Mar. He that will give good words to thee will flatter
Beneath abhorring. What would you have, you curs,
That like nor peace nor war? The one affrights you,
The other makes you proud. He that trusts to you,
Where he should find you lions, finds you hares;
Where foxes, geese. You are no surer, no,
Than is the coal of fire upon the ice,
Or hailstone in the sun. Your virtue is
To make him worthy whose offense subdues him,
And curse that justice did it. Who deserves greatness
Deserves your hate; and your affections are
A sick man's appetite, who desires most that
Which would increase his evil. He that depends
Upon your favors swims with fins of lead,
And hews down oaks with rushes. Hang ye! Trust ye?
With every minute you do change a mind,
And call him noble, that was now your hate;
Him vild, that was your garland. What's the matter,
That in these several places of the city
You cry against the noble Senate, who
(Under the gods) keep you in awe, which else
Would feed on one another? What's their seeking?
Men. For corn at their own rates, whereof they say
The city is well stor'd.
Mar. Hang 'em! They say?
They'll sit by th' fire, and presume to know
What's done i' th' Capitol; who's like to rise,
Who thrives, and who declines; side factions, and give out
Conjectural marriages, making parties strong,
And feebling such as stand not in their liking
Below their cobbled shoes. They say there's grain enough?
Would the nobility lay aside their ruth
And let me use my sword, I'd make a quarry
With thousands of these quarter'd slaves, as high
As I could pick my lance.
Men. Nay, these are almost thoroughly persuaded;
For though abundantly they lack discretion,
Yet are they passing cowardly. But I beseech you,
What says the other troop?
Mar. They are dissolv'd. Hang 'em!
They said they were an-hungry; sigh'd forth proverbs—
That hunger broke stone walls, that dogs must eat,
That meat was made for mouths, that the gods sent not
Corn for the rich men only. With these shreds
They vented their complainings, which being answer'd,
And a petition granted them—a strange one,
To break the heart of generosity
And make bold power look pale—they threw their caps
As they would hang them on the horns a' th' moon,
[Shouting] their emulation.
Men. What is granted them?
Mar. Five tribunes to defend their vulgar wisdoms,
Of their own choice. One's Junius Brutus,
Sicinius Velutus, and I know not—'Sdeath,
The rabble should have first [unroof'd] the city
Ere so prevail'd with me; it will in time
Win upon power, and throw forth greater themes

138. nerves: sinews, muscles.
139. natural competency: amount sufficient for their nature.
145. flour: choice and nourishing portion.
146. bran: husks, refuse. **150. disgest:** digest.
151. weal . . . common: public welfare.
159. rascal: (1) wretch; (2) thin, inferior animal (commonly applied to deer, but here apparently to a hunting-dog). **blood:** condition.
161. stiff: (1) stout; (2) stubbornly borne.
163. The one side: one side or the other. **bale:** disaster.
166. scabs: (1) sores; (2) scurvy fellows.
174. virtue: characteristic excellence.
175. whose . . . him: whose own fault has ruined him.
176. did it: i.e. that punished his fault.
183. now: just now, a moment before. **184. vild:** vile, base.
187. which else: who otherwise.
193. side: take sides with. **give out:** report.
194. marriages: i.e. political alliances. **making parties strong:** reporting parties to be strong.
195. feebling: reporting to be feeble. **196. cobbled:** ill-mended.
197. ruth: compassion. **198. quarry:** heap of dead bodies.
199. quarter'd: cut into quarters (as traitors were), slaughtered.
200. pick: pitch. **203. passing:** surpassingly, extremely.
205. an-hungry: hungry. **206. dogs:** i.e. even dogs.
211. break . . . generosity: be the death of the patricians.
214. emulation: envious pleasure.
215. their vulgar wisdoms: i.e. those wise plebeians (ironically analogous to such formations as *their worships* or *their honors*).
217. 'Sdeath: by God's (Christ's) death.
220. Win upon power: encroach further upon authority.
220–21. throw . . . arguing: make greater demands to be urged by rebel uprisings.

For insurrection's arguing.
Men. This is strange.
Mar. Go get you home, you fragments!

Enter a MESSENGER *hastily.*

Mess. Where's Caius Martius?
Mar. Here. What's the matter?
Mess. The news is, sir, the Volsces are in arms.
Mar. I am glad on't, then we shall ha' means to vent
Our musty superfluity. See, our best elders.

Enter SICINIUS VELUTUS, JUNIUS BRUTUS, COMINIUS, TITUS LARTIUS, *with other* SENATORS.

1. Sen. Martius, 'tis true that you have lately told us,
The Volsces are in arms.
Mar. They have a leader,
Tullus Aufidius, that will put you to't.
I sin in envying his nobility;
And were I any thing but what I am,
I would wish me only he.
Com. You have fought together?
Mar. Were half to half the world by th' ears, and he
Upon my party, I'd revolt, to make
Only my wars with him. He is a lion
That I am proud to hunt.
1. Sen. Then, worthy Martius,
Attend upon Cominius to these wars.
Com. It is your former promise.
Mar. Sir, it is,
And I am constant. Titus [Lartius], thou
Shalt see me once more strike at Tullus' face.
What, art thou stiff? Stand'st out?
Lart. No, Caius Martius,
I'll lean upon one crutch, and fight with t' other,
Ere stay behind this business.
Men. O, true-bred!
[1.] Sen. Your company to th' Capitol, where I know
Our greatest friends attend us.
Lart. [*To Cominius.*] Lead you on.
[*To Martius.*] Follow Cominius; we must follow you,
Right worthy you priority.
Com. Noble Martius!
[1.] Sen. [*To the Citizens.*] Hence to your homes, be gone!
Mar. Nay, let them follow.
The Volsces have much corn; take these rats thither
To gnaw their garners. Worshipful mutiners,
Your valor puts well forth; pray follow.

Exeunt. Citizens steal away. Manent Sicinius and Brutus.

Sic. Was ever man so proud as is this Martius?
Bru. He has no equal.
Sic. When we were chosen tribunes for the people—
Bru. Mark'd you his lip and eyes?
Sic. Nay, but his taunts.
Bru. Being mov'd, he will not spare to gird the gods.
Sic. Bemock the modest moon.
Bru. The present wars devour him! he is grown
Too proud to be so valiant.
Sic. Such a nature,
Tickled with good success, disdains the shadow
Which he treads on at noon. But I do wonder
His insolence can brook to be commanded
Under Cominius.
Bru. Fame, at the which he aims,
In whom already he's well grac'd, cannot
Better be held nor more attain'd than by
A place below the first; for what miscarries
Shall be the general's fault, though he perform
To th' utmost of a man, and giddy censure
Will then cry out of Martius, "O, if he
Had borne the business!"
Sic. Besides, if things go well,
Opinion that so sticks on Martius shall
Of his demerits rob Cominius.
Bru. Come.
Half all Cominius' honors are to Martius,
Though Martius earn'd them not; and all his faults
To Martius shall be honors, though indeed
In aught he merit not.
Sic. Let's hence, and hear
How the dispatch is made, and in what fashion,
More than his singularity, he goes
Upon this present action.
Bru. Let's along. *Exeunt.*

[SCENE II]

Enter TULLUS AUFIDIUS *with* SENATORS *of Corioles.*

1. Sen. So, your opinion is, Aufidius,
That they of Rome are ent'red in our counsels,
And know how we proceed.
Auf. Is it not yours?
What ever have been thought [on] in this state
That could be brought to bodily act ere Rome
Had circumvention? 'Tis not four days gone
Since I heard thence; these are the words—I think
I have the letter here; yes, here it is:

225. vent: excrete, get rid of.
229. put you to't: push you hard, make you exert yourselves.
232. together: against one another.
233. Were . . . ears: if one half of the world were at war with the other half. **234. Upon my party:** on the same side as myself.
235. with: against. **239. constant:** true to my word.
241. stiff: resistant, opposed (but Lartius' answer quibbles on the sense "stiff with age"). **out:** aside, aloof.
247. Right . . . priority: you well deserve to take precedence.
250. mutiners: mutineers, rebels.
251. puts well forth: makes a fine show.

256. gird: scoff at. **259. to be:** of being.
260. Tickled with: flattered by. **good success.** Not redundant for the Elizabethans; success = *outcome*, whether good or bad.
262. brook: endure. **262–63. be commanded Under:** rank below.
264. whom: which. **268. giddy censure:** flighty popular judgment.
271. Opinion . . . on: the high reputation that so firmly adheres to.
272. demerits: merits (both words formerly meant "deserts," whether good or bad).
278. More . . . singularity: apart from his usual idiosyncrasies.

I.ii. Location: Corioles. The Senate-house.
2. ent'red in: initiated into, privy to.
6. circumvention: means to circumvent.

[*Reads.*] "They have press'd a power, but it is not known
Whether for east or west. The dearth is great,
The people mutinous; and it is rumor'd,
Cominius, Martius your old enemy
(Who is of Rome worse hated than of you),
And Titus Lartius, a most valiant Roman,
These three lead on this preparation
Whither 'tis bent. Most likely 'tis for you;
Consider of it."

1. Sen. Our army's in the field.
We never yet made doubt but Rome was ready
To answer us.

Auf. Nor did you think it folly
To keep your great pretenses veil'd till when
They needs must show themselves, which in the hatching,
It seem'd, appear'd to Rome. By the discovery
We shall be short'ned in our aim, which was
To take in many towns ere (almost) Rome
Should know we were afoot.

2. Sen. Noble Aufidius,
Take your commission, hie you to your bands,
Let us alone to guard Corioles.
If they set down before 's, for the remove
Bring up your army; but, I think, you'll find
Th' have not prepar'd for us.

Auf. O, doubt not that,
I speak from certainties. Nay more,
Some parcels of their power are forth already,
And only hitherward. I leave your honors.
If we and Caius Martius chance to meet,
'Tis sworn between us we shall ever strike
Till one can do no more.

All. The gods assist you!

Auf. And keep your honors safe!

1. Sen. Farewell.

2. Sen. Farewell.

All. Farewell. *Exeunt omnes.*

[Scene III]

Enter Volumnia *and* Virgilia, *mother and wife to Martius; they set them down on two low stools and sew.*

Vol. I pray you, daughter, sing, or express yourself in a more comfortable sort. If my son were my husband, I should freelier rejoice in that absence wherein he won honor than in the embracements of his bed where he would show most love. When yet he was but tender-bodied and the only son of my womb; when youth with comeliness pluck'd all gaze his way; when for a day of kings' entreaties a mother should not sell him an hour from her beholding; I, considering how honor would become such a person, that it was no better than picture-like to hang by th' wall, if renown made it not stir, was pleas'd to let him seek danger where he was like to find fame. To a cruel war I sent him, from whence he return'd, his brows bound with oak. I tell thee, daughter, I sprang not more in joy at first hearing he was a man-child than now in first seeing he had prov'd himself a man.

Vir. But had he died in the business, madam, how then?

Vol. Then his good report should have been my son; I therein would have found issue. Hear me profess sincerely: had I a dozen sons, each in my love alike, and none less dear than thine and my good Martius, I had rather had eleven die nobly for their country than one voluptuously surfeit out of action.

Enter a Gentlewoman.

Gent. Madam, the Lady Valeria is come to visit you.

Vir. Beseech you give me leave to retire myself.

Vol. Indeed you shall not.
Methinks I hear hither your husband's drum;
See him pluck Aufidius down by th' hair;
As children from a bear, the Volsces shunning him.
Methinks I see him stamp thus, and call thus:
"Come on, you cowards, you were got in fear,
Though you were born in Rome!" His bloody brow
With his mail'd hand then wiping, forth he goes,
Like to a harvest-man [that's] task'd to mow
Or all or lose his hire.

Vir. His bloody brow? O Jupiter, no blood!

Vol. Away, you fool! it more becomes a man
Than gilt his trophy. The breasts of Hecuba,
When she did suckle Hector, look'd not lovelier
Than Hector's forehead when it spit forth blood
At Grecian sword, [contemning]. Tell Valeria
We are fit to bid her welcome. *Exit Gentlewoman.*

Vir. Heavens bless my lord from fell Aufidius!

Vol. He'll beat Aufidius' head below his knee,
And tread upon his neck.

Enter Valeria *with an* Usher *and a* Gentlewoman.

Val. My ladies both, good day to you.

Vol. Sweet madam.

Vir. I am glad to see your ladyship.

Val. How do you both? You are manifest house-keepers. What are you sewing here? A fine spot, in good faith. How does your little son?

Vir. I thank your ladyship; well, good madam.

9. press'd a power: conscripted forces.
15. preparation: prepared force, army.
16. Whither 'tis bent: to whatever destination it is directed toward.
20. pretenses: designs. **23. be short'ned in:** fall short of.
24. take in: capture.
28. set . . . 's: lay siege to us. **remove:** raising of the siege.
30. prepar'd for: raised this army against. **32. parcels:** parts.
35. ever strike: keep on fighting.

I.iii. Location: Rome. The house of Martius.
1–2. express yourself: appear, behave.
2. comfortable sort: cheerful fashion.

10. person: handsome body.
12. made . . . stir: did not animate it.
15. oak. Symbol of heroism in battle. **16. now:** i.e. then.
20. report: reputation. **21–22. profess:** avow, declare.
29. hither: from here. **33. got:** begotten.
36–37. that's . . . hire: i.e. who has agreed that he will either do the whole job of mowing or receive no wages at all.
40. gilt: gilding, gold. **trophy:** monument. **Hecuba:** queen of Troy. Hector was the most valorous of her fifty sons.
44. fit: ready.
51–52. manifest house-keepers: i.e. obviously staying at home to-day.
52. spot: embroidered figure.

Vol. He had rather see the swords and hear a drum than look upon his schoolmaster.

Val. A' my word, the father's son. I'll swear 'tis a very pretty boy. A' my troth, I look'd upon him a' We'n'sday half an hour together; h'as such a confirm'd countenance. I saw him run after a gilded butter-fly, and when he caught it, he let it go again, and after it again, and over and over he comes, and up again; catch'd it again: or whether his fall enrag'd him, or how 'twas, he did so set his teeth and tear it. O, I warrant, how he mammock'd it!

Vol. One on 's father's moods.

Val. Indeed la, 'tis a noble child.

Vir. A crack, madam.

Val. Come, lay aside your stitchery, I must have you play the idle huswife with me this afternoon.

Vir. No, good madam, I will not out of doors.

Val. Not out of doors?

Vol. She shall, she shall.

Vir. Indeed no, by your patience; I'll not over the threshold till my lord return from the wars.

Val. Fie, you confine yourself most unreasonably. Come, you must go visit the good lady that lies in.

Vir. I will wish her speedy strength, and visit her with my prayers; but I cannot go thither.

Vol. Why, I pray you?

Vir. 'Tis not to save labor, nor that I want love.

Val. You would be another Penelope: yet they say, all the yarn she spun in Ulysses' absence did but fill [Ithaca] full of moths. Come, I would your cambric were sensible as your finger, that you might leave pricking it for pity. Come, you shall go with us.

Vir. No, good madam, pardon me, indeed I will not forth.

Val. In truth la, go with me, and I'll tell you excellent news of your husband.

Vir. O, good madam, there can be none yet.

Val. Verily, I do not jest with you; there came news from him last night.

Vir. Indeed, madam?

Val. In earnest, it's true; I heard a senator speak it. Thus it is: the Volsces have an army forth; against whom Cominius the general is gone, with one part of our Roman power. Your lord and Titus Lartius are set down before their city Corioles; they nothing doubt prevailing, and to make it brief wars. This is true, on mine honor, and so I pray go with us.

Vir. Give me excuse, good madam, I will obey you in every thing hereafter.

Vol. Let her alone, lady; as she is now, she will but disease our better mirth.

Val. In troth, I think she would. Fare you well then. Come, good sweet lady. Prithee, Virgilia, turn thy solemnness out a' door, and go along with us.

Vir. No, at a word, madam; indeed I must not. I wish you much mirth.

Val. Well, then farewell.

Exeunt Ladies [with Usher].

[Scene IV]

Enter Martius, Titus Lartius, *with Drum and Colors, with* Captains *and* Soldiers, *as before the city Corioles; to them a* Messenger.

Mar. Yonder comes news: a wager they have met.
Lart. My horse to yours, no.
Mar. 'Tis done.
Lart. Agreed.
Mar. Say, has our general met the enemy?
Mess. They lie in view, but have not spoke as yet.
Lart. So, the good horse is mine.
Mar. I'll buy him of you.
Lart. No, I'll nor sell nor give him; lend you him I will
For half a hundred years. Summon the town.
Mar. How far off lie these armies?
Mess. Within this mile and half.
Mar. Then shall we hear their 'larum, and they ours.
Now, Mars, I prithee make us quick in work,
That we with smoking swords may march from hence
To help our fielded friends! Come, blow thy blast.

They sound a parley. Enter two Senators *with others on the walls of Corioles.*

Tullus Aufidius, is he within your walls?
1. Sen. No, nor a man that fears you less than he,
That's lesser than a little. (*Drum afar off.*) Hark, our drums
Are bringing forth our youth. We'll break our walls
Rather than they shall pound us up; our gates,
Which yet seem shut, we have but pinn'd with rushes,
They'll open of themselves. (*Alarum far off.*) Hark you, far off!
There is Aufidius. List what work he makes
Amongst your cloven army.
Mar. O, they are at it!
Lart. Their noise be our instruction. Ladders ho!

Enter the Army *of the Volsces.*

Mar. They fear us not, but issue forth their city.
Now put your shields before your hearts, and fight
With hearts more proof than shields. Advance, brave Titus!
They do disdain us much beyond our thoughts,
Which makes me sweat with wrath. Come on, my fellows!
He that retires, I'll take him for a Volsce,
And he shall feel mine edge.

Alarum. The Romans are beat back to their trenches.

59. h'as: he has. **confirm'd:** resolute, determined.
65. mammock'd: tore to pieces. **66. on 's:** of his.
68. crack: rascal. **81. want:** am deficient in.
82. Penelope: faithful wife of Ulysses. She held off suitors during his absence by saying that she must first finish her weaving, which she secretly unravelled every night.
84. moths: i.e. idle consumers, parasites. **85. sensible:** sensitive
105. disease: make uneasy, spoil. **109. at a word:** once for all.

I.iv. Location: Before Corioles.
4. spoke: engaged. **9. 'larum:** alarum, trumpet call to arms.
12. fielded: on the battlefield. **s.d. parley:** trumpet signal for a conference. **17. pound:** pen.
22. our instruction: an example to us.
25. proof: of tested strength, stout. **29. edge:** sword.

Enter MARTIUS *cursing.*

Mar. All the contagion of the south light on you,
You shames of Rome! you herd of—Biles and plagues
Plaster you o'er, that you may be abhorr'd
Farther than seen, and one infect another
Against the wind a mile! You souls of geese,
That bear the shapes of men, how have you run
From slaves that apes would beat! Pluto and hell!
All hurt behind! backs red, and faces pale
With flight and agued fear! Mend and charge home,
Or, by the fires of heaven, I'll leave the foe
And make my wars on you. Look to't; come on!
If you'll stand fast, we'll beat them to their wives,
As they us to our trenches. Follow 's.

Another alarum. [The Volsces fly,] and Martius follows them to [the] gates.

So, now the gates are ope; now prove good seconds:
'Tis for the followers fortune widens them,
Not for the fliers. Mark me, and do the like.

Enter the gates.

1. Sold. Foolhardiness, not I.
2. Sold. Nor I. *[Martius] is shut in.*
1. Sold. See, they have shut him in.

Alarum continues.

All. To th' pot, I warrant him.

Enter TITUS LARTIUS.

Lart. What is become of Martius?
All. Slain, sir, doubtless.
1. Sold. Following the fliers at the very heels,
With them he enters; who upon the sudden
Clapp'd to their gates. He is himself alone,
To answer all the city.
Lart. O noble fellow!
Who sensibly outdares his senseless sword,
And when it bows, stand'st up. Thou art left, Martius—
A carbuncle entire, as big as thou art,
Were not so rich a jewel. Thou wast a soldier
Even to [Cato's] wish, not fierce and terrible
Only in strokes, but, with thy grim looks and
The thunder-like percussion of thy sounds,
Thou mad'st thine enemies shake, as if the world
Were feverous and did tremble.

Enter MARTIUS *bleeding, assaulted by the enemy.*

1. Sold. Look, sir.
Lart. O, 'tis Martius!
Let's fetch him off, or make remain alike.

They fight, and all enter the city.

30. south: south wind (thought to bear pestilence).
31. Biles: boils.
38. agued: shivering (as if with malarial fever). **Mend:** (1) regain your health (continuing the figure in *agued*); (2) reform your battle lines. **home:** to the heart of their defenses.
42 s.d. follows: pursues. **43. seconds:** helpers.
47. th' pot: i.e. destruction.
53. Who . . . sword: who, though sensitive to pain, is bolder than his sword, which is not.
54. bows: bends. **stand'st up:** i.e. refusest to bow (yield). **left:** deserted. Some editors emend to *lost*, following Singer.
55. carbuncle: a kind of precious stone.
57. Cato: Cato the Censor, Roman moralist and reformer.
62. fetch . . . alike: rescue him or stay to share his fate.

[SCENE V]

Enter certain ROMANS *with spoils.*

1. Rom. This will I carry to Rome.
2. Rom. And I this.
3. Rom. A murrain on't! I took this for silver.

Exeunt. Alarum continues still afar off.

Enter MARTIUS *and* TITUS [LARTIUS] *with a Trumpet.*

Mar. See here these movers that do prize their hours
At a crack'd drachme! Cushions, leaden spoons,
Irons of a doit, doublets that hangmen would
Bury with those that wore them, these base slaves,
Ere yet the fight be done, pack up. Down with them!
And hark, what noise the general makes! To him!
There is the man of my soul's hate, Aufidius,
Piercing our Romans; then, valiant Titus, take
Convenient numbers to make good the city,
Whilst I, with those that have the spirit, will haste
To help Cominius.
Lart. Worthy sir, thou bleed'st,
Thy exercise hath been too violent for
A second course of fight.
Mar. Sir, praise me not;
My work hath yet not warm'd me. Fare you well.
The blood I drop is rather physical
Than dangerous to me. To Aufidius thus
I will appear, and fight.
Lart. Now the fair goddess Fortune
Fall deep in love with thee, and her great charms
Misguide thy opposers' swords! Bold gentleman!
Prosperity be thy page.
Mar. Thy friend no less
Than those she placeth highest! So farewell.
Lart. Thou worthiest Martius! *[Exit Martius.]*
Go sound thy trumpet in the market-place;
Call thither all the officers a' th' town,
Where they shall know our mind. Away! *Exeunt.*

[SCENE VI]

Enter COMINIUS, *as it were in retire, with* SOLDIERS.

Com. Breathe you, my friends. Well fought; we are come off
Like Romans, neither foolish in our stands
Nor cowardly in retire. Believe me, sirs,
We shall be charg'd again. Whiles we have strook,

I.v. Location: Corioles. A street.
3. murrain: cattle plague. **s.d. Trumpet:** trumpeter.
4. movers. Ironic, of men who should be moving but who hang about looting. **prize their hours:** value their time. Many editors adopt Rowe's emendation *prize their honors.*
5. drachme: drachma, small Greek coin.
6. of a doit: worth a doit (very small coin). **hangmen.** A hangman was entitled to the clothing of those he executed.
12. Convenient: suitable. **make good:** make sure of.
16. course: round. **praise me:** appraise me, estimate my strength.
18. physical: healthful. **21. charms:** spells.
23. Prosperity . . . page: success attend you.
24. those: i.e. friend to those.

I.vi Location: Near the camp of Cominius.
o.s.d. retire: withdrawal, retreat.
1. Breathe: rest. **are come off:** have left the field.
2. foolish: foolhardy. **4. strook:** struck, fought.

By interims and conveying gusts we have heard
The charges of our friends. The Roman gods,
Lead their successes as we wish our own,
That both our powers, with smiling fronts encount'ring,
May give you thankful sacrifice.

Enter a MESSENGER.

Thy news?

Mess. The citizens of Corioles have issued,
And given to Lartius and to Martius battle.
I saw our party to their trenches driven,
And then I came away.

Com. Though thou speakest truth,
Methinks thou speak'st not well. How long is't since?

Mess. Above an hour, my lord.

Com. 'Tis not a mile; briefly we heard their drums.
How couldst thou in a mile confound an hour,
And bring thy news so late?

Mess. Spies of the Volsces
Held me in chase, that I was forc'd to wheel
Three or four miles about, else had I, sir,
Half an hour since brought my report.

Enter MARTIUS.

Com. Who's yonder,
That does appear as he were flea'd? O gods,
He has the stamp of Martius, and I have
Before-time seen him thus.

Mar. Come I too late?

Com. The shepherd knows not thunder from a tabor
More than I know the sound of Martius' tongue
From every meaner man.

Mar. Come I too late?

Com. Ay, if you come not in the blood of others,
But mantled in your own.

Mar. O! let me clip ye
In arms as sound as when I woo'd, in heart
As merry as when our nuptial day was done
And tapers burnt to bedward!

Com. Flower of warriors,
How is't with Titus Lartius?

Mar. As with a man busied about decrees:
Condemning some to death, and some to exile;
Ransoming him, or pitying, threat'ning th' other;
Holding Corioles in the name of Rome,
Even like a fawning greyhound in the leash,
To let him slip at will.

Com. Where is that slave
Which told me they had beat you to your trenches?
Where is he? Call him hither.

Mar. Let him alone,

He did inform the truth. But for our gentlemen,
The common file (a plague—tribunes for them!),
The mouse ne'er shunn'd the cat as they did budge
From rascals worse than they.

Com. But how prevail'd you?

Mar. Will the time serve to tell? I do not think.
Where is the enemy? Are you lords a' th' field?
If not, why cease you till you are so?

Com. Martius,
We have at disadvantage fought, and did
Retire to win our purpose.

Mar. How lies their battle? Know you on which side
They have plac'd their men of trust?

Com. As I guess, Martius,
Their bands i' th' vaward are the [Antiates,]
Of their best trust; o'er them Aufidius,
Their very heart of hope.

Mar. I do beseech you,
By all the battles wherein we have fought,
By th' blood we have shed together, by th' vows
We have made to endure friends, that you directly
Set me against Aufidius and his Antiates,
And that you not delay the present, but,
Filling the air with swords advanc'd and darts,
We prove this very hour.

Com. Though I could wish
You were conducted to a gentle bath
And balms applied to you, yet dare I never
Deny your asking. Take your choice of those
That best can aid your action.

Mar. Those are they
That most are willing. If any such be here
(As it were sin to doubt) that love this painting
Wherein you see me smear'd; if any fear
[Lesser] his person than an ill report;
If any think brave death outweighs bad life,
And that his country's dearer than himself;
Let him alone, or so many so minded,
Wave thus to express his disposition,
And follow Martius.

They all shout and wave their swords, take him up in their arms, and cast up their caps.

O, me alone! make you a sword of me?
If these shows be not outward, which of you
But is four Volsces? None of you but is
Able to bear against the great Aufidius
A shield as hard as his. A certain number
(Though thanks to all) must I select from all; the rest
Shall bear the business in some other fight
(As cause will be obey'd). Please you to march,

5. By . . . gusts: at intervals, by gusts of wind which bore the sounds.
6. The Roman gods. A form of vocative.
7. successes: outcomes, fortunes.
8. fronts: (1) front lines; (2) faces.
16. briefly: a short time ago. **17. confound:** waste.
22. flea'd: flayed. **24. Before-time:** on earlier occasions.
25. tabor: small drum. **29. clip:** embrace.
32. burnt to bedward: lighted the way to bed (?) or burned low, indicating the arrival of bedtime (?).
36. pitying: i.e. releasing without ransom.
39. let him slip: release him.

42. inform: report. **gentlemen.** Ironical.
43. common file: plebeian soldiers. **44. budge:** flinch.
50. to . . . purpose: i.e. for reasons of strategy.
51. battle: battle line.
53. vaward: vanguard. **Antiates:** citizens of Antium.
58. to endure: always to remain. **60. present:** affair in hand.
62. prove: try. **70. his person:** i.e. injury to himself.
76. O . . . me. Coriolanus seems to be protesting that the other volunteers are equally worthy of being lifted up and regarded as swords against the enemy.
77. outward: merely external, insincere.
83. cause . . . obey'd: occasion demands.

And four shall quickly draw out my command,
Which men are best inclin'd.
Com. March on, my fellows!
Make good this ostentation, and you shall
Divide in all with us. *Exeunt.*

[SCENE VII]

TITUS LARTIUS, *having set a guard upon Corioles, going with Drum and Trumpet toward Cominius and Caius Martius, enters with a* LIEUTENANT, *other* SOLDIERS, *and a* SCOUT.

Lart. So, let the ports be guarded; keep your duties,
As I have set them down. If I do send, dispatch
Those centuries to our aid; the rest will serve
For a short holding. If we lose the field,
We cannot keep the town.
Lieu. Fear not our care, sir.
Lart. Hence; and shut your gates upon 's.
Our guider, come, to th' Roman camp conduct us.
Exeunt.

[SCENE VIII]

Alarum as in battle. Enter MARTIUS *and* AUFIDIUS *at several doors.*

Mar. I'll fight with none but thee, for I do hate thee
Worse than a promise-breaker.
Auf. We hate alike:
Not Afric owns a serpent I abhor
More than thy fame and envy. Fix thy foot.
Mar. Let the first budger die the other's slave,
And the gods doom him after!
Auf. If I fly, Martius,
Hollow me like a hare.
Mar. Within these three hours, Tullus,
Alone I fought in your Corioles walls,
And made what work I pleas'd. 'Tis not my blood
Wherein thou seest me mask'd; for thy revenge
Wrench up thy power to th' highest.
Auf. Wert thou the Hector
That was the whip of your bragg'd progeny
Thou shouldst not scape me here.
Here they fight, and certain Volsces come in the aid of Aufidius. Martius fights till they be driven in breathless.
Officious, and not valiant, you have sham'd me
In your condemned seconds. [*Exeunt.*]

84. four. Some editors, following Capell, read *I*, arguing that Coriolanus would not depute the choice of men to others.
86. ostentation: showing (not pejorative).

I.vii. Location: Before the gates of Corioles.
1. ports: gates. **3. centuries:** companies of a hundred.
5. Fear not: have no anxiety about.

I.viii. Location: Near the Roman camp.
o.s.d. several: different. **4. fame and envy:** hated reputation.
7. Hollow: hollo, hunt with loud cries.
12. the whip . . . progeny: the most effective soldier among your boasted Trojan ancestors.
14. Officious: offering unwanted help.
15. In . . . seconds: by your futile attempts to support me.

[SCENE IX]

Flourish. Alarum. A retreat is sounded. Enter, at one door, COMINIUS, *with the* ROMANS; *at another door,* MARTIUS *with his arm in a scarf.*

Com. If I should tell thee o'er this thy day's work,
Thou't not believe thy deeds: but I'll report it
Where senators shall mingle tears with smiles;
Where great patricians shall attend and shrug,
I' th' end admire; where ladies shall be frighted,
And gladly quak'd, hear more; where the dull tribunes,
That with the fusty plebeians hate thine honors,
Shall say against their hearts, "We thank the gods
Our Rome hath such a soldier."
Yet cam'st thou to a morsel of this feast,
Having fully din'd before.

Enter TITUS [LARTIUS] *with his power, from the pursuit.*

Lart. O general!
Here is the steed, we the caparison.
Hadst thou beheld—
Mar. Pray now, no more. My mother,
Who has a charter to extol her blood,
When she does praise me grieves me. I have done
As you have done—that's what I can; induc'd
As you have been—that's for my country:
He that has but effected his good will
Hath overta'en mine act.
Com. You shall not be
The grave of your deserving; Rome must know
The value of her own. 'Twere a concealment
Worse than a theft, no less than a traducement,
To hide your doings, and to silence that
Which, to the spire and top of praises vouch'd,
Would seem but modest; therefore I beseech you,
In sign of what you are, not to reward
What you have done, before our army hear me.
Mar. I have some wounds upon me, and they smart
To hear themselves rememb'red.
Com. Should they not,
Well might they fester 'gainst ingratitude,
And tent themselves with death. Of all the horses—
Whereof we have ta'en good and good store—of all
The treasure in this field achiev'd and city,
We render you the tenth, to be ta'en forth,
Before the common distribution, at
Your only choice.
Mar. I thank you, general;
But cannot make my heart consent to take

I.ix. Location: Scene continues.
o.s.d. scarf: sling. **2. Thou't:** thou wouldst.
4. attend and shrug: listen incredulously. **5. admire:** marvel.
6. quak'd: made to tremble, agitated. **7. fusty:** mouldy, smelly.
8. hearts: inclinations, wills.
10. Yet . . . feast: yet this feast was a mere morsel to you (*of* = in).
12. caparison: mere trappings. **14. charter:** special privilege.
18. will: intention. **19. overta'en:** surpassed.
19–20. be . . . deserving: bury your deserts (in your modesty).
22. traducement: slander. **24. vouch'd:** affirmed.
25. modest: moderate, scarcely adequate.
26–27. In . . . done: i.e. what I shall say will be merely a recognition of your worth, not a reward for your achievement.
29. not: i.e. not be memorialized (*rememb'red*).
31. tent . . . death: i.e. have no remedy except death. *Tent* = probe, clean with a "tent" or roll of linen; i.e. cure.
32. good and good store: excellent beasts and plenty of them.

A bribe to pay my sword. I do refuse it,
And stand upon my common part with those
That have beheld the doing.

A long flourish. They all cry, "Martius! Martius!", cast up their caps and lances. Cominius and Lartius stand bare.

May these same instruments, which you profane,
Never sound more! When drums and trumpets shall
I' th' field prove flatterers, let courts and cities be
Made all of false-fac'd soothing!
When steel grows soft as the parasite's silk,
Let him be made an overture for th' wars!
No more, I say! For that I have not wash'd
My nose that bled, or foil'd some debile wretch—
Which, without note, here's many else have done—
You [shout] me forth
In acclamations hyperbolical,
As if I lov'd my little should be dieted
In praises sauc'd with lies.

Com. Too modest are you;
More cruel to your good report than grateful
To us that give you truly. By your patience,
If 'gainst yourself you be incens'd, we'll put you
(Like one that means his proper harm) in manacles,
Then reason safely with you. Therefore be it known,
As to us, to all the world, that Caius Martius
Wears this war's garland; in token of the which,
My noble steed, known to the camp, I give him,
With all his trim belonging; and from this time,
For what he did before Corioles, call him,
With all th' applause and clamor of the host,
Martius Caius Coriolanus! Bear
Th' addition nobly ever!

Flourish. Trumpets sound, and drums.

Omnes. Martius Caius Coriolanus!

Cor. I will go wash;
And when my face is fair, you shall perceive
Whether I blush or no; howbeit, I thank you.
I mean to stride your steed, and at all times
To undercrest your good addition
To th' fairness of my power.

Com. So, to our tent;
Where, ere we do repose us, we will write
To Rome of our success. You, Titus Lartius,
Must to Corioles back. Send us to Rome
The best, with whom we may articulate
For their own good and ours.

Lart. I shall, my lord.

Cor. The gods begin to mock me. I, that now
Refus'd most princely gifts, am bound to beg
Of my lord general.

Com. Take't, 'tis yours. What is't?

Cor. I sometime lay here in Corioles
At a poor man's house; he us'd me kindly.
He cried to me; I saw him prisoner;
But then Aufidius was within my view,
And wrath o'erwhelm'd my pity. I request you
To give my poor host freedom.

Com. O, well begg'd!
Were he the butcher of my son, he should
Be free as is the wind. Deliver him, Titus.

Lart. Martius, his name?

Cor. By Jupiter, forgot!
I am weary, yea, my memory is tir'd.
Have we no wine here?

Com. Go we to our tent.
The blood upon your visage dries, 'tis time
It should be look'd to. Come. *Exeunt.*

[Scene X]

A flourish. Cornets. Enter Tullus Aufidius *bloody, with two or three* Soldiers.

Auf. The town is ta'en!

[*1.*] *Sold.* 'Twill be deliver'd back on good condition.

Auf. Condition?
I would I were a Roman, for I cannot,
Being a Volsce, be that I am. Condition?
What good condition can a treaty find
I' th' part that is at mercy? Five times, Martius,
I have fought with thee; so often hast thou beat me;
And wouldst do so, I think, should we encounter
As often as we eat. By th' elements,
If e'er again I meet him beard to beard,
He's mine, or I am his. Mine emulation
Hath not that honor in't it had; for where
I thought to crush him in an equal force,
True sword to sword, I'll potch at him some way,
Or wrath or craft may get him.

[*1.*] *Sold.* He's the devil.

Auf. Bolder, though not so subtle. My valor's poison'd
With only suff'ring stain by him; for him
Shall fly out of itself. Nor sleep nor sanctuary,
Being naked, sick, nor fane nor Capitol,
The prayers of priests nor times of sacrifice,

39. stand upon: insist on.
40. beheld. This sounds sarcastic, and some editors read *upheld.*
s.d. flourish: trumpet fanfare. **bare:** bareheaded.
44. soothing: flattery.
46. overture. Hard to explain. Sisson takes it to mean "herald"—let the parasite summon men to war. Many editors adopt Tyrwhitt's emendation *coverture*—let silk supersede armor as martial garb. Moore Smith conjectures *officer*—let the parasite become a soldier.
48. foil'd: thrown down. **debile:** weak.
49. without note: unobserved. **50. shout me forth:** acclaim me.
52. dieted: fed, fattened. **53. In:** by. **55. give:** report.
57. means . . . harm: intends to do himself an injury.
62. his trim belonging: the equipment that goes with him.
66. addition: added title. **69. fair:** clean.
72. undercrest: support (as in armorial bearings the shield supports the crest), i.e. strive to be worthy of.
73. fairness . . . power: best of my ability.
77. The best: their principal men. **articulate:** arrange terms.

82. sometime lay: once lodged.
84. cried: cried out (during the fighting). **89. Deliver:** free.

I.x. Location: The camp of the Volsces.
2. condition: terms.
5. that I am: what I am, i.e. proud and honorable.
7. I' . . . mercy: on the conquered side.
12. emulation: rivalry. **13. where:** whereas.
15. potch: thrust. **16. Or:** either.
18. stain: loss of lustre, impairment.
19. fly . . . itself: deviate sharply from its natural course. **Nor sleep.** Aufidius begins listing the circumstances that would formerly have restrained him from attacking his foe; the first would be to happen upon him sleeping.
20. naked: i.e. unarmed. **fane:** temple.

Embarquements all of fury, shall lift up
Their rotten privilege and custom 'gainst
My hate to Martius. Where I find him, were it
At home, upon my brother's guard, even there,
Against the hospitable canon, would I
Wash my fierce hand in 's heart. Go you to th' city,
Learn how 'tis held, and what they are that must
Be hostages for Rome.
 [*1.*] *Sold.* Will not you go?
 Auf. I am attended at the cypress grove. I pray you
('Tis south the city mills) bring me word thither
How the world goes, that to the pace of it
I may spur on my journey.
 [*1.*] *Sold.* I shall, sir. [*Exeunt.*]

ACT II, [SCENE I]

Enter MENENIUS *with the two Tribunes of the people,* SICINIUS *and* BRUTUS.

Men. The augurer tells me we shall have news to-night.

Bru. Good or bad?

Men. Not according to the prayer of the people, for they love not Martius.

Sic. Nature teaches beasts to know their friends.

Men. Pray you, who does the wolf love?

Sic. The lamb.

Men. Ay, to devour him, as the hungry plebeians would the noble Martius.

Bru. He's a lamb indeed, that baes like a bear.

Men. He's a bear indeed, that lives like a lamb. You two are old men: tell me one thing that I shall ask you.

Both. Well, sir.

Men. In what enormity is Martius poor in, that you two have not in abundance?

Bru. He's poor in no one fault, but stor'd with all.

Sic. Especially in pride.

Bru. And topping all others in boasting.

Men. This is strange now. Do you two know how you are censur'd here in the city, I mean of us a' th' right-hand file? do you?

Both. Why? how are we censur'd?

Men. Because you talk of pride now—will you not be angry?

Both. Well, well, sir, well.

Men. Why, 'tis no great matter; for a very little thief of occasion will rob you of a great deal of patience. Give your dispositions the reins and be angry at your pleasures; at the least, if you take it as a pleasure to you in being so. You blame Martius for being proud?

Bru. We do it not alone, sir.

Men. I know you can do very little alone, for your helps are many, or else your actions would grow wondrous single; your abilities are too infant-like for doing much alone. You talk of pride: O that you could turn your eyes toward the napes of your necks and make but an interior survey of your good selves! O that you could!

Both. What then, sir?

Men. Why then you should discover a brace of unmeriting, proud, violent, testy magistrates (alias fools) as any in Rome.

Sic. Menenius, you are known well enough too.

Men. I am known to be a humorous patrician, and one that loves a cup of hot wine with not a drop of allaying Tiber in't; said to be something imperfect in favoring the first complaint, hasty and tinder-like upon too trivial motion; one that converses more with the buttock of the night than with the forehead of the morning. What I think, I utter, and spend my malice in my breath. Meeting two such wealsmen as you are (I cannot call you Lycurguses), if the drink you give me touch my palate adversely, I make a crooked face at it. I [cannot] say your worships have deliver'd the matter well, when I find the ass in compound with the major part of your syllables; and though I must be content to bear with those that say you are reverend grave men, yet they lie deadly that tell you have good faces. If you see this in the map of my microcosm, follows it that I am known well enough too? What harm can your beesom conspectuities glean out of this character, if I be known well enough too?

Bru. Come, sir, come, we know you well enough.

Men. You know neither me, yourselves, nor any thing. You are ambitious for poor knaves' caps and legs. You wear out a good wholesome forenoon in hearing a cause between an orange-wife and a forset-seller, and then rejourn the controversy of threepence to a second day of audience. When you are hearing a matter between party and party, if you chance to be pinch'd with the colic, you make faces like mummers, set up the bloody flag against all pa-

22. **Embarquements . . . of:** restraints . . . upon.
23. **rotten:** (henceforth) enfeebled. **privilege and custom:** traditional immunity.
25. **At home:** in my own house. **upon:** under. **guard:** protection.
26. **hospitable canon:** law of hospitality.
28. **what:** who, of what rank. 30. **attended:** waited for.
32. **to:** in accordance with.

II.i. Location: Rome. A public place.
4. **Not . . . people:** not what the people have prayed for.
6. **beasts:** i.e. even beasts. 16. **enormity:** vice.
22. **censur'd:** judged.
23. **right-hand file:** i.e. patricians (literally, those who take the most honorable place in battle).
28–30. **a very . . . patience:** i.e. it takes only a trifling occasion to make you lose your patience.
37. **single:** feeble. 47. **humorous:** whimsical, eccentric.
49. **allaying Tiber:** diluting water.
49–50. **something . . . complaint:** somewhat at fault in accepting one complainant's version of a dispute without hearing the other side.
50. **tinder-like:** blazing up easily. 51. **motion:** cause.
51–53. **converses . . . morning:** i.e. is more familiar with late nights than with early rising. 54. **wealsmen:** statesmen.
55. **Lycurguses.** Lycurgus was the legendary Spartan lawgiver.
55–57. **if . . . it:** i.e. if I don't like what you say, I make it clear that I don't. 57. **deliver'd:** reported.
58–59. **the ass . . . syllables:** an element of the fool in all you say (with play in *ass in compound* on the grammatical sense "words compounded with *-as*, e.g. *whereas*").
62–63. **the map . . . microcosm:** my face (reflecting the notion of man as a reflection in little of the universe or macrocosm).
64. **beesom:** blinded (more usually spelled *bisson*). **conspectuities:** eyesight. 68–69. **caps and legs:** uncappings and bowings.
70. **orange-wife:** female fruit-vendor.
71. **forset-seller:** seller of taps for broaching barrels. **rejourn:** adjourn, postpone.
75. **mummers:** players in dumb shows. **set . . . flag:** declare war.

tience, and in roaring for a chamber-pot, dismiss the controversy bleeding, the more entangled by your hearing. All the peace you make in their cause is calling both the parties knaves. You are a pair of strange ones.

Bru. Come, come, you are well understood to be a perfecter giber for the table than a necessary bencher in the Capitol.

Men. Our very priests must become mockers if they shall encounter such ridiculous subjects as you are. When you speak best unto the purpose, it is not worth the wagging of your beards, and your beards deserve not so honorable a grave as to stuff a botcher's cushion, or to be entomb'd in an ass's pack-saddle. Yet you must be saying Martius is proud; who, in a cheap estimation, is worth all your predecessors since Deucalion, though peradventure some of the best of 'em were hereditary hangmen. God-den to your worships; more of your conversation would infect my brain, being the herdsmen of the beastly plebeians. I will be bold to take my leave of you.

Brutus and Sicinius [go] aside.

Enter VOLUMNIA, VIRGILIA, *and* VALERIA.

How now, my as fair as noble ladies—and the moon, were she earthly, no nobler—whither do you follow your eyes so fast?

Vol. Honorable Menenius, my boy Martius approaches. For the love of Juno, let's go.

Men. Ha? Martius coming home?

Vol. Ay, worthy Menenius, and with most prosperous approbation.

Men. Take my cap, Jupiter, [*tosses it up*] and I thank thee. Hoo! Martius coming home?

Two Ladies [*Vir., Val.*]. Nay, 'tis true.

Vol. Look, here's a letter from him; the state hath another, his wife another, and, I think, there's one at home for you.

Men. I will make my very house reel to-night. A letter for me?

Vir. Yes certain, there's a letter for you, I saw't.

Men. A letter for me! it gives me an estate of seven years' health, in which time I will make a lip at the physician. The most sovereign prescription in Galen is but empiricutic, and, to this preservative, of no better report than a horse-drench. Is he not wounded? he was wont to come home wounded.

Vir. O no, no, no.

Vol. O, he is wounded, I thank the gods for't.

Men. So do I too, if it be not too much. Brings 'a victory in his pocket? The wounds become him.

Vol. On 's brows. Menenius, he comes the third time home with the oaken garland.

Men. Has he disciplin'd Aufidius soundly?

Vol. Titus Lartius writes they fought together, but Aufidius got off.

Men. And 'twas time for him too, I'll warrant him that; and he had stay'd by him, I would not have been so fidius'd for all the chests in Corioles, and the gold that's in them. Is the Senate possess'd of this?

Vol. Good ladies, let's go.—Yes, yes, yes; the Senate has letters from the general, wherein he gives my son the whole name of the war. He hath in this action outdone his former deeds doubly.

Val. In troth, there's wondrous things spoke of him.

Men. Wondrous ! ay, I warrant you, and not without his true purchasing.

Vir. The gods grant them true!

Vol. True? pow, waw.

Men. True? I'll be sworn they are true. Where is he wounded? [*To the Tribunes.*] God save your good worships! Martius is coming home; he has more cause to be proud.—Where is he wounded?

Vol. I' th' shoulder and i' th' left arm. There will be large cicatrices to show the people, when he shall stand for his place. He receiv'd in the repulse of Tarquin seven hurts i' th' body.

Men. One i' th' neck, and two i' th' thigh—there's nine that I know.

Vol. He had, before this last expedition, twenty-five wounds upon him.

Men. Now it's twenty-seven; every gash was an enemy's grave. (*A shout and flourish.*) Hark, the trumpets.

Vol. These are the ushers of Martius: before him he carries noise, and behind him he leaves tears:
Death, that dark spirit, in 's nervy arm doth lie,
Which, being advanc'd, declines, and then men die.

A sennet. Trumpets sound. Enter COMINIUS *the General, and* TITUS LARTIUS; *between them,* CORIOLANUS, *crown'd with an oaken garland; with* CAPTAINS *and* SOLDIERS *and a* HERALD.

Her. Know, Rome, that all alone Martius did fight
Within Corioles gates; where he hath won,
With fame, a name to Martius Caius; these
In honor follows Coriolanus.
Welcome to Rome, renowned Coriolanus!

Sound. Flourish.

All. Welcome to Rome, renowned Coriolanus!

Cor. No more of this, it does offend my heart;
Pray now, no more.

Com. Look, sir, your mother!

Cor. O!

77. **bleeding:** unhealed, i.e. not adjudicated.
82. **giber . . . table:** witty table-companion. **necessary bencher:** useful judge. 85. **subjects:** creatures.
88. **botcher:** mender of old clothes.
90–91. **in . . . estimation:** i.e. to rate him at the lowest.
92. **Deucalion:** the Noah of classical myth.
93. **God-den:** good evening.
103–4. **with . . . approbation:** having won golden opinions.
114. **gives . . . of:** endows me with.
115. **make . . . at:** i.e. defy. 116. **sovereign:** efficacious.
117. **Galen:** famous Greek physician of the second century A.D. **empiricutic:** quackish. **to:** in comparison with.
118. **horse-drench:** dose for horses. 122. **'a:** he.
130. **and:** if. 131. **fidius'd:** Aufidiused, i.e. thrashed.
132. **possess'd:** informed. 135. **name:** honor, credit.
140. **purchasing:** earning, deserving.
142. **pow, waw:** pooh, pooh; i.e. of course they are true.
148. **cicatrices:** scars. 149. **his place:** i.e. the consulship.
149–50. **repulse of Tarquin.** Tarquin Superbus, having been expelled from Rome after his son's rape of Lucrece, led an army against the city in an attempt to regain the kingship, but was defeated. See II.ii.87–98. 160. **nervy:** sinewy.
161. **advanc'd:** raised. **declines:** descends.
161 s.d. **sennet:** trumpet signal announcing an important personage.
164. **With:** together with. **to:** in addition to.

You have, I know, petition'd all the gods
For my prosperity! *Kneels.*
Vol. Nay, my good soldier, up;
My gentle Martius, worthy Caius, and
By deed-achieving honor newly nam'd—
What is it?—Coriolanus must I call thee?—
But O, thy wife!
Cor. My gracious silence, hail!
Wouldst thou have laugh'd had I come coffin'd home,
That weep'st to see me triumph? Ah, my dear,
Such eyes the widows in Corioles wear,
And mothers that lack sons.
Men. Now the gods crown thee!
[*Cor.*] And live you yet? [*To Valeria.*] O my sweet lady, pardon.
Vol. I know not where to turn. O, welcome home;
And welcome, general, and y' are welcome all.
Men. A hundred thousand welcomes! I could weep,
And I could laugh; I am light, and heavy. Welcome!
A curse begin at very root on 's heart,
That is not glad to see thee! [You] are three
That Rome should dote on; yet, by the faith of men,
We have some old crab-trees here at home that will not
Be grafted to your relish. Yet welcome, warriors;
We call a nettle but a nettle, and
The faults of fools but folly.
Com. Ever right.
Cor. Menenius, ever, ever.
Her. Give way there, and go on!
Cor. [*To Volumnia and Virgilia.*] Your hand, and yours!
Ere in our own house I do shade my head,
The good patricians must be visited,
From whom I have receiv'd not only greetings,
But with them change of honors.
Vol. I have lived
To see inherited my very wishes
And the buildings of my fancy; only
There's one thing wanting, which I doubt not but
Our Rome will cast upon thee.
Cor. Know, good mother,
I had rather be their servant in my way
Than sway with them in theirs.
Com. On, to the Capitol!
Flourish. Cornets. Exeunt in state, as before. Brutus and Sicinius [*come forward*].
Bru. All tongues speak of him, and the bleared sights
Are spectacled to see him. Your prattling nurse
Into a rapture lets her baby cry
While she chats him; the kitchen malkin pins

171. **prosperity:** success.
173. **deed-achieving honor:** honor achieved by deeds.
184. **light:** merry. **heavy:** sad.
188. **old crab-trees:** old crab apple trees, i.e. sour old men.
189. **grafted to:** implanted with. **your relish:** (1) liking for you; (2) your agreeable taste (which would sweeten their sourness).
190–91. **We . . . folly:** we have to face the fact that we can't change a nettle's unpleasant nature, and that fools will be fools.
198. **change of honors:** new honors. 199. **inherited:** realized.
204. **sway with:** rule over.
205–6. **bleared . . . spectacled:** dim-sighted old people put on their spectacles. 207. **rapture:** fit.
208. **chats:** chatters about. **malkin:** slattern.

Her richest lockram 'bout her reechy neck,
Clamb'ring the walls to eye him; stalls, bulks, windows
Are smother'd up, leads fill'd, and ridges hors'd
With variable complexions, all agreeing
In earnestness to see him. Seld-shown flamens
Do press among the popular throngs, and puff
To win a vulgar station; our veil'd dames
Commit the war of white and damask in
Their nicely gawded cheeks to th' wanton spoil
Of Phoebus' burning kisses—such a poother
As if that whatsoever god who leads him
Were slily crept into his human powers,
And gave him graceful posture.
Sic. On the sudden,
I warrant him consul.
Bru. Then our office may,
During his power, go sleep.
Sic. He cannot temp'rately transport his honors
From where he should begin and end, but will
Lose those he hath won.
Bru. In that there's comfort.
Sic. Doubt not
The commoners, for whom we stand, but they
Upon their ancient malice will forget
With the least cause these his new honors, which
That he will give them make I as little question
As he is proud to do't.
Bru. I heard him swear,
Were he to stand for consul, never would he
Appear i' th' market-place, nor on him put
The napless vesture of humility,
Nor, showing (as the manner is) his wounds
To th' people, beg their stinking breaths.
Sic. 'Tis right.
Bru. It was his word. O, he would miss it rather
Than carry it but by the suit of the gentry to him
And the desire of the nobles.
Sic. I wish no better
Than have him hold that purpose and to put it
In execution.
Bru. 'Tis most like he will.
Sic. It shall be to him then as our good wills:
A sure destruction.
Bru. So it must fall out

209. **lockram:** cheap linen fabric. **reechy:** dirty.
210. **bulks:** stall-like structures in front of shops.
211. **leads:** leaded roofs. **ridges:** rooftops. **hors'd:** bestridden.
212. **variable complexions:** all sorts of people. **agreeing:** alike.
213. **Seld-shown flamens:** priests who rarely appear in public.
214. **popular:** plebeian, vulgar. **puff:** pant, i.e. strive.
215. **vulgar station:** good place in the crowd. 216. **damask:** red.
217. **nicely gawded:** prettily made-up (?). Some editors read *nicely guarded,* "carefully protected (at other times)." **wanton spoil:** (1) careless destruction; (2) amorous despoiling (leading to *kisses* in the next line).
218. **Phoebus' burning kisses:** the sun's heat. **poother:** pother, commotion. 220. **human powers:** body.
221. **graceful posture:** i.e. more than human grace of bearing.
225. **and end:** i.e. to where he should end.
228. **Upon . . . malice:** because of their long-standing ill-will.
229. **With . . . cause:** on the slightest provocation. **which:** i.e. which cause. 234. **napless:** threadbare. 236. **breaths:** voices, votes.
237. **miss it:** go without the consulship.
238. **carry:** achieve. **but:** except, otherwise than.
242. **as . . . wills:** as we desire.

To him, or our authorities, for an end.
We must suggest the people in what hatred
He still hath held them; that to 's power he would
Have made them mules, silenc'd their pleaders, and
Dispropertied their freedoms, holding them,
In human action and capacity,
Of no more soul nor fitness for the world
Than camels in their war, who have their provand
Only for bearing burthens, and sore blows
For sinking under them.

Sic. This, as you say, suggested
At some time when his soaring insolence
Shall teach the people—which time shall not want,
If he be put upon't, and that's as easy
As to set dogs on sheep—will be his fire
To kindle their dry stubble; and their blaze
Shall darken him for ever.

Enter a MESSENGER.

Bru. What's the matter?

Mess. You are sent for to the Capitol. 'Tis thought
That Martius shall be consul.
I have seen the dumb men throng to see him, and
The blind to hear him speak. Matrons flung gloves,
Ladies and maids their scarfs and handkerchers,
Upon him as he pass'd; the nobles bended,
As to Jove's statue, and the commons made
A shower and thunder with their caps and shouts.
I never saw the like.

Bru. Let's to the Capitol,
And carry with us ears and eyes for th' time,
But hearts for the event.

Sic. Have with you. *Exeunt.*

[SCENE II]

Enter two OFFICERS *to lay cushions, as it were in the Capitol.*

1. Off. Come, come, they are almost here. How many stand for consulships?

2. Off. Three, they say; but 'tis thought of every one Coriolanus will carry it.

1. Off. That's a brave fellow; but he's vengeance proud, and loves not the common people.

2. Off. Faith, there hath been many great men that have flatter'd the people, who ne'er lov'd them; and there be many that they have lov'd, they know not wherefore; so that, if they love they know not why, they hate upon no better a ground. Therefore, for Coriolanus neither to care whether they love or hate him manifests the true knowledge he has in their

244. **for an end:** ultimately. 245. **suggest:** insinuate to.
246. **still:** always. **to 's power:** so far as he could.
247. **pleaders:** i.e. those who argue their case, the tribunes.
248. **Dispropertied:** dispossessed them of.
251. **provand:** provender.
255. **teach:** i.e. show the truth about him to. Some editors adopt Hanmer's emendation *touch*. **want:** be lacking, fail to come.
256. **put upon't:** provoked to it.
269. **th' time:** the present time. 270. **event:** outcome.

II.ii. **Location:** Rome. The Capitol.
5. **vengeance:** terribly. 8. **who:** i.e. the people. 13. **in:** of.

disposition, and out of his noble carelessness lets them plainly see't.

1. Off. If he did not care whether he had their love or no, he wav'd indifferently 'twixt doing them neither good nor harm; but he seeks their hate with greater devotion than they can render it him, and leaves nothing undone that may fully discover him their opposite. Now, to seem to affect the malice and displeasure of the people is as bad as that which he dislikes, to flatter them for their love.

2. Off. He hath deserv'd worthily of his country, and his ascent is not by such easy degrees as those who, having been supple and courteous to the people, bonneted, without any further deed to have them at all into their estimation and report. But he hath so planted his honors in their eyes and his actions in their hearts that for their tongues to be silent and not confess so much were a kind of ingrateful injury; to report otherwise were a malice that, giving itself the lie, would pluck reproof and rebuke from every ear that heard it.

1. Off. No more of him, he's a worthy man. Make way, they are coming.

A sennet. Enter the PATRICIANS *and the Tribunes of the people* [SICINIUS *and* BRUTUS], LICTORS *before them;* CORIOLANUS, MENENIUS, COMINIUS *the Consul. Sicinius and Brutus take their places by themselves. Coriolanus stands.*

Men. Having determin'd of the Volsces and
To send for Titus Lartius, it remains,
As the main point of this our after-meeting,
To gratify his noble service that
Hath thus stood for his country; therefore please you,
Most reverend and grave elders, to desire
The present consul and last general
In our well-found successes, to report
A little of that worthy work perform'd
By Martius Caius Coriolanus, whom
We met here both to thank and to remember
With honors like himself. [*Coriolanus sits.*]

1. Sen. Speak, good Cominius:
Leave nothing out for length, and make us think
Rather our state's defective for requital
Than we to stretch it out. [*To the Tribunes.*] Masters a' th' people,
We do request your kindest ears, and after,
Your loving motion toward the common body

14. **noble carelessness:** patrician lack of concern.
17. **wav'd:** would fluctuate.
20–21. **discover . . . opposite:** show that he is their enemy.
21. **affect:** desire.
27. **bonneted:** took off their caps. **have them:** gain their way.
28. **estimation and report:** good opinion.
32. **giving . . . lie:** proclaiming itself a liar, being manifestly untrue.
36. s.d. **Lictors:** attendants upon the magistrates.
37. **determin'd of:** decided what to do about.
40. **gratify:** reward. 43. **last:** late.
44. **well-found:** happily met with.
48. **like himself:** i.e. befitting his deeds.
50–51. **Rather . . . out:** that our state lacks means to reward him adequately rather than that we lack willingness to extend the means it possesses.
53. **loving:** friendly, favorable. **motion:** urging, influence.

To yield what passes here.
Sic. We are convented
Upon a pleasing treaty, and have hearts
Inclinable to honor and advance
The theme of our assembly.
Bru. Which the rather
We shall be blest to do, if he remember
A kinder value of the people than
He hath hereto priz'd them at.
Men. That's off, that's off;
I would you rather had been silent. Please you
To hear Cominius speak?
Bru. Most willingly;
But yet my caution was more pertinent
Than the rebuke you give it.
Men. He loves your people,
But tie him not to be their bedfellow.
Worthy Cominius, speak.
Coriolanus rises and offers to go away.
Nay, keep your place.
[1.] Sen. Sit, Coriolanus; never shame to hear
What you have nobly done.
Cor. Your honors' pardon;
I had rather have my wounds to heal again
Than hear say how I got them.
Bru. Sir, I hope
My words disbench'd you not?
Cor. No, sir; yet oft,
When blows have made me stay, I fled from words.
You sooth'd not, therefore hurt not; but your people,
I love them as they weigh—
Men. Pray now, sit down.
Cor. I had rather have one scratch my head i' th' sun
When the alarum were struck than idly sit
To hear my nothings monster'd. *Exit Coriolanus.*
Men. Masters of the people,
Your multiplying spawn how can he flatter—
That's thousand to one good one—when you now see
He had rather venture all his limbs for honor
Than [one on 's] ears to hear it? Proceed, Cominius.
Com. I shall lack voice: the deeds of Coriolanus
Should not be utter'd feebly. It is held
That valor is the chiefest virtue, and
Most dignifies the haver; if it be,
The man I speak of cannot in the world
Be singly counterpois'd. At sixteen years,
When Tarquin made a head for Rome, he fought
Beyond the mark of others. Our then dictator,
Whom with all praise I point at, saw him fight,
When with his Amazonian [chin] he drove
The bristled lips before him. He bestrid
An o'erpress'd Roman, and i' th' consul's view
Slew three opposers. Tarquin's self he met,
And struck him on his knee. In that day's feats,
When he might act the woman in the scene,
He prov'd best man i' th' field, and for his meed
Was brow-bound with the oak. His pupil age
Man-ent'red thus, he waxed like a sea,
And in the brunt of seventeen battles since
He lurch'd all swords of the garland. For this last,
Before and in Corioles, let me say,
I cannot speak him home. He stopp'd the fliers,
And by his rare example made the coward
Turn terror into sport; as weeds before
A vessel under sail, so men obey'd
And fell below his stem. His sword, death's stamp,
Where it did mark, it took; from face to foot
He was a thing of blood, whose every motion
Was tim'd with dying cries. Alone he ent'red
The mortal gate of th' city, which he painted
With shunless destiny; aidless came off,
And with a sudden reinforcement struck
Corioles like a planet. Now all's his,
When by and by the din of war gan pierce
His ready sense; then straight his doubled spirit
Requick'ned what in flesh was fatigate,
And to the battle came he, where he did
Run reeking o'er the lives of men, as if
'Twere a perpetual spoil; and till we call'd
Both field and city ours, he never stood
To ease his breast with panting.
Men. Worthy man!
[1.] Sen. He cannot but with measure fit the honors
Which we devise him.
Com. Our spoils he kick'd at,
And look'd upon things precious as they were
The common muck of the world. He covets less
Than misery itself would give, rewards
His deeds with doing them, and is content
To spend the time to end it.
Men. He's right noble.
Let him be call'd for.
[1.] Sen. Call Coriolanus.
Off. He doth appear.

54. yield: assent to. **passes:** receives sanction. **convented:** convened.
55. treaty: matter for discussion. **58. blest:** happy.
59. value: valuation. **60. off:** not pertinent.
71. My . . . not: it was not my words that made you leave your seat.
73. sooth'd: flattered.
74. as they weigh: in accordance with their worth.
76. alarum were struck: call to arms was sounded.
77. nothings monster'd: trifling feats treated like something outside the ordinary course of nature.
87. singly counterpois'd: equalled by any other single man.
88. made . . . for: raised a force to reconquer.
91. Amazonian: i.e. beardless. The Amazons were female warriors.
93. o'erpress'd: overwhelmed. **95. on his knee:** to his knees.
96. he . . . scene: i.e. he was still young enough to have played women's roles in the theatre. **97. meed:** reward.
99. Man-ent'red: initiated into manhood. **101. lurch'd:** robbed.
103. speak him home: praise him duly.
107. stem: bow. **stamp:** die (for stamping an impression).
108. took: killed. **109. motion:** movement.
110. tim'd with: accompanied regularly by. **111. mortal:** fatal.
112. shunless destiny: i.e. the blood of enemies unable to escape their doom.
113–14. struck . . . planet. Planets of malign influences were said to "strike" men. **115. gan:** began to.
116. ready sense: quick hearing. **doubled:** renewed.
117. Requick'ned: gave new life to. **fatigate:** weary.
119. reeking: steaming (with the blood of his victims).
120. perpetual spoil: endless slaughter.
121. stood: stood still, stopped.
123. with measure: becomingly (i.e. no honor would be too great for him). **124. kick'd at:** spurned.
127. misery: wretched poverty.
127–29. rewards . . . end it: finds reward for his feats in the satisfaction of doing them, and asks no payment for the time so spent beyond the pleasure of passing it in such a fashion.

Enter CORIOLANUS.

Men. The Senate, Coriolanus, are well pleas'd
To make thee consul.
Cor. I do owe them still
My life and services.
Men. It then remains
That you do speak to the people.
Cor. I do beseech you,
Let me o'erleap that custom; for I cannot
Put on the gown, stand naked, and entreat them
For my wounds' sake to give their suffrage. Please you
That I may pass this doing.
Sic. Sir, the people
Must have their voices; neither will they bate
One jot of ceremony.
Men. Put them not to't.
Pray you go fit you to the custom, and
Take to you, as your predecessors have,
Your honor with your form.
Cor. It is a part
That I shall blush in acting, and might well
Be taken from the people.
Bru. Mark you that.
Cor. To brag unto them, "Thus I did, and thus!"
Show them th' unaching scars which I should hide,
As if I had receiv'd them for the hire
Of their breath only!
Men. Do not stand upon't.
We recommend to you, tribunes of the people,
Our purpose to them, and to our noble consul
Wish we all joy and honor.
Senators. To Coriolanus come all joy and honor!
Flourish cornets. Then exeunt. Manent Sicinius and Brutus.
Bru. You see how he intends to use the people.
Sic. May they perceive 's intent! He will require them
As if he did contemn what he requested
Should be in them to give.
Bru. Come, we'll inform them
Of our proceedings here on th' market-place;
I know they do attend us. [*Exeunt.*]

[SCENE III]

Enter seven or eight CITIZENS.

1. Cit. Once if he do require our voices, we ought not to deny him.

2. Cit. We may, sir, if we will.

3. Cit. We have power in ourselves to do it, but it is a power that we have no power to do; for if he show

133. **still**: ever. 136. **o'erleap**: skip, omit.
137. **naked**: exposed. 139. **pass**: omit.
140. **voices**: votes. **bate**: dispense with.
141. **Put . . . to't**: do not provoke them.
149. **your form**: the formality you must go through with.
149. **hire**: wages.
150. **breath**: i.e. votes. **stand upon't**: be unyielding about it.
151. **recommend**: commit, entrust. 156. **require**: solicit.
157. **contemn**: think it hateful (that).

II.iii. Location: Rome. The Forum.
1. **Once if**: if indeed. 5. **no power**: i.e. no moral right.

us his wounds and tell us his deeds, we are to put our tongues into those wounds and speak for them; so, if he tell us his noble deeds, we must also tell him our noble acceptance of them. Ingratitude is monstrous, and for the multitude to be ingrateful were to make a monster of the multitude; of the which we being members, should bring ourselves to be monstrous members.

1. Cit. And to make us no better thought of, a little help will serve; for once we stood up about the corn, he himself stuck not to call us the many-headed multitude.

3. Cit. We have been call'd so of many, not that our heads are some brown, some black, some abram, some bald, but that our wits are so diversely color'd; and truly I think if all our wits were to issue out of one skull, they would fly east, west, north, south, and their consent of one direct way should be at once to all the points a' th' compass.

2. Cit. Think you so? Which way do you judge my wit would fly?

3. Cit. Nay, your wit will not so soon out as another man's will; 'tis strongly wadg'd up in a block-head; but if it were at liberty, 'twould sure southward.

2. Cit. Why that way?

3. Cit. To lose itself in a fog, where being three parts melted away with rotten dews, the fourth would return for conscience' sake to help to get thee a wife.

2. Cit. You are never without your tricks; you may, you may.

3. Cit. Are you all resolv'd to give your voices? But that's no matter, the greater part carries it, I say. If he would incline to the people, there was never a worthier man.

Enter CORIOLANUS *in a gown of humility, with* MENENIUS.

Here he comes, and in the gown of humility, mark his behavior. We are not to stay all together, but to come by him where he stands, by ones, by twos, and by threes. He's to make his requests by particulars, wherein every one of us has a single honor, in giving him our own voices with our own tongues; therefore follow me, and I'll direct you how you shall go by him.

All. Content, content. [*Exeunt Citizens.*]

Men. O sir, you are not right. Have you not known
The worthiest men have done't?
Cor. What must I say?
"I pray, sir"—Plague upon't! I cannot bring
My tongue to such a pace. "Look, sir, my wounds!
I got them in my country's service, when
Some certain of your brethren roar'd, and ran

14–15. **a little . . . serve**: very little will suffice.
15. **once . . . up**: when we took a stand.
16. **stuck not**: did not hesitate.
18. **of**: by. 19. **abram**: auburn, reddish-brown.
23. **consent of**: agreement about. 28. **wadg'd**: wedged.
32. **rotten**: unwholesome.
32–33. **the fourth . . . wife**. The joke is obscure.
34–35. **you may**: i.e. keep it up. 37. **greater part**: majority.
38. **incline to**: favor.
43. **by particulars**: to each individually. 44. **single**: individual.

From th' noise of our own drums."

Men. O me, the gods!
You must not speak of that. You must desire them
To think upon you.

Cor. Think upon me? Hang 'em,
I would they would forget me, like the virtues
Which our divines lose by 'em.

Men. You'll mar all.
I'll leave you. Pray you speak to 'em, I pray you,
In wholesome manner. *Exit.*

Enter three of the Citizens.

Cor. Bid them wash their faces,
And keep their teeth clean. So, here comes a brace.—
You know the cause, sir, of my standing here.

3. Cit. We do, sir, tell us what hath brought you to't.

Cor. Mine own desert.

2. Cit. Your own desert!

Cor. Ay, [not] mine own desire.

3. Cit. How, not your own desire?

Cor. No, sir, 'twas never my desire yet to trouble the poor with begging.

3. Cit. You must think, if we give you any thing, we hope to gain by you.

Cor. Well then, I pray, your price a' th' consulship?

1. Cit. The price is, to ask it kindly.

Cor. Kindly, sir, I pray let me ha't. I have wounds to show you, which shall be yours in private. Your good voice, sir, what say you?

2. Cit. You shall ha't, worthy sir.

Cor. A match, sir. There's in all two worthy voices begg'd. I have your alms, adieu.

3. Cit. But this is something odd.

2. Cit. And 'twere to give again—but 'tis no matter. *Exeunt* [*Citizens*].

Enter two other Citizens.

Cor. Pray you now, if it may stand with the tune of your voices that I may be consul, I have here the customary gown.

[*4.*] *Cit.* You have deserv'd nobly of your country, and you have not deserv'd nobly.

Cor. Your enigma?

[*4.*] *Cit.* You have been a scourge to her enemies, you have been a rod to her friends; you have not indeed lov'd the common people.

Cor. You should account me the more virtuous that I have not been common in my love. I will, sir, flatter my sworn brother, the people, to earn a dearer estimation of them; 'tis a condition they account gentle. And since the wisdom of their choice is rather to have my hat than my heart, I will practice the insinuating nod and be off to them most counterfeitly; that is, sir, I will counterfeit the bewitchment of some popular man, and give it bountiful to the desirers. Therefore beseech you I may be consul.

[*5.*] *Cit.* We hope to find you our friend; and therefore give you our voices heartily.

[*4.*] *Cit.* You have receiv'd many wounds for your country.

Cor. I will not seal your knowledge with showing them. I will make much of your voices, and so trouble you no farther.

Both [*Cit.*] The gods give you joy, sir, heartily! [*Exeunt Citizens.*]

Cor. Most sweet voices!
Better it is to die, better to starve,
Than crave the hire which first we do deserve.
Why in this woolvish [toge] should I stand here
To beg of Hob and Dick, that does appear,
Their needless vouches? Custom calls me to't.
What custom wills, in all things should we do't,
The dust on antique time would lie unswept,
And mountainous error be too highly heap'd
For truth to o'erpeer. Rather than fool it so,
Let the high office and the honor go
To one that would do thus. I am half through:
The one part suffered, the other will I do.

Enter three Citizens *more.*

Here come moe voices.—
Your voices? For your voices I have fought;
Watch'd for your voices; for your voices bear
Of wounds two dozen odd; battles thrice six
I have seen, and heard of; for your voices have
Done many things, some less, some more. Your voices?
Indeed I would be consul.

[*6.*] *Cit.* He has done nobly, and cannot go without any honest man's voice.

[*7.*] *Cit.* Therefore let him be consul. The gods give him joy, and make him good friend to the people!

All. Amen, amen. God save thee, noble consul! [*Exeunt Citizens.*]

Cor. Worthy voices!

Enter Menenius *with* Brutus *and* Sicinius.

Men. You have stood your limitation, and the tribunes
Endue you with the people's voice. Remains
That, in th' official marks invested, you
Anon do meet the Senate.

Cor. Is this done?

Sic. The custom of request you have discharg'd.
The people do admit you and are summon'd

56. think upon you: bear you in mind.
58. lose by 'em: i.e. uselessly urge upon them in sermons.
60. wholesome: reasonable, suitable (but Coriolanus' reply rises from the sense "conducive to health"). **77. yours:** i.e. shown to you.
80. A match: it's a deal. **83. And:** if. **85. stand:** accord.
97. condition: quality. **gentle:** courteous.
99. my hat: i.e. outward manifestations of courtesy from me.
100. be off: take off my hat. **counterfeitly:** falsely, hypocritically.
101–2. popular man: demagogue. **108. seal:** confirm.
114. crave . . . deserve: ask for the wages we have already earned.
115. woolvish. Probably a variant of *woolish*, "of coarse wool." Many editors read *wolvish*, with some such meaning as "incongruous with my true nature" (like the sheepskin worn by the wolf in Aesop's fable); others read *woolless*. **toge:** toga.
116. that does appear: as they turn up.
117. vouches: attestations.
121. o'erpeer: be seen over. **fool it:** play the fool.
125. moe: more. **127. Watch'd:** kept watch.
138. limitation: prescribed time. **139. Endue:** endow.
140. official marks: insignia of office.

To meet anon, upon your approbation.
Cor. Where? at the Senate-house?
Sic. There, Coriolanus.
Cor. May I change these garments?
Sic. You may, sir.
Cor. That I'll straight do; and, knowing myself again,
Repair to th' Senate-house.
Men. I'll keep you company. Will you along?
Bru. We stay here for the people.
Sic. Fare you well.
Exeunt Coriolanus and Menenius.
He has it now; and by his looks, methinks,
'Tis warm at 's heart.
Bru. With a proud heart he wore his humble weeds.
Will you dismiss the people?

Enter the PLEBEIANS.

Sic. How now, my masters, have you chose this man?
1. Cit. He has our voices, sir.
Bru. We pray the gods he may deserve your loves.
2. Cit. Amen, sir. To my poor unworthy notice,
He mock'd us when he begg'd our voices.
3. Cit. Certainly,
He flouted us downright.
1. Cit. No, 'tis his kind of speech, he did not mock us.
2. Cit. Not one amongst us, save yourself, but says
He us'd us scornfully. He should have show'd us
His marks of merit, wounds receiv'd for 's country.
Sic. Why, so he did, I am sure.
All [*Cit.*] No, no; no man saw 'em.
3. Cit. He said he had wounds, which he could show in private;
And with his hat, thus waving it in scorn,
"I would be consul," says he; "aged custom,
But by your voices, will not so permit me;
Your voices therefore." When we granted that,
Here was "I thank you for your voices, thank you,
Your most sweet voices. Now you have left your voices,
I have no further with you." Was not this mockery?
Sic. Why either were you ignorant to see't,
Or, seeing it, of such childish friendliness
To yield your voices?
Bru. Could you not have told him
As you were lesson'd: when he had no power,
But was a petty servant to the state,
He was your enemy, ever spake against
Your liberties and the charters that you bear
I' th' body of the weal; and now, arriving
A place of potency and sway o' th' state,
If he should still malignantly remain
Fast foe to th' plebeii, your voices might
Be curses to yourselves? You should have said
That as his worthy deeds did claim no less

144. **upon your approbation:** to confirm your election.
173. **further:** further business. 174. **ignorant:** too dull.
180. **charters:** rights and privileges.
181. **body . . . weal:** commonwealth. **arriving:** attaining to.

Than what he stood for, so his gracious nature
Would think upon you for your voices, and
Translate his malice towards you into love,
Standing your friendly lord.
Sic. Thus to have said,
As you were fore-advis'd, had touch'd his spirit
And tried his inclination; from him pluck'd
Either his gracious promise, which you might,
As cause had call'd you up, have held him to;
Or else it would have gall'd his surly nature,
Which easily endures not article
Tying him to aught; so putting him to rage,
You should have ta'en th' advantage of his choler,
And pass'd him unelected.
Bru. Did you perceive
He did solicit you in free contempt
When he did need your loves; and do you think
That his contempt shall not be bruising to you
When he hath power to crush? Why, had your bodies
No heart among you? Or had you tongues to cry
Against the rectorship of judgment?
Sic. Have you
Ere now denied the asker; and now again,
Of him that did not ask but mock, bestow
Your su'd-for tongues?
3. Cit. He's not confirm'd, we may deny him yet.
2. Cit. And will deny him.
I'll have five hundred voices of that sound.
1. Cit. I twice five hundred, and their friends to piece 'em.
Bru. Get you hence instantly, and tell those friends
They have chose a consul that will from them take
Their liberties, make them of no more voice
Than dogs, that are as often beat for barking
As therefore kept to do so.
Sic. Let them assemble;
And on a safer judgment all revoke
Your ignorant election. Enforce his pride,
And his old hate unto you; besides, forget not
With what contempt he wore the humble weed,
How in his suit he scorn'd you; but your loves,
Thinking upon his services, took from you
Th' apprehension of his present portance,
Which most gibingly, ungravely, he did fashion
After the inveterate hate he bears you.
Bru. Lay
A fault on us, your tribunes, that we labor'd
(No impediment between) but that you must
Cast your election on him.
Sic. Say you chose him

187. **what . . . for:** the office he sought. 191. **touch'd:** tested.
194. **As . . . up:** as occasion required of you.
195. **gall'd:** rubbed sore, irritated.
196. **easily . . . article:** doesn't easily endure stipulation.
200. **free:** unconcealed.
204. **heart.** Here, the organ of wisdom.
204–5. **to . . . judgment:** capable of uttering what was contrary to the dictates of common sense.
205–6. **Have . . . asker:** haven't you on earlier occasions said no to someone who asked for your votes. 207. **Of:** on.
212. **piece:** augment. 218. **safer:** sounder.
219. **Enforce:** emphasize.
224. **apprehension:** understanding. **portance:** bearing.
225. **ungravely:** not seriously. 226. **After:** in accordance with.
227. **A fault:** the blame.
228. **No impediment between:** permitting nothing to hinder.

More after our commandment than as guided
By your own true affections, and that your minds,
Preoccupied with what you rather must do
Than what you should, made you against the grain
To voice him consul. Lay the fault on us.

Bru. Ay, spare us not. Say we read lectures to you,
How youngly he began to serve his country,
How long continued, and what stock he springs of—
The noble house o' th' Martians; from whence came
That Ancus Martius, Numa's daughter's son,
Who after great Hostilius here was king;
Of the same house Publius and Quintus were,
That our best water brought by conduits hither,
[And Censorinus that was so surnam'd,]
And nobly named so, twice being censor,
Was his great ancestor.

Sic. One thus descended,
That hath beside well in his person wrought
To be set high in place, we did commend
To your remembrances; but you have found,
Scaling his present bearing with his past,
That he's your fixed enemy, and revoke
Your sudden approbation.

Bru. Say you ne'er had done't
(Harp on that still) but by our putting on;
And presently, when you have drawn your number,
Repair to th' Capitol.

All. We will so. Almost all
Repent in their election. *Exeunt Plebeians.*

Bru. Let them go on;
This mutiny were better put in hazard
Than stay, past doubt, for greater.
If, as his nature is, he fall in rage
With their refusal, both observe and answer
The vantage of his anger.

Sic. To th' Capitol, come.
We will be there before the stream o' th' people;
And this shall seem, as partly 'tis, their own,
Which we have goaded onward. *Exeunt.*

ACT III, [Scene I]

Cornets. Enter Coriolanus, Menenius, *all the* Gentry, Cominius, Titus Lartius, *and other* Senators.

Cor. Tullus Aufidius then had made new head?

233. **against the grain:** contrary to your natural inclination.
239. **Numa:** Roman king who succeeded Romulus, founder of the city. 242. **conduits:** aqueducts.
243. **And . . . surnam'd.** This line, constructed by N. Delius to fill an obvious gap in F1, rests upon the passage in North's Plutarch which Shakespeare was following closely at this point: "Of the same house were Publius, and Quintus, who brought Rome their best water they had by conducts. Censorinus also came of that familie, that was so surnamed, bicause the people had chosen him Censor twise." Various editors solve the difficulty in various ways.
244. **censor:** one of two officials who supervised the census and had general oversight of the conduct of citizens.
249. **Scaling:** weighing. 251. **sudden:** hasty.
252. **putting on:** urging. 253. **presently:** immediately. **drawn your number:** collected your crowd.
256–57. **This . . . greater:** it is wiser to run a risk with this mob of rebels than to delay until we can raise a larger one that would make the outcome certain (?) or it is better to take the risk of this uprising than to wait for a later time when the trouble will certainly be more serious (?). 259–60. **answer The vantage:** make good use.

Lart. He had, my lord, and that it was which caus'd
Our swifter composition.

Cor. So then the Volsces stand but as at first,
Ready, when time shall prompt them, to make road
Upon 's again.

Com. They are worn, Lord Consul, so
That we shall hardly in our ages see
Their banners wave again.

Cor. Saw you Aufidius?

Lart. On safeguard he came to me, and did curse
Against the Volsces for they had so vildly
Yielded the town. He is retired to Antium.

Cor. Spoke he of me?

Lart. He did, my lord.

Cor. How? What?

Lart. How often he had met you, sword to sword;
That of all things upon the earth he hated
Your person most; that he would pawn his fortunes
To hopeless restitution, so he might
Be call'd your vanquisher.

Cor. At Antium lives he?

Lart. At Antium.

Cor. I wish I had a cause to seek him there,
To oppose his hatred fully. Welcome home.

Enter Sicinius *and* Brutus.

Behold, these are the tribunes of the people,
The tongues o' th' common mouth. I do despise them!
For they do prank them in authority,
Against all noble sufferance.

Sic. Pass no further.

Cor. Hah? what is that?

Bru. It will be dangerous to go on—no further.

Cor. What makes this change?

Men. The matter?

Com. Hath he not pass'd the noble and the common?

Bru. Cominius, no.

Cor. Have I had children's voices?

[1.] Sen. Tribunes, give way, he shall to th' market-place.

Bru. The people are incens'd against him.

Sic. Stop,
Or all will fall in broil.

Cor. Are these your herd?
Must these have voices, that can yield them now,
And straight disclaim their tongues? What are your offices?
You being their mouths, why rule you not their teeth?
Have you not set them on?

Men. Be calm, be calm.

Cor. It is a purpos'd thing, and grows by plot,
To curb the will of the nobility.

III.i. Location: Rome. A street.
1. **made new head:** raised a new force.
3. **composition:** coming to terms. 5. **road:** inroad, invasion.
7. **ages:** lifetimes. 9. **On safeguard:** under safe-conduct.
10. **for:** because.
16. **To . . . restitution:** beyond hope of recovery.
23. **prank them:** deck themselves out.
24. **Against . . . sufferance:** beyond what a patrician can tolerate.
33. **in broil:** into tumult. 35. **offices:** functions, duties.
38. **purpos'd:** planned, prearranged.

Suffer't, and live with such as cannot rule,
Nor ever will be ruled.
Bru. Call't not a plot.
The people cry you mock'd them; and of late,
When corn was given them gratis, you repin'd,
Scandall'd the suppliants for the people, call'd them
Time-pleasers, flatterers, foes to nobleness.
Cor. Why, this was known before.
Bru. Not to them all.
Cor. Have you inform'd them sithence?
Bru. How? I inform them?
Com. You are like to do such business.
Bru. Not unlike
Each way to better yours.
Cor. Why then should I be consul? By yond clouds,
Let me deserve so ill as you, and make me
Your fellow tribune.
Sic. You show too much of that
For which the people stir. If you will pass
To where you are bound, you must inquire your way,
Which you are out of, with a gentler spirit,
Or never be so noble as a consul,
Nor yoke with him for tribune.
Men. Let's be calm.
Com. The people are abus'd, set on. This palt'ring
Becomes not Rome; nor has Coriolanus
Deserv'd this so dishonor'd rub, laid falsely
I' th' plain way of his merit.
Cor. Tell me of corn!
This was my speech, and I will speak't again—
Men. Not now, not now.
[1.] Sen. Not in this heat, sir, now.
Cor. Now, as I live, I will.
My nobler friends, I crave their pardons.
For the mutable, rank-scented meiny, let them
Regard me as I do not flatter, and
Therein behold themselves. I say again,
In soothing them we nourish 'gainst our Senate
The cockle of rebellion, insolence, sedition,
Which we ourselves have plough'd for, sow'd, and scatter'd,
By mingling them with us, the honor'd number,
Who lack not virtue, no, nor power, but that
Which they have given to beggars.
Men. Well, no more.
[1.] Sen. No more words, we beseech you.
Cor. How? no more?
As for my country I have shed my blood,
Not fearing outward force, so shall my lungs
Coin words till their decay against those measles
Which we disdain should tetter us, yet sought
The very way to catch them.
Bru. You speak a' th' people
As if you were a god, to punish; not
A man of their infirmity.
Sic. 'Twere well
We let the people know't.
Men. What, what? His choler?
Cor. Choler?
Were I as patient as the midnight sleep,
By Jove, 'twould be my mind!
Sic. It is a mind
That shall remain a poison where it is;
Not poison any further.
Cor. Shall remain?
Hear you this Triton of the minnows? Mark you
His absolute "shall"?
Com. 'Twas from the canon.
Cor. "Shall"?
O [good] but most unwise patricians! why,
You grave but reakless senators, have you thus
Given Hydra here to choose an officer,
That with his peremptory "shall," being but
The horn and noise o' th' monster's, wants not spirit
To say he'll turn your current in a ditch,
And make your channel his? If he have power,
Then vail your ignorance; if none, awake
Your dangerous lenity. If you are learn'd,
Be not as common fools; if you are not,
Let them have cushions by you. You are plebeians,
If they be senators; and they are no less,
When, both your voices blended, the great'st taste
Most palates theirs. They choose their magistrate,
And such a one as he, who puts his "shall,"
His popular "shall," against a graver bench
Than ever frown'd in Greece. By Jove himself,
It makes the consuls base; and my soul aches
To know, when two authorities are up,
Neither supreme, how soon confusion
May enter 'twixt the gap of both, and take
The one by th' other.
Com. Well, on to th' market-place.
Cor. Whoever gave that counsel, to give forth
The corn a' th' store-house gratis, as 'twas us'd
Sometime in Greece—
Men. Well, well, no more of that.
Cor. Though there the people had more absolute pow'r,

40. Suffer't, and: if you put up with it, you will have to.
44. Scandall'd: defamed. **47. sithence:** since.
48–49. Not . . . yours: in any case I'm likely to do my business better than you would do yours (if you were consul).
53. stir: are roused.
53–54. If . . . bound: if you want to reach your destination (the consulship). **55. are out of:** have lost.
58. abus'd: deceived. **set on:** incited. **palt'ring:** trickery.
60. dishonor'd: shameful. **rub:** impediment (term from the game of bowls). **falsely:** dishonestly. **61. plain:** clear, open.
66. meiny: common herd, multitude.
67. Regard . . . flatter: see me in my true, non-flattering character.
68. behold themselves: see the truth about themselves.
70. cockle: weed. **78. measles:** plague-spots.
79. tetter us: loathsomely disfigure our skin.
82. of their infirmity: sharing their human shortcomings.
86. mind: opinion.
89. Triton: a minor sea-god, trumpeter to Neptune.
90. from the canon: contrary to the law, in excess of his authority.
93. Given: empowered. **Hydra:** a many-headed beast, i.e. the multitude.
95. horn and noise: noisy horn (continuing the Triton figure).
96. turn . . . in: divert . . . into.
98. vail your ignorance: submit yourselves in your stupidity. **awake:** rouse yourselves from. **99. learn'd:** wise.
101. have . . . you: i.e. sit beside you in the Senate.
103–4. the great'st . . . theirs: the dominant flavor comes from them, i.e. their votes decide.
106. popular: plebeian. **graver bench:** more august deliberative body. **109. up:** in action. **110. confusion:** anarchy.
111. 'twixt . . . both: into the gap between the two. **take:** overthrow. **112. by:** by the agency of. **114. us'd:** customary.

I say they nourish'd disobedience, fed
The ruin of the state.
Bru. Why shall the people give
One that speaks thus their voice?
Cor. I'll give my reasons,
More worthier than their voices. They know the corn
Was not our recompense, resting well assur'd
They ne'er did service for't; being press'd to th' war,
Even when the navel of the state was touch'd,
They would not thread the gates. This kind of service
Did not deserve corn gratis. Being i' th' war,
Their mutinies and revolts, wherein they show'd
Most valor, spoke not for them. Th' accusation
Which they have often made against the Senate,
All cause unborn, could never be the native
Of our so frank donation. Well, what then?
How shall this bosom multiplied digest
The Senate's courtesy? Let deeds express
What's like to be their words: "We did request it,
We are the greater pole, and in true fear
They gave us our demands." Thus we debase
The nature of our seats and make the rabble
Call our cares fears; which will in time
Break ope the locks a' th' Senate, and bring in
The crows to peck the eagles.
Men. Come, enough.
Bru. Enough, with over-measure.
Cor. No, take more!
What may be sworn by, both divine and human,
Seal what I end withal! This double worship,
Where [one] part does disdain with cause, the other
Insult without all reason; where gentry, title, wisdom,
Cannot conclude but by the yea and no
Of general ignorance—it must omit
Real necessities, and give way the while
To unstable slightness. Purpose so barr'd, it follows
Nothing is done to purpose. Therefore beseech you—
You that will be less fearful than discreet;
That love the fundamental part of state
More than you doubt the change on't; that prefer
A noble life before a long, and wish
To jump a body with a dangerous physic
That's sure of death without it—at once pluck out
The multitudinous tongue; let them not lick
The sweet which is their poison. Your dishonor
Mangles true judgment, and bereaves the state
Of that integrity which should become't;
Not having the power to do the good it would,
For th' ill which doth control't.
Bru. H'as said enough.
Sic. H'as spoken like a traitor, and shall answer
As traitors do.
Cor. Thou wretch, despite o'erwhelm thee!
What should the people do with these bald tribunes?
On whom depending, their obedience fails
To th' greater bench. In a rebellion,
When what's not meet, but what must be, was law,
Then were they chosen; in a better hour,
Let what is meet be said it must be meet,
And throw their power i' th' dust.
Bru. Manifest treason!
Sic. This a consul? No!
Bru. The aediles ho!

Enter an Aedile.

Let him be apprehended.
Sic. Go call the people [*exit Aedile*], in whose name myself
Attach thee as a traitorous innovator,
A foe to th' public weal. Obey, I charge thee,
And follow to thine answer.
Cor. Hence, old goat!
All [*Patricians*]. We'll surety him.
Com. Ag'd sir, hands off.
Cor. Hence, rotten thing! or I shall shake thy bones
Out of thy garments.
Sic. Help, ye citizens!

Enter a rabble of Plebeians *with the* Aediles.

Men. On both sides more respect.
Sic. Here's he that would take from you all your power.
Bru. Seize him, aediles!
All [*Plebeians*]. Down with him, down with him!
2. Sen. Weapons, weapons, weapons!
They all bustle about Coriolanus.
[*All*.] Tribunes!—Patricians!—Citizens!—What ho!—
Sicinius!—Brutus!—Coriolanus!—Citizens!—
Peace, peace, peace!—Stay, hold, peace!
Men. What is about to be? I am out of breath,
Confusion's near, I cannot speak. You, tribunes
To th' people! Coriolanus, patience!
Speak, good Sicinius.
Sic. Hear me, people, peace!
All [*Plebeians*]. Let's hear our tribune; peace! Speak, speak, speak!
Sic. You are at point to lose your liberties.
Martius would have all from you; Martius,
Whom late you have nam'd for consul.
Men. Fie, fie, fie!

121. recompense: payment for their service.
122. press'd: conscripted.
123. navel: i.e. very centre. **touch'd:** threatened.
124. thread: pass through.
129. All cause unborn: completely without justification. **native:** origin, cause. **130. frank:** freely given.
131. bosom multiplied: manifold stomach.
134. pole: poll, number of heads. **137. cares:** concern (for them).
142. Seal: confirm. **withal:** with. **double worship:** divided authority. **144. without:** beyond. **gentry:** aristocratic birth.
145. conclude: take decisions.
148. Purpose: thoughtful administration.
150. discreet: prudent, wise.
151. fundamental . . . state: basic nature of our government.
152. doubt . . . on't: i.e. fear revolution. **154. jump:** risk.
156. multitudinous tongue: the tongue of the many-headed beast, i.e. the tribunes. **157. dishonor:** (present) dishonorable state.
162. answer: answer for it. **163. despite:** contempt.
164. bald: trifling. **166. greater bench:** i.e. the Senate.
167. When . . . law: when we had to do not what was right but what was necessary.
169. Let . . . be meet: i.e. let it be decided that what should properly be done shall be done.
172. aediles: police officers in the service of the tribunes.
174. Attach: arrest. **innovator:** revolutionary.
176. to thine answer: to answer the charges against you.
193. at . . . lose: on the point of losing.

This is the way to kindle, not to quench.
[*1.*] *Sen.* To unbuild the city, and to lay all flat.
Sic. What is the city but the people?
All [*Plebeians*]. True,
The people are the city.
Bru. By the consent of all, we were establish'd
The people's magistrates.
All [*Plebeians*]. You so remain.
Men. And so are like to do.
Com. That is the way to lay the city flat,
To bring the roof to the foundation,
And bury all, which yet distinctly ranges,
In heaps and piles of ruin.
Sic. This deserves death.
Bru. Or let us stand to our authority,
Or let us lose it. We do here pronounce,
Upon the part o' th' people, in whose power
We were elected theirs, Martius is worthy
Of present death.
Sic. Therefore lay hold of him;
Bear him to th' rock Tarpeian, and from thence
Into destruction cast him.
Bru. Aediles, seize him!
All Plebeians. Yield, Martius, yield!
Men. Hear me one word,
Beseech you, tribunes, hear me but a word.
Aediles. Peace, peace!
Men. [*To Brutus.*] Be that you seem, truly your country's friend,
And temp'rately proceed to what you would
Thus violently redress.
Bru. Sir, those cold ways,
That seem like prudent helps, are very poisonous
Where the disease is violent.—Lay hands upon him,
And bear him to the rock.
Coriolanus draws his sword.
Cor. No, I'll die here.
There's some among you have beheld me fighting;
Come, try upon yourselves what you have seen me.
Men. Down with that sword! Tribunes, withdraw a while.
Bru. Lay hands upon him.
Men. Help Martius, help!
You that be noble, help him, young and old!
All [*Plebeians*]. Down with him, down with him!
In this mutiny the Tribunes, the Aediles, and the People are beat in [*and*] *exeunt.*
Men. [*To Coriolanus.*] Go, get you to [your] house; be gone, away!
All will be naught else.
2. Sen. Get you gone.
[*Cor.*] Stand fast,
We have as many friends as enemies.
Men. Shall it be put to that?
[*1.*] *Sen.* The gods forbid!

I prithee, noble friend, home to thy house;
Leave us to cure this cause.
Men. For 'tis a sore upon us
You cannot tent yourself. Be gone, beseech you.
[*Com.*] Come, sir, along with us.
[*Cor.*] I would they were barbarians, as they are,
Though in Rome litter'd; not Romans, as they are not,
Though calved i' th' porch o' th' Capitol!
[*Men.*] Be gone!
Put not your worthy rage into your tongue;
One time will owe another.
Cor. On fair ground
I could beat forty of them.
Men. I could myself
Take up a brace o' th' best of them, yea, the two tribunes.
Com. But now 'tis odds beyond arithmetic,
And manhood is call'd foolery when it stands
Against a falling fabric. Will you hence
Before the tag return, whose rage doth rend
Like interrupted waters, and o'erbear
What they are us'd to bear?
Men. Pray you be gone.
I'll try whether my old wit be in request
With those that have but little. This must be patch'd
With cloth of any color.
Com. Nay, come away.
Exeunt Coriolanus and Cominius [*with others*].
[*A*] *Patrician.* This man has marr'd his fortune.
Men. His nature is too noble for the world;
He would not flatter Neptune for his trident,
Or Jove for 's power to thunder. His heart's his mouth;
What his breast forges, that his tongue must vent,
And, being angry, does forget that ever
He heard the name of death. *A noise within.*
Here's goodly work!
[*A*] *Patrician.* I would they were a-bed!
Men. I would they were in Tiber! What the vengeance,
Could he not speak 'em fair?
Enter Brutus *and* Sicinius *with the rabble again.*
Sic. Where is this viper
That would depopulate the city and
Be every man himself?
Men. You worthy tribunes—
Sic. He shall be thrown down the Tarpeian rock
With rigorous hands. He hath resisted law,
And therefore law shall scorn him further trial
Than the severity of the public power,
Which he so sets at nought.
1. Cit. He shall well know
The noble tribunes are the people's mouths,
And we their hands.

205. distinctly ranges: extends in orderly ranks.
207. stand to: maintain stoutly.
209. Upon . . . o': as spokesmen for. **in:** by.
211. present: immediate.
212. rock Tarpeian: precipice on the Capitoline Hill from which offenders against the state were hurled to their deaths at the order of the tribunes. **220. helps:** remedies.
230. naught: lost, ruined. **232. put:** driven.

234. cause: case. **235. tent:** probe, cure.
241. One . . . another: i.e. we shall have a good time to make up for this bad one. **243. Take up:** take on, cope with.
245–46. manhood . . . fabric: valor becomes folly when it opposes a collapsing building. **247. tag:** rabble.
248. interrupted waters: waters that have burst their banks. **o'erbear:** overwhelm. **249. bear:** endure, submit to.
250. request: demand.
262. speak 'em fair: speak courteously to them.

All [Plebeians]. He shall, sure on't.
Men. Sir, sir—
Sic. Peace!
Men. Do not cry havoc where you should but hunt
With modest warrant.
Sic. Sir, how comes't that you
Have holp to make this rescue?
Men. Hear me speak!
As I do know the consul's worthiness,
So can I name his faults.
Sic. Consul? what consul?
Men. The consul Coriolanus.
Bru. He consul!
All [Plebeians]. No, no, no, no, no.
Men. If, by the tribunes' leave, and yours, good people,
I may be heard, I would crave a word or two,
The which shall turn you to no further harm
Than so much loss of time.
Sic. Speak briefly then,
For we are peremptory to dispatch
This viperous traitor. To eject him hence
Were but one danger, and to keep him here
Our certain death; therefore it is decreed
He dies to-night.
Men. Now the good gods forbid
That our renowned Rome, whose gratitude
Towards her deserved children is enroll'd
In Jove's own book, like an unnatural dam
Should now eat up her own!
Sic. He's a disease that must be cut away.
Men. O, he's a limb that has but a disease:
Mortal, to cut it off; to cure it, easy.
What has he done to Rome that's worthy death?
Killing our enemies, the blood he hath lost
(Which, I dare vouch, is more than that he hath
By many an ounce) he dropp'd it for his country;
And what is left, to lose it by his country
Were to us all that do't and suffer it
A brand to th' end a' th' world.
Sic. This is clean kam.
Bru. Merely awry. When he did love his country,
It honor'd him.
Men. The service of the foot,
Being once gangren'd, is not then respected
For what before it was.
Bru. We'll hear no more.
Pursue him to his house and pluck him thence,
Lest his infection, being of catching nature,
Spread further.
Men. One word more, one word:
This tiger-footed rage, when it shall find
The harm of unscann'd swiftness, will (too late)
Tie leaden pounds to 's heels. Proceed by process,
Lest parties (as he is belov'd) break out,
And sack great Rome with Romans.
Bru. If it were so—
Sic. What do ye talk?
Have we not had a taste of his obedience—
Our aediles smote, ourselves resisted? Come.
Men. Consider this: he has been bred i' th' wars
Since 'a could draw a sword, and is ill school'd
In bolted language; meal and bran together
He throws without distinction. Give me leave,
I'll go to him, and undertake to bring him
Where he shall answer, by a lawful form
(In peace), to his utmost peril.
1. Sen. Noble tribunes,
It is the humane way. The other course
Will prove too bloody; and the end of it
Unknown to the beginning.
Sic. Noble Menenius,
Be you then as the people's officer.
Masters, lay down your weapons.
Bru. Go not home.
Sic. Meet on the market-place. We'll attend you there;
Where if you bring not Martius, we'll proceed
In our first way.
Men. I'll bring him to you.
[To the Senators.] Let me desire your company. He must come,
Or what is worst will follow.
[1.] Sen. Pray you let's to him.
Exeunt omnes.

[Scene II]

Enter Coriolanus *with* Nobles.

Cor. Let them pull all about mine ears, present me
Death on the wheel, or at wild horses' heels,
Or pile ten hills on the Tarpeian rock,
That the precipitation might down stretch
Below the beam of sight, yet will I still
Be thus to them.
Noble. You do the nobler.
Cor. I muse my mother
Does not approve me further, who was wont
To call them woollen vassals, things created
To buy and sell with groats, to show bare heads
In congregations, to yawn, be still, and wonder,
When one but of my ordinance stood up
To speak of peace or war.

Enter Volumnia.

I talk of you:
Why did you wish me milder? Would you have me

273. cry havoc: give the signal for general slaughter.
274. modest: moderate.
275. holp: helped. **rescue:** illegal removal of a prisoner from custody. **284. peremptory:** resolved.
285. eject him hence: exile him.
286. one. Most editors emend to *our*. **290. deserved:** deserving.
295. Mortal: certain death. **300. by:** at the hands of.
302. brand: stigma. **clean kam:** completely twisted.
303. Merely: utterly. **311. unscann'd:** unconsidered, thoughtless.
312. pounds: weights. **process:** legal means.

313. parties: factions. **314. with:** by means of.
315. What: why.
320. bolted: sifted, refined. **meal and bran:** flour and husks.
324. to . . . peril: at risk of the severest penalty.

III.ii. Location: Rome. The house of Coriolanus.
4. precipitation: steepness. **5. beam:** range. **7. muse:** marvel.
9. woollen vassals: coarsely clad slaves.
10. groats: small coins worth fourpence.
11. congregations: assemblies of people. **yawn:** gape (with awe).
12. ordinance: rank.

False to my nature? Rather say, I play
The man I am.
Vol. O, sir, sir, sir,
I would have had you put your power well on
Before you had worn it out.
Cor. Let go.
Vol. You might have been enough the man you are,
With striving less to be so. Lesser had been
The [thwartings] of your dispositions, if
You had not show'd them how ye were dispos'd
Ere they lack'd power to cross you.
Cor. Let them hang!
Vol. Ay, and burn too.

Enter MENENIUS *with the* SENATORS.

Men. Come, come, you have been too rough, something too rough;
You must return and mend it.
[*1.*] *Sen.* There's no remedy,
Unless, by not so doing, our good city
Cleave in the midst and perish.
Vol. Pray be counsell'd.
I have a heart as little apt as yours,
But yet a brain that leads my use of anger
To better vantage.
Men. Well said, noble woman!
Before he should thus stoop to th' [herd], but that
The violent fit a' th' time craves it as physic
For the whole state, I would put mine armor on,
Which I can scarcely bear.
Cor. What must I do?
Men. Return to th' tribunes.
Cor. Well, what then? what then?
Men. Repent what you have spoke.
Cor. For them? I cannot do it to the gods,
Must I then do't to them?
Vol. You are too absolute,
Though therein you can never be too noble,
But when extremities speak. I have heard you say
Honor and policy, like unsever'd friends,
I' th' war do grow together; grant that, and tell me
In peace what each of them by th' other lose
That they combine not there.
Cor. Tush, tush!
Men. A good demand.
Vol. If it be honor in your wars to seem
The same you are not, which, for your best ends,
You adopt your policy, how is it less or worse
That it shall hold companionship in peace
With honor, as in war, since that to both
It stands in like request?
Cor. Why force you this?
Vol. Because that now it lies you on to speak

18. **Let go:** enough of that.
23. **Ere . . . power:** until it was beyond their power. **cross:** thwart.
26. **no remedy:** no help for it.
28. **Cleave . . . midst:** split down the middle. 29. **apt:** docile.
33. **craves . . . physic:** demands it as medicine.
35. **bear:** bear the weight of, move in.
42. **policy:** shrewd management. **unsever'd:** inseparable.
48. **adopt:** adopt as.
51. **It . . . request:** it is equally necessary. **force:** urge.
52. **lies you on:** is incumbent on you.

To th' people; not by your own instruction,
Nor by th' matter which your heart prompts you,
But with such words that are but roted in
Your tongue, though but bastards, and syllables
Of no allowance, to your bosom's truth.
Now, this no more dishonors you at all
Than to take in a town with gentle words,
Which else would put you to your fortune and
The hazard of much blood.
I would dissemble with my nature where
My fortunes and my friends at stake requir'd
I should do so in honor. I am in this
Your wife, your son, these senators, the nobles;
And you will rather show our general louts
How you can frown, than spend a fawn upon 'em
For the inheritance of their loves and safeguard
Of what that want might ruin.
Men. Noble lady!
—Come go with us, speak fair. You may salve so,
Not what is dangerous present, but the loss
Of what is past.
Vol. I prithee now, my son,
Go to them, with this bonnet in thy hand,
And thus far having stretch'd it (here be with them),
Thy knee bussing the stones (for in such business
Action is eloquence, and the eyes of th' ignorant
More learned than the ears), waving thy head,
Which often thus correcting thy stout heart,
Now humble as the ripest mulberry
That will not hold the handling: or say to them,
Thou art their soldier, and, being bred in broils,
Hast not the soft way which, thou dost confess,
Were fit for thee to use as they to claim,
In asking their good loves, but thou wilt frame
Thyself, forsooth, hereafter theirs, so far
As thou hast power and person.
Men. This but done,
Even as she speaks, why, their hearts were yours;
For they have pardons, being ask'd, as free
As words to little purpose.
Vol. Prithee now,
Go, and be rul'd; although I know thou hadst rather
Follow thine enemy in a fiery gulf
Than flatter him in a bower.

Enter COMINIUS.

Here is Cominius.
Com. I have been i' th' market-place; and, sir, 'tis fit

53. **own instruction:** self-direction.
55. **roted:** learned by rote, memorized.
57. **Of . . . to:** unacknowledged by. 59. **take in:** capture.
60. **put . . . fortune:** force you to take your chances (in battle).
64. **in honor:** in compliance with the demands of honor. **am in this:** speak in this for. 68. **inheritance:** possession.
69. **that want:** i.e. lack of their loves.
70. **salve:** remedy. 71. **Not:** not only.
74. **here . . . them:** go about it in this fashion.
75. **bussing:** kissing. 77. **waving:** continually bowing.
78. **correcting:** chastening. **stout:** proud.
79. **humble:** abase, let droop. 80. **hold:** bear.
83. **they:** for them. 85. **theirs:** as they would like.
85–86. **so . . . person:** so far as in you lies. 87. **Even:** exactly.
88. **as free:** i.e. which they will bestow as liberally. 91. **in:** into.
92. **bower:** arbor.

You make strong party, or defend yourself
By calmness or by absence. All's in anger.
Men. Only fair speech.
Com. I think 'twill serve, if he
Can thereto frame his spirit.
Vol. He must, and will.
Prithee now say you will, and go about it.
Cor. Must I go show them my unbarb'd sconce? Must I
With my base tongue give to my noble heart
A lie that it must bear? Well, I will do't;
Yet, were there but this single plot to lose,
This mould of Martius, they to dust should grind it
And throw't against the wind. To th' market-place!
You have put me now to such a part which never
I shall discharge to th' life.
Com. Come, come, we'll prompt you.
Vol. I prithee now, sweet son, as thou hast said
My praises made thee first a soldier, so,
To have my praise for this, perform a part
Thou hast not done before.
Cor. Well, I must do't.
Away, my disposition, and possess me
Some harlot's spirit! My throat of war be turn'd,
Which quier'd with my drum, into a pipe
Small as an eunuch, or the virgin voice
That babies lull asleep! The smiles of knaves
Tent in my cheeks, and schoolboys' tears take up
The glasses of my sight! A beggar's tongue
Make motion through my lips, and my arm'd knees,
Who bow'd but in my stirrup, bend like his
That hath receiv'd an alms! I will not do't,
Lest I surcease to honor mine own truth,
And by my body's action teach my mind
A most inherent baseness.
Vol. At thy choice then.
To beg of thee, it is my more dishonor
Than thou of them. Come all to ruin, let
Thy mother rather feel thy pride than fear
Thy dangerous stoutness; for I mock at death
With as big heart as thou. Do as thou list;
Thy valiantness was mine, thou suck'st it from me;
But owe thy pride thyself.
Cor. Pray be content.
Mother, I am going to the market-place;
Chide me no more. I'll mountebank their loves,

94. make strong party: hold up your side well.
99. unbarb'd: unprotected, bare (*barb* = protective covering for a war-horse). **sconce:** head (jocose).
102. this single plot: only this piece of earth, i.e. only myself.
103. mould: (1) bodily form; (2) earth.
105–6. part . . . discharge: role . . . act (hence *prompt* in line 107 and *perform a part* in line 109).
106. to th' life: realistically, convincingly.
112. harlot's: knave's. **throat of war:** martial voice.
113. quier'd: choired, made harmonious music. **pipe:** piping voice.
114. Small: thin and high-pitched.
115. babies lull: lulls dolls.
116. Tent: encamp. **take up:** take over, occupy (military term, as in "occupied territory"). **117. The glasses . . . sight:** my eyes.
121. surcease: cease. **123. inherent:** inhering, ineradicable.
126–27. feel . . . stoutness: suffer the consequences of your stubborn pride than fear its dangers.
128. big heart: great courage. **list:** please. **130. owe:** own.
132. mountebank: win by clever talk (like an itinerant quack cajoling his hearers into buying his remedies).

Cog their hearts from them, and come home belov'd
Of all the trades in Rome. Look, I am going.
Commend me to my wife. I'll return consul,
Or never trust to what my tongue can do
I' th' way of flattery further.
Vol. Do your will. *Exit Volumnia.*
Com. Away, the tribunes do attend you. Arm yourself
To answer mildly; for they are prepar'd
With accusations, as I hear, more strong
Than are upon you yet.
Cor. The word is "mildly." Pray you let us go.
Let them accuse me by invention; I
Will answer in mine honor.
Men. Ay, but mildly.
Cor. Well, mildly be it then. Mildly! *Exeunt.*

[Scene III]

Enter Sicinius *and* Brutus.

Bru. In this point charge him home, that he affects
Tyrannical power. If he evade us there,
Enforce him with his envy to the people,
And that the spoil got on the Antiates
Was ne'er distributed.

Enter an Aedile.

What, will he come?
Aed. He's coming.
Bru. How accompanied?
Aed. With old Menenius and those senators
That always favor'd him.
Sic. Have you a catalogue
Of all the voices that we have procur'd,
Set down by th' pole?
Aed. I have; 'tis ready.
Sic. Have you collected them by tribes?
Aed. I have.
Sic. Assemble presently the people hither;
And when they hear me say, "It shall be so
I' th' right and strength a' th' commons," be it either
For death, for fine, or banishment, then let them,
If I say fine, cry "Fine!"; if death, cry "Death!";
Insisting on the old prerogative
And power i' th' truth a' th' cause.
Aed. I shall inform them.
Bru. And when such time they have begun to cry,
Let them not cease, but with a din confus'd
Enforce the present execution
Of what we chance to sentence.
Aed. Very well.

133. Cog: beguile. **135. Commend me:** give my love.
138. Arm: prepare. **142. word:** watchword.
143. accuse . . . invention: invent charges against me.
144. in: consistently with.

III.iii. Location: Rome. The Forum.
1. charge him home: press your charge against him to the limit. **affects:** desires, aims at.
3. Enforce . . . to: charge him strenuously with ill-will toward.
4. got on: wrested from.
10. by th' pole: by the poll (head), individually.
12. presently: at once. **18. truth:** justice. **cause:** case.

Sic. Make them be strong, and ready for this hint
When we shall hap to give't them.
Bru. Go about it. [*Exit Aedile.*]
Put him to choler straight, he hath been us'd
Ever to conquer, and to have his worth
Of contradiction. Being once chaf'd, he cannot
Be rein'd again to temperance; then he speaks
What's in his heart, and that is there which looks
With us to break his neck.

Enter CORIOLANUS, MENENIUS, *and* COMINIUS, *with others* [SENATORS *and* PATRICIANS].

Sic. Well, here he comes.
Men. Calmly, I do beseech you.
Cor. Ay, as an hostler, that [for th'] poorest piece
Will bear the knave by th' volume. Th' honor'd gods
Keep Rome in safety, and the chairs of justice
Supplied with worthy men! plant love among 's!
[Throng] our large temples with the shows of peace,
And not our streets with war!
1. Sen. Amen, amen.
Men. A noble wish.

Enter the AEDILE *with the* PLEBEIANS.

Sic. Draw near, ye people.
Aed. List to your tribunes. Audience! peace, I say!
Cor. First hear me speak.
Both Tri. Well, say. Peace ho!
Cor. Shall I be charg'd no further than this present?
Must all determine here?
Sic. I do demand
If you submit you to the people's voices,
Allow their officers, and are content
To suffer lawful censure for such faults
As shall be prov'd upon you.
Cor. I am content.
Men. Lo, citizens, he says he is content.
The warlike service he has done, consider; think
Upon the wounds his body bears, which show
Like graves i' th' holy churchyard.
Cor. Scratches with briers,
Scars to move laughter only.
Men. Consider further:
That when he speaks not like a citizen,
You find him like a soldier; do not take
His rougher [accents] for malicious sounds,
But as I say, such as become a soldier
Rather than envy you.
Com. Well, well, no more.
Cor. What is the matter
That being pass'd for consul with full voice,
I am so dishonor'd that the very hour
You take it off again?
Sic. Answer to us.
Cor. Say then; 'tis true, I ought so.
Sic. We charge you, that you have contriv'd to take
From Rome all season'd office, and to wind
Yourself into a power tyrannical,
For which you are a traitor to the people.
Cor. How? traitor?
Men. Nay, temperately; your promise.
Cor. The fires i' th' lowest hell fold in the people!
Call me their traitor, thou injurious tribune!
Within thine eyes sate twenty thousand deaths,
In thy hands clutch'd as many millions, in
Thy lying tongue both numbers, I would say
"Thou liest" unto thee with a voice as free
As I do pray the gods.
Sic. Mark you this, people?
All [*Plebeians*]. To th' rock, to th' rock with him!
Sic. Peace!
We need not put new matter to his charge.
What you have seen him do, and heard him speak,
Beating your officers, cursing yourselves,
Opposing laws with strokes, and here defying
Those whose great power must try him—even this
So criminal, and in such capital kind,
Deserves th' extremest death.
Bru. But since he hath
Serv'd well for Rome—
Cor. What do you prate of service?
Bru. I talk of that, that know it.
Cor. You?
Men. Is this the promise that you made your mother?
Com. Know, I pray you—
Cor. I'll know no further.
Let them pronounce the steep Tarpeian death,
Vagabond exile, fleaing, pent to linger
But with a grain a day, I would not buy
Their mercy at the price of one fair word,
Nor check my courage for what they can give,
To have't with saying "Good morrow."
Sic. For that he has
(As much as in him lies) from time to time
Envied against the people, seeking means
To pluck away their power, as now at last
Given hostile strokes, and that not in the presence
Of dreaded justice, but on the ministers
That doth distribute it—in the name a' th' people,
And in the power of us the tribunes, we,
Even from this instant, banish him our city,
In peril of precipitation
From off the rock Tarpeian, never more
To enter our Rome gates. I' th' people's name,
I say it shall be so.
All [*Plebeians*]. It shall be so, it shall be so. Let him away!
He's banish'd, and it shall be so.

26. **worth**: pennyworth, i.e. full share.
27. **contradiction**: answering back.
29. **looks**: promises, seems likely.
30. **With us**: in our estimation. 32. **piece**: coin.
33. **bear the knave**: tolerate being called a knave. **by th' volume**: enough times to fill a book.
43. **determine**: be brought to a conclusion. **demand**: ask.
45. **Allow**: acknowledge the authority of.
57. **envy you**: show malice toward you. 58. **matter**: cause.
59. **with full voice**: unanimously.
63. **contriv'd**: plotted. 64. **season'd**: established.
69. **their traitor**: a traitor to them. **injurious**: insulting.
70. **Within**: i.e. if within. **sate**: sat.
73. **free**: unrestrained.
89. **fleaing**: flaying. **pent**: imprisoned. 92. **courage**: spirit.
95. **Envied**: shown malice. 97. **not**: not merely.

Com. Hear me, my masters, and my common friends—
Sic. He's sentenc'd; no more hearing.
Com. Let me speak.
I have been consul, and can show [for] Rome
Her enemies' marks upon me. I do love
My country's good with a respect more tender,
More holy and profound, than mine own life,
My dear wive's estimate, her womb's increase
And treasure of my loins; then if I would
Speak that—
Sic. We know your drift. Speak what?
Bru. There's no more to be said, but he is banish'd
As enemy to the people and his country.
It shall be so.
All [Plebeians]. It shall be so, it shall be so. 119
Cor. You common cry of curs, whose breath I hate
As reek a' th' rotten fens, whose loves I prize
As the dead carcasses of unburied men
That do corrupt my air—I banish you!
And here remain with your uncertainty!
Let every feeble rumor shake your hearts!
Your enemies, with nodding of their plumes,
Fan you into despair! Have the power still
To banish your defenders, till at length
Your ignorance (which finds not till it feels,
Making but reservation of yourselves,
Still your own foes) deliver you as most
Abated captives to some nation
That won you without blows! Despising,
For you, the city, thus I turn my back;
There is a world elsewhere.
Exeunt Coriolanus, Cominius, cum aliis [Menenius, Senators, and Patricians].
Aed. The people's enemy is gone, is gone!
All [Plebeians]. Our enemy is banish'd, he is gone! Hoo! hoo!
They all shout and throw up their caps.
Sic. Go see him out at gates, and follow him,
As he hath follow'd you, with all despite;
Give him deserv'd vexation. Let a guard
Attend us through the city.
All [Plebeians]. Come, come, let's see him out at gates, come.
The gods preserve our noble tribunes! Come.
Exeunt.

ACT IV, [Scene I]

Enter Coriolanus, Volumnia, Virgilia, Menenius, Cominius, *with the young* Nobility *of Rome.*

Cor. Come leave your tears: a brief farewell. The beast
With many heads butts me away. Nay, mother,

Where is your ancient courage? You were us'd
To say extremities was the trier of spirits,
That common chances common men could bear,
That when the sea was calm all boats alike
Show'd mastership in floating; fortune's blows
When most strook home, being gentle wounded craves
A noble cunning. You were us'd to load me
With precepts that would make invincible
The heart that conn'd them.
Vir. O heavens! O heavens!
Cor. Nay, I prithee, woman—
Vol. Now the red pestilence strike all trades in Rome,
And occupations perish!
Cor. What, what, what!
I shall be lov'd when I am lack'd. Nay, mother,
Resume that spirit when you were wont to say,
If you had been the wife of Hercules,
Six of his labors you'ld have done, and sav'd
Your husband so much sweat. Cominius,
Droop not, adieu. Farewell, my wife, my mother,
I'll do well yet. Thou old and true Menenius,
Thy tears are salter than a younger man's,
And venomous to thine eyes. My sometime general,
I have seen thee stern, and thou hast oft beheld
Heart-hard'ning spectacles; tell these sad women
'Tis fond to wail inevitable strokes,
As 'tis to laugh at 'em. My mother, you wot well
My hazards still have been your solace, and
Believe't not lightly—though I go alone,
Like to a lonely dragon, that his fen
Makes fear'd and talk'd of more than seen—your son
Will or exceed the common or be caught
With cautelous baits and practice.
Vol. My first son,
Whither [wilt] thou go? Take good Cominius
With thee a while. Determine on some course
More than a wild exposture to each chance
That starts i' th' way before thee.
Cor. O the gods!
Com. I'll follow thee a month, devise with thee
Where thou shalt rest, that thou mayst hear of us
And we of thee; so if the time thrust forth
A cause for thy repeal, we shall not send
O'er the vast world to seek a single man,
And lose advantage, which doth ever cool
I' th' absence of the needer.
Cor. Fare ye well!
Thou hast years upon thee, and thou art too full
Of the wars' surfeits to go rove with one
That's yet unbruis'd. Bring me but out at gate.
Come, my sweet wife, my dearest mother, and
My friends of noble touch; when I am forth,
Bid me farewell, and smile. I pray you come.

112. respect: regard. **114. wive's estimate:** wife's reputation. **120. cry:** pack. **121. reek:** unwholesome vapor, miasma. **124. uncertainty:** insecurity (since they banish their defender). **127. still:** ever, continually. **129. finds:** learns. **feels:** suffers. **130. Making . . . yourselves:** excepting only yourselves (from banishment). **132. Abated:** humiliated. **134. For you:** on your account. **135 s.d. cum aliis:** with others.

IV.i. Location: Rome. Before a gate of the city.

3. ancient: former.
7–9. fortune's . . . cunning: i.e. to bear like a gentleman the severest blows of fortune requires a very high order of accomplishment.
26. fond: foolish. **27. wot:** know.
33. cautelous: crafty. **practice:** treachery.
36. exposture: exposure. **37. starts:** springs up.
38. follow: accompany. **41. repeal:** recall.
43. advantage: the opportune moment.
44. the needer: the man who needs to seize the opportunity.
49. noble touch: proved nobleness.

While I remain above the ground, you shall
Hear from me still, and never of me aught
But what is like me formerly.
Men. That's worthily
As any ear can hear. Come, let's not weep.
If I could shake off but one seven years
From these old arms and legs, by the good gods
I'ld with thee every foot.
Cor. Give me thy hand.
Come. *Exeunt.*

[SCENE II]

Enter the two Tribunes, SICINIUS *and* BRUTUS, *with the* AEDILE.

Sic. Bid them all home, he's gone; and we'll no further.
The nobility are vexed, whom we see have sided
In his behalf.
Bru. Now we have shown our power,
Let us seem humbler after it is done
Than when it was a-doing.
Sic. Bid them home.
Say their great enemy is gone, and they
Stand in their ancient strength.
Bru. Dismiss them home. [*Exit Aedile.*]
Here comes his mother.

Enter VOLUMNIA, VIRGILIA, *and* MENENIUS.

Sic. Let's not meet her.
Bru. Why?
Sic. They say she's mad.
Bru. They have ta'en note of us; keep on your way.
Vol. O, y' are well met. The hoarded plague a' th' gods
Requite your love!
Men. Peace, peace, be not so loud.
Vol. If that I could for weeping, you should hear—
Nay, and you shall hear some. [*To Brutus.*] Will you be gone?
Vir. [*To Sicinius.*] You shall stay too. I would I had the power
To say so to my husband.
Sic. Are you mankind?
Vol. Ay, fool, is that a shame? Note but this fool.
Was not a man my father? Hadst thou foxship
To banish him that strook more blows for Rome
Than thou hast spoken words?
Sic. O blessed heavens!
Vol. Moe noble blows than ever thou wise words,
And for Rome's good. I'll tell thee what—yet go!
Nay, but thou shalt stay too. I would my son
Were in Arabia, and thy tribe before him,
His good sword in his hand.
Sic. What then?
Vir. What then?
He'ld make an end of thy posterity.
Vol. Bastards and all!
Good man, the wounds that he does bear for Rome!
Men. Come, come, peace.
Sic. I would he had continued to his country
As he began, and not unknit himself
The noble knot he made.
Bru. I would he had.
Vol. "I would he had"? 'Twas you incens'd the rabble;
Cats, that can judge as fitly of his worth
As I can of those mysteries which heaven
Will not have earth to know.
Bru. Pray let's go.
Vol. Now pray, sir, get you gone;
You have done a brave deed. Ere you go, hear this:
As far as doth the Capitol exceed
The meanest house in Rome, so far my son,
This lady's husband here—this (do you see?)
Whom you have banish'd—does exceed you all.
Bru. Well, well, we'll leave you.
Sic. Why stay we to be baited
With one that wants her wits? *Exeunt Tribunes.*
Vol. Take my prayers with you.
I would the gods had nothing else to do
But to confirm my curses! Could I meet 'em
But once a day, it would unclog my heart
Of what lies heavy to't.
Men. You have told them home,
And, by my troth, you have cause. You'll sup with me?
Vol. Anger's my meat; I sup upon myself,
And so shall starve with feeding. Come, let's go.
[*To Virgilia.*] Leave this faint puling, and lament as I do,
In anger, Juno-like. Come, come, come.
Exeunt [*Volumnia and Virgilia*].
Men. Fie, fie, fie! *Exit.*

[SCENE III]

Enter a ROMAN *and a* VOLSCE, [*meeting*].

Rom. I know you well, sir, and you know me. Your name, I think, is Adrian.

Vols. It is so, sir. Truly, I have forgot you.

Rom. I am a Roman, and my services are, as you are, against 'em. Know you me yet?

Vols. Nicanor? no.

Rom. The same, sir.

Vols. You had more beard when I last saw you, but your favor is well appear'd by your tongue. What's the news in Rome? I have a note from the Volscian state to find you out there. You have well sav'd me a day's journey.

Rom. There hath been in Rome strange insurrections; the people against the senators, patricians, and nobles.

IV.ii. Location: Rome. A street near the gate.
16. mankind: masculine (since you rail in so unfeminine a manner). Volumnia takes it in the sense "human."
18. foxship: low cunning (more appropriate to a fox than to "mankind").
24. in Arabia: i.e. in some desert spot where no one would intervene.

47. unclog: disburden.
IV.iii. Location: A highway between Rome and Antium.
4–5. my . . . 'em: i.e. he is working for the Volsces.
9. your . . . appear'd: your face is manifested, i.e. your identity is proved. **10. a note:** instructions.

Vols. Hath been! is it ended then? Our state thinks not so; they are in a most warlike preparation, and hope to come upon them in the heat of their division.

Rom. The main blaze of it is past, but a small thing would make it flame again; for the nobles receive so to heart the banishment of that worthy Coriolanus, that they are in a ripe aptness to take all power from the people, and to pluck from them their tribunes for ever. This lies glowing, I can tell you, and is almost mature for the violent breaking out.

Vols. Coriolanus banish'd?

Rom. Banish'd, sir.

Vols. You will be welcome with this intelligence, Nicanor.

Rom. The day serves well for them now. I have heard it said, the fittest time to corrupt a man's wife is when she's fall'n out with her husband. Your noble Tullus Aufidius [will] appear well in these wars, his great opposer Coriolanus being now in no request of his country.

Vols. He cannot choose. I am most fortunate thus accidentally to encounter you. You have ended my business, and I will merrily accompany you home.

Rom. I shall, between this and supper, tell you most strange things from Rome, all tending to the good of their adversaries. Have you an army ready, say you?

Vols. A most royal one: the centurions and their charges, distinctly billeted, already in th' entertainment, and to be on foot at an hour's warning.

Rom. I am joyful to hear of their readiness, and am the man, I think, that shall set them in present action. So, sir, heartily well met, and most glad of your company.

Vols. You take my part from me, sir, I have the most cause to be glad of yours.

Rom. Well, let us go together. *Exeunt.*

[Scene IV]

Enter Coriolanus *in mean apparel, disguis'd and muffled.*

Cor. A goodly city is this Antium. City,
'Tis I that made thy widows; many an heir
Of these fair edifices 'fore my wars
Have I heard groan and drop. Then know me not,
Lest that thy wives with spits and boys with stones
In puny battle slay me.

Enter a Citizen.

'Save you, sir.

Cit. And you.

Cor. Direct me, if it be your will,
Where great Aufidius lies. Is he in Antium?

Cit. He is, and feasts the nobles of the state

25. **glowing:** smouldering.
37. **choose:** do otherwise (than appear well).
43. **centurions:** commanders of units of a hundred men.
44. **distinctly billeted:** separately enrolled.
44–45. **in th' entertainment:** mobilized. 47. **present:** immediate.

IV.iv. **Location:** Antium. Before the house of Aufidius.
3. **'fore my wars:** in the face of my onslaughts.
6. **'Save:** God save. 8. **lies:** lives.

At his house this night.

Cor. Which is his house, beseech you?

Cit. This here before you.

Cor. Thank you, sir, farewell.
Exit Citizen.
O world, thy slippery turns! Friends now fast sworn,
Whose double bosoms seems to wear one heart,
Whose hours, whose bed, whose meal and exercise
Are still together, who twin, as 'twere, in love
Unseparable, shall within this hour,
On a dissension of a doit, break out
To bitterest enmity; so, fellest foes,
Whose passions and whose plots have broke their sleep
To take the one the other, by some chance,
Some trick not worth an egg, shall grow dear friends
And interjoin their issues. So with me,
My birthplace [hate] I, and my love's upon
This enemy town. I'll enter. If he slay me,
He does fair justice; if he give me way,
I'll do his country service. *Exit.*

[Scene V]

Music plays. Enter a Servingman.

1. Serv. Wine, wine, wine! What service is here? I think our fellows are asleep. [*Exit.*]

Enter another Servingman.

2. Serv. Where's Cotus? my master calls for him. Cotus! *Exit.*

Enter Coriolanus.

Cor. A goodly house! The feast smells well, but I
Appear not like a guest.

Enter the First Servingman.

1. Serv. What would you have, friend? whence are you? Here's no place for you; pray go to the door. *Exit.*

Cor. I have deserv'd no better entertainment
In being Coriolanus.

Enter Second Servant.

2. Serv. Whence are you, sir? Has the porter his eyes in his head, that he gives entrance to such companions? Pray get you out.

Cor. Away!

2. Serv. Away? Get you away.

Cor. Now th' art troublesome.

2. Serv. Are you so brave? I'll have you talk'd with anon.

Enter Third Servingman; *the* First, [*entering,*] *meets him.*

12. **slippery turns:** fickle changes. 15. **still:** always.
17. **On . . . doit:** falling into disagreement over a trifle (*doit* = a very small coin). 18. **fellest:** fiercest. 21. **trick:** trifling matter.
22. **interjoin their issues:** make common cause (?) or intermarry their children (?). 25. **give me way:** yield to my request.

IV.v. **Location:** Antium. The house of Aufidius.
2. **fellows:** fellow servants. 9. **entertainment:** reception.
12–13. **companions:** low fellows. 17. **brave:** saucy.

3. Serv. What fellow's this?

1. Serv. A strange one as ever I look'd on. I cannot get him out o' th' house. Prithee call my master to him.

3. Serv. What have you to do here, fellow? Pray you avoid the house.

Cor. Let me but stand, I will not hurt your hearth.

3. Serv. What are you?

Cor. A gentleman.

3. Serv. A marv'llous poor one.

Cor. True, so I am.

3. Serv. Pray you, poor gentleman, take up some other station; here's no place for you. Pray you avoid. Come.

Cor. Follow your function, go, and batten on cold bits. *Pushes him away from him.*

3. Serv. What, you will not? Prithee tell my master what a strange guest he has here.

2. Serv. And I shall. *Exit Second Servingman.*

3. Serv. Where dwell'st thou?

Cor. Under the canopy.

3. Serv. Under the canopy?

Cor. Ay.

3. Serv. Where's that?

Cor. I' th' city of kites and crows.

3. Serv. I' th' city of kites and crows? What an ass it is! Then thou dwell'st with daws too?

Cor. No, I serve not thy master.

3. Serv. How, sir? do you meddle with my master?

Cor. Ay, 'tis an honester service than to meddle with thy mistress. Thou prat'st, and prat'st; serve with thy trencher. Hence!

Beats him away. [*Exit Third Servingman.*]

Enter Aufidius *with the* [Second] Servingman.

Auf. Where is this fellow?

2. Serv. Here, sir. I'd have beaten him like a dog, but for disturbing the lords within.

[*First and Second Servingmen stand aside.*]

Auf. Whence com'st thou? What wouldst thou?
Thy name?
Why speak'st not? Speak, man: what's thy name?

Cor. [*Unmuffling.*] If, Tullus,
Not yet thou know'st me, and, seeing me, dost not
Think me for the man I am, necessity
Commands me name myself.

Auf. What is thy name?

Cor. A name unmusical to the Volscians' ears,
And harsh in sound to thine.

Auf. Say, what's thy name?
Thou hast a grim appearance, and thy face
Bears a command in't; though thy tackle's torn,
Thou show'st a noble vessel. What's thy name?

Cor. Prepare thy brow to frown. Know'st thou me
yet?

Auf. I know thee not. Thy name?

Cor. My name is Caius Martius, who hath done
To thee particularly, and to all the Volsces,

Great hurt and mischief; thereto witness may
My surname, Coriolanus. The painful service,
The extreme dangers, and the drops of blood
Shed for my thankless country are requited
But with that surname—a good memory
And witness of the malice and displeasure
Which thou shouldst bear me. Only that name remains;
The cruelty and envy of the people,
Permitted by our dastard nobles, who
Have all forsook me, hath devour'd the rest,
And suffer'd me by th' voice of slaves to be
Hoop'd out of Rome. Now this extremity
Hath brought me to thy hearth; not out of hope
(Mistake me not) to save my life, for if
I had fear'd death, of all the men i' th' world
I would have 'voided thee; but in mere spite,
To be full quit of those my banishers,
Stand I before thee here. Then if thou hast
A heart of wreak in thee, that wilt revenge
Thine own particular wrongs, and stop those maims
Of shame seen through thy country, speed thee straight
And make my misery serve thy turn. So use it
That my revengeful services may prove
As benefits to thee; for I will fight
Against my cank'red country with the spleen
Of all the under fiends. But if so be
Thou dar'st not this, and that to prove more fortunes
Th' art tir'd, then, in a word, I also am
Longer to live most weary, and present
My throat to thee and to thy ancient malice;
Which not to cut would show thee but a fool,
Since I have ever followed thee with hate,
Drawn tuns of blood out of thy country's breast,
And cannot live but to thy shame, unless
It be to do thee service.

Auf. O Martius, Martius!
Each word thou hast spoke hath weeded from my heart
A root of ancient envy. If Jupiter
Should from yond cloud speak divine things,
And say "'Tis true," I'd not believe them more
Than thee, all-noble Martius. Let me twine
Mine arms about that body, where against
My grained ash an hundred times hath broke,
And scarr'd the moon with splinters. Here I cleep
The anvil of my sword, and do contest
As hotly and as nobly with thy love
As ever in ambitious strength I did
Contend against thy valor. Know thou first,
I lov'd the maid I married; never man
Sigh'd truer breath; but that I see thee here,
Thou noble thing, more dances my rapt heart

23. **avoid:** leave.
32. **Follow your function:** go about your business. **batten:** grow fat.
38. **canopy:** i.e. sky. 42. **kites and crows:** i.e. birds of prey.
44. **daws:** jackdaws (foolish birds). 49. **trencher:** wooden platter.
61. **a command:** authority. 62. **Thou show'st:** you appear to be.
66. **particularly:** personally (so also *particular* = personal in line 86).

68. **painful:** laborious. 71. **memory:** reminder.
78. **Hoop'd:** whooped, shouted. 82. **mere spite:** pure hatred.
83. **be . . . of:** settle in full my account with.
85. **wreak:** vengeance.
86–87. **maims Of shame:** shameful injuries.
91. **cank'red:** ulcerous. **spleen:** rage. 92. **under:** i.e. of hell.
93. **dar'st.** Schmidt gives examples of *dare* "passing . . . into the sense of *will*," and possibly that is the sense here. **prove:** try.
96. **ancient malice:** long-standing enmity.
108. **grained ash:** spear. 109. **cleep:** clip, embrace.
110. **anvil . . . sword:** i.e. the body of Coriolanus, on which his sword has been sharpened.
116. **dances . . . heart:** makes my heart leap with rapture.

Than when I first my wedded mistress saw
Bestride my threshold. Why, thou Mars, I tell thee,
We have a power on foot; and I had purpose
Once more to hew thy target from thy brawn,
Or lose mine arm for't. Thou hast beat me out
Twelve several times, and I have nightly since
Dreamt of encounters 'twixt thyself and me;
We have been down together in my sleep,
Unbuckling helms, fisting each other's throat,
And wak'd half dead with nothing. Worthy Martius,
Had we no other quarrel else to Rome but that
Thou art thence banish'd, we would muster all
From twelve to seventy, and pouring war
Into the bowels of ungrateful Rome,
Like a bold flood o'er-beat. O, come, go in,
And take our friendly senators by th' hands,
Who now are here, taking their leaves of me,
Who am prepar'd against your territories,
Though not for Rome itself.

Cor. You bless me, gods!

Auf. Therefore, most absolute sir, if thou wilt have
The leading of thine own revenges, take
Th' one half of my commission, and set down—
As best thou art experienc'd, since thou know'st
Thy country's strength and weakness—thine own ways:
Whether to knock against the gates of Rome,
Or rudely visit them in parts remote,
To fright them, ere destroy. But come in,
Let me commend thee first to those that shall
Say yea to thy desires. A thousand welcomes!
And more a friend than e'er an enemy;
Yet, Martius, that was much. Your hand; most welcome!

Exeunt [Coriolanus and Aufidius]. The First and Second Servingmen [come forward].

1. Serv. Here's a strange alteration!

2. Serv. By my hand, I had thought to have strooken him with a cudgel, and yet my mind gave me his clothes made a false report of him.

1. Serv. What an arm he has! he turn'd me about with his finger and his thumb as one would set up a top.

2. Serv. Nay, I knew by his face that there was something in him. He had, sir, a kind of face, methought—I cannot tell how to term it.

1. Serv. He had so, looking as it were—Would I were hang'd but I thought there was more in him than I could think.

2. Serv. So did I, I'll be sworn. He is simply the rarest man i' th' world.

1. Serv. I think he is; but a greater soldier than he, you wot one.

2. Serv. Who, my master?

1. Serv. Nay, it's no matter for that.

2. Serv. Worth six on him.

1. Serv. Nay, not so neither; but I take him to be the greater soldier.

2. Serv. Faith, look you, one cannot tell how to say that. For the defense of a town, our general is excellent.

1. Serv. Ay, and for an assault too.

Enter the THIRD SERVINGMAN.

3. Serv. O slaves, I can tell you news—news, you rascals!

Both [*1.*, *2. Serv.*]. What, what, what? Let's partake.

3. Serv. I would not be a Roman, of all nations; I had as live be a condemn'd man.

Both [*1.*, *2. Serv.*]. Wherefore? wherefore?

3. Serv. Why, here's he that was wont to thwack our general, Caius Martius.

1. Serv. Why do you say "thwack our general"?

3. Serv. I do not say "thwack our general," but he was always good enough for him.

2. Serv. Come, we are fellows and friends: he was ever too hard for him; I have heard him say so himself.

1. Serv. He was too hard for him, directly to say the troth on't, before Corioles; he scotch'd him and notch'd him like a carbinado.

2. Serv. And he had been cannibally given, he might have boil'd and eaten him too.

1. Serv. But more of thy news.

3. Serv. Why, he is so made on here within as if he were son and heir to Mars; set at upper end o' th' table; no question ask'd him by any of the senators but they stand bald before him. Our general himself makes a mistress of him, sanctifies himself with 's hand, and turns up the white o' th' eye to his discourse. But the bottom of the news is, our general is cut i' th' middle, and but one half of what he was yesterday; for the other has half by the entreaty and grant of the whole table. He'll go, he says, and sowl the porter of Rome gates by th' ears. He will mow all down before him, and leave his passage poll'd.

2. Serv. And he's as like to do't as any man I can imagine.

3. Serv. Do't? he will do't; for look you, sir, he has as many friends as enemies; which friends, sir, as it were, durst not (look you, sir) show themselves (as we term it) his friends whilest he's in directitude.

1. Serv. Directitude? What's that?

3. Serv. But when they shall see, sir, his crest up again and the man in blood, they will out of their burrows, like conies after rain, and revel all with him.

1. Serv. But when goes this forward?

3. Serv. To-morrow, to-day, presently; you shall have the drum strook up this afternoon. 'Tis, as it

120. target: shield. **brawn:** brawny arm.
131. o'er-beat: beat (all) down.
134. am prepar'd: have a force ready. **136. absolute:** perfect.
138. my commission: the forces under my command. **set down:** determine. **144. commend:** present.
150. gave: told. **153. set up:** spin.
158. but I thought: if I didn't think.
162–63. a greater . . . one: you know one soldier greater than he (i.e. Aufidius). For *he, you wot one* most editors read *he you wot on,* which reverses the sense: Coriolanus is a greater soldier than you know who (Aufidius).

165. it's . . . that: never mind about names.
176. as live: as lief, as soon. **186. scotch'd:** slashed.
187. carbinado: carbonado, meat sliced and scored for broiling.
188. And: if. **191. so made on:** made so much of.
194. bald: bareheaded.
195. sanctifies . . . hand: touches his hand as if it conveyed a blessing.
197. bottom: final item. **200. sowl:** drag, yank.
202. poll'd: shorn, cleared.
208. directitude: blunder for *discredit* or some such word.
211. in blood: in full vigor. **212. conies:** rabbits.
214. presently: right now.

were, a parcel of their feast, and to be executed ere they wipe their lips.

2. Serv. Why then we shall have a stirring world again. This peace is nothing but to rust iron, increase tailors, and breed ballad-makers.

1. Serv. Let me have war, say I, it exceeds peace as far as day does night; it's sprightly, [waking], audible, and full of vent. Peace is a very apoplexy, lethargy, mull'd, deaf, [sleepy], insensible, a getter of more bastard children than war's a destroyer of men.

2. Serv. 'Tis so, and as wars, in some sort, may be said to be a ravisher, so it cannot be denied but peace is a great maker of cuckolds.

1. Serv. Ay, and it makes men hate one another.

3. Serv. Reason: because they then less need one another. The wars for my money! I hope to see Romans as cheap as Volscians.—They are rising, they are rising.

Both [1., 2. Serv.]. In, in, in, in! *Exeunt.*

[SCENE VI]

Enter the two Tribunes, SICINIUS *and* BRUTUS.

Sic. We hear not of him, neither need we fear him;
His remedies are tame—the present peace
And quietness of the people, which before
Were in wild hurry. Here do we make his friends
Blush that the world goes well, who rather had,
Though they themselves did suffer by't, behold
Dissentious numbers pest'ring streets, than see
Our tradesmen singing in their shops, and going
About their functions friendly.

Enter MENENIUS.

Bru. We stood to't in good time. Is this Menenius?
Sic. 'Tis he, 'tis he. O, he is grown most kind of late.
Hail, sir!
Men. Hail to you both!
Sic. Your Coriolanus
Is not much miss'd but with his friends;
The commonwealth doth stand, and so would do,
Were he more angry at it.
Men. All's well; and might have been much better, if
He could have temporiz'd.
Sic. Where is he, hear you?
Men. Nay, I hear nothing; his mother and his wife
Hear nothing from him.

Enter three or four CITIZENS.

All [Citizens]. The gods preserve you both!

Sic. Good-en, our neighbors.
Bru. Good-en to you all, good-en to you all.
1. Cit. Ourselves, our wives, and children, on our knees,
Are bound to pray for you both.
Sic. Live, and thrive!
Bru. Farewell, kind neighbors! We wish'd Coriolanus
Had lov'd you as we did.
All [Citizens]. Now the gods keep you!
Both Tri. Farewell, farewell. *Exeunt Citizens.*
Sic. This is a happier and more comely time
Than when these fellows ran about the streets,
Crying confusion.
Bru. Caius Martius was
A worthy officer i' th' war, but insolent,
O'ercome with pride, ambitious past all thinking,
Self-loving—
Sic. And affecting one sole throne,
Without assistance.
Men. I think not so.
Sic. We should by this, to all our lamentation,
If he had gone forth consul, found it so.
Bru. The gods have well prevented it, and Rome
Sits safe and still without him.

Enter an AEDILE.

Aed. Worthy tribunes,
There is a slave, whom we have put in prison,
Reports the Volsces with two several powers
Are ent'red in the Roman territories,
And with the deepest malice of the war
Destroy what lies before 'em.
Men. 'Tis Aufidius,
Who, hearing of our Martius' banishment,
Thrusts forth his horns again into the world,
Which were inshell'd when Martius stood for Rome,
And durst not once peep out.
Sic. Come, what talk you
Of Martius?
Bru. Go see this rumorer whipt. It cannot be
The Volsces dare break with us.
Men. Cannot be?
We have record that very well it can,
And three examples of the like hath been
Within my age. But reason with the fellow,
Before you punish him, where he heard this,
Lest you shall chance to whip your information,
And beat the messenger who bids beware
Of what is to be dreaded.
Sic. Tell not me!
I know this cannot be.
Bru. Not possible.

Enter a MESSENGER.

Mess. The nobles in great earnestness are going

216. **parcel:** integral part. 222. **waking:** i.e. alert.
223. **audible:** sharp-eared. **full of vent:** bursting with vitality. **apoplexy:** paralysis.
224. **lethargy:** torpor. **mull'd:** stupefied. **getter:** begetter.
233. **rising:** getting up from the table.

IV.vi. Location: Rome. A public place.
2. **remedies:** means of redress. 4. **hurry:** commotion.
7. **pest'ring:** blocking. 10. **stood to't:** took a firm stand.

20. **Good-en:** good evening.
32. **affecting . . . throne:** desiring to rule alone.
33. **assistance:** associates.
39. **several powers:** separate armies.
44–45. **horns . . . inshell'd.** The figure is of a snail.
45. **stood:** fought. 52. **reason:** talk.
54. **your information:** i.e. one who informs you truly.

All to the Senate-house; some news is coming
That turns their countenances.
Sic. 'Tis this slave—
Go whip him 'fore the people's eyes—his raising,
Nothing but his report.
Mess. Yes, worthy sir,
The slave's report is seconded, and more,
More fearful, is deliver'd.
Sic. What more fearful?
Mess. It is spoke freely out of many mouths—
How probable I do not know—that Martius,
Join'd with Aufidius, leads a power 'gainst Rome,
And vows revenge as spacious as between
The young'st and oldest thing.
Sic. This is most likely!
Bru. Rais'd only that the weaker sort may wish
Good Martius home again.
Sic. The very trick on't.
Men. This is unlikely: he and Aufidius can
No more atone than violent'st contrariety.

Enter [another] MESSENGER.

[2.] *Mess.* You are sent for to the Senate.
A fearful army, led by Caius Martius
Associated with Aufidius, rages
Upon our territories, and have already
O'erborne their way, consum'd with fire, and took
What lay before them.

Enter COMINIUS.

Com. O, you have made good work!
Men. What news? what news?
Com. You have holp to ravish your own daughters, and
To melt the city leads upon your pates,
To see your wives dishonor'd to your noses—
Men. What's the news? what's the news?
Com. Your temples burned in their cement, and
Your franchises, whereon you stood, confin'd
Into an auger's bore.
Men. Pray now, your news?—
You have made fair work, I fear me.—Pray, your news?
If Martius should be join'd [wi' th'] Volscians—
Com. If?
He is their god; he leads them like a thing
Made by some other deity than Nature,
That shapes man better; and they follow him
Against us brats with no less confidence
Than boys pursuing summer butterflies,
Or butchers killing flies.
Men. You have made good work,
You and your apron-men; you that stood so much

Upon the voice of occupation and
The breath of garlic-eaters!
Com. He'll shake
Your Rome about your ears.
Men. As Hercules
Did shake down mellow fruit. You have made fair work!
Bru. But is this true, sir?
Com. Ay, and you'll look pale
Before you find it other. All the regions
Do smilingly revolt, and who resists
Are mock'd for valiant ignorance,
And perish constant fools. Who is't can blame him?
Your enemies and his find something in him.
Men. We are all undone, unless
The noble man have mercy.
Com. Who shall ask it?
The tribunes cannot do't for shame; the people
Deserve such pity of him as the wolf
Does of the shepherds. For his best friends, if they
Should say, "Be good to Rome," they charg'd him even
As those should do that had deserv'd his hate,
And therein show'd like enemies.
Men. 'Tis true;
If he were putting to my house the brand
That should consume it, I have not the face
To say, "Beseech you cease." You have made fair hands,
You and your crafts! You have crafted fair!
Com. You have brought
A trembling upon Rome, such as was never
S' incapable of help.
[*Both*] *Tri.* Say not we brought it.
Men. How? Was't we? We lov'd him, but like beasts
And cowardly nobles gave way unto your clusters,
Who did hoot him out o' th' city.
Com. But I fear
They'll roar him in again. Tullus Aufidius,
The second name of men, obeys his points
As if he were his officer. Desperation
Is all the policy, strength, and defense
That Rome can make against them.

Enter a troop of CITIZENS.

Men. Here come the clusters.
And is Aufidius with him? You are they
That made the air unwholesome, when you cast
Your stinking greasy caps in hooting at
Coriolanus' exile. Now he's coming,
And not a hair upon a soldier's head
Which will not prove a whip. As many coxcombs
As you threw caps up will he tumble down,
And pay you for your voices. 'Tis no matter;
If he could burn us all into one coal,

59. coming: in process of coming in. **60. turns:** alters.
61. raising: invention, fabrication (cf. *Rais'd* in line 70).
64. deliver'd: reported.
68. as . . . between: so comprehensive as to include.
73. atone: be reconciled.
78. O'erborne their way: surged over everything in their way.
82. leads: lead roofs.
85. burned . . . cement: i.e. burned to the ground.
86. franchises: political rights. **stood:** insisted.
86–87. confin'd . . . bore: shrunk until they could be accommodated in the smallest aperture (literally, in a hole drilled by an auger).
93. brats: insignificant creatures. **96. apron-men:** artisans.

97. occupation: workingmen. **105. constant:** loyal.
112. charg'd: would be urging. **114. show'd:** would look.
117. made fair hands: done a fine job.
118. crafts: (1) artisans; (2) stratagems. **crafted:** (1) wrought; (2) intrigued.
120. S': so. **help:** remedy. **122. clusters:** mobs.
125. second . . . men: man second in renown. **points:** directions.
134. coxcombs: fools' heads.

We have deserv'd it.
Omnes [*Citizens*]. Faith, we hear fearful news.
1. Cit. For mine own part,
When I said banish him, I said 'twas pity.
2. Cit. And so did I.
3. Cit. And so did I; and, to say the truth, so did very many of us. That we did, we did for the best, and though we willingly consented to his banishment, yet it was against our will.
Com. Y' are goodly things, you voices!
Men. You have made
Good work, you and your cry! Shall 's to the Capitol?
Com. O ay, what else?
Exeunt both [*Cominius and Menenius*].
Sic. Go, masters, get you home, be not dismay'd.
These are a side that would be glad to have
This true which they so seem to fear. Go home,
And show no sign of fear.
1. Cit. The gods be good to us! Come, masters, let's home. I ever said we were i' th' wrong when we banish'd him.
2. Cit. So did we all. But come, let's home.
Exeunt Citizens.
Bru. I do not like this news.
Sic. Nor I.
Bru. Let's to the Capitol. Would half my wealth
Would buy this for a lie!
Sic. Pray let's go. *Exeunt Tribunes.*

[Scene VII]

Enter Aufidius *with his* Lieutenant.

Auf. Do they still fly to th' Roman?
Lieu. I do not know what witchcraft's in him, but
Your soldiers use him as the grace 'fore meat,
Their talk at table, and their thanks at end;
And you are dark'ned in this action, sir,
Even by your own.
Auf. I cannot help it now,
Unless by using means I lame the foot
Of our design. He bears himself more proudlier,
Even to my person, than I thought he would
When first I did embrace him; yet his nature
In that's no changeling, and I must excuse
What cannot be amended.
Lieu. Yet I wish, sir
(I mean for your particular), you had not
Join'd in commission with him; but either
Have borne the action of yourself, or else
To him had left it soly.
Auf. I understand thee well, and be thou sure,
When he shall come to his account, he knows not
What I can urge against him. Although it seems,
And so he thinks, and is no less apparent
To th' vulgar eye, that he bears all things fairly,
And shows good husbandry for the Volscian state,
Fights dragon-like, and does achieve as soon
As draw his sword; yet he hath left undone
That which shall break his neck, or hazard mine,
When e'er we come to our account.
Lieu. Sir, I beseech you, think you he'll carry Rome?
Auf. All places yields to him ere he sits down,
And the nobility of Rome are his.
The senators and patricians love him too;
The tribunes are no soldiers, and their people
Will be as rash in the repeal, as hasty
To expel him thence. I think he'll be to Rome
As is the aspray to the fish, who takes it
By sovereignty of nature. First he was
A noble servant to them, but he could not
Carry his honors even. Whether ['twas] pride,
Which out of daily fortune ever taints
The happy man; whether [defect] of judgment,
To fail in the disposing of those chances
Which he was lord of; or whether nature,
Not to be other than one thing, not moving
From th' casque to th' cushion, but commanding peace
Even with the same austerity and garb
As he controll'd the war; but one of these
(As he hath spices of them all, not all,
For I dare so far free him) made him fear'd,
So hated, and so banish'd; but he has a merit
To choke it in the utt'rance. So our [virtues]
Lie in th' interpretation of the time,
And power, unto itself most commendable,
Hath not a tomb so evident as a chair
T' extol what it hath done.
One fire drives out one fire; one nail, one nail;
Rights by rights fouler, strengths by strengths do fail.
Come, let's away. When, Caius, Rome is thine,
Thou art poor'st of all; then shortly art thou mine.
Exeunt.

ACT V, [Scene I]

Enter Menenius, Cominius, Sicinius [*and*] Brutus, *the two Tribunes, with others.*

143. **That:** what. 147. **cry:** pack. 150. **side:** faction.
IV.vii. Location: A camp near Rome.
5. **dark'ned:** put in the shade, eclipsed. **action:** campaign.
6. **your own:** i.e. your own act in receiving Coriolanus (?) or your own men (?).
13. **for your particular:** with respect to your own interest.
14. **commission:** command. 16. **soly:** solely.

21. **bears:** conducts, executes. 22. **husbandry:** management.
27. **carry:** conquer. 28. **sits down:** lays siege.
32. **rash . . . repeal:** impetuous in recalling him.
34. **aspray:** osprey, fish hawk (to which fish were said to surrender themselves without attempting to escape).
35. **sovereignty of nature:** natural supremacy.
37. **Carry . . . even:** bear the weight of his honors without losing his balance. 38. **daily fortune:** continuous success.
39. **happy:** lucky.
41. **nature:** i.e. his temperament (which did not allow him to behave differently in war and peace).
43. **casque:** military helmet. **cushion:** seat in the Senate.
44. **austerity and garb:** stern demeanor.
46. **spices:** tastes, tinctures. **not all:** not all in full measure.
47. **so . . . him:** absolve him to that extent.
48. **So . . . so:** because feared . . . because hated.
49. **it:** i.e. the sentence of banishment (?) or the recital of his faults (?).
51–53. **power . . . done:** honorable achievement, despite the value it has in itself, derives less from its own completed purposes than from what is said of it by those who commend it publicly.
55. **by rights:** i.e. by other rights. **fouler:** i.e. become fouler, are made to seem less fair. Most editors emend to *falter* (Dyce) or *founder* (*Malone; Johnson conj.*).

V.i. Location: Rome. A public place.

Men. No, I'll not go. You hear what he hath said
Which was sometime his general, who loved him
In a most dear particular. He call'd me father;
But what o' that? Go you that banish'd him
A mile before his tent, fall down, and knee
The way into his mercy. Nay, if he coy'd
To hear Cominius speak, I'll keep at home.

Com. He would not seem to know me.

Men. Do you hear?

Com. Yet one time he did call me by my name.
I urg'd our old acquaintance, and the drops
That we have bled together. Coriolanus
He would not answer to; forbade all names;
He was a kind of nothing, titleless,
Till he had forg'd himself a name a' th' fire
Of burning Rome.

Men. Why, so; you have made good work!
A pair of tribunes that have wrack'd for Rome
To make coals cheap! A noble memory!

Com. I minded him how royal 'twas to pardon
When it was less expected. He replied,
It was a bare petition of a state
To one whom they had punish'd.

Men. Very well.
Could he say less?

Com. I offered to awaken his regard
For 's private friends. His answer to me was,
He could not stay to pick them in a pile
Of noisome musty chaff. He said 'twas folly,
For one poor grain or two, to leave unburnt
And still to nose th' offense.

Men. For one poor grain or two?
I am one of those; his mother, wife, his child,
And this brave fellow too: we are the grains,
You are the musty chaff, and you are smelt
Above the moon. We must be burnt for you.

Sic. Nay, pray be patient. If you refuse your aid
In this so never-needed help, yet do not
Upbraid 's with our distress. But sure if you
Would be your country's pleader, your good tongue,
More than the instant army we can make,
Might stop our countryman.

Men. No; I'll not meddle.

Sic. Pray you go to him.

Men. What should I do?

Bru. Only make trial what your love can do
For Rome, towards Martius.

Men. Well, and say that Martius
Return me, as Cominius is return'd,
Unheard—what then?
But as a discontented friend, grief-shot
With his unkindness? Say't be so?

Sic. Yet your good will
Must have that thanks from Rome, after the measure
As you intended well.

Men. I'll undertake't.
I think he'll hear me. Yet, to bite his lip
And hum at good Cominius much unhearts me.
He was not taken well, he had not din'd:
The veins unfill'd, our blood is cold, and then
We pout upon the morning, are unapt
To give or to forgive; but when we have stuff'd
These pipes and these conveyances of our blood
With wine and feeding, we have suppler souls
Than in our priest-like fasts: therefore I'll watch him
Till he be dieted to my request,
And then I'll set upon him.

Bru. You know the very road into his kindness,
And cannot lose your way.

Men. Good faith, I'll prove him,
Speed how it will. I shall ere long have knowledge
Of my success. *Exit.*

Com. He'll never hear him.

Sic. Not?

Com. I tell you, he does sit in gold, his eye
Red as 'twould burn Rome; and his injury
The jailer to his pity. I kneel'd before him;
'Twas very faintly he said, "Rise"; dismiss'd me
Thus, with his speechless hand. What he would do
He sent in writing after me; what he would not,
Bound with an oath to yield to his conditions;
So that all hope is vain,
Unless his noble mother and his wife,
Who, as I hear, mean to solicit him
For mercy to his country. Therefore let's hence,
And with our fair entreaties haste them on. *Exeunt.*

[Scene II]

Enter Menenius *to the* Watch *or* Guard.

1. Watch. Stay! Whence are you?

2. Watch. Stand, and go back.

Men. You guard like men, 'tis well. But, by your leave,
I am an officer of state, and come
To speak with Coriolanus.

1. Watch. From whence?

Men. From Rome.

1. Watch. You may not pass, you must return; our general
Will no more hear from thence.

2. Watch. You'll see your Rome embrac'd with fire before
You'll speak with Coriolanus.

Men. Good my friends,

1–3. he . . . He: i.e. Cominius . . . Coriolanus.
3. In . . . particular: with deep personal affection.
5. knee: crawl. **6. coy'd:** disdained.
8. would . . . know: gave no sign of recognizing.
16. wrack'd: racked, striven (?). Some editors emend *wrack'd for* to *wrack'd* (i.e. ruined) *fair*.
20. bare: worthless, paltry. **23. offered:** made an attempt.
25. stay . . . them: take time to search them out.
28. still . . . offense: constantly to smell the offensive matter.
34. so never-needed: never before so sorely needed.
37. instant: raised on the spur of the moment.
44. grief-shot: grief-stricken.

46. after the measure: in proportion.
50. taken well: approached at a favorable time.
57. dieted . . . request: fed, and so in the mood to listen to my request.
60. prove: try. **62. success:** results (whether good or bad).
63. in gold: on a golden throne.
69. Bound: i.e. on condition that we bind ourselves (?).
71. Unless: except for.

V.ii. Location: The Volscian camp before Rome.

If you have heard your general talk of Rome
And of his friends there, it is lots to blanks
My name hath touch'd your ears: it is Menenius.

1. Watch. Be it so, go back. The virtue of your name
Is not here passable.

Men. I tell thee, fellow,
Thy general is my lover. I have been
The book of his good acts, whence men have read
His fame unparallel'd, happily amplified;
For I have ever verified my friends
(Of whom he's chief) with all the size that verity
Would without lapsing suffer. Nay, sometimes,
Like to a bowl upon a subtle ground,
I have tumbled past the throw; and in his praise
Have (almost) stamp'd the leasing. Therefore, fellow,
I must have leave to pass.

1. Watch. Faith, sir, if you had told as many lies in his behalf as you have utter'd words in your own, you should not pass here; no, though it were as virtuous to lie as to live chastely. Therefore go back.

Men. Prithee, fellow, remember my name is Menenius, always factionary on the party of your general.

2. Watch. Howsoever you have been his liar, as you say you have, I am one that, telling true under him, must say you cannot pass. Therefore go back.

Men. Has he din'd, canst thou tell? for I would not speak with him till after dinner.

1. Watch. You are a Roman, are you?

Men. I am, as thy general is.

1. Watch. Then you should hate Rome, as he does. Can you, when you have push'd out your gates the very defender of them, and, in a violent popular ignorance, given your enemy your shield, think to front his revenges with the easy groans of old women, the virginal palms of your daughters, or with the palsied intercession of such a decay'd dotant as you seem to be? Can you think to blow out the intended fire your city is ready to flame in, with such weak breath as this? No, you are deceiv'd; therefore back to Rome, and prepare for your execution. You are condemn'd; our general has sworn you out of reprieve and pardon.

Men. Sirrah, if thy captain knew I were here, he would use me with estimation.

1. Watch. Come, my captain knows you not.

Men. I mean, thy general.

1. Watch. My general cares not for you. Back, I say, go; lest I let forth your half-pint of blood. Back, that's the utmost of your having, back!

Men. Nay, but, fellow, fellow—

Enter CORIOLANUS *with* AUFIDIUS.

Cor. What's the matter?

Men. Now, you companion! I'll say an arrant for you. You shall know now that I am in estimation; you shall perceive that a Jack guardant cannot office me from my son Coriolanus. Guess but [by] my entertainment with him if thou stand'st not i' th' state of hanging, or of some death more long in spectatorship and crueller in suffering; behold now presently, and swound for what's to come upon thee. [*To Coriolanus.*] The glorious gods sit in hourly synod about thy particular prosperity, and love thee no worse than thy old father Menenius does! O my son, my son! thou art preparing fire for us; look thee, here's water to quench it. I was hardly mov'd to come to thee; but being assur'd none but myself could move thee, I have been blown out of your gates with sighs, and conjure thee to pardon Rome and thy petitionary countrymen. The good gods assuage thy wrath, and turn the dregs of it upon this varlet here—this, who like a block hath denied my access to thee.

Cor. Away!

Men. How? away?

Cor. Wife, mother, child I know not. My affairs
Are servanted to others; though I owe
My revenge properly, my remission lies
In Volscian breasts. That we have been familiar,
Ingrate forgetfulness shall poison rather
Than pity note how much. Therefore be gone.
Mine ears against your suits are stronger than
Your gates against my force. Yet, for I loved thee,
Take this along, I writ it for thy sake,
[*Gives a letter.*]
And would have sent it. Another word, Menenius,
I will not hear thee speak. This man, Aufidius,
Was my belov'd in Rome; yet thou behold'st!

Auf. You keep a constant temper.

Exeunt. Manent the Guard and Menenius.

1. Watch. Now, sir, is your name Menenius?

2. Watch. 'Tis a spell, you see, of much power. You know the way home again.

1. Watch. Do you hear how we are shent for keeping your greatness back?

2. Watch. What cause do you think I have to swound?

Men. I neither care for th' world nor your general; for such things as you, I can scarce think there's any, y' are so slight. He that hath a will to die by

10. lots to blanks: winning tickets to non-winning tickets, i.e. absolutely certain. **12. virtue**: power.
13. passable: (1) current (used of valid coinage); (2) able to gain you passage. **14. my lover**: my friend, one well-disposed toward me.
16. happily: haply, perhaps. **17. verified**: testified to the worth of.
18. with . . . size: to the full extent.
20. bowl: ball in the game of bowls. **subtle**: deceptive, full of irregularities to deflect the bowl.
21. tumbled . . . throw: unintentionally overshot the mark.
22. stamp'd the leasing: given the stamp of truth to a lie, i.e. exaggerated his virtues. **24. if**: even if.
27. lie. With sexual quibble, as shown by the contrast with *live chastely*. **29. factionary on**: an adherent to. **39. out**: out at.
40–41. in . . . ignorance: by the stupidity of a violent mob.
42. front: confront, meet.
43. palms: i.e. hands extended in entreaty. **44. dotant**: dotard.
51. Sirrah: term of address to inferiors.
52. use: treat. **estimation**: esteem.

60. companion: base fellow. **say an arrant**: deliver a message.
62. Jack guardant: ill-mannered guard. **office**: officiously keep.
64. entertainment with: reception by. **67. swound**: swoon.
72. hardly: with difficulty.
78. block: (1) blockhead; (2) obstruction.
83. servanted: made subject.
83–84. I . . . properly: my revenge is in my own hands. **remission**: power to pardon. **94. constant temper**: resolute mind.
98. shent: scolded.

himself fears it not from another. Let your general do his worst. For you, be that you are, long; and your misery increase with your age! I say to you, as I was said to, "Away!" *Exit.*

1. Watch. A noble fellow, I warrant him.

2. Watch. The worthy fellow is our general. He's the rock, the oak not to be wind-shaken. *Exit Watch.*

[Scene III]

Enter Coriolanus *and* Aufidius [*with others*].

Cor. We will before the walls of Rome to-morrow
Set down our host. My partner in this action,
You must report to th' Volscian lords, how plainly
I have borne this business.
Auf. Only their ends
You have respected; stopp'd your ears against
The general suit of Rome; never admitted
A private whisper, no, not with such friends
That thought them sure of you.
Cor. This last old man,
Whom with a crack'd heart I have sent to Rome,
Lov'd me above the measure of a father,
Nay, godded me indeed. Their latest refuge
Was to send him; for whose old love I have
(Though I show'd sourly to him) once more offer'd
The first conditions, which they did refuse
And cannot now accept, to grace him only
That thought he could do more: a very little
I have yielded to. Fresh embassies and suits,
Nor from the state nor private friends, hereafter
Will I lend ear to. (*Shout within.*) Ha? what shout is this?
Shall I be tempted to infringe my vow
In the same time 'tis made? I will not.

Enter [*in mourning habits*] Virgilia, Volumnia, Valeria, *young* Martius, *with* Attendants.

My wife comes foremost; then the honor'd mould
Wherein this trunk was fram'd, and in her hand
The grandchild to her blood. But out, affection,
All bond and privilege of nature, break!
Let it be virtuous to be obstinate.
What is that curtsy worth? or those doves' eyes,
Which can make gods forsworn? I melt, and am not
Of stronger earth than others. My mother bows,
As if Olympus to a molehill should
In supplication nod; and my young boy
Hath an aspect of intercession, which
Great Nature cries, "Deny not." Let the Volsces
Plough Rome and harrow Italy, I'll never
Be such a gosling to obey instinct, but stand
As if a man were author of himself,
And knew no other kin.

105. himself: his own hand.
106. be . . . long: i.e. may you have the misfortune of remaining your contemptible selves through a long lifetime.

V.iii. Location: The Volscian camp. The tent of Coriolanus.
3. plainly: openly, honestly. **4. borne:** conducted.
11. godded: idolized. **latest:** last. **13. show'd:** acted.
22–23. mould . . . trunk: (1) form . . . body; (2) earth . . . stem.
32. aspect of intercession: pleading look. **35. to:** as to.

Vir. My lord and husband!
Cor. These eyes are not the same I wore in Rome.
Vir. The sorrow that delivers us thus chang'd
Makes you think so.
Cor. Like a dull actor now
I have forgot my part, and I am out,
Even to a full disgrace. Best of my flesh,
Forgive my tyranny; but do not say
For that, "Forgive our Romans." O, a kiss
Long as my exile, sweet as my revenge!
Now, by the jealous queen of heaven, that kiss
I carried from thee, dear; and my true lip
Hath virgin'd it e'er since. You gods, I [prate],
And the most noble mother of the world
Leave unsaluted. Sink, my knee, i' th' earth; *Kneels.*
Of thy deep duty more impression show
Than that of common sons.
Vol. O, stand up blest!
Whilst with no softer cushion than the flint
I kneel before thee, and unproperly
Show duty as mistaken all this while
Between the child and parent. [*Kneels.*]
Cor. What's this?
Your knees to me? to your corrected son? [*Raises her.*]
Then let the pibbles on the hungry beach
Fillop the stars; then let the mutinous winds
Strike the proud cedars 'gainst the fiery sun,
Murd'ring impossibility, to make
What cannot be, slight work.
Vol. Thou art my warrior,
I [holp] to frame thee. Do you know this lady?
Cor. The noble sister of Publicola,
The moon of Rome, chaste as the icicle
That's curdied by the frost from purest snow
And hangs on Dian's temple—dear Valeria!
Vol. This is a poor epitome of yours,
Which by th' interpretation of full time
May show like all yourself.
Cor. The god of soldiers,
With the consent of supreme Jove, inform
Thy thoughts with nobleness, that thou mayst prove
To shame unvulnerable, and stick i' th' wars
Like a great sea-mark, standing every flaw,
And saving those that eye thee!
Vol. Your knee, sirrah.

39. delivers: presents.
41. out: at a loss for words (like an actor who has "dried up").
43. tyranny: cruelty.
46. jealous . . . heaven: Juno, guardian of marriage.
48. virgin'd it: lived chastely. **51. duty:** filial piety, reverence.
54. unproperly: in a way that has not been characteristic of me.
57. corrected: chastened (by Volumnia's words and act).
58. pibbles: pebbles. **hungry:** barren.
59. Fillop: fillip, strike smartly against.
61. Murd'ring impossibility: i.e. making anything possible.
65. moon. Symbolic of chastity, since the moon-goddess was one aspect of Diana, patroness of virgins.
66. curdied: congealed, frozen.
68. epitome: summary (referring to the young Martius, his father in little).
69. by . . . time: when time has made plain all that it contains.
71. inform: inspire, imbue. **73. stick:** stand out.
74. sea-mark: conspicuous object that guides mariners (cf. *landmark*).
standing: withstanding. **flaw:** squall.
75. saving . . . thee: bringing to safety all who use you as a guide (continuing the figure of the sea-mark).

Cor. That's my brave boy!
Vol. Even he, your wife, this lady, and myself
Are suitors to you.
Cor. I beseech you peace;
Or, if you'd ask, remember this before:
The thing I have forsworn to grant may never
Be held by you denials. Do not bid me
Dismiss my soldiers, or capitulate
Again with Rome's mechanics. Tell me not
Wherein I seem unnatural; desire not
T' allay my rages and revenges with
Your colder reasons.
Vol. O, no more, no more!
You have said you will not grant us any thing;
For we have nothing else to ask but that
Which you deny already. Yet we will ask,
That, if you fail in our request, the blame
May hang upon your hardness, therefore hear us.
Cor. Aufidius, and you Volsces, mark, for we'll
Hear nought from Rome in private. [*Sits.*] Your request?
Vol. Should we be silent and not speak, our raiment
And state of bodies would bewray what life
We have led since thy exile. Think with thyself
How more unfortunate than all living women
Are we come hither; since that thy sight, which should
Make our eyes flow with joy, hearts dance with comforts,
Constrains them weep and shake with fear and sorrow,
Making the mother, wife, and child to see
The son, the husband, and the father tearing
His country's bowels out. And to poor we
Thine enmity's most capital; thou barr'st us
Our prayers to the gods, which is a comfort
That all but we enjoy. For how can we,
Alas! how can we, for our country pray,
Whereto we are bound, together with thy victory,
Whereto we are bound? Alack, or we must lose
The country, our dear nurse, or else thy person,
Our comfort in the country. We must find
An evident calamity, though we had
Our wish, which side should win; for either thou
Must as a foreign recreant be led
With manacles through our streets, or else
Triumphantly tread on thy country's ruin,
And bear the palm for having bravely shed
Thy wife and children's blood. For myself, son,
I purpose not to wait on fortune till
These wars determine. If I cannot persuade thee
Rather to show a noble grace to both parts
Than seek the end of one, thou shalt no sooner
March to assault thy country than to tread
(Trust to't, thou shalt not) on thy mother's womb
That brought thee to this world.
Vir. Ay, and mine,
That brought you forth this boy, to keep your name
Living to time.
Boy. 'A shall not tread on me;
I'll run away till I am bigger, but then I'll fight.
Cor. Not of a woman's tenderness to be,
Requires nor child nor woman's face to see.
I have sate too long. [*Rises.*]
Vol. Nay, go not from us thus.
If it were so that our request did tend
To save the Romans, thereby to destroy
The Volsces whom you serve, you might condemn us,
As poisonous of your honor. No, our suit
Is that you reconcile them: while the Volsces
May say, "This mercy we have show'd," the Romans,
"This we receiv'd"; and each in either side
Give the all-hail to thee, and cry, "Be blest
For making up this peace!" Thou know'st, great son,
The end of war's uncertain; but this certain,
That, if thou conquer Rome, the benefit
Which thou shalt thereby reap is such a name
Whose repetition will be dogg'd with curses;
Whose chronicle thus writ: "The man was noble,
But with his last attempt he wip'd it out,
Destroy'd his country, and his name remains
To th' ensuing age abhorr'd." Speak to me, son.
Thou hast affected the [fine] strains of honor,
To imitate the graces of the gods:
To tear with thunder the wide cheeks a' th' air,
And yet to [charge] thy sulphur with a bolt
That should but rive an oak. Why dost not speak?
Think'st thou it honorable for a noble man
Still to remember wrongs? Daughter, speak you;
He cares not for your weeping. Speak thou, boy;
Perhaps thy childishness will move him more
Than can our reasons. There's no man in the world
More bound to 's mother, yet here he lets me prate
Like one i' th' stocks.—Thou hast never in thy life
Show'd thy dear mother any courtesy,
When she, poor hen, fond of no second brood,
Has cluck'd thee to the wars, and safely home
Loaden with honor. Say my request's unjust,
And spurn me back; but if it be not so,
Thou art not honest, and the gods will plague thee
That thou restrain'st from me the duty which
To a mother's part belongs.—He turns away.
Down, ladies; let us shame him with our knees.
To his surname Coriolanus 'longs more pride
Than pity to our prayers. Down! an end,
This is the last. So, we will home to Rome,
And die among our neighbors.—Nay, behold 's!
This boy, that cannot tell what he would have,
But kneels and holds up hands for fellowship,

80–81. The thing . . . denials: i.e. you must not construe as a denial of your requests my refusal to grant what I have sworn never to grant.
82. capitulate: come to terms. **83. mechanics:** artisans.
90. fail in: refuse. **94. Should we:** even if we should.
95. bewray: reveal. **104. capital:** deadly.
111. find: experience. **112. evident:** certain.
114. recreant: traitor, deserter. **120. determine:** end.
121. grace: indulgence, mercy.
124. Trust . . . not. In sense this parenthesis follows *sooner*, line 122.

131. sate: sat, i.e. listened.
146. attempt: enterprise. **it:** i.e. his nobility.
150. graces: merciful qualities.
152. charge: load. **sulphur:** lightning. **bolt:** thunderbolt (thought to be the destructive agency in thunderstorms).
153. but . . . oak: i.e. do only trifling damage.
155. Still: forever. **156. cares not for:** is unaffected by.
166. honest: honorable. **167. restrain'st:** withholdest.
170. 'longs: belongs. **172. So:** very well; so be it.
174. cannot . . . have: doesn't understand what he is asking for.
175. for fellowship: merely to keep us company.

Does reason our petition with more strength
Than thou hast to deny't.—Come, let us go.
This fellow had a Volscian to his mother;
His wife is in Corioles, and his child
Like him by chance.—Yet give us our dispatch.
I am hush'd until our city be afire,
And then I'll speak a little.

[*Coriolanus*] *holds her by the hand, silent.*

Cor. O mother, mother!
What have you done? Behold, the heavens do ope,
The gods look down, and this unnatural scene
They laugh at. O my mother, mother! O!
You have won a happy victory to Rome;
But, for your son, believe it—O, believe it—
Most dangerously you have with him prevail'd,
If not most mortal to him. But let it come.
Aufidius, though I cannot make true wars,
I'll frame convenient peace. Now, good Aufidius,
Were you in my stead, would you have heard
A mother less? or granted less, Aufidius?

Auf. I was mov'd withal.

Cor. I dare be sworn you were;
And, sir, it is no little thing to make
Mine eyes to sweat compassion. But, good sir,
What peace you'll make, advise me. For my part,
I'll not to Rome, I'll back with you, and pray you
Stand to me in this cause.—O mother! wife!

Auf. [*Aside.*] I am glad thou hast set thy mercy and thy honor
At difference in thee. Out of that I'll work
Myself a former fortune.

Cor. [*To Volumnia, Virgilia, etc.*] Ay, by and by;
But we will drink together; and you shall bear
A better witness back than words, which we,
On like conditions, will have counter-seal'd.
Come enter with us. Ladies, you deserve
To have a temple built you. All the swords
In Italy, and her confederate arms,
Could not have made this peace. *Exeunt.*

[Scene IV]

Enter Menenius *and* Sicinius.

Men. See you yond coign a' th' Capitol, yond cornerstone?

Sic. Why, what of that?

Men. If it be possible for you to displace it with your little finger, there is some hope the ladies of Rome, especially his mother, may prevail with him. But I say there is no hope in't; our throats are sentenc'd, and stay upon execution.

Sic. Is't possible that so short a time can alter the condition of a man?

Men. There is differency between a grub and a butterfly, yet your butterfly was a grub. This Martius is grown from man to dragon: he has wings, he's more than a creeping thing.

Sic. He lov'd his mother dearly.

Men. So did he me; and he no more remembers his mother now than an eight-year-old horse. The tartness of his face sours ripe grapes. When he walks, he moves like an engine, and the ground shrinks before his treading. He is able to pierce a corslet with his eye, talks like a knell, and his hum is a battery. He sits in his state, as a thing made for Alexander. What he bids be done is finish'd with his bidding. He wants nothing of a god but eternity and a heaven to throne in.

Sic. Yes, mercy, if you report him truly.

Men. I paint him in the character. Mark what mercy his mother shall bring from him. There is no more mercy in him than there is milk in a male tiger, that shall our poor city find. And all this is long of you.

Sic. The gods be good unto us!

Men. No, in such a case the gods will not be good unto us. When we banish'd him, we respected not them; and, he returning to break our necks, they respect not us.

Enter a Messenger.

Mess. Sir, if you'd save your life, fly to your house.
The plebeians have got your fellow tribune,
And hale him up and down, all swearing, if
The Roman ladies bring not comfort home,
They'll give him death by inches.

Enter another Messenger.

Sic. What's the news?

[2.] *Mess.* Good news, good news! The ladies have prevail'd,
The Volscians are dislodg'd, and Martius gone.
A merrier day did never yet greet Rome,
No, not th' expulsion of the Tarquins.

Sic. Friend,
Art thou certain this is true? Is't most certain?

[2.] *Mess.* As certain as I know the sun is fire.
Where have you lurk'd, that you make doubt of it?
Ne'er through an arch so hurried the blown tide,
As the recomforted through th' gates. Why, hark you!

Trumpets, hoboys, drums beat, all together.

The trumpets, sackbuts, psalteries, and fifes,
Tabors and cymbals, and the shouting Romans,

176. reason: argue. **178. to:** for.
179. his child: i.e. this boy, supposed his child. Many editors read *this child.*
180. dispatch: dismissal; i.e. you must at least speak to do that.
189. mortal: fatally. **191. convenient:** fitting.
199. Stand to: support.
201–2. work . . . fortune: regain my former standing (as sole commander). **204. A better . . . words:** i.e. a written treaty.
208. her confederate arms: the weapons of her allies.

V.iv. Location: Rome. A street near a gate.
1. coign: corner.

8. stay upon: await. **10. condition:** nature.
19. engine: instrument of war. **20. corslet:** body armor.
21. battery: artillery bombardment.
22. state: chair of state. **as . . . Alexander:** like an image of Alexander the Great.
23. finish'd . . . bidding: accomplished as soon as he speaks.
23–24. wants nothing: lacks no attribute.
25. mercy: i.e. he lacks mercy. **29. long of:** because of.
32. respected: considered, regarded. **41. dislodg'd:** decamped.
47. blown: swollen. **48 s.d. hoboys:** oboes.
49. sackbuts: trombones. **psalteries:** stringed instruments resembling zithers.

Make the sun dance. Hark you! *A shout within.*
Men. This is good news.
I will go meet the ladies. This Volumnia
Is worth of consuls, senators, patricians,
A city full; of tribunes such as you,
A sea and land full. You have pray'd well to-day.
This morning for ten thousand of your throats
I'd not have given a doit. Hark, how they joy!
Sound still with the shouts.
Sic. First, the gods bless you for your tidings; next,
Accept my thankfulness.
[2.] *Mess.* Sir, we have all
Great cause to give great thanks.
Sic. They are near the city?
[2.] *Mess.* Almost at point to enter.
Sic. We'll meet them
And help the joy. *Exeunt.*

[Scene V]

Enter two Senators *with Ladies* [Volumnia, Virgilia, Valeria], *passing over the stage, with other* Lords.

[*1.*] *Sen.* Behold our patroness, the life of Rome!
Call all your tribes together, praise the gods,
And make triumphant fires! Strew flowers before them!
[Unshout] the noise that banish'd Martius!
Repeal him with the welcome of his mother.
Cry, "Welcome, ladies, welcome!"
All. Welcome, ladies,
Welcome!
A flourish with drums and trumpets. [*Exeunt.*]

[Scene VI]

Enter Tullus Aufidius *with* Attendants.

Auf. Go tell the lords a' th' city I am here.
Deliver them this paper. Having read it,
Bid them repair to th' market-place, where I,
Even in theirs and in the commons' ears,
Will vouch the truth of it. Him I accuse
The city ports by this hath enter'd, and
Intends t' appear before the people, hoping
To purge himself with words. Dispatch.
[*Exeunt Attendants.*]

Enter three or four Conspirators *of Aufidius' faction.*

Most welcome!
1. Consp. How is it with our general?
Auf. Even so
As with a man by his own alms empoison'd,
And with his charity slain.
2. Consp. Most noble sir,
If you do hold the same intent wherein
You wish'd us parties, we'll deliver you
Of your great danger.
Auf. Sir, I cannot tell,
We must proceed as we do find the people.
3. Consp. The people will remain uncertain whilst
'Twixt you there's difference; but the fall of either
Makes the survivor heir of all.
Auf. I know it;
And my pretext to strike at him admits
A good construction. I rais'd him, and I pawn'd
Mine honor for his truth; who being so heighten'd,
He watered his new plants with dews of flattery,
Seducing so my friends; and, to this end,
He bow'd his nature, never known before
But to be rough, unswayable, and free.
3. Consp. Sir, his stoutness
When he did stand for consul, which he lost
By lack of stooping—
Auf. That I would have spoke of:
Being banish'd for't, he came unto my hearth,
Presented to my knife his throat. I took him;
Made him joint-servant with me; gave him way
In all his own desires; nay, let him choose
Out of my files, his projects to accomplish,
My best and freshest men; serv'd his designments
In mine own person; holp to reap the fame
Which he did end all his, and took some pride
To do myself this wrong; till at the last
I seem'd his follower, not partner, and
He wag'd me with his countenance as if
I had been mercenary.
1. Consp. So he did, my lord.
The army marvell'd at it, and in the last,
When he had carried Rome and that we look'd
For no less spoil than glory—
Auf. There was it;
For which my sinews shall be stretch'd upon him:
At a few drops of women's rheum, which are
As cheap as lies, he sold the blood and labor
Of our great action; therefore shall he die,
And I'll renew me in his fall. But hark!
Drums and trumpets sounds, with great shouts of the people.
1. Consp. Your native town you enter'd like a post,
And had no welcomes home, but he returns
Splitting the air with noise.
2. Consp. And patient fools,
Whose children he hath slain, their base throats tear
With giving him glory.
3. Consp. Therefore at your vantage,
Ere he express himself or move the people
With what he would say, let him feel your sword,
Which we will second. When he lies along,
After your way his tale pronounc'd shall bury

V.v. Location: Scene continues.
4. Unshout: annul with your shouts.

V.vi. Location: Corioles. A public place.
5. Him: he whom. 11. with: by. 13. parties: allies.

19. pretext to strike: motive for striking.
20. pawn'd: pledged. 25. free: admitting no restraint.
26. stoutness: stubborn pride. 31. joint-servant: partner.
33. files: ranks. 36. end: garner.
39. wag'd . . . countenance: paid me with his favor, patronized me.
41. in the last: finally. 42. carried: (all but) conquered.
44. upon: against. 45. At: for, at the cost of. rheum: tears.
49. post: (mere) messenger.
53. at your vantage: seizing your opportunity.
56. along: prostrate.
57. After . . . pronounc'd: your version of the story.

His reasons with his body.
Auf. Say no more.
Here come the lords.

Enter the Lords *of the city.*

All Lords. You are most welcome home.
Auf. I have not deserv'd it.
But, worthy lords, have you with heed perused
What I have written to you?
All [*Lords.*] We have.
1. Lord. And grieve to hear't.
What faults he made before the last, I think
Might have found easy fines; but there to end
Where he was to begin, and give away
The benefit of our levies, answering us
With our own charge, making a treaty where
There was a yielding—this admits no excuse.
Auf. He approaches, you shall hear him.

Enter Coriolanus *marching with Drum and Colors, the* Commoners *being with him.*

Cor. Hail, lords! I am return'd your soldier;
No more infected with my country's love
Than when I parted hence, but still subsisting
Under your great command. You are to know
That prosperously I have attempted, and
With bloody passage led your wars even to
The gates of Rome. Our spoils we have brought home
Doth more than counterpoise a full third part
The charges of the action. We have made peace
With no less honor to the Antiates
Than shame to th' Romans; and we here deliver,
Subscrib'd by th' consuls and patricians,
Together with the seal a' th' Senate, what
We have compounded on.
Auf. Read it not, noble lords,
But tell the traitor, in the highest degree
He hath abus'd your powers.
Cor. "Traitor"? How now?
Auf. Ay, traitor, Martius!
Cor. "Martius"?
Auf. Ay, Martius, Caius Martius! Dost thou think
I'll grace thee with that robbery, thy stol'n name
Coriolanus, in Corioles?
You lords and heads a' th' state, perfidiously
He has betray'd your business, and given up,
For certain drops of salt, your city Rome,
I say "your city," to his wife and mother,
Breaking his oath and resolution like
A twist of rotten silk, never admitting
Counsel a' th' war; but at his nurse's tears
He whin'd and roar'd away your victory,
That pages blush'd at him, and men of heart
Look'd wond'ring each at others.

Cor. Hear'st thou, Mars?
Auf. Name not the god, thou boy of tears!
Cor. Ha?
Auf. No more.
Cor. Measureless liar, thou hast made my heart
Too great for what contains it. "Boy"? O slave!
Pardon me, lords, 'tis the first time that ever
I was forc'd to scold. Your judgments, my grave lords,
Must give this cur the lie; and his own notion—
Who wears my stripes impress'd upon him, that
Must bear my beating to his grave—shall join
To thrust the lie unto him.
1. Lord. Peace both, and hear me speak.
Cor. Cut me to pieces, Volsces, men and lads,
Stain all your edges on me. "Boy," false hound!
If you have writ your annals true, 'tis there
That, like an eagle in a dove-cote, I
[Flutter'd] your Volscians in Corioles.
Alone I did it. "Boy"!
Auf. Why, noble lords,
Will you be put in mind of his blind fortune,
Which was your shame, by this unholy braggart,
'Fore your own eyes and ears?
All Consp. Let him die for't.
All People. Tear him to pieces! Do it presently!—He kill'd my son!—My daughter!—He kill'd my cousin Marcus!—He kill'd my father!
2. Lord. Peace ho! no outrage, peace!
The man is noble, and his fame folds in
This orb o' th' earth. His last offenses to us
Shall have judicious hearing. Stand, Aufidius,
And trouble not the peace.
Cor. O that I had him,
With six Aufidiuses, or more, his tribe,
To use my lawful sword!
Auf. Insolent villain!
All Consp. Kill, kill, kill, kill, kill him!
Draw the Conspirators, and kills Martius, who falls; Aufidius stands on him.
Lords. Hold, hold, hold, hold!
Auf. My noble masters, hear me speak.
1. Lord. O Tullus!
2. Lord. Thou hast done a deed whereat valor will weep.
3. Lord. Tread not upon him. Masters all, be quiet,
Put up your swords.
Auf. My lords, when you shall know (as in this rage,
Provok'd by him, you cannot) the great danger
Which this man's life did owe you, you'll rejoice
That he is thus cut off. Please it your honors
To call me to your Senate, I'll deliver
Myself your loyal servant, or endure
Your heaviest censure.
1. Lord. Bear from hence his body,

58. His reasons: his own explanations.
63. faults he made: wrongs he committed.
64. easy fines: light penalties.
66–67. answering . . . charge: i.e. leaving us to pay the expenses.
68. yielding: surrender.
77. Doth . . . part: exceed by a full third.
78. action: campaign. **81. Subscrib'd:** signed.
83. compounded: agreed. **98. heart:** spirit.

106. notion: consciousness of the truth. **112. edges:** swords.
113. there: i.e. recorded there.
117. blind fortune: pure good luck.
120. presently: now. **124. folds in:** enwraps, covers.
126. judicious: judicial. **Stand:** hold, stop.
137. did owe: had in store for. **139. deliver:** prove.
141. censure: judgment, sentence.

And mourn you for him. Let him be regarded
As the most noble corse that ever herald
Did follow to his urn.
2. Lord. His own impatience
Takes from Aufidius a great part of blame.
Let's make the best of it.
Auf. My rage is gone,
And I am struck with sorrow. Take him up.
Help, three a' th' chiefest soldiers; I'll be one.
Beat thou the drum, that it speak mournfully;
Trail your steel pikes. Though in this city he
Hath widowed and unchilded many a one,
Which to this hour bewail the injury,
Yet he shall have a noble memory.
Assist.
Exeunt, bearing the body of Martius. A dead march sounded.

148. be one: i.e. make the fourth.

153. memory: memorial.

NOTE ON THE TEXT

The First Folio (1623) is the sole authority for *Coriolanus*; all later editions are derived from that source. Some disagreement persists about the exact nature of the printer's copy behind the F1 text, although there is near consensus that it must have been relatively close to Shakespeare's "foul papers." Nevertheless, Dover Wilson and Brockbank caution that there is insufficient evidence to determine whether the printer's copy was Shakespeare's "foul papers" (Parker) or a scribal transcript of the "foul papers" (Williams, Bowers). Jowett/Taylor also argue for a scribal transcript, but probably of the official prompt-book, not of the "foul papers," a view that approximates that of Greg who says, "There can be no doubt that behind F lies a very carefully prepared author's manuscript," one that "could have been used as a prompt-book," but, he adds, "there is no evidence that it was." Even the two or three notations in the F1 text that suggest the hand of the book-keeper may after all be nothing more than the book-keeper's anticipatory jottings on the "foul papers" in preparation for making the prompt-book.

The stage directions are notably descriptive in terms of stage action; entrances and exits are, as a rule, carefully marked; and there is almost no ambiguity or confusion in the use of speech-prefixes. Apparently, however, the Folio compositors (here both A and B) had difficulty at times in reading Shakespeare's hand, and the F1 text contains an unusually large number of readings requiring emendation. There is also a good deal of mislineation in the verse. Whether this mislineation reflects the state of Shakespeare's manuscript or is the result of compositorial manipulation (sometimes necessitated by the limiting width of the Folio column or the exigencies of cast-off copy) is a matter of debate; probably the compositors may be held responsible for a substantial share of it. A few characteristically Shakespearean spellings have been pointed out: *one* confused with *on*, *shoot* for *shout*, and *Scicinius* for *Sicinius* (see Textual Notes, for example, at I.i.16, 214, II.i.204 s.d., V.v.4).

For further information, see: E. K. Chambers, *William Shakespeare*, 2 vols. (Oxford, 1930); W. W. Greg, *The Shakespeare First Folio* (Oxford, 1955); Fredson Bowers, *On Editing Shakespeare and the Elizabethan Dramatists* (Philadelphia, 1955); Philip Williams, "New Approaches to Textual Problems in Shakespeare," *SB*, VIII (1956) 3–14; J. D. Wilson, ed., New Shakespeare *Coriolanus* (Cambridge, 1960),; Philip Brockbank, ed., New Arden *Coriolanus* (London, 1976); Stanley Wells, Gary Taylor, John Jowett, and William Montgomery, *William Shakespeare: A Textual Companion* (Oxford, 1987); R. B. Parker, ed., New Oxford *Coriolanus* (Oxford, 1994).

TEXTUAL NOTES

Dramatis personae: *subs. as first given in Rowe, with some additions by later editors*
Act-scene division: *F1 marks acts only, except I.i; other scene divisions from Rowe and later editors (see first note to each scene); present act-scene arrangement as a whole first established by Dyce*

I.i

Location: *Pope*
7 **First, you know]** *Cornwall (in Cambridge)*; First you know, *F1*
16 **on]** *F3*; one *F1*
28 **s.p. 1. Cit.]** *Malone conj.*; All. *F1*
35 **s.p. 2. Cit.]** *Malone*; All. *F1*
44 **accusations;]** *Rowe*; Accusations *F1*
56 **matter?]** *Johnson*; matter *F1*
57, 64, etc. **s.pp. 1. Cit.]** *Capell*; 2 Cit. *or* 2 Citizen. *F1*
66 **you. For your wants,]** *Rowe (subs.)*; you for your wants. *F1*
70 **takes,]** *Rowe*; takes: *F1*
79 **indeed!]** *Theobald (subs.)*; indeed, *F1*
92 **stale't]** *Theobald*; scale't *F1*
93–5 **Well . . . deliver.]** *as prose, Capell*; *as verse, F1*
100 **cupboarding]** *Pope (after Rowe)*; cubbording *F1*
103 **And,]** *Malone*; And *F1*
104 **appetite]** *F4 (subs.)*; appetite; *F1*
105 **body.]** *Rowe*; body, *F1*
105 **answer'd—]** *Rowe*; answer'd. *F1*
107 **you.]** *Theobald (subs.)*; you *F1*
110 **tauntingly]** *F4*; taintingly *F1*
114 **answer—what?]** *Theobald (subs.)*; answer: What *F1*
115 **kingly-crowned]** *hyphen, Warburton*
120 **'Fore me]** *Theobald*; Foreme *F1*
126 **awhile,]** *Capell (subs.)*; awhile; *F1*
127 **this,]** *F4*; this *F1*
140–1 **once"— . . . belly,]** *W. A. Wright (in Cambridge)*; once / (You . . . Belly) *F1*
145 **flour]** *Knight*; Flowre *F1*
172 **geese. You are]** *Theobald (subs.)*; Geese you are: *F1*
178 **sick man's]** *F4 (subs.)*; sickmans *F1*
205 **an-hungry]** *hyphen, Capell*
205 **proverbs—]** *Rowe (subs.)*; Prouerbes *F1*
206 **hunger broke]** *F3*; Hunger-broke *F1*
206 **eat,]** *F4*; eate *F1*
208 **rich men]** *F3*; Richmen *F1*
214 **Shouting]** *Pope*; Shooting *F1*
218 **unroof'd]** *Theobald*; vnroo'st *F1*
221 **insurrection's]** *Theobald*; Insurrections *F1*
224, 228 **Volsces]** *Collier (so Plutarch)*; Volcies *and* Volces *F1* (*Volces generally throughout*)
226 **s.d. Junius Brutus, Cominius]** *F4* (Cominius *F2*); Annius Brutus Cominisn *F1* (*sn is a turned us ligature*)
239 **Lartius]** *Rowe*; Lucius *F1*
241, 245 **s.pp. Lart.]** *Neilson*; Tit. *F1*
244, 248 **s.pp. 1. Sen.]** *Rowe*; Sen. *F1*
245, 246 **s.dd. To Cominius., To Martius.]** *Cambridge (after Malone conj.)*
248 **s.d. To the Citizens.]** *Rowe*
251 **s.d. Manent]** *F2*; Manet *F1*
259–63 **Such . . . Cominius.]** *as verse, Pope*; *as prose, F1*

I.ii

I.ii] *Rowe*
Location: *Pope, Capell (subs.)*
o.s.d. Corioles] *Keightley (so Plutarch)*; Coriolus *F1*
4 **on]** *F3*; one *F1*
9 **s.d. Reads.]** *Theobald (subs.)*
9 **press'd]** *Capell*; prest *F1*
27–8 **Corioles. . . . before 's,]** *F4 (subs.)*; Corioles . . . before's: *F1*

I.iii

I.iii] *Rowe*

Location: *Theobald*
8 **kings'**] *Theobald;* Kings *F1*
36 **that's**] *Rowe (after F2 thats);* that *F1*
40 **trophy**] *F2;* Trophe *F1*
43 **sword, contemning. Tell**] *Seymour conj.;* sword. *Contenning,* tell *F1*
59 **h'as**] *F4;* ha's *F1*
71 **No . . . doors.**] *as prose, Pope; as verse, F1*
81 **s.p. Vir.**] *F3;* Vlug. *F1*
84 **Ithaca**] *F3;* Athica *F1*
94 **madam?**] *F3;* Madam. *F1*
96 **Volsces**] *Collier;* Volcies *F1*
104–10 **Let . . . mirth.**] *as prose, Pope; as verse, F1*
104 **lady; . . . now,**] *Pope (after F4);* Ladie, . . . now: *F1*
111 **s.d. with Usher**] *ed.*

I.iv

I.iv] *Rowe*
Location: *Steevens (subs., after Rowe)*
o.s.d., 12 **s.d. Corioles**] *Keightley;* Corialus *F1*
13, 20 **Aufidius**] *F2* (Auffidius); Auffidious *F1*
17 **up;**] *F4;* vp *F1*
19 **s.d. Alarum far off.**] *placed as in Globe; after* off! *l. 19, F1*
19 **off!**] *Dyce;* off *F1*
31 **of—**] *Johnson;* of *F1*
42 **trenches. Follow 's.**] *Collier conj.;* Trenches followes. *F1*
42 **s.d. The Volsces fly,**] *Globe (after Capell)*
42 **s.d. the**] *F3*
42 **s.d. gates.**] *Theobald;* gates, and is shut in. *F1*
45 **s.d. gates**] *F2;* Gati *F1*
46 **s.d. Martius is shut in.**] *Dyce (from F1 s.d. at l. 42)*
48 **s.p. Lart.**] *Rowe;* Tit. *F1*
54 **Martius—**] *Rowe;* Martius, *F1*
55 **entire,**] *F3 (subs.);* intire: *F1*
56 **Were**] *F3;* Weare *F1*
57 **Cato's**] *Theobald (from Plutarch);* Calues *F1*

I.v

I.v] *Capell*
Location: *Capell (subs.)*
7 **them,**] *F4;* them. *F1*
8 **up.**] *Johnson;* vp, *F1*
9 **him!**] *Knight;* him *F1*
10, 19 **Aufidius**] *F2* (Auffidius); Auffidious *F1*
22 **swords! Bold gentleman!**] *Rowe (subs.);* swords, Bold Gentleman: *F1*
25 **Martius!**] *Capell;* Martius, *F1*
25 **s.d. Exit Martius.**] *Capell*

I.vi

I.vi] *Capell*
Location: *Capell (after Pope)*
9 **s.d. Enter a Messenger.**] *placed as in Collier; after l. 9, F1*
24 **Before-time**] *hyphen, Hanmer*
30 **woo'd, in heart**] *Globe (after Theobald);* woo'd in heart; *F1*
43 **plague!—tribunes**] *Johnson (after Rowe);* plague-Tribunes *F1*
46 **tell?**] *F3;* tell, *F1*
53 **Antiates**] *Pope;* Antients *F1*
54, 79 **Aufidius**] *F2* (Auffidius); Auffidious *F1*
59 **Aufidius**] *F2* (Auffidius); Affidius *F1*
59 **Antiates**] *Pope;* Antiats *F1*
60–1 **but, . . . advanc'd**] *Rowe (subs.);* (but . . . aduanc'd) *F1*
70 **Lesser**] *F3;* Lessen *F1*
72 **himself;**] *Johnson;* himselfe, *F1*
73 **alone, or**] *F4* (alone, (or,); alone: Or *F1*
76 **O, me alone!**] *Dyce;* Oh me alone, *F1*

I.vii

I.vii] *Sisson (after Capell)*
Location: *Capell (after Pope)*
o.s.d. **Corioles**] *F2* (Coriolus); Carioles *F1*
4 **holding.**] *F3;* holding, *F1*
7 **s.d. Exeunt.**] *Pope;* Exit *F1*

I.viii

I.viii] *Capell*
Location: *Pelican (after Pope)*
10 **mask'd;**] *Rowe;* maskt, *F1*
15 **s.d. Exeunt.**] *Hanmer*

I.ix

I.ix] *Capell*
Location: *ed. (after Wilson)*
32 **store—of all**] *Capell (subs., after Rowe);* store of all, *F1*
33 **achiev'd**] *F3;* atchieued *F1*
41 **May**] *Capell; Mar.* May *F1 (repeated s.p.)*
47 **more,**] *F4;* more *F1*
50 **shout**] *F4;* shoot *F1 (cf. I.i.214)*
53 **praises sauc'd**] *Hanmer;* prayses, sawc'st *F1*
65, 67 **Martius**] *F3;* Marcus *F1*
68, 79, 82, 90 **s.pp. Cor.**] *Steevens;* Martius. *F1*
74 **Where,**] *F4;* Where *F1*
76 **back.**] *Rowe (subs.);* backe, *F1*
83 **kindly.**] *F3;* kindly, *F1*

I.x

I.x] *Capell*
Location: *Pope*
2, 16, etc. **s.pp. 1. Sold.**] *Capell;* Sould., Sol., *or* Soul. *F1*
15 **sword,**] *Pope;* Sword: *F1*
17 **valor's**] *F3;* valors *F1*
19–20 **itself. . . . sick,**] *Rowe (subs.);* it selfe, . . . sicke; *F1*
30 **cypress**] *Rowe;* Cyprus *F1*
33 **s.d. Exeunt.**] *Rowe*

II.i

II.i] *Rowe;* Actus Secundus. *F1*
Location: *Capell (after Rowe)*
1 **augurer**] *F2;* Agurer *F1*
18 **with all**] *F3;* withall *F1*
23 **right-hand**] *hyphen, Steevens*
24 **how are**] *F2;* ho ware *F1*
25 **now—**] *Capell;* now, *F1*
31 **pleasures; . . . least,**] *Theobald;* pleasures (at the least) *F1*
33 **proud?**] *Capell;* proud. *F1*
51 **upon too**] *Rowe;* vppon, to *F1*
54 **wealsmen**] *F3;* Weales men *F1*
57 **it.**] *F2;* it, *F1*
61 **cannot**] *Capell;* can *F1*
62 **faces.**] *F2 (subs.);* faces, *F1*
64 **beesom**] *F3;* beesome *F1 (eds. read* bisson *after Theobald)*
86 **are. . . . purpose,**] *F4 (subs.);* are, . . . purpose. *F1*
96 **s.d. go**] *Globe; F1 s.d. reads:* Bru. and Scic. Aside.
96 **s.d. Volumnia**] *F2;* Volumina *F1*
105 **s.d. tosses it up**] *Keightley (subs., after Johnson conj.)*
107 **s.pp. Vir., Val.**] *Capell*
111–2 **I . . . me?**] *as prose, Pope; as verse, F1*
122 **'a**] *Theobald;* a *F1*
144 **wounded?**] *Theobald;* wounded, *F1*
144 **s.d. To the Tribunes.**] *Theobald*
156 **s.d. A . . . flourish.**] *placed as in Capell; after* trumpets. *l. 157, F1*
158–9 **These . . . tears:**] *as prose, Pope; as verse, F1*
161 **s.d. Lartius**] *F2;* Latius *F1 (Plutarch uses both forms)*
165 **follows Coriolanus**] *Steevens;* followes Martius Caius Coriolanus *F1*
168–71 **No . . . prosperity!**] *as verse, Pope; as prose, F1*
174 **it?—Coriolanus**] *Johnson;* it (Coriolanus) *F1*
178 **wear**] *F2;* were *F1*
180 **s.p. Cor.**] *Theobald;* Com. *F1*
180 **s.d. To Valeria.**] *Theobald*
186 **You**] *F2;* Yon *F1*
189 **relish**] *F2;* Rallish *F1*
194 **s.d. To . . . Virgilia.**] *Capell (subs.)*
204 **s.d. Brutus . . . forward.**] *Theobald;* Enter Brutus and Scicinius. *F1 (with* Scicin. *or* Scici. *as s.pp. throughout rest of scene and sporadically through III.i.211)*
213 **flamens**] *Hanmer;* Flamins *F1*
220, 249 **human**] *Rowe;* humane *F1*
222–3 **Then . . . sleep.**] *as verse, Pope; as prose, F1*
226 **not**] *Knight;* not, *F1*
234 **napless**] *Rowe;* Naples *F1*
239–41 **I . . . execution.**] *as verse, Pope (after Rowe); as prose, F1*
242–3 **It . . . destruction.**] *as verse, Rowe; as prose, F1*
255–7 **people— . . . sheep—**] *Pope (subs.);* People, . . . Sheepe, *F1*
263 **flung**] *F3;* flong *F1*

II.ii

II.ii] *Capell*
Location: *Pope*
25 **ascent**] *F2;* assent *F1*
48 **s.d. Coriolanus sits.**] *Neilson*
50 **state's**] *F4;* states *F1*
51 **s.d. To the Tribunes.**] *Globe (after Capell)*
52 **after,**] *F3;* after *F1*
54–66 **We . . . speak.**] *as verse, Pope; as prose, F1*
67, 123 **s.pp. 1. Sen.**] *Rowe;* Senat. *F1*
68 **honors'**] *Theobald;* Honors *F1*
78–81 **flatter— . . . it?**] *Capell (subs.);* flatter? . . . one, . . . it. *F1*
81 **one on 's**] *F3;* on ones *F1*
91 **chin**] *F3;* Shinne *F1*
92 **bristled**] *Rowe;* brizled *F1*
108 **took; . . . foot**] *Tyrwhitt conj.;* tooke from face to foot: *F1*
123–4 **He . . . him.**] *as verse, Rowe; as prose, F1*
130 **s.p. 1. Sen.**] *Capell;* Senat. *F1*
132–5 **The . . . people.**] *as verse, Rowe; as prose, F1*
138 **suffrage**] *F4;* sufferage *F1*
147 **thus!**] *Theobald (subs., after F3);* thus *F1*
153 **s.p. Senators.**] *Dyce;* Senat. *F1*
153 **s.d. Manent**] *F4;* Manet *F1*
160 **s.d. Exeunt.**] *Rowe*

II.iii

II.iii] *Capell*
Location: *Theobald*
21 **color'd**] *F3;* Coulord *F1*
41 **all together**] *F3;* altogether *F1*
47 **s.d. Exeunt Citizens.**] *Capell (after Rowe)*
49–50 **say? . . . sir"—**] *Theobald (subs.);* say, . . . Sir? *F1*
67 **not**] *F3;* but *F1*
68 **How,**] *F4;* How *F1*
76 **Kindly,**] *F4;* Kindly *F1*
84 **s.d. Citizens**] *Capell (subs.)*
88, 106 **s.pp. 4. Cit.**] *Globe;* 1. *F1*
91 **s.p. 4. Cit.**] *Cambridge;* 1. *F1*
104 **s.p. 5. Cit.**] *Globe;* 2. *F1*
111 **s.p. Cit.**] *Malone*
111 **s.d. Exeunt Citizens.**] *Rowe (subs.)*
114 **hire**] *F2;* higher *F1*
115 **toge**] *Steevens conj.;* tongue *F1*
116 **appear,**] *F4;* appeere *F1*
117 **vouches?**] *F4;* Vouches: *F1*
118 **wills, . . . things**] *Pope;* wills . . . things, *F1*
118 **do't,**] *Theobald;* doo't? *F1*
132 **s.p. 6. Cit.**] *Globe;* 1. Cit. *F1*
134 **s.p. 7. Cit.**] *Globe;* 2. Cit. *F1*
136 **s.d. Exeunt Citizens.**] *Rowe (subs.)*
165 **s.p. Cit.**] *Singer*
185 **yourselves?**] *Reed;* your selues. *F1*
197 **aught;**] *Rowe (subs.);* ought, *F1*
243 **And . . . surnam'd,**] *Delius (from Plutarch); there is clearly a lacuna in F1*
244 **named so,**] *Steevens* (named *Delius*); nam'd, so *F1*
257 **stay,**] *Capell;* stay *F1*
263 **onward**] *F4;* on-ward *F1*

III.i

III.i] *Rowe;* Actus Tertius. *F1*
Location: *Theobald (subs.)*
o.s.d. **Lartius**] *F2;* Latius *F1 (with* Latius. *as s.p. throughout scene; Plutarch uses both forms)*

31, 63, 75, 197, 232 s.pp. **1. Sen.]** *Capell;* Senat. *or* Sena. *F1*
33 **herd]** *F3;* Heard *F1*
44 **suppliants]** *F4;* Suppliants: *F1*
58 **abus'd, set on.]** *Rowe (subs.);* abus'd: set on, *F1*
71 **plough'd]** *Rowe;* plowed *F1*
89 **minnows]** *Pope;* Minnoues *F1 (in italics)*
91 **good]** *Theobald conj.;* God! *F1*
92 **reakless]** *ed.;* wreaklesse *F1*
95 **monster's]** *Delius;* Monsters *F1*
98 **vail]** *F4;* vale *F1*
117 **disobedience, fed]** *F4 (after F3* disobedience: fed); disobedience: fed, *F1*
126 **Their]** *F3;* There *F1*
131 **bosom multiplied]** *Hanmer;* Bosome-multiplied *F1*
140 **over-measure]** *hyphen, Capell*
141 **human]** *F4;* Humane *F1*
143 **Where one]** *Rowe;* Whereon *F1*
146 **ignorance—]** *Capell;* Ignorance, *F1*
161–2 **H'as . . . H'as]** *F4;* Has . . . Ha's *F1*
166 **bench. . . . rebellion,]** *Pope;* Bench, . . . Rebellion: *F1*
172 **aediles]** *F3;* Ediles *F1 (sporadically throughout)*
172 s.d. **Enter an Aedile.]** *placed as in Globe; after l. 171, F1*
173 s.d. **exit Aedile]** *Collier*
177 s.p. **All Patricians.]** *Kittredge;* All. *F1*
179 **Help,]** *Malone;* Helpe *F1*
183, 192, etc. s.pp. **All Plebeians.]** *Kittredge;* All. *F1*
185 s.p. **All.]** *Globe; F1 apparently continues ll. 185–6 to* 2 Sen. *and assigns only l. 187 to* All.
189 **Confusion's]** *F3;* Confusions *F1*
191 **people, peace!]** *Rowe (subs., after F4);* People peace. *F1*
195–201 **Fie . . . magistrates.]** *as verse, Pope; as prose, F1*
217 s.d. **To Brutus.]** *Globe*
226–7 **Help . . . old!]** *as verse, Capell; as prose, F1*
228 s.d. **and exeunt]** *Sisson; F1 places* Exeunt. *after* him! *l. 228*
229 s.d. **To Coriolanus.]** *Neilson-Hill*
229 **your]** *Rowe;* our *F1*
230 s.p. **Cor.]** *Warburton;* Com. *F1*
236 s.p. **Com.]** *F2;* Corio. *F1*
237 s.p. **Cor.]** *Tyrwhitt conj.;* Mene. *F1*
239 s.p. **Men.]** *Tyrwhitt conj.; lines continued as part of preceding speech, F1*
242–3 **I . . . tribunes.]** *as verse, Capell; as prose, F1*
252 s.d. **with others]** *Capell (subs.)*
253, 260 s.p. **A Patrician.]** *Neilson;* Patri. *F1*
264 **himself?]** *F3;* himself *F1*
269 **nought]** *F4;* naught *F1*
271 **shall,]** *Malone;* shall *F1*
271 **on't]** *Pope;* ont *F1;* out *F2*
274 **comes't]** *Capell;* com'st *F1*
294 **disease:]** *Rowe (subs.);* Disease *F1*
310 **tiger-footed rage]** *Pope;* Tiger-footed-rage *F1*
314 **so—]** *F3;* so? *F1*
317 **smote,]** *F3* (smot,); smot: *F1*
319 **ill school'd]** *Capell;* ill-school'd *F1*
322 **him]** *Pope;* him in peace, *F1*
333 s.d. **To the Senators.]** *Hanmer*
334 s.p. **1. Sen.]** *Rowe;* Sena. *F1*

III.ii

III.ii] *Capell*
Location: *Pope*
9 **woollen]** *Rowe;* Wollen *F1*
13 s.d. **Enter Volumnia.]** *placed as in Collier; after* them. *l. 6, F1*
21 **thwartings]** *Theobald;* things *F1 (Sisson's* taxings *is graphically appealing but does not fit* cross you *in l. 23 so well as Theobald's reading)*
25–6 **Come . . . it.]** *as verse, Pope; as prose, F1*
26 s.p. **1. Sen.]** *Capell;* Sen. *F1*
32 **herd]** *Theobald;* heart *F1*
38 **them?]** *F3;* them, *F1*
55 **roted]** *Malone;* roated *F1*
65 **son, . . . nobles;]** *Warburton conj. (subs.);* Sonne: . . . Nobles, *F1*
69 **lady!]** *Rowe;* Lady, *F1*
85 **theirs, so far]** *Capell;* theirs so farre, *F1*
96–7 **I . . . spirit.]** *as verse, Rowe; as prose, F1*
101 **bear? Well,]** *Pope;* beare well? *F1*
102 **plot to lose,]** *Theobald;* Plot, to loose *F1*
113 **drum, . . . pipe]** *Pope (after Rowe);* Drumme into a Pipe, *F1*

III.iii

III.iii] *Capell*
Location: *Pope*
4 **Antiates]** *Pope;* Antiats *F1*
5 s.d. **Enter an Aedile.]** *placed as in Capell; after l. 5, F1*
24 s.d. **Exit Aedile.]** *Pope*
30 s.d. **Senators and Patricians]** *Capell*
32 **for th']** *F2;* fourth *F1*
35 **among 's!]** *Dyce (after Capell);* amongs *F1*
36 **Throng]** *Theobald;* Through *F1*
47 **you?]** *F4;* you. *F1*
55 **accents]** *Theobald conj.;* Actions *F1*
55 **sounds,]** *Malone;* sounds: *F1*
68 **hell fold]** *F2;* hell. Fould *F1*
70–2 **deaths, . . . numbers,]** *F3 (subs.);* deaths / In thy hands clutcht: as many Millions in / Thy lying tongue, both numbers. *F1*
74 **this,]** *F4;* this *F1*
75, 106, etc. s.pp. **All Plebeians.]** *Kittredge;* All. *F1*
80 **him—even]** *Capell (subs.);* him. / Euen *F1*
99 **it—in]** *Theobald (subs.);* it. In *F1*
110 **for]** *Theobald;* from *F1*
133–4 **blows! Despising . . . city,]** *Capell;* blowes, despising / For you the City. *F1*
135 s.d. **cum aliis]** *F3;* with Cumalijs *F1*
135 s.d. **Menenius . . . Patricians]** *Capell (subs.)*
137 **Hoo! hoo!]** *F3 (subs.);* Hoo, oo. *F1*
137 s.d. **They . . . caps.]** *placed as in Capell; after s.d. at l. 135, F1*
139 **despite;]** *Capell;* despight *F1*

IV.i

IV.i] *Rowe;* Actus Quartus. *F1*
Location: *Theobald (subs.)*
5 **chances]** *F4;* chances. *F1*
23 **sometime]** *Theobald;* (sometime) *F1*
24 **thee]** *F3;* the *F1*
34 **wilt]** *Capell;* will *F1*
35 **a while]** *F2;* awhile *F1*
46 **wars']** *Steevens;* warres *F1*

IV.ii

IV.ii] *Pope*
Location: *Capell (subs.)*
7 s.d. **Exit Aedile.]** *Capell*
12 **Requite]** *F3;* requit *F1*
14 s.d. **To Brutus.]** *Johnson*
15 s.d. **To Sicinius.]** *Johnson*
20 **words?]** *Hanmer;* words. *F1*
21 **words,]** *Rowe;* words. *F1*
22 **good.]** *Capell (after Rowe);* good, *F1*
33 **"I . . . had"?]** *quotes, Staunton*
41 **here—]** *ed.,* heere; *F1*
42 **banish'd—]** *Wilson;* banish'd, *F1*
44 s.d. **Exeunt]** *F4;* Exit *F1*
49 **me?]** *F3;* me. *F1*
50 **Anger's]** *F4;* Angers *F1*
52 s.d. **To Virgilia.]** *Hanmer*
52 **faint puling]** *Rowe;* faint-puling *F1*
53 s.d. **Volumnia and Virgilia]** *Cambridge*

IV.iii

IV.iii] *Pope*
Location: *Malone (after Capell)*
o.s.d. **meeting]** *Capell*
6 **Nicanor?]** *F3;* Nicanor: *F1*
34 **will]** *F2;* well *F1*
44 **charges, distinctly billeted,]** *Steevens (after F4 and Capell);* charges distinctly billetted *F1*

IV.iv

IV.iv] *Capell*
Location: *Capell*
6 s.d. **Enter a Citizen.]** *placed as in Dyce; after l. 6, F1*
7–8 **Direct . . . Antium?]** *as verse, Capell (after Pope); as prose, F1*
9–10 **He . . . night.]** *as verse, Johnson; as prose, F1*
23 **hate . . . love's]** *Capell;* haue . . . loues *F1*

IV.v

IV.v] *Capell*
Location: *Rowe (subs.)*
2 s.d. **Exit.]** *Rowe*
3 **master]** *F4;* M. *F1*
7–8 **What . . . door.]** *as prose, Pope; as verse, F1 (?)*
9–10 **I . . . Coriolanus.]** *as verse, Capell; as prose, F1*
18 s.d. **entering]** *ed. (after Sisson)*
19 **fellow's]** *F3;* Fellowes *F1*
44 **is!]** *Pope;* is, *F1*
49 s.d. **Exit Third Servingman.]** *Globe*
49 s.d. **Second]** *Capell*
52 s.d. **First . . . aside.]** *ed. (after Capell)*
54 s.d. **Unmuffling.]** *Capell*
54–7 **If . . . myself.]** *as verse, Pope; as prose, F1*
70–1 **requited . . . surname—]** *Rowe (subs.);* requitted: . . . Surname, *F1*
73 **me.]** *Collier;* me, *F1*
79 **hearth;]** *Capell;* Harth, *F1*
138–40 **down— . . . weakness—]** *Capell;* downe . . . weaknesse, *F1*
140 **ways:]** *Rowe (subs.);* waies *F1*
147 s.d. **Coriolanus and Aufidius]** *Capell*
147 s.d. **The . . . forward.]** *ed. (after Capell);* Enter two of the Seruingmen. *F1*
150 **strooken]** *Capell;* stroken *F1*
155 **methought—]** *Rowe;* me thought, *F1*
157 **were—]** *Rowe;* were, *F1*
162–3 **I . . . one.]** *as prose, Pope; as verse, F1*
174, 177 s.pp. **1., 2. Serv.]** *Malone (after Capell)*
175 **Roman,]** *Pope;* Roman *F1*
185–6 **him, . . . Corioles;]** *ed.;* him directly, to say the Troth on't before Corioles, *F1*
200 **sowl]** *Rowe;* sole *F1*
202 **poll'd]** *Rowe;* poul'd *F1*
214 **presently;]** *Johnson (subs.);* presently, *F1*
222 **sprightly, waking]** *Pope;* sprightly walking *F1*
224 **sleepy]** *F3;* sleepe *F1*
225 **war's]** *Rowe;* warres *F1*
235 s.p. **1., 2. Serv.]** *Cambridge*

IV.vi

IV.vi] *Pope*
Location: *Theobald*
2 **tame—]** *Sisson (after Rowe);* tame, *F1*
12–7 **Your . . . temporiz'd.]** *as verse, Capell; as prose, F1*
19, 25 s.pp. **All Citizens.]** *Kittredge;* All. *F1*
20, 21 (twice) **Good-en]** *Kittredge;* Gooden *F1*
31 **ambitious . . . thinking,]** *F4;* Ambitious, . . . thinking *F1*
32 **Self-loving—]** *Capell;* Selfe-louing. *F1*
34 **lamentation]** *F2;* Lamention *F1*
48 **whipt.]** *Pope;* whipt, *F1*
61 **'fore]** *F3;* fore *F1*
69 **likely!]** *Theobald;* likely. *F1*
73 s.d. **another]** *Hanmer*
74 s.p. **2. Mess.]** *Hanmer;* Mes. *F1*
85 **cement]** *F4;* Ciment *F1*
89 **wi' th']** *Alexander;* with *F1*
96 **apron-men]** *hyphen, F4*
120 s.p. **Both Tri.]** *Dyce;* Tri. *F1*
137 **one]** *F2;* oue *F1*
138 s.p. **Citizens]** *Dyce*
143 **us.]** *Rowe (subs.);* vs, *F1*
148 s.d. **Cominius and Menenius]** *Capell*
156 s.d. **Exeunt Citizens.]** *Warburton;* Exit Cit. *F1*

IV.vii

IV.vii] *Capell*
Location: *Theobald (subs., after Pope)*
19 **him.]** *Capell (after Pope);* him, *F1*
35 **First]** *Capell;* First, *F1*
37 **'twas]** *F3;* 'was *F1*
39 **defect]** *F2;* detect *F1*

43 casque] *Steevens;* Caske *F1*
46–7 them all, . . . him)] *Hanmer;* them all) . . him, *F1*
49 virtues] *F2;* Vertue *F1*

V.i

V.i] *Rowe;* Actus Quintus. *F1*
Location: *Rowe, Theobald*
62 Not?] *F3;* Not. *F1*

V.ii

V.ii] *Rowe*
Location: *Theobald, Capell*
2–6 You . . . thence.] *as verse, Pope; as prose, F1*
16 happily] *F3;* happely *F1*
37 am,] *F4;* am *F1*
51–2 Sirrah . . . estimation.] *as prose, Pope; as verse, F1*
63 Coriolanus. Guess] *Pope (subs.);* Coriolanus, guesse *F1*
63 by] *Malone (after Hanmer)*
64 him] *Thirlby conj. (subs.);* him: *F1*
66 suffering;] *Hanmer;* suffering, *F1*
68 s.d. To Coriolanus.] *Globe (after Pope)*
87 pity . . . much.] *Theobald;* pitty: Note how much, *F1*
90 s.d. Gives a letter.] *Pope*
94 s.d. Manent] *F2;* Manet *F1*
96–7 'Tis . . . again.] *as prose, Pope; as verse, F1*
110–1 The . . . wind-shaken.] *as prose, F4; as verse, F1*

V.iii

V.iii] *Pope*
Location: *Sisson (after Capell)*
o.s.d. with others] *Capell (subs.)*
17 to] *F2;* too *F1*
17 embassies] *F4;* Embasses *F1*
19 s.d. Shout within.] *placed as in Capell; after l. 19, F1*
21 s.d. in mourning habits] *Malone (after Capell)*
27 doves'] *Steevens;* Doues *F1*
48 prate] *Theobald conj.;* pray *F1*
50 Sink, my knee,] *Theobald;* Sinke my knee *F1*
56 s.d. Kneels.] *Rowe*
57 s.d. Raises her.] *Wilson*
60 sun,] *Collier;* Sun: *F1*
63 holp] *Pope;* hope *F1*
70 soldiers,] *F3;* Souldiers: *F1*
93 s.d. Sits.] *Capell (subs.)*
101 see] *Theobald;* see, *F1*
104 enmity's] *F4;* enmities *F1*
109 bound?] *F4;* bound: *F1*
131 s.d. Rises.] *Capell (subs.)*
141 war's] *F3;* Warres *F1*
149 fine] *Johnson;* fiue *F1*
152 charge] *Theobald;* change *F1*
154 noble man] *F2;* Nobleman *F1*
163 cluck'd] *F2;* clock'd *F1*
163 wars,] *F2;* Warres: *F1*
169 him with] *F3;* him with him with *F1*
169 knees.] *F4;* knees *F1*
170 'longs] *F4;* longs *F1*
182 s.d. Coriolanus] *ed.*
192 stead] *F4;* steed *F1*
200 s.d. Aside.] *Rowe*
202 s.d. To . . . etc.] *Rowe*

V.iv

V.iv] *Pope*
Location: *Wilson (subs.)*
1 coign] *Capell;* Coin *F1*
28 male tiger] *Pope;* male-Tyger *F1*
40, 45, etc. s.pp. 2. Mess.] *Dyce;* Mess. *or* Mes. *F1*
48 s.d. all together] *Rowe;* altogether *F1*
50 cymbals] *F4;* Symboles *F1*
60 city?] *F3;* City. *F1*

V.v

V.v] *Dyce*
Location: *ed. (after all eds. before Dyce)*
o.s.d. Volumnia . . . Valeria] *Dyce (subs.)*
1 s.p. 1. Sen.] *Capell;* Sena. *F1*
3 fires! Strew] *Pope (subs.);* fires, strew *F1*
4 Unshout] *Rowe;* Vnshoot *F1*
7 s.d. Exeunt.] *F2*

V.vi

V.vi] *Dyce*
Location: *Theobald*
5 accuse] *F4;* accuse: *F1*
8 s.d. Exeunt Attendants.] *Malone (after Capell)*
9–11 Even . . . slain.] *as verse, Pope; as prose, F1*
33 projects to accomplish,] *F3;* proiects, to accomplish *F1*
39 wag'd] *F3;* wadg'd *F1*
43 spoil than glory—] *F3 (subs.);* Spoile, then Glory. *F1*
44 him:] *F4;* him, *F1*
56–7 second. . . . way] *Theobald;* second, . . . way. *F1*
62 s.p. All Lords.] *Stevens (subs.);* All. *F1*
84 traitor,] *Theobald;* Traitor *F1*
92–3 Rome, . . . city,] *F3 (subs.);* Rome: . . . City *F1*
105 scold] *Rowe;* scoul'd *F1*
111 Volsces,] *F3* (Volcies); Volces *F1*
115 Flutter'd] *F3;* Flatter'd *F1*
116 it. "Boy"!] *Rowe;* it, Boy. *F1*
118 braggart,] *Rowe;* Braggart? *F1*
128 more, his] *Theobald;* more: / His *F1*
130 s.d. Draw] *Kittredge;* Draw both *F1*
133 him.] *Rowe (subs.);* him *F1*
154 s.d. sounded.] Sounded. / FINIS. *F1*

Timon of Athens

TIMON OF ATHENS has usually been regarded as a poor relation of the major tragedies. Hazlitt commended its intensity and directness of purpose, but his praise woke few echoes until the present century, when several critics, notably G. Wilson Knight in *The Wheel of Fire*, not merely championed the play but argued that it has something like central importance in the interpretation of Shakespeare. Although there has been a subsequent revival of interest, a high proportion of comment has been devoted to textual matters and to various theories of collaboration or revision, so that *Timon* has probably had less attention from literary critics than any other of the tragedies except *Titus Andronicus*.

The play first achieved print in the Folio of 1623, where it occupies the position—between *Romeo and Juliet* and *Julius Caesar*—which was originally reserved for *Troilus and Cressida*. That play was indeed already in part printed when copyright difficulties (later surmounted) compelled Jaggard to withdraw it, and copies of the Folio with the original leaf having the end of *Romeo* on one side and the beginning of *Troilus* on the reverse side survive. There is a gap in the page numbering between *Timon* and *Julius Caesar* which corresponds exactly to the difference in length between the printed text of *Timon* and that of *Troilus*, almost half again as long, as it eventually appeared between the Histories and the Tragedies. It is clear that the emergency over *Troilus* presented Jaggard with an awkward technical problem which he could solve only imperfectly.

Whether *Timon* would have been left out altogether if that emergency had not arisen it is impossible to say for certain. It has long been known that *Timon* has unusual imperfections. There is much difficulty over the lineation of the verse, not all of which can be explained by the compositor's vagaries. There are also indications of loose ends and careless writing. One explanation is that the text we have is an abandoned draft, for some reason never given final revision. Another, which is at present more in favor, is that the play was a collaboration, probably with Thomas Middleton, to whom recent scholarship attributes about one third of the play, including I.ii and III. i–vi. The evidence for this view is strong but not incontrovertible. Elaborate investigation of the language of the play suggests that it should be dated between *King Lear* and *Macbeth*.

Whether the difficulties arose from incomplete collaboration or from the use by compositors of foul papers, it must be said that some are not as baffling as some critics have suggested. There is, for instance, no real difficulty in the behavior of Ventidius, who does not differ from Timon's other friends in offering him money and help only when they are not needed; and although the relation to the main plot of the Alcibiades story may not be explicitly stated, few will have much difficulty in inferring it, and it seems too bold to say positively that something is missing or awry. But there are undoubtedly speeches, such as that of Alcibiades to the senators at III.v.40–58, and that of Flavius before Timon's cave at IV.iii.458–71, which strike one as rough and unfinished; the introduction of the Fool in II.ii seems to have small point in the play as it stands (though the same may be said of the Fool in *Othello*); and in a final version Apemantus' announcement of the arrival of the Poet and the Painter (IV.ii.351) would presumably have been cancelled, since their arrival is so long delayed. Having two epitaphs for Timon before him in Plutarch, Shakespeare transcribed them both (V.iv.70–73) and, since one contradicts the other, would have cancelled one in making a final version. Finally, Shakespeare had clearly not made up his mind about the value of the Athenian talent. He uses different values inconsistently, and in III.ii three times writes "so many," as if he intended to go back and fill in the appropriate number; however this muddle arose, it seems obvious that it would have been sorted out for an acting version.

The date of the play is very uncertain. Many scholars, including Bradley and J. C. Maxwell, hold that its affinities with *King Lear* make most probable a date near 1605. Others, on the whole more plausibly, associate *Timon* with *Antony and Cleopatra* and *Coriolanus*. Shakespeare had recently been working closely on Plutarch's *Life of Antony*, and there are traces in the play of the *Life of Alcibiades*, which is the parallel life to that of Coriolanus. One may also note the similarity between the two "beast-gods," Coriolanus and Timon; and the style of the verse—though since the play is unrevised one cannot build even as much as usual on this—seems closest to *Coriolanus*. Without any certainty, then, one may conjecture 1607–8.

The principal source of the play is North's translation of Plutarch's *Life of Antony*. After his defeat at Actium, Antony "forsook the city and company of his friends, and built him a house in the sea by the Isle of Pharos . . . and dwelt there, as a man that banished himself from all men's company: saying that he would lead Timon's life, because he had the like wrong offered him, that was before offered unto Timon: and that for the unthankfulness of those he had done good unto, and whom he took to be his friends, he was angry with all men, and would trust no man." Plutarch goes on to tell the story of Timon of Athens, called "Misanthropus," and Alcibiades, whom Timon cherished as a source of harm to Athens. He mentions the railing with Apemantus, and Timon's invitation to Athenians to hang themselves on his fig tree. Finally he says that Timon was buried "upon the Sea side," and that the tide compassed the tomb about. The epitaph read:

> Here lies a wretched corse, of wretched soul bereft,
> Seek not my name: a plague consume you wicked wretches left.

And Plutarch also quotes a later epitaph by Callimachus:

> Here lie I, Timon, who alive all living men did hate,
> Pass by, and curse thy fill: but pass, and stay not here thy gait.

These verses Shakespeare uses, almost word for word, in the concluding scene.

This misanthropic episode in Antony's life is entirely omitted from *Antony and Cleopatra*, but Shakespeare must have read it, though probably not for the first time, when he was planning that play.

Plutarch says nothing of Timon's having lost great riches and honor, nor does he send him out into the wilderness. In his *Life of Alcibiades* he offered hints as to that character's ambitions, his love of women (including a courtesan called Timandra), and his last-minute decision to spare a penitent Athens the pains of military conquest. Shakespeare also borrowed various names from different parts of the *Lives*, and especially from that of Antony. And since Plutarch's Antony had himself pointed out resemblances between his life and Timon's, Shakespeare took the hint and gave his Timon traits borrowed from Antony, for example his uncalculating generosity. But in this instance Plutarch gave him little more than the basic idea of the play, and he sought more help in Lucian's dialogue *Timon the Misanthrope*. This work had not been translated into English, but was available in Latin, French, and Italian versions. A recent study suggests plausibly that Shakespeare made direct use of a French translation by Filbert Bretin, published in 1582/3. Lucian treats of Timon's last days, when he digs for hire; although he claims to be better off now than he was as a rich and flattered man, the gods arrange that he should find gold, and soon his false friends seek him out again. Timon drives them away with stones. Although Lucian refers to instances of Timon's earlier munificence, he is chiefly concerned with the Timon that Shakespeare treats in the second half of his play. His dialogue had already been used by Italian writers, but it is unlikely that Shakespeare knew them.

He does, however, seem to have known an English academic play called *Timon*, which was not published until 1842. The date of this play is unknown, but it is probably though not certainly earlier than Shakespeare's, and the similarities, which include a fake banquet and a faithful steward, make it fairly certain either that Shakespeare had seen it or that the plays had a common source, now lost.

There is not much doubt that the opening scene of *Timon of Athens* survives in its finished state, and it ought to provide our chief clue to the design of a play which is, however unfinished, schematic to an unusual degree. The dialogue between Poet and Painter with which the work opens is based on the *paragone* of Renaissance Italy. This was a formalized controversy about the status of the painter in society, especially in relation to that of the poet. The arguments in favor of giving the painter higher status depended largely upon the neo-Platonic view, first expressed in this connection by Leonardo da Vinci, that sight is the supreme sense, and that the painter's blend of science and imagination gives a truer rendering than poetry of the reality that underlies appearance. Shakespeare gives a sample of the conventional arguments, and the Painter's portrait of Timon is valued because it represents better than nature itself can his true magnanimity. The Poet puts his case, explaining that his work expresses the useful moral warning that Timon, despite his glorious estate, is subject to Fortune; and the Painter counters this by his claim that such moralizing may be more succinctly expressed in allegorical pictures.

Timon shows how the arguments of the *paragone* relate to the themes of the play when (I.i.156–60) he endorses the view that painting represents not the false outside of a man, but his true nature. We should remember that the motives of the Painter and the Poet are just as corrupt as those of the other attendants; and the full relevance of the opening scene is not understood until they make their appearance in the second half of the play, when Timon is rumored to be rich again. Then he can use the language of art criticism ironically, implying that what the Painter draws is "counterfeit" not in the innocent technical usage, but in the moral sense; as to the Poet, he is, as Plato first remarked, a liar by trade. Despite their claims to insight they are all "outside"; he, stripped of the outward trappings of magnanimity, is a misanthrope. We must see the two scenes in relation to one another; perhaps the connections would have been strengthened in a revised text.

We learn early that Timon's generosity is based upon a false estimate of his own nature, and of his followers. He is unaware that he is buying love and admiration. Deceived by appearance and false protestation, he fails to see that the principal motive of everybody, from the Senate down, is greed. This unworldliness is made to seem blameworthy but not altogether ignoble; the Steward sees Timon's folly but continues to love him, whereas Apemantus, who indicates a brute reality under the fair seeming, is no more intended to propose a totally acceptable point of view than his counterpart Thersites in *Troilus and Cressida*. He is "opposite to humanity," and his Cynic philosophy has made him more dog than man. Yet, excessively misanthropic as he is, his purpose is constantly to remind us of the wild excess that characterizes Timon in both halves of the play, and the absurdity of his assumptions concerning human behavior in a world ruled by greed and usury. We are not to love or to sympathize much with Timon; he is one of the "minimized" heroes, like Coriolanus. But his excesses appear absurd at least in part because of the baseness of his contemporaries, and there is a kind of ruinous splendor in his conduct which reminds us that Shakespeare is always capable of observing the fineness in excess. "Unwisely, not ignobly, have I given" (II.ii.174) is a modest and acceptable account of Timon's behavior.

Shakespeare is even willing to indicate comparisons between the treachery of Timon's friends and the betrayal of Christ by Judas. These persistent allusions are perhaps the most remarkable single feature of the play. "It grieves me to see so many dip their meat in one man's blood" (I.ii.40–41); "the fellow that sits next him, now parts bread with him, pledges the breath of him in a divided draught, is the readiest man to kill him" (I.ii.46–49); "Who can call him / His friend that dips in the same dish?" (III.ii.65–66). And there are other references to the flatterers "eating" Timon. Wilson Knight was obviously justified in staging the banquet scenes (I.ii, III.vi) so that they resembled the Last Supper of the painters. The second of these scenes is sometimes held to be unfinished, but this view is less acceptable if one reflects that they derive their point largely from the contrast between them. At the first, all is sensual gratification, a theme reinforced by the masque of Amazons, which is in iconographical terms a Banquet of Sense, with connotations of baseness and loss of virtue. The second banquet, where only water is served, is a total reversal, a banquet unattractive to the senses, and subversive of ceremony, which has proved to be merely "outward"; Shakespeare deliberately chose tasteless, colorless, odorless water in place of the stones painted to resemble artichokes which figure in the other *Timon* play.

The play was evidently designed to consist of two halves illustrating contrasting modes of excess. Timon knows no mean, only extremes; and this has rightly been called the most Aristotelian of Shakespeare's plots. Despite the cunning diversification of the texture, which prevents the monotony so many similar passages might have induced, the series of interviews between Timon's servants and his false friends which constitutes the bulk of Act III shows how simple the scheme of the play is; and the second half consists of a procession of visitors to a static Timon. There is almost no development here, since Timon from the outset represents an extreme of misanthropy. Little is left to be done save the exploration and definition of Timon's state, and this lacks dramatic dynamism. Shakespeare seeks to achieve some symmetry by postponing the visit of the Poet and the Painter to the last possible moment, before, in accordance with rudimentary plot requirements, Timon rejects the appeal of the senators and dies.

Clearly it was a harder task to show Timon as beastly than to show him as godlike—a dichotomy, specific to men incapable of adjusting themselves to society, that was Shakespeare's concern both here and in *Coriolanus*. At the beginning of what we know as Act IV (there are no act divisions in the Folio text) he already speaks in tones of absolute misanthropy, praying for the overthrow of all order and the confounding of Athenian humanity. The curse extends beyond Athens to the world at large; the whole of society is poisoned by greed for gold. Figures from money-exchange, and from the goldsmith's trade, recur throughout the play. Gold becomes the sole test of honor, replacing that native worth in which Timon had formerly trusted, and which his very name may be said to represent. Greek *timè*, or *timos*, means both "personal honor" and "value," the price of a thing. And the noun *timoria* means both "assistance" and "vengeance." Timon, as it were, is exploring the etymology of his own name when his criterion shifts from an assumption of personal integrity in everybody to a knowledge that everything has its price in gold, and that this is the world's "honor."

His visitors provide Timon with exempla for misanthropic sermons. The courtesans represent a second form of usury, since prostitution is lending the body out at interest. Timon thinks of the diseases which this usury brings upon the world. Alcibiades himself exemplifies honor in its military aspect—murder, anger, and rapine. The interview with Apemantus is crucial. He is a cruel version of Lear's Fool, and tells Timon a harsh truth: "The middle of humanity thou never knewest, but the extremity of both ends" (IV.iii.300–301). Timon has no longer the magnanimity which enabled him to accept Apemantus as a king accepts a licensed fool; he now rails at him in his own terms. The strangely perverted anacreontics at IV.iii.435 ff.—"I'll example you with thievery: The sun's a thief," etc.—represent an inordinate hatred, a conversion of the imagery of pleasure to the purposes of hatred. They do not say that the whole creation is a system of luxurious thieving; what they imply, when we allow for Timon's hysteria, is that the ordinary conditions of life (which friendship and generous conduct could mitigate) are such that men can slip into a natural condition in which all created things are at enmity with one another.

The presence of Alcibiades in the play is justified by the implicit contrast between him and Timon in their reactions to the ingratitude of Athens. At first he is as angry as Timon, and he knows why the Senate is inhumane: usury—"good business"—has become the sole object of life. His reward for telling the senators so is banishment; but he does not go off alone to eat roots and curse society; he collects his troops and comes like some Richmond or Malcolm against the corrupted city. He will restore order, using mercy with justice, the olive with the sword.

It may be that the Alcibiades of the play (or indeed the Alcibiades of history) is not a very serviceable emblem of the mean between the extremes exampled by Timon; if so, that is a flaw in the play as it stands. It would, however, be unwise to argue that Shakespeare is at fault in neglecting to make us feel very intensely sympathetic to Timon. This is not a *Hamlet*: it is a tragedy of ideas, much more schematic than *Hamlet*. Shakespeare is trying, not to focus attention upon the fall of greatness, but to explore the affinity between the image a great man may see of himself in the magnanimous glass of a flatterer, and the misanthropy that colors the world as he sees it in the mirror of his own avoidable misfortune. Public usury and private ostentation are plainly seen as faults for which society and its victim share the guilt. Remedy lies, if anywhere, in Alcibiades' course of action, not in self-exile and universal hatred. Failure to be Honor itself (by a misunderstanding of the terms of such an appointment) is not an excuse for amateur Cynicism; the alternative to being a great man is not bestiality. Timon should not emulate Apemantus, and in any case to do so is impossible, since that is a trade he must have been born to.

So strident is the tone of declamatory hatred in the second half of *Timon* that some critics accuse Shakespeare of a loss of control, even suggesting that to have written this play and left it in a rough state could have been a consequence of some mental disorder. But these thin harsh tones are the tones of Timon's hysteria, not Shakespeare's; and the verse no more than the structure of the play suggests loss of control or the indulgence of some private loathing. Wherever the verse is thoroughly finished, as in the first scene, we recognize the authentic idiom of the later Shakespeare, characteristic even in its ellipses and obscurities. In fact, we cannot hope to know the reason for the abandonment of the work at so late a stage. Perhaps the lack of a true climax at the end of the play made it seem finally unsatisfactory to the playwright. Whatever the explanation, it obviously had nothing to do with loss of power or control.

Frank Kermode

The Life of Timon of Athens

The Actors' Names

Timon of Athens
Lucius *and* Lucullus } *two flattering lords*
Sempronius, *another flattering lord*
Ventidius, *one of Timon's false friends*
Alcibiades, *an Athenian captain*
Apemantus, *a churlish philosopher*
[Flavius, *steward to Timon*]
Flaminius, *one of Timon's servants*
Servilius, *another*
[Lucilius, *another*]
Caphis, Philotus, Titus, Hortensius, *several servants to usurers*
[Servants *to Varro, Isidore, and Lucius, usurers, and Timon's creditors*]

Poet, Painter, Jeweller, Merchant
[Old Athenian
Three Strangers (*one named* Hostilius)
Page
Fool

Phrynia } *mistresses to Alcibiades*]
Timandra }

Cupid
Certain Maskers [*as Amazons*]

Certain Senators [*and other* Lords, Officers, Soldiers,] *certain Thieves* [*the* Banditti,] *with divers other* Servants *and* Attendants

[Scene: *Athens, and the neighboring woods*]

ACT I, Scene I

Enter Poet, Painter, Jeweller, Merchant, *at several doors.*

Poet. Good day, sir.
Pain. I am glad y' are well.
Poet. I have not seen you long, how goes the world?
Pain. It wears, sir, as it grows.
Poet. Ay, that's well known;
But what particular rarity? What strange,
Which manifold record not matches? See,
Magic of bounty! all these spirits thy power
Hath conjur'd to attend. I know the merchant.
Pain. I know them both; th' other's a jeweller.
Mer. O, 'tis a worthy lord.
Jew. Nay, that's most fix'd.
Mer. A most incomparable man, breath'd, as it were,
To an untirable and continuate goodness;
He passes.
Jew. I have a jewel here—
Mer. O, pray let's see't. For the Lord Timon, sir?
Jew. If he will touch the estimate. But for that—
Poet. [*Reciting to himself.*]
"When we for recompense have prais'd the vild,
It stains the glory in that happy verse
Which aptly sings the good."
Mer. [*Looking on the jewel.*] 'Tis a good form.
Jew. And rich. Here is a water, look ye.
Pain. You are rapt, sir, in some work, some dedication
To the great lord.
Poet. A thing slipp'd idlely from me.
Our poesy is as a [gum], which [oozes]
From whence 'tis nourish'd. The fire i' th' flint
Shows not till it be strook; our gentle flame
Provokes itself and like the current flies
Each bound it chases. What have you there?
Pain. A picture, sir. When comes your book forth?

Words and passages enclosed in square brackets in the text above are either emendations of the copy-text or additions to it. The Textual Notes immediately following the play cite the earliest authority for every such change or insertion and supply the reading of the copy-text wherever it is emended in this edition.

I.i. Location: Athens. Timon's house.
2. long: for a long time.
3. wears: wears away, wears out. **grows:** grows older.
5. Which . . . matches: i.e. for which the records, though full, offer no precedent. **6. bounty:** generosity (Timon's).
7. conjur'd: summoned by a magic spell. **9. fix'd:** certain.
10. breath'd: trained by exercise.
11. continuate: continuous, habitual. **goodness:** bounty.
12. passes: excels. **14. touch the estimate:** meet the price.
15. vild: vile. **16. happy:** (more) appropriate to its occasion.
17. aptly: fitly, i.e. truthfully. **form:** shape.
18. water: lustre. **19. rapt:** engrossed. **23. gentle:** noble.
24. Provokes itself: i.e. needs no external stimulus, as the flint does. **flies:** seeks to escape from.
25. bound: bank. **chases:** i.e. seems to direct itself toward. Many editors adopt Theobald's emendation *chafes*, "frets against."

Poet. Upon the heels of my presentment, sir.
Let's see your piece.
Pain. 'Tis a good piece.
Poet. So 'tis. This comes off well and excellent.
Pain. Indifferent.
Poet. Admirable! How this grace
Speaks his own standing! What a mental power
This eye shoots forth! How big imagination
Moves in this lip! To th' dumbness of the gesture
One might interpret.
Pain. It is a pretty mocking of the life.
Here is a touch; is't good?
Poet. I will say of it,
It tutors nature. Artificial strife
Lives in these touches, livelier than life.

Enter certain SENATORS [*and pass over*].

Pain. How this lord is followed!
Poet. The senators of Athens, happy men!
Pain. Look, moe!
Poet. You see this confluence, this great flood of visitors.
I have, in this rough work, shap'd out a man
Whom this beneath world doth embrace and hug
With amplest entertainment. My free drift
Halts not particularly, but moves itself
In a wide sea of wax; no levell'd malice
Infects one comma in the course I hold,
But flies an eagle flight, bold, and forth on,
Leaving no tract behind.
Pain. How shall I understand you?
Poet. I will unbolt to you.
You see how all conditions, how all minds,
As well of glib and slipp'ry creatures as
Of grave and austere quality, tender down
Their services to Lord Timon. His large fortune,
Upon his good and gracious nature hanging,
Subdues and properties to his love and tendance
All sorts of hearts; yea, from the glass-fac'd flatterer
To Apemantus, that few things loves better
Than to abhor himself; even he drops down
The knee before him, and returns in peace
Most rich in Timon's nod.
Pain. I saw them speak together.
Poet. Sir, I have upon a high and pleasant hill
Feign'd Fortune to be thron'd. The base o' th' mount
Is rank'd with all deserts, all kind of natures,
That labor on the bosom of this sphere
To propagate their states. Amongst them all,
Whose eyes are on this sovereign lady fix'd,
One do I personate of Lord Timon's frame,
Whom Fortune with her ivory hand wafts to her,
Whose present grace to present slaves and servants
Translates his rivals.
Pain. 'Tis conceiv'd to scope.
This throne, this Fortune, and this hill, methinks,
With one man beckon'd from the rest below,
Bowing his head against the steepy mount
To climb his happiness, would be well express'd
In our condition.
Poet. Nay, sir, but hear me on:
All those which were his fellows but of late—
Some better than his value—on the moment
Follow his strides, his lobbies fill with tendance,
Rain sacrificial whisperings in his ear,
Make sacred even his stirrup, and through him
Drink the free air.
Pain. Ay, marry, what of these?
Poet. When Fortune in her shift and change of mood
Spurns down her late beloved, all his dependants
Which labor'd after him to the mountain's top
Even on their knees and [hands], let him [slip] down,
Not one accompanying his declining foot.
Pain. 'Tis common:
A thousand moral paintings I can show
That shall demonstrate these quick blows of Fortune's
More pregnantly than words. Yet you do well
To show Lord Timon that mean eyes have seen
The foot above the head.

Trumpets sound. Enter LORD TIMON, *addressing himself courteously to every suitor,* [*a* MESSENGER *from Ventidius talking with him;* LUCILIUS *and other* SERVANTS *following*].

Tim. Imprison'd is he, say you?

27. **Upon . . . presentment:** as soon as I have presented the poem (to Timon). 30. **Indifferent:** not bad.
31. **Speaks . . . standing:** expresses the dignity of the sitter (probably Timon). 32. **big:** largely.
33–34. **To . . . interpret:** i.e. the gesture, though silent, is so expressive that one could easily supply words to fit.
35. **mocking:** imitation.
37. **Artificial strife:** the striving of art (to outdo nature).
38. **Lives:** achieves the level of life, equals nature. **livelier than life:** more lifelike than life itself.
40. **happy men:** i.e. the senators are fortunate in being friends of Timon. Many editors accept Theobald's emendation of *men* to *man*—Timon is fortunate in having senators among his "followers."
41. **moe:** more.
44. **beneath world.** Cf. "under globe" in *King Lear*, II.ii.163. In the Ptolemaic astronomy the earth was seen as under the moon's sphere, and the sublunary region was the only part of the universe subject to change. 45. **drift:** flow of meaning.
46. **particularly:** at particular persons.
46–47. **moves . . . wax:** i.e. ranges widely, as in writing not limited by the small size of the wax tablet used (?). A much disputed passage.
47. **levell'd:** aimed (at a single person). 48. **comma:** detail.
49. **flies:** it flies, i.e. my course is. 50. **tract:** trace, track.
51. **unbolt:** unlock, lay open.
52. **conditions:** temperaments, characters. 54. **tender down:** offer.
57. **properties . . . tendance:** makes his own to love him and attend on him.
58. **glass-fac'd:** mirror-faced (because he reflects the desires and moods of the flattered).
61. **returns:** departs.
65. **rank'd . . . deserts:** lined with men of all degrees of merit.
67. **propagate:** multiply. **states:** fortunes.
69. **personate:** represent. **frame:** mental and physical nature.
70. **ivory:** white. **wafts:** waves, beckons.
71. **Whose:** i.e. Fortune's. **grace:** favor (to the man representing Timon).
71–72. **to . . . rivals:** transforms his rivals instantly into slaves and servants. 72. **to scope:** fittingly.
77. **our condition:** i.e. the human condition (but some take it to mean the painter's profession).
79. **better . . . value:** worth more than he.
80. **his . . . tendance:** i.e. crowd into his house to offer their services.
81. **sacrificial:** i.e. worshipful.
82. **Make . . . stirrup:** i.e. perform with reverence even the menial duty of helping him to mount his horse.
82–83. **through . . . air:** act as if it were by his courtesy that they breathed the air (which we know to be free).
83. **marry:** indeed (originally the name of the Virgin Mary used as an oath). 90. **moral:** allegorical.
92. **pregnantly:** cogently. 93. **mean:** lowly.
94. **The foot . . . head:** i.e. the great man falling headlong.

Mess. Ay, my good lord, five talents is his debt,
His means most short, his creditors most strait.
Your honorable letter he desires
To those have shut him up, which failing,
Periods his comfort.
Tim. Noble Ventidius! Well;
I am not of that feather to shake off
My friend when he must need me. I do know him
A gentleman that well deserves a help,
Which he shall have. I'll pay the debt and free him.
Mess. Your lordship ever binds him.
Tim. Commend me to him. I will send his ransom,
And being enfranchis'd, bid him come to me;
'Tis not enough to help the feeble up,
But to support him after. Fare you well.
Mess. All happiness to your honor! *Exit.*

Enter an OLD ATHENIAN.

Old Ath. Lord Timon, hear me speak.
Tim. Freely, good father.
Old Ath. Thou hast a servant nam'd Lucilius.
Tim. I have so. What of him?
Old Ath. Most noble Timon, call the man before thee.
Tim. Attends he here, or no? Lucilius!
Lucil. Here, at your lordship's service.
Old Ath. This fellow here, Lord Timon, this thy creature,
By night frequents my house. I am a man
That from my first have been inclin'd to thrift,
And my estate deserves an heir more rais'd
Than one which holds a trencher.
Tim. Well; what further?
Old Ath. One only daughter have I, no kin else,
On whom I may confer what I have got.
The maid is fair, a' th' youngest for a bride,
And I have bred her at my dearest cost
In qualities of the best. This man of thine
Attempts her love. I prithee, noble lord,
Join with me to forbid him her resort,
Myself have spoke in vain.
Tim. The man is honest.
Old Ath. Therefore he will be, Timon.
His honesty rewards him in itself,
It must not bear my daughter.
Tim. Does she love him?
Old Ath. She is young and apt.
Our own precedent passions do instruct us
What levity's in youth.

95. talents. A talent might be taken, very roughly, as $2000 in modern money. On Shakespeare's understanding of its value, see the introduction. **96. strait:** unyielding, insistent.
98. those: those who. **99. Periods:** puts an end to.
100. feather: type, disposition.
104. binds: ties him to gratitude (by freeing him).
105. Commend me: express my regards.
108. But: i.e. but it is necessary also.
116. creature: dependent (contemptuous).
119. more rais'd: of higher social status.
120. holds a trencher: i.e. waits at table (*trencher* = wooden dish).
123. a' th' youngest: i.e. barely old enough (*a'* = of).
125. qualities: accomplishments. **128. honest:** honorable.
129. Therefore . . . be: i.e. that being so, he will do the honorable thing in this case (and leave my daughter alone).
131. bear: carry with it. **132. apt:** impressionable.
133. precedent: experienced in the past.

Tim. [*To Lucilius.*] Love you the maid?
Lucil. Ay, my good lord, and she accepts of it.
Old Ath. If in her marriage my consent be missing,
I call the gods to witness, I will choose
Mine heir from forth the beggars of the world,
And dispossess her all.
Tim. How shall she be endowed,
If she be mated with an equal husband?
Old Ath. Three talents on the present; in future, all.
Tim. This gentleman of mine hath serv'd me long;
To build his fortune I will strain a little,
For 'tis a bond in men. Give him thy daughter;
What you bestow, in him I'll counterpoise,
And make him weigh with her.
Old Ath. Most noble lord,
Pawn me to this your honor, she is his.
Tim. My hand to thee, mine honor on my promise.
Lucil. Humbly I thank your lordship. Never may
That state or fortune fall into my keeping,
Which is not owed to you!
Exit [with Old Athenian].
Poet. Vouchsafe my labor, and long live your lordship!
Tim. I thank you, you shall hear from me anon.
Go not away. What have you there, my friend?
Pain. A piece of painting, which I do beseech
Your lordship to accept.
Tim. Painting is welcome.
The painting is almost the natural man;
For since dishonor traffics with man's nature,
He is but outside; these pencill'd figures are
Even such as they give out. I like your work,
And you shall find I like it. Wait attendance
Till you hear further from me.
Pain. The gods preserve ye!
Tim. Well fare you, gentleman; give me your hand.
We must needs dine together.—Sir, your jewel
Hath suffered under praise.
Jew. What, my lord, dispraise?
Tim. A mere saciety of commendations;
If I should pay you for't as 'tis extoll'd,
It would unclew me quite.
Jew. My lord, 'tis rated
As those which sell would give; but you well know,
Things of like value differing in the owners
Are prized by their masters. Believe't, dear lord,
You mend the jewel by the wearing it.
Tim. Well mock'd.

139. all: entirely. **How . . . endowed:** what dowry shall she have.
141. on the present: immediately.
144. bond in: duty of friendship among.
147. Pawn . . . honor: if you will give me your word of honor to do this.
151. owed to you: (1) acknowledged as issuing from your generosity; (2) due to you as a debt.
152. Vouchsafe: deign to accept. **158. traffics:** has dealings.
159. but outside: only what he lets appear. **pencill'd:** painted.
165. suffered under: i.e. been overwhelmed by. (The Jeweller misunderstands.) **166. mere saciety:** utter satiety.
168. unclew: undo.
169. As . . . give: at the price the seller would be ready to pay for it.
171. prized . . . masters: valued according to the status of their wearers. **172. mend:** increase the value of.
173. Well mock'd: an excellent performance.

Enter APEMANTUS.

Mer. No, my good lord, he speaks the common tongue
Which all men speak with him.

Tim. Look who comes here; will you be chid?

Jew. We'll bear, with your lordship.

Mer. He'll spare none.

Tim. Good morrow to thee, gentle Apemantus!

Apem. Till I be gentle, stay thou for thy good morrow—
When thou art Timon's dog, and these knaves honest.

Tim. Why dost thou call them knaves? thou know'st them not.

Apem. Are they not Athenians?

Tim. Yes.

Apem. Then I repent not.

Jew. You know me, Apemantus?

Apem. Thou know'st I do, I call'd thee by thy name.

Tim. Thou art proud, Apemantus.

Apem. Of nothing so much as that I am not like Timon.

Tim. Whither art going?

Apem. To knock out an honest Athenian's brains.

Tim. That's a deed thou't die for.

Apem. Right, if doing nothing be death by th' law.

Tim. How lik'st thou this picture, Apemantus?

Apem. The best, for the innocence.

Tim. Wrought he not well that painted it?

Apem. He wrought better that made the painter, and yet he's but a filthy piece of work.

Pain. Y' are a dog.

Apem. Thy mother's of my generation; what's she, if I be a dog?

Tim. Wilt dine with me, Apemantus?

Apem. No; I eat not lords.

Tim. And thou shouldst, thou'dst anger ladies.

Apem. O, they eat lords; so they come by great bellies.

Tim. That's a lascivious apprehension.

Apem. So thou apprehend'st it, take it for thy labor.

Tim. How dost thou like this jewel, Apemantus?

Apem. Not so well as plain-dealing, which will not cast a man a doit.

Tim. What dost thou think 'tis worth?

Apem. Not worth my thinking. How now, poet?

Poet. How now, philosopher?

Apem. Thou liest.

Poet. Art not one?

Apem. Yes.

Poet. Then I lie not.

Apem. Art not a poet?

Poet. Yes.

Apem. Then thou liest: look in thy last work, where thou hast feign'd him a worthy fellow.

Poet. That's not feign'd, he is so.

Apem. Yes, he is worthy of thee, and to pay thee for thy labor. He that loves to be flatter'd is worthy o' th' flatterer. Heavens, that I were a lord!

Tim. What wouldst do then, Apemantus?

Apem. E'en as Apemantus does now: hate a lord with my heart.

Tim. What, thyself?

Apem. Ay.

Tim. Wherefore?

Apem. That I had no angry wit to be a lord. Art not thou a merchant?

Mer. Ay, Apemantus.

Apem. Traffic confound thee, if the gods will not!

Mer. If traffic do it, the gods do it.

Apem. Traffic's thy god, and thy god confound thee!

Trumpet sounds. Enter a MESSENGER.

Tim. What trumpet's that?

Mess. 'Tis Alcibiades, and some twenty horse,
All of companionship.

Tim. Pray entertain them, give them guide to us.
[*Exeunt some Attendants.*]
You must needs dine with me; go not you hence
Till I have thank'd you. When dinner's done,
Show me this piece. I am joyful of your sights.

Enter ALCIBIADES *with the rest.*

Most welcome, sir!

Apem. So, so; [there!]
Aches contract and starve your supple joints!
That there should be small love amongst these sweet knaves,
And all this courtesy! The strain of man's bred out
Into baboon and monkey.

Alcib. Sir, you have sav'd my longing, and I feed
Most hungerly on your sight.

Tim. Right welcome, sir!
Ere we depart, we'll share a bounteous time
In different pleasures. Pray you let us in.
Exeunt [*all but Apemantus*].

Enter two LORDS.

1. Lord. What time a' day is't, Apemantus?

Apem. Time to be honest.

174. **the common tongue:** what everybody says.
177. **bear, with:** suffer along with.
186–87. **thy name:** i.e. knave. 193. **thou't:** thou wilt.
196. **innocence:** harmlessness (in which, he implies, it differs from real life).
200. **a dog.** Alluding to Apemantus' being a cynic philosopher; *cynic* is derived from the Greek word for "dog."
201. **of my generation:** (1) my coeval; (2) of my species.
204. **eat not lords:** i.e. do not consume their substance.
205. **And:** if.
208. **apprehension:** (1) interpretation; (2) seizure.
211. **plain-dealing.** Alluding to the saying "Plain dealing is a jewel."
212. **cast.** Almost all editors adopt the F3 reading *cost,* but *cast* receives some support from a longer variant of the proverb quoted just above: "Plain dealing is a jewel, but they that use it die beggars." Possibly Apemantus plays on both senses to contrast the conventional advantage (it makes one no poorer) with what he sees as the true advantage (it makes one no richer). **doit:** small coin worth a fraction of a penny.
222. **Then thou liest.** Because poets only feign truth.
234. **no . . . lord:** that in being a lord I forfeited the angry wit (which I have now). Many editors emend *no angry wit,* adopting Theobald's *so hungry a wit* or Deighton's *my angry will.*
237. **Traffic:** trade, business. **confound:** ruin.
242. **of companionship:** in one party.
243. **entertain:** receive, welcome. 246. **of your sights:** to see you.
248. **Aches.** Pronounced *aitches.* **starve:** paralyze, wither.
250. **courtesy:** display of politeness. **bred out:** degenerated.
252. **sav'd my longing:** brought to fruition my passionate desire.
254. **depart:** part.
255. **different:** various. **let us in:** let us go in.

1. Lord. That time serves still.
Apem. The most accursed thou, that still omit'st it.
2. Lord. Thou art going to Lord Timon's feast?
Apem. Ay, to see meat fill knaves, and wine heat fools.
2. Lord. Fare thee well, fare thee well.
Apem. Thou art a fool to bid me farewell twice.
2. Lord. Why, Apemantus?
Apem. Shouldst have kept one to thyself, for I mean to give thee none.
1. Lord. Hang thyself!
Apem. No, I will do nothing at thy bidding; make thy requests to thy friend.
2. Lord. Away, unpeaceable dog, or I'll spurn thee hence!
Apem. I will fly, like a dog, the heels a' th' ass. [*Exit.*]
1. Lord. He's opposite to humanity. [Come], shall we in
And taste Lord Timon's bounty? he outgoes
The very heart of kindness.
2. Lord. He pours it out: Plutus, the god of gold,
Is but his steward. No meed but he repays
Sevenfold above itself; no gift to him
But breeds the giver a return exceeding
All use of quittance.
1. Lord. The noblest mind he carries
That ever govern'd man.
2. Lord. Long may he live in fortunes! Shall we in?
[*1. Lord.*] I'll keep you company. *Exeunt.*

[Scene II]

Hoboys playing loud music. A great banquet serv'd in, [Flavius *and others attending;*] *and then enter* Lord Timon, *the* States, *the Athenian* Lords, [Alcibiades, *and*] Ventidius, *which Timon redeem'd from prison. Then comes, dropping after all,* Apemantus, *discontentedly, like himself.*

Ven. Most honored Timon,
It hath pleas'd the gods to remember my father's age,
And call him to long peace.
He is gone happy, and has left me rich.
Then, as in grateful virtue I am bound
To your free heart, I do return those talents,
Doubled with thanks and service, from whose help
I deriv'd liberty.
Tim. O, by no means,
Honest Ventidius. You mistake my love;

I gave it freely ever, and there's none
Can truly say he gives if he receives.
If our betters play at that game, we must not dare
To imitate them; faults that are rich are fair.
Ven. A noble spirit!
Tim. Nay, my lords,
Ceremony was but devis'd at first
To set a gloss on faint deeds, hollow welcomes,
Recanting goodness, sorry ere 'tis shown;
But where there is true friendship, there needs none.
Pray sit, more welcome are ye to my fortunes
Than my fortunes to me. [*They sit.*]
1. Lord. My lord, we always have confess'd it.
Apem. Ho, ho, confess'd it? Hang'd it, have you not?
Tim. O, Apemantus, you are welcome.
Apem. No;
You shall not make me welcome.
I come to have thee thrust me out of doors.
Tim. Fie, th' art a churl. Ye have got a humor there
Does not become a man, 'tis much to blame.
They say, my lords, "*Ira furor brevis est*,"
But yond man is very angry. Go,
Let him have a table by himself,
For he does neither affect company,
Nor is he fit for't indeed.
Apem. Let me stay at thine apperil, Timon. I come to observe, I give thee warning on't.
Tim. I take no heed of thee; th' art an Athenian, therefore welcome. I myself would have no power; prithee let my meat make thee silent.
Apem. I scorn thy meat, 'twould choke me; for I should ne'er flatter thee. O you gods! what a number of men eats Timon, and he sees 'em not! It grieves me to see so many dip their meat in one man's blood, and all the madness is, he cheers them up too.
I wonder men dare trust themselves with men.
Methinks they should invite them without knives:
Good for their meat, and safer for their lives.
There's much example for't: the fellow that sits next him, now parts bread with him, pledges the breath of him in a divided draught, is the readiest man to kill him; 't 'as been prov'd. If I were a huge man, I should fear to drink at meals,

258. still: always.
259. omit'st: fail to take advantage of.
261. meat: food. **270. spurn:** kick.
273. opposite to: hostile to (?) or the reverse of (?).
274. outgoes: goes beyond.
277. meed: merit, service (?) or gift (?). **repays:** rewards.
280. use of quittance: customary rates of repayment. *Use* means both "usual practice" and "interest."

I.ii. Location: Athens. A banqueting-room in Timon's house.
o.s.d. Hoboys: oboes. **States:** rulers of the state, here the senators.
like himself: in his ordinary clothes; not attempting to be ceremonious.
6. free: generous.

12. our betters: those in higher positions of authority, i.e. the senators.
13. faults . . . rich: the faults of rich people.
16. faint: half-hearted.
18. none: i.e. no ceremony.
21. confess'd: declared. Apemantus quibbles on the word.
22. confess'd . . . not. Echo of the proverb "Confess and be hanged."
26. humor: disposition.
28. Ira . . . est: anger is a brief madness.
29. very angry: i.e. his anger cannot be called a *brief* madness. Many editors follow Rowe in reading *ever angry.*
31. affect: like. **33. thine apperil:** your own risk.
36. would . . . power: i.e. do not desire the power to make you silent (which the rule of hospitality forbids).
38–39. for . . . thee: i.e. for it is provided for flatterers, and I would be aware that I hadn't paid for it in flattery.
42. all the madness: the height of his madness. **cheers them up:** encourages them.
44. without knives. In Shakespeare's day guests brought their own knives. **45. Good . . . meat:** i.e. the guests would eat less.
48. divided draught: shared drink.
49. huge: great, of high rank.

Lest they should spy my windpipe's dangerous notes:
Great men should drink with harness on their throats.

Tim. My lord, in heart; and let the health go round.

2. Lord. Let it flow this way, my good lord.

Apem. Flow this way? A brave fellow! he keeps his tides well. Those healths will make thee and thy state look ill, Timon.
Here's that which is too weak to be a sinner,
Honest water, which ne'er left man i' th' mire.
This and my food are equals, there's no odds;
Feasts are too proud to give thanks to the gods.

Apemantus' grace.

Immortal gods, I crave no pelf,
I pray for no man but myself.
Grant I may never prove so fond,
To trust man on his oath or bond;
Or a harlot for her weeping,
Or a dog that seems a-sleeping,
Or a keeper with my freedom,
Or my friends, if I should need 'em.
Amen. So fall to't:
Rich men sin, and I eat root.

[*Eats and drinks.*]

Much good dich thy good heart, Apemantus!

Tim. Captain Alcibiades, your heart's in the field now.

Alcib. My heart is ever at your service, my lord.

Tim. You had rather be at a breakfast of enemies than a dinner of friends.

Alcib. So they were bleeding new, my lord, there's no meat like 'em; I could wish my best friend at such a feast.

Apem. Would all those flatterers were thine enemies then, that then thou mightst kill 'em—and bid me to 'em!

1. Lord. Might we but have that happiness, my lord, that you would once use our hearts, whereby we might express some part of our zeals, we should think ourselves for ever perfect.

Tim. O, no doubt, my good friends, but the gods themselves have provided that I shall have much help from you: how had you been my friends else? Why have you that charitable title from thousands, did not you chiefly belong to my heart? I have told more of you to myself than you can with modesty speak in your own behalf; and thus far I confirm you. O you gods, think I, what need we have any friends, if we should ne'er have need of 'em? They were the most needless creatures living, should we ne'er have use for 'em; and would most resemble sweet instruments hung up in cases, that keeps their sounds to themselves. Why, I have often wish'd myself poorer, that I might come nearer to you. We are born to do benefits; and what better or properer can we call our own than the riches of our friends? O, what a precious comfort 'tis to have so many like brothers commanding one another's fortunes! O, joy's e'en made away ere't can be born! Mine eyes cannot hold out water, methinks. To forget their faults, I drink to you.

Apem. Thou weep'st to make them drink, Timon.

2. Lord. Joy had the like conception in our eyes,
And at that instant like a babe sprung up.

Apem. Ho, ho! I laugh to think that babe a bastard.

3. Lord. I promise you, my lord, you mov'd me much.

Apem. Much! *Sound tucket* [*within*].

Tim. What means that trump?

Enter Servant.

How now?

Serv. Please you, my lord, there are certain ladies most desirous of admittance.

Tim. Ladies? what are their wills?

Serv. There comes with them a forerunner, my lord, which bears that office to signify their pleasures.

Tim. I pray let them be admitted. [*Exit Servant.*]

Enter Cupid.

Cup. Hail to thee, worthy Timon, and to all
That of his bounties taste! The five best senses
Acknowledge thee their patron, and come freely
To gratulate thy plenteous bosom. There,
Taste, touch, all, pleas'd from thy table rise;
They only now come but to feast thine eyes.

Tim. They're welcome all, let 'em have kind admittance.
Music, make their welcome! [*Exit Cupid.*]

[*1. Lord.*] You see, my lord, how ample y' are belov'd.

[*Music. Enter* Cupid] *with the masque of* Ladies, [*as*] *Amazons, with lutes in their hands, dancing and playing.*

Apem. Hoy-day,
What a sweep of vanity comes this way!
They dance? they are madwomen.
Like madness is the glory of this life,
As this pomp shows to a little oil and root.
We make ourselves fools to disport ourselves,

51. notes: i.e. indications of its position (as the man drinks with his head thrown back); but with play on the sense "musical notes."
52. harness: armor.
53. in heart: heartily (spoken as a kind of toast). **55. brave:** fine.
56. tides: times (with a jibe at the Second Lord's use of *flow*).
59. i' th' mire: i.e. in difficulties.
61. Feasts: i.e. the men who give and attend feasts.
64. fond: foolish. **68. keeper:** jailer. **72. dich:** may it do.
76–77. of . . . of: consisting of . . . with. **78. So:** provided.
85. use our hearts: ask some service of our love.
87. perfect: completely happy.
91. charitable: loving. **from thousands:** (only you) out of thousands.
94. confirm you: confirm your claims to be worthy friends.
95. what: why.

106. made away: i.e. dissolved in tears. **born:** put into words.
109. Thou . . . drink: i.e. you exude liquid to give them an occasion for absorbing liquid.
110. had . . . eyes: had its inception in the same way with tears.
112. a bastard: i.e. having no legitimate source.
114 s.d. tucket: trumpet call.
120. which . . . office: whose function is.
121 s.d. Enter Cupid: i.e. as the presenter of the masque.
125. gratulate: salute. **plenteous:** generous. **There.** Most editors adopt Theobald's emendation *Th' ear*, and in line 126 many emend *all* to *smell* (following Theobald) or read *smell, all* (following Steevens). **127. They:** i.e. the maskers.
134. Like: similar. **glory:** vainglory, ostentation.
135. As . . . root: as the magnificence of this feast shows itself to be in comparison with the basic necessities.

And spend our flatteries to drink those men
Upon whose age we void it up again
With poisonous spite and envy.
Who lives that's not depraved or depraves?
Who dies that bears not one spurn to their graves
Of their friends' gift?
I should fear those that dance before me now
Would one day stamp upon me. 'T 'as been done;
Men shut their doors against a setting sun.

The Lords rise from table, with much adoring of Timon, and to show their loves, each single out an Amazon, and all dance, men with women, a lofty strain or two to the hoboys, and cease.

Tim. You have done our pleasures much grace, fair ladies,
Set a fair fashion on our entertainment,
Which was not half so beautiful and kind;
You have added worth unto't and lustre,
And entertain'd me with mine own device.
I am to thank you for't.

1. [Lady]. My lord, you take us even at the best.

Apem. Faith, for the worst is filthy, and would not hold taking, I doubt me.

Tim. Ladies, there is an idle banquet attends you,
Please you to dispose yourselves.

All Ladies. Most thankfully, my lord.

Exeunt [Cupid and Ladies].

Tim. Flavius!

Flav. My lord?

Tim. The little casket bring me hither.

Flav. Yes, my lord. [*Aside.*] More jewels yet?
There is no crossing him in 's humor,
Else I should tell him well (i' faith, I should),
When all's spent, he'ld be cross'd then, and he could.
'Tis pity bounty had not eyes behind,
That man might ne'er be wretched for his mind.

Exit.

1. Lord. Where be our men?

Serv. Here, my lord, in readiness.

2. Lord. Our horses!

[*Enter* FLAVIUS *with the casket.*]

Tim. O my friends! I have one word
To say to you. Look you, my good lord,
I must entreat you honor me so much
As to advance this jewel; accept it and wear it,
Kind my lord.

1. Lord. I am so far already in your gifts—

All. So are we all.

Enter a SERVANT.

Serv. My lord, there are certain nobles of the Senate
Newly alighted, and come to visit you.

Tim. They are fairly welcome. [*Exit Servant.*]

Flav. I beseech your honor,
Vouchsafe me a word, it does concern you near.

Tim. Near? why then another time I'll hear thee.
I prithee let's be provided to show them entertainment.

Flav. [*Aside.*] I scarce know how.

Enter another SERVANT.

[2.] Serv. May it please your honor, Lord Lucius
(Out of his free love) hath presented to you
Four milk-white horses, trapp'd in silver.

Tim. I shall accept them fairly; let the presents
Be worthily entertain'd. [*Exit Servant.*]

Enter a third SERVANT.

How now? what news?

3. Serv. Please you, my lord, that honorable gentleman, Lord Lucullus, entreats your company tomorrow to hunt with him, and has sent your honor two brace of greyhounds.

Tim. I'll hunt with him, and let them be receiv'd,
Not without fair reward. [*Exit Servant.*]

Flav. [*Aside.*] What will this come to?
He commands us to provide, and give great gifts,
And all out of an empty coffer;
Nor will he know his purse, or yield me this,
To show him what a beggar his heart is,
Being of no power to make his wishes good.
His promises fly so beyond his state
That what he speaks is all in debt: he owes
For ev'ry word. He is so kind that he now
Pays interest for't; his land's put to their books.
Well, would I were gently put out of office
Before I were forc'd out!
Happier is he that has no friend to feed
Than such that do e'en enemies exceed.
I bleed inwardly for my lord. *Exit.*

Tim. You do yourselves
Much wrong, you bate too much of your own merits.
Here, my lord, a trifle of our love.

2. Lord. With more than common thanks I will receive it.

3. Lord. O, he's the very soul of bounty!

Tim. And now I remember, my lord, you gave
Good words the other day of a bay courser
I rode on. 'Tis yours, because you lik'd it.

[3.] Lord. O, I beseech you pardon me, my lord, in that.

137. **drink:** (1) drink the health of; (2) consume (cf. *eats* in line 40 above and *eat* in I.i.204). 138. **age:** old age.
139. **envy:** malice. 141. **spurn:** blow, injury. 142. **gift:** giving.
145 s.d. **adoring:** reverential saluting. 148. **kind:** gracious.
150. **mine own device:** this allegorical entertainment which you have composed especially for me (?). Less probably, Timon may be acknowledging that he himself devised the entertainment.
152. **take . . . best:** rate us at the most favorable valuation.
154. **hold taking:** bear handling (being rotten). **doubt me:** fear.
155. **idle:** trifling. **banquet:** dessert, refreshment.
156. **dispose yourselves:** take your places.
160. **crossing:** opposing. **humor:** inclination, caprice.
161. **well:** i.e. forthrightly.
162. **he'ld be cross'd:** he'd like to have his debts cancelled. **and:** if.
164. **for his mind:** i.e. because of his generous impulses.
170. **advance:** increase the value of (by accepting).

176. **fairly:** courteously. In line 182 the word may include the implication that the gift will be handsomely rewarded; cf. line 191, "Not without fair reward."
183. **trapp'd in silver:** wearing silver-mounted trappings.
185. **worthily entertain'd:** fittingly received.
197. **state:** estate, means.
200. **put . . . books:** i.e. mortgaged to the very people to whom he makes gifts.
204. **Than . . . exceed:** than he who has such friends as do him more harm than enemies.
206. **bate . . . of:** undervalue too much.
213. **pardon . . . that:** i.e. permit me to decline that too generous gift.

Tim. You may take my word, my lord; I know no man
Can justly praise but what he does affect.
I weigh my friend's affection with mine own.
I'll tell you true, I'll call to you.
All Lords. O, none so welcome.
Tim. I take all and your several visitations
So kind to heart, 'tis not enough to give;
Methinks, I could deal kingdoms to my friends,
And ne'er be weary. Alcibiades,
Thou art a soldier, therefore seldom rich,
It comes in charity to thee; for all thy living
Is 'mongst the dead, and all the lands thou hast
Lie in a pitch'd field.
Alcib. Ay, defil'd land, my lord.
1. Lord. We are so virtuously bound—
Tim. And so
Am I to you.
2. Lord. So infinitely endear'd—
Tim. All to you. Lights, more lights!
1. Lord. The best of happiness,
Honor, and fortunes keep with you, Lord Timon!
Tim. Ready for his friends.
Exeunt Lords [*and others. Apemantus and Timon remain*].
Apem. What a coil's here!
Serving of becks and jutting-out of bums!
I doubt whether their legs be worth the sums
That are given for 'em. Friendship's full of dregs;
Methinks false hearts should never have sound legs.
Thus honest fools lay out their wealth on curtsies.
Tim. Now, Apemantus, if thou wert not sullen,
I would be good to thee.
Apem. No, I'll nothing; for if I should be brib'd too, there would be none left to rail upon thee, and then thou wouldst sin the faster. Thou giv'st so long, Timon (I fear me), thou wilt give away thyself in paper shortly. What needs these feasts, pomps, and vainglories?
Tim. Nay, and you begin to rail on society once, I am sworn not to give regard to you. Farewell, and come with better music. *Exit.*
Apem. So; thou wilt not hear me now, thou shalt not then. I'll lock thy heaven from thee.
O that men's ears should be
To counsel deaf, but not to flattery! *Exit.*

215. **affect:** like.
216. **weigh . . . with:** regard my friend's wishes as equal in importance to. 217. **to:** on.
218. **all . . . several:** your joint and individual.
223. **It . . . thee:** to give to you is genuine charity. **living:** (1) means; (2) existence.
225. **pitch'd field:** battlefield. **defil'd.** A quibble on *pitch'd* ("He that touches pitch shall be defiled," Ecclesiasticus 13:1); perhaps also playing on *filed* = with soldiers drawn up in ranks.
230. **coil:** fuss.
231. **Serving of becks:** bowing.
232. **legs:** (1) limbs; (2) bows.
234. **sound:** i.e. able to make bows.
242. **in paper:** i.e. in promissory notes because there are no valuables left.
244. **and . . . once:** if once you begin to attack friendly companionship. 247. **So:** very well.
248. **thy heaven:** i.e. my saving advice.

[ACT II, SCENE I]

Enter a SENATOR [*with papers in his hand*].

Sen. And late, five thousand; to Varro and to Isidore
He owes nine thousand, besides my former sum,
Which makes it five and twenty. Still in motion
Of raging waste? It cannot hold, it will not.
If I want gold, steal but a beggar's dog
And give it Timon, why, the dog coins gold.
If I would sell my horse and buy twenty moe
Better than he, why, give my horse to Timon,
Ask nothing, give it him, it foals me straight
And able horses. No porter at his gate,
But rather one that smiles and still invites
All that pass by. It cannot hold, no reason
Can sound his state in safety. Caphis ho!
Caphis, I say!

Enter CAPHIS.

Caph. Here, sir, what is your pleasure?
Sen. Get on your cloak and haste you to Lord Timon;
Importune him for my moneys, be not ceas'd
With slight denial; nor then silenc'd when
"Commend me to your master" and the cap
Plays in the right hand, thus—but tell him
My uses cry to me; I must serve my turn
Out of mine own. His days and times are past,
And my reliances on his fracted dates
Have smit my credit. I love and honor him,
But must not break my back to heal his finger.
Immediate are my needs, and my relief
Must not be toss'd and turn'd to me in words,
But find supply immediate. Get you gone,
Put on a most importunate aspect,
A visage of demand; for I do fear,
When every feather sticks in his own wing,
Lord Timon will be left a naked gull,
Which flashes now a phoenix. Get you gone.
Caph. I go, sir.
Sen. Ay, go, sir; take the bonds along with you,
And have the dates in. Come!
Caph. I will, sir.
Sen. Go. *Exeunt.*

[SCENE II]

Enter Steward [FLAVIUS] *with many bills in his hand.*

Flav. No care, no stop, so senseless of expense,

II.i. Location: Athens. A senator's house.
1. **late:** lately. 4. **hold:** last. 5. **steal:** I need only steal.
9. **foals me straight:** bears foals straightway.
10. **able horses:** i.e. not foals, either, but full-grown horses. **porter:** i.e. one who keeps people out. 12. **reason:** i.e. rational person.
13. **sound . . . safety:** i.e. estimate his estate as safe.
16. **ceas'd:** put off. 20. **uses:** needs, business undertakings.
21. **His . . . past:** the terms of his loans have expired.
22. **fracted:** broken. **dates:** due dates for repayment (so also in line 35). 23. **smit:** damaged.
26. **toss'd and turn'd:** hit back to me (metaphor from tennis).
30. **every . . . wing:** i.e. every creditor has taken what is due him.
31. **gull:** (1) unfledged bird; (2) dupe, fool.

II.ii. Location: Athens. Before Timon's house.

That he will neither know how to maintain it,
Nor cease his flow of riot. Takes no accompt
How things go from him, nor [resumes] no care
Of what is to continue. Never mind
Was to be so unwise, to be so kind.
What shall be done, he will not hear, till feel.
I must be round with him, now he comes from hunting.
Fie, fie, fie, fie!

Enter CAPHIS [*and the* SERVANTS *of*] *Isidore and Varro.*

Caph. Good even, Varro. What,
You come for money?
Var. [*Serv.*] Is't not your business too?
Caph. It is; and yours too, Isidore?
Isid. [*Serv.*] It is so.
Caph. Would we were all discharg'd!
Var. [*Serv.*] I fear it.
Caph. Here comes the lord.

Enter TIMON *and his* TRAIN [*with* ALCIBIADES].

Tim. So soon as dinner's done, we'll forth again,
My Alcibiades.—With me, what is your will?
Caph. My lord, here is a note of certain dues.
Tim. Dues? Whence are you?
Caph. Of Athens here, my lord.
Tim. Go to my steward.
Caph. Please it your lordship, he hath put me off
To the succession of new days this month.
My master is awak'd by great occasion
To call upon his own, and humbly prays you
That with your other noble parts you'll suit
In giving him his right.
Tim. Mine honest friend,
I prithee but repair to me next morning.
Caph. Nay, good my lord—
Tim. Contain thyself, good friend.
Var. [*Serv.*] One Varro's servant, my good lord—
Isid. [*Serv.*] From Isidore;
He humbly prays your speedy payment.
Caph. If you did know, my lord, my master's wants—
Var. [*Serv.*] 'Twas due on forfeiture, my lord, six weeks
And past.
Isid. [*Serv.*] Your steward puts me off, my lord,
And I am sent expressly to your lordship.
Tim. Give me breath.
I do beseech you, good my lords, keep on,
I'll wait upon you instantly.
[*Exeunt Alcibiades and Lords.*]
[*To Flavius.*] Come hither. Pray you,
How goes the world, that I am thus encount'red

With clamorous demands of debt, broken bonds,
And the detention of long since due debts,
Against my honor?
Flav. Please you, gentlemen,
The time is unagreeable to this business.
Your importunacy cease till after dinner,
That I may make his lordship understand
Wherefore you are not paid.
Tim. Do so, my friends. See them well entertain'd.
[*Exit.*]
Flav. Pray draw near. *Exit.*

Enter APEMANTUS *and* FOOL.

Caph. Stay, stay, here comes the Fool with Apemantus, let's ha' some sport with 'em.

Var. [*Serv.*] Hang him, he'll abuse us.

Isid. [*Serv.*] A plague upon him, dog!

Var. [*Serv.*] How dost, Fool?

Apem. Dost dialogue with thy shadow?

Var. [*Serv.*] I speak not to thee.

Apem. No, 'tis to thyself. [*To the Fool.*] Come away.

Isid. [*Serv.*] [*To Varro's Servant.*] There's the Fool hangs on your back already.

Apem. No, thou stand'st single, th' art not on him yet.

Caph. Where's the Fool now?

Apem. He last ask'd the question. Poor rogues, and usurers' men, bawds between gold and want!

All [*Serv.*] What are we, Apemantus?

Apem. Asses.

All [*Serv.*] Why?

Apem. That you ask me what you are, and do not know yourselves. Speak to 'em, Fool.

Fool. How do you, gentlemen?

All [*Serv.*] Gramercies, good Fool; how does your mistress?

Fool. She's e'en setting on water to scald such chickens as you are. Would we could see you at Corinth!

Apem. Good, gramercy.

Enter PAGE.

Fool. Look you, here comes my master's page.

Page. [*To the Fool.*] Why, how now, captain? what do you in this wise company? How dost thou, Apemantus?

2. know: find out.
3. riot: extravagant revelling. **accompt:** account.
4–5. resumes . . . continue: takes no care for means to continue.
6. Was to be: was fated to be. **to be:** as to be (?) or in being (?).
7. feel: (he) suffers. **8. round:** plain, blunt.
12. discharg'd: paid. **I fear it:** i.e. I'm afraid we won't be.
20. To . . . month: i.e. from one day to the next for the past month.
21. awak'd . . . occasion: aroused by great needs which have arisen.
22. his own: i.e. what is rightfully due him. **23. suit:** be consistent.
30. on forfeiture: under penalty of forfeit for non-payment on due date. **34. keep on:** go on ahead.
36. How . . . world: what on earth is going on.

37. debt, broken. Some editors omit *debt*, in view of the metrical irregularity and the occurrence of *debts* in line 38; others, following Steevens, read *date-broke*, i.e. overdue.
38. detention: non-payment. **39. Against:** to the detriment of.
53. 'tis to thyself: you speak to yourself (when you say "How dost, Fool?"). Apemantus thus calls Varro's servant a fool.
54–55. There's . . . already: i.e. Apemantus' rejoinder has already attached the name "fool" to you.
56–57. single: by yourself. **th' art . . . yet:** i.e. you're not on his back yet. Apemantus thus calls Isidore's servant a fool.
58. Where's . . . now: i.e. whose back is the Fool on now.
59. He . . . question. Apemantus thus calls Caphis a fool.
67. Gramercies: many thanks.
69. scald. A method of removing feathers from poultry. The Fool alludes to loss of hair from venereal disease and to its treatment by "sweating." His mistress is a bawd or a prostitute.
70. Corinth: brothel, or brothel district. (The city of Corinth was notorious for prostitutes.)
72, 101. master's. Many editors read *mistress'*, following Theobald, but the Fool and the Page could have had both a master and a mistress; cf. Boult in *Pericles*, who calls the Pander master and the Bawd mistress (IV.vi.159–60).

Apem. Would I had a rod in my mouth, that I might answer thee profitably.

[*Page.*] Prithee, Apemantus, read me the superscription of these letters, I know not which is which.

Apem. Canst not read?

Page. No.

Apem. There will little learning die then that day thou art hang'd. This is to Lord Timon, this to Alcibiades. Go, thou wast born a bastard, and thou't die a bawd.

Page. Thou wast whelp'd a dog, and thou shalt famish a dog's death. Answer not, I am gone. *Exit.*

Apem. E'en so thou outrun'st grace. Fool, I will go with you to Lord Timon's.

Fool. Will you leave me there?

Apem. If Timon stay at home. You three serve three usurers?

All [*Serv.*] Ay, would they serv'd us!

Apem. So would I—as good a trick as ever hangman serv'd thief.

Fool. Are you three usurers' men?

All [*Serv.*] Ay, Fool.

Fool. I think no usurer but has a fool to his servant; my mistress is one, and I am her fool. When men come to borrow of your masters, they approach sadly, and go away merry; but they enter my master's house merrily, and go away sadly. The reason of this?

Var. [*Serv.*] I could render one.

Apem. Do it then, that we may account thee a whoremaster and a knave, which notwithstanding, thou shalt be no less esteem'd.

Var. [*Serv.*] What is a whoremaster, Fool?

Fool. A fool in good clothes, and something like thee. 'Tis a spirit; sometime't appears like a lord, sometime like a lawyer, sometime like a philosopher, with two stones moe than 's artificial one. He is very often like a knight; and, generally, in all shapes that man goes up and down in from fourscore to thirteen, this spirit walks in.

Var. [*Serv.*] Thou art not altogether a fool.

Fool. Nor thou altogether a wise man; as much foolery as I have, so much wit thou lack'st.

Apem. That answer might have become Apemantus.

All [*Serv.*] Aside, aside, here comes Lord Timon.

Enter TIMON *and Steward* [FLAVIUS].

Apem. Come with me, Fool, come.

Fool. I do not always follow lover, elder brother, and woman; sometime the philosopher.

[*Exeunt Apemantus and Fool.*]

Flav. Pray you walk near, I'll speak with you anon. *Exeunt* [*Servants*].

Tim. You make me marvel wherefore ere this time
Had you not fully laid my state before me,
That I might so have rated my expense
As I had leave of means.

Flav. You would not hear me;
At many leisures I [propos'd].

Tim. Go to!
Perchance some single vantages you took,
When my indisposition put you back,
And that unaptness made your minister
Thus to excuse yourself.

Flav. O my good lord,
At many times I brought in my accompts,
Laid them before you; you would throw them off,
And say you [found] them in mine honesty.
When for some trifling present you have bid me
Return so much, I have shook my head, and wept;
Yea, 'gainst th' authority of manners, pray'd you
To hold your hand more close. I did endure
Not seldom, nor no slight checks, when I have
Prompted you in the ebb of your estate
And your great flow of debts. My lov'd lord,
Though you hear now (too late), yet now's a time:
The greatest of your having lacks a half
To pay your present debts.

Tim. Let all my land be sold.

Flav. 'Tis all engag'd, some forfeited and gone,
And what remains will hardly stop the mouth
Of present dues. The future comes apace;
What shall defend the interim? and at length
How goes our reck'ning?

Tim. To Lacedaemon did my land extend.

Flav. O my good lord, the world is but a word;
Were it all yours to give it in a breath,
How quickly were it gone!

Tim. You tell me true.

Flav. If you suspect my husbandry or falsehood,
Call me before th' exactest auditors,
And set me on the proof. So the gods bless me,
When all our offices have been oppress'd
With riotous feeders, when our vaults have wept
With drunken spilth of wine, when every room
Hath blaz'd with lights and bray'd with minstrelsy,

77. **answer thee profitably:** i.e. chastise you with my words, to your profit. 84. **thou't:** thou wilt. 87. **famish:** die.
88. **thou outrun'st grace:** i.e. you flee from the instruction that might save you (cf. I.ii.248).
91. **If . . . home:** i.e. if I leave Timon there, I'll leave a fool there.
98. **I . . . servant.** Implying that any servant to a usurer is a fool.
106. **no less esteem'd.** A slur at Athenian morals.
111. **stones:** testicles. **artificial one:** i.e. the philosopher's stone (alchemical).
121. **elder brother:** i.e. the son who inherits; and so, like lovers and women, the most profitable kind of person for the Fool to cultivate.

126. **rated:** estimated.
127. **As . . . means:** in accordance with my resources.
128. **propos'd:** attempted (to tell you). **Go to:** exclamation of impatience or indignation. 129. **vantages:** opportunities.
130. **indisposition:** disinclination to listen.
131–32. **that . . . yourself:** you used my unwillingness to listen on those few occasions as an excuse for not trying again.
138. **'gainst . . . manners:** contrary to what good manners required.
139. **more close:** tighter.
140. **seldom:** infrequent. **checks:** rebukes.
141. **Prompted you:** told you what you ought to do. **in:** in the matter of. 143. **a time:** i.e. a time at least to tell you.
144. **The greatest . . . having:** your possessions at the most sanguine estimate. 146. **engag'd:** mortgaged.
148. **present dues:** debts now due.
149. **What . . . interim:** i.e. what preparation can we make against the onslaught of debts that will be coming due in the near future. **at length:** in the long run. 151. **Lacedaemon:** Sparta.
155. **my . . . falsehood:** i.e. that my management has been dishonest. Some editors emend *or* to *of.* 157. **on:** to.
158. **offices:** kitchens and other service departments. **oppress'd:** taxed to the limit. 159. **With:** by, because of.
160. **spilth:** spilling. 161. **bray'd:** resounded noisily.

I have retir'd me to a wasteful cock,
And set mine eyes at flow.

Tim. Prithee no more.

Flav. Heavens, have I said, the bounty of this lord!
How many prodigal bits have slaves and peasants
This night englutted! Who is not Timon's?
What heart, head, sword, force, means, but is Lord Timon's?
Great Timon! noble, worthy, royal Timon!
Ah, when the means are gone that buy this praise,
The breath is gone whereof this praise is made.
Feast-won, fast-lost; one cloud of winter show'rs,
These flies are couch'd.

Tim. Come, sermon me no further.
No villainous bounty yet hath pass'd my heart;
Unwisely, not ignobly, have I given.
Why dost thou weep? Canst thou the conscience lack
To think I shall lack friends? Secure thy heart;
If I would broach the vessels of my love,
And try the argument of hearts, by borrowing,
Men and men's fortunes could I frankly use
As I can bid thee speak.

Flav. Assurance bless your thoughts!

Tim. And in some sort these wants of mine are crown'd,
That I account them blessings; for by these
Shall I try friends. You shall perceive how you
Mistake my fortunes; I am wealthy in my friends.
Within there! [Flaminius!] Servilius!

Enter three Servants [Flaminius, Servilius, *and another*].

Servants. My lord? My lord?

Tim. I will dispatch you severally: [*to Servilius*] you to Lord Lucius; [*to Flaminius*] to Lord Lucullus you—I hunted with his honor to-day; [*to the other*] you to Sempronius. Commend me to their loves; and I am proud, say, that my occasions have found time to use 'em toward a supply of money. Let the request be fifty talents.

Flam. As you have said, my lord.

[*Exeunt the three Servants.*]

Flav. [*Aside.*] Lord Lucius and Lucullus? Humh!

Tim. Go you, sir, to the senators—
Of whom, even to the state's best health, I have
Deserv'd this hearing—bid 'em send o' th' instant
A thousand talents to me.

Flav. I have been bold
(For that I knew it the most general way)

To them to use your signet and your name,
But they do shake their heads, and I am here
No richer in return.

Tim. Is't true? Can 't be?

Flav. They answer, in a joint and corporate voice,
That now they are at fall, want treasure, cannot
Do what they would, are sorry; you are honorable,
But yet they could have wish'd—they know not—
Something hath been amiss—a noble nature
May catch a wrench—would all were well—'tis pity—
And so, intending other serious matters,
After distasteful looks, and these hard fractions,
With certain half-caps and cold-moving nods,
They froze me into silence.

Tim. You gods, reward them!
Prithee, man, look cheerly. These old fellows
Have their ingratitude in them hereditary:
Their blood is cak'd, 'tis cold, it seldom flows;
'Tis lack of kindly warmth they are not kind;
And nature, as it grows again toward earth,
Is fashion'd for the journey, dull and heavy.
Go to Ventidius. (Prithee be not sad,
Thou art true and honest; ingeniously I speak,
No blame belongs to thee.) Ventidius lately
Buried his father, by whose death he's stepp'd
Into a great estate. When he was poor,
Imprison'd, and in scarcity of friends,
I clear'd him with five talents. Greet him from me,
Bid him suppose some good necessity
Touches his friend, which craves to be rememb'red
With those five talents. That had, give't these fellows
To whom 'tis instant due. Nev'r speak or think
That Timon's fortunes 'mong his friends can sink.

Flav. I would I could not think it! That thought is bounty's foe;
Being free itself, it thinks all others so. *Exeunt.*

[ACT III, Scene I]

Flaminius *waiting to speak with a lord* [*Lucullus*] *from his master, enters a* Servant *to him.*

Serv. I have told my lord of you, he is coming down to you.

Flam. I thank you, sir.

Enter Lucullus.

Serv. Here's my lord.

Lucul. [*Aside.*] One of Lord Timon's men? A gift, I warrant. Why, this hits right; I dreamt of a silver

162–63. retir'd . . . flow: i.e. withdrawn to sit beside one of the flowing barrels and added my tears to its waste.
165. prodigal bits: lavishly provided delicacies.
166. is not: i.e. does not declare himself.
171. fast-lost: (1) quickly lost; (2) lost when fasting supersedes feasting. **172. are couch'd:** go into hiding.
175. conscience: good sense, judgment. **176. Secure:** set at ease.
177. broach: tap. **178. try . . . hearts:** test avowals of love.
179. frankly: as freely.
180. Assurance . . . thoughts: may your hopes be blessed by proving well founded. **181. crown'd:** given great dignity.
182. That: so that.
191–92. occasions . . . time: needs . . . occasion.
197. to . . . health: i.e. by my contributions to the welfare of the state.
200. general: usual (?) or comprehensive, i.e. offering the possibility of the largest loan (?).

201. signet: seal (as proof of authority to act).
205. at fall: at a low ebb. **want treasure:** lack funds.
209. catch a wrench: suffer a twist from its proper direction.
210. intending: pretending (?) or busying themselves with (?).
211. distasteful: indicating their distaste. **hard fractions:** harsh fragments of sentences.
212. half-caps: grudging salutes. **cold-moving:** (1) stiff (as if with benumbed muscles); (2) importing coldness.
216. cak'd: congealed. Old age was associated with the melancholy humor, described in the traditional physiology as dry and cold.
217. kindly: natural. **221. ingeniously:** sincerely, unfeignedly.
233. free: generous.

III.i. Location: Athens. Lucullus' house.
6. hits right: fits perfectly.

basin and ew'r to-night.—Flaminius, honest Flaminius, you are very respectively welcome, sir. Fill me some wine. [*Exit Servant.*] And how does that honorable, complete, free-hearted gentleman of Athens, thy very bountiful good lord and master?

Flam. His health is well, sir.

Lucul. I am right glad that his health is well, sir; and what hast thou there under thy cloak, pretty Flaminius?

Flam. Faith, nothing but an empty box, sir, which, in my lord's behalf, I come to entreat your honor to supply; who, having great and instant occasion to use fifty talents, hath sent to your lordship to furnish him, nothing doubting your present assistance therein.

Lucul. La, la, la, la! "nothing doubting," says he? Alas, good lord! a noble gentleman 'tis, if he would not keep so good a house. Many a time and often I ha' din'd with him, and told him on't, and come again to supper to him of purpose to have him spend less, and yet he would embrace no counsel, take no warning by my coming. Every man has his fault, and honesty is his. I ha' told him on't, but I could ne'er get him from't.

Enter SERVANT *with wine.*

Serv. Please your lordship, here is the wine.

Lucul. Flaminius, I have noted thee always wise. Here's to thee.

Flam. Your lordship speaks your pleasure.

Lucul. I have observ'd thee always for a towardly prompt spirit—give thee thy due—and one that knows what belongs to reason; and canst use the time well, if the time use thee well. Good parts in thee! [*To Servant.*] Get you gone, sirrah. [*Exit Servant.*] Draw nearer, honest Flaminius. Thy lord's a bountiful gentleman, but thou art wise, and thou know'st well enough (although thou com'st to me) that this is no time to lend money, especially upon bare friendship without security. Here's three solidares for thee; good boy, wink at me, and say thou saw'st me not. Fare thee well.

Flam. Is't possible the world should so much differ,
And we alive that lived? Fly, damned baseness,
To him that worships thee!
[*Throwing the money back.*]

Lucul. Ha? now I see thou art a fool, and fit for thy master. *Exit Lucullus.*

Flam. May these add to the number that may scald thee!
Let molten coin be thy damnation,
Thou disease of a friend, and not himself!
Has friendship such a faint and milky heart,
It turns in less than two nights? O you gods!
I feel my master's passion. This slave
Unto his honor has my lord's meat in him;
Why should it thrive and turn to nutriment
When he is turn'd to poison?
O, may diseases only work upon't!
And when he's sick to death, let not that part of nature
Which my lord paid for, be of any power
To expel sickness, but prolong his hour! *Exit.*

[SCENE II]

Enter LUCIUS *with three* STRANGERS.

Luc. Who, the Lord Timon? He is my very good friend, and an honorable gentleman.

1. Stran. We know him for no less, though we are but strangers to him. But I can tell you one thing, my lord, and which I hear from common rumors, now Lord Timon's happy hours are done and past, and his estate shrinks from him.

Luc. Fie, no, do not believe it; he cannot want for money.

2. Stran. But believe you this, my lord, that not long ago one of his men was with the Lord Lucullus to borrow so many talents, nay, urg'd extremely for't, and show'd what necessity belong'd to't, and yet was denied.

Luc. How?

2. Stran. I tell you, denied, my lord.

Luc. What a strange case was that! Now before the gods, I am asham'd on't. Denied that honorable man? There was very little honor show'd in't. For my own part, I must needs confess, I have receiv'd some small kindnesses from him, as money, plate, jewels, and such like trifles—nothing comparing to his—yet had he mistook him and sent to me, I should ne'er have denied his occasion so many talents.

Enter SERVILIUS.

Ser. See, by good hap, yonder's my lord; I have sweat to see his honor. My honor'd lord—

Luc. Servilius? You are kindly met, sir. Fare thee well, commend me to thy honorable virtuous lord, my very exquisite friend.

Ser. May it please your honor, my lord hath sent—

Luc. Ha? what has he sent? I am so much endear'd to that lord: he's ever sending. How shall I thank him, think'st thou? And what has he sent now?

Ser. H'as only sent his present occasion now, my

8. respectively: particularly.
10. complete: endowed with all good qualities. **18. supply:** fill.
23. keep . . . house: offer such lavish hospitality.
25. of purpose: with the express purpose (of persuading him).
27. honesty: generosity.
33. speaks your pleasure: is pleased to say so.
34. towardly: well-disposed. **37. parts:** traits.
38. sirrah: term of address used to inferiors.
43. solidares: coins (of Shakespeare's invention, from Latin *solidus*).
44. wink: shut your eyes.
46–47. so . . . lived: i.e. be so changed in a single lifetime.
52. Let . . . damnation: may you be killed (and your soul sent to hell) by having molten gold poured down your throat.

55. turns: sours.
57. Unto . . . him: i.e. much to his honor has been a guest at Timon's table. Some editors change *Unto his honor* to *Unto this hour*, after Pope; some, following F1 lineation, take the phrase back to the end of line 62 and explain *slave unto his honor* as an ironic description of Lucullus. (It would better fit Sempronius; see III.iii.28.)
63. his hour: i.e. his time of suffering before death.

III.ii. Location: Athens. A public place.
22. his: i.e. what Lucullus has received.
23. mistook . . . me: i.e. by mistake sent his messenger to me, who owed him less (instead of to Lucullus).
25. hap: luck. **34. H'as:** he has.

lord; requesting your lordship to supply his instant use with so many talents.

Luc. I know his lordship is but merry with me;
He cannot want fifty—five hundred talents.

Ser. But in the mean time he wants less, my lord.
If his occasion were not virtuous,
I should not urge it half so faithfully.

Luc. Dost thou speak seriously, Servilius?

Ser. Upon my soul, 'tis true, sir.

Luc. What a wicked beast was I to disfurnish myself against such a good time, when I might ha' shown myself honorable! How unluckily it happ'ned that I should purchase the day before for a little part, and undo a great deal of honor! Servilius, now before the gods, I am not able to do (the more beast, I say!)—I was sending to use Lord Timon myself, these gentlemen can witness; but I would not, for the wealth of Athens, I had done't now. Commend me bountifully to his good lordship, and I hope his honor will conceive the fairest of me, because I have no power to be kind. And tell him this from me, I count it one of my greatest afflictions, say, that I cannot pleasure such an honorable gentleman. Good Servilius, will you befriend me so far as to use mine own words to him?

Ser. Yes, sir, I shall. *Exit Servilius.*

Luc. [*Calling after him.*] I'll look you out a good
turn, Servilius.—
True, as you said, Timon is shrunk indeed,
And he that's once denied will hardly speed. *Exit.*

1. Stran. Do you observe this, Hostilius?

2. Stran. Ay, too well.

1. Stran. Why, this is the world's soul, and just of
the same piece
Is every flatterer's sport. Who can call him
His friend that dips in the same dish? for, in
My knowing, Timon has been this lord's father,
And kept his credit with his purse;
Supported his estate, nay, Timon's money
Has paid his men their wages. He ne'er drinks
But Timon's silver treads upon his lip,
And yet—O, see the monstrousness of man
When he looks out in an ungrateful shape!—
He does deny him (in respect of his)
What charitable men afford to beggars.

3. Stran. Religion groans at it.

1. Stran. For mine own part,
I never tasted Timon in my life,
Nor came any of his bounties over me
To mark me for his friend; yet, I protest,
For his right noble mind, illustrious virtue,
And honorable carriage,
Had his necessity made use of me,
I would have put my wealth into donation,
And the best half should have return'd to him,
So much I love his heart. But I perceive
Men must learn now with pity to dispense,
For policy sits above conscience. *Exeunt.*

47–48. **for . . . honor:** what brings me little honor, and (thus) lose a chance to win a great deal of honor. 50. **use:** borrow from.
53–54. **conceive . . . me:** regard me in the most favorable light.
62. **speed:** prosper.
65. **sport:** mockery. Many editors adopt Theobald's reading *spirit*.
68. **kept his credit:** maintained Lucius' credit.
71. **treads:** rests its weight.
74. **in . . . his:** in proportion to his resources.
77. **tasted Timon:** i.e. sampled his generosity.
79. **protest:** avow. 81. **carriage:** conduct.
83. **put . . . donation:** regarded my wealth as a gift (from Timon).

87. **policy:** shrewd dealing.

[Scene III]

Enter a third Servant *with* Sempronius, *another of Timon's friends.*

Sem. Must he needs trouble me in't—hum!—
'bove all others?
He might have tried Lord Lucius or Lucullus;
And now Ventidius is wealthy too,
Whom he redeem'd from prison. All these
Owes their estates unto him.

Serv. My lord,
They have all been touch'd and found base metal,
For they have all denied him.

Sem. How? Have they denied him?
Has Ventidius and Lucullus denied him,
And does he send to me? Three? Humh!
It shows but little love or judgment in him.
Must I be his last refuge? His friends, like physicians,
Thrive, give him over; must I take th' cure upon
me?
H'as much disgrac'd me in't, I'm angry at him,
That might have known my place. I see no sense
for't,
But his occasions might have wooed me first;
For, in my conscience, I was the first man
That e'er received gift from him;
And does he think so backwardly of me now,
That I'll requite it last? No!
So it may prove an argument of laughter
To th' rest, and 'mongst lords [I] be thought a fool.
I'd rather than the worth of thrice the sum
H'ad sent to me first, but for my mind's sake;
I'd such a courage to do him good. But now return,
And with their faint reply this answer join:
Who bates mine honor shall not know my coin. *Exit.*

Serv. Excellent! your lordship's a goodly villain. The devil knew not what he did when he made man politic; he cross'd himself by't; and I cannot think but, in the end, the villainies of man will set him clear. How fairly this lord strives to appear foul! takes virtuous copies to be wicked; like those that under hot

III.iii. Location: Athens. Sempronius' house.
6. **touch'd:** tested (by being rubbed on a touchstone, to see whether they are gold or base metal).
12. **Thrive . . . over:** i.e. thrive on his money but declare his case hopeless and make no effort to help him.
14–15. **I . . . first:** I see no reason why, in his need, he did not apply to me first.
18. **think . . . me:** i.e. think me so slow and reluctant.
20. **argument of:** matter for.
23. **but . . . sake:** if only because of my good will toward him.
24. **courage:** heart, i.e. desire.
26. **bates:** undervalues (?) or diminishes (?).
29. **politic:** crafty. **cross'd:** thwarted.
30. **set him clear:** i.e. make the devil look innocent.
31. **How fairly:** with what an appearance of virtue.
31–32. **takes . . . wicked:** for his wicked ends models himself on the virtuous.

ardent zeal would set whole realms on fire; of such a nature is his politic love.
This was my lord's best hope, now all are fled,
Save only the gods. Now his friends are dead,
Doors, that were ne'er acquainted with their wards
Many a bounteous year, must be employ'd
Now to guard sure their master.
And this is all a liberal course allows:
Who cannot keep his wealth must keep his house.
Exit.

[Scene IV]

Enter Varro's [*two* Servants], *meeting* [Titus *and*] *others, all* [*servants of*] *Timon's creditors, to wait for his coming out. Then enter Lucius'* [Servant] *and* Hortensius.

[*1.*] *Var. Serv.* Well met, good morrow, Titus and Hortensius.
Tit. The like to you, kind Varro.
Hor. Lucius!
What, do we meet together?
Luc. [*Serv.*] Ay, and I think
One business does command us all; for mine
Is money.
Tit. So is theirs and ours.

Enter Philotus.

Luc. [*Serv.*] And, sir, Philotus too!
Phi. Good day at once.
Luc. [*Serv.*] Welcome, good brother.
What do you think the hour?
Phi. Laboring for nine.
Luc. [*Serv.*] So much?
Phi. Is not my lord seen yet?
Luc. [*Serv.*] Not yet.
Phi. I wonder on't, he was wont to shine at seven.
Luc. [*Serv.*] Ay, but the days are wax'd shorter with him.
You must consider that a prodigal course
Is like the sun's, but not like his recoverable,
I fear. 'Tis deepest winter in Lord Timon's purse;
That is, one may reach deep enough and yet
Find little.
Phi. I am of your fear for that.
Tit. I'll show you how t' observe a strange event.
Your lord sends now for money.
Hor. Most true, he does.
Tit. And he wears jewels now of Timon's gift,
For which I wait for money.
Hor. It is against my heart.

32–33. **those . . . fire:** i.e. those who cause great disturbances in the state for religious ends.
37. **wards:** locks. 39. **guard . . . master:** i.e. from arrest for debt.
40. **liberal:** generous.
41. **keep . . . keep:** preserve . . . remain inside.

III.iv. Location: Athens. Timon's house.
7. **at once:** to you all. 11. **wax'd:** become.
13. **like . . . recoverable.** The sun moves lower in the sky when winter comes; but, unlike the prodigal, it can regain its height the next year.
20. **money:** i.e. the loan which Timon cannot repay, since he spent it on jewels for Hortensius' master.

Luc. [*Serv.*] Mark how strange it shows,
Timon in this should pay more than he owes;
And e'en as if your lord should wear rich jewels
And send for money for 'em.
Hor. I'm weary of this charge, the gods can witness.
I know my lord hath spent of Timon's wealth,
And now ingratitude makes it worse than stealth.
[*1.*] *Var.* [*Serv.*] Yes, mine's three thousand crowns; what's yours?
Luc. [*Serv.*] Five thousand mine.
[*1.*] *Var.* [*Serv.*] 'Tis much deep, and it should seem by th' sum
Your master's confidence was above mine,
Else surely his had equall'd.

Enter Flaminius.

Tit. One of Lord Timon's men.
Luc. [*Serv.*] Flaminius? Sir, a word. Pray is my lord ready to come forth?
Flam. No, indeed he is not.
Tit. We attend his lordship; pray signify so much.
Flam. I need not tell him that, he knows you are too diligent. [*Exit.*]

Enter Steward [Flavius] *in a cloak, muffled.*

Luc. [*Serv.*] Ha! is not that his steward muffled so?
He goes away in a cloud; call him, call him.
Tit. Do you hear, sir?
2. Var. [*Serv.*] By your leave, sir—
Flav. What do ye ask of me, my friend?
Tit. We wait for certain money here, sir.
Flav. Ay,
If money were as certain as your waiting,
'Twere sure enough.
Why then preferr'd you not your sums and bills
When your false masters eat of my lord's meat?
Then they could smile, and fawn upon his debts,
And take down th' int'rest into their glutt'nous maws.
You do yourselves but wrong to stir me up,
Let me pass quietly.
Believe't, my lord and I have made an end:
I have no more to reckon, he to spend.
Luc. [*Serv.*] Ay, but this answer will not serve.
Flav. If 'twill not serve, 'tis not so base as you,
For you serve knaves. [*Exit.*]
1. Var. [*Serv.*] How? what does his cashier'd worship mutter?
2. Var. [*Serv.*] No matter what, he's poor, and that's revenge enough. Who can speak broader than he that has no house to put his head in? Such may rail against great buildings.

25. **charge:** commission. 27. **stealth:** stealing.
31. **above mine:** i.e. greater than my master's confidence.
32. **his had equall'd:** i.e. my master's loan would have equalled your master's.
42. **in a cloud:** (1) as if covered by a cloud; (2) in a state of gloom.
49. **preferr'd:** proffered, presented.
50. **eat:** ate (pronounced *et*).
55. **made an end:** parted company. 60. **cashier'd:** dismissed.
63. **broader:** more freely.

Enter SERVILIUS.

Tit. O, here's Servilius; now we shall know some answer.

Ser. If I might beseech you, gentlemen, to repair some other hour, I should derive much from't; for take't of my soul, my lord leans wondrously to discontent. His comfortable temper has forsook him, he's much out of health, and keeps his chamber.

Luc. [*Serv.*] Many do keep their chambers are not sick;
And if it be so far beyond his health,
Methinks he should the sooner pay his debts,
And make a clear way to the gods.

Ser. Good gods!

Tit. We cannot take this for answer, sir.

Flam. (*Within.*) Servilius, help! My lord, my lord!

Enter TIMON *in a rage*, [FLAMINIUS *following*].

Tim. What, are my doors oppos'd against my passage?
Have I been ever free, and must my house
Be my retentive enemy? my jail?
The place which I have feasted, does it now
(Like all mankind) show me an iron heart?

Luc. [*Serv.*] Put in now, Titus.

Tit. My lord, here is my bill.

Luc. [*Serv.*] Here's mine.

[*Hor.*] And mine, my lord.

[*Both*] *Var.* [*Serv.*] And ours, my lord.

Phi. All our bills.

Tim. Knock me down with 'em, cleave me to the girdle!

Luc. [*Serv.*] Alas, my lord—

Tim. Cut my heart in sums.

Tit. Mine, fifty talents.

Tim. Tell out my blood.

Luc. [*Serv.*] Five thousand crowns, my lord.

Tim. Five thousand drops pays that. What yours? and yours?

1. Var. [*Serv.*] My lord—

2. Var. [*Serv.*] My lord—

Tim. Tear me, take me, and the gods fall upon you! *Exit Timon.*

Hor. Faith, I perceive our masters may throw their caps at their money. These debts may well be call'd desperate ones, for a madman owes 'em. *Exeunt.*

Enter TIMON [*and* FLAVIUS].

Tim. They have e'en put my breath from me, the slaves.
Creditors? Devils!

Flav. My dear lord—

68. **repair:** come back. 71. **comfortable:** cheerful.
73. **are:** who are.
74. **if . . . health:** if he has indeed passed beyond good health.
76. **clear:** unencumbered. **the gods:** i.e. heaven.
82. **feasted:** made festive (?) or feasted in (?).
90. **Knock . . . girdle.** Timon quibbles on *bills* in the sense "watchmen's pikes."
92. **sums:** i.e. sufficient pieces to make up the sums demanded.
94. **Tell out:** count out drop by drop.
100–101. **throw . . . at:** give up all hope of.

Tim. What if it should be so?

Flav. My lord—

Tim. I'll have it so. My steward!

Flav. Here, my lord.

Tim. So fitly? Go, bid all my friends again,
Lucius, Lucullus, and Sempronius—all.
I'll once more feast the rascals.

Flav. O my lord,
You only speak from your distracted soul;
There's not so much left to furnish out
A moderate table.

Tim. Be it not in thy care;
Go, I charge thee, invite them all, let in the tide
Of knaves once more; my cook and I'll provide.
Exeunt.

[SCENE V]

Enter three SENATORS *at one door*, ALCIBIADES *meeting them, with* ATTENDANTS.

1. Sen. My lord, you have my voice to't; the fault's
Bloody; 'tis necessary he should die.
Nothing emboldens sin so much as mercy.

2. Sen. Most true; the law shall bruise 'em.

Alcib. Honor, health, and compassion to the Senate!

1. Sen. Now, captain?

Alcib. I am an humble suitor to your virtues;
For pity is the virtue of the law,
And none but tyrants use it cruelly.
It pleases time and fortune to lie heavy
Upon a friend of mine, who in hot blood
Hath stepp'd into the law, which is past depth
To those that (without heed) do plunge into't.
He is a man (setting his fate aside)
Of comely virtues;
Nor did he soil the fact with cowardice
([An] honor in him which buys out his fault),
But with a noble fury and fair spirit,
Seeing his reputation touch'd to death,
He did oppose his foe;
And with such sober and unnoted passion
He did behoove his anger, ere 'twas spent,
As if he had but prov'd an argument.

1. Sen. You undergo too strict a paradox,
Striving to make an ugly deed look fair.
Your words have took such pains as if they labor'd

106. **What . . . so:** i.e. suppose I do it. (Timon has just conceived the idea of the banquet of III.vi.) 114. **to:** as to.
115. **Be . . . care:** that's not your responsibility.

III.v. Location: Athens. The Senate-house.
1. **voice to't:** vote in favor of it. 4. **'em:** i.e. sinners.
8. **virtue:** excellence, merit.
12–13. **past depth To:** over the head of.
14. **his fate:** i.e. the deed he was fated to do. Some editors read *his* (or *this*) *fault*, after Warburton and Pope. 16. **fact:** deed.
17. **buys out:** redeems.
19. **touch'd to death:** threatened with fatal injury.
21. **unnoted:** i.e. so well under control as to be without visible symptoms.
22. **behoove:** make seemly. Most editors adopt Rowe's emendation *behave*, i.e. manage, regulate.
24. **undergo:** undertake. **strict:** forced.

To bring manslaughter into form, and set quarrelling
Upon the head of valor; which indeed
Is valor misbegot, and came into the world
When sects and factions were newly born.
He's truly valiant that can wisely suffer
The worst that man can breathe, and make his wrongs
His outsides, to wear them like his raiment, carelessly,
And ne'er prefer his injuries to his heart,
To bring it into danger.
If wrongs be evils and enforce us kill,
What folly 'tis to hazard life for ill!
Alcib. My lord—
1. Sen. You cannot make gross sins look clear;
To revenge is no valor, but to bear.
Alcib. My lords, then, under favor, pardon me
If I speak like a captain.
Why do fond men expose themselves to battle,
And not endure all threats? sleep upon't,
And let the foes quietly cut their throats
Without repugnancy? If there be
Such valor in the bearing, what make we
Abroad? Why then, women are more valiant
That stay at home, if bearing carry it;
And the ass more captain than the lion, the fellow
Loaden with irons wiser than the judge,
If wisdom be in suffering. O my lords,
As you are great, be pitifully good.
Who cannot condemn rashness in cold blood?
To kill, I grant, is sin's extremest gust,
But in defense, by mercy, 'tis most just.
To be in anger is impiety;
But who is man that is not angry?
Weigh but the crime with this.
2. Sen. You breathe in vain.
Alcib. In vain? His service done
At Lacedaemon and Byzantium
Were a sufficient briber for his life.
1. Sen. What's that?
Alcib. Why, [I] say, my lords, h'as done fair service,
And slain in fight many of your enemies.
How full of valor did he bear himself
In the last conflict, and made plenteous wounds!
2. Sen. He has made too much plenty with ['em].
He's a sworn rioter; he has a sin that often
Drowns him and takes his valor prisoner.
If there were no foes, that were enough
To overcome him. In that beastly fury
He has been known to commit outrages
And cherish factions. 'Tis inferr'd to us,
His days are foul and his drink dangerous.
1. Sen. He dies.
Alcib. Hard fate! he might have died in war.
My lords, if not for any parts in him—
Though his right arm might purchase his own time
And be in debt to none—yet more to move you,
Take my deserts to his, and join 'em both;
And for I know your reverend ages love
Security, I'll pawn my victories, all
My honor to you, upon his good returns.
If by this crime he owes the law his life,
Why, let the war receive't in valiant gore,
For law is strict, and war is nothing more.
1. Sen. We are for law, he dies, urge it no more
On height of our displeasure. Friend, or brother,
He forfeits his own blood that spills another.
Alcib. Must it be so? It must not be. My lords,
I do beseech you know me.
2. Sen. How?
Alcib. Call me to your remembrances.
3. Sen. What?
Alcib. I cannot think but your age has forgot me,
It could not else be I should prove so base
To sue and be denied such common grace.
My wounds ache at you.
1. Sen. Do you dare our anger?
'Tis in few words, but spacious in effect:
We banish thee for ever.
Alcib. Banish me?
Banish your dotage, banish usury,
That makes the Senate ugly!
1. Sen. If after two days' shine Athens contain thee,
Attend our weightier judgment. And not to swell our spirit,
He shall be executed presently. *Exeunt* [*Senators*].
Alcib. Now the gods keep you old enough that you may live
Only in bone, that none may look on you!
I'm worse than mad. I have kept back their foes,
While they have told their money, and let out
Their coin upon large interest—I myself
Rich only in large hurts. All those, for this?
Is this the balsom that the usuring Senate
Pours into captains' wounds? Banishment!
It comes not ill; I hate not to be banish'd,
It is a cause worthy my spleen and fury,

27. bring . . . into form: make . . . a formal procedure.
27–28. set . . . head: treat quarrelling as a subdivision of.
28. which: i.e. quarrelling. **33. carelessly:** unconcernedly.
34. prefer: present. **38. clear:** innocent.
40. under favor: by your leave. **42. fond:** foolish.
45. repugnancy: fighting back. **46. make:** do.
47. Abroad: away from home.
48. bearing. With play on "childbearing" and "bearing men in sexual intercourse."
49. more captain than: superior to. **fellow.** Many editors adopt Theobald's conjecture *felon*. **52. pitifully:** compassionately.
54. sin's extremest gust: "the utmost degree of appetite for sin" (Johnson) (?) or sin's utmost violence (metaphor from wind) (?).
55. by mercy: mercifully interpreted.
57. not: i.e. never. **61. briber:** giver of bribes.
66. He . . . 'em: he has used them as an excuse for too much riotous living (?).
67. sworn rioter: inveterate reveller. **sin:** i.e. drunkenness.
69. If: even if.
72. cherish factions: support subversive elements. **inferr'd:** alleged.
75. parts: good qualities.
76. purchase. Beginning a financial figure that continues throughout the speech. **his own time:** the right to his natural term of life.
79. for: because.
80. Security: (1) safety; (2) collateral for a loan.
81. upon: as a guarantee of. **good returns:** (1) high profit; (2) good behavior. **86. On . . . our:** on pain of our highest.
87. another: another's.
94. common grace: i.e. a favor you might be expected to grant any man.
101. Attend . . . judgment: expect our severer sentence. **spirit:** anger. **102. presently:** immediately.
104. Only in bone: i.e. as mere skeletons.
106. told: counted. **109. balsom:** balsam, healing ointment.

That I may strike at Athens. I'll cheer up
My discontented troops, and lay for hearts.
'Tis honor with most lands to be at odds;
Soldiers should brook as little wrongs as gods. *Exit.*

[SCENE VI]

[*Music. Tables set out:* SERVANTS *attending.*] *Enter divers friends [of Timon,* SENATORS *and other* LORDS,] *at several doors.*

1. [*Lord*]. The good time of day to you, sir.

2. [*Lord*]. I also wish it to you. I think this honorable lord did but try us this other day.

1. [*Lord*]. Upon that were my thoughts tiring when we encount'red. I hope it is not so low with him as he made it seem in the trial of his several friends.

2. [*Lord*]. It should not be, by the persuasion of his new feasting.

1. [*Lord*]. I should think so. He hath sent me an earnest inviting, which many my near occasions did urge me to put off; but he hath conjur'd me beyond them, and I must needs appear.

2. [*Lord*]. In like manner was I in debt to my importunate business, but he would not hear my excuse. I am sorry, when he sent to borrow of me, that my provision was out.

1. [*Lord*]. I am sick of that grief too, as I understand how all things go.

2. [*Lord*]. Every man here's so. What would he have borrow'd of you?

1. [*Lord*]. A thousand pieces.

2. [*Lord*]. A thousand pieces?

1. [*Lord*]. What of you?

2. [*Lord*]. He sent to me, sir—Here he comes.

Enter TIMON *and* ATTENDANTS.

Tim. With all my heart, gentlemen both; and how fare you?

1. [*Lord*]. Ever at the best, hearing well of your lordship.

2. [*Lord*]. The swallow follows not summer more willing than we your lordship.

Tim. [*Aside.*] Nor more willingly leaves winter, such summer birds are men.—Gentlemen, our dinner will not recompense this long stay; feast your ears with the music awhile, if they will fare so harshly o' th' trumpet's sound; we shall to't presently.

1. [*Lord*]. I hope it remains not unkindly with your lordship that I return'd you an empty messenger.

Tim. O, sir, let it not trouble you.

2. [*Lord*]. My noble lord—

114. **lay for hearts:** win their support (literally, ambush affections).
116. **brook . . . gods:** not endure wrongs any more than gods do.

III.vi. Location: Athens. A banqueting-room in Timon's house.
4. **tiring:** eagerly feeding (term from falconry).
7. **by the persuasion:** on the evidence.
10. **near occasions:** pressing engagements. 11. **put off:** decline.
11–12. **conjur'd . . . them:** summoned me with an urgency exceeding theirs. 13. **in debt to:** subject to the demands of.
16. **out:** exhausted. 18. **how . . . go:** the way things really are.
25. **With . . . heart:** my cordial greetings. 33. **stay:** wait.
34. **fare . . . o':** partake of such rough fare as.

Tim. Ah, my good friend, what cheer?

The banket brought in.

2. [*Lord*]. My most honorable lord, I am e'en sick of shame that, when your lordship this other day sent to me, I was so unfortunate a beggar.

Tim. Think not on't, sir.

2. [*Lord*]. If you had sent but two hours before—

Tim. Let it not cumber your better remembrance. —Come, bring in all together!

2. [*Lord*]. All cover'd dishes!

1. [*Lord*]. Royal cheer, I warrant you.

3. [*Lord*]. Doubt not that, if money and the season can yield it.

1. [*Lord*]. How do you? What's the news?

3. [*Lord*]. Alcibiades is banish'd: hear you of it?

Both [*1., 2. Lords*]. Alcibiades banish'd?

3. [*Lord*]. 'Tis so, be sure of it.

1. [*Lord*]. How? how?

2. [*Lord*]. I pray you, upon what?

Tim. My worthy friends, will you draw near?

3. [*Lord*]. I'll tell you more anon. Here's a noble feast toward.

2. [*Lord*]. This is the old man still.

3. [*Lord*]. Will't hold? will't hold?

2. [*Lord*]. It does; but time will—and so—

3. [*Lord*]. I do conceive.

Tim. Each man to his stool, with that spur as he would to the lip of his mistress; your diet shall be in all places alike. Make not a city feast of it, to let the meat cool ere we can agree upon the first place; sit, sit. The gods require our thanks.

You great benefactors, sprinkle our society with thankfulness. For your own gifts, make yourselves prais'd; but reserve still to give, lest your deities be despis'd. Lend to each man enough, that one need not lend to another; for were your godheads to borrow of men, men would forsake the gods. Make the meat be belov'd more than the man that gives it. Let no assembly of twenty be without a score of villains. If there sit twelve women at the table, let a dozen of them be—as they are. The rest of your fees, O gods—the senators of Athens, together with the common [lag] of people—what is amiss in them, you gods, make suitable for destruction. For these my present friends, as they are to me nothing, so in nothing bless them, and to nothing are they welcome.

Uncover, dogs, and lap!

[*The dishes are uncovered and seen to be full of warm water.*]

Some speak. What does his lordship mean?

Some other. I know not.

Tim. May you a better feast never behold,

43. **so . . . beggar:** so unlucky as to be out of money.
46. **cumber . . . remembrance:** interfere with happier memories.
48. **cover'd dishes.** Promising particularly good food.
57. **upon what:** for what cause. 60. **toward:** forthcoming.
61. **old:** same. 62. **hold:** last. 63. **will:** i.e. will tell.
64. **conceive:** understand you.
67. **a city feast:** an official banquet (with seating strictly by rank).
72. **reserve still:** always keep back (something).
79. **fees:** property (?) or those who hold their lives in fee from you (?). 81. **lag:** tag end. 82. **For:** as for.

You knot of mouth-friends! Smoke and lukewarm water
Is your perfection. This is Timon's last,
Who, stuck and spangled [with your] flatteries,
Washes it off, and sprinkles in your faces
Your reeking villainy.
[*Throwing the water in their faces.*]
Live loath'd, and long,
Most smiling, smooth, detested parasites,
Courteous destroyers, affable wolves, meek bears,
You fools of fortune, trencher-friends, time's flies,
Cap-and-knee slaves, vapors, and minute-jacks!
Of man and beast the infinite malady
Crust you quite o'er! What, dost thou go?
Soft, take thy physic first—thou too—and thou;
Stay, I will lend thee money, borrow none.
[*Throws the dishes at them, and drives them out.*]
What? all in motion? Henceforth be no feast
Whereat a villain's not a welcome guest.
Burn house! sink Athens! henceforth hated be
Of Timon man and all humanity! *Exit.*

Enter the SENATORS *with other* LORDS [*again*].

1. [*Lord*]. How now, my lords?

2. [*Lord*]. Know you the quality of Lord Timon's fury?

3. [*Lord*]. Push, did you see my cap?

4. [*Lord*]. I have lost my gown.

1. [*Lord*]. He's but a mad lord, and nought but humors sways him. He gave me a jewel th' other day, and now he has beat it out of my hat. Did you see my jewel?

[*3. Lord.*] Did you see my cap?

[*2. Lord.*] Here 'tis.

4. [*Lord*]. Here lies my gown.

1. [*Lord*]. Let's make no stay.

2. [*Lord*]. Lord Timon's mad.

3. [*Lord*]. I feel't upon my bones.

4. [*Lord*]. One day he gives us diamonds, next day stones. *Exeunt the Senators* [*and other Lords*].

[ACT IV, SCENE I]

Enter TIMON.

Tim. Let me look back upon thee. O thou wall
That girdles in those wolves, dive in the earth,
And fence not Athens! Matrons, turn incontinent!

Obedience, fail in children! Slaves and fools,
Pluck the grave wrinkled Senate from the bench,
And minister in their steads! To general filths
Convert o' th' instant, green virginity!
Do't in your parents' eyes! Bankrupts, hold fast;
Rather than render back, out with your knives,
And cut your trusters' throats! Bound servants, steal;
Large-handed robbers your grave masters are,
And pill by law. Maid, to thy master's bed,
Thy mistress is o' th' brothel! [Son] of sixteen,
Pluck the lin'd crutch from thy old limping sire,
With it beat out his brains! Piety, and fear,
Religion to the gods, peace, justice, truth,
Domestic awe, night-rest, and neighborhood,
Instruction, manners, mysteries, and trades,
Degrees, observances, customs, and laws,
Decline to your confounding contraries;
And yet confusion live! Plagues incident to men,
Your potent and infectious fevers heap
On Athens, ripe for stroke! Thou cold sciatica,
Cripple our senators, that their limbs may halt
As lamely as their manners! Lust, and liberty,
Creep in the minds and marrows of our youth,
That 'gainst the stream of virtue they may strive,
And drown themselves in riot! Itches, blains,
Sow all th' Athenian bosoms, and their crop
Be general leprosy! Breath, infect breath,
That their society (as their friendship) may
Be merely poison! Nothing I'll bear from thee
But nakedness, thou detestable town!
Take thou that too, with multiplying bans!
Timon will to the woods, where he shall find
Th' unkindest beast more kinder than mankind.
The gods confound (hear me, you good gods all)
Th' Athenians both within and out that wall!
And grant, as Timon grows, his hate may grow
To the whole race of mankind, high and low!
Amen. *Exit.*

[SCENE II]

Enter Steward [FLAVIUS] *with two or three* SERVANTS.

1. Serv. Hear you, Master Steward, where's our master?

89. **mouth-friends**: friends won by being fed (cf. *trencher-friends* line 96) (?) or people falsely professing friendship (?). **Smoke**: steam; as applied to the false friends, "hot air."
90. **your perfection**: what suits you best. 94. **detested**: detestable.
96. **fools of fortune**: creatures completely controlled (like puppets) by fortune; *fools* = playthings. **time's flies**: i.e. creatures who come only in summer, when times are good (cf. II.ii.171–72).
97. **Cap-and-knee slaves**: base fellows always raising their hats and bowing. **minute-jacks**: time-servers (a jack was the figure striking the bell in a clock). 98. **the infinite**: i.e. each and every.
99. **Crust**: cover with scabs. 100. **Soft**: not so fast.
105. **Of**: by. 107. **quality**: occasion, cause.
109. **Push**: pish, pshaw.
111. **mad**: given to mad tricks (but the word means "insane" in line 119).
111–12. **nought . . . him**: he is governed wholly by caprice.
IV.i. Location: Outside the walls of Athens.

6. **general filths**: common prostitutes.
7. **Convert**: change (intransitive). **green virginity**: young virgins.
10. **Bound**: under bond to serve for a specified term.
11. **Large-handed**: taking without restraint.
12. **pill**: plunder. 14. **lin'd**: padded. 15. **fear**: religious awe.
16. **Religion to**: reverence for.
17. **Domestic awe**: respect due to parents and seniors in the family. **neighborhood**: neighborly feeling.
18. **mysteries**: trades, crafts. 19. **Degrees**: ranks.
20. **confounding contraries**: opposites that will produce chaos (*confound* = ruin utterly).
21. **yet confusion live**: nevertheless (though everything is destroyed) let destruction continue. 23. **cold**: i.e. incident to age (?).
24. **halt**: limp. 25. **liberty**: license.
27. **stream**: current. **strive**: struggle (to swim).
28. **riot**: licentious living. **blains**: sores, blisters.
29. **Sow**: sow themselves in.
31. **their**: i.e. the Athenians'. **society**: association with one another.
32. **merely**: entirely. **bear**: carry away.
34. **that too.** He is tearing off his clothes. **bans**: curses.
IV.ii. Location: Athens. Timon's house.

Are we undone, cast off, nothing remaining?
Flav. Alack, my fellows, what should I say to you?
Let me be recorded by the righteous gods,
I am as poor as you.
1. Serv. Such a house broke?
So noble a master fall'n, all gone, and not
One friend to take his fortune by the arm,
And go along with him.
2. Serv. As we do turn our backs
From our companion thrown into his grave,
So his familiars to his buried fortunes
Slink all away, leave their false vows with him,
Like empty purses pick'd; and his poor self,
A dedicated beggar to the air,
With his disease of all-shunn'd poverty,
Walks, like contempt, alone. More of our fellows.

Enter other SERVANTS.

Flav. All broken implements of a ruin'd house.
3. Serv. Yet do our hearts wear Timon's livery,
That see I by our faces; we are fellows still,
Serving alike in sorrow. Leak'd is our bark,
And we, poor mates, stand on the dying deck,
Hearing the surges threat; we must all part
Into this sea of air.
Flav. Good fellows all,
The latest of my wealth I'll share amongst you.
Where ever we shall meet, for Timon's sake
Let's yet be fellows. Let's shake our heads, and say,
As 'twere a knell unto our master's fortunes,
"We have seen better days." Let each take some;
[*Giving them money.*]
Nay, put out all your hands. Not one word more:
Thus part we rich in sorrow, parting poor.
Embrace, and part several ways.
O, the fierce wretchedness that glory brings us!
Who would not wish to be from wealth exempt,
Since riches point to misery and contempt?
Who would be so mock'd with glory, or to live
But in a dream of friendship,
To have his pomp, and all what state compounds,
But only painted, like his varnish'd friends?
Poor honest lord, brought low by his own heart,
Undone by goodness! Strange, unusual blood,
When man's worst sin is, he does too much good!
Who then dares to be half so kind again?
For bounty, that makes gods, do still mar men.
My dearest lord, blest to be most accurs'd,
Rich only to be wretched, thy great fortunes
Are made thy chief afflictions. Alas, kind lord,
He's flung in rage from this ingrateful seat

5. broke: gone bankrupt.
7. his fortune: i.e. him in his ill-fortune.
10. his familiars . . . fortunes: those friends who were so close to his fortunes now dead.
13. dedicated . . . air: i.e. beggar dedicated, or solely devoted, to the open air.
15. like contempt: as if he were contemptibility itself. **fellows:** fellow workers, associates (as also in lines 18, 22, 25).
20. dying: sinking. **23. latest:** last.
28. all your hands: the hands of all of you.
30. glory: greatness, high estate.
35. what . . . compounds: that splendor is composed of.
38. blood: nature. **40. again:** i.e. in future.
42. to be: only to be.

Of monstrous friends; nor has he with him to
Supply his life, or that which can command it.
I'll follow and inquire him out.
I'll ever serve his mind with my best will;
Whilst I have gold, I'll be his steward still. *Exit.*

[SCENE III]

Enter TIMON *in the woods.*

Tim. O blessed breeding sun, draw from the earth
Rotten humidity; below thy sister's orb
Infect the air! Twinn'd brothers of one womb,
Whose procreation, residence, and birth
Scarce is dividant, touch them with several fortunes,
The greater scorns the lesser. Not nature
(To whom all sores lay siege) can bear great fortune
But by contempt of nature.
Raise me this beggar, and deny't that lord,
The [senator] shall bear contempt hereditary,
The beggar native honor.
It is the paster lards the brother's sides,
The want that makes him [lean]. Who dares? who dares
In purity of manhood stand upright
And say, "This man's a flatterer"? If one be,
So are they all; for every grize of fortune
Is smooth'd by that below. The learned pate
Ducks to the golden fool. All's obliquy;
There's nothing level in our cursed natures
But direct villainy. Therefore be abhorr'd
All feasts, societies, and throngs of men!
His semblable, yea, himself, Timon disdains;
Destruction fang mankind! Earth, yield me roots!
[*Digging.*]
Who seeks for better of thee, sauce his palate
With thy most operant poison! What is here?
Gold? Yellow, glittering, precious gold?
No, gods, I am no idle votarist;
Roots, you clear heavens! Thus much of this will make

46–47. to . . . life: i.e. what is necessary to sustain life.

IV.iii. Location: Before Timon's cave in the woods, near the sea-shore.
1. from the earth: i.e. out of the earth and into the air (to infect the atmosphere).
2. Rotten humidity: dampness that causes rot. **thy sister's:** i.e. the moon's. See note on I.i.44.
5. dividant: capable of differentiation. **touch:** test. **several:** different.
6–8. Not . . . nature: human nature, subject to all kinds of evils, cannot bear prosperity without behaving in a manner which shows its contempt for the merely natural; i.e. a man raised by fortune out of the normal miseries of nature despises those who continue in them.
9. deny't: withhold such advancement from. Some editors emend to *deject*.
10–11. The senator . . . honor: i.e. the senator will be scorned and the beggar honored, as if each had been born to his new station.
12–13. It . . . lean: i.e. that one brother prospers and the other does not, is entirely explained by the quality of their luck. Many editors follow Singer in adopting Collier's famous conjecture *rother's* (= ox's) for *brother's*; others, with Warburton, read *wether's*.
12. paster: pasture. **16. grize:** step, level.
17. smooth'd: flattered.
18. Ducks: bows. **golden:** rich. **obliquy:** obliquity (perhaps by confusion with *obloquy*).
22. His semblable: anything resembling him, i.e. his fellow man.
23. fang: seize. **25. operant:** potent.
27. idle votarist: one who makes a vow lightly.
28. clear: pure.

Black white, foul fair, wrong right,
Base noble, old young, coward valiant.
Ha, you gods! why this? what this, you gods? Why, this
Will lug your priests and servants from your sides,
Pluck stout men's pillows from below their heads.
This yellow slave
Will knit and break religions, bless th' accurs'd,
Make the hoar leprosy ador'd, place thieves,
And give them title, knee, and approbation
With senators on the bench. This is it
That makes the wappen'd widow wed again;
She, whom the spittle-house and ulcerous sores
Would cast the gorge at, this embalms and spices
To th' April day again. Come, damn'd earth,
Thou common whore of mankind, that puts odds
Among the rout of nations, I will make thee
Do thy right nature. (*March afar off.*) Ha? a drum?
Th' art quick,
But yet I'll bury thee; thou't go, strong thief,
When gouty keepers of thee cannot stand.
Nay, stay thou out for earnest. [*Keeping some gold.*]

Enter ALCIBIADES, *with Drum and Fife, in warlike manner, and* PHRYNIA *and* TIMANDRA.

Alcib. What art thou there? speak.
Tim. A beast, as thou art. The canker gnaw thy heart,
For showing me again the eyes of man!
Alcib. What is thy name? Is man so hateful to thee,
That art thyself a man?
Tim. I am Misanthropos, and hate mankind.
For thy part, I do wish thou wert a dog,
That I might love thee something.
Alcib. I know thee well;
But in thy fortunes am unlearn'd and strange.
Tim. I know thee too, and more than that I know thee
I not desire to know. Follow thy drum,
With man's blood paint the ground, gules, gules.
Religious canons, civil laws are cruel;
Then what should war be? This fell whore of thine
Hath in her more destruction than thy sword,
For all her cherubin look.
Phry. Thy lips rot off!
Tim. I will not kiss thee, then the rot returns
To thine own lips again.
Alcib. How came the noble Timon to this change?
Tim. As the moon does, by wanting light to give:
But then renew I could not, like the moon;
There were no suns to borrow of.
Alcib. Noble Timon,
What friendship may I do thee?
Tim. None, but to
Maintain my opinion.
Alcib. What is it, Timon?
Tim. Promise me friendship, but perform none. If thou wilt not promise, the gods plague thee, for thou art a man! If thou dost perform, confound thee, for thou art a man!
Alcib. I have heard in some sort of thy miseries.
Tim. Thou saw'st them, when I had prosperity.
Alcib. I see them now, then was a blessed time.
Tim. As thine is now, held with a brace of harlots.
Timan. Is this th' Athenian minion, whom the world
Voic'd so regardfully?
Tim. Art thou Timandra?
Timan. Yes.
Tim. Be a whore still. They love thee not that use thee;
Give them diseases, leaving with thee their lust.
Make use of thy salt hours, season the slaves
For tubs and baths, bring down rose-cheek'd youth
To the [tub-]fast and the diet.
Timan. Hang thee, monster!
Alcib. Pardon him, sweet Timandra, for his wits
Are drown'd and lost in his calamities.
I have but little gold of late, brave Timon,
The want whereof doth daily make revolt
In my penurious band. I have heard, and griev'd,
How cursed Athens, mindless of thy worth,
Forgetting thy great deeds when neighbor states,
But for thy sword and fortune, trod upon them—
Tim. I prithee beat thy drum and get thee gone.
Alcib. I am thy friend, and pity thee, dear Timon.
Tim. How dost thou pity him whom thou dost trouble?
I had rather be alone.
Alcib. Why, fare thee well;
Here is some gold for thee.
Tim. Keep it, I cannot eat it.
Alcib. When I have laid proud Athens on a heap—
Tim. Warr'st thou 'gainst Athens?
Alcib. Ay, Timon, and have cause.
Tim. The gods confound them all in thy conquest,
And thee after, when thou hast conquer'd!
Alcib. Why me, Timon?
Tim. That by killing of villains
Thou wast born to conquer my country.

29. foul: ugly. **31. what:** for what, why.
33. Pluck . . . heads. "Alludes to the custom of drawing away the pillow to allow a dying man to die more easily. 'Stout' implies that gold will hasten on their way even those who are not at their last gasp." (Warburton, quoted by Maxwell.)
36. place: give office to. **37. knee:** i.e. deference.
38. With: i.e. on a level with. **39. wappen'd:** worn-out sexually.
40–41. spittle-house . . . at: hospital patients and sufferers from running sores would be sickened by.
43–44. puts . . . nations: creates dissensions among different peoples.
45. Do . . . nature: act in accordance with your true nature, i.e. create trouble. **quick:** swift in action (with quibble on the sense "alive").
46. thou't: thou wilt. **go:** walk, get about.
48. earnest: token payment, pledge. **50. canker:** ulcerous growth.
54. Misanthropos: i.e. a hater of mankind.
56. something: a little.
57. unlearn'd: uninformed. **strange:** ignorant.
60. gules: red (heraldic term). **62. fell:** deadly.
64. cherubin: angelic.

68. wanting: lacking. **71. but:** except.
74–76. If . . . man: i.e. if you refuse to make false promises, or if you make promises and carry them out, damn you anyway, because you are a man. **77. in some sort:** to some extent.
80. held with: i.e. bound to.
81. Athenian minion: darling of Athens.
82. Voic'd so regardfully: spoke of so respectfully.
86. salt: lascivious.
87–88. tubs . . . diet. Referring to treatments for venereal diseases.
93. penurious: poverty-stricken. **96. trod:** would have trodden.
102. on a heap: in ruins.

Put up thy gold. Go on—here's gold—go on;
Be as a planetary plague when Jove
Will o'er some high-vic'd city hang his poison
In the sick air. Let not thy sword skip one.
Pity not honor'd age for his white beard,
He is an usurer. Strike me the counterfeit matron,
It is her habit only that is honest,
Herself's a bawd. Let not the virgin's cheek
Make soft thy trenchant sword; for those milk paps,
That through the window[-bars] bore at men's eyes,
Are not within the leaf of pity writ,
But set them down horrible traitors. Spare not the babe,
Whose dimpled smiles from fools exhaust their mercy;
Think it a bastard, whom the oracle
Hath doubtfully pronounc'd the throat shall cut,
And mince it sans remorse. Swear against objects,
Put armor on thine ears and on thine eyes,
Whose proof nor yells of mothers, maids, nor babes,
Nor sight of priests in holy vestments bleeding,
Shall pierce a jot. There's gold to pay thy soldiers,
Make large confusion; and thy fury spent,
Confounded be thyself! Speak not, be gone.

Alcib. Hast thou gold yet? I'll take the gold thou givest me,
Not all thy counsel.

Tim. Dost thou, or dost thou not, heaven's curse upon thee!

Both [*Phry.*, *Timan.*]. Give us some gold, good Timon; hast thou more?

Tim. Enough to make a whore forswear her trade,
And to make whores, a bawd. Hold up, you sluts,
Your aprons mountant. You are not oathable,
Although I know you'll swear, terribly swear
Into strong shudders and to heavenly agues
Th' immortal gods that hear you. Spare your oaths;
I'll trust to your conditions, be whores still.
And he whose pious breath seeks to convert you,
Be strong in whore, allure him, burn him up,
Let your close fire predominate his smoke,
And be no turncoats; yet may your pains six months
Be quite contrary. And thatch your poor thin roofs
With burthens of the dead—some that were hang'd,
No matter; wear them, betray with them. Whore still,
Paint till a horse may mire upon your face:
A pox of wrinkles!

Both [*Phry.*, *Timan.*]. Well, more gold—what then?
Believe't that we'll do any thing for gold.

Tim. Consumptions sow
In hollow bones of man, strike their sharp shins,
And mar men's spurring. Crack the lawyer's voice,
That he may never more false title plead,
Nor sound his quillets shrilly; hoar the flamen,
That [scolds] against the quality of flesh
And not believes himself. Down with the nose,
Down with it flat; take the bridge quite away
Of him that, his particular to foresee,
Smells from the general weal. Make curl'd-pate ruffians bald,
And let the unscarr'd braggarts of the war
Derive some pain from you. Plague all,
That your activity may defeat and quell
The source of all erection. There's more gold.
Do you damn others, and let this damn you,
And ditches grave you all!

Both [*Phry.*, *Timan.*]. More counsel with more money, bounteous Timon.

Tim. More whore, more mischief first; I have given you earnest.

Alcib. Strike up the drum towards Athens! Farewell, Timon!
If I thrive well, I'll visit thee again.

Tim. If I hope well, I'll never see thee more.

Alcib. I never did thee harm.

Tim. Yes, thou spok'st well of me.

Alcib. Call'st thou that harm?

Tim. Men daily find it. Get thee away, and take
Thy beagles with thee.

Alcib. We but offend him. Strike!

[*Drum beats.*] *Exeunt* [*Alcibiades, Phrynia, and Timandra*].

Tim. That nature being sick of man's unkindness
Should yet be hungry! Common mother, thou [*Digging.*]
Whose womb unmeasurable and infinite breast
Teems and feeds all; whose self-same mettle,

108. Put up: put away.
109. planetary: caused by a malignant planet.
114. habit: dress, outward behavior.
117. window-bars: lattice of her window (?) or open-work squares of her bodice (?).
118. within . . . writ: i.e. on the list of things that are to be spared.
120. exhaust: draw out.
122. doubtfully: ambiguously or obscurely.
123. sans remorse: without pity. **Swear against objects:** take an oath not to heed objections.
125. Whose proof: the impenetrability of which (armor).
128. large confusion: widespread destruction.
132. Dost . . . not: whether you do or not.
134. forswear: i.e. retire from.
135. to . . . bawd: i.e. make a bawd retire from her trade of turning women into whores.
136. mountant: rising. (A coinage on the analogy of such heraldic terms as *rampant*; he means "hold up your skirts—which you're accustomed enough to doing—to receive the gold.") **oathable:** fit to be trusted on your oath.
140. conditions: characters. **still:** always.
143. close: hidden. **predominate:** overmaster. **his smoke:** i.e. his "pious breath."
144. pains . . . months. Obscure; perhaps referring to abnormal menstrual pain.
145–46. thatch . . . dead: cover your heads (the hair being lost through disease) with wigs made from the hair of the dead.
148. mire upon: bog down in. **149. of:** on.
151. Consumptions. Used of all wasting disease, including syphilis.
152. In hollow bones: i.e. in bones which become hollow in consequence.
155. quillets: quibbles. **hoar the flamen:** whiten (with disease) the priest; with a quibble on *hoar/whore.*
156. quality of flesh: fleshly nature, carnality.
157. Down . . . nose. The decay of the nasal bone was a conspicuous effect of syphilis.
159. particular: private gain. **foresee:** provide for.
160. Smells . . . weal: loses the scent of the public welfare.
161. unscarr'd . . . war: those who boast of their war service but have no scar to show for it. **163. quell:** destroy.
164. erection. With obvious double meaning.
166. grave: entomb.
168. whore: i.e. activity as whore. **earnest:** token payment.
171. If . . . well: if my hope is realized.
174. find it: discover that it is.
175. beagles: small hunting dogs, i.e. the prostitutes.
176. sick of: satiated with. **179. Teems:** bears. **mettle:** spirit.

Whereof thy proud child (arrogant man) is puff'd,
Engenders the black toad and adder blue,
The gilded newt and eyeless venom'd worm,
With all th' abhorred births below crisp heaven
Whereon Hyperion's quick'ning fire doth shine:
Yield him who all the human sons do hate,
From forth thy plenteous bosom, one poor root!
Ensear thy fertile and conceptious womb,
Let it no more bring out ingrateful man!
Go great with tigers, dragons, wolves, and bears,
Teem with new monsters, whom thy upward face
Hath to the marbled mansion all above
Never presented!—O, a root, dear thanks!—
Dry up thy marrows, vines, and plough-torn leas,
Whereof ingrateful man, with liquorish draughts
And morsels unctious, greases his pure mind,
That from it all consideration slips—

Enter APEMANTUS.

More man? Plague, plague!
Apem. I was directed hither. Men report
Thou dost affect my manners, and dost use them.
Tim. 'Tis then, because thou dost not keep a dog,
Whom I would imitate. Consumption catch thee!
Apem. This is in thee a nature but infected,
A poor unmanly melancholy sprung
From change of future. Why this spade? this place?
This slave-like habit? and these looks of care?
Thy flatterers yet wear silk, drink wine, lie soft,
Hug their diseas'd perfumes, and have forgot
That ever Timon was. Shame not these woods
By putting on the cunning of a carper.
Be thou a flatterer now, and seek to thrive
By that which has undone thee; hinge thy knee,
And let his very breath whom thou'lt observe
Blow off thy cap; praise his most vicious strain,
And call it excellent. Thou wast told thus;
Thou gav'st thine ears (like tapsters that bade welcome)
To knaves and all approachers. 'Tis most just
That thou turn rascal; hadst thou wealth again,
Rascals should have't. Do not assume my likeness.
Tim. Were I like thee, I'd throw away myself.
Apem. Thou hast cast away thyself, being like thyself,
A madman so long, now a fool. What, think'st
That the bleak air, thy boisterous chamberlain,
Will put thy shirt on warm? Will these moist trees,
That have outliv'd the eagle, page thy heels
And skip when thou point'st out? Will the cold brook,
Candied with ice, caudle thy morning taste
To cure thy o'ernight's surfeit? Call the creatures
Whose naked natures live in all the spite
Of wreakful heaven, whose bare unhoused trunks,
To the conflicting elements expos'd,
Answer mere nature; bid them flatter thee.
O, thou shalt find—
Tim. A fool of thee. Depart.
Apem. I love thee better now than e'er I did.
Tim. I hate thee worse.
Apem. Why?
Tim. Thou flatter'st misery.
Apem. I flatter not, but say thou art a caitiff.
Tim. Why dost thou seek me out?
Apem. To vex thee.
Tim. Always a villain's office, or a fool's.
Dost please thyself in't?
Apem. Ay.
Tim. What, a knave too?
Apem. If thou didst put this sour cold habit on
To castigate thy pride, 'twere well; but thou
Dost it enforcedly. Thou'dst courtier be again,
Wert thou not beggar. Willing misery
Outlives incertain pomp, is crown'd before:
The one is filling still, never complete;
The other, at high wish. Best state, contentless,
Hath a distracted and most wretched being,
Worse than the worst, content.
Thou shouldst desire to die, being miserable.
Tim. Not by his breath that is more miserable.
Thou art a slave, whom Fortune's tender arm
With favor never clasp'd, but bred a dog.
Hadst thou like us from our first swath proceeded
The sweet degrees that this brief world affords
To such as may the passive drugs of it
Freely [command], thou wouldst have plung'd thyself
In general riot, melted down thy youth
In different beds of lust, and never learn'd
The icy precepts of respect, but followed

180. puff'd: inflated with pride.
182. eyeless venom'd worm: probably the blindworm, wrongly believed to be poisonous.
183. abhorred: abhorrent. **crisp:** clear (?) or wavy (with clouds) (?).
184. Hyperion: the sun. **quick'ning:** life-giving.
187. Ensear: dry up. **conceptious:** conceiving, prolific.
189. Go great: be pregnant. **190. upward face:** i.e. surface.
191. marbled mansion: i.e. heaven. *Marbled* is variously explained as "shining" or "enduring, changeless." **192. dear:** heartfelt.
193. marrows . . . leas: i.e. the vineyards and fields of grain which can be regarded as the vital strength (*marrows*) of the earth's body.
194. liquorish: sweet.
195. unctious: unctuous, richly fat. **greases:** makes gross.
196. consideration: reflection. **205. habit:** garb.
207. perfumes: i.e. perfumed mistresses.
209. cunning: craft, profession. **carper:** cynic.
212. observe: pay court to.
214. Thou . . . thus: this is what you used to be told.
217. rascal: (1) rogue; (2) deer in poor condition, isolated from the herd.
222. chamberlain: body-servant.
224. page: follow attentively like pages.
225. skip . . . out: i.e. leap to do your bidding.
226. Candied: crusted over (as with sugar). **caudle . . . taste:** serve you a warm soothing drink in the morning.
227. o'ernight's: last night's.
229. wreakful: vengeful. **trunks:** bodies.
231. Answer mere nature: contend with stark nature.
232. of: in. **235. caitiff:** wretch.
242–43. Willing . . . before: poverty when voluntarily undergone is a securer state than luxury with all its uncertainties, and achieves its desires sooner.
245. at high wish: at the height of its desires.
247. Worse . . . content: worse than the meanest state which is contentedly accepted. **249. his breath:** the advice of him.
252. swath: swaddling-clothes. **proceeded:** passed through (university term).
254. passive drugs. Schmidt explains as "all things in passive subserviency to salutary as well as pernicious purposes" (since *drug* was frequently used of poison as well as of healing substances); but *drugges* (the reading of F1) was also a variant spelling of *drudges*, which most editors take to be the probable meaning here.
258. icy . . . respect: the cold admonitions of reason.

The sug'red game before thee. But myself,
Who had the world as my confectionary,
The mouths, the tongues, the eyes, and hearts of men
At duty, more than I could frame employment;
That numberless upon me stuck as leaves
Do on the oak, have with one winter's brush
Fell from their boughs, and left me open, bare,
For every storm that blows—I to bear this,
That never knew but better, is some burthen:
Thy nature did commence in sufferance, time
Hath made thee hard in't. Why shouldst thou hate men?
They never flatter'd thee. What hast thou given?
If thou wilt curse, thy father (that poor rag)
Must be thy subject, who in spite put stuff
To some she-beggar and compounded thee
Poor rogue hereditary. Hence, be gone!
If thou hadst not been born the worst of men,
Thou hadst been a knave and flatterer.

Apem. Art thou proud yet?

Tim. Ay, that I am not thee.

Apem. I, that I was
No prodigal.

Tim. I, that I am one now.
Were all the wealth I have shut up in thee,
I'ld give thee leave to hang it. Get thee gone.
That the whole life of Athens were in this!
Thus would I eat it. [*Eating a root.*]

Apem. Here, I will mend thy feast.
[*Offering him another.*]

Tim. First mend [my] company, take away thyself.

Apem. So I shall mend mine own, by th' lack of thine.

Tim. 'Tis not well mended so, it is but botch'd;
If not, I would it were.

Apem. What wouldst thou have to Athens?

Tim. Thee thither in a whirlwind. If thou wilt,
Tell them there I have gold; look, so I have.

Apem. Here is no use for gold.

Tim. The best, and truest;
For here it sleeps, and does no hired harm.

Apem. Where liest a' nights, Timon?

Tim. Under that's above me.
Where feed'st thou a' days, Apemantus?

Apem. Where my stomach finds meat, or, rather, where I eat it.

Tim. Would poison were obedient and knew my mind!

Apem. Where wouldst thou send it?

Tim. To sauce thy dishes.

Apem. The middle of humanity thou never knew-est, but the extremity of both ends. When thou wast in thy gilt and thy perfume, they mock'd thee for too much curiosity; in thy rags thou know'st none, but art despis'd for the contrary. There's a medlar for thee, eat it.

Tim. On what I hate I feed not.

Apem. Dost hate a medlar?

Tim. Ay, though it look like thee.

Apem. And th' hadst hated meddlers sooner, thou shouldst have lov'd thyself better now. What man didst thou ever know unthrift that was belov'd after his means?

Tim. Who, without those means thou talk'st of, didst thou ever know belov'd?

Apem. Myself.

Tim. I understand thee: thou hadst some means to keep a dog.

Apem. What things in the world canst thou nearest compare to thy flatterers?

Tim. Women nearest, but men—men are the things themselves. What wouldst thou do with the world, Apemantus, if it lay in thy power?

Apem. Give it the beasts, to be rid of the men.

Tim. Wouldst thou have thyself fall in the confusion of men, and remain a beast with the beasts?

Apem. Ay, Timon.

Tim. A beastly ambition, which the gods grant thee t' attain to! If thou wert the lion, the fox would beguile thee; if thou wert the lamb, the fox would eat thee; if thou wert the fox, the lion would suspect thee, when peradventure thou wert accus'd by the ass; if thou wert the ass, thy dullness would torment thee, and still thou liv'dst but as a breakfast to the wolf; if thou wert the wolf, thy greediness would afflict thee, and oft thou shouldst hazard thy life for thy dinner; wert thou the unicorn, pride and wrath would confound thee and make thine own self the conquest of thy fury; wert thou a bear, thou wouldst be kill'd by the horse; wert thou a horse, thou wouldst be seiz'd by the leopard; wert thou a leopard, thou wert germane to the lion, and the spots of thy kindred were jurors on thy life; all thy safety were remotion and thy defense absence. What beast couldst thou be, that were not subject to a beast? And what a beast art thou already, that seest not thy loss in transformation!

Apem. If thou couldst please me with speaking to me, thou mightst have hit upon it here. The commonwealth of Athens is become a forest of beasts.

259. sug'red game: enticing quarry.
260. confectionary: place where sweets are made.
262. At duty: awaiting my command. **frame:** devise (for).
263. That: i.e. they that. **265. Fell:** fallen.
268. sufferance: suffering.
269. made . . . in't: hardened you to it. **282. mend:** improve.
285. botch'd: badly mended (because he is still in his own company).
286. If . . . were. Obscure; perhaps "I wish your company were truly mended—by your death."
287. What . . . have: i.e. what report shall I take back, what message will you send (but Timon replies with a quibble).
291. hired: suborned. **292. that's:** what is.
303. curiosity: fastidiousness.
304. medlar: small apple-like fruit, eaten when partly decayed.
308. like thee: i.e. decayed. **309. And:** if.
311. after: (1) in accordance with; (2) after the loss of.
316–17. thou . . . dog: i.e. since only a dog could love you, you must once have had means enough to keep a dog.
329. beguile: deceive by craft.
331. when . . . wert: if you happened to be.
333. liv'dst: wouldst live.
336. unicorn. Caught by being tricked into charging a tree and embedding its horn deeply.
340. wert germane: wouldst be german, i.e. akin, related.
341–42. the spots . . . life: the crimes of your relatives would be reasons for condemning you to death.
342. all . . . remotion: your only safety would lie in removing yourself to some other place.
345. thy . . . transformation: what you would lose by being changed to an animal.

Tim. How has the ass broke the wall, that thou art out of the city?

Apem. Yonder comes a poet and a painter; the plague of company light upon thee! I will fear to catch it, and give way. When I know not what else to do, I'll see thee again.

Tim. When there is nothing living but thee, thou shalt be welcome. I had rather be a beggar's dog than Apemantus.

Apem. Thou art the cap of all the fools alive.
Tim. Would thou wert clean enough to spit upon!
Apem. A plague on thee, thou art too bad to curse!
Tim. All villains that do stand by thee are pure.
Apem. There is no leprosy but what thou speak'st.
Tim. If I name thee.
I'll beat thee, but I should infect my hands.
Apem. I would my tongue could rot them off!
Tim. Away, thou issue of a mangy dog!
Choler does kill me that thou art alive;
I swound to see thee.
Apem. Would thou wouldst burst!
Tim. Away, thou tedious rogue!
I am sorry I shall lose a stone by thee.
[*Throws a stone at him.*]
Apem. Beast!
Tim. Slave!
Apem. Toad!
Tim. Rogue, rogue, rogue!
I am sick of this false world, and will love nought
But even the mere necessities upon't.
Then, Timon, presently prepare thy grave;
Lie where the light foam of the sea may beat
Thy grave-stone daily; make thine epitaph,
That death in me at others' lives may laugh.
[*To the gold.*] O thou sweet king-killer, and dear divorce
'Twixt natural [son] and [sire]! thou bright defiler
Of Hymen's purest bed! thou valiant Mars!
Thou ever young, fresh, lov'd, and delicate wooer,
Whose blush doth thaw the consecrated snow
That lies on Dian's lap! thou visible god,
That sold'rest close impossibilities,
And mak'st them kiss! that speak'st with every tongue
To every purpose! O thou touch of hearts,
Think thy slave man rebels, and by thy virtue
Set them into confounding odds, that beasts
May have the world in empire!
Apem. Would 'twere so!
But not till I am dead. I'll say th' hast gold;
Thou wilt be throng'd to shortly.

351. **Yonder . . . painter.** Their entry is long postponed; probably Shakespeare had second thoughts but neglected to delete this line.
358. **cap:** chief. 361. **are pure:** i.e. seem pure by contrast.
368. **swound:** swoon. 376. **even:** only. **mere:** bare.
377. **presently:** without delay.
382. **natural:** i.e. bound by ties of nature.
383. **Hymen:** god of marriage. **Mars.** Alluding to Mars' adultery with Venus.
385–86. **Whose . . . lap:** i.e. whose glow overpowers the most steadfast chastity.
387. **close:** tightly. **impossibilities:** things (otherwise) incapable of being brought together.
389. **touch:** touchstone. 390. **virtue:** power.
391. **them:** i.e. men. **into confounding odds:** at strife that will destroy them.

Tim. Throng'd to?
Apem. Ay.
Tim. Thy back, I prithee.
Apem. Live, and love thy misery.
Tim. Long live so, and so die. I am quit.
Apem. Moe things like men! eat, Timon, and abhor [them]. *Exit Apemantus.*

Enter the BANDITTI.

1. Ban. Where should he have this gold? It is some poor fragment, some slender ort of his remainder. The mere want of gold, and the falling-from of his friends, drove him into this melancholy.

2. Ban. It is nois'd he hath a mass of treasure.

3. Ban. Let us make the assay upon him. If he care not for't, he will supply us easily; if he covetously reserve it, how shall 's get it?

2. Ban. True; for he bears it not about him, 'tis hid.
1. Ban. Is not this he?
All [*Other Banditti*]. Where?
2. Ban. 'Tis his description.
3. Ban. He; I know him.
All [*Banditti*]. 'Save thee, Timon.
Tim. Now, thieves?
All [*Banditti*]. Soldiers, not thieves.
Tim. Both too, and women's sons.
All [*Banditti*]. We are not thieves, but men that much do want.
Tim. Your greatest want is, you want much of meat.
Why should you want? Behold, the earth hath roots;
Within this mile break forth a hundred springs;
The oaks bear mast, the briers scarlet heps;
The bounteous huswife Nature on each bush
Lays her full mess before you. Want? why want?
1. Ban. We cannot live on grass, on berries, water,
As beasts and birds and fishes.
Tim. Nor on the beasts themselves, the birds and fishes;
You must eat men. Yet thanks I must you con
That you are thieves profess'd, that you work not
In holier shapes; for there is boundless theft
In limited professions. Rascal thieves,
Here's gold. Go, suck the subtle blood o' th' grape,
Till the high fever seethe your blood to froth,
And so scape hanging. Trust not the physician,
His antidotes are poison, and he slays
Moe than you rob. Take wealth and lives together,
Do, [villains,] do, since you protest to do't.

396. **quit:** rid (of you).
397. **Moe:** (here come) more. Many editors follow Hanmer in giving this line to Timon.
398. **Where . . . have:** where can he have got.
399. **ort:** scrap. 400. **mere:** utter.
403. **assay:** trial (used to determine the amount of precious metal in ore or alloy). 411. **'Save:** God save.
415. **want:** lack. Timon plays on the word in his reply: "Your greatest feeling of lack is occasioned by the fact that you desire a great deal to eat."
419. **mast:** acorns, beech nuts, and other fruits of forest trees. **heps:** hips, fruit of the wild rose.
420. **huswife:** housewife. 421. **mess:** meal. 425. **con:** offer.
427. **holier shapes:** more respectable guises.
428. **limited:** restricted, officially regulated.
431. **scape hanging:** i.e. by dying of drink. 434. **protest:** profess.

Like workmen, I'll example you with thievery:
The sun's a thief, and with his great attraction
Robs the vast sea; the moon's an arrant thief,
And her pale fire she snatches from the sun;
The sea's a thief, whose liquid surge resolves
The moon into salt tears; the earth's a thief,
That feeds and breeds by a composture stol'n
From gen'ral excrement; each thing's a thief.
The laws, your curb and whip, in their rough power
Has uncheck'd theft. Love not yourselves, away,
Rob one another. There's more gold. Cut throats,
All that you meet are thieves. To Athens go,
Break open shops; nothing can you steal
But thieves do lose it. Steal less for this I give you,
And gold confound you howsoe'er! Amen.

3. Ban. H'as almost charm'd me from my profession, by persuading me to it.

1. Ban. 'Tis in the malice of mankind that he thus advises us, not to have us thrive in our mystery.

2. Ban. I'll believe him as an enemy, and give over my trade.

1. Ban. Let us first see peace in Athens. There is no time so miserable but a man may be true.

Exeunt Thieves [*the Banditti*].

Enter the Steward [Flavius] *to Timon.*

Flav. O you gods!
Is yond despis'd and ruinous man my lord?
Full of decay and failing? O monument
And wonder of good deeds evilly bestow'd!
What an alteration of honor has desp'rate want made!
What vilder thing upon the earth than friends,
Who can bring noblest minds to basest ends!
How rarely does it meet with this time's guise,
When man was wish'd to love his enemies!
Grant I may ever love, and rather woo
Those that would mischief me than those that do!
H'as caught me in his eye, I will present
My honest grief unto him; and as my lord,
Still serve him with my life. My dearest master!

Tim. Away! what art thou?

Flav. Have you forgot me, sir?

Tim. Why dost ask that? I have forgot all men.
Then, if thou [grant'st] th' art a man, I have forgot thee.

Flav. An honest poor servant of yours.

Tim. Then I know thee not.
I never had honest man about me, I; all

I kept were knaves, to serve in meat to villains.

Flav. The gods are witness,
Nev'r did poor steward wear a truer grief
For his undone lord than mine eyes for you.

Tim. What, dost thou weep? Come nearer. Then I love thee,
Because thou art a woman, and disclaim'st
Flinty mankind, whose eyes do never give
But thorough lust and laughter. Pity's sleeping:
Strange times, that weep with laughing, not with weeping!

Flav. I beg of you to know me, good my lord,
T' accept my grief, and whilst this poor wealth lasts
To entertain me as your steward still.

Tim. Had I a steward
So true, so just, and now so comfortable?
It almost turns my dangerous nature wild.
Let me behold thy face. Surely, this man
Was born of woman.
Forgive my general and exceptless rashness,
You perpetual-sober gods! I do proclaim
One honest man—mistake me not, but one;
No more, I pray—and he's a steward.
How fain would I have hated all mankind,
And thou redeem'st thyself. But all, save thee,
I fell with curses.
Methinks thou art more honest now than wise;
For, by oppressing and betraying me,
Thou mightst have sooner got another service;
For many so arrive at second masters,
Upon their first lord's neck. But tell me true
(For I must ever doubt, though ne'er so sure),
Is not thy kindness subtle, covetous,
If not a usuring kindness, and, as rich men deal gifts,
Expecting in return twenty for one?

Flav. No, my most worthy master, in whose breast
Doubt and suspect, alas, are plac'd too late;
You should have fear'd false times when you did feast:
Suspect still comes where an estate is least.
That which I show, heaven knows, is merely love,
Duty, and zeal to your unmatched mind,
Care of your food and living; and believe it,
My most honor'd lord,
For any benefit that points to me,
Either in hope or present, I'd exchange
For this one wish, that you had power and wealth
To requite me by making rich yourself.

Tim. Look thee, 'tis so. Thou singly honest man,
Here, take; the gods out of my misery
Has sent thee treasure. Go, live rich and happy,
But thus condition'd: thou shalt build from men;

435. Like . . . thievery: i.e. as one does in instructing practitioners of any craft, I'll furnish you with instances of your profession, thievery.
439. resolves: dissolves. **441. composture:** compost, manure.
444. uncheck'd theft: unlimited power to thieve.
448–49. Steal . . . howsoe'er: if you steal less because of the gold I am giving you, may gold destroy you whatever happens.
452. the malice: i.e. his hatred. **453. mystery:** trade, craft.
454. as: i.e. as I would believe.
456. Let . . . peace: let us wait until the war is over (and prospects for stealing are less good). **457. true:** honest.
459. ruinous: in ruins.
460–61. monument And wonder: wonderful monument, awesome memorial.
465–66. How . . . enemies: i.e. how excellently (*rarely*) does the command to love our enemies suit the fashion of this age.
468. Those . . . do: those who frankly intend my harm rather than those who harm me (while falsely professing friendship).

478. serve in: serve. **484. give:** yield tears.
485. thorough: through. **489. entertain:** employ.
491. comfortable: comforting.
492. wild: insane. Most editors read *mild*, following Hanmer.
495. exceptless: making no exception. **499. fain:** gladly.
500. And . . . thyself: but you deliver yourself (from the all-embracing hatred intended). **501. fell:** strike down. **504. service:** position..
506. Upon . . . neck: i.e. by treading down their first employer.
509. If not. These words are usually, and perhaps rightly, omitted by editors, following Pope.
512. suspect: suspicion. **515. merely:** purely.
523. singly: (1) uniquely; (2) sincerely.
526. thus condition'd: on these conditions. **from:** remote from.

Hate all, curse all, show charity to none,
But let the famish'd flesh slide from the bone
Ere thou relieve the beggar. Give to dogs
What thou deniest to men. Let prisons swallow 'em,
Debts wither 'em to nothing; be men like blasted woods,
And may diseases lick up their false bloods!
And so farewell and thrive.

Flav. O, let me stay,
And comfort you, my master.

Tim. If thou hat'st curses,
Stay not; fly, whilst thou art blest and free.
Ne'er see thou man, and let me ne'er see thee.

Exeunt [*severally*].

[ACT V, SCENE I]

Enter POET *and* PAINTER; [TIMON *watching them from his cave*].

Pain. As I took note of the place, it cannot be far
Where he abides.

Poet. What's to be thought of him?
Does the rumor hold for true that he's
So full of gold?

Pain. Certain. Alcibiades reports it;
[Phrynia] and [Timandra] had gold of him.
He likewise enrich'd poor straggling soldiers with
Great quantity. 'Tis said he gave unto
His steward a mighty sum.

Poet. Then this breaking of his
Has been but a try for his friends?

Pain. Nothing else.
You shall see him a palm in Athens again, and flourish
With the highest. Therefore, 'tis not amiss
We tender our loves to him in this suppos'd
Distress of his; it will show honestly in us,
And is very likely to load our purposes
With what they travail for, if it be
A just and true report that goes of his having.

Poet. What have you now to present unto him?

Pain. Nothing at this time but my visitation;
Only I will promise him an excellent piece.

Poet. I must serve him so too: tell him of an intent
That's coming toward him.

Pain. Good as the best.
Promising is the very air o' th' time;
It opens the eyes of expectation.
Performance is ever the duller for his act,
And but in the plainer and simpler kind of people
The deed of saying is quite out of use.
To promise is most courtly and fashionable;
Performance is a kind of will or testament
Which argues a great sickness in his judgment
That makes it.

Enter TIMON *from his cave*.

Tim. [*Aside.*] Excellent workman! thou canst not paint a man
So bad as is thyself.

Poet. I am thinking
What I shall say I have provided for him.
It must be a personating of himself;
A satire against the softness of prosperity,
With a discovery of the infinite flatteries
That follow youth and opulency.

Tim. [*Aside.*] Must thou needs
Stand for a villain in thine own work?
Wilt thou whip thine own faults in other men?
Do so, I have gold for thee.

Poet. Nay, let's seek him:
Then do we sin against our own estate,
When we may profit meet, and come too late.

Pain. True:
When the day serves, before black-corner'd night,
Find what thou want'st by free and offer'd light.
Come.

Tim. [*Aside.*] I'll meet you at the turn. What a god's gold
That he is worshipp'd in a baser temple
Than where swine feed!
'Tis thou that rig'st the bark and plough'st the foam,
Settlest admired reverence in a slave.
To thee be [worship], and thy saints for aye
Be crown'd with plagues, that thee alone obey!
Fit I meet them. [*Coming forward.*]

Poet. Hail, worthy Timon!

Pain. Our late noble master!

Tim. Have I once liv'd to see two honest men?

Poet. Sir,
Having often of your open bounty tasted,
Hearing you were retir'd, your friends fall'n off,
Whose thankless natures (O abhorred spirits!)
Not all the whips of heaven are large enough—
What, to you,
Whose star-like nobleness gave life and influence
To their whole being! I am rapt and cannot cover
The monstrous bulk of this ingratitude
With any size of words.

Tim. Let it go naked, men may see't the better.
You that are honest, by being what you are
Make them best seen and known.

Pain. He and myself
Have travail'd in the great show'r of your gifts,
And sweetly felt it.

Tim. Ay, you are honest [men].

Pain. We are hither come to offer you our service.

Tim. Most honest men! Why, how shall I requite you?

531. blasted: blighted, withered.

V.i. Location: The woods, before Timon's cave.
8. breaking: bankruptcy. **9. try:** test.
13. show honestly: appear honorable. **14. load:** reward.
16. having: wealth.
18. visitation: visit. Shakespeare knew the word *visit* only as a verb.
24. his act: its performance.
26. deed of saying: fulfillment of promise.

34. himself: i.e. his case. **36. discovery:** exposure.
38. Stand: be a model.
44. black-corner'd: obscuring things as in dark corners.
45. free and offer'd: offered freely.
47. meet . . . turn. Obscure; perhaps "play you at your own game" (Maxwell).
51. Settlest . . . slave: causes a slave to admire and venerate his master. **52. saints:** devotees. **56. once:** actually, indeed.
63. influence: i.e. astral influence.
64. rapt: carried out of myself, at a loss for words.
66. size: quantity. **69. them:** i.e. ungrateful men.

Can you eat roots and drink cold water? No?
Both. What we can do, we'll do, to do you service.
Tim. Y' are honest men; y' have heard that I have gold,
I am sure you have. Speak truth, y' are honest men.
Pain. So it is said, my noble lord, but therefore
Came not my friend nor I.
Tim. Good honest men! Thou draw'st a counterfeit
Best in all Athens; th' art indeed the best,
Thou counterfeit'st most lively.
Pain. So, so, my lord.
Tim. E'en so, sir, as I say.—And, for thy fiction,
Why, thy verse swells with stuff so fine and smooth
That thou art even natural in thine art.
But for all this, my honest-natur'd friends,
I must needs say you have a little fault;
Marry, 'tis not monstrous in you, neither wish I
You take much pains to mend.
Both. Beseech your honor
To make it known to us.
Tim. You'll take it ill.
Both. Most thankfully, my lord.
Tim. Will you indeed?
Both. Doubt it not, worthy lord.
Tim. There's never a one of you but trusts a knave
That mightily deceives you.
Both. Do we, my lord?
Tim. Ay, and you hear him cog, see him dissemble,
Know his gross patchery, love him, feed him,
Keep in your bosom; yet remain assur'd
That he's a made-up villain.
Pain. I know none such, my lord.
Poet. Nor I.
Tim. Look you, I love you well, I'll give you gold,
Rid me these villains from your companies;
Hang them, or stab them, drown them in a draught,
Confound them by some course, and come to me,
I'll give you gold enough.
Both. Name them, my lord, let's know them.
Tim. You that way and you this; but two in company;
Each man apart, all single and alone,
Yet an arch-villain keeps him company.
[*To one.*] If where thou art, two villains shall not be,
Come not near him. [*To the other.*] If thou wouldst not reside
But where one villain is, then him abandon.—
Hence, pack! there's gold; you came for gold, ye slaves.
[*To one.*] You have work for me; there's payment, hence!
[*To the other.*] You are an alcumist, make gold of that.
Out, rascal dogs!
Exeunt [*both, driven out by Timon, who retires to his cave*].

Enter Steward [FLAVIUS] *and two* SENATORS.

Flav. It is vain that you would speak with Timon;
For he is set so only to himself,
That nothing but himself which looks like man
Is friendly with him.
1. Sen. Bring us to his cave.
It is our part and promise to th' Athenians
To speak with Timon.
2. Sen. At all times alike
Men are not still the same; 'twas time and griefs
That fram'd him thus. Time with his fairer hand,
Offering the fortunes of his former days,
The former man may make him. Bring us to him,
And [chance] it as it may.
Flav. Here is his cave.
Peace and content be here! Lord Timon! Timon,
Look out and speak to friends. Th' Athenians
By two of their most reverend Senate greet thee.
Speak to them, noble Timon.

Enter TIMON *out of his cave.*

Tim. Thou sun that comforts, burn! Speak and be hang'd.
For each true word, a blister, and each false
Be as a cantherizing to the root o' th' tongue,
Consuming it with speaking!
1. Sen. Worthy Timon—
Tim. Of none but such as you, and you of Timon.
1. Sen. The senators of Athens greet thee, Timon.
Tim. I thank them, and would send them back the plague,
Could I but catch it for them.
1. Sen. O, forget
What we are sorry for ourselves in thee.
The senators with one consent of love
Entreat thee back to Athens, who have thought
On special dignities, which vacant lie,
For thy best use and wearing.
2. Sen. They confess
Toward thee forgetfulness too general gross;
Which now the public body, which doth seldom
Play the recanter, feeling in itself
A lack of Timon's aid, hath [sense] withal
Of it own fall, restraining aid to Timon,

78–79. **therefore . . . I:** it was not for that reason that we came.
80. **counterfeit:** portrait (but Timon intends also the fraudulent sense).
82. **Thou . . . lively:** (1) you paint very realistically; (2) you are a living counterfeit. **So, so:** passably.
83–84. **fiction, swells, stuff, smooth.** These are all words capable of being taken in two ways.
85. **thou . . . art:** (1) your art equals nature; (2) the feigning of your art reveals your own nature. 95. **cog:** cheat.
96. **patchery:** knavery. 98. **made-up:** complete.
102. **draught:** privy. 103. **Confound:** get rid of.
106. **two in company:** i.e. each still in company with another.
109. **shall not:** are not to. 112. **pack:** be off.
114. **alcumist:** alchemist. **that.** Probably a thrown stone; another may have been the "payment" of line 113.
117. **set . . . to:** so completely intent upon.
119. **friendly with:** congenial to.
120. **our . . . Athenians:** i.e. the part we have promised the Athenians we will play.
122. **still the same.** Synonymous with *At all times alike.* **griefs:** grievances.
123. **fram'd:** shaped, i.e. altered. 126. **chance it:** let it turn out.
133. **cantherizing.** On this form, for which most editors substitute *cauterizing*, see the Textual Notes. 139. **in thee:** in your case.
140. **one . . . love:** a single loving voice.
144. **general gross:** obvious to everybody.
147. **hath sense withal:** becomes aware at the same time.
148. **it:** its. **fall:** decline, defection from virtue. **restraining:** in holding back.

And send forth us to make their sorrowed render,
Together with a recompense more fruitful
Than their offense can weigh down by the dram;
Ay, even such heaps and sums of love and wealth
As shall to thee blot out what wrongs were theirs,
And write in thee the figures of their love,
Ever to read them thine.
Tim. You witch me in it;
Surprise me to the very brink of tears.
Lend me a fool's heart and a woman's eyes,
And I'll beweep these comforts, worthy senators.
1. Sen. Therefore so please thee to return with us,
And of our Athens, thine and ours, to take
The captainship, thou shalt be met with thanks,
Allow'd with absolute power, and thy good name
Live with authority; so soon we shall drive back
Of Alcibiades th' approaches wild,
Who, like a boar too savage, doth root up
His country's peace.
2. Sen. And shakes his threat'ning sword
Against the walls of Athens.
1. Sen. Therefore, Timon—
Tim. Well, sir, I will; therefore I will, sir, thus:
If Alcibiades kill my countrymen,
Let Alcibiades know this of Timon,
That Timon cares not. But if he sack fair Athens,
And take our goodly aged men by th' beards,
Giving our holy virgins to the stain
Of contumelious, beastly, mad-brain'd war,
Then let him know, and tell him Timon speaks it,
In pity of our aged and our youth,
I cannot choose but tell him that I care not,
And let him take't at worst—for their knives care not,
While you have throats to answer. For myself,
There's not a whittle in th' unruly camp
But I do prize it at my love before
The [reverend'st] throat in Athens. So I leave you
To the protection of the prosperous gods,
As thieves to keepers.
Flav. Stay not, all's in vain.
Tim. Why, I was writing of my epitaph;
It will be seen to-morrow. My long sickness
Of health and living now begins to mend,
And nothing brings me all things. Go, live still;
Be Alcibiades your plague, you his,
And last so long enough!
1. Sen. We speak in vain.
Tim. But yet I love my country, and am not
One that rejoices in the common wrack,
As common bruit doth put it.

149. sorrowed render: sorrowful acknowledgement.
150. fruitful: abundant.
151. weigh . . . dram: outweigh even if measured out to the last fraction of an ounce. **153. theirs:** of their doing.
154. figures: (1) shapes, signs; (2) amounts. **of their love:** that show how much they love you. **156. Surprise:** overcome.
159. so: if it. **162. Allow'd:** endowed.
174. contumelious: insolent.
178. take't at worst: put the worst construction on it.
179. answer: be answerable, suffer the consequences.
180. whittle: clasp-knife. **unruly:** rebel. **181. at:** in.
183. prosperous: propitious.
184. keepers: jailers (who "protect" thieves for the hangman).
188. nothing: i.e. death. **193. bruit:** rumor.

1. Sen. That's well spoke.
Tim. Commend me to my loving countrymen—
1. Sen. These words become your lips as they pass thorough them.
2. Sen. And enter in our ears like great triumphers
In their applauding gates.
Tim. Commend me to them,
And tell them that, to ease them of their griefs,
Their fears of hostile strokes, their aches, losses,
Their pangs of love, with other incident throes
That nature's fragile vessel doth sustain
In life's uncertain voyage, I will some kindness do them:
I'll teach them to prevent wild Alcibiades' wrath.
1. Sen. I like this well, he will return again.
Tim. I have a tree, which grows here in my close,
That mine own use invites me to cut down,
And shortly must I fell it. Tell my friends,
Tell Athens, in the sequence of degree,
From high to low throughout, that whoso please
To stop affliction, let him take his haste,
Come hither, ere my tree hath felt the axe,
And hang himself. I pray you do my greeting.
Flav. Trouble him no further, thus you still shall find him.
Tim. Come not to me again, but say to Athens,
Timon hath made his everlasting mansion
Upon the beached verge of the salt flood,
Who once a day with his embossed froth
The turbulent surge shall cover; thither come,
And let my grave-stone be your oracle.
Lips, let four words go by and language end!
What is amiss, plague and infection mend!
Graves only be men's works, and death their gain!
Sun, hide thy beams, Timon hath done his reign.
Exit Timon.
1. Sen. His discontents are unremovably
Coupled to nature.
2. Sen. Our hope in him is dead. Let us return,
And strain what other means is left unto us
In our dear peril.
1. Sen. It requires swift foot. *Exeunt.*

[Scene II]

Enter two other Senators *with a* Messenger.

[3.] *Sen.* Thou hast painfully discover'd; are his files
As full as thy report?
Mess. I have spoke the least.

203. prevent: forestall, thwart.
205. close: enclosure. **208. degree:** rank.
216. beached verge: beach at the edge.
217. Who. Object of *cover* (line 218); the sense here is probably "which" (as often) rather than "whom." **embossed:** foaming.
219. oracle: i.e. source of wisdom. **220. four.** Indefinite.
225. Coupled to nature: made part of his nature.
227. strain: exert to the limit. **228. dear:** extreme, dire.

V.ii. Location: Before the walls of Athens.
1. painfully discover'd: reconnoitred painstakingly (?) or revealed distressing news (?).
2. spoke the least: given the most conservative estimate.

Besides, his expedition promises
Present approach.

[*4.*] *Sen.* We stand much hazard if they bring not
Timon.

Mess. I met a courier, one mine ancient friend,
Whom, though in general part we were oppos'd,
Yet our old love made a particular force,
And made us speak like friends. This man was riding
From Alcibiades to Timon's cave
With letters of entreaty, which imported
His fellowship i' th' cause against your city,
In part for his sake mov'd.

Enter the other SENATORS.

[*3.*] *Sen.* Here come our brothers.

[*1.*] *Sen.* No talk of Timon, nothing of him expect.
The enemy's drum is heard, and fearful scouring
Doth choke the air with dust. In, and prepare:
Ours is the fall, I fear, our foes the snare. *Exeunt.*

[SCENE III]

Enter a SOLDIER *in the woods, seeking Timon.* [*A rude tomb seen.*]

Sold. By all description this should be the place.
Who's here? Speak ho! No answer? What is this?
[*Reads.*] "Timon is dead, who hath outstretch'd his
span:
Some beast read this; there does not live a man."
Dead, sure, and this his grave. What's on this tomb
I cannot read; the character I'll take with wax;
Our captain hath in every figure skill,
An ag'd interpreter, though young in days.
Before proud Athens he's set down by this,
Whose fall the mark of his ambition is. *Exit.*

[SCENE IV]

Trumpets sound. Enter ALCIBIADES *with his powers before Athens.*

Alcib. Sound to this coward and lascivious town
Our terrible approach. *Sounds a parley.*

The SENATORS *appear upon the walls.*

Till now you have gone on and fill'd the time
With all licentious measure, making your wills
The scope of justice; till now myself and such
As slept within the shadow of your power
Have wander'd with our travers'd arms, and breath'd
Our sufferance vainly. Now the time is flush,
When crouching marrow in the bearer strong
Cries (of itself) "No more!" Now breathless wrong
Shall sit and pant in your great chairs of ease,
And pursy insolence shall break his wind
With fear and horrid flight.

1. Sen. Noble and young—
When thy first griefs were but a mere conceit,
Ere thou hadst power or we had cause of fear,
We sent to thee to give thy rages balm,
To wipe out our ingratitude with loves
Above their quantity.

2. Sen. So did we woo
Transformed Timon to our city's love
By humble message and by promis'd means.
We were not all unkind, nor all deserve
The common stroke of war.

1. Sen. These walls of ours
Were not erected by their hands from whom
You have receiv'd your grief; nor are they such
That these great tow'rs, trophies, and schools should
fall
For private faults in them.

2. Sen. Nor are they living
Who were the motives that you first went out;
Shame, that they wanted cunning in excess,
Hath broke their hearts. March, noble lord,
Into our city with thy banners spread;
By decimation, and a tithed death,
If thy revenges hunger for that food
Which nature loathes, take thou the destin'd tenth,
And by the hazard of the spotted die
Let die the spotted.

1. Sen. All have not offended;
For those that were, it is not square to take
On those that are, revenge; crimes, like lands,
Are not inherited. Then, dear countryman,
Bring in thy ranks, but leave without thy rage;

3. **expedition:** speed.
7. **Whom.** Syntactically superfluous. **general part:** public quarrel.
8. **partic**[illegible] [illegible]ersonal.
[illegible]**ted:** the import of which was (possibly with some [illegible] sense of *importuned*, "besought").
[illegible]operation, participation.
[illegible] undertaken partly in his (Timon's) behalf.
[illegible]rying about.
[illegible]itors read *foe's* (or *foes'*), perhaps rightly.

[illegible]e woods, before Timon's cave.
[illegible]reat these lines as part of the Soldier's comment; [illegible]e finds two inscriptions, one in his own language, [illegible]age or an alphabet unintelligible to him. More [illegible]cture that Shakespeare composed these lines as [illegible]n had second thoughts about both its wording [illegible] text, but neglected to delete the first version. [illegible]–73.
[illegible] reached the utmost limit of his allotted time.
[illegible]**an:** i.e. all men are beasts.
6. **character:** lettering. 7. **figure:** kind of writing.
8. **ag'd:** i.e. experienced. 10. **mark:** goal.

V.iv. **Location:** Before the walls of Athens.

4. **all licentious measure:** the utmost degree of license.
5. **scope:** measure.
7. **travers'd arms.** Probably in a military sense, "small arms held in a non-firing position"; possibly "folded arms," signifying dejection. **breath'd:** voiced. 8. **flush:** at flood, i.e. ripe for action.
9. **crouching:** (formerly) submissive. **marrow:** vital strength.
10. **breathless wrong:** wrongdoers breathless with fear.
12. **pursy:** short-winded. 13. **horrid:** terrified.
14. **griefs:** grievances. **conceit:** idea.
18. **Above their quantity:** i.e. greater than your griefs and rages.
20. **means:** terms of reconciliation (?) or wealth (?).
24. **they.** Many editors follow Theobald in emending *grief* to *griefs*, to provide a plural antecedent for *they*. But *they* can refer to those who aggrieved Timon, as *them* in line 26 does.
25. **trophies:** monuments.
27. **motives . . . out:** instigators of your banishment.
28. **Shame . . . excess.** Obscure; probably "shame at finding themselves (unexpectedly) deficient in the extremes of low cunning."
31. **tithed death:** the killing of one person in ten (synonymous with *decimation*). 34. **die.** Singular of *dice*.
35. **spotted:** guilty. 36. **square:** just.
37–38. **like . . . not:** are not, like lands.
39. **without:** outside.

Spare thy Athenian cradle and those kin
Which in the bluster of thy wrath must fall
With those that have offended; like a shepherd,
Approach the fold and cull th' infected forth,
But kill not all together.
2. Sen. What thou wilt,
Thou rather shalt enforce it with thy smile
Than hew to't with thy sword.
1. Sen. Set but thy foot
Against our rampir'd gates and they shall ope,
So thou wilt send thy gentle heart before,
To say thou't enter friendly.
2. Sen. Throw thy glove,
Or any token of thine honor else,
That thou wilt use the wars as thy redress
And not as our confusion, all thy powers
Shall make their harbor in our town till we
Have seal'd thy full desire.
Alcib. Then there's my glove;
[Descend,] and open your uncharged ports.
Those enemies of Timon's and mine own
Whom you yourselves shall set out for reproof
Fall, and no more; and to atone your fears
With my more noble meaning, not a man
Shall pass his quarter, or offend the stream
Of regular justice in your city's bounds,
But shall be remedied to your public laws
At heaviest answer.
Both. 'Tis most nobly spoken.
Alcib. Descend, and keep your words.
[*The Senators descend and open the gates.*]
Enter [Soldier *as*] *a Messenger.*
[*Sold.*] My noble general, Timon is dead,
Entomb'd upon the very hem o' th' sea,
And on his grave-stone this insculpture, which
With wax I brought away, whose soft impression
Interprets for my poor ignorance.
Alcib. (*Reads the epitaph.*) "Here lies a wretched corse, of wretched soul bereft;
Seek not my name: a plague consume you, wicked caitiffs left!
Here lie I, Timon, who, alive, all living men did hate;
Pass by and curse thy fill, but pass and stay not here thy gait."
These well express in thee thy latter spirits:
Though thou abhorr'dst in us our human griefs,
Scorn'dst our brains' flow, and those our droplets which
From niggard nature fall, yet rich conceit
Taught thee to make vast Neptune weep for aye
On thy low grave, on faults forgiven. Dead
Is noble Timon, of whose memory
Hereafter more. Bring me into your city,
And I will use the olive with my sword:
Make war breed peace, make peace stint war, make each
Prescribe to other as each other's leech.
Let our drums strike. *Exeunt.*

41. bluster: tempest.
47. rampir'd: strengthened against attack, as by ramparts.
48. So: if only. **53. make their harbor:** be quartered.
54. seal'd: satisfied. **55. uncharged ports:** unassailed gates.
58. atone: appease.
59. meaning: intention. **man:** i.e. soldier of mine.
60. pass his quarter: go beyond his assigned area.
62. remedied: handed over for punishment. Some editors adopt Dyce's emendation *render'd.*
63. At heaviest answer: to pay the severest penalty.
67. insculpture: inscription.
70–73. As the introduction points out, these lines bring together two separate epitaphs in Plutarch's account of Timon; since they are contradictory, Shakespeare would certainly have deleted or revised in a final version. **70. corse:** corpse.
76. brains' flow: i.e. tears.
77. rich conceit: ingenious fancy.
82. use . . . sword: combine peace with war.
83. stint: stop. **84. leech:** physician.

NOTE ON THE TEXT

The First Folio (1623) is the only authority for *Timon of Athens*; all later editions are derived from that source.

In addition to the general impression that the play (particularly the last half) gives of having been abandoned by Shakespeare in an unfinished state (see Ellis-Fermor), there is considerable evidence scattered throughout the F1 text of the use of "foul papers" as copy-text: various kinds of confusion in character designations (Textual Notes, I.i o.s.d., II.ii; the problem of Flavius as the name for the Steward); difficulties in scene development (I.ii.130 s.d., IV.iii [see first note to V.i]); faulty verse lineation; misarrangement of verse as prose and of prose as verse; the appearance of descriptive and permissive stage directions (I.i.94, I.ii o.s.d., 145, III.i o.s.d., III.iv.77, III.vi o.s.d., IV.iii o.s.d.); and the absence of any notations suggestive of a prompter's hand. There is some disagreement, however, as to whether the F1 text was set directly from Shakespeare's "foul papers" (Greg, Maxwell) or from a transcript of them (Williams). H. J. Oliver tries to argue that both views are partially correct, that is, that parts of the play (I.i.174–283, I.ii, III.ii.–v, sections of IV.iii, including 463–536, and V.i), too "foul" in the autograph for use by a compositor, were set from a transcript of the "foul papers," prepared perhaps by Ralph Crane, and that the remainder was set from the "foul papers" themselves. (For Crane's scribal characteristics, see the "Note on the Text" to *The Tempest*; Howard-Hill and Lake deny Crane's involvement).

Until comparatively recently, the most generally accepted view held that *Timon* was the unaided (though uncompleted) work of Shakespeare (Greg, Maxwell, Oliver). Building, however, on earlier studies (see particularly Sykes) which claimed that *Timon* was either a collaboration between Shakespeare and one or more other playwrights or a revision by another hand (or hands) of Shakespeare's unfinished first draft (Thomas Middleton, John Day, George Chapman, George Wilkins, or Thomas Heywood are among those proposed), Jowett/Taylor (1993), basing their decision on further internal evidence advanced by Lake, Jackson, and Holdsworth, claim that the play must be considered as a collaboration between Shakespeare and Middleton. Holdsworth (as reported in the Oxford *Textual Companion*) assigns about a third of the play to Middleton: I.i.273–83 (?); I.ii; II.ii.1–45 (?); III.i–v; III.vi.1–35, 106–21; IV.ii.1–29 (?), 30–48; IV.iii.458–536 (and Middleton's hand may also be seen in II.ii after line 119). Smith, however, using, among others, most of the same attribution tests as Lake, Jackson, and Jowett/Taylor, suggests that Jowett/Taylor "might have been more cautious [in focusing on Middleton only] and perhaps attributed the play to 'Shakespeare *et al.*' without attempting to resolve *alii* into names of dramatists." He also suggests that Middleton may have played a scribal role like that played by Anthony Munday in *Sir Thomas More* (see the Introduction to *More*). Although Sykes' attribution techniques are now frequently dismissed, his assignment of the Timon/Apemantus prose dialogue in I.i, II.ii, and IV.iii to John Day should perhaps be given further consideration.

For further information, see: William Wells, "*Timon of Athens*," *N & Q*, 12th. ser., VI (1920), 266–9; H. D. Sykes, *Sidelights on Elizabethan Drama* (Oxford, 1924); Una Ellis-Fermor, "*Timon of Athens*: An Unfinished Play," *RES*, XVIII (1924), 270–83; W. W. Greg, *The Shakespeare First Folio* (Oxford, 1955); Philip Williams, "New Approaches to Textual Problems in Shakespeare," *SB*, VIII (1956), 3–14; J. C. Maxwell, ed., New Shakespeare *Timon of Athens* (Cambridge, 1957); H. J. Oliver, ed., New Arden *Timon of Athens* (London, rev. ed., 1963); T. H. Howard-Hill, "Ralph Crane's Parentheses," *N & Q*, CCX (1966), 334–40; G. R. Hibbard, ed., New Penguin *Timon of Athens* (Harmondsworth, Middlesex, 1970); D. J. Lake, *The Canon of Thomas Middleton's Plays* (Cambridge, 1975); MacD. P. Jackson, *Studies in Attribution: Middleton and Shakespeare* (Salzburg, 1979); Stanley Wells, Gary Taylor, John Jowett, and William Montgomery, *William Shakespeare: A Textual Companion* (Oxford, 1987); M. W. A. Smith, "The Authorship of *Timon of Athens*," *Text*, V (1991), 195–240; John Jowett and Gary Taylor, "'With New Additions': Theatrical Interpolation in *Measure for Measure* [and *Timon*]," in Gary Taylor and John Jowett, *Shakespeare Reshaped, 1606–1623* (Oxford 1993).

TEXTUAL NOTES

Dramatis personae: *as in F1, following the play, with changes in order and some additions by Rowe and later editors*
Philotus] *Capell;* Philo. *F1*
Hortensius] *F2;* Hortensis *F1 (F1 includes a* Lucius *among the* Seruants to Vsurers*)*
the Banditti] *Knight*
Act-scene division: *F1 marks only I.i; other act-scene divisions from Rowe and later editors (see first note to each scene); present act-scene arrangement as a whole first established by Dyce*

I.i

Location: *Rowe*
o.s.d. **Merchant]** *Johnson;* Merchant, and Mercer *F1 (perhaps Shakespeare intended a separate character in the Mercer, but he has no lines unless the ambiguous s.p.* Mer. *at ll. 9, 10, etc. is intended to designate him instead of the Merchant;* Mer.*, however, must refer to a single character in the scene as it is set up in F1)*
5 **matches?]** *Pope;* matches: *F1*
12 **here—]** *Collier;* heere. *F1*
15 s.d. **Reciting to himself.]** *Globe (after Warburton conj.)*
17 s.d. **Looking . . . jewel.]** *Pope*
19–20 **You . . . lord.]** *as verse, Pope; as prose, F1*
21 **gum]** *Pope;* Gowne *F1*
21 **oozes]** *Johnson;* vses *F1*
33 **lip! To]** *F2 (subs.);* Lip, to *F1*
38 s.d. **and pass over]** *Capell*
47 **wax;]** *Theobald;* wax, *F1*
72 **conceiv'd to scope.]** *Johnson (after Theobald);* conceyu'd, to scope *F1*
78–9 **late— . . . value—]** *Capell;* late, . . . valew; *F1*
87 **hands]** *F2;* hand *F1*
87 **slip]** *Rowe;* sit *F1*
91 **Fortune's]** *Malone;* Fortunes *F1*
94 s.d. **a . . . following]** *Globe (after Capell)*
99 **Ventidius! Well]** *Rowe;* Ventidius well *F1*
106 **enfranchis'd]** *Pope;* enfranchized *F1*
110 s.p. **Old Ath.]** *F4;* Oldm. *or* Old. *F1 (throughout scene)*
129 **be, Timon.]** *Theobald (after Warburton; comma, F4);* be Timon, *F1*
134 **levity's]** *F3;* leuities *F1*
134 s.d. **To Lucilius.]** *Johnson*
151 s.d. **with Old Athenian]** *Theobald (subs.)*
173 s.d. **Apemantus]** *F4;* Apermantus *F1 sporadically throughout; see "Note on the Text")*
177 **bear,]** *Steevens;* beare *F1*
179 **morrow—]** *ed. (after Warburton);* morrow. *F1*
181 **Why . . . not.]** *as verse, Pope; as prose, F1*
188 **Apemantus.]** *F3;* Apemantus? *F1*
201 **mother's]** *F4;* Mothers *F1*
206–7 **O . . . bellies.]** *as prose, Pope; as verse, F1*
209 **So . . . labor.]** *as prose, Pope; as verse, F1*
209 **So]** *F3;* So, *F1*
214 **Not . . . poet?]** *as prose, Pope; as verse, F1*
222 **Then thou liest:]** *as prose, Pope; as verse, F1*
223 **feign'd]** *F2;* fegin'd *F1*
234–5 **That . . . merchant?]** *as prose, Capell; as verse, F1*
239 **Traffic's]** *F4;* Traffickes *F1*
240 **trumpet's]** *F3;* Trumpets *F1*
243 s.d. **Exeunt some Attendants.]** *Capell*
245 **dinner's]** *F3;* dinners *F1*
246 **piece.]** *F3;* peece, *F1*
247–51 **So . . . monkey.]** *as verse, Capell; as prose, F1*
247 **there!]** *Capell;* their *F1*
250 **man's]** *F3;* mans *F1*
254 **depart]** *F2;* depatt *F1*
255 s.d. **all but Apemantus]** *Capell (after Rowe)*
260 **feast?]** *Capell;* Feast. *F1*
268–71 **No . . . hence!]** *as prose, Pope; as verse, F1*
272 s.d. **Exit.]** *Hanmer*
273 **Come]** *F2;* Comes *F1*
279 **return]** *Rowe (subs.);* returne: *F1*
283 s.p. **1. Lord.]** *Capell (after Rowe)*

I.ii

I.ii] *Capell*
Location: *Cambridge (after Theobald)*
o.s.d. **Flavius . . . attending]** *Capell (subs.)*
o.s.d. **Alcibiades]** *Johnson*
o.s.d. **Ventidius]** *F4;* Ventigius *F1 (throughout scene and sporadically elsewhere; see "Note on the Text")*
20 s.d. **They sit.]** *Rowe*
36 **power;]** *Rowe (subs.);* power, *F1*
49 **prov'd.]** *Rowe (subs.);* proued, *F1*
51–2 **Lest . . . throats.]** *as verse, Rowe; as prose, F1*
51 **notes:]** *Rowe;* noates, *F1*
71 s.d. **Eats and drinks.]** *Johnson*
73 **Captain]** *Hanmer;* Captaine, *F1*
82 **'em—]** *Sisson;* 'em: *F1*
91–2 **thousands, did]** *Theobald;* thousands? Did *F1*
105 **joy's]** *Kittredge;* ioyes, *F1*
107 **methinks. To . . . faults,]** *Rowe;* me thinks to . . . Faults. *F1 (pointing after* thinks *uncertain)*
113 **Much!]** *Pope;* Much. *F1*
113 s.d. **within]** *Capell; for F1 s.d. see l. 130*
s.d. **(Amazons . . . playing)** *below*
115 s.d. **Enter Servant.]** *placed as in Dyce; after l. 115, F1*
116–7 **Please . . . admittance.]** *as prose, Pope; as verse, F1*
121 s.d. **Exit Servant.]** *Kittredge*
121 s.d. **Enter Cupid.]** *Capell;* Enter Cupid with the Maske of Ladies. *F1 (see l. 130 s.d.)*
122–5 **Hail . . . bosom.]** *as verse, Rann (after Pope); as prose, F1*
125–6 **There, . . . all]** *Oliver (subs.);* There tast, touch all *F1*
128–9 **They're . . . welcome!]** *as verse, F3 (?); as prose, F1*
128 **welcome]** *F2;* wecome *F1*
129 **Music,]** *Capell;* Musicke *F1*
129 s.d. **Exit Cupid.]** *Capell*
130 s.p. **1. Lord.]** *Capell;* Luc. *F1*
130 s.d. **Music. Enter Cupid]** *Capell*
130 s.d. **with . . . Ladies]** *from F1 s.d. after l. 121 (see above); placed as in Capell*
130 s.d. **as]** *Theobald*
130 s.d. **Amazons . . . playing]** *from F1 s.d. after l. 113:* Sound Tucket. Enter the Maskers of Amazons, with Lutes in their hands, dauncing and playing.*; placed as in Capell*
152 s.p. **1. Lady.]** *Heath conj.;* 1 Lord. *F1*
157 s.d. **Cupid and Ladies]** *Capell*
159 s.d. **Aside.]** *Johnson*
167 s.d. **Enter . . . casket.]** *Globe (after Capell); F1 has* Enter Flauius. *after* welcome. *l. 176*
174–7 **My . . . near.]** *as verse, Capell; as prose, F1*
176 s.d. **Exit Servant.]** *Kittredge*
180, 191 s.dd. **Aside.]** *Johnson*
181 s.p. **2. Serv.]** *Rowe;* Ser. *F1*
185, 191 s.dd. **Exit Servant.]** *Kittredge*
210–2 **And . . . it.]** *as verse, Steevens (after Capell); as prose, F1*
212 **rode]** *F3;* rod *F1*
213 s.p. **3. Lord.]** *Capell conj.;* 1. L. *F1*
214–7 **You . . . you.]** *as verse, Johnson; as prose, F1*
216 **friend's]** *Warburton;* Friends *F1*
225 **Ay]** *Malone;* I *F1*
230 s.d. **and others]** *Kittredge*
230 s.d. **Apemantus . . . remain.]** *ed. (after Cambridge)*
230–3 **What . . . 'em.]** *as verse, Rowe; as prose, F1*
230 **coil's]** *Rowe;* coiles *F1*
231 **jutting-out]** *hyphen, Dyce*

II.i

II.i] *Rowe*
Location: *Capell (subs.)*

o.s.d. with . . . hand] *Capell*
34 Ay, go, sir;] *Pope (subs.)*; I go sir? *F1*

II.ii

II.ii] *Rowe*
Location: *Capell (subs., after Rowe)*
1 s.p. Flav.] *Rowe*; Stew. *F1 (throughout)*
4 resumes] *Rowe*; resume *F1*
5 mind] *F2*; minde, *F1*
9 s.d. and . . . of] *Johnson*
10 s.p. Var. Serv.] *Malone*; Var. *F1 (throughout scene)*
11 s.p. Isid. Serv.] *Malone*; Isid. *F1 (throughout scene)*
13 s.d. with Alcibiades] *Capell (subs.)*
26 lord—] *Rowe*; Lord. *F1*
27–8 From . . . payment.] *as verse, Capell; as prose, F1*
30–1 'Twas . . . past.] *as verse, Capell; as prose, F1*
35 s.d. Exeunt . . . Lords.] *Capell (subs.)*
35 s.d. To Flavius.] *Johnson*
44 s.d. Exit.] *Pope*
53 s.d. To the Fool.] *Johnson*
54 s.d. To Varro's Servant.] *Malone (after Johnson)*
61 s.p. All Serv.] *Malone (after Capell)*; Al. *F1 (or* All. *throughout scene)*
71 Good!] *Rowe*; Good, *F1*
73 s.d. To the Fool.] *Johnson*
78 s.p. Page.] *F4*; Boy. *F1*
91–2 If . . . usurers?] *as prose, Capell; as verse, F1*
93 Ay,] *Capell (subs.)*; I *F1*
94–5 So . . . thief.] *as prose, Pope; as verse, F1*
105 notwithstanding,] *Theobald*; notwithstanding *F1*
109 sometime't] *F3*; sometime t' *F1*
116–7 Nor . . . lack'st.] *as prose, Pope; as verse, F1*
122 s.d. Exeunt . . . Fool.] *Capell*
123 s.d. Servants] *Capell (after Theobald)*
128 propos'd] *F2*; propose *F1*
134 you;] *Rowe*; you, *F1*
135 found] *F2*; sound *F1*
135 honesty.] *Rowe*; honestie, *F1*
143 time:] *Theobald (subs.)*; time, *F1*
171 Feast-won] *hyphen, Pope*
171 fast-lost] *hyphen, Theobald*
185 Flaminius] *Rowe*; Flauius *F1*
185 s.d. Flaminius . . . another] *Rowe (subs.)*
186 s.p. Servants.] *Dyce*; Ser. *F1*
186 lord? My lord?] *Dyce*; Lord, my Lord. *F1*
187, 188, 189 s.dd. to Servilius, to Flaminius, to the other] *Kittredge*
194 s.d. Exeunt . . . Servants.] *Dyce (subs.)*
195 s.d. Aside.] *Capell*
197 health,] *F3*; health; *F1*
205 treasure,] *F2*; Treature *F1*
211 looks,] *F4*; lookes; *F1*
211 fractions,] *F3*; Fractions *F1*
212 cold-moving] *hyphen, Theobald*
214 cheerly] *F3*; cheerely *F1*

III.i

III.i] *Rowe*
Location: *Theobald*
5 s.d. Aside.] *Johnson*
9 s.d. Exit Servant.] *Capell*
38 s.d. To Servant.] *Pope*
38 s.d. Exit Servant.] *Capell (after Theobald)*
48 s.d. Throwing . . . back.] *Rowe (subs.)*
57 honor has] *F4*; Honor, / Has *F1*

III.ii

III.ii] *Pope*
Location: *Capell (after Theobald)*
3 s.p. 1. Stran.] *Rowe*; 1 *F1 (throughout scene)*
10 s.p. 2. Stran.] *Rowe*; 2 *F1 (throughout scene)*
34 H'as] *F4*; Has *F1*
38 fifty—five] *Deighton*; fifty fiue *F1*
49 beast,] *Theobald*; beast *F1*
60 s.d. Calling after him.] *Oliver (after Pyle)*
76 s.p. 3. Stran.] *Rowe*; 3 *F1*

III.iii

III.iii] *Pope*
Location: *Capell*
6 base metal] *F4*; Base-Mettle *F1*
13 H'as] *Rowe*; Has *F1*
21 I] *F2*
23 H'ad] *F4*; Had *F1*

III.iv

III.iv] *Pope*
Location: *Capell (subs., after Rowe)*
o.s.d. two Servants] *Capell*; man *F1*
o.s.d. Titus and] *Rowe (subs.)*
o.s.d. servants of] *Rowe*
o.s.d. Lucius' Servant] *Malone (subs., after Rowe)*; Lucius *F1*
1 s.p. 1. Var. Serv.] *Capell (subs.)*; Var. man. *F1*
2 Lucius!] *Dyce*; Lucius, *F1*
3 s.p. Luc. Serv.] *Malone*; Luci. *F1 (or* Luc. *throughout scene)*
3 What,] *Capell*; what *F1*
6 And, sir,] *Oliver*; And sir *F1*
14–6 'Tis . . . little.] *as verse, Pope; as prose, F1*
28, 30 s.pp. 1. Var. Serv.] *Capell (subs.)*; Varro. *F1*
40 s.d. Exit.] *Steevens (after Capell)*
44, 62, 98 s.pp. 2. Var. Serv.] *Globe*; 2. Varro. *or* 2. Var. *F1*
58 If] *F4*; If't *F1*
59 s.d. Exit.] *Rowe*
60, 97 s.pp. 1. Var. Serv.] *Malone*; 1. Varro. *and* 1. Var. *F1*
78 help!] *Rowe (subs.)*; helpe, *F1*
78 s.d. Flaminius following] *Capell*
87 s.p. Hor.] *Capell*; 1. Var. *F1*
88 s.p. Both Var.. Serv.] *Malone (after Capell)*; 2. Var. *F1*
102 s.d. and Flavius] *Rowe*
103–4 They . . . Devils!] *as verse, Capell; as prose, F1*
111 Sempronius—all.] *F2 (subs.)*; Sempronius Vllorxa: All, *F1 (first two words in italics)*
112–5 O . . . table.] *as verse, Pope; as prose, F1*

III.v

III.v] *Capell*
Location: *Theobald*
1 fault's] *F3*; faults *F1*
6 Now, Captain?] *Capell*; Now Captaine. *F1*
17 An] *Johnson*; And *F1*
50 judge,] *Rowe*; Iudge? *F1*
51 suffering.] *F2*; suffering, *F1*
52 good.] *Rowe (subs.)*; good, *F1*
62 I] *F2*
62 h'as] *F4*; ha's *F1*
66 'em] *F2*; him *F1*
79 And, . . . know] *Capell*; And . . . know, *F1*
102 s.d. Senators] *Capell (subs.)*
107 interest—] *Rowe (subs.)*; interest. *F1*

III.vi

III.vi] *Capell*
Location: *Globe (after Capell)*
o.s.d. Music . . . attending.] *Capell (subs.)*
o.s.d. of Timon] *Kittredge*
o.s.d. Senators] *Capell*
o.s.d. and other Lords] *ed. (after Capell)*
1, 2, etc. s.pp. 1. Lord. . . . 2. Lord., etc.] *Capell* (1. Senator. *etc., Rowe;* 1. Friend. *etc., Kittredge*); 1 . . . 2 . . . 3 . . . 4 *F1 (throughout scene)*
19 here's] *F4*; heares *F1*
31 s.d. Aside.] *Johnson*
34 awhile, if] *Collier*; awhile; If *F1*
51 it.] *F3*; it *F1*
54 s.p. 1., 2. Lords.] *Capell (subs.)*
60 toward.] *F3*; toward *F1*
62 Will't hold? will't] *F4*; Wilt hold? Wilt *F1*
63 will—and so—] *Steevens (after Johnson)*; will, and so. *F1*
79 be—as] *Steevens*; bee as *F1*
81 lag] *Rowe*; legge *F1*
85 s.d. The . . . water.] *Johnson (subs.)*
91 with your] *Hanmer*; you with *F1*
93 s.d. Throwing . . . faces.] *Johnson*
93 long,] *Rowe*; long *F1*
97 Cap-and-knee slaves] *Pope*; Cap and knee-Slaues *F1*
97 minute-jacks] *hyphen, Pope*
101 s.d. Throws . . . out.] *Rowe (subs., after l. 100); placed as in Capell*
105 s.d. again] *ed. (after Pope)*
115 s.p. 3. Lord.] *Capell*; 2 *F1*
116 s.p. 2. Lord.] *Capell*; 3 *F1*
120 s.d. and other Lords] *ed.*

IV.i

IV.i] *Rowe*
Location: *Rowe*
4 Obedience,] *Alexander*; Obedience *F1*
4 fools,] *Capell*; Fooles *F1*
6 steads! . . . filths] *Theobald (subs.;* steads *F4)*; steeds, to generall Filthes. *F1*
7 instant,] *Pope*; Instant *F1*
8–9 fast; . . . back,] *Theobald*; fast . . . backe; *F1*
13 Son] *F2*; Some *F1*
33 town!] *F2 (subs.)*; Towne, *F1*

IV.ii

IV.ii] *Rowe*
Location: *Rowe*
1, 5, 8, 17 s.pp. 1. Serv. . . . 2. Serv. . . . 3. Serv.] *Rowe*; 1 . . . 2 . . . 3 *F1*
14 all-shunn'd] *hyphen, Pope*
27 s.d. Giving them money.] *Collier (after Pope)*

IV.iii

IV.iii] *Rowe*
Location: *Kittredge (after Rowe, Capell, Globe)*
3 Twinn'd] *Pope*; Twin'd *F1*
10 senator] *Rowe*; Senators *F1*
12 paster] *ed.*; Pastour *F1*
12 lards] *Rowe*; Lards, *F1*
13 lean] *F2*; leaue *F1*
15 say] *F2*; fay *F1*
15 man's] *F3*; mans *F1*
23 fang] *Johnson*; phang *F1*
23 s.d. Digging.] *Rowe (subs.)*
41 at,] *Pope*; at. *F1*
48 s.d. Keeping some gold.] *Pope*
54 Misanthropos] *F2*; Misantropos *F1*
70–2 Noble . . . Timon?] *as verse, Steevens (after Capell); as prose, F1*
84–8 Be . . . diet.] *as verse, Pope; as prose, F1*
88 tub-fast] *Warburton*; Fubfast *F1*
96 them—] *Rowe*; them. *F1*
99 dost] *F3*; doest *F1*
117 window-bars] *Johnson conj.*; window Barne *F1*
122 pronounc'd] *Pope*; pronounced *F1*
130–1 Hast . . . counsel.] *as verse, Capell (after Pope); as prose, F1*
133, 149, 167 s.pp. Phry., Timan.] *Steevens (after Capell)*
145 contrary.] *F2*; contrary, *F1*
149 gold—] *Rowe*; Gold, *F1*
156 scolds] *Rowe*; scold'st *F1*
167–70 More . . . again.] *as verse, Pope; as prose, F1*
175 s.d. Drum beats.] *Johnson*
175 s.d. Alcibiades . . . Timandra] *Theobald*
177 s.d. Digging.] *Johnson (before l. 176); placed as in Malone*
185 human] *Rowe*; humane *F1*
221 What,] *Pope*; what *F1*
233 e'er] *Rowe*; ere *F1*
243 Outlives] *Rowe*; Out-liues: *F1*
255 command,] *Rowe (comma, Johnson)*; command'st: *F1*
261–2 men At duty,] *Theobald (after Pope)*; men, / At duty *F1*
271 curse,] *Pope*; curse; *F1*
282 s.d. Eating a root.] *Rowe*
282 s.d. Offering him another.] *Johnson*
283 my] *Rowe*; thy *F1*
293 a' days] *F3*; a-dayes *F1*
304, 307 medlar] *Theobald*; medler *F1*

346–8 If . . . beasts.] *as prose, Pope; as irregular verse, F1*
351–7 Yonder . . . Apemantus.] *as prose, Theobald (after Pope); as irregular verse, F1*
363 thee.] *Theobald (subs.);* thee, *F1*
368 swound] *F3;* swoond *F1*
370 s.d. Throws . . . him.] *Capell (subs.)*
381 s.d. To the gold.] *Pope (subs.)*
382 son and sire] *Rowe;* Sunne and fire *F1*
384 ever] *Rowe;* euer, *F1*
384 lov'd] *Pope;* loued *F1*
390 slave man] *Rowe;* slaue-man *F1*
394 to . . . to] *Rowe;* too . . . too *F1*
397 them] *Rowe;* then *F1*
398, 402, etc. s.pp. 1. Ban. . . . 2. Ban. . . . 3. Ban.] *Rowe;* 1 . . . 2 . . . 3 *F1*
400 falling-from] *hyphen, Capell*
402 It . . . treasure.] *as prose, Pope; as verse, F1*
406 True . . . hid.] *as prose, Pope; as verse, F1*
408 s.p. Other Banditti] *ed. (after Knight)*
410 He;] *Rowe;* He? *F1*
411, 413, 415 s.pp. Banditti.] *Knight*
412 Now, thieves?] *Capell (after Theobald);* Now Theeues. *F1*
430 seethe] *Collier;* seeth *F1*
434 villains] *Collier MS;* Villaine *F1*
448 less] *Globe;* lesse, *F1*
450 H'as] *F3;* Has *F1*
453 us,] *Rowe;* vs *F1*
454–5 I'll . . . trade.] *as prose, Pope; as verse, F1*
457 s.d. Exeunt] *F2;* Exit *F1*
469 H'as] *F4;* Has *F1*
474 grant'st] *Capell (after Pope);* grunt'st *F1*
474 man,] *F2;* man. *F1*
477 I;] *Capell;* I *F1*
496 perpetual-sober] *hyphen, Hanmer*
536 s.d. Exeunt severally.] *Theobald;* Exit *F1*

V.i

V.i] *Capell. The act break before the entry of the Poet and Painter conflicts with the reference to their approach at IV.iii.351; on the other hand, at V.i.8 (as here marked) the Painter refers to Timon's gift of money to Flavius, something he could not know unless we suppose some passage of time after IV.iii.536. Apparently Shakespeare originally intended to introduce the Poet and Painter after Apemantus' exit at IV.iii.397; he then added the visits of the Banditti and Flavius and forgot to cancel the reference to the Poet and Painter at IV.iii.351.*
Location: *Capell (subs.)*
o.s.d. Timon . . . cave.] *Dyce*
1–2 As . . . abides.] *as verse, F2; as prose, F1*
5 Phrynia] *Rowe (after F2* Phrinia); Phrinica *F1*
5 Timandra] *F2;* Timandylo *F1*
31, 37, 47 s.dd. Aside.] *Capell*
44 serves, . . . night,] *Theobald* (serves, *Pope*); serues . . . night; *F1*
45 want'st] *Capell;* want'st, *F1*
47 god's] *F3;* Gods *F1*
52 worship] *Rowe;* worshipt *F1*
52 aye] *Rowe;* aye: *F1*
54 s.d. Coming forward.] *Malone (subs., after Capell)*
61 enough—] *Rowe;* enough. *F1*
67 go naked,] *Theobald;* go, / Naked *F1*
71 men] *F2;* man *F1*
98 made-up villain] *F3;* made-vp-Villaine *F1*
100 gold,] *F4;* Gold *F1*
107 apart] *F3;* a part *F1*
109 s.d. To one.] *Neilson (after Pope)*
110 s.d. To the other.] *Neilson (after Pope)*
110 reside] *Rowe;* recide *F1*
113 s.d. To one.] *ed.*
114 s.d. To the other.] *ed.*
115 s.d. both . . . cave] *Staunton (after Rowe)*
126 chance] *F3;* chanc'd *F1*
133 cantherizing] *The F1 reading here retained may be a compositorial misreading of* Cautherizing *(and Rowe, following F2–4* Catherizing*, emended to* cauterizing*), but there is a good possibility that Shakespeare was thinking of the action of dried powder of cantharides (Spanish flies), used by doctors in cauterizing with caustics, and thus produced either intentionally or by confusion the portmanteau form* cantherizing. *The clue to his train of thought, as Maxwell notes, lies in the word* blister *in the preceding line (cf. Robert Copeland,* The Questionary of Chirurgeons, *1541: "Some other [forms of cauterizing employing more gentle caustics] thyrleth more lyghtly and make no scarres, but blysters as canterides, . . ."; and Francis Bacon,* Sylva Sylvarum, *1626: "No marvel though Cantharides have such a Corrosive and Cauterizing quality."). It is a curious coincidence, pointed out by the Cambridge editors, and perhaps significant, that Copeland, the first to discuss in English the process of cauterization or searing, regularly spells the various forms of the word with* n *instead of* u *(i.e.* cantere, canterysing, canterysacyon, canterysed*). The word appears nowhere else in Shakespeare in either form.*
147 sense] *Rowe* (sence); since *F1*
150 Together] *Rowe;* Together, *F1*
162 Allow'd] *Pope;* Allowed *F1*
182 reverend'st] *F2;* reuerends *F1*
199 aches,] *F4;* Aches *F1*
200 throes] *F4;* throwes *F1*
209 whoso] *Rowe;* who so *F1*
224–5 His . . . nature.] *as verse, Capell; as prose, F1*

V.ii

V.ii] *Dyce*
Location: *Globe (after Pope)*
1, 13 s.pp. 3. Sen.] *Sisson;* 1 *F1*
5 s.p. 4. Sen.] *Sisson;* 2 *F1*
14 s.p. 1. Sen.] *Capell;* 3 *F1*
15 enemy's] *Delius;* Enemies *F1*

V.iii

V.iii] *Dyce*
Location: *Sisson (after Capell)*
o.s.d. A . . . seen.] *Capell*
2 Who's] *F3;* Whose *F1*
3 s.d. Reads.] *Staunton*
3–4 "Timon . . . man."] *quotes, Staunton*
7 skill,] *F2;* skill; *F1*

V.iv

V.iv] *Dyce*
Location: *Theobald*
10 "No more!"] *Theobald (subs.);* no more: *F1*
23 their] *F2;* rhier *F1*
28 Shame, . . . excess,] *F2 (subs.);* (Shame that they wanted, cunning in excesse) *F1*
30–1 spread; . . . death,] *Theobald;* spred, . . . death; *F1*
38 inherited.] *Rowe;* inherited, *F1*
42 offended;] *Pope;* offended, *F1*
44 all together] *F3;* altogether *F1*
47 ope,] *Collier;* ope: *F1*
52 confusion, all] *Johnson;* Confusion: All *F1*
55 Descend] *F2;* Defend *F1*
64 s.d. The . . . gates.] *Malone (after Capell)*
64 s.d. Soldier as] *Theobald (subs.)*
65 s.p. Sold.] *Theobald;* Mes. *F1*
75 human] *Rowe;* humane *F1*
76 brains'] *Dyce;* Braines *F1*
85 s.d. Exeunt.] Exeunt. / FINIS. *F1*

The morris-dance. Engraving from Malone's *Shakespeare* (1790), Vol. V, of a mid-fifteenth-century window at Betley in Staffordshire. The morris-dance, an early medieval folk dance associated with the sword-dance and the May-game (note the maypole in the centre of the window), is of uncertain origin, though possibly native to England. The number and character of the dancers varied. More or less standard figures that attended the actual dancers, who are distinguished by wearing bells on their legs, were a fool or clown (No. 12), a hobby-horse (No. 5), and a "Maid Marian" (No. 2). Musical accompaniment was furnished by a taborer who also played on a pipe (No. 9). Apart from Maid Marian, the Robin Hood association, probably a comparatively late addition to the morris-dance tradition, is here represented by Robin Hood as the hobby-horse (note the ladle he carries for making collections from the spectators) and Friar Tuck (No. 3). A morris-dance with a rather different cast of characters occurs in *The Two Noble Kinsmen* (III.v), and a woodcut of Kemp's one-man morris from London to Norwich may be seen in Plate 11. (*The Huntington Library, San Marino, California*)

Pericles, Prince of Tyre

On the twentieth of May in 1608 Edward Blount entered in the Stationers' Register "A booke called the booke of Pericles prynce of Tyre," but he did not publish a quarto of the play. The form of the entry indicates that he had in his possession the official playhouse copy ("the book"), which he was presumably entering on behalf of the actors' company for "blocking" purposes—that is, to prevent anyone else from publishing it—but if so his effort was unsuccessful, for the next year a "bad" quarto, with Shakespeare's name on the title-page, was printed by Henry Gosson. Meanwhile a novel by George Wilkins, *The Painful Adventures of Pericles, Prince of Tyre*, had appeared in 1608, described as "the true History of the Play of Pericles, as it was lately presented by the worthy and ancient Poet John Gower"; this play is said to have been performed "by the King's Majesty's Players," that is, by Shakespeare's company. The Venetian and French ambassadors, Zorzi Giustinian and Antoine de la Boderie, together saw a performance of the play in London sometime between May 1606 and November 1608. A conjectural date of 1607 or early 1608 would accord well with these facts.

The quarto of 1609 was reprinted three times before the publication of the First Folio in 1623, and twice more in 1630 and 1635; but the First Folio itself does not include *Pericles*, even though Blount, who had originally registered the play, was one of the chief promoters of the volume. The reason is not clear. It may have been that Shakespeare was not considered the author of the whole play, though this consideration did not exclude *Henry VIII*, now generally thought to be the joint work of Shakespeare and John Fletcher. Or perhaps the good text entered in 1608 had been lost by 1623 and the editors were unwilling to represent their dead friend with so corrupt a text as the only one available, that of the quartos—just such a text as the "stolne, and surreptitious copies, maimed, and deformed by the frauds and stealthes of iniurious imposters," which Heminge and Condell complain of in their address to the reader in the First Folio. Whatever the reason, *Pericles* did not appear among Shakespeare's collected plays until the second issue (1664) of the Third Folio, which reprinted the text of the 1635 quarto. Included in the Fourth Folio and in Rowe's edition, it was rejected by succeeding editors until Malone admitted it to the canon at the end of the eighteenth century.

Almost all readers and spectators will sense a marked difference between the first two acts and the last three acts of the play, and various explanations have been offered for this difference. Philip Edwards has argued that it arose in the course of transmission of the text. *Pericles* is a "reported" text, not based upon an author's or a playhouse manuscript, and Edwards postulated two different reporters, one much better than the other. This view, though considered seriously by scholars, has been generally rejected in favor of dual authorship—but dual authorship of what kind? It is difficult to believe that a play so disparate in its parts could have been the result of a planned collaboration in which Shakespeare was one of the partners, particularly if we take *Henry VIII* and *The Two Noble Kinsmen* to be examples of what such collaboration actually produced. A much likelier hypothesis is that Shakespeare revised a play by another hand.

There was much patching and revising of old plays for revival at this period, when a rather old-fashioned type of play, dealing in the strange and wonderful adventures typical of romantic narrative, gained a fresh vogue. The old play *Mucedorus*, for example, was revived, apparently by Shakespeare's own company, with additions by an unidentified writer, and was enormously successful both on the stage and in reprints of the expanded text. Shakespeare may have taken in hand another such play, or he may have undertaken to improve a more recent script written to satisfy the new demand. He seems to have given a few touches to the first two acts but to have left them standing largely as the original author had written them—perhaps, as has been suggested, because in these acts the emphasis is largely on political ideas—what it takes to be a good ruler—and Shakespeare had already worked out this theme in his history plays and was no longer attracted by it. But when his interest was aroused by the situation at the beginning of Act III, he began to rewrite completely, and thereafter he focused on the "painful" adventures of Pericles and Marina, contrasting and elaborating the story of a father and the story of a daughter. Who the author of Acts I and II may have been is entirely a matter of conjecture. George Wilkins, the author of *The Painful Adventures*, has been suggested, but this is most unlikely, nor have other proposed candidates—among them Thomas Heywood and John Day—won acceptance.

The story of *Pericles* is a version of one of the most popular of all romantic narratives, the tale of Apollonius of Tyre. It has been traced back to the fifth century A.D. and probably originated as a still earlier Greek novel; it circulated widely in the Middle Ages, and in oral tradition it has survived into modern times. The writer of *Pericles* drew his material from two different retellings of the story. One was the fourteenth-century poet John Gower's *Confessio Amantis*, Book VIII (available in an edition of 1554), which had been Shakespeare's source years before when he adapted the story in the "hapless Egeon" frame of *The Comedy of Errors*. The other was Laurence Twine's prose romance called *The Pattern of Painful Adventures . . . That Befell unto Prince Apollonius*, written apparently as early as 1576, when it was registered for publication, but now known only in an undated edition probably from the mid-1590's and in a reprint of 1607. The plot of *Pericles* draws jointly upon the two sources, but with greater use of Gower than Twine, in much the same manner throughout—evidence that what Shakespeare reworked was a complete play, not, as has been argued, a two-act fragment to which he added three acts more, or three acts of his own which he relinquished to another hand for completion. The play's debt to Gower, regarded in Shakespeare's time as an old-fashioned poet, is acknowledged and partly apologized for by his role as Chorus or presenter, done in a quaintly naive style.

One other source should be mentioned. The name of Prince Pericles, not found in any earlier version of the Apollonius story, is probably borrowed from Sidney's *Arcadia*, in which Pyrocles is a principal character. Two episodes of the play apparently derive from adventures of Pyrocles in the *Arcadia*: one is the appearance of the hero in rusty armor to participate in a tournament (in Gower and Twine the hero displays his physical prowess in other ways); the other is Marina's somewhat surprisingly detailed description of her father's behavior in the tempest during which she was born (IV.i.52 ff.), which corresponds to Pyrocles' actions in a storm at sea.

The corruption of the text, and the uncertainty about the authorship of Acts I and II, prevent a sustained and consistent view of the style of the play. Some passages are clearly in Shakespeare's elegiac manner as it appears later in *Cymbeline* and *The Winter's Tale*, such as Marina's lament for her nurse Lychorida:

> No; I will rob Tellus of her weed
> To strow thy green with flowers. The yellows, blues,
> The purple violets, and marigolds,
> Shall as a carpet hang upon thy grave
> While summer days doth last. (IV.i.13–17)

Pericles' adieu to his dead wife in the storm is similar, in imagery, to certain passages in *The Tempest*:

> A terrible child-bed hast thou had, my dear,
> No light, no fire. Th' unfriendly elements
> Forget thee utterly, nor have I time
> To give thee hallow'd to thy grave, but straight
> Must cast thee, scarcely coffin'd, in the ooze,
> Where, for a monument upon thy bones,
> The e'er-remaining lamps, the belching whale
> And humming water must o'erwhelm thy corpse,
> Lying with simple shells. (III.i.56–64)

The style and imagery occasionally recall the tragedies, as in the philosophic brooding of a passage which might have come from *King Lear*:

> The blind mole casts
> Copp'd hills towards heaven, to tell the earth is throng'd
> By man's oppression, and the poor worm doth die for't. (I.i.100–102)

This passage is so Shakespearean that scholars refuse to ascribe it to the author of the first two acts; it must be one of the "touches" which the master supposedly added to the text of the original. Other passages, sententious rhyming couplets, suggest the manner of earlier plays, and indeed these passages fit more decorously with the antique style of Gower's prologues. How much the playwright's style, and his conception of the quaint character of the romantic tale he was dramatizing, were influenced by Gower may be suggested by a sample of the old writer's verse from the 1554 edition of *Confessio Amantis*:

> To ship he goth, his wife with childe,
> The whiche was ever meke and milde
> And wolde not departe hym fro,
> Such love was betwene hem two.
> Lichorida for hir office
> Was take, whiche was a norice [nurse],
> To wende with this yonge wife,

To whom was shape a wofull life.
Within a tyme, as it betid,
Whan theï were in the sea amid,
Out of the north thei see a cloude,
The storme arose, the wyndes loude
Shei blewen many a dredefull blaste,
The welken was all overcaste;
The darke night the soune [sun] hath under,
There was a great tempest of thunder.

The characterization is often as naive and uncomplicated as the verse. Though some modern critics, seeking in the play the theme of expiration and forgiveness that was to appear in the later romances, have supposed that Pericles is tainted by his experience at the court of Antiochus, or that his marriage to Thaisa is an offense to Diana for which he must pay the penalty, the natural view is that Pericles is not very fully characterized but that he is essentially blameless, a "man on whom perfections wait."

The lost Marina, a model of innocence and virtue, the precursor of Shakespeare's Perdita and Miranda, can yet teach her father Pericles something about patience. Pericles speaks to her in terms curiously reminiscent of the projection of the lovelorn Viola in *Twelfth Night* (II.iv.107 ff.):

Tell thy story;
If thine, considered, prove the thousand part
Of my endurance, thou art a man, and I
Have suffered like a girl. Yet thou dost look
Like Patience gazing on kings' graves, and smiling
Extremity out of act. (V.i.134–39)

She has also some attributes of Cordelia, another "lost" daughter who in the end saves her father from madness. Her role is often that of the helpless victim of fortune, but in the brothel scenes she defends herself courageously and denounces the evil of the place in positive terms. It is no clinging, romantic heroine who says to Boult, as he is preparing to rape her:

Thou hold'st a place for which the pained'st fiend
Of hell would not in reputation change.
Thou art the damned door-keeper to every
Custrel that comes inquiring for his Tib.
To the choleric fisting of every rogue
Thy ear is liable; thy food is such
As hath been belch'd on by infected lungs.
(IV.vi.163–69)

Thaisa, the lost wife, who is resurrected through the remarkable medical skill of Cerimon, is less prominent, since once she is saved she does not seek Pericles but retires to a nunnery. Why? The plot of romantic fiction will have it so. Probability and plausibility must give way to the demands of the marvellous and the spectacular. Thaisa has some character, which she shows in declaring for Pericles, the stranger knight, over all her other suitors. In the last scene her words suddenly take on resonance as a summing-up of the whole action of which she has been a part:

Did you not name a tempest,
A birth, and death? (V.iii.33–34)

Among the evil characters, Antiochus and his daughter form an obvious contrast with the good Simonides and his daughter Thaisa; but near the end of the play a subtler thematic contrast is suggested by Pericles' address to Marina: "Thou that beget'st him that did thee beget" (V.i.195). Dionyza, in I.iv an obedient echoer of her husband's lamentations, emerges unexpectedly in IV.i as the wicked stepmother of folklore, like the Queen in Cymbeline, and in IV.iii as kin to Goneril in the contempt she pours upon Cleon for his horror at her evil deed.

The Bawd, the Pandar, and Boult are the representatives of a world of vice which Shakespeare had explored more minutely in *Measure for Measure.* In this play the brothel scenes serve, not only as danger for Marina, but also as realistic-comic relief from the romantic remoteness of the main plot of the play.

The technique of *Pericles* exploits the typical elements of romance. The hero has been on the stage for only sixty lines when he proclaims:

Like a bold champion I assume the lists,
Nor ask advice of any other thought
But faithfulness and courage. (I.i.61–63)

as he prepares to answer a riddle at the risk of his life. His "painful adventures" include all kinds of spectacular events—flight from a king who seeks his life, a shipwreck of which he is the only survivor, winning a wife by gallant display in a tournament, losing her in a tempest at sea, regaining her years later, when their daughter is grown. The surprises come not only from extraordinary events, but from sudden changes of heart in the characters, even the minor ones. Human behavior is full of pretense and manipulation—as when Simonides in II.v pretends to oppose the match between his daughter Thaisa and the stranger Pericles (as Prospero later feigns opposition to the love of Ferdinand and Miranda) but actually brings it about. That scene aroused the indignation of the great eighteenth-century editor of Shakespeare, George Steevens, who expressed "the most supreme contempt of it." In his view "It is impossible not to wish that the knights had horsewhipped Simonides, and that Pericles had kicked him off the stage." A modern critic, G. Wilson Knight, on the other hand, speaks of the scene's "delightful conclusion" and thinks Simonides is "a grand person."

From any realistic point of view, the spectacular scenes of *Pericles* are of course utter nonsense. But some modern critics have turned their attention beyond the surface of the drama and looked for symbolic meanings. The plot shows a rough and violent world in which purity and innocence miraculously survive and triumph. There are the themes of the tempest, of rebirth, of resurrection. The finding of what has been lost is often connected with larger reflections on the emergence of harmony from discord. Imagery related to jewels is especially common in the last three acts of the play. Presiding over a turbulent world of tempest, shipwreck, abandonment, and loss, in which purity, value, royalty, and beauty are rescued and reunited, are the deities Neptune and Diana, inscrutable but finally beneficent.

Pericles, though it is now interesting as the first of Shakespeare's late romances, must have struck his contemporaries as a reversion (clearly a welcome one) to an old-fashioned type of play. Its popularity is strongly attested to. In addition to its lively history of quarto publication, there are four notices of performances before 1642 and several references to the play as a popular success, including a sour one from Ben Jonson, who called it a "mouldy tale." It was the first Shakespearean play produced after the Restoration, but its seventeenth-century popularity did not last into the eighteenth and nineteenth centuries. In our time it has shared with other minor Shakespearean plays in a revival of interest, and the reunion-recognition of Pericles and Marina is sometimes felt to be comparable to that of Lear and Cordelia.

Hallett Smith

The poet John Gower as Chorus in *Pericles*. From the title-page of George Wilkins, *The Painful Adventures of Pericles, Prince of Tyre* (1608). It is highly unlikely that this picture is a serious representation of the actor who played Gower's role of Chorus or presenter in Shakespeare's *Pericles*, even though Wilkins' little novel is in part probably based on Shakespeare's play as it was acted by the King's Men at the Globe (1607–8).

(By permission of the Harvard College Library)

Pericles, Prince of Tyre

[Dramatis Personae

Gower, *as Chorus*

Antiochus, *King of Antioch*
Pericles, *Prince of Tyre*
Helicanus } *two lords of Tyre*
Escanes }
Simonides, *King of Pentapolis*
Cleon, *Governor of Tharsus*
Lysimachus, *Governor of Mytilene*
Cerimon, *a lord of Ephesus*
Thaliard, *a lord of Antioch*
Philemon, *servant to Cerimon*
Leonine, *a murderer, servant to Dionyza*
Marshal

Pander
Boult, *his servant*
Another Servant

Daughter of Antiochus
Dionyza, *wife to Cleon*
Thaisa, *daughter to Simonides*
Marina, *daughter to Pericles and Thaisa*
Lychorida, *nurse to Marina*
Bawd

Diana, *a goddess appearing to Pericles*

Lords, Ladies, Knights, Gentlemen, Sailors, Pirates, Fishermen, *and* Messengers

Scene: *In several eastern Mediterranean countries*]

[ACT I]

Enter Gower.

[*Gow.*] To sing a song that old was sung,
From ashes ancient Gower is come,
Assuming man's infirmities,
To glad your ear and please your eyes.
It hath been sung at festivals,
On ember-eves and holy[-ales];
And lords and ladies in their lives
Have read it for restoratives.
The purchase is to make men glorious,
Et bonum quo antiquius, eo melius.
If you, born in those latter times,
When wit's more ripe, accept my rhymes,
And that to hear an old man sing
May to your wishes pleasure bring,
I life would wish, and that I might
Waste it for you like taper-light.
This' Antioch, then; Antiochus the Great
Built up this city for his chiefest seat,
The fairest in all Syria—
I tell you what mine authors say.
This king unto him took a peer,
Who died and left a female heir,
So buxom, blithe, and full of face
As heaven had lent her all his grace;
With whom the father liking took,
And her to incest did provoke—
Bad child, worse father, to entice his own
To evil should be done by none.
But custom what they did begin
Was with long use account'd no sin.
The beauty of this sinful dame
Made many princes thither frame
To seek her as a bedfellow,
In marriage pleasures playfellow;
Which to prevent he made a law,
To keep her still and men in awe,
That whoso ask'd her for his wife,
His riddle told not, lost his life.
So for her many [a] wight did die,

Words and passages enclosed in square brackets in the text above are either emendations of the copy-text or additions to it. The Textual Notes immediately following the play cite the earliest authority for every such change or insertion and supply the reading of the copy-text wherever it is emended in this edition.

I.Cho.1. old: of old.
3. Assuming man's infirmities: putting on (again) mortal human form.
6. ember-eves: eves of certain fast-days. **holy-ales**: rural festivals.
8. for restoratives: in place of healing medicines.
9. purchase: profit.
10. Et . . . melius: and the older a good thing is, the better.
13. that. Equivalent to a repetition of *if* (line 11).
16. Waste: expend.
17. This': this is. **21. peer**: wife of rank equal to his own.
23. buxom: lively. **full of face**: i.e. beautiful.
24. As: as if. **his**: its.
28. should: that should (a type of elision very frequent in this play).
29. custom: by custom. Many editors adopt Malone's emendation of *But* to *By*. **32. frame**: direct their course. **36. still**: always.
38. told: guessed.

As yon grim looks do testify.
[*Points to the heads of the unsuccessful suitors, displayed above.*]
What now ensues, to the judgment of your eye
I give my cause, who best can justify. *Exit.*

[Scene I]

Enter Antiochus, Prince Pericles, *and* Followers.

Ant. Young Prince of Tyre, you have at large received
The danger of the task you undertake.
Per. I have, Antiochus, and with a soul
Embold'ned with the glory of her praise,
Think death no hazard in this enterprise. *Music.*
Ant. Bring in our daughter, clothed like a bride
For embracements even of Jove himself;
At whose conception, till Lucina reigned,
Nature this dowry gave: to glad her presence,
The senate-house of planets all did sit,
To knit in her their best perfections.

Enter Antiochus' Daughter.

Per. See where she comes, apparelled like the spring,
Graces her subjects, and her thoughts the king
Of every virtue gives renown to men!
Her face the book of praises, where is read
Nothing but curious pleasures, as from thence
Sorrow were ever ras'd, and testy wrath
Could never be her mild companion.
You gods that made me man, and sway in love,
That have inflam'd desire in my breast
To taste the fruit of yon celestial tree
(Or die in th' adventure), be my helps,
As I am son and servant to your will,
To compass such a [boundless] happiness!
Ant. Prince Pericles—
Per. That would be son to great Antiochus.
Ant. Before thee stands this fair Hesperides,
With golden fruit, but dangerous to be touch'd;
For death-like dragons here affright thee hard.
Her face, like heaven, enticeth thee to view
Her countless glory, which desert must gain;
And which without desert because thine eye

42. **give my cause**: submit my case. **justify**: give a favorable verdict (?).

I.i. **Location**: Antioch. The palace.
1. **at large received**: learned in full detail.
8. **At . . . reigned**: i.e. from her conception to her birth. Lucina was the Roman goddess of childbirth.
9. **dowry**: gift (namely, that all the planets were in the most favorable positions for the child). **glad**: make gladsome.
14. **gives**: that gives.
15. **book of praises**: compendium of everything worth praise.
16. **curious**: exquisite. **as**: as though.
17. **ever ras'd**: forever erased.
18. **her mild companion**: the companion of her serene self.
19. **sway**: govern. 22. **adventure**: venture, hazardous attempt.
27. **Hesperides**: properly, the daughters of Hesperus who, together with a dragon, protected the garden where Hercules plucked golden apples; but here, as often, used of the garden itself. The image begins in line 21.
31. **countless glory**: i.e. innumerable beauties (like stars in the heavens). The adjective implies a collective sense for *glory*.

Presumes to reach, all the whole heap must die.
Yon sometimes famous princes, like thyself,
Drawn by report, advent'rous by desire,
Tell thee, with speechless tongues and semblance pale,
That without covering, save yon field of stars,
Here they stand martyrs, slain in Cupid's wars;
And with dead cheeks advise thee to desist
For going on death's net, whom none resist.
Per. Antiochus, I thank thee, who hath taught
My frail mortality to know itself,
And by those fearful objects to prepare
This body, like to them, to what I must;
For death remembered should be like a mirror,
Who tells us life's but breath, to trust it error.
I'll make my will then, and as sick men do,
Who know the world, see heaven, but feeling woe,
Gripe not at earthly joys as erst they did;
So I bequeath a happy peace to you
And all good men, as every prince should do;
My riches to the earth from whence they came;
[*To the Princess.*] But my unspotted fire of love to you.
Thus ready for the way of life or death,
I wait the sharpest blow, Antiochus.
[*Ant.*] Scorning advice, read the conclusion then;
Which read and not expounded, 'tis decreed,
As these before thee, thou thyself shalt bleed.
Daugh. Of all 'say'd yet, mayst thou prove prosperous!
Of all 'say'd yet, I wish thee happiness!
Per. Like a bold champion I assume the lists,
Nor ask advice of any other thought
But faithfulness and courage. [*Reads.*]

The Riddle

I am no viper, yet I feed
On mother's flesh which did me breed.
I sought a husband, in which labor
I found that kindness in a father.
He's father, son, and husband mild;
I mother, wife—and yet his child.
How they may be, and yet in two,
As you will live, resolve it you.

[*Aside.*] Sharp physic is the last. But O you powers!
That gives heaven countless eyes to view men's acts,
Why cloud they not their sights perpetually,
If this be true which makes me pale to read it?
[*Aside to the Princess.*] Fair glass of light, I lov'd you, and could still,
Were not this glorious casket stor'd with ill.

33. **heap**: mass, i.e. body. 34. **sometimes**: formerly.
35. **advent'rous by desire**: (made) rash by passion.
40. **For**: from, or, perhaps, for fear of (both senses occur).
44. **what I must**: whatever proves necessary.
45. **remembered**: called to mind.
49. **Gripe**: grip, grasp. **erst**: formerly.
56. **conclusion**: riddle (with play on the sense "end").
59. **'say'd**: who have assayed (i.e. attempted).
61. **lists**: tournament ground.
64. **viper**. The viper's young were believed to eat their way out of their mother's body. 70. **in two**: be only two people.
72. **Sharp . . . last**: the final condition—"as you will live"—is bitter medicine.
76. **glass**: mirror (reflecting external light, but dark within; cf. line 77). 77. **casket**: jewel box.

But I must tell you, now my thoughts revolt,
For he's no man on whom perfections wait
That, knowing sin within, will touch the gate.
You are a fair viol, and your sense the strings;
Who, finger'd to make man his lawful music,
Would draw heaven down, and all the gods to hearken;
But being play'd upon before your time,
Hell only danceth at so harsh a chime.
Good sooth, I care not for you.

Ant. Prince Pericles, touch not, upon thy life,
For that's an article within our law,
As dangerous as the rest. Your time's expir'd,
Either expound now, or receive your sentence.

Per. Great King,
Few love to hear the sins they love to act;
'Twould braid yourself too near for me to tell it.
Who has a book of all that monarchs do,
He's more secure to keep it shut than shown;
For vice repeated is like the wand'ring wind,
Blows dust in others' eyes, to spread itself;
And yet the end of all is bought thus dear,
The breath is gone, and the sore eyes see clear
To stop the air would hurt them. The blind mole casts
Copp'd hills towards heaven, to tell the earth is throng'd
By man's oppression, and the poor worm doth die for't.
Kings are earth's gods; in vice their law's their will;
And if Jove stray, who dares say Jove doth ill?
It is enough you know, and it is fit,
What being more known grows worse, to smother it.
All love the womb that their first being bred,
Then give my tongue like leave to love my head.

Ant. [*Aside.*] Heaven, that I had thy head! He has found the meaning.
But I will gloze with him.—Young Prince of Tyre,
Though by the tenor of [our] strict edict,
Your exposition misinterpreting,
We might proceed to [cancel] of your days;
Yet hope, succeeding from so fair a tree
As your fair self, doth tune us otherwise.
Forty days longer we do respite you;
If by which time our secret be undone,
This mercy shows we'll joy in such a son;
And until then your entertain shall be
As doth befit our honor and your worth.

[*Exeunt.*] *Manet Pericles solus.*

Per. How courtesy would seem to cover sin,
When what is done is like an hypocrite,
The which is good in nothing but in sight!
If it be true that I interpret false,
Then were it certain you were not so bad
As with foul incest to abuse your soul;
Where now you['re] both a father and a son
By your [uncomely] claspings with your child
(Which pleasures fits a husband, not a father),
And she an eater of her mother's flesh
By the defiling of her parent's bed;
And both like serpents are, who though they feed
On sweetest flowers, yet they poison breed.
Antioch, farewell, for wisdom sees those men
Blush not in actions blacker than the night
Will ['schew] no course to keep them from the light.
One sin, I know, another doth provoke:
Murther's as near to lust as flame to smoke;
Poison and treason are the hands of sin,
Ay, and the targets to put off the shame;
Then lest my life be cropp'd to keep you clear,
By flight I'll shun the danger which I fear. *Exit.*

Enter ANTIOCHUS.

Ant. He hath found the meaning,
For which we mean to have his head.
He must not live to trumpet forth my infamy,
Nor tell the world Antiochus doth sin
In such a loathed manner;
And therefore instantly this prince must die,
For by his fall my honor must keep high.
Who attends us there?

Enter THALIARD.

Thal. Doth your Highness call?

Ant. Thaliard—you are of our chamber, Thaliard,
And our mind partakes her private actions
To your secrecy; and for your faithfulness
We will advance you, Thaliard. Behold,
Here's poison and here's gold; we hate the Prince
Of Tyre, and thou must kill him. It fits thee not
To ask the reason why, because we bid it.
Say, is it done?

Thal. My lord, 'tis done.

Ant. Enough.

Enter a MESSENGER.

Let your breath cool yourself, telling your haste.

Mess. My lord, Prince Pericles is fled. [*Exit.*]

Ant. As thou
Wilt live, fly after, and like an arrow shot
From a well-experienc'd archer hits the mark
His eye doth level at, so thou never return
Unless thou say Prince Pericles is dead.

Thal. My lord,
If I can get him within my pistol's length,

81. sense: senses (a collective singular).
86. Good sooth: in truth.
87. touch not. Antiochus presumably misinterprets some movement made by Pericles. **93. braid:** upbraid.
96. repeated: i.e. reported.
97. Blows: which blows. **others' eyes.** Lines 99–100 make clear that the "others" are those whose vice is talked about. **to spread:** in spreading.
100. To . . . air: how to stop the air which.
101. Copp'd: peaked. **throng'd:** overwhelmed.
102. worm: i.e. creature. **110. gloze:** talk deceptively.
112. Your . . . misinterpreting: since your explanation interprets incorrectly. **113. cancel:** termination.
114. hope: i.e. hope (actually, fear) that you will yet answer correctly. **succeeding . . . tree:** i.e. issuing from so excellent a prospective stem of royal progeny for me (this meaning seems implied by both *succeeding* and *tree*).
117. undone: unravelled, solved. **121. seem:** dissemble.

123. sight: appearance. **128. uncomely:** improper, unseemly.
131. parent's. The singular form is supported by Wilkins; see the Textual Notes. **135. Blush:** who blush. **136. 'schew:** eschew.
140. targets: shields. **put:** ward.
141. clear: free from suspicion.
151. of our chamber: i.e. one of my most trusted retainers (*our* is the royal plural). **152. partakes:** imparts.
159. Let . . . haste: "let the breath you are panting out to cool yourself also express the reason for your haste" (Maxwell).
163. level: aim. **166. length:** range.

I'll make him sure enough; so farewell to your Highness.
[*Ant.*] Thaliard, adieu! [*Exit Thaliard.*] Till Pericles be dead,
My heart can lend no succor to my head. [*Exit.*]

[SCENE II]

Enter PERICLES *with his* LORDS.

Per. Let none disturb us. [*Exeunt Lords.*] Why should this change of thoughts,
The sad companion, dull-ey'd melancholy,
[Be my] so us'd a guest as not an hour
In the day's glorious walk or peaceful night,
The tomb where grief should sleep, can breed me quiet?
Here pleasures court mine eyes, and mine eyes shun them,
And danger, which I fear'd, is at Antioch,
Whose arm seems far too short to hit me here.
Yet neither pleasure's art can joy my spirits,
Nor yet the other's distance comfort me.
Then it is thus: the passions of the mind,
That have their first conception by misdread,
Have after-nourishment and life by care;
And what was first but fear what might be done,
Grows elder now, and cares it be not done.
And so with me: the great Antiochus,
'Gainst whom I am too little to contend,
Since he's so great can make his will his act,
Will think me speaking, though I swear to silence;
Nor boots it me to say I honor [him],
If he suspect I may dishonor him;
And what may make him blush in being known,
He'll stop the course by which it might be known.
With hostile forces he'll o'erspread the land,
And with [th' ostent] of war will look so huge,
Amazement shall drive courage from the state,
Our men be vanquish'd ere they do resist,
And subjects punish'd that ne'er thought offense:
Which care of them, not pity of myself—
Who [am] no more but as the tops of trees,
Which fence the roots they grow by and defend them—
Makes both my body pine and soul to languish,
And punish that before that he would punish.

Enter [HELICANUS *and*] *all the* LORDS *to Pericles.*

1. Lord. Joy and all comfort in your sacred breast!
2. Lord. And keep your mind, till you return to us,

Peaceful and comfortable!
Hel. Peace, peace, and give experience tongue.
They do abuse the King that flatter him,
For flattery is the bellows blows up sin,
The thing the which is flattered, but a spark
To which that [blast] gives heat and stronger glowing;
Whereas reproof, obedient and in order,
Fits kings as they are men, for they may err.
When Signior Sooth here does proclaim peace,
He flatters you, makes war upon your life.
Prince, pardon me, or strike me, if you please,
I cannot be much lower than my knees. [*Kneels.*]
Per. All leave us else; but let your cares o'erlook
What shipping and what lading's in our haven,
And then return to us. [*Exeunt Lords.*] Helicanus, thou
Hast mov'd us. What seest thou in our looks?
Hel. An angry brow, dread lord.
Per. If there be such a dart in princes' frowns,
How durst thy tongue move anger to our face?
Hel. How dares the plants look up to heaven, from whence
They have their nourishment?
Per. Thou knowest I have power
To take thy life from thee.
Hel. I have ground the axe myself,
Do but you strike the blow.
Per. Rise, prithee rise. Sit down. Thou art
No flatterer. I thank thee for't, and heaven forbid
That kings should let their ears hear their faults hid!
Fit counsellor and servant for a prince,
Who by thy wisdom makes a prince thy servant,
What wouldst thou have me do?
Hel. To bear with patience
Such griefs as you yourself do lay upon yourself.
Per. Thou speak'st like a physician, Helicanus,
That ministers a potion unto me
That thou wouldst tremble to receive thyself.
Attend me then: I went to Antioch,
Where, as thou know'st, against the face of death
I sought the purchase of a glorious beauty,
From whence an issue I might propagate,
Are arms to princes and bring joys to subjects.
Her face was to mine eye beyond all wonder;
The rest (hark in thine ear) as black as incest,
Which by my knowledge found, the sinful father
Seem'd not to strike, but smooth. But thou know'st this,
'Tis time to fear when tyrants seems to kiss.
Which fear so grew in me, I hither fled,
Under the covering of a careful night,
Who seem'd my good protector, and being here,
Bethought what was past, what might succeed.
I knew him tyrannous, and tyrants' [fears]
Decrease not, but grow faster than the years;

167. make him sure: render him harmless, i.e. kill him.

I.ii. Location: Tyre. The palace.
1. us. Royal plural. **change of thoughts**: changed state of mind.
3. us'd: accustomed. **as**: that. **4. day's**: i.e. sun's.
8. arm . . . short. Alluding to the proverb "Kings have long arms."
12. misdread: fear of evil. **13. care**: anxiety.
15. cares . . . done: is anxious to keep it from being done.
18. can: that he can (or, alternatively, *he's* = he who is).
20. boots: avails. **22. in being known**: if it were to become known.
25. ostent: display. **26. Amazement**: consternation.
31. fence: protect.
35. till you return. The lords have no knowledge of Pericles' intention to travel; see I.iii.16–18. Nor is there any apparent reason for the following remarks by Helicanus on flattery. Most commentators postulate major textual dislocations in this scene.

38. abuse: use ill, wrong. **39. blows**: that blows.
44. Signior Sooth: Sir Flattery (one who talks soothingly).
48. o'erlook: look over, survey. **49. lading**: cargo.
51. mov'd: angered.
62. let . . . hid: listen to talk that hides their faults, i.e. to flattery.
72. purchase: acquisition.
74. Are arms: who are weapons. The plural verb requires that *an issue* be interpreted in the plural sense "offspring, children."
78. smooth: gloss over. **81. careful**: protective.
83. Bethought. Supply *me*. **succeed**: follow.

And should he [doubt]'t, as no doubt he doth,
That I should open to the list'ning air
How many worthy princes' bloods were shed
To keep his bed of blackness unlaid ope,
To lop that doubt, he'll fill this land with arms,
And make pretense of wrong that I have done him;
When all, for mine, if I may call offense,
Must feel war's blow, who spares not innocence:
Which love to all, of which thyself art one,
Who now reprov'dst me for't—

Hel. Alas, sir!

Per. Drew sleep out of mine eyes, blood from my cheeks,
Musings into my mind, with thousand doubts
How I might stop this tempest ere it came,
And finding little comfort to relieve them,
I thought it princely charity to grieve for them.

Hel. Well, my lord, since you have given me leave to speak,
Freely will I speak. Antiochus you fear,
And justly too, I think, you fear the tyrant,
Who either by public war or private treason
Will take away your life.
Therefore, my lord, go travel for a while,
Till that his rage and anger be forgot,
Or till the Destinies do cut his thread of life.
Your rule direct to any; if to me,
Day serves not light more faithful than I'll be.

Per. I do not doubt thy faith;
But should he wrong my liberties in my absence?

Hel. We'll mingle our bloods together in the earth,
From whence we had our being and our birth.

Per. Tyre, I now look from thee then, and to Tharsus
Intend my travel, where I'll hear from thee,
And by whose letters I'll dispose myself.
The care I had and have of subjects' good
On thee I lay, whose wisdom's strength can bear it.
I'll take thy word for faith, not ask thine oath:
Who shuns not to break one will crack [them] both;
But in our orbs [we'll] live so round and safe,
That time of both this truth shall ne'er convince,
Thou show'dst a subject's shine, I a true prince'.

Exeunt.

[SCENE III]

Enter THALIARD *solus.*

Thal. So this is Tyre, and this the court. Here must I kill King Pericles; and if I do it not, I am sure to be hang'd at home. 'Tis dangerous. Well, I perceive he was a wise fellow and had good discretion that, being bid to ask what he would of the king, desir'd he might know none of his secrets. Now do I see he had some reason for't; for if a king bid a man be a villain, he's bound by the indenture of his oath to be one. Husht! here comes the lords of Tyre.

Enter HELICANUS, ESCANES, *with other* LORDS.

Hel. You shall not need, my fellow peers of Tyre,
Further to question me of your king's departure.
His seal'd commission, left in trust with me,
Does speak sufficiently he's gone to travel.

Thal. [*Aside.*] How? the King gone?

Hel. If further yet you will be satisfied
Why (as it were unlicens'd of your loves)
He would depart, I'll give some light unto you.
Being at Antioch—

Thal. [*Aside.*] What from Antioch?

Hel. Royal Antiochus, on what cause I know not,
Took some displeasure at him, at least he judg'd so;
And doubting lest he had err'd or sinn'd,
To show his sorrow, he'd correct himself;
So puts himself unto the shipman's toil,
With whom each minute threatens life or death.

Thal. [*Aside.*] Well, I perceive
I shall not be hang'd now, although I would;
But since he's gone, the King's seas must please:
He scap'd the land to perish at the sea.
I'll present myself.—Peace to the lords of Tyre!

[*Hel.*] Lord Thaliard from Antiochus is welcome.

Thal. From him I come
With message unto princely Pericles,
But since my landing I have understood
Your lord has [betook] himself to unknown travels;
Now message must return from whence it came.

Hel. We have no reason to desire it,
Commended to our master, not to us;
Yet ere you shall depart, this we desire,
As friends to Antioch, we may feast in Tyre.

Exeunt.

[SCENE IV]

Enter CLEON, *the Governor of Tharsus, with his wife* [DIONYZA] *and others.*

Cle. My Dionyza, shall we rest us here,
And by relating tales of others' griefs,
See if 'twill teach us to forget our own?

Dion. That were to blow at fire in hope to quench it,

86. doubt't: suspect it, fear it. **89. unlaid ope:** undisclosed.
92. all: everyone. **mine . . . offense:** my offense, if I may call it that. **93. who:** which. **95. now:** just now.
100. grieve for them. Many editors regularize rhyme and metre by emending to *grieve them* (*grieve* = grieve for). **109. direct:** assign.
112. should he: what if he should. **my liberties:** my subjects' freedom (?) or my royal rights (?). **116. Intend:** purpose, direct.
122. A line is apparently lost after 121. **orbs:** orbits, i.e. spheres of action. **round:** honestly (but with play on "circular" suggested by *orbs*).
123. time . . . convince: time shall never refute this truth concerning both of us. **124. shine:** honor, glory. **prince':** prince's.

I.iii. Location: Tyre. The palace.
2. and if: if.

4. he: that man (the poet Philippides, who made this answer to King Lysimachus of Thrace). **8. indenture:** contract.
16. unlicens'd . . . loves: without the consent of you, his loving subjects. (This contradicts I.ii.34–36.)
21. doubting lest: fearing that.
26. although I would: even if I wished it.
27. please: do their pleasure with him (?) or please the King by destroying him (?). Text probably corrupt in lines 27–28; most editors, following Dyce, read *the King's ears it must please*, and *seas* (line 28) for a rhyme with *please*.
36. desire it: ask what it is.
37. Commended: since it is sent.

I.iv. Location: Tharsus. The Governor's house.

For who digs hills because they do aspire
Throws down one mountain to cast up a higher.
O my distressed lord, even such our griefs are;
Here they are but felt, and seen with mischief's eyes,
But like to groves, being topp'd, they higher rise.

Cle. O Dionyza!
Who wanteth food and will not say he wants it,
Or can conceal his hunger till he famish?
Our tongues and sorrows to sound deep our woes
Into the air, our eyes to weep, till tongues
Fetch breath that may proclaim them louder, that
If heaven slumber, while their creatures want,
They may awake their helpers to comfort them.
I'll then discourse our woes, felt several years,
And wanting breath to speak, help me with tears.

Dion. I'll do my best, sir.

Cle. This Tharsus, o'er which I have the government,
A city on whom plenty held full hand,
For riches strew'd herself even in her streets;
Whose towers bore heads so high they kiss'd the clouds,
And strangers ne'er beheld but wond'red at;
Whose men and dames so jetted and adorn'd,
Like one another's glass to trim them by;
Their tables were stor'd full, to glad the sight,
And not so much to feed on as delight;
All poverty was scorn'd, and pride so great,
The name of help grew odious to repeat.

Dion. O, 'tis too true.

Cle. But see what heaven can do by this our change:
These mouths who, but of late, earth, sea, and air
Were all too little to content and please,
Although they gave their creatures in abundance,
As houses are defil'd for want of use,
They are now starv'd for want of exercise;
Those palates who, not yet [two summers] younger,
Must have inventions to delight the taste,
Would now be glad of bread and beg for it;
Those mothers who, to nousle up their babes,
Thought nought too curious, are ready now
To eat those little darlings whom they lov'd.
So sharp are hunger's teeth, that man and wife
Draw lots who first shall die to lengthen life.
Here stands a lord, and there a lady weeping;
Here many sink, yet those which see them fall
Have scarce strength left to give them burial.
Is not this true?

Dion. Our cheeks and hollow eyes do witness it.

Cle. O, let those cities that of plenty's cup
And her prosperities so largely taste,
With their superfluous riots, hear these tears!

The misery of Tharsus may be theirs.

Enter a Lord.

Lord. Where's the Lord Governor?

Cle. Here.
Speak out thy sorrows which [thou] bring'st in haste,
For comfort is too far for us to expect.

Lord. We have descried, upon our neighboring shore,
A portly sail of ships make hitherward.

Cle. I thought as much.
One sorrow never comes but brings an heir
That may succeed as his inheritor;
And so in ours, some neighboring nation,
Taking advantage of our misery,
[Hath] stuff'd the hollow vessels with their power
To beat us down, the which are down already,
And make a conquest of unhappy me,
Whereas no glory's got to overcome.

Lord. That's the least fear; for by the semblance
Of their white flags display'd, they bring us peace,
And come to us as favorers, not as foes.

Cle. Thou speak'st like [him's] untutor'd to repeat:
Who makes the fairest show means most deceit.
But bring they what they will and what they can,
What need we [fear]?
Our ground's the lowest, and we are half way there.
Go tell their general we attend him here,
To know for what he comes, and whence he comes,
And what he craves.

Lord. I go, my lord. [*Exit.*]

Cle. Welcome is peace, if he on peace consist;
If wars, we are unable to resist.

Enter Pericles *with* [Lord *and*] Attendants.

Per. Lord Governor, for so we hear you are,
Let not our ships and number of our men
Be like a beacon fir'd t' amaze your eyes.
We have heard your miseries as far as Tyre,
And seen the desolation of your streets;
Nor come we to add sorrow to your tears,
But to relieve them of their heavy load;
And these our ships, you happily may think
Are like the Troyan horse was stuff'd within
With bloody veins, expecting overthrow,
Are stor'd with corn to make your needy bread,
And give them life whom hunger starv'd half dead.

Omnes. The gods of Greece protect you!
And we'll pray for you.

Per. Arise, I pray you, rise.
We do not look for reverence but for love,

5. aspire: rise up. **8. mischief's:** calamity's.
9. topp'd: cut back, pruned. **11. wanteth:** lacks.
13–17. The text is corrupt beyond restoration, but the general sense is clear. **19. wanting:** when I run out of.
22. on whom: over which.
23. herself. *Riches* is singular (from French *richesse*).
26. jetted: strutted.
27. glass: mirror, i.e. model. **trim them:** adorn themselves.
31. repeat: mention. **33. by . . . change.** Modifies *see.*
39. two summers. See the Textual Notes.
40. inventions: novel concoctions.
42. nousle up: nurture tenderly. **43. curious:** choice.
54. superfluous riots: excessively wasteful living.

61. portly sail: stately fleet. **67. power:** soldiers.
70. Whereas . . . overcome: where no glory can be gained by conquering.
74. him's . . . repeat: a man who has never been taught to recite (the following proverb), i.e. who does not know that it is true.
78. Our. Many editors emend to *The* (so Q4) or *On* (Maxwell).
83. on peace consist: intends peace. **87. amaze:** terrify.
92. you: which you. **happily:** haply, perhaps.
93. was: which was.
94. bloody veins: i.e. the bloodthirsty Greek soldiers concealed in the wooden horse at Troy. **expecting overthrow.** This phrase may modify *you* (line 93) or may refer to the Greeks in the wooden horse, in the sense "awaiting conquest (of Troy)."
95. corn: grain. **your needy:** for your needy people.

And harborage for ourself, our ships, and men.
Cle. The which when any shall not gratify,
Or pay you with unthankfulness in thought,
Be it our wives, our children, or ourselves,
The curse of heaven and men succeed their evils!
Till when—the which I hope shall ne'er be seen—
Your Grace is welcome to our town and us.
Per. Which welcome we'll accept; feast here awhile,
Until our stars that frown lend us a smile. *Exeunt.*

[ACT II]

Enter Gower.

[*Gow.*] Here have you seen a mighty king
His child, I wis, to incest bring;
A better prince and benign lord,
That will prove aweful both in deed and word.
Be quiet then, as men should be,
Till he hath pass'd necessity.
I'll show you those in troubles reign,
Losing a mite, a mountain gain.
The good in conversation,
To whom I give my benison,
Is still at Tharsus, where each man
Thinks all is writ he [speken] can;
And, to remember what he does,
Build his statue to make him glorious.
But tidings to the contrary
Are brought your eyes; what need speak I?

Dumb Show

Enter at one door Pericles *talking with* Cleon; *all the* Train *with them. Enter at another door a* Gentleman *with a letter to Pericles; Pericles shows the letter to Cleon; Pericles gives the Messenger a reward and knights him. Exit Pericles at one door and Cleon at another.*

Good Helicane, that stay'd at home,
Not to eat honey like a drone
From others' labors; for though he strive
To killen bad, keep good alive,
And to fulfill his prince' desire,
[Sends word] of all that haps in Tyre:
How Thaliard came full bent with sin

101. **gratify:** show gratitude for. 102. **in:** even in.

II.Cho.2. **I wis:** I know—a common misunderstanding of *iwis*, "certainly." 4. **aweful:** deserving of respect.
6. **pass'd necessity:** undergone extreme hardship (?) or followed the course of his destiny (?).
7. **those . . . reign:** that those who reign amid troubles. Some editors, following Deighton, emend *troubles* to *trouble's* to produce the meaning "those who under the domination of trouble."
9. **The good in conversation:** the virtuous (man), i.e. Pericles; *conversation* = behavior.
12. **all . . . can:** every word he speaks is gospel. The archaic ending of *speken* is seen again in *killen* (line 20), *been* (line 28), and elsewhere.
13. **remember:** commemorate.
15. **to the contrary:** of a nature to change the situation (?).
17–22. This passage is obviously corrupt. Of the various emendations proposed, the simplest (Kittredge's) is to drop *for* (line 19) and indicate lines 18–21 as a parenthesis.
23. **bent with:** intent upon.

And hid intent to murder him;
And that in Tharsus was not best
Longer for him to make his rest.
He, doing so, put forth to seas,
Where when men been, there's seldom ease,
For now the wind begins to blow;
Thunder above, and deeps below,
Makes such unquiet, that the ship
Should house him safe is wrack'd and split,
And he, good prince, having all lost,
By waves from coast to coast is toss'd.
All perishen of man, of pelf,
Ne aught escapend but himself;
Till Fortune, tir'd with doing bad,
Threw him ashore, to give him glad.
And here he comes. What shall be next,
Pardon old Gower—this long's the text. [*Exit.*]

[Scene I]

Enter Pericles *wet.*

Per. Yet cease your ire, you angry stars of heaven!
Wind, rain, and thunder, remember earthly man
Is but a substance that must yield to you;
And I (as fits my nature) do obey you.
Alas, the seas hath cast me on the rocks,
Wash'd me from shore to shore, and left [me] breath
Nothing to think on but ensuing death.
Let it suffice the greatness of your powers
To have bereft a prince of all his fortunes;
And having thrown him from your wat'ry grave,
Here to have death in peace is all he'll crave.

Enter three Fishermen.

1. Fish. What [ho,] Pilch!
2. Fish. Ha, come and bring away the nets!
1. Fish. What, Patch-breech, I say!
3. Fish. What say you, master?
1. Fish. Look how thou stir'st now! Come away, or I'll fetch th' with a wanion.
3. Fish. Faith, master, I am thinking of the poor men that were cast away before us even now.
1. Fish. Alas, poor souls, it griev'd my heart to hear what pitiful cries they made to us to help them, when, well-a-day, we could scarce help ourselves.
3. Fish. Nay, master, said not I as much when I saw the porpas how he bounc'd and tumbled? They say they're half fish, half flesh. A plague on them, they

24. **hid:** hidden, secret (?) or simply the past tense of *hide* (?). On this line see the Textual Notes.
27. **doing so:** i.e. acting in accordance with the warning.
32. **Should:** which should.
35. **All . . . pelf:** all the men and property perish.
36. **Ne aught escapend:** nothing escaping. 38. **glad:** gladness.
40. **this . . . text:** i.e. the text of my speech is this long and no longer. Many editors read *'longs* = belongs to (the text of the play proper).

II.i. Location: Pentapolis. The seashore.
12. **Pilch.** The name (or nickname) means a leather garment.
13. **bring away:** bring along at once. Cf. *come away* (= come right along) in line 16.
16. **how thou stir'st:** how speedy you are (ironic).
17. **th':** thee. **wanion:** vengeance.
19. **before us:** before our eyes. 22. **well-a-day:** alas.
24. **porpas:** porpoise, proverbial predictor of storms.

ne'er come but I look to be wash'd. Master, I marvel how the fishes live in the sea.

1. Fish. Why, as men do a-land; the great ones eat up the little ones. I can compare our rich misers to nothing so fitly as to a whale: 'a plays and tumbles, driving the poor fry before him, and at last devour them all at a mouthful. Such whales have I heard on a' th' land, who never leave gaping till they swallow'd the whole parish, church, steeple, bells, and all.

Per. [*Aside.*] A pretty moral.

3. Fish. But, master, if I had been the sexton, I would have been that day in the belfry.

2. Fish. Why, man?

3. Fish. Because he should have swallow'd me too, and when I had been in his belly, I would have kept such a jangling of the bells, that he should never have left till he cast bells, steeple, church, and parish up again. But if the good King Simonides were of my mind—

Per. [*Aside.*] Simonides?

3. Fish. We would purge the land of these drones, that rob the bee of her honey.

Per. [*Aside.*] How from the [finny] subject of the sea
These fishers tell the infirmities of men,
And from their wat'ry empire recollect
All that may men approve or men detect!—
Peace be at your labor, honest fishermen.

2. Fish. Honest, good fellow, what's that? If it be a day fits you, search out of the calendar, and nobody look after it.

Per. May see the sea hath cast upon your coast—

2. Fish. What a drunken knave was the sea to cast thee in our way!

Per. A man whom both the waters and the wind,
In that vast tennis-court, hath made the ball
For them to play upon, entreats you pity him.
He asks of you that never us'd to beg.

1. Fish. No, friend, cannot you beg? Here's them in our country of Greece gets more with begging than we can do with working.

2. Fish. Canst thou catch any fishes then?

Per. I never practic'd it.

2. Fish. Nay then thou wilt starve sure; for here's nothing to be got now-a-days unless thou canst fish for't.

Per. What I have been I have forgot to know,
But what I am, want teaches me to think on:
A man throng'd up with cold, my veins are chill,
And have no more of life than may suffice

30. 'a: he. **31. devour:** devours. **32. on:** of.
33. a': on. **leave gaping:** shut their mouths.
42. cast: vomited (as also in line 57). **48. subject:** citizenry.
51. approve: commend. **detect:** expose.
53–55. If . . . it. Textually corrupt. Malone postulated the loss of a line in which Pericles says "good day" to the fishermen. If so, the Second Fisherman replies that if the day fits Pericles' miserable condition, it should be dropped from the calendar; no one would miss it. Some editors, following Steevens, emend *search* to *scratch't*.
55. after: for. **56. May:** you may.
60. tennis-court. Referring to court tennis, an older form of the game, played, like squash, in an enclosed court. Tennis furnished a common figure for the buffetings and rapid shifts of fortune.
62. us'd: was accustomed.
69–70. fish for't: i.e. get it by trickery.
73. throng'd up: overwhelmed.

To give my tongue that heat to ask your help;
Which if you shall refuse, when I am dead,
For that I am a man, pray you see me buried.

1. Fish. Die, keth 'a? Now gods forbid't, and I have a gown here! Come put it on, keep thee warm. Now, afore me, a handsome fellow! Come, thou shalt go home, and we'll have flesh for [holidays], fish for fasting-days, and, moreo'er, puddings and flap-jacks, and thou shalt be welcome.

Per. I thank you, sir.

2. Fish. Hark you, my friend. You said you could not beg?

Per. I did but crave.

2. Fish. But crave? Then I'll turn craver too, and so I shall scape whipping.

Per. Why, are [your] beggars whipt then?

2. Fish. O, not all, my friend, not all; for if all your beggars were whipt, I would wish no better office than to be beadle. But, master, I'll go draw up the net. [*Exit with Third Fisherman.*]

Per. [*Aside.*] How well this honest mirth becomes their labor!

1. Fish. Hark you, sir; do you know where ye are?

Per. Not well.

1. Fish. Why, I'll tell you. This [is] call'd Pentapolis, and our king the good Simonides.

Per. The good Simonides, do you call him?

1. Fish. Ay, sir, and he deserves so to be call'd for his peaceable reign and good government.

Per. He is a happy king, since he gains from his subjects the name of good by his government. How far is his court distant from this shore?

1. Fish. Marry, sir, half a day's journey. And I'll tell you, he hath a fair daughter, and to-morrow is her birthday, and there are princes and knights come from all parts of the world to just and tourney for her love.

Per. Were my fortunes equal to my desires, I could wish to make one there.

1. Fish. O, sir, things must be as they may; and what a man cannot get, he may lawfully deal for his wive's soul.

Enter the two [*other*] FISHERMEN *drawing up a net.*

2. Fish. Help, master, help! here's a fish hangs in the net, like a poor man's right in the law; 'twill hardly come out. Ha, bots on't, 'tis come at last, and 'tis turn'd to a rusty armor.

Per. An armor, friends? I pray you let me see it.
Thanks, Fortune, yet, that after all [thy] crosses,
Thou givest me somewhat to repair myself;
And though it was mine own, part of my heritage,
Which my dead father did bequeath to me,
With this strict charge, even as he left his life,

77. For that: because. **78. keth 'a:** quoth he. **and:** if.
80. afore me: by my faith. **87. crave:** request.
89. whipping. The regular punishment for able-bodied beggars.
93. beadle: official who administered corporal punishment.
95. becomes: suits.
107. Marry: indeed (originally the name of the Virgin Mary used as an oath). **110. just:** joust.
114–15. he . . . soul. Not satisfactorily explained; no doubt the text is corrupt. **118. bots:** i.e. a plague (actually, a disease of horses).
121. crosses: thwartings, adverse actions.

"Keep it, my Pericles, it hath been a shield
'Twixt me and death"—and pointed to this brace—
"For that it sav'd me, keep it. In like necessity—
The which the gods protect thee [from!—] may defend thee."
It kept where I kept, I so dearly lov'd it,
Till the rough seas, that spares not any man,
Took it in rage, though calm'd have given't again.
I thank thee for't. My shipwrack now's no ill,
Since I have here my father gave in his will.

1. Fish. What mean you, sir?

Per. To beg of you, kind friends, this coat of worth,
For it was sometime target to a king;
I know it by this mark. He loved me dearly,
And for his sake I wish the having of it;
And that you'd guide me to your sovereign's court,
Where with it I may appear a gentleman;
And if that ever my low fortunes better,
I'll pay your bounties; till then, rest your debtor.

1. Fish. Why, wilt thou tourney for the lady?

Per. I'll show the virtue I have borne in arms.

1. Fish. Why, d' ye take it, and the gods give thee good an't!

2. Fish. Ay, but hark you, my friend, 'twas we that made up this garment through the rough seams of the waters. There are certain condolements, certain vails. I hope, sir, if you thrive, you'll remember from whence you had them.

Per. Believe't, I will.
By your furtherance I am cloth'd in steel,
And, spite of all the [rapture] of the sea,
This jewel holds his building on my arm.
Unto thy value I will mount myself
Upon a courser, whose [delightful] steps
Shall make the gazer joy to see him tread.
Only, my friend, I yet am unprovided
Of a pair of bases.

2. Fish. We'll sure provide. Thou shalt have my best gown to make thee a pair; and I'll bring thee to the court myself.

Per. Then honor be but a goal to my will,
This day I'll rise, or else add ill to ill. [*Exeunt.*]

[Scene II]

Enter Simonides, *with attendance,* [Lords,] *and* Thaisa.

Sim. Are the knights ready to begin the triumph?

127. **brace**: armor for the arm. 130. **kept**: lodged.
134. **my father**: what my father.
137. **target**: shield; here, protection (cf. *shield* in line 126).
143. **pay your bounties**: repay your generosity.
145. **virtue**: quality, expertness. 147. **an't**: on it, i.e. of it.
150. **condolements**: apparently a malapropism connected with *doles*, "shares of loot."
151. **vails**: perquisites, "extras" picked up in addition to regular wages. 152. **them**: i.e. the pieces of armor.
155. **rapture**: plundering. 156. **his building**: its fixed place.
157. **thy**: i.e. the jewel's.
161. **pair of bases**: skirtlike garment worn by a mounted knight.

II.ii. See the Textual Notes for significant variations in Wilkins' description of this scene.
Location: Pentapolis. The entrance to the lists. A covered platform at one side.
1. **triumph**: public festivity or spectacle; here, tournament.

1. Lord. They are, my liege,
And stay your coming to present themselves.

Sim. Return them, we are ready; and our daughter here,
In honor of whose birth these triumphs are,
Sits here like beauty's child, whom nature gat
For men to see, and seeing wonder at. [*Exit a Lord.*]

Thai. It pleaseth you, my royal father, to express
My commendations great, whose merit's less.

Sim. It's fit it should be so, for princes are
A model which heaven makes like to itself.
As jewels lose their glory if neglected,
So princes their renowns if not respected.
'Tis now your honor, daughter, to entertain
The labor of each knight in his device.

Thai. Which, to preserve mine honor, I'll perform.

The First Knight *passes by* [*and his* Page *presents his shield to the Princess*].

Sim. Who is the first that doth prefer himself?

Thai. A knight of Sparta, my renowned father,
And the device he bears upon his shield
Is a black Ethiope reaching at the sun;
The word: "*Lux tua vita mihi.*"

Sim. He loves you well that holds his life of you.

The Second Knight [*passes by*].

Who is the second that presents himself?

Thai. A prince of Macedon, my royal father,
And the device he bears upon his shield
Is an armed knight that's conquered by a lady;
The motto thus, in Spanish: "*Piu per dolcera que per força.*"

Third Knight [*passes by*].

Sim. And with the third?

Thai. The third, of Antioch;
And his device, a wreath of chivalry;
The word: "*Me* [*pompae*] *provexit apex.*"

Fourth Knight [*passes by*].

Sim. What is the fourth?

Thai. A burning torch that's turned upside down;
The word: "*Qui me alit, me extinguit.*"

Sim. Which shows that beauty hath his power and will,
Which can as well inflame as it can kill.

Fift Knight [*passes by*].

Thai. The fift, an hand environed with clouds,
Holding out gold that's by the touchstone tried;

3. **stay**: await. 4. **Return**: answer. 6. **gat**: begot.
14. **honor**: i.e. duty exacted by honor. **entertain**: receive.
15. **device**: emblem. 17. **prefer**: present.
21. **word**: motto. **Lux . . . mihi**: Thy light is life to me.
27. **Piu . . . força**: More by gentleness than by strength. (The motto is in a kind of Italian-Portuguese-Spanish.)
29. **wreath of chivalry**: a circlet formed of a twisted band, or of two bands of different colors twisted together.
30. **Me . . . apex**: The crown of the triumph has led me on.
33. **Qui . . . extinguit**: Who feeds me extinguishes me.
34. **his**: its. 36, 40. **fift, sixt**: fifth, sixth.
37. **touchstone**: flint on which gold was rubbed to test its purity. Tried gold was a symbol of fidelity.

The motto thus: "*Sic spectanda fides.*"

Sixt Knight, [Pericles, *as he passes by, himself presents his device to the Princess*].

Sim. And what's
The sixt and last, the which the knight himself
With such a graceful courtesy delivered?
Thai. He seems to be a stranger; but his present is
A withered branch, that's only green at top;
The motto: "*In hac spe vivo.*"
Sim. A pretty moral:
From the dejected state wherein he is,
He hopes by you his fortunes yet may flourish.
1. Lord. He had need mean better than his outward show
Can any way speak in his just commend;
For by his rusty outside he appears
To have practic'd more the whipstock than the lance.
2. Lord. He well may be a stranger, for he comes
To an honor'd triumph strangely furnished.
3. Lord. And on set purpose let his armor rust
Until this day, to scour it in the dust.
Sim. Opinion's but a fool, that makes us scan
The outward habit by the inward man.
But stay, the knights are coming, we will withdraw
Into the gallery. [*Exeunt.*]

Great shouts [*within,*] *and all cry,* "The mean knight!"

[Scene III]

[*A banquet prepared.*] *Enter the King* [Simonides, Thaisa, Marshal, Lords, Ladies, Attendants,] *and* Knights, *from tilting.*

Sim. Knights,
To say you're welcome were superfluous.
[To] place upon the volume of your deeds,
As in a title-page, your worth in arms,
Were more than you expect, or more than's fit,
Since every worth in show commends itself.
Prepare for mirth, for mirth becomes a feast.
You are princes and my guests.
Thai. But you, my knight and guest,
To whom this wreath of victory I give,
And crown you king of this day's happiness.
Per. 'Tis more by fortune, lady, than my merit.
Sim. Call it by what you will, the day is your,
And here, I hope, is none that envies it.
In framing an artist, art hath thus decreed,
To make some good, but others to exceed,

And you are her labor'd scholar. Come, queen a' th' feast—
For, daughter, so you are—here take your place.
[*To the Marshal.*] Marshal, the rest, as they deserve their grace.
Knights. We are honor'd much by good Simonides.
Sim. Your presence glads our days. Honor we love,
For who hates honor hates the gods above.
Marshal. Sir, yonder is your place.
Per. Some other is more fit.
1. Knight. Contend not, sir, for we are gentlemen
Have neither in our hearts nor outward eyes
[Envied] the great, nor shall the low despise.
Per. You are right courteous knights.
Sim. Sit, sir, sit.
[*Aside.*] By Jove, I wonder, that is king of thoughts,
These cates resist me, he not thought upon.
Thai. [*Aside.*] By Juno, that is queen of marriage,
All viands that I eat do seem unsavory,
Wishing him my meat. [*To Simonides.*] Sure he's a gallant gentleman.
Sim. [*To Thaisa.*] He's but a country gentleman:
H'as done no more than other knights have done,
H'as broken a staff or so; so let it pass.
Thai. [*Aside.*] To me he seems like diamond to glass.
Per. [*Aside.*] [Yon] king's to me like to my father's picture,
Which tells [me] in that glory once he was;
Had princes sit like stars about his throne,
And he the sun for them to reverence;
None that beheld him but, like lesser lights,
Did vail their crowns to his supremacy;
Where now his [son's] like a glow-worm in the night,
The which hath fire in darkness, none in light:
Whereby I see that Time's the king of men,
He's both their parent, and he is their grave,
And gives them what he will, not what they crave.
Sim. What, are you merry, knights?
Knights. Who can be other in this royal presence?
Sim. Here, with a cup that's [stor'd] unto the brim—
As do you love, fill to your mistress' lips—
We drink this health to you.
Knights. We thank your Grace.
Sim. Yet pause awhile,
Yon knight doth sit too melancholy,
As if the entertainment in our court
Had not a show might countervail his worth.
Note it not you, Thaisa?
Thai. What is't
To me, my father?
Sim. O, attend, my daughter:
Princes in this should live like gods above,

38. Sic . . . fides: So should faith be tested. **41. courtesy:** bow. **42. present:** device presented. **44. In . . . vivo:** In this hope I live. **45. moral:** symbolic import. **49. commend:** commendation. **50–51. he . . . lance:** i.e. he looks more like a cart-driver than a knight. **52. stranger:** foreigner. **55. scour . . . dust.** Implying that he will certainly be overthrown. **56. Opinion:** popular judgment (considered superficial). **56–57. scan . . . man.** The intended meaning is clear but the text is apparently corrupt. Some editors replace *by* with *for* (= in order to discover). 59 s.d. **mean:** lowly, of undistinguished appearance.

II.iii. Location: Pentapolis. The palace.
6. in show: by displaying itself in actions (not words). **7. becomes:** befits. **13. your:** yours. **14. envies:** resents. **15. framing:** making.

17. labor'd: labored-over, perfected. **19. grace:** favor. **23. yonder.** The Marshal points to a place of honor, near the King and the Princess. **25. Have:** who have. **28. wonder:** marvel. **29. cates resist me:** delicacies do not appeal to me. **31. unsavory:** tasteless. **32. meat:** food. **34, 35. H'as:** he has. **36. to:** compared with. **38. that:** such, similar. **42. vail:** take off as a sign of submission. **56. might countervail:** which could equal.

Who freely give to every one that come
To honor them;
And princes not doing so are like to gnats,
Which make a sound, but kill'd are wond'red at.
Therefore to make his entrance more sweet,
Here, say we drink this standing-bowl of wine to him.
Thai. Alas, my father, it befits not me
Unto a stranger knight to be so bold.
He may my proffer take for an offense,
Since men take women's gifts for impudence.
Sim. How?
Do as I bid you, or you'll move me else.
Thai. [*Aside.*] Now by the gods, he could not please me better.
Sim. And furthermore tell him, we desire to know of him
Of whence he is, his name, and parentage.
Thai. The King my father, sir, has drunk to you—
Per. I thank him.
Thai. Wishing it so much blood unto your life.
Per. I thank both him and you, and pledge him freely.
Thai. And further, he desires to know of you
Of whence you are, your name, and parentage.
Per. A gentleman of Tyre, my name, Pericles,
My education been in arts and arms;
Who, looking for adventures in the world,
Was by the rough seas reft of ships and men,
And after shipwrack driven upon this shore.
Thai. He thanks your Grace; names himself Pericles,
A gentleman of Tyre,
Who only by misfortune of the seas
Bereft of ships and men, cast on this shore.
Sim. Now by the gods, I pity his misfortune,
And will awake him from his melancholy.
Come, gentlemen, we sit too long on trifles,
And waste the time, which looks for other revels.
Even in your armors, as you are address'd,
Will well become a soldier's dance.
I will not have excuse with saying this,
Loud music is too harsh for ladies' heads,
Since they love men in arms as well as beds.
They dance.
So, this was well ask'd, 'twas so well perform'd.
Come, sir, here's a lady that wants breathing too,
And I have heard you knights of Tyre
Are excellent in making ladies trip,
And that their measures are as excellent.
Per. In those that practice them they are, my lord.
Sim. O, that's as much as you would be denied
Of your fair courtesy. *They* [*Knights and Ladies*] *dance.*
Unclasp, unclasp:
Thanks, gentlemen, to all, all have done well;
[*To Pericles.*] But you the best.—Pages and lights, to conduct
These knights unto their several lodgings! [*To Pericles.*] Yours, sir,
We have given order be next our own.
Per. I am at your Grace's pleasure.
[*Sim.*] Princes, it is too late to talk of love,
And that's the mark I know you level at.
Therefore each one betake him to his rest;
To-morrow all for speeding do their best. *Exeunt.*

63. **are wond'red at:** create surprise (that so small an insect could have made such a loud sound). 71. **move me:** make me angry.
82. **been:** has been. 92. **sit:** i.e. spend. 94. **address'd:** attired.
95. **Will:** you will.
97. **Loud music.** If, as Malone suggested, this refers to the clashing of armor, the wordplay of *in arms* in line 98 gains point.
99. **this . . . ask'd:** I did well to ask this.
100. **breathing:** gentle exercise.
102–3. **trip . . . measures:** dance lightly . . . stately dances (with obvious double-entendre).
105–6. **that's . . . courtesy:** i.e. that's no more than a denial of your skill out of politeness (?).
113. **level:** aim.
115. **for speeding:** to be successful, i.e. in their wooing of the Princess.

[Scene IV]

Enter Helicanus *and* Escanes.

Hel. No, Escanes, know this of me,
Antiochus from incest lived not free;
For which, the most high gods not minding longer
To withhold the vengeance that they had in store,
Due to this heinous capital offense,
Even in the height and pride of all his glory,
When he was seated in a chariot
Of an inestimable value, and his daughter with him,
A fire from heaven came and shrivell'd up
Those bodies, even to loathing; for they so stunk,
That all those eyes ador'd them ere their fall
Scorn now their hand should give them burial.
Esca. 'Twas very strange.
Hel. And yet but justice; for though
This king were great, his greatness was no guard
To bar heaven's shaft, but sin had his reward.
Esca. 'Tis very true.

Enter two or three Lords.

1. Lord. See, not a man in private conference
Or council has respect with him but he.
2. Lord. It shall no longer grieve without reproof.
3. Lord. And curs'd be he that will not second it.
1. Lord. Follow me then. Lord Helicane, a word.
Hel. With me? and welcome. Happy day, my lords.
1. Lord. Know that our griefs are risen to the top,
And now at length they overflow their banks.
Hel. Your griefs, for what? Wrong not your prince you love.
1. Lord. Wrong not yourself then, noble Helicane;
But if the Prince do live, let us salute him,
Or know what ground's made happy by his breath.
If in the world he live, we'll seek him out;
If in his grave he rest, we'll find him there;
And be resolved he lives to govern us,

II.iv. Location: Tyre. The Governor's house.
3. **minding:** being minded. 11. **ador'd:** which adored.
14. **great:** strong, powerful.
18. **respect:** influence. **he:** i.e. Escanes.
19. **grieve:** aggrieve. **reproof:** protest.
23. **griefs:** grievances. 31. **resolved:** satisfied, made certain.

Or dead, give 's cause to mourn his funeral,
And leave us to our free election.
2. Lord. Whose death indeed the strongest in our censure,
And knowing this kingdom is without a head—
Like goodly buildings left without a roof
Soon fall to ruin—your noble self,
That best know how to rule and how to reign,
We thus submit unto—our sovereign.
Omnes. Live, noble Helicane!
Hel. Try honor's cause; forbear your suffrages.
If that you love Prince Pericles, forbear.
Take I your wish, I leap into the seas,
Where's hourly trouble for a minute's ease.
A twelvemonth longer let me entreat you
To forbear the absence of your king;
If in which time expir'd he not return,
I shall with aged patience bear your yoke.
But if I cannot win you to this love,
Go search like nobles, like noble subjects,
And in your search spend your adventurous worth;
Whom if you find, and win unto return,
You shall like diamonds sit about his crown.
1. Lord. To wisdom he's a fool that will not yield;
And since Lord Helicane enjoineth us,
We with our travels will endeavor.
Hel. Then you love us, we you, and we'll clasp hands:
When peers thus knit, a kingdom ever stands.
[*Exeunt.*]

[Scene V]

Enter the King [Simonides,] *reading of a letter, at one door; the* Knights *meet him.*

1. Knight. Good morrow to the good Simonides.
Sim. Knights, from my daughter this I let you know,
That for this twelvemonth she'll not undertake
A married life.
Her reason to herself is only known,
Which from her by no means can I get.
2. Knight. May we not get access to her, my lord?
Sim. Faith, by no means, she hath so strictly tied
Her to her chamber, that 'tis impossible.
One twelve moons more she'll wear Diana's livery;
This by the eye of Cynthia hath she vowed,
And on her virgin honor will not break it.
3. Knight. Loath to bid farewell, we take our leaves.
[*Exeunt Knights.*]
Sim. So,
They are well dispatch'd; now to my daughter's letter.
She tells me here, she'll wed the stranger knight,

Or never more to view nor day nor light.
'Tis well, mistress, your choice agrees with mine;
I like that well. Nay, how absolute she's in't,
Not minding whether I dislike or no!
Well, I do commend her choice,
And will no longer have it be delayed.
Soft, here he comes, I must dissemble it.

Enter Pericles.

Per. All fortune to the good Simonides!
Sim. To you as much! Sir, I am beholding to you
For your sweet music this last night. I do
Protest my ears were never better fed
With such delightful pleasing harmony.
Per. It is your Grace's pleasure to commend,
Not my desert.
Sim. Sir, you are music's master.
Per. The worst of all her scholars, my good lord.
Sim. Let me ask you one thing:
What do you think of my daughter, sir?
Per. A most virtuous princess.
Sim. And she is fair too, is she not?
Per. As a fair day in summer; wondrous fair.
Sim. Sir, my daughter thinks very well of you,
Ay, so well, that you must be her master,
And she will be your scholar; therefore look to it.
Per. I am unworthy for her schoolmaster.
Sim. She thinks not so; peruse this writing else.
Per. [*Aside.*] What's here?
A letter that she loves the knight of Tyre!
'Tis the King's subtilty to have my life.—
O, seek not to entrap me, gracious lord,
A stranger and distressed gentleman,
That never aim'd so high to love your daughter,
But bent all offices to honor her.
Sim. Thou hast bewitch'd my daughter, and thou art
A villain.
Per. By the gods, I have not.
Never did thought of mine levy offense;
Nor never did my actions yet commence
A deed might gain her love or your displeasure.
Sim. Traitor, thou liest.
Per. Traitor?
Sim. Ay, traitor.
Per. Even in his throat—unless it be the King—
That calls me traitor, I return the lie.
Sim. [*Aside.*] Now by the gods, I do applaud his courage.
Per. My actions are as noble as my thoughts,
That never relish'd of a base descent.
I came unto your court for honor's cause,
And not to be a rebel to her state;
And he that otherwise accounts of me,
This sword shall prove he's honor's enemy.

34. the strongest: (being) most probable. **censure:** judgment.
36. Like: as.
41. Try honor's cause: i.e. maintain the code of honor. **forbear your suffrages:** withhold your pledges of allegiance (to me).
43. Take I: if I accede to. **46. forbear:** put up with (?).
49. love: act of kindness.

II.v. Location: Pentapolis. The palace.
10. wear Diana's livery: remain the servant of Diana, goddess of virginity. **11. Cynthia:** Diana in her aspect as the moon-goddess.

17. nor . . . nor: neither . . . nor. **19. absolute:** positive.
25. beholding: beholden, indebted. **39. look to it:** be prepared.
41. else: i.e. if you don't believe it. **44. subtilty:** trick.
47. to: as to. **48. bent all offices:** directed all my services.
52. levy. Apparently misused for *level (at)*; see I.i.163, II.iii.113.
54. might: which might. **60. relish'd:** had a trace of.
62. her: i.e. honor's. Some editors emend to *your* on the strength of Wilkins' "not to be a rebell to his [Simonides'] State."

Sim. No?
Here comes my daughter, she can witness it.

Enter THAISA.

Per. Then as you are as virtuous as fair,
Resolve your angry father if my tongue
Did e'er solicit, or my hand subscribe
To any syllable that made love to you.
Thai. Why, sir, say if you had, who takes offense
At that would make me glad?
Sim. Yea, mistress, are you so peremptory?
(*Aside.*) I am glad on't with all my heart.—
I'll tame you; I'll bring you in subjection.
Will you, not having my consent,
Bestow your love and your affections
Upon a stranger? (*aside*) who, for aught I know,
May be (nor can I think the contrary)
As great in blood as I myself.—
Therefore hear you, mistress, either frame
Your will to mine—and you, sir, hear you—
Either be rul'd by me, or I'll make you—
Man and wife.
Nay come, your hands and lips must seal it too;
And being join'd, I'll thus your hopes destroy,
And for further grief—God give you joy!
What, are you both pleased?
Thai. Yes, if you love me, sir.
Per. Even as my life my blood that fosters it.
Sim. What, are you both agreed?
Ambo. Yes, if't please your Majesty.
Sim. It pleaseth me so well that I will see you wed,
And then with what haste you can, get you to bed.
Exeunt.

[ACT III]

Enter GOWER.

[*Gow.*] Now sleep yslacked hath the rout,
No din but snores [the house about],
Made louder by the o'erfed breast
Of this most pompous marriage-feast.
The cat, with eyne of burning coal,
Now couches from the mouse's hole;
And [crickets] sing at the oven's mouth,
Are the blither for their drouth.
Hymen hath brought the bride to bed,
Where, by the loss of maidenhead,
A babe is moulded. Be attent,
And time that is so briefly spent
With your fine fancies quaintly [eche]:
What's dumb in show I'll plain with speech.

[DUMB SHOW]

Enter PERICLES *and* SIMONIDES, *at one door, with* ATTENDANTS. *A* MESSENGER *meets them, kneels, and gives Pericles a letter. Pericles shows it Simonides; the Lords kneel to him. Then enter* THAISA *with child, with* LYCHORIDA, *a nurse. The King shows her the letter; she rejoices. She and Pericles take leave of her father, and depart* [*with Lychorida and their Attendants. Then exeunt Simonides and the rest*].

By many a dern and painful perch,
Of Pericles the careful search,
By the four opposing [coigns]
Which the world together joins,
Is made with all due diligence
That horse and sail and high expense
Can stead the quest. At last from Tyre,
Fame answering the most strange inquire,
To th' court of King Simonides
Are letters brought, the tenor these:
Antiochus and his daughter dead,
The men of Tyrus on the head
Of Helicanus would set on
The crown of Tyre, but he will none.
The mutiny he there hastes t' oppress,
Says to 'em, if King Pericles
Come not home in twice six moons,
He, obedient to their dooms,
Will take the crown. The sum of this,
Brought hither to Pentapolis,
Yravished the regions round,
And every one with claps can sound,
"Our heir-apparent is a king!
Who dreamt? who thought of such a thing?"
Brief, he must hence depart to Tyre:
His queen, with child, makes her desire—
Which who shall cross?—along to go.
Omit we all their dole and woe.
Lychorida, her nurse, she takes,
And so to sea. Their vessel shakes
On Neptune's billow; half the flood
Hath their keel cut. But fortune, mov'd,
Varies again; the grisled north
Disgorges such a tempest forth,
That, as a duck for life that dives,
So up and down the poor ship drives.
The lady shrieks, and well-a-near
Does fall in travail with her fear;
And what ensues in this fell storm
Shall for itself itself perform.
I nill relate, action may
Conveniently the rest convey,
Which might not what by me is told.
In your imagination hold

68. Resolve: satisfy. **72. that**: that which.
73. peremptory: determined. **81. frame**: conform.

III.Cho.1. yslacked: reduced to inactivity. **rout**: crowd.
4. pompous: magnificent. **5. eyne**: eyes.
6. from: near, not immediately in front of. Often emended to *'fore*.
8. blither . . . drouth: happier for their dryness.
9. Hymen: god of marriage. **11. attent**: attentive.
13. quaintly eche: skillfully eke out. **14. plain**: make plain.

15. dern . . . perch: dreary and difficult stretch of land.
17. coigns: corners. **21. stead**: help.
22. Fame: rumor. **most strange inquire**: inquiry in the most remote places. **32. dooms**: judgments.
33. sum: gist (as in *sum and substance*).
35. Yravished: enraptured.
36. can: gan, began to. **sound**: declare. **39. Brief**: in short.
45–46. half . . . cut: i.e. they have made half the voyage.
47. grisled: grisly, grim. **51. well-a-near**: alas.
53. fell: cruel, violent. **55. nill**: will not.
57. Which . . . told: which (i.e. action) could not represent the part of the story that I have related. **58. hold**: suppose.

This stage the ship, upon whose deck
The seas-toss'd Pericles appears to speak. [*Exit.*]

[SCENE I]

Enter PERICLES *a-shipboard.*

Per. The god of this great vast, rebuke these surges,
Which wash both heaven and hell; and thou that hast
Upon the winds command, bind them in brass,
Having call'd them from the deep! O, still
Thy deaf'ning, dreadful thunders, gently quench
Thy nimble, sulphurous flashes!—O, how, Lychorida!
How does my queen?—[Thou] storm, venomously
Wilt thou spet all thyself? The seaman's whistle
Is as a whisper in the ears of death,
Unheard.—Lychorida!—Lucina, O!
Divinest patroness, and [midwife] gentle
To those that cry by night, convey thy Deity
Aboard our dancing boat, make swift the pangs
Of my queen's travails!—Now, Lychorida!

Enter LYCHORIDA [*with an infant*].

Lyc. Here is a thing too young for such a place,
Who, if it had conceit, would die, as I
Am like to do. Take in your arms this piece
Of your dead queen.
Per. How? How, Lychorida?
Lyc. Patience, good sir, do not assist the storm.
Here's all that is left living of your queen:
A little daughter. For the sake of it
Be manly, and take comfort.
Per. O you gods!
Why do you make us love your goodly gifts
And snatch them straight away? We here below
Recall not what we give, and therein may
Use honor with you.
Lyc. Patience, good sir,
Even for this charge.
Per. Now, mild may be thy life!
For a more blusterous birth had never babe.
Quiet and gentle thy conditions! for
Thou art the rudeliest welcome to this world
That ever was prince's child. Happy what follows!
Thou hast as chiding a nativity
As fire, air, water, earth, and heaven can make
To herald thee from the womb. Even at the first
Thy loss is more than can thy portage quit

With all thou canst find here. Now the good gods
Throw their best eyes upon't!

Enter two SAILORS.

1. Sail. What courage, sir? God save you!
Per. Courage enough. I do not fear the flaw,
It hath done to me the worst. Yet for the love
Of this poor infant, this fresh new sea-farer,
I would it would be quiet.

1. Sail. Slack the bolins there!—Thou wilt not, wilt thou? Blow, and split thyself.

2. Sail. But sea-room, and the brine and cloudy billow kiss the moon, I care not.

1. Sail. Sir, your queen must overboard. The sea works high, the wind is loud, and will not lie till the ship be clear'd of the dead.

Per. That's your superstition.

1. Sail. Pardon us, sir; with us at sea it hath been still observ'd, and we are strong in [custom]; therefore briefly yield 'er, for she must overboard straight.

Per. As you think meet. Most wretched queen!
Lyc. Here she lies, sir.
Per. A terrible child-bed hast thou had, my dear,
No light, no fire. Th' unfriendly elements
Forgot thee utterly, nor have I time
To give thee hallow'd to thy grave, but straight
Must cast thee, scarcely coffin'd, in [the ooze],
Where, for a monument upon thy bones,
The [e'er-]remaining lamps, the belching whale
And humming water must o'erwhelm thy corpse,
Lying with simple shells. O Lychorida,
Bid Nestor bring me spices, ink and [paper],
My casket and my jewels; and bid Nicander
Bring me the satin coffin. Lay the babe
Upon the pillow. Hie thee, whiles I say
A priestly farewell to her. Suddenly, woman.
[*Exit Lychorida.*]

2. Sail. Sir, we have a chest beneath the hatches, caulk'd and bitum'd ready.

Per. I thank thee. Mariner, say, what coast is this?
2. Sail. We are near Tharsus.
Per. Thither, gentle mariner,
Alter thy course for Tyre. When canst thou reach it?
2. Sail. By break of day, if the wind cease.
Per. O, make for Tharsus!
There will I visit Cleon, for the babe
Cannot hold out to Tyrus. There I'll leave it
At careful nursing. Go thy ways, good mariner,
I'll bring the body presently. *Exeunt.*

III.i. Location: On a ship at sea.
1. **vast**: desolate expanse. 8. **spet**: spit.
12. **thy Deity.** A title formed like *your Majesty.*
16. **conceit**: understanding.
19. **assist the storm**: augment the wind and rain with your cries and tears. 24. **straight**: at once.
25. **Recall not**: do not take back. **therein**: in that respect.
26. **Use honor**: deal honorably (?). Many editors, following Steevens, read *Vie honor* = contend in honor.
27. **for**: for the sake of. **charge**: care, i.e. the baby.
29. **conditions**: circumstances.
30–33. See the Textual Notes for a possibly Shakespearean phrase preserved in Wilkins.
34–36. **Even . . . here**: i.e. your loss at the very beginning (your mother's death) is more than can ever be compensated for by your native endowments plus all the benefits that may befall you during your life. *Portage* = what a sailor was entitled to place aboard as part of the cargo when his voyage began.

37. **Throw . . . eyes**: direct their most auspicious influence.
39. **flaw**: squall. 43. **bolins**: bowlines.
45. **But sea-room**: so long as we have space to maneuver without going on the rocks. **and**: if.
48. **works**: seethes, rages. **lie**: subside.
52. **still**: always.
59. **give . . . grave**: bury you with religious services.
60. **ooze**: bed of the sea. 61. **for**: in place of.
62. **The.** Most editors, following Steevens, emend to *And.* **e'er-remaining**: perpetually burning. **belching**: blowing.
67. **coffin**: coffer. 69. **Suddenly**: quickly.
71. **bitum'd**: caulked with pitch.
74–75. **Thither . . . Tyre**: i.e. change your present course, with Tyre as its destination, and make for Tharsus. Many editors emend *for* to *from.* 80. **Go thy ways**: go along (a stock phrase).
81. **presently**: straightaway.

[Scene II]

Enter Lord Cerimon *with a* Servant [*and another* Man, *both storm-beaten*].

Cer. Philemon, ho!

Enter Philemon.

Phil. Doth my lord call?
Cer. Get fire and meat for these poor men.
[*Exit Philemon.*]
'T 'as been a turbulent and stormy night.
Serv. I have been in many; but such a night as this
Till now I ne'er endured.
Cer. Your master will be dead ere you return,
There's nothing can be minist'red to nature
That can recover him. [*To the other Man.*] Give this to the pothecary,
And tell me how it works.
[*Exeunt Servant and other Man.*]

Enter two Gentlemen.

1. Gent. Good morrow.
2. Gent. Good morrow to your lordship.
Cer. Gentlemen,
Why do you stir so early?
1. Gent. Sir,
Our lodgings, standing bleak upon the sea,
Shook as the earth did quake;
The very principals did seem to rend,
And all to topple. Pure surprise and fear
Made me to quit the house.
2. Gent. That is the cause we trouble you so early,
'Tis not our husbandry.
Cer. O, you say well.
1. Gent. But I much marvel that your lordship, having
Rich tire about you, should at these early hours
Shake off the golden slumber of repose.
'Tis most strange
Nature should be so conversant with pain,
Being thereto not compelled.
Cer. I hold it ever
Virtue and cunning were endowments greater
Than nobleness and riches. Careless heirs
May the two latter darken and expend;
But immortality attends the former,
Making a man a god. 'Tis known, I ever
Have studied physic; through which secret art,
By turning o'er authorities, I have,
Together with my practice, made familiar
To me and to my aid the blest infusions
That dwells in vegetives, in metals, stones;
And can speak of the disturbances
That nature works, and of her cures; which doth give me
A more content in course of true delight
Than to be thirsty after tottering honor,
Or tie my pleasure up in silken bags,
To please the fool and death.
2. Gent. Your honor has through Ephesus pour'd forth
Your charity, and hundreds call themselves
Your creatures, who by you have been restored;
And not your knowledge, your personal pain, but even
Your purse, still open, hath built Lord Cerimon
Such strong renown as time shall never—

Enter two or three [Servants] *with a chest.*

[*1.*] *Serv.* So, lift there.
Cer. What's that?
[*1.*] *Serv.* Sir, even now
Did the sea toss up upon our shore this chest.
'Tis of some wrack.
Cer. Set't down, let's look upon't.
2. Gent. 'Tis like a coffin, sir.
Cer. What e'er it be,
'Tis wondrous heavy. Wrench it open straight.
If the sea's stomach be o'ercharg'd with gold,
'Tis a good constraint of fortune it belches upon us.
2. Gent. 'Tis so, my lord.
Cer. How close 'tis caulk'd and [bitum'd]!
Did the sea cast it up?
[*1.*] *Serv.* I never saw so huge a billow, sir,
As toss'd it upon shore.
Cer. Wrench it open.
Soft! It smells most sweetly in my sense.
2. Gent. A delicate odor.
Cer. As ever hit my nostril. So, up with it.
O you most potent gods! what's here? a corse?
2. Gent. Most strange.
Cer. Shrouded in cloth of state, balm'd and entreasur'd
With full bags of spices! A passport too!
Apollo, perfect me in the characters!
[*Reads from a scroll.*]
"Here I give to understand,
If e'er this coffin drives a-land,
I, King Pericles, have lost
This queen, worth all our mundane cost.
Who finds her, give her burying,
She was the daughter of a king.
Besides this treasure for a fee,
The gods requite his charity!"
If thou livest, Pericles, thou hast a heart
That ever cracks for woe! This chanc'd to-night.
2. Gent. Most likely, sir.

III.ii. Location: Ephesus. Cerimon's house.
9. recover: cure, restore to health. **15. as:** as if.
16. principals: main rafters.
20. husbandry: thrifty habits (which would include rising early).
22. tire: furnishings. **25. pain:** toil.
26. hold it ever: have always believed.
27. cunning: skill, expertness. **28. nobleness:** noble birth.
32. physic: medicine.
35. aid: assistant(s). **36. vegetives:** herbs.
39. more: greater. **40. tottering honor:** unstable fame.
41. tie . . . bags: find my pleasure in money hoarded in silken bags.
42. the fool: i.e. anyone foolish enough to take pleasure in wealth, which death inevitably deprives him of. **46. not:** not only.
55. good . . . fortune: benefit which Fortune constrained the sea to confer. **63. corse:** corpse. **65. cloth of state:** magnificent fabric.
67. perfect . . . characters: enable me to read the writing. (Apollo was the patron of scholars as well as of physicians.)
71. mundane cost: worldly treasure.
77. ever cracks: is forever broken. Some editors, with support from Wilkins, read *even cracks.* **to-night:** last night.

Cer. Nay, certainly to-night,
For look how fresh she looks! They were too rough
That threw her in the sea. Make a fire within.
Fetch hither all my boxes in my closet.
[*Exit a Servant.*]
Death may usurp on nature many hours,
And yet the fire of life kindle again
The o'erpress'd spirits. I heard of an Egyptian
That had nine hours lien dead,
Who was by good appliance recovered.

Enter one with [*boxes,*] *napkins, and fire.*

Well said, well said. The fire and cloths.
The rough and woeful music that we have,
Cause it to sound, beseech you.
The [vial] once more. How thou stir'st, thou block!
The music there! I pray you give her air.
Gentlemen, this queen will live. Nature awakes,
A warmth [breathes] out of her. She hath not been
Entranc'd above five hours. See how she gins
To blow into life's flower again!
1. Gent. The heavens,
Through you, increase our wonder, and sets up
Your fame for ever.
Cer. She is alive; behold
Her eyelids, cases to those heavenly jewels
Which Pericles hath lost, begin to part
Their fringes of bright gold. The diamonds
Of a most praised water doth appear,
To make the world twice rich. Live, and make
Us weep to hear your fate, fair creature,
Rare as you seem to be. *She moves.*
Thai. O dear Diana,
Where am I? Where's my lord? What world is this?
2. Gent. Is not this strange?
1. Gent. Most rare.
Cer. Hush, my gentle neighbors!
Lend me your hands. To the next chamber bear her.
Get linen. Now this matter must be look'd to,
For her relapse is mortal. Come, come;
And Aesculapius guide us!
They carry her away. Exeunt omnes.

[Scene III]

Enter Pericles *at Tharsus with* Cleon *and* Dionyza [*and* Lychorida *with* Marina *in her arms*].

Per. Most honor'd Cleon, I must needs be gone.
My twelve months are expir'd, and Tyrus stands
In a litigious peace. You and your lady

79. **rough:** i.e. hasty. 84. **o'erpress'd:** overcome.
84–86. **I . . . recovered.** See the Textual Notes.
85. **lien:** lain. 86. **appliance:** treatment.
87. **Well said:** well done.
88. **rough:** harsh, discordant. See the Textual Notes.
90. **How thou stir'st.** See note on II.i.16.
94. **Entranc'd:** unconscious. **gins:** begins.
95. **blow:** blossom. 101. **water:** lustre.
109. **is mortal:** would be fatal. 110. **Aesculapius:** god of healing.

III.iii. **Location:** Tharsus. The Governor's house.
3. **litigious:** marked by bickering.

Take from my heart all thankfulness! The gods
Make up the rest upon you!
Cle. Your shakes of fortune, though they haunt you mortally,
Yet glance full wond'ringly on us.
Dion. O your sweet queen!
That the strict fates had pleas'd you had brought her hither
To have blest mine eyes with her!
Per. We cannot but obey
The powers above us. Could I rage and roar
As doth the sea she lies in, yet the end
Must be as 'tis. My gentle babe Marina, whom,
For she was born at sea, I have nam'd so, here
I charge your charity withal; leaving her
The infant of your care, beseeching you
To give her princely training, that she may be
Manner'd as she is born.
Cle. Fear not, my lord, but think
Your Grace, that fed my country with your corn,
For which the people's prayers still fall upon you,
Must in your child be thought on. If neglection
Should therein make me vile, the common body,
By you reliev'd, would force me to my duty;
But if to that my nature need a spur,
The gods revenge it upon me and mine
To the end of generation!
Per. I believe you,
Your honor and your goodness teach me to't
Without your vows. Till she be married, madam,
By bright Diana, whom we honor, all
[Unscissor'd] shall this hair of mine remain,
Though I show [ill] in't. So I take my leave.
Good madam, make me blessed in your care
In bringing up my child.
Dion. I have one myself,
Who shall not be more dear to my respect
Than yours, my lord.
Per. Madam, my thanks and prayers.
Cle. We'll bring your Grace e'en to the edge a' th' shore,
Then give you up to the mask'd Neptune and
The gentlest winds of heaven.
Per. I will embrace
Your offer. Come, dearest madam. O, no tears,
Lychorida, no tears.
Look to your little mistress, on whose grace
You may depend hereafter. Come, my lord. [*Exeunt.*]

4. **Take:** receive. 5. **upon:** to.
6–7. **Your . . . us:** i.e. your changes of fortune, which follow you fatally, also affect us in a strange way (?). The passage is probably corrupt; most editors emend *shakes* to *shafts* or *strokes*, *haunt* to *hurt*, and *wond'ringly* to *woundingly*.
13. **For:** because. 14. **withal:** with.
17. **as . . . born:** in accordance with her high birth.
20. **neglection:** neglect. 21. **common body:** populace.
25. **To . . . generation:** i.e. until the human race dies out; *generation* = procreation. 26. **to't:** to do so. 33. **respect:** regard, attention.
36. **mask'd:** i.e. wearing a different aspect from the one he has displayed to you before. 40. **grace:** favor.

[Scene IV]

Enter Cerimon *and* Thaisa.

Cer. Madam, this letter and some certain jewels
Lay with you in your coffer, which are
At your command. Know you the character?
Thai. It is my lord's.
That I was shipp'd at sea I well remember,
Even on my [eaning] time, but whether there
Delivered, by the holy gods
I cannot rightly say. But since King Pericles,
My wedded lord, I ne'er shall see again,
A vestal livery will I take me to,
And never more have joy.
Cer. Madam, if this you purpose as ye speak,
Diana's temple is not distant far,
Where you may abide till your date expire.
Moreover if you please a niece of mine
Shall there attend you.
Thai. My recompense is thanks, that's all,
Yet my good will is great, though the gift small.
Exeunt.

[ACT IV]

Enter Gower.

[*Gow.*] Imagine Pericles arriv'd at Tyre,
Welcom'd and settled to his own desire.
His woeful queen we leave at Ephesus,
Unto Diana there 's a votaress.
Now to Marina bend your mind,
Whom our fast-growing scene must find
At Tharsus, and by Cleon train'd
In music's letters, who hath gain'd
Of education all the grace,
Which makes [her] both th' [heart] and place
Of general wonder. But alack,
That monster Envy, oft the wrack
Of earned praise, Marina's life
[Seeks] to take off by treason's knife,
And in this kind: our Cleon hath
One daughter, and a full-grown wench,
Even [ripe] for marriage [rite]; this maid
Hight Philoten, and it is said
For certain in our story, she
Would ever with Marina be:
Be't when they weav'd the sleided silk
With fingers long, small, white as milk;
Or when she would with sharp needle wound
The cambric, which she made more sound
By hurting it; or when to th' lute
She sung, and made the night[-bird] mute,
That still records with moan; or when

III.iv. Location: Ephesus. Cerimon's house.
3. character: handwriting. **6. eaning time**: time of childbirth.
10. vestal livery: nun's habit. **14. date**: term of life.

IV.Cho.4. 's: as.
6. scene: play. **8. music's letters**: the study of music.
10–11. heart . . . wonder: "very centre of heartfelt wonder" (Deighton). **12. wrack**: destruction. **14. treason's**: treachery's.
15. kind: manner. **18. Hight**: is called.
21. sleided: separated into threads. **22. small**: slender.
26. night-bird: nightingale. **27. still records**: always sings.

She would with rich and constant pen
Vail to her mistress Dian; still
This Philoten contends in skill
With absolute Marina: so
The dove of Paphos might with the crow
Vie feathers white. Marina gets
All praises, which are paid as debts,
And not as given. This so darks
In Philoten all graceful marks,
That Cleon's wife, with envy rare,
A present murderer does prepare
For good Marina, that her daughter
Might stand peerless by this slaughter.
The sooner her vile thoughts to stead,
Lychorida, our nurse, is dead,
And cursed Dionyza hath
The pregnant instrument of wrath
Prest for this blow. The unborn event
I do commend to your content;
Only I carried winged time
Post [on] the lame feet of my rhyme,
Which never could I so convey,
Unless your thoughts went on my way.
Dionyza does appear,
With Leonine, a murtherer. *Exit.*

[Scene I]

Enter Dionyza *with* Leonine.

Dion. Thy oath remember, thou hast sworn to do't.
'Tis but a blow, which never shall be known.
Thou canst not do a thing in the world so soon
To yield thee so much profit. Let not conscience,
Which is but cold in flaming, thy [lone] bosom
Inflame too nicely, nor let pity, which
Even women have cast off, melt thee, but be
A soldier to thy purpose.
Leon. I will do't, but yet she is a goodly creature.
Dion. The fitter then the gods should have her.
Here she comes weeping for her only mistress' death.
Thou art resolv'd?
Leon. I am resolv'd.

Enter Marina *with a basket of flowers.*

Mar. No; I will rob Tellus of her weed
To strow thy green with flowers. The yellows, blues,

28. constant: faithful, devoted. **29. Vail**: pay homage.
31. absolute: perfect.
32. The . . . with the. Emended by many editors to *With* (or *With the*) . . . *the.* **dove of Paphos.** Doves drew the chariot of Venus, one of whose chief centres of worship was Paphos in Cyprus.
34–35. are . . . given: are felt to be owing to her, not given as compliments. **35. darks**: obscures.
37. envy rare: resentment of extraordinary intensity.
41. stead: aid. **44. pregnant**: compliant, receptive.
45. Prest: ready. **event**: outcome.
46. commend . . . content: i.e. present to you for your pleasure.
48. Post: post-haste.

IV.i. Location: Tharsus. Near the seashore.
4–6. Let . . . nicely: i.e. do not let conscience, usually cold, inflame your heart with foolish scruples. But the text is corrupt, and many emendations have been proposed.
11. only mistress': i.e. Lychorida's.
13. Tellus: the earth. **weed**: garment. **14. green**: i.e. grave.

The purple violets, and marigolds,
Shall as a carpet hang upon thy grave
While summer days doth last. Ay me! poor maid,
Born in a tempest when my mother died,
This world to me is a lasting storm,
Whirring me from my friends.

Dion. How now, Marina, why do you keep alone?
How chance my daughter is not with you? Do not
Consume your blood with sorrowing; have you
A nurse of me. Lord, how your favor's chang'd
With this unprofitable woe! Come
Give me your flowers, ere the sea mar it.
Walk with Leonine, the air is quick there,
And it pierces and sharpens the stomach. Come,
Leonine, take her by the arm, walk with her.

Mar. No, I pray you,
I'll not bereave you of your servant.

Dion. Come, come,
I love the King your father, and yourself,
With more than foreign heart. We every day
Expect him here: when he shall come and find
Our paragon to all reports thus blasted,
He will repent the breadth of his great voyage,
Blame both my lord and me, that we have taken
No care to your best courses. Go, I pray you,
Walk, and be cheerful once again, reserve
That excellent complexion, which did steal
The eyes of young and old. Care not for me,
I can go home alone.

Mar. Well, I will go,
But yet I have no desire to it.

Dion. Come, come, I know 'tis good for you.
Walk half an hour, Leonine, at the least.
Remember what I have said.

Leon. I warrant you, madam.

Dion. I'll leave you, my sweet lady, for a while.
Pray walk softly, do not heat your blood.
What, I must have care of you.

Mar. My thanks, sweet madam.
[*Exit Dionyza.*]
Is this wind westerly that blows?

Leon. South-west.

Mar. When I was born, the wind was north.

Leon. Was't so?

Mar. My father, as nurse says, did never fear,
But cried "Good seamen!" to the sailors, galling
His kingly hands haling ropes,
And clasping to the mast, endur'd a sea
That almost burst the deck.

Leon. When was this?

20. Whirring: whirling, blowing.
23. Consume . . . sorrowing. Sighing was believed to thin the blood and shorten life.
23–24. have . . . me: take me for your nurse, i.e. let me succeed Lychorida in your affections. **24. favor:** face, appearance.
26. it: i.e. the bouquet. Many editors, following Hudson, read the line *Give me your flowers. On the sea-margent* (i.e. sea-margin, beach), thus making *there* in line 27 more intelligible.
27. quick: invigorating. **28. stomach:** appetite.
31. bereave: deprive.
33. With . . . heart: i.e. as if you were members of my own family.
35. Our . . . blasted: our universally acknowledged model of beauty thus withered. **38. courses:** interests. **39. reserve:** guard.
41. Care not for: don't worry about. **46. warrant:** assure.
53. galling: rubbing sore. **54. haling:** pulling.

Mar. When I was born.
Never was waves nor wind more violent,
And from the ladder-tackle washes off
A canvas-climber. "Ha!" says one, "wolt out?"
And with a dropping industry they skip
From [stem] to stern. The boatswain whistles, and
The master calls, and trebles their confusion.

Leon. Come say your prayers.

Mar. What mean you?

Leon. If you require a little space for prayer,
I grant it. Pray, but be not tedious, for
The gods are quick of ear, and I am sworn
To do my work with haste.

Mar. Why will you kill me?

Leon. To satisfy my lady.

Mar. Why would she have me kill'd now?
As I can remember, by my troth,
I never did her hurt in all my life.
I never spake bad word, nor did ill turn
To any living creature. Believe me law,
I never kill'd a mouse, nor hurt a fly;
I trod upon a worm against my will,
But I wept for't. How have I offended,
Wherein my death might yield her any profit,
Or my life imply her any danger?

Leon. My commission
Is not to reason of the deed, but do't.

Mar. You will not do't for all the world, I hope.
You are well-favored, and your looks foreshow
You have a gentle heart. I saw you lately
When you caught hurt in parting two that fought;
Good sooth, it show'd well in you. Do so now.
Your lady seeks my life, come you between,
And save poor me, the weaker.

Leon. I am sworn,
And will dispatch.

Enter PIRATES.

1. Pirate. Hold, villain! [*Leonine runs away.*]

2. Pirate. A prize, a prize!

3. Pirate. Half-part, mates, half-part. Come, let's
have her aboard suddenly.
Exit [*Marina dragged out by the Pirates*].

Enter LEONINE.

Leon. These roguing thieves serve the great pirate Valdes,
And they have seiz'd Marina. Let her go!
There's no hope she will return. I'll swear she's dead,
And thrown into the sea. But I'll see further:
Perhaps they will but please themselves upon her,
Not carry her aboard. If she remain,
Whom they have ravish'd must by me be slain. *Exit.*

61. wolt out: so you want to get out (addressed either to the wind, as if it were striving to free itself from some restraint, or, with brutal levity, to the man overboard).
62. dropping: dripping. **68. tedious:** long-winded.
73. As: as far as. **76. law:** la (an exclamation).
85. well-favored: handsome. **foreshow:** show forth.
91. dispatch: do it, and quickly.
93. prize: booty.
94. Half-part: i.e. we'll go shares.
95. suddenly: quickly.
98. hope: i.e. possibility.

[Scene II]

Enter the three bawds [Pander, Bawd, *and* Boult].

Pand. Boult!

Boult. Sir?

Pand. Search the market narrowly, Meteline is full of gallants. We lost too much money this mart by being too wenchless.

Bawd. We were never so much out of creatures. We have but poor three, and they can do no more than they can do; and they with continual action are even as good as rotten.

Pand. Therefore let's have fresh ones, what e'er we pay for them. If there be not a conscience to be us'd in every trade, we shall never prosper.

Bawd. Thou say'st true. 'Tis not our bringing up of poor bastards—as I think, I have brought up some eleven—

Boult. Ay, to eleven, and brought them down again. But shall I search the market?

Bawd. What else, man? The stuff we have, a strong wind will blow it to pieces, they are so pitifully sodden.

Pand. Thou sayest true, there's two unwholesome, a' conscience. The poor Transylvanian is dead that lay with the little baggage.

Boult. Ay, she quickly poop'd him, she made him roast-meat for worms. But I'll go search the market. *Exit.*

Pand. Three or four thousand chequins were as pretty a proportion to live quietly, and so give over.

Bawd. Why to give over, I pray you? Is it a shame to get when we are old?

Pand. O, our credit comes not in like the commodity, nor the commodity wages not with the danger; therefore if in our youths we could pick up some pretty estate, 'twere not amiss to keep our door hatch'd. Besides, the sore terms we stand upon with the gods will be strong with us for giving o'er.

Bawd. Come, other sorts offend as well as we.

Pand. As well as we! ay, and better too; we offend worse. Neither is our profession any trade, it's no calling. But here comes Boult.

Enter Boult *with the* Pirates *and* Marina.

Boult. Come your ways, my masters. You say she's a virgin?

[*1. Pirate.*] O, sir, we doubt it not.

Boult. Master, I have gone through for this piece you see. If you like her, so; if not, I have lost my earnest.

Bawd. Boult, has she any qualities?

Boult. She has a good face, speaks well, and has excellent good clothes; there's no farther necessity of qualities can make her be refus'd.

Bawd. What's her price, Boult?

Boult. I cannot be bated one doit of a thousand pieces.

Pand. Well, follow me, my masters, you shall have your money presently. Wife, take her in, instruct her what she has to do, that she may not be raw in her entertainment. [*Exeunt Pander and Pirates.*]

Bawd. Boult, take you the marks of her, the color of her hair, complexion, height, her age, with warrant of her virginity, and cry, "He that will give most shall have her first." Such a maidenhead were no cheap thing, if men were as they have been. Get this done as I command you.

Boult. Performance shall follow. *Exit.*

Mar. Alack that Leonine was so slack, so slow!
He should have strook, not spoke; or that these pirates,
Not enough barbarous, had not o'erboard thrown me
For to seek my mother!

Bawd. Why lament you, pretty one?

Mar. That I am pretty.

Bawd. Come, the gods have done their part in you.

Mar. I accuse them not.

Bawd. You are light into my hands, where you are like to live.

Mar. The more my fault
To scape his hands where I was to die.

Bawd. Ay, and you shall live in pleasure.

Mar. No.

Bawd. Yes indeed shall you, and taste gentlemen of all fashions. You shall fare well, you shall have the difference of all complexions. What do you stop your ears?

Mar. Are you a woman?

Bawd. What would you have me be, and I be not a woman?

Mar. An honest woman, or not a woman.

Bawd. Marry, whip the gosling, I think I shall

IV.ii. Location: Mytilene. A brothel.
3. Meteline: Mytilene. **4. mart:** market-time.
7. poor three: three poor specimens.
16. to eleven: to the age of eleven. **18. stuff:** goods.
20. sodden: boiled, i.e. sweated in the powdering tub (the current treatment for venereal disease).
24. poop'd him: did for him (by infecting him with venereal disease).
26. chequins: gold coins.
27. proportion: portion. **give over:** retire.
29. get: make money. **30. credit:** reputation.
30–31. commodity: profit.
31. wages not with: is not commensurate with.
33. keep . . hatch'd: i.e. shut up shop. A hatch is the lower half of a divided door; to keep this closed is to exclude the public.
34. sore: sorry, wretched. **35. strong:** a strong inducement.
36. sorts: i.e. classes of workmen.
38. trade: recognized type of business.
39. calling: (1) synonymous with *trade;* (2) occupation that God has called us to labor in (alluding to the doctrine of "calling" or "vocation").
43. gone through: struck a bargain. **piece:** girl (slang).
45. earnest: down payment to bind the agreement.
48–49. necessity of qualities: requisite qualities. **can:** which (i.e. the lack of which) can.
51. be . . . of: get the price reduced a doit (the coin of smallest value) below. But *bated* normally means simply "reduced"; hence editors from Dyce onward have usually emended *I* to *It.*
54. presently: immediately. **55. raw:** "green," inexperienced.
56. entertainment: reception (of customers).
63. Performance shall follow: (1) I shall carry out your orders; (2) I guarantee results.
70. the gods . . . you: i.e. you have no reason to complain of your natural endowments.
72. are light: have lighted, have chanced to fall.
72–73. are . . . live: will in all likelihood remain. On the strength of this line, most editors adopt Q4's reading *like to die* in line 75.
74. fault: misfortune.
80. difference: variety. **complexions:** colors of skin (as in line 58), i.e. races, nationalities (?) or, more generally, temperaments, i.e. kinds (?). **What:** why. **83. and:** if. **85. honest:** chaste.
86. whip the gosling: i.e. confound the silly young creature.

have something to do with you. Come, you're a young foolish sapling, and must be bow'd as I would have you.

Mar. The gods defend me!

Bawd. If it please the gods to defend you by men, then men must comfort you, men must feed you, men stir you up. Boult's return'd.

[*Enter* BOULT.]

Now, sir, hast thou cried her through the market?

Boult. I have cried her almost to the number of her hairs, I have drawn her picture with my voice.

Bawd. And I prithee tell me, how dost thou find the inclination of the people, especially of the younger sort?

Boult. Faith, they listen'd to me as they would have hearken'd to their father's testament. There was a Spaniard's mouth wat'red, and he went to bed to her very description.

Bawd. We shall have him here to-morrow with his best ruff on.

Boult. To-night, to-night. But, mistress, do you know the French knight that cow'rs i' the hams?

Bawd. Who, Monsieur Verollus?

Boult. Ay, he, he offer'd to cut a caper at the proclamation, but he made a groan at it, and swore he would see her to-morrow.

Bawd. Well, well, as for him, he brought his disease hither; here he does but repair it. I know he will come in our shadow, to scatter his crowns in the sun.

Boult. Well, if we had of every nation a traveller, we should lodge them with this sign.

Bawd. [*To Marina.*] Pray you come hither a while. You have fortunes coming upon you. Mark me: you must seem to do that fearfully which you commit willingly, despise profit where you have most gain. To weep that you live as ye do makes pity in your lovers; seldom but that pity begets you a good opinion, and that opinion a mere profit.

Mar. I understand you not.

Boult. O, take her home, mistress, take her home. These blushes of hers must be quench'd with some present practice.

[*Bawd.*] Thou sayest true, i' faith, so they must: for your bride goes to that with shame which is her way to go with warrant.

Boult. Faith, some do, and some do not. But, mistress, if I have bargain'd for the joint—

Bawd. Thou mayst cut a morsel off the spit.

Boult. I may so.

Bawd. Who should deny it? Come, young one, I like the manner of your garments well.

Boult. Ay, by my faith, they shall not be chang'd yet.

Bawd. Boult, spend thou that in the town. Report what a sojourner we have; you'll lose nothing by custom. When nature fram'd this piece, she meant thee a good turn; therefore say what a paragon she is, and thou hast the harvest out of thine own report.

Boult. I warrant you, mistress, thunder shall not so awake the beds of eels as my giving out her beauty stirs up the lewdly inclin'd. I'll bring home some to-night.

Bawd. Come your ways, follow me.

Mar. If fires be hot, knives sharp, or waters deep,
Untied I still my virgin knot will keep.
Diana aid my purpose!

Bawd. What have we to do with Diana? Pray you, will you go with us? *Exeunt.*

[SCENE III]

Enter CLEON *and* DIONYZA.

Dion. Why [are] you foolish? Can it be undone?

Cle. O Dionyza, such a piece of slaughter
The sun and moon ne'er look'd upon!

Dion. I think you'll turn a child again.

Cle. Were I chief lord of all this spacious world,
I'd give it to undo the deed. O lady,
Much less in blood than virtue, yet a princess
To equal any single crown a' th' earth
I' th' justice of compare! O villain Leonine!
Whom thou hast pois'ned too.
If thou hadst drunk to him, 't 'ad been a kindness
Becoming well thy [fact]. What canst thou say
When noble Pericles shall demand his child?

Dion. That she is dead. Nurses are not the fates,
To foster it, not ever to preserve.
She died at night; I'll say so. Who can cross it?
Unless you play the [pious] innocent,
And for an honest attribute cry out,
"She died by foul play."

Cle. O, go to. Well, well,
Of all the faults beneath the heavens, the gods
Do like this worst.

Dion. Be one of those that thinks

87. **something to do:** some trouble.
93. **cried her:** advertised her attractions.
94–95. **almost . . . hairs:** i.e. more times than I can count (?) or in the minutest detail (?). 100. **and:** as if (?).
105. **cow'rs . . . hams.** As a result of syphilis (French *vérole,* whence the knight's name).
107. **offer'd:** made as if to. **cut a caper:** leap into the air and clap his heels together.
110–11. **he . . . hither.** The English commonly referred to syphilis as "the French disease." 111. **repair:** renew.
112. **in our shadow:** to the privacy of our house. **in the sun:** in the presence of the radiantly beautiful Marina (?). Many editors emend *in* to *of*; *crowns of the sun* = French gold coins. In either case, *scatter his crowns* plays on the notion of loss of hair from syphilis.
114. **lodge . . . sign:** attract them with the picture of Marina (cf. line 95) as our sign. Brothels, like inns and shops, were often identified by signs displaying a picture. 121. **mere:** clear.
123. **take her home:** take her inside (?) or make her understand you (?). 128. **with warrant:** lawfully.
135–36. **they . . . yet.** Prostitutes wore distinctive dress. Marina's garments indicate her virginity, which will bring a higher price for her.
138–39. **by custom:** by our getting customers.
139. **piece:** masterpiece (probably with ironic admixture of the perjorative slang sense "girl").
142–43. **thunder . . . eels.** Thunder supposedly roused eels from the mud and made them easier to catch.

IV.iii. Location: Tharsus. The Governor's house.
6. **lady:** i.e. Marina. 9. **I' . . . compare:** in a just comparison.
11. **drunk to him:** i.e. pledged him in the same poison.
12. **fact:** deed, crime.
14–15. **Nurses . . . preserve.** Text corrupt; many editors have conjectured the loss of a line after 14. Excellent sense is made by Vaughan's MS emendation (recorded by Maxwell in the 1969 issue of his New Cambridge edition): "Nurses are not the fates. / To foster is not ever to preserve [i.e. to keep alive forever]."
16. **cross:** contradict. 18. **attribute:** reputation.
19. **O . . . well.** These inappropriately mild exclamations suggest textual corruption. Wilkins at this point says: "But *Cleon* rather cursing than commending this obduracy in her. . . ."

The petty wrens of Tharsus will fly hence
And open this to Pericles. I do shame
To think of what a noble strain you are,
And of how coward a spirit.

Cle. To such proceeding
Who ever but his approbation added,
Though not his [prime] consent, he did not flow
From honorable courses.

Dion. Be it so then,
Yet none does know but you how she came dead,
Nor none can know, Leonine being gone.
She did [distain] my child, and stood between
Her and her fortunes. None would look on her,
But cast their gazes on Marina's face;
Whilest ours was blurted at and held a mawkin
Not worth the time of day. It pierc'd me thorough,
And though you call my course unnatural,
You not your child well loving, yet I find
It greets me as an enterprise of kindness
Perform'd to your sole daughter.

Cle. Heavens forgive it!

Dion. And as for Pericles,
What should he say? We wept after her hearse,
And yet we mourn. Her monument
Is almost finished, and her epitaphs
In glitt'ring golden characters express
A general praise to her, and care in us
At whose expense 'tis done.

Cle. Thou art like the harpy,
Which to betray, dost with thine angel's face
Seize with thine eagle's talents.

Dion. Y' are like one that superstitiously
Do swear to th' gods that winter kills the flies,
But yet I know you'll do as I advise. [*Exeunt.*]

[Scene IV]

[*Enter* Gower *before the monument of Marina at Tharsus.*]

Gow. Thus time we waste, and long leagues make short;
Sail seas in cockles, have and wish but for't,
Making, to take our imagination,
From bourn to bourn, region to region.
By you being pardoned, we commit no crime
To use one language in each several clime
Where our scenes seems to live. I do beseech you

To learn of me, who stand [i' th'] gaps to teach you,
The stages of our story. Pericles
Is now again thwarting [the] wayward seas,
Attended on by many a lord and knight,
To see his daughter, all his live's delight.
Old Helicanus goes along. Behind
Is left to govern it, you bear in mind,
Old Escanes, whom Helicanus late
Advanc'd in time to great and high estate.
Well-sailing ships and bounteous winds have brought
This king to Tharsus—think [his] pilot thought,
So with his steerage shall your thoughts [grow on]—
To fetch his daughter home, who first is gone.
Like motes and shadows see them move a while,
Your ears unto your eyes I'll reconcile.

[Dumb Show]

Enter Pericles *at one door with all his* Train; Cleon *and* Dionyza *at the other. Cleon shows Pericles the tomb; whereat Pericles makes lamentation, puts on sackcloth, and in a mighty passion departs.* [*Then exeunt Cleon and Dionyza.*]

See how belief may suffer by foul show!
This borrowed passion stands for true old woe;
And Pericles, in sorrow all devour'd,
With sighs shot through and biggest tears o'er-show'r'd,
Leaves Tharsus and again embarks. He swears
Never to wash his face, nor cut his hairs;
He [puts] on sackcloth, and to sea. He bears
A tempest, which his mortal vessel tears,
And yet he rides it out. Now please you wit
The epitaph is for Marina writ
By wicked Dionyza.

[*Reads the inscription on Marina's monument.*]

"The fairest, sweetest, and best lies here,
Who withered in her spring of year.
She was of Tyrus the King's daughter,
On whom foul death hath made this slaughter.
Marina was she call'd, and at her birth,
Thetis, being proud, swallowed some part a' th' earth.
Therefore the earth, fearing to be o'erflowed,
Hath Thetis' birth-child on the heavens bestowed;
Wherefore she does, and swears she'll never stint,
Make raging battery upon shores of flint."
No visor does become black villainy
So well as soft and tender flattery.
Let Pericles believe his daughter's dead,

23. open: reveal.
26. but . . . added: i.e. was an accessory after the fact.
27. prime: original.
28. courses: stream beds. Many editors emend to *sources*, following Dyce. **31. distain:** stain, i.e. cause to seem ugly by comparison.
34. blurted at: mocked. **mawkin:** malkin, slattern.
35. thorough: through. **38. greets:** presents itself to.
46. harpy: rapacious creature with the face of a woman and the claws of a bird of prey. **48. talents:** talons.
49–50. Y' are . . . flies: you are one of those fearful souls so afraid of divine punishment that you foolishly swear to the gods that winter and not you was responsible for the death of the flies.

IV.iv.1. waste: cause to disappear, i.e. telescope.
2. cockles: scallop shells. **have . . . for't:** obtain something by merely wishing for it.
3. Making: proceeding. **to take:** by taking, i.e. by means of (?). Cf. *To use* (= by using) in line 6. **4. bourn:** boundary, frontier.

8. stand i': fill up. **10. thwarting:** crossing. **12. live's:** life's.
18. think . . . thought: imagine that thought is his pilot.
19. with his steerage: by thought's pilotage (?) or with Pericles' voyage (?). **20. first:** already.
21. motes: specks in the sunlight. **22. s.d. passion:** fit of grief.
23. suffer . . . show: be deluded by evil dissembling.
24. borrowed: i.e. pretended (by Dionyza and Cleon). **true old.** Many editors emend to *true-ow'd* = truly owned, genuine.
30. A tempest . . . tears: i.e. mental torment which almost kills him.
31. wit: know. **32. is:** which is.
35. See the Textual Notes for Wilkins' extra couplet following this line.
39. Thetis: properly, a sea-nymph, Achilles' mother; here, as elsewhere, confused with the sea-goddess Tethys, wife of Oceanus. **proud.** Because Marina was born at sea (and is hence "Thetis' birth-child," line 41). **42. she:** i.e. Thetis. **stint:** cease.
43. Make . . . flint: storm against rocky shores.

And bear his courses to be ordered
By Lady Fortune, while our [scene] must play
His daughter's woe and heavy well-a-day
In her unholy service. Patience then,
And think you now are all in Metelin. *Exit.*

[SCENE V]

Enter two GENTLEMEN.

1. Gent. Did you ever hear the like?

2. Gent. No, nor never shall do in such a place as this, she being once gone.

1. Gent. But to have divinity preach'd there! did you ever dream of such a thing?

2. Gent. No, no. Come, I am for no more bawdy-houses. Shall 's go hear the vestals sing?

1. Gent. I'll do any thing now that is virtuous, but I am out of the road of rutting for ever. *Exeunt.*

[SCENE VI]

Enter three bawds [PANDER, BAWD, *and* BOULT].

Pand. Well, I had rather than twice the worth of her she had ne'er come here.

Bawd. Fie, fie upon her, she's able to freeze the god Priapus, and undo a whole generation. We must either get her ravish'd or be rid of her. When she should do for clients her fitment, and do me the kindness of our profession, she has me her quirks, her reasons, her master reasons, her prayers, her knees, that she would make a puritan of the devil, if he should cheapen a kiss of her.

Boult. Faith, I must ravish her, or she'll disfurnish us of all our cavalleria, and make our swearers priests.

Pand. Now the pox upon her green-sickness for me!

Bawd. Faith, there's no way to be rid on't but by the way to the pox. Here comes the Lord Lysimachus disguis'd.

Boult. We should have both lord and lown, if the peevish baggage would but give way to customers.

Enter LYSIMACHUS.

Lys. How now? how a dozen of virginities?

Bawd. Now the gods to bless your honor!

Boult. I am glad to see your honor in good health.

Lys. You may so, 'tis the better for you that your resorters stand upon sound legs. How now? wholesome iniquity have you, that a man may deal withal and defy the surgeon?

Bawd. We have here one, sir, if she would—but there never came her like in Meteline.

Lys. If she'd do the deeds of darkness, thou wouldst say.

Bawd. Your honor knows what 'tis to say well enough.

Lys. Well, call forth, call forth.

Boult. For flesh and blood, sir, white and red, you shall see a rose, and she were a rose indeed, if she had but—

Lys. What, prithee?

Boult. O, sir, I can be modest. [*Exit.*]

Lys. That [dignifies] the renown of a bawd, no less than it gives a good report to a number to be chaste.

Bawd. Here comes that which grows to the stalk, never pluck'd yet, I can assure you.

[*Enter* BOULT *with* MARINA.]

Is she not a fair creature?

Lys. Faith, she would serve after a long voyage at sea. Well, there's for you, leave us.

Bawd. I beseech your honor give me leave a word, and I'll have done presently.

Lys. I beseech you do.

Bawd. [*Aside to Marina.*] First, I would have you note, this is an honorable man.

Mar. I desire to find him so, that I may worthily note him.

Bawd. Next, he's the governor of this country, and a man whom I am bound to.

Mar. If he govern the country, you are bound to him indeed, but how honorable he is in that, I know not.

Bawd. Pray you, without any more virginal fencing, will you use him kindly? He will line your apron with gold.

Mar. What he will do graciously, I will thankfully receive.

Lys. Ha' you done?

Bawd. My lord, she's not pac'd yet, you must take some pains to work her to your manage. Come, we will leave his honor and her together. Go thy ways.

[*Exeunt Bawd, Pander, and Boult.*]

Lys. Now, pretty one, how long have you been at this trade?

Mar. What trade, sir?

Lys. Why, I cannot name['t] but I shall offend.

Mar. I cannot be offended with my trade. Please you to name it.

Lys. How long have you been of this profession?

Mar. E'er since I can remember.

47. bear . . . ordered: suffer his way of life to be shaped.
49. well-a-day: lamentation.

IV.v. Location: Mytilene. The brothel.
4. divinity: theology. **7. vestals**: virgin priestesses.

IV.vi. Location: Scene continues.
4. Priapus: a god of fertility and generation.
6. fitment: duty. **do me**: do, perform (a colloquialism).
7. has me: has, comes up with. **quirks**: quibbles.
10. cheapen: bargain for.
12. cavalleria: cavaliers. **our swearers**: our profane customers (?) or customers who swear by us (?).
13. green-sickness: an anemic condition in girls, usually associated with moodiness and obstinacy. **18. lown**: low fellow.
19. peevish: perverse, obstinate. **20. how a**: how much for a.
21. the gods: i.e. I pray the gods.

24. resorters: customers.
24–25. wholesome iniquity: i.e. a healthy prostitute.
31. what . . . say: what my meaning is.
35–36. if . . . but. Boult refrains from saying "a thorn"—all she lacks is sexual experience.
39. That . . . renown: modesty in speech enhances the reputation.
40. gives . . . chaste: gives some people an (undeserved) reputation for being chaste. **50. note**: notice. **54. bound**: obligated.
55. bound: subject. **60. graciously**: honorably and courteously.
63. pac'd: broken, trained. **64. manage**: manege, horsemanship.
69. but . . . offend: without offending.

Lys. Did you go to't so young? were you a gamester at five, or at seven?

Mar. Earlier too, sir, if now I be one.

Lys. Why, the house you dwell in proclaims you to be a creature of sale.

Mar. Do you know this house to be a place of such resort, and will come into't? I hear say you're of honorable parts, and are the governor of this place.

Lys. Why, hath your principal made known unto you who I am?

Mar. Who is my principal?

Lys. Why, your herb-woman, she that sets seeds and roots of shame and iniquity. O, you have heard something of my power, and so stand [aloof] for more serious wooing. But I protest to thee, pretty one, my authority shall not see thee, or else look friendly upon thee. Come bring me to some private place. Come, come.

Mar. If you were born to honor, show it now;
If put upon you, make the judgment good
That thought you worthy of it.

Lys. How's this? how's this? Some more, be sage.

Mar. For me,
That am a maid, though most ungentle fortune
Have plac'd me in this sty, where since I came,
Diseases have been sold dearer than physic—
That the gods
Would set me free from this unhallowed place,
Though they did change me to the meanest bird
That flies i' th' purer air!

Lys. I did not think
Thou couldst have spoke so well, ne'er dreamt thou couldst.
Had I brought hither a corrupted mind,
Thy speech had altered it. Hold, here's gold for thee.
Persever in that clear way thou goest,
And the gods strengthen thee!

Mar. The good gods preserve you!

Lys. For me, be you thoughten
That I came with no ill intent, for to me
The very doors and windows savor vilely.
Fare thee well, thou art a piece of virtue, and
I doubt not but thy training hath been noble.
Hold, here's more gold for thee.
A curse upon him, die he like a thief,
That robs thee of thy goodness! If thou dost
Hear from me, it shall be for thy good.

[*Enter* BOULT.]

Boult. I beseech your honor one piece for me.

Lys. Avaunt, thou damned door-keeper!
Your house, but for this virgin that doth prop it,
Would sink and overwhelm you. Away! [*Exit.*]

Boult. How's this? We must take another course with you! If your peevish chastity, which is not worth a breakfast in the cheapest country under the cope, shall undo a whole household, let me be gelded like a spaniel. Come your ways.

Mar. Whither would you have me?

Boult. I must have your maidenhead taken off, or the common hangman shall execute it. Come your [ways]. We'll have no more gentlemen driven away. Come your ways, I say.

Enter bawds [BAWD *and* PANDER].

Bawd. How now, what's the matter?

Boult. Worse and worse, mistress, she has here spoken holy words to the Lord Lysimachus.

Bawd. O abominable!

Boult. [She] makes our profession as it were to stink afore the face of the gods.

Bawd. Marry, hang her up for ever!

Boult. The nobleman would have dealt with her like a nobleman, and she sent him away as cold as a snowball, saying his prayers too.

Bawd. Boult, take her away, use her at thy pleasure. Crack the glass of her virginity, and make the rest malleable.

Boult. And if she were a thornier piece of ground than she is, she shall be plough'd.

Mar. Hark, hark, you gods!

Bawd. She conjures, away with her! Would she had never come within my doors. Marry, hang you! She's born to undo us. Will you not go the way of womenkind? Marry, come up, my dish of chastity with rosemary and bays!

[*Exeunt Bawd and Pander.*]

Boult. Come, mistress, come your [ways] with me.

Mar. Whither wilt thou have me?

Boult. To take from you the jewel you hold so dear.

Mar. Prithee tell me one thing first.

Boult. Come now, your one thing.

Mar. What canst thou wish thine enemy to be?

Boult. Why, I could wish him to be my master, or rather, my mistress.

Mar. Neither of these are so bad as thou art,
Since they do better thee in their command.
Thou hold'st a place for which the pained'st fiend
Of hell would not in reputation change.
Thou art the damned door-keeper to every
Custrel that comes inquiring for his Tib.
To the choleric fisting of every rogue
Thy ear is liable; thy food is such
As hath been belch'd on by infected lungs.

Boult. What would you have me do? Go to the wars, would you? where a man may serve seven years

74. go to't: copulate.
79–116. See the Textual Notes for Wilkins' much fuller account of the conversation between Marina and Lysimachus.
81. parts: qualities. **82. principal**: employer.
88–89. my authority: i.e. I in my official capacity (as upholder of the law). **93. put upon you**: bestowed, not inherited.
105. had: would have. **106. clear**: virtuous.
108. be you thoughten: believe. **111. piece**: masterpiece.
123. cope: canopy (of the sky). **144. And if**: even if.
150. Marry, come up: an indignant or derisive exclamation, implying that Marina is putting on airs.
151. with . . . bays: i.e. showily garnished.
158. What . . . be: what wickedness would you wish on your enemy, i.e. what is the greatest wickedness you can imagine.
159–60. my . . . mistress: i.e. as wicked as my master is, or, still worse, my mistress.
162. they . . . command: they have the advantage of you (their slave) in being your employers, i.e. they can make you do things they wouldn't do themselves. **166. Custrel**: coistrel, knave.
167. choleric fisting: angry beating.

for the loss of a leg, and have not money enough in the end to buy him a wooden one?

Mar. Do any thing but this thou doest. Empty
Old receptacles, or common shores, of filth,
Serve by indenture to the common hangman:
Any of these ways are yet better than this;
For what thou professest, a baboon, could he speak,
Would own a name too dear. That the gods
Would safely deliver me from this place!
Here, here's gold for thee.
If that thy master would gain by me,
Proclaim that I can sing, weave, sew, and dance,
With other virtues, which I'll keep from boast,
And will undertake all these to teach.
I doubt not but this populous city will
Yield many scholars.

Boult. But can you teach all this you speak of?

Mar. Prove that I cannot, take me home again
And prostitute me to the basest groom
That doth frequent your house.

Boult. Well, I will see what I can do for thee. If I can place thee, I will.

Mar. But amongst honest [women].

Boult. Faith, my acquaintance lies little amongst them. But since my master and mistress hath bought you, there's no going but by their consent. Therefore I will make them acquainted with your purpose, and I doubt not but I shall find them tractable enough. Come, I'll do for thee what I can; come your ways.

Exeunt.

[ACT V]

Enter GOWER.

[*Gow.*] Marina thus the brothel scapes, and chances
Into an honest house, our story says.
She sings like one immortal, and she dances
As goddess-like to her admired lays.
Deep clerks she dumbs, and with her neele composes
Nature's own shape of bud, bird, branch, or berry,
That even her art sisters the natural roses;
Her inkle, silk, [twin] with the rubied cherry,
That pupils lacks she none of noble race,
Who pour their bounty on her; and her gain
She gives the cursed bawd. Here we her place,
And to her father turn our thoughts again,
Where we left him, on the sea. We there him [lost],
Where, driven before the winds, he is arriv'd
Here where his daughter dwells, and on this coast
Suppose him now at anchor. The city striv'd
God Neptune's annual feast to keep, from whence
Lysimachus our Tyrian ship espies,
His banners sable, trimm'd with rich expense,
And to him in his barge with fervor hies.
In your supposing once more put your sight:
Of heavy Pericles think this his bark;
Where what is done in action, more, if might,
Shall be discover'd, please you sit and hark. *Exit.*

[SCENE I]

[*On board Pericles' ship, off Mytilene. A close pavilion on deck, with a curtain before it;* PERICLES *within it, reclined on a couch*]. *Enter* HELICANUS; *to him two* SAILORS, [*one of Tyre, the other of Mytilene*].

[*Tyr.*] *Sail.* [*To the Sailor of Mytilene.*] Where is
Lord Helicanus? He can resolve you.
O, here he is.—
Sir, there is a barge put off from Meteline,
And in it is Lysimachus the governor,
Who craves to come aboard. What is your will?

Hel. That he have his. Call up some gentlemen.

[*Tyr.*] *Sail.* Ho, gentlemen! my lord calls.

Enter two or three GENTLEMEN.

1. Gent. Doth your lordship call?

Hel. Gentlemen, there is some of worth would
come aboard;
I pray greet him fairly.

[*Exeunt Gentlemen and the two Sailors.*]

Enter LYSIMACHUS [*and* LORDS *with the* GENTLEMEN *and the* TYRIAN SAILOR].

[*Tyr.*] *Sail.* Sir,
This is the man that can, in aught you would,
Resolve you.

Lys. Hail, reverent sir! The gods preserve you!

Hel. And you, to outlive the age I am,
And die as I would do.

Lys. You wish me well.
Being on shore, honoring of Neptune's triumphs,
Seeing this goodly vessel ride before us,
I made to it to know of whence you are.

Hel. First, what is your place?

Lys. I am the governor of this place you lie before.

Hel. Sir,
Our vessel is of Tyre, in it the King,
A man who for this three months hath not spoken
To any one, nor taken sustenance
But to prorogue his grief.

Lys. Upon what ground is his distemperature?

Hel. 'Twould be too tedious to repeat,
But the main grief springs from the loss
Of a beloved daughter and a wife.

Lys. May we not see him?

Hel. You may,

175. **shores:** sewers. 176. **by indenture:** i.e. as an apprentice.
179. **Would . . . dear:** would say that it was beneath the dignity of baboons.
184. **virtues:** accomplishments. 187. **scholars:** pupils.

V.Cho.4. **lays:** songs.
5. **Deep . . . dumbs:** she silences profound scholars (with her wisdom). **neele:** needle. 7. **That:** so that. **sisters:** i.e. resembles closely.
8. **inkle:** tape, linen thread.
14. **Where.** Many editors emend to *Whence.*
16. **striv'd:** i.e. outdid itself. This past tense surrounded by present forms suggests textual corruption.

21. **In your supposing:** under the control of your imagination.
22. **heavy:** sad. 23. **if might:** if that were possible.
24. **discover'd:** displayed.

V.1 o.s.d. **close pavilion:** tentlike enclosure.
1. **resolve:** inform, satisfy.
9. **some of worth:** some noble person. 26. **prorogue:** prolong.
27. **distemperature:** disturbance of mind.

But bootless is your sight; he will not speak
To any.
[*Lys.*] Yet let me obtain my wish.
[*Hel.*] Behold him. [*Pericles discovered.*] This was a goodly person,
Till the disaster that, one mortal [night,]
Drove him to this.
Lys. Sir King, all hail! The gods preserve you!
Hail, royal sir!
Hel. It is in vain, he will not speak to you.
[*1.*] *Lord.* Sir,
We have a maid in Meteline, I durst wager,
Would win some words of him.
Lys. 'Tis well bethought.
She questionless with her sweet harmony,
And other chosen attractions, would allure
And make a batt'ry through his [deafen'd] parts,
Which now are midway stopp'd.
She is all happy as the fairest of all,
And [with] her fellow maids, [is] now upon
The leavy shelter that abuts against
The island's side.
[*Gives an order to a Lord, who goes out.*]
Hel. Sure all effectless; yet nothing we'll omit
That bears recovery's name. But since your kindness
We have stretch'd thus far, let us beseech you
That for our gold we may provision have,
Wherein we are not destitute for want,
But weary for the staleness.
Lys. O sir, a courtesy
Which if we should deny, the most just God
For every graff would send a caterpillar,
And so inflict our province. Yet once more
Let me entreat to know at large the cause
Of your king's sorrow.
Hel. Sit, sir, I will recount it to you,
But see, I am prevented.

[*Enter* LORD *with* MARINA *and a young* LADY.]

Lys. O, here's
The lady that I sent for. Welcome, fair one!
—Is't not a goodly [presence]?
Hel. She's a gallant lady.
Lys. She's such a one that were I well assur'd
Came of a gentle kind and noble stock,
I['d] wish no better choice, and think me rarely to wed.
Fair [one], all goodness that consists in beauty,
Expect even here, where is a kingly patient,
If that thy prosperous and artificial [feat]

33. bootless . . . sight: it will do no good for you to see him.
38. this: i.e. this condition. **46. chosen:** choice.
47. make . . . parts: force an entry through his shut ears.
48. midway stopp'd: i.e. messages get only halfway through to him.
53. all effectless: entirely useless.
54. bears recovery's name: bears the name of cure. *Recovery* does not mean, as now, "regaining health" but "restoring (someone) to health"; so in line 76 *in his recovery* = in recovering (i.e. curing) him. Cf. *recover him* at III.ii.9. **57, 58. for:** because of.
58. staleness: monotony. **60. graff:** grafted plant.
61. inflict: afflict. **62. at large:** fully. **64. prevented:** forestalled.
68. gentle kind. Synonymous with *noble stock.*
69. think . . . wed: consider that I was making a remarkably good marriage.
70. all . . . beauty: i.e. as good as you are beautiful. *Consists* = inheres, resides.
72. If . . . feat: i.e. if your feat of skill is successful (*prosperous*) and.

Can draw him but to answer thee in aught,
Thy sacred physic shall receive such pay
As thy desires can wish.
Mar. Sir, I will use
My utmost skill in his recovery, provided
That none but I and my companion maid
Be suffered to come near him.
Lys. Come, let us leave her,
And the gods make her prosperous!
[*They withdraw. Marina sings*] *the Song.*
Lys. [*Advances.*] [Mark'd] he your music?
Mar. No, nor look'd on us.
Lys. See, she will speak to him.
Mar. Hail, sir! my lord, lend ear.
Per. Hum, ha! [*Pushing her roughly back.*]
Mar. I am a maid,
My lord, that ne'er before invited eyes,
But have been gaz'd on like a comet. She speaks,
My lord, that, may be, hath endur'd a grief
Might equal yours, if both were justly weigh'd.
Though wayward fortune did malign my state,
My derivation was from ancestors
Who stood equivalent with mighty kings,
But time hath rooted out my parentage,
And to the world and awkward casualties
Bound me in servitude. [*Aside.*] I will desist,
But there is something glows upon my cheek,
And whispers in mine ear, "Go not till he speak."
Per. My fortunes—parentage—good parentage—
To equal mine—was it not thus? What say you?
Mar. I said, my lord, if you did know my parentage,
You would not do me violence.
Per. I do think so. Pray you turn your eyes upon me.
You're like something that—What country[-woman]?
Here of these [shores]?
Mar. No, nor of any [shores],
Yet I was mortally brought forth, and am
No other than I appear.
Per. I am great with woe, and shall deliver weeping.
My dearest wife was like this maid, and such a one
My daughter might have been. My queen's square brows,
Her stature to an inch, as wand-like straight,
As silver-voic'd, her eyes as jewel-like
And [cas'd] as richly, in pace another Juno;
Who starves the ears she feeds, and makes them hungry,
The more she gives them speech. Where do you live?
Mar. Where I am but a stranger. From the deck
You may discern the place.
Per. Where were you bred?
And how achiev'd you these endowments which

85. invited eyes: asked to be looked at.
89. did . . . state: had a malignant effect on my condition.
91. equivalent: equal in power.
93. awkward casualties: adverse accidents.
102. What country-woman: of what country.
103–5. No . . . appear: i.e. I was not born in any country, yet I am human, not a supernatural being in disguise.
106. great: (1) full; (2) pregnant. **deliver:** (1) speak; (2) give birth.
111. cas'd: enclosed (cf. III.ii.98–100). **pace:** gait, carriage.

You make more rich to owe?
Mar. If I should tell my history, it would seem
Like lies disdain'd in the reporting.
Per. Prithee speak.
Falseness cannot come from thee, for thou lookest
Modest as Justice, and thou seemest a [palace]
For the crown'd Truth to dwell in. I will believe thee,
And make [my] senses credit thy relation
To points that seem impossible, for thou lookest
Like one I lov'd indeed. What were thy friends?
Didst thou not [say], when I did push thee back—
Which was when I perceiv'd thee—that thou cam'st
From good descending?
Mar. So indeed I did.
Per. Report thy parentage. I think thou saidst
Thou hadst been toss'd from wrong to injury,
And that thou thoughts' thy griefs might equal mine,
If both were opened.
Mar. Some such thing
I said, and said no more but what my thoughts
Did warrant me was likely.
Per. Tell thy story;
If thine, considered, prove the thousand part
Of my endurance, thou art a man, and I
Have suffered like a girl. Yet thou dost look
Like Patience gazing on kings' graves, and smiling
Extremity out of act. What were thy friends?
How lost thou [them?] Thy name, my most kind
virgin?
Recount, I do beseech thee. Come sit by me.
Mar. My name is Marina.
Per. O, I am mock'd,
And thou by some incensed god sent hither
To make the world to laugh at me.
Mar. Patience, good sir!
Or here I'll cease.
Per. Nay, I'll be patient.
Thou little know'st how thou dost startle me
To call thyself Marina.
Mar. The name
Was given me by one that had some power,
My father, and a king.
Per. How, a king's daughter?
And call'd Marina?
Mar. You said you would believe me,
But not to be a troubler of your peace,
I will end here.
Per. But are you flesh and blood?
Have you a working pulse, and are no fairy?
Motion? Well, speak on. Where were you born?
And wherefore call'd Marina?

117. to owe: in possessing.
119. in the reporting: even as they are being told.
123. credit thy relation: believe your story.
125. friends: relations. **131. thoughts':** thought'st.
132. opened: revealed. **135. thousand:** thousandth.
136. my endurance: what I have endured.
138–39. smiling . . . act: rendering the greatest calamity powerless with a smile. **153. working:** beating.
153–54. no fairy? Motion? Perhaps *no* is to be taken as applying to both nouns, with *Motion* signifying "puppet"; this would give the same sense as Steevens' emendation *no fairy? No motion?*, which many editors adopt. Others, following Mason's conjecture, read *no fairy motion?* (i.e. "not a puppet formed by enchantment?"). Various other alterations have been proposed.

Mar. Call'd Marina
For I was born at sea.
Per. At sea! what mother?
Mar. My mother was the daughter of a king,
Who died the minute I was born,
As my good nurse Lychorida hath oft
Delivered weeping.
Per. O, stop there a little!
[*Aside.*] This is the rarest dream that e'er dull'd sleep
Did mock sad fools withal. This cannot be
My daughter—buried!—Well, where were you bred?
I'll hear you more, to th' bottom of your story,
And never interrupt you.
Mar. You scorn. Believe me, 'twere best I did give
o'er.
Per. I will believe you by the syllable
Of what you shall deliver. Yet give me leave:
How came you in these parts? Where were you bred?
Mar. The King my father did in Tharsus leave
me,
Till cruel Cleon, with his wicked wife,
Did seek to murther me; and having wooed
A villain to attempt it, who having drawn to do't,
A crew of pirates came and rescued me;
Brought me to Meteline. But, good sir,
Whither will you have me? Why do you weep? It
may be
You think me an imposture. No, good faith;
I am the daughter to King Pericles,
If good King Pericles be.
[*Per.*] Ho, Helicanus!
Hel. Calls my lord?
Per. Thou art a grave and noble counsellor,
Most wise in general, tell me if thou canst,
What this maid is, or what is like to be,
That thus hath made me weep.
Hel. I know not, but
Here's the regent, sir, of Meteline
Speaks nobly of her.
Lys. She never would tell
Her parentage; being demanded that,
She would sit still and weep.
Per. O Helicanus, strike me, honored sir,
Give me a gash, put me to present pain,
Lest this great sea of joys rushing upon me
O'erbear the shores of my mortality,
And drown me with their sweetness. O, come hither,
Thou that beget'st him that did thee beget;
Thou that wast born at sea, buried at Tharsus,
And found at sea again! O Helicanus,
Down on thy knees, thank the holy gods as loud
As thunder threatens us. This is Marina.
What was thy mother's name? Tell me but that,
For truth can never be confirm'd enough,
Though doubts did ever sleep.
Mar. First, sir, I pray,
What is your title?
Per. I am Pericles of Tyre; but tell me now

167. by the syllable: i.e. to the letter. **172. wooed:** persuaded.
173. drawn: i.e. drawn his sword.
176. Whither . . . me: to what end are you questioning me.
177. imposture: impostor (a variant spelling).

My drown'd queen's name, as in the rest you said
Thou hast been godlike perfit,
The heir of kingdoms, and another [life]
To Pericles thy father.
Mar. Is it no more to be your daughter than
To say my mother's name was Thaisa?
Thaisa was my mother, who did end
The minute I began.
Per. Now blessing on thee! rise, th' art my child.
Give me fresh garments. Mine own Helicanus,
She is not dead at Tharsus as she should have been
By savage Cleon. She shall tell thee all,
When thou shalt kneel, and justify in knowledge
She is thy very princess. Who is this?
Hel. Sir, 'tis the governor of Meteline,
Who, hearing of your melancholy state,
Did come to see you.
Per. I embrace you.
Give me my robes. I am wild in my beholding.
O heavens bless my girl! But hark, what music?
Tell Helicanus, my Marina, tell him
O'er, point by point, for yet he seems to dote,
How sure you are my daughter. But what music?
Hel. My lord, I hear none.
Per. None?
The music of the spheres! List, my Marina.
Lys. It is not good to cross him, give him way.
Per. Rarest sounds! do ye not hear?
Lys. Music, my lord? I hear.
Per. Most heavenly music!
It nips me unto list'ning, and thick slumber
Hangs upon mine eyes. Let me rest. [*Sleeps.*]
Lys. A pillow for his head.
So leave him all. Well, my companion friends,
If this but answer to my just belief,
I'll well remember you. [*Exeunt all but Pericles.*]

DIANA [*appears to Pericles as in a vision*].

Dia. My temple stands in Ephesus, hie thee thither,
And do upon mine altar sacrifice.
There, when my maiden priests are met together
Before the people all,
Reveal how thou at sea didst lose thy wife.
To mourn thy crosses, with thy daughter's, call
And give them repetition to the [life].
Or perform my bidding, or thou livest in woe;
Do't, and happy, by my silver bow!
Awake, and tell thy dream. [*Disappears.*]
Per. Celestial Dian, goddess argentine,
I will obey thee. Helicanus!

206. godlike perfit: as perfectly informed as if you had a god's faculty of knowing.
209. Is . . . be: i.e. is nothing required to establish myself as.
215. should have been: was reported to be (?) or was intended to be (?); perhaps a telescoping of both notions.
217. When: whereupon. **justify in knowledge:** assure yourself completely. **222. beholding:** appearance (?).
225. dote: be slow to understand (?). Most editors from Malone onward read *doubt*. **226. sure:** certainly.
234. nips: urges (?).
245. crosses: tribulations. **call:** lift your voice.
246. give . . . life: repeat them exactly as they happened.
247. Or: either. **250. argentine:** silvery.

[*Enter* HELICANUS, LYSIMACHUS, *and* MARINA.]
Hel. Sir?
Per. My purpose was for Tharsus, there to strike
The inhospitable Cleon, but I am
For other service first. Toward Ephesus
Turn our blown sails; eftsoons I'll tell thee why.
[*To Lysimachus.*] Shall we refresh us, sir, upon your shore,
And give you gold for such provision
As our intents will need?
Lys. Sir,
With all my heart, and, when you come ashore,
I have another [suit].
Per. You shall prevail,
Were it to woo my daughter, for it seems
You have been noble towards her.
Lys. Sir, lend me your arm.
Per. Come, my Marina. *Exeunt.*

[SCENE II]

[*The Temple of Diana at Ephesus;* THAISA *standing near the altar, as high priestess; a number of* VIRGINS *on each side;* CERIMON *and other inhabitants of Ephesus attending. Enter* GOWER.]

Gow. Now our sands are almost run,
More a little, and then dumb.
This, my last boon, give me,
For such kindness must relieve me:
That you aptly will suppose
What pageantry, what feats, what shows,
What minstrelsy, and pretty din,
The regent made in Metelin,
To greet the King. So he thrived
That he is promis'd to be wived
To fair Marina, but in no wise
Till he had done his sacrifice,
As Dian bade; whereto being bound,
The interim, pray you, all confound.
In feather'd briefness sails are fill'd,
And wishes fall out as they're will'd.
At Ephesus the temple see,
Our King and all his company.
That he can hither come so soon
Is by your fancies' thankful doom. [*Exit.*]

[SCENE III]

[*Enter* PERICLES *with his Train:* LYSIMACHUS, HELICANUS, MARINA, *and a* LADY.]

Per. Hail, Dian! to perform thy just command,
I here confess myself the King of Tyre,

255. eftsoons: soon.

V.ii.5. aptly: readily. **12. he:** i.e. Pericles.
14. confound: destroy, i.e. blot from your minds.
15. In feather'd briefness: with winged speed.
20. thankful doom: judgment deserving gratitude.

V.iii. Location: Scene continues.
1. just: exact.

Who frighted from my country, did wed
At Pentapolis the fair Thaisa.
At sea in child-bed died she, but brought forth
A maid-child call'd Marina, whom, O goddess,
Wears yet thy silver livery. She at Tharsus
Was nurs'd with Cleon, who at fourteen years
He sought to murder, but her better stars
Brought her to Meteline, 'gainst whose shore
Riding, her fortunes brought the maid aboard us,
Where, by her own most clear remembrance, she
Made known herself my daughter.

Thai. Voice and favor!
You are, you are—O royal Pericles! [*Faints.*]

Per. What means the [nun]? She dies, help, gentlemen!

Cer. Noble sir,
If you have told Diana's altar true,
This is your wife.

Per. Reverent appearer, no,
I threw her overboard with these very arms.

Cer. Upon this coast, I warrant you.

Per. 'Tis most certain.

Cer. Look to the lady; O, she's but overjoy'd.
Early in blustering morn this lady was
Thrown upon this shore. I op'd the coffin,
Found there rich jewels, recovered her, and plac'd her
Here in Diana's temple.

Per. May we see them?

Cer. Great sir, they shall be brought you to my house,
Whither I invite you. Look, Thaisa is
Recovered.

Thai. O, let me look!
If he be none of mine, my sanctity
Will to my sense bend no licentious ear,
But curb it, spite of seeing. O my lord,
Are you not Pericles? Like him you spake,
Like him you are! Did you not name a tempest,
A birth, and death?

Per. The voice of dead Thaisa!

Thai. That Thaisa am I, supposed dead
And drown'd.

Per. Immortal Dian!

Thai. Now I know you better.
When we with tears parted Pentapolis,
The King my father gave you such a ring.
[*Points to his ring.*]

Per. This, this. No more, you gods! your present kindness
Makes my past miseries sports. You shall do well
That on the touching of her lips I may
Melt, and no more be seen. O, come, be buried
A second time within these arms.

Mar. My heart
Leaps to be gone into my mother's bosom.
[*Kneels to Thaisa.*]

Per. Look who kneels here! Flesh of thy flesh, Thaisa,
Thy burden at the sea, and call'd Marina
For she was yielded there.

Thai. Blest, and mine own!

Hel. Hail, madam, and my queen!

Thai. I know you not.

[*Per.*] You have heard me say, when I did fly from Tyre,
I left behind an ancient substitute.
Can you remember what I call'd the man?
I have nam'd him oft.

Thai. 'Twas Helicanus then.

Per. Still confirmation!
Embrace him, dear Thaisa, this is he.
Now do I long to hear how you were found,
How possibly preserved, and who to thank
(Besides the gods) for this great miracle.

Thai. Lord Cerimon, my lord; this man,
Through whom the gods have shown their power; that can
From first to last resolve you.

Per. Reverent sir,
The gods can have no mortal officer
More like a god than you. Will you deliver
How this dead queen relives?

Cer. I will, my lord.
Beseech you first, go with me to my house,
Where shall be shown you all was found with her;
How she came plac'd here in the temple;
No needful thing omitted.

Per. Pure Dian,
[I] bless thee for thy vision, and will offer
Night-oblations to thee. Thaisa,
This prince, the fair-betrothed of your daughter,
Shall marry her at Pentapolis. And now
This ornament
Makes me look dismal will I clip to form,
And what this fourteen years no razor touch'd,
To grace thy marriage-day, I'll beautify.

Thai. Lord Cerimon hath letters of good credit, sir,
My father's dead.

Per. Heavens make a star of him! Yet there, my queen,
We'll celebrate their nuptials, and ourselves
Will in that kingdom spend our following days.
Our son and daughter shall in Tyrus reign.
Lord Cerimon, we do our longing stay
To hear the rest untold. Sir, lead 's the way.
[*Exeunt.*]

[*Enter*] Gower.

[*Gow.*] In Antiochus and his daughter you have heard
Of monstrous lust the due and just reward.
In Pericles, his queen and daughter, seen,
Although assail'd with fortune fierce and keen,

11. Riding: as we were riding at anchor. **13. favor:** appearance.
18. Reverent: reverend (so also in line 61). These forms were interchangeable. **24. recovered:** revived.
30. sense: i.e. sense of sight.
31. spite of seeing: no matter what I see.
38. parted: departed from. **42. That:** if.

48. yielded: born. **61. resolve you:** answer all your questions.
73. ornament: i.e. his hair and beard.
74. Makes: which makes. **77. credit:** trustworthiness.
79. there: i.e. in Pentapolis.
83. do . . . stay: are postponing the satisfaction of our desire.

Virtue [preserv'd] from fell destruction's blast,
Led on by heaven, and crown'd with joy at last.
In Helicanus may you well descry
A figure of truth, of faith, of loyalty.
In reverend Cerimon there well appears
The worth that learned charity aye wears.
For wicked Cleon and his wife, when fame
Had spread his cursed deed, the honor'd name
Of Pericles to rage the city turn,
That him and his they in his palace burn;
The gods for murder seemed so content
To punish, although not done, but meant.
So, on your patience evermore attending,
New joy wait on you! Here our play has ending.
[*Exit.*]

NOTE ON THE TEXT

The textual situation in *Pericles* is extremely unsatisfactory. The play was first published in quarto in 1609 (Q1) in a form which there is every reason to believe represents a memorially reconstructed version; in other words, Q1 is a "bad" quarto. Unfortunately Q1 is our only substantive text of *Pericles,* all later texts being derived from it at one or more removes. *Pericles* is thus the only play in the Shakespeare canon for which no comparatively authoritative text has survived. A second quarto (Q2) appeared also in 1609, reprinted from Q1, and four more quarto editions, each deriving from the immediately preceding edition (except Q6, which was partly printed from a copy of Q4), were published in 1611 (Q3), 1619 (Q4), 1630 (Q5), and 1635 (Q6). *Pericles* was not included in the First Folio (1623), but was added, along with six other plays, now considered non-Shakespearean, in the second issue (1664) of the Third Folio (F3), printed from a copy of Q6. It was also included in the Fourth Folio (1685) in a text based on F3. Q4 and, to a lesser extent, F3 show evidence of an attempt here and there to improve the text, but there is no reason to suppose that the new readings of either text represent anything more than well-intentioned guesswork; Q4 also restores to verse a good many passages misprinted as prose in Q1.

Among a number of bibliographical peculiarities in Q1, one deserves special notice. It has been shown by Philip Edwards that three compositors and probably two printing houses worked on setting up the text (two men in one printing house [Thomas Creede], working alternately, though not by casting off copy, producing sheets B, F, G, H, I, and one in another [William White], producing sheets A, C, D, E—the printer being distinguished by the use of different sets of running titles). Because sheet B begins and ends at points not easily determinable in advance by a printer casting off copy, it has been suggested by John Crow (in Maxwell's edition) that what we now have as sheet B must in fact be a resetting of an original sheet B set by the compositor who set sheets A, C, D, E. The reason for this resetting of an entire sheet is beyond our recall, unless a copy of Q1 containing the canceled sheet should yet turn up, but it is important to recognize that this stretch of text (I.i.159–I.iv.92) is probably one remove farther from the manuscript than the rest of Q1.

An editor of *Pericles* has one source of external aid in a little novel by George Wilkins called *The Painfull Adventures of Pericles Prince of Tyre* (1608). This account describes itself on the title-page as "Being The true History of the Play of *Pericles,* as it was lately presented by the worthy and ancient Poet Iohn Gower." Later Wilkins mentions the "Play" in question as having been "by the Kings Maiesties Players excellently presented," that is, by Shakespeare's company. There is some disagreement about the exact relation of Wilkins's novel to Q1. Some believe that Wilkins based his book on an *Ur-Pericles* play by an unknown author or authors (Wilkins himself, John Day, and Thomas Heywood, individually or in collaboration, have been suggested; Wilkins, however, is increasingly being accepted as at least part author [see Jowett/Taylor, Jackson, Smith]) and that this play was the source of the version now associated with Shakespeare. Others, whether they accept the probable use of an *Ur-Pericles* as Shakespeare's source or assert Shakespeare's sole authorship of the play, believe that Wilkins' novel was derived directly from the Shakespearean version as it was acted at the Globe, the version of which Q1 is a memorially reported text. Such evidence as there is seems to favor the second view. Whichever view is taken, however, Wilkins' novel is clearly a botch job, drawing heavily and directly, where his memory of his dramatic source seems to have failed him, on Laurence Twine's *The Patterne of Painefull Adventures . . . that befell unto Prince Apollonius* (1594), a second edition of which appeared in 1607. Twine's account, presumably in its earlier sixteenth-century edition, had served, together with Gower's version of the tale in the *Confessio Amantis,* as the principal source of either Shakespeare's or, perhaps more probably, an earlier *Pericles* play.

Despite the unsatisfactory state of Wilkins' novel, itself a memorial reconstruction like Q1, it nevertheless serves to restore the text of the play at a number of points (see Textual Notes, I.i.128, 131, I.iv.39, II.Cho.22, II.i.48, 155, etc.), and Wilkins' claim of a direct relationship between *Pericles* as acted at the Globe and his *Painfull Aduentures* and the presence of what seem to be numerous verse fossils in his narrative prose have led several scholars (Edwards, H. F. Brooks [in Hoeniger], Bullough, Taylor, Jackson) to attempt the reconstruction, from Wilkins' account, of patches of dialogue (even a short scene; see below) which would appear at some points to have been parts of the original play (see Textual Notes, II.ii, III.i.30–3, IV.vi.79–166). An example of such reconstruction from the New Oxford *Works* (1986, modern spelling text; *Pericles,* edited by Taylor and Mac. D. P. Jackson) will illustrate the sort of reconstruction proposed. There, for the first time, a considerable number of such passages derived from Wilkins are admitted into the text proper—dangerous, perhaps, but challenging. For example, the following passage from Wilkins (Chapter 6) becomes the basis for a new scene in the Oxford text (following II.iv in Q):

Prince *Pericles* having had . . . his lodging directed next adjoyning to the kings bed-chamber, whereas all the other Princes uppon their comming to their lodgings betooke themselves to their pillowes, . . . he of the Gentlemen that attended him, . . . desired that hee might be left private, onely that for his instant solace they would pleasure him with some delightfull instrument, with which, and his former practise hee intended to passe away the tediousnesse of the night insteade of more fitting slumbers. His wil was presently obeyed in all things . . . the Instrument is brought him, and as hee had formerly wished, the Chamber is disfurnished of any other company but himselfe, where presently hee beganne to compell such heavenly voyces from the sencelesse workemanship, as if *Apollo* himselfe had now beene fingering on it, . . . [King Simonides is awakened by the music and listens with great delight, a reaction vouched for in the play proper in II.v.25–8.] But day that hath still that soveraigntie to drawe backe the empire of the night, though a while shee in darknesse usurpe, brought the morning on, . . .

From the raw, but suggestive, material above, the Oxford editors extract the following short verse scene (numbered scene 8a in their text).

Enter Pericles with Gentlemen with lights

FIRST GENTLEMAN
Here is your lodging, sir.
PERICLES — Pray leave me private.
Only for instant solace pleasure me
With some delightful instrument, with which,
And with my former practice, I intend
To pass away the tediousness of night,
Though slumbers were more fitting.
FIRST GENTLEMAN — Presently.
Exit First Gentleman
SECOND GENTLEMAN
Your will's obeyed in all things, for our master
Commanded you be disobeyed in nothing.
Enter First Gentleman with a stringed instrument
PERICLES
I thank you. Now betake you to your pillows,
And to the nourishment of quiet sleep.
Exeunt Gentlemen.
Pericles plays and sings
Day—that hath still that sovereignty to draw back
The empire of the night, though for a while
In darkness she usurp—brings morning on.
I will go give his grace that salutation
Morning requires of me. *Exit with instrument.*

In dealing editorially with such a corrupt copy-text as that furnished by Q1, the present text has adopted a more than usually conservative attitude toward emendation and has allowed some probably corrupt passages to stand unchanged. The most commonly accepted emendations are pointed out in the explanatory notes.

For further information, see: W. W. Greg, *The Editorial Problem in Shakespeare* (Oxford, rev. ed., 1951); Philip Edwards, "An Approach to the Problem of *Pericles*," *S Sur*, V (1952), 25–49; Kenneth Muir, ed., George Wilkins, *The Painfull Aduentures of Pericles* (Liverpool, 1953); J. C. Maxwell, ed., New Shakespeare *Pericles* (Cambridge, 1956); F. D. Hoeniger, ed., New Arden *Pericles* (London, 1963); Geoffrey Bullough, ed., Laurence Twine's *The Patterne of Painefull Adventures* in *Narrative and Dramatic Sources of Shakespeare*, VI (London, 1966), 423–82 [also contains Wilkins' *Painfull Adventures*, 492–548]; S. Musgrove, "The First Quarto of *Pericles* Reconsidered," *SQ*, XXIX (1978), 389–406; Gary Taylor, "The Transmission of *Pericles*," *PBSA*, LXXX (1986), 193–217; M. W. A. Smith, "The Authorship of *Pericles:* New Evidence for Wilkins," *Literary and Linguistic Computing*, II (1987), 221–30, and "The Authorship of Acts I and II of *Pericles*: A New Approach Using First Words of Speeches," *Computers and the Humanities* XXII (1988), 23–41; Stanley Wells, Gary Taylor, John Jowett, William Montgomery, *William Shakespeare: A Textual Companion* (Oxford, 1987); MacD. P. Jackson, "*Pericles*, Acts I and II: New Evidence for George Wilkins," *N & Q*, n.s., XXXVII (1990), 102–06, "George Wilkins and the First Two Acts of *Pericles*: New Evidence from Function Words," *Literary and Linguistic Computing*, VI (1991), 155–63, and "Rhyming in *Pericles:* More Evidence of Dual Authorship," *SB*, XLVI (1993), 239–49.

TEXTUAL NOTES

Title: Pericles . . . Tyre] The Late And much admired Play, Called Pericles, Prince of Tyre. With the true Relation of the whole Historie, aduentures, and fortunes of the said Prince: As also, The no lesse strange, and worthy accidents, in the Birth and Life, of his Daughter Mariana. As it hath been diuers and sundry times acted by his Maiesties Seruants, at the Globe on the Banck-side. By William Shakespeare. *Q1 (title-page)*

Dramatis personae: *subs. as given in Malone (after F3)*

Governor of Mytilene] *Malone;* Governor of Metaline *F3*

Act-scene division: *none in Q1–6; F3 designates I.i and thereafter acts only, marking, however, Act III at the present III.iii, Act IV at the present IV.iv, and Act V following the present V.i.239; other act-scene divisions from Malone and later editors (see the first note to each scene); present act-scene arrangement as a whole first established by Globe*

I.Cho.

Act I] *F3* (Actus Primus. Scena Prima.)
1 s.p. **Gow.]** *Neilson*
6 **ember-eves]** *hyphen, Malone*
6 **holy-ales]** *Farmer conj. (hyphen, Steevens);* Holydayes *Q1*
11 **those]** these *Q2*
12 **wit's]** *Rowe;* Witts *Q1*
16 **taper-light]** *hyphen, Q2*
17 **This' Antioch, then;]** *Round (subs., in Henry Irving Shakespeare);* This Antioch, then *Q1*
37 **whoso]** *Pope;* who so *Q1*
38 **told not,]** *Q2;* tould, not *Q1*
39 **a]** *F3;* of *Q1*
40 s.d. **Points . . . above.]** *ed. (after Round in Henry Irving Shakespeare)*

I.i

I.i] *Malone*
Location: *Malone*
o.s.d. **Followers]** *Q2;* fellowers *Q1*
5 s.d. **Music.]** *as s.d., Malone; as opening word of l. 6, Q1*
10 **senate-house]** *Q2 (hyphen, Malone);* Seanate house *Q1*
13 **king]** *Malone;* King, *Q1*
17 **ras'd]** *Malone;* racte *Q1*
24 **boundless]** *Rowe;* bondlesse *Q1*
29 **death-like]** *hyphen, Malone (after Theobald)*
53 s.d. **To the Princess.]** *Rowe (subs.)*
56 s.p. **Ant.]** *Malone; om. Q1, unless* (Antiochus) *at end of l. 55 was intended as s.p. and misread by the compositor as the conclusion of Pericles' speech*
59, 60 **'say'd]** *Knight (after Percy conj.);* sayd *Q1*
62 **advice]** *Q3;* aduise *Q1*
63 s.d. **Reads.]** *Steevens (subs.); cf. Wilkins'* read aloude
64–71 **I . . . you.]** *verbatim in Wilkins, except* that *for* which, *l. 65*
72 **Aside.]** *Cambridge*
76 **Aside . . . Princess.]** *ed.*
99–100 **clear . . . them.]** *Mason conj.;* cleare: . . . them, *Q1*
105 **fit,]** *Malone;* fit; *Q1*
106 **known grows]** *Malone;* knowne, growes *Q1*
109 s.d. **Aside.]** *Steevens*
111 **our]** *F3;* your *Q1*
113 **cancel of]** *Malone (after F3* cancel off*);* counsell of *Q1*
116 **forty]** *so Wilkins;* thirtie *in Twine*
120 s.d. **Exeunt.]** *Malone;* Exit. *Q4*
127 **you're]** *F3 (subs.);* you *Q1*
128 **uncomely]** *Delius conj. (from Wilkins:* hee was become both father, sonne, and husband by his vncomely and abhorred actions with his own child); vntimely *Q1* (OED *does not record the required sense of* improper *which earlier authorities had assigned to the word in this context*)
131 **parent's]** *Rowe;* Parents *Q1 (the singular seems to be borne out by Wilkins'* mothers)
136 **'schew]** *Malone conj.;* shew *Q1*
142 s.d.] *Hoeniger here indicates a new scene*
151 **Thaliard—]** *ed.;* Thaliard, *Q1*
157 **why, because]** *Malone;* why? / Because *Q1*
158–64 **Enough . . . dead.]** *as verse, Malone; as prose, Q1*
158 s.d. **Enter a Messenger.]** *placed as in Dyce; after* 'tis done. *l. 158, Q1*
160 s.d. **Exit.]** *Malone*
165–7 **My . . . Highness.]** *as verse, Dyce; as prose, Q1*
168 s.p. **Ant.]** *Q4*

168 s.d. **Exit Thaliard.**] *Dyce (after Rowe)*
169 s.d. **Exit.**] *Q2*

I.ii

I.ii] *Malone*
Location: *Malone (subs.)*
1 s.d. **Exeunt Lords.**] *Kittredge*
3 **Be my]** *Dyce;* By me *Q1*
5 **quiet?]** *Malone;* quiet, *Q1*
10 **me.]** *Q2 (subs.);* me, *Q1*
13 **after-nourishment]** *hyphen, Malone*
13 **care;]** *Q2;* care *Q1*
16 **me:]** *Q4 (subs.);* me *Q1*
20 **him]** *Rowe*
25 **th' ostent]** *Tyrwhitt conj.;* the stint *Q1*
30 **am]** *Farmer conj.;* once *Q1*
33 s.d. **Helicanus and]** *Dyce*
41 **blast]** *Mason conj.;* sparke *Q1*
43 **err.]** *Rowe (subs.);* erre, *Q1*
44 **Signior Sooth]** *F3;* signior sooth *Q1*
46 **pardon]** *Q2;* paadon *Q1*
47 s.d. **Kneels.**] *Collier*
50 s.d. **Exeunt Lords.**] *Malone*
50 **Helicanus]** *Q2* (Hellicanus); Hellicans *Q1 (Q1 usually spells* Hellicanus; *Wilkins, either* Helycanus *or* Helicanus)
65–6 **To . . . yourself.]** *as verse, Knight (after Q4); as prose, Q1*
68 **me]** *Q2* (me,); me: *Q1*
71 **Where, as]** *Q2* (Where as); Whereas *Q1*
73 **propagate]** *Q6;* propogate *Q1 (a possible, if erroneous, form; cf.* Romeo and Juliet *(Q2), I.i.187)*
76 **(hark . . . ear)]** *Q2;* harke . . . eare, *Q1*
84 **fears]** *F4;* feare *Q1*
86 **doubt't]** *ed. (after Steevens conj.* doubt it); do'ot *Q1*
95 **for't—]** *Malone (subs.);* fort. *Q1*
103 **think,]** *Rowe;* thinke *Q1*
105–10 **Will . . . be.]** *as verse, Rowe; as prose, Q1*
109 **any;]** *Malone;* anie, *Q1*
116 **travel]** *F3;* trauaile *Q1*
118 **subjects']** *Malone;* subiects *Q1*
121 **them]** *Maxwell; F3 inserts* sure *after* will
122 **we'll]** *Malone;* will *Q1;* we *Q2*
124 **prince']** *Maxwell;* Prince *Q1*
124 s.d. **Exeunt.**] *Rowe;* Exit. *Q1*

I.iii

I.iii] *Malone*
Location: *Malone (subs.)*
10–39] *As verse, Rowe and Malone; as prose, Q1*
10 **fellow peers]** *Steevens;* fellow-Peers *Q1*
12 **seal'd]** *Rowe;* sea- / led *Q1*
13 **travel]** *Q4;* trauaile *Q1*
14, 18, 25 s.dd. **Aside.**] *Malone*
16 **unlicens'd]** *Q4;* vnlicensed *Q1*
17 **depart,]** *Malone;* depart? *Q1*
17 **you.]** *Q4;* you, *Q1*
30 s.p. **Hel.**] *Q4*
34 **betook]** *Q2;* betake *Q1*
34 **travels]** *F3;* trauailes *Q1*
39 s.d. **Exeunt.**] *Q2;* Exit. *Q1*

I.iv

I.iv] *Malone*
Location: *Steevens (subs.)*
5 **aspire]** *Q4* (aspire,); aspire? *Q1*
10 **Dionyza!]** *ed. (after Malone);* Dioniza. *Q1 (Wilkins* Dyonysa)
13 **deep]** *Malone;* deepe: *Q1*
14 **weep,]** *Q3;* weepe. *Q1*
39 **palates]** *Malone;* pallats *Q1*
39 **two summers]** *Mason conj.;* too sauers *Q1 (despite the support of Wilkins'* two summers younger, *which is, however, applied to* their City, *the connection between* palates *and* savors *in Q1 suggests that perhaps the original text did not follow Wilkins; Maxwell notes that the equivalent of two blank-verse lines follows the phrase in Wilkins' prose:* did so excell in pompe and bore a state, whom all hir neighbors enuied for her greatnes,)
42 **nousle]** *Steevens;* nouzell *Q1*
57–9 **Here . . . expect.]** *as verse, Malone; as prose, Q1*
58 **thou]** *Q3;* thee *Q1*
60–1 **We . . . hitherward.]** *as verse, Q4; as prose, Q1*
67 **Hath]** *Rowe;* That *Q1*
70 **glory's]** *Malone;* glories *Q1*
71–3 **That's . . . foes.]** *as verse, Malone (after Rowe); as prose, Q1*
74 **him's]** *Malone;* himnes *Q1*
77–8 **fear? . . . lowest,]** *Malone (subs., after Q4* feare, the ground's the lowest,); leaue our grounds the lowest? *Q1*
78–81 **and . . . craves.]** *as verse, Malone (after Rowe); as prose, Q1*
81 **craves.]** *Q3;* craues? *Q1*
82 s.d. **Exit.**] *Malone*
84 s.d. **Lord and]** *Hoeniger (subs.)*
96 **hunger starv'd]** *Q4;* hunger-staru'd *Q1*
105 **ne'er]** *Q2* (nere); neare *Q1*

II.Cho.

Act II] *F3*
1 s.p. **Gow.**] *Q4*
2 **I wis]** *Q4;* I'wis *Q1*
11 **Tharsus]** *Q5;* Tharstill *Q1*
12 **speken]** *White;* spoken *Q1*
17 **Helicane]** *Malone;* Helicon *Q1*
20 **alive,]** *Craig;* alive: *Q1*
21 **prince']** *Malone;* prince *Q1*
22 **Sends word]** *Steevens conj. (after Theobald conj.: Wilkins uses* send word *in the identical context);* Sau'd one *Q1*
23 **Thaliard]** *Q2;* Thaliart *Q1* (Thalyart *or* Thaliart *is the spelling in Wilkins)*
24 **hid intent to murder]** *Q1 (c) reads* had intent to murder; *Q1 (u) reads* hid in Tent to murdred; *Q2 reads* hid intent to murder *(apparently an independent correction of Q1 (u), which Q2 was following at this point); Q1 (u)* hid *seems preferable and did not bother the Q2 compositor; Maxwell suggests that the Q1 corrector in dealing with* murdred *may have concealed an original form such as* murdren
25 **Tharsus]** *F3;* Tharsis *Q1*
35 **man,]** *F3;* man *Q1*
36 **aught]** *Steevens;* ought *Q1*
38 **ashore]** *F3;* a shore *Q1*
40 **this long's]** thus long's *F3;* this 'longs *Theobald conj.*
40 s.d. **Exit.**] *Malone*

II.i

II.i] *Malone*
Location: *Malone (subs.)*
1 **heaven!]** *Malone;* heauen, *Q1*
6 **me]** *Malone;* my *Q1*
12 **ff.]** *Fishermen's speeches largely as irregular verse, Q1; as prose, Malone*
12 etc. s.pp. **1. Fish. . . . 2. Fish. . . . 3. Fish.**] *Rowe;* 1. . . . 2. . . . 3. *Q1*
12 **ho, Pilch!]** *Malone;* to pelch? *Q1*
17 **fetch th']** *Pelican;* fetch'th *Q1;* fetch thee *Q4*
27 **sea.]** *Malone;* Sea? *Q1*
35, 45, 48 s.dd. **Aside.**] *Dyce*
48 **finny]** *Steevens (after 1734 ed.; supported by Wilkins'* finny subiects); fenny *Q1*
53 **Honest,]** *Q2;* Honest *Q1*
55 **it.]** *Malone;* it? *Q1*
78 **keth 'a]** *ed.;* ke-tha *Q1*
81 **holidays]** *Malone;* all day *Q1*
82 **moreo'er]** *Farmer conj.;* more; or *Q1*
90 **your]** *Q4* (all your); you *Q1*
94 s.d. **Exit . . . Fisherman.**] *Dyce (after Malone)*
95 s.d. **Aside.**] *Dyce*
99 **is]** *Q2;* I *Q1*
99 **Pentapolis]** *Rowe (so Wilkins);* Pantapoles *Q1*
115 s.d. **other]** *Pelican*
120 **it.]** *Q4;* it? *Q1*
121 **yet]** *Q2;* yeat *Q1*
121 **thy]** *Delius (from Wilkins'* all her crosses)
123 **own,]** *Q5;* owne *Q1*
127 **brace]** *Malone;* brayse *Q1*
128 **sav'd]** *Malone;* saued *Q1*
128 **it.]** *Malone (subs.);* it *Q1*
129 **from!—]** *Dyce (after Malone);* Fame *Q1*
142 **fortunes]** *Mason conj. (Wilkins:* if euer his fortunes came to their ancient height); fortune's *Q1*
146 **d' ye]** *Sisson (from Q1 (u)* Di'e); *Q1 (c) alters to* do'e
155 **rapture]** *Rowe (Wilkins:* a Iewel, whom all the raptures of the sea could not bereaue from his arme); rupture *Q1*
158 **delightful]** *F3;* delight *Q1*
166 s.d. **Exeunt.**] *Rowe*

II.ii

II.ii] *Malone*
Location: *ed.; Wilkins' circumstantial description of this scene (not in Twine) differs from the play in a number of ways and suggests that the Q1 text has been shortened and is open to question at several points:* This is the day, this *Symonides* Court, where the King himselfe, with the Princesse his daughter, haue placed themselues in a Gallery, to beholde the triumphes of seuerall Princes, who in honour of the Princes[s] birth day, but more in hope to haue her loue, came purposely thither, to approoue their chiualrie. They thus seated, and Prince *Pericles,* as well as his owne prouiding, and the Fishermens care could furnish him, likewise came to the court. In this maner also 5. seuerall princes (their horses richly caparasoned, but themselues more richly armed, their Pages before them bearing their Deuices on their shields) entred then the Tilting place. The first a prince of *Macedon,* and the Deuice hee bore vpon his shield, was a blacke Ethiope reaching at the Sunne, the word, *Lux tua vita mihi:* which being by the knights Page deliuered to the Lady, and from her presented to the King her father, hee made playne to her the meaning of each imprese: and for this first, it was, that the Macedonian Prince loued her so well hee helde his life of her. The second, a Prince of *Corinth,* and the Deuice hee bare vpon his shield was a wreathe of Chiualry, the word, *Me pompae prouexet apex,* the desire of renowne drew him to this enterprise. The third of *Antioch,* and his Deuice was an armed Knight, being conquered by a Lady, the word, *Pue per dolcera qui per sforsa:* more by lenitie than by force. The fourth of *Sparta,* and the Deuice he bare was a mans arme enuironed with a cloude, holding out golde thats by the touchstone tride, the word, *Sic spectanda fides,* so faith is to be looked into. The fift of *Athens,* and his Deuice was a flaming Torche turned downeward, the word, *Qui me alit me extinguit,* that which giues me life giues me death. The sixt and last was *Pericles* Prince of *Tyre,* who hauing neither Page to deliuer his shield, nor shield to deliuer, making his Deuice according to his fortunes, which was a withered Braunch being onely greene at the top, which prooued the abating of his body, decayed not the noblenesse of his minde, his word, *In hac spe viuo,* In that hope I liue. Himselfe with a most gracefull curtesie presented it vnto her, which shee as curteously receiued, whilest the Peeres attending on the King forbare not to scoffe, both at his presence, and the present hee brought, being himselfe in a rusty Armour, the Caparison of his horse of plaine country russet, and his owne Bases but the skirtes of a poore Fishermans coate, which the King mildely reproouing them for, hee tolde them, that as Vertue was not to be approoued by wordes, but by actions, so the outward habite was the least table of the inward minde, and counselling them not to condemne ere they had cause to

accuse: . . . To be short, both of Court and Commons, the praises of none were spoken of, but of the meane Knights (for by any other name he was yet vnknowne to any.)
o.s.d. **Lords**] *Malone*
1 s.p. **Sim.**] *Malone;* King. *Q1 (throughout)*
7 s.d. **Exit a Lord.**] *Malone*
16 s.d. **and . . . Princess**] *Malone (subs.; from Wilkins)*
22, 27, 30, 35 s.dd. **passes by**] *Malone (subs.)*
27 **Piu**] *Malone;* Pue *Q1 (Wilkins)*
27 **dolcera**] *Rowe (Wilkins);* doleera *Q1*
27 **que**] *Malone;* kee *Q1*
27 **força**] *Maxwell;* forsa *Q1*
29 **chivalry**] *Q2 (Wilkins);* Chiually *Q1*
30 **pompae**] *Steevens conj. (Wilkins);* Pompey *Q1*
35 s.d. **Fift**] *Q4;* 5. *Q1*
38 s.d. **Sixt**] *Q4;* 6. *Q1*
38 s.d. **Pericles . . . Princess.**] *ed. (after Malone and Hoeniger)*
45 **moral:**] *Q2 (subs.);* morrall *Q1*
53 **strangely**] *Q2;* strangly *Q1*
53 **furnished**] *Malone;* furnisht *Q1*
59 s.d. **Exeunt.**] *Rowe*
59 s.d. **within**] *Dyce*

II.iii

II.iii] *Malone*
Location: *Malone*
o.s.d. **A banquet prepared.**] *Malone*
o.s.d. **Simonides . . . Attendants**] *Malone (subs.;* Marshal *added, Craig;* Ladies *added, Kittredge)*
3 **To**] *F4;* I *Q1*
13 **your**] yours *Q3*
19 s.d. **To the Marshal.**] *ed.*
19 **Marshal,**] *Hoeniger;* Martiall *Q1*
26 **Envied**] *Trent conj. (in Maxwell);* Enuies *Q1;* Enuie *Q4*
28, 30, 36, 37 s.dd. **Aside.**] *Cambridge*
32 s.d. **To Simonides.**] *Hoeniger*
33 s.d. **To Thaisa.**] *Hoeniger*
34, 35 **H'as**] *ed.;* ha's *Q1*
37 **Yon king's**] *Q2;* You Kings *Q1*
38 **me**] *Q4*
43 **son's**] *Malone;* sonne *Q1*
50 **stor'd**] *Steevens conj.;* stur'd *Q1*
65 **standing-bowl**] *hyphen, Steevens*
72 s.d. **Aside.**] *Rowe*
96 **this**] *Malone;* this, *Q1;* that *Q4*
106 s.d. **Knights and Ladies**] *Malone; s.d. after l. 106, Q1; places as in Dyce*
108 s.d. **To Pericles.**] *Malone*
109 s.d. **To Pericles.**] *Neilson*
112 s.p. **Sim.**] *Q4* (King.)
115 s.d. **Exeunt.**] *Malone*

II.iv

II.iv] *Malone*
Location: *Malone (subs.)*
10 **Those**] their *Wilkins*
18 **council**] *Malone;* counsaile *Q1*
19 **reproof**] *Q2;* reprofe *Q1*
22 **welcome. Happy**] *Malone (subs., after Q2* welcome, happy); welcome happy *Q1*
34 **indeed**] *Sisson (after Malone;* indeed, *Q4);* in deed, *Q1*
34 **censure**] *Q2;* sensure *Q1*
39 **unto—**] *Malone;* vnto *Q1*
40 **Live,**] *F3;* Liue *Q1*
58 s.d. **Exeunt.**] *Rowe;* Exit. *Q4*

II.v

II.v] *Malone*
Location: *Malone (subs.)*
13 s.d. **Exeunt Knights.**] *Dyce (after Malone);* Exit. *Q2*
38 **Ay**] *Malone;* I *Q1*
42, 58 s.dd. **Aside.**] *Malone*
47 **aim'd**] *Q4;* aymed *Q1*
71 **offense**] *Malone (after Q4);* offence? *Q1*
74 s.d. **Aside.**] *placed as in Q4; after l. 75, Q1*
76 **you, not**] *Q4;* you not, *Q1*
78 s.d. **aside**] *placed as in Q4; after l. 79, Q1*
83 **you—**] *Q4;* you, *Q1*

III.Cho.

Act III] *Malone*
1 s.p. **Gow.**] *Malone*
2 **the house about**] *Malone;* about the house *Q1*
7 **crickets**] *Rowe;* Cricket *Q1*
10 **Where, by**] *Rowe;* Whereby *Q1*
13 **eche**] *Malone;* each *Q1*
14 s.d. **Dumb Show**] *this heading from Q5*
14 s.d. **with . . . rest**] *Dyce (after Malone)*
17 **coigns**] *Rowe;* Crignes *Q1*
21 **stead**] *Malone;* steed *Q1*
21 **quest. At . . . Tyre,**] *Rowe (subs.);* quest at last from Tyre: *Q1*
34 **Pentapolis**] *Q6;* Penlapolis *Q1*
35 **Yravished**] *Steevens conj.;* Iranyshed *Q1*
40–1 **desire— . . . cross?—**] *Malone (subs.);* desire, . . . crosse *Q1*
57 **not**] *Malone;* not? *Q1*
57–8 **told. . . . hold**] *Malone* (told; *Q5);* told, . . . hold: *Q1*
60 **seas-toss'd**] *ed.* (Sea-tost *Rowe);* seas tost *Q1*
60 s.d. **Exit.**] *Q5*

III.i

III.i] *Malone*
Location: *Malone*
o.s.d. **a-shipboard**] *hyphen, Kittredge*
7 **Thou storm,**] *Malone;* then storme *Q1*
8 **spet**] *Kittredge;* speat *Q1*
10 **Unheard.—Lychorida!—**] *Malone;* Vnheard Lychorida? *Q1*
11 **patroness**] *Q4;* patronesse *Q1*
11 **midwife**] *Steevens conj.;* my wife *Q1*
14 s.d. **with an infant**] *Steevens*
30–3 **Thou . . . make**] *cf. Wilkins:* Poore inch of Nature (quoth he) thou arte as rudely welcome to the worlde, as euer Princesse Babe was, and hast as chiding a natiuitie, as fire, ayre, earth, and water can affoord thee, *(the first four words are felt to have a decidedly Shakespearean quality)*
34 **herald**] *Steevens conj.;* harould *Q1*
45–6 **But . . . not.**] *as prose, F3; as verse, Q1*
47–53 **Sir . . . straight.**] *as prose, Malone; as verse, Q1*
52 **custom**] *Boswell conj.;* easterne *Q1*
53 **for . . . straight.**] *arranged as in Malone; Q1 gives as part of Pericles' next speech, following* meet. *l. 54*
60 **the ooze**] *Steevens conj.;* oare *Q1*
62 **e'er-remaining**] *Globe;* ayre remayning *Q1*
65 **paper**] *Q2;* Taper *Q1*
69 s.d. **Exit Lychorida.**] *Malone*
70–1 **Sir . . . ready.**] *as prose, Malone; as verse, Q1*
70 **chest**] *Q2;* Chist *Q1 (throughout)*
81 s.d. **Exeunt.**] *Rowe;* Exit. *Q1*

III.ii

III.ii] *Malone*
Location: *Malone (subs.)*
o.s.d. **and . . . storm-beaten**] *Hoeniger (subs.)*
3 s.d. **Exit Philemon.**] *Hoeniger (after l. 4); placed by ed.*
6 **ne'er**] *F3;* neare *Q1*
9 s.d. **To . . . Man.**] *Hoeniger (subs.)*
10 s.d. **Exeunt . . . Man.**] *Hoeniger (subs.)*
18 **quit**] *Malone;* quite *Q1;* leaue *Q4*
29 **expend**] *Wilkins'* dispend *may preserve the original*
43 **pour'd**] *Malone;* Poured *Q1*
48 **shall never—**] *Malone;* shall neuer. *Q1;* neuer shall decay. *Q4*
48 s.d. **Servants**] *Malone*
49, 58 s.pp. **1. Serv.**] *Dyce;* Seru. *and* Ser. *Q1*
56 **bitum'd**] *Malone (so Wilkins; see III.i.71);* bottomed *Q1*
59–60 **open. Soft!**] *Knight (subs., after Malone);* open soft; *Q1;* open; *Q4*
65–7 **Shrouded . . . characters!**] *as verse, Q4 (after Q3); as prose, Q1*
65 **balm'd**] *Q4;* balmed *Q1*
65 **entreasur'd**] *Malone;* entreasured *Q1*
66 **too!**] *Malone;* to *Q1*
67 s.d. **Reads . . . scroll.**] *Malone (subs.)*
74 **Besides**] *Q4;* Besides, *Q1*
75 **requite**] *Q2;* requit *Q1*
77 **woe! This**] *F3 (subs.);* woe, this *Q1*
81 s.d. **Exit a Servant.**] *Dyce*
84–6 **I . . . recovered.**] *eds. have felt that the text here is corrupt and that Wilkins preserves something close to the original:* I haue read of some Egyptians, who after foure houres death, (if man may call it so) haue raised impouerished bodies, like to this, vnto their former health, . . *(the blank verse movement of Wilkins' prose is obvious)*
86 s.d. **boxes,**] *Dyce*
87 **cloths**] *Pope;* clothes *Q1*
88 **rough**] *Q1 probably corrupt here; Delius' conj.* still *receives some support from Wilkins'* they should commaund some still musicke to sound *but is graphically very difficult*
90 **vial**] *Q4;* Violl *Q1*
92–3 **awakes, . . . breathes**] *Steevens conj. (subs.);* awakes a warmth breath *Q1*
97 **behold,**] *Malone;* behold *Q1*
103 **weep to**] *Rowe;* weepe. / To *Q1*
110 **Aesculapius**] *Q2* (Esculapius); Escelapius *Q1*

III.iii

III.iii] *Malone;* Actus Tertius. *F3*
Location: *Dyce (subs., after Malone)*
o.s.d. **Pericles at Tharsus**] *Q4;* Pericles, Atharsus *Q1*
o.s.d. **and . . . arms**] *Dyce (after Malone)*
1–3 **Most . . . peace.**] *as verse, Malone (after Q4); as prose, Q1*
6 **haunt**] *Q2;* hant *Q1*
7–9 **O . . . her!**] *as verse, Rowe (after Q3); as prose, Q1*
13 **nam'd**] *Rowe;* named *Q1*
20 **on.**] *Rowe (subs.);* on, *Q1*
29 **Unscissor'd . . . hair**] *Steevens (Wilkins* vncisserd); vnsisterd . . . heyre *Q1*
30 **ill**] *Malone conj.;* will *Q1 (the emendation is supported by Wilkins'* himselfe in all vncomely)
32 s.p. **Dion.**] *Q1 catchword reads* Cler.
32–4 **I . . . lord.**] *as verse, Malone (after Rowe); as prose, Q1*
35 s.p. **Cle.**] *Q4;* Cler. *Q1*
35–41 **We'll . . . lord.**] *as verse, Malone; as prose, Q1*
39 **Lychorida**] *Q2;* Licherida *Q1*
41 s.d. **Exeunt.**] *Rowe*

III.iv

III.iv] *Malone*
Location: *Malone (subs.)*
o.s.d. **Thaisa**] *Q4;* Tharsa *Q1* (Tharsia *in Twine)*
4 s.p. **Thai.**] *Q4;* Thar. *Q1*
4–11 **It . . . joy.**] *as verse, Steevens (after Rowe); as prose, Q1*
4 **lord's.**] *F4 (subs.);* Lords, *Q1*
6 **eaning**] *F3;* learning *Q1*
10 **vestal**] *F3;* vastall *Q1*
12 s.p. **Cer.**] *Q6;* Cler. *Q1*
17 s.p. **Thai.**] *Q4;* Thin. *Q1*
18 s.d. **Exeunt.**] *Rowe;* Exit. *Q1*

IV.Cho.

Act IV] *Malone*
1 s.p. **Gow.**] *Q4*
10 **her**] *Steevens conj.;* hie *Q1*
10 **th' heart**] *ed. (after Steevens conj.* the heart); the art *Q1*
14 **Seeks**] *Rowe;* Seeke *Q1*
15–6 **kind: . . . wench,**] *colon, Dyce conj.; Q1 is obviously corrupt, since the lack of rhyme breaks the couplet pattern; Steevens suggests reading:* kind hath our Cleon / One daughter, and a wench full grown,
17 **ripe**] *Q2;* right *Q1*
17 **rite**] *Collier;* sight *Q1*
21 **Be't**] *F3;* Beet *Q1*
21 **sleided**] *Malone;* sleded *Q1*
26 **night-bird**] *Malone;* night bed *Q1*
29 **Dian; still**] *Malone;* Dian still, *Q1*

44 **wrath]** *F3;* wrath. *Q1*
45 **blow.]** *Malone;* blow, *Q1*
48 **on]** *Q2;* one *Q1*

IV.i

IV.i] *Malone*
Location: *Malone (subs.)*
Scene largely prose in Q1, except for ll. 10–12, 21–9; as verse, basically Rowe
5 **lone]** *ed.;* loue *Q1*
19 **is]** is like *Q4*
24 **me.]** *Q4 (reading* You haue . . . me.); me? *Q1*
24 **favor's]** *Q4;* fauours *Q1*
33 **heart.]** *Q4 (subs.);* heart, *Q1*
45 **least.]** *Q4;* least, *Q1*
47 **while.]** *Q4 (subs.);* while, *Q1*
49 **s.d. Exit Dionyza.]** *Malone (after Rowe)*
51 **Was't]** *F3;* Wast *Q1*
52 **nurse]** *Q2;* nutse *Q1 (but* nurse *in Praetorius and Ashbee facsimiles may represent a corrected state)*
55 **endur'd]** *Rowe;* endured *Q1*
60 **ladder-tackle]** *hyphen, Rowe*
61 **canvas-climber]** *hyphen, Malone*
63 **stem]** *Malone;* sterne *Q1*
89 **life, come]** *Q2;* life Come, *Q1*
92 **s.d. Leonine runs away.]** *Malone*
94 **Half-part . . . half-part]** *hyphens, Malone*
95 **s.d. Marina . . . Pirates]** *ed. (after Pelican)*
99 **sea.]** *Rowe (subs.);* Sea, *Q1*

IV.ii

IV.ii] *Dyce*
Location: *Malone (subs.)*
o.s.d. Pander, Bawd, and Boult] *F3 (subs.)*
2 **Sir?]** *Dyce;* Sir. *Q1*
3 **Meteline]** *ed. (so Wilkins);* Mettelyne *Q1*
4 **much]** *Q2;* much much *Q1*
14 **bastards—]** *Dyce;* bastards, *Q1*
15 **eleven—]** *Malone;* eleuen. *Q1*
16 **Ay,]** *Malone;* I *Q1*
26 **chequins]** *Malone;* Checkins *Q1*
41 **virgin?]** *Q4;* virgin. *Q1*
42 **s.p. 1. Pirate.]** *Malone (after Rowe);* Sayler. *Q1*
54 **presently]** *Q2;* presenly *Q1*
56 **s.d. Exeunt . . . Pirates.]** *Malone*
64–7 **Alack . . . mother!]** *as verse, Q4; as prose, Q1*
74–5 **The . . . die.]** *as verse, Q4; as prose, Q1*
75 **was]** was like *Q4*
76 **pleasure]** *Q2;* peasure *Q1*
86 **Marry]** *Q4;* Marie *Q1*
88 **gosling]** *Q4;* Gosseling *Q1*
92 **s.d. Enter Boult.]** *Q4*
105 **i' the]** *Q4 (subs.);* ethe *Q1*
107 **he, he]** he *Q4*
115 **s.d. To Marina.]** *Globe*
116 **you. Mark]** *Malone;* you, marke *Q1*
120 **lovers; seldom]** *Malone;* Louers seldome, *Q1*
126 **s.p. Bawd.]** *F3;* Mari. *Q1*
150 **s.d. Exeunt.]** *F3;* Exit. *Q1*

IV.iii

IV.iii] *Dyce*
Location: *Dyce (subs., after Malone)*
1 **are]** *Q4;* ere *Q1*
4 **child]** *Q3;* chidle *Q1*
5–46 **Were . . . done.]** *as verse, Malone; as prose, Q1*
8–9 **earth I' th']** *Malone (subs.);* earth- / ith *Q1;* earth, in the *Q4*
11 **'t 'ad]** *ed. (after Dyce);* tad *Q1*
12 **fact]** *Dyce conj.;* face *Q1*
17 **pious]** *Mason conj. (so Wilkins);* impious *Q1*
19 **to.]** *Pope (subs.);* too, *Q1*
27 **prime]** *Dyce;* prince *Q1*
30 **know,]** *F3;* knowe *Q1*
31 **distain]** *Steevens conj.;* disdaine *Q1*
33 **Marina's]** *Q2 (subs.);* Marianas *Q1*
47 **dost]** *Q4;* doest *Q1*
49 **Y' are]** *Sisson;* Yere *Q1*
51 **s.d. Exeunt.]** *Rowe;* Exit. *Q4*

IV.iv

IV.iv] *Globe;* Actus Quartus. *F3*
o.s.d. Enter Gower] *F3*
o.s.d. before . . . Tharsus] *Malone*
3 **Making,]** *Malone;* Making *Q1*
8 **i' th']** *Steevens conj.;* with *Q1*
8 **you,]** *Malone (after F4);* you. *Q1*
9 **story.]** *Malone;* storie *Q1*
10 **the]** *Q2;* thy *Q1*
13–4 **along. Behind . . . mind,]** *Daniel conj.;* along behind, . . . mind. *Q1*
15 **Escanes]** *F3;* Escenes *Q1* (Eschines *Wilkins)*
17 **Well-sailing]** *hyphen, Malone*
18–9 **Tharsus— . . . on—]** *Malone;* Tharsus, thinke this . . . grone *Q1*
20 **gone.]** *F4 (subs.);* gone *Q1*
22 **s.d. Dumb Show]** *this heading from Malone*
22 **s.d. lamentation]** *Q2;* lamentatton *Q1*
22 **s.d. Then . . . Dionyza.]** *Globe (after Malone)*
23 **See]** *Dyce;* Gowr. See *Q1 (repeated s.p.)*
26 **o'ershow'r'd,]** *F4;* ore-showr'd. *Q1*
29 **puts . . . bears]** *Malone;* put . . . Sea he beares, *Q1*
30 **tears,]** *Rowe;* teares. *Q1*
31 **wit]** *Malone;* wit: *Q1*
31–3 **Now . . . Dionyza.]** Now take we our way / To the Epitaph for *Marina,* writ by *Dionizia. Q4 (Q3 had confused the lines by printing* wi : *[the* t *failing to print] and* write)
33 **s.d. Reads . . . monument.]** *Malone*
35 **Who . . . year.]** *following this line Wilkins gives:* In Natures garden, though by growth a Bud, Shee was the chiefest flower, she was good.
47 **ordered]** *Q4;* ordered; *Q1*
48 **scene]** *Malone;* Steare *Q1*
49 **well-a-day]** *F4 (subs.);* welladay. *Q1*
51 **Metelin]** *ed.;* Mittelin *Q1*

IV.v

IV.v] *Malone*
Location: *Pelican (after Malone)*
6 **no.]** *Rowe (subs.);* no, *Q1*
9 **s.d. Exeunt.]** *F3;* Exit. *Q1*

IV.vi

IV.vi] *Malone*
Location: *ed. (after Pelican)*
o.s.d. Enter . . . Boult.] *Malone (subs.);* Enter Bawdes 3. *Q1*
9 **puritan]** *Q4;* Puri-/taine *Q1 (in italics)*
12 **cavalleria]** *anon. conj. (in Cambridge);* Caualereea *Q1*
13 **green-sickness]** *hyphen, Rowe*
23 **may so,]** *Q4;* may, so *Q1*
38 **s.d. Exit.]** *Craig (after Dyce)*
39 **dignifies]** *Q4;* dignities *Q1*
41–7 **Here . . . presently.]** *as prose, Malone; as verse, Q1*
42 **s.d. Enter . . . Marina.]** *Dyce (after Q4* Enter Marina.)
49 **s.d. Aside to Marina.]** *Malone (subs.)*
65 **s.d. Exeunt . . . Boult.]** *Malone (after Q4* Exit Baud.)
69 **name't]** *F3;* name *Q1*
77 **Why,]** *Malone;* Why? *Q1*
79–116] *The following passage from Wilkins may well contain a more faithful account of Shakespeare's original development of the episode than Q1 (note the so-called verse fossils in the prose):* Then gentle Sir, quoth shee, since heauen hath been so gratious, to restore me from death, let not their good to me, be a meanes for you, to be author of my more misfortune. But the Gouernour suspecting these teares, but to be some new cunning, which her matron the Bawde had instructed her in, to drawe him to a more large expence: He as freely tolde her so, and now beganne to be more rough with her, vrging her, that he was the Gouernour, whose authoritie coulde wincke at those blemishes, her selfe, and that sinnefull house could cast vppon her, or his displeasure punish at his owne pleasure, which displeasure of mine, thy beauty shall not priuiledge thee from, nor my affection, which hath drawen me vnto this place abate, if thou with further lingering withstand me. By which wordes, she vnderstanding him to be as confident in euill, as she was constant in good, she intreated him but to be heard, and thus she beganne. / If as you say (my Lorde) you are the Gouernour, let not your authoritie, which should teach you to rule others, be the meanes to make you mis-gouerne your selfe: If the eminence of your place came vnto you by discent, and the royalty of your blood, let not your life prooue your birth a bastard: If it were throwne vpon you by opinion, make good, that opinion was the cause to make you great. What reason is there in your Iustice, who hath power ouer all, to vndoe any? If you take from mee mine honour, you are like him, that make a gappe into forbidden ground, after whome too many enter, and you are guiltie of all their euilles: my life is yet vnspotted, my chastitie vnstained in thought. Then if your violence deface this building, the workemanship of heauen, made vp for good, and not to be the exercise of sinnes intemperaunce, you do kill your owne honour, abuse your owne iustice, and impouerish me. Why quoth *Lysimachus,* this house wherein thou liuest, is euen the receptacle of all mens sinnes, and nurse of wickednesse, and how canst thou then be otherwise than naught, that liuest in it? It is not good, answered *Marina,* when you that are the Gouernour, who should liue well, the better to be bolde to punish euill, doe knowe that there is such a roofe, and yet come vnder it. Is there a necessitie (my yet good Lord) if there be fire before me, that I must strait then thither flie and burne my selfe? Or if suppose this house, (which too too many feele such houses are) should be the Doctors patrimony, and Surgeons feeding; folowes it therefore, that I must needs infect my self to giue them maintenance? O my good Lord, kill me, but not deflower me, punish me how you please, so you spare my chastitie, and since it is all the dowry that both the Gods haue giuen, and men haue left to me, do not you take it from me; make me your seruant, I will willingly obey you; make mee your bondwoman, I will accompt it freedome; let me be the worst that is called vile, so I may still liue honest, I am content: or if you thinke it is too blessed a happinesse to haue me so, let me euen now, now in this minute die, and Ile accompt my death more happy than my birth. With which wordes (being spoken vpon her knees) while her eyes were the glasses that carried the water of her mis-hap, the good Gentlewoman being mooued, hee lift her vp with his hands, and euen then imbraced her in his hart, saying aside: Now surely this is Virtues image, or rather, Vertues selfe, sent downe from heauen, a while to raigne on earth, to teach vs what we should be. So in steede of willing her to drie her eyes, he wiped the wet himselfe off, and could haue found in his heart, with modest thoughts to haue kissed her, but that hee feared the offer would offend her. This onely hee sayde, Lady, for such your vertues are, a farre more worthy stile your beuty challenges, and no way lesse your beauty can promise me that you are, I hither came with thoughtes intemperate, foule and deformed, the which your paines so well hath laued, that they are now white, continue still to all so, and for my parte, who hither came but to haue payd the price, a peece of golde for your virginitie, now giue you twenty to releeue your

honesty. It shall become you still to be euen as you are, a peece of goodnesse, the best wrought vppe, that euer Nature made, and if that any shall inforce you ill, if you but send to me, I am your friend.

87 aloof] *Rowe;* aloft *Q1*
92–116 If . . . good.] *as verse, Rowe; as prose, Q1*
99 That] O that *Q4*
108–9 For . . . That] For my part, *Q4*
115 dost] *Q4;* doest *Q1*
116 s.d. Enter Boult.] *Dyce (after Malone)*
118–20 Avaunt . . . Away!] *as verse, Rowe; as prose, Q1*
119 doth] *Q4;* doeth *Q1*
120 s.d. Exit.] *Rowe*
129 ways] *Dyce;* way *Q1*
130 s.d. Bawd and Pander] *Maxwell*
134 abominable] *F3;* abhominable *Q1*
135 She] *Rowe;* He *Q1*
137 Marry] *Q4;* Marie *Q1 (in italics)*
138, 139 nobleman] *Q4;* Noble man *Q1*
150 womenkind] *Q2 (subs.);* wemen-kinde *Q1*
151 s.d. Exeunt . . . Pander.] *Maxwell (after Q4* Exit.)
152 ways] *F3;* way *Q1*
161 ff.] *Marina's speeches as verse, Rowe; as prose, Q1*
166 Custrel] *Kittredge;* custerell *Q1*
175 common shores] *Globe;* common-shores *Q1*
179 That] Oh, that *Q4*
191 doth] *Q4;* doeth *Q1*
194 women] *Q3;* woman *Q1*

V.Cho.

Act V] *Malone*
1 s.p. Gow.] *Malone*
2 honest house] *Q4;* Honest-house *Q1 (in italics)*
6 berry,] *F3;* berry. *Q1*
7 roses;] *Malone;* Roses *Q1*
8 silk,] *Q2;* Silke *Q1*
8 twin] *Malone;* Twine, *Q1*
11 Here] Leaue *Q4*
13 on . . . lost] *Malone;* on the Sea, wee there him left *Q1;* at sea, tumbled and tost *Q4*
14 Where] And *Q4*
17 annual] *Q4;* Annuall *Q1 (in italics)*
20 hies.] *Q4;* hyes, *Q1*
21 sight:] *Malone (subs.);* sight, *Q1*
23 more,] *Malone;* more *Q1*

V.i

V.i] *Malone*
Scene is prose in Q1 through prevented. *l. 64, verse to* wish. *l. 75, and thereafter a mixture of prose and irregular verse; converted to verse largely by Malone, a few lines by Rowe, Steevens, and Collier*
o.s.d. On . . . couch.] *Malone*
o.s.d. one . . . Mytilene] *ed. (after Malone)*
1, 11 s.pp. Tyr. Sail.] *Malone;* 1. Say. *Q1*
1 s.d. To . . . Mytilene.] *Malone*
2–3 is.—Sir,] *Rowe (subs.);* is Sir, *Q1*
3, 175, 186, 219 Meteline] *ed.;* Metaline *Q1*
7 s.p. Tyr. Sail.] *Malone;* 2. Say. *Q1*
8 Doth] *Q2;* Doeth *Q1*
10 s.d. Exeunt . . . Sailors.] *Kittredge (after Malone)*
10 s.d. and . . . Sailor] *Malone (subs., entering also the second sailor)*
16 well.] *F3 (subs.);* well, *Q1*
33 bootless is] *Q4;* bootlesse. Is *Q1*
33 sight; he] *Malone;* sight, hee *Q1 (c);* sight see, *Q1 (u)*
35 s.p. Lys.] *Q4 (om.* Yet*); line continued to Helicanus, Q1*
36 s.p. Hel.] *Q4;* Lys. *Q1*
36 s.d. Pericles discovered.] *Malone*
37 Till] *Q4; Hell.* Till *Q1*
37 night,] *Malone;* wight *Q1*
42 s.p. 1. Lord.] *Malone;* Lord. *Q1*
43 Meteline] *ed.;* Metiliue *Q1;* Metaline *Q2*
47 deafen'd] *Malone;* defend *Q1*
50 with] *Malone*
50 is] *Malone*
52 s.d. Gives . . . out.] *Kittredge (subs., after Malone)*
63 s.p. Hel.] *Q2;* Holl. *Q1*
64 s.d. Enter . . . Lady.] *Kittredge (after Malone);* Enter Marina. *Q2*
65–6 one!—Is't] *Q4 (subs.);* one, ist *Q1*
66 presence] *Malone;* present *Q1*
69 I'd] *Q4;* I do *Q1*
70 one] *Malone;* on *Q1*
72 feat] *Percy conj.;* fate *Q1*
79 s.d. They withdraw.] *Maxwell*
79 s.d. Marina sings] *Malone (an inferior 20-line song appears at this point in Twine and Wilkins)*
80 s.d. Advances.] *Maxwell*
80 Mark'd] *Q4;* Marke *Q1*
83 s.d. Pushing . . . back.] *Cambridge conj. (suggested by l. 100 and by Wilkins'* in this rash distemperature, strucke her on the face*)*
86 gaz'd] *Malone;* gazed *Q1*
87 endur'd] *Malone;* endured *Q1*
91 equivalent] *F4;* equiuolent *Q1*
93 awkward] *Q2;* augward *Q1*
94 s.d. Aside.] *Malone*
97–8 fortunes— . . . mine—] *Malone (subs.);* fortunes, parentage, good parentage, to equall mine, *Q1*
102 You're] *Sisson;* your *Q1;* y'are *Q4*
102 that—What] *Malone;* that, what *Q1*
102 country-woman?] Q6 *(question mark, Malone);* Countrey women *Q1*
103 Here . . . shores? . . . shores,] *Malone (from Charlemont conj.);* heare . . . shewes? / . . . shewes, *Q1*
109 wand-like straight] *Q4;* wandlike-straight *Q1*
111 cas'd] *Malone;* caste *Q1*
114 stranger.] *Pope (subs.);* straunger *Q1;* stranger, *Q6*
121 palace] *Malone (after Lillo's adaptation);* Pallas *Q1 (in italics; a barely possible reading)*
123 my] *Q4*
125 lov'd] *Rowe;* loued *Q1*
126 say] *Malone;* stay *Q1*
126–7 back— . . . thee—] *Malone (subs.);* backe, . . thee *Q1*
131 thoughts'] *Maxwell;* thoughts *Q1;* thought'st *F3*
137 dost] *Q4;* doest *Q1*
140 thou them? Thy] *Malone;* thou thy *Q1*
146 dost] *Pope;* doest *Q1*
149 daughter?] *Steevens;* daughter, *Q1*
154 Motion? Well] *F3;* Motion well *Q1*
156 sea!] *Q4;* sea, *Q1*
159 Lychorida] *Q4;* Licherida *Q1*
161 s.d. Aside.] *Malone*
161 dull'd] *Maxwell;* duld *Q1;* dull *Q4*
163 daughter—buried!] *F3 (subs.);* daughter, buried; *Q1*
166 scorn.] *Dyce (subs.);* scorne, *Q1*
178 daughter] *Q2;* dsughter *Q1*
180 s.p. Per.] *Q4;* Hell. *Q1*
188 parentage; being] *F4 (subs.);* parentage, Being *Q1*
188 demanded that,] *Q4;* demaunded, that *Q1*
200 me but that,] *Q4;* me, but that *Q1*
202 First] *Q2;* Frist *Q1*
207 life] *Mason conj.;* like *Q1*
210 Thaisa?] *Q4;* Thaisa, *Q1*
214 garments.] *Malone;* garments, *Q1*
214 own,] *Steevens;* owne *Q1*
223–4 music? Tell] *Steevens (after Malone);* Musicke tell, *Q1*
228 None?] *Q4;* None, *Q1*
235 s.d. Sleeps.] *Malone (subs.)*
239 s.d. Exeunt . . . Pericles.] *Dyce (after Malone)*
239 s.d. Diana . . . vision.] *Globe (after Rowe);* Diana. *Q1;* Actus Quintus. / Diana. *F3*
246 life] *Malone (Charlemont conj.);* like *Q1*
248 bow!] *Dyce;* bow, *Q1*
249 s.d. Disappears.] *Malone (subs.)*
250 argentine] *Malone;* Argentine *Q1 (in italics)*
251 thee.] *Q4 (subs.);* thee *Q1*
251 s.d. Enter . . . Marina.] *Dyce (after Malone)*
251 Sir?] *Dyce;* Sir. *Q1*
256 s.d. To Lysimachus.] *Malone*
261 suit] *Malone;* sleight *Q1*

V.ii

V.ii] *Staunton*
o.s.d. The . . . attending.] *Malone (subs.) for V.iii; placed as in Maxwell*
o.s.d. Enter Gower.] *Q4*
8–9 Metelin, . . . King.] *Q4 (subs.;* Metelin *ed.);* Metalin. . . King, *Q1*
12 sacrifice,] *Q4;* sacrifice. *Q1*
13 bade;] *Rowe (subs.);* bad, *Q1*
14 interim, pray you,] *Malone;* Interim pray, you *Q1 (*Interim *in italics)*
15 fill'd] *F3;* fild *Q1*
16 will'd] *F3;* wild *Q1*
20 fancies'] *W. S. Walker conj.;* fancies *Q1*
20 s.d. Exit.] *Q4*

V.iii

V.iii] *Malone*
Location: *ed. (after Maxwell)*
o.s.d. Enter . . . Lady.] *Malone (after Q4)*
3–82 Who . . . reign.] *as verse, Rowe; as prose, Q1*
14 s.d. Faints.] *Rowe (subs.)*
15 nun] *Collier;* mum *Q1;* woman *Q4*
28–9 look! If] *Malone (after Rowe);* looke if *Q1*
37 Immortal] *Q4;* I mortall *Q1*
39 s.d. Points . . . ring.] *Cowden Clarke*
40 this . . . gods!] *Malone (subs.);* this, . . . gods, *Q1*
45 s.d. Kneels to Thaisa.] *Malone*
50 s.p. Per.] *F3;* Hell. *Q1*
59–60 lord; . . . power;] *Malone;* Lord, . . . power, *Q1*
69 I] *Malone*
70 Night-oblations] *hyphen, Malone*
70 thee.] *Q4 (subs.);* thee *Q1*
71 fair-betrothed] *hyphen, Malone*
77 credit,] *Q4;* credit. *Q1*
79 Heavens] *so Q1, but catchword reads* Heauen
84 s.d. Exeunt.] *Q4* (Exeunt omnes.); *Q1 reads* FINIS. *(and again after l. 102)*
84 s.d. Enter] *Q4*
85 s.p. Gow.] *Malone*
87 Pericles,] *Rowe;* Pericles *Q1*
88 keen,] *Q2;* keene. *Q1*
89 preserv'd] *Malone (after 1734 ed.);* preferd *Q1*
90 Led] *Q2;* Lead *Q1*
99 seemed] *Q4;* seemde *Q1*
102 s.d. Exit.] *Malone;* FINIS. *Q1*

Cymbeline

CYMBELINE is set in the same pre-Christian, semi-legendary period of English history as *King Lear*. The gods are Roman gods, and the chief of them, Jupiter, appears in the play in a spectacular vision scene, to assure the hero of his eventual happiness. The ways of the gods are mysterious, but they are beneficent in the end, and the penitent hero and patient heroine will find themselves reunited in happiness after many hazardous adventures.

Laud we the gods,
And let our crooked smokes climb to their nostrils
From our blest altars

is the benediction spoken by the King at the end of the play.

Cymbeline was first published in the Folio of 1623 as the last play in that volume; it is there classified as a tragedy, which of course it is not, but the Folio has no category called Romances. The two other romances included in it appear among the Comedies, *The Tempest* first and *The Winter's Tale* last in that section; perhaps it was thought that a play with a British king as its title character belonged to the more elevated genre of tragedy, despite its happy ending. *Cymbeline* follows *Pericles* in the order of composition, and it is probably a little, but not much, earlier in date than *The Winter's Tale*; 1609–10 cannot be far wrong. The first reference to it is by Dr. Simon Forman, who saw a performance sometime before his death in September 1611—perhaps between April 20 and 30 of that year, since his recollections of the performance are recorded in his journal between two entries bearing those dates. (See Appendix C, Number 20, below) Shakespeare's company acquired the Blackfriars as a private theatre in 1608, and the plays of the next few years, *Cymbeline*, *The Winter's Tale*, and *The Tempest*, doubtless reflect a deliberate policy to present plays which would be popular both there and in the public theatre, the Globe, where Dr. Forman saw *Cymbeline* and *The Winter's Tale*. That *Cymbeline* pleased courtly tastes is suggested by the second reference we have to it, in the office book of the Master of the Revels for January 1, 1634, which states that the play was performed at court on that date by the King's players and was well liked by the King.

The tradition to which *Cymbeline* belongs is that of romance, and examples of the type can be found in both popular and courtly literature. The prologue to an old play of the Queen's players, *Sir Clyomon and Clamydes*, published in 1599 but apparently written ten or fifteen years before that, describes the general nature of the type:

Wherein the froward chances oft, of Fortune
  you shall see,
Wherein the cheerful countenance of good successes be;
Wherein true lovers findeth joy, with hugie
  heaps of care,
Wherein as well as famous facts, ignomious
  placed are;
Wherein the just reward of both is manifestly
  shown,
That virtue from the root of vice might openly
  be known.

This crude and naive play has some interesting resemblances to *Cymbeline*. In it there is a cowardly knight who goes to seek his lady wearing the armor of his successful rival, as Cloten searches for Imogen in the wilds of Wales dressed in the clothing of Posthumus. A princess finds a grave which she mistakenly thinks is that of her lover, as Imogen thinks the headless body of Cloten is that of her husband Posthumus. She is about to kill herself when Providence descends and prevents her, much as Jupiter descends to reassure Posthumus. She dresses as a page, and in this disguise uses a French name, just as Imogen gives the name Richard du Champ for her deceased master.

Another old play, *The Rare Triumphs of Love and Fortune*, performed in 1582 and printed in 1589, is also an example of dramatic romance which has striking resemblances to *Cymbeline*. The lovers are named Fidelia and Hermione (whence perhaps Fidele of *Cymbeline* and—the name being changed from a man's to a woman's—Hermione of *The Winter's Tale*). Fidelia is a princess, like Imogen, and Hermione an orphan brought up at court, like Posthumus. A villain gets the hero banished, and Fidelia, journeying to meet him, receives hospitality in a cave from a courtier who had been wrongfully banished by her father. The plot situations and even the characters in *Cymbeline* were accordingly familiar fare for Shakespeare's audience, and the strange, even absurd improbabilities that trouble a modern reader were common and acceptable.

Shakespeare had recently turned to the greatest Elizabethan prose romance, Sidney's *Arcadia*, for the subplot of *King Lear*, and the reading of that aristocratic romance perhaps suggested to him that the material of the old romantic plays could be transformed into something suitable for both courtly and popular audiences. The old play *Mucedorus*, based upon the *Arcadia*, was acted, with some additions, before the King at Whitehall on Shrove Sunday night in 1610 by Shakespeare's company. Perhaps its comedy and some such spectacular business as a live bear helped it to regain favor, but it maintained its position as "the most popular Elizabethan play" by its utilization of good old reliable romance motifs.

A romantic plot could appropriately be set in the earliest period of British history as Shakespeare read of it in Holinshed's *Chronicles*. The legendary Brutus, after whom Britain was supposedly named, had a wife named Innogen (which Forman says is the name of Shakespeare's heroine) and a grandfather named Posthumus. In his third book Holinshed tells of Cymbeline or Kymbeline, who ruled about the time of Christ and who was brought up in Rome and knighted by Augustus Caesar there. In his "History of Scotland," which Shakespeare had read for *Macbeth*, Holinshed mentions the sending of an embassy from Augustus to Cymbeline, and he also tells the story of a ploughman and his two sons who turn the tide of battle ("A narrow lane, an old man, and two boys"). Shakespeare drew some further details from *A Mirror for Magistrates* (1578 and 1587 eds.).

The first dramatic development in *Cymbeline*, after the banishment of Posthumus, is the wager on the question of Imogen's fidelity to her husband. This popular motif, widespread in medieval literature, is best known as the ninth story of the second day in Boccaccio's *Decameron*. No English translation was available to Shakespeare, but he could have read the tale in a French rendering, if not in Italian; he certainly read the English translation of a German version of it called *Frederick of Jennen*. Modern critics have often found the situation a distasteful one, for, as W. W. Lawrence says, "Nowadays we feel that to give a villain a chance to attempt to seduce one's wife, for the sake of proving to him and to others her unassailable chastity, would be the height of folly, and of cruelty to her. But the Middle Ages thought otherwise; they believed that a virtue exaggerated, as it seems to us, beyond reason, was a virtue magnified." Accordingly, the character of Posthumus should be viewed in a chivalric context, and his behavior, up to the time he is deceived by the villain Jachimo, considered fully worthy of the high reputation he enjoys in Britain and abroad. Such plot devices from an older convention had been used by Shakespeare in the so-called "problem comedies" such as *All's Well* and *Measure for Measure*, and the consequences of the wager provide particularly appropriate material for the typical stage effects of romance or tragicomedy.

It was formerly thought that Beaumont and Fletcher, the great practitioners and definers of tragicomedy on the Jacobean stage, had influenced Shakespeare by the success of their play *Philaster* to try the same sort of thing in *Cymbeline*, *The Winter's Tale*, and *The Tempest*. But it now seems that the influence, if any, was the other way. For *Pericles* probably comes before *Philaster*, and *Cymbeline* develops naturally from *Pericles*. Furthermore the characteristic effects of tragicomedy as practiced by Beaumont and Fletcher are different from those produced by Shakespeare. In *Philaster* there is a pervasive feeling of the presence of evil in a courtly-pastoral environment; innocence and virtue live as close neighbors to the kind of vice that incites the satirist's sharpest lines. The events are sensational, as indeed they are in *Cymbeline*, but Beaumont and Fletcher depend upon surprise whereas Shakespeare depends upon the more complex effects of awareness and anticipation. The audience knows that Guiderius and Arviragus are Imogen's brothers, though the three of them do not; it knows while the dirge is sung that Imogen is not dead, though the singers do not; it knows that the headless body dressed in Posthumus' clothes is Cloten's, though Imogen does not. In *Philaster* the hero stabs the page, Bellario, in a fit of insane jealousy, and neither he nor the audience knows until afterward that Bellario is really a woman in disguise. Tragicomedy of this sort verges on melodrama, but in Shakespeare's play, though it contains sensational incidents enough—a princess in disguise finding her long-lost brothers in the mountains of Wales, an Italian villain hiding in a chest in a lady's bedroom, the taking of a medicine which, as in *Romeo and Juliet*, produces apparent death, the descent of Jupiter on an eagle in answer to the prayers of the ghosts of the hero's parents, the defeat of a Roman army by an old man and two boys in a narrow lane—the tone and atmosphere of the play produce a mood of reconciliation to things as they are.

Theodore Spencer contrasted these late plays with Shakespeare's tragedies. "In the tragedies," he says, "the appearance might be good, but the reality—the lust of Gertrude, the hypocrisy of Goneril and Regan, the crown of Scotland, and, to Timon, all mankind—was evil. In the last plays the appearance may be evil, but the reality is good." The reconciliation of Imogen with her husband and father, the reunion of Cymbeline with his long-lost sons and their faithful guardian, the harmonious settlement of the quarrel with Rome, all take place in a surprising way and yet as if it were all perfectly natural. The course of events is a riddle—the lion's whelp embracing tender air and an old oak regaining its lost branches—but the outcome is serenity itself: "Britain be fortunate and flourish in peace and plenty."

The play is not tightly constructed. It has two plots, the story of what happened to the princess Imogen and the story of what happened to her brothers. Although the two strands meet when Imogen and then Cloten come to Belarius' cave, there is little interaction until, just before the end, all the characters are brought geographically together and the audience can watch, with a kind of amused wonder, the unravelling of all the misunderstandings. Hazlitt praised V.v as one of the great revelation scenes:

> The business of the plot evidently thickens in the last act: the story moves forward with increasing rapidity at every step; its various ramifications are drawn from the most distant points to the same centre; the principal characters are brought together, and placed in very crucial situations; and the fate of almost every person in the drama is made to depend on the solution of a single circumstance—the answer of Iachimo to the question of Imogen respecting the obtaining of the ring from Posthumus.

The lack of connection between the plots means that once the wager story is complete, Posthumus, who is supposed to be the hero, is off the stage for a remarkably long time. But the neglect of the hero means more attention to the heroine, and nineteenth-century critics who could not abide the play fell in love with Imogen. She is one of Shakespeare's good women, loving and faithful, patient to an almost incredible degree, but sharp at seeing the flaws in a seducer's arguments and vigorous in defense of the dignity of a princess. Yet she wistfully notes how tired she gets on her way to Milford, and she swears pretty feminine oaths like " 'Od's pittikins." The name she adopts in her disguise as a page, Fidele, is the true emblem of her character.

The evil in *Cymbeline* is not of the profound kind Shakespeare explores in the tragedies. The villains Cloten and his mother the Queen are easily disposed of by the natural forces which seem to guarantee the eventual triumph of virtue and peace. Cloten, whose name is pronounced *Clotten* to rhyme with *rotten* and to permit the word-play on *clotpole* (IV.ii.184), is a combination of absurd vanity and boorishness; he is a bully and a numbskull. "Not Hercules could have knocked out his brains, for he had none" (IV.ii.114–15). His closest relation is Thurio in *The Two Gentlemen of Verona*. His mother, an amateur pharmacist who poisons dogs and cats for practice and for fun, is closer to the cruel stepmother of folk tales than she is to Lady Macbeth. Indeed, the play's closest correspondence with *Macbeth* is found in the philosophic gaoler of Act V, who, with his reflections on drink and on life and death, is a fellow of the Porter in the earlier play.

Jachimo is required by the story of the wager to play a villain's part, and he is an Italian. But he is no Iago, with a reputation for plain-speaking and honesty to hide the deepest venom of the human heart. Jachimo is a cavalier, adept at flowery speech, a sportsman under the Italian code, who looks down upon the British and finds himself beaten in the battle by what looks like the humblest of them. But even though he is an Italian, he is a gentleman, "bold Jachimo," brother of the Duke of Siena; he is capable of repentance and deserving of forgiveness from a generous adversary.

Some modern critics of the play, including Granville-Barker, find Shakespeare's technique faulty with respect to the soliloquies, especially those of minor characters. Pisanio's soliloquy at IV.iii.36–46 is a summary of the situation, in the manner of the oldest convention of soliloquy, but it is also of thematic value: "The heavens still must work"; "Fortune brings in some boats that are not steer'd." There must be no impatience with the slow, complicated working-out of the ways of Fortune. Moreover, Pisanio is under suspicion as a servant who shifts his loyalties, and the audience must not mistake him for a double-dealer such as Subtle Shift in *Sir Clyomon and Clamydes*. So he justifies himself: "Wherein I am false, I am honest; not true, to be true." Granville-Barker sees Shakespeare's development as leading to the use of the soliloquy as "a vehicle for the intimate thought and emotion of his chief characters only, and to let its plot-forwarding seem quite incidental to this." But in the romances there are diverse plot-elements which can only be conveyed in soliloquy; often the traditional romantic play used them in a very naive and overinformative way. An audience that had seen *Sir Clyomon and Clamydes*, *The Rare Triumphs of Love and Fortune*, and *Mucedorus* would not be concerned over the long expository soliloquy of Belarius (III.iii.79–107) which explains the meaning of the first Welsh scene, provides information about the beginning of the whole story, and at last tells us why this play is called *Cymbeline*. We should not attribute to a weakening of Shakespeare's powers, or to his supposed boredom (imagined by Lytton Strachey), dramatic traits that simply come from a different tradition.

The plot is complex, but the characters are not. The play can be theatrically effective. Much depends upon the atmosphere. It is a strange and distant world, though in it there appear oddly familiar touches of character and behavior. *Cymbeline* is an example of what Marianne Moore has described as poetic creation —"imaginary gardens with real toads in them."

The poetry of *Cymbeline* is most explicit in the two incomparable songs, "Hark, hark, the lark," usually considered the finest aubade in the English language, and the poignant dirge for the supposedly dead Fidele, "Fear no more the heat o' th' sun," quite possibly the most resonant lyric lines Shakespeare ever composed. The verse of the dialogue is typical of Shakespeare's last period. The rhythm is loose, the images are freer and less integrated than in the tragedies. The adaptability of the verse to scene-painting, character portrayal, and action, often mixed together, is very remarkable. A good example is Jachimo's speech in Imogen's bedroom, II.ii.11–51.

'Tis her breathing that
Perfumes the chamber thus. The flame o' th' taper
Bows toward her, and would under-peep her lids,
To see th' enclosed lights, now canopied
Under these windows, white and azure lac'd
With blue of heaven's own tinct.

Here is the scene evoked by poetic description. It is followed immediately by the dramatic, psychologically persuasive irregularity of

But my design!
To note the chamber, I will write all down:
Such and such pictures; there the window; such
Th' adornment of her bed; the arras, figures,
Why, such and such; and the contents o' th' story.

The speech ends with a rhetorical flamboyance reminiscent of *Macbeth* and Marlowe's *Faustus*:

Swift, swift, you dragons of the night, that dawning
May bare the raven's eye! I lodge in fear;
Though this a heavenly angel, hell is here.

Perhaps nothing is sustained in *Cymbeline*, but there is plenty of variety of mood and tone and poetic intensity. There is imagery from a variety of sources: birds, as when Posthumus is referred to as an eagle and Imogen is thought of as a phoenix; commercial transactions, buying, selling, going into debt, perhaps because in Boccaccio and *Frederick of Jennen* the participants in the wager episode were merchants; trees and fruit, as when old Belarius describes his fall from Cymbeline's favor,

Then was I as a tree
Whose boughs did bend with fruit; but in one night,
A storm or robbery (call it what you will)
Shook down my mellow hangings, nay, my leaves,
And left me bare to weather. (III.iii.60–64)

And the reunion embrace of Posthumus and Imogen is marked by

Hang there like fruit, my soul,
Till the tree die! (V.v.263–64)

The variety and vitality of the imagery in the play enhance its poetic, as distinct from dramatic, interest. One is not surprised that it was Tennyson's favorite among all of Shakespeare's plays.

The closer attention paid to imagery and style in recent years and perhaps also a less proprietary attitude toward Shakespeare have now resulted in a general willingness to attribute all of *Cymbeline* to him. Earlier critics often wished to attribute the vision scene to another writer, because of its doggerel verse. But Shakespeare was quite capable of writing this kind of verse for a special purpose, and the pageant-like character of the scene no doubt explains that special purpose. Furthermore, the continuity of image and vocabulary between the vision and other scenes strongly suggests that they are all by the same hand.

The unity of *Cymbeline* was apparent to Bernard Shaw, who nevertheless wrote a substitute fifth act for the play in order to bring it to an end without such absurdities as the identification of a long-lost child by a birthmark, a plot device so stale that it was ridiculed in nineteenth-century farce. "Plot has always been the curse of serious drama," wrote Shaw,

and indeed of serious literature of any kind. It is so out of place there that Shakespear never could invent one. Unfortunately, instead of taking Nature's hint and discarding plots, he borrowed them all over the place and got into trouble through having to unravel them in the last act. The more childish spectators may find some delight in the revelation that Polydore and Cadwal are Imogen's long-lost brothers and Cymbeline's long-lost sons; that Iachimo is now an occupant of the penitent form and very unlike his old self; and that Imogen is so dutiful that she accepts her husband's attempt to have her murdered with affectionate docility. I cannot share these infantile joys.

Whether these plot developments are "infantile joys" or not, they are the very stuff of romance, and anyone who reads romance for what it is, or sees it in the theatre for what it distinctively offers, must accept them.

Hallett Smith

Cymbeline

[Dramatis Personae

Cymbeline, *King of Britain*
Cloten, *son to the Queen by a former husband*
Posthumus Leonatus, *a gentleman, husband to Imogen*
Belarius, *a banished lord disguised under the name of Morgan*
Guiderius, Arviragus — *sons to Cymbeline, disguised under the names of Polydore and Cadwal, supposed sons to Morgan*
Philario, *friend to Posthumus*; Jachimo, *friend to Philario* — *Italians*
Caius Lucius, *general of the Roman forces*
Pisanio, *servant to Posthumus*
Cornelius, *a physician*
Philarmonus, *a soothsayer*
Roman Captain

Two British Captains
Frenchman, *friend to Philario*
Two Lords *of Cymbeline's court*
Two Gentlemen *of the same*
Two Jailers

Apparitions

Queen, *wife to Cymbeline*
Imogen, *daughter to Cymbeline by a former Queen*
Helen, *a lady attending on Imogen*

Lords, Ladies, Roman Senators, Tribunes, Dutchman, Spaniard, Musicians, Officers, Captains, Soldiers, Messengers, *and other* Attendants

Scene: *Britain; Italy*]

ACT I, Scene I

Enter two Gentlemen.

1. Gent. You do not meet a man but frowns. Our bloods
No more obey the heavens than our courtiers'
Still seem as does the King's.
2. Gent. But what's the matter?
1. Gent. His daughter, and the heir of 's kingdom (whom
He purpos'd to his wive's sole son—a widow
That late he married), hath referr'd herself
Unto a poor but worthy gentleman. She's wedded,
Her husband banish'd, she imprison'd: all
Is outward sorrow, though I think the King
Be touch'd at very heart.
2. Gent. None but the King?
1. Gent. He that hath lost her too; so is the Queen,
That most desir'd the match. But not a courtier,
Although they wear their faces to the bent
Of the King's looks, hath a heart that is not
Glad at the thing they scowl at.
2. Gent. And why so?
1. Gent. He that hath miss'd the Princess is a thing
Too bad for bad report; and he that hath her
(I mean, that married her, alack, good man!
And therefore banish'd) is a creature such
As, to seek through the regions of the earth
For one his like, there would be something failing
In him that should compare. I do not think
So fair an outward and such stuff within
Endows a man but he.
2. Gent. You speak him far.
1. Gent. I do extend him, sir, within himself,
Crush him together rather than unfold
His measure duly.
2. Gent. What's his name and birth?
1. Gent. I cannot delve him to the root: his father
Was call'd Sicilius, who did join his honor
Against the Romans with Cassibelan,
But had his titles by Tenantius, whom
He serv'd with glory and admir'd success:
So gain'd the sur-addition Leonatus;

Words and passages enclosed in square brackets in the text above are either emendations of the copy-text or additions to it. The Textual Notes immediately following the play cite the earliest authority for every such change or insertion and supply the reading of the copy-text wherever it is emended in this edition.

I.i. Location: Britain. The grounds of Cymbeline's palace.
1–2. **Our . . . heavens:** our dispositions do not reflect more completely the influence of the heavenly bodies.
2. **courtiers':** i.e. courtiers' faces (see lines 12–14).
5. **purpos'd to:** intended for. **wive's:** wife's.
6. **referr'd:** assigned, given. 13. **bent:** inclination, cast.
22. **him . . . compare:** the man chosen as comparable with him.
23. **stuff:** substance; but the sense "fabric" leads into the figure of lines 26–27. 24. **speak him far:** go far in praising him.
25. **I . . . himself:** i.e. I go far yet stay well within the bounds of his merits. 28. **delve . . . root:** give a full account of his lineage.
29. **honor:** military prowess.
33. **sur-addition:** added name. **Leonatus:** lion-born.

And had (besides this gentleman in question)
Two other sons, who in the wars o' th' time
Died with their swords in hand; for which their father,
Then old and fond of issue, took such sorrow
That he quit being, and his gentle lady,
Big of this gentleman, our theme, deceas'd
As he was born. The King he takes the babe
To his protection, calls him Posthumus Leonatus,
Breeds him and makes him of his bedchamber,
Puts to him all the learnings that his time
Could make him the receiver of, which he took,
As we do air, fast as 'twas minist'red,
And in 's spring became a harvest; liv'd in court
(Which rare it is to do) most prais'd, most lov'd,
A sample to the youngest, to th' more mature
A glass that feated them, and to the graver
A child that guided dotards. To his mistress
(For whom he now is banish'd), her own price
Proclaims how she esteem'd him; and his virtue
By her election may be truly read,
What kind of man he is.

2. Gent. I honor him
Even out of your report. But pray you tell me,
Is she sole child to th' King?

1. Gent. His only child.
He had two sons (if this be worth your hearing,
Mark it), the eldest of them at three years old,
I' th' swathing clothes the other, from their nursery
Were stol'n, and to this hour no guess in knowledge
Which way they went.

2. Gent. How long is this ago?

1. Gent. Some twenty years.

2. Gent. That a king's children should be so convey'd,
So slackly guarded, and the search so slow,
That could not trace them!

1. Gent. Howsoe'er 'tis strange,
Or that the negligence may well be laugh'd at,
Yet is it true, sir.

2. Gent. I do well believe you.

1. Gent. We must forbear. Here comes the gentleman,
The Queen, and Princess. *Exeunt.*

Enter the Queen, Posthumus, *and* Imogen.

Queen. No, be assur'd you shall not find me, daughter,
After the slander of most stepmothers,
Evil-ey'd unto you. You're my prisoner, but
Your jailer shall deliver you the keys
That lock up your restraint. For you, Posthumus,
So soon as I can win th' offended King,
I will be known your advocate. Marry, yet
The fire of rage is in him, and 'twere good
You lean'd unto his sentence with what patience
Your wisdom may inform you.

Post. Please your Highness,
I will from hence to-day.

Queen. You know the peril.
I'll fetch a turn about the garden, pitying
The pangs of barr'd affections, though the King
Hath charg'd you should not speak together. *Exit.*

Imo. O
Dissembling courtesy! How fine this tyrant
Can tickle where she wounds! My dearest husband,
I something fear my father's wrath, but nothing
(Always reserv'd my holy duty) what
His rage can do on me. You must be gone,
And I shall here abide the hourly shot
Of angry eyes, not comforted to live,
But that there is this jewel in the world
That I may see again.

Post. My queen, my mistress!
O lady, weep no more, lest I give cause
To be suspected of more tenderness
Than doth become a man. I will remain
The loyall'st husband that did e'er plight troth.
My residence in Rome at one [Philario's],
Who to my father was a friend, to me
Known but by letter; thither write, my queen,
And with mine eyes I'll drink the words you send,
Though ink be made of gall.

Enter Queen.

Queen. Be brief, I pray you.
If the King come, I shall incur I know not
How much of his displeasure. [*Aside.*] Yet I'll move him
To walk this way. I never do him wrong
But he does buy my injuries, to be friends;
Pays dear for my offenses. [*Exit.*]

Post. Should we be taking leave
As long a term as yet we have to live,
The loathness to depart would grow. Adieu!

Imo. Nay, stay a little:
Were you but riding forth to air yourself,
Such parting were too petty. Look here, love,
This diamond was my mother's. Take it, heart,
But keep it till you woo another wife,
When Imogen is dead.

Post. How, how? another?
You gentle gods, give me but this I have,
And cere up my embracements from a next

37. fond of issue: doting on his children (?).
42. of his bedchamber: one of his personal attendants.
43. time: years, age. **48. sample**: example.
49. glass: mirror. **feated them**: "'reflected them as feat—i.e. elegant—', with the implication that they then proceeded to emulate what they saw" (Maxwell).
50. dotards: i.e. even the oldest (?). **To**: as for.
51. her own price: what she paid for him—her father's disfavor and its consequences. **53. election**: choice. **59. swathing**: swaddling.
60. in knowledge: leading to knowledge of (?).
63. convey'd: carried off, stolen.
66. laugh'd at: thought incredible. **68. forbear**: withdraw.
71. After the slander: in accordance with the slanderous repute.
74. your restraint: what restrains you, i.e. your prison.
76. Marry: indeed (originally the name of the Virgin Mary used as an oath). **78. lean'd unto**: bent to, obeyed.
79. inform you: imbue you with.
86. something . . . nothing: somewhat . . . not at all.
87. reserv'd: excepted. **duty**: i.e. duty as a wife (which the King could bring to an end by annulling the marriage).
90. not . . . live: finding no comfort in living.
93–95. lest . . . man: i.e. lest I weep too (*become* = befit).
105. buy . . . friends: i.e. mistake my injuries for benefits.
116. cere up: wrap in cerecloth (waxed linen used for burial garments); perhaps with play (as *bonds* in line 117 suggests) on sealing with wax.

With bonds of death! [*Puts on the ring.*] Remain, remain thou here,
While sense can keep it on. And, sweetest, fairest,
As I my poor self did exchange for you,
To your so infinite loss, so in our trifles
I still win of you. For my sake wear this:
It is a manacle of love, I'll place it
Upon this fairest prisoner.
[*Putting a bracelet upon her arm.*]

Imo. O the gods!
When shall we see again?

Enter CYMBELINE *and* LORDS.

Post. Alack, the King!

Cym. Thou basest thing, avoid hence, from my sight!
If after this command thou fraught the court
With thy unworthiness, thou diest. Away!
Thou'rt poison to my blood.

Post. The gods protect you,
And bless the good remainders of the court!
I am gone. *Exit.*

Imo. There cannot be a pinch in death
More sharp than this is.

Cym. O disloyal thing,
That shouldst repair my youth, thou heap'st
A year's age on me.

Imo. I beseech you, sir,
Harm not yourself with your vexation,
I am senseless of your wrath; a touch more rare
Subdues all pangs, all fears.

Cym. Past grace? obedience?

Imo. Past hope, and in despair, that way past grace.

Cym. That mightst have had the sole son of my queen!

Imo. O blessed, that I might not! I chose an eagle,
And did avoid a puttock.

Cym. Thou took'st a beggar, wouldst have made my throne
A seat for baseness.

Imo. No, I rather added
A lustre to it.

Cym. O thou vild one!

Imo. Sir,
It is your fault that I have lov'd Posthumus:
You bred him as my playfellow, and he is
A man worth any woman; overbuys me
Almost the sum he pays.

Cym. What? art thou mad?

Imo. Almost, sir: heaven restore me! Would I were

118. sense: sensory powers, ability to feel.
121. still: always. **125. avoid hence:** begone.
126. fraught: burden. **129. remainders of:** persons remaining at.
130. pinch: pang. **132. repair:** restore.
135. senseless of: insensible to. **touch more rare:** more exquisite pain (i.e. that of being parted from Posthumus).
136. grace: sense of duty. Imogen takes it up in the meaning "heavenly grace, redemption."
139. blessed. In antithesis with *past grace*, i.e. damned, in line 137. **might not:** was able not to.
140. puttock: kite (regarded as a bird of ignoble nature).
143. vild: vile, base.
146–47. overbuys . . . pays: pays a price for me that is almost entirely in excess of my value.

A neat-herd's daughter, and my Leonatus
Our neighbor shepherd's son!

Enter QUEEN.

Cym. Thou foolish thing!
[*To the Queen.*] They were again together; you have done
Not after our command. Away with her,
And pen her up.

Queen. Beseech your patience. Peace,
Dear lady daughter, peace! Sweet sovereign,
Leave us to ourselves, and make yourself some comfort
Out of your best advice.

Cym. Nay, let her languish
A drop of blood a day, and being aged
Die of this folly! *Exit* [*with Lords*].

Enter PISANIO.

Queen. Fie, you must give way.
Here is your servant. How now, sir? What news?

Pis. My lord your son drew on my master.

Queen. Hah?
No harm, I trust, is done?

Pis. There might have been,
But that my master rather play'd than fought
And had no help of anger. They were parted
By gentlemen at hand.

Queen. I am very glad on't.

Imo. Your son's my father's friend, he takes his part
To draw upon an exile. O brave sir!
I would they were in Afric both together,
Myself by with a needle, that I might prick
The goer-back. Why came you from your master?

Pis. On his command. He would not suffer me
To bring him to the haven; left these notes
Of what commands I should be subject to,
When't pleas'd you to employ me.

Queen. This hath been
Your faithful servant. I dare lay mine honor
He will remain so.

Pis. I humbly thank your Highness.

Queen. Pray walk awhile.

Imo. [*To Pisanio.*] About some half hour hence,
Pray you speak with me. You shall, at least,
Go see my lord aboard. For this time leave me.
Exeunt.

SCENE [II]

Enter CLOTEN *and two* LORDS.

1. Lord. Sir, I would advise you to shift a shirt; the violence of action hath made you reek as a sacrifice. Where air comes out, air comes in; there's none abroad so wholesome as that you vent.

156. advice: consideration.
165. takes his part: sides with him (?) or acts in character (?).
167. in Afric: i.e. in some desert spot where no one would stop the combat. **174. lay:** wager.

I.ii. Location: Britain. The grounds of Cymbeline's palace.
1. shift: change. **2. reek:** emit vapors.
4. abroad: outside you. **vent:** give off.

Clo. If my shirt were bloody, then to shift it. Have I hurt him?

2. Lord. [*Aside.*] No, faith; not so much as his patience.

1. Lord. Hurt him? His body's a passable carcass, if he be not hurt; it is a throughfare for steel, if it be not hurt.

2. Lord. [*Aside.*] His steel was in debt, it went o' th' backside the town.

Clo. The villain would not stand me.

2. Lord. [*Aside.*] No, but he fled forward still, toward your face.

1. Lord. Stand you? You have land enough of your own, but he added to your having, gave you some ground.

2. Lord. [*Aside.*] As many inches as you have oceans. Puppies!

Clo. I would they had not come between us.

2. Lord. [*Aside.*] So would I, till you had measur'd how long a fool you were upon the ground.

Clo. And that she should love this fellow, and refuse me!

2. Lord. [*Aside.*] If it be a sin to make a true election, she is damn'd.

1. Lord. Sir, as I told you always: her beauty and her brain go not together. She's a good sign, but I have seen small reflection of her wit.

2. Lord. [*Aside.*] She shines not upon fools, lest the reflection should hurt her.

Clo. Come, I'll to my chamber. Would there had been some hurt done!

2. Lord. [*Aside.*] I wish not so, unless it had been the fall of an ass, which is no great hurt.

Clo. You'll go with us?

1. Lord. I'll attend your lordship.

Clo. Nay, come, let's go together.

2. Lord. Well, my lord. *Exeunt.*

SCENE [III]

Enter IMOGEN *and* PISANIO.

Imo. I would thou grew'st unto the shores o' th' haven,
And questionedst every sail. If he should write
And I not have it, 'twere a paper lost
As offer'd mercy is. What was the last
That he spake to thee?
Pis. It was his queen, his queen!
Imo. Then wav'd his handkerchief?
Pis. And kiss'd it, madam.
Imo. Senseless linen, happier therein than I!
And that was all?
Pis. No, madam; for so long
As he could make me with [this] eye or ear
Distinguish him from others, he did keep
The deck, with glove or hat or handkerchief
Still waving, as the fits and stirs of 's mind
Could best express how slow his soul sail'd on,
How swift his ship.
Imo. Thou shouldst have made him
As little as a crow, or less, ere left
To after-eye him.
Pis. Madam, so I did.
Imo. I would have broke mine eye-strings, crack'd them, but
To look upon him, till the diminution
Of space had pointed him sharp as my needle;
Nay, followed him till he had melted from
The smallness of a gnat to air, and then
Have turn'd mine eye and wept. But, good Pisanio,
When shall we hear from him?
Pis. Be assur'd, madam,
With his next vantage.
Imo. I did not take my leave of him, but had
Most pretty things to say. Ere I could tell him
How I would think on him at certain hours
Such thoughts and such; or I could make him swear
The shes of Italy should not betray
Mine interest and his honor; or have charg'd him,
At the sixt hour of morn, at noon, at midnight,
T' encounter me with orisons, for then
I am in heaven for him; or ere I could
Give him that parting kiss which I had set
Betwixt two charming words, comes in my father,
And like the tyrannous breathing of the north
Shakes all our buds from growing.

Enter a LADY.

Lady. The Queen, madam,
Desires your Highness' company.
Imo. Those things I bid you do, get them dispatch'd,
And I will attend the Queen.
Pis. Madam, I shall. *Exeunt.*

SCENE [IV]

Enter PHILARIO, JACHIMO, *a* FRENCHMAN, *a* DUTCHMAN, *and a* SPANIARD.

Jach. Believe it, sir, I have seen him in Britain. He

9. passable: (1) pretty good; (2) allowing unobstructed passage (to a rapier).
12–13. His . . . town: his rapier behaved like a debtor, slinking along back streets; i.e. it avoided the main street (the "throughfare" of Posthumus' body).
14. stand me: stand his ground before me. **15. still:** continually.
18–19. gave . . . ground: fell back (with obvious pun).
20–21. As many . . . oceans: i.e. none. Perhaps *inches* puns on the sense "islands," but Shakespeare elsewhere uses the word in that sense only in a place-name that he found in his source ("Saint Colme's inch," *Macbeth*, I.ii.61).
27–28. true election: correct choice (with pun on the theological sense of *election*).
30. go not together: do not match. **sign:** appearance.
31. wit: intelligence.
38. You'll . . . us. Cloten now takes notice of the Second Lord, who has been lagging behind.

I.iii. Location: Britain. Cymbeline's palace.
4. As . . . is: i.e. as precious as pardon to a condemned man (?) or as God's mercy to a sinner (?).
17. eye-strings. It was thought that the eye muscles or tendons could break from excessive strain.
24. With . . . vantage: at his first opportunity (*next* = nearest).
30. interest: right, claim. **31. sixt:** sixth.
32. encounter . . . orisons: join me in prayers.
35. charming: carrying a charm or spell (against danger or evil).
36. north: north wind.

I.iv. Location: Rome. Philario's house.

was then of a crescent note, expected to prove so worthy as since he hath been allow'd the name of. But I could then have look'd on him without the help of admiration, though the catalogue of his endowments had been tabled by his side, and I to peruse him by items.

Phi. You speak of him when he was less furnish'd than now he is with that which makes him both without and within.

French. I have seen him in France. We had very many there could behold the sun with as firm eyes as he.

Jach. This matter of marrying his king's daughter, wherein he must be weigh'd rather by her value than his own, words him, I doubt not, a great deal from the matter.

French. And then his banishment.

Jach. Ay, and the approbation of those that weep this lamentable divorce under her colors are wonderfully to extend him, be it but to fortify her judgment, which else an easy battery might lay flat, for taking a beggar without less quality. But how comes it he is to sojourn with you? How creeps acquaintance?

Phi. His father and I were soldiers together, to whom I have been often bound for no less than my life.

Enter POSTHUMUS.

Here comes the Britain. Let him be so entertain'd amongst you as suits with gentlemen of your knowing to a stranger of his quality. I beseech you all be better known to this gentleman, whom I commend to you as a noble friend of mine. How worthy he is I will leave to appear hereafter, rather than story him in his own hearing.

French. Sir, we have known together in Orleance.

Post. Since when I have been debtor to you for courtesies, which I will be ever to pay and yet pay still.

French. Sir, you o'errate my poor kindness, I was glad I did atone my countryman and you. It had been pity you should have been put together, with so mortal a purpose as then each bore, upon importance of so slight and trivial a nature.

Post. By your pardon, sir, I was then a young traveller, rather shunn'd to go even with what I heard than in my every action to be guided by others' experiences: but upon my mended judgment (if I offend [not] to say it is mended) my quarrel was not altogether slight.

French. Faith, yes, to be put to the arbiterment of swords, and by such two that would by all likelihood have confounded one the other, or have fall'n both.

Jach. Can we, with manners, ask what was the difference?

French. Safely, I think; 'twas a contention in public, which may, without contradiction, suffer the report. It was much like an argument that fell out last night, where each of us fell in praise of our country mistresses; this gentleman at that time vouching (and upon warrant of bloody affirmation) his to be more fair, virtuous, wise, chaste, constant, qualified, and less attemptable than any the rarest of our ladies in France.

Jach. That lady is not now living; or this gentleman's opinion by this worn out.

Post. She holds her virtue still, and I my mind.

Jach. You must not so far prefer her 'fore ours of Italy.

Post. Being so far provok'd as I was in France, I would abate her nothing, though I profess myself her adorer, not her friend.

Jach. As fair and as good—a kind of hand-in-hand comparison—had been something too fair and too good for any lady in Brittany. If she went before others I have seen, as that diamond of yours outlustres many I have beheld, I could not [but] believe she excell'd many. But I have not seen the most precious diamond that is, nor you the lady.

Post. I prais'd her as I rated her: so do I my stone.

Jach. What do you esteem it at?

Post. More than the world enjoys.

Jach. Either your unparagon'd mistress is dead, or she's outpriz'd by a trifle.

Post. You are mistaken: the one may be sold or given, or if there were wealth enough for the [purchase], or merit for the gift; the other is not a thing for sale, and only the gift of the gods.

Jach. Which the gods have given you?

Post. Which, by their graces, I will keep.

Jach. You may wear her in title yours; but you know strange fowl light upon neighboring ponds. Your ring may be stol'n too: so your brace of unprizable estimations, the one is but frail and the other casual. A cunning thief, or a (that way) accomplish'd courtier, would hazard the winning both of first and last.

Post. Your Italy contains none so accomplish'd a courtier to convince the honor of my mistress, if in the holding or loss of that you term her frail. I do

2. **crescent note**: increasing reputation.
5. **admiration**: astonishment.
6. **tabled**: set down in a table or list.
12. **behold the sun.** Supposedly the eagle could stare at the sun without blinking. Posthumus is here again associated with the king of birds, as at I.i.139.
16–17. **words . . . matter**: causes him to be described in terms very wide of the truth.
20. **colors**: banners (i.e. on Imogen's side). The military imagery is continued in *fortify* and *battery*.
23. **without less quality**: i.e. of no rank (a kind of double negative). The phrase has been much emended. 28. **Britain**: Briton.
35. **known together**: been acquainted. **Orleance**: Orleans.
39. **atone**: reconcile. 40. **put together**: opposed (in a duel).
41. **mortal**: deadly, dangerous. **importance**: import, matter.
44. **shunn'd . . . even**: refused to agree. 46. **upon**: i.e. even upon.
49. **arbiterment**: settlement. 51. **confounded**: destroyed.
55. **contradiction**: objection. **suffer**: allow of. 57. **in**: into.
57–58. **our country mistresses**: the lady each of us loves in his own country.
59. **upon . . . affirmation**: pledging to back it up with a duel.
60. **qualified**: endowed with good qualities.
60–61. **attemptable**: seduceable.
63. **by . . . out**: by now no longer what it was. 64. **mind**: opinion.
65. **prefer her**: advance her claims.
68. **would . . . nothing**: would not lower my valuation of her in the slightest. 69. **friend**: lover, i.e. paramour.
70–71. **As . . . comparison**: i.e. a comparison claiming equality, not superiority. 72. **Brittany**: Britain.
79. **enjoys**: possesses. Jachimo quibbles on the other sense.
83. **or if**: if either.
88. **wear . . . yours**: have a legal right to her.
90–91. **your . . . estimations**: the two objects that you esteem priceless. 91. **casual**: subject to accident. 95. **convince**: overthrow.

nothing doubt you have store of thieves; notwithstanding, I fear not my ring.

Phi. Let us leave here, gentlemen.

Post. Sir, with all my heart. This worthy signior, I thank him, makes no stranger of me: we are familiar at first.

Jach. With five times so much conversation, I should get ground of your fair mistress; make her go back, even to the yielding, had I admittance, and opportunity to friend.

Post. No, no.

Jach. I dare thereupon pawn the moi'ty of my estate to your ring, which in my opinion o'ervalues it something. But I make my wager rather against your confidence than her reputation; and to bar your offense herein too, I durst attempt it against any lady in the world.

Post. You are a great deal abus'd in too bold a persuasion, and I doubt not you sustain what y' are worthy of by your attempt.

Jach. What's that?

Post. A repulse, though your attempt (as you call it) deserve more—a punishment too.

Phi. Gentlemen, enough of this. It came in too suddenly, let it die as it was born, and I pray you be better acquainted.

Jach. Would I had put my estate and my neighbor's on th' approbation of what I have spoke!

Post. What lady would you choose to assail?

Jach. Yours, whom in constancy you think stands so safe. I will lay you ten [thousand] ducats to your ring, that, commend me to the court where your lady is, with no more advantage than the opportunity of a second conference, and I will bring from thence that honor of hers which you imagine so reserv'd.

Post. I will wage against your gold, gold to it. My ring I hold dear as my finger, 'tis part of it.

Jach. You are a friend, and therein the wiser. If you buy ladies' flesh at a million a dram, you cannot preserve it from tainting. But I see you have some religion in you, that you fear.

Post. This is but a custom in your tongue; you bear a graver purpose, I hope.

Jach. I am the master of my speeches, and would undergo what's spoken, I swear.

Post. Will you? I shall but lend my diamond till your return. Let there be covenants drawn between 's. My mistress exceeds in goodness the hugeness of your unworthy thinking. I dare you to this match: here's my ring.

Phi. I will have it no lay.

Jach. By the gods, it is one. If I bring you no sufficient testimony that I have enjoy'd the dearest bodily part of your mistress, my ten thousand ducats are yours, so is your diamond too. If I come off and leave her in such honor as you have trust in, she your jewel, this your jewel, and my gold are yours—provided I have your commendation for my more free entertainment.

Post. I embrace these conditions, let us have articles betwixt us. Only, thus far you shall answer: if you make your voyage upon her and give me directly to understand you have prevail'd, I am no further your enemy; she is not worth our debate. If she remain unseduc'd, you not making it appear otherwise, for your ill opinion and th' assault you have made to her chastity, you shall answer me with your sword.

Jach. Your hand—a covenant. We will have these things set down by lawful counsel, and straight away for Britain, lest the bargain should catch cold and starve. I will fetch my gold and have our two wagers recorded.

Post. Agreed. [*Exeunt Posthumus and Jachimo.*]

French. Will this hold, think you?

Phi. Signior Jachimo will not from it. Pray let us follow 'em. *Exeunt.*

SCENE [V]

Enter QUEEN, LADIES, *and* CORNELIUS.

Queen. Whiles yet the dew's on ground, gather those flowers;
Make haste. Who has the note of them?
[*1.*] *Lady.* I, madam.
Queen. Dispatch. *Exeunt Ladies.*
Now, master doctor, have you brought those drugs?
Cor. Pleaseth your Highness, ay. Here they are, madam. [*Presenting a small box.*]
But I beseech your Grace, without offense
(My conscience bids me ask), wherefore you have
Commanded of me these most poisonous compounds,
Which are the movers of a languishing death,
But though slow, deadly.
Queen. I wonder, doctor,
Thou ask'st me such a question. Have I not been
Thy pupil long? Hast thou not learn'd me how
To make perfumes? distill? preserve? yea so,
That our great King himself doth woo me oft
For my confections? Having thus far proceeded
(Unless thou think'st me devilish) is't not meet
That I did amplify my judgment in
Other conclusions? I will try the forces
Of these thy compounds on such creatures as
We count not worth the hanging (but none human),
To try the vigor of them, and apply

97. store: plenty. **98. fear:** fear for.
99. leave: stop the discussion.
101–2. familiar at first: on easy terms from the start. **106. to:** as a.
108. moi'ty: half. **114. abus'd:** deceived.
114–15. persuasion: opinion. **115. sustain:** will sustain.
124. approbation: proof. **127. lay:** wager.
128. commend me: i.e. give me a letter of introduction.
132. to it: to match it.
134. a friend: i.e. a paramour (which Posthumus has denied in line 69). Jachimo implies that Posthumus has good reason to doubt Imogen's virtue and hence refuses to wager the ring.
137. that: since. **fear.** Jachimo plays on two senses: (1) feel religious awe; (2) are fearful. **141. undergo:** undertake.
147. I . . . lay: i.e. I will not allow the wager.

155. free entertainment: ready reception.
158. directly: straightforwardly. **167. starve:** die.
171. from: depart from.

I.v. Location: Britain. Cymbeline's palace.
2. note: list. **12. learn'd:** taught.
15. confections: mixtures (of drugs).
18. conclusions: experiments. **try:** test.

Allayments to their act, and by them gather
Their several virtues and effects.
Cor. Your Highness
Shall from this practice but make hard your heart;
Besides, the seeing these effects will be
Both noisome and infectious.
Queen. O, content thee.

Enter Pisanio.

[*Aside.*] Here comes a flattering rascal, upon him
Will I first work. He's for his master,
And enemy to my son.—How now, Pisanio?
Doctor, your service for this time is ended,
Take your own way.
Cor. [*Aside.*] I do suspect you, madam,
But you shall do no harm.
Queen. [*To Pisanio.*] Hark thee, a word.
Cor. [*Aside.*] I do not like her. She doth think she has
Strange ling'ring poisons. I do know her spirit,
And will not trust one of her malice with
A drug of such damn'd nature. Those she has
Will stupefy and dull the sense awhile,
Which first (perchance) she'll prove on cats and dogs,
Then afterward up higher; but there is
No danger in what show of death it makes,
More than the locking up the spirits a time,
To be more fresh, reviving. She is fool'd
With a most false effect; and I the truer,
So to be false with her.
Queen. No further service, doctor,
Until I send for thee.
Cor. I humbly take my leave. *Exit.*
Queen. Weeps she still, say'st thou? Dost thou think in time
She will not quench, and let instructions enter
Where folly now possesses? Do thou work.
When thou shalt bring me word she loves my son,
I'll tell thee on the instant thou art then
As great as is thy master—greater, for
His fortunes all lie speechless, and his name
Is at last gasp. Return he cannot, nor
Continue where he is. To shift his being
Is to exchange one misery with another,
And every day that comes comes to decay
A day's work in him. What shalt thou expect
To be depender on a thing that leans?
Who cannot be new built, nor has no friends
So much as but to prop him?
[*The Queen drops the box; Pisanio takes it up.*]
Thou tak'st up
Thou know'st not what; but take it for thy labor.
It is a thing I made, which hath the King
Five times redeem'd from death. I do not know
What is more cordial. Nay, I prithee take it,
It is an earnest of a farther good
That I mean to thee. Tell thy mistress how
The case stands with her; do't as from thyself.
Think what a chance thou changest on, but think
Thou hast thy mistress still; to boot, my son,
Who shall take notice of thee. I'll move the King
To any shape of thy preferment, such
As thou'lt desire; and then myself, I chiefly,
That set thee on to this desert, am bound
To load thy merit richly. Call my women.
Think on my words. *Exit Pisanio.*
A sly and constant knave,
Not to be shak'd; the agent for his master,
And the remembrancer of her to hold
The hand-fast to her lord. I have given him that
Which, if he take, shall quite unpeople her
Of liegers for her sweet; and which she after,
Except she bend her humor, shall be assur'd
To taste of too.

Enter Pisanio *and* Ladies.

So, so. Well done, well done.
The violets, cowslips, and the primeroses,
Bear to my closet. Fare thee well, Pisanio;
Think on my words. *Exeunt Queen and Ladies.*
Pis. And shall do.
But when to my good lord I prove untrue,
I'll choke myself. There's all I'll do for you. *Exit.*

Scene [VI]

Enter Imogen *alone.*

Imo. A father cruel, and a step-dame false,
A foolish suitor to a wedded lady
That hath her husband banish'd. O, that husband!
My supreme crown of grief, and those repeated
Vexations of it! Had I been thief-stol'n,
As my two brothers, happy! but most miserable
Is the [desire] that's glorious. Blessed be those,
How mean soe'er, that have their honest wills,
Which seasons comfort. Who may this be? Fie!

Enter Pisanio *and* Jachimo.

Pis. Madam, a noble gentleman of Rome,
Comes from my lord with letters.
Jach. Change you, madam:
The worthy Leonatus is in safety

22. Allayments . . . act: antidotes to their action.
26. content thee: set your mind at rest.
28. This metrically irregular line has been variously emended; for example, some editors read *He's factor for.*
36. damn'd: damnable.
43. false: deceiving. **truer:** more honest.
47. quench: cool off. **instructions:** good advice.
54. being: place of abode. **56. decay:** destroy.
58. leans: "inclines towards its fall" (Johnson).

64. cordial: restorative. **65. earnest:** first payment.
68. chance . . . on: change in your fortunes has come to you by chance.
73. set . . . desert: urged you to this action which will deserve reward.
77–78. remembrancer . . . lord: her official reminder to remain true to her marriage bond.
80. liegers . . . sweet: ambassadors in the service of her lover.
81. bend her humor: alter her inclination.
83. primeroses: primroses.

I.vi. Location: Britain. Cymbeline's palace.
3. That . . . banish'd: who has had her husband taken away from her.
4. repeated: enumerated.
7. desire that's glorious: yearning for great things (?) or yearning of one in an exalted position (?). **8. wills:** desires.
9. seasons: gives relish to.
11. Comes: who comes. **Change you:** alter your expression.

And greets your Highness dearly. [*Presents a letter.*]
Imo. Thanks, good sir,
You're kindly welcome.
Jach. [*Aside.*] All of her that is out of door most
rich!
If she be furnish'd with a mind so rare,
She is alone th' Arabian bird, and I
Have lost the wager. Boldness be my friend;
Arm me audacity from head to foot,
Or like the Parthian I shall flying fight—
Rather, directly fly.
Imo. (*Reads.*) "He is one of the noblest note, to whose kindnesses I am most infinitely tied. Reflect upon him accordingly, as you value your trust—
Leonatus."
So far I read aloud—
But even the very middle of my heart
Is warm'd by th' rest—and take it thankfully.
You are as welcome, worthy sir, as I
Have words to bid you, and shall find it so
In all that I can do.
Jach. Thanks, fairest lady.
What, are men mad? Hath nature given them eyes
To see this vaulted arch and the rich crop
Of sea and land, which can distinguish 'twixt
The fiery orbs above, and the twinn'd stones
Upon the number'd beach, and can we not
Partition make with spectacles so precious
'Twixt fair and foul?
Imo. What makes your admiration?
Jach. It cannot be i' th' eye: for apes and monkeys
'Twixt two such shes would chatter this way, and
Contemn with mows the other; nor i' th' judgment:
For idiots in this case of favor would
Be wisely definite; nor i' th' appetite:
Sluttery, to such neat excellence oppos'd,
Should make desire vomit emptiness,
Not so allur'd to feed.
Imo. What is the matter, trow?
Jach. The cloyed will—
That satiate yet unsatisfied desire, that tub
Both fill'd and running—ravening first the lamb,
Longs after for the garbage.
Imo. What, dear sir,
Thus raps you? Are you well?

15. out of door: external, visible.
17. th' Arabian bird: the phoenix, i.e. uniquely excellent.
20. Parthian. The mounted archers of Parthia shot arrows while retreating. **22. note**: reputation. **23–24. Reflect upon**: regard.
33. vaulted arch: sky. **crop**: harvest.
35. twinn'd: looking exactly alike.
36. number'd: numerous, i.e. abounding in "twinn'd stones" (?). Many editors follow Theobald in emending to *unnumbered*, i.e. numberless.
37. Partition: discrimination. **spectacles so precious**: organs of sight so keenly sensitive.
38. admiration: astonishment, wonder.
40. chatter this way: i.e. indicate their preference for Imogen.
41. mows: grimaces.
42. case of favor: question concerning beauty.
43. Be wisely definite: make a wise decision.
44. neat: elegant. **oppos'd**: placed in contrast.
45. make . . . emptiness: make sexual desire feel satiated to the point of revulsion without being fed.
47. trow: do you think. **The cloyed will**: lust, i.e. the lustful man (contrasted with normal sexual appetite).
49. running: running out, emptying itself. **ravening**: eating voraciously. **51. raps**: transports.

Jach. Thanks, madam, well. [*To Pisanio.*] Beseech
you, sir,
Desire my man's abode where I did leave him:
He's strange and peevish.
Pis. I was going, sir,
To give him welcome. *Exit.*
Imo. Continues well my lord? His health, beseech
you?
Jach. Well, madam.
Imo. Is he dispos'd to mirth? I hope he is.
Jach. Exceeding pleasant; none a stranger there
So merry and so gamesome. He is call'd
The Britain reveller.
Imo. When he was here,
He did incline to sadness, and oft-times
Not knowing why.
Jach. I never saw him sad.
There is a Frenchman his companion, one
An eminent monsieur that it seems much loves
A Gallian girl at home. He furnaces
The thick sighs from him, whiles the jolly Britain
(Your lord, I mean) laughs from 's free lungs; cries "O,
Can my sides hold, to think that man, who knows
By history, report, or his own proof,
What woman is, yea, what she cannot choose
But must be, will 's free hours languish for
Assured bondage?"
Imo. Will my lord say so?
Jach. Ay, madam, with his eyes in flood with
laughter.
It is a recreation to be by
And hear him mock the Frenchman. But heavens
know
Some men are much to blame.
Imo. Not he, I hope.
Jach. Not he; but yet heaven's bounty towards him
might
Be us'd more thankfully. In himself, 'tis much;
In you, which I account his, beyond all talents.
Whilst I am bound to wonder, I am bound
To pity too.
Imo. What do you pity, sir?
Jach. Two creatures heartily.
Imo. Am I one, sir?
You look on me; what wrack discern you in me
Deserves your pity?
Jach. Lamentable! What,
To hide me from the radiant sun, and solace
I' th' dungeon by a snuff!

53. Desire . . . abode: ask my servant to remain.
54. strange and peevish: unfamiliar with the place and of undependable temper. **59. none a stranger**: no (other) foreigner.
62. sadness: seriousness. **66. Gallian**: Gallic.
67. thick: frequent. **68. from . . . lungs**: i.e. unrestrainedly.
70. proof: experience.
72. languish: give up to languishing. *Languish* has a secondary meaning "be sexually frustrated"; *free* in the same line means both "independent" and "licentious," and Jachimo's earlier *gamesome*, *reveller*, *jolly* suggest not only gaiety but sexual looseness.
79. In . . . much: i.e. heaven's bounty has been great with respect to his personal endowments.
80. In you: i.e. heaven's bounty in giving him you. **talents**: his own heaven-given qualities. **84. wrack**: ruin, loss.
86. solace: find pleasure.
87. snuff: smoking candle-end. The image is developed in lines 109–10.

Imo. I pray you, sir,
Deliver with more openness your answers
To my demands. Why do you pity me?
Jach. That others do
(I was about to say) enjoy your—But
It is an office of the gods to venge it,
Not mine to speak on't.
Imo. You do seem to know
Something of me, or what concerns me: pray you—
Since doubting things go ill often hurts more
Than to be sure they do; for certainties
Either are past remedies, or, timely knowing,
The remedy then born—discover to me
What both you spur and stop.
Jach. Had I this cheek
To bathe my lips upon; this hand, whose touch
(Whose every touch) would force the feeler's soul
To th' oath of loyalty; this object, which
Takes prisoner the wild motion of mine eye,
Firing it only here; should I (damn'd then)
Slaver with lips as common as the stairs
That mount the Capitol; join gripes with hands
Made hard with hourly falsehood (falsehood, as
With labor); then by-peeping in an eye
Base and illustrious as the smoky light
That's fed with stinking tallow: it were fit
That all the plagues of hell should at one time
Encounter such revolt.
Imo. My lord, I fear,
Has forgot Britain.
Jach. And himself. Not I
Inclin'd to this intelligence pronounce
The beggary of his change; but 'tis your graces
That from my mutest conscience to my tongue
Charms this report out.
Imo. Let me hear no more.
Jach. O dearest soul! your cause doth strike my heart
With pity that doth make me sick. A lady
So fair, and fasten'd to an empery
Would make the great'st king double—to be partner'd
With tomboys hir'd with that self exhibition
Which your own coffers yield; with diseas'd ventures
That play with all infirmities for gold
Which rottenness can lend nature; such boil'd stuff
As well might poison poison. Be reveng'd,
Or she that bore you was no queen, and you
Recoil from your great stock.
Imo. Reveng'd?
How should I be reveng'd? If this be true
(As I have such a heart that both mine ears
Must not in haste abuse), if it be true,
How should I be reveng'd?
Jach. Should he make me
Live, like Diana's priest, betwixt cold sheets,
Whiles he is vaulting variable ramps,
In your despite, upon your purse—revenge it.
I dedicate myself to your sweet pleasure,
More noble than that runagate to your bed,
And will continue fast to your affection,
Still close as sure.
Imo. What ho, Pisanio!
Jach. Let me my service tender on your lips.
Imo. Away, I do condemn mine ears that have
So long attended thee. If thou wert honorable,
Thou wouldst have told this tale for virtue, not
For such an end thou seek'st—as base as strange.
Thou wrong'st a gentleman, who is as far
From thy report as thou from honor, and
Solicits here a lady that disdains
Thee and the devil alike. What ho, Pisanio!
The King my father shall be made acquainted
Of thy assault. If he shall think it fit
A saucy stranger in his court to mart
As in a Romish stew, and to expound
His beastly mind to us, he hath a court
He little cares for and a daughter who
He not respects at all. What ho, Pisanio!
Jach. O happy Leonatus! I may say,
The credit that thy lady hath of thee
Deserves thy trust, and thy most perfect goodness
Her assur'd credit. Blessed live you long,
A lady to the worthiest sir that ever
Country call'd his; and you his mistress, only
For the most worthiest fit. Give me your pardon.
I have spoke this to know if your affiance
Were deeply rooted, and shall make your lord,
That which he is, new o'er; and he is one
The truest manner'd, such a holy witch
That he enchants societies into him;
Half all [men's] hearts are his.
Imo. You make amends.
Jach. He sits 'mongst men like a [descended] god;
He hath a kind of honor sets him off,
More than a mortal seeming. Be not angry,
Most mighty Princess, that I have adventur'd
To try your taking of a false report, which hath
Honor'd with confirmation your great judgment

92. office: function. **95. doubting:** fearing, suspecting.
97. timely knowing: if one knows in time.
98. discover: make known.
99. What . . . stop: what you simultaneously urge toward utterance and restrain from utterance (a figure from horsemanship).
104. Firing: giving fire to. **106. gripes:** grips, claspings.
109. illustrious: lacking lustre.
112. Encounter: fall upon. **revolt:** faithlessness.
113–14. Not . . . intelligence: it is not through any inclination to tell this news that I.
115. beggary . . . change: i.e. his change to worthlessness.
116. conscience: inner knowledge. **120. empery:** empire.
121. double: twice as powerful as before. **partner'd:** i.e. made to share your rights.
122. tomboys: strumpets. **self exhibition:** very allowance of money.
123. ventures: things risked for commercial profit.
124. play: (1) gambol; (2) toy carelessly.
125. Which. The antecedent is *infirmities*. **boil'd stuff:** women who had taken the sweating treatment for venereal disease.

128. Recoil: degenerate. **130. As:** i.e. I say "if," for.
131. in haste abuse: wrong by overhasty acceptance of what they hear. **134. vaulting variable ramps:** mounting various trollops.
135. your despite: contempt of you. **137. runagate:** renegade.
139. close: secret. **147. Solicits:** solicitest. **151. mart:** bargain.
152. stew: brothel. **157. credit . . . of:** trust . . . in.
161. call'd his: called its own.
165. new o'er: over again.
165–66. one . . . manner'd: above all others honorably behaved.
166. witch: wizard. **167. societies:** social groups. **into:** to.
168. Half . . . his: i.e. every man has given him half his heart.
171. More . . . seeming: seeming more than a mortal (?) or more than a human being (?). Possibly a = *a'*, "of," and the line means "(honor) which seems more than human."

In the election of a sir so rare,
Which you know cannot err. The love I bear him
Made me to fan you thus, but the gods made you
(Unlike all others) chaffless. Pray your pardon.
Imo. All's well, sir. Take my pow'r i' th' court for yours.
Jach. My humble thanks. I had almost forgot
T' entreat your Grace but in a small request,
And yet of moment too, for it concerns:
Your lord, myself, and other noble friends
Are partners in the business.
Imo. Pray, what is't?
Jach. Some dozen Romans of us and your lord
(The best feather of our wing) have mingled sums
To buy a present for the Emperor;
Which I (the factor for the rest) have done
In France. 'Tis plate of rare device, and jewels
Of rich and exquisite form, their values great,
And I am something curious, being strange,
To have them in safe stowage. May it please you
To take them in protection?
Imo. Willingly;
And pawn mine honor for their safety. Since
My lord hath interest in them, I will keep them
In my bedchamber.
Jach. They are in a trunk,
Attended by my men. I will make bold
To send them to you, only for this night;
I must aboard to-morrow.
Imo. O no, no.
Jach. Yes, I beseech; or I shall short my word
By length'ning my return. From Gallia
I cross'd the seas on purpose and on promise
To see your Grace.
Imo. I thank you for your pains:
But not away to-morrow!
Jach. O, I must, madam.
Therefore I shall beseech you, if you please
To greet your lord with writing, do't to-night.
I have outstood my time, which is material
To th' tender of our present.
Imo. I will write.
Send your trunk to me, it shall safe be kept,
And truly yielded you. You're very welcome.
Exeunt.

ACT II, SCENE I

Enter CLOTEN *and the two* LORDS.

Clo. Was there ever man had such luck? when I kiss'd the jack upon an up-cast, to be hit away! I had a hundred pound on't; and then a whoreson jack-an-apes must take me up for swearing, as if I borrow'd mine oaths of him and might not spend them at my pleasure.

1. Lord. What got he by that? You have broke his pate with your bowl.

2. Lord. [*Aside.*] If his wit had been like him that broke it, it would have run all out.

Clo. When a gentleman is dispos'd to swear, it is not for any standers-by to curtal his oaths. Ha?

2. Lord. No, my lord; [*aside*] nor crop the ears of them.

Clo. Whoreson dog! I gave him satisfaction! Would he had been one of my rank!

2. Lord. [*Aside.*] To have smell'd like a fool.

Clo. I am not vex'd more at any thing in th' earth; a pox on't! I had rather not be so noble as I am. They dare not fight with me because of the Queen my mother. Every Jack slave hath his bellyful of fighting, and I must go up and down like a cock that nobody can match.

2. Lord. [*Aside.*] You are cock and capon too, and you crow, cock, with your comb on.

Clo. Sayest thou?

2. Lord. It is not fit [your] lordship should undertake every companion that you give offense to.

Clo. No, I know that; but it is fit I should commit offense to my inferiors.

2. Lord. Ay, it is fit for your lordship only.

Clo. Why, so I say.

1. Lord. Did you hear of a stranger that's come to court [to-]night?

Clo. A stranger, and I not know on't?

2. Lord. [*Aside.*] He's a strange fellow himself, and knows it not.

1. Lord. There's an Italian come, and 'tis thought one of Leonatus' friends.

Clo. Leonatus? a banish'd rascal; and he's another, whatsoever he be. Who told you of this stranger?

1. Lord. One of your lordship's pages.

Clo. Is it fit I went to look upon him? Is there no derogation in't?

2. Lord. You cannot derogate, my lord.

Clo. Not easily, I think.

2. Lord. [*Aside.*] You are a fool granted, therefore your issues, being foolish, do not derogate.

Clo. Come, I'll go see this Italian. What I have lost to-day at bowls I'll win to-night of him. Come; go.

2. Lord. I'll attend your lordship.
Exeunt [*Cloten and First Lord*].
That such a crafty devil as is his mother
Should yield the world this ass! a woman that
Bears all down with her brain, and this her son

176. Which: who, i.e. Posthumus.
177. fan: winnow; the figure is continued in ***chaffless,*** line 178.
182. concerns: is of importance. Most editors drop the colon and either read ***lord;*** in line 183 or interpret ***Are*** in line 184 as "Who are."
188. factor: agent. **189. jewels:** pieces of jewelry.
191. something curious: somewhat anxious. **strange:** a foreigner.
195. interest: share, right. **200. short:** fall short of.
207. outstood: outstayed. **208. tender:** giving.

II.i. Location: Britain. The grounds of Cymbeline's palace.
2. kiss'd the jack. In the game of bowls, the jack is the target ball, and to kiss it is to roll one's own ball close enough to touch it. **up-cast:** final throw.

4. take me up: rebuke me.
9. run all out. Implying that Cloten's brains are water.
11. curtal: curtail, cut off. **16. smell'd.** Punning on ***rank.***
20. Jack slave: knavish fellow.
23. capon: (1) castrated cock; (2) foolish fellow (leading to the play on ***comb*** = cock's-comb, fool's cap); (3) cap-on (anticipating ***comb on***). **26–27. undertake:** take on. **27. companion:** fellow.
28–29. commit offense to: take the offensive against (with unintended second sense "excrete upon"). **43. derogation:** loss of dignity.
44. You cannot derogate: (1) nothing can lessen your dignity; (2) you have no dignity to lose.
47. issues: offspring, i.e. words and actions.
54. Bears all down: carries all before her.

Cannot take two from twenty, for his heart,
And leave eighteen. Alas, poor Princess,
Thou divine Imogen, what thou endur'st,
Betwixt a father by thy step-dame govern'd,
A mother hourly coining plots, a wooer
More hateful than the foul expulsion is
Of thy dear husband, than that horrid act
Of the divorce he'ld make. The heavens hold firm
The walls of thy dear honor; keep unshak'd
That temple, thy fair mind, that thou mayst stand
T' enjoy thy banish'd lord and this great land! *Exit.*

Scene II

Enter Imogen *in her bed, and a* Lady. [*A trunk in one corner.*]

Imo. Who's there? My woman? Helen?
Lady. Please you, madam.
Imo. What hour is it?
Lady. Almost midnight, madam.
Imo. I have read three hours then. Mine eyes are weak.
Fold down the leaf where I have left. To bed.
Take not away the taper, leave it burning;
And if thou canst awake by four o' th' clock,
I prithee call me. Sleep hath seiz'd me wholly.
[*Exit Lady.*]
To your protection I commend me, gods,
From fairies and the tempters of the night
Guard me, beseech ye.
Sleeps. Jachimo from the trunk.
Jach. The crickets sing, and man's o'erlabor'd sense
Repairs itself by rest. Our Tarquin thus
Did softly press the rushes ere he waken'd
The chastity he wounded. Cytherea,
How bravely thou becom'st thy bed! fresh lily,
And whiter than the sheets! That I might touch!
But kiss, one kiss! Rubies unparagon'd,
How dearly they do't! 'Tis her breathing that
Perfumes the chamber thus. The flame o' th' taper
Bows toward her, and would under-peep her lids,
To see th' enclosed lights, now canopied
Under these windows, white and azure lac'd
With blue of heaven's own tinct. But my design!
To note the chamber, I will write all down:
[*Takes out his tables.*]
Such and such pictures; there the window; such
Th' adornment of her bed; the arras, figures,
Why, such and such; and the contents o' th' story.
Ah, but some natural notes about her body,
Above ten thousand meaner moveables

55. for his heart: for the life of him.

II.ii. Location: Britain. Imogen's bedchamber.
9. fairies: here, malignant spirits.
12. Our: i.e. Roman. **Tarquin:** the ravisher of Lucrece.
13. rushes: reeds for floor coverings. **14. Cytherea:** Venus.
15. bravely: beautifully. **18. do't:** i.e. kiss each other.
24 s.d. tables: memorandum-book.
26. arras: wall-hangings. **figures:** carvings.
27. story: room (?) or narrative represented on the arras (?).
28. notes: marks. **29. moveables:** articles of furniture.

Would testify, t' enrich mine inventory.
O sleep, thou ape of death, lie dull upon her,
And be her sense but as a monument,
Thus in a chapel lying! Come off, come off;
[*Taking off her bracelet.*]
As slippery as the Gordian knot was hard!
'Tis mine, and this will witness outwardly,
As strongly as the conscience does within,
To th' madding of her lord. On her left breast
A mole cinque-spotted, like the crimson drops
I' th' bottom of a cowslip. Here's a voucher,
Stronger than ever law could make; this secret
Will force him think I have pick'd the lock and ta'en
The treasure of her honor. No more: to what end?
Why should I write this down that's riveted,
Screw'd to my memory? She hath been reading late
The tale of Tereus; here the leaf's turn'd down
Where Philomele gave up. I have enough;
To th' trunk again, and shut the spring of it.
Swift, swift, you dragons of the night, that dawning
May bare the raven's eye! I lodge in fear;
Though this a heavenly angel, hell is here.
Clock strikes.
One, two, three: time, time! *Exit* [*into the trunk*].

Scene III

Enter Cloten *and* Lords.

1. Lord. Your lordship is the most patient man in loss, the most coldest that ever turn'd up ace.

Clo. It would make any man cold to lose.

1. Lord. But not every man patient after the noble temper of your lordship. You are most hot and furious when you win.

Clo. Winning will put any man into courage. If I could get this foolish Imogen, I should have gold enough. It's almost morning, is't not?

1. Lord. Day, my lord.

Clo. I would this music would come. I am advis'd to give her music a' mornings; they say it will penetrate.

Enter Musicians.

Come on, tune. If you can penetrate her with your fingering, so; we'll try with tongue too. If none will do, let her remain; but I'll never give o'er. First, a very excellent good conceited thing; after, a wonderful

31. dull: heavy.
32. be . . . monument: let her be as insensible as an effigy on a tomb.
34. Gordian knot: intricate knot which the Phrygian king Gordius tied and defied anyone to untie. Alexander the Great cut it with a stroke of his sword. **36. conscience:** consciousness.
38. cinque-spotted: having five spots. **39. voucher:** proof.
45. Tereus: a Thracian king who raped his sister-in-law Philomela and cut out her tongue. **46. gave up:** was forced to yield.
49. bare . . . eye. The raven was believed to sleep facing east and to waken at sunrise.

II.iii. Location: Britain. An antechamber adjoining Imogen's apartments.
2. coldest: coolest. **ace:** losing throw at dice (with pun on *ass*).
3. cold: disappointed. **11. music:** group of musicians.
12–13. penetrate: affect deeply (with indecent pun following).
17. conceited: full of fanciful invention (describing an elaborate piece for several instruments).

sweet air, with admirable rich words to it—and then let her consider.

Song

Hark, hark, the lark at heaven's gate sings,
And Phoebus gins arise,
His steeds to water at those springs
On chalic'd flow'rs that lies;
And winking Mary-buds begin to ope
their golden eyes;
With every thing that pretty is, my lady
sweet, arise:
Arise, arise!

[*Clo.*] So, get you gone. If this penetrate, I will consider your music the better; if it do not, it is a [vice] in her ears, which horsehairs and calves'-guts, nor the voice of unpav'd eunuch to boot, can never amend. [*Exeunt Musicians.*]

Enter Cymbeline *and* Queen.

2. Lord. Here comes the King.

Clo. I am glad I was up so late, for that's the reason I was up so early. He cannot choose but take this service I have done fatherly.—Good morrow to your Majesty, and to my gracious mother!

Cym. Attend you here the door of our stern
daughter?
Will she not forth?

Clo. I have assail'd her with musics, but she vouchsafes no notice.

Cym. The exile of her minion is too new,
She hath not yet forgot him. Some more time
Must wear the print of his remembrance on't,
And then she's yours.

Queen. You are most bound to th' King,
Who lets go by no vantages that may
Prefer you to his daughter. Frame yourself
To orderly [solicits], and be friended
With aptness of the season; make denials
Increase your services; so seem as if
You were inspir'd to do those duties which
You tender to her; that you in all obey her,
Save when command to your dismission tends,
And therein you are senseless.

Clo. Senseless? not so.

[*Enter a* Messenger.]

Mess. So like you, sir, ambassadors from Rome;
The one is Caius Lucius.

Cym. A worthy fellow,
Albeit he comes on angry purpose now;
But that's no fault of his. We must receive him
According to the honor of his sender,
And towards himself, his goodness forespent on us,
We must extend our notice. Our dear son,
When you have given good morning to your mistress,
Attend the Queen and us; we shall have need
T' employ you towards this Roman. Come, our queen.
Exeunt [*all but Cloten*].

Clo. If she be up, I'll speak with her; if not,
Let her lie still and dream. [*Knocks.*] By your leave
ho!
I know her women are about her; what
If I do line one of their hands? 'Tis gold
Which buys admittance (oft it doth), yea, and makes
Diana's rangers false themselves, yield up
Their deer to th' stand o' th' stealer; and 'tis gold
Which makes the true man kill'd and saves the thief;
Nay, sometime hangs both thief and true man. What
Can it not do, and undo? I will make
One of her women lawyer to me, for
I yet not understand the case myself.
By your leave. *Knocks.*

Enter a Lady.

Lady. Who's there that knocks?

Clo. A gentleman.

Lady. No more?

Clo. Yes, and a gentlewoman's son.

Lady. That's more
Than some, whose tailors are as dear as yours,
Can justly boast of. What's your lordship's pleasure?

Clo. Your lady's person. Is she ready?

Lady. Ay,
To keep her chamber.

Clo. There is gold for you,
Sell me your good report.

Lady. How, my good name? or to report of you
What I shall think is good?—The Princess.

Enter Imogen.

Clo. Good morrow, fairest: sister, your sweet
hand. [*Exit Lady.*]

Imo. Good morrow, sir. You lay out too much
pains
For purchasing but trouble. The thanks I give
Is telling you that I am poor of thanks,
And scarce can spare them.

Clo. Still I swear I love you.

Imo. If you but said so, 'twere as deep with me.
If you swear still, your recompense is still
That I regard it not.

Clo. This is no answer.

Imo. But that you shall not say I yield being silent,
I would not speak. I pray you spare me. Faith,

18. air: song for a single voice, accompanied.
21. Phoebus: the sun-god. **gins:** begins to.
23. chalic'd: cup-shaped.
24. winking Mary-buds: closed marigold buds.
28. consider: reward (?) or deem (?).
29. horsehairs and calves'-guts: bowstrings and fiddlestrings.
30. unpav'd: without stones (i.e. testicles), castrated.
41. minion: darling. **45. vantages:** favorable occasions.
46. Prefer: recommend.
47–48. be . . . season: take advantage of appropriate times. **denials:** i.e. Imogen's refusals.
53. senseless: insensible (but Cloten misunderstands).
54. So like you: if it please you.

59. forespent: having previously been bestowed.
69. Diana's rangers: gamekeepers of Diana, i.e. maidens vowed to chastity.
70. stand: station from which a hunter shoots game (with sexual pun).
71. true: honest. **75. understand:** i.e. know how to manage.
81. ready: dressed (with following quibble).
91. deep: binding. Shakespeare frequently applies this adjective to oaths. **92. still:** continually.

I shall unfold equal discourtesy
To your best kindness; one of your great knowing
Should learn, being taught, forbearance.
Clo. To leave you in your madness, 'twere my sin;
I will not.
Imo. Fools are not mad folks.
Clo. Do you call me fool?
Imo. As I am mad, I do.
If you'll be patient, I'll no more be mad;
That cures us both. I am much sorry, sir,
You put me to forget a lady's manners
By being so verbal; and learn now, for all,
That I, which know my heart, do here pronounce
By th' very truth of it, I care not for you,
And am so near the lack of charity
To accuse myself I hate you; which I had rather
You felt than make't my boast.
Clo. You sin against
Obedience, which you owe your father. For
The contract you pretend with that base wretch,
One bred of alms and foster'd with cold dishes,
With scraps o' th' court, it is no contract, none;
And though it be allowed in meaner parties
(Yet who than he more mean?) to knit their souls
(On whom there is no more dependancy
But brats and beggary) in self-figur'd knot,
Yet you are curb'd from that enlargement by
The consequence o' th' crown, and must not foil
The precious note of it with a base slave,
A hilding for a livery, a squire's cloth,
A pantler—not so eminent.
Imo. Profane fellow!
Wert thou the son of Jupiter, and no more
But what thou art besides, thou wert too base
To be his groom. Thou wert dignified enough,
Even to the point of envy, if 'twere made
Comparative for your virtues, to be styl'd
The under-hangman of his kingdom, and hated
For being preferr'd so well.
Clo. The south-fog rot him!
Imo. He never can meet more mischance than come
To be but nam'd of thee. His mean'st garment
That ever hath but clipt his body, is dearer
In my respect than all the hairs above thee,
Were they all made such men. How now, Pisanio?

96. unfold equal discourtesy: display discourtesy equal.
98. forbearance: desisting (but Cloten takes the word in the sense "withdrawal").
101. Fools . . . folks: i.e. I may be a fool for wasting words with you, but I am not insane (?). An obscure passage that has been variously explained.
106. verbal: talkative (instead of maintaining silence as I would prefer; cf. lines 95–96). **110. To . . . hate:** accuse myself of hating.
116. meaner: of humbler rank.
118–19. On . . . But: of whose marriage there is no greater consequence than. **119. self-figur'd:** tied by yourself.
120. enlargement: freedom of action.
121. consequence . . . crown: i.e. consequences of your being heir to the throne. **foil:** defile, dishonor. **122. note:** distinction.
123. hilding . . . livery: worthless fellow fit only to wear a servant's clothing. **124. pantler:** pantry servant.
128–29. if . . . virtues: i.e. if your rank and his corresponded to your respective qualities.
131. preferr'd so well: advanced so high. **south-fog:** fog brought by the south wind (which was commonly regarded as unwholesomely damp).
134. clipt: embraced. **135. respect:** regard.

Enter Pisanio.

Clo. "His garments"? Now the devil—
Imo. To Dorothy my woman hie thee presently.
Clo. "His garment"?
Imo. I am sprited with a fool,
Frighted, and ang'red worse. Go bid my woman
Search for a jewel that too casually
Hath left mine arm. It was thy master's. Shrew me
If I would lose it for a revenue
Of any king's in Europe! I do think
I saw't this morning; confident I am,
Last night 'twas on mine arm; I kiss'd it:
I hope it be not gone to tell my lord
That I kiss aught but he.
Pis. 'Twill not be lost.
Imo. I hope so; go and search. [*Exit Pisanio.*]
Clo. You have abus'd me.
"His meanest garment"?
Imo. Ay, I said so, sir;
If you will make't an action, call witness to't.
Clo. I will inform your father.
Imo. Your mother too.
She's my good lady, and will conceive, I hope,
But the worst of me. So I leave [you,] sir,
To th' worst of discontent. *Exit.*
Clo. I'll be reveng'd.
"His mean'st garment"? Well. *Exit.*

Scene IV

Enter Posthumus *and* Philario.

Post. Fear it not, sir. I would I were so sure
To win the King as I am bold her honor
Will remain hers.
Phi. What means do you make to him?
Post. Not any; but abide the change of time,
Quake in the present winter's state, and wish
That warmer days would come. In these fear'd [hopes]
I barely gratify your love; they failing,
I must die much your debtor.
Phi. Your very goodness and your company
O'erpays all I can do. By this, your king
Hath heard of great Augustus. Caius Lucius
Will do 's commission throughly. And I think
He'll grant the tribute, send th' arrearages,
Or look upon our Romans, whose remembrance
Is yet fresh in their grief.
Post. I do believe

138. presently: immediately. **139. sprited with:** haunted by.
142. Shrew me: beshrew me, mischief take me.
149. so: i.e. that it will not be lost. Modern idiom would require *not.*
151. action: law case.
153. my good lady: i.e. well disposed toward me. Perhaps *hope* is similarly ironical, but it was frequently used in the neutral sense "expect." **conceive:** think.

II.iv. Location: Rome. Philario's house.
2. bold: confident. **3. means:** i.e. overtures.
6. fear'd: mixed with fear. **7. gratify:** requite.
12. throughly: thoroughly.
13. He: i.e. Cymbeline. **arrearages:** back payments of tribute.
14. Or: ere (as in *or ere* = before), sooner than (?). But the commoner meaning "or else" makes good sense.
15. their grief: the Britons' grief (?) or the grief inflicted by the Romans (?).

(Statist though I am none, nor like to be)
That this will prove a war; and you shall hear
The legion now in Gallia sooner landed
In our not-fearing Britain than have tidings
Of any penny tribute paid. Our countrymen
Are men more order'd than when Julius Caesar
Smil'd at their lack of skill, but found their courage
Worthy his frowning at. Their discipline
(Now wing-led with their courages) will make known
To their approvers they are people such
That mend upon the world.

Enter Jachimo.

Phi. See! Jachimo!
Post. The swiftest harts have posted you by land,
And winds of all the corners kiss'd your sails,
To make your vessel nimble.
Phi. Welcome, sir.
Post. I hope the briefness of your answer made
The speediness of your return.
Jach. Your lady
Is one of the fairest that I have look'd upon.
Post. And therewithal the best, or let her beauty
Look thorough a casement to allure false hearts,
And be false with them.
Jach. Here are letters for you.
Post. Their tenure good, I trust.
Jach. 'Tis very like.
[*Phi.*] Was Caius Lucius in the Britain court
When you were there?
Jach. He was expected then,
But not approach'd.
Post. All is well yet.
Sparkles this stone as it was wont, or is't not
Too dull for your good wearing?
Jach. If I have lost it,
I should have lost the worth of it in gold.
I'll make a journey twice as far, t' enjoy
A second night of such sweet shortness which
Was mine in Britain, for the ring is won.
Post. The stone's too hard to come by.
Jach. Not a whit,
Your lady being so easy.
Post. Make [not], sir,
Your loss your sport. I hope you know that we
Must not continue friends.
Jach. Good sir, we must,
If you keep covenant. Had I not brought
The knowledge of your mistress home, I grant
We were to question farther; but I now
Profess myself the winner of her honor,
Together with your ring; and not the wronger
Of her or you, having proceeded but
By both your wills.

16. **Statist:** statesman.
24. **wing-led:** reinforced, supported on the right and left flanks. Most editors follow F2 in reading *mingled.*
25. **their approvers:** those who put them to the test.
26. **That . . . world:** as improve their reputation in the eyes of the world. 27. **posted:** sped. 28. **corners:** quarters.
30. **your answer:** the answer you received. 36. **tenure:** tenor.
39. **All . . . yet.** Presumably a comment on the letter which Posthumus has glanced through. 51. **knowledge:** carnal knowledge.
52. **question:** dispute, i.e. duel.

Post. If you can make't apparent
That you have tasted her in bed, my hand
And ring is yours; if not, the foul opinion
You had of her pure honor gains or loses
Your sword or mine, or masterless leave both
To who shall find them.
Jach. Sir, my circumstances,
Being so near the truth as I will make them,
Must first induce you to believe; whose strength
I will confirm with oath, which I doubt not
You'll give me leave to spare when you shall find
You need it not.
Post. Proceed.
Jach. First, her bedchamber
(Where I confess I slept not, but profess
Had that was well worth watching), it was hang'd
With tapestry of silk and silver; the story
Proud Cleopatra, when she met her Roman,
And Cydnus swell'd above the banks, or for
The press of boats or pride. A piece of work
So bravely done, so rich, that it did strive
In workmanship and value, which I wonder'd
Could be so rarely and exactly wrought,
Since the true life on't was—
Post. This is true;
And this you might have heard of here, by me,
Or by some other.
Jach. More particulars
Must justify my knowledge.
Post. So they must,
Or do your honor injury.
Jach. The chimney
Is south the chamber, and the chimney-piece
Chaste Dian bathing. Never saw I figures
So likely to report themselves. The cutter
Was as another Nature, dumb; outwent her,
Motion and breath left out.
Post. This is a thing
Which you might from relation likewise reap,
Being, as it is, much spoke of.
Jach. The roof o' th' chamber
With golden cherubins is fretted. Her andirons
(I had forgot them) were two winking Cupids
Of silver, each on one foot standing, nicely
Depending on their brands.
Post. This is her honor!
Let it be granted you have seen all this (and praise
Be given to your remembrance), the description
Of what is in her chamber nothing saves
The wager you have laid.

60. **leave:** let it leave (?). Many editors emend to *leaves.*
61. **circumstances:** particulars. 65. **spare:** omit.
68. **that:** what. **watching:** staying awake for.
70. **her.** Probably stressed. Jachimo suggests that he was Imogen's Roman, as Antony was Cleopatra's. 71. **or for:** either because of.
73. **bravely:** splendidly.
73–74. **it . . . value:** it was a question whether the workmanship or the material was the more valuable. 79. **justify:** confirm.
83. **So . . . themselves:** such speaking likenesses.
83–84. **The cutter . . . dumb:** the carver made figures as natural as living ones, except that they could not speak.
86. **relation:** hearsay. 88. **fretted:** carved.
89. **winking:** i.e. blind.
91. **Depending . . . brands:** leaning on their torches.
93. **remembrance:** power of memory.

Jach. Then if you can
[*Showing the bracelet.*]
Be pale, I beg but leave to air this jewel. See!
And now 'tis up again. It must be married
To that your diamond, I'll keep them.
Post. Jove—
Once more let me behold it. Is it that
Which I left with her?
Jach. Sir (I thank her), that.
She stripp'd it from her arm. I see her yet:
Her pretty action did outsell her gift,
And yet enrich'd it too. She gave it me, and said
She priz'd it once.
Post. May be she pluck'd it off
To send it me.
Jach. She writes so to you? doth she?
Post. O no, no, no, 'tis true. Here, take this too,
[*Gives the ring.*]
It is a basilisk unto mine eye,
Kills me to look on't. Let there be no honor
Where there is beauty; truth, where semblance; love,
Where there's another man. The vows of women
Of no more bondage be to where they are made
Than they are to their virtues, which is nothing.
O, above measure false!
Phi. Have patience, sir,
And take your ring again, 'tis not yet won.
It may be probable she lost it; or
Who knows if one her women, being corrupted,
Hath stol'n it from her?
Post. Very true,
And so I hope he came by't. Back my ring!
Render to me some corporal sign about her,
More evident than this; for this was stol'n.
Jach. By Jupiter, I had it from her arm.
Post. Hark you, he swears; by Jupiter he swears.
'Tis true—nay, keep the ring—'tis true. I am sure
She would not lose it. Her attendants are
All sworn and honorable. They induc'd to steal it?
And by a stranger? No, he hath enjoy'd her.
The cognizance of her incontinency
Is this. She hath bought the name of whore thus dearly.
There, take thy hire, and all the fiends of hell
Divide themselves between you!
Phi. Sir, be patient.
This is not strong enough to be believ'd
Of one persuaded well of.
Post. Never talk on't:
She hath been colted by him.
Jach. If you seek
For further satisfying, under her breast
(Worthy her pressing) lies a mole, right proud
Of that most delicate lodging. By my life,
I kiss'd it, and it gave me present hunger
To feed again, though full. You do remember

97. up: put away. **102. outsell**: exceed in value.
107. basilisk: fabulous serpent which was believed to kill by its glance. **111. where**: i.e. those to whom.
115. probable: provable. **116. one**: one of.
120. evident: conclusive.
121. By Jupiter. A solemn oath in context.
127. cognizance: badge worn by retainers to show what master they served. **132. persuaded well of**: well reputed.
135. her: i.e. the breast's.

This stain upon her?
Post. Ay, and it doth confirm
Another stain, as big as hell can hold,
Were there no more but it.
Jach. Will you hear more?
Post. Spare your arithmetic, never count the turns.
Once, and a million!
Jach. I'll be sworn.
Post. No swearing:
If you will swear you have not done't, you lie,
And I will kill thee if thou dost deny
Thou'st made me cuckold.
Jach. I'll deny nothing.
Post. O that I had her here, to tear her limb-meal!
I will go there and do't, i' th' court, before
Her father. I'll do something— *Exit.*
Phi. Quite besides
The government of patience! You have won.
Let's follow him, and pervert the present wrath
He hath against himself.
Jach. With all my heart. *Exeunt.*

[Scene V]

Enter Posthumus.

Post. Is there no way for men to be, but women
Must be half-workers? We are all bastards,
And that most venerable man which I
Did call my father, was I know not where
When I was stamp'd. Some coiner with his tools
Made me a counterfeit; yet my mother seem'd
The Dian of that time. So doth my wife
The nonpareil of this. O vengeance, vengeance!
Me of my lawful pleasure she restrain'd,
And pray'd me oft forbearance; did it with
A pudency so rosy the sweet view on't
Might well have warm'd old Saturn; that I thought her
As chaste as unsunn'd snow. O, all the devils!
This yellow Jachimo, in an hour—was't not?—
Or less—at first? Perchance he spoke not, but
Like a full-acorn'd boar, a German [one],
Cried "O!" and mounted; found no opposition
But what he look'd for should oppose and she
Should from encounter guard. Could I find out
The woman's part in me—for there's no motion
That tends to vice in man, but I affirm
It is the woman's part: be it lying, note it,
The woman's; flattering, hers; deceiving, hers;
Lust and rank thoughts, hers, hers; revenges, hers;
Ambitions, covetings, change of prides, disdain,
Nice longing, slanders, mutability,

147. limb-meal: limb from limb. **149. besides**: beyond.
150. government: control. **151. pervert**: divert.

II.v. Location: Scene continues.
2. half-workers: collaborators (in procreation).
11. pudency: modesty. **14. yellow**: sallow.
15. at first: right away.
18. what . . . oppose: what he expected to find placed against him (with bitter pun on two senses of *opposition*).
20. motion: impulse.
25. change of prides: one extravagance after another.
26. Nice longing: wanton appetites.

All faults that name, nay, that hell knows,
Why, hers, in part or all; but rather, all;
For even to vice
They are not constant, but are changing still:
One vice but of a minute old, for one
Not half so old as that. I'll write against them,
Detest them, curse them; yet 'tis greater skill
In a true hate, to pray they have their will:
The very devils cannot plague them better. *Exit.*

ACT III, SCENE I

Enter in state CYMBELINE, QUEEN, CLOTEN, *and* LORDS *at one door, and at another*, CAIUS LUCIUS *and* ATTENDANTS.

Cym. Now say, what would Augustus Caesar with us?
Luc. When Julius Caesar (whose remembrance yet
Lives in men's eyes, and will to ears and tongues
Be theme and hearing ever) was in this Britain,
And conquer'd it, Cassibelan, thine uncle
(Famous in Caesar's praises, no whit less
Than in his feats deserving it), for him
And his succession granted Rome a tribute,
Yearly three thousand pounds, which, by thee, lately
Is left untender'd.
Queen. And to kill the marvel,
Shall be so ever.
Clo. There be many Caesars,
Ere such another Julius. Britain's a world
By itself, and we will nothing pay
For wearing our own noses.
Queen. That opportunity
Which then they had to take from 's, to resume
We have again. Remember, sir, my liege,
The kings your ancestors, together with
The natural bravery of your isle, which stands
As Neptune's park, ribb'd and pal'd in
With oaks unscalable and roaring waters,
With sands that will not bear your enemies' boats,
But suck them up to th' topmast. A kind of conquest
Caesar made here, but made not here his brag
Of "Came, and saw, and overcame." With shame
(The first that ever touch'd him) he was carried
From off our coast, twice beaten; and his shipping
(Poor ignorant baubles!) on our terrible seas,
Like egg-shells mov'd upon their surges, crack'd
As easily 'gainst our rocks. For joy whereof
The fam'd Cassibelan, who was once at point
(O giglet Fortune!) to master Caesar's sword,
Made Lud's-Town with rejoicing fires bright,

27. **name:** have a name.
30. **still:** continuously. 33. **skill:** sagacity.

III.i. Location: Britain. Cymbeline's palace.
10. **kill the marvel:** put an end to the surprise (by making nonpayment the rule).
14. **our own noses.** A rude jibe at the Roman nose. See lines 36–37 below. 15. **resume:** take back. 16. **liege:** sovereign.
20. **oaks.** Many editors adopt Theobald's emendation *rocks*.
30–31. **at point . . . to master:** on the point . . . of mastering.
31. **giglet:** loose woman.
32. **Lud's-Town:** London. Lud was Cymbeline's grandfather, and the town was erroneously supposed to have been named after him.

And Britains strut with courage.
Clo. Come, there's no more tribute to be paid. Our kingdom is stronger than it was at that time; and (as I said) there is no moe such Caesars. Other of them may have crook'd noses, but to owe such straight arms, none.
Cym. Son, let your mother end.
Clo. We have yet many among us can gripe as hard as Cassibelan. I do not say I am one; but I have a hand. Why tribute? Why should we pay tribute? If Caesar can hide the sun from us with a blanket, or put the moon in his pocket, we will pay him tribute for light; else, sir, no more tribute, pray you now.
Cym. You must know,
Till the injurious Romans did extort
This tribute from us, we were free. Caesar's ambition,
Which swell'd so much that it did almost stretch
The sides o' th' world, against all color here
Did put the yoke upon 's; which to shake off
Becomes a warlike people, whom we reckon
Ourselves to be. We do say then to Caesar,
Our ancestor was that Mulmutius which
Ordain'd our laws, whose use the sword of Caesar
Hath too much mangled, whose repair and franchise
Shall (by the power we hold) be our good deed,
Though Rome be therefore angry. Mulmutius made our laws,
Who was the first of Britain which did put
His brows within a golden crown and call'd
Himself a king.
Luc. I am sorry, Cymbeline,
That I am to pronounce Augustus Caesar
(Caesar, that hath moe kings his servants than
Thyself domestic officers) thine enemy.
Receive it from me then: war and confusion
In Caesar's name pronounce I 'gainst thee; look
For fury not to be resisted. Thus defied,
I thank thee for myself.
Cym. Thou art welcome, Caius.
Thy Caesar knighted me; my youth I spent
Much under him; of him I gather'd honor,
Which he to seek of me again, perforce,
Behooves me keep at utterance. I am perfect
That the Pannonians and Dalmatians for
Their liberties are now in arms, a president
Which not to read would show the Britains cold.
So Caesar shall not find them.
Luc. Let proof speak.
Clo. His Majesty bids you welcome. Make pastime with us a day or two, or longer. If you seek us afterwards in other terms, you shall find us in our salt-water girdle. If you beat us out of it, it is yours;

36. **moe:** more. 37. **owe:** own.
39. **end:** finish what she has to say. 40. **gripe:** grip.
47. **injurious:** insulting.
50. **against all color:** without even a pretense of right. Perhaps *color* puns on *collar*, the *yoke* of the next line.
56. **franchise:** free exercise. 65. **confusion:** destruction.
67. **Thus defied:** i.e. this official declaration of hostilities having been delivered. 71. **he . . . of:** his seeking to take back from.
72. **keep at utterance:** defend to the death (from French *à outrance*). **perfect:** fully informed. 74. **president:** precedent.
75. **cold:** lacking spirit.

if you fall in the adventure, our crows shall fare the better for you; and there's an end.

Luc. So, sir.

Cym. I know your master's pleasure and he mine:
All the remain is "Welcome!" *Exeunt.*

Scene II

Enter Pisanio *reading of a letter.*

Pis. How? of adultery? Wherefore write you not
What monsters her accuse? Leonatus!
O master, what a strange infection
Is fall'n into thy ear! What false Italian
(As poisonous tongu'd as handed) hath prevail'd
On thy too ready hearing? Disloyal? No.
She's punish'd for her truth, and undergoes,
More goddess-like than wife-like, such assaults
As would take in some virtue. O my master,
Thy mind to her is now as low as were
Thy fortunes. How? that I should murther her,
Upon the love and truth and vows which I
Have made to thy command? I, her? Her blood?
If it be so to do good service, never
Let me be counted serviceable. How look I
That I should seem to lack humanity
So much as this fact comes to? [*Reading.*] "Do't; the letter
That I have sent her, by her own command
Shall give thee opportunity." O damn'd paper,
Black as the ink that's on thee! Senseless bauble,
Art thou a feodary for this act, and look'st
So virgin-like without? Lo here she comes.

Enter Imogen.

I am ignorant in what I am commanded.

Imo. How now, Pisanio?

Pis. Madam, here is a letter from my lord.

Imo. Who, thy lord? That is my lord Leonatus?
O, learn'd indeed were that astronomer
That knew the stars as I his characters;
He'ld lay the future open. You good gods,
Let what is here contain'd relish of love,
Of my lord's health, of his content—yet not
That we two are asunder; let that grieve him:
Some griefs are med'cinable, that is one of them,
For it doth physic love—of his content,
All but in that! Good wax, thy leave. Blest be
You bees that make these locks of counsel! Lovers
And men in dangerous bonds pray not alike;
Though forfeiters you cast in prison, yet
You clasp young Cupid's tables. Good news, gods!
[*Reads.*] "Justice, and your father's wrath, should he take me in his dominion, could not be so cruel to me as you, O the dearest of creatures, would even renew me with your eyes. Take notice that I am in Cambria, at Milford-Haven; what your own love will out of this advise you, follow. So he wishes you all happiness, that remains loyal to his vow, and your increasing in love.
Leonatus Posthumus."
O for a horse with wings! Hear'st thou, Pisanio?
He is at Milford-Haven. Read, and tell me
How far 'tis thither. If one of mean affairs
May plod it in a week, why may not I
Glide thither in a day? Then, true Pisanio,
Who long'st like me to see thy lord; who long'st
(O let me bate!)—but not like me—yet long'st,
But in a fainter kind—O, not like me,
For mine's beyond beyond—say, and speak thick
(Love's counsellor should fill the bores of hearing,
To th' smothering of the sense), how far it is
To this same blessed Milford. And by th' way
Tell me how Wales was made so happy as
T' inherit such a haven. But first of all,
How we may steal from hence; and for the gap
That we shall make in time, from our hence-going
And our return, to excuse. But first, how get hence.
Why should excuse be born or ere begot?
We'll talk of that hereafter. Prithee speak,
How many [score] of miles may we well rid
'Twixt hour and hour?

Pis. One score 'twixt sun and sun,
Madam, 's enough for you—and too much too.

Imo. Why, one that rode to 's execution, man,
Could never go so slow. I have heard of riding wagers,
Where horses have been nimbler than the sands
That run i' th' clock's behalf. But this is fool'ry.
Go, bid my woman feign a sickness, say
She'll home to her father; and provide me presently
A riding-suit, no costlier than would fit
A franklin's huswife.

Pis. Madam, you're best consider.

Imo. I see before me, man; nor here, [nor] here,
Nor what ensues, but have a fog in them
That I cannot look through. Away, I prithee,
Do as I bid thee. There's no more to say:
Accessible is none but Milford way. *Exeunt.*

81. adventure: venture, risky undertaking.
85. All the remain: all that remains to be said.

III.ii. Location: Britain. Cymbeline's palace.
7. truth: fidelity. **undergoes:** endures, i.e. holds out against.
9. take in: conquer. **10. to her:** compared with hers.
12. Upon: in consequence of. **17. fact:** deed, crime.
20. Senseless bauble: insentient trifle. **21. feodary:** accomplice.
23. I . . . commanded: i.e. I will give no hint of what I have been ordered to do.
27. astronomer: astrologer. **28. characters:** handwriting.
30. relish: taste. **31. not:** not content.
33. are med'cinable: have medicinal value, are salutary.
34. physic: make healthy, strengthen.
35. Good . . . leave. She breaks the seal.
36. of counsel: for private matters.
37. in dangerous bonds: bound by risky contracts (also sealed with wax).
39. Cupid's tables: i.e. love letters; *tables* = writing tablets.
41. as: but that. **43. Cambria:** Wales.
50. of mean affairs: having unimportant business.
54. bate: abate, modify. **56. thick:** rapidly.
57. bores of hearing: ears. **58. sense:** sense of hearing.
59. by: on.
62–64. for . . . excuse. The syntax reflects Imogen's excitement.
65. or ere begot: before (the need for it is) begotten.
67. rid: dispose of. Most editors follow F2 in reading *ride.*
71. riding: i.e. racing.
73. i' . . . behalf: in place of the clock, i.e. in an hourglass.
77. franklin's huswife: small landowner's housewife.
78. nor . . . here: neither on this side nor on that.
79. what ensues: the road behind (?) or what will happen after I reach Milford-Haven (?). If the latter, *before me* in line 78 means "immediately before me," i.e. the road to Milford-Haven, but not beyond.

Scene III

Enter [*from their cave*] Belarius, Guiderius, *and* Arviragus.

Bel. A goodly day not to keep house with such
Whose roof's as low as ours! [Stoop,] boys, this gate
Instructs you how t' adore the heavens, and bows you
To a morning's holy office. The gates of monarchs
Are arch'd so high that giants may jet through
And keep their impious turbands on without
Good morrow to the sun. Hail, thou fair heaven!
We house i' th' rock, yet use thee not so hardly
As prouder livers do.
Gui. Hail, heaven!
Arv. Hail, heaven!
Bel. Now for our mountain sport: up to yond hill,
Your legs are young; I'll tread these flats. Consider,
When you above perceive me like a crow,
That it is place which lessens and sets off,
And you may then revolve what tales I have told you
Of courts, of princes, of the tricks in war.
This service is not service, so being done,
But being so allowed. To apprehend thus
Draws us a profit from all things we see;
And often, to our comfort, shall we find
The sharded beetle in a safer hold
Than is the full-wing'd eagle. O, this life
Is nobler than attending for a check;
Richer than doing nothing for a [bable];
Prouder than rustling in unpaid-for silk:
Such gain the cap of him that makes him fine,
Yet keeps his book uncross'd. No life to ours.
Gui. Out of your proof you speak; we poor unfledg'd
Have never wing'd from view o' th' nest, nor [know] not
What air's from home. Happ'ly this life is best,
If quiet life be best; sweeter to you
That have a sharper known; well corresponding
With your stiff age; but unto us it is
A cell of ignorance, travelling a-bed,
A prison, or a debtor that not dares
To stride a limit.
Arv. What should we speak of
When we are old as you? When we shall hear
The rain and wind beat dark December, how,

III.iii. Location: Wales. Before the cave of Belarius.
1. **keep house:** stay indoors.
4. **morning's holy office:** morning prayers. 5. **jet:** strut.
6. **impious turbands.** In the old romances giants were often Saracens.
8. **use . . . hardly:** treat . . . badly.
9. **prouder livers:** those who live more splendidly.
12. **like:** i.e. as small as. 13. **place:** position. **sets off:** enhances.
16. **This service:** this or that (i.e. any) act of service. **so being done:** because it was performed as a service.
17. **allowed:** accepted, acknowledged.
20. **sharded:** wing-cased. **hold:** stronghold.
22. **attending . . . check:** doing courtly service only to be rebuked.
23. **bable:** bauble, trifle.
25. **gain . . . fine:** win the approval of the man who dresses fashionably (?). Some editors, following Rowe, read *makes them* and explain, "receive the respectful salute of their tailor."
26. **book uncross'd:** record of debts uncancelled.
27. **proof:** experience. 29. **Happ'ly:** haply, perhaps.
33. **a-bed:** i.e. in imagination.
35. **stride a limit:** overstep a boundary (beyond which he will be liable to arrest).

In this our pinching cave, shall we discourse
The freezing hours away? We have seen nothing.
We are beastly: subtle as the fox for prey,
Like warlike as the wolf for what we eat;
Our valor is to chase what flies. Our cage
We make a choir, as doth the prison'd bird,
And sing our bondage freely.
Bel. How you speak!
Did you but know the city's usuries,
And felt them knowingly; the art o' th' court,
As hard to leave as keep; whose top to climb
Is certain falling, or so slipp'ry that
The fear's as bad as falling; the toil o' th' war,
A pain that only seems to seek out danger
I' th' name of fame and honor which dies i' th' search,
And hath as oft a sland'rous epitaph
As record of fair act; nay, many times
Doth ill deserve by doing well; what's worse,
Must curtsy at the censure. O boys, this story
The world may read in me: my body's mark'd
With Roman swords, and my report was once
First with the best of note. Cymbeline lov'd me,
And when a soldier was the theme, my name
Was not far off. Then was I as a tree
Whose boughs did bend with fruit; but in one night,
A storm or robbery (call it what you will)
Shook down my mellow hangings, nay, my leaves,
And left me bare to weather.
Gui. Uncertain favor!
Bel. My fault being nothing (as I have told you oft)
But that two villains, whose false oaths prevail'd
Before my perfect honor, swore to Cymbeline
I was confederate with the Romans. So
Followed my banishment, and this twenty years
This rock and these demesnes have been my world,
Where I have liv'd at honest freedom, paid
More pious debts to heaven than in all
The fore-end of my time. But up to th' mountains!
This is not hunters' language. He that strikes
The venison first shall be the lord o' th' feast,
To him the other two shall minister,
And we will fear no poison, which attends
In place of greater state. I'll meet you in the valleys.
Exeunt [*Guiderius and Arviragus*].
How hard it is to hide the sparks of nature!
These boys know little they are sons to th' King,
Nor Cymbeline dreams that they are alive.
They think they are mine, and though train'd up thus meanly
I' th' cave [wherein they] bow, their thoughts do hit
The roofs of palaces, and nature prompts them
In simple and low things to prince it much
Beyond the trick of others. This Polydore,
The heir of Cymbeline and Britain, who
The King his father call'd Guiderius—Jove!
When on my three-foot stool I sit and tell
The warlike feats I have done, his spirits fly out

38. **pinching:** confining (?) or nippingly cold (?).
50. **pain:** labor. 54. **deserve:** earn.
55. **curtsy . . . censure:** bow to the verdict.
86. **trick:** habit, manner.

Into my story; say, "Thus mine enemy fell,
And thus I set my foot on 's neck," even then
The princely blood flows in his cheek, he sweats,
Strains his young nerves, and puts himself in posture
That acts my words. The younger brother, Cadwal,
Once Arviragus, in as like a figure
Strikes life into my speech, and shows much more
His own conceiving.—Hark, the game is rous'd!—
O Cymbeline, heaven and my conscience knows
Thou didst unjustly banish me; whereon,
At three and two years old, I stole these babes,
Thinking to bar thee of succession, as
Thou refts me of my lands. Euriphile,
Thou wast their nurse; they took thee for their mother,
And every day do honor to her grave.
Myself, Belarius, that am Morgan call'd,
They take for natural father.—The game is up. *Exit.*

Scene IV

Enter Pisanio *and* Imogen.

Imo. Thou toldst me, when we came from horse, the place
Was near at hand. Ne'er long'd my mother so
To see me first, as I have now. Pisanio! man!
Where is Posthumus? What is in thy mind
That makes thee stare thus? Wherefore breaks that sigh
From th' inward of thee? One but painted thus
Would be interpreted a thing perplex'd
Beyond self-explication. Put thyself
Into a havior of less fear, ere wildness
Vanquish my staider senses. What's the matter?
Why tender'st thou that paper to me with
A look untender? If't be summer news,
Smile to't before; if winterly, thou need'st
But keep that count'nance still. My husband's hand!
That drug-damn'd Italy hath outcraftied him,
And he's at some hard point. Speak, man, thy tongue
May take off some extremity, which to read
Would be even mortal to me.

Pis. Please you read,
And you shall find me, wretched man, a thing
The most disdain'd of fortune.

Imo. (*Reads.*) "Thy mistress, Pisanio, hath play'd the strumpet in my bed; the testimonies whereof lies bleeding in me. I speak not out of weak surmises, but from proof as strong as my grief and as certain as I expect my revenge. That part thou, Pisanio, must act for me, if thy faith be not tainted with the breach of hers. Let thine own hands take away her life. I shall give thee opportunity at Milford-Haven. She hath my letter for the purpose; where, if thou fear to strike and to make me certain it is done, thou art the pander to her dishonor and equally to me disloyal."

Pis. What shall I need to draw my sword, the paper
Hath cut her throat already! No, 'tis slander,
Whose edge is sharper than the sword, whose tongue
Outvenoms all the worms of Nile, whose breath
Rides on the posting winds and doth belie
All corners of the world. Kings, queens, and states,
Maids, matrons, nay, the secrets of the grave
This viperous slander enters. What cheer, madam?

Imo. False to his bed? What is it to be false?
To lie in watch there, and to think on him?
To weep 'twixt clock and clock? If sleep charge nature,
To break it with a fearful dream of him,
And cry myself awake? That's false to 's bed? is it?

Pis. Alas, good lady!

Imo. I false? Thy conscience witness! Jachimo,
Thou didst accuse him of incontinency;
Thou then look'dst like a villain; now methinks
Thy favor's good enough. Some jay of Italy
(Whose mother was her painting) hath betray'd him.
Poor I am stale, a garment out of fashion,
And for I am richer than to hang by th' walls,
I must be ripp'd. To pieces with me! O!
Men's vows are women's traitors. All good seeming,
By thy revolt, O husband, shall be thought
Put on for villainy; not born where't grows,
But worn a bait for ladies.

Pis. Good madam, hear me.

Imo. True honest men being heard, like false Aeneas,
Were in his time thought false; and Sinon's weeping
Did scandal many a holy tear, took pity
From most true wretchedness. So thou, Posthumus,
Wilt lay the leaven on all proper men;
Goodly and gallant shall be false and perjur'd
From thy great fail.—Come, fellow, be thou honest,
Do thou thy master's bidding. When thou seest him,
A little witness my obedience. Look
I draw the sword myself, take it, and hit
The innocent mansion of my love, my heart.
Fear not, 'tis empty of all things but grief.
Thy master is not there, who was indeed
The riches of it. Do his bidding, strike.
Thou mayst be valiant in a better cause,
But now thou seem'st a coward.

Pis. Hence, vile instrument!
Thou shalt not damn my hand.

Imo. Why, I must die;
And if I do not by thy hand, thou art

94. nerves: sinews.
96. in . . . figure: as graphically as his brother.
105. her: "of 'their mother, as they suppose it to be'" (Malone).
107. up: roused (cf. line 98).

III.iv. Location: Wales. Country near Milford-Haven.
3. have: i.e. have longing to see Posthumus.
7. perplex'd: distressed. **9. of less fear:** less fearsome.
15. drug-damn'd: damned for its use of poisons. **outcraftied him:** been too much for him with its craftiness.
16. hard point: dangerous crisis.
35. worms: serpents.
37. states: statesmen. **41. in watch:** awake.
42. 'twixt . . . clock: hour by hour. **charge:** overburden, prove too much for. **49. favor:** countenance. **jay:** strumpet.
50. Whose . . . painting: i.e. who is the creature of her cosmetics.
52. for . . . than: because I am too fine. **55. revolt:** faithlessness.
56. not . . . grows: not natural but assumed.
58, 59. Aeneas, Sinon. Types of deceivers. Aeneas deserted Dido; Sinon betrayed Troy to the Greeks.
60. scandal: make disreputable.
62. lay . . . men: discredit all honorable men, as sour dough spoils other dough. **66. A little witness:** testify briefly to.

No servant of thy master's. Against self-slaughter
There is a prohibition so divine
That cravens my weak hand. Come, here's my heart:
Something's [afore't]. Soft, soft, we'll no defense,
Obedient as the scabbard. What is here?
The scriptures of the loyal Leonatus,
All turn'd to heresy? Away, away,
Corrupters of my faith! you shall no more
Be stomachers to my heart. Thus may poor fools
Believe false teachers. Though those that are betray'd
Do feel the treason sharply, yet the traitor
Stands in worse case of woe. And thou, Posthumus,
That didst set up my disobedience 'gainst the King
My father, and [make] me put into contempt the suits
Of princely fellows, shalt hereafter find
It is no act of common passage, but
A strain of rareness; and I grieve myself
To think, when thou shalt be disedg'd by her
That now thou tirest on, how thy memory
Will then be pang'd by me. Prithee dispatch,
The lamb entreats the butcher. Where's thy knife?
Thou art too slow to do thy master's bidding
When I desire it too.
Pis. O gracious lady!
Since I receiv'd command to do this business
I have not slept one wink.
Imo. Do't, and to bed then.
Pis. I'll wake mine eyeballs [out] first.
Imo. Wherefore then
Didst undertake it? Why hast thou abus'd
So many miles with a pretense? this place?
Mine action? and thine own? our horses' labor?
The time inviting thee? the perturb'd court
For my being absent? whereunto I never
Purpose return. Why hast thou gone so far,
To be unbent when thou hast ta'en thy stand,
Th' elected deer before thee?
Pis. But to win time
To lose so bad employment, in the which
I have consider'd of a course. Good lady,
Hear me with patience.
Imo. Talk thy tongue weary, speak.
I have heard I am a strumpet, and mine ear,
Therein false strook, can take no greater wound,
Nor tent to bottom that. But speak.
Pis. Then, madam,
I thought you would not back again.
Imo. Most like,
Bringing me here to kill me.
Pis. Not so, neither;
But if I were as wise as honest, then
My purpose would prove well. It cannot be
But that my master is abus'd. Some villain,
Ay, and singular in his art, hath done you both
This cursed injury.
Imo. Some Roman courtezan?
Pis. No, on my life.
I'll give but notice you are dead, and send him
Some bloody sign of it; for 'tis commanded
I should do so. You shall be miss'd at court,
And that will well confirm it.
Imo. Why, good fellow,
What shall I do the while? where bide? how live?
Or in my life what comfort, when I am
Dead to my husband?
Pis. If you'll back to th' court—
Imo. No court, no father, nor no more ado
With that harsh, noble, simple nothing,
That Cloten, whose love-suit hath been to me
As fearful as a siege.
Pis. If not at court,
Then not in Britain must you bide.
Imo. Where then?
Hath Britain all the sun that shines? day? night?
Are they not but in Britain? I' th' world's volume
Our Britain seems as of it, but not in't;
In a great pool a swan's nest. Prithee think
There's livers out of Britain.
Pis. I am most glad
You think of other place. Th' ambassador,
Lucius the Roman, comes to Milford-Haven
To-morrow. Now, if you could wear a mind
Dark as your fortune is, and but disguise
That which, t' appear itself, must not yet be
But by self-danger, you should tread a course
Pretty and full of view; yea, happily, near
The residence of Posthumus; so nigh, at least,
That though his actions were not visible, yet
Report should render him hourly to your ear
As truly as he moves.
Imo. O, for such means,
Though peril to my modesty, not death on't,
I would adventure.
Pis. Well then, here's the point:
You must forget to be a woman; change
Command into obedience; fear and niceness
(The handmaids of all women, or more truly
Woman it pretty self) into a waggish courage,

78. **cravens:** makes cowardly. 79. **Soft:** hold on.
80. **Obedient:** i.e. as ready to receive the sword.
81. **scriptures:** letters, with play on the sense "sacred books."
84. **stomachers:** ornamental chest-coverings worn to fill in the front opening of the bodice.
91–92. **no . . . rareness:** no common occurrence, but the product of rare qualities.
93–94. **be . . . tirest on:** have the edge of your appetite taken off by her on whom you now feed ravenously (a continuation of the eagle imagery associated with Posthumus throughout, but now with emphasis not on the bird's regal nature, as earlier, but on its predatory aspect).
95. **pang'd:** tortured.
101. **wake . . . out:** keep awake until my eyes drop out.
108. **be unbent:** have your bow unbent, i.e. refuse to shoot.
109. **elected:** chosen. 114. **strook:** struck.
115. **tent . . . that:** probe that wound to the bottom.
116. **back:** go back (to the court).
120. **abus'd:** deceived. 121. **singular:** unmatched.
132. This metrically defective line may be corrupt; it has been variously emended.
138. **Our . . . in't:** i.e. Britain is only a page, and a detached page at that. 144. **Dark:** obscured (?) or lowly (?).
145. **That:** i.e. the fact that she is a woman. **appear itself:** show itself undisguised.
147. **Pretty . . . view:** pleasant and with good prospects. **happily:** haply, perchance (but since such a chance would be a fortunate one, the intended sense may include the modern meaning).
153. **adventure:** take extreme risks.
154–55. **change . . . obedience.** Not because women command and men obey, but because Imogen will be changing from high rank to low. 155. **niceness:** fastidiousness.
157. **it:** its. **waggish:** roguish.

Ready in gibes, quick-answer'd, saucy, and
As quarrellous as the weasel; nay, you must
Forget that rarest treasure of your cheek,
Exposing it (but O, the harder heart!
Alack, no remedy!) to the greedy touch
Of common-kissing Titan, and forget
Your laborsome and dainty trims, wherein
You made great Juno angry.
Imo. Nay, be brief:
I see into thy end, and am almost
A man already.
Pis. First, make yourself but like one.
Forethinking this, I have already fit
('Tis in my cloak-bag) doublet, hat, hose, all
That answer to them. Would you in their serving
(And with what imitation you can borrow
From youth of such a season) 'fore noble Lucius
Present yourself, desire his service, tell him
Wherein you're happy, which will make him know,
If that his head have ear in music, doubtless
With joy he will embrace you; for he's honorable,
And doubling that, most holy. Your means abroad—
You have me, rich, and I will never fail
Beginning nor supplyment.
Imo. Thou art all the comfort
The gods will diet me with. Prithee away,
There's more to be consider'd; but we'll even
All that good time will give us. This attempt
I am soldier to, and will abide it with
A prince's courage. Away, I prithee.
Pis. Well, madam, we must take a short farewell,
Lest being miss'd, I be suspected of
Your carriage from the court. My noble mistress,
Here is a box, I had it from the Queen,
What's in't is precious. If you are sick at sea,
Or stomach-qualm'd at land, a dram of this
Will drive away distemper. To some shade,
And fit you to your manhood. May the gods
Direct you to the best!
Imo. Amen! I thank thee.
Exeunt [severally].

SCENE V

Enter CYMBELINE *[attended]*, QUEEN, CLOTEN, LUCIUS, *and* LORDS.

Cym. Thus far, and so farewell.
Luc. Thanks, royal sir.
My emperor hath wrote I must from hence,
And am right sorry that I must report ye
My master's enemy.
Cym. Our subjects, sir,
Will not endure his yoke; and for ourself
To show less sovereignty than they, must needs
Appear unkinglike.
Luc. So, sir. I desire of you
A conduct overland to Milford-Haven.
Madam, all joy befall your Grace, and you!
Cym. My lords, you are appointed for that office;
The due of honor in no point omit.
So farewell, noble Lucius.
Luc. Your hand, my lord.
Clo. Receive it friendly; but from this time forth
I wear it as your enemy.
Luc. Sir, the event
Is yet to name the winner. Fare you well.
Cym. Leave not the worthy Lucius, good my lords,
Till he have cross'd the Severn. Happiness!
Exit Lucius [with Lords].
Queen. He goes hence frowning; but it honors us
That we have given him cause.
Clo. 'Tis all the better,
Your valiant Britains have their wishes in it.
Cym. Lucius hath wrote already to the Emperor
How it goes here. It fits us therefore ripely
Our chariots and our horsemen be in readiness.
The pow'rs that he already hath in Gallia
Will soon be drawn to head, from whence he moves
His war for Britain.
Queen. 'Tis not sleepy business,
But must be look'd to speedily and strongly.
Cym. Our expectation that it would be thus
Hath made us forward. But, my gentle queen,
Where is our daughter? She hath not appear'd
Before the Roman, nor to us hath tender'd
The duty of the day. She [looks] us like
A thing more made of malice than of duty,
We have noted it. Call her before us, for
We have been too slight in sufferance.
[Exit a Messenger.]
Queen. Royal sir,
Since the exile of Posthumus, most retir'd
Hath her life been; the cure whereof, my lord,
'Tis time must do. Beseech your Majesty,
Forbear sharp speeches to her. She's a lady
So tender of rebukes that words are [strokes],
And strokes death to her.

Enter a MESSENGER.

Cym. Where is she, sir? How
Can her contempt be answer'd?
Mess. Please you, sir,
Her chambers are all lock'd, and there's no answer
That will be given to th' loud of noise we make.

161. the harder heart. Variously explained as referring to Posthumus, to Pisanio (who thinks the very recital of these changes is brutal), and to Imogen (who must harden her heart as well as tan her face).
163. Titan: the sun. **164. laborsome:** elaborate.
165. angry: i.e. jealous. **168. fit:** ready.
170. answer to: are needed to go along with. **in their serving:** aided by them. **172. season:** age.
173. his service: service under him.
174. Wherein you're happy: what accomplishments you have. **make him know:** convince him.
175. If . . . music: i.e. if he can appreciate your musical voice.
176. embrace: receive into his service.
177. Your means: as for your financial needs.
181. even: keep pace with.
183. soldier to: enlisted in, committed to.
185. short: hasty (not "for a short time").
187. carriage: removal.

III.v. Location: Britain. Cymbeline's palace.

7. So. A polite way of closing the subject.
14. event: outcome. **22. It . . . ripely:** it is high time.
25. drawn to head: assembled. **moves:** launches.
29. forward: well advanced in preparation. **32. looks:** looks at.
35. slight in sufferance: mild in tolerating (her behavior).
44. loud: loudness.

Queen. My lord, when last I went to visit her,
She pray'd me to excuse her keeping close,
Whereto constrain'd by her infirmity,
She should that duty leave unpaid to you
Which daily she was bound to proffer. This
She wish'd me to make known; but our great court
Made me to blame in memory.

Cym. Her doors lock'd?
Not seen of late? Grant, heavens, that which I fear
Prove false! *Exit.*

Queen. Son, I say, follow the King.

Clo. That man of hers, Pisanio, her old servant,
I have not seen these two days.

Queen. Go, look after. *Exit [Cloten].*
Pisanio, thou that stand'st so for Posthumus!
He hath a drug of mine; I pray his absence
Proceed by swallowing that; for he believes
It is a thing most precious. But for her,
Where is she gone? Haply despair hath seiz'd her;
Or wing'd with fervor of her love, she's flown
To her desir'd Posthumus. Gone she is
To death or to dishonor, and my end
Can make good use of either. She being down,
I have the placing of the British crown.

Enter CLOTEN.

How now, my son?

Clo. 'Tis certain she is fled.
Go in and cheer the King, he rages, none
Dare come about him.

Queen. [*Aside.*] All the better. May
This night forestall him of the coming day!
Exit Queen.

Clo. I love and hate her; for she's fair and royal,
And that she hath all courtly parts more exquisite
Than lady, ladies, woman, from every one
The best she hath, and she, of all compounded,
Outsells them all. I love her therefore, but
Disdaining me and throwing favors on
The low Posthumus slanders so her judgment
That what's else rare is chok'd; and in that point
I will conclude to hate her, nay indeed,
To be reveng'd upon her. For when fools shall—

Enter PISANIO.

Who is here? What, are you packing, sirrah?
Come hither. Ah, you precious pandar! Villain,
Where is thy lady? In a word, or else
Thou art straightway with the fiends.

Pis. O, good my lord!

Clo. Where is thy lady? or, by Jupiter,
I will not ask again. Close villain,
I'll have this secret from thy heart, or rip
Thy heart to find it. Is she with Posthumus?
From whose so many weights of baseness cannot
A dram of worth be drawn.

Pis. Alas, my lord,
How can she be with him? When was she miss'd?
He is in Rome.

Clo. Where is she, sir? Come nearer.
No farther halting. Satisfy me home,
What is become of her?

Pis. O, my all-worthy lord!

Clo. All-worthy villain!
Discover where thy mistress is, at once,
At the next word. No more of "worthy lord"!
Speak, or thy silence on the instant is
Thy condemnation and thy death.

Pis. Then, sir:
This paper is the history of my knowledge
Touching her flight. [*Presenting a letter.*]

Clo. Let's see't. I will pursue her
Even to Augustus' throne.

Pis. [*Aside.*] Or this, or perish.
She's far enough, and what he learns by this
May prove his travel, not her danger.

Clo. Humh!

Pis. [*Aside.*] I'll write to my lord she's dead. O Imogen,
Safe mayst thou wander, safe return again!

Clo. Sirrah, is this letter true?

Pis. Sir, as I think.

Clo. It is Posthumus' hand, I know't. Sirrah, if thou wouldst not be a villain, but do me true service, undergo those employments wherein I should have cause to use thee with a serious industry, that is, what villainy soe'er I bid thee do, to perform it directly and truly, I would think thee an honest man. Thou shouldst neither want my means for thy relief nor my voice for thy preferment.

Pis. Well, my good lord.

Clo. Wilt thou serve me? For since patiently and constantly thou hast stuck to the bare fortune of that beggar Posthumus, thou canst not, in the course of gratitude, but be a diligent follower of mine. Wilt thou serve me?

Pis. Sir, I will.

Clo. Give me thy hand, here's my purse. Hast any of thy late master's garments in thy possession?

Pis. I have, my lord, at my lodging, the same suit he wore when he took leave of my lady and mistress.

Clo. The first service thou dost me, fetch that suit hither. Let it be thy first service, go.

Pis. I shall, my lord. *Exit.*

Clo. Meet thee at Milford-Haven! (I forgot to ask him one thing, I'll remember't anon.) Even there, thou villain Posthumus, will I kill thee. I would these garments were come. She said upon a time (the bitterness of it I now belch from my heart) that she held the very garment of Posthumus in more respect than my noble and natural person, together with the adornment of my qualities. With that suit upon my back will I ravish her; first kill him, and in her eyes; there shall

56. stand'st: standest up.
69. forestall: deprive. She hopes that the King's fit of rage will be fatal. **70–71. for . . . that:** because . . . because.
72. Than . . . woman: "than any lady, than all ladies, than all womankind" (Johnson). **74. Outsells:** exceeds in value.
76. slanders: discredits.
80. packing: scheming. **sirrah:** term of address to an inferior.
81. pandar. As agent between Imogen and Posthumus.
85. Close: secretive.

91. Come nearer: answer more directly.
92. home: completely. **95. Discover:** reveal.
131. one thing: i.e. how long ago Imogen left (see lines 148–49).
135. more respect: higher regard.

she see my valor, which will then be a torment to her contempt. He on the ground, my speech of insultment ended on his dead body, and when my lust hath din'd (which, as I say, to vex her I will execute in the clothes that she so prais'd), to the court I'll knock her back, foot her home again. She hath despis'd me rejoicingly, and I'll be merry in my revenge.

Enter Pisanio [*with the clothes*].

Be those the garments?

Pis. Ay, my noble lord.

Clo. How long is't since she went to Milford-Haven?

Pis. She can scarce be there yet.

Clo. Bring this apparel to my chamber. That is the second thing that I have commanded thee. The third is, that thou wilt be a voluntary mute to my design. Be but duteous, and true preferment shall tender itself to thee. My revenge is now at Milford; would I had wings to follow it! Come, and be true. *Exit.*

Pis. Thou bid'st me to my loss; for true to thee
Were to prove false, which I will never be
To him that is most true. To Milford go,
And find not her whom thou pursuest. Flow, flow,
You heavenly blessings, on her! This fool's speed
Be cross'd with slowness; labor be his meed. *Exit.*

Scene VI

Enter Imogen *alone* [*in boy's clothes*].

Imo. I see a man's life is a tedious one,
I have tir'd myself; and for two nights together
Have made the ground my bed. I should be sick,
But that my resolution helps me. Milford,
When from the mountain top Pisanio show'd thee,
Thou wast within a ken. O Jove, I think
Foundations fly the wretched: such, I mean,
Where they should be reliev'd. Two beggars told me
I could not miss my way. Will poor folks lie,
That have afflictions on them, knowing 'tis
A punishment or trial? Yes; no wonder,
When rich ones scarce tell true. To lapse in fullness
Is sorer than to lie for need; and falsehood
Is worse in kings than beggars. My dear lord,
Thou art one o' th' false ones. Now I think on thee,
My hunger's gone; but even before, I was
At point to sink for food. But what is this?
Here is a path to't; 'tis some savage hold.
I were best not call; I dare not call; yet famine,
Ere clean it o'erthrow nature, makes it valiant.
Plenty and peace breeds cowards; hardness ever
Of hardiness is mother. Ho! who's here?
If any thing that's civil, speak; if savage,
Take or lend. Ho! No answer? Then I'll enter.
Best draw my sword; and if mine enemy
But fear the sword like me, he'll scarcely look on't.
Such a foe, good heavens! *Exit* [*to the cave*].

Enter Belarius, Guiderius, *and* Arviragus.

Bel. You, Polydore, have prov'd best woodman, and
Are master of the feast. Cadwal and I
Will play the cook and servant, 'tis our match.
The sweat of industry would dry and die,
But for the end it works to. Come, our stomachs
Will make what's homely savory; weariness
Can snore upon the flint, when resty sloth
Finds the down pillow hard. Now peace be here,
Poor house, that keep'st thyself!

Gui. I am throughly weary.

Arv. I am weak with toil, yet strong in appetite.

Gui. There is cold meat i' th' cave, we'll browse on that
Whilst what we have kill'd be cook'd.

Bel. [*Looking into the cave.*] Stay, come not in.
But that it eats our victuals, I should think
Here were a fairy.

Gui. What's the matter, sir?

Bel. By Jupiter, an angel! or if not,
An earthly paragon! Behold divineness
No elder than a boy!

Enter Imogen.

Imo. Good masters, harm me not.
Before I enter'd here I call'd, and thought
To have begg'd or bought what I have took. Good troth,
I have stol'n nought, nor would not, though I had found
Gold strew'd i' th' floor. Here's money for my meat,
I would have left it on the board so soon
As I had made my meal, and parted with
Pray'rs for the provider.

Gui. Money, youth?

Arv. All gold and silver rather turn to dirt,
As 'tis no better reckon'd, but of those
Who worship dirty gods.

Imo. I see you're angry.
Know, if you kill me for my fault, I should
Have died had I not made it.

Bel. Whither bound?

Imo. To Milford-Haven.

Bel. What's your name?

Imo. Fidele, sir. I have a kinsman who
Is bound for Italy; he embark'd at Milford;
To whom being going, almost spent with hunger,
I am fall'n in this offense.

Bel. Prithee, fair youth,
Think us no churls; nor measure our good minds
By this rude place we live in. Well encounter'd!

144. foot: kick. **162. cross'd:** frustrated. **meed:** reward.

III.vi. Location: Wales. Before the cave of Belarius.
6. within a ken: in sight.
7. Foundations . . . wretched: charitable institutions are never at hand when people most need them. **11. trial:** test of virtue.
12. lapse in fullness: sin in prosperity. **13. sorer:** worse.
16. but even: only a moment. **17. for:** for lack of.
18. hold: fastness. **21. hardness:** hardship. **23. civil:** civilized.

24. Take or lend: rob me or give me food. **25. and if:** if.
27. Such a foe: i.e. send me a foe as timid as myself.
28. woodman: woodsman, hunter. **30. match:** agreement.
33. homely: plain. **34. resty:** idle.
36. that keep'st thyself: i.e. that is empty. **throughly:** thoroughly.
38. browse: nibble. **47. Good troth:** in truth.
57. made: committed. **63. in:** into.

'Tis almost night, you shall have better cheer
Ere you depart, and thanks to stay and eat it.
Boys, bid him welcome.
Gui. Were you a woman, youth,
I should woo hard but be your groom in honesty:
I bid for you as I do buy.
Arv. I'll make't my comfort
He is a man, I'll love him as my brother:
And such a welcome as I'ld give to him
After long absence, such is yours. Most welcome!
Be sprightly, for you fall 'mongst friends.
Imo. [*Aside.*] 'Mongst friends?
If brothers: would it had been so, that they
Had been my father's sons, then had my prize
Been less, and so more equal ballasting
To thee, Posthumus.
Bel. He wrings at some distress.
Gui. Would I could free't!
Arv. Or I, what e'er it be,
What pain it cost, what danger. Gods!
Bel. Hark, boys. [*Whispering.*]
Imo. Great men,
That had a court no bigger than this cave,
That did attend themselves and had the virtue
Which their own conscience seal'd them, laying by
That nothing-gift of differing multitudes,
Could not outpeer these twain. Pardon me, gods!
I'ld change my sex to be companion with them,
Since Leonatus' false.
Bel. It shall be so.
Boys, we'll go dress our hunt. Fair youth, come in.
Discourse is heavy, fasting; when we have supp'd,
We'll mannerly demand thee of thy story,
So far as thou wilt speak it.
Gui. Pray draw near.
Arv. The night to th' owl and morn to th' lark less welcome.
Imo. Thanks, sir.
Arv. I pray draw near. *Exeunt.*

Scene VII

Enter two Roman Senators *and* Tribunes.

1. Sen. This is the tenor of the Emperor's writ:
That since the common men are now in action
'Gainst the Pannonians and Dalmatians,
And that the legions now in Gallia are
Full weak to undertake our wars against
The fall'n-off Britains, that we do incite
The gentry to this business. He creates
Lucius proconsul; and to you the tribunes,
For this immediate levy, he commands
His absolute commission. Long live Caesar!
[1.] Tri. Is Lucius general of the forces?
2. Sen. Ay.
[1.] Tri. Remaining now in Gallia?
1. Sen. With those legions
Which I have spoke of, whereunto your levy
Must be supplyant. The words of your commission
Will tie you to the numbers and the time
Of their dispatch.
[1.] Tri. We will discharge our duty. *Exeunt.*

Act IV, Scene I

Enter Cloten *alone.*

Clo. I am near to th' place where they should meet, if Pisanio have mapp'd it truly. How fit his garments serve me! Why should his mistress, who was made by him that made the tailor, not be fit too? the rather (saving reverence of the word) for 'tis said a woman's fitness comes by fits. Therein I must play the workman. I dare speak it to myself, for it is not vain-glory for a man and his glass to confer in his own chamber—I mean, the lines of my body are as well drawn as his; no less young, more strong, not beneath him in fortunes, beyond him in the advantage of the time, above him in birth, alike conversant in general services, and more remarkable in single oppositions; yet this imperceiverant thing loves him in my despite. What mortality is! Posthumus, thy head, which now is growing upon thy shoulders, shall within this hour be off, thy mistress enforc'd, thy garments cut to pieces before [her] face: and all this done, spurn her home to her father, who may (happily) be a little angry for my so rough usage; but my mother, having power of his testiness, shall turn all into my commendations. My horse is tied up safe; out, sword, and to a sore purpose! Fortune put them into my hand! This is the very description of their meeting-place, and the fellow dares not deceive me. *Exit.*

Scene II

Enter Belarius, Guiderius, Arviragus, *and* Imogen *from the cave.*

Bel. [*To Imogen.*] You are not well. Remain here in the cave,

69. but be: but I'd be, i.e. before I'd fail to be.
70. I bid . . . buy: i.e. you can depend upon my words (?). The line may be corrupt and has been variously emended, e.g. "Bid [*or* And bid] for you as I'd buy." **72. him:** i.e. my brother.
75. If brothers: i.e. yes, clearly friends, since they have offered me the affection of brothers (?).
76. prize: price, value (as heir to the throne), with play on the sense "captured treasure ship," a figure continued in *ballasting* in line 77.
78. wrings: writhes. **83. attend:** wait on. **virtue:** merit.
84. conscience: self-knowledge. **seal'd:** assured.
85. nothing-gift: worthless gift, i.e. adulation which adds nothing to their merit. **differing:** fickle. **86. outpeer:** surpass.
88. Leonatus' false: Leonatus is false (?) or Leonatus' infidelity (?).

III.vii. Location: Rome. A public place.
6. fall'n-off: revolted. **9. commands:** commends, entrusts.
10. absolute commission: unrestricted authorization to act.
14. supplyant: auxiliary.
15. tie you to: give you precise instructions as to.

IV.i. Location: Wales. Before the cave of Belarius.
5. saving . . . word. Cloten apologizes for his indecent puns on the word *fit*. **for:** because. **6. fitness:** sexual inclination.
11. fortunes: chances for good luck (?).
11–12. advantage . . . time: cultural and social opportunities (?) or worldly experience (?). **13. general services:** battles.
13–14. single oppositions: single combats or duels.
14. imperceiverant: unperceptive, undiscriminating.
15. mortality: human life. **19. happily:** perhaps.
21. power of: control over. **23. sore:** grievous.

IV.ii. Location: Scene continues.

We'll come to you after hunting.
Arv. [*To Imogen.*] Brother, stay here.
Are we not brothers?
Imo. So man and man should be,
But clay and clay differs in dignity,
Whose dust is both alike. I am very sick.
Gui. Go you to hunting, I'll abide with him.
Imo. So sick I am not, yet I am not well;
But not so citizen a wanton as
To seem to die ere sick. So please you, leave me,
Stick to your journal course: the breach of custom
Is breach of all. I am ill, but your being by me
Cannot amend me; society is no comfort
To one not sociable. I am not very sick,
Since I can reason of it. Pray you trust me here,
I'll rob none but myself, and let me die,
Stealing so poorly.
Gui. I love thee; I have spoke it;
How much the quantity, the weight as much,
As I do love my father.
Bel. What? how? how?
Arv. If it be sin to say so, sir, I yoke me
In my good brother's fault. I know not why
I love this youth, and I have heard you say,
Love's reason's without reason. The bier at door,
And a demand who is't shall die, I'ld say
"My father, not this youth."
Bel. [*Aside.*] O noble strain!
O worthiness of nature! breed of greatness!
Cowards father cowards and base things sire base:
Nature hath meal and bran, contempt and grace.
I'm not their father, yet who this should be
Doth miracle itself, lov'd before me.—
'Tis the ninth hour o' th' morn.
Arv. Brother, farewell.
Imo. I wish ye sport.
Arv. You health. [*To Belarius.*] So please you, sir.
Imo. [*Aside.*] These are kind creatures. Gods, what lies I have heard!
Our courtiers say all's savage but at court.
Experience, O, thou disprov'st report!
Th' imperious seas breeds monsters; for the dish,
Poor tributary rivers as sweet fish.
I am sick still, heart-sick. Pisanio,
I'll now taste of thy drug. [*Swallows some.*]
Gui. I could not stir him.
He said he was gentle, but unfortunate;
Dishonestly afflicted, but yet honest.
Arv. Thus did he answer me; yet said hereafter
I might know more.
Bel. To th' field, to th' field!
We'll leave you for this time, go in, and rest.
Arv. We'll not be long away.
Bel. Pray, be not sick,
For you must be our huswife.
Imo. Well or ill,
I am bound to you.
Bel. And shalt be ever. *Exit* [*Imogen to the cave*].
This youth, how e'er distress'd, appears he hath had
Good ancestors.
Arv. How angel-like he sings!
Gui. But his neat cookery! he cut our roots in characters,
And sauc'd our broths, as Juno had been sick
And he her dieter.
Arv. Nobly he yokes
A smiling with a sigh, as if the sigh
Was that it was for not being such a smile;
The smile mocking the sigh, that it would fly
From so divine a temple to commix
With winds that sailors rail at.
Gui. I do note
That grief and patience, rooted in them both,
Mingle their spurs together.
Arv. Grow [patience],
And let the stinking elder, grief, untwine
His perishing root with the increasing vine.
Bel. It is great morning. Come away!—Who's there?

Enter CLOTEN.

Clo. I cannot find those runagates, that villain
Hath mock'd me. I am faint.
Bel. "Those runagates"?
Means he not us? I partly know him, 'tis
Cloten, the son o' th' Queen. I fear some ambush.
I saw him not these many years, and yet
I know 'tis he. We are held as outlaws. Hence!
Gui. He is but one. You and my brother search
What companies are near. Pray you away,
Let me alone with him.
[*Exeunt Belarius and Arviragus.*]
Clo. Soft, what are you
That fly me thus? Some villain mountainers?
I have heard of such. What slave art thou?
Gui. A thing
More slavish did I ne'er than answering
A slave without a knock.
Clo. Thou art a robber,

4. clay and clay: i.e. different persons. **dignity:** estimation, rank.
5. dust: i.e. what remains of the body after death. With lines 4–5 cf. lines 246–49.
8. so . . . wanton: i.e. so "soft." Both *citizen* (= city-bred) and *wanton* (= spoiled child) imply habituation to an easy existence.
10. journal: daily. **14. reason:** talk sensibly.
16. Stealing so poorly: i.e. robbing none but myself.
17. How: as.
19–20. yoke . . . fault: declare myself guilty of the same fault my brother has committed.
24. strain: lineage, inherited character.
27. meal and bran: flour and husks.
28–29. who . . . me: i.e. that this youth, whoever he is, should be loved more than I is miraculous.
35. imperious: imperial (in contrast to *tributary*, line 36).
36. as sweet fish: i.e. breed as sweet fish as the sea breeds.
38. stir him: persuade him (to tell his story).
39. gentle: well-born.
46. bound: indebted. Belarius puns on the sense "tied by affection."
47. appears: shows. **49. characters:** letters, shapes.
50. as: as if.
57. them: i.e. the smile and the sigh. Many editors, following Pope, read *him*. **58. spurs:** roots.
59. stinking elder. There was a tradition that Judas hanged himself on an elder tree. **untwine:** cease to twine (?). Alternatively, *with . . . vine* in line 60 may mean "as the vine (i.e. patience) increases."
60. perishing: destructive. **61. great morning:** broad daylight.
62. runagates: runaways, i.e. Posthumus and Imogen.
64. I . . . him: he looks familiar. **67. held:** regarded.
71. mountainers: mountaineers (often, as here, implying criminality, since the mountains offered hiding places for outlaws).

A law-breaker, a villain. Yield thee, thief.
Gui. To who? to thee? What art thou? Have not I
An arm as big as thine? a heart as big?
Thy words I grant are bigger; for I wear not
My dagger in my mouth. Say what thou art;
Why I should yield to thee.
Clo. Thou villain base,
Know'st me not by my clothes?
Gui. No, nor thy tailor, rascal,
Who is thy grandfather! he made those clothes,
Which (as it seems) make thee.
Clo. Thou precious varlet,
My tailor made them not.
Gui. Hence then, and thank
The man that gave them thee. Thou art some fool,
I am loath to beat thee.
Clo. Thou injurious thief,
Hear but my name, and tremble.
Gui. What's thy name?
Clo. Cloten, thou villain.
Gui. Cloten, thou double villain, be thy name,
I cannot tremble at it. Were it Toad, or Adder, Spider,
'Twould move me sooner.
Clo. To thy further fear,
Nay, to thy mere confusion, thou shalt know
I am son to th' Queen.
Gui. I am sorry for't; not seeming
So worthy as thy birth.
Clo. Art not afeard?
Gui. Those that I reverence, those I fear—the wise:
At fools I laugh, not fear them.
Clo. Die the death!
When I have slain thee with my proper hand,
I'll follow those that even now fled hence,
And on the gates of Lud's-Town set your heads.
Yield, rustic mountaineer. *Fight and exeunt.*

Enter Belarius *and* Arviragus.

Bel. No company's abroad?
Arv. None in the world. You did mistake him sure.
Bel. I cannot tell; long is it since I saw him,
But time hath nothing blurr'd those lines of favor
Which then he wore. The snatches in his voice,
And burst of speaking, were as his. I am absolute
'Twas very Cloten.
Arv. In this place we left them.
I wish my brother make good time with him,
You say he is so fell.
Bel. Being scarce made up,
I mean, to man, he had not apprehension
Of roaring terrors; for defect of judgment
Is oft the cause of fear.

Enter Guiderius [*with Cloten's head*].

But see, thy brother.
Gui. This Cloten was a fool, an empty purse,
There was no money in't. Not Hercules
Could have knock'd out his brains, for he had none.
Yet I not doing this, the fool had borne
My head as I do his.
Bel. What hast thou done?
Gui. I am perfect what: cut off one Cloten's head,
Son to the Queen (after his own report),
Who call'd me traitor, mountaineer, and swore
With his own single hand he'ld take us in,
Displace our heads where (thanks, [ye] gods!) they grow,
And set them on Lud's-Town.
Bel. We are all undone.
Gui. Why, worthy father, what have we to lose,
But that he swore to take, our lives? The law
Protects not us; then why should we be tender
To let an arrogant piece of flesh threat us,
Play judge and executioner all himself,
For we do fear the law? What company
Discover you abroad?
Bel. No single soul
Can we set eye on; but in all safe reason
He must have some attendants. Though his [humor]
Was nothing but mutation, ay, and that
From one bad thing to worse, not frenzy, not
Absolute madness could so far have rav'd
To bring him here alone; although perhaps
It may be heard at court that such as we
Cave here, hunt here, are outlaws, and in time
May make some stronger head, the which he hearing
(As it is like him), might break out and swear
He'ld fetch us in; yet is't not probable
To come alone, either he so undertaking,
Or they so suffering. Then on good ground we fear,
If we do fear this body hath a tail
More perilous than the head.
Arv. Let ord'nance
Come as the gods foresay it; howsoe'er,
My brother hath done well.
Bel. I had no mind
To hunt this day; the boy Fidele's sickness
Did make my way long forth.
Gui. With his own sword,
Which he did wave against my throat, I have ta'en

81. know'st . . . clothes: can't you see from my clothes that I come from the court.
82. grandfather. A jest on the old proverb that it takes two or three (later nine) tailors to make a man.
83. precious varlet: arrant knave.
86. injurious: insulting. **thief:** malefactor.
92. mere confusion: utter ruin. **95. fear:** hold in awe.
97. proper: own. **100. rustic:** i.e. boorish.
101. abroad: about.
104. lines of favor: facial lineaments.
105. snatches: catches, hesitations.
106. absolute: positive. **107. very Cloten:** Cloten himself.
108. make . . . with: do well against.
109. fell: aggressive, dangerous.

109–12. Being . . . fear. Compressed and obscure; perhaps the meaning is: "I consider him dangerous because even when he was still a youth (when he might well have been timorous, for youthful deficiency of judgment is often the cause of fear) he was afraid of nothing." Among the numerous emendations proposed are *th' effect* for *defect* (line 111) and *cess* for *cause* (line 112).
118. I . . . what: I can tell you exactly what.
121. take us in: overpower us. **122. where:** from where.
129. For: because. **132. humor:** disposition, nature.
133. mutation: changeableness. **139. head:** armed force.
142. To: that he would. **143. suffering:** permitting.
145. ord'nance: what is ordained. **147. mind:** inclination.
149. my . . . forth: my way forth seem long.

His head from him. I'll throw't into the creek
Behind our rock, and let it to the sea,
And tell the fishes he's the Queen's son, Cloten.
That's all I reak. *Exit.*

Bel. I fear 'twill be reveng'd.
Would, Polydore, thou hadst not done't! though valor
Becomes thee well enough.

Arv. Would I had done't!
So the revenge alone pursu'd me. Polydore,
I love thee brotherly, but envy much
Thou hast robb'd me of this deed. I would revenges,
That possible strength might meet, would seek us through
And put us to our answer.

Bel. Well, 'tis done.
We'll hunt no more to-day, nor seek for danger
Where there's no profit. I prithee to our rock,
You and Fidele play the cooks. I'll stay
Till hasty Polydore return, and bring him
To dinner presently.

Arv. Poor sick Fidele!
I'll willingly to him. To gain his color
I'ld let a parish of such Clotens blood,
And praise myself for charity. *Exit.*

Bel. O thou goddess,
Thou divine Nature, thou thyself thou blazon'st
In these two princely boys! They are as gentle
As zephyrs blowing below the violet,
Not wagging his sweet head; and yet as rough,
Their royal blood enchaf'd, as the rud'st wind
That by the top doth take the mountain pine
And make him stoop to th' vale. 'Tis wonder
That an invisible instinct should frame them
To royalty unlearn'd, honor untaught,
Civility not seen from other, valor
That wildly grows in them but yields a crop
As if it had been sow'd. Yet still it's strange
What Cloten's being here to us portends,
Or what his death will bring us.

Enter GUIDERIUS.

Gui. Where's my brother?
I have sent Cloten's clotpole down the stream
In embassy to his mother. His body's hostage
For his return. *Solemn music.*

Bel. My ingenious instrument
(Hark, Polydore), it sounds! But what occasion
Hath Cadwal now to give it motion? Hark!

Gui. Is he at home?

Bel. He went hence even now.

Gui. What does he mean? Since death of my dear'st mother

It did not speak before. All solemn things
Should answer solemn accidents. The matter?
Triumphs for nothing, and lamenting toys,
Is jollity for apes, and grief for boys.
Is Cadwal mad?

Enter ARVIRAGUS *with* IMOGEN *[as] dead, bearing her in his arms.*

Bel. Look, here he comes,
And brings the dire occasion in his arms
Of what we blame him for.

Arv. The bird is dead
That we have made so much on. I had rather
Have skipp'd from sixteen years of age to sixty,
To have turn'd my leaping time into a crutch,
Than have seen this.

Gui. O sweetest, fairest lily!
My brother wears thee not the one half so well
As when thou grew'st thyself.

Bel. O melancholy,
Who ever yet could sound thy bottom? find
The ooze, to show what coast thy sluggish [crare]
Mightst easil'est harbor in? Thou blessed thing,
Jove knows what man thou mightst have made; but I,
Thou diedst, a most rare boy, of melancholy.
How found you him?

Arv. Stark, as you see;
Thus smiling, as some fly had tickled slumber,
Not as death's dart being laugh'd at; his right cheek
Reposing on a cushion.

Gui. Where?

Arv. O' th' floor;
His arms thus leagu'd. I thought he slept, and put
My clouted brogues from off my feet, whose rudeness
Answer'd my steps too loud.

Gui. Why, he but sleeps!
If he be gone, he'll make his grave a bed.
With female fairies will his tomb be haunted,
And worms will not come to thee.

Arv. With fairest flowers
Whilst summer lasts and I live here, Fidele,
I'll sweeten thy sad grave. Thou shalt not lack
The flower that's like thy face, pale primrose, nor
The azur'd harebell, like thy veins; no, nor
The leaf of eglantine, whom not to slander,
Outsweet'ned not thy breath. The raddock would,
With charitable bill (O bill, sore shaming
Those rich-left heirs that let their fathers lie
Without a monument!), bring thee all this,
Yea, and furr'd moss besides. When flow'rs are none,
To winter-ground thy corse—

Gui. Prithee have done,

154. reak: reck, care.
157. So: so that. **160. possible:** our potential. **through:** out.
161. put . . . answer: force us to retaliate. **165. hasty:** rash.
167. gain: restore.
170. thou . . . blazon'st: you display your very self.
174. enchaf'd: heated in anger. **177. frame:** shape.
179. Civility: civilized behavior. **seen:** i.e. imitated.
180. wildly: spontaneously, without deliberate cultivation.
184. clotpole: clotpoll, blockhead (with play on Cloten's name, showing that it was pronounced *Clotten*).
186. ingenious: mechanical (?) or, more generally, skillfully made (?).

192. answer: be in response to, match. **accidents:** events.
193. lamenting toys: wailing about trifles. Guiderius supposes that the elegiac music he hears is for Cloten's death.
204. sound thy bottom: plumb your depth.
205. crare: small trading vessel. **207. I:** I know.
209. Stark: stiff.
211. Not . . . at: i.e. not as if he were laughing at death's dart.
213. leagu'd: crossed. **214. clouted:** hobnailed.
220. sweeten: make fragrant.
223. eglantine: honeysuckle. **slander:** depreciate.
224. raddock: ruddock, robin redbreast, traditionally a coverer of graves. **229. winter-ground:** cover in winter.

And do not play in wench-like words with that
Which is so serious. Let us bury him,
And not protract with admiration what
Is now due debt. To th' grave!

Arv. Say, where shall 's lay him?

Gui. By good Euriphile, our mother.

Arv. Be't so;
And let us, Polydore, though now our voices
Have got the mannish crack, sing him to th' ground,
As once to our mother; use like note and words,
Save that Euriphile must be Fidele.

Gui. Cadwal,
I cannot sing. I'll weep, and word it with thee;
For notes of sorrow out of tune are worse
Than priests and fanes that lie.

Arv. We'll speak it then.

Bel. Great griefs, I see, med'cine the less; for Cloten
Is quite forgot. He was a queen's son, boys,
And though he came our enemy, remember
He was paid for that. Though mean and mighty, rotting
Together, have one dust, yet reverence
(That angel of the world) doth make distinction
Of place 'tween high and low. Our foe was princely,
And though you took his life, as being our foe,
Yet bury him as a prince.

Gui. Pray you fetch him hither.
Thersites' body is as good as Ajax',
When neither are alive.

Arv. If you'll go fetch him,
We'll say our song the whilst. Brother, begin.
[*Exit Belarius.*]

Gui. Nay, Cadwal, we must lay his head to th' east,
My father hath a reason for't.

Arv. 'Tis true.

Gui. Come on then, and remove him.

Arv. So. Begin.

SONG

Gui. Fear no more the heat o' th' sun,
Nor the furious winter's rages,
Thou thy worldly task hast done,
Home art gone, and ta'en thy wages.
Golden lads and girls all must,
As chimney-sweepers, come to dust.

Arv. Fear no more the frown o' th' great,
Thou art past the tyrant's stroke;
Care no more to clothe and eat,
To thee the reed is as the oak.
The sceptre, learning, physic, must
All follow this and come to dust.

Gui. Fear no more the lightning-flash.
Arv. Nor th' all-dreaded thunder-stone.
Gui. Fear not slander, censure rash.
Arv. Thou hast finish'd joy and moan.
Both. All lovers young, all lovers must
Consign to thee and come to dust.

Gui. No exorciser harm thee.
Arv. Nor no witchcraft charm thee.
Gui. Ghost unlaid forbear thee.
Arv. Nothing ill come near thee.
Both. Quiet consummation have,
And renowned be thy grave.

Enter BELARIUS *with the body of Cloten.*

Gui. We have done our obsequies. Come lay him down.

Bel. Here's a few flow'rs, but 'bout midnight, more:
The herbs that have on them cold dew o' th' night
Are strewings fitt'st for graves. Upon their faces.
You were as flow'rs, now wither'd; even so
These herblets shall, which we upon you strew.
Come on, away, apart upon our knees.
The ground that gave them first has them again:
Their pleasures here are past, so [is] their pain.
Exeunt [Belarius, Guiderius, and Arviragus].

Imo. (*Awakes.*) Yes, sir, to Milford-Haven, which is the way?
I thank you. By yond bush? Pray how far thither?
'Od's pittikins! can it be six mile yet?
I have gone all night. Faith, I'll lie down and sleep.
[*Sees the body of Cloten.*]
But soft! no bedfellow! O gods and goddesses!
These flow'rs are like the pleasures of the world;
This bloody man, the care on't. I hope I dream;
For so I thought I was a cave-keeper,
And cook to honest creatures. But 'tis not so.
'Twas but a bolt of nothing, shot at nothing,
Which the brain makes of fumes. Our very eyes
Are sometimes like our judgments, blind. Good faith,
I tremble still with fear; but if there be
Yet left in heaven as small a drop of pity
As a wren's eye, fear'd gods, a part of it!
The dream's here still; even when I wake, it is
Without me, as within me; not imagin'd, felt.
A headless man? The garments of Posthumus?
I know the shape of 's leg; this is his hand,
His foot Mercurial, his Martial thigh,

230. wench-like: womanish. Such flower passages in Shakespeare are usually spoken by women. **232. admiration:** wonder.
242. fanes: temples.
248. angel . . . world: i.e. messenger from heaven to the earth.
252. Thersites, Ajax. Symbols of meanness and heroism respectively. Thersites was the most contemptible of the Greeks before Troy, Ajax one of the mightiest Greek warriors.
255. lay . . . east. A pre-Christian touch. **263. As:** like.
268. physic: medical science.
269. this. Emended by some editors to *thee*.
271. thunder-stone: thunderbolt, thought of as an actual stone.
275. Consign to thee: accept the same terms with you. Some editors read *Consign to this*, i.e. submit to death.
276. exorciser: raiser of spirits.
285. Upon their faces. This raises a difficulty in view of Cloten's decapitation. Dover Wilson suggested that the words may represent an inserted revision of line 284, which would have read "The herbs that have cold dew upon their faces."
287. shall: i.e. shall become withered.
288. apart . . . knees: let us pray elsewhere.
293. 'Od's pittikins: diminutive of "God's pity."
294. gone: walked. **298. cave-keeper:** cave-dweller.
300. bolt: arrow.
301. fumes. It was believed that bodily vapors ascending to the brain were the cause of dreams and fantasies.
305. As . . . eye: i.e. as a tear shed by a wren.
310. Mercurial . . . Martial: like Mercury's . . . like Mars'.

The brawns of Hercules; but his Jovial face—
Murther in heaven? How? 'Tis gone. Pisanio,
All curses madded Hecuba gave the Greeks,
And mine to boot, be darted on thee! Thou,
Conspir'd with that irregulous devil Cloten,
Hath here cut off my lord. To write and read
Be henceforth treacherous! Damn'd Pisanio
Hath with his forged letters (damn'd Pisanio!)
From this most bravest vessel of the world
Strook the main-top! O Posthumus, alas,
Where is thy head? Where's that? Ay me! where's that?
Pisanio might have kill'd thee at the heart
And left this head on. How should this be? Pisanio?
'Tis he and Cloten. Malice and lucre in them
Have laid this woe here. O, 'tis pregnant, pregnant!
The drug he gave me, which he said was precious
And cordial to me, have I not found it
Murd'rous to th' senses? That confirms it home.
This is Pisanio's deed, and Cloten. O!
Give color to my pale cheek with thy blood,
That we the horrider may seem to those
Which chance to find us. O, my lord! my lord!
[*Falls on the body.*]

Enter Lucius, Captains, *and a* Soothsayer.

Cap. To them the legions garrison'd in Gallia,
After your will, have cross'd the sea, attending
You here at Milford-Haven with your ships.
They are here in readiness.
Luc. But what from Rome?
Cap. The Senate hath stirr'd up the confiners
And gentlemen of Italy, most willing spirits
That promise noble service; and they come
Under the conduct of bold Jachimo,
Sienna's brother.
Luc. When expect you them?
Cap. With the next benefit o' th' wind.
Luc. This forwardness
Makes our hopes fair. Command our present numbers
Be muster'd; bid the captains look to't. Now, sir,
What have you dream'd of late of this war's purpose?
Sooth. Last night the very gods show'd me a vision
(I fast and pray'd for their intelligence) thus:
I saw Jove's bird, the Roman eagle, wing'd
From the spungy south to this part of the west,
There vanish'd in the sunbeams, which portends
(Unless my sins abuse my divination)
Success to th' Roman host.
Luc. Dream often so,
And never false. Soft ho, what trunk is here?
Without his top? The ruin speaks that sometime
It was a worthy building. How? a page?
Or dead, or sleeping on him? But dead rather;
For nature doth abhor to make his bed
With the defunct, or sleep upon the dead.
Let's see the boy's face.
Cap. He's alive, my lord.
Luc. He'll then instruct us of this body. Young one,
Inform us of thy fortunes, for it seems
They crave to be demanded. Who is this
Thou mak'st thy bloody pillow? Or who was he
That (otherwise than noble nature did)
Hath alter'd that good picture? What's thy interest
In this sad wrack? How came't? Who is't?
What art thou?
Imo. I am nothing; or if not,
Nothing to be were better. This was my master,
A very valiant Britain, and a good,
That here by mountaineers lies slain. Alas,
There is no more such masters. I may wander
From east to occident, cry out for service,
Try many, all good; serve truly; never
Find such another master.
Luc. 'Lack, good youth!
Thou mov'st no less with thy complaining than
Thy master in bleeding. Say his name, good friend.
Imo. Richard du Champ. [*Aside.*] If I do lie and do
No harm by it, though the gods hear, I hope
They'll pardon it.—Say you, sir?
Luc. Thy name?
Imo. Fidele, sir.
Luc. Thou dost approve thyself the very same;
Thy name well fits thy faith; thy faith thy name.
Wilt take thy chance with me? I will not say
Thou shalt be so well master'd, but be sure
No less belov'd. The Roman Emperor's letters,
Sent by a consul to me, should not sooner
Than thine own worth prefer thee. Go with me.
Imo. I'll follow, sir. But first, and't please the gods,
I'll hide my master from the flies, as deep
As these poor pickaxes can dig; and when
With wild wood-leaves and weeds I ha' strew'd his grave,
And on it said a century of prayers
(Such as I can) twice o'er, I'll weep and sigh,
And leaving so his service, follow you,
So please you entertain me.
Luc. Ay, good youth,
And rather father thee than master thee.
My friends,
The boy hath taught us manly duties. Let us
Find out the prettiest daisied plot we can,
And make him with our pikes and partisans
A grave. Come, arm him. Boy, he's preferr'd
By thee to us, and he shall be interr'd
As soldiers can. Be cheerful; wipe thine eyes:
Some falls are means the happier to arise. *Exeunt.*

311. brawns: muscles. **Jovial:** like Jupiter's.
312. Murther in heaven: i.e. since this godlike man is dead.
313. Hecuba: queen of Troy when it was won by the Greeks.
315. Conspir'd: conspiring. **irregulous:** lawless.
324. lucre: i.e. greed. **325. pregnant:** obvious.
333. To: in addition to.
337. confiners: inhabitants.
341. Sienna's: the Duke of Sienna's.
347. fast: fasted. **349. spungy:** spongy, damp.
351. abuse: make false.
380. approve: prove.
386. prefer: recommend (so also in line 400). **387. and't:** if it.
389. pickaxes: i.e. her fingers. **394. entertain:** employ.
399. pikes: spears. **partisans:** long-handled weapons with broad blades. **400. arm him:** lift him up.

Scene III

Enter Cymbeline, Lords, *and* Pisanio [*with* Attendants].

Cym. Again; and bring me word how 'tis with her.
[*Exit an Attendant.*]
A fever with the absence of her son;
A madness, of which her life's in danger. Heavens,
How deeply you at once do touch me! Imogen,
The great part of my comfort, gone; my queen
Upon a desperate bed, and in a time
When fearful wars point at me; her son gone,
So needful for this present! It strikes me, past
The hope of comfort. But for thee, fellow,
Who needs must know of her departure, and
Dost seem so ignorant, we'll enforce it from thee
By a sharp torture.
Pis. Sir, my life is yours,
I humbly set it at your will; but, for my mistress,
I nothing know where she remains, why gone,
Nor when she purposes return. Beseech your Highness,
Hold me your loyal servant.
[*1.*] *Lord.* Good my liege,
The day that she was missing he was here;
I dare be bound he's true and shall perform
All parts of his subjection loyally. For Cloten,
There wants no diligence in seeking him,
And will, no doubt, be found.
Cym. The time is troublesome.
[*To Pisanio.*] We'll slip you for a season, but our jealousy
Does yet depend.
[*1.*] *Lord.* So please your Majesty,
The Roman legions, all from Gallia drawn,
Are landed on your coast, with a supply
Of Roman gentlemen, by the Senate sent.
Cym. Now for the counsel of my son and queen!
I am amaz'd with matter.
[*1.*] *Lord.* Good my liege,
Your preparation can affront no less
Than what you hear of. Come more, for more you're ready;
The want is but to put those pow'rs in motion
That long to move.
Cym. I thank you. Let's withdraw,
And meet the time as it seeks us. We fear not
What can from Italy annoy us, but
We grieve at chances here. Away!
Exeunt [*all but Pisanio*].
Pis. I heard no letter from my master since
I wrote him Imogen was slain. 'Tis strange.
Nor hear I from my mistress, who did promise
To yield me often tidings. Neither know I
What is betide to Cloten, but remain
Perplex'd in all. The heavens still must work.
Wherein I am false, I am honest; not true, to be true.
These present wars shall find I love my country,
Even to the note o' th' King, or I'll fall in them.
All other doubts, by time let them be clear'd,
Fortune brings in some boats that are not steer'd.
Exit.

IV.iii. Location: Britain. Cymbeline's palace.
2. with: caused by. 4. touch: afflict. 11. seem: pretend to be.
19. subjection: duty as a subject. 20. wants: lacks.
21. troublesome. A much stronger word than in modern usage; so also *annoy* in line 34. 22. slip: release. jealousy: suspicion.
23. depend: hang (over you).
28. amaz'd with matter: confused with all there is to do.
29. preparation: forces now in arms.
29–30. affront . . . of: confront the number reported.
30. Come more: if more (Romans) come.

40. is betide: has happened. 44. note: notice.

Scene IV

Enter Belarius, Guiderius, *and* Arviragus.

Gui. The noise is round about us.
Bel. Let us from it.
Arv. What pleasure, sir, [find we] in life, to lock it
From action and adventure?
Gui. Nay, what hope
Have we in hiding us? This way, the Romans
Must or for Britains slay us or receive us
For barbarous and unnatural revolts
During their use, and slay us after.
Bel. Sons,
We'll higher to the mountains, there secure us.
To the King's party there's no going. Newness
Of Cloten's death (we being not known, not muster'd
Among the bands) may drive us to a render
Where we have liv'd, and so extort from 's that
Which we have done, whose answer would be death
Drawn on with torture.
Gui. This is, sir, a doubt
In such a time nothing becoming you,
Nor satisfying us.
Arv. It is not likely
That when they hear their Roman horses neigh,
Behold their quarter'd fires, have both their eyes
And ears so cloy'd importantly as now,
That they will waste their time upon our note,
To know from whence we are.
Bel. O, I am known
Of many in the army. Many years,
Though Cloten then but young, you see, not wore him
From my remembrance. And besides, the King
Hath not deserv'd my service nor your loves,
Who find in my exile the want of breeding,
The certainty of this hard life, aye hopeless
To have the courtesy your cradle promis'd,
But to be still hot summer's tanlings and
The shrinking slaves of winter.
Gui. Than be so,
Better to cease to be. Pray, sir, to th' army.
I and my brother are not known; yourself
So out of thought, and thereto so o'ergrown,
Cannot be question'd.

IV.iv. Location: Wales. Before the cave of Belarius.
5. or for: either as. 6. revolts: rebels, traitors.
7. During their use: for as long as we are useful to them.
11. render: confession. 13. answer: consequence.
18. quarter'd fires: campfires.
19. cloy'd importantly: fully occupied with urgent matters.
20. upon our note: in noticing us.
27. certainty: i.e. impossibility of getting away from.
28. courtesy: cultivated existence.
33. thereto: in addition. o'ergrown: bearded (?) or grown old (?).

Arv. By this sun that shines,
I'll thither. What thing is't that I never
Did see man die, scarce ever look'd on blood,
But that of coward hares, hot goats, and venison!
Never bestrid a horse, save one that had
A rider like myself, who ne'er wore rowel
Nor iron on his heel! I am asham'd
To look upon the holy sun, to have
The benefit of his blest beams, remaining
So long a poor unknown.
Gui. By heavens, I'll go.
If you will bless me, sir, and give me leave,
I'll take the better care; but if you will not,
The hazard therefore due fall on me by
The hands of Romans!
Arv. So say I, amen.
Bel. No reason I, since of your lives you set
So slight a valuation, should reserve
My crack'd one to more care. Have with you, boys!
If in your country wars you chance to die,
That is my bed too, lads, and there I'll lie.
Lead, lead! [*Aside.*] The time seems long, their blood thinks scorn
Till it fly out and show them princes born. *Exeunt.*

ACT V, Scene I

Enter Posthumus *alone* [*with a bloody handkerchief*].

Post. Yea, bloody cloth, I'll keep thee, for I wish'd
Thou shouldst be color'd thus. You married ones,
If each of you should take this course, how many
Must murther wives much better than themselves
For wrying but a little! O Pisanio,
Every good servant does not all commands;
No bond, but to do just ones. Gods, if you
Should have ta'en vengeance on my faults, I never
Had liv'd to put on this; so had you saved
The noble Imogen to repent, and strook
Me, wretch, more worth your vengeance. But alack,
You snatch some hence for little faults; that's love,
To have them fall no more: you some permit
To second ills with ills, each elder worse,
And make them dread it, to the doers' thrift.
But Imogen is your own, do your best wills,
And make me blest to obey. I am brought hither
Among th' Italian gentry, and to fight
Against my lady's kingdom. 'Tis enough
That, Britain, I have kill'd thy mistress; peace,
I'll give no wound to thee. Therefore, good heavens,
Hear patiently my purpose: I'll disrobe me
Of these Italian weeds and suit myself
As does a Britain peasant; so I'll fight
Against the part I come with; so I'll die

35. What thing: i.e. what a disgraceful thing. **37. hot:** lustful.
46. hazard therefore due: fate merited by my disobedience.
50. crack'd: weakened with age. **51. country:** country's.

V.i. Location: Britain. The Roman camp.
5. wrying: deviating from virtue.
9. put on: instigate (?) or take upon myself (?).
14. elder: i.e. later. **15. thrift:** profit. **23. suit:** clothe.
25. part: party, side.

For thee, O Imogen, even for whom my life
Is every breath a death; and thus, unknown,
Pitied nor hated, to the face of peril
Myself I'll dedicate. Let me make men know
More valor in me than my habits show.
Gods, put the strength o' th' Leonati in me!
To shame the guise o' th' world, I will begin
The fashion: less without and more within. *Exit.*

Scene II

Enter Lucius, Jachimo, *and the Roman army at one door, and the Britain army at another;* Leonatus Posthumus *following, like a poor soldier. They march over and go out. Then enter again, in skirmish,* Jachimo *and* Posthumus: *he vanquisheth and disarmeth Jachimo, and then leaves him.*

Jach. The heaviness and guilt within my bosom
Takes off my manhood. I have belied a lady,
The Princess of this country; and the air on't
Revengingly enfeebles me, or could this carl,
A very drudge of nature's, have subdu'd me
In my profession? Knighthoods and honors, borne
As I wear mine, are titles but of scorn.
If that thy gentry, Britain, go before
This lout as he exceeds our lords, the odds
Is that we scarce are men and you are gods. *Exit.*

The battle continues, the Britains fly, Cymbeline *is taken: then enter, to his rescue,* Belarius, Guiderius, *and* Arviragus.

Bel. Stand, stand! we have th' advantage of the ground,
The lane is guarded. Nothing routs us but
The villainy of our fears.
Gui., Arv. Stand, stand, and fight!

Enter Posthumus *and seconds the Britains. They rescue Cymbeline and exeunt. Then enter* Lucius, Jachimo, *and* Imogen.

Luc. Away, boy, from the troops, and save thyself;
For friends kill friends, and the disorder's such
As war were hoodwink'd.
Jach. 'Tis their fresh supplies.
Luc. It is a day turn'd strangely. Or betimes
Let's reinforce, or fly. *Exeunt.*

Scene III

Enter Posthumus *and a* Britain Lord.

Lord. Cam'st thou from where they made the stand?

28. Pitied: neither pitied.
30. habits: garments. **32. guise:** custom.

V.ii. Location: Britain. Field between the British and Roman camps.
3. on't: of it. **4. carl:** churl, peasant.
7. of scorn: contemptible. **8. go before:** surpass.
16. As: as if. **hoodwink'd:** blindfolded.
17. Or betimes: either promptly.

V.iii. Location: Scene continues.

Post. I did,
Though you it seems come from the fliers?
Lord. I did.
Post. No blame be to you, sir, for all was lost
But that the heavens fought; the King himself
Of his wings destitute, the army broken,
And but the backs of Britains seen, all flying
Through a strait lane; the enemy full-hearted,
Lolling the tongue with slaught'ring—having work
More plentiful than tools to do't—strook down
Some mortally, some slightly touch'd, some falling
Merely through fear, that the strait pass was damm'd
With dead men hurt behind, and cowards living
To die with length'ned shame.
Lord. Where was this lane?
Post. Close by the battle, ditch'd, and wall'd with turf,
Which gave advantage to an ancient soldier
(An honest one, I warrant), who deserv'd
So long a breeding as his white beard came to,
In doing this for 's country. Athwart the lane,
He, with two striplings (lads more like to run
The country base than to commit such slaughter,
With faces fit for masks, or rather fairer
Than those for preservation cas'd, or shame),
Made good the passage, cried to those that fled,
"Our Britain's harts die flying, not our men.
To darkness fleet souls that fly backwards. Stand,
Or we are Romans and will give you that
Like beasts which you shun beastly, and may save
But to look back in frown. Stand, stand!" These three,
Three thousand confident, in act as many—
For three performers are the file when all
The rest do nothing—with this word "Stand, stand!"
Accommodated by the place, more charming
With their own nobleness, which could have turn'd
A distaff to a lance, gilded pale looks;
Part shame, part spirit renew'd, that some, turn'd coward
But by example (O, a sin in war,
Damn'd in the first beginners!), gan to look
The way that they did, and to grin like lions
Upon the pikes o' th' hunters. Then began
A stop i' th' chaser; a retire; anon
A rout, confusion thick. Forthwith they fly
Chickens, the way which they [stoop'd] eagles; slaves,
The strides [they] victors made: and now our cowards,
Like fragments in hard voyages, became
The life o' th' need. Having found the back door open
Of the unguarded hearts, heavens, how they wound
Some slain before, some dying, some their friends
O'erborne i' th' former wave. Ten chas'd by one
Are now each one the slaughter-man of twenty.
Those that would die or ere resist are grown
The mortal bugs o' th' field.
Lord. This was strange chance.
A narrow lane, an old man, and two boys!
Post. Nay, do not wonder at it; you are made
Rather to wonder at the things you hear
Than to work any. Will you rhyme upon't,
And vent it for a mock'ry? Here is one:
"Two boys, an old man (twice a boy), a lane,
Preserv'd the Britains, was the Romans' bane."
Lord. Nay, be not angry, sir.
Post. 'Lack, to what end?
Who dares not stand his foe, I'll be his friend;
For if he'll do as he is made to do,
I know he'll quickly fly my friendship too.
You have put me into rhyme.
Lord. Farewell, you're angry. *Exit.*
Post. Still going? This is a lord! O noble misery,
To be i' th' field, and ask "what news?" of me!
To-day how many would have given their honors
To have sav'd their carcasses! took heel to do't,
And yet died too! I, in mine own woe charm'd,
Could not find death where I did hear him groan,
Nor feel him where he strook. Being an ugly monster,
'Tis strange he hides him in fresh cups, soft beds,
Sweet words; or hath moe ministers than we
That draw his knives i' th' war. Well, I will find him;
For being now a favorer to the Britain,
No more a Britain, I have resum'd again
The part I came in. Fight I will no more,
But yield me to the veriest hind that shall
Once touch my shoulder. Great the slaughter is
Here made by th' Roman; great the answer be
Britains must take. For me, my ransom's death.
On either side I come to spend my breath;
Which neither here I'll keep nor bear again,
But end it by some means for Imogen.

4. But: if it had not been for the fact.
7. full-hearted: with high courage and confidence.
8. Lolling the tongue: with their tongues hanging out (like wild beasts). **10. touch'd:** wounded.
12. hurt behind: i.e. wounded while fleeing.
13. length'ned: extended through the remainder of their lives.
16. honest: worthy.
16–17. deserv'd . . . to: "deserved to live so long as to breed his long white beard" (Schmidt). Others prefer the sense "deserved to be supported (or cherished) in the future for as many years as his white beard showed he had already lived."
20. country base: prisoner's base, a children's game.
21. fit for masks: i.e. worthy to be protected against sun and wind.
22. those . . . shame: i.e. ladies' faces masked to preserve their complexions, or for modesty.
26. are Romans: i.e. will behave like Romans.
27–28. may . . . frown: may avert if you turn and face the enemy boldly.
29. Three . . . many: as confident, and performing as much, as three thousand.
30. file: number of men constituting the depth from front to rear of a line formation; here, entire force.
32. charming: i.e. exerting what seemed like magic, working their spell.
33–34. turn'd . . . lance: i.e. transformed a housewife into a soldier.
34. gilded: restored color to. Blood was often called "golden."
35. Part . . . renew'd: shame revived some, courage others.
37. first beginners: those who first set the example.
38. they: i.e. the three. **grin:** bare their teeth.
40. chaser: i.e. those hunting the Britons like animals.
41–42. Forthwith . . . eagles: "immediately they retrace like chickens the path down which they had recently advanced like swooping eagles" (Knight). **44. fragments:** bits of food.
51. mortal bugs: deadly terrors.
56. vent it: i.e. circulate the rhyme.
57. twice a boy: in his second childhood. **60. stand:** withstand.
64. Still going: always running away. **noble misery:** wretched specimen of the nobility.
68. charm'd: protected by a spell (cf. "leading a charmed life").
72. moe: more, i.e. other.
74. being: since death is. In line 75 *No more a Britain* refers to Posthumus. **77. hind:** peasant.
78. touch my shoulder: arrest me. **79. answer:** retaliation.

Enter two [Britain] Captains *and Soldiers.*

1. [*Cap.*] Great Jupiter be prais'd! Lucius is taken.
'Tis thought the old man and his sons were angels.
2. [*Cap.*] There was a fourth man, in a silly habit,
That gave th' affront with them.
1. [*Cap.*] So 'tis reported;
But none of 'em can be found. Stand! who's there?
Post. A Roman,
Who had not now been drooping here, if seconds
Had answer'd him.
2. [*Cap.*] Lay hands on him; a dog!
A leg of Rome shall not return to tell
What crows have peck'd them here. He brags his service
As if he were of note. Bring him to th' King.

Enter Cymbeline, Belarius, Guiderius, Arviragus, Pisanio, *and Roman captives. The Captains present Posthumus to Cymbeline, who delivers him over to a* Jailer. [*Then exeunt omnes.*]

Scene IV

Enter Posthumus *and* [*two*] Jailer[s].

[*1.*] *Jail.* You shall not now be stol'n, you have locks upon you;
So graze, as you find pasture.
2. Jail. Ay, or a stomach. [*Exeunt Jailers.*]
Post. Most welcome, bondage! for thou art a way,
I think, to liberty; yet am I better
Than one that's sick o' th' gout, since he had rather
Groan so in perpetuity than be cur'd
By th' sure physician, death, who is the key
T' unbar these locks. My conscience, thou art fetter'd
More than my shanks and wrists. You good gods, give me
The penitent instrument to pick that bolt,
Then free for ever! Is't enough I am sorry?
So children temporal fathers do appease;
Gods are more full of mercy. Must I repent,
I cannot do it better than in gyves,
Desir'd more than constrain'd. To satisfy,
If of my freedom 'tis the main part, take
No stricter render of me than my all.
I know you are more clement than vild men,
Who of their broken debtors take a third,
A sixt, a tenth, letting them thrive again
On their abatement. That's not my desire.
For Imogen's dear life take mine, and though
'Tis not so dear, yet 'tis a life; you coin'd it.
'Tween man and man they weigh not every stamp;

86. **silly habit:** rustic garb. 90. **seconds:** supporters.
91. **answer'd him:** followed his example.

V.iv. Location: Britain. A stockade in the British camp.
10. **The penitent . . . bolt:** the key of penitence to unlock the shackles on my conscience.
15. **constrain'd:** forced on me. **satisfy:** make atonement.
16. **freedom:** being freed from sin. 17. **render:** restitution.
19. **broken:** bankrupt. 21. **abatement:** reduced principal.
23. **so dear:** as valuable as hers.
24. **'Tween . . . stamp:** in business dealings men don't weigh every coin (to make sure that it contains the full amount of metal).

Though light, take pieces for the figure's sake;
You rather, mine being yours; and so, great pow'rs,
If you will take this audit, take this life,
And cancel these cold bonds. O Imogen,
I'll speak to thee in silence. [*Sleeps.*]

Solemn music. Enter (*as in an apparition*) Sicilius Leonatus, *father to Posthumus, an old man, attired like a warrior; leading in his hand an ancient* Matron, *his wife and mother to Posthumus, with music before them. Then, after other music, follows the two young* Leonati, *brothers to Posthumus, with wounds as they died in the wars. They circle Posthumus round as he lies sleeping.*

Sici. No more, thou Thunder-master, show
Thy spite on mortal flies:
With Mars fall out, with Juno chide,
That thy adulteries
Rates and revenges.
Hath my poor boy done aught but well,
Whose face I never saw?
I died whilst in the womb he stay'd
Attending nature's law;
Whose father then (as men report
Thou orphans' father art)
Thou shouldst have been, and shielded him
From this earth-vexing smart.
Moth. Lucina lent not me her aid,
But took me in my throes,
That from me was Posthumus ripp'd,
Came crying 'mongst his foes,
A thing of pity!
Sici. Great nature, like his ancestry,
Moulded the stuff so fair,
That he deserv'd the praise o' th' world,
As great Sicilius' heir.
1. Bro. When once he was mature for man,
In Britain where was he
That could stand up his parallel,
Or fruitful object be
In eye of Imogen, that best
Could deem his dignity?
Moth. With marriage wherefore was he mock'd,
To be exil'd, and thrown
From Leonati seat, and cast
From her his dearest one,
Sweet Imogen?
Sici. Why did you suffer Jachimo,
Slight thing of Italy,
To taint his nobler heart and brain
With needless jealousy,

25. **for . . . sake:** because they are stamped with a representation of the king's head (which assures their negotiability).
26. **You . . . yours:** you should accept the light coin of my life all the more readily because the figure stamped on it is your own (man being made in God's image). 27. **take this audit:** accept this accounting.
28. **bonds:** (1) contract by which the term of life is held; (2) binding ropes of conscience; (3) prison fetters. 34. **Rates:** rebukes.
38. **Attending nature's law:** i.e. awaiting birth in accordance with nature's decree.
39–40. **Whose . . . art.** An echo of Psalm 68:5, where God is declared to be father of the fatherless.
42. **earth-vexing smart:** suffering that plagues mortals.
43. **Lucina:** goddess of childbirth. 49. **stuff:** substance.
57. **deem:** judge. 64. **Slight:** worthless.

And to become the geck and scorn
O' th' other's villainy?
2. Bro. For this from stiller seats we came,
Our parents and us twain,
That striking in our country's cause
Fell bravely and were slain,
Our fealty and Tenantius' right
With honor to maintain.
1. Bro. Like hardiment Posthumus hath
To Cymbeline perform'd.
Then, Jupiter, thou king of gods,
Why hast thou thus adjourn'd
The graces for his merits due,
Being all to dolors turn'd?
Sici. Thy crystal window ope; look out;
No longer exercise
Upon a valiant race thy harsh
And potent injuries.
Moth. Since, Jupiter, our son is good,
Take off his miseries.
Sici. Peep through thy marble mansion, help,
Or we poor ghosts will cry
To th' shining synod of the rest
Against thy deity.
Brothers. Help, Jupiter, or we appeal,
And from thy justice fly.

JUPITER *descends in thunder and lightning, sitting upon an eagle: he throws a thunderbolt. The Ghosts fall on their knees.*

Jup. No more, you petty spirits of region low,
Offend our hearing; hush! How dare you ghosts
Accuse the Thunderer, whose bolt, you know,
Sky-planted, batters all rebelling coasts?
Poor shadows of Elysium, hence, and rest
Upon your never-withering banks of flow'rs.
Be not with mortal accidents oppress'd,
No care of yours it is, you know 'tis ours.
Whom best I love, I cross; to make my gift,
The more delay'd, delighted. Be content,
Your low-laid son our godhead will uplift.
His comforts thrive, his trials well are spent.
Our Jovial star reign'd at his birth, and in
Our temple was he married. Rise, and fade.
He shall be lord of Lady Imogen,
And happier much by his affliction made.
This tablet lay upon his breast, wherein
Our pleasure his full fortune doth confine,
[*Jupiter drops a tablet.*]
And so away! No farther with your din
Express impatience, lest you stir up mine.
Mount, eagle, to my palace crystalline. *Ascends.*
Sici. He came in thunder, his celestial breath
Was sulphurous to smell; the holy eagle
Stoop'd, as to foot us. His ascension is
More sweet than our blest fields. His royal bird
Prunes the immortal wing, and cloys his beak,
As when his god is pleas'd.
All. Thanks, Jupiter!
Sici. The marble pavement closes, he is enter'd
His radiant roof. Away, and, to be blest,
Let us with care perform his great behest.
[*The Ghosts*] *vanish* [*after placing the tablet on Posthumus' breast*].
Post. [*Waking.*] Sleep, thou hast been a grandsire and begot
A father to me; and thou hast created
A mother and two brothers. But (O scorn!)
Gone! they went hence so soon as they were born.
And so I am awake. Poor wretches that depend
On greatness' favor dream as I have done,
Wake, and find nothing. But, alas, I swerve.
Many dream not to find, neither deserve,
And yet are steep'd in favors; so am I,
That have this golden chance and know not why.
What fairies haunt this ground? A book? O rare one,
Be not, as is our fangled world, a garment
Nobler than that it covers! Let thy effects
So follow, to be most unlike our courtiers,
As good as promise!

(*Reads.*) "When as a lion's whelp shall, to himself unknown, without seeking find, and be embrac'd by a piece of tender air; and when from a stately cedar shall be lopp'd branches, which, being dead many years, shall after revive, be jointed to the old stock, and freshly grow; then shall Posthumus end his miseries, Britain be fortunate and flourish in peace and plenty."

'Tis still a dream, or else such stuff as madmen
Tongue and brain not; either both or nothing,
Or senseless speaking, or a speaking such
As sense cannot untie. Be what it is,
The action of my life is like it, which
I'll keep, if but for sympathy.

Enter [FIRST] JAILER.

[*1.*] *Jail.* Come, sir, are you ready for death?
Post. Overroasted rather; ready long ago.

[*1.*] *Jail.* Hanging is the word, sir. If you be ready for that, you are well cook'd.

Post. So if I prove a good repast to the spectators, the dish pays the shot.

[*1.*] *Jail.* A heavy reckoning for you, sir. But the comfort is, you shall be call'd to no more payments, fear no more tavern-bills, which are often the sadness of parting, as the procuring of mirth. You come in faint for want of meat, depart reeling with too much drink; sorry that you have paid too much, and sorry that you are paid too much; purse and brain both

67. **geck**: dupe. 69. **stiller seats**. See lines 97–98.
75. **Like hardiment**: deeds of equal valor.
78. **adjourn'd**: delayed. 89. **synod**: assembly of the gods.
99. **accidents**: events. 102. **delighted**: (the more) delighted in.
104. **spent**: ended. 105. **Our Jovial star**: the planet Jupiter.
109. **This tablet**. Lines 133–35 indicate that this is an inscribed sheet within elaborate covers.
116. **Stoop'd . . . us**: swooped as if to seize us in its claws.

118. **Prunes**: preens. **cloys**: claws (?). 125. **scorn**: mockery.
129. **swerve**: err. 130. **to find**: of finding.
133. **rare**: exceptionally fine. 134. **fangled**: given to finery.
138. **When as**: when. 146. **Tongue**: speak. **brain**: understand. **either both**: one of the two (?). 147. **Or**: either.
148. **sense cannot untie**: reason cannot interpret.
150. **sympathy**: i.e. the similarity between my life and it.
153. **Hanging**. With punning reference to hanging meat.
156. **the dish . . . shot**: (1) the food is worth what it costs (*shot* = reckoning, bill); (2) I (as the "repast") pay the reckoning, i.e. settle the account. 163. **paid**: subdued (by drink).

empty; the brain the heavier for being too light, the purse too light, being drawn of heaviness. O, of this contradiction you shall now be quit. O, the charity of a penny cord! it sums up thousands in a trice. You have no true debitor and creditor but it: of what's past, is, and to come, the discharge. Your neck, sir, is pen, book, and counters; so the acquittance follows.

Post. I am merrier to die than thou art to live.

[*1.*] *Jail.* Indeed, sir, he that sleeps feels not the toothache; but a man that were to sleep your sleep, and a hangman to help him to bed, I think he would change places with his officer; for, look you, sir, you know not which way you shall go.

Post. Yes indeed do I, fellow.

[*1.*] *Jail.* Your death has eyes in 's head then; I have not seen him so pictur'd. You must either be directed by some that take upon them to know, or to take upon yourself that which I am sure you do not know, or jump the after-inquiry on your own peril; and how you shall speed in your journey's end, I think you'll never return to tell one.

Post. I tell thee, fellow, there are none want eyes to direct them the way I am going, but such as wink and will not use them.

[*1.*] *Jail.* What an infinite mock is this, that a man should have the best use of eyes to see the way of blindness! I am sure hanging's the way of winking.

Enter a MESSENGER.

Mess. Knock off his manacles, bring your prisoner to the King.

Post. Thou bring'st good news, I am call'd to be made free.

[*1.*] *Jail.* I'll be hang'd then.

Post. Thou shalt be then freer than a jailer; no bolts for the dead. [*Exeunt Posthumus and Messenger.*]

[*1.*] *Jail.* Unless a man would marry a gallows and beget young gibbets, I never saw one so prone. Yet, on my conscience, there are verier knaves desire to live, for all he be a Roman; and there be some of them too that die against their wills. So should I, if I were one. I would we were all of one mind, and one mind good. O, there were desolation of jailers and gallowses! I speak against my present profit, but my wish hath a preferment in't. *Exit.*

SCENE V

Enter CYMBELINE, BELARIUS, GUIDERIUS, ARVIRAGUS, PISANIO, *and* LORDS, [OFFICERS, *and* ATTENDANTS].

164. heavier: sleepier. **165. drawn:** emptied.
168. debitor and creditor: account book, or accountant.
170. counters: metal disks used in calculations.
175. officer: executioner.
178–79. death . . . pictur'd. Alluding to the common representation of Death as a figure with a skull for a head.
180. take upon them: profess. **182. jump:** hazard.
184. one. Perhaps a variant spelling of *on* = of.
186. wink: close the eyes. **194. made free:** i.e. executed.
199. prone: eager (to die).
201–2. Roman . . . wills. The Romans were commonly represented as having the Stoic's indifference to death.
206. preferment: promotion (to a more dignified role than jailer).

V.v. Location: Britain. Cymbeline's tent in the British camp.

Cym. Stand by my side, you whom the gods have made
Preservers of my throne. Woe is my heart
That the poor soldier that so richly fought,
Whose rags sham'd gilded arms, whose naked breast
Stepp'd before targes of proof, cannot be found.
He shall be happy that can find him, if
Our grace can make him so.
Bel. I never saw
Such noble fury in so poor a thing;
Such precious deeds in one that promis'd nought
But beggary and poor looks.
Cym. No tidings of him?
Pis. He hath been search'd among the dead and living;
But no trace of him.
Cym. To my grief, I am
The heir of his reward, [*to Belarius, Guiderius, and Arviragus*] which I will add
To you, the liver, heart, and brain of Britain,
By whom, I grant, she lives. 'Tis now the time
To ask of whence you are. Report it.
Bel. Sir,
In Cambria are we born, and gentlemen.
Further to boast were neither true nor modest,
Unless I add, we are honest.
Cym. Bow your knees.
Arise my knights o' th' battle. I create you
Companions to our person, and will fit you
With dignities becoming your estates.

Enter CORNELIUS *and* LADIES.

There's business in these faces. Why so sadly
Greet you our victory? You look like Romans,
And not o' th' court of Britain.
Cor. Hail, great King!
To sour your happiness, I must report
The Queen is dead.
Cym. Who worse than a physician
Would this report become? But I consider,
By med'cine life may be prolong'd, yet death
Will seize the doctor too. How ended she?
Cor. With horror, madly dying, like her life,
Which (being cruel to the world) concluded
Most cruel to herself. What she confess'd
I will report, so please you. These her women
Can trip me, if I err, who with wet cheeks
Were present when she finish'd.
Cym. Prithee say.
Cor. First, she confess'd she never lov'd you; only
Affected greatness got by you, not you;
Married your royalty, was wife to your place,
Abhorr'd your person.
Cym. She alone knew this;
And but she spoke it dying, I would not
Believe her lips in opening it. Proceed.

5. targes of proof: shields of tested strength.
7. grace: favor. **14. liver . . . brain:** i.e. the very life.
20. knights . . . battle: knights created on the battlefield in recognition of extraordinary valor.
22. estates: (new) rank. **35. trip:** refute, correct.
38. Affected: loved. **41. but:** except that.
42. opening: revealing.

Cor. Your daughter, whom she bore in hand to love
With such integrity, she did confess
Was as a scorpion to her sight, whose life,
But that her flight prevented it, she had
Ta'en off by poison.

Cym. O most delicate fiend!
Who is't can read a woman? Is there more?

Cor. More, sir, and worse. She did confess she had
For you a mortal mineral, which, being took,
Should by the minute feed on life, and ling'ring,
By inches waste you. In which time she purpos'd,
By watching, weeping, tendance, kissing, to
O'ercome you with her show, and in time
(When she had fitted you with her craft) to work
Her son into th' adoption of the crown;
But failing of her end by his strange absence,
Grew shameless desperate; open'd (in despite
Of heaven and men) her purposes; repented
The evils she hatch'd were not effected; so
Despairing died.

Cym. Heard you all this, her women?

Ladies. We did, so please your Highness.

Cym. Mine eyes
Were not in fault, for she was beautiful;
Mine ears, that [heard] her flattery, nor my heart,
That thought her like her seeming. It had been vicious
To have mistrusted her; yet, O my daughter,
That it was folly in me, thou mayst say,
And prove it in thy feeling. Heaven mend all!

Enter LUCIUS, JACHIMO, [*the* SOOTHSAYER,] *and other Roman prisoners* [*guarded*]; LEONATUS [POSTHUMUS] *behind, and* IMOGEN.

Thou com'st not, Caius, now for tribute; that
The Britains have ras'd out, though with the loss
Of many a bold one, whose kinsmen have made suit
That their good souls may be appeas'd with slaughter
Of you their captives, which ourself have granted;
So think of your estate.

Luc. Consider, sir, the chance of war, the day
Was yours by accident. Had it gone with us,
We should not, when the blood was cool, have threaten'd
Our prisoners with the sword. But since the gods
Will have it thus, that nothing but our lives
May be call'd ransom, let it come. Sufficeth
A Roman with a Roman's heart can suffer.
Augustus lives to think on't; and so much
For my peculiar care. This one thing only
I will entreat: my boy, a Britain born,
Let him be ransom'd. Never master had
A page so kind, so duteous, diligent,
So tender over his occasions, true,
So feat, so nurse-like. Let his virtue join
With my request, which I'll make bold your Highness
Cannot deny. He hath done no Britain harm,
Though he have serv'd a Roman. Save him, sir,
And spare no blood beside.

Cym. I have surely seen him;
His favor is familiar to me. Boy,
Thou hast look'd thyself into my grace,
And art mine own. I know not why, wherefore,
To say "Live, boy." Ne'er thank thy master. Live;
And ask of Cymbeline what boon thou wilt,
Fitting my bounty and thy state, I'll give it;
Yea, though thou do demand a prisoner,
The noblest ta'en.

Imo. I humbly thank your Highness.

Luc. I do not bid thee beg my life, good lad,
And yet I know thou wilt.

Imo. No, no, alack,
There's other work in hand. I see a thing
Bitter to me as death; your life, good master,
Must shuffle for itself.

Luc. The boy disdains me,
He leaves me, scorns me. Briefly die their joys
That place them on the truth of girls and boys.
Why stands he so perplex'd?

Cym. What wouldst thou, boy?
I love thee more and more; think more and more
What's best to ask. Know'st him thou look'st on? Speak,
Wilt have him live? Is he thy kin? thy friend?

Imo. He is a Roman, no more kin to me
Than I to your Highness; who, being born your vassal,
Am something nearer.

Cym. Wherefore ey'st him so?

Imo. I'll tell you, sir, in private, if you please
To give me hearing.

Cym. Ay, with all my heart,
And lend my best attention. What's thy name?

Imo. Fidele, sir.

Cym. Thou'rt my good youth—my page;
I'll be thy master. Walk with me; speak freely.

[*Cymbeline and Imogen talk apart.*]

Bel. Is not this boy reviv'd from death?

Arv. One sand another
Not more resembles that sweet rosy lad
Who died, and was Fidele. What think you?

Gui. The same dead thing alive.

Bel. Peace, peace, see further. He eyes us not, forbear.
Creatures may be alike; were't he, I am sure
He would have spoke to us.

Gui. But we [saw] him dead.

Bel. Be silent; let's see further.

Pis. [*Aside.*] It is my mistress.
Since she is living, let the time run on
To good or bad.

[*Cymbeline and Imogen come forward.*]

Cym. Come, stand thou by our side,
Make thy demand aloud. [*To Jachimo.*] Sir, step you forth;

43. **bore in hand:** pretended.
47. **delicate:** subtle, crafty. 50. **mortal mineral:** deadly poison.
55. **fitted you:** moulded you to her purpose.
56. **adoption . . . crown:** official recognition by you as heir to the throne. 65. **vicious:** wrong (weaker than the modern sense).
68. **in thy feeling:** by feeling it, i.e. by the suffering it has caused you.
74. **think . . . estate:** give thought to your spiritual state (in preparation for death). 83. **peculiar care:** personal concern.
87. **occasions:** needs. 88. **feat:** deft.

92. **And:** even if you.
93. **favor:** face. 103. **thing:** i.e. the ring on Jachimo's finger.

Give answer to this boy, and do it freely,
Or by our greatness, and the grace of it
(Which is our honor), bitter torture shall
Winnow the truth from falsehood.—[On,] speak to him.

Imo. My boon is, that this gentleman may render
Of whom he had this ring.

Post. [*Aside.*] What's that to him?

Cym. That diamond upon your finger, say
How came it yours?

Iach. Thou'lt torture me to leave unspoken that
Which, to be spoke, would torture thee.

Cym. How? me?

Iach. I am glad to be constrain'd to utter that
Which torments me to conceal. By villainy
I got this ring. 'Twas Leonatus' jewel,
Whom thou didst banish; and—which more may grieve thee,
As it doth me—a nobler sir ne'er liv'd
'Twixt sky and ground. Wilt thou hear more, my lord?

Cym. All that belongs to this.

Iach. That paragon, thy daughter,
For whom my heart drops blood, and my false spirits
Quail to remember—Give me leave, I faint.

Cym. My daughter? what of her? Renew thy strength;
I had rather thou shouldst live while nature will
Than die ere I hear more. Strive, man, and speak.

Iach. Upon a time—unhappy was the clock
That strook the hour!—it was in Rome—accurs'd
The mansion where!—'twas at a feast—O would
Our viands had been poison'd, or at least
Those which I heav'd to head!—the good Posthumus
(What should I say? He was too good to be
Where ill men were, and was the best of all
Amongst the rar'st of good ones), sitting sadly,
Hearing us praise our loves of Italy
For beauty that made barren the swell'd boast
Of him that best could speak; for feature, laming
The shrine of Venus or straight-pight Minerva,
Postures beyond brief nature; for condition,
A shop of all the qualities that man
Loves woman for, besides that hook of wiving,
Fairness which strikes the eye—

Cym. I stand on fire:
Come to the matter.

Iach. All too soon I shall,
Unless thou wouldst grieve quickly. This Posthumus,
Most like a noble lord in love and one
That had a royal lover, took his hint,
And (not dispraising whom we prais'd; therein
He was as calm as virtue) he began
His mistress' picture, which by his tongue being made,
And then a mind put in't, either our brags
Were crak'd of kitchen trulls, or his description
Prov'd us unspeaking sots.

Cym. Nay, nay, to th' purpose.

Iach. Your daughter's chastity—there it begins.
He spake of her, as Dian had hot dreams,
And she alone were cold; whereat I, wretch,
Made scruple of his praise, and wager'd with him
Pieces of gold 'gainst this which then he wore
Upon his honor'd finger, to attain
In suit the place of 's bed and win this ring
By hers and mine adultery. He, true knight,
No lesser of her honor confident
Than I did truly find her, stakes this ring,
And would so, had it been a carbuncle
Of Phoebus' wheel; and might so safely, had it
Been all the worth of 's car. Away to Britain
Post I in this design. Well may you, sir,
Remember me at court, where I was taught
Of your chaste daughter the wide difference
'Twixt amorous and villainous. Being thus quench'd
Of hope, not longing, mine Italian brain
Gan in your duller Britain operate
Most vildly; for my vantage, excellent;
And to be brief, my practice so prevail'd,
That I return'd with simular proof enough
To make the noble Leonatus mad,
By wounding his belief in her renown
With tokens thus, and thus; averring notes
Of chamber-hanging, pictures, this her bracelet
(O cunning, how I got[']t!), nay, some marks
Of secret on her person, that he could not
But think her bond of chastity quite crack'd,
I having ta'en the forfeit. Whereupon—
Methinks I see him now—

Post. [*Advancing.*] Ay, so thou dost,
Italian fiend! Ay me, most credulous fool,
Egregious murtherer, thief, any thing
That's due to all the villains past, in being,
To come! O, give me cord, or knife, or poison,
Some upright justicer! Thou, King, send out
For torturers ingenious; it is I
That all th' abhorred things o' th' earth amend
By being worse than they. I am Posthumus,
That kill'd thy daughter—villain-like, I lie—
That caus'd a lesser villain than myself,
A sacrilegious thief, to do't. The temple
Of virtue was she; yea, and she herself.
Spit, and throw stones, cast mire upon me, set

139. to leave: for leaving.
151. live . . . will: live out your natural life, i.e. have your death sentence revoked. **163. feature:** form, figure.
163–64. laming . . . Venus: making the image of Venus seem by comparison a cripple.
164. straight-pight: straight-pitched, i.e. erect.
165. brief: i.e. in comparison with the immortal gods. **condition:** character. **166. shop:** storehouse.
167. hook of wiving: bait for marriage. **172. hint:** occasion.
176. put in't: inserted into the picture.
177. crak'd: boastfully spoken. **trulls:** wenches.
178. unspeaking sots: fools unable to describe beauty.
182. Made scruple: expressed doubt.
184. honor'd finger: finger which was thereby honored.
185. In suit: by urging my suit.
189–90. a carbuncle . . . wheel: a ruby on the wheel of the sun-god's chariot (which according to Ovid was so decorated).
192. Post: hasten. **194. Of:** by.
197. duller Britain. An ancient theory held that northern climates make men dull-witted. **199. practice:** treacherous scheme.
200. simular: pretended. **202. renown:** good name.
203. averring: citing.
208. forfeit: i.e. what was forfeited by the broken bond—her sexual favors. **214. justicer:** justice.
216. That . . . amend: who make all loathed things look better.
221. she herself: virtue herself.

The dogs o' th' street to bay me; every villain
Be call'd Posthumus Leonatus, and
Be villainy less than 'twas! O Imogen!
My queen, my life, my wife! O Imogen,
Imogen, Imogen!
Imo. Peace, my lord, hear, hear—
Post. Shall 's have a play of this? Thou scornful page,
There lie thy part. [*Striking her; she falls.*]
Pis. O gentlemen, help
Mine and your mistress! O my Lord Posthumus,
You ne'er kill'd Imogen till now! Help, help!
Mine honor'd lady!
Cym. Does the world go round?
Post. How comes these staggers on me?
Pis. Wake, my mistress!
Cym. If this be so, the gods do mean to strike me
To death with mortal joy.
Pis. How fares my mistress?
Imo. O, get thee from my sight,
Thou gav'st me poison. Dangerous fellow, hence!
Breathe not where princes are.
Cym. The tune of Imogen!
Pis. Lady,
The gods throw stones of sulphur on me, if
That box I gave you was not thought by me
A precious thing. I had it from the Queen.
Cym. New matter still.
Imo. It poison'd me.
Cor. O gods!
I left out one thing which the Queen confess'd,
Which must approve thee honest. "If Pisanio
Have," said she, "given his mistress that confection
Which I gave him for cordial, she is serv'd
As I would serve a rat."
Cym. What's this, Cornelius?
Cor. The Queen, sir, very oft importun'd me
To temper poisons for her, still pretending
The satisfaction of her knowledge only
In killing creatures vild, as cats and dogs
Of no esteem. I, dreading that her purpose
Was of more danger, did compound for her
A certain stuff, which, being ta'en, would cease
The present pow'r of life, but in short time
All offices of nature should again
Do their due functions. Have you ta'en of it?
Imo. Most like I did, for I was dead.
Bel. My boys,
There was our error.
Gui. This is sure Fidele.
Imo. Why did you throw your wedded lady [from] you?
Think that you are upon a rock, and now
Throw me again. [*Embracing him.*]
Post. Hang there like fruit, my soul,
Till the tree die!
Cym. How now, my flesh? my child?

233. staggers: dizziness.
238. tune: voice. **240. stones of sulphur:** thunderbolts.
245. approve: prove. **250. temper:** mix. **255. cease:** halt.
262. upon a rock: i.e. like a shipwrecked sailor reaching safety (?). Most editors emend *rock* to *lock*, i.e. a wrestling hold.

What, mak'st thou me a dullard in this act?
Wilt thou not speak to me?
Imo. [*Kneeling.*] Your blessing, sir.
Bel. [*To Guiderius and Arviragus.*] Though you did love this youth, I blame ye not,
You had a motive for't.
Cym. My tears that fall
Prove holy water on thee! Imogen,
Thy mother's dead.
Imo. I am sorry for't, my lord.
Cym. O, she was naught; and long of her it was
That we meet here so strangely; but her son
Is gone, we know not how, nor where.
Pis. My lord,
Now fear is from me, I'll speak troth. Lord Cloten,
Upon my lady's missing, came to me
With his sword drawn, foam'd at the mouth, and swore,
If I discover'd not which way she was gone,
It was my instant death. By accident
I had a feigned letter of my master's
Then in my pocket, which directed him
To seek her on the mountains near to Milford,
Where, in a frenzy, in my master's garments
(Which he enforc'd from me), away he posts
With unchaste purpose, and with oath to violate
My lady's honor. What became of him
I further know not.
Gui. Let me end the story:
I slew him there.
Cym. Marry, the gods forefend!
I would not thy good deeds should from my lips
Pluck a hard sentence. Prithee, valiant youth,
Deny't again.
Gui. I have spoke it, and I did it.
Cym. He was a prince.
Gui. A most incivil one. The wrongs he did me
Were nothing prince-like; for he did provoke me
With language that would make me spurn the sea
If it could so roar to me. I cut off 's head,
And am right glad he is not standing here
To tell this tale of mine.
Cym. I am sorrow for thee;
By thine own tongue thou art condemn'd, and must
Endure our law. Thou'rt dead.
Imo. That headless man
I thought had been my lord.
Cym. Bind the offender,
And take him from our presence.
Bel. Stay, sir King.
This man is better than the man he slew,
As well descended as thyself, and hath
More of thee merited than a band of Clotens
Had ever scar for. [*To the Guard.*] Let his arms alone,
They were not born for bondage.
Cym. Why, old soldier:

268. motive: cause.
271. naught: wicked. **long of:** owing to. **280. directed:** led.
288. thy good deeds: i.e. you who have performed so well in battle.
290. again. A sense still seen in "go and come back again."
297. tell . . . mine: i.e. say that he cut off my head. **I am sorrow.** Cf. "I am woe" in *The Tempest*, V.i.139.
305. Had . . . for: ever merited for their battle wounds.

Wilt thou undo the worth thou art unpaid for,
By tasting of our wrath? How of descent
As good as we?
Arv. In that he spake too far.
Cym. And thou shalt die for't.
Bel. We will die all three
But I will prove that two on 's are as good
As I have given out him. My sons, I must
For mine own part unfold a dangerous speech,
Though haply well for you.
Arv. Your danger's ours.
Gui. And our good his.
Bel. Have at it then, by leave:
Thou hadst, great King, a subject who
Was call'd Belarius.
Cym. What of him? He is
A banish'd traitor.
Bel. He it is that hath
Assum'd this age: indeed a banish'd man,
I know not how a traitor.
Cym. Take him hence,
The whole world shall not save him.
Bel. Not too hot.
First pay me for the nursing of thy sons,
And let it be confiscate all, so soon
As I have receiv'd it.
Cym. Nursing of my sons?
Bel. I am too blunt and saucy: here's my knee.
Ere I arise, I will prefer my sons;
Then spare not the old father. Mighty sir,
These two young gentlemen, that call me father,
And think they are my sons, are none of mine;
They are the issue of your loins, my liege,
And blood of your begetting.
Cym. How? my issue?
Bel. So sure as you your father's. I, old Morgan,
Am that Belarius whom you sometime banish'd.
Your pleasure was my [mere] offense, my punishment
Itself, and all my treason: that I suffer'd
Was all the harm I did. These gentle princes
(For such and so they are) these twenty years
Have I train'd up; those arts they have as I
Could put into them. My breeding was, sir, as
Your Highness knows. Their nurse, Euriphile
(Whom for the theft I wedded), stole these children
Upon my banishment; I mov'd her to't,
Having receiv'd the punishment before
For that which I did then. Beaten for loyalty
Excited me to treason. Their dear loss,
The more of you 'twas felt, the more it shap'd
Unto my end of stealing them. But, gracious sir,
Here are your sons again, and I must lose
Two of the sweet'st companions in the world.
The benediction of these covering heavens
Fall on their heads like dew! for they are worthy

311. But I will: if I do not. **on 's:** of us.
313. For . . . part. Modifies *dangerous.*
315. Have at it: I'll go at it; here goes.
319. Assum'd: reached. **326. prefer:** advance.
334. Your pleasure: i.e. what it pleased you to think and proclaim. **was . . . offense:** constituted an entire offense.
336. all . . . did: the only wrong I had anything to do with.
344. Beaten: being beaten. **345. dear:** heartfelt, grievous.
346–47. shap'd . . . of: fitted my purpose in.

To inlay heaven with stars.
Cym. Thou weep'st, and speak'st.
The service that you three have done is more
Unlike than this thou tell'st. I lost my children;
If these be they, I know not how to wish
A pair of worthier sons.
Bel. Be pleas'd awhile:
This gentleman, whom I call Polydore,
Most worthy prince, as yours, is true Guiderius;
This gentleman, my Cadwal, Arviragus,
Your younger princely son. He, sir, was lapp'd
In a most curious mantle, wrought by th' hand
Of his queen mother, which for more probation
I can with ease produce.
Cym. Guiderius had
Upon his neck a mole, a sanguine star,
It was a mark of wonder.
Bel. This is he,
Who hath upon him still that natural stamp.
It was wise nature's end in the donation,
To be his evidence now.
Cym. O, what, am I
A mother to the birth of three? Ne'er mother
Rejoic'd deliverance more. Blest pray you be,
That after this strange starting from your orbs,
You may reign in them now! O Imogen,
Thou hast lost by this a kingdom.
Imo. No, my lord;
I have got two worlds by't. O my gentle brothers,
Have we thus met? O, never say hereafter
But I am truest speaker. You call'd me brother,
When I was but your sister; I you brothers,
When we were so indeed.
Cym. Did you e'er meet?
Arv. Ay, my good lord.
Gui. And at first meeting lov'd,
Continu'd so, until we thought he died.
Cor. By the Queen's dram she swallow'd.
Cym. O rare instinct!
When shall I hear all through? This fierce abridgment
Hath to it circumstantial branches, which
Distinction should be rich in. Where? how liv'd you?
And when came you to serve our Roman captive?
How parted with your [brothers]? How first met them?
Why fled you from the court? and whither? These,
And your three motives to the battle, with
I know not how much more, should be demanded,
And all the other by-dependances,
From chance to chance; but nor the time nor place
Will serve our long interrogatories. See,

354. Unlike: incredible. **361. curious:** exquisitely made.
362. probation: proof. **364. sanguine:** blood-red.
365. of wonder: wonderful.
367. end . . . donation: purpose in bestowing it.
368. To . . . evidence: that it should testify to his identity.
370. deliverance. The subject of *Rejoic'd.*
371. starting . . . orbs: shooting from your spheres.
372. reign: (1) exert astrological influence; (2) have kingly power.
382. fierce abridgment: drastically compressed account.
383. branches: ramifications.
384. Distinction . . . in: as they are distinguished should prove to be abundant. **388. your three motives:** the motives of you three.
390. by-dependances: circumstances growing out of (literally, hanging from) these. **391. chance:** event.

Posthumus anchors upon Imogen;
And she (like harmless lightning) throws her eye
On him, her brothers, me, her master, hitting
Each object with a joy; the counterchange
Is severally in all. Let's quit this ground,
And smoke the temple with our sacrifices.
[*To Belarius*.] Thou art my brother, so we'll hold thee
ever.

Imo. You are my father too, and did relieve me
To see this gracious season.

Cym. All o'erjoy'd,
Save these in bonds. Let them be joyful too,
For they shall taste our comfort.

Imo. My good master,
I will yet do you service.

Luc. Happy be you!

Cym. The forlorn soldier, that [so] nobly fought,
He would have well becom'd this place, and grac'd
The thankings of a king.

Post. I am, sir,
The soldier that did company these three
In poor beseeming; 'twas a fitment for
The purpose I then follow'd. That I was he,
Speak, Jachimo. I had you down and might
Have made you finish.

Jach. [*Kneeling*.] I am down again;
But now my heavy conscience sinks my knee,
As then your force did. Take that life, beseech you,
Which I so often owe; but your ring first,
And here the bracelet of the truest princess
That ever swore her faith.

Post. Kneel not to me.
The pow'r that I have on you is to spare you;
The malice towards you, to forgive you. Live,
And deal with others better.

Cym. Nobly doom'd!
We'll learn our freeness of a son-in-law:
Pardon's the word to all.

Arv. [*To Posthumus*.] You holp us, sir,
As you did mean indeed to be our brother;
Joy'd are we that you are.

Post. Your servant, Princes. Good my lord of
Rome,
Call forth your soothsayer. As I slept, methought
Great Jupiter, upon his eagle back'd,
Appear'd to me, with other spritely shows
Of mine own kindred. When I wak'd, I found
This label on my bosom, whose containing
Is so from sense in hardness, that I can
Make no collection of it. Let him show
His skill in the construction.

Luc. Philarmonus!

Sooth. Here, my good lord.

Luc. Read, and declare the meaning.

397. **severally in all**: from individual to every other individual.
400. **relieve**: deliver, as a town from a siege. Cf. III.iv.133–34.
405. **forlorn**: lost, missing.
409. **beseeming**: appearance. **fitment**: suitable disguise.
412. **finish**: die. 415. **often**: many times over.
420. **doom'd**: judged. 421. **freeness**: nobility.
422. **holp**: helped. 428. **spritely**: ghostly. 430. **label**: paper.
431. **from . . . hardness**: difficult to understand.
432. **collection**: interpretation.
433. **the construction**: construing it.

[*Sooth*.] (*Reads*.) "When as a lion's whelp shall, to himself unknown, without seeking find, and be embrac'd by a piece of tender air; and when from a stately cedar shall be lopp'd branches, which, being dead many years, shall after revive, be jointed to the old stock, and freshly grow; then shall Posthumus end his miseries, Britain be fortunate and flourish in peace and plenty."
Thou, Leonatus, art the lion's whelp;
The fit and apt construction of thy name,
Being *Leo-natus*, doth import so much.
[*To Cymbeline*.] The piece of tender air, thy virtuous
daughter,
Which we call *mollis aer*, and *mollis aer*
We term it *mulier*; [*to Posthumus*] which *mulier* I divine
Is this most constant wife, who, even now,
Answering the letter of the oracle,
Unknown to you, unsought, were clipt about
With this most tender air.

Cym. This hath some seeming.

Sooth. The lofty cedar, royal Cymbeline,
Personates thee; and thy lopp'd branches point
Thy two sons forth; who, by Belarius stol'n,
For many years thought dead, are now reviv'd,
To the majestic cedar join'd, whose issue
Promises Britain peace and plenty.

Cym. Well,
My peace we will begin. And, Caius Lucius,
Although the victor, we submit to Caesar,
And to the Roman empire, promising
To pay our wonted tribute, from the which
We were dissuaded by our wicked queen,
Whom heavens, in justice both on her and hers,
Have laid most heavy hand.

Sooth. The fingers of the pow'rs above do tune
The harmony of this peace. The vision
Which I made known to Lucius, ere the stroke
Of yet this scarce-cold battle, at this instant
Is full accomplish'd: for the Roman eagle,
From south to west on wing soaring aloft,
Lessen'd herself, and in the beams o' th' sun
So vanish'd; which foreshow'd our princely eagle,
Th' imperial Caesar, should again unite
His favor with the radiant Cymbeline,
Which shines here in the west.

Cym. Laud we the gods,
And let our crooked smokes climb to their nostrils
From our blest altars. Publish we this peace
To all our subjects. Set we forward. Let
A Roman and a British ensign wave
Friendly together. So through Lud's-Town march,
And in the temple of great Jupiter
Our peace we'll ratify; seal it with feasts.
Set on there! Never was a war did cease
(Ere bloody hands were wash'd) with such a peace.

Exeunt.

447. **mollis aer**: gentle air. This false etymology for Latin *mulier*, "woman," is older than Shakespeare.
450. **Answering**: agreeing with.
451. **were**: you were. **clipt**: embraced.
452. **seeming**: likelihood.
464. **Whom**: on whom. **hers**: i.e. Cloten.
469. **yet this**: this yet. 484. **Set on**: start up.

NOTE ON THE TEXT

The First Folio (1623) is the only authority for *Cymbeline*; all later texts are derived from that source. The copy behind the F1 text (set by Compositors B and E) is a scribal transcript, probably by Ralph Crane, of a manuscript at one remove from Shakespeare's "foul papers"; but there is nothing in the text to rule out or substantiate the possibility that the transcript behind Crane's transcript was the official prompt-book.

J. C. Maxwell was the first to suggest that the scribe responsible for the F1 copy may have been Ralph Crane, who, it is generally accepted, prepared special transcripts for the F1 texts of *The Winter's Tale* and the first three (or four) plays in F1 (see "Note on the Text" to *The Tempest* and Howard-Hill). A number of Crane's characteristics are present: a considerable, though lighter than in some other Crane transcripts, use of parentheses, as well as of uncommon hyphenated forms (especially adjective-plus-noun; see Textual Notes, I.iv.57–8, I.vi.17, 66, II.iii.71, II.iv.19, II.v.26, III.i.32, IV.ii.226, 398, V.v.469), so-called Jonsonian elisions (see, e.g., F1, I.vi.28, III.ii.58–59, IV.ii.328), employment of the forms *o'th'* and *you're* in preference to *a' th'* and *y'are*, and regular act-scene division, but Crane's most distinctive scribal mannerism, the hyphenating of verb and following pronoun or preposition, is completely absent. It may be added that one typical Crane spelling, *dampn'd*, had been changed to *damn'd* in the process of stop-press correction at I.vi.104. Jowett/Taylor accept Crane's hand in the F1 printer's copy and offer further supporting evidence. Honigmann first noticed that the F1 text suddenly shifts from "O" (Shakespeare's preferred form) to "Oh" after II.iv, a change which, it is agreed, cannot be compositorial (see also Taylor/Wells); this means, Honigmann suggests, that a second scribe took over at this point in the manuscript copy from which Crane worked in preparing the play for F1. That the second hand must almost certainly have figured in Crane's copy, and not in the F1 copy, is strongly supported by the fact that Crane's general scribal characteristics appear equally in both sections of the F1 text.

The text as a whole is a clean one and presents comparatively few textual difficulties.

For further information, see: W. W. Greg, *The Shakespeare First Folio* (Oxford, 1955): J. M. Nosworthy, ed., New Arden *Cymbeline* (London, 1955); J. C. Maxwell, ed., New Shakespeare *Cymbeline* (Cambridge, 1960 [see my review in *JEGP*, LX (1961), 327–9]; E. A. J. Honigmann, "On the Indifferent and One-Way Variants in Shakespeare." The *Library*, 5th. ser., XXII (1967), 189–204; T. H. Howard-Hill, *Ralph Crane and Some Shakespeare First Folio Comedies* (Charlottesville, Va., 1972); Stanley Wells, Gary Taylor, et al., *William Shakespeare: A Textual Companion* (Oxford, 1987); John Jowett and Gary Taylor, "'With New Additions': Theatrical Interpolation in *Measure for Measure* (Appendix I)." in Gary Taylor and John Jowett, *Shakespeare Reshaped* (Oxford, 1993).

TEXTUAL NOTES

Title: Cymbeline] The Tragedie of Cymbeline. *F1*
Dramatis personae: *subs. as first given by Rowe*
Imogen] *This name may be a scribal or compositorial misreading of* Innogen, *the name of the wife of Brute, first ruler of Britain.* Innogen *appears as the name of Leonato's wife, a ghost character, in* Much Ado, *I.i o.s.d., and Simon Forman records the name as* Innogen *in his description of a performance of* Cymbeline *witnessed by him before September 12, 1611 (see Appendix B, Number 20).*
Act-scene division: *from F1, with the following exceptions: F1 divides the present I.i. into two scenes, breaking after l. 69 (and hence designates I.ii-vi as I.iii-vii), marks no scene division at II.v, and divides III.vi into two scenes, breaking after l. 27 (and hence designates III.vii as III.viii); adjustments by Rowe and later editors (see notes to these scenes below); present act-scene arrangement as a whole first established by Dyce*

I.i

Location: *ed. (after Rowe, Capell)*
2 **courtiers']** *Steevens (after Johnson* courtiers';); Courtiers: *F1*
3 **King's]** *Rowe;* Kings *F1*
4, 10 **s.pp. 1. Gent. . . . 2. Gent.]** *Rowe;* 1. . . . 2 *F1 (throughout rest of scene)*
30 **Cassibelan]** *F2 (so Holinshed);* Cassibulan *F1*
58–9 **old, . . . other,]** *Rowe;* old . . . cloathes, the other *F1*
65 **Howsoe'er]** *F3;* Howsoere, *F1*
69 **s.d. Exeunt.]** *following this s.d. F1 marks a new scene:* Scena Secunda.; *Rowe first continued the scene unbroken*
97 **Philario's]** *Rowe;* Filorio's *F1*
103 **s.d. Aside.]** *Rowe*
104 **wrong]** *Cambridge;* wrong, *F1*
106 **s.d. Exit.]** *Rowe*
116 **cere]** *Steevens conj.;* seare *F1*
117 **s.d. Puts . . . ring.]** *Rowe (subs.)*
119 **my poor self]** *Pope;* (my poore selfe) *F1*
123 **s.d. Putting . . . arm.]** *Rowe*
150 **neighbor shepherd's]** *Capell;* Neighbour-Shepheards *F1*
151 **s.d. To the Queen.]** *Theobald*
158 **s.d. with Lords]** *Dyce (subs.)*
169 **goer-back]** *hyphen, Pope*
177 **s.d. To Pisanio.]** *Craig*

I.ii

I.ii] *Dyce;* Scena Tertia. *F1*
Location: *ed. (after Capell)*
o.s.d. Cloten] *Rowe;* Clotten *F1 (throughout until IV.ii, thereafter* Cloten; *the form* Clotten *represents the pronunciation: cf.* Clotens Clot-pole *at IV.ii.184 in F1)*
1, 7 **s.pp. 1. Lord. . . . 2. Lord.]** *Rowe;* 1. . . . 2 *F1 (through II.iii)*
5–6 **If . . . him?]** *as prose, Capell; as verse, F1*
7, 12, 15 **s.dd. Aside.]** *Theobald*
17–9 **Stand . . . ground.]** *as prose, Pope; as verse, F1*
20, 23, 27, 32, 36 **s.dd. Aside.]** *Pope*
21 **oceans. Puppies!]** *Capell;* Oceans (Puppies.) *F1*
32–3 **Sha . . . her.]** *as prose, Rowe; as verse, F1*

I.iii

I.iii] *Dyce;* Scena Quarta. *F1*
Location: *Capell (subs.)*
9 **this]** *Theobald (after Warburton);* his *F1*

I.iv

I.iv] *Dyce;* Scena Quinta. *F1*
Location: *Rowe, Capell*
o.s.d. Jachimo] *Capell;* Iachimo *F1 (throughout)*
47 **not]** *Rowe*
57–8 **country mistresses]** *Theobald;* Country-Mistresses *F1*
67 **France,]** *Rowe;* France: *F1*
70–1 **good— . . . comparison—]** *Capell (subs., after Theobald);* good: . . . comparison, *F1*
72–3 **others]** *Pope;* others. *F1*
74 **but]** *Malone*
80 **mistress]** *F2;* Mistirs *F1*
83 **purchase]** *Rowe;* purchases *F1*
90 **too:]** *Rowe (subs.);* too, *F1*
95 **mistress,]** *Collier;* Mistris: *F1*
96 **frail.]** *Pope (subs.);* fraile, *F1*
99 **gentlemen.]** *F2;* Gentlemen? *F1*
112 **too]** *F3;* to *F1*
118 **repulse,]** *F4;* Repulse *F1*
123 **estate]** *F2;* Fstate *F1*
123 **neighbor's]** *Pope;* Neighbors *F1*
127 **thousand]** *F3;* thousands *F1*
128 **that,]** *Theobald;* that *F1*
134 **therein]** *F2;* there in *F1*
135 **ladies']** *Warburton;* Ladies *F1*
136 **preserve]** *F2;* preseure *F1*
169 **s.d. Exeunt . . . Jachimo.]** *Theobald*
171–2 **Signior . . . 'em.]** *as prose, Capell; as verse, F1*

I.v

I.v] *Dyce;* Scena Sexta. *F1*
Location: *Rowe*
2 **s.p. 1. Lady.]** *Theobald;* Lady. *F1*
3 **s.d. Exeunt]** *F2;* Exit *F1*
5 **s.d. Presenting . . . box.]** *Malone (after Capell)*
9 **death,]** *Cambridge;* death: *F1*
20 **human]** *Rowe;* humane *F1*
27, 31 **s.dd. Aside.]** *Rowe*
32 **s.d. To Pisanio.]** *Rowe*
33 **s.d. Aside.]** *Capell (after Johnson)*
60 **s.d. The . . . up.]** *Malone (after Capell, Johnson)*
69 **still;]** *Rowe;* still, *F1*
75 **s.d. Exit Pisanio.]** *placed as in Capell; after l. 74, F1*
77 **her]** *Dyce;* her, *F1*
80 **liegers]** *Hanmer;* Leidgers *F1*
83 **primeroses]** *Kittredge;* Prime-Roses *F1*
85 **s.d. Exeunt]** *Theobald;* Exit *F1*

I.vi

I.vi] *Dyce;* Scena Septima. *F1*
Location: *Capell (subs.)*
2 **wedded lady]** *F2;* Wedded-Lady *F1*
7 **desire]** *F2;* desires *F1*
8 **soe'er]** *Pope;* so ere *F1*
13 **s.d. Presents a letter.]** *Johnson (subs.)*
15 **s.d. Aside.]** *Pope*
17 **Arabian bird]** *F4;* Arabian-Bird *F1*
24 **trust—]** *Boswell;* trust. *F1*
26–8 **aloud— . . . rest—]** *Vaughan conj.;* aloud. . . . rest, *F1*

37 spectacles] F3; Spectales F1
44 excellence oppos'd,] Rowe; Excellence, oppos'd F1
52 s.d. To Pisanio.] Rowe (after peevish. l. 54); placed as in Globe
66 Gallian girl] Pope; Gallian-Girle F1
72 languish for] Steevens; languish: / For F1
76 heavens] F2; Heauen's F1
80 his,] Staunton (subs.); his F1
94–8 you— . . . born—] Pope (subs.); you . . . borne. F1 (born. F3)
108 by-peeping] hyphen, Knight
113 himself.] Rowe (subs.); himselfe, F1
122 hir'd] Rowe; hyr'd, F1
134 ramps,] Capell; Rampes F1
156 Leonatus!] Capell; Leonatus F1; Leonatus, F3
168 men's] F2; men F1
169 descended] F2; defended F1
191 strange,] F2; strange F1
193 protection?] Theobald; protection. F1
194 safety.] Pope; safety, F1
204 to-morrow!] Knight; to morrow. F1

II.i

Location: ed. (after Capell)
8, 12, 35 s.dd. Aside.] Theobald
11 standers-by] hyphen, Pope
16, 46 s.dd. Aside.] Pope
20 bellyful] Capell (belly-full); belly full F1
23 s.d. Aside.] Rowe
24 crow,] Theobald; crow F1
26 your] F3; you F1
33 to-night] F2; night F1
51 s.d. Exeunt . . . Lord.] Capell; Exit. F1
61 husband, than] F4 (after F2 husband, Then); Husband. Then F1
62 make.] Theobald (subs.); make F1
63 honor;] Rowe; Honour. F1
65 s.d. Exit.] Capell; Exeunt. F1

II.ii

Location: Rowe (subs.)
o.s.d. A . . . corner.] Rowe (subs.)
1 woman?] Kittredge; woman: F1
1 Helen] F3; Helene F1
7 seiz'd] F2; ceiz'd F1
7 s.d. Exit Lady.] Rowe
16 touch!] Capell; touch, F1
20 lids,] Rowe; lids. F1
23 design!] ed.; designe? F1 (u); designe. F1 (c)
24 s.d. Takes . . . tables.] Collier MS
33 s.d. Taking . . . bracelet.] Rowe
34 Gordian knot] Pope (subs.); Gordian-knot F1
36 within,] Rowe; within: F1
43 down] Kittredge; downe, F1
49 bare] Theobald conj.; beare F1
49 fear;] Capell; feare, F1
50 angel,] Rowe; Angell: F1
51 s.d. into the trunk] Rowe

II.iii

Location: Capell (subs., after Theobald)
7 s.p. Clo.] from F1 catchword
17 after,] Pope; after F1
24 eyes;] Theobald; eyes F1
27 s.p. Clo.] Dyce
29 vice] Rowe; voyce F1
31 amend] F2; amed F1
31 s.d. Exeunt Musicians.] Theobald
37 daughter?] Rowe; daughter F1; daughter. F3
47 solicits] F2; solicity F1
53 s.d. Enter a Messenger.] Rowe
63 s.d. all but Cloten] Globe (after Capell)
65 s.d. Knocks.] Theobald
71 true man] Pope; True-man F1
72 true man] Steevens; True-man F1
77 more?] Rowe; more. F1
86 fairest: sister,] Theobald; fairest, Sister F1
86 s.d. Exit Lady.] Capell (after l. 85); placed as in Dyce
97 kindness] F2; kinduesse F1
110 myself] Neilson; my selfe, F1
112 father.] Rowe (subs.); Father, F1
122 it] Pope; it; F1
128 envy,] F2; Enuie. F1
134 body,] F2; body; F1
135 hairs] F2; Heires F1
137 devil—] Theobald; diuell. F1
144 king's] Rowe; Kings F1
145 am,] F4; am. F1
149 s.d. Exit Pisanio.] Capell
154 you,] F3; your F1

II.iv

Location: Rowe, Capell
6 hopes] F2; hope F1
19 not-fearing Britain] Rowe; not-fearing-Britaine F1
24 wing-led] mingled F2
26 See! Jachimo!] Capell; see Iachimo. F1
37 s.p. Phi.] Capell; Post. F1
39 yet.] Rowe; yet, F1
46 stone's] Rowe; Stones F1
47 not] F2; note F1
55 her or you,] F2 (subs.); her, or you F1
57 you] F2; yon F1
62 near] F4; nere F1
71 Cydnus] Theobald; Sidnus F1
84 Nature, dumb;] Warburton (after Theobald); Nature dumbe, F1
95 s.d. Showing the bracelet.] Rowe (subs.)
102 action] Rowe; Action, F1
106 s.d. Gives the ring.] Johnson
116 one] one of F2
117 her?] Knight; her. F1
128 dearly.] F3; deerly F1
142 arithmetic] F2 (subs.); Arethmaticke F1
149 something—] Rowe; something. F1

II.v

II.v] Capell
Location: ed. (after Theobald)
16 full-acorn'd] hyphen, Pope
16 German one] Rowe; Iarmen on F1
18 for] Pope; for, F1
20 me—] Pope; me, F1
26 Nice longing] Capell; Nice-longing F1
28 all;] F2 (all.); all F1

III.i

Location: Pope (after Rowe)
o.s.d. Caius] Rowe; Caius, F1
5 Cassibelan] F2 (so Holinshed); Cassibulan F1 (throughout scene)
21 enemies'] Warburton; Enemies F1
32 rejoicing fires] Rowe; reioycing-Fires F1
41 Cassibelan.] Theobald (subs.); Cassibulan, F1
50 here] Pope; heere, F1
53 be. We do say] Malone; be, we do. Say F1
59 Britain] Knight; Britaine, F1
80 salt-water girdle] Rowe; Salt-water-Girdle F1
85 remain] Theobald (subs.); Remaine, F1

III.ii

Location: ed. (after Rowe)
14 so] Pope; so, F1
17 s.d. Reading.] Rowe
17–8 Do't; the letter] Rowe (subs., as part of the letter); Doo't: The Letter. F1 (not in italics as part of the letter)
21 feodary] Capell; Foedarie F1
31–4 content— . . . love—] Theobald (subs.); content: . . . Loue, F1
37 alike;] F2 (alike.); alike, F1
38 forfeiters] Hanmer; Forfeytours F1
40 s.d. Reads.] Rowe (subs.)
42 you, . . . creatures,] Rowe; you: (oh . . . Creatures) F1
55 kind—] Rowe; kinde. F1
56 beyond beyond] Ritson conj.; beyond, beyond F1
64 get] F2; ger F1
67 score] F2; store F1
67 rid] ride F2
70 execution] F2 (Execntion); Excution F1
78 here, nor here,] F2; heere, not heere; F1
79 ensues,] Rowe; ensues F1

III.iii

Location: Pope, Pelican (after Sisson)
o.s.d. from their cave] Capell (subs.)
1 day] Capell; day, F1
1 such] Theobald; such, F1
2 Stoop] Hanmer; Sleepe F1
6 turbands] F2; Turbonds F1
10 sport:] Capell; sport, F1
10 hill,] F4; hill F1
20 sharded beetle] F3; sharded-Beetle F1
23 bable] ed. (after Rowe bauble); Babe F1
25 him] Knight; him, F1
28 know] F2; knowes F1
33 travelling a-bed] Rowe; trauailing a bed F1
37 December, how] Hanmer; December? How F1
43 choir] Pope; Quire F1
45 city's] F3; Citties F1
71 paid] Rowe; payed F1
74 hunters'] Theobald; Hunters F1
78 s.d. Guiderius and Arviragus] Theobald
83 wherein they bow,] Warburton; whereon the Bowe F1
83 hit] F3; hit, F1
86 Polydore] Steevens (after Rowe); Paladour F1
88 Guiderius—Jove!] Capell; Guiderius. Ioue, F1
91–2 "Thus . . . neck,"] quotes, Theobald
106 Morgan] F2; Mergan F1

III.iv

Location: Steevens
6 One] Cambridge; One, F1
28 Milford-Haven] hyphen, Rowe
33 already!] ed.; alreadie? F1
44 false] F2; falfe F1
49 favor's] Rowe; fauours F1
60 tear,] Globe; teare: F1
79 afore't] Rowe; a-foot F1
89 make] Malone; makes F1
101 out] Johnson conj.
139 swan's nest.] Rowe (hyphen dropped, F3); Swannes-nest, F1
165 brief:] F2; breefe? F1
167–8 one. . . . this,] Rowe; one, . . . this. F1
173 service,] Theobald; seruice: F1
174 happy,] F3; happy: F1
178 me,] Capell; me F1
182–3 attempt . . . to] Rowe; attempt, . . . too F1
193 s.d. severally] Theobald

III.v

Location: Rowe (subs.)
o.s.d. attended] Kittredge (after Globe)
17 s.d. with Lords] Malone (subs., after Capell); &c F1
32 looks us] Johnson; looke vs F1; lookes as F2
35 s.d. Exit a Messenger.] Kittredge (after Theobald)
40 strokes,] F2; stroke;, F1
52 Grant,] Capell; Grant F1
55 s.d. Exit Cloten.] Capell; Exit. F1 (after days. l. 55)
56 Posthumus!] Rowe; Posthumus, F1
58 that;] Rowe; that. F1
68 s.d. Aside.] S. Walker conj.
81 pandar!] Capell; Pandar, F1
100 s.d. Presenting a letter.] Malone (after Capell)
101 s.d. Aside.] Rowe
104 s.d. Aside.] Theobald
112 do, . . . it] Theobald; do . . . it, F1
140 insultment] F2; insulment F1
145 s.d. with the clothes] Rowe (subs.)

III.vi

Location: Capell (after Rowe)
o.s.d. in boy's clothes] Rowe
12 rich ones] Rowe; Rich-ones F1
27 s.d. to the cave] Rowe (subs.)
27 s.d. Enter . . . Arviragus.] preceding this entry F1 marks a new scene: Scena Septima.; Rowe first continued the scene unbroken
32 to] F2; too F1
35 down pillow] Pope; Downe-pillow F1
39 s.d. Looking . . . cave.] Rowe (subs.)
52 Money, youth?] Rowe; Money? Youth. F1
65 encounter'd!] Pope; encounter'd, F1
67 depart,] F3; depart; F1
69 hard] Knight; hard, F1

72–3 **him . . . absence,]** *Knight;* him / (After long absence) *Fi*
74 **s.d. Aside.]** *Rowe*
80 **s.d. Whispering.]** *Rowe*
84–5 **them, . . . multitudes,]** *Johnson;* them: . . . Multitudes *Fl*
88 **Leonatus']** *S. Walker conj.;* Leonatus *Fl*

III.vii

III.vii] *Steevens;* Scena Octaua. *Fl*
Location: *Rowe, Dyce*
11, 12, 16 **s.pp. 1. Tri.]** *Dyce;* Tri. *Fl*
14 **supplyant]** *Capell;* suppliant *Fl*

IV.i

Location: *Sisson*
7 **workman.]** *Theobald (subs.);* Workman, *Fl*
14 **imperceiverant]** *Dyce;* imperseuerant *Fl*
18 **her]** *Warburton conj.;* thy *Fl*

IV.ii

Location: *ed. (after Rowe)*
1 **s.d. To Imogen.]** *Capell*
2 **s.d. To Imogen.]** *Theobald*
22 **reason's]** *Rowe (after F2);* reason's, *Fl*
24 **s.d. Aside.]** *Capell*
26, 27] *Marked with gnomic quotes, Fl*
31 **s.d. To Belarius.]** *S. Walker conj.*
32 **s.d. Aside.]** *Johnson*
35 **imperious]** *F3;* emperious *Fl*
38 **s.d. Swallows some.]** *Dyce (after Rowe)*
46 **s.d. Imogen . . . cave]** *Theobald; s.d. after* you. *l. 46, Fl; placed as in Capell*
49–51 **he . . . dieter.]** *continued to Guiderius, Capell; assigned to* Arui. *in Fl (Fl assigns also the next speech to Arviragus)*
50 **sauc'd]** *F2* (sawc't); sawc'st *Fl*
58 **patience]** *Rowe;* patient *Fl*
59 **stinking elder]** *F3;* stinking-Elder *Fl*
70 **s.d. Exeunt . . . Arviragus.]** *Rowe*
71 **villain mountainers]** *F3; hyphenated in Fl*
80 **thee.]** *Ingleby (in Cambridge);* thee? *Fl*
81 **rascal,]** *F2;* Rascall: *Fl*
82 **grandfather!]** *ed.;* Grandfather? *Fl*
89 **villain,]** *Theobald;* Villaine *Fl*
90 **it. Were]** *Rowe (subs.);* it, were *Fl*
112 **s.d. with Cloten's head]** *Theobald*
112 **see,]** *Theobald;* see *Fl*
122 **ye]** *Johnson;* the *Fl*
128–9 **himself, . . . law?]** *Johnson;* himselfe? . . . Law. *Fl*
132 **humor]** *Theobald;* Honor *Fl*
153 **Cloten.]** *Pope;* Cloten, *Fl*
167 **him.]** *Rowe (subs.);* him, *Fl*
186 **ingenious]** *Rowe;* ingenuous *Fl*
195 **s.d. as]** *Capell*
205 **crare]** *Sympson conj. (in Steevens);* care *Fl*
213 **leagu'd.]** *Pope (subs.);* leagu'd, *Fl*
221 **face, pale primrose]** *Rowe;* face. Pale-Primrose *Fl*
226 **rich-left heirs]** *Rowe;* rich-left-heyres *Fl*
254 **s.d. Exit Belarius.]** *Capell*
257 **So. Begin.]** *Capell (subs.);* So, begin. *Fl*
263 **chimney-sweepers,]** *Pope;* Chimney-Sweepers *Fl*
287 **herblets]** *Capell* (herb'lets); Herbelets *Fl*
290 **is]** *Pope;* are *Fl*
290 **s.d. Belarius . . . Arviragus]** *Capell*
294 **s.d. Sees . . . Cloten.]** *Rowe (subs., after l. 295); placed as in Craig*
295 **bedfellow!]** *Rowe;* Bedfellow? *Fl*
305 **eye,]** *Pope;* eye; *Fl*
310 **Martial]** *F3;* martiall *Fl*
314 **Thou,]** *Pope;* thou *Fl*
323 **be?]** *Capell;* be, *Fl*
332 **s.d. Falls . . . body.]** *Globe*
377 **s.d. Aside.]** *Rowe*
398 **daisied plot]** *Capell;* Dazied-Plot *Fl*

IV.iii

Location: *Theobald (after Rowe)*
o.s.d. with Attendants] *Capell (subs.)*
1 **s.d. Exit an Attendant.]** *Capell (subs.)*
16, 23 **s.pp. 1. Lord.]** *Capell;* Lord. *Fl*
22 **s.d. To Pisanio.]** *Johnson*
27 **queen!]** *Theobald;* Queen, *Fl*
28 **s.p. 1. Lord.]** *Malone;* Lord. *Fl*
32 **withdraw,]** *Theobald;* withdraw *Fl*
35 **s.d. all but Pisanio]** *Dyce (after Hanmer)*

IV.iv

Location: *Capell*
2–3 **find we . . . adventure?]** *F2;* we finde . . . Aduenture. *Fl*
8 **us.]** *F4;* v.. *or* v,. *(comma broken) Fl (?);* us *F2*
26 **breeding,]** *Capell;* Breeding; *Fl*
27 **hard]** *F2;* heard *Fl*
30 **Than]** *F4;* Then *Fl*
38 **horse, save one]** *Capell (subs.);* Horse saue one, *Fl*
43 **go.]** *Rowe (subs.);* go, *Fl*
49 **valuation]** *F2;* valewation *Fl*
53 **s.d. Aside.]** *Hanmer*

V.i

Location: *Dyce (after Rowe)*
o.s.d. with . . . handkerchief] *Rowe*
1 **wish'd]** *Pope;* am wisht *Fl*
15 **doers']** *Theobald;* dooers *Fl*
32–3 **begin The fashion:]** *Dyce (subs., after Theobald);* begin, / The fashion *Fl*

V.ii

Location: *Capell*
5 **nature's]** *Rowe;* Natures *Fl*

V.iii

Location: *ed. (after Rowe)*
7 **lane;]** *Theobald;* Lane, *Fl*
12 **dead men]** *Rowe;* deadmen *Fl*
23 **fled,]** *F2;* fled. *Fl*
24 **harts]** *Theobald;* hearts *Fl*
29–31 **many— . . . nothing—with]** *Pope (subs.);* many: . . . nothing. With *Fl*
42 **stoop'd]** *Rowe;* stopt *Fl*
42 **slaves,]** *Pope;* Slaues *Fl*
43 **they]** *Theobald;* the *Fl*
46 **hearts,]** *Rowe;* hearts: *Fl*
46–8 **wound . . . Ten]** *Theobald (subs.; before, F2);* wound, . . . before some . . . waue, ten *Fl*
57 **old man]** *F4;* Oldman *Fl*
65 **"what news?"]** *Globe;* what newes *Fl*
82 **again]** *Pope;* agen *Fl (for the rhyme)*
83 **s.d. Britain]** *Kittredge (after Theobald)*
84, 87 **s.pp. 1. Cap.]** *Rowe;* 1 *Fl*
86, 91 **s.pp. 2. Cap.]** *Rowe;* 2 *Fl*
91 **dog!]** *Theobald;* Dogge, *Fl*
94 **s.d. Then exeunt omnes.]** *Globe (after Theobald)*

V.iv

Location: *ed. (after Pelican)*
o.s.d. two] *Rowe*
1 **s.p. 1. Jail.]** *Rowe;* Gao. *Fl*
2 **s.d. Exeunt Jailers.]** *Rowe*
15 **constrain'd.]** *Rowe (subs.);* constrain'd, *Fl*
23 **it.]** *Rowe (subs.);* it, *Fl*
25 **figure's]** *F3;* figures *Fl*
29 **s.d. Sleeps.]** *Rowe*
29 **s.d. apparition]** *F2;* Apparation *Fl*
40 **orphans']** *Theobald;* Orphanes *Fl*
46 **foes,]** *Pope;* Foes. *Fl*
67 **geck]** *Capell;* geeke *Fl*
81 **look]** *F2;* looke, / looke *Fl*
81 **out;]** *Rowe;* out, *Fl;* out *F2*
110 **s.d. Jupiter . . . tablet.]** *Rowe (after l. 109); placed by ed.*
122 **s.d. The Ghosts]** *Capell*
122 **s.d. after . . . breast]** *ed.*
123 **s.d. Waking.]** *Theobald*
126 **Gone!]** *Capell (after Rowe);* Gone, *Fl*
128 **greatness']** *Theobald;* Greatnesse, *Fl*
128 **favor dream]** *Rowe (subs.);* Fauour; Dreame *Fl*
150 **s.d. First]** *Dyce*
151, 153, etc. **s.pp. 1. Jail.]** *Capell;* Gao. *Fl*
153 **sir.]** *Pope (subs.);* Sir, *Fl*
169 **sir]** *F2;* Sis *Fl*
197 **s.d. Exeunt . . . Messenger.]** *Theobald;* Exeunt. *F2*
206 **s.d. Exit.]** *F2;* Exeunt. *Fl*

V.v

Location: *ed. (after Rowe)*
o.s.d. Officers, and Attendants] *Capell*
13 **s.d. to . . . Arviragus]** *Rowe*
54 **and]** yes and *F2*
62 **s.p. Ladies.]** *Cambridge;* La. *Fl*
64 **heard]** *F3;* heare *Fl*
68 **s.d. the Soothsayer, . . . guarded]** *Capell*
96 **master.]** *Capell (subs.);* Master, *Fl*
118 **page;]** *Theobald;* Page *Fl*
119 **s.d. Cymbeline . . . apart.]** *Theobald (subs.)*
124 **forbear.]** *Steevens (subs.);* forbeare *Fl*
126 **saw]** *Rowe;* see *Fl*
127 **s.d. Aside.]** *Rowe*
129 **s.d. Cymbeline . . . forward.]** *Theobald*
130 **s.d. To Jachimo.]** *Rowe*
134 **On,]** *F3;* One *Fl*
136 **s.d. Aside.]** *Capell*
150 **strength;]** *Theobald;* strength *Fl;* strength, *F4*
171 **lord in love]** *Pope;* Lord, in loue, *Fl*
177 **kitchen trulls]** *Capell;* Kitchin-Trulles *Fl*
197 **operate]** *F2;* operare *Fl*
205 **got't]** *ed. (after F2* got it); got *Fl*
208–9 **Whereupon— . . . now—]** *Johnson (after Rowe);* Whereupon, . . . now. *Fl*
209 **s.d. Advancing.]** *Rowe (subs.)*
210 **Ay]** *Rowe;* Aye *Fl*
212 **being,]** *Rowe;* being *Fl*
214 **Thou,]** *Theobald;* Thou *Fl*
229 **s.d. Striking . . . falls.]** *Rowe*
233 **Wake,]** *Rowe;* Wake *Fl*
245 **Pisanio]** *F2;* Pasanio *Fl*
261 **from]** *Rowe;* fro *Fl*
263 **s.d. Embracing him.]** *Malone (after Hanmer)*
266 **s.d. Kneeling.]** *Rowe*
267 **s.d. To . . . Arviragus.]** *Pope*
269 **holy water]** *Capell;* holy-water *Fl*
300 **lord.]** *F4;* Lord *Fl*
305 **s.d. To the Guard.]** *Theobald*
310 **three]** *Cowden Clarke;* three, *Fl*
311 **on 's]** *F2;* one's *Fl*
315 **leave.]** *Pope;* leaue *Fl*
331 **issue?]** *Rowe;* Issue. *Fl*
334 **mere]** *Tyrwhitt conj.;* neere *Fl*
335 **treason:]** *Pope;* Treason *Fl*
351 **like]** *F2;* liks *Fl*
367 **end . . . donation,]** *Capell (after Rowe);* end, . . . donation *Fl*
368 **what,]** *Dyce;* what *Fl*
370 **Blest]** *Dyce (after Rowe);* Blest, *Fl*
378 **we]** ye *Rowe*
378 **e'er]** *Rowe;* ere *Fl*
386 **brothers]** *Rowe;* Brother *Fl*
387 **whither? These,]** *Theobald;* whether these? *Fl*
388 **battle,]** *Theobald;* Battaile? *Fl*
391 **chance;]** *Theobald (subs.);* chance? *Fl*
395 **him, . . . me,]** *Rowe;* him: . . . Me: *Fl*
395 **master,]** *Rowe;* Master *Fl*
399 **s.d. To Belarius.]** *Rowe*
400 **me]** *Rowe;* me: *Fl*
405 **so]** *F2;* no *Fl*
412 **s.d. Kneeling.]** *Hanmer (subs.)*
422 **s.d. To Posthumus.]** *Capell*
428 **spritely]** *Steevens;* sprightly *Fl*
435 **s.p. Sooth.]** *Capell*
445 **Leo-natus]** *Capell;* Leonatus *Fl*
446 **s.d. To Cymbeline.]** *Theobald*
448 **s.d. to Posthumus]** *Sisson (after Capell)*
451 **you,]** *Rowe;* you *Fl*
469 **scarce-cold battle]** *Rowe;* scarse-cold-Battaile *Fl*
485 **s.d. Exeunt.]** Exeunt. / FINIS. *Fl*

The Winter's Tale

THE WINTER'S TALE was seen by Dr. Simon Forman, who left a record of a performance at the Globe on May 15, 1611.[1] Later in the same year, in November, the account book of the Office of the Revels noted a performance at court, by the King's Players, of a play called "Ye Winters night Tayle." How much earlier than its first known performance *The Winter's Tale* was written is a matter of surmise, but for a number of reasons it is supposed to be later than *Cymbeline*. One of these reasons is that Shakespeare uses comically, in this play, a bit of source material he had put aside as unsuitable for *Cymbeline*; it is the description of the frightful fate to be meted out to the poor Clown, according to Autolycus in IV.iv.783–91. Accordingly *The Winter's Tale* is generally dated 1610–11. It was first published in the Folio of 1623.

The first three acts of *The Winter's Tale* are a dramatization of the corresponding portion of Robert Greene's novel *Pandosto* (1588), or, as it was later called, *Dorastus and Fawnia*. This romantic tale proclaims as its purpose the displaying of the evils of jealousy. Greene's jealous king, Pandosto of Bohemia, is changed into Leontes of Sicilia (with a corresponding change of Egistus of Sicilia into Polixenes of Bohemia), and Shakespeare's reason for switching the countries is a matter of some critical interest. He saw a relation between the plot of the lost flower girl and the classical story of Proserpina:

> O Proserpina,
> For the flow'rs now, that, frighted, thou let'st fall
> From Dis's waggon! (IV.iv.116–18)

The Proserpina legend was of course set in Sicily. But the exchanging of countries led Shakespeare to set the action of III.iii on the non-existent sea-coast of Bohemia, to the scorn of Ben Jonson and other pedants. (It is not always noted that Greene, too, gave Bohemia a sea-coast.) Some details seem to have come from Francis Sabie's versified renderings of *Pandosto* called *The Fisherman's Tale* and *Flora's Fortune* (1595). More important are links to Shakespeare's own work just preceding *The Winter's Tale*. *Pericles* had featured the reunion of a king with his lost wife and daughter, with the dramatic emphasis upon the discovery of the daughter, Marina. In *The Winter's Tale* the reunion with the daughter is passed over lightly and the disclosure of the supposedly dead wife is made a theatrical spectacle. It is an instance of Shakespeare as an artist declining to repeat himself. In so far as *Cymbeline* is the story of Posthumus, that play looks forward to the jealousy and repentance of Leontes in *The Winter's Tale*. And the world of oracles and dream visions, rustics and royalty, strange disguisings and the revelation of identity after many years, remains generally similar through these late plays.

Structurally, *The Winter's Tale* falls into two parts, each ending in a sensational scene. In the first, the dramatic force is the insane jealousy of Leontes, apparently unmotivated, a kind of disease. Shakespeare deliberately eliminates some of the possible justification for the King's suspicion which was a part of his source. Here is no study such as he had already made in *Othello* of the gradual poisoning of a mind; the seizure is sudden, inexplicable to impartial observers, and so complete that it makes Leontes denounce the holy oracle as a liar. Some critics have maintained that Leontes is already jealous when the play begins, and even that he himself has been a secret lecher and is

[1] For Forman's accounts of *Macbeth* and *Cymbeline* as well as *The Winter's Tale*, see Appendix C, Number 20, below.

therefore particularly susceptible to jealousy. But this is reading too much into the play. A failure to understand the clear meaning of Leontes' speech at I.ii.138–46 has caused much difficulty; one modern critic refers to it as Leontes' "mysterious, mumbling half-soliloquy."

> Affection! thy intention stabs the centre.
> Thou dost make possible things not so held,
> Communicat'st with dreams (how can this be?),
> With what's unreal thou co-active art,
> And fellow'st nothing. Then 'tis very credent
> Thou mayst co-join with something, and thou dost
> (And that beyond commission), and I find it
> (And that to the infection of my brains
> And hard'ning of my brows).

The crucial word is *affection*, which in Shakespeare often means "sexual desire" and is usually so explained in this passage. But here it is much more plausibly *affectio*, in the sense used by Cicero, which Cooper's Latin dictionary (1584 ed.) defines as "a disposition or mutation happening to bodie or minde: trouble of minde." Leontes is accordingly talking not about the supposed passion of Hermione and Polixenes, but about his own jealousy, as Macbeth in soliloquy talks about his vaulting ambition.

The dignified patience of the accused queen, Hermione, makes necessary the presence of some other character to express resistance to Leontes' tyranny, so Shakespeare creates Paulina, who in her fearless assertion of her mistress' innocence is reminiscent of Emilia in the final scene of *Othello*, and in her later manipulation of affairs toward a happy ending recalls the capable women in the problem comedies. The faithful Camillo is a stock type—the courtier who is loyal to the better side of his sovereign's character rather than to his present passionate rage. Antigonus, with his more short-sighted loyalty, is individualized by being made, as Dover Wilson points out, a rather "horsy" character, and he is of course immortalized by his sensational departure from the play: "Exit pursued by a bear."

The second major part of the play does not depend primarily upon the plot details of *Pandosto*. Its highlight is a delightful pastoral celebration, festive, joyous, and comic, with a characteristically Shakespearean mingling of romantic love and pleasant fooling. The transition from the serious, melodramatic first part to the gay pastoral scenes is summarized in the words of the old shepherd to his son, the Clown: "Now bless thyself; thou met'st with things dying, I with things new-born." He refers to the discovery of an abandoned baby in contrast to Antigonus' fate in the jaws of a bear and his shipmates' destruction in a tempest. But his words have a wider significance. The first part is the traditional winter's tale—"a sad tale's best for winter," says the young prince Mamillius, who will die while only a boy. The festive scenes set in Bohemia (an English Arcadia, really) celebrate new life, new growth and beauty, the awakening of spring. Autolycus establishes the tone with his first song:

> When daffadils begin to peer,
> With heigh, the doxy over the dale!
> Why, then comes in the sweet o' the year,
> For the red blood reigns in the winter's pale.
> (IV.iii.1–4)

In the first part of the play young people are the victims of the evil in their elders: Mamillius dies and Perdita is abandoned. In the second part a regeneration like that of spring has taken place and the young are triumphant. In the great sheep-shearing scene (IV.iv, one of the longest in Shakespeare) we are observers of a celebration like the traditional popular Whitsun-ale, a folk festival in which two young people were chosen to be specially dressed and act as king and queen. There was eating, drinking, and merrymaking, with the older people looking on. Each young fellow was supposed to treat his girl with a ribbon or favor, and there was usually a jester to provide merriment.

Perdita is the queen of such a festival; as Florizel points out, her special costume transforms her:

> no shepherdess, but Flora
> Peering in April's front. This your sheep-shearing
> Is as a meeting of the petty gods,
> And you the queen on't. (IV.iv.2–5)

There was usually some license in the behavior of the merrymakers at Whitsun-ales, and Perdita shows more than once her awareness of the fact, as when she says:

> Methinks I play as I have seen them do
> In Whitsun pastorals. Sure this robe of mine
> Does change my disposition. (IV.iv.133–35)

Such remarks only throw into higher relief her modesty and innocence.

The Winter's Tale is an interesting contrast to John Fletcher's *The Faithful Shepherdess*, which had been produced by the King's Men a year or two earlier and had been a pronounced failure. In his preface to the published version, Fletcher explained what he had been trying to do—write tragicomedy—and why the play failed—the audience expected something different from what it got. The people expected, he said, "a play of country hired shepherds in gray cloaks, with curtailed dogs in strings"—in other words, low, realistic characters like Shakespeare's Shepherd, Clown, and Autolycus. They insisted on the traditional folk elements of festival, too, and, says Fletcher, "missing Whitsun-ales, cream, wassail and morris-dances, [they] began to be angry." Shakespeare made no such mistake. There are two dances, several ballads, and a catch. He gave his audience what it wanted in such generous profusion as to make clear that it was what he enjoyed too.

If Shakespeare, intentionally or not, taught his colleagues Beaumont and Fletcher a lesson in the successful writing of pastoral, he adopted their kind of melodramatic surprise for the conclusion of his play. In his source, *Pandosto*, the falsely accused queen does die; but for a happier ending a reunion like that in Shakespeare's earlier *Pericles* must be brought about.

In that play a supposedly dead wife, as well as a supposedly dead daughter, is restored to a king. But the audience knows that the queen is still alive; only Pericles is surprised. Shakespeare, by keeping the audience as well as Leontes in ignorance of Hermione's survival, makes possible the grand, theatrical statue scene. The scene in which Leontes recognizes his lost daughter Perdita is only reported, in order to save emotional tension for Leontes' recovery of Hermione. There are obvious suggestions of the Pygmalion story in the statue scene as there are of the Proserpina story in connection with Perdita. Although the posing of a woman as a statue may seem silly enough to a reader, Shakespeare's audience was accustomed to it in the court masques, and the scene has proved strikingly effective on the public stage.

The characterization of Perdita is the glory of the fourth act. Her charming modesty and diffidence about her role as the humble sweetheart of a disguised prince make her hold back as mistress of the feast and her father's hostess, until she is gently reproached by the shepherd. Her bestowal of flowers on the guests involves her in a discussion with the disguised king, Polixenes, on the question of nature and artifice, a major theme of this part of the play. She fears and distrusts anything that is not natural, and though Polixenes gives her the standard humanistic answer in defense of art,

> Yet Nature is made better by no mean
> But Nature makes that mean; so over that art
> Which you say adds to Nature, is an art
> That Nature makes, (IV.iv.89–92)

she nevertheless rejects artificially crossed flowers as she would reject cosmetics. Though she is, unknown to herself, a princess, yet she is a child of nature. (Ironically, Polixenes in his argument unconsciously undermines his own case against the marriage of a prince with a shepherdess.) She is almost, but not quite, an egalitarian; when she has been denounced by Polixenes as "this knack" and threatened with torture and death, she says,

> I was not much afeard; for once or twice
> I was about to speak, and tell him plainly
> The self-same sun that shines upon his court
> Hides not his visage from our cottage, but
> Looks on alike. (IV.iv.442–46)

Yet she is no rebel against the artificial barriers which rank puts in the way of her happiness. Her conclusion is:

> This dream of mine
> Being now awake, I'll queen it no inch farther,
> But milk my ewes, and weep. (IV.iv.448–50)

After Florizel has assured her of his faith, she is resolute, even against Camillo's warnings that love flourishes in prosperity but alters in affliction. She stoutly replies,

> I think affliction may subdue the cheek,
> But not take in the mind. (IV.iv.576–77)

Shakespeare has made out of his "queen of curds and cream" something of a Stoic hero.

The rogue Autolycus is one of literature's great comic characters. His work is by preference disreputable; he thoroughly enjoys his calling and is an artist at it. He is, like Falstaff, a philosopher of roguery, but he is less of a casuist. He is Mercurial, a snapper-up of unconsidered trifles, and he has a merry heart which carries him all the way. He prefers cheating to robbery, as less risky and painful. He is as exuberant about the stupidities of men as P. T. Barnum was to be, and, like every good showman, he has a varied repertory. His first triumph in the play is the enactment of one of the old cony-catching tricks described by Greene in his underworld pamphlets. It may have given Shakespeare a kind of Autolycan pleasure to use as a source for both the main plot and the subplot of his play that same Greene who had attacked him so bitterly twenty years before as "an upstart crow, beautified with our feathers." Autolycus sells his trinkets and tawdry wares, and plies his customers with his broadside ballads until they are anesthetized for his purse-cutting. He makes the most of every opportunity; as he says, "Every lane's end, every shop, church, session, hanging, yields a careful man work" (IV.iv.685–86). Yet an ironic comic force manipulates him in the play, making him an instrument of good in spite of himself, and he is finally dependent for favor on those rustics he has fleeced and patronized.

Irving Babbitt used to say that two lines of Camillo's, "a wild dedication of yourselves / To unpath'd waters, undream'd shores" (IV.iv.566–67), are the most romantic lines in English literature. There are many passages in the fourth act of *The Winter's Tale* that might compete for the designation. The same characteristically Shakespearean romantic feeling that informs *A Midsummer Night's Dream* is apparent here —a yearning for English flowers and the intimacy of the English countryside in the context of classical mythology and legend:

> daffadils,
> That come before the swallow dares, and take
> The winds of March with beauty; violets, dim,
> But sweeter than the lids of Juno's eyes,
> Or Cytherea's breath; pale primeroses,
> That die unmarried, ere they can behold
> Bright Phoebus in his strength (a malady
> Most incident to maids); bold oxlips, and
> The crown imperial; lilies of all kinds
> (The flow'r-de-luce being one). (IV.iv.118–27)

Such passages are Shakespeare's arias for his romantic heroines; when the prince Arviragus uses such language in *Cymbeline*, his brother chides him for playing in wench-like words.

Even the rustics in *The Winter's Tale* are not confined to comic dialogue, though some of Shakespeare's finest prose is put into the mouths of Autolycus and the Clown. It is the old shepherd who evokes, in verse more active and compact than that lovely stuff in the flower-catalogue, the picture of his old wife, when she lived, presiding at a feast:

> This day she was both pantler, butler, cook,
> Both dame and servant; welcom'd all, serv'd all;
> Would sing her song, and dance her turn; now here,
> At upper end o' th' table, now i' th' middle;
> On his shoulder, and his; her face o' fire
> With labor, and the thing she took to quench it
> She would to each one sip. (IV.iv.56–62)

The run-on lines, the shifting accent, the repetition, all contribute to the feeling of bustle and scurry that animates the scene.

A very different effect is conveyed by the strange, anti-rhythmical verse which Shakespeare uses for Hermione's prologue to her defense after the indictment, in formal prose, is made against her at the trial:

> Since what I am to say must be but that
> Which contradicts my accusation, and
> The testimony on my part no other
> But what comes from myself, it shall scarce boot me
> To say "Not guilty." Mine integrity,
> Being counted falsehood, shall (as I express it)
> Be so receiv'd. (III.ii.22–28)

Another passage, the speech of the Chorus which bridges the early scenes at the Sicilian court and the later pastoral scenes in Bohemia, shows how the freedom of movement from line to line which characterizes Shakespeare's late verse can operate even in rhymed couplets:

> I, that please some, try all, both joy and terror
> Of good and bad, that makes and unfolds error,
> Now take upon me, in the name of Time,
> To use my wings. Impute it not a crime
> To me, or my swift passage, that I slide
> O'er sixteen years and leave the growth untried
> Of that wide gap, since it is in my pow'r
> To o'erthrow law, and in one self-born hour
> To plant and o'erwhelm custom. (IV.i.1–9)

The Winter's Tale was popular at the Jacobean and Caroline court, but its loose construction and the improbabilities of its plot drew censure from the sterner critics. Ben Jonson wrote, in his preface to *Bartholomew Fair* (published 1631), that he was loath to make Nature afraid in his plays—that is, to violate probability, naturalness, credibility—"like those that beget *Tales*, *Tempests*, and such-like drolleries." That he specifically knew *The Winter's Tale* is clear from his jibing at the notion of a shipwreck in Bohemia in his conversations with Drummond, 1618–19.

The earliest criticisms of the play were neo-classical objections to its violation of the unities. It is a play of the type Sidney had had in mind when, perhaps as early as 1580, he objected in his *Defense of Poesy* (published 1595) to plays

> where you shall have Asia of the one side, and Afric of the other, and so many other under-kingdoms, that the Player, when he comes in, must ever begin telling where he is, or else the tale will not be conceived. Now you shall have three ladies walk to gather flowers, and then we must believe the stage to be a garden. By and by we hear news of shipwreck in the same place, then we are to blame if we accept it not for a rock. . . . Now of time they are much more liberal. For ordinary it is, that two young princes fall in love, after many adverses she is got with child, delivered of a fair boy; he is lost, groweth a man, falleth in love and is ready to get another child, and all this in two hours' space; which, how absurd it is in sense, even sense may imagine, and art hath taught and all ancient examples justified . . .

Samuel Johnson's great defense of the dramatic imagination, which destroyed the doctrine of the unities, was not published until 1765.

Modern criticism of the play has tended to emphasize its symbolic aspects, often reading into it significant religious meanings and sometimes even regarding it as allegory. The "Christianization" of this play has gone almost as far as has that of *Measure for Measure*. But the overt religious references are mainly pagan, and considerable straining of the language, structure, and atmosphere of the play is required to make a specifically Christian doctrinal statement of it.

At the other end of the scale, critics have directed their attacks upon the ludicrous stage business indicated by the direction "Exit pursued by a bear"; the abruptness and artificiality of the Father Time chorus beginning Act IV; the crude shifts to clear the stage in the Florizel-Perdita-Camillo-Autolycus sequence toward the end of IV.iv; the use of "messenger" speeches (V.ii) to report the identification of Perdita as the lost princess; and, of course, the statue scene. They argue that Shakespeare was hurried, negligent, or bored, worn out perhaps by writing all those histories and tragedies. One recent critic, Nevill Coghill, has ingeniously defended the play on all these points, maintaining that the stagecraft of *The Winter's Tale* "is as novel, subtle, and revolutionary as it had been a few years before in *Antony and Cleopatra*, but in an entirely different way."

One of the most curious pieces of stage business is the bear. Was it a real one or an actor in a bear suit? The authorities cannot agree. There were bears, real or feigned, in contemporary masques and in the revival of *Mucedorus*, that extremely popular old play, and of course there were tame bears in London as well as the fierce ones used for bear-baiting. But, as Wilson Knight reminds us, Shakespeare may have cared little about who played the bear, man or animal; he was dramatizing, as he so often did, his own imagery:

> Thou think'st 'tis much that this contentious storm
> Invades us to the skin; so 'tis to thee;
> But where the greater malady is fix'd,
> The lesser is scarce felt. Thou'dst shun a bear,
> But if [thy] flight lay toward the roaring sea,
> Thou'dst meet the bear i' th' mouth.
> (*King Lear*, III.iv.6–11)

Most of the critical problems disappear if we remember the play's title and its meaning. George Peele's *Old Wive's Tale*, the earliest Elizabethan romantic play that can be called in any sense a masterpiece, is "a winter's tale to drive away the time," and in *Macbeth* Shakespeare speaks of "A woman's story at a winter's fire / Authoriz'd by her grandam" (III.iv.64–65). Winter's tales were not supposed to have credibility, consistency, or conciseness. In the words of the Third Gentleman (V.ii.61–63), *The Winter's Tale* is "like an old tale still, which will have matter to rehearse, though credit be asleep and not an ear open."

Hallett Smith

The Winter's Tale

The Names of the Actors

Leontes, *King of Sicilia*
Mamillius, *young prince of Sicilia*
Camillo, Antigonus, Cleomines, Dion — *four lords of Sicilia*
Polixenes, *King of Bohemia*
Florizel, *prince of Bohemia*
Archidamus, *a lord of Bohemia*
Old Shepherd, *reputed father of Perdita*
Clown, *his son*
Autolycus, *a rogue*
[Mariner]
[Jailer]

Hermione, *queen to Leontes*
Perdita, *daughter to Leontes and Hermione*
Paulina, *wife to Antigonus*
Emilia, *a lady* [*attending on Hermione*]
[Mopsa, Dorcas — *shepherdesses*]

[Time, *as Chorus*]

Other Lords *and* Gentlemen, [Ladies, Officers,] *and* Servants, Shepherds, *and* Shepherdesses

[Scene: *Sicilia and Bohemia*]

ACT I, Scene I

Enter Camillo *and* Archidamus.

Arch. If you shall chance, Camillo, to visit Bohemia on the like occasion whereon my services are now on foot, you shall see (as I have said) great difference betwixt our Bohemia and your Sicilia.

Cam. I think, this coming summer, the King of Sicilia means to pay Bohemia the visitation which he justly owes him.

Arch. Wherein our entertainment shall shame us: we will be justified in our loves; for indeed—

Cam. Beseech you—

Arch. Verily, I speak it in the freedom of my knowledge: we cannot with such magnificence—in so rare—I know not what to say—We will give you sleepy drinks, that your senses (unintelligent of our insufficience) may, though they cannot praise us, as little accuse us.

Cam. You pay a great deal too dear for what's given freely.

Arch. Believe me, I speak as my understanding instructs me, and as mine honesty puts it to utterance.

Cam. Sicilia cannot show himself overkind to Bohemia. They were train'd together in their childhoods; and there rooted betwixt them then such an affection, which cannot choose but branch now. Since their more mature dignities and royal necessities made separation of their society, their encounters (though not personal) hath been royally attorney'd with interchange of gifts, letters, loving embassies, that they have seem'd to be together, though absent; shook hands, as over a vast; and embrac'd as it were from the ends of oppos'd winds. The heavens continue their loves!

Arch. I think there is not in the world either malice or matter to alter it. You have an unspeakable comfort of your young prince Mamillius: it is a gentleman of the greatest promise that ever came into my note.

Cam. I very well agree with you in the hopes of him; it is a gallant child; one that, indeed, physics the subject, makes old hearts fresh. They that went on crutches ere he was born desire yet their life to see him a man.

Arch. Would they else be content to die?

Words and passages enclosed in square brackets in the text above are either emendations of the copy-text or additions to it. The Textual Notes immediately following the play cite the earliest authority for every such change or insertion and supply the reading of the copy-text wherever it is emended in this edition.

I.i. Location: Sicilia. The palace of Leontes.
6. **Bohemia:** the King of Bohemia (a frequent usage).
8. **shame us:** i.e. by falling short of your entertainment of us.
9. **be . . . loves:** make up for it by our affection.
14. **unintelligent:** unaware.
24. **branch:** send out shoots, i.e. flourish.
27. **attorney'd:** performed by proxy. 30. **vast:** wide expanse.
31. **ends . . . winds:** i.e. opposite corners of the earth.
36. **into my note:** under my observation.
38–39. **physics the subject:** acts as a restorative medicine to the populace.

Cam. Yes; if there were no other excuse why they should desire to live.

Arch. If the King had no son, they would desire to live on crutches till he had one. *Exeunt.*

Scene II

Enter Leontes, Hermione, Mamillius, Polixenes, Camillo, [*and* Attendants].

Pol. Nine changes of the wat'ry star hath been
The shepherd's note since we have left our throne
Without a burthen. Time as long again
Would be fill'd up, my brother, with our thanks,
And yet we should, for perpetuity,
Go hence in debt. And therefore, like a cipher
(Yet standing in rich place), I multiply
With one "We thank you" many thousands moe
That go before it.

Leon. Stay your thanks a while,
And pay them when you part.

Pol. Sir, that's to-morrow.
I am question'd by my fears of what may chance
Or breed upon our absence, that may blow
No sneaping winds at home, to make us say,
"This is put forth too truly." Besides, I have stay'd
To tire your royalty.

Leon. We are tougher, brother,
Than you can put us to't.

Pol. No longer stay.

Leon. One sev'nnight longer.

Pol. Very sooth, to-morrow.

Leon. We'll part the time between 's then; and in that
I'll no gainsaying.

Pol. Press me not, beseech you, so.
There is no tongue that moves, none, none i' th' world,
So soon as yours could win me. So it should now,
Were there necessity in your request, although
'Twere needful I denied it. My affairs
Do even drag me homeward; which to hinder
Were (in your love) a whip to me; my stay,
To you a charge and trouble. To save both,
Farewell, our brother.

Leon. Tongue-tied our queen? Speak you.

Her. I had thought, sir, to have held my peace until
You had drawn oaths from him not to stay. You, sir,
Charge him too coldly. Tell him you are sure

All in Bohemia's well; this satisfaction
The by-gone day proclaim'd. Say this to him,
He's beat from his best ward.

Leon. Well said, Hermione.

Her. To tell he longs to see his son were strong;
But let him say so then, and let him go;
But let him swear so, and he shall not stay,
We'll thwack him hence with distaffs.
Yet of your royal presence I'll adventure
The borrow of a week. When at Bohemia
You take my lord, I'll give him my commission
To let him there a month behind the gest
Prefix'd for 's parting; yet, good deed, Leontes,
I love thee not a jar o' th' clock behind
What lady she her lord. You'll stay?

Pol. No, madam.

Her. Nay, but you will?

Pol. I may not, verily.

Her. Verily?
You put me off with limber vows; but I,
Though you would seek t' unsphere the stars with oaths,
Should yet say, "Sir, no going." Verily,
You shall not go; a lady's "verily" is
As potent as a lord's. Will you go yet?
Force me to keep you as a prisoner,
Not like a guest: so you shall pay your fees
When you depart, and save your thanks. How say you?
My prisoner? or my guest? By your dread "verily,"
One of them you shall be.

Pol. Your guest then, madam.
To be your prisoner should import offending,
Which is for me less easy to commit
Than you to punish.

Her. Not your jailer then,
But your kind hostess. Come, I'll question you
Of my lord's tricks and yours when you were boys.
You were pretty lordings then?

Pol. We were, fair queen,
Two lads that thought there was no more behind
But such a day to-morrow as to-day,
And to be boy eternal.

Her. Was not my lord
The verier wag o' th' two?

Pol. We were as twinn'd lambs that did frisk i' th' sun,
And bleat the one at th' other. What we chang'd
Was innocence for innocence; we knew not

I.ii. Location: Sicilia. The palace of Leontes.
1. wat'ry star: moon. 2. we. Royal plural.
3. burthen: burden, i.e. occupant.
5–6. yet . . . debt: even after that we should depart in your debt forever.
6–7. like . . . place: i.e. having no value in itself, yet capable of multiplying the value of the numbers that stand before it.
8. moe: more.
11–14. I . . . truly: I am concerned about what may happen at home, by chance or as a direct result of my absence—concerned lest biting (*sneaping*) winds may blow (i.e. forces hostile to me may be active) to make me say my fears were well-founded.
15–16. We . . . to't: I can withstand your extremest pressure, i.e. you couldn't stay long enough to tire me.
18. part the time: i.e. split the difference (of one week).
19. I'll no gainsaying: I'll take no denial.
22–23. although . . . it: even if I had pressing reason to refuse it.
25. in . . . whip: though a sign of your love, a punishment.
26. charge: expense.

31–32. this . . . proclaim'd: this reassuring news was heard from Bohemia yesterday.
33. beat . . . ward: forced from his best defensive position. The combat imagery goes back to *Charge* (line 30).
34. tell: tell us.
38. adventure: risk (since she must stand ready to repay the loan with interest).
40. take: charm. commission: authorization.
41. let him: permit him to remain. gest: a stop on a royal journey; here, appointed day.
42. Prefix'd: set in advance. good deed: in truth.
43. jar: tick. 44. What lady she: any lady whatever.
47. limber: limp, flabby.
53. fees. Jailers claimed a fee from prisoners upon their release.
57. import offending: imply that I had committed some offense.
63. behind: beyond, to come. 66. verier wag: greater rascal.
67. twinn'd: exactly alike. 68. chang'd: exchanged.

The doctrine of ill-doing, nor dream'd
That any did. Had we pursu'd that life,
And our weak spirits ne'er been higher rear'd
With stronger blood, we should have answer'd heaven
Boldly, "Not guilty"; the imposition clear'd,
Hereditary ours.
Her. By this we gather
You have tripp'd since.
Pol. O my most sacred lady,
Temptations have since then been born to 's: for
In those unfledg'd days was my wife a girl;
Your precious self had then not cross'd the eyes
Of my young playfellow.
Her. Grace to boot!
Of this make no conclusion, lest you say
Your queen and I are devils. Yet go on,
Th' offenses we have made you do we'll answer,
If you first sinn'd with us, and that with us
You did continue fault, and that you slipp'd not
With any but with us.
Leon. Is he won yet?
Her. He'll stay, my lord.
Leon. At my request he would not.
Hermione, my dearest, thou never spok'st
To better purpose.
Her. Never?
Leon. Never, but once.
Her. What? have I twice said well? When was't before?
I prithee tell me; cram 's with praise, and make 's
As fat as tame things. One good deed dying tongueless
Slaughters a thousand waiting upon that.
Our praises are our wages. You may ride 's
With one soft kiss a thousand furlongs ere
With spur we heat an acre. But to th' goal:
My last good deed was to entreat his stay;
What was my first? It has an elder sister,
Or I mistake you. O, would her name were Grace!
But once before I spoke to th' purpose? when?
Nay, let me have't; I long.
Leon. Why, that was when
Three crabbed months had sour'd themselves to death,
Ere I could make thee open thy white hand,
[And] clap thyself my love; then didst thou utter,
"I am yours for ever."
Her. 'Tis Grace indeed.
Why, lo you now! I have spoke to th' purpose twice:

73. stronger blood: i.e. the passions of maturity.
74–75. the imposition . . . ours: even original sin being remitted (because our wills would never have been corrupted).
78. unfledg'd: immature.
80. Grace to boot: heavenly grace help me.
81. Of . . . conclusion: don't follow out that line of reasoning to its logical end. **83. answer:** answer for.
84, 85. that. Takes on the sense of *If* (line 84); a common usage in Elizabethan English.
85. fault: offense, sin.
91. cram 's: cram us. Hermione speaks for herself and all women.
92. tongueless: without praise.
93. waiting upon that: i.e. which would have followed that if it had been praised.
96. heat: race over. **goal:** point aimed at, purpose.
99. would . . . Grace: i.e. may it prove to have been a virtuous action (with a backward glance at lines 76–86).
104. clap: pledge by handclasp.

The one for ever earn'd a royal husband;
Th' other for some while a friend.
[*Gives her hand to Polixenes.*]
Leon. [*Aside.*] Too hot, too hot!
To mingle friendship far is mingling bloods.
I have *tremor cordis* on me; my heart dances,
But not for joy; not joy. This entertainment
May a free face put on, derive a liberty
From heartiness, from bounty, fertile bosom,
And well become the agent; 't may—I grant.
But to be paddling palms and pinching fingers,
As now they are, and making practic'd smiles,
As in a looking-glass; and then to sigh, as 'twere
The mort o' th' deer—O, that is entertainment
My bosom likes not, nor my brows! Mamillius,
Art thou my boy?
Mam. Ay, my good lord.
Leon. I' fecks!
Why, that's my bawcock. What? [hast] smutch'd thy nose?
They say it is a copy out of mine. Come, captain,
We must be neat; not neat, but cleanly, captain:
And yet the steer, the heckfer, and the calf
Are all call'd neat.—Still virginalling
Upon his palm?—How now, you wanton calf,
Art thou my calf?
Mam. Yes, if you will, my lord.
Leon. Thou want'st a rough pash and the shoots that I have,
To be full like me; yet they say we are
Almost as like as eggs; women say so—
That will say any thing. But were they false
As o'er-dy'd blacks, as wind, as waters, false
As dice are to be wish'd by one that fixes
No bourn 'twixt his and mine, yet were it true
To say this boy were like me. Come, sir page,
Look on me with your welkin eye. Sweet villain!
Most dear'st! my collop! Can thy dam?—may't be?—
Affection! thy intention stabs the centre.
Thou dost make possible things not so held,
Communicat'st with dreams (how can this be?),
With what's unreal thou co-active art,
And fellow'st nothing. Then 'tis very credent
Thou mayst co-join with something, and thou dost

110. tremor cordis: fluttering of the heart.
111. entertainment: courtesy to a guest. **112. free:** innocent.
113. heartiness: warmheartedness. **fertile bosom:** generous affection.
118. mort . . . deer: horn blast announcing the death of the hunted deer.
119. brows. Alluding to the common Elizabethan notion that a cuckold grew horns. **120. I' fecks:** in faith.
121. bawcock: fine fellow (French *beau coq*).
123. not neat. Leontes' mind leaps from the sense "tidy" to the sense "cattle," and he rejects the term because cattle have horns.
124. heckfer: heifer.
125. virginalling: fingering, as when playing the virginals.
126. wanton: sportive.
128. rough pash: shaggy head. **shoots:** horns.
129. full: entirely.
132. o'er-dy'd blacks: black things painted over with another color.
134. bourn: boundary. **136. welkin:** like the sky, i.e. blue.
137. collop: bit of meat cut from a larger piece, i.e. portion of my own flesh.
138. Affection: *affectio*, a sudden, unexplained change in mind and body; here, jealousy. **intention:** intensity. **centre:** heart (?) or core of existence (?). **139. not so held:** not supposed possible.
142. fellow'st nothing: you associate yourself with what is non-existent. **credent:** credible.

(And that beyond commission), and I find it
(And that to the infection of my brains
And hard'ning of my brows).
Pol. What means Sicilia?
Her. He something seems unsettled.
Pol. How? my lord?
Leon. What cheer? How is't with you, best brother?
Her. You look
As if you held a brow of much distraction.
Are you mov'd, my lord?
Leon. No, in good earnest.
How sometimes nature will betray its folly!
Its tenderness! and make itself a pastime
To harder bosoms! Looking on the lines
Of my boy's face, methoughts I did recoil
Twenty-three years, and saw myself unbreech'd
In my green velvet coat, my dagger muzzled,
Lest it should bite its master, and so prove
(As [ornament] oft does) too dangerous.
How like (methought) I then was to this kernel,
This squash, this gentleman. Mine honest friend,
Will you take eggs for money?
Mam. No, my lord, I'll fight.
Leon. You will? Why, happy man be 's dole!
My brother,
Are you so fond of your young prince as we
Do seem to be of ours?
Pol. If at home, sir,
He's all my exercise, my mirth, my matter;
Now my sworn friend, and then mine enemy;
My parasite, my soldier, statesman, all.
He makes a July's day short as December,
And with his varying childness cures in me
Thoughts that would thick my blood.
Leon. So stands this squire
Offic'd with me. We two will walk, my lord,
And leave you to your graver steps. Hermione,
How thou lov'st us, show in our brother's welcome;
Let what is dear in Sicily be cheap.
Next to thyself and my young rover, he's
Apparent to my heart.
Her. If you would seek us,
We are yours i' th' garden. Shall 's attend you there?
Leon. To your own bents dispose you; you'll be found,
Be you beneath the sky. [*Aside.*] I am angling now,
Though you perceive me not how I give line.
Go to, go to!
How she holds up the neb! the bill to him!
And arms her with the boldness of a wife
To her allowing husband!
[*Exeunt Polixenes, Hermione, and Attendants.*]
Gone already!
Inch-thick, knee-deep, o'er head and ears a fork'd one!
Go play, boy, play. Thy mother plays, and I
Play too, but so disgrac'd a part, whose issue
Will hiss me to my grave: contempt and clamor
Will be my knell. Go play, boy, play. There have been
(Or I am much deceiv'd) cuckolds ere now,
And many a man there is (even at this present,
Now, while I speak this) holds his wife by th' arm,
That little thinks she has been sluic'd in 's absence,
And his pond fish'd by his next neighbor—by
Sir Smile, his neighbor. Nay, there's comfort in't,
Whiles other men have gates, and those gates open'd,
As mine, against their will. Should all despair
That have revolted wives, the tenth of mankind
Would hang themselves. Physic for't there's none.
It is a bawdy planet, that will strike
Where 'tis predominant; and 'tis pow'rful—think it—
From east, west, north, and south. Be it concluded,
No barricado for a belly. Know't,
It will let in and out the enemy,
With bag and baggage. Many thousand on 's
Have the disease, and feel't not. How now, boy?
Mam. I am like you, [they] say.
Leon. Why, that's some comfort.
What? Camillo there?
Cam. Ay, my good lord.
Leon. Go play, Mamillius, thou'rt an honest man.
[*Exit Mamillius.*]
Camillo, this great sir will yet stay longer.
Cam. You had much ado to make his anchor hold,
When you cast out, it still came home.
Leon. Didst note it?
Cam. He would not stay at your petitions, made
His business more material.
Leon. Didst perceive it?
[*Aside.*] They're here with me already, whisp'ring, rounding:
"Sicilia is a so-forth." 'Tis far gone,
When I shall gust it last.—How came't, Camillo,
That he did stay?
Cam. At the good Queen's entreaty.
Leon. At the Queen's be't; "good" should be pertinent,
But so it is, it is not. Was this taken
By any understanding pate but thine?

144. commission: what is authorized. **find:** experience.
147. something seems: seems somewhat.
148. What . . . brother. Many editors assign this speech to Polixenes.
150. mov'd: angry. **152. pastime:** source of mirth.
154. methoughts: it seemed to me (a variant of *methought*). **recoil:** go back.
155–56. unbreech'd . . . coat: i.e. not old enough to wear men's clothes. **159. kernel:** seed.
160. squash: unripe pea pod. **honest:** worthy.
161. take . . . money: allow yourself to be imposed upon.
163. happy . . . dole: may his lot be that of a happy man (proverbial).
166. matter: interest. **170. childness:** childish ways.
171. thick my blood: make me melancholy.
171–72. So . . . Offic'd: this boy holds the same position.
177. Apparent: heir apparent, i.e. closest.
179. found. With pun on the sense "found out."
182. Go to: a common expression of reproof or admonition.
183. neb: mouth. **185. allowing:** approving.
186. fork'd: horned.
187–89. Go . . . grave. Leontes puns on three senses of *play*: (1) amuse yourself, (2) engage in sexual dalliance, (3) act a part; and on three senses of *issue*: (1) outcome, (2) offspring, (3) exit.
195. next: nearest. **199. revolted:** unfaithful.
201–2. strike . . . predominant: exercise a harmful influence when it is in the ascendant. **204. barricado:** fortification.
206. on 's: of us. **214. still came home:** always failed to hold.
217. They're . . . me: people are aware of my situation. **rounding:** whispering. **218. so-forth:** you-know-what.
219. gust: taste, i.e. perceive. Leontes means, "Everybody must know it, for I know it, and the husband is always the last to find out."
222. so it is: as things stand. **taken:** perceived.

For thy conceit is soaking, will draw in
More than the common blocks. Not noted, is't,
But of the finer natures? By some severals
Of head-piece extraordinary? Lower messes
Perchance are to this business purblind? Say.
Cam. Business, my lord? I think most understand
Bohemia stays here longer.
Leon. Ha?
Cam. Stays here longer.
Leon. Ay, but why?
Cam. To satisfy your Highness and the entreaties
Of our most gracious mistress.
Leon. Satisfy?
Th' entreaties of your mistress? Satisfy?
Let that suffice. I have trusted thee, Camillo,
With all the nearest things to my heart, as well
My chamber-counsels, wherein, priest-like, thou
Hast cleans'd my bosom: I from thee departed
Thy penitent reform'd. But we have been
Deceiv'd in thy integrity, deceiv'd
In that which seems so.
Cam. Be it forbid, my lord!
Leon. To bide upon't: thou art not honest; or
If thou inclin'st that way, thou art a coward,
Which hoxes honesty behind, restraining
From course requir'd; or else thou must be counted
A servant grafted in my serious trust
And therein negligent; or else a fool,
That seest a game play'd home, the rich stake drawn,
And tak'st it all for jest.
Cam. My gracious lord,
I may be negligent, foolish, and fearful:
In every one of these no man is free
But that his negligence, his folly, fear,
Among the infinite doings of the world,
Sometime puts forth. In your affairs, my lord,
If ever I were willful-negligent,
It was my folly; if industriously
I play'd the fool, it was my negligence,
Not weighing well the end; if ever fearful
To do a thing, where I the issue doubted,
Whereof the execution did cry out
Against the non-performance, 'twas a fear
Which oft infects the wisest: these, my lord,
Are such allow'd infirmities that honesty
Is never free of. But beseech your Grace
Be plainer with me, let me know my trespass
By its own visage. If I then deny it,
'Tis none of mine.
Leon. Ha' not you seen, Camillo
(But that's past doubt; you have, or your eye-glass

224. conceit is soaking: intelligence is highly absorbent.
225. blocks: blockheads. **226. severals**: individuals.
227. Lower messes: those lower at the dining table, i.e. lower in rank? A mess was originally a group of four served from the same dishes.
228. purblind: completely blind.
233. Satisfy. Leontes interprets the word in a sexual sense.
237. chamber-counsels: private concerns. **242. bide**: dwell, insist.
244. hoxes: hamstrings.
248. home: i.e. in dead seriousness. **drawn**: won.
251. free: guiltless. **254. puts forth**: shows itself.
256. industriously: deliberately.
263. allow'd: acknowledged. **that**: as.
266. By . . . visage: i.e. in such a fashion that I can recognize it.
267. Ha': have. **268. eye-glass**: lens of the eye.

Is thicker than a cuckold's horn), or heard
(For to a vision so apparent rumor
Cannot be mute), or thought (for cogitation
Resides not in that man that does not think)
My wife is slippery? If thou wilt confess,
Or else be impudently negative,
To have nor eyes nor ears nor thought, then say
My wife's a [hobby]-horse, deserves a name
As rank as any flax-wench that puts to
Before her troth-plight: say't and justify't.
Cam. I would not be a stander-by to hear
My sovereign mistress clouded so, without
My present vengeance taken. 'Shrew my heart,
You never spoke what did become you less
Than this; which to reiterate were sin
As deep as that, though true.
Leon. Is whispering nothing?
Is leaning cheek to cheek? is meeting noses?
Kissing with inside lip? stopping the career
Of laughter with a sigh (a note infallible
Of breaking honesty)? horsing foot on foot?
Skulking in corners? wishing clocks more swift?
Hours, minutes? noon, midnight? and all eyes
Blind with the pin and web but theirs, theirs only,
That would unseen be wicked? Is this nothing?
Why then the world and all that's in't is nothing,
The covering sky is nothing, Bohemia nothing,
My wife is nothing, nor nothing have these nothings,
If this be nothing.
Cam. Good my lord, be cur'd
Of this diseas'd opinion, and betimes,
For 'tis most dangerous.
Leon. Say it be, 'tis true.
Cam. No, no, my lord.
Leon. It is: you lie, you lie!
I say thou liest, Camillo, and I hate thee,
Pronounce thee a gross lout, a mindless slave,
Or else a hovering temporizer, that
Canst with thine eyes at once see good and evil,
Inclining to them both. Were my wive's liver
Infected as her life, she would not live
The running of one glass.
Cam. Who does infect her?
Leon. Why, he that wears her like her medal hanging
About his neck, Bohemia—who, if I
Had servants true about me, that bare eyes
To see alike mine honor as their profits

269. thicker: more opaque. **cuckold's horn.** Horn, which in thin sheets is nearly transparent, offers a natural comparison, but in Leontes' mind *horn* is immediately equated with *cuckold's horn.*
270. vision so apparent: sight so plain. **272. think**: think so.
274. impudently: shamelessly. **275. nor eyes**: neither eyes.
276. hobby-horse: loose woman. **277. puts to**: copulates.
281. present: instant. **'Shrew**: beshrew, curse.
283–84. which . . . true: repeating this would be as sinful as her adultery if it were a fact, which it isn't. **286. career**: full gallop.
288. honesty: chastity. **horsing**: mounting and moving up and down. **291. pin and web**: cataract. **297. betimes**: quickly.
298. Say it be: suppose it is (dangerous).
302. hovering: wavering.
304–5. liver . . . life. Some editors read *life . . . liver*, arguing that her liver (regarded as the seat of the passions) *was* fatally infected. But the sense may be "If her body were as seriously diseased as her behavior is." **306. glass**: hourglass.
307. like her medal: i.e. as he might wear her medallion portrait.
309. bare: bore.

(Their own particular thrifts), they would do that
Which should undo more doing; ay, and thou,
His cupbearer—whom I from meaner form
Have bench'd and rear'd to worship, who mayst see
Plainly as heaven sees earth and earth sees heaven,
How I am gall'd—mightst bespice a cup,
To give mine enemy a lasting wink;
Which draught to me were cordial.

Cam. Sir, my lord,
I could do this, and that with no rash potion,
But with a ling'ring dram that should not work
Maliciously, like poison; but I cannot
Believe this crack to be in my dread mistress
(So sovereignly being honorable).
I have lov'd thee—

Leon. Make that thy question, and go rot!
Dost think I am so muddy, so unsettled,
To appoint myself in this vexation, sully
The purity and whiteness of my sheets
(Which to preserve is sleep, which being spotted
Is goads, thorns, nettles, tails of wasps),
Give scandal to the blood o' th' Prince my son
(Who I do think is mine and love as mine),
Without ripe moving to't? Would I do this?
Could man so blench?

Cam. I must believe you, sir.
I do, and will fetch off Bohemia for't;
Provided that, when he's remov'd, your Highness
Will take again your queen as yours at first,
Even for your son's sake, and thereby for sealing
The injury of tongues in courts and kingdoms
Known and allied to yours.

Leon. Thou dost advise me
Even so as I mine own course have set down.
I'll give no blemish to her honor, none.

Cam. My lord,
Go then; and with a countenance as clear
As friendship wears at feasts, keep with Bohemia
And with your queen. I am his cupbearer:
If from me he have wholesome beverage,
Account me not your servant.

Leon. This is all:
Do't, and thou hast the one half of my heart;
Do't not, thou split'st thine own.

Cam. I'll do't, my lord.

Leon. I will seem friendly, as thou hast advis'd me.
Exit.

Cam. O miserable lady! But for me,
What case stand I in? I must be the poisoner
Of good Polixenes, and my ground to do't
Is the obedience to a master; one
Who, in rebellion with himself, will have
All that are his so too. To do this deed,
Promotion follows. If I could find example
Of thousands that had struck anointed kings
And flourish'd after, I'ld not do't; but since
Nor brass nor stone nor parchment bears not one,
Let villainy itself forswear't. I must
Forsake the court. To do't, or no, is certain
To me a break-neck. Happy star reign now!
Here comes Bohemia.

Enter Polixenes.

Pol. This is strange; methinks
My favor here begins to warp. Not speak?
Good day, Camillo.

Cam. Hail, most royal sir!

Pol. What is the news i' th' court?

Cam. None rare, my lord.

Pol. The King hath on him such a countenance
As he had lost some province and a region
Lov'd as he loves himself. Even now I met him
With customary compliment, when he,
Wafting his eyes to th' contrary and falling
A lip of much contempt, speeds from me, and
So leaves me to consider what is breeding
That changes thus his manners.

Cam. I dare not know, my lord.

Pol. How, dare not? Do not? Do you know, and dare not?
Be intelligent to me, 'tis thereabouts:
For to yourself, what you do know, you must,
And cannot say you dare not. Good Camillo,
Your chang'd complexions are to me a mirror
Which shows me mine chang'd too; for I must be
A party in this alteration, finding
Myself thus alter'd with't.

Cam. There is a sickness
Which puts some of us in distemper, but
I cannot name the disease, and it is caught
Of you that yet are well.

Pol. How caught of me?
Make me not sighted like the basilisk.
I have look'd on thousands, who have sped the better
By my regard, but kill'd none so. Camillo,
As you are certainly a gentleman, thereto
Clerk-like experienc'd, which no less adorns
Our gentry than our parents' noble names,

311. **particular thrifts**: personal gains.
313. **meaner form**: lower degree.
314. **bench'd**: given official status. **rear'd to worship**: raised to a position of dignity. 316. **gall'd**: rubbed sore.
318. **were cordial**: would be curative. 319. **rash**: quick-acting.
321. **Maliciously**: violently. 322. **crack**: flaw. **dread**: revered.
323. **So . . . honorable**: who is so supremely honorable.
324. **Make . . . rot**: if you're going to take that line, go and be damned.
325. **muddy**: i.e. disturbed in mind (synonymous with *unsettled*).
326. **appoint**: place. 332. **ripe**: full, ample.
333. **blench**: swerve (from rational behavior).
334. **fetch off.** Perhaps deliberately ambiguous: (1) kill; (2) bear off, rescue (cf. *bear'st . . . off*, line 462). So also *remov'd*, line 335; and see lines 346–47. 337. **sealing**: silencing.
344. **keep**: keep company. 351. **for**: as for.
355–56. **Who . . . too**: who, because he has turned against his better nature, would have all his subjects do so too. 357. **If**: even if.
362. **To . . . no**: either to kill Polixenes, or not to kill him.
363. **a break-neck**: i.e. fatal. **Happy**: propitious.
365. **warp**: change for the worse. 367. **rare**: remarkable.
369. **As**: as if.
372. **Wafting . . . contrary**: averting his eyes. **falling**: letting droop.
374. **breeding**: hatching.
377. **Do not**: i.e. do you mean you do not.
378. **intelligent**: communicative, informative. **'tis thereabouts**: that's getting near it, i.e. telling me is probably what you dare not do.
379–80. **what . . . not**: what you know, you know perforce; daring doesn't enter into it.
388. **basilisk**: fabulous serpent whose glance killed.
389–90. **sped . . . regard**: fared the better for my look.
391. **gentleman**: man of gentle birth. **thereto**: in addition to that.
392. **Clerk-like experienc'd**: having the experience of an educated man. 393. **gentry**: status as gentlemen.

In whose success we are gentle, I beseech you,
If you know aught which does behove my knowledge
Thereof to be inform'd, imprison't not
In ignorant concealment.
Cam. I may not answer.
Pol. A sickness caught of me, and yet I well?
I must be answer'd. Dost thou hear, Camillo,
I conjure thee, by all the parts of man
Which honor does acknowledge, whereof the least
Is not this suit of mine, that thou declare
What incidency thou dost guess of harm
Is creeping toward me; how far off, how near,
Which way to be prevented, if to be;
If not, how best to bear it.
Cam. Sir, I will tell you,
Since I am charg'd in honor and by him
That I think honorable. Therefore mark my counsel,
Which must be ev'n as swiftly followed as
I mean to utter it; or both yourself and me
Cry lost, and so good night!
Pol. On, good Camillo.
Cam. I am appointed him to murther you.
Pol. By whom, Camillo?
Cam. By the King.
Pol. For what?
Cam. He thinks, nay, with all confidence he swears,
As he had seen't or been an instrument
To vice you to't, that you have touch'd his queen
Forbiddenly.
Pol. O then, my best blood turn
To an infected jelly, and my name
Be yok'd with his that did betray the Best!
Turn then my freshest reputation to
A savor that may strike the dullest nostril
Where I arrive, and my approach be shunn'd,
Nay, hated too, worse than the great'st infection
That e'er was heard or read!
Cam. Swear his thought over
By each particular star in heaven, and
By all their influences, you may as well
Forbid the sea for to obey the moon
As or by oath remove or counsel shake
The fabric of his folly, whose foundation
Is pil'd upon his faith, and will continue
The standing of his body.
Pol. How should this grow?
Cam. I know not; but I am sure 'tis safer to
Avoid what's grown than question how 'tis born.
If therefore you dare trust my honesty,
That lies enclosed in this trunk which you
Shall bear along impawn'd, away to-night!
Your followers I will whisper to the business,
And will by twos and threes at several posterns
Clear them o' th' city. For myself, I'll put
My fortunes to your service, which are here
By this discovery lost. Be not uncertain,
For by the honor of my parents, I
Have utt'red truth; which if you seek to prove,
I dare not stand by; nor shall you be safer
Than one condemn'd by the King's own mouth—thereon
His execution sworn.
Pol. I do believe thee:
I saw his heart in 's face. Give me thy hand,
Be pilot to me, and thy places shall
Still neighbor mine. My ships are ready, and
My people did expect my hence departure
Two days ago. This jealousy
Is for a precious creature: as she's rare,
Must it be great; and as his person's mighty,
Must it be violent; and as he does conceive
He is dishonor'd by a man which ever
Profess'd to him, why, his revenges must
In that be made more bitter. Fear o'ershades me.
Good expedition be my friend, and comfort
The gracious queen, part of his theme, but nothing
Of his ill-ta'en suspicion! Come, Camillo,
I will respect thee as a father, if
Thou bear'st my life off. Hence! Let us avoid.
Cam. It is in mine authority to command
The keys of all the posterns. Please your Highness
To take the urgent hour. Come, sir, away. *Exeunt.*

394. **In whose success**: in succession from whom.
395–96. **does . . . inform'd**: would be advantageous for me to learn.
397. **ignorant concealment**: concealment in pretended ignorance (?) or concealment which would keep me ignorant (?).
400. **parts**: duties. 403. **incidency**: likelihood.
405. **if to be**: if it can be prevented.
411. **good night**: farewell forever. 412. **him**: the person.
416. **vice**: screw or force, as with the carpenter's tool; with implication of evil arising from the sense "wrongdoing."
419. **his . . . Best**: that of Judas, the betrayer of Jesus.
424. **Swear . . . over**: swear that his suspicion is false.
428. **or by . . . or**: either by . . . or by.
429. **fabric**: construction.
430. **pil'd . . . faith**: based upon his firm conviction.
430–31. **continue . . . body**: last as long as his body does.
431. **How . . . grow**: how can this have come about.
435. **trunk**: (1) body; (2) container.
436. **impawn'd**: as a pledge (of my good faith).
438. **posterns**: back gates. 441. **discovery**: disclosure.
443. **prove**: test.
448–49. **thy . . . mine**: your position will always be close to the throne.
456. **Profess'd**: professed friendship. 458. **expedition**: speed.
458–60. **comfort . . . suspicion**: (may my speedy departure) ease the situation of the Queen, who is involved in the King's misconception but is entirely innocent of what he suspects.
462. **avoid**: be off.
465. **take . . . hour**: seize this critical moment.

ACT II, Scene I

Enter Hermione, Mamillius, Ladies.

Her. Take the boy to you; he so troubles me,
'Tis past enduring.
[1.] Lady. Come, my gracious lord,
Shall I be your playfellow?
Mam. No, I'll none of you.
[1.] Lady. Why, my sweet lord?
Mam. You'll kiss me hard and speak to me as if
I were a baby still.—I love you better.
2. Lady. And why so, my lord?
Mam. Not for because
Your brows are blacker, yet black brows they say
Become some women best, so that there be not
Too much hair there, but in a semicircle,
Or a half-moon made with a pen.

II.i. Location: Sicilia. The palace of Leontes.

2. Lady. Who taught' this?
Mam. I learn'd it out of women's faces. Pray now
What color are your eyebrows?
[1.] Lady. Blue, my lord.
Mam. Nay, that's a mock. I have seen a lady's nose
That has been blue, but not her eyebrows.
[1.] Lady. Hark ye,
The Queen your mother rounds apace: we shall
Present our services to a fine new prince
One of these days, and then you'ld wanton with us,
If we would have you.
2. Lady. She is spread of late
Into a goodly bulk. Good time encounter her!
Her. What wisdom stirs amongst you? Come, sir, now
I am for you again. Pray you sit by us,
And tell 's a tale.
Mam. Merry, or sad, shall't be?
Her. As merry as you will.
Mam. A sad tale's best for winter. I have one
Of sprites and goblins.
Her. Let's have that, good sir.
Come on, sit down, come on, and do your best
To fright me with your sprites; you're pow'rful at it.
Mam. There was a man—
Her. Nay, come sit down; then on.
Mam. Dwelt by a churchyard. I will tell it softly,
Yond crickets shall not hear it.
Her. Come on then,
And give't me in mine ear.

[*Enter*] Leontes, Antigonus, Lords, [*and others*].

Leon. Was he met there? his train? Camillo with him?
[1.] Lord. Behind the tuft of pines I met them; never
Saw I men scour so on their way. I ey'd them
Even to their ships.
Leon. How blest am I
In my just censure! in my true opinion!
Alack, for lesser knowledge! how accurs'd
In being so blest! There may be in the cup
A spider steep'd, and one may drink; depart,
And yet partake no venom (for his knowledge
Is not infected), but if one present
Th' abhorr'd ingredient to his eye, make known
How he hath drunk, he cracks his gorge, his sides,
With violent hefts. I have drunk, and seen the spider.
Camillo was his help in this, his pandar.
There is a plot against my life, my crown;
All's true that is mistrusted. That false villain
Whom I employ'd was pre-employ'd by him:
He has discover'd my design, and I
Remain a pinch'd thing; yea, a very trick

11. taught': taught you. **18. wanton:** play.
31. crickets: i.e. the chattering ladies. **35. scour:** hurry.
37. censure: judgment.
38. for lesser knowledge: would that I knew less.
39–45. There . . . hefts. An old superstition about spiders.
44. gorge: throat. **45. hefts:** heavings, retchings.
48. mistrusted: suspected. **50. discover'd:** disclosed.
51. pinch'd: tormented (?) or manipulated (?).

For them to play at will. How came the posterns
So easily open?
[1.] Lord. By his great authority,
Which often hath no less prevail'd than so
On your command.
Leon. I know't too well.
Give me the boy. I am glad you did not nurse him.
Though he does bear some signs of me, yet you
Have too much blood in him.
Her. What is this? Sport?
Leon. Bear the boy hence, he shall not come about her.
Away with him! and let her sport herself
With that she's big with, for 'tis Polixenes
Has made thee swell thus.
Her. But I'ld say he had not;
And I'll be sworn you would believe my saying,
Howe'er you lean to th' nayward.
Leon. You, my lords,
Look on her, mark her well; be but about
To say she is a goodly lady, and
The justice of your hearts will thereto add
'Tis pity she's not honest—honorable.
Praise her but for this her without-door form
(Which on my faith deserves high speech) and straight
The shrug, the hum or ha (these petty brands
That calumny doth use—O, I am out—
That mercy does, for calumny will sear
Virtue itself), these shrugs, these hums and ha's,
When you have said she's goodly, come between
Ere you can say she's honest: but be't known
(From him that has most cause to grieve it should be)
She's an adult'ress.
Her. Should a villain say so,
The most replenish'd villain in the world,
He were as much more villain: you, my lord,
Do but mistake.
Leon. You have mistook, my lady,
Polixenes for Leontes. O thou thing!
Which I'll not call a creature of thy place,
Lest barbarism (making me the precedent)
Should a like language use to all degrees,
And mannerly distinguishment leave out
Betwixt the prince and beggar. I have said
She's an adult'ress, I have said with whom:
More—she's a traitor, and Camillo is
A federary with her, and one that knows
What she should shame to know herself,
But with her most vild principal—that she's
A bed-swerver, even as bad as those
That vulgars give bold'st titles; ay, and privy
To this their late escape.
Her. No, by my life,
Privy to none of this. How will this grieve you,
When you shall come to clearer knowledge, that

64. to th' nayward: in the opposite direction.
66. goodly: beautiful. **68. honest:** chaste.
69. without-door: external. **72. out:** in error.
75. come between: interrupt, i.e. break off.
79. replenish'd: complete.
83. Which . . . place: a name I will not apply to anyone of your rank.
90. federary: confederate. **92. vild principal:** vile partner.
94. vulgars . . . titles: common people call by the bluntest names.

You thus have publish'd me! Gentle my lord,
You scarce can right me throughly, then, to say
You did mistake.
Leon. No; if I mistake
In those foundations which I build upon,
The centre is not big enough to bear
A schoolboy's top. Away with her, to prison!
He who shall speak for her is afar off guilty
But that he speaks.
Her. There's some ill planet reigns;
I must be patient, till the heavens look
With an aspect more favorable. Good my lords,
I am not prone to weeping, as our sex
Commonly are, the want of which vain dew
Perchance shall dry your pities; but I have
That honorable grief lodg'd here which burns
Worse than tears drown. Beseech you all, my lords,
With thoughts so qualified as your charities
Shall best instruct you, measure me; and so
The King's will be perform'd!
Leon. Shall I be heard?
Her. Who is't that goes with me? Beseech your Highness
My women may be with me, for you see
My plight requires it. Do not weep, good fools,
There is no cause. When you shall know your mistress
Has deserv'd prison, then abound in tears
As I come out; this action I now go on
Is for my better grace. Adieu, my lord,
I never wish'd to see you sorry, now
I trust I shall. My women, come, you have leave.
Leon. Go, do our bidding; hence!
[*Exit Queen guarded, with Ladies.*]
[*1.*] *Lord.* Beseech your Highness call the Queen again.
Ant. Be certain what you do, sir, lest your justice
Prove violence, in the which three great ones suffer,
Yourself, your queen, your son.
[*1.*] *Lord.* For her, my lord,
I dare my life lay down—and will do't, sir,
Please you t' accept it—that the Queen is spotless
I' th' eyes of heaven and to you—I mean,
In this which you accuse her.
Ant. If it prove
She's otherwise, I'll keep my stables where
I lodge my wife; I'll go in couples with her;
Than when I feel and see her no farther trust her;
For every inch of woman in the world,
Ay, every dram of woman's flesh is false,
If she be.
Leon. Hold your peaces.
[*1.*] *Lord.* Good my lord—
Ant. It is for you we speak, not for ourselves.
You are abus'd, and by some putter-on
That will be damn'd for't. Would I knew the villain,
I would land-damn him. Be she honor-flaw'd,
I have three daughters: the eldest is eleven;
The second and the third, nine, and some five;
If this prove true, they'll pay for't. By mine honor,
I'll geld 'em all; fourteen they shall not see
To bring false generations. They are co-heirs,
And I had rather glib myself than they
Should not produce fair issue.
Leon. Cease, no more.
You smell this business with a sense as cold
As is a dead man's nose; but I do see't, and feel't,
As you feel doing thus [*grasps his arm*]—and see withal
The instruments that feel.
Ant. If it be so,
We need no grave to bury honesty,
There's not a grain of it the face to sweeten
Of the whole dungy earth.
Leon. What? lack I credit?
[*1.*] *Lord.* I had rather you did lack than I, my lord,
Upon this ground; and more it would content me
To have her honor true than your suspicion,
Be blam'd for't how you might.
Leon. Why, what need we
Commune with you of this, but rather follow
Our forceful instigation? Our prerogative
Calls not your counsels, but our natural goodness
Imparts this; which if you—or stupefied
Or seeming so in skill—cannot, or will not,
Relish a truth like us, inform yourselves
We need no more of your advice. The matter,
The loss, the gain, the ord'ring on't, is all
Properly ours.
Ant. And I wish, my liege,
You had only in your silent judgment tried it,
Without more overture.
Leon. How could that be?
Either thou art most ignorant by age,
Or thou wert born a fool. Camillo's flight,
Added to their familiarity
(Which was as gross as ever touch'd conjecture,
That lack'd sight only, nought for approbation
But only seeing, all other circumstances
Made up to th' deed), doth push on this proceeding.
Yet, for a greater confirmation
(For in an act of this importance 'twere
Most piteous to be wild), I have dispatch'd in post
To sacred Delphos, to Apollo's temple,

98. publish'd: publicly proclaimed. **Gentle my**: my noble.
99. throughly: thoroughly, fully. **to say**: by saying.
102. centre: earth.
104–5. afar . . . speaks: indirectly guilty merely for speaking.
113. qualified: tempered. **114. measure**: judge.
115. heard: obeyed.
118. fools. Often, as here, a term of affection and pity.
122. better grace: greater honor (when I am vindicated).
134–35. I'll . . . wife. Meaning uncertain; perhaps "I'll guard (*keep*) my wife as I guard my horses" or "I'll keep my wife away from men as watchfully as I keep my mares from my stallions."
135. in . . . her: i.e. constantly beside her, as if we were two dogs leashed together. **139. she**: i.e. Hermione.

141. abus'd: deceived. **putter-on**: inciter.
143. land-damn. The word occurs only here and has not been satisfactorily explained. **148. false generations**: illegitimate children.
149. glib: castrate.
154. instruments: (1) Leontes' fingers; (2) Hermione and Polixenes.
159. Upon this ground: in this matter.
163. instigation: motive for action.
163–64. Our prerogative . . . counsels: I am under no obligation to consult you.
166. seeming . . . skill: cunningly pretending to be so.
167. Relish: taste, i.e. perceive. **169. on't**: of it.
170. liege: sovereign. **172. overture**: public disclosure.
176. gross: palpable, manifest. **touch'd conjecture**: conjecture reached to. **177. approbation**: proof. **179. Made up**: added up.
182. wild: rash. **post**: haste. **183. Delphos.** See note on III.i.2.

Cleomines and Dion, whom you know
Of stuff'd sufficiency. Now, from the oracle
They will bring all, whose spiritual counsel had,
Shall stop or spur me. Have I done well?

[*1.*] *Lord.* Well done, my lord.

Leon. Though I am satisfied, and need no more
Than what I know, yet shall the oracle
Give rest to th' minds of others—such as he,
[*Points at Antigonus.*]
Whose ignorant credulity will not
Come up to th' truth. So have we thought it good
From our free person she should be confin'd,
Lest that the treachery of the two fled hence
Be left her to perform. Come follow us,
We are to speak in public; for this business
Will raise us all.

Ant. [*Aside.*] To laughter, as I take it,
If the good truth were known. *Exeunt.*

Scene II

Enter Paulina, *a* Gentleman, [*and* Attendants].

Paul. The keeper of the prison, call to him;
Let him have knowledge who I am. [*Exit Gentleman.*]
Good lady,
No court in Europe is too good for thee,
What dost thou then in prison?

[*Enter* Gentleman *with the*] Jailer.

Now, good sir,
You know me, do you not?

Jail. For a worthy lady,
And one who much I honor.

Paul. Pray you then,
Conduct me to the Queen.

Jail. I may not, madam:
To the contrary I have express commandment.

Paul. Here's ado, to lock up honesty
And honor from th' access of gentle visitors.
Is't lawful, pray you, to see her women?
Any of them? Emilia?

Jail. So please you, madam,
To put apart these your attendants, I
Shall bring Emilia forth.

Paul. I pray now call her.—
Withdraw yourselves.
[*Exeunt Gentleman and Attendants.*]

Jail. And, madam, I must
Be present at your conference.

Paul. Well; be't so; prithee. [*Exit Jailer.*]
Here's such ado to make no stain a stain
As passes coloring.

[*Enter* Jailer *with*] Emilia.

Dear gentlewoman,
How fares our gracious lady?

Emil. As well as one so great and so forlorn
May hold together. On her frights and griefs
(Which never tender lady hath borne greater)
She is, something before her time, deliver'd.

Paul. A boy?

Emil. A daughter, and a goodly babe,
Lusty and like to live. The Queen receives
Much comfort in't; says, "My poor prisoner,
I am innocent as you."

Paul. I dare be sworn.
These dangerous, unsafe lunes i' th' King, beshrew
them!
He must be told on't, and he shall. The office
Becomes a woman best. I'll take't upon me.
If I prove honey-mouth'd, let my tongue blister;
And never to my red-look'd anger be
The trumpet any more. Pray you, Emilia,
Commend my best obedience to the Queen.
If she dares trust me with her little babe,
I'll show't the King, and undertake to be
Her advocate to th' loud'st. We do not know
How he may soften at the sight o' th' child:
The silence often of pure innocence
Persuades when speaking fails.

Emil. Most worthy madam,
Your honor and your goodness is so evident
That your free undertaking cannot miss
A thriving issue. There is no lady living
So meet for this great errand. Please your ladyship
To visit the next room, I'll presently
Acquaint the Queen of your most noble offer,
Who but to-day hammered of this design,
But durst not tempt a minister of honor,
Lest she should be denied.

Paul. Tell her, Emilia,
I'll use that tongue I have. If wit flow from't
As boldness from my bosom, let't not be doubted
I shall do good.

Emil. Now be you blest for it!
I'll to the Queen.—Please you, come something nearer.

Jail. Madam, if't please the Queen to send the babe,
I know not what I shall incur to pass it,
Having no warrant.

Paul. You need not fear it, sir.
This child was prisoner to the womb, and is
By law and process of great Nature thence
Freed and enfranchis'd, not a party to
The anger of the King, nor guilty of
(If any be) the trespass of the Queen.

Jail. I do believe it.

Paul. Do not you fear. Upon mine honor, I
Will stand betwixt you and danger. *Exeunt.*

185. stuff'd sufficiency: full competence.
189. satisfied: free from doubt.
193. we. Note the shift to the royal plural.
194. From: away from. **free:** freely accessible.
195. treachery: i.e. the "plot against my life" (line 45).
198. raise: rouse.

II.ii. Location: Sicilia. A prison.
18. coloring: (1) dyeing; (2) excusing.

21. On: in consequence of. **28. lunes:** fits of lunacy.
29. The office: i.e. that duty. **30. Becomes:** befits.
31. my tongue blister. Lying was supposed to blister the tongue.
32. red-look'd: flushing. **34. Commend:** deliver.
37. to th' loud'st: at the top of my voice. **42. free:** generous.
43. thriving issue: successful result.
45. presently: immediately. **47. hammered of:** shaped, worked out.
48. tempt . . . honor: i.e. solicit any person of standing to undertake it. **50. wit:** wisdom.

SCENE III

Enter LEONTES; SERVANTS [*keeping the door*].

Leon. Nor night, nor day, no rest. It is but weakness
To bear the matter thus—mere weakness. If
The cause were not in being—part o' th' cause,
She th' adult'ress; for the harlot king
Is quite beyond mine arm, out of the blank
And level of my brain, plot-proof; but she
I can hook to me—say that she were gone,
Given to the fire, a moi'ty of my rest
Might come to me again. Who's there?
[*1.*] *Serv.* [*Advancing.*] My lord?
Leon. How does the boy?
[*1.*] *Serv.* He took good rest to-night;
'Tis hop'd his sickness is discharg'd.
Leon. To see his nobleness,
Conceiving the dishonor of his mother!
He straight declin'd, droop'd, took it deeply,
Fasten'd and fix'd the shame on't in himself,
Threw off his spirit, his appetite, his sleep,
And downright languish'd. Leave me solely; go,
See how he fares. [*Exit First Servant.*] Fie, fie, no thought of him;
The very thought of my revenges that way
Recoil upon me: in himself too mighty,
And in his parties, his alliance. Let him be,
Until a time may serve. For present vengeance,
Take it on her. Camillo and Polixenes
Laugh at me; make their pastime at my sorrow:
They should not laugh if I could reach them, nor
Shall she, within my pow'r.

Enter PAULINA [*with a child*]; ANTIGONUS *and* LORDS [*endeavoring to hold her back*].

[*1.*] *Lord.* You must not enter.
Paul. Nay, rather, good my lords, be second to me.
Fear you his tyrannous passion more, alas,
Than the Queen's life? A gracious innocent soul,
More free than he is jealous.
Ant. That's enough.
[*2.*] *Serv.* Madam—he hath not slept to-night, commanded
None should come at him.
Paul. Not so hot, good sir,
I come to bring him sleep. 'Tis such as you,
That creep like shadows by him, and do sigh
At each his needless heavings, such as you
Nourish the cause of his awaking. I
Do come with words as medicinal as true,
Honest as either, to purge him of that humor
That presses him from sleep.
Leon. [What] noise there, ho?
Paul. No noise, my lord, but needful conference

II.iii. Location: Sicilia. The palace of Leontes.
4. harlot: lewd (formerly used of either sex).
5–6. blank And level. Both nouns mean "aim"; literally, *blank* = bull's-eye of a target.
8. Given . . . fire. The punishment for treason, which a queen's adultery would amount to. **moi'ty:** portion. **15. on't:** of it.
17. solely: alone. **18. him:** i.e. Polixenes.
27. be second to: support. **30. free:** innocent.
36. awaking: wakefulness. **38. humor:** distemper.

About some gossips for your Highness.
Leon. How?
Away with that audacious lady! Antigonus,
I charg'd thee that she should not come about me:
I knew she would.
Ant. I told her so, my lord,
On your displeasure's peril and on mine,
She should not visit you.
Leon. What? canst not rule her?
Paul. From all dishonesty he can. In this,
Unless he take the course that you have done—
Commit me for committing honor—trust it,
He shall not rule me.
Ant. La you now, you hear!
When she will take the rein I let her run,
[*Aside.*] But she'll not stumble.
Paul. Good my liege, I come—
And I beseech you hear me, who professes
Myself your loyal servant, your physician,
Your most obedient counsellor; yet that dares
Less appear so, in comforting your evils,
Than such as most seem yours—I say, I come
From your good queen.
Leon. Good queen?
Paul. Good queen, my lord, good queen, I say good queen,
And would by combat make her good, so were I
A man, the worst about you.
Leon. Force her hence.
Paul. Let him that makes but trifles of his eyes
First hand me. On mine own accord I'll off,
But first I'll do my errand. The good queen
(For she is good) hath brought you forth a daughter—
Here 'tis—commends it to your blessing.
[*Laying down the child.*]
Leon. Out!
A mankind witch! Hence with her, out o' door!
A most intelligencing bawd!
Paul. Not so.
I am as ignorant in that, as you
In so entit'ling me; and no less honest
Than you are mad; which is enough, I'll warrant
(As this world goes), to pass for honest.
Leon. Traitors!
Will you not push her out? [*To Antigonus.*] Give her the bastard,
Thou dotard, thou art woman-tir'd; unroosted
By thy Dame Partlet here. Take up the bastard,
Take't up, I say; give't to thy crone.
Paul. For ever
Unvenerable be thy hands, if thou

41. gossips: baptismal sponsors (for the baby).
49. Commit: imprison. **for committing honor:** i.e. for honorable behavior which you misjudge as a crime, just as in Hermione's case.
56. comforting: condoning. **57. yours:** i.e. your loyal servants.
61. by combat. A reference to trial by combat as a means of proving innocence or guilt. **make her good:** make good her assertion of innocence. **62. worst:** least worthy.
68. mankind: masculine, i.e. behaving with unwomanly violence.
69. intelligencing bawd: spying go-between (for the Queen and Polixenes).
71. entit'ling. A contraction of the old spelling *entituling*. **honest:** chaste.
75. woman-tir'd: henpecked. *Tire* = tear with the beak (a term from falconry). **unroosted:** pushed off the roost.
76. Partlet: traditional name for a hen.

Tak'st up the Princess by that forced baseness
Which he has put upon't!
Leon. He dreads his wife.
Paul. So I would you did; then 'twere past all doubt
You'ld call your children yours.
Leon. A nest of traitors!
Ant. I am none, by this good light.
Paul. Nor I, nor any
But one that's here—and that's himself; for he
The sacred honor of himself, his queen's,
His hopeful son's, his babe's, betrays to slander,
Whose sting is sharper than the sword's, and will not
(For as the case now stands, it is a curse
He cannot be compell'd to't) once remove
The root of his opinion, which is rotten
As ever oak or stone was sound.
Leon. A callat
Of boundless tongue, who late hath beat her husband,
And now baits me! This brat is none of mine,
It is the issue of Polixenes.
Hence with it, and together with the dam
Commit them to the fire!
Paul. It is yours:
And might we lay th' old proverb to your charge,
So like you, 'tis the worse. Behold, my lords,
Although the print be little, the whole matter
And copy of the father—eye, nose, lip,
The trick of 's frown, his forehead, nay, the valley,
The pretty dimples of his chin and cheek, his smiles,
The very mould and frame of hand, nail, finger.
And thou, good goddess Nature, which hast made it
So like to him that got it, if thou hast
The ordering of the mind too, 'mongst all colors
No yellow in't, lest she suspect, as he does,
Her children not her husband's!
Leon. A gross hag!
And, lozel, thou art worthy to be hang'd,
That wilt not stay her tongue.
Ant. Hang all the husbands
That cannot do that feat, you'll leave yourself
Hardly one subject.
Leon. Once more, take her hence.
Paul. A most unworthy and unnatural lord
Can do no more.
Leon. I'll ha' thee burnt.
Paul. I care not:
It is an heretic that makes the fire,
Not she which burns in't. I'll not call you tyrant;
But this most cruel usage of your queen
(Not able to produce more accusation

79. forced baseness: wrongfully imposed name of bastard.
83. by . . . light: by my eyesight (a common oath).
91. callat: scold.
93. baits: harasses, as dogs do bears; with a pun on *beat* (line 92), then pronounced *bait*.
101. trick: characteristic expression. **valley:** cleft of the chin (?).
105. got: begot.
107. yellow. Symbolic of jealousy.
107–8. lest . . . husband's. It has been pointed out that this would be an odd effect of suspicion of one's husband. Perhaps the wording reflects Paulina's excitement.
109. lozel: scoundrel (addressed to Antigonus).
115–16. It . . . in't: i.e. it is the guilt of the condemned that makes the fire an act of justice, not the mere fact that a woman is burned.

Than your own weak-hing'd fancy) something savors
Of tyranny, and will ignoble make you,
Yea, scandalous to the world.
Leon. On your allegiance,
Out of the chamber with her! Were I a tyrant,
Where were her life? She durst not call me so,
If she did know me one. Away with her!
Paul. I pray you do not push me, I'll be gone.
Look to your babe, my lord, 'tis yours. Jove send her
A better guiding spirit! What needs these hands?
You, that are thus so tender o'er his follies,
Will never do him good, not one of you.
So, so. Farewell, we are gone. *Exit.*
Leon. Thou, traitor, hast set on thy wife to this.
My child? Away with't! Even thou, that hast
A heart so tender o'er it, take it hence,
And see it instantly consum'd with fire.
Even thou, and none but thou. Take it up straight.
Within this hour bring me word 'tis done
(And by good testimony), or I'll seize thy life,
With what thou else call'st thine. If thou refuse
And wilt encounter with my wrath, say so;
The bastard brains with these my proper hands
Shall I dash out. Go, take it to the fire,
For thou set'st on thy wife.
Ant. I did not, sir.
These lords, my noble fellows, if they please,
Can clear me in't.
Lords. We can. My royal liege,
He is not guilty of her coming hither.
Leon. You're liars all.
[*1.*] *Lord.* Beseech your Highness, give us better credit.
We have always truly serv'd you, and beseech'
So to esteem of us; and on our knees we beg
(As recompense of our dear services
Past and to come) that you do change this purpose,
Which being so horrible, so bloody, must
Lead on to some foul issue. We all kneel.
Leon. I am a feather for each wind that blows.
Shall I live on to see this bastard kneel
And call me father? Better burn it now
Than curse it then. But be it; let it live.
It shall not neither. [*To Antigonus.*] You, sir, come you hither:
You that have been so tenderly officious
With Lady Margery, your midwife there,
To save this bastard's life—for 'tis a bastard,
So sure as this beard's grey—what will you adventure
To save this brat's life?
Ant. Any thing, my lord,
That my ability may undergo
And nobleness impose; at least thus much:
I'll pawn the little blood which I have left
To save the innocent—any thing possible.
Leon. It shall be possible. Swear by this sword
Thou wilt perform my bidding.

127. What . . . hands: no need to push me. **140. proper:** own.
147. credit: belief. **148. beseech':** beseech you.
150. dear: heartfelt, deeply loyal.
160. Lady Margery. Perhaps equivalent to *Dame Partlet* (line 76), since *margery-prater* is recorded as a slang term for "hen."
162. this beard. Probably Antigonus'. **adventure:** risk.

Ant. I will, my lord.
Leon. Mark and perform it—seest thou? for the fail
Of any point in't shall not only be
Death to thyself but to thy lewd-tongu'd wife,
Whom for this time we pardon. We enjoin thee,
As thou art liegeman to us, that thou carry
This female bastard hence, and that thou bear it
To some remote and desert place quite out
Of our dominions, and that there thou leave it
(Without more mercy) to it own protection,
And favor of the climate. As by strange fortune
It came to us, I do in justice charge thee,
On thy soul's peril, and thy body's torture,
That thou commend it strangely to some place
Where chance may nurse or end it. Take it up.
Ant. I swear to do this—though a present death
Had been more merciful. Come on, poor babe.
Some powerful spirit instruct the kites and ravens
To be thy nurses! Wolves and bears, they say,
Casting their savageness aside, have done
Like offices of pity. Sir, be prosperous
In more than this deed does require! And blessing
Against this cruelty fight on thy side,
Poor thing, condemn'd to loss! *Exit [with the child].*
Leon. No! I'll not rear
Another's issue.

Enter a SERVANT.

Serv. Please' your Highness, posts
From those you sent to th' oracle are come
An hour since. Cleomines and Dion,
Being well arriv'd from Delphos, are both landed,
Hasting to th' court.
[1.] Lord. So please you, sir, their speed
Hath been beyond accompt.
Leon. Twenty-three days
They have been absent. 'Tis good speed; foretells
The great Apollo suddenly will have
The truth of this appear. Prepare you, lords,
Summon a session, that we may arraign
Our most disloyal lady; for as she hath
Been publicly accus'd, so shall she have
A just and open trial. While she lives
My heart will be a burthen to me. Leave me,
And think upon my bidding. *Exeunt.*

ACT III, SCENE I

Enter CLEOMINES *and* DION.

Cleo. The climate's delicate, the air most sweet,
Fertile the isle, the temple much surpassing
The common praise it bears.
Dion. I shall report,
For most it caught me, the celestial habits
(Methinks I so should term them) and the reverence
Of the grave wearers. O, the sacrifice!
How ceremonious, solemn, and unearthly
It was i' th' off'ring!
Cleo. But of all, the burst
And the ear-deaf'ning voice o' th' oracle,
Kin to Jove's thunder, so surpris'd my sense,
That I was nothing.
Dion. If th' event o' th' journey
Prove as successful to the Queen (O be't so!)
As it hath been to us rare, pleasant, speedy,
The time is worth the use on't.
Cleo. Great Apollo
Turn all to th' best! These proclamations,
So forcing faults upon Hermione,
I little like.
Dion. The violent carriage of it
Will clear or end the business. When the oracle
(Thus by Apollo's great divine seal'd up)
Shall the contents discover, something rare
Even then will rush to knowledge. Go; fresh horses!
And gracious be the issue! *Exeunt.*

SCENE II

Enter LEONTES, LORDS, OFFICERS.

Leon. This sessions (to our great grief we pronounce)
Even pushes 'gainst our heart—the party tried,
The daughter of a king, our wife, and one
Of us too much belov'd. Let us be clear'd
Of being tyrannous, since we so openly
Proceed in justice, which shall have due course,
Even to the guilt or the purgation.
Produce the prisoner.
Off. It is his Highness' pleasure that the Queen
Appear in person here in court.

[Enter] HERMIONE *(as to her trial)*, [PAULINA, *and*] LADIES *[attending]*.

Silence!
Leon. Read the indictment.
Off. [*Reads.*] "Hermione, queen to the worthy Leontes, King of Sicilia, thou art here accused and arraigned of high treason, in committing adultery with Polixenes, King of Bohemia, and conspiring with Camillo to take away the life of our sovereign lord the King, thy royal husband: the pretense whereof being by circumstances partly laid open, thou, Hermione,

170. fail: failure (the regular Elizabethan form).
174. liegeman: loyal subject. **178. it:** its.
182. commend: commit. **strangely . . . place:** i.e. to some foreign place. The same sense of *strange* is present in *strange fortune* (line 179), where Leontes must intend not only "extraordinary" but also "brought about by a foreigner."
190. In more: in more ways (?) or to a greater degree (?). **require:** deserve. **192. loss:** destruction.
193. Please': please it, i.e. may it please. **posts:** speedy messengers.
198. accompt: record, i.e. precedent. **200. suddenly:** at once.
202. session: trial.

III.i. Location: Sicilia. On the road.

2. isle. Shakespeare follows his source *Pandosto* in locating Apollo's oracle on "the isle of Delphos"—perhaps a confusion of Delphi with the island of Delos, the god's reputed birthplace.
4. caught: charmed. **habits:** garments.
10. surpris'd: overwhelmed. **11. event:** outcome.
17. carriage: handling. **19. great divine:** chief priest.
20. discover: reveal.

III.ii. Location: Sicilia. A court of justice.
4. Of: by. **7. purgation:** exculpation. **17. pretense:** design.

contrary to the faith and allegiance of a true subject, didst counsel and aid them, for their better safety, to fly away by night."

Her. Since what I am to say must be but that
Which contradicts my accusation, and
The testimony on my part no other
But what comes from myself, it shall scarce boot me
To say "Not guilty." Mine integrity,
Being counted falsehood, shall (as I express it)
Be so receiv'd. But thus, if pow'rs divine
Behold our human actions (as they do),
I doubt not then but innocence shall make
False accusation blush, and tyranny
Tremble at patience. You, my lord, best know
([Who] least will seem to do so) my past life
Hath been as continent, as chaste, as true,
As I am now unhappy; which is more
Than history can pattern, though devis'd
And play'd to take spectators. For behold me,
A fellow of the royal bed, which owe
A moi'ty of the throne, a great king's daughter,
The mother to a hopeful prince, here standing
To prate and talk for life and honor 'fore
Who please to come and hear. For life, I prize it
As I weigh grief, which I would spare; for honor,
'Tis a derivative from me to mine,
And only that I stand for. I appeal
To your own conscience, sir, before Polixenes
Came to your court, how I was in your grace,
How merited to be so; since he came,
With what encounter so uncurrent I
Have strain'd t' appear thus; if one jot beyond
The bound of honor, or in act or will
That way inclining, hard'ned be the hearts
Of all that hear me, and my near'st of kin
Cry fie upon my grave!

Leon. I ne'er heard yet
That any of these bolder vices wanted
Less impudence to gainsay what they did
Than to perform it first.

Her. That's true enough,
Though 'tis a saying, sir, not due to me.

Leon. You will not own it.

Her. More than mistress of
Which comes to me in name of fault, I must not
At all acknowledge. For Polixenes
(With whom I am accus'd), I do confess
I lov'd him as in honor he requir'd;
With such a kind of love as might become
A lady like me; with a love even such,
So, and no other, as yourself commanded;
Which not to have done I think had been in me
Both disobedience and ingratitude
To you and toward your friend, whose love had spoke,
Even since it could speak, from an infant, freely,
That it was yours. Now for conspiracy,
I know not how it tastes, though it be dish'd
For me to try how. All I know of it
Is that Camillo was an honest man;
And why he left your court, the gods themselves
(Wotting no more than I) are ignorant.

Leon. You knew of his departure, as you know
What you have underta'en to do in 's absence.

Her. Sir,
You speak a language that I understand not.
My life stands in the level of your dreams,
Which I'll lay down.

Leon. Your actions are my dreams.
You had a bastard by Polixenes,
And I but dream'd it. As you were past all shame
(Those of your fact are so), so past all truth;
Which to deny concerns more than avails; for as
Thy brat hath been cast out, like to itself,
No father owning it (which is indeed
More criminal in thee than it), so thou
Shalt feel our justice; in whose easiest passage
Look for no less than death.

Her. Sir, spare your threats.
The bug which you would fright me with, I seek.
To me can life be no commodity;
The crown and comfort of my life, your favor,
I do give lost, for I do feel it gone,
But know not how it went. My second joy
And first-fruits of my body, from his presence
I am barr'd, like one infectious. My third comfort
(Starr'd most unluckily) is from my breast
(The innocent milk in it most innocent mouth)
Hal'd out to murther; myself on every post
Proclaim'd a strumpet; with immodest hatred
The child-bed privilege denied, which 'longs
To women of all fashion; lastly, hurried
Here to this place, i' th' open air, before
I have got strength of limit. Now, my liege,
Tell me what blessings I have here alive,
That I should fear to die? Therefore proceed.
But yet hear this—mistake me not; no life
(I prize it not a straw), but for mine honor,
Which I would free—if I shall be condemn'd
Upon surmises (all proofs sleeping else
But what your jealousies awake), I tell you

25. boot: profit. **35. which:** which unhappiness.
36. history: story. **pattern:** show a precedent for.
37. take: charm. **38. which owe:** who own.
39. moi'ty: share (?) or half (?)
42–43. For . . . spare: as for life, I rate it as I rate grief, and would as willingly give it up.
44. a derivative: something to be handed on. **mine:** my children.
45. stand: make a stand, fight.
46. conscience: consideration, judgment.
49. encounter so uncurrent: conduct so unlawful.
50. strain'd: transgressed. **thus:** i.e. on trial for adultery.
55–56. wanted Less: i.e. were more wanting in. *Less* (where a modern ear expects *More*) intensifies the idea of deficiency in *wanted.*
58. due: applicable. **59. mistress:** possessor.
60. fault: ordinary human failings (not any of the "bolder vices" of line 56). **63. he requir'd:** was his due.

72. dish'd: served up, placed before me.
76. Wotting: knowing, i.e. if they know.
81. level: aim. **dreams:** fantasies, delusions.
85. Those . . . fact: those who commit the crime that you have committed.
86. concerns . . . avails: costs more effort than it will repay.
87. like to itself: i.e. appropriately for a bastard.
90–91. in . . . death. A threat of torture in addition to death.
92. bug: bugbear, bogey. **93. commodity:** benefit.
95. give: account.
99. Starr'd most unluckily: born under unlucky stars. **100. it:** its.
101. post. Public notices were placed on posts.
102. immodest: immoderate. **103. 'longs:** belongs.
104. all fashion: every rank.
106. got . . . limit: i.e. regained customary strength following child-birth. **111. free:** clear.

'Tis rigor and not law. Your honors all,
I do refer me to the oracle:
Apollo be my judge!
[*1.*] *Lord.* This your request
Is altogether just; therefore bring forth,
And in Apollo's name, his oracle.
[*Exeunt certain Officers.*]
Her. The Emperor of Russia was my father.
O that he were alive, and here beholding
His daughter's trial! that he did but see
The flatness of my misery, yet with eyes
Of pity, not revenge!

[*Enter* OFFICERS *with*] CLEOMINES, DION.

Off. You here shall swear upon this sword of justice,
That you, Cleomines and Dion, have
Been both at Delphos, and from thence have brought
This seal'd-up oracle, by the hand deliver'd
Of great Apollo's priest; and that since then
You have not dar'd to break the holy seal
Nor read the secrets in't.
Cleo., Dion. All this we swear.
Leon. Break up the seals, and read.
Off. [*Reads.*] "Hermione is chaste, Polixenes blameless, Camillo a true subject, Leontes a jealous tyrant, his innocent babe truly begotten, and the King shall live without an heir, if that which is lost be not found."
Lords. Now blessed be the great Apollo!
Her. Praised!
Leon. Hast thou read truth?
Off. Ay, my lord, even so
As it is here set down.
Leon. There is no truth at all i' th' oracle.
The sessions shall proceed; this is mere falsehood.

[*Enter a* SERVANT.]

Serv. My lord the King! the King!
Leon. What is the business?
Serv. O sir, I shall be hated to report it!
The Prince your son, with mere conceit and fear
Of the Queen's speed, is gone.
Leon. How? gone?
Serv. Is dead.
Leon. Apollo's angry, and the heavens themselves
Do strike at my injustice. [*Hermione swoons.*] How now there?
Paul. This news is mortal to the Queen. Look down
And see what death is doing.
Leon. Take her hence;
Her heart is but o'ercharg'd; she will recover.
I have too much believ'd mine own suspicion.
Beseech you tenderly apply to her
Some remedies for life.
[*Exeunt Paulina and Ladies with Hermione.*]
Apollo, pardon
My great profaneness 'gainst thine oracle!
I'll reconcile me to Polixenes,
New woo my queen, recall the good Camillo,
Whom I proclaim a man of truth, of mercy;
For being transported by my jealousies
To bloody thoughts, and to revenge, I chose
Camillo for the minister to poison
My friend Polixenes; which had been done,
But that the good mind of Camillo tardied
My swift command, though I with death and with
Reward did threaten and encourage him,
Not doing it and being done. He (most humane
And fill'd with honor) to my kingly guest
Unclasp'd my practice, quit his fortunes here
(Which you knew great), and to the hazard of
All incertainties himself commended,
No richer than his honor. How he glisters
Through my rust! and how his piety
Does my deeds make the blacker!

[*Enter* PAULINA.]

Paul. Woe the while!
O, cut my lace, lest my heart, cracking it,
Break too!
[*1.*] *Lord.* What fit is this, good lady?
Paul. What studied torments, tyrant, hast for me?
What wheels? racks? fires? What flaying? boiling
In leads or oils? What old or newer torture
Must I receive, whose every word deserves
To taste of thy most worst? Thy tyranny,
Together working with thy jealousies
(Fancies too weak for boys, too green and idle
For girls of nine), O, think what they have done,
And then run mad indeed—stark mad! for all
Thy by-gone fooleries were but spices of it.
That thou betrayedst Polixenes, 'twas nothing—
That did but show thee, of a fool, inconstant,
And damnable ingrateful; nor was't much
Thou wouldst have poison'd good Camillo's honor,
To have him kill a king—poor trespasses,
More monstrous standing by; whereof I reckon
The casting forth to crows thy baby-daughter
To be or none or little—though a devil
Would have shed water out of fire ere done't;
Nor is't directly laid to thee, the death
Of the young Prince, whose honorable thoughts
(Thoughts high for one so tender) cleft the heart
That could conceive a gross and foolish sire
Blemish'd his gracious dam; this is not, no,
Laid to thy answer: but the last—O lords,
When I have said, cry "Woe!"—the Queen, the Queen,
The sweet'st, dear'st creature's dead, and vengeance for't
Not dropp'd down yet.
[*1.*] *Lord.* The higher pow'rs forbid!

114. rigor: tyranny. **122. flatness:** completeness.
141. mere: utter. **144. conceit and fear:** anxious thoughts.
145. speed: fortune.

167. Unclasp'd my practice: disclosed my plot.
169. commended: committed.
170. No richer than: taking nothing with him except. **glisters:** shines. **184. spices:** slight foretastes. **186. of:** for.
189. poor: trivial.
190. standing by: to follow (?) or standing beside them for comparison (?) **196. tender:** young.
200. said: i.e. said what I have to say.

Paul. I say she's dead; I'll swear't. If word nor oath
Prevail not, go and see. If you can bring
Tincture or lustre in her lip, her eye,
Heat outwardly or breath within, I'll serve you
As I would do the gods. But, O thou tyrant!
Do not repent these things, for they are heavier
Than all thy woes can stir; therefore betake thee
To nothing but despair. A thousand knees,
Ten thousand years together, naked, fasting,
Upon a barren mountain, and still winter
In storm perpetual, could not move the gods
To look that way thou wert.
Leon. Go on, go on;
Thou canst not speak too much, I have deserv'd
All tongues to talk their bitt'rest.
[*1.*] *Lord.* Say no more.
Howe'er the business goes, you have made fault
I' th' boldness of your speech.
Paul. I am sorry for't.
All faults I make, when I shall come to know them,
I do repent. Alas, I have show'd too much
The rashness of a woman; he is touch'd
To th' noble heart. What's gone and what's past help
Should be past grief. Do not receive affliction
At my petition; I beseech you, rather
Let me be punish'd, that have minded you
Of what you should forget. Now, good my liege,
Sir, royal sir, forgive a foolish woman.
The love I bore your queen—lo, fool again!—
I'll speak of her no more, nor of your children;
I'll not remember you of my own lord,
Who is lost too. Take your patience to you,
And I'll say nothing.
Leon. Thou didst speak but well
When most the truth; which I receive much better
Than to be pitied of thee. Prithee bring me
To the dead bodies of my queen and son.
One grave shall be for both; upon them shall
The causes of their death appear (unto
Our shame perpetual). Once a day I'll visit
The chapel where they lie, and tears shed there
Shall be my recreation. So long as nature
Will bear up with this exercise, so long
I daily vow to use it. Come, and lead me
To these sorrows. *Exeunt.*

Scene III

Enter Antigonus [*and*] *a* Mariner [*with the*] *babe.*

Ant. Thou art perfect then, our ship hath touch'd upon
The deserts of Bohemia?
Mar. Ay, my lord, and fear
We have landed in ill time: the skies look grimly,
And threaten present blusters. In my conscience,
The heavens with that we have in hand are angry,
And frown upon 's.
Ant. Their sacred wills be done! Go get aboard;
Look to thy bark, I'll not be long before
I call upon thee.
Mar. Make your best haste, and go not
Too far i' th' land; 'tis like to be loud weather.
Besides, this place is famous for the creatures
Of prey that keep upon't.
Ant. Go thou away,
I'll follow instantly.
Mar. I am glad at heart
To be so rid o' th' business. *Exit.*
Ant. Come, poor babe.
I have heard (but not believ'd) the spirits o' th' dead
May walk again. If such thing be, thy mother
Appear'd to me last night; for ne'er was dream
So like a waking. To me comes a creature,
Sometimes her head on one side, some another—
I never saw a vessel of like sorrow,
So fill'd, and so becoming; in pure white robes,
Like very sanctity, she did approach
My cabin where I lay; thrice bow'd before me,
And (gasping to begin some speech) her eyes
Became two spouts; the fury spent, anon
Did this break from her: "Good Antigonus,
Since fate (against thy better disposition)
Hath made thy person for the thrower-out
Of my poor babe, according to thine oath,
Places remote enough are in Bohemia,
There weep and leave it crying; and for the babe
Is counted lost for ever, Perdita
I prithee call't. For this ungentle business,
Put on thee by my lord, thou ne'er shalt see
Thy wife Paulina more." And so, with shrieks,
She melted into air. Affrighted much,
I did in time collect myself and thought
This was so, and no slumber. Dreams are toys,
Yet for this once, yea, superstitiously,
I will be squar'd by this. I do believe
Hermione hath suffer'd death, and that
Apollo would (this being indeed the issue
Of King Polixenes) it should here be laid,
Either for life or death, upon the earth
Of its right father. Blossom, speed thee well!
[*Laying down the child, with a scroll.*]
There lie, and there thy character; there these,
[*Placing a bundle beside it.*]
Which may, if Fortune please, both breed thee, pretty,
And still rest thine. [*Thunder.*] The storm begins.
Poor wretch,
That for thy mother's fault art thus expos'd
To loss, and what may follow! Weep I cannot,

209. woes: lamentations. **stir:** move. **212. still:** always.
214. that . . . wert: in your direction.
223–24. Do . . . petition: let not my prayer for vengeance bring down suffering upon you. **225. minded:** reminded.
230. remember: remind.

III.iii. Location: Bohemia. The sea-coast.
1. perfect: certain.

4. present: immediate. **conscience:** opinion.
5. that . . . hand: what we are doing. **13. keep upon't:** inhabit it.
22. becoming: i.e. beautiful in sorrow. **32. for:** because.
33. Perdita: i.e. the lost one. **34. ungentle:** ignoble.
39. toys: trifles. **41. squar'd:** ruled.
47. character: writing, i.e. written statement which will later prove her identity (see V.ii.33–35). **these:** i.e. gold and jewels.
48–49. breed . . . thine: pay for your bringing up and still leave something over. **51. Weep I cannot.** See line 32.

But my heart bleeds; and most accurs'd am I
To be by oath enjoin'd to this. Farewell!
The day frowns more and more; thou'rt like to have
A lullaby too rough. I never saw
The heavens so dim by day. A savage clamor!
Well may I get aboard! This is the chase;
I am gone for ever. *Exit pursued by a bear.*

[*Enter*] Shepherd.

Shep. I would there were no age between ten and three-and-twenty, or that youth would sleep out the rest; for there is nothing in the between but getting wenches with child, wronging the ancientry, stealing, fighting— [*Horns.*] Hark you now! Would any but these boil'd-brains of nineteen and two-and-twenty hunt this weather? They have scar'd away two of my best sheep, which I fear the wolf will sooner find than the master. If any where I have them, 'tis by the sea-side, browsing of ivy. Good luck, and't be thy will! What have we here? Mercy on 's, a barne? A very pretty barne! A boy, or a child, I wonder? A pretty one, a very pretty one: sure some scape. Though I am not bookish, yet I can read waiting-gentlewoman in the scape. This has been some stair-work, some trunk-work, some behind-door-work. They were warmer that got this than the poor thing is here. I'll take it up for pity, yet I'll tarry till my son come; he hallow'd but even now. Whoa-ho-hoa!

Enter Clown.

Clo. Hilloa, loa!

Shep. What? art so near? If thou'lt see a thing to talk on when thou art dead and rotten, come hither. What ail'st thou, man?

Clo. I have seen two such sights, by sea and by land! But I am not to say it is a sea, for it is now the sky, betwixt the firmament and it you cannot thrust a bodkin's point.

Shep. Why, boy, how is it?

Clo. I would you did but see how it chafes, how it rages, how it takes up the shore! But that's not to the point. O, the most piteous cry of the poor souls! Sometimes to see 'em, and not to see 'em; now the ship boring the moon with her mainmast, and anon swallow'd with yest and froth, as you'd thrust a cork into a hogshead. And then for the land-service, to see how the bear tore out his shoulder-bone, how he cried to me for help, and said his name was Antigonus, a nobleman. But to make an end of the ship, to see how the sea flap-dragon'd it; but, first, how the poor souls roar'd, and the sea mock'd them; and how the poor gentleman roar'd, and the bear mock'd him, both roaring louder than the sea or weather.

Shep. Name of mercy, when was this, boy?

Clo. Now, now; I have not wink'd since I saw these sights. The men are not yet cold under water, nor the bear half din'd on the gentleman. He's at it now.

Shep. Would I had been by, to have help'd the old man!

Clo. I would you had been by the ship side, to have help'd her; there your charity would have lack'd footing.

Shep. Heavy matters, heavy matters! But look thee here, boy. Now bless thyself: thou met'st with things dying, I with things new-born. Here's a sight for thee; look thee, a bearing-cloth for a squire's child! Look thee here, take up, take up, boy; open't. So, let's see—it was told me I should be rich by the fairies. This is some changeling; open't; what's within, boy?

Clo. You're a [made] old man; if the sins of your youth are forgiven you, you're well to live. Gold, all gold!

Shep. This is fairy gold, boy, and 'twill prove so. Up with't, keep it close. Home, home, the next way. We are lucky, boy, and to be so still requires nothing but secrecy. Let my sheep go. Come, good boy, the next way home.

Clo. Go you the next way with your findings; I'll go see if the bear be gone from the gentleman and how much he hath eaten. They are never curst but when they are hungry. If there be any of him left, I'll bury it.

Shep. That's a good deed. If thou mayest discern by that which is left of him what he is, fetch me to th' sight of him.

Clo. Marry, will I; and you shall help to put him i' th' ground.

Shep. 'Tis a lucky day, boy, and we'll do good deeds on't. *Exeunt.*

ACT IV, Scene I

Enter Time, *the Chorus.*

Time. I, that please some, try all, both joy and terror
Of good and bad, that makes and unfolds error,
Now take upon me, in the name of Time,
To use my wings. Impute it not a crime
To me, or my swift passage, that I slide
O'er sixteen years and leave the growth untried

62. ancientry: old people. **64. boil'd-brains:** senseless creatures.
70. barne: bairn, child. **child:** girl. **72. scape:** sexual escapade.
74. trunk-work: secret affair involving a trunk (perhaps with play on *trunk* = body).
75. got: begot. **78 s.d. Clown:** rustic. **86. bodkin's:** needle's.
89. takes up: rebukes. **93. yest:** yeast, foam.
94. the land-service: (1) what was taking place ashore (literally, military service on land, in contrast to naval service); (2) the dish that was being served up ashore.
98. flap-dragon'd: swallowed as if it had been a flap-dragon (a raisin floating on burning brandy).

110–11. would . . . footing: would have lacked a firm foothold (such as the land would provide), with pun on the sense "would not have founded a charitable institution."
115. bearing-cloth: rich cloth in which an infant was borne to its baptism. **118. changeling:** child left by fairies.
121. well to live: well-to-do, with pun on the sense "living in virtue."
124. close: secret. It was bad luck to talk about gifts from the fairies. **125. be so still:** go on being so.
127. next: nearest, shortest. **130. curst:** fierce.
136. Marry: indeed (originally the name of the Virgin Mary used as an oath).

IV.i.1. try: test.
6. leave . . . untried: leave unexamined the developments.

Of that wide gap, since it is in my pow'r
To o'erthrow law, and in one self-born hour
To plant and o'erwhelm custom. Let me pass
The same I am, ere ancient'st order was,
Or what is now receiv'd. I witness to
The times that brought them in; so shall I do
To th' freshest things now reigning, and make stale
The glistering of this present, as my tale
Now seems to it. Your patience this allowing,
I turn my glass, and give my scene such growing
As you had slept between. Leontes leaving—
Th' effects of his fond jealousies so grieving
That he shuts up himself—imagine me,
Gentle spectators, that I now may be
In fair Bohemia, and remember well,
I mentioned a son o' th' King's, which Florizel
I now name to you; and with speed so pace
To speak of Perdita, now grown in grace
Equal with wond'ring. What of her ensues
I list not prophesy; but let Time's news
Be known when 'tis brought forth. A shepherd's daughter,
And what to her adheres, which follows after,
Is th' argument of Time. Of this allow,
If ever you have spent time worse ere now;
If never, yet that Time himself doth say,
He wishes earnestly you never may. *Exit.*

Scene II

Enter Polixenes *and* Camillo.

Pol. I pray thee, good Camillo, be no more importunate. 'Tis a sickness denying thee any thing; a death to grant this.

Cam. It is fifteen years since I saw my country; though I have for the most part been air'd abroad, I desire to lay my bones there. Besides, the penitent King, my master, hath sent for me, to whose feeling sorrows I might be some allay (or I o'erween to think so), which is another spur to my departure.

Pol. As thou lov'st me, Camillo, wipe not out the rest of thy services by leaving me now. The need I have of thee, thine own goodness hath made. Better not to have had thee than thus to want thee. Thou, having made me businesses which none without thee can sufficiently manage, must either stay to execute them thyself, or take away with thee the very services thou hast done; which if I have not enough consider'd (as too much I cannot), to be more thankful to thee

8. **self-born:** self-same.
9–11. **Let . . . receiv'd:** i.e. accept me as the same before civilization began and right now. 14. **glistering:** brightness, freshness.
15. **seems to it:** i.e. seems stale in comparison with the present.
16. **glass:** hourglass (regularly carried by Time in conventional representations). 17. **As:** as if. 18. **fond:** foolish.
22. **I . . . King's.** The mention of Polixenes' son in I.ii is part of "Time's news" (line 26). 23. **pace:** proceed.
25. **Equal with wond'ring:** to a degree that creates admiring wonderment. 26. **list not:** do not wish to. 28. **adheres:** relates.
29. **argument:** subject matter.

IV.ii. Location: Bohemia. The palace of Polixenes.
5. **been air'd:** lived. 8. **o'erween:** am conceited enough.
13. **want:** lack, i.e. lose. 17. **consider'd:** rewarded.

shall be my study, and my profit therein the heaping friendships. Of that fatal country Sicilia, prithee speak no more, whose very naming punishes me with the remembrance of that penitent (as thou call'st him) and reconcil'd king, my brother, whose loss of his most precious queen and children are even now to be afresh lamented. Say to me, when saw'st thou the Prince Florizel, my son? Kings are no less unhappy, their issue not being gracious, than they are in losing them when they have approv'd their virtues.

Cam. Sir, it is three days since I saw the Prince. What his happier affairs may be, are to me unknown; but I have (missingly) noted, he is of late much retir'd from court, and is less frequent to his princely exercises than formerly he hath appear'd.

Pol. I have consider'd so much, Camillo, and with some care, so far that I have eyes under my service which look upon his removedness; from whom I have this intelligence, that he is seldom from the house of a most homely shepherd, a man, they say, that from very nothing, and beyond the imagination of his neighbors, is grown into an unspeakable estate.

Cam. I have heard, sir, of such a man, who hath a daughter of most rare note. The report of her is extended more than can be thought to begin from such a cottage.

Pol. That's likewise part of my intelligence; but (I fear) the angle that plucks our son thither. Thou shalt accompany us to the place, where we will (not appearing what we are) have some question with the shepherd; from whose simplicity I think it not uneasy to get the cause of my son's resort thither. Prithee be my present partner in this business, and lay aside the thoughts of Sicilia.

Cam. I willingly obey your command.

Pol. My best Camillo! We must disguise ourselves. *Exeunt.*

Scene III

Enter Autolycus *singing.*

[*Aut.*] When daffadils begin to peer,
With heigh, the doxy over the dale!
Why, then comes in the sweet o' the year,
For the red blood reigns in the winter's pale.
The white sheet bleaching on the hedge,
With hey, the sweet birds, O how they sing!

19–20. **heaping friendships:** piling up of kind services.
22. **as . . . him:** to use your own word (no implication of doubt is intended).
27. **being gracious:** having princely qualities.
28. **approv'd:** proved. 31. **missingly:** aware of missing him.
35–36. **eyes . . . removedness:** spies who watch him in his retirement from court. 37. **intelligence:** news. **from:** away from.
38. **homely:** plain, simple.
40. **unspeakable:** unutterable, i.e. beyond reckoning.
42. **note:** distinction. 46. **angle:** baited hook.
48. **question:** conversation. 49. **uneasy:** difficult.

IV.iii. Location: Bohemia. A road near the Shepherd's cottage.
1. **daffadils:** daffodils. **peer:** peep out.
2. **doxy:** beggar's wench.
4. **pale:** (1) paleness; (2) area of royal authority.

Doth set my pugging tooth an edge,
For a quart of ale is a dish for a king.

The lark, that tirra-lyra chaunts,
With heigh, [with heigh,] the thrush and the jay!
Are summer songs for me and my aunts,
While we lie tumbling in the hay.

I have serv'd Prince Florizel, and in my time wore three-pile, but now I am out of service.

But shall I go mourn for that, my dear?
The pale moon shines by night;
And when I wander here and there,
I then do most go right.

If tinkers may have leave to live,
And bear the sow-skin bouget,
Then my account I well may give,
And in the stocks avouch it.

My traffic is sheets; when the kite builds, look to lesser linen. My father nam'd me Autolycus, who being, as I am, litter'd under Mercury, was likewise a snapper-up of unconsider'd trifles. With die and drab I purchas'd this caparison, and my revenue is the silly cheat. Gallows and knock are too powerful on the highway. Beating and hanging are terrors to me. For the life to come, I sleep out the thought of it. A prize, a prize!

Enter CLOWN.

Clo. Let me see: every 'leven wether tods, every tod yields pound and odd shilling; fifteen hundred shorn, what comes the wool to?

Aut. [*Aside.*] If the springe hold, the cock's mine.

Clo. I cannot do't without compters. Let me see: what am I to buy for our sheep-shearing feast? Three pound of sugar, five pound of currants, rice—what will this sister of mine do with rice? But my father hath made her mistress of the feast, and she lays it on. She hath made me four and twenty nosegays for the shearers (three-man song-men all, and very good ones), but they are most of them means and bases; but one Puritan amongst them, and he sings psalms to hornpipes. I must have saffron to color the warden pies; mace; dates, none—that's out of my note; nutmegs, seven; a race or two of ginger, but that I may beg; four pounds of pruins, and as many of raisins o' th' sun.

Aut. O that ever I was born! [*Grovelling on the ground.*]

Clo. I' th' name of me—

Aut. O, help me, help me! Pluck but off these rags; and then, death, death!

Clo. Alack, poor soul, thou hast need of more rags to lay on thee, rather than have these off.

Aut. O sir, the loathsomeness of them offend me more than the stripes I have receiv'd, which are mighty ones and millions.

Clo. Alas, poor man, a million of beating may come to a great matter.

Aut. I am robb'd, sir, and beaten; my money and apparel ta'en from me, and these detestable things put upon me.

Clo. What, by a horseman, or a footman?

Aut. A footman, sweet sir, a footman.

Clo. Indeed, he should be a footman by the garments he has left with thee. If this be a horseman's coat, it hath seen very hot service. Lend me thy hand, I'll help thee. Come, lend me thy hand.

Aut. O good sir, tenderly, O!

Clo. Alas, poor soul!

Aut. O good sir, softly, good sir! I fear, sir, my shoulder-blade is out.

Clo. How now? canst stand?

Aut. Softly, dear sir; [*picking his pocket*] good sir, softly. You ha' done me a charitable office.

Clo. Dost lack any money? I have a little money for thee.

Aut. No, good sweet sir; no, I beseech you, sir. I have a kinsman not past three quarters of a mile hence, unto whom I was going. I shall there have money, or any thing I want. Offer me no money, I pray you, that kills my heart.

Clo. What manner of fellow was he that robb'd you?

Aut. A fellow, sir, that I have known to go about with troll-my-dames. I knew him once a servant of the Prince. I cannot tell, good sir, for which of his virtues it was, but he was certainly whipt out of the court.

Clo. His vices, you would say; there's no virtue whipt out of the court. They cherish it to make it stay there; and yet it will no more but abide.

Aut. Vices, I would say, sir. I know this man well; he hath been since an ape-bearer, then a process-server, a bailiff, then he compass'd a motion of the Prodigal Son, and married a tinker's wife within a mile where my land and living lies; and, having

7. pugging: thieving. **set . . . an edge**: set . . . on edge, i.e. sharpen make keen. **11. aunts**: i.e. whores. **14. three-pile**: costly velvet.
20. bouget: budget, i.e. wallet or bag.
22. avouch it: testify to my thieving trade.
23–24. My . . . linen. Autolycus steals sheets which have been left to dry on hedges; the kite at nesting-time steals smaller pieces of linen.
24. Autolycus. The ancient Autolycus, Ulysses' grandfather, was the son of Mercury, god of thieves, and was himself an expert thief.
25. litter'd under Mercury: (1) begotten by Mercury; (2) born when the planet Mercury was in the ascendant.
26–27. With . . . caparison: dice and women have reduced me to these rags. **27. revenue**: source of income.
28. silly cheat: petty swindle (?) or cheating the simple (?). **knock**: beating. **30. For**: as for.
31. A prize: booty, something for the taking.
32. every . . . tods: every eleven sheep produce a tod (28 pounds) of wool. The Clown and his father will get over £143 at this shearing; they are very prosperous shepherds.
35. springe: snare. **cock**: woodcock, a proverbially silly bird.
36. compters: counters, metal disks used in calculating.
42. three-man song-men: singers of catches or rounds for three voices.
43. means: tenors. **44–45. hornpipes**: dance tunes.

45–46. warden pies: pies made of winter pears.
46. out . . . note: crossed off my list. **47. race**: root.
48. pruins: prunes. **48–49. o' th' sun**: sun-dried.
72. softly: gently.
87. troll-my-dames: a game resembling bagatelle.
93. abide: stay briefly.
95. ape-bearer: exhibitor of a tame monkey.
96. compass'd: got possession of (?) or contrived (?) or took on tour (?). **motion**: puppet show.

flown over many knavish professions, he settled only in rogue. Some call him Autolycus.

Clo. Out upon him! prig, for my life, prig! He haunts wakes, fairs, and bear-baitings.

Aut. Very true, sir; he, sir, he. That's the rogue that put me into this apparel.

Clo. Not a more cowardly rogue in all Bohemia. If you had but look'd big, and spit at him, he'ld have run.

Aut. I must confess to you, sir, I am no fighter. I am false of heart that way, and that he knew, I warrant him.

Clo. How do you now?

Aut. Sweet sir, much better than I was: I can stand and walk. I will even take my leave of you, and pace softly towards my kinsman's.

Clo. Shall I bring thee on the way?

Aut. No, good-fac'd sir, no, sweet sir.

Clo. Then fare thee well, I must go buy spices for our sheep-shearing. *Exit.*

Aut. Prosper you, sweet sir! Your purse is not hot enough to purchase your spice. I'll be with you at your sheep-shearing too. If I make not this cheat bring out another, and the shearers prove sheep, let me be unroll'd, and my name put in the book of virtue!

Song

Jog on, jog on, the foot-path way,
And merrily hent the stile-a;
A merry heart goes all the day,
Your sad tires in a mile-a. *Exit.*

Scene IV

Enter Florizel, Perdita.

Flo. These your unusual weeds to each part of you
Does give a life; no shepherdess, but Flora
Peering in April's front. This your sheep-shearing
Is as a meeting of the petty gods,
And you the queen on't.

Per. Sir, my gracious lord,
To chide at your extremes it not becomes me.
O, pardon, that I name them! Your high self,
The gracious mark o' th' land, you have obscur'd
With a swain's wearing, and me, poor lowly maid,
Most goddess-like prank'd up. But that our feasts
In every mess have folly, and the feeders
Digest['t] with a custom, I should blush
To see you so attir'd—sworn, I think,
To show myself a glass.

Flo. I bless the time
When my good falcon made her flight across
Thy father's ground.

Per. Now Jove afford you cause!
To me the difference forges dread; your greatness
Hath not been us'd to fear. Even now I tremble
To think your father, by some accident,
Should pass this way as you did. O, the Fates!
How would he look to see his work, so noble,
Vildly bound up? What would he say? Or how
Should I, in these my borrowed flaunts, behold
The sternness of his presence?

Flo. Apprehend
Nothing but jollity. The gods themselves
(Humbling their deities to love) have taken
The shapes of beasts upon them. Jupiter
Became a bull and bellow'd; the green Neptune
A ram and bleated; and the fire-rob'd god,
Golden Apollo, a poor humble swain,
As I seem now. Their transformations
Were never for a piece of beauty rarer,
Nor in a way so chaste, since my desires
Run not before mine honor, nor my lusts
Burn hotter than my faith.

Per. O but, sir,
Your resolution cannot hold when 'tis
Oppos'd (as it must be) by th' pow'r of the King.
One of these two must be necessities,
Which then will speak, that you must change this purpose,
Or I my life.

Flo. Thou dear'st Perdita,
With these forc'd thoughts I prithee darken not
The mirth o' th' feast. Or I'll be thine, my fair,
Or not my father's; for I cannot be
Mine own, nor any thing to any, if
I be not thine. To this I am most constant,
Though destiny say no. Be merry, gentle!
Strangle such thoughts as these with any thing
That you behold the while. Your guests are coming:
Lift up your countenance, as it were the day
Of celebration of that nuptial, which
We two have sworn shall come.

Per. O Lady Fortune,
Stand you auspicious!

Flo. See, your guests approach,
Address yourself to entertain them sprightly,
And let's be red with mirth.

101. prig: thief. **102. wakes:** village festivals.
106. look'd big: put on a bold front.
114. bring . . . way: go part of the way with you.
122. unroll'd: struck from the roll of thieves.
124. hent: grasp (in order to leap over).

IV.iv. Location: Bohemia. Before the Shepherd's cottage.
1. unusual weeds: unaccustomed garments.
2. Flora: goddess of flowers.
3. Peering . . . front: peeping out in early April.
6. extremes: exaggerations.
8. gracious . . . land: one whose graces cause him to be noted by everybody (like Hamlet, "Th' observ'd of all observers").
9. swain's wearing: country youth's garb.
10. prank'd up: bedecked.
11. mess: group (see note on I.ii.227).
12. Digest't . . . custom: i.e. accept it because they have become used to it.
13–14. sworn . . . glass: i.e. dedicated to showing me what I ought to see if I looked in a mirror—one dressed in rustic attire. Many editors follow Theobald in emending *sworn* to *swoon*, which makes easy sense: "faint if I were to see myself in a mirror."
17. difference: i.e. disparity in rank.
22. bound up: i.e. clothed (a metaphor from bookbinding).
23. flaunts: bits of finery.
27–30. Jupiter . . . swain. The references are to Jupiter's wooing of Europa, Neptune's wooing of Theopane, and Apollo's role in the wooing of Alcestis by Admetus.
32. a piece . . . rarer: a woman more beautiful than you.
33. Nor . . . chaste: nor for a purpose so chaste (since he intends marriage).
40. Or . . . life: i.e. or I will have to undergo some harsh change in my life. **41. forc'd:** farfetched. **42. Or:** either. **49. as:** as if.
53. Address: prepare. **entertain:** receive. **54. red:** flushed.

[*Enter*] SHEPHERD, CLOWN, POLIXENES [*and*] CAMILLO [*disguised*], MOPSA, DORCAS, SERVANTS.

Shep. Fie, daughter, when my old wife liv'd, upon
This day she was both pantler, butler, cook,
Both dame and servant; welcom'd all, serv'd all;
Would sing her song, and dance her turn; now here,
At upper end o' th' table, now i' th' middle;
On his shoulder, and his; her face o' fire
With labor, and the thing she took to quench it
She would to each one sip. You are retired,
As if you were a feasted one and not
The hostess of the meeting. Pray you bid
These unknown friends to 's welcome, for it is
A way to make us better friends, more known.
Come, quench your blushes, and present yourself
That which you are, mistress o' th' feast. Come on,
And bid us welcome to your sheep-shearing,
As your good flock shall prosper.

Per. [*To Polixenes.*] Sir, welcome.
It is my father's will I should take on me
The hostess-ship o' th' day. [*To Camillo.*] You're welcome, sir.
Give me those flow'rs there, Dorcas. Reverend sirs,
For you there's rosemary and rue; these keep
Seeming and savor all the winter long.
Grace and remembrance be to you both,
And welcome to our shearing!

Pol. Shepherdess
(A fair one are you!), well you fit our ages
With flow'rs of winter.

Per. Sir, the year growing ancient,
Not yet on summer's death, nor on the birth
Of trembling winter, the fairest flow'rs o' th' season
Are our carnations and streak'd gillyvors
(Which some call Nature's bastards). Of that kind
Our rustic garden's barren, and I care not
To get slips of them.

Pol. Wherefore, gentle maiden,
Do you neglect them?

Per. For I have heard it said,
There is an art which in their piedness shares
With great creating Nature.

Pol. Say there be;
Yet Nature is made better by no mean
But Nature makes that mean; so over that art
Which you say adds to Nature, is an art
That Nature makes. You see, sweet maid, we marry
A gentler scion to the wildest stock,
And make conceive a bark of baser kind
By bud of nobler race. This is an art
Which does mend Nature—change it rather; but
The art itself is Nature.

Per. So it is.

Pol. Then make [your] garden rich in gillyvors,
And do not call them bastards.

Per. I'll not put
The dibble in earth to set one slip of them;
No more than were I painted I would wish
This youth should say 'twere well, and only therefore
Desire to breed by me. Here's flow'rs for you:
Hot lavender, mints, savory, marjorum,
The marigold, that goes to bed wi' th' sun,
And with him rises weeping. These are flow'rs
Of middle summer, and I think they are given
To men of middle age. Y' are very welcome.

Cam. I should leave grazing, were I of your flock,
And only live by gazing.

Per. Out, alas!
You'ld be so lean, that blasts of January
Would blow you through and through. Now, my fair'st friend,
I would I had some flow'rs o' th' spring that might
Become your time of day—and yours, and yours,
That wear upon your virgin branches yet
Your maidenheads growing. O Proserpina,
For the flow'rs now, that, frighted, thou let'st fall
From Dis's waggon! daffadils,
That come before the swallow dares, and take
The winds of March with beauty; violets, dim,
But sweeter than the lids of Juno's eyes,
Or Cytherea's breath; pale primeroses,
That die unmarried, ere they can behold
Bright Phoebus in his strength (a malady
Most incident to maids); bold oxlips, and
The crown imperial; lilies of all kinds
(The flow'r-de-luce being one). O, these I lack,
To make you garlands of, and my sweet friend,
To strew him o'er and o'er!

Flo. What? like a corse?

Per. No, like a bank, for love to lie and play on;
Not like a corse; or if—not to be buried,
But quick and in mine arms. Come, take your flow'rs.
Methinks I play as I have seen them do
In Whitsun pastorals. Sure this robe of mine
Does change my disposition.

Flo. What you do
Still betters what is done. When you speak, sweet,
I'ld have you do it ever; when you sing,
I'ld have you buy and sell so; so give alms;
Pray so; and for the ord'ring your affairs,
To sing them too. When you do dance, I wish you
A wave o' th' sea, that you might ever do
Nothing but that; move still, still so,
And own no other function. Each your doing

56. **pantler**: pantry servant.
60. **On his . . . his**: at one man's . . . another man's.
75. **Seeming and savor**: color and scent.
76. **Grace and remembrance.** Symbolized by rue and rosemary respectively. 82. **gillyvors**: gillyflowers, pinks. 85. **slips**: cuttings.
86. **For**: because.
87. **art**: i.e. the gardener's skill in cross-breeding. **piedness**: variegated color. 89. **mean**: means.

100. **dibble**: small implement used to make holes in the soil for planting.
104. **Hot.** Meaning here uncertain. Contemporary herbalists classified some herbs as hot, others as cold. **marjorum**: marjoram.
116–18. **Proserpina . . . waggon.** Proserpina, Ceres' daughter, was gathering flowers when Pluto (Dis) saw her and carried her in his chariot to the underworld to become his queen.
119. **take**: bewitch.
122. **Cytherea's**: Venus'. **primeroses**: primroses.
124. **Phoebus**: the sun-god. 127. **flow'r-de-luce**: fleur-de-lis.
129. **corse**: corpse. 132. **quick**: alive.
134. **Whitsun pastorals**: May games and dances, with Robin Hood and Maid Marian as leading characters. Perdita thinks of them as somewhat indecent and is surprised at herself, a modest girl, for talking in their vein.
143. **Each your doing**: the manner in which you perform each act.

(So singular in each particular)
Crowns what you are doing in the present deeds,
That all your acts are queens.

Per. O Doricles,
Your praises are too large. But that your youth,
And the true blood which peeps fairly through't,
Do plainly give you out an unstain'd shepherd,
With wisdom I might fear, my Doricles,
You woo'd me the false way.

Flo. I think you have
As little skill to fear as I have purpose
To put you to't. But come, our dance, I pray.
Your hand, my Perdita. So turtles pair
That never mean to part.

Per. I'll swear for 'em.

Pol. This is the prettiest low-born lass that ever
Ran on the green-sord. Nothing she does, or seems,
But smacks of something greater than herself,
Too noble for this place.

Cam. He tells her something
That makes her blood look on't. Good sooth, she is
The queen of curds and cream.

Clo. Come on. Strike up.

Dor. Mopsa must be your mistress; marry, garlic,
To mend her kissing with!

Mop. Now in good time!

Clo. Not a word, a word, we stand upon our manners.
Come, strike up. [*Music.*]

Here a dance of Shepherds and Shepherdesses.

Pol. Pray, good shepherd, what fair swain is this
Which dances with your daughter?

Shep. They call him Doricles, and boasts himself
To have a worthy feeding; but I have it
Upon his own report, and I believe it.
He looks like sooth. He says he loves my daughter.
I think so too; for never gaz'd the moon
Upon the water as he'll stand and read
As 'twere my daughter's eyes; and to be plain,
I think there is not half a kiss to choose
Who loves another best.

Pol. She dances featly.

Shep. So she does any thing, though I report it
That should be silent. If young Doricles
Do light upon her, she shall bring him that
Which he not dreams of.

Enter SERVANT.

Serv. O master! if you did but hear the pedlar at the door, you would never dance again after a tabor and pipe; no, the bagpipe could not move you. He sings

several tunes faster than you'll tell money; he utters them as he had eaten ballads and all men's ears grew to his tunes.

Clo. He could never come better; he shall come in. I love a ballad but even too well, if it be doleful matter merrily set down, or a very pleasant thing indeed and sung lamentably.

Serv. He hath songs for man or woman, of all sizes; no milliner can so fit his customers with gloves. He has the prettiest love-songs for maids, so without bawdry, which is strange; with such delicate burthens of dildos and fadings, "jump her and thump her"; and where some stretch-mouth'd rascal would (as it were) mean mischief, and break a foul gap into the matter, he makes the maid to answer, "Whoop, do me no harm, good man"—puts him off, slights him, with "Whoop, do me no harm, good man."

Pol. This is a brave fellow.

Clo. Believe me, thou talkest of an admirable conceited fellow. Has he any unbraided wares?

Serv. He hath ribbons of all the colors i' th' rainbow; points more than all the lawyers in Bohemia can learnedly handle, though they come to him by th' gross; inkles, caddises, cambrics, lawns. Why, he sings 'em over as they were gods or goddesses: you would think a smock were a she-angel, he so chaunts to the sleeve-hand and the work about the square on't.

Clo. Prithee bring him in, and let him approach singing.

Per. Forewarn him that he use no scurrilous words in 's tunes. [*Exit Servant.*]

Clo. You have of these pedlars, that have more in them than you'ld think, sister.

Per. Ay, good brother, or go about to think.

Enter AUTOLYCUS *singing*.

[*Aut.*] Lawn as white as driven snow,
Cypress black as e'er was crow,
Gloves as sweet as damask roses,
Masks for faces and for noses;
Bugle-bracelet, necklace amber,
Perfume for a lady's chamber;
Golden quoifs and stomachers
For my lads to give their dears;

144. singular: distinctively yours.
146. Doricles: Florizel's assumed name. **152. skill:** reason.
154. turtles: turtledoves (symbolic of constancy in love).
157. green-sord: greensward.
160. makes . . . on't: makes her blush. Most editors emend *on't* to *out*. **Good sooth:** in truth.
163. Now . . . time: an expression of indignation.
168. boasts: he boasts.
169. feeding: pasture lands, i.e. landed estate.
171. looks like sooth: gives the impression of being an honest man.
176. another: the other. **featly:** gracefully.
179. light upon: choose. **182. tabor:** small drum.
184. tell: count.
185. ballads: here, the individual sheets on which ballads were printed and offered for sale. On Autolycus' stock of these "broadsides" see lines 259ff. below.
194–95. burthens . . . thump her: ballad refrains. Actually, those commended by the servant allude to male sex organs, orgasms, and erotic play, so that his examples absurdly contradict his "so without bawdry." **196. stretch-mouth'd:** foul-mouthed.
197–98. break . . . matter: introduce obscenity.
198–99. Whoop . . . man. A line from a popular ballad. The original words are lost, but the tune survives, along with several later ballads set to it. **201. brave:** splendid.
202–3. admirable conceited: wonderfully clever.
203. unbraided: fresh.
205. points: laces to fasten hose to doublet (with a pun on the sense "arguments").
207. inkles: linen tapes. **caddises:** worsted tapes for garters.
210. sleeve-hand: wrist-band. **square on't:** yoke of it.
215. You have: there are some.
217. go about: intend. **s.d. Autolycus.** He is disguised with a beard (see lines 713–14, where he removes it). **219. Cypress:** filmy crepe.
220. sweet. Gloves were often perfumed.
222. Bugle-bracelet: bracelet made of black beads.
224. quoifs: coifs, tight caps. **stomachers:** ornamental chest-coverings worn to fill in the front opening of the bodice.

Pins and poking-sticks of steel;
What maids lack from head to heel:
Come buy of me, come; come buy,
come buy,
Buy, lads, or else your lasses cry:
Come buy.

Clo. If I were not in love with Mopsa, thou shouldst take no money of me, but being enthrall'd as I am, it will also be the bondage of certain ribbons and gloves.

Mop. I was promis'd them against the feast, but they come not too late now.

Dor. He hath promis'd you more than that, or there be liars.

Mop. He hath paid you all he promis'd you. May be he has paid you more, which will shame you to give him again.

Clo. Is there no manners left among maids? Will they wear their plackets where they should bear their faces? Is there not milking-time? when you are going to bed? or kill-hole? to whistle [off] these secrets, but you must be tittle-tattling before all our guests? 'Tis well they are whisp'ring. Clamor your tongues, and not a word more.

Mop. I have done. Come, you promis'd me a tawdry-lace and a pair of sweet gloves.

Clo. Have I not told thee how I was cozen'd by the way, and lost all my money?

Aut. And indeed, sir, there are cozeners abroad, therefore it behooves men to be wary.

Clo. Fear not thou, man, thou shalt lose nothing here.

Aut. I hope so, sir, for I have about me many parcels of charge.

Clo. What hast here? Ballads?

Mop. Pray now buy some. I love a ballet in print, a-life, for then we are sure they are true.

Aut. Here's one to a very doleful tune, how a usurer's wife was brought to bed of twenty money-bags at a burthen, and how she long'd to eat adders' heads, and toads carbonado'd.

Mop. Is it true, think you?

Aut. Very true, and but a month old.

Dor. Bless me from marrying a usurer!

Aut. Here's the midwive's name to't, one Mistress

226. **poking-sticks**: metal rods used to iron fluted ruffs.
232–34. **being . . . gloves**: since I have been taken prisoner by love, certain ribbons and gloves must also be taken prisoner, i.e. be bought and bound up in a parcel. 235. **against**: before, in readiness for.
237–38. **He . . . liars**: i.e. the rumor is that he has promised to marry you.
240–41. **more . . . again**: i.e. an illegitimate child.
243–44. **wear . . . faces**: i.e. disclose their most private affairs (?). *Plackets* = slits in petticoats.
245. **kill-hole**: kiln-hole, fireplace. **whistle off**: release (term from falconry).
247. **Clamor.** The sense must be "silence." The word has been connected by some with *clammer*, a term in bell-ringing. Others emend to *Charm a'* or *Clam a'*.
250. **tawdry-lace**: bright neckerchief. *Tawdry* is a corruption of the name of Saint Audrey, whose feast day was celebrated with a fair at which showy articles of dress were sold.
251. **cozen'd**: cheated. 257. **hope so**: i.e. hope you are right.
258. **parcels of charge**: valuable articles. 260. **ballet**: ballad.
261. **a-life**: on my life.
265. **carbonado'd**: sliced and scored across for broiling.

Tale-porter, and five or six honest wives that were present. Why should I carry lies abroad?

Mop. Pray you now buy it.

Clo. Come on, lay it by; and let's first see moe ballads. We'll buy the other things anon.

Aut. Here's another ballad, of a fish that appear'd upon the coast on We'n'sday the fourscore of April, forty thousand fadom above water, and sung this ballad against the hard hearts of maids. It was thought she was a woman, and was turn'd into a cold fish for she would not exchange flesh with one that lov'd her. The ballad is very pitiful, and as true.

Dor. Is it true too, think you?

Aut. Five justices' hands at it, and witnesses more than my pack will hold.

Clo. Lay it by too. Another.

Aut. This is a merry ballad, but a very pretty one.

Mop. Let's have some merry ones.

Aut. Why, this is a passing merry one and goes to the tune of "Two maids wooing a man." There's scarce a maid westward but she sings it. 'Tis in request, I can tell you.

Mop. We can both sing it. If thou'lt bear a part, thou shalt hear; 'tis in three parts.

Dor. We had the tune on't a month ago.

Aut. I can bear my part, you must know 'tis my occupation. Have at it with you.

Song

Aut. Get you hence, for I must go
Where it fits not you to know.
Dor. Whither? *Mop.* O, whither?
Dor. Whither?
Mop. It becomes thy oath full well,
Thou to me thy secrets tell.
Dor. Me too; let me go thither.

Mop. Or thou goest to th' grange, or mill.
Dor. If to either, thou dost ill.
Aut. Neither. *Dor.* What, neither?
Aut. Neither.
Dor. Thou hast sworn my love to be.
Mop. Thou hast sworn it more to me:
Then whither goest? say, whither?

Clo. We'll have this song out anon by ourselves. My father and the gentlemen are in sad talk, and we'll not trouble them. Come bring away thy pack after me. Wenches, I'll buy for you both. Pedlar, let's have the first choice. Follow me, girls.

[*Exit with Dorcas and Mopsa.*]

Aut. And you shall pay well for 'em.

Song

Will you buy any tape,
Or lace for your cape,
My dainty duck, my dear-a?
Any silk, any thread,
Any toys for your head
Of the new'st and fin'st, fin'st wear-a?

273. **moe**: more. 303. **grange**: farm. 310. **sad**: serious.
319. **toys**: trifling ornaments.

Come to the pedlar,
Money's a meddler,
That doth utter all men's ware-a. *Exit.*

[*Enter* SERVANT.]

Serv. Master, there is three carters, three shepherds, three neat-herds, three swine-herds, that have made themselves all men of hair. They call themselves Saltiers, and they have a dance which the wenches say is a gallimaufry of gambols, because they are not in't; but they themselves are o' th' mind (if it be not too rough for some that know little but bowling) it will please plentifully.

Shep. Away! we'll none on't. Here has been too much homely foolery already. I know, sir, we weary you.

Pol. You weary those that refresh us. Pray let's see these four threes of herdsmen.

Serv. One three of them, by their own report, sir, hath danc'd before the King; and not the worst of the three but jumps twelve foot and a half by th' squier.

Shep. Leave your prating. Since these good men are pleas'd, let them come in; but quickly now.

Serv. Why, they stay at door, sir. [*Exit.*]

Here a dance of twelve Satyrs.

Pol. O, father, you'll know more of that hereafter.
[*To Camillo.*] Is it not too far gone? 'Tis time to part them.
He's simple, and tells much. [*To Florizel.*] How now, fair shepherd?
Your heart is full of something that does take
Your mind from feasting. Sooth, when I was young,
And handed love as you do, I was wont
To load my she with knacks. I would have ransack'd
The pedlar's silken treasury, and have pour'd it
To her acceptance; you have let him go,
And nothing marted with him. If your lass
Interpretation should abuse, and call this
Your lack of love or bounty, you were straited
For a reply, at least if you make a care
Of happy holding her.

Flo. Old sir, I know
She prizes not such trifles as these are.
The gifts she looks from me are pack'd and lock'd
Up in my heart, which I have given already,
But not deliver'd. O, hear me breathe my life
Before this ancient sir, whom, it should seem,
Hath sometime lov'd! I take thy hand, this hand,
As soft as dove's down and as white as it,
Or Ethiopian's tooth, or the fann'd snow that's bolted
By th' northern blasts twice o'er.

Pol. What follows this?
How prettily th' young swain seems to wash
The hand was fair before! I have put you out.
But to your protestation; let me hear
What you profess.

Flo. Do, and be witness to't.

Pol. And this my neighbor too?

Flo. And he, and more
Than he, and men—the earth, the heavens, and all:
That were I crown'd the most imperial monarch,
Thereof most worthy, were I the fairest youth
That ever made eye swerve, had force and knowledge
More than was ever man's, I would not prize them
Without her love; for her, employ them all,
Commend them and condemn them to her service,
Or to their own perdition.

Pol. Fairly offer'd.

Cam. This shows a sound affection.

Shep. But, my daughter,
Say you the like to him?

Per. I cannot speak
So well, nothing so well; no, nor mean better.
By th' pattern of mine own thoughts I cut out
The purity of his.

Shep. Take hands, a bargain!
And, friends unknown, you shall bear witness to't:
I give my daughter to him, and will make
Her portion equal his.

Flo. O, that must be
I' th' virtue of your daughter. One being dead,
I shall have more than you can dream of yet,
Enough then for your wonder. But come on,
Contract us 'fore these witnesses.

Shep. Come, your hand;
And, daughter, yours.

Pol. Soft, swain, awhile, beseech you.
Have you a father?

Flo. I have; but what of him?

Pol. Knows he of this?

Flo. He neither does, nor shall.

Pol. Methinks a father
Is at the nuptial of his son a guest
That best becomes the table. Pray you once more,
Is not your father grown incapable
Of reasonable affairs? is he not stupid
With age and alt'ring rheums? Can he speak? hear?
Know man from man? dispute his own estate?
Lies he not bed-rid? and again does nothing
But what he did being childish?

Flo. No, good sir;
He has his health, and ampler strength indeed
Than most have of his age.

Pol. By my white beard,
You offer him, if this be so, a wrong
Something unfilial. Reason my son
Should choose himself a wife, but as good reason
The father (all whose joy is nothing else

323. **utter:** put to sale. 326. **of hair:** wearing skins of animals.
327. **Saltiers:** i.e. satyrs (but probably with additional sense "leapers"; *sault* = jump, as in *somersault*).
328. **gallimaufry:** jumble, hodgepodge.
339. **squier:** square, foot-rule. 348. **handed:** was involved in.
352. **nothing marted:** done no business.
353. **Interpretation should abuse:** should misinterpret.
354. **were straited:** would be hard pressed.
355–56. **make . . . her:** are seriously concerned to keep her happy.
358. **looks:** looks for. 364. **bolted:** sifted.

367. **was:** which was. **put you out:** interrupted your recital.
377–78. **Commend . . . perdition:** commend them to her service, or, if denied that, condemn them to destruction.
391. **Soft:** not so fast.
398. **reasonable:** requiring the exercise of reason.
399. **alt'ring rheums:** debilitating diseases.
400. **dispute:** discuss. **estate:** state, condition.
406. **Reason:** it is reasonable that.

But fair posterity) should hold some counsel
In such a business.
Flo. I yield all this;
But for some other reasons, my grave sir,
Which 'tis not fit you know, I not acquaint
My father of this business.
Pol. Let him know't.
Flo. He shall not.
Pol. Prithee let him.
Flo. No, he must not.
Shep. Let him, my son. He shall not need to grieve
At knowing of thy choice.
Flo. Come, come, he must not.
Mark our contract.
Pol. Mark your divorce, young sir,
[*Discovering himself.*]
Whom son I dare not call. Thou art too base
To be [acknowledg'd]. Thou, a sceptre's heir,
That thus affects a sheep-hook! Thou, old traitor,
I am sorry that by hanging thee I can
But shorten thy life one week. And thou, fresh piece
Of excellent witchcraft, whom of force must know
The royal fool thou cop'st with—
Shep. O, my heart!
Pol. I'll have thy beauty scratch'd with briers and made
More homely than thy state. For thee, fond boy,
If I may ever know thou dost but sigh
That thou no more shalt see this knack (as never
I mean thou shalt), we'll bar thee from succession,
Not hold thee of our blood, no, not our kin,
Farre than Deucalion off. Mark thou my words.
Follow us to the court. Thou, churl, for this time,
Though full of our displeasure, yet we free thee
From the dead blow of it. And you, enchantment—
Worthy enough a herdsman, yea, him too,
That makes himself (but for our honor therein)
Unworthy thee—if ever, henceforth, thou
These rural latches to his entrance open,
Or [hoop] his body more with thy embraces,
I will devise a death as cruel for thee
As thou art tender to't. *Exit.*
Per. Even here undone!
I was not much afeard; for once or twice
I was about to speak, and tell him plainly
The self-same sun that shines upon his court
Hides not his visage from our cottage, but
Looks on alike. Will't please you, sir, be gone?
I told you what would come of this. Beseech you
Of your own state take care. This dream of mine

410. **yield**: concede. 418. **dare**: will.
420. **affects**: affectest, desirest.
422–23. **fresh . . . witchcraft**: fair young creature skilled in witchcraft. She is at once bewitchingly beautiful and a wicked witch. In line 434 *enchantment* has precisely the same duality of meaning.
423. **whom of force**: who necessarily. 424. **cop'st**: dealest.
426. **homely**: (1) ugly (with reference to *beauty*); (2) humble (with reference to *state* = station). **fond**: foolish.
428. **knack**: crafty contriver.
431. **Farre . . . off**: more remote in kinship than Deucalion (the Noah of classical myth and hence the ancestor of all mankind).
432. **churl.** He addresses the Shepherd. 434. **dead**: death-dealing.
435. **Worthy**: worthy of.
436. **but . . . therein**: except that my royal honor comes into it, i.e. except that he is the king's son.
448. **Of . . . care**: have a proper care for your high station.

Being now awake, I'll queen it no inch farther,
But milk my ewes, and weep.
Cam. Why, how now, father?
Speak ere thou diest.
Shep. I cannot speak, nor think,
Nor dare to know that which I know. [*To Florizel.*]
O sir,
You have undone a man of fourscore three,
That thought to fill his grave in quiet; yea,
To die upon the bed my father died,
To lie close by his honest bones; but now
Some hangman must put on my shroud and lay me
Where no priest shovels in dust. [*To Perdita.*] O cursed wretch,
That knew'st this was the Prince, and wouldst adventure
To mingle faith with him!—Undone, undone!
If I might die within this hour, I have liv'd
To die when I desire. *Exit.*
Flo. Why look you so upon me?
I am but sorry, not afeard; delay'd,
But nothing alt'red. What I was, I am:
More straining on for plucking back, not following
My leash unwillingly.
Cam. Gracious my lord,
You know [your] father's temper. At this time
He will allow no speech (which I do guess
You do not purpose to him) and as hardly
Will he endure your sight as yet, I fear.
Then till the fury of his Highness settle
Come not before him.
Flo. I not purpose it.
I think Camillo?
Cam. Even he, my lord.
Per. How often have I told you 'twould be thus!
How often said my dignity would last
But till 'twere known!
Flo. It cannot fail, but by
The violation of my faith, and then
Let nature crush the sides o' th' earth together,
And mar the seeds within! Lift up thy looks.
From my succession wipe me, father, I
Am heir to my affection.
Cam. Be advis'd.
Flo. I am—and by my fancy. If my reason
Will thereto be obedient, I have reason;
If not, my senses, better pleas'd with madness,
Do bid it welcome.
Cam. This is desperate, sir.
Flo. So call it; but it does fulfill my vow;
I needs must think it honesty. Camillo,
Not for Bohemia, nor the pomp that may
Be thereat gleaned, for all the sun sees, or
The close earth wombs, or the profound seas hides
In unknown fadoms, will I break my oath
To this my fair belov'd. Therefore, I pray you,
As you have ever been my father's honor'd friend,
When he shall miss me (as, in faith, I mean not

459. **adventure**: dare.
465. **for plucking back**: for having been dragged back.
477. **then**: i.e. when that happens. 481. **Be advis'd**: take thought.
482. **fancy**: love.

To see him any more), cast your good counsels
Upon his passion. Let myself and Fortune
Tug for the time to come. This you may know,
And so deliver: I am put to sea
With her who here I cannot hold on shore;
And most opportune to her need I have
A vessel rides fast by, but not prepar'd
For this design. What course I mean to hold
Shall nothing benefit your knowledge, nor
Concern me the reporting.

Cam. O my lord,
I would your spirit were easier for advice,
Or stronger for your need.

Flo. Hark, Perdita! [*Drawing her aside.*]
[*To Camillo.*] I'll hear you by and by.

Cam. He's irremovable,
Resolv'd for flight. Now were I happy if
His going I could frame to serve my turn,
Save him from danger, do him love and honor,
Purchase the sight again of dear Sicilia
And that unhappy king, my master, whom
I so much thirst to see.

Flo. Now, good Camillo,
I am so fraught with curious business that
I leave out ceremony.

Cam. Sir, I think
You have heard of my poor services, i' th' love
That I have borne your father?

Flo. Very nobly
Have you deserv'd. It is my father's music
To speak your deeds; not little of his care
To have them recompens'd as thought on.

Cam. Well, my lord,
If you may please to think I love the King,
And through him what's nearest to him, which is
Your gracious self, embrace but my direction,
If your more ponderous and settled project
May suffer alteration. On mine honor,
I'll point you where you shall have such receiving
As shall become your Highness, where you may
Enjoy your mistress—from the whom, I see,
There's no disjunction to be made, but by
(As heavens forefend!) your ruin—marry her,
And with my best endeavors in your absence,
Your discontenting father strive to qualify,
And bring him up to liking.

Flo. How, Camillo,
May this (almost a miracle) be done?
That I may call thee something more than man,
And after that trust to thee.

Cam. Have you thought on
A place whereto you'll go?

Flo. Not any yet:
But as th' unthought-on accident is guilty
To what we wildly do, so we profess
Ourselves to be the slaves of chance, and flies
Of every wind that blows.

Cam. Then list to me.
This follows, if you will not change your purpose
But undergo this flight: make for Sicilia,
And there present yourself and your fair princess
(For so I see she must be) 'fore Leontes.
She shall be habited as it becomes
The partner of your bed. Methinks I see
Leontes opening his free arms, and weeping
His welcomes forth; asks thee there, son, forgiveness,
As 'twere i' th' father's person; kisses the hands
Of your fresh princess; o'er and o'er divides him
'Twixt his unkindness and his kindness: th' one
He chides to hell, and bids the other grow
Faster than thought or time.

Flo. Worthy Camillo,
What color for my visitation shall I
Hold up before him?

Cam. Sent by the King your father
To greet him and to give him comforts. Sir,
The manner of your bearing towards him, with
What you (as from your father) shall deliver,
Things known betwixt us three, I'll write you down,
The which shall point you forth at every sitting
What you must say; that he shall not perceive
But that you have your father's bosom there,
And speak his very heart.

Flo. I am bound to you.
There is some sap in this.

Cam. A course more promising
Than a wild dedication of yourselves
To unpath'd waters, undream'd shores, most certain
To miseries enough; no hope to help you,
But as you shake off one, to take another;
Nothing so certain as your anchors, who
Do their best office, if they can but stay you
Where you'll be loath to be. Besides you know,
Prosperity's the very bond of love,
Whose fresh complexion and whose heart together
Affliction alters.

Per. One of these is true:
I think affliction may subdue the cheek,
But not take in the mind.

Cam. Yea? say you so?
There shall not at your father's house these seven years
Be born another such.

Flo. My good Camillo,
She's as forward of her breeding as
She is i' th' rear 'our birth.

497. Tug . . . come: contend for the future.
498. deliver: report.
500. her. Some editors emend to *our*, arguing that the compositor picked up *her* from the preceding line.
505. easier for: more open to. **507. irremovable:** immovable.
514. curious: demanding care.
520. as thought on: in accordance with his high estimation of them.
524. ponderous: weighty. **525. suffer:** admit of.
530. forefend: forfend, forbid.
532. discontenting: discontented, angry. **qualify:** appease.
533. liking: approval.

538–39. as . . . do: i.e. as the unexpected discovery is responsible for whatever course we must rashly undertake.
548. free: generous, welcoming. **555. color:** pretext, explanation.
561. point you forth: direct you. **sitting:** conference.
563. bosom: inmost thoughts.
565. sap: vitality, i.e. promise of success.
573. bond: uniting tie or force. **577. take in:** subdue.
578–79. There . . . such. Probably spoken to Florizel: "Even in the royal palace people of Perdita's quality are not often born." *These seven years* = for a long time to come (not a definite period).
580. forward . . . breeding: far in advance of her upbringing.
581. 'our: of our, i.e. of my.

Cam. I cannot say 'tis pity
She lacks instructions, for she seems a mistress
To most that teach.

Per. Your pardon, sir; for this
I'll blush you thanks.

Flo. My prettiest Perdita!
But O, the thorns we stand upon! Camillo,
Preserver of my father, now of me,
The medicine of our house, how shall we do?
We are not furnish'd like Bohemia's son,
Nor shall appear in Sicilia.

Cam. My lord,
Fear none of this. I think you know my fortunes
Do all lie there. It shall be so my care
To have you royally appointed, as if
The scene you play were mine. For instance, sir,
That you may know you shall not want—one word.

[*They talk aside.*]

Enter AUTOLYCUS [*laughing*].

Aut. Ha, ha, what a fool Honesty is! and Trust, his sworn brother, a very simple gentleman! I have sold all my trompery; not a counterfeit stone, not a ribbon, glass, pomander, brooch, table-book, ballad, knife, tape, glove, shoe-tie, bracelet, horn-ring, to keep my pack from fasting. They throng who should buy first, as if my trinkets had been hallow'd and brought a benediction to the buyer; by which means I saw whose purse was best in picture, and what I saw, to my good use I remember'd. My clown (who wants but something to be a reasonable man) grew so in love with the wenches' song, that he would not stir his pettitoes till he had both tune and words, which so drew the rest of the herd to me that all their other senses stuck in ears. You might have pinch'd a placket, it was senseless; 'twas nothing to geld a codpiece of a purse; I would have fil'd keys off that hung in chains. No hearing, no feeling, but my sir's song, and admiring the nothing of it. So that in this time of lethargy I pick'd and cut most of their festival purses; and had not the old man come in with a whoobub against his daughter and the King's son, and scar'd my choughs from the chaff, I had not left a purse alive in the whole army.

[*Camillo, Florizel, and Perdita come forward.*]

Cam. Nay, but my letters, by this means being there
So soon as you arrive, shall clear that doubt.

Flo. And those that you'll procure from King Leontes?

Cam. Shall satisfy your father.

Per. Happy be you!
All that you speak shows fair.

Cam. Who have we here? [*Seeing Autolycus.*]
We'll make an instrument of this; omit
Nothing may give us aid.

Aut. [*Aside.*] If they have overheard me now—why, hanging.

Cam. How now, good fellow? why shak'st thou so?
Fear not, man, here's no harm intended to thee.

Aut. I am a poor fellow, sir.

Cam. Why, be so still; here's nobody will steal that from thee. Yet for the outside of thy poverty we must make an exchange; therefore discase thee instantly (thou must think there's a necessity in't) and change garments with this gentleman. Though the pennyworth on his side be the worst, yet hold thee, there's some boot. [*Giving money.*]

Aut. I am a poor fellow, sir. [*Aside.*] I know ye well enough.

Cam. Nay, prithee dispatch. The gentleman is half [flea'd] already.

Aut. Are you in earnest, sir? [*Aside.*] I smell the trick on't.

Flo. Dispatch, I prithee.

Aut. Indeed I have had earnest, but I cannot with conscience take it.

Cam. Unbuckle, unbuckle.

[*Florizel and Autolycus exchange garments.*]

Fortunate mistress (let my prophecy
Come home to ye!), you must retire yourself
Into some covert. Take your sweetheart's hat
And pluck it o'er your brows, muffle your face,
Dismantle you, and (as you can) disliken
The truth of your own seeming, that you may
(For I do fear eyes over) to shipboard
Get undescried.

Per. I see the play so lies
That I must bear a part.

Cam. No remedy.
Have you done there?

Flo. Should I now meet my father,
He would not call me son.

Cam. Nay, you shall have no hat.
[*Giving it to Perdita.*]
Come, lady, come. Farewell, my friend.

Aut. Adieu, sir.

Flo. O Perdita! what have we twain forgot?
Pray you a word.

Cam. [*Aside.*] What I do next shall be to tell the King
Of this escape, and whither they are bound;
Wherein my hope is I shall so prevail
To force him after; in whose company
I shall re-view Sicilia, for whose sight
I have a woman's longing.

Flo. Fortune speed us!
Thus we set on, Camillo, to th' sea-side.

587. medicine: restorative. **589. appear:** appear so.
597. trompery: trumpery, cheap wares.
598. pomander: scent-ball. **table-book:** notebook.
601. hallow'd: sacred, like holy relics. **603. picture:** looks.
605. wants but something: lacks only one thing.
607. pettitoes: toes (of a pig).
609. stuck in ears: were devoted to listening.
610. senseless: insensible.
611. codpiece: baglike flap on the front of Elizabethan breeches.
613. nothing: nonsense (with pun on *noting*, i.e. tune, pronounced similarly). **614. lethargy:** coma. **616. whoobub:** hubbub.
617. choughs: crows or jackdaws.

632. outside . . . poverty: i.e. your ragged clothes.
633. discase: undress. **635–36. pennyworth:** bargain.
637. some boot: something in addition.
640. dispatch: make haste.
641. flea'd: flayed, skinned, i.e. undressed.
645. earnest: first payment.
648–49. let . . . ye: i.e. may I prove a true prophet in calling you fortunate. **652. disliken:** alter, falsify.
654. eyes over: spying eyes.

Cam. The swifter speed the better.

Exit [with Florizel and Perdita].

Aut. I understand the business, I hear it. To have an open ear, a quick eye, and a nimble hand, is necessary for a cutpurse; a good nose is requisite also, to smell out work for th' other senses. I see this is the time that the unjust man doth thrive. What an exchange had this been, without boot! What a boot is here, with this exchange! Sure the gods do this year connive at us, and we may do any thing extempore. The Prince himself is about a piece of iniquity: stealing away from his father with his clog at his heels. If I thought it were a piece of honesty to acquaint the King withal, I would not do't. I hold it the more knavery to conceal it; and therein am I constant to my profession.

Enter CLOWN *and* SHEPHERD.

Aside, aside, here is more matter for a hot brain. Every lane's end, every shop, church, session, hanging, yields a careful man work.

Clo. See, see; what a man you are now! There is no other way but to tell the King she's a changeling, and none of your flesh and blood.

Shep. Nay, but hear me.

Clo. Nay—but hear me.

Shep. Go to then.

Clo. She being none of your flesh and blood, your flesh and blood has not offended the King, and so your flesh and blood is not to be punish'd by him. Show those things you found about her, those secret things, all but what she has with her. This being done, let the law go whistle; I warrant you.

Shep. I will tell the King all, every word, yea, and his son's pranks too; who, I may say, is no honest man, neither to his father nor to me, to go about to make me the King's brother-in-law.

Clo. Indeed brother-in-law was the farthest off you could have been to him, and then your blood had been the dearer by I know how much an ounce.

Aut. [*Aside.*] Very wisely, puppies!

Shep. Well; let us to the King. There is that in this farthel will make him scratch his beard.

Aut. [*Aside.*] I know not what impediment this complaint may be to the flight of my master.

Clo. Pray heartily he be at' palace.

Aut. [*Aside.*] Though I am not naturally honest, I am so sometimes by chance. Let me pocket up my pedlar's excrement. [*Takes off his false beard.*] How now, rustics, whither are you bound?

Shep. To th' palace, and it like your worship.

Aut. Your affairs there? what? with whom? the condition of that farthel? the place of your dwelling? your names? your ages? of what having? breeding? and any thing that is fitting to be known—discover.

Clo. We are but plain fellows, sir.

675. **without:** even without.
679. **clog:** impediment (slang for a wife). 681. **withal:** with it.
692. **to:** ahead. 708. **farthel:** bundle. 711. **at':** at the.
714. **excrement:** outgrowth (of hair). 716. **and it like:** if it please.
719. **having:** property.
721. **plain.** With following pun on the sense "smooth."

Aut. A lie; you are rough and hairy. Let me have no lying. It becomes none but tradesmen, and they often give us soldiers the lie, but we pay them for it with stamped coin, not stabbing steel, therefore they do not give us the lie.

Clo. Your worship had like to have given us one, if you had not taken yourself with the manner.

Shep. Are you a courtier, and't like you, sir?

Aut. Whether it like me or no, I am a courtier. Seest thou not the air of the court in these enfoldings? Hath not my gait in it the measure of the court? Receives not thy nose court-odor from me? Reflect I not on thy baseness court-contempt? Think'st thou, for that I insinuate, [that] toze from thee thy business, I am therefore no courtier? I am courtier cap-a-pe, and one that will either push on or pluck back thy business there; whereupon I command thee to open thy affair.

Shep. My business, sir, is to the King.

Aut. What advocate hast thou to him?

Shep. I know not, and't like you.

Clo. Advocate's the court-word for a pheasant. Say you have none.

Shep. None, sir; I have no pheasant cock, nor hen.

Aut. How blessed are we that are not simple men!
Yet nature might have made me as these are,
Therefore I will not disdain.

Clo. This cannot be but a great courtier.

Shep. His garments are rich, but he wears them not handsomely.

Clo. He seems to be the more noble in being fantastical. A great man, I'll warrant; I know by the picking on 's teeth.

Aut. The farthel there? What's i' th' farthel? Wherefore that box?

Shep. Sir, there lies such secrets in this farthel and box, which none must know but the King, and which he shall know within this hour, if I may come to th' speech of him.

Aut. Age, thou hast lost thy labor.

Shep. Why, sir?

Aut. The King is not at the palace. He is gone aboard a new ship to purge melancholy and air himself; for if thou be'st capable of things serious, thou must know the King is full of grief.

Shep. So 'tis said, sir—about his son, that should have married a shepherd's daughter.

Aut. If that shepherd be not in hand-fast, let him fly. The curses he shall have, the tortures he shall feel, will break the back of man, the heart of monster.

Clo. Think you so, sir?

724. **give . . . lie:** (1) practice a deception on us; (2) call us liar (hence Autolycus' reference to "stabbing steel," the soldier's revenge for an insult).
725. **therefore:** i.e. because we pay for it (and so they cannot be said to give it).
727–28. **Your . . . manner:** i.e. you almost told us an untruth (i.e. that the tradesmen had *given* you the lie) but you caught yourself in time. *With the manner* = in the act. 731–32. **enfoldings:** garments.
732. **measure:** stately stride.
735. **insinuate:** pry. **toze:** tease out.
736. **cap-a-pe:** from head to foot.
742. **pheasant.** The Clown confuses the two kinds of court. A pheasant or other bird was often given as a bribe to a judge.
764. **if . . . capable of:** if you know anything about.
768. **hand-fast:** custody.

Aut. Not he alone shall suffer what wit can make heavy and vengeance bitter; but those that are germane to him (though remov'd fifty times) shall all come under the hangman; which though it be great pity, yet it is necessary. An old sheep-whistling rogue, a ram-tender, to offer to have his daughter come into grace! Some say he shall be ston'd; but that death is too soft for him, say I. Draw our throne into a sheep-cote!—all deaths are too few, the sharpest too easy.

Clo. Has the old man e'er a son, sir, do you hear, and't like you, sir?

Aut. He has a son, who shall be flay'd alive; then 'nointed over with honey, set on the head of a wasp's nest; then stand till he be three quarters and a dram dead; then recover'd again with aqua-vitae or some other hot infusion; then, raw as he is (and in the hottest day prognostication proclaims), shall he be set against a brick-wall, the sun looking with a southward eye upon him, where he is to behold him with flies blown to death. But what talk we of these traitorly rascals, whose miseries are to be smil'd at, their offenses being so capital? Tell me (for you seem to be honest plain men) what you have to the King. Being something gently consider'd, I'll bring you where he is aboard, tender your persons to his presence, whisper him in your behalfs; and if it be in man besides the King to effect your suits, here is man shall do it.

Clo. He seems to be of great authority. Close with him, give him gold; and though authority be a stubborn bear, yet he is oft led by the nose with gold. Show the inside of your purse to the outside of his hand, and no more ado. Remember "ston'd," and "flay'd alive."

Shep. And't please you, sir, to undertake the business for us, here is that gold I have. I'll make it as much more, and leave this young man in pawn till I bring it you.

Aut. After I have done what I promis'd?

Shep. Ay, sir.

Aut. Well, give me the moi'ty. Are you a party in this business?

Clo. In some sort, sir; but though my case be a pitiful one, I hope I shall not be flay'd out of it.

Aut. O, that's the case of the shepherd's son. Hang him, he'll be made an example.

Clo. Comfort, good comfort! We must to the King, and show our strange sights. He must know 'tis none of your daughter, nor my sister; we are gone else. Sir, I will give you as much as this old man does when the business is perform'd, and remain (as he says) your pawn till it be brought you.

Aut. I will trust you. Walk before toward the sea-side, go on the right hand, I will but look upon the hedge, and follow you.

Clo. We are bless'd in this man, as I may say, even bless'd.

Shep. Let's before, as he bids us. He was provided to do us good. [*Exeunt Shepherd and Clown.*]

Aut. If I had a mind to be honest, I see Fortune would not suffer me: she drops booties in my mouth. I am courted now with a double occasion: gold and a means to do the Prince my master good; which who knows how that may turn back to my advancement? I will bring these two moles, these blind ones, aboard him. If he think it fit to shore them again, and that the complaint they have to the King concerns him nothing, let him call me rogue for being so far officious, for I am proof against that title, and what shame else belongs to't. To him will I present them, there may be matter in it. *Exit.*

772. **wit**: ingenuity. 773. **germane**: related.
776. **sheep-whistling**: whistling after (i.e. tending) sheep.
778. **grace**: favor. 785. **a dram**: i.e. a little more.
786. **aqua-vitae**: brandy.
788. **prognostication**: prediction in the almanac.
790–91. **with . . . death.** A kind of punishment the Spaniards used on Negroes and Indians.
794–95. **Being . . . consider'd**: for a gentlemanly consideration, i.e. a generous bribe.
800. **Close**: come to an agreement. 812. **moi'ty**: half.
814. **case**: (1) plight; (2) skin. 820. **gone else**: done for otherwise.
833. **occasion**: opportunity.
837. **aboard him**: to him aboard his ship. **shore**: put ashore.
840. **proof against**: invulnerable to.

ACT V, SCENE I

Enter LEONTES, CLEOMINES, DION, PAULINA, SERVANTS.

Cleo. Sir, you have done enough, and have perform'd
A saint-like sorrow. No fault could you make
Which you have not redeem'd; indeed paid down
More penitence than done trespass. At the last
Do as the heavens have done, forget your evil,
With them, forgive yourself.

Leon. Whilest I remember
Her and her virtues, I cannot forget
My blemishes in them, and so still think of
The wrong I did myself; which was so much
That heirless it hath made my kingdom, and
Destroy'd the sweet'st companion that e'er man
Bred his hopes out of.

Paul. True, too true, my lord.
If, one by one, you wedded all the world,
Or, from the all that are, took something good
To make a perfect woman, she you kill'd
Would be unparallel'd.

Leon. I think so. Kill'd?
She I kill'd? I did so; but thou strik'st me
Sorely, to say I did. It is as bitter
Upon thy tongue as in my thought. Now, good now,
Say so but seldom.

Cleo. Not at all, good lady.
You might have spoken a thousand things that would
Have done the time more benefit, and grac'd
Your kindness better.

Paul. You are one of those
Would have him wed again.

Dion. If you would not so,
You pity not the state, nor the remembrance
Of his most sovereign name; consider little

V.1. Location: Sicilia. The palace of Leontes.
19. **good now**: i.e. please. 22. **grac'd**: befitted.
25. **remembrance**: perpetuation (through an heir).

What dangers, by his Highness' fail of issue,
May drop upon his kingdom, and devour
Incertain lookers-on. What were more holy
Than to rejoice the former queen is well?
What holier than, for royalty's repair,
For present comfort, and for future good,
To bless the bed of majesty again
With a sweet fellow to't?

Paul. There is none worthy,
Respecting her that's gone. Besides, the gods
Will have fulfill'd their secret purposes;
For has not the divine Apollo said,
Is't not the tenor of his oracle,
That King Leontes shall not have an heir
Till his lost child be found? Which that it shall,
Is all as monstrous to our human reason
As my Antigonus to break his grave,
And come again to me; who, on my life,
Did perish with the infant. 'Tis your counsel
My lord should to the heavens be contrary,
Oppose against their wills. [*To Leontes.*] Care not for issue,
The crown will find an heir. Great Alexander
Left his to th' worthiest; so his successor
Was like to be the best.

Leon. Good Paulina,
Who hast the memory of Hermione,
I know, in honor, O, that ever I
Had squar'd me to thy counsel! then, even now,
I might have look'd upon my queen's full eyes,
Have taken treasure from her lips—

Paul. And left them
More rich for what they yielded.

Leon. Thou speak'st truth:
No more such wives, therefore no wife. One worse,
And better us'd, would make her sainted spirit
Again possess her corpse, and on this stage
(Where we offenders now) appear soul-vex'd,
And begin, "Why to me—?"

Paul. Had she such power,
She had just cause.

Leon. She had, and would incense me
To murther her I married.

Paul. I should so:
Were I the ghost that walk'd, I'ld bid you mark
Her eye, and tell me for what dull part in't
You chose her; then I'ld shriek, that even your ears
Should rift to hear me, and the words that follow'd
Should be "Remember mine."

Leon. Stars, stars,
And all eyes else dead coals! Fear thou no wife;
I'll have no wife, Paulina.

Paul. Will you swear
Never to marry but by my free leave?

Leon. Never, Paulina, so be bless'd my spirit!

Paul. Then, good my lords, bear witness to his oath.

Cleo. You tempt him overmuch.

Paul. Unless another,
As like Hermione as is her picture,
Affront his eye.

Cleo. Good madam—

Paul. I have done.
Yet if my lord will marry—if you will, sir,
No remedy but you will—give me the office
To choose you a queen. She shall not be so young
As was your former, but she shall be such
As (walk'd your first queen's ghost) it should take joy
To see her in your arms.

Leon. My true Paulina,
We shall not marry till thou bid'st us.

Paul. That
Shall be when your first queen's again in breath;
Never till then.

Enter a SERVANT.

Serv. One that gives out himself Prince Florizel,
Son of Polixenes, with his princess (she
The fairest I have yet beheld), desires access
To your high presence.

Leon. What with him? He comes not
Like to his father's greatness. His approach,
So out of circumstance and sudden, tells us
'Tis not a visitation fram'd, but forc'd
By need and accident. What train?

Serv. But few,
And those but mean.

Leon. His princess, say you, with him?

Serv. Ay; the most peerless piece of earth, I think,
That e'er the sun shone bright on.

Paul. O Hermione,
As every present time doth boast itself
Above a better gone, so must thy grave
Give way to what's seen now! Sir, you yourself
Have said and writ so, but your writing now
Is colder than that theme, "She had not been,
Nor was not to be equall'd"—thus your verse
Flow'd with her beauty once. 'Tis shrewdly ebb'd,
To say you have seen a better.

Serv. Pardon, madam:
The one I have almost forgot—your pardon—
The other, when she has obtain'd your eye,
Will have your tongue too. This is a creature,
Would she begin a sect, might quench the zeal
Of all professors else, make proselytes
Of who she but bid follow.

Paul. How? not women?

Serv. Women will love her, that she is a woman
More worth than any man; men, that she is
The rarest of all women.

Leon. Go, Cleomines;

29. Incertain lookers-on: i.e. citizens who cannot decide between rival claimants of the crown. **30. well:** i.e. in heaven.
35. Respecting: compared to.
36. have . . . purposes: have their secret purposes fulfilled.
41. monstrous: unnatural, i.e. incredible.
46. Care not for: do not be anxious about.
52. squar'd me to: ruled myself by. **59. now:** i.e. now are.
66. rift: split.
73. tempt: press. **75. Affront:** confront.
88. What: who, what company.
90. out of circumstance: without ceremony.
91. fram'd: planned. **93. mean:** of low rank.
94. piece of earth: mortal. **102. shrewdly:** grievously.
108. all professors else: all who professed other faiths, i.e. worshippers of all other deities.

Yourself, assisted with your honor'd friends,
Bring them to our embracement.
Exeunt [*Cleomines and others*].
Still, 'tis strange
He thus should steal upon us.
Paul. Had our prince,
Jewel of children, seen this hour, he had pair'd
Well with this lord; there was not full a month
Between their births.
Leon. Prithee no more; cease. Thou know'st
He dies to me again when talk'd of. Sure
When I shall see this gentleman, thy speeches
Will bring me to consider that which may
Unfurnish me of reason. They are come.

Enter FLORIZEL, PERDITA, CLEOMINES, *and others.*

Your mother was most true to wedlock, Prince,
For she did print your royal father off,
Conceiving you. Were I but twenty-one,
Your father's image is so hit in you
(His very air) that I should call you brother,
As I did him, and speak of something wildly
By us perform'd before. Most dearly welcome!
And your fair princess—goddess! O! alas,
I lost a couple, that 'twixt heaven and earth
Might thus have stood, begetting wonder, as
You, gracious couple, do; and then I lost
(All mine own folly) the society,
Amity too, of your brave father, whom
(Though bearing misery) I desire my life
Once more to look on him.
Flo. By his command
Have I here touch'd Sicilia, and from him
Give you all greetings that a king (at friend)
Can send his brother; and but infirmity
(Which waits upon worn times) hath something seiz'd
His wish'd ability, he had himself
The lands and waters 'twixt your throne and his
Measur'd to look upon you; whom he loves
(He bade me say so) more than all the sceptres,
And those that bear them, living.
Leon. O my brother,
Good gentleman! the wrongs I have done thee stir
Afresh within me, and these thy offices,
So rarely kind, are as interpreters
Of my behind-hand slackness.—Welcome hither,
As is the spring to th' earth. And hath he too
Expos'd this paragon to th' fearful usage
(At least ungentle) of the dreadful Neptune,
To greet a man not worth her pains, much less
Th' adventure of her person?
Flo. Good my lord,
She came from Libya.

123. **Unfurnish**: divest.
127. **hit**: precisely achieved. 129. **wildly**: madly, exuberantly.
137. **my life**: i.e. to go on living long enough.
138. **him.** Redundant in modern syntax.
140. **at friend**: in friendship. 141. **but**: except for the fact that.
142. **waits . . . times**: attends old age.
142–43. **seiz'd . . . ability**: i.e. reduced his strength to less than he would wish it. 145. **Measur'd**: journeyed over.
149. **offices**: attentions. 150. **rarely**: extraordinarily.
150–51. **interpreters Of**: commentators on.
156. **adventure**: hazard.

Leon. Where the warlike Smalus,
That noble honor'd lord, is fear'd and lov'd?
Flo. Most royal sir, from thence; from him, whose daughter
His tears proclaim'd his, parting with her; thence
(A prosperous south-wind friendly) we have cross'd,
To execute the charge my father gave me
For visiting your Highness. My best train
I have from your Sicilian shores dismiss'd;
Who for Bohemia bend, to signify
Not only my success in Libya, sir,
But my arrival, and my wife's, in safety
Here, where we are.
Leon. The blessed gods
Purge all infection from our air whilest you
Do climate here! You have a holy father,
A graceful gentleman, against whose person
(So sacred as it is) I have done sin,
For which the heavens, taking angry note,
Have left me issueless; and your father's bless'd
(As he from heaven merits it) with you,
Worthy his goodness. What might I have been,
Might I a son and daughter now have look'd on,
Such goodly things as you?

Enter a LORD.

Lord. Most noble sir,
That which I shall report will bear no credit,
Were not the proof so nigh. Please you, great sir,
Bohemia greets you from himself by me;
Desires you to attach his son, who has
(His dignity and duty both cast off)
Fled from his father, from his hopes, and with
A shepherd's daughter.
Leon. Where's Bohemia? speak.
Lord. Here, in your city; I now came from him.
I speak amazedly, and it becomes
My marvel and my message. To your court
Whiles he was hast'ning (in the chase, it seems,
Of this fair couple), meets he on the way
The father of this seeming lady, and
Her brother, having both their country quitted
With this young prince.
Flo. Camillo has betray'd me;
Whose honor and whose honesty till now
Endur'd all weathers.
Lord. Lay't so to his charge:
He's with the King your father.
Leon. Who? Camillo?
Lord. Camillo, sir; I spake with him; who now
Has these poor men in question. Never saw I
Wretches so quake: they kneel, they kiss the earth;
Forswear themselves as often as they speak.
Bohemia stops his ears, and threatens them
With divers deaths in death.

170. **climate**: reside. 171. **graceful**: full of noble qualities.
182. **attach**: arrest.
183. **dignity and duty**: i.e. obligations as a prince and as a son.
187. **amazedly**: confusedly.
187–88. **it . . . message**: my confused speech befits my bewilderment and the news I have to tell. 198. **in question**: under examination.
199. **kiss the earth**: i.e. abase themselves on the ground.
202. **deaths in death**: tortures.

Per. O my poor father!
The heaven sets spies upon us, will not have
Our contract celebrated.
Leon. You are married?
Flo. We are not, sir, nor are we like to be.
The stars, I see, will kiss the valleys first;
The odds for high and low's alike.
Leon. My lord,
Is this the daughter of a king?
Flo. She is,
When once she is my wife.
Leon. That "once," I see, by your good father's speed,
Will come on very slowly. I am sorry,
Most sorry, you have broken from his liking,
Where you were tied in duty; and as sorry
Your choice is not so rich in worth as beauty,
That you might well enjoy her.
Flo. Dear, look up.
Though Fortune, visible an enemy,
Should chase us with my father, pow'r no jot
Hath she to change our loves. Beseech you, sir,
Remember since you ow'd no more to time
Than I do now. With thought of such affections,
Step forth mine advocate. At your request
My father will grant precious things as trifles.
Leon. Would he do so, I'ld beg your precious mistress,
Which he counts but a trifle.
Paul. Sir, my liege,
Your eye hath too much youth in't. Not a month
'Fore your queen died, she was more worth such gazes
Than what you look on now.
Leon. I thought of her,
Even in these looks I made. [*To Florizel.*] But your petition
Is yet unanswer'd. I will to your father.
Your honor not o'erthrown by your desires,
I am friend to them and you. Upon which errand
I now go toward him; therefore follow me,
And mark what way I make. Come, good my lord.
Exeunt.

Scene II

Enter Autolycus *and a* Gentleman.

Aut. Beseech you, sir, were you present at this relation?

1. Gent. I was by at the opening of the farthel, heard the old shepherd deliver the manner how he found it; whereupon, after a little amazedness, we were all commanded out of the chamber; only this, methought, I heard the shepherd say, he found the child.

Aut. I would most gladly know the issue of it.

1. Gent. I make a broken delivery of the business; but the changes I perceiv'd in the King and Camillo were very notes of admiration. They seem'd almost, with staring on one another, to tear the cases of their eyes. There was speech in their dumbness, language in their very gesture; they look'd as they had heard of a world ransom'd, or one destroy'd. A notable passion of wonder appear'd in them; but the wisest beholder, that knew no more but seeing, could not say if th' importance were joy or sorrow; but in the extremity of the one, it must needs be.

Enter another Gentleman.

Here comes a gentleman that happily knows more. The news, Rogero?

2. Gent. Nothing but bonfires. The oracle is fulfill'd; the King's daughter is found. Such a deal of wonder is broken out within this hour that ballad-makers cannot be able to express it.

Enter another Gentleman.

Here comes the Lady Paulina's steward, he can deliver you more. How goes it now, sir? This news, which is call'd true, is so like an old tale, that the verity of it is in strong suspicion. Has the King found his heir?

3. Gent. Most true, if ever truth were pregnant by circumstance. That which you hear you'll swear you see, there is such unity in the proofs. The mantle of Queen Hermione's; her jewel about the neck of it; the letters of Antigonus found with it, which they know to be his character; the majesty of the creature in resemblance of the mother; the affection of nobleness which nature shows above her breeding; and many other evidences proclaim her, with all certainty, to be the King's daughter. Did you see the meeting of the two kings?

2. Gent. No.

3. Gent. Then have you lost a sight which was to be seen, cannot be spoken of. There might you have beheld one joy crown another, so and in such manner that it seem'd sorrow wept to take leave of them, for their joy waded in tears. There was casting up of eyes, holding up of hands, with countenance of such distraction that they were to be known by garment, not by favor. Our king, being ready to leap out of himself for joy of his found daughter, as if that joy were now become a loss, cries, "O, thy mother, thy mother!"; then asks Bohemia forgiveness; then embraces his son-in-law; then again worries he his daughter with clipping her. Now he thanks the old shepherd, which stands by like a weather-bitten

207. The odds . . . alike: i.e. prince and shepherdess are equally the playthings of fortune (?). If *high and low* includes also the meaning "false dice," the implication is that fortune is a cheater against whom it is impossible to win. **214. worth:** rank.
219–20. since . . . now: when you were my age.
220. With . . . affections: recalling how it felt to be in love.
230. Your . . . desires: if your desires are not incompatible with your honor (?) or if your passion has not prematurely overcome your chastity (?). **233. way:** progress.

V.ii. Location: Sicilia. Before the palace of Leontes.
4. deliver: report.

9. broken: fragmentary.
11. notes of admiration: exclamation marks (*admiration* = wonder).
12. cases: lids. **17. seeing:** what he saw.
18. importance: import.
18–19. in . . . be: it was certainly the extreme degree of one or the other. **20. happily:** haply, perhaps.
30–31. pregnant by circumstance: made convincing by detailed evidence. **35. character:** handwriting.
36. affection of: natural inclination toward.
37. breeding: rearing.
47. countenance: demeanor (?) or countenances (?).
47–48. of such distraction: so altered by emotion.
49. favor: face, features. **54. clipping:** embracing.

conduit of many kings' reigns. I never heard of such another encounter, which lames report to follow it, and undoes description to do it.

2. Gent. What, pray you, became of Antigonus, that carried hence the child?

3. Gent. Like an old tale still, which will have matter to rehearse, though credit be asleep and not an ear open: he was torn to pieces with a bear. This avouches the shepherd's son, who has not only his innocence (which seems much) to justify him, but a handkerchief and rings of his that Paulina knows.

1. Gent. What became of his bark and his followers?

3. Gent. Wrack'd the same instant of their master's death, and in the view of the shepherd; so that all the instruments which aided to expose the child were even then lost when it was found. But O, the noble combat that 'twixt joy and sorrow was fought in Paulina! She had one eye declin'd for the loss of her husband, another elevated that the oracle was fulfill'd. She lifted the Princess from the earth, and so locks her in embracing, as if she would pin her to her heart, that she might no more be in danger of losing.

1. Gent. The dignity of this act was worth the audience of kings and princes, for by such was it acted.

3. Gent. One of the prettiest touches of all, and that which angled for mine eyes (caught the water though not the fish), was when, at the relation of the Queen's death (with the manner how she came to't bravely confess'd and lamented by the King), how attentiveness wounded his daughter, till (from one sign of dolor to another) she did (with an "Alas!"), I would fain say, bleed tears; for I am sure my heart wept blood. Who was most marble there chang'd color; some swounded, all sorrow'd. If all the world could have seen't, the woe had been universal.

1. Gent. Are they return'd to the court?

3. Gent. No. The Princess hearing of her mother's statue, which is in the keeping of Paulina—a piece many years in doing and now newly perform'd by that rare Italian master, Julio Romano, who, had he himself eternity and could put breath into his work, would beguile Nature of her custom, so perfectly he is her ape. He so near to Hermione hath done Hermione that they say one would speak to her and stand in hope of answer. Thither with all greediness of affection are they gone, and there they intend to sup.

2. Gent. I thought she had some great matter there in hand, for she hath privately twice or thrice a day, ever since the death of Hermione, visited that remov'd house. Shall we thither, and with our company piece the rejoicing?

56. conduit: i.e. because he is weeping too.
58. do: i.e. describe; *undoes . . . it* = utterly defies description.
62. credit: belief. **63. with:** by.
65. innocence: simple-mindedness.
78. she: i.e. Perdita. **losing:** being lost.
86. attentiveness: listening to it. **96. perform'd:** completed.
97. Julio Romano: the name of an actual Italian artist (died 1546).
99. beguile . . . custom: drive Nature out of business.
100. ape: imitator.
102–3. greediness of affection: i.e. eagerness arising out of love.
103. sup. Perhaps concluding the figure in *greediness*—satisfy their hunger to see it. **108. piece:** augment.

1. Gent. Who would be thence that has the benefit of access? Every wink of an eye some new grace will be born. Our absence makes us unthrifty to our knowledge. Let's along. *Exeunt [Gentlemen].*

Aut. Now, had I not the dash of my former life in me, would preferment drop on my head. I brought the old man and his son aboard the Prince; told him I heard them talk of a farthel, and I know not what; but he at that time, overfond of the shepherd's daughter (so he then took her to be), who began to be much sea-sick, and himself little better, extremity of weather continuing, this mystery remain'd undiscover'd. But 'tis all one to me; for had I been the finder-out of this secret, it would not have relish'd among my other discredits.

Enter Shepherd *and* Clown.

Here come those I have done good to against my will, and already appearing in the blossoms of their fortune.

Shep. Come, boy, I am past moe children, but thy sons and daughters will be all gentlemen born.

Clo. You are well met, sir. You denied to fight with me this other day, because I was no gentleman born. See you these clothes? Say you see them not and think me still no gentleman born. You were best say these robes are not gentlemen born. Give me the lie, do; and try whether I am not now a gentleman born.

Aut. I know you are now, sir, a gentleman born.

Clo. Ay, and have been so any time these four hours.

Shep. And so have I, boy.

Clo. So you have. But I was a gentleman born before my father; for the King's son took me by the hand, and call'd me brother; and then the two kings call'd my father brother; and then the Prince, my brother, and the Princess, my sister, call'd my father father; and so we wept; and there was the first gentleman-like tears that ever we shed.

Shep. We may live, son, to shed many more.

Clo. Ay; or else 'twere hard luck, being in so preposterous estate as we are.

Aut. I humbly beseech you, sir, to pardon me all the faults I have committed to your worship, and to give me your good report to the Prince my master.

Shep. Prithee, son, do; for we must be gentle, now we are gentlemen.

Clo. Thou wilt amend thy life?

Aut. Ay, and it like your good worship.

Clo. Give me thy hand: I will swear to the Prince thou art as honest a true fellow as any is in Bohemia.

Shep. You may say it, but not swear it.

Clo. Not swear it, now I am a gentleman? Let boors and franklins say it, I'll swear it.

Shep. How if it be false, son?

Clo. If it be ne'er so false, a true gentleman may

111–12. unthrifty . . . knowledge: wasteful of a chance to increase our store of knowledge. **113. dash:** black mark, stain.
122. relish'd: had a pleasing taste.
148. preposterous: blunder for *prosperous* (but closer to the truth than the Clown knows).
157. honest . . . true: worthy . . . honest.
160. boors and franklins: peasants and small landowners.

swear it in the behalf of his friend; and I'll swear to the Prince thou art a tall fellow of thy hands, and that thou wilt not be drunk; but I know thou art no tall fellow of thy hands, and that thou wilt be drunk; but I'll swear it, and I would thou wouldst be a tall fellow of thy hands.

Aut. I will prove so, sir, to my power.

Clo. Ay, by any means prove a tall fellow. If I do not wonder how thou dar'st venture to be drunk, not being a tall fellow, trust me not. Hark, the kings and the princes, our kindred, are going to see the Queen's picture. Come, follow us; we'll be thy good masters.
Exeunt.

Scene III

Enter Leontes, Polixenes, Florizel, Perdita, Camillo, Paulina, Lords, *etc.*

Leon. O grave and good Paulina, the great comfort
That I have had of thee!
Paul. What, sovereign sir,
I did not well, I meant well. All my services
You have paid home; but that you have vouchsaf'd,
With your crown'd brother and these your contracted
Heirs of your kingdoms, my poor house to visit,
It is a surplus of your grace, which never
My life may last to answer.
Leon. O Paulina,
We honor you with trouble; but we came
To see the statue of our queen. Your gallery
Have we pass'd through, not without much content
In many singularities; but we saw not
That which my daughter came to look upon,
The statue of her mother.
Paul. As she liv'd peerless,
So her dead likeness, I do well believe,
Excels what ever yet you look'd upon,
Or hand of man hath done; therefore I keep it
[Lonely], apart. But here it is; prepare
To see the life as lively mock'd as ever
Still sleep mock'd death. Behold, and say 'tis well.
[*Paulina draws a curtain, and discovers*] *Hermione*
[*standing*] *like a statue.*
I like your silence, it the more shows off
Your wonder; but yet speak. First, you, my liege;
Comes it not something near?
Leon. Her natural posture!
Chide me, dear stone, that I may say indeed
Thou art Hermione; or rather, thou art she
In thy not chiding; for she was as tender
As infancy and grace. But yet, Paulina,
Hermione was not so much wrinkled, nothing
So aged as this seems.
Pol. O, not by much.
Paul. So much the more our carver's excellence,
Which lets go by some sixteen years, and makes her
As she liv'd now.
Leon. As now she might have done,
So much to my good comfort as it is
Now piercing to my soul. O, thus she stood,
Even with such life of majesty (warm life,
As now it coldly stands), when first I woo'd her!
I am asham'd; does not the stone rebuke me
For being more stone than it? O royal piece,
There's magic in thy majesty, which has
My evils conjur'd to remembrance, and
From thy admiring daughter took the spirits,
Standing like stone with thee.
Per. And give me leave,
And do not say 'tis superstition, that
I kneel, and then implore her blessing. Lady,
Dear queen, that ended when I but began,
Give me that hand of yours to kiss.
Paul. O, patience!
The statue is but newly fix'd; the color's
Not dry.
Cam. My lord, your sorrow was too sore laid on,
Which sixteen winters cannot blow away,
So many summers dry. Scarce any joy
Did ever so long live; no sorrow
But kill'd itself much sooner.
Pol. Dear my brother,
Let him that was the cause of this have pow'r
To take off so much grief from you as he
Will piece up in himself.
Paul. Indeed, my lord,
If I had thought the sight of my poor image
Would thus have wrought you (for the stone is mine),
I'ld not have show'd it.
Leon. Do not draw the curtain.
Paul. No longer shall you gaze on't, lest your fancy
May think anon it moves.
Leon. Let be, let be.
Would I were dead but that methinks already—
What was he that did make it? See, my lord,
Would you not deem it breath'd? and that those veins
Did verily bear blood?
Pol. Masterly done!
The very life seems warm upon her lip.
Leon. The fixure of her eye has motion in't,
As we are mock'd with art.
Paul. I'll draw the curtain.
My lord's almost so far transported that
He'll think anon it lives.
Leon. O sweet Paulina,
Make me to think so twenty years together!
No settled senses of the world can match
The pleasure of that madness. Let't alone.

164. tall . . . hands: valiant fellow.
169. to my power: to the best of my ability.

V.iii. Location: Sicilia. Paulina's house.
4. paid home: rewarded fully.
8. last to answer: last long enough for me to make an adequate return. **12. singularities:** rarities.
19. lively mock'd: realistically imitated.

38. piece: work of art.
40. conjur'd: summoned up (as a magician summons evil spirits).
41. admiring: wonderstruck. **spirits:** vital forces.
47. fix'd: i.e. painted.
56. piece . . . himself: make part of himself.
58. wrought: moved.
62. but . . . already: if it doesn't seem to me already (that it moves).
67. The fixure . . . in't: i.e. her eye, though stationary, seems to move.
68. As . . . with: in such a way that we are deluded by.
72. settled: stable, sane.

Paul. I am sorry, sir, I have thus far stirr'd you; but
I could afflict you farther.
Leon. Do, Paulina;
For this affliction has a taste as sweet
As any cordial comfort. Still methinks
There is an air comes from her. What fine chisel
Could ever yet cut breath? Let no man mock me,
For I will kiss her.
Paul. Good my lord, forbear.
The ruddiness upon her lip is wet;
You'll mar it if you kiss it; stain your own
With oily painting. Shall I draw the curtain?
Leon. No! not these twenty years.
Per. So long could I
Stand by, a looker-on.
Paul. Either forbear,
Quit presently the chapel, or resolve you
For more amazement. If you can behold it,
I'll make the statue move indeed, descend,
And take ycu by the hand; but then you'll think
(Which I protest against) I am assisted
By wicked powers.
Leon. What you can make her do,
I am content to look on; what to speak,
I am content to hear; for 'tis as easy
To make her speak as move.
Paul. It is requir'd
You do awake your faith. Then, all stand still.
On; those that think it is unlawful business
I am about, let them depart.
Leon. Proceed;
No foot shall stir.
Paul. Music! awake her! strike! [*Music.*]
'Tis time; descend; be stone no more; approach;
Strike all that look upon with marvel. Come;
I'll fill your grave up. Stir; nay, come away;
Bequeath to death your numbness; for from him
Dear life redeems you. You perceive she stirs.
[*Hermione comes down.*]
Start not; her actions shall be holy, as
You hear my spell is lawful. Do not shun her
Until you see her die again, for then
You kill her double. Nay, present your hand.
When she was young, you woo'd her; now, in age,
Is she become the suitor?
Leon. O, she's warm!
If this be magic, let it be an art
Lawful as eating.
Pol. She embraces him.
Cam. She hangs about his neck.
If she pertain to life let her speak too.
Pol. Ay, and make it manifest where she has liv'd,
Or how stol'n from the dead.
Paul. That she is living,
Were it but told you, should be hooted at
Like an old tale; but it appears she lives,
Though yet she speak not. Mark a little while.
Please you to interpose, fair madam, kneel,
And pray your mother's blessing. Turn, good lady,
Our Perdita is found.
Her. You gods, look down
And from your sacred vials pour your graces
Upon my daughter's head! Tell me, mine own,
Where hast thou been preserv'd? where liv'd? how found
Thy father's court? for thou shalt hear that I,
Knowing by Paulina that the oracle
Gave hope thou wast in being, have preserv'd
Myself to see the issue.
Paul. There's time enough for that;
Least they desire (upon this push) to trouble
Your joys with like relation. Go together,
You precious winners all; your exultation
Partake to every one. I, an old turtle,
Will wing me to some wither'd bough, and there
My mate (that's never to be found again)
Lament till I am lost.
Leon. O, peace, Paulina!
Thou shouldst a husband take by my consent,
As I by thine a wife: this is a match,
And made between 's by vows. Thou hast found mine,
But how, is to be question'd; for I saw her
(As I thought) dead; and have (in vain) said many
A prayer upon her grave. I'll not seek far
(For him, I partly know his mind) to find thee
An honorable husband. Come, Camillo,
And take her by the hand, whose worth and honesty
Is richly noted; and here justified
By us, a pair of kings. Let's from this place.
What? look upon my brother. Both your pardons,
That e'er I put between your holy looks
My ill suspicion. This' your son-in-law,
And son unto the King, whom heavens directing
Is troth-plight to your daughter. Good Paulina,
Lead us from hence, where we may leisurely
Each one demand, and answer to his part
Perform'd in this wide gap of time, since first
We were dissever'd. Hastily lead away.
Exeunt.

77. cordial: heartwarming. **85. forbear:** withdraw.
86. presently: at once.
96. On; those. Many editors emend to *Or those.*
98. strike: strike up. **100. upon:** on. **106. then:** i.e. if you do.
107. double: a second time.

129–30. Least . . . relation: the last thing they want, at this critical moment, is to trouble your happiness with such an account.
132. Partake to: share with. **turtle:** turtledove (symbol of faithful love). **145. justified:** confirmed. **148. holy:** chaste.
149. This': this is.

NOTE ON THE TEXT

The First Folio (1623) is the only authority for *The Winter's Tale*; all later editions are derived from that source. The F1 text, it is widely agreed, was printed from a transcript made by Ralph Crane, scrivener to the King's Men, and probably specially prepared for the printer. Most of Crane's scribal characteristics (see the "Note on the Text" to *The Tempest*) are clearly apparent in the printed text (see, e.g., Textual Notes, I.i.3, 10, I.ii.l, 254, II.i.61, 179, II.iii.16, III.ii.11, IV.iii.32, 41, IV.iv.83, 88, 195, 273, 577, 737, V.i.120, V.iii.21, 49); moreover the list of "The Names of the Actors," the careful act-scene division, and the use of "massed entries," though not entirely consistent, link this play with *The Merry Wives of Windsor* and *The Two Gentlemen of Verona,* both generally agreed to have been printed from Crane transcripts. (On the "massed entry" technique see the "Note on the Text" to *The Two Gentlemen.*)

It is not clear what sort of manuscript lies behind Crane's transcript: Greg suggests "foul papers" and Wells/Taylor suggest authorial "fair copy," probably a prompt-book. But nothing in the text suggests any use of the official prompt-book; indeed, an entry in the *Office Book* of Sir Henry Herbert, Master of the Revels, strongly suggests that the company's prompt-book was lost at the time copy was needed for F1. The entry reads: "For the king's players. An olde play called *Winter's Tale,* formerly allowed of by Sir George Bucke, and likewyse by mee on Mr. Hemmings his worde that there was nothing prophane added or reformed, thogh the allowed booke was missinge; and therefore I returned itt without a fee, this 19 of August, 1623." (Quoted from Malone's *Shakspeare* (1790), Vol. I, Pt.ii, p. 226, the original *Office Book* being since lost.)

Since the F1 text of *The Winter's Tale* had most probably been printed off by December 1622 (Hinman), E. E. Willoughby's suggestion (in Wilson) that the "booke" submitted to Herbert in 1623 may well have consisted of F1 sheets marked up by the book-keeper for use as the prompt-book is perhaps more credible than Greg allows. See, for example, the so-called Padua First Folio prompt-books of *Macbeth* and *Measure for Measure* (pre-Restoration) and the copy of the Third Folio (1663/4), in which some ten plays were annotated as prompt-books (c. 1674–85) for use in the Smock Alley Theatre in Dublin (G. B. Evans, ed., *Shakespearean Prompt-Books of the Seventeenth Century,* 8 vols., 1960–96).

It has been claimed, with some likelihood, that the "dance of twelve Satyrs" in IV.iv and its introductory lines (324–42) are an addition, which was inserted, perhaps, at a Court performance of *The Winter's Tale* (5 November 1611) as part of the festivities arranged for the coming marriage of Princess Elizabeth with the Elector Palatine, an addition imitating a similar dance of ten (or twelve) satyrs in Ben Jonson's masque, *Oberon, The Fairy Prince,* performed 1 January 1611. Certainly this short episode is completely detachable without affecting the surrounding text and Polixenes' first line after the dance (343) shows no consciousness of the dance action but is addressed to the old Shepherd, whose son (the Clown) has shortly before remarked (310) that the Shepherd is "in sad talk" with the "gentlemen" (i.e., Polixenes and Camillo).

Some suggestive, but inconclusive, evidence has been interpreted to suggest (see J. E. Ballard and W. M. Fox as cited in Greg) that Hermione's intensely moving and dramatic "resurrection" scene, with which the play concludes (V.iii), represents a change in Shakespeare's original intention—that is, he had intended to make the reunion between Leontes and Perdita the final climactic episode, thus leaving Hermione dead as in Robert Greene's *Pandosto* (1588), Shakespeare's principal source, and, seemingly, as in Antigonus' reaction to her ghostlike appearance in III.iii.15–46. In *Pandosto,* Bellaria (=Hermione), having been declared guiltless of adultery with Egistus (=Polixenes) by the Oracle of Delphos, dies from grief when news is brought of the sudden death of her son, little Garinter (=Mamillius). Since, then, (1) Shakespeare must have known how Greene had dealt with Bellaria and because Simon Forman, who witnessed a performance of *The Winter's Tale* at the Globe on 15 May 1611 (see Appendix C, No. 20), fails to mention Hermione's surprise survival, it may be argued that the performance of the play concluded with a scene showing the reunion of Leontes and Perdita. (2) Antigonus interprets the apparition of Hermione, in pure white robes "like very sanctity," that appeared to him in a kind of waking dream to mean that she has died (III.iii.15–46). (3) The reunion of Leontes and Perdita, a naturally climactic scene toward which Acts IV and V would seem, inevitably, to be leading, is, instead of being shown, merely reported by several gentlemen, who describe the event in considerable detail. The arguments advanced above, however, are not perhaps so persuasive as they may at first appear (compare Pafford's discussion). (1) Forman, although he fails to mention Hermione's "resurrection," also fails to report her death. Moreover, he makes no reference to Paulina, an important character not found in *Pandosto,* and it would be absurd to suggest she was also an afterthought and played no part in the play as seen by Forman. (2) Antigonus' belief that it must have been Hermione's ghost that had appeared to him may also be explained as a clever piece of Shakespearean legerdemain intended to make the audience temporarily forget Hermione and hence eventually to heighten the dramatic tension generated by the surprise ending. (3) The use of what is called "reported action" to describe, instead of show, the reunion of Leontes and Perdita is, perhaps, the strongest of the three points discussed above, but, like the first two points, it remains essentially speculative. In other words, an opposite supposition is similarly probable and unprovable: namely, Shakespeare, always intending to end the play with Hermione's "rebirth," realized that the plot-line, as he was developing it, required the prior reunion of Leontes and Perdita and that to show two reunion scenes almost back to back would surely result in reducing the second to an anticlimax, and he thus wisely chose to play down the first by using the distancing "reported action" technique.

The F1 text is unusually clean and good and presents few problems to the editor.

For further information, see: J. D. Wilson, ed., New Shakespeare *The Winter's Tale* (Cambridge, 1931) [Wilson's theory that the F1 text is based on a transcript made up from players' parts is no longer accepted]; W. W. Greg, *The Shakespeare First Folio* (Oxford, 1955); Charlton Hinman, *The Printing and Proof-Reading of the First Folio,* 2 vols. (Oxford, 1963); J. H. P. Pafford, ed., New Arden *The Winter's Tale* (London, 1953; rev. 1965); E. A. J. Honigmann, "On the Indifferent and One-Way Variants in Shakespeare," *The Library,* 5th. ser., XXII (1967), 189–204; Stanley Wells, Gary Taylor, et al., *William Shakespeare: A Textual Companion* (Oxford, 1987).

TEXTUAL NOTES

Dramatis personae: *as given in F1, following the play, with a few additions by Rowe and later eds.*
Mamillius] *F3* (Mamilius); Mamillus *F1*
Act-scene division: *from F1*

I.i

Location: *Theobald (after Rowe)*
3 **on foot]** *F4;* on-foot *F1*
10 **Beseech]** *Capell;* 'Beseech *F1 (sporadically throughout)*
19 **Believe]** *F3;* 'Beleeue *F1*

I.ii

Location: *Capell (subs.)*
o.s.d. **and Attendants]** *Theobald*
1 **wat'ry star]** *F4;* Watry-Starre *F1*
32 **by-gone day]** *Rowe;* by-gone-day *F1*
32 **proclaim'd.]** *Rowe (subs.);* proclaym'd, *F1*
42 **good deed]** *Capell;* good-deed *F1;* good-heed *F2*
50 **"verily" is]** *F3 (subs.);* Verely' is *F1*
67 **twinn'd]** *Rowe;* twyn'd *F1*
104 **And]** *F2;* A *F1*
106 **lo you]** *Rowe;* lo-you *F1*
108 s.d. **Gives . . . Polixenes.]** *Capell*
108 s.d. **Aside.]** *Rowe*
121 **hast]** *Capell;* has't *F1*
124 **heckfer]** *ed.;* Heycfer *F1*
129 **full]** *Pope;* full, *F1*
137 **be?—]** *Rowe (question mark, Hanmer);* be *F1*
138 **Affection!]** *Steevens;* Affection? *F1*
141 **unreal]** *Theobald conj.;* vnreall: *F1*
154 **recoil]** *F3;* requoyle *F1*
158 **ornament]** *Capell;* Ornaments *F1*
180 s.d. **Aside.]** *Rowe (subs.; after l. 182); placed as in Dyce*
185 s.d. **Exeunt . . . Attendants.]** *Rowe (after l. 184); placed as in Cambridge*
203 **south.]** *Johnson;* South, *F1*
208 **they]** *F2*
211 s.d. **Exit Mamillius.]** *Rowe*
217 s.d. **Aside.]** *Hanmer*
254 **forth. . . . lord,]** *Theobald;* forth in your affaires (my Lord.) *F1*
276 **hobby-horse]** *Rowe;* Holy-Horse *F1*
285 **meeting]** *F4;* meating *F1*
305 **Infected . . . life,]** *Capell (after Rowe);* Infected (as her life) *F1*
307 **medal]** *Rowe;* Medull *F1*
312 **ay]** *Capell;* I *F1*
371 **compliment]** *Rowe;* complement *F1*
403 **guess]** *F3;* ghesse *F1*
421 **nostril]** *F3;* Nosthrill *F1*
462 **off. Hence!]** *Wilson (subs.);* off, hence: *F1*

II.i

Location: *Theobald (subs.)*
o.s.d. **Enter . . . Ladies.]** *Rowe* (Mamillus); Enter Hermione, Mamillius, Ladies: Leontes, Antigonus, Lords. *F1 (the first of the "massed entries"; Leontes, Antigonus, and the Lords actually enter later in the scene)*
2, 4, etc. s.pp. **1. Lady.]** *Rowe;* Lady. *F1*
27 **Come on . . . come on]** *Rowe;* Come-on . . . come-on *F1*
32 s.d. **Enter . . . others.]** *Capell (after Rowe);* Enter L. *F2*
33 **Was . . . him?]** *as verse, Warburton (after Rowe); as prose, F1*
34, 53, etc. s.pp. **1. Lord.]** *Capell;* Lord. *F1*
35 **ey'd]** *Rowe;* eyed *F1*
38 **knowledge!]** *Capell (subs.);* knowledge, *F1*
61 **big with]** *F3;* big-with *F1*
69 **without-door form]** *Rowe;* without-dore-Forme *F1*
71 **petty brands]** *Hanmer;* Petty-brands *F1*
104 **afar off]** *F4;* a farre-off *F1*
125 s.d. **Exit . . . Ladies.]** *Theobald*
136 **Than]** *Pope;* Then *F1*
141 **putter-on]** *hyphen, Rowe*
145 **nine,]** *Theobald;* nine: *F1*
147 **geld]** *Rowe;* gell'd *F1*
152 **dead man's]** *Rowe;* dead-mans *F1*
153 s.d. **grasps his arm]** *Hanmer (subs.)*
157 **dungy earth]** *Rowe;* dungy-earth *F1*
160 **true than]** *Dyce* (than *F4*); true, then *F1*
160 **suspicion,]** *Collier;* suspition *F1*
179 **push on]** *F2;* push-on *F1*
182 **have]** *F2;* hane *F1*
185 **stuff'd sufficiency]** *F3;* stuff'd-sufficiency *F1*
191 s.d. **Points at Antigonus.]** *Furness conj.*
198 s.d. **Aside.]** *Hanmer*

II.ii

Location: *Pope*
o.s.d. **Enter . . . Attendants.]** *Hanmer (after Rowe);* Enter Paulina, a Gentleman, Gaoler, Emilia. *F1*
2 s.d. **Exit Gentleman.]** *Rowe (after l. 1); placed as in Dyce*
4 s.d. **Enter . . . Jailer.]** *Rowe (after* not? *l. 5); placed as in Johnson*
15 s.d. **Exeunt . . . Attendants.]** *Theobald (subs.)*
16 s.d. **Exit Jailer.]** *Capell (subs.)*
18 s.d. **Enter . . . Emilia.]** *Capell (subs.);* Enter Emilia. *F2 (opposite ll. 16–7)*
19 **gracious]** *F2;* gtacious *F1*
34 **Queen.]** *Capell (subs.);* Queene, *F1*
45 **presently]** *F2;* presenrly *F1*
51 **let't]** *F3;* le't *F1*

II.iii

Location: *Pope (subs.)*
o.s.d. **Enter . . . door.]** *ed.,* Enter Leontes, Seruants, Paulina, Antigonus, and Lords. *F1 (F1 enters Paulina again at l. 26)*
2 **weakness.]** *Collier;* weaknesse, *F1*
4 **harlot king]** *Capell;* harlot-King *F1*
9, 10 s.pp. **1. Serv.]** *Cambridge (after Capell);* Ser. *F1*
9 **Advancing.]** *Capell*
13 **mother!]** *ed.;* Mother. *F1*
16 **Threw off]** *F3;* Threw-off *F1*
18 s.d. **Exit First Servant.]** *Theobald (subs.; after l. 17); placed as in Capell*
26 s.d. **with a child]** *Rowe*
26 s.d. **endeavoring . . . back]** *ed. (after Wilson)*
26 s.p. **1. Lord.]** *Malone;* Lord. *F1*
31 s.p. **2. Serv.]** *Cambridge (after Capell);* Ser. *F1*
39 **What]** *F2;* Who *F1*
50 **La you]** *Capell (subs.);* La-you *F1*
52 s.d. **Aside.]** *Wilson*
52–7 **come— . . . yours.—]** *Capell (after Rowe);* come: . . . yours. *F1*
61 **good, so]** *Theobald;* good so, *F1*
67 s.d. **Laying . . . child.]** *Rowe*
74 s.d. **To Antigonus.]** *Rowe*
112 **more,]** *Theobald;* more *F1*
140 **bastard brains]** *Theobald;* Bastard-braynes *F1*
147, 197 s.pp. **1. Lord.]** *Capell;* Lord. *F1*
162 **grey—what]** *Pope;* gray. What *F1*
192 s.d. **with the child]** *Rowe*

III.i

Location: *Kittredge (after Capell)*
12 **successful]** *F2;* snccessefull *F1*
18 **business.]** *Theobald (subs.);* Businesse, *F1*
20 **discover,]** *Johnson;* discouer: *F1*

III.ii

Location: *Theobald*
o.s.d. **Enter . . . Officers.]** *Theobald (subs.);* Enter Leontes, Lords, Officers: Hermione (as to her Triall) Ladies: Cleomines, Dion. *F1*
10 s.d. **Enter . . . attending.]** *Theobald (subs.; after* Silence! *l. 10); placed as in Wilson*
10 **Silence!]** *Rowe; in italics as s.d., F1*
12 s.d. **Reads.]** *Capell*
29 **human]** *Rowe;* humane *F1*
33 **Who]** *Rowe;* Whom *F1*
41 **'fore]** *Pope;* fore *F1*
97 **first-fruits]** *hyphen, Rowe*
105 **Here]** *Pope;* Here, *F1*
116, 174, etc. s.pp. **1. Lord.]** *Capell;* Lord. *F1*
118 s.d. **Exeunt certain Officers.]** *Capell*
123 s.d. **Enter . . . Dion.]** *Capell (subs.);* Enter Dion and Cleomines. *F2 (after l. 116)*
132 s.d. **Reads.]** *Capell*
141 s.d. **Enter a Servant.]** *Rowe*
147 s.d. **Hermione swoons.]** *Rowe (subs.)*
153 s.d. **Exeunt . . . Hermione.]** *Rowe (after l. 150); placed subs. as in Malone*
156 **woo]** *F2;* woe *F1*
172 s.d. **Enter Paulina.]** *Rowe*
179–81 **tyranny, Together . . . (Fancies]** *Theobald (subs., after Pope);* Tyranny (Together . . . Fancies *F1*
205 **eye,]** *Rowe;* eye *F1;* eye; *F4*
238 **perpetual).]** *Rowe (subs.);* perpetuall) *F1*

III.iii

Location: *Pope, Kittredge (after Rowe)*
o.s.d. **Enter . . . babe.]** *ed. (after Rowe);* Enter Antigonus, A Marriner, Babe, Sheepe-heard, and Clowne. *F1*
11 **Too far]** *F3;* Too-farre *F1*
21 **sorrow,]** *Capell;* sorrow *F1*
29 **thrower-out]** *F2;* Thower-out *F1*
46 s.d. **Laying . . . scroll.]** *Kittredge (after Rowe)*
47 s.d. **Placing . . . it.]** *Johnson (subs.)*
49 s.d. **Thunder.]** *Wilson*
49 **begins.]** *Rowe (subs.);* beginnes, *F1*
58 s.d. **Enter a Shepherd.]** *F2*
61 **in the between]** *Pope;* (in the betweene) *F1*
63 **fighting—Hark]** *Rowe;* fighting, hearke *F1*
63 s.d. **Horns.]** *White*
65 **scar'd]** *Rowe;* scarr'd *F1*
68 **Good luck]** *F4;* Good-lucke *F1*
69 **will!]** *Kittredge (after Theobald);* will) *F1*
114 **new-born]** *hyphen, Theobald*
120 **made]** *Theobald;* mad *F1*

IV.i

17–9 **leaving— . . . himself—]** *Staunton;* leauing . . . himselfe. *F1*

IV.ii

Location: *Pope, Capell*
13 **thee.]** *Rowe;* thee, *F1*
54 **Camillo!]** *Theobald;* Camillo, *F1*
55 **Exeunt.]** *Rowe;* Exit *F1*

IV.iii

Location: *Malone*
1 s.p. **Aut.]** *Capell*
10 **with heigh,]** *F2*
15 **my dear?]** *Pope;* (my deere) *F1*
17 **here and there,]** *F4;* here, and there *F1;* here and there *F3*
22 **avouch it]** *F3;* auouch-it *F1*
32 **'leven wether]** *Malone;* Leauen-weather *F1*
35 s.d. **Aside.]** *Rowe*
37 **sheep-shearing feast]** *Rowe;* Sheepe-shearing-Feast *F1*
38 **currants]** *Rowe;* Currence *F1*
41 **made me]** *F3;* made-me *F1*
50 s.d. **Grovelling . . . ground.]** *Rowe*
51 **me—]** *Rowe;* me. *F1*
62 **detestable]** *F2;* derestable *F1*
75 s.d. **picking his pocket]** *Capell*
77 **Dost]** *F3;* Doest *F1*
115 **good-fac'd]** *hyphen, Theobald*
123 **Jog on, jog on]** *Rowe;* Iog-on, Iog-on *F1*

IV.iv

Location: *Sisson (after Theobald)*
o.s.d. **Enter . . . Perdita.]** *Rowe;* Enter Florizell, Perdita, Shepherd, Clowne, Polixenes, Camillo, Mopsa, Dorcas, Seruants, Autolicus. *F1*
2 **Does]** *Rowe;* Do's *F1*

5 Sir,] *Pope;* Sir: *F1*
12 Digest't] *ed. (after* Disgest it *F2);* Digest *F1*
29 fire-rob'd god] *Rowe;* Fire-roab'd-God *F1*
32 beauty] *Rowe;* beauty, *F1*
54 s.d. Enter . . . Servants.] *placed as in Capell;* Enter All. *F2 (after* auspicious! *l. 52)*
54 s.d. **disguised]** *Rowe*
55 liv'd,] *Rowe;* liu'd: *F1*
70 s.d. **To Polixenes.]** *Malone (after Rowe)*
72 s.d. **To Camillo.]** *Malone*
83 bastards). Of] *Rowe (subs.);* bastards) of *F1*
84 garden's] *F2;* Gardens *F1*
88 creating Nature] *F4;* creating-Nature *F1*
93 scion] *Steevens;* Sien *F1*
98 your] *F2;* you *F1*
105 wi' th'] *Capell (subs.);* with' *F1*
115 virgin branches] *Capell;* Virgin-branches *F1*
134 Whitsun pastorals] *Johnson;* Whitson-Pastorals *F1*
162–3 Mopsa . . . with!] *as verse, Capell; as prose, F1*
165 s.d. **Music.]** *Capell (after l. 155); placed as in Malone*
195 jump her] *F4;* Iump-her *F1*
195 thump her] *F3;* thump-her *F1*
214 s.d. **Exit Servant.]** *Capell*
218 s.p. **Aut.]** *Capell*
245 off] *Hanmer;* of *F1*
249 promis'd] *F2;* ptomis'd *F1*
261 a-life] *Tyrwhitt conj.;* a life *F1*
273 Come on] *F2;* Come-on *F1*
297–8] *In F1 the first line of the song is preceded by* Song *and the second line by* Aut.*; arranged as in Rowe*
310 gentlemen] *Rowe;* Gent. *F1*
313 s.d. **Exit . . . Mopsa.]** *Dyce*
316 cape] *F2;* Crpe *F1*
323 s.d. **Enter Servant.]** *Rowe (subs.)*
336 four threes] *Capell;* foure-threes *F1*
340 prating.] *Rowe (subs.);* prating, *F1*
342 s.d. **Exit.]** *Capell*
344 s.d. **To Camillo.]** *Cambridge*
345 s.d. **To Florizel.]** *Craig*
355 reply, at least] *Dyce (after Theobald);* reply at least, *F1*
363 dove's down] *F2;* Doues-downe *F1*
381 better.] *Rowe;* better *F1*
389 come on] *Rowe;* come-on *F1*
390 'fore] *F2;* fore *F1*
401 again] *Capell;* againe, *F1*
417 s.d. **Discovering himself.]** *Rowe*
419 acknowledg'd] *F2;* acknowledge *F1*
428 shalt] *Rowe;* shalt neuer *F1*
437 thee—] *Capell;* thee. *F1*
439 hoop] *Pope;* hope *F1*
446 Will't] *Hanmer;* Wilt *F1*
452 s.d. **To Florizel.]** *Rowe*
458 shovels in] *Rowe;* shouels-in *F1*
458 s.d. **To Perdita.]** *Rowe*
467 your] *F2;* my *F1*
468 guess] *Rowe;* ghesse *F1*
470 sight as yet,] *Hanmer;* sight, as yet *F1*
473 think, Camillo?] *Johnson;* think Camillo. *F1*
482–3 fancy. . . . obedient,] *Theobald (after Rowe);* fancie, . . . obedient: *F1*
490 seas hides] *F2* (hide); seas, hides *F1*
494 (as, in] *Rowe (subs.);* as (in *F1*
506 s.d. **Drawing her aside.]** *Capell*
507 s.d. **To Camillo.]** *Theobald*
549 there,] *ed.;* there *F1*
577 take in] *F4;* take-in *F1*
583 sir; for this] *Hanmer;* Sir, for this, *F1*
594 s.d. **They talk aside.]** *Rowe*
594 s.d. **laughing]** *ed.*
606 wenches'] *Johnson;* Wenches *F1*
611 fil'd] *F3;* fill'd *F1*
611 off] *F3;* of *F1*
615 old man] *F3;* old-man *F1*
618 s.d. **Camillo . . . forward.]** *Theobald*
623 s.d. **Seeing Autolycus.]** *Theobald*
626 s.d. **Aside.]** *Theobald*
628–9 How . . . thee.] *as prose, Malone; as verse, F1*
637 s.d. **Giving money.]** *Dyce (after Capell)*
638, 642 s.dd. **Aside.]** *Johnson; indicated by parentheses, F1*
641 flea'd] *Rowe;* fled *F1*
647 s.d. **Florizel . . . garments.]** *Capell*
658 s.d. **Giving . . . Perdita.]** *Capell*
662, 706 s.dd. **Aside.]** *Rowe*
669 s.d. **with . . . Perdita]** *Capell (subs.)*
709, 712 s.dd. **Aside.]** *Capell*
714 s.d. **Takes . . . beard.]** *Steevens (after Capell)*
730 like] *F2;* lke *F1*
735 that toze] *Alexander (subs.);* at toaze *F1*
737 push on] *Pope;* push-on *F1*
737 pluck back] *Theobald (after Rowe);* pluck-back *F1*
773 germane] *Theobald;* Iermaine *F1*
776 sheep-whistling] *F2;* Sheepe-whistiing *F1*
786 aqua-vitae] *F2;* Aquavite *F1*
791–2 traitorly rascals] *Theobald;* Traitorly-Rascals *F1*
830 s.d. **Exeunt . . . Clown.]** *Rowe;* Exeunt. *F2*
842 s.d. **Exit.]** *Rowe;* Exeunt. *F1*

V.i

Location: *Pope, Capell*
o.s.d. **Enter . . . Servants.]** *Rowe;* Enter Leontes, Cleomines, Dion, Paulina, Seruants: Florizel, Perdita. *F1*
5 done,] *Theobald;* done; *F1*
12 of. / Paul. True, too] *Theobald;* of, true. / *Paul.* Too *F1*
29 lookers-on] *hyphen, Capell*
31 holier than,] *Capell (subs.;* than *F4);* holyer, then *F1*
41 human] *Pope;* humane *F1*
44, 52 counsel] *Pope;* councell *F1*
46 s.d. **To Leontes.]** *Theobald*
59 now) appear] *Theobald;* now appeare) *F1*
61 just] *F3;* iust such *F1*
75 madam— / Paul. I have done.] *Capell;* Madame, I haue done. *F1 (continued to Cleomines)*
114 s.d. **Exeunt . . . others.]** *Dyce (after Capell);* Exit. *F1 (after* us. *l. 115)*
120 talk'd of] *F4;* talk'd-of *F1*
160 his,] *Hanmer;* his *F1*
211 come on] *Rowe;* come-on *F1*
228 s.d. **To Florizel.]** *Theobald*

V.ii

Location: *Capell*
78 losing] *F2;* loosing *F1*
90 marble] *F3;* Marble, *F1*
112 s.d. **Exeunt Gentlemen.]** *Capell;* Exit. *F1*

V.iii

Location: *Pope*
o.s.d. **Paulina, Lords]** *Rowe;* Paulina: Hermione (like a Statue:) Lords *F1*
18 Lonely] *Hanmer;* Louely *F1*
20 s.d. **Paulina . . . statue.]** *Rowe (after F1 o.s.d.)*
21 shows off] *F2* (shewes); shewes-off *F1*
22 speak.] *Johnson;* speake, *F1*
31 go by] *F4;* goe-by *F1*
49 laid on] *Rowe;* lay'd-on *F1*
55 take off] *F2;* take-off *F1*
62 already—] *Rowe;* alreadie. *F1*
85 Stand by] *F2;* Stand-by *F1*
98 s.d. **Music.]** *Rowe*
103 s.d. **Hermione comes down.]** *Rowe*
112 neck.] *Theobald (subs.);* necke, *F1*
115 dead.] *Capell;* dead? *F1*
122 vials] *Pope;* Viols *F1*
126 the] *F2;* rhe *F1*
128 time] *F2;* ttme *F1*
128–9 that; Least] *F2;* that, / Least *F1;* that; / Lest *F3*
149 This'] *W. S. Walker conj.;* This *F1*
155 s.d. **Exeunt.]** Exeunt. *[list of actors]* FINIS. *F1*

A royal picnic. From George Turberville, *The Noble Art of Venery* (1575). Queen Elizabeth is here pictured at a hunt picnic in a forest clearing. Note that the Queen eats alone, waited on by the Gentlemen of her Chamber, while her Maids in Waiting stand behind her. Some relaxation in the royal presence is indicated by the group of gentlemen seated on the ground (to the right) eating their lunch. (*The Huntington Library, San Marino, California*)

The Tempest

THE TEMPEST is primarily a play for the theatre. It has a spectacular storm scene at the beginning, scenes of magic manipulation of people and of things, a masque of goddesses, spirits in the form of a pack of hounds, a half-domesticated monster, and characters who can go about invisible to other characters. The hero is a man who puts on shows. And the play is full of music.

Our first knowledge of it comes from a performance. There is a record of a production at court on November 1, 1611. It must have been a fairly new play then, because it draws on some travel accounts which were not available in England before the autumn of 1610. A date of composition can thus be more definitely fixed for *The Tempest* than for most plays of Shakespeare. We hear of it again as a play produced in the winter of 1612–13 as part of the festivities at court to celebrate the marriage of the Princess Elizabeth to the Elector Palatine. *The Tempest*, like *A Midsummer Night's Dream*, is very appropriate for a wedding. It was first published in the Folio of 1623, where it was given the place of honor as the opening piece in the collection, perhaps because it was the most recent of the comedies and had been popular on the stage.

It might be said that the title of the play should be *The Island* rather than *The Tempest*, for the storm occupies only the first scene of the play and the island pervades all of it. The magic island is an old theme in folklore and literature, and Shakespeare certainly knew many treatments of it. In his play, the magic of the island comes from Prospero's "art," it seems, and the nature of that "art" must be clearly understood. It is white magic, not black, in that the magician uses only some secret powers of nature, which he has learned after laborious study; he does not call up evil spirits, as the black magician does, nor does he make compacts with the devil and jeopardize his immortal soul, as Marlowe's Dr. Faustus does. Shakespeare's Prospero is represented as a scholar, a man for whom his library in Milan had been dukedom large enough. Although Prospero's magic and the actions of his minister Ariel determine the events of the play, the island itself has a history that begins before his coming. It had earlier been ruled by the black magic of the witch Sycorax, who for her evil deeds had been marooned on the island and had "littered" there her son Caliban. The spirit Ariel, because he had refused to perform her evil commands, she had incarcerated in a cloven pine, and afterwards she had died. The "hag-born whelp" and the spirit groaning in his prison were the sole inhabitants when Prospero and the child Miranda arrived.

The location of the island is ambiguous. In some aspects it is a Mediterranean island, which the shipwrecked party reaches on its way from Tunis to Naples. In other ways it reflects the Bermuda described in two printed pamphlets and a manuscript letter which Shakespeare read.

An expedition of the Virginia Company set sail from Plymouth on June 2, 1609. On July 24 the fleet was scattered by a storm. The vessels arrived at Jamestown in August, all except the flagship, which had carried the admiral, Sir George Somers, and the future governor of Virginia, Sir Thomas Gates. The flagship, called the *Sea Adventure*, was presumed to be lost. But on May 23, 1610, to the astonishment of the colonists, two small pinnaces appeared at Jamestown carrying the complement of the *Sea Adventure*. Somers and his men had run aground on the island of Bermuda, sedulously avoided by sailors because of dire reports which circulated concerning it, causing it to be called the Isle of Devils. The English found no devils there; instead the island proved to be delightful, furnishing them with food, shelter, and wood to build the pinnaces for the remainder of their voyage. The news of their survival and safety naturally created a sensation. Sylvester Jourdain, a member of the crew, published a pamphlet called *A Discovery of the Bermudas, Otherwise Called the Isle of Devils*, and the Virginia Company published its own account in *The True Declaration of the Estate of the Colony in Virginia*. Another report, by William Strachey of the *Sea Adventure*, dated July 15, 1610, circulated in manuscript; it was called *The True Repertory of the Wrack and Redemption of Sir Thomas Gates*, and was eventually published in 1625 in *Purchas His Pilgrims*.

Two of these pamphlets mention Dido and Aeneas as early colonizers, and this may be related in some way to Shakespeare's mixing the atmosphere of a Mediterranean island with that of a New World discovery. (It may also have some connection with the rather pointless quibbling about "Widow Dido" in II.i.77–102.) For all the Mediterranean locale, there are such reminders of the voyages of discovery as Trinculo's remark about the curiosity of the English, that "when they will not give a doit to relieve a lame beggar, they will lay out ten to see a dead Indian" (II.i.31–33), and Ariel recalls (I.ii.227–29) that once at midnight Prospero had called him to fetch dew from "the still-vex'd Bermoothes" (the always-stormy Bermudas).

Another influence from the New World came indirectly. One of Montaigne's essays, which Shakespeare read in John Florio's translation of 1603, is called "Of the Cannibals." It is essentially Montaigne's praise of primitive American Indian society, as he has heard it described by explorers. (*Cannibal* derives from *Carib* and originally had no connection with the eating of human flesh.) He thinks of it as an ideal state, superior to Plato's republic:

> It is a nation, would I answer Plato, that hath no kind of traffic, no knowledge of letters, no intelligence of numbers, no name of magistrate, nor of politic superiority; no use of service, of riches, or of poverty; no contracts, no successions, no partitions, no occupation but idle; no respect of kindred but common, no apparel but natural, no manuring of lands, no use of wine, corn, or metal.

This is obviously the source of Gonzalo's description of his ideal commonwealth in II.i.148–69. It would be too much to say, although it has been said, that Shakespeare's Caliban (an obvious anagram of Cannibal), described in the Folio dramatis personae as "a salvage and deformed slave," is the playwright's refutation of Montaigne's primitivism.

The question "What is natural?" is an important concern in *King Lear*, and Shakespeare continues to develop the interest in his later romances, *Cymbeline*, *The Winter's Tale*, and *The Tempest*. "Nothing natural I ever saw so noble," says Miranda on her first view of Ferdinand. But the word *natural* had many meanings in Shakespeare's English. In *The Tempest*, of course, a major concern is identifying what is *natural* and what is *supernatural*. Prospero, with his "art" or, as we would call it, science, can move from one realm to the other. But nature, in medieval and Renaissance thought, was defined by the old word *kind*, and this included *human* nature. Human nature was (and is) notoriously capable of the most noble and the most despicable behavior. Is the action of a brother in deposing a prince "natural"? Is it natural to serve only your own interests and care nothing for those of others? Is the *natural* man a Caliban, with no innate moral concerns or ability to comprehend the interests and needs of others? He aspires to freedom, which for him may mean only self-indulgence, but Ariel yearns for a kind of self-indulgent freedom too, and he is specifically set apart from human nature. Caliban is beyond the lower limits of human nature, for he is the offspring of a witch and the devil. Whether he can be morally regenerated or not is something of a puzzle, but at least he can say of himself

> What a thrice-double ass
> Was I to take this drunkard for a god,
> And worship this dull fool! (V.i.296–98)

One of the major themes of *The Tempest* is that of reality and illusion. From the time the shipwrecked men set foot on dry land they never know whether to trust their eyes or not, or, indeed, whether to trust their ears, for Ariel can deceive both the senses of sight and hearing. At the simplest level this is of course mere magic; a magician is someone who can make things appear and disappear. On the comic side we see Stephano thinking that the four legs of Trinculo and Caliban are the limbs of a four-legged monster, and we see Caliban taking the drunken Stephano for a god and getting pickled on his liquor. Ferdinand and Miranda have the delightful illusions of lovers, taking each other for goddess and spirit at first sight, but as they are young and in love the assumption has to be that reality will not be very different for them. Prospero's dry remark on Miranda's excitement over a hitherto unknown world is as far as the comic spirit is allowed to go:

> *Miranda.* O wonder!
> How many goodly creatures are there here!
> How beauteous mankind is! O brave new world
> That has such people in't!
> *Prospero.* 'Tis new to thee.
> (V.i.181–84)

There is a further, philosophic dimension to this theme of illusion and reality. Shakespeare is very fond of likening life to a play; it is a metaphor or simile equally at home in comedy and tragedy, in *As You Like It* and *Macbeth*. Acting is creating illusions; the actor is a "shadow." But in one of the greatest passages in *The Tempest*, or indeed in all of Shakespeare, we are told that what we take for concrete physical reality will turn out to be an illusion too:

Our revels now are ended. These our actors
(As I foretold you) were all spirits, and
Are melted into air, into thin air,
And like the baseless fabric of this vision,
The cloud-capp'd tow'rs, the gorgeous palaces,
The solemn temples, the great globe itself,
Yea, all which it inherit, shall dissolve,
And like this insubstantial pageant faded
Leave not a rack behind. We are such stuff
As dreams are made on; and our little life
Is rounded with a sleep. (IV.i.148–58)

Since Prospero, by virtue of his "art," his magic, is all-powerful on the island, since the other characters are subject to him, there arises inevitably the theme of servitude and freedom. His principal agent is Ariel, who owes to him his release from the dreadful imprisonment imposed by Sycorax—"a torment / To lay upon the damn'd." Ariel is a spirit of air, eager to be free and unconfined, but serving a limited indenture to Prospero, his liberator. His function in the action somewhat resembles that of Puck in *A Midsummer Night's Dream*, but his character is quite different. Though he is naturally restless in his servitude and eager to follow summer merrily, yet there is a delicacy and eagerness about him which is quite unlike Puck. He says, "What shall I do? say what? what shall I do?" and again, "Was't well done?" and "Do you love me, master?" Prospero calls him his tricksy Ariel and his dainty spirit. He is not as interested in being a practical joker as Puck is, though he can mislead men by mimicry and by his magic as well as his fire. He would never say, "Lord, what fools these mortals be!" but rather says that he would sympathize with the charmed prisoners if he were human. He earns his freedom, though Prospero is somewhat reluctant to let him go.

At the other extreme is Caliban, whose work is physical as befits his capacity. He resents his servitude bitterly; his first words in the play are "There's wood enough within." His rebellion against Prospero is futile, he realizes, because the magician's power is enough to control his mother's god, Setebos. But he finds a potential deliverer, so he thinks, in Stephano. It is only liquor that Stephano can provide, but that inspires the drunken declaration of independence in which Caliban cries, "Freedom, high-day! high-day, freedom! freedom, high-day, freedom!" (II.ii.186–87).

In immediate juxtaposition with this drunken hilarity is the scene of Ferdinand, King of Naples (as he believes himself to be), ignominiously carrying logs at the command of Prospero. Far from rebelling at his servitude, Ferdinand accepts it gladly:

This my mean task
Would be as heavy to me as odious, but
The mistress which I serve quickens what's dead,
And makes my labors pleasures. (III.i.4–7)

The conspiracy of Antonio and Sebastian, which is an extension of Antonio's seizure of Prospero's dukedom long before the play opens, has to do with rebellion against authority, usurpation of power, and these have to do with freedom and servitude. Gonzalo's description of an ideal commonwealth, with maximum freedom and minimum control, is not irrelevant. In a comedy, faithful service is rewarded, and those who have seized, or plan to seize, power to which they are not entitled will be frustrated. The drunkard who would be king of the island fetches up in a foul-smelling horsepond.

What powers there are above us is not a question asked insistently in the late romances as it is in such tragedies as *Hamlet* and *King Lear*. The real wielder of power in the play is Prospero himself. He is dependent upon his books and upon time, but, as his farewell to magic in V.i.33–57 indicates, there are few limitations to his power until he renounces it. Like Medea in Ovid's *Metamorphoses*, he controls sea and air, mountains and trees, the noonday sun and even graves. (He also controls some tiny English countryside fairies that Medea never heard of.) But Prospero admits that Providence preserved him and his daughter in the "rotten carcass of a butt," and he seems to undergo a kind of spiritual education during the play which an absolute power could not undergo. His forgiveness of his enemies shows the process:

Though with their high wrongs I am strook to th' quick,
Yet, with my nobler reason, 'gainst my fury
Do I take part. The rarer action is
In virtue than in vengeance. They being penitent,
The sole drift of my purpose doth extend
Not a frown further. (V.i.25–30)

Though the island is a magic place, Shakespeare makes its landscape specific and credible; he provides more details than the authors of the reports on Bermuda. It has "fresh springs, brine-pits, barren place and fertile" (I.ii.338). If necessary, a person could survive on "fresh-brook mussels, wither'd roots and husks / Wherein the acorn cradled" (I.ii.464–65). The native knew where to find berries, nuts, crab apples, and scamels from the rock, whatever they are (II.ii.160, 167–72). Caliban says there are bogs, fens, and flats (II.ii.2) and there is at least one open place, as in *King Lear*, which affords no shelter in a storm. It is apparently mixed wilderness and meadow, since it has "Tooth'd briers, sharp furzes, pricking goss [i.e. gorse], and thorns" (IV.i.180), yet in some places the grass grows "lush and lusty" and is green after a storm (II.i.53–54)—or so it appears to Gonzalo. But it has often been noticed that the island looks different to the different people who find themselves in it. Gonzalo also expects that there an innocent existence could be led without sweat or endeavor, but apparently much wood must be carried to provide fuel. Another curiosity is that there is a horsepond (IV.i.182, 199) but no horses.

Time is more prominent in the play than place. Prospero's magic depends, of course, upon precise timing.

I find my zenith doth depend upon
A most auspicious star, whose influence

If now I court not, but omit, my fortunes
Will ever after droop. (I.ii.181–84)

His first concern, after the business of the storm, is about time. Ariel knows vaguely that it is afternoon, but Prospero says that noon is past

At least two glasses. The time 'twixt six and now
Must by us both be spent most preciously.
(I.ii.240–41)

He emphasizes "the present business"; he keeps reminding himself and others that it is "at this hour," or even at this moment, that something must be done. Ariel is incredibly swift in his errands, as he must be to serve such an exacting and time-conscious master. The word *now* occurs seventy-nine times in the course of the play. In *The Tempest* truly "the past is prologue" and the present is what matters. Structure, action, and language combine to reinforce the effect.

The play is unusual among the works of Shakespeare in that it follows the unities of time and place; only the early *Comedy of Errors* is as compact. Neoclassical critics like Sir Philip Sidney and Ben Jonson insisted that a play should cover an action not longer than one day and preferably shorter, and should be set in a single place. That Shakespeare took a more flexible view may be seen in *The Winter's Tale*, the play of his which probably just preceded *The Tempest*: it begins before the birth of Perdita and ends about the time of her marriage, and it divides its action between Sicily and Bohemia. *Pericles*, the first of the romances, has an even longer time-span and a much more widely ranging locale. Some critics say that in *The Tempest* Shakespeare was merely showing people like Ben Jonson that he could follow the unities if he wanted to. It is perhaps more likely that, having treated *in extenso* the story of a father and a daughter both in *Pericles* and in *The Winter's Tale*, he preferred here to concentrate on the final stage of his plot.

Whatever the reason, his decision meant that information about the antecedent action must be conveyed in some way to the audience. The stir and bustle of the first scene is therefore followed by a long scene consisting largely of exposition, a species of discourse which is inherently undramatic. Shakespeare acknowledges the danger when he has Prospero several times accuse Miranda of not attending while he tells his story. But in fact Miranda is as far as possible from dozing off (until her father sends her into a magic slumber at the conclusion of their conversation), and Shakespeare keeps the audience similarly alert with a technical resourcefulness which merits close observation. The exposition is completed in the confrontations between Prospero and Ariel and between Prospero and Caliban. Here the information conveyed to the audience is already familiar to the two whom Prospero addresses, but it is rendered dramatic by the conflict between him and each of his servants. The contrast between Ariel and Caliban is strikingly brought out, but their kinship as servants to a testy and autocratic master given to abusive language emerges as well.

Actually, there is not very much plot in *The Tempest*. There is the love of Ferdinand and Miranda, which Prospero has to pretend to oppose (though we know he doesn't), lest it all seem too easy to the lovers. And there are the two conspiracies, but Prospero is so powerful and so well informed that we can feel little suspense about the outcome of either one. Each of the three strands of plot, however, leads up to a spectacle, and in this way, by theatrical means, Shakespeare makes up for the lack of dramatic tension. The disappearing banquet, the masque of the classical goddesses, and the three drunks parading in stolen finery offer variety and display.

Because the play has so little plot and yet makes so great an effect, some commentators suppose that it is allegorical—that there is another plot behind the one we see. Nineteenth-century critics suggested that Prospero stands for Shakespeare himself and the magic is his dramatic art; alternatively, the play is a psychological allegory in which Prospero stands for Imagination, Ariel is Fancy, and Caliban is brute Understanding. Another theory is that Ferdinand stands for John Fletcher, Shakespeare's younger colleague just beginning to write for the King's Men, and Miranda stands for Art. A twentieth-century commentator interprets the play as an initiation ritual and a portrayal of the fall and redemption of man. In this version Caliban becomes "the Tempter who is Desire" and Miranda becomes Wisdom. Still another view is that the play is an allegory of the struggles within the Christian church at the time of the Reformation. Quite recently Prospero has been defined as "the mind of European civilization casting off the shackles, and the false hopes, and the terrors of magical daemonology." These theories are constructed because the play is so suggestive, because its atmosphere so strongly stimulates the imagination. Their danger is that they may distract attention from the literary qualities that are inside the play and not outside it.

The verse of *The Tempest* is typical of Shakespeare's final period. It exhibits wide variety, from the stylized rhymed couplets of the masque to the loose rhythms of the dramatic dialogue:

Full many a lady
I have ey'd with best regard, and many a time
Th' harmony of their tongues hath into bondage
Brought my too diligent ear. For several virtues
Have I lik'd several women, never any
With so full soul but some defect in her
Did quarrel with the noblest grace she ow'd,
And put it to the foil. But you, O you,
So perfect and so peerless, are created
Of every creature's best! (III.i.39–48)

It has sometimes caused surprise that Caliban usually speaks verse though his companions Stephano and Trinculo speak prose. This is not to be taken as indicating that Caliban is more of a poet than they; he is a grotesque but not a comic character, and he is associated with the background of the magic island, which is created largely by poetry. He tells Prospero that the benefit of his having learned language is that he can curse; but to him is assigned also one of the loveliest passages in the play:

> Be not afeard, the isle is full of noises,
> Sounds, and sweet airs, that give delight and hurt not.
> Sometimes a thousand twangling instruments
> Will hum about mine ears; and sometime voices,
> That if I then had wak'd after long sleep,
> Will make me sleep again, and then in dreaming,
> The clouds methought would open, and show riches
> Ready to drop upon me, that when I wak'd
> I cried to dream again. (III.ii.135–43)

Like the isle, the play is full of music. Short as it is, it contains more songs than any other play in the canon; there is also a considerable amount of instrumental music. Ferdinand is first brought on the stage drawn by one of Ariel's songs; he asserts that the music that crept by him on the waters allayed both their fury and his sorrow. The magical beauty of "Full fadom five thy father lies" would seem to set an almost impossible standard for the lyrics of the rest of the play, but "Where the bee sucks, there suck I" and the rollicking "The master, the swabber, the boatswain, and I" are as superb of their kind. Contemporary settings for the first two of these survive, composed by Robert Johnson, lutenist to the King; perhaps he also supplied the rest of the music for the play.

The Tempest—"this almost miraculous drama," as Coleridge called it—has been greatly loved, both by audiences and by readers. One evidence of its tremendous appeal to the imagination is that it has been part of the inspiration for such vastly different poems as Milton's *Comus*, T. S. Eliot's *The Waste Land*, and W. H. Auden's *The Sea and the Mirror*.

Hallett Smith

A fiery spirit. Watercolor sketch by Inigo Jones. Jones created this costume sketch for sixteen "fiery spirits" in Thomas Campion's *The Lords' Masque*, which was presented at court in 1613 in honor of the marriage of the Lady Elizabeth, James I's daughter, to the Elector Palatine. *The Tempest* was also presented as part of the same celebrations. Campion describes the costume as follows: "their attires being alike composed of flames, with fiery wings and bases, bearing in either hand a torch of virgin wax." From the sketch we get some suggestion of how a spirit character like Ariel may have been presented in *The Tempest*. (*Devonshire Collection, Chatsworth. Reproduced by permission of the Trustees of the Chatsworth Settlement.*)

The Tempest

Names of the Actors

Alonso, *King of Naples*
Sebastian, *his brother*
Prospero, *the right Duke of Milan*
Antonio, *his brother, the usurping Duke of Milan*
Ferdinand, *son to the King of Naples*
Gonzalo, *an honest old councillor*
Adrian *and* Francisco, *lords*
Caliban, *a savage and deformed slave*
Trinculo, *a jester*
Stephano, *a drunken butler*
Master of a Ship

Boatswain
Mariners
Miranda, *daughter to Prospero*

Ariel, *an airy spirit*
Iris, Ceres, Juno, Nymphs, Reapers — *spirits*
[*Other* Spirits *attending on Prospero*]

The Scene: [*A ship at sea;*] *an uninhabited island*

ACT I, Scene I

A tempestuous noise of thunder and lightning heard. Enter a Ship-Master *and a* Boatswain.

Mast. Boatswain!

Boats. Here, master; what cheer?

Mast. Good; speak to th' mariners. Fall to't, yarely, or we run ourselves aground. Bestir, bestir. *Exit.*

Enter Mariners.

Boats. Heigh, my hearts! cheerly, cheerly, my hearts! yare, yare! Take in the topsail. Tend to th' master's whistle.—Blow till thou burst thy wind, if room enough!

Enter Alonso, Sebastian, Antonio, Ferdinando, Gonzalo, *and others.*

Alon. Good boatswain, have care. Where's the master? Play the men.

Boats. I pray now keep below.

Ant. Where is the master, bos'n?

Boats. Do you not hear him? You mar our labor. Keep your cabins; you do assist the storm.

Gon. Nay, good, be patient.

Boats. When the sea is. Hence! What cares these roarers for the name of king? To cabin! silence! trouble us not.

Gon. Good, yet remember whom thou hast aboard.

Boats. None that I more love than myself. You are a councillor; if you can command these elements to silence, and work the peace of the present, we will not hand a rope more. Use your authority. If you cannot, give thanks you have liv'd so long, and make yourself ready in your cabin for the mischance of the hour, if it so hap.—Cheerly, good hearts!—Out of our way, I say. *Exit.*

Gon. I have great comfort from this fellow. Methinks he hath no drowning mark upon him, his complexion is perfect gallows. Stand fast, good Fate, to his hanging, make the rope of his destiny our cable, for our own doth little advantage. If he be not born to be hang'd, our case is miserable. *Exeunt.*

Enter Boatswain.

Boats. Down with the topmast! yare! lower, lower!

Words and passages enclosed in square brackets in the text above are either emendations of the copy-text or additions to it. The Textual Notes immediately following the play cite the earliest authority for every such change or insertion and supply the reading of the copy-text wherever it is emended in this edition.

Names of the Actors. salvage: savage.

I.i. Location: On a ship at sea.
3. Good. An acknowledgment of the boatswain's reply. The punctuation differentiates this from the *good* in line 15, which means "good fellow." **4. yarely:** smartly, nimbly. **6. Tend:** attend.
7–8. Blow . . . enough. He addresses the storm. **if room enough:** so long as we have sea-room, i.e. space in which to maneuver without going aground. **10. Play:** ply, urge on (?).

17. roarers: (1) turbulent waves; (2) rowdies.
21. councillor: member of the King's council.
22. the present: the present occasion; but *present* may be a mistake for *presence*, i.e. the King's presence or presence chamber.
28–30. Methinks . . . gallows. Alluding to the proverb "He that is born to be hanged need fear no drowning."
29–30. complexion: appearance (as reflecting his temperament).
31–32. make . . . advantage: make the rope that will hang him our anchor chain, since our actual one now does us little good.

bring her to try with main-course. (*A cry within.*) A plague upon this howling! they are louder than the weather, or our office.

Enter SEBASTIAN, ANTONIO, *and* GONZALO.

Yet again? What do you here? Shall we give o'er and drown? Have you a mind to sink?

Seb. A pox o' your throat, you bawling, blasphemous, incharitable dog!

Boats. Work you then.

Ant. Hang, cur! hang, you whoreson, insolent noisemaker! We are less afraid to be drown'd than thou art.

Gon. I'll warrant him for drowning, though the ship were no stronger than a nutshell, and as leaky as an unstanch'd wench.

Boats. Lay her a-hold, a-hold! Set her two courses off to sea again! Lay her off.

Enter MARINERS *wet.*

Mariners. All lost! To prayers, to prayers! All lost! [*Exeunt.*]

Boats. What, must our mouths be cold?

Gon. The King and Prince at prayers, let's assist them,
For our case is as theirs.

Seb. I am out of patience.

Ant. We are merely cheated of our lives by drunkards.
This wide-chopp'd rascal—would thou mightst lie drowning
The washing of ten tides!

Gon. He'll be hang'd yet,
Though every drop of water swear against it,
And gape at wid'st to glut him.

A confused noise within: "Mercy on us!"—
"We split, we split!"—"Farewell, my wife and children!"—
"Farewell, brother!"—"We split, we split, we split!"
[*Exit Boatswain.*]

Ant. Let's all sink wi' th' King.

Seb. Let's take leave of him. *Exit* [*with Antonio*].

Gon. Now would I give a thousand furlongs of sea for an acre of barren ground, long heath, brown [furze], any thing. The wills above be done! but I would fain die a dry death. *Exit.*

SCENE II

Enter PROSPERO *and* MIRANDA.

Acting
Spectacle
played out by
Ariel

Mir. If by your art, my dearest father, you have
Put the wild waters in this roar, allay them.

35. **bring . . . main-course:** keep her close to the wind by means of the mainsail. 37. **office:** duties. 38. **give o'er:** give up.
46. **warrant him for:** guarantee him against.
49. **a-hold:** a-hull, close to the wind.
49–50. **Set . . . sea:** i.e. set her mainsail and foresail so as to get her out to sea. 56. **merely:** utterly. 57. **wide-chopp'd:** wide-jawed.
58. **ten tides.** Pirates were hanged on shore and left until three tides had washed over them.
60. **gape . . . him:** open its mouth to the widest to gulp him down.
66. **heath . . . furze:** heather . . . gorse (plants that grow in poor soil).
67. **fain:** gladly.

I.ii. Location: An island. Before Prospero's cell.
1. **art:** magic.

The sky it seems would pour down stinking pitch,
But that the sea, mounting to th' welkin's cheek,
Dashes the fire out. O! I have suffered
With those that I saw suffer. A brave vessel
(Who had, no doubt, some noble creature in her)
Dash'd all to pieces! O, the cry did knock
Against my very heart. Poor souls, they perish'd.
Had I been any God of power, I would
Have sunk the sea within the earth or ere
It should the good ship so have swallow'd, and
The fraughting souls within her.

Pros. Be collected,
No more amazement. Tell your piteous heart
There's no harm done.

Mir. O woe the day!

Pros. No harm:
I have done nothing, but in care of thee
(Of thee my dear one, thee my daughter), who
Art ignorant of what thou art, nought knowing
Of whence I am, nor that I am more better
Than Prospero, master of a full poor cell,
And thy no greater father.

Mir. More to know
Did never meddle with my thoughts.

Pros. 'T:s time
I should inform thee farther. Lend thy hand,
And pluck my magic garment from me. So,
[*Lays down his mantle.*]
Lie there, my art. Wipe thou thine eyes, have comfort.
The direful spectacle of the wrack, which touch'd
The very virtue of compassion in thee,
I have with such provision in mine art
So safely ordered that there is no soul—
No, not so much perdition as an hair
Betid to any creature in the vessel
Which thou heardst cry, which thou saw'st sink. Sit down,
For thou must now know farther.

Mir. You have often
Begun to tell me what I am, but stopp'd
And left me to a bootless inquisition,
Concluding, "Stay: not yet."

Pros. The hour's now come,
The very minute bids thee ope thine ear.
Obey, and be attentive. Canst thou remember
A time before we came unto this cell?
I do not think thou canst, for then thou wast not
Out three years old.

Mir. Certainly, sir, I can.

Pros. By what? by any other house, or person?

4. **welkin's:** sky's. **cheek:** (1) face; (2) side of a grate.
6. **brave:** splendid. 11. **or ere:** before.
13. **fraughting:** forming the cargo. **collected:** composed.
14. **amazement:** terror. **piteous:** pitying.
19. **more better:** of higher rank (common Elizabethan double comparative). 20. **full:** very.
21. **no greater:** i.e. of no loftier position than is implied by his "full poor cell."
22. **meddle with:** mingle with, enter. 26. **wrack:** shipwreck.
27. **virtue:** essence. 28. **provision:** foresight.
29. **soul—.** The sentence changes its course in what follows, but the sense is plain. 30. **perdition:** loss. 31. **Betid:** happened.
35. **bootless inquisition:** useless inquiry. 38. **Obey:** i.e. listen.
41. **Out:** fully.

Of any thing the image, tell me, that
Hath kept with thy remembrance.
Mir. 'Tis far off;
And rather like a dream than an assurance
That my remembrance warrants. Had I not
Four, or five, women once that tended me?
Pros. Thou hadst; and more, Miranda. But how is it
That this lives in thy mind? What seest thou else
In the dark backward and abysm of time?
If thou rememb'rest aught ere thou cam'st here,
How thou cam'st here thou mayst.
Mir. But that I do not.
Pros. Twelve year since, Miranda, twelve year since,
Thy father was the Duke of Milan and
A prince of power.
Mir. Sir, are not you my father?
Pros. Thy mother was a piece of virtue, and
She said thou wast my daughter; and thy father
Was Duke of Milan, and his only heir
And princess no worse issued.
Mir. O the heavens,
What foul play had we, that we came from thence?
Or blessed was't we did?
Pros. Both, both, my girl.
By foul play (as thou say'st) were we heav'd thence,
But blessedly holp hither.
Mir. O, my heart bleeds
To think o' th' teen that I have turn'd you to,
Which is from my remembrance! Please you, farther.
Pros. My brother and thy uncle, call'd Antonio—
I pray thee mark me—that a brother should
Be so perfidious!—he whom next thyself
Of all the world I lov'd, and to him put
The manage of my state, as at that time
Through all the signories it was the first,
And Prospero the prime duke, being so reputed
In dignity, and for the liberal arts
Without a parallel; those being all my study,
The government I cast upon my brother,
And to my state grew stranger, being transported
And rapt in secret studies. Thy false uncle—
Dost thou attend me?
Mir. Sir, most heedfully.
Pros. Being once perfected how to grant suits,
How to deny them, who t' advance, and who
To trash for overtopping, new created
The creatures that were mine, I say, or chang'd 'em,
Or else new form'd 'em; having both the key
Of officer and office, set all hearts i' th' state

45. assurance: certainty.
46. remembrance warrants: memory guarantees.
50. backward . . . time: abyss of the past.
56. piece: masterpiece. **virtue:** chastity.
59. no worse issued: no less noble in birth.
63. blessedly holp: providentially helped.
64. teen: sorrow, trouble. **turn'd you to:** reminded you of.
65. from: out of.
71. signories: city states. **72. prime:** chief, first in rank.
79. perfected: expert in.
81. trash for overtopping: restrain from becoming too powerful. Two images are combined here: *trash* = check a hunting dog from going too fast; *overtopping* = growing too high. **82. or:** either.
83. key: (1) key to office; (2) tuning key.

To what tune pleas'd his ear, that now he was
The ivy which had hid my princely trunk,
And suck'd my verdure out on't. Thou attend'st not!
Mir. O, good sir, I do.
Pros. I pray thee mark me.
I, thus neglecting worldly ends, all dedicated
To closeness and the bettering of my mind
With that which, but by being so retir'd,
O'er-priz'd all popular rate, in my false brother
Awak'd an evil nature, and my trust,
Like a good parent, did beget of him
A falsehood in its contrary, as great
As my trust was, which had indeed no limit,
A confidence sans bound. He being thus lorded,
Not only with what my revenue yielded,
But what my power might else exact—like one
Who having into truth, by telling of it,
Made such a sinner of his memory
To credit his own lie—he did believe
He was indeed the Duke, out o' th' substitution,
And executing th' outward face of royalty
With all prerogative. Hence his ambition growing—
Dost thou hear?
Mir. Your tale, sir, would cure deafness.
Pros. To have no screen between this part he play'd
And him he play'd it for, he needs will be
Absolute Milan—me (poor man) my library
Was dukedom large enough: of temporal royalties
He thinks me now incapable; confederates
(So dry he was for sway) wi' th' King of Naples
To give him annual tribute, do him homage,
Subject his coronet to his crown, and bend
The dukedom yet unbow'd (alas, poor Milan!)
To most ignoble stooping.
Mir. O the heavens!
Pros. Mark his condition, and th' event, then tell me
If this might be a brother.
Mir. I should sin
To think but nobly of my grandmother.
Good wombs have borne bad sons.
Pros. Now the condition.
This King of Naples, being an enemy
To me inveterate, hearkens my brother's suit,
Which was, that he in lieu o' th' premises,
Of homage, and I know not how much tribute,
Should presently extirpate me and mine
Out of the dukedom, and confer fair Milan
With all the honors on my brother; whereon,

87. verdure: vigor, vitality. **on't:** of it. **90. closeness:** seclusion.
92. O'er-priz'd . . . rate: had greater worth than any vulgar evaluation would place upon it.
94. good parent. That a good parent often bred a bad child was proverbial.
97. sans: without. **lorded:** i.e. established in a position of power.
100. into: unto, against (*into truth* modifies *sinner*).
102. To: as to. **103. out:** as a result.
107–8. no . . . for: i.e. no separation between acting as Duke and being Duke. **109. Absolute Milan:** actual Duke of Milan.
110. temporal royalties: practical administration.
111. confederates: makes alliance. **112. dry:** thirsty.
117. condition: compact. **event:** outcome.
123. lieu . . . premises: return for the pledge.
125. presently extirpate: immediately remove.

A treacherous army levied, one midnight
Fated to th' purpose, did Antonio open
The gates of Milan, and i' th' dead of darkness
The ministers for th' purpose hurried thence
Me and thy crying self.
Mir. Alack, for pity!
I, not remememb'ring how I cried out then,
Will cry it o'er again. It is a hint
That wrings mine eyes to't.
Pros. Hear a little further,
And then I'll bring thee to the present business
Which now's upon 's; without the which this story
Were most impertinent.
Mir. Wherefore did they not
That hour destroy us?
Pros. Well demanded, wench;
My tale provokes that question. Dear, they durst not,
So dear the love my people bore me; nor set
A mark so bloody on the business; but
With colors fairer painted their foul ends.
In few, they hurried us aboard a bark,
Bore us some leagues to sea, where they prepared
A rotten carcass of a butt, not rigg'd,
Nor tackle, sail, nor mast, the very rats
Instinctively have quit it. There they hoist us,
To cry to th' sea, that roar'd to us; to sigh
To th' winds, whose pity, sighing back again,
Did us but loving wrong.
Mir. Alack, what trouble
Was I then to you!
Pros. O, a cherubin
Thou wast that did preserve me. Thou didst smile,
Infused with a fortitude from heaven,
When I have deck'd the sea with drops full salt,
Under my burthen groan'd, which rais'd in me
An undergoing stomach, to bear up
Against what should ensue.
Mir. How came we ashore?
Pros. By Providence divine.
Some food we had, and some fresh water, that
A noble Neapolitan, Gonzalo,
Out of his charity, who being then appointed
Master of this design, did give us, with
Rich garments, linens, stuffs, and necessaries,
Which since have steaded much; so of his gentleness,
Knowing I lov'd my books, he furnish'd me
From mine own library with volumes that
I prize above my dukedom.
Mir. Would I might
But ever see that man!
Pros. Now I arise. [*Puts on his robe.*]
Sit still, and hear the last of our sea-sorrow:
Here in this island we arriv'd, and here
Have I, thy schoolmaster, made thee more profit
Than other princes can, that have more time
For vainer hours, and tutors not so careful.
Mir. Heavens thank you for't! And now I pray
you, sir,
For still 'tis beating in my mind, your reason
For raising this sea-storm?
Pros. Know thus far forth:
By accident most strange, bountiful Fortune
(Now my dear lady) hath mine enemies
Brought to this shore; and by my prescience
I find my zenith doth depend upon
A most auspicious star, whose influence
If now I court not, but omit, my fortunes
Will ever after droop. Here cease more questions.
Thou art inclin'd to sleep; 'tis a good dullness,
And give it way. I know thou canst not choose.
[*Miranda sleeps.*]
Come away, servant, come; I am ready now,
Approach, my Ariel. Come.

Enter ARIEL.

Ari. All hail, great master, grave sir, hail! I come
To answer thy best pleasure; be't to fly,
To swim, to dive into the fire, to ride
On the curl'd clouds. To thy strong bidding, task
Ariel, and all his quality.
Pros. Hast thou, spirit,
Perform'd to point the tempest that I bade thee?
Ari. To every article.
I boarded the King's ship; now on the beak,
Now in the waist, the deck, in every cabin,
I flam'd amazement. Sometime I'ld divide,
And burn in many places; on the topmast,
The yards and boresprit, would I flame distinctly,
Then meet and join. Jove's lightning, the precursors
O' th' dreadful thunder-claps, more momentary
And sight-outrunning were not; the fire and cracks
Of sulphurous roaring the most mighty Neptune
Seem to besiege, and make his bold waves tremble,
Yea, his dread trident shake.
Pros. My brave spirit!
Who was so firm, so constant, that this coil
Would not infect his reason?
Ari. Not a soul
But felt a fever of the mad, and play'd
Some tricks of desperation. All but mariners
Plung'd in the foaming brine, and quit the vessel;
Then all afire with me, the King's son, Ferdinand,

131. **ministers:** agents. 134. **hint:** occasion.
135. **wrings:** (1) constrains; (2) extracts moisture from.
138. **impertinent:** irrelevant.
143. **With . . . ends:** i.e. undertook to accomplish the same end by less violent means. 144. **In few:** in short. 146. **butt:** tub.
151. **Did . . . wrong:** i.e. only added to our discomfort.
155. **deck'd:** (1) adorned; (2) covered.
156. **which:** i.e. Miranda's smile.
157. **undergoing stomach:** courage to endure.
165. **steaded:** been of use. **gentleness:** character proper to one of high birth and cultivation. 167. **volumes:** i.e. books of magic.

172. **more profit:** profit more.
173. **princes.** The title "prince" could be used to honor either sex.
176. **beating:** working violently.
179. **my dear lady:** i.e. favorable to me.
181. **zenith:** height of fortune.
182. **influence:** power (astrological term). 183. **omit:** ignore.
185. **good dullness:** timely sleepiness.
187. **Come away:** come here.
193. **quality:** (1) skill; (2) cohorts, minor spirits under him.
194. **to point:** in detail. 196. **beak:** prow.
198. **flam'd amazement:** struck terror by appearing as the flamelike phenomenon called St. Elmo's fire or the corposant.
200. **boresprit:** bowsprit. **distinctly:** in separate places.
206. **brave:** splendid. 207. **coil:** uproar.
209. **of the mad:** such as madmen have.
212. **Then . . . me.** Many editors repunctuate lines 211–12 so as to make this phrase modify *vessel* rather than *son*.

With hair up-staring (then like reeds, not hair),
Was the first man that leapt; cried, "Hell is empty,
And all the devils are here."
Pros. Why, that's my spirit!
But was not this nigh shore?
Ari. Close by, my master.
Pros. But are they, Ariel, safe?
Ari. Not a hair perish'd;
On their sustaining garments not a blemish,
But fresher than before; and as thou badst me,
In troops I have dispers'd them 'bout the isle.
The King's son have I landed by himself,
Whom I left cooling of the air with sighs,
In an odd angle of the isle, and sitting,
His arms in this sad knot.
Pros. Of the King's ship,
The mariners, say how thou hast dispos'd,
And all the rest o' th' fleet.
Ari. Safely in harbor
Is the King's ship, in the deep nook, where once
Thou call'dst me up at midnight to fetch dew
From the still-vex'd Bermoothes, there she's hid;
The mariners all under hatches stowed,
Who, with a charm join'd to their suff'red labor,
I have left asleep; and for the rest o' th' fleet
(Which I dispers'd), they all have met again,
And are upon the Mediterranean float
Bound sadly home for Naples,
Supposing that they saw the King's ship wrack'd,
And his great person perish.
Pros. Ariel, thy charge
Exactly is perform'd; but there's more work.
What is the time o' th' day?
Ari. Past the mid season.
Pros. At least two glasses. The time 'twixt six and now
Must by us both be spent most preciously.
Ari. Is there more toil? Since thou dost give me pains,
Let me remember thee what thou hast promis'd,
Which is not yet perform'd me.
Pros. How now? moody?
What is't thou canst demand?
Ari. My liberty.
Pros. Before the time be out? No more!
Ari. I prithee,
Remember I have done thee worthy service,
Told thee no lies, made thee no mistakings, serv'd
Without or grudge or grumblings. Thou did promise
To bate me a full year.
Pros. Dost thou forget
From what a torment I did free thee?
Ari. No.

213. up-staring: standing on end.
218. sustaining garments: garments that bore them up in the water.
224. in . . . knot: i.e. crossed thus (Ariel illustrates with a gesture). Crossed arms indicated melancholy.
227. nook: inlet, small bay.
229. still-vex'd Bermoothes: always stormy Bermuda islands.
231. with a charm: by means of a magic spell. **their suff'red labor:** the labor they have endured.
234. float: flood, sea. **239. mid season:** noon.
240. glasses: hourglasses. **242. pains:** duties, chores.
243. remember: remind. **250. bate:** remit.

Pros. Thou dost; and think'st it much to tread the ooze
Of the salt deep,
To run upon the sharp wind of the north,
To do me business in the veins o' th' earth
When it is bak'd with frost.
Ari. I do not, sir.
Pros. Thou liest, malignant thing! Hast thou forgot
The foul witch Sycorax, who with age and envy
Was grown into a hoop? Hast thou forgot her?
Ari. No, sir.
Pros. Thou hast. Where was she born? Speak. Tell me.
Ari. Sir, in Argier.
Pros. O, was she so? I must
Once in a month recount what thou hast been,
Which thou forget'st. This damn'd witch Sycorax,
For mischiefs manifold, and sorceries terrible
To enter human hearing, from Argier
Thou know'st was banish'd; for one thing she did
They would not take her life. Is not this true?
Ari. Ay, sir.
Pros. This blue-ey'd hag was hither brought with child,
And here was left by th' sailors. Thou, my slave,
As thou report'st thyself, was then her servant,
And for thou wast a spirit too delicate
To act her earthy and abhorr'd commands,
Refusing her grand hests, she did confine thee,
By help of her more potent ministers,
And in her most unmitigable rage,
Into a cloven pine, within which rift
Imprison'd, thou didst painfully remain
A dozen years; within which space she died,
And left thee there, where thou didst vent thy groans
As fast as mill-wheels strike. Then was this island
(Save for the son that [she] did litter here,
A freckled whelp, hag-born) not honor'd with
A human shape.
Ari. Yes—Caliban her son.
Pros. Dull thing, I say so; he, that Caliban
Whom now I keep in service. Thou best know'st
What torment I did find thee in; thy groans
Did make wolves howl, and penetrate the breasts
Of ever-angry bears. It was a torment
To lay upon the damn'd, which Sycorax
Could not again undo. It was mine art,
When I arriv'd and heard thee, that made gape
The pine, and let thee out.
Ari. I thank thee, master.
Pros. If thou more murmur'st, I will rend an oak
And peg thee in his knotty entrails till
Thou hast howl'd away twelve winters.
Ari. Pardon, master,

252. ooze: mud at sea-bottom.
255. veins: underground streams, which were thought to correspond to veins of the body. **256. bak'd:** hardened.
258. envy: malice. **261. Argier:** Algiers.
269. blue-ey'd: with dark circles around the eyes.
272. for: because. **274. hests:** commands.
281. mill-wheels: i.e. the clappers on mill-wheels.
292. gape: open wide. **295. his:** its.

I will be correspondent to command
And do my spriting gently.
Pros. Do so; and after two days
I will discharge thee.
Ari. That's my noble master!
What shall I do? say what? what shall I do?
Pros. Go make thyself like a nymph o' th' sea; be subject
To no sight but thine and mine, invisible
To every eyeball else. Go take this shape
And hither come in't. Go. Hence with diligence!
Exit [Ariel].
Awake, dear heart, awake! Thou hast slept well,
Awake!
Mir. The strangeness of your story put
Heaviness in me.
Pros. Shake it off. Come on,
We'll visit Caliban my slave, who never
Yields us kind answer.
Mir. 'Tis a villain, sir,
I do not love to look on.
Pros. But as 'tis,
We cannot miss him. He does make our fire,
Fetch in our wood, and serves in offices
That profit us. What ho! slave! Caliban!
Thou earth, thou! speak.
Cal. (*Within.*) There's wood enough within.
Pros. Come forth, I say, there's other business for thee.
Come, thou tortoise, when?

Enter Ariel *like a water-nymph.*

Fine apparition! My quaint Ariel,
Hark in thine ear.
Ari. My lord, it shall be done. *Exit.*
Pros. Thou poisonous slave, got by the devil himself
Upon thy wicked dam, come forth!

Enter Caliban.

Cal. As wicked dew as e'er my mother brush'd
With raven's feather from unwholesome fen
Drop on you both! A south-west blow on ye,
And blister you all o'er!
Pros. For this, be sure, to-night thou shalt have cramps,
Side-stitches, that shall pen thy breath up; urchins
Shall, for that vast of night that they may work,
All exercise on thee; thou shalt be pinch'd
As thick as honeycomb, each pinch more stinging
Than bees that made 'em.
Cal. I must eat my dinner.
This island's mine by Sycorax my mother,

297. **correspondent:** obedient.
298. **do . . . gently:** perform my tasks as a spirit ungrudgingly.
307. **Heaviness:** drowsiness. 311. **miss:** do without.
316. **when:** a common expression of impatience. s.d. **like:** in the shape of. 317. **quaint:** clever, ingenious. 321. **wicked:** harmful.
323. **south-west:** southwest wind, thought to bring pestilence.
326. **urchins:** hedgehogs; here, goblins in the shape of hedgehogs.
327. **for . . . work:** during that long and desolate period of darkness during which they are permitted to perform their mischief. It was thought that malignant spirits lost their power with the coming of day.
330. **'em:** i.e. cells of the honeycomb.

Which thou tak'st from me. When thou cam'st first,
Thou strok'st me and made much of me, wouldst give me
Water with berries in't, and teach me how
To name the bigger light, and how the less,
That burn by day and night; and then I lov'd thee
And show'd thee all the qualities o' th' isle,
The fresh springs, brine-pits, barren place and fertile.
Curs'd be I that did so! All the charms
Of Sycorax, toads, beetles, bats, light on you!
For I am all the subjects that you have,
Which first was mine own king; and here you sty me
In this hard rock, whiles you do keep from me
The rest o' th' island.
Pros. Thou most lying slave,
Whom stripes may move, not kindness! I have us'd thee
(Filth as thou art) with human care, and lodg'd thee
In mine own cell, till thou didst seek to violate
The honor of my child.
Cal. O ho, O ho, would't had been done!
Thou didst prevent me; I had peopled else
This isle with Calibans.
Mir. Abhorred slave,
Which any print of goodness wilt not take,
Being capable of all ill! I pitied thee,
Took pains to make thee speak, taught thee each hour
One thing or other. When thou didst not, savage,
Know thine own meaning, but wouldst gabble like
A thing most brutish, I endow'd thy purposes
With words that made them known. But thy vild race
(Though thou didst learn) had that in't which good natures
Could not abide to be with; therefore wast thou
Deservedly confin'd into this rock,
Who hadst deserv'd more than a prison.
Cal. You taught me language, and my profit on't
Is, I know how to curse. The red-plague rid you
For learning me your language!
Pros. Hag-seed, hence!
Fetch us in fuel, and be quick, thou'rt best,
To answer other business. Shrug'st thou, malice?
If thou neglect'st, or dost unwillingly
What I command, I'll rack thee with old cramps,
Fill all thy bones with aches, make thee roar
That beasts shall tremble at thy din.
Cal. No, pray thee.
[*Aside.*] I must obey. His art is of such pow'r,
It would control my dam's god, Setebos,
And make a vassal of him.
Pros. So, slave, hence! *Exit Caliban.*

Enter Ferdinand; *and* Ariel, *invisible, playing and singing.*

345. **stripes:** lashes. 346. **human:** humane.
351 s.p. **Mir.** Some editors make Prospero the speaker.
358. **vild:** vile. **race:** nature.
364. **red-plague:** plague that produces red sores. **rid:** destroy.
365. **learning:** teaching. 366. **thou'rt best:** you had better.
369. **old:** i.e. such as old people have.
370. **aches.** Pronounced *aitches.*
374 s.d. **invisible.** Ariel is of course visible to the audience but he wears a costume which by convention makes him invisible to other persons on the stage, except Prospero.

ARIEL['s] SONG

Come unto these yellow sands,
And then take hands:
Curtsied when you have, and kiss'd,
The wild waves whist:
Foot it featly here and there,
And, sweet sprites, [the burthen bear].
Hark, hark!
Burthen, dispersedly, [*within*]. Bow-wow.
The watch-dogs bark!
[*Burthen, dispersedly, within.*] Bow-wow.
Hark, hark, I hear
The strain of strutting chanticleer:
Cry [*within*]. Cock-a-diddle-dow.

Fer. Where should this music be? I' th' air, or th' earth?
It sounds no more; and sure it waits upon
Some god o' th' island. Sitting on a bank,
Weeping again the King my father's wrack,
This music crept by me upon the waters,
Allaying both their fury and my passion
With its sweet air; thence I have follow'd it,
Or it hath drawn me rather. But 'tis gone.
No, it begins again.

ARIEL['s] SONG

Full fadom five thy father lies,
Of his bones are coral made:
Those are pearls that were his eyes:
Nothing of him that doth fade,
But doth suffer a sea-change
Into something rich and strange.
Sea-nymphs hourly ring his knell:
Burthen [*within*]. Ding-dong.
Hark now I hear them—ding-dong bell.

Fer. The ditty does remember my drown'd father.
This is no mortal business, nor no sound
That the earth owes. I hear it now above me.
Pros. The fringed curtains of thine eye advance,
And say what thou seest yond.
Mir. What, is't a spirit?
Lord, how it looks about! Believe me, sir,
It carries a brave form. But 'tis a spirit.
Pros. No, wench, it eats, and sleeps, and hath such senses
As we have—such. This gallant which thou seest
Was in the wrack; and but he's something stain'd
With grief (that's beauty's canker), thou mightst call him
A goodly person. He hath lost his fellows,
And strays about to find 'em.
Mir. I might call him
A thing divine, for nothing natural

378. **whist**: being hushed. 379. **featly**: nimbly.
380. **the burthen bear**: bear the burden, i.e. the bass undersong.
382. **dispersedly**: from several directions.
393. **passion**: sorrow. 397. **fadom**: fathom.
406. **ditty**: words of the song. **remember**: commemorate.
408. **owes**: owns. 409. **advance**: raise.
412. **brave**: excellent, splendid.
415. **but**: except that. **something stain'd**: somewhat disfigured.
416. **canker**: worm that eats blossoms.

I ever saw so noble.
Pros. [*Aside.*] It goes on, I see,
As my soul prompts it. Spirit, fine spirit, I'll free thee
Within two days for this.
Fer. Most sure, the goddess
On whom these airs attend! Vouchsafe my pray'r
May know if you remain upon this island,
And that you will some good instruction give
How I may bear me here. My prime request,
Which I do last pronounce, is (O you wonder!)
If you be maid, or no?
Mir. No wonder, sir,
But certainly a maid.
Fer. My language? heavens!
I am the best of them that speak this speech,
Were I but where 'tis spoken.
Pros. How? the best?
What wert thou, if the King of Naples heard thee?
Fer. A single thing, as I am now, that wonders
To hear thee speak of Naples. He does hear me,
And that he does I weep. Myself am Naples,
Who with mine eyes (never since at ebb) beheld
The King my father wrack'd.
Mir. Alack, for mercy!
Fer. Yes, faith, and all his lords, the Duke of Milan
And his brave son being twain.
Pros. [*Aside.*] The Duke of Milan
And his more braver daughter could control thee,
If now 'twere fit to do't. At the first sight
They have chang'd eyes. Delicate Ariel,
I'll set thee free for this.—A word, good sir,
I fear you have done yourself some wrong; a word.
Mir. Why speaks my father so ungently? This
Is the third man that e'er I saw; the first
That e'er I sigh'd for. Pity move my father
To be inclin'd my way!
Fer. O, if a virgin,
And your affection not gone forth, I'll make you
The Queen of Naples.
Pros. Soft, sir, one word more.
[*Aside.*] They are both in either's pow'rs; but this swift business
I must uneasy make, lest too light winning
Make the prize light.—One word more: I charge thee
That thou attend me. Thou dost here usurp
The name thou ow'st not, and hast put thyself
Upon this island as a spy, to win it
From me, the lord on't.
Fer. No, as I am a man.
Mir. There's nothing ill can dwell in such a temple.
If the ill spirit have so fair a house,

420. **It**: i.e. the charm. 423. **airs**: i.e. the music he has heard.
426. **prime**: first, most important.
428. **maid**: i.e. a human maiden, not a goddess.
430. **best**: first in rank.
433. **single**: solitary (because he thinks that he and the King are one and the same), but he probably has in mind also the senses "deserted" and "helpless." 435. **Naples**: King of Naples.
436. **at ebb**: dry (a part of the continued sea-imagery in the play).
439. **his brave son.** Not mentioned elsewhere in the play.
440. **control**: refute. 442. **chang'd eyes**: exchanged loving looks.
444. **done . . . wrong.** An ironically polite way of charging him with lying. 452. **uneasy**: difficult.
452–53. **light . . . light**: easy . . . lightly esteemed.
457. **on't**: of it.

Good things will strive to dwell with't.
Pros. Follow me.—
Speak not you for him; he's a traitor.—Come,
I'll manacle thy neck and feet together.
Sea-water shalt thou drink; thy food shall be
The fresh-brook mussels, wither'd roots, and husks
Wherein the acorn cradled. Follow.
Fer. No,
I will resist such entertainment till
Mine enemy has more pow'r.
He draws, and is charmed from moving.
Mir. O dear father,
Make not too rash a trial of him, for
He's gentle, and not fearful.
Pros. What, I say,
My foot my tutor? Put thy sword up, traitor,
Who mak'st a show but dar'st not strike, thy conscience
Is so possess'd with guilt. Come, from thy ward,
For I can here disarm thee with this stick,
And make thy weapon drop.
Mir. Beseech you, father.
Pros. Hence! hang not on my garments.
Mir. Sir, have pity,
I'll be his surety.
Pros. Silence! one word more
Shall make me chide thee, if not hate thee. What,
An advocate for an impostor? Hush!
Thou think'st there is no more such shapes as he,
Having seen but him and Caliban. Foolish wench,
To th' most of men this is a Caliban,
And they to him are angels.
Mir. My affections
Are then most humble; I have no ambition
To see a goodlier man.
Pros. [*To Ferdinand.*] Come on, obey:
Thy nerves are in their infancy again
And have no vigor in them.
Fer. So they are.
My spirits, as in a dream, are all bound up.
My father's loss, the weakness which I feel,
The wrack of all my friends, nor this man's threats
To whom I am subdu'd, are but light to me,
Might I but through my prison once a day
Behold this maid. All corners else o' th' earth
Let liberty make use of; space enough
Have I in such a prison.
Pros. [*Aside.*] It works. [*To Ferdinand.*] Come on.—
Thou hast done well, fine Ariel! [*To Ferdinand.*] Follow me.
[*To Ariel.*] Hark what thou else shalt do me.
Mir. Be of comfort,
My father's of a better nature, sir,
Than he appears by speech. This is unwonted

466. entertainment: treatment.
467 s.d. charmed: magically prevented.
469. gentle: of high birth. **fearful:** cowardly.
470. foot: i.e. subordinate (Miranda).
472. ward: position of defense. **473. stick:** staff.
481. To: in comparison with. **482. affections:** inclinations.
485. nerves: sinews. **487. spirits:** vital powers.
496. do me: do for me.

Which now came from him.
Pros. Thou shalt be as free
As mountain winds; but then exactly do
All points of my command.
Ari. To th' syllable.
Pros. [*To Ferdinand.*] Come, follow. [*To Miranda.*] Speak not for him. *Exeunt.*

ACT II, Scene I

Enter Alonso, Sebastian, Antonio, Gonzalo, Adrian, Francisco, *and others.*

Gon. Beseech you, sir, be merry; you have cause
(So have we all) of joy; for our escape
Is much beyond our loss. Our hint of woe
Is common: every day some sailor's wife,
The masters of some merchant, and the merchant
Have just our theme of woe; but for the miracle
(I mean our preservation), few in millions
Can speak like us. Then wisely, good sir, weigh
Our sorrow with our comfort.
Alon. Prithee peace.
Seb. He receives comfort like cold porridge.
Ant. The visitor will not give him o'er so.
Seb. Look, he's winding up the watch of his wit, by and by it will strike.
Gon. Sir—
Seb. One. Tell.
Gon. When every grief is entertain'd that's offer'd,
Comes to th' entertainer—
Seb. A dollar.
Gon. Dolor comes to him indeed, you have spoken truer than you purpos'd.
Seb. You have taken it wiselier than I meant you should.
Gon. Therefore, my lord—
Ant. Fie, what a spendthrift is he of his tongue!
Alon. I prithee spare.
Gon. Well, I have done. But yet—
Seb. He will be talking.
Ant. Which, of he or Adrian, for a good wager, first begins to crow?
Seb. The old cock.
Ant. The cock'rel.
Seb. Done. The wager?
Ant. A laughter.
Seb. A match!
Adr. Though this island seem to be desert—
Seb. Ha, ha, ha!

II.i. Location: Another part of the island.
3. hint: occasion.
5. masters . . . the merchant: chief officers of some merchant vessel, and the owner of it. **9. with:** against.
10. porridge: broth. There is an underlying pun on *peace* (line 9) and *pease*, i.e. peas, a common ingredient of porridge.
11. visitor: minister who visits the sick and bereaved, i.e. would-be comforter. **15. Tell:** count.
17. entertainer: sufferer. Sebastian puns on the sense "innkeeper."
18. dollar: a continental coin. **19. Dolor:** sorrow.
30. old cock: i.e. Gonzalo. **31. cock'rel:** i.e. Adrian.
33. laughter: a laugh (perhaps with pun on the sense "a sitting of eggs," consistent with the poultry imagery).
35. desert: uninhabited.
36. Ha, ha, ha. Antonio wins the bet, since Adrian spoke first. The winner was entitled to laugh. Accordingly most editors reverse the speech prefixes for lines 36 and 37.

Ant. So: you're paid!

Adr. Uninhabitable, and almost inaccessible—

Seb. Yet—

Adr. Yet—

Ant. He could not miss't.

Adr. It must needs be of subtle, tender, and delicate temperance.

Ant. Temperance was a delicate wench.

Seb. Ay, and a subtle, as he most learnedly deliver'd.

Adr. The air breathes upon us here most sweetly.

Seb. As if it had lungs, and rotten ones.

Ant. Or, as 'twere perfum'd by a fen.

Gon. Here is every thing advantageous to life.

Ant. True, save means to live.

Seb. Of that there's none, or little.

Gon. How lush and lusty the grass looks! How green!

Ant. The ground indeed is tawny.

Seb. With an eye of green in't.

Ant. He misses not much.

Seb. No; he doth but mistake the truth totally.

Gon. But the rariety of it is—which is indeed almost beyond credit—

Seb. As many vouch'd rarieties are.

Gon. That our garments, being (as they were) drench'd in the sea, hold notwithstanding their freshness and glosses, being rather new dy'd than stain'd with salt water.

Ant. If but one of his pockets could speak, would it not say he lies?

Seb. Ay, or very falsely pocket up his report.

Gon. Methinks our garments are now as fresh as when we put them on first in Afric, at the marriage of the King's fair daughter Claribel to the King of Tunis.

Seb. 'Twas a sweet marriage, and we prosper well in our return.

Adr. Tunis was never grac'd before with such a paragon to their queen.

Gon. Not since widow Dido's time.

Ant. Widow? a pox o' that! How came that widow in? Widow Dido!

Seb. What if he had said "widower Aeneas" too? Good Lord, how you take it!

Adr. "Widow Dido," said you? You make me study of that. She was of Carthage, not of Tunis.

Gon. This Tunis, sir, was Carthage.

Adr. Carthage?

Gon. I assure you, Carthage.

Ant. His word is more than the miraculous harp.

Seb. He hath rais'd the wall, and houses too.

Ant. What impossible matter will he make easy next?

Seb. I think he will carry this island home in his pocket, and give it his son for an apple.

Ant. And sowing the kernels of it in the sea, bring forth more islands.

Gon. Ay.

Ant. Why, in good time.

Gon. Sir, we were talking that our garments seem now as fresh as when we were at Tunis at the marriage of your daughter, who is now queen.

Ant. And the rarest that e'er came there.

Seb. Bate, I beseech you, widow Dido.

Ant. O, widow Dido? Ay, widow Dido.

Gon. Is not, sir, my doublet as fresh as the first day I wore it? I mean, in a sort.

Ant. That "sort" was well fish'd for.

Gon. When I wore it at your daughter's marriage?

Alon. You cram these words into mine ears against
The stomach of my sense. Would I had never
Married my daughter there! for coming thence,
My son is lost and (in my rate) she too,
Who is so far from Italy removed
I ne'er again shall see her. O thou mine heir
Of Naples and of Milan, what strange fish
Hath made his meal on thee?

Fran. Sir, he may live.
I saw him beat the surges under him,
And ride upon their backs. He trod the water,
Whose enmity he flung aside, and breasted
The surge most swoll'n that met him. His bold head
'Bove the contentious waves he kept, and oared
Himself with his good arms in lusty stroke
To th' shore, that o'er his wave-worn basis bowed,
As stooping to relieve him. I not doubt
He came alive to land.

Alon. No, no, he's gone.

Seb. Sir, you may thank yourself for this great loss,
That would not bless our Europe with your daughter,
But rather loose her to an African,
Where she, at least, is banish'd from your eye,
Who hath cause to wet the grief on't.

Alon. Prithee peace.

Seb. You were kneel'd to, and importun'd otherwise
By all of us, and the fair soul herself
Weigh'd between loathness and obedience, at

41. miss't: (1) escape saying "yet"; (2) avoid the island.
43. temperance: climate. Antonio puns on the word as a girl's name.
55. tawny: parched tan or yellow. **56. eye:** spot.
59. rariety. Perhaps this spelling indicates an unusual pronunciation of the word by Gonzalo, which Sebastian mimics.
61. vouch'd: guaranteed true.
68. pocket up: conceal, suppress. One who failed to challenge a lie or an insult was said to "pocket up" the injury. **76. to:** for.
78–79. Widow . . . Dido. Antonio's vigorous reaction has been variously explained. Dido was indeed a widow, and Aeneas a widower, when they met, and perhaps Antonio is laughing at what he considers Gonzalo's prudery in referring to her as widow rather than as Aeneas' mistress. *Widow* could also be used of a wife separated from or deserted by her husband, and Antonio may be laughing at Gonzalo for prudish evasion of the fact that the deserted Dido was not Aeneas' wife.
84. This . . . Carthage. Tunis and Carthage were separate cities, though not far apart.
87. miraculous harp: the legendary harp of Amphion, which raised the walls of Thebes. Gonzalo's error has created a whole new city.
93. kernels: seeds.
95. Ay. Probably a reassertion of the identity of the two cities. Antonio responds with a sarcastic expression of approbation.
101. Bate: except. **104. in a sort:** comparatively.
107–8. You . . . sense. The image is of someone being fed against his will; *stomach* = appetite. **110. rate:** opinion.
121. his wave-worn basis: its foundation hollowed by the action of the sea. **125. That:** you who.
126. loose. With second (perhaps primary) sense "lose," often spelled *loose*.
131–32. Weigh'd . . . bow: weighed in the scale her unwillingness to marry and her duty of obedience to her father, to see which would prevail.

Which end o' th' beam should bow. We have lost your son,
I fear for ever. Milan and Naples have
Moe widows in them of this business' making
Than we bring men to comfort them.
The fault's your own.

Alon. So is the dear'st o' th' loss.

Gon. My Lord Sebastian,
The truth you speak doth lack some gentleness,
And time to speak it in. You rub the sore,
When you should bring the plaster.

Seb. Very well.

Ant. And most chirurgeonly.

Gon. It is foul weather in us all, good sir,
When you are cloudy.

Seb. Fowl weather?

Ant. Very foul.

Gon. Had I plantation of this isle, my lord—

Ant. He'd sow't with nettle-seed.

Seb. Or docks, or mallows.

Gon. And were the king on't, what would I do?

Seb. Scape being drunk, for want of wine.

Gon. I' th' commonwealth I would, by contraries,
Execute all things; for no kind of traffic
Would I admit; no name of magistrate;
Letters should not be known; riches, poverty,
And use of service, none; contract, succession,
Bourn, bound of land, tilth, vineyard, none;
No use of metal, corn, or wine, or oil;
No occupation, all men idle, all;
And women too, but innocent and pure;
No sovereignty—

Seb. Yet he would be king on't.

Ant. The latter end of his commonwealth forgets the beginning.

Gon. All things in common nature should produce
Without sweat or endeavor: treason, felony,
Sword, pike, knife, gun, or need of any engine,
Would I not have; but nature should bring forth,
Of it own kind, all foison, all abundance,
To feed my innocent people.

Seb. No marrying 'mong his subjects?

Ant. None, man, all idle—whores and knaves.

Gon. I would with such perfection govern, sir,
T' excel the golden age.

Seb. 'Save his Majesty!

Ant. Long live Gonzalo!

Gon. And—do you mark me, sir?

Alon. Prithee no more; thou dost talk nothing to me.

Gon. I do well believe your Highness, and did it to minister occasion to these gentlemen, who are of such sensible and nimble lungs that they always use to laugh at nothing.

Ant. 'Twas you we laugh'd at.

Gon. Who, in this kind of merry fooling, am nothing to you; so you may continue, and laugh at nothing still.

Ant. What a blow was there given!

Seb. And it had not fall'n flat-long.

Gon. You are gentlemen of brave mettle; you would lift the moon out of her sphere, if she would continue in it five weeks without changing.

Enter ARIEL [*invisible*], *playing solemn music.*

Seb. We would so, and then go a-batfowling.

Ant. Nay, good my lord, be not angry.

Gon. No, I warrant you, I will not adventure my discretion so weakly. Will you laugh me asleep, for I am very heavy?

Ant. Go sleep, and hear us.

[*All sleep except Alonso, Sebastian, and Antonio.*]

Alon. What, all so soon asleep! I wish mine eyes
Would, with themselves, shut up my thoughts. I find
They are inclin'd to do so.

Seb. Please you, sir,
Do not omit the heavy offer of it.
It seldom visits sorrow; when it doth,
It is a comforter.

Ant. We two, my lord,
Will guard your person while you take your rest,
And watch your safety.

Alon. Thank you. Wondrous heavy.

[*Alonso sleeps. Exit Ariel.*]

Seb. What a strange drowsiness possesses them!

Ant. It is the quality o' th' climate.

Seb. Why
Doth it not then our eyelids sink? I find not
Myself dispos'd to sleep.

Ant. Nor I, my spirits are nimble.
They fell together all, as by consent;
They dropp'd, as by a thunder-stroke. What might,
Worthy Sebastian, O, what might—? No more—
And yet methinks I see it in thy face,
What thou shouldst be. Th' occasion speaks thee, and
My strong imagination sees a crown
Dropping upon thy head.

Seb. What? art thou waking?

Ant. Do you not hear me speak?

Seb. I do, and surely
It is a sleepy language, and thou speak'st
Out of thy sleep. What is it thou didst say?
This is a strange repose, to be asleep
With eyes wide open—standing, speaking, moving—

134. Moe: more. **136. dear'st:** most heartfelt.
139. time: appropriate occasion. **141. chirurgeonly:** like a surgeon.
143. Fowl. Sebastian's pun returns to the imagery of lines 28–31.
144. plantation: colonization, but the following speakers take up the word in the sense "planting."
148. contraries: the opposite of what is customary.
149. traffic: business, trade. **151. Letters:** learning, literacy.
152. service: servanthood, serving of some by others. **succession:** inheritance, hereditary privilege.
153. Bourn: boundary, i.e. division of land among individual owners. **tilth:** tillage. **154. corn:** grain.
162. pike: spear. **engine:** instrument of war.
164. it: its. **foison:** plenty. **169. 'Save:** God save.

173. minister occasion: give opportunity.
174. sensible and nimble: sensitive and lively.
181. And: if. **flat-long:** with the sword blade flat, not on edge.
185. a-batfowling: bird-hunting with sticks (*bats*) at night. He suggests that they would use the moon as their lantern.
187–88. adventure . . . weakly: risk my reputation for good sense by getting angry at such superficial fellows. **189. heavy:** drowsy.
190. hear us: i.e. listen to our laughter.
194. omit . . . offer: neglect the opportunity sleepiness provides.
195. visits. See note to II.i.11.
207. speaks thee: calls upon you (to seize the opportunity).

And yet so fast asleep.
Ant. Noble Sebastian,
Thou let'st thy fortune sleep—die, rather; wink'st
Whiles thou art waking.
Seb. Thou dost snore distinctly,
There's meaning in thy snores.
Ant. I am more serious than my custom; you
Must be so too, if heed me; which to do,
Trebles thee o'er.
Seb. Well; I am standing water.
Ant. I'll teach you how to flow.
Seb. Do so. To ebb
Hereditary sloth instructs me.
Ant. O!
If you but knew how you the purpose cherish
Whiles thus you mock it! how, in stripping it,
You more invest it! Ebbing men, indeed,
Most often, do so near the bottom run
By their own fear or sloth.
Seb. Prithee say on.
The setting of thine eye and cheek proclaim
A matter from thee; and a birth, indeed,
Which throes thee much to yield.
Ant. Thus, sir:
Although this lord of weak remembrance, this
Who shall be of as little memory
When he is earth'd, hath here almost persuaded
(For he's a spirit of persuasion, only
Professes to persuade) the King his son's alive,
'Tis as impossible that he's undrown'd,
As he that sleeps here swims.
Seb. I have no hope
That he's undrown'd.
Ant. O, out of that no hope
What great hope have you! No hope, that way, is
Another way so high a hope that even
Ambition cannot pierce a wink beyond,
But doubt discovery there. Will you grant with me
That Ferdinand is drown'd?
Seb. He's gone.
Ant. Then tell me,
Who's the next heir of Naples?
Seb. Claribel.
Ant. She that is Queen of Tunis; she that dwells
Ten leagues beyond man's life; she that from Naples
Can have no note, unless the sun were post—
The Man i' th' Moon's too slow—till new-born chins
Be rough and razorable; she that from whom
We all were sea-swallow'd, though some cast again

216. **wink'st**: keep your eyes shut.
221. **Trebles thee o'er**: triples your fortune. **standing water**: i.e. indecisive, going neither forward nor back.
223. **Hereditary sloth**: natural laziness. 224. **cherish**: enrich.
226. **invest**: dress up. 229. **setting**: fixed look.
231. **throes**: causes labor pains.
232. **this lord**: i.e. Gonzalo. **of weak remembrance**: having a short memory (perhaps alluding to Gonzalo's lapse in identifying Tunis with Carthage); with following shift to the sense "remembered only briefly after death." 234. **earth'd**: buried.
235–36. **only . . . persuade**: has no function except to persuade. Gonzalo is a privy councillor.
240. **that way**: i.e. with respect to Ferdinand's being undrowned.
242. **wink**: glimpse.
243. **doubt discovery there**: is uncertain of seeing clearly even there.
247. **Ten . . . life**: thirty miles farther than a lifetime's journey.
248. **note**: news. **post**: messenger. 250. **from**: coming from.
251. **cast**: (1) cast up; (2) cast as actors.

(And by that destiny) to perform an act
Whereof what's past is prologue, what to come
In yours and my discharge.
Seb. What stuff is this? How say you?
'Tis true, my brother's daughter 's Queen of Tunis,
So is she heir of Naples; 'twixt which regions
There is some space.
Ant. A space whose ev'ry cubit
Seems to cry out, "How shall that Claribel
Measure us back to Naples? Keep in Tunis,
And let Sebastian wake." Say this were death
That now hath seiz'd them, why, they were no worse
Than now they are. There be that can rule Naples
As well as he that sleeps; lords that can prate
As amply and unnecessarily
As this Gonzalo; I myself could make
A chough of as deep chat. O that you bore
The mind that I do! what a sleep were this
For your advancement! Do you understand me?
Seb. Methinks I do.
Ant. And how does your content
Tender your own good fortune?
Seb. I remember
You did supplant your brother Prospero.
Ant. True.
And look how well my garments sit upon me,
Much feater than before. My brother's servants
Were then my fellows, now they are my men.
Seb. But, for your conscience?
Ant. Ay, sir; where lies that? If 'twere a kibe,
'Twould put me to my slipper; but I feel not
This deity in my bosom. Twenty consciences,
That stand 'twixt me and Milan, candied be they,
And melt ere they molest! Here lies your brother,
No better than the earth he lies upon,
If he were that which now he's like—that's dead,
Whom I with this obedient steel, three inches of it,
Can lay to bed for ever; whiles you, doing thus,
To the perpetual wink for aye might put
This ancient morsel, this Sir Prudence, who
Should not upbraid our course. For all the rest,
They'll take suggestion as a cat laps milk;
They'll tell the clock to any business that
We say befits the hour.
Seb. Thy case, dear friend,
Shall be my president: as thou got'st Milan,
I'll come by Naples. Draw thy sword. One stroke
Shall free thee from the tribute which thou payest,
And I the King shall love thee.
Ant. Draw together;
And when I rear my hand, do you the like,
To fall it on Gonzalo.
Seb. O, but one word. [*They talk apart.*]

254. **discharge**: performance.
257. **cubit**: measure of about 20 inches.
259. **Measure us**: i.e. travel over the cubits.
260. **wake**: i.e. awake to fortune.
265–66. **make . . . chat**: train a jackdaw to speak as wisely as he. Jackdaws were taught to speak. 269. **content**: inclination.
270. **Tender**: regard. 273. **feater**: more gracefully.
276. **kibe**: chilblain. 277. **put me to**: make me wear.
279. **Milan**: the dukedom of Milan. **candied**: sugared.
285. **wink**: sleep. 288. **suggestion**: evil prompting.
289. **tell . . . to**: i.e. agree that the time sorts with.
291. **president**: precedent. 296. **fall it**: let it fall.

Enter Ariel [*invisible*], *with music and song.*

Ari. My master through his art foresees the danger
That you, his friend, are in, and sends me forth
(For else his project dies) to keep them living.
Sings in Gonzalo's ear.

While you here do snoring lie,
Open-ey'd conspiracy
His time doth take.
If of life you keep a care,
Shake off slumber, and beware.
Awake, awake!

Ant. Then let us both be sudden.
Gon. [*Waking.*] Now, good angels
Preserve the King! [*Wakes Alonso.*]
Alon. Why, how now, ho! Awake? Why are you drawn?
Wherefore this ghastly looking?
Gon. What's the matter?
Seb. Whiles we stood here securing your repose,
Even now, we heard a hollow burst of bellowing
Like bulls, or rather lions. Did't not wake you?
It strook mine ear most terribly.
Alon. I heard nothing.
Ant. O, 'twas a din to fright a monster's ear,
To make an earthquake; sure it was the roar
Of a whole herd of lions.
Alon. Heard you this, Gonzalo?
Gon. Upon mine honor, sir, I heard a humming
(And that a strange one too) which did awake me.
I shak'd you, sir, and cried. As mine eyes open'd,
I saw their weapons drawn. There was a noise,
That's verily. 'Tis best we stand upon our guard,
Or that we quit this place. Let's draw our weapons.
Alon. Lead off this ground, and let's make further search
For my poor son.
Gon. Heavens keep him from these beasts!
For he is sure i' th' island.
Alon. Lead away.
Ari. Prospero my lord shall know what I have done.
So, King, go safely on to seek thy son. *Exeunt.*

Scene II

Enter Caliban *with a burthen of wood. A noise of thunder heard.*

Cal. All the infections that the sun sucks up
From bogs, fens, flats, on Prosper fall, and make him
By inch-meal a disease! His spirits hear me,
And yet I needs must curse. But they'll nor pinch,
Fright me with urchin-shows, pitch me i' th' mire,
Nor lead me, like a fire-brand, in the dark
Out of my way, unless he bid 'em; but
For every trifle are they set upon me,

302. time: opportunity. **310. securing:** guarding.
313. strook: struck. **319. cried:** called out.

II.ii. Location: Another part of the island.
3. By inch-meal: inch by inch. Cf. *piecemeal.*
5. urchin-shows: sights of goblins in the shape of hedgehogs.
6. like a fire-brand: in the shape of a will-o'-the-wisp.

Sometime like apes that mow and chatter at me,
And after bite me; then like hedgehogs which
Lie tumbling in my barefoot way, and mount
Their pricks at my footfall; sometime am I
All wound with adders, who with cloven tongues
Do hiss me into madness.

Enter Trinculo.

Lo, now lo,
Here comes a spirit of his, and to torment me
For bringing wood in slowly. I'll fall flat,
Perchance he will not mind me.

Trin. Here's neither bush nor shrub to bear off any weather at all. And another storm brewing, I hear it sing i' th' wind. Yond same black cloud, yond huge one, looks like a foul bumbard that would shed his liquor. If it should thunder as it did before, I know not where to hide my head. Yond same cloud cannot choose but fall by pailfuls. What have we here? a man or a fish? dead or alive? _A fish, he smells like a fish; a very ancient and fish-like smell; a kind of, not-of-the-newest poor-John. A strange fish! Were I in England now (as once I was) and had but this fish painted, not a holiday fool there but would give a piece of silver. There would this monster make a man; any strange beast there makes a man. When they will not give a doit to relieve a lame beggar, they will lay out ten to see a dead Indian. Legg'd like a man; and his fins like arms! Warm, o' my troth! I do now let loose my opinion, hold it no longer: this is no fish, but an islander, that hath lately suffer'd by a thunderbolt. [*Thunder.*] Alas, the storm is come again! My best way is to creep under his gaberdine; there is no other shelter hereabout. Misery acquaints a man with strange bedfellows; I will here shroud till the dregs of the storm be past.

Enter Stephano, *singing,* [*a bottle in his hand*].

Ste. "I shall no more to sea, to sea,
Here shall I die ashore—"
This is a very scurvy tune to sing at a man's funeral.
Well, here's my comfort. *Drinks.*
(*Sings.*) "The master, the swabber, the boatswain, and I,
The gunner and his mate,
Lov'd Mall, Meg, and Marian, and Margery,
But none of us car'd for Kate;
For she had a tongue with a tang,
Would cry to a sailor, 'Go hang!'
She lov'd not the savor of tar nor of pitch,
Yet a tailor might scratch her where e'er she did itch.
Then to sea, boys, and let her go hang!"

9. mow: make faces. **13. wound:** twined about.
17. mind: notice. **18. bear off:** ward off.
21. bumbard: bombard, leather bottle. **22. his:** its.
27. poor-John: cheap dried fish.
29. painted: i.e. on a sign hung outside a booth at a fair to attract customers, with the monster exhibited within.
30. make a man: make a man's fortune, with obvious punning sense "be indistinguishable from an Englishman."
32. doit: coin of trifling value. **34. o' my troth:** by my faith.
35. hold it: hold it back. **38. gaberdine:** cloak.
40. dregs: lees (recurring to the image of the rain as liquor poured from a jug).

This is a scurvy tune too; but here's my comfort. *Drinks.*

Cal. Do not torment me! O!

Ste. What's the matter? Have we devils here? Do you put tricks upon 's with salvages and men of Inde? Ha? I have not scap'd drowning to be afeard now of your four legs; for it hath been said, "As proper a man as ever went on four legs cannot make him give ground"; and it shall be said so again while Stephano breathes at' nostrils.

Cal. The spirit torments me! O!

Ste. This is some monster of the isle with four legs, who hath got (as I take it) an ague. Where the devil should he learn our language? I will give him some relief, if it be but for that. If I can recover him, and keep him tame, and get to Naples with him, he's a present for any emperor that ever trod on neat's-leather.

Cal. Do not torment me, prithee. I'll bring my wood home faster.

Ste. He's in his fit now, and does not talk after the wisest. He shall taste of my bottle; if he have never drunk wine afore, it will go near to remove his fit. If I can recover him, and keep him tame, I will not take too much for him; he shall pay for him that hath him, and that soundly.

Cal. Thou dost me yet but little hurt; thou wilt anon, I know it by thy trembling. Now Prosper works upon thee.

Ste. Come on your ways. Open your mouth; here is that which will give language to you, cat. Open your mouth; this will shake your shaking, I can tell you, and that soundly. You cannot tell who's your friend. Open your chaps again. [*Caliban drinks.*]

Trin. I should know that voice; it should be—but he is drown'd; and these are devils. O, defend me!

Ste. Four legs and two voices; a most delicate monster! His forward voice now is to speak well of his friend; his backward voice is to utter foul speeches and to detract. If all the wine in my bottle will recover him, I will help his ague. Come. [*Caliban drinks again.*] Amen! I will pour some in thy other mouth.

Trin. Stephano!

Ste. Doth thy other mouth call me? Mercy, mercy! This is a devil, and no monster. I will leave him, I have no long spoon.

Trin. Stephano! If thou beest Stephano, touch me, and speak to me; for I am Trinculo—be not afeard—thy good friend Trinculo.

Ste. If thou beest Trinculo, come forth. I'll pull thee by the lesser legs. If any be Trinculo's legs, these are they. Thou art very Trinculo indeed! How cam'st thou to be the siege of this moon-calf? Can he vent Trinculos?

Trin. I took him to be kill'd with a thunder-stroke. But art thou not drown'd, Stephano? I hope now thou art not drown'd. Is the storm overblown? I hid me under the dead moon-calf's gaberdine for fear of the storm. And art thou living, Stephano? O Stephano, two Neapolitans scap'd!

Ste. Prithee do not turn me about, my stomach is not constant.

Cal. [*Aside.*] These be fine things, and if they be not sprites.
That's a brave god, and bears celestial liquor.
I will kneel to him.

Ste. How didst thou scape? How cam'st thou hither? Swear by this bottle how thou cam'st hither—I escap'd upon a butt of sack which the sailors heav'd o'erboard—by this bottle, which I made of the bark of a tree with mine own hands since I was cast ashore.

Cal. I'll swear upon that bottle to be thy true subject, for the liquor is not earthly.

Ste. Here; swear then how thou escap'dst.

Trin. Swom ashore, man, like a duck. I can swim like a duck, I'll be sworn.

Ste. Here, kiss the book. [*Passing the bottle.*] Though thou canst swim like a duck, thou art made like a goose.

Trin. O Stephano, hast any more of this?

Ste. The whole butt, man. My cellar is in a rock by th' sea-side, where my wine is hid. How now, moon-calf? how does thine ague?

Cal. Hast thou not dropp'd from heaven?

Ste. Out o' th' moon, I do assure thee. I was the Man i' th' Moon, when time was.

Cal. I have seen thee in her, and I do adore thee.
My mistress show'd me thee, and thy dog, and thy bush.

Ste. Come, swear to that; kiss the book. I will furnish it anon with new contents. Swear. [*Caliban drinks.*]

Trin. By this good light, this is a very shallow monster! I afeard of him? A very weak monster! The Man i' th' Moon? A most poor credulous monster! Well drawn, monster, in good sooth!

Cal. I'll show thee every fertile inch o' th' island;
And I will kiss thy foot. I prithee be my god.

Trin. By this light, a most perfidious and drunken monster! When 's god's asleep, he'll rob his bottle.

Cal. I'll kiss thy foot. I'll swear myself thy subject.

Ste. Come on then; down, and swear.

56. Do . . . me. Caliban takes Stephano for a spirit sent by Prospero to plague him.
58. put tricks upon 's: delude us with a conjuror's or showman's devices. **salvages:** savages. **Inde:** India.
60–61. As . . . legs. Stephano adapts a proverbial expression by substituting *four* for *two. Proper* = handsome. **63. at':** at the.
68. for that: i.e. because he knows our language. **recover:** restore.
70. neat's-leather: cowhide.
76–77. I will . . . much: whatever I can take for him won't be too much. **77. hath:** gets.
79–80. thou wilt anon: i.e. you will hurt me more very soon.
82–83. here . . . cat. Alluding to the proverb "Liquor will make a cat talk." **86. chaps:** jaws. **89. delicate:** ingenious.
99. long spoon. Alluding to the proverb "He must have a long spoon that will eat with the devil."

106. siege: excrement. **moon-calf:** monstrosity, creature born misshapen because of lunar influence. **107. vent:** emit.
116. and if: if. **121. butt of sack:** barrel of Spanish wine.
128. Swom: swam.
130. kiss the book. Trinculo has taken his oath on the bottle, not on the customary Bible. Stephano means "Take a drink."
139. when time was: once upon a time.
141. dog . . . bush. The man in the moon was placed there in punishment for gathering firewood on Sunday.
147. Well drawn: that's a good long draught you've taken. **sooth:** truth.

Trin. I shall laugh myself to death at this puppy-headed monster. A most scurvy monster! I could find in my heart to beat him—

Ste. Come, kiss.

Trin. But that the poor monster's in drink. An abominable monster!

Cal. I'll show thee the best springs; I'll pluck thee berries;
I'll fish for thee, and get thee wood enough.
A plague upon the tyrant that I serve!
I'll bear him no more sticks, but follow thee,
Thou wondrous man.

Trin. A most ridiculous monster, to make a wonder of a poor drunkard!

Cal. I prithee let me bring thee where crabs grow;
And I with my long nails will dig thee pig-nuts,
Show thee a jay's nest, and instruct thee how
To snare the nimble marmazet. I'll bring thee
To clust'ring filberts, and sometimes I'll get thee
Young scamels from the rock. Wilt thou go with me?

Ste. I prithee now lead the way without any more talking. Trinculo, the King and all our company else being drown'd, we will inherit here. Here! bear my bottle. Fellow Trinculo, we'll fill him by and by again.

Cal. (*Sings drunkenly.*) Farewell, master; farewell, farewell!

Trin. A howling monster; a drunken monster!

Cal. No more dams I'll make for fish,
Nor fetch in firing
At requiring,
Nor scrape trenchering, nor wash dish.
'Ban, 'Ban, Ca-Caliban
Has a new master, get a new man.
Freedom, high-day! high-day, freedom! freedom, high-day, freedom!

Ste. O brave monster! lead the way. *Exeunt.*

ACT III, Scene I

Enter Ferdinand *bearing a log.*

Fer. There be some sports are painful, and their labor
Delight in them [sets] off; some kinds of baseness
Are nobly undergone; and most poor matters
Point to rich ends. This my mean task
Would be as heavy to me as odious, but
The mistress which I serve quickens what's dead,
And makes my labors pleasures. O, she is
Ten times more gentle than her father's crabbed;
And he's compos'd of harshness. I must remove
Some thousands of these logs, and pile them up,

167. crabs: crab apples. **168. pig-nuts:** peanuts.
170. marmazet: marmoset (a small monkey).
172. scamels. Meaning unknown, but apparently either shellfish or rock-inhabiting birds. Some editors emend to *sea-mels*, i.e. sea-mews.
183. trenchering: trenchers, wooden plates.

III.i. Location: Before Prospero's cell.
1. are painful: that are laborious.
1–2. their . . . off: their laboriousness increases our pleasure in them (?) or our pleasure in them offsets their laboriousness (?).
2. baseness: menial activity. **6. quickens:** brings to life.

Upon a sore injunction. My sweet mistress
Weeps when she sees me work, and says such baseness
Had never like executor. I forget;
But these sweet thoughts do even refresh my labors,
Most [busil'est] when I do it.

Enter Miranda, *and* Prospero [*at a distance, unseen*].

Mir. Alas, now pray you
Work not so hard. I would the lightning had
Burnt up those logs that you are enjoin'd to pile!
Pray set it down, and rest you. When this burns,
'Twill weep for having wearied you. My father
Is hard at study; pray now rest yourself,
He's safe for these three hours.

Fer. O most dear mistress,
The sun will set before I shall discharge
What I must strive to do.

Mir. If you'll sit down,
I'll bear your logs the while. Pray give me that,
I'll carry it to the pile.

Fer. No, precious creature,
I had rather crack my sinews, break my back,
Than you should such dishonor undergo,
While I sit lazy by.

Mir. It would become me
As well as it does you; and I should do it
With much more ease, for my good will is to it,
And yours it is against.

Pros. [*Aside.*] Poor worm, thou art infected!
This visitation shows it.

Mir. You look wearily.

Fer. No, noble mistress, 'tis fresh morning with me
When you are by at night. I do beseech you—
Chiefly that I might set it in my prayers—
What is your name?

Mir. Miranda.—O my father,
I have broke your hest to say so.

Fer. Admir'd Miranda,
Indeed the top of admiration! worth
What's dearest to the world! Full many a lady
I have ey'd with best regard, and many a time
Th' harmony of their tongues hath into bondage
Brought my too diligent ear. For several virtues
Have I lik'd several women, never any
With so full soul but some defect in her
Did quarrel with the noblest grace she ow'd,
And put it to the foil. But you, O you,
So perfect and so peerless, are created
Of every creature's best!

Mir. I do not know
One of my sex; no woman's face remember,
Save, from my glass, mine own; nor have I seen
More that I may call men than you, good friend,

11. sore injunction: harsh command.
13. like: such, i.e. such a noble.
15. Most . . . it: when I am working hardest.
19. weep: i.e. exude resin.
32. visitation: (1) visit; (2) attack of plague (carrying on the medical figure in *infected*).
37. hest: command. **Admir'd Miranda.** A pun, since *Miranda* = admired, i.e. wondered at. **40. best regard:** highest approval.
42, 43. several: particular. **45. ow'd:** owned.
46. foil: (1) contrast; (2) defeat.

And my dear father. How features are abroad
I am skilless of; but by my modesty
(The jewel in my dower), I would not wish
Any companion in the world but you;
Nor can imagination form a shape,
Besides yourself, to like of. But I prattle
Something too wildly, and my father's precepts
I therein do forget.

Fer. I am, in my condition,
A prince, Miranda; I do think, a king
(I would, not so!), and would no more endure
This wooden slavery than to suffer
The flesh-fly blow my mouth. Hear my soul speak:
The very instant that I saw you, did
My heart fly to your service, there resides,
To make me slave to it, and for your sake
Am I this patient log-man.

Mir. Do you love me?

Fer. O heaven, O earth, bear witness to this sound,
And crown what I profess with kind event
If I speak true! if hollowly, invert
What best is boded me to mischief! I,
Beyond all limit of what else i' th' world,
Do love, prize, honor you.

Mir. I am a fool
To weep at what I am glad of.

Pros. [*Aside.*] Fair encounter
Of two most rare affections! Heavens rain grace
On that which breeds between 'em!

Fer. Wherefore weep you?

Mir. At mine unworthiness, that dare not offer
What I desire to give; and much less take
What I shall die to want. But this is trifling,
And all the more it seeks to hide itself,
The bigger bulk it shows. Hence, bashful cunning,
And prompt me, plain and holy innocence!
I am your wife, if you will marry me;
If not, I'll die your maid. To be your fellow
You may deny me, but I'll be your servant,
Whether you will or no.

Fer. My mistress, dearest,
And I thus humble ever.

Mir. My husband then?

Fer. Ay, with a heart as willing
As bondage e'er of freedom. Here's my hand.

Mir. And mine, with my heart in't. And now farewell
Till half an hour hence.

Fer. A thousand, thousand!

Exeunt [*Ferdinand and Miranda severally*].

Pros. So glad of this as they I cannot be,
Who are surpris'd [withal]; but my rejoicing
At nothing can be more. I'll to my book,
For yet ere supper-time must I perform
Much business appertaining. *Exit.*

52. **abroad**: elsewhere.
53. **skilless**: ignorant. 59. **condition**: rank.
62. **wooden slavery**: being compelled to carry wood.
63. **blow**: defile. 69. **kind event**: favorable outcome.
70. **hollowly**: insincerely.
70–71. **invert . . . to mischief**: turn . . . to ill fortune.
71. **boded**: destined. 79. **want**: be without.
81. **bashful cunning**: coyness.
84. **maid**: handmaiden. **fellow**: mate.
91. **thousand**: i.e. thousand farewells.
93. **withal**: with it, i.e. by it.

Scene II

Enter Caliban, Stephano, *and* Trinculo.

Ste. Tell not me. When the butt is out, we will drink water—not a drop before; therefore bear up and board 'em. Servant-monster, drink to me.

Trin. Servant-monster? the folly of this island! They say there's but five upon this isle: we are three of them; if th' other two be brain'd like us, the state totters.

Ste. Drink, servant-monster, when I bid thee. Thy eyes are almost set in thy head.

Trin. Where should they be set else? He were a brave monster indeed if they were set in his tail.

Ste. My man-monster hath drown'd his tongue in sack. For my part, the sea cannot drown me; I swam, ere I could recover the shore, five and thirty leagues off and on. By this light, thou shalt be my lieutenant, monster, or my standard.

Trin. Your lieutenant if you list, he's no standard.

Ste. We'll not run, Monsieur Monster.

Trin. Nor go neither; but you'll lie like dogs, and yet say nothing neither.

Ste. Moon-calf, speak once in thy life, if thou beest a good moon-calf.

Cal. How does thy honor? Let me lick thy shoe. I'll not serve him, he is not valiant.

Trin. Thou liest, most ignorant monster, I am in case to justle a constable. Why, thou debosh'd fish thou, was there ever man a coward that hath drunk so much sack as I to-day? Wilt thou tell a monstrous lie, being but half a fish and half a monster?

Cal. Lo, how he mocks me! Wilt thou let him, my lord?

Trin. "Lord," quoth he? That a monster should be such a natural!

Cal. Lo, lo again. Bite him to death, I prithee.

Ste. Trinculo, keep a good tongue in your head. If you prove a mutineer—the next tree! The poor monster's my subject, and he shall not suffer indignity.

Cal. I thank my noble lord. Wilt thou be pleas'd to hearken once again to the suit I made to thee?

Ste. Marry, will I; kneel, and repeat it. I will stand, and so shall Trinculo.

III.ii. Location: Another part of the island.
1. **out**: empty.
2–3. **bear . . . 'em**: stand firm and attack. Stephano uses naval jargon as an encouragement to drink.
4. **folly of**: low level of intellect on.
9. **set**: sunk out of sight. Trinculo puns on the sense "placed."
16. **standard**: standard-bearer.
17. **no standard**: i.e. unable to stand.
18. **run**: i.e. run from the enemy.
19. **go**: walk. **lie**: (1) lie down; (2) tell lies; (3) excrete (with a backward glance at *run* in the sense "urinate" and perhaps at *standard* in the sense "conduit").
26. **case**: fit condition. **debosh'd**: debauched.
33. **natural**: idiot. The point is that a monster is by definition "unnatural."
40. **Marry**: indeed (originally the name of the Virgin Mary used as an oath).

Enter Ariel, *invisible.*

Cal. As I told thee before, I am subject to a tyrant,
A sorcerer, that by his cunning hath
Cheated me of the island.

Ari. Thou liest.

Cal. Thou liest, thou jesting monkey thou!
I would my valiant master would destroy thee.
I do not lie.

Ste. Trinculo, if you trouble him any more in 's tale, by this hand, I will supplant some of your teeth.

Trin. Why, I said nothing.

Ste. Mum then, and no more.—Proceed.

Cal. I say by sorcery he got this isle;
From me he got it. If thy greatness will
Revenge it on him—for I know thou dar'st,
But this thing dare not—

Ste. That's most certain.

Cal. Thou shalt be lord of it, and I'll serve thee.

Ste. How now shall this be compass'd? Canst thou bring me to the party?

Cal. Yea, yea, my lord. I'll yield him thee asleep,
Where thou mayst knock a nail into his head.

Ari. Thou liest, thou canst not.

Cal. What a pied ninny's this! Thou scurvy patch!
I do beseech thy greatness, give him blows,
And take his bottle from him. When that's gone,
He shall drink nought but brine, for I'll not show him
Where the quick freshes are.

Ste. Trinculo, run into no further danger; interrupt the monster one word further, and by this hand, I'll turn my mercy out o' doors, and make a stock-fish of thee.

Trin. Why, what did I? I did nothing. I'll go farther off.

Ste. Didst thou not say he lied?

Ari. Thou liest.

Ste. Do I so? Take thou that. [*Beats Trinculo.*] As you like this, give me the lie another time.

Trin. I did not give the lie. Out o' your wits, and hearing too? A pox o' your bottle! this can sack and drinking do. A murrain on your monster, and the devil take your fingers!

Cal. Ha, ha, ha!

Ste. Now forward with your tale.—Prithee stand further off.

Cal. Beat him enough. After a little time
I'll beat him too.

Ste. Stand farther.—Come, proceed.

Cal. Why, as I told thee, 'tis a custom with him
I' th' afternoon to sleep. There thou mayst brain him,
Having first seiz'd his books; or with a log
Batter his skull, or paunch him with a stake,
Or cut his wezand with thy knife. Remember
First to possess his books; for without them
He's but a sot, as I am; nor hath not
One spirit to command: they all do hate him
As rootedly as I. Burn but his books.
He has brave utensils (for so he calls them)
Which when he has a house, he'll deck withal.
And that most deeply to consider is
The beauty of his daughter. He himself
Calls her a nonpareil. I never saw a woman
But only Sycorax my dam and she;
But she as far surpasseth Sycorax
As great'st does least.

Ste. Is it so brave a lass?

Cal. Ay, lord, she will become thy bed, I warrant,
And bring thee forth brave brood.

Ste. Monster, I will kill this man. His daughter and I will be king and queen—'save our Graces! and Trinculo and thyself shall be viceroys. Dost thou like the plot, Trinculo?

Trin. Excellent.

Ste. Give me thy hand. I am sorry I beat thee; but while thou liv'st keep a good tongue in thy head.

Cal. Within this half hour will he be asleep.
Wilt thou destroy him then?

Ste. Ay, on mine honor.

Ari. This will I tell my master.

Cal. Thou mak'st me merry; I am full of pleasure,
Let us be jocund. Will you troll the catch
You taught me but while-ere?

Ste. At thy request, monster, I will do reason, any reason. Come on, Trinculo, let us sing. *Sings.*

"Flout 'em and [scout] 'em,
And scout 'em and flout 'em!
Thought is free."

Cal. That's not the tune.

Ariel plays the tune on a tabor and pipe.

Ste. What is this same?

Trin. This is the tune of our catch, play'd by the picture of Nobody.

Ste. If thou beest a man, show thyself in thy likeness. If thou beest a devil, take't as thou list.

Trin. O, forgive me my sins!

Ste. He that dies pays all debts. I defy thee. Mercy upon us!

Cal. Art thou afeard?

Ste. No, monster, not I.

Cal. Be not afeard, the isle is full of noises,
Sounds, and sweet airs, that give delight and hurt not.
Sometimes a thousand twangling instruments
Will hum about mine ears; and sometime voices,
That if I then had wak'd after long sleep,
Will make me sleep again, and then in dreaming,
The clouds methought would open, and show riches
Ready to drop upon me, that when I wak'd
I cried to dream again.

Ste. This will prove a brave kingdom to me, where I shall have my music for nothing.

Cal. When Prospero is destroy'd.

55. this thing: i.e. Trinculo.
63. pied . . . patch: foolish . . . fool (from the multicolored garb of the professional fool). **67. quick freshes:** fresh-water springs.
70. stock-fish: dried cod, so stiff it had to be beaten before cooking.
80. murrain: a disease of cattle. **90. paunch:** stab in the belly.
91. wezand: windpipe. **93. sot:** fool.

96. utensils: furnishings.
97. withal: with. **117. troll the catch:** sing the round.
118. but while-ere: a short time ago.
121. Flout: deride. **scout:** jeer at. **124 s.d. tabor:** small drum.
127. picture of Nobody: traditional image of a man with arms and legs but no torso; but Trinculo means an invisible agency.
129. take't . . . list: do as you please (a challenge).
135. noises: musical sounds. **137. twangling.** An invented word.

Ste. That shall be by and by. I remember the story.

Trin. The sound is going away. Let's follow it, and after do our work.

Ste. Lead, monster, we'll follow. I would I could see this taborer; he lays it on.

Trin. Wilt come? I'll follow Stephano. *Exeunt.*

Scene III

Enter Alonso, Sebastian, Antonio, Gonzalo, Adrian, Francisco, *etc.*

Gon. By'r lakin, I can go no further, sir,
My old bones aches. Here's a maze trod indeed
Through forth-rights and meanders! By your patience,
I needs must rest me.

Alon. Old lord, I cannot blame thee,
Who am myself attach'd with weariness
To th' dulling of my spirits. Sit down, and rest.
Even here I will put off my hope, and keep it
No longer for my flatterer. He is drown'd
Whom thus we stray to find, and the sea mocks
Our frustrate search on land. Well, let him go.

Ant. [*Aside to Sebastian.*] I am right glad that he's so out of hope.
Do not for one repulse forgo the purpose
That you resolv'd t' effect.

Seb. [*Aside to Antonio.*] The next advantage
Will we take throughly.

Ant. [*Aside to Sebastian.*] Let it be to-night,
For now they are oppress'd with travail, they
Will not, nor cannot, use such vigilance
As when they are fresh.

Seb. [*Aside to Antonio.*] I say to-night. No more.

Solemn and strange music; and Prosper *on the top, invisible.*

Alon. What harmony is this? My good friends, hark!

Gon. Marvellous sweet music!

Enter several strange Shapes, *bringing in a banket; and dance about it with gentle actions of salutations; and inviting the King, etc., to eat, they depart.*

Alon. Give us kind keepers, heavens! what were these?

Seb. A living drollery. Now I will believe
That there are unicorns; that in Arabia
There is one tree, the phoenix' throne, one phoenix
At this hour reigning there.

Ant. I'll believe both;
And what does else want credit, come to me,
And I'll be sworn 'tis true. Travellers ne'er did lie,
Though fools at home condemn 'em.

Gon. If in Naples
I should report this now, would they believe me?
If I should say I saw such [islanders]
(For, certes, these are people of the island),
Who though they are of monstrous shape, yet note
Their manners are more gentle, kind, than of
Our human generation you shall find
Many, nay, almost any.

Pros. [*Aside.*] Honest lord,
Thou hast said well; for some of you there present
Are worse than devils.

Alon. I cannot too much muse
Such shapes, such gesture, and such sound expressing
(Although they want the use of tongue) a kind
Of excellent dumb discourse.

Pros. [*Aside.*] Praise in departing.

Fran. They vanish'd strangely.

Seb. No matter, since
They have left their viands behind; for we have stomachs.
Will't please you taste of what is here?

Alon. Not I.

Gon. Faith, sir, you need not fear. When we were boys,
Who would believe that there were mountaineers,
Dew-lapp'd, like bulls, whose throats had hanging at 'em
Wallets of flesh? or that there were such men
Whose heads stood in their breasts? which now we find
Each putter-out of five for one will bring us
Good warrant of.

Alon. I will stand to, and feed,
Although my last, no matter, since I feel
The best is past. Brother, my lord the Duke,
Stand to, and do as we.

Thunder and lightning. Enter Ariel, *like a harpy, claps his wings upon the table, and with a quaint device the banquet vanishes.*

Ari. You are three men of sin, whom Destiny,
That hath to instrument this lower world
And what is in't, the never-surfeited sea
Hath caus'd to belch up you; and on this island
Where man doth not inhabit—you 'mongst men
Being most unfit to live. I have made you mad;
And even with such-like valor men hang and drown
Their proper selves.

147. by and by: immediately.

III.iii. Location: Another part of the island.
1. By'r lakin: by our Ladykin, i.e. the Virgin Mary.
3. forth-rights: straight paths. **5. attach'd**: seized. **8. for**: as.
12. for: because of. **14. throughly**: thoroughly.
17 s.d. top. Probably the third level of the tiring-house.
19 s.d. banket: banquet, i.e. light repast.
20. kind keepers: guardian angels.
21. living drollery: puppet show with live actors.
25. want credit: lack credence.

30. certes: certainly. **31. monstrous**: abnormal, unnatural.
36. muse: wonder at.
39. Praise in departing: i.e. don't judge until you see the conclusion (proverbial). **41. stomachs**: appetites.
45. Dew-lapp'd: with pouches of skin hanging from the neck (probably alluding to travellers' tales about goiter among Swiss mountaineers).
46–47. men . . . breasts. A common travellers' tale. See *Othello*, I.iii.144–45.
48. Each . . . one. Travellers deposited a sum of money at home to be repaid fivefold if they returned, forfeited if they did not.
49. stand to: take the risk. **51. best**: i.e. best part of life.
52 s.d. like a harpy: in the shape of a harpy, a rapacious monster with the face of a woman and the wings and claws of a bird of prey.
with . . . device: by means of an ingenious stage mechanism.
54. to: for.
59. such-like valor: i.e. the valor of madness, very different from true courage. **60. proper**: own.

[*Alonso, Sebastian, etc. draw their swords.*]
You fools! I and my fellows
Are ministers of Fate. The elements,
Of whom your swords are temper'd, may as well
Wound the loud winds, or with bemock'd-at stabs
Kill the still-closing waters, as diminish
One dowle that's in my plume. My fellow ministers
Are like invulnerable. If you could hurt,
Your swords are now too massy for your strengths,
And will not be uplifted. But remember
(For that's my business to you) that you three
From Milan did supplant good Prospero,
Expos'd unto the sea (which hath requit it)
Him, and his innocent child; for which foul deed
The pow'rs, delaying (not forgetting), have
Incens'd the seas and shores—yea, all the creatures,
Against your peace. Thee of thy son, Alonso,
They have bereft; and do pronounce by me
Ling'ring perdition (worse than any death
Can be at once) shall step by step attend
You and your ways, whose wraths to guard you from—
Which here, in this most desolate isle, else falls
Upon your heads—is nothing but heart's sorrow,
And a clear life ensuing.

He vanishes in thunder; then, to soft music, enter the SHAPES *again, and dance, with mocks and mows, and carrying out the table.*

Pros. Bravely the figure of this harpy hast thou
Perform'd, my Ariel; a grace it had, devouring.
Of my instruction hast thou nothing bated
In what thou hadst to say; so with good life,
And observation strange, my meaner ministers
Their several kinds have done. My high charms work,
And these, mine enemies, are all knit up
In their distractions. They now are in my pow'r;
And in these fits I leave them, while I visit
Young Ferdinand, whom they suppose is drown'd,
And his and mine lov'd darling. [*Exit above.*]

Gon. I' th' name of something holy, sir, why stand you
In this strange stare?

Alon. O, it is monstrous! monstrous!
Methought the billows spoke, and told me of it;
The winds did sing it to me, and the thunder,
That deep and dreadful organ-pipe, pronounc'd
The name of Prosper; it did base my trespass.
Therefore my son i' th' ooze is bedded; and
I'll seek him deeper than e'er plummet sounded,
And with him there lie mudded. *Exit.*

Seb. But one fiend at a time,
I'll fight their legions o'er.

Ant. I'll be thy second.
Exeunt [*Sebastian and Antonio*].

Gon. All three of them are desperate: their great guilt
(Like poison given to work a great time after)
Now gins to bite the spirits. I do beseech you
(That are of suppler joints) follow them swiftly,
And hinder them from what this ecstasy
May now provoke them to.

Adr. Follow, I pray you. *Exeunt omnes.*

ACT IV, SCENE I

Enter PROSPERO, FERDINAND, *and* MIRANDA.

Pros. If I have too austerely punish'd you,
Your compensation makes amends, for I
Have given you here a third of mine own life,
Or that for which I live; who once again
I tender to thy hand. All thy vexations
Were but my trials of thy love, and thou
Hast strangely stood the test. Here, afore heaven,
I ratify this my rich gift. O Ferdinand,
Do not smile at me that I boast her [off],
For thou shalt find she will outstrip all praise
And make it halt behind her.

Fer. I do believe it
Against an oracle.

Pros. Then, as my [gift], and thine own acquisition
Worthily purchas'd, take my daughter. But
If thou dost break her virgin-knot before
All sanctimonious ceremonies may
With full and holy rite be minist'red,
No sweet aspersion shall the heavens let fall
To make this contract grow; but barren hate,
Sour-ey'd disdain, and discord shall bestrew
The union of your bed with weeds so loathly
That you shall hate it both. Therefore take heed,
As Hymen's lamps shall light you.

Fer. As I hope
For quiet days, fair issue, and long life,
With such love as 'tis now, the murkiest den,

62. whom: which.
64. still-closing: always closing as soon as parted.
65. dowle: small feather. **66. like:** similarly.
71. requit it: repaid the act (by casting you up here).
77. perdition: ruin.
79. whose: i.e. those of the "pow'rs" of line 73.
81. is . . . sorrow: there is no means except repentance.
82. clear: sinless. **s.d. mocks and mows:** mocking gestures and grimaces. **84. devouring:** i.e. making the banquet disappear.
85. bated: omitted. **86. life:** realism.
87. observation strange: exceptional care. **meaner:** i.e. inferior to Ariel. **88. several kinds:** individual parts.
89–90. knit . . . distractions: entangled in their madness.
94–95. why . . . stare. Gonzalo has not heard Ariel's speech.
96. it: i.e. my sin. **99. base:** bass, i.e. utter in a deep voice.
100. Therefore: therefor, i.e. in consequence of his trespass.

103. o'er: one after another.
106. gins . . . spirits: begins to cause mental anguish.
108. ecstasy: fit of madness.

IV.i. Location: Before Prospero's cell.
3. a third . . . life. Various explanations have been put forward: for example, that the other two parts have been his dukedom and his books, or his late wife and his personal interests; or that Miranda represents his future, the other two parts being his past and his present; or that he has spent a third of his life on Miranda's education.
7. strangely: wonderfully well.
9. boast her off: i.e. praise her so highly. **11. halt:** limp.
12. Against an oracle: even if an oracle should declare otherwise.
16. sanctimonious: sacred, holy.
18. aspersion: i.e. blessing; literally, sprinkling, as of rain that promotes fertility and growth.
19. grow: be fruitful (as contrasted with *barren*).
21. weeds. Instead of the flowers with which the marriage bed was customarily strewn.
23. As . . . you: i.e. as you desire happiness in your marriage. The symbolic torch of Hymen, god of marriage, was supposed to promise happiness if it burned with a clear flame, the opposite if it smoked.

The most opportune place, the strong'st suggestion
Our worser genius can, shall never melt
Mine honor into lust, to take away
The edge of that day's celebration,
When I shall think or Phoebus' steeds are founder'd
Or Night kept chain'd below.

Pros. Fairly spoke.
Sit then and talk with her, she is thine own.
What, Ariel! my industrious servant, Ariel!

Enter ARIEL.

Ari. What would my potent master? here I am.

Pros. Thou and thy meaner fellows your last service
Did worthily perform; and I must use you
In such another trick. Go bring the rabble
(O'er whom I give thee pow'r) here to this place.
Incite them to quick motion, for I must
Bestow upon the eyes of this young couple
Some vanity of mine art. It is my promise,
And they expect it from me.

Ari. Presently?

Pros. Ay, with a twink.

Ari. Before you can say "come" and "go,"
And breathe twice, and cry "so, so,"
Each one, tripping on his toe,
Will be here with mop and mow.
Do you love me, master? no?

Pros. Dearly, my delicate Ariel. Do not approach
Till thou dost hear me call.

Ari. Well; I conceive. *Exit.*

Pros. Look thou be true; do not give dalliance
Too much the rein. The strongest oaths are straw
To th' fire i' th' blood. Be more abstenious,
Or else good night your vow!

Fer. I warrant you, sir,
The white cold virgin snow upon my heart
Abates the ardor of my liver.

Pros. Well.
Now come, my Ariel, bring a corollary,
Rather than want a spirit. Appear, and pertly!
No tongue! all eyes! Be silent. *Soft music.*

Enter IRIS.

Iris. Ceres, most bounteous lady, thy rich leas
Of wheat, rye, barley, fetches, oats, and pease;
Thy turfy mountains, where live nibbling sheep,
And flat meads thatch'd with stover, them to keep;
Thy banks with pioned and twilled brims,

Which spungy April at thy hest betrims,
To make cold nymphs chaste crowns; and thy broom-groves,
Whose shadow the dismissed bachelor loves,
Being lass-lorn; thy pole-clipt vineyard,
And thy sea-marge, sterile and rocky-hard,
Where thou thyself dost air—the Queen o' th' sky,
Whose wat'ry arch and messenger am I,
Bids thee leave these, and with her sovereign Grace,
Here on this grass-plot, in this very place,
To come and sport. [Her] peacocks fly amain.
Juno descends [*slowly in her car*].
Approach, rich Ceres, her to entertain.

Enter CERES.

Cer. Hail, many-colored messenger, that ne'er
Dost disobey the wife of Jupiter;
Who with thy saffron wings upon my flow'rs
Diffusest honey-drops, refreshing show'rs,
And with each end of thy blue bow dost crown
My bosky acres and my unshrubb'd down,
Rich scarf to my proud earth—why hath thy Queen
Summon'd me hither, to this short-grass'd green?

Iris. A contract of true love to celebrate,
And some donation freely to estate
On the bless'd lovers.

Cer. Tell me, heavenly bow,
If Venus or her son, as thou dost know,
Do now attend the Queen? Since they did plot
The means that dusky Dis my daughter got,
Her and her blind boy's scandall'd company
I have forsworn.

Iris. Of her society
Be not afraid. I met her Deity
Cutting the clouds towards Paphos; and her son
Dove-drawn with her. Here thought they to have done
Some wanton charm upon this man and maid,
Whose vows are, that no bed-right shall be paid
Till Hymen's torch be lighted; but in vain,
Mars's hot minion is return'd again;
Her waspish-headed son has broke his arrows,
Swears he will shoot no more, but play with sparrows,
And be a boy right out.

[JUNO *alights*.]

Cer. Highest Queen of state,

26. **suggestion**: temptation.
27. **Our . . . can**: our bad angel is capable of.
30. **or . . . founder'd**: either the sun-god's horses have gone lame (because the day is so long).
37. **trick**: ingenious device (technical term in pageantry). **rabble**: troop of inferior spirits. 41. **vanity**: show, delusive appearance.
42. **Presently**: immediately. 43. **with a twink**: in a twinkling.
47. **mop and mow**: gesture and grimace. 50. **conceive**: understand.
53. **abstenious**: abstemious.
56. **liver**. Supposed seat of the passions. 57. **corollary**: extra.
58. **want**: lack. **pertly**: briskly.
59. **No tongue**. Any speech from the spectators would make the spirits vanish. Cf. lines 126–27. s.d. **Iris**: goddess of the rainbow and Juno's messenger.
60. **Ceres**: goddess of agriculture. **leas**: meadows, cultivated land.
61. **fetches**: vetch, a fodder plant. 63. **stover**: hay for winter use.
64. **pioned and twilled**: undercut by the stream and retained by interwoven branches.
65. **spungy**: spongy, i.e. wet.
66. **cold**: chaste. **broom**: a kind of shrub bearing yellow flowers.
67. **dismissed bachelor**: rejected suitor.
68. **pole-clipt**: poll-clipped, i.e. with top growth pruned back (?). If *clipt* means (as often) "embraced," the sense could be "enclosed by a fence of poles" or "with poles entwined by the vines."
70. **Queen . . . sky**: Juno.
74. **peacocks**. Juno's sacred birds, which drew her chariot. **amain**: swiftly. 75. **entertain**: receive.
81. **bosky**: wooded. **down**: upland. 85. **estate**: bestow.
87. **son**: Cupid, the "blind boy" of line 90.
89. **Dis**: Pluto, ruler of the underworld (hence *dusky*), who carried off Ceres' daughter Proserpine to be his queen.
90. **scandall'd**: scandalous.
93. **Paphos**: place in Cyprus sacred to Venus.
94. **Dove-drawn**. Venus' chariot was drawn by her sacred doves.
94–95. **done . . . charm**: cast some unchaste spell.
98. **hot minion**: lustful mistress. **Venus and Mars were lovers. return'd**: i.e. to Paphos. 99. **waspish-headed**: peevish.
100. **sparrows**. Like doves, sacred to Venus. Sparrows were proverbially lecherous.
101. **right out**: outright. **Highest . . . state**: most majestic queen.

Great Juno, comes, I know her by her gait.
Juno. How does my bounteous sister? Go with me
To bless this twain, that they may prosperous be,
And honor'd in their issue. *They sing.*
Juno. Honor, riches, marriage-blessing,
Long continuance, and increasing,
Hourly joys be still upon you!
Juno sings her blessings on you.
[*Cer.*] Earth's increase, foison plenty,
Barns and garners never empty;
Vines with clust'ring bunches growing,
Plants with goodly burthen bowing;
Spring come to you at the farthest
In the very end of harvest!
Scarcity and want shall shun you,
Ceres' blessing so is on you.
Fer. This is a most majestic vision, and
Harmonious charmingly. May I be bold
To think these spirits?
Pros. Spirits, which by mine art
I have from their confines call'd to enact
My present fancies.
Fer. Let me live here ever;
So rare a wond'red father and a wise
Makes this place Paradise.

Juno and Ceres whisper, and send Iris on employment.

Pros. Sweet now, silence!
Juno and Ceres whisper seriously;
There's something else to do. Hush and be mute,
Or else our spell is marr'd.
Iris. You nymphs, call'd Naiades, of the windring brooks,
With your sedg'd crowns and ever-harmless looks,
Leave your crisp channels, and on this green land
Answer your summons; Juno does command.
Come, temperate nymphs, and help to celebrate
A contract of true love; be not too late.

Enter certain NYMPHS.

You sunburn'd sicklemen, of August weary,
Come hither from the furrow and be merry.
Make holiday; your rye-straw hats put on,
And these fresh nymphs encounter every one
In country footing.

Enter certain REAPERS, *properly habited: they join with the Nymphs in a graceful dance, towards the end whereof Prospero starts suddenly, and speaks; after which, to a strange, hollow, and confused noise, they heavily vanish.*

Pros. [*Aside.*] I had forgot that foul conspiracy
Of the beast Caliban and his confederates
Against my life. The minute of their plot
Is almost come. [*To the Spirits.*] Well done, avoid; no more.
Fer. This is strange. Your father's in some passion
That works him strongly.
Mir. Never till this day
Saw I him touch'd with anger, so distemper'd.
Pros. You do look, my son, in a mov'd sort,
As if you were dismay'd; be cheerful, sir.
Our revels now are ended. These our actors
(As I foretold you) were all spirits, and
Are melted into air, into thin air,
And like the baseless fabric of this vision,
The cloud-capp'd tow'rs, the gorgeous palaces,
The solemn temples, the great globe itself,
Yea, all which it inherit, shall dissolve,
And like this insubstantial pageant faded
Leave not a rack behind. We are such stuff
As dreams are made on; and our little life
Is rounded with a sleep. Sir, I am vex'd;
Bear with my weakness, my old brain is troubled.
Be not disturb'd with my infirmity.
If you be pleas'd, retire into my cell,
And there repose. A turn or two I'll walk
To still my beating mind.
Fer., *Mir.* We wish your peace.
Pros. [*To Ariel.*] Come with a thought. [*To Ferdinand and Miranda.*] I thank thee.
Exeunt [*Ferdinand and Miranda*].
Ariel! come.

Enter ARIEL.

Ari. Thy thoughts I cleave to. What's thy pleasure?
Pros. Spirit,
We must prepare to meet with Caliban.
Ari. Ay, my commander. When I presented Ceres,
I thought to have told thee of it, but I fear'd
Lest I might anger thee.
Pros. Say again, where didst thou leave these varlots?
Ari. I told you, sir, they were red-hot with drinking,
So full of valor that they smote the air
For breathing in their faces; beat the ground
For kissing of their feet; yet always bending
Towards their project. Then I beat my tabor,
At which like unback'd colts they prick'd their ears,
Advanc'd their eyelids, lifted up their noses
As they smelt music. So I charm'd their ears
That calf-like they my lowing follow'd through

102. gait: i.e. regal bearing. **108. still:** always.
110. foison plenty: plentiful abundance.
115. In . . . harvest: i.e. without intervening winter.
119. charmingly: enchantingly, magically.
123. wond'red: (1) to be wondered at; (2) able to perform wonders; (3) possessed of that wonder, Miranda (see note to III.i.37).
124. Sweet now, silence. Addressed to Miranda, who is about to speak.
128. windring: winding and wandering (apparently a coinage of Shakespeare's). **129. ever-harmless:** ever-innocent.
130. crisp: rippling. **132. temperate:** chaste.
137. fresh: young and beautiful. **encounter:** meet.
138. footing: dance. **s.d. heavily:** reluctantly.
142. avoid: be gone. **144. works:** agitates.
146. mov'd sort: troubled state.
148. revels: festivity, entertainment.
151. baseless fabric: structure without physical foundation.
154. which it inherit: who occupy it.
155. insubstantial: without material substance.
156. rack: wisp of cloud. **157. on:** of.
158. rounded: surrounded. **164. with:** at the summons of.
167. presented: represented, took the part of (?).
170. varlots: varlets, ruffians.
174–75. bending . . . project: pursuing their purpose—the murder of Prospero. **176. unback'd:** never ridden, unbroken.
177. Advanc'd: raised. **178. As:** as if.

Tooth'd briers, sharp furzes, pricking goss, and thorns,
Which ent'red their frail shins. At last I left them
I' th' filthy-mantled pool beyond your cell,
There dancing up to th' chins, that the foul lake
O'erstunk their feet.

Pros. This was well done, my bird.
Thy shape invisible retain thou still.
The trumpery in my house, go bring it hither,
For stale to catch these thieves.

Ari. I go, I go. *Exit.*

Pros. A devil, a born devil, on whose nature
Nurture can never stick; on whom my pains,
Humanely taken, all, all lost, quite lost;
And as with age his body uglier grows,
So his mind cankers. I will plague them all,
Even to roaring.

Enter ARIEL, *loaden with glistering apparel, etc.*

Come, hang [them on] this line.

[*Prospero and Ariel remain, invisible.*] *Enter* CALIBAN, STEPHANO, *and* TRINCULO, *all wet.*

Cal. Pray you tread softly, that the blind mole may not
Hear a foot fall; we now are near his cell.

Ste. Monster, your fairy, which you say is a harmless fairy, has done little better than play'd the Jack with us.

Trin. Monster, I do smell all horse-piss, at which my nose is in great indignation.

Ste. So is mine. Do you hear, monster? If I should take a displeasure against you, look you—

Trin. Thou wert but a lost monster.

Cal. Good my lord, give me thy favor still.
Be patient, for the prize I'll bring thee to
Shall hoodwink this mischance; therefore speak softly,
All's hush'd as midnight yet.

Trin. Ay, but to lose our bottles in the pool—

Ste. There is not only disgrace and dishonor in that, monster, but an infinite loss.

Trin. That's more to me than my wetting; yet this is your harmless fairy, monster!

Ste. I will fetch off my bottle, though I be o'er ears for my labor.

Cal. Prithee, my king, be quiet. Seest thou here,
This is the mouth o' th' cell. No noise, and enter.
Do that good mischief which may make this island
Thine own for ever, and I, thy Caliban,
For aye thy foot-licker.

Ste. Give me thy hand. I do begin to have bloody thoughts.

Trin. O King Stephano! O peer! O worthy Stephano! look what a wardrobe here is for thee!

Cal. Let it alone, thou fool, it is but trash.

Trin. O, ho, monster! we know what belongs to a frippery. O King Stephano!

Ste. Put off that gown, Trinculo. By this hand, I'll have that gown.

Trin. Thy Grace shall have it.

Cal. The dropsy drown this fool! what do you mean
To dote thus on such luggage? Let['t] alone
And do the murther first. If he awake,
From toe to crown he'll fill our skins with pinches,
Make us strange stuff.

Ste. Be you quiet, monster. Mistress line, is not this my jerkin? Now is the jerkin under the line. Now, jerkin, you are like to lose your hair, and prove a bald jerkin.

Trin. Do, do; we steal by line and level, and't like your Grace.

Ste. I thank thee for that jest; here's a garment for't. Wit shall not go unrewarded while I am king of this country. "Steal by line and level" is an excellent pass of pate; there's another garment for't.

Trin. Monster, come put some lime upon your fingers, and away with the rest.

Cal. I will have none on't. We shall lose our time,
And all be turn'd to barnacles, or to apes
With foreheads villainous low.

Ste. Monster, lay-to your fingers. Help to bear this away where my hogshead of wine is, or I'll turn you out of my kingdom. Go to, carry this.

Trin. And this.

Ste. Ay, and this.

A noise of hunters heard. Enter divers SPIRITS *in shape of dogs and hounds, hunting them about; Prospero and Ariel setting them on.*

Pros. Hey, Mountain, hey!

Ari. Silver! there it goes, Silver!

Pros. Fury, Fury! there, Tyrant, there! hark, hark!

[*Caliban, Stephano, and Trinculo are driven out.*]

Go, charge my goblins that they grind their joints
With dry convulsions, shorten up their sinews
With aged cramps, and more pinch-spotted make them
Than pard or cat o' mountain.

Ari. Hark, they roar!

Pros. Let them be hunted soundly. At this hour
Lies at my mercy all mine enemies.
Shortly shall all my labors end, and thou
Shalt have the air at freedom. For a little
Follow, and do me service. *Exeunt.*

180. **goss:** gorse. 182. **filthy-mantled:** covered with dirty scum.
186. **trumpery:** showy finery (the "glistering apparel" of line 193 s.d.).
187. **stale:** bait. 192. **cankers:** becomes malignant.
193. **line:** lime tree, linden.
194. **mole.** Thought to have sensitive hearing.
197. **Jack:** (1) knave; (2) jack-o'-lantern, i.e. will-o'-the-wisp.
206. **hoodwink:** make you blind to.
222. **peer.** Referring to the old ballad "King Stephen was a worthy peer," quoted in *Othello*, II.iii.89–96.
226. **frippery:** secondhand-clothes shop. 230. **drown:** suffocate.
231. **luggage:** encumbering trash.
236. **jerkin:** a kind of jacket. **under the line.** With pun on the sense "south of the equator." The joke involves the popular idea that travellers to tropical countries lost their hair through fevers, or from scurvy resulting from lack of fresh food on the long voyage.
239. **Do, do:** an expression of approval, equivalent to "bravo." **by . . . level:** with plumb-line and carpenter's level, i.e. with professional skill (continuing the puns on *line*). **and't like:** if it please.
244. **pass:** thrust (a fencing term). **pate:** i.e. wit.
245. **lime:** sticky substance; thieves were jokingly said to have lime on their fingers.
248. **barnacles:** a kind of geese traditionally supposed to develop from the shellfish so named. 249. **villainous:** wretchedly.
252. **Go to:** expression of exhortation or reproof, equivalent to "come, come!" 257. **hark:** "sic 'em!"
259. **dry convulsions.** Precisely what sort of painful seizure is meant here is uncertain. 260. **aged:** such as old people have.
261. **pard:** leopard. **cat o' mountain:** catamount, wildcat.

ACT V, SCENE I

Enter PROSPERO *in his magic robes, and* ARIEL.

Pros. Now does my project gather to a head:
My charms crack not; my spirits obey; and Time
Goes upright with his carriage. How's the day?
Ari. On the sixt hour, at which time, my lord,
You said our work should cease.
Pros. I did say so,
When first I rais'd the tempest. Say, my spirit,
How fares the King and 's followers?
Ari. Confin'd together
In the same fashion as you gave in charge,
Just as you left them; all prisoners, sir,
In the line-grove which weather-fends your cell;
They cannot boudge till your release. The King,
His brother, and yours, abide all three distracted,
And the remainder mourning over them,
Brimful of sorrow and dismay; but chiefly
Him that you term'd, sir, "the good old Lord Gonzalo,"
His tears runs down his beard like winter's drops
From eaves of reeds. Your charm so strongly works 'em
That if you now beheld them, your affections
Would become tender.
Pros. Dost thou think so, spirit?
Ari. Mine would, sir, were I human.
Pros. And mine shall.
Hast thou, which art but air, a touch, a feeling
Of their afflictions, and shall not myself,
One of their kind, that relish all as sharply
Passion as they, be kindlier mov'd than thou art?
Though with their high wrongs I am strook to th' quick,
Yet, with my nobler reason, 'gainst my fury
Do I take part. The rarer action is
In virtue than in vengeance. They being penitent,
The sole drift of my purpose doth extend
Not a frown further. Go, release them, Ariel.
My charms I'll break, their senses I'll restore,
And they shall be themselves.
Ari. I'll fetch them, sir.
Exit. [*Prospero traces a magic circle with his staff.*]
Pros. Ye elves of hills, brooks, standing lakes, and groves,
And ye that on the sands with printless foot
Do chase the ebbing Neptune, and do fly him
When he comes back; you demi-puppets that
By moonshine do the green sour ringlets make,
Whereof the ewe not bites; and you whose pastime
Is to make midnight mushrumps, that rejoice
To hear the solemn curfew: by whose aid
(Weak masters though ye be) I have bedimm'd
The noontide sun, call'd forth the mutinous winds,
And 'twixt the green sea and the azur'd vault
Set roaring war; to the dread rattling thunder
Have I given fire, and rifted Jove's stout oak
With his own bolt; the strong-bas'd promontory
Have I made shake, and by the spurs pluck'd up
The pine and cedar. Graves at my command
Have wak'd their sleepers, op'd, and let 'em forth
By my so potent art. But this rough magic
I here abjure; and when I have requir'd
Some heavenly music (which even now I do)
To work mine end upon their senses that
This airy charm is for, I'll break my staff,
Bury it certain fadoms in the earth,
And deeper than did ever plummet sound
I'll drown my book. *Solemn music.*

Here enters ARIEL *before; then* ALONSO, *with a frantic gesture, attended by* GONZALO; SEBASTIAN *and* ANTONIO *in like manner, attended by* ADRIAN *and* FRANCISCO. *They all enter the circle which Prospero had made, and there stand charm'd; which Prospero observing, speaks.*

A solemn air, and the best comforter
To an unsettled fancy, cure thy brains,
Now useless, [boil'd] within thy skull! There stand,
For you are spell-stopp'd.
Holy Gonzalo, honorable man,
Mine eyes, ev'n sociable to the show of thine,
Fall fellowly drops. The charm dissolves apace,
And as the morning steals upon the night,
Melting the darkness, so their rising senses
Begin to chase the ignorant fumes that mantle
Their clearer reason. O good Gonzalo,
My true preserver, and a loyal sir
To him thou follow'st! I will pay thy graces
Home both in word and deed. Most cruelly
Didst thou, Alonso, use me and my daughter;
Thy brother was a furtherer in the act.
Thou art pinch'd for't now, Sebastian. Flesh and blood,
You, brother mine, that [entertain'd] ambition,
Expell'd remorse and nature, whom, with Sebastian
(Whose inward pinches therefore are most strong),
Would here have kill'd your king, I do forgive thee,

V.i. Location: Before Prospero's cell.
3. Goes . . . carriage: walks upright under what he is carrying (because his burden of coming events has been greatly lightened).
4. On: approaching. **sixt:** sixth. On the time, see I.ii.240–41.
10. weather-fends: serves as windbreak for.
11. boudge: budge, stir. **your release:** i.e. their release by you.
12. distracted: out of their wits. **17. eaves of reeds:** thatched roofs.
18. affections: inclinations, bent of mind.
21. touch. Synonymous with *feeling*.
23. relish: experience. **all:** quite.
24. kindlier: (1) more sympathetically; (2) more naturally (as "one of their kind"). **27. take part:** side. **rarer:** finer, nobler.
36. demi-puppets: quasi-puppets, i.e. creatures of small size.
37. green sour ringlets: so-called "fairy rings" in grass, actually caused by mushrooms.
39. mushrumps: mushrooms, supposed because of their rapid growth to be made by elves during the night.
40. curfew. Supposedly spirits could be abroad only between curfew (9 p.m.) and the first cockcrow; cf. I.ii.327.
41. Weak: i.e. as compared with the powerful demons summoned up by black magic. **45. rifted:** split. **47. spurs:** roots.
50. rough: i.e. capable of producing the violent effects just described (?). **51. requir'd:** requested.
53. their senses that: the senses of those whom.
54. airy charm: i.e. the music.
57 s.d. frantic gesture: insane demeanor. **58. and:** i.e. which is.
59. thy brains. The first sentence is addressed to Alonso, the next to all six now within the circle.
60. boil'd: i.e. made useless by passion.
63. sociable: sympathetic. **show:** appearance.
64. Fall: let fall.
67. ignorant fumes: fumes that make them uncomprehending.
70–71. pay . . . Home: reward your favors fully.
76. remorse: pity. **nature:** natural feeling.
77. therefore: therefor, to that end.

Unnatural though thou art.—Their understanding
Begins to swell, and the approaching tide
Will shortly fill the reasonable [shores]
That now lie foul and muddy. Not one of them
That yet looks on me, or would know me! Ariel,
Fetch me the hat and rapier in my cell.
[*Exit Ariel, and returns immediately.*]
I will discase me, and myself present
As I was sometime Milan. Quickly, spirit,
Thou shalt ere long be free.
Ariel sings and helps to attire him.
[*Ari.*] Where the bee sucks, there suck I,
In a cowslip's bell I lie;
There I couch when owls do cry.
On the bat's back I do fly
After summer merrily.
Merrily, merrily shall I live now,
Under the blossom that hangs on the bough.
Pros. Why, that's my dainty Ariel! I shall miss thee,
But yet thou shalt have freedom. So, so, so.
To the King's ship, invisible as thou art;
There shalt thou find the mariners asleep
Under the hatches. The master and the boatswain
Being awake, enforce them to this place;
And presently, I prithee.
Ari. I drink the air before me, and return
Or ere your pulse twice beat. *Exit.*
Gon. All torment, trouble, wonder, and amazement
Inhabits here. Some heavenly power guide us
Out of this fearful country!
Pros. Behold, sir King,
The wronged Duke of Milan, Prospero.
For more assurance that a living prince
Does now speak to thee, I embrace thy body,
And to thee and thy company I bid
A hearty welcome.
Alon. Whe'er thou beest he or no,
Or some enchanted trifle to abuse me
(As late I have been), I not know. Thy pulse
Beats as of flesh and blood; and since I saw thee,
Th' affliction of my mind amends, with which
I fear a madness held me. This must crave
(And if this be at all) a most strange story.
Thy dukedom I resign, and do entreat
Thou pardon me my wrongs. But how should Prospero
Be living, and be here?
Pros. [*To Gonzalo.*] First, noble friend,
Let me embrace thine age, whose honor cannot
Be measur'd or confin'd.
Gon. Whether this be,
Or be not, I'll not swear.
Pros. You do yet taste

81. reasonable shores: shores of reason, i.e. minds.
85. discase me: take off my magician's robe.
86. As . . . Milan: dressed as I formerly was as Duke of Milan.
96. So, so, so. Probably an expression of approval as Ariel finishes attiring him. **101. presently:** at once.
108. a living prince: i.e. not a spirit.
112. enchanted trifle: trick of magic. **abuse:** deceive.
116–17. This . . . story: this demands, if it is really taking place, an extraordinary explanation.
121. thine age: i.e. thy reverend self.
121–22. cannot . . . confin'd: i.e. is immeasurable and boundless.

Some subtleties o' th' isle, that will [not] let you
Believe things certain. Welcome, my friends all!
[*Aside to Sebastian and Antonio.*] But you, my brace of lords, were I so minded,
I here could pluck his Highness' frown upon you
And justify you traitors. At this time
I will tell no tales.
Seb. [*Aside.*] The devil speaks in him.
Pros. No.
For you, most wicked sir, whom to call brother
Would even infect my mouth, I do forgive
Thy rankest fault—all of them; and require
My dukedom of thee, which perforce, I know
Thou must restore.
Alon. If thou beest Prospero,
Give us particulars of thy preservation,
How thou hast met us here, whom three hours since
Were wrack'd upon this shore; where I have lost
(How sharp the point of this remembrance is!)
My dear son Ferdinand.
Pros. I am woe for't, sir.
Alon. Irreparable is the loss, and patience
Says, it is past her cure.
Pros. I rather think
You have not sought her help, of whose soft grace
For the like loss I have her sovereign aid,
And rest myself content.
Alon. You the like loss?
Pros. As great to me as late, and supportable
To make the dear loss, have I means much weaker
Than you may call to comfort you; for I
Have lost my daughter.
Alon. A daughter?
O heavens, that they were living both in Naples,
The King and Queen there! That they were, I wish
Myself were mudded in that oozy bed
Where my son lies. When did you lose your daughter?
Pros. In this last tempest. I perceive these lords
At this encounter do so much admire
That they devour their reason, and scarce think
Their eyes do offices of truth, their words
Are natural breath; but howsoev'r you have
Been justled from your senses, know for certain
That I am Prospero, and that very duke
Which was thrust forth of Milan, who most strangely
Upon this shore (where you were wrack'd) was landed,
To be the lord on't. No more yet of this,
For 'tis a chronicle of day by day,
Not a relation for a breakfast, nor
Befitting this first meeting. Welcome, sir;
This cell's my court. Here have I few attendants,
And subjects none abroad. Pray you look in.
My dukedom since you have given me again,
I will requite you with as good a thing,

124. subtleties: illusions, with play (as *taste* suggests) on the word as applied to fancy confections representing actual objects or allegorical figures. **128. justify:** prove.
142. of . . . grace: by whose mercy. **145. late:** recent.
146. dear: deeply felt. **150. That:** provided that.
154. admire: marvel.
155. devour their reason. Presumably referring to the open-mouthed astonishment in which their rational powers are lost.
156. do . . . truth: function accurately. **160. of:** from.
167. abroad: i.e. elsewhere on the island.

At least bring forth a wonder, to content ye
As much as me my dukedom.

Here Prospero discovers FERDINAND *and* MIRANDA *playing at chess.*

Mir. Sweet lord, you play me false.
Fer. No, my dearest love,
I would not for the world.
Mir. Yes, for a score of kingdoms you should wrangle,
And I would call it fair play.
Alon. If this prove
A vision of the island, one dear son
Shall I twice lose.
Seb. A most high miracle!
Fer. Though the seas threaten, they are merciful;
I have curs'd them without cause. [*Kneels.*]
Alon. Now all the blessings
Of a glad father compass thee about!
Arise, and say how thou cam'st here.
Mir. O wonder!
How many goodly creatures are there here!
How beauteous mankind is! O brave new world
That has such people in't!
Pros. 'Tis new to thee.
Alon. What is this maid with whom thou wast at play?
Your eld'st acquaintance cannot be three hours.
Is she the goddess that hath sever'd us,
And brought us thus together?
Fer. Sir, she is mortal;
But by immortal Providence she's mine.
I chose her when I could not ask my father
For his advice, nor thought I had one. She
Is daughter to this famous Duke of Milan,
Of whom so often I have heard renown,
But never saw before; of whom I have
Receiv'd a second life; and second father
This lady makes him to me.
Alon. I am hers.
But O, how oddly will it sound that I
Must ask my child forgiveness!
Pros. There, sir, stop.
Let us not burthen our remembrances with
A heaviness that's gone.
Gon. I have inly wept,
Or should have spoke ere this. Look down, you gods,
And on this couple drop a blessed crown!
For it is you that have chalk'd forth the way
Which brought us hither.
Alon. I say amen, Gonzalo!
Gon. Was Milan thrust from Milan, that his issue
Should become kings of Naples? O, rejoice
Beyond a common joy, and set it down
With gold on lasting pillars: in one voyage
Did Claribel her husband find at Tunis,
And Ferdinand, her brother, found a wife
Where he himself was lost; Prospero, his dukedom
In a poor isle; and all of us, ourselves,
When no man was his own.
Alon. [*To Ferdinand and Miranda.*] Give me your hands.
Let grief and sorrow still embrace his heart
That doth not wish you joy!
Gon. Be it so, amen!

Enter ARIEL, *with the* MASTER *and* BOATSWAIN *amazedly following.*

O, look, sir, look, sir, here is more of us.
I prophesied, if a gallows were on land,
This fellow could not drown. Now, blasphemy,
That swear'st grace o'erboard, not an oath on shore?
Hast thou no mouth by land? What is the news?
Boats. The best news is, that we have safely found
Our king and company; the next, our ship—
Which, but three glasses since, we gave out split—
Is tight and yare, and bravely rigg'd as when
We first put out to sea.
Ari. [*Aside to Prospero.*] Sir, all this service
Have I done since I went.
Pros. [*Aside to Ariel.*] My tricksy spirit!
Alon. These are not natural events, they strengthen
From strange to stranger. Say, how came you hither?
Boats. If I did think, sir, I were well awake,
I'ld strive to tell you. We were dead of sleep,
And (how we know not) all clapp'd under hatches,
Where, but even now, with strange and several noises
Of roaring, shrieking, howling, jingling chains,
And moe diversity of sounds, all horrible,
We were awak'd; straightway, at liberty;
Where we, in all our trim, freshly beheld
Our royal, good, and gallant ship; our master
Cap'ring to eye her. On a trice, so please you,
Even in a dream, were we divided from them,
And were brought moping hither.
Ari. [*Aside to Prospero.*] Was't well done?
Pros. [*Aside to Ariel.*] Bravely, my diligence.
Thou shalt be free.
Alon. This is as strange a maze as e'er men trod,
And there is in this business more than nature
Was ever conduct of. Some oracle
Must rectify our knowledge.
Pros. Sir, my liege,
Do not infest your mind with beating on
The strangeness of this business. At pick'd leisure,
Which shall be shortly, single I'll resolve you

171 s.d. discovers: discloses (by pulling aside a curtain).
174. Yes . . . wrangle: i.e. certainly you should do so for the world; in fact, for less than the world—for twenty kingdoms you ought to do your utmost against me. **176. vision:** i.e. illusion.
186. eld'st: longest possible. **200. heaviness:** grief.
205. Milan . . . Milan: the Duke . . . the city.
212–13. all . . . own: we all found ourselves when every man was deluded. **214. still:** ever.
214–15. his heart That: the heart of anyone who.
215 s.d. amazedly: as in a maze, in bewilderment.
218. blasphemy: blasphemous fellow. Cf. *diligence* (= diligent creature) in line 241.
219. That . . . o'erboard: who are profane enough to make heavenly grace forsake the ship.
223. glasses: i.e. hours. **gave out:** reported.
224. yare: shipshape. **226. tricksy:** ingenious, adroit.
227–28. strengthen . . . stranger: increase in strangeness.
230. of sleep: asleep. **234. moe:** more.
235. at liberty: i.e. no longer under hatches. **238. On:** in.
240. moping: in a daze. **244. conduct:** conductor.
245. liege: sovereign. **246. infest:** annoy.
247. pick'd: i.e. convenient.
248. single: by myself (without an oracle).

(Which to you shall seem probable) of every
These happen'd accidents; till when, be cheerful
And think of each thing well. [*Aside to Ariel.*] Come hither, spirit.
Set Caliban and his companions free;
Untie the spell. [*Exit Ariel.*] How fares my gracious sir?
There are yet missing of your company
Some few odd lads that you remember not.

Enter ARIEL, *driving in* CALIBAN, STEPHANO, *and* TRINCULO *in their stol'n apparel.*

Ste. Every man shift for all the rest, and let no man take care for himself; for all is but fortune. *Coraggio*, bully-monster, *coraggio!*

Trin. If these be true spies which I wear in my head, here's a goodly sight.

Cal. O Setebos, these be brave spirits indeed!
How fine my master is! I am afraid
He will chastise me.

Seb. Ha, ha!
What things are these, my Lord Antonio?
Will money buy 'em?

Ant. Very like; one of them
Is a plain fish, and no doubt marketable.

Pros. Mark but the badges of these men, my lords,
Then say if they be true. This misshapen knave—
His mother was a witch, and one so strong
That could control the moon, make flows and ebbs,
And deal in her command without her power.
These three have robb'd me, and this demi-devil
(For he's a bastard one) had plotted with them
To take my life. Two of these fellows you
Must know and own, this thing of darkness I
Acknowledge mine.

Cal. I shall be pinch'd to death.

Alon. Is not this Stephano, my drunken butler?

Seb. He is drunk now. Where had he wine?

Alon. And Trinculo is reeling ripe. Where should they
Find this grand liquor that hath gilded 'em?
How cam'st thou in this pickle?

Trin. I have been in such a pickle since I saw you last that I fear me will never out of my bones. I shall not fear fly-blowing.

Seb. Why, how now, Stephano?

Ste. O, touch me not, I am not Stephano, but a cramp.

Pros. You'ld be king o' the isle, sirrah?

Ste. I should have been a sore one then.

Alon. This is a strange thing as e'er I look'd on.
[*Pointing to Caliban.*]

Pros. He is as disproportion'd in his manners
As in his shape. Go, sirrah, to my cell;
Take with you your companions. As you look
To have my pardon, trim it handsomely.

Cal. Ay, that I will; and I'll be wise hereafter,
And seek for grace. What a thrice-double ass
Was I to take this drunkard for a god,
And worship this dull fool!

Pros. Go to, away!

Alon. Hence, and bestow your luggage where you found it.

Seb. Or stole it, rather.
[*Exeunt Caliban, Stephano, and Trinculo.*]

Pros. Sir, I invite your Highness and your train
To my poor cell, where you shall take your rest
For this one night; which, part of it, I'll waste
With such discourse as, I not doubt, shall make it
Go quick away—the story of my life,
And the particular accidents gone by
Since I came to this isle. And in the morn
I'll bring you to your ship, and so to Naples,
Where I have hope to see the nuptial
Of these our dear-belov'd solemnized,
And thence retire me to my Milan, where
Every third thought shall be my grave.

Alon. I long
To hear the story of your life, which must
Take the ear strangely.

Pros. I'll deliver all,
And promise you calm seas, auspicious gales,
And sail so expeditious, that shall catch
Your royal fleet far off. [*Aside to Ariel.*] My Ariel, chick,
That is thy charge. Then to the elements
Be free, and fare thou well!—Please you draw near.
Exeunt omnes.

EPILOGUE

Spoken by PROSPERO.

Now my charms are all o'erthrown,
And what strength I have's mine own,
Which is most faint. Now 'tis true,
I must be here confin'd by you,
Or sent to Naples. Let me not,
Since I have my dukedom got,
And pardon'd the deceiver, dwell
In this bare island by your spell,
But release me from my bands
With the help of your good hands.
Gentle breath of yours my sails

249. probable: satisfactory. **250. accidents:** occurrences.
255. odd: unaccounted for.
256. Every . . . rest. Stephano drunkenly inverts the proverbial "Every man for himself." **257. Coraggio:** courage (Italian).
259. true spies: reliable observers (eyes).
262. fine: splendidly dressed (in his ducal robes).
267. badges: insignia for servants, indicating what master they served. Stephano and Trinculo are of course dressed in stolen garments. **268. true:** honest.
271. her command: i.e. the moon's authority. **without her power:** beyond the moon's influence.
280. gilded 'em: flushed their faces (a common connection between blood and gold). Possibly *grand liquor* contains an alchemical allusion to the long-sought elixir that could transform base substances to gold.
281. pickle: predicament.
282. pickle: preservative (the horse urine of the pool being equivalent to vinegar).
284. fly-blowing: infestation by maggots (to which unpickled meat would be subject).

288. sirrah: form of address to an inferior.
289. sore: (1) harsh; (2) pain-wracked. **303. waste:** use up.
314. Take: enchant. **deliver:** report. **316. sail:** voyage.
319. draw near: i.e. enter the cell.

Epi. **9. bands:** bonds. **10. hands:** i.e. applause. The noise of clapping would break the charm.
11. Gentle breath: a favorable breeze (produced by hands clapping).

Must fill, or else my project fails,
Which was to please. Now I want
Spirits to enforce, art to enchant,
And my ending is despair,
Unless I be reliev'd by prayer,
Which pierces so, that it assaults
Mercy itself, and frees all faults.
As you from crimes would pardon'd be,
Let your indulgence set me free. *Exit.*

13. want: lack. **16. prayer:** i.e. this petition.

17. assaults: storms the ear of. **18. frees:** remits. **19. crimes:** sins.

NOTE ON THE TEXT

The First Folio (1623) is the only authority for *The Tempest*; all later texts are derived from that source. As was first demonstrated by Dover Wilson, following a suggestion of F. P. Wilson's, the manuscript underlying the F1 text was a transcript made from some form of Shakespeare's autograph (either "foul papers" or possibly slightly revised "fair copy") by Ralph Crane, a scrivener known to have been employed by the King's Men. It also seems likely that this transcript was prepared at the request of William or Isaac Jaggard expressly as copy for F1. Whether Shakespeare's manuscript had ever been used as a prompt-book is uncertain; no unambiguous evidence of playhouse association occurs in the F1 text. The text is unusually clean and offers few serious problems to the editor.

Since it is now believed that not only *The Tempest* but also *The Two Gentlemen of Verona, The Merry Wives of Windsor, The Winter's Tale,* probably *Measure for Measure* and *Cymbeline,* and possibly parts of *2 Henry IV* and *Timon of Athens* were printed from transcripts by Ralph Crane, his distinguishing characteristics as a scribe are worth noticing here. These are: (1) Regular and intelligent division of the play into acts and scenes. (2) A list of dramatis personae at the end of each play, except *Measure for Measure* and *Cymbeline.* For *Measure for Measure* such a list would have required a separate page in F1 and may have been omitted by the compositor for that reason; lack of space may also explain the absence of one for *Cymbeline,* which ends halfway down the final page of F1 and had to be followed by a colophon and, for appearance's sake, a printer's ornament. (3) Use of the "massed entry" technique (see "Note on the Text" to *The Two Gentlemen of Verona*), found only in *The Two Gentlemen of Verona, The Merry Wives of Windsor,* and *The Winter's Tale.* (4) Heavy use of parentheses for parenthetical and appositive phrases, single words of address, and exclamations. (5) Frequent use of hyphenated forms, many of unusual pattern, perhaps the most distinctive being verb plus pronoun (in *The Tempest,* for example, *wide-chopt-rascall, sty-me, dark-backward, peg-thee, red-plague, flat-long, bemockt-at-Stabs, like-vulnerable, hearts-sorrow, Turphie-Mountaines, greene-Land, borne-Deuille, oo-zie*). (6) Generally careful and heavy punctuation (colons and semicolons) and fairly consistent use of the apostrophe to mark elided syllables or shortened forms (*'bove* for *above, 'Pray* for *I pray, 'pox* for *a pox, 'Save* for *God save*). There is also an occasional use of what W. W. Greg has called "Jonsonian elision" in such forms as *I'am, I'prethee,* and (in *Cymbeline*) *to' th'.* (7) A preference for *o'th'* over *a th',* and an occasional use of *you'r* or *you're* for *y'are.* Although singly some of these characteristics can be found here and there in other F1 texts, the combined appearance of four or five of them in any text may fairly be taken as strong evidence of Crane's hand in the manuscript copy. For a more detailed and inclusive study of Crane's scribal characteristics, see Howard-Hill.

As the Textual Notes indicate, the F1 text shows some apparent confusion in the printing of prose as verse in a number of the speeches of Trinculo and Stephano (II.ii, III.ii, and the last parts of IV.i and V.i) and of verse as prose in two or three of Caliban's speeches. Kermode suggests that the prose-as-verse anomaly in the speeches of Trinculo and Stephano may best be laid at the door of the compositors (B and D [or F?] for quire A, sigs. A4, A5; and C and D [or F] for quire B, sigs. B2 and B3^v), who, having cast off their copy inaccurately, found it necessary to stretch it by breaking single prose lines into two shorter lines in order to fill out the page. So far as the problem in quire A is concerned, this is an appealing explanation, because, as Hinman shows, the six formes of quire A were not composed and printed off in the order usually employed by the F1 printers. But the theory encounters difficulties when it is applied to quire B, which, unlike quire A, employed the regular F1 composing and printing-off order (i.e., beginning with the third inner forme of the quire, B3^v and B4^r), since the speeches in question do not fall on pages where the compositors might be expected to have found themselves with too much space on their hands. The few instances where Caliban's verse appears as prose do not pose a comparable problem and may most easily be explained as the result of revision in Shakespeare's manuscript, the intention of which was misinterpreted by Crane.

Shakespeare's authorship of the somewhat flat and plodding masque in IV.i has often been questioned (other suggested authors are Francis Beaumont, George Chapman, or Thomas Heywood), but more recent opinion (Chambers, Kermode, Jowett, and Orgel) tends to accept it as by Shakespeare, arguing that it is an integral part of the play from the first, thus rejecting Lawrence's suggestion that the masque had been added for the second Court performance (perhaps 27 December 1612) as part of the festivities arranged for the espousal and marriage of Princess Elizabeth to Frederick V, Elector Palatine. One stage direction in the masque, (*"Iuno descends."*), which F1 places in the left margin opposite lines 72–3, has troubled editors. Based on the argument that a descent beginning at this point distracts the audience from attending to the speeches of Iris and Ceres (76–101) which immediately follow, Theobald moved Juno's descent to follow line 101, while some editors (e.g., Capell, Dyce, Globe, Kittredge) dispense with her descent altogether, simply entering her after line 101. Most recently, however, Jowett/Wells and Orgel, postpone the actual descent, but show Juno appearing *"in the air"* following line 72 (Orgel, line 74), where she "floats" until alighting from her "machine" after line 101 (Orgel, after 102). Since there is little difference, so far as distraction is concerned, between slowly descending and dangling uneasily in midair, the present text preserves F1's *"Iuno descends."* following line 72, adding *"slowly in her car"* (after Collier) and lets her "alight" after the first half of line 101.

Among Shakespeare's plays, generally, except for *Henry VIII,* the stage directions in *The Tempest* are the most detailed and directive/prescriptive of action and reaction. This may be in part a result of the play's close relation to the

Court masque (which contained elaborate stage directions) and in part Shakespeare's attempt to "direct" after his retirement to Stratford. It has also been shown, however, that to some small extent, as Greg suggested, the stage directions seem to reveal the hand of someone, other than the author, who has witnessed a performance of the play. That someone is almost certainly Crane, who, from the evidence of other Crane transcripts, is known to have "improved" the original stage directions in the course of transcribing. See Roberts and Jowett and such examples as: III.iii.52 s.d. "*with a quaint device*" and 82 s.d. "*with mocks and mows*"; IV.i.138 s.d. "*to a strange, hollow, and confused noise, they heavily vanish*"; V.i.57 s.d. "*with a frantic gesture.*"

For further information, see W. J. Lawrence, "The Masque in *The Tempest,*" *The Fortnightly Review,* n.s. CVII (1920), 941–6; F. P. Wilson, "Ralph Crane, Scrivener to the King's Players," *The Library,* 4th. sec., VII (1926–27), 194–215; J. D. Wilson, ed., New Shakespeare *The Tempest* and *The Winter's Tale* (Cambridge, 1921 and 1931); E. K. Chambers, *Shakespearean Gleanings* (Oxford, 1944); W. W. Greg, *The Shakespeare First Folio* (Oxford, 1955); Frank Kermode, ed., New Arden *The Tempest* (London, rev. ed., 1958); Charlton Hinman, *The Printing and Proof-Reading of the First Folio of Shakespeare,* 2 vols. (Oxford, 1963); T. H. Howard-Hill, *Ralph Crane and Some Shakespeare First Folio Comedies* (Charlottesville, Va., 1972) and "The Compositors of Shakespeare's Folio Comedies," *SB,* XXVI (1973), 61–106; J. A. Roberts, "Ralph Crane and the Text of *The Tempest,*" *S St,* XIII (1980), 213–33; John Jowett, "New Created Creatures: Ralph Crane and the Stage Directions in *The Tempest,*" *S Sur,* XXXVI (1983), 107–20; Stephen Orgel, ed., New Oxford *The Tempest* (Oxford, 1987); Stanley Wells, Gary Taylor, John Jowett, and William Montgomery, *William Shakespeare: A Textual Companion* (Oxford, 1987).

TEXTUAL NOTES

Dramatis personae: *as given in F1, following the play, with slight additions by later editors*
Act-scene division: *from F1*

I.i

Location: *Pope*
5 **hearts! cheerly]** *Capell* (hearts; cheerly); hearts, cheerely *F1* (*F4 and eds. until Capell om.* cheerely)
5 **cheerly, my]** *F2* (*comma, Theobald*); cheerely my *F1*
8 s.d. **Antonio]** *Theobald;* Anthonio *F1* (*throughout*)
21 **councillor]** *Wilson;* Counsellor *F1*
26 **Cheerly]** *F4;* Cheerely *F1*
33 s.d. **Exeunt.]** *Theobald;* Exit. *F1*
35 s.d. **A cry within.]** *placed as in Johnson; in F1 follows* plague (*see next note*)
36 **plague]** *Pope;* plague—— *F1*
37 s.d. **Enter . . . Gonzalo.]** *placed as in Capell; in F1 follows* A cry within. (*see note to l. 35 s.d.*)
51 s.p. **Mariners.]** *Dyce;* Mari. *F1*
52 s.d. **Exeunt.]** *Theobald*
54–5 **The . . . theirs.]** *as verse, Pope; as prose, F1*
54 **Prince]** *F4;* Prince, *F1*
55 **I am]** *Steevens;* I'am *F1*
57–8 **This . . . tides!]** *as verse, Pope; as prose, F1*
57 **wide-chopp'd rascal]** *F4;* wide-chopt-rascall *F1*
60–2 **"Mercy . . . split!"]** *first marked as part of the* confused noise within *by Capell; apparently part of Gonzalo's speech, F1*
62 s.d. **Exit Boatswain.]** *Dyce*
63 **wi' th']** *White;* with' *F1*
64 s.d. **with Antonio]** *Cambridge* (*subs.*)
66 **furze]** *Rowe;* firrs *F1*

I.ii

Location: *Pope, Theobald*
15 **woe]** *Pope;* woe, *F1*
24 s.d. **Lays . . . mantle.]** *Pope*
29 **soul—]** *Steevens;* soule *F1;* soul, *F3*
50 **dark backward]** *F3;* dark-backward *F1*
54 **Milan]** *Rowe* (Millan); Millaine *F1* (*throughout*)
59 **princess]** *Knight;* Princesse; *F1*
62 **foul play]** *F3;* fowle-play *F1*
77 **studies.]** *F4* (*subs.*); studies, *F1*
91 **that which, . . . retir'd,]** *Pope;* that, which . . . retir'd *F1*
99 **exact—]** *Capell;* exact. *F1*
107 **screen]** *F4;* Schreene *F1*
109 **Milan—me]** *Wilson;* Millaine, Me *F1*
110 **royalties]** *F2;* roalties *F1*
112 **wi' th']** *Rowe;* with *F1*
113–4 **homage, . . . crown,]** *F3* (Crowne, *F2*); homage / Subiect his Coronet, to his Crowne *F1*
159 **divine.]** *F4* (*subs.*); diuine, *F1*
169 **arise.]** *Pope* (*subs.*); arise, *F1*
169 s.d. **Puts . . . robe.]** *Collier MS* (*subs.*)
173 **princes]** *Rowe;* Princesse *F1*
181 **zenith]** *Capell;* Zenith *F1* (*in italics*)
186 s.d. **Miranda sleeps.]** *Theobald*
203 **sight-outrunning]** *Capell;* sight out-running *F1*
265, 284, 346 **human]** *F4;* humane *F1*
282 **she]** *Rowe;* he *F1*
286 **service.]** *F2* (*subs.*); seruice, *F1*
295 **peg thee]** *F2;* peg-thee *F1*
304 s.d. **Ariel]** *Rowe*
305 **Awake]** *Rowe; Pro.* Awake *F1* (*repeated s.p.*)
327 **Shall, . . . work,]** *Rowe;* Shall . . . night, . . . worke *F1*
342 **sty me]** *Rowe;* sty-me *F1*
372 s.d. **Aside.]** *Johnson*
375, 397 **song headings Ariel's]** *F3;* Ariel *F1*
377 **kiss'd,]** *Rowe;* kist *F1*
380 **the burthen bear]** *Pope* (*after Davenant-Dryden*); beare the burthen *F1*
381–7 **Hark . . . Cock-a-diddle-dow.]** *arranged as by Capell* (*and Daniel, l. 387*); Burthen dispersedly. / *Harke, harke, bowgh wawgh: the watch-Dogges barke, / bowgh-wawgh. / Ar. Hark, hark, I heare, the straine of strutting Chanticlere / cry cockadidle-dowe. F1*
382, 384, 404 s.dd. **within]** *Bullen*
390–1 **island. . . . wrack,]** *Pope;* Iland, . . . wracke. *F1*
410 **What,]** *ed.* (*after Daniel*); What *F1*
420 s.d. **Aside.]** *Pope*
439 s.d. **Aside.]** *Collier MS*
451 s.d. **Aside.]** *Capell*
459 **ill spirit]** *F4;* ill-spirit *F1*
484 s.d. **To Ferdinand.]** *Wilson*
494 s.d. **Aside.]** *Capell*
494, 495 s.dd. **To Ferdinand.]** *Cambridge*
496 s.d. **To Ariel.]** *Theobald*
502 s.d. **To Ferdinand.]** *Craig*
502 s.d. **To Miranda.]** *Munro*

II.i

Location: *Pope*
16 **entertain'd]** *Rowe;* entertaind, *F1*
16 **offer'd,]** *Capell;* offer'd *F1*
18 **dollar]** *Capell;* dollor *F1*
28–9 **Which . . . crow?]** *as prose, Pope; as verse, F1*
53–4 **How lush . . . green!]** *as prose, Pope; as verse, F1*
95 **Ay]** *Rowe;* I *F1*
106 **marriage?]** *Capell;* marriage. *F1*
153 **Bourn]** *Rowe;* Borne *F1*
170 **And—]** *Cambridge;* And *F1*
182 **mettle]** *Capell;* mettal *F1*
184 s.d. **invisible]** *Malone*
190 s.d. **All . . . Antonio.]** *Capell* (*subs., after Rowe*)
198 s.d. **Alonso sleeps.]** *Capell*
198 s.d. **Exit Ariel.]** *Malone*
203 **consent;]** *Capell;* consent *F1*
231 **throes]** *Pope;* throwes *F1*
278 **Twenty]** *F3;* 'Twentie *F1*
296 s.d. **They talk apart.]** *Capell*
296 s.d. **invisible]** *Capell*
306 s.d. **Waking.]** *Dyce*
307 s.d. **Wakes Alonso.]** *Neilson*

II.ii

Location: *Pope*
14 s.d. **Enter Trinculo.]** *placed as in Rowe; in margin opposite ll. 14, 15, F1*
29 **holiday fool]** *F3* (*subs.*); holiday-foole *F1*
37 s.d. **Thunder.]** *Capell*
41 s.d. **a . . . hand]** *Capell*
44–5 **This . . . comfort.]** *as prose, Pope; as verse, F1*
55 **This . . . comfort.]** *as prose, Pope; as verse, F1*
57 **What's . . . here?]** *as prose, Pope; as verse, F1*
86 s.d. **Caliban drinks.]** *Collier MS*
87 **I . . . be—]** *as prose, Pope; as verse, F1*
87 **be—]** *F2;* be, *F1*
93–4 s.d. **Caliban drinks again.]** *Wilson*
116 s.d. **Aside.]** *Dyce*
116–8 **These . . . him.]** *as verse, Johnson; as prose, F1*
119–20 **How didst . . . hither?]** *as prose, Pope; as verse, F1*
124 **ashore]** *F3;* a'- / shore *F1*
130 s.d. **Passing the bottle.]** *Neilson-Hill* (*after Craig*)
135–6 **How . . . ague?]** *as prose, Pope; as verse, F1*
143 s.d. **Caliban drinks.]** *Collier*
146–7 **The . . . sooth!]** *as prose, Pope; as verse, F1*
148–9 **I'll . . . god.]** *as verse, Johnson; as prose, F1*
156 **him—]** *Pope;* him. *F1*
158–9 **But . . . monster!]** *as prose, Pope; as verse, F1*
159 **abominable]** *F4;* abhominable *F1*
160–1 **I'll . . . enough.]** *as verse, Pope; as prose, F1*
163–4 **I'll . . . man.]** *as verse, Pope; as prose, F1*
167–72 **I . . . me?]** *as verse, Pope; as prose, F1*
178 s.p. **Cal. (Sings drunkenly.)]** *given as* Caliban Sings drunkenly. *above l. 178, F1*

III.i

Location: *Theobald* (*after Pope*)
2 **sets]** *Rowe;* set *F1*
15 **busil'est]** *Kermode* (busilest, *after Bulloch conj.* busiliest); busie lest, *F1*
15 s.d. **at . . . unseen]** *Rowe*
25 **No,]** *Rowe;* No *F1*
31 s.d. **Aside.]** *Capell*

34–5 **you—Chiefly]** *Pope (subs., after Rowe)*; you / Cheefely, *F1*
61 **would,]** *Theobald;* would *F1*
62 **wooden]** *F2* (woodden); wodden *F1*
74 **s.d. Aside.]** *Capell*
91 **s.d. Ferdinand . . . severally]** *Capell*
93 **withal]** *Theobald;* with all *F1*

III.ii

Location: *Pope*
15 **on.]** *Cambridge;* on, *F1*
15–6 **lieutenant, monster]** *Rowe;* Lieutenant Monster *F1*
40–1 **Marry . . . Trinculo.]** *as prose, Pope; as verse, F1*
48–9 **Trinculo . . . teeth.]** *as prose, Pope; as verse, F1*
52 **isle;]** *Theobald;* Isle *F1*
54–5 **him—for . . . not—]** *Theobald (subs.);* him, (for . . . dar'st) . . . not. *F1*
58–9 **How . . . party?]** *as prose, Pope; as verse, F1*
68 **Trinculo . . . danger.]** *as prose, Pope; as verse, F1*
72–3 **Why . . . off.]** *as prose, Pope; as verse, F1*
76–7 **Do . . . time.]** *probably meant as prose, Pope; as verse, F1*
76 **s.d. Beats Trinculo.]** *Rowe (subs.)*
78–81 **I . . . fingers!]** *as prose, Pope; as verse, F1*
80 **murrain]** *F3;* murren *F1*
108–9 **Dost . . . Trinculo?]** *as prose, Pope; as verse, F1*
111–2 **Give . . . head.]** *as prose, Pope; as verse, F1*
119–20 **At . . . sing.]** *as prose, Pope; as verse, F1*
121 **scout]** *Rowe;* cout *F1*
128–9 **If . . . list.]** *as prose, Pope; as verse, F1*
144–52 **This . . . Stephano.]** *as prose, Pope; as verse, F1*

III.iii

Location: *Theobald (after Pope)*
2 **aches]** *Sisson;* akes *F1;* ake *F2*
11 **s.d. Aside to Sebastian.]** *Hanmer*
13, 17 **s.dd. Aside to Antonio.]** *Capell*
14 **s.d. Aside to Sebastian.]** *Capell*
17 **s.d. Solemn . . . invisible.]** *placed as in Pope; after* fresh. *l. 17, F1*
19 **s.d. Enter . . . depart.]** *placed as in Wilson; part of s.d. at l. 17, F1*
29 **islanders]** *F2;* Islands *F1*
33 **human]** *Rowe;* humaine *F1*
34, 39 **s.dd. Aside.]** *Capell*
35 **present]** *Rowe;* present; *F1;* present, *F2*
42 **Will't]** *Pope;* Wilt *F1*
48 **putter-out]** *hyphen, Capell*
52 **to]** *F4;* too *F1*
60 **s.d. Alonso . . . swords.]** *Cambridge (after Hanmer)*
63 **bemock'd-at stabs]** *Rowe;* bemockt-at-Stabs *F1*
64 **still-closing]** *hyphen, Pope*
65 **plume]** *Rowe;* plumbe *F1*
66 **like invulnerable]** *Rowe;* like-invulnerable *F1*
81 **heart's sorrow]** *Pope (after Rowe);* hearts-sorrow *F1*
82 **s.d. to . . . enter]** *Rowe;* (to soft Musicke.) Enter *F1*
93 **s.d. Exit above.]** *Theobald*
103 **s.d. Sebastian and Antonio]** *Malone*

IV.i

Location: *Capell (after Pope)*
9 **off]** *F2;* of *F1*
13 **gift]** *Rowe;* guest *F1*
17 **rite]** *Rowe;* right *F1*
25 **love . . . now,]** *Rowe;* loue, . . . now *F1*
52 **rein]** *F4;* raigne *F1*
59 s.d. **Soft music.]** *placed as in Pope; after l. 58, F1*
62 **turfy mountains]** *F2;* Turphie-Mountaines *F1*
63 **thatch'd]** *Rowe;* thetchd *F1*
74 **Her]** *Rowe;* here *F1*
74 s.d. **slowly . . . car]** *ed. (after Collier MS and Wilson); s.d. in margin opposite ll. 72, 73, F1*
83 **short-grass'd]** *F3 (hyphen, Rowe);* short gras'd *F1*
90 **blind boy's]** *F3 (subs.);* blind-Boyes *F1*
101 s.d. **Juno alights.]** *Wilson*
106 **marriage-blessing]** *Theobald;* marriage, blessing *F1*
110 s.p. **Cer.]** *Theobald; lines continued to Juno, F1*
123 **wise]** *some copies of F1 may read* wife
124 s.d. **Juno . . . employment.]** *placed as in Capell; after l. 127, F1*
125 **seriously;]** *F4;* seriously, *F1*
130 **green land]** *Warburton;* Greene-Land *F1*
134 **sicklemen,]** *F4;* Sicklemen *F1*
136 **holiday]** *Capell;* holly day *F1*
139 **s.d. Aside.]** *Johnson*
142 **s.d. To the Spirits.]** *Johnson*
147 **sir.]** *Pope (subs.);* Sir, *F1*
160 **infirmity.]** *F4 (subs.);* infirmitie, *F1*
162 **repose.]** *F3 (subs.);* repose, *F1*
164 **s.d. To Ariel.]** *ed.*
164 **s.d. To . . . Miranda.]** *ed.*
164 **thee. Ariel! come.]** *ed. (after Kermode);* thee *Ariel*: come. *F1*
164 **s.d. Exeunt . . . Miranda.]** *ed.;* Exit. *F1 (after l. 163)*
173 **princes]** *Rowe;* Princesse *F1 (a Crane spelling of* Princes)
180 **furzes]** *Rowe;* firzes *F1*
182 **filthy-mantled]** *hyphen, Cambridge*
188 **born devil]** *F4* (born *F3*); borne-Deuill *F1*
193 s.d. **Enter . . . etc.]** *placed as in Dyce; after l. 193, F1*
193 **them on]** *Rowe;* on them *F1*
193 s.d. **Prospero . . . invisible.]** *Capell (after Theobald)*
193 **s.d. Enter . . . wet.]** *placed as in Capell; in F1 follows* etc. *in preceding s.d.*
194–5 **Pray . . . cell.]** *as verse, Rowe; as prose, F1*
196–202 **Monster . . . you—]** *as prose, Pope; as verse, F1*
206 **hoodwink]** *F3;* hudwinke *F1*
211–4 **That's . . . labor.]** *as prose, Pope; as verse, F1*
220–1 **Give . . . thoughts.]** *as prose, Pope; as verse, F1*
222–3 **O . . . thee!]** *probably meant as prose, Pope; as verse, F1*
226 **frippery.]** *Theobald (subs.);* frippery, *F1*
231 **Let't]** *Rann;* let's *F1*
250 **lay-to]** *hyphen, Steevens*
257 **s.d. Caliban . . . out.]** *Theobald (subs.)*

V.i

Location: *Theobald*
10 **line-grove]** *Collier;* Line-groue *F1 (in italics)*
14 **Brimful]** *F4 (subs.);* Brim full *F1*
20 **human]** *Rowe;* humane *F1*
32 **s.d. Prospero . . . staff.]** *Wilson*
35 **ebbing Neptune]** *F3;* ebbing-Neptune *F1*
39 **midnight mushrumps]** *ed.;* midnight-Mushrumps *F1; hyphen om. F4* (midnight Mushromes)
46 **strong-bas'd]** *hyphen, Pope*
54 **airy charm]** *F3;* Ayrie-charme *F1*
60 **boil'd]** *Rowe;* boile *F1*
72 **Didst]** *F1 catchword;* Did *F1*
75 **entertain'd]** *F2;* entertaine *F1*
81 **shores]** *Malone;* shore *F1*
84 **s.d. Exit . . . immediately.]** *Theobald (after l. 85); placed as in Capell*
88 **s.p. Ari.]** *Craig*
111 **Whe'er]** *Capell;* Where *F1*
120 **s.d. To Gonzalo.]** *Wilson*
124 **not]** *F3;* nor *F1*
126 **s.d. Aside . . . Antonio.]** *Johnson*
129 **s.d. Aside.]** *Johnson*
151 **oozy]** *Rowe;* oo-zie *F1*
179 **s.d. Kneels.]** *Theobald*
191 **advice]** *F4;* aduise *F1*
213 **s.d. To . . . Miranda.]** *Hanmer*
219 **shore?]** *Pope;* shore, *F1*
224 **tight]** *Rowe;* tyte *F1*
225, 240 **s.dd. Aside to Prospero.]** *Capell*
226, 241, 251 **s.dd. Aside to Ariel.]** *Capell*
241 **my diligence. Thou]** *F4 (subs.);* (my diligence) thou *F1*
248 **Which . . . shortly, single]** *Pope;* (Which . . . shortly single) *F1*
253 **s.d. Exit Ariel.]** *Capell*
256–8 **Every . . . coraggio!]** *as prose, Pope; as verse, F1*
258 **coraggio]** *F2;* Corasio *F1*
272 **robb'd]** *F3;* robd *F1*
282–4 **I . . . fly-blowing.]** *as prose, Pope; as verse, F1*
290 **s.d. Pointing to Caliban.]** *Steevens*
296 **thrice-double]** *hyphen, Theobald*
300 **s.d. Exeunt . . . Trinculo.]** *Capell*
314 **strangely]** *F2;* starngely *F1*
317 **s.d. Aside to Ariel.]** *Capell*

Epilogue

2 **own,]** *F2;* owne. *F1*
14 **enforce, art]** *Rowe;* enforce: Art *F1*
20 **s.d. Exit.]** Exit. *[list of actors]* FINIS. *F1*

The Two Noble Kinsmen

The Two Noble Kinsmen is the one play in this volume for which divided authorship can be argued partly on the basis of external evidence. The radical difference between the two parts of *Pericles* forces the conclusion that they are by separate hands, and stylistic differences are the basis of persuasive showings that *Henry VIII* is the product of collaboration, but for *The Two Noble Kinsmen* we have an entry in the Stationers' Register and the title-page of a quarto to assert that two authors were involved. The play was entered on April 8, 1634, as "a Tragi Comedy . . . by John ffletcher and William Shakespeare," and the title-page of the quarto that appeared later that year says that the play had been presented at the Blackfriars "by the Kings Maiesties servants, with great applause," and that it was "Written by the memorable Worthies of their time; Mr. John Fletcher, and Mr. William Shakespeare, Gent[lemen]." Such statements cannot always be taken at face value; but John Waterson, the publisher of the 1634 quarto, was a reputable printer and bookseller who brought out other plays belonging to the King's Men, his quarto was based upon a theatre manuscript that must have been made available by them, and from them he would have had reliable information about the authorship of the play.

Yet *The Two Noble Kinsmen* has not often, until recently, been included in collected editions of Shakespeare's plays. It does not appear in the First Folio of 1623, and in this it is like *Pericles*. But there is a good likelihood that *Pericles* was excluded because no satisfactory text was available; whereas the text of *The Two Noble Kinsmen* that Waterson was able to obtain in 1634 was excellent. Moreover, we know from a scrap of paper from the King's Office of the Revels that the play was in repertory in 1619 and was being considered for performance at court; and two actors' names which have slipped into the text show that there was a revival in the mid-1620's. A good text would therefore have been at hand in 1623, and it is hard to resist the conclusion that its non-appearance in the Folio is somehow related to the facts of authorship. It is argued by some that dual authorship in itself would not have been a reason for exclusion, since *Henry VIII* was included. Unless the minority view is correct which denies Fletcher a part in that history play, the answer may be simply that the company knew Shakespeare to have had the controlling hand in the one play, Fletcher in the other. But this is pure conjecture.

The Two Noble Kinsmen was reprinted in the Beaumont and Fletcher Second Folio of 1679 (which included many plays in which Fletcher had collaborated with other dramatists) and since then has appeared in all collected editions of Beaumont and Fletcher. Editors of Shakespeare's works have been less hospitable, for although critics have commonly seen two hands in the play, by no means the majority have believed that one of them is Shakespeare's. Claims have been advanced for Beaumont, Massinger, and others as Fletcher's collaborator in the play. The most recent full-length study, Paul Bertram's *Shakespeare and "The Two Noble Kinsmen"* (1965), argues, on the other hand, that Shakespeare wrote the whole play. Bertram has won few followers, but the case for Shakespeare as part-author, which has never been without strong adherents, has recently gained ground. In the present edition the play is accepted as a collaborative work by Fletcher and Shakespeare.

For almost a century and a half, since William

Spalding's pioneering article in 1833, scholars have attempted to distinguish between Fletcher's and Shakespeare's scenes in the play. The criteria used include metrical characteristics, vocabulary and word-compounding, incidence of certain contractions, kinds and uses of imagery, and characteristic lines of certain types. When evidence from these various elements converges in agreement, critics have been able to assign authorship with some, but of course not complete, confidence. According to their findings, the play divides up roughly as follows:

I.i–II.i	Shakespeare (but I.iv, v uncertain)
II.ii–vi	Fletcher
III.i	Shakespeare
III.ii–V.i.33	Fletcher (but IV.ii uncertain)
V.i.34–173	Shakespeare
V.ii	Fletcher
V.iii, iv	Shakespeare

Fletcher is usually given the prologue and epilogue and the pretty song at the beginning of the first scene.

A number of indications place the play in the year 1613. The Schoolmaster's entertainment in III.v is borrowed from the second antimasque in Beaumont's *Inner Temple and Gray's Inn Mask*, which was presented at Whitehall on February 20, 1613; the same professional dancers probably appeared in both productions. In *Bartholomew Fair* (1614) Ben Jonson refers to a dramatic character named Palamon. And there is reason to believe that Shakespeare was collaborating with Fletcher in 1613 on *Henry VIII* and a lost play called *Cardenio*.

The Two Noble Kinsmen is a dramatization of Chaucer's "Knight's Tale." Shakespeare had drawn on the same tale years before, for some details of his treatment of Theseus and Hippolyta in *A Midsummer Night's Dream*. The story is not inherently dramatic, though it lends itself readily to rhetorical elaboration and pageantry. The cousins Palamon and Arcite, at first devoted friends, then deadly foes because of their rivalry for the love of Emilia, cannot be sharply distinguished one from the other; and the outcome is the result of the whim of the gods, or rather, the special interests of individual gods.

The material is well suited to the tastes of the audience for which Shakespeare wrote his romances, and there are many links between this and the previous plays. As old Gower is the source for *Pericles*, his contemporary Chaucer is the source for the *Kinsmen*. Thebes and Athens are as remote as Antioch, Tharsus, Mytilene, and Ephesus. The gods are invoked and their favors are granted; in this, of course, we are in the same world as in *Cymbeline* and *The Winter's Tale*. Nothing is too strange or improbable to be accepted, not the interruption of Theseus' wedding ceremony for a military expedition, nor the courtesy of two deadly foes who arm each other before conflict, nor the gratuitous accident which kills the victor before he can claim his prize. There is less variety but as much strangeness as there was in the world of *Pericles*. The picture of innocence in the midst of corruption, exploited both in the scene introducing Palamon and Arcite in Thebes (I.ii) and in the long account by Emilia of her girlhood friendship with Flavina (I.iii.55–82), is a part of the same vision we see in Marina, Imogen, Perdita, and Miranda. And Leontes and Polixenes look back to the innocence of their boyhood years (*The Winter's Tale*, I.ii.62 ff.).

The chief alteration made in Chaucer's narrative is the addition of the subplot of the Jailer's daughter, who complicates the love-triangle by falling in love with Palamon, effecting his escape from prison, and going mad for unrequited love of him. (In the "Knight's Tale" Palamon, with the aid of a friend, escapes by plying the jailer with drugged wine.) Moreover, she also has a suitor in love with her, and we see the kind of "cross-eyed Cupid" situation which Shakespeare had used in *A Midsummer Night's Dream* and *As You Like It*. This does not necessarily mean that her addition to the plot or the conception of her role in it was Shakespeare's idea. She is introduced in a scene (II.i) generally assigned to him, but the scenes in which she is developed (II.iv, vi, III.ii, iv–v, IV.i, iii, V.ii) are Fletcher's. Reminiscences of Ophelia are numerous and striking, but Fletcher's plays show many such resemblances to Shakespeare's. The extended sentimentality of the daughter's situation and the coarseness of the doctor's suggested cure by seduction are far more characteristic of Fletcher than of Shakespeare.

Shakespeare's scenes are marked by his characteristic use of imagery and by some typical image-clusters: for example, the association of *kites* (carrion-eating hawks) with *ravens*, *crows*, *dead*, *slain*, *kings* in I.i.39–50, and the elaborate association of the word *hum* with *death*, *food*, *sleep*, *music*, *song*, *flowers*, *wealth*, *ears*, *spirit*, *bastardy* in I.iii.66–82. Furthermore, Shakespeare's manner with images, as well as the imagery itself, is different from Fletcher's. Charles Lamb described Fletcher and his senior collaborator as follows:

> His [Fletcher's] ideas move slow; his versification, though sweet, is tedious; it stops every moment; he lays line upon line, making up one after the other, adding image to image so deliberately that we see where they join: Shakespeare mingles everything, he runs line into line, embarrasses sentences and metaphors; before one idea has burst its shell, another is hatched and clamorous for disclosure.

The play depends heavily upon rhetoric and upon theatrical scenes. The first grand spectacle, the wedding procession of Theseus and Hippolyta, is interrupted by the pleas of the three "blubber'd queens" for aid against Creon, who has refused rites of burial to the three slain kings. In Chaucer the oldest queen speaks for all three, addressing herself to Theseus, who quickly consents. The purpose is to initiate the action that will bring Palamon and Arcite to Athens as prisoners of Theseus. Shakespeare, expanding about forty lines in Chaucer to two hundred, exploits the possibilities of the scene with an elaborately patterned succession of speeches involving all three queens and Theseus, Hippolyta, and Emilia.

Similarly, in the last act, the big event of the plot is the combat between Palamon and Arcite, but the drama allows that to take place off stage and gives theatrical prominence to the knight's prayers before the altars of Mars and Venus, and Emilia's before the altar of Diana. Palamon's prayer to Venus (V.i.77–136) is especially remarkable. Alfred Harbage has wittily commented that "it is difficult to see what Venus could have done with this client except refer him to Diana."

DeQuincey, in his treatise on rhetoric, has given these passages the most ardent praise that they have ever received:

> The first and last acts . . . of *Two Noble Kinsmen*—which in point of composition is perhaps the most superb work in the language and beyond all doubt from the loom of Shakespeare—would have been the most gorgeous rhetoric, had they not happened to be something far better. The supplication of the widowed queens to Theseus, the invocations of their tutelar divinities by Palamon and Arcite, the death of Arcite, etc., are furnished in a more elaborate style of excellence than any other almost of Shakespeare's most felicitous scenes. In their first intention they were perhaps merely rhetorical; but the furnace of composition has transmuted their substance.

The play deals in a curious way with the theme of innocence and experience, and the conflict between sexual desire and duty. Theseus postpones nuptial pleasures for a military duty, but neither Palamon nor Arcite can subordinate his love to any other consideration. Emilia seems sexless in her inability to express a preference for one suitor over another, yet the Jailer's daughter, who is all sex, and who has had no difficulty in fixing her choice upon Palamon, is finally satisfied with a substitute for him. The characters move from a state of innocence, which is presexual, into an area of experience where the will seems totally irrelevant to the way things will turn out. What Arcite says early in the play (I.ii.113–16) proves at the end to have been prophetic of the whole course of action:

> Let th' event,
> That never-erring arbitrator, tell us
> When we know all ourselves, and let us follow
> The becking of our chance.

Hallett Smith

The Two Noble Kinsmen

[Dramatis Personae

Theseus, *Duke of Athens*
Pirithous, *an Athenian general*
Artesius, *an Athenian captain*
Palamon } *nephews to Creon, King of Thebes*
Arcite }
Valerius
Six Knights
Herald
Jailer (*also called* Keeper)
Wooer *to the Jailer's Daughter*
Doctor
Brother } *to the Jailer*
Friends }
Gentleman

Gerrold, *a schoolmaster*

Hymen

Hippolyta, *an Amazon, bride to Theseus*
Emilia, *her sister*
Three Queens
Jailer's Daughter
Waiting-Woman *to Emilia*

Nymphs

Countrymen, Country Girls, Messengers, Taborer, Boy, Executioner, Guard, Servant, Attendants

Scene: *Athens and the neighborhood; Thebes and the neighborhood*]

PROLOGUE

Flourish.

New plays and maidenheads are near akin—
Much follow'd both, for both much money gi'n,
If they stand sound and well; and a good play
(Whose modest scenes blush on his marriage-day,
And shake to lose his honor) is like her
That after holy tie and first night's stir,
Yet still is modesty, and still retains
More of the maid to sight than husband's pains.
We pray our play may be so; for I am sure
It has a noble breeder and a pure,
A learned, and a poet never went
More famous yet 'twixt Po and silver Trent.
Chaucer (of all admir'd) the story gives;
There constant to eternity it lives.
If we let fall the nobleness of this,
And the first sound this child hear be a hiss,
How will it shake the bones of that good man,
And make him cry from under ground, "O, fan
From me the witless chaff of such a writer
That blasts my bays and my fam'd works makes lighter
Than Robin Hood!" This is the fear we bring;
For to say truth, it were an endless thing,
And too ambitious, to aspire to him,
Weak as we are, and almost breathless swim
In this deep water. Do but you hold out
Your helping hands, and we shall tack about
And something do to save us. You shall hear
Scenes, though below his art, may yet appear
Worth two hours' travail. To his bones sweet sleep!
Content to you! If this play do not keep
A little dull time from us, we perceive
Our losses fall so thick we must needs leave.

Flourish.

ACT I, [Scene I]

Enter Hymen *with a torch burning; a* Boy, *in a white robe, before, singing and strewing flow'rs; after Hymen, a* Nymph, *encompass'd in her tresses, bearing*

Words and passages enclosed in square brackets in the text above are either emendations of the copy-text or additions to it. The Textual Notes immediately following the play cite the earliest authority for every such change or insertion and supply the reading of the copy-text wherever it is emended in this edition.

Pro. o.s.d. **Flourish:** trumpet fanfare. 2. **gi'n:** given.
4. **his:** its. 5. **shake . . . honor:** tremble at losing its virginity.
8. **to sight:** visible. **pains:** exertions. 15. **let fall:** fail to sustain.

20. **blasts my bays:** blights my fame as a poet. **lighter:** more trivial.
21. **Than Robin Hood:** i.e. than some popular ballad or tale.
22. **endless:** fruitless.
25–26. **hold . . . hands:** i.e. assist us with your applause.
28. **Scenes:** scenes which. 31. **dull:** slack.
32. **Our losses.** Variously explained; perhaps a reference to the burning of the Globe in 1613. **leave:** leave off acting.

I.i. Location: Athens. Before the temple.
o.s.d. **Hymen:** god of marriage. **encompass'd . . . tresses:** with her hair hanging loose about her (symbolic of virginity).

a wheaten garland; then THESEUS, *between two other* NYMPHS *with wheaten chaplets on their heads; then* HIPPOLYTA, *the bride, led by* [PIRITHOUS], *and another holding a garland over her head (her tresses likewise hanging); after her,* EMILIA, *holding up her train;* [ARTESIUS *and* ATTENDANTS]. *Music.*

THE SONG [*by the* BOY].

Roses, their sharp spines being gone,
Not royal in their smells alone,
  But in their hue;
Maiden pinks, of odor faint,
Daisies smell-less, yet most quaint,
  And sweet thyme true;

Primrose, first-born child of Ver,
Merry spring-time's harbinger,
  With her bells dim;
Oxlips in their cradles growing,
Marigolds on death-beds blowing,
  Larks'-heels trim;

All dear Nature's children sweet,
Lie 'fore bride and bridegroom's
  feet, *Strew flowers.*
  Blessing their sense;
Not an [angel] of the air,
Bird melodious, or bird fair,
  Is absent hence.

The crow, the sland'rous cuckoo, nor
The boding raven, nor [chough hoar],
  Nor chatt'ring pie,
May on our bridehouse perch or sing,
Or with them any discord bring,
  But from it fly.

Enter three QUEENS, *in black, with veils stain'd, with imperial crowns. The first Queen falls down at the foot of Theseus; the second falls down at the foot of Hippolyta; the third before Emilia.*

1. Queen. For pity's sake and true gentility's,
Hear and respect me.
2. Queen. For your mother's sake,
And as you wish your womb may thrive with fair ones,
Hear and respect me.
3. Queen. Now for the love of him whom Jove hath mark'd
The honor of your bed, and for the sake
Of clear virginity, be advocate
For us and our distresses! This good deed
Shall raze you out o' th' book of trespasses
All you are set down there.

5. quaint: pretty, fine. **7. Ver:** spring.
9. her bells. Skeat's emendation *harebells* is tempting. **dim:** pale in color. **11. death-beds:** i.e. graves. **blowing:** blooming.
12. Larks'-heels: larkspur.
16. angel . . . air: i.e. bird of good omen.
19. sland'rous. The cuckoo supposedly called out "Cuckold!" to men, slandering their innocent wives.
20. chough hoar: crow with grey topknot. **21. pie:** magpie.
24 s.d. stain'd: dyed, dark. **25. gentility's:** nobility's.
26. respect: give attention to.
29. whom: to (or for) whom. **mark'd:** appointed, destined.
31. clear: pure, innocent.
33–34. raze . . . there: i.e. erase all your sins from the record.

The. Sad lady, rise.
Hip. Stand up.
Emil. No knees to me.
What woman I may stead that is distress'd
Does bind me to her.
The. What's your request? Deliver you for all.
1. Queen. We are three queens, whose sovereigns fell before
The wrath of cruel Creon; who endured
The beaks of ravens, talents of the kites,
And pecks of crows in the foul fields of Thebes.
He will not suffer us to burn their bones,
To urn their ashes, nor to take th' offense
Of mortal loathsomeness from the blest eye
Of holy Phoebus, but infects the winds
With stench of our slain lords. O, pity, Duke,
Thou purger of the earth, draw thy fear'd sword
That does good turns to th' world; give us the bones
Of our dead kings, that we may chapel them;
And of thy boundless goodness take some note
That for our crowned heads we have no roof,
Save this which is the lion's, and the bear's,
And vault to every thing!
The. Pray you kneel not;
I was transported with your speech, and suffer'd
Your knees to wrong themselves. I have heard the fortunes
Of your dead lords, which gives me such lamenting
As wakes my vengeance and revenge for 'em.
King Capaneus was your lord. The day
That he should marry you, at such a season
As now it is with me, I met your groom
By Mars's altar. You were that time fair;
Not Juno's mantle fairer than your tresses,
Nor in more bounty spread her. Your wheaten wreath
Was then nor thresh'd nor blasted; Fortune at you
Dimpled her cheek with smiles. Hercules our kinsman
(Then weaker than your eyes) laid by his club;
He tumbled down upon his [Nemean] hide,
And swore his sinews thaw'd. O grief and time,
Fearful consumers, you will all devour!
1. Queen. O, I hope some god,
Some god hath put his mercy in your manhood,
Whereto he'll infuse pow'r, and press you forth
Our undertaker.
The. O, no knees, none, widow!
Unto the helmeted Bellona use them,

36. stead: aid. **38. Deliver:** report.
40. Creon: king of Thebes after Oedipus, whose uncle he was. He denied burial to Oedipus' son Polynices and the kings who had fallen with him in the military expedition known as the Seven against Thebes.
41. talents: talons.
44–46. take . . . Phoebus: i.e. remove their rotting bodies from the sunlight. **50. chapel:** i.e. entomb (as in a chapel).
54. vault: arched roof, i.e. the sky.
55. transported: carried away.
64. in . . . spread: more luxuriantly covered.
65. blasted: blighted, withered.
67. weaker than: i.e. conquered by.
68. his Nemean hide: the skin of the Nemean lion, which Hercules slew as one of his twelve labors.
69. sinews thaw'd: muscles turned to water.
73. Whereto: in addition to which.
74. undertaker: champion; literally, one who takes up an action on another's behalf. **75. Bellona:** goddess of war.

And pray for me your soldier.
Troubled I am. *Turns away.*
2. Queen. Honored Hippolyta,
Most dreaded Amazonian, that hast slain
The scythe-tusk'd boar; that with thy arm, as strong
As it is white, wast near to make the male
To thy sex captive, but that this thy lord,
Born to uphold creation in that honor
First Nature styl'd it in, shrunk thee into
The bound thou wast o'erflowing, at once subduing
Thy force and thy affection; soldieress
That equally canst poise sternness with pity,
Whom now I know hast much more power on him
Than ever he had on thee, who ow'st his strength,
And his love too, who is a servant for
The tenor of [thy] speech; dear glass of ladies,
Bid him that we, whom flaming war doth scorch,
Under the shadow of his sword may cool us;
Require him he advance it o'er our heads;
Speak't in a woman's key—like such a woman
As any of us three; weep ere you fail;
Lend us a knee;
But touch the ground for us no longer time
Than a dove's motion when the head's pluck'd off;
Tell him, if he i' th' blood-siz'd field lay swoll'n,
Showing the sun his teeth, grinning at the moon,
What you would do.
Hip. Poor lady, say no more:
I had as lief trace this good action with you
As that whereto I am going, and never yet
Went I so willing way. My lord is taken
Heart-deep with your distress. Let him consider.
I'll speak anon.
3. Queen. O, my petition was *Kneel to Emilia.*
Set down in ice, which by hot grief uncandied
Melts into drops; so sorrow wanting form
Is press'd with deeper matter.
Emil. Pray stand up,
Your grief is written in your cheek.
3. Queen. O, woe,
You cannot read it there. There, through my tears,
Like wrinkled pebbles in a [glassy] stream,
You may behold 'em. Lady, lady, alack!
He that will all the treasure know o' th' earth
Must know the centre too; he that will fish
For my least minnow, let him lead his line
To catch one at my heart. O, pardon me,
Extremity, that sharpens sundry wits,
Makes me a fool.
Emil. Pray you say nothing, pray you.

82–83. honor . . . in: dignity that Nature in the beginning invested it with, i.e. the primacy of man over woman.
84. bound: boundary, due limits (of womanly behavior).
86. poise: balance. **88. ow'st:** ownest.
89–90. is . . . speech: i.e. will faithfully perform whatever your speech imports. **90. glass:** mirror, i.e. model.
93. Require him: ask of him that.
99. blood-siz'd: covered with coagulated blood.
102. trace: traverse, follow out.
107. ice: i.e. cold formality. **uncandied:** thawed.
108–9. so . . . matter: i.e. thus grief is made more oppressive by its inability to express itself.
113. 'em: i.e. her eyes, in which her grief can be more clearly read.
115. know the centre: dig deep into the earth.
116. lead: weight with lead. **118. sundry wits:** some minds.

Who cannot feel nor see the rain, being in't,
Knows neither wet nor dry. If that you were
The ground-piece of some painter, I would buy you
T' instruct me 'gainst a capital grief indeed—
Such heart-pierc'd demonstration! but alas,
Being a natural sister of our sex,
Your sorrow beats so ardently upon me
That it shall make a counter-reflect 'gainst
My brother's heart, and warm it to some pity,
Though it were made of stone. Pray have good comfort.
The. Forward to th' temple. Leave not out a jot
O' th' sacred ceremony.
1. Queen. O, this celebration
Will long last and be more costly than
Your suppliants' war! Remember that your fame
Knolls in the ear o' th' world; what you do quickly
Is not done rashly; your first thought is more
Than others' labored meditance; your premeditating
More than their actions. But, O Jove, your actions,
Soon as they [move,] as asprays do the fish,
Subdue before they touch. Think, dear Duke, think
What beds our slain kings have!
2. Queen. What griefs our beds
That our dear lords have none!
3. Queen. None fit for th' dead:
Those that with cords, knives, drams, precipitance,
Weary of this world's light, have to themselves
Been death's most horrid agents, humane grace
Affords them dust and shadow.
1. Queen. But our lords
Lie blist'ring 'fore the visitating sun,
And were good kings when living.
The. It is true; and I will give you comfort
To give your dead lords graves; the which to do
Must make some work with Creon.
1. Queen. And that work presents itself to th' doing:
Now 'twill take form, the heats are gone to-morrow.
Then, bootless toil must recompense itself
With its own sweat; now he's secure,
Not dreams we stand before your puissance
Wrinching our holy begging in our eyes
To make petition clear.
2. Queen. Now you may take him
Drunk with his victory.
3. Queen. And his army full
Of bread and sloth.

122. ground-piece: preliminary sketch (?) or two-dimensional representation (?). **123. capital:** killing.
124. heart-pierc'd: heart-piercing.
125. natural. As opposed to the creation of an artist.
134. Knolls: tolls, rings.
138. asprays: ospreys, fish hawks. It was said that fish, on seeing an osprey fly overhead, turned over as if dead and allowed themselves to be taken.
142. drams: i.e. poisons. **precipitance:** leaping from high places.
144. humane. Perhaps no more than a variant spelling of *human*, as often. **grace:** mercy.
146. visitating: visiting with destructive effects (cf. "visitation of the plague"). **149. To give:** by giving.
151. presents . . . doing: stands ready for performance.
152. take form: receive impression (like heated metal). Cf. the proverbial "Strike while the iron is hot."
154. secure: without suspicion.
155. your puissance: your powerful self.
156. Wrinching: rinsing. **157. clear:** (1) clean, pure; (2) manifest.

The. Artesius, that best knowest
How to draw out, fit to this enterprise,
The prim'st for this proceeding, and the number
To carry such a business, forth and levy
Our worthiest instruments, whilst we dispatch
This grand act of our life, this daring deed
Of fate in wedlock.

1. Queen. Dowagers, take hands,
Let us be widows to our woes; delay
Commends us to a famishing hope.

All [Queens]. Farewell.

2. Queen. We come unseasonably; but when could grief
Cull forth, as unpang'd judgment can, fitt'st time
For best solicitation?

The. Why, good ladies,
This is a service, whereto I am going,
Greater than any [war]; it more imports me
Than all the actions that I have foregone,
Or futurely can cope.

1. Queen. The more proclaiming
Our suit shall be neglected. When her arms,
Able to lock Jove from a synod, shall
By warranting moonlight corslet thee—O, when
Her twinning cherries shall their sweetness fall
Upon thy tasteful lips, what wilt thou think
Of rotten kings or blubber'd queens? what care
For what thou feel'st not? what thou feel'st being able
To make Mars spurn his drum. O, if thou couch
But one night with her, every hour in't will
Take hostage of thee for a hundred, and
Thou shalt remember nothing more than what
That banket bids thee to!

Hip. Though much unlike
You should be so transported, as much sorry
I should be such a suitor; yet I think
Did I not by th' abstaining of my joy,
Which breeds a deeper longing, cure their surfeit
That craves a present med'cine, I should pluck
All ladies' scandal on me. Therefore, sir, *[Kneels.]*
As I shall here make trial of my pray'rs,
Either presuming them to have some force,
Or sentencing for aye their vigor dumb,
Prorogue this business we are going about, and hang
Your shield afore your heart, about that neck
Which is my fee, and which I freely lend
To do these poor queens service.

All Queens. [*To Emilia.*] O, help now!
Our cause cries for your knee.

Emil. [*Kneels.*] If you grant not
My sister her petition, in that force,
With that celerity and nature, which
She makes it in, from henceforth I'll not dare
To ask you any thing, nor be so hardy
Ever to take a husband.

The. Pray stand up. [*They rise.*]
I am entreating of myself to do
That which you kneel to have me. Pirithous,
Lead on the bride; get you and pray the gods
For success and return; omit not any thing
In the pretended celebration. Queens,
Follow your soldier. [*To Artesius.*] As before, hence you,
And at the banks of [Aulis] meet us with
The forces you can raise, where we shall find
The moi'ty of a number for a business
More bigger-look'd. [*Exit Artesius.*]
[*To Hippolyta.*] Since that our theme is haste,
I stamp this kiss upon thy currant lip.
Sweet, keep it as my token. Set you forward,
For I will see you gone.

Exeunt [*slowly*] *towards the temple.*

Farewell, my beauteous sister. Pirithous,
Keep the feast full, bate not an hour on't.

Pir. Sir,
I'll follow you at heels; the feast's solemnity
Shall want till your return.

The. Cousin, I charge you
Boudge not from Athens. We shall be returning
Ere you can end this feast, of which I pray you
Make no abatement. Once more, farewell all.

1. Queen. Thus dost thou still make good
The tongue o' th' world.

2. Queen. And earn'st a deity
Equal with Mars.

3. Queen. If not above him, for
Thou being but mortal makest affections bend
To godlike honors; they themselves, some say,
Groan under such a mast'ry.

160. draw out: select. **fit to:** suitable for.
164–65. daring . . . fate: deed which challenges fate.
166. Let . . . woes: "let us be widows to our woes, as well as to our husbands; for as Creon has left our dead lords unburied, so our woes have been left unburied by Theseus" (Littledale).
167. Commends: commits, consigns.
172. more imports me: concerns me more seriously.
173. foregone: done in the past. **174. cope:** have to do with.
176. lock . . . synod: keep Jove from a meeting of the gods.
177. warranting: giving authorization.
178. fall: let fall. **179. tasteful:** tasting.
179–80. what . . . Of: what thought will you give to.
180. blubber'd: tear-stained.
182. his drum: i.e. the signal for battle.
184. Take . . . for: i.e. commit you to.
186. banket: banquet. **bids:** invites. **much unlike:** it is highly unlikely.
187–88. as . . . suitor: i.e. and it would be equally regrettable if I should persuade you to such behavior.
190. surfeit: sickness caused by excess (of grief).
191. craves . . . med'cine: requires immediate remedy.
192. scandal: reproach. **195. dumb:** to silence.
196. Prorogue: postpone.
198. is my fee: belongs to me (cf. line 88).
201. in that force: with the same vigor.
202. celerity and nature: natural celerity, i.e. kindly quickness of response. **204. hardy:** bold, rash. **208. get you:** set forward.
210. pretended: intended.
211. your soldier: i.e. Theseus.
214–15. The moi'ty . . . bigger-look'd: (part) of a force sufficient for a bigger undertaking than this willbe.
216. currant. With play (as indicated by *stamp*) on *current*, used of coins that circulated freely in trade (cf. *currency*), identified by the device stamped on them.
217. my token: (1) a reminder of me; (2) a token of my ownership (continuing the wordplay).
218 s.d. Exeunt . . . temple. Apparently the procession begins to move at this point and passes from sight after line 225, leaving on stage only Theseus, the Queens, and attendants.
220. full: fully. **bate:** abate. **on:** of.
221. solemnity: splendor.
222. want: be lacking (?) or be incomplete (?).
223. Boudge: budge.
227. tongue . . . world: what everyone says of you.
229. affections: passions, sexual desires. **bend:** yield, give way.
230. godlike honors: honorable deeds worthy of a god.
231. Groan . . . mast'ry: i.e. are slaves to the appetites.

The. As we are men
Thus should we do, being sensually subdu'd
We lose our human title. Good cheer, ladies.
Now turn we towards your comforts.
Flourish. Exeunt.

SCENE II

Enter PALAMON *and* ARCITE.

Arc. Dear Palamon, dearer in love than blood,
And our prime cousin, yet unhard'ned in
The crimes of nature—let us leave the city
Thebes, and the temptings in't, before we further
Sully our gloss of youth:
And here to keep in abstinence we shame
As in incontinence; for not to swim
I' th' aid o' th' current were almost to sink,
At least to frustrate striving, and to follow
The common stream, 'twould bring us to an eddy
Where we should turn or drown; if labor through,
Our gain but life and weakness.
Pal. Your advice
Is cried up with example. What strange ruins,
Since first we went to school, may we perceive
Walking in Thebes! scars and bare weeds
The gain o' th' martialist, who did propound
To his bold ends honor and golden ingots,
Which though he won, he had not; and now flurted
By peace, for whom he fought, who then shall offer
To Mars's so scorn'd altar? I do bleed
When such I meet, and wish great Juno would
Resume her ancient fit of jealousy
To get the soldier work, that peace might purge
For her repletion, and retain anew
Her charitable heart, now hard, and harsher
Than strife or war could be.
Arc. Are you not out?
Meet you no ruin but the soldier in
The cranks and turns of Thebes? You did begin
As if you met decays of many kinds.
Perceive you none that do arouse your pity
But th' unconsider'd soldier?
Pal. Yes, I pity
Decays where e'er I find them, but such most
That sweating in an honorable toil
Are paid with ice to cool 'em.

Arc. 'Tis not this
I did begin to speak of. This is virtue
Of no respect in Thebes. I spake of Thebes,
How dangerous, if we will keep our honors,
It is for our residing; where every evil
Hath a good color; where ev'ry seeming good's
A certain evil; where not to be ev'n jump
As they are, here were to be strangers, and
Such things to be, mere monsters.
Pal. 'Tis in our power
(Unless we fear that apes can tutor 's) to
Be masters of our manners. What need I
Affect another's gait, which is not catching
Where there is faith? or to be fond upon
Another's way of speech, when by mine own
I may be reasonably conceiv'd; sav'd too,
Speaking it truly? Why am I bound
By any generous bond to follow him
Follows his tailor, haply so long until
The follow'd make pursuit? Or let me know
Why mine own barber is unblest, with him
My poor chin too, for 'tis not scissor'd just
To such a favorite's glass? What canon is there
That does command my rapier from my hip,
To dangle't in my hand, or to go tiptoe
Before the street be foul? Either I am
The forehorse in the team, or I am none
That draw i' th' sequent trace. These poor slight sores
Need not a plantin; that which rips my bosom
Almost to th' heart's—
Arc. Our uncle Creon.
Pal. He,
A most unbounded tyrant, whose successes
Makes heaven unfear'd, and villainy assured
Beyond its power there's nothing; almost puts
Faith in a fever, and deifies alone
Voluble chance; who only attributes
The faculties of other instruments
To his own nerves and act; commands men service,
And what they win in't, boot and glory; [one]
That fears not to do harm; good, dares not. Let
The blood of mine that's sib to him be suck'd
From me with leeches! let them break and fall
Off me with that corruption!
Arc. Clear-spirited cousin,
Let's leave his court, that we may nothing share

232. sensually subdu'd: slaves to the senses.
233. human title: right to be called men (rather than animals).

I.ii. Location: Thebes. The palace.
2. our prime cousin: my nearest kinsman, i.e. "dearer in blood" than anyone else.
2–3. yet . . . nature. For the idea that maturity inevitably brings loss of innocence, see especially *The Winter's Tale*, I.ii.67ff.
6–7. here . . . incontinence: living here is shameful, whether one lives virtuously or wickedly. **8. I' . . . current:** with the current.
9. frustrate striving: i.e. be unable to make any forward progress.
11. turn: i.e. be caught up in the eddy and carried round and round.
13. cried up with: supported by.
15. scars . . . weeds: battle scars and ragged garments.
16–17. propound . . . ends: set before himself as the objectives of his courage. **18. flurted:** scorned, cast aside.
21–22. Juno . . . jealousy. Juno was the prompter of many wars, including the Trojan war. **22. ancient:** former.
23–24. purge . . . repletion: take medicine to cure the effects of overeating. **24. retain:** take into service.
26. out: on a false scent, off the point.
28. cranks and turns: winding streets.

39. color: appearance. **40. ev'n jump:** exactly.
41. strangers: aliens. **42. mere:** utter.
43. that . . . 's: i.e. that we will learn to imitate what we see.
44. What: why. **46. faith:** fidelity to oneself.
48. conceiv'd: understood.
50. generous bond: obligation of honorable conduct.
51. Follows: i.e. who follows the advice of.
52. make pursuit: i.e. for unpaid bills. **54. for:** because.
55. glass: mirror, i.e. pattern. **canon:** law.
57–58. go . . . foul: i.e. walk in a mincing fashion suitable only for picking one's way through a dirty street.
60. sequent trace: team that follows.
61. plantin: plantain, an herb used as an application for superficial wounds.
63. unbounded: without limits, absolute.
65–66. puts . . . fever: enfeebles religious faith.
67. Voluble: rolling (alluding to Fortune's wheel), i.e. constantly changing.
67–69. only . . . act: attribute all that others are able to accomplish to his own prowess alone (*nerves* = sinews).
70. boot: profit. **72. sib:** akin.

Of his loud infamy; for our milk
Will relish of the pasture, and we must
Be vile, or disobedient—not his kinsmen
In blood unless in quality.
Pal. Nothing truer.
I think the echoes of his shames have deaf'd
The ears of heav'nly justice. Widows' cries
Descend again into their throats, and have not
Due audience of the gods.

Enter VALERIUS.

Valerius!
Val. The King calls for you; yet be leaden-footed
Till his great rage be off him. Phoebus, when
He broke his whipstock and exclaim'd against
The horses of the sun, but whisper'd, to
The loudness of his fury.
Pal. Small winds shake him.
But what's the matter?
Val. Theseus (who where he threats appalls) hath sent
Deadly defiance to him, and pronounces
Ruin to Thebes; who is at hand to seal
The promise of his wrath.
Arc. Let him approach.
But that we fear the gods in him, he brings not
A jot of terror to us. Yet what man
Thirds his own worth (the case is each of ours),
When that his action's dregg'd with mind assur'd
'Tis bad he goes about.
Pal. Leave that unreason'd.
Our services stand now for Thebes, not Creon.
Yet to be neutral to him were dishonor;
Rebellious to oppose; therefore we must
With him stand to the mercy of our fate,
Who hath bounded our last minute.
Arc. So we must.
Is't said this war's afoot? or it shall be,
On fail of some condition?
Val. 'Tis in motion,
The intelligence of state came in the instant
With the defier.
Pal. Let's to the King, who were he
A quarter carrier of that honor which
His enemy come in, the blood we venture
Should be as for our health, which were not spent,
Rather laid out for purchase. But alas,
Our hands advanc'd before our hearts, what will
The fall o' th' stroke do damage?
Arc. Let th' event,
That never-erring arbitrator, tell us
When we know all ourselves, and let us follow
The becking of our chance. *Exeunt.*

SCENE III

Enter PIRITHOUS, HIPPOLYTA, EMILIA.

Pir. No further.
Hip. Sir, farewell. Repeat my wishes
To our great lord, of whose success I dare not
Make any timorous question; yet I wish him
Excess and overflow of power, and't might be,
To dure ill-dealing fortune. Speed to him,
Store never hurts good governors.
Pir. Though I know
His ocean needs not my poor drops, yet they
Must yield their tribute there. My precious maid,
Those best affections that the heavens infuse
In their best-temper'd pieces, keep enthron'd
In your dear heart!
Emil. Thanks, sir. Remember me
To our all-royal brother, for whose speed
The great Bellona I'll solicit; and
Since in our terrene state petitions are not
Without gifts understood, I'll offer to her
What I shall be advis'd she likes. Our hearts
Are in his army, in his tent.
Hip. In 's bosom.
We have been soldiers, and we cannot weep
When our friends don their helms, or put to sea,
Or tell of babes broach'd on the lance, or women
That have sod their infants in (and after eat them)
The brine they wept at killing 'em. Then if
You stay to see of us such spinsters, we
Should hold you here for ever.
Pir. Peace be to you
As I pursue this war, which shall be then
Beyond further requiring. *Exit Pirithous.*
Emil. How his longing
Follows his friend: since his depart, his sports,
Though craving seriousness and skill, pass'd slightly
His careless execution, where nor gain

76. loud: resounding (cf. "echoes of his shames," line 80).
76–77. our . . . pasture: i.e. our behavior must be affected by our environment, as milk must taste (*relish*) of what the cow eats.
79. quality: character.
86. whipstock: here, whip. The allusion is probably to Apollo's anger after the death of his son Phaëthon, who came to grief when he attempted to drive the chariot of the sun. **87. to:** compared with.
89. matter: subject, occasion (of his anger).
94. the gods in him: i.e. the fact that he comes as an instrument of divine justice. **95. what:** whatsoever, i.e. any.
96. Thirds: reduces to a third.
97–98. dregg'd . . . about: clogged by the certainty that he is acting in a bad cause. **99. stand . . . for:** are in support . . . of.
100. Yet to be: to continue. **101. Rebellious:** i.e. treasonable.
102. stand to: abide by, entrust ourselves to.
103. bounded . . . minute: ordained the moment of our death (?) or ordained the course of our lives to their last moment (?).
105. fail: failure, rejection.
106. intelligence of state: official notice.
110. for our health. Therapeutic bloodletting was common. **spent:** wasted.

111. laid . . . purchase: invested in the expectation of profit.
112. before: farther than.
112–13. what . . . do damage: what damage . . . do.
113. event: outcome.

I.iii. Location: Before the gates of Athens.
2. dare. Schmidt gives examples of *dare* "passing . . . into the sense of *will.*" **4. and't might be:** if necessary.
5. dure: endure, hold out against.
6. Store . . . governors: plenty never handicaps good managers.
9. affections: inclinations, bents of mind.
10. best-temper'd pieces: best-fashioned works, i.e. finest persons.
12. speed: success. **20. broach'd:** spitted.
21. sod: seethed, boiled. **eat:** eaten.
23. spinsters: women who spin, i.e. housewives.
25–26. which . . . requiring: which (i.e. peace) need not thereafter be further invoked (since victory will be ours).
27. his depart: Theseus' departure.
28–29. pass'd . . . execution: were executed carelessly as if they were trifles.

Made him regard, or loss consider, but
Playing o'er business in his hand, another
Directing in his head, his mind nurse equal
To these so diff'ring twins. Have you observ'd him
Since our great lord departed?
Hip. With much labor;
And I did love him for't. They two have cabin'd
In many as dangerous as poor a corner,
Peril and want contending, they have skiff'd
Torrents whose roaring tyranny and power
I' th' least of these was dreadful, and they have
Fought out together where death's self was lodg'd;
Yet fate hath brought them off. Their knot of love
Tied, weav'd, entangled, with so true, so long,
And with a finger of so deep a cunning,
May be outworn, never undone. I think
Theseus cannot be umpire to himself,
Cleaving his conscience into twain and doing
Each side like justice, which he loves best.
Emil. Doubtless
There is a best, and reason has no manners
To say it is not you. I was acquainted
Once with a time when I enjoy'd a playfellow;
You were at wars when she the grave enrich'd,
Who made too proud the bed, took leave o' th' moon
(Which then look'd pale at parting) when our count
Was each aleven.
Hip. 'Twas [Flavina].
Emil. Yes.
You talk of Pirithous' and Theseus' love:
Theirs has more ground, is more maturely season'd,
More buckled with strong judgment, and their needs
The one of th' other may be said to water
Their intertangled roots of love, but I
And she (I sigh and spoke of) were things innocent,
Lov'd for we did, and like the elements
That know not what nor why, yet do effect
Rare issues by their operance, our souls
Did so to one another. What she lik'd
Was then of me approv'd, what not, condemn'd,
No more arraignment. The flow'r that I would pluck
And put between my breasts (O then but beginning
To swell about the blossom), she would long
Till she had such another, and commit it
To the like innocent cradle, where phoenix-like
They died in perfume. On my head no toy
But was her pattern, her affections (pretty,
Though happily her careless [wear]) I followed
For my most serious decking. Had mine ear

34. labor: diligence.
37. contending: i.e. as to which was the severer hardship.
39. I' . . . these: at their minimum.
44. outworn: worn out by the passage of time, i.e. destroyed by death.
46. conscience: private thoughts.
47. which: i.e. Pirithous or Hippolyta.
52. bed: i.e. grave (cf. I.i.11). **took . . . moon.** The moon-goddess, Diana, was the patroness of maidens. **54. aleven:** eleven.
56. ground: foundation. **57. buckled:** supported.
61. for we did: simply because we did. **the elements:** i.e. earth, air, fire, and water, the basic constituents of all material things.
63. Rare issues: wonderful results. **65. of:** by.
66. No more arraignment: without further examination.
70–71. phoenix-like . . . perfume. The phoenix immolated itself on a pyre of aromatic wood and was reborn from the ashes.
71. toy: trifling ornament.
72. her affections: what she took a fancy to.
73. happily: haply, perhaps.

Stol'n some new air, or at adventure humm'd [one]
From musical coinage, why, it was a note
Whereon her spirits would sojourn (rather dwell on)
And sing it in her slumbers. This rehearsal
(Which, [ev'ry] innocent wots well, comes in
Like old importment's bastard) has this end,
That the true love 'tween maid and maid may be
More than in sex [dividual].
Hip. Y' are out of breath,
And this high-speeded pace is but to say
That you shall never (like the maid Flavina)
Love any that's call'd man.
Emil. I am sure I shall not.
Hip. Now alack, weak sister,
I must no more believe thee in this point
(Though in't I know thou dost believe thyself)
Than I will trust a sickly appetite,
That loathes even as it longs. But sure, my sister,
If I were ripe for your persuasion, you
Have said enough to shake me from the arm
Of the all-noble Theseus, for whose fortunes
I will now in and kneel, with great assurance
That we, more than his Pirithous, possess
The high throne in his heart.
Emil. I am not
Against your faith, yet I continue mine. *Exeunt.*

SCENE IV

Cornets. A battle strook within; then a retrait; flourish. Then enter THESEUS, *victor,* [*with his* LORDS]. *The three* QUEENS *meet him and fall on their faces before him.*

1. Queen. To thee no star be dark.
2. Queen. Both heaven and earth
Friend thee for ever.
3. Queen. All the good that may
Be wish'd upon thy head, I cry amen to't.
The. Th' impartial gods, who from the mounted heavens
View us their mortal herd, behold who err,
And in their time chastise. Go and find out
The bones of your dead lords, and honor them
With treble ceremony; rather than a gap
Should be in their dear rites, we would supply't.
But those we will depute which shall invest
You in your dignities, and even each thing
Our haste does leave imperfect. So adieu,
And heaven's good eyes look on you! *Exeunt Queens.*

[*Enter* HERALD *with* ATTENDANTS *bearing* PALAMON *and* ARCITE *on two hearses.*]

75. at adventure: by chance. **76. note:** melody.
79. wots: knows.
80. old . . . bastard: "a feeble counterpart of the old passion (*emportement*)" (Herford).
82. in sex dividual: between persons of different sex.
91. ripe for: at a stage of development to be affected by.

I.iv. Location: The field of battle before Thebes.
o.s.d. Cornets: small horns, made of wood. **strook:** struck, fought. **retrait:** retreat, trumpet signal for withdrawal of forces.
1. dark: i.e. unfavorable. **9. dear:** precious to me.
11. even: make even, rectify. **13 s.d. hearses:** portable biers.

What are those?
Her. Men of great quality, as may be judg'd
By their appointment. Some of Thebes have told 's
They are sisters' children, nephews to the King.
The. By th' helm of Mars, I saw them in the war,
Like to a pair of lions smear'd with prey,
Make lanes in troops aghast. I fix'd my note
Constantly on them; for they were a mark
Worth a god's view. What [was't that prisoner] told me
When I inquired their names?
Her. [Wi'] leave, they're called
Arcite and Palamon.
The. 'Tis right—those, those.
They are not dead?
Her. Nor in a state of life; had they been taken
When their last hurts were given, 'twas possible
They might have been recovered. Yet they breathe
And have the name of men.
The. Then like men use 'em.
The very lees of such (millions of rates)
Exceed the wine of others. All our surgeons
Convent in their behoof, our richest balms,
Rather than niggard, waste; their lives concern us
Much more than Thebes is worth. Rather than have 'em
Freed of this plight, and in their morning state
(Sound and at liberty), I would 'em dead;
But forty thousand fold we had rather have 'em
Prisoners to us than death. Bear 'em speedily
From our kind air, to them unkind, and minister
What man to man may do; for our sake more,
Since I have known frights, fury, friends' behests,
Love's provocations, zeal, a mistress' task,
Desire of liberty, a fever, madness,
Hath set a mark which nature could not reach to
Without some imposition, sickness in will
[O'er-]wrastling strength in reason. For our love,
And great Apollo's mercy, all our best
Their best skill tender.—Lead into the city,
Where having bound things scatter'd, we will post
To Athens ['fore] our army.
Flourish. Exeunt, [Attendants bearing Palamon and Arcite].

Scene V

Music. Enter the Queens *with the hearses of their Knights in a funeral solemnity, etc.*

14. great quality: high rank. **15. appointment:** accoutrements.
19. note: notice. **28. men:** i.e. not corpses.
29. lees of such: dregs of men of this type. **millions of rates:** by a multiple of millions. **31. Convent:** call together.
32. niggard: be stingy with.
38. unkind. Fresh air was thought bad for wounds.
40. frights, fury. Dyce's emendation *fight's fury* is tempting; so also Skeat's reading *zeal in* for *zeal*, in line 41. **43. mark:** goal.
44. some imposition: i.e. the compulsion of some external stimulus (such as those just listed).
44–45. sickness . . . reason: i.e. since without such "imposition" feebleness of will defeats the capabilities of reason.
46. Apollo's. Apollo was the god of healing.
48. post: ride with speed.

I.v. Location: The field of battle.

[Song]

Urns and odors bring away,
Vapors, sighs, darken the day;
Our dole more deadly looks than dying;
Balms, and gums, and heavy cheers,
Sacred vials fill'd with tears,
And clamors through the wild air flying!

Come all sad and solemn shows,
That are quick-ey'd pleasure's foes!
We convent nought else but woes:
We convent, etc.

3. Queen. This funeral path brings to your household's grave:
Joy seize on you again! Peace sleep with him!
2. Queen. And this to yours.
1. Queen. Yours this way. Heavens lend
A thousand differing ways to one sure end.
3. Queen. This world's a city full of straying streets,
And death's the market-place, where each one meets.
Exeunt severally.

Act II, Scene I

Enter Jailer *and* Wooer.

Jail. I may depart with little, while I live; something I may cast to you, not much. Alas, the prison I keep, though it be for great ones, yet they seldom come: before one salmon, you shall take a number of minnows. I am given out to be better lin'd than it can appear to me report is a true speaker. I would I were really that I am deliver'd to be. Marry, what I have (be it what it will) I will assure upon my daughter at the day of my death.

Wooer. Sir, I demand no more than your own offer, and I will estate your daughter in what I have promis'd.

Jail. Well, we will talk more of this when the solemnity is past. But have you a full promise of her? When that shall be seen, I tender my consent.

Enter Daughter *[with strewings].*

Wooer. I have, sir. Here she comes.

Jail. Your friend and I have chanc'd to name you here, upon the old business. But no more of that now; so soon as the court hurry is over, we will have an end of it. I' th' mean time, look tenderly to the two prisoners. I can tell you they are princes.

Daugh. These strewings are for their chamber. 'Tis pity they are in prison, and 'twere pity they should be out. I do think they have patience to make any

3. dole: sorrow.
4. gums: aromatic substances. **heavy cheers:** mournful countenances.

II.i. Location: Athens. The palace garden, overlooked by the windows of a prison.
1. depart with: part with, spare.
5. given . . . lin'd: reputed to be richer.
7. that: what. **deliver'd:** reported. **Marry:** to be sure (originally the name of the Virgin Mary used as an oath).
14 s.d. strewings: rushes for floor covering.
19. tenderly: carefully.

adversity asham'd. The prison itself is proud of 'em; and they have all the world in their chamber.

Jail. They are fam'd to be a pair of absolute men.

Daugh. By my troth, I think fame but stammers 'em, they stand a grise above the reach of report.

Jail. I heard them reported in the battle to be the only doers.

Daugh. Nay, most likely, for they are noble suff'rers. I marvel how they would have look'd had they been victors, that with such a constant nobility enforce a freedom out of bondage, making misery their mirth, and affliction a toy to jest at.

Jail. Do they so?

Daugh. It seems to me they have no more sense of their captivity than I of ruling Athens. They eat well, look merrily, discourse of many things, but nothing of their own restraint and disasters. Yet sometime a divided sigh, martyr'd as 'twere i' th' deliverance, will break from one of them; when the other presently gives it so sweet a rebuke that I could wish myself a sigh to be so chid, or at least a sigher to be comforted.

Wooer. I never saw 'em.

Jail. The Duke himself came privately in the night, and so did they. What the reason of it is, I know not.

Enter PALAMON *and* ARCITE *above.*

Look yonder they are! That's Arcite looks out.

Daugh. No, sir, no, that's Palamon. Arcite is the lower of the twain; you may perceive a part of him.

Jail. Go to, leave your pointing. They would not make us their object. Out of their sight.

Daugh. It is a holiday to look on them. Lord, the diff'rence of men!

Exeunt [*Jailer, Wooer, and Daughter*].

SCENE II

Pal. How do you, noble cousin?
Arc. How do you, sir?
Pal. Why, strong enough to laugh at misery
And bear the chance of war yet. We are prisoners
I fear for ever, cousin.
Arc. I believe it,
And to that destiny have patiently
Laid up my hour to come.
Pal. O cousin Arcite,
Where is Thebes now? where is our noble country?
Where are our friends and kindreds? Never more
Must we behold those comforts, never see
The hardy youths strive for the games of honor,
Hung with the painted favors of their ladies,
Like tall ships under sail; then start amongst 'em
And as an east wind leave 'em all behind us,
Like lazy clouds, whilst Palamon and Arcite,
Even in the wagging of a wanton leg,
Outstripp'd the people's praises, won the garlands,
Ere they have time to wish 'em ours. O, never
Shall we two exercise, like twins of honor,
Our arms again, and feel our fiery horses
Like proud seas under us. Our good swords now
(Better the red-ey'd god of war nev'r [ware]),
[Ravish'd] our sides, like age must run to rust,
And deck the temples of those gods that hate us;
These hands shall never draw 'em out like lightning
To blast whole armies more.
Arc. No, Palamon,
Those hopes are prisoners with us. Here we are,
And here the graces of our youths must wither
Like a too-timely spring. Here age must find us,
And which is heaviest, Palamon, unmarried.
The sweet embraces of a loving wife,
Loaden with kisses, arm'd with thousand Cupids,
Shall never clasp our necks; no issue know us;
No figures of ourselves shall we ev'r see
To glad our age, and like young eagles teach 'em
Boldly to gaze against bright arms, and say,
"Remember what your fathers were, and conquer!"
The fair-ey'd maids shall weep our banishments,
And in their songs curse ever-blinded Fortune
Till she for shame see what a wrong she has done
To youth and nature. This is all our world:
We shall know nothing here but one another,
Hear nothing but the clock that tells our woes;
The vine shall grow, but we shall never see it;
Summer shall come, and with her all delights,
But dead-cold winter must inhabit here still.
Pal. 'Tis too true, Arcite. To our Theban hounds,
That shook the aged forest with their echoes,
No more now must we hallow; no more shake
Our pointed javelins, whilst the angry swine
Flies like a Parthian quiver from our rages,
Struck with our well-steel'd darts. All valiant uses
(The food and nourishment of noble minds)
In us two here shall perish; we shall die
(Which is the curse of honor) lastly
Children of grief and ignorance.
Arc. Yet, cousin,
Even from the bottom of these miseries,
From all that fortune can inflict upon us,
I see two comforts rising, two mere blessings,
If the gods please—to hold here a brave patience,
And the enjoying of our griefs together.
Whilst Palamon is with me, let me perish
If I think this our prison.

25. have . . . world: i.e. create a whole world of their own.
26. fam'd: rumored. **absolute:** perfect.
27. stammers: i.e. gives a defective account of.
28. grise: step. **30. only:** supreme.
31–32. are noble suff'rers: bear nobly what others do to them. *Do* and *suffer* form a common antithetical pair.
39. look merrily: look merry (the regular Elizabethan idiom).
40. restraint: imprisonment. **41. divided:** half-uttered.
42. presently: at once. **50. lower:** shorter.
51. Go to: an expression of reproach, equivalent to "come, come."
51–52. would . . . object: don't want to look at us.

II.ii. Location: Scene continues. (See the Textual Notes.)
6. Laid . . . come: reserved the rest of my life. **10. for:** in.

15. in . . . leg: i.e. running carelessly (with the easy grace required of a true courtier). *Wanton* = sportive, carefree.
21. ware: wore. **22. Ravish'd:** snatched from.
28. too-timely: too early. **29. which is heaviest:** what is saddest.
34. like young eagles. It was thought that eagles could gaze at the sun without being blinded. **42. tells:** counts.
48. hallow: halloo. **49. swine:** i.e. wild boars.
50. Parthian quiver: quiver of a mounted Parthian archer (who shot while retreating). **51. uses:** practices. **58. mere:** pure.

Pal. Certainly
'Tis a main goodness, cousin, that our fortunes
Were twin'd together. 'Tis most true, two souls
Put in two noble bodies, let 'em suffer
The gall of hazard, so they grow together,
Will never sink; they must not, say they could;
A willing man dies sleeping, and all's done.
Arc. Shall we make worthy uses of this place
That all men hate so much?
Pal. How, gentle cousin?
Arc. Let's think this prison holy sanctuary
To keep us from corruption of worse men.
We are young and yet desire the ways of honor,
That liberty and common conversation,
The poison of pure spirits, might, like women,
Woo us to wander from. What worthy blessing
Can be, but our imaginations
May make it ours? And here being thus together,
We are an endless mine to one another;
We are one another's wife, ever begetting
New births of love; we are father, friends, acquaintance;
We are, in one another, families:
I am your heir, and you are mine; this place
Is our inheritance. No hard oppressor
Dare take this from us; here with a little patience
We shall live long, and loving. No surfeits seek us;
The hand of war hurts none here, nor the seas
Swallow their youth. Were we at liberty,
A wife might part us lawfully, or business,
Quarrels consume us, envy of ill men
Crave our acquaintance; I might sicken, cousin,
Where you should never know it, and so perish
Without your noble hand to close mine eyes,
Or prayers to the gods. A thousand chances,
Were we from hence, would sever us.
Pal. You have made me
(I thank you, cousin Arcite) almost wanton
With my captivity. What a misery
It is to live abroad, and every where!
'Tis like a beast, methinks. I find the court here,
I am sure, a more content, and all those pleasures
That woo the wills of men to vanity
I see through now, and am sufficient
To tell the world 'tis but a gaudy shadow
That old Time, as he passes by, takes with him.
What had we been, old in the court of Creon,
Where sin is justice, lust and ignorance
The virtues of the great ones? Cousin Arcite,
Had not the loving gods found this place for us,
We had died as they do, ill old men, unwept,
And had their epitaphs, the people's curses.
Shall I say more?
Arc. I would hear you still.
Pal. Ye shall.
Is there record of any two that lov'd
Better than we do, Arcite?
Arc. Sure there cannot.
Pal. I do not think it possible our friendship
Should ever leave us.
Arc. Till our deaths it cannot,

Enter Emilia *and her* Woman *[below].*

And after death our spirits shall be led
To those that love eternally. Speak on, sir.
[Emil.] This garden has a world of pleasures in't.
What flow'r is this?
Woman. 'Tis call'd narcissus, madam.
Emil. That was a fair boy certain, but a fool
To love himself. Were there not maids enough?
Arc. Pray forward.
Pal. Yes.
Emil. Or were they all hard-hearted?
Woman. They could not be to one so fair.
Emil. Thou wouldst not.
Woman. I think I should not, madam.
Emil. That's a good wench!
But take heed to your kindness though.
Woman. Why, madam?
Emil. Men are mad things.
Arc. Will ye go forward, cousin?
Emil. Canst not thou work such flowers in silk, wench?
Woman. Yes.
Emil. I'll have a gown full of 'em, and of these:
This is a pretty color, will't not do
Rarely upon a skirt, wench?
Woman. Dainty, madam.
Arc. Cousin, cousin, how do you, sir? why, Palamon!
Pal. Never till now I was in prison, Arcite.
Arc. Why, what's the matter, man?
Pal. Behold, and wonder!
By heaven, she is a goddess.
Arc. Ha!
Pal. Do reverence;
She is a goddess, Arcite.
Emil. Of all flow'rs
Methinks a rose is best.
Woman. Why, gentle madam?
Emil. It is the very emblem of a maid;
For when the west wind courts her gently,
How modestly she blows, and paints the sun
With her chaste blushes! When the north comes near her,
Rude and impatient, then, like chastity,
She locks her beauties in her bud again,
And leaves him to base briers.
Woman. Yet, good madam,
Sometimes her modesty will blow so far she falls for't.

63. main goodness: major benefit, great blessing.
66. gall of hazard: bitterness of fortune. **so:** provided that.
68. A willing . . . sleeping: to the man who is reconciled to his fate, death is as easy as falling asleep. **73. yet:** still.
74. common conversation: having dealings with everybody.
79. mine: source of riches. **90. envy:** malice. **ill:** evil.
91. Crave our acquaintance: intrude upon us (?). Suggested emendations of *Crave* include *Grave* (= bury, i.e. destroy) and *Craze* (= crack, damage). **98. abroad:** not confined.
100. more content: greater contentment. **111. still:** forever.

120–21. a fair . . . himself. Narcissus, who fell in love with his own reflection in the water and was drowned when he tried to embrace it, was turned into the flower that bears his name.
122. forward: go on talking. **130. Rarely:** beautifully.
139. blows: opens. **paints:** i.e. calls up a picture of.
143. briers: wild roses (regarded as weeds). **144. for't:** as a result.

A maid, if she have any honor, would be loath
To take example by her.
Emil. Thou art wanton.
Arc. She is wondrous fair.
Pal. She is all the beauty extant.
Emil. The sun grows high, let's walk in. Keep these flowers,
We'll see how near art can come near their colors.
I am wondrous merry-hearted, I could laugh now.
Woman. I could lie down, I am sure.
Emil. And take one with you?
Woman. That's as we bargain, madam.
Emil. Well, agree then.
Exeunt Emilia and Woman.
Pal. What think you of this beauty?
Arc. 'Tis a rare one.
Pal. Is't but a rare one?
Arc. Yes, a matchless beauty.
Pal. Might not a man well lose himself and love her?
Arc. I cannot tell what you have done; I have,
Beshrew mine eyes for't! Now I feel my shackles.
Pal. You love her then?
Arc. Who would not?
Pal. And desire her?
Arc. Before my liberty.
Pal. I saw her first.
Arc. That's nothing.
Pal. But it shall be.
Arc. I saw her too.
Pal. Yes, but you must not love her.
Arc. I will not, as you do—to worship her
As she is heavenly and a blessed goddess;
I love her as a woman, to enjoy her.
So both may love.
Pal. You shall not love at all.
Arc. Not love at all! who shall deny me?
Pal. I, that first saw her; I, that took possession
First with mine eye of all those beauties in her
Reveal'd to mankind. If thou lov'st her,
Or entertain'st a hope to blast my wishes,
Thou art a traitor, Arcite, and a fellow
False as thy title to her. Friendship, blood,
And all the ties between us, I disclaim
If thou once think upon her.
Arc. Yes, I love her,
And if the lives of all my name lay on it,
I must do so; I love her with my soul;
If that will lose ye, farewell, Palamon.
I say again, I love, and in loving her maintain
I am as worthy and as free a lover,
And have as just a title to her beauty,
As any Palamon or any living
That is a man's son.
Pal. Have I call'd thee friend?

146. wanton: "naughty," improper.
151. lie down. An old card game, "Laugh and lay down," prompted many mildly indecent puns.
157. Beshrew: curse (a mild oath).
172. title: claim to a right of possession, or the right itself (the word occurs in these legal senses a number of times in the play).
175. all my name: my whole family. lay: depended.
179. free: noble.

Arc. Yes, and have found me so. Why are you mov'd thus?
Let me deal coldly with you: am not I
Part of [your] blood, part of your soul? You have told me
That I was Palamon, and you were Arcite.
Pal. Yes.
Arc. Am not I liable to those affections,
Those joys, griefs, angers, fears, my friend shall suffer?
Pal. Ye may be.
Arc. Why then would you deal so cunningly,
So strangely, so unlike a noble kinsman,
To love alone? Speak truly: do you think me
Unworthy of her sight?
Pal. No; but unjust
If thou pursue that sight.
Arc. Because another
First sees the enemy, shall I stand still,
And let mine honor down, and never charge?
Pal. Yes, if he be but one.
Arc. But say that one
Had rather combat me?
Pal. Let that one say so,
And use thy freedom; else, if thou pursuest her,
Be as that cursed man that hates his country,
A branded villain.
Arc. You are mad.
Pal. I must be—
Till thou art worthy, Arcite, it concerns me,
And in this madness if I hazard thee
And take thy life, I deal but truly.
Arc. Fie, sir!
You play the child extremely. I will love her,
I must, I ought to do so, and I dare—
And all this justly.
Pal. O that now, that now
Thy false-self and thy friend had but this fortune
To be one hour at liberty, and grasp
Our good swords in our hands, I would quickly teach thee
What 'twere to filch affection from another!
Thou art baser in it than a cutpurse.
Put but thy head out of this window more,
And as I have a soul, I'll nail thy life to't!
Arc. Thou dar'st not, fool, thou canst not, thou art feeble.
Put my head out? I'll throw my body out,
And leap the garden, when I see her next,
And pitch between her arms to anger thee.
Enter KEEPER [*above*].
Pal. No more; the keeper's coming. I shall live
To knock thy brains out with my shackles.
Arc. Do.
Keep. By your leave, gentlemen.
Pal. Now, honest keeper?
Keep. Lord Arcite, you must presently to th' Duke;
The cause I know not yet.

183. mov'd: angered. 184. coldly: calmly.
202. hazard thee: put you in hazard.
216. leap: leap into. 217. pitch: take up a fixed position.

Arc. I am ready, keeper.
Keep. Prince Palamon, I must awhile bereave you
Of your fair cousin's company.
Exeunt Arcite and Keeper.
Pal. And me too,
Even when you please, of life. Why is he sent for?
It may be he shall marry her; he's goodly,
And like enough the Duke hath taken notice
Both of his blood and body. But his falsehood!
Why should a friend be treacherous? If that
Get him a wife so noble and so fair,
Let honest men ne'er love again. Once more
I would but see this fair one. Blessed garden,
And fruit and flowers more blessed, that still blossom
As her bright eyes shine on ye, would I were,
For all the fortune of my life hereafter,
Yon little tree, yon blooming apricock!
How I would spread, and fling my wanton arms
In at her window! I would bring her fruit
Fit for the gods to feed on; youth and pleasure,
Still as she tasted, should be doubled on her,
And if she be not heavenly, I would make her
So near the gods in nature, they should fear her;
And then I am sure she would love me.

Enter KEEPER [*above*].

How now, keeper,
Where's Arcite?
Keep. Banish'd. Prince Pirithous
Obtained his liberty; but never more,
Upon his oath and life, must he set foot
Upon this kingdom.
Pal. [*Aside.*] He's a blessed man!
He shall see Thebes again, and call to arms
The bold young men that when he bids 'em charge,
Fall on like fire. Arcite shall have a fortune,
If he dare make himself a worthy lover,
Yet in the field to strike a battle for her;
And if he lose her then, he's a cold coward.
How bravely may he bear himself to win her,
If he be noble Arcite—thousand ways!
Were I at liberty, I would do things
Of such a virtuous greatness that this lady,
This blushing virgin, should take manhood to her
And seek to ravish me.
Keep. My lord, for you
I have this charge too—
Pal. To discharge my life?
Keep. No, but from this place to remove your lordship;
The windows are too open.
Pal. Devils take 'em
That are so envious to me! Prithee kill me.
Keep. And hang for't afterward!
Pal. By this good light,
Had I a sword, I would kill thee.
Keep. Why, my lord?
Pal. Thou bring'st such pelting scurvy news continually,
Thou art not worthy life. I will not go.
Keep. Indeed you must, my lord.
Pal. May I see the garden?
Keep. No.
Pal. Then I am resolv'd, I will not go.
Keep. I must
Constrain you then; and for you are dangerous
I'll clap more irons on you.
Pal. Do, good keeper.
I'll shake 'em so, ye shall not sleep,
I'll make ye a new morris. Must I go?
Keep. There is no remedy.
Pal. [*Aside.*] Farewell, kind window.
May rude wind never hurt thee! O my lady,
If ever thou hast felt what sorrow was,
Dream how I suffer!—Come; now bury me.
Exeunt Palamon and Keeper.

226. **goodly:** handsome.
228. **blood and body:** high birth and handsome appearance.
236. **apricock:** apricot. 250. **fortune:** chance.
258. **take . . . her:** i.e. take the initiative in wooing.
263. **envious:** malicious.
266. **pelting:** paltry. 268. **May I:** shall I be able to.
273. **a new morris:** a new kind of morris-dance (with rattling fetters replacing the bells traditionally worn by the dancers). See the illustration showing morris-dancers on page 1526.

SCENE III

Enter ARCITE.

Arc. Banish'd the kingdom? 'Tis a benefit,
A mercy I must thank 'em for; but banish'd
The free enjoying of that face I die for—
O, 'twas a studied punishment, a death
Beyond imagination! such a vengeance
That were I old and wicked, all my sins
Could never pluck upon me. Palamon!
Thou hast the start now; thou shalt stay and see
Her bright eyes break each morning 'gainst thy window,
And let in life into thee; thou shalt feed
Upon the sweetness of a noble beauty,
That nature nev'r exceeded, nor nev'r shall.
Good gods! what happiness has Palamon!
Twenty to one, he'll come to speak to her,
And if she be as gentle as she's fair,
I know she's his; he has a tongue will tame tempests,
And make the wild rocks wanton. Come what can come,
The worst is death: I will not leave the kingdom.
I know mine own but a heap of ruins,
And no redress there. If I go, he has her.
I am resolv'd another shape shall make me,
Or end my fortunes. Either way, I am happy:
I'll see her, and be near her, or no more. [*Retires.*]

Enter four COUNTRY PEOPLE, *and one with a garland before them.*

1. Coun. My masters, I'll be there, that's certain.
2. Coun. And I'll be there.
3. Coun. And I.

II.iii. Location: The country near Athens.
9. break: begin to shine (as in *daybreak*).
21. another shape: a disguise.

4. Coun. Why then have with ye, boys! 'Tis but a chiding.
Let the plough play to-day, I'll tickle't out
Of the jades' tails to-morrow.
1. Coun. I am sure
To have my wife as jealous as a turkey.
But that's all one, I'll go through, let her mumble.
2. Coun. Clap her aboard to-morrow night, and stow her,
And all's made up again.
3. Coun. Ay, do but put
A fescue in her fist, and you shall see her
Take a new lesson out, and be a good wench.
Do we all hold against the Maying?
4. Coun. Hold?
What should ail us?
3. Coun. Arcas will be there.
2. Coun. And Sennois,
And Rycas, and three better lads nev'r danc'd
Under green tree; and [ye] know what wenches, ha?
But will the dainty domine, the schoolmaster,
Keep touch, do you think? for he does all, ye know.
3. Coun. He'll eat a horn-book ere he fail. Go to!
The matter's too far driven between him
And the tanner's daughter to let slip now;
And she must see the Duke, and she must dance too.
4. Coun. Shall we be lusty?
2. Coun. All the boys in Athens
Blow wind i' th' breech on 's, and here I'll be,
And there I'll be, for our town, and here again,
And there again. Ha, boys, heigh for the weavers!
1. Coun. This must be done i' th' woods.
4. Coun. O, pardon me!
2. Coun. By any means; our thing of learning [says] so—
Where he himself will edify the Duke
Most parlously in our behalfs. He's excellent i' th' woods,
Bring him to th' plains, his learning makes no cry.
3. Coun. We'll see the sports, then every man to 's tackle!
And, sweet companions, let's rehearse by any means
Before the ladies see us, and do sweetly,
And God knows what may come on't.
4. Coun. Content. The sports
Once ended, we'll perform. Away, boys, and hold!
Arc. [*Comes forward.*] By your leaves, honest friends: pray you, whither go you?

27. have with ye: an expression of readiness to join in or go along. **'Tis . . . chiding:** it will cost no more than a scolding.
32. Clap her aboard . . . stow her: go aboard her . . . fill up her hold.
34. fescue: (1) a teacher's pointer; (2) slang for "penis" (the scene is full of obvious sexual double entendre).
35. Take . . . out: learn a new lesson.
36. hold against: stick to our arrangements about.
37. What . . . us: what would induce us to do otherwise.
40. dainty domine: finicky schoolmaster.
41. Keep touch: hold to his promise. **he does all:** i.e. we can do nothing without him.
42. horn-book: primer; a single printed page protected by a transparent sheet of horn.
47. Blow . . . 's: i.e. will be unable to keep up with us.
49. weavers. The craft to which he apparently belongs.
50. pardon me: a conventional expression of disagreement.
51. any: all. **53. parlously:** cleverly.
54. makes no cry: doesn't show itself off (?) or elicits no acclaim (?).

4. Coun. Whither? why, what a question's that?
Arc. Yes, 'tis a question
To me that know not.
3. Coun. To the games, my friend.
2. Coun. Where were you bred you know it not?
Arc. Not far, sir.
Are there such games to-day?
1. Coun. Yes, marry, are there;
And such as you never saw. The Duke himself
Will be in person there.
Arc. What pastimes are they?
2. Coun. Wrastling and running.—'Tis a pretty fellow.
3. Coun. Thou wilt not go along?
Arc. Not yet, sir.
4. Coun. Well, sir,
Take your own time. Come, boys.
1. Coun. My mind misgives me
This fellow has a veng'ance trick o' th' hip,
Mark how his body's made for't.
2. Coun. I'll be hang'd though
If he dare venture. Hang him, plum porridge!
He wrastle? he roast eggs! Come let's be gone, lads.
Exeunt four [*Countrymen*].
Arc. This is an offer'd opportunity
I durst not wish for. Well I could have wrestled,
The best men call'd it excellent; and run
Swifter than wind upon a field of corn,
Curling the wealthy ears, never flew. I'll venture,
And in some poor disguise be there. Who knows
Whether my brows may not be girt with garlands,
And happiness prefer me to a place
Where I may ever dwell in sight of her? *Exit Arcite.*

SCENE IV

Enter JAILER'S DAUGHTER *alone.*

Daugh. Why should I love this gentleman? 'Tis odds
He never will affect me. I am base,
My father the mean keeper of his prison,
And he a prince. To marry him is hopeless;
To be his whore is witless. Out upon't!
What pushes are we wenches driven to
When fifteen once has found us! First, I saw him:
I, seeing, thought he was a goodly man;
He has as much to please a woman in him
(If he please to bestow it so) as ever
These eyes yet look'd on. Next, I pitied him;
And so would any young wench o' my conscience

61. what a: what kind of.
69–70. My . . . hip: I suspect that this fellow is confoundedly good at wrestling.
72. plum porridge: concoction of stewed plums and other ingredients; here, expressive of contempt.
73. he roast eggs: i.e. he is fitter for a job in the kitchen.
75. could have wrestled: have known how to wrestle.
77. corn: wheat.
78. wealthy: rich, abundant. **never.** Modern idiom would require *ever.* **81. happiness prefer:** good fortune advance.

II.iv. Location: Athens. The prison.
2. affect: love. **base:** low-born (so also *mean* in line 3).
6. pushes: extremities.

That ever dream'd, or vow'd her maidenhead
To a young handsome man. Then, I lov'd him,
Extremely lov'd him, infinitely lov'd him;
And yet he had a cousin, fair as he too;
But in my heart was Palamon, and there,
Lord, what a coil he keeps! To hear him
Sing in an evening, what a heaven it is!
And yet his songs are sad ones. Fairer spoken
Was never gentleman. When I come in
To bring him water in a morning, first
He bows his noble body, then salutes me thus:
"Fair gentle maid, good morrow. May thy goodness
Get thee a happy husband!" Once he kiss'd me—
I lov'd my lips the better ten days after.
Would he would do so ev'ry day! He grieves much,
And me as much to see his misery.
What should I do to make him know I love him,
For I would fain enjoy him? Say I ventur'd
To set him free? what says the law then?
Thus much for law or kindred! I will do it,
And this night, or to-morrow, he shall love me. *Exit.*

Scene [V]

This short flourish of cornets, and shouts within. Enter Theseus, Hippolyta, Pirithous, Emilia, Arcite *[disguised,] with a garland, etc.*

The. You have done worthily. I have not seen,
Since Hercules, a man of tougher sinews.
What e'er you are, you run the best, and wrastle,
That these times can allow.
Arc. I am proud to please you.
The. What country bred you?
Arc. This; but far off, prince.
The. Are you a gentleman?
Arc. My father said so;
And to those gentle uses gave me life.
The. Are you his heir?
Arc. His youngest, sir.
The. Your father
Sure is a happy sire then. What proves you?
Arc. A little of all noble qualities:
I could have kept a hawk, and well have hollow'd
To a deep cry of dogs; I dare not praise
My feat in horsemanship, yet they that knew me
Would say it was my best piece; last, and greatest,
I would be thought a soldier.
The. You are perfect.
Pir. Upon my soul, a proper man!
Emil. He is so.
Pir. How do you like him, lady?

18. coil he keeps: turmoil he keeps up.
30. would fain: am eager to.

II.v. Location: Athens. An open place.
2. sinews: muscles. 4. allow: admit of, i.e. show.
7. to . . . life: i.e. bred me to gentlemanly pursuits.
9. What proves you: i.e. what gentlemanly skills can you show in proof. 10. qualities: accomplishments.
11. could have kept: have known how to maintain and manage.
12. deep cry: loud-voiced pack. dare not: i.e. hesitate to.
14. Would: used to. my best piece: what I was best at.
15. perfect: complete (in a gentleman's skills).
16. proper: handsome.

Hip. I admire him;
I have not seen so young a man so noble
(If he say true) of his sort.
Emil. Believe
His mother was a wondrous handsome woman,
His face, methinks, goes that way.
Hip. But his body
And fiery mind illustrate a brave father.
Pir. Mark how his virtue, like a hidden sun,
Breaks through his baser garments.
Hip. He's well got sure.
The. What made you seek this place, sir?
Arc. Noble Theseus,
To purchase name, and do my ablest service
To such a well-found wonder as thy worth,
For only in thy court, of all the world,
Dwells fair-ey'd honor.
Pir. All his words are worthy.
The. Sir, we are much indebted to your travel,
Nor shall you lose your wish. Pirithous,
Dispose of this fair gentleman.
Pir. Thanks, Theseus.—
What e'er you are, y' are mine, and I shall give you
To a most noble service—to this lady,
This bright young virgin. Pray observe her goodness.
You have honor'd her fair birthday with your virtues,
And as your due y' are hers. Kiss her fair hand, sir.
Arc. Sir, y' are a noble giver. Dearest beauty,
Thus let me seal my vow'd faith. *[Kisses Emilia's hand.]* When your servant
(Your most unworthy creature) but offends you,
Command him die, he shall.
Emil. That were too cruel.
If you deserve well, sir, I shall soon see't.
Y' are mine, and somewhat better than your rank I'll use you.
Pir. I'll see you furnish'd, and because you say
You are a horseman, I must needs entreat you
This afternoon to ride, but 'tis a rough one.
Arc. I like him better, prince, I shall not then
Freeze in my saddle.
The. Sweet, you must be ready,
And you, Emilia, and you, friend, and all,
To-morrow, by the sun, to do observance
To flow'ry May, in Dian's wood. Wait well, sir,
Upon your mistress. Emily, I hope
He shall not go afoot.
Emil. That were a shame, sir,
While I have horses.—Take your choice, and what
You want at any time, let me but know it.
If you serve faithfully, I dare assure you
You'll find a loving mistress.
Arc. If I do not,

17. admire: marvel at. 19. sort: rank.
22. illustrate: shed lustre on (?) or make clear, i.e. give evidence of (?). 23. virtue: excellence. 24. well got: nobly begotten.
26. purchase name: win reputation.
27. well-found: well-attested.
30. travel: (1) journey hither; (2) travail, effort (in the games).
35. observe: pay homage to, hold in reverential regard.
43. rank: position (as my servant). 44. furnish'd: equipped.
50. by the sun: by sunrise. 55. want: lack, need.
57. loving: benevolent.

Let me find that my father ever hated,
Disgrace and blows.
The. Go lead the way; you have won it.
It shall be so; you shall receive all dues
Fit for the honor you have won; 'twere wrong else.
Sister, beshrew my heart, you have a servant
That if I were a woman, would be master,
But you are wise.
Emil. I hope too wise for that, sir.
Flourish. Exeunt omnes.

Scene VI

Enter Jailer's Daughter *alone.*

Daugh. Let all the dukes and all the devils roar,
He is at liberty! I have ventur'd for him,
And out I have brought him to a little wood
A mile hence. I have sent him where a cedar,
Higher than all the rest, spreads like a plane
Fast by a brook, and there he shall keep close
Till I provide him files and food, for yet
His iron bracelets are not off. O Love,
What a stout-hearted child thou art! My father
Durst better have endur'd cold iron than done it.
I love him beyond love and beyond reason,
Or wit, or safety. I have made him know it.
I care not, I am desperate. If the law
Find me, and then condemn me for't, some wenches,
Some honest-hearted maids, will sing my dirge,
And tell to memory my death was noble,
Dying almost a martyr. That way he takes
I purpose is my way too. Sure he cannot
Be so unmanly as to leave me here.
If he do, maids will not so easily
Trust men again. And yet he has not thank'd me
For what I have done; no, not so much as kiss'd me;
And that, methinks, is not so well; nor scarcely
Could I persuade him to become a freeman,
He made such scruples of the wrong he did
To me and to my father. Yet I hope,
When he considers more, this love of mine
Will take more root within him. Let him do
What he will with me, so he use me kindly,
For use me so he shall, or I'll proclaim him,
And to his face, no man. I'll presently
Provide him necessaries, and pack my clothes up,
And where there is a path of ground I'll venture,
So he be with me. By him, like a shadow,
I'll ever dwell. Within this hour the whoobub
Will be all o'er the prison. I am then
Kissing the man they look for. Farewell, father;
Get many more such prisoners and such daughters,
And shortly you may keep yourself. Now to him!
[Exit.]

58. **find that:** experience what.
59. **won it:** i.e. earned the right to lead the procession.

II.vi. **Location:** Athens. Before the prison.
5. **plane:** plane tree. 6. **close:** concealed. 8. **Love:** Cupid.
10. **cold iron:** shackles (?) or death by stabbing or beheading (?).
12. **wit:** good sense. 14. **Find me:** discover what I have done.
29. **so:** provided that. **kindly:** (1) gently; (2) in the way of nature (*kind*), i.e. sexually.
33. **path of ground:** path on ground, i.e. ground that permits passage.
35. **whoobub:** hubbub.
39. **keep yourself:** have only yourself to look after (?) or guard yourself, i.e. be a prisoner in your own prison (?).

ACT III, Scene I

Cornets in sundry places. Noise and hallowing, as people a-Maying. Enter Arcite *alone.*

Arc. The Duke has lost Hippolyta; each took
A several land. This is a solemn rite
They owe bloom'd May, and the Athenians pay it
To th' heart of ceremony. O queen Emilia,
Fresher than May, sweeter
Than her gold buttons on the boughs, or all
Th' enamell'd knacks o' th' mead or garden! yea
(We challenge too) the bank of any nymph,
That makes the stream seem flowers! thou, O jewel
O' th' wood, o' th' world, hast likewise blest a [place]
With thy sole presence. In thy rumination
That I, poor man, might eftsoons come between
And chop on some cold thought! Thrice-blessed chance,
To drop on such a mistress, expectation
Most guiltless on't. Tell me, O Lady Fortune
(Next after Emily my sovereign), how far
I may be proud. She takes strong note of me,
Hath made me near her; and this beauteous morn
(The prim'st of all the year) presents me with
A brace of horses; two such steeds might well
Be by a pair of kings back'd, in a field
That their crowns' titles tried. Alas, alas,
Poor cousin Palamon, poor prisoner, thou
So little dream'st upon my fortune that
Thou think'st thyself the happier thing to be
So near Emilia. Me thou deem'st at Thebes,
And therein wretched, although free. But if
Thou knew'st my mistress breath'd on me, and that
I ear'd her language, liv'd in her eye, O coz,
What passion would enclose thee!

Enter Palamon, *as out of a bush, with his shackles; bends his fist at Arcite.*

Pal. Traitor kinsman,
Thou shouldst perceive my passion, if these signs
Of prisonment were off me, and this hand
But owner of a sword! By all oaths in one,
I, and the justice of my love, would make thee
A confess'd traitor! O thou most perfidious
That ever gently look'd! the [void'st] of honor
That ev'r bore gentle token! falsest cousin

III.i. **Location:** A forest near Athens.
2. **several:** separate, different. **land:** territory (?) or laund, opening in the forest (?). 4. **heart:** highest degree. 6. **buttons:** buds.
7. **knacks:** ornaments, i.e. flowers. 12. **eftsoons:** soon.
13. **chop on:** thrust (myself) into (?) or exchange (myself) for (?). **cold:** chaste. 14. **drop on:** happen upon.
15. **guiltless on't:** free of it.
21–22. **field . . . tried:** battlefield where their conflicting claims to the crown were being decided.
36. **gently look'd:** bore a noble appearance (identical in meaning with *bore gentle token* in line 37).

That ever blood made kin, call'st thou her thine?
I'll prove it in my shackles, with these hands
Void of appointment, that thou li'st, and art
A very thief in love, a chaffy lord,
Nor worth the name of villain! Had I a sword,
And these house-clogs away—
Arc. Dear cousin Palamon—
Pal. Cozener Arcite, give me language such
As thou hast show'd me feat.
Arc. Not finding in
The circuit of my breast any gross stuff
To form me like your blazon, holds me to
This gentleness of answer: 'tis your passion
That thus mistakes, the which to you being enemy,
Cannot to me be kind. Honor and honesty
I cherish and depend on, howsoev'r
You skip them in me, and with them, fair coz,
I'll maintain my proceedings. Pray be pleas'd
To show in generous terms your griefs, since that
Your question's with your equal, who professes
To clear his own way with the mind and sword
Of a true gentleman.
Pal. That thou durst, Arcite!
Arc. My coz, my coz, you have been well advertis'd
How much I dare; y'ave seen me use my sword
Against th' advice of fear. Sure, of another
You would not hear me doubted, but your silence
Should break out, though i' th' sanctuary.
Pal. Sir,
I have seen you move in such a place which well
Might justify your manhood; you were call'd
A good knight and a bold. But the whole week's not fair
If any day it rain. Their valiant temper
Men lose when they incline to treachery,
And then they fight like compell'd bears, would fly
Were they not tied.
Arc. Kinsman, you might as well
Speak this and act it in your glass, as to
His ear which now disdains you.
Pal. Come up to me,
Quit me of these cold gyves, give me a sword
Though it be rusty, and the charity
Of one meal lend me; come before me then,
A good sword in thy hand, and do but say
That Emily is thine, I will forgive
The trespass thou hast done me, yea, my life
If then thou carry't, and brave souls in shades
That have died manly, which will seek of me
Some news from earth, they shall get none but this—
That thou art brave and noble.
Arc. Be content,
Again betake you to your hawthorn house.
With counsel of the night, I will be here
With wholesome viands; these impediments
Will I file off; you shall have garments, and
Perfumes to kill the smell o' th' prison; after,
When you shall stretch yourself, and say but, "Arcite,
I am in plight," there shall be at your choice
Both sword and armor.
Pal. O you heavens, dares any
So noble bear a guilty business? None
But only Arcite; therefore none but Arcite
In this kind is so bold.
Arc. Sweet Palamon—
Pal. I do embrace you and your offer. For
Your offer do't I only, sir; your person
Without hypocrisy I may not wish
More than my sword's edge on't.
Wind horns [off]. Cornets.
Arc. You hear the horns:
Enter your [musit], lest this match between 's
Be cross'd ere met. Give me your hand, farewell.
I'll bring you every needful thing. I pray you
Take comfort and be strong.
Pal. Pray hold your promise;
And do the deed with a bent brow. Most certain
You love me not; be rough with me, and pour
This oil out of your language. By this air,
I could for each word give a cuff, my stomach
Not reconcil'd by reason.
Arc. Plainly spoken,
Yet pardon me hard language. When I spur
My horse, I chide him [not]; content and anger
In me have but one face. *Wind horns [within].*
Hark, sir, they call
The scatter'd to the banket. You must guess
I have an office there.
Pal. Sir, your attendance
Cannot please heaven, and I know your office
Unjustly is achiev'd.
Arc. If a good title,
I am persuaded this question, sick between 's,
By bleeding must be cur'd. I am a suitor
That to your sword you will bequeath this plea,
And talk of it no more.
Pal. But this one word:
You are going now to gaze upon my mistress,
For note you, mine she is—
Arc. Nay then—
Pal. Nay, pray you—
You talk of feeding me to breed me strength;
You are going now to look upon a sun
That strengthens what it looks on; there you have

40. appointment: here, weapon. **41. chaffy:** worthless.
43. house-clogs: i.e. fetters. **45. feat:** deed.
47. blazon: description (of me). **52. skip:** pass over, deny.
54. show . . . griefs: make known your grievances in the language proper to gentlemen. **55. question:** dispute. **56. clear:** justify.
58. advertis'd: made acquainted with.
61–62. your . . . out: you would speak out (in my defense).
63. place which: situation as.
67. incline: yield (?) or bow, stoop (?).
68. would: which would. **72. Quit me of:** free me from.
78. carry't: prevail, defeat me.
83. With . . . night: confiding only in the night, i.e. alone at night.
88. in plight: in condition, ready.
96 s.d. Wind: sound. **Cornets.** Perhaps (as Bertram argues) this direction is the book-keeper's intended substitution for *horns* (as for *Trumpets* in V.iii.55 s.d.).
97. musit: gap in a hedge or thicket.
98. cross'd: thwarted. **101. bent:** frowning.
104. stomach: rage. **106. pardon me:** excuse me from.
108. but one face: the same appearance.
109. banket: banquet, light repast.
110. office: place, assigned duty. **115. plea:** suit (legal sense).

A vantage o'er me, but enjoy't till
I may enforce my remedy. Farewell.
Exeunt [severally].

Scene II

Enter Jailer's Daughter *alone*.

Daugh. He has mistook the [brake] I meant, is gone
After his fancy. 'Tis now well-nigh morning;
No matter, would it were perpetual night,
And darkness lord o' th' world! Hark, 'tis a wolf!
In me hath grief slain fear, and but for one thing,
I care for nothing, and that's Palamon.
I reak not if the wolves would jaw me, so
He had this file. What if I hallow'd for him?
I cannot hallow. If I whoop'd, what then?
If he not answer'd, I should call a wolf,
And do him but that service. I have heard
Strange howls this livelong night; why may't not be
They have made prey of him? He has no weapons,
He cannot run, the jingling of his gyves
Might call fell things to listen, who have in them
A sense to know a man unarm'd, and can
Smell where resistance is. I'll set it down
He's torn to pieces. They howl'd many together,
And then they [fed] on him. So much for that,
Be bold to ring the bell. How stand I then?
All's char'd when he is gone. No, no, I lie:
My father's to be hang'd for his escape,
Myself to beg, if I priz'd life so much
As to deny my act, but that I would not,
Should I try death by dozens. I am mop'd:
Food took I none these two days—
Sipp'd some water. I have not clos'd mine eyes
Save when my lids scour'd off their [brine]. Alas,
Dissolve, my life, let not my sense unsettle
Lest I should drown, or stab, or hang myself.
O state of nature, fail together in me,
Since thy best props are warp'd! So which way now?
The best way is, the next way to a grave;
Each errant step beside is torment. Lo
The moon is down, the crickets chirp, the screech-owl
Calls in the dawn! All offices are done
Save what I fail in. But the point is this—
An end, and that is all. *Exit*.

Scene III

Enter Arcite *with meat, wine, and files*.

III.ii. Location: The forest.
1. brake: thicket. 2. After his fancy: as his fancy directs.
7. reak: reck, care. jaw: gnaw. 15. fell: savage.
17. set it down: take it as settled.
20. bell: i.e. passing-bell (for a death).
21. All's char'd: all tasks are ended (*chare = chore*).
25. try . . . dozens: experience death many times (or in many ways).
mop'd: dazed, bewildered. 29. sense: reason.
31. together: altogether. 33. next: nearest.
34. errant: i.e. deviating from "the next way to a grave."
36. offices: tasks.

III.iii. Location: The forest.

Arc. I should be near the place. Ho, cousin Palamon!

Enter Palamon.

Pal. Arcite?
Arc. The same. I have brought you food and files.
Come forth and fear not, here's no Theseus.
Pal. Nor none so honest, Arcite.
Arc. That's no matter,
We'll argue that hereafter. Come, take courage,
You shall not die thus beastly. Here, sir, drink—
I know you are faint—then I'll talk further with you.
Pal. Arcite, thou mightst now poison me.
Arc. I might;
But I must fear you first. Sit down, and good now
No more of these vain parleys; let us not,
Having our ancient reputation with us,
Make talk for fools and cowards. To your health, etc.
[*Drinks*.]
Pal. Do.
Arc. Pray sit down then, and let me entreat you
By all the honesty and honor in you,
No mention of this woman. 'Twill disturb us,
We shall have time enough.
Pal. Well, sir, I'll pledge you. [*Drinks*.]
Arc. Drink a good hearty draught, it breeds good blood, man.
Do not you feel it thaw you?
Pal. Stay, I'll tell you
After a draught or two more.
Arc. Spare it not,
The Duke has more, coz. Eat now.
Pal. Yes. [*Eats*.]
Arc. I am glad
You have so good a stomach.
Pal. I am gladder
I have so good meat to't.
Arc. Is't not mad lodging
Here in the wild woods, cousin?
Pal. Yes, for [them]
That have wild consciences.
Arc. How tastes your victuals?
Your hunger needs no sauce, I see.
Pal. Not much.
But if it did, yours is too tart, sweet cousin.
What is this?
Arc. Venison.
Pal. 'Tis a lusty meat.
Give me more wine. Here, Arcite, to the wenches
We have known in our days! The Lord Steward's daughter—
Do you remember her?
Arc. After you, coz.

4. matter: i.e. topic for discussion just now.
6. beastly: like an animal. 9. good now: please.
11. ancient: former (?) or long-established (?).
21. stomach: appetite. Palamon plays on the sense "anger" and on literal and figurative senses of *meat*.
22. mad: wild. 24. wild: uncivilized.
25. sauce. Proverbially "Hunger is the best sauce." Palamon takes up the word in the sense "insolence." 27. lusty: fortifying.

Pal. She lov'd a black-hair'd man.
Arc. She did so; well, sir?
Pal. And I have heard some call him Arcite, and—
Arc. Out with't, faith!
Pal. She met him in an arbor:
What did she there, coz? play o' th' virginals?
Arc. Something she did, sir.
Pal. Made her groan a month for't;
Or two, or three, or ten.
Arc. The Marshal's sister
Had her share too, as I remember, cousin,
Else there be tales abroad. You'll pledge her?
Pal. Yes.
Arc. A pretty brown wench 'tis. There was a time
When young men went a-hunting, and a wood,
And a broad beech; and thereby hangs a tale.
Heigh-ho!
Pal. For Emily, upon my life! Fool,
Away with this strain'd mirth! I say again,
That sigh was breath'd for Emily. Base cousin,
Dar'st thou break first?
Arc. You are wide.
Pal. By heaven and earth,
There's nothing in thee honest.
Arc. Then I'll leave you;
You are a beast now.
Pal. As thou mak'st me, traitor!
Arc. There's all things needful, files and shirts and perfumes.
I'll come again some two hours hence and bring
That that shall quiet all.
Pal. A sword and armor.
Arc. Fear me not. You are now too foul; farewell.
Get off your trinkets, you shall want nought.
Pal. Sirrah—
Arc. I'll hear no more. *Exit.*
Pal. If he keep touch, he dies for't. *Exit.*

Scene IV

Enter Jailer's Daughter.

Daugh. I am very cold, and all the stars are out too,
The little stars and all, that look like aglets.
The sun has seen my folly. Palamon!
Alas, no; he's in heaven. Where am I now?
Yonder's the sea, and there's a ship. How't tumbles!
And there's a rock lies watching under water;
Now, now, it beats upon it—now, now, now!
There's a leak sprung, a sound one. How they cry!

34. virginals: a keyboard instrument; its name prompted much bawdy wordplay, as here.
35. Something: somewhat, to a certain extent.
38. tales: false accounts. **39. brown:** brunette.
42. Heigh-ho. A sigh.
45. break: break agreement. **wide:** wide of the mark, mistaken.
50. quiet: settle, write paid to.
51. Fear: doubt. **foul:** offensive.
52. trinkets: i.e. shackles. **Sirrah:** term of address used to inferiors, hence insulting here. **53. touch:** promise.
III.iv. Location: The forest.
2. aglets: spangles. **8. a sound one:** a good big one.

[Open] her before the wind! you'll lose all else.
Up with a course or two, and tack about, boys!
Good night, good night, y' are gone. I am very hungry:
Would I could find a fine frog! he would tell me
News from all parts o' th' world. Then would I make
A carreck of a cockleshell, and sail
By east and north-east to the King of Pigmies,
For he tells fortunes rarely. Now my father,
Twenty to one, is truss'd up in a trice
To-morrow morning; I'll say never a word. *Sing.*
"For I'll cut my green coat a foot above my knee,
And I'll clip my yellow locks an inch below mine e'e.
Hey, nonny, nonny, nonny.

"He s' buy me a white cut, forth for to ride,
And I'll go seek him through the world that is so wide.
Hey, nonny, nonny, nonny."

O for a prick now, like a nightingale,
To put my breast against! I shall sleep like a top else.
Exit.

Scene [V]

Enter a Schoolmaster [Gerrold], *four* Countrymen [*as morris-dancers*] *and* [*another as the*] Bavian, [*five*] Wenches, *with a* Taborer.

School. Fie, fie,
What tediosity and disensanity
Is here among ye! Have my rudiments
Been labor'd so long with ye, milk'd unto ye,
And by a figure, even the very plum-broth
And marrow of my understanding laid upon ye,
And do you still cry, "Where?" and "How?" and "Wherefore?"
You most coarse frieze capacities, ye [jane] judgments,
Have I said, "Thus let be," and "There let be,"
And "Then let be," and no man understand me?
Proh Deum, medius fidius, ye are all dunces!
For why, here stand I; here the Duke comes; there are you,
Close in the thicket. The Duke appears, I meet him
And unto him I utter learned things,
And many figures; he hears, and nods, and hums,

9. Open her: let her run. **10. course:** sail.
14. carreck: carrack, large cargo ship.
17. is . . . trice: is to be hanged promptly. **20. e'e:** eye.
22. He s': he shall. **cut:** gelding (?) or dock-tailed horse (?).
25. prick: thorn. It was supposed that the nightingale kept itself from falling asleep at night like other birds by pressing its breast against a thorn.
III.v. Location: The forest.
o.s.d. Bavian: one of the morris-dancers who was costumed as an ape; his name apparently derives from *baboon.* **Taborer:** player of a tabor or small drum.
2. disensanity: insanity (*dis-* is intensive).
5. figure: figure of speech.
5, 6. plum-broth, marrow. Used metaphorically for "vital part, essence."
8. coarse frieze capacities: crude homespun minds. Frieze is a rough woollen cloth. **jane:** jean, cheap cotton cloth.
11. Proh . . . fidius: O God! so help me heaven.
13. Close: out of sight.

And then cries, "Rare!" and I go forward. At length
I fling my cap up; mark there! Then do you,
As once did Meleager and the boar,
Break comely out before him; like true lovers,
Cast yourselves in a body decently,
And sweetly, by a figure, trace and turn, boys.
1. Coun. And sweetly we will do it, Master Gerrold.
2. Coun. Draw up the company. Where's the taborer?
3. Coun. Why, Timothy!
Taborer. Here, my mad boys, have at ye!
School. But I say, where's their women?
4. Coun. Here's Friz and Maudline.
2. Coun. And little Luce with the white legs, and bouncing Barbary.
1. Coun. And freckled Nell—that never fail'd her master.
School. Where be your ribands, maids? Swim with your bodies,
And carry it sweetly and deliverly,
And now and then a favor and a frisk.
Nell. Let us alone, sir.
School. Where's the rest o' th' music?
3. Coun. Dispers'd as you commanded.
School. Couple then,
And see what's wanting. Where's the Bavian?
My friend, carry your tail without offense
Or scandal to the ladies; and be sure
You tumble with audacity and manhood,
And when you bark, do it with judgment.
Bavian. Yes, sir.
School. *Quo usque tandem?* Here is a woman wanting.
4. Coun. We may go whistle; all the fat's i' th' fire.
School. We have, as learned authors utter, wash'd a tile,
We have been *fatuus*, and labored vainly.
2. Coun. This is that scornful piece, that scurvy hilding,
That gave her promise faithfully she would
Be here, Cicely the sempster's daughter.
The next gloves that I give her shall be dogskin;
Nay, and she fail me once—You can tell, Arcas,
She swore by wine and bread she would not break.
School. An eel and woman,
A learned poet says, unless by th' tail
And with thy teeth thou hold, will either fail.
In manners this was false position.
1. Coun. A fire ill take her does she flinch now?
3. Coun. What
Shall we determine, sir?
School. Nothing,
Our business is become a nullity,
Yea, and a woeful and a piteous nullity.
4. Coun. Now when the credit of our town lay on it,
Now to be frampal, now to piss o' th' nettle!
Go thy ways, I'll remember thee, I'll fit thee!

Enter JAILER'S DAUGHTER.

Daugh. [*Sings.*] "The *George Alow* came from the south,
From the coast of Barbary-a;
And there he met with brave gallants of war,
By one, by two, by three-a.

"Well hail'd, well hail'd, you jolly gallants!
And whither now are you bound-a?
O, let me have your company
Till [I] come to the sound-a."

"There was three fools fell out about an howlet:
The one said it was an owl,
The other he said nay,
The third he said it was a hawk,
And her bells were cut away."

3. Coun. There's a dainty mad woman, master,
Comes i' th' nick, as mad as a March hare.
If we can get her dance, we are made again.
I warrant her, she'll do the rarest gambols.
1. Coun. A mad woman? We are made, boys!
School. And are you mad, good woman?
Daugh. I would be sorry else.
Give me your hand.
School. Why?
Daugh. I can tell your fortune.
You are a fool. Tell ten—I have pos'd him. Buzz!
Friend, you must eat no white bread; if you do,
Your teeth will bleed extremely. Shall we dance ho?
I know you, y' are a tinker. Sirrah tinker,
Stop no more holes but what you should.

16. go forward: continue.
18. Meleager: mythical Greek hero who slew the Calydonian boar (a singularly inept comparison for the rustic actors).
19. comely: fittingly, decorously (so also *decently* in line 20). **like true lovers:** i.e. each man arm in arm with his girl (?). Cf. "Couple then" in line 32.
20. Cast . . . body: group yourselves for the dance.
21. trace: go through your steps.
24. have at ye: come ahead, I'm ready for you.
29. deliverly: nimbly.
30. favor: a kiss (?) or a graceful pose (?). **frisk:** skip or leap.
31. Let us alone: leave it to us. **music:** musicians.
32. Dispers'd: scattered here and there. **Couple:** pair up.
38. Quo usque tandem: how long then (from the opening sentence of Cicero's first oration against Catiline: "How long [or how far], Catiline, will you abuse our patience?")
39. We . . . whistle: there's nothing we can do about it (proverbial). **all . . . fire:** all our work has come to nothing (proverbial; the modern meaning is different).
40. wash'd a tile: i.e. labored in vain (from a Latin proverbial expression, *laterem lavare*). **41. fatuus:** foolish.
42. hilding: worthless creature. **44. sempster's:** seamstress'.
45. dogskin: i.e. cheap ones of inferior leather. **46. and:** if.
47. break: break promise.
48–50. An eel . . . fail. Proverbial, not from "a learned poet."
50. either: both.
51. In . . . position: this was as great a defect in good manners as a false proposition is in logic.
52. fire ill take: venereal rash infect.
57. frampal: perverse. **piss . . . nettle:** be in a bad temper (a proverbial expression).
58. fit thee: see that you get what you deserve.
59–66. The George Alow . . . sound-a. Probably quoted or adapted from a ballad entitled "The George Aloo and the Swifte-stake" (i.e. Sweepstake) which was entered in the Stationers' Register in 1611.
67–71. There . . . away. Earliest known version of a popular nursery rhyme. **67. howlet:** owlet.
71. bells. Attached to a hawk to lessen the danger of losing it.
79. Tell ten. A folkways sanity test was to make someone count his fingers. **pos'd:** stumped.

School. *Dii boni!*
A tinker, damsel?
Daugh. Or a conjurer.
Raise me a devil now, and let him play
Qui passa o' th' bells and bones.
School. Go take her,
And fluently persuade her to a peace.
"*Et opus exegi, quod nec Jovis ira, nec ignis*"—
Strike up, and lead her in.
2. Coun. Come, lass, let's trip it.
Daugh. I'll lead.
3. Coun. Do, do.
School. Persuasively and cunningly. *Wind horns.*
Away, boys!
I hear the horns. Give me some meditation,
And mark your cue. *Exeunt all but Schoolmaster.*
Pallas inspire me!

Enter Theseus, Pirithous, Hippolyta, Emilia, Arcite, *and* Train.

The. This way the stag took.
School. Stay, and edify.
The. What have we here?
Pir. Some country sport, upon my life, sir.
[*The.*] Well, sir, go forward, we will edify.
Ladies, sit down, we'll stay it.
School. Thou doughty Duke, all hail! All hail, sweet ladies!
The. This is a cold beginning.
School. If you but favor, our country pastime made is.
We are a few of those collected here
That ruder tongues distinguish villager,
And to say verity, and not to fable,
We are a merry rout, or else a rable,
Or company, or, by a figure, choris,
That 'fore thy dignity will dance a morris.
And I, that am the rectifier of all,
By title paedagogus, that let fall
The birch upon the breeches of the small ones,
And humble with a ferula the tall ones,
Do here present this machine, or this frame,
And, dainty Duke, whose doughty dismal fame
From Dis to Daedalus, from post to pillar,
Is blown abroad, help me, thy poor well-willer,
And with thy twinkling eyes look right and straight
Upon this mighty *Morr*—of mickle weight—
Is—now comes in, which being glu'd together
Makes *Morris*, and the cause that we came hither.
The body of our sport, of no small study,
I first appear, though rude, and raw, and muddy,
To speak, before thy noble Grace, this tenner;
At whose great feet I offer up my penner.
The next, the Lord of May and Lady bright,
The Chambermaid and Servingman, by night
That seek out silent hanging. Then mine Host
And his fat spouse, that welcomes to their cost
The galled traveller, and with a beck'ning
Informs the tapster to inflame the reck'ning.
Then the beast-eating Clown, and next the Fool,
The Bavian, with long tail and eke long tool,
Cum multis aliis that make a dance.
Say "Ay," and all shall presently advance.
The. Ay, ay, by any means, dear domine.
Pir. Produce.
[*School.*] (*Knock for school.*) *Intrate, filii;* come forth, and foot it.

Enter the Dance. *Music. Dance.*

Ladies, if we have been merry,
And have pleas'd [ye] with a derry,
And a derry, and a down,
Say the schoolmaster's no clown.
Duke, if we have pleas'd [thee] too
And have done as good boys should do,
Give us but a tree or twain
For a Maypole, and again,
Ere another year run out,
We'll make thee laugh and all this rout.
The. Take twenty, domine.—How does my sweet heart?
Hip. Never so pleas'd, sir.
Emil. 'Twas an excellent dance, and for a preface,
I never heard a better.
The. Schoolmaster, I thank you.
One see 'em all rewarded.
Pir. And here's something [*Gives money.*]
To paint your pole withal.
The. Now to our sports again.
School. May the stag thou hunt'st stand long,
And thy dogs be swift and strong!
May they kill him without lets,
And the ladies eat his dowsets!
[*Exeunt Theseus and his company.*] *Wind horns.*

83. Dii boni: good gods.
86. Qui passa. A popular tune. **bones.** Clapped together as an accompaniment for rustic dancing.
87. fluently . . . peace: quickly get her to agree.
88. Et . . . ignis: a version of Ovid, *Metamorphoses*, XV.871: "And I have built a work which neither the wrath of Jove nor fire [will destroy]."
93. meditation: thoughtful attention (?) or opportunity to consider what I want to say (?).
95. edify: be edified. **99. stay:** stay to see.
101. cold. Playing on a different meaning of *hail.*
107. choris: chorus.
109. rectifier: director (?) or corrector (as described in the next three lines) (?).
112. ferula: cane.
113. machine, frame. Both words mean "contrivance" or "device."
114. dismal: creating dismay (in your enemies).
115. Dis, Daedalus. Dis was god of the underworld and Daedalus the Cretan artist-craftsman who built the labyrinth in which the Minotaur was enclosed; but the names are apparently chosen for their alliterative value.
118–20. It has been suggested that the Schoolmaster first holds up a board bearing the syllable *Morr* (or possibly the figure of a Moor) and then places beside it a second board with the syllable *Is.*
118. mickle: great. **123. tenner:** tenor, import.
124. my penner: my pen-case, i.e. what I have penned.
127. hanging: wall-hanging or curtain (to conceal their love-making).
128. their. The sense seems to require *his,* but possibly *traveller* (line 129) is to be taken as a collective plural.
129. galled: sore (from walking or riding).
130. inflame the reck'ning: pad the bill.
131. beast: beest, the milk a cow gives soon after calving.
132. tool: penis. **133. Cum multis aliis:** with many others.
137. s.d. school: i.e. the dancers. **Intrate, filii:** enter, my sons.
139, 140. derry, down: common expressions in song refrains.
150. preface: prologue.
154. stand: stand out (against the dogs), i.e. give you good sport.
156. lets: hindrances.
157. dowsets: doucets, testicles of deer.

Come, we are all made. *Dii deaeque omnes!*
Ye have danc'd rarely, wenches. *Exeunt.*

SCENE [VI]

Enter PALAMON *from the bush.*

Pal. About this hour my cousin gave his faith
To visit me again, and with him bring
Two swords and two good armors. If he fail,
He's neither man nor soldier. When he left me,
I did not think a week could have restor'd
My lost strength to me, I was grown so low
And crestfall'n with my wants. I thank thee, Arcite,
Thou art yet a fair foe; and I feel myself,
With this refreshing, able once again
To out-dure danger. To delay it longer
Would make the world think, when it comes to hearing,
That I lay fatting like a swine, to fight,
And not a soldier: therefore this blest morning
Shall be the last; and that sword he refuses,
If it but hold, I kill him with. 'Tis justice.
So, love and fortune for me!

Enter ARCITE *with armors and swords.*

O, good morrow.
Arc. Good morrow, noble kinsman.
Pal. I have put you
To too much pains, sir.
Arc. That too much, fair cousin,
Is but a debt to honor, and my duty.
Pal. Would you were so in all, sir! I could wish ye
As kind a kinsman as you force me find
A beneficial foe, that my embraces
Might thank ye, not my blows.
Arc. I shall think either,
Well done, a noble recompense.
Pal. Then I shall quit you.
Arc. Defy me in these fair terms, and you show
More than a mistress to me; no more anger,
As you love any thing that's honorable.
We were not bred to talk, man. When we are arm'd
And both upon our guards, then let our fury,
Like meeting of two tides, fly strongly from us,
And then to whom the birthright of this beauty
Truly pertains (without obbraidings, scorns,
Despisings of our persons, and such poutings,
Fitter for girls and schoolboys) will be seen,
And quickly, yours or mine. Will't please you arm, sir?
Or if you feel yourself not fitting yet
And furnish'd with your old strength, I'll stay, cousin,
And ev'ry day discourse you into health,
As I am spar'd. Your person I am friends with,
And I could wish I had not said I lov'd her,

Though I had died; but loving such a lady
And justifying my love, I must not fly from't.
Pal. Arcite, thou art so brave an enemy
That no man but thy cousin's fit to kill thee.
I am well and lusty, choose your arms.
Arc. Choose you, sir.
Pal. Wilt thou exceed in all, or dost thou do it
To make me spare thee?
Arc. If you think so, cousin,
You are deceived, for as I am a soldier,
I will not spare you.
Pal. That's well said.
Arc. You'll find it.
Pal. Then as I am an honest man, and love
With all the justice of affection,
I'll pay thee soundly. This I'll take.
Arc. That's mine then.
I'll arm you first.
Pal. Do. Pray thee tell me, cousin,
Where got'st thou this good armor?
Arc. 'Tis the Duke's,
And to say true, I stole it. Do I pinch you?
Pal. No.
Arc. Is't not too heavy?
Pal. I have worn a lighter,
But I shall make it serve.
Arc. I'll buckle't close.
Pal. By any means.
Arc. You care not for a grand-guard?
Pal. No, no, we'll use no horses. I perceive
You would fain be at that fight.
Arc. I am indifferent.
Pal. Faith, so am I. Good cousin, thrust the buckle
Through far enough.
Arc. I warrant you.
Pal. My casque now.
Arc. Will you fight bare-arm'd?
Pal. We shall be the nimbler.
Arc. But use your gauntlets though. Those are o' th' least;
Prithee take mine, good cousin.
Pal. Thank you, Arcite.
How do I look? am I fall'n much away?
Arc. Faith, very little. Love has us'd you kindly.
Pal. I'll warrant thee, I'll strike home.
Arc. Do, and spare not.
I'll give you càuse, sweet cousin.
Pal. Now to you, sir.
Methinks this armor's very like that, Arcite,
Thou wor'st that day the three kings fell, but lighter.
Arc. That was a very good one, and that day,
I well remember, you outdid me, cousin;
I never saw such valor. When you charg'd
Upon the left wing of the enemy,
I spurr'd hard to come up, and under me
I had a right good horse.
Pal. You had indeed,
A bright bay, I remember.

158. Dii deaeque omnes: all gods and goddesses.

III.vi. Location: The forest.
10. out-dure: outlast. **24. quit:** requite.
31. birthright: right destined for one of us at birth.
32. pertains: belongs. **obbraidings:** upbraidings.
37. stay: wait.

42. justifying: knowing myself justified in.
58. grand-guard: chest-guard used by mounted knights.
60. fain . . . fight: i.e. like to fight on horseback. **am indifferent:** have no preference. **64. o' th' least:** i.e. too small.

Arc. Yes, but all
Was vainly labor'd in me; you outwent me,
Nor could my wishes reach you. Yet a little
I did by imitation.
Pal. More by virtue.
You are modest, cousin.
Arc. When I saw you charge first,
Methought I heard a dreadful clap of thunder
Break from the troop.
Pal. But still before that flew
The lightning of your valor. Stay a little;
Is not this piece too strait?
Arc. No, no, 'tis well.
Pal. I would have nothing hurt thee but my sword,
A bruise would be dishonor.
Arc. Now I am perfect.
Pal. Stand off then.
Arc. Take my sword, I hold it better.
Pal. I thank ye. No, keep it, your life lies on it.
Here's one, if it but hold, I ask no more
For all my hopes. My cause and honor guard me!
Arc. And me my love!
They bow several ways; then advance and stand.
Is there aught else to say?
Pal. This only, and no more: thou art mine aunt's son,
And that blood we desire to shed is mutual,
In me, thine, and in thee, mine. My sword
Is in my hand, and if thou kill'st me,
The gods and I forgive thee. If there be
A place prepar'd for those that sleep in honor,
I wish his weary soul that falls may win it.
Fight bravely, cousin. Give me thy noble hand.
Arc. Here, Palamon: this hand shall never more
Come near thee with such friendship.
Pal. I commend thee.
Arc. If I fall, curse me, and say I was a coward,
For none but such dare die in these just trials.
Once more farewell, my cousin.
Pal. Farewell, Arcite.
Fight. Horns within; they stand.
Arc. Lo, cousin, lo, our folly has undone us.
Pal. Why?
Arc. This is the Duke, a-hunting as I told you.
If we be found, we are wretched. O, retire
For honor's sake, and safely presently
Into your bush again, sir. We shall find
Too many hours to die in, gentle cousin.
If you be seen, you perish instantly
For breaking prison, and I, if you reveal me,
For my contempt. Then all the world will scorn us,
And say we had a noble difference,
But base disposers of it.
Pal. No, no, cousin,
I will no more be hidden, nor put off
This great adventure to a second trial.
I know your cunning, and I know your cause.
He that faints now, shame take him! Put thyself
Upon thy present guard—
Arc. You are not mad?
Pal. Or I will make th' advantage of this hour
Mine own; and what to come shall threaten me
I fear less than my fortune. Know, weak cousin,
I love Emilia, and in that I'll bury
Thee and all crosses else.
Arc. Then come what can come,
Thou shalt know, Palamon, I dare as well
Die as discourse or sleep. Only this fears me,
The law will have the honor of our ends.
Have at thy life!
Pal. Look to thine own well, Arcite.
Fight again. Horns.
Enter THESEUS, HIPPOLYTA, EMILIA, PIRITHOUS, *and* TRAIN.
The. What ignorant and mad malicious traitors
Are you, that 'gainst the tenor of my laws
Are making battle, thus like knights appointed,
Without my leave and officers of arms?
By Castor, both shall die.
Pal. Hold thy word, Theseus.
We are certainly both traitors, both despisers
Of thee and of thy goodness. I am Palamon,
That cannot love thee, he that broke thy prison—
Think well what that deserves; and this is Arcite,
A bolder traitor never trod thy ground,
A falser nev'r seem'd friend. This is the man
Was begg'd and banish'd, this is he contemns thee
And what thou dar'st do; and in this disguise,
Against [thy] own edict, follows thy sister,
That fortunate bright star, the fair Emilia,
Whose servant (if there be a right in seeing,
And first bequeathing of the soul to) justly
I am, and which is more, dares think her his.
This treachery, like a most trusty lover,
I call'd him now to answer. If thou be'st,
As thou art spoken, great and virtuous,
The true decider of all injuries,
Say, "Fight again!" and thou shalt see me, Theseus,
Do such a justice thou thyself wilt envy.
Then take my life, I'll woo thee to't.
Pir. O heaven,
What more than man is this!
The. I have sworn.
Arc. We seek not
Thy breath of mercy, Theseus. 'Tis to me
A thing as soon to die as thee to say it,
And no more mov'd. Where this man calls me traitor,
Let me say thus much: if in love be treason
In service of so excellent a beauty,
As I love most, and in that faith will perish,

81. virtue: i.e. your own endowments. **86. strait:** tight.
88. perfect: complete, ready. **89. hold:** think.
93 s.d. several ways: in different directions.
103. commend: honor.
115. contempt: disobedience (of the order for his banishment).
119. adventure: venture.
121. faints: is fainthearted, draws back.
123. Or: i.e. either I am mad or.
125. fortune: i.e. fortune in this fight.
127. crosses: obstacles. **129. fears me:** makes me fearful.
135. officers of arms: officials in charge of tournaments, which were conducted according to a strict etiquette.
136. Castor. Castor and his twin brother Pollux were sons of Leda by Zeus. **Hold:** keep. **137–38. despisers Of:** disobedient to.
143. begg'd: petitioned for (by Pirithous; see II.ii.244–45).

As I have brought my life here to confirm it,
As I have serv'd her truest, worthiest,
As I dare kill this cousin that denies it,
So let me be most traitor, and ye please me.
For scorning thy edict, Duke, ask that lady
Why she is fair, and why her eyes command me
Stay here to love her; and if she say "traitor,"
I am a villain fit to lie unburied.
Pal. Thou shalt have pity of us both, O Theseus,
If unto neither thou show mercy. Stop,
As thou art just, thy noble ear against us;
As thou art valiant, for thy cousin's soul,
Whose twelve strong labors crown his memory,
Let 's die together, at one instant, Duke.
Only a little let him fall before me,
That I may tell my soul he shall not have her.
The. I grant your wish, for to say true, your cousin
Has ten times more offended, for I gave him
More mercy than you found, sir, your offenses
Being no more than his. None here speak for 'em,
For ere the sun set, both shall sleep for ever.
Hip. Alas, the pity! Now or never, sister,
Speak, not to be denied. That face of yours
Will bear the curses else of after-ages
For these lost cousins.
Emil. In my face, dear sister,
I find no anger to 'em, nor no ruin:
The misadventure of their own eyes kill 'em;
Yet that I will be woman, and have pity,
My knees shall grow to th' ground but I'll get mercy.
Help me, dear sister, in a deed so virtuous
The powers of all women will be with us.
Most royal brother— [*They kneel.*]
Hip. Sir, by our tie of marriage—
Emil. By your own spotless honor—
Hip. By that faith,
That fair hand, and that honest heart you gave me—
Emil. By that you would have pity in another,
By your own virtues infinite—
Hip. By valor,
By all the chaste nights I have ever pleas'd you—
The. These are strange conjurings.
Pir. Nay then I'll in too. [*Kneels.*]
By all our friendship, sir, by all our dangers,
By all you love most—wars, and this sweet lady—
Emil. By that you would have trembled to deny
A blushing maid—
Hip. By your own eyes, by strength,
In which you swore I went beyond all women,
Almost all men, and yet I yielded, Theseus—
Pir. To crown all this, by your most noble soul,
Which cannot want due mercy, I beg first.
Hip. Next hear my prayers.
Emil. Last let me entreat, sir.
Pir. For mercy.
Hip. Mercy.
Emil. Mercy on these princes.

172. **of:** on.
175. **thy cousin's.** Referring to Hercules, who according to one tradition was Theseus' kinsman.
198. **By . . . another:** by whatever you would invoke to arouse pity in someone else.
209. **want:** be wanting in.

The. Ye make my faith reel. Say I felt
Compassion to 'em both, how would you place it?
Emil. Upon their lives; but with their banishments.
The. You are a right woman, sister, you have pity,
But want the understanding where to use it.
If you desire their lives, invent a way
Safer than banishment. Can these two live,
And have the agony of love about 'em,
And not kill one another? Every day
They'ld fight about you; hourly bring your honor
In public question with their swords. Be wise then
And here forget 'em; it concerns your credit
And my oath equally. I have said they die;
Better they fall by th' law than one another.
Bow not my honor.
Emil. O my noble brother,
That oath was rashly made, and in your anger,
Your reason will not hold it. If such vows
Stand for express will, all the world must perish.
Beside, I have another oath 'gainst yours,
Of more authority, I am sure more love,
Not made in passion neither, but good heed.
The. What is it, sister?
Pir. Urge it home, brave lady.
Emil. That you would nev'r deny me any thing
Fit for my modest suit and your free granting.
I tie you to your word now; if ye fall in't,
Think how you maim your honor
(For now I am set a-begging, sir, I am deaf
To all but your compassion), how their lives
Might breed the ruin of my name; opinion,
Shall any thing that loves me perish for me?
That were a cruel wisdom. Do men proin
The straight young boughs that blush with thousand blossoms,
Because they may be rotten? O Duke Theseus,
The goodly mothers that have groan'd for these,
And all the longing maids that ever lov'd,
If your vow stand, shall curse me and my beauty,
And in their funeral songs for these two cousins
Despise my cruelty, and cry woe worth me,
Till I am nothing but the scorn of women.
For heaven's sake save their lives, and banish 'em.
The. On what conditions?
Emil. Swear 'em never more
To make me their contention, or to know me,
To tread upon thy dukedom, and to be,
Where ever they shall travel, ever strangers
To one another.
Pal. I'll be cut a-pieces
Before I take this oath. Forget I love her?
O all ye gods, despise me then. Thy banishment
I not mislike, so we may fairly carry
Our swords and cause along; else, never trifle,

212. **make . . . reel:** make my constancy to my oath waver.
215. **right:** true, typical. 222. **question:** controversy.
226. **Bow:** bend, cause to yield.
227. **rashly:** impulsively, without due thought.
228. **hold:** maintain. 229. **express will:** inflexible determination.
235. **free:** honorable. 236. **fall:** fail. 240. **opinion:** consider.
241. **for me:** on my account. 242. **proin:** prune.
244. **be:** become. 249. **worth:** befall.
253. **know:** remember (?). Cf. line 257.

But take our lives, Duke. I must love, and will,
And for that love must and dare kill this cousin,
On any piece the earth has.
The. Will you, Arcite,
Take these conditions?
Pal. He's a villain then.
Pir. These are men!
Arc. No, never, Duke. 'Tis worse to me than begging
To take my life so basely. Though I think
I never shall enjoy her, yet I'll preserve
The honor of affection, and die for her,
Make death a devil.
The. What may be done? for now I feel compassion.
Pir. Let it not fall again, sir.
The. Say, Emilia,
If one of them were dead, as one must, are you
Content to take th' other to your husband?
They cannot both enjoy you. They are princes
As goodly as your own eyes, and as noble
As ever fame yet spoke of. Look upon 'em,
And if you can love, end this difference.
I give consent.—Are you content too, princes?
Both. With all our souls.
The. He that she refuses
Must die then.
Both. Any death thou canst invent, Duke.
Pal. If I fall from that mouth, I fall with favor,
And lovers yet unborn shall bless my ashes.
Arc. If she refuse me, yet my grave will wed me,
And soldiers sing my epitaph.
The. Make choice then.
Emil. I cannot, sir, they are both too excellent:
For me, a hair shall never fall of these men.
Hip. What will become of 'em?
The. Thus I ordain it,
And by mine honor, once again it stands,
Or both shall die: you shall both to your country,
And each within this month, accompanied
With three fair knights, appear again in this place,
In which I'll plant a pyramid; and whether,
Before us that are here, can force his cousin
By fair and knightly strength to touch the pillar,
He shall enjoy her; the other lose his head,
And all his friends; nor shall he grudge to fall,
Nor think he dies with interest in this lady.
Will this content ye?
Pal. Yes. Here, cousin Arcite,
I am friends again till that hour.
Arc. I embrace ye.
The. Are you content, sister?
Emil. Yes, I must, sir,
Else both miscarry.
The. Come shake hands again then,
And take heed, as you are gentlemen, this quarrel

270. Make: though you make. **272. fall:** diminish.
282. from that mouth: in consequence of what she says.
293. whether: whichever of the two.
297. all his friends: i.e. they shall lose their heads too. **grudge to fall:** feel that he dies unjustly.
298. interest in: rightful claim to. **302. miscarry:** perish.

Sleep till the hour prefix'd, and hold your course.
Pal. We dare not fail thee, Theseus.
The. Come, I'll give ye
Now usage like to princes and to friends.
When ye return, who wins I'll settle here;
Who loses, yet I'll weep upon his bier. *Exeunt.*

ACT IV, SCENE I

Enter JAILER *and his* FRIEND.

Jail. Hear you no more? Was nothing said of me
Concerning the escape of Palamon?
Good sir, remember.
1. Friend. Nothing that I heard,
For I came home before the business
Was fully ended. Yet I might perceive,
Ere I departed, a great likelihood
Of both their pardons; for Hippolyta,
And fair-ey'd Emily, upon their knees
Begg'd with such handsome pity, that the Duke
Methought stood staggering whether he should follow
His rash oath, or the sweet compassion
Of those two ladies; and to second them,
That truly noble prince Pirithous,
Half his own heart, set in too, that I hope
All shall be well. Neither heard I one question
Of your name, or his scape.
Jail. Pray heaven it hold so!

Enter SECOND FRIEND.

2. Friend. Be of good comfort, man; I bring you news,
Good news.
Jail. They are welcome.
2. Friend. Palamon has clear'd you,
And got your pardon, and discover'd how
And by whose means he escap'd, which was your daughter's,
Whose pardon is procur'd too; and the prisoner—
Not to be held ungrateful to her goodness—
Has given a sum of money to her marriage,
A large one, I'll assure you.
Jail. Ye are a good man
And ever bring good news.
1. Friend. How was it ended?
2. Friend. Why, as it should be: they that nev'r begg'd
But they prevail'd, had their suits fairly granted:
The prisoners have their lives.
1. Friend. I knew 'twould be so.
2. Friend. But there be new conditions, which you'll hear of
At better time.
Jail. I hope they are good.
2. Friend. They are honorable,
How good they'll prove, I know not.
1. Friend. 'Twill be known.

IV.i. Location: Athens. The prison.
10. staggering: wavering. **16. scape:** escape.
19. discover'd: revealed.

Enter Wooer.

Wooer. Alas, sir, where's your daughter?
Jail. Why do you ask?
Wooer. O sir, when did you see her?
2. Friend. How he looks!
Jail. This morning.
Wooer. Was she well? was she in health?
Sir, when did she sleep?
1. Friend. These are strange questions.
Jail. I do not think she was very well, for, now
You make me mind her, but this very day
I ask'd her questions, and she answered me
So far from what she was, so childishly,
So sillily, as if she were a fool,
An innocent, and I was very angry.
But what of her, sir?
Wooer. Nothing but my pity.
But you must know it, and as good by me
As by another that less loves her.
Jail. Well, sir?
1. Friend. Not right?
2. Friend. Not well?
Wooer. No, sir, not well:
'Tis too true, she is mad.
1. Friend. It cannot be.
Wooer. Believe you'll find it so.
Jail. I half suspected
What you told me. The gods comfort her!
Either this was her love to Palamon,
Or fear of my miscarrying on his scape,
Or both.
Wooer. 'Tis likely.
Jail. But why all this haste, sir?
Wooer. I'll tell you quickly. As I late was angling
In the great lake that lies behind the palace,
From the far shore, thick set with reeds and sedges,
As patiently I was attending sport,
I heard a voice, a shrill one; and attentive
I gave my ear, when I might well perceive
'Twas one that sung, and by the smallness of it,
A boy or woman. I then left my angle
To his own skill, came near, but yet perceiv'd not
Who made the sound, the rushes and the reeds
Had so encompass'd it. I laid me down
And list'ned to the words she sung, for then
Through a small glade cut by the fishermen,
I saw it was your daughter.
Jail. Pray go on, sir.
Wooer. She sung much, but no sense; only I heard her
Repeat this often, "Palamon is gone,
Is gone to th' wood to gather mulberries.
I'll find him out to-morrow."
1. Friend. Pretty soul!
Wooer. "His shackles will betray him, he'll be taken,
And what shall I do then? I'll bring a bevy,
A hundred black-ey'd maids that love as I do,

37. **make me mind:** put me in mind of.
39. **what she was:** i.e. her usual manner. 41. **innocent:** idiot.
50. **miscarrying on:** coming to grief because of.
55. **attending:** awaiting. 58. **smallness:** high pitch. 60. **his:** its.

With chaplets on their heads of daffadillies,
With cherry lips and cheeks of damask roses,
And all we'll dance an antic 'fore the Duke,
And beg his pardon." Then she talk'd of you, sir:
That you must lose your head to-morrow morning,
And she must gather flowers to bury you,
And see the house made handsome. Then she sung
Nothing but "Willow, willow, willow," and between
Ever was "Palamon, fair Palamon,"
And "Palamon was a tall young man." The place
Was knee-deep where she sat; her careless tresses
A [wreath] of bulrush rounded; about her stuck
Thousand fresh water-flowers of several colors,
That methought she appear'd like the fair nymph
That feeds the lake with waters, or as Iris
Newly dropp'd down from heaven. Rings she made
Of rushes that grew by, and to 'em spoke
The prettiest posies—"Thus our true love's tied,"
"This you may loose, not me," and many a one;
And then she wept, and sung again, and sigh'd,
And with the same breath smil'd, and kiss'd her hand.
2. Friend. Alas, what pity it is!
Wooer. I made in to her.
She saw me, and straight sought the flood. I sav'd her,
And set her safe to land; when presently
She slipp'd away, and to the city made
With such a cry and swiftness that, believe me,
She left me far behind her. Three or four
I saw from far off cross her—one of 'em
I knew to be your brother; where she stay'd,
And fell, scarce to be got away. I left them with her,
And hither came to tell you.

Enter Brother, Daughter, *and others.*

Here they are.
Daugh. [*Sings.*]
"May you never more enjoy the light," etc.
Is not this a fine song?
Broth. O, a very fine one!
Daugh. I can sing twenty more.
Broth. I think you can.
Daugh. Yes, truly, can I. I can sing "The Broom,"
And "Bonny Robin." Are not you a tailor?
Broth. Yes.
Daugh. Where's my wedding gown?
Broth. I'll bring it to-morrow.
Daugh. Do, very [rearly], I must be abroad else,
To call the maids and pay the minstrels,
For I must lose my maidenhead by cocklight,
'Twill never thrive else. *Sings.*
"O fair, O sweet," etc.
Broth. You must ev'n take it patiently.

75. **antic:** grotesque dance. 76. **beg his:** beg for Palamon's.
80. **"Willow, willow, willow."** In *Othello*, IV.iii.26–57, Desdemona sings a version of this song. 82. **tall:** excellent, valiant.
85. **several:** various. 87. **Iris:** goddess of the rainbow.
90. **posies:** mottoes, often inscribed in rings (derived from *poesies*).
91. **loose.** A common variant of *lose*, but the first posy shows that the second may mean, "This you may untie, but not my love."
95. **straight:** straightway. 100. **cross:** intercept.
101. **stay'd:** stopped.
108. **"Bonny Robin."** In *Hamlet*, IV.v.187, Ophelia sings a line of this song. 110. **rearly:** early. **abroad:** away from home.
112. **cocklight:** at cockcrow, early daylight.
113. **'Twill never thrive:** things will never go well.

Jail. 'Tis true.
Daugh. Good ev'n, good men. Pray did you ever hear
Of one young Palamon?
Jail. Yes, wench, we know him.
Daugh. Is't not a fine young gentleman?
Jail. 'Tis, love.
Broth. By no mean cross her, she is then distemper'd
[Far] worse than now she shows.
1. Friend. Yes, he's a fine man.
Daugh. O, is he so? You have a sister?
1. Friend. Yes.
Daugh. But she shall never have him, tell her so,
For a trick that I know. Y' had best look to her,
For if she see him once, she's gone—she's done,
And undone in an hour. All the young maids
Of our town are in love with him, but I laugh at 'em
And let 'em all alone. Is't not a wise course?
1. Friend. Yes.
Daugh. There is at least two hundred now with child by him—
There must be four. Yet I keep close for all this,
Close as a cockle. And all these must be boys,
He has the trick on't; and at ten years old
They must be all gelt for musicians,
And sing the wars of Theseus.
2. Friend. This is strange.
Daugh. As ever you heard, but say nothing.
1. Friend. No.
Daugh. They come from all parts of the dukedom to him.
I'll warrant ye he had not so few last night
As twenty to dispatch. He'll tickle't up
In two hours, if his hand be in.
Jail. She's lost
Past all cure.
Broth. Heaven forbid, man!
Daugh. [*To the Jailer.*] Come hither, you are a wise man.
1. Friend. Does she know him?
[2.] *Friend.* No, would she did!
Daugh. You are master of a ship?
Jail. Yes.
Daugh. Where's your compass?
Jail. Here.
Daugh. Set it to th' north.
And now direct your course to th' wood, where Palamon
Lies longing for me. For the tackling
Let me alone. Come weigh, my hearts, cheerly!
All. Owgh, owgh, owgh! 'Tis up! The wind's fair.

119. cross: contradict.
119–20. is . . . shows: will in that case become far more disordered than she shows herself to be now. **123. For:** because of.
130. close: close-mouthed.
131. cockle. Cf. *clam* in modern parlance.
132. on't: i.e. of begetting nothing but male children.
133. gelt for musicians: castrated so that their voices won't change.
138. tickle't up: bring it to a satisfying conclusion.
139. if . . . in: if he is in good form. **145. tackling:** rigging.
146. Let me alone: leave that to me. **weigh:** weigh anchor.
147. Owgh. Apparently they imitate the sound of the wind in the sails.

Top the bowling! Out with the mainsail!
Where's your whistle, master?
Broth. Let's get her in.
Jail. Up to the top, boy!
Broth. Where's the pilot?
1. Friend. Here.
Daugh. What ken'st thou?
2. Friend. A fair wood.
Daugh. Bear for it, master.
Tack about! *Sings.*
"When Cynthia with her borrowed light," etc.
Exeunt.

Scene II

Enter Emilia *alone, with two pictures.*

Emil. Yet I may bind those wounds up, that must open
And bleed to death for my sake else. I'll choose,
And end their strife. Two such young handsome men
Shall never fall for me; their weeping mothers,
Following the dead-cold ashes of their sons,
Shall never curse my cruelty. Good heaven,
What a sweet face has Arcite! If wise Nature,
With all her best endowments, all those beauties
She sows into the births of noble bodies,
Were here a mortal woman, and had in her
The coy denials of young maids, yet doubtless
She would run mad for this man. What an eye,
Of what a fiery sparkle and quick sweetness,
Has this young prince! Here Love himself sits smiling.
Just such another wanton Ganymede
Set [Jove] afire with, and enforc'd the god
Snatch up the goodly boy and set him by him,
A shining constellation. What a brow,
Of what a spacious majesty, he carries,
Arch'd like the great-ey'd Juno's, but far sweeter,
Smoother than Pelops' shoulder! Fame and Honor
Methinks from hence, as from a promontory
Pointed in heaven, should clap their wings and sing
To all the under world the loves and fights
Of gods and such men near 'em. Palamon
Is but his foil, to him, a mere dull shadow;
He's swarth and meagre, of an eye as heavy
As if he had lost his mother; a still temper,
No stirring in him, no alacrity,
Of all this sprightly sharpness, not a smile.

148. Top the bowling: tighten the bowline.
151. What ken'st thou: what do you see.
153. Cynthia: i.e. the moon.

IV.ii. Location: Athens. The palace.
4. fall for me: perish on my account.
11. coy: modest. **14. Here:** i.e. in his eye.
15. Just such another: an eye just like this. **Ganymede:** a beautiful youth carried off by Zeus to be his cupbearer.
18. constellation. Ganymede was turned into Aquarius.
21. Pelops: Tantalus' son, whose left shoulder had been replaced by an ivory one.
22–23. promontory Pointed: peaked eminence.
25. near 'em: i.e. rivalling their exploits in love and war.
26. his foil: one who sets him off by contrast. **to:** in comparison with (as also in line 44).
27. swarth: dark-complexioned. **heavy:** dull, lacklustre.
28. still temper: temperament lacking in animation.
30. this: i.e. Arcite's.

Yet these that we count errors may become him:
Narcissus was a sad boy, but a heavenly.
O, who can find the bent of woman's fancy?
I am a fool, my reason is lost in me;
I have no choice, and I have lied so lewdly
That women ought to beat me. On my knees
I ask thy pardon: Palamon, thou art alone
And only beautiful, and these the eyes,
These the bright lamps of beauty, that command
And threaten Love, and what young maid dare cross 'em?
What a bold gravity, and yet inviting,
Has this brown manly face! O Love, this only
From this hour is complexion. Lie there, Arcite,
Thou art a changeling to him, a mere gipsy,
And this the noble body. I am sotted,
Utterly lost. My virgin's faith has fled me;
For if my brother but even now had ask'd me
Whether I lov'd, I had run mad for Arcite;
Now if my sister—more for Palamon.
Stand both together: now, come ask me, brother—
Alas, I know not! Ask me now, sweet sister—
I may go look! What a mere child is fancy,
That having two fair gauds of equal sweetness,
Cannot distinguish, but must cry for both!

Enter GENTLEMAN.

How now, sir?
Gent. From the noble Duke your brother,
Madam, I bring you news. The knights are come.
Emil. To end the quarrel?
Gent. Yes.
Emil. Would I might end first!
What sins have I committed, chaste Diana,
That my unspotted youth must now be soil'd
With blood of princes? and my chastity
Be made the altar where the lives of lovers—
Two greater and two better never yet
Made mothers joy—must be the sacrifice
To my unhappy beauty?

Enter THESEUS, HIPPOLYTA, PIRITHOUS, *and* ATTENDANTS.

The. Bring 'em in
Quickly, by any means, I long to see 'em.—
Your two contending lovers are return'd,
And with them their fair knights. Now, my fair sister,
You must love one of them.
Emil. I had rather both,
So neither for my sake should fall untimely.
The. Who saw 'em?
Pir. I a while.
Gent. And I.

Enter [MESSENGER].

The. From whence come you, sir?
Mess. From the knights.
The. Pray speak,
You that have seen them, what they are.
Mess. I will, sir,
And truly what I think. Six braver spirits
Than these they have brought (if we judge by the outside)
I never saw nor read of. He that stands
In the [first] place with Arcite, by his seeming
Should be a stout man, by his face a prince
(His very looks so say him), his complexion
Nearer a brown than black; stern, and yet noble,
Which shows him hardy, fearless, proud of dangers.
The circles of his eyes show [fire] within him,
And as a heated lion, so he looks;
His hair hangs long behind him, black and shining
Like ravens' wings; his shoulders broad and strong,
Arm'd long and round, and on his thigh a sword
Hung by a curious baldrick, when he frowns
To seal his will with. Better, o' my conscience,
Was never soldier's friend.
The. Thou hast well describ'd him.
Pir. Yet a great deal short,
Methinks, of him that's first with Palamon.
The. Pray speak him, friend.
Pir. I guess he is a prince too,
And if it may be, greater; for his show
Has all the ornament of honor in't.
He's somewhat bigger than the knight he spoke of,
But of a face far sweeter; his complexion
Is, as a ripe grape, ruddy. He has felt
Without doubt what he fights for, and so apter
To make this cause his own. In's face appears
All the fair hopes of what he undertakes,
And when he's angry, then a settled valor
(Not tainted with extremes) runs through his body,
And guides his arm to brave things. Fear he cannot,
He shows no such soft temper. His head's yellow,
Hard-hair'd, and curl'd, thick twin'd like ivy[-tods],
Not to undo with thunder. In his face
The livery of the warlike maid appears,
Pure red and white, for yet no beard has blest him;
And in his rolling eyes sits victory,
As if she ever meant to [crown] his valor.
His nose stands high, a character of honor;
His red lips, after fights, are fit for ladies.
Emil. Must these men die too?
Pir. When he speaks, his tongue
Sounds like a trumpet. All his lineaments

32. sad: serious. **33. bent**: tendency.
35. choice: discrimination. **lewdly**: ignorantly.
37. alone: peerless.
44. changeling: child exchanged for another by the fairies; hence, often an ugly or deformed creature. **gipsy**. Ordinarily used of a dark-skinned person, but it is Palamon who is "swarth," though Arcite has black hair (see III.iii.31–32). Perhaps *changeling* suggested *gipsy*, since gipsies were also thought to steal children.
45. am sotted: have become utterly stupid.
46. virgin's faith: dedication to a virgin's life.
52. look: i.e. look for an answer, since I have none.
53. gauds: toys, knickknacks.

77. stout: valorous. **80. proud**: scornful.
82. heated: angry.
85. Arm'd . . . round: with long, well-muscled arms.
86. curious baldrick: skillfully made belt.
86–87. when . . . with: to execute his purpose when he is angry.
97. what . . . for: i.e. love.
99. All . . . hopes: complete confidence of success.
104. Hard-hair'd. Meaning uncertain. **ivy-tods**: ivy bushes.
105. undo: be undone, i.e. disheveled.
106. livery . . . maid: distinctive badge of the servants of Bellona, goddess of war.

Are as a man would wish 'em, strong and clean.
He wears a well-steel'd axe, the staff of gold.
His age some five and twenty.
Mess. There's another,
A little man, but of a tough soul, seeming
As great as any. Fairer promises
In such a body yet I never look'd on.
Pir. O, he that's freckle-fac'd?
Mess. The same, my lord.
Are they not sweet ones?
Pir. Yes, they are well.
Mess. Methinks,
Being so few and well dispos'd, they show
Great and fine art in nature. He's white-hair'd,
Not wanton white, but such a manly color
Next to an aborn; tough and nimble set,
Which shows an active soul; his arms are brawny,
Lin'd with strong sinews; to the shoulder-piece
Gently they swell, like women new conceiv'd,
Which speaks him prone to labor, never fainting
Under the weight of arms; stout-hearted, still,
But when he stirs, a tiger. He's grey-ey'd,
Which yields compassion where he conquers; sharp
To spy advantages, and where he finds 'em,
He's swift to make 'em his. He does no wrongs,
Nor takes none. He's round-fac'd, and when he smiles
He shows a lover, when he frowns, a soldier.
About his head he wears the winner's oak,
And in it stuck the favor of his lady.
His age some six and thirty. In his hand
He bears a charging-staff emboss'd with silver.
The. Are they all thus?
Pir. They are all the sons of honor.
The. Now as I have a soul I long to see 'em.
Lady, you shall see men fight now.
Hip. I wish it,
But not the cause, my lord. They would show
Bravely about the titles of two kingdoms.
'Tis pity love should be so tyrannous.
O my soft-hearted sister, what think you?
Weep not, till they weep blood. Wench, it must be.
The. You have steel'd 'em with your beauty.—
Honor'd friend,
To you I give the field; pray order it,
Fitting the persons that must use it.
Pir. Yes, sir.
The. Come, I'll go visit 'em. I cannot stay—
Their fame has fir'd me so—till they appear.
Good friend, be royal.
Pir. There shall want no bravery.
Emil. Poor wench, go weep, for whosoever wins
Loses a noble cousin for thy sins. *Exeunt.*

123. **white-hair'd:** fair-haired.
124. **wanton white:** effeminately blond. 125. **aborn:** auburn.
128. **new conceiv'd:** newly pregnant. 130. **still:** when he is at rest.
136. **shows:** exhibits. 140. **charging-staff:** lance.
144–45. **They . . . titles:** they would be fitting combatants in a fight to determine the rightful ruler.
150. **the field:** management of the tournament.
152. **stay:** wait. 153. **Their fame:** the report of them.
154. **be royal:** do everything on a kingly scale. **bravery:** magnificence.

Scene III

Enter Jailer, Wooer, Doctor.

Doct. Her distraction is more at some time of the moon than at other some, is it not?

Jail. She is continually in a harmless distemper, sleeps little, altogether without appetite, save often drinking, dreaming of another world and a better; and what broken piece of matter soe'er she's about, the name Palamon lards it, that she farces ev'ry business withal, fits it to every question.

Enter Daughter.

Look where she comes, you shall perceive her behavior.

Daugh. I have forgot it quite; the burden on't was "Down-a, down-a," and penn'd by no worse man than Giraldo, Emilia's schoolmaster. He's as fantastical, too, as ever he may go upon 's legs, for in the next world will Dido see Palamon, and then will she be out of love with Aeneas.

Doct. What stuff's here? poor soul!

Jail. Ev'n thus all day long.

Daugh. Now for this charm that I told you of, you must bring a piece of silver on the tip of your tongue, or no ferry. Then, if it be your chance to come where the blessed spirits—as there's a sight now! We maids that have our livers perish'd, crack'd to pieces with love, we shall come there, and do nothing all day long but pick flowers with Proserpine. Then will I make Palamon a nosegay, then let him mark me—then—

Doct. How prettily she's amiss! Note her a little further.

Daugh. Faith, I'll tell you; sometime we go to barley-break, we of the blessed. Alas, 'tis a sore life they have i' th' tother place, such burning, frying, boiling, hissing, howling, chatt'ring, cursing! O, they have shrowd measure! take heed: if one be mad, or hang or drown themselves, thither they go—Jupiter bless us!—and there shall we be put in a cauldron of lead and usurers' grease, amongst a whole million of cutpurses, and there boil like a gammon of bacon that will never be enough. *Exit.*

Doct. How her brain coins!

[*Enter* Daughter.]

Daugh. Lords and courtiers that have got maids with child, they are in this place. They shall stand in fire up to the nav'l, and in ice up to th' heart, and there th' offending part burns, and the deceiving part freezes: in troth a very grievous punishment, as one would

IV.iii. Location: Athens. The prison.
7. **lards it:** is inserted into it (like strips of fat into lean meat—a term from cookery). **farces:** stuffs (another culinary term).
8. **withal:** with it. 11. **burden:** bass undersong.
13. **fantastical:** full of fancies.
21. **ferry:** i.e. Charon's ferry across the river Styx to the underworld.
23. **livers.** The liver was thought to be the seat of the passions.
31. **barley-break:** a game played by men and girls in couples. One couple, said to be "in hell," had to try to catch the others.
34. **shrowd:** shrewd, i.e. harsh (literally, cursed). **measure:** meting-out, i.e. punishment.
37. **usurers' grease:** fat sweated out by usurers.
39. **enough:** i.e. thoroughly cooked. 40. **coins:** invents.

think, for such a trifle. Believe me, one would marry a leprous witch to be rid on't, I'll assure you.

Doct. How she continues this fancy! 'Tis not an engraff'd madness, but a most thick and profound melancholy.

Daugh. To hear there a proud lady and a proud city-wife howl together! I were a beast and I'ld call it good sport. One cries, "O, this smoke!" [th'] other, "This fire!" One cries, "O, that ever I did it behind the arras!" and then howls; th' other curses a suing fellow and her garden-house. *Sings.*

"I will be true, my stars, my fate," etc.

Exit Daughter.

Jail. What think you of her, sir?

Doct. I think she has a perturb'd mind, which I cannot minister to.

Jail. Alas, what then?

Doct. Understand you she ever affected any man ere she beheld Palamon?

Jail. I was once, sir, in great hope she had fix'd her liking on this gentleman, my friend.

Wooer. I did think so too, and would account I had a great penn'worth on't to give half my state that both she and I at this present stood unfeignedly on the same terms.

Doct. That intemp'rate surfeit of her eye hath distemper'd the other senses. They may return and settle again to execute their preordain'd faculties, but they are now in a most extravagant vagary. This you must do: confine her to a place where the light may rather seem to steal in than be permitted. Take upon you, young sir her friend, the name of Palamon, say you come to eat with her, and to commune of love. This will catch her attention, for this her mind beats upon; other objects that are inserted 'tween her mind and eye become the pranks and friskins of her madness. Sing to her such green songs of love as she says Palamon hath sung in prison. Come to her, stuck in as sweet flowers as the season is mistress of, and thereto make an addition of some other compounded odors which are grateful to the sense. All this shall become Palamon, for Palamon can sing, and Palamon is sweet, and ev'ry good thing. Desire to eat with her, [carve] her, drink to her, and still among intermingle your petition of grace and acceptance into her favor. Learn what maids have been her companions and play-feres, and let them repair to her with Palamon in their mouths, and appear with tokens, as if they suggested for him. It is a falsehood she is in, which is with falsehoods to be combated. This may bring her to eat, to sleep, and reduce what's now out of square in her into their former law and regiment. I have seen it approv'd, how many times I know not, but to make the number more I have great hope in this. I will, between the passages of this project, come in with my appliance. Let us put it in execution; and hasten the success, which doubt not will bring forth comfort. *Exeunt.*

49. **engraff'd:** implanted, firmly established.
52. **were . . . and:** should be . . . if. 55. **arras:** wall-hanging.
56. **suing:** pleading. 62. **affected:** loved.
67. **great penn'worth:** splendid bargain. **state:** estate, possessions.
71. **distemper'd:** unbalanced, deranged.
73. **extravagant:** wandering beyond established bounds. **vagary:** wandering (overlapping the meaning of *extravagant*, which contains the same root).
74–75. **light . . . permitted.** Darkness was considered highly therapeutic for the insane.
80. **pranks and friskins:** freakish tricks and frolickings.
81. **green:** youthful (cf. "young lays of love," V.i.89).
82–83. **stuck in:** decked with.
84–85. **compounded odors:** mixed perfumes.
85. **grateful:** pleasing. 86. **become:** fit, be consistent with.
88. **carve her:** carve for her. **still among:** all the while.
91. **play-feres:** playmates. 92–93. **suggested:** pleaded love.
94. **bring:** induce.
95. **reduce:** bring back, restore. **square:** order, balance.
96. **regiment:** rule. 97. **approv'd:** demonstrated.
99. **passages:** events. **appliance:** treatment.
100. **success:** outcome.

ACT V, Scene I

[*Three altars erected—to Mars, Venus, and Diana.*]
Flourish. Enter Theseus, Pirithous, Hippolyta, Attendants.

The. Now let 'em enter, and before the gods
Tender their holy prayers. Let the temples
Burn bright with sacred fires, and the altars
In hallowed clouds commend their swelling incense
To those above us. Let no due be wanting;
They have a noble work in hand will honor
The very powers that love 'em.

Flourish of cornets. Enter Palamon *and* Arcite *and their* Knights.

Pir. Sir, they enter.

The. You valiant and strong-hearted enemies,
You royal germane foes, that this day come
To blow that nearness out that flames between ye,
Lay by your anger for an hour, and dove-like,
Before the holy altars of your helpers,
The all-fear'd gods, bow down your stubborn bodies.
Your ire is more than mortal; so your help be;
And as the gods regard ye, fight with justice.
I'll leave you to your prayers, and betwixt ye
I part my wishes.

Pir. Honor crown the worthiest!

Exeunt Theseus and his Train.

Pal. The glass is running now that cannot finish
Till one of us expire. Think you but thus,
That were there aught in me which strove to show
Mine enemy in this business, were't one eye
Against another, arm oppress'd by arm,
I would destroy th' offender, coz, I would,
Though parcel of myself. Then from this gather
How I should tender you.

Arc. I am in labor
To push your name, your ancient love, our kindred,
Out of my memory; and i' th' self-same place
To seat something I would confound. So hoist we

V.i. Location: Athens. An open place.
4. **commend:** commit. 9. **germane:** related by kinship.
10. **nearness:** close relationship.
15. **as . . . ye:** since you will fight under the eyes of the gods.
17. **part my wishes:** divide my good wishes.
20. **show:** show itself. 24. **parcel:** a part.
25. **tender:** treat. 26. **kindred:** kinship.
28. **something . . . confound:** i.e. the idea of you as an enemy whom I want to destroy.

The sails that must these vessels port even where
The heavenly limiter pleases.
Pal. You speak well.
Before I turn, let me embrace thee, cousin.
[*They embrace.*]
This I shall never do again.
Arc. One farewell.
Pal. Why, let it be so; farewell, coz.
Arc. Farewell, sir.
Exeunt Palamon and his Knights.
Knights, kinsmen, lovers, yea, my sacrifices,
True worshippers of Mars, whose spirit in you
Expels the seeds of fear, and th' apprehension
Which still is farther off it, go with me
Before the god of our profession. There
Require of him the hearts of lions and
The breath of tigers, yea, the fierceness too,
Yea, the speed also—to go on, I mean,
Else wish we to be snails. You know my prize
Must be dragg'd out of blood; force and great feat
Must put my garland on, where she sticks
The queen of flowers. Our intercession then
Must be to him that makes the camp a cestron
Brimm'd with the blood of men. Give me your aid
And bend your spirits towards him.
They [advance to the altar of Mars and fall on their faces; then] kneel.
Thou mighty one, that with thy power hast turn'd
Green Neptune into purple, [. . . .]
Comets prewarn, whose havoc in vast field
Unearthed skulls proclaim, whose breath blows down
The teeming Ceres' foison, who dost pluck
With hand armipotent from forth blue clouds
The mason'd turrets, that both mak'st and break'st
The stony girths of cities: me thy pupil,
Youngest follower of thy drum, instruct this day
With military skill, that to thy laud
I may advance my streamer, and by thee
Be styl'd the lord o' th' day. Give me, great Mars,
Some token of thy pleasure.
Here they fall on their faces as formerly, and there is heard clanging of armor, with a short thunder, as the burst of a battle, whereupon they all rise and bow to the altar.
O great corrector of enormous times,
Shaker of o'er-rank states, thou grand decider
Of dusty and old titles, that heal'st with blood
The earth when it is sick, and cur'st the world

29. port: carry (?) or bring to port (?).
30. limiter: i.e. ordainer of our ends. **34. lovers:** friends.
36. th' apprehension: i.e. even the idea of fear.
37. Which . . . it: "the idea of fear is farther from fear itself than its 'seeds' or first beginnings are" (Leech).
38. of our profession: whose worshippers we profess ourselves to be.
39. Require: ask. **41. go on:** advance.
42. Else: otherwise, i.e. in retreat. **46. cestron:** cistern.
50. There is an obvious gap in the sense here. Seward, followed by most later editors, inserted "whose approach" at the end of the line.
53. Ceres: goddess of agriculture. **foison:** plenty. **pluck:** pull down.
54. armipotent: strong in arms. **from . . . clouds:** i.e. from high in the sky.
56. girths: walls. **57. instruct:** inform, furnish.
59. advance my streamer: raise my banner. **60. styl'd:** named.
62. enormous: degenerate.
63. o'er-rank: grossly overgrown, swollen by excess.

O' th' plurisy of people! I do take
Thy signs auspiciously, and in thy name
To my design march boldly.—Let us go. *Exeunt.*

Enter Palamon *and his* Knights, *with the former observance.*

Pal. Our stars must glister with new fire, or be
To-day extinct. Our argument is love,
Which if the goddess of it grant, she gives
Victory too. Then blend your spirits with mine,
You whose free nobleness do make my cause
Your personal hazard. To the goddess Venus
Commend we our proceeding, and implore
Her power unto our party.
Here they [advance to the altar of Venus, and fall on their faces; then] kneel, as formerly.
Hail, sovereign queen of secrets, who hast power
To call the fiercest tyrant from his rage,
And weep unto a girl; that hast the might,
Even with an eye-glance, to choke Mars's drum
And turn th' alarm to whispers; that canst make
A cripple flourish with his crutch, and cure him
Before Apollo; that mayst force the king
To be his subject's vassal, and induce
Stale gravity to dance; the poll'd bachelor,
Whose youth, like wanton boys through bonfires,
Have skipp'd thy flame, at seventy thou canst catch,
And make him, to the scorn of his hoarse throat,
Abuse young lays of love. What godlike power
Hast thou not power upon? To Phoebus thou
Add'st flames, hotter than his; the heavenly fires
Did scorch his mortal son, thine him. The huntress
All moist and cold, some say, began to throw
Her bow away, and sigh. Take to thy grace
Me thy vow'd soldier, who do bear thy yoke
As 'twere a wreath of roses, yet is heavier
Than lead itself, stings more than nettles. I
Have never been foul-mouth'd against thy law,
Nev'r reveal'd secret, for I knew none—would not,
Had I kenn'd all that were. I never practiced
Upon man's wife, nor would the libels read
Of liberal wits. I never at great feasts
Sought to betray a beauty, but have blush'd
At simp'ring sirs that did. I have been harsh

66. plurisy: plethora, excess (a variant spelling of *pleurisy*, based on a supposed derivation from Latin *plus*, stem *plur-*, meaning "more" or "overmuch").
70. To-day. Modifies the whole sentence. **extinct:** extinguished.
73. free nobleness: noble generosity.
75. Commend: commit, entrust. **76. party:** side.
77. secrets. Secrecy was a cardinal virtue in the love code, as later lines in the speech indicate.
79. weep: make him weep. **unto a girl:** like a girl (?) or until he becomes as weak as a girl (?). **80. choke:** silence.
81. alarm: call to arms.
82. flourish with: brandish.
83. Before Apollo: i.e. sooner than the god of medicine himself.
85. poll'd: bald. **86. wanton:** frolicsome.
87. skipp'd: i.e. skipped over without being burned.
88. scorn: mockery (from those who hear him).
92. his mortal son: Phaëthon; see the note to I.ii.86. **huntress:** Diana, goddess of chastity. The allusion is to her love for the shepherd Endymion.
99. knew none: i.e. had never been in love.
100. kenn'd: known. **100–101. practiced Upon:** seduced.
101. libels: i.e. slanderous misrepresentations of love.
102. liberal: licentious.
103. betray: disclose the private affairs of.

To large confessors, and have hotly ask'd them
If they had mothers; I had one, a woman,
And women 'twere they wrong'd. I knew a man
Of eighty winters—this I told them—who
A lass of fourteen brided. 'Twas thy power
To put life into dust: the aged cramp
Had screw'd his square foot round,
The gout had knit his fingers into knots,
Torturing convulsions from his globy eyes
Had almost drawn their spheres, that what was life
In him seem'd torture. This anatomy
Had by his young fair fere a boy, and I
Believ'd it was his, for she swore it was,
And who would not believe her? Brief, I am
To those that prate and have done, no companion;
To those that boast and have not, a defier;
To those that would and cannot, a rejoicer.
Yea, him I do not love that tells close offices
The foulest way, nor names concealments in
The boldest language. Such a one I am,
And vow that lover never yet made sigh
Truer than I. O then, most soft sweet goddess,
Give me the victory of this question, which
Is true love's merit, and bless me with a sign
Of thy great pleasure.

Here music is heard; doves are seen to flutter. They fall again upon their faces, then on their knees.

O thou that from eleven to ninety reign'st
In mortal bosoms, whose chase is this world,
And we in herds thy game, I give thee thanks
For this fair token, which being laid unto
Mine innocent true heart, arms in assurance
My body to this business.—Let us rise
And bow before the goddess. Time comes on.

They bow. Exeunt.

Still music of records. Enter EMILIA *in white, her hair about her shoulders, [and wearing] a wheaten wreath; one in white holding up her train, her hair stuck with flowers; one before her carrying a silver hind, in which is convey'd incense and sweet odors, which being set upon the altar [of Diana], her maids standing aloof, she sets fire to it; then they curtsy and kneel.*

Emil. O sacred, shadowy, cold, and constant queen,
Abandoner of revels, mute, contemplative,
Sweet, solitary, white as chaste, and pure
As wind-fann'd snow, who to thy female knights
Allow'st no more blood than will make a blush,
Which is their order's robe: I here, thy priest,
Am humbled 'fore thine altar. O, vouchsafe,
With that thy rare green eye—which never yet
Beheld thing maculate—look on thy virgin,

105. **large confessors:** i.e. boasters of sexual conquests; *large* signifies both that they boast much and that their boasts are gross.
110. **aged:** incident to old age.
111. **square . . . round:** straight . . . askew. 114. **spheres:** sockets.
115. **anatomy:** skeleton. 116. **fere:** mate. 118. **Brief:** in brief.
122. **close offices:** secret affairs.
123. **nor names concealments:** nor him who tells things that should be concealed. 127. **question:** conflict.
129 s.d. **doves.** Sacred to Venus. 131. **chase:** hunting ground.
136 s.d. **Still . . . records:** soft music played on recorders.
145. **maculate:** spotted, unclean.

And, sacred silver mistress, lend thine ear
(Which nev'r heard scurril term, into whose port
Ne'er ent'red wanton sound) to my petition,
Season'd with holy fear. This is my last
Of vestal office; I am bride-habited,
But maiden-hearted. A husband I have 'pointed,
But do not know him. Out of two I should
Choose one, and pray for his success, but I
Am guiltless of election. Of mine eyes
Were I to lose one, they are equal precious,
I could doom neither; that which perish'd should
Go to't unsentenc'd. Therefore, most modest queen,
He of the two pretenders that best loves me
And has the truest title in't, let him
Take off my wheaten garland, or else grant
The file and quality I hold I may
Continue in thy band.

Here the hind vanishes under the altar, and in the place ascends a rose tree, having one rose upon it.

See what our general of ebbs and flows
Out from the bowels of her holy altar
With sacred act advances: but one rose!
If well inspir'd, this battle shall confound
Both these brave knights, and I, a virgin flow'r,
Must grow alone, unpluck'd.

Here is heard a sudden twang of instruments, and the rose falls from the tree, [which vanishes under the altar].

The flow'r is fall'n, the tree descends. O mistress,
Thou here dischargest me. I shall be gather'd,
I think so, but I know not thine own will:
Unclasp thy mystery.—I hope she's pleas'd,
Her signs were gracious. *They curtsy and exeunt.*

SCENE II

Enter DOCTOR, JAILER, *and* WOOER *in habit of Palamon.*

Doct. Has this advice I told you done any good upon her?
Wooer. O, very much; the maids that kept her company
Have half persuaded her that I am Palamon.
Within this half hour she came smiling to me,
And ask'd me what I would eat, and when I would kiss her.
I told her, presently, and kiss'd her twice.
Doct. 'Twas well done. Twenty times had been far better,
For there the cure lies mainly.
Wooer. Then she told me
She would watch with me to-night, for well she knew
What hour my fit would take me.

147. **port:** portal. 148. **wanton:** lewd.
150. **bride-habited:** dressed as a bride.
151. **'pointed:** appointed, destined for me.
154. **election:** choice. 158. **pretenders:** claimants.
161. **file and quality:** rank and condition.
163. **general . . . flows.** Diana, as moon-goddess, governed the tides.
166. **If well inspir'd:** if this sign is from the goddess (?) or if I interpret correctly (?). **confound:** destroy.

V.ii. Location: Athens. The prison.
6. **presently:** immediately. 9. **watch:** sit up.

Doct. Let her do so,
And when your fit comes, fit her home, and presently.
Wooer. She would have me sing.
Doct. You did so?
Wooer. No.
Doct. 'Twas very ill done then.
You should observe her ev'ry way.
Wooer. Alas,
I have no voice, sir, to confirm her that way.
Doct. That's all one, if ye make a noise.
If she entreat again, do any thing,
Lie with her, if she ask you.
Jail. Ho there, doctor!
Doct. Yes, in the way of cure.
Jail. But first, by your leave,
I' th' way of honesty.
Doct. That's but a niceness.
Nev'r cast your child away for honesty.
Cure her first this way; then if she will be honest,
She has the path before her.
Jail. Thank ye, doctor.
Doct. Pray bring her in
And let's see how she is.
Jail. I will, and tell her
Her Palamon stays for her; but, doctor,
Methinks you are i' th' wrong still. *Exit Jailer.*
Doct. Go, go!
You fathers are fine fools. Her honesty!
And we should give her physic till we find that—
Wooer. Why, do you think she is not honest, sir?
Doct. How old is she?
Wooer. She's eighteen.
Doct. She may be,
But that's all one, 'tis nothing to our purpose.
What e'er her father says, if you perceive
Her mood inclining that way that I spoke of,
Videlicet, the way of flesh—you have me?
Wooer. Yet very well, sir.
Doct. Please her appetite,
And do it home; it cures her *ipso facto*
The melancholy humor that infects her.
Wooer. I am of your mind, doctor.

Enter JAILER, DAUGHTER, MAID.

Doct. You'll find it so. She comes. Pray [humor] her. [*Wooer retires.*]
Jail. Come, your love Palamon stays for you, child,
And has done this long hour, to visit you.
Daugh. I thank him for his gentle patience,
He's a kind gentleman, and I am much bound to him.
Did you nev'r see the horse he gave me?
Jail. Yes.
Daugh. How do you like him?
Jail. He's a very fair one.
Daugh. You never saw him dance?
Jail. No.
Daugh. I have often.
He dances very finely, very comely,
And for a jig, come cut and long tail to him,
He turns ye like a top.
Jail. That's fine indeed.
Daugh. He'll dance the morris twenty mile an hour,
And that will founder the best hobby-horse
(If I have any skill) in all the parish,
And gallops to the [tune] of "Light a' love."
What think you of this horse?
Jail. Having these virtues,
I think he might be brought to play at tennis.
Daugh. Alas, that's nothing.
Jail. Can he write and read too?
Daugh. A very fair hand, and casts himself th' accounts
Of all his hay and provender. That hostler
Must rise betime that cozens him. You know
The chestnut mare the Duke has?
Jail. Very well.
Daugh. She is horribly in love with him, poor beast,
But he is like his master, coy and scornful.
Jail. What dowry has she?
Daugh. Some two hundred bottles,
And twenty strike of oats, but he'll ne'er have her.
He lisps in 's neighing able to entice
A miller's mare, he'll be the death of her.
Doct. What stuff she utters!
Jail. Make curtsy, here your love comes.
[*Wooer comes forward.*]
Wooer. Pretty soul,
How do ye? That's a fine maid! There's a curtsy!
Daugh. Yours to command i' th' way of honesty.
How far is't now to th' end o' th' world, my masters?
Doct. Why, a day's journey, wench.
Daugh. Will you go with me?
Wooer. What shall we do there, wench?
Daugh. Why, play at stoolball:
What is there else to do?
Wooer. I am content,
If we shall keep our wedding there.
Daugh. 'Tis true,
For there, I will assure you, we shall find
Some blind priest for the purpose that will venture
To marry us, for here they are nice and foolish.
Besides, my father must be hang'd to-morrow,
And that would be a blot i' th' business.
Are not you Palamon?
Wooer. Do not you know me?

11. fit her home: give her complete service.
14. observe: obey, humor.
16. That's all one: that makes no difference.
20. honesty: chastity. **niceness:** fastidious scruple.
23. the path: i.e. the option of marriage. **29. And:** if.
35. Videlicet: namely. **have:** understand.
37. ipso facto: by the very act.

49. come . . . him: i.e. no matter what horse he is compared with (*cut* = a horse with a docked tail; hence *cut and long tail* = all horses).
52. founder: lame. **hobby-horse:** one of the morris-dancers who was costumed to represent a horse and who imitated a horse's movements. **53. have any skill:** know anything.
54. "Light a' love": a well-known song, referred to in *Much Ado about Nothing*, III.iv.44, and *The Two Gentlemen of Verona*, I.ii.80.
60. rise betime: get up very early. **cozens:** cheats (by padding the accounts). **63. coy:** standoffish. **64. bottles:** bales of hay.
65. strike: measures (usually bushels).
67. miller's mare: i.e. a dull stolid beast plodding in a circle to turn the mill-wheel.
74. stoolball: a not very strenuous ball game, hence suitable for men and women to play together. **79. nice:** too particular.

Daugh. Yes, but you care not for me. I have nothing
But this poor petticoat and two coarse smocks.
Wooer. That's all one, I will have you.
Daugh. Will you surely?
Wooer. Yes, by this fair hand, will I.
Daugh. We'll to bed then.
Wooer. Ev'n when you will. [*Kisses her.*]
Daugh. O, sir, you would fain be nibbling.
Wooer. Why do you rub my kiss off?
Daugh. 'Tis a sweet one,
And will perfume me finely against the wedding.
Is not this your cousin Arcite?
Doct. Yes, sweet heart,
And I am glad my cousin Palamon
Has made so fair a choice.
Daugh. Do you think he'll have me?
Doct. Yes, without doubt.
Daugh. Do you think so too?
Jail. Yes.
Daugh. We shall have many children.—Lord, how y' are grown!
My Palamon I hope will grow too, finely,
Now he's at liberty. Alas, poor chicken,
He was kept down with hard meat and ill lodging,
But I'll kiss him up again.

Enter a MESSENGER.

Mess. What do you here? You'll lose the noblest sight
That ev'r was seen.
Jail. Are they i' th' field?
Mess. They are.
You bear a charge there too.
Jail. I'll away straight.
I must ev'n leave you here.
Doct. Nay, we'll go with you,
I will not lose the fight.
Jail. How did you like her?
Doct. I'll warrant you within these three or four days
I'll make her right again. [*To the Wooer.*] You must not from her,
But still preserve her in this way.
Wooer. I will.
Doct. Let's get her in.
Wooer. Come, sweet, we'll go to dinner,
And then we'll play at cards.
Daugh. And shall we kiss too?
Wooer. A hundred times.
Daugh. And twenty?
Wooer. Ay, and twenty.
Daugh. And then we'll sleep together?
Doct. Take her offer.
Wooer. Yes, marry, will we.
Daugh. But you shall not hurt me.
Wooer. I will not, sweet.
Daugh. If you do, love, I'll cry. *Exeunt.*

84. smocks: undergarments. **89. against:** in preparation for.
97. hard meat: coarse food. **101. bear a charge:** have duties.
103. How . . . her: what did you think of her condition.

SCENE III

Flourish. Enter THESEUS, HIPPOLYTA, EMILIA, PIRITHOUS, *and some* ATTENDANTS.

Emil. I'll no step further.
Pir. Will you lose this sight?
Emil. I had rather see a wren hawk at a fly
Than this decision. Ev'ry blow that falls
Threats a brave life, each stroke laments
The place whereon it falls, and sounds more like
A bell than blade. I will stay here,
It is enough my hearing shall be punish'd
With what shall happen—'gainst the which there is
No deafing—but to hear, not taint mine eye
With dread sights it may shun.
Pir. Sir, my good lord,
Your sister will no further.
The. O, she must.
She shall see deeds of honor in their kind
Which sometime show well, pencill'd. Nature now
Shall make and act the story, the belief
Both seal'd with eye and ear. You must be present,
You are the victor's meed, the price and garland
To crown the question's title.
Emil. Pardon me,
If I were there, I'ld wink.
The. You must be there;
This trial is as 'twere i' th' night, and you
The only star to shine.
Emil. I am extinct,
There is but envy in that light which shows
The one the other. Darkness, which ever was
The dam of Horror, who does stand accurs'd
Of many mortal millions, may even now,
By casting her black mantle over both,
That neither could find other, get herself
Some part of a good name, and many a murther
Set off whereto she's guilty.
Hip. You must go.
Emil. In faith, I will not.
The. Why, the knights must kindle
Their valor at your eye. Know, of this war
You are the treasure, and must needs be by
To give the service pay.
Emil. Sir, pardon me,
The title of a kingdom may be tried
Out of itself.
The. Well, well then, at your pleasure.
Those that remain with you could wish their office
To any of their enemies.
Hip. Farewell, sister,
I am like to know your husband 'fore yourself
By some small start of time. He whom the gods
Do of the two know best, I pray them he

V.iii. Location: The forest; near the place of combat.
6. bell: passing-bell. **12. kind:** true nature, actuality.
13. show well, pencill'd: i.e. are impressive even in an artist's rendering.
15. seal'd with: certified by. **16. price:** prize.
17. question's title: right which is in dispute.
18. wink: keep my eyes shut. **20. star . . . extinct.** Cf. V.i.69–70.
21. envy: malice. **23. dam:** mother.
28. Set off: offset, compensate for.
34. Out of itself: outside the kingdom. **39. know:** know to be.

Be made your lot.
Exeunt Theseus, Hippolyta, Pirithous, etc.
Emil. Arcite is gently visag'd; yet his eye
Is like an engine bent, or a sharp weapon
In a soft sheath; mercy and manly courage
Are bedfellows in his visage. Palamon
Has a most menacing aspect, his brow
Is grav'd, and seems to bury what it frowns on,
Yet sometime 'tis not so, but alters to
The quality of his thoughts; long time his eye
Will dwell upon his object; melancholy
Becomes him nobly. So does Arcite's mirth,
But Palamon's sadness is a kind of mirth,
So mingled as if mirth did make him sad,
And sadness merry; those darker humors that
Stick misbecomingly on others, on [him]
Live in fair dwelling.
Cornets. Trumpets sound as to a charge.
Hark how yon spurs to spirit do incite
The princes to their proof! Arcite may win me,
And yet may Palamon wound Arcite to
The spoiling of his figure. O, what pity
Enough for such a chance? If I were by,
I might do hurt, for they would glance their eyes
Toward my seat, and in that motion might
Omit a ward, or forfeit an offense,
Which crav'd that very time. It is much better
I am not there. O, better never born
Than minister to such harm!
Cornets. A great cry and noise within, crying "A Palamon!"

Enter SERVANT.

What is the chance?
Serv. The cry's "A Palamon!"
Emil. Then he has won. 'Twas ever likely:
He look'd all grace and success, and he is
Doubtless the prim'st of men. I prithee run
And tell me how it goes.
Shout and cornets. Crying "A Palamon!" [*within*].
Serv. Still "Palamon!"
Emil. Run and inquire. [*Exit Servant.*]
Poor servant, thou hast lost.
Upon my right side still I wore thy picture,
Palamon's on the left. Why so, I know not;
I had no end in't else; chance would have it so.
On the sinister side the heart lies; Palamon
Had the best-boding chance.
Another cry, and shout within, and cornets.
This burst of clamor
Is sure th' end o' th' combat.

Enter SERVANT.

Serv. They said that Palamon had Arcite's body
Within an inch o' th' pyramid, that the cry

42. **engine bent:** instrument of war ready for action (as a bow is bent). 46. **grav'd:** engraved, furrowed; with play on the sense "containing graves." 47. **to:** in accordance with. 49. **his:** its.
55 s.d. **Cornets. Trumpets.** See note to III.i.96 s.d.
59. **spoiling . . . figure:** permanent crippling of his body.
63. **ward:** defensive position. **forfeit an offense:** lose a chance to attack. 72. **servant:** lover, i.e. Arcite. 75. **end:** purpose.
76. **sinister:** left. 77. **best-boding:** most auspicious.

Was general "A Palamon!"; but anon
Th' assistants made a brave redemption, and
The two bold titlers at this instant are
Hand to hand at it.
Emil. Were they metamorphis'd
Both into one—O why? there were no woman
Worth so compos'd a man! Their single share,
Their nobleness peculiar to them, gives
The prejudice of disparity, value's shortness,
To any lady breathing.
Cornets. Cry within, "Arcite, Arcite!"
More exulting?
"Palamon" still?
Serv. Nay, now the sound is "Arcite."
Emil. I prithee lay attention to the cry;
Set both thine ears to th' business.
Cornets. A great shout and cry, "Arcite! victory!"
Serv. The cry is
"Arcite!" and "victory!" Hark, "Arcite! victory!"
The combat's consummation is proclaim'd
By the wind instruments.
Emil. Half-sights saw
That Arcite was no babe. God's lid, his richness
And costliness of spirit look'd through him, it could
No more be hid in him than fire in flax,
Than humble banks can go to law with waters
That drift-winds force to raging. I did think
Good Palamon would miscarry, yet I knew not
Why I did think so. Our reasons are not prophets
When oft our fancies are. They are coming off.
Alas, poor Palamon! *Cornets.*

Enter THESEUS, HIPPOLYTA, PIRITHOUS, ARCITE *as victor, and* ATTENDANTS, *etc.*

The. Lo, where our sister is in expectation,
Yet quaking and unsettled. Fairest Emily,
The gods by their divine arbitrement
Have given you this knight: he is a good one
As ever strook at head. Give me your hands.
Receive you her, you him, be plighted with
A love that grows as you decay.
Arc. Emily,
To buy you I have lost what's dearest to me
Save what is bought, and yet I purchase cheaply,
As I do rate your value.
The. O loved sister,
He speaks now of as brave a knight as e'er
Did spur a noble steed. Surely the gods
Would have him die a bachelor, lest his race
Should show i' th' world too godlike. His behavior
So charm'd me that methought Alcides was
To him a sow of lead. If I could praise
Each part of him to th' all I have spoke, your Arcite

82. **redemption:** rescue. 83. **titlers:** contestants for the title.
84. **Were they metamorphis'd:** if only they were metamorphosed.
86–89. **Their . . . breathing:** i.e. the nobleness of either taken singly outweighs the value of any lady alive.
95. **Half-sights:** mere glances.
96. **God's lid.** A common oath ("by God's [Christ's] eyelid").
99. **go to law:** i.e. contest. 100. **drift:** driving.
119. **Alcides:** Hercules.
120. **To:** in comparison with. **sow:** heavy mass.
121. **to . . . spoke:** to the same extent that I have praised him in general.

Did not lose by't; for he that was thus good
Encount'red yet his better. I have heard
Two emulous Philomels beat the ear o' th' night
With their contentious throats, now one the higher,
Anon the other, then again the first,
And by and by out-breasted, that the sense
Could not be judge between 'em. So it far'd
Good space between these kinsmen; till heavens did
Make hardly one the winner.—Wear the girlond
With joy that you have won.—For the subdu'd,
Give them our present justice, since I know
Their lives but pinch 'em. Let it here be done.
The scene's not for our seeing, go we hence,
Right joyful, with some sorrow.—Arm your prize,
I know you will not loose her.—Hippolyta,
I see one eye of yours conceives a tear,
The which it will deliver.

Emil. Is this winning?
O all you heavenly powers, where is [your] mercy?
But that your wills have said it must be so,
And charge me live to comfort this unfriended,
This miserable prince, that cuts away
A life more worthy from him than all women,
I should and would die too.

Hip. Infinite pity
That four such eyes should be so fix'd on one
That two must needs be blind for't!

The. So it is. *Flourish. Exeunt.*

Scene IV

[*A block ready.*] *Enter* Palamon *and his* Knights *pinion'd*, Jailer, Executioner, *etc.*, Guard.

[*Pal.*] There's many a man alive that hath outliv'd
The love o' th' people, yea, i' th' self-same state
Stands many a father with his child. Some comfort
We have by so considering: we expire,
And not without men's pity; to live still,
Have their good wishes; we prevent
The loathsome misery of age, beguile
The gout and rheum, that in lag hours attend
For grey approachers; we come towards the gods
Young and unwapper'd, not halting under crimes
Many and stale. That sure shall please the gods
Sooner than such, to give us nectar with 'em,
For we are more clear spirits. My dear kinsmen,
Whose lives (for this poor comfort) are laid down,
You have sold 'em too too cheap.

1. Knight. What ending could be
Of more content? O'er us the victors have

Fortune, whose title is as momentary
As to us death is certain. A grain of honor
They not o'erweigh us.

2. Knight. Let us bid farewell;
And with our patience anger tott'ring Fortune,
Who at her certain'st reels.

3. Knight. Come! Who begins?

Pal. Ev'n he that led you to this banket shall
Taste to you all. [*To the Jailer.*] Ah ha, my friend, my friend,
Your gentle daughter gave me freedom once;
You'll see't done now for ever. Pray how does she?
I heard she was not well; her kind of ill
Gave me some sorrow.

Jail. Sir, she's well restor'd,
And to be married shortly.

Pal. By my short life,
I am most glad on't. 'Tis the latest thing
I shall be glad of, prithee tell her so.
Commend me to her, and to piece her portion
Tender her this. [*Gives purse.*]

1. Knight. Nay, let's be offerers all.

2. Knight. Is it a maid?

Pal. Verily I think so,
A right good creature, more to me deserving
Than I can quite or speak of.

All Knights. Commend us to her.
They give their purses.

Jail. The gods requite you all, and make her thankful!

Pal. Adieu; and let my life be now as short
As my leave-taking. *Lies on the block.*

[*3.*] *Knight.* Lead, courageous cousin.

1., 2. Knights. We'll follow cheerfully.

A great noise within crying "Run! Save! Hold!"

Enter in haste a Messenger.

Mess. Hold, hold! O, hold, hold, hold!

Enter Pirithous *in haste.*

Pir. Hold ho! It is a cursed haste you made
If you have done so quickly. Noble Palamon,
The gods will show their glory in a life
That thou art yet to lead.

Pal. Can that be, when
Venus I have said is false? How do things fare?

Pir. Arise, great sir, and give the tidings ear
[*Palamon rises.*]
That are most [dearly] sweet and bitter.

Pal. What
Hath wak'd us from our dream?

Pir. List then: your cousin,
Mounted upon a steed that Emily
Did first bestow on him—a black one, owing
Not a hair-worth of white, which some will say
Weakens his price, and many will not buy

122. Did: would. **124. Philomels:** nightingales.
127. out-breasted: outsung.
129. Good space: for a considerable time.
130. hardly: barely, by a very slight margin. **girlond:** garland.
132. present: immediate. **133. pinch:** are painful to.
135. Arm: embrace. **136. loose.** See the note to IV.i.91.

V.iv. Location: The same.
5–6. to . . . wishes: we have their good wishes that we might go on living. **6. prevent:** forestall. **7. beguile:** cheat.
8. rheum: catarrh. **lag:** last, laggard. **attend:** wait, watch.
9. grey approachers: old men who come their way.
10. unwapper'd: unworn, undebilitated. **halting:** moving laboriously. **crimes:** sins.

20–21. tott'ring . . . reels. Alluding to the instability of Fortune (cf. "Voluble chance" at I.ii.67).
23. Taste . . . all: act as taster for you all, i.e. be first to die.
25. see't done: see freedom given to me. **29. latest:** last.
31. piece her portion: augment her dowry. **35. quite:** requite.
47. dearly: intensely. **50. owing:** owning.

His goodness with this note; which superstition
Here finds allowance—on this horse is Arcite
Trotting the stones of Athens, which the calkins
Did rather tell than trample; for the horse
Would make his length a mile, if't pleas'd his rider
To put pride in him. As he thus went counting
The flinty pavement, dancing as 'twere to th' music
His own hoofs made (for as they say from iron
Came music's origin), what envious flint,
Cold as old Saturn, and like him possess'd
With fire malevolent, darted a spark,
Or what fierce sulphur else, to this end made,
I comment not—the hot horse, hot as fire,
Took toy at this, and fell to what disorder
His power could give his will, bounds, comes on end,
Forgets school-doing, being therein train'd,
And of kind manage; pig-like he whines
At the sharp rowel, which he frets at rather
Than any jot obeys; seeks all foul means
Of boist'rous and rough jad'ry, to disseat
His lord that kept it bravely. When nought serv'd,
When neither curb would crack, girth break, nor diff'ring plunges
Disroot his rider whence he grew, but that
He kept him 'tween his legs, on his hind hoofs
[. . . .] on end he stands,
That Arcite's legs, being higher than his head,
Seem'd with strange art to hang. His victor's wreath
Even then fell off his head; and presently
Backward the jade comes o'er, and his full poise
Becomes the rider's load. Yet is he living,
But such a vessel 'tis that floats but for
The surge that next approaches. He much desires
To have some speech with you. Lo he appears.

Enter Theseus, Hippolyta, Emilia, Arcite *in a chair.*

Pal. O miserable end of our alliance!
The gods are mighty, Arcite. If thy heart,
Thy worthy, manly heart, be yet unbroken,
Give me thy last words; I am Palamon,
One that yet loves thee dying.

Arc. Take Emilia,
And with her all the world's joy. Reach thy hand;
Farewell. I have told my last hour; I was false,
Yet never treacherous. Forgive me, cousin.
One kiss from fair Emilia.—'Tis done.
Take her. I die. [*Dies.*]

Pal. Thy brave soul seek Elysium!

Emil. I'll close thine eyes, prince; blessed souls be with thee!
Thou art a right good man, and while I live,
This day I give to tears.

53. note: distinctive feature. **54. allowance:** credence, support.
55. calkins: part of the horseshoe that is turned down.
56. tell: count, i.e. touch lightly.
57. make . . . mile: make his paces a mile long.
65. comment: speculate on.
66. toy at: capricious or unaccountable aversion to.
69. manage: manege, training. **70. rowel:** spur.
72. jad'ry: behavior of a jade, an inferior horse.
73. it: i.e. his seat. **bravely:** in fine style.
77. On this line see the Textual Notes. **81. poise:** weight.
83–84. floats . . . approaches: is still afloat but will sink under the next wave. **92. false:** i.e. to friendship; see lines 116–18.
98. This day: i.e. the anniversary of this day.

Pal. And I to honor.

The. In this place first you fought; ev'n very here
I sund'red you. Acknowledge to the gods
Our thanks that you are living.
His part is play'd, and though it were too short,
He did it well; your day is length'ned, and
The blissful dew of heaven does arrouse you.
The powerful Venus well hath grac'd her altar,
And given you your love. Our master Mars
[Hath] vouch'd his oracle, and to Arcite gave
The grace of the contention. So the deities
Have show'd due justice.—Bear this hence.
[*Arcite is carried out.*]

Pal. O cousin,
That we should things desire which do cost us
The loss of our desire! that nought could buy
Dear love but loss of dear love!

The. Never fortune
Did play a subtler game. The conquer'd triumphs,
The victor has the loss; yet in the passage
The gods have been most equal. Palamon,
Your kinsman hath confess'd the right o' th' lady
Did lie in you, for you first saw her, and
Even then proclaim'd your fancy. He restor'd her
As your stol'n jewel, and desir'd your spirit
To send him hence forgiven. The gods my justice
Take from my hand, and they themselves become
The executioners. Lead your lady off;
And call your lovers from the stage of death,
Whom I adopt my friends. A day or two
Let us look sadly, and give grace unto
The funeral of Arcite, in whose end
The visages of bridegrooms we'll put on
And smile with Palamon; for whom an hour,
But one hour since, I was as dearly sorry
As glad of Arcite; and am now as glad
As for him sorry. O you heavenly charmers,
What things you make of us! For what we lack
We laugh, for what we have are sorry, still
Are children in some kind. Let us be thankful
For that which is, and with you leave dispute
That are above our question. Let's go off,
And bear us like the time. *Flourish. Exeunt.*

EPILOGUE

I would now ask ye how ye like the play,
But as it is with schoolboys, cannot say;
I am cruel fearful. Pray yet stay a while,

104. arrouse: sprinkle, fall gently upon.
107. vouch'd: made good. **114. passage:** proceeding.
115. equal: just.
120–21. my . . . hand: take from me my judicial function.
122. The executioners: those who execute justice.
123. lovers: friends, companion knights. **stage of death:** scaffold.
126. in whose end: at the end of which.
131. charmers: casters of spells.
133. laugh: i.e. are happy in anticipation.
135. with . . . dispute: cease to dispute with you.
137. bear . . . time: comport ourselves as the occasion demands (sadly for the funeral, then happily for the wedding).

Epi. 2. say: speak.
3. cruel fearful: dreadfully anxious. **stay a while:** i.e. wait a bit before you applaud or hiss.

And let me look upon ye. No man smile?
Then it goes hard, I see. He that has
Lov'd a young handsome wench then, show his face—
'Tis strange if none be here—and if he will
Against his conscience, let him hiss, and kill
Our market. 'Tis in vain, I see, to stay ye;
Have at the worst can come, then! Now what say ye?
And yet mistake me not: I am not bold,
We have no such cause. If the tale we have told
(For 'tis no other) any way content ye
(For to that honest purpose it was meant ye),
We have our end; and ye shall have ere long
I dare say many a better, to prolong
Your old loves to us. We, and all our might,
Rest at your service. Gentlemen, good night.
Flourish.

8. Against his conscience: hypocritically.
10. Have . . . worst: let come the worst that.
17. all our might: all we can do.

NOTE ON THE TEXT

The only authority for *The Two Noble Kinsmen* is the quarto published in 1634 (Q), printed by Thomas Cotes for John Waterson, and set by two compositors (see Waller, Werstine, Bowers), in which the play is ascribed to "the memorable Worthies of their time; Mr. John Fletcher, and Mr. William Shakespeare. Gent. [=Gentlemen]." All later editions are derived from that source. The play was included, printed essentially without change from Q, in the Second Folio (here F) of Beaumont and Fletcher's works in 1679. The problems raised by dual authorship (i.e., what parts of the play may most probably be assigned to Shakespeare or Fletcher, a few parts [e.g., II.i, IV.iii] being of uncertain or possibly mixed authorship) are discussed in the Introduction.

Scholars have become increasingly unwilling to commit themselves concerning the provenience of the manuscript copy underlying the Q text. Several views have been advanced. F. O. Waller argues for the use of some form of the "foul papers" which had earlier been annotated by the company's book-keeper, Edward Knight, for a revival of the play in 1625–26. In Waller's opinion, the text of Q shows too many of the stigmata associated with "foul papers" (confusions in the text and stage directions, some permissive stage directions, inconsistencies in speech-prefixes, etc.) to have been derived from an actual prompt-book. He suggests that the copy-text was either an intermediate transcript of Fletcher's and Shakespeare's "foul papers" or a composite copy prepared by combining a transcript of Fletcher's "foul papers" with Shakespeare's original "foul papers." The reason for proposing a transcript as copy for at least the scenes usually ascribed to Fletcher is the relatively small number of Fletcher's characteristic *ye*-forms as compared with *you*-forms in those scenes. That Shakespeare's "foul papers" were used directly is suggested (a) by textual difficulties and confusions in those scenes usually ascribed to Shakespeare and (b) by the occurrence in those scenes of certain spellings which may perhaps be considered characteristically Shakespearean: *angle* (for *angel*), I.i.16; *cizd* (for *siz'd*), I.i.99; *boudge* (for *budge*), I.i.223; *Cizard* (for *scissor'd*), I.ii.54; *on* (for *one*), I.ii.70, I.iii.75; *a eleven* (a compositorial confusion of the Shakespearean *a leven*), I.iii.54; *ceaze* (for *seize*), I.v.12; *Wrinching* (for *rinsing*), I.i.156 (cf. *wrenching* in *Henry VIII*, I.i.167, a Shakespearean scene). Proudfoot points out that in Act I (usually assigned to Shakespeare) the name *Pirithous* is trisyllabic, but that elsewhere (in parts assigned to Fletcher) it is accorded a quadrisyllabic accentuation. Shakespeare, he also notes, strongly favored the spelling *Pirithous,* Fletcher, *Perithous*.

Q contains an exceptional number of prompt notes (by Edward Knight; Montgomery/Taylor argue for an earlier layer of theatrical annotation, but see below). These are usually printed in the margins of the text in Q; see Textual Notes, I.iii.58–64, I.iv.26, II.v o.s.d., III.i o.s.d., III.v.64–5, III.vi.93 (perhaps authorial). Two actors of small roles are also named: *Curtis.* (probably Curtis Greville) at IV.ii.70 s.d. and V.iii o.s.d. and *T. Tucke:* (Thomas Tuckfield) at V.iii o.s.d.

Montgomery/Taylor question the use of any transcript and accept Waller's belief that Shakespeare's "foul papers" underlie his parts of the Q text. Moreover, they question the necessity of proposing the use of a transcript of Fletcher's "foul papers," instead of the "foul papers" themselves, arguing that the comparatively small number of *ye* as opposed to *you* forms in Fletcher's sections of the text may most probably be laid to a house policy followed by Cotes' compositors. They also argue that both sets of "foul papers" had earlier (c. 1613) been annotated by the company's book-keeper preparatory to the transcription of the official prompt-book and that these same "foul papers," the original prompt-book being lost or otherwise unavailable, were later further annotated by Edward Knight for a 1625–6 revival. Bowers, however, who finds no evidence for a pre-Knight annotation, believes that "the evidence as a whole is definitely against annotated foul papers as printer's copy and for a transcript of some sort from these papers, whether or not a full-fledged prompt-book" (a statement essentially endorsed by Waith).

Some slight revision may be signalled by (1) the repeated entry for Emilia at IV.ii.54, following her long opening soliloquy, which may suggest either that the soliloquy was a Fletcherian afterthought or that the soliloquy, which, as Montgomery/Taylor note, clashes with the later characterization of Emilia in another soliloquy (by Shakespeare) in V.iii.41–66, had been marked for omission, a marking overlooked by the compositor; and (2) Q's lack of a stage direction for the re-entry of the Jailor's daughter following her exit at IV.iii.39 (she reappears almost immediately after line 40), again suggests that the daughter's speech (41–7) on court immorality may have been another Fletcherian afterthought. See a detailed discussion of these points by Montgomery/Taylor and Bowers.

Since F, although it makes a number of fairly obvious corrections, is basically a reprint of Q, its substantial agreement with Q may be assumed where it is not otherwise cited in the Textual Notes.

For further information, see: for Littledale, Rolfe, Sympson, Theobald, Tonson, Weber, see Abbreviations; W. W. Greg, *The Editorial Problem in Shakespeare* (Oxford, rev. ed., 1951) and *The Shakespeare First Folio* (Oxford, 1955); F. O. Waller, "Printer's Copy for *The Two Noble Kinsmen,*"

SB, XI (1958), 61–84; Paul Bertram, *Shakespeare and "The Two Noble Kinsmen"* (New Brunswick, 1965); Clifford Leech, ed., *The Two Noble Kinsmen* (New York, 1966); G. R. Proudfoot, ed., *The Two Noble Kinsmen* (Lincoln, Nebr., 1970); N. W. Bawcutt, New Penguin *Two Noble Kinsmen* (Harmondsworth, Middlesex, 1977); Stanley Wells, Gary Taylor, William Montgomery, and John Jowett, *William Shakespeare: A Textual Companion* (Oxford, 1987); F. T. Bowers, ed., *The Two Noble Kinsmen in The Dramatic Works in the Beaumont and Fletcher Canon*, VII (Cambridge, 1989); E. M. Waith, ed., New Oxford *The Two Noble Kinsmen* (Oxford, 1989); Paul Werstine, "On the Compositors of *The Two Noble Kinsmen*," in *Shakespeare, Fletcher and "The Two Noble Kinsmen*," ed., C. H. Frey (Columbia, Mo., 1989).

TEXTUAL NOTES

Dramatis personae: *subs. as first given in F, with some expansion by later eds.*
Act-scene division: *from Q, with the numbering adjusted at I.i (Q marks act only), II.v (Q repeats in error the numbering II.iv), III.v-vi (misnumbered III.vi-vii in Q); see first note to each of these scenes*

Prologue

1 akin] *F;* a kin *Q*
2 gi'n] *F;* g'yn *Q*
23 him,] *Littledale;* him; *Q*
26 tack] *F;* take *Q*
29 travail] *Dyce;* travell *Q*

I.i

I.i] *F;* Actus Primus. *Q*
Location: *Weber*
o.s.d. Pirithous] *Theobald;* Theseus *Q*
o.s.d. Artesius and Attendants] *Weber*
o.s.d. Music.] *placed as in Kittredge; after heading* The Song *in Q*
o.s.d. by the Boy] *Dyce*
7 Primrose, first-born] *Tonson (hyphen, Seward);* Prim-rose first borne, *Q*
13–4 children sweet, Lie] *F;* children: sweete- / Ly *Q*
16 angel] *F;* angle *Q*
20 chough hoar] *Seward;* Clough hee *Q*
25 pity's . . . gentility's] *Seward;* pitties . . gentilities *Q*
42 Thebes] *Colman;* Thebs *Q (throughout)*
59 lord.] *Colman;* Lord *Q*
62 Mars's] *F;* Marsis *Q*
62 altar.] *F (subs.);* Altar, *Q*
63 mantle] *Tonson;* Mantle *Q in (italics)*
68 Nemean] *Theobald;* Nenuan *Q*
75 helmeted Bellona] *Tonson;* Helmeted-Belona *Q*
79 scythe-tusk'd boar] *Tonson (scythe Colman);* Sith-tuskd-Bore *Q*
83 styl'd] *Knight (after Weber);* stilde *Q;* 'stilled *Leech*
90 thy] *Seward;* the *Q*
99 blood-siz'd] *Seward (hyphen, F);* blood cizd *Q*
104 willing] *Seward;* willing, *Q*
105 Heart-deep] *hyphen, Seward*
112 glassy] *Theobald;* glasse *Q*
119 you.] *Dyce (subs., after Colman);* you, *Q*
121 dry.] *Theobald (subs.);* dry, *Q*
123–4 indeed— . . . demonstration!] *Seward;* indeed . . . demonstration; *Q*
124 heart-pierc'd] *hyphen, F*
127 counter-reflect] *hyphen, F*
133 suppliants'] *Colman;* Suppliants *Q*
138 move,] *F;* mooves *Q*
142 drams,] *Seward;* drams *Q*
155 dreams] *Tonson;* dreames, *Q*
160 out,] *F;* out *Q*
167 s.p. Queens.] *Weber*
169 unpang'd] *Seward;* unpanged *Q*
172 war] *Theobald;* was *Q*
175 neglected.] *Seward (subs.);* neglected, *Q*
178 twinning] *Theobald;* twyning *Q*
192 s.d. Kneels.] *Weber (after l. 186); placed as in Kittredge*
199 s.d. To Emilia.] *Weber*
199 now!] *Colman (after Tonson);* now *Q*
200 s.d. Kneels.] *Dyce*
205 s.d. They rise.] *Dyce (subs.)*
211 soldier. As before,] *Mason conj.;* Soldier (as before) *Q*
211 s.d. To Artesius.] *Dyce*
212 Aulis] *Theobald;* Anly *Q*
214 number] *Kittredge;* number, *Q*
215 bigger-look'd] *hyphen, Dyce*
215 s.d. Exit Artesius.] *Weber*
215 s.d. To Hippolyta.] *Dyce*
218 s.d. slowly] *ed.*
233 human] *Dyce;* humane *Q*
234 s.d. Flourish.] *placed as in Weber; after l. 233, Q*

I.ii

Location: *ed. (after Weber)*
20 Mars's] *F;* Marsis *Q*
42 be,] *Nicholson (in Littledale);* be *Q*
55 canon] *Seward;* Cannon *Q*
57 tiptoe] *Tonson (subs.);* tip toe *Q*
65 power there's nothing;] *Seward;* power: there's nothing, *Q*
70 glory; one] *Ingram (in Littedale);* glory on; *Q*
83 s.d. Enter Valerius.] *placed as in F; after l. 82, Q*
87 whisper'd, to] *Colman;* whisperd too *Q*
97 action's dregg'd] *Seward;* actions dregd, *Q*
105 motion,] *Tonson;* motion *Q*

I.iii

Location: *Weber*
12 all-royal] *hyphen, F*
16 advis'd] *F;* advised *Q*
17 army,] *F;* Army *Q*
35 for't.] *Tonson (subs.);* fort, *Q;* for't, *F*
40 death's self] *Colman (apostrophe, F);* Deaths-selfe *Q*
54 aleven] *ed. (after F. O. Waller);* a eleven *Q;* eleven *F*
54 Flavina] *Seward (cf. l. 84);* Flauia *Q*
54 Yes.] *Colman;* Yes *Q;* Yes, *F*
58–64] *In left margin Q has an anticipative prompter's note for the next scene:* 2. Hearses ready with Palamon: and Arcite: the 3. Queenes. Theseus: and his Lordes ready.
65–6 condemn'd, . . . arraignment.] *Seward (subs.);* condemd . . . arraignement, *Q*
66 pluck] *F;* plncke *Q*
67 (O then] *Seward (subs.);* oh (then *Q*
73 careless wear)] *Seward;* careles, were, *Q*
74 decking.] *Seward (subs.);* decking, *Q*
75 one] *Seward conj.;* on *Q*
76 musical] *F;* misicall *Q*
79 ev'ry innocent] *Lamb (in* Specimens*);* fury-innocent *Q;* sorry innocence *Bertram conj. (after Sympson)*
79–80 well, . . . bastard)] *Weber;* well) . . . bastard, *Q*
82 dividual] *Seward;* individuall *Q*
82 out] *F;* ont *Q*
83 high-speeded pace] *Colman;* high speeded-pace *Q*
94 kneel,] *Colman;* kneele *Q*
94 assurance] *Dyce;* assurance, *Q*
95 Pirithous] *Dyce (after Tonson);* Pirothous *Q*

I.iv

Location: *Weber*
o.s.d. Cornets.] *placed as in Skeat; precedes scene division in Q*
o.s.d. within] *F;* withim *Q*
o.s.d. with his Lords] *from prompter's note in Q at I.iii.58–64*
6 chastise] *F;* chastice *Q*
9 rites] *Seward;* rights *Q*
9 supply't] *F;* suppl'it *Q*
13 s.d. Exeunt Queens.] *placed as in Dyce; after l. 13, Q*
13 s.d. Enter . . . hearses.] *ed. (after Dyce and prompter's note at I.iii.58–64)*
21 was't that prisoner] *Dyce;* prisoner was't that *Q*
22 Wi'] *Dyce;* We *Q*
23 those.] *Colman;* those *Q*
26] *In left margin Q has an anticipative prompter's note for the next scene:* 3. Hearses ready.
28 'em.] *Colman (subs., after Tonson);* 'em *Q*
32 niggard, waste;] *Colman (subs.);* niggard wast, *Q*
33 worth.] *Seward (subs.);* worth, *Q*
39 do;] *Seward;* do *Q*
40 friends' behests] *Seward (subs.);* friends, beheastes *Q*
41 Love's] *Seward;* Loves, *Q*
45 O'er-wrastling] *ed. (after Bertram);* Or wrastling *Q*
45 reason.] *Seward;* reason, *Q*
49 'fore] *Theobald;* for *Q*
49 s.d. Flourish.] *placed as in Weber; after l. 48, Q*
49 s.d. Attendants . . . Arcite] *Dyce*

I.v

Location: *Skeat (subs., after Weber)*
o.s.d. Music.] *placed as in Skeat; precedes scene division in Q*
o.s.d. Song] *Skeat*
3 dying;] *Dyce (after Colman);* dying *Q*
12 seize] *F;* ceaze *Q*

II.i

Location: *ed. (after Weber)*
Whole scene as verse in Q; as prose, Weber
1 live; something] *Colman;* live, some thing *Q*
6 appear] *Tonson;* appeare, *Q*
14 s.d. with strewings] *Dyce (after Weber); Q s.d. after l. 13; placed as in Weber*
17 that now;] *Colman (subs.);* that. Now, *Q*
47 s.d. Enter . . . above.] *placed as in Weber; after l. 46, Q*
54 s.d. Jailer . . . Daughter] *Dyce*

II.ii

Location: *ed. (after Weber)*
1] *Preceding Palamon's opening speech Q reads* Enter Palamon, and Arcite in prison.*; the present arrangement, by which Palamon and Arcite remain on stage above from their entry at II.i.47, was first adopted by Weber*
11 Hung . . . ladies,] *Tonson;* (Hung . . . Ladies) *Q*
20 us.] *Theobald (subs.);* us, *Q*
21 ware] *Dyce (after Theobald);* were *Q*
22 Ravish'd] *Theobald;* Bravishd *Q*
48 hallow] *ed.;* halloa *Q*
59 please—] *Brooke (subs.);* please, *Q*
68 sleeping] *F;* sseeping *Q (?)*
105 been,] *Colman;* bin *Q*
106 lust and ignorance] *Tonson (subs.);* lust, and ignorance, *Q*
115 s.d. below] *Weber*
118 s.p. Emil.] *Theobald; line continued to Arcite, Q (s.p.* Emil. *at l. 119 in Q)*
129 will't] *F;* wilt *Q*

130 **Dainty, madam]** *Tonson;* Deinty Madam *Q*
148 **in.]** *Colman (subs.);* in, *Q*
156 **done;]** *Colman;* done, *Q*
157 **for't! Now]** *Colman;* for't, now *Q*
162 **her]** *Seward (subs.);* her; *Q*
164 **I . . . her.]** *Tonson (subs.);* (I . . . her) *Q*
185 **your]** *F;* you *Q*
200 **be—]** *ed.;* be. *Q*
217 **s.d. above]** *Leech; Q s.d. after l. 211; placed as in Weber*
234 **bright]** *F;* brighr *Q*
243 **s.d. above]** *Leech; Q s.d. after l. 242; placed as in Weber*
247, 274 **s.dd. Aside.]** *Dyce*
260 **life?]** *Tonson;* life. *Q*
268 **you]** *F;* yon *Q*

II.iii

Location: *Dyce (after Weber)*
20 **there.]** *Tonson (subs.);* there, *Q*
23 **s.d. Retires.]** *Kittredge*
23 **s.d. garland]** *F;* Garlon *Q*
24, 25, 26, 27 **s.pp. 1. Coun. . . . 2. Coun. . . . 3. Coun. . . . 4. Coun.]** *Seward;* 1. . . . 2. . . . 3. . . . 4. *Q (throughout scene)*
32 **stow]** *Colman;* stoa *Q*
39 **ye]** *Seward;* yet *Q*
41 **all,]** *Tonson;* all *Q*
42–59 **He'll . . . hold!]** *as verse, Seward; as prose, Q*
51 **means;]** *Colman;* meanes *Q*
51 **says]** *Seward;* sees *Q*
60 **s.d. Comes forward.]** *Kittredge*
62, 64 **games]** *Tonson;* Games *Q (in italics)*
68 **along?]** *Tonson;* along. *Q*
72 **venture.]** *Colman (subs.);* venture, *Q*
72 **eggs!]** *Littledale;* eggs. *Q*
73 **s.d. Countrymen]** *Seward*
75 **Well]** *Seward;* Well, *Q*

II.iv

Location: *Weber (subs.)*
20 **sad ones]** *Seward;* sad-ones *Q*

II.v

II.v] *Colman;* Scaena 4. *Q*
Location: *Weber (subs.)*
o.s.d. **This . . . within.]** *prompter's note in left margin, Q*
o.s.d. **disguised]** *Weber*
11 **hollow'd]** *ed.;* holloa'd *Q*
16 **s.p. Pir.]** *Dyce;* Per. *Q (or Perith. throughout scene)*
28 **For]** *F;* Fo *Q*
31 **Pirithous]** *Dyce;* Perithous *Q*
39 **s.d. Kisses Emilia's hand.]** *Dyce*
53 **afoot]** *Tonson;* a foote *Q*
61 **else.]** *F;* else, *Q*
64 **s.d. Flourish.]** *placed as in Dyce; after* wise. *l. 64, Q*

II.vi

Location: *Dyce (after Weber)*
4 **hence.]** *Seward (subs.);* hence, *Q*
12 **it.]** *Colman (subs.);* it *Q*
15 **dirge,]** *Tonson;* Dirge. *Q*
31 **no man]** *F;* no-man *Q*
39 **s.d. Exit.]** *Colman*

III.i

Location: *Dyce (after Weber)*
o.s.d. **Cornets . . . a-Maying.]** *prompter's note in right margin, Q*
o.s.d. **a-Maying]** *hyphen, Colman*
2 **rite]** *Colman;* Right *Q*
10 **place]** *Theobald;* pace *Q*
11 **presence.]** *Seward (subs.);* presence, *Q*
36 **look'd! . . . honor]** *Sympson* (honor *Tonson*); lookd the voides of honour. *Q*
43 **house-clogs]** *hyphen, Seward*
63 **place]** *Kittredge;* place, *Q*
70 **this]** *Kittredge;* this, *Q*
82 **house.]** *Seward (subs.);* house, *Q*
93–4 **offer. . . . sir;]** *Colman (subs.);* offer, . . . Sir *Q*
96 **s.d. off. Cornets.]** *ed. (after Bertram);* of Cornets. *Q; Q s.d. after l. 95; placed as in Colman*
97 **musit]** *Knight,* Musicke *Q*
101 **brow.]** *Tonson (subs.);* brow, *Q*
101 **certain]** *F;* crtaine *Q*
106 **language.]** *Colman (subs.);* language, *Q*
107 **not]** *F;* nor *Q*
108 **s.d. within]** *ed.; Q s.d. after l. 106; placed as in Weber*
119 **strength;]** *Colman (subs., after Tonson);* strength *Q*
123 **s.d. severally]** *Dyce*

III.ii

Location: *ed. (after Weber)*
1 **mistook]** *Seward;* mistooke; *Q*
1 **brake]** *Theobald conj.;* Beake *Q*
7 **reak]** *ed.;* wreake *Q*
14 **jingling]** *Colman;* Iengling *Q*
19 **fed]** *F;* feed *Q*
25 **dozens]** *Theobald;* dussons *Q*
26 **days—]** *Littledale;* daies. *Q*
28 **brine]** *Tonson;* bine *Q*
29 **Dissolve,]** *Colman;* Dissolue *Q*
37 **this—]** *Kittredge;* this *Q*

III.iii

Location: *ed. (after Weber)*
1 **place. Ho,]** *Tonson (subs.);* place, hoa. *Q*
2 **Arcite?]** *F;* Arcite. *Q*
6–7 **drink— . . . faint—]** *ed.;* drinke . . . faint, *Q*
12 **s.d. Drinks.]** *Weber*
16 **s.d. Drinks.]** *Dyce*
20 **s.d. Eats.]** *Dyce*
23 **them]** *F;* then *Q*
26 **tart,]** *Seward;* tart: *Q*
31 **sir?]** *Colman;* Sir. *Q*
40 **a-hunting]** *hyphen, Colman*
52 **Sirrah—]** *Colman;* Sir ha: *Q*

III.iv

Location: *ed. (after Weber)*
9 **Open]** *J. Freehafer (in ELN);* Vpon *Q*
10 **tack]** *F;* take *Q*
19 **a foot]** *Tonson;* afoote *Q*
20 **e'e]** *Weber;* eie *Q*
22 **He s']** *Littledale;* He's *Q*
23 **wide.]** *F;* wide *Q*
25 **now,]** *Knight;* now *Q*

III.v

III.v] *Tonson;* Scaena 6. *Q*
Location: *ed. (after Weber)*
o.s.d. **Gerrold]** *Colman*
o.s.d. **as morris-dancers]** *Weber*
o.s.d. **another as the]** *Dyce*
o.s.d. **Bavian]** *Seward;* Baum *Q*
o.s.d. **five]** *Weber;* 2. or 3 *Q*
1–21 **Fie, . . . boys.]** *as verse, Seward; as prose, Q*
8 **jane]** *Dyce;* jave *Q*
21 **figure, trace]** *Colman (subs.);* figure trace, *Q*
22, 23, 24, 25 **s.pp. 1. Coun. . . . 2. Coun. . . . 3. Coun. . . . 4. Coun.]** *Colman;* 1. . . . 2. . . . 3. . . . 4. *Q (throughout scene)*
26 **Barbary]** *F;* Barbery *Q*
27 **freckled]** *F;* freckeled *Q*
38 **tandem]** *F;* taudem *Q*
46 **once—]** *Colman;* once, *Q*
50 **fail.]** *Seward;* faile, *Q*
59 **s.p. Daugh.]** *placed as in F; opposite l. 60, Q*
59 **s.d. Sings.]** *Weber (subs.)*
59 **George Alow]** *as name of ship, Kittredge;* George alow *Q*
60 **Barbary-a]** *hyphen here and in ll. 62, 64, 66, Colman*
64–5] *In left margin Q has an anticipative prompter's note for the next scene:* Chaire and stooles out.
66 **I]** *Tonson*
72–5 **There's . . . gambols.]** *as verse, Seward; as prose, Q*
72 **master]** *Weber;* Mr. *Q;* Magister *Seward*
79 **ten—]** *Seward;* ten, *Q*
79 **Buzz!]** *Tonson (subs.);* Buz *Q*
82 **Sirrah]** *Colman;* Sir ha *Q*
86 **Qui passa]** *Weber;* Quipassa *Q*
92 **s.d. Wind horns.]** *placed as in Leech; after l. 90, Q*
94 **s.d. Exeunt . . . Schoolmaster.]** *placed as in Dyce; after l. 92, Q*
97 **s.p. Pir.]** *Dyce;* Per. *Q (throughout scene)*
98 **s.p. The.]** *F;* Per. *Q*
102 **favor,]** *Tonson;* favour; *Q*
102 **is.]** *Weber;* is, *Q*
107 **choris]** *Littledale;* Choris *Q (in italics)*
118–20 **Morr . . . Is . . . Morris]** *italics, Colman*
118 **weight—]** *Dyce (after Colman);* waight *Q*
120 **hither]** *F;* hether *Q*
133 **aliis]** *F;* aliijs *Q*
134 **"Ay"]** *Tonson (subs.);* I *Q*
135 **Ay, ay]** *Tonson;* I, I *Q*
137 **s.p. School.]** *Colman* (Ger.)
137 **s.d. school]** Schoolm. *F (Q s.d.* Knocke for Schoole. Enter the Dance. *is a prompter's notation in left margin, beginning opposite l. 137; redistributed by ed.)*
137 **s.d. Music. Dance.]** *placed as in Leech; after l. 136, Q*
139 **ye]** *Seward;* thee *Q*
142 **thee]** *F;* three *Q*
151 **you]** *F;* yon *Q*
152 **s.d. Gives money.]** *Dyce*
157 **s.d. Exeunt . . . company.]** *Dyce (subs.)*
157 **s.d. Wind horns.]** *placed as in Dyce; after* made. *l. 158, Q*

III.vi

III.vi] *Tonson;* Scaena 7. *Q*
Location: *ed. (after Weber)*
10 **out-dure]** *hyphen, F*
12 **fight,]** *Tonson;* fight *Q*
16 **So, love]** *Colman (after Tonson);* So love, *Q*
16 **s.d. Enter . . . swords.]** *placed as in Kittredge; after l. 16, Q*
28 **man.]** *Colman (subs.);* man, *Q*
35 **Will't]** *Knight;* wilt *Q*
39 **spar'd.]** *Tonson (subs.);* spard, *Q*
58 **grand-guard]** *hyphen, Seward*
77 **indeed,]** *Tonson;* indeede *Q*
93 **s.d. They . . . stand.]** *author's or prompter's note in left margin, Q (point of insertion marked with star after* love!*)*
108 **a-hunting]** *hyphen, Colman*
108 **you.]** *Colman (subs.);* you, *Q*
111 **again, sir.]** *Seward (subs.);* agen; Sir *Q*
131 **s.d. Pirithous]** *Dyce;* Perithous *Q (and* Per. *as s.p. throughout scene)*
145 **thy]** *Dyce;* this *Q*
151 **be'st]** *F;* bee'st *Q*
173 **mercy.]** *Colman (subs.);* mercy, *Q*
174–5 **us; . . . valiant,]** *Colman;* us, . . . valiant; *Q*
186 **Speak,]** *Colman;* Speake *Q*
195 **s.d. They kneel.]** *Weber*
201 **s.d. Kneels.]** *Weber*
203 **wars,]** *Tonson;* warres; *Q*
228 **it.]** *Tonson (subs.);* it, *Q*
238 **a-begging]** *hyphen, Colman*
251 **heaven's]** *Theobald (subs.);* heavens *Q*
256 **a-pieces]** *hyphen, Colman*
286 **excellent:]** *Tonson (subs.);* excellent *Q*
293 **whether,]** *Tonson;* whether *Q*

IV.i

Location: *Weber (subs.)*
3 **sir,]** *Tonson;* Sir *Q*
11 **oath]** *F;* o'th *Q*
13 **Pirithous]** *Dyce;* Perithous *Q*
16 **s.d. Enter Second Friend.]** *placed as in Dyce; after* scape. *l. 16, Q*
31 **s.d. Enter Wooer.]** *placed as in Weber; after* not. *l. 31, Q*
46 **'Tis]** *Tonson;* Woo. Tis *Q (repeated s.p.)*
63 **sung]** *F;* song *Q*
65 **sir.]** *Tonson;* Sir? *Q*
74 **cherry lips]** *F;* cherry-lips *Q*
75 **antic]** *Tonson;* Antique *Q*
83 **knee-deep]** *hyphen, Colman*
84 **wreath]** *Seward;* wreake *Q*

85 **water-flowers]** *hyphen, Knight*
90–1 **"Thus . . . me,"]** *as two separate posies, Theobald*
103 s.d. **Enter . . . others.]** *placed as in Kittredge: after l. 102, Q*
104 s.d. **Sings.]** *Weber*
108 **Bonny]** *F;* Bony *Q*
110 **rearly]** *Sympson;* rarely *Q*
111 **minstrels,]** *Tonson;* Minstrels *Q*
112 **cocklight,]** *Hopkinson;* cocklight *Q*
113 s.d. **Sings.]** *placed as in Knight; after l. 114, Q*
120 **Far]** *Tonson;* For *Q*
121 **sister?]** *Colman;* Sister. *Q*
123 **know.]** *Colman (subs.);* know, *Q*
124 **gone—]** *Colman (subs.);* gone, *Q*
136 **him.]** *Colman (subs.);* him, *Q*
141 s.d. **To the Jailer.]** *ed.*
142 s.p. **2. Friend.]** *F;* 1. Fr. *Q*
146 **cheerly]** *F;* cheerely *Q*
147 s.p. **All.]** *Leech takes this s.p. as part of the Daughter's speech and reads* cheerly all!, *thus continuing ll. 147–8* (. . . master?) *to the Daughter*
152 **Tack]** *F;* take *Q*

IV.ii

Location: *Weber (subs.)*
5 **dead-cold]** *hyphen, Colman*
14 **smiling.]** *Colman (subs.);* smyling, *Q*
16 **Jove]** *Sympson;* Love *Q*
16 **afire]** *Tonson;* a fire *Q*
20 **great-ey'd]** *hyphen, Seward*
40 **'em?]** *Theobald;* 'em *Q*
44 **gipsy,]** *Colman;* Gipsey. *Q*
49 **Palamon.]** *F;* Palamon, *Q*
52 **fancy]** *Tonson;* Fancie *Q (in italics)*
54 s.d. **Enter Gentleman.]** *Tonson (subs.);* Enter Emil. and Gent. *Q*
55 **How]** *Colman; Emil.* How *Q (repeated s.p.)*
64 s.d. **Pirithous]** *Dyce;* Perithous *Q (and* Per. *as s.p. throughout scene)*
70 s.d. **Enter Messenger.]** *F (after l. 69; here placed as in Weber);* Enter Messengers. Curtis. *Q (after l. 69; Curtis is probably Curtis Greville, who played the part of the Messenger; the name is picked up in F)*
76 **first]** *F;* fitst *Q*
81 **fire]** *Heath conj.;* faire *Q*
86 **baldrick,]** *Seward;* Bauldricke; *Q*
87 **with.]** *Seward (subs.);* with, *Q*
88 **soldier's]** *Colman;* Souldiers *Q*
91 **guess]** *Tonson;* ghesse *Q*
104 **Hard-hair'd]** *hyphen, Colman*
104 **ivy-tods]** *Littledale;* Ivy tops *Q*
109 **crown]** *Seward;* corect *Q*
127 **shoulder-piece]** *hyphen, F*
140 **charging-staff]** *hyphen, Colman*
153 **so— . . . appear.]** *Tonson (subs.);* so; . . . appeare, *Q*

IV.iii

Location: *Weber (subs.)*
1–39 **Her . . . enough.]** *as prose, Seward; as irregular verse, Q*
8 s.d. **Enter Daughter.]** *placed as in Weber; after* business *l. 8, Q*
12 **Down-a, down-a]** *hyphens, Colman*
18 s.p. **Jail.]** *F;* Ioy. *Q*
22 **there's]** *F;* the'rs *Q*
32 **th' tother]** *ed.;* th / Thother *Q;* i' th' / Other *F*
40 s.d. **Enter Daughter.]** *Leech*
46 **trifle.]** *Colman (subs.);* Trifle, *Q*
53–4 **th' other]** *Dyce;* another *Q*
62–101 **Understand . . . comfort.]** *as prose, Seward; as irregular verse, Q*
67 **penn'worth]** *F (subs.);* Pen-worth *Q*
88 **carve]** *F;* crave *Q*
91 **play-feres]** *Rolfe;* play-pheeres *Q*

V.i

Location: *Skeat*
o.s.d. **Three . . . Diana.]** *Kittredge (subs.)*
o.s.d. **Flourish.]** *placed as in Weber; before* Exeunt. *at end of IV.iii, Q*
o.s.d. **Pirithous]** *Dyce;* Perithous *Q (and* Per. *as s.p., ll. 7, 17)*
7 s.d. **Flourish of cornets.]** *placed as in Weber; after l. 5, Q*
9 **germane]** *Colman;* German *Q*
17 s.d. **Exeunt]** *Tonson;* Exit *Q*
31 s.d. **They embrace.]** *Dyce*
33 s.d. **Exeunt . . . Knights.]** *placed as in Seward; after* coz! *l. 33, Q*
48 s.d. **advance . . . then]** *Dyce (after Weber)*
50 **Neptune]** *F;* Nepture *Q*
50 **purple, ...]** *one or more words missing in Q; Seward supplies* whose approach
54 **armipotent]** *Theobald;* armenypotent *Q*
65 **cur'st]** *Theobald;* curst *Q*
68 **design march boldly.]** *Tonson (subs.);* designe; march boldly, *Q*
76 s.d. **advance . . . then]** *Dyce*
80 **Mars's]** *Tonson;* Marsis *Q*
85 **poll'd]** *Seward (subs.);* pould *Q*
91 **his;]** *Seward;* his *Q*
116 **fere]** *Rolfe;* pheare *Q*
118 **Brief,]** *Weber (subs.);* briefe *Q*
119–21 **done, . . . rejoicer.]** *F;* done; no Companion / To . . . not; a defyer / To . . . cannot; a Rejoycer, *Q*
124 **language.]** *Colman (subs.);* language, *Q*
130 **O]** *Colman; Pal.* O *Q (repeated s.p.)*
136 s.d. **They bow.]** *placed as in Weber; after l. 134, Q*
136 s.d. **and wearing]** *Dyce*
136 s.d. **of Diana]** *Dyce*
150 **bride-habited]** *hyphen, F*
151 **'pointed]** *Colman;* pointed *Q*
152 **him.]** *Seward (subs.);* him, *Q*
154 **election.]** *Dyce;* election *Q*
165 **rose!]** *Dyce (after Colman);* Rose, *Q*
168 s.d. **which . . . altar]** *Dyce*

V.ii

Location: *Dyce (after Weber)*
2 **kept]** *F;* hept *Q*
5 **ask'd]** *F;* asked *Q*
6 **her, presently]** *F;* her / Presently *Q*
32 **purpose.]** *Tonson (subs.);* purpose, *Q*
35 **way . . . me?]** *Colman; way of flesh,* you have me. *Q*
40 **humor]** *Theobald;* honour *Q*
40 s.d. **Wooer retires.]** *ed.*
54 **tune]** *Theobald;* turne *Q*
69 s.d. **Wooer comes forward.]** *ed.*
72 **end]** *F;* eud *Q*
74 **stoolball]** *F (subs.);* stoole ball *Q*
81 **business.]** *Tonson;* businesse *Q*
84 **two]** *F;* too *Q*
87 s.d. **Kisses her.]** *Dyce*
105 s.d. **To the Wooer.]** *ed.*
109–10 **twenty? . . . together?]** *Colman;* twenty. . . . together. *Q*
111 **Yes,]** *Colman;* Yes *Q*

V.iii

Location: *Skeat (subs., after Dyce)*
o.s.d. **Flourish.]** *placed as in Dyce; before* Exeunt. *at end of V.ii, Q*
o.s.d. **Pirithous]** *Dyce;* Perithous *Q*
o.s.d. **Attendants]** *Seward;* Attendants, T, Tucke: Curtis. *Q (the first actor referred to is Thomas Tuckfield; for Curtis, see IV.ii.70)*
1 s.p. **Pir.]** *Dyce;* Per. *Q*
3 **decision. Ev'ry]** *F (subs.);* decision ev'ry; *Q*
8–9 **happen— . . . hear,]** *Colman (subs.);* happen, . . . deaffing, but to heare; *Q*
13 **well,]** *Heath conj.;* well *Q*
16 **garland]** *F;* garlond *Q*
54 **him]** *Seward;* them *Q*
66 s.d. **Cornets. . . . Palamon!"]** *placed as in Weber; after l. 64, Q*
66 s.d. **Enter Servant.]** *placed as in Kittredge; after l. 66, Q*
71 s.d. **within]** *Dyce*
72 s.d. **Exit Servant.]** *Dyce (subs.)*
74 **left]** *F;* leff *Q*
75 **in't else;]** *Mason conj.;* in't; else *Q*
77 **best-boding]** *hyphen, Seward*
77 s.d. **Another . . . cornets.]** *placed as in Weber; after l. 75, Q*
88 **disparity, value's shortness,]** *Colman;* disparity values shortnes *Q*
89 s.d. **Cornets. . . . Arcite!"]** *placed as in Dyce; after l. 88, Q*
92 s.d. **Cornets. . . . victory!"]** *placed as in Weber; after l. 91, Q*
95 **Half-sights]** *hyphen, Colman*
100 **drift-winds]** *hyphen, Weber*
121 **all]** *F;* all; *Q*
127 **out-breasted]** *hyphen, F*
139 **your]** *F;* you *Q*
146 s.d. **Flourish.]** *placed as in Kittredge; after* deliver. *l. 138, Q*

V.iv

Location: *ed. (after Dyce)*
o.s.d. **A block ready.]** *Littledale*
1 s.p. **Pal.]** *Tonson*
6 **wishes;]** *Theobald;* wishes, *Q*
10 **unwapper'd, not]** *Tonson;* unwapper'd not, *Q*
23 s.d. **To the Jailer.]** *ed.*
32 s.d. **Gives purse.]** *Dyce*
35 **quite]** *Weber;* quight *Q*
36 **requite]** *F;* requight *Q*
38 **leave-taking]** *hyphen, Tonson*
38 s.p. **3. Knight.]** *ed.;* 1. K. *Q*
38 **courageous]** *F;* couragiour *Q*
46 s.d. **Palamon rises.]** *Dyce*
47 **dearly]** *Seward;* early *Q*
51 **hair-worth]** *hyphen, Colman*
55 **calkins]** *Colman;* Calkins *Q (in italics)*
68 **school-doing]** *hyphen, Tonson*
77 **. . . on]** *Q leaves the first two-thirds of the line blank, presumably indicating the omission of several illegible words; or, as F. O. Waller suggests,* on . . . stands *may be a revision of* on his hind hoofes *immediately above in the preceding line*
87 **mighty, Arcite.]** *Brooke (subs.);* mightie Arcite, *Q*
95 s.d. **Dies.]** *Colman*
104 **arrouse]** *Littledale (subs.);* arowze *Q*
107 **Hath]** *Hopkinson;* Hast *Q;* Has *Tonson*
109 s.d. **Arcite . . . out.]** *Kittredge*
133 **sorry, still]** *ed. (after Weber);* sorry still, *Q*

Epilogue

2 **say;]** *Kittredge (subs.);* say, *Q*
11 **bold,]** *ed.;* bold *Q*
18 s.d. **Flourish.]** Florish. / FINIS. *Q*

Edward III

If Shakespeare had not written at least some of *Edward III*, most readers would argue that he certainly should have. All those plays about the politics of the reigns of Edward's descendants, from Richard II to Henry VIII, and (by implication) Elizabeth I and James I, cry out for some analogous dramatic treatment of the founding father and his rule. The play itself was registered 1 December 1595 and was published for Cuthbert Burby, the publisher of *Love's Labor's Lost* Q1 (1598) and *Romeo and Juliet* Q2 (1599) in 1596, as *The Raigne of King Edward the third: As it hath bin sundrie times plaied about the Citie of London.* A second quarto appeared in 1599, but in spite of its touted popularity, there is no evidence of further production. In 1656, a catalogue by Rogers and Ley ascribed it to Shakespeare, but as they also thought he had written Marlowe's *Edward the Second* among other clearly already-spoken-for texts, it remained for Capell on the title page of his *Prolusions*; *or Select Pieces of Ancient Poetry* (1760) to make the first serious statement that it was a play "thought to be writ by Shakespeare." But if Capell and those on the growing list of subsequent scholars and critics are right, why was the play not claimed by Shakespeare's company, and why not included in the Folio of 1623 (a fate also suffered by *Pericles* and *The Two Noble Kinsmen*)? The answer now generally given is that it was politically incorrect in the extreme with its

> bitterly satirical presentation of King David of Scotland and Sir William Douglas, who are also the objects of the pointed irony of the Countess of Salisbury [I.ii.60–80], while in the last scene of the play King David is led prisoner on the stage [V.i.64 ff.]. The play was presumably forbidden, and the 1599 reprint can be taken as an attempt by the publisher to get some profit from a play that was no longer to be seen on the stage [and scarcely so *au courant* as the newly written and staged analogous historical play, *Henry V*]. The suppression of the play would of course be maintained even more rigidly after the advent, in 1603, to the throne of England, of King James of Scotland. . . . So, after a time, the vetoed play would have been completely forgotten, and Heminges and Condell would not include it in the 1623 Folio, as they did those other early histories and comedies that were still alive on the stage. (Giorgio Melchiori, *Shakespeare's Garter Plays: "Edward III" to "Merry Wives of Windsor"* [1994], 117–18)

The work itself combines elements of both the chronicle drama and the morality play. There is no stress on the providential theme of Tudor historiography found in the First Tetralogy, nor is there a focus on the principle of succession in England. There is no truly tragic element but, in general, a far more benign, even optimistic view of humanity than is found elsewhere in Shakespeare's work. There is no clear villain deserving of the audience's animus, no specifically duplicitous or hostile figure like Queen Margaret or Joan of Arc or Richard of Gloucester. There is a series of historical events taken primarily from Jean Froissart's *Chronicles* and presented one after the other with no concern about violating the dramatic unities of time and place—moving from England to France, from land to sea to land, from 1340 to 1346 to 1356—with not even the slightest hesitation or appeal for a muse of fire to transcend the limitations of the Elizabethan stage. Inserted into this pageant of military achievement is an episode drawn from Froissart (Sir John Bouchier, Lord Berners' translation, 1523–25) and, to a lesser extent, William Painter's novel 46 in *The Palace of Pleasure Beautified* (1575), in which King Edward nearly succumbs to the temptation to violate the beautiful wife of the Earl of Salisbury. The fissure that separates this episode of love and lust (the section of the play considered most Shakespearean) from the large military portion of the play is closed up in part by imagery (e.g., the Countess's "winning of the sun" of Edward at II.ii.68 and the Froissart-given "winning the sun" tactic at Sluys and Crécy), but chiefly by the similarity of theme: King Edward, the conqueror of the French, must first be the conqueror of his own appetitive self. Having triumphed first over this more difficult enemy, he finds, with the help of his son the Black Prince, that he can vanquish the French relatively easily (though not without a momentary fright as to the safety of the young Black Prince at Poitiers). Because of the presence of this balance of internal and external battles and the repeated stress on the necessity of keeping one's oaths and vows, the play as a whole has from the time of Tillyard, more than a half-century ago, to almost the current moment with Melchiori been considered to have as its

> unifying structural element . . . the education of princes. In fact, the theme is pursued. The authors [sic] went to the trouble of borrowing a marginal episode found only in Froissart (Book I, chapter CXXXV: "How sir Gaultier of Manny rode through all France by safe conduct to Calys"), changing the names of the characters involved to provide another example of the education of a Prince, this time Charles, the French Dauphin: Villiers, a French nobleman, teaches a lesson to Prince Charles by threatening to go back to prison unless the Prince grants the Earl of Salisbury a safe-conduct, which Villiers had promised to procure in exchange for his freedom—see *Edward III*, IV.i.[19–43] and IV.iii.[1–56], as well as IV.v.[56–126] where the Prince teaches the same lesson to his father, the King of the French, who wants to detain Salisbury on his way to join King Edward at Calais (Melchiori, 126–7).

Self-mastery is a theme ubiquitous in the Shakespearean canon, and the particular issue of illicit sexual desire on the part of a person with military or executive power occurs quite frequently. Parallels of vocabulary and imagery with *Edward III*, *The Rape of Lucrece*, and *Measure for Measure* (especially Angelo's temptation scenes in II.ii and II.iv) are striking, particularly those that make up clusters or semi-clusters, "groups of unconsciously associated words which reappear in play after play" (Kenneth Muir, *Shakespeare as Collaborator* [1960], 20). Still other echoes and anticipations of Shakespearean language reverberate between the Countess scenes and a network made up of the early plays and poems, *Venus and Adonis*, *The Rape of Lucrece*, *Romeo and Juliet*, *Love's Labor's Lost*, the Sonnets, and *A Midsummer Night's Dream* (V. Østerberg, "The 'Countess Scenes' of *Edward the Third*," *Shakespeare-Jahrbuch*, LXV [1929], 49–91). The political part of the play, with its insulting French and resourceful English, anticipates motifs and images in *Henry V*. There are also a good many interesting elements, interesting especially in terms of the probable date of composition, connecting with *Richard III* (1592–93). The omen of the ravens and the misinterpreted prophecies prefigure those of *Julius Caesar* and *Macbeth*, respectively.

Telling against the idea of Shakespeare's authorship of the whole drama—holding aside the additional fact that much of the play, however otherwise impressive, often lacks the full metaphorical vividness of typical Shakespearean verse—are matters of source use, the near-total absence of comedy, and the all-too-easy successful moral resolutions. As to source, while it is quite characteristic for Shakespeare to take a marginal or minor element in his historical sources and develop theme and character from it, as in the instance of Walter Manny and his safe-conduct, from Book I of Froissart, the fact of the matter is that Shakespeare is a notorious recidivist and if he had used Froissart as early as 1592–95, we would expect to see frequent subsequent use of the French chronicler; however, we don't. There is the earlier reference in the Duke of Alencon's statement in *1 Henry VI*:

> Froissart, a countryman of ours, records
> England all Olivers and Rolands bred
> During the time Edward the Third did reign.
> (I.ii.29–31)

Further, it may be that Froissart contributed to the character of Gaunt in *King Richard II*, though that possibility remains debatable (see the review of the arguments for Froissart and *King Richard II* in Muir, *The Sources of Shakespeare's Plays* [1977], 47 ff.). It is, of course, conceivable that Holinshed and Plutarch were such large works that, later in his career, Shakespeare simply had little need and time for yet another lengthy text—conceivable, but not likely.

As for the absent-comedy issue, Shakespeare need not have been obliged to add comedy to the play or to those parts of the play he was responsible for, but perhaps, in order to create some humor, the reader could pump more air into the king's embarrassed witticism, "What, thinkest thou I did bid thee praise a horse?" at II.i.98 (itself a nice anticipation of *Henry V*, III.vii.39 ff.) and his humorous criticism of his scribe Lodwick's comparing the Countess to the biblical Judith who slew Holofernes: "O monstrous line! Put in the next a sword, / And I shall woo her to cut off my head" (II.i.170–1). The clearest answer is that he need not have added any comedy nor been any the less Shakespeare, for the lyrical *Richard II* (1595–6), about Edward III's grandson, clearly has no laughter or comedy in it.

Perhaps the most intransigent feature of *Edward III* insofar as acceptance of Shakespeare as the author of the whole text is concerned, and, to a somewhat lesser degree, as the author of the Countess scenes (I.ii, II.i, and II.ii) and IV.iv, is the ease with which moral reversals occur, always from the corrupt to the ethically appropriate. The opposing French, who are prepared to override the oaths of their vassals, or even Edward III, who appears quite happy to execute the Burghers of Calais until advised to be merciful by Queen Philippe, are given few lines to show a tortured or even passionate struggle to reach a position true and good. Each of the political leaders learns a lesson in moral virtue: not only, as Tillyard first noted in his *Shakespeare's History Plays* (1944), is King Edward himself taught by the Countess and, in the matter of the Burghers of Calais, by his wife Queen Philippe, who in turn is led to accept and perhaps even value the independence and courage of the esquire John Copland, while the Black Prince is instructed by Audley about facing death with equanimity. Not only do King John and Charles of Normandy learn about the inviolability of oaths, but Salisbury learns from Villiers how right he has been to trust the word of a fellow knight, even if that knight is French. This stress on moral education "makes the play something of a sermon" (Eliot Slater, *The Problem of* The Reign of King Edward III: *A Statistical Approach* [1988], 9).

One might say that the Shakespearean argument stands or falls on the Countess scenes and the struggle there of King Edward to show himself better than an English Tarquin, and that the depth and vividness of the articulation of that struggle are parallel to the treatment of the analogous problem of Angelo in *Measure for Measure*—even if the parallels show the differences in intensity and moral result. Angelo in the first part of the later play is one of Shakespeare's supreme portraits in psychological realism. King Edward's difficulties are less gripping, not because the genre of the history play somehow did not admit of extended vivid moral analysis and inner tension (for such examples are seen in the sleepless Henry IV, or his son, the nocturnally peripatetic Henry V), but merely because the scenes are earlier by several years of work and progress in the capacity to dramatize motivation.

The problem remains that the parallelism of plots in *Edward III*, in their neatness and simplicity, their inner and outer triumphs, and their multiple near-violations of oaths, are quite different from even such ostensibly parallel plots as those of *1* and *2 Henry IV* and *King Lear.* But this lack of subtlety and the only intermittent flashes of Shakespearean concentration, especially of language, are explicable if we assume that Shakespeare had a hand in revising a play already rather fully worked out, and that he had, *pace* Swinburne, more than a finger in the Countess scenes and IV.iv. The time spent on this revision, however, was enough to create a play more interesting than almost any historical drama written by Shakespeare's contemporaries and short only of his own mature histories in brilliance.

The authors of various stylometric tests have lately provided statistical arguments for sole authorship of *Edward III*, that author being Shakespeare (e.g., Slater and, with caution, M. W. A. Smith), and Jonathan Hope observes in his *The Authorship of Shakespeare's Plays: A Sociolinguistic Study* (1994): "Nothing in the findings of this study offers a serious challenge to the status of *Edward III* as the best candidate from the apocryphal plays for inclusion in the canon" (137). So too does Richard Proudfoot in his 1985 British Academy lecture, the clearest critical argument yet.

Each reader, of course, will make his or her own judgment on the evidence provided by the text itself. Whatever the judgment, the play is likely to give genuine delight. A substantial number, but by no means all, of the parallels with Shakespeare's canonically accepted plays and poems are pointed out in the commentary notes.

J. J. M. Tobin

The Reign of King Edward the Third

[Dramatis Personae

King Edward the Third
Edward, Prince of Wales, *his son*
Earl of Warwick
Earl of Derby
Earl of Salisbury
Lord Audley
Lord Percy
Lodwick, *King Edward's secretary*
Sir William Mountague
Sir John Copland
Robert, Count of Artois
Earl of Mountford
Two English Esquires
An English Herald
Gobin de Grey
John the Second, King of France
Charles, Duke of Normandy, *his son*
Philip, *his second son*
Duke of Lorraine
Villiers, *a French Lord*
King of Bohemia
A Polish Captain
Six Merchants of Calais
Six poor men of Calais
Two Citizens *of Calais*
Two French Captains
Another Captain
A French Mariner
Three French Heralds
Four other Frenchmen
David the Second, King of Scotland
Earl Douglas
Two Scottish Messengers
Philippe, Queen of England
Countess of Salisbury
A French Woman
Attendants, Soldiers

Scene: *England, Flanders, and France*]

[Act I, Scene I]

Enter King Edward, Derby, Prince Edward, [Warwick,] Audley, *and* Artois.

K. Edw. Robert of Artois, banish'd though thou be
From France, thy native country, yet with us
Thou shalt retain as great a signiory;
For we create thee Earl of Richmond here:
And now go forwards with our pedigree.
Who next succeeded Philip [le] Beau?
Art. Three sons of his, which all [successively],
Did sit upon their father's regal throne;
Yet died and left no issue of their loins.
K. Edw. But was my mother sister unto those?
Art. She was, my lord, and only Isabel
Was all the daughters that this Philip had,
Whom afterward your father took to wife,
And from the fragrant garden of her womb
Your gracious self, the flower of Europe's hope,
Derived is inheritor to France.
But [note] the rancor of rebellious minds:
When thus the linage of [le] Beau was out,
The French obscur'd your mother's privilege,
And, though she were the next of blood, proclaimed
John of the house of Valois, now their King:
The reason was, they say, the realm of France,
Replete with princes of great parentage,
Ought not admit a governor to rule,

Words and passages enclosed in square brackets in the text above are either emendations of the copy-text or additions to it. The Textual Notes immediately following the play cite the earliest authority for every such change or insertion and supply the reading of the copy-text wherever it is emended in this edition.

I.i. Location: London. A room of state in the palace.
1. **Robert of Artois.** Philip the Sixth's brother-in-law, who supported the claims of Edward to the French throne after he himself had been indicted for treachery against his aunt, Mahaut, in the matter of the inheritance of Artois. Elizabethans pronounced "Artois" to rhyme with "boys."
3. **signiory:** lordship, rights and privileges of a feudal lord. Othello speaks of "My services which I have done the signiory," *Othello*, I.ii.18.
6. **Philip le Beau:** Philip IV (called the "Fair"). Elizabethans pronounced "Beau" to rhyme with "new."
7. **Three sons . . . successively:** Lewis X (called "Hutin"), Philip V (called the "Long"), Charles V (called the "Fair"), each succeeding the other in linear succession.
11–12. **Isabel / Was . . . had.** Cf. Viola/Cesario, "I am all the daughters of my father's house," *Twelfth Night*, II.iv.120.
14. **garden of her womb.** Cf. Sonnet 16.6–7.
17. **rancor of rebellious minds.** Cf. *Richard III*, II.ii.117.
18. **linage of le Beau . . . out.** Philip le Beau's three sons had no issue and Isabel, his daughter, being a woman, was passed over in favor of Philip of Valois, instituting the second branch of the Capet royal family. In the play, Philip's son, John II, is now reigning in France, even though, historically, he ascended to the throne only in 1350, his father having been king at the time of the battles of Sluys (1340) and Crécy (1346). **linage:** lineage (variant form).
19. **obscur'd . . . privilege:** hid (out of sight) your mother's right.

Except he be descended of the male;
And that's the special ground of their contempt,
Wherewith they study to exclude your Grace;
But they shall find that forged ground of theirs
To be but dusty heaps of brittle sand.
Perhaps it will be thought a heinous thing,
That I, a Frenchman, should discover this,
But heaven I call to record of my vows,
It is not hate, nor any private wrong,
But love unto my country and the right
Provokes my tongue thus lavish in report.
You are the lineal watch[man] of our peace,
And John of Valois indirectly climbs:
What then should subjects but embrace their King?
Ah, wherein may our duty more be seen,
Than striving to rebate a tyrant's pride,
And place the true shepherd of our commonwealth?
K. Edw. This counsel, Artois, like to fructful showers,
Hath added growth unto my dignity,
And, by the fiery vigor of thy words,
Hot courage is engend'red in my breast,
Which heretofore was rak'd in ignorance,
But now doth mount with golden wings of fame,
And will approve fair Isabel's descent
Able to yoke their stubborn necks with steel
That spurn against my sovereignty in France.
Sound a horn.
A messenger!—Lord Audley, know from whence.
[*Exit Audley, who returns.*]
Aud. The Duke of Lorraine, having cross'd the seas,
Entreats he may have conference with your Highness.
K. Edw. Admit him, lords, that we may hear the news.
[*Exeunt Lords, who then return with the Duke of Lorraine, attended.*]
Say, Duke of Lorraine, wherefore art thou come?
Lor. The most renowned Prince, King John of France,
Doth greet thee, Edward, and by me commands

That, for so much as by his liberal gift
The Guyenne dukedom is entail'd to thee,
Thou do him lowly homage for the same.
And for that purpose, here I summon thee
Repair to France within these forty days,
That there, according as the custom is,
Thou mayst be sworn true liegeman to our King,
Or else thy title in that province dies,
And he himself will repossess the place.
K. Edw. See how occasion laughs me in the face!
No sooner minded to prepare for France,
But straight I am invited; nay, with threats
Upon a penalty enjoin'd to come.
'Twere but a childish part to say him nay.—
Lorraine, return this answer to thy lord:
I mean to visit him as he requests,
But how? Not servilely dispos'd to bend,
But like a conqueror to make him bow.
His lame, unpolish'd shifts are come to light,
And truth hath pull'd the vizard from his face
That set a [gloss] upon his arrogance.
Dare he command a fealty in me?
Tell him the crown that he usurps is mine,
And where he sets his foot he ought to kneel.
'Tis not a petty dukedom that I claim,
But all the whole dominions of the realm,
Which, if with grudging he refuse to yield,
I'll take away those borrow'd plumes of his,
And send him naked to the wilderness.
Lor. Then, Edward, here, in spite of all thy lords,
I do pronounce defiance to thy face.
P. Edw. Defiance, Frenchman! we rebound it back
Even to the bottom of thy master's throat,
And, be it spoke with reverence of the King,
My gracious father, and these other lords,
I hold thy message but as scurrilous,
And him that sent thee, like the lazy drone

25. **Except . . . male.** Cf. Canterbury's lengthy speech of justification in *Henry V*, I.ii.33 ff. and its repudiation of the Salic law argument.
26. **ground . . . contempt:** reason for their disobedience (in relation to your claim of sovereignty).
31. **discover:** reveal.
32. **to record of:** as witness to.
35. **Provokes:** urges, stirs up.
35. **lavish:** unrestrained, unstinting.
36. **lineal watchman:** guardian by true descent (i.e., from Isabel). Cf. Canterbury's "That fair Isabel, his grandmother / Was lineal of the Lady Ermengare," *Henry V*, I.ii.81–2.
37. **indirectly:** unfairly, deviously.
38. **subjects but:** i.e., subjects (do) except (elliptical).
40. **rebate:** repress.
41. **place:** install (as the true leader and protector).
42. **fructful:** fruitful (variant form).
43. **dignity:** position (as a royal claimant).
46. **rak'd in:** buried under.
48–9. **will approve . . . Able:** make good, will prove that fair Isabel's descent is appropriate.
50. **spurn against:** oppose with scorn (literally kick against).
52. **Duke of Lorraine.** Leader of the old Frankish duchy at the center of which are the three bishoprics of Metz, Toul, and Verdun.
59. **entail'd:** settled upon you by entail (i.e., secured to you and your heirs).
60. **do . . . homage:** as a vassal humbly make a public acknowledgment of allegiance to him.
64. **liegeman:** vassal sworn to the service and support of his liege lord.
67. **occasion . . . face:** a fortunate opportunity offers itself to me (with probable reference both to the more modest instance of Fortune smiling upon one (cf. *Hamlet*, I.iii.54) and the celebrated emblem of seizing Occasion's forelock).
69. **straight:** immediately, at once.
70. **upon a penalty:** under threat of punishment.
74. **dispos'd:** inclined, prepared.
76. **lame unpolish'd shifts:** weak, limping, poorly conceived expedients.
77. **vizard:** disguising mask (primarily, the visor on a knight's helmet).
78. **gloss:** fair and deceptive appearance.
79. **fealty:** vassal's sworn faith to his liege lord.
81. **where . . . foot:** wherever he treads.
81. **And where . . . kneel.** Cf. *Sir Thomas More* (ll. 110–13 in the scene in Hand D, generally accepted as Shakespeare's): "and your unreverent knees, / Make them your feet. To kneel to be forgiven / Is safer wars than ever you can make, / Whose discipline is riot."
85. **borrow'd plumes:** falsely assumed finery (see Aesop).
86. **naked:** defenseless.
87. **in spite of:** despite the (threatening) presence of. Possibly a misreading of "sight" (Capell), an easier reading.
89. **Defiance, . . . back.** Cf. the structure and rhythm of *1 Henry VI*, IV.vii.54: "Submission, Dolphin? 'tis a mere French word."
91. **with reverence of:** with all proper respect to.
93. **but as scurrilous:** merely the message of a buffoon or fool.
94. **drone:** sluggard, idler, do-nothing. Cf. *2 Henry VI*, IV.i.109.

Crept up by stealth unto the eagle's nest;
From whence we'll shake him with so rough a storm,
As others shall be warned by his harm.
War. Bid him leave off the lion's case he wears,
Lest, meeting with the lion in the field,
He chance to tear him piecemeal for his pride.
Art. The soundest counsel I can give his Grace
Is to surrender ere he be constrain'd:
A voluntary mischief hath less scorn
Than when reproach with violence is borne.
Lor. Regenerate traitor, viper to the place
Where thou [wast] fost'red in thine infancy,
Bearest thou a part in this conspiracy?
He draws his sword.
K. Edw. [*Draws his.*] Lorraine, behold the sharpness of this steel:
Fervent desire that sits against my heart
Is far more thorny-pricking than this blade,
That, with the nightingale, I shall be scarr'd
As oft as I dispose myself to rest,
Until my colors be display'd in France.
This is thy final answer; so be gone.
Lor. It is not that, nor any English brave,
Afflicts me so, as doth his poison'd view,
That is most false, should most of all be true.
[*Exeunt Lorraine and attendants.*]
K. Edw. Now, [lords], our fleeting bark is under sail:
Our gage is thrown, and war is soon begun,
But not so quickly brought unto an end.

Enter [SIR WILLIAM] MOUNTAGUE.

But wherefore comes Sir William Mountague?
How stands the league between the Scot and us?
Moun. Crack'd and dissever'd, my renowned lord:
The treacherous King no sooner was inform'd
Of your withdrawing of your army back,
But straight, forgetting of his former oath,
He made invasion on the bordering towns:
Berwick is won, Newcastle spoil'd and lost;
And now the tyrant hath begirt with siege
The castle of Roxborough, where enclos'd
The Countess Salisbury is like to perish.
K. Edw. That is thy daughter, Warwick, is it not,
Whose husband hath in Britain serv'd so long
About the planting of Lord Mountford there?
War. It is, my lord.
K. Edw. Ignoble David, hast thou none to grieve
But silly ladies with thy threat'ning arms?
But I will make you shrink your snaily horns.—
First, therefore, Audley, this shall be thy charge:
Go levy footmen for our wars in France.
And, Ned, take muster of our men at arms:
In every shire elect a several band;
Let them be soldiers of a lusty spirit,
Such as dread nothing but dishonor's blot.
Be wary, therefore, since we do commence
A famous war, and with so mighty a nation.
Derby, be thou embassador for us
Unto our father-in-law, the Earl of Hainault:
Make him acquainted with our enterprise,
And likewise will him, with our own allies
That are in Flanders, to solicit, too,
The Emperor of Almaigne in our name.
Myself, whilst you are jointly thus employ'd,
Will with these forces that I have at hand
March and once more repulse the traitorous Scot.
But, sirs, be resolute: we shall have wars
On every side:— and, Ned, thou must begin
Now to forget thy study and thy books
And ure thy shoulders to an armor's weight.
P. Edw. As cheerful sounding to my youthful spleen
This tumult is of war's increasing broils,
As at the coronation of a king
The joyful clamors of the people are,
When "Ave, Caesar!" they pronounce aloud.
Within this school of honor I shall learn,
Either to sacrifice my foes to death,
Or in a rightful quarrel spend my breath.
Then cheerfully forward! each a several way:
In great affairs 'tis naught to use delay. *Exeunt.*

95. **eagle's nest:** royal throne (the eagle being considered the king of birds).
98. **lion's case:** lion's skin. (The lion was considered the king of beasts. Cf. *Henry V*, IV.iii.93 and note.) Lorraine seems to have some such symbolic coat over his armor, as does Austria with that stolen from Richard the Lion-hearted in *King John*, III.i.113–29.
99. **meeting . . . field:** encountering a real lion (Edward III) on the battlefield.
100. **piecemeal for:** piece by piece because of.
101: **his grace:** i.e., John, the French king.
103. **voluntary . . . scorn:** misfortune accepted voluntarily results in less contempt or derision.
105. **Regenerate:** degenerate (only citation in *O.E.D.*; Tyrrell's *Degenerate* may be right).
105–6. **viper . . . fost'red:** vipers were believed to kill their mothers by eating their way through the maternal entrails.
109. **Fervent . . . heart:** burning longing that presses against my heart.
111. **That . . . scarr'd:** so that like the nightingale I shall be wounded. Cf. *The Rape of Lucrece*, 1135 ff.
113. **colors:** flags, ensigns.
115. **brave:** boast.
116. **his poison'd view:** sight of this morally corrupted man.
117. **That . . . true:** i.e., the sight or appearance of which is (in fact) most deceptive, which, of all things, should be most truthful (since Lorraine, though a native of France, was a traitor as an ally of England).
119. **gage is thrown:** pledge (e.g., a glove) has been cast down (as a challenge).
121–69. Cf. George Peele's *Edward I* (1593; Malone Society ed.), lines 2182–2251.
122. **league:** compact, peace treaty.
128. **spoil'd:** pillaged, plundered.
133. **Britain:** Brittany (Bretagne).
134. **planting . . . Mountford:** setting up Mountford in position (to cause trouble for the French). Cf. *Richard II*, V.i.63. On Mountford, see IV.i o.s.d.
137. **silly:** helpless, defenseless.
138. **shrink . . . horns:** pull in his snail-like horns (i.e., retreat). Cf. *Venus and Adonis*, 1033–34: "Or as the snail, whose tender horns being hit, / Shrinks backward in his shelly cave with pain."
141. **take muster:** determine the number of and inspect.
142. **In every . . . band:** in each county pick out a specially selected body of footsoldiers.
148. **Earl of Hainault:** leader of the territory east of Artois, south of Lille, the westernmost part of the Holy Roman Empire with Cambrai as its major city. Cf. *Richard III*, I.iv.49 for Clarence's mention of "my great father-in-law, renowned Warwick."
152. **Almaigne:** Germany.
159. **ure:** accustom.
160. **spleen:** hot, proud temper.
161. **broils:** disturbances, quarrels. Cf. *Macbeth*, I.ii.6: "Say to the king the knowledge of the broil."
164. **"Ave, Caesar!":** Hail, Caesar!
167. **spend my breath:** i.e., die.
168. **several:** separate.
169. **naught:** hurtful, bad.

[SCENE II]

Enter the COUNTESS [OF SALISBURY, *upon the walls*].

[*Count.*] Alas, how much in vain my poor eyes gaze
For succor that my sovereign should send!
Ah, cousin Mountague, I fear thou wants
The lively spirit sharply to solicit,
With vehement suit, the King in my behalf:
Thou dost not tell him what a grief it is
To be the scornful captive to a Scot;
Either to be woo'd with broad untuned oaths,
Or forc'd by rough insulting barbarism.
Thou dost not tell him, if he here prevail,
How much they will deride us in the north,
And in their vild, uncivil, skipping jigs
Bray forth their conquest and our overthrow,
Even in the barren, bleak, and fruitless air.

Enter [KING] DAVID *and* DOUGLAS, LORRAINE, [*and others*].

I must withdraw: the everlasting foe
Comes to the wall. I'll closely step aside,
And list their babble, blunt and full of pride.
[*Retiring behind the works.*]

K. Dav. My Lord of Lorraine, to our brother of France
Commend us, as the man in Christendom
That we [most] reverence and entirely love.
Touching your embassage, return and say
That we with England will not enter parley,
Nor never make fair weather, or take truce,
But burn their neighbor towns, and so persist
With eager [roads] beyond their city York:
And never shall our bonny riders rest,
Nor [rusting] canker have the time to eat
Their light-borne snaffles nor their nimble [spurs],
Nor lay aside their jacks of gymold mail,
Nor hang their staves of grained Scottish ash
In peaceful wise upon their city walls,
Nor from their button'd tawny leathern belts
Dismiss their biting whinyards, till your King
Cry out "Enough! spare England now for pity."
Farewell, and tell him that you leave us here
Before this castle: say, you came from us
Even when we had that yielded to our hands.

Lor. [I] take my leave, and fairly will return
Your acceptable greeting to my King. *Exit Lorraine.*

K. Dav. Now, Douglas, to our former task again,
For the division of this certain spoil.

Doug. My liege, I crave the lady, and no more.

K. Dav. Nay, soft ye, sir; first I must make my choice,
And first I do bespeak her for myself.

[*Doug*]. Why then, my liege, let me enjoy her jewels.

K. Dav. Those are her own, still liable to her,
And who inherits her hath those withal.

Enter a SCOT, [*as a messenger*,] *in haste.*

Mes. My liege, as we were pricking on the hills
To fetch in booty, marching hitherward
We might descry a mighty host of men.
The sun, reflecting on the armor, showed
A field of plate, a wood of pikes advanced.
Bethink your Highness speedily herein:
An easy march within four hours will bring
The hindmost rank unto this place, my liege.

K. Dav. Dislodge, dislodge! it is the King of England.

Doug. Jemmy, my man, saddle my bonny black.

K. Dav. Mean'st thou to fight, Douglas? we are too weak.

Doug. I know it well, my liege, and therefore fly.

Count. [*Coming forward.*] My lords of Scotland, will ye stay and drink?

K. Dav. She mocks at us, Douglas. I cannot endure it.

Count. Say, good my lord, which is he must have the lady,
And which her jewels? I am sure, my lords,
Ye will not hence 'till you have shar'd the spoils.

K. Dav. She heard the messenger, and heard our talk;
And now that comfort makes her scorn at us.

I.ii. Location: Roxborough. Before the castle.
2. **should:** (1) ought to, is bound to; (2) may be expected to.
3. **Mountague.** Historically, the first Earl of Salisbury, a confidant of the King, instrumental in the capture of Mortimer, lover of Edward's mother (see Marlowe's *Edward II*), and subsequently a warrior in the struggles in France.
7. **be the scornful . . . Scot:** as a prisoner to be scorned by a Scot.
8. **broad untuned:** indecent, harsh sounding.
9. **forc'd:** overpowered. **barbarism:** rudeness, coarseness.
12. **vild:** vile (variant form).
12. **skipping jigs:** lightweight mocking jokes or jibes. The phrasing of the Countess's scorn at being the captive of a Scot anticipates the Sergeant's reference to Macbeth's having "Compell'd these skipping kerns to trust their heels" (*Macbeth*, I.ii.30).
13. **Bray forth.** Cf. *Hamlet*, I.iv.11: "The kettle-drum and trumpet thus bray out."
14. **fruitless:** infertile (repeats "barren" = unproductive).
14. **Even . . . air.** Cf. "Upon my head they plac'd a *fruitless* crown, / And put a *barren* sceptre in my gripe," (*Macbeth*, III.i.60–61). "Bleak air" occurs in both *As You Like It*, II.vi.15 and *Timon of Athens*, IV.iii.222.
16. **closely:** covertly.
21. **embassage:** ambassadorial mission or message.
22. **enter parley:** begin to debate terms for a truce.
23. **make fair weather:** agree amicably. Cf. *King John*, V.i.21.
25. **eager roads:** fierce raids.
26. **bonny:** comely, good-looking.
27. **rusting canker:** corrupting sore or ulcer. Cf. *Venus and Adonis*, 767, "cank'ring rust."
28. **snaffles:** form of bridle bit, exerting less control than one provided with a curb (hence "light-borne").
29. **jacks of gymold mail:** coats of double-ringed chain mail.
32. **button'd:** fastened with buttons.
33. **Dismiss:** remove, discard.
33. **whinyards:** swords.
37. **that:** i.e., the castle.
41. **certain spoil:** assured booty or plunder.
43. **soft ye:** not so fast, slow up.
46. **still liable:** always (legally) belonging.
48. **pricking:** spurring, galloping. Cf. *The Faerie Queene*, Bk. I, Canto 1, line 1.
51–52. **The sun . . . advanced.** Cf. "And now a wood / Comes toward Dunsinane . . . I begin to be a-weary of the sun," *Macbeth*, V.v.44–45, 48.
52. **plate:** plate-armor.
52. **pikes advanced:** long steel-headed spear-like weapons at the ready.
62–63. **Say . . . jewels.** Cf. *The Merchant of Venice*, IV.i.174 for Portia's query, "Which is the merchant here? and which the Jew?"
66. **comfort:** reinforcement, relief.

[Enter] another MESSENGER.

Mes. Arm, my good lord! O, we are all surpris'd!
[Count.] After the French embassador, my liege,
And tell him that you dare not ride to York:
Excuse it, that your bonny horse is lame.
K. Dav. [She] heard that, too: intolerable grief!
Woman, farewell. Although I do not stay—
Exeunt Scots.
Count. 'Tis not for fear: and yet you run away.—
O happy comfort, welcome to our house!
The confident and boist'rous boasting Scot,
That swore before my walls they would not back
For all the armed power of this land,
With faceless fear, that ever turns his back,
Turn'd hence again the blasting north-east wind,
Upon the bare report and name of arms!

Enter MOUNTAGUE *[and others].*

O summer's day! see where my cousin comes.
Moun. How fares my aunt? We are not Scots:
Why do you shut your gates against your friends?
Count. Well may I give a welcome, cousin, to thee,
For thou com'st well to chase my foes from hence.
Moun. The King himself is come in person hither.
Dear aunt, descend, and gratulate his Highness.
Count. How may I entertain his Majesty,
To show my duty and his dignity?
[Exit from the walls.]

[Flourish.] *Enter* KING EDWARD, WARWICK, ARTOIS, *with others.*

K. Edw. What, are the stealing foxes fled and gone
Before we could uncouple at their heels?
War. They are, my liege, but, with a cheerful cry,
Hot hounds and hardy chase them at the heels.

Enter COUNTESS, *[attended].*

K. Edw. This is the Countess, Warwick, is it not?
War. Even she, [my] liege, whose beauty tyrant's fear,
As a May blossom with pernicious winds,
Hath sullied, wither'd, overcast, and done.
K. Edw. Hath she been fairer, Warwick, than she is?
War. My gracious King, fair is she not at all,
If that herself were by to stain herself,
As I have seen her when she was herself.
K. Edw. *[Aside.]* What strange enchantment [lurk'd] in those her eyes,
When they excell'd this excellence they have,
That now her dim decline hath power to draw
My subject eyes from piercing majesty
To gaze on her with doting admiration.
Count. *[Kneels.]* In duty lower than the ground I kneel,
And for my dull knees bow my feeling heart
To witness my obedience to your Highness,
With many millions of a subject's thanks
For this your royal presence, whose approach
Hath driven war and danger from my gate.
K. Edw. Lady, stand up. I come to bring thee peace,
However thereby I have purchas'd war.
Count. No war to you, my liege: the Scots are gone,
And gallop home toward Scotland with their hate.
[K. Edw.] *[Aside.]* Lest yielding here I pine in shameful love.—
Come, we'll pursue the Scots. Artois, away!
Count. A little while, my gracious sovereign, stay,
And let the power of a mighty king
Honor our roof. My husband in the wars,
When he shall hear it, will triumph for joy:
Then, dear my liege, now niggard not thy state,
Being at the wall, enter our homely gate.
K. Edw. Pardon me, Countess, I will come no near;
I dream'd to-night of treason, and I fear.
Count. Far from this place let ugly treason lie!
K. Edw. *[Aside.]* No farther off than her conspiring eye,
Which shoots infected poison in my heart,
Beyond repulse of wit or cure of art.
Now in the sun alone it doth not lie
With light to take light from a mortal eye;
For here [two] day stars, that mine eyes would see,

68. **embassador:** ambassador (variant form).
70. **Excuse it:** make the excuse.
78. **faceless fear . . . back:** i.e., fear is faceless because all one can see is its back.
81. **O summer's day:** O what a fortunate (or happy) day.
85. **well:** at the right moment.
89. **show . . . dignity:** pay my homage (to the King) in a way worthy of his high estate.
91. **uncouple:** literally, release the hounds from being coupled together, let them run free (a hunting metaphor for giving free rein to soldiers).
92. **cry:** i.e., the yelping of hunting dogs.
93. **This . . . not.** Froissart (Berners, Chapter LXXVII) describes the meeting between the Countess and the King: "Assone as the lady knewe of ye kynges comyng, she set opyn the gates, and ca[m]e out so richely be sene, that euery man maueyled of her beauty, and coude nat cease to regarde her noblenes with her great beauty, and the gracyous wordes and countenaunce that she made: when she came to the kyng, she knelyd downe to the yerth thankyng hym of his socours, and so ledde hym into the castell, to make hym chere and honour, as she that coude ryght well do it."
97. **done:** ruined.
99–101. **My gracious . . . herself.** Cf. Richard and Anne in *Richard III*, I.ii.84–87.
100. **stain:** blemish (by comparison).
103. **excell'd . . . have:** overmatched their present excellence.
104. **That:** so that.
105. **subject . . . majesty:** (changed) my (now) captivated eyes from (their customary) penetrating regal gaze.
108. **for:** as representative of (my feeling heart).
114. **thereby . . . war:** in so coming I have brought war (with the Scots) upon myself.
117. **yielding . . . pine:** surrendering myself here (as a prisoner), I languish.
122. **triumph:** rejoice.
123. **niggard . . . state:** do not be ungenerous with your (1) greatness, (2) power (as a king).
125. **no near:** no nearer.
126. **I dream'd.** Cf. *Romeo and Juliet*, I.iv.49–50.
128. **conspiring:** inspiring treason (against marital faith). The expression *conspiring eye* leads into a description which parallels *Romeo and Juliet*, III.ii.46–7.
129. **shoots.** The eye was believed to emit rays.
130. **Beyond . . . art:** past the mind's powers to resist or medicine's capacity to cure.
132. **take . . . eye:** blind a man's eye.
133. **would:** desire to.

More than the sun, steals mine own light from me.
Contemplative desire! desire to be
In contemplation that may master thee.—
Warwick, Artois, to horse, and let's away!

Count. What might I speak to make my sovereign stay?

K. Edw. What needs a tongue to such a speaking eye,
That more persuades than winning oratory?

Count. Let not thy presence, like the April sun,
Flatter our earth, and suddenly be done.
More happy do not make our outward wall
Than thou wilt grace our inner house withal.
Our house, my liege, is like a country swain,
Whose habit rude, and manners blunt and plain,
Presageth nought, yet inly beautified
With bounty's riches and fair hidden pride;
For where the golden ore doth buried lie,
The ground, undeck'd wth nature's tapestry,
Seems barren, sere, unfertile, fructless, dry;
And where the upper turf of earth doth boast
His pride, perfumes, and parti-color'd cost,
Delve there, and find this issue and their pride
To spring from ordure and corruption's side:
But to make up my all too long compare,
These ragged walls no testimony are
What is within, but, like a cloak, doth hide
From weather's [waste] the under-garnish'd pride.
More gracious than my terms can let thee be,
Entreat thyself to stay a while with me.

K. Edw. [*Aside.*] As wise as fair! what fond fit can be heard,
When wisdom keeps the gate as beauty's guard?—
Countess, albeit my business urgeth me,
It shall attend, while I attend on thee.—
Come on, my lords, here will I host to-night.

Exeunt.

134. **More . . . sun:** even more than the sun (blinds one).
135. **contemplative desire:** an apparent oxymoron, but meaning meditative emotion directed to the attainment of the desired object (the Countess).
136. **master thee:** subdue desire.
139. **what . . . tongue to.** For a calculated use of the language of eyes, see *King Lear*, IV.v.25: "She gave strange eliads and most speaking looks." Cf. also *The Rape of Lucrece*, 29 ff., 268, and 561–3.
145. **swain:** lover.
146. **habit rude:** rustic clothing.
147. **Presageth nought:** predicts, promises nothing (of worth).
147. **inly beautified:** is made beautiful within. Cf. *Hamlet*, II.ii.110–11.
148, 153, 154, 159. **pride:** splendor, magnificence.
150. **undeck'd . . . tapestry:** unadorned by nature's decorated carpet of grass and flowers.
151. **sere:** withered. Cf. Macbeth, V.iii.23.
151. **fructless:** fruitless (variant form).
153. **parti-color'd cost:** variously colored (1) pomp. (2) riches. Shakespeare associates "cost" with "pride" in Sonnets 64.2 and 91.10.
154. **Delve . . . find:** dig there and you will find.
154. **issue:** result.
155. **ordure:** dung.
155. **side:** space, area.
156. **make up . . . compare:** conclude . . . comparison.
159. **under-garnish'd:** too slightly defended.
160. **my terms . . . be:** (better than) my words can allow you to stay.
162. **fond . . . heard:** foolish fear (of treason; see l. 126) can be given audience.
163. **albeit:** although.
165. **attend . . . attend on:** wait . . . wait upon.
166. **host:** be a guest. A nice example of the antithetical sense of primal words.

[ACT II, Scene I]

[*Enter* Lodwick.]

[*Lod.*] I might perceive his eye in her eye lost,
His ear to drink her sweet tongue's utterance,
And changing passion, like inconstant clouds
That rack upon the carriage of the winds,
Increase and die, in his disturbed cheeks.
Lo, when she blush'd, even then did he look pale,
As if her cheeks, by some enchanted power,
Attracted had the cherry blood from his;
Anon, with reverent fear, when she grew pale,
His [cheeks] put on their scarlet ornaments,
But no more like her oriental red
Than brick to coral, or live things to dead.
Why did he then thus counterfeit her looks?
If she did blush, 'twas tender modest shame,
Being in the sacred presence of a king;
If he did blush, 'twas red immodest shame,
To [vail] his eyes amiss, being a king:
If she look'd pale, 'twas silly woman's fear,
To bear herself in presence of a king;
If he look'd pale, it was with guilty fear,
To dote amiss, being a mighty king.
Then Scottish wars farewell: I fear 'twill prove
A ling'ring English siege of peevish love.
Here comes his Highness, walking all alone.

[*Lodwick stands aside.*]

Enter King Edward.

K. Edw. She is grown more fairer far since I came [hither],
Her voice more silver every word than other,
Her wit more fluent. What a strange discourse
Unfolded she of David and his Scots!
"Even thus," quoth she, "he spake,"—and then spoke broad

II.i. Location: Roxborough. Gardens of the castle.
1. **might perceive:** was able to observe.
2. **sweet tongue's utterance.** Cf. *Romeo and Juliet*, II.ii.58–9: "My ears have yet not drunk a hundred words / Of thy tongue's uttering"
3. **changing passion:** different strong emotion.
4. **rack . . . carriage:** drive upon the conveyance.
5. **Increase and die:** i.e., fluctuate, grow and expire.
6 ff. **Lo, when she blushed.** Cf. for the significance of change in facial coloring and "the oscillatory rhetoric—marked by the recurring He-She" (Østerberg), *Venus and Adonis*, 35 ff., 49 ff., 73 ff., 345 ff., and 589 ff.; *The Rape of Lucrece*, 54 ff., 257 ff., and 736 ff.; and *Love's Labor's Lost*, I.ii.99 ff.
7. **enchanted:** magical.
9. **Anon, with . . . pale:** straightaway, when her cheeks grew pale from reverent fear (being in the King's presence).
10. **scarlet ornaments:** i.e., blushes. Cf. Sonnet 142.6.
11. **oriental:** brilliantly lustrous.
11–12. **But no more . . . coral.** Cf. Sonnet 130.1–2.
13. **counterfeit:** imitate (to deceive), forge.
14. **tender modest shame:** the result of sensitive and modest fear of offending against propriety.
17. **To vail . . . amiss:** i.e., causing him to look down, avoiding her.
18. **silly:** (1) lowly; (2) foolish; (3) defenseless.
19. **To bear herself:** i.e., as how to behave.
21. **To dote amiss:** to be foolishly and wrongly in love.
23. **peevish:** (1) silly; (2) mischievous; (3) perverse.
25. **more fairer.** Elizabethan double comparative = more fair.
26. **silver . . . other:** soft-toned, musical with every word. "Silver" was regularly associated with musical sound (cf. *Romeo and Juliet*, IV.v.128–43).
27. **wit:** great mental capacity (expressed in speaking).
29. **quoth:** said.
29. **broad:** i.e., in Lowland Scottish dialect.

With epithetes and accents of the Scot,
But somewhat better than the Scot could speak:
"And thus," quoth she,—and answer'd then herself;
For who could speak like her? but she herself
Breathes from the wall an angel's note from heaven
Of sweet defiance to her barbarous foes.
When she would talk of peace, methinks her tongue
Commanded war to prison; when of war,
It waken'd Caesar from his Roman grave
To hear war beautified by her discourse.
Wisdom is foolishness but in her tongue,
Beauty a slander but in her fair face:
There is no summer but in her cheerful looks,
Nor frosty winter but in her disdain.
I cannot blame the Scots that did besiege her,
For she is all the treasure of our land,
But call them cowards that they ran away,
Having so rich and fair a cause to stay.—
Art thou there, Lodwick? [*Lodwick comes forward.*]
Give me ink and paper.
Lod. I will, my liege.
K. Edw. And bid the lords hold on their play at chess,
For we will walk and meditate alone.
Lod. I will, my sovereign. [*Exit.*]
K. Edw. This fellow is well read in poetry,
And hath a lusty and persuasive spirit:
I will acquaint him with my passion,
Which he shall shadow with a veil of lawn,
Through which the queen of beauty's queen shall see
Herself the ground of my infirmity.

Enter LODWICK.

Hast thou pen, ink, and paper ready, Lodwick?
Lod. Ready, my liege.
K. Edw. Then in the summer arbor sit by me,
Make it our council house, or cabinet:
Since green our thoughts, green be the conventicle,
Where we will ease us by disburd'ning them.
Now, Lodwick, invocate some golden muse
To bring thee hither an enchanted pen,
That may for sighs set down true sighs indeed,
Talking of grief to make thee ready groan;
And when thou writest of tears, encouch the word,
Before and after, with such sweet laments
That it my raise drops in a Tartar's eye,
And make a flint-heart Scythian pitiful;
For so much moving hath a poet's pen.
Then, if thou be a poet, move thou so,
And be enriched by thy [sovereign's] love:
For if the touch of sweet concordant strings
Could force attendance in the ears of hell,
How much more shall the strains of poet's wit
[Beguile] and ravish soft and humane minds?
[*Lod.*] To whom, my lord, shall I direct my style?
K. Edw. To one that shames the fair and sots the wise,
Whose body [as] an abstract, or a brief,
Contains each general virtue in the world.
Better than "beautiful," thou must begin,
Devise for fair a fairer word than fair,
And every ornament that thou wouldest praise
Fly it a pitch above the soar of praise;
For flattery fear thou not to be convicted,
For were thy admiration ten times more,
Ten times ten thousand more [the] worth exceeds
Of that thou art to praise, [thy] praise's worth.
Begin, I will to contemplate the while.
Forget not to set down, how passionate,
How heart-sick, and how full of languishment
Her beauty makes me.
[*Lod.*] [Write] I to a woman?
K. Edw. What beauty else could triumph [o'er] me,
Or who but women do our love lays greet?
What, thinkest thou I did bid thee praise a horse?
[*Lod.*] Of what condition or estate she is,
'Twere requisite that I should know, my lord.
K. Edw. Of such estate, that hers is as a throne,
And my estate the footstool where she treads:
Then mayst thou judge what her condition is
By the proportion of her mightiness.
Write on, while I peruse her in my thoughts:
Her voice to music or the nightingale—
To music every summer-leaping swain
Compares his sunburnt lover, when she speaks;
And why should I speak of the nightingale?

30. **epithetes:** terms, expressions (variant form).
31. **better:** more articulately, clearly (perhaps, less "broadly").
40, 41, 42, 43. **but:** except.
45. **all:** alone, above everything else.
50. **hold on:** continue.
53. **well read:** very knowledgeable.
54. **lusty:** lively.
58. **ground of:** reason for.
61. **summer arbor:** trellis-work covered with vines and climbing shrubs (for shade) in summertime.
63. **conventicle:** meeting place (with some suggestion of secrecy).
65. **invocate:** call upon (poets in classical times and in the imitative Renaissance frequently began their poems by "invocating" their muse).
66. **enchanted:** magic.
68. **ready:** readily, quickly.
69. **encouch:** (1) inlay (a nonce use); (2) surround.
71. **Tartar's:** savage's (Tartars, like Scythians [see below], were stereotypically of a rough and violent disposition).
73. **moving:** power of exciting (the emotions).
77. **Could . . . hell:** an allusion to the myth of Orpheus and Eurydice, emblematic of the power of poetry.
78. **strains . . . wit:** lines of poets' inspiration.
80. **style:** literary composition.
81. **shames . . . wise:** puts the beautiful to shame and makes fools of the wise.
82. **abstract . . . brief:** summary . . . epitome. Cf. *Richard III*, IV.iv.28; *Hamlet*, II.ii.524; and especially *King John*, II.i.101–3.
84. **Better . . . begin:** To begin you must find a word more appropriate than merely "beautiful" (i.e., "fair").
85. **Devise for fair:** invent in the place of beauty, beautiful.
87. **pitch . . . praise:** above the highest point praise can attain.
88. **For:** so far as.
92. **I will . . . while:** I will (go) to meditate meanwhile.
97. **love lays greet:** love poems salute ("lays" were usually written to be sung).
98. **praise a horse.** Cf. *Henry V*, III.vii.7–65.
99. **condition or estate:** social position or rank.
101. **throne:** i.e. "throne" = state (with play on "estate"; see note on 99).
104. **By . . . mightiness:** by the comparative extent of her great powers (to influence).
105. **peruse:** describe, examine (in meditating upon).
107. **summer-leaping swain:** country youth who, in summer, jumps up and down for joy.
108. **lover.** Applied to both men and women in Elizabethan times.

The nightingale sings of adulterate wrong,
And that compar'd is too satirical;
For sin, though sin, would not be so esteem'd,
But, rather, virtue sin, sin virtue deem'd.
Her hair far softer than the silkworm's twist,
Like to a flattering glass, doth make more fair
The yellow amber.—"Like a flattering glass"
Comes in too soon; for writing of her eyes
I'll say, that like a glass they catch the sun,
And thence the hot reflection doth rebound
Against my breast, and burns my heart within.
Ah, what a world of descant make my soul
Upon this voluntary ground of love.—
Come, Lodwick, hast thou turn'd thy ink to gold?
If not, write but in letters capital
My mistress' name, and it will gild thy paper.
Read, [Lodwick], read:
Fill thou the empty hollows of mine ears
With the sweet hearing of thy poetry.
Lod. I have not to a period brought her praise.
K. Edw. Her praise is as my love, both infinite,
Which apprehend such violent extremes
That they disdain an ending period.
Her beauty hath no match but my affection:
Hers more than most, mine most, and more than more;
Hers more to praise than tell the sea by drops:
Nay, more, than drop the massy earth by sands,
And [sand] by [sand] print them in memory.
Then wherefore talkest thou of a period
To that which craves unended admiration?
Read! let us hear.
Lod. "More fair and chaste than is the queen of shades,"—
K. Edw. That [line] hath two faults, gross and palpable.
Comparest thou her to the pale queen of night,
Who, being set in dark, seems therefore light?
What is she, when the sun lifts up his head,
But like a fading taper, dim and dead?
My love shall brave the eye of heaven at noon,
And, being unmask'd, outshine the golden sun.
Lod. What is the other fault, my sovereign lord?
K. Edw. Read o'er the line again.
Lod. "More fair and chaste,"—
K. Edw. I did not bid thee talk of chastity,
To ransack so the [treasure] of her mind,
For I had rather have her chas'd, than chaste.
Out with the moon-line! I will none of it;
And let me have her liken'd to the sun:
Say, she hath thrice more splendor than the sun,
That her perfections emulates the sun,
That she breeds sweets as plenteous as the sun,
That she doth thaw cold winter like the sun,
That she doth cheer fresh summer like the sun,
That she doth dazzle gazers like the sun,
And, in this application to the sun,
Bid her be free and general as the sun,
Who smiles upon the basest weed that grows,
As lovingly as on the fragrant rose.—
Let's see what follows that same moonlight line.
Lod. "More fair and chaste than is the [queen] of shades,
More bold in constancy"—
K. Edw. In constancy! than who?
Lod. —"than Judith was."
K. Edw. Oh monstrous line! Put in the next a sword,
And I shall woo her to cut off my head.
Blot, blot, good Lodwick. Let us hear the next.
Lod. There's all that yet is done.
K. Edw. I thank thee then, thou hast done little ill;
But what is done is passing, passing ill.
No, let the captain talk of boist'rous war,
The prisoner of emured dark constraint;
The sick man best sets down the pangs of death,
The man that starves, the sweetness of a feast,
The frozen soul, the benefit of fire,

110. **nightingale . . . wrong.** An allusion to the Philomela, Procne, and Tereus myth; cf. *Titus Andronicus*, II.iii.43 and elsewhere; Sonnet 102.7; *A Midsummer Night's Dream*, II.ii.13,24; *Cymbeline*, II.ii.46; and *The Rape of Lucrece*, 1079, 1128.
111. **that compar'd . . . satirical:** i.e., using that as a comparison comes too close to comparing (my love) to something that deserves condemnation.
112. **would . . . esteem'd:** would prefer not to be so judged (i.e., as a sin).
113. **But . . . deem'd:** but preferably (that) virtue be considered as sin and sin as virtue.
114. **twist:** finely spun thread.
115–6. **Like . . . amber:** (her hair itself) acting as a flattering mirror, making already fair (i.e., yellow amber) even fairer. Blonde hair was generally considered as one of the distinguishing marks of beauty in a woman (cf. Sonnets 127 and 130).
119. **thence:** i.e., from the burning glass of her eyes.
121. **a world of descant:** a great deal of musical harmony or composition.
122. **voluntary ground:** spontaneous plainsong or melody (with ironic pun).
124. **write . . . capital.** Cf. Malvolio, *Twelfth Night*, II.v.120 ff.
127. **Fill thou . . . ears.** Cf. *Romeo and Juliet*, III.v.3: "That pierc'd the fearful hollow of thine ear."
129. **to a period:** to an end (with play on "period" = complete complex sentence).
131. **apprehend:** embrace, comprehend.
132. **disdain . . . period:** scorn any final expression.
133. **affection:** love, passion (also in the pejorative sense of "lust").
135. **tell:** count.
136. **more, than drop:** more than by the measure of a "drop" (i.e., by something even smaller and more numerous, the liquid version of a grain of sand).
139. **craves:** demands.
143. **queen of night:** Cynthia, the moon goddess.
147–48. **My love . . . sun.** Cf. *Romeo and Juliet*, II.ii.3 ff.
152. **ransack . . . mind:** examine thoroughly the (moral) richness of her thought.
153. **chas'd:** pursued (used mainly for the feeble pun on "chaste").
155–63. **And let . . . sun.** These nine lines all ending in "sun" illustrate the rhetorical figure called *epistrophe*.
157. **emulates.** Northern plural in *s* not uncommon in Elizabethan English (see Abbott, 333).
158. **sweets:** i.e., sweet things (pleasures, delights; perfumes).
160. **cheer:** (1) animate; (2) inspire.
162. **application . . . sun:** the applying of the sun metaphor to the Countess.
163. **free and general:** liberal and common or open to all.
164. **basest:** meanest, lowliest. Cf. Sonnet 94.12.
169. **Judith.** See the story of the Israelite heroine in the Book of Judith in the Apocrypha. She charms and then decapitates the Assyrian general Holofernes (the parallel figure to King Edward here), whose "heart was whole moved: for he burnt in desire toward her." (Bishops', Judith 12:16).
172. **Blot:** eliminate, efface.
174. **done little ill:** i.e., the little (you have) done is badly done.
175. **passing:** exceedingly.
177. **emured:** immured, enclosed, confined (variant form).
178. **sets down:** relates, records.
180. **soul:** person.

And every grief his happy opposite:
Love cannot sound well but in lovers' tongues.
Give me the pen and paper: I will write.

Enter [the] COUNTESS.

But soft, here comes the treasurer of my spirit.—
Lodwick, thou know'st not how to draw a battle;
These wings, these flankers, and these squadrons
Argue in thee defective discipline:
Thou shouldest have plac'd this here, this other here.
Count. Pardon my boldness, my thrice-gracious [lord]:
Let my intrusion here be call'd my duty,
That comes to see my sovereign how he fares.
K. Edw. [*To Lodwick.*] Go, draw the same, I tell thee in what form.
[*Lod.*] I go. [*Exit.*]
Count. Sorry I am to see my liege so sad.
What may thy subject do, to drive from thee
Thy gloomy consort, sullen melancholy?
K. Edw. Ah, lady, I am blunt and cannot straw
The flowers of solace in a ground of shame.
Since I came hither, Countess, I am wronged.
Count. Now God forbid that any in my house
Should think my sovereign wrong! Thrice-gentle King,
Acquaint me with [thy] cause of discontent.
K. Edw. How near then shall I be to remedy?
Count. As near, my liege, as all my woman's power
Can pawn itself to buy thy remedy.
K. Edw. If thou speak'st true, then have I my redress:
Engage thy power to redeem my joys,
And I am joyful, Countess; else I die.
Count. I will, my liege.
K. Edw. Swear, Countess, that thou wilt.
Count. By heaven, I will.
K. Edw. Then take thyself a little way aside,
And tell thyself, a king doth dote on thee:
Say that within thy power [it] doth lie
To make him happy, and that thou hast sworn
To give him all the joy within thy power.

181. **his:** its.
184. **treasurer:** keeper, preserver.
185. **draw:** design, lay out plans for. Edward pretends after the Countess's entry to have been talking of military strategy. From the time of Ovid and before, military metaphors were frequently used in describing love encounters.
186. **wings:** divisions on each side of the main body of an army.
186. **flankers:** (1) fortifications placed so as to command the flank of an enemy; (2) soldiers so placed.
187. **discipline:** training (in military matters).
188. **shouldest . . . here.** Edward points to a supposed battle plan being held by Lodwick.
190. **duty:** courtesy properly due to a superior.
192. **draw the same:** i.e., the battle plan mentioned in l. 185, but with a play on "same" referring to what Lodwick had actually been engaged in.
192. **I tell . . . form:** i.e., as in the model the King suggested in ll. 186–8.
196. **consort:** companion.
196. **sullen.** Q1–2 read "sullome," possibly a spelling for "solemn"; Capell's "sullen," however, is probably more suitable for the context.
197. **straw.** Variant form of "strew."
205. **pawn:** pledge.
206. **redress:** (1) remedy; (2) relief.
207. **redeem:** (1) fulfill; (2) repair.
212. **dote:** love wildly (usually descriptive of foolish infatuation).

Do this, and tell me when I shall be happy.
Count. All this is done, my thrice-dread sovereign.
That power of love, that I have power to give,
Thou hast with all devout obedience:
Employ me how thou wilt in proof thereof.
K. Edw. Thou hear'st me say that I do dote on thee.
Count. If on my beauty, take it if thou canst,
Though little, I do prize it ten times less;
If on my virtue, take it if thou canst,
For virtue's store by giving doth augment;
Be it on what it will, that I can give
And thou canst take away, inherit it.
K. Edw. It is thy beauty that I would enjoy.
Count. O, were it painted, I would wipe it off
And [dispossess] myself to give it thee;
But, sovereign, it is solder'd to my life:
Take one and both, for like an humble shadow
It haunts the sunshine of my summer's life.
[*K. Edw.*] But thou mayst [lend] it me to sport withal.
Count. As easy may my intellectual soul
Be lent away, and yet my body live,
As lend my body, palace to my soul,
Away from her and yet retain my soul.
My body is her bower, her court, her abbey,
And she an angel pure, divine, unspotted.
If I should [lend] her house, my lord, to thee,
I kill my poor soul, and my poor soul me.
K. Edw. Did'st thou not swear to give me what I would?
Count. I did, my liege, so what you would I could.
K. Edw. I wish no more of thee than thou mayst give,
Nor beg I do not, but I rather buy:
That is, thy love; and for that love of thine
In rich exchange I tender to thee mine.
Count. But that your lips were sacred, my lord,
You would profane the holy name of love.
That love you offer me you cannot give,
For Caesar owes that tribute to his queen;
That love you beg of me I cannot give,
For Sarah owes that duty to her lord.

217. **thrice-dread:** thrice-revered.
219. **devout:** devoted.
225. **virtue's . . . augment.** Cf. *Romeo and Juliet*, II.ii.133–5.
226. **Be . . . will:** Let it be whatever it may be.
231. **solder'd:** bonded.
232. **Take . . . both:** i.e., if you take one (beauty), you also take the other (life).
233. **haunts . . . life:** accompanies it as part of the happiness of my life no longer in its youth (spring).
234. **sport withal:** amuse myself (sexually) with.
235. **intellectual soul:** i.e., the spiritual faculty as distinct from the physical body, and also that part of the soul distinguished from the appetitive faculty of the will. Cf. this image of the soul and its house in *The Rape of Lucrece*, 1156–7, 1163 ff.
239. **My body . . . abbey.** Cf. *The Taming of the Shrew*, V.ii.146: "Thy husband is thy lord, thy life, thy keeper."
243. **what I would:** whatever I desired.
244. **so:** so long as.
246. **but:** except for the fact.
249. **But . . . sacred:** except for the fact that your lips are indeed divinely consecrated (as belonging to a king appointed by God).
252. **Caesar.** A term for king; here Edward. Cf. *The Taming of the Shrew*, V.ii.152–6.
254. **Sarah.** An allusion to 1 Peter 3: 5–6: "After this manner in the old time did the holy women also, which trusted in God, tire themselves being obedient unto their husbands. Even as Sarah obeyed Abraham, calling him husband . . . " (Bishops').

He that doth clip or counterfeit your stamp
Shall die, my lord: and will your sacred self
Commit high treason against the King of Heaven
To stamp his image in forbidden metal,
Forgetting your allegiance and your oath?
In violating marriage' sacred law
You break a greater honor than yourself.
To be a king is of a younger house
Than to be married: your progenitor,
Sole-reigning Adam on the universe,
By God was honor'd for a married man,
But not by him anointed for a king.
It is a penalty to break your statutes,
Though not enacted with your Highness' hand:
How much more to infringe the holy act,
Made by the mouth of God, seal'd with His hand!
I know my sovereign, in my husband's love,
Who now doth loyal service in his wars,
Doth but to try the wife of Salisbury,
Whether she will hear a wanton's tale or no,
Lest being therein guilty by my stay,
From that, not from my liege, I turn away. *Exit.*

K. Edw. Whether is her beauty by her words divine,
Or are her words sweet chaplains to her beauty?
Like as the wind doth beautify a sail,
And as a sail becomes the unseen wind,
So do her words her beauties, beauty words.
O that I were a honey-gathering bee
To bear the comb of virtue from [this] flower,
And not a poison-sucking envious spider
To turn the [juice] I take to deadly venom!
Religion is austere, and beauty gentle;

Too [strict] a guardian for so fair a [ward].
O that she were as is the air to me!
Why, so she is, for when I would embrace her,
This do I—and catch nothing but myself.
I must enjoy her, for I cannot beat
With reason and reproof fond love away.

Enter WARWICK.

Here comes her father: I will work with him,
To bear my colors in this field of love.

War. How is it that my sovereign is so sad?
May I, with pardon, know your Highness' grief,
And that my old endeavor will remove it,
It shall not cumber long your majesty.

K. Edw. A kind and voluntary gift thou profferest,
That I was forward to have begg'd of thee.
But O thou world, great nurse of flattery,
Why dost thou tip men's tongues with golden words,
And peise their deeds with weight of heavy lead,
That fair performance cannot follow promise?
O that a man might hold the heart's close book
And choke the lavish tongue when it doth utter
The breath of falsehood not charact'red there!

War. Far be it from the honor of my age,
That I should owe bright gold, and render lead!
Age is a cynic, not a flatterer.
I say again, that if I knew your grief,
And that by me it may be lessened,
My proper harm should buy your Highness' good.

K. Edw. These are the vulgar tenders of false men
That never pay the duty of their words.
Thou wilt not stick to swear what thou hast said,
But when thou knowest my grief's condition,
This rash-disgorged vomit of thy word
Thou wilt eat up again, and leave me helpless.

War. By heaven, I will not, though your Majesty

255. **clip . . . stamp.** Refers to the criminal practice of clipping slivers of gold or silver from an unmilled coin (see p. 841); "stamp" = a coin struck with the King's (or Queen's) head on the obverse; if clipped "within the ring" (i.e., within the circle surounding the King's head), a coin was no longer legal tender.
259. **allegiance:** (1) sworn duty of a liege lord to his subjects; (2) duty to God.
259. **oath:** (1) marriage vow; (2) pledge taken on becoming king.
262. **house:** lineage.
264. **on:** of. Cf. the line with *Romeo and Juliet*, III.ii.94: "Sole monarch of the universal earth."
265. **for:** for being.
266. **anointed:** consecrated (on becoming king by being rubbed with holy oil).
267. **penalty:** act deserving punishment, crime.
268. **enacted . . . hand:** officially decreed (by Parliament) during your reign.
269. **act:** decree.
270. **seal'd . . . hand:** i.e., in the marriage rite.
271. **in . . . love:** out of love for my husband.
273. **try:** test, prove.
274. **will hear . . . tale:** will pay heed to a lascivious person's story (invented to deceive). Cf. Jachimo's in *Cymbeline*, I.vi.157–68.
275. **being . . . stay:** giving the appearance of being ready to accede to such a wanton invitation by remaining to listen to it. Cf. *Cymbeline*, I.vi.141–2.
280. **becomes:** accords with, befits. Cf. *A Midsummer Night's Dream*, II.i.128–9.
281. **So . . . words:** in the same way her words accord with her beauties, her beauty with her words.
282–5. **bee . . . spider.** There was a popular belief that everything natural contained the seeds of both "good" and "evil," with the value depending on how the entity was used. Cf. *Romeo and Juliet*, II.iii.1–30.
283. **comb:** honeycomb.
286. **Religion . . . gentle:** religion is strict or harsh but beauty is pliant and easily manipulated.

287. **guardian . . . ward:** literally, legal guardian for so beautiful a minor (here used figuratively; cf. "chaplains" in l. 278).
288. **as . . . air:** free, available, open.
291. **enjoy:** possess sexually. Cf. *The Rape of Lucrece*, 489 ff. and 512: "'Lucrece,' quoth he, 'this night I must enjoy thee'."
292. **fond:** doting, foolish.
293. **work with him:** get him to cooperate (with me).
294. **bear . . . love:** (military metaphor) carry my flag or standard on this battleground of love.
297. **And:** if.
298. **cumber long:** long trouble, distress.
300. **forward:** ready, eager.
301. **nurse:** nourisher.
303. **peise:** weigh down.
304. **That:** so that.
305. **hold . . . book:** control the secret feelings of the heart.
306. **lavish:** loose, licentious.
307. **breath of falsehood:** lying utterance.
307. **charact'red:** (figuratively) inscribed in the heart (cf. Sonnet 108.1–2).
308. **honor . . . age:** sense of allegiance to what is right and proper to one of my years.
310. **cynic:** one disposed to sneer at the sincerity of human motives and actions.
313. **My . . . should:** injury to myself would.
314: **vulgar tenders:** ordinary, usual offers (to undertake something). Cf. *Hamlet*, I.iii.103–9.
316. **stick:** hesitate. Cf. *2 Henry IV*, I.iii.97–100.
317. **grief's condition:** what my sickness or unhappiness demands (to effect a cure).
318–9. **rash-disgorged . . . again:** i.e., over-hastily made promise, which, like a dog returning to its vomit, you will eat up again. Cf. *2 Henry IV*, I.iii.95–9.

Did bid me run upon your sword and die.
[*K. Edw.*] Say that my grief is no way medicinable,
But by the loss and bruising of thine honor?
War. If nothing but that loss may vantage you,
I would [accompt] that loss my vantage too.
K. Edw. Think'st that thou canst [unswear] thy oath again?
War. I cannot, nor I would not, if I could.
K. Edw. But if thou dost, what shall I say to thee?
War. What may be said to any perjur'd villain
That [breaks] the sacred warrant of an oath.
K. Edw. What wilt thou say to one that breaks an oath?
War. That he hath broke his faith with God and man,
And from them both stands excommunicate.
K. Edw. What office were it to suggest a man
To break a lawful and religious vow?
War. An office for the devil, not for man.
K. Edw. That devil's office must thou do for me,
Or break thy oath, or cancel all the bonds
Of love and duty 'twixt thyself and me:
And therefore, Warwick, if thou art thyself
The lord and master of thy word and oath,
Go to thy daughter, and in my behalf
Command her, woo her, win her any ways
To be my mistress and my secret love.
I will not stand to hear thee make reply:
Thy oath break hers, or let thy sovereign die. *Exit.*
[*War.*] O doting King! [O] detestable office!
Well may I tempt myself to wrong myself,
When he hath sworn me by the name of God
To break a vow made by the name of God.
What if I swear by this right hand of mine
To cut this right hand off? the better way
Were to profane the idol than confound it.
But neither will I do: I'll keep mine oath,
And to my daughter make a recantation
Of all the virtue I have preach'd to her:
I'll say, she must forget her husband, Salisbury,
If she remember to embrace the King;
I'll say, an oath may easily be broken,
But not so easily pardon'd, being broken;
I'll say, it is true charity to love,
But not true love to be so charitable;
I'll say, his greatness may bear out the shame,
But not his kingdom can buy out the sin;
I'll say, it is my duty to persuade,
But not her honesty to give consent.

Enter [the] COUNTESS.

See where she comes! Was never father had,
Against his child, an embassage so bad.
Count. My lord and father, I have sought for you:
My mother and the peers importune you
To keep in [presence] of his majesty,
And do your best to make his Highness merry.
War. [*Aside.*] How shall I enter in this graceless arrant?
I must not call her child, for where's the father
That will in such a suit seduce his child?
Then, "wife of Salisbury," shall I so begin?
No, he's my friend, and where is found the friend
That will do friendship such indamagement?
[*To the Countess.*] Neither my daughter, nor my dear friend's wife,
I am not Warwick, as thou think'st I am,
But an attorney from the court of hell,
That thus have hous'd my spirit in his form,
To do a message to thee from the King:
The mighty King of England dotes on thee:
He that hath power to take away thy life
Hath power to take thy honor, then consent
To pawn thine honor rather than thy life.
Honor is often lost and got again,
But life, once gone, hath no recovery.
The sun that withers hay doth nourish grass;
The King that would distain thee will advance thee.
The poets write, that great Achilles' spear
Could heal the wound it made: the moral is,
What mighty men misdo they can amend.
The lion doth become his bloody jaws
And grace his foragement by being mild,
When vassal fear lies trembling at his feet;
The King will in his glory hide thy shame,

323. **But:** except.
324. **vantage:** profit.
324–25 ff. **If . . . too.** Cf. Sonnet 88.3, 8–14.
329–30. **What . . . oath.** Cf. the problem of oath-breaking in *Love's Labor's Lost*, IV.iii.358 ff.
330. **warrant:** pledge.
333. **excommunicate:** cut off from membership in church (and, here, society).
334. **What . . . man:** what kind of action or undertaking would it be to tempt a man.
340. **if . . . thyself:** if you are truly, within yourself.
345. **stand:** wait.
347. **doting:** foolishly infatuated.
348. **wrong:** (1) injure; (2) dishonor.
348–50. **Well . . . God.** Cf. *King John*, III.i. 288–89.
349. **sworn me:** made me swear.
353. **profane . . . it:** desecrate the thing adored rather than destroy it.
355–6. **make a recantation:** disavow; retract.
356. **virtue:** (1) morality; (2) chastity.
357–66. **I'll say . . . consent.** These ten lines are a form of the rhetorical figure called *anaphora*, here alternate, every other line beginning with "I'll."
361. **true charity:** (1) an honest expression of natural affection; (2) spontaneous goodness (with play on "charity" = love).
362. **so charitable:** generous, tender-hearted to such an extreme extent.
363. **bear . . . shame:** i.e., make the shame tolerable.
364. **kingdom:** i.e., wealth.
366. **not her honesty:** not according with her honorable (1) conduct, (2) chastity.
368. **embassage:** mission.
370. **importune:** urge.
373. **arrant:** errand (variant form).
375. **suit:** petition.
381. **attorney:** agent (acting for someone else).
387. **pawn:** stake, risk.
391. **distain:** defile, dishonor.
392. **Achilles' spear.** An allusion to the legend of King Telephos of Mysia, a son of Hercules, who was wounded in battle by Achilles. The wound would not heal until Ulysses pointed out that if the spear were to be applied to the wound itself, the injury would, by a kind of homeopathic medicine, heal. So it was that, by some scrapings of Achilles' spear, the supplicant Telephos was cured. Cf. *2 Henry VI*, V.i.100–01, where York says, speaking of himself: "Whose smile and frown, like to Achilles' spear, / Is able with the change to kill and cure."
395. **doth become:** looks well with.
395–97. **The lion . . . feet.** Cf. *Love's Labor's Lost*, IV.i.90–1: "Submissive fall his princely feet before, / And he from forage will incline to play."
396. **grace his foragement:** confer honor on him as a hunter. Lions disdain a weak or cowering prey.
397. **vassal:** slavish.

And those that gaze on him to find out thee
Will lose their eyesight looking in the sun.
What can one drop of poison harm the sea,
Whose hugy vastures can digest the ill,
And make it lose his operation?
The King's great name will temper [thy] misdeeds,
And give the bitter [potion] of reproach
A sug'red, sweet, and most delicious taste;
Besides, it is no harm to do the thing
Which without shame could not be left undone.
Thus have I, in his Majesty's behalf,
Apparell'd sin in virtuous sentences,
And dwell upon thy answer in his suit.
Count. Unnatural besiege! Woe me unhappy,
To have escap'd the danger of my foes,
And to be ten times worse invir'd by friends!
Hath he no means to stain my honest blood
But to corrupt the author of my blood
To be his scandalous and vile solicitor?
No marvel though the branches be then infected,
When poison hath encompassed the root;
No marvel though the leprous infant die,
When the stern dame envenometh the dug.
Why then, give sin a passport to offend,
And youth the dangerous rein of liberty;
Blot out the strict forbidding of the law,
And cancel every canon that prescribes
A shame for shame, or penance for offence.
No, let me die, if his too boist'rous will
Will have it so, before I will consent
To be an actor in his graceless lust.
War. Why now thou speak'st as I would have thee speak,
And mark how I unsay my words again:
An honorable grave is more esteem'd
Than the polluted closet of a king;
The greater man, the greater is the thing,
Be it good or bad, that he shall undertake;
An unreputed mote, flying in the sun,
Presents a greater substance than it is;
The freshest summer's day doth soonest taint
The loathed carrion that it seems to kiss;
Deep are the blows made with a mighty axe;
That sin doth ten times aggravate itself
That is committed in a holy place;
An evil deed done by authority
Is sin and subornation; deck an ape
In tissue, and the beauty of the robe
Adds but the greater scorn unto the beast.
A spacious field of reasons could I urge
Between his [glory], daughter, and thy shame:
That poison shows worst in a golden cup;
Dark night seems darker by the lightning flash;
Lilies that fester smell far worse than weeds;
And every glory that inclines to sin
The shame is treble by the opposite.
So leave I with my blessing in thy bosom,
Which then convert to a most heavy curse,
When thou convertest from honor's golden name
To the black faction of bed-blotting shame. [*Exit.*]
Count. I'll follow thee; and when my mind turns so,
My body sink my soul in endless woe! [*Exit.*]

[SCENE II]

Enter at one door DERBY *from France; at another door* AUDLEY, *with a Drum.*

Derby. Thrice-noble Audley, well encount'red here.
How is it with our sovereign and his peers?
Aud. 'Tis full a fortnight since I saw his Highness,
What time he sent me forth to muster men,
Which I accordingly have done, and bring them hither
In fair array before his Majesty.
What news, my Lord of Derby, from the Emperor?
Derby. As good as we desire: the Emperor
Hath yielded to his Highness friendly aid,
And makes our King Lieutenant General
In all his lands and large dominions.
Then *via*! for the spacious bounds of France.

399. **find out:** spy out, discover.
400. **Will . . . sun.** Cf. *Love's Labor's Lost*, I.i.77 ff.
401–403. **What . . . sea.** Cf. the similarity of thought in *The Rape of Lucrece*, 527–32.
402. **hugy vastures:** immense spaces.
403. **operation:** efficacy.
404. **temper:** mitigate.
407. **do the thing:** have sexual intercourse.
408. **shame:** severe reproach (because intercourse is the only means by which the human race can survive). Cf. *Romeo and Juliet*, I.i.210–11; Sonnet 9.14, and Thomas Wilson, *The Arte of Rhetorique*, 1553 (ed. T. J. Derrick, p. 137).
410. **virtuous sentences:** righteous precepts.
411. **dwell upon:** await.
414. **invir'd:** beleaguered.
415. **honest:** (1) virtuous; (2) chaste. See *Hamlet*, III.i.102–114.
418. **though:** if.
419. **encompassed:** encircled (looks back to "besiege" and "invir'd").
420. **leprous:** skin-diseased.
421. **dame.** Variant of "dam" = mother.
422. **passport:** warrant.
423. **rein:** manage, control. Q1's "reigne" (= power, sway) is perhaps a possible reading.
423. **liberty:** license, sexual indulgence, Cf. Sonnet 41.1.
425. **canon:** (moral) law, decree.
429. **graceless:** merciless, depraved.
431. **unsay . . . again:** take back what I have been saying.
432–53. **An honorable grave . . . opposite.** Cf. this sustained collection of proverbial wisdom with *Othello*, I.iii.202–20.
433. **closet:** private apartment.
434. **The . . . thing.** Cf. *The Rape of Lucrece*, 1004 ff., beginning "The mightier man, the mightier is the thing."
436–37. **An unreputed . . . is:** an insignificant speck drifting against the sun appears to be larger and more substantial than it really is.
439. **carrion:** dead and putrefying flesh. Cf. *Hamlet*, II.ii.182: "a good kissing carrion."
441. **doth . . . itself:** makes itself ten times worse.
444. **subornation:** corruption by bribery or undue influence.
445. **tissue:** rich cloth often interwoven with gold and silver threads.
446. **Adds . . . beast:** makes the beast more greatly scorned.
447. **spacious . . . reasons:** wide range of wise sayings, observations.
448. **Between:** i.e., to illustrate the difference between.
451. **Lilies . . . weeds:** lilies (which are beautiful flowers) smell worse when decaying than mere unattractive vegetation (weeds). This line is repeated verbatim in Sonnet 94.14, and ll. 452–3 are a variant statement of 94:13: "For sweetest things turn sourest by their deeds." The line seems to ignore the fact that lilies are ill-smelling to begin with.
453. **is treble:** i.e., is made three times worse.
457. **bed-blotting shame:** i.e., an offense staining the (purity of) the marriage bed.
458. **turns so:** i.e., to the behavior of the "black faction" of l. 457.

II.ii. Location: Roxborough. A room in the castle.
o.s.d. **Drum:** drummer.
4. **What time:** at the time that.
12. ***via*!:** be off, up and away (Italian).

Aud. What, doth his Highness leap to hear these news?
Derby. I have not yet found time to open them.
The King is in his closet malcontent;
For what I know not, but he gave in charge,
Till after dinner none should interrupt him.
The Countess Salisbury, and her father Warwick,
Artois, and all, look underneath the brows.
Aud. Undoubtedly, then, something is amiss.
[Trumpets within.]
Derby. The trumpets sound: the King is now abroad.

Enter the King.

[Aud.] Here comes his Highness.
Derby. Befall my sovereign all my sovereign's wish!
K. Edw. Ah, that thou wert a witch to make it so!
Derby. The Emperor greeteth you.
[Presenting letters.]
K. Edw. *[Aside.]* Would it were the Countess!
Derby. And hath accorded to your Highness' suit.
K. Edw. *[Aside.]* Thou liest: she hath not, but I would she had.
Aud. All love and duty to my lord the King!
K. Edw. *[Aside.]* Well, all but one is none.— What news with you?
Aud. I have, my liege, levied those horse and foot,
According as your charge, and brought them hither.
K. Edw. Then let those foot trudge hence upon those horse,
According to our discharge, and be gone.
Derby, I'll look upon the Countess' mind anon.
Derby. The Countess' mind, my liege?
K. Edw. I mean the Emperor. Leave me alone.
Aud. What is his mind?
Derby. Let's leave him to his humor.
Exeunt [Derby and Audley].
K. Edw. Thus from the heart's [abundance] speaks the tongue:
Countess for Emperor: and, indeed, why not?
She is as imperator over me, and I to her
Am as a kneeling vassal that observes
The pleasure or displeasure of her eye.

Enter Lodwick.

What says the more than Cleopatra's match
To Caesar now?
Lod. That yet, my liege, ere night
She will resolve your Majesty. *[Drum within.]*
K. Edw. What drum is this that thunders forth this march,
To start the tender Cupid in my bosom?
Poor sheepskin! how it brawls with him that beateth it.
Go, break the thund'ring parchment bottom out,
And I will teach it to conduct sweet lines
Unto the bosom of a heavenly nymph;
For I will use it as my writing paper,
And so reduce him from a scolding drum
To be the herald and dear counsel-bearer
Betwixt a goddess and a mighty king.
Go, bid the drummer learn to touch the lute,
Or hang him in the braces of his drum,
For now we think it an uncivil thing
To trouble heaven with such harsh resounds.
Away! *Exit [Lodwick].*
The quarrel that I have requires no arms
But these of mine, and these shall meet my foe
In a deep march of penetrable groans;
My eyes shall be my arrows, and my sighs
Shall serve me as the vantage of the wind,
To whirl away my sweetest artillery.
Ah, but alas, she wins the sun of me,
For that is she herself, and thence it comes
That poets term the wanton warrior blind;
But love hath eyes as judgment to his steps,
Till too much loved glory dazzles them.

Enter Lodwick.

How now!
Lod. My liege, the drum that strook the lusty march
Stands with Prince Edward, your thrice-valiant son.

Enter Prince Edward.

K. Edw. I see the boy. *[Exit Lodwick.]* *[Aside.]*
O how his mother's face,
Modell'd in his, corrects my stray'd desire,
And rates my heart, and chides my thievish eye,
Who being rich enough in seeing her,
Yet [seeks] elsewhere; and basest theft is that
Which cannot cloak itself on poverty.—

13. **these news:** these tidings.
14. **open them:** disclose them (to the King).
15. **malcontent:** discontented, restless.
16. **gave in charge:** ordered.
19. **look . . . brows:** frown.
21. **trumpets:** (1) trumpeters; (2) their instruments.
30. **all . . . none:** all love and duty, except from the Countess, amounts to nothing.
31. **horse and foot:** cavalry and infantry.
33. **trudge hence upon:** be off immediately after.
38. **his humor:** i.e., his present "malcontent" mood (perhaps with reference to the doctrine of the "four humours" [blood, phlegm, choler, melancholy], the relative mixture of which fluids determined the nature of a person's temperament, "melancholy" in Edward's case).
39. **abundance:** overflowing.
41. **imperator:** general, absolute ruler. Cf. *Venus and Adonis,* 101 ff.
42. **observes:** watches (with careful attention in order to judge how she reacts).
46. **resolve:** inform.
48. **Cupid:** the god of love, used metaphorically for "love."
49. **brawls . . . it:** (1) clamors, (2) scolds as he beats it.
51. **lines:** verses.
54. **reduce:** change.
57. **touch:** play on, finger.
58. **braces:** leather cords which regulate the tension of the drumskin.
60. **resounds:** resonances.
64. **penetrable:** penetrating.
68. **wins . . . me:** gets the better of me by having the sun (i.e. herself) shine in my face. See the same situation of the sun in the face of the French at Crécy and note Shakespeare's use of the image in *Love's Labor's Lost,* IV.iii.366, for masculine advantage: "In conflict that you get the sun of them."
70. **wanton warrior:** Cupid.
71. **as . . . steps:** as a guide to his actions.
74. **strook.** Variant form of "struck."
74. **drum:** drummer.
75. **Stands with:** makes common cause with.
78. **rates:** chides, reproves.
79. **Who:** which.
81. **cloak . . . poverty:** excuse itself on the grounds of poverty.

Now boy, what news?
P. Edw. I have assembled, my dear lord and father,
The choicest buds of all our English blood
For our affairs to France; and here we come
To take direction from your majesty.
K. Edw. [*Aside.*] Still do I see in him delineate
His mother's visage: those his eyes are hers,
Who looking wistly on me make me blush,
For faults against themselves give evidence:
Lust [is] a fire; and [men], like [lanthorns], show
Light lust within themselves, even through themselves.
Away, loose silks [of] wavering vanity!
Shall the large limit of fair Brittany
By me be overthrown; and shall I not
Master this little mansion of myself?
Give me an armor of eternal steel:
I go to conquer kings; and shall I not then
Subdue myself, and be my enemy's friend?
It must not be.— Come, boy, forward, advance!
Let's with our colors sweet the air of France!

Enter LODWICK.

Lod. My liege, the Countess, with a smiling cheer,
Desires access unto your Majesty.
K. Edw. [*Aside.*] Why, there it goes! that very smile of hers
Hath ransom'd captive France, and set the King,
The Dolphin, and the peers at liberty.—
Go, leave me, Ned, and revel with thy friends.
Exit Prince.
[*Aside.*] Thy mother is but black, and thou, like her,
Dost put it in my mind how foul she is.—
Go, fetch the Countess hither in thy hand
And let her chase away these winter clouds,
For she gives beauty both to heaven and earth!
Exit Lodwick.
The sin is more to hack and hew poor men
Than to embrace in an unlawful bed
The register of all rarieties
Since leathern Adam till this youngest hour.

Enter [*the*] COUNTESS, [*escorted by* LODWICK].

Go, Lodwick, put thy hand into [my] purse;
Play, spend, give, riot, waste; do what thou wilt,
So thou wilt hence a while and leave me here.
[*Exit Lodwick.*]
Now my soul's playfellow, art thou come
To speak the more than heavenly word of "yea"
To my objection in thy beauteous love?
Count. My father, on his blessing, hath commanded—
K. Edw. That thou shalt yield to me.
Count. Ay, dear my liege, your due.
K. Edw. And that, my dearest love, can be no less
Than right for right, and render love for love.
Count. Than wrong for wrong, and endless hate for hate.
But sith I see your Majesty so bent,
That my unwillingness, my husband's love,
Your high estate, nor no respect respected
Can be my help, but that your mightiness
Will overbear and awe these dear regards,
I bind my discontent to my content,
And what I would not, I'll compel "I will,"
Provided that yourself remove those lets
That stand between your Highness' love and mine.
K. Edw. Name [them], fair Countess, and, by heaven, I will.
Count. It is their lives that stand between our love
That I would have chok'd up, my sovereign.
K. Edw. Whose lives, my lady?
Count. My thrice-loving liege,
Your Queen and Salisbury, my wedded husband,
Who living have that title in our love
That we cannot bestow but by their death.
K. Edw. Thy opposition is beyond our law.
Count. So is your desire. If the law
Can hinder you to execute the one,
Let it forbid you to attempt the other.
I cannot think you love me as you say,
Unless you do make good what you have sworn.
[*K. Edw.*] No more: thy husband and the Queen shall die.
Fairer thou art by far than Hero was,
Beardless Leander not so strong as I:
He swom an easy current for his love,
But I will [through] a [Hellespont] of blood

84. **buds:** i.e., youths.
89. **wistly:** intently.
90. **For:** because.
91. **lanthorns:** lanterns.
92. **Light:** fickle, unsteady (with play on light shining from the flame in a lantern).
93. **Loose . . . vanity:** unchaste silk trappings of vacillating self-conceit (with play on "silk" as being lustrous or iridescent).
98–9. **shall I . . . friend?:** (if that is so) must I not, therefore, first conquer myself, or, failing to do so, become a friend to my enemy (by supporting him). Capell drops "not", thereby giving an easier reading, but "shall I not then / Subdue" picks up "shall I not / Master" in ll. 95–6.
102. **cheer:** countenance.
106. **Dolphin.** English form of "Dauphin" = French heir apparent.
108. **but black:** comparatively swarthy (in contrast to the Countess).
109. **foul:** ugly.
110. **in thy hand:** by your hand.
113. **more:** greater, heavier.
115. **register:** index.
116. **leathern Adam:** i.e., Adam dressed in skins. See Genesis 3:21: "Unto Adam also, and to his wife, did the Lord God make garments of skins, and he put them on." (Bishops').
116. **youngest hour:** present hour (i.e., now). Cf. *1 Henry IV*, II.iv.93–5: ". . . since the old days of goodman Adam to the pupil age of this present twelve a'clock at midnight."
122. **objection:** suit, request.
123. **on his blessing:** i.e., his blessing depends upon my compliance.
127. **render:** return (supplying "to yield" following "Than" at the beginning of the line).
128. **Than:** (if that is so,) then.
129. **sith:** since.
131. **no respect respected:** no thoughtful consideration being taken into account.
133. **awe . . . regards:** subdue these precious considerations.
134. **I . . . content:** I make a compromise out of what I desire and don't desire.
135. **I'll compel "I will":** i.e., I will make myself say "I will."
136. **lets:** obstacles.
140. **chok'd up:** killed (literally, suffocated, strangled).
143. **title:** rightful claim.
145. **opposition . . . law:** objection or counter-proposal is beyond the limit of our laws (i.e., it is against all law, civil or religious).
147. **to execute:** in executing.
152–56. **Hero . . . lies.** The tragic love story of Hero and Leander, with the latter drowning as he swam (across the Hellespont) toward the former, is featured in several Elizabethan works, including Marlowe and Chapman's *Hero and Leander* (1598), Nashe's *Lenten Stuffe* (1599), and *As You Like It* (1599), IV.i.100–06.
154. **swom:** swam (variant form). Cf. *The Two Gentlemen of Verona*, I.i.25: "And yet you never swom the Hellespont."

To arrive at Sestos where my Hero lies.
Count. Nay, you'll do more; you'll make the river, too,
With their heart-bloods that keep our love asunder,
Of which my husband and your wife are twain.
K. Edw. Thy beauty makes them guilty of their death,
And gives in evidence that they shall die;
Upon which verdict I, their judge, condemn them.
Count. [*Aside.*] O perjur'd beauty! more corrupted judge!
When to the great star-chamber o'er our heads
The universal sessions calls to count
This packing evil, we both shall tremble for it.
K. Edw. What says my fair love? is she resolute?
Count. Resolute to be dissolv'd, and therefore this:
Keep but thy word, great King, and I am thine.
Stand where thou dost: I'll part a little from thee—
And see how I will yield me to thy hands.
[*Turning suddenly upon him and showing two daggers.*]
Here by my side doth hang my wedding knives:
Take thou the one, and with it kill thy Queen,
And learn by me to find her where she lies;
And with this other I'll dispatch my love,
Which now lies fast asleep within my heart.
When they are gone, then I'll consent to love.
Stir not, lascivious King, to hinder me:
My resolution is more nimbler far
Than thy prevention can be in my rescue;
And if thou stir, I strike; therefore stand still,
And hear the choice that I will put thee to:
[*Kneels.*] Either swear to leave thy most unholy suit,
And never henceforth to solicit me,
Or else, by heaven, this sharp-pointed knife
Shall stain thy earth with that which thou [wouldst] stain,
My poor chaste blood. Swear, Edward, swear,
Or I will strike and die before thee here.
K. Edw. Even by that power I swear, that gives me now
The power to be ashamed of myself,
I never mean to part my lips again
In any words that tends to such a suit.

157. **river:** i.e., the Hellespont (actually a strait rather than a river).
158. **heart-bloods:** vital life bloods.
160. **Thy . . . death.** Cf. *Richard III*, I.ii.117 ff.
161. **gives . . . die:** furnishes evidence to condemn them to death.
164. **star-chamber:** the heavens (with play on the Court of Star-chamber, a criminal court made up of the King's Council, hence under control of the monarch [here Edward]).
165. **universal sessions:** the Last Judgment, Doomsday (when all of human kind shall be brought before God for judgment).
165. **count:** account, reckoning.
166. **packing evil:** evil conspiracy ("pack" = conspire).
167. **resolute:** (1) resolved; (2) constant.
168. **be dissolv'd:** be destroyed.
170–88. **Stand . . . here.** Cf. *Romeo and Juliet*, IV.i.50–67.
172. **wedding knives:** small knives for domestic use, worn by a bride.
174. **learn . . . lies.** Since there is no evidence that the Queen has accompanied the King, "where she lies" has to be considered metaphorically: learn through my action where the Queen really resides (in your heart) even as my husband resides in my heart; these knives can kill our spouses, but only as we kill ourselves. The King may not have felt that the Queen does reside in his breast, but he perceives the suicidal nature of the Countess's argument and moves to forestall her, only to be met by her demand that he surrender his quest or face her death.
179. **more nimbler.** Double comparative for emphasis.
192. **tends.** A northern plural form in *s*.

Arise, true English lady, whom our isle
May better boast of than ever Roman might
Of her, whose ransack'd treasury hath task'd
The vain endeavor of so many pens.
Arise, and be my fault thy honor's fame,
Which after-ages shall enrich thee with.
I am awaked from this idle dream.—
Warwick, my son, Derby, Artois, and Audley,
Brave warriors all, where are you all this while?

Enter all.

Warwick, I make thee Warden of the North:—
Thou, Prince of Wales, and Audley, straight to sea;
Scour to Newhaven; some there stay for me;—
Myself, Artois, and Derby will through Flanders
To greet our friends there, and to crave their aid.
This night will scarce suffice me to discover
My folly's siege against a faithful lover;
For, ere the sun shall [gild] the eastern sky,
We'll wake him with our martial harmony.

Exeunt.

[ACT III, SCENE I]

Enter KING JOHN OF FRANCE, *his two Sons,* CHARLES OF NORMANDY *and* PHILIP, *and the* DUKE OF LORRAINE.

K. John. Here, till our navy of a thousand sail
Have made a breakfast to our foe by sea,
Let us encamp to wait their happy speed.—
Lorraine, what readiness is Edward in?
How hast thou heard that he provided is
Of martial furniture for this exploit?
Lor. To lay aside unnecessary soothing,
And not to spend the time in circumstance,
'Tis bruited for a certainty, my lord,
That he's exceeding strongly fortified.
His subjects flock as willingly to war,
As if unto a triumph they were led.
P. Cha. England was wont to harbor malcontents,
Bloodthirsty and seditious Catilines,
Spendthrifts, and such as gape for nothing else
But changing and alteration of the state;

195. **ransack'd treasury:** violated virtue. Cf. *Titus Andronicus*, II.i.131.
196. **vain . . . pens:** unsuccessful effort of many writers. Aside from Shakespeare, the Lucrece story is told by, among others, William Painter, *The Palace of Pleasure* (1575), a text which also contains a version of the Countess-Edward story. The story also appeared in what was probably the earliest version (c. 1592) of Thomas Heywood's play *The Rape of Lucrece*.
195–96. **her . . . pens:** a reference to the Roman matron Lucrece, wife of Collatinus, who was raped by Tarquinius Superbus; perhaps also an allusion to Shakespeare's poem *The Rape of Lucrece* (1594).
197. **be my fault . . . fame:** let my offense contribute to the fame of your (unviolated) honor.
199. **I am . . . dream.** Cf. *2 Henry IV*, V.v.51.
204. **Scour:** hasten.
207. **discover:** reveal, disclose.
208. **lover:** i.e., the Countess.

III.i. Location: Flanders. The French camp.
2. **made . . . to:** eaten up; perhaps an early version of "ate their lunch."
6. **martial furniture:** military equipment, stores.
7. **soothing:** humoring.
8. **circumstance:** (unimportant) detail.
9. **bruited:** noised abroad.
10. **fortified:** armed against attack.
14. **Catilines.** Like Lucius Sergius Catiline (d. 62 B.C.), Roman conspirator against whom Cicero spoke before the Senate.
15. **gape:** long for.
15–6. **gape . . . state.** Refers perhaps to the several Roman Catholic conspiracies against Queen Elizabeth.

And is it possible that they are now
So loyal in themselves?
Lor. All but the Scot, who solemnly protests,
As heretofore I have inform'd his grace,
Never to sheathe his sword or take a truce.
K. John. Ah, that's the anch'rage of some better hope;
But on the other side, to think what friends
King Edward hath retain'd in Netherland
Among those ever-bibbing epicures,
Those frothy Dutchmen, puff'd with double beer,
That drink and swill in every place they come,
Doth not a little aggravate mine ire;
Besides, we hear the Emperor conjoins,
And stalls him in his own authority.
But all the mightier that their number is,
The greater glory reaps the victory.
Some friends have we, beside [domestic] power:
The stern Polonian and the warlike Dane,
The King of Boheme and of Sicily,
Are all become confederates with us,
And, as I think, are marching hither apace.
[*Drums within.*]
But soft, I hear the music of their drums,
By which I guess that their approach is near.

Enter the King of Bohemia, *with* Danes, *and a* Polonian Captain *with other* Soldiers, [*some* Muscovites,] *another way.*

K. of Boh. King John of France, as league and neighborhood
Requires, when friends are any way distress'd,
I come to aid thee with my country's force.
Pol. Cap. And from great Moscow, fearful to the Turk,
And lofty Poland, nurse of hardy men,
I bring these servitors to fight for thee,
Who willingly will venture in thy cause.
K. John. Welcome, Bohemian King, and welcome all!
This your great kindness I will not forget.
Besides your plentiful rewards in crowns,
That from our treasury ye shall receive,
There comes a hare-brain'd nation, deck'd in pride,
The spoil of whom will be a treble [gain].
And now my hope is full, my joy complete:
At sea we are as puissant as the force
Of Agamemnon in the haven of Troy;
By land with Xerxes we compare of strength,
Whose soldiers drank up rivers in their thirst.
Then, Bayard-like, blind overweening Ned,
To reach at our imperial diadem,
Is either to be swallow'd of the waves,
Or hack'd a-pieces when thou comest ashore.

Enter [*a* Mariner].

Mar. Near to the coast I have [descried], my lord,
As I was busy in my watchful charge,
The proud armado of King Edward's ships,
Which at the first, far off when I did ken,
Seem'd, as it were, a grove of wither'd pines;
But drawing near, their glorious bright aspect,
Their streaming ensigns wrought of color'd silk,
Like to a meadow full of sundry flowers,
Adorns the naked bosom of the earth:
Majestical the order of their course,
Figuring the horned circle of the moon;
And on the top-gallant of the admiral,
And likewise all the handmaids of his train,
The arms of England and of France unite
Are quart'red equally by herald's art;
Thus tightly carried with a merry gale,
They plough the ocean hitherward amain.
[*K. John.*] Dare he already crop the flower-de-luce?
I hope, the honey being gather'd thence,
He, with the spider, afterward approach'd,
Shall suck forth deadly venom from the leaves.—
But where's [our] navy? how are they prepared
To wing themselves against this flight of ravens?
Mar. They, having knowledge brought them by the scouts,
Did break from anchor straight, and puff'd with rage,
No otherwise than were their sails with wind,
Made forth, as when the empty eagle flies

19. **Scot:** i.e., King David.
24. **Netherland.** Here refers to Flanders, then part of the Netherlands.
25. **ever-bibbing epicures:** always-drinking hedonists. Shakespeare uses "epicure" in several forms, perhaps most famously in *Antony and Cleopatra*, II.i.24–5, where Sextus Pompeius hopes that the "epicurean cooks [will] / Sharpen with cloyless sauce his [Antony's] appetite."
26. **frothy:** transferred epithet from the beer to the beer drinkers.
26. **double:** strong.
28. **ire:** anger.
29–30. **conjoins . . . authority:** joins with him and invests him with the right to command in his name.
33. **beside domestic power:** in addition to the strength furnished by our native country.
34. **stern Polonian:** fierce Pole.
35. **King of Boheme:** i.e., King of Bohemia. Historically, this is the celebrated blind John who died at the battle of Crécy.
35. **Sicily:** i.e., King Peter, son of Frederick III, succeeded in 1337.
37. **apace:** swiftly.
54. **puissant:** mighty, powerful.
55. **Agamemnon:** commander-in-chief of the invading Greeks against the Trojans. King John has his analogy reversed, inasmuch as it is the English who, like the Greeks, are invading.
56. **Xerxes:** Persian king (486–465 B.C.), son of Darius, bridged the Hellespont, invaded Greece, destroyed the Spartans at Thermopylae, but was ultimately defeated in the naval battle of Salamis and the land battle of Platea and forced to withdraw to Persia; another unfortunate analogy drawn by King John.
58. **Bayard-like:** self-confidently, recklessly (from Bayard, a magical horse given by Charlemagne to Rinaldo).
58. **overweening:** presumptuous.
63. **charge:** assigned duty.
64. **armado:** fleet of ships (variant of "armada"); used with allusion to the Spanish Armada of 1588; see l. 72.
65. **ken:** see.
72. **Figuring . . . moon:** The Spanish Armada, in the English Channel, sailed in half-moon formation.
73. **admiral:** the flag-ship carrying the admiral or commander-in-chief.
75. **unite:** united.
77. **tightly:** trimly, unwaterlogged.
78. **amain:** at full speed.
79. **flower-de-luce:** Floral symbol of France (English form of *fleur-de-lis*).
81. **afterward approach'd:** i.e., (he, having cropped the flower) being later encountered.
84. **ravens:** crow-like birds considered noisy, unlucky, thievish; i.e., the English. Looks forward to the metaphor of "war" as a raven (III.ii.49–50) and, ironically, to the ill-omened "flight of ravens" that foretells the defeat of the French at Crécy (IV.v.22 ff.).

To satisfy his hungry griping maw.
K. John. There's for thy news. [*Giving money.*] Return unto thy bark,
And if thou scape the bloody stroke of war,
And do survive the conflict, come again,
And let us hear the manner of the fight.—
Exit [*Mariner*].
Mean space, my lords, 'tis best we be dispers'd
To several places, lest they chance to land:
First you, my lord, with your Bohemian troops
Shall pitch your battles on the lower hand;
My eldest son, the Duke of Normandy,
Together with this aid of Muscovites,
Shall climb the higher ground another way;
Here, in the middle coast, betwixt you both,
Philip, my youngest boy, and I will lodge.
So, lords, be gone, and look unto your charge:
You stand for France, an empire fair and large.
Exeunt [*Prince Charles, Lorraine, Bohemia, and the other forces*].
Now tell me Philip, what is [thy] concept,
Touching the challenge that the English make?
P. Phil. I say, my lord, claim Edward what he can,
And bring he ne'er so plain a pedigree,
'Tis you are in possession of the crown,
And that's the surest point of all the law;
But were it not, yet, ere he should prevail,
I'll make a conduit of my dearest blood,
Or chase those straggling upstarts home again.
K. John. Well said, young Philip! Call for bread and wine,
That we may cheer our stomachs with repast,
To look our foes more sternly in the face.

[*A table, etc. brought in.* KING JOHN *and* PRINCE PHILIP *sit down to it.*] *The battle heard afar off.*

Now is begun the heavy day at sea.
Fight, Frenchmen, fight! be like the field of bears,
When they defend their younglings in their caves.
Steer, angry Nemesis, the happy helm,
That with the sulphur battles of your rage
The English fleet may be dispers'd and sunk.
Shot [*heard*].
P. Phil. O father, how this echoing cannon-shot,
Like sweet harmony, disgests my cates!
K. John. Now, boy, thou hearest what thund'ring terror 'tis
To buckle for a kingdom's sovereignty:
The earth with giddy trembling when it shakes,

89. **griping maw:** pinching stomach.
101. **coast:** position.
105. **concept:** conceit, thought (variant form).
110. **surest . . . law.** Cf. the proverb "Possession is eleven (nine) points of the law" (Tilley, P487, earliest citation).
112. **conduit:** fountain.
118–9. **bears, . . . younglings:** i.e., like bears when they fight to defend their young.
120. **Nemesis:** personified principle of retribution.
121. **sulphur.** an ingredient of gunpowder.
123. **cannon-shot,** Basically an anachronism, since, though Edward III, for the first time in Europe, is reported to have introduced bombards (an early and unsatisfactory form of small cannon), at the battle of Crécy, gunpowder was not seriously employed in naval or land warfare until later in the century.
124. **disgests my cates:** digests (variant form) my food.
126. **buckle:** combat, fight.

Or when the exhalations of the air
Breaks in extremity of lightning flash,
Affrights not more than kings, when they dispose
To show the rancor of their high-swoll'n hearts.
Retreat [*sounded*].
Retreat is sounded; one side hath the worse.
O, if it be the French, sweet Fortune, turn,
And in thy turning change the forward winds,
That, with advantage of a [favoring] sky,
Our men may vanquish and [the other] fly.

Enter [*the*] MARINER.

My heart misgives—say, mirror of pale death,
To whom belongs the honor of this day?
Relate, I pray thee, if thy breath will serve,
The sad discourse of this discomfiture.
Mar. I will, my lord.
My gracious sovereign, France hath ta'en the foil,
And boasting Edward triumphs with success.
These iron-hearted navies,
When last I was reporter to your Grace,
Both full of angry spleen, of hope and fear,
Hasting to meet each other in the face,
At last conjoin'd, and by their admiral
Our admiral encount'red many shot;
By this, the other, that beheld these twain
Give earnest-penny of a further wrack,
Like fiery dragons took their haughty flight;
And likewise meeting, from their smoky wombs
Sent many grim embassadors of death.
Then 'gan the day to turn to gloomy night,
And darkness did as well enclose the quick
As those that were but newly reft of life.
No leisure serv'd for friends to bid farewell,
And if it had, the hideous noise was such
As each to other seemed deaf and dumb.
Purple the sea, whose channel fill'd as fast
With streaming gore that from the maimed fell,
As did her gushing moisture break into
The cranny cleftures of the through-shot planks.
Here flew a head dissever'd from the trunk;
There mangled arms and legs were toss'd aloft,
As when a whirlwind takes the summer dust
And scatters it in middle of the air.

128. **exhalations:** meteors.
129. **Breaks.** Northern plural form.
129. **in extremity:** with the intensity.
130. **affrights:** terrifies.
130. **dispose:** prepare.
131. **rancor:** hatred.
135. **favoring sky:** (1) favorable wind and weather conditions; (2) heaven's blessing.
137. **mirror:** mirror image.
142. **foil:** defeat. The Mariner here (and to some extent earlier in 62–78), the Fourth Frenchman (III.ii.46–76), and Audley (IV.iv.10–39) serve as the Messenger of classical drama, reporting off-stage action.
146. **spleen:** (1) malice; (2) courage.
147. **in the face:** i.e., face to face.
149. **shot:** shots (collective singular).
150. **other:** others (i.e., the captains of the other ships).
151. **earnest-penny:** surety.
151. **wrack:** injury, disaster.
156. **quick:** living.
157. **reft:** bereft, robbed.
164. **cranny cleftures:** fissure cracks, splittings. Capell's emendation "cranny'd" is easier, but doesn't avoid the tautology of the phrase. *O.E.D.* does not record any instance of "cranny" used as an adjective.

Then might ye see the reeling vessels split,
And tottering sink into the ruthless flood,
Until their lofty tops were seen no more.
All shifts were tried, both for defense and hurt;
And now the effect of valor and of [fear],
Of resolution and of cowardice,
We lively pictur'd: how the one for fame,
The other by compulsion, laid about.
Much did the [*Nonpareille*], that brave ship;
So did the *Black Snake* of Bullen, than which
A bonnier vessel never yet spread sail.
But all in vain: both sun, the [wind] and tide
Revolted all unto our foemen's side,
That we perforce were fain to give them way;
And they are landed. Thus my tale is done:
We have untimely lost, and they have won.

K. John. Then rests there nothing, but with present speed
To join our several forces all in one
And bid them battle ere they range too far.—
Come, gentle Philip, let us hence depart:
This soldier's words have pierc'd thy father's heart.
Exeunt.

[SCENE II]

Enter two FRENCHMEN, *a* WOMAN, *and two little children; meet them another* [FRENCH CITIZEN].

[3] *Fr.* Well met, my masters. How now, what's the news?
And wherefore are ye laden thus with stuff?
What, is it quarter-day, that you remove,
And carry bag and baggage, too?

[1] *Fr.* Quarter-day, ay and quartering [day], I fear.
Have [ye] not heard the news that flies abroad?

[3] *Fr.* What news?

[2] *Fr.* How the French navy is destroy'd at sea,
And that the English army is arrived.

[3] *Fr.* What then?

[1] *Fr.* What then, quoth you? why, is't not time to fly,

170. **ruthless:** pitiless.
172. **shifts:** expedients, devices.
175. **We lively pictur'd:** we illustrated in a lifelike manner. Capell's emendation "Were" for "We" is difficult to explain graphically, though a tempting emendation.
176. **by compulsion:** i.e., because under attack.
177–78. ***Nonpareille . . . Black Snake.*** Two ships on the French side. Shakespeare uses "nonpareil" (= without equal) five times.
178. **Bullen:** Boulogne (indicating the English pronunciation).
182. **That we perforce:** so that we from necessity.
184. **untimely:** as the result of bad conditions.
185. **present:** immediate.
187. **bid them battle:** challenge them to fight.

III.ii. Location: Picardy. Fields near Crécy.
1–4. **Well . . . too.** Cf. *Sir Thomas More* (ll. 74–6 in the scene in Hand D, generally accepted as Shakespeare's, also describing fugitives): "Imagine that you see the wretched strangers, / Their babies at their backs, with their poor luggage / Plodding to th' ports and coasts for transportation."
3. **quarter-day:** rent-day.
5. **quartering day:** the day when we may be cut up into quarters (cf. the phrase "hanged, drawn, and quartered," the punishment executed upon traitors).

When envy and destruction is so nigh?

[3] *Fr.* Content thee, man: they are far enough from hence,
And will be met, I warrant ye, to their cost,
Before they break so far into the realm.

[1] *Fr.* Ay, so the grasshopper doth spend the time
In mirthful jollity, till winter come,
And then too late he would redeem his time,
When frozen cold hath nipt his careless head.
He that no sooner will provide a cloak,
Than when he sees it doth begin to rain,
May, peradventure, for his negligence,
Be throughly wash'd when he suspects it not.
We that have charge, and such a train as this,
Must look in time to look for them and us,
Lest, when we would, we cannot be relieved.

[3] *Fr.* Belike you then depair of ill success,
And think your country will be subjugate.

[2] *Fr.* We cannot tell; 'tis good to fear the worst.

[3] *Fr.* Yet rather fight, than like unnatural sons
Forsake your loving parents in distress.

[1] *Fr.* Tush, they that have already taken arms
Are many fearful millions in respect
Of that small handful of our enemies;
But 'tis a rightful quarrel must prevail:
Edward is son unto our late king's sister,
Where John Valois is three degrees removed.

Woman. Besides, there goes a prophecy abroad,
Publish'd by one that was a friar once,
Whose oracles have many times prov'd true;
And now he says, "The time will shortly come,
Whenas a lion, roused in the west,
Shall carry hence the flower-de-luce of France."
These, I can tell ye, and such like surmises
Strike many Frenchmen cold unto the heart.

Enter a [*fourth*] FRENCHMAN, [*in haste*].

[4 *Fr.*] Fly, countrymen and citizens of France!
Sweet-flow'ring peace, the root of happy life,
Is quite abandon'd and expuls'd the land:
In stead of whom [ransack-]constraining war
Sits like to ravens upon your houses' tops;
Slaughter and mischief walk within your streets,
And unrestrain'd make havoc as they pass,
The form whereof even now myself beheld
Upon this fair mountain, whence I came;
For so far off as I directed mine eyes

12. **envy:** ill will, mischief.
18. **would redeem:** would like to recover.
22. **peradventure:** perhaps.
23. **throughly:** thoroughly.
24. **have charge:** are in a position of responsibility.
24. **train:** group of followers.
25. **look . . . us:** look out for them and ourselves.
28. **subjugate:** subjugated, enslaved.
32. **Tush.** An exclamation of contempt or disagreement.
33. **fearful:** terrifying.
33–34. **in respect/Of:** compared with.
35. **quarrel:** occasion of complaint (note the device of making a Frenchman admit the justice of Edward's claim).
39. **Publish'd:** made public.
42. **Whenas a lion:** when a lion (king of beasts, i.e., Edward).
49. **ransack-constraining war:** war which compels plundering and devastation.

I might perceive five cities all on fire,
Cornfields and vineyards burning like an oven;
And, as the [reeking] vapor in the wind
Turn'd but aside, I likewise might discern
The poor inhabitants, escap'd the flame,
Fall numberless upon the soldiers' pikes.
Three ways these dreadful ministers of wrath
Do tread the measures of their tragic march:
Upon the right hand comes the conquering king,
Upon the left [his] hot unbridled son,
And in the midst our nation's glittering host;
All which, though distant, yet conspire in one
To leave a desolation where they come.
Fly, therefore, citizens, if you be wise,
Seek out some habitation further off;
Here if you stay, your wives will be abused,
Your treasure shar'd before your weeping eyes.
Shelter you yourselves, for now the storm doth rise.
Away, away! methinks I hear their drums.
Ah wretched France, I greatly fear thy fall;
Thy glory shaketh like a tottering wall. [*Exeunt.*]

[SCENE III]

Enter KING EDWARD *and the* EARL OF DERBY, *with* SOLDIERS, *and* GOBIN DE GREY.

K. Edw. Where's the Frenchman, by whose cunning guide
We found the shallow of this river [Somme],
And had direction how to pass the sea?
Gob. Here, my good lord.
K. Edw. How art thou call'd? tell me thy name.
Gob. Gobin de Grey, if please your Excellence.
K. Edw. Then, Gobin, for the service thou hast done
We here enlarge and give thee liberty;
And for recompence, beside this good,
Thou shalt receive five hundred marks in gold.—
I know not how, we should have met our son,
Whom now in heart I wish I might behold.

Enter ARTOIS.

[*Art.*] Good news, my lord: the Prince is hard at hand,
And with him comes Lord Audley and the rest,
Whom since our landing we could never meet.

[*Drums sound.*] *Enter* PRINCE EDWARD, LORD AUDLEY, *and* SOLDIERS.

K. Edw. Welcome, fair Prince! How hast thou sped, my son,
Since thy arrival on the coast of France?
P. Edw. Successfully, I thank the gracious heavens.
Some of their strongest cities we have won,
As [Harflew], [Lo], [Crotaye], and Carentigne,
And others wasted, leaving at our heels
A wide apparent field and beaten path
For solitariness to progress in.
Yet those that would submit we kindly pard'ned;
For who in scorn refus'd our proffer'd peace
Endur'd the penalty of sharp revenge.
K. Edw. Ah France, why shouldst thou be [thus] obstinate
Against the kind embracement of thy friends?
How gently had we thought to touch thy breast,
And set our foot upon thy tender mould,
But that in froward and disdainful pride,
Thou, like a skittish and untamed colt,
Dost start aside and strike us with thy heels.—
But tell me, Ned, in all thy warlike course
Hast thou not seen the usurping King of France?
P. Edw. Yes, my good lord, and not two hours ago,
With full a hundred thousand fighting men,
Upon the one side with the river's bank,
And [I] on the other; [with] his multitudes
I fear'd he would have cropp'd our smaller power;
But happily, perceiving your approach,
He hath withdrawn himself to Cressy plains,
Where, as it seemeth by his good array,
He means to bid us battle presently.
K. Edw. He shall be welcome: that's the thing we crave.

[*Drums.*] *Enter* KING JOHN, [*the*] DUKES OF NORMANDY *and* LORRAINE, [*the*] KING OF BOHEME, *young* [PRINCE] PHILIP, *and* SOLDIERS.

K. John. Edward, know that John, the true King of France,
Musing thou shouldst encroach upon his land,
And in thy tyrannous proceeding slay
His faithful subjects and subvert his towns,
Spits in thy face; and in this manner following
Upbraids thee with thine arrogant intrusion:
First, I condemn thee for a fugitive,

58. **reeking:** smoky.
63. **tread the measures:** march in formation (a dance metaphor).
67. **in one:** together, between them.

III.iii. Location: Picardy. Fields near Crécy.
1. **guide:** guidance. Given the earlier tangled reference to the Persian Wars, Gobin may be considered a French Ephialtes. Froissart (Berners, Chapter CXXVI) tells of "a varlet called Gobyn a Grace, who stept forthe and sayde to the kyng, sir, I promyse you on the ieopardy of my head, I shall bringe you to suche a place where as ye and all your hoost shall passe the ryuer of Some without paryll."
3. **pass the sea:** make a landing.
8. **enlarge:** release.
9. **good:** benefit.
10. **marks:** gold or silver coins equivalent to half or two-thirds of a pound sterling.
11. **I . . . how:** I don't know why I think so but.
13. **hard at hand:** close by.
16. **sped:** succeeded.
20. **Harflew . . . Carentigne:** Harfleur, Saint Lo, Crotay, Carentigne, cities in northwest France.
22. **apparent:** conspicuous, plainly to be seen.
23. **solitariness:** emptiness (the vacuum produced by the ravages of war).
25. **For who:** so far as those who.
31. **But that:** if it had not been that.
31. **froward:** perversely unreasonable.
38. **with:** along.
39. **And I . . . multitudes.** A crux. Q1–2 place King John's forces on both banks of the Somme, whereas, historically, John was on one side (the Crécy side) and King Edward on the opposite bank; the reading here adopted takes Q1–2 "both" as a misreading of "with" (Capell), but retains Q1–2 "And" (as in Collier).
40. **cropp'd:** cut off.
42. **Cressy.** English form of Crécy.
48. **tyrannous proceeding:** tyrannical advance.
51. **with:** because of.

A thievish pirate, and a needy mate,
One that hath either no abiding place,
Or else, inhabiting some barren soil,
Where neither herb or fruitful grain is had,
Dost altogether live by pilfering;
Next, insomuch thou hast infring'd thy faith,
Broke league and solemn covenant made with me,
I hold thee for a false pernicious wretch;
And last of all, although I scorn to cope
With one [so much] inferior to myself,
Yet in respect thy thirst is all for gold,
[Thy] labor rather to be fear'd than loved,
To satisfy thy lust in either part,
Here am I come, and with me have I brought
Exceeding store of treasure, pearl and coin.
Leave therefore now to persecute the weak,
And, armed, ent'ring conflict with the arm'd,
Let it be seen, 'mongst other petty thefts,
How thou canst win this pillage manfully.
K. Edw. If gall or wormwood have a pleasant taste,
Then is thy salutation honey-sweet;
But as the one hath no such property,
So is the other most satirical.
Yet wot how I regard thy worthless taunts:
If thou have utt'red them to foil my fame,
Or dim the reputation of my birth,
Know that thy wolvish barking cannot hurt;
If slily to insinuate with the world,
And with a strumpet's artificial line
To paint thy vicious and deformed cause,
Be well assur'd the counterfeit will fade,
And in the end thy foul defects be seen;
But if thou didst it to provoke me on,
As who should say I were but timorous,
Or coldly negligent did need a spur,
Bethink thyself how slack I was at sea;
Now, since my landing, I have won no towns,
Enter'd no further but upon the coast,
And there have ever since securely slept;
But if I have been otherwise employ'd,
Imagine, Valois, whether I intend
To skirmish, not for pillage, but for the crown
Which thou dost wear; and that I vow to have,
Or one of us shall fall into [his] grave.
P. Edw. Look not for cross invectives at our hands,
Or railing execrations of despite.
Let creeping serpents, [hid] in hollow banks,
Sting with their tongues, we have remorseless swords,
And they shall plead for us and our affairs.
Yet thus much briefly, by my father's leave:
As all the immodest poison of thy throat
Is scandalous and most notorious lies,
And our pretended quarrel is truly just,
So end the battle when we meet to-day;
May either of us prosper and prevail,
Or, luckless curs'd, receive eternal shame.
K. Edw. That needs no further question, and I know
His conscience witnesseth it is my right.—
Therefore, Valois, say, wilt thou yet resign,
Before the sickle's thrust into the corn,
Or that enkindled fury turn to flame?
K. John. Edward, I know what right thou hast in France,
And ere I basely will resign my crown,
This champion field shall be a pool of blood,
And all our prospect as a slaughterhouse.
P. Edw. Ay, that approves thee, tyrant, what thou art:
No father, king, or shepherd of thy realm,
But one that tears her entrails with thy hands,
And, like a thirsty tiger, suck'st her blood.
Aud. You peers of France, why do you follow him
That is so prodigal to spend your lives?
P. Cha. Whom should they follow, aged impotent,
But he that is their true-born sovereign?
K. Edw. Upbraid'st thou him, because within his face
Time hath engrav'd deep characters of age?
Know that these grave scholars of experience,
Like stiff-grown oaks, will stand immovable
When whirlwind quickly turns up younger trees.
Derby. Was ever any of thy father's house
King, but thyself, before this present time?
Edward's great linage, by the mother's side,
Five hundred years hath held the sceptre up.
Judge, then, conspirators, by this descent,
Which is the true-born sovereign, this or that?
P. [Phil.] Father, range your battles, prate no more:

53. **needy mate:** impoverished fellow (who, at home, lacks all the necessities of life).
58. **infring'd thy faith:** broken thy faith (as a sworn liegeman to King John for the dukedom of Guyenne; see I.i.59–66).
65. **lust . . . part:** desire, appetite on either score.
68. **Leave . . . weak:** cease persecuting the weak (i.e., the towns that have fallen to Prince Edward).
69. **armed . . . arm'd:** being armed, fight with those who are also armed.
71. **manfully:** like a man (not preying on the weak).
72. **If gall . . . honey-sweet:** if gall or wormwood have a pleasing taste (which they don't), then your "greeting" is honey-sweet (which it isn't). Cf. *Hamlet,* III.ii.181 and *The Rape of Lucrece,* 889, 893.
74–75. **one . . . other:** i.e., gall or wormwood . . . salutation.
75. **satirical.** Used in the sense of bitterly critical.
76. **wot:** know.
81. **artificial line:** false stroke (of cosmetic painting).
83. **counterfeit:** pretense (with play on "counterfeit" = picture, portrait).
86. **As . . . timorous:** as one who should say I was being merely fearful.
88. **slack:** moderate.
89. **Now . . . landing:** Now, after landing. Capell (generally followed) reads "How" to parallel the "how" in l. 88.
91. **securely:** (1) free from care; (2) carelessly.
92. **otherwise employ'd:** i.e., than in capturing towns.
97. **cross invectives:** counter-denunciations.
98. **railing . . . despite:** abusive curses of (1) anger, (2) scorn, contempt.
100. **remorseless:** pitiless.
103. **immodest:** arrogant, boastful.
105. **pretended:** stated.
108. **luckless:** unhappily, unfortunately.
112. **Before . . . corn:** i.e., before action is taken.
113. **enkindled:** burning.
116. **champion:** open, level.
117. **prospect:** view.
123. **prodigal:** wastefully lavish.
126. **Upbraid'st.** Q1's "Obraidst" is a recognized but corrupt variant form.
127. **deep characters:** deep wrinkles.
128. **grave scholars:** i.e., the "deep characters" (with play on "characters" = things written).
137. **range your battles:** set up your battle formations.
137. **prate:** talk idly.

These English fain would spend the time in words,
That, night approaching, they might escape unfought.
K. John. Lords and my loving subjects, [now's] the time
That your intended force must bide the touch.
Therefore, my friends, consider this in brief:
He that you fight for is your natural King;
He against whom you fight a foreigner;
He that you fight for rules in clemency,
And reins you with a mild and gentle bit;
He against whom you fight, if he prevail,
Will straight enthrone himself in tyranny,
Make slaves of you, and with a heavy hand
Curtal and curb your sweetest liberty.
Then, to protect your country and your King,
Let but the haughty courage of your hearts
Answer the number of your able hands,
And we shall quickly chase these fugitives;
For what's this Edward but a belly-god,
A tender and lascivious wantonness,
That th'other day was almost dead for love?
And what, I pray you, is his goodly guard?
Such as, but scant them of their chines of beef,
And take away their downy feather-beds,
And presently they are as resty-stiff,
As 'twere a many over-ridden jades.
Then, Frenchmen, scorn that such should be your lords,
And rather bind ye them in captive bands.
All French. Vive le roi! God save King John of France!
K. John. Now, on this plain of Cressy spread yourselves:
And, Edward, when thou darest, begin the fight.
[*Exeunt King John, his train, and Soldiers.*]
K. Edw. We presently will meet thee, John of France:—
And, English lords, let us resolve [this] day,
Either to clear us of that scandalous crime,
Or be entombed in our innocence.—
And, Ned, because this battle is the first
That ever yet thou foughtest in pitched field,
As ancient custom is of martialists,
To dub thee with the type of chivalry,
In solemn manner we will give thee arms.
Come, therefore, heralds: orderly bring forth
A strong attirement for the Prince, my son.

[*Flourish.*] *Enter four Heralds bringing in a coat-armor, a helmet, a lance, and a shield.* [*The first Herald delivers the armor to* King Edward, *who puts it on his son.*]

Edward Plantagenet, in the name of God,
As with this armor I impale thy breast,
So be thy noble unrelenting heart
Wall'd in with flint of matchless fortitude
That never base affections enter there:
Fight and be valiant; conquer where thou com'st!—
Now follow, lords, and do him honor too.
Derby. [*Receiving the helmet from the second Herald.*]
Edward Plantagenet, Prince of Wales,
As I do set this helmet on thy head,
Wherewith the chamber of [thy] brain is fenc'd,
So may thy temples with Bellona's hand
Be still adorn'd with laurel victory:
Fight and be valiant; conquer where thou com'st!
Aud. [*Receiving the lance from the third Herald.*]
Edward Plantagenet, Prince of Wales,
Receive this lance into thy manly hand;
Use it in fashion of a brazen pen
To draw forth bloody stratagems in France,
And print thy valiant deeds in honor's book:
Fight and be valiant; [conquer] where thou com'st!
Art. [*Receiving the shield from the fourth Herald.*]
Edward Plantagenet, Prince of Wales,
Hold, take this target, wear it on thy arm,
And may the view thereof, like Perseus' shield,
Astonish and transform thy gazing foes
To senseless images of meagre death:
Fight and be valiant; conquer where thou com'st!
K. Edw. Now wants there nought but knighthood, which deferr'd
We leave, till thou hast won it in the field.
[*P. Edw.*] My gracious father, and ye forward peers,
This honor you have done me animates
And cheers my green yet-scarce-appearing strength
With comfortable good-presaging signs,
No otherwise than did old Jacob's words,
Whenas he breath'd his blessings on his sons.
These hallow'd gifts of yours when I profane,

141. **intended . . . touch:** attending army (now waiting) must endure the test of its courage (i.e., whether it is, in the metaphor taken from metallurgy, true gold or not).
150. **Curtal:** curtail, abridge (variant form).
155. **belly-god:** glutton given to sensual satisfaction.
156. **tender:** weak, soft.
156. **wantonness:** wanton. Lines 156–7 are an indication that the thematic substance of the Countess scenes and the rest of the play are rather more integrated than some critics suggest.
158. **goodly guard:** handsome (used ironically) body of soldiers.
159. **scant . . . beef:** deprive them of their fleshy backs of beef. Cf. *2 Henry VI*, IV.x.57.
161. **resty-stiff:** sluggish, indolent, rigidly unmoving.
164. **captive bands:** bonds of captivity.
165. ***Vive le roi!*:** (long) live the king!
170. **clear . . . crime:** free us from that scandalous accusation. (see ll. 60–3, 159–62).
171. **be . . . innocence:** i.e., die, trying to prove that we are innocent of alleged "crime."
173. **pitched field:** field set in array for joining battle.
174. **martialists:** men learned in military custom. Cf. the character of Fluellen in *Henry V*.
175. **dub . . . chivalry:** invest you with the distinguishing stamp of one living under the knightly code.
178. **strong attirement:** stout, well-made equipment, furnishings.
180. **impale:** enclose for defense.
181. **unrelenting:** firmly constant.
189. **Bellona:** goddess of war (cf. *Macbeth*, I.ii.54).
190. **laurel victory:** triumph honored with a crown of laurel.
195. **draw forth:** trace out, design.
199. **target:** shield.
200. **Perseus' shield.** Anyone looking upon Perseus' shield was turned to stone (because of the presence on the shield of the head of the Gorgon Medusa). This version of the myth is a variant of the standard story which has the head as a feature of the shield only when Perseus presented the petrifying object to his benefactress Athena, and it ever after appeared on her aegis.
201. **gazing:** staring, gaping.
206. **forward:** eager.
210. **Jacob's words.** See Genesis 49.
211. **Whenas:** when.

Or use them not to glory of my God,
To patronage the fatherless and poor,
Or for the benefit of England's peace,
Be numb my joints! wax feeble both mine arms!
Wither my heart! that, like a sapless tree,
I may remain the map of infamy!
K. Edw. Then [thus] our steel'd battles shall be ranged:
The leading of the vaward, Ned, is thine;
To dignify whose lusty spirit the more,
We temper it with Audley's gravity,
That courage and experience join'd in one,
Your manage may be second unto none;
For the main battles, I will guide myself;
And, Derby, in the rearward march behind:
That orderly dispos'd and set in 'ray,
Let us to horse; and God grant us the day! *Exeunt.*

[SCENE IV]

Alarum. Enter a many FRENCHMEN, *flying; after them* PRINCE EDWARD [*and English* SOLDIERS], *running. Then enter* KING JOHN *and* [*the*] DUKE OF LORRAINE.

K. John. O Lorraine, say, what mean our men to fly?
Our number is far greater than our foe's.
Lor. The garrison of Genoaes, my lord,
That came from Paris, weary with their march,
Grudging to be suddenly employ'd,
No sooner in the forefront took their place,
But, straight retiring, so dismay'd the rest
As likewise they betook themselves to flight,
In which, for haste to make a safe escape,
More in the clustering throng are press'd to death
Than by the enemy a thousand-fold.
K. John. O hapless fortune! let us yet assay
If we can counsel some of them to stay. [*Exeunt.*]

[SCENE V]

[*Drums.*] *Enter* KING EDWARD *and* AUDLEY.

K. Edw. Lord Audley, whiles our son is in the chase,

214. **patronage:** defend, support.
218. **map of infamy:** the very picture of shame.
220. **vaward:** forefront.
222. **temper:** (1) blend; (2) curb.
224. **manage:** management, handling.
225. **For . . . myself:** so far as the main battalions are concerned, I will guide them myself.
226. **rearward:** that part of the army stationed behind the main body.
227. **'ray:** array.

III.iv. Location: Picardy. Fields near Crécy.
3. **garrison of Genoaes:** Genoan troops. Froissart (Berners, Chapter CXXX) writes, "Of the batayle of Cressy bytwene the kyng of England the french kyng. . . . Ther were of the genowayes crosbowes, about a fiftene thousand, but they were so wery of goyng a fote that day a six leages armed with their crosbowes, that they sayde to their constables, We be nat well ordred to fyght this day, for we be nat in the case to do any great ded of armes, we have more nede of rest . . . Whan the genowayes felte the arowes persynge through heedes, armes and brestes, many of them cast downe their crosbowes, and dyde cutte their strynges and retourned dysconfited."
5. **Grudging to be:** discontented about being.
11. **thousand-fold:** thousand times.
12. **hapless:** unlucky.

III.v. Location: Picardy. Fields near Crécy.
1. **whiles:** while.

Withdraw our powers unto this little hill,
And here a season let us breathe ourselves.
Aud. I will, my lord. *Exit. Sound retreat.*
K. Edw. Just-dooming heaven, whose secret providence
To our gross judgment is inscrutable,
How are we bound to praise Thy wondrous works,
That hast this day given way unto the right,
And made the wicked stumble at themselves!

Enter ARTOIS.

[*Art.*] Rescue, King Edward! rescue for thy son!
K. Edw. Rescue, Artois? What, is he prisoner,
Or by violence fell beside his horse?
Art. Neither, my lord, but narrowly beset
With turning Frenchmen, whom he did pursue,
As 'tis impossible that he should scape,
Except your Highness presently descend.
K. Edw. Tut, let him fight: we gave him arms today,
And he is laboring for a knighthood, man.

Enter DERBY.

Derby. The Prince, my lord, the Prince! O succor him!
He's close encompass'd with a world of odds.
K. Edw. Then will he win a world of honor, too,
If he by valor can redeem him thence;
If not, what remedy? We have more sons
Than one to comfort our declining age.

Enter AUDLEY.

Aud. Renowned Edward, give me leave, I pray,
To lead my soldiers where I may relieve
Your Grace's son, in danger to be slain:
The snares of French, like emmets on a bank,
Muster about him, whilst he, lion-like,
Entangled in the net of their assaults,
Franticly rends and bites the woven toil;
But all in vain, he cannot free himself.
K. Edw. Audley, content; I will not have a man,
On pain of death, sent forth to succor him.
This is the day ordain'd by destiny
To season his courage with those grievous thoughts,

3. **breathe ourselves:** catch our breath.
6. **gross:** inferior, coarse.
7. **How . . . bound:** i.e. how obligated we are.
10. **Rescue . . . rescue.** Froissart (Berners, Chapter CXXX) describes the King's response: "Than the kynge sayde, Is my sonne deed or hurt, or on the yerthe felled? No sir, quoth the knyght, but he is hardely matched, wherefore he hathe nede of your ayde. Well, sayde the kyng, retourne to him and to them that sent you hyther, and say to them, that they sende no more to me for any adventure that falleth, as long as my soone is alyve; and also say to the[m], that they suffre hym this day to wynne his spurres."
12. **fell beside:** fallen along side of.
14. **turning Frenchmen:** Frenchmen who have turned back to fight after initially retreating (or, possibly, traitorous French allies).
16. **Except:** unless.
20. **world of odds:** infinite number of disadvantages.
28. **emmets:** ants.
31. **toil:** snare, trap.
36. **season:** mature.
36. **those grievous thoughts:** i.e., the sense of danger and death that he must be feeling.

That, if he breaketh out, Nestor's years on earth,
Will make him savor still of this exploit.
Derby. Ah, but he shall not live to see those days.
K. Edw. Why then his epitaph is lasting praise.
Aud. Yet, good my lord, 'tis too much willfulness,
To let his blood be spilt that may be sav'd.
K. Edw. Exclaim no more, for none of you can tell
Whether a borrow'd aid will serve, or no.
Perhaps he is already slain or ta'en:
And dare a falcon when she's in her flight,
And ever after she'll be haggard-like.
Let Edward be deliver'd by our hands,
And still in danger he'll expect the like;
But if himself himself redeem from thence,
He will have vanquish'd, cheerful, death and fear,
And ever after dread their force no more
Than if they were but babes or captive slaves.
Aud. [*Aside.*] O cruel father!—Farewel, Edward, then.
Derby. Farewel, sweet Prince, the hope of chivalry!
Art. O would my life might ransom him from death! [*Retreat sounded.*]
K. Edw. But soft, methinks I hear
The dismal charge of trumpets' loud retreat.
All are not slain, I hope, that went with him;
Some will return with tidings, good or bad.

[*Flourish.*] *Enter* Prince Edward *in triumph, bearing in his hand his shivered lance;* [*his sword and battered armor carried before him*], *and* [*the body of*] *the* King of Boheme, *wrapped in the colors. They run and embrace him.*

Aud. O joyful sight! victorious Edward lives!
Derby. Welcome, brave Prince!
K. Edw. Welcome, Plantagenet!
P. Edw. *(Kneel and kiss his father's hand.)*
First having done my duty as beseemed,
Lords, I regreet you all with hearty thanks.
And now behold, after my winter's toil,
My painful voyage on the boist'rous sea
Of war's devouring gulfs and steely rocks,
I bring my fraught unto the wished port,
My summer's hope, my travail's sweet reward;
And here with humble duty I present
This sacrifice, this first-fruit of my sword,
Cropp'd and cut down even at the gate of death,
The King of Boheme, father, whom I slew,
[Whose thousands] had intrench'd me round about,
And lay as thick upon my batter'd crest,
As on an anvil, with their ponderous glaives;
Yet marble courage still did underprop;
And when my weary arms with often blows,
Like the continual-laboring woodman's axe
That is enjoin'd to fell a load of oaks,
Began to falter, straight I would recover
My gifts you gave me, and my zealous vow:
And then new courage made me fresh again,
That in despite I [carv'd] my passage forth,
And put the multitude to speedy flight.
Lo, [thus] hath Edward's hand fill'd your request,
And done, I hope, the duty of a knight.
K. Edw. Ay, well thou hast deserv'd a knighthood, Ned:
And, therefore, with thy sword, yet reeking warm
His sword borne by a soldier; [*the King takes it and knights him*].
With blood of those that fought to be thy bane,
Arise, Prince Edward, trusty knight at arms.
This day thou hast confounded me with joy,
And prov'd thyself fit heir unto a king.
P. Edw. Here is a note, my gracious lord, of those
That in this conflict of our foes were slain:
Eleven princes of esteem, fourscore barons,
A hundred and twenty knights, and thirty thousand
Common soldiers; and of our men a thousand.
[*K. Edw.*] Our God be praised!—Now, John of France, I hope
Thou knowest King Edward for no wantonness
No love-sick cockney, nor his soldiers jades.—
But which way is the fearful King escap'd?
P. Edw. Towards Poictiers, noble father, and his sons.
K. Edw. Ned, thou and Audley shall pursue them still;
Myself and Derby will to Callice straight,
And there begirt that haven town with siege.
Now lies it on an upshot: therefore strike,
And wistly follow whiles the game's on foot.
What picture's this?
P. Edw. [*Pointing to the colors.*] A pelican, my lord,
Wounding her bosom with her crooked beak,
That so her nest of young ones might be fed
With drops of blood that issue from her heart;
The motto, *Sic et vos*: "And so should you." *Exeunt.*

37. **Nestor's years.** Nestor was a Homeric hero famous both for his wisdom and his great age; he figures as a character in *Troilus and Cressida*.
38. **savor still:** relish forever.
46. **dare:** daze (by means of a reflecting mirror).
47. **haggard-like:** wild, untrained, undisciplined. Cf., e.g., *The Taming of the Shrew*, IV.i.93 and IV.ii.39.
49. **still:** ever after.
58. **charge:** order.
63. **beseemed:** was fitting
64. **regreet:** greet once again.
68. **fraught:** lading, cargo.
69. **travail:** painful labor.
75. **crest:** (1) helmet; (2) plume of feathers or horseshair fixed on a helmet.
76. **ponderous glaives:** weighty swords.
80. **enjoin'd:** required.
81. **recover:** recall to mind.
84. **That in despite:** so that in rage, anger.
89. **reeking:** steaming, smoking.
90. **bane:** destruction, ruin.
92. **confounded:** overpowered, consumed.
100. **for no wantonness:** not because of any (amorous) sportiveness.
101. **jades:** poor, worn-out horses.
105. **Callice:** Calais (as pronounced in Elizabethan England).
106. **begirt . . . town:** encircle that harbor town.
107. **lies . . . upshot:** it (all) depends on the outcome.
108. **wistly:** with close attention, intently.
108. **whiles . . . foot:** while the sport is in progress. Cf. *1 Henry VI*, I.iii.278 and *Henry V*, III.i.32.
109–113. **A pelican . . . you:** Compare *Hamlet*, IV.v.147: "life-rend'ring pelican" and, especially, *Richard II*, II.i.124–7, where Gaunt links himself with Edward III and indicts his nephew Richard: "For that I was his father Edward's son, / That blood already, like the pelican, / Hast thou tapp'd out and drunkenly carous'd." See Plate 22.

[ACT IV, Scene I]

Enter Lord Mountford *with a coronet in his hand; with him the* Earl of Salisbury.

Mount. My Lord of Salisbury, since by [your] aid
Mine enemy, Sir Charles of Blois, is slain,
And I again am quietly possess'd
In Britain's dukedom, know that I resolve,
For this kind furtherance of your King and you,
To swear allegiance to his Majesty:
In sign whereof receive this coronet;
Bear it unto him, and withal mine oath,
Never to be but Edward's faithful friend.
Sal. I take it, Mountford: thus I hope, ere long,
The whole dominions of the realm of France
Will be surrend'red to his conquering hand.
Exit [Mountford].
Now, if I knew but safely how to pass,
I would to Callice gladly meet his Grace,
Whither I am by letters certified
[That] he intends to have his host remov'd.
It shall be so: this policy will serve.—
Ho, who's within? Bring Villiers to me.
Enter Villiers.
Villiers, thou knowest thou art my prisoner,
And that I might for ransom, if I would,
Require of thee a hundred thousand francs,
Or else retain and keep thee captive still;
But so it is, that, for a smaller charge,
Thou mayst be quit, and if thou wilt thyself;
And this it is: procure me but a passport
Of Charles, the Duke of Normandy, that I
Without restraint may have recourse to Callice
Through all the countries where he hath to do;
Which thou mayst easily obtain, I think,
By reason I have often heard thee say,
He and thou were students once together;
And then thou shalt be set at liberty.
How sayest thou? wilt thou undertake to do it?
Vill. I will, my lord, but I must speak with him.
Sal. Why, so thou shalt; take horse and post from hence.
Only before thou goest, swear by thy faith,
That if thou canst not compass my desire,
Thou wilt return, my prisoner, back again;
And that shall be sufficient warrant for me.
Vill. To that condition I agree, my lord,
And will unfeignedly perform the same.
Sal. Farewel, Villiers. *Exit [Villiers].*
Thus once I mean to try a Frenchman's faith. *Exit.*

IV.i. Location: Bretagne. The English camp.
o.s.d. **Lord Mountford.** John, Count of Mountford (a part of Brittany),the son of Yolanda, the heiress of the Mountfords, and Arthur II, Duke of Brittany, claimed Brittany in opposition to Charles of Blois and succeeded in acquiring the entire duchy. He allied himself with Edward III in spite of the judgment of the Parliament of Paris that to Charles belonged the Duchy of Brittany. See Froissart, Chapters LXVIII, LXIX, *et seq.*
4. **Britain:** Brittany (Bretagne).
5. **furtherance:** support, help.
7. **coronet:** a small crown (one suitable to a duke and sent as a symbol of his fealty to King Edward).
8. **withal:** therewith.
13. **pass:** get there.
14. **to:** at or in.
16. **host:** army.
18. **Villiers.** The episode is based on Froissart (Berners, Chapter CXXXV), who describes how Sir Gaultier (i.e., Walter) of Manny (= the Earl of Salisbury in the play) asked his prisoner, an unnamed knight of Normandy (= Villiers), on the promise that he would free the knight without ransom, to procure a passport from the Duke of Normandy, his kinsman, for himself and twenty men to enable them to pass through enemy territory and join King Edward at Calais, The name "Villiers" is unhistorical in this context.
21. **francs:** fourteenth-century French gold coins weighing about sixty grains.
23. **smaller charge:** i.e., than the hundred thousand franks.
24. **quit . . . thyself:** released (from the amount of the ransom), and yourself freed if you wish.
25. **but:** only.
28. **countries . . . do:** regions, districts in which he acts (as a ruler).
35. **post:** hasten.
43. **once:** for one time only.

[Scene II]

Enter King Edward *and* Derby, *with* Soldiers.

K. Edw. Since they refuse our proffer'd league, my lord,
And will not ope their gates and let us in,
We will intrench ourselves on every side,
That neither victuals nor supply of men
May come to succor this accursed town:
Famine shall combat where our swords are stopp'd.
Derby. The promis'd aid that made them stand aloof
Is now retir'd and gone another way:
It will repent them of their stubborn will.
Enter six poor Frenchmen.
But what are these poor ragged slaves, my lord?
K. Edw. Ask what they are; it seems they come from Callice.
Derby. You wretched patterns of despair and woe,
What are you? living men, or gliding ghosts
Crept from your graves to walk upon the earth?
Poor [Fr.] No ghosts, my lord, but men that breathe a life
Far worse than is the quiet sleep of death:
We are distressed poor inhabitants
That long have been diseased, sick, and lame;
And now, because we are not fit to serve,
The captain of the town hath thrust us forth,
That so expense of victuals may be saved.
K. Edw. A charitable deed no doubt, and worthy praise!
But how do you imagine then to speed?

IV.ii. Location: Picardy. The English camp before Calais.
1. **league:** compact, alliance.
2. **ope:** open.
6. **combat . . . stopp'd:** fight for us (here) where our swords won't work (because of the resistance of the city's walls).
7. **stand aloof:** take no part in agreeing to capitulate.
10. **poor . . . slaves.** Froissart (Berners, Chapter CXXXIII) describes this moment of royal magnanimity: "Whan the capten of Calys sawe that maner of thorder of thengleysshmen: than he constrayned all poore and meane peple to yssue out of the towne . . . and as they passed through ye hoost they were demaunded why they departed and they answered and sayde, bycause they had nothyng to lyve on. Than the kynge . . . gave them mete and drinke to dyner, and every person ii.d. [i.e., two pence] sterlyng in almes . . . ."
23. **speed:** fare, be treated.

We are your enemies: in such a case
We can no less but put ye to the sword,
Since, when we proffer'd truce, it was refus'd.
[*Poor Fr.*] And if your Grace no otherwise vouchsafe,
As welcome death is unto us as life.
K. Edw. Poor silly men, much wrong'd and more distress'd!
Go, Derby, go, and see they be reliev'd;
Command that victuals be appointed them,
And give to every one five crowns apiece.
[*Exeunt Derby and Frenchmen.*]
The lion scorns to touch the yielding prey,
And Edward's sword must [flesh] itself in such
As willful stubborness hath made perverse.

Enter Lord Percy.

Lord Percy, welcome! What's the news in England?
Per. The Queen, my lord, comes here to your Grace,
And from her Highness, and the Lord Vicegerent,
I bring this happy tidings of success:
David of Scotland, lately up in arms,
Thinking, belike, he soonest should prevail,
Your Highness being absent from the realm,
Is by the fruitful service of your peers
And painful travel of the Queen herself,
That, big with child, was every day in arms,
Vanquish'd, subdu'd, and taken prisoner.
K. Edw. Thanks, Percy, for thy news with all my heart.
What was he took him prisoner in the field?
Per. [An] esquire, my lord, John Copland is his name;
Who since, entreated by her Majesty,
Denies to make surrender of his prize
To any but unto your grace alone:
Whereat the Queen is grievously displeas'd.
K. Edw. Well then, we'll have a pursuivant [dispatch'd]
To summon Copland hither out of hand;
And with him he shall bring his prisoner king.
Per. The [Queen's], my lord, herself by this at sea,
And purposeth, as soon as wind will serve,

27. **And if . . . vouchsafe:** unless your Grace deigns to do something else.
29. **silly:** simple, harmless.
31. **be appointed them:** granted to them.
34. **flesh:** bloody. Q1–2's reading "fresh" satisfied editors until Delius and may, perhaps, be taken as meaning "refresh its thirst (for blood)."
35. **perverse:** obstinate.
37. **comes here.** This is the somewhat metrically awkward reading of Q1–2 and receives some support from ll. 57–9 below. Capell, however, emended to "commends her," perhaps correctly.
38. **Lord Vicegerent:** i.e., Warwick, who in II.ii.203 was appointed Warden of the North by Edward (i.e., his deputy = "vicegerent").
39. **this happy tidings:** this good news ("tidings" was often treated as a singular).
43. **fruitful service:** i.e., service that has produced good results.
44. **travel:** journeying. Perhaps, however, since "travel" and "travail" were then interchangeable spellings, Q1's "travell," given the context, should be treated as "travail" = hardship, labor.
48. **What was he:** Of what rank was he?
49. **esquire:** young man, generally of aristocratic birth, who served a knight. The form "esquire" is used throughout because that form, rather than "squire," is the Q1 form used throughout the text proper.
51. **Denies:** refuses.
54. **pursuivant:** royal messenger (empowered with a warrant).
55. **out of hand:** immediately.

To land at Callice and to visit you.
K. Edw. She shall be welcome; and, to wait her coming,
I'll pitch my tent near to the sandy shore.

Enter a [French] Captain.

[*F. Capt.*] The burgesses of Callice, mighty King,
Have, by a council, willingly decreed
To yield the town and castle to your hands,
Upon condition it will please your Grace
To grant them benefit of life and goods.
K. Edw. They will so! then, belike, they may command,
Dispose, elect, and govern as they list.
No, sirrah, tell them, since they did refuse
Our princely clemency at first proclaimed,
They shall not have it now, although they would;
[I] will accept of nought but fire and sword,
Except, within these two days, six of them,
That are the wealthiest merchants in the town,
Come naked all but for their linen shirts,
With each a halter hang'd about his neck,
And prostrate yield themselves upon their knees,
To be afflicted, hang'd, or what I please:
And so you may inform their masterships.
Exeunt [*King Edward, Percy, and Soldiers*].
[*F.*] *Capt.* Why this it is to trust a broken staff.
Had we not been persuaded, John our King
Would with his army have reliev'd the town,
We had not stood upon defiance so;
But now 'tis past that no man can recall,
And better some do go to wrack than all. *Exit.*

[Scene III]

Enter Charles of Normandy *and* Villiers.

P. Cha. I wonder, Villiers, thou shouldest importune me
For one that is our deadly enemy.
Vill. Not for his sake, my gracious lord, so much
Am I become an earnest advocate,
As that thereby my ransom will be quit.
P. Cha. Thy ransom, man! why needest thou talk of that?
Art thou not free? and are not all occasions

61–79. **I'll . . . masterships.** Froissart (Berners, Chapter CXLVI) describes this celebrated scene: ". . . sir Gaultyer of Manny ye shall goo and say to the capytayne . . . that they lette sixe of the chiefe burgesses of the towne come out bare heeded, bare foted and bare legged, and in their shertes, with haulters about their neckes, with the kayes of the towne and castell in their handes, and lette theym sixe yelde themselfe to my wyll."
62. **burgesses:** members of the town council.
67. **They . . . belike:** They *will* indeed! then they probably (think).
69. **sirrah:** a form of "sir," used for inferiors, often as a mark of contempt.
71. **they would:** i.e., they would like clemency.
73. **Except:** unless.
78. **afflicted:** grievously treated, punished.
79. **masterships.** Here used sarcastically as they are anything but "masters" of the situation.
83. **stood upon:** insisted on.
85. **wrack:** ruin, disaster.

IV.iii. Location: Poitiers. Fields near Poitiers. The French camp; tent of the Duke of Normandy.
2. **For one:** on behalf of one (i.e. the Earl of Salisbury).

That happen for advantage of our foes
To be accepted of, and stood upon?

Vill. No, good my lord, except the same be just;
For profit must with honor be commix'd,
Or else our actions are but scandalous.
But letting pass these intricate objections,
Will't please your Highness to subscribe or no?

P. Cha. Villiers, I will not, nor I cannot do it:
Salisbury shall not have his will so much
To claim a passport how it pleaseth himself.

Vill. Why, then I know the extremity, my lord:
I must return to prison whence I came.

P. Cha. Return! I hope thou wilt not.
What bird that hath escap'd the fowler's gin
Will not be ware how she's ensnar'd again?
Or what is he so senseless and secure,
That, having hardly pass'd a dangerous gulf,
Will put himself in peril there again?

Vill. Ah, but it is mine oath, my gracious lord,
Which I in conscience may not violate,
Or else a kingdom should not draw me hence.

P. Cha. Thine oath? why, that doth bind thee to abide.
Hast thou not sworn obedience to thy Prince?

Vill. In all things that uprightly he commands:
But either to persuade or threaten me
Not to perform the covenant of my word
Is lawless, and I need not to obey.

P. Cha. Why, is it lawful for a man to kill,
And not to break a promise with his foe?

Vill. To kill, my lord, when war is once proclaim'd,
So that our quarrel be for wrongs receiv'd,
No doubt is lawfully permitted us;
But in an oath we must be well advis'd
How we do swear; and when we once have sworn,
Not to infringe it though we die therefore:
Therefore, my lord, as willing I return
As if I were to fly to paradise. [*Going.*]

P. Cha. Stay, my Villiers! thine honorable mind
Deserves to be eternally admir'd.
Thy suit shall be no longer thus deferr'd:
Give me the paper, I'll subscribe to it;
And wheretofore I lov'd thee as Villiers,
Hereafter I'll embrace thee as myself.
Stay, and be still in favor with thy lord.

Vill. I humbly thank your Grace. I must dispatch,
And send this passport first unto the Earl,
And then I will attend your Highness' pleasure.

P. Cha. Do so, Villiers; and Charles, when he hath need,
Be such his soldiers, howsoever he speed.
Exit Villiers.

Enter King John.

K. John. Come, Charles, and arm thee; Edward is entrapp'd,
The Prince of Wales is fall'n into our hands,
And we have compass'd him; he cannot scape.

P. Cha. But will your Highness fight to-day?

K. John. What else, my son? he's scarce eight thousand strong,
And we are threescore thousand at the least.

P. Cha. I have a prophecy, my gracious lord,
Wherein is written what success is like
To happen us in this outrageous war:
It was deliver'd me at Cressy's field
By one that is an aged hermit there.
[*Reads.*] "When feather'd fowl shall make thine army tremble,
And flint-stones rise and break the battle 'ray,
Then think on him that doth not now dissemble,
For that shall be the hapless dreadful day:
Yet in the end, thy foot thou shalt advance
As far in England as thy foe in France."

K. John. By this, it seems, we shall be fortunate:
For as it is impossible that stones
Should ever rise and break the battle 'ray,
Or airy fowl make men in arms to quake,
So is it like we shall not be subdu'd;
Or say this might be true, yet in the end,
Since he doth promise we shall drive him hence
And forage their country as they have done ours,
By this revenge that loss will seem the less.
But all are frivolous fancies, toys and dreams:
Once we are sure we have ensnar'd the son,
Catch we the father after how we can. *Exeunt.*

8. **for advantage of:** for (our) advantage over.
9. **stood upon:** made use of.
10. **except the same:** unless such occasions.
13. **intricate:** perplexingly involved.
14. **subscribe:** agree.
18. **extremity:** final outcome.
21. **fowler's gin:** birdcatcher's net or snare.
23. **secure:** careless.
24. **hardly:** (1) painfully; (2) barely.
28. **Or else:** otherwise.
33. **covenant . . . word:** contract mutually agreed upon.
38. **So that:** so long as.
40–41. **we . . . swear:** consider carefully under what circumstances we are swearing.
51. **still:** forever.
56. **Be . . . speed:** may his soldiers be like Villiers, whether or not he is successful in war.
59. **compass'd:** surrounded.
63. **prophecy.** As is usually true of prophecies, this prophecy is ambiguous: King John will set foot in England, but only as a prisoner.
65. **outrageous:** violent, excessively hurtful, atrocious.
69. **flint-stones.** Holinshed (1587 edition) describes the prophecy on the eve of Poitiers: "Here is to be remembred, that when (as Thomas Walsingham writeth) this cardinall of Piergort was sent from the pope to trauell betwixt the parties for a peace to be had, and that the pope exhorted him verie earnestlie to shew his vttermost diligence and indeuour therein: at his setting foorth to go on that message, the said cardinall (as was said) made this answer: Most blessed father (said he) either we will persuade them to peace and quietnesse, either else shall the verie flintstones crie out of it. But this he spake not of himselfe, as it was supposed, but being a prelate in that time, he prophesied what should follow; for when the English archers had bestowed all their arrowes vpon their enimies, they tooke vp pebles from the place where they stood, being full of those kind of stones, and approching to their enimies, they threw the same with such violence on them, that lighting against their helmets, armor, and targets, they made a great ringing noise, so that the cardinals prophesie was fulfilled, that he would either persuade a peace, or else the stones should crie out thereof."
69. **break . . . 'ray:** break up the order of battle (i.e., make the soldiers retreat in disorder).
71. **hapless:** unlucky.
75–6. **impossible . . . rise.** Cf. *Macbeth*, IV.i.78 ff.
79. **this . . . true:** i.e., that the French might be subdued.
81. **forage:** plunder.
85. **after . . . can:** afterwards in whatever way we can.

[SCENE IV]

Enter PRINCE EDWARD, AUDLEY, *and others.*

P. Edw. Audley, the arms of death embrace us round,
And comfort have we none, save that to die
We pay sour earnest for a sweeter life.
At Cressy field our clouds of warlike smoke
Chok'd up those French mouths, and dissever'd them;
But now their multitudes of millions hide,
Masking, as 'twere, the beauteous burning sun,
Leaving no hope to us but sullen dark
And eyeless terror of all-ending night.
Aud. This sudden, mighty, and expedient head
That they have made, fair Prince, is wonderful.
Before us in the valley lies the King,
Vantag'd with all that heaven and earth can yield;
His party stronger battled than our whole:
His son, the braving Duke of Normandy,
Hath trimm'd the mountain on our right hand up
In shining plate, that now the aspiring hill
Shows like a silver quarry or an orb,
Aloft the which the banners, bannerettes,
And new-replenish'd pendants cuff the air
And beat the winds, that for their gaudiness
Struggles to kiss them; on our left hand lies
Philip, the younger issue of the King,
Coating the other hill in such array
That all his gilded upright pikes do seem
Straight trees of gold, the [pendants] leaves,
And their device of antique heraldry,
Quart'red in colors, seeming sundry fruits,
Makes it the orchard of the Hesperides.
Behind us, [too], the hill doth bear his height,
For like a half-moon, opening but one way,
It rounds us in; there at our backs are lodg'd
The fatal cross-bows, and the battle there
Is govern'd by the rough Chatillion.
Then thus it stands: the valley for our flight
The King binds in; the hills on either hand
Are proudly royalized by his sons;
And on the hill behind stands certain death
In pay and service with Chatillion.
P. Edw. Death's name is much more mighty than his deeds:
Thy parcelling this power hath made it more:
As many sands as these my hands can hold
Are but my handful of so many sands;
Then, all the world—and call it but a power—
Easily ta'en up, and quickly thrown away;
But if I stand to count them, sand by sand,
The number would confound my memory
And make a thousand millions of a task,
Which, briefly, is no more indeed than one.
These quarters, squadrons, and these regiments,
Before, behind us, and on either hand,
Are but a power: when we name a man,
His hand, his foot, his head hath several strengths;
And being all but one self instant strength,
Why, all this many, Audley, is but one,
And we can call it all but one man's strength.
He that hath far to go, tells it by miles;
If he should tell the steps, it kills his heart;
The drops are infinite that make a flood,
And yet, thou knowest, we call it but a rain.
There is but one France, one King of France,
That France has no more kings; and that same King
Hath but the puissant legion of one king;
And we have one: then apprehend no odds,
For one to one is fair equality.

Enter an HERALD *from* KING JOHN.

What tidings, messenger? be plain and brief.
Her. The King of France, my sovereign lord and master,
Greets by me his foe, the Prince of Wales:
If thou call forth a hundred men of name,

IV.iv. Location: Poitiers. Fields near Poitiers. The English camp.
1. **arms of death.** Note the play on metaphorical "arms" and military weaponry.
3. **sour . . . life:** unpleasant foretaste in order to have a sweeter life (in heaven).
5. **dissever'd:** divided.
10. **expedient head:** speedy advance.
13. **Vantag'd:** benefited.
14. **battled:** armed (for battle).
15. **braving:** boastful.
17. **plate:** plate armor.
18. **orb.** Here perhaps used for the moon (shining and silvery).
19. **bannerettes:** pennants, small banners.
20. **new-replenish'd pendants:** newly puffed up or filled out (by the winds).
20. **cuff:** buffet.
21. **for:** because of.
21–2. **winds, . . . kiss them.** Cf. *Antony and Cleopatra*, II.ii.191–205.
22. **struggles.** A northern plural form (see Abbott, 333).
24. **Coating:** covering. The Q1–2 reading "Coting" may perhaps mean (as Moore Smith suggests) "lining the side of."
29. **orchard . . . Hesperides:** garden of the island of the Hesperides, or the nymphs themselves called the Hesperides, who guarded the golden apples in the garden with the help of a never-sleeping dragon. It was one of the labors of Hercules to capture some of these apples, and the situation of the English here at Poitiers by implication requires similarly heroic measures. Cf. *Love's Labor's Lost*, IV.iii.337–8 and note.
30. **bear his height:** i.e., as a powerful threat.
34. **Chatillion.** Perhaps the son of Gaucher of Chatillon, Lord of Crecy and Constable of France, as well as, from 1290, Lord of Chatillon-sur-Marne and, from 1303, Count of Porcien; or perhaps (as Lapides suggests) Louis de Blois, called Louis de Chatillion, who was killed at the battle of Crecy (1346). Holinshed (1587 ed.) writes of "Guie de Chatillon master of the crosbowes in France," who led a rebellion in Ponthieu some thirteen years after Poitiers.
37. **royaliz'd.** Made so by the presence of the French princes.
41. **parcelling:** division into separate parts.
42–56. **As . . . strength.** The argument of these lines depends upon a willing suspension of reality in order to count the very numerous French force as a single entity and therefore manageable, inasmuch as the English army is also a single entity considered as an "army," whatever its numerical makeup. See the analogous manipulation of arithmetic and reality in *Henry V*, Prologue, esp. 15–25.
50. **quarters:** (?) army divisions.
53. **several strengths:** different powers.
54. **being . . . strength:** being a single power acting entirely together (Hopkinson).
57–65. **He . . . equality.** These lines continue the rhetorical argument of the manageable whole versus the apparently unconquerable multiplicity.
57. **tells:** counts, reckons.
63. **puissant:** powerful, as in the "imaginary puissance" of *Henry V*, Prologue 25.
67–122. **The King . . . gone.** Cf. this episode of the three Heralds, each bearing a taunting message to Prince Edward, with the Dauphin's gift of tennis balls to the young King Henry (*Henry V*, I.ii.245–57) and Henry's answer (I.ii.258–97).

Of lords, knights, esquires, and English gentlemen,
And with thyself and those kneel at his feet,
He straight will fold his bloody colors up,
And ransom shall redeem lives forfeited;
If not, this day shall drink more English blood
Than e'er was buried in our British earth.
What is the answer to his proffer'd mercy?
P. Edw. This heaven that covers France contains the mercy
That draws from me submissive orisons;
That such base breath should vanish from my lips
To urge the plea of mercy to a man,
The Lord forbid! Return, and tell the King,
My tongue is made of steel, and it shall beg
My mercy on his coward burgonet;
Tell him, my colors are as red as his,
My men as bold, our English arms as strong:
Return him my defiance in his face.
Her. I go. [*Exit.*]

Enter another [HERALD].

P. Edw. What news with thee?
Her. The Duke of Normandy, my lord and master,
Pitying thy youth is so engirt with peril,
By me hath sent a nimble-jointed jennet,
As swift as ever yet thou didst bestride,
And therewithal he counsels thee to fly,
Else Death himself hath sworn that thou shalt die.
P. Edw. Back with the beast unto the beast that sent him!
Tell him, I cannot sit a coward's horse;
Bid him to-day bestride the jade himself,
For I will stain my horse quite o'er with blood,
And double gild my spurs, but I will catch him.
So tell the cap'ring boy, and get thee gone.
[*Exit Herald.*]

Enter another [HERALD].

Her. Edward of Wales: Philip, the second son
To the most mighty Christian King of France,
Seeing thy body's living date expir'd,
All full of charity and Christian love,
Commends this book, full fraught with prayers,
To thy fair hand; and for thy hour of life
Entreats thee that thou meditate therein
And arm thy soul for her long journey towards.
Thus have I done his bidding, and return.
P. Edw. Herald of Philip, greet thy lord from me:
All good that he can send I can receive;
But think'st thou not, the unadvised boy
Hath wrong'd himself in [thus] far tendering me?
Happily, he cannot pray without the book;
I think him no divine extemporal:
Then render back this commonplace of prayer
To do himself good in adversity.
Besides, he knows not my sins' quality,
And therefore knows no prayers for my avail.
Ere night his prayer may be, to pray to God
To put it in my heart to hear his prayer;
So tell the courtly wanton and be gone.
Her. I go. [*Exit.*]
P. Edw. How confident their strength and number makes them!—
Now, Audley, sound those silver wings of thine,
And let those milk-white messengers of Time
Show thy time's learning in this dangerous time.
Thyself art busy and bit with many broils,
And stratagems forepast with iron pens
Are texted in thine honorable face:
Thou art a married man in this distress,
But danger woos me as a blushing maid.
Teach me an answer to this perilous time.
Aud. To die is all as common as to live:
The one in choice, the other holds in chase;
For from the instant we begin to live
We do pursue and hunt the time to die:
First bud we, then we blow, and after seed;
Then presently we fall, and as a shade
Follows the body, so we follow death.
If, then, we hunt for death, why do we fear it?
If we fear it, why do we follow it?
If we do fear, how can we shun it?
If we do fear, with fear we do but aid
The thing we fear to seize on us the sooner;

72. **bloody colors.** Probably an allusion to Christopher Marlowe's *1 Tamburlaine*, IV.i.48ff.
75. **British earth:** Brittany.
77–78. **This heaven . . . orisons:** i.e. only heaven (God) could make me offer submissive prayers for mercy.
80. **to a man:** i.e., it is one thing to ask mercy of God, quite another to ask it of a mere mortal.
82–83. **beg . . . burgonet:** my sword ("tongue of steel") will "beg" (sarcastic) for mercy upon his coward's helmet.
91–95. **jennet . . . beast.** These words are brought together in *Othello*, I.i.113, 116–17.
99. **double . . . spurs:** doubly gild my spurs with blood.
100. **cap'ring:** prancing about (etymologically the Duke of Normandy's jade has become a goat). Q2's "carping" (= prating or fault-finding) is commonly, perhaps rightly, adopted.
103. **living date:** time of life.
105. **full fraught:** filled full of.
106. **hour of life:** i.e., the single hour now apparently left him.
108. **towards:** i.e., up to heaven.
113. **thus far tendering:** going so far as to present.
114. **Happily:** variant form of "haply" = perhaps.
115. **divine extemporal:** minister who prays without a text or preparation (perhaps a jibe at the Puritans, who repudiated the Anglican Book of Common Prayer).
116. **commonplace:** commonplace book (a mere collection of quoted passages).
118. **sins' quality:** the nature of my sins. Cf. Sonnet 121. 5–8, in which the theme of judgment by others who "count bad what I think good" is treated.
122. **courtly wanton:** over-indulged, spoiled child of the court.
125. **sound . . . wings.** Meaning questionable; perhaps referring to the sweetness of Audley's eloquence (W. G. Stone), "silver" being commonly used to describe the sound of music, as in *Romeo and Juliet*, IV.v.128: "Then music with her silver sound"; or to the silvered cheeks of the old man (Moore Smith), which, with "those milk-white messengers of Time" (i.e., his grey hairs) in l. 126, may be taken to refer to the wisdom proper to his experience and venerable age.
128. **busy . . . broils:** actively engaged in and lacerated by many fights. Capell's emendation ("bruis'd" for "busy") is commonly adopted.
129–30. **stratagems . . . texted:** the results of previous enemy strategies, written with iron pens, are shown in your scarred visage ("iron pens" = swords).
135. **The one . . . chase:** the one we would choose (life), the other (death) continually pursuing (us).
138. **blow . . . seed:** blossom and then run to seed.
139. **shade:** shadow.
141. **why . . . it?** Cf. *Julius Caesar*: II.ii.32–7.

If we fear not, then no resolved proffer
Can overthrow the limit of our fate:
For whether ripe or rotten, drop we shall,
As we do draw the lottery of our doom.

P. Edw. Ah, good old man, a thousand thousand armors
These words of thine have buckled on my back.
Ah, what an idiot hast thou made of life,
To seek the thing it fears; and how disgrac'd
The imperial victory of murd'ring Death!
Since all the lives his conquering arrows strike
Seek him, and he not them, to shame his glory.
I will not give a penny for a life,
Nor half a halfpenny to shun grim death,
Since for to live is but to seek to die,
And dying but beginning of new life.
Let come the hour when He that rules it will,
To live or die I hold indifferent. *Exeunt.*

[Scene V]

Enter King John *and* [Prince] Charles.

K. John. A sudden darkness hath defac'd the sky,
The winds are crept into their caves for fear,
The leaves move not, the world is hush'd and still,
The birds cease singing, and the wand'ring brooks
Murmur no wonted greeting to their shores;
Silence attends some wonder and expecteth
That heaven should pronounce some prophecy.
Where or from whom proceeds this silence, Charles?

P. Cha. Our men with open mouths and staring eyes
Look on each other, as they did attend
Each other's words, and yet no creature speaks:
A tongue-tied fear hath made a midnight hour,
And speeches sleep through all the waking regions.

K. John. But now the pompous sun in all his pride
Look'd through his golden coach upon the world,
And on a sudden hath he hid himself,
That now the under earth is as a grave,
Dark, deadly, silent, and uncomfortable.
A clamor of ravens.
Hark! what a deadly outcry do I hear?

P. Cha. Here comes my brother Philip.

K. John. All dismay'd.

[*Enter* Prince Philip.]

What fearful words are those thy looks presage?

P. [Phil.] A flight! a flight!

K. John. Coward, what flight? thou liest, there needs no flight.

P. [Phil.] A flight!

K. John. Awake thy craven powers, and tell on
The substance of that very fear indeed,
Which is so ghastly printed in thy face.
What is the matter?

P. [Phil.] A flight of ugly ravens
Do croak and hover o'er our soldiers' heads
And keep in triangles and corner'd squares
Right as our forces are embattled.
With their approach there came this sudden fog
Which now hath hid the airy [floor] of heaven
And made at noon a night unnatural
Upon the quaking and dismayed world:
In brief, our soldiers have let fall their arms
And stand like metamorphos'd images,
Bloodless and pale, one gazing on another.

K. John. [*Aside.*] Ay, now I call to mind the prophecy,
But I must give no entrance to a fear.—
Return, and hearten up these yielding souls.
Tell them, the ravens, seeing them in arms,
So many fair against a famish'd few,
Come but to dine upon their handy-work
And prey upon the carrion that they kill:
For when we see a horse laid down to die,
Although not dead, the ravenous birds
Sit watching the departure of his life;
Even so these ravens, for the carcases
Of those poor English that are mark'd to die,
Hover about; and if they cry to us,
'Tis but for meat that we must kill for them.
Away, and comfort up my soldiers,
And sound the trumpets, and at once dispatch
This little business of a silly fraud.
Exit Prince [Philip].

Another noise. Salisbury *brought in by a* French Captain.

[Fr.] Cap. Behold, my liege, this knight and forty mo,

146–47. **no resolved . . . fate:** no determined effort can upset or change the fixed time when we are fated [to die].
148. **whether ripe or rotten.** Cf. *As You Like It*, II.vii.26–7.
149. **As . . . doom:** i.e., in accordance with the chance lot we are dealt, which determines the date of our death.
151. **buckled on my back.** Cf. *Richard III*, III.vii.228: "Since you will buckle Fortune on my back."
152. **idiot . . . life:** Cf. *1 Henry IV*, V.iv.81–3.
156. **shame his glory:** put his boasting to shame.
161. **He . . . will:** i.e., God wills it to be.
162. **hold indifferent:** consider impartially.

IV.v. Location: Poitiers. Fields near Poitiers. The French camp.
2. **winds . . . caves:** The four winds in classical mythology resided in a cave or caves when inactive. Cf. *2 Henry VI*, III.ii.88–89: "What did I then, but curs'd the gentle gusts, / And he that loos'd them forth their brazen caves."
6. **attends:** awaits.
10. **as . . . attend:** as if they did listen for.
12. **A tongue-tied . . . hour:** a silent fear of impending danger has turned the time into that of the ever-so-quiet middle of the night. Cf. *The Rape of Lucrece*, 1625: "the dreadful dead of dark midnight" and *Titus Andronicus*, II.iii.99: "at dead time of the night."
14. **But . . . sun:** only a moment ago the magnificent sun.
17. **under earth:** i.e., the earth which is below or beneath the sun in position, size, and magnificence.

21. **presage:** predict.
25. **craven:** abjectly frightened, scared.
28. **flight of ugly ravens.** Cf. the ravens, crows, and kites which replace the encouraging eagles in *Julius Caesar*, V.i.79–88. Froissart (Berners, Chapter CXXX) describes the scene: "Also the same season there fell a great rayne and a clyps, with a terryble thonder, and before the rayne ther came fleyng ouer bothe batayls a great nombre of crowes, for feare of the tempest commynge. Than anone the eyre beganne to waxe clere, and the sonne to shyne fayre and bright; the which was right in the Frenchmens eyen, and on the Englyshhmens backes."
31. **Right . . . embattled:** in the same battle formations as our forces.
37. **stand . . . images:** stand as if transformed into statues.
43. **fair:** sound, uninjured.
54–5. **dispatch . . . fraud:** get rid of, dismiss this small matter arising out of a foolish misconception ("fraud" refers to the prophecy as King John would now wish it to be interpreted).
56. **mo:** more (in number).

Of whom the better part are slain and fled,
With all endeavor sought to break our ranks,
And make their way to the encompass'd Prince.
Dispose of him as please your majesty.

K. John. Go, and the next bough, soldier, that thou seest
Disgrace it with his body presently;
For I do hold a tree in France too good
To be the gallows of an English thief.

Sal. My Lord of Normandy, I have your pass
And warrant for my safety through this land.

P. Cha. Villiers procur'd it for thee, did he not?

Sal. He did.

P. Cha. And it is current, thou shalt freely pass.

K. John. Ay, freely to the gallows to be hang'd,
Without denial or impediment.
Away with him!

[*P. Cha.*] I hope your Highness will not so disgrace me,
And dash the virtue of my seal-at-arms.
He hath my never-broken name to show,
Charact'red with this princely hand of mine;
And rather let me leave to be a prince
Than break the stable verdict of a prince.
I do beseech you, let him pass in quiet.

K. John. Thou and thy word lie both in my command:
What canst thou promise that I cannot break?
Which of these twain is greater infamy,
To disobey thy father, or thyself?
Thy word, nor no man's, may exceed his power;
Nor that same man doth never break his word
That keeps it to the utmost of his power.
The breach of faith dwells in the soul's consent,
Which if thyself without consent do break
Thou art not charged with the breach of faith.—
Go hang him, for thy license lies in me,
And my constraint stands the excuse for thee.

P. Cha. What, am I not a soldier in my word?
Then arms adieu, and let them fight that list.
Shall I not give my girdle from my waist,
But with a guardian I shall be controll'd
To say I may not give my things away?
Upon my soul, had Edward, Prince of Wales,
Engag'd his word, writ down his noble hand,
For all your knights to pass his father's land,
The royal King, to grace his warlike son,
Would not alone safe conduct give to them,

74. **virtue:** both (1) moral value and (2) power.
75. **name:** (1) word; (2) good name.
76. **Charact'red:** inscribed (i.e., the "passport" has been both sealed [l. 74] and signed by him).
78. **stable verdict:** unchangeable decision, promise.
80–91. **Thou . . . thee.** These lines devoted to analysis of moral responsiblity are analogous to those of the King, Bates, and Williams in *Henry V*, IV.1.126 ff.
88. **without consent:** i.e., without your own consent.
91. **constraint:** coercion. The line sums up the argument of this pretty piece of royal casuistry.
93. **list:** wish to.
94. **girdle:** belt used to carry a weapon.
94–95. **Shall . . . say:** may I not give away my military belt from my waist, without being reprehended by an overseer who will say . . .
100. **grace:** honor.
101. **not alone:** not only. Cf. *Hamlet*, I.ii.77: "'Tis not alone my inky cloak, good mother."

But with all bounty feasted them and theirs.

K. John. Dwell'st thou on presidents? Then be it so.—
Say, Englishman, of what degree thou art.

Sal. An Earl in England, though a prisoner here,
And those that know me call me Salisbury.

K. John. Then, Salisbury, say whither thou art bound.

Sal. To Callice, where my liege, King Edward, is.

K. John. To Callice, Salisbury? Then to Callice pack,
And bid the King prepare a noble grave
To put his princely son, black Edward, in.
And as thou travel'st westward from this place,
Some two leagues hence there is a lofty hill,
Whose top seems topless, for the embracing sky
Doth hide his high head in her azure bosom;
Upon whose tall top, when thy foot attains,
Look back upon the humble vale beneath
(Humble of late, but now made proud with arms),
And thence behold the wretched Prince of Wales
Hoop'd with a bond of iron round about.
After which sight to Callice spur amain,
And say the Prince was smother'd and not slain;
And tell the King, this is not all his ill,
For I will greet him ere he thinks I will.
Away, be gone! The smoke but of our shot
Will choke our foes, though bullets hit them not.
[*Exeunt.*]

[SCENE VI]

Alarum. Enter PRINCE EDWARD *and* ARTOIS.

Art. How fares your Grace? Are you not shot, my lord?

P. Edw. No, dear Artois, but chok'd with dust and smoke,
And stepp'd aside for breath and fresher air.

Art. Breathe, then, and to it again. The amazed French
Are quite distract with gazing on the crows;
And were our quivers full of shafts again,
Your Grace should see a glorious day of this.
O for more arrows, Lord! that's our want.

P. Edw. Courage, Artois! a fig for feather'd shafts,
When feather'd fowls do bandy on our side.
What need we fight, and sweat, and keep a coil,

103. **presidents.** Variant form of "precedents."
111. **black:** malignant, devilish (from the perspective of the French, Edward's sobriquet did not derive from complexion, but from the color of his armor and the terrifying effect he had upon his enemies).
113. **two leagues:** equal to about six miles.
115. **his:** its.
117. **vale:** valley.
118. **Humble of late:** until recently humble.
120. **bond.** Variant form of "band."
121. **amain:** with full speed.

IV.vi. Location: Poitiers. A part of the field of battle.
4. **Breathe . . . again.** Cf. *1 Henry IV*, II.iv.249: "Well, breathe a while, and then to it again."
5. **distract:** distracted, confused. **crows:** i.e., the flight of ravens.
9. **attainted:** infected.
10. **bandy:** fight. Cf. *Titus Andronicus*, I.i.312: "One fit to bandy with thy lawless sons."
11. **keep a coil:** make or keep up such a disturbance or fuss.

When railing crows out-scold our adversaries?
Up, up Artois! the ground itself is arm'd
[With] fire-containing flint; command our bows
To hurl away their pretty-colour'd yew,
And to it with stones. Away, Artois, away!
My soul doth prophesy we win the day. *Exeunt.*

[SCENE VII]

Alarum. Enter KING JOHN.

[*K. John.*] Our multitudes are in themselves confounded,
Dismayed, and distraught. Swift-starting fear
Hath buzz'd a cold dismay through all our army,
And every petty disadvantage prompts
The fear-possessed abject soul to fly.
Myself, whose spirit is steel to their dull lead
(What with recalling of the prophecy,
And that our native stones from English arms
Rebel against us), find myself attainted
With strong surprise of weak and yielding fear.

Enter [PRINCE] CHARLES.

[*P. Cha.*] Fly, father, fly! the French do kill the French!
Some that would stand let drive at some that fly;
Our drums strike nothing but discouragement,
Our trumpets sound dishonor and retire;
The spirit of fear, that feareth nought but death,
Cowardly works confusion on itself.

Enter [PRINCE] PHILIP.

[*P. Phil.*] Pluck out your eyes, and see not this day's shame!
An arm hath beat an army: one poor David
Hath with a stone foil'd twenty stout Goliahs:
Some twenty naked starvelings with small flints
Hath driven back a puissant host of men,
Array'd and fenc'd in all accomplements.
K. John. Mordieu! they quoit at us and kill us up;
No less than forty thousand wicked elders
Have forty lean slaves this day ston'd to death.
P. Cha. O that I were some other countryman!
This day hath set derision on the French,
And all the world [will] blurt and scorn at us.
K. John. What, is there no hope left?
P. [*Phil.*] No hope but death to bury up our shame.
K. John. Make up once more with me: the twentith part
Of those that live are men enow to quail
The feeble handful on the adverse part.
P. Cha. Then, charge again: if heaven be not opos'd,
We cannot lose the day.
K. John. On! away! *Exeunt.*

[SCENE VIII]

[*Alarum.*] *Enter* AUDLEY, *wounded, and rescued by two* [ESQUIRES].

[1] *Esq.* How fares my lord?
Aud. Even as a man may do
That dines at such a bloody feast as this.
[2] *Esq.* I hope, my lord, that is no mortal scar.
Aud. No matter if it be: the count is cast,
And, in the worst, ends but a mortal man.
Good friends, convey me to the princely Edward,
That, in the crimson bravery of my blood,
I may become him with saluting him;
I'll smile and tell him that this open scar
Doth end the harvest of his Audley's war.
Retreat sounded. Exeunt.

[SCENE IX]

Enter PRINCE EDWARD [*in triumph, with his* SOLDIERS *and some French* SOLDIERS], *all with ensigns spread;* KING JOHN [*and* PRINCE] CHARLES [*as prisoners*].

P. Edw. Now John in France, and lately John of France,
Thy bloody ensigns are my captive colors;

12. **railing:** scolding.
14. **fire-containing flint.** When flint is struck it gives off sparks.
14. **bows:** bowmen.
16. **to . . . stones:** begin hurling stones (this fulfills the prophecy; see IV.iii.68–73).

IV.vii. Scene continues.
2. **distraught:** distracted, much confused.
5. **abject soul:** cast down, dispirited person.
9. **attainted:** infected.
10. **strong surprise:** powerful and unexpected attack.
12. **stand:** continue to make a stand (i.e., fight).
13. **discouragement:** i.e., retreat.
14. **retire:** retreat.
17. **Pluck out your eyes.** Cf. *King Lear*, III.vii.57.
18–19. **David . . . Goliahs.** See 1 Samuel 17:4–54.
22. **fenc'd . . . accomplements:** armed with all things that complete a soldier's equipment.
23. **Mordieu!:** French oath, "(By the) death of God"; English equivalent "'Sdeath" = God's death. Cf. Warwick's ejaculation "Mort dieu" in *2 Henry VI*, I.i.123.
23. **quoit at us:** throw stones (as in the game of quoits) at us as targets.
24. **forty thousand wicked elders.** Some say this is an allusion to the legend of Susannah (in the Apocrypha); this seems unlikely. More probably, it is an allusion to 1 Kings 21, and the unjust stoning to death of Naboth by the elders who were inveigled into their killing by Jezebel, the wife of Ahab, who coveted the vineyard of the victim, a vineyard inherited from Naboth's fathers.

28. **blurt:** "make a contemptuous puffing gesture with the lips" (*O.E.D.*).
31. **Make . . . me:** rally (the soldiers) again with me.
31. **twentith:** twentieth (variant form).
32. **enow:** enough.
33. **adverse part:** opposing side.

IV.viii. Location: Scene continues.
4. **count is cast:** (final) reckoning is determined (i.e., the day of my death is already set). Cf. IV.v.146–47 and note.
7. **crimson bravery:** fine garment of my blood.
8. **become him with:** honor him in.
10. **harvest . . . war:** final reaping and ingathering (like a harvest home of Audley's military career in the service of king and country).

IV.ix. Location: Poitou. The English Camp.
1–2. **Now John . . . colors.** Richard Proudfoot in his British Academy lecture points out how here the dramatist follows Holinshed rather than Froissart, who offers a magnanimous response by Prince Edward to the defeated John: "Sir, methynke ye ought to rejoyse, though the journey be nat as ye wolde have had it, for this day ye have wonne the hygh renome of prowes and have past this day in valyantnesse all other of your partie: sir, I say natte this to mocke you, for all that be on our partie that sawe every mannes dedes, ar playnly acorded by true sentence to gyve you the price and chapellette."
2. **colors:** ensigns, flags.

And you, high-vaunting Charles of Normandy,
That once to-day sent me a horse to fly,
Are now the subjects of my clemency.
Fie lords! is it not a shame that English boys,
Whose early days are yet not worth a beard,
Should in the bosom of your kingdom thus,
One against twenty, beat you up together?

K. John. Thy fortune, not thy force, hath conquer'd us.

P. Edw. An argument that heaven aids the right.

[*Enter* ARTOIS, *with* PRINCE PHILIP.]

See, see! Artois doth bring with him along
The late good-council-giver to my soul.—
Welcome, Artois, and welcome Philip, too:
Who now of you or I have need to pray?
Now is the proverb verified in you:
Too bright a morning breeds a low'ring day.

Sound trumpets. Enter AUDLEY, [*led by the two* ESQUIRES].

But say, what grim discouragement comes here?
Alas, what thousand armed men of France
Have writ that note of death in Audley's face?
Speak thou, that wooest death with thy careless smile
And look'st so merrily upon thy grave,
As if thou wert enamor'd on thine end,
What hungry sword hath so bereav'd thy face,
And lopp'd a true friend from my loving soul?

Aud. O Prince, thy sweet bemoaning speech to me
Is as a mournful knell to one dead-sick.

P. Edw. Dear Audley, if my tongue ring out thy end,
My arms shall be [thy] grave. What may I do
To win thy life, or to revenge thy death?
If thou wilt drink the blood of captive kings,
Or that it were restorative, command
A [health] of kings' blood, and I'll drink to thee.
If honor may dispense for thee with death,
The never-dying honor of this day
Share wholly, Audley, to thyself, and live.

Aud. Victorious Prince—that thou art so, behold
A Caesar's fame in king's captivity—
If I could hold dim death but at a bay,
Till I did see my liege, thy [royal] father,
My soul should yield this castle of my flesh,
This mangled tribute, with all willingness
To darkness, consummation, dust, and worms.

P. Edw. Cheerly, bold man! thy soul is all too proud
To yield her city for one little breach,
Should be divorced from her earthly spouse
By the soft temper of a Frenchman's sword.
Lo, to repair thy life, I give to thee
Three thousand marks a year in English land.

Aud. I take thy gift, to pay the debts I owe:
These two poor esquires redeem'd me from the French
With lusty and dear hazard of their lives:
What thou hast given me, I give to them;
And, as thou lovest me, Prince, lay thy consent
To this bequeath in my last testament.

P. Edw. Renowned Audley, live, and have from me
This gift twice doubled, to these esquires and thee:
But live or die, what thou hast given away
To these and theirs shall lasting freedom stay.—
Come, gentlemen, I will see my friend bestowed
Within an easy litter; then we'll march
Proudly toward Callice with triumphant pace
Unto my royal father; and there bring
The tribute of my wars, fair France his King. *Exeunt.*

[ACT V, SCENE I]

Enter KING EDWARD, QUEEN PHILIPPE, DERBY, [*and*] SOLDIERS.

K. Edw. No more, Queen Philippe, pacify yourself:
Copland, except he can excuse his fault,
Shall find displeasure written in our looks.—
And now unto this proud resisting town:
Soldiers, assault! I will no longer stay
To be deluded by their false delays;
Put all to sword, and make the spoil your own.
[*Trumpets sound a charge.*]

Enter six CITIZENS [*of* CALAIS] *in their shirts, barefoot, with halters about their necks.*

3. **high-vaunting:** loud-boasting.
7. **early:** youthful.
9. **together:** increasingly, continuously.
17. **Too . . . day.** See Tilley, M1175; cf. *Venus and Adonis*, 453–6; *Richard II*, III.iii.62–7; and *1 Henry IV*, V.i.1–7.
17. **low'ring:** dark, threatening.
24. **bereav'd:** plundered.
26. **bemoaning:** lamenting.
27. **knell:** funeral bell.
28–9. **Dear . . . grave.** cf. *1 Henry VI*, IV.vii.52: "Now my old arms are young John Talbot's grave."
28. **ring out:** sound forth (like a funeral bell).
34. **If . . . death:** if honor might exempt you from dying.
36. **Share wholly:** possess unshaped.
38. **Caesar's . . . captivity:** the fame of Julius Caesar in having a king as your prisoner.
39. **hold . . . bay:** hold death at baying distance, not letting it come in for the kill (a hunting metaphor).
42–43. **mangled . . . dust, and worms.** Cf. *1 Henry IV*, V.iv.85–86, 96.
43. **consummation:** death.
46. **Should:** (or) should. Perhaps, however, one or more preceding lines have been lost (Moore Smith).
47. **soft temper:** inferior quality.
49. **Three . . . land:** The dramatist has multiplied the Prince's generosity six-fold. Froissart (Berners, Chapter CLXV) describes this scene: "than he [Audley] called eyght of his servantes, and caused them to bere hym in his lytter to the place wereas the prince was. Than the prince tooke hym in his armes and kyst him and made hym great chere and sayd, Sir James, . . . to thyntent to furnysshe you the better to pursue the warres, I retayne you for ever to be my knight with fyve hundred markes of yerely revenewes, the which I shall assigne you on myne herytage in Englande."
52. **lusty . . . hazard:** vigorous and costly risk.
55. **bequeath:** bequest.
59. **shall . . . stay:** shall remain freely theirs in the future.
61. **easy:** comfortable, restful.
64. **tribute:** duty-offering. **France his:** = France's.

V.i. Location: Picardy. The English camp before Calais.
2. **except:** unless.
7. **spoil:** plunder, booty.

All [*Cit.*] Mercy, King Edward! mercy, gracious lord!
K. Edw. Contemptuous villains! call ye now for truce?
Mine ears are stopp'd against your bootless cries.
Sound drums, alarum! [*Alarum.*] Draw, threat'ning swords!
[1 *Cit.*] Ah, noble Prince, take pity on this town,
And hear us, mighty King!
We claim the promise that your Highness made;
The two days' respite is not yet expir'd,
And we are come with willingness to bear
What tortering death or punishment you please,
So that the trembling multitude be saved.
K. Edw. My promise? well, I do confess as much;
But I require the chiefest citizens,
And men of most account, that should submit.
You, peradventure, are but servile grooms,
Or some felonious robbers on the sea,
Whom, apprehended, law would execute,
Albeit severity lay dead in us.
No, no; ye cannot overreach us thus.
2[*Cit.*] The sun, dread lord, that in the western fall
Beholds us now low brought through misery,
Did in the orient purple of the morn
Salute our coming forth, when we were known;
Or may our portion be with damned fiends.
K. Edw. If it be so, then let our covenant stand:
We take possession of the town in peace;
But for yourselves, look you for no remorse,
But, as imperial justice hath decreed,
Your bodies shall be dragg'd about these walls,
And after feel the stroke of quartering steel:
This is your doom.— Go, soldiers, see it done.
Q. Phil. Ah, be more mild unto these yielding men!
It is a glorious thing to stablish peace,
And kings approach the nearest unto God
By giving life and safety unto men.
As thou intendest to be King of France,
So let her people live to call thee king;
For what the sword cuts down, or fire hath spoil'd,
Is held in reputation none of ours.
K. Edw. Although experience teach us this is true,
That peacefull quietness brings most delight
When most of all abuses are controll'd,
Yet, insomuch it shall be known that we
As well can master our affections
As conquer other by the dint of sword,
Philippe, prevail; we yield to thy request:
These men shall live to boast of clemency;
And, Tyranny, strike terror to thyself.
2[*Cit.*] Long live your Highness! happy be your reign!
K. Edw. Go, get you hence: return unto the town;
And if this kindness hath deserv'd your love,
Learn then to reverence Edward as your King.
Exeunt [*Citizens*].
Now might we hear of our affairs abroad,
We would, till gloomy winter were o'erspent,
Dispose our men in garrison a while.—
But who comes here?

Enter COPLAND *and* KING DAVID.

Derby. Copland, my lord, and David, King of Scots.
K. Edw Is this the proud presumptuous esquire of the north
That would not yield his prisoner to my Queen?
Cop. I am, my liege, a northen esquire, indeed,
But neither proud nor insolent, I trust.
K. Edw. What mov'd thee then to be so obstinate
To contradict our royal Queen's desire?
Cop. No willful disobedience, mighty lord,
But my desert and public law at arms:
I took the King myself in single fight,
And, like a soldier, would be loth to lose
The least preeminence that I had won;
And Copland, straight upon your Highness' charge,
Is come to France, and with a lowly mind
Doth vail the bonnet of his victory.
Receive, dread lord, the custom of my fraught,
The wealthy tribute of my laboring hands,
Which should long since have been surrend'red up,
Had but your gracious self been there in place.

8–54. **Mercy . . . clemency.** Froissart (Berners, Chapter CXLVI) describes this scene with the queen's intervention: " . . . we submyt oure self clerely into your wyll and pleasure, to save the resydue of the peple of Calays, . . . Sir, we beseche your grace to haue mercy and pytie on us through your hygh nobles: than all the erles and barownes, and other that were there, wept for pytie . . . . Than he commaunded their heedes to be stryken of: than every man requyred the kyng for mercy but he wolde here no man in that behalfe: . . . Than the quene . . . kneled down and sore wepyng, sayd, A gentyll sir . . . now I humbly requyre you . . . for the love of me, that ye woll take mercy of these sixe burgesses. The kyng . . . sayd, A dame, I wold ye had ben as nowe in some other place, ye make suche request to me that I can nat deny you. . . ."
9. **Contemptuous:** contemptible.
10. **bootless:** useless.
17. **tortering:** torturing (variant form).
22. **peradventure . . . grooms:** are perhaps only cringing servants.
25. **albeit:** although.
26. **overreach:** get the better of.
29. **orient:** resplendent, lustrous.
30. **when . . . known:** when we were once recognized as substantial citizens.
31. **portion:** lot, fate.
36. **dragg'd . . . walls.** The allusion to Achilles' treatment of the body of Hector suggests a hardness in Edward which is historically accurate, but a hardness softened by his response to the subsequent appeal by the Queen.
37. **quartering.** Note the frequency of forms of this term allowing for puns in the play on dismemberment, renting, and heraldic emblems of dynastic alliances.
38. **doom:** both "sentence" and "fate."

41–2. **kings . . . men.** Cf. Tilley, M898 and *The Merchant of Venice*, IV.i.193–7.
46. **held . . . ours:** i.e., (must be) considered as no gain or advantage to us.
51. **affections:** passions.
52. **dint:** stroke.
64. **David, King of Scots.** Cf. the similar unhistorical mention of David's being brought to France in *Henry V*, I.ii.160–62.
67–82. **I am . . . place.** Copland's defense anticipates in tone and appeal to dignity the argument of Hotspur in *1 Henry IV*, I.iii.29 ff.
67. **northen:** northern (variant form).
78. **vail:** doff.
79. **custom . . . fraught:** the duty levied on my cargo (a nautical trading image appropriate to Copland's having brought his prisoner across the sea to France).

Q. Phil. But, Copland, thou didst scorn the King's command,
Neglecting our commission in his name.
Cop. His name I reverence, but his person more:
His name shall keep me in allegiance still,
But to his person I will bend my knee.
K. Edw. I pray thee, Philippe, let displeasure pass.
This man doth please me, and I like his words:
For what is he that will attempt great deeds
And lose the glory that ensues the same?
All rivers have recourse unto the sea,
And Copland's faith, relation to his King.—
Kneel therefore down; now rise, King Edward's knight:
And to maintain thy state, I freely give
Five hundred marks a year to thee and thine.

Enter SALISBURY.

Welcome, Lord Salisbury. What news from Britain?
Sal. This, mighty King: the country we have won;
And Charles de Mountford, Regent of that place,
Presents your Highness with this coronet,
Protesting true allegiance to your Grace.
K. Edw. We thank thee for thy service, valiant Earl;
Challenge our favor, for we owe it thee.
Sal. But now, my lord, as this is joyful news,
So must my voice be tragical again,
And I must sing of doleful accidents.
K. Edw. What, have our men the overthrow at Poictiers?
Or is our son beset with too much odds?
Sal. He was, my lord; and as my worthless self,
With forty other serviceable knights,
Under safe-conduct of the Dolphin's seal,
Did travel that way, finding him distress'd,
A troop of lances met us on the way,
Surpris'd, and brought us prisoners to the King;
Who, proud of this, and eager of revenge,
Commanded straight to cut off all our heads:
And surely we had died, but that the Duke,
More full of honor than his angry sire,
Procur'd our quick deliverance from thence;
But ere we went, "Salute your King," quoth he,
"Bid him provide a funeral for his son:
To-day our sword shall cut his thread of life;
And sooner than he thinks, we'll be with him
To quittance those displeasures he hath done."
This said, we pass'd, not daring to reply:
Our hearts were dead, ours looks diffus'd and wan;
Wand'ring, at last we climb'd unto a hill,
From whence, although our grief were much before,
Yet now to see the occasion with our eyes
Did thrice so much increase our heaviness;
For there, my lord, O there, we did descry
Down in a valley how both armies lay.
The French had cast their trenches like a ring,
And every barricado's open front
Was thick emboss'd with brazen ordinance:
Here stood a battle of ten thousand horse,
There twice as many pikes in quadrant-wise;
Here cross-bows and deadly-wounding darts,
And in the midst, like to a slender point
Within the compass of the horizon
(As 'twere a rising bubble in the sea,
A hazel wand amidst a wood of pines,
Or as a bear fast chain'd unto a stake),
Stood famous Edward, still expecting when
Those dogs of France would fasten on his flesh.
Anon, the death-procuring knell begins:
Off go the cannons, that with trembling noise
Did shake the very mountain where they stood;
Then sound the trumpets' clangor in the air;
The battles join, and when we could no more
Discern the difference 'twixt the friend and foe,
So intricate the dark confusion was,
Away we turn'd our watery eyes, with sighs
As black as powder fuming into smoke.
And thus, I fear, unhappy have I told
The most untimely tale of Edward's fall.
Q. Phil. Ah me, is this my welcome into France?
Is this the comfort that I look'd to have,
When I should meet with my beloved son?
Sweet Ned, I would thy mother in the sea
Had been prevented of this mortal grief.
K. Edw. Content thee, Philippe; 'tis not tears will serve
To call him back, if he be taken hence.
Comfort thyself, as I do, gentle Queen,
With hope of sharp, unheard-of, dire revenge.—
He bids me to provide his funeral,
And so I will; but all the peers in France

85. **person:** the actual self.
91. **ensues:** follows from.
92. **have recourse unto:** flow toward.
93. **relation:** (has similar) recourse.
99. **Charles de Mountford]** Historically, John not Charles (see the note at IV.i. o.s.d.).
103. **Challenge:** claim.
111. **Dolphin's seal:** Dauphin's official signet.
113. **troop of lances:** horse-troop of lancers (lance = a long wooden shaft with an iron or steel head).
122. **thread of life.** Stock image derived from the classical myth of the three Fates, Clotho, Lachesis, and Atropos, who, respectively, spin, hold, and cut the life-line of each human being.
124. **quittance:** repay.
125. **pass'd:** departed.
126. **diffus'd and wan:** confused, distracted, and very pale and sickly.
129. **occasion:** state of affairs.
130. **heaviness:** weight of grief.
134. **barricado's:** barrier's.
135. **emboss'd . . . ordinance:** bristling with brass cannon.
137. **quadrant-wise:** in square form.
142. **hazel wand:** a slender, supple rod, suggestive of the youth of the Black Prince.
144. **still:** continually, ever.
145. **dogs.** In bear-baiting, dogs were set upon the bear, which was chained to a stake (see above, l. 143).
149. **clangor.** *O.E.D.* defines the term as "a loud, resonant ringing sound" and illustrates the definition by reference to *3 Henry VI*, II.iii.18, "Like to a dismal clangor heard from far."
152. **intricate:** perplexing.
160–1. **thy mother . . . grief:** i.e., Queen Philippe wishes she had been drowned, thus forestalling this killing sorrow.
161. **prevented:** deprived of.
166. **He:** King John (see l. 121).

Shall mourners be and weep out bloody tears
Until their empty veins be dry and sere.
The pillars of his hearse shall be [their] bones,
The mould that covers him, their city' ashes,
His knell, the groaning cries of dying men,
And, in the stead of tapers on his tomb,
An hundred fifty towers shall burning blaze,
While we bewail our valiant son's decease.

After a flourish sounded within, enter an HERALD.

Her. Rejoice, my lord, ascend the imperial throne!
The mighty and redoubted Prince of Wales,
Great servitor to bloody Mars in arms,
The Frenchman's terror, and his country's fame,
Triumphant rideth like a Roman peer;
And lowly at his stirrup comes afoot
King John of France, together with his son,
In captive bonds, whose diadem he brings
To crown thee with and to proclaim thee King.
K. Edw. Away with mourning! Philippe, wipe thine eyes.—
Sound, trumpets! welcome in Plantagenet!

[*A grand flourish.*] *Enter* PRINCE EDWARD, [*with*] KING JOHN [*and* PRINCE] PHILIP, [*as prisoners*], AUDLEY, [*and*] ARTOIS.

As things long lost, when they are found again,
So doth my son rejoice his father's heart,
For whom even now my soul was much perplex'd.
Q. Phil. Be this a token to express my joy,
For inward passions will not let me speak. *Kiss him.*
P. Edw. My gracious father, here receive the gift,
[*Presenting the crown of France.*]
This wreath of conquest and reward of war,
Got with as mickle peril of our lives
As e'er was thing of price before this day;
Install your Highness in your proper right:
And herewithal I render to your hands
These prisoners, chief occasion of our strife.
K. Edw. So, John of France, I see you keep your word:
You promis'd to be sooner with ourself
Than we did think for, and 'tis so indeed;
But had you done at first as now you do,
How many civil towns had stood untouch'd
That now are turn'd to ragged heaps of stones?
How many people's lives mightst thou have sav'd
That are untimely sunk into their graves?

169. **sere:** withered.
170. **hearse:** *O.E.D.* 2.a. "an elaborate framework originally intended to carry a large number of lighted tapers and other decorations over the bier or coffin while placed in the church at the funerals of distinguished persons."
171. **mould:** clods of earth.
172. **knell:** the ringing of the funeral bell.
177. **redoubted:** (1) dreaded; (2) reverenced.
178. **servitor:** squire.
179. **The Frenchman's terror.** Cf. *1 Henry VI*, I.iv.42, II.ii.17, IV.ii.16, IV.vii.77–8; see also Nashe (Appendix C, No. 12).
186. **Plantagenet:** the Prince of Wales, who by his courage has proven himself a fit member of the ruling family that began in England with Henry II.
193. **mickle:** deliberately archaic term for "great."
203. **civil:** well-governed.

K. John. Edward, recount not things irrevocable;
Tell me what ransom thou requirest to have?
K. Edw. Thy ransom, John, hereafter shall be known;
But first to England thou must cross the seas
To see what entertainment it affords:
Howe'er it falls, it cannot be so bad
As ours hath been since we arriv'd in France.
K. John. Accursed man! of this I was foretold,
But did misconster what the prophet told.
P. Edw. Now, father, this petition Edward makes—
[*Kneels in prayer.*] To Thee whose grace hath been his strongest shield,
That as Thy pleasure chose me for the man
To be the instrument to show Thy power,
So Thou wilt grant, that many princes more,
Bred and brought up within that little isle,
May still be famous for like victories!
And for my part, the bloody scars I bear,
The weary nights that I have watch'd in field,
The dangerous conflicts I have often had,
The fearful menaces were proffer'd me,
The heat and cold, and what else might displease,
I wish were now redoubled twenty-fold,
So that hereafter ages, when they read
The painful traffic of my tender youth,
Might thereby be inflam'd with such resolve,
As not the territories of France alone,
But likewise Spain, Turkey, and what countries else
That justly would provoke fair England's ire,
Might at their presence tremble and retire.
K. Edw. Here, English lords, we do proclaim a rest,
An intercession of our painful arms:
Sheath up your swords, refresh your weary limbs,
Peruse your spoils; and after we have breath'd
A day or two within this haven town,
God willing, then for England we'll be shipp'd;
Where, in a happy hour, I trust we shall
Arrive, three kings, two princes, and a queen.
[*Exeunt.*]

FINIS.

215. **misconster:** misconstrue, mistake the meaning of (variant form).
216. **father:** i.e., King Edward, but it is possible that we should read "Father" = God.
217. **Thee.** The Prince is addressing the deity with his "petition" for future English successes on the battlefield.
230. **traffic:** dealings.
234. **justly:** deservedly.
237. **intercession:** intermission.
239. **Peruse:** survey. **breath'd:** paused to catch our breath.
243. **three kings . . . queen:** i.e., King Edward, King John, and, unhistorically, King David; Prince Edward and Prince Philip (but not Prince Charles, who, also unhistorically, has been shown as captured at the battle of Poitiers in IV. ix above); and Queen Philippe.

NOTE ON THE TEXT

The basic authority for the text of *Edward III* is the quarto (Q1) published in 1596 by Cuthbert Burby, who had entered the play in the Stationers' Register on 1 December 1595/6, where it was entitled "Edward the Third and the Blacke Prince their warres with Kinge John of Fraunce." The printer appears to have been Thomas Scarlet. Burby published a second edition (Q2) in 1599 printed by Simon Stafford (see Greg and Lapides for detailed bibliographical descriptions).

Q1, as Greg and Lapides note, employs an unusual pattern of signature notation and fails to indent the speech-prefixes, idiosyncrasies that, among books printed in England, appear elsewhere only in another play printed by Scarlet (*A Knack to Know an Honest Man,* 1596). Lapides believes that the printer's copy for Q1 was authorial (i.e., a Shakespearean holograph), since he accepts the view that the play is the work of a single author and that author, Shakespeare. He bases his case for the most part on variations in the speech-prefixes as they apply to the same character and on the use of abrupt, imperative stage directions. Leaving aside, for the moment, the precise nature of the printer's copy, whether authorial or scribal, it should be noted that, despite variations in the use of speech-prefixes (e.g., *King, K. Ed., Ki.,* and *K.E.* for King Edward), the speech-prefixes are generally unambiguous (the *Lo./Lor.* confusion in II.i is almost certainly compositorial or, possibly, scribal) and that, overall, the state of the Q1 text may reflect copy that represents some stage in the preparation of the official prompt-book, a stage that would help to explain the occasional use of imperative stage directions, which (*pace* Lapides) one may associate with theatrical rather than authorial or scribal copy.

Two small but intriguing pieces of textual evidence may now be considered, since both not only bear on the provenience of the Q1 copy, but appear to offer new links between Shakespeare and *Edward III.* The first is connected with four compositorial misreadings (see II.i.91, 202, 404; III.i.105) in which a contracted manuscript form of "thy" (i.e., "y^{i}" or "y^{ie}") is misread as a contracted manuscript form of "their" (i.e., "y^{r}" or "y^{er}"), in both of which "y" represents a debased form of the Old English "þ"= "th", as for example, in the then commonly used contraction "y^{e}" for "the". With one exception, such a misreading occurs nowhere else in the accepted Shakespeare canon, most significantly not in those plays or poems believed to have been set up from Shakespeare's holograph copy (e.g., *Romeo and Juliet* Q2, *Hamlet* Q2, *Venus and Adonis* Q1) or in the 147-line scene in *Sir Thomas More* now generally viewed as being in Shakespeare's own hand (i.e., Hand D). The exception occurs in Thomas Thorpe's 1609 edition (Q) of Shakespeare's Sonnets printed by George Eld, in which there are some fifteen examples of the "thy/their" misreading. In the case of the Sonnets these misreadings, given the absence of any other examples in Shakespeare's other texts (or, so far as I know, outside the Shakespeare canon, except for *Edward III*), are taken as evidence that the printer's copy underlying the 1609 Sonnets was, at least for the most part, scribal, not authorial (see Evans, New Cambridge Sonnets, pp. 280–82, where the possible interrelations between *Edward III* and the Sonnets are also discussed). Thus, allowing for the unlikely possibility of simple coincidence and considering the common "Shakespeare" link (assuming, of course, that, as most now agree, Shakespeare had a major hand in the play, particularly the Countess scenes, I.ii, II.i–ii, as well as IV.iv), the "thy/their" connection strongly suggests that the same scribe was involved in at least some parts of the printer's copy for both *Edward III* and the Sonnets and may be taken to point to scribal copy for some sections of the manuscript copy behind the Q1 text.

The second "Shakespeare" link, although it is necessarily ambiguous in relation to the nature of the printer's copy, concerns just three Q1 spellings that suggest, graphically, that Shakespeare had a "hand" in the play. Hand D in *Sir Thomas More* (see above) drops the final *e* in "obedience" (ll. 39, 94, 113, 114), in "insolence" (l. 81), in "office" (l. 98) and in "France" (l. 121, there spelled "ffraunc"). In *Edward III* we find "present" for "presence" (II.i.15) and "aboundant" for "aboundance" (II.ii.39), errors best explained by postulating for both spellings a final *c* in the manuscript copy, a letter which, in the Secretary script that Shakespeare (and most of his contemporaries) used, is very easily mistaken for *t* (cf. *Romeo and Juliet* [Q2], V.iii.107, "pallat" for "pallace"). The third spelling actually illustrates the dropped *e* form: "recompenc" (III.iii.9). Again, if we admit Shakespeare's involvement, either he or a scribe may here be implicated, though, given the "thy/their" scribal confusion, a scribe seems the more likely. Obviously, the whole question of the printer's copy (authorial or scribal) needs further study.

Q1 was carelessly printed, full of typographical errors (see the Textual Notes), and wildly punctuated—punctuation that we may safely assume is in large part compositorial. The great majority of verse lines are end-stopped with indiscriminately used commas, colons, and periods, which are peppered about without any serious attention to syntax or meaning. Some press-correction was undertaken (see Lapides, pp. 66–67), but none of the press-variants is significantly substantive. The sudden appearance of entry stage directions in large roman type, instead of the usual italic type, on sigs. E1^{v} and E2 (inner forme), obviously introduced, as Greg noted, to fill up space, suggests that Q1 was probably set up from cast-off copy and printed by formes rather than *seriatim.* Q2 corrects a number of Q1's errors and improves the punctuation. Only a selection of Q2 variants is included in the Textual Notes.

Q1 violates the metrical distinction between accented and unaccented final *-ed* forms, a spelling convention usually observed with at least some care, to such a degree that the unaccented *'d* form has been silently adopted within the line when Q1 uses a metrically awkward (sometimes impossible) accented form; only at the end of a line has a Q1 accented *-ed* form been retained, because in that position it may represent an author's intended stress, an intention probably more often honored in speaking verse than we now recognize. Q1's fairly frequent *in-* prefix forms (e.g. "inchanted" [I.ii.7], a recognized obsolete variant form of "enchanted") have also been silently converted to the standard modern *en-* form.

For further information, see: Edward Capell, ed., *Edward III* in *Prolusions; or select Pieces of ancient Poetry* (London, 1760); Henry Tyrrell, ed., *Edward III* in *The Doubtful Plays of Shakespeare* (London, [1851]); Nicolaus Delius, ed., *Edward III* in *The Leopold Shakspere* (London [1877]); J. P. Collier, ed., *Edward III* (London, 1878); Karl Warnke and Ludwig Proescholdt, eds., *Edward III* in *Shakespearian Plays* (Halle, 1883); E. A. Hopkinson, ed., *Edward III* (London, 1891; 2nd ed. [greatly enlarged] 1911); G. C. Moore Smith, ed., *Edward III* (London, 1897); Tucker Brooke, ed., *Edward III* in *The Shakespeare Apocrypha* (Oxford, 1908); Alfred Hart, *Shakespeare and the Homilies* (Melbourne, 1934); W. W. Greg, *A Bibliography of the English Printed Drama to the Restoration,* Vol. I (London, 1939); Kenneth Muir, *Shakespeare as Collaborator* (London, 1960); R. L. Armstrong, ed., *Edward III* in *Six Early Plays Related to the Shakespeare Canon,* ed., E. B. Everitt (Copenhagen,

1965); Fred Lapides, ed., *The Raigne of King Edward the Third* (New York, 1980); Richard Proudfoot, *"The Reign of King Edward the Third* (1596) and Shakespeare," *Proceedings of the British Academy* (for 1985), LXXI (1986), 159–85; George Parfitt, ed., Nottingham Drama Series *Edward III* (Nottingham, 1985); Louis Ule, ed., *A Concordance to the Shakespeare Apocrypha*, 3 vols. (Hildesheim, 1987); R. Matthews and T. Merriam,"A Bard by Any Other Name," *New Scientist*, XII (1994), 23–7; Eric Sams, ed., *Shakespeare's "Edward III": An Early Play Restored to the Canon* (Yale, 1996) [unfortunately, appeared too late to be consulted].

TEXTUAL NOTES

Title: **The . . . Third**] The Raigne of King Edward the third: As it hath bin sundrie times plaied about the Citie of London. *Q1 (title-page).*
Dramatis Personae: *subs. as first given by Capell*
Act-scene division: *none in Q1–2; essentially that of Capell, who, however, treats IV.vi-viii as a single scene; present arrangement, Warnke/Proescholdt*

I.i

I.i] *Capell*
Location: *Capell*
o.s.d. **Warwick]** *Capell*
6 **le Beau]** *Capell;* of Bew *Q1–2*
7 **successively]** *Capell;* successefully *Q1–2*
17 **note]** *Q2;* not *Q1*
18 **linage]** lineage *Tyrrell* (variant form)
18 **le Beau]** *Capell;* of Bew *Q1–2*
30 **Perhaps]** *Q2; Art:* Perhaps *Q1*
36 **watchman]** *Capell;* watchmen *Q1–2*
41 **And]** *om. Capell*
46 **rak'd]** *Capell;* rakt *Q1;* rakte *Q2;* rack'd *Moore Smith*
51 s.d. **Exit . . . returns.]** *Capell*
54 s.d. **Exeunt . . . attended.]** *Capell (subs.);* Enter a Messenger Lorrayne. *Q1–2, after l. 51*
58 **much]** *Q2;* mnch *Q1*
71 **childish]** foolish *Q2*
76 **shifts]** *Q2;* shists *Q1*
78 **gloss]** *Q2;* glasse *Q1*
87 **spite]** sight *Capell conj.*
89 **Frenchman!]** *Collier;* French man *Q1;* French man? *Q2*
105 **Regenerate]** Degenerate *Tyrrell*
106 **wast]** *Q2;* was *Q1*
108 s.d. **Draws his.]** *Capell (subs.)*
117 s.d. **Exeunt . . . attendants.]** *Capell (subs.)*
118 **lords]** *Capell;* Lord *Q1–2*
120 s.d. **Sir William]** *Capell*
121–2] *These lines assigned to Mountford in Q1; corrected, Q2*
126 **straight,]** *Capell;* straight *Q1–2*
134 **Mountford]** *Tyrrell;* Mounefort *Q1–2*
169 **naught]** *Q2;* nought *Q1*
169 s.d. **Exeunt.]** *Q2;* Exunt.] *Q1*

I.ii

I.ii] *Capell*
Location: *Capell*
o.s.d. **of . . . walls.]** *Capell*
1 s.p. **Count.]** *Capell*
3 **Ah]** *Q2; A Q1*
3 **wants]** *want'st Q2*
4 **spirit]** *Q2;* spirirt *Q1*
14 s.d. **and others]** *Capell*
17 s.d. **Retiring . . . works.]** *Capell*
20 **most]** *Q2;* must *Q1*
25 **roads]** *Capell;* Rods *Q1*
27 **rusting]** *Capell;* rust in *Q1*
28 **spurs]** *Q2;* spurre *Q1*
34 **"Enough . . . pity."]** *quoted, Capell*
38 **I]** *Q2; om. Q1*
45 s.p. **Doug.]** *Q2;* Da. *Q1*
47 s.d. **as a messenger,]** *ed.*
58 **Douglas?]** *Q2;* Duglas *Q1*
66 s.d. **Enter another]** *Q2;* Annother *Q1*
68 s.p. **Count.]** *Capell*
71 **She]** *Capell;* He *Q1–2*
72 s.d. **Exeunt]** *Q2;* Exunt *Q1*
80 s.d. **and others]** *Capell*
81] *Line assigned to Mountague in Q1–2; corrected, Capell*
89 s.d. **Exit . . . walls.]** *Capell (subs.)*
89 s.d. **Flourish.]** *Capell*
93 s.d. **attended.]** *Capell*
95 **my]** *Q2*
95 **tyrant's]** *Capell;* tyrants *Q1–2*
96 **with]** which *Q2*
102, 117, 128 s.dd. **Aside.]** *Capell*
102 **lurk'd]** Q2; lurke *Q1*
104 **her]** their *Capell conj.*
117 s.p. **K. Edw.]** *Q2; om. Q1, which continues ll. 117–18 to the Countess*
133 **two]** *Q2;* to *Q1*
135 **desire! . . . be]** *Delius; (after Capell);* desire, . . . be, *Q1–2*
144 **inner]** inward *Q2*
153 **pride]** proud *Capell;* pied *Capell conj.*
157 **testimony]** *Q2;* testomie *Q1*
159 **waste]** *Delius;* West *Q1–2*
162 s.d. **Aside.]** *ed.*

II.i

II.i] *Capell*
Location: *Capell*
o.s.d. **Lodwick]** *The disyllabic form is adopted throughout; the form* Lodowick *occurs, except in II.i.59, only in Q1–2 stage directions*
1 s.p. **Lod.]** *Q2;* Lor. *Q1*
10 **cheeks]** *Capell;* cheeke *Q1–2*
11 **oriental]** *Q2;* oryent all *Q1*
15 **presence]** *Q2;* present *Q1*
17 **vail]** *Capell;* waile *Q1–2*
24 s.d. **Lodwick stands aside.]** *ed. (after Collier)*
25 **hither]** *Q2;* thither *Q1*
33 **her? . . . herself]** *Q2;* her . . . herselfe: *Q1*
48 **there]** *Q2;* thete *Q1*
48 s.d. **Lodwick comes forward.]** *ed. (after Collier)*
52 s.d. **Exit.]** *Capell*
57 **beauty's queen]** *Capell;* beauties Queene *Q1–2*
59 **Hast]** *Capell; Ki:* Hast *Q1; King Ed.* Hast *Q2*
59 **Lodwick]** *Moore Smith;* Lodowike *Q1;* Lodow. *Q2*
71 **Tartar's]** *Capell;* Torters *Q1–2*
75 **sovereign's]** *Q2* (soueraignes)*;* soueraigne *Q1*
79 **Beguile]** *Q2;* Beguild *Q1*
79 **humane]** humaine *Q2;* human *Moore Smith*
80 s. p. **Lod.]** *Q2;* Lor. *Q1*
82 **as]** *Capell;* is *Q1–2*
84 **"beautiful,"]** *quoted, ed. (after Armstrong)*
90 **the]** *Q2;* thy *Q1*
91 **thy]** *Capell;* their *Q1–2*
91 **praise's]** *Capell;* praises *Q1–2*
92 **Begin, I]** *Capell;* Beginne I *Q1–2*
95 s.p. **Lod.]** *Q2;* Lor. *Q1*
95 **Write]** *Q2;* Writ *Q1*
96 **o'er]** *ed. (after Q2);* on *Q1;* over *Q2*
98 **thinkest]** *Q2;* thinekst *Q1*
99 s.p. **Lod.]** *Q2;* Lor. *Q1*
105 *Following this line, Moore Smith suggests that a line or two has dropped out.*
116 **"Like . . . glass"]** *quoted, Capell*
116 **amber.]** *Q2* (subs.); Amber *Q1*
124–26] *Two lines in Q1–2, ending* name . . . read; *present arrangement, Warnke and Proescholdt*
126 **Lodwick]** *Warnke and Proescholdt;* Lorde *Q1–2*
134, 135 **Hers]** Her's *Collier*
137 **sand by sand]** *Capell;* said, by said, *Q1–2*
141 **"More . . . shades,"]** *quoted Capell*
142 **line]** *Q2;* loue *Q1*
150 **"More . . . chaste,"]** *quoted, Capell*
152 **treasure]** *Capell;* treason *Q1–2*
156 **Say,]** *Capell;* Say *Q1–2*
167–68 **"More . . . constancy"]** *quoted, Capell*
167 **queen]** *Capell;* louer *Q1–2*
169 **"than Judith was."]** *quoted, Capell*
174 **then,]** *Q2;* then *Q1*
184 **treasurer]** treasure *Q2*
189 **lord]** *Capell;* Lords *Q1–2*
192 s.d. **To Lodwick.]** *ed.*
193 s.p. **Lod.]** *Q2;* Lor. *Q1*
193 s.d. **Exit.]** *Capell*
196 **sullen]** *Capell;* sullome *Q1–2*
201 **wrong! . . . king,]** *Capell;* wrong, . . . King: *Q1–2*
202] *Line given to King Edward in Q1; corrected, Q2*
202 **Aquaint]** *Q2;* Aquant *Q1*
202 **thy]** *ed.;* theyr *Q1;* your *Q2*
210 **Countess]** *Q2;* Counties *Q1*
213 **it]** *Capell*
220 **Employ]** *Capell;* Inploy *Q1;* Imploy *Q2*
228 **beauty]** *Q2;* beauie *Q1*
230 **dispossess]** *Q2;* disposse *Q1*
234 s.p. **K. Edw.]** *Q2; om. Q1, which continues the line to the Countess*
234 **lend]** *Q2;* leue *Q1*
241 **lend]** *Q2;* leaue *Q1*
260 **marriage']** *Delius;* mariage *Q1–2*
260 **sacred]** *Q2;* secred *Q1*
275 **guilty]** *Q2;* giulty *Q1*
283 **this]** *Capell;* his *Q1–2*
285 **juice]** *Capell;* vice *Q1–2*
287 **Too strict]** *Q2;* To stricke *Q1*
287 **ward]** *Capell;* weed *Q1–2*
299 **profferest]** offerest *Q2*
310 **cynic]** *Q2;* cyncke *Q1*
311 **if I]** *Q2;* I if *Q1*
312 **lessened]** *Capell;* lesned *Q1–2*
314–15] *Lines continued to Warwick in Q1–2; corrected, Cappell*
322–23] *Lines continued to Warwick in Q1; corrected, Q2*
322 s.p. **K. Edw.]** *Q2; om. Q1*
325 **accompt]** *ed.;* accomplish *Q1;* account *Q2*
326 **unswear]** *Capell;* answere *Q1–2*
330 **breaks]** *Q2;* breake *Q1*
347 s.p. **War.]** *Q2; assigned to King Edward in Q1*
347 **O]** *Capell;* or *Q1–2*
371 **presence]** *Q2;* promise *Q1*
372 s.d. **Aside.]** *Warnke and Proescholdt*
378 **such]** *Q2;* snch *Q1*
379 s.d. **To the Countess.]** *Warnke and Proescholdt*
390 **doth]** *Q2;* goth *Q1*
404 **thy]** *Capell;* their *Q1*
405 **potion]** *Q2;* portion *Q1*
414 **invir'd]** *Capell;* inuierd *Q1–2*
423 **rein]** *Q2;* reigne *Q1*
448 **glory]** *Capell;* gloomie *Q1–2*
457 s.d. **Exit.]** *Capell*
458 **I'll]** *Q2;* Ils *Q1*
459 s.d. **Exit.]** *Capell;* Exeunt. *Q1–2*

II.ii

II.ii] *Capell*
o.s.d. **France]** *Q2;* Eraunce *Q1*
7] *line given to King Edward in Q1; correctly continued to Audley, Q2*
13 **these]** this *Q2*
20 s.d. **Trumpets within.]** *Capell (subs.)*
21 s.d. **Enter the King.]** *Follows l. 20 in Q1–2; corrected Capell*
22 s.p. **Aud. Hast]** *Q2* (Awd.), *Ar.* Hhere *Q1*
25 s.d. **Presenting letters.]** *Capell*
26, 28 s.dd. **Aside.]** *Warnke and Proescholdt*
30 s.dd. **Aside.]** *ed.*

32 **as**] to *Q2*
38 **is**] Is in *Q2*
38 s.d. **Exeunt . . . Audley.**] *Capell* (Exeunt *Q2*); Exunt. *Q1*
39 **abundance**] *Delius;* aboundant *Q1–2*
44 **What**] *Capell; Ki:* What *Q1; Kin.* What *Q2*
46 s.d. **Drum within.**] Capell
50, 57 **Go,**] *Capell;* Go *Q1–2*
60–61] *One line in Q1–2; rearranged, Capell*
60 **with**] *Q2;* wrth *Q1*
61 s.d. **Exit Lodwick.**] *Q2;* Exit. *Q1*
72 s.d. **Enter Ludwick.**] *Follows l. 73 in Q1–2; rearranged, Capell*
73 **How now!**] *Precedes Lodwick's entry in Q1–2; rearranged, Capell*
74 **strook**] *Capell;* stroke *Q1–2*
76 s.d. **Exit Lodwick.**] *ed. (after Capell)*
76 s.d. **Aside.**] *ed.*
77 **Modell'd**] Molded *Q2*
80 **seeks**] *Q2;* seeke *Q1*
85 **to**] in *Q2*
87 s.d. **Aside.**] *ed.*
89 **make**] made *Q2*
91 **Lust . . . men . . . lanthorns**] *Capell;* Lust as a fire, and me like lanthorne *Q1–2*
93 **of**] *Q2;* or *Q1*
94 **Brittany**] *Q2* (Britany); Brittayne *Q1*
98 **not**] *om. Capell*
101 **sweet**] sweep *Capell;* beat *Delius;* sweat *Collier*
104, 108 s.dd. **Aside.**] *ed.*
107, 115 **Go,**] *Q2;* Go *Q1*
111. **these**] those *Q2*
112 s.d. **Exit Lodwick.**] *Follows l. 110 in Q1–2; rearranged, Capell*
116 s.d. **escorted by Lodwick**] *ed. (after Capell)*
117 **my**] *Capell;* thy *Q1–2*
119 s.d. **Exit Lodwick.**] *Capell*
121 **"yea"**] *quoted, Collier*
125 **Ay**] *Capell;* I *Q1–2*
127 **render**] tender *Capell*
135 **"I will,"**] *quoted, Armstrong*
138 **them**] *Capell;* then *Q1–2*
141 **thrice-loving**] *Q2 (hyphen, Delius);* thrice loning *Q1*
151 s.p. **K. Edw.**] *Q2; om. Q1*
151 **more: thy**] *Q2;* mor, ethy *Q1*
155 **through**] *Q2;* throng *Q1*
155 **Hellespont**] *Tyrrell;* hellie spout *Q1;* helly, spoute *Q2*
156 **Sestos**] *Capell;* Cestus *Q1–2*
158 **heart-bloods**] *Capell;* hart bloods *Q1;* heart bloods *Q2*
163 s.d. **Aside.**] *Warnke and Proescholdt*
166 **evil**] ill *Capell conj.*
168 **therefore**] *Q2;* therefote *Q1*
171 s.d. **Turning . . . daggers.**] *Capell*
172 **knives**] *Q2;* knifes *Q1*
183 s.d. **Kneels.**] *ed. (after Capell, but following* heaven *in l. 185)*
186 **wouldst**] *Q2;* would *Q1*
209 **gild**] *Capell;* guide *Q1–2*

III.i

III.i] *Capell*
Location: *Capell*
17–18 *Two lines, ending* possible . . . themselves *Q1; corrected Capell*
33 **domestic**] *Capell;* drum stricke *Q1;* drumsticke *Q2*
35 **Sicily**] *Capell;* Cycelie *Q1*
37 s.d. **Drums within.**] *Capell (subs.)*
39 s.d. **some Muscovites**] *ed. (after Capell)*
52 **gain**] *Q2;* game *Q1*
61 s.d. **a Mariner**] *Q2 (subs.)*
62 **descried**] *Q2;* discribde *Q1*
79 s.p. **K. John.**] *Q2: speech continued to the Mariner, Q1*
83 **our**] *Q2;* out *Q1*
90 **There's**] *Q2;* Thees *Q1*
90 s.d. **Giving money.**] *ed. (after Capell)*
93 s.d. **Mariner**] *Q2*
99 **Together**] *Q2;* **Togeither** *Q1*
104 s.d. **Prince . . . forces**] *Capell; following l. 103, Q1–2;* Exeunt. *Q2;* Exunt. *Q1*
105 **thy**] *Q2;* their *Q1*
116 s.d. **A table . . . it.**] *Capell*
116 s.d. **heard**] *Q2;* hard *Q1*
120 **Steer**] *Capell;* Stir *Q1–2 (variant form of "Steer")*
122 s.d. **heard**] *Collier*
125 s.p. **K. John.**] *Q2; catchword, Q1*
131 s.d. **sounded**] *Collier; s.d. following l. 132, Q1–2; corrected, Capell*
134 **forward**] froward *Q2*
135 **favoring**] *Q2;* sauouring *Q1*
136 **the other**] *Capell;* thither *Q1;* th'other *Q2*
164 **cranny**] cranny'd *Capell*
165 **dissever'd**] *Q2* (disseuered); dissuuered *Q1*
168 **middle**] *Q2;* middle *Q1*
173 **fear**] *Capell;* force *Q1–2*
174 **of cowardice**] *Q2;* of a cowardize *Q1*
175 **We**] Were *Capell*
177 **Nonpareille**] *Capell;* Nomper illa *Q1–2*
180 **wind**] *Q2;* wine *Q1*

III.ii

III.ii] *Capell*
Location: *Capell*
o.s.d. **Frenchmen, . . . children; meet . . . Citizen.**] *ed.;* French men, . . . Children, meet them another Citizens. *Q1;* Frenchmen; . . . children meet them, and other Citizens. *Q2*
1, 7, 10, 13, 27, 30 s.pp. **3 Fr.**] *ed;* One: *Q1–2*
5, 11, 16, 32 s.pp. **1 Fr.**] *ed;* Two: *Q1–2*
5 **ay**] *Capell;* I *Q1–2*
5 **day**] *Q2;* pay *Q1*
6 **ye**] *Q2;* we *Q1*
8, 29 s.pp. **2 Fr.**] *ed.;* Three. *Q1–2*
16 **Ay**] *Cappell;* I *Q1–2*
27 **ill**] all *Capell*
41–3 "The . . . France."] *quoted, Capell*
43 **flower-de-luce**] *Q2 (hyphen, Capell);* fleur deluce *Q1*
46 s.p. **4 Fr.**] *Capell; om. Q1–2*
49 **ransack-constraining**] *Capell;* ransackt constraining *Q1–2*
58 **reeking**] *Capell conj.;* leaking *Q1–2*
59 **Turn'd**] *Capell (subs.);* I tourned *Q1–2*
65 **his**] *Q2;* is *Q1*
67 **distant,**] *Q2;* distant *Q1*
76 s.d. **Exeunt.**] *Q2*

III.iii

III.iii] *Capell*
Location: *Capell*
2 **Somme**] *Capell;* Sone *Q1–2*
9 **recompence**] *Q2;* recompenc
13 s.p. **Art.**] *Q2; om. Q1, which continues the speech to the King*
20 **Harflew**] *Brooke;* Harslen *Q1–2;* Harfleur *Capell*
20 **Lo**] *Capell;* Lie *Q1–2*
20 **Crotaye**] *Warnke and Proescholdt;* Crotag *Q1–2;* Crotage *Capell*
25 **proffer'd**] *Q2* (proffered); poffered *Q1*
27 **thus**] *Q2;* this *Q1*
36 **hours**] *Q2;* owers *Q1*
38 **with**] 'o *Capell;* of *Moore Smith*
39 **And I . . . other; with**] *Collier (after Capell);* And on the other both *Q1–2;* I on the other; with *Capell*
51 **Upbraids**] *Q2;* Obraids *Q1*
60 **false**] most *Q2*
62 **so much**] *Capell;* such *Q1–2;* such, [so] *Collier*
64 **Thy**] *Q2;* they *Q1*
70 **'mongst**] *Q2 (subs.);* mongest *Q1*
89 **Now**] How *Capell*
90 **the**] thy *Q2*
96 **his**] *Q2;* this *Q1*
99 **hid**] *Q2;* hide *Q1*
118 **Ay**] *Capell;* I *Q1–2*
126 **Upbraid'st**] *Q2;* Obraidst *Q1*
131–32] *Lines end* king . . . time *in Q1–2; rearranged, Capell*
134 **held**] kept *Q2*
137 s.p. **Phil.**] *Q2; om. Q1*
138 **words**] *Q2;* wodrs *Q1*
140 **now's**] *Capell;* knowes *Q1–2*
161 **resty-stiff**] *hyphen, Capell*
165 s.d. **French**] *Capell (subs);* Fra. *Q1–2*
167 s.d. **Exeunt . . . Soldiers.**] *Collier (subs., after Capell)*
169 **this**] *Capell;* the *Q1–2*
178 s.d. **Flourish.**] *Capell*
178 s.d. **The first . . . son.**] *Capell (subs.)*
179 **Edward**] *Capell; Kin:* Edward *Q1; K. Ed.* Edward *Q2*
186 s.d. **Receiving . . . Herald.**] *Capell*
188 **thy**] *Capell;* this *Q1–2*
192 s.d. **Receiving . . . Herald.**] *Capell*
193 **manly**] manlike *Q2*
197 **conquer**] *Q2;* vanquish *Q1*
198 s.d. **Receiving . . . Herald.**] *Capell*
198 **Plantagenet**] *Q2;* Plantagener *Q1*
203 **conquer**] *Q2;* couquer *Q1*
206 s.p. **P. Edw.**] *Q2*
209 **presaging**] *Q2;* persaging *Q1*
219 **thus**] *Q2;* this *Q1*

III.iv

III.iv] *Capell*
Location: *Capell*
o.s.d. **and English Soldiers**] *Capell (subs.)*
3 **Genoaes**] Genoeses *Capell;* Genoese *Collier;* Genoa's *Moore Smith*
5 **be**] be so *Capell*
13 s.d. **Exeunt.**] *Q2*

III.v

III.v] *Capell*
Location: *Capell*
o.s.d. **Drums**] *Capell*
2 **our**] your *Q2*
10 s.p. **Art.**] *Q2*
29 **whilst**] *Capell;* whilest *Q1–2*
47 **haggard-like**] *Q2 (hyphen, Capell);* huggard like *Q1*
51 **vanquish'd, cheerful,**] *Capell;* vanquisht cheerefull *Q1–2*
54 s.d. **Aside.**] *ed. (after Capell)*
56 s.d. **Retreat sounded.**] *Capell*
60 s.d. **Flourish.**] *Capell*
60 s.d. **his . . . him**] *Capell (subs.)*
60 s.d. **the body of**] *Capell*
69 **travail's**] *ed.;* travels *Q1–2;* travel's *Capell*
74 **Whose thousands**] *Capell;* Whom you sayd *Q1–2;* Who you saw *Anon. (in Collier)*
75 **lay**] laid *Anon. conj.*
81 **recover**] remember *Capell*
84 **carv'd**] *Q2;* craud *Q1*
86 **thus**] *Q2;* this *Q1*
88 **Ay**] *Capell;* I *Q1–2*
89 s.d. **the King . . . him**] *ed. (after Capell); Q1 s.d. opposite ll. 85–86; repositioned as here by Q2*
90 **fought**] sought *Tyrrell*
96–98] *Lines arranged as in Q1–2; rearranged by Capell, ending* fourscore . . . knights . . . soldiers . . . thousand
98 **Common**] Priuate *Q2*
99 s.p. **K. Edw.**] *Q2*
109 **What**] *Q2; Ki.* What *Q1*
109 s.d. **Pointing . . . colors.**] *Capell*
114 **"And . . . you."**] *quoted, Capell*

IV.i

IV.i] *Capell*
Location: *Capell*
1 **your**] *Q2;* our *Q1*
4 **Britain's**] *Q2;* Btitaines *Q1*
10 **Mountford**] *Q2;* Mountfort *Q1*
12 s.d. **Mountford**] *Capell*
16 **That**] *Capell;* Yet *Q1–2*
18 **who's**] *Q2;* whose *Q1*
19 **knowest**] *Q2;* kuowest *Q1*
24 **enemies:**] *Capell (subs.)* enemies *Q1;* enemies, *Q2*
39 **me**] thee *Capell*
42 s.d. **Exit Villiers.**] *Capell; s.d. follows l. 41 in Q1–2; adjusted, Capell*

IV.ii

IV.ii] *Capell*
Location: *Capell*
2 **their**] the *Q2*
4 **neither**] *Q2;* neithet *Q1*
9 s.d. **Enter . . . Frenchmen.**] *Follows l. 6 in Q1–2; rearranged, Capell*
12 **patterns**] partners *Q2*
13 **or**] *Q2;* er *Q1*
14 **your**] ye *Q2*
15 s.p. **Poor Fr.**] *ed.;* Poore. *Q1–2;* l. F. *Capell*
25 **ye**] you *Q2*

27 s.p. **Poor Fr.**] *ed.;* So. *Q1;* Poore. *Q2;* 1. F. *Capell*
32 s.d. **Exeunt . . . Frenchmen.**] *Capell*
34 **flesh**] *Delius conj.;* fresh *Q1–2*
36 **Lord**] *Capell; Ki:* Lord *Q1; K.E.* Lord *Q2*
37 **comes here**] commends her *Capell*
43 **fruitful**] faithfull *Q2*
49 **An esquire**] *ed.;* A Esquire *Q1;* A squire *Q2*
53 **grievously**] *Q2;* greouously *Q1*
54 **dispatch'd**] *Q2* (dispatcht)*;* dispatch *Q1*
57 **queen's**] *Q2;* Queene *Q1*
61 s.d. **French**] *Capell*
62 s.p. **F. Capt.**] *Q2* (Captaine.)*; om. Q1*
72 **I will**] *Q2;* Will *Q1*
79 s.d. **King . . . Soldiers**] *ed. (after Capell)*
80 s.p. **F. Capt.**] *ed.;* Cap. *Q1;* Captaine. *Q2*

IV.iii

IV.iii] *Capell*
Location: *Capell*
18 **lord**] *Q2;* Loid *Q1*
22 **be ware**] *Capell;* beware *Q1–2*
44 s.d. **Going.**] *Capell*
66 **Cressy's**] *Q2* (Cressyes)*;* Cresses *Q1;* Cressi' *Capell*
68 s.d. **Reads.**] *Capell*
68–73 **"When . . . France."**] *quoted, Capell*
83 **frivolous**] *Q2;* fryuolous, *Q1 (a possible reading)*

IV.iv

IV.iv] *Capell*
Location: *Capell*
24 **Coating**] *Capell;* Coting *Q1–2*
26 **the pendants**] *Warnke and Proescholdt;* the pendant *Q1–2;* the pendant streamers, *Capell;* with pendant *Collier*
28 **sundry**] *Q2;* sundy *Q1*
30 **too**] *Capell;* two *Q1–2*
30 **bear**] rear *Collier conj.*
41 **more.**] *Capell;* more, *Q1;* more *Q2*
44 **world— . . . power—**] *Capell;* world, . . . power: *Q1;* world, . . . power, *Q2*
50 **squadrons**] *Q2;* spuadrons *Q1*
66 **What**] *Q2; Pr:* What *Q1*
68 **Greets by me**] Greets thus by me *Capell;* Greeteth by me *Collier*
69 **a**] an *Q2*
70 **esquires**] Squires *Q2*
81 **the**] thy *Q2*
87 s.d. **Exit.**] *Q2*
87, 100 s.d. **Herald**] *Capell*
100 **cap'ring**] carping *Q2*
100 s.d. **Exit Herald.**] *Capell*
105 **prayers**] holy prayers *Capell*
113 **thus**] *Q2;* this *Q1*
114 **Happily**] Haply *Q2*
118 **sins'**] *ed.;* sinnes *Q1–2;* sin's *Capell*
123 s.d. **Exit.**] *Q2*
125 **wings**] strings *Delius*
128 **busy and bit**] bruis'd and bent *Capell*
130 **texted**] texed *Q2*

IV.v

IV.v] *Capell*
Location: *Capell*
20–21 **All . . . presage?**] *One line in Q1; divided* words . . . presage *Q2; divided as here, Capell*
22, 24, 28, s.pp. **Phil.**] *Q2* (Phillp.)
20 s.d. **Enter Prince Philip.**] *Capell*
31 **embattled**] *Tyrrell;* embatteled *Q1–Q2*
33 **floor**] *Capell;* flower *Q1–2*
39 s.d. **Aside.**] *ed. (after Capell)*
39 **Ay**] *Capell;* I *Q1–2*
47 **Although**] Although he be *Capell*
55 s.d. **Philip**] *Capell*
63 **For**] *Q2;* Eor *Q1*
70 s.p. **K. John.**] *Q2;* En: Io: *Q1*
70 **Ay**] *Capell;* I *Q1–2*
73 s.p. **P. Cha.**] *Q2;* Vil. *Q1*
107 **whither**] *Q2;* whether *Q1*
120 **bond**] band *Q2*
126 s.d. **Exeunt.**] *Delius;* Exit. *Q1; om. Q2*

IV.vi

IV.vi] *Capell*
Location: *Capell*
14 **With**] *Capell*

IV.vii

IV.vi] *Warnke and Proescholdt*
Location: *ed. (after Capell)*
1 s.p. **K. John.**] *Q2*
11 s.p. **P. Cha.**] *Q2*
17 s.p. **P. Phil.**] *Q2*
23 **quoit**] *Capell;* quait *Q1–2*
28 **will**] *Q2;* wilt *Q1*
30 s.p. **P. Phil.**] *Q2* (Phil.)*;* Pr: *Q1*
31 **twentith**] twentieth *Q2*

IV.viii

IV.viii] *Warnke and Proescholdt*
Location: *ed. (after Capell)*
o.s.d. **Alarum.**] *Capell (subs.)*
o.s.d. **Esquires**] *Q2;* squirs *Q1*
1 s.p. 1. **Esq.**] *Capell;* Esq. *Q1;* Esquires. *Q2*
3 s.p. 2. **Esq.**] *Capell;* Esq. *Q1;* Esquire. *Q2*
10 s.d. **Exeunt.**] *Q2;* Ex. *Q1*
10 **s.d. Retreat sounded.**] *Placed as in Capell; follows o.s.d. of Scene ix in Q1–2*

IV.ix

IV.ix] *Capell*
Location: *Capell*
o.s.d. **in . . . Soldiers**] *ed. (after Capell)*
o.s.d. **as prisoners**] *Capell (subs.)*
6 **is it**] is't *Q2*
11 s.d. **Enter . . . Philip.**] *Capell*
17 s.d. **led . . . Esquires**] *Capell*
22 **thy**] *Q2;* thv *Q1*
26 **bemoaning**] becoming *Moore Smith*
29 **thy**] *Q2* the *Q1*
33 **health**] *Capell;* Heath *Q1–2*
33 **kings'**] *ed.;* kings *Q1–2;* king's *Capell*
38 **king's**] *Collier;* kings *Q1–2;* kings' *Capell*
40 **royal**] *Capell;* loyall *Q1–2*
60 **I will**] Ile *Q2*
64 s.d. **Exeunt.**] *Q2;* Ex. *Q1*

V.i

V.i] *Moore Smith (after Capell)*
Location: *Capell*
o.s.d. **Philippe**] *Armstrong;* Phillip *Q1;* Philip *Q2;* Philippa *Capell*
1 **Philippe**] *Capell;* Phillip *Q1;* Philip *Q2*
7 s.d. **Trumpets . . . charge.**] *Collier (after Capell)*
7 s.d. **Enter . . . necks.**] *Placed as in Q2;* precedes o.s.d., *Q1*
7 s.d. **of Calais**] *Collier*
8 s.p. **All Cit.**] *Armstrong;* All: *Q1–2*
11 s.d. **Alarum.**] *Hopkinson*
12 s.p. **1 Cit.**] *Capell;* All: *Q1–2*
27, 56 s.pp. **2 Cit.**] *Capell;* Two: *Q1–2*
38 **doom**] *Q2;* dome *Q1*
44 **her**] thy *Q2*
59 s.d. **Exeunt Citizens.**] *Capell;* Ex. *Q1;* Exit. *Q2*
65 **esquire**] 'squire *Capell*
72 **at**] of *Q2*
78 **vail**] *Q2;* vale *Q1*
90 **attempt**] *Q2;* attmpt *Q1*
96 s.d. **Enter Salisbury.**] *Follows l. 97 in Q1; rearranged Q2*
99 **Charles**] John *Capell*
109 **worthless**] *Q2;* worthltsse *Q1*
120–4 **"Salute . . . done."**] *quoted, Capell*
136 **thousand**] *Q2;* tstousand *Q1*
170 **their**] *Delius;* his *Q1–2*
171 **city'**] *Capell;* Citie *Q1–2;* cities' *Delius*
185 **mourning, Philippe!**] *Collier;* mourning Philip, *Q1;* mourning, Philip, *Q2*
186 s.d. **A grand flourish.**] *Collier (after Capell)*
186 s.d. **as prisoners**] *Collier (subs.)*
187 **As**] *Q2; Ki:* As *Q1*
191 s.d. **Kiss her.**] *Placed as in Collier; after l. 190 in Q1–2*
192 s.d. **Presenting . . . France.**] *Collier (after Capell)*
205 **mightst thou**] might you *Q2*
216 **makes—**] *Capell;* makes, *Q1;* makes *Q2*
217 s.d. **Kneels in prayer.**] *ed. (after Capell)*
217 **Thee**] *Capell;* thee *Q1–2*
218, 219 **Thy**] *ed.;* thy *Q1–2*
220 **Thou**] *ed.;* thou *Q1–2*

Sir Thomas More

The Additions Ascribed to Shakespeare

THE TWO PASSAGES here reproduced in type facsimile are very widely accepted as the work of Shakespeare. They form part of a manuscript play (British Library, Harleian MS. 7368) described on the first (binding) leaf as *The Booke of Sir Thomas Moore.* Properly, however, the title is *Sir Thomas Moore*, "The Booke" being a theatrical term for the official theatre copy, usually the prompt-book.

The play was first edited by Alexander Dyce for the Shakespeare Society as early as 1844, but it aroused no great interest until 1871, when Richard Simpson (in *Notes and Queries*) suggested that three sections of the play were by Shakespeare and, moreover, that these parts of the manuscript were actually in Shakespeare's autograph. Careful investigation by later scholars, although it has rejected Simpson's claim for Shakespeare's authorship of one of these sections (the revised More-Faulkner scene), has generally endorsed his claim for the other two passages so far as authorship is concerned. It has shown, however, that only one of the passages, the 147 lines dealing with More's handling of the insurgent mob, has any likelihood of being in Shakespeare's handwriting.

The manuscript as a whole offers a variety of complex problems, some of them insoluble. In its present state it represents a heavily revised version of the original play, and six different hands (not including that of Sir Edmund Tilney, the Master of the Revels) can readily be distinguished: Hand S (Anthony Munday's), Hand A (Henry Chettle's), Hand B (probably Thomas Heywood's), Hand C (that of a professional scribe/book-keeper),[1] Hand D (now almost universally accepted as Shakespeare's), Hand E (Thomas Dekker's). Originally the manuscript (containing sixteen leaves) was written throughout by Anthony Munday (S) and almost certainly represented a "fair copy" of the play as composed by himself, or in collaboration with Chettle (see Jowett, who assigns to him at least scenes i, ii, vii, x, xiii), and perhaps Dekker. Objections to this form of the play seem to have arisen from at least two quarters. First, members of the company for which the play was written appear to have made professional criticisms which led to revisions; and, second, Sir Edmund Tilney, for political reasons, called for very substantial deletions and revisions, as evidenced particularly by a note at the beginning of the play (fol. 3^{r}): "<Le>aue o<ut . . . .> ye insur<rection> wholy & ye Cause ther off & <b>egin w^{t} Sr Tho: Moore att ye mayors sessions w^{t} A reportt afterwardę off his good servic' don being' Shriue off Londõ vppõ a mutiny Agaynst ye Lũbardę only by A shortt reportt & nott otherwise att your own perrilles E Tyllney"—an order which would imply the deletion of something like a quarter of the play! Unfortunately, it is not clear whether Tilney censored the play once or twice, nor is it at all apparent to what extent, if any, the substantial revisions should be connected with Tilney's official strictures, since the revisions generally fail to meet them (see below). Thus it is uncertain at what point, or even exactly why, Shakespeare (if indeed Hand D is his) was called in (there is nothing to suggest that he was originally connected with the play) to revise the insurrection scene. From the vagueness of the speech-prefixes in the earlier part of D's contribution, it is obvious that he gave little attention to the actual names of the members of the "commons" who

[1]Tannenbaum's suggestion that Hand C is Thomas Kyd's has received no acceptance. Hand C has, however, been identified with that of the scribe in two theatrical "plots": Richard Tarlton's *2 Seven Deadly Sins* (c. 1592) and a fragmentary "plot" that may belong to a lost play, Thomas Dekker's *Fortune's Tennis* (c. 1602–3).

take part in the scene and was unconcerned about the exact distribution of their speeches—that, in fact, he was generally ignorant of the play as a whole.

The dating of both Munday's transcript of *More* and the revisions and additions is open to question. Aside from the question of Shakespeare's authorship of Additions II and III (see below), three other material and teasing questions call for answers: (1) When was the original play, as transcribed by Munday, written? (2) When were the additions and other revisions introduced? (3) At what point and how often was the play manuscript submitted to Sir Edmund Tilney, Master of the Revels from 1579 to 1610? There is general agreement that the original play was most probably written in 1592–3, years in which the London merchants and shopkeepers had surreptitiously circulated various libels against "strangers" then living and conducting business in London (e.g., French, Flemish, Dutch, and Lombards), who, supported by the City authorities and the Court, were viewed as posing a serious threat to the native English business ventures. Apparently, they even incited their apprentices and journeymen to violence (not without some reason) against these "aliens," and attempted, unsuccessfully, to force the House of Commons to pass a bill that would protect them from such "foreign" competition and misuse. It has been suggested that such contemporary events reminded Munday (described by Francis Meres as "our best plotter") of the quite detailed account in Holinshed's *Chronicles* (1587 ed.) of the so-called Ill May Day riot of 1517 (also directed against "strangers"), in which, historically, More, unlike the fictional More in the play, tried and failed to control and win over the rioters and was allowed no credit for persuading King Henry to pardon the insurgents. Shapiro's redating of the holograph manuscript of Munday's play entitled *John a' Kent*, formerly dated 1596, to about 1590 has given additional support to an early date for Munday's *More* transcript, particularly since handwriting experts have convincingly demonstrated that Munday's handwriting in *More* is closer to his hand in *John a' Kent* than in another Munday holograph manuscript, *The Heaven of the Mind*, written in 1602. The only piece of evidence that may be taken to suggest a date in 1596 or later, at least for Munday's transcript, is its inclusion of More's so-called "urinal witticism" (V.iii.17–26), which occurs in none of the recognized sources of the play and is otherwise recorded only in Sir John Harington's *Metamorphosis of Ajax* not published until 1596. Here, however, any general agreement ceases.

Answers to the second and third questions are essentially speculative and are best treated together. Gabrieli and Melchiori (1990) point out that no less than five such "speculations" have been advanced: (1) Upon completion, Munday's unrevised transcript was submitted to Tilney, while at the same time, for theatrical reasons, the actors and associated dramatists were making their own revisions and additions; these, when Tilney's harsh verdict was received, simply abandoned the play (Metz). (2) (a) Upon completion, Munday's transcript was submitted to Tilney, who, influenced by the recent riot, censored all references to prison-breaking, street brawls, and general trouble with prentices; (b) Tilney returned the "book," and Shakespeare, Chettle, and Heywood, with Hand C's help, make what they think are the necessary revisions and return the manuscript, pretty much in its present state, to Tilney; (c) Tilney then objected to the Ill May Day scene in his marginal note on the first page of the text (fol. 3^{r}, see above); (d) with the closing of the theatres in early 1593 because of the plague, the company lost interest and gave up any thought of production (Blayney). (3) Munday's transcript, Hand D's addition, and perhaps Chettle's revision were submitted to Tilney in 1592–3, the remainder of the revisions and additions being made sometime after 1603 as further preparation perhaps for a performance by Prince Henry's (earlier the Admiral's) Men (McMillin). (4) Munday's transcript was censored by Tilney in 1593–5; as a result the play was shelved until around 1603, when the additions and revisions were undertaken for a possible revival by the Chamberlain's/King's Men, Shakespeare's company (Taylor). (5) All additions and revisions were made before the manuscript was submitted to Tilney in 1593–4, at which time he allowed the revisions, but refused to allow Hand D's Ill May Day scene and part of scene x (i.e., IV.i.81–105); the play was probably never produced (Gabrieli/Melchiori).

The principal differences among these five hypotheses concern, for the most part, the dating of the revisions and additions—whether early, 1592–4, or late, 1600–4. An early date (1592) is argued for by Blayney, who claims that the basic text of *More* and Hand D's Addition II (ascribed to Shakespeare) appear to have influenced Henry Chettle when he wrote *Kind-Harts Dreame* (1593, but entered in the Stationers' Register 8 December 1592), in which he apologizes to Shakespeare for Robert Greene's attack on him in his *Groats-worth of witte* (1592; see Appendix C, No. 9). A later date, however, seems to be supported by: (1) linguistic and vocabulary studies which place both Munday's uncensored transcript and Additions II and III around 1600–2 (Nosworthy and [for the additions only] Jackson); (2) the clustering in Additions II and III of echoes from, or anticipations of, ideas and verbal parallels found in Shakespeare's plays written between about 1600 and 1607–8 (i.e., between *Hamlet* and *Coriolanus;* see the commentary notes and R. W. Chambers, Spurgeon, Taylor); and (3) the comparative poetic, dramatic, and metrical maturity of Additions II and III, which associate them with Shakespeare's middle period, 1596–1604 (Harrison, Collins, Lake).

The first of the two passages claimed as Shakespeare's (the 147 lines in Hand D dealing with More and the rebellious commons) is here technically designated as Addition II (C–D) to allow for the necessary inclusion of the opening stage direction in Hand C at the bottom of fol. 7^{v}. It occupies the whole of fols. 8–9ʳ (three pages), fol.9ᵛ being blank except for a speech prefix ("all") and what appears to be a capital "C", both in Hand D. The second passage, Addition III (C) (a 21-line soliloquy by More, in Hand C), was written on a separate slip of paper and then pasted onto the lower half of fol. 11ᵛ, presumably by C.

The evidence advanced to connect Shakespeare with the two passages commonly attributed to him is significantly of various kinds. The handwriting of Addition II has been painstakingly compared with the six genuine Shakespeare signatures and the only other two words known to be in Shakespeare's hand ("By me" in his will) by the eminent paleographer Sir E. Maunde Thompson and declared in his view to be that of Shakespeare. But the material for comparison is so limited that an absolute verdict on the basis of the handwriting alone in some minds remains unresolved (see, however, Dawson). More persuasive than the handwriting analysis, perhaps, is the surprisingly large number of uncommon spelling links between Addition II and the several quarto and First Folio texts which other evidence leads us to believe were set up from Shakespeare's autograph manuscripts, usually from his "foul papers" (see, below, the notes to lines 2, 8, 28, 39, 50, 53, 62, 128, 136). Shakespeare's authorship of both passages is also strongly substantiated by what R. W. Chambers calls "the expression of ideas" (see, below, in Addition II the notes to lines 10–11, 12, 39–40, 72–87, 77, 104–13, 112–14, 121–22; in Addition III, lines 1, 9, 13–18, 15, 17–18, 19–21), and by studies of the vocabulary (see, below, in Addition II the notes to lines 5, 7, 18, 86, 115; in Addition III, lines 9, 11, 16, 19), the imagery (see the references above under "expression of ideas"), and the metrical characteristics. The real strength of the case for Shakespeare's authorship of these two passages rests, then, not on any single piece or kind of evidence but on the quite remarkable manner in which several independent lines of approach support and reinforce one another in pointing to a single conclusion—the "hand" of Shakespeare.

If Hand D is indeed Shakespeare's, the 147 lines of Addition II are of extraordinary interest for a number of reasons. Since the lines give every appearance of being an authorial first draft, with vague and carelessly used speech-prefixes and with deletions and insertions made in the process of composition and even one example of "first thoughts" left uncancelled (line 62), they afford us a unique view of what Shakespeare's "foul papers" may have looked like and of the kinds of problems which such copy posed for a scribe preparing a prompt-book or for an Elizabethan printer. We may, for example, note the careless omission of More (and others) in the stage direction at lines 24–25 (see below), a carelessness which is reflected in a number of instances in Shakespeare's printed texts, and difficulties of other kinds can be shown to arise from just the sort of *currente calamo* changes and insertions evident in Addition II. One passage in particular (lines 112–14) was left by D in such a seemingly unresolved tangle that C, the professional scribe who had the responsibility of tidying up the various revisions and fitting them into the original form of the play, felt forced to delete most of it and bridge the gap with a short line of his own. How mislineation in the printed texts could arise may be seen in lines 94–95 (four lines written as two) or in lines 114 and 147 (each a line and a half as one). We can see also how Shakespeare's handwriting and idiosyncratic spelling may have caused misreadings by a compositor (or scribe) (see, below, the notes to lines 8, 28, 39, 53, 62). And the almost complete absence of punctuation, or the wrong punctuation (lines 123, 137), suggests how easily a compositor (or scribe) working from such manuscript copy could be misled and confuse the sense in a well-meant attempt to clarify it. Compared even with the comparatively light and uncertain punctuation of S (Munday) or E (Dekker), the general lack of punctuation in D's lines is conspicuous. In this connection it is interesting to note the almost complete absence of pointing in C's transcription of Addition III. C's punctuation in Addition IV, for example, where he is transcribing from Dekker's revision of the scene, reflects the fuller pointing of his copy.

As a play *Sir Thomas More* is negligible. It belongs to a group of chronicle histories or semi-historical dramas on well-known English figures, plays like *The Life and Death of the Lord Cromwell* (of unknown authorship), *The True and Honorable History of the Life of Sir John Oldcastle* (by Munday, Drayton, Wilson, and Hathaway), *The Famous History of Sir Thomas Wyat* (by Dekker and Webster), all ranging in date from about 1599 to 1604, and, to some extent, the later *Henry VIII* (Shakespeare and Fletcher). In its bourgeois sympathies it is also related to a comedy like Dekker's *The Shoemakers' Holiday*. The life of More, his rise from Sheriff of London to Lord Chancellor of England with his fall and execution, affords the loose plot line of the play. Except, however, for D's insurrection scene, it never rises above more or less competent mediocrity, though in the theatre the rough humor and bustle of the earlier scenes leading up to the revolt and the pathetically presented death of More might well have been successful enough in their kind. One other scene is of special interest to the student of Tudor drama. It contains a miniature morality play called The *Marriage of Wit and Wisdom*, having nothing to do with the extant morality play of that name, but based on a scene from *Lusty Juventus*, with a prologue partly derived from *The Disobedient Child*. This interlude is acted before More's guests and he himself plays an extempore role in it.

The present texts of Addition II and Addition III are based on a firsthand examination of the British Library manuscript, with reference to the facsimiles reproduced by J. S. Farmer (Tudor Facsimile Texts, 1910) and E. M. Thompson (*Shakespeare's Handwriting*, 1916) and the transcripts by Alexander Dyce (Shakespeare Society, 1844), Tucker Brooke (*Shakespeare Apocrypha*, 1910), W. W. Greg (Malone

Society, 1911, and *Shakespeare's Hand in "Sir Thomas More,"* 1923, Addition II only), and R. C. Bald (*Shakespeare Survey*, II, 1949, Addition II only). Pointed brackets are used to indicate readings which are either doubtful or taken from Dyce's transcript, the manuscript at these points having deteriorated since Dyce's time. Readings in boldface type are changes or additions made by C in D's work; readings crossed through in the actual speeches indicate deletions or changes made by D himself, unless otherwise noted in the commentary. A modernized text of Additions II and III has been included; lineation in this version follows that of the manuscript text.

The important Gabrieli/Melchiori edition of *Sir Thomas More* (1990) makes certain changes in its edited text of Addition II that call for brief comment. They argue that Hand C misinterpreted the intentions of Hand D (hereafter identified as that of Shakespeare) at several points. (1) Shakespeare, they say, meant to enter More and the Sergeant at Arms, as well as Sherwin, the "other Sheriff," Palmer, and Cholmley at the beginning of his revision of the original uncensored scene, characters that Hand C failed to include in his entering stage direction added at the foot of fol. 7^v because Shakespeare fails to enter More later following lines 24–5, when the Lord Mayor, Surrey, and Shrewsbury enter. The introduction of the Sergeant at Arms at the beginning of the scene is most probably justified, since Hand C seems confused, entering him, apparently as an afterthought, in his opening stage direction and again following line 16, at which point Shakespeare had assigned him a single line. The inclusion of Sherwin is also probably justified (see my note on lines 26, 30). But the entry of the other characters (particularly More) at the opening of the scene is open to question: (a) in dramatic terms it is surely unlikely that a central character like More (or for that matter the "other Sheriff") would merely stand around doing and saying nothing during twenty-three lines of insurgent grumbling; (b) in the preceding scene (II.ii), a scene preserved only in Hand C's transcript (the original now lost Guildhall scene, of which this is a revision), More is closely associated with the Lord Mayor, Shrewsbury, Surrey, Palmer, and Cholmley, and in discussing the incipient riot, says "Let's to these simple men," thus clearly preparing for their later confrontation with the rioters following line 23 in Addition II; (c) Gabrieli/Melchiori claim that More's first speech (line 39), which comes thirteen lines after the entrance of the Lord Mayor, etc. (following line 25), implies that More has been present from the opening of the scene, but it equally well describes what More et al. have heard and seen since their entry following line 25; (d) in the play's principal source (Holinshed), More arrives on the scene after the "maior and shiriffes." (2) Gabrieli/Melchiori include the "other Sheriff" (London had two Sheriffs) to accommodate Shakespeare's speech-prefix "Sher" at line 26, which Hand C reassigns to "Maior" (i.e., the Lord Mayor, who has just entered). The assignment of line 26 to "Sheriff" may be justified (Holinshed, as noted above, records that "shiriffes" were present before More appeared), but two points should be noted: (a) Shakespeare uses only one form of "Shrieue" throughout Addition II (see my note on lines 26, 30, and 41) and one would expect a speech-prefix for "Shrieve" to match that form of the word; (b) in Holinshed the "maior and Shiriffes were present there, and made proclamation in the kings name, but nothing was obeied." If a "Sheriff" was present from the opening of the scene, why does he say nothing until line 26 when the Lord Mayor, etc., enter? If the speech-prefix "Sher" does indeed stand for "Sheriff", perhaps to distinguish it from a speech-prefix for Shrewsbury, the Sheriff should, most probably, be entered along with the Lord Mayor instead of at the beginning of the scene. (3) Gabrieli/Melchiori suggest, correctly I think, that when Shakespeare added "all no no no no no Shrewsbury shr" to line 38 that he intended the speech-prefix "all" to refer to the second group of speakers who are also refusing to listen to Surrey by calling on Shrewsbury and that Hand C, misunderstanding Shakespeare's intention, deleted the second "all" speech-prefix. Compare Shakespeare's use of similar duplicated "all" speech-prefixes for lines 48 and 49, which Hand C inconsistently leaves untouched, and to lines 141 and 142, where Hand C, probably mistakenly, alters the second "all" to "Linco".

For further information, and for the source of most of the annotation of the text, see: E. M. Thompson, *Shakespeare's Handwriting* (Oxford, 1916); A. W. Pollard, W. W. Greg, E. M. Thompson, J. D. Wilson, R. W. Chambers, *Shakespeare's Hand in the Play of "Sir Thomas More"* (Cambridge, 1923); G. B. Harrison, "The Date of *Sir Thomas More,*" *RES*, I (1925), 337–9; E. K. Chambers, *William Shakespeare*, 2 vols. (Oxford, 1930); Caroline Spurgeon, "The Imagery in the *Sir Thomas More* Fragment," *RES*, VI (1930), 257–70; R. W. Chambers, "Some Sequences of Thought in Shakespeare and in the 147 Lines of *Sir Thomas More,*" *MLR*, XXVI (1931), 251–80, and *Man's Unconquerable Mind* (London, 1939), 204–49; R. C. Bald, "Addition III of *Sir Thomas More,*" *RES*, VII (1931), 67–69, and "*The Booke of Sir Thomas More* and Its Problems," *S. Sur*, II (1949), 44–65; D. C. Collins, "On the Date of *Sir Thomas More,*" *RES*, X (1934), 401–11; J. M. Nosworthy, "Shakespeare and *Sir Thomas More,*" *RES*, n.s. VI (1955), 12–25; I. A. Shapiro, "The Significance of a Date," *S. Sur.*, VIII (1955), 100–105; Harold Jenkins, "Supplement to the [Malone Society] Introduction," Malone Society *Collections*, VI (1961), 179–92; A. C. Partridge, *Orthography in Shakespeare and Elizabethan Drama* (London, 1964); Thomas Clayton, *The "Shakespearean" Addition in "The Booke of Sir Thomas Moore": Some Aids to Scholarly and Critical Shakespearean Studies*, Shakespeare Studies, Monograph Series, I (Dubuque, Iowa, 1969); P. W. M. Blayney, "*The Book of Sir Thomas Moore*, Re-Examined," *SP*, LXIX (1972), 167–91; M. L. Hays, "Shakespeare's Hand in *Sir Thomas More*: Some Aspects of the Paleographic Argument," *S. St.*, VIII (1975), 241–53; D. J. Lake,

"The Date of the 'Sir Thomas More' Additions by Dekker and Shakespeare," *N & Q*, n.s., XXIV (1977), 114–16; MacD. P. Jackson, "Linguistic Evidence for the Date of Shakespeare's Addition to *Sir Thomas More*," *N & Q*, n.s., XXV (1978), 154–6; G. H. Metz, "The Master of the Revels and *The Booke of Sir Thomas Moore*," *SQ*, XXXIII (1982), 493–5; Giorgio Melchiori, "Hand D in *Sir Thomas More*: An Essay in Misinterpretation," *S. Sur.*, XXXVIII (1985), 101–14, "'The Booke of Sir Thomas Moore,' A Chronology of Revision," *SQ*, XXXVII (1986), 291–308, and "The Master of the Revels and the Date of the Additions to *The Book of Sir Thomas More*," in *Shakespeare: Text, Language, Criticism*, eds., B. Fabian and K. Tetzeli von Rosador (Zurich, 1987), 164–79; Scott McMillin, *The Elizabethan Theatre and 'The Book of Sir Thomas More'* (Ithaca, N.Y., 1986); Stanley Wells, Gary Taylor, et al., *William Shakespeare: A Textual Companion* (Oxford, 1987); T. H. Howard-Hill ed., *Shakespeare and "Sir Thomas More": Essays on the Play and Its Shakespearian Interest* (Cambridge, 1989) [an important collection; see essays by T. H. Howard-Hill, 1–10; G. H. Metz, 11–44; W. B. Long, 45–56; Scott McMillin, 57–76; Giorgio Melchiori, 77–100; Gary Taylor, 101–30; John Jowett, 131–50; C. R. Forker, 151–70; J. W. Velz, 171–96]; G. E. Dawson, "Shakespeare's Handwriting," *S. Sur.*, XLII (1990).

The comparatively small minority position against Shakespeare's authorship may be consulted in: Alexander Green, "The Apocryphal *Sir Thomas More* and the Shakespeare Holograph," *American Journal of Philology*, XXXIX (1918), 229–67; L. L. Schücking, "Shakespeare and *Sir Thomas More*," *RES*, I (1925), 40–59; S. A. Tannenbaum, *"The Booke of Sir Thomas Moore," A Bibliotic Study* (New York, 1927) and *Shakespere and "Sir Thomas Moore"* (New York, 1929); Brents Stirling, *The Populace in Shakespeare* (New York, 1949); C. A. Chillington, "Playwrights at Work: Henslowe's, not Shakespeare's, *Book of Sir Thomas More*," *ELR*, X (1980), 439–79 [attempts, unconvincingly, to attribute Addition II to John Webster; see Forker]; Paul Ramsey, "The Literary Evidence for Shakespeare as Hand D in the Manuscript Play *Sir Thomas More*: A Re-re-consideration," *The Upstart Crow*, XI (1991), 131–55.

Two modern-spelling texts of the complete play are: (1) ed., Harold Jenkins in *The Complete Works of Shakespeare*, ed., C. J. Sisson (London, [1954]); (2) Vittorio Gabrieli and Giorgio Melchiori, eds., *Sir Thomas More* (Manchester University Press, 1990).

G. Blakemore Evans

[The action leading up to Addition II may be summarized as follows: the commons, led by John Lincoln, Williamson and his wife Doll, George and Ralph Betts (the latter also called the Clown), and Sherwin, are shown as ill-treated and properly outraged by the high-handed and illegal actions of certain of the foreign groups in London, who, for economic reasons, have been allowed by the authorities to flout the law and to make life miserable for honest Englishmen; they determine to stage a bloody revolt on the following May Day, in which the "aliens" will be massacred and their houses burned; word of the revolt is brought to the authorities, and Thomas More, then a Sheriff of London, is prevailed upon to address the angry commons in an attempt to stem the rebellion by persuasion rather than arms.]

Enter Lincoln · Doll · Clown · Georg betts williamſon others And A ſergaunt at armes [fol. 7ᵛ]

Lincolne — Peace heare me, he that will not ſee ⟨a red⟩ hearing at a harry grote, butter at a levenpence a pou⟨nde meale at⟩ nyne ſhillingȩ a Buſhell and Beeff at fower nob⟨les a ſtone lyſ⟩t to me [fol. 8ʳ]

~~other~~ Geo bett — yt will Come to that paſſe yf ſtrain⟨gers be ſu⟩fferd mark him

Linco — our Countrie is a great eating Country, argo they eate more in our Countrey then they do in their owne

~~other~~ betts clow — by a half penny loff a day troy waight

Linc — they bring in ſtraing rootes, which is meerly to the vndoing of poor prentizes, for whatȩ ~~a watrie~~ a ſorry p̷ſnyp to a good hart

~~oth~~ willian — traſh traſh,: they breed ſore eyes and tis enough to infect the Cytty wᵗ the palſey

Lin — nay yt has infected yt wᵗ the palſey, for theiſe baſterdȩ of dung as you knowe they growe in Dvng haue infected vs, and yt is our infeccion will make the Cytty ſhake which p̷tly Coms through the eating of p̷ſnyps

~~o~~ Clown · betts — trewe and pumpions togeather

Enter ſeriant — what ſay youᵘ to t⟨he⟩ mercy of the king do youᵘ refuſe yt

Lin — youᵘ woold haue ⟨vs⟩ vppon thipp woold youᵘ no marry do we not, we accept of the kingȩ mercy but wee will ſhowe no mercy vppõ the ſtraingers

feriaunt — youᵘ ar the ſimpleſt thingȩ that eu̾ ſtood in ſuch a queſtion

o.s.d. Enter . . . armes] In C's italic hand, at bottom of fol. 7ᵛ. C also enters the "sergaunt at armes" after line 16 below.
1–2. harry grote] small silver coin worth fourpence coined in the reign of Henry VIII.
2. a levenpence] For this unusual spelling of *eleven*, see also *The Merchant of Venice* (Q1), II.ii.162; *Romeo and Juliet* (Q2), I.iii.35; *Love's Labor's Lost* (Q1), III.i.171; *Hamlet* (Q2), I.ii.251; *Troilus and Cressida* (Q), III.iii.295; and the peculiar form "a eleuen" (a compositor's misreading of "a leven") in *Romeo and Juliet* (F1), I.iii.35, and *The Two Noble Kinsmen* (Q), I.iii.54 (a Shakespearean section). **shillingȩ]** The character ȩ, used frequently by D, is a common secretary form for final *-es*.
3. nobles] gold coins worth about five shillings in Shakespeare's time. **stone]** measure of weight, fourteen pounds (still used in England in stating the weight of men or animals).
4. straingers] foreigners.
5. argo] corruption of *ergo* (Latin, "therefore"). Cf. *2 Henry VI*, IV.ii.29, and the analogous form "argall" in *Hamlet*, V.i.19. No other example of "argo" has been found in contemporary drama outside of *2 Henry VI*.
6. then] than. A very common spelling; it occurs again in line 112 (cancelled).
7. half penny loff] Cf. *2 Henry VI*, IV.ii.65–66. R. W. Chambers notes the following points of likeness between the Cade scenes and this section of Addition II: (a) the entrance of the rebel leader haranguing his followers and commanding silence; (b) the enumeration of things which go to make up the budgets of the poor, with false economics based on the halfpenny loaf, and (c) the logic-chopping with "argo"; (d) the statement of the grievance of the rioters, there through the misuse of honest sheepskin, here tnrough parsnips, and (e) the absurd statements about the corruption spread by these "innovations"; (f) the fun and merry good humor coupled with merciless savagery; (g) the instability of the rioters. The combination produces an effect of mingled humor and horror. **troy waight]** the standard system used for determining the weight of jewels and precious metals, also for weighing bread.

Enter LINCOLN, DOLL, CLOWN [RALPH BETTS], GEORGE BETTS, WILLIAMSON, *others* [PRENTICES].

Lincoln. Peace, hear me! He that will not see a red herring at a Harry groat, butter at alevenpence a pound, meal at nine shillings a bushel, and beef at four nobles a stone, list to me.

Betts. It will come to that pass if strangers be suffer'd. Mark him.

Lincoln. Our country is a great eating country, argo they eat more in our country than they do in their own.

Clown. By a halfpenny loaf a day, troy weight.

Lincoln. They bring in strange roots, which is merely to the undoing of poor prentices, for what's a sorry parsnip to a good heart?

Williamson. Trash, trash; they breed sore eyes and 'tis enough to infect the city with the palsy.

Lincoln. Nay, it has infected it with the palsy, for these bastards of dung—as you know they grow in dung—have infected us, and it is our infection will make the city shake, which partly comes through the eating of parsnips.

Clown. True, and pumpions together.

Enter SERGEANT-AT-ARMS.

Sergeant. What say you to the mercy of the King? Do you refuse it?

Lincoln. You would have us upon th' hip, would you? No, marry, do we not; we accept of the King's mercy, but we will show no mercy upon the strangers.

Sergeant. You are the simplest things that ever stood in such a question.

8. straing] foreign. This form occurs in *A Lover's Complaint*, line 303, and may explain the possible misprint "straying" for "strange" in *Love's Labor's Lost* (Q1), V.ii.763. Cf. the consistent spelling "strainger" throughout Addition II. **meerly]** entirely, altogether.

9. what . . . hart] i.e. what good is a [watery] miserable parsnip to a young fellow of spirit (an apprentice). **psnyp]** parsnip or persnip. The *p* with a stroke through its tail is a common contraction for *per* (see "pceaue", line 92) and *par* (see "ptly", line 14; "pdon", line 143). The concerted attack on the parsnip (and "pumpion") which follows seems to be a purely comic ploy to make the "reasons" of the commons appear even more absurd. In the first place, parsnips were not "straing [foreign] rootes"; in the second place, John Gerard in his *Herbal* (1597, p. 811) finds many virtues in the cultivated garden parsnip ("good for the stomacke, kidneies, bladder and lungs"), though he admits it is "somwhat windie." D's substitution of "a sorry" for "a watrie" is interesting, since parsnips were not, according to Gerard, particularly watery.

10 trash,:] The pointing here is uncertain (as in several other instances). Greg (1911) first read "trash;" but later (1923) as given here. The comma seems clear, but there is some doubt about the following colon.

10–11. sore eyes . . . palsey] Cf. the association of palsy and raw eyes in *Troilus and Cressida*, V.i.19–20.

11. w^{t}] with. Cf. lines 12, 51, 75, 108; the commoner form "wth" is used in lines 22, 85.

12. basterdę of dung] illegitimate products of artificial (hence unnatural) horticulture. Cf. *The Winter's Tale*, IV.iv.82–103.

14. ptly] partly.

16. pumpions] pumpkins. Gerard also gives a good bill of health to pumpkins.

18. vppon thipp] upon the hip, i.e. at a disadvantage. Cf. *The Merchant of Venice*, I.iii.46, IV.i.334; *Othello*, II.i.305. With "thipp" cf. "thappostle", line 94, "thoffendor", line 123. **marry]** indeed (originally the name of the Virgin Mary used as an oath).

19. vppõ] upon. The mark over the "o" (called a tilde or tittle) usually indicates the omission of *n* or *m*, but see the note on line 73.

21. eu] ever. The symbol over the "u" is a common contraction for *er*. **stood . . . question]** remained obstinate in such a dispute.

now prenty
Lin how ſay yo^{u} prentiſſes ſymple downe wth him
all prentiſſes ſymple prentiſſes ſymple
Enter the L maier Surrey
Shrewſbury
~~Sher~~ **Maior** hold in the kingꝭ name hold
Surrey frendꝭ maſters Countrymen
mayer peace how peace I ~~ſh~~ Charg yo^{u} keep the peace
Shro· my maſters Countrymen
~~Sher~~ **Williamson** The noble Earle of Shrewſbury lettꝭ hear him
Ge bettꝭ weele heare the Earle of Surrey
Linc the earle of Shrewſbury
bettꝭ weele heare both
all both both both both
Linc Peace I ſay peace ar yo^{u} men of Wiſdome ~~ar~~ or
what ar yo^{u}
Surr ~~But~~ what yo^{u} will haue them but not men of Wiſdome
all weele not heare my L of Surrey, ~~all~~ no no no no no
Shrewſbury ſhr
moor whiles they ar ore the banck of their obedyenc
thus will they bere downe all thingꝭ
Linc Shreiff moor ſpeakes ſhall we heare ſhreef moor ſpeake
Doll Lettꝭ heare him a keepes a plentyfull ſhrevaltry, and a made my
Brother Arther watchin⟨s⟩ Seriant Safes yeoman letꝭ heare
ſhreeve moore
all Shreiue moor moor more Shreue moore
moor ⟨ev⟩en by the rule yo^{u} haue among yor fealues [fol. 8^{v}]
Comand ſtill audience
all ⟨S⟩urrey Sury
all moor moor
Lincolne bettꝭ peace peace ſcilens peace

22. **prenty**] The reading of this word is doubtful. It is presumably intended as an abbreviated form for "prentices" "how . . . prenty" is an insertion in Hand D.
23.] The small x-mark following this line in the ms is in pencil and appears to be modern.
26, 30. ~~**Sher**~~] It has been suggested that "Sher" at line 26 is D's careless error for "Shre" (Shrewsbury), but this view is complicated by two facts: C substituted "Maior" not "Shre", and D repeated "Sher" at line 30 as a speech-prefix to a line that could not possibly belong to Shrewsbury (C there substituted "Williamson"). Some part of the confusion may have arisen from a character named Sherwin (assuming that D knew of his existence), a goldsmith, who is associated with the rebels in the earlier scenes, and who is present in the later and original part of this scene. Since Sherwin is a moderate, line 30 would fit him perfectly, though line 26 is unlikely for him.
27–30. **frends . . . him**] Cf. *Julius Caesar*, III.ii.53–55, 72–73.
28. **mayer**] Although this speech-prefix appears to be in Hand D, the ink looks much closer to that used by C. The omission of the rule after line 27 suggests that this speech-prefix may have been added after the others, which would perhaps explain the different ink. **how**] ho. This spelling (or "howe") occurs six times in *Hamlet* (Q2) and once each in *The Merchant of Venice* (Q1), *A Midsummer Night's Dream* (Q1), and *Antony and Cleopatra*. Such a spelling could lead to a misunderstanding by the compositor, as it most probably did in *The Merchant of Venice* (Q1), V.i.109.
30. ~~**Sher**~~ **Williamson**] The first part of C's "Williamson" is written over D's "Sher". **Shrewsbury**] The *e* may well be an *o*; also in l. 32.
35–36. **ar . . . you**] i.e. are you, or are you not, men of wisdom?
38. ~~**all**~~ **no . . . shr**] This is an addition in Hand D. The speech-prefix "all" was probably deleted by C, since it duplicates the earlier speech-prefix. Cf. the repeated speech-prefixes at line 49, also in Hand D, and at line 142, there changed to "Linco" by C.

Lincoln. How say you now, [prentices]? Prentices simple! Down with him!

All. Prentices simple, prentices simple!

Enter the Lord Mayor, Surrey, Shrewsbury, [More, Palmer, *and* Cholmeley].

Mayor. Hold, in the King's name hold!

Surrey. Friends, masters, countrymen—

Mayor. Peace ho, peace, I charge you keep the peace!

Shrewsbury. My masters, countrymen—

Williamson. The noble Earl of Shrewsbury, let's hear him.

Betts. We'll hear the Earl of Surrey.

Lincoln. The Earl of Shrewsbury.

Betts. We'll hear both.

All. Both, both, both, both!

Lincoln. Peace, I say, peace! Are you men of wisdom or what are you?

Surrey. What you will have them, but not men of wisdom.

All. We'll not hear my Lord of Surrey, no, no, no, no, no! Shrewsbury, Shrewsbury!

More. Whiles they are o'er the bank of their obedience,
Thus will they bear down all things.

Lincoln. Shrieve More speaks. Shall we hear Shrieve More speak?

Doll. Let's hear him. 'A keeps a plentiful shrievaltry, and 'a made my brother Arthur Watchins Sergeant Safe's yeoman. Let's hear Shrieve More.

All. Shrieve More, More, More, Shrieve More!

More. Even by the rule you have among yourselves,
Command still audience.

All [1]. Surrey, Surrey!

All [2]. More, More!

Lincoln, Betts. Peace, peace, silence, peace!

39–40. whiles . . . thinge] Cf. *Coriolanus,* III.i.246–49; *Troilus and Cressida,* I.iii.110–13; *Hamlet,* IV.v.100–103; *The Two Noble Kinsmen,* I.i.81–85 (a Shakespearean section).

39. obedyenc] obedience. See lines 94, 113, 114, and cf. "offyc" in line 98. The omission of final *e* after *c* may be reflected in the probable misprint "pallat" for "palace" in *Romeo and Juliet* (Q2), V.iii.107, final *c* being very easily misread as *t* in secretary hand. A similar explanation may lie behind the unusual form "precepit" for "precipice" in *Henry VIII,* V.i.139 (a Shakespearean section), though *O.E.D.* recognizes the rare form "precipit".

41. Shreiff] Note the five different spellings of this word within five lines. The form "shrieve" occurs only twice in the canon: *All's Well,* IV.iii.187, and *2 Henry IV* (Q), IV.iv.99. Hall (*Chronicle,* ed. 1809, pp. 588–89) uses "shrife"; Holinshed (*Chronicles,* ed. 1808, III, 620–21) uses "shiriffe". Note also the three different spellings of "country" in lines 5–6 and of "More" in line 45.

42. a . . . shrevaltry] i.e. he maintains a generous table as sheriff. Cf. "a good howskeeper" in line 58. *O.E.D.* records only one earlier use of *shrievalty* (1502); the form with *r* seems to be unique to D. Shakespeare does not employ the word in his acknowledged work. **yeoman]** The "o" seems to have been written over some other letter by C.

45.] Greg (1923) suggests that D added this line and speech-prefix (including the short rule above) somewhat later.

46. rule] i.e. such authority as you recognize.

47. still audience] quiet hearing.

50. scilens] silence. This spelling occurs eighteen times in *2 Henry IV* (Q) and, except here, apparently nowhere else in the literature of the period. Cf. "Sceneca" for "Seneca" (*Hamlet* [Q2], II.ii.400), "Scicion" for "Sicyon" (*Antony and Cleopatra,* I.ii.113, 114, 119), and "Scicinius" for "Sicinius" (*Coriolanus,* II.i.204 s.d., also in speech-prefixes).

moor   Yo^{u} that haue voyce and Credyt w^{t} the ~~mv~~ nvmber
Comaund them to a ſtilnes

Lincolne   a plaigue on them they will not hold their peace the deule
Cannot rule them

moor   Then what a rough and ryotous charge haue yo^{u}
to Leade thoſe that the deule Cannot rule
good maſters heare me ſpeake

Doll   I byth mas will we moor thart a good howſkeeper and I
thanck thy good worſhip for my Brother Arthur watchins

all   peace peace

moor   look what yo^{u} do offend yo^{u} Cry vppõ
that is the peace; not ⟨on⟩ of yo^{u} heare preſent
had there ſuch fellowes lyvd when yo^{u} wer babes
that coold haue topt the peace, as nowe yo^{u} woold
the peace wherin yo^{u} haue till nowe growne vp
had bin tane from yo^{u}, and the bloody tymes
coold not haue brought yo^{u} to ~~theiſe~~ the ſtate of men
alas poor thingȩ what is yt yo^{u} haue gott
although we graunt yo^{u} geat the thing yo^{u} ſeeke

~~D~~Bett   marry the removing of the ſtraingers wch cannot chooſe but
much ~~helpe~~ advauntage the poor handycraftes of the Cytty

moor   graunt them remoued and graunt that this yor ~~y~~ noyce
hath Chidd downe all the matie of Ingland
ymagin that yo^{u} ſee the wretched ſtraingers
their babyes at their backȩ, ~~and~~ w^{t} their poor lugage
plodding tooth portȩ and coſtȩ for tranſportacion
and that yo^{u} ſytt as kingȩ in your deſyres
aucthoryty quyte ſylenct by yor braule
and yo^{u} in ruff of yor ~~yo~~ opynions clothd
what had yo^{u} gott;· Ile tell yo^{u}, yo^{u} had taught
how inſolenc and ſtrong hand ſhoold prevayle
how orderd ſhoold be quelld, and by this patterne
not on of yo^{u} ſhoold lyve an aged man
for other ruffians as their fancies wrought
wth ſealf ſame hand ſealf reaſons and ſealf right
woold ſhark on yo^{u} and men lyke ravenous fiſhes
woold feed on on another

Doll   before god thatȩ as trewe as the goſpell

~~Bettȩ~~ lincoln   nay this a ſound fellowe I tell yo^{u} lets mark him

51. **the nvmber]** the crowd. Cf. *Julius Caesar*, III.ii.4, and *Coriolanus*, IV.vi.7.

53, 56. **deule]** devil. An unusual spelling. Cf. *Romeo and Juliet* (Q2), II.iv.1, III.i.103; *Henry V* (F1), II.iii.31, 35; *Hamlet* (Q2), III.ii.129; also, the misprint "deale" for "deule" in *Hamlet* (Q2), II.ii.599, where *u* has been misread as *a*.

55. **charge]** military command.

61. **what]** that which.

62. **peace;]** The semicolon is not clear; possibly a comma.

62–67. **not . . . men]** There is syntactical difficulty in these lines. The phrase "not . . . present" seems to hang unresolved, requiring something like "had been alive" to complete it. Essentially the same thought is then repeated in lines 66–67, and later, lines 80–87. A dash (Jenkins) after "woold" (line 64) helps to clarify the sense at this point.

62. **on]** one. Cf. lines 83, 87, 91. This spelling, not as unusual as some of the others noted, occurs a number of times in texts believed to have been printed from some form of Shakespeare's autograph, both in the "good" quartos and in the First Folio. See the note on "Iarmen", line 128.

64. **topt]** cut off (as it were the head).

67. **coold . . . men]** i.e. would not have permitted you to reach manhood.

70. **~~D~~Bett]** D began to write the speech-prefix "Doll", deleted the "D" and wrote "Bett"; C further crossed through "D".

More. You that have voice and credit with the number,
Command them to a stillness.

Lincoln. A plague on them, they will not hold their peace. The dev'l cannot rule them.

More. Then what a rough and riotous charge have you
To lead those that the dev'l cannot rule.
Good masters, hear me speak.

Doll. Ay, by th' mass, will we, More. Th' art a good house-keeper and I thank thy good worship for my brother Arthur Watchins.

All. Peace, peace!

More. Look what you do offend you cry upon,
That is the peace; not one of you here present,
Had there such fellows liv'd when you were babes,
That could have topp'd the peace, as now you would,
The peace wherein you have till now grown up
Had been ta'en from you, and the bloody times
Could not have brought you to the state of men.
Alas, poor things, what is it you have got
Although we grant you get the thing you seek?

Betts. Marry, the removing of the strangers, which cannot choose but much advantage the poor handicrafts of the city.

More. Grant them removed and grant that this your noise
Hath chid down all the majesty of England,
Imagine that you see the wretched strangers,
Their babies at their backs, with their poor luggage
Plodding to th' ports and coasts for transportation,
And that you sit as kings in your desires,
Authority quite silenc'd by your brawl,
And you in ruff of your opinions cloth'd,
What had you got? I'll tell you: you had taught
How insolence and strong hand should prevail,
How [order] should be quell'd, and by this pattern
Not one of you should live an aged man,
For other ruffians, as their fancies wrought,
With self-same hand, self reasons, and self right,
Would shark on you, and men like ravenous fishes
Would feed on one another.

Doll. Before God, that's as true as the gospel.

Lincoln. Nay, this' a sound fellow, I tell you, let's mark him.

72–87. **graunt . . . another]** Cf. *Hamlet*, IV.v.100–103; *Troilus and Cressida*, I.iii.110–24; *King Lear* (Q1), IV.ii.46–50; *Coriolanus*, I.i.164–88. R. W. Chambers points out how the sequence of thought in Addition II and *Troilus and Cressida* is the same: (a) degree neglected, (b) the flood surging over its banks (see above, lines 39–40), (c) the doing to death of the aged or babes, (d) cannibal monsters; and further how parts of the sequence are reflected in *Hamlet* (a, b), in *King Lear* (c, d), and in *Coriolanus* (a, b, d).
73. **matie]** majesty. Cf. lines 101, 121. The tilde over the "t" (present in the form in line 101) indicating the abbreviation is lacking here (and in line 121). Cf. the frequent misprint in *Romeo and Juliet* (Q2) of "kismen" for "kinsmen". 76. **tooth]** to th'. Cf. "byth", line 58.
77. **that . . . desyres]** Cf. Sonnet 37, lines 5–7.
78. **braule]** noisy disturbance.
79. **in ruff]** in height of pride, with a play (picked up in "clothd") on the starched neckwear worn generally by members of the upper class. This kind of metaphorical association has been pointed out as characteristically Shakespearean.
82. **orderd]** Although "ordere" is required for the sense, the final letter seems certainly a *d*.
86. **shark]** prey. Shakespeare uses the verb only once, in *Hamlet*, I.i.98.
89. **this]** this is. Cf. *A Midsummer Night's Dream* (Q1), IV.i.128; *Hamlet* (Q2), III.iii.137; *King Lear*, IV.vi.183; *The Winter's Tale*, V.iii.149.

moor Let me ſett vp before yor thoughts good freindꝭ
on ſuppoſytion, which if yo^{u} will marke
yo^{u} ſhall ꝑceaue howe horrible a ſhape
your ynnovation beres, firſt tis a ſinn
which oft thappoſtle did forwarne vs of vrging obedienc to authory⟨ty⟩
and twere ~~in~~ no error yf I told yo^{u} all yo^{u} wer in armes gainſt g⟨od⟩

all marry god forbid that [fol. 9^{r}]

moo nay certainly yo^{u} ar
for to the king god hath his offyc lent
of dread of Iuſtyce, power and Comaund
hath bid him rule, and willd yo^{u} to obay
and to add ampler maţie to this
he ~~god~~ hath not ~~le~~ only lent the king his figure
his throne ~~his~~ & ſword, but gyven him his owne name
calls him a god on earth, what do yo^{u} then
ryſing gainſt him that god himſealf enſtalls
but ryſe gainſt god, what do yo^{u} to yor ſowles
in doing this o deſperat ~~ar~~ as you are·
waſh your foule mynds w^{t} teares and thoſe ſame handꝭ
that yo^{u} lyke rebells lyft againſt the peace
lift vp for peace, and your vnreuerent knees
~~that~~ make them your feet to kneele to be forgyven
~~is ſafer warrs, then euer yo^{u} can make~~
~~in in to yor obedienc·~~
~~whoſe diſcipline is ryot~~; ~~why euen yor warrs hurly~~
tell me but this
~~cannot ꝑceed but by obedienc~~ what rebell captaine
n
as mutyes ar incident, by his name
can ſtill the rout who will obay ~~th~~ a traytor
or howe can well that ꝑclamation founde
when ther is no adicion but a rebell
to quallyfy a rebell, youle put downe ſtraingers
kill them cutt their throts poſſeſſe their howſes
and leade the maţie of lawe in liom
~~alas alas~~
to ſlipp him lyke a hound; ~~ſayeng~~ ſay nowe the king
as he is clement,. yf thoffendor moorne
ſhoold ſo much com to ſhort of your great treſpas
as but to banyſh yo^{u}, whether woold yo^{u} go·
what Country by the nature of yor error
ſhoold gyve you harber go yo^{u} to ffraunc or flanders
to any Iarman ꝑvince, ~~to~~ ſpane or portigall
nay any where ~~why yo^{u}~~ that not adheres to Ingland

92. **ꝑceaue]** perceive.
93. **ynnovation]** rebellion, insurrection. Three of Shakespeare's four acknowledged uses of this word (including the form *innovator*) have this pejorative sense. As used in *Hamlet* (II.ii.333), the word may also, according to some interpretations of the passage, bear this meaning.
94. **thappostle]** th' apostle, i.e. St. Paul. See Romans 13: 1–5.
98. **offyc]** office, position of authority.
99. **of dread of Iustyce]** i.e. of dread, of justice. *Dread* here means the fear and reverence due to the king as God's substitute (cf. line 104, "a god on earth").
103. **~~his~~ &]** The "&" is actually written across "his".
104–13. **what . . . ~~ryot~~]** Cf. *Coriolanus*, I.i.64–74.
110. **and your]** "and" seems to have been lightly crossed through; certainly another word, smudged and pretty much illegible, has been interlined by D above "your". The obvious word would be "bend", as suggested by Maunde Thompson, but Greg (1923) believed that the first letter is "h" (a conclusion reached independently by the present editor) and that it is followed by "ye". The "ye" is more doubtful, however, and it may be suggested that what follows the "h" is "yde" (i.e. hide), a word that makes acceptable sense in the context. It is possible that D changed his mind, hence the smudging, and decided to revert to the original "and".
112–14. **~~is~~ . . . ~~obedienc~~]** The only word cancelled by D in this passage is "warrs" in line 113, which he replaced by "hurly"; the remainder seems to have been crossed through by C, who then interlined "tell me but this" in an attempt to bridge the gap he had created. The passage as D left it, though confusing enough in appearance, makes good sense and is more or less metrical. Where C went wrong, not surprisingly (Dyce did also), was in failing to understand that something like a full stop is required after "feet" in line 111, and that "to kneele to be forgyven" is meant to be the subject of "is" at the begin-

More. Let me set up before your thoughts, good friends,
[One] supposition, which if you will mark
You shall perceive how horrible a shape
Your innovation bears: first, 'tis a sin
Which oft th' apostle did forewarn us of, urging obedience to authority,
And 'twere no error if I told you all you were in arms 'gainst God.

All. Marry, God forbid that!

More. Nay, certainly you are,
For to the King God hath his office lent
Of dread, of justice, power and command,
Hath bid him rule, and will'd you to obey;
And to add ampler majesty to this
He hath not only lent the King his figure,
His throne and sword, but given him his own name,
Calls him a god on earth. What do you then,
Rising 'gainst him that God himself installs,
But rise 'gainst God? What do you to your souls
In doing this, O desperate as you are?
Wash your foul minds with tears, and those same hands
That you like rebels lift against the peace
Lift up for peace, and your unreverent knees,
Make them your feet. To kneel to be forgiven
Is safer wars than ever you can make,
Whose discipline is riot. In, in to your obedience! Why, even your hurly
Cannot proceed but by obedience. [Tell me but this:] what rebel captain,
As mutines are incident, by his name
Can still the rout? Who will obey a traitor?
Or how can well that proclamation sound
When there is no addition but a rebel
To qualify a rebel? You'll put down strangers,
Kill them, cut their throats, possess their houses,
And lead the majesty of law in lyam
To slip him like a hound; alas, alas, say now the King,
As he is clement if th' offender mourn,
Should so much come too short of your great trespass
As but to banish you, whither would you go?
What country by the nature of your error
Should give you harbor? Go you to France or Flanders,
To any German province, Spain or Portigal,
Nay, any where that not adheres to England,

ning of line 112. Modernized, the whole passage would then read: "To kneel to be forgiven / Is safer wars than ever you can make / Whose discipline is riot. In, in to your obedience! / Why, even your hurly cannot proceed / But by obedience." With the cancelled "~~you~~ . . . ~~ryot~~" (lines 112–13) cf. *2 Henry VI*, IV.ii.189–90.

114. **~~pceed~~**] proceed. The *p* with a left hook on its tail is a common contraction for *pro* (see "pclamation", line 117; "pvince", line 128; "pcure", line 143).

115. **mutyes**] (n interlined above) mutines, an obsolete form of *mutinies*. Cf. *King John*, II.i.378; *Hamlet*, V.ii.6. D, however, may have intended the *n* to follow the *t*, giving a form *mut'nies* ("mutinies" Jenkins). **incident**] likely to happen. 116. **rout**] disorderly crowd.

118. **ther**] This word seems to have been altered from "their", possibly by C. **adicion**] addition, i.e. title.

119. **quallyfy**] afford a recognized status to.

121–22. **leade . . . , hound**] Cf. *Coriolanus*, I.vi.37–9; *The Taming of the Shrew*, V.ii.52.

121. **liom**] leash. The word does not occur in Shakespeare's acknowledged work.

122. **slipp him**] release him (when it suits you to allow him to hunt). **~~alas alas~~**] D interlined "alas alas" above a cancelled "~~sayeng~~"; C then crossed through "alas alas", presumably for metrical reasons.

123. **moorne**] mourn, i.e. repent.

125. **whether**] whither, a very common spelling.

126. **by**] in view of.

128. **Iarman**] German. See *2 Henry IV* (Q), II.i.145; and cf. "a Iarmen on" (i.e. a German one) in *Cymbeline*, II.v.16, and "Iermane" in *Love's Labor's Lost* (Q1), III.i.190. **pvince**] province.

129. **not adheres to**] is not in accord with (in manners, speech, customs, etc.). Shakespeare uses this verb five times; only Bacon, according to *O.E.D.*, used it earlier (1597).

why yo^{u} muſt needꝭ be ſtraingers; woold yo^{u} be pleaſd
to find a nation of ſuch barbarous temper
that breaking out in hiddious violence
woold not afoord yo^{u}, an abode on earth
whett their deteſted knyves againſt yor throtes
ſpurne yo^{u} lyke doggꝭ, and lyke as yf that god
owed not nor made not yo^{u}, nor that the elamentꝭ
wer not all appropriat to ~~their~~ yor Comfortꝭ.
but Charterd vnto them, what woold yo^{u} thinck
to be thus vſd, this is the ſtraingers caſe
all and this your momtaniſh inhumanyty

fayth a faies trewe letts ~~vs~~ do as we may be doon by

~~all~~ **Linco** weele be ruld by yo^{u} maſter moor yf youle ſtand our
freind to ꝑcure our ꝑdon

moor Submyt yo^{u} to theiſe noble gentlemen
entreate their mediation to the kinge
gyve vp yor ſealf to forme obay the maieſtrate
and thers no doubt, but mercy may be found yf yo^{u} ſo ſeek ⟨yt⟩

[The remainder of the scene, in Hand S, shows the success of More's oratory in persuading the rioters to throw themselves on the King's mercy and the consequent knighting of More for his good service.

Addition III seems to have been intended to introduce More's state of mind shortly after he was made Lord Chancellor of England. Written in Hand C on a slip of paper, it is pasted on to the manuscript at the bottom of fol. 11^{v} immediately preceding the scene (Addition IV, revised throughout by Dekker, but largely in Hand C) in which More deals with the comic ruffian Faulkner and meets Erasmus for the first time.]

Enter moore

It is in heaven that I am thus and thus
And that wch we prophanlie terme o^{r} fortuns
Is the proviſion of the power aboue
fitted and ſhapte Iuſt to that ſtrength of nature
wch we are borne good god good god
that I from ſuch an humble bench of birth
ſhould ſtepp as twere vp to my Countries head
And give the law out ther I in my fathers lif
to take prerogative and tyth of knees
from elder kinſmen and him bynd by my place

131. **barbarous]** The second *r* has been altered (by D) from a *b*.
135. **spurne . . . doggꝭ]** In the context of "straingers" above (line 130), cf. *The Merchant of Venice*, I.iii.118–19.
136. **owed not]** did not acknowledge as belonging to him. **elamentꝭ]** For the spelling with *a*, cf. *Love's Labor's Lost* (Q1), IV.iii.326; *Hamlet* (Q2), IV.vii.180.
137. **appropriat]** particularly assigned.
138. **Charterd]** reserved as a privilege.
140. **momtanish]** Meaning not known; possibly a carelessly written "mountanish" (Dyce) with the meaning "mountainous" (i.e. barbarous); or, less probably, a form of "Mohammetanish," implying un-Christian and hence merciless. For the sense in "mountanish", see *Twelfth Night*, IV.i.47–49. **all]** Speech-prefix for line 141 has been placed a line too high.
141. **~~vs~~]** Deleted by C.
143. **ꝑcure]** procure. **ꝑdon]** pardon.

144–47. **Submyt . . . yt]** The original form of these lines, all that has survived of that part of the scene rewritten by D, appears on fol. 10^{r} (Hand S): "To persist in it, is present ⟨deat⟩h. bu⟨t if⟩ you yee⟨ld yourselues⟩, no doubt, what ⟨punish⟩ / ment you (in simplicitie haue incurred, his highnesse in mercie will moste ⟨graciously⟩ / pardon." Although these lines appear to be prose in the MS, they were probably intended as four verse lines.
146. **forme]** orderly and proper behavior (according to law).
147.] This is the last line on fol. 9^{r}. Greg (1911) says that fol. 9^{v} is blank. Although hitherto unquestioned, his statement is not entirely accurate. In the upper left corner of fol. 9^{v} appears in Hand D "all / C". "all" is clearly a speech-prefix and was intended perhaps to link with the first speech of the original scene retained on fol. 10^{r} ("All. we yeeld, and desire his highnesse mercie."). The "C", which appears slightly to the left below "all", is less certain as a reading and no interpretation suggests itself.

Why, you must needs be strangers; would you be pleas'd
To find a nation of such barbarous temper
That breaking out in hideous violence
Would not afford you an abode on earth,
Whet their detested knives against your throats,
Spurn you like dogs, and like as if that God
Owed not nor made not you, nor that the elements
Were not all appropriate to your comforts,
But charter'd unto them? What would you think
To be thus us'd? This is the strangers' case
And this your [mountainish] inhumanity.

All. Faith, 'a says true. Let's us do as we may be done by.

Lincoln. We'll be rul'd by you, Master More, if you'll stand our friend to procure our pardon.

More. Submit you to these noble gentlemen,
Entreat their mediation to the King,
Give up yourself to form, obey the magistrate,
And there's no doubt but mercy may be found if you so seek it.

Enter More.

[*More.*] It is in heaven that I am thus and thus,
And that which we profanely term our fortunes
Is the provision of the power above,
Fitted and shap'd just to that strength of nature
Which we are born [withal]. Good God, good God,
That I from such an humble bench of birth
Should step as 'twere up to my country's head
And give the law out there. I in my father's life
To take prerogative and tithe of knees
From elder kinsmen, and him bind by my place

1. It . . . thus] Cf. *Othello*, I.iii.319–20: "'tis in ourselves that we are thus and thus."

5. borne] Some word seems to have dropped out after "borne" in C's transcript. Dyce suggested *withal* (regularly used in place of *with* in final position in a relative clause, as here), which would mend both syntax and metre.

6. such . . . birth] This phrase offers difficulties of interpretation. It would seem to mean "such lowly birth," but if so More is intentionally exaggerating, since his father, Sir John More, was a respected judge. Given this interpretation, the use of "bench" and "head" (line 7) suggests that the author has in mind the image of moving from the foot of the table (below the salt), where people of more menial station were placed, to a position as host (or lord) at the head. But it is better, perhaps, to take "bench" in its legal sense (More was elected as a bencher of Lincoln's Inn in 1509, and, as a practicing lawyer, had been associated with "the bench" for some years before) and to interpret "bench of birth" as "place of beginnings as a lawyer" when compared with his recent elevation (1529) to the Lord Chancellorship ("my Countries head", line 7). Shakespeare uses "bench" in both the non-legal and legal senses. Cf. particularly *The Winter's Tale*, I.ii.313–14.

9. prerogative . . . knees] Bald compares *Troilus and Cressida*, I.iii.106–7, and *Richard II*, I.iv.33. "tyth" (i.e. tithe) must mean simply "tribute" without reference to its basic meaning of "one tenth," but *O.E.D.* does not record this more general sense. Note "vnreverent knees" and "kneele" in Addition II (lines 110–11). Jenkins notes that Shakespeare, in both *Lear* and *Coriolanus*, is deeply concerned with the proper relations between parents and children, and that there, as here, the "kneeling" image is used to express that concern.

10. bynd . . . place] constrain through my position ("bynd" in the sense of "constrain with legal authority" carries on the legal language).

to give the ſmooth and dexter way to me
that owe it him by nature, ſure thes things
not phiſickt by reſpecte might turne o^{r} bloud
to much Coruption· but moore. the more thou haſt
ether of honor office wealth and calling
wch might ~~aeee~~ accite thee to embrace and hugg them
the more doe thou in ſerpents natures thinke them
feare ther gay ſkinns wth thought of ther ſharpe ſtate
And lett this be thy maxime, to be greate
Is when the thred of hazard is once Spuñ
A bottom great woond vpp greatly vndonn·

11. dexter] right-hand (to walk on the right of a person was to have the position of honor). Shakespeare uses the word only in *Troilus and Cressida*, IV.v.128.
13. phisickt by respecte] tempered by reflection.
13–18. turne . . . state] Cf. the association of "distemp'red blood", "adders", and "corrupted" nature in *Troilus and Cressida*, II.ii.168–77.
14. moore.] The period is questionable. The play on "moore" and "more" (continued in line 17) has been pointed out as very much in Shakespeare's manner.
15. honor . . . calling] Cf. the accumulation of nouns in *Richard II*, III.ii.172–73; *Troilus and Cressida*, I.iii.86–88; *Macbeth*, V.iii.25; and in lines 98–99 of Addition II.
16. accite] arouse, excite. Twice used by Shakespeare in *2 Henry IV*, II.ii.60, V.ii.141, and once in *Titus Andronicus*, I.i.27.
17–18. more . . . state] With these and the preceding lines cf. *Julius Caesar*, II.i.14–15: "It is the bright day that brings forth the adder, / And that craves wary walking."
17. in serpents natures] like serpents in their natures.

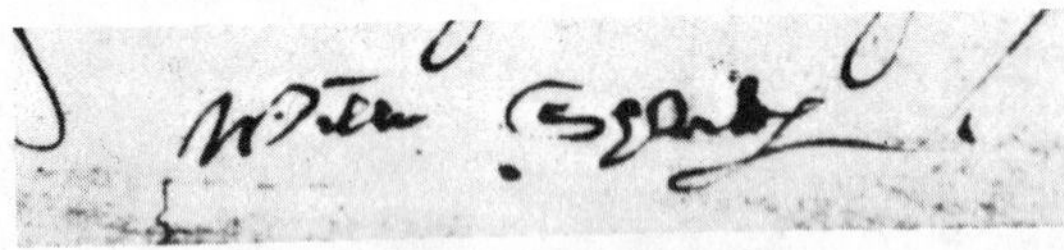

Willm̃ (*or* Wilm) Shakp

From the Belott-Mountjoy deposition, May 11, 1612; in the Public Record Office, London [REQ4/1]

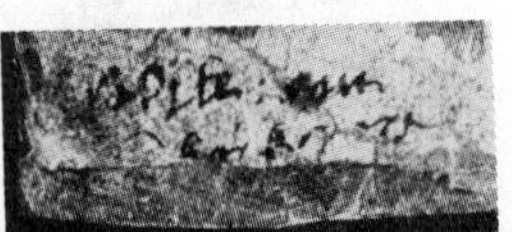

William Shakspere

From the first sheet of Shakespeare's will, March 25, 1616; in the Public Record Office [PROB1/4]; see below, Appendix C, Number 5

William Shakspẽ

From the conveyance for the Blackfriars property, March 10, 1613; in the Guildhall Library, London

Wm Shakspẽ

From the mortgage deed for the Blackfriars property, March 11, 1613; in the British Museum, London (*By permission of The British Library*)

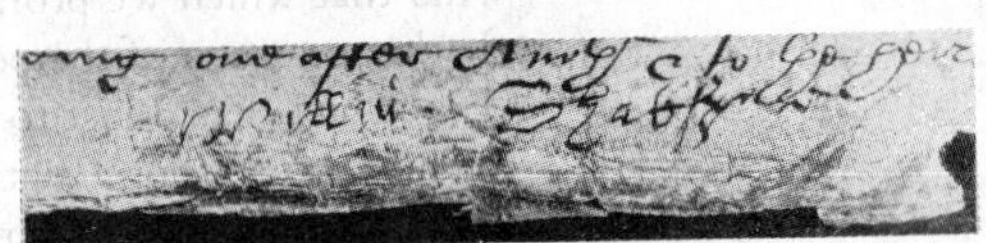

Willm̃ Shakspere

From the second sheet of Shakespeare's will

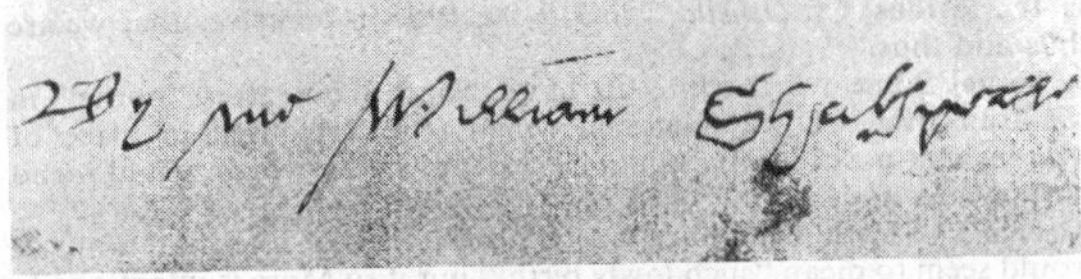

By me William Shakspeare

From the third and last sheet of Shakespeare's will

The six genuine signatures of William Shakespeare

To give the smooth and dexter way to me
That owe it him by nature. Sure these things
Not physick'd by respect might turn our blood
To much corruption. But, More, the more thou hast
Either of honor, office, wealth, and calling,
Which might accite thee to embrace and hug them,
The more do thou in serpents' natures think them,
Fear their gay skins with thought of their sharp state,
And let this be thy maxime: to be great
Is, when the thread of hazard is once spun,
A bottom great wound up, greatly undone.

18. feare . . . state] i.e. learn to fear (doubt, distrust) their appealing appearance ("gay skinns") by thinking of their dangerous inner nature ("sharpe state"). This "feare . . . wth" construction is awkward and finds no parallel in Shakespeare's use of the verb. **sharpe state]** i.e. it is the nature of serpents to sting.

19. maxime] rule of conduct. Shakespeare uses the word only in *Troilus and Cressida*, I.ii.292.

19–21. to . . . vndonn] A difficult passage. The sense seems to be something like this: To be great, after a man has overcome all the dangers of attaining greatness (i.e. has spun "the thred of hazard" and wound it up on Fortune's clew into one great ball), is to fall (allow the thread to unwind) only in a great cause. Cf. *Hamlet*, IV.iv.53–56; Nosworthy considers this an exceedingly significant parallel.

20. Spuñ] The tilde may imply the doubling of the *n* ("Spunn"; cf. "undonn", line 21) or be simply a non-significant flourish. Cf. *2 Henry VI*, IV.ii.29: "Argo, their thread of life is spun.", a passage that seems to have been in D's mind in Addition II, line 5.

21. bottom] either the clew on which to wind thread, or a ball of wound thread (with some suggestion, perhaps, of "foundation").

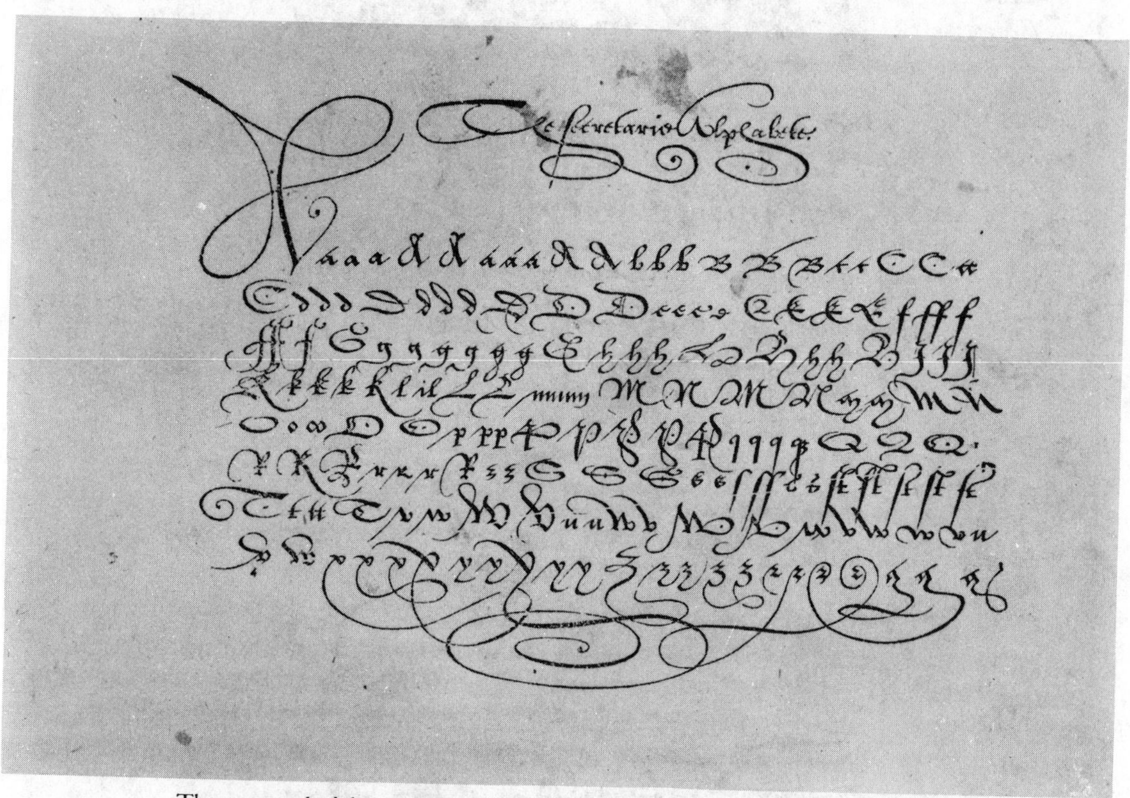

The engraved alphabet above (from John de Beau Chesne and John Baildon, *A Book Containing Divers Sorts of Hands* [1615?]) illustrates the commonest letter-forms, both capital and small, of the so-called "secretary" hand, which is exemplified both by Shakespeare's six known signatures (opposite) and by Hand D (Shakespeare's?) in *Sir Thomas More* (see the next three pages). The most widely used of several styles of handwriting in Shakespeare's England, it was gradually superseded in the course of the seventeenth century by the "italic" hand, the ancestor of our modern script. (*By permission of the Harvard College Library*)

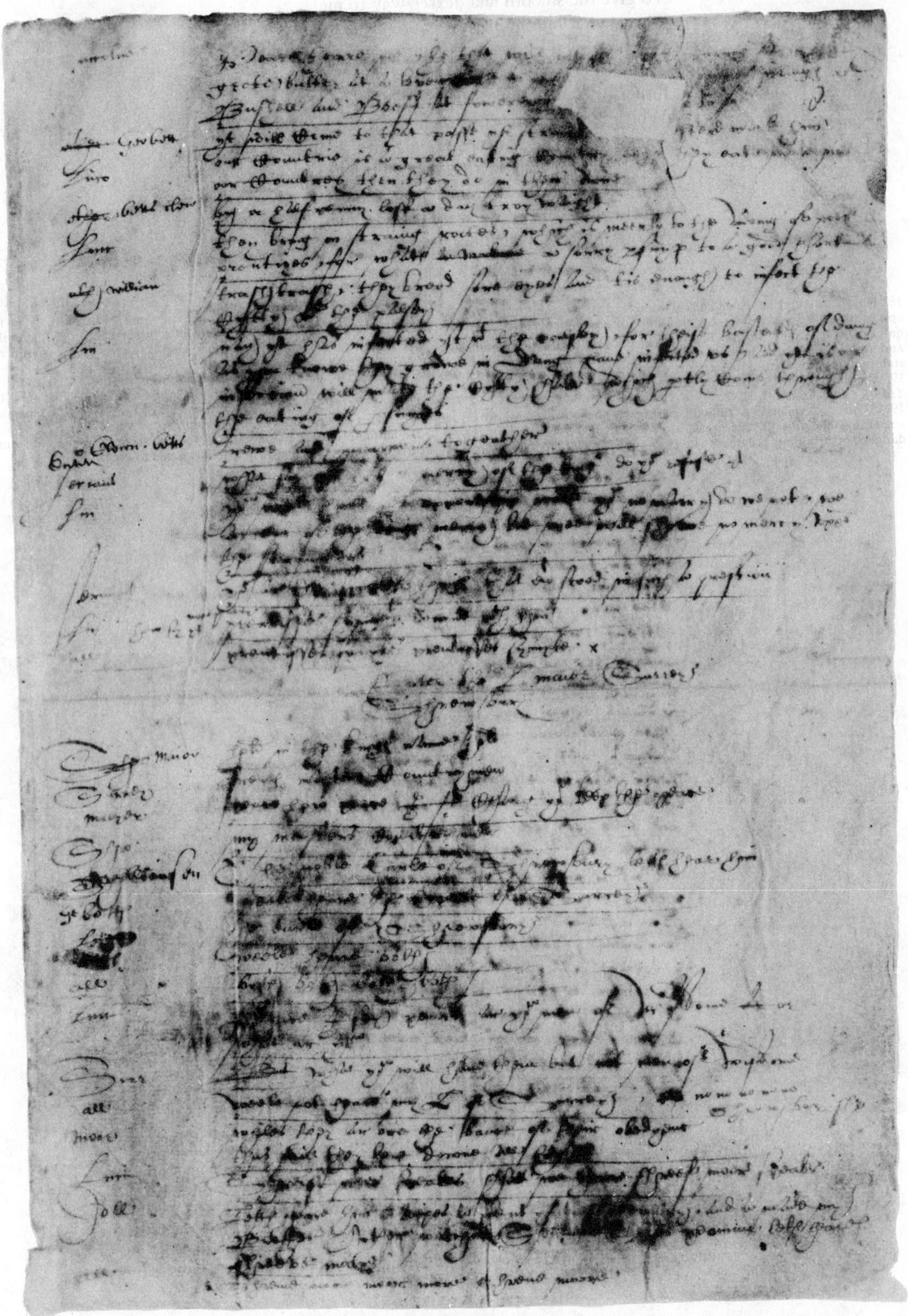

Sir Thomas More, Addition IID; Br. Mus. Harl. MS. 7368, fol. 8r (actual size, 12½ by 8¼ inches)
(By permission of the British Library)

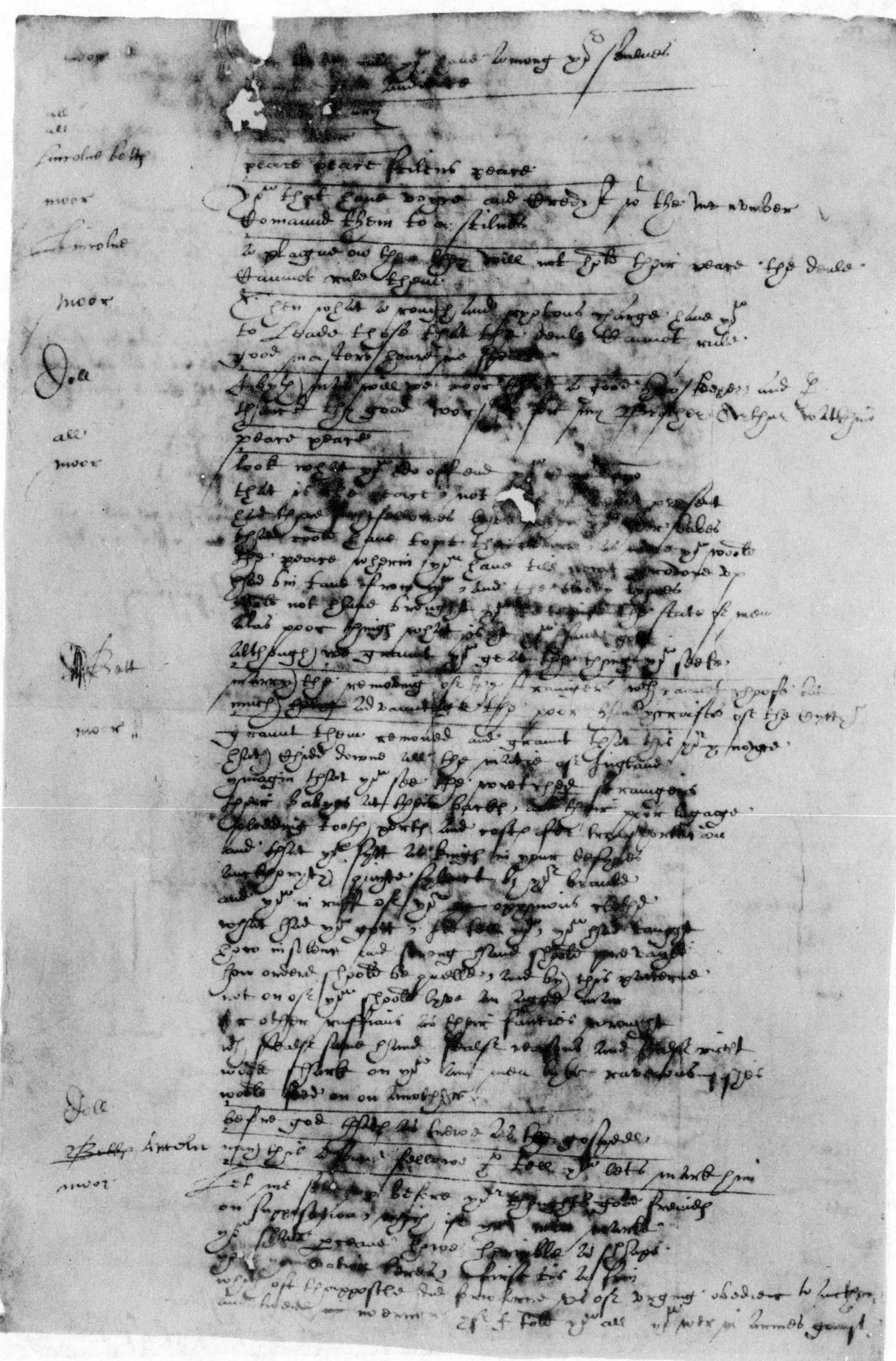

Sir Thomas More, Addition IID; Br. Mus. Harl. MS. 7368, fol. 8v

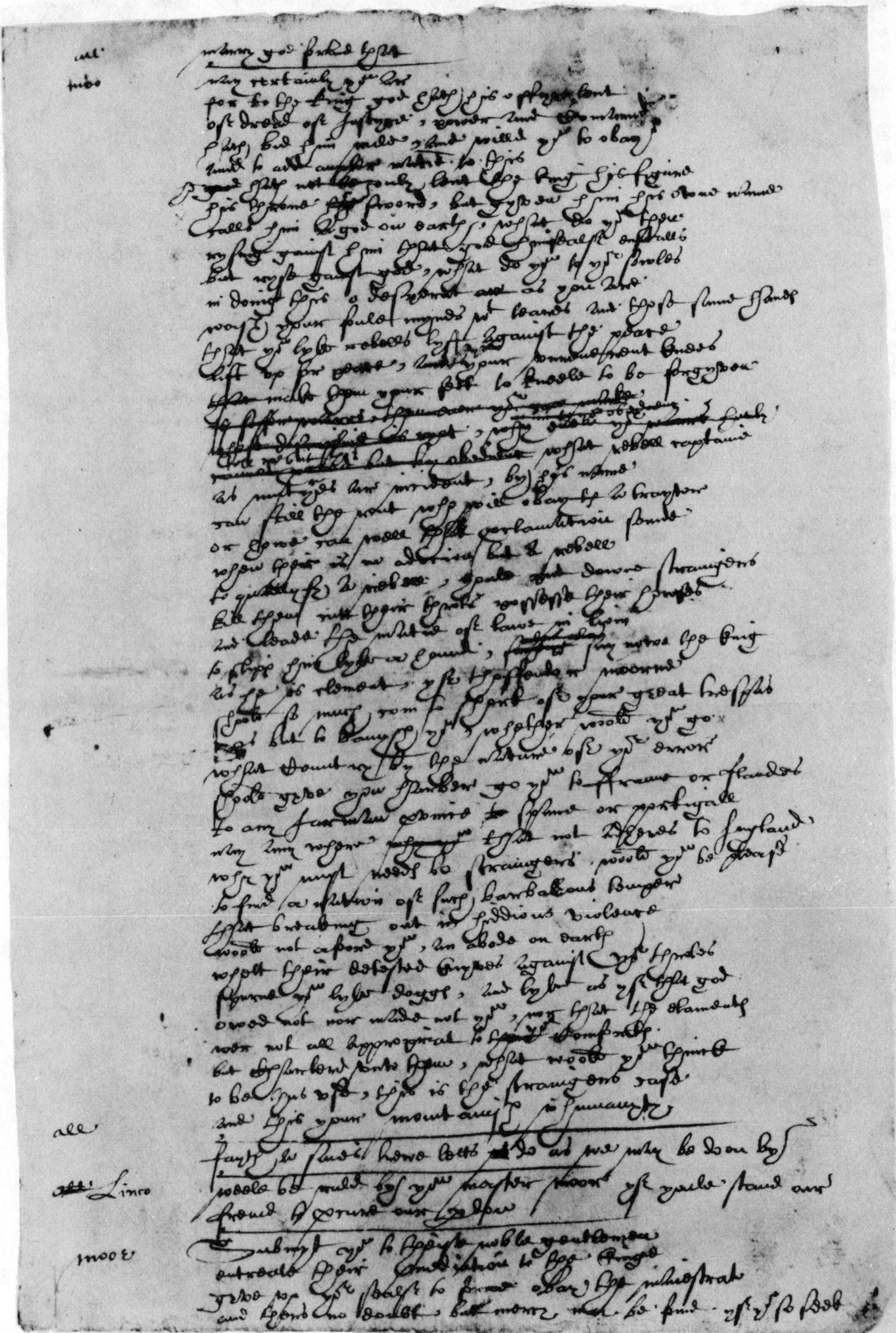

Sir Thomas More, Addition IID; Br. Mus. Harl. MS. 7368, fol. 9r

THE POEMS

Venus and Adonis

The Rape of Lucrece

Sonnets

A Lover's Complaint

The Passionate Pilgrim

The Phoenix and Turtle

A Funeral Elegy by W. S.

Venus and Adonis

In his dedication to the Earl of Southampton, Shakespeare calls *Venus and Adonis* "the first heir of my invention." These words need not mean that he had written no plays earlier—merely that *Venus and Adonis* was his first published literary or poetical work (plays were in a different category). The poem was entered in the Stationers' Register on April 18, 1593. The most probable date of composition is the latter part of 1592, when the theatres were closed because of the plague, though some earlier editors used to fancy that Shakespeare had written it in Stratford and brought it with him when he came up to London. There is no evidence for this supposition unless it can be found in some undeniable rural touches in the poem and the fact that it was published by Richard Field, who had come from Stratford.

Venus and Adonis belongs to a genre of Ovidian mythological-erotic poems, a type which the poet well knew would appeal to the Italianate tastes of a young nobleman like Southampton. In Marlowe's play *Edward II* (1591) the King's favorite, Gaveston, soliloquizes about the surest way to please his sovereign:

I must have wanton poets, pleasant wits,
Musicians, that with touching of a string
May draw the pliant king which way I please.
Music and poetry is his delight:
Therefore I'll have Italian masks by night,
Sweet speeches, comedies, and pleasing shows;
And in the day, when he shall walk abroad,
Like sylvan nymphs my pages shall be clad;
My men, like satyrs grazing on the lawns,
Shall with their goat-feet dance an antic hay.
Sometimes a lovely boy in Dian's shape,
With hair that gilds the water as it glides,
Crownets of pearl about his naked arms,
And in his sportful hands an olive tree,
To hide those parts that men delight to see,
Shall bathe him in a spring; and there, hard by,
One like Actaeon peeping through the grove
Shall by the angry goddess be transform'd,
And running in the likeness of a hart
By yelping hounds pull'd down, and seem to die—
Such sights as these best please his Majesty.
(I.i.51–71)

And in one of Shakespeare's own plays, *The Taming of the Shrew*, when the servants are trying to persuade Christopher Sly that he is a lord, they assume that he will like mythological-erotic art:

Dost thou love pictures? We will fetch thee straight
Adonis painted by a running brook,
And Cytherea all in sedges hid,
Which seem to move and wanton with her breath,
Even as the waving sedges play with wind.
(Induction ii.49–53)

Ovid seems to have been Shakespeare's favorite poet, as he was of the Elizabethans generally. The material for *Venus and Adonis* comes principally from Book X of Ovid's *Metamorphoses*, but the story as told there has been modified in Shakespeare's version by influences from Ovid's treatment of the Salmacis-Hermaphroditus story in Book IV and the Narcissus story in Book III. This conflation of Ovidian stories was not peculiar to Shakespeare nor original with him.

The verse form, a six-line stanza, had been used by Thomas Lodge in 1589 in an Ovidian poem called *Scilla's Metamorphosis, Interlaced with the Unfortunate*

Love of Glaucus, the title-page of which proclaims it "very fit for young courtiers to peruse and coy dames to remember." Lodge exploits the situation of a reluctant young man being wooed by an ardent maiden, and he has a couple of stanzas about Venus and Adonis. Shakespeare could have found enough hints in Lodge, then, to stimulate his writing of the poem, though there are other treatments of the story, particularly one by Spenser (*The Faerie Queene*, III.i.xxxiv ff.), which he may have known.

Whether he yet knew the finest of all the English mythological-erotic poems is uncertain, because we cannot be positive about the date of composition of Marlowe's unfinished *Hero and Leander*. This poem, in couplets, describes the love affair of two mythical figures, supremely beautiful but complete novices in love. The plot is simple and the narrative rapid. What gives the poem its distinctive quality is the combination of lavish descriptive and narrative decoration with gravely mocking asides. The final effect is not ironic, however; these asides merely limit the romantic feeling of the poem. They are characteristically Ovidian. Marlowe's poem fits the requirements of the Italianate entertainment perfectly.

Venus and Adonis, whether or not it was written in imitation of or competition with *Hero and Leander*, is an Ovidian poem that does not fully succeed. In the person of Adonis it presents the reluctance, innocence, and naïveté which Ovid and Marlowe had used so successfully for erotic effect; unfortunately, Shakespeare's hunter seems rather less a creature of myth than a bashful country boy from Stratford. That Shakespeare retained much of his country taste and outlook may be seen from the celebrated description of the horse, the account of the coursing of the hare, and the images of the dive-dapper, the snail, and the lark. But this material is difficult to harmonize with the elements of classical myth (as Shakespeare was to do perfectly when he came to write *A Midsummer Night's Dream*). Similarly unadapted to the requirements of the genre was the rhetorical tradition which caused Shakespeare to put a large part of the poem into extended discourses by Venus, for example the long argumentative speech that begins at line 95. Here for eighty lines she discusses Mars, her own charms, Narcissus, torches, jewels, herbs, and the laws of nature which require propagation (much like the arguments in the first seventeen of Shakespeare's sonnets), so that instead of realizing evoked physical beauty we are listening to a lecture.

We may take as conventional modesty Shakespeare's reference to *Venus and Adonis* as "my unpolish'd lines" and the promise of "some graver labor" if his first effort pleased Southampton. Yet it is clear that contemporaries read the poem for what it is, an Italianate entertainment. Gabriel Harvey noted that the younger sort took much delight in it, and there are many expressions of the belief that, as Hyder Rollins put it, "Shakespeare's poems were the favorite reading of loose and degenerate people, and that, as a consequence, they led to looseness and degeneracy." As late as 1601 a character in a Cambridge play (*The Return from Parnassus, Part 2*, II.i) says that Shakespeare would be a better writer

> Could but a graver subject him content,
> Without love's foolish, lazy languishment.

Of all Shakespeare's works, *Venus and Adonis* was the most popular during his lifetime. It was printed in at least nine editions (with half a dozen more by 1636); there are more allusions to it than to any other work of the author; and in the decade after its publication a swarm of imitations, of it and *Hero and Leander*, appeared.

Modern criticism of *Venus and Adonis* begins with Coleridge, who used the poem to illustrate his ideas about the early signs of genius in a poet and about the distinction between fancy and imagination. He did much to bring the non-dramatic poems to the attention of lovers of Shakespeare. Hazlitt, however, declared that the poet's genius was entirely dramatic. "The two poems of Venus and Adonis and of Tarquin and Lucrece," he wrote, "appear to us like a couple of ice-houses. They are about as hard, as glittering, and as cold." (Elizabethans thought just the opposite—that *Venus and Adonis* is, if anything, a bit too warm.)

Modern criticism has often floundered by failing to place the poem rightly in its genre. Since the older tradition stretching back into the Middle Ages was to moralize and allegorize Ovidian myth, some modern critics have strained to interpret *Venus and Adonis* as a moral or philosophical allegory. (If Shakespeare had intended it to be that, he would surely not have promised Southampton "some graver labor" in his next attempt.) Others, more bewildered still, have maintained that the poem is primarily comic or is a piece of savage irony.

Read as a mythological-erotic poem, *Venus and Adonis* is a vivid and fluent example of the type, not as successful as Marlowe's *Hero and Leander* but interesting in its own right for several reasons. It shows what kind of artist Shakespeare was at this early stage of his career; it demonstrates, as Coleridge pointed out, the artistic and intellectual potentialities of its author. And it prefigures, to the perceptive reader, some of Shakespeare's future triumphs. The inclusion of homely, rural, earthy details in a Renaissance narrative of a mythical world may be a blemish on *Venus and Adonis* as a work of art in a particular literary kind, but it was perhaps a necessity for the writer who would later create Bottom and Falstaff and Juliet's nurse.

Hallett Smith

Venus and Adonis

Vilia miretur vulgus: mihi flauus Apollo
Pocula Castalia plena ministret aqua.

TO THE RIGHT HONORABLE HENRIE WRIOTHESLEY,

EARLE OF SOUTHAMPTON, AND BARON OF TITCHFIELD.

Right Honourable, I know not how I shall offend in dedicating my vnpolisht lines to your Lordship, nor how the worlde will censure mee for choosing so strong a proppe to support so weake a burthen, onelye if your Honour seeme but pleased, I account my selfe highly praised, and vowe to take aduantage of all idle houres, till I haue honoured you with some grauer labour. But if the first heire of my inuention proue deformed, I shall be sorie it had so noble a god-father: and neuer after eare so barren a land, for feare it yeeld me still so bad a haruest, I leaue it to your Honourable suruey, and your Honor to your hearts content, which I wish may alwaies answere your owne wish, and the worlds hopefull expectation.

Your Honors in all dutie,
William Shakespeare.

Even as the sun with purple-color'd face
Had ta'en his last leave of the weeping morn,
Rose-cheek'd Adonis hied him to the chase;
Hunting he lov'd, but love he laugh'd to scorn.
  Sick-thoughted Venus makes amain unto him,
  And like a bold-fac'd suitor gins to woo him.

"Thrice fairer than myself," thus she began,
"The field's chief flower, sweet above compare,
Stain to all nymphs, more lovely than a man,
More white and red than doves or roses are,
  Nature, that made thee with herself at strife,
  Saith that the world hath ending with thy life.

"Vouchsafe, thou wonder, to alight thy steed,
And rein his proud head to the saddle-bow;
If thou wilt deign this favor, for thy meed
A thousand honey secrets shalt thou know.
  Here come and sit, where never serpent hisses,
  And being set, I'll smother thee with kisses;

"And yet not cloy thy lips with loath'd saciety,
But rather famish them amid their plenty,
Making them red, and pale, with fresh variety—
Ten kisses short as one, one long as twenty.
  A summer's day will seem an hour but short,
  Being wasted in such time-beguiling sport."

With this she seizeth on his sweating palm,
The president of pith and livelihood,
And trembling in her passion, calls it balm,
Earth's sovereign salve, to do a goddess good.
  Being so enrag'd, desire doth lend her force
  Courageously to pluck him from his horse.

Over one arm the lusty courser's rein,
Under her other was the tender boy,
Who blush'd, and pouted in a dull disdain,
With leaden appetite, unapt to toy;

Motto. Vilia . . . aqua. These lines, which appear on the title-page, are from Ovid's *Amores*, I.xv.35–36. Marlowe's translation runs: "Let base-conceited wits admire vile things, / Fair Phoebus lead me to the Muses' springs."

Dedication. The original spelling is here retained. censure: judge. eare: cultivate.

2. the weeping morn: i.e. the goddess of the dawn, weeping because the sun-god has left her bed. 3. hied him: hastened.
5. Sick-thoughted: lovesick. makes amain: hastens.
9. Stain . . . nymphs: one who eclipses the nymphs in beauty.
11. made . . . strife: strove to surpass herself in creating you.
15. meed: reward. 16. honey: sweet.

19. saciety: satiety. 24. wasted: spent.
25. sweating palm. A moist hand supposedly indicated sometimes (as here) youth, sometimes (as in line 143 but certainly not here) an amorous disposition.
26. president: precedent, i.e. evidence, sign. pith and livelihood: energy and vitality.
28. sovereign: most potent. 29. enrag'd: mad with desire.
30. Courageously: lustfully. pluck: pull, drag.
34. unapt to toy: not ready to dally amorously.

She red and hot as coals of glowing fire,
He red for shame, but frosty in desire.

The studded bridle on a ragged bough
Nimbly she fastens (O how quick is love!);
The steed is stalled up, and even now
To tie the rider she begins to prove.
Backward she push'd him, as she would be thrust,
And govern'd him in strength, though not in lust.

So soon was she along as he was down,
Each leaning on their elbows and their hips.
Now doth she stroke his cheek, now doth he frown,
And gins to chide, but soon she stops his lips,
And kissing speaks, with lustful language broken,
"If thou wilt chide, thy lips shall never open."

He burns with bashful shame, she with her tears
Doth quench the maiden burning of his cheeks;
Then with her windy sighs and golden hairs
To fan and blow them dry again she seeks.
He saith she is immodest, blames her miss;
What follows more, she murthers with a kiss.

Even as an empty eagle, sharp by fast,
Tires with her beak on feathers, flesh, and bone,
Shaking her wings, devouring all in haste,
Till either gorge be stuff'd, or prey be gone;
Even so she kiss'd his brow, his cheek, his chin,
And where she ends, she doth anew begin.

Forc'd to content, but never to obey,
Panting he lies, and breatheth in her face.
She feedeth on the steam, as on a prey,
And calls it heavenly moisture, air of grace,
Wishing her cheeks were gardens full of flowers,
So they were dew'd with such distilling showers.

Look how a bird lies tangled in a net,
So fast'ned in her arms Adonis lies;
Pure shame and aw'd resistance made him fret,
Which bred more beauty in his angry eyes.
Rain added to a river that is rank
Perforce will force it overflow the bank.

Still she entreats, and prettily entreats,
For to a pretty ear she tunes her tale.
Still is he sullen, still he low'rs and frets,
'Twixt crimson shame and anger ashy-pale.
Being red, she loves him best, and being white,
Her best is better'd with a more delight.

Look how he can, she cannot choose but love,
And by her fair immortal hand she swears
From his soft bosom never to remove
Till he take truce with her contending tears,
Which long have rain'd, making her cheeks all wet,
And one sweet kiss shall pay this comptless debt.

Upon this promise did he raise his chin,
Like a dive-dapper peering through a wave,
Who being look'd on, ducks as quickly in;
So offers he to give what she did crave,
But when her lips were ready for his pay,
He winks, and turns his lips another way.

Never did passenger in summer's heat
More thirst for drink than she for this good turn.
Her help she sees, but help she cannot get,
She bathes in water, yet her fire must burn.
"O, pity," gan she cry, "flint-hearted boy,
'Tis but a kiss I beg, why art thou coy?

"I have been wooed, as I entreat thee now,
Even by the stern and direful god of war,
Whose sinowy neck in battle ne'er did bow,
Who conquers where he comes in every jar,
Yet hath he been my captive, and my slave,
And begg'd for that which thou unask'd shalt have.

"Over my altars hath he hung his lance,
His batt'red shield, his uncontrolled crest,
And for my sake hath learn'd to sport and dance,
To toy, to wanton, dally, smile, and jest,
Scorning his churlish drum, and ensign red,
Making my arms his field, his tent my bed.

"Thus he that overrul'd I overswayed,
Leading him prisoner in a red rose chain;
Strong-temper'd steel his stronger strength obeyed,
Yet was he servile to my coy disdain.
O, be not proud, nor brag not of thy might,
For mast'ring her that foil'd the god of fight.

"Touch but my lips with those fair lips of thine—
Though mine be not so fair, yet are they red—
The kiss shall be thine own as well as mine.
What seest thou in the ground? hold up thy head,
Look in mine eyeballs, there thy beauty lies;
Then why not lips on lips, since eyes in eyes?

"Art thou asham'd to kiss? then wink again,
And I will wink, so shall the day seem night.
Love keeps his revels where there are but twain;
Be bold to play, our sport is not in sight;
These blue-vein'd violets whereon we lean
Never can blab, nor know not what we mean.

"The tender spring upon thy tempting lip
Shows thee unripe; yet mayst thou well be tasted.

39. **stalled:** tied (as in a stall). 40. **prove:** try. 43. **along:** lying beside him. 53. **miss:** fault. 55. **sharp by fast:** hungry from fasting. 56. **Tires . . . on:** tears ravenously . . . at. 58. **gorge:** stomach. 61. **content:** content himself, submit. **obey:** i.e. respond as she wishes. 66. **So:** provided that. **distilling:** gently dropping. 67. **Look how:** just as. 69. **aw'd:** daunted. 71. **rank:** brim-full. 78. **more:** greater.

82. **take truce:** come to terms, make peace. 84. **comptless:** beyond reckoning. 86. **dive-dapper:** little grebe, a water bird. 87. **Who:** which. 90. **winks:** shuts his eyes. 91. **passenger:** traveller on foot. 99. **sinowy:** sinewy. 100. **jar:** fight. 104. **uncontrolled:** unconquered. **crest:** i.e. helmet. 112. **coy:** aloof. 114. **foil'd:** overthrew. 124. **not in sight:** unobserved. 127. **tender spring:** soft down.

Make use of time, let not advantage slip,
Beauty within itself should not be wasted.
  Fair flowers that are not gath'red in their prime
  Rot, and consume themselves in little time.

"Were I hard-favor'd, foul, or wrinkled old,
Ill-nurtur'd, crooked, churlish, harsh in voice,
O'erworn, despised, rheumatic, and cold,
Thick-sighted, barren, lean, and lacking juice,
  Then mightst thou pause, for then I were not for thee,
  But having no defects, why dost abhor me?

"Thou canst not see one wrinkle in my brow,
Mine eyes are grey, and bright, and quick in turning;
My beauty as the spring doth yearly grow,
My flesh is soft and plump, my marrow burning,
  My smooth moist hand, were it with thy hand felt,
  Would in thy palm dissolve, or seem to melt.

"Bid me discourse, I will enchant thine ear,
Or like a fairy, trip upon the green,
Or like a nymph, with long dishevelled hair,
Dance on the sands, and yet no footing seen.
  Love is a spirit all compact of fire,
  Not gross to sink, but light, and will aspire.

"Witness this primrose bank whereon I lie,
These forceless flowers like sturdy trees support me;
Two strengthless doves will draw me through the sky,
From morn till night, even where I list to sport me.
  Is love so light, sweet boy, and may it be
  That thou should think it heavy unto thee?

"Is thine own heart to thine own face affected?
Can thy right hand seize love upon thy left?
Then woo thyself, be of thyself rejected;
Steal thine own freedom, and complain on theft.
  Narcissus so himself himself forsook,
  And died to kiss his shadow in the brook.

"Torches are made to light, jewels to wear,
Dainties to taste, fresh beauty for the use,
Herbs for their smell, and sappy plants to bear:
Things growing to themselves are growth's abuse.
  Seeds spring from seeds, and beauty breedeth beauty;
  Thou wast begot, to get it is thy duty.

"Upon the earth's increase why shouldst thou feed,
Unless the earth with thy increase be fed?
By law of nature thou art bound to breed,
That thine may live, when thou thyself art dead;
  And so in spite of death thou dost survive,
  In that thy likeness still is left alive."

By this the love-sick queen began to sweat,
For where they lay the shadow had forsook them,
And Titan, tired in the midday heat,
With burning eye did hotly overlook them,
  Wishing Adonis had his team to guide,
  So he were like him, and by Venus' side.

And now Adonis, with a lazy sprite,
And with a heavy, dark, disliking eye,
His low'ring brows o'erwhelming his fair sight,
Like misty vapors when they blot the sky,
  Souring his cheeks, cries, "Fie, no more of love!
  The sun doth burn my face, I must remove."

"Ay me," quoth Venus, "young, and so unkind,
What bare excuses mak'st thou to be gone!
I'll sigh celestial breath, whose gentle wind
Shall cool the heat of this descending sun;
  I'll make a shadow for thee of my hairs;
  If they burn too, I'll quench them with my tears.

"The sun that shines from heaven shines but warm,
And lo I lie between that sun and thee;
The heat I have from thence doth little harm,
Thine eye darts forth the fire that burneth me,
  And were I not immortal, life were done,
  Between this heavenly and earthly sun.

"Art thou obdurate, flinty, hard as steel?
Nay, more than flint, for stone at rain relenteth.
Art thou a woman's son and canst not feel
What 'tis to love, how want of love tormenteth?
  O, had thy mother borne so hard a mind,
  She had not brought forth thee, but died unkind.

"What am I that thou shouldst contemn me this?
Or what great danger dwells upon my suit?
What were thy lips the worse for one poor kiss?
Speak, fair, but speak fair words, or else be mute.
  Give me one kiss, I'll give it thee again,
  And one for int'rest, if thou wilt have twain.

"Fie, liveless picture, cold and senseless stone,
Well-painted idol, image dull and dead,
Statuë contenting but the eye alone,
Thing like a man, but of no woman bred!
  Thou art no man, though of a man's complexion,
  For men will kiss even by their own direction."

This said, impatience chokes her pleading tongue,
And swelling passion doth provoke a pause.

133. hard-favor'd, foul: ill-featured, ugly.
135. O'erworn: worn by time. **136. Thick-sighted:** dim-sighted.
140. grey. What we call blue.
141. as . . . grow: i.e. is always in its prime.
142. burning: sexually ardent. **146. trip:** dance.
148. footing: footprint. **149. compact:** composed.
150. aspire: rise. **152. forceless:** weak, fragile.
154. list: wish. **156. heavy:** dull, tedious.
157. to . . . affected: in love with your own face.
158. upon thy left: i.e. by clasping your left hand. **160. on:** of.
166. to themselves: i.e. for no purpose outside themselves.
168. get it: beget beauty (in a child). With this stanza and the next compare the theme of Sonnets 1–17.

175. By this: by this time. **177. Titan:** the sun-god. **178. overlook:** survey. **179. his team:** the horses that drew his chariot.
181. sprite: spirit. **185. Souring his cheeks:** scowling.
187. unkind: unrelenting. **188. bare:** poor, thin.
197. done: destroyed.
200. stone . . . relenteth. Referring to the proverbial saying that drops of water wear away the hardest stone. **205. this:** thus.
207. What: in what respect, how.
211. liveless: inanimate. **senseless:** insensible.
215. complexion: outward appearance. **216. direction:** inclination.

Red cheeks and fiery eyes blaze forth her wrong;
Being judge in love, she cannot right her cause.
And now she weeps, and now she fain would speak,
And now her sobs do her intendments break.

Sometime she shakes her head, and then his hand,
Now gazeth she on him, now on the ground;
Sometime her arms infold him like a band:
She would, he will not in her arms be bound;
And when from thence he struggles to be gone,
She locks her lily fingers one in one.

"Fondling," she saith, "since I have hemm'd thee here
Within the circuit of this ivory pale,
I'll be a park, and thou shalt be my deer:
Feed where thou wilt, on mountain, or in dale;
Graze on my lips, and if those hills be dry,
Stray lower, where the pleasant fountains lie.

"Within this limit is relief enough,
Sweet bottom grass and high delightful plain,
Round rising hillocks, brakes obscure and rough,
To shelter thee from tempest and from rain;
Then be my deer, since I am such a park,
No dog shall rouse thee, though a thousand bark."

At this Adonis smiles as in disdain,
That in each cheek appears a pretty dimple;
Love made those hollows, if himself were slain,
He might be buried in a tomb so simple,
Foreknowing well, if there he came to lie,
Why, there Love liv'd, and there he could not die.

These lovely caves, these round enchanting pits,
Open'd their mouths to swallow Venus' liking.
Being mad before, how doth she now for wits?
Struck dead at first, what needs a second striking?
Poor queen of love, in thine own law forlorn,
To love a cheek that smiles at thee in scorn!

Now which way shall she turn? what shall she say?
Her words are done, her woes the more increasing;
The time is spent, her object will away,
And from her twining arms doth urge releasing.
"Pity," she cries, "some favor, some remorse!"
Away he springs, and hasteth to his horse.

But lo from forth a copse that neighbors by,
A breeding jennet, lusty, young, and proud,
Adonis' trampling courser doth espy;
And forth she rushes, snorts, and neighs aloud.
The strong-neck'd steed, being tied unto a tree,
Breaketh his rein, and to her straight goes he.

Imperiously he leaps, he neighs, he bounds,
And now his woven girths he breaks asunder;
The bearing earth with his hard hoof he wounds,
Whose hollow womb resounds like heaven's thunder;
The iron bit he crusheth 'tween his teeth,
Controlling what he was controlled with.

His ears up-prick'd, his braided hanging mane
Upon his compass'd crest now stand on end,
His nostrils drink the air, and forth again
As from a furnace, vapors doth he send;
His eye, which scornfully glisters like fire,
Shows his hot courage and his high desire.

Sometime he trots, as if he told the steps,
With gentle majesty and modest pride;
Anon he rears upright, curvets, and leaps,
As who should say, "Lo thus my strength is tried;
And this I do to captivate the eye
Of the fair breeder that is standing by."

What recketh he his rider's angry stir,
His flattering "Holla," or his "Stand, I say"?
What cares he now for curb, or pricking spur,
For rich caparisons, or trappings gay?
He sees his love, and nothing else he sees,
For nothing else with his proud sight agrees.

Look when a painter would surpass the life
In limning out a well-proportioned steed,
His art with nature's workmanship at strife,
As if the dead the living should exceed;
So did this horse excel a common one,
In shape, in courage, color, pace, and bone.

Round-hoof'd, short-jointed, fetlocks shag and long,
Broad breast, full eye, small head, and nostril wide,
High crest, short ears, straight legs and passing strong,
Thin mane, thick tail, broad buttock, tender hide:
Look what a horse should have he did not lack,
Save a proud rider on so proud a back.

Sometime he scuds far off, and there he stares,
Anon he starts at stirring of a feather;
To bid the wind a base he now prepares,
And whe'er he run, or fly, they know not whether;
For through his mane and tail the high wind sings,
Fanning the hairs, who wave like feath'red wings.

He looks upon his love, and neighs unto her,
She answers him, as if she knew his mind;

219. blaze forth: (1) proclaim; (2) show by flaming.
220. Being . . . cause: although she is love's arbiter she cannot win her own case. **222. intendments:** intended words.
225. band: bond, fetter. **229. Fondling:** foolish one.
230. pale: fence. **231. park:** deer preserve. **235. relief:** pasture.
236. bottom grass: grass growing in a valley.
237. brakes: thickets. **240. rouse:** drive from cover.
242. That: so that. **243. if:** so that if.
244. simple: plain, unadorned.
257. remorse: compassion.
260. breeding jennet: small Spanish mare.
267. bearing earth: earth that bears him (?) or earth that receives the hoofbeats (?).
272. his compass'd crest: the arched ridge of his neck. **stand.** Plural as referring to the hairs composing the mane (cf. line 306).
276. hot courage: lust. **277. told:** counted.
279. curvets: hops on his hind legs.
280. tried: tested, proved. **283. stir:** agitation.
284. flattering: cajoling, coaxing. **Holla:** stop, hold.
289. Look when: just as when.
290. limning out: painting, drawing.
292. dead: i.e. inanimate. **294. bone:** frame.
299. Look what: whatever.
303. bid . . . base: play a running game with the wind.
304. whe'er: whether. **whether:** which of the two.

Being proud as females are, to see him woo her,
She puts on outward strangeness, seems unkind,
Spurns at his love, and scorns the heat he feels,
Beating his kind embracements with her heels.

Then like a melancholy malcontent,
He vails his tail that like a falling plume
Cool shadow to his melting buttock lent;
He stamps, and bites the poor flies in his fume.
His love, perceiving how he was enrag'd,
Grew kinder, and his fury was assuag'd.

His testy master goeth about to take him,
When lo the unback'd breeder, full of fear,
Jealous of catching, swiftly doth forsake him,
With her the horse, and left Adonis there.
As they were mad unto the wood they hie them,
Outstripping crows that strive to overfly them.

All swoll'n with chafing, down Adonis sits,
Banning his boist'rous and unruly beast;
And now the happy season once more fits
That love-sick Love by pleading may be blest;
For lovers say, the heart hath treble wrong
When it is barr'd the aidance of the tongue.

An oven that is stopp'd, or river stay'd,
Burneth more hotly, swelleth with more rage;
So of concealed sorrow may be said,
Free vent of words love's fire doth assuage,
But when the heart's attorney once is mute,
The client breaks, as desperate in his suit.

He sees her coming, and begins to glow,
Even as a dying coal revives with wind,
And with his bonnet hides his angry brow,
Looks on the dull earth with disturbed mind,
Taking no notice that she is so nigh,
For all askance he holds her in his eye.

O what a sight it was wistly to view,
How she came stealing to the wayward boy,
To note the fighting conflict of her hue,
How white and red each other did destroy!
But now her cheek was pale, and by and by
It flash'd forth fire, as lightning from the sky.

Now was she just before him as he sat,
And like a lowly lover down she kneels;
With one fair hand she heaveth up his hat,
Her other tender hand his fair cheek feels:
His tend'rer cheek receives her soft hand's print,
As apt as new-fall'n snow takes any dint.

O what a war of looks was then between them!
Her eyes petitioners to his eyes suing,
His eyes saw her eyes as they had not seen them,
Her eyes wooed still, his eyes disdain'd the wooing;
And all this dumb play had his acts made plain
With tears which chorus-like her eyes did rain.

Full gently now she takes him by the hand,
A lily prison'd in a jail of snow,
Or ivory in an alablaster band,
So white a friend engirts so white a foe:
This beauteous combat, willful and unwilling,
Showed like two silver doves that sit a-billing.

Once more the engine of her thoughts began:
"O fairest mover on this mortal round,
Would thou wert as I am, and I a man,
My heart all whole as thine, thy heart my wound!
For one sweet look thy help I would assure thee,
Though nothing but my body's bane would cure thee."

"Give me my hand," saith he, "why dost thou feel it?"
"Give me my heart," saith she, "and thou shalt have it.
O, give it me, lest thy hard heart do steel it,
And being steel'd, soft sighs can never grave it.
Then love's deep groans I never shall regard,
Because Adonis' heart hath made mine hard."

"For shame," he cries, "let go, and let me go,
My day's delight is past, my horse is gone,
And 'tis your fault I am bereft him so.
I pray you hence, and leave me here alone,
For all my mind, my thought, my busy care,
Is how to get my palfrey from the mare."

Thus she replies: "Thy palfrey, as he should,
Welcomes the warm approach of sweet desire;
Affection is a coal that must be cool'd,
Else suffer'd it will set the heart on fire.
The sea hath bounds, but deep desire hath none,
Therefore no marvel though thy horse be gone.

"How like a jade he stood, tied to the tree,
Servilely master'd with a leathern rein!
But when he saw his love, his youth's fair fee,
He held such petty bondage in disdain,
Throwing the base thong from his bending crest,
Enfranchising his mouth, his back, his breast.

"Who sees his true-love in her naked bed,
Teaching the sheets a whiter hue than white,

310. strangeness: aloofness, coldness.
311. Spurns: kicks. **314. vails**: lowers.
319. testy: angry. **goeth about**: tries.
320. unback'd: never ridden, unbroken.
321. Jealous of catching: fearful of being caught. **323. As**: as if.
324. overfly them: remain over them in flight (?) or fly faster than they can run (?). **325. swoll'n with chafing**: puffed with anger.
326. Banning: cursing.
335. heart's attorney: heart's advocate or pleader, i.e. tongue.
336. breaks. With pun on the sense "goes bankrupt."
339. bonnet: hat. **343. wistly**: intently. **354. dint**: impression.
357. as: as if.
359. his: its. This dumb show, or drama without words, was explained by her tears, which served as Chorus to interpret the action.
363. alablaster: alabaster. **band**: bond, fetter (as in line 225).
364. engirts: encloses. **367. the engine . . . thoughts**: her tongue.
368. mortal round: earth. **370. my wound**: wounded like mine.
372. bane: destruction. **375. steel**: turn to steel.
376. grave: engrave, make an impression on.
387. Affection: passion. **coal**: ember.
388. suffer'd: allowed to persist.
391. jade: spiritless nag. **393. fee**: rightful reward.
397. in . . . bed: i.e. naked in her bed. A common Elizabethan expression. Night clothes were not worn.

But when his glutton eye so full hath fed,
His other agents aim at like delight?
Who is so faint that dares not be so bold
To touch the fire, the weather being cold?

"Let me excuse thy courser, gentle boy,
And learn of him, I heartily beseech thee,
To take advantage on presented joy;
Though I were dumb, yet his proceedings teach thee.
O, learn to love, the lesson is but plain,
And once made perfect, never lost again."

"I know not love," quoth he, "nor will not know it,
Unless it be a boar, and then I chase it;
'Tis much to borrow, and I will not owe it;
My love to love is love but to disgrace it,
For I have heard it is a life in death,
That laughs and weeps, and all but with a breath.

"Who wears a garment shapeless and unfinish'd?
Who plucks the bud before one leaf put forth?
If springing things be any jot diminish'd,
They wither in their prime, prove nothing worth;
The colt that's back'd and burthen'd being young,
Loseth his pride, and never waxeth strong.

"You hurt my hand with wringing, let us part,
And leave this idle theme, this bootless chat;
Remove your siege from my unyielding heart,
To love's alarms it will not ope the gate;
Dismiss your vows, your feigned tears, your flatt'ry,
For where a heart is hard they make no batt'ry."

"What, canst thou talk?" quoth she, "hast thou a tongue?
O would thou hadst not, or I had no hearing!
Thy mermaid's voice hath done me double wrong;
I had my load before, now press'd with bearing:
Melodious discord, heavenly tune harsh sounding,
Ears' deep sweet music, and heart's deep sore wounding.

"Had I no eyes but ears, my ears would love
That inward beauty and invisible,
Or were I deaf, thy outward parts would move
Each part in me that were but sensible;
Though neither eyes nor ears to hear nor see,
Yet should I be in love by touching thee.

"Say that the sense of feeling were bereft me,
And that I could not see, nor hear, nor touch,
And nothing but the very smell were left me,
Yet would my love to thee be still as much,
For from the stillitory of thy face excelling
Comes breath perfum'd, that breedeth love by smelling.

"But O, what banquet wert thou to the taste,
Being nurse and feeder of the other four!
Would they not wish the feast might ever last,
And bid Suspicion double-lock the door,
Lest Jealousy, that sour unwelcome guest,
Should by his stealing in disturb the feast?"

Once more the ruby-color'd portal open'd,
Which to his speech did honey passage yield,
Like a red morn, that ever yet betoken'd
Wrack to the seaman, tempest to the field,
Sorrow to shepherds, woe unto the birds,
Gusts and foul flaws to herdmen and to herds.

This ill presage advisedly she marketh:
Even as the wind is hush'd before it raineth,
Or as the wolf doth grin before he barketh,
Or as the berry breaks before it staineth,
Or like the deadly bullet of a gun,
His meaning struck her ere his words begun.

And at his look she flatly falleth down,
For looks kill love, and love by looks reviveth:
A smile recures the wounding of a frown.
But blessed bankrout that by love so thriveth!
The silly boy, believing she is dead,
Claps her pale cheek, till clapping makes it red;

And all amaz'd, brake off his late intent,
For sharply he did think to reprehend her,
Which cunning Love did wittily prevent:
Fair fall the wit that can so well defend her!
For on the grass she lies as she were slain,
Till his breath breatheth life in her again.

He wrings her nose, he strikes her on the cheeks,
He bends her fingers, holds her pulses hard,
He chafes her lips, a thousand ways he seeks
To mend the hurt that his unkindness marr'd,
He kisses her, and she by her good will
Will never rise, so he will kiss her still.

The night of sorrow now is turn'd to day:
Her two blue windows faintly she upheaveth,
Like the fair sun, when in his fresh array
He cheers the morn, and all the earth relieveth;
And as the bright sun glorifies the sky,
So is her face illumin'd with her eye,

400. agents: senses, organs.
408. made perfect: learned thoroughly, got by heart.
412. My . . . it: my only desire with respect to love is a desire to discredit it.
414. with a breath: in the same breath, simultaneously.
417. springing: growing, immature. **424. alarms:** attacks.
426. batt'ry: breach in a fortification.
429. mermaid's: siren's. **430. press'd:** oppressed, overburdened.
434. That . . . invisible: i.e. his voice.
435. deaf: i.e. deaf as well as blind.
436. sensible: i.e. tactually sensitive.
443. stillitory: still (used in manufacturing perfume). **excelling:** supremely beautiful.
448. Suspicion: i.e. watchfulness against danger.
454. Wrack: shipwreck. **456. flaws:** blasts of wind.
457. advisedly: attentively. **459. grin:** show his teeth.
466. blessed: fortunate. **bankrout:** bankrupt. **love.** W. S. Walker's proposed emendation *loss* is tempting. **thriveth:** becomes prosperous. **467. silly:** simple, naive.
469. all amaz'd: in utter confusion. **471. wittily:** cleverly.
472. Fair fall: good fortune befall.
478. marr'd: i.e. caused, to her injury.
480. so . . . still: provided that he will never stop kissing her.

Whose beams upon his hairless face are fix'd,
As if from thence they borrowed all their shine.
Were never four such lamps together mix'd,
Had not his clouded with his brow's repine;
But hers, which through the crystal tears gave light,
Shone like the moon in water seen by night.

"O, where am I?" quoth she, "in earth or heaven,
Or in the ocean drench'd, or in the fire?
What hour is this? or morn or weary even?
Do I delight to die, or life desire?
But now I liv'd, and life was death's annoy,
But now I died, and death was lively joy.

"O, thou didst kill me, kill me once again.
Thy eyes' shrowd tutor, that hard heart of thine,
Hath taught them scornful tricks, and such disdain
That they have murd'red this poor heart of mine,
And these mine eyes, true leaders to their queen,
But for thy piteous lips no more had seen.

"Long may they kiss each other for this cure!
O, never let their crimson liveries wear!
And as they last, their verdour still endure,
To drive infection from the dangerous year!
That the star-gazers, having writ on death,
May say, the plague is banish'd by thy breath.

"Pure lips, sweet seals in my soft lips imprinted,
What bargains may I make, still to be sealing?
To sell myself I can be well contented,
So thou wilt buy, and pay, and use good dealing,
Which purchase if thou make, for fear of slips,
Set thy seal manual on my wax-red lips.

"A thousand kisses buys my heart from me,
And pay them at thy leisure, one by one.
What is ten hundred touches unto thee?
Are they not quickly told, and quickly gone?
Say for non-payment that the debt should double,
Is twenty hundred kisses such a trouble?"

"Fair queen," quoth he, "if any love you owe me,
Measure my strangeness with my unripe years;
Before I know myself, seek not to know me,
No fisher but the ungrown fry forbears;
The mellow plum doth fall, the green sticks fast,
Or being early pluck'd, is sour to taste.

"Look the world's comforter with weary gait
His day's hot task hath ended in the west;
The owl (night's herald) shrieks, 'tis very late;
The sheep are gone to fold, birds to their nest,
And coal-black clouds that shadow heaven's light
Do summon us to part, and bid good night.

"Now let me say 'Good night,' and so say you;
If you will say so, you shall have a kiss."
"Good night," quoth she, and ere he says "Adieu,"
The honey fee of parting tend'red is;
Her arms do lend his neck a sweet embrace;
Incorporate then they seem, face grows to face;

Till breathless he disjoin'd, and backward drew
The heavenly moisture, that sweet coral mouth,
Whose precious taste her thirsty lips well knew,
Whereon they surfeit, yet complain on drouth;
He with her plenty press'd, she faint with dearth,
Their lips together glued, fall to the earth.

Now quick desire hath caught the yielding prey,
And glutton-like she feeds, yet never filleth;
Her lips are conquerors, his lips obey,
Paying what ransom the insulter willeth;
Whose vultur thought doth pitch the price so high
That she will draw his lips' rich treasure dry.

And having felt the sweetness of the spoil,
With blindfold fury she begins to forage;
Her face doth reek and smoke, her blood doth boil,
And careless lust stirs up a desperate courage,
Planting oblivion, beating reason back,
Forgetting shame's pure blush and honor's wrack.

Hot, faint, and weary, with her hard embracing,
Like a wild bird being tam'd with too much handling,
Or as the fleet-foot roe that's tir'd with chasing,
Or like the froward infant still'd with dandling,
He now obeys, and now no more resisteth,
While she takes all she can, not all she listeth.

What wax so frozen but dissolves with temp'ring,
And yields at last to every light impression?
Things out of hope are compass'd oft with vent'ring,
Chiefly in love, whose leave exceeds commission;
Affection faints not like a pale-fac'd coward,
But then woos best when most his choice is froward.

When he did frown, O had she then gave over,
Such nectar from his lips she had not suck'd.
Foul words and frowns must not repel a lover;
What though the rose have prickles, yet 'tis pluck'd!
Were beauty under twenty locks kept fast,
Yet love breaks through, and picks them all at last.

For pity now she can no more detain him;
The poor fool prays her that he may depart.

490. repine: repining, discontent. **494. drench'd**: immersed.
497. death's annoy: i.e. painful as death.
498. lively joy: i.e. joyful as life.
500. shrowd: shrewd, harsh. **506. wear**: wear out, fade.
507. verdour: verdure; here, freshness and fragrance, like that of herbs used to combat contagion.
509. writ on death: i.e. predicted death by plague in their almanacs.
515. slips: error or fraud, which would be avoided in the contract by an identifying seal (*seal manual*). **520. told**: counted.
523. owe: bear. **524. strangeness**: coldness. **with**: by.
526. but . . . forbears: who does not throw back the small fish.
540. Incorporate: made into one body.
550. insulter: vaunting conqueror.
551. vultur: vulture, i.e. ravenous. **555. reek**: steam.
556. careless: heedless, without concern for consequences.
557. oblivion: i.e. forgetfulness of all other considerations.
558. wrack: ruin. **562. froward**: fretful.
565. temp'ring: warming and working between thumb and finger.
567. out of: beyond. **compass'd**: brought to pass.
568. leave: liberty, license. **commission**: warrant, authorization.
570. choice: chosen one. **froward**: obstinate, contrary.
573. Foul: hard, disagreeable. **578. poor fool.** A term of pity.

She is resolv'd no longer to restrain him,
Bids him farewell, and look well to her heart,
The which, by Cupid's bow she doth protest,
He carries thence incaged in his breast.

"Sweet boy," she says, "this night I'll waste in sorrow,
For my sick heart commands mine eyes to watch.
Tell me, Love's master, shall we meet to-morrow?
Say, shall we, shall we? wilt thou make the match?"
He tells her no, to-morrow he intends
To hunt the boar with certain of his friends.

"The boar!" quoth she, whereat a sudden pale,
Like lawn being spread upon the blushing rose,
Usurps her cheek; she trembles at his tale,
And on his neck her yoking arms she throws.
She sinketh down, still hanging by his neck,
He on her belly falls, she on her back.

Now is she in the very lists of love,
Her champion mounted for the hot encounter;
All is imaginary she doth prove,
He will not manage her, although he mount her,
That worse than Tantalus' is her annoy,
To clip Elysium and to lack her joy.

Even so poor birds, deceiv'd with painted grapes,
Do surfeit by the eye and pine the maw;
Even so she languisheth in her mishaps,
As those poor birds that helpless berries saw.
The warm effects which she in him finds missing
She seeks to kindle with continual kissing.

But all in vain, good queen, it will not be;
She hath assay'd as much as may be prov'd.
Her pleading hath deserv'd a greater fee;
She's Love, she loves, and yet she is not lov'd.
"Fie, fie," he says, "you crush me, let me go,
You have no reason to withhold me so."

"Thou hadst been gone," quoth she, "sweet boy, ere this,
But that thou toldst me thou wouldst hunt the boar.
O, be advis'd, thou know'st not what it is
With javeling's point a churlish swine to gore,
Whose tushes never sheath'd he whetteth still,
Like to a mortal butcher bent to kill.

"On his bow-back he hath a battle set
Of bristly pikes that ever threat his foes,
His eyes like glow-worms shine when he doth fret,
His snout digs sepulchres where e'er he goes;
Being mov'd, he strikes, what e'er is in his way,
And whom he strikes his crooked tushes slay.

"His brawny sides, with hairy bristles armed,
Are better proof than thy spear's point can enter;
His short thick neck cannot be easily harmed;
Being ireful, on the lion he will venter.
The thorny brambles and embracing bushes,
As fearful of him, part, through whom he rushes.

"Alas, he nought esteems that face of thine,
To which Love's eyes pays tributary gazes,
Nor thy soft hands, sweet lips, and crystal eyne,
Whose full perfection all the world amazes,
But having thee at vantage (wondrous dread!)
Would root these beauties as he roots the mead.

"O, let him keep his loathsome cabin still!
Beauty hath nought to do with such foul fiends.
Come not within his danger by thy will,
They that thrive well take counsel of their friends.
When thou didst name the boar, not to dissemble,
I fear'd thy fortune, and my joints did tremble.

"Didst thou not mark my face? was it not white?
Sawest thou not signs of fear lurk in mine eye?
Grew I not faint, and fell I not downright?
Within my bosom, whereon thou dost lie,
My boding heart pants, beats, and takes no rest,
But like an earthquake, shakes thee on my breast.

"For where Love reigns, disturbing Jealousy
Doth call himself Affection's sentinel,
Gives false alarms, suggesteth mutiny,
And in a peaceful hour doth cry, 'Kill, kill!'
Distemp'ring gentle Love in his desire,
As air and water do abate the fire.

"This sour informer, this bate-breeding spy,
This canker that eats up Love's tender spring,
This carry-tale, dissentious Jealousy,
That sometime true news, sometime false doth bring,
Knocks at my heart, and whispers in mine ear,
That if I love thee, I thy death should fear;

"And more than so, presenteth to mine eye
The picture of an angry chafing boar,
Under whose sharp fangs, on his back doth lie
An image like thyself, all stain'd with gore,

580. look well to: take good care of. **581. protest:** affirm, vow.
583. waste: spend. **584. watch:** stay open.
589. pale: pallor. **590. lawn:** fine white linen.
595. lists: enclosed area where tournaments were held.
597. All . . . prove: all she experiences is imaginary.
598. manage her: put her through her paces (term from horsemanship).
599. Tantalus'. Tantalus was punished in the underworld by insatiable hunger and thirst; food and water receded whenever he tried to eat or drink.
600. clip Elysium: embrace bliss (Elysium was the heaven of classical mythology).
601. birds . . . grapes. An incident, first related by Pliny, connected with a painting by the Greek artist Zeuxis.
602. pine the maw: starve the stomach.
604. helpless: affording no help or nourishment.
605. effects: manifestations.
608. assay'd, prov'd. Both words mean "tried."
616. javeling's: javelin's. **617. tushes:** tusks.
618. mortal: deadly. **bent to kill:** bent on killing.

619. battle: martial array (literally, line of armed men).
623. mov'd: angered. **626. proof:** armor.
628. venter: venture, dare (to make assault).
633. eyne: eyes (old plural, already archaic in the sixteenth century).
636. root: root up. **637. keep:** keep to, remain in. **cabin:** den.
642. fear'd: feared for. **645. downright:** forthwith.
649. Jealousy: fear of loss. **651. suggesteth mutiny:** incites discord.
652. Kill, kill. An ancient battle-cry.
653. Distemp'ring: quenching. **654. abate:** extinguish.
655. bate-breeding: strife-breeding.
656. canker: cankerworm. **spring:** young shoot.

Whose blood upon the fresh flowers being shed,
Doth make them droop with grief and hang the head.

"What should I do, seeing thee so indeed,
That tremble at th' imagination?
The thought of it doth make my faint heart bleed,
And fear doth teach it divination:
I prophesy thy death, my living sorrow,
If thou encounter with the boar to-morrow.

"But if thou needs wilt hunt, be rul'd by me,
Uncouple at the timorous flying hare,
Or at the fox which lives by subtilty,
Or at the roe which no encounter dare;
Pursue these fearful creatures o'er the downs,
And on thy well-breath'd horse keep with thy hounds.

"And when thou hast on foot the purblind hare,
Mark the poor wretch, to overshut his troubles,
How he outruns the wind, and with what care
He cranks and crosses with a thousand doubles:
The many musits through the which he goes
Are like a labyrinth to amaze his foes.

"Sometime he runs among a flock of sheep,
To make the cunning hounds mistake their smell,
And sometime where earth-delving conies keep,
To stop the loud pursuers in their yell,
And sometime sorteth with a herd of deer:
Danger deviseth shifts, wit waits on fear.

"For there his smell with others being mingled,
The hot scent-snuffing hounds are driven to doubt,
Ceasing their clamorous cry till they have singled
With much ado the cold fault cleanly out;
Then do they spend their mouths: echo replies,
As if another chase were in the skies.

"By this, poor Wat, far off upon a hill,
Stands on his hinder-legs with list'ning ear,
To hearken if his foes pursue him still.
Anon their loud alarums he doth hear,
And now his grief may be compared well
To one sore sick that hears the passing bell.

"Then shalt thou see the dew-bedabbled wretch
Turn, and return, indenting with the way;
Each envious brier his weary legs do scratch,
Each shadow makes him stop, each murmur stay,
For misery is trodden on by many,
And being low, never reliev'd by any.

674. Uncouple: unleash the dogs. **677. fearful:** timid.
679. purblind: dim-sighted. Hares were thought to have weak vision.
680. overshut: conclude (or perhaps a variant spelling of *overshoot*, "run beyond"). **682. cranks:** twists and turns.
683. musits: gaps in hedges. **684. amaze:** bewilder.
687. earth-delving conies: rabbits that dig burrows. **keep:** live.
689. sorteth: consorts.
690. shifts: tricks, stratagems. **waits:** attends.
694. cold fault: lost scent. **697. Wat:** traditional name for a hare.
700. alarums: calls to attack.
702. sore: very. **passing bell:** bell tolled for one who has just died.
703. dew-bedabbled: sprinkled with dew.
704. indenting: zigzagging. **705. envious:** malicious.

"Lie quietly, and hear a little more,
Nay, do not struggle, for thou shalt not rise.
To make thee hate the hunting of the boar,
Unlike myself thou hear'st me moralize,
Applying this to that, and so to so,
For love can comment upon every woe.

"Where did I leave?" "No matter where," quoth he,
"Leave me, and then the story aptly ends;
The night is spent." "Why, what of that?" quoth she.
"I am," quoth he, "expected of my friends,
And now 'tis dark, and going I shall fall."
"In night," quoth she, "desire sees best of all.

"But if thou fall, O then imagine this,
The earth, in love with thee, thy footing trips,
And all is but to rob thee of a kiss.
Rich preys make true men thieves; so do thy lips
Make modest Dian cloudy and forlorn,
Lest she should steal a kiss and die forsworn.

"Now of this dark night I perceive the reason:
Cynthia for shame obscures her silver shine,
Till forging Nature be condemn'd of treason,
For stealing moulds from heaven that were divine,
Wherein she fram'd thee, in high heaven's despite,
To shame the sun by day, and her by night.

"And therefore hath she brib'd the Destinies
To cross the curious workmanship of Nature,
To mingle beauty with infirmities,
And pure perfection with impure defeature,
Making it subject to the tyranny
Of mad mischances and much misery:

"As burning fevers, agues pale and faint,
Life-poisoning pestilence, and frenzies wood,
The marrow-eating sickness, whose attaint
Disorder breeds by heating of the blood;
Surfeits, impostumes, grief, and damn'd despair
Swear Nature's death for framing thee so fair.

"And not the least of all these maladies
But in one minute's fight brings beauty under;
Both favor, savor, hue, and qualities,
Whereat th' impartial gazer late did wonder,
Are on the sudden wasted, thaw'd, and done,
As mountain snow melts with the midday sun.

"Therefore despite of fruitless chastity,
Love-lacking vestals, and self-loving nuns,

712. moralize: point morals, make applications.
724. preys: spoils. **true:** honest.
725. Dian: Diana, the moon-goddess. Venus is saying that the moon is covered with clouds and explaining why.
726. forsworn: i.e. with her vow of virginity broken.
728. Cynthia: another name for Diana.
729. forging: counterfeiting.
731–32. she . . . her: Nature . . . Cynthia.
731. in . . . despite: in defiance of high heaven.
734. cross: frustrate. **curious:** beautifully wrought.
736. defeature: disfigurement. **740. wood:** mad.
741. attaint: infection. **743. impostumes:** abscesses.
747. favor: beauty of form and feature.
748. th' impartial gazer: i.e. even the observer not influenced by love.
749. thaw'd: dissolved, dissipated.
751. despite of: in defiance of. **fruitless:** barren.

That on the earth would breed a scarcity
And barren dearth of daughters and of sons,
Be prodigal: the lamp that burns by night
Dries up his oil to lend the world his light.

"What is thy body but a swallowing grave,
Seeming to bury that posterity
Which by the rights of time thou needs must have,
If thou destroy them not in dark obscurity?
If so, the world will hold thee in disdain,
Sith in thy pride so fair a hope is slain.

"So in thyself thyself art made away,
A mischief worse than civil home-bred strife,
Or theirs whose desperate hands themselves do slay,
Or butcher sire that reaves his son of life.
Foul cank'ring rust the hidden treasure frets,
But gold that's put to use more gold begets."

"Nay then," quoth Adon, "you will fall again
Into your idle over-handled theme.
The kiss I gave you is bestow'd in vain,
And all in vain you strive against the stream,
For by this black-fac'd night, desire's foul nurse,
Your treatise makes me like you worse and worse.

"If love have lent you twenty thousand tongues,
And every tongue more moving than your own,
Bewitching like the wanton mermaids' songs,
Yet from mine ear the tempting tune is blown;
For know my heart stands armed in mine ear,
And will not let a false sound enter there,

"Lest the deceiving harmony should run
Into the quiet closure of my breast,
And then my little heart were quite undone,
In his bedchamber to be barr'd of rest.
No, lady, no, my heart longs not to groan,
But soundly sleeps, while now it sleeps alone.

"What have you urg'd that I cannot reprove?
The path is smooth that leadeth on to danger.
I hate not love, but your device in love,
That lends embracements unto every stranger.
You do it for increase: O strange excuse!
When reason is the bawd to lust's abuse.

"Call it not love, for Love to heaven is fled,
Since sweating Lust on earth usurp'd his name,
Under whose simple semblance he hath fed
Upon fresh beauty, blotting it with blame;
Which the hot tyrant stains, and soon bereaves,
As caterpillars do the tender leaves.

"Love comforteth like sunshine after rain,
But Lust's effect is tempest after sun;

762. **Sith**: since. 763. **made away**: destroyed.
766. **reaves**: robs. 767. **frets**: eats away.
772. **stream**: current. 774. **treatise**: discourse.
777. **mermaids'**: i.e. sirens'. 782. **closure**: enclosure.
787. **reprove**: refute. 789. **device**: plan of conduct.
795. **whose**: i.e. Love's. **simple semblance**: innocent appearance.
796. **blotting**: soiling. 797. **bereaves**: spoils.

Love's gentle spring doth always fresh remain,
Lust's winter comes ere summer half be done;
Love surfeits not, Lust like a glutton dies;
Love is all truth, Lust full of forged lies.

"More I could tell, but more I dare not say,
The text is old, the orator too green,
Therefore in sadness, now I will away;
My face is full of shame, my heart of teen,
Mine ears, that to your wanton talk attended,
Do burn themselves for having so offended."

With this he breaketh from the sweet embrace
Of those fair arms which bound him to her breast,
And homeward through the dark laund runs apace,
Leaves Love upon her back, deeply distress'd.
Look how a bright star shooteth from the sky,
So glides he in the night from Venus' eye,

Which after him she darts, as one on shore
Gazing upon a late embarked friend,
Till the wild waves will have him seen no more,
Whose ridges with the meeting clouds contend;
So did the merciless and pitchy night
Fold in the object that did feed her sight.

Whereat amaz'd as one that unaware
Hath dropp'd a precious jewel in the flood,
Or stonish'd as night-wand'rers often are,
Their light blown out in some mistrustful wood,
Even so confounded in the dark she lay,
Having lost the fair discovery of her way.

And now she beats her heart, whereat it groans,
That all the neighbor caves, as seeming troubled,
Make verbal repetition of her moans;
Passion on passion deeply is redoubled:
"Ay me!" she cries, and twenty times, "Woe, woe!"
And twenty echoes twenty times cry so.

She marking them begins a wailing note,
And sings extemporally a woeful ditty,
How love makes young men thrall, and old men dote,
How love is wise in folly, foolish witty.
Her heavy anthem still concludes in woe,
And still the choir of echoes answer so.

Her song was tedious, and outwore the night,
For lovers' hours are long, though seeming short;
If pleas'd themselves, others they think delight
In such-like circumstance, with such-like sport.
Their copious stories, oftentimes begun,
End without audience, and are never done.

806. **green**: young, inexperienced.
807. **in sadness**: seriously, in truth.
808. **teen**: vexation. 813. **laund**: glade.
823. **amaz'd**: confounded. **unaware**: inadvertently.
825. **stonish'd**: dismayed.
826. **mistrustful**: creating apprehension.
828. **fair . . . way**: i.e. the one who gave light to her path (*discovery* = discoverer, i.e. revealer). 832. **Passion**: lamentation.
839. **heavy**: melancholy.

For who hath she to spend the night withal,
But idle sounds resembling parasits,
Like shrill-tongu'd tapsters answering every call,
Soothing the humor of fantastic wits?
  She says, " 'Tis so," they answer all, " 'Tis so,"
  And would say after her, if she said "No."

Lo here the gentle lark, weary of rest,
From his moist cabinet mounts up on high,
And wakes the morning, from whose silver breast
The sun ariseth in his majesty,
  Who doth the world so gloriously behold
  That cedar tops and hills seem burnish'd gold.

Venus salutes him with this fair good morrow:
"O thou clear god, and patron of all light,
From whom each lamp and shining star doth borrow
The beauteous influence that makes him bright,
  There lives a son that suck'd an earthly mother,
  May lend thee light, as thou dost lend to other."

This said, she hasteth to a myrtle grove,
Musing the morning is so much o'erworn,
And yet she hears no tidings of her love.
She hearkens for his hounds and for his horn;
  Anon she hears them chaunt it lustily,
  And all in haste she coasteth to the cry.

And as she runs, the bushes in the way,
Some catch her by the neck, some kiss her face,
Some twin'd about her thigh to make her stay.
She wildly breaketh from their strict embrace,
  Like a milch doe, whose swelling dugs do ache,
  Hasting to feed her fawn hid in some brake.

By this she hears the hounds are at a bay,
Whereat she starts like one that spies an adder
Wreath'd up in fatal folds just in his way,
The fear whereof doth make him shake and shudder;
  Even so the timorous yelping of the hounds
  Appalls her senses, and her spirit confounds.

For now she knows it is no gentle chase,
But the blunt boar, rough bear, or lion proud,
Because the cry remaineth in one place,
Where fearfully the dogs exclaim aloud;
  Finding their enemy to be so curst,
  They all strain court'sy who shall cope him first.

This dismal cry rings sadly in her ear,
Through which it enters to surprise her heart,
Who overcome by doubt, and bloodless fear,
With cold-pale weakness numbs each feeling part:
  Like soldiers when their captain once doth yield,
  They basely fly, and dare not stay the field.

Thus stands she in a trembling ecstasy,
Till cheering up her senses all dismay'd,
She tells them 'tis a causeless fantasy,
And childish error that they are afraid;
  Bids them leave quaking, bids them fear no more—
  And with that word, she spied the hunted boar,

Whose frothy mouth bepainted all with red,
Like milk and blood being mingled both together,
A second fear through all her sinews spread,
Which madly hurries her she knows not whither;
  This way she runs, and now she will no further,
  But back retires to rate the boar for murther.

A thousand spleens bear her a thousand ways,
She treads the path that she untreads again;
Her more than haste is mated with delays,
Like the proceedings of a drunken brain,
  Full of respects, yet nought at all respecting,
  In hand with all things, nought at all effecting.

Here kennell'd in a brake she finds a hound,
And asks the weary caitiff for his master,
And there another licking of his wound,
'Gainst venom'd sores the only sovereign plaster,
  And here she meets another sadly scowling,
  To whom she speaks, and he replies with howling.

When he hath ceas'd his ill-resounding noise,
Another flap-mouth'd mourner, black and grim,
Against the welkin volleys out his voice;
Another, and another, answer him,
  Clapping their proud tails to the ground below,
  Shaking their scratch'd ears, bleeding as they go.

Look how the world's poor people are amazed
At apparitions, signs, and prodigies,
Whereon with fearful eyes they long have gazed,
Infusing them with dreadful prophecies;
  So she at these sad signs draws up her breath,
  And sighing it again, exclaims on Death.

"Hard-favor'd tyrant, ugly, meagre, lean,
Hateful divorce of love"—thus chides she Death—
"Grim-grinning ghost, earth's worm, what dost thou
  mean
To stifle beauty, and to steal his breath?

847. withal: with.
848. parasits: parasites, i.e. yes-men, repeating her words.
849. tapsters: waiters in taverns.
850. Soothing . . . wits: indulging the whims of capricious minds.
854. moist cabinet: i.e. dewy nest. **860. clear:** bright, shining.
866. Musing: wondering. **o'erworn:** i.e. advanced.
869. chaunt it: sound. **870. coasteth:** runs in the direction of.
873. twin'd. Most editors read *twine*, following Q7.
874. strict: tight.
877. at a bay: i.e. faced by the quarry, which has turned to make a stand. **884. blunt:** rough. **887. curst:** savage, vicious.
888. strain court'sy: i.e. are exceedingly polite in deferring to one another. **cope:** encounter. **889. dismal:** ill-boding.
890. surprise: assail, take possession of.
894. stay the field: stand against the onslaught.
895. ecstasy: violent agitation of mind.
906. rate: berate. **907. spleens:** impulses.
908. untreads: retraces. **909. mated:** frustrated.
911. Full . . . respecting: full of consideration, but not really considering anything. **912. In hand:** busied. **914. caitiff:** wretch.
916. only: i.e. best. **plaster:** i.e. curative application.
921. welkin: sky. **926. prodigies:** abnormal events.
928. Infusing . . . prophecies: i.e. imparting to them the character of dire omens. **930. exclaims on:** rails at.
932. divorce: divorcer, i.e. terminator.
933. worm. Destroyer of the rose, symbol of beauty.

Who when he liv'd, his breath and beauty set
Gloss on the rose, smell to the violet.

"If he be dead—O no, it cannot be,
Seeing his beauty, thou shouldst strike at it:
O yes, it may, thou hast no eyes to see,
But hatefully at randon dost thou hit.
Thy mark is feeble age, but thy false dart
Mistakes that aim, and cleaves an infant's heart.

"Hadst thou but bid beware, then he had spoke,
And hearing him, thy power had lost his power.
The Destinies will curse thee for this stroke:
They bid thee crop a weed, thou pluck'st a flower.
Love's golden arrow at him should have fled,
And not Death's ebon dart to strike him dead.

"Dost thou drink tears, that thou provok'st such weeping?
What may a heavy groan advantage thee?
Why hast thou cast into eternal sleeping
Those eyes that taught all other eyes to see?
Now Nature cares not for thy mortal vigor,
Since her best work is ruin'd with thy rigor."

Here overcome, as one full of despair,
She vail'd her eyelids, who like sluices stopp'd
The crystal tide that from her two cheeks fair
In the sweet channel of her bosom dropp'd;
But through the flood-gates breaks the silver rain,
And with his strong course opens them again.

O how her eyes and tears did lend and borrow!
Her eye seen in the tears, tears in her eye,
Both crystals, where they view'd each other's sorrow,
Sorrow that friendly sighs sought still to dry;
But like a stormy day, now wind, now rain,
Sighs dry her cheeks, tears make them wet again.

Variable passions throng her constant woe,
As striving who should best become her grief;
All entertain'd, each passion labors so,
That every present sorrow seemeth chief,
But none is best; then join they all together,
Like many clouds consulting for foul weather.

By this, far off, she hears some huntsman hallow;
A nurse's song ne'er pleas'd her babe so well.
The dire imagination she did follow
This sound of hope doth labor to expel,
For now reviving joy bids her rejoice,
And flatters her it is Adonis' voice.

Whereat her tears began to turn their tide,
Being prison'd in her eye, like pearls in glass,
Yet sometimes falls an orient drop beside,
Which her cheek melts, as scorning it should pass
To wash the foul face of the sluttish ground,
Who is but drunken when she seemeth drown'd.

O hard-believing love, how strange it seems!
Not to believe, and yet too credulous:
Thy weal and woe are both of them extremes;
Despair and hope makes thee ridiculous:
The one doth flatter thee in thoughts unlikely,
In likely thoughts the other kills thee quickly.

Now she unweaves the web that she hath wrought,
Adonis lives, and Death is not to blame;
It was not she that call'd him all to naught;
Now she adds honors to his hateful name:
She clepes him king of graves, and grave for kings,
Imperious supreme of all mortal things.

"No, no," quoth she, "sweet Death, I did but jest,
Yet pardon me, I felt a kind of fear
When as I met the boar, that bloody beast,
Which knows no pity, but is still severe;
Then, gentle shadow (truth I must confess),
I rail'd on thee, fearing my love's decesse.

"'Tis not my fault, the boar provok'd my tongue,
Be wreak'd on him, invisible commander;
'Tis he, foul creature, that hath done thee wrong,
I did but act, he's author of thy slander.
Grief hath two tongues, and never woman yet
Could rule them both without ten women's wit."

Thus hoping that Adonis is alive,
Her rash suspect she doth extenuate,
And that his beauty may the better thrive,
With Death she humbly doth insinuate;
Tells him of trophies, statues, tombs, and stories
His victories, his triumphs, and his glories.

"O Jove," quoth she, "how much a fool was I,
To be of such a weak and silly mind,
To wail his death who lives, and must not die
Till mutual overthrow of mortal kind!
For he being dead, with him is beauty slain,
And beauty dead, black chaos comes again.

"Fie, fie, fond love, thou art as full of fear
As one with treasure laden, hemm'd with thieves;
Trifles, unwitnessed with eye or ear,
Thy coward heart with false bethinking grieves."
Even at this word she hears a merry horn,
Whereat she leaps, that was but late forlorn.

940. randon: random. **941. mark:** target. **944. his:** its.
953. cares not for: is no longer apprehensive about. **mortal:** deadly.
956. vail'd: lowered. **969. entertain'd:** admitted.
972. consulting for: cooperating to bring about.
973. hallow: halloo, shout. **981. orient:** shining.

983. foul: dirty.
988. Despair and hope: i.e. the rapid alternation of despair and hope (hence the singular verb).
993. all to naught: thoroughly wicked. **995. clepes:** calls.
996. Imperious supreme: imperial sovereign.
999. When as: when.
1000. still severe: always merciless. **1001. shadow:** spectre.
1002. decesse: decease. **1004. wreak'd:** revenged.
1006. I . . . act: I was only the agent.
1010. rash suspect: overhasty suspicion.
1012. insinuate: ingratiate herself. **1013. stories:** relates.
1018. mutual: common, universal.
1023. unwitnessed with: not attested by.
1026. leaps: jumps for joy.

As falcons to the lure, away she flies,
The grass stoops not, she treads on it so light,
And in her haste unfortunately spies
The foul boar's conquest on her fair delight,
Which seen, her eyes [as] murd'red with the view,
Like stars asham'd of day, themselves withdrew;

Or as the snail, whose tender horns being hit,
Shrinks backward in his shelly cave with pain,
And there, all smoth'red up, in shade doth sit,
Long after fearing to creep forth again;
So at his bloody view her eyes are fled
Into the deep-dark cabins of her head,

Where they resign their office, and their light,
To the disposing of her troubled brain,
Who bids them still consort with ugly night,
And never wound the heart with looks again,
Who like a king perplexed in his throne,
By their suggestion, gives a deadly groan.

Whereat each tributary subject quakes,
As when the wind imprison'd in the ground,
Struggling for passage, earth's foundation shakes,
Which with cold terror doth men's minds confound.
This mutiny each part doth so surprise
That from their dark beds once more leap her eyes,

And being open'd, threw unwilling light
Upon the wide wound that the boar had trench'd
In his soft flank, whose wonted lily white
With purple tears, that his wound wept, [was] drench'd.
No flow'r was nigh, no grass, herb, leaf, or weed,
But stole his blood, and seem'd with him to bleed.

This solemn sympathy poor Venus noteth,
Over one shoulder doth she hang her head;
Dumbly she passions, franticly she doteth,
She thinks he could not die, he is not dead;
Her voice is stopp'd, her joints forget to bow,
Her eyes are mad that they have wept till now.

Upon his hurt she looks so steadfastly,
That her sight dazzling makes the wound seem three,
And then she reprehends her mangling eye,
That makes more gashes where no breach should be.
His face seems twain, each several limb is doubled,
For oft the eye mistakes, the brain being troubled.

"My tongue cannot express my grief for one,
And yet," quoth she, "behold two Adons dead!
My sighs are blown away, my salt tears gone,
Mine eyes are turn'd to fire, my heart to lead:
Heavy heart's lead, melt at mine eyes' red fire,
So shall I die by drops of hot desire.

"Alas, poor world, what treasure hast thou lost!
What face remains alive that's worth the viewing?
Whose tongue is music now? what canst thou boast
Of things long since, or any thing ensuing?
The flowers are sweet, their colors fresh and trim,
But true sweet beauty liv'd and died with him.

"Bonnet nor veil henceforth no creature wear!
Nor sun nor wind will ever strive to kiss you:
Having no fair to lose, you need not fear,
The sun doth scorn you, and the wind doth hiss you.
But when Adonis liv'd, sun and sharp air
Lurk'd like two thieves, to rob him of his fair.

"And therefore would he put his bonnet on,
Under whose brim the gaudy sun would peep;
The wind would blow it off, and being gone,
Play with his locks; then would Adonis weep;
And straight, in pity of his tender years,
They both would strive who first should dry his tears.

"To see his face the lion walk'd along
Behind some hedge, because he would not fear him;
To recreate himself when he hath song,
The tiger would be tame, and gently hear him;
If he had spoke, the wolf would leave his prey,
And never fright the silly lamb that day.

"When he beheld his shadow in the brook,
The fishes spread on it their golden gills;
When he was by, the birds such pleasure took,
That some would sing, some other in their bills
Would bring him mulberries and ripe-red cherries:
He fed them with his sight, they him with berries.

"But this foul, grim, and urchin-snouted boar,
Whose downward eye still looketh for a grave,
Ne'er saw the beauteous livery that he wore—
Witness the entertainment that he gave.
If he did see his face, why then I know
He thought to kiss him, and hath kill'd him so.

"'Tis true, 'tis true, thus was Adonis slain:
He ran upon the boar with his sharp spear,
Who did not whet his teeth at him again,
But by a kiss thought to persuade him there;
And nousling in his flank, the loving swine
Sheath'd unaware the tusk in his soft groin.

1027. lure: bait used in training hawks.
1031. as. See the Textual Notes.
1032. asham'd of: put to shame by.
1041. still consort: always keep company.
1043. Who: which, i.e. the heart. **perplexed:** deeply troubled.
1044. suggestion: incitement.
1045. tributary subject: i.e. subordinate member (of her body).
1046–47. As . . . shakes. The standard Elizabethan explanation of earthquakes. **1049. surprise:** overcome by sudden attack.
1054. was. See the Textual Notes.
1059. passions: suffers (or manifests) grief.
1062. till now: before now, i.e. for lesser cause.
1083. fair: beauty. **1091. straight:** straightway.
1094. would not fear: didn't want to frighten.
1095. song: sung. (In sense, *To recreate himself* follows *song.*)
1098. silly: innocent, harmless.
1105. urchin-snouted: hedgehog-snouted (exact force uncertain).
1107. livery: outward appearance.
1108. entertainment: reception, treatment.
1114. persuade: win over (?); or *persuade him there* may mean "persuade him to remain there."

"Had I been tooth'd like him, I must confess,
With kissing him I should have kill'd him first,
But he is dead, and never did he bless
My youth with his, the more am I accurs'd."
With this she falleth in the place she stood,
And stains her face with his congealed blood.

She looks upon his lips, and they are pale,
She takes him by the hand, and that is cold,
She whispers in his ears a heavy tale,
As if they heard the woeful words she told;
She lifts the coffer-lids that close his eyes,
Where lo, two lamps burnt out in darkness lies;

Two glasses, where herself herself beheld
A thousand times, and now no more reflect,
Their virtue lost, wherein they late excell'd,
And every beauty robb'd of his effect.
"Wonder of time," quoth she, "this is my spite,
That thou being dead, the day should yet be light.

"Since thou art dead, lo here I prophesy,
Sorrow on love hereafter shall attend;
It shall be waited on with jealousy,
Find sweet beginning, but unsavory end;
Ne'er settled equally, but high or low,
That all love's pleasure shall not match his woe.

"It shall be fickle, false, and full of fraud,
Bud, and be blasted, in a breathing while,
The bottom poison, and the top o'erstraw'd
With sweets that shall the truest sight beguile;
The strongest body shall it make most weak,
Strike the wise dumb, and teach the fool to speak.

"It shall be sparing, and too full of riot,
Teaching decrepit age to tread the measures;
The staring ruffian shall it keep in quiet,
Pluck down the rich, enrich the poor with treasures;
It shall be raging mad, and silly mild,
Make the young old, the old become a child.

"It shall suspect where is no cause of fear,
It shall not fear where it should most mistrust,
It shall be merciful, and too severe,
And most deceiving when it seems most just;
Perverse it shall be, where it shows most toward,
Put fear to valor, courage to the coward.

"It shall be cause of war and dire events,
And set dissension 'twixt the son and sire,
Subject and servile to all discontents,
As dry combustious matter is to fire.
Sith in his prime, Death doth my love destroy,
They that love best, their loves shall not enjoy."

By this the boy that by her side lay kill'd
Was melted like a vapor from her sight,
And in his blood that on the ground lay spill'd,
A purple flow'r sprung up, check'red with white,
Resembling well his pale cheeks and the blood
Which in round drops upon their whiteness stood.

She bows her head, the new-sprung flow'r to smell,
Comparing it to her Adonis' breath,
And says within her bosom it shall dwell,
Since he himself is reft from her by death.
She crops the stalk, and in the breach appears
Green-dropping sap, which she compares to tears.

"Poor flow'r," quoth she, "this was thy father's guise—
Sweet issue of a more sweet-smelling sire—
For every little grief to wet his eyes;
To grow unto himself was his desire,
And so 'tis thine, but know it is as good
To wither in my breast as in his blood.

"Here was thy father's bed, here in my breast;
Thou art the next of blood, and 'tis thy right.
Lo in this hollow cradle take thy rest,
My throbbing heart shall rock thee day and night;
There shall not be one minute in an hour
Wherein I will not kiss my sweet love's flow'r."

Thus weary of the world, away she hies,
And yokes her silver doves, by whose swift aid
Their mistress mounted through the empty skies,
In her light chariot, quickly is convey'd,
Holding their course to Paphos, where their queen
Means to immure herself, and not be seen.

1127. coffer-lids: lids to treasure-chests.
1131. virtue: power (to see and to reflect).
1133. spite: vexation, grief.
1142. a breathing while: the time required to draw breath, a moment.
1143. o'erstraw'd: strewn over.
1147. sparing: parsimonious. **full of riot:** prodigal, extravagant.
1148. tread the measures: dance.
1149. staring: glaring, furious.
1156. just: honest, trustworthy.
1157. Perverse: obstinate, contrary. **toward:** compliant, willing.
1177. guise: manner, habit.
1193. Paphos: Venus' city in Cyprus.

NOTE ON THE TEXT

Venus and Adonis was printed for the first time in 1593 (Q1) by Richard Field, one of the best printers of the period. Only a single copy of this edition (now in the Bodleian Library) has survived. The poem was immensely popular and went through a large number of editions in the sixteenth and seventeenth centuries. In the enumeration of Hyder Rollins (New Variorum edition), they are as follows: Q2 (1594), Q3 (1595?), Q4 (1596), Q5 (1599), Q6 (1599) Q7 (1602?), Q8 (1602), Q9 (1602), Q10 (1617), Q11 (1620), Q12 (1627), Q13 (1630?), Q14 (1630), Q15 (1636), Q16

(1675)—all editions after Q2 being in fact not quartos but octavos.

In view of the apparently authorized nature of the publication of *Venus and Adonis*, and of *Lucrece* in the following year by the same printer, each with a formal dedication to the Earl of Southampton, there is every reason to postulate author's manuscript as the basis of the Q1 text; and many critics have felt that there is a strong probability that Shakespeare himself, day by day, superintended the proofreading in Field's printing house. At any rate, Q1 is printed with exceptional care, only two substantive readings (ll. 1031, 1054) requiring emendation. These readings, both of which occur on the inner forme of sheet G, probably represent carelessness in Shakespeare's manuscript rather than compositor's errors, but it is possible that if other copies of Q1 had survived, they might show a corrected state of G inner. Indeed, the Q2 corrections of some of the few punctuation and literal errors in Q1 may actually have originated in corrected states of Q1. The Q1 text affords no especially characteristic Shakespearean spellings.

For further information, see: H. E. Rollins, ed., New Variorum *Poems* (Philadelphia, 1938); F. T. Prince, ed., New Arden *Poems* (London, 1960); J. C. Maxwell, ed., New Shakespeare *Poems* (Cambridge, 1966); Stanley Wells, Gary Taylor, et al., *William Shakespeare: A Textual Companion* (Oxford, 1987); John Roe, ed., New Cambridge *Poems* (Cambridge, 1992).

TEXTUAL NOTES

Motto: Vilia . . . aqua.] *from Q1 title-page*
6 bold-fac'd] *hyphen, Q11*
8 field's] *Capell MS;* fields *Q1*
11 Nature,] *Gildon;* Nature *Q1*
25 seizeth] *Q5;* ceazeth *Q1*
28 good.] *Q4* (good:); good, *Q1*
51 hairs] *Q14;* heares *Q1 (again in ll. 147, 191)*
58 prey] *Q7;* pray *Q1 (throughout)*
76 ashy-pale] *hyphen, Malone*
103 hung] *Q4;* hong *Q1*
115–6 mine— . . . red—] *Dyce (after Lintott);* mine, . . . red, *Q1*
138 dost] *Q6;* doest *Q1*
158 seize] *Q5;* ceaze *Q1*
173 dost] *Q5;* doest *Q1*
185 Souring] *Q2* (Sowring); So wring *Q1*
193 shines but] *Altered to* shineth but *in an apparently contemporary hand in the unique copy of Q1*
198 earthly] *The same hand as in line 193 inserts* this *before* earthly
208 Speak,] *Q7;* Speake *Q1*
213 Statuë] *ed.;* Statüe *Q1*
231 deer] *Q5;* deare *Q1*
235 Within] *Q2;* Witin *Q1*
239 deer] *Q6;* deare *Q1*
271 up-prick'd] *hyphen, Gildon*
290 limning] *Q16;* limming *Q1*
290 well-proportioned] *hyphen, Staunton*
295 Round-hoof'd] *hyphen, Gildon*
301 and] *Q2;* aud *Q1*
324 Outstripping] *Q6;* Out stripping *Q1*
343 was,] *Capell MS;* was *Q1*
343 view] *Q5,* view, *Q1*
354 new-fall'n] *hyphen, Q11*
366 a-billing] *hyphen, Bell*
393 But] *Q2;* Bnt *Q1*
406 thee.] *Q6;* thee *Q1*
430 bearing:] *State Poems;* bearing, *Q1*
432 Ears'] *Prince;* Eares *Q1*
448 double-lock] *hyphen, State Poems*
472 Fair fall] *Q11;* Faire-fall *Q1*
476 fingers,] *Q2;* fingers. *Q1*
490 brow's] *Collier;* browes *Q1*
503 eyes,] *Q6;* eyes *Q1*
554 blindfold] *Q9* (blind-fold); blind fold *Q1*
599 Tantalus'] *Malone;* Tantalus *Q1*
610 Love] *State Poems;* loue *Q1*
620 bristly] *Q6;* brisly *Q1*
621 fret,] *Q5;* fret *Q1*
638 nought] *Q9;* nanght *Q1;* naught *Q2*
645 downright] *Lintott;* downe right *Q1*
646 dost] *Q5;* doest *Q1*
678 well-breath'd] *hyphen, Q9*
695 mouths] *Q5;* mouth's *Q1*
724 true men] *Boswell;* true-men *Q1*
748 th' impartial] *Q2;* the th'impartiall *Q1*
749 thaw'd] *Q4;* thawed *Q1*
754 sons] *Q2;* suns *Q1*
758 posterity] *Capell MS;* posteritie. *Q1*
774 you] *Q5;* you, *Q1*
777 mermaids'] *ed.;* Marmaids *Q1*
789 device] *Q10;* deuise *Q1*
823 amaz'd] *Q3;* amas'd *Q1*
825 night-wand'rers] *hyphen, Q11*
834 so.] *Q2;* so, *Q1*
837 young men] *Q2;* yong-men *Q1*
840 choir] *Gildon;* quier *Q1*
864 dost] *Q5;* doest *Q1*
876 brake.] *Q2;* brake, *Q1*
888 court'sy] *Q12;* curt'sie *Q1*
900 boar,] *Globe;* boare. *Q1*
919 ill-resounding] *hyphen, Q12*
924 scratch'd ears] *Q7;* scratcht-eares *Q1*
925 how] *Q3;* how, *Q1*
931 Hard-favor'd] *hyphen, Q10* (Hard-fauoured)
933 earth's worm] *Q3* (earths worme); earths-worme *Q1*
933 mean] *Q6;* meane? *Q1*
940 dost] *Q5;* doest *Q1*
973 this,] *Q6;* this *Q1*
980 eye,] *Q12;* eye: *Q1*
984 drunken] *Q3;* dronken *Q1*
985 hard-believing] *hyphen, Q9*
993 naught] *Q7;* nought *Q1*
1013 stories] *Malone;* stories, *Q1*
1031 as] *Q3;* are *Q1*
1035 And there,] *Q16;* And, there *Q1*
1038 head,] *Malone;* head. *Q1*
1050 eyes,] *Q5;* eies. *Q1*
1054 was] *Q7;* had *Q1*
1068 troubled.] *Q2;* troubled *Q1*
1073 lead,] *Capell MS;* lead *Q1*
1101 by,] *Q3;* by *Q1*
1132 robb'd] *Murden;* robd *Q1*
1168 sprung] *Q2;* sproong *Q1*
1171 new-sprung] *Q10;* new-sprong *Q1*
1178 sweet-smelling] *hyphen, Q10*
1194] *This line followed by* FINIS *in Q1*

The Rape of Lucrece

Thirteen months after *Venus and Adonis*, on May 9, 1594, "a book intituled *the Ravyshement of Lucrece*" was entered on the Stationers' Register. The quarto that soon followed bears the title *Lucrece* on its title-page, but the heading immediately preceding the poem, as well as the running-title throughout, is *The Rape of Lucrece*. Whether the title-page reflects Shakespeare's final choice is of course impossible to say. Like its predecessor, the poem was printed by Richard Field (though this time for another publisher, John Harrison, to whom Field now also transferred *Venus and Adonis*) and is dedicated to the Earl of Southampton. It is obviously the "graver labor" promised by Shakespeare to Southampton if his first poem proved acceptable. That the poem, and its author, had found favor with the Earl seems evident from the much more intimate tone of the second dedication; as Tucker Brooke said, "There is no other Elizabethan dedication like this."

Lucrece is indeed a graver labor; it celebrates a heroine of chastity rather than the amorous advances of the Queen of Love to a bashful country sportsman. As Gabriel Harvey, Spenser's friend, remarked in a marginal note, sometime later, "The younger sort takes much delight in Shakespeare's *Venus and Adonis*, but his *Lucrece*, and his tragedy of *Hamlet, Prince of Denmark*, have it in them to please the wiser sort."

Lucrece proved to be popular; it went through at least six editions in Shakespeare's lifetime. The poem belongs to a genre that was very much in vogue in the 'nineties, both with poets and readers. In 1592 Samuel Daniel published as an appendage to his sonnet cycle *Delia* a poem called *The Complaint of Rosamond*, an adaptation of the old complaint poems of the *Mirror for Magistrates* tradition to more modern, and more feminine, tastes. Fair Rosamond, the mistress of Henry II, was poisoned by his jealous queen; the poem is the complaint of her ghost. She attributes her downfall to nature, youth, and beauty, and she appeals for sympathy and for rescue from oblivion.

Shakespeare followed Daniel in choosing the seven-line rhyme royal or *Troilus* stanza for his complaint poem; it was the verse form recommended in the critical treatises for tragic matters, complaints, and testaments. Some similarities in phrasing make clear that Shakespeare had read and been influenced by Daniel's poem. But he abandoned the old form of the complaining ghost because he wanted to make the poem more dramatic.

Taking the plot from Livy's history of Rome and Ovid's *Fasti* (and perhaps from English versions in Chaucer's *Legend of Good Women* and William Painter's *Palace of Pleasure*), he plunged into the middle of the story with a scene of action. The preceding events are narrated in the Argument. The two protagonists are not complex characters; they are saint and devil, the embodiments of good and evil found in the old morality plays. In the confrontation between them Shakespeare employs all the rhetoric at his command, making the debate into a kind of dramatic dialogue. The subsequent declamations of Lucrece display the kind of rhetorical extravagance which Kyd and Marlowe had made popular on the stage and which Shakespeare had found useful for his lamenting queens in *Richard III* and would employ again in Constance's speeches in *King John*.

There are some anticipations of *Lucrece* in the earlier *Venus and Adonis*. One of Adonis' speeches seems to catch the imagery which will later pervade the graver labor:

Call it not love, for Love to heaven is fled,
Since sweating Lust on earth usurp'd his name,
Under whose simple semblance he hath fed
Upon fresh beauty, blotting it with blame;
Which the hot tyrant stains, and soon bereaves,
As caterpillars do the tender leaves. (793–98)

Moreover, the peculiar image used to describe Venus' lust, the "vulture thought" of line 551, becomes in Tarquin "his vulture folly, / A swallowing gulf that even in plenty wanteth" (lines 556–57). The imagery in *Lucrece* is more elaborate and insistent than that in *Venus and Adonis*. The figures range from conventional similes, like the comparison of sexual appetite to fire hidden in embers, to the bizarre image in

Even so his sighs, his sorrows, make a saw,
To push grief on, and back the same grief draw.
(1672–73)

Some of them are simple and merely decorative, but others are quite fully developed and begin to show those traits which mark Shakespeare's dramatic (as opposed to merely poetic) imagery, so often thought to be the product of his work on the great tragedies. The conceit of Lucrece's breasts as "maiden" worlds, subject only to their proper lord (lines 407–8), develops into the picture of a "maiden" castle under siege in lines 428–41, 463–83. The identification of Lucrece with Philomela the nightingale is obvious enough, since both were ravished, but Shakespeare's four stanzas (lines 1121–48) create a rather complex symbol of birds and music.

The most expanded and elaborate conceit is the digression of some two hundred lines on the siege of Troy (lines 1366–1568). A passage of this sort is a convention in the complaint form: Daniel's Rosamond also examines a work of art, in this instance a casket. Shakespeare's description is minute, with careful attention to pictorial details and to matters of artistic technique, though for all his care the commentators are still arguing about whether the obviously very large picture is a tapestry or a painting. The justification of the digression is that some time should elapse in order to allow the messenger to get to Ardea and Collatine to return home; it is a need that would be especially apparent to a playwright. But the identification of grief with Hecuba, queen of Troy, remained in Shakespeare's mind and he used it again in the play brought to court by the travelling actors in *Hamlet*.

The atmosphere of the night of Tarquin's crime also powerfully occupied Shakespeare's imagination:

Now stole upon the time the dead of night,
When heavy sleep had clos'd up mortal eyes;
No comfortable star did lend his light,
No noise but owls' and wolves' death-boding cries;
Now serves the season that they may surprise
The silly lambs: pure thoughts are dead and still,
While lust and murder wakes to stain and kill.
(162–68)

About a decade later he evoked some of the same images to accompany a Scottish murderer on his way to the bedroom of a king:

Now o'er the one half world
Nature seems dead, and wicked dreams abuse
The curtain'd sleep; witchcraft celebrates
Pale Hecat's off'rings; and wither'd Murther,
Alarum'd by his sentinel, the wolf,
Whose howl's his watch, thus with his stealthy pace,
With Tarquin's ravishing strides, towards his design
Moves like a ghost. (*Macbeth*, II.i.49–56)

Lucrece is interesting for its exploitation of the possibilities of a currently popular type, the complaint poem, and especially for Shakespeare's rhetorical and declamatory passages, so evocative of the stage. But the poem is also valuable as a precursor of Shakespeare's mature tragedies, not only with respect to his imagery, but also in his conception of honor, his handling of the tragic dilemma of the protagonist, and his portrayal of evil.

Hallett Smith

The Rape of Lucrece

TO THE RIGHT HONOVRABLE, HENRY WRIOTHESLEY,

EARLE OF SOUTHHAMPTON, AND BARON OF TITCHFIELD.

The loue I dedicate to your Lordship is without end: wherof this Pamphlet without beginning is but a superfluous Moity. The warrant I haue of your Honourable disposition, not the worth of my vntutord Lines makes it assured of acceptance. What I haue done is yours, what I haue to doe is yours, being part in all I haue, deuoted yours. Were my worth greater, my duety would shew greater, meane time, as it is, it is bound to your Lordship; To whom I wish long life still lengthned with all happinesse.

Your Lordships in all duety.
William Shakespeare.

THE ARGUMENT

Lucius Tarquinius (for his excessive pride surnamed Superbus), after he had caused his own father-in-law Servius Tullius to be cruelly murd'red, and contrary to the Roman laws and customs, not requiring or staying for the people's suffrages, had possessed himself of the kingdom, went, accompanied with his sons and other noblemen of Rome, to besiege Ardea; during which siege, the principal men of the army meeting one evening at the tent of Sextus Tarquinius, the King's son, in their discourses after supper every one commended the virtues of his own wife; among whom Collatinus extolled the incomparable chastity of his wife Lucretia. In that pleasant humor they all posted to Rome, and intending by their secret and sudden arrival to make trial of that which every one had before avouched, only Collatinus finds his wife (though it were late in the night) spinning amongest her maids; the other ladies were all found dancing and revelling, or in several disports; whereupon the noblemen yielded Collatinus the victory, and his wife the fame. At that time Sextus Tarquinius being inflamed with Lucrece' beauty, yet smothering his passions for the present, departed with the rest back to the camp; from whence he shortly after privily withdrew himself, and was (according to his estate) royally entertained and lodged by Lucrece at Collatium. The same night he treacherously stealeth into her chamber, violently ravish'd her, and early in the morning speedeth away. Lucrece, in this lamentable plight, hastily dispatcheth messengers, one to Rome for her father, another to the camp for Collatine. They came, the one accompanied with Junius Brutus, the other with Publius Valerius; and finding Lucrece attired in mourning habit, demanded the cause of her sorrow. She, first taking an oath of them for her revenge, revealed the actor, and whole manner of his dealing, and withal suddenly stabbed herself. Which done, with one consent they all vowed to root out the whole hated family of the Tarquins; and bearing the dead body to Rome, Brutus acquainted the people with the doer and manner of the vile deed; with a bitter invective against the tyranny of the King, wherewith the people were so moved, that with one consent and a general acclamation the Tarquins were all exiled, and the state government changed from kings to consuls.

From the besieged Ardea all in post,
Borne by the trustless wings of false desire,
Lust-breathed Tarquin leaves the Roman host,
And to Collatium bears the lightless fire,
Which in pale embers hid, lurks to aspire,
  And girdle with embracing flames the waist
  Of Collatine's fair love, Lucrece the chaste.

Happ'ly that name of "chaste" unhapp'ly set
This bateless edge on his keen appetite;
When Collatine unwisely did not let
To praise the clear unmatched red and white

Dedication. The original spelling is here retained. **Pamphlet**: short composition. **without beginning.** The poem begins in the middle of the action. **superfluous Moity**: a portion that runs over. **warrant**: assurance.

Argument 4. **requiring**: requesting. 5. **suffrages**: vote of approval. 13. **pleasant humor**: merry state of mind. **posted**: rode swiftly. 19. **disports**: pastimes. 25. **estate**: rank.

1. **post**: haste. 2. **trustless**: treacherous.
3. **Lust-breathed**: inspired by lust.
4. **lightless**: i.e. smouldering unseen. 5. **aspire**: rise.
8. **Happ'ly**: haply, perhaps.
9. **bateless**: not to be blunted.
10. **let**: forbear.

Which triumph'd in that sky of his delight;
 Where mortal stars as bright as heaven's beauties,
 With pure aspects did him peculiar duties.

For he the night before, in Tarquin's tent,
Unlock'd the treasure of his happy state;
What priceless wealth the heavens had him lent
In the possession of his beauteous mate;
Reck'ning his fortune at such high proud rate
 That kings might be espoused to more fame,
 But king nor peer to such a peerless dame.

O happiness enjoy'd but of a few,
And if possess'd, as soon decay'd and done
As is the morning's silver melting dew
Against the golden splendor of the sun!
An expir'd date, cancell'd ere well begun.
 Honor and beauty, in the owner's arms,
 Are weakly fortress'd from a world of harms.

Beauty itself doth of itself persuade
The eyes of men without an orator;
What needeth then apology be made
To set forth that which is so singular?
Or why is Collatine the publisher
 Of that rich jewel he should keep unknown
 From thievish ears because it is his own?

Perchance his boast of Lucrece' sov'reignty
Suggested this proud issue of a king;
For by our ears our hearts oft tainted be;
Perchance that envy of so rich a thing,
Braving compare, disdainfully did sting
 His high-pitch'd thoughts, that meaner men should vaunt
 That golden hap which their superiors want.

But some untimely thought did instigate
His all too timeless speed, if none of those.
His honor, his affairs, his friends, his state,
Neglected all, with swift intent he goes
To quench the coal which in his liver glows.
 O rash false heat, wrapp'd in repentant cold,
 Thy hasty spring still blasts and ne'er grows old!

When at Collatium this false lord arrived,
Well was he welcom'd by the Roman dame,
Within whose face beauty and virtue strived
Which of them both should underprop her fame.
When virtue bragg'd, beauty would blush for shame;
 When beauty boasted blushes, in despite
 Virtue would stain that o'er with silver white.

But beauty, in that white entituled
From Venus' doves, doth challenge that fair field;
Then virtue claims from beauty beauty's red,
Which virtue gave the golden age to gild
Their silver cheeks, and call'd it then their shield,
 Teaching them thus to use it in the fight,
 When shame assail'd, the red should fence the white.

This heraldry in Lucrece' face was seen,
Argued by beauty's red and virtue's white;
Of either's color was the other queen,
Proving from world's minority their right;
Yet their ambition makes them still to fight,
 The sovereignty of either being so great
 That oft they interchange each other's seat.

This silent war of lilies and of roses,
Which Tarquin view'd in her fair face's field,
In their pure ranks his traitor eye encloses,
Where lest between them both it should be kill'd,
The coward captive vanquished doth yield
 To those two armies that would let him go,
 Rather than triumph in so false a foe.

Now thinks he that her husband's shallow tongue,
The niggard prodigal that prais'd her so,
In that high task hath done her beauty wrong,
Which far exceeds his barren skill to show.
Therefore that praise which Collatine doth owe,
 Enchanted Tarquin answers with surmise,
 In silent wonder of still-gazing eyes.

This earthly saint, adored by this devil,
Little suspecteth the false worshipper:
For unstain'd thoughts do seldom dream on evil;
Birds never lim'd no secret bushes fear.
So guiltless she securely gives good cheer
 And reverend welcome to her princely guest,
 Whose inward ill no outward harm express'd.

For that he color'd with his high estate,
Hiding base sin in pleats of majesty;
That nothing in him seem'd inordinate,
Save sometime too much wonder of his eye,
Which having all, all could not satisfy;
 But poorly rich, so wanteth in his store,
 That cloy'd with much, he pineth still for more.

12. sky: i.e. Lucrece's face.
13. mortal stars: i.e. her eyes. **heaven's beauties:** the actual stars.
14. aspects: (1) looks; (2) position and influence (of stars). **peculiar:** exclusive, belonging to him only. **22. of:** by.
23. done: destroyed.
26. date: period of time. The combination of *date* and *cancell'd* reappears at lines 934–35 and 1720. **31. apology:** defense.
32. singular: unique. **33. publisher:** proclaimer.
37. Suggested: tempted. **issue:** son.
40. Braving compare: defying comparison.
42. hap: fortune. **want:** lack.
44. timeless: unseasonable, with a pun on "rapid."
45. state: position.
47. liver. Thought to be the seat of the passions.
49. blasts: withers, fails to grow.
56. stain: dye.
57–58. entituled From: having a claim derived from.
58. field: (1) background in heraldic coats of arms; (2) battlefield.
60. golden age: the age of innocence. **gild.** Gold and red were often considered equivalent in Elizabethan English. For references to blood as golden see *King John*, II.i.316; *Macbeth*, II.ii.56, II.iii.112.
63. fence: defend. **67. from world's minority:** since the time of the world's infancy (the golden age of line 60).
82. owe. Because his praise was less than her due.
83. answers: compensates for. **surmise:** imagination.
88. lim'd: caught by a sticky substance rubbed on branches.
89. securely: without anxiety, suspecting nothing wrong.
90. reverend: revering. **92. color'd:** disguised.
93. pleats: concealing folds. **94. That:** so that.
97. store: plenty.

But she that never cop'd with stranger eyes,
Could pick no meaning from their parling looks,
Nor read the subtle shining secrecies
Writ in the glassy margents of such books.
She touch'd no unknown baits, nor fear'd no hooks,
  Nor could she moralize his wanton sight,
  More than his eyes were open'd to the light.

He stories to her ears her husband's fame,
Won in the fields of fruitful Italy;
And decks with praises Collatine's high name,
Made glorious by his manly chivalry,
With bruised arms and wreaths of victory.
  Her joy with heav'd-up hand she doth express,
  And wordless so greets heaven for his success.

Far from the purpose of his coming thither,
He makes excuses for his being there.
No cloudy show of stormy blust'ring weather
Doth yet in his fair welkin once appear,
Till sable Night, mother of dread and fear,
  Upon the world dim darkness doth display,
  And in her vaulty prison stows the day.

For then is Tarquin brought unto his bed,
Intending weariness with heavy sprite;
For after supper long he questioned
With modest Lucrece, and wore out the night.
Now leaden slumber with live's strength doth fight,
  And every one to rest himself betakes,
  Save thieves, and cares, and troubled minds that wakes.

As one of which doth Tarquin lie revolving
The sundry dangers of his will's obtaining;
Yet ever to obtain his will resolving,
Though weak-built hopes persuade him to abstaining:
Despair to gain doth traffic oft for gaining,
  And when great treasure is the meed proposed,
  Though death be adjunct, there's no death supposed.

Those that much covet are with gain so fond,
That what they have not, that which they possess,
They scatter and unloose it from their bond,
And so by hoping more they have but less,
Or gaining more, the profit of excess
  Is but to surfeit, and such griefs sustain
  That they prove bankrout in this poor rich gain.

The aim of all is but to nurse the life
With honor, wealth, and ease, in waning age;
And in this aim there is such thwarting strife
That one for all, or all for one, we gage:
As life for honor in fell battle's rage,
  Honor for wealth, and oft that wealth doth cost
  The death of all, and all together lost.

So that in vent'ring ill we leave to be
The things we are, for that which we expect;
And this ambitious foul infirmity,
In having much, torments us with defect
Of that we have: so then we do neglect
  The thing we have, and all for want of wit,
  Make something nothing by augmenting it.

Such hazard now must doting Tarquin make,
Pawning his honor to obtain his lust,
And for himself himself he must forsake.
Then where is truth, if there be no self-trust?
When shall he think to find a stranger just,
  When he himself himself confounds, betrays
  To sland'rous tongues and wretched hateful days?

Now stole upon the time the dead of night,
When heavy sleep had clos'd up mortal eyes;
No comfortable star did lend his light,
No noise but owls' and wolves' death-boding cries;
Now serves the season that they may surprise
  The silly lambs: pure thoughts are dead and still,
  While lust and murder wakes to stain and kill.

And now this lustful lord leapt from his bed,
Throwing his mantle rudely o'er his arm,
Is madly toss'd between desire and dread;
Th' one sweetly flatters, th' other feareth harm,
But honest fear, bewitch'd with lust's foul charm,
  Doth too too oft betake him to retire,
  Beaten away by brain-sick rude desire.

His falchion on a flint he softly smiteth,
That from the cold stone sparks of fire do fly,
Whereat a waxen torch forthwith he lighteth,
Which must be lodestar to his lustful eye;
And to the flame thus speaks advisedly:
  "As from this cold flint I enforc'd this fire,
  So Lucrece must I force to my desire."

Here pale with fear he doth premeditate
The dangers of his loathsome enterprise;
And in his inward mind he doth debate
What following sorrow may on this arise.
Then looking scornfully, he doth despise
  His naked armor of still-slaughtered lust,
  And justly thus controls his thoughts unjust:

99. **cop'd with**: encountered. **stranger**: a stranger's.
100. **parling**: speaking, persuading. 102. **margents**: margins.
104. **moralize**: interpret. **sight**: looking.
105. **More than**: more than that. 106. **stories**: tells.
110. **bruised arms**: dented armor. 116. **welkin**: sky.
121. **Intending**: pretending. **heavy**: dull, drowsy. **sprite**: spirit.
122. **questioned**: conversed. 124. **live's**: life's.
126. **wakes**: are wakeful.
128. **will**: (1) volition; (2) sexual desire. 131. **traffic**: bargain.
132. **meed proposed**: reward anticipated.
133. **adjunct**: consequent. **supposed**: thought of.
134. **fond**: infatuated.
135. **what**: for what (?). Some editors emend *That what* to *For what*.
136. **bond**: possession. 140. **bankrout**: bankrupt.

144. **gage**: risk, stake. 145. **fell**: fierce.
150. **this . . . infirmity**: this foul infirmity, ambition.
151. **defect**: supposed deficiency. 155. **doting**: loving excessively.
157. **for . . . forsake**: for the sake of his lustful self he must abandon his honorable self. 158. **no self-trust**: not even truth to oneself.
160. **confounds**: destroys.
164. **comfortable**: comforting. **his**: its.
167. **silly**: innocent. 168. **stain**: taint, defile.
174. **too too oft**: very frequently. **him**: himself. **retire**: fall back.
176. **falchion**: scimitar, curved sword.
179. **lodestar**: guiding star. 180. **advisedly**: deliberately.
188. **His . . . lust**: his useless (*naked* = unarmed) armor against fear—his lust—which is continually (*still*) slaughtered by its own fulfillment. 189. **controls**: attempts to check, reproves.

"Fair torch, burn out thy light, and lend it not
To darken her whose light excelleth thine;
And die, unhallowed thoughts, before you blot
With your uncleanness that which is divine;
Offer pure incense to so pure a shrine:
Let fair humanity abhor the deed
That spots and stains love's modest snow-white weed.

"O shame to knighthood, and to shining arms!
O foul dishonor to my household's grave!
O impious act including all foul harms!
A martial man to be soft fancy's slave!
True valor still a true respect should have;
Then my digression is so vile, so base,
That it will live engraven in my face.

"Yea, though I die, the scandal will survive,
And be an eye-sore in my golden coat;
Some loathsome dash the herald will contrive,
To cipher me how fondly I did dote;
That my posterity, sham'd with the note,
Shall curse my bones, and hold it for no sin
To wish that I their father had not been.

"What win I if I gain the thing I seek?
A dream, a breath, a froth of fleeting joy.
Who buys a minute's mirth to wail a week?
Or sells eternity to get a toy?
For one sweet grape who will the vine destroy?
Or what fond beggar, but to touch the crown,
Would with the sceptre straight be strooken down?

"If Collatinus dream of my intent,
Will he not wake, and in a desp'rate rage
Post hither, this vile purpose to prevent?
This siege that hath engirt his marriage,
This blur to youth, this sorrow to the sage,
This dying virtue, this surviving shame,
Whose crime will bear an ever-during blame.

"O, what excuse can my invention make
When thou shalt charge me with so black a deed?
Will not my tongue be mute, my frail joints shake?
Mine eyes forgo their light, my false heart bleed?
The guilt being great, the fear doth still exceed;
And extreme fear can neither fight nor fly,
But coward-like with trembling terror die.

"Had Collatinus kill'd my son or sire,
Or lain in ambush to betray my life,
Or were he not my dear friend, this desire
Might have excuse to work upon his wife,
As in revenge or quittal of such strife;
But as he is my kinsman, my dear friend,
The shame and fault finds no excuse nor end.

"Shameful it is: ay, if the fact be known;
Hateful it is: there is no hate in loving;
I'll beg her love: but she is not her own;
The worst is but denial and reproving.
My will is strong, past reason's weak removing:
Who fears a sentence or an old man's saw
Shall by a painted cloth be kept in awe."

Thus graceless holds he disputation
'Tween frozen conscience and hot burning will,
And with good thoughts makes dispensation,
Urging the worser sense for vantage still;
Which in a moment doth confound and kill
All pure effects, and doth so far proceed
That what is vile shows like a virtuous deed.

Quoth he, "She took me kindly by the hand,
And gaz'd for tidings in my eager eyes,
Fearing some hard news from the warlike band
Where her beloved Collatinus lies.
O how her fear did make her color rise!
First red as roses that on lawn we lay,
Then white as lawn, the roses took away.

"And how her hand, in my hand being lock'd,
Forc'd it to tremble with her loyal fear!
Which strook her sad, and then it faster rock'd,
Until her husband's welfare she did hear;
Whereat she smiled with so sweet a cheer
That had Narcissus seen her as she stood,
Self-love had never drown'd him in the flood.

"Why hunt I then for color or excuses?
All orators are dumb when beauty pleadeth,
Poor wretches have remorse in poor abuses,
Love thrives not in the heart that shadows dreadeth,
Affection is my captain, and he leadeth;
And when his gaudy banner is display'd,
The coward fights, and will not be dismay'd.

"Then childish fear avaunt, debating die!
Respect and reason wait on wrinkled age!
My heart shall never countermand mine eye.
Sad pause and deep regard beseems the sage;
My part is youth, and beats these from the stage.
Desire my pilot is, beauty my prize,
Then who fears sinking where such treasure lies?"

As corn o'ergrown by weeds, so heedful fear
Is almost chok'd by unresisted lust.

196. weed: garment (i.e. chastity).
198. my household's grave: the tomb of my ancestors.
200. fancy's: love's.
201. a true respect: a consideration for what true valor is.
202. digression: transgression.
205. golden coat: honored coat of arms.
206. dash: stroke of pen or brush.
207. To . . . dote: to display how foolishly I took leave of my senses.
208. note: stigma, brand. **214. toy:** frivolous trifle.
217. with: by. **straight:** straightway.
221. engirt: surrounded, besieged. **222. blur:** blot.
224. ever-during: everlasting.
236. quittal: requital. **239. fact:** deed, crime.
244. sentence, saw. Both words mean "moral saying."
245. Shall . . . awe: will be intimidated by moralizing scenes or mottoes on a wall hanging. **248. makes dispensation:** dispenses.
251. effects: workings, impulses. **258. lawn:** fine linen.
264. cheer: expression. **267. color:** pretext.
271. Affection: passion. **273. The coward:** i.e. even the coward.
275. Respect: reflection, consideration of consequences (so also *regard* in line 277). **wait on:** attend, accompany.
277. Sad pause: serious deliberation.
279. prize: ship or rich cargo captured at sea. **281. corn:** grain.

Away he steals with open list'ning ear,
Full of foul hope, and full of fond mistrust;
Both which, as servitors to the unjust,
So cross him with their opposite persuasion,
That now he vows a league, and now invasion.

Within his thought her heavenly image sits,
And in the self-same seat sits Collatine.
That eye which looks on her confounds his wits;
That eye which him beholds, as more divine,
Unto a view so false will not incline,
But with a pure appeal seeks to the heart,
Which once corrupted takes the worser part;

And therein heartens up his servile powers,
Who flatt'red by their leader's jocund show,
Stuff up his lust, as minutes fill up hours;
And as their captain, so their pride doth grow,
Paying more slavish tribute than they owe.
By reprobate desire thus madly led,
The Roman lord marcheth to Lucrece' bed.

The locks between her chamber and his will,
Each one by him enforc'd retires his ward;
But as they open they all rate his ill,
Which drives the creeping thief to some regard.
The threshold grates the door to have him heard;
Night-wand'ring weasels shriek to see him there;
They fright him, yet he still pursues his fear.

As each unwilling portal yields him way,
Through little vents and crannies of the place
The wind wars with his torch to make him stay,
And blows the smoke of it into his face,
Extinguishing his conduct in this case;
But his hot heart, which fond desire doth scorch,
Puffs forth another wind that fires the torch.

And being lighted, by the light he spies
Lucretia's glove, wherein her needle sticks.
He takes it from the rushes where it lies,
And griping it, the needle his finger pricks,
As who should say, "This glove to wanton tricks
Is not inur'd; return again in haste,
Thou seest our mistress' ornaments are chaste."

But all these poor forbiddings could not stay him,
He in the worst sense consters their denial:
The doors, the wind, the glove that did delay him,
He takes for accidental things of trial;
Or as those bars which stop the hourly dial,
Who with a ling'ring stay his course doth let,
Till every minute pays the hour his debt.

"So, so," quoth he, "these lets attend the time,
Like little frosts that sometime threat the spring,
To add a more rejoicing to the prime,
And give the sneaped birds more cause to sing.
Pain pays the income of each precious thing:
Huge rocks, high winds, strong pirates, shelves and sands
The merchant fears, ere rich at home he lands."

Now is he come unto the chamber door
That shuts him from the heaven of his thought,
Which with a yielding latch, and with no more,
Hath barr'd him from the blessed thing he sought.
So from himself impiety hath wrought,
That for his prey to pray he doth begin,
As if the heavens should countenance his sin.

But in the midst of his unfruitful prayer,
Having solicited th' eternal power
That his foul thoughts might compass his fair fair,
And they would stand auspicious to the hour,
Even there he starts: quoth he, "I must deflow'r;
The powers to whom I pray abhor this fact,
How can they then assist me in the act?

"Then Love and Fortune be my gods, my guide!
My will is back'd with resolution.
Thoughts are but dreams till their effects be tried,
The blackest sin is clear'd with absolution;
Against love's fire fear's frost hath dissolution.
The eye of heaven is out, and misty night
Covers the shame that follows sweet delight."

This said, his guilty hand pluck'd up the latch,
And with his knee the door he opens wide.
The dove sleeps fast that this night-owl will catch;
Thus treason works ere traitors be espied.
Who sees the lurking serpent steps aside;
But she sound sleeping, fearing no such thing,
Lies at the mercy of his mortal sting.

Into the chamber wickedly he stalks,
And gazeth on her yet unstained bed.
The curtains being close, about he walks,
Rolling his greedy eyeballs in his head.
By their high treason is his heart misled,
Which gives the watch-word to his hand full soon
To draw the cloud that hides the silver moon.

Look as the fair and fiery-pointed sun,
Rushing from forth a cloud, bereaves our sight,

287. **league:** armistice, peace treaty. 293. **seeks:** applies, appeals.
295. **servile powers:** i.e. senses, appetites.
296. **Who:** which. **leader's:** i.e. the heart's.
303. **retires his ward:** withdraws its guard.
304. **rate his ill:** reproach his wickedness (by creaking).
307. **weasels.** Kept in houses to catch rats and mice.
308. **his fear:** the intention that causes him to fear.
313. **conduct:** guide. 318. **rushes:** reeds used as floor covering.
319. **griping:** grasping. **needle.** Pronounced *neeld.*
321. **inur'd:** accustomed. 324. **consters:** construes, interprets.
326. **accidental . . . trial:** mere casual events (not forebodings) that test his determination. 327. **bars . . . dial:** i.e. minute-marks on a clock-face, at which the hand, travelling in jerks, paused slightly. *Bars* plays on "lines" and "impediments."

328. **let:** hinder, interrupt. Cf. *lets* (= hindrances) in line 330.
330. **attend the time:** are natural to the occasion.
332. **more:** greater. **prime:** spring.
333. **sneaped:** nipped with cold.
334. **pays . . . of:** is the price of obtaining. 335. **shelves:** sandbanks.
341. **So . . . wrought:** impiety has brought him so far from his natural self. 346. **fair fair:** virtuous beauty.
347. **they:** i.e. (that) the heavenly powers. 349. **fact:** deed, crime.
356. **out:** put out, extinguished. 365. **stalks:** steals.
367. **close:** closed. 372. **Look:** just. 373. **bereaves:** takes away.

Even so the curtain drawn, his eyes begun
To wink, being blinded with a greater light:
Whether it is that she reflects so bright
That dazzleth them, or else some shame supposed,
But blind they are, and keep themselves enclosed.

O had they in that darksome prison died,
Then had they seen the period of their ill!
Then Collatine again by Lucrece' side
In his clear bed might have reposed still.
But they must ope, this blessed league to kill,
And holy-thoughted Lucrece to their sight
Must sell her joy, her life, her world's delight.

Her lily hand her rosy cheek lies under,
Coz'ning the pillow of a lawful kiss;
Who therefore angry seems to part in sunder,
Swelling on either side to want his bliss;
Between whose hills her head entombed is;
Where like a virtuous monument she lies,
To be admir'd of lewd unhallowed eyes.

Without the bed her other fair hand was,
On the green coverlet, whose perfect white
Show'd like an April daisy on the grass,
With pearly sweat resembling dew of night.
Her eyes like marigolds had sheath'd their light,
And canopied in darkness sweetly lay,
Till they might open to adorn the day.

Her hair like golden threads play'd with her breath—
O modest wantons, wanton modesty!—
Showing life's triumph in the map of death,
And death's dim look in life's mortality.
Each in her sleep themselves so beautify,
As if between them twain there were no strife,
But that life liv'd in death, and death in life.

Her breasts like ivory globes circled with blue,
A pair of maiden worlds unconquered,
Save of their lord no bearing yoke they knew,
And him by oath they truly honored.
These worlds in Tarquin new ambition bred,
Who like a foul usurper went about
From this fair throne to heave the owner out.

What could he see but mightily he noted?
What did he note but strongly he desired?
What he beheld, on that he firmly doted,
And in his will his willful eye he tired.
With more than admiration he admired
Her azure veins, her alablaster skin,
Her coral lips, her snow-white dimpled chin.

As the grim lion fawneth o'er his prey,
Sharp hunger by the conquest satisfied,
So o'er this sleeping soul doth Tarquin stay,
His rage of lust by gazing qualified;
Slak'd, not suppress'd, for standing by her side,
His eye, which late this mutiny restrains,
Unto a greater uproar tempts his veins.

And they like straggling slaves for pillage fighting,
Obdurate vassals fell exploits effecting,
In bloody death and ravishment delighting,
Nor children's tears nor mothers' groans respecting,
Swell in their pride, the onset still expecting.
Anon his beating heart, alarum striking,
Gives the hot charge, and bids them do their liking.

His drumming heart cheers up his burning eye,
His eye commends the leading to his hand;
His hand as proud of such a dignity,
Smoking with pride, march'd on, to make his stand
On her bare breast, the heart of all her land;
Whose ranks of blue veins, as his hand did scale,
Left their round turrets destitute and pale.

They must'ring to the quiet cabinet
Where their dear governess and lady lies,
Do tell her she is dreadfully beset,
And fright her with confusion of their cries.
She much amaz'd breaks ope her lock'd-up eyes,
Who peeping forth this tumult to behold,
Are by his flaming torch dimm'd and controll'd.

Imagine her as one in dead of night
From forth dull sleep by dreadful fancy waking,
That thinks she hath beheld some ghastly sprite,
Whose grim aspect sets every joint a-shaking;
What terror 'tis! but she in worser taking,
From sleep disturbed, heedfully doth view
The sight which makes supposed terror true.

Wrapp'd and confounded in a thousand fears,
Like to a new-kill'd bird she trembling lies;
She dares not look, yet winking there appears
Quick-shifting antics, ugly in her eyes.
Such shadows are the weak brain's forgeries,
Who angry that the eyes fly from their lights,
In darkness daunts them with more dreadful sights.

His hand that yet remains upon her breast
(Rude ram, to batter such an ivory wall!)

375. wink: shut. **380. period:** termination. **382. clear:** pure.
383. league: alliance, union. **387. Coz'ning:** cheating, depriving.
389. to want: at being deprived of.
390. entombed. On ancient tombs the head of the recumbent effigy often rests on a pillow. The image continues in *monument*, line 391.
397. marigolds. Said to "go to bed wi' th' sun" (*The Winter's Tale*, IV.iv.105). **401. wantons:** sportive creatures.
402. map: picture. It was a commonplace that sleep is a picture of death.
408. maiden. This term was applied to a secure castle which will admit its lord but not a foe. It prepares for the extended military conceit in lines 428–41 and again in lines 464–83.
417. will: lust. **tired:** made to feed ravenously (?) or wearied (?).
418. admiration: wonder. **admired:** marvelled at.
419. alablaster: alabaster. **424. qualified:** diluted, moderated.
426. late: lately, a moment before.
427. veins: i.e. passions. **429. fell:** savage, cruel.
432. pride: sexual heat. **still:** constantly, at every moment.
433. alarum: signal for attack. **436. commends:** commits.
438. Smoking: steaming. **442. cabinet:** i.e. the heart.
443. governess: ruler. **448. controll'd:** overpowered.
452. joint: member, limb. **453. taking:** agitation, fright.
458. winking: with eyes closed. **459. antics:** grotesque figures.
464. Rude: rough, violent. **ram:** battering ram.

May feel her heart (poor citizen!) distress'd,
Wounding itself to death, rise up and fall,
Beating her bulk, that his hand shakes withal.
  This moves in him more rage and lesser pity
  To make the breach and enter this sweet city.

First like a trumpet doth his tongue begin
To sound a parley to his heartless foe,
Who o'er the white sheet peers her whiter chin,
The reason of this rash alarm to know,
Which he by dumb demeanor seeks to show;
  But she with vehement prayers urgeth still
  Under what color he commits this ill.

Thus he replies: "The color in thy face,
That even for anger makes the lily pale,
And the red rose blush at her own disgrace,
Shall plead for me and tell my loving tale.
Under that color am I come to scale
  Thy never-conquered fort; the fault is thine,
  For those thine eyes betray thee unto mine.

"Thus I forestall thee, if thou mean to chide,
Thy beauty hath ensnar'd thee to this night,
Where thou with patience must my will abide—
My will that marks thee for my earth's delight,
Which I to conquer sought with all my might;
  But as reproof and reason beat it dead,
  By thy bright beauty was it newly bred.

"I see what crosses my attempt will bring,
I know what thorns the growing rose defends,
I think the honey guarded with a sting:
All this beforehand counsel comprehends.
But Will is deaf and hears no heedful friends;
  Only he hath an eye to gaze on beauty,
  And dotes on what he looks, 'gainst law or duty.

"I have debated, even in my soul,
What wrong, what shame, what sorrow I shall breed,
But nothing can affection's course control,
Or stop the headlong fury of his speed.
I know repentant tears ensue the deed,
  Reproach, disdain, and deadly enmity,
  Yet strive I to embrace mine infamy."

This said, he shakes aloft his Roman blade,
Which like a falcon tow'ring in the skies,
Coucheth the fowl below with his wings' shade,
Whose crooked beak threats, if he mount, he dies:
So under his insulting falchion lies
  Harmless Lucretia, marking what he tells
  With trembling fear, as fowl hear falcons' bells.

"Lucrece," quoth he, "this night I must enjoy thee;
If thou deny, then force must work my way,
For in thy bed I purpose to destroy thee.
That done, some worthless slave of thine I'll slay,
To kill thine honor with thy live's decay;
  And in thy dead arms do I mean to place him,
  Swearing I slew him, seeing thee embrace him.

"So thy surviving husband shall remain
The scornful mark of every open eye;
Thy kinsmen hang their heads at this disdain,
Thy issue blurr'd with nameless bastardy;
And thou, the author of their obloquy,
  Shalt have thy trespass cited up in rhymes,
  And sung by children in succeeding times.

"But if thou yield, I rest thy secret friend:
The fault unknown is as a thought unacted.
A little harm done to a great good end
For lawful policy remains enacted.
The poisonous simple sometime is compacted
  In a pure compound; being so applied,
  His venom in effect is purified.

"Then for thy husband and thy children's sake,
Tender my suit; bequeath not to their lot
The shame that from them no device can take,
The blemish that will never be forgot,
Worse than a slavish wipe, or birth-hour's blot;
  For marks descried in men's nativity
  Are nature's faults, not their own infamy."

Here with a cockatrice' dead-killing eye
He rouseth up himself, and makes a pause;
While she, the picture of pure piety,
Like a white hind under the gripe's sharp claws,
Pleads in a wilderness where are no laws,
  To the rough beast that knows no gentle right,
  Nor aught obeys but his foul appetite.

But when a black-fac'd cloud the world doth threat,
In his dim mist th' aspiring mountains hiding,
From earth's dark womb some gentle gust doth get,
Which blow these pitchy vapors from their biding,
Hind'ring their present fall by this dividing;
  So his unhallowed haste her words delays,
  And moody Pluto winks while Orpheus plays.

Yet, foul night-waking cat, he doth but dally,
While in his hold-fast foot the weak mouse panteth.
Her sad behavior feeds his vulture folly,

467. **bulk**: body. **that**: so that. **withal**: therewith.
469. **make the breach**: break through the fortification.
471. **parley**: trumpet summons to a discussion of terms. **heartless**: lacking courage, frightened. 473. **rash alarm**: sudden attack.
474. **dumb demeanor**: dumb show.
476. **color**: pretext. In line 477 Tarquin quibbles on the meaning "hue," in line 481 on "military banner." 491. **crosses**: troubles.
493. **think the honey**: know the honey is. 497. **looks**: looks on.
503. **disdain**: disgrace, ignominy. 506. **tow'ring**: flying high.
507. **Coucheth**: causes to cower and lie close.
508. **Whose**: i.e. the falcon's. **crooked**: curved. **he**: i.e. the fowl.
509. **insulting**: exulting in conquest.
511. **bells**. Attached to a falcon's legs to help the owner find him.

522. **nameless bastardy**: i.e. the suspicion that they are illegitimate and have no right to Collatine's name.
524. **rhymes**: i.e. broadside ballads, often based upon sensational events or scandals. 526. **rest**: remain.
530. **simple**: drug. **compacted**: combined. 534. **Tender**: regard.
537. **slavish wipe**: slave's brand. **birth-hour's blot**: disfiguring birthmark.
540. **cockatrice**: basilisk, fabled to have the power of killing by its glance.
543. **gripe**: griffin (a fabulous beast, half lion, half eagle) or perhaps vulture or eagle. 549. **get**: make its way. 550. **biding**: place.
551. **present**: immediate. 552. **delays**: delay.
553. **Pluto . . . plays**. Orpheus charmed the ears of Pluto with his music when he went to the underworld to retrieve his wife Eurydice.
winks: sleeps. 556. **folly**: depravity.

A swallowing gulf that even in plenty wanteth.
His ear her prayers admits, but his heart granteth
No penetrable entrance to her plaining:
Tears harden lust, though marble [wear] with raining.

Her pity-pleading eyes are sadly fixed
In the remorseless wrinkles of his face;
Her modest eloquence with sighs is mixed,
Which to her oratory adds more grace.
She puts the period often from his place,
And midst the sentence so her accent breaks,
That twice she doth begin ere once she speaks.

She conjures him by high almighty Jove,
By knighthood, gentry, and sweet friendship's oath,
By her untimely tears, her husband's love,
By holy human law, and common troth,
By heaven and earth, and all the power of both,
That to his borrowed bed he make retire,
And stoop to honor, not to foul desire.

Quoth she, "Reward not hospitality
With such black payment as thou hast pretended;
Mud not the fountain that gave drink to thee,
Mar not the thing that cannot be amended.
End thy ill aim before thy shoot be ended;
He is no woodman that doth bend his bow
To strike a poor unseasonable doe.

"My husband is thy friend, for his sake spare me;
Thyself art mighty, for thine own sake leave me;
Myself a weakling, do not then ensnare me;
Thou look'st not like deceit, do not deceive me.
My sighs like whirlwinds labor hence to heave thee.
If ever man were mov'd with woman's moans,
Be moved with my tears, my sighs, my groans.

"All which together, like a troubled ocean,
Beat at thy rocky and wrack-threat'ning heart,
To soften it with their continual motion;
For stones dissolv'd to water do convert.
O, if no harder than a stone thou art,
Melt at my tears and be compassionate!
Soft pity enters at an iron gate.

"In Tarquin's likeness I did entertain thee;
Hast thou put on his shape to do him shame?
To all the host of heaven I complain me:
Thou wrong'st his honor, wound'st his princely name.
Thou art not what thou seem'st, and if the same,
Thou seem'st not what thou art, a god, a king;
For kings like gods should govern every thing.

"How will thy shame be seeded in thine age
When thus thy vices bud before thy spring?
If in thy hope thou dar'st do such outrage,
What dar'st thou not when once thou art a king?
O, be rememb'red, no outrageous thing
From vassal actors can be wip'd away;
Then kings' misdeeds cannot be hid in clay.

"This deed will make thee only lov'd for fear,
But happy monarchs still are fear'd for love;
With foul offenders thou perforce must bear,
When they in thee the like offenses prove.
If but for fear of this, thy will remove;
For princes are the glass, the school, the book,
Where subjects' eyes do learn, do read, do look.

"And wilt thou be the school where Lust shall learn?
Must he in thee read lectures of such shame?
Wilt thou be glass wherein it shall discern
Authority for sin, warrant for blame,
To privilege dishonor in thy name?
Thou back'st reproach against long-living laud,
And mak'st fair reputation but a bawd.

"Hast thou command? by him that gave it thee,
From a pure heart command thy rebel will;
Draw not thy sword to guard iniquity,
For it was lent thee all that brood to kill.
Thy princely office how canst thou fulfill,
When pattern'd by thy fault foul Sin may say
He learn'd to sin, and thou didst teach the way?

"Think but how vile a spectacle it were
To view thy present trespass in another.
Men's faults do seldom to themselves appear,
Their own transgressions partially they smother:
This guilt would seem death-worthy in thy brother.
O how are they wrapp'd in with infamies
That from their own misdeeds askaunce their eyes!

"To thee, to thee, my heav'd-up hands appeal,
Not to seducing lust, thy rash relier.
I sue for exil'd majesty's repeal,
Let him return, and flatt'ring thoughts retire,
His true respect will prison false desire,
And wipe the dim mist from thy doting eyne,
That thou shalt see thy state, and pity mine."

"Have done," quoth he, "my uncontrolled tide
Turns not, but swells the higher by this let.
Small lights are soon blown out, huge fires abide,
And with the wind in greater fury fret.
The petty streams that pay a daily debt

562. **wrinkles**: i.e. frowns. 564. **oratory**: pleading.
565. **his place**: its proper position in the sentence.
569. **gentry**: gentle birth and breeding. 574. **stoop**: bow, yield.
576. **pretended**: offered, proposed.
579. **shoot be ended**: shot be executed, arrow be discharged.
580. **woodman**: hunter, sportsman. 592. **convert**: change.
603. **seeded**: fruited, matured.
605. **in thy hope**: while you are still heir to the throne.
607. **be rememb'red**: bear in mind.
608. **vassal actors**: i.e. kings' subjects who perpetrate outrages.
609. **in clay**: i.e. even after death. 615. **glass**: mirror.
622. **back'st**: supportest. **laud**: praise.
634. **partially**: with partiality toward themselves.
637. **askaunce**: avert.
639. **thy rash relier**: which you rashly rely on.
640. **repeal**: recall.
642. **respect**: consideration, judgment. **prison**: imprison, put restraints on.
643. **eyne**: eyes (old plural, already archaic in Shakespeare's day).
648. **fret**: rage.

To their salt sovereign, with their fresh falls' haste
  Add to his flow, but alter not his taste."

"Thou art," quoth she, "a sea, a sovereign king,
And lo there falls into thy boundless flood
Black lust, dishonor, shame, misgoverning,
Who seek to stain the ocean of thy blood.
If all these petty ills shall change thy good,
  Thy sea within a puddle's womb is hearsed,
  And not the puddle in thy sea dispersed.

"So shall these slaves be king, and thou their slave;
Thou nobly base, they basely dignified;
Thou their fair life, and they thy fouler grave;
Thou loathed in their shame, they in thy pride.
The lesser thing should not the greater hide:
  The cedar stoops not to the base shrub's foot,
  But low shrubs wither at the cedar's root.

"So let thy thoughts, low vassals to thy state"—
"No more," quoth he, "by heaven, I will not hear thee.
Yield to my love, if not, enforced hate,
In stead of love's coy touch, shall rudely tear thee;
That done, despitefully I mean to bear thee
  Unto the base bed of some rascal groom,
  To be thy partner in this shameful doom."

This said, he sets his foot upon the light,
For light and lust are deadly enemies;
Shame folded up in blind concealing night,
When most unseen, then most doth tyrannize.
The wolf hath seiz'd his prey, the poor lamb cries,
  Till with her own white fleece her voice controll'd
  Entombs her outcry in her lips' sweet fold.

For with the nightly linen that she wears
He pens her piteous clamors in her head,
Cooling his hot face in the chastest tears
That ever modest eyes with sorrow shed.
O that prone lust should stain so pure a bed!
  The spots whereof could weeping purify,
  Her tears should drop on them perpetually.

But she hath lost a dearer thing than life,
And he hath won what he would lose again;
This forced league doth force a further strife,
This momentary joy breeds months of pain,
This hot desire converts to cold disdain;
  Pure Chastity is rifled of her store,
  And Lust, the thief, far poorer than before.

Look as the full-fed hound or gorged hawk,
Unapt for tender smell, or speedy flight,
Make slow pursuit, or altogether balk
The prey wherein by nature they delight,
So surfeit-taking Tarquin fares this night:
  His taste delicious, in digestion souring,
  Devours his will, that liv'd by foul devouring.

657. hearsed: entombed. **669. coy:** gentle.
671. rascal groom: baseborn servant. **684. prone:** eager.
685. could weeping: if weeping could. **689. league:** peace treaty.
692. store: possessions. **695. tender:** sensitive.
696. balk: turn aside from.

O, deeper sin than bottomless conceit
Can comprehend in still imagination!
Drunken Desire must vomit his receipt
Ere he can see his own abomination.
While Lust is in his pride, no exclamation
  Can curb his heat, or rein his rash desire,
  Till like a jade, Self-will himself doth tire.

And then with lank and lean discolor'd cheek,
With heavy eye, knit brow, and strengthless pace,
Feeble Desire, all recreant, poor, and meek,
Like to a bankrout beggar wails his case:
The flesh being proud, Desire doth fight with Grace,
  For there it revels, and when that decays,
  The guilty rebel for remission prays.

So fares it with this fault-full lord of Rome,
Who this accomplishment so hotly chased,
For now against himself he sounds this doom,
That through the length of times he stands disgraced;
Besides, his soul's fair temple is defaced,
  To whose weak ruins muster troops of cares,
  To ask the spotted princess how she fares.

She says her subjects with foul insurrection
Have batter'd down her consecrated wall,
And by their mortal fault brought in subjection
Her immortality, and made her thrall
To living death and pain perpetual;
  Which in her prescience she controlled still,
  But her foresight could not forestall their will.

Ev'n in this thought through the dark night he stealeth,
A captive victor that hath lost in gain,
Bearing away the wound that nothing healeth,
The scar that will despite of cure remain,
Leaving his spoil perplex'd in greater pain.
  She bears the load of lust he left behind,
  And he the burthen of a guilty mind.

He like a thievish dog creeps sadly thence,
She like a wearied lamb lies panting there;
He scowls and hates himself for his offense,
She desperate with her nails her flesh doth tear;
He faintly flies, sweating with guilty fear;
  She stays, exclaiming on the direful night,
  He runs, and chides his vanish'd loath'd delight.

He thence departs a heavy convertite,
She there remains a hopeless castaway;
He in his speed looks for the morning light,

701. conceit: intellectual power.
703. his receipt: what he has swallowed.
705. in his pride: in heat. **exclamation:** protest, reproach.
707. jade: undisciplined horse. **710. recreant:** craven.
713. revels: indulges itself.
716. accomplishment: fulfillment (of his desire).
717. doom: judgment, sentence.
721. spotted princess: i.e. his soul.
722–28. Cf. Sonnet 146. **724. mortal:** deadly.
727. Which: who, i.e. her subjects, the senses. **controlled:** commanded.
733. spoil: prey, victim. **perplex'd:** distraught.
740. faintly: with faint heart.
741. exclaiming on: vehemently reproaching.
743. convertite: penitent.

She prays she never may behold the day:
"For day," quoth she, "night's scapes doth open lay,
And my true eyes have never practic'd how
To cloak offenses with a cunning brow.

"They think not but that every eye can see
The same disgrace which they themselves behold;
And therefore would they still in darkness be,
To have their unseen sin remain untold;
For they their guilt with weeping will unfold,
And grave, like water that doth eat in steel,
Upon my cheeks what helpless shame I feel."

Here she exclaims against repose and rest,
And bids her eyes hereafter still be blind;
She wakes her heart by beating on her breast,
And bids it leap from thence, where it may find
Some purer chest to close so pure a mind.
Frantic with grief thus breathes she forth her spite
Against the unseen secrecy of night:

"O comfort-killing Night, image of hell,
Dim register and notary of shame,
Black stage for tragedies and murthers fell,
Vast sin-concealing chaos, nurse of blame!
Blind muffled bawd, dark harbor for defame,
Grim cave of death, whisp'ring conspirator
With close-tongu'd treason and the ravisher!

"O hateful, vaporous, and foggy Night,
Since thou art guilty of my cureless crime,
Muster thy mists to meet the eastern light,
Make war against proportion'd course of time;
Or if thou wilt permit the sun to climb
His wonted height, yet ere he go to bed,
Knit poisonous clouds about his golden head.

"With rotten damps ravish the morning air;
Let their exhal'd unwholesome breaths make sick
The life of purity, the supreme fair,
Ere he arrive his weary noontide prick,
And let thy musty vapors march so thick
That in their smoky ranks his smoth'red light
May set at noon, and make perpetual night.

"Were Tarquin Night, as he is but Night's child,
The silver-shining queen he would distain;
Her twinkling handmaids too (by him defil'd)
Through Night's black bosom should not peep again.
So should I have co-partners in my pain,
And fellowship in woe doth woe assuage,
As palmers' chat makes short their pilgrimage.

"Where now I have no one to blush with me,
To cross their arms and hang their heads with mine,
To mask their brows and hide their infamy,
But I alone, alone must sit and pine,
Seasoning the earth with show'rs of silver brine,
Mingling my talk with tears, my grief with groans,
Poor wasting monuments of lasting moans.

"O Night, thou furnace of foul reeking smoke!
Let not the jealous Day behold that face,
Which underneath thy black all-hiding cloak
Immodestly lies martyr'd with disgrace.
Keep still possession of thy gloomy place,
That all the faults which in thy reign are made
May likewise be sepulcher'd in thy shade.

"Make me not object to the tell-tale Day:
The light will show, character'd in my brow,
The story of sweet chastity's decay,
The impious breach of holy wedlock vow;
Yea, the illiterate that know not how
To cipher what is writ in learned books,
Will cote my loathsome trespass in my looks.

"The nurse to still her child will tell my story,
And fright her crying babe with Tarquin's name;
The orator to deck his oratory
Will couple my reproach to Tarquin's shame;
Feast-finding minstrels, tuning my defame,
Will tie the hearers to attend each line,
How Tarquin wronged me, I Collatine.

"Let my good name, that senseless reputation,
For Collatine's dear love be kept unspotted:
If that be made a theme for disputation,
The branches of another root are rotted,
And undeserv'd reproach to him allotted,
That is as clear from this attaint of mine
As I ere this was pure to Collatine.

"O unseen shame, invisible disgrace!
O unfelt sore, crest-wounding private scar!
Reproach is stamp'd in Collatinus' face,
And Tarquin's eye may read the mot afar,
How he in peace is wounded, not in war.
Alas, how many bear such shameful blows,
Which not themselves but he that gives them knows!

"If, Collatine, thine honor lay in me,
From me by strong assault it is bereft:
My honey lost, and I, a drone-like bee,
Have no perfection of my summer left,
But robb'd and ransack'd by injurious theft.
In thy weak hive a wand'ring wasp hath crept,
And suck'd the honey which thy chaste bee kept.

747. scapes: transgressions, i.e. sexual offenses.
752. still: forever. **754. unfold:** reveal, betray.
755. grave: engrave. **water:** aqua fortis, acid.
761. close: enclose. **762. spite:** grievance. **768. defame:** infamy.
774. proportion'd: i.e. with its ordered relationship between day and night. **780. life:** essence. **supreme fair:** i.e. the sun.
781. prick: mark on a clock face. **786. distain:** defile.
791. palmers': pilgrims'. **792. Where:** whereas.
793. cross their arms. Folded arms signalized melancholy; so did a hat pulled low over the forehead (see line 794).

800. jealous: suspicious, spying out faults.
804. in . . . made: are committed at night.
806. object: i.e. visible; literally, a thing perceived.
807. character'd: written. **808. decay:** ruin.
811. cipher: decipher. **812. cote:** notice, observe.
817. Feast-finding: seeking out feasts at which to perform.
820. senseless: unfelt, intangible.
828. crest-wounding: injuring one's coat of arms, therefore one's honor. The crest is the device above the shield. **830. mot:** motto.

"Yet am I guilty of thy honor's wrack,
Yet for thy honor did I entertain him;
Coming from thee, I could not put him back,
For it had been dishonor to disdain him.
Besides, of weariness he did complain him,
And talk'd of virtue: O unlook'd-for evil,
When virtue is profan'd in such a devil!

"Why should the worm intrude the maiden bud?
Or hateful cuckoos hatch in sparrows' nests?
Or toads infect fair founts with venom mud?
Or tyrant folly lurk in gentle breasts?
Or kings be breakers of their own behests?
But no perfection is so absolute,
That some impurity doth not pollute.

"The aged man that coffers up his gold
Is plagu'd with cramps and gouts and painful fits,
And scarce hath eyes his treasure to behold,
But like still-pining Tantalus he sits,
And useless barns the harvest of his wits;
Having no other pleasure of his gain
But torment that it cannot cure his pain.

"So then he hath it when he cannot use it,
And leaves it to be mast'red by his young,
Who in their pride do presently abuse it;
Their father was too weak, and they too strong,
To hold their cursed-blessed fortune long.
The sweets we wish for turn to loathed sours
Even in the moment that we call them ours.

"Unruly blasts wait on the tender spring,
Unwholesome weeds take root with precious flow'rs,
The adder hisses where the sweet birds sing,
What virtue breeds iniquity devours:
We have no good that we can say is ours,
But ill-annexed Opportunity
Or kills his life or else his quality.

"O Opportunity, thy guilt is great!
'Tis thou that execut'st the traitor's treason;
Thou sets the wolf where he the lamb may get;
Whoever plots the sin, thou 'point'st the season;
'Tis thou that spurn'st at right, at law, at reason,
And in thy shady cell, where none may spy him,
Sits Sin, to seize the souls that wander by him.

"Thou makest the vestal violate her oath,
Thou blowest the fire when temperance is thaw'd,
Thou smother'st honesty, thou murth'rest troth,
Thou foul abettor, thou notorious bawd,
Thou plantest scandal, and displacest laud.
Thou ravisher, thou traitor, thou false thief,
Thy honey turns to gall, thy joy to grief.

"Thy secret pleasure turns to open shame,
Thy private feasting to a public fast,
Thy smoothing titles to a ragged name,
Thy sug'red tongue to bitter wormwood taste;
Thy violent vanities can never last.
How comes it then, vile Opportunity,
Being so bad, such numbers seek for thee?

"When wilt thou be the humble suppliant's friend,
And bring him where his suit may be obtained?
When wilt thou sort an hour great strifes to end?
Or free that soul which wretchedness hath chained?
Give physic to the sick, ease to the pained?
The poor, lame, blind, halt, creep, cry-out for thee,
But they ne'er meet with Opportunity.

"The patient dies while the physician sleeps,
The orphan pines while the oppressor feeds,
Justice is feasting while the widow weeps,
Advice is sporting while infection breeds.
Thou grant'st no time for charitable deeds.
Wrath, envy, treason, rape, and murther's rages,
Thy heinous hours wait on them as their pages.

"When Truth and Virtue have to do with thee,
A thousand crosses keep them from thy aid:
They buy thy help, but Sin ne'er gives a fee,
He gratis comes, and thou art well apaid,
As well to hear as grant what he hath said.
My Collatine would else have come to me
When Tarquin did, but he was stay'd by thee.

"Guilty thou art of murther and of theft,
Guilty of perjury and subornation,
Guilty of treason, forgery, and shift,
Guilty of incest, that abomination;
An accessary by thine inclination
To all sins past and all that are to come,
From the creation to the general doom.

"Misshapen Time, copesmate of ugly Night,
Swift subtle post, carrier of grisly care,
Eater of youth, false slave to false delight,
Base watch of woes, sin's pack-horse, virtue's snare!
Thou nursest all, and murth'rest all that are.
O, hear me then, injurious shifting Time,
Be guilty of my death, since of my crime.

"Why hath thy servant Opportunity
Betray'd the hours thou gav'st me to repose?
Cancell'd my fortunes, and enchained me
To endless date of never-ending woes?
Time's office is to fine the hate of foes,

851. **tyrant folly:** cruel depravity. 853. **absolute:** complete.
858. **still-pining:** always starving. Tantalus was punished in the underworld by the sight of food and drink which eternally eluded his grasp. 859. **barns:** stores up. 864. **presently:** at once.
874. **ill-annexed:** joined to it with evil consequences. **Opportunity:** occasion offered by chance.
875. **Or:** either. **his:** its, i.e. good's. **quality:** nature.
879. **'point'st:** appointest. 884. **temperance:** self-control.
885. **honesty:** chastity. **troth:** fidelity.
892. **smoothing:** flattering. **ragged:** in tatters; i.e. disgraced.
899. **sort:** arrange, select. 905. **pines:** starves.
907. **Advice:** medical counsel. The reference is to the plague.
912. **crosses:** hindrances. 914. **apaid:** satisfied.
919. **subornation:** the crime of inducing another to commit a crime.
920. **shift:** wicked device. 925. **copesmate:** companion.
926. **subtle post:** crafty messenger. **carrier:** deliveryman. **grisly:** grim, terrible.
928. **watch of woes:** i.e. one who announces woes as regularly as watchmen cry the hours. 935. **date:** duration, term.
936. **fine:** end.

To eat up errors by opinion bred,
Not spend the dowry of a lawful bed.

"Time's glory is to calm contending kings,
To unmask falsehood, and bring truth to light,
To stamp the seal of time in aged things,
To wake the morn, and sentinel the night,
To wrong the wronger till he render right,
To ruinate proud buildings with thy hours,
And smear with dust their glitt'ring golden tow'rs;

"To fill with worm-holes stately monuments,
To feed oblivion with decay of things,
To blot old books, and alter their contents,
To pluck the quills from ancient ravens' wings,
To dry the old oak's sap, and cherish springs,
To spoil antiquities of hammer'd steel,
And turn the giddy round of Fortune's wheel;

"To show the beldame daughters of her daughter,
To make the child a man, the man a child,
To slay the tiger that doth live by slaughter,
To tame the unicorn and lion wild,
To mock the subtle in themselves beguil'd,
To cheer the ploughman with increaseful crops,
And waste huge stones with little water-drops.

"Why work'st thou mischief in thy pilgrimage,
Unless thou couldst return to make amends?
One poor retiring minute in an age
Would purchase thee a thousand thousand friends,
Lending him wit that to bad debtors lends:
O this dread night, wouldst thou one hour come back,
I could prevent this storm, and shun thy wrack!

"Thou ceaseless lackey to eternity,
With some mischance cross Tarquin in his flight.
Devise extremes beyond extremity,
To make him curse this cursed crimeful night.
Let ghastly shadows his lewd eyes affright,
And the dire thought of his committed evil
Shape every bush a hideous shapeless devil.

"Disturb his hours of rest with restless trances,
Afflict him in his bed with bedred groans;
Let there bechance him pitiful mischances
To make him moan, but pity not his moans;
Stone him with hard'ned hearts harder than stones,
And let mild women to him lose their mildness,
Wilder to him than tigers in their wildness.

"Let him have time to tear his curled hair,
Let him have time against himself to rave,
Let him have time of Time's help to despair,
Let him have time to live a loathed slave,
Let him have time a beggar's orts to crave,
And time to see one that by alms doth live
Disdain to him disdained scraps to give.

"Let him have time to see his friends his foes,
And merry fools to mock at him resort;
Let him have time to mark how slow time goes
In time of sorrow, and how swift and short
His time of folly and his time of sport;
And ever let his unrecalling crime
Have time to wail th' abusing of his time.

"O Time, thou tutor both to good and bad,
Teach me to curse him that thou taught'st this ill.
At his own shadow let the thief run mad,
Himself himself seek every hour to kill.
Such wretched hands such wretched blood should spill;
For who so base would such an office have
As sland'rous deathsman to so base a slave?

"The baser is he, coming from a king,
To shame his hope with deeds degenerate;
The mightier man, the mightier is the thing
That makes him honor'd, or begets him hate;
For greatest scandal waits on greatest state.
The moon being clouded presently is miss'd,
But little stars may hide them when they list.

"The crow may bathe his coal-black wings in mire,
And unperceiv'd fly with the filth away,
But if the like the snow-white swan desire,
The stain upon his silver down will stay.
Poor grooms are sightless night, kings glorious day;
Gnats are unnoted wheresoe'er they fly,
But eagles gaz'd upon with every eye.

"Out, idle words, servants to shallow fools,
Unprofitable sounds, weak arbitrators!
Busy yourselves in skill-contending schools,
Debate where leisure serves with dull debaters;
To trembling clients be you mediators.
For me, I force not argument a straw,
Since that my case is past the help of law.

"In vain I rail at Opportunity,
At Time, at Tarquin, and uncheerful Night,
In vain I cavil with mine infamy,
In vain I spurn at my confirm'd despite:
This helpless smoke of words doth me no right.
The remedy indeed to do me good
Is to let forth my foul defiled blood.

"Poor hand, why quiver'st thou at this decree?
Honor thyself to rid me of this shame,

937. opinion: popular belief. **938. spend:** dissipate.
948. blot: erase, destroy.
949. ravens. Traditionally long-lived.
950. springs: young shoots. **953. beldame:** old woman.
957. the subtle . . . beguil'd: the crafty who fall victim to their own schemes. **962. retiring:** returning. **974. trances:** fits.
975. bedred: bedridden.

985. orts: scraps of food. **993. unrecalling:** unrecallable.
1001. sland'rous deathsman: despicable executioner.
1007. presently: at once.
1013. sightless: rendering everything invisible.
1018. in . . . schools: i.e. among those who argue to exhibit their verbal skill.
1020. clients: those who have hired advocates to plead their cases in court. **1021. force:** value.
1024. uncheerful: cheerless, dismal. **1027. helpless:** yielding no help.
1031. to rid: by ridding.

For if I die, my honor lives in thee,
But if I live, thou liv'st in my defame.
Since thou couldst not defend thy loyal dame,
And wast afeard to scratch her wicked foe,
Kill both thyself and her for yielding so."

This said, from her betumbled couch she starteth,
To find some desp'rate instrument of death,
But this no slaughter-house no tool imparteth,
To make more vent for passage of her breath,
Which thronging through her lips, so vanisheth
As smoke from Aetna, that in air consumes,
Or that which from discharged cannon fumes.

"In vain," quoth she, "I live, and seek in vain
Some happy mean to end a hapless life.
I fear'd by Tarquin's falchion to be slain,
Yet for the self-same purpose seek a knife;
But when I fear'd, I was a loyal wife:
So am I now—O no, that cannot be,
Of that true type hath Tarquin rifled me.

"O, that is gone for which I sought to live,
And therefore now I need not fear to die.
To clear this spot by death (at least) I give
A badge of fame to slander's livery,
A dying life to living infamy.
Poor helpless help, the treasure stol'n away,
To burn the guiltless casket where it lay!

"Well, well, dear Collatine, thou shalt not know
The stained taste of violated troth;
I will not wrong thy true affection so,
To flatter thee with an infringed oath;
This bastard graff shall never come to growth.
He shall not boast who did thy stock pollute,
That thou art doting father of his fruit.

"Nor shall he smile at thee in secret thought,
Nor laugh with his companions at thy state,
But thou shalt know thy int'rest was not bought
Basely with gold, but stol'n from forth thy gate.
For me, I am the mistress of my fate,
And with my trespass never will dispense,
Till life to death acquit my forc'd offense.

"I will not poison thee with my attaint,
Nor fold my fault in cleanly coin'd excuses;
My sable ground of sin I will not paint,
To hide the truth of this false night's abuses.
My tongue shall utter all, mine eyes like sluices,
As from a mountain spring that feeds a dale,
Shall gush pure streams to purge my impure tale."

By this, lamenting Philomele had ended
The well-tun'd warble of her nightly sorrow,
And solemn night with slow sad gait descended
To ugly hell, when lo the blushing morrow
Lends light to all fair eyes that light will borrow;
But cloudy Lucrece shames herself to see,
And therefore still in night would cloist'red be.

Revealing day through every cranny spies,
And seems to point her out where she sits weeping,
To whom she sobbing speaks: "O eye of eyes,
Why pry'st thou through my window? Leave thy peeping,
Mock with thy tickling beams eyes that are sleeping;
Brand not my forehead with thy piercing light,
For day hath nought to do what's done by night."

Thus cavils she with every thing she sees:
True grief is fond and testy as a child,
Who wayward once, his mood with nought agrees.
Old woes, not infant sorrows, bear them mild;
Continuance tames the one, the other wild,
Like an unpractic'd swimmer plunging still,
With too much labor drowns for want of skill.

So she, deep drenched in a sea of care,
Holds disputation with each thing she views,
And to herself all sorrow doth compare;
No object but her passion's strength renews;
And as one shifts, another straight ensues:
Sometime her grief is dumb and hath no words,
Sometime 'tis mad and too much talk affords.

The little birds that tune their morning's joy
Make her moans mad with their sweet melody,
For mirth doth search the bottom of annoy,
Sad souls are slain in merry company,
Grief best is pleas'd with grief's society;
True sorrow then is feelingly suffic'd
When with like semblance it is sympathiz'd.

'Tis double death to drown in ken of shore,
He ten times pines that pines beholding food,
To see the salve doth make the wound ache more,
Great grief grieves most at that would do it good;
Deep woes roll forward like a gentle flood,
Who being stopp'd, the bounding banks o'erflows;
Grief dallied with nor law nor limit knows.

"You mocking birds," quoth she, "your tunes entomb
Within your hollow swelling feathered breasts,
And in my hearing be you mute and dumb,

1034. **loyal dame:** chaste mistress.
1039. **imparteth:** affords. 1045. **mean:** means.
1050. **true type:** stamp of virtue. 1053. **To clear:** by clearing.
1054. **badge:** the device worn by servants on their livery to show who their master was. **fame:** good reputation. 1062. **graff:** graft.
1067. **int'rest:** property. 1069. **For me:** for my part.
1070. **with . . . dispense.** *Dispense with* = give dispensation to, i.e. pardon, excuse. See also lines 1279, 1704.
1073. **fold:** wrap, i.e. try to conceal. **cleanly coin'd:** i.e. counterfeiting purity.
1074. **sable ground:** black surface on a heraldic shield.

1079. **By this:** by this time. **Philomele.** In the classical legend Philomela was raped by her brother-in-law Tereus, who then cut out her tongue. She was changed into the nightingale.
1084. **shames:** is ashamed.
1090. **tickling:** cajoling, stirring up to pleasure.
1092. **do:** do with. 1094. **fond:** foolish. **testy:** peevishly fretful.
1096. **them:** themselves.
1109. **search:** probe, sound. **annoy:** grief, misery.
1112–13. **is . . . sympathiz'd:** has its adequate company when it is associated with similar grief. 1114. **ken:** sight.
1117. **would:** which would. 1120. **dallied:** trifled.
1121–34. Many technical terms from music are used here, some of them in a punning way (e.g. *restless,* line 1124).

My restless discord loves no stops nor rests;
A woeful hostess brooks not merry guests.
  Relish your nimble notes to pleasing ears,
  Distress likes dumps when time is kept with tears.

"Come, Philomele, that sing'st of ravishment,
Make thy sad grove in my dishevell'd hair;
As the dank earth weeps at thy languishment,
So I at each sad strain will strain a tear,
And with deep groans the diapason bear;
  For burthen-wise I'll hum on Tarquin still,
  While thou on Tereus descants better skill.

"And whiles against a thorn thou bear'st thy part
To keep thy sharp woes waking, wretched I,
To imitate thee well, against my heart
Will fix a sharp knife to affright mine eye,
Who if it wink shall thereon fall and die.
  These means, as frets upon an instrument,
  Shall tune our heart-strings to true languishment.

"And for, poor bird, thou sing'st not in the day,
As shaming any eye should thee behold,
Some dark deep desert seated from the way,
That knows not parching heat nor freezing cold,
Will we find out; and there we will unfold
  To creatures stern, sad tunes to change their kinds;
  Since men prove beasts, let beasts bear gentle minds."

As the poor frighted deer that stands at gaze,
Wildly determining which way to fly,
Or one encompass'd with a winding maze,
That cannot tread the way out readily,
So with herself is she in mutiny,
  To live or die which of the twain were better,
  When life is sham'd and death reproach's debtor.

"To kill myself," quoth she, "alack, what were it,
But with my body my poor soul's pollution?
They that lose half with greater patience bear it
Than they whose whole is swallowed in confusion.
That mother tries a merciless conclusion,
  Who having two sweet babes, when death takes one,
  Will slay the other, and be nurse to none.

1126. Relish: (1) make pleasing; (2) sing with elaborate ornamentation. **pleasing:** capable of being pleased by them.
1127. dumps: slow, mournful songs.
1132. diapason: bass accompaniment an octave lower.
1133. burthen-wise: like a bass accompaniment.
1134. descants: descantest. To descant is to sing freely in the treble over a ground bass. **better skill:** more skillfully (?).
1135–36. against . . . waking. The nightingale was thought to keep itself awake for its nocturnal singing by pressing its breast against a thorn.
1139. Who: which, i.e. the heart. **if it wink:** i.e. if the eye closes in sleep.
1140. frets: stops on the fingerboard of a string instrument.
1142. for: because. **thou . . . day.** A popular but erroneous belief.
1144. desert . . . way: deserted place situated far from any road.
1147. stern: savage. **kinds:** natures.
1149. at gaze: looking this way and that in bewilderment (?).
1153. mutiny: conflict.
1155. death reproach's debtor: i.e. suicide would bring reproach upon her.
1157. with my body: i.e. along with my body's pollution.
1159. confusion: ruin. **1160. conclusion:** experiment.

"My body or my soul, which was the dearer,
When the one pure, the other made divine?
Whose love of either to myself was nearer,
When both were kept for heaven and Collatine?
Ay me, the bark pill'd from the lofty pine,
  His leaves will wither and his sap decay;
  So must my soul, her bark being pill'd away.

"Her house is sack'd, her quiet interrupted,
Her mansion batter'd by the enemy,
Her sacred temple spotted, spoil'd, corrupted,
Grossly engirt with daring infamy:
Then let it not be call'd impiety,
  If in this blemish'd fort I make some hole
  Through which I may convey this troubled soul.

"Yet die I will not till my Collatine
Have heard the cause of my untimely death,
That he may vow, in that sad hour of mine,
Revenge on him that made me stop my breath.
My stained blood to Tarquin I'll bequeath,
  Which by him tainted shall for him be spent,
  And as his due writ in my testament.

"My honor I'll bequeath unto the knife
That wounds my body so dishonored.
'Tis honor to deprive dishonor'd life,
The one will live, the other being dead.
So of shame's ashes shall my fame be bred,
  For in my death I murther shameful scorn:
  My shame so dead, mine honor is new born.

"Dear lord of that dear jewel I have lost,
What legacy shall I bequeath to thee?
My resolution, love, shall be thy boast,
By whose example thou reveng'd mayst be.
How Tarquin must be us'd, read it in me:
  Myself thy friend will kill myself thy foe,
  And for my sake serve thou false Tarquin so.

"This brief abridgment of my will I make:
My soul and body to the skies and ground,
My resolution, husband, do thou take,
Mine honor be the knife's that makes my wound,
My shame be his that did my fame confound;
  And all my fame that lives disbursed be
  To those that live and think no shame of me.

"Thou, Collatine, shalt oversee this will;
How was I overseen that thou shalt see it!
My blood shall wash the slander of mine ill;
My live's foul deed, my life's fair end shall free it.
Faint not, faint heart, but stoutly say, 'So be it';
  Yield to my hand, my hand shall conquer thee:
  Thou dead, both die, and both shall victors be."

1165. Whose . . . either: love of which of the two.
1167. pill'd: stripped off.
1173. daring: i.e. unrestrained, shameless.
1186. deprive: rob, take away.
1188. So . . . bred. Alluding to the phoenix, a legendary bird which died in flames and arose from its own ashes.
1195. us'd: dealt with. **1205. oversee:** supervise the execution of.
1206. overseen: deceived, betrayed into a fault.

This plot of death when sadly she had laid,
And wip'd the brinish pearl from her bright eyes,
With untun'd tongue she hoarsely calls her maid,
Whose swift obedience to her mistress hies;
For fleet-wing'd duty with thought's feathers flies.
Poor Lucrece' cheeks unto her maid seem so
As winter meads when sun doth melt their snow.

Her mistress she doth give demure good morrow,
With soft slow tongue, true mark of modesty,
And sorts a sad look to her lady's sorrow
(For why her face wore sorrow's livery),
But durst not ask of her audaciously,
Why her two suns were cloud-eclipsed so,
Nor why her fair cheeks over-wash'd with woe.

But as the earth doth weep, the sun being set,
Each flow'r moist'ned like a melting eye,
Even so the maid with swelling drops gan wet
Her circled eyne, enforc'd by sympathy
Of those fair suns set in her mistress' sky,
Who in a salt-wav'd ocean quench their light,
Which makes the maid weep like the dewy night.

A pretty while these pretty creatures stand,
Like ivory conduits coral cesterns filling:
One justly weeps, the other takes in hand
No cause, but company of her drops spilling.
Their gentle sex to weep are often willing,
Grieving themselves to guess at others' smarts,
And then they drown their eyes, or break their hearts.

For men have marble, women waxen minds,
And therefore are they form'd as marble will;
The weak oppress'd, th' impression of strange kinds
Is form'd in them by force, by fraud, or skill.
Then call them not the authors of their ill,
No more than wax shall be accounted evil,
Wherein is stamp'd the semblance of a devil.

Their smoothness, like a goodly champaign plain,
Lays open all the little worms that creep;
In men, as in a rough-grown grove, remain
Cave-keeping evils that obscurely sleep.
Through crystal walls each little mote will peep;
Though men can cover crimes with bold stern looks,
Poor women's faces are their own faults' books.

No man inveigh against the withered flow'r,
But chide rough winter that the flow'r hath kill'd;
Not that devour'd, but that which doth devour,
Is worthy blame. O, let it not be hild
Poor women's faults that they are so fulfill'd
With men's abuses: those proud lords to blame
Make weak-made women tenants to their shame.

The president whereof in Lucrece view,
Assail'd by night with circumstances strong
Of present death, and shame that might ensue
By that her death, to do her husband wrong.
Such danger to resistance did belong
That dying fear through all her body spread,
And who cannot abuse a body dead?

By this, mild patience bid fair Lucrece speak
To the poor counterfeit of her complaining:
"My girl," quoth she, "on what occasion break
Those tears from thee, that down thy cheeks are raining?
If thou dost weep for grief of my sustaining,
Know, gentle wench, it small avails my mood;
If tears could help, mine own would do me good.

"But tell me, girl, when went" (and there she stay'd
Till after a deep groan) "Tarquin from hence?"
"Madam, ere I was up," replied the maid,
"The more to blame my sluggard negligence.
Yet with the fault I thus far can dispense:
Myself was stirring ere the break of day,
And ere I rose was Tarquin gone away.

"But, lady, if your maid may be so bold,
She would request to know your heaviness."
"O, peace," quoth Lucrece, "if it should be told,
The repetition cannot make it less;
For more it is than I can well express,
And that deep torture may be call'd a hell,
When more is felt than one hath power to tell.

"Go get me hither paper, ink, and pen,
Yet save that labor, for I have them here.—
What should I say?—One of my husband's men
Bid thou be ready, by and by, to bear
A letter to my lord, my love, my dear.
Bid him with speed prepare to carry it,
The cause craves haste, and it will soon be writ."

Her maid is gone, and she prepares to write,
First hovering o'er the paper with her quill.
Conceit and grief an eager combat fight,
What wit sets down is blotted straight with will;
This is too curious-good, this blunt and ill:
Much like a press of people at a door,
Throng her inventions, which shall go before.

1212. **plot:** plan. 1215. **hies:** hastens.
1219. **demure:** modest, sober. 1221. **sorts:** fits.
1222. **For why:** because. 1229. **circled:** rounded.
1233. **pretty while:** considerable time. 1234. **cesterns:** cisterns.
1235. **justly:** with cause. **takes in hand:** entertains.
1236. **No . . . spilling:** i.e. no reason to weep except to keep her weeping mistress company. 1241. **will:** i.e. will have it.
1242. **strange kinds:** natures unlike their own.
1247. **smoothness:** i.e. open natures. **champaign:** level and open.
1248. **Lays open:** reveals. **little worms:** i.e. petty faults.
1250. **Cave-keeping:** i.e. concealed, like beasts keeping to their lairs. **obscurely:** in darkness, unseen.
1257. **hild:** held.
1258. **fulfill'd:** filled up. 1261. **president:** precedent, example.
1263. **present:** instant, immediate (so also in line 1307).
1266. **dying:** i.e. destroying the power to resist, paralyzing.
1269. **counterfeit:** copy, replica.
1272. **of my sustaining:** borne by me.
1279. **with . . . dispense.** See the note on line 1070.
1283. **know your heaviness:** learn the cause of your grief.
1285. **repetition:** recital. 1298. **Conceit:** thought.
1299. **wit:** intellect. **blotted:** cancelled. **will:** feeling.
1300. **curious-good:** elaborately artistic.
1302. **go before:** take precedence.

At last she thus begins: "Thou worthy lord
Of that unworthy wife that greeteth thee,
Health to thy person; next, vouchsafe t' afford
(If ever, love, thy Lucrece thou wilt see)
Some present speed to come and visit me.
  So I commend me from our house in grief,
  My woes are tedious, though my words are brief."

Here folds she up the tenure of her woe,
Her certain sorrow writ uncertainly.
By this short schedule Collatine may know
Her grief, but not her grief's true quality.
She dares not thereof make discovery,
  Lest he should hold it her own gross abuse,
  Ere she with blood had stain'd her stain'd excuse.

Besides, the life and feeling of her passion
She hoards, to spend when he is by to hear her,
When sighs and groans and tears may grace the fashion
Of her disgrace, the better so to clear her
From that suspicion which the world might bear her.
  To shun this blot, she would not blot the letter
  With words, till action might become them better.

To see sad sights moves more than hear them told,
For then the eye interprets to the ear
The heavy motion that it doth behold,
When every part a part of woe doth bear.
'Tis but a part of sorrow that we hear.
  Deep sounds make lesser noise than shallow fords,
  And sorrow ebbs, being blown with wind of words.

Her letter now is seal'd, and on it writ,
"At Ardea to my lord with more than haste."
The post attends, and she delivers it,
Charging the sour-fac'd groom to hie as fast
As lagging fowls before the northern blast.
  Speed more than speed but dull and slow she deems:
  Extremity still urgeth such extremes.

The homely villain cur'sies to her low,
And blushing on her with a steadfast eye,
Receives the scroll without or yea or no,
And forth with bashful innocence doth hie.
But they whose guilt within their bosoms lie
  Imagine every eye beholds their blame,
  For Lucrece thought he blush'd to see her shame,

When, seely groom, God wot, it was defect
Of spirit, life, and bold audacity.
Such harmless creatures have a true respect
To talk in deeds, while others saucily
Promise more speed, but do it leisurely;
  Even so this pattern of the worn-out age
  Pawn'd honest looks, but laid no words to gage.

His kindled duty kindled her mistrust,
That two red fires in both their faces blazed;
She thought he blush'd, as knowing Tarquin's lust,
And blushing with him, wistly on him gazed;
Her earnest eye did make him more amazed.
  The more she saw the blood his cheeks replenish,
  The more she thought he spied in her some blemish.

But long she thinks till he return again,
And yet the duteous vassal scarce is gone;
The weary time she cannot entertain,
For now 'tis stale to sigh, to weep, and groan.
So woe hath wearied woe, moan tired moan,
  That she her plaints a little while doth stay,
  Pausing for means to mourn some newer way.

At last she calls to mind where hangs a piece
Of skillful painting, made for Priam's Troy,
Before the which is drawn the power of Greece,
For Helen's rape the city to destroy,
Threat'ning cloud-kissing Ilion with annoy,
  Which the conceited painter drew so proud,
  As heaven (it seem'd) to kiss the turrets bow'd.

A thousand lamentable objects there,
In scorn of nature, art gave liveless life:
Many a dry drop seem'd a weeping tear,
Shed for the slaught'red husband by the wife;
The red blood reek'd, to show the painter's strife,
  And dying eyes gleam'd forth their ashy lights,
  Like dying coals burnt out in tedious nights.

There might you see the laboring pioner
Begrim'd with sweat, and smeared all with dust,
And from the tow'rs of Troy there would appear
The very eyes of men through loop-holes thrust,
Gazing upon the Greeks with little lust.
  Such sweet observance in this work was had,
  That one might see those far-off eyes look sad.

In great commanders, grace and majesty
You might behold triumphing in their faces;
In youth, quick bearing and dexterity;

1307. present: instant, immediate.
1310. tenure: tenor, purport, i.e. summary statement.
1311. uncertainly: without definite details.
1312. schedule: document. **1314. discovery:** revelation.
1316. her stain'd excuse: the explanation of her shame.
1317. passion: violent grief.
1319. fashion: fashioning forth, i.e. relating (?) or shape, appearance (?). **1322. blot . . . blot:** stain . . . mar. **1324. hear:** to hear.
1326. heavy motion: sad action (but *motion* can mean specifically "puppet show," a sense made likely here by *interprets* [line 1325], which can mean "explains mute dramatic action").
1327. a part . . . bear: (1) supports a portion of the woe; (2) sings a woeful part (in the musical sense); (3) plays a woeful role.
1329. sounds: straits, narrow passages of water.
1333. post attends: messenger is waiting.
1334. sour-fac'd: sullen-looking.
1335. lagging: late to migrate, hence flying fast to avoid winter.
1338. homely: simple, unpolished. **villain:** servant. **cur'sies:** bows. **1339. blushing . . . eye:** i.e. looking steadily at her but blushing at the same time (from bashfulness).

1345. seely: silly, i.e. simple. **1347. respect:** care.
1350. pattern . . . age: i.e. example of what servants were like in the good old days.
1351. Pawn'd: gave as security. **to gage:** in pledge.
1355. wistly: intently. **1356. amazed:** confused, embarrassed.
1361. entertain: spend usefully. **1367. made for:** representing.
1368. drawn: arrayed, ranged. **power:** army.
1370. cloud-kissing Ilion: i.e. lofty-towered Troy. **annoy:** harm, injury. **1371. conceited:** ingenious, imaginative.
1377. reek'd: steamed. **strife:** i.e. effort to surpass nature.
1380. pioner: soldier of the lowest rank whose function was to perform manual labor. **1384. lust:** liking.
1385. sweet observance: pleasing lifelikeness.
1389. quick: lively.

And here and there the painter interlaces
Pale cowards, marching on with trembling paces,
  Which heartless peasants did so well resemble,
  That one would swear he saw them quake and
    tremble.

In Ajax and Ulysses, O what art
Of physiognomy might one behold!
The face of either cipher'd either's heart,
Their face their manners most expressly told:
In Ajax' eyes blunt rage and rigor roll'd,
  But the mild glance that sly Ulysses lent
  Showed deep regard and smiling government.

There pleading might you see grave Nestor stand,
As 'twere encouraging the Greeks to fight,
Making such sober action with his hand,
That it beguil'd attention, charm'd the sight.
In speech it seem'd his beard, all silver white,
  Wagg'd up and down, and from his lips did fly
  Thin winding breath, which purl'd up to the sky.

About him were a press of gaping faces,
Which seem'd to swallow up his sound advice,
All jointly list'ning, but with several graces,
As if some mermaid did their ears entice,
Some high, some low, the painter was so nice;
  The scalps of many, almost hid behind,
  To jump up higher seem'd to mock the mind.

Here one man's hand lean'd on another's head,
His nose being shadowed by his neighbor's ear;
Here one being throng'd bears back, all boll'n and red,
Another, smother'd, seems to pelt and swear,
And in their rage such signs of rage they bear,
  As but for loss of Nestor's golden words,
  It seem'd they would debate with angry swords.

For much imaginary work was there,
Conceit deceitful, so compact, so kind,
That for Achilles' image stood his spear,
Grip'd in an armed hand, himself behind
Was left unseen, save to the eye of mind:
  A hand, a foot, a face, a leg, a head
  Stood for the whole to be imagined.

And from the walls of strong-besieged Troy,
When their brave hope, bold Hector, march'd to field,
Stood many Troyan mothers, sharing joy
To see their youthful sons bright weapons wield,
And to their hope they such odd action yield
  That through their light joy seemed to appear
  (Like bright things stain'd) a kind of heavy fear.

And from the strond of Dardan, where they fought,
To Simois' reedy banks the red blood ran,
Whose waves to imitate the battle sought
With swelling ridges, and their ranks began
To break upon the galled shore, and than
  Retire again, till meeting greater ranks,
  They join, and shoot their foam at Simois' banks.

To this well-painted piece is Lucrece come,
To find a face where all distress is stell'd.
Many she sees where cares have carved some,
But none where all distress and dolor dwell'd,
Till she despairing Hecuba beheld,
  Staring on Priam's wounds with her old eyes,
  Which bleeding under Pyrrhus' proud foot lies.

In her the painter had anatomiz'd
Time's ruin, beauty's wrack, and grim care's reign;
Her cheeks with chops and wrinkles were disguis'd,
Of what she was, no semblance did remain.
Her blue blood chang'd to black in every vein,
  Wanting the spring that those shrunk pipes had fed,
  Show'd life imprison'd in a body dead.

On this sad shadow Lucrece spends her eyes,
And shapes her sorrow to the beldame's woes,
Who nothing wants to answer her but cries,
And bitter words to ban her cruel foes;
The painter was no god to lend her those,
  And therefore Lucrece swears he did her wrong,
  To give her so much grief, and not a tongue.

"Poor instrument," quoth she, "without a sound,
I'll tune thy woes with my lamenting tongue,
And drop sweet balm in Priam's painted wound,
And rail on Pyrrhus that hath done him wrong,
And with my tears quench Troy that burns so long,
  And with my knife scratch out the angry eyes
  Of all the Greeks that are thine enemies.

"Show me the strumpet that began this stir,
That with my nails her beauty I may tear.
Thy heat of lust, fond Paris, did incur
This load of wrath that burning Troy doth bear;
Thy eye kindled the fire that burneth here,
  And here in Troy, for trespass of thine eye,
  The sire, the son, the dame, and daughter die.

"Why should the private pleasure of some one
Become the public plague of many moe?
Let sin, alone committed, light alone
Upon his head that hath transgressed so;
Let guiltless souls be freed from guilty woe.
  For one's offense why should so many fall,
  To plague a private sin in general?

1392. heartless: cowardly.
1396. cipher'd: expressed. **1398. blunt:** rough.
1400. regard: deliberation. **government:** self-possession.
1407. purl'd: flowed with whirling motion.
1411. mermaid: i.e. siren.
1412. high . . . low: tall . . . short. **nice:** particular.
1414. To . . . mind: i.e. were so realistically painted as to tempt the spectator to jump up in order to get a better look at them.
1417. throng'd: pressed by the throng. **bears:** pushes. **boll'n:** puffed (with anger). **1418. pelt:** scold.
1422. imaginary: imaginative.
1423. compact: economical. **kind:** natural.
1425. Grip'd: gripped.
1436. strond: strand, shore. **Dardan:** Dardania, a name for the district in which Troy was located.
1437. Simois: a river near Troy.
1440. galled: worn away. **than:** then.
1444. stell'd: placed, fixed (?) or steeled, i.e. engraved (?).
1450. anatomiz'd: laid open, shown distinctly.
1452. chops: cracks. **disguis'd:** disfigured beyond recognition.
1457. shadow: painted form. **1459. wants:** lacks.
1460. ban: curse. **1471. stir:** tumult. **1479. moe:** more.
1484. To . . . general: i.e. to punish everybody for the sin of one.

"Lo here weeps Hecuba, here Priam dies,
Here manly Hector faints, here Troilus sounds,
Here friend by friend in bloody channel lies,
And friend to friend gives unadvised wounds,
And one man's lust these many lives confounds.
Had doting Priam check'd his son's desire,
Troy had been bright with fame, and not with fire."

Here feelingly she weeps Troy's painted woes,
For sorrow, like a heavy hanging bell,
Once set on ringing, with his own weight goes;
Then little strength rings out the doleful knell:
So Lucrece, set a-work, sad tales doth tell
To pencill'd pensiveness and color'd sorrow;
She lends them words, and she their looks doth borrow.

She throws her eyes about the painting round,
And who she finds forlorn, she doth lament.
At last she sees a wretched image bound,
That piteous looks to Phrygian shepherds lent;
His face, though full of cares, yet show'd content;
Onward to Troy with the blunt swains he goes,
So mild that patience seem'd to scorn his woes.

In him the painter labor'd with his skill
To hide deceit, and give the harmless show
An humble gait, calm looks, eyes wailing still,
A brow unbent, that seem'd to welcome woe,
Cheeks neither red nor pale, but mingled so
That blushing red no guilty instance gave,
Nor ashy pale the fear that false hearts have.

But like a constant and confirmed devil,
He entertain'd a show so seeming just,
And therein so ensconc'd his secret evil,
That jealousy itself could not mistrust
False creeping craft and perjury should thrust
Into so bright a day such black-fac'd storms,
Or blot with hell-born sin such saint-like forms.

The well-skill'd workman this mild image drew
For perjur'd Sinon, whose enchanting story
The credulous old Priam after slew;
Whose words like wildfire burnt the shining glory
Of rich-built Ilion, that the skies were sorry,
And little stars shot from their fixed places,
When their glass fell wherein they view'd their faces.

This picture she advisedly perus'd,
And chid the painter for his wondrous skill,

1486. sounds: swoons. **1487. channel:** kennel, gutter.
1488. unadvised: unintentional. **1497. color'd:** painted.
1502. piteous: pitying. **to . . . lent:** in . . . inspired.
1503. content: acquiescence, acceptance. **1504. blunt:** rough.
1505. patience: i.e. his patience. **scorn:** scoff at, make light of.
1507. harmless show: outwardly harmless figure.
1511. guilty instance: sign of guilt.
1514. entertain'd a show: maintained an appearance.
1515. ensconc'd: concealed.
1516. jealousy: suspicion. **mistrust:** suspect.
1521. Sinon: the Greek who persuaded the Trojans to admit the wooden horse that caused the fall of Troy. **enchanting:** casting a spell, i.e. deluding. **1526. glass:** mirror.
1527. advisedly: with careful consideration.

Saying, some shape in Sinon's was abus'd:
So fair a form lodg'd not a mind so ill.
And still on him she gaz'd, and gazing still,
Such signs of truth in his plain face she spied,
That she concludes the picture was belied.

"It cannot be," quoth she, "that so much guile"—
She would have said, "can lurk in such a look";
But Tarquin's shape came in her mind the while,
And from her tongue "can lurk" from "cannot" took:
"It cannot be" she in that sense forsook,
And turn'd it thus, "It cannot be, I find,
But such a face should bear a wicked mind.

"For even as subtile Sinon here is painted,
So sober-sad, so weary, and so mild
(As if with grief or travail he had fainted),
To me came Tarquin armed to beguild
With outward honesty, but yet defil'd
With inward vice: as Priam him did cherish,
So did I Tarquin, so my Troy did perish.

"Look, look how list'ning Priam wets his eyes,
To see those borrowed tears that Sinon sheeds!
Priam, why art thou old, and yet not wise?
For every tear he falls a Troyan bleeds;
His eye drops fire, no water thence proceeds;
Those round clear pearls of his, that move thy pity,
Are balls of quenchless fire to burn thy city.

"Such devils steal effects from lightless hell,
For Sinon in his fire doth quake with cold,
And in that cold, hot burning fire doth dwell;
These contraries such unity do hold
Only to flatter fools, and make them bold:
So Priam's trust false Sinon's tears doth flatter,
That he finds means to burn his Troy with water."

Here all enrag'd, such passion her assails
That patience is quite beaten from her breast;
She tears the senseless Sinon with her nails,
Comparing him to that unhappy guest
Whose deed hath made herself herself detest.
At last she smilingly with this gives o'er;
"Fool, fool," quoth she, "his wounds will not be sore."

Thus ebbs and flows the current of her sorrow,
And time doth weary time with her complaining;
She looks for night, and then she longs for morrow,
And both she thinks too long with her remaining.
Short time seems long in sorrow's sharp sustaining;
Though woe be heavy, yet it seldom sleeps,
And they that watch see time how slow it creeps;

1529. some . . . abus'd: someone else is painted there and slanderously called Sinon. **1532. plain:** open, honest.
1533. belied: proved false.
1544. armed: prepared, equipped. **beguild:** variant of *beguile*, like *vild* for *vile* (?). Among various emendations of *armed to beguild* the most popular has been *armed; so beguil'd* (i.e. guileful).
1549. sheeds: sheds. **1551. falls:** lets fall.
1564. senseless: insensible. **1565. unhappy:** bringing misfortune.
1574. heavy: distressing, with quibble on the sense "sleepy."
1575. watch: are wakeful.

Which all this time hath overslipp'd her thought,
That she with painted images hath spent,
Being from the feeling of her own grief brought
By deep surmise of others' detriment,
Losing her woes in shows of discontent.
It easeth some, though none it ever cured,
To think their dolor others have endured.

But now the mindful messenger, come back,
Brings home his lord and other company,
Who finds his Lucrece clad in mourning black,
And round about her tear-distained eye
Blue circles stream'd, like rainbows in the sky.
These water-galls in her dim element
Foretell new storms to those already spent;

Which when her sad-beholding husband saw,
Amazedly in her sad face he stares:
Her eyes, though sod in tears, look'd red and raw,
Her lively color kill'd with deadly cares.
He hath no power to ask her how she fares.
Both stood like old acquaintance in a trance,
Met far from home, wond'ring each other's chance.

At last he takes her by the bloodless hand,
And thus begins: "What uncouth ill event
Hath thee befall'n, that thou dost trembling stand?
Sweet love, what spite hath thy fair color spent?
Why art thou thus attir'd in discontent?
Unmask, dear dear, this moody heaviness,
And tell thy grief, that we may give redress."

Three times with sighs she gives her sorrow fire,
Ere once she can discharge one word of woe;
At length address'd to answer his desire,
She modestly prepares to let them know
Her honor is ta'en prisoner by the foe,
While Collatine and his consorted lords
With sad attention long to hear her words.

And now this pale swan in her wat'ry nest
Begins the sad dirge of her certain ending:
"Few words," quoth she, "shall fit the trespass best,
Where no excuse can give the fault amending.
In me moe woes than words are now depending,
And my laments would be drawn out too long
To tell them all with one poor tired tongue.

"Then be this all the task it hath to say:
Dear husband, in the interest of thy bed
A stranger came, and on that pillow lay
Where thou wast wont to rest thy weary head,
And what wrong else may be imagined
By foul enforcement might be done to me,
From that, alas, thy Lucrece is not free.

"For in the dreadful dead of dark midnight,
With shining falchion in my chamber came
A creeping creature, with a flaming light,
And softly cried, 'Awake, thou Roman dame,
And entertain my love, else lasting shame
On thee and thine this night I will inflict,
If thou my love's desire do contradict.

" 'For some hard-favor'd groom of thine,' quoth he,
'Unless thou yoke thy liking to my will,
I'll murther straight, and then I'll slaughter thee,
And swear I found you where you did fulfill
The loathsome act of lust, and so did kill
The lechers in their deed. This act will be
My fame, and thy perpetual infamy.'

"With this I did begin to start and cry,
And then against my heart he set his sword,
Swearing, unless I took all patiently,
I should not live to speak another word;
So should my shame still rest upon record,
And never be forgot in mighty Rome
Th' adulterate death of Lucrece and her groom.

"Mine enemy was strong, my poor self weak
(And far the weaker with so strong a fear),
My bloody judge forbod my tongue to speak,
No rightful plea might plead for justice there.
His scarlet lust came evidence to swear
That my poor beauty had purloin'd his eyes,
And when the judge is robb'd, the prisoner dies.

"O, teach me how to make mine own excuse,
Or (at the least) this refuge let me find:
Though my gross blood be stain'd with this abuse,
Immaculate and spotless is my mind;
That was not forc'd, that never was inclin'd
To accessary yieldings, but still pure
Doth in her poison'd closet yet endure."

Lo here the hopeless merchant of this loss,
With head declin'd, and voice damm'd up with woe,
With sad set eyes, and wretched arms across,
From lips new waxen pale begins to blow
The grief away that stops his answer so;
But wretched as he is he strives in vain,
What he breathes out, his breath drinks up again.

As through an arch the violent roaring tide
Outruns the eye that doth behold his haste,
Yet in the eddy boundeth in his pride
Back to the strait that forc'd him on so fast
(In rage sent out, recall'd in rage, being past),

1580. shows of discontent: painted representations of sorrow.
1583. mindful: careful, dutiful.
1588. water-galls: fragments of rainbow. **element:** sky.
1589. to: in addition to. **1592. sod:** steeped.
1598. uncouth: unknown, strange. **1600. spite:** injury.
1602. moody: melancholy.
1604–5. Three . . . woe. The figure is of the firing of a gun.
1606. address'd: ready. **1610. sad:** serious.
1611. swan. An allusion to the old notion that the swan, which is not a singing bird, sings once, beautifully, just before its death.
1619. in the interest: to claim possession.
1632. hard-favor'd: ugly. **1648. forbod:** forbade.
1658. accessary yieldings: voluntary yieldings that would make her an accessory to the crime.
1660. merchant . . . loss: i.e. owner who has suffered this loss.
1662. wretched arms across. Crossed or folded arms traditionally betokened grief. Some editors emend *wretched* to *wreathed*, following W. S. Walker. **1663. new waxen:** newly turned.

Even so his sighs, his sorrows, make a saw,
To push grief on, and back the same grief draw.

Which speechless woe of his poor she attendeth,
And his untimely frenzy thus awaketh:
"Dear lord, thy sorrow to my sorrow lendeth
Another power; no flood by raining slaketh.
My woe too sensible thy passion maketh
More feeling-painful: let it then suffice
To drown [one] woe, one pair of weeping eyes.

"And for my sake when I might charm thee so,
For she that was thy Lucrece, now attend me:
Be suddenly revenged on my foe,
Thine, mine, his own. Suppose thou dost defend me
From what is past: the help that thou shalt lend me
Comes all too late, yet let the traitor die,
For sparing justice feeds iniquity.

"But ere I name him, you fair lords," quoth she
(Speaking to those that came with Collatine),
"Shall plight your honorable faiths to me
With swift pursuit to venge this wrong of mine,
For 'tis a meritorious fair design
To chase injustice with revengeful arms:
Knights, by their oaths, should right poor ladies' harms."

At this request, with noble disposition
Each present lord began to promise aid,
As bound in knighthood to her imposition,
Longing to hear the hateful foe bewray'd.
But she that yet her sad task hath not said,
The protestation stops: "O, speak," quoth she,
"How may this forced stain be wip'd from me?

"What is the quality of my offense,
Being constrain'd with dreadful circumstance?
May my pure mind with the foul act dispense,
My low-declined honor to advance?
May any terms acquit me from this chance?
The poisoned fountain clears itself again,
And why not I from this compelled stain?"

With this they all at once began to say,
Her body's stain her mind untainted clears,
While with a joyless smile she turns away
The face, that map which deep impression bears
Of hard misfortune, carv'd [in it] with tears.
"No, no," quoth she, "no dame hereafter living
By my excuse shall claim excuse's giving."

Here with a sigh as if her heart would break,
She throws forth Tarquin's name: "He, he," she says,
But more than "he" her poor tongue could not speak,
Till after many accents and delays,
Untimely breathings, sick and short assays,
She utters this, "He, he, fair lords, 'tis he,
That guides this hand to give this wound to me."

Even here she sheathed in her harmless breast
A harmful knife, that thence her soul unsheathed;
That blow did bail it from the deep unrest
Of that polluted prison where it breathed.
Her contrite sighs unto the clouds bequeathed
Her winged sprite, and through her wounds doth fly
Live's lasting date from cancell'd destiny.

Stone-still, astonish'd with this deadly deed,
Stood Collatine, and all his lordly crew,
Till Lucrece' father that beholds her bleed,
Himself on her self-slaught'red body threw,
And from the purple fountain Brutus drew
The murd'rous knife, and as it left the place,
Her blood, in poor revenge, held it in chase;

And bubbling from her breast, it doth divide
In two slow rivers, that the crimson blood
Circles her body in on every side,
Who like a late-sack'd island vastly stood
Bare and unpeopled in this fearful flood.
Some of her blood still pure and red remain'd,
And some look'd black, and that false Tarquin stain'd.

About the mourning and congealed face
Of that black blood a wat'ry rigol goes,
Which seems to weep upon the tainted place,
And ever since, as pitying Lucrece' woes,
Corrupted blood some watery token shows,
And blood untainted still doth red abide,
Blushing at that which is so putrefied.

"Daughter, dear daughter," old Lucretius cries,
"That life was mine which thou hast here deprived.
If in the child the father's image lies,
Where shall I live now Lucrece is unlived?
Thou wast not to this end from me derived.
If children predecease progenitors,
We are their offspring, and they none of ours.

"Poor broken glass, I often did behold
In thy sweet semblance my old age new born,
But now that fair fresh mirror dim and old

1672. saw: the tool of that name, moving back and forth.
1673. To push . . . draw: by pushing . . . drawing.
1675. his . . . awaketh: i.e. tries to arouse him with the following words from his ill-timed state of benumbed distraction.
1677. Another power: added intensity.
1678. sensible: keenly felt. **passion:** violent grief.
1683. suddenly: immediately.
1687. sparing: i.e. overmerciful. **feeds iniquity:** i.e. encourages further wrongdoing.
1697. her imposition: the duty she has imposed upon them.
1698. bewray'd: revealed.
1699. her . . . said: has not completed her sad task of speaking.
1702. quality: nature. **1705. advance:** i.e. raise again.
1713. in it. See the Textual Notes.
1719. accents: sounds expressive of emotion.
1720. Untimely: irregular. **assays:** attempts.
1723. harmless: guiltless.
1729. Live's lasting date: everlasting life (*date* = duration, term), i.e. her immortal part. **cancell'd destiny:** earthly life, now terminated, i.e. her mortal body.
1730. astonish'd: struck dumb, stunned.
1734. Brutus. Lucius Junius Brutus, whose brother had been killed by the tyrant Tarquin, father of Lucrece's ravisher, pretended idiocy to escape a like fate. See lines 1807–16.
1740. vastly: laid waste, desolate.
1745. rigol: ring, circle. **1754. unlived:** deprived of life.

Shows me a bare-bon'd death by time outworn.
O, from thy cheeks my image thou hast torn,
And shiver'd all the beauty of my glass,
That I no more can see what once I was!

"O Time, cease thou thy course and last no longer,
If they surcease to be that should survive.
Shall rotten Death make conquest of the stronger,
And leave the falt'ring feeble souls alive?
The old bees die, the young possess their hive:
Then live, sweet Lucrece, live again and see
Thy father die, and not thy father thee!"

By this starts Collatine as from a dream,
And bids Lucretius give his sorrow place,
And then in key-cold Lucrece' bleeding stream
He falls, and bathes the pale fear in his face,
And counterfeits to die with her a space,
Till manly shame bids him possess his breath,
And live to be revenged on her death.

The deep vexation of his inward soul
Hath serv'd a dumb arrest upon his tongue,
Who mad that sorrow should his use control,
Or keep him from heart-easing words so long,
Begins to talk, but through his lips do throng
Weak words, so thick come in his poor heart's aid,
That no man could distinguish what he said.

Yet sometime "Tarquin" was pronounced plain,
But through his teeth, as if the name he tore.
This windy tempest, till it blow up rain,
Held back his sorrow's tide, to make it more.
At last it rains, and busy winds give o'er;
Then son and father weep with equal strife,
Who should weep most, for daughter or for wife.

The one doth call her his, the other his,
Yet neither may possess the claim they lay.
The father says, "She's mine." "O, mine she is,"
Replies her husband, "do not take away
My sorrow's interest, let no mourner say
He weeps for her, for she was only mine,
And only must be wail'd by Collatine."

"O," quoth Lucretius, "I did give that life
Which she too early and too late hath spill'd."
"Woe, woe," quoth Collatine, "she was my wife,
I owed her, and 'tis mine that she hath kill'd."
"My daughter!" and "My wife!" with clamors fill'd
The dispers'd air, who holding Lucrece' life,
Answer'd their cries, "My daughter!" and "My wife!"

Brutus, who pluck'd the knife from Lucrece' side,
Seeing such emulation in their woe,
Began to clothe his wit in state and pride,
Burying in Lucrece' wound his folly's show.
He with the Romans was esteemed so
As seely jeering idiots are with kings,
For sportive words, and utt'ring foolish things.

But now he throws that shallow habit by,
Wherein deep policy did him disguise,
And arm'd his long-hid wits advisedly,
To check the tears in Collatinus' eyes.
"Thou wronged lord of Rome," quoth he, "arise,
Let my unsounded self, suppos'd a fool,
Now set thy long-experienc'd wit to school.

"Why, Collatine, is woe the cure for woe?
Do wounds help wounds, or grief help grievous deeds?
Is it revenge to give thyself a blow
For his foul act by whom thy fair wife bleeds?
Such childish humor from weak minds proceeds;
Thy wretched wife mistook the matter so,
To slay herself, that should have slain her foe.

"Courageous Roman, do not steep thy heart
In such relenting dew of lamentations,
But kneel with me and help to bear thy part,
To rouse our Roman gods with invocations,
That they will suffer these abominations
(Since Rome herself in them doth stand disgraced)
By our strong arms from forth her fair streets chased.

"Now by the Capitol that we adore,
And by this chaste blood so unjustly stained,
By heaven's fair sun that breeds the fat earth's store,
By all our country rights in Rome maintained,
And by chaste Lucrece' soul that late complained
Her wrongs to us, and by this bloody knife,
We will revenge the death of this true wife."

This said, he strook his hand upon his breast,
And kiss'd the fatal knife to end his vow;
And to his protestation urg'd the rest,
Who wond'ring at him, did his words allow.
Then jointly to the ground their knees they bow,
And that deep vow which Brutus made before,
He doth again repeat, and that they swore.

When they had sworn to this advised doom,
They did conclude to bear dead Lucrece thence,
To show her bleeding body thorough Rome,
And so to publish Tarquin's foul offense;
Which being done with speedy diligence,
The Romans plausibly did give consent
To Tarquin's everlasting banishment.

1761. **death:** death's head, skull. 1766. **surcease:** cease.
1774. **key-cold:** cold as metal. 1775. **pale fear:** fearful pallor.
1780. **dumb arrest:** order to be silent.
1784. **so thick:** in such numbers. 1791. **strife:** striving.
1797. **interest:** claim. 1801. **late:** recently.
1803. **owed:** owned. 1809. **state:** dignity.

1810. **folly's show:** appearance of folly.
1812. **seely:** silly, simple. **idiots:** i.e. court fools.
1814. **shallow habit:** i.e. pretense of shallowness (*habit* = cloak).
1819. **unsounded:** unplumbed, of unknown depth.
1825. **humor:** capricious behavior.
1829. **relenting:** softening. 1832. **suffer:** allow.
1834. **chased:** to be chased. 1837. **fat:** fertile.
1838. **our country rights:** the rights of our country.
1844. **to his protestation:** to take the same oath he had sworn.
1845. **allow:** approve.
1849. **advised doom:** considered judgment.
1851. **thorough:** throughout. 1852. **publish:** make public.
1854. **plausibly:** with applause.

NOTE ON THE TEXT

The Rape of Lucrece, perhaps better called simply *Lucrece* as on the title-page of the first quarto (Q1), was printed in 1594 by Richard Field, the printer of *Venus and Adonis*, for John Harrison. Though less popular than *Venus and Adonis*, it passed through a number of editions in the sixteenth and seventeenth centuries. In the enumeration of Hyder Rollins (New Variorum edition), they are as follows: Q2 (1598), Q3 (1600), Q4 (1600), Q5 (1607), Q6 (1616), Q7 (1624), Q8 (1632), Q9 (1655)—all editions after Q1 being in fact octavos.

The text of Q1 is carefully printed, only one substantive reading (l. 1713) needing correction; and the conditions controlling such a text may be supposed to have been the same as those outlined in the "Note on the Text" to *Venus and Adonis*. The textual situation for *Lucrece*, however, is somewhat sounder than for *Venus and Adonis* with its single surviving exemplar of the first edition, for there are eleven known copies (two imperfect) of Q1, showing press corrections in sheets B (see Textual Notes, ll. 24, 31, 50, 125–6), I (ll. 1182, 1335), K (l. 1350), and M (l. 1832).

Q1 contains only two forms which may perhaps be considered characteristic Shakespearean spellings: *bedred* for *bedrid* (l. 975) and *on* for *one* (l. 1680). The first, an unusual form, occurs also in Q1 of *Love's Labor's Lost* (I.i.138) and Q2 of *Hamlet* (I.ii.29), both believed to have been set up from some form of Shakespeare's "foul papers."

For further information, see the works cited for *Venus and Adonis*.

TEXTUAL NOTES

Title: **The . . . Lucrece**] *from heading of poem and running-titles in Q1;* Lucrece. *Q1 title-page*
Argument 7, 20 **noblemen**] *as two words, Q1*
4 **Collatium**] *Malone;* Colatium *Q1* (*throughout; but see l. 50 below*)
7, 10, etc. **Collatine's, Collatine**] *Malone* (*sporadically in Q5, etc.*); Colatines, Colatine *Q1* (*throughout*)
8 **Happ'ly**] *ed.;* Hap'ly *Q1*
8 **unhapp'ly**] *Prince;* vnhap'ly *Q1*
17 **priceless**] *Q3;* priselesse *Q1*
23 **decay'd**] *Q6;* decayed *Q1*
23 **done**] *Malone;* done: *Q1*
24 **morning's**] *Q1* (c); morning *Q1* (*u*)
27 **owner's**] *State Poems;* owners *Q1*
31 **apology**] *Q1* (*u*); Apologies *Q1* (c)
41 **high-pitch'd**] *Gildon;* high picht *Q1;* high pitcht *Q2*
50 **Collatium**] *Malone;* Colatium *Q1* (*u*); Colatia *Q1* (c) (Collatia *is the proper form historically, but except for this one reading, doubtless a non-authorial correction, Q1 everywhere uses the form* Colatium, *i.e.* Collatium; *see l. 4 and Argument, l. 26*)
50 **arrived**] *Q1* (c); ariued *Q1* (*u*)
56 **o'er**] *Q6* (o're); ore *Q1;* or'e *Q5*
57–8 **entituled . . . doves,**] *Gildon* (*subs.*); entituled, . . . doues *Q1*
59 **beauty's**] *State Poems;* Beauties *Q1*
65 **beauty's . . . virtue's**] *Gildon;* Beauties . . . Vertues *Q1*
74 **kill'd,**] *Q2;* kild. *Q1*
80 **wrong,**] *Q7;* wrong. *Q1*
84 **still-gazing**] *hyphen, Malone*
87–8 **For . . . fear.**] *with gnomic quotes, Q1*
111 **heav'd-up**] *Q3;* heaued-vp *Q1*
125–6 **himself betakes, . . . wakes.**] *Q1* (*u*); themselues betake, . . . wake. *Q1* (c)
129 **resolving,**] *Q9;* resoluing. *Q1*
130 **abstaining:**] *Capell MS;* abstaining *Q1;* abstaining. *Q3*
135 **possess,**] *Q6;* possesse *Q1*
145 **battle's**] *Bell;* battailes *Q1*
147 **all together**] *Q8;* altogether *Q1*
151 **much,**] *Q3;* much *Q1*
161 **sland'rous**] *Q4* (slanderous); sclandrous *Q1* (*the spelling with* c *used in all forms throughout*)
163 **sleep**] *Q2;* sleeep *Q1*
165 **owls' and wolves'**] *Capell MS;* Owles, & wolues *Q1*
188 **still-slaughtered**] *hyphen, Malone*
200 **fancy's**] *State Poems;* fancies *Q1*
217 **strooken**] *ed.* (*after Capell MS*); stroken *Q1*
298 **captain,**] *Q5;* Captaine: *Q1*
347 **hour,**] *Q3;* howre. *Q1*
360 **night-owl**] *hyphen, Q7*
372 **fiery-pointed**] *hyphen, Sewell*
395 **Show'd**] *England's Parnassus* (*1600*), *Q8;* Showed *Q1*
431 **mothers'**] *Capell MS;* mothers *Q1*
440 **scale,**] *Q3;* scale. *Q1*
446 **lock'd-up**] *hyphen, Gildon*
452 **a-shaking**] *hyphen, Bell*
459 **antics**] *State Poems;* Antiques *Q1*
460 **Such . . . forgeries,**] *with gnomic quotes, Q1*
460 **weak brain's**] *Q6* (*subs.*); weake-brains *Q1*
482 **never-conquered**] *hyphen, Q3*
507 **wings'**] *Capell MS;* wings *Q1*
509 **falchion**] *Malone* (*after Ewing*); Fauchion *Q1* (*so in ll. 1046, 1626*)
511 **falcons'**] *Capell MS;* Faulcons *Q1*
515 **slay,**] *Q2;* slay. *Q1*
528 **A . . . end**] *with gnomic quotes, Q1*
530 **The . . . compacted**] *with gnomic quotes, Q1*
535 **device**] *Q6;* deuise *Q1*
540 **dead-killing**] *hyphen, Q3*
549 **dark womb**] *Q5;* dark-womb *Q1*
560 **Tears . . . raining.**] *with gnomic quotes, Q1*
560 **wear**] *Capell MS;* were *Q1*
571 **human**] *State Poems;* humaine *Q1*
598 **me:**] *Kittredge;* me. *Q1*
609 **kings'**] *Capell MS;* Kings *Q1*
620 **blame,**] *Malone;* blame? *Q1*
621 **name?**] *Capell MS;* name. *Q1*
624 **thee,**] *State Poems;* thee *Q1*
628 **fulfill,**] *Gildon;* fulfill? *Q1*
630 **way?**] *Capell MS;* way. *Q1*
638 **heav'd-up**] *hyphen, Gildon*
650 **sovereign, . . . haste**] *Dyce* (*after Malone*); soueraigne . . . hast, *Q1*
650 **falls'**] *Capell MS;* fals *Q1*
665 **low shrubs**] *Q3;* low-shrubs *Q1*
666 **state"—**] *Capell MS;* state, *Q1*
668 **not,**] *Q5;* not *Q1*
704 **abomination**] *State Poems;* abhomination *Q1*
709 **knit brow**] *Q3;* knit-brow *Q1*
729 **dark night**] *Q5;* dark-night *Q1*
779 **unwholesome**] *Q2* (vnholesome); vnholdsome *Q1*
786 **silver-shining**] *hyphen, State Poems*
831–2 **How . . . blows,**] *with gnomic quotes, Q1*
838 **robb'd**] *Gildon;* rob'd *Q1*
846 **virtue: . . . evil,**] *Gildon* (*subs., after Q8*); Vertue (O . . . euill,) *Q1*
846 **unlook'd-for**] *hyphen, Ewing*
853 **But . . . absolute,**] *with gnomic quotes, Q1*
858 **still-pining**] *hyphen, Capell MS*
867–8 **The . . . ours.**] *with gnomic quotes, Q1*
874 **ill-annexed**] *hyphen, Q3*
879 **'point'st**] *Malone;* poinst *Q1*
907 **Advice**] *Gildon;* Aduise *Q1*
917 **stay'd**] *Q3;* staied *Q1*
921 **abomination**] *Q9;* abhomination *Q1*
922 **inclination**] *Q3;* inclination. *Q1*
950 **oak's**] *State Poems;* oakes *Q1*
959 **water-drops**] *hyphen, State Poems*
975 **bedred**] *cf.* Hamlet, *I.ii.29;* Love's Labor's Lost, *I.i.138*
1009 **bathe**] *Q3;* bath *Q1*
1018 **skill-contending**] *hyphen, Q3*
1039 **slaughter-house**] *hyphen, Q7*
1048 **fear'd,**] *Q3;* fear'd *Q1*
1079 **this,**] *Gildon;* this *Q1*
1103 **passion's**] *Gildon;* passions *Q1*
1109–18 **For . . . flood,**] *with gnomic quotes, Q1*
1112 **suffic'd**] *Malone;* suffiz'd *Q1*
1125 **A . . . guests.**] *with gnomic quotes, Q1*
1126 **Relish**] *Q4;* Ralish *Q1*
1127 **Distress . . . tears.**] *with gnomic quotes, Q1*
1129 **hair**] *Q4;* heare *Q1*
1147 **kinds;**] *Q9* (kinds:); kinds, *Q1*
1155 **reproach's**] *Capell MS;* reproches *Q1*
1163–6 **dearer, . . . Collatine?**] *Sewell;* dearer? . . . deuine, . . . nearer? . . . Colatine: *Q1*
1182 **by**] *Q1* (c); for *Q1* (*u*)
1193 **resolution, love,**] *Q3;* resolution loue *Q1*
1200 **resolution, husband,**] *Q3* (*subs.*); resolution Husband *Q1*
1216 **For . . . flies.**] *with gnomic quotes, Q1*
1220 **slow tongue**] *Q3;* slow-tongue *Q1*
1224 **cloud-eclipsed**] *hyphen, Q3*
1226 **weep,**] *State Poems;* weepe *Q1*
1229 **eyne, enforc'd**] *Q8;* eien inforst, *Q1*
1231 **salt-wav'd**] *hyphen, Q3*
1247 **smoothness,**] *Gildon;* smoothnesse; *Q1*
1249 **remain**] *Q3;* remaine. *Q1*
1263 **ensue**] *Capell MS;* insue. *Q1*
1264 **wrong.**] *Q3* (wrong:); wrong, *Q1*
1265 **belong**] *Q8;* belong: *Q1*
1268 **this,**] *Capell MS;* this *Q1*
1276 **hence?**] *Q3;* hence, *Q1*
1284 **"O . . . Lucrece,**] *Q3* (*subs.*); (O peace quoth Lucrece) *Q1*
1293 **dear.**] *State Poems* (*subs.*); Deare, *Q1*
1300 **curious-good**] *hyphen, Capell MS*
1312 **schedule**] *Q8;* Cedule *Q1*
1317 **Besides,**] *Q8;* Besides *Q1*
1318 **hoards, to spend**] *Sewell;* hoords to spend, *Q1*
1335 **blast**] *Q1* (c); blasts *Q1* (*u*)
1344 **shame,**] *Malone;* shame. *Q1*
1350 **this . . . the**] the . . . this *in four copies of Q1; this is a possible reading, and it is not certain which reading represents the corrected state*
1370, 1524 **Ilion**] *Q4;* Illion *Q1*
1386 **far-off**] *Gildon;* farre of *Q1;* farre off *Q3*
1389 **quick bearing**] *Malone;* quick-bearing, *Q1*
1406 **Wagg'd**] *Q9;* Wag'd *Q1*
1423 **compact,**] *Q4;* compact *Q1*
1429 **strong-besieged**] *hyphen, Sewell*
1443 **well-painted**] *hyphen, State Poems*
1444 **stell'd**] *Gildon;* steld *Q1*

1450 **anatomiz'd]** *Q8;* anathomiz'd *Q1*
1473 **lust, fond Paris,]** *Q3;* lust fond Paris *Q1*
1482 **woe.]** *Q3;* woe, *Q1*
1483–4 **fall, . . . general?]** *Sewell;* fall? . . . generall. *Q1*
1496 **a-work]** *hyphen, Gildon*
1522 **slew;]** *Gildon;* slew. *Q1*
1523 **wildfire]** *Q8* (wild-fire); wild fire *Q1*
1537 **took:]** *Gildon;* tooke *Q1*
1542 **sober-sad]** *hyphen, Capell MS*
1546 **vice: . . . cherish,]** *Q5;* vice, . . . cherish: *Q1*
1557 **cold,]** *Malone;* cold *Q1*
1573 **sorrow's]** *Ewing;* sorrowes *Q1*
1579 **others']** *Malone;* others *Q1*
1590 **sad-beholding]** *hyphen, Sewell*
1644 **Rome]** *Q3;* Roome *Q1*
1652 **robb'd]** *Gildon;* rob'd *Q1*
1660 **here]** *Q5;* heare *Q1*
1670–1 **fast (In . . . past),]** *ed.;* fast: / In . . . past, *Q1*
1671 **rage,]** *Malone;* rage *Q1*
1672 **sorrows,]** *Capell MS;* sorrowes *Q1*
1679 **feeling-painful]** *hyphen, Malone*
1680 **one]** *Q3;* on *Q1*
1684 **own.]** *State Poems (subs.);* own, *Q1*
1685 **past:]** *Malone;* past, *Q1*
1687 **For . . . iniquity.]** *with gnomic quotes, Q1*
1705 **low-declined]** *hyphen, Q9*
1713 **in it]** *Capell MS;* it in *Q1*
1715 **excuse's]** *Malone;* excuses *Q1*
1730 **Stone-still]** *hyphen, Q8*
1740 **late-sack'd]** *hyyhen, Malone*
1768 **falt'ring]** *Gildon;* foultring *Q1*
1773 **Lucretius]** *Q2;* Lucrecius *Q1*
1789, 1797 **sorrow's]** *State Poems;* sorrowes *Q1*
1804 **fill'd]** *Gildon;* fild *Q1*
1820 **long-experienc'd]** *hyphen, Capell MS*
1821 **Why,]** *Gildon;* Why *Q1*
1832 **abominations]** *State Poems;* abhominations. *Q1 (the Yale Elizabethan Club copy of Q1 omits the period and represents a late corrected state of sheet M, not recorded by Rollins)*
1851 **Rome]** *Q3;* Roome *Q1*
1853 **done]** *Malone;* done, *Q1*
1855] *This line followed by* FINIS. *in Q1*

Lucrece and Tarquin. From an engraving by J. C. Visscher after David Vinckeboons. The four scenes shown above are from a dramatic representation, staged in Amsterdam in 1609, of the events that culminated in the expulsion of the Tarquins and the founding of the Roman Republic. Readily recognizable here are (1) Tarquin compelling Lucrece with threats of death; (2) Lucrece on the point of stabbing herself; (3) Collatine and the other lords in consternation at her suicide; (4) the Tarquins being driven from Rome. *(Rijksmuseum, Amsterdam)*

Sonnets

SHAKESPEARE'S SONNETS were published, under that title, in 1609 by Thomas Thorpe and distributed through two booksellers, William Aspley and John Wright. Quite evidently the publication was not authorized nor seen through the press by the author, for the text is considerably worse than the texts of *Venus and Adonis* and *Lucrece* and there is no dedication by the author. Instead there is a cryptic dedication by the publisher to a mysterious "Mr. [Master] W. H." who is described as "the only begetter" of the sonnets and is wished "all happiness and that eternity promised by our ever-living poet."

The obscure wording of the dedication has led to much conjecture but has permitted no certainty. If, as has been argued, "the only begetter" means merely the person who got or procured the sonnets for the printer, it seems odd that the publisher should wish him immortality for his pains, especially since his name is not revealed by the initials. If Master W. H. is not the mere procurer of the text of the poems, but the young man who is promised immortality in some of them (for example, 55, 60, 63, 81, 107), his identity remains obscure, though two noblemen who were certainly patrons of Shakespeare at some time in his life are the favorite candidates of the commentators. William Herbert, third Earl of Pembroke, was one of the dedicatees of the First Folio in 1623 and is said there by Heminge and Condell, Shakespeare's fellows, to have valued Shakespeare's works and prosecuted both them, and him when he was alive, with much favor. His initials are right, but it would have been disrespectful for a common publisher to call an Earl "Master," and there is no evidence of any connection between Shakespeare and Pembroke as early as the most probable dating of the composition of the sonnets would require. Henry Wriothesley, third Earl of Southampton, was certainly a patron of Shakespeare's in the early 1590's, as the dedications to *Venus and Adonis* and *Lucrece* show. The second dedication, especially, suggests a certain degree of intimacy, and it ends with the phrase "all happiness" which Thorpe invoked on Master W. H. The initials, if they are Southampton's, are transposed, and again rank is slighted, but it should be admitted that Thorpe was not trying to reveal to the public the identity of W. H. Many other candidates have been proposed, with rather less plausibility.

Shakespeare's sonnets, or some of them, were circulating in manuscript for a decade before their publication, for Francis Meres referred in 1598 to "his sugared sonnets among his private friends," and in the next year two of them (138 and 144) appeared in a miscellaneous collection called *The Passionate Pilgrim.* Attempts have been made to date the sonnets from supposed topical references in them, but no such references are indisputably clear, even in Sonnet 107, which obviously alludes to contemporary events. On grounds of style and verbal correspondences with the plays and non-dramatic poems, the period of 1592 to 1595 or 1596, with the possibility of occasional later sonnets, would seem satisfactory to most Shakespearean scholars.

The order in which the 154 sonnets are printed in Thorpe's edition cannot be said to have the authority of the poet himself, but attempts by various editors to rearrange them have failed to carry conviction to others, and the original order is therefore followed in most modern editions. In this arrangement, the first 126 sonnets seem to be addressed to a young man, beloved of the poet, of superior beauty and rank but of somewhat questionable morals and constancy. In the first seventeen sonnets the young man is urged to marry and beget children. The attitude of the poet toward the friend is one of love and admiration, deference and possessiveness, but it is not at all a sexual passion. Sonnet 20 makes quite clear the difference between the platonic love of a man for a man, more often expressed in the sixteenth century than the twentieth, and any kind of homosexual attachment.

The sonnets numbered 127–152 form a less coherent group. They involve a mistress of the poet's, a mysterious "Dark Lady"—i.e. not blonde, as the current fashion in beauty preferred—who is sensual, promiscuous, and irresistible. The poet's attitude toward her is frankly lustful, with occasional pangs of conscience and feelings of revulsion. Apparently, to judge by the key sonnet 144, the Dark Lady seduced the poet's friend, and the poet's reaction is one of concern for the friend rather than ordinary jealousy. Identification of a real person with the Dark Lady is more difficult even than identification of the friend; some commentators who confidently assert that the young man is Southampton or Pembroke or another believe that the name of the mistress will never be known. Some of the sonnets in the first series (35, 40, 41, 42) apparently refer to the liaison between the friend and the lady, and so we cannot assume that the two groups, or sonnets within a group, are in chronological order.

Several sonnets addressed to the friend (79, 80, 83, 86, and perhaps 21) refer to another poet who is a rival for the friend's esteem, and several others (78, 82, 84, 85) make clear that the friend is a subject of praise by many poets. Who the particular rival poet was is still another question to which various answers have been given, none with much supporting evidence. Those commentators who feel that Shakespeare would apply the phrase "the proud full sail of his great verse" (86.1) to none of his contemporaries but Marlowe must date the sonnets, or the events behind them, quite early, for Marlowe died in 1593. Chapman is another favorite, partly because references in sonnet 86 may have some connection with his *Shadow of Night* (1594). Yet no one has found any evidence that either Chapman or Marlowe wrote verse to either Southampton or Pembroke. Much Elizabethan verse which never reached print has not survived; it is perhaps by the merest accident that Thorpe got hold of Shakespeare's sonnets and published them. Accordingly, the rival poet (if he was a real person) and his works may well be forever lost in the dark backward and abysm of time.

The two final sonnets in Thorpe's edition do not, apparently, belong to either the friend or the Dark Lady sequence. They are translations, or adaptations, of some version of a Greek epigram, and they evidently refer to the hot springs at Bath. There is no sufficient ground for denying, as some have tried to do, their authorship to Shakespeare.

An agnostic position with respect to the biographical significance of Shakespeare's sonnets may not be one which is permanently satisfying to hold. It rests upon the rather dry and academic principle that there is insufficient evidence to warrant a positive conclusion. Yet it does encourage the focusing of attention upon what is surely most important about the sonnets—their literary quality and characteristics.

The composition of sonnet cycles was a European vogue, an imitation of Petrarch's famous cycles to Laura. The fad reached England not long before 1590; it flourished there to such an extent that some twelve hundred sonnets have survived in print from the last decade of the century. Individual sonnets, translated or imitated from Petrarch or his followers, had of course been published in England earlier, from the time of Wyatt and Surrey on. But the cycle, with a thread of story and a named lady, who usually gave her name—Delia, Idea, Diana, Phillis, or the like—to the series itself, was introduced into England by the publication of Sidney's *Astrophel and Stella* in 1591. It had been written as early as 1582, but until its publication it was known only to a small circle of intimates. Many English poets of the nineties composed sonnet cycles: Spenser, Daniel, Drayton, and a host of minor versifiers.

The conventions of the sonnet cycle offered ample opportunity for poets to display their wit and ingenuity. One of the conventions was a disclaimer of conventionality and a pretense of originality. Standard themes were the lady's coldness and the poet's despair, a blazon or catalogue of the lady's beauties, invocations to sleep, and assertions of the immortality of verse. Some of the sonnet cycles reveal in part an autobiographical narrative or situation, and the lady can be identified with a real person—Penelope, Lady Rich, in Sidney's, and the poet's wife, Elizabeth, in Spenser's. In others the lady is the poet's patroness or even a wholly imaginary figure.

Sidney's *Astrophel and Stella* is distinguished by its vivid dramatization of moods, its colloquial directness, and its energy. Spenser's cycle *Amoretti* is notable for its musical qualities, its emblematic imagery, and its deep Platonic and Christian feeling. Drayton's *Idea's Mirror* strives for originality by drawing images from unusual sources—bookkeeping, the alphabet, celestial numbers—and offers the reader a quite bewildering rhetorical and metaphorical variety.

Shakespeare's series, though it is well within the general tradition of Elizabethan sonnet cycles, is nevertheless in several ways unique. The principal person addressed by the poet is not a woman but a young man; the Dark Lady, when she appears, is vastly different from the Delias and Celias of Petrarchan convention. More important, the depths of moral and esthetic contemplation in Shakespeare's sonnets are far more profound than we find in any other Elizabethan cycle. The best of these poems could only have been written by the man who wrote *Romeo and Juliet*, *Macbeth*, and *King Lear*.

With three exceptions (99, 126, and 145) Shakespeare uses the sonnet in the popular English form, first fully developed by Surrey, of three quatrains and a couplet. The rhetorical organization most commonly follows this structure also, though occasionally Shakespeare varies it. The couplet usually ties the sonnet to one of the general themes of the series, leaving the quatrains free to develop the poetic intensity which makes the separate sonnets so memorable.

Naive readers sometimes wonder how Shakespeare could have boasted of the immortality of his poems when he did not publish them himself and they came into print only by some accident or the deviousness of the publisher Thorpe. The answer is that the theme was a conventional one. Samuel Daniel's *Delia* (1591, 1592), for example, contains seven sonnets on this subject. Shakespeare has eight (15, 18, 19, 55, 60, 63, 81, 101); some are no better than many a contemporary could have written (81, 101), but others, such as "Not marble nor the gilded monuments" (55) and "Like as the waves make towards the pibbled shore" (60), bear the unmistakable stamp of his genius. The conventional boast of the immortality of verse, far older than the sonnet fad, prompted Shakespeare to meditations on time and mutability as the destroyers of the evanescent beauty of nature and of youth. The passing of the seasons was also a conventional theme; Spenser's cycle can be followed as a kind of calendar. Shakespeare has one sonnet (104) which mentions that he has known the fair friend for three years, but the seasons are transformed into symbols of the lover's moods in a marvellous trio of sonnets (97, 98, 99). Another favorite theme of Shakespeare's is the parable of the talents, as given in Matthew 25:14–30. This gospel text, popular with Elizabethan preachers, especially of the Puritan sort, seems to have haunted Shakespeare's memory. It transforms his imagery about lending, interest, repayment, and fulfillment of contract, conventional enough in itself, into something more profound and searching:

Farewell, thou art too dear for my possessing,
And like enough thou know'st thy estimate;
The charter of thy worth gives thee releasing;
My bonds in thee are all determinate.
. . . .
Thyself thou gav'st, thy own worth then not
  knowing,
Or me, to whom thou gav'st it, else mistaking,
So thy great gift, upon misprision growing,
Comes home again, on better judgment making.
(87.1–4, 9–12)

It is of course interesting to see Shakespeare drawing imagery from his own profession in a sonnet like 23, "As an unperfect actor on the stage," but there seems to be something more personal in the three sonnets (110, 111, 112) in which the poet confesses that he has gone here and there, made himself a motley to the view, gored his own thoughts, and sold cheap what is most dear. The cause of all this, he says, is his fortune which made him earn his living in a public way, which in turn vulgarized him:

Thence comes it that my name receives a brand,
And almost thence my nature is subdu'd
To what it works in, like the dyer's hand.
(111.5–7)

The brand on his name he also calls a vulgar scandal stamped upon his brow. To what particular event these poems refer we cannot now even guess intelligently, but it does not matter. We have the results in the expression of guilt and shame felt by the man who was so often referred to by his contemporaries as "gentle" (i.e. gentlemanly) Shakespeare.

When the subject is sex, as it is in some twenty sonnets of the Dark Lady series, Shakespeare's tone varies from the rapture of *Romeo and Juliet* to the disgust evident in *Hamlet* and *Troilus and Cressida*. Sonnet 129 is an anatomy of lust, with the sombre conclusion

All this the world well knows, yet none knows well
To shun the heaven that leads men to this hell.

By and large the situation is an inferno, made explicit in the summary sonnet 144, "Two loves I have of comfort and despair." Yet we cannot be sure that the final tone is one of renunciation of the body, because there is no certainty about the order of the sonnets. Sonnet 146, "Poor soul, the centre of my sinful earth," would make a satisfactory conclusion if the story is to end that way, but unfortunately Sonnet 151, the nearest thing to indecency in the series, comes after it.

Shakespeare's sonnets constitute a vast landscape of metaphor, surprising often because it seems to anticipate the atmosphere of some of the later plays. In this landscape are some vividly recognizable figures—the poet, the friend, the Dark Lady, and, more indefinite, the rival poet. One should be content with this and not try to make the poems into more literal statements than they are. It is risky to reach the conclusion that Shakespeare is aged merely because he seems to say that he is in Sonnets 22, 62, 73, and 138. Young men, particularly poets, often feel older than they are. And it is foolish—yet it has been done—to suppose that Shakespeare was actually lame because of the third line in Sonnet 37. "More folly has been written about the sonnets than about any other Shakespearean topic" was the judicious estimate of E. K. Chambers in 1930; there seems to be little reason to modify the statement now. Much of this folly arises from a failure to apprehend the deeply metaphorical nature of Shakespeare's language. The sonnets are not allegories to be translated or puzzled out; they are explorations of the human spirit in confrontation with time, death, change, love, lust, and beauty—remembrance of things past and the prophetic soul of the wide world dreaming on things to come.

Shakespeare's sonnets were published when the vogue for sonnets was long past; for thirty years thereafter, so far as we know, the public ignored them. In 1640 John Benson published a curious volume called *Poems Written by Wil. Shakespeare*, which contains all but eight of the sonnets, as well as *The Phoenix and Turtle*, *A Lover's Complaint*, all the poems in the third edition of *The Passionate Pilgrim*, and other poems by various writers. The sonnets were rearranged, in many cases combined into longer "poems," given titles, and altered so that most of those addressed to the young man were made to seem addressed to a woman. Benson's text has no authority and his volume is quite evidently a fraudulent publisher's venture. Nevertheless, for nearly 150 years it was the basis for what the world knew of Shakespeare's sonnets. In 1780 Edmond Malone published the first reliable text and commentary.

Critical appraisal of the sonnets lagged even more conspicuously. George Steevens, who with Malone and Capell made the greatest contribution to Shakespearean scholarship in the eighteenth century, declared of the sonnets in 1793 that "the strongest act of Parliament that could be framed would fail to compel readers into their service." Part of this attitude was prejudice against the sonnet form itself, a neo-classical rejection which can be traced back to Thomas Campion and Ben Jonson in Shakespeare's lifetime. Though Milton wrote some great sonnets, the form was generally scorned until Wordsworth and Keats demonstrated again that it is capable, in the hands of a master, of the greatest poetic expression. Unfortunately, as soon as the literary climate was right for the appreciation of the sonnets as poetry, the attraction of the biographical mystery in the background proved overwhelming. From the first published guess as to the identity of the fair friend—Pembroke, by James Boaden in 1837—until about a century later, the poetry was obscured by the mystery. "With this key [the sonnet] Shakespeare unlocked his heart," wrote Wordsworth, to which Browning retorted, "If so, the less Shakespeare he." About the end of the century the leading Shakespeare authority, Sir Sidney Lee, after some abrupt changes of opinion, settled firmly on the doctrine that the sonnets are purely conventional literary exercises, without any biographical significance. This view was comforting to some, but others found it unacceptable, either because it tainted the poems with insincerity or because it frustrated the scholar's indigenous detective instinct. Curiosity about the biographical mystery has by no means subsided, but now it seems possible to read the poems with major interest in their literary quality.

Hallett Smith

Sonnets

TO . THE . ONLIE . BEGETTER . OF .
THESE . INSVING . SONNETS .
Mr. W. H. ALL . HAPPINESSE .
AND . THAT . ETERNITIE .
PROMISED .
BY .
OVR . EVER-LIVING . POET .
WISHETH .
THE . WELL-WISHING .
ADVENTVRER . IN .
SETTING .
FORTH .

T. T.

[1]

From fairest creatures we desire increase,
That thereby beauty's rose might never die,
But as the riper should by time decease,
His tender heir might bear his memory:
But thou, contracted to thine own bright eyes,
Feed'st thy light's flame with self-substantial fuel,
Making a famine where abundance lies,
Thyself thy foe, to thy sweet self too cruel.
Thou that art now the world's fresh ornament,
And only herald to the gaudy spring,
Within thine own bud buriest thy content,
And, tender chorl, mak'st waste in niggarding:
  Pity the world, or else this glutton be,
  To eat the world's due, by the grave and thee.

Words enclosed in square brackets in the text above are emendations of the copy-text. The Textual Notes record in every instance the reading of the copy-text and the earliest authority for the emendation here adopted.

Dedication. T.T. These are the initials of Thomas Thorpe, publisher of the 1609 quarto. On Mr. W. H., see the introduction.

1.1. **creatures**: created things of every kind. **increase**: fruit, progeny. 4. **tender**: youthful.
5. **contracted**: betrothed or married (perhaps with additional sense of "restricted"). 6. **self-substantial**: of your own substance.
10. **only**: unique, peerless. **gaudy**: bright, sparkling, like a gaud (jewel).
11. **content**: (1) what is contained, i.e. potential fatherhood; (2) contentment.
12. **tender chorl**: youthful churl—an oxymoron, since churls (ill-natured and niggardly men) are typically represented as old. The youth (as the line goes on to say) commits extravagance, not by the prodigality characteristic of young men, but by hoarding.
14. **the world's due**: what you owe the world (increase, offspring). **by . . . thee**: (eaten) by you, in refusing to marry and beget, and by the grave, in consuming you and your potential offspring.

2

When forty winters shall besiege thy brow,
And dig deep trenches in thy beauty's field,
Thy youth's proud livery, so gaz'd on now,
Will be a totter'd weed of small worth held:
Then being ask'd, where all thy beauty lies,
Where all the treasure of thy lusty days,
To say within thine own deep-sunken eyes
Were an all-eating shame, and thriftless praise.
How much more praise deserv'd thy beauty's use,
If thou couldst answer, "This fair child of mine
Shall sum my count, and make my old excuse,"
Proving his beauty by succession thine.
  This were to be new made when thou art old,
  And see thy blood warm when thou feel'st it cold.

3

Look in thy glass and tell the face thou viewest,
Now is the time that face should form another,
Whose fresh repair if now thou not renewest,
Thou dost beguile the world, unbless some mother.

2.3. **proud livery**: gorgeous dress.
4. **totter'd weed**: tattered garment. 6. **lusty**: fresh and vigorous.
8. **all-eating shame**: shameful gluttony. Cf. Sonnet 1.13–14. **thriftless praise**: (1) unprofitable praise; (2) praise for thriftlessness.
9. **use**: (1) employment; (2) investment, lending for interest.
11. **sum . . . excuse**: add up my account and justify me in my age.
12. **Proving . . . thine**: proving that his beauty is technically and legally yours because he derived it from you.

3.3. **repair**: condition.
4. **beguile**: cheat. **unbless some mother**: deprive some woman of the blessing of motherhood.

For where is she so fair whose unear'd womb
Disdains the tillage of thy husbandry?
Or who is he so fond will be the tomb,
Of his self-love, to stop posterity?
Thou art thy mother's glass, and she in thee
Calls back the lovely April of her prime,
So thou through windows of thine age shalt see,
Despite of wrinkles, this thy golden time.
  But if thou live rememb'red not to be,
  Die single, and thine image dies with thee.

4

Unthrifty loveliness, why dost thou spend
Upon thyself thy beauty's legacy?
Nature's bequest gives nothing, but doth lend,
And being frank she lends to those are free:
Then, beauteous niggard, why dost thou abuse
The bounteous largess given thee to give?
Profitless usurer, why dost thou use
So great a sum of sums, yet canst not live?
For having traffic with thyself alone,
Thou of thyself thy sweet self dost deceive,
Then how when Nature calls thee to be gone,
What acceptable audit canst thou leave?
  Thy unus'd beauty must be tomb'd with thee,
  Which used lives th' executor to be.

5

Those hours that with gentle work did frame
The lovely gaze where every eye doth dwell
Will play the tyrants to the very same,
And that unfair which fairly doth excel:
For never-resting time leads summer on
To hideous winter and confounds him there,
Sap check'd with frost and lusty leaves quite gone,
Beauty o'ersnow'd and bareness every where:
Then were not summer's distillation left
A liquid prisoner pent in walls of glass,
Beauty's effect with beauty were bereft,
Nor it nor no remembrance what it was.

5. unear'd: unploughed. The sexual metaphor is very common.
6. husbandry: (1) cultivation; (2) marital duties.
7. so fond will: so foolish that he will. **8. Of:** because of.
9. glass: mirror. **10. prime:** springtime, youth.
11. windows . . . age: i.e. children, who in his old age will permit him a view of what he was in youth.
13. remembr'red . . . be: i.e. to be forgotten.

4.1. spend: use up.
2. thy beauty's legacy: your inheritance of beauty.
4. frank: generous. **are free:** who are bountiful.
5. abuse: misuse. **7. use:** have the use of; but there is an implicit contrast with another common meaning, "lay out at interest, invest profitably" (as in *unus'd* and *used* in lines 13, 14), in terms of which the youth's use is, paradoxically, non-use.
8. live: (1) gain a livelihood; (2) remain alive (through offspring).
9. traffic: commerce, dealings. **10. deceive:** cheat.
14. lives: i.e. would survive in the person of your child.

5.1. gentle work: (1) kindly operation; (2) refined workmanship.
2. gaze: object of gazing.
4. unfair: unbeautify. **fairly:** in beauty.
6. confounds: destroys.
9. summer's distillation: the distillation of summer flowers, perfumes.
11. effect: product. **with:** along with. **were bereft:** would be lost.
12. Nor . . . no: (leaving behind) neither beauty nor any.

  But flowers distill'd, though they with winter meet,
  Leese but their show, their substance still lives sweet.

6

Then let not winter's ragged hand deface
In thee thy summer ere thou be distill'd:
Make sweet some vial; treasure thou some place
With beauty's treasure ere it be self-kill'd.
That use is not forbidden usury,
Which happies those that pay the willing loan;
That's for thyself to breed another thee,
Or ten times happier be it ten for one;
Ten times thyself were happier than thou art,
If ten of thine ten times refigur'd thee,
Then what could death do if thou shouldst depart,
Leaving thee living in posterity?
  Be not self-will'd, for thou art much too fair
  To be death's conquest and make worms thine heir.

7

Lo in the orient when the gracious light
Lifts up his burning head, each under eye
Doth homage to his new-appearing sight,
Serving with looks his sacred majesty,
And having climb'd the steep-up heavenly hill,
Resembling strong youth in his middle age,
Yet mortal looks adore his beauty still,
Attending on his golden pilgrimage:
But when from highmost pitch, with weary car,
Like feeble age he reeleth from the day,
The eyes ('fore duteous) now converted are
From his low tract and look another way:
  So thou, thyself outgoing in thy noon,
  Unlook'd on diest unless thou get a son.

8

Music to hear, why hear'st thou music sadly?
Sweets with sweets war not, joy delights in joy.
Why lov'st thou that which thou receiv'st not gladly,
Or else receiv'st with pleasure thine annoy?
If the true concord of well-tuned sounds,
By unions married, do offend thine ear,
They do but sweetly chide thee, who confounds

14. Leese: lose.

6.1. ragged: rough. **3. treasure:** enrich.
5. use: lending money at interest.
6. happies: makes happy. **pay . . . loan:** willingly repay the loan.
10. refigur'd: reportrayed, copied.
13. self-will'd: (1) obstinate; (2) leaving no inheritance beyond yourself.

7.1. gracious: kingly. **2. under:** i.e. earthly.
4. Serving: worshipping (cf. *divine service*).
5. steep-up: high and precipitous.
9. car: chariot (of the sun-god).
11. converted: turned. **12. tract:** track, path.
13. thyself . . . noon: passing the zenith of your beauty.
14. get: beget.

8.1. Music to hear: you whose voice is music. **sadly:** gravely, without showing pleasure. **4. thine annoy:** what bores you.
6. unions: i.e. harmonious blending. **7. confounds:** destroyest.

In singleness the parts that thou shouldst bear.
Mark how one string, sweet husband to another,
Strikes each in each by mutual ordering;
Resembling sire, and child, and happy mother,
Who all in one, one pleasing note do sing:
Whose speechless song, being many, seeming one,
Sings this to thee, "Thou single wilt prove none."

9

Is it for fear to wet a widow's eye
That thou consum'st thyself in single life?
Ah! if thou issueless shalt hap to die,
The world will wail thee like a makeless wife,
The world will be thy widow and still weep,
That thou no form of thee hast left behind,
When every private widow well may keep,
By children's eyes, her husband's shape in mind.
Look what an unthrift in the world doth spend
Shifts but his place, for still the world enjoys it,
But beauty's waste hath in the world an end,
And kept unus'd, the user so destroys it:
No love toward others in that bosom sits
That on himself such murd'rous shame commits.

10

For shame deny that thou bear'st love to any,
Who for thyself art so unprovident.
Grant, if thou wilt, thou art belov'd of many,
But that thou none lov'st is most evident;
For thou art so possess'd with murd'rous hate,
That 'gainst thyself thou stick'st not to conspire,
Seeking that beauteous roof to ruinate
Which to repair should be thy chief desire.
O, change thy thought, that I may change my mind!
Shall hate be fairer lodg'd than gentle love?
Be as thy presence is gracious and kind,
Or to thyself at least kind-hearted prove:
Make thee another self for love of me,
That beauty still may live in thine or thee.

11

As fast as thou shalt wane, so fast thou grow'st,
In one of thine, from that which thou departest,
And that fresh blood which youngly thou bestow'st
Thou mayst call thine, when thou from youth convertest.
Herein lives wisdom, beauty, and increase,
Without this, folly, age, and cold decay.
If all were minded so, the times should cease,
And threescore year would make the world away.
Let those whom nature hath not made for store,
Harsh, featureless, and rude, barrenly perish:
Look whom she best endow'd she gave the more;
Which bounteous gift thou shouldst in bounty cherish.
She carv'd thee for her seal, and meant thereby,
Thou shouldst print more, not let that copy die.

12

When I do count the clock that tells the time,
And see the brave day sunk in hideous night;
When I behold the violet past prime,
And sable curls [all] silver'd o'er with white;
When lofty trees I see barren of leaves,
Which erst from heat did canopy the herd,
And summer's green all girded up in sheaves
Borne on the bier with white and bristly beard:
Then of thy beauty do I question make
That thou among the wastes of time must go,
Since sweets and beauties do themselves forsake,
And die as fast as they see others grow,
And nothing 'gainst Time's scythe can make defense
Save breed, to brave him when he takes thee hence.

13

O that you were yourself! but, love, you are
No longer yours than you yourself here live:
Against this coming end you should prepare,
And your sweet semblance to some other give.
So should that beauty which you hold in lease
Find no determination; then you were
[Yourself] again after yourself's decease,
When your sweet issue your sweet form should bear.
Who lets so fair a house fall to decay,
Which husbandry in honor might uphold
Against the stormy gusts of winter's day
And barren rage of death's eternal cold?
O, none but unthrifts: dear my love, you know
You had a father, let your son say so.

8. singleness: (1) solo performance; (2) unmarried state. **parts . . . bear:** (1) harmony in which you should bear a part; (2) roles of husband and father that you should be playing.
9–10. one . . . ordering. Referring to the double strings of the lute, one of which vibrates sympathetically when the other is plucked.
12. note: music or harmony, not in unison.
13. Whose: i.e. the strings'. **speechless:** wordless.
14. Thou . . . none. Alluding to the proverbial "One is no number."

9.4. makeless: mateless, widowed. **5. still:** always.
7. private: individual. **9. Look what:** whatever.
10. his: its. **11. beauty's waste:** wasted beauty.
12. the user: i.e. the one who had it to use.
14. murd'rous shame: shameful act of murder.

10.6. stick'st not: dost not hesitate. **conspire:** have evil designs.
8. repair: keep in repair. **9. thought:** intention. **mind:** opinion (of you). **11. presence:** appearance.

11.2. one of thine: a child of yours. **from that which:** in that from which.
3. youngly: in youth. **4. convertest:** changest.
7. minded so: of your mind (to remain childless). **times:** i.e. successive generations of men. **9. store:** a stock to draw upon.
10. Harsh: displeasing to the eye. **featureless:** ill-favored, ugly. **rude:** crudely formed. **11. Look whom:** whomever.
12. in bounty: i.e. by being bountiful.
14. copy: original (as in *printer's copy*).

12.2. brave: splendid, beautiful. **4. sable:** black, dark.
8. bier: i.e. harvest cart. **9. question make:** discuss with myself.
10. wastes of time: things wasted or destroyed by time.
14. breed: offspring. **brave:** defy.

13.1. yourself: i.e. your own, not subject to time and change.
3. Against: in expectation of.
6. determination: end (legal term).
10. husbandry: prudent management (with obvious pun).
11. winter's day: time when winter reigns.
12. barren rage: ravaging which produces barrenness.

14

Not from the stars do I my judgment pluck,
And yet methinks I have astronomy,
But not to tell of good or evil luck,
Of plagues, of dearths, or seasons' quality;
Nor can I fortune to brief minutes tell,
'Pointing to each his thunder, rain, and wind,
Or say with princes if it shall go well
By oft predict that I in heaven find.
But from thine eyes my knowledge I derive,
And, constant stars, in them I read such art
As truth and beauty shall together thrive
If from thyself to store thou wouldst convert;
Or else of thee this I prognosticate,
Thy end is truth's and beauty's doom and date.

15

When I consider every thing that grows
Holds in perfection but a little moment;
That this huge stage presenteth nought but shows
Whereon the stars in secret influence comment;
When I perceive that men as plants increase,
Cheered and check'd even by the self-same sky,
Vaunt in their youthful sap, at height decrease,
And wear their brave state out of memory:
Then the conceit of this inconstant stay
Sets you most rich in youth before my sight,
Where wasteful Time debateth with Decay
To change your day of youth to sullied night,
And all in war with Time for love of you,
As he takes from you, I ingraft you new.

16

But wherefore do not you a mightier way
Make war upon this bloody tyrant Time?
And fortify yourself in your decay
With means more blessed than my barren rhyme?
Now stand you on the top of happy hours,
And many maiden gardens, yet unset,
With virtuous wish would bear your living flowers,
Much liker than your painted counterfeit:
So should the lines of life that life repair
Which this time's pencil, or my pupil pen,

14.1. judgment pluck: draw conclusions.
2. have astronomy: understand astrology.
5. minutes: i.e. short periods of time.
8. oft predict: frequent signs and omens.
10–11. read . . . As: gather such knowledge as that.
12. store: plenty (progeny). **convert:** change.
14. date: limit of duration.

15.2. Holds: stays, as in *hold still*. **4. secret:** occult.
6. Cheered and check'd: urged forward and held back.
7. Vaunt: exult. **sap:** vigor.
8. brave: splendid. **out of memory:** until forgotten (that it ever was "brave"). **9. conceit:** conception, idea.
11. debateth: fights. **with:** together with.
12. sullied: soiled, blackened.
14. ingraft you new: renew you by grafting, implant beauty in you again (by my verse).

16.4 blessed: productive of happy results, effectual.
5. on the top: at the height. **6. unset:** unplanted.
8. counterfeit: portrait.
9. lines of life: living lines (of offspring) in contrast to the lines of a painter or poet. **10. pencil:** paint brush.

Neither in inward worth nor outward fair
Can make you live yourself in eyes of men.
To give away yourself keeps yourself still,
And you must live drawn by your own sweet skill.

17

Who will believe my verse in time to come
If it were fill'd with your most high deserts?
Though yet heaven knows it is but as a tomb
Which hides your life, and shows not half your parts.
If I could write the beauty of your eyes,
And in fresh numbers number all your graces,
The age to come would say, "This poet lies,
Such heavenly touches ne'er touch'd earthly faces."
So should my papers (yellowed with their age)
Be scorn'd, like old men of less truth than tongue,
And your true rights be term'd a poet's rage,
And stretched metre of an antique song:
But were some child of yours alive that time,
You should live twice, in it and in my rhyme.

18

Shall I compare thee to a summer's day?
Thou art more lovely and more temperate:
Rough winds do shake the darling buds of May,
And summer's lease hath all too short a date;
Sometime too hot the eye of heaven shines,
And often is his gold complexion dimm'd,
And every fair from fair sometime declines,
By chance or nature's changing course untrimm'd:
But thy eternal summer shall not fade,
Nor lose possession of that fair thou ow'st,
Nor shall Death brag thou wand'rest in his shade,
When in eternal lines to time thou grow'st.
So long as men can breathe or eyes can see,
So long lives this, and this gives life to thee.

19

Devouring Time, blunt thou the lion's paws,
And make the earth devour her own sweet brood;
Pluck the keen teeth from the fierce tiger's [jaws],
And burn the long-liv'd phoenix in her blood;
Make glad and sorry seasons as thou fleet'st,
And do what e'er thou wilt, swift-footed Time,
To the wide world and all her fading sweets:
But I forbid thee one most heinous crime,
O, carve not with thy hours my love's fair brow,

11. fair: beauty.

17.4. parts: admirable qualities.
6. numbers: verses. **8. touches:** brush strokes.
11. true rights: due praise. **rage:** *furor poeticus*, inspiration. Cf. *fury*, Sonnet 100.3. **12. stretched metre:** poetic exaggeration.

18.1. a summer's day: i.e. the summer season.
2. temperate: of even temperature.
4. lease: allotted time. **date:** duration.
7. fair . . . fair: beautiful thing . . . beauty.
8. untrimm'd: divested of beauty. **10. ow'st:** ownest.
12. to . . . grow'st: you become inseparably engrafted upon time.

19.4. phoenix. Reputed to live five hundred (or, by other accounts, a thousand) years, and then to die in flames. **in her blood:** i.e. in the full vigor of life (a hunting term).

Nor draw no lines there with thine antique pen;
Him in thy course untainted do allow,
For beauty's pattern to succeeding men.
 Yet do thy worst, old Time: despite thy wrong,
 My love shall in my verse ever live young.

20

A woman's face with Nature's own hand painted
Hast thou, the master mistress of my passion;
A woman's gentle heart but not acquainted
With shifting change as is false women's fashion;
An eye more bright than theirs, less false in rolling,
Gilding the object whereupon it gazeth;
A man in hue all hues in his controlling,
Which steals men's eyes and women's souls amazeth.
And for a woman wert thou first created,
Till Nature as she wrought thee fell a-doting,
And by addition me of thee defeated,
By adding one thing to my purpose nothing.
 But since she prick'd thee out for women's pleasure,
 Mine be thy love, and thy love's use their treasure.

21

So is it not with me as with that Muse
Stirr'd by a painted beauty to his verse,
Who heaven itself for ornament doth use,
And every fair with his fair doth rehearse,
Making a couplement of proud compare
With sun and moon, with earth and sea's rich gems,
With April's first-born flowers, and all things rare
That heaven's air in this huge rondure hems.
O, let me, true in love, but truly write,
And then believe me, my love is as fair
As any mother's child, though not so bright
As those gold candles fix'd in heaven's air:
 Let them say more that like of hearsay well,
 I will not praise that purpose not to sell.

22

My glass shall not persuade me I am old,
So long as youth and thou are of one date,

10. antique: (1) old; (2) antic, drawing fantastic lines.
11. untainted: (1) undefiled; (2) untouched by a weapon (a term from tilting, presumably suggested by *in thy course*). **allow:** allow to remain.

20.1. with . . . hand: i.e. without any aid from cosmetics (*with* = by). **2. master mistress:** a paradox which the sonnet elaborates. Some editors join the two words with a hyphen. **passion:** (1) strong feeling, love; (2) love poem. **5. rolling:** roving.
7. hue: shape, form. The line may be corrupt; various editors have emended *A man in hue* to *A woman's hue* or *A maiden hue; his* then = its. **all . . . controlling:** i.e. surpassing all other forms.
10. a-doting: in love (with additional suggestion of folly or irrationality). **11. defeated:** deprived. **12. nothing:** of no value.
13. prick'd thee out: marked you out (with sexual quibble).
14. use: (1) physical enjoyment; (2) interest, as contrasted with capital.

21.1. Muse: i.e. poet. **2. painted:** dependent on cosmetics.
4. every . . . rehearse: compares his lady with every beautiful thing.
5. compare: comparison. **8. rondure:** sphere.
13. hearsay: conventional or trite expressions.
14. that purpose not: who (= since I) do not intend.

22.2. of one date: the same age.

But when in thee time's furrows I behold,
Then look I death my days should expiate.
For all that beauty that doth cover thee
Is but the seemly raiment of my heart,
Which in thy breast doth live, as thine in me:
How can I then be elder than thou art?
O, therefore, love, be of thyself so wary
As I, not for myself, but for thee will,
Bearing thy heart, which I will keep so chary
As tender nurse her babe from faring ill.
 Presume not on thy heart when mine is slain,
 Thou gav'st me thine not to give back again.

23

As an unperfect actor on the stage,
Who with his fear is put besides his part,
Or some fierce thing replete with too much rage,
Whose strength's abundance weakens his own heart,
So I, for fear of trust, forget to say
The perfect ceremony of love's [rite],
And in mine own love's strength seem to decay,
O'ercharg'd with burthen of mine own love's might.
O, let my books be then the eloquence
And dumb presagers of my speaking breast,
Who plead for love, and look for recompense,
More than that tongue that more hath more express'd.
 O, learn to read what silent love hath writ:
 To hear with eyes belongs to love's fine wit.

24

Mine eye hath play'd the painter and hath [stell'd]
Thy beauty's form in table of my heart;
My body is the frame wherein 'tis held,
And perspective it is best painter's art.
For through the painter must you see his skill,
To find where your true image pictur'd lies,
Which in my bosom's shop is hanging still,
That hath his windows glazed with thine eyes.
Now see what good turns eyes for eyes have done:
Mine eyes have drawn thy shape, and thine for me
Are windows to my breast, wherethrough the sun
Delights to peep, to gaze therein on thee.
 Yet eyes this cunning want to grace their art,
 They draw but what they see, know not the heart.

4. expiate: end.
10. will: i.e. will be wary of myself, will take care of myself.
11. Bearing: because I bear. **chary:** carefully.
13. Presume not on: do not count on getting back.

23.1. unperfect: not completely knowing his part.
2. is . . . part: is unable to speak his lines.
5. for . . . trust: fearing to trust myself, lacking self-confidence. **forget:** forget how. **6. rite:** ritual. **7. decay:** grow weak.
9. books. Citing Sonnet 85, many editors prefer Sewell's emendation *looks*. If *books* is the correct reading, it may mean these sonnets, or, if the addressee is Southampton, the two poems *Venus and Adonis* and *Lucrece*.
10. presagers: presenters, as in the dumb show of a play.
12. more express'd: expressed more often or more fully.

24.1. stell'd: placed, fixed.
2. table: panel on which a picture is painted.
4. perspective: either a glass prism through which the painter (= the eye, line 1) looks at the object, or the technique of composition to suggest distance; perhaps both. **8. his:** its. **glazed:** glassed in.
13. want: lack. **grace:** beautify.

25

Let those who are in favor with their stars
Of public honor and proud titles boast,
Whilst I whom fortune of such triumph bars
Unlook'd for joy in that I honor most.
Great princes' favorites their fair leaves spread
But as the marigold at the sun's eye,
And in themselves their pride lies buried,
For at a frown they in their glory die.
The painful warrior famoused for [fight],
After a thousand victories once foil'd,
Is from the book of honor rased quite,
And all the rest forgot for which he toil'd.
Then happy I that love and am beloved
Where I may not remove, nor be removed.

26

Lord of my love, to whom in vassalage
Thy merit hath my duty strongly knit,
To thee I send this written ambassage
To witness duty, not to show my wit;
Duty so great, which wit so poor as mine
May make seem bare, in wanting words to show it,
But that I hope some good conceit of thine
In thy soul's thought (all naked) will bestow it;
Till whatsoever star that guides my moving
Points on me graciously with fair aspect,
And puts apparel on my tottered loving,
To show me worthy of [thy] sweet respect:
Then may I dare to boast how I do love thee,
Till then, not show my head where thou mayst prove me.

27

Weary with toil, I haste me to my bed,
The dear repose for limbs with travel tired,
But then begins a journey in my head
To work my mind, when body's work's expired;
For then my thoughts (from far where I abide)
Intend a zealous pilgrimage to thee,
And keep my drooping eyelids open wide,
Looking on darkness which the blind do see;
Save that my soul's imaginary sight
Presents [thy] shadow to my sightless view,
Which like a jewel hung in ghastly night,
Makes black night beauteous, and her old face new.
Lo thus by day my limbs, by night my mind,
For thee, and for myself, no quiet find.

25.4 Unlook'd for: unexpectedly. **that:** what. **6. But:** only.
9. painful: toiling with pain. **fight.** Some editors retain the reading of the 1609 quarto, *worth*, and in line 11 emend *quite* to *forth*.
11. rased: erased, blotted out. **12. rest:** i.e. earlier victories.

26.3. ambassage: message. **4. wit:** i.e. poetic ability.
7. good conceit: favorable opinion.
8. all naked. Continues *bare*, line 6. **bestow:** provide hospitality for, lodge. **11. tottered:** tattered.
12. respect: consideration. **14. prove:** test, try.

27.1. toil: toilsome journeying (cf. Sonnet 28, 7–8).
4. To work: to cause to work. **6. Intend:** set out upon.
9. imaginary: imagining. **10. shadow:** image.
11. ghastly: terrifying.

28

How can I then return in happy plight
That am debarr'd the benefit of rest?
When day's oppression is not eas'd by night,
But day by night and night by day oppress'd;
And each (though enemies to [either's] reign)
Do in consent shake hands to torture me,
The one by toil, the other to complain
How far I toil, still farther off from thee.
I tell the day, to please him, thou art bright,
And dost him grace when clouds do blot the heaven;
So flatter I the swart-complexion'd night,
When sparkling stars twire not thou [gild'st] th' even:
But day doth daily draw my sorrows longer,
And night doth nightly make grief's length seem stronger.

29

When in disgrace with Fortune and men's eyes
I all alone beweep my outcast state,
And trouble deaf heaven with my bootless cries,
And look upon myself and curse my fate,
Wishing me like to one more rich in hope,
Featur'd like him, like him with friends possess'd,
Desiring this man's art, and that man's scope,
With what I most enjoy contented least;
Yet in these thoughts myself almost despising,
Haply I think on thee, and then my state
(Like to the lark at break of day arising
From sullen earth) sings hymns at heaven's gate,
For thy sweet love rememb'red such wealth brings,
That then I scorn to change my state with kings.

30

When to the sessions of sweet silent thought
I summon up remembrance of things past,
I sigh the lack of many a thing I sought,
And with old woes new wail my dear time's waste;
Then can I drown an eye (unus'd to flow)
For precious friends hid in death's dateless night,
And weep afresh love's long since cancell'd woe,
And moan th' expense of many a vanish'd sight;
Then can I grieve at grievances foregone,
And heavily from woe to woe tell o'er

28.1. plight: state. **6. shake hands:** seal a compact.
7. complain: make me complain.
11. flatter: gratify. **swart:** black, dark.
12. When: i.e. by telling him that when. **twire:** peep. **even:** evening.

29.1. disgrace: disfavor.
6. Featur'd: i.e. handsome. **like him, like him:** like another, like a third.
7. art: literary skill (?). **scope:** intellectual range.
10. state: i.e. mental or emotional state, mood.
12. sullen: (1) dull, heavy; (2) sombre.
14. state. The word here adds to its meaning in line 10 the sense "throne."

30.3. sigh: bemoan.
4. my . . . waste: the destruction of the best part of my life.
6. dateless: without termination.
7. cancell'd: paid in full (with tears). **8. expense:** loss.
9. foregone: past. **10. heavily:** sadly. **tell:** count.

The sad account of fore-bemoaned moan,
Which I new pay as if not paid before:
  But if the while I think on thee, dear friend,
  All losses are restor'd, and sorrows end.

31

Thy bosom is endeared with all hearts
Which I by lacking have supposed dead,
And there reigns love and all love's loving parts,
And all those friends which I thought buried.
How many a holy and obsequious tear
Hath dear religious love stol'n from mine eye
As interest of the dead, which now appear
But things remov'd that hidden in [thee] lie!
Thou art the grave where buried love doth live,
Hung with the trophies of my lovers gone,
Who all their parts of me to thee did give:
That due of many now is thine alone.
  Their images I lov'd I view in thee,
  And thou (all they) hast all the all of me.

32

If thou survive my well-contented day,
When that churl Death my bones with dust shall cover,
And shalt by fortune once more re-survey
These poor rude lines of thy deceased lover,
Compare them with the bett'ring of the time,
And though they be outstripp'd by every pen,
Reserve them for my love, not for their rhyme,
Exceeded by the height of happier men.
O then voutsafe me but this loving thought:
"Had my friend's Muse grown with this growing age,
A dearer birth than this his love had brought
To march in ranks of better equipage;
  But since he died and poets better prove,
  Theirs for their style I'll read, his for his love."

33

Full many a glorious morning have I seen
Flatter the mountain tops with sovereign eye,
Kissing with golden face the meadows green,
Gilding pale streams with heavenly alcumy;
Anon permit the basest clouds to ride
With ugly rack on his celestial face,
And from the forlorn world his visage hide,
Stealing unseen to west with this disgrace:

31.1. **endeared**: enriched.
5. **obsequious**: dutiful in performing funeral rites.
6. **religious**: dutiful, devoted.
7. **interest**: right. **which**: who. 8. **remov'd**: absent.
10. **trophies**: memorials. **lovers**: friends (a common Elizabethan usage; cf. Sonnet 32.4). 11. **parts**: shares.
14. **all they**: comprising all of them.

32.1. **my well-contented day**: i.e. the day of my death, at which I shall not repine.
5. **bett'ring . . . time**: i.e. improved writing of that day.
7. **Reserve**: preserve, treasure up. **rhyme**: i.e. poetic excellence.
8. **happier**: more gifted. 9. **voutsafe**: vouchsafe.
12. **equipage**: equipment and dress (a common expression for literary production).

33.4. **alcumy**: alchemy. 5. **Anon**: soon. **basest**: darkest.
6. **rack**: vaporous mass or streamer.

Even so my sun one early morn did shine
With all-triumphant splendor on my brow,
But out, alack, he was but one hour mine,
The region cloud hath mask'd him from me now.
  Yet him for this my love no whit disdaineth:
  Suns of the world may stain, when heaven's sun staineth.

34

Why didst thou promise such a beauteous day,
And make me travel forth without my cloak,
To let base clouds o'ertake me in my way,
Hiding thy brav'ry in their rotten smoke?
'Tis not enough that through the cloud thou break,
To dry the rain on my storm-beaten face,
For no man well of such a salve can speak
That heals the wound, and cures not the disgrace;
Nor can thy shame give physic to my grief,
Though thou repent, yet I have still the loss,
Th' offender's sorrow lends but weak relief
To him that bears the strong offense's [cross].
  Ah, but those tears are pearl which thy love sheeds,
  And they are rich, and ransom all ill deeds.

35

No more be griev'd at that which thou hast done:
Roses have thorns, and silver fountains mud,
Clouds and eclipses stain both moon and sun,
And loathsome canker lives in sweetest bud.
All men make faults, and even I in this,
Authorizing thy trespass with compare,
Myself corrupting, salving thy amiss,
Excusing [thy] sins more than [thy] sins are;
For to thy sensual fault I bring in sense—
Thy adverse party is thy advocate—
And 'gainst myself a lawful plea commence.
Such civil war is in my love and hate,
  That I an accessary needs must be
  To that sweet thief which sourly robs from me.

36

Let me confess that we two must be twain,
Although our undivided loves are one:
So shall those blots that do with me remain,
Without thy help, by me be borne alone.
In our two loves there is but one respect,
Though in our lives a separable spite,

11. **out, alack**: alas. 12. **region**: of the upper air.
14. **stain**: lose brightness.

34.3. **base**: dark.
4. **brav'ry**: splendor. **rotten smoke**: foul vapors.
9. **shame**: remorse. 12. **cross**: affliction. 13. **sheeds**: sheds.

35.3. **stain**: dim. 4. **canker**: rose worm.
6. **Authorizing**: justifying. **compare**: comparisons (such as those in lines 2–4).
7. **Myself . . . amiss**: i.e. spreading excuses over your trespass in an attempt to cure it and corrupting myself by doing so.
8. **Excusing . . . are**: i.e. worse in excusing your sins than you are in sinning. 9. **sense**: reason. 14. **sourly**: with bitter effect.

36.5. **respect**: focus of attention.
6. **separable spite**: spiteful separation.

Which though it alter not love's sole effect,
Yet doth it steal sweet hours from love's delight.
I may not evermore acknowledge thee,
Lest my bewailed guilt should do thee shame,
Nor thou with public kindness honor me,
Unless thou take that honor from thy name.
  But do not so, I love thee in such sort,
  As thou being mine, mine is thy good report.

37

As a decrepit father takes delight
To see his active child do deeds of youth,
So I, made lame by Fortune's dearest spite,
Take all my comfort of thy worth and truth.
For whether beauty, birth, or wealth, or wit,
Or any of these all, or all, or more,
Intitled in [thy] parts do crowned sit,
I make my love ingrafted to this store:
So then I am not lame, poor, nor despis'd,
Whilst that this shadow doth such substance give,
That I in thy abundance am suffic'd,
And by a part of all thy glory live.
  Look what is best, that best I wish in thee:
  This wish I have, then ten times happy me!

38

How can my Muse want subject to invent
While thou dost breathe, that pour'st into my verse
Thine own sweet argument, too excellent
For every vulgar paper to rehearse?
O, give thyself the thanks if aught in me
Worthy perusal stand against thy sight,
For who's so dumb that cannot write to thee,
When thou thyself dost give invention light?
Be thou the tenth Muse, ten times more in worth
Than those old nine which rhymers invocate,
And he that calls on thee, let him bring forth
Eternal numbers to outlive long date.
  If my slight Muse do please these curious days,
  The pain be mine, but thine shall be the praise.

39

O, how thy worth with manners may I sing,
When thou art all the better part of me?
What can mine own praise to mine own self bring?
And what is't but mine own when I praise thee?
Even for this, let us divided live,
And our dear love lose name of single one,
That by this separation I may give
That due to thee which thou deserv'st alone.
O absence, what a torment wouldst thou prove,
Were it not thy sour leisure gave sweet leave
To entertain the time with thoughts of love,
Which time and thoughts so sweetly dost deceive,
  And that thou teachest how to make one twain,
  By praising him here who doth hence remain!

40

Take all my loves, my love, yea, take them all,
What hast thou then more than thou hadst before?
No love, my love, that thou mayst true love call,
All mine was thine, before thou hadst this more.
Then if for my love thou my love receivest,
I cannot blame thee for my love thou usest,
But yet be blam'd, if thou this self deceivest
By willful taste of what thyself refusest.
I do forgive thy robb'ry, gentle thief,
Although thou steal thee all my poverty;
And yet love knows it is a greater grief
To bear love's wrong than hate's known injury.
  Lascivious grace, in whom all ill well shows,
  Kill me with spites, yet we must not be foes.

41

Those pretty wrongs that liberty commits
When I am sometime absent from thy heart,
Thy beauty and thy years full well befits,
For still temptation follows where thou art.
Gentle thou art, and therefore to be won,
Beauteous thou art, therefore to be assailed;
And when a woman woos, what woman's son
Will sourly leave her till [she] have prevailed?
Ay me, but yet thou mightst my seat forbear,
And chide thy beauty and thy straying youth,
Who lead thee in their riot even there
Where thou art forc'd to break a twofold truth:
  Hers by thy beauty tempting her to thee,
  Thine by thy beauty being false to me.

7. **sole:** (1) unique; (2) creating oneness.
9. **not evermore:** never henceforth. **acknowledge:** indicate that I know. 14. **As:** that. The final couplet also ends Sonnet 96.

37.3. **made lame:** i.e. disabled. **dearest spite:** direst injury.
4. **comfort:** delight. **of:** from, in. 5. **wit:** intellect.
7. **Intitled . . . sit:** rightfully enjoy first place among your good qualities.
8. **make . . . to:** engraft my love upon. **store:** accumulation of riches. 13. **Look what:** whatever.

38.1. **want . . . invent:** lack subject matter for writing.
3. **argument:** theme, subject.
4. **paper:** piece of writing. **rehearse:** recite.
5. **in me:** of my writing. 6. **stand against:** meet.
7. **dumb:** destitute of matter.
12. **numbers:** verses. **date:** duration.
13. **curious:** critical. 14. **pain:** effort, labor.

39.1. **manners:** proper modesty.

5. **for:** because of. 11. **entertain:** occupy, while away.
12. **thoughts:** i.e. melancholy thoughts (a common meaning). **dost.** The subject is a supplied *thou*, standing for *absence*, line 9. Many editors emend to *doth* (good Elizabethan usage with a plural subject).
deceive: beguile away. 13. **that:** were it not that.
14. **praising him here:** i.e. making him seem present to me here as I utter his praises.

40.5–6. **if . . . usest:** if for love of me you receive my love (mistress), I cannot blame you because (*for*) you use her (i.e. have intercourse with her; cf. the noun *use* in Sonnet 20.14).
7. **this self:** this one of your selves, i.e. the poet.
8. **willful taste:** sexual enjoyment. **thyself:** your true self, yourself at your best (?). 10. **my poverty:** the little I possess.
12. **known:** open, undissembled.
14. **spites:** injuries, outrages.

41.1. **pretty:** sportive. **liberty:** license, loose behavior.
4. **still:** continuously.
9. **my seat:** the place that belongs to me, i.e. my monopoly of sexual rights. 11. **riot:** wantonness. 12. **truth:** pledge of fidelity.

42

That thou hast her, it is not all my grief,
And yet it may be said I lov'd her dearly;
That she hath thee is of my wailing chief,
A loss in love that touches me more nearly.
Loving offenders, thus I will excuse ye:
Thou dost love her because thou know'st I love her,
And for my sake even so doth she abuse me,
Suff'ring my friend for my sake to approve her.
If I lose thee, my loss is my love's gain,
And losing her, my friend hath found that loss;
Both find each other, and I lose both twain,
And both for my sake lay on me this cross.
  But here's the joy, my friend and I are one;
  Sweet flattery! then she loves but me alone.

43

When most I wink, then do mine eyes best see,
For all the day they view things unrespected,
But when I sleep, in dreams they look on thee,
And darkly bright, are bright in dark directed.
Then thou, whose shadow shadows doth make bright,
How would thy shadow's form form happy show
To the clear day with thy much clearer light,
When to unseeing eyes thy shade shines so!
How would (I say) mine eyes be blessed made
By looking on thee in the living day,
When in dead night [thy] fair imperfect shade
Through heavy sleep on sightless eyes doth stay!
  All days are nights to see till I see thee,
  And nights bright days when dreams do show thee me.

44

If the dull substance of my flesh were thought,
Injurious distance should not stop my way,
For then despite of space I would be brought,
From limits far remote, where thou dost stay.
No matter then although my foot did stand
Upon the farthest earth remov'd from thee,
For nimble thought can jump both sea and land
As soon as think the place where he would be.
But ah, thought kills me that I am not thought,
To leap large lengths of miles when thou art gone,
But that, so much of earth and water wrought,
I must attend time's leisure with my moan,
Receiving [nought] by elements so slow
But heavy tears, badges of either's woe.

45

The other two, slight air and purging fire,
Are both with thee, where ever I abide;
The first my thought, the other my desire,
These present-absent with swift motion slide.
For when these quicker elements are gone
In tender embassy of love to thee,
My life being made of four, with two alone
Sinks down to death, oppress'd with melancholy;
Until live's composition be recured
By those swift messengers return'd from thee,
Who even but now come back again, assured
Of [thy] fair health, recounting it to me.
  This told, I joy, but then no longer glad,
  I send them back again and straight grow sad.

46

Mine eye and heart are at a mortal war,
How to divide the conquest of thy sight:
Mine eye my heart [thy] picture's sight would bar,
My heart mine eye the freedom of that right.
My heart doth plead that thou in him dost lie
(A closet never pierc'd with crystal eyes),
But the defendant doth that plea deny,
And says in him [thy] fair appearance lies.
To ['cide] this title is impanelled
A quest of thoughts, all tenants to the heart,
And by their verdict is determined
The clear eye's moiety and the dear heart's part—
  As thus: mine eye's due is [thy] outward part,
  And my heart's right [thy] inward love of heart.

47

Betwixt mine eye and heart a league is took,
And each doth good turns now unto the other:
When that mine eye is famish'd for a look,
Or heart in love with sighs himself doth smother,
With my love's picture then my eye doth feast,
And to the painted banquet bids my heart;
Another time mine eye is my heart's guest,
And in his thoughts of love doth share a part.
So either by thy picture or my love,
Thyself away are present still with me,
For thou [not] farther than my thoughts canst move,

42.7. abuse: wrong. **8. approve:** test, experience sexually.
9. love's: mistress's. **12. cross:** affliction.

43.1. wink: close my eyes (in sleep).
2. unrespected: unconsidered, unnoticed.
4. darkly bright: lighted though closed (?) or mysteriously lighted (?). **are . . . directed:** see clearly in the darkness.
5. shadow: image. **shadows:** darkness.
6. thy shadow's form: the form that casts your shadow. The line means "What a gladdening sight your actual presence would make."
14. me: to me.

44.1. dull: heavy. **4. limits:** regions. **where:** to where.
9. thought. The first *thought* may mean "melancholy" (cf. Sonnet 39.12).
11. earth and water. Heavy in comparison with the other two elements, air and fire. **wrought:** fashioned, composed.
12. attend . . . moan: wait, lamenting, until time has leisure to unite us.
14. either's: i.e. both earth's and water's (since his tears are heavy like earth and wet like water).

45.1. slight: unsubstantial.
9. live's: life's. **composition:** the proper balance of the four elements in the humors, which was thought to produce health. **recured:** restored.

46.1. mortal: deadly.
2. conquest . . . sight: the right to look at your image. A real portrait may be involved here, rather than the imaginary one of Sonnet 24.
4. freedom: free enjoyment, privilege.
6. crystal: clear, penetrating. **9. 'cide:** decide, award.
10. quest: inquest or jury. **12. moiety:** share.

47.1. league is took: peace treaty is arranged. **10. still:** always.

And I am still with them, and they with thee;
Or if they sleep, thy picture in my sight
Awakes my heart to heart's and eye's delight.

48

How careful was I, when I took my way,
Each trifle under truest bars to thrust,
That to my use it might unused stay
From hands of falsehood, in sure wards of trust!
But thou, to whom my jewels trifles are,
Most worthy comfort, now my greatest grief,
Thou best of dearest, and mine only care,
Art left the prey of every vulgar thief.
Thee have I not lock'd up in any chest,
Save where thou art not, though I feel thou art,
Within the gentle closure of my breast,
From whence at pleasure thou mayst come and part,
And even thence thou wilt be stol'n, I fear,
For truth proves thievish for a prize so dear.

49

Against that time (if ever that time come)
When I shall see thee frown on my defects,
When as thy love hath cast his utmost sum,
Call'd to that audit by advis'd respects;
Against that time when thou shalt strangely pass,
And scarcely greet me with that sun, thine eye,
When love converted from the thing it was
Shall reasons find of settled gravity:
Against that time do I insconce me here
Within the knowledge of mine own desert,
And this my hand against myself uprear,
To guard the lawful reasons on thy part.
To leave poor me thou hast the strength of laws,
Since why to love I can allege no cause.

50

How heavy do I journey on the way,
When what I seek (my weary travel's end)
Doth teach that ease and that repose to say,
"Thus far the miles are measur'd from thy friend."

48.1. took my way: started on my journey.
2. truest: most trustworthy.
4. wards: safes. Cf. *wardrobe*. **5. to:** in comparison with.
6. worthy: precious. **grief:** cause of mental distress (because he is absent and in danger of being stolen).
7. mine only care: the only thing I care about.
8. vulgar: common.
9. chest: (1) coffer; (2) breast. **12. part:** depart.
14. truth: i.e. honesty itself, the antithesis of thievery.

49.1. Against: in preparation for.
3. When as: when. **cast . . . sum:** made its final reckoning.
4. advis'd respects: thoughtful consideration.
5. strangely: like a stranger.
8. of settled gravity: of sufficient weight (to justify the change [?] or for dignified reserve [?]). **9. insconce:** shelter.
10. desert: i.e. lack of desert.
11. this . . . uprear. As if to swear as a witness.
12. guard . . . part: i.e. testify that your reasons are lawful.
14. why to love: why you should love me. **allege no cause:** plead no lawful reason.

50.1. heavy: sad(ly).
3. ease . . . repose: accommodation (at an inn) . . . bed.

The beast that bears me, tired with my woe,
Plods [dully] on, to bear that weight in me,
As if by some instinct the wretch did know
His rider lov'd not speed, being made from thee.
The bloody spur cannot provoke him on,
That sometimes anger thrusts into his hide,
Which heavily he answers with a groan,
More sharp to me than spurring to his side,
For that same groan doth put this in my mind:
My grief lies onward and my joy behind.

51

Thus can my love excuse the slow offense
Of my dull bearer, when from thee I speed:
From where thou art, why should I haste me thence?
Till I return, of posting is no need.
O, what excuse will my poor beast then find,
When swift extremity can seem but slow?
Then should I spur though mounted on the wind,
In winged speed no motion shall I know.
Then can no horse with my desire keep pace;
Therefore desire (of [perfect'st] love being made)
Shall neigh (no dull flesh) in his fiery race,
But love, for love, thus shall excuse my jade:
Since from thee going he went willful-slow,
Towards thee I'll run, and give him leave to go.

52

So am I as the rich whose blessed key
Can bring him to his sweet up-locked treasure,
The which he will not ev'ry hour survey,
For blunting the fine point of seldom pleasure.
Therefore are feasts so solemn and so rare,
Since seldom coming, in the long year set,
Like stones of worth they thinly placed are,
Or captain jewels in the carcanet.
So is the time that keeps you as my chest,
Or as the wardrobe which the robe doth hide,
To make some special instant special blest,
By new unfolding his imprison'd pride.
Blessed are you whose worthiness gives scope,
Being had, to triumph, being lack'd, to hope.

53

What is your substance, whereof are you made,
That millions of strange shadows on you tend?
Since every one hath, every one, one shade,

6. dully: slowly. **weight:** i.e. of grief.
8. being made. Modifies *speed*. **from:** away from.

51.1. slow offense: offense of slowness. **4. posting:** riding fast.
6. swift extremity: extreme of swiftness.
8. In . . . know: even the speed of flight would seem to me like standing still. **14. go:** walk.

52.1. blessed: fortunate, producing happiness.
4. For blunting: lest he blunt. **seldom:** infrequent.
5. solemn: ceremonious. **8. captain:** principal. **carcanet:** necklace. **12. his:** its. **pride:** splendor.
13–14. gives . . . hope: enables me, when you are present, to rejoice, and when you are absent, to hope for your return.

53.2. tend: attend. **3. shade:** shadow.

And you, but one, can every shadow lend:
Describe Adonis, and the counterfeit
Is poorly imitated after you;
On Helen's cheek all art of beauty set,
And you in Grecian tires are painted new;
Speak of the spring and foison of the year,
The one doth shadow of your beauty show,
The other as your bounty doth appear,
And you in every blessed shape we know.
  In all external grace you have some part,
  But you like none, none you, for constant heart.

54

O how much more doth beauty beauteous seem
By that sweet ornament which truth doth give!
The rose looks fair, but fairer we it deem
For that sweet odor which doth in it live.
The canker-blooms have full as deep a dye
As the perfumed tincture of the roses,
Hang on such thorns, and play as wantonly,
When summer's breath their masked buds discloses;
But for their virtue only is their show,
They live unwoo'd, and unrespected fade,
Die to themselves. Sweet roses do not so,
Of their sweet deaths are sweetest odors made:
  And so of you, beauteous and lovely youth,
  When that shall vade, by verse distills your truth.

55

Not marble nor the gilded [monuments]
Of princes shall outlive this pow'rful rhyme,
But you shall shine more bright in these contents
Than unswept stone, besmear'd with sluttish time.
When wasteful war shall statues overturn,
And broils root out the work of masonry,
Nor Mars his sword nor war's quick fire shall burn
The living record of your memory.
'Gainst death and all-oblivious enmity
Shall you pace forth; your praise shall still find room,
Even in the eyes of all posterity
That wear this world out to the ending doom.
  So till the judgment that yourself arise,
  You live in this, and dwell in lovers' eyes.

4. can . . . lend: can cast all manner of shadows (here used in the sense of "shadowy images" or "reflections," such as those specified in lines 5–11). **5. counterfeit:** portrait (in words).
8. tires: attire. **9. foison:** season of plenty, harvest.

54.2. truth: (1) constancy; (2) essence, reality.
5. canker-blooms: wild roses, regarded as weeds.
6. tincture: dye, color. **7. wantonly:** sportively.
8. discloses: opens.
9. for: because. **only . . . show:** consists only of their appearance.
10. unrespected: disregarded.
13. lovely: lovable, in contrast to line 10.
14. When . . . truth: when your external beauty fades, verse will distill and preserve your essential beauty. (Many editors emend *by* to *my*.)

55.3. these contents: what is contained in these sonnets.
4. Than . . . time: than in a memorial stone, dulled by time, which like a lazy housemaid (*sluttish*) has not swept it.
5. wasteful: laying waste, devastating.
6. broils: tumults, uprisings.
7. Nor: neither. **Mars his sword:** Mars' sword [shall destroy].
9. all-oblivious enmity: oblivion, hostile to everything.
13. judgment that: Judgment Day, when.

56

Sweet love, renew thy force, be it not said
Thy edge should blunter be than appetite,
Which but to-day by feeding is allay'd,
To-morrow sharp'ned in his former might.
So, love, be thou: although to-day thou fill
Thy hungry eyes even till they wink with fullness,
To-morrow see again, and do not kill
The spirit of love with a perpetual dullness:
Let this sad int'rim like the ocean be
Which parts the shore, where two contracted new
Come daily to the banks, that when they see
Return of love, more blest may be the view;
  As call it winter, which being full of care,
  Makes summer's welcome thrice more wish'd, more rare.

57

Being your slave, what should I do but tend
Upon the hours and times of your desire?
I have no precious time at all to spend,
Nor services to do, till you require.
Nor dare I chide the world-without-end hour,
Whilst I, my sovereign, watch the clock for you,
Nor think the bitterness of absence sour,
When you have bid your servant once adieu.
Nor dare I question with my jealious thought
Where you may be, or your affairs suppose,
But like a sad slave stay and think of nought
Save where you are how happy you make those.
  So true a fool is love that in your will
  (Though you do any thing) he thinks no ill.

58

That god forbid that made me first your slave
I should in thought control your times of pleasure,
Or at your hand th' account of hours to crave,
Being your vassal bound to stay your leisure.
O, let me suffer (being at your beck)
Th' imprison'd absence of your liberty,
And patience, tame to sufferance, bide each check,
Without accusing you of injury.
Be where you list, your charter is so strong,

56.1. love: the feeling of love. **6. wink:** close in sleep.
9. int'rim: interval.
10. parts the shore: separates the shores. **contracted new:** newly engaged. **11. banks:** shores. **12. love:** the loved one.
13. As: as appropriately. Many editors emend to *Or*.
14. rare: precious.

57.4. require: demand. **8. servant:** (1) slave; (2) lover.
9. question: discuss. **jealious:** jealous.
10. suppose: make conjectures about. **11. sad:** sober.
13. true: constant. **fool:** one who tamely submits. **will:** pleasure, particularly of the senses. The word is capitalized in the 1609 quarto. There may be a pun on the name Will (i.e. Shakespeare); see the note on Sonnet 135.1.

58.2. control: regulate (?) or reprove (?).
3. th' account of: an accounting for. **to crave:** i.e. should crave.
4. stay: await.
6. imprison'd: imprisoning (since it shuts me away from you). **of:** arising from. **liberty:** (1) freedom; (2) libertine behavior (cf. Sonnet 41.1).
7. tame to sufferance: trained to endure anything. **bide each check:** submit to each rebuke. **9. list:** please. **charter:** privilege.

That you yourself may privilege your time
To what you will, to you it doth belong
Your self to pardon of self-doing crime.
 I am to wait, though waiting so be hell,
 Not blame your pleasure, be it ill or well.

59

If there be nothing new, but that which is
Hath been before, how are our brains beguil'd,
Which laboring for invention bear amiss
The second burthen of a former child!
O that record could with a backward look,
Even of five hundreth courses of the sun,
Show me your image in some antique book,
Since mind at first in character was done!
That I might see what the old world could say
To this composed wonder of your frame,
Whether we are mended, or whe'er better they,
Or whether revolution be the same.
 O, sure I am the wits of former days
 To subjects worse have given admiring praise.

60

Like as the waves make towards the pibbled shore,
So do our minutes hasten to their end,
Each changing place with that which goes before,
In sequent toil all forwards do contend.
Nativity, once in the main of light,
Crawls to maturity, wherewith being crown'd,
Crooked eclipses 'gainst his glory fight,
And Time that gave doth now his gift confound.
Time doth transfix the flourish set on youth,
And delves the parallels in beauty's brow,
Feeds on the rarities of nature's truth,
And nothing stands but for his scythe to mow:
 And yet to times in hope my verse shall stand,
 Praising thy worth, despite his cruel hand.

61

Is it thy will thy image should keep open
My heavy eyelids to the weary night?
Dost thou desire my slumbers should be broken,
While shadows like to thee do mock my sight?
Is it thy spirit that thou send'st from thee
So far from home into my deeds to pry,
To find out shames and idle hours in me,
The scope and tenure of thy jealousy?
O no, thy love, though much, is not so great,
It is my love that keeps mine eye awake,
Mine own true love that doth my rest defeat,
To play the watchman ever for thy sake.
 For thee watch I, whilst thou dost wake elsewhere,
 From me far off, with others all too near.

62

Sin of self-love possesseth all mine eye,
And all my soul, and all my every part;
And for this sin there is no remedy,
It is so grounded inward in my heart.
Methinks no face so gracious is as mine,
No shape so true, no truth of such account,
And for myself mine own worth do define,
As I all other in all worths surmount.
But when my glass shows me myself indeed,
Beated and chopp'd with tann'd antiquity,
Mine own self-love quite contrary I read;
Self so self-loving were iniquity.
 'Tis thee (myself) that for myself I praise,
 Painting my age with beauty of thy days.

63

Against my love shall be as I am now
With Time's injurious hand crush'd and o'erworn,
When hours have drain'd his blood and fill'd his brow
With lines and wrinkles, when his youthful morn
Hath travell'd on to age's steepy night,
And all those beauties whereof now he's king
Are vanishing, or vanish'd out of sight,
Stealing away the treasure of his spring;
For such a time do I now fortify
Against confounding age's cruel knife,
That he shall never cut from memory
My sweet love's beauty, though my lover's life.
 His beauty shall in these black lines be seen,
 And they shall live, and he in them still green.

64

When I have seen by Time's fell hand defaced
The rich proud cost of outworn buried age;

10. **privilege**: license, assign.
12. **self-doing**: done by yourself. 13. **am to**: must.

59.3. **laboring**: (1) toiling; (2) in labor. **for invention**: to create something new, but particularly in a literary sense. Cf. Sonnet 38.1, 8.
6. **hundreth**: hundred. **courses . . . sun**: years.
8. **Since . . . done**: since thought was first recorded in writing.
10. **composed wonder**: wonderful composition. **frame**: shape, form.
11. **are mended**: have made progress. **whe'er**: whether.
12. **revolution . . . same**: i.e. the change of times makes no difference.
13. **wits**: talented writers.

60.1. **pibbled**: pebbled. 3. **changing place with**: taking the place of.
4. **In sequent toil**: toiling one after another in close succession. **forwards**: forward. **contend**: struggle.
5. **Nativity**: i.e. the new-born child. **main**: vast expanse.
7. **Crooked**: malignant. 8. **confound**: destroy.
9. **transfix the flourish**: pierce through the outward decoration.
10. **delves the parallels**: digs the furrows.
11. **Feeds . . . truth**: consumes the most precious things true nature produces. 12. **nothing . . . mow**: i.e. everything in nature is subject to his scythe. 13. **in hope**: future. **stand**: endure.

61.8. **scope and tenure**: intent and purport. **jealousy**: suspicion.
11. **defeat**: destroy. 13. **watch**: (1) stand guard; (2) stay awake all night. **wake**: revel at night.

62.8. **As**: as if (?) or in such a way that (?). **other**: others.
10. **Beated**: beaten, battered. Cf. *storm-beaten*, Sonnet 34.6. **chopp'd**: chapped, cracked. **tann'd antiquity**: old age which dries and darkens the skin. Cf. Sonnet 115.7. 13. **for**: as.

63.1. **Against**: in anticipation of the time when.
2. **crush'd and o'erworn**: crumpled and worn bare.
5. **steepy**: precipitous (referring to the dropping of the sun at sunset).
9. **fortify**: prepare defenses. 10. **confounding**: destroying.
12. **though**: i.e. though he will cut. 14. **green**: young and fair.

64.1. **fell**: savage, cruel.
2. **The rich . . . age**: i.e. the monuments of antiquity which were once magnificent, proud, and costly.

When sometime lofty towers I see down rased,
And brass eternal slave to mortal rage;
When I have seen the hungry ocean gain
Advantage on the kingdom of the shore,
And the firm soil win of the wat'ry main,
Increasing store with loss, and loss with store;
When I have seen such interchange of state,
Or state itself confounded to decay,
Ruin hath taught me thus to ruminate,
That Time will come and take my love away.
  This thought is as a death, which cannot choose
  But weep to have that which it fears to lose.

65

Since brass, nor stone, nor earth, nor boundless sea,
But sad mortality o'ersways their power,
How with this rage shall beauty hold a plea,
Whose action is no stronger than a flower?
O how shall summer's honey breath hold out
Against the wrackful siege of batt'ring days,
When rocks impregnable are not so stout,
Nor gates of steel so strong, but Time decays?
O fearful meditation! where, alack,
Shall Time's best jewel from Time's chest lie hid?
Or what strong hand can hold his swift foot back?
Or who his spoil [of] beauty can forbid?
  O none, unless this miracle have might,
  That in black ink my love may still shine bright.

66

Tir'd with all these, for restful death I cry:
As to behold desert a beggar born,
And needy nothing trimm'd in jollity,
And purest faith unhappily forsworn,
And gilded honor shamefully misplac'd,
And maiden virtue rudely strumpeted,
And right perfection wrongfully disgrac'd,
And strength by limping sway disabled,
And art made tongue-tied by authority,
And folly (doctor-like) controlling skill,
And simple truth miscall'd simplicity,
And captive good attending captain ill:
  Tir'd with all these, from these would I be gone,
  Save that to die, I leave my love alone.

3. sometime: formerly, once.
4. eternal. Modifies *brass.* **mortal rage:** the destructive power of mortality. Cf. Sonnet 65.1–3. **7. win of:** gain at the expense of.
8. store: abundance, plenty. **9. state:** condition.
10. state: (1) greatness; (2) apparent stability itself. **confounded:** reduced. **14. to have:** at having.

65.1. Since: i.e. since there is neither.
3. with this rage: against this destructive power. **hold a plea:** maintain a plea (a legal figure, continued in *action* in line 4).
6. wrackful: destructive. **8. decays:** causes (them) to decay.
10. from Time's chest: i.e. away from the danger of being locked up in Time's chest. **12. spoil:** ravaging.

66.1. these: the following. **2. As:** namely.
3. needy nothing: bare insignificance (the opposite of *desert*). **jollity:** gaudy dress. **4. unhappily forsworn:** evilly betrayed.
8. limping sway: incompetent authority. **9. art:** letters, learning.
10. doctor-like: pretending to wisdom. **controlling:** dominating.
11. simplicity: foolishness.
12. attending: following as a subordinate.

67

Ah, wherefore with infection should he live,
And with his presence grace impiety,
That sin by him advantage should achieve,
And lace itself with his society?
Why should false painting imitate his cheek,
And steal dead seeing of his living hue?
Why should poor beauty indirectly seek
Roses of shadow, since his rose is true?
Why should he live, now Nature bankrout is,
Beggar'd of blood to blush through lively veins,
For she hath no exchequer now but his,
And proud of many, lives upon his gains?
  O, him she stores, to show what wealth she had
  In days long since, before these last so bad.

68

Thus is his cheek the map of days outworn,
When beauty liv'd and died as flowers do now,
Before these bastard signs of fair were born,
Or durst inhabit on a living brow;
Before the golden tresses of the dead,
The right of sepulchres, were shorn away,
To live a second life on second head;
Ere beauty's dead fleece made another gay:
In him those holy antique hours are seen,
Without all ornament, itself and true,
Making no summer of another's green,
Robbing no old to dress his beauty new,
  And him as for a map doth Nature store,
  To show false Art what beauty was of yore.

69

Those parts of thee that the world's eye doth view
Want nothing that the thought of hearts can mend;
All tongues (the voice of souls) give thee that [due],
Utt'ring bare truth, even so as foes commend.
[Thy] outward thus with outward praise is crown'd,
But those same tongues that give thee so thine own,
In other accents do this praise confound
By seeing farther than the eye hath shown.
They look into the beauty of thy mind,
And that in guess they measure by thy deeds,
Then, churls, their thoughts (although their eyes were
      kind)

67.1. with infection: in a time of moral corruption.
4. lace: adorn. **6. dead seeing:** the lifeless appearance.
7. poor: inferior, defective. **indirectly:** falsely, wrongfully (?) or at second hand (?).
8. Roses of shadow: painted roses. **9. bankrout:** bankrupt.
11. For: since. Many editors emend *veins, . . . gains?* (lines 10, 12) to *veins? . . . gains.*; *For* then = because.
12. proud: i.e. though making a proud boast. **gains:** endowment (of beauty). **13. stores:** preserves, keeps alive.
14. last: latest, i.e. present.

68.1. map: picture. **2. as . . . now:** i.e. naturally.
3. fair: beauty. **4. inhabit:** dwell.
6. The right of: rightfully belonging to.
9. antique hours: ancient times.
10. all: any. **13. store:** preserve.

69.2. Want nothing: have no lack.
6. thine own: your due. **7. confound:** destroy.

To thy fair flower add the rank smell of weeds:
But why thy odor matcheth not thy show,
The [soil] is this, that thou dost common grow.

70

That thou are blam'd shall not be thy defect,
For slander's mark was ever yet the fair;
The ornament of beauty is suspect,
A crow that flies in heaven's sweetest air.
So thou be good, slander doth but approve
[Thy] worth the greater, being woo'd of time,
For canker vice the sweetest buds doth love,
And thou present'st a pure unstained prime.
Thou hast pass'd by the ambush of young days,
Either not assail'd, or victor being charg'd,
Yet this thy praise cannot be so thy praise
To tie up envy, evermore enlarg'd:
If some suspect of ill mask'd not thy show,
Then thou alone kingdoms of hearts shouldst owe.

71

No longer mourn for me when I am dead
Than you shall hear the surly sullen bell
Give warning to the world that I am fled
From this vile world with vildest worms to dwell;
Nay, if you read this line, remember not
The hand that writ it, for I love you so,
That I in your sweet thoughts would be forgot,
If thinking on me then should make you woe.
O, if (I say) you look upon this verse,
When I (perhaps) compounded am with clay,
Do not so much as my poor name rehearse,
But let your love even with my life decay;
Lest the wise world should look into your moan,
And mock you with me after I am gone.

72

O, lest the world should task you to recite
What merit liv'd in me that you should love
After my death, dear love, forget me quite,
For you in me can nothing worthy prove;
Unless you would devise some virtuous lie,
To do more for me than mine own desert,
And hang more praise upon deceased I
Than niggard truth would willingly impart:
O, lest your true love may seem false in this,
That you for love speak well of me untrue,
My name be buried where my body is,
And live no more to shame nor me nor you.
For I am sham'd by that which I bring forth,
And so should you, to love things nothing worth.

73

That time of year thou mayst in me behold
When yellow leaves, or none, or few, do hang
Upon those boughs which shake against the cold,
Bare [ruin'd] choirs, where late the sweet birds sang.
In me thou seest the twilight of such day
As after sunset fadeth in the west,
Which by and by black night doth take away,
Death's second self, that seals up all in rest.
In me thou seest the glowing of such fire
That on the ashes of his youth doth lie,
As the death-bed whereon it must expire,
Consum'd with that which it was nourish'd by.
This thou perceiv'st, which makes thy love more strong,
To love that well, which thou must leave ere long.

74

But be contented when that fell arrest
Without all bail shall carry me away,
My life hath in this line some interest,
Which for memorial still with thee shall stay.
When thou reviewest this, thou dost review
The very part was consecrate to thee:
The earth can have but earth, which is his due,
My spirit is thine, the better part of me.
So then thou hast but lost the dregs of life,
The prey of worms, my body being dead,
The coward conquest of a wretch's knife,
Too base of thee to be remembered.
The worth of that is that which it contains,
And that is this, and this with thee remains.

75

So are you to my thoughts as food to life,
Or as sweet-season'd showers are to the ground;

14. soil: (1) ground, basis; (2) blemish. **common:** low, base, prostitute (with quibble on the sense "wild, uncultivated," suggested by *weeds* in line 12).

70.1. are: art. **2. mark:** target.
3. suspect: suspicion (so also in line 13).
4. crow. Often cited as a foul or evil bird.
5. So: provided that. **approve:** prove.
6. being . . . time: i.e. since you are courted by the world.
7. canker: the rose worm. **9. ambush . . . days:** i.e. temptations that lie in wait for inexperienced youth.
10. charg'd. Synonymous with *assail'd*. **11. so:** sufficiently.
12. envy: malice. **evermore enlarg'd:** always at large.
13. mask'd . . . show: did not partly obscure your attractiveness.
14. owe: own.

71.2. bell. The passing bell would toll once for each year of the dead man's life.
4. vile world. A conventional expression, not used with full emphasis. Cf. line 13. **vildest:** vilest. **8. make:** cause.
10. compounded: mingled. **11. rehearse:** repeat.
12. even with: at the same time as.
14. with me: i.e. for loving me (not "together with me").

72.4. prove: demonstrate by evidence.

10. untrue: untruly. **13. I . . . forth.** Presumably a reference to his theatrical activities and plays, not to these sonnets.
14. should you: would you certainly be shamed. **to love:** for loving.

73.4. late: lately, not long ago. **8. seals:** closes. **10. That:** as.

74.1. be contented: do not repine. **fell:** cruel. With the image in lines 1–2 cf. *Hamlet*, V.ii.336–37: "this fell sergeant, Death, / Is strict in his arrest."
3. line: poetry. Cf. Sonnet 71.5. **interest:** share, participation.
4. still: always. **6. part was:** part of me which was.
11. a wretch's knife: i.e. the weapon of "that churl Death" (Sonnet 32.2). **12. of:** by.
13. The worth . . . contains: i.e. the only value of the body is that it contains the spirit.

75.2. sweet-season'd: coming in the sweet season, spring.

And for the peace of you I hold such strife
As 'twixt a miser and his wealth is found:
Now proud as an enjoyer, and anon
Doubting the filching age will steal his treasure;
Now counting best to be with you alone,
Then better'd that the world may see my pleasure;
Sometime all full with feasting on your sight,
And by and by clean starved for a look;
Possessing or pursuing no delight
Save what is had or must from you be took.
  Thus do I pine and surfeit day by day,
  Or gluttoning on all, or all away.

76

Why is my verse so barren of new pride?
So far from variation or quick change?
Why with the time do I not glance aside
To new-found methods and to compounds strange?
Why write I still all one, ever the same,
And keep invention in a noted weed,
That every word doth almost [tell] my name,
Showing their birth, and where they did proceed?
O, know, sweet love, I always write of you,
And you and love are still my argument;
So all my best is dressing old words new,
Spending again what is already spent:
  For as the sun is daily new and old,
  So is my love still telling what is told.

77

Thy glass will show thee how thy beauties [wear],
Thy dial how thy precious minutes waste,
The vacant leaves thy mind's imprint will bear,
And of this book this learning mayst thou taste.
The wrinkles which thy glass will truly show,
Of mouthed graves will give thee memory;
Thou by thy dial's shady stealth mayst know
Time's thievish progress to eternity.
Look what thy memory cannot contain
Commit to these waste [blanks], and thou shalt find
Those children nurs'd, deliver'd from thy brain,
To take a new acquaintance of thy mind.
  These offices, so oft as thou wilt look,
  Shall profit thee, and much enrich thy book.

3. peace of you: i.e. peace that comes from love of you.
6. Doubting: fearing that. **filching age**: thieving time.
12. took: derived. **13. pine and surfeit**: starve and overeat.
14. Or: either. **all away**: nothing to feed on.

76.1. pride: ornament. **2. quick change**: i.e. facile innovation.
3. time: current fashion.
4. compounds: kinds of literary composition (?) or compound words (?). **5. still**: always (so also in lines 10, 14).
6. invention: imagination, or poetic creation. **noted weed**: well-known garment. **8. where**: whence. **10. argument**: theme.

77.1. glass: mirror. **wear**: wear away. **2. dial**: sun-dial.
3. vacant leaves: blank leaves of a notebook accompanying the sonnet. **thy mind's imprint**: your thoughts, written in the book.
6. mouthed: gaping, ready to devour. **memory**: reminder.
7. shady stealth: stealing shadow.
9. Look what: whatever. **10. waste**: empty.
11. nurs'd: cared for, i.e. preserved. **deliver'd**: which are delivered.
12. take . . . of: i.e. yield fresh meaning to.
13. offices: duties (perhaps with a suggestion of the sense "religious observances").

78

So oft have I invok'd thee for my Muse,
And found such fair assistance in my verse,
As every alien pen hath got my use,
And under thee their poesy disperse.
Thine eyes, that taught the dumb on high to sing,
And heavy ignorance aloft to fly,
Have added feathers to the learned's wing,
And given grace a double majesty.
Yet be most proud of that which I compile,
Whose influence is thine, and born of thee:
In others' works thou dost but mend the style,
And arts with thy sweet graces graced be;
  But thou art all my art, and dost advance
  As high as learning my rude ignorance.

79

Whilst I alone did call upon thy aid,
My verse alone had all thy gentle grace,
But now my gracious numbers are decay'd,
And my sick Muse doth give another place.
I grant, sweet love, thy lovely argument
Deserves the travail of a worthier pen,
Yet what of thee thy poet doth invent
He robs thee of, and pays it thee again.
He lends thee virtue, and he stole that word
From thy behavior; beauty doth he give,
And found it in thy cheek; he can afford
No praise to thee but what in thee doth live.
  Then thank him not for that which he doth say,
  Since what he owes thee, thou thyself dost pay.

80

O how I faint when I of you do write,
Knowing a better spirit doth use your name,
And in the praise thereof spends all his might,
To make me tongue-tied, speaking of your fame.
But since your worth (wide as the ocean is)
The humble as the proudest sail doth bear,
My saucy bark (inferior far to his)
On your broad main doth willfully appear.
Your shallowest help will hold me up afloat,
Whilst he upon your soundless deep doth ride,
Or (being wrack'd) I am a worthless boat,
He of tall building and of goodly pride.

78.3. As: that. **alien pen**: other poet. **got my use**: adopted my practice.
4. under thee: under your patronage. **disperse**: circulate.
5. on high: aloud. **6. aloft to fly**: i.e. to get off the ground.
7. added . . . wing: i.e. enabled learned poets who were already making high flights to fly still higher. **8. grace**: majesty.
9. compile: compose. **10. influence**: (sole) inspiration.
12. arts: learning. **graces**: pleasing qualities.
13. advance: raise up.

79.4. give another place: yield its place to another.
5. thy lovely argument: the theme of your lovableness.
6. travail: labor. **11. afford**: offer.

80.1. faint: grow weak and dispirited.
2. better spirit: more gifted poet. **6. as**: as well as.
8. willfully: perversely, i.e. against reason (?) or at will, freely (?).
10. soundless: unfathomed.
12. tall building: large and strong construction. **pride**: splendor.

Then if he thrive and I be cast away,
The worst was this: my love was my decay.

81

Or I shall live your epitaph to make,
Or you survive when I in earth am rotten;
From hence your memory death cannot take,
Although in me each part will be forgotten.
Your name from hence immortal life shall have,
Though I (once gone) to all the world must die;
The earth can yield me but a common grave,
When you entombed in men's eyes shall lie;
Your monument shall be my gentle verse,
Which eyes not yet created shall o'er-read,
And tongues to be your being shall rehearse,
When all the breathers of this world are dead;
You still shall live (such virtue hath my pen)
Where breath most breathes, even in the mouths of men.

82

I grant thou wert not married to my Muse,
And therefore mayest without attaint o'erlook
The dedicated words which writers use
Of their fair subject, blessing every book.
Thou art as fair in knowledge as in hue,
Finding thy worth a limit past my praise,
And therefore art enforc'd to seek anew
Some fresher stamp of the time-bettering days.
And do so, love; yet when they have devis'd
What strained touches rhetoric can lend,
Thou, truly fair, wert truly sympathiz'd
In true plain words by thy true-telling friend;
And their gross painting might be better us'd
Where cheeks need blood, in thee it is abus'd.

83

I never saw that you did painting need,
And therefore to your fair no painting set;
I found (or thought I found) you did exceed
The barren tender of a poet's debt;
And therefore have I slept in your report,
That you yourself, being extant, well might show
How far a modern quill doth come too short,
Speaking of worth, what worth in you doth grow.
This silence for my sin you did impute,
Which shall be most my glory being dumb,
For I impair not beauty being mute,
When others would give life and bring a tomb.
There lives more life in one of your fair eyes
Than both your poets can in praise devise.

84

Who is it that says most, which can say more
Than this rich praise, that you alone are you,
In whose confine immured is the store
Which should example where your equal grew?
Lean penury within that pen doth dwell
That to his subject lends not some small glory,
But he that writes of you, if he can tell
That you are you, so dignifies his story.
Let him but copy what in you is writ,
Not making worse what nature made so clear,
And such a counterpart shall fame his wit,
Making his style admired every where.
You to your beauteous blessings add a curse,
Being fond on praise, which makes your praises worse.

85

My tongue-tied Muse in manners holds her still,
While comments of your praise, richly compil'd,
Reserve their character with golden quill
And precious phrase by all the Muses fil'd.
I think good thoughts whilst other write good words,
And like unlettered clerk still cry "Amen"
To every hymn that able spirit affords
In polish'd form of well-refined pen.
Hearing you prais'd, I say, "'Tis so, 'tis true,"
And to the most of praise add something more,
But that is in my thought, whose love to you
(Though words come hindmost) holds his rank before.
Then others for the breath of words respect,
Me for my dumb thoughts, speaking in effect.

14. decay: ruin.

81.1. Or: whether.
3. From hence: (1) from the earth; (2) from this poetry (as in line 5).
4. in . . . part: all that I am.
11. to be: future. **rehearse:** recite.
12. breathers: living people. **world:** time, generation.
13. virtue: power.

82.2. attaint: dishonor. **o'erlook:** peruse.
3. dedicated: devoted. **writers:** i.e. other writers.
4. blessing every book: i.e. gracing every such book by your perusal.
5. hue: appearance. **6. limit:** extent, reach.
8. Some . . . days: some more up-to-date imprint of this era of progress. **11. sympathiz'd:** matched. **14. abus'd:** misapplied.

83.2. fair: beauty. **set:** applied.
4. tender: offering. **debt:** i.e. payment.
5. slept . . . report: neglected to praise you. **6. That:** because.
7. modern: ordinary, commonplace.
8. what worth: i.e. to describe such worth as.
12. tomb. Cf. Sonnet 17.3–4.

84.1. which: who.
3–4. In . . . grew: i.e. within whom is contained the treasure (of beauty) which would be required to produce another example of beauty equal to you. **10. clear:** glorious.
11. counterpart: copy. **fame:** make famous.
13. curse: (1) an ill quality (in your own character); (2) a great vexation (for your would-be praisers).
14. Being fond: doting. **makes . . . worse:** (1) diminishes the praise due you; (2) encourages poets to go beyond the simple description that would be your best praise. Various annotators, believing that the sense requires the second meaning here (and in the gloss for *curse*), suspect corruption in *Being fond on*.

85.1. in . . . still: politely keeps silent.
2. comments: elaborations. **compil'd:** composed.
3. Reserve their character: treasure up their writing (?). The passage may be corrupt, and many emendations have been proposed, e.g. *Receive their character*. **4. fil'd:** polished, refined.
5. other: others.
6. unlettered clerk: illiterate assistant to a priest.
10. most: utmost. **11. in my thought:** i.e. silent.
12. before: i.e. before all others, in first place.
13. respect: take notice of, regard.
14. speaking in effect: having the same effect as speaking.

86

Was it the proud full sail of his great verse,
Bound for the prize of all-too-precious you,
That did my ripe thoughts in my brain inhearse,
Making their tomb the womb wherein they grew?
Was it his spirit, by spirits taught to write
Above a mortal pitch, that struck me dead?
No, neither he, nor his compeers by night
Giving him aid, my verse astonished.
He, nor that affable familiar ghost
Which nightly gulls him with intelligence,
As victors of my silence cannot boast;
I was not sick of any fear from thence:
  But when your countenance fill'd up his line,
  Then lack'd I matter, that enfeebled mine.

87

Farewell, thou art too dear for my possessing,
And like enough thou know'st thy estimate;
The charter of thy worth gives thee releasing;
My bonds in thee are all determinate.
For how do I hold thee but by thy granting,
And for that riches where is my deserving?
The cause of this fair gift in me is wanting,
And so my patent back again is swerving.
Thyself thou gav'st, thy own worth then not knowing,
Or me, to whom thou gav'st it, else mistaking,
So thy great gift, upon misprision growing,
Comes home again, on better judgment making.
  Thus have I had thee as a dream doth flatter:
  In sleep a king, but waking no such matter.

88

When thou shalt be dispos'd to set me light,
And place my merit in the eye of scorn,
Upon thy side against myself I'll fight,
And prove thee virtuous, though thou art forsworn.
With mine own weakness being best acquainted,
Upon thy part I can set down a story
Of faults conceal'd, wherein I am attainted,
That thou in losing me shall win much glory.
And I by this will be a gainer too,
For bending all my loving thoughts on thee,
The injuries that to myself I do,
Doing thee vantage, double-vantage me.
  Such is my love, to thee I so belong,
  That for thy right myself will bear all wrong.

89

Say that thou didst forsake me for some fault,
And I will comment upon that offense;
Speak of my lameness, and I straight will halt,
Against thy reasons making no defense.
Thou canst not, love, disgrace me half so ill,
To set a form upon desired change,
As I'll myself disgrace, knowing thy will:
I will acquaintance strangle and look strange,
Be absent from thy walks, and in my tongue
Thy sweet beloved name no more shall dwell,
Lest I (too much profane) should do it wrong,
And haply of our old acquaintance tell.
  For thee, against myself I'll vow debate,
  For I must ne'er love him whom thou dost hate.

90

Then hate me when thou wilt, if ever, now,
Now while the world is bent my deeds to cross,
Join with the spite of fortune, make me bow,
And do not drop in for an after-loss.
Ah, do not, when my heart hath scap'd this sorrow,
Come in the rearward of a conquer'd woe;
Give not a windy night a rainy morrow,
To linger out a purpos'd overthrow.
If thou wilt leave me, do not leave me last,
When other petty griefs have done their spite,
But in the onset come, so [shall] I taste
At first the very worst of fortune's might;
  And other strains of woe, which now seem woe,
  Compar'd with loss of thee will not seem so.

91

Some glory in their birth, some in their skill,
Some in their wealth, some in their body's force,
Some in their garments, though new-fangled ill,
Some in their hawks and hounds, some in their horse;
And every humor hath his adjunct pleasure,
Wherein it finds a joy above the rest,
But these particulars are not my measure,
All these I better in one general best.

86.2. prize: capture (used of a ship, particularly a rich cargo-ship, taken at sea). **3. inhearse:** bury. **6. pitch:** height.
7. compeers: associates (the "spirits" of line 5).
8. astonished: stunned, paralyzed. **9. ghost:** spirit.
10. gulls: deceptively provides. **intelligence:** late news, ideas.
13. your . . . line: (1) your acceptance of his poetry compensated for anything wanting in it; (2) your beauty became the subject of his verse.

87.1. dear: precious. **2. estimate:** value.
3. charter of: privilege conferred by. **4. determinate:** expired.
8. patent: title. **swerving:** returning.
10. mistaking: i.e. overestimating.
11. upon misprision growing: originating in error.
12. making: being made (by you).
13–14. dream, flatter, king. A Shakespearean image cluster. Cf. *Romeo and Juliet*, II.ii.140–41, V.i.1–5.

88.1. set me light: rate me slightingly, depreciate me.
3. Upon thy side: in support of your case. **6. part:** side.
7. conceal'd: not publicly known. **attainted:** disgraced.
12. vantage: advantage.

89.2. comment: enlarge, expatiate.
3. Speak . . . halt: i.e. ascribe to me any defect, and I will at once (*straight*) assume it. *Halt* = limp. **4. reasons:** assertions.
5. disgrace: discredit. **6. form:** plausible appearance.
8. acquaintance strangle: put an end to our familiarity. **strange:** like a stranger. **13. debate:** warfare.

90.2. cross: frustrate.
4. drop . . . after-loss: come in unexpectedly to inflict a second loss on me.
6. in . . . woe: following a woe I have managed to survive.
8. linger out: protract. **13. strains:** kinds and degrees.

91.3. new-fangled ill: fashionably ugly.
4. horse. A common plural.
5. humor: temperament. **his:** its. **adjunct:** attendant, related.
7. measure: i.e. criterion of happiness. **8. better:** surpass.

Thy love is [better] than high birth to me,
Richer than wealth, prouder than garments' cost,
Of more delight than hawks or horses be;
And having thee, of all men's pride I boast:
  Wretched in this alone, that thou mayst take
  All this away, and me most wretched make.

92

But do thy worst to steal thyself away,
For term of life thou art assured mine,
And life no longer than thy love will stay,
For it depends upon that love of thine.
Then need I not to fear the worst of wrongs,
When in the least of them my life hath end;
I see a better state to me belongs
Than that which on thy humor doth depend.
Thou canst not vex me with inconstant mind,
Since that my life on thy revolt doth lie;
O, what a happy title do I find,
Happy to have thy love, happy to die!
  But what's so blessed-fair that fears no blot?
  Thou mayst be false, and yet I know it not.

93

So shall I live, supposing thou art true,
Like a deceived husband, so love's face
May still seem love to me, though alter'd new:
Thy looks with me, thy heart in other place.
For there can live no hatred in thine eye,
Therefore in that I cannot know thy change.
In many's looks the false heart's history
Is writ in moods and frowns and wrinkles strange;
But heaven in thy creation did decree
That in thy face sweet love should ever dwell;
What e'er thy thoughts or thy heart's workings be,
Thy looks should nothing thence but sweetness tell.
  How like Eve's apple doth thy beauty grow,
  If thy sweet virtue answer not thy show!

94

They that have pow'r to hurt, and will do none,
That do not do the thing they most do show,
Who moving others, are themselves as stone,
Unmoved, cold, and to temptation slow,
They rightly do inherit heaven's graces,
And husband nature's riches from expense;
They are the lords and owners of their faces,
Others but stewards of their excellence.
The summer's flow'r is to the summer sweet,
Though to itself it only live and die,
But if that flow'r with base infection meet,
The basest weed outbraves his dignity:
  For sweetest things turn sourest by their deeds;
  Lilies that fester smell far worse than weeds.

95

How sweet and lovely dost thou make the shame
Which, like a canker in the fragrant rose,
Doth spot the beauty of thy budding name!
O, in what sweets dost thou thy sins enclose!
That tongue that tells the story of thy days
(Making lascivious comments on thy sport)
Cannot dispraise but in a kind of praise,
Naming thy name blesses an ill report.
O, what a mansion have those vices got
Which for their habitation chose out thee,
Where beauty's veil doth cover every blot,
And all things turns to fair that eyes can see!
  Take heed, dear heart, of this large privilege,
  The hardest knife ill us'd doth lose his edge.

96

Some say thy fault is youth, some wantonness,
Some say thy grace is youth and gentle sport;
Both grace and faults are lov'd of more and less:
Thou mak'st faults graces that to thee resort.
As on the finger of a throned queen
The basest jewel will be well esteem'd,
So are those errors that in thee are seen
To truths translated, and for true things deem'd.
How many lambs might the stern wolf betray,
If like a lamb he could his looks translate!
How many gazers mightst thou lead away,
If thou wouldst use the strength of all thy state!
  But do not so, I love thee in such sort,
  As thou being mine, mine is thy good report.

97

How like a winter hath my absence been
From thee, the pleasure of the fleeting year!
What freezings have I felt, what dark days seen!
What old December's bareness every where!
And yet this time remov'd was summer's time,

10. **prouder:** more an object of pride.
12. **of . . . boast:** I boast of having the equivalent of all other sources of pride put together.

92.8. **humor:** fancy, caprice.
10. **my . . . lie:** i.e. your desertion would kill me.
11. **happy title:** right to be called happy.
13. **that fears:** as to fear.

93.2. **love's face:** the appearance of love (but by line 4 *face* has become literal). 3. **new:** i.e. to something new.
8. **moods:** moody expressions. **wrinkles strange:** unfriendly scowls.
14. **answer . . . show:** does not match your appearance.

94.2. **the thing . . . show:** what their appearance strongly implies.
4. **cold:** dispassionate.
5. **rightly do inherit:** i.e. make proper use of (*inherit* = possess, enjoy).
6. **husband . . . expense:** keep the riches of nature (physical beauty) from wasteful expenditure or loss.
8. **stewards:** i.e. dispensers, distributors.
10. **to . . . only:** to itself alone it. With the line cf. Sonnet 54.11.
12. **outbraves:** surpasses in splendor. **his dignity:** its worth.
14. **Lilies . . . weeds.** This line occurs also in *The Reign of King Edward III* (II.i.451).

95.3. **name:** reputation. 6. **sport:** amorous dalliance.
8. **blesses:** graces, makes favorable. 9. **mansion:** dwelling place.

96.2. **sport.** Cf. Sonnet 95.6. *Wantonness* in line 1 is synonymous.
3. **of . . . less:** i.e. by persons of all ranks.
8. **translated:** transformed. 9. **stern:** savage.
12. **the strength . . . state:** all your power.
13–14. **But . . . report.** The same couplet ends Sonnet 36.

97.5. **time remov'd:** time of separation.

The teeming autumn, big with rich increase,
Bearing the wanton burthen of the prime,
Like widowed wombs after their lords' decease:
Yet this abundant issue seem'd to me
But hope of orphans and unfathered fruit,
For summer and his pleasures wait on thee,
And thou away, the very birds are mute;
Or if they sing, 'tis with so dull a cheer
That leaves look pale, dreading the winter's near.

98

From you have I been absent in the spring,
When proud-pied April (dress'd in all his trim)
Hath put a spirit of youth in every thing,
That heavy Saturn laugh'd and leapt with him.
Yet nor the lays of birds, nor the sweet smell
Of different flowers in odor and in hue,
Could make me any summer's story tell,
Or from their proud lap pluck them where they grew;
Nor did I wonder at the lily's white,
Nor praise the deep vermilion in the rose,
They were but sweet, but figures of delight,
Drawn after you, you pattern of all those.
Yet seem'd it winter still, and, you away,
As with your shadow I with these did play.

99

The forward violet thus did I chide:
Sweet thief, whence didst thou steal thy sweet that smells,
If not from my love's breath? The purple pride
Which on thy soft cheek for complexion dwells
In my love's veins thou hast too grossly dy'd.
The lily I condemned for thy hand,
And buds of marjerom had stol'n thy hair;
The roses fearfully on thorns did stand,
[One] blushing shame, another white despair;
A third, nor red nor white, had stol'n of both,
And to his robb'ry had annex'd thy breath,
But for his theft in pride of all his growth
A vengeful canker eat him up to death.
More flowers I noted, yet I none could see
But sweet or color it had stol'n from thee.

100

Where art thou, Muse, that thou forget'st so long
To speak of that which gives thee all thy might?
Spend'st thou thy fury on some worthless song,
Dark'ning thy pow'r to lend base subjects light?
Return, forgetful Muse, and straight redeem
In gentle numbers time so idly spent;
Sing to the ear that doth thy lays esteem,
And gives thy pen both skill and argument.
Rise, resty Muse, my love's sweet face survey,
If Time have any wrinkle graven there;
If any, be a satire to decay,
And make Time's spoils despised every where.
Give my love fame faster than Time wastes life,
So thou prevent'st his scythe and crooked knife.

101

O truant Muse, what shall be thy amends
For thy neglect of truth in beauty dy'd?
Both truth and beauty on my love depends;
So dost thou too, and therein dignified.
Make answer, Muse, wilt thou not haply say,
"Truth needs no color with his color fix'd,
Beauty no pencil, beauty's truth to lay;
But best is best, if never intermix'd"?
Because he needs no praise, wilt thou be dumb?
Excuse not silence so, for't lies in thee
To make him much outlive a gilded tomb,
And to be prais'd of ages yet to be.
Then do thy office, Muse; I teach thee how
To make him seem long hence, as he shows now.

102

My love is strength'ned, though more weak in seeming,
I love not less, though less the show appear;
That love is merchandiz'd whose rich esteeming
The owner's tongue doth publish every where.
Our love was new, and then but in the spring,
When I was wont to greet it with my lays,
As Philomel in summer's front doth sing,
And stops [her] pipe in growth of riper days:
Not that the summer is less pleasant now
Than when her mournful hymns did hush the night,
But that wild music burthens every bough,
And sweets grown common lose their dear delight.

6. big: pregnant.
7. the wanton . . . prime: the children of wanton springtime, i.e. the crops then planted. **11. his:** its.
13. with . . . cheer: i.e. in so melancholy a fashion.

98.2. proud-pied: brilliantly multi-colored. **trim:** finery.
4. heavy: melancholy, morose. The planet Saturn was associated with gloom and sluggishness.
5. Yet nor: yet neither.
6. different flowers: flowers varied.
7. summer's story: pleasant narrative. **11. figures:** symbols.
14. shadow: portrait. **these:** i.e. the flowers. See Sonnet 99.

99.1. The . . . chide. An extra, introductory line. **forward:** early, a common epithet for the violet. **2. sweet:** scent.
5. grossly: obviously.
6. for: i.e. for stealing its whiteness from.
7. marjerom: marjoram. The line has been variously explained as referring to the color (dark auburn?) or the scent of the hair, or to its tight ringlets.
11. to . . . annex'd: to his robbery had added the theft of (?) or to his stolen attributes had added (?).
13. eat: was eating.

100.3. fury: poetic inspiration. Cf. *rage*, Sonnet 17.11.
4. Dark'ning: debasing. **6. gentle numbers:** noble verses.
8. argument: subject matter. **9. resty:** lazy. **10. If:** to see if.
11. If . . . decay: i.e. if you find any, compose satires on the ruins of time (*satire* = satirist). **12. spoils:** ravages.
13. faster. "Used in the senses swiftly and firmly at the same time" (Schmidt).
14. prevent'st: frustratest. **crooked knife:** curved blade (another way of saying "scythe").

101.6. no color with: i.e. no artificial color added to (with play on *color* = false pretense). **his:** its. **fix'd:** native, unchangeable.
7. pencil: painter's brush. **lay:** apply color to (a technical term).
8. intermix'd: adulterated. **12. of:** by. **13. office:** function.

102.3. merchandiz'd: commercialized. **esteeming:** valuation.
4. publish: advertise.
7. Philomel: the nightingale. **front:** beginning. **11. wild:** unrestrained, profuse. **burthens:** (1) loads; (2) provides choruses from.

Therefore like her, I sometime hold my tongue,
Because I would not dull you with my song.

103

Alack, what poverty my Muse brings forth,
That having such a scope to show her pride,
The argument all bare is of more worth
Than when it hath my added praise beside.
O, blame me not if I no more can write!
Look in your glass, and there appears a face
That overgoes my blunt invention quite,
Dulling my lines, and doing me disgrace.
Were it not sinful then, striving to mend,
To mar the subject that before was well?
For to no other pass my verses tend
Than of your graces and your gifts to tell;
  And more, much more than in my verse can sit,
  Your own glass shows you, when you look in it.

104

To me, fair friend, you never can be old,
For as you were when first your eye I ey'd,
Such seems your beauty still. Three winters cold
Have from the forests shook three summers' pride,
Three beauteous springs to yellow autumn turn'd
In process of the seasons have I seen,
Three April perfumes in three hot Junes burn'd,
Since first I saw you fresh, which yet are green.
Ah, yet doth beauty, like a dial hand,
Steal from his figure, and no pace perceiv'd,
So your sweet hue, which methinks still doth stand,
Hath motion, and mine eye may be deceiv'd;
  For fear of which, hear this, thou age unbred:
  Ere you were born was beauty's summer dead.

105

Let not my love be call'd idolatry,
Nor my beloved as an idol show,
Since all alike my songs and praises be
To one, of one, still such, and ever so.
Kind is my love to-day, to-morrow kind,
Still constant in a wondrous excellence,
Therefore my verse, to constancy confin'd,
One thing expressing, leaves out difference.
"Fair," "kind," and "true" is all my argument,
"Fair," "kind," and "true" varying to other words,
And in this change is my invention spent,
Three themes in one, which wondrous scope affords.

14. **dull:** satiate.

103.2. **pride:** splendor. 3. **argument:** subject.
6. **glass:** mirror. 7. **overgoes:** surpasses. **blunt:** clumsy.
11. **pass:** issue, end. 13. **sit:** reside.

104.6. **process:** the progression. 9. **dial hand:** watch hand.
10. **figure:** (1) numeral on the dial; (2) shape. **and . . . perceiv'd:** i.e. with imperceptible motion.
11. **still:** unmoving, i.e. unchanged. 13. **unbred:** unborn.

105.4. **still:** always. 8. **difference:** variety.
11. **change:** verbal variation. **invention:** inventiveness. **spent:** used up.

  "Fair," "kind," and "true" have often liv'd alone,
  Which three till now never kept seat in one.

106

When in the chronicle of wasted time
I see descriptions of the fairest wights,
And beauty making beautiful old rhyme
In praise of ladies dead and lovely knights,
Then in the blazon of sweet beauty's best,
Of hand, of foot, of lip, of eye, of brow,
I see their antique pen would have express'd
Even such a beauty as you master now.
So all their praises are but prophecies
Of this our time, all you prefiguring,
And for they look'd but with divining eyes,
They had not still enough your worth to sing:
  For we which now behold these present days
  Have eyes to wonder, but lack tongues to praise.

107

Not mine own fears, nor the prophetic soul
Of the wide world, dreaming on things to come,
Can yet the lease of my true love control,
Suppos'd as forfeit to a confin'd doom.
The mortal moon hath her eclipse endur'd,
And the sad augurs mock their own presage,
Incertainties now crown themselves assur'd,
And peace proclaims olives of endless age.
Now with the drops of this most balmy time
My love looks fresh, and Death to me subscribes,
Since spite of him I'll live in this poor rhyme,
While he insults o'er dull and speechless tribes;
  And thou in this shalt find thy monument,
  When tyrants' crests and tombs of brass are spent.

108

What's in the brain that ink may character
Which hath not figur'd to thee my true spirit?

13. **alone:** separately. 14. **kept seat:** resided.

106.1. **wasted:** bygone. 2. **wights:** persons.
5. **blazon:** poetic catalogue. 8. **master:** possess, command.
11. **for:** because. **divining:** prophetic (not actually beholding).
12. **still:** yet. Often emended to *skill* (i.e. knowledge).
13. **we:** i.e. even we. 14. **praise:** i.e. praise worthily.

107.3. **lease:** term.
4. **forfeit . . . doom:** subject to a limited duration.
5. **mortal moon.** Usually interpreted as a reference to Queen Elizabeth, after the virgin moon-goddess Diana. A great many explanations of lines 5–8 have been proposed, and in consequence the sonnet has been assigned to a wide range of dates, but there is no general agreement about what events are referred to.
6. **the sad . . . presage:** the pessimistic astrologers now ridicule their own earlier predictions.
7. **Incertainties . . . assur'd:** desirable events, once doubtful, are now crowned with certainty.
8. **peace . . . age:** peace, symbolized by olive branches, seems perpetual.
9. **Now . . . time:** the dew of this happy time has been like a balm, so that now . . . 10. **subscribes:** surrenders.
12. **insults:** triumphs. **dull and speechless:** i.e. non-literary. **tribes:** races.
14. **spent:** wasted away by the passage of time.

108.1. **character:** write. 2. **figur'd:** portrayed.

What's new to speak, what now to register,
That may express my love, or thy dear merit?
Nothing, sweet boy, but yet like prayers divine,
I must each day say o'er the very same,
Counting no old thing old, thou mine, I thine,
Even as when first I hallowed thy fair name.
So that eternal love in love's fresh case
Weighs not the dust and injury of age,
Nor gives to necessary wrinkles place,
But makes antiquity for aye his page,
  Finding the first conceit of love there bred,
  Where time and outward form would show it dead.

109

O, never say that I was false of heart,
Though absence seem'd my flame to qualify;
As easy might I from myself depart
As from my soul which in thy breast doth lie:
That is my home of love; if I have rang'd,
Like him that travels I return again,
Just to the time, not with the time exchang'd,
So that myself bring water for my stain.
Never believe, though in my nature reign'd
All frailties that besiege all kinds of blood,
That it could so preposterously be stain'd,
To leave for nothing all thy sum of good;
  For nothing this wide universe I call,
  Save thou, my rose, in it thou art my all.

110

Alas, 'tis true, I have gone here and there,
And made myself a motley to the view,
Gor'd mine own thoughts, sold cheap what is most dear,
Made old offenses of affections new;
Most true it is that I have look'd on truth
Askaunce and strangely: but by all above,
These blenches gave my heart another youth,
And worse essays prov'd thee my best of love.
Now all is done, have what shall have no end,
Mine appetite I never more will grind
On newer proof, to try an older friend,
A god in love, to whom I am confin'd.
  Then give me welcome, next my heaven the best,
  Even to thy pure and most most loving breast.

3. now. Often emended to *new*. **register:** record.
9. case: covering, garment. **10. Weighs not:** disregards.
11. place: consideration. **12. antiquity:** old age.
13. first . . . love: i.e. love as strong as when it was first felt. **bred:** generated.

109.2. qualify: reduce, temper.
7. Just: punctual. **exchang'd:** changed.
10. blood: sensual nature. **12. for:** in exchange for.

110.2. motley: clown. **3. Gor'd:** wounded deeply.
4. Made . . . new: i.e. transgressed against old friendships by my conduct of new ones. **5. truth:** fidelity.
6. Askaunce and strangely: obliquely and coldly.
7. blenches: turnings aside, swervings away (from constancy). Cf. Shakespeare's use of *blench* as a verb in, e.g., *Troilus and Cressida*, II.ii.68, and *The Winter's Tale*, I.ii.333.
8. worse essays: experiments in what was inferior.
10–11. grind . . . proof: sharpen on new experience. **11. try:** test.

111

O, for my sake do you [with] Fortune chide,
The guilty goddess of my harmful deeds,
That did not better for my life provide
Than public means which public manners breeds.
Thence comes it that my name receives a brand,
And almost thence my nature is subdu'd
To what it works in, like the dyer's hand.
Pity me then, and wish I were renew'd,
Whilst like a willing patient I will drink
Potions of eisel 'gainst my strong infection,
No bitterness that I will bitter think,
Nor double penance, to correct correction.
  Pity me then, dear friend, and I assure ye,
  Even that your pity is enough to cure me.

112

Your love and pity doth th' impression fill
Which vulgar scandal stamp'd upon my brow,
For what care I who calls me well or ill,
So you o'er-green my bad, my good allow?
You are my all the world, and I must strive
To know my shames and praises from your tongue;
None else to me, nor I to none alive,
That my steel'd sense or changes right or wrong.
In so profound abysm I throw all care
Of others' voices, that my adder's sense
To critic and to flatterer stopped are.
Mark how with my neglect I do dispense:
  You are so strongly in my purpose bred
  That all the world besides methinks are dead.

113

Since I left you, mine eye is in my mind,
And that which governs me to go about
Doth part his function, and is partly blind,
Seems seeing, but effectually is out;
For it no form delivers to the heart
Of bird, of flow'r, or shape which it doth [latch].

111.2. harmful: wrong (not necessarily causing harm).
4. public means: subsistence through pleasing the public. **public manners:** vulgar conduct.
5. name: reputation. **brand:** mark of disgrace.
8. renew'd: cured.
10. Potions of eisel: draught of vinegar (which was commonly taken to avoid the plague and other diseases).
12. correct correction: add punishment to punishment.
14. Even . . . pity: that very pity of yours.

112.1. th' impression fill: efface the brand. **2. vulgar:** public.
4. o'er-green: cover, as with grass. **allow:** approve.
7–8. None . . . wrong: for me there are no others alive who can change my hardened sensibilities, whether for better or for worse.
10. adder's sense: i.e. deaf ears. The adder supposedly stopped its ears; see Psalm 58:4. **11. critic:** fault-finder.
12. with . . . dispense: I excuse my indifference (to others' opinions).
13. so . . . bred: so firmly a part of all my pursuits.

113.1. mine . . . mind: i.e. the eye I see with is my mind's eye.
2. that . . . about: i.e. my physical eye.
3. part: divide. The eye was supposed to have two functions: (1) to receive images and (2) to transmit them to the mind. His eye performs the first of these functions but not the second. **his:** its (so also in lines 7 and 8).
4. effectually is out: in effect is out (like a light), i.e. blinded.
5. heart: i.e. mind. **6. latch:** catch sight of.

Of his quick objects hath the mind no part,
Nor his own vision holds what it doth catch;
For if it see the rud'st or gentlest sight,
The most sweet favor or deformed'st creature,
The mountain or the sea, the day or night,
The crow or dove, it shapes them to your feature.
  Incapable of more, replete with you,
  My most true mind thus maketh mine untrue.

114

Or whether doth my mind being crown'd with you
Drink up the monarch's plague, this flattery?
Or whether shall I say mine eye saith true,
And that your love taught it this alcumy,
To make of monsters and things indigest
Such cherubins as your sweet self resemble,
Creating every bad a perfect best
As fast as objects to his beams assemble?
O, 'tis the first, 'tis flatt'ry in my seeing,
And my great mind most kingly drinks it up;
Mine eye well knows what with his gust is 'greeing,
And to his palate doth prepare the cup.
  If it be poison'd, 'tis the lesser sin
  That mine eye loves it and doth first begin.

115

Those lines that I before have writ do lie,
Even those that said I could not love you dearer,
Yet then my judgment knew no reason why
My most full flame should afterwards burn clearer.
But reckoning Time, whose million'd accidents
Creep in 'twixt vows, and change decrees of kings,
Tan sacred beauty, blunt the sharp'st intents,
Divert strong minds to th' course of alt'ring things:
Alas, why, fearing of Time's tyranny,
Might I not then say, "Now I love you best,"
When I was certain o'er incertainty,
Crowning the present, doubting of the rest?
  Love is a babe, then might I not say so,
  To give full growth to that which still doth grow.

116

Let me not to the marriage of true minds
Admit impediments; love is not love
Which alters when it alteration finds,
Or bends with the remover to remove.
O no, it is an ever-fixed mark
That looks on tempests and is never shaken;
It is the star to every wand'ring bark,
Whose worth's unknown, although his highth be taken.
Love's not Time's fool, though rosy lips and cheeks
Within his bending sickle's compass come,
Love alters not with his brief hours and weeks,
But bears it out even to the edge of doom.
  If this be error and upon me proved,
  I never writ, nor no man ever loved.

117

Accuse me thus: that I have scanted all
Wherein I should your great deserts repay,
Forgot upon your dearest love to call,
Whereto all bonds do tie me day by day;
That I have frequent been with unknown minds,
And given to time your own dear-purchas'd right;
That I have hoisted sail to all the winds
Which should transport me farthest from your sight.
Book both my willfulness and errors down,
And on just proof surmise accumulate;
Bring me within the level of your frown,
But shoot not at me in your wakened hate:
  Since my appeal says I did strive to prove
  The constancy and virtue of your love.

118

Like as to make our appetites more keen,
With eager compounds we our palate urge,
As to prevent our maladies unseen,
We sicken to shun sickness when we purge;
Even so being full of your ne'er-cloying sweetness,
To bitter sauces did I frame my feeding,
And sick of welfare, found a kind of meetness
To be diseas'd ere that there was true needing.
Thus policy in love, t' anticipate

7. quick objects: fleeting perceptions.
10. favor: face. **12. feature:** likeness.
14. true: constant. **maketh mine untrue.** Sometimes explained as "creates my untruth (i.e. delusion)," but most editors emend to produce the expected contrast between *mind* and *eye*: e.g. *maketh* (or *mak'th*) *mine eye untrue, maketh m' eye untrue*, etc.

114.1, 3. Or whether. Introducing alternatives.
1. crown'd with you: make a king by your presence.
2. this: "this objectionable thing" (Tucker). **flattery:** falsification of the truth for the sake of pleasing the hearer.
5. indigest: chaotic, shapeless.
6. cherubins: angelic forms.
8. beams: i.e. gaze. The eye was thought to cast out beams of light.
9. 'tis . . . seeing: my eye is flattering my mind.
11. what . . . 'greeing: what is agreeable to the mind's taste.
13–14. 'tis . . . That: the sin is made less by the fact that.
14. doth first begin: drinks of it first (alluding to the function of the king's taster).

115.5–8. But . . . things. A suspended construction. These details are summed up in *Time's tyranny*, line 9.
5. reckoning: (1) considering; (2) counting. **million'd:** multiplied into millions. **7. Tan.** See Sonnet 62.10.
10. Might . . . say: could . . . rightly say.
13. then: therefore. **say so:** rightly say, "Now I love you best."
14. To give: i.e. because to say so was to ascribe.

116.2. Admit impediments. An echo of the marriage service: "If any of you know cause or just impediment why these persons should not be joined together . . ." **4. bends . . . remove.** Cf. Sonnet 25.14.
5. mark: sea-mark (cf. *landmark*).
8. Whose . . . taken: whose height above the horizon is known for purposes of navigation, but whose internal riches (or influence upon the earth) cannot be known.
9. fool: object of mockery, victim.
10. bending: curved. **compass:** range. **11. his:** Time's.
12. bears it out: endures. **edge of doom:** brink of Doomsday.

117.1. scanted: neglected, fallen short in.
5. frequent: familiar. **unknown minds:** strangers.
6. given to time: i.e. wasted (?) or given to the world, i.e. to other people (?). **10. on . . . accumulate:** add suspicion to proof.
11. level: range, aim.
13. appeal: plea (to a judge). **I . . . prove:** my purpose was to test.

118.2. eager: sour, sharp.
3. prevent: forestall, ward off (so also *anticipate* in line 9).
4. purge: take a cathartic.
7. sick of welfare: gorged with happiness.
9. policy: (supposed) shrewd dealing.

The ills that were not, grew to faults assured,
And brought to medicine a healthful state
Which, rank of goodness, would by ill be cured.
But thence I learn, and find the lesson true,
Drugs poison him that so fell sick of you.

119

What potions have I drunk of Siren tears
Distill'd from limbecks foul as hell within,
Applying fears to hopes, and hopes to fears,
Still losing when I saw myself to win!
What wretched errors hath my heart committed,
Whilst it hath thought itself so blessed never!
How have mine eyes out of their spheres been fitted
In the distraction of this madding fever!
O benefit of ill, now I find true
That better is by evil still made better,
And ruin'd love when it is built anew
Grows fairer than at first, more strong, far greater.
So I return rebuk'd to my content,
And gain by ills thrice more than I have spent.

120

That you were once unkind befriends me now,
And for that sorrow which I then did feel
Needs must I under my transgression bow,
Unless my nerves were brass or hammered steel.
For if you were by my unkindness shaken
As I by yours, y' have pass'd a hell of time,
And I, a tyrant, have no leisure taken
To weigh how once I suffered in your crime.
O that our night of woe might have rememb'red
My deepest sense, how hard true sorrow hits,
And soon to you, as you to me then, tend'red
The humble salve which wounded bosoms fits!
But that your trespass now becomes a fee,
Mine ransoms yours, and yours must ransom me.

121

'Tis better to be vile than vile esteemed,
When not to be receives reproach of being,
And the just pleasure lost, which is so deemed
Not by our feeling, but by others' seeing.
For why should others' false adulterate eyes
Give salutation to my sportive blood?
Or on my frailties why are frailer spies,
Which in their wills count bad what I think good?
No, I am that I am, and they that level
At my abuses reckon up their own;
I may be straight though they themselves be bevel;
By their rank thoughts my deeds must not be shown,
Unless this general evil they maintain:
All men are bad and in their badness reign.

122

Thy gift, thy tables, are within my brain
Full character'd with lasting memory,
Which shall above that idle rank remain
Beyond all date, even to eternity;
Or at the least, so long as brain and heart
Have faculty by nature to subsist,
Till each to raz'd oblivion yield his part
Of thee, thy record never can be miss'd.
That poor retention could not so much hold,
Nor need I tallies thy dear love to score;
Therefore to give them from me was I bold,
To trust those tables that receive thee more:
To keep an adjunct to remember thee
Were to import forgetfulness in me.

123

No! Time, thou shalt not boast that I do change:
Thy pyramids built up with newer might
To me are nothing novel, nothing strange;
They are but dressings of a former sight.
Our dates are brief, and therefore we admire
What thou dost foist upon us that is old,
And rather make them born to our desire
Than think that we before have heard them told.
Thy registers and thee I both defy,
Not wond'ring at the present, nor the past,
For thy records and what we see doth lie,
Made more or less by thy continual haste.
This I do vow and this shall ever be,
I will be true despite thy scythe and thee.

11. brought to medicine: prescribed drugs for.
12. rank: too full. **would . . . be:** was . . . to be.

119.1. Siren tears: the tears of a seductive and dangerous woman.
2. limbecks: alembics, stills.
3. Applying. Used in the medical sense.
4. Still: always. **saw myself:** expected. **7. fitted:** driven by fits.
8. distraction: madness. **madding:** maddening, producing lunacy.

120.2. for: because of. **4. nerves:** sinews, tendons.
8. weigh: consider. **crime:** offense.
9. woe: estrangement. **remember'red:** reminded.
12. humble salve: salve of humility, i.e. acknowledgment of wrongdoing and remorse. **fits:** befits.
13. that your trespass: that transgression of yours. **fee:** payment, compensation. **14. ransoms:** redeems, excuses.

121.1. vile esteemed: (to be) thought vile.
2. When . . . being: i.e. when innocence is accused of vileness.
3. just: legitimate. **so:** i.e. vile.
4. by others' seeing: in the view of others. **5. For why:** why.
6. Give salutation to: greet familiarly, as an equal. **sportive:** licentious. **7. why are:** i.e. why should there be.
8. in their wills: arbitrarily (?) or lasciviously (?).
9. that: what. **level:** aim. **10. abuses:** misdeeds.
11. bevel: slanting, deviating from uprightness.
12. rank: foul. **shown:** interpreted. **13. general:** universal.

122.1. tables: writing tablets. **2. character'd:** written. **with:** by.
3. idle rank: useless category (of actual tablets as compared to those of memory). **6. Have faculty:** are able.
7. raz'd: obliterating everything. **8. miss'd:** lost.
9. retention: retainer (the actual tablet).
10. tallies: sticks on which accounts were recorded by notching or cutting. **score:** keep account of.
11. them: i.e. the paper "tables."
12. those tables: i.e. the tablet of memory.
13. adjunct: aid, assistant. **14. import:** imply.

123.2. pyramids: i.e. imposing structures. **3. nothing:** not at all.
4. dressings . . . sight: reconstructions of what has been seen before.
5. dates: lifetimes. **admire:** wonder at.
7. make: deem. **born . . . desire:** i.e. the new things we would like to see. **8. told:** told of. **9. registers:** records. **11. doth:** i.e. do.
12. Made . . . less: i.e. made to seem more impressive or less impressive than they actually were.

124

If my dear love were but the child of state,
It might for Fortune's bastard be unfather'd,
As subject to Time's love, or to Time's hate,
Weeds among weeds, or flowers with flowers gather'd.
No, it was builded far from accident;
It suffers not in smiling pomp, nor falls
Under the blow of thralled discontent,
Whereto th' inviting time our fashion calls;
It fears not policy, that heretic,
Which works on leases of short-numb'red hours,
But all alone stands hugely politic,
That it nor grows with heat, nor drowns with show'rs.
  To this I witness call the fools of Time,
  Which die for goodness, who have liv'd for crime.

125

Were't aught to me I bore the canopy,
With my extern the outward honoring,
Or laid great bases for eternity,
Which proves more short than waste or ruining?
Have I not seen dwellers on form and favor
Lose all, and more, by paying too much rent,
For compound sweet forgoing simple savor,
Pitiful thrivers, in their gazing spent?
No, let me be obsequious in thy heart,
And take thou my oblation, poor but free,
Which is not mix'd with seconds, knows no art,
But mutual render, only me for thee.
  Hence, thou suborn'd informer, a true soul
  When most impeach'd stands least in thy control.

124.1. **dear love**: intense feeling of love. **but**: merely. **state**: (1) circumstance; (2) high station (of the loved one).
2. **for . . . unfather'd**: i.e. have no parent but Fortune, hence be solely under Fortune's control.
4. **Weeds . . . gather'd**: i.e. worthless or precious as chance dictates.
5. **accident**: effects of chance events. 6. **suffers**: alters.
7. **the blow . . . discontent**: the blows of fortune which make one a slave to grief.
8. **Whereto . . . calls**: to which (both "smiling pomp" and, in turn, "thralled discontent") the present time summons us to accommodate our condition.
9. **policy, that heretic**: i.e. the sort of prudence that has no true faith; material self-interest.
10. **works . . . hours**: i.e. operates with a view to immediate gains.
11. **hugely politic**: i.e. prudent in the largest sense, since not vulnerable to chance.
12. **heat**: sunshine, i.e. good fortune.
13. **fools**: victims, playthings. Cf. Sonnet 116.9. Line 14 is widely supposed to allude topically to specific "fools of Time," but none of the attempted identifications has been generally accepted.

125.1. **Were't . . . me**: would it be anything to me if. **bore the canopy**: carried a ceremonial canopy over a royal person in a procession; figuratively, paid public homage.
2. **extern**: exterior, external action.
3. **bases for eternity**: i.e. foundations for (supposedly) eternal memorials.
5. **dwellers on**: those who make much of (with quibble on "tenants of," which suggests the figure in the next line). **form and favor**: (1) courtly behavior and status; (2) figure and face.
7. **For . . . savor**: i.e. for elaborate ceremony forgoing simple sincerity.
8. **Pitiful thrivers**: pitiful in their gains (since what they gain is without value). **gazing**: courtly observance.
9. **be obsequious**: pay court, render devotion.
10. **oblation**: offering.
11. **seconds**: elements of secondary importance, adulterants. **art**: artifice, craft.
12. **render**: return, exchange.
13. **suborn'd informer**: paid spy, i.e. Jealousy, who prompted the charges the poet is answering in lines 1–8.
14. **impeach'd**: accused.

126

O thou, my lovely boy, who in thy power
Dost hold Time's fickle glass, his sickle, hour;
Who hast by waning grown, and therein show'st
Thy lovers withering as thy sweet self grow'st;
If Nature (sovereign mistress over wrack)
As thou goest onwards still will pluck thee back,
She keeps thee to this purpose, that her skill
May Time disgrace and wretched [minutes] kill.
Yet fear her, O thou minion of her pleasure,
She may detain, but not still keep, her treasure!
Her audit (though delay'd) answer'd must be,
And her quietus is to render thee.

127

In the old age black was not counted fair,
Or if it were it bore not beauty's name;
But now is black beauty's successive heir,
And beauty slander'd with a bastard shame,
For since each hand hath put on nature's power,
Fairing the foul with art's false borrow'd face,
Sweet beauty hath no name, no holy bow'r,
But is profan'd, if not lives in disgrace.
Therefore my mistress' eyes are raven black,
Her eyes so suited, and they mourners seem
At such who, not born fair, no beauty lack,
Sland'ring creation with a false esteem:
  Yet so they mourn, becoming of their woe,
  That every tongue says beauty should look so.

128

How oft when thou, my music, music play'st
Upon that blessed wood whose motion sounds
With thy sweet fingers when thou gently sway'st
The wiry concord that mine ear confounds,
Do I envy those jacks that nimble leap
To kiss the tender inward of thy hand,
Whilst my poor lips, which should that harvest reap,
At the wood's boldness by thee blushing stand.
To be so tickled they would change their state
And situation with those dancing chips,
O'er whom [thy] fingers walk with gentle gait,
Making dead wood more blest than living lips:

126.2. **glass**: mirror (in which Time's ravaging of beauty can be viewed) (?). The line may be corrupt. **hour**: hourglass (?).
3. **by waning grown**: grown more beautiful with the passing of time.
5. **wrack**: ruin. 6. **still**: continually.
8. **minutes kill**: render powerless the passage of minutes.
9. **minion**: darling, favorite. 10. **still**: always, forever.
11. **audit**: final accounting. **answer'd**: settled, paid.
12. **quietus**: (means of) settlement. **render**: surrender.

127.1. **the old age**: the good old days. **black**: dark hair and eyes. **fair**: beautiful (with quibble on "blonde").
3. **is . . . heir**: black has succeeded to the title of beauty.
4. **beauty . . . shame**: (blonde) beauty now suffers the disgrace of illegitimacy (through cosmetics). 5. **put on**: assumed.
6. **Fairing the foul**: making beautiful the ugly.
9, 10. **eyes, eyes**. Many editors emend one of these to *hairs* or *brows*.
10. **so suited**: dressed in the same color. 13. **becoming of**: gracing.

128.2. **wood**: keys of the spinet or virginals. 3. **sway'st**: governest.
4. **confounds**: i.e. overcomes with delight.
5. **jacks**: i.e. keys (an inaccurate use of the term, which properly refers to the plectrums that pluck the strings when activated by pressure on the keys).

Since saucy jacks so happy are in this,
Give them [thy] fingers, me thy lips to kiss.

129

Th' expense of spirit in a waste of shame
Is lust in action, and till action, lust
Is perjur'd, murd'rous, bloody, full of blame,
Savage, extreme, rude, cruel, not to trust,
Enjoy'd no sooner but despised straight,
Past reason hunted, and no sooner had,
Past reason hated as a swallowed bait
On purpose laid to make the taker mad:
[Mad] in pursuit and in possession so,
Had, having, and in quest to have, extreme,
A bliss in proof, and prov'd, [a] very woe,
Before, a joy propos'd, behind, a dream.
All this the world well knows, yet none knows well
To shun the heaven that leads men to this hell.

130

My mistress' eyes are nothing like the sun;
Coral is far more red than her lips' red;
If snow be white, why then her breasts are dun;
If hairs be wires, black wires grow on her head.
I have seen roses damask'd, red and white,
But no such roses see I in her cheeks,
And in some perfumes is there more delight
Than in the breath that from my mistress reeks.
I love to hear her speak, yet well I know
That music hath a far more pleasing sound;
I grant I never saw a goddess go,
My mistress when she walks treads on the ground.
And yet, by heaven, I think my love as rare
As any she belied with false compare.

131

Thou art as tyrannous, so as thou art,
As those whose beauties proudly make them cruel;
For well thou know'st to my dear doting heart
Thou art the fairest and most precious jewel.
Yet in good faith some say that thee behold,
Thy face hath not the power to make love groan;
To say they err I dare not be so bold,
Although I swear it to myself alone.
And to be sure that is not false I swear,
A thousand groans, but thinking on thy face,

13. saucy jacks. With a quibble on the sense "impertinent fellows."

129.1. expense: expenditure, dissipation. **spirit:** vital energy. **waste of shame:** shameful waste.
4. extreme: violent. **rude:** brutal. **trust:** be trusted.
11. in proof: while being experienced.

130.1. nothing: not at all. **3. dun:** dark, swarthy.
5. damask'd: mingled red and white.
8. reeks: is exhaled (without pejorative connotation).
11. go: walk. **13. rare:** admirable, extraordinary.
14. she: woman. **belied:** misrepresented. **compare:** comparison.

131.1. tyrannous: cruel, pitiless. **so . . . art:** i.e. being black and not fair. **2. proudly:** with justified pride.
3. dear: fond, loving. **7. say:** i.e. say publicly.
9. to be sure: as proof.
10. but thinking on: when I do no more than think of.

One on another's neck, do witness bear
Thy black is fairest in my judgment's place.
In nothing art thou black save in thy deeds,
And thence this slander as I think proceeds.

132

Thine eyes I love, and they as pitying me,
Knowing thy heart torment me with disdain,
Have put on black, and loving mourners be,
Looking with pretty ruth upon my pain.
And truly not the morning sun of heaven
Better becomes the grey cheeks of th' east,
Nor that full star that ushers in the even
Doth half that glory to the sober west,
As those two [mourning] eyes become thy face.
O, let it then as well beseem thy heart
To mourn for me, since mourning doth thee grace,
And suit thy pity like in every part.
Then will I swear beauty herself is black,
And all they foul that thy complexion lack.

133

Beshrew that heart that makes my heart to groan
For that deep wound it gives my friend and me;
Is't not enough to torture me alone,
But slave to slavery my sweet'st friend must be?
Me from myself thy cruel eye hath taken,
And my next self thou harder hast engrossed:
Of him, myself, and thee I am forsaken,
A torment thrice threefold thus to be crossed.
Prison my heart in thy steel bosom's ward,
But then my friend's heart let my poor heart bail;
Whoe'er keeps me, let my heart be his guard,
Thou canst not then use rigor in my jail:
And yet thou wilt, for I being pent in thee,
Perforce am thine, and all that is in me.

134

So now I have confess'd that he is thine,
And I myself am mortgag'd to thy will,
Myself I'll forfeit, so that other mine
Thou wilt restore to be my comfort still:
But thou wilt not, nor he will not be free,

11. One . . . neck: in rapid succession.
12. black: dark complexion. **13. black:** i.e. not fair, ugly.
14. this slander: i.e. in line 6. **proceeds:** originates.

132.2. torment: i.e. to torment (infinitive construction). Many editors emend to *torments*. **4. ruth:** pity. **6. becomes:** graces.
8. Doth: gives, lends (so also in line 11). **sober:** subdued in color.
10. beseem: become. **11. grace:** beauty.
12. suit: (1) dress; (2) fit. **every part:** i.e. your heart (line 2) as well as your eyes. **14. foul:** ugly.

133.1. Beshrew: a plague on (a very mild imprecation).
6. next: nearest, second. **harder:** more securely. **engrossed:** monopolized. **8. crossed:** afflicted. **9. ward:** prison cell.
10. bail: liberate by suffering in its place.
11. keeps me: is my jailer. **his guard:** my friend's guardhouse.
12. rigor: harsh extreme of the law. **13. pent:** imprisoned.

134.1. confess'd: acknowledged.
2. will: (1) wishes; (2) pleasure, particularly sexual.
3. so: provided that. **that other mine:** my other self.
5. will not: does not will to.

For thou art covetous, and he is kind;
He learn'd but surety-like to write for me
Under that bond that him as fast doth bind.
The statute of thy beauty thou wilt take,
Thou usurer, that put'st forth all to use,
And sue a friend came debtor for my sake,
So him I lose through my unkind abuse.
  Him have I lost, thou hast both him and me,
  He pays the whole, and yet am I not free.

135

Whoever hath her wish, thou hast thy *Will*,
And *Will* to boot, and *Will* in overplus;
More than enough am I that vex thee still,
To thy sweet will making addition thus.
Wilt thou, whose will is large and spacious,
Not once vouchsafe to hide my will in thine?
Shall will in others seem right gracious,
And in my will no fair acceptance shine?
The sea, all water, yet receives rain still,
And in abundance addeth to his store,
So thou being rich in *Will* add to thy *Will*
One will of mine to make thy large *Will* more.
  Let no unkind, no fair beseechers kill;
  Think all but one, and me in that one *Will*.

136

If thy soul check thee that I come so near,
Swear to thy blind soul that I was thy *Will*,
And will, thy soul knows, is admitted there;
Thus far for love my love-suit, sweet, fulfill.
Will will fulfill the treasure of thy love,
Ay, fill it full with wills, and my will one.
In things of great receipt with ease we prove
Among a number one is reckon'd none:
Then in the number let me pass untold,
Though in thy store's account I one must be,
For nothing hold me, so it please thee hold
That nothing me, a something sweet to thee.
  Make but my name thy love, and love that still,
  And then thou lovest me, for my name is *Will*.

137

Thou blind fool, Love, what dost thou to mine eyes,
That they behold and see not what they see?
They know what beauty is, see where it lies,
Yet what the best is take the worst to be.
If eyes, corrupt by over-partial looks,
Be anchor'd in the bay where all men ride,
Why of eyes' falsehood hast thou forged hooks,
Whereto the judgment of my heart is tied?
Why should my heart think that a several plot,
Which my heart knows the wide world's common place?
Or mine eyes seeing this, say this is not,
To put fair truth upon so foul a face?
  In things right true my heart and eyes have erred,
  And to this false plague are they now transferred.

138

When my love swears that she is made of truth,
I do believe her, though I know she lies,
That she might think me some untutor'd youth,
Unlearned in the world's false subtilties.
Thus vainly thinking that she thinks me young,
Although she knows my days are past the best,
Simply I credit her false-speaking tongue;
On both sides thus is simple truth suppress'd.
But wherefore says she not she is unjust?
And wherefore say not I that I am old?
O, love's best habit is in seeming trust,
And age in love loves not t' have years told.
  Therefore I lie with her, and she with me,
  And in our faults by lies we flattered be.

139

O, call not me to justify the wrong
That thy unkindness lays upon my heart,
Wound me not with thine eye but with thy tongue,
Use power with power, and slay me not by art.
Tell me thou lov'st elsewhere, but in my sight,
Dear heart, forbear to glance thine eye aside;
What need'st thou wound with cunning when thy might
Is more than my o'erpress'd defense can bide?
Let me excuse thee: ah, my love well knows
Her pretty looks have been mine enemies,
And therefore from my face she turns my foes,
That they elsewhere might dart their injuries:

6. **kind:** generous. 7. **surety-like:** as guarantor. **write:** endorse. 8. **bond:** (1) mortgage; (2) rope or chain. **bind:** (1) obligate; (2) tie. 9. **statute:** full amount secured under a bond. 10. **use:** (1) interest; (2) sexual activity. 11. **came:** who became. 12. **my unkind abuse:** your unkind deceiving of me.

135.1. **Will:** (1) wishes; (2) carnal desire; (3) one or more persons named Will. This sonnet and Nos. 136 and 143 involve elaborate punning on the word. The proverb "A woman will have her will" (understood carnally) is implied. 3. **still:** continually. 13. **Let . . . kill:** do not kill with unkindness any of your wooers.

136.1. **If . . . near:** if this bold address to you (Sonnet 135) causes your conscience to reproach you. 5. **fulfill the treasure:** fill full the treasury. 7. **receipt:** capacity. 8. **one . . . none.** Playing on the proverb "One is no number." 9. **untold:** uncounted. 10. **store's account:** inventory (of lovers). 13. **still:** always.

137.4. **what . . . be:** take the worst for the best. 5. **over-partial:** prejudiced. 6. **bay . . . ride:** harbor open to any ship (common slang for a loose woman). 7. **falsehood:** deception, delusion. 9. **that . . . plot:** that to be private property. 10. **common place:** common land, open to everyone. 13. **erred:** i.e. by adjudging them false. 14. **false plague:** plague of seeing false things (which I adjudge true).

138. Another version of this sonnet is the first poem in *The Passionate Pilgrim*. 1. **truth:** fidelity, constancy. 2. **believe:** i.e. appear to believe. 7. **Simply:** in my pretended simpleness. 8. **simple:** pure. 9. **unjust:** untrue. 11. **habit . . . trust:** deportment consists of apparent fidelity. 12. **told:** counted. 13. **lie with:** lie to (with obvious pun).

139.3. **with thine eye:** i.e. by casting it on others (line 6). 4. **with power:** i.e. openly and directly. **by art:** artfully, deviously. 7. **What:** why. 8. **bide:** stand up against. 10. **pretty looks:** wanton glances. 11. **my foes:** i.e. her "pretty looks."

Yet do not so, but since I am near slain,
Kill me outright with looks, and rid my pain.

140

Be wise as thou art cruel, do not press
My tongue-tied patience with too much disdain,
Lest sorrow lend me words, and words express
The manner of my pity-wanting pain.
If I might teach thee wit, better it were,
Though not to love, yet, love, to tell me so,
As testy sick men, when their deaths be near,
No news but health from their physicians know;
For if I should despair, I should grow mad,
And in my madness might speak ill of thee;
Now this ill-wresting world is grown so bad,
Mad slanderers by mad ears believed be.
That I may not be so, nor thou belied,
Bear thine eyes straight, though thy proud heart go wide.

141

In faith, I do not love thee with mine eyes,
For they in thee a thousand errors note,
But 'tis my heart that loves what they despise,
Who in despite of view is pleas'd to dote;
Nor are mine ears with thy tongue's tune delighted,
Nor tender feeling to base touches prone,
Nor taste, nor smell, desire to be invited
To any sensual feast with thee alone;
But my five wits nor my five senses can
Dissuade one foolish heart from serving thee,
Who leaves unsway'd the likeness of a man,
Thy proud heart's slave and vassal wretch to be:
Only my plague thus far I count my gain,
That she that makes me sin awards me pain.

142

Love is my sin, and thy dear virtue hate,
Hate of my sin, grounded on sinful loving:
O, but with mine compare thou thine own state,
And thou shalt find it merits not reproving,
Or if it do, not from those lips of thine,
That have profan'd their scarlet ornaments,
And seal'd false bonds of love as oft as mine,
Robb'd others' beds' revenues of their rents.
Be it lawful I love thee as thou lov'st those
Whom thine eyes woo as mine importune thee.
Root pity in thy heart, that when it grows,
Thy pity may deserve to pitied be.
If thou dost seek to have what thou dost hide,
By self-example mayst thou be denied.

143

Lo as a careful huswife runs to catch
One of her feathered creatures broke away,
Sets down her babe and makes all swift dispatch
In pursuit of the thing she would have stay;
Whilst her neglected child holds her in chase,
Cries to catch her whose busy care is bent
To follow that which flies before her face,
Not prizing her poor infant's discontent;
So run'st thou after that which flies from thee,
Whilst I, thy babe, chase thee afar behind,
But if thou catch thy hope, turn back to me,
And play the mother's part, kiss me, be kind.
So will I pray that thou mayst have thy *Will*,
If thou turn back and my loud crying still.

144

Two loves I have of comfort and despair,
Which like two spirits do suggest me still:
The better angel is a man right fair,
The worser spirit a woman color'd ill.
To win me soon to hell, my female evil
Tempteth my better angel from my [side],
And would corrupt my saint to be a devil,
Wooing his purity with her foul pride.
And whether that my angel be turn'd fiend
Suspect I may, yet not directly tell,
But being both from me, both to each friend,
I guess one angel in another's hell.
Yet this shall I ne'er know, but live in doubt,
Till my bad angel fire my good one out.

145

Those lips that Love's own hand did make
Breath'd forth the sound that said "I hate"

14. rid: destroy, end.

140.4. manner: nature. **pity-wanting:** unpitied. **5. wit:** wisdom.
6. Though . . . so: to say you love me even though you don't.
7. testy: fretful, peevish. **8. know:** hear.
11. ill-wresting: that puts a bad construction on everything.
13. so: i.e. mad. **belied:** slandered.
14. wide: wide of the mark (term from archery), i.e. astray.

141.4. in . . . view: despite the evidence of vision.
6. Nor . . . prone: i.e. nor (is) my delicate sense of touch desirous of sexual contact with you.
9. five wits: intellectual faculties (usually listed as common wit, memory, fantasy, imagination, and judgment).
11. Who . . . man: i.e. the heart, which should control the body, has deserted it, leaving it ungoverned, the mere likeness of a man.
13. thus far: to the following extent.
14. pain: penance, punishment.

142.1. dear: most valued.
2. grounded. Modifies *Hate*. **sinful loving:** i.e. the fact that my love is sinful. **4. it:** i.e. my love.

7. seal'd. The comparison of lips to the red wax used for sealing documents is a common figure.
9. Be it lawful: let it be considered lawful that.
12. deserve: make you worthy.
13. what . . . hide: what you refuse to show, i.e. pity.

143.1. careful: busy, full of cares. **huswife:** housewife (probably pronounced *hussif*).
8. Not prizing: disregarding. **discontent:** grief, complaining.
13. Will. Cf. Sonnets 135, 136. **14. still:** silence.

144. Another version of this sonnet is the second poem in *The Passionate Pilgrim*. **1. comfort.** Cf. Sonnet 48.6.
2. suggest: urge (toward comfort or despair). **still:** constantly.
4. color'd ill: i.e. dark. Cf. Sonnets 127, 132.
8. pride: wantonness.
11. from me: away from me. **both . . . friend:** each a friend to the other.
14. fire . . . out: drive . . . out (with quibble on the sense "infect with venereal disease").

To me that languish'd for her sake;
But when she saw my woeful state,
Straight in her heart did mercy come,
Chiding that tongue that, ever sweet,
Was us'd in giving gentle doom,
And taught it thus anew to greet:
"I hate" she alter'd with an end
That follow'd it as gentle day
Doth follow night, who like a fiend
From heaven to hell is flown away:
  "I hate" from hate away she threw,
  And sav'd my life, saying "not you."

146

Poor soul, the centre of my sinful earth,
[. . . .] these rebel pow'rs that thee array,
Why dost thou pine within and suffer dearth,
Painting thy outward walls so costly gay?
Why so large cost, having so short a lease,
Dost thou upon thy fading mansion spend?
Shall worms, inheritors of this excess,
Eat up thy charge? Is this thy body's end?
Then, soul, live thou upon thy servant's loss,
And let that pine to aggravate thy store;
Buy terms divine in selling hours of dross;
Within be fed, without be rich no more:
  So shalt thou feed on Death, that feeds on men,
  And Death once dead, there's no more dying then.

147

My love is as a fever, longing still
For that which longer nurseth the disease,
Feeding on that which doth preserve the ill,
Th' uncertain sickly appetite to please.
My reason, the physician to my love,
Angry that his prescriptions are not kept,
Hath left me, and I desperate now approve
Desire is death, which physic did except.
Past cure I am, now reason is past care,
And frantic mad with evermore unrest;
My thoughts and my discourse as madmen's are,
At randon from the truth vainly express'd;
  For I have sworn thee fair, and thought thee bright,
  Who art as black as hell, as dark as night.

145.7. **doom:** judgment, decision.
13. **from hate:** from hateful meaning.

146.2. In the 1609 quarto this line begins with the apparently inadvertent repetition of the last three words of line 1. *Thrall to, Hemm'd with, Fool'd by, Feeding* are four of many conjectural restorations of the lost first foot. **these rebel pow'rs:** i.e. rebellious flesh and blood. **array:** clothe. 5. **cost:** amount.
6. **mansion:** dwelling. 8. **charge:** expense.
9. **thy servant's:** i.e. the body's.
10. **that:** i.e. the body. **pine:** starve, dwindle. **aggravate thy store:** enrich your resources.
11. **terms divine:** i.e. everlasting life.

147.1. **still:** continuously.
3. **preserve the ill:** maintain the illness.
7. **approve:** learn by experience, demonstrate.
8. **Desire . . . except:** that desire, which refused medical treatment (from reason), is fatal.
9. **care:** medical care (of me). The line is an inversion of the proverb "Past cure, past care."
12. **randon:** random. **vainly:** idly, to no rational purpose.

148

O me! what eyes hath Love put in my head,
Which have no correspondence with true sight,
Or if they have, where is my judgment fled,
That censures falsely what they see aright?
If that be fair whereon my false eyes dote,
What means the world to say it is not so?
If it be not, then love doth well denote
Love's eye is not so true as all men's: no,
How can it? O, how can Love's eye be true,
That is so vex'd with watching and with tears?
No marvel then though I mistake my view,
The sun itself sees not till heaven clears.
  O cunning Love, with tears thou keep'st me blind,
  Lest eyes well seeing thy foul faults should find.

149

Canst thou, O cruel, say I love thee not,
When I against myself with thee partake?
Do I not think on thee when I forgot
Am of myself, all tyrant for thy sake?
Who hateth thee that I do call my friend?
On whom frown'st thou that I do fawn upon?
Nay, if thou low'r'st on me, do I not spend
Revenge upon myself with present moan?
What merit do I in myself respect,
That is so proud thy service to despise,
When all my best doth worship thy defect,
Commanded by the motion of thine eyes?
  But, love, hate on, for now I know thy mind:
  Those that can see thou lov'st, and I am blind.

150

O, from what pow'r hast thou this pow'rful might
With insufficiency my heart to sway,
To make me give the lie to my true sight,
And swear that brightness doth not grace the day?
Whence hast thou this becoming of things ill,
That in the very refuse of thy deeds
There is such strength and warrantise of skill
That in my mind thy worst all best exceeds?
Who taught thee how to make me love thee more,
The more I hear and see just cause of hate?
O, though I love what others do abhor,
With others thou shouldst not abhor my state.

148.2. **correspondence:** agreement. 4. **censures:** judges.
7. **denote:** indicate.
8. **men's: no.** Many editors emend to *men's no;* if they are correct, *Love's eye* contains a quibble on *Love's ay*.
10. **watching:** staying awake at night. 11. **my view:** what I see.

149.2. **partake:** take sides. 3. **forgot:** forgotten.
4. **all tyrant:** i.e. complete tyrant to myself (?). Some editors read *all-tyrant* and construe it as a vocative, paralleling *O cruel* in line 1.
9. **respect:** value. 10. **thy . . . despise:** as to scorn to serve you.
11. **defect:** insufficiency. See Sonnet 150.
14. **Those . . . lov'st:** you love people who can see.

150.1. **pow'r:** supernatural being.
2. **With insufficiency:** by means of your shortcomings. **sway:** rule.
3. **give the lie:** say "you lie."
5. **becoming . . . ill:** ability to make defects seem attractive.
6. **in . . . deeds:** in your unworthiest behavior.
7. **warrantise:** pledge, surety.

If thy unworthiness rais'd love in me,
More worthy I to be belov'd of thee.

151

Love is too young to know what conscience is,
Yet who knows not conscience is born of love?
Then, gentle cheater, urge not my amiss,
Lest guilty of my faults thy sweet self prove:
For thou betraying me, I do betray
My nobler part to my gross body's treason;
My soul doth tell my body that he may
Triumph in love; flesh stays no farther reason,
But rising at thy name doth point out thee
As his triumphant prize. Proud of this pride,
He is contented thy poor drudge to be,
To stand in thy affairs, fall by thy side.
No want of conscience hold it that I call
Her "love" for whose dear love I rise and fall.

152

In loving thee thou know'st I am forsworn,
But thou art twice forsworn, to me love swearing;
In act thy bed-vow broke, and new faith torn
In vowing new hate after new love bearing.
But why of two oaths' breach do I accuse thee,
When I break twenty? I am perjur'd most,
For all my vows are oaths but to misuse thee,
And all my honest faith in thee is lost;
For I have sworn deep oaths of thy deep kindness,
Oaths of thy love, thy truth, thy constancy,
And to enlighten thee gave eyes to blindness,
Or made them swear against the thing they see;

151.1. too young: Cf. Sonnet 115.13.
1, 2. conscience: "(1) moral sense and understanding; (2) guilty 'knowing'" (Tucker). **3. urge:** stress. **amiss:** fault, sin.
6. nobler part: soul. **8. stays:** awaits. **reason:** talk.
10. triumphant: to be enjoyed in triumph. **Proud of:** swelling with. **pride:** sexual ardor. **12. stand:** (1) serve; (2) be erect.

152.1. am forsworn: i.e. have broken my marriage vows.
3. bed-vow: marriage vows. **faith:** trust. **torn.** The "new faith" is represented as a contractual document.
7. misuse: belie, misrepresent. **9. of:** i.e. asserting.
11. enlighten: shed lustre upon.
11–12. gave . . . see: i.e. pretended to see what I did not see, or denied seeing what was manifest.

For I have sworn thee fair: more perjur'd eye,
To swear against the truth so foul a lie!

153

Cupid laid by his brand and fell asleep;
A maid of Dian's this advantage found,
And his love-kindling fire did quickly steep
In a cold valley-fountain of that ground;
Which borrow'd from this holy fire of Love
A dateless lively heat, still to endure,
And grew a seething bath, which yet men prove
Against strange maladies a sovereign cure.
But at my mistress' eye Love's brand new fired,
The boy for trial needs would touch my breast;
I sick withal the help of bath desired,
And thither hied, a sad distemper'd guest;
But found no cure: the bath for my help lies
Where Cupid got new fire—my mistress' [eyes].

154

The little Love-god, lying once asleep,
Laid by his side his heart-inflaming brand,
Whilst many nymphs that vow'd chaste life to keep
Came tripping by, but in her maiden hand
The fairest votary took up that fire,
Which many legions of true hearts had warm'd,
And so the general of hot desire
Was sleeping by a virgin hand disarm'd.
This brand she quenched in a cool well by,
Which from Love's fire took heat perpetual,
Growing a bath and healthful remedy
For men diseas'd, but I, my mistress' thrall,
Came there for cure, and this by that I prove:
Love's fire heats water, water cools not love.

13. eye. With a quibble on *I*, to which many editors emend *eye.*

153.1. brand: torch.
2. maid of Dian's: votaress of Diana, goddess of chastity. **advantage:** opportunity. **6. dateless:** endless. **still:** always.
7. grew: became. **seething:** boiling. **10. for trial:** to test it.
11. withal: from that.
12. hied: hastened. **distemper'd:** ill.

154.9. by: nearby. **11. Growing:** becoming.
13. this: the following proposition.

NOTE ON THE TEXT

The sole authority for the text of all but two of the Sonnets (and for *"A Lover's Complaint"*: see the "Note on the Text" to that poem) is the quarto volume (Q) printed by George Eld for Thomas Thorpe in 1609 and entitled *Shake-speares Sonnets. Neuer before Imprinted.* Sonnets 138 and 144 had been published earlier in that heterogeneous collection, *The Passionate Pilgrim* (?1599), but even for these two poems Q must be considered the basic text.

The authority of the manuscript copy-text used by Thorpe has been the subject of endless debate (see Rollins, Jackson, Evans). Whatever its provenience, the manuscript would seem to have been a single more or less homogeneous collection, not, like *The Passionate Pilgrim,* one assembled from a variety of sources. There is a possibility, though not a strong one, that this manuscript was in Shakespeare's autograph. More probably it was a transcript by another hand or hands. In any case, although it is highly unlikely that Shakespeare authorized the publication (in contrast to the editions of *Venus and Adonis* and *Lucrece*), the resulting text, as Hyder Rollins has shown, is not as faulty or unreliable as some earlier scholars have liked to insist.

Until lately, much praise has been lavished on the sensitivity and poetic intelligence displayed by the punctuation in Q, qualities that were attributed to Shakespeare's own "pointing hand." MacD. P. Jackson, however, in a seminal compositor study of Q (1975) established beyond question that Q's punctuation was, probably almost wholly, the work of two compositors (A and B), each of whom had his own characteristic (and not always very sensitive) style. Thus, with a single blow, Jackson exposed a lot of wishful thinking and exploded another Shakespeare myth. See also a detailed discussion of Q's punctuation and other characteristics in Evans.

Katherine Duncan-Jones, in another important study (1983), has helped to establish the overall integrity of Q by showing that the two anacreontic Cupid sonnets (153 and 154) and *"A Lover's Complaint"* form a more or less regular coda also found in a number of other contemporary sonnet sequences by Samuel Daniel (1593), Thomas Lodge (1593), Giles Fletcher the Elder (1593), Edmund Spenser (1595), and Richard Barnfield (1595). This sonnet sequence pattern, consequently, suggests that the Q ordering of the sonnets generally, an order so often, and futilely, rearranged in so many essentially contradictory sequences (see Rollins, II, 113–16), may also represent some authorial intention.

The Sonnets (with the exception of 18, 19, 43, 56, 75, 76, 96, 126) and *"A Lover's Complaint"* were again published, piratically printed from Q, by John Benson in 1640, in a volume entitled *Poems: Written by Wil. Shake-speare. Gent.* In this collection the sonnets were rearranged, grouped under invented titles, and indiscriminately combined with the contents of the third edition (1612) of *The Passionate Pilgrim.*

For further information, see: H. E. Rollins, ed., New Variorum *Sonnets,* 2 vols. (Philadelphia, 1944); A. H. Carter, "The Publication of Shakespeare's *Sonnets* of 1609," *Joseph Quincy Adams Memorial Studies*, ed. J. G. McManaway, et al. (Washington, 1948), 409–28; Edward Hubler, ed., *Shakespeare's Songs and Poems* (New York, 1959); Martin Seymour-Smith, ed., *Shakespeare's Sonnets* (London, 1963); W. G. Ingram and Theodore Redpath, eds., *Shakespeare's Sonnets* (London, 1964); J. D. Wilson, ed., New Shakespeare *Sonnets* (Cambridge, 1966); MacD. P. Jackson, "Punctuation and the Compositors of Shakespeare's *Sonnets, 1609,*" *The Library*, 5th. ser., XXX (1975), 1–24; Stephen Booth, ed., *Shakespeare's Sonnets* (Yale, 1977; rev. 1978); Randall McLeod, "A Technique of Headline Analysis, with Application to Shakespeare's *Sonnets*," *SB*, XXXII (1979), 197–210; Katherine Duncan-Jones, "Was the 1609 *Shakespeares Sonnets* Really Unauthorized?", *RES*, n.s., XXXIV (1983), 151–71; Stanley Wells, "New Readings in Shakespeare's Sonnets," in *Elizabethan and Modern Studies*, ed., J. P. Vander Motten (R. U. G., 1985), 317–22; Gary Taylor, "Some Manuscripts of Shakespeare's Sonnets," *The Bulletin of the John Rylands Library*, LXVIII (1985), 210–46; John Kerrigan, ed., New Penguin *The Sonnets* and *A Lover's Complaint* (Harmondsworth, Middlesex, 1986); Stanley Wells, Gary Taylor, et al., *William Shakespeare: A Textual Companion* (Oxford, 1987); G. B. Evans, ed., New Cambridge *The Sonnets* (Cambridge, 1996).

TEXTUAL NOTES

1

Numbered by Benson; unnumbered, Q
2 rose] *Gildon;* Rose *Q (in italics)*
6 self-substantial] *hyphen, Gildon*
12 And, tender chorl,] *Capell MS;* And tender chorle *Q*

2

7 deep-sunken] *hyphen, Gildon*
10–1 "This ... excuse,"] *quotes, Capell MS*
14 cold.] *Benson;* could, *Q*

3

2 another] *Gildon;* an other *Q (generally)*
4 dost] doo'st *Q (or* doost *frequently)*
8 self-love,] *Gildon (hyphen, Lintott);* selfe loue *Q*

4

12 audit] *Murden;* Audit *Q (in italics)*

5

5 never-resting] *hyphen, Gildon*

6

1 ragged] *Gildon;* wragged *Q*
4 beauty's] *Benson (subs.);* beautits *Q*
4 self-kill'd] *hyphen, Gildon*
13 self-will'd] *Gildon;* selfe-wild *Q*

7

3 new-appearing] *hyphen, Murden*
5 steep-up] *hyphen, Gildon*

8

9 string,] *Gildon;* string *Q*
14 thee,] *Gildon;* thee *Q*

10

2 unprovident.] *Gildon (subs.);* vnprovident *Q*
12 kind-hearted] *hyphen, Gildon*

11

6 this,] *Gildon;* this *Q*

12

4 all] *Malone;* or *Q*
14 breed, ... him] *Gildon;* breed ... him, *Q*

13

1 but, love,] *Gildon;* but loue *Q*
7 Yourself] *Benson;* You selfe *Q*
13 unthrifts: ... love,] *Gildon;* vnthrifts, ... loue *Q*
13 know] *Gildon;* know, *Q*

14

4 seasons'] *Capell MS;* seasons *Q*
5 minutes] *Benson* (minuts); mynuits *Q*
6 'Pointing] *W. S. Walker conj.;* Pointing *Q*
10 And, constant stars,] *Capell MS;* And constant stars *Q*

15

8 wear] *Gildon;* were *Q*
13 you,] *Gildon;* you *Q*

16

10 this ... pen,] *Gildon;* this (Times pensel or my pupill pen) *Q*
12 men,] *Gildon;* men, *Q*
14 skill.] *Benson;* skill, *Q*

17

2 fill'd] *Gildon;* fild *Q*
12 metre] *Gildon;* miter *Q*
14 twice, in it] *Capell MS (subs.);* twise in it, *Q*

18

11 wand'rest] *Wyndham;* wandr'st *Q*
14 thee.] *Benson;* thee, *Q*

19

3 jaws] *Capell MS;* yawes *Q*
4 long-liv'd] *hyphen, Capell MS*
13 Time:] *Capell MS (subs.);* Time *Q*

20

2 Hast] *Benson;* Haste *Q*
6 gazeth;] *Gildon (subs.);* gazeth, *Q*
7 hues] *Malone;* Hews *Q (in italics)*
10 a-doting] *hyphen, Malone*

21

6 sea's] *Gildon;* seas *Q*
9 me, ... love,] *Gildon;* me ... loue *Q*

22

3 furrows] *Benson;* forrwes *Q (a possible variant form)*
9 therefore, love,] *Sewell;* therefore loue *Q*

23

6 rite] *Malone;* right *Q*
14 with ... wit] *Benson;* wit ... wiht *Q*

24

1 stell'd] *Capell MS;* steeld *Q*
9 good turns] *Gildon;* good-turnes *Q*
12 thee.] *Gildon;* thee *Q*
13 art,] *Gildon;* art *Q*

25

9 fight] *Theobald conj.;* worth *Q (Theobald also suggested that alternatively one might read* forth *for* quite *in l. 11)*

26

12 thy] *Capell MS;* their *Q*

27

2 travel] *Gildon;* trauaill *Q*
10 thy] *Capell MS;* their *Q*
11 hung ... night,] *Malone;* (hunge ... night) *Q*

28

5 either's] *Malone;* ethers *Q*
9 day, ... him,] *Malone;* Day ... him *Q*
11 swart-complexion'd] *hyphen, Gildon*
12 gild'st] *Sewell;* guil'st *Q*
14 stronger.] *Lintott;* stronger *Q*

29

4 fate,] *Malone;* fate. *Q*
11–2 arising . . . earth)] *Malone* (*after Gildon*); arising) . . . earth *Q*

30

4 time's] *Gildon;* times *Q*
7 afresh] *Gildon;* a fresh *Q*

31

8 thee] *Gildon;* there *Q*
11 give:] *Sewell* (*subs.*); giue, *Q*

32

1 well-contented] *hyphen, Gildon*
3 re-survey] *Lintott* (*subs.*); re-suruay: *Q*

33

10 all-triumphant] *hyphen, S. Walker conj.*
14 staineth] *Benson;* stainteh *Q*

34

2 travel] *Gildon;* trauaile *Q*
12 cross] *Capell MS;* losse *Q*

35

7 corrupting,] *Gildon;* corrupting *Q*
8 thy . . . thy] *Capell MS;* their . . . their *Q*
9–10 sense— . . . advocate—] *Malone* (*subs.*); sence, . . . Aduocate, *Q*
11 commence.] *Malone* (*subs.*); commence, *Q*
14 me.] *Benson;* me, *Q*

37

6–7 more, . . . parts] *Malone* (*after Gildon*); more / . . . parts, *Q*
7 thy] *Capell MS;* their *Q*

39

7 give] *Lintott;* giue: *Q*
12 deceive,] *Malone* (*subs.*); deceiue. *Q*

40

6 thee] *Knight;* thee, *Q*
14 spites,] *ed.;* spights *Q*

41

8 she] *Malone;* he *Q* (*a possible, but unlikely, reading*)
9 Ay] *Gildon;* Aye *Q*

42

12 cross.] *Lintott* (*subs.*); crosse *Q*
14 flattery!] *Ewing* (*Capell MS*); flattery, *Q*

43

10 day,] *Capell MS;* day? *Q*
11 thy] *Capell MS;* their *Q*
14 me.] *Benson;* me, *Q*

44

9 thought,] *Gildon;* thought *Q*
12 attend time's] *Gildon* (*after Lintott*); attend, times *Q*
12 moan,] *Neilson;* mone. *Q*
13 nought] *Gildon* (*subs.*); naughts *Q*

45

4 present-absent] *hyphen, Malone*
11 assured] *Benson;* assured, *Q*
12 thy] *Gildon;* their *Q*

46

3, 8, 13, 14 thy] *Capell MS;* their *Q*
4 freedom] *Benson;* freeedome *Q*
9 'cide] *Gildon;* side *Q*

47

2 other:] *Gildon;* other, *Q*
4 smother,] *Malone;* smother; *Q*
10 Thyself] *Benson;* Thy seife *Q* (*possibly corrected in one copy*)
11 not] *Benson;* nor *Q*

49

12 part.] *Brooke;* part, *Q*

50

2 travel's] *Gildon;* trauels *Q*
6 dully] *Benson;* duly *Q*
8 speed,] *Malone;* speed *Q*

51

3 thence?] *Gildon;* thence, *Q*
10 perfect'st] *Dyce;* perfects *Q*
11 neigh (no dull flesh)] *Malone;* naigh noe dull flesh *Q*
13 willful-slow] *hyphen, Malone*

52

8 carcanet] *Capell MS;* carconet *Q*

53

3 one hath,] *Malone;* one, hath *Q*
5 Adonis, . . . counterfeit] *Lintott;* Adonis . . . counterfet, *Q*

55

1 monuments] *Malone;* monument *Q*
5 statues] *Malone;* Statues *Q* (*in italics*)
7 burn] *Gildon;* burne: *Q*
9 all-oblivious] *hyphen, Malone*
9 enmity] *Gildon;* emnity *Q*

56

3 allay'd] *Malone;* alaied *Q*
5 So, love,] *Capell MS;* So loue *Q*
9 int'rim] *Malone* (interim); Intrim *Q* (*in italics*)
11 see] *Capell MS;* see: *Q*
14 summer's] *Capell MS;* Sommers *Q*

57

5 world-without-end] *hyphens, Capell MS*
12 are] *E. B. Reed;* are, *Q*
13 will] *Murden;* Will *Q*

58

4 vassal] *Gildon;* vassail *Q*
7 patience, . . . sufferance,] *Gildon;* patience tame, to sufferance *Q*

59

1 is] *Gildon;* is, *Q*
11 whe'er] *Neilson* (*after Capell MS*); where *Q*

60

5 light,] *Lintott;* light. *Q*
13 hope] *Collier;* hope, *Q*

61

14 off] *Gildon;* of *Q*

62

11 self-love] *hyphen, Lintott*
11 read;] *Collier;* read *Q*
12 self-loving] *hyphen, Gildon*
14 days.] *Lintott;* daies, *Q*

63

3 fill'd] *Lintott;* fild *Q*
5 travell'd] *Gildon;* trauaild *Q*

64

10 confounded] *Sewell;* confounded, *Q*

65

12 of] *Malone;* or *Q*

66

11 simple truth] *Gildon;* simple-Truth *Q*
12 captive good] *Gildon;* captiue-good *Q*

68

7 a second] *Benson;* a scond *Q*
7 head;] *Malone;* head, *Q*

69

3 due] *Capell MS;* end *Q*
5 Thy] *Capell MS;* Their *Q*
11 Then, churls,] *Capell MS* (*subs.*); Then churls *Q*
14 soil] *Benson;* solye *Q*
14 dost] *Gildon;* doest *Q*

70

5 approve] *Lintott;* approue, *Q*
6 Thy] *Capell MS;* Their *Q*
8 unstained] *Benson;* vnstayined *Q*
12 enlarg'd] *Gentleman;* inlarged *Q*

71

1 dead] *Knight;* dead, *Q*
2 Than] *Malone;* Then *Q*

72

3 forget] *Benson;* for get *Q*

73

2 few,] *Capell MS;* few *Q*
4 ruin'd] *Benson;* rn'wd *Q*
4 choirs] *Malone;* quiers *Q*

74

2 Without] *Benson;* With out *Q*
5 dost] *Benson;* doest *Q*
8 me.] *Gildon;* me, *Q*
12 remembered] *Gildon;* remembred *Q*

75

2 sweet-season'd] *hyphen, Malone*
14 away.] *Benson;* away, *Q*

76

4 new-found] *hyphen, Malone*
7 tell] *Capell MS;* fel *Q*
14 told.] *Malone;* told, *Q*

77

1 wear] *Gildon;* were *Q*
10 blanks] *Theobald conj.;* blacks *Q*

78

3 alien] *Murden;* Alien *Q* (*in italics*)
7 learned's] *Gildon;* learneds *Q*

79

9 word] *Lintott;* word, *Q*
10 behavior;] *Gildon;* behauiour, *Q*
14 pay.] *Benson;* pay, *Q*

80

9 afloat] *Sewell* (*subs.*); a floate *Q*

81

8 lie;] *Gildon* (*subs.*); lye, *Q*
12 dead;] *Sewell;* dead, *Q*

82

8 time-bettering] *hyphen, Gildon*
9 so,] *Capell MS;* so *Q*
10 rhetoric] *Benson;* Rhethorick *Q*
12 true-telling] *hyphen, Gildon*

84

4 grew?] *Capell MS;* grew, *Q*

86

2 all-too-precious] *Capell MS* (*hyphens, Gildon*); (all to precious) *Q*
13 fill'd] *Gildon;* fild *Q*

88

1 dispos'd] *Benson;* dispode *Q*
7 attainted,] *Capell MS;* attainted: *Q*
12 double-vantage] *hyphen, Capell MS*

89

7 will:] *Capell MS;* wil, *Q*
9 walks, . . . tongue] *Gildon;* walkes . . . tongue, *Q*

90

4 after-loss] *hyphen, Sewell*
11 shall] *Benson;* stall *Q*

91

2 body's] *Capell MS;* bodies *Q*
9 better] *Benson;* bitter *Q*
10 garments'] *Capell MS;* garments *Q*

92

6 end;] *Gildon;* end, *Q*
7 see] *Lintott;* see, *Q*
10 lie;] *Gildon;* lie, *Q*
13 blessed-fair] *hyphen, Malone*

93

5 there] *Gildon;* their *Q*
10 dwell;] *Gildon;* dwell, *Q*

95

4 dost] *Gildon;* doest *Q*

96

11 mightst] *Lintott;* might *Q*

97

8 lords'] *Capell MS;* Lords *Q*
14 winter's] *Gildon;* Winters *Q*

98

2 proud-pied] *hyphen, Ewing*
9 lily's] *Capell MS;* Lillies *Q*
11 were] *Benson;* weare *Q*
13 and,] *Capell MS;* and *Q*

99

3–4 breath? The . . . dwells] *Gildon;* breath, the . . . dwells? *Q*
5 dy'd.] *Gildon;* died, *Q*
9 One] *Sewell;* Our *Q*
15 color] *Benson;* culler *Q*

100

11 satire] *Malone;* Satire *Q (in italics)*
14 prevent'st] *Gildon;* preuenst *Q*
14 scythe] *Ewing (after Sewell);* sieth *Q*

101

2 dy'd] *Gildon;* di'd *Q*
6–8 "Truth . . . intermix'd"] *quotes, Malone*
13 Muse;] *Capell MS;* Muse, *Q*

102

1 seeming,] *Butler;* seeming *Q*
8 her] *Housman;* his *Q*

104

8 fresh,] *Gildon;* fresh *Q*
12 deceiv'd] *Gentleman;* deceaued *Q*
14 born] *Gildon;* borne *Q*

105

13 alone,] *Malone;* alone. *Q*

106

5 beauty's] *Gildon;* beauties *Q*

108

14 dead.] *Benson;* dead, *Q*

109

5 love;] *Sewell;* loue, *Q*
8 stain.] *Gildon;* staine, *Q*
14 thou,] *Gildon;* thou *Q*

110

6 Askaunce] *ed.;* Asconce *Q*
8 love.] *Gildon;* loue, *Q*

111

1 with] *Gildon;* wish *Q*

112

8 wrong.] *Gildon;* wrong, *Q*
9 abysm] *Murden;* Abisme *Q (in italics)*
10 others'] *Capell MS;* others *Q*
14 methinks are] *Capell MS (subs.);* me thinkes y'are *Q*

113

6 latch] *Malone;* lack *Q*
10 sweet favor] *Benson;* sweet-fauor *Q*
13 more, replete] *Gildon;* more repleat, *Q*

114

4 alcumy] *ed.;* Alcumie *Q (in italics)*
11 'greeing] *Gildon;* greeing *Q*

115

10 "Now . . . best,"] *quotes, Malone*

116

5 ever-fixed] *hyphen, Gildon*
8 highth] *Capell MS;* higth *Q*

117

6 dear-purchas'd] *hyphen, Sewell*
10 surmise] *Knight;* surmise, *Q*
10 accumulate] *Gildon;* accumilate *Q*
14 love.] *Benson;* loue *Q*

118

5 ne'er-cloying] *Theobald conj.;* nere cloying *Q*
10 were not,] *Gildon;* were, not *Q*
12 Which, . . . goodness,] *Malone;* Which . . . goodnesse *Q*

119

10 is] *Lintott;* is *Q*

120

11 then,] *W. S. Walker conj.;* then *Q*

121

4, 5 others'] *Capell MS;* others *Q*
11 bevel;] *Gildon;* beuel *Q*

122

1 Thy] *Benson;* TThy *Q*

123

7 born] *Gildon;* borne *Q*

124

2 unfather'd] *Sewell;* vnfathered *Q*
9 heretic] *Murden;* Hereticke *Q (in italics)*
10 short-numb'red] *hyphen, Capell MS*
13 fools] *Benson;* foles *Q*

125

6–7 rent, . . . sweet] *Malone (comma, Sewell);* rent . . . sweet; *Q*
8 spent?] *Capell MS;* spent. *Q*
13 informer] *Murden;* Informer *Q (in italics)*

126

2 Dost] *Capell MS;* Doest *Q*
5 mistress] *Capell MS;* misteres *Q*
7 skill] *Lintott;* skill. *Q*
8 minutes] *Malone (after Capell MS);* mynuit *Q*
11 audit] *Malone;* Audite *Q (in italics)*
12 quietus] *Malone;* Quietus *Q (in italics)*
12] *Q, surely mistakenly, indicates what it considers to be two missing lines following l. 12 by two pairs of parentheses, spaced out the full line length and set one above the other.*

127

2 were] *Benson;* weare *Q*
7 bow'r] *ed.;* boure *Q*
9 mistress'] *Benson (subs.);* Mistersse *Q*
13 mourn,] *Lintott;* mourne *Q*

128

1 thou, my music,] *Capell MS;* thou my musike *Q*
3 sway'st] *Capell MS;* swayst, *Q*
11 thy] *Gildon;* their *Q*
12 lips:] *Capell MS;* lips, *Q*
14 thy] *Benson;* their *Q*

129

9 Mad] *Gildon;* Made *Q*
10 quest to have,] *Capell MS;* quest, to haue *Q*
11 prov'd, a] *Malone (after Sewell);* proud and *Q*
12 Before, . . . behind,] *Ridley (after Bell);* Before a ioy proposd behind *Q*

130

2 Coral] *Gildon;* Currall *Q*
2 lips'] *Capell MS;* lips *Q*

131

9 swear,] *Malone;* sweare *Q*

132

9 mourning] *Gildon;* morning *Q*

135

1 Whoever] *Gildon;* Who euer *Q*

136

4 love-suit, sweet,] *Capell MS;* loue-sute sweet *Q*
6 Ay] *Capell MS;* I *Q*
7 prove] *Dyce;* prooue, *Q*
10 store's] *Gildon;* stores *Q*
11 hold] *Gildon;* hold, *Q*

137

11 not,] *Sewell;* not *Q*

138

A variant version of this sonnet is the first poem in The Passionate Pilgrim
7 false-speaking] *hyphen, Sewell*

140

4 pity-wanting] *hyphen, Gildon*
5 were] *Benson;* weare *Q*
6 yet, love,] *Capell MS (subs.);* yet loue *Q*
7 sick men] *Gildon;* sick-men *Q*
11 ill-wresting] *hyphen, Lintott*
13 belied] *Gildon;* be lyde *Q*

142

8 Robb'd] *Gildon;* Robd *Q*
8 beds'] *Oulton conj.;* beds *Q*
14 self-example] *hyphen, Gildon*

143

10 afar] *Gildon;* a farre *Q*

144

A variant version of this sonnet is the second poem in The Passionate Pilgrim
2 suggest] *Passionate Pilgrim;* sugiest *Q*
6 side] *Passionate Pilgrim;* sight *Q*
9 fiend] *Passionate Pilgrim;* finde *Q*
11 me,] *Lintott;* me *Q*
12 guess] *Gildon;* gesse *Q*

145

8 anew] *Gildon;* a new *Q*

146

2 . . . .] *the Q compositor here inadvertently repeated the last three words of l. 1* (My sinfull earth), *apparently in place of a two-syllable word or two monosyllables*

147

7 approve] *Dyce;* approoue, *Q*
11 madmen's] *Gildon (subs.);* mad mens *Q*

151

2 born] *Lintott;* borne *Q*
7 may] *Lintott;* may, *Q*
10 prize.] *Gildon (subs.);* prize, *Q*
14 "love"] *Dyce;* loue, *Q*

152

2 forsworn,] *Capell MS;* forsworne *Q*
2 swearing;] *Gildon;* swearing, *Q*
3 torn] *Neilson;* torne, *Q*
14 so] *Benson;* fo *Q*

153

1 asleep] *Benson;* a sleepe *Q*
8 strange] *Benson;* strang *Q*
14 eyes] *Benson;* eye *Q*

154

1 asleep] *Gildon;* a sleepe *Q*
2 heart-inflaming] *hyphen, Capell MS*
3 vow'd] *Benson;* vou'd *Q*
14] *This line followed by* FINIS. *in Q*

A Lover's Complaint

A Lover's Complaint was published in 1609 in the same volume with Shakespeare's sonnets. Its attribution to Shakespeare therefore depends upon the publisher, Thomas Thorpe. Modern scholars who deny that Shakespeare wrote *A Lover's Complaint* point out that Thorpe's edition was unauthorized and that he was accordingly an unscrupulous publisher; but it is not necessarily true that a publisher who will bring out a book without the author's permission will also deceive the public about the author's name. William Jaggard and John Benson did so attempt to deceive the public, but Thorpe is not to be classed with them. His only attribution to Shakespeare, other than *A Lover's Complaint*, was the sonnets, and in that attribution he was right.

Considerations of style and literary quality have also been brought to bear. The language of the poem is highly mannered; in the relatively short space of 329 lines there are twenty-three words, mainly Latinisms, which Shakespeare does not use elsewhere. But Shakespeare does, sometimes, in his undisputed writings use a special vocabulary—for example, in the prologue to *Troilus and Cressida* and in *The Phoenix and Turtle*. And if we suggest that *A Lover's Complaint* could not be by Shakespeare because it is not good enough for him, we are depending too heavily upon subjective judgment; moreover, the poem has been highly praised by some critics as well as despised by others.

External evidence bearing on the date is completely lacking. The poem is never referred to by a contemporary. There was a vogue of complaint poems about women in the 1590's; Shakespeare's *Lucrece* is closely related to the genre. In 1592 Samuel Daniel appended to his sonnet cycle *Delia* a poem called *The Complaint of Rosamond*, and a year later Thomas Lodge published his sonnet cycle *Phillis* with a companion piece, *The Complaint of Elstred*; so there was nothing peculiar about attaching a complaint poem to a collection of sonnets. What *is* unusual about *A Lover's Complaint* is that the lady is not named, is not a historical character. It is also somewhat unusual in having three characters, the "I" of the poem, the girl, and the old man.

The verse form is the rhyme royal stanza of seven lines, which Shakespeare used in *Lucrece*. The speech of the girl is very rhetorical, and the reported pleas of her lover as well as her own lamentings are full of highly wrought conceits. The poem is characteristically Elizabethan. The extravagance of the sentiments and the fantastic elaboration of the imagery were more palatable to sixteenth-century taste than they are to our own. Yet occasionally a modern reader will perceive a flash of something that may have gone into the creation of *Romeo and Juliet*:

> O father, what a hell of witchcraft lies
> In the small orb of one particular tear!

The poem is not a major work in any sense; it is an exercise in a popular literary form; it may even be unfinished. If it is by Shakespeare, it neither detracts from his achievement nor adds anything to it.

Hallett Smith

A Lover's Complaint

From off a hill whose concave womb reworded
A plaintful story from a sist'ring vale,
My spirits t' attend this double voice accorded,
And down I laid to list the sad-tun'd tale,
Ere long espied a fickle maid full pale
Tearing of papers, breaking rings a-twain,
Storming her world with sorrow's wind and rain.

Upon her head a platted hive of straw,
Which fortified her visage from the sun,
Whereon the thought might think sometime it saw
The carcass of a beauty spent and done.
Time had not scythed all that youth begun,
Nor youth all quit, but spite of heaven's fell rage,
Some beauty peep'd through lettice of sear'd age.

Oft did she heave her napkin to her eyne,
Which on it had conceited characters,
Laund'ring the silken figures in the brine
That seasoned woe had pelleted in tears,
And often reading what contents it bears;
As often shriking undistinguish'd woe,
In clamors of all size, both high and low.

Sometimes her levell'd eyes their carriage ride,
As they did batt'ry to the spheres intend;
Sometime diverted their poor balls are tied
To th' orbed earth; sometimes they do extend
Their view right on; anon their gazes lend
To every place at once, and no where fix'd,
The mind and sight distractedly commix'd.

Her hair, nor loose nor tied in formal plat,
Proclaim'd in her a careless hand of pride;
For some untuck'd descended her sheav'd hat,
Hanging her pale and pined cheek beside;
Some in her threaden fillet still did bide,
And true to bondage would not break from thence,
Though slackly braided in loose negligence.

A thousand favors from a maund she drew,
Of amber, crystal, and of beaded jet,
Which one by one she in a river threw,
Upon whose weeping margent she was set,
Like usury applying wet to wet,
Or monarch's hands that lets not bounty fall
Where want cries some, but where excess begs all.

Of folded schedules had she many a one,
Which she perus'd, sigh'd, tore, and gave the flood,
Crack'd many a ring of posied gold and bone,
Bidding them find their sepulchres in mud,
Found yet moe letters sadly penn'd in blood,
With sleided silk feat and affectedly
Enswath'd and seal'd to curious secrecy.

These often bath'd she in her fluxive eyes,
And often kiss'd, and often [gan] to tear;
Cried, "O false blood, thou register of lies,
What unapproved witness dost thou bear!
Ink would have seem'd more black and damned here!"
This said, in top of rage the lines she rents,
Big discontent so breaking their contents.

A reverend man that graz'd his cattle nigh,
Sometime a blusterer that the ruffle knew
Of court, of city, and had let go by
The swiftest hours, observed as they flew,
Towards this afflicted fancy fastly drew,
And privileg'd by age desires to know
In brief the grounds and motives of her woe.

So slides he down upon his grained bat,
And comely distant sits he by her side,

Words enclosed in square brackets in the text above are emendations of the copy-text. The Textual Notes record in every instance the reading of the copy-text and the earliest authority for the emendation here adopted.

1. reworded: repeated, echoed.
3. attend: listen to. **accorded**: agreed. **5. fickle**: i.e. agitated.
8. platted hive: i.e. woven hat. **9. fortified**: protected.
10. thought: i.e. thinker, thoughtful observer.
11. carcass: decaying remnant.
13. all quit: left every part. **fell**: cruel.
14. lettice: lattice. **sear'd**: dried-up.
15. heave: raise. **napkin**: handkerchief. **eyne**: eyes (an old plural, already archaic in Shakespeare's time).
16. conceited characters: fanciful designs.
18. seasoned: matured (with quibble on "salted," suggested by *brine*).
20. shriking: shrieking. **undistinguish'd woe**: inarticulate cries of woe.
22. levell'd . . . ride. The image, continued in line 23, is of a cannon; *levell'd* = aimed. **23. As**: as if.
30. careless . . . pride: hand indifferent to proud appearance.
31. sheav'd: straw.
33. threaden fillet: ribbon binding the hair.
36. favors: love tokens. **maund**: basket.
37. beaded jet: jet beads. (The quarto reading *bedded* may be a variant spelling of *beaded*, but some editors explain it as meaning "embedded" or "inlaid.") **39. weeping margent**: marshy bank.
40. usury: i.e. adding money to money. **42. cries**: cries out for.
43. schedules: sheets bearing writing, i.e. letters.
45. posied: inscribed with posies, or mottoes. **47. moe**: more.
48. sleided: separated into threads. **feat**: featly, delicately. **affectedly**: lovingly. **49. curious**: careful. **50. fluxive**: flowing.
53. unapproved: not confirmed by trial, i.e. false.
57. reverend: aged.
58. Sometime: formerly. **ruffle**: bustling and pretentious activity.
61. afflicted fancy: lady afflicted by love.
64. slides . . . upon: he lets himself down by means of. **grained**: showing the grain of the wood, i.e. worn, furrowed (?) or forked (*O.E.D.*)(?). **bat**: staff.
65. comely distant: at a decorous distance.

When he again desires her, being sat,
Her grievance with his hearing to divide:
If that from him there may be aught applied
Which may her suffering ecstasy assuage,
'Tis promis'd in the charity of age.

"Father," she says, "though in me you behold
The injury of many a blasting hour,
Let it not tell your judgment I am old,
Not age, but sorrow, over me hath power;
I might as yet have been a spreading flower,
Fresh to myself, if I had self-applied
Love to myself, and to no love beside.

"But woe is me, too early I attended
A youthful suit—it was to gain my grace;
O, one by nature's outwards so commended
That maidens' eyes stuck over all his face.
Love lack'd a dwelling and made him her place;
And when in his fair parts she did abide,
She was new lodg'd and newly deified.

"His browny locks did hang in crooked curls,
And every light occasion of the wind
Upon his lips their silken parcels hurls.
What's sweet to do, to do will aptly find:
Each eye that saw him did enchant the mind,
For on his visage was in little drawn
What largeness thinks in Paradise was sawn.

"Small show of man was yet upon his chin,
His phoenix down began but to appear
Like unshorn velvet on that termless skin,
Whose bare outbragg'd the web it seem'd to wear;
Yet showed his visage by that cost more dear,
And nice affections wavering stood in doubt
If best were as it was, or best without.

"His qualities were beauteous as his form,
For maiden-tongu'd he was, and thereof free;
Yet if men mov'd him, was he such a storm
As oft 'twixt May and April is to see,
When winds breathe sweet, unruly though they be.
His rudeness so with his authoriz'd youth
Did livery falseness in a pride of truth.

"Well could he ride, and often men would say,
'That horse his mettle from his rider takes;
Proud of subjection, noble by the sway,
What rounds, what bounds, what course, what stop he
makes!'
And controversy hence a question takes,
Whether the horse by him became his deed,
Or he his manage by th' well-doing steed.

"But quickly on this side the verdict went:
His real habitude gave life and grace
To appertainings and to ornament,
Accomplish'd in himself, not in his case;
All aids, themselves made fairer by their place,
[Came] for additions, yet their purpos'd trim
Piec'd not his grace but were all grac'd by him.

"So on the tip of his subduing tongue
All kind of arguments and question deep,
All replication prompt and reason strong,
For his advantage still did wake and sleep.
To make the weeper laugh, the laugher weep,
He had the dialect and different skill,
Catching all passions in his craft of will,

"That he did in the general bosom reign
Of young, of old, and sexes both enchanted,
To dwell with him in thoughts, or to remain
In personal duty, following where he haunted.
Consents bewitch'd, ere he desire, have granted,
And dialogu'd for him what he would say,
Ask'd their own wills and made their wills obey.

"Many there were that did his picture get
To serve their eyes, and in it put their mind,
Like fools that in th' imagination set
The goodly objects which abroad they find
Of lands and mansions, theirs in thought assign'd,
And laboring in moe pleasures to bestow them
Than the true gouty landlord which doth owe them.

"So many have that never touch'd his hand
Sweetly suppos'd them mistress of his heart.
My woeful self that did in freedom stand,
And was my own fee-simple (not in part),
What with his art in youth and youth in art,
Threw my affections in his charmed power,
Reserv'd the stalk and gave him all my flower.

67. **divide**: share. 69. **suffering ecstasy**: violent fit of grief.
72. **blasting**: blighting. 75. **spreading**: opening.
79. **grace**: favor.
80. **O.** Editors usually emend to *Of*. **nature's outwards**: external appearance bestowed by nature.
81. **stuck over.** Equivalent to "were glued (or riveted) to."
86. **occasion**: chance occurrence, i.e. stirring.
88. **What's . . . find**: what is pleasant to do will readily find people to perform it.
90–91. **on . . . sawn**: i.e. his face showed in miniature what is supposed to have existed in full magnitude in Eden. *Sawn* is variously glossed as "seen" and "sown, i.e. spread."
93. **phoenix**: i.e. uniquely beautiful.
94. **termless**: indescribable (?) or youthful, untouched by time (?).
95. **bare outbragg'd**: bareness surpassed. **web**: covering.
96. **cost**: (1) ornament; (2) expense. **dear**: (1) endearing, beloved; (2) costly.
97. **nice**: precise, carefully discriminating. **affections**: inclinations, bents of mind.
100. **maiden-tongu'd**: mild-spoken. **free**: innocent.
101. **mov'd**: angered.
104–5. **His . . . truth**: his roughness, excused by his youth, thus dressed his falseness in a proud display of truth.

108. **sway**: control.
109. **rounds . . . stop.** All tricks of the manage, or elaborate horsemanship. 110. **takes**: takes up.
111–12. **Whether . . . steed**: i.e. whether the horse performed with such grace because of his rider's horsemanship, or whether the rider was able to display such horsemanship because the horse performed so well. 114. **real habitude**: essential quality, personality.
116. **case**: conditions and circumstances.
118. **trim**: adornment. 119. **Piec'd**: mended, augmented.
122. **replication prompt**: quick reply.
125. **dialect . . . skill**: various skills in discourse.
126. **craft of will**: i.e. power to carry his point, persuasive faculty.
127. **That**: so that. 130. **haunted**: frequented.
131. **Consents**: consenting persons. 137. **objects**: sights.
139. **laboring . . . them**: exerting themselves more to derive pleasure from them. 140. **owe**: own.
144. **was . . . part**: i.e. was in complete (not partial) control of myself (as of land in freehold). 146. **charmed**: exerting a spell.

"Yet did I not as some my equals did
Demand of him, nor being desired yielded;
Finding myself in honor so forbid,
With safest distance I mine honor shielded.
Experience for me many bulwarks builded
Of proofs new-bleeding which remain'd the foil
Of this false jewel, and his amorous spoil.

"But ah, who ever shunn'd by precedent
The destin'd ill she must herself assay,
Or forc'd examples 'gainst her own content
To put the by-past perils in her way?
Counsel may stop a while what will not stay;
For when we rage, advice is often seen
By blunting us to make our wits more keen.

"Nor gives it satisfaction to our blood
That we must curb it upon others' proof,
To be forbod the sweets that seems so good
For fear of harms that preach in our behoof.
O appetite, from judgment stand aloof!
The one a palate hath that needs will taste,
Though Reason weep and cry, 'It is thy last.'

"For further I could say this man's untrue,
And knew the patterns of his foul beguiling,
Heard where his plants in others' orchards grew,
Saw how deceits were gilded in his smiling,
Knew vows were ever brokers to defiling,
Thought characters and words merely but art,
And bastards of his foul adulterate heart.

"And long upon these terms I held my city,
Till thus he gan besiege me: 'Gentle maid,
Have of my suffering youth some feeling pity
And be not of my holy vows afraid.
That's to ye sworn to none was ever said,
For feasts of love I have been call'd unto,
Till now did ne'er invite nor never vow.

" 'All my offenses that abroad you see
Are errors of the blood, none of the mind;
Love made them not, with acture they may be,
Where neither party is nor true nor kind:
They sought their shame that so their shame did find,
And so much less of shame in me remains
By how much of me their reproach contains.

" 'Among the many that mine eyes have seen,
Not one whose flame my heart so much as warmed,
Or my affection put to th' smallest teen,
Or any of my leisures ever charmed.
Harm have I done to them but ne'er was harmed,
Kept hearts in liveries, but mine own was free,
And reign'd commanding in his monarchy.

" 'Look here what tributes wounded fancies sent me,
Of pallid pearls and rubies red as blood:
Figuring that they their passions likewise lent me
Of grief and blushes, aptly understood
In bloodless white and the encrimson'd mood,
Effects of terror and dear modesty,
Encamp'd in hearts but fighting outwardly.

" 'And lo behold these talents of their hair,
With twisted metal amorously impleach'd,
I have receiv'd from many a several fair,
Their kind acceptance weepingly beseech'd,
With th' annexions of fair gems enrich'd,
And deep-brain'd sonnets that did amplify
Each stone's dear nature, worth, and quality.

" 'The diamond? why, 'twas beautiful and hard,
Whereto his invis'd properties did tend;
The deep-green em'rald, in whose fresh regard
Weak sights their sickly radiance do amend;
The heaven-hu'd sapphire and the opal blend
With objects manifold: each several stone,
With wit well blazon'd, smil'd or made some moan.

" 'Lo all these trophies of affections hot,
Of pensiv'd and subdu'd desires the tender,
Nature hath charg'd me that I hoard them not,
But yield them up where I myself must render:
That is to you, my origin and ender;
For these of force must your oblations be,
Since I their altar, you enpatron me.

" 'O then advance (of yours) that phraseless hand,
Whose white weighs down the airy scale of praise,
Take all these similes to your own command,
[Hallowed] with sighs that burning lungs did raise;
What me, your minister, for you obeys,

148. **my equals:** i.e. other girls of my own age and station.
149. **being desired:** i.e. the first time he asked me.
153. **proofs new-bleeding:** i.e. examples of those he had recently injured. **foil:** dark background showing off a jewel.
156. **assay:** make trial of.
157. **forc'd:** urged. **content:** i.e. supposed happiness.
158. **in her way:** i.e. as hindrances. 159. **stay:** stop permanently.
160. **rage:** are driven by passion. 161. **blunting:** repressing.
162. **blood:** passion. 163. **proof:** experience.
164. **forbod:** forbidden.
165. **in our behoof:** to benefit us, for our good.
169. **say . . . untrue:** tell of this man's faithlessness.
170. **patterns:** examples. 171. **orchards:** gardens.
173. **brokers:** i.e. panders.
174. **characters and words:** written and spoken words. **art:** artifice.
176. **city:** citadel, stronghold.
182. **vow.** Many editors emend to *woo.*
185. **with acture:** i.e. by mere physical act. **be:** be made.
189. **how much:** i.e. how much less, how little.

192. **teen:** sorrow. 195. **in liveries:** i.e. as servants.
199. **Figuring:** symbolizing. 204. **talents:** i.e. riches.
205. **impleach'd:** entwined.
206. **many . . . fair:** many different beautiful ladies.
209. **amplify:** go into detail about.
212. **his:** its. **invis'd:** unseen (?). The word does not occur elsewhere. 214. **radiance:** power of vision.
215–16. **blend . . . manifold:** blended of various colors (?). A common sense of *object* is "something presented to the sight."
217. **blazon'd:** described, catalogued (in the "deep-brain'd sonnets").
218. **affections:** passions.
219. **pensiv'd:** saddened. **tender:** offering.
222. **ender:** conclusion.
223. **of force:** perforce. **your oblations:** offerings to you.
224. **Since . . . me:** i.e. since I am the altar on which they are offered and you are the patron saint to whom the altar is dedicated.
225. **phraseless:** indescribably beautiful.
226. **weighs . . . praise:** i.e. cannot be adequately praised (the figure is of a balance, with the whiteness outweighing the praise, however eloquent).
227. **similes:** i.e. the symbolic gems with the poems explaining the symbolism. 229. **minister:** agent, servant.

Works under you, and to your audit comes
Their distract parcels in combined sums.

" 'Lo this device was sent me from a nun,
Or sister sanctified, of holiest note,
Which late her noble suit in court did shun,
Whose rarest havings made the blossoms dote,
For she was sought by spirits of richest coat,
But kept cold distance, and did thence remove
To spend her living in eternal love.

" 'But, O my sweet, what labor is't to leave
The thing we have not, mast'ring what not strives,
Playing the place which did no form receive,
Playing patient sports in unconstrained gyves?
She that her fame so to herself contrives,
The scars of battle scapeth by the flight,
And makes her absence valiant, not her might.

" 'O, pardon me, in that my boast is true:
The accident which brought me to her eye
Upon the moment did her force subdue,
And now she would the caged cloister fly:
Religious love put out religion's eye.
Not to be tempted would she be enur'd,
And now to tempt all liberty [procur'd].

" 'How mighty then you are, O, hear me tell!
The broken bosoms that to me belong
Have emptied all their fountains in my well,
And mine I pour your ocean all among:
I strong o'er them, and you o'er me being strong,
Must for your victory us all congest,
As compound love to physic your cold breast.

" 'My parts had pow'r to charm a sacred [nun],
Who disciplin'd, ay, dieted in grace,
Believ'd her eyes when they t' assail begun,
All vows and consecrations giving place.
O most potential love! vow, bond, nor space
In thee hath neither sting, knot, nor confine,
For thou art all, and all things else are thine.

" 'When thou impressest, what are precepts worth
Of stale example? When thou wilt inflame,
How coldly those impediments stand forth
Of wealth, of filial fear, law, kindred, fame!
Love's arms are peace, 'gainst rule, 'gainst sense, 'gainst shame,
And sweetens, in the suff'ring pangs it bears,
The aloes of all forces, shocks, and fears.

" 'Now all these hearts that do on mine depend,
Feeling it break, with bleeding groans they pine,
And supplicant their sighs to you extend
To leave the batt'ry that you make 'gainst mine,
Lending soft audience to my sweet design,
And credent soul to that strong-bonded oath
That shall prefer and undertake my troth.'

"This said, his wat'ry eyes he did dismount,
Whose sights till then were levell'd on my face,
Each cheek a river running from a fount
With brinish current downward flow'd apace:
O how the channel to the stream gave grace!
Who glaz'd with crystal gate the glowing roses
That flame through water which their hue encloses.

"O father, what a hell of witchcraft lies
In the small orb of one particular tear!
But with the inundation of the eyes
What rocky heart to water will not wear?
What breast so cold that is not warmed here?
[O] cleft effect! cold modesty, hot wrath,
Both fire from hence and chill extincture hath.

"For lo his passion, but an art of craft,
Even there resolv'd my reason into tears,
There my white stole of chastity I daff'd,
Shook off my sober guards and civil fears;
Appear to him as he to me appears,
All melting, though our drops this diff'rence bore:
His poison'd me, and mine did him restore.

"In him a plenitude of subtle matter,
Applied to cautels, all strange forms receives,
Of burning blushes, or of weeping water,
Or sounding paleness; and he takes and leaves,
In either's aptness as it best deceives,
To blush at speeches rank, to weep at woes,
Or to turn white and sound at tragic shows;

"That not a heart which in his level came
Could scape the hail of his all-hurting aim,

230. **audit**: accounting. 231. **distract**: separate.
234. **suit**: attendance.
235. **havings**: endowments. **blossoms**: young courtiers.
236. **coat**: coat of arms, i.e. descent, family.
238. **living**: lifetime. 240. **strives**: resists.
241. **Playing**. A mistake, obviously imported by the compositor or scribe from the following line. Of many emendations, the most widely accepted is Malone's *Paling* = fencing, enclosing (as in a cloister). **the place . . . receive**: i.e. the heart on which no lover had made an impression (?).
242. **Playing . . . gyves**: pretending to endure patiently fetters which have not been imposed against one's will (or *unconstrained* may mean "unconstraining"). 243. **fame**: reputation.
245. **makes . . . might**: i.e. gets her reputation for valiant resistance from mere absence, not from her actual power to resist.
250. **Religious**: devoted.
251. **enur'd**: inured, hardened. Many editors read *immur'd*.
252. **to . . . liberty**. It is uncertain whether *all* modifies *liberty* or is the object of *tempt* (*tempt all* = venture everything, or experience the whole of love). 254. **bosoms**: i.e. hearts.
255. **well**: spring, stream. 257. **strong**: victorious.
258. **for**: in consequence of. **congest**: gather together.
259. **physic**: cure. 260. **parts**: qualities.
261. **dieted**: i.e. strictly regulated.
262. **assail**: i.e. assail her heart.
264. **potential**: powerful. **space**: i.e. limitation of space, confinement.
267. **impressest**: conscriptest. 271. **peace**: i.e. victorious.
272. **sweetens**: i.e. love sweetens. 273. **aloes**: i.e. bitterness.
275. **bleeding groans**. It was thought that every sigh drew a drop of blood from the heart.
280. **prefer**: put forward. **undertake**: guarantee.
281–82. **dismount . . . face**. With this figure from artillery compare lines 22–23 and see lines 309–10 below.
286. **Who**: which, i.e. the stream. **gate**: i.e. barrier (like a protective layer of glass). 289. **particular**: single.
296. **resolv'd**: dissolved. 297. **daff'd**: doffed, put off.
298. **civil**: grave. 302. **subtle matter**: craft, cunning.
303. **cautels**: deceits.
305. **sounding**: swooning (so also *sound* in line 308).
307. **rank**: gross. 309. **level**: range.

Showing fair nature is both kind and tame;
And veil'd in them did win whom he would maim.
Against the thing he sought he would exclaim:
When he most burnt in heart-wish'd luxury,
He preach'd pure maid, and prais'd cold chastity.

"Thus merely with the garment of a Grace
The naked and concealed fiend he cover'd,
That th' unexperient gave the tempter place,
Which like a cherubin above them hover'd.
Who, young and simple, would not be so lover'd?
Ay me, I fell, and yet do question make
What I should do again for such a sake.

"O, that infected moisture of his eye,
O, that false fire which in his cheek so glowed,
O, that forc'd thunder from his heart did fly,
O, that sad breath his spungy lungs bestowed,
O, all that borrowed motion seeming owed,
Would yet again betray the fore-betray'd,
And new pervert a reconciled maid!"

311. Showing . . . is: i.e. falsely representing his nature as.
312. them: i.e. kindness and tameness. 314. luxury: lust.
317. concealed. This word anticipates *cover'd*; the meaning is that he covered his fiendish nature so that it was concealed.
318. unexperient: inexperienced. place: i.e. entry.
319. Which . . . cherubin: who looking like a cherub.
321. question make: i.e. ask myself. 323. infected: infectious.
325. forc'd: not natural, false. from: which from.
326. spungy: spongy. 327. owed: i.e. his own.
329. reconciled: repentant.

NOTE ON THE TEXT

"*A Lover's Complaint*" was first published by Thomas Thorpe at the end (sigs. K1v–L2v) of *Shake-speares Sonnets* in 1609. This edition, here designated as Q, is our only authority for the text. The poem was reprinted, with text pirated from Q, in John Benson's 1640 edition of Shakespeare's *Poems* (see "Note on the Text" to the Sonnets, above).

As a result of the important and comparatively recent work of Jackson, Duncan-Jones, and Kerrigan, "A Lover's Complaint" is now generally accepted as by Shakespeare and recognized as an integral part of the sonnet sequence as a whole (see "Note on the Text" to the Sonnets). The date of composition is probably c. 1602–4.

For further information, see: H. E. Rollins, ed., New Variorum *Poems* (Philadelphia, 1938); MacD. P. Jackson, *Shakespeare's "A Lover's Complaint," Its Date and Authenticity* (University of Auckland, 1965); J. C. Maxwell, ed., New Shakespeare *Poems* (Cambridge, 1966); Katherine Duncan-Jones, "Was the 1609 *Shake-speares Sonnets* Really Unauthorized?", *RES*, n.s., XXXIV (1983), 151–71; John Kerrigan, ed., New Penguin *The Sonnets* and *A Lover's Complaint* (Harmondsworth, Middlesex, 1986); Stanley Wells, Gary Taylor, et al., *William Shakespeare: A Textual Companion* (Oxford, 1987); John Roe, ed., New Cambridge *Poems* (Cambridge, 1992).

TEXTUAL NOTES

4 **sad-tun'd]** *hyphen, Capell MS*
6 **a-twain]** *hyphen, Sewell*
7 **sorrow's]** *Gildon;* sorrowes, *Q*
12 **scythed]** *Gildon (subs.);* sithed *Q*
26 **gazes]** *Benson;* gases *Q*
28 **commix'd]** *Benson;* commxit *Q*
31 **sheav'd]** *Capell MS;* sheu'd *Q*
33 **threaden]** *Gildon;* threeden *Q*
37 **amber,]** *Benson;* amber *Q*
37 **beaded]** *Gildon;* bedded *Q (a possible variant form of* beaded)
41 **monarch's]** *Gildon;* Monarches *Q*
51 **gan]** *Malone (subs.);* gaue *Q*
55 **said,]** *Gildon;* said *Q*
56 **discontent]** *Gildon;* discontent, *Q*
59 **court,]** *Benson;* Court *Q*
60 **hours,]** *Dyce;* houres *Q*
64 **grained]** *Gildon;* greyned *Q*
76 **self-applied]** *hyphen, Gildon*
79 **suit—]** *Malone (subs.);* suit *Q*
80 **O,]** *Capell MS;* O *Q; most eds. adopt Tyrwhitt's conj.* Of
81 **maidens']** *Capell MS;* maidens *Q*
87 **hurls.]** *Gildon;* hurles, *Q*
95 **wear]** *Benson;* were *Q*
100 **maiden-tongu'd]** *hyphen, Gildon*
107 **takes;]** *Benson;* takes *Q*
109 **course,]** *Benson;* course *Q*
109 **makes!]** *Gildon;* makes *Q*
112 **manage]** *Capell MS;* mannad'g *Q*
112 **well-doing]** *hyphen, Benson*
118 **Came]** *Sewell;* Can *Q*
122 **strong,]** *Gildon*, strong *Q*
123 **sleep.]** *Sewell (subs.);* sleep, *Q*
124 **weep,]** *Capell MS;* weepe: *Q*
126 **will,]** *Benson;* will. *Q*
130 **haunted.]** *Gildon (subs.);* haunted, *Q*
131 **Consents]** *Malone;* Consent's *Q*
131 **desire,]** *Malone;* desire *Q*
142 **of]** *Benson;* os *Q*
144 **fee-simple]** *hyphen, Sewell*
153 **new-bleeding]** *hyphen, Malone*
160 **advice]** *Benson;* aduise *Q*
173 **vows were]** *Lintott;* vowes, wer e *Q*
181 **unto,]** *Gildon;* vnto *Q*
186 **kind:]** *Gildon;* kind, *Q*
189 **contains.]** *Benson;* containes, *Q*
197 **here]** *Benson;* heare *Q*
198 **pallid]** *Gildon;* palyd *Q*
204 **hair]** *Benson;* heir *Q*
205 **metal]** *Gildon;* mettle *Q*
209 **deep-brain'd]** *hyphen, Gildon*
213 **deep-green]** *hyphen, Capell MS*
215 **heaven-hu'd]** *hyphen, Gildon*
227 **similes]** *Gildon;* similies *Q*
228 **Hallowed]** *Capell MS (subs.);* Hollowed *Q*
229 **me, your minister,]** *Collier;* me your minister *Q*
233 **sanctified,]** *Gildon (subs.);* sanctified *Q*
242 **unconstrained]** *Gildon;* vnconstraind *Q*
242 **gyves]** *Malone;* giues *Q*
252 **procur'd]** *Benson;* procure *Q*
260 **nun]** *Capell MS;* Sunne *Q*
261 **ay]** *Capell MS;* I *Q*
265 **confine,]** *Gildon;* confine *Q*
270 **wealth,]** *Benson;* wealth *Q*
270 **kindred,]** *Benson;* kindred *Q*
273 **aloes]** *Murden;* Alloes *Q (in italics)*
279 **strong-bonded]** *hyphen, Capell MS*
284 **flow'd]** *Gildon;* flowed *Q*
284 **apace]** *Benson;* a pace *Q*
286 **roses]** *Malone;* Roses, *Q*
287 **encloses.]** *Benson (subs.);* incloses, *Q*
290 **eyes]** *Gildon;* eies: *Q*
293 **O]** *Gildon;* Or *Q*
293 **modesty,]** *Benson;* modesty *Q*
293 **wrath,]** *Gildon;* wrath: *Q*
297 **daff'd]** *Malone;* daft *Q*
299 **appears,]** *Gildon;* appeares: *Q*
303 **cautels]** *Malone (after Capell MS);* Cautills *Q*
306 **deceives,]** *Sewell;* deceiues: *Q*
308 **shows;]** *Malone;* showes. *Q*
310 **all-hurting]** *hyphen, Gildon*
312 **veil'd]** *Gildon;* vaild *Q*
312 **maim.]** *Gildon (subs.);* maime, *Q*
319–20 **hover'd. . . . lover'd?]** *Gildon (subs.);* houerd, . . . louerd. *Q*
321 **Ay me,]** *Capell MS;* Aye me *Q*
324 **glowed]** *Collier;* glowd *Q*
328 **fore-betray'd]** *Benson;* fore-betrayed *Q*
329] *This line followed by* FINIS. *in Q*

The Passionate Pilgrim

The Passionate Pilgrim is a miscellany of poems by various authors, known and unknown. The first edition has survived only in a fragment containing the text of poems I–IV, XVI–XVIII. The title-page is missing and the date is therefore uncertain. The second edition, which was set up from the first, survives in two complete copies and a fragment. Its title-page reads: "The Passionate Pilgrime. by W. Shakespeare. At London. Printed for W. Iaggard, and are to be sold by W. Leake, at the Greyhound in Paules Churchyard. 1599."

The publisher Jaggard may have simply published a manuscript commonplace book which attributed the poems to Shakespeare or he may have fraudulently put Shakespeare's name on the title-page to attract customers. In view of his behavior later, the second alternative is by no means unlikely. Five poems in the book are certainly by Shakespeare, as we know from their appearance elsewhere. Two (I and II) are his sonnets 138 and 144, in rather inferior texts. The other three (III, V, and XVI) had already appeared in *Love's Labor's Lost* (IV.iii.58–71, IV.ii.105–18, and IV.iii.99–118 respectively). Four of the remaining poems are known to be by other authors. VIII and XX had been published in 1598 by Richard Barnfield, in his *Poems in Divers Humors* appended to *The Encomion of Lady Pecunia*. XI had been published by Bartholomew Griffin in his *Fidessa* in 1596. The first four stanzas of XIX are a very inferior version of Christopher Marlowe's great pastoral lyric "The Passionate Shepherd to His Love," which had not been printed before but was to appear in its full text, properly attributed to Marlowe, in *England's Helicon* (1600); it is there followed by "The Nymph's Reply to the Shepherd," attributed since the seventeenth century to Sir Walter Raleigh, from which the final stanza of XIX is taken.

The other poems, of no very remarkable quality, are of unknown authorship. XVII had appeared in Thomas Weelkes' *Madrigals* in 1597, but Weelkes composed the music, not the words. Of some interest are IV, VI, and IX, which, like XI, are sonnets having to do with the legend of Venus and Adonis. Since XI is known to be by Bartholomew Griffin, the others are sometimes assigned to him also, but there is no proof. It used to be thought that IV, VI, and IX might be trial efforts by Shakespeare before he wrote his *Venus and Adonis*, but this theory has now been generally abandoned. In IV and VI Venus is called Cytherea, as she is in *The Taming of the Shrew* (Induction ii.51), but this is hardly evidence that Shakespeare wrote the sonnets. The motif of Venus watching Adonis bathe, a conflation of two Ovidian stories, was the property of no single poet, Shakespeare or another; it appears, for example, in Spenser's *Faerie Queene* (III.i.xxxvi).

The unassigned poem which readers have shown the greatest inclination to claim for Shakespeare is XII, but there is nothing to support the attribution. It reappeared, with additional stanzas, in Thomas Deloney's *Garland of Good Will* in 1631. There were earlier editions of this book, now lost, but whether XII was in them we have no way of knowing. Deloney died about 1600, and posthumous editions of his ballad collections, like the *Garland*, contain poems not of his writing.

Thirteen years after the second edition, in 1612, Jaggard brought out a third, with some added material. The title-page reads: "The Passionate Pilgrime. Or Certaine Amorous Sonnets, betweene Venus and Adonis, newly corrected and augmented. By W. Shakespeare. The third edition. Where-unto is newly added two Love-Epistles, the first from Paris to Hellen, and Hellens answere back to Paris. Printed by W. Iaggard. 1612." Actually, the poems "newly added" number not two but nine, all by Thomas Heywood, and all lifted from his *Troia Britannica*, which Jaggard had published in 1609. Heywood promptly made a public protest, in his *Apology for Actors*, expressing concern lest the world think that he had stolen the poems and published them as his own in *Troia Britannica* and that Shakespeare, to do himself right, had later published them under his own name. It was not so, said Heywood; the poems were not worthy of Shakespeare, and he knew that Shakespeare was much offended with Jaggard for making such wrongful use of his name. This protest, and perhaps one from Shakespeare, forced Jaggard to replace the title-page in the unsold copies of the third edition with one which omitted Shakespeare's name entirely.

The Passionate Pilgrim adds nothing to our knowledge of Shakespeare's work, but it tells us something about his reputation and about the vagaries of publishers of his time.

Hallett Smith

The Passionate Pilgrim

[I]

When my love swears that she is made of truth,
I do believe her (though I know she lies)
That she might think me some untutor'd youth,
Unskillful in the world's false forgeries.
Thus vainly thinking that she thinks me young,
Although I know my years be past the best,
I smiling credit her false-speaking tongue,
Outfacing faults in love with love's ill rest.
But wherefore says my love that she is young?
And wherefore say not I that I am old?
O, love's best habit's in a soothing tongue,
And age in love, loves not to have years told.
  Therefore I'll lie with love, and love with me,
  Since that our faults in love thus smother'd be.

[II]

Two loves I have, of comfort and despair,
That like two spirits do suggest me still:
My better angel is a man (right fair),
My worser spirit a woman (color'd ill).
To win me soon to hell, my female evil
Tempteth my better angel from my side;
And would corrupt my saint to be a devil,
Wooing his purity with her fair pride.
And whether that my angel be turn'd fiend,
Suspect I may (yet not directly tell):
For being both to me, both to each friend,
I guess one angel in another's hell:
  The truth I shall not know, but live in doubt,
  Till my bad angel fire my good one out.

[III]

Did not the heavenly rhetoric of thine eye,
'Gainst whom the world could not hold argument,
Persuade my heart to this false perjury?
Vows for thee broke deserve not punishment.
A woman I forswore; but I will prove,
Thou being a goddess, I forswore not thee:
My vow was earthly, thou a heavenly love;
Thy grace being gain'd cures all disgrace in me.
My vow was breath, and breath a vapor is,
Then thou, fair sun, that on this earth doth shine,
[Exhal'st] this vapor vow, in thee it is:
If broken, then it is no fault of mine.
  If by me broke, what fool is not so wise
  To break an oath, to win a paradise?

[IV]

Sweet Cytherea, sitting by a brook
With young Adonis, lovely, fresh, and green,
Did court the lad with many a lovely look,
Such looks as none could look but beauty's queen.
She told him stories to delight his [ear];
She show'd him favors to allure his eye;
To win his heart she touch'd him here and there—
Touches so soft still conquer chastity.
But whether unripe years did want conceit,
Or he refus'd to take [her] figured proffer,
The tender nibbler would not touch the bait,
But smile and jest at every gentle offer.
  Then fell she on her back, fair queen, and toward:
  He rose and ran away, ah, fool too froward!

[V]

If love make me forsworn, how shall I swear to love?
O, never faith could hold, if not to beauty vowed:
Though to myself forsworn, to thee I'll constant prove;
Those thoughts to me like oaks, to thee like osiers bowed.
Study his bias leaves, and makes his book thine eyes,
Where all those pleasures live that art can comprehend.
If knowledge be the mark, to know thee shall suffice:
Well learned is that tongue that well can thee commend,
All ignorant that soul that sees thee without wonder,

Words enclosed in square brackets in the text above are emendations of the copy-text. The Textual Notes record in every instance the reading of the copy-text and the earliest authority for the emendation here adopted.

I. Cf. Sonnet 138.
2. believe: i.e. pretend to believe. **4. forgeries:** deceits.
8. Outfacing . . . rest. Not satisfactorily explained. Sonnet 138 substitutes an entirely different line.
11. habit: behavior, deportment. **soothing:** flattering.
12. told: counted. **13. lie with:** lie to (with obvious pun).

II. Cf. Sonnet 144.
2. suggest: urge (toward comfort or despair). **still:** continually.
4. color'd ill: i.e. dark. **8. pride:** sexual attraction.
11. being . . . friend: since both of them are friends of mine and friends to each other. **14. fire . . . out:** drive . . . out (with quibble on the sense "infect with venereal disease").

III. Cf. *Love's Labor's Lost*, IV.iii.58–71.
2. whom: which.
11. Exhal'st: drawest up. **13. so wise:** wise enough.

IV.**1. Cytherea:** Venus. **2. green:** young. **3. lovely:** loving.
8. still: always. **9. want conceit:** lack understanding.
10. figured: indicated by signs and gestures.
13. toward: willing, compliant. **14. froward:** perverse, resisting.

V. Cf. *Love's Labor's Lost*, IV.ii.105–18.
4. osiers: willows.
5. Study . . . leaves: i.e. the student abandons his inclination (to learning). **6. art:** learning. **7. mark:** target, goal.

Which is to me some praise, that I thy parts admire.
Thine eye Jove's lightning seems, thy voice his dreadful thunder,
Which, not to anger bent, is music and sweet fire.
Celestial as thou art, O, do not love that wrong:
To sing heaven's praise with such an earthly tongue.

[VI]

Scarce had the sun dried up the dewy morn,
And scarce the herd gone to the hedge for shade,
When Cytherea (all in love forlorn)
A longing tarriance for Adonis made
Under an osier growing by a brook,
A brook where Adon us'd to cool his spleen.
Hot was the day, she hotter that did look
For his approach, that often there had been.
Anon he comes, and throws his mantle by,
And stood stark naked on the brook's green brim.
The sun look'd on the world with glorious eye,
Yet not so wistly as this queen on him.
He spying her, bounc'd in, whereas he stood;
"O Jove," quoth she, "why was not I a flood?"

[VII]

Fair is my love, but not so fair as fickle,
Mild as a dove, but neither true nor trusty,
Brighter than glass, and yet as glass is brittle,
Softer than wax, and yet as iron rusty:
A lily pale, with damask dye to grace her,
None fairer, nor none falser to deface her.

Her lips to mine how often hath she joined,
Between each kiss her oaths of true love swearing!
How many tales to please me hath she coined,
Dreading my love, the loss whereof still fearing!
Yet in the mids of all her pure protestings,
Her faith, her oaths, her tears, and all were jestings.

She burnt with love, as straw with fire flameth,
She burnt out love, as soon as straw out-burneth;
She fram'd the love, and yet she foil'd the framing,
She bade love last, and yet she fell a-turning.
Was this a lover, or a lecher whether?
Bad in the best, though excellent in neither.

[VIII]

If music and sweet poetry agree,
As they must needs (the sister and the brother),
Then must the love be great 'twixt thee and me,
Because thou lov'st the one, and I the other.
Dowland to thee is dear, whose heavenly touch
Upon the lute doth ravish human sense;
Spenser to me, whose deep conceit is such
As passing all conceit, needs no defense.
Thou lov'st to hear the sweet melodious sound
That Phoebus' lute, the queen of music, makes;
And I in deep delight am chiefly drown'd
When as himself to singing he betakes.
One god is god of both (as poets feign),
One knight loves both, and both in thee remain.

[IX]

Fair was the morn when the fair queen of love,
[. . . . . . .]
Paler for sorrow than her milk-white dove,
For Adon's sake, a youngster proud and wild,
Her stand she takes upon a steep-up hill.
Anon Adonis comes with horn and hounds;
She, silly queen, with more than love's good will,
Forbade the boy he should not pass those grounds.
"Once," quoth she, "did I see a fair sweet youth
Here in these brakes deep-wounded with a boar,
Deep in the thigh, a spectacle of ruth!
See, in my thigh," quoth she, "here was the sore."
She showed hers, he saw more wounds than one,
And blushing fled, and left her all alone.

[X]

Sweet rose, fair flower, untimely pluck'd, soon vaded,
Pluck'd in the bud, and vaded in the spring!
Bright orient pearl, alack, too timely shaded!
Fair creature, kill'd too soon by death's sharp sting!
Like a green plum that hangs upon a tree,
And falls (through wind) before the fall should be.

I weep for thee, and yet no cause I have,
For why: thou lefts me nothing in thy will;
And yet thou lefts me more than I did crave,
For why: I craved nothing of thee still.
O yes, dear friend, I pardon crave of thee,
Thy discontent thou didst bequeath to me.

[XI]

Venus, with Adonis sitting by her,
Under a myrtle shade began to woo him.
She told the youngling how god Mars did try her,

13. do . . . wrong: do not desire to do such a wrong as (?) or do not do love such a wrong as (?). The line must be corrupt, since clearly it is not the "celestial" one but the poet who is chargeable with the wrong specified in line 14.

VI.4. **tarriance:** tarrying, waiting.
6. **spleen.** Thought to be the source of body heat.
12. **wistly:** intently. 13. **whereas:** from where.
14. **flood:** body of water.

VII.5. **damask:** red or pink.
6. **nor . . . her:** nor, to her shame, is anyone more false.
10. **Dreading . . . fearing:** constantly fearing that she would lose my love, and dreading the thought.
15. **fram'd:** built. **foil'd:** destroyed.
17. **whether:** which of the two.

VIII.3. **thee.** Barnfield (see the introduction) addressed this sonnet to "R. L."
5. **Dowland:** John Dowland (1563?–?1626), composer and lutenist.
7–8. **conceit . . . conceit:** imaginative power . . . conception.
10. **Phoebus'.** Phoebus Apollo was the god of music and poetry (see line 13).
12. **When as:** when. **singing.** With reference to the words rather than the music. 14. **One knight.** Not certainly identified.

IX.2. The defective rhyme scheme indicates that a line is missing.
5. **steep-up:** steeply rising. 7. **silly:** poor, pitiable.
8. **pass:** cross. 11. **ruth:** pity.

X.1. **vaded:** faded.
3. **orient:** lustrous. **timely:** early. **shaded:** darkened.
8. **For why:** for this reason. **lefts:** leftst.
12. **discontent:** unhappiness.

And as he fell to her, she fell to him.
"Even thus," quoth she, "the warlike god embrac'd me,"
And then she clipt Adonis in her arms;
"Even thus," quoth she, "the warlike god unlac'd me,"
As if the boy should use like loving charms;
"Even thus," quoth she, "he seized on my lips,"
And with her lips on his did act the seizure:
And as she fetched breath, away he skips,
And would not take her meaning nor her pleasure.
Ah, that I had my lady at this bay:
To kiss and clip me till I run away!

[XII]

Crabbed age and youth cannot live together:
Youth is full of pleasance, age is full of care,
Youth like summer morn, age like winter weather,
Youth like summer brave, age like winter bare.
Youth is full of sport, age's breath is short,
Youth is nimble, age is lame,
Youth is hot and bold, age is weak and cold,
Youth is wild, and age is tame.
Age, I do abhor thee, youth, I do adore thee:
O, my love, my love is young!
Age, I do defy thee. O sweet shepherd, hie thee,
For methinks thou stays too long.

[XIII]

Beauty is but a vain and doubtful good,
A shining gloss that vadeth suddenly,
A flower that dies when first it gins to bud,
A brittle glass that's broken presently:
A doubtful good, a gloss, a glass, a flower,
Lost, vaded, broken, dead within an hour.

And as goods lost are seld or never found,
As vaded gloss no rubbing will refresh,
As flowers dead lie withered on the ground,
As broken glass no cement can redress:
So beauty blemish'd once, for ever lost,
In spite of physic, painting, pain, and cost.

[XIV]

Good night, good rest, ah, neither be my share!
She bade good night that kept my rest away,
And daff'd me to a cabin hang'd with care,
To descant on the doubts of my decay.
"Farewell," quoth she, "and come again to-morrow."
Fare well I could not, for I supp'd with sorrow.

Yet at my parting sweetly did she smile,
In scorn or friendship, nill I conster whether.
'T may be she joy'd to jest at my exile,
'T may be again, to make me wander thither:
"Wander," a word for shadows like myself,
As take the pain but cannot pluck the pelf.

Lord, how mine eyes throw gazes to the east!
My heart doth charge the watch; the morning rise
Doth cite each moving sense from idle rest,
Not daring trust the office of mine eyes.
While Philomela sits and sings, I sit and mark,
And wish her lays were tuned like the lark.

For she doth welcome daylight with her ditty,
And drives away dark dreaming night.
The night so pack'd, I post unto my pretty;
Heart hath his hope, and eyes their wished sight:
Sorrow chang'd to solace, and solace mix'd with sorrow;
For why, she sight, and bade me come to-morrow.

Were I with her, the night would post too soon,
But now are minutes added to the hours;
To spite me now, each minute seems [a moon],
Yet not for me, shine sun to succor flowers!
Pack night, peep day; good day, of night now borrow:
Short night to-night, and length thyself to-morrow.

Sonnets to Sundry Notes of Music

[XV]

It was a lording's daughter, the fairest one of three,
That liked of her master, as well as well might be,
Till looking on an Englishman, the fairest that eye could see,
Her fancy fell a-turning.
Long was the combat doubtful, that love with love did fight,
To leave the master loveless, or kill the gallant knight:
To put in practice either, alas, it was a spite
Unto the silly damsel!
But one must be refused; more mickle was the pain,
That nothing could be used, to turn them both to gain,
For of the two the trusty knight was wounded with disdain:
Alas, she could not help it!

XI.6. **clipt**: hugged. 12. **her pleasure**: i.e. the pleasure she offered. 13. **at this bay**: in such an encounter at close quarters (a term from hunting).

XII.2. **pleasance**: gaiety. 4. **brave**: splendidly dressed. 11. **defy**: despise. **hie thee**: hasten. 12. **stays**: delayest.

XIII.4. **presently**: at once. 7. **seld**: seldom. 10. **redress**: repair. 12. **pain**: labor.

XIV.3. **daff'd**: sent off, dismissed. **cabin**: small room. 4. **descant**: compose variations on. **doubts**: fears. 6. **Fare**. With quibble on the sense "eat."

8. **nill I**: I will not. **conster**: construe, interpret. **whether**: which of the two.
10. **again**: on the other hand (but most editors emend *be again*, to *be, again*). 12. **As**: who. **pelf**: riches, i.e. reward.
14. **charge the watch**: tell the watchman to proclaim dawn (?).
15. **cite**: summon.
17. **Philomela**: the nightingale. **sits and**. It has been observed that sense and metre would be improved by the omission of these words. Various attempts have also been made to mend the metre of line 20.
21. **pack'd**: gone. **post**: hasten. 24. **sight**: sighed.
30. **Short . . . to-morrow**: shorten the night to-night (by borrowing from the end of it), and (thus) lengthen yourself to-morrow.

XV.1. **lording's**: lord's. 2. **master**: tutor.
8. **silly**: poor, pitiable. 9. **mickle**: great. 10. **used**: done.

Thus art with arms contending was victor of the day,
Which by a gift of learning did bear the maid away:
Then lullaby, the learned man hath got the lady gay,
For now my song is ended.

[XVI]

On a day (alack the day!)
Love, whose month was ever May,
Spied a blossom passing fair,
Playing in the wanton air.
Through the velvet leaves the wind
All unseen gan passage find,
That the lover, sick to death,
Wish'd himself the heavens' breath.
"Air," quoth he, "thy cheeks may blow,
Air, would I might triumph so!
But (alas) my hand hath sworn
Ne'er to pluck thee from thy [thorn],
Vow (alack) for youth unmeet,
Youth, so apt to pluck a sweet.
Thou for whom Jove would swear
Juno but an Ethiope were,
And deny himself for Jove,
Turning mortal for thy love."

[XVII]

My flocks feed not, my ewes breed not,
My rams speed not, all is amiss;
Love is dying, faith's defying,
Heart's denying, causer of this.
All my merry jigs are quite forgot,
All my lady's love is lost, God wot.
Where her faith was firmly fix'd in love,
There a nay is plac'd without remove.
One silly cross wrought all my loss,
O frowning Fortune, cursed, fickle dame!
For now I see inconstancy
More in women than in men remain.

In black mourn I, all fears scorn I,
Love hath forlorn me, living in thrall;
Heart is bleeding, all help needing,
O cruel speeding, fraughted with gall.
My shepherd's pipe can sound no deal,
My wether's bell rings doleful knell,
My curtal dog, that wont to have play'd,
Plays not at all, but seems afraid;
With sighs so deep procures to weep,
In howling wise, to see my doleful plight.
How sighs resound through heartless ground,
Like a thousand vanquish'd men in bloody fight!

Clear wells spring not, sweet birds sing not,
Green plants bring not forth their dye;
Herds stands weeping, flocks all sleeping,
Nymphs [back] peeping fearfully.
All our pleasure known to us poor swains,
All our merry meetings on the plains,
All our evening sport from us is fled,
All our love is lost, for Love is dead.
Farewell, sweet [lass], thy like ne'er was
For a sweet content, the cause of all my [moan].
Poor Corydon must live alone,
Other help for him I see that there is none.

[XVIII]

When as thine eye hath chose the dame,
And stall'd the deer that thou shouldst strike,
Let reason rule things worthy blame,
As well as fancy, partial might.
Take counsel of some wiser head,
Neither too young nor yet unwed.

And when thou com'st thy tale to tell,
Smooth not thy tongue with filed talk,
Lest she some subtile practice smell—
A cripple soon can find a halt—
But plainly say thou lov'st her well,
And set her person forth to sale.

And to her will frame all thy ways,
Spare not to spend, and chiefly there
Where thy desert may merit praise,
By ringing in thy lady's ear.
The strongest castle, tower, and town,
The golden bullet beats it down.

Serve always with assured trust,
And in thy suit be humble true;
Unless thy lady prove unjust,
Press never thou to choose anew.
When time shall serve, be thou not slack
To proffer, though she put thee back.

What though her frowning brows be bent,
Her cloudy looks will calm yer night,
And then too late she will repent,
That thus dissembled her delight;
And twice desire, yer it be day,
That which with scorn she put away.

What though she strive to try her strength,
And ban and brawl, and say thee nay,

13. art: learning.

XVI. Cf. *Love's Labor's Lost*, IV.iii.99–118.
4. wanton: frolicsome. **7. That:** so that.
16. Ethiope: blackamoor.

XVII.2. **speed:** thrive. **3. defying:** rejection. **9. cross:** mishap.
14. forlorn me: made me forlorn.
16. speeding: faring. **fraughted:** loaded. **17. no deal:** not at all.
19. curtal: with docked tail. **wont . . . play'd:** used to be playful.
21. procures: manages. **23. heartless:** barren, desolate.
24. vanquish'd: men vanquished in.

25. wells: springs.

XVIII.2. **stall'd:** got within range of.
4. fancy: love. **partial:** biased, unable to be objective. **might:** power. **8. filed:** polished, studied.
9. practice: deception. **10. find a halt:** detect a limp.
12. set . . . sale: i.e. praise her qualities (like a salesman exhibiting his goods to the best advantage). Some editors regularize the rhyme by emending *sale* to *sell*, without change in the meaning; many read *thy* for *her*, i.e. show yourself in the most favorable light.
21. unjust: untrue. **23. time:** occasion.
24. proffer: make advances. **26. yer:** ere. **28. dissembled her delight:** pretended to be displeased. **32. ban:** curse.

Her feeble force will yield at length,
When craft hath taught her thus to say:
"Had women been so strong as men,
In faith, you had not had it then."

The wiles and guiles that women work,
Dissembled with an outward show,
The tricks and toys that in them lurk,
The cock that treads them shall not know.
Have you not heard it said full oft,
A woman's nay doth stand for nought?

Think women still to strive with men,
To sin and never for to saint:
There is no heaven, [be] holy then,
When time with age shall them attaint.
Were kisses all the joys in bed,
One woman would another wed.

But soft, enough—too much, I fear—
Lest that my mistress hear my song;
She will not stick to round me on th' [ear],
To teach my tongue to be so long.
Yet will she blush, here be it said,
To hear her secrets so bewray'd.

[XIX]

Live with me and be my love,
And we will all the pleasures prove
That hills and valleys, dales and fields,
And all the craggy mountains yield.

There will we sit upon the rocks,
And see the shepherds feed their flocks,
By shallow rivers, by whose falls
Melodious birds sing madrigals.

There will I make thee a bed of roses,
With a thousand fragrant posies,
A cap of flowers, and a kirtle
Embroidered all with leaves of myrtle;

A belt of straw and ivy buds,
With coral clasps and amber studs:
And if these pleasures may thee move,
Then live with me, and be my love.

LOVE'S ANSWER

If that the world and love were young,
And truth in every shepherd's tongue,
These pretty pleasures might me move,
To live with thee and be thy love.

[XX]

As it fell upon a day,
In the merry month of May,
Sitting in a pleasant shade,
Which a grove of myrtles made,
Beasts did leap and birds did sing,
Trees did grow and plants did spring;
Every thing did banish moan,
Save the nightingale alone.
She, poor bird, as all forlorn,
Lean'd her breast up-till a thorn,
And there sung the dolefull'st ditty,
That to hear it was great pity.
"Fie, fie, fie," now would she cry,
"Tereu, tereu," by and by;
That to hear her so complain,
Scarce I could from tears refrain;
For her griefs, so lively shown,
Made me think upon mine own.
Ah, thought I, thou mourn'st in vain,
None takes pity on thy pain.
Senseless trees, they cannot hear thee,
Ruthless bears, they will not cheer thee.
King Pandion, he is dead:
All thy friends are lapp'd in lead;
All thy fellow birds do sing,
Careless of thy sorrowing.
Whilst as fickle Fortune smil'd,
Thou and I were both beguil'd.
Every one that flatters thee
Is no friend in misery.
Words are easy, like the wind,
Faithful friends are hard to find:
Every man will be thy friend,
Whilst thou hast wherewith to spend;
But if store of crowns be scant,
No man will supply thy want.
If that one be prodigal,
Bountiful they will him call;
And with such-like flattering,
"Pity but he were a king!"
If he be addict to vice,
Quickly him they will entice;
If to women he be bent,
They have at commandement.
But if Fortune once do frown,
Then farewell his great renown;
They that fawn'd on him before
Use his company no more.
He that is thy friend indeed,
He will help thee in thy need:
If thou sorrow, he will weep;
If thou wake, he cannot sleep;
Thus of every grief in heart
He with thee doth bear a part.
These are certain signs to know
Faithful friend from flatt'ring foe.

43. Think: expect. **44. saint:** play the saint.
45. There: i.e. in women, or in dealings with them.
51. round . . . ear: take me to task. **54. bewray'd:** revealed.

XIX.**2. prove:** try, experience. **11. kirtle:** gown.

XX.**10. up-till:** upon, against.
14. Tereu, tereu. The cry conventionally ascribed to the nightingale, from the name of Tereus, the Thracian king who in the classical story raped Philomela and cut out her tongue.
21. Senseless: insensible.
23. Pandion: Philomela's father, a king of Athens.
40. but he were: that he is not.
44. have at commandement: i.e. can easily command women for his use. **52. wake:** be sleepless.

NOTE ON THE TEXT

The two earliest editions of *The Passionate Pilgrim* were printed by William Jaggard, the first possibly in 1598 but more probably in 1599, the second in 1599. The first, an octavo (O1), survives only in a fragment (parts of sheets A and C) in the Folger Shakespeare Library, and it was not until 1939, as the result of a careful study by J. Q. Adams, that these sheets were recognized as without question the remnant of a first edition (Hyder Rollins, for example, in his New Variorum *Poems*, 1938, though admitting their possible priority, treats these sheets in his collations as representing a second edition). Because of the fragmentary state of the surviving O1 text (it contains only the poems numbered i–v, xvi–xviii in the present edition), the second edition (O2) must serve as copy-text for a number of the poems (as indicated in the Textual Notes). In 1612 Jaggard printed a third edition (O3), based on O2 but much enlarged by the addition of nine poems by Thomas Heywood. The contents of O3 were later scattered, without any apparent system, throughout the edition of Shakespeare's *Poems* published by John Benson in 1640 (see "Note on the Text" to the Sonnets).

For further information, see: H. E. Rollins, ed., New Variorum *Poems* (Philadelphia, 1938) and ed., *The Passionate Pilgrim* [facsimile of O3] (New York, 1940); J. Q. Adams, ed., *The Passionate Pilgrim* [facsimile of O1] (New York, 1939); F. T. Prince, ed., New Arden *Poems* (London, 1960); J. C. Maxwell, ed., New Shakespeare *Poems* (Cambridge, 1966); Stanley Wells, Gary Taylor, et al., *William Shakespeare: A Textual Companion* (Oxford, 1987); John Roe, ed., New Cambridge Shakespeare *Poems* (Cambridge, 1992).

TEXTUAL NOTES

Numbering: *poems unnumbered in O1–2; present numbering as a whole from Neilson; for numbers of individual poems, see notes below*

I

A variant version of Sonnet 138
I] *Collier*
7 false-speaking] *hyphen, Sewell*
8 love] *Sewell (Folger MS. 2071.7);* loue, *O1*

II

A variant version of Sonnet 144
II] *Collier*
11 me, both] *Gildon (after Benson);* me; both, *O1*
12 guess] *Lintott;* ghesse *O1*

III

A variant version of a sonnet in Love's Labor's Lost, *IV.iii.58–71*
III] *Collier*
3 perjury?] *Love's Labor's Lost;* periury; *O1*
11 Exhal'st] *Love's Labor's Lost;* Exhalt *O1;* Exhale *O2 (possibly the reading should be* Exhal'd)

IV

IV] *Collier*
5 ear] *Folger MS. 1.8;* eares *O1*
10 her] *O2;* his *O1*
13 toward:] *Sewell (subs.);* toward *O1*

V

A variant version of a sonnet in Love's Labor's Lost, *IV.ii.105–18*
V] *Collier*
8 commend,] *O2;* commend. *O1*
11 Thine] *O2;* Thin *O1*
14 heaven's] *Gildon;* heauens *O1*

VI

Copy-text, O2
VI] *Collier*
13 in, . . . stood;] *Malone;* in (whereas he stood) *O2*

VII

Copy-text, O2
VII] *Malone*
1 fickle,] *Benson;* fickle. *O2*
14 out-burneth] *hyphen, Malone*
16 a-turning] *hyphen, Hudson*

VIII

A sonnet by Richard Barnfield
Copy-text, O2
VIII] *Collier*
6 human] *Gildon;* humane *O2*

IX

Copy-text, O2
IX] *Collier*
2] *Line apparently lacking; omission first noted by Malone*
5 steep-up] *hyphen, Gildon*

X

Copy-text, O2
X] *Collier*

XI

Probably by Bartholomew Griffin
Copy-text, O2
XI] *Collier*
1 with Adonis] and yong Adonis *Griffin's Fidessa, Folger MS. 1.8*
4 she fell] so fell she *Griffin's Fidessa, Folger MS. 1.8*

XII

Copy-text, O2
XII] *Collier*

XIII

Copy-text, O2
XIII] *Collier*
10 cement] *Gildon (subs.);* symant *O2*

XIV

Copy-text, O2
XIV] *Craig*
11 "Wander," a word] *Malone;* Wander (a word) *O2*
14 watch;] *Gildon;* watch, *O2*
19 ditty] *O3;* ditte *O2*
27 a moon] *Steevens conj.;* an houre *O2*

XV

Copy-text, O2
XV] *Neilson*
4 a-turning] *hyphen, Hudson*
9 refused;] *Dyce;* refused, *O2*
15 lullaby,] *Malone (after Sewell);* lullaby *O2*

XVI

A variant version of a poem in Love's Labor's Lost, *IV.iii.99–118*
XVI] *Neilson*
2 ever] *Love's Labor's Lost;* ener *O1*
2 May,] *Benson;* May: *O1*
8 heavens'] *ed.;* heauens *O1*
12 pluck] *Love's Labor's Lost;* pruck *O1*
12 thorn] *England's Helicon;* throne *O1*
13 alack] *Love's Labor's Lost;* allcke *O1*

XVII

XVII] *Neilson*
3 defying] *O2;* defieng *O1*
4 denying] *O3;* denieng *O1;* nenying *O2*
7 love,] *O2;* loue: *O1*
10 Fortune,] *Weelkes' Madrigals;* fortune *O1*
13 mourn] *Weelkes' Madrigals;* morne *O1*
18 knell] *O2;* kuell *O1*
21 weep,] *O2;* weepe *O1*
22 plight.] *Gildon (subs.);* plight, *O1*
24 vanquish'd] *O2;* vanpuisht *O1*
28 back] *Weelkes' Madrigals;* blacke *O1*
33 lass] *Weelkes' Madrigals;* loue *O1*
33 was] *Malone;* was, *O1*
34 content,] *Weelkes' Madrigals;* content *O1*
34 moan] *England's Helicon;* woe *O1*

XVIII

XVIII] *Neilson*
2 stall'd] *Gildon;* stalde *O1*
4 fancy, partial might.] *Malone (subs.);* fancy (partyall might) *O1*
13–24] *These two stanzas follow l. 36 in O2–3*
20 humble] *O2;* hnmble *O1*
22 anew] *O1* (auew); a new *O2*
32 nay,] *Lintott;* nay: *O1*
36 not] *O2;* uot *O1*
45 be] *Folger MS. 2071.7;* by *O1*
46 attaint.] *Gildon;* attaint, *O1*
48 another] *O2;* an other *O1*
49 soft,] *Capell MS;* soft *O1*
51 th' ear] *O3* (th'ere); th'are *O1*

XIX

A version of a lyric by Christopher Marlowe, with one stanza of Sir Walter Raleigh's (?) answer
Copy-text, O2
XIX] *Neilson*
4 yield] yeeldes *England's Helicon*
10 posies] *England's Helicon;* poses *O2*
12 Embroidered] *Neilson (after Gildon);* Imbrodered *O2*

XX

By Richard Barnfield
Copy-text, O2
XX] *Keightley*
13 cry,] *Pepys ballad;* cry *O2*
36 want.] *Barnfield's Poems;* want *O2*
40 "Pity . . . king!"] *in quotes, Malone*
47 before] *Hudson;* before. *O2*
54 doth] *Benson;* doeth *O2*

The Phoenix and Turtle

SHAKESPEARE OFTEN REFERS in his plays to the phoenix, that legendary bird of Arabia which lived in a nest of spices and perfumes and died in flames only to rise again from its own ashes. The attribute of the bird which recalled it to Shakespeare's mind was its uniqueness: only one phoenix was ever alive at any particular time. Shakespeare's poem *The Phoenix and Turtle* is unique among his works—there is nothing else like it.

It appeared in 1601 as one of a collection of poems on the same subject appended to Robert Chester's *Love's Martyr, or Rosalin's Complaint, Allegorically Shadowing the Truth of Love, in the Constant Fate of the Phoenix and Turtle.* These appended poems are called, on their separate title-page, "diverse poetical essays on the former subject . . . done by the best and chiefest of our modern writers, with their names subscribed to their particular works: never before extant." The first two are signed *Vatum Chorus,* as if the poems spoke for all the contributors; the next, *Ignoto.* Shakespeare's poem follows, with his name appended, and then come signed poems by John Marston, George Chapman, and Ben Jonson.

As the phoenix was famous for its beauty and rarity, the turtledove was renowned for its constancy in love. Poems about birds were traditionally allegorical, and Robert Chester announces on his title-page that *Love's Martyr* allegorically shadows the truth of love. But the allegorical meaning of Shakespeare's poem is by no means clear. Some critics have thought that the phoenix and the turtle darkly hint at Queen Elizabeth (who was often represented symbolically by the phoenix) and the Earl of Essex. Others have thought the chaste and loving birds must represent Sir John Salusbury, to whom *Love's Martyr* and the appended poems are dedicated, and his lady; alternative candidates are the Earl and Countess of Bedford. But Shakespeare's poem does not reflect the same situation as certain of the other poems; it clearly states that the phoenix and turtle left no posterity, whereas Marston celebrates their offspring, "a most exact wondrous creature, arising out of the Phoenix and Turtledove's ashes."

The poem is in three sections. The first five stanzas call up a funeral procession of birds to mourn; the next eight stanzas are an anthem, presumably sung by the mourners, in which Reason is confounded by Love as exemplified in the phoenix and the turtle. The final section, in a different verse form, is a *threnos* or *threne*—a lament for the dead—composed by Reason.

The language of the middle section is highly technical; it is the scholastic language used in discussions of the three Persons of the Trinity. The phoenix legend was a recognized subject for paradox, especially the paradoxes associated with love and death. As John Donne puts it in "The Canonization,"

> The phoenix riddle hath more wit
> By us: we two being one, are it.

Looking for references to things outside the poem is probably less profitable than to pay attention to the way the poem works. It turns in upon itself. The richly evocative, but traditional, catalogue of birds in the beginning gives way to the intensely active and dramatic statements of the paradoxes in the anthem, and these in turn yield to the monumental lyric simplicity and dignity of the threnos. Beginning with the concrete specifications of the mourners, the poem moves into the abstract so far that an abstraction within the poem, Reason, cries out and composes a song which solemnly declares the burial of the abstractions Truth and Beauty and returns to the specific and concrete:

Truth may seem, but cannot be,
Beauty brag, but 'tis not she,
Truth and Beauty buried be.

To this urn let those repair
That are either true or fair;
For these dead birds sigh a prayer.

What began with a trumpet call ends in a sigh. The strictest economy of means has brought all this about in only sixty-seven lines.

Hallett Smith

"Death is now the Phoenix' nest." From Geffrey Whitney, *A Choice of Emblems* (1586). The phoenix, a favorite emblem for unique perfection, was a creation of classical mythology. Born in the Arabian desert, only a single phoenix existed at any one time. It lived between five and six hundred years, and when its cycle was completed burned itself to death atop a pyre of aromatic twigs, which, once ignited by the sun, was kept blazing by the beating of the phoenix' wings. Out of the ashes emerged a new phoenix, self-generated. Usually Shakespeare treats the phoenix myth with conventional poetic deference, but in *The Tempest* he cites it as an example (with the unicorn) of something ordinarily unbelievable. Sebastian exclaims, in amazement at having witnessed the introduction of Prospero's magic banquet: "Now I will believe / That there are unicorns; that in Arabia / There is one tree, the phoenix' throne, one phoenix / At this hour reigning there" (III. iii. 21–24).

[The Phoenix and Turtle]

Let the bird of loudest lay,
On the sole Arabian tree,
Herald sad and trumpet be,
To whose sound chaste wings obey.

But thou shriking harbinger,
Foul precurrer of the fiend,
Augur of the fever's end,
To this troop come thou not near.

From this session interdict
Every fowl of tyrant wing,
Save the eagle, feath'red king;
Keep the obsequy so strict.

Let the priest in surplice white,
That defunctive music can,
Be the death-divining swan,
Lest the requiem lack his right.

And thou treble-dated crow,
That thy sable gender mak'st
With the breath thou giv'st and tak'st,
'Mongst our mourners shalt thou go.

Here the anthem doth commence:
Love and Constancy is dead,
Phoenix and the Turtle fled
In a mutual flame from hence.

So they loved as love in twain
Had the essence but in one,
Two distincts, division none:
Number there in love was slain.

Hearts remote, yet not asunder;
Distance and no space was seen
'Twixt this Turtle and his queen:
But in them it were a wonder.

So between them love did shine,
That the Turtle saw his right
Flaming in the Phoenix' sight;
Either was the other's mine.

Property was thus appalled,
That the self was not the same;
Single nature's double name
Neither two nor one was called.

Reason, in itself confounded,
Saw division grow together,
To themselves yet either neither,
Simple were so well compounded:

That it cried, "How true a twain
Seemeth this concordant one!
Love hath reason, Reason none,
If what parts, can so remain."

Whereupon it made this threne
To the Phoenix and the Dove,
Co-supremes and stars of love,
As chorus to their tragic scene.

THRENOS

Beauty, Truth, and Rarity,
Grace in all simplicity,
Here enclos'd, in cinders lie.

Title. Turtle: turtledove (symbolic of constancy in love).
1. bird . . . lay. Of uncertain identity, but clearly not the phoenix, though the "sole Arabian tree" of line 2 suggests the traditional habitat of the phoenix (see *The Tempest*, III.iii.22–24). **lay:** song.
3. sad: solemn, grave. **trumpet:** trumpeter.
4. To . . . obey. *Obey to* was idiomatic Elizabethan English.
5. shriking harbinger: i.e. the screech owl, foreteller of death.
6. precurrer: forerunner. **7. Augur . . . end:** i.e. presager of death.
10. fowl . . . wing: bird of prey.
11. eagle, feath'red king. The eagle was considered symbolically the king of birds, as the lion was king of beasts.
14. defunctive: funereal. **can:** knows, is skilled in.
15. death-divining swan. According to legend the swan could foresee its own death; only then could it sing.
16. his right: its due ceremony.
17. treble-dated: living as long as three ordinary lifetimes.
18. sable gender: black offspring.
19. breath . . . tak'st. Alluding to the belief that crows conceived at the bill.
25–28. So . . . slain: their love was such that although they were two persons they had but one essence; they were separate yet undivided; their love made the very concept of number meaningless.
29. remote: at a distance from each other.
32. But . . . wonder: it would have been amazing in anyone but them.
33. So: in such a way.
34. his right: what was peculiarly his own, his own nature.
35. sight: eyes.
36. mine: own, i.e. self. Cf. Sonnet 134.3, "that other mine," i.e. my other self.
37–38. Property . . . same: property (essential quality) was thus impaired since self (single nature) had been altered.
41–44. Reason . . . compounded: reason, which can discriminate separate entities, is confounded by the paradox of united division, neither one being either one or both, and the single having become the thoroughly mingled.
47–48. Love . . . remain: i.e. reason surrenders to love as more reasonable, if what is separate can remain joined.
49. threne: threnody, funeral song. *Threnos* (following line 52) is the same word in its Greek form.
51. Co-supremes: joint sovereigns (continuing the two-in-one and one-in-two theme).
53. Truth: fidelity in love. **Rarity:** uncommon excellence.

Death is now the Phoenix' nest,
And the Turtle's loyal breast
To eternity doth rest.

Leaving no posterity,
'Twas not their infirmity,
It was married chastity.

Truth may seem, but cannot be,
Beauty brag, but 'tis not she,
Truth and Beauty buried be.

To this urn let those repair
That are either true or fair;
For these dead birds sigh a prayer.

56. Death . . . nest. The phoenix was believed to make a funeral pyre of its own nest and to be miraculously reborn from the ashes, but now death has finally claimed it.

62–64. Truth . . . be: i.e. what seems to be fidelity, and what claims to be beauty, may hereafter appear, but they will be impostors; the reality is buried with the phoenix and the turtledove.

NOTE ON THE TEXT

"The Phoenix and Turtle," without title, was first printed among a number of commendatory poems appended to Robert Chester's *Loues Martyr* in 1601 (sigs. $Z3^v$–$Z4^v$). Apart from a reissue of the original sheets in 1611, the poem next appeared in John Benson's 1640 edition of Shakespeare's *Poems* (see "Note on the Text" to the Sonnets). Benson took his text from the *Loues Martyr* printing, and hence the 1601 edition (Q1) here serves as copy-text. The poem was first given a title in two Boston editions published in 1807, in both of which it was called "The Phoenix and the Turtle." The slightly different title used here derives from the general title-page of *Loues Martyr*, where the phrase "the Phoenix and Turtle" appears twice, though it should be noted that on the separate title-page to the added poems, "Done by the best and chiefest of our moderne writers," the phrase becomes "the Turtle and Phoenix."

For further information, see: H. E. Rollins, ed., New Variorum *Poems* (Philadelphia, 1938); F. T. Prince, ed., New Arden *Poems* (London, 1960); W. H. Matchett, *"The Phoenix and the Turtle," Shakespeare's Poem and "Loues Martyr"* (The Hague, 1965); J. C. Maxwell, ed., New Shakespeare *Poems* (Cambridge, 1966); Stanley Wells, Gary Taylor, et al., *William Shakespeare: A Textual Companion* (Oxford, 1987); John Roe, ed., New Cambridge *Poems* (Cambridge, 1992).

TEXTUAL NOTES

Title: The Phoenix and Turtle] ***see "Note on the Text"***
3 be,] ***Benson;*** **be:** ***Q1***
13 surplice] ***Gildon;*** **Surples** ***Q1***
17 treble-dated] ***hyphen, Gildon***
39 nature's] ***Malone;*** **Natures** ***Q1***
67] ***This line is followed in Q1 by*** **William Shake-speare.**

A Funeral Elegy

by W. S

(a poem recently suggested to be by Shakespeare; see, however, p. 1895)

Funeral Elegy by W. S. is a straightforward lament of the early death (by murder, as we know from legal records) of William Peter of Exeter in Devonshire, a twenty-nine-year-old, Oxford-educated husband and father. It is impossible to judge the depth of grief felt by the poet, whoever he was, and today it does not seem an appropriate question to ask, but it is certainly clear that, in his effort to immortalize his friend, the poet had no leisure for fiction or for remote or even proximate allusions to classical mythology, with the single exception of the "*Genius*" (499), the guardian angel who was prevented by a higher force from protecting William Peter. The poet does use his Bible, for important allusions to Genesis, for the death of the innocent Abel; to St. Matthew, for Christ's punning assignment of St. Peter as the foundation of the Church; and to Revelation, for reference to the Book of Life and to the "saints before the everlasting throne" (391), best known poetically in *Lycidas.* He has a knowledge of rhetorical devices and uses, among them *apostrophe* (to the deceased in lines 197 and 538—compare Daniel's "O Noble Devonshire") and once to the overconfident youths who should heed the example of Peter (483); *anadiplosis,* the beginning of a phrase with the words which have ended the previous phrase (531–32, with a turn that would have done the Seymour Bushe of *Ulysses* proud); personification (of death and time in several instances, especially 422 and 518); rhetorical questions (269–72 and 388–90); and *paronomasia* ("endeavors," 4, "suiting," 95, and "*Drew*," 341).

The form of the poem seems modelled upon Samuel Daniel's *A Funeral Poem upon the Death of the late noble Earl of Devonshire* (1606), with its succession of quatrains in iambic pentameter interspersed with infrequent summary couplets. However, the Earl's wealth and military achievements, the nature of his death by plague, and his meeting it "smilingly" were of no use to W. S. in his poem about a private person of modest means who was killed suddenly.

Among English writers, he seems to know, in addition to *A Funeral Poem . . . Devonshire,* Daniel's *The Complaint of Rosamond* (for possible influences of which, see "Notes to the Text"), although the poet makes no use of the device of having the deceased return to make her or his own complaint. He may have known Sidney's *Arcadia,* where there is a "seeled dove," here made into a simile by W. S. at 451. He uses Chaucerian elements in parts of the poem. These do not include irony, which is an attitude absent from the elegy, but line 90 recalls the virtues of the Knight in Chaucer's idealized portrait in the General Prologue, line 73; lines 315–16 with their moral statement and syntactical structure echo the typical Chaucerian descriptive method; and, perhaps in an antithetical response to Daniel's wealthy, aristocratic subject, the poet reminds us that gentle is as gentle does (461–70), as *The Wife of Bath's Tale* had shown us long ago. And there are parallels with Shakespearean passages.

There is no dallying with false surmise in the poem; there is no imagery of regeneration, neither floral nor aquatic. Peter is dead and lives in heaven and, with luck, in this poem. There is no metamorphosis. There is, however, the identification of the deceased with Christ in an attempt to demonstrate the falsity of the view that the nature of the end of life reveals the nature of the quality of that life. Indeed, the central theme of the poem is that it is a mistake, even an act of malice, to lose sight of the exemplary life Peter has led by imagining that his bloody death reflected anything other than the madness of his killer. Had it not been for his moral principles, which led him to enrage his killer, he would still be alive (329–335). This central theme is the reverse of the idea used by Daniel in his funeral poem, which stresses the notion that the end crowns all. In Daniel's theatrical metaphor, the last scene of Devonshire's active life glorifies the whole.

There are several subsidiary themes in the *Elegy* by W. S.: that the poem is a sacrifice, an offering up in homage to the deceased, by one who during the life of William Peter had failed to express his love fully; that confident youth should note the example of William Peter, who, for all his virtues, could not protect himself from the unexpected arrival of death (indeed, the poem is both sacrificial offering and admonitory lesson); and that virtue need not be the province solely of the well-born or well-off. Further, as is often the case with elegists, the lament for the dead includes a self-centered element, whether in the merely conventional suggestion that the recipient of the elegy would have done the same poetic duty for the giver (compare 236) or in an even more substantial way. W. S. refers with special pain to a "witless sin" (144)—a description of an offense committed either ignorantly by himself or foolishly by others at Oxford, which resulted in poisoning the poet's reputation. Later in the poem, referring to his current state of misfortune, he says that he hopes to learn from (presumably) that experience of his youth (557–560). He concludes that, whatever his own fate—which seems to be one in which he is in disgrace with Fortune and men's eyes (569–74)—he hopes that the deceased will live forever in this poem.

All of this would be of only modest interest to users of an edition of Shakespeare, even those interested in minor Jacobean elegiac verse, were it not for those two potent initials "W. S." and the devoted work of a single scholar, Donald W. Foster, without whose efforts, it seems fair to say, few having read the poem would have identified the poem or the initials as those of William Shakespeare. The argument for Shakespeare's authorship began modestly enough in Foster's *Elegy by W. S.* (1989), a study that stopped short of claiming absolutely that "W. S." was William Shakespeare, gave even-handed arguments for William Strachey as the author, and devoted some pages to the case against Shakespeare. The book was rightly praised as a model of attribution study. More recently, Professor Foster, together with some other critics, including Professor Richard Abrams, has come to the position that the elegy is clearly by Shakespeare.[1] When these critics expressed this opinion in scholarly seminars at the end of 1995, the *New York Times* celebrated the discovery of a new Shakespearean text, and there followed in the *TLS* in January through April of 1996 a spirited exchange of views, with Abrams and then Foster leading the forces for the new candidate and Stanley Wells, Katherine Duncan-Jones, and, most vigorously, Brian Vickers resisting.[2]

A number of converging arguments are made for including *A Funeral Elegy* in the Shakespearean canon, itself a complex structure which has undergone expansion (and fitful attempts at contraction) over the centuries. Some of these arguments are more attractive than others. They include: 1) the similarity "in language and format" (Foster, 1989, 81) of the dedication of the *Elegy* to William Peter's brother John with that of *The Rape of Lucrece* to the Earl of Southampton; 2) the fact that the publisher, Thomas Thorpe, and the printer, George Eld, are the publisher and printer of Shakespeare's Sonnets of 1609; 3) the poem's prosody, in particular the high percentage of instances of enjambment, i.e., run-on lines (though enjambment, in a modernized text, is often the result of editorial judgment); 4) its rhyme, which, presumably as a consequence of the poet's delight in enjambment, is seldom sought after at the expense of natural syntax; 5) its diction; 6) its spelling; 7) its accidence, including "a relatively high frequency of superlatives" (Foster, 1989, 108); 8) its syntax, which demonstrates a fondness for hendiadys, the grammatical tactic of expressing an idea by using two nouns and a conjunction rather than an adjective and a substantive noun (frequent in *Hamlet*, e.g., "fantasy and trick of fame" [IV.iv.61]) as well as an unusual habit of using "who" as a relative with inanimate objects where we would expect "which"; 9) certain thematic and verbal affinities, parallels that seem, to supporters of the idea that W. S. is William Shakespeare, to be particularly striking between the *Elegy* and *Richard II* and, less surprisingly, between *Elegy* and those Shakespearean parts of the nearly contemporaneous *Henry VIII*[3]; 10) the connection of early seventeenth-century absences from college by William Peter at times when Shakespeare's company, with, presumably, Shakespeare, was in Oxford; 11) the Sonnet links with William Peter as both the "Will" of Sonnets 135 and 136 and the "young man" who figures throughout the sequence (although champions of W. S. as Shakespeare point out that the argument that William Peter is the same young man is not an essential component to the larger argument that W. S. is William Shakespeare); and 12) common sources, especially Samuel Daniel, who is, in the judgment of Foster, Shakespeare's "mentor-poet."[4]

[1]See the paired articles by Foster, "*A Funeral Elegy*: W[illiam] S[hakespeare]'s 'best-speaking witnesses,'" *PMLA* CXI (Oct. 1996), 1080–1105 and by Abrams, "W[illiam] S[hakespeare]'s *Funeral Elegy* and the Turn from the Theatrical," *SEL* XXXVI (Spring, 1996), 435–60.

[2]Stanley Wells, "In Memory of Master William Peter," *TLS* (26 Jan. 1996), 28; Richard Abrams, "In Defence of W. S.," *TLS* (9 Feb. 1996), 25–26; Wells, Letter to Editor, *TLS* (16 Feb., 1996), 17; Brian Vickers, "Whose thumbprints?" *TLS* (8 March 1996), 16–18; Abrams, Letter to the Editor, *TLS* (22 March 1996), 17; Katherine Duncan-Jones and Donald Foster, Letters to the Editor, *TLS* (29 March 1996), 17; Vickers, Letter to the Editor, *TLS* (12 April 1996), 17.

[3]Readers will find in the footnotes to the text parallels drawn by Foster and others to *Richard II* and *Henry VIII*, parallels representative of the similarities seen by proponents of Shakespeare's authorship of the *Elegy*.

[4]Parallels drawn by Foster between *A Funeral Elegy* and *The Complaint of Rosamond* are included in the notes to the poem. The editors have also added parallels from Daniel's *A Funeral Poem upon the Death of the late noble Earl of Devonshire* (1606).

In this multifaceted argument that *A Funeral Elegy* is by William Shakespeare and that the canon of his works must be expanded, there is a vexing and ironic parallel with the anti-Stratfordians, who wish to deprive Shakespeare of the entire canon. There is the same unquestioned sincerity, the same zeal and alertness to detail. In the case of the supporters of the *Elegy*, despite all the interconnecting lines of possible evidence there remains the basic recalcitrance of the poem itself. It has little of the philosophical tolerance and psychological profundity that we expect in Shakespeare's work; more importantly, it has none of the metaphoric genius that makes Shakespeare Shakespeare. Supporters of the elegy, who, in making their case, have sometimes put very great weight on the subjunctive mood, have adopted an argument that critics might call a version of the fallacy of imitative form (as used, for instance, in the defense of the dullness of Chaucer's *Parson's Tale* as deliberate on the part of the poet in order to replicate the tediousness of the sermons of a fourteenth-century priest). In this application, so the argument goes, the absence of any anticipated Shakespearean metaphoric vibrancy can be explained by Shakespeare's recognition of the role that heightened imagination had had in the murder of William Peter and how, accordingly, a poem full of vivid language belonging to the creative imagination would be a work improper in style and guilty of, at the least, faulty decorum. That is, to some supporters the absence of metaphoric language is both a stylistic and a moral choice. This argument has impressed some as an elegant solution to the problem of the prevalence of quite undistinguished verse, and others as memorable casuistry.

The current state of affairs may perhaps be best illustrated by another work of literary detection by Foster. In 1996, the publication and success of *Primary Colors* by "Anonymous," a *roman à clef* about Bill Clinton's 1992 campaign for the presidential nomination, led to speculation as to the author's identity. Professor Foster was asked to apply the same strategies he had used in his investigation of *A Funeral Elegy* in order to determine which of a number of likely candidates was the author of the novel. Foster concluded by a study of the reportorial writings of Joe Klein of *Newsweek* magazine that they corresponded to the stylistic thumbprints of *Primary Colors*, long before Mr. Klein himself admitted authorship.

Such a success may lead us to credit still more easily the notion that those ever-so-important letters "W. S." do stand for "William Shakespeare," but, for purposes of understanding the magnetic power of magical names and the role of the subjective and political, even in the case of expansion of the canon, we should also recall from another political primary the celebrated anecdote of the opponent who told the inexperienced brother of President Kennedy, "If your name were Edward Moore and not Edward Moore Kennedy, your candidacy would be a joke." Many voters thought this judgment too harsh. Some thought it fair—but history tells us who won. See the immediately following pages for *A Funeral Elegy* by W. S.

In 1989, Donald W. Foster suggested that "A Funeral Elegy" by "W.S." was possibly the work of William Shakespeare, a claim he, supported by Richard Abrams, pressed categorically in the mid 1990s, a position that sparked a great deal of controversy (see the footnotes on p. 1894 and the "Note on the Text"). Recently, however, thanks to the work of Brian Vickers and G.D. Monserrat (for specific references, see the "Note on the Text") a final verdict on the authorship of "A Funeral Elegy" has been rendered, a verdict that both Foster and Abrams have accepted (see "A Scholar Recants on His Shakespeare Discovery," *NY Times*, June 20, 2002, pp. B1 and B5): "A Funeral Elegy" is not by Shakepeare but was written by John Ford, best known as a dramatist, who also wrote a number of non-dramatic poems, all of which brim with anticipations of, or echoes from, thought and linguistic parallels all too rife in "A Funeral Elegy." It has been suggested that the tempting initials "W.S." may best be explained as those of a close friend of William Peter who employed Ford to ghost-write "A Funeral Elegy" and whose initials just happened to be "W.S."

The case of "A Funeral Elegy" will, we may safely assume, go down in the history of the many attempts to add to the canon of Shakepeare's work as one of the most stimulating and educational of all. It has much to tell us of the intertwined roles of the media, especially newspapers, of publishers in their competitive quest for completeness, of the world's too great readiness to accept computer technology as the best analytical instrument in these matters, as well as of editorial skepticism balanced with a proper sense of fair play in the market place of ideas. The application of rather traditional scholarly tools to give us new and unquestionable evidence has provided a comic ending to this story of an opinion held not all that wisely but too well.

J. J. M. Tobin

A Funeral Elegy

TO MASTER JOHN PETER

OF BOWHAY IN DEVON, ESQ.

The love I bore to your brother, and will do to his memory, hath crav'd from me this last duty of a friend; I am herein but a second to the privilege of *Truth*, who can warrant more in his behalf than I undertook to deliver. Exercise in this kind I will little affect, and am less addicted to, but there must be miracle in that labor, which, to witness my remembrance to this departed gentleman, I would not willingly undergo; yet whatsoever is here done, is done to him, and to him only. For whom, and whose sake, I will not forget to remember any friendly respects to you, or to any of those that have lov'd him for himself, and himself for his deserts.

W. S.

Since *Time*, and his predestinated end,
Abridg'd the circuit of his hopeful days,
Whiles both his *Youth* and *Virtue* did intend
The good endeavors of deserving praise,
What memorable monument can last,
Whereon to build his never-blemish'd name
But his own worth, wherein his life was grac'd,
Sith as [that] ever he maintain'd the same?
Oblivion in the darkest day to come,
When sin shall tread on merit in the dust,
Cannot rase out the lamentable tomb
Of his *Short-liv'd deserts*, but still they must,
Even in the hearts and memories of men,
Claim fit *Respect*, that they, in every limb
Rememb'ring what he was, with comfort then
May pattern out *One truly good* by him.
For he was truly good, if honest care
Of harmless conversation may commend
A life free from such stains as follies are,
Ill recompensed only in his end.
Nor can the tongue of him who lov'd him least
(If there can be minority of love
To one superlative above the rest
Of many men in steady faith) reprove
His constant temper, in the equal weight
Of *thankfulness* and *kindness*: *Truth* doth leave
Sufficient proof, he was, in every right,
As kind to *give*, as thankful to *receive*.
The curious eye, of a quick-brain'd survey,
Could scantly find a mote amidst the sun
Of his too-short'ned days, or make a prey
Of any faulty errors he had done:
Not that he was above the spleenful sense
And spite of malice, but for that he had
Warrant enough in his own innocence
Against the sting of some in nature bad.
Yet who is he so absolutely blest
That lives incompass'd in a mortal frame,
Sometime in reputation not oppress'd
By some in nothing famous but defame?
Such in the *By-path* and the *Ridge-way* lurk
That leads to ruin, in a smooth pretense
Of what they do to be a special work
Of singleness, not tending to offense;
Whose very virtues are, not to detract
Whiles hope remains of gain (base fee of slaves),
Despising, chiefly, men in fortunes wrack'd—
But death to such gives unrememb'red graves.
Now therein liv'd he happy, if to be
Free from detraction happiness it be.
His younger years gave comfortable hope
To hope for comfort in his riper youth,
Which (harvest-like) did yield again the crop

1. **his:** i.e., William Peter's.
3. **Whiles:** while.
7. **wherein . . . grac'd.** Cf. Samuel Daniel's *The Complaint of Rosamond*, 46: "Whereby thou might'st be graced."
9–12. **Oblivion . . . *deserts*.** Cf. *Richard II*, II.iii.74–75: "'tis not my meaning / To rase one title of your honor out."
11. **rase out:** remove by scraping.
12. ***Short-liv'd deserts.*** Critics who find ambiguity in the attitude the poet has toward the deceased read this expression as a perjorative description of Peter's only modestly consistent morality rather than, as genre and context would seem to suggest, a statement of the brevity of his life, a life that was one of desert.
30. **mote:** speck.
33. **spleenful:** irritable.
41. ***Ridge-way:*** a road or way along the crest of a hill.
42. **pretense:** a false claim or profession.
44. **singleness:** sincerity, integrity
50. **detraction:** calumny. Cf. Samuel Daniel's *A Funeral Poem* (B3[v]) where Daniel in an apostrophe to envy writes of the frustrations of "detraction."

Of *Education*, better'd in his truth.
Those noble twins of heaven-infused races,
Learning and *Wit*, refined in their kind,
Did jointly both in their peculiar graces
Enrich the curious temple of his mind:
Indeed a temple, in whose precious white
Sat *Reason*, by *Religion* oversway'd,
Teaching his other senses, with delight,
How *Piety* and *Zeal* should be obey'd:
Not fruitlessly in prodigal expense,
Wasting his best of time, but so content
With *Reason's golden Mean* to make defense
Against the assault of youth's encouragement;
As not the tide of this surrounding age
(When now his Father's death had freed his will)
Could make him subject to the drunken rage
Of such whose only glory is their ill.
He from the happy knowledge of the wise
Draws virtue to reprove secured fools,
And shuns the glad sleights of insnaring vice
To spend his spring of days in sacred schools.
Here gave he diet to the sick desires
That, day by day, assault the weaker man;
And with fit moderation still retires
From what doth batter virtue now and than.
But that I not intend in full discourse
To progress out his life, I could display
A *Good man* in each part exact, and force
The common voice to warrant what I say:
For if his fate and heaven had decreed
That full of days he might have liv'd to see
The grave in peace, the times that should succeed
Had been best-speaking witnesses with me,
Whose conversation, so untouch'd, did move
Respect most in itself, as who would scan
His honesty and worth, by them might prove
He was a kind, true, perfect gentleman—
Not in the outside of disgraceful folly
Courting opinion, with unfit disguise
Affecting fashions, nor addicted wholly
To unbeseeming, blushless vanities:
»But suiting so his habit and desire
»As that his *Virtue* was his best *Attire*.
Not in the waste of many idle words
Car'd he to be heard talk; nor in the float
Of fond conceit (such as this age affords),
By vain discourse, upon himself to dote;
For his becoming silence gave such grace
To his judicious parts, as what he spake
Seem'd rather answers (which the wise imbrace)
Than busy questions such as talkers make.
And though his qualities might well deserve
Just commendation, yet his furnish'd mind
Such harmony of goodness did preserve
As nature never built in better kind;
Knowing the best, and therefore not presuming
In knowing, but for that it was the best,
Ever within himself free choice resuming
Of true perfection, in a perfect breast;
So that his mind and body made an inn,
The one to lodge the other, both like fram'd
For fair conditions, guests that soonest win
Applause: in generality well fam'd,
If trim behavior, gestures mild, discreet
Endeavors, modest speech, beseeming mirth,
True friendship, active grace, persuasion sweet,
Delightful love, innated from his birth,
Acquaintance unfamiliar, carriage just,
Offenseless resolution, wish'd sobriety,
Clean-temper'd moderation, steady trust,
Unburthen'd conscience, unfeign'd piety;
If these, or all of these, knit fast in one
Can merit praise, then justly may we say,
Not any from this frailer stage is gone
Whose name is like to live a longer day—
Though not in eminent courts, or places great
For popular concourse, yet in that soil
Where he injoy'd his birth, life, death, and seat,
Which now sits mourning his untimely spoil.
And as much glory is it to be good
For private persons, in their private home,
As those descended from illustrious blood
In public view of greatness, whence they come.
Though I, rewarded with some sadder taste
Of knowing shame, by feeling it have prov'd
My country's thankless misconstruction cast
Upon my name and credit, both unlov'd
By some whose fortunes, sunk into the wane
Of Plenty and Desert, have strove to win
Justice by wrong, and sifted to imbane
My reputation with a witless sin;
Yet Time, the father of unblushing truth,

57. **peculiar:** individual.
58. **curious:** beautifully wrought.
60. **Sat.** The Q reading "Sot" is a possible dialect form found in Leicestershire and Warwickshire; *O.E.D.* cites a London provenience.
62. ***Zeal.*** Cf. *A Funeral Poem* (C2) for the earl's "fervent zeal."
63. **prodigal:** extravagantly wasteful. Cf. Luke 15: 11–32.
66. **encouragement:** incitement.
72. **secured:** careless, overconfident.
73. **insnaring:** ensnaring (variant form).
75. **diet:** regimen, a restrictive course. Cf. the analysis of Pompey Bum in *Measure for Measure,* II.i.110–12: "that such a one were past cure of the thing you wot of, unless they kept very good diet."
78. **than.** A common variant of *then,* used here (as often) to rhyme with *man.* Cf. l. 434.
80. **progress out:** follow out in detail.
82. **warrant:** guarantee as true.
95–96. These gnomic quotation marks are inserted in order to draw attention to proverbial wisdom.
95. **habit:** disposition (with play on "suiting" and "attire"). Cf. *A Funeral Poem* (B2): "But in what noble fashion he did sute / This action."
98. **float:** flood.
103. **imbrace:** embrace (variant form).
108. **As nature . . . kind.** Cf. *Richard II,* II.i.43: "built by nature for herself."
112. **Of true . . . breast.** Cf. *Richard II,* I.iii.96: "Truth hath a quiet breast."
113–16. **his mind . . . Applause.** Cf. *Richard II,* V.i.13–15: "thou most beauteous inn, / Why should hard-favor'd grief be lodg'd in thee, / When triumph is become an alehouse guest?"
118. **beseeming:** becoming, seemly.
120. **innated:** naturally endowed with.
121. **unfamiliar:** ceremonious. **carriage:** conduct, deportment.
127. **stage.** The metaphor that all the world is a drama and we are all players is an ancient one and particularly frequent in the Renaissance. Cf. *A Funeral Poem* (B3ᵛ): "The last scene of his act of life . . . / Which gives th' applause to all."
129–36. **Though . . . come.** Cf. *Henry VIII,* II.iii.19–22: "'tis better to be lowly born, / And range with humble livers in content, / Than to be perk'd up in a glist'ring grief / And wear a golden sorrow."
131. **injoy'd:** enjoyed (variant form).
132. **spoil:** destruction, ruin.
141. **wane:** decline, diminution.
143. **imbane:** poison (variant form of *embane*).

May one day lay ope malice which hath cross'd it,
And right the hopes of my indanger'd youth,
Purchasing credit in the place I lost it.
Even in which place the subject of the verse
(Unhappy matter of a mourning style,
Which now that subject's merits doth rehearse)
Had education and new being; while
By fair demeanor he had won repute
Amongst the All of all that lived there,
For that his actions did so wholly suit
With worthiness, still memorable here.
The many hours till the day of doom
Will not consume his life and hapless end,
For should he lie obscur'd without a tomb,
Time would to time his honesty commend;
Whiles parents to their children will make known,
And they to their posterity impart,
How such a man was sadly overthrown
By a hand guided by a cruel heart:
»Whereof as many as shall hear that sadness
»Will blame the one's hard fate, the other's madness;
Whiles such as do recount that tale of woe,
Told by remembrance of the wisest heads,
Will in the end conclude the matter so,
As they will all go weeping to their beds.
For when the world lies winter'd in the storms
Of fearful consummation, and lays down
Th' unsteady change of his fantastic forms,
Expecting ever to be overthrown;
When the proud height of much affected sin
Shall ripen to a head, and in that pride
End in the miseries it did begin,
And fall amidst the glory of his tide:
Then in a book where every work is writ
Shall this man's actions be reveal'd, to show
The gainful fruit of well-imployed wit,
Which paid to heaven the debt that it did owe.
Here shall be reckon'd up the constant faith,
Never untrue, where once he love profess'd;
Which is a miracle in men (one saith)
Long sought, though rarely found, and he is best,
»Who can make friendship, in those times of
change,
»Admired more for being firm than strange.
When those weak houses of our brittle flesh
Shall ruin'd be by death, our grace and strength,
Youth, memory, and shape that made us fresh
Cast down, and utterly decay'd at length;
When all shall turn to dust from whence we came
And we low level'd in a narrow grave,
What can we leave behind us but a name,
Which, by a life well led, may honor have?
Such honor, O thou youth untimely lost,
Thou didst deserve and hast; for though thy soul
Hath took her flight to a diviner coast,
Yet here on earth thy fame lives ever whole,
In every heart seal'd up, in every tongue
Fit matter to discourse, no day prevented
That pities not thy sad and sudden wrong,
Of all alike beloved and lamented.
And I here to thy memorable worth,
In this last act of friendship, sacrifice
My love to thee, which I could not set forth
In any other habit of disguise.
Although I could not learn (whiles yet thou wert)
To speak the language of a servile breath,
My truth stole from my tongue into my heart,
Which shall not thence be sund'red, but in death.
And I confess my love was too remiss
That had not made thee know how much I priz'd
thee;
But that mine error was, as yet it is,
To think love best in silence: for I siz'd thee
By what I would have been, not only ready
In telling I was thine, but, being so,
By some effect to show it. He is steady
Who seems less than he is in open show.
Since then I still reserv'd to try the worst,
Which hardest fate and time thus can lay on me:
T' inlarge my thoughts was hindered at first,
While thou hadst life; I took this task upon me,
To register with mine unhappy pen
Such duties as it owes to thy desert,
And set thee as a President to Men,
And limn thee to the world but as thou wert:
Not hir'd, as heaven can witness in my soul,
By vain conceit to please such ones as know it;
Nor servile to be lik'd, free from control,
Which, pain to many men, I do not owe it.
But here I trust I have discharged now

148. **the place:** Oxford.
158. **hapless:** luckless.
167–70. **such . . . beds.** Cf. *Richard II*, V.i.41–45: "let them tell thee tales / Of woeful ages long ago betid; / And ere thou bid good night, to quite their griefs, / Tell thou the lamentable tale of me, / And send the hearers weeping to their beds."
171. **winter'd:** blasted, deadened.
172. **consummation:** destruction.
173–74. **Th' unsteady . . . overthrown:** The fluctuating variety of its imaginary matrices awaiting always (its) final destruction. These forms are analogous to "nature's germains" in *Macbeth*, IV.i.59 and Spenser's "uncouth forms which none yet ever knew" in the Gardens of Adonis, *The Faerie Queene*, III.vi.35.2.
173. **his:** its.
178. **tide:** time.
179. **in a book.** The Book of Life, containing the names of those who shall inherit eternal life, referred to in Revelation 20:12. The less virtuous are registered in other volumes. Cf. *Richard II*, IV.i.274–75: "When I do see the very book indeed / Where all my sins are writ."
181. **well-imployed:** well-employed (variant form) **wit:** reason.
188. **strange:** cold, reserved.
194. **And we . . . grave.** Cf. *Richard II*, III.ii.140: "And lie full low, grav'd in the hollow ground."
194–96. **in a narrow grave . . . have?** Cf. *Richard II*, II.i.137–38: "Convey me . . . to my grave; / Love they to live that love and honor have."
201. **seal'd up:** closed securely.
202. **prevented:** yet to come.
209–13. **Although I . . . too remiss.** Cf. *Richard II*, III.ii.33–35, 184–85: "we are too remiss, / Whilst Bullingbrook, through our security, / Grows strong and great in substance and in power." and "[To] fight and die is death destroying death, / Where fearing dying pays death servile breath." Cf. also *Richard II*, V.v.97: "What my tongue dares not, that my heart shall say."
212. **sund'red:** severed.
216. **siz'd:** measured, estimated.
219. **effect:** result, action, deed. Cf. l. 246.
223. **inlarge:** enlarge (variant form).
225. **unhappy:** unfortunate, unworthy (conventional modesty).
227. **President:** precedent (variant form).
228. **limn:** sketch, portray.
230. **conceit:** opinion, notion.
230. **it.** The antecedent of "it," here and in line 232, is not clear.
232. **do not owe it:** have no obligation to it; I am independent of others' control.

Shakespeare's Plays in Performance

At right, C. Walter Hodges' model of the second Globe Theatre (1614), on view at Harvard University's Theatre Collection, shows the Globe stage with its pillared canopy (called "the heavens"), the two stage entry-doors, the inner stage (or "discovery space"), and the upper stage. Also shown are the three gallery levels and the forefront of the "pit" (as it was later called) where the "groundlings" stood. Compare the contemporary sketch of the Swan Theatre in Plate 8. Below, the exterior of the newly reconstructed Globe Theatre, which opened unofficially on the South Bank of the Thames in the summer of 1996, with a performance of *The Two Gentlemen of Verona*. See Appendixes A and B for further discussion of the subjects illustrated in these eight pages.

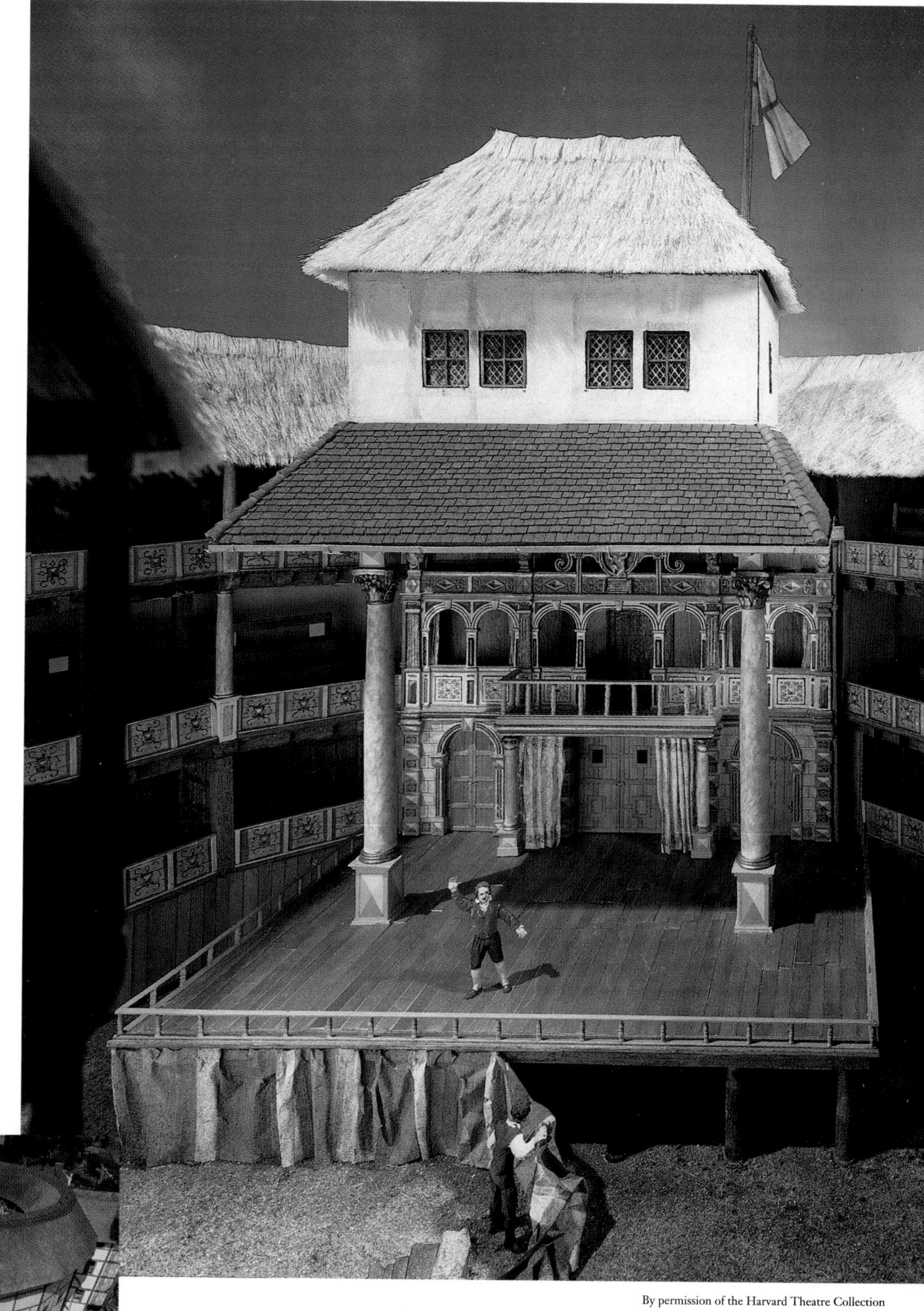

By permission of the Harvard Theatre Collection

Richard Kalina/Shakespeare's Globe

Photofest

By permission of the Harvard Theatre Collection

Photofest

Three *Hamlets* (this page). Above left, Sir Laurence Olivier's film production, 1948. Here Olivier, as Hamlet, addresses Queen Gertrude, played by Eileen Herlie, in I.ii.85–6: "But I have that within which passes show, / These but the trappings and the suits of woe." One of several nineteenth-century actresses who essayed major Shakespearean male roles, Sarah Bernhardt (above right) played Hamlet in a French stage production in 1899, at the age of 54. Here she addresses the skull of the late court jester in V.i: "Hélas, le pauvre Yorick! . . ." In the final scene of the play, she kissed the dead Gertrude's hair. At left, in Franco Zeffirelli's 1990 film version, a distraught Queen Gertrude, played by Glenn Close, embraces the Prince (Mel Gibson) in the closet scene (III.iv). This version of the play cuts out Fortinbras.

Non-English film productions (opposite page). In the German silent film of *Othello*, top left (1922), Emil Jannings as Othello meditates upon murder at the bedside of the sleeping Desdemona (Ica Lenkeffy) before strangling—not smothering—her. The production also featured a hypnotically repulsive Iago played by Werner Krauss. At top right, Grigori Kozintsev's 1970 Russian-language film of *King Lear* shows the awakened and calmed Lear (Yuri Yarvet) comforted by Cordelia (V. Shendrikova). In this profoundly moving interpretation Lear is not merely "a man more sinned against than sinning," but the representative of all sinful and suffering mankind. At right, *Throne of Blood*, Akira Kurosawa's Japanese film version of *Macbeth*, 1957. Here Washizu (Macbeth), played by Toshiro Mifune, is stunned at realizing the enormity of his deed. He sits beside the container of water that Asaji (Lady Macbeth, played by Isuzu Yamada) believes will cleanse their bloodied hands.

Museum of Modern Art Film Stills Archive

RIA-Novosti/Sovfoto

Museum of Modern Art Film Stills Archive

American Film Institute

Photofest

PLATE 35

At left, Frederick Warde's 1912 movie version of *Richard III*, considered to be the first complete American feature and believed lost until 1996. This still from I.ii catches the moment following Richard's brilliantly outrageous wooing when Lady Anne finally capitulates. In Franco Zeffirelli's 1968 film of *Romeo and Juliet* (shown below left), Lady Capulet (Natasha Parry) talks to the fourteen-year-old Juliet (Olivia Hussey) of marriage, supported by the Nurse (Pat Heywood). This memorable film values spectacle above verbal poetry. Peter Brook's stage production of *A Midsummer Night's Dream* for the Royal Shakespeare Company, 1970–71, shown at right, continues to influence Shakespearean productions in its stripping of scenery and concentration on the language. Here, Alan Howard as Oberon and John Kane as Puck, on the production's celebrated trapezes. Below, Trevor Nunn's stage production of *Macbeth* for the RSC, 1976. Here Ian McKellen as Macbeth consults the Weird Sisters. All action was constrained within the circle inscribed on the floor; actors not in a scene watched from outside the circle.

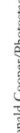

© Donald Cooper/Photostage

The Shakespeare Centre Library, Stratford-upon-Avon

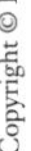

Above, a *Richard II* for television, directed by David Giles for the British Broadcasting Corporation, 1978. Derek Jacobi portrayed a vain, self-pitying, and finally courageous Richard II, and Sir John Gielgud, perhaps the leading Shakespearean actor of the last sixty years, played a moving John of Gaunt in the inaugural season of *The Shakespeare Plays* on public television. Sir Anthony Hopkins and Judi Dench played the aging and attractive lovers in a stage production of *Antony and Cleopatra* (shown at left) directed by Peter Hall at the Royal National Theatre, 1987. Transvestites in Mistress Overdone's nightclub (opposite, top) embody the decadence of Vienna in Michael Bogdanov's stage production of *Measure for Measure* at the Stratford Festival Theatre, Stratford, Ontario, 1985. Simon Bradbury, standing at center and pointing, played Pompey; Patricia Collins, seated on stool, played Overdone. At the age of 28, Kenneth Branagh revived Shakespearean film-making by attempting a role regarded as the province of Olivier. Less overtly patriotic than Olivier's, Branagh's 1989 *Henry V* (at right) reflected the disillusionment of the post-Falklands (and post-Vietnam) era.

David Cooper/Courtesy of Stratford Festival Archives

Photofest

Michal Daniel

At left, Teagle F. Bougere as an intelligent Caliban displays hostility to Patrick Stewart's Prospero for dispossessing him of his Caribbean island in this multicultural stage production of *The Tempest*, directed by George C. Wolfe for the New York Shakespeare Festival in Central Park, 1995. The final wedding scene from Kenneth Branagh's 1993 film of *Much Ado about Nothing* (below) glows with the high spirits that enthralled critics and popular audiences. The cast included Denzel Washington as Don Pedro, Branagh as Benedick, and Emma Thompson as Beatrice.

Photofest

(Fair lovely branch too soon cut off) to thee
My constant and irrefragable vow,
As, had it chanc'd, thou mightst have done to me;
But that no merit strong enough of mine
Had yielded store to thy well-abled quill
Whereby t' enroll my name, as this of thine,
Hows'e'er inriched by thy plenteous skill.
Here, then, I offer up to memory
The value of my talent (precious man),
Whereby if thou live to posterity,
Though 't be not as I would, 'tis as I can:
»In minds from whence endeavor doth proceed,
»A ready will is taken for the deed.
Yet ere I take my longest, last farewell
From thee, fair mark of sorrow, let me frame
Some ampler work of thank, wherein to tell
What more thou didst deserve than in thy name,
And free thee from the scandal of such senses
As in the rancor of unhappy spleen
Measure thy course of life, with false pretenses
Comparing by thy death what thou hast been:
»So in his mischiefs is the world accurs'd;
»It picks out matter to inform the worst,
The willful blindness that hoodwinks the eyes
Of men in-wrapped in an earthy veil
Makes them most ignorantly exercise
And yield to humor when it doth assail;
Whereby the candle, and the body's light,
Darkens the inward eyesight of the mind,
Presuming still it sees, even in the night
Of that same ignorance which makes them blind.
Hence conster they with corrupt commentaries,
Proceeding from a nature as corrupt,
The text of malice, which so often varies
As 'tis by seeming reason underpropp'd.
O! whither tends the lamentable spite
Of this world's teenful apprehension,
Which understands all things amiss, whose light
Shines not amidst the dark of their dissension?
True 'tis, this man (whiles yet he was a man)
Sooth'd not the current of besotted fashion,
Nor could digest, as some loose mimics can,
An empty sound of overweening passion,
So much to be made servant to the base
And sensual aptness of dis-union'd vices,
To purchase commendation by disgrace,
Whereto the world and heat of sin intices.
But in a safer contemplation,
Secure in what he knew, he ever chose
The ready way to commendation
By shunning all invitements strange of those
Whose illness is, the necessary praise
Must wait upon their actions; only rare
In being rare in shame, which strives to raise
Their name by doing what they do not care,
As if the free commission of their ill
Were even as boundless as their prompt desires;
Only like lords, like subjects to their will,
Which their fond dotage ever more admires.
He was not so: but in a serious awe,
Ruling the little order'd commonwealth
Of his *own self*, with honor to the law
That gave peace to his bread, bread to his health;
Which ever he maintain'd in sweet content
And pleasurable rest, wherein he joy'd
A monarchy of comfort's government,
Never until his last to be destroy'd.
For in the *Vineyard* of heaven-favor'd learning
(Where he was double-honor'd in degree)
His observation and discreet discerning
Had taught him in both fortunes to be free;
Whence now retir'd home, to a home indeed
The home of his condition and estate,
He well provided 'gainst the hand of need,

234. **Fair . . . cut off.** Cf. *Richard II*, I.ii.15–20: "branches by the Destinies cut; / . . . One flourishing branch . . . / Is hack'd down." and Marlowe's *Dr. Faustus*, the concluding epilogue.
235. **irrefragable:** unbreakable.
238. **well-abled quill.** Cf. Sonnet 85.7–8: "To every hymn that able spirit affords / In polish'd form of well-refined pen."
240. **inriched:** enriched (variant form).
243. **posterity.** Cf. *A Funeral Poem* (B2v): "A Trophy . . . that will stay / To all posterityes."
248. **mark:** target.
249. **thank:** grateful acknowledgement.
251–53. **free . . . pretenses.** Cf. *Henry VIII*, V.i.131–3: "At what ease / Might corrupt minds procure knaves as corrupt / To swear against you?" **pretenses:** allegations.
255–56. **So . . . worst.** Cf. *Henry VIII*, I.i.102, 104–06: "I advise you . . . . that you read / The Cardinal's malice and his potency / Together." Cf. also I.ii.81–85: "What we oft do best, / By sick interpreters (once weak ones) is / Not ours, or not allow'd; what worst, as oft, / Hitting a grosser quality, is cried up / For our best act," and *1 Henry IV*, V.i.139: "Detraction will not suffer it." **his:** its (the world's).
256. **inform the worst:** shape everything in the most negative light.
258. **in-wrapped:** enwrapped (variant form).
260. **humor:** whim, caprice.
263. **still:** always.
265–67. **Hence . . . varies.** Cf. *Henry VIII*, I.ii.71–75: "If I am, / Traduc'd by ignorant tongues, which neither know / My faculties nor person, yet will be / The chronicles of my doing, let me say / 'Tis but the fate of place."
265. **conster:** interpret, construe (variant form).
265–66. **with . . . corrupt.** Cf. *Henry VIII*, IV.ii.141–47: "Have follow'd both my fortunes faithfully, / Of which there is not one, I dare avow / (And now I should not lie), but will deserve, / For virtue and true beauty of the soul, / For honesty and decent carriage / A right good husband (let him be a noble), / And sure those men are happy that shall have 'em."

270. **teenful:** painful, distressing.
271. **amiss:** wrongly.
274. **Sooth'd:** flattered, approved. **besotted:** stupefying, doting.
275. **disgest:** endure, put up with (variant form of *digest*).
280. **intice:** entice (variant form).
281. **contemplation.** Here a word of five syllables, *-ion* being frequently pronounced disyllabically at this time for metrical reasons.
284. **invitements:** allurements.
284. **strange:** immoral. In seventeenth-century English, a "strange woman" was a harlot.
286–87. **only rare . . . shame:** unusual only in being extraordinarily shameful.
288. **by doing . . . care:** in not caring what they do.
290. **prompt:** ready.
291. **Only . . . will.** A seemingly gratuitous slur upon aristocrats who while lords of others are themselves subjects of their own appetite, a greater lord—and so are those with "prompt desires."
292. **fond dotage:** foolish stupidity (an intentional tautology for emphasis).
293. **serious awe:** solemn dread mingled with veneration (as of God).
294. **little.** An adjective modifying "commonwealth," rather than an adverb modifying "order'd."
294–99. **Ruling . . . comfort's government.** Cf. *Richard II*, III.iv.34–36: "Cut off the heads of too fast growing sprays, / That look too lofty in our commonwealth: / All must be even in our government."
296. **bread:** sustenance.
301. ***Vineyard* of heaven-favor'd learning:** Oxford University.
302. **double-honor'd in degree.** Peter had earned a B.A. and an M.A. at Oxford University.
304. **both fortunes:** two different kinds of life (domestic and university).
306. **condition and estate:** rank and fortune.

Whence young men sometime grow unfortunate;
His disposition, by the bonds of unity,
So fast'ned to his reason that it strove
With understanding's grave immunity
To purchase from all hearts a steady love;
Wherein not any one thing comprehends
Proportionable note of what he was,
Than that he was so constant to his friends
As he would no occasion overpass
Which might make known his unaffected care,
In all respects of trial, to unlock
His bosom and his store, which did declare
That Christ was his, and he was *Friendship's Rock*:
A Rock of *Friendship* figur'd in his name,
Fore-showing what he was, and what should be,
Most true presage; and he discharg'd the same
In every act of perfect amity—
Though in the complemental phrase of words,
He never was addicted to the vain
Of boast, such as the common breath affords;
He was in use most fast, in tongue most plain,
Nor amongst all those virtues that for ever
Adorn'd his reputation will be found
One greater than his *Faith*, which did persever,
Where once it was protested, alway sound.
Hence sprung the deadly fuel that reviv'd
The rage which wrought his end, for had he been
Slacker in love, he had been longer liv'd,
And not oppress'd by wrath's unhappy sin—
By wrath's unhappy sin, which unadvis'd
Gave death for free good will and wounds for love.
Pity it was that blood had not been priz'd
At higher rate, and reason set above
Most unjust choler, which untimely *Drew*
Destruction on itself; and most unjust,
Robb'd virtue of a follower so true
As time can boast of, both for *love* and *trust*:
»So henceforth all (great glory to his blood)
»Shall be but seconds to him, being good;
»The wicked end their honor with their sin
»In death, which only then the good begin.
Lo here a lesson by experience taught
For men whose pure simplicity hath drawn
Their trust to be betray'd by being caught
Within the snares of making truth a pawn;
Whiles it, not doubting whereinto it enters,
Without true proof and knowledge of a friend,
Sincere in singleness of heart, adventers
To give fit cause, ere love begin to end:
»His unfeign'd friendship where it least was sought,
»Him to a fatal timeless ruin brought;
Whereby the life that purity adorn'd
With real merit, by this sudden end
Is in the mouth of some, in manners scorn'd,
Made questionable, for they do intend,
According to the tenor of the saw
Mistook (if not observ'd, writ long ago
When men were only led by *Reason's* law),
That *Such as is the end, the life proves so.*
Thus *He*, who to the universal lapse
Gave sweet redemption, off'ring up his blood
To conquer death by death, and loose the traps
Of Hell, even in the triumph that it stood:
He thus, for that his guiltless life was spilt
By death, which was made subject to the curse,
Might in like manner be reprov'd of guilt
In his pure life, for that his end was worse.
But O far be it, our unholy lips
Should so profane the Deity above
As thereby to ordain revenging whips
Against the day of *Judgment* and of *Love*;
The hand that lends us honor in our days
May shorten when it please, and justly take
Our honor from us many sundry ways,
As best becomes that wisdom did us make.
The second brother, who was next begot
Of all that ever were begotten yet,
Was by a hand in vengeance rude and hot
Sent innocent to be in heaven set;
Whose fame the Angels in melodious quires
Still witness to the world; then why should he,
Well-profited in excellent desires,
Be more rebuk'd, who had like destiny?

311. **With . . . grave immunity:** either (1) together with judgment's sober freedom (from error) or (2) against judgment's oppressive license (toward error).
314. **Proportionable note:** commensurate recognition.
317. **unaffected:** genuine, sincere.
318. **all . . . trial:** all aspects relative to temptation or testing.
319. **store:** treasury of good.
320. **That Christ was his.** An oddly pious phrasing from the usually religiously inscrutable Shakespeare. "Rock" is to be understood after "his"; cf. 1 Corinthians 10:4.
321. **Rock . . . name.** Cf. Matthew 16:18: "And I say also unto thee, that thou art Peter [Gk. *Petros*] and upon this rocke [Gk. *petra*] I will build my Church: and the gates of hell shall not prevaile against it" (AV).
323. **presage:** portent.
325. **complemental:** (1) self-congratulatory; (2) complimentary.
326–7. **vain / Of boast:** vanity of bragging, or, taking "vain" as a contemporary spelling of "vein," habit of bragging.
327. **common breath:** vulgar speech.
328. **fast:** steadfast.
331. **persever:** continue constant, persevere (variant form).
332. **protested:** affirmed, declared.
332. **alway sound:** ever sincere.
338. **free:** unconditional.
341. ***Drew.*** Pun on the family name of William Peter's murderer, Edward Drew.
348. **only . . . begin:** i.e., the righteous only start to achieve their highest honor when they die.
352. **making truth a pawn:** giving a pledge of truth (to a person unworthy of it, i.e., Edward Drew).
353–54. **not doubting . . . friend:** truth without question, freely, gives itself to someone without asking for proof that he or she is indeed a friend.
355. **adventers:** adventures (variant form).
357. **sought:** asked for or, perhaps, looked for.
361. **manners scorn'd:** conduct (which is) contemned.
363. **tenor:** meaning. **saw:** adage. Cf. Tilley, E116.
364. **if not observ'd:** if (even then) not followed.
365. **only . . . *Reason's* law:** that is, without benefit of the insights of Faith.
367–74. Compares Christ and William Peter as men whose lives ended bloodily but whose deaths are no indictment of their morally unblemished lives.
367. **universal lapse:** i.e., original sin, which was inherited by all human beings as a result of Adam's sin.
373. **reprov'd of guilt:** accused of sin.
374. **for that:** because.
378. **Against:** in anticipation of. ***of Love:*** (the day) of entry into God's love (= heaven).
379. **The hand:** i.e., of God.
383. **The second brother:** Abel, in Genesis 4:8.
386–98. This heavenly choir and the saints washed white in the blood of the lamb are rather pre-Miltonic.
387. **quires:** choirs.
390. **had like destiny.** He like Abel was murdered.

Those Saints before the everlasting throne,
Who sit with crowns of glory on their heads,
Wash'd white in blood, from earth hence have not gone
All to their joys in quiet on their beds,
But tasted of the sour-bitter scourge
Of torture and affliction ere they gained
Those blessings which their sufferance did urge,
Whereby the grace fore-promis'd they attained.
Let then the false suggestions of the froward,
Building large castles in the empty air,
By suppositions fond and thoughts untoward
(Issues of discontent and sick despair),
Rebound gross arguments upon their heart
That may disprove their malice, and confound
Uncivil loose opinions, which insert
Their souls into the roll that doth unsound
Betraying policies, and show their brains,
Unto their shame, ridiculous; whose scope
Is envy, whose endeavors fruitless pains,
In nothing surely prosperous, but hope;
And that same hope, so lame, so unprevailing,
It buries self-conceit in weak opinion;
Which being cross'd, gives matter of bewailing
Their vain designs, on whom want hath dominion.
Such, and of such condition, may devise
Which way to wound with defamation's spirit
(Close-lurking whispers' hidden forgeries)
His taintless goodness, his desertful merit.
But whiles the minds of men can judge sincerely,
Upon assured knowledge, his repute
And estimation shall be rumor'd clearly
In equal worth: Time shall to time renew 't.
The Grave, that in his ever-empty womb
For ever closes up the unrespected,
Who, when they die, die all, shall not intomb
His pleading best perfections as neglected.
They to his notice in succeeding years
Shall speak for him when he shall lie below;
When nothing but his memory appears
Of what he was, then shall his virtues grow.
His being but a private man in rank
(And yet not rank'd beneath a gentleman)
Shall not abridge the commendable thank
Which wise posterity shall give him than;
For *Nature*, and his therein happy *Fate*,
Ordain'd that by his quality of mind
T' ennoble that best part, although his state
Were to a lower blessedness confin'd.
Blood, pomp, state, honor, glory, and command,
Without fit ornaments of disposition,
Are in themselves but heathenish and profane,
And much more peaceful is a mean condition,
Which, underneath the roof of safe content,
Feeds on the bread of rest, and takes delight
To look upon the labors it hath spent
For its own sustenance, both day and night;
Whiles others, plotting which way to be great,
How to augment their portion and ambition,
Do toil their giddy brains, and ever sweat
For popular applause and power's commission.
But one in honors, like a seeled dove,
Whose inward eyes are dimm'd with dignity,
Does think most safety doth remain above,
And seeks to be secure by mounting high:
»Whence, when he falls, who did erewhile aspire,
»Falls deeper down, for that he climbed higher.
Now men who in a lower region live
Exempt from danger of authority
Have fittest times in *Reason's rules* to thrive,
Not vex'd with envy of priority:
»And those are much more noble in the mind
»Than many that have nobleness by kind.
Birth, blood, and ancestors are none of ours,
Nor can we make a proper challenge to them,
But virtues and perfections in our powers
Proceed most truly from us, if we do them.
Respective titles or a gracious style,
With all what men in eminence possess,
Are, without ornaments to praise them, vile:
The beauty of the mind is nobleness,
And such as have that beauty well deserve
Eternal characters, that after death

393. **Wash'd white in blood.** Cf. Revelation 7:14.
395. **sour-bitter scourge.** An echo of Christ's passion. Cf. Matthew 27:26, 34.
395–400. **the . . . air.** Cf. *The Complaint of Rosamond*, 265–66: "beauty's scourge, hell to the fair, / To leave the sweet, for castles in the air."
397. **sufferance did urge:** suffering did recommend or claim.
399. **froward:** perverse.
401. **fond . . . untoward:** foolish . . . unruly.
405. **insert:** enter.
406–07. **Their souls . . . policies:** their (own) souls into the list which does (reveal) treacherous actions (as) wicked.
408. **scope:** outlook.
412. **self-conceit . . . opinion:** self-understanding in poor judgment.
413. **Which . . . bewailing.** Cf. *The Complaint of Rosamond*, 32: "And being dead, gives matter to bewail."
423–24. **The Grave . . . unrespected.** Cf. *Richard II*, II.i.82–83: "a grave, / Whose hollow womb inherits nought but bones."
425–26. **shall not . . . neglected:** i.e., his best perfections that plead on his behalf shall not be buried as if they were disregarded.
433. **commendable thank:** grateful approval.
435–38. **For *Nature* . . . confin'd.** Virtue is not a matter of aristocratic birth.
435. ***Fate:*** the determined course of his life (i.e., up to his death).
437. **state:** social rank.
440. **fit . . . disposition:** appropriate qualities of character.
441. **in themselves . . . profane.** Foster emends "profane" to "profan'd" in order to make a rhyme with "command" (l. 439), but "in themselves" calls for an adjective to match "heathenish" because the above attributes ("Blood, pomp," etc.) are what they are in their very nature (i.e., "in themselves") and have not been made so by external agency. Occasionally such imperfect rhymes may be found elsewhere in Elizabethan-Jacobean verse.
442. **mean:** middle-rank.
444. **Feeds . . . rest.** Cf. *Richard II*, III.i.21: "Eating the bitter bread of banishment."
450. **commission:** active authority.
451. **seeled dove:** pigeon with eyelids stitched closed. *O.E.D.* cites Sidney's *Arcadia*, "Now she brought them to see a sealed Dove, who the blinder she was, the higher she strove."
452. **dignity:** (concern for) status.
454–56. **seeks . . . higher.** Cf. *Henry VIII*, III.ii.368–72: "There is, betwixt that smile we would aspire to, / That sweet aspect of princes, and their ruin, / More pangs and fears than wars or women have; / And when he falls, he falls like Lucifer, / Never to hope again."
460. **priority:** precedence.
462. **kind:** relation, ancestry.
464. **proper challenge:** fitting claim.
466. **do them:** act on them.
467. **Respective:** worthy of respect.
467. **style:** manner.
469. **ornaments:** virtues.
472. **Eternal characters:** everlasting words engraved on a memorial.

Remembrance of their worth we may preserve
So that their glory die not with their breath.
Else what avails it in a goodly strife
Upon this face of earth here to contend,
The good t' exceed the wicked in their life,
Should both be like obscured in their end?
Until which end, there is none rightly can
Be termed happy, since the happiness
Depends upon the *goodness* of the man,
Which afterwards his praises will express.
Look hither then, you that enjoy the youth
Of your best days, and see how unexpected
Death can betray your jollity to ruth
When death you think is least to be respected!
The person of this model here set out
Had all that youth and happy days could give him,
Yet could not all encompass him about
Against th' assault of *Death*, who to relieve him
Strook home but to the frail and mortal parts
Of his humanity, but could not touch
His flourishing and fair long-liv'd deserts,
Above *Fate's* reach, his singleness was such;
So that he dies but once, but doubly lives,
Once in his proper *self*, then in his *name*;
Predestinated *Time*, who all deprives,
Could never yet deprive him of the same.
And had the *Genius* which attended on him
Been possibilited to keep him safe
Against the rigor that hath overgone him,
He had been to the public use a staff,
Leading by his example in the path
Which guides to doing well, wherein so few
The proneness of this age to error hath
Informed rightly in the courses true.
As then the loss of one, whose inclination
Strove to win love in general, is sad,
So specially his friends, in soft compassion,
Do feel the greatest loss they could have had.
Amongst them all, she, who those nine of years
Liv'd fellow to his counsels and his bed,
Hath the most share in loss: for I in hers
Feel what distemperature this chance hath bred.
The chaste embracements of conjugal love,
Who in a mutual harmony concent,
Are so impatient of a strange remove
As meager *Death* itself seems to lament,
And weep upon those cheeks which nature fram'd
To be delightful orbs in whom the force
Of lively sweetness plays, so that asham'd
Death often pities his unkind divorce.
Such was the separation here constrain'd
(Well-worthy to be term'd a *rudeness* rather),
For in his life his love was so unfeign'd
As he was both an husband and a father:
The one in firm affection, and the other
In careful providence, which ever strove
With joint assistance to grace one another
With every helpful furtherance of love.
But since the sum of all that can be said
Can be but said that *He was good*, which wholly
Includes all excellence can be display'd
In praise of virtue and reproach of folly:
  His due deserts, this sentence on him gives,
  He died in life, yet in his death he lives.
Now runs the method of this doleful song,
In accents brief, to thee, *O thou deceas'd!*
To whom those pains do only all belong
As witnesses I did not love thee least.
For could my worthless brain find out but how
To raise thee from the sepulchre of dust,
Undoubtedly thou shouldst have partage now
Of life with me; and heaven be counted just
If to a supplicating soul it would
Give life anew, by giving life again
Where life is miss'd; whereby discomfort should
Right his old griefs, and former joys retain,
Which now with thee are leapt into thy tomb
And buried in that hollow vault of woe,
Expecting yet a more severer doom
Than Time's strict flinty hand will let 'em know.
And now if I have level'd mine account,
And reckon'd up in a true measur'd score
Those perfect graces which were ever wont
To wait on thee alive, I ask no more,
But shall hereafter in a poor content
Immure those imputations I sustain,

475–78. **Else . . . end.** Cf. *Lycidas*, ll. 64–69.
479–80. **Until . . . happy.** This is a Christianized version of the classical adage that no man is to be counted happy until he is dead.
483–85. **Look hither . . . youth . . . ruth.** Cf. Milton, *Lycidas*, 163–64: "Look homeward angel now, and melt with ruth. / And O ye dolphins, waft the helpless youth."
485. **ruth:** sorrow.
486. **When . . . respected.** Cf. *The Complaint of Rosamond*, 558: "Forth breaks reproach when we least think thereon."
486. **respected:** concerned about.
489–90. **Yet . . . *Death*.** Cf. *The Complaint of Rosamond*, 346–47: "This dreadful danger, which thou seest is laid, / Wherein thy shame doth compass thee about."
491. **Strook:** struck (variant form).
494. **singleness:** uniqueness.
496. **proper:** own.
497. **Predestinated:** appointed.
499. ***Genius*:** guardian spirit. Cf. *A Funeral Poem* (B1[v]): "England's *Genius*."
500. **possibilited:** enabled. Not recorded in *O.E.D.*
505. **proneness:** inclination.
511. **nine.** As William Peter married in January of 1609, this may be a misprint for "three," or an instance of ignorance on the part of W. S., or, as some would argue, in spite of the claims of genre and decorum, evidence that "she" is someone other than the living widow Margaret Peter.
514. **distemperature:** disorder (psychological).
516. **concent:** "sing together" (i.e., agree).
517. **strange remove:** unexpected separation.
518. **meager:** lean.
522. **pities . . . divorce:** feels sorry for his unnatural separating of the couple.
524. ***rudeness*:** violence.
525. **unfeign'd:** sincere.
528. **providence:** provision for the future.
536. ***He . . . lives*.** A standard expression of one of the central paradoxes of Christianity.
537. **method:** arrangement.
539. **pains:** (poetic) efforts.
543. **partage:** a portion or share.
550. **And buried . . . woe.** Cf. *Richard II*, III.ii.140: "And lie full low, grav'd in the hollow ground."
551. **more severer:** Double comparatives are not uncommon in Elizabethan usage. **doom:** judgment. Cf. *Richard II*, I.iii.148: "for thee remains a heavier doom."
553. **level'd:** settled. **account:** Cf. *A Funeral Poem* (C2): "And thus Great [Patrone] of my muse have I / Paid thee my vowes, and fairely cleer'd th' accounts."
558. **Immure:** wall up. **imputations:** accusations. **sustain:** Cf. *A Funeral Poem* (A[v]): "The benefite thou gav'st me to sustaine / My humble life."

Learning my days of youth so to prevent
As not to be cast down by them again:
Only those hopes which *Fate* denies to grant
In full possession to a captive heart,
Who, if it were in plenty, still would want
Before it may enjoy his better part;
From which detain'd, and banish'd in th' exile
Of dim misfortune, has none other prop
Whereon to lean and rest itself the while
But the weak comfort of the hapless, *Hope*;
And *Hope* must in despite of fearful change
Play in the strongest closet of my breast,
Although perhaps I ignorantly range,
And court opinion in my deep'st unrest.
But whither doth the stream of my mischance
Drive me beyond myself? Fast friend, soon lost,
Long may thy worthiness thy name advance
Amongst the virtuous and deserving most,
  Who herein hast forever happy prov'd:
  In *life* thou liv'dst, in *death* thou died'st *belov'd.*

FINIS.

563. **want:** desire.
564. **part:** lot (being in heaven).
569. **in . . . fearful change.** Cf. *Richard II*, II.iv.11: "prophets whisper fearful change."
570. **closet:** inner chamber; treasure chest.
573–74. **But . . . friend.** Cf. *Henry VIII*, I.i.141–3: "We may outrun / By violent swiftness that which we run at, / And lose by overrunning."

NOTE ON THE TEXT

Thomas Thorpe entered *A Funerall Elegye* on the Stationers' Register on 13 February 1612, barely nineteen days after the murder of William Peter on 25 January 1612. As in his edition of Shakespeare's Sonnets (1609), Thorpe employed George Eld as printer and published the *Elegy* sometime later in 1612. Of this edition only two copies are known to be extant, one in the Bodleian Library, the second in the Balliol College Library. Donald Foster records, from a collation of these two copies, four press variants, the corrected state appearing in the Balliol copy: in the inner forme of sig. C, l. 421 (C1^v) "rumor'd" for "rumor"; l. 469 (C2) "without" for "withour"; l. 552 (C3^v) "'em" for "'m"; and the auxiliary "haue" (l. 553 [C3^v]), which had been omitted from the Bodleian copy.

Substantively, Eld's text is generally sound, but the punctuation, in great part most probably the work of the compositor(s), is heavy and not infrequently misleading or simply wrong. Since, as Foster says, the volume was printed "from copy apparently supplied by the author" (i.e., authorial copy), it is important to present a conservative text that preserves so far as possible its authorial "flavor." The present text, therefore, retains the author's italics and gnomic quotation marks, as well as some apparently characteristic Elizabethan variant spelling forms (e.g., "incompassed"; "insnaring"; "injoy'd"; "than" for "then," rhyming with "man"; "president" for "precedent"; "imbane"; "imbrace").

For further information, see: Donald W. Foster, *Elegy by W. S.: A Study in Attribution* (University of Delaware Press, 1989) [referred to in the Textual Notes as *Foster*[1]], and "*A Funeral Elegy:* W[illiam] S[hakesspeare]]'s 'Best-Speaking Witness'," *PMLA*, CXI (1996), 1080–1105 [referred to in the Textual Notes as *Foster*[2]]; Brian Vickers, *Counterfeiting Shakespeare: Evidence, Authorship, and John Ford's "Funerall Elegye"* (Cambridge, 2002); G.D. Monserrat, "'A Funeral Elegy:" Ford, W.S., and Shakespeare," *RES*, New Series, LIII, Number 210 (2002), 186–203.

TEXTUAL NOTES

Title: **A FVNERALL / Elegye / *In memory of the late Vertuous / Maister* William Peeter / of Whipton neere / Excester. / *By W. S.*** *Q (title-page); A Funerall Elegie. Q (drop-title)*
[All lemmata in the following textual notes are taken from *Foster*[2], unless assigned to the present editor.]
Dedication: 6 any] my *ed. conj.*
6 **never-blemish'd name**] neuer blemisht name? *Q*
7 **grac'd,**] *ed.;* grac't? *Q;* grac'd—*Foster*
8 **that**] *Foster (after ed.);* it *Q*
8 **same?**] same. *Q*
12 ***deserts,***] *ed.; desert's*: *Q;* deserts; *Foster*
29 **quick-brain'd**] quick brain'd *Q*
38 **frame,**] frame? *Q*
39 **oppress'd**] opprest? *Q*
41 ***Ridge-way***] *Ridg-way Q;* ridgway *Foster*[1] Ridgeway *Foster*[2]
44 **offense;**] offence. *Q*
45 **are, not to detract**] are not to detract, *Q*
47 **wrack'd—**] wrackt, *Q*
49–50 **Now . . . be.**] *indented, Foster*
55 **heaven-infused**] heaven infused *Q*
56 **kind,**] *ed.;* kind: *Q;* kind *Foster*
60 **Sat**] Sot *Q*
62 **obey'd:**] *ed.;* obey'd. *Q;* obey'd— *Foster*
78 **than**] then *Foster*
91–2 **folly / Courting opinion, . . . disguise**] *ed.;* folly / Courting Opinion, . . . disguise; *Q;* folly, / Courting opinion . . . disguise, *Foster*
90 **gentleman—**] gentleman. *Q*
116 **Applause:**] *ed.;* Applause, *Q;* Applause; *Foster*
128 **day—**] day. *Q*
147 **indanger'd**] *ed.;* indangered *Q;* endangered *Foster*
150 **style,**] *ed. (after Foster);* stile) *Q*
151 **rehearse)**] rehearse, *Q*
164 **heart:**] *ed.;* heart. *Q, Foster*
182 **paid**] payed *Q*
183 **reckon'd**] reckoned *Q*
194 **low level'd**] low-level'd *Foster*
195 **name,**] name? *Q*
200 **whole,**] whole. *Q*
228 **wert:**] *ed.;* wert. *Q;* wert— *Foster*
233 **Which, pain . . . men,**] Which paine . . . men *Q*
236 **me,**] *ed.;* mee. *Q;* me— *Foster*
240 **Hows'e'er**] *ed.;* How s'ere *Q, Foster*
253 **life, with . . . pretenses**] life (with . . . pretenses) *Q*
258 **in-wrapped**] enwrapped *Foster*
269 **whither**] whether *Q*
270 **apprehension,**] apprehension? *Q*
284 **invitements**] inuitemens *Q*
285 **the**] that *ed. conj.*
294 **order'd**] *ed.;* ordered *Q, Foster*
301 **heaven-favor'd**] *ed.;* heauen-fauoured *Q, Foster*
305 **home, . . . indeed**] home; . . . indeed; *Q*
308 **young men**] yong-men *Q*
321 **figur'd**] *ed.;* figured *Q, Foster*
323 **presage;**] presage, *Q*
327 **affords;**] affoords, *Q*
336 **sin—**] sinne. *Q*
338 **love.**] loue *Q*
346 **him,**] him *Q*
363–65 **According . . . Mistook (if . . . ago . . . law),**] (According . . . Mistooke, if . . . agoe) . . . law, *Q*
366 **That *Such* . . . *so***] *ed.* (*after Foster*); *That such . . . so. Q;* That "Such . . . so." *Foster*
386 **set;**] *ed.;* set. *Q;* set— *Foster*
406 **roll**] roule *Q*
406 **unsound**] unfound *ed. conj.*
410 **hope;**] *ed.;* hope. *Q;* hope— *Foster*
412 **self-conceit**] selfe conceit *Q*
417 **Close-lurking**] Close lurking *Q*
417 **whispers'**] *ed.;* whispers *Q;* whisper's *Foster;* whispers, *ed. conj.*

422 **worth:**] *ed.;* worth, *Q;* worth— *Foster*
423 **Grave,**] grave, *Foster*[1]; Grave— *Foster*[2]
423 **ever-empty**] euer empty *Q*
425 **all,**] *Foster*[1]; all; *Q;* all— *Foster*[2]
435 **than**] then *Foster*
441 **profane**] *ed.;* prophane *Q;* profan'd *Foster*
477 **good**] goood *Q*
486 **respected!**] respected?
489 **all encompass**] all-encompass *Foster*
490 ***Death***] *ed.;* death *Q, Foster*
494 ***Fate's***] *ed.;* fates *Q;* fate's *Foster*
494 **such;**] *ed.;* such. *Q;* such— *Foster*
516 **concent**] *ed.;* consent *Q, Foster*
518 ***Death***] *ed.;* Death *Q;* death *Foster*
518 **lament,**] lament. *Q*
524 **term'd**] termed *Q, Foster*[2]
540 **witnesses**] witnesles *Q*
544 **just**] iust: *Q*
549 **leapt**] leap'd *Foster*[2]
551 ***Fate***] *ed.;* fate *Q, Foster*
552 **Time's**] *ed.;* times *Q;* time's *Foster*
554 **measur'd**] *ed.;* measured *Q, Foster*
557–60 **But . . . again;**] (But . . . again)— *Foster*
568 **hapless,**] haplesse *Q*
573 **whither**] *ed.;* whether *Q, Foster*
574 **myself? Fast**] *ed.;* my selfe: fast *Q;* myself, fast *Foster*

Appendix A

Shakespeare's Plays in Performance

From 1660 to 1971

Charles H. Shattuck

When King Charles II returned from exile in 1660, the theatrical prohibition imposed by the Puritans eighteen years earlier came to an end. In August of that year the King assigned monopolist control of theatrical activity to two courtiers, Thomas Killigrew and Sir William Davenant.

Killigrew (1612–83), a close companion to the King ("a merry droll," Samuel Pepys called him), was to direct the first company, called the King's Men, and he claimed performance rights to the then most attractive pre-Commonwealth plays. These included Ben Jonson's plays, Beaumont and Fletcher's, and James Shirley's, but very few of Shakespeare's, for Shakespeare had long since dropped out of fashion on account of his antiquated manners, morals, language, and wit. Davenant (1606–68), who for various reasons stood in the suburbs of the King's favor, was assigned the second company, called the Duke's Men, and of the very few plays to which he got performance rights, nine were by Shakespeare: *The Tempest*, *Measure for Measure*, *Much Ado about Nothing*, *Twelfth Night*, *Henry VIII*, *Romeo and Juliet*, *King Lear*, *Macbeth*, and *Hamlet*.

THE RESTORATION PLAYHOUSE: SCENES AND MACHINES

In taking on so heavy a burden of Shakespeare, Davenant may have been moved by filial piety, for, as everybody knew, he was Shakespeare's godson, and gossip proclaimed an even nearer relationship. In any case, he did not intend merely to revive these plays; he would "reforme" them and make them "fitt"—that is, would trim, augment, rewrite, and embellish them in whatever ways were necessary to bring them up to sophisticated modern taste. To begin with, however, he had another winning trick to play—a fundamental reformation of the physical stage.

As a provider of masques at the court of Charles I, he had become an expert in stage scenery, and in this new age he was determined to introduce the delights of scenery to the general public. So while his company marked time in temporary quarters, he busied himself equipping a tennis court building in Lincoln's Inn Fields with a kind of stage hitherto unknown in England. It was not actually a new conception, but a patching together of two old ones. It retained the broad open platform with side entering doors which actors had been accustomed to in the playhouses of Elizabethan times. But behind this platform, where formerly there had stood the tiring-house wall with its shallow inner stages or discovery places, Davenant substituted the scene house of the Stuart masques—a sizable room, framed by a proscenium arch, in which moveable painted scenery and stage machines could be displayed. From Davenant's day until very recently, all our theatres have pretty much followed Davenant's pattern, so that Arthur Nethercot in his biography of Davenant has called this first theatre in Lincoln's Inn Fields "the most influential single playhouse in English stage history."

The basic system for displaying and changing scenery in Davenant's theatre (and for two centuries after his time) was the wing-and-shutter system. At either side of the stage, and spaced throughout its depth, there lay on the floor, parallel to the curtain line, sets of grooves in which flat scenic pieces stood and moved onstage or offstage. The floor grooves were matched by overhead grooves which held the scenic pieces erect. Each groove contained three or four "cuts" to accommodate so many scenic pieces. If the scene to be represented was, for instance, a Chamber, the far wall of the Chamber, with its windows, draperies, pictures, and other decorations, would be painted upon a pair of broad flats (shutters) standing in one of the upstage grooves, say the fourth, and meeting at centre. The side walls of the Chamber would be painted in perspective on pairs of narrow flats (wings) standing at the sides of the stage in the third, second, and first grooves. The spectator sitting along the centre axis of the auditorium (the royal box at that time was at centre) would receive a perfect illusion of the three sides of a room. Suppose, then, the scene to follow was a Forest. While the Chamber scene was playing, shutters and wings representing the Forest would have been placed in the cuts next behind the Chamber pieces. When the moment for scene change came, the prompter blew a tiny whistle and eight stage hands (called "carpenters") instantly drew off the six Chamber wings and two Chamber shutters. In the wink of an eye, and as if by magic, the spectators were transported from Chamber to Forest.

Davenant's vision of what scenery ought to be was grandiose, and his theatre in Lincoln's Inn Fields was too small to accommodate it. In 1671, three years after his death, his heirs built a theatre in Dorset Garden which was twice as large—its scene house measuring fifty feet from proscenium arch to back wall, its scenic pieces standing nearly thirty feet tall. Killigrew followed Davenant's lead, of course: his Theatre Royal in Drury Lane—built in 1663, burned and rebuilt in 1674—was equipped for scenes.

What effect, then, did scenery have upon the staging of Shakespeare? On some plays not much. When Pepys first saw *Hamlet* "done with scenes very well" it did not occur to him to describe those scenes. *Hamlet*, *Othello*, *Twelfth Night*, *The Merry Wives of Windsor*—and, of course, the new comedies of Etherege and his followers—could be backed by indoor and outdoor scenes which made their necessary statements without drawing attention from the acting or the play. But those plays which could be forced into the condition of masque or opera spurred Davenant and his followers to astonishing scenic achievements. In his version of *Macbeth*, the Witches danced and flew, the cauldron and the cave sank into the earth, and Hecate was carried aloft in a cloud machine. *The Tempest* opened with a mighty storm: just off a rocky coast a ship tossed about in a "Tempestuous Sea in perpetual agitation"; horrid spirits filled the sky and flew down among the sailors; as the ship sank amid lightning and thunderclaps, a shower of fire fell upon it. An opera called *The Fairy Queen*, concocted out of *A Midsummer Night's Dream*, was the nine days' wonder of 1692. Four times in the course of it the stage was transformed into a wondrous setting for a masque-like entertainment—a Fairy Land, an Enchanted Lake, a Garden of Fountains, a Chinese Garden. Late in the play the goddess Juno arrived to bless the bridal beds, floating down in a car drawn by peacocks. While music played, the peacocks spread their tails, filling the whole width of the stage and concealing a scene change going on behind them.

An occasional folly like this *Fairy Queen* (it cost £3000 to produce) would matter little, but what has mattered very much to the after-history of Shakespeare production is the simple fact that a scene house was attached to the dramatic stage. Once it stood there it had to be filled—not merely a temptation but a downright compulsion to scenic elaboration. Eventually producers would actually delete Shakespeare's finest descriptive verses whenever they thought that their scene painters could show the thing better. Eventually the scene house swallowed up the great platform itself, pulling the actors back behind the arch, subordinating them to the composition of the "picture." Richard Flecknoe perceived the danger of the course at once. "That which makes our Stage the better," he wrote in 1664, "makes our Plays the worse perhaps, they striving now to make them more for sight, than hearing." Not until our own century have we begun to escape from Davenant's delusion. As William Poel spent a lifetime preaching and as Tyrone Guthrie demonstrated at the Canadian Stratford, Shakespeare's plays need little more than to be well acted in an open space: they *can* stand alone.

SHAKESPEARE IMPROVED

Davenant was poet and playwright as well as builder and decorator, with thoroughly up-to-date ideas of what a play might contain, how its parts should be set in balance, how to unify its tone, how to drive home its lessons, and what language it should be cast in. His triumphant assaults upon *Macbeth* and *The Tempest* educated a host of followers in how to "reforme and make fitt" some two dozen more of Shakespeare's plays.

In producing *Macbeth* he swept out a raft of minor characters, cancelled the Porter's vulgar maunderings, and expanded the matter of the Witches to the proportions of an anti-masque. His most artful contribution was to invent new actions which meaningfully parallel those given by Shakespeare. The ghost of Banquo, which haunts Macbeth when his courage is lowest, is balanced by the ghost of Duncan, which haunts Lady Macbeth when she is slipping toward nightmare and death. Lady Macduff becomes Davenant's spokesman of moral tidings, and through several wholly new scenes she is built up into an opposite number to wicked Lady Macbeth.

His improvements upon the language of the play, though ruinous to its poetic vigor, were quite in tune with the best efforts of the age to free English from "luxury and redundance," to eliminate metaphor in the interests of scientific exactitude, and to establish principles of appropriateness and decorum. Tragic heroes, since they dwelt in the highest social strata, could not utter anything "low." Thus Davenant's King Duncan does not cry out, "What bloody man is that?" but "What aged man is that?" For the rude wording of "Screw your courage to the sticking place," his Lady Macbeth substitutes "Bring your courage to the fatal place." Macbeth does not call his lady "dearest chuck," but "my dear." When in the final act Shakespeare's Macbeth rages at a frightened messenger, "The devil damn thee black, thou cream-fac'd loon! / Where got'st thou that goose-look?", Davenant's Macbeth, mindful of his dignity, can muster only, "Now Friend, what means thy change of Countenance?"

Davenant's revision of *The Tempest*, in which John Dryden collaborated, employs the same system of parallelism and balance which had netted two ghosts and two heroines in *Macbeth*. As counterpart to Shakespeare's woman who has never seen a man (Miranda), he invented a man who has never seen a woman (Hippolito). To provide a mate for Hippolito, he gave Miranda a sister, called Dorinda. With Ferdinand to make up a fourth, these innocents are shown experiencing love between the sexes as if in a playful version of the Garden of Eden.

For the last hundred years it has been the fashion to denounce this *Tempest* in severest terms—"a licentious farce," "the worst perversion of Shakespeare in the two-century history of such atrocities"—but this is Bardolatry gone mad. The Dryden-Davenant *Tempest* is simply an ingenious Augustan romp over Shakespearean materials—"elegant frivolity," as one London critic called it on the occasion of the Old Vic revival in 1959. One can no more quarrel with it than with the romance of *Daphnis and Chloe*, and we can well understand Dryden's testimony that the idea "so pleas'd me, that I never writ anything with more delight."

Few of the other improved versions have much to recommend them, although we can usually understand why they pleased the audiences of their day. Dryden's *Troilus and Cressida* genuinely improves the sequence of scenes and clears up that portion of the dialogue (especially the verbal roundabouts of the Greek generals) which seemed to Dryden "so pester'd with Figurative expressions that it is as affected as it is obscure." But in the long run he spoiled the play by "purifying" Cressida: she becomes a mere romantic heroine, blameless, a pitiful victim of circumstance. Thomas Shadwell reworked *Timon of Athens* and "made it into a play" by adding women and a love story, but in doing so he undercut Timon's credibility as a misanthrope. Thomas Otway, with typical Augustan insensitivity to sentiment, converted *Romeo and Juliet* into *The Fall of Caius Marius*, removing the love story from sunny warm Verona to classical cold Rome, and subordinating it to an overplot of political factionalism. The two most notorious, because longest-lived, improvements were Nahum Tate's *King Lear* and Colley Cibber's *Richard III*. Tate suppressed Lear's Fool, inserted a silly love story between Cordelia and Edgar, embroidered upon Edmund's sexual misdoings, and imposed a happy ending. His rewriting of the dialogue was mindless. Yet this version, variously modified, held the stage in England until Macready displaced it in 1838, and in America it lasted a generation longer. Cibber's *Richard III* persisted on stages well into the twentieth century. By eliminating Margaret, Clarence, and several lesser figures, by heightening Richard's villainy with additional scenes, some original and some borrowed from other plays, and by raising the number of Richard's soliloquies from four to eleven, Cibber focused Shakespeare's sprawling work into a shapely one-man melodrama, a favorite vehicle for generations of starring tragedians.

RESTORATION ACTORS AND ACTING

The Restoration stage was manned by great actors. Colley Cibber, who joined the profession in 1690, devoted two chapters of his autobiography to describing a baker's dozen of its most brilliant members, contending that no other stage in history could boast a company of such variety and skill. Chief among them, in executive ability as well as art, was Thomas Betterton (1635–1710). When Davenant died in 1668, Betterton became principal manager of the Duke's Men, and after 1682 he directed the United Company. Competent in comic roles, he was superb in tragedy, and such witnesses as Addison, Steele, and Rowe sustain Cibber's opinion that his Hamlet, Macbeth, Othello, and Brutus were inimitable. He could make great music out of even the maddest rants that Nahum Tate patched onto Shakespeare, and Cibber's praise of his vocal control is a classic of theatre criticism:

> In the just delivery of poetical numbers, particularly where the sentiments are pathetick, it is scarce credible upon how minute an article of sound depends their greatest beauty or inaffection. The voice of a singer is not more strictly ty'd to time and tune than that of an actor in theatrical elocution. The least syllable too long or too slightly dwelt upon in a period depreciates it to nothing; which very syllable if rightly touch'd shall, like the heightening stroke of light from a master's pencil, give life and spirit to the whole. I never heard a line in tragedy come from Betterton wherein my judgment, my ear, and my imagination were not fully satisfy'd; which, since his time, I cannot equally say of any one actor whatsoever.

Yet another token of Betterton's artistry was his preference for attentive silence over applause: "There were many ways of deceiving an audience into a loud one," he would say; "but to keep them husht and quiet was an applause that only truth and merit could arrive at."

A major innovation in this period was the introduction of the *actress*. When Charles II issued his letters patent he made it plain that thereafter women's parts could be (must be?) played by women. He seems to have intended this, along with the suppression of "profane, obscene, and scurrilous passages" in plays, as part of an overall *moral* reform, but of course the event did not altogether conform to the expectation. From the beginning the attraction of the actresses was rather grossly sexual, and although the best of them, such as Mrs. Betterton, Elizabeth Barry, and Anne Bracegirdle, developed into great artists, for many a young woman entering the profession the stage was but a way station along the high road to some kind keeper's bed or the downward path to a brothel. As for the Shakespearean drama, it may be questioned whether the introduction of actresses, any more than the introduction of painted scenery, was a genuine benefit. Shakespeare wrote his women's roles to be performed by boys: they call for emotional vigor, strength of character, and braininess—that is, qualities of which both sexes can show examples—more than for femininity and sex appeal—as, indeed, certain modern experiments with all-male casts have demonstrated. As a matter of fact, the availability of actresses may have worked *against* the staging of some of Shakespeare's best "she" roles. To capitalize on sex appeal the playwrights wrote new plays with risqué scenes in them, but Beatrice and Viola appeared only rarely, and Rosalind, Hermione and Perdita, Helena of *All's Well*, and Cleopatra were not seen at all.

THE EIGHTEENTH CENTURY: FORMALISM, REALISM, AND THE CLASSIC MODE

The stage history of Shakespeare between the death of Betterton in 1710 and the emergence of Garrick in 1741 has about it a sense of interim. The actors were worthy—Barton Booth, Robert Wilks, Mary Ann Porter for tragedy, Colley Cibber and Nance Oldfield for comedy—but none of them stands in the front rank of fame, and even in their own day they were overshadowed by the remembered excellence of their masters. To a considerable extent, too, their art, except in broadest comedy, was hemmed in by fashionable demand for "dignity" in posture and movement, and "tone" (a musical monotony approaching *recitatif*) in speaking. Practitioners of this "neoclassical" style, of whom James Quin is the most notorious, seemed to be playing Shakespeare's tragic heroes in straitjackets.

As for the stage repertory of Shakespeare, the canon had been pretty thoroughly sifted. Fifteen of the plays had settled into stock—some essentially Shakespearean in form and substance, some in the fancy garments fitted to them by their "improvers"; the rest had gone on the shelf. The great roles had all been created. There seemed to be nothing for the actors to do but endlessly repeat what the Betterton generation had done aforetime.

A few years before Garrick arrived on the scene, however, a gradual but conspicuous Shakespeare revival got under way. In 1737 there began a long series of Shakespeare performances "At the Desire of several Ladies of Quality." We do not know who these ladies were, but Shakespeare himself sent a letter to the *Daily Advertiser*, posted from Elysium, to thank them for their interest in his works. In the same year a sudden and harsh government censorship cut down the number of *new* plays, and the managers, forced to depend on revivals, found Shakespeare their strongest card. In 1740 the fashion of "breeches parts" prompted some one at Drury Lane to remember Rosalind and Viola, and thus for the first time since Shakespeare's day *As You Like It* and *Twelfth Night* found an audience. In February of 1741 Charles Macklin (c. 1700–97) enacted his astonishingly "real" Shylock in a restoration of *The Merchant of Venice*. Toward the end of that season *All's Well That Ends Well* and *The Winter's Tale* were revived at Goodman's Fields. Thus within one season five Shakespeares were restored to the repertory, and a Shakespeare "boom" was under way.

We are to this day so dazzled by the reputation of David Garrick (1717–79) that we are all too ready to concede his valuation of himself as the prime advocate of Shakespeare in his age. In the prologue to one of his "restorations" he declared:

> 'Tis my chief wish, my joy, my only plan
> To lose no drop of that immortal man.

For the most part, his public took him at his word—but not his old friend Dr. Johnson. When Boswell once argued that Johnson should have mentioned Garrick in his *Preface* to Shakespeare, on the grounds that Garrick had "brought Shakespeare into notice," the Doctor's gruff rejoinder was, "Sir, to allow that would be to lampoon the age."

Garrick's most celebrated feat of restoration was to stage *Macbeth* "as written by Shakespeare." The phrase was a startling one, at least inside the profession, and it prompted James Quin's plaintive query, "Don't I play *Macbeth* as Shakespeare wrote it?" Garrick replaced Davenant's flat language with Shakespeare's and discarded the foolish Lady Macduff scenes. These were indeed improvements. Yet he cut some two hundred seventy lines of the original, retained Davenant's additions to the Witches, and added a moralizing dying speech for the hero. His partial restoration of *King Lear* was next in importance: insofar as possible he used Shakespeare's language, yet he dared not reintroduce the Fool or drop the Cordelia-Edgar love affair or restore the tragic ending. He staged *Antony and Cleopatra* in a version prepared by Edward Capell—an ambitious effort which should have been a significant one, but it lasted for only six performances. His own arrangement of *Cymbeline*, cunningly tailored for the picture-frame stage, worked better, and in fact remained the standard acting version for decades.

He tampered with texts almost as much as he restored them. His *Romeo and Juliet*, which held the stage for a century, was much admired for its "original" ending (which Garrick got from Theophilus Cibber who got it from Thomas Otway), in which Juliet wakes before Romeo dies and the lovers enjoy a rapturous but brief reunion. He made an opera of *The Tempest* and another of *A Midsummer Night's Dream*. He knocked down *The Taming of the Shrew* into an afterpiece called *Catherine and Petruchio*, and *The Winter's Tale* into another called *Florizel and Perdita*. Near the end of his career he "rescued" *Hamlet* from the "rubbish of the fifth act." In order to get rid of the gravediggers—the vulgar *fossoyeurs* whom Voltaire had inveighed against for destroying the tragic tone—he brought Hamlet home in the midst of the Claudius-Laertes conspiracy and killed off the tragic figures then and there, only keeping Laertes alive to share the government of Denmark with Horatio.

Garrick's real service to Shakespeare was not so much through his tentative and sometimes wrong-headed attention to the texts, but rather through his splendid acting. From his first London performances of Richard III in the fall of 1741, it was clear to all that here was an actor who would cut through the stilted formalism of the neo-classic school and get to the particularities of his characters. Eight months earlier his friend Charles Macklin had ushered in the new realism with his Shylock, played with all the bold starts and contrasts to be expected of a hard-crusted, cunning usurer, and with none of what Macklin called the "hoity-toity" intoning which was supposed to be the mark of serious acting. This had been a significant breakthrough. But Macklin, limited by harsh voice, physique, and temper, was unable to carry the campaign much beyond this one role. Garrick, blessed with flexibility, could extend the realistic method to almost every corner of the repertory. Though a very small man, he could fill such soldierly figures as Macbeth and Richard III, and he could express the overwhelming passions of King Lear. He excelled in comedy: the gaiety of his Benedick matched the brilliance of his Hamlet; his dirty, foolish Abel Drugger in *The Alchemist* delighted audiences as much as his graceful, romantic Romeo.

His voice was clear and agreeable, and though not loud it carried well, so that even his softest utterance was heard in every part of the auditorium. He concentrated upon meaningfulness, and we know of many a point at which he strove for the exact emphasis, pause, and intonation that would convey exact logical relationships and exact shades of feeling. Sometimes he was accused of sacrificing poetry for meaning's sake—of overusing the run-on line, of breaking down pentameters into scatterings of minute phrases. It is possible, however, that those who objected on this score were addicted to the intoning of the older school, and would have held him to manners of speaking which neither we nor Shakespeare's own audience would find tolerable.

He spent immense care upon *transitions*—those moments in a play when he could electrify the audience by instantaneous transformation from one attitude to another. In confronting the ghost of Banquo in *Macbeth* he made a transition from high conviviality to staring horror. In the Tent Scene in *Richard III* he exhibited in quick succession terror, manliness, physical anguish, and self-pity. In his King Lear, rage and grief and indignation and pride and distress followed upon each other in lightning alternation, and his descent into madness was marked by most careful gradations.

All that he did and said on the stage was planned to the minutest detail, and he once told an aspiring actor that if he could not make love to "a table, chair, or marble slab, as well as to the finest woman in the world," he would never reach the top of the profession. Dr. Johnson took this to mean that he acted without emotional commitment: "Punch has no feelings." But Garrick was very much aware of the importance of "fire." In the famous rivalry between the French actress Dumesnil, who depended wholly on passion to sustain her, and Clairon, whose every effect was controlled by intellect, Garrick came down on the side of Clairon; but privately he declared his fear that Clairon's "heart has none of those instantaneous feelings, that life-blood, that keen sensibility, that bursts out at once from genius, and like electrical fire, shoots through the veins, marrow, bones and all, of every spectator."

It is difficult to understand how, after Garrick had charmed an entire generation with his energy, sparkle, and infinite variety, the next generation could tender its allegiance to the solemn, inflexible John Philip Kemble (1757–1823), who dominated the stage of Drury Lane Theatre from 1783 to 1802 and Covent Garden from 1803 to 1817. Garrick's art, like Shakespeare's, was grounded in particularities; Kemble's art, closely akin to the esthetics of Sir Joshua Reynolds, aimed at the *suppression* of particularities. In one of his presidential addresses to the Royal Academy, Reynolds actually dwelt upon the necessity of *unnaturalness* in the art of acting, arguing that everything on the stage must be "raised and enlarged beyond its natural state" in order that its full effect be experienced by the spectator. When Reynolds referred to "the deliberate and stately step, the studied grace of action, which seems to enlarge the dimensions of the actor, and alone to fill the stage," he doubtless expected to remind his hearers of the nobly Roman Kemble. The deliberation and statuesqueness of Kemble sometimes amused, sometimes infuriated the rising critics of the Romantic age. William Hazlitt accounted for his slow movement by likening him to a marble statue: "the least trip in his gait, or discomposure of his balance, would be sure to fracture some of his limbs." Leigh Hunt compared his syllable-by-syllable vocal delivery to an apothecary's drop-by-drop measuring out of laudanum.

One external circumstance—the enlargement of the London theatres—certainly contributed to Kemble's deliberateness. Drury Lane, which had held an audience of 2000, was rebuilt in 1794 to hold 3611. About the same time Covent Garden was expanded to hold about 3000. In such vast halls subtleties were out of the question. Facial expression, except the coarsest grimaces, would not carry beyond the middle of the pit. Soft voices would not be heard; rapid speech would not be understood. Thus the actors were driven into that slow and heavy enunciation, with each phrase marked off by strong pause, which we associate with stump oratory. Gesture, stride, and stance had to be "grand" if they were to be noticed, and Sir Joshua's formula of "unnaturalness" became more necessary than ever.

Kemble had almost no aptitude for comedy. His Benedick strained patience; his Charles Surface in *The School for Scandal* was known as "Charles's Martyrdom." He was too cold and formal to play lovers. "The thoughtful strength of his features," says his biographer James Boaden, "was at variance with the juvenile passion." His Othello was cold, logical, reasonable, as if the actor took literally the character's estimate of himself as "one not easily jealous." As King Lear he smothered the passions under a fussy accumulation of the external marks of age, so that he seemed to Charles Lamb only "an old man tottering about the stage with a walking-stick."

Yet unquestionably he was impressive in many parts, and his greatness lay, it appears, in the concentrated intensity he brought to those roles in which he could make one strong passion run all one way—jealous Leontes, proud Coriolanus, gloomy Macbeth, dangerous Posthumus, melancholy Hamlet, malignant King John. He excelled in roles sustained by stoicism or unrelaxing dignity—Wolsey, the Duke in *Measure for Measure*, and Brutus. Near the end of his career he revived Addison's *Cato*, and his rendering of that motionless, flavorless, textbook-stoic hero became one of his *chefs-d'œuvre*.

Kemble enjoyed a reputation for "scholarship," and was said to study Shakespeare "critically." But of the twenty-six Shakespeares that he staged, the texts of comparatively few show the results of such study. Many of them are little more than Garrick's versions or others which he found in Bell's *Shakespeare*, tinkered in minor ways—small cuts and restorations and the addition of proper names to hitherto anonymous characters. In his *King Lear* he bypassed Garrick's restorations and reverted wholly to the language of Tate. For *The Tempest* he substituted an operatic hodgepodge of his own concocting. He mingled into the latter acts of *Coriolanus* stuff from James Thomson's play of the same name.

It is clear that he did study *Hamlet* thoroughly, and he must be credited with restoring dozens of true readings in place of the false ones which generations of actors had let into the text. He adapted three plays—*All's Well That Ends Well*, *Measure for Measure*, and *Twelfth Night*—without spoiling them: by judicious transposing of certain scenes and passages, as Garrick had done with *Cymbeline*, he fitted these plays to the esthetic of the picture-frame stage.

Following eighteenth-century practice Kemble usually mounted his Shakespeares with stock sets, but occasionally he got up special productions. For the opening of Drury Lane in 1794 he offered a gorgeously appointed *Macbeth*, with new scenes, special music, and huge choruses of sprites and witches to sing it. In his last years at Drury Lane he staged wholly new productions of *Cymbeline* and *The Winter's Tale*. His Covent Garden productions of *Coriolanus*, *Cato*, and *Julius Caesar* were held to be correct re-creations of both the costume and the architecture of Imperial Rome.

He was the first actor-manager in the English theatre who systematically published his acting versions, and between 1789 and 1815 he issued them repeatedly. These books were purchased not only by playgoers but by other actors and managers, who found them to be the handiest instruments with which to act and stage the plays. Editors of later acting editions, such as Elizabeth Inchbald and William Oxberry, derived their texts from Kemble's. Thus he came to be for his own time and for at least a generation longer, in the words of Herschel Baker, "the arbiter, *par excellence*, of Shakespeare on the stage."

Those restless, younger-generation critics who did not care for Kemble himself could still be attracted to his theatre by the brilliant company he kept about him—in the Drury Lane years the comic actresses Elizabeth Farren and Dorothy Jordan; at Covent Garden the drunken genius George Frederick Cooke (1756–1812), a brute of a man who happened also to be the best Richard III, Iago, Shylock, and Falstaff in the business. Foremost in Kemble's company, of course, was his sister Sarah Siddons (1755–1831). Magnificent in stature and voice, she was far more fiery and flexible than he. "Power was seated on her brow," said Hazlitt; "passion emanated from her breast." Her Lady Macbeth was described as a kind of "sister to Milton's Lucifer"; her Volumnia exuded an almost drunken pride in her son Coriolanus. She was capable of tenderness and pathos, too, in the bereaved Constance in *King John* and the dying Katharine in *Henry VIII*. Her Desdemona expressed a "violet-like sweetness."

NINETEENTH-CENTURY REALISM

But the younger generation found their own man one January night in 1814 when a fireball burst upon the stage of Drury Lane Theatre—Edmund Kean in Shylock. Kean (1787–1833) was as unlike Kemble as could be imagined. His Shylock was all innovation. He wore a black beard, not a red one. His manner was not merely vindictive: it was shot through with humor—a sardonic chuckling which startled his hearers into new recognitions of Shylock's cynicism and menace. His swift movement, his flashing black eyes, and above all his astonishing *transitions* reminded old playgoers of Garrick or suggested to young ones that the art of acting was being re-created before their eyes.

Shylock was only aperitif. Three weeks later Kean exhibited his full line of histrionic wares in *Richard III*. And here, as Harold Hillebrand summarized the evidence:

> The little tragedian was in everything he did prodigious. He was the master virtuoso who swept through the gamut of moods, throwing his hearers, with each change, into new ecstasies. His technical dexterity alone was amazing. There was nothing here of the noble dignity, the statuesque poses, the measured declamation of Kemble; here were the thunder and lightning, here were storms and bursts of sunlight, here were the colors of the rainbow and the terrible shadows of crime and death.

A month later he dared Hamlet, the test role for tragic actors, and in those days peculiarly the property of John Philip Kemble. His brightness and agility were less useful to him on this occasion, but he worked up two moments of pathos which won the audience's affection. On the lines "I'll call thee Hamlet, King, father, royal Dane," he put so much love into the word "father" that many in the audience broke into tears. At the end of the scene with Ophelia, having shouted, "To a nunnery, go," and reached the exit, he returned, took her hand tenderly, and kissed it. These two sentimental points became part of the stage Hamlet tradition. In May and June he capped the season with a run of *Othello*, playing hero and villain on alternate nights. His Iago was acclaimed at once for its briskness, cordiality, gaiety, and wit; his Othello was eventually regarded as his masterpiece.

Kean had faults, of course. Indeed, to confirmed Kembleites he had nothing else. John Taylor, the journalist friend of Kemble, called him a "*Humbug*" and a "*Pot-House Actor*," whose art was a "low, vulgar art, without dignity or elevated conception of character." One of his most powerful instruments—his facial expression—actually worked against him. Hazlitt had observed that in the play of his features "you see the writhing and coiling up of the passions before they make their serpent-spring; the lightning of his eye precedes the hoarse burst of thunder from his voice." So it was for those who sat in the pit close to the stage. But in the vastness of Drury Lane Theatre, the hundreds who sat in the galleries and farther boxes got none of this, and Kean appeared to them to be meaninglessly and affectedly stretching out his pauses.

Kean was by temperament a lone wolf, a rebel against society and the system, and he was by no means an organizer or a leader. He could never direct a company or manage a theatre. Thus his influence upon the staging of Shakespeare was limited to the establishing of his romantic style of acting.

As the nineteenth century progressed, Shakespeare production responded on all fronts to the rising spirit of realism, to the pursuit of truth conceived as *fact*. The actors, beginning with Kean and his lightning flashes of psychological revelation, sought to discover hitherto unrecognized facts about the appetencies and motivations of the characters they played. Responding to the advances of Shakespeare scholarship, actor-managers bowed down to the fact of "the book" and with rising fervor proclaimed their allegiance to the "true text." New developments in historical and archeological research and, of course, the popularity of historical fiction promoted a theatrical response to the facts of history—a striving after "historical accuracy" in *mise-en-scène*.

The scholarly Kemble had been interested in history, especially in classical antiquity—up to a point. When his learned friend Sir Walter Scott once snatched the "tragic" ostrich plumes from his Macbeth headdress and replaced them with a "correct" eagle feather, he was delighted; but a programmed campaign of historical accuracy would have been irrelevant to his kind of art. When someone asked him why he did not stage *Julius Caesar* in the plain architecture of republican Rome rather than in the glamorized Rome of the Emperors, he protested, "Why, if I did, sir, they would call me an antiquary."

No such scruple deterred his younger brother Charles (1775–1854), who succeeded to the Covent Garden management. In 1823, when planning a revival of *King John*, Charles Kemble commissioned young James Robinson Planché to costume the play according to authentic historical models. In consultation with Sir Samuel Meyrick, Francis Douce, and other experts on ancient dress and armor, Planché based his designs on the evidence of tomb effigies, royal seals, and illuminated manuscripts. The actors were put off at first by the unfamiliar garb—especially the flat-topped helmets, which they called stewpans—but the public, well instructed by the massive list of "authorities" listed in the playbill, was delighted. The critics urged Kemble to apply the same principle to all of Shakespeare's histories, and a few months later he offered *1 Henry IV* in authentic costumes and authentic scenery as well. His *Cymbeline* of 1827 tickled the Londoners' imagination with its claims to reconstruct the features of daily life among their ancestors "before their Subjugation by the Romans", and flattered their erudition with its playbill appeal to the writings of Julius Caesar, Pliny, Suetonius, Diodorus Siculus, and Dionysius of Halicarnassus.

A decade later William Charles Macready (1793–1873) launched his campaign to present "the plays of our divine Shakespeare fitly illustrated." Between 1837 and 1839 at Covent Garden and between 1841 and 1843 at Drury Lane he got up special productions of nearly a dozen of them. A sketch has been preserved of the opening scene of *King Lear*—a low, broad Saxon hall, the walls made of squared blocks of stone and hung with shields, spears, and hunting horns. Through one of the large arched openings in the rear wall could be seen in the middle distance a temple suggestive of Stonehenge. The scenery of Macready's *Coriolanus* re-created Rome of the fifth century B. C. Along the streets were primitive temples flanked by thatch-covered huts; residential rooms were of undecorated brickwork; the only ornament in the Senate chamber was a statue of the legendary wolf suckling Romulus and Remus. The *Times* on this occasion congratulated the public on these educated insights into the truths of history. "Fifty years ago," the reviewer pointed out, "no manager would have thought of distinguishing different periods of ancient history; a Roman was a Roman; . . . Julius Caesar and Coriolanus lived comfortably in houses of precisely the same fashion." The particular glory of Macready's *Henry V* was the scenic illustration of the Choruses: each Chorus was backed by a painted screen, which either moved (as, for instance, to show the passage of the English fleet across the Channel), or melted magically from still-life into acted scene (the beginning of the siege of Harfleur).

Macready's efforts to "restore the true text" were not in fact numerous, but they were well advertised, and they seem to have won him as much fame as did his "fit illustrations." By "restoration" he did not, of course, mean performance of the inviolate text, but only the deletion of all language inserted by earlier "improvers," and performance of as much of the original as time and decency permitted. His *King Lear*, which he brought out in 1838, contained no Tate, but only two-thirds of Shakespeare. He suppressed all lines which he thought unintelligible or sacrilegious or obscene. He suppressed the blinding of Gloucester, which would have been too painful for his audience to endure, and Gloucester's attempt to leap from the cliff, which probably seemed too eccentric and possibly comic. He almost suppressed the Fool, fearing that it would "weary or annoy or distract the spectator," but a few weeks before the opening his stage manager convinced him that this "fragile, hectic, beautiful-faced, half-idiot-looking boy" (so Macready conceived the Fool) might be realized if a woman played it. Accordingly the role was stripped of all its indelicacies and most of its comic touches and assigned to Priscilla Horton, whose Fool was all tenderness and pathos.

When he produced *The Tempest* he eliminated the Dorinda-Hippolito complex and all other traces of the Davenant and Dryden treatment. He gave *As You Like It* for the first time on record in a true if bowdlerized text, restoring to the First Lord his second-act speeches, which for the last hundred years had been usurped by Jaques, and banishing the Cuckoo Song, which had long ago been borrowed from *Love's Labor's Lost* for its teasing allusions to cuckoldry.

Bulwer-Lytton called Macready "a great metaphysical actor," meaning presumably that his acting suggested intense mental rather than physical activity. Macready had certainly trained to achieve this effect. In order to eliminate physical excesses he would repeat the most impassioned speeches of Othello, Lear, Hamlet, or Macbeth while lying on the floor or standing against a wall with his hands tied to his body. To eliminate mere noise he would repeat these passages in a whisper. He would rehearse before a mirror, not in order to plan facial expressions but to get rid of them and to make sure that the "intense passion should speak from the eyes alone." The result of such exercises was that, at best, he could communicate powerful emotional impulses like a mesmerist while employing a minimum of external means. Lady Pollock testifies to his "metaphysical" success in *Macbeth*: "his wandering, unsettled tone did more than all the efforts of those who played the witches in showing the supernatural at work"; and "when he spoke 'into the air,' we could almost see the hags pass away, and like a wreath of vapour dissolve into the invisible element." He put the greatest store upon total identification with the character he was playing, and herein lies the measure of his involvement with the esthetics of realism. "I cannot act Macbeth without *being Macbeth*," he would say, and the most determined Method actor of our own day could say no more. He declared that the highest reach of the player's art "is to fathom the depths of the character, to trace its latent motives, to feel its finest quiverings of emotion, to comprehend the thoughts that are hidden under words, and thus possess oneself of the actual mind of the individual man."

In 1844 Samuel Phelps (1804–78), who had acted under Macready for several seasons, went into management at Sadler's Wells. The Wells, an old theatre in the working-class district of Islington, was traditionally a melodrama house catering to a supposedly vulgar public, and there, against all odds, Phelps offered a program of "the legitimate." He succeeded remarkably, and he did so without playing down to his audiences or cheapening his art in any way. His management lasted eighteen years. He staged thirty-one Shakespeares, nearly sixty other plays then regarded as classics, and over thirty serious plays of modern vintage. Merely to list his Shakespearean restorations is to acknowledge his courage and integrity. He was the first to displace Cibber's *Richard III* with a purely Shakespearean version. His *King Lear*, some five hundred lines longer than Macready's, restored most of the Fool's lines, and Phelps assigned the Fool to a male actor. In *Macbeth* he cancelled the chorus of singing witches, and reintroduced the drunken Porter, the assassins' attack upon Lady Macduff, and the bringing in of Macbeth's head on a pole. He staged *Timon of Athens* purged of improvements and a bowdlerized but spectacular *Pericles*. He staged a Shakespearean version of *Antony and Cleopatra*, which since Kemble's time had been cross-bred with Dryden's *All for Love*. Madame Vestris had anticipated him in revivals of *A Midsummer Night's Dream* and *Love's Labor's Lost*, but his versions were far superior to hers. He followed Ben Webster in staging the entire *Taming of the Shrew*, including the Induction, and followed Charlotte Cushman in restoring the proper ending to *Romeo and Juliet*.

Though limited financially, Phelps strove to emulate Macready's best work in *mise-en-scène*. In scenes of the supernatural, by darkening the stage and by clever use of gauzes he rendered the comings and goings of ghosts and witches truly mysterious. In the last act of *Richard III* he avoided the many scene shifts from camp to camp by setting Richard's tent and Richmond's at either side of the stage and separating them by a brook which flowed downstage from a grove of trees in the central distance. He ended *Timon of Athens* with a panoramic depiction of a journey from Timon's forest hiding-place to his tomb beside the city. His most celebrated staging was that of *A Midsummer Night's Dream*. The three acts in the fairy-haunted forest were seen through a green gauze, behind which, by a nice manipulation of sliding flats, one scene melted into another almost imperceptibly. The lovers moved from glade to glade, with now and then a distant view of sea or city; and the fairies, shadowy figures neither winged nor spangled, drifted in and out of the foliage like true spirits of the woodland.

Much of Phelps's success was owing to his extraordinary versatility as an actor. If he lacked something of Macready's intensity and subtlety, he certainly matched his old master in conscientiousness. Physically he was superior to Macready—his face and figure handsomer, his natural voice richer and more musical. He mastered all the tragic roles except the young romantics, and he was a fine comedian, too, as Macready was not. Thanks to his goodly stature his comic range greatly exceeded Garrick's: he was a splendidly absurd Malvolio, a thoroughly idiotic Armado, and a shrewd Falstaff. In *2 Henry IV* he demonstrated his versatility by playing both the dying King and Master Shallow in the same performance. His comic masterpiece was sweet bully Bottom.

From 1850 to 1859, while Phelps was working up his last ten Shakespeares for the Islingtonians, the theatrical cynosure of fashionable London was the Princess's Theatre in Oxford Street, where Charles Kean (1811–68) was developing "historical accuracy" to the farthest possible limits. So prestigious had Kean become that even Her Majesty patronized him—not only by attendance at his theatre, but by making him Director of the Windsor Theatricals: during each Christmas season Kean took one or more of his own productions and commandeered those of other managements to entertain the royal family at Windsor Castle.

Kean was not a first-rate Shakespearean actor. His forte was adapted French melodrama (*Louis XI*, *The Corsican Brothers*, *The Courier of Lyons*) and modern domestic drama, and when he played a major tragic role he rarely seemed to "fathom the depth of the character" in the Macready manner, but rather to decorate its surfaces with little realistic touches in the manner of genre painting. "We see in Mr. Charles Kean," said one critic, "a very Dutch transcript, graphic and real, but utterly devoid of heroic proportions."

His major contribution to Shakespeare production was to load it with the fruits of historical research. In 1859, at a banquet in Kean's honor, the Duke of Newcastle declared him to be "one of the greatest archaeologists of the day." The remark was cheered. The Duke went on:

> He has had a reason for everything; there is nothing which he introduces upon the stage for which he has not authority, and you may see living presentations of Shakespeare's characters, with the exact costume, the exact scenery, the exact furniture of the rooms which, there is every reason to believe, from pictures and other sources, existed at the time Shakespeare represented.

He specialized in the English history plays—seven of them, counting *Macbeth* and *King Lear*. His *Macbeth* in 1853 was the occasion of his first "Fly Leaf" to the audience, a solemnly erudite document which—invoking the authority of Sir Samuel Meyrick and Charles Hamilton Smith the antiquaries, George Godwin the architect, the histories of Strabo and Pliny, the Eyrbiggia Saga, and the Latin *Life of St. Columba*—instructed the public in a great many things they did not need to know, including the domestic arrangements and dressing habits of Boadicea, Harold Hardrada, Harold II, Thorlef of Iceland, and the Scottish kings Alexander, David, and Roderick of Strathclyde.

His *Henry VIII* was "a succession of historical pictures, in which every person, group, and movement is modelled from life . . . embodied from the minute descriptions of those who had seen, known, and lived with the characters introduced." The dialogue of the final act was much curtailed in order to make time for a panoramic journey down the Thames from Westminster to the Greyfriars Church at Greenwich, where the christening of the Infant Elizabeth took place. Between the third and fourth acts of *Richard II* he staged the usurper's entry into London with Richard as prisoner: over six hundred supernumeraries represented the guards, the officials, the entertainers, the seven Guilds, and the cheering bystanders of the scene. In *Henry V* he staged Henry's triumphal return to London (Chorus to Act V), "carefully following the account of an eye-witness, whose MS. has been preserved." All these and countless more scenic splendors were carefully recorded in Kean's playbills, fly leaves, published acting versions, and souvenir prompt-books, and in his two-volume *Life and Times* compiled by one of the officers in the Princess's Theatre and published in the year that Kean concluded his management.

SHAKESPEARE IN AMERICA

Shakespeare in America in earliest times was a spin-off from the theatres of London, and usually from the humblest theatres. Lewis Hallam and his "select Company of Comedians" who performed America's first *Merchant of Venice* at Williamsburg in 1752 were theatrical nobodies in their homeland, hardly more distinguished than any other lot of provincial strollers. By the end of the century, though, theatre in America was well enough established that London actors of talent and repute would make the crossing, either to become permanent residents or to reap a quick golden harvest as visiting stars. In 1795 young Thomas Abthorpe Cooper (1776–1849), after a promising debut at Covent Garden, was persuaded to emigrate: his beauty of voice and person, his classic style, and the excellence of his Hamlet and Macbeth soon fixed his reputation as America's leading tragic actor. Mary Ann Duff, the "American Siddons" whose exploits in tragedy are legendary, came in 1810. J. W. Wallack, a handsome young actor of the Kemble school, who in fact resembled and rivalled Cooper, came in 1818. In 1821 came Junius Brutus Booth, the fiery and erratic rival to Kean, whose Richard III, Iago, and Shylock enlivened American stages for the next three decades.

The more renowned London Shakespeareans who visited America on starring expeditions undoubtedly contributed to the growth of American taste, and as a rule they were well rewarded for their efforts. The great George Frederick Cooke, who came in 1810, was immensely admired when he was sober enough to play; but he seems to have dissipated his earnings almost as fast as he got them, and he died before he could go home. Edmund Kean came twice—in 1820 at the peak of his fame and in 1825 when, although his reputation was stained by the scandal of his recent sex exploits, he could still command Yankee audiences and inspire young actors with whom he came in contact. His son Charles, whose talent was milder, met milder responses in 1831, 1839, and 1845. Macready first came in 1826 at a point in his career when his talents shone in Virginius and William Tell as much as in Shakespearean work; again in 1843, just after his final term of London management when his reputation was at its highest; and finally in 1848–49, when his feud with Edwin Forrest exploded into the frightful Astor Place Riots. The happiest visitation, perhaps, was that of Charles Kemble and his daughter Fanny in 1832–34. They charmed the best society, and their performances—his Hamlet, their joint appearances as Romeo and Juliet and Benedick and Beatrice—were so pleasing that, as their host Philip Hone declared, they improved the tone of the New York stage and renewed public respect for it.

In the 1820's and 1830's there began to emerge a line of native-born actors, whose attitudes and energies constituted what came to be known as the "American style." The hallmarks of this style included extraordinary emotional intensity and physical power, brilliant elocution, and bold projection of fairly uncomplicated readings of character and theme. Edwin Forrest (1806–72), the greatest of the first generation of native actors, was a massive man, whose voice could shake theatre walls when he let it out in anger, yet could be brought down to the tenderest murmur. Stage scenes of high passion cost him no special effort, for he was passionate by nature. He loathed the "foreign aristocrat" Macready and he loved his friend James Oakes with equal fervor; he loved Catherine Sinclair ardently when he married her and hated her even more ardently once he decided she was an adulteress. He attracted an enormous following, especially among the male population and the Bowery Boys, for whom he was a champion of Americanism and Democracy; in polite society he was increasingly regarded as a rather vulgar giant.

He could play grandly those roles that matched his own nature. He was no Romeo, and his Hamlet succeeded only at the elocutionary level, for he could not enter sympathetically into a character who let thought immobilize him from action. His Macbeth, too, was unconvincing: as a brawny soldier he could not be awed by witches. His Coriolanus was magnificent—not that he sympathized with Coriolanus' anti-democratic bias, but that his own fierce assertiveness lent itself to the role. He was overwhelming in Othello, especially after the breakup of his marriage in 1850, when Othello's experience became his own. His masterwork was King Lear, with whom he openly claimed identity as one "more sinned against than sinning." He did not "play" Lear, he insisted. "I *play* Hamlet, Richard, Shylock, Virginius, if you please; but, by God, sir! I *am* Lear!"

James Henry Hackett (1800–71), who specialized in comic Yankee characters, was also a Shakespearean of sorts. He studied Hamlet, Lear, and Iago, and during Edmund Kean's second American visit he made a special study of all of Kean's line-readings and stage business in *Richard III*. But Hackett's one great role was Falstaff, which he played in both *The Merry Wives of Windsor* and *1* and *2 Henry IV* all over America and sometimes abroad.

It was not so much a comical Falstaff that Hackett projected as a *moralizing* one, an example of wickedness put down. In his playbills of *The Merry Wives* he would affix the subtitle *Falstaff Outwitted by Women*, and would explain that he was about to exhibit a "vain old coxcomb" deservedly abused and "exposed to the laughter and ridicule of all observers." To Londoners, who had long since absolved Falstaff from moral responsibility and taken him to their hearts as a jolly old fun-lover, Hackett's intentions were almost unintelligible. The London critics regarded him as a brainy but tiresome provincial, some two or three generations behind the times in art and manners. Hackett grumbled back at them in letters to the press that he had forgotten more about Falstaff than Sir Oracle had ever known, and he went on to instruct young men (like Prince Hal) not to become "corrupted by intimacy with old and vicious company"; and to teach companions of the mighty not to minister to the vices of their patrons "lest they too, like Falstaff, be left to die in despair."

The female counterpart to Edwin Forrest was America's greatest tragic actress, Charlotte Cushman (1816–76). Cushman's voice, like Forrest's, was powerful, and with it she could express a vast range of emotions. Trained in youth as a singer, she had broken her voice by overstraining it, and it had become fascinatingly husky. In scenes of deep passion, physical agony, and death, it was inimitable. A skilled elocutionist, she extracted great music and vivid meaning from Shakespeare's language. Like Forrest, too, she was powerfully built—tall, big-boned, broad-shouldered. Her face with its square forehead, flattish nose, and strong square jaw was downright mannish.

Her roles ran to the "heavies," of course—Mrs. Haller in *The Stranger*, Belvidera in *Venice Preserv'd*, and her famous Meg Merrilies in *Guy Mannering*. In Shakespeare she gave up the Ophelias and Cordelias after her earliest years, only occasionally resorted to Beatrice or Rosalind, and specialized in Lady Macbeth and Queen Katharine in *Henry VIII*. Few actors of Macbeth could hold their own against her, and the pathos as well as the majesty of her dying Katharine was unforgettable. But Shakespeare's women were not enough for her. During a London engagement in 1845 she played Romeo, and played it with more earnestness and believability than any male actor had brought to the part since Garrick's time. A few years later she undertook Hamlet, and sometimes she played Cardinal Wolsey. These essays in transvestism were artistically in dead earnest, and they were much admired.

None of these three leading American actors showed much interest in the contemporary English efforts at correct mounting, nor even in efforts to restore Shakespeare's texts. All three claimed to be "scholarly," but the meaning of the word grows dim in the light of their practices. Although Forrest actually owned a First Folio, for the stage he used the acting versions published by Oxberry, Cumberland, French, and others. Hackett claimed that he traced every word of his roles back through modern editions to the earliest printed texts in order to determine the author's precise meanings; yet the text of his *Merry Wives* was only that of an 1824 operatic version with the songs left out. Miss Cushman restored the proper ending to *Romeo and Juliet*, but seems not otherwise to have troubled overmuch about textual authenticity. As for the arts of *mise-en-scène*, none of the three was a producer, and for their starring performances they appear to have been contented with whatever Chamber, Palace, Street, and Wood sets any theatre would have in stock. Forrest positively hated what he called "scene painter's drama," and once in Philadelphia when he was about to play Hamlet and found the stage arranged with scenery from Edwin Booth's production, he made the stage manager remove it before he would go on.

Through the early half of the century American audiences wanted their Shakespeare heroically acted, but asked no more of the "accessories" than that they be reasonably in keeping. Scenery was not in itself a draw. Charles Kean discovered this in 1846 when he attempted to educate New York playgoers in the delights of "historical accuracy" and found them dismayingly uneducable. His *Richard III* at the Park Theatre—done "with a wealth of scenery and a degree of historical accuracy never even dreamed of hitherto on the American stage," says G. C. D. Odell—closed in three weeks, and his even more lavish *King John* barely eked out sixteen performances.

Not until the soft revolution in American cultural life in the 1850's, when Tennysonian neo-Romanticism spread across the Atlantic and infused the American artistic establishment, could American playgoers be persuaded to look beyond the actor to the scenery which enclosed him. It was Edwin Booth (1833–93), after he won a firm hold on the New York stage in 1860, who turned taste around and persuaded the public to settle for his own relatively quiet acting and to appreciate stage scenery.

Booth, being slight and lithe rather than brawny, learned as an actor to avoid mere violence, to capitalize on good looks and a beautiful voice, to create bonds of sympathy with his audience, to charm them before he overwhelmed them. His forte was tragedy. Oddly enough, in spite of his personal beauty he could not play stage lovers, and the critics laughed him out of Romeo. Othello and Macbeth were too much for him physically, although on occasion he could rise to those roles through sheer intensity of playing. Richard III, Brutus, Shylock, and Richard II were well within his range, and his Iago, which became a saturnine comic character as he played it, was exactly right. He did not undertake Lear until past midway in his career, but thereafter it was held in high esteem. The Shakespearean role he was especially identified with, of course, was his deep-brooding, passionate Hamlet.

In 1861 Booth spent a season in England, where he heard much about the "authentic" stagings which Charles Kean had recently mounted at the Princess's; and thus when he took up management at the Winter Garden in New York a few years later, his ambition was to emulate Kean. His first production was *Hamlet*. "Some of the pictures in the play will be what has never been used on any stage in America," he wrote to a friend, "and I doubt if Kean did anything like it." This was the "Hundred Nights Hamlet" of 1864–65, painted by John Thorne and Charles Witham. Everything about it was claimed to be authentically tenth-century Norman and historically appropriate to Hamlet's Elsinore. The press, astonished by its beauty and completeness, recognized that for the first time in America the play was staged "with due regard to external effect."

When the Winter Garden burned, Booth built his own theatre, its stage equipped with hydraulic engines to change scenery by the "rise-and-sink" system—an improvement over the traditional "wing-and-groove" system—by which the scenic pieces would move vertically instead of horizontally. Witham and old Henry Hilliard, a veteran scene painter from Kean's Princess's Theatre, labored for a year or more to prepare sets for the plays Booth expected to bring out. First came *Romeo and Juliet* in 1869. "Scene painting in such hands as those of Messrs. Witham and Hilliard becomes a fine art," said the critic of the *World*. "In the first scene we have not a house, nor a row, but a whole square of the Gothic architecture of Italy reproduced with a pains and a patience which would have brought forth plaudits if only a tithe of it had been exhibited." Booth was congratulated for at last bringing to Shakespeare the scenic splendor which other managements wasted on such trash as *The Black Crook*.

Other particularly well-mounted Shakespeares at Booth's Theatre included *Hamlet*, *The Winter's Tale*, and *Julius Caesar*; but by 1873 Booth was in such desperate financial straits that he withdrew from management and took to the road. Thereafter he devoted his energies solely to acting, accepting whatever scenic investiture his managers or employers would provide. At one time he became as embittered against the arts of *mise-en-scène* as Edwin Forrest had been. He complained from London in 1881 that "the actor's art is judged by his costume and the scenery. If they are not 'esthetic' (God save the mark!) he makes no stir. . . . Chas. Kean, Fechter, & Irving have feasted the Londoners so richly that they cannot relish undecorated dishes."

THE VICTORIAN FLOWERING

In 1861 London was visited by an astonishing Hamlet and Othello. The French actor Charles Albert Fechter (1824–79) had changed residence and language and was undertaking to revolutionize English tragic acting. Fechter was a master of the up-to-date realism of French drawing-room drama (he had created Armand Duval in *La Dame aux Camélias*), and it seemed to him that what most English Shakespeareans were doing on stages was unreal, inhuman, and simply outlandish. What he objected to was vividly described by the contemporary English critic George Henry Lewes in his analysis of the "conventional" actor who cannot *be* the part and therefore tries to *act* it:

> Instead of allowing a strong feeling to express itself through its natural signs, he seizes upon the conventional signs . . . his lips will curl, his brow wrinkle, his eyes be thrown up, his forehead be slapped, or he will grimace, rant, and "take the stage," in the style which has become traditional, but which was never seen off the stage; and thus he runs through the gamut of sounds and signs which bear as remote an affinity to any real expressions as the pantomimic conventions of ballet-dancers.

Fechter would reject all that, would domesticate tragic acting, would make Hamlet and Othello as much like Armand Duval as possible. He would get down to *particularities*—not so much, however, those particularities intrinsic to the characters, which Garrick had brought out, but the particularities of "coat-and-waistcoat" behavior common in the daily life of nineteenth-century gentlemen, which he would then *impose upon* the Shakespearean characters.

Much of the Hamlet role was amenable to the Fechter treatment, for a good deal of the time Hamlet is, or can be construed to be, the relaxed and polished courtier. Fechter's foreign accent was mildly distracting, of course, and there were some famous blunders. When the Ghost said he came to "whet" Hamlet's blunted purpose, Fechter thought he meant to "wet"—i.e. to damp down—Hamlet's over-inflamed purpose. He supposed that Hamlet's "worse remains behind" was a reference to the "remains" of Polonius, dead behind the arras. He read the "To be or not to be" soliloquy at great speed, with sword in hand, as if it was his intention to commit suicide then and there. In his effort to avoid conventional declamation he generally sacrificed the music of Hamlet's language, and the character he projected was rather outgoing and cheery than melancholy. Yet Lewes thought that for refinement, feminine delicacy, and vacillation this was one of the very best Hamlets he had ever seen.

But Fechter's Othello was for Lewes one of the worst. In order to gentlemanize Othello, Fechter simply acted against the text. Shakespeare's Othello is ageing and black; Fechter made him young and prettily sun-tanned. Shakespeare's Othello is a military general, universally respected for his dignity and command; Fechter's Othello lolled and lay on chairs and sofas, leaned on Iago and pawed him, and affably shook hands with everyone he met. He gallantly kissed Desdemona's hand when he should have been embracing her passionately, played idly with her curls when he should have been eyeing her with suspicion, and busied himself with paperwork at his desk when he should have been showing deepest concern for the dark insinuations which Iago was pouring into his ears. As Lewes summed up Fechter's fundamental error, "In his desire to be effective by means of small details of 'business,' he has entirely frittered away the great effects of the drama."

The Fechter method, abetted by the rise of cup-and-saucer drama and eventually of post-Ibsen realism, became the wave of the future, giving to many Shakespearean actors precedent for the near-abandonment of musical verse-speaking, the infinite multiplication of tricky bits of stage business, and the substitution of personality-projection for serious interpretation of character.

During the final quarter of the century the London stage was dominated by Henry Irving (1838–1905), the first English actor to be knighted, who enjoyed immense prestige not only at home but in America, too, where he trouped his full productions eight times. His success as an actor was due partly to the intensity with which he conceived and projected his not always sound but always "interesting" characterizations, partly to his striking, almost demonic personality, partly to his very faults—his queer and unmelodious voice and erratic pronunciations, his lean ascetic face, his angular gestures and crooked gait (like that of "a fretful man trying to get very quickly over a plowed field")—which so fascinated beholders that they came to be accepted almost as trademarks of his excellence.

Bernard Shaw would claim that Irving couldn't play Shakespeare's characters but only versions of himself, and that he used Shakespeare's texts as mere quarries for the makings of original romantic dramas in which to exhibit characters of his own creation. As a friendlier critic would put it, Irving strove to re-imagine the characters in new terms. Thus, his Hamlet was impeded from action not so much by weakness of will as by excessive tenderness: he almost obliterated the revenge motif as he emphasized Hamlet's passionate but impossible love for Ophelia. In Macbeth he rejected the usual conception of the haunted, craven villain. He could see no vulgarity in Cardinal Wolsey, but ennobled him. His majestic, patriarchal Shylock was not Shakespeare's at all, Shaw says, although it was so much more interesting than the original that it played Shakespeare off the stage.

His productions were pictorially gorgeous. He paid lip service to the old doctrine of historical accuracy, but he never let History get in the way of Beauty. Costumes were made of the richest fabrics, and many journals carried special articles on them, as if the play were first of all a costume show. In *Macbeth* the four hundred or so costumes of the supporting actors and supernumeraries were dull brown, rust, and earth-colored to set off Irving's own, which were of gold damask, blue silk, brick-red silk, and rose velvet, with blue, green, red, and yellow glass studdings. Of the many dresses worn by Ellen Terry as Lady Macbeth, the "beetle wing" dress is famous, having been immortalized in John Singer Sargent's portrait of Miss Terry in the role: it consisted of a claret and gold mantle worn over a green silk dress which had actual green beetle wings sewed all over its front panel.

Irving commissioned such distinguished artists as Ford Madox Brown and Lawrence Alma-Tadema to design his scenery; and the best of scene painters, including William Telbin, Joseph Harker, and Hawes Craven, painted it. Most of the thirteen scenes of

Irving's famous *Much Ado about Nothing* were only painted drops, but they were executed so skillfully and lighted so cunningly as to create perfect illusions of depth and solidity. The grandest of the "built" scenes was the interior of the cathedral at Messina, which Irving himself described as:

> Telbin's masterpiece, with its real built-out round pillars thirty feet high, its canopied roof of crimson plush from which hung the golden lamps universally used in Italian cathedrals, its painted canopy overhanging the altar, its great ironwork gates, its altar with cases of flowers and flaming candles rising to a height of eighteen feet, its stained glass windows and statues of saints.

At times, of course, the pursuit of beauty violated good sense, and now and then a critic would rouse himself to question the proceedings. In *Macbeth*, for instance, some thought it rather late in the day to be reviving Davenant's songs for the Witches, for no apparent reason but to bring on a chorus of sixty white-clad spirits to sing them. After *Cymbeline*, a reviewer teased the management for pretending to historical accuracy while showing a first-century Imogen reading herself to sleep (and turning down the page to mark her place) from what is obviously a printed book. In reviewing *Richard III* for the *Athenaeum*, Joseph Knight declared that the representation was all that could be desired, the views of London striking and picturesque, the scenes of combat as realistic as possible—but somehow from the midst of all this esthetic perfection the spirit of tragedy had fled, or was choked to death by "naturalism—the false god of these later days." It goes without saying that Irving cut his texts relentlessly—Shaw's word was "disembowelled"—in order to make time for so much elaborate scenery.

About the turn of the century leadership in Shakespeare production in London passed from Irving to Herbert Beerbohm Tree (1853–1917), and "spectacular" Shakespeare moved into its most opulent and essentially final phase. Except in the cinema, Shakespeare as historical fact or as pictorial illustration would hardly survive the 1914–18 war.

In 1898, in his beautiful new theatre called Her Majesty's, Tree staked his claim to preeminence with a spectacular *Julius Caesar*. Thereafter he would add a Shakespeare to his repertory nearly every season, until by 1914 he had done seventeen of them. And every spring from 1905 to 1913 he conducted a Shakespeare Festival, in which he revived his own productions and sometimes invited in those of neighbor companies.

Shakespeare at Tree's theatre was less magisterial than at Irving's, and it was more likely to be fun. Tree himself was a playful and humorous man—witty, whimsical, dandiacal. He loved to play characters who are, in Desmond MacCarthy's phrase, "the play-actors of their own emotions." Of his serious roles Richard II and King John were ideally suited to his personality. His Macbeth and Othello were inadequate. He never attempted King Lear. He was at heart a comedian, a character actor, a makeup artist specializing in the eccentric.

As a producer he "loved" Shakespeare, or what he thought was Shakespeare, and decked out the plays with extraordinary ingenuity. Shaw maintained that for Tree the real Shakespeare didn't exist; that a Shakespearean play was only an "ancient, dusty, mouldy, empty house which it is his business to furnish, decorate, and housewarm with an amusing entertainment." Scenery was lavish, of course; the most expert of old-school scene painters created for his productions stage worlds which were the ultimate in make-believe. For *Antony and Cleopatra* he actually built "the barge she sat in," with its purple sails, golden poop, and silver oars, and moved it onto the stage. Throne rooms of the English history plays were lofty chambers topped by fan vaulting or hammerbeam roofs, their walls tapestried, their furnishings authentically medieval or Tudor. Out of any three-to-four-hour performance, upwards of forty-five minutes was consumed in changing these cumbersome sets, and to accommodate them, Tree, like Irving before him, cut and rearranged the texts freely.

He loved tricky business, tableaux, and dumb shows. In *King John* he staged the signing of Magna Carta, which Shakespeare never thought of. In *Twelfth Night* Malvolio was accompanied by four lesser Malvolios, dressed exactly like him and repeating his actions. In *Richard II*, when the power passed to the usurper, Richard's pet hound crossed the stage and licked the new king's hand. In *A Midsummer Night's Dream* real rabbits nibbled the grass of the floorcloth. In *The Tempest*, Caliban (Tree played Caliban in a marvellous monster make-up) chewed a dead fish, shooed flies off his master Stephano, and at the final curtain was seen watching Prospero's ship disappear in the distance, stretching his arms out after it lovingly: "The night falls, and Caliban is left alone on the lonely rock. He is a King once more."

Tree often helped Shakespeare along with music. The actress who played Oberon not only spoke the passage beginning "I know a bank where the wild thyme blows" but then sang it. King Duncan, having dined at Inverness, was escorted to his chamber by a harper and a band of singers who lulled him to sleep with a hymn. At Hamlet's death his soul was wafted upward by an angelic chorus singing him to his rest.

Tree's faith in his method was never shaken. When about 1912 the idea of a National Theatre was being seriously considered, Tree confidently expected to be appointed to the directorship. Younger rivals like Harley Granville Barker, who espoused more "modern" methods, were in his eyes nothing but "humbug." "What one wants," he declared, sublimely indifferent to the theatrical revolution which would soon discredit all he had stood for, "is sincerity, directness and a reverence for Shakespeare."

THE MODERNIST REVOLT

With the rise of modern scholarship and criticism, with the growth of educated readership, an ever greater number of Shakespeare lovers were coming to perceive that Shakespeare the playwright knew his business, and that on the stage the dramatic essences of his plays should be realized, not diluted or smothered. In certain literary and academic circles Tree's methods were denounced. Yet it is easier for critics to attack bad methods than for artists to create good methods and win acceptance for them. No one in Tree's lifetime managed to break his hold on the favor of the general public.

Of his opponents inside the profession, the most persistent was the saintly monomaniac William Poel (1852–1934), whose life in the theatre was a never-ending campaign to recover the playing conditions of the Elizabethan stage. Poel did not ask for a literal reconstruction of an Elizabethan playhouse. He required only a broad open platform, a curtained inner space for discoveries, and some sort of "above" for scenes in balconies or on castle walls. Costumes were to be, for the most part, standard Elizabethan. The actors must be lighted from the front and above, not from footlights. Speech was to be swift and continuous, not interrupted for "business"; it was to be musical; by firm underscoring of key words it was to be meaningful. He preferred actors who were novices, not old hands, because they saved him the labor of eradicating their professional bad habits. (Of Henry Irving he said, "I wouldn't give him five pounds a week.") He did not seek "runs" but got up plays for one or two or half a dozen performances. Between 1881 and 1932 he accomplished nearly seventy productions of Shakespeare and other English classics and a dozen classics of foreign origin.

Poel's aim with Shakespeare was always to act him "naturally and appealingly from the full text as in a modern drama." Or so he said. It is not easy to square his practice with his principle: he bowdlerized shockingly, lopped out passages which got in the way of the story, and on occasion slashed texts as wildly as an Irving or Tree would do. Even so, Shakespeare without theatrical trappings was immensely attractive to many distinguished, if somewhat bookish, Shakespeare lovers—among them Edmund Gosse, Stopford Brooke, Israel Gollancz, F. J. Furnivall, Sir Sidney Lee, and W. J. Lawrence. Granville Barker would call Poel "one of the greatest and finest influences in the English theatre." Bernard Shaw approved his platform productions enthusiastically. The painter Byam Shaw said, "I only wish that others would follow your noble example and allow us to listen to Shakespeare instead of looking at what Mr. So-and-so thinks is like a sunset or a cherry tree."

Poel rejected scenery altogether, but in the early years of this century, when the esthetics of post-impressionism were on the rise, it was the theatrical revolution fomented by Gordon Craig (1872–1966) which would prevail. Craig too was hostile to realistic scenery, but not to *stage decoration*, which must produce essences rather than pictures, not facts but feelings and ideas. Just as the easel painters—Whistler and Steer and Sickert—had learned to paint for the sake of painting, to abandon story-telling and message-bearing, to relinquish to photographers the literal imitation of surfaces, so Craig turned away from representational *mise-en-scène*, and in the very few productions he achieved in London between *Dido and Aeneas* in 1900 and *Much Ado about Nothing* in 1903, he initiated the new stagecraft and rang the knell of the old.

To measure the distance between the old art and the new we need only to contemplate the Church Scene in *Much Ado* as Henry Irving had staged it in 1882 (see above, page 1811) alongside Craig's. Being short of funds and having barely three weeks to produce the entire play, Craig created the church out of one light shining downward, one large cross over an altar, and some tall painted curtains. A critic described it as follows:

> Stage and auditorium are in utter darkness at first. The music of an organ swells out from the gloom of the stage. Then a shaft of light suddenly illuminates the jewelled patriarchal cross on the altar just beyond the centre of the scene; a mysterious blueness, vague, translucent, like the blue of atmospheric space, grows out of the darkness beyond the altar; a warmer glow suffuses the whole stage; dim forms of worshippers take shape and colour; arched mosaic columns spring up on either side; and so, little by little, with the cross, the altar, the priest, and Claudio and Hero for the central group there grows out of darkness a scene of Byzantine splendour. It is as though one were within the walls of a vast cathedral with a vista beyond the altar that seems to soar outward and upward into illimitable space.

No one today, outside of film studios, would attempt to recreate the Irving church, but Craig's would still pass for excellent on any stage.

After *Much Ado* Craig had only one flirtation with the London theatre. Tree, of all people, invited him to do the scenery for *Macbeth*. When Craig submitted his models, Tree was delighted with them. Later, however, he let his regular scene painter, Joseph Harker, persuade him that if the sets were built to scale no theatre would be tall enough to contain them. Some of the models were destroyed. Craig, angered at this, sued for damages. The case was settled out of court.

On July 14, 1911, a dinner was given in Craig's honor at the Café Royal. "Some two hundred of Craig's supporters thronged to this dinner," says Denis Bablet; "writers, painters and musicians formed the majority, there were not many theatre people."

In 1912 Harley Granville Barker (1877–1946) was the ideal person to take up the cause of modernizing Shakespeare production. Having been through the famous Vedrenne-Barker stand at the Royal Court, where he had staged thirty-two plays by seventeen playwrights, from Euripides to Galsworthy, including a good many plays of Bernard Shaw, he was a thoroughly experienced director. He was as devoted a Shakespearean as Poel (indeed, far more dedicated to the text); and he was sufficiently abreast of esthetic fashions to keep pace with Craig's best ideas.

In September of 1912, at the Savoy Theatre, he opened *The Winter's Tale.* The battle lines formed. From one side, cries of outrage: it wasn't Shakespeare, it was post-impressionism; the settings were meaningless; the garish costumes were half Beardsley, half Russian ballet; the speech was unintelligible gabbling; and "every actor or actress who had ever played in Shakespeare would loathe and hate this method of doing it." From the other side, John Palmer declared in the *Saturday Review* that it was the first production since Burbage that Shakespeare would recognize as his own, and urged all playgoers to visit the Savoy in order "to recover for the first time on a modern West End stage something of the strength, glamour, and delicacy of Shakespeare himself."

Barker arranged his stage in three levels. Several feet behind the proscenium arch he erected a smaller arch which framed the equivalent of an Elizabethan inner stage, elevated four steps above the main stage. In front of the main stage two steps dropped down to a platform built out over the orchestra pit. He abolished footlights and lighted the actors mainly from lamps attached to the front of the dress circle.

The "stage decoration" was executed by Norman Wilkinson. Leontes' palace was indicated by dull gold curtains across the back of the stage, divided into three sections by white pilasters. The scene in Bohemia showed at upstage centre a neat little thatched cottage. Lesser scenes were played in front of non-representational curtains. The costumes, by Albert Rutherston, were exotic in design and bold in color—emerald, magenta, lemon, cerise. Barker staged the entire text—all but six of the some three thousand lines—about a thousand more lines than any audience had to listen to in an evening at Tree's theatre. His actors did *not* gabble, but with utmost care to bring out the sense of their lines they spoke swiftly, and they wasted no time on stage business between the lines. Indeed, Palmer declared Henry Ainley's Leontes to be "the finest piece of Shakespearean acting I have ever seen. It was absolutely in the spirit of the platform stage, and Shakespeare's seventeenth century audience would have risen to him in wildest admiration." Henry Massingham of the *Nation* declared that "Mr. Barker has at one stroke destroyed the old way of playing Shakespeare and reopened the theatre to thousands who were instinctively repelled from it by the superior refinement of their taste in musical and representative art."

The thousands did not respond, however: *The Winter's Tale* lost a good deal of money. But *Twelfth Night*, which replaced it in the evening bill on November 15, ran to a hundred and thirty-seven performances, successful in every way. Now everybody praised Barker. Again the actors spoke speedily and spoke the entire text, but since the play was more familiar and the language less complex than in *The Winter's Tale*, there were no complaints about intelligibility. Incrustations of clownery which had been settling onto the "comic" scenes for a century and a half were scraped away, and the actors created their roles "from the book" rather than from tradition. Palmer said of Henry Ainley that he "is the first Malvolio of this generation that does not seem to have walked onto the stage from some municipal museum of theatrical bric-a-brac. He does not, like so many of his predecessors, give one the impression that he has just been dusted and taken down."

About a year later, in February of 1914, came Barker's production of *A Midsummer Night's Dream*, forever memorable because of the Barker-Wilkinson fancy of presenting the fairies all in gold. Not only were their dresses golden, but arms, legs, faces, and hair were painted with gold paint. The forest scene was made up of a green grassy mound at centre stage, high in the air above it a wide circle of flowers from which hung a gauze canopy glittering with fireflies, and at the back of the stage loosely folded curtains of purple, green, and blue. Most splendid in this setting, said the *Times*, was Oberon:

> The golden Oberon, Mr. Dennis Neilson-Terry, is a figure of slim, noble, and giorgionesque beauty. His movements are grace itself. His voice, with the familiar family *timbre*, is the very voice for some of the most beautiful lines Shakespeare ever wrote. This Oberon, for the first time, dominates not only the scene, but the whole play, informs it with graciousness and majesty (fairy majesty, golden majesty) and exquisite rhythmic beauty.

The figure of Puck, as played by Dion Calthrop, made a fierce counterpoint. By no means a gentle, playful Ariel figure, he seemed rather a sinister hobgoblin out of English folklore. His dress was scarlet, his huge wig yellow with red berries in it, and he moved fiercely and spoke in harsh tones. The lovers and the hard-handed men received their due of praise, but always, the *Times* said, "the mind goes back to the golden fairies, and one's memories of this production must always be golden memories."

In 1920 the American theatre historian G. C. D. Odell, having praised the late Beerbohm Tree unstintingly ("Let us here lay a wreath on the tomb of the brave believer in Shakespeare and the theatre"), and having dismissed with scorn both the "new" staging of Gordon Craig and the revival of the Elizabethan platform stage by William Poel, loosed a full-scale attack upon Barker's *Dream*, which he had seen when Barker brought it to New York. "I hope," Odell concluded, "that this silly and vulgar way of presenting Shakespeare died with all the other vain, frivolous, un-simple things burnt up by the great war-conflagration."

THE FESTIVAL THEATRES

The death of Beerbohm Tree in 1917 wiped out the last commercial management in London which regularly offered "spectacular" Shakespeare. Barker withdrew from the practical theatre altogether and Craig had exiled himself to Italy. Thus to Shakespeare-lovers of all persuasions the future must have looked bleak. As a matter of fact Shakespeare production in the future would be more plentiful and at its best much more satisfying than ever in the past; only it would not depend upon old style actor-managers, commercial speculators, or lonely artist-pioneers. England, and eventually America also, would see the rise of theatrical organizations, often referred to as "festival theatres," whose central if not sole concern would be the production of Shakespeare. Control of these organizations would as a rule be vested in a board of governors, so that survival would not depend upon the life, whim, or fortune of any single person. London's Old Vic, for instance, between 1914 and 1963 sponsored Shakespeare for fifty seasons. The number of its productions was three hundred and forty-seven. About fifteen principal or supervising directors succeeded one another, and the actual stage direction was done by nearly fifty different persons. Within this pattern, now common in festival theatres, individual artists come and go, policies change, artistic quality and box-office prosperity fluctuate, but the enterprise goes on.

The Old Vic came to maturity in the 1930's under the successive directorships of Harcourt Williams (1880–1957) and Tyrone Guthrie (1900–71), when it launched the careers of such major Shakespearean actors as John Gielgud, Ralph Richardson, Peggy Ashcroft, Maurice Evans, Alec Clunes, Laurence Olivier, and Vivien Leigh. In a resurgence of energy in the 1950's it put through a Five Year Plan to stage every play in the Folio. Michael Benthall conducted the Plan, and Michael Hordern, Richard Burton, Claire Bloom, John Neville, Paul Rogers, Barbara Jefford, and others carried the burden of the acting. In 1963 the Old Vic organization ceased to exist, and the Old Vic Theatre became the temporary home of the National Theatre, headed by Sir Laurence Olivier (b. 1907). During its first decade the National staged half a dozen distinctive Shakespeare productions.

The oldest modern festival is that at Stratford-upon-Avon, which dates from 1879 when the first Shakespeare Memorial Theatre was dedicated, the gift of the Flower family of Stratford. In the nineteenth century and down to 1919, while the Memorial Theatre was served briefly each spring (and in later years each summer also) by the provincial company of F. R. Benson (1858–1939), its festival was barely noticed by the London press. Nor in the 1920's was the solider program of W. Bridges-Adams (1889–1965) looked upon by fashionable Londoners as much more than the dull labors of a country "rep" company. The burning of the old theatre in 1926 and the dedication of the new one in 1932 were newsworthy events, of course, and Bridges-Adams attracted a good deal of transatlantic attention when he trouped his company to America in a series of fund-raising tours. Through the 1930's, under the scholarly but somewhat pedestrian direction of B. Iden Payne (b. 1881), Stratford continued to mark time, its even tenor broken only occasionally by the astonishing productions of Theodore Komisarjevsky (1882–1954).

Finally in the 1950's, under the leadership of Anthony Quayle (b. 1913) and Glen Byam Shaw (b. 1904), abetted by the brilliant directing of Peter Brook, Peter Hall, Douglas Seale, and Tyrone Guthrie, Stratford arrived at a climax of excellence. The finest actors in England came there to play, and every season boasted its share of masterpiece productions.

In 1960 Peter Hall (b. 1930) assumed the post of artistic director, to be joined presently by Michel St. Denis and Peter Brook. Hall effected a change of name from the "Memorial" Theatre to the Royal Shakespeare Theatre and Company (RSC), and he fulfilled an old dream of the governing board by acquiring a base in London: the Aldwych has provided a year-round home not only for Shakespeare but for modern drama also.

The Canadian Shakespeare Festival was established at Stratford, Ontario, in 1953, with Tyrone Guthrie in command. Guthrie had long since been attracted toward a Poelesque faith in the open stage for Shakespeare, and in collaboration with Tanya Moiseiwitsch he designed for the Canadian Stratford a spacious platform backed by a neutral scenic facade, the audience ranged in a curve around three sides of the platform. For the first seasons, while the arrangement was being tested, audience and stage were housed under a tent, but in 1957 the tent was replaced by a permanent and very handsome building. Walter Kerr has called it "the only really new stage and the only really new actor-audience experience of the last hundred years on this continent."

Guthrie served as artistic director for three seasons and set a pattern which still more or less obtains: a central core of Shakespeare productions with one or two other classic or masterpiece plays to vary the pace; the leading roles sometimes played by guest stars but the bulk of the work by native Canadians, who are given ever more demanding roles as their skills mature. After Guthrie left, Michael Langham (b. 1919) directed the theatre for twelve years, to be succeeded in turn by Jean Gascon from the Théâtre du Nouveau Monde of Montreal.

One must admire the decorum of the Ontario operation: the dedication of its officers, the beauty of the building and its grounds, the growth of the company. One senses throughout the Stratford community a pride of ownership and an awareness that their theatre is a contribution to the nation's well-being.

The American Shakespeare Festival Theatre was conceived by the late Lawrence Langner (1890–1962) of Theatre Guild Incorporated, and built in 1955 at Stratford, Connecticut. Langner doubtless assumed that proximity to New York City—its pool of talent, its financial resources, and its carriage trade—would ensure the theatre's success. Unfortunately the ills of Broadway are as communicable as its strengths, and though the Connecticut theatre has kept going, much of its work has disappointed knowledgeable critics.

The building itself is disappointing. Whereas the Canadian theatre began as a stage for performing Shakespeare, planned by one of the most experienced directors in the business, and only after this stage had been well tested was a shell built around it, the

Connecticut theatre began with the shell. Handsome from the outside—tall, polygonal, wood-covered—it tells us clearly that we are about to enter a "genuine" Elizabethan playhouse. But once inside we realize that the exterior is only an architectural caprice: we are seated in a merely modern (i.e. nineteenth-century) theatre, facing a conventional proscenium arch behind which is a conventional stage house for the display of scenery.

New York could supply plenty of actors, of course, but almost none who are experienced Shakespeareans, because for more than half a century New York has had no continuing classic theatre to promote classic acting. The critics of Connecticut productions have instinctively recognized this when they have praised a Richard Waring or a John Colicos for expert verse-reading—the one English-born, the other Canadian-trained, and neither of them subject to the speech habits of Broadway.

There have been valuable events, of course: Philip Bosco's Coriolanus, Morris Carnovsky's Shylock and King Lear, John Houseman's production of *All's Well That Ends Well*. But far too often (though they have no monopoly of this vice) the Stratford directors substitute gimmick for interpretation: Beatrice on her hands and knees under a table, "walking" it about the garden scene the better to overhear Hero's confidences; Richard II with his head all to one side pretending to be a Christ-figure; Duke Senior doing setting-up exercises; Sir Oliver Martext arriving on a bicycle; the King of Navarre as Hindu guru to whom the young romantics come for lessons in meditation.

The New York Shakespeare Festival, which operates in an open air theatre in Central Park, is vigorously democratic. Its producer, Joseph Papp (b. 1921) a hardhitting and unstoppable loner up from the slums of Brooklyn, a dedicated exponent of theatre as a social force, has achieved by sheer will power what committees of millionaires could never bring off—theatre for the people. Admission is free, and some two thousand spectators, many of whom have never seen Shakespeare under any other conditions, attend nightly. Papp has taken whatever money he could find (never enough, but he gets by), from wealthy donors, from foundations, from City Hall, and he has staged an average of three Shakespeares each summer since 1957.

In reviewing the plays of the 1962 season Alice Griffin declared that Papp's festival could "take its place with the major professional Shakespearian festivals of the world." The productions lacked polish, to be sure, and few of the actors were adepts in the classical style, but the productions "have about them a spirit of creativity, imagination, and excitement that gives unity and importance to the venture that has been lacking so far in America's other professional Shakespeare festival, at Stratford, Connecticut." Three years later Mrs. Griffin observed again how free the Papp productions were of those fanciful stunts which continued to multiply in Connecticut. Papp's directors, she said, have "approached Shakespeare with great honesty, letting the merits of the play speak clearly for themselves, rather than overloading the play with such tricks as changes of period, devices which call attention to themselves rather than to the action and dialogue, and the general 'hoking up' which modern productions often employ."

The compliments were, of course, premature. As early as 1966, when Papp himself directed an *All's Well That Ends Well* with unhelpful cross-reference to the then fashionable *Marat/Sade*, the New York Shakespeare Festival showed signs of catching up with faddish modes of "interpretation." The next year *Titus Andronicus* was turned into a sort of Artaudian ritual with overtones of Kabuki. *Twelfth Night* has been set at the turn of the present century. *The Two Gentlemen of Verona* has become a musical, and *Much Ado about Nothing* a jolly romp about Teddy Roosevelt's America, with ragtime bands, canoeing in the park, a steam-powered automobile, and free beer.

"INTERPRETING" SHAKESPEARE: SIX MODES AND MASTERS

Muriel St. Clare Byrne once declared that after the work of Granville Barker, "the most important single contribution to the history of modern Shakespearian production" was the modern-dress *Hamlet* which appeared at the Kingsway in London in August 1925. This *Hamlet* was the creation of Sir Barry Jackson (1879–1961), sponsor of the Birmingham Repertory Theatre, and his director H. K. Ayliff. It was by no means as a stunt that Sir Barry stripped the play of sables and reclothed it in dinner jackets, but an earnest experiment to discover whether our appreciation of it might not be reinvigorated if we could hear it and view it freed of time-worn non-essentials. He would explain that he was only "going back to Garrick," or reverting to Shakespeare's own practices—that is to say, he was bypassing the romantic tone and antiquarian debris imposed upon the play during the nineteenth century, and treating it as if it were a contemporary action. "Give Hamlet a dinner jacket," noted Richard Jennings of the *Spectator*, "he will no longer dare to keep the table waiting while he tells his tale. He will leave his mouthings and begin."

The actors were wonderfully responsive to their garments. As Hamlet, Colin Keith-Johnston was, in Ivor Brown's words, "a loose-tongued, bawdy-minded, and savage product of youthful disenchantment." It was a narrow and special Hamlet, to be sure, but this very narrowness, along with the cigarettes, wrist watches, short skirts, and syncopated music, served as the attention-pricks exactly needed by the audience of that day: as Miss Byrne put it, it "shocked them into thinking."

Unfortunately, that sort of shock wore off very quickly. Modern-dress Shakespeare became the fashion, or rather, a craze, which spread epidemically on both sides of the ocean. Presently what mattered to a good many Shakespeare directors was not so much the actors or even the book, but a properties crew that could supply telephones, motor cars, cocktail shakers, shooting sticks, golf clubs, wireless sets, Colt revolvers, and roller skates.

In the long run, however, it was not so much the specifics of modern dress that mattered in Sir Barry Jackson's experiment, but the fact that he freed the theatre from its century-long obsession with "historical accuracy." From then on directors could (as, indeed, Granville Barker had already done) stage and dress a play in *any* mode, including the fashions of any historical period, which would enhance the play's meaning. But freedom bred license, too, and it is sometimes to be wondered whether Sir Barry's experiment really freed the theatre or only opened its Pandora's box. As early as 1934 Harold Child was complaining that "the age shows signs of wanting merely to find some way of playing Shakespeare that has never been tried before . . . and tricks are played with the construction and the tone of the plays every whit as daring as those of Tate and Cibber." The annals are shot through with directorial irrelevancies, of which anyone can make his own bouquet. In 1953 Michael Benthall staged *All's Well* at the Old Vic as a farcical comic strip, with Molièresque doctors surrounding the sick King, who indulged in spasms of vomiting. In Canada in 1954 Tyrone Guthrie turned *The Shrew* into a shoot-'em-up Western. In London in 1955 the American artist Isamu Noguchi decorated *King Lear* with abstract expressionist costumes and geometrical scenic pieces which slid, hovered, and turned in ways amusing in themselves but by no means expressive of the tragedy. In 1961 at Stratford, Connecticut, Jack Landau presented *Troilus and Cressida* as a dramatization of the War between the States. In 1965 at London's National Theatre, Franco Zeffirelli "had fun" with *Much Ado*—and undercut its fundamental seriousness—by plastering it with *lazzi* borrowed from the daily life of modern Sicily. When Shakespeare is approached by the "stunts-and-games" method, it is not uncommon to find that the stunts and games are brought off with zest and skill, because they are within reach of the actors' understanding; but that the Shakespeare is ill understood, ineptly performed, and in consequence worse than boring.

Yet anachronism and other devices of interpretation are not crimes unless they are badly used. The pleasantest accounts come to us of "period" productions that seem to have been true illuminations: Peter Brook's *Love's Labor's Lost* à la Watteau at Stratford-upon-Avon in 1946; Michael Benthall's Victorian *Hamlet* at Stratford in 1948; Michael Langham's Victorian *Much Ado* at the Canadian Stratford in 1958 and his modern dress *Timon* in 1963; Jonathan Miller's Victorian *Merchant of Venice* at the National in 1970. There are no rules to this game. Only the imponderables—talent and taste and discretion, and above all a sure hold of the play's essentials—make the difference between illumination and impertinence.

One of the most startling interpreters (many then said "traducers") of Shakespeare in England was Theodore Komisarjevsky, whose half dozen productions in the 1930's enlivened what was otherwise a rather humdrum decade at Stratford-upon-Avon. His *Merchant of Venice* in 1932 was at once a masque, a farce, and a Venetian harlequinade. His *Macbeth* in 1933 dispensed with the supernatural, rendered the tragic experience as neurosis and nightmare, and bodied it forth in modern military dress and walls of aluminium. In 1935 he set *The Merry Wives of Windsor* in a comic picture-book background of nineteenth-century Vienna. In 1936 he undertook *Lear*, and forsaking his habits of embroidery, stripped it to essentials: the scenery was a massive flight of steps rising from the curtain line toward the cyclorama, where marvellously effective though simple lighting effects created storm and fair weather. The bold acting and severe costumes were exactly tuned to the spirit of the play. *Lear* was Komisarjevsky's Shakespearean masterpiece. In 1938 his *Comedy of Errors* was brilliant farce, unlocalized and timeless. In 1939 his *Taming of the Shrew* combined the physical high jinks of *commedia dell'arte* with the full-bottomed wigs and fancy dress of the English Restoration. When reactionary critics objected to Komisarjevsky's fast-and-loose handlings of Shakespeare, he answered with well-informed asperity. He dismissed the appeal to "tradition" as meaningless. "The accepted method of performing Shakespeare is based upon a mixture of the French romanticists and the heavy German declamatory style. To my mind this makes merely nonsense; they do not mix." And he would claim that his *Merry Wives* got more laughs from Shakespeare's lines than any previous production of the play—because "it is faithful in word and gesture to Shakespeare."

Tyrone Guthrie, when he was a young beginner, declared against modern dress, but eventually he learned to use it with great distinction. In his Old Vic *Hamlet* in the fall of 1938, while carefully excluding the prop-list trivia which had fascinated so many directors, he achieved beauty and dignity through the color and line of modern court dress. The women wore low-cut and sweeping evening gowns, with tiaras and jewelled necklaces; the men dress suits with colorful sashes, orders, and court swords. Against this elegant background, or amidst the gaudy costumes of the Players, the figure of Hamlet, casually garbed in black and purple, showed in fine contrast. The Ghost wore a modern military overcoat and plain helmet, and the Gravediggers modern workmen's clothes. It rained on the day of Ophelia's funeral, and everyone remembers the "dreary vista of wet umbrellas and dripping mackintoshes." In Canada in 1953 and again at Stratford-upon-Avon in 1959 Guthrie used much the same costume plan for his revivals of *All's Well That Ends Well*.

Costume of earlier periods, too, served him to high esthetic and intellectual advantage. His early Victorian *Midsummer Night's Dream* in 1937 was designed to unite "the words of Shakespeare, the music of Mendelssohn, and the architecture of the Old Vic," and it would have pleased the late proprietress of the Old Vic, Lilian Baylis, who had once exclaimed, "I like my fairies gauzy." Ninette de Valois composed flying ballets in the romantic manner for a company of fairies, winged and white-clad. The Titania who led them was Vivien Leigh, "beautiful as a fairy princess, silver of tongue and meltingly seductive," in her poses reminiscent of the ballerina Taglioni. Oberon was played by the actor-dancer-mime Robert Helpmann, white-faced, green-clad, horned, reminding some observers of a great dangerous insect. Oliver Messel's forest scenery was a true Victorian fairyland. And in the midst of this the moon face of Ralph Richardson expressed the naiveté and authority of Bottom. The exquisite verse-speaking, the gossamer music, the rare pictorial beauty worked such magic that the crustiest of anti-sentimental critics surrendered to it.

Guthrie could use anachronism effectively, too, to assist Shakespeare in dismantling the glamorous pretensions of love and war. His *Troilus and Cressida* at the Old Vic in 1956 was aptly set in the very last era when war still seemed a romantic adventure—late Edwardian times. It was a war between a decadent Ruritanian Troy and its Prussian-like Greek invaders. The Trojans wore gay yellow tunics and shiny brass helmets topped by yellow plumes; the helmets of the Greeks were spiked and severe. Cressida in riding habit, Helen as a torchy *femme fatale* with cigarettes and cocktail glass, and Pandarus, silver-haired and wearing morning suit and grey Ascot top hat, neatly symbolized the futile elegance of the Trojans. On the Greek side the overbearing Agamemnon, the imperviously boobish Ajax, the sullen Achilles lolling at the door of his tent expressed relentless and tyrannical power. Thersites was particularly credible as a war correspondent in civilian trenchcoat and cap, equipped with notebook and camera, spreading his virulent commentary up and down the theatre aisles as well as on the stage. The ending of the production, suddenly Brechtian, showed the smoking cannon that had done down the walls of Troy, and under the pall of smoke a shabby Pandarus sitting on his suitcases packed for the road, plaintively bequeathing us his "diseases."

Such brilliant conceptions as these, and the unfailing assurance of their execution, won for Guthrie the reputation of foremost Shakespearean producer of his day. Besides an unerring sense in casting he seems to have inspired actors to give better than their known best in performance, and to have earned the trust and respect from performers that musicians accord to great conductors. His one conspicuous weakness was sometimes analyzed as a fear of audiences, sometimes as simple addiction to gag, sometimes as egotistic insistence on putting his personal mark upon every work. He rarely played Shakespeare whole and straight, but would in greater or lesser ways "hoke him up." In *All's Well That Ends Well*, for instance, he thought nothing of eliminating Lavatch the clown entirely, of translating the Italian military actions into the North African campaigns of World War II, and inserting a farcical business of a military inspection by an idiotic modern general. Purists deplored these interventions of Guthrian fancy. Right or wrong, Guthrie persisted to the end in refusing to bore the "average man in the street" in order to satisfy "the pedantic minority."

Peter Brook (b. 1925), who appears to have inherited the Guthrie mantle, is far more radical in his approach to Shakespeare—far less obviously the popular showman and far more determinedly the original and all-mastering Producer that Gordon Craig once prophesied would "save the English stage." He has directed at least ten Shakespeares; his international reputation depends upon three—*Titus Andronicus* (1955–57), *King Lear* (1962–63), and *A Midsummer Night's Dream* (1970–73). Unquestionably Brook is a genius. Whether he is a great Shakespearean, or, rather, a great theatrician who from time to time improvises on Shakespearean materials, will long be debated. "I am more easily bored with Shakespeare," he has said, "and have suffered more ghastly evenings with him, than with any dramatist I know." The reason for this is what he calls "Deadly Theatre"—the "old formulae, old methods, old jokes, old effects." He insists ever more urgently in getting beyond surface realities to inner realities, and for Shakespeare this has meant an increasing stripping away of visual realism and the substitution of abstract forms from other media, culminating in the white box full of circus performers who enacted *A Midsummer Night's Dream.*

Brook's *Titus Andronicus*, as we look back upon it, was comparatively conventional. Taking up what is commonly regarded as Shakespeare's worst play, Brook assembled at Stratford-upon-Avon a magnificent cast led by Sir Laurence Olivier, Anthony Quayle, Vivien Leigh, and Maxine Audley, and in gorgeously gloomy scenery which he himself designed, accompanied by an elaborate score of *musique concrète* which he composed, conducted that company to a theatrical triumph. Wherever necessary he "saved Shakespeare from himself," cutting lines which would have provoked laughter because of their crudity, suppressing literal bloodshed, but, as Muriel St. Clare Byrne observed, using color, light, and form "to work on our imaginations to create a more potent horror." From the opening sacrifice of Tamora's son, the rape of Lavinia, the chopping-off of Titus' hand, Titus' horrendous howl at his recognition scene, the shooting of arrows into the palace walls, Aaron's murder of the Nurse, to the final Thyestean feast, Brook used every normal means (which presumably he would now disown as the "old" means) to express the agony and horror of this play. In 1957 he toured it with the same company to Paris, Venice, Belgrade, Zagreb, Vienna, and Warsaw—and in Warsaw he provided the critic Jan Kott with one of "the five greatest theatrical experiences of my life."

By 1962 Brook had read in Jan Kott's *Shakespeare Our Contemporary* the chapter entitled "*King Lear*; or *Endgame*," and in the autumn of that year he staged at Stratford-upon-Avon a relentlessly Beckettian production of that play. It was an "epic unfolding of the nature of the absurdity of the human condition." In an abstract staging of tall whitish screens and strange shapes of rusted metal, Paul Scofield acted out the most deliberately cruel destruction of a man that

Brook could imagine. Deliberately Brook removed from the text every touch of pity or sympathy, every sign of catharsis, every hope of redemption. Again his work was greeted by a storm of critical enthusiasm, not only in England, but in Paris, the Balkan countries, Moscow, and finally New York. Yet here and there a cautionary objection was heard. It is all very well, wrote Robert Speaight in the *Shakespeare Quarterly*, for Brook to stage a play which is not about redemption but about despair. But that is Brook's play, not Shakespeare's. He ought not to mutilate the play to make his own point. Two cuts which Speaight found deplorable were the compassionate lines of the servants after the blinding of Gloucester, and Edmund's sudden impulse to do good just before his death. A vicious bit of business which Brook invented without textual excuse was to show Edgar lugging the dead Edmund into the wings "like a slaughtered pig." Much as Speaight admits to admiration of Brook's technical skill, it "was rather like watching a great surgeon at work in a delicate operation": one had not much pity for the patient. Nine years later, it may be noted, Speaight thought rather better of Brook's *King Lear* film.

The stage of Brook's *A Midsummer Night's Dream* was a white-walled room, lighted with white light, and containing swings, trapezes, and ladders. Strange music filled the air. The characters were circus performers. "It must be *your* imagination then," says Hippolyta in the play, and so it was. By removing every expectable visual item from the stage, Brook compelled the spectator to recreate the world of the play in his own mind, even as its first spectators had to recreate it in the non-illusionistic theatre of the 1590's. Brook's actors seem to have realized the humanity of the characters with remarkable warmth, and many hearers found the lines of the play better spoken than they had ever known. According to the *Times* Brook had discovered the genuine essence of the play, its Platonic Form, and hence had given us not a mere copy of it but a true production.

In the wake of Peter Brook comes his sometime assistant, Charles Marowitz, whose own productions send us into a swift plunge down a steep place. His game with *Hamlet* in 1966 and other tragedies since then has been to disassemble the text and put it together again (actions occurring in random order, characters taking each other's speeches) in such ways as to break up the "relentless *narrativeness*, the impregnable closed circuit of story-lines," which has locked away from us the multitudinous possibilities of the mythic material. Some of these possibilities which Marowitz has chosen to express are: a boundless contempt for Hamlet (a parlor liberal and paralyzed intellectual, a very bad actor playing badly the role of scholar, courtier, soldier, poet, lover); a view of Ophelia as a frustrated Lolita ("a sexual convenience passed methodically from one peer to the other and even turning up in Claudius' bed"); the Ghost as a vengeful old wretch whose reign ruined Denmark; Horatio as "the most obnoxious Yes-man in the Shakespearian canon." The Marowitz method need not, of course, adopt the Marowitz themes, and an occasional "disassembled" production may very well work upon audiences, even as Sir Barry Jackson's innovation of modern dress worked long ago, to "shock them into thinking."

After Marowitz comes Joseph Papp, who concocted his "*Naked*" *Hamlet* to open his Public Theatre in New York in 1968. It is an utterly zany vaudeville, less in earnest than Marowitz's version and more obviously meant to be amusing in its mixtures of language, its topical references, and its clowneries. Hamlet appears sometimes in his underwear, sometimes in a white suit and black beret, sometimes in baggy pants and leather jacket. Sometimes he is Hamlet, sometimes a ventriloquist's dummy, sometimes a Puerto Rican peanut vendor. Ophelia is more than ready for sex, and most of her songs are grouped and delivered as a nightclub entertainment. The Ghost wears a white union-suit, tennis shoes, and a battered combat helmet—or sometimes a Wagnerian helmet with huge golden horns. Claudius is a lewd and drunken general, attended by guards in olive-drab fatigues. The play opens with Hamlet reading in bed. He is reading *Hamlet*. He is handcuffed, and his bed is a coffin, which stands like a cradle at the foot of the Royal Bed where Claudius and Gertrude are sleeping. The play-within-the-play is conducted as a wild party, with funny hats, practical jokes, balloons, streamers, plenty of booze, and a sex-fumble between Claudius and Ophelia in the coffin. Hamlet breaks up the party by shooting Claudius, who storms off stage shouting, "I don't have to take that kind of crap." At the end of the play a single pistol, loaded and reloaded, is passed from character to character and fired repeatedly until everyone is dead.

Both the Marowitz and the Papp *Hamlets* were ecstatically received by young and cultish audiences and denounced as crimes against good taste by most publishing critics. Librarians do not shelve these *Hamlets* with Shakespeare: they catalogue them as original plays.

At the end of an enthusiastic account of Brook's *A Midsummer Night's Dream* J. C. Trewin acknowledges that this particularly theatricalist way with the play is not really imitable: "Moonlight will be silver again, and the Duke's oak will rise." And even Marowitz pauses to remind us that what he has done to *Hamlet* has not displaced the original: "A spliced-up *Hamlet* doesn't destroy the play forever; just as a beautiful woman who is raped isn't barred from future domestic felicity." The play is always there in the book, and there will always be directors and actors whose peculiar delight will be to bring it to us in the most forthright, unobtrusive, and perhaps even *conventional* style, so that our attention is hardly at all distracted from the play to the manner of its performance.

STRIKING A BALANCE

We shall always owe especial allegiance to such directors as Glen Byam Shaw, who give us Shakespeare "straight." During his tenure at Stratford-upon-Avon (1953–59), Shaw brought off a round dozen Shakespeares, none of them revolutionary or even modish but surely among the most satisfying of this past generation. He loves actors and loves the text, and has a knack for bringing out the best of both. As the actress Yvonne Mitchell once wrote, "He talks in the actor's language, which would, I suppose, approximate to an architect being able to tell a builder how to lay the stones which will build a cathedral, but leaving him free to make his own gargoyles. Glen is full of invention, but the invention is never a 'clever idea.' It springs directly from the words in the play, but few people are imaginative enough to have seen it for themselves." His *Merry Wives of Windsor* in 1955 sparkled with exactly this kind of invention. In the first place, he dared answer the call of the text for April or wintry weather: Windsor was snow-clad. The forms and colors of the scenery, designed by Motley, expressed the gaiety of the piece—a Street Scene consisting of bright brown cut-out houses, a school, a church, which flew down on wires or slipped into view on rolling stages; the Field near Frogmore a bright backcloth of snow-covered gardens and houses with Windsor Castle rising distantly on the hill. Countless bits of business derived from close reading of the text—even a dance by Sackerson the bear—enlivened the actors' games.

In *Macbeth*, in the same year, having secured Olivier and Vivien Leigh for the leads, Shaw agreed with them that for once it was the actors' job, rather than the designer's, to create the atmosphere. Thus the sets and costumes were conventionally functional, hardly to be noticed; the actors took the lead, with Shaw's skillfully inconspicuous supervision, in creating what is commonly recognized as the most successful *Macbeth* of the twentieth century. One noticed how in the handling of the Witches, or in the butchery of the Macduff family, Shaw brought those parts of the play into perfect harmony with the parts controlled by Olivier and Leigh.

In reporting the 1957 *As You Like It*, with Peggy Ashcroft (Shaw always had a way of bringing into his Stratford net the best actors in the kingdom), Muriel St. Clare Byrne declared that the fundamental virtue in Shaw's work is "a trust in his author and his actors, in straight playing and in a direct and uncomplicated approach to character." She remarked, too, on his "gift for eliciting most happily conceived little portraits from his small-part actors, which give depth to the picture and admirable support to the strikingly fresh and individualized character work of his leading players." All in all, Miss Byrne declared, it was *As You Like It* "exactly as I like it."

SHAKESPEARE ON FILM: THE SILENT ERA

In our own century the most significant mutation of Shakespeare has been from stage to film, a phenomenon which, with the growth of film technology (*movement* plus *sound* plus *color*), has given us increasing pleasure. In recent years, however, as film esthetics have grown more sophisticated—as strong-minded directors have introduced more avant-garde camera techniques and imposed upon the texts more insistently "modern" interpretations—filmed Shakespeare has provoked heated argument among the critics, sometimes even sharp hostility.

The appreciation of filmed Shakespeare is troubled by certain confusions which are not always understood by critics and hardly even occur to the average box-office patron. In the first place, because of the similarities between stage and film, it is easy to overlook the difference—to assume that the film of a Shakespeare play *is* that play; and since the film version is quicker, brighter, nearer, and easier to take in, we can easily be persuaded that it is "better than" a stage version or than the play in the book. In order to judge a Shakespeare film fairly we must measure it evenhandedly against two standards: its validity as film art and its validity as an interpretation of the original play. The partisan film enthusiast and the partisan Shakespearean will argue at cross-purposes *ad infinitum* unless each acknowledges the other's premises.

Because Shakespeare presented his stories somewhat episodically (as everyone else did in the theatre of his day), film enthusiasts have made a sort of patron saint of him, have called him the first and best of scenario-writers, and assured us ten thousand times that "if he were alive today" he would be writing for the studios rather than the stage. As a matter of fact, though, most of Shakespeare's supposed "episodes" are sustained flights of dramatic action, to be viewed uninterruptedly from a single point of view. We do not object to this on the living stage: as the action grows we concentrate on it the more intently. When the action is filmed, however, we expect the camera to busy itself on our behalf. It must leap and glide about the scene, reporting the action from every thinkable angle and vantage, breaking down the single long episode into a dozen brief ones. Unless our interest is titillated by this ceaseless change, boredom sets in. The camera does our thinking, our concentrating and discriminating, for us.

Film enthusiasts seize with delight Shakespeare's acknowledgment that his "cockpit" could not hold "the vasty fields of France." The film screen can do just that, and it does. It "opens out" the play, and shows us actual scenery and whole events that Shakespeare could only describe or refer to. Here, of course, the film-makers bypass the basic Shakespearean art, which is verbal, and substitute for it their film art, which is pictorial. Shakespeare calls upon us to make our own images—to *imagine*:

> Piece out our imperfections with your thoughts;
> Into a thousand parts divide one man,
> And make imaginary puissance.

But in the presence of a film there is neither time nor need for imagining. We merely *look*, as the film-makers parade their casts of thousands before us, or lead us like sightseers through the Doge's palace or the Cotswold hills or fitted-up grandeurs of ancient Rome. What the film-makers thus achieve in fullest measure is exactly what stage producers in the nineteenth century longed to achieve and could not: factual realism. Since the innovative stagings of Gordon Craig and Granville-Barker, most modern stage producers have abandoned factual realism as unessential to the art of the play.

The intimacy of film art is another point of pride with film enthusiasts. The camera brings the actors so close to us that they communicate meaning and feeling by the minutest variations of facial expression, movement, or sound. Sometimes they deliver soliloquies without opening their lips, and a face set in brown study tells us that "To be or not to be" is not speech at all but only inward thinking. Often, indeed, language becomes superfluous and is scanted in favor of glance or shrug or touch or smile. Shakespeare never intended quite such intimate communication, of course. He wrote plays for open-air stages and stages in great halls, where meaning and feeling had to be projected strongly. He wrote vocal scores of continuous rhetoric—elegant verse and high-styled prose—which demand the full range of great voices for utterance. He expected, too, that his actors would use their whole bodies vigorously, athletically, with grand and unmistakable gestures. The modern stage requires the same kind (if not degree) of projective power. Film, however, for the most part does not, and much of what excels upon the stage appears quite false when the camera records it.

One especial value of filmed Shakespeare in these days is that by presenting Shakespearean material in easily pleasing form it may attract to the plays a good many who have hitherto avoided them, supposing them tedious or too difficult. It once was otherwise. When the film industry was in its infancy the film producers turned naturally to Shakespeare because they needed stories which audiences already knew and thus could follow through pantomime alone: in those days the Shakespeare plays (some of them at least), being regularly performed on stages, were familiar to nearly everyone. The number of *silent* Shakespeares brought out in the first three decades of the century runs into the hundreds. These include some seventeen *Hamlets*, ten *Julius Caesars*, eight *Macbeths*, ten *Merchant of Venices*, sixteen *Othellos*, twenty *Romeo and Juliets*.

The earliest films were extremely brief, and only the most telling actions were shown. A *Hamlet* made in France in 1907 ran about ten minutes. The ten Shakespeares made by Vitagraph, an American company, in 1908–9 were all one-reelers lasting little over fifteen minutes. They were very wooden, too, or would seem so to us. More often than not the filming was done in studios, with painted drops in lieu of real scenery. None of the manipulative camera techniques—panning, tracking, zooming, and so forth—which are by now the basics of film art had yet been dreamed of. The camera stood still in front of the set and the actors presented themselves before its fixed, cyclopic eye.

By 1911 multiple-reel films came into being, and the idea of "features," as opposed to "shorts," was catching on. In London, where staged Shakespeare was still common in West End theatres, the actor-managers could sometimes be persuaded to take their productions before the camera. Sir Herbert Beerbohm Tree's *Henry VIII*, which had been the cynosure of the 1910–11 season, was filmed—or, rather, five major scenes of it were filmed—in about five reels, to be exhibited throughout England. Although the prints were called in and burned once the showings were completed, in one of Tree's obituary notices six years later this *Henry VIII* was remembered as "one of the finest picture plays ever produced, and really the origin of the superfilms." In 1913 Arthur Bourchier, a well-known Macbeth, and his wife Violet Vanbrugh joined a German film company at Heidelberg, where they made a feature-length *Macbeth*. In 1913 also, Sir Johnston Forbes-Robertson, whose Hamlet was the most celebrated of that generation, submitted to the camera under a producer named Cecil Hepworth. Much care went into that *Hamlet* film. Whereas Tree's *Henry VIII* was shot in a studio during the course of an afternoon, Hepworth kept his *Hamlet* company together for at least three weeks, tripping them about to various parts of southern England where he had found ideal locations for the outdoor scenes. Forbes-Robertson skillfully underplayed Hamlet for the camera, and, in the words of Robert Hamilton Ball, "the rugged, though sensitive face, the deepest piercing eyes, the grace and significance of the figure in action create a sustained intensity in the film." It is six reels and plays for an hour and forty minutes. Two other feature films of those days were *The Merchant of Venice*, made in 1916 by Matheson Lang, who was a famous Shylock; and *Hamlet* in 1917, by the Italian star Ruggero Ruggeri.

It should be remembered, of course, that in the silent-film era language was no barrier, and no matter where a film was made it was quite as intelligible to one national audience as another. Down to the war years French and Italian producers traded heavily in Shakespearean themes, and English-speaking audiences could enjoy the Shylock of Harry Baur, the Othello of Ferruccio Garavaglia, the Lear and Shylock of Ermete Novelli as thoroughly as the same roles played by their countrymen. Many Italian films were especially attractive to northern audiences because of their "authentic" locales—a *Romeo and Juliet* filmed in the streets and palazzi of Verona, a *Merchant* or *Othello* in Venice. A Danish-made *Hamlet* was staged in and about the palace at Helsingor, which at least sentimentally passes for Shakespeare's Elsinore.

In America before and during the war years the movie industry, though it lacked front-line Shakespearean actors, was busily experimenting in film technology, expanding its financial structure, and developing those advertising techniques for which it would become notorious. As early as 1913 Thomas Alva Edison's device for producing sound film, called the Kinetophone, was tried in public. It failed, and the American Talking Picture Company withdrew it, but the incident reminds us that sound was desired and the problems of achieving it were under study long before it came to pass. It was obvious to all that film could not justly serve drama of literary worth until it could deliver the language of which drama is made.

In 1914 the American tragedian Frederick Warde made a quaint attempt to fill the need for sound by means of an "Illustrated dramalogue of Shakespeare's historical play *Richard III*." Warde, who had long before acted in support of Edwin Booth and for many years after that managed his own Shakespeare company, had just played Richard in a five-reel spectacular of Shakespeare's play (a Cibberized version). According to the publicity releases this *Richard III* had cost $30,000 to produce, and involved "1500 People, 200 Horses, 5 Distinct Battle Scenes, A Three-Masted Warship, Crowded with Soldiers, on Real Water," etc. Warde went on tour with this film, delivering a brief lecture before the showing began, reciting the more famous passages of dialogue between the reels, and commenting on the actions of the play as they silently proceeded on the screen. Critics praised his offering as "the best combination moving picture entertainment" yet known, but Warde could lecture in only one theatre at a time, and his effort contributed nothing to the potential needs of the mass audience.

Warde seems to have been the only American Shakespearean of stature available to the producers during these years when full-length films were becoming possible, and he was aging. His last Shakespeare film was a *King Lear*, made when he was sixty-five, during the Shakespeare tercentenary in 1916—"unquestionably the best silent version made of *King Lear*," says Robert Hamilton Ball. It was advertised as "A Drama of Powerful Heart Interest Staged in Barbaric Splendour." In order to fill the talent gap, a Hollywood company engaged Beerbohm Tree in 1916 and featured him in an expensive *Macbeth*: though flatteringly reviewed, it was a box-office failure. Two other American-made Shakespeares during the tercentenary were both of *Romeo and Juliet*: Metro issued one, announced as costing $250,000, featuring Francis X. Bushman; a rival producer named William Fox hastily (and secretly) got up another, with "an incomparable cast of more than 2500 persons," featuring Theda Bara. Even this early, it appears, film as an art form was yielding to the appeal of matinee idols and the competitive dirty tricks of "show-business."

After the 1914–18 war the film industry grew by leaps and bounds, but the filming of Shakespeare abruptly declined. In Hollywood it was almost forgotten. The film studios developed their own breed of directors, actors, writers, and technicians, none of them concerned for the "legitimate" drama. Techniques of lighting, handling the camera, cutting, and montage were increasingly subtilized, but Shakespeare was not needed to test these improvements. Audiences increased in geometrical progression, but the greater the box office the less was the call for entertainment of finer substance than historical spectacle, spy-thriller, sentimental romance, and custard-pie farce. That part of the audience which might want literary drama had come to realize that performance of such plays with the words left out was a mockery.

Only in Germany did serious filming of Shakespeare go on. A very celebrated *Hamlet*—or version of *Hamlet*—was made there in 1920, with the Danish actress Asta Nielsen in the title role. This was not the usual transvestite game, as when Sarah Siddons or Charlotte Cushman or Sarah Bernhardt had put on Hamlet's tights. It was a totally new conception of the play: Hamlet was a woman—a princess who for reasons of state was disguised as a prince. This strange notion did not originate with Nielsen or her scenarist, but had been broached forty years earlier by an obscure American critic named Edward Vining, in a book called *The Mystery of Hamlet*. Vining had been impressed by the almost womanly delicacy of Hamlet, and after exhaustive testing of the character against the Rosalinds, Violas, and Portias who assume masculine disguise for comic purposes, he concluded that during early stages of the composition of *Hamlet* Shakespeare had intended to turn this favorite situation to tragic uses. The film based on Vining's notion pleased a wide European (though not American) audience. Asta Nielsen was a powerful tragic actress, who could express intense passion with a very minimum of physical action—an ideal actress for the camera and an ideal she-Hamlet.

Three other German Shakespeares of the 1920's are memorable. In 1922 Emil Jannings and Werner Krauss played hero and villain in a curiously violent *Othello*, which was enthusiastically praised in America as well as Europe. *Der Kaufmann von Venedig* (but in English called *The Jew of Mestri*), made in 1923, is another free rewriting of Shakespeare, the most noticeable feature of which is the renaming of many of the characters: Shylock becomes Mordecai, Portia becomes Beatrice, Jessica becomes Rachela, etc. Werner Krauss made an impressive Mordecai. All that we know about *Ein Sommernachtstraum*, made in 1925, piques our curiosity. Apparently it was a satiric or parodistic reworking of the *Dream*, done in modern dress, with saucy captions by the poet Klabund, ribald actions by Werner Krauss in the role of Bottom the Weaver, and lascivious leering by Valeska Gert, a female pantomimist who played Puck. The Berlin censors marked it "Forbidden for juveniles." One glimpses in these bits of information about it reflections of the morally shaken world of Bertolt Brecht, the rowdiness and freakishness that inspired Brecht's *Jungle of the Cities* or the *Dreigroschenoper*. Curiously, too, the film anticipates the savagely "absurdist" reading of the play by Jan Kott a long generation later.

THE ADVENT OF SOUND FILM

When sound film became a practical reality in the late 1920's, we might have expected a swift renascence of filmed Shakespeare, but it did not come to pass.

After the hundreds of silent Shakespeares made before 1930, hardly three dozen notable Shakespeares with sound have been made since then. The audience for Shakespeare, which once could be taken for granted, had for various reasons dwindled and slipped away, and it could not easily be reconstituted. Language itself was an inhibiting factor. In America most of the actors of silent film were not trained speakers, much less trained verse-speakers, and badly spoken Shakespeare was worse than none at all. Such classic actors as we still had were mostly based in New York City, three thousand miles and temperamentally even farther from the film factories of Hollywood. Continental producers generally refrained from filming the plays in their own languages since they could no longer, as in the silent days, enjoy a lively export trade. And there arose, too, the great dilemma, which can never be finally resolved, of verbal vs. pictorial art. Shakespeare's plays are too word-filled (including words which no one understands any more) to make good pictures. To cut his language drastically would alienate the intelligentsia, who in those days thought little enough of film art anyway; to keep his language whole and unmended would drive away the general public.

The first experiment, in 1929, was the Pickford Corporation's *The Taming of the Shrew*, directed by Sam Taylor and starring Mary Pickford and Douglas Fairbanks. A jovial affair, it relied less upon literary substance than upon the hurling about of furniture in the slapstick style common to Hollywood farces of the 1920's. Laurence Irving, who designed its handsome Italian villa sets, has recalled the report that the studio was "turning it into a comedy"; and says that Taylor hired a pair of gagmen to inject some clownery whenever the dialogue sagged. Taylor got himself much laughed at for the famous credit line, "Written by William Shakespeare with additional dialogue by Sam Taylor."

Six years passed between the first sound film of Shakespeare and the second: in 1935 Warner Brothers brought out Max Reinhardt's famed conception of *A Midsummer Night's Dream*, which he had been nurturing for a quarter of a century through stage productions in Germany, England, and America. The film is a badly mixed bag, ponderous and disjunctive, on the whole a pretentious failure. Reinhardt's romantic attitudes led him to overemphasize the fairy element, and although the film is more than two hours long, barely half the lines are spoken, the time being much taken up by merely decorative pantomime and dance. The ballet company, which might look well on a stage, is very unfairylike on the screen—"pretty girls in white gauze and sturdy gentlemen with wings strapped to their shoulders," observed one critic. The scenery, too, especially Theseus' palace, is stagey. The lovers were misdirected—the ladies excessively tearful, the gentlemen (one of them was the song-and-dance man Dick Powell) excessively jolly. The clowns were badly cast, probably because Reinhardt, being new to Hollywood, was not wise to the actors' qualities. Hugh Herbert and Frank McHugh did well enough as Snout and Quince, but Joe E. Brown could play only himself, a poor likeness of timorous Flute-Thisbe; and the tight little, tough little voice and figure of James Cagney were miles away from Bottom the Weaver.

In 1936 Irving Thalberg produced and George Cukor directed *Romeo and Juliet* for MGM. Norma Shearer and Leslie Howard were the starring actors. This was Shakespeare in the "supercolossal" manner. The Hollywood-built Verona covered a hundred acres, and everywhere the camera looked it discovered views straight out of romantic storybooks. Many of the sets and dresses were copied from Botticelli, Bellini, Carpaccio, and other Renaissance painters. As one enraptured critic exclaimed, "the screen has gloriously released the play from the limitations of the stage," and "Shakespeare would have gloried in the medium." (The farther we get from Shakespeare's Globe Playhouse, the more noisily we congratulate ourselves and invoke Shakespeare's approval.) However extravagant, this was the first successful sound film of Shakespeare, and it is the only one from the 1930's which we can still look at and listen to with more pleasure than fret. The decor, though plushy, is handsome and in harmony with itself, and it expresses eloquently the "romantic beauty" it intends to express. Howard and Shearer were more than twice the ages of the characters they were playing, but being adult and intelligent actors they spoke the language of the lovers with professional competence—thoughtfully, sensitively, gracefully. The supporting company included such fine performers as Basil Rathbone, a tiger-cat of a Tybalt; John Barrymore, a rowdily satyric Mercutio; Edna Mae Oliver as the Nurse, a touch too lace-curtain, perhaps, but wonderfully comical when her false dignity was assailed; and Andy Devine, who played Peter "with a frog's voice and a canary's heart." Although this *Romeo and Juliet* is by now only a period piece, its earnestness, good taste, and careful workmanship still command respect.

SHAKESPEARE FILMS SINCE WORLD WAR II

Toward the end of World War II, leadership in the filming of Shakespeare suddenly passed from America to England, and into the hands of Laurence Olivier, who was then swiftly rising toward leadership of the English theatrical profession. Between 1944 and 1955 Olivier directed and starred in films of *Henry V*, *Hamlet*, and *Richard III*, all three now commonly accepted as classics. *Henry V*, which was the earliest of these, is probably in the long run the most satisfactory. The original play—not a very subtle one but rather a historical pageant concocted by Shakespeare to set off the attractive aspects of a hero king—lends itself readily to the film medium. The play cries out for picturization, and indeed as long ago as 1839 William Charles Macready at Covent Garden Theatre was illustrating the choral interludes with "moving pictures" called dioramas. Olivier's film designers,

Roger Furze and others, considered several possible modes of decor and discovered how to use them all in a cunning cyclical pattern. First, in order to ground the work in its time, they give us an aerial view of Elizabethan London and bring the camera down upon the Globe Playhouse, where the opening dialogue is played. Then, to take us back to the early fifteenth century, they resort to painted sets reminiscent of illuminations in a medieval Book of Hours. Here the color photography is particularly apt in recreating the vivid palette of medieval miniature painters. When the action moves to camp and battlefield, the decor widens out into real landscapes. Then in the last section it returns to a series of painted sets and finally to a view of the Globe while the end captions are being shown. In preparing the scenario Olivier and his collaborators excused King Henry from some of his more questionable actions—his bloody threats against the citizens of Harfleur, his order to kill the French prisoners—and emphasized his patriotism and generalship. With such a play at such a time (1944 was the year of the Allied invasion of Normandy), this sort of bowdlerization was expectable. Olivier's performance of the King is superb. He is brainy, majestic, and straightforward, and he uses the Shakespearean language for its maximum worth. As he once explained to Roger Manvell, he had discovered a special technique for handling heroic or climactic language which runs exactly counter to traditional film practice: whereas in most film climaxes the camera draws in very close to the actor and enlarges his face, and the actor reduces his voice and movement to a minimum, Olivier sent the camera farther away so that he could let out his voice to full power. Thus, such oratorical high points as the Saint Crispin's Day speech are as richly vocalized as they would be upon a stage. At the opposite extreme, for the brooding soliloquy "Upon the King," the camera not only draws near but, as it were, melts into the King: we *become* the King, seeing with his eyes as the camera moves slowly through the camp at night.

Olivier's *Hamlet*, made in 1948, is a far subtler work than his *Henry V*, but as a treatment of the original play it is less satisfying. Scenically it is excellent. In response to the play's imagery, the sets, largely palace interiors of Norman architecture, are confining, and the choice of black and white photography was appropriate to the tone of the play. The camera work is artful, expressive, and steady. Bosley Crowther personified the camera moving around the palace as "a silent observer of great events, eager not to miss any." The acting of the entire company is excellent, and, as we expect in Olivier films, all the language is delivered faultlessly. It is the scenario, prepared by Olivier and the critic Alan Dent, which has aroused certain objections. The cuts are severe and sometimes astonishing, and the theme of the play is sorely oversimplified. In a necessarily abbreviated text one does not expect to find the soliloquy of "How all occasions do inform against me," but to lose "Oh, what a rogue and peasant slave am I" is to lose too much. The omission of Fortinbras was long the tradition of the stage itself, but we really cannot dispense with Rosencrantz and Guildenstern, not because of what they themselves perform but because of the fine bitter things which they provoke. As for the play's theme, it is not too far amiss to apply to Hamlet his own discourse on the tragic flaw—"the vicious mole of nature" and "the stamp of one defect"—but it is a condescension to public simple-mindedness for Olivier to declare at the beginning of the film that "This is the tragedy of a man who could not make up his mind." Then, too, invoking the wisdom of popular psychoanalysis, the film implies that this is also the tragedy of a man suffering a mother-fixation. In casting Eileen Herlie as the Queen, Olivier chose an actress fitter to play Hamlet's mistress than his mother, and the persistence with which the camera's eye peers and peers again into Gertrude's bedroom emphasizes this second "interpretation" embarrassingly much.

In Olivier's third film, *Richard III*, made in 1955, he returned to the high coloring and bold histrionics of political pageantry and melodrama. It is a thoroughly enjoyable work, as unsubtle as the play from which it derives, providing an expensive setting for Olivier's own tour de force performance of the monster-hero. Shakespeare's vast text is much cut and rearranged freely, with scenes added that did not occur to Shakespeare. Evidently Colley Cibber's version of the play was used to guide the arrangement, and one or two of Cibber's original lines are incorporated. None of this matters: we enjoy the piece without debating its fine points. But it is the least significant film of Olivier's three.

Among the Shakespeare films made since Olivier's early work, the following are memorable for one quality or another: the John Houseman-Joseph Mankiewicz *Julius Caesar* (1953), a fairly conventional treatment with interesting performances by James Mason, John Gielgud, and Marlon Brando; the Sergei Yutkevitch *Othello* (1955), an elaborately pictorial version, marred by one or two naive touches near the end, as for instance when in his fury Othello's eyes are made to glitter, or when his hair suddenly turns white; Akira Kurosawa's *Throne of Blood* (1957), a totally free reworking of the *Macbeth* story in terms of Japanese folklore and ancient history, in which realistic acting is crossed with conventions of Noh; Grigori Kozintsev's *Hamlet* (1964), an explosively energetic version which the director claims to have organized around five sets of elemental images—stone, iron, fire, sea, and earth; Orson Welles's *Chimes at Midnight*, or *Falstaff* (1965), a somewhat chaotic but widely praised anthology of Falstaff passages taken from the several plays; Peter Hall's *A Midsummer Night's Dream* (1969), a light-hearted, low-budget treatment, filmed with a company of Stratford actors in the rain, frost, and mist of a late September in Warwickshire.

Something like a school or movement in modern film-making which has impinged upon the filming of Shakespeare is the "neo-realism" of two Italians who have directed English actors on location in Italy,

Renato Castellani and Franco Zeffirelli. Both these men are intensely interested in pictorial imagery and know where to find striking scenery in Italian towns and countryside; both strive for energy, speed, and even violence in their action scenes; and both are so insistent upon "natural" speaking that they are indifferent or even hostile to Shakespeare's poetry. Castellani's *Romeo and Juliet* (1954), which took top honors at the Venice Film Festival, is a tourists' remembrancer of golden Italian vistas. The Capulet ball is staged in the Ca' d'Oro in Venice; the duel takes place before the Duomo in Siena; Friar Laurence gathers herbs outside the walls of Montagnana; the death scenes occur in the handsomest of all crypts in the church of San Zeno in Verona. Life in the streets is zestful, and the brawls that take place there are wild and bloody. The casting, however, was haphazard: Laurence Harvey, perhaps because of faulty direction, seems to have been inadequate to Romeo, and Juliet was assigned to a lovely young blonde who had no acting experience and was incapable of verse. Castellani slashed out scenes and verse passages that slowed the action, and invented other scenes to speed it up. He so far flattened the language into prose that here and there in bridge scenes the lesser actors break out with whatever words come into their heads.

Zeffirelli has pursued neo-realism much farther. "I am a crusader against boredom, bad taste, and stupidity in theatre," he has declared. In 1966 he demonstrated his notions of taste in a filming of *The Taming of the Shrew*, starring Richard Burton and Elizabeth Taylor, which would make the old Pickford-Fairbanks *Shrew* look positively staid. Except for one or two of Petruchio's speeches and Kate's final lecture, language mainly gives way to swaggering and drunken bellowing on Burton's part, and to yelps and squawks on Miss Taylor's. The wedding scene, which Shakespeare *describes* with some wit, is acted out in all imaginable coarseness. In one memorable scene which somehow took place in a barn, Petruchio tumbled Kate into a bin full of wool. Zeffirelli's *Romeo and Juliet*, issued in 1968, is a far better film—indeed, within the limits of his esthetic it is a serious attempt to realize the play in cinematic equivalents. Yet it is marred by meddling. The opening street brawl, for instance, builds up to a grand fury, but this is achieved in the cutting room by such a frenetic popping of images that one can hardly tell who is doing what to whom. In order to "naturalize" the story, Zeffirelli cast the leading roles to a pair of adolescents. These youngsters "act themselves" with considerable charm, the fifteen-year-old Juliet "listens" with remarkably sensitive facial expression, and sentence by sentence they speak nicely. They are not capable of sustained flights of rhetoric, however, and their long speeches are fragmented between bits of stage business or are simply omitted. Their "love" is expressed not so much by words as by prolonged bouts of nuzzling and gurgling, puppy fashion. The actor of Mercutio brings to his role an almost crazy interpretation—at times so high-strung that instead of the lines written for him he cries out, "Blah! blah! blah!" He overacts the Queen Mab speech wildly, and when he comes to its serene coda he warps it into an anguished *cri de coeur*: it appears that he is suffering an unsatisfiable lust for Romeo. When interviewed on this subject, Zeffirelli further revealed that Mercutio is a self-portrait of Shakespeare.

Whatever values accrue from these neo-realists—their inventiveness, their vitality, their rejection of academic stodginess, their popular appeal—we cannot take their work with Shakespeare to be very significant. One wishes they would confine themselves to pantomime or dance or any other *wordless* art. Their persistent disregard, and sometimes wreckage, of Shakespeare's language disqualifies them from serious consideration.

Two plays of greater weight than *Romeo and Juliet* or *The Shrew* have yielded films which suggest a more dangerous way in which directors can damage Shakespeare: by imposing perverse and reductive interpretations. Roman Polanski's *Macbeth*, completed in 1971, was much heralded in advance because of its conception of the Macbeths as young and attractive rather than middle-aged and forbidding. This, together with the promise of a few nude scenes, roused lively expectations. When the film appeared, critics on every hand acknowledged it to be handsomely directed and very well acted, and many of them emphasized that the language was spoken with intelligence and skill. Yet they were appalled. In earlier films Polanski had exhibited his Gothic taste for mystic rites, witchcraft, blood, and Satan-worship. Now, it appeared, he was not so much interpreting *Macbeth* as imposing upon *Macbeth* his own vision of evil, his personal despair in the face of existence. What he had given us was a pair of beautiful but damned creatures who murder efficiently and without compunction until they have risen to the summit of political power. There is nothing noble or even fundamentally decent about them and there never was: corrupt from the beginning, they are capable only of corruption and of generating corruption around them. All that they are or do, wrote Paul Zimmerman, "seems a pretext for closeups of knives and geysers of blood from men, women, and children. No chance to revel in gore is passed up. We watch bodies crushed and mutilated by spiked clubs, limbs severed, hands bathed in crimson, necks broken, heads lopped off. The horror is unremitting." A generation ago we should have labelled such a film Grand Guignol and dismissed it. Since then, however, we have had to acknowledge Dachau, and it is understandable that such horrors fester in the imagination of central Europeans like Jan Kott and Roman Polanski. It profits nothing, however, to reduce Shakespeare's tragedy to Grand Guignol, or Dachau, or the Manson murders.

When Peter Brook staged *King Lear* at Stratford-upon-Avon and across Europe in the early 1960's, it was greeted with clamorous enthusiasm, and only occasional voices objected to the ethical nihilism which he read into the play. When he filmed it in 1969, he made his bleak message so much more emphatic—partly through the locale he chose, which was northern Jutland in sub-zero weather—that many film critics were violently alienated. There could be no doubt now that his vision of the play was Jan Kott's, whose essay equating *Lear* with Beckett's *Endgame* contains such sentences as these:

> In *King Lear* the stage is empty throughout; there is nothing except the cruel earth, where man goes on his journey from the cradle to the grave. . . . There are no longer kings and subjects, fathers and children, husbands and wives. There are only huge Renaissance monsters, devouring each other like beasts of prey. . . . People murder, butcher and torture one another, commit adultery and fornication, divide kingdoms. . . . All that remains at the end of this gigantic pantomime is the earth—empty and bleeding.

Brook is charged with reducing *King Lear* to mere Theatre of Cruelty; with suppressing Lear's greatness and minimizing all good, even in Cordelia, so that the Shakespearean pattern of Lear being brought down by tragic flaw, then redeemed, then brought down again by external forces is simply lost sight of. From the beginning of the film Lear is a mean, paltry old man, surrounded by a soulless, vicious family and court; and once the film is under way, as Pauline Kael has said, there is no development, the camera only grinds on. We cannot sense tragedy at work here, for nothing is destroyed that was worth saving: it is all trash to the chopping machine. Jan Kott is doubtless correct in recognizing that Beckett's *Godot* and *Endgame* and *Act Without Words* are derivable from *King Lear*, or are nihilistic restatements of *Lear* material; it is not in order, however, to reverse the process and derive Shakespeare's play from Beckett's. In attempting to do so, Brook has in fact betrayed Shakespeare and Beckett both: he has banished their humor and their compassion; he has prevented emotional involvement and denied catharsis.

No one would question the technical proficiency of Brook or Polanski. What they set out to do in film they do supremely well. Both, too, are profoundly in earnest, and they decline to play to the box office. Yet the finer their skills, the more rigorously must we test their Shakespeare films for validity. Brook himself once said that Shakespeare could not be filmed, by which he meant that the "straight" versions then in favor, like Olivier's, were little more than records of stage actors at work. Somehow, he implied, the essence of the play must be extracted and transmuted into film language which will be as free and suggestive as was the original on Shakespeare's bare stage. Perhaps Brook has achieved this miracle for the contemporary *stage* with his *A Midsummer Night's Dream* on trapezes: a chorus of critics have said so. His film of *King Lear*, however, is not free and suggestive, but partial, limiting, and mean, and although Brook more than anyone in the business is likely to invent a validly transcendent way of filming Shakespeare, we must abide the time.

Appendix B

Shakespeare's Plays in Performance

From 1970

William T. Liston

Since the first edition of *The Riverside Shakespeare* was published in 1974, several important developments have taken place with respect to the performance of Shakespeare, though much has remained constant, of course. Shakespeare is still the world's most popular playwright, as a glance at any listing of theatre productions will attest. The *World Shakespeare Bibliography*, published annually by *Shakespeare Quarterly*, lists hundreds of productions throughout the world each year, by commercial theatres as well as by the numerous non-profit theatres and Shakespeare festivals. And these productions are reviewed by the popular press as well as by scholarly journals.

In an important essay composed at the beginning of the present decade Michael Jamieson wrote:

> There have been, broadly speaking, four movements in the history of Shakespeare in performance—the first dominated by the adapters, the second by the great players of the eighteenth- and nineteenth-century stage, the third by that international figure of the twentieth-century theatre, the director, and the fourth by the technological revolution of film, television, and video. (p. 53)

All of these movements were treated extensively by Charles H. Shattuck in his essay in the first edition of *The Riverside Shakespeare*. (See Appendix A.) This continuation of his work will necessarily deal with only the last two.

As has been widely noted, productions in recent decades have more often than not been identified with the director rather than the leading actors: for example, the Brook *A Midsummer Night's Dream*, the Barton *Richard II*, the Bogdanov *Romeo and Juliet*, the Phillips *As You Like It*. With respect to the technological revolution, probably the most important of the three media mentioned has been the videorecording, dependent though it is on the other two. Its pervasiveness has made great performances of Shakespeare's plays accessible to millions who might never have the opportunity or the inclination to attend a stage production. *Great Performances* is, in fact, the apt title of an anthology videotape of a selection of scenes from Royal Shakespeare Company productions of the mid-1990s.

Television productions have been particularly plentiful during the last two decades, most evident in the production and broadcast of all thirty-seven plays in the canon over a period of slightly more than seven years (1978–1985) by the British Broadcasting Corporation. Yet Anthony Davies has concluded "that while the videos have become a part of Shakespeare teaching programmes in school classrooms, the most obvious consequence of the BBC-TV Shakespeare series has been the publication of much writing by academics for academics" (Davies and Wells, p. 15). True though the statement may be, teachers have increasingly come to appreciate the immediate comprehension by students of what is funny in a comic scene, for example, when they see and hear the scene performed by a professional company of actors.

Comparatively few Shakespearean motion pictures appeared during the seventies and eighties, however, until Kenneth Branagh's films of both *Henry V* and *Much Ado about Nothing*, with himself as Henry and Benedick, and Emma Thompson as Katherine and Beatrice, reached large audiences, as did Franco Zeffirelli's *Hamlet* with Mel Gibson as the prince.

Another significant development during this period has been the respect accorded to performance. In an essay on this topic, Roger Warren cites two main contributions of the twentieth-century stage to the interpretation of Shakespeare: the playing, complete, of the history plays of both tetralogies as interrelated units, bringing out unexpectedly rich roles (Bullingbrook and Queen Margaret, for example) and themes (power politics), and the establishment of *Love's Labor's Lost* "as one of Shakespeare's major plays," something that had not been suspected until the productions of Tyrone Guthrie at the Old Vic in

1936 and of John Barton for the Royal Shakespeare Company in 1965 and 1978 (pp. 268–70). He might have added the "Watteau-esque" production with Paul Scofield as Armado, directed by Peter Brook in his debut at the Shakespeare Memorial Theatre in 1946.

Titus Andronicus has also been reclaimed from the Table of Contents page by performance, notably by Brook's stylized production of 1955 in Stratford with Laurence Olivier as Titus and Vivien Leigh as Lavinia. Closer to our own time, and possibly even more influential, was Deborah Warner's uncut 1987–88 production for the RSC, in the Swan Theatre in Stratford. The powerful realism of the production in this relatively small and intimate theatre, and in The Pit at the Barbican Centre, the RSC's London home, spoke to the modern consciousness of the violence of rape (Bate, pp. 62–66). Productions in 1989 at the Stratford, New York, and New Jersey Shakespeare Festivals attest to the renewed interest in the play on stage, as does Julie Taymore's 1994 production at the Theatre for a New Audience in New York.

Without doubt, however, Peter Brook's 1970 *Midsummer Night's Dream* for the RSC established the primacy of performance as the medium for appreciating Shakespeare. Charles H. Shattuck in his essay above acclaims the production on several levels, and Sally Beauman in her history of the Royal Shakespeare Company calls it "the most celebrated of all RSC productions": "It became the most discussed, most written about, most analysed, and most imitated Shakespearian production of the century" (pp. 301, 304).

Setting the production in a white-walled gymnasium, Brook eschewed realism and, paradoxically, illusion. Trapezes, ladders, and ropes constituted most of the scenery. By refusing to provide the traditional forest, Brook forced the audience to see and hear the play in the language, which all critics agree was beautifully and meaningfully spoken. In essence, the production was a working out of Brook's 1968 book *The Empty Space*. One of the highest tributes to the production, because of her general reluctance to credit so-called Director's Theatre, is Helen Gardner's. She found the production "wonderfully liberating and imaginative":

> The young lovers were teenagers and Helena looked and behaved just like the gawky, awkward one who gets left out. The mechanicals were in deadly earnest over their play and acted it with touching conviction, which made the court's reception of it seem less like condescending patronage and more like genuine enjoyment. At the end the performers ran down the aisles of the theatre with the audience stretching out their hands to shake hands as they passed in greeting and thanks. I put out mine with the others.

Not having read Brook's explanation of his indebtedness to the theories of Jan Kott, Gardner

> had no idea that I was witnessing a sex-orgy, that Oberon was punishing his wife Titania by making her commit bestiality, or that, in the persons of Oberon and Titania, Theseus and Hippolyta [whose roles were doubled] were working out their own sexual problems, or any of the dreary absurdities and solemn nonsense with which Kott had smeared the play. The play, as performed, simply defeated, by the beauty of the language and the high spirits of the performers, the supposed meaning as far as I was concerned. Little was cut, the atmosphere of gaiety and magic was sustained, the intended implications of the doubling and some additional business could be passed over and I felt free to enjoy the play. I did not feel directed. (pp. 70–71)

Adrian Noble's *A Midsummer Night's Dream*, thoroughly theatrical and set in a red rather than a white box, captivated audiences in 1996 as it harked back to Brook's *Dream* of a quarter-century earlier.

Concomitant with this rise in the importance of performance as a tool of interpretation has grown the discipline of performance criticism. Indeed, one is now likely to hear the word *script* where one has been used to hearing *text*. In the last two decades a great many books—including several series of books—have been published on specific performances of Shakespearean plays and of the actors' interpretations of major roles.

Political considerations (in both broad and narrow senses) have become increasingly important in performance. Productions on the continent regularly suggest a political relevance (which does not always assure a good production) to almost every play produced. These political overtones can frequently illuminate a play without violating it, as in the case of Michael Bogdanov's 1991 *Coriolanus* for the English Shakespeare Company, which made the populace the focus of the production "with no disrespect to Michael Pennington's subtle and powerful performance as Coriolanus" (Holland, p. 132). The parallels to the dissolution of communist governments in Eastern Europe were obvious in, among other things, the large "Democratie" banner unfurled in the opening scene, understood to imply "Solidarity."

Equally important is the (by now) well-established practice of color-blind, multi-racial casting, a consequence of multiculturalism. The Stratford Festival Theatre has been criticized (possibly unfairly) for not seeking out people of color so assiduously as it might; but nonwhite faces have had at least a minor representation there for several years. Hugh Quarshie of the Royal Shakespeare Company (Antony in *Julius Caesar*, 1995), Franchelle Stewart Dorn of The Shakespeare Theatre in Washington (Cleopatra, 1988; Queen Elizabeth in *Richard III*, 1990), and Derrick Lee Weeden (a commanding Coriolanus in a powerful production set in "the imminently feudal future" at the Oregon Shakespeare Festival, 1996), among many others, all attest to the validity of incorporating actors in Shakespearean productions without regard to skin tone.

A question arises as to just what is the essence of a Shakespearean play in performance. Traditionally, Shakespeare has been valued above all for his language: Scholars and theatre-goers in general can not only recite "To be or not to be" but can describe how Gielgud and Olivier and Burton delivered the lines. Yet it is not unusual for a Shakespearean film to contain only a third of the lines preserved in print. And how necessary is it that the lines be delivered in English? Michael Billington, the knowledgeable critic of *The Guardian*, wrote not long ago that "If I had only three hours left to spend in a theatre before I died, I think I would choose to spend it watching the Ninagawa *Macbeth*," which was performed at Britain's National Theatre in 1987 (1992, p. 25). He was not alone in being moved by the "mythic power" of this production, set in sixteenth-century Japan, spoken in Japanese (although at the 1990 production at the Brooklyn Academy of Music English was available on head-phones). And of course there are the highly regarded Japanese film versions of *Macbeth* (*Throne of Blood*, 1957) and *King Lear* (*Ran*, 1985) by Akira Kurosawa, both very free adaptations of Shakespeare, as well as the *King Lear* (1970) directed by Grigori Kozintsev, in a Russian translation by Boris Pasternak, with music by Dimitri Shostakovich, highly admired for its fidelity to Shakespeare's intent.

Finally, the reconstruction of the Globe Theatre in Southwark nears completion. About the time the first edition of *The Riverside Shakespeare* was going to press, performances were given under a canopy at a temporary Bankside Globe Playhouse (1972) near, but not on the site of, the original Globe, under the aegis of Sam Wanamaker, with the expectation of a functioning permanent playhouse by 1975. Now Wanamaker's dream is about to be realized, posthumously: An artistic director has been appointed, and performances are soon to be given on a stage and under conditions that replicate as closely as possible those of performances given almost four hundred years ago in the Jacobean Globe.

In this survey of Shakespearean production of the last quarter-century, the intent will be to focus on the plays themselves, and, with occasional exceptions, to concentrate on those productions that have provided new interpretations of the plays and on those that have been major influences on other productions. Since most of the major productions have been mounted by long-established companies specializing in Shakespeare, the emphasis is necessarily on the offerings of those companies, first in England and then in the United States and Canada, with, however, some attention to the productions of other companies or theatres. There follows a look at major television and film productions, and, ultimately, an overview of the reconstruction of the Globe Theatre. (Note: Photos of several of the productions described in Appendixes A and B and of the reconstructed Globe Theatre appear in Plates 32–39.)

SHAKESPEARE IN ENGLAND

The Royal Shakespeare Company

In *Shakespeare Observed*, Samuel Crowl asserts "that we have been living in a golden age of British theatre, and nowhere is that more apparent than in the variety of intelligent and illuminating approaches to Shakespeare spawned by Peter Hall and the directors who came to join him at the RSC and their successors" (pp. 100–01). Hall founded the Royal Shakespeare Company in 1960, four years after he had first worked at Stratford, and he ran the company until 1968. During his tenure, Hall brought in such directors as Peter Brook, John Barton, Trevor Nunn, and Terry Hands, who were to continue their association with the RSC at least into the 1990s. Barton, still active, has directed more than fifty separate productions, including *The Wars of the Roses*, that he and Hall, jointly, adapted from the three parts of *Henry VI* and *Richard III* in the early 1960s, and which inspired mountings of the cycle by both the RSC and the English Shakespeare Company in the ensuing decades.

Barton's *Richard II* (1973) was equally significant. After the cast came on stage in rehearsal clothes, Richard Pasco and Ian Richardson chose their costumes from the racks, nightly alternating the roles of Richard and Bullingbrook. This opening established the theatricality of the production, an effect which was carried further by the wearing of hobby-horses about their waists by Mowbray and Bullingbrook during the tournament scene. The abstract set consisted of parallel stairways at either side supporting a mechanized platform that moved up and down as needed for such scenes as Richard's deposition. Those unlucky enough to have seen only one performance still argue that the choice of actors for Richard and Bullingbrook on that evening achieved the ideal in casting.

Some of the most stimulating RSC productions of the 1970s originated in The Other Place, a corrugated-iron hut converted in 1974 from a rehearsal room to a studio theatre seating 140. Nunn, who succeeded Hall as artistic director in 1969, put the young Buzz Goodbody in charge, and the space was an immediate success with both non-Shakespearean and Shakespearean work. Goodbody's modern-dress *Hamlet* with Ben Kingsley in 1975 was one of the decade's strongest productions of the play: "It rewardingly investigated the complexity of personal and family relationships in the play, indicating that the RSC was now moving away from the epic style of the Sixties, with its emphasis on relationships of state, to the interior world of the plays, to the network of cousins, brothers, fathers, daughters, and sons which provides a focus for the wider events" (Beauman, pp. 329–30). The intelligence of the directing appealed to a modern audience.

The other triumph of 1975 was Terry Hands's *Henry V* with Alan Howard, which played more than a hundred times in the main theatre in Stratford and then went on tour in Europe and New York. The production was infused with irony and ambiguity: The actions of the King, "himself wracked with self-doubts," and the rest of the scruffy cast played against the glorious account of the Chorus. "The battle itself became not the jingoistic vanquishing of the French, but the victory of a united group of men over a hierarchic and entrenched society; when the French died, trapped in [designer] Farrah's glorious golden armour, they died visibly imprisoned in the symbol of a way of life and set of assumptions that they—unlike the English—had been unable to escape." The quietly played St. Crispin's Day speech made its "moment of unification completely convincing: It was the visible welling-up of an *esprit de corps* that was closer to the vision of a Fanon than a Kitchener" (Beauman, pp. 328–29). It was a production, Shattuck wrote, that "received more unqualified praise than any other RSC production since Brook's *King Lear*" (Andrews, p. 659). Like Barton's *Richard II*, *Henry V* found its New York home at the Brooklyn Academy of Music during the years 1974–76.

Following the success of *Henry V*, Hands mounted the *Henry VI* plays in 1976, and to similar acclaim. Whereas John Barton, with Peter Hall, had extensively rewritten the plays for their famed *Wars of the Roses* cycle of 1962—reducing the three *Henry VI* plays to two, entitled *Henry VI* and *Edward IV*, and following them with *Richard III*—Hands presented the trilogy without adaptation. With Alan Howard as a King Henry VI who understood the folly of the world in which he lived and Anton Lesser as a Richard of Gloucester representing that deformed society, the production changed our perceptions of the plays. Not the least discovery was the number and variety of good roles in the trilogy, as well as confirmation of the dramatic power of the plays to captivate an audience. Hands's *Coriolanus* in the same season, with Alan Howard in the title role, gave "that notoriously difficult play its most thrilling production in recent memory" (Beauman, p. 342); it later toured France and Germany.

Trevor Nunn's *Macbeth* at The Other Place in 1976 was one of the most striking productions the play has ever received. Nunn had a circle painted in the center of the floor, and actors not involved in the action would step outside the circle and watch. This patently theatrical device not only heightened audience consciousness of the theatrical process, but it also exerted a sense of a closed world tightly circumscribed by magical forces. For those who saw this *Macbeth*, the performances of Ian McKellen and Judi Dench were unforgettable. Its filming for television preserved the intimacy of the small theatre.

In the main theatre (and subsequently at the Aldwych), Judi Dench's performance in *Much Ado about Nothing* (1976) confirmed, for Stanley Wells, "that she is the finest Shakespearean actress of her generation with a deeply felt Beatrice to Donald Sinden's ebullient Benedick in a production by John Barton that surprisingly illuminated the play's social structure by setting it in British India" (Andrews, p. 627). A few years later, Terry Hands's 1982 *Much Ado about Nothing*, with Derek Jacobi and Sinead Cusack, entranced New Yorkers when it came to Broadway in 1984.

During the 1980s, the RSC provided two strikingly thought-provoking productions of *Richard III*. The first of these stemmed, at least partly, from the visit of a troupe of Soviet Georgian actors, in 1979, to the Edinburgh Festival, and later, to the Roundhouse in London, with "a version" of *Richard III* performed in the Georgian language. "Directed by Robert Sturua, with Ramaz Chkhikvadze as Richard, the production proved to be one of the extraordinary interpretations of this half-century, revealing how successful an expressionist approach to *Richard III* can be" (Colley, pp. 230–32). "Sturua himself justified the many cuts and alterations by claiming 'theatre doesn't serve the author but society. Our productions will step over the corpses of the philologists'" (Maria Tarsitano, quoted in Colley, p. 233).

Of Bill Alexander's 1984 *Richard III* with Anthony Sher in the title role, Hugh Richmond wrote, "the whole production was conceived in the context of high, even envious admiration of the *Richard III* presented during the recent visits to Britain of the Rustaveli company from Russian Georgia" (p. 108). The result of this adulation was a production that devalued the language and the specific shared culture of English history. What the production is most famous for in the memories of all who have seen it or pictures of it is Sher, on elbow crutches, a "bottled spider." "It is going to be hard," Michael Billington wrote, "to displace the image of this mobile, runtish, grasshopper-quick figure who, with his two crutches and two dependent cloak tails, seems to be the fastest thing in England on six legs" (1985, p. 10). Sher used the crutches as weapons and even, during his wooing of the Lady Anne, as a symbolic phallus.

More satisfying to many traditionalists was Anton Lesser's Richard in Adrian Noble's nine-hour cycle of three plays that he entitled *The Plantagenets* (1988), consisting of *Henry VI* and *The Rise of Edward IV* edited from the three parts of *Henry VI*, as well as *Richard III*. At the end of *Edward IV*, the actors froze on stage, and a spotlighted Richard declared "Now!," the first word of his opening soliloquy in the culminating play, to proclaim his moment in the sun (Colley, p. 253). Praised for his irony and craftiness, Lesser brought the focus of the role back to the language rather than the visual effects, while the company was praised for its ensemble playing.

Michael Bogdanov's 1986 *Romeo and Juliet* (or, as it was called by some wags, "Alfa-Romeo") was a notably disturbing production. Modernized in dress and setting, as is typical of Bogdanov, it earned its sobriquet from the presence of an Alfa Romeo, driven on stage during the opening gang fight. Mercutio jumped on its hood to avoid being attacked with a chain-flail by Tybalt: No one of that young generation would risk scratching the paint of the trendy sports car. The production dramatized, according to Dennis Kennedy, "Foucauldian visions of the complicity of knowledge and power." At the end, "The Prince entered, a man of power dressed to kill, and TV lights flared as microphones were stuck in his face. What he spoke, astoundingly, were the opening eight lines of the prologue—the Chorus's lines, which had been omitted—but changed into the past tense, and read from a notecard" (*Looking at Shakespeare* pp. 297–98). The directorial concept so overshadowed the play that the young lovers, Sean Bean and Niamh Cusack, are only lightly noticed in reviews.

Trevor Nunn's *Othello*, in 1989, may be the defining production of that difficult play. For it, The Other Place was transformed into a nineteenth-century barracks, though it served equally well for non-military locations. Willard White, a Jamaican-born opera singer, acquitted himself well as Othello in his first non-singing role: He had the size and the bearing as well as the voice for the role. But, as usual, it was Iago who dominated the audience's attention. Ian McKellen played the Ancient with absolute directness (but betrayed more than a hint of repression), so that his duping of Othello did not demean the general, reducing him to a fool—always a danger in the relationship. Robert Cushman saw Iago's character deriving from "a corroded bisexuality; he can fascinate his wife Emilia without loving her, and he himself is dazzled by Othello." Zoë Wanamaker as Emilia commanded attention with her sturdy presence while earning sympathy as well. Desdemona, played by the young Imogen Stubbs, was entirely credible: attractive, naively flirtatious, and vulnerable. The videotape of the production (1990) makes no pretense to be a film: The Other Place is undisguisedly The Other Place; McKellen delivers his soliloquies quietly into the camera, without gloating, without seeming to take any particular pleasure in what he is doing, without revealing any insight into his nature or his motives.

Sam Mendes, while still in his twenties, made his RSC debut directing *Troilus and Cressida* in the Swan in 1990. This theatre, built on the model of a Jacobean cockpit playhouse, was constructed in 1986 by converting a rehearsal space in the Shakespeare Memorial Theatre expressly to stage plays by Shakespeare's contemporaries as well as by himself. Long but not very wide, and without a center aisle, the theatre makes the audience conscious of other audience members, encouraging a kind of complicity in the action. Intended by Trevor Nunn to encourage directors to work without sets, the Swan makes itself the set. For at least one scene in *Troilus*, Mendes had "the top brass, up aloft, away from it all, at the Swan's highest level, surveying the carnage while dogs bark in the distance in anticipation of the carrion" (Smallwood, p. 358). In a "theatrically exciting, and consistently intelligent" production, Ralph Fiennes as Troilus faced the role's "naive heroics and immature self-absorption admirably" (p. 357).

At the age of thirty-two, Kenneth Branagh, who had played Henry V and other roles, including Laertes, for the RSC in 1984, returned in 1992 to play the fourth *Hamlet* of his career, in a production, directed by Adrian Noble and designed by Bob Crowley, that pleased critics and audiences alike. "To hear Branagh read lines that had only been words on a page before and make them so *clear* was worth the trip to London," wrote H. R. Coursen (p. 26). Set just before World War I, in a design inspired by Ingmar Bergman's film *Fanny and Alexander*, the production "emphasized the domestic over the political, family over state," and offered the first polite, mature Hamlet in more than a decade, "including Branagh's own for the Renaissance Theatre Company in 1988" (Crowl, 1994, p. 5).

Not all has been smooth, however. In 1989, the RSC shut down its Barbican Centre productions because of a severe deficit, although Hands was able to raise adequate private and public funds quickly to resume the operation. And in 1995, Adrian Noble stunned the Corporation of London, the owners of the Barbican Centre, by announcing that the Royal Shakespeare Company would cut its London season to a half-year and would spend the rest of the year touring. The Royal Shakespeare Company is nevertheless a vigorous company, long acclaimed for the highest quality of Shakespearean production, and its continued excellence is not likely to be in jeopardy, despite recent cuts in government funding. Its devotees around the world, many of whom make an annual visit to immerse themselves in Shakespeare performance at its best, will not suffer a diminution of the RSC's offerings or quality without vigorous protest, buttressed by equally vigorous support.

The Royal National Theatre

The dream of a National Theatre in England was finally realized in 1961, when Laurence Olivier was appointed director, and performances began at the Old Vic in 1963. During the Olivier era, Jonathan Miller directed Olivier himself in *The Merchant of Venice* in 1970, and then in 1973 directed him again in the role for television. The setting was the top-hatted banking community of Victorian London, with Olivier modeling himself on Disraeli. By cutting Shylock's anti-Christian lines, and by making the Belmont plot rather silly, Miller presented Shylock as an outsider who, though quirky, had justifiable reasons for seeking revenge against the upper-class Christian bigots. Reluctantly calling this "the key production of its period," John Gross wrote that he did so not because it was the best, but "because it was the one which established the principle that a director is free to do whatever he likes with the play" (p. 329).

Peter Hall succeeded Olivier as director in 1973, and three years later the company moved into its new building on the South Bank. Hall's production of *Hamlet* with Albert Finney opened on the proscenium Lyttelton stage on 16 March 1976; the other two theatres, the thrust-stage Olivier, and the flexible Cottesloe, opened by the end of the year.

Among Hall's several productions of Shakespeare at the National, his modern-dress 1984–85 *Coriolanus* with Ian McKellen, which also played in Athens, Greece, was notable. Kristina Bedford characterized the production as primarily intellectual, and thought that McKellen offered "too civilized a portrayal of Coriolanus," but concluded that "no other interpretation would be consistent with the style of the overall production" (pp. 166–68). She found that "as Tullus Aufidius, Greg Hicks captures the animalistic violence that lurks under the skin of the most rational of military strategists" (p. 171).

Antony and Cleopatra (1987), the last production Hall directed on the Olivier stage, was universally applauded. In summarizing it, Gerald Berkowitz wrote that "Anthony Hopkins and Judi Dench played middle-aged lovers past their most passionate years but bound together by memories" (p. 496). Michael Bryant and Tim Piggott-Smith brought their considerable powers to the already strong cast as Enobarbus and Caesar respectively. "This production," David Bevington wrote, "perhaps shows contemporary staging of *Antony and Cleopatra* at its best, less insistent on star performances and on a romantic vision of the lovers than on a cohesiveness that can unify the play's irony and transcendence into something approaching a singleness of vision" (p. 70). In 1988, his final year with the National, Hall staged *The Winter's Tale*, *Cymbeline*, and *The Tempest*.

When Hall resigned in 1988, the year the National became the Royal National Theatre in celebration of its Silver Jubilee, he was succeeded by Richard Eyre, a director experienced in Shakespearean production. Eyre had, for example, directed Jonathan Pryce as a Hamlet if not mad at least epileptic at the Royal Court Theatre in 1980. Pryce had played not only the Prince but his father's Ghost as well, his Hamlet having internalized the Ghost and seeming to vomit forth its lines. Probably Eyre's best known Shakespearean production at the RNT is his 1990 fascist *Richard III*, set in the 1930s, with Ian McKellen modeling his Richard, more or less, on Hitler (with a touch of Stalin and his withered arm) and speaking with a Sandhurst accent. Because of a good many special effects and brilliant gimmickry, including a toy electric train to the Finland Station, the production fascinated audiences and, on the whole, pleased critics. Encouraged by the success of the production, McKellen later turned it into a film (1996, made with director Richard Locraine because of Eyre's previous commitments elsewhere).

Canadian director Robert Lepage's RNT production of *A Midsummer Night's Dream* (1992–93) began with the four lovers together in a hospital bed in a mud-puddle. The play was their three-and-a-half-hour dream, or, rather, as George Geckle put it, a "mudsummer nightmare." Heavily indebted to Freud, Jung, and Jan Kott, it was "the most innovative *Dream* since Peter Brook's," and as a production it was equally liked and loathed. What most disturbed viewers, according to Geckle, was the loss of the poetry to the acrobatics (Angela Laurier, who played Puck, was a Canadian circus performer) and difficulty hearing over the sloshing water (pp. 27–28).

Deborah Warner's *Richard II* in the Cottesloe in 1995 may have owed something to Barry Kyle's RSC version a few years earlier. Hildegard Bechtler's design established the setting as a church, with much chanting and incense. Fiona Shaw, with cropped hair (the men were able to wear their hair long), was a smiling and playful Richard, continually checking a hand mirror, who forced Bullingbrook to play patty-cake with her to pick up the crown she had placed at his feet. The most surprising aspect of the production, however, was the conception of Bullingbrook. David Threlfall, hesitant, sometimes almost sniveling, fearful before Richard's anointed power, hardly seemed the man to take Richard's throne. Finally, though the production pleased many, it was not possible to forget that Richard was Fiona Shaw.

In 1996, Trevor Nunn, who had taken over the Royal Shakespeare Company at the age of 28 in 1969, was appointed to succeed Eyre at the RNT in October 1997.

The English Shakespeare Company

In 1985, Michael Bogdanov and Michael Pennington founded the English Shakespeare Company as a touring group, with the intent of challenging the conservatism of the Royal Shakespeare Company and the National Theatre. They dissolved the company in 1994. Their most famous productions were their cycle of seven history plays (out of a possible eight, covering the period 1398–1485), which they titled *The Wars of the Roses*. In their first season, 1986–87, they presented *The Henrys*, which consisted of both parts of *Henry IV* and *Henry V*, three plays in all. So successful were the productions that in the following year they added *Richard II* to begin the saga, and then reduced the three *Henry VI* plays to two, entitled *Henry VI House of Lancaster* and *Henry VI House of York*, and concluded with *Richard III*. This *Wars of the Roses* cycle differed from the Hall-Barton productions of the early 1960s (originally just the *Henry VI* plays and *Richard III*) and the Hands productions of the 1970s (originally just the six Henry plays) in that neither of those groupings of all eight plays was performed by a single cast as a continuous cycle (Crowl, 1992, pp. 142–43). The twenty-two-hour cycle toured the world, as well as the United Kingdom.

Pennington played Prince Hal and Henry V in *The Henrys* (the two parts of *Henry IV* and *Henry V*, 1986–87); for *The Wars of the Roses*, he retained these roles and added Richard II, Jack Cade, and others. Andrew Jarvis developed Richard of Gloucester into Richard III, also playing Hotspur. The "monumental Falstaffs" of John Woodvine and Barry Stanton, Barbara Hodgdon wrote, were destined "to outlive the productions of which they were such an essential part" (p. 143).

Sets were minimal and costumes eclectic, a mix of medieval and contemporary battle dress along with some costuming from other periods. Football hooligans with a "Fuck the Frogs" banner embarked for France in *Henry V*; and though Richard III was dressed in a double-breasted pin-striped suit (it is said that in a Bogdanov production the bad guys are always the ones in suits), he and Richmond fought their climactic duel in full medieval armor, in filmic slow motion and to the accompaniment of Samuel

Barber's "Adagio for Strings." The music obviously alluded to the film *Platoon*, the sort of allusion Bogdanov, heavily influenced by popular culture in general and by film in particular, frequently makes. The entire cycle was videotaped during performance in Swansea, in 1989.

In general, war was presented without glory, as the pastime of rowdies and thugs. Critical and popular acceptance was mixed: Some viewers thought the productions a desecration of Shakespeare, an abandonment of classicism, while others found the plays revivified, a confirmation of their timelessness. Sheridan Morley wrote that "Bogdanov's productions are aimed by the young at the young. . . . Never mind the intelligence, feel the energy" (quoted in Hodgdon, p. 144).

In 1992, the English Shakespeare Company again visited the United States after touring the United Kingdom, this time with *Macbeth*, set on a rehearsal stage cluttered with a shopping cart and trash, that the witches picked through. A mobile crane of the sort usually called a cherry picker dominated the stage. Costuming was again eclectic, very much modern, as were the automatic weapons. Banquo wore an equestrian costume as he went for his last ride and made one of his entrances during the banquet scene via the cherry picker. Duncan, supplied with a throne also via the cherry picker in his first appearance, arrived at Macbeth's "pleasant seat" clad much in the style of Sherlock Holmes. For the decade of its existence, the English Shakespeare Company was a vigorous force in Shakespearean production, mounting thought-provoking productions of *Coriolanus*, *The Winter's Tale*, *Twelfth Night*, and many others, as well as those discussed here. Veteran theatre-goers will recognize the company's continuing influence chiefly in productions that challenge the political status quo.

Other Companies

Cheek by Jowl was founded in 1981 by director Declan Donnellan and designer Nick Ormerod. Its all-male *As You Like It* enjoyed great acclaim at the Sixth International Theatre Festival at the State University of New York in Stony Brook in July of 1991, and later the same year in London. It stimulated audiences on several continents before returning to New York in 1994 at the Brooklyn Academy of Music. Critics were agreed that there was nothing gimmicky about the production, although there were suggestions of homosexual desire, as is frequently the case in contemporary productions of the cross-dressing comedies. Adrian Lester, the black male who played Rosalind, was universally praised for his grace in the role, and the multicultural casting occasioned little comment. Of the company's 1994 *Measure for Measure*, Mel Gussow wrote that the simple black-and-white production "on an almost bare stage, pierces to the ethical heart of the matter." Hearing Isabella's pleas, Adam Kotz, as Angelo, was thoroughly contemporary without forsaking Shakespeare: "Calculating his demands—favor for favor, measure for measure—he becomes an embodiment of sexual harassment," Gussow notes (p. 72).

Peter Hall had left the RNT in 1988 to start his own Peter Hall Company, and one of his company's first productions was *The Merchant of Venice*, staged both in London's West End and in New York in 1989, with Dustin Hoffman as Shylock giving "a quietly authoritative performance (*not* small-scale as all the London critics had it), only overstretched by the rhetoric of the trial scene" (Cushman, p. C9).

When in 1994 Hall came to direct *Hamlet* at the newly named Gielgud Theatre (which ceded the name "Globe" to the reconstruction of Shakespeare's theatre in progress in Southwark), he had already directed the play twice before: with David Warner for the Royal Shakespeare Company in 1965, a production that became famous despite poor initial reviews, and with Albert Finney at the National Theatre in 1976, the opening production in the new building. Alan Franks quotes Hall's reflections on this sequence.

> I had no idea, when we were doing the Warner *Hamlet*, that we were in effect doing the 1960s flower-power version, the man of apathy. . . . As far as I was concerned, we were just doing the play. Then with Albert Finney at the National, I also had no idea that we were dealing with quite such ferocious bitterness. This was the previous decade's dream gone wrong. Albert was a black, angry Hamlet, carrying round this really terrible weight of crushed hopes. And I think that in that time, in the 1970s, there was a strong sense of expectations unfulfilled.

In his *Diaries*, Hall claimed that the Finney production was "the closest I have reached to the heart of a Shakespeare play in my own estimation," in part because "the production is the closest I've ever got to a unified style of verse speaking which is right" (Goodwin, p. 199).

Hall's third *Hamlet* (1994–95), with Stephen Dillane, focused chiefly on the relations between Hamlet and fathers: Michael Pennington as both insecure Claudius and regal ghost and Donald Sinden as a fear-inspiring "bureaucratic bully" in the role of Polonius (Crowl, 1995, p. 19). Pennington was praised as much as Dillane for the excellence of the production.

SHAKESPEARE IN THE UNITED STATES

Shakespeare Festivals

In the summer of 1990, Felicia Londré gathered information on about half of the eighty U.S. Shakespeare festivals she had identified, and visited eleven. She found most of them to be Shakespeare-in-the-park festivals that prospered by stressing accessibility, achieved, among other means, by catering to the ethnic diversity of their audiences. Many relied on donations rather than charging admission.

Chief among such festivals, certainly, is the New York Shakespeare Festival, founded by the populist Joseph Papp in 1954 and under his direction until his death in 1991. (For more on the founding and early history of the New York Shakespeare Festival, see Appendix A.) Papp was succeeded by Joanne Akalaitis, who was fired by the board two years later, in 1993, and was succeeded by George C. Wolfe. The NYSF record is uneven.

To bring the plays to the people, Papp put them on not only in the Delacorte Theatre in Central Park, but in various other city parks as well. And, in recognition of the ethnic diversity of New York, the casting has been vigorously color-blind and multicultural. At various times Papp had under his control several indoor spaces as well. In 1966 he established the Public Theatre in what had been the Astor Library on Lafayette Street, which now includes the Newman and Anspacher theatres as venues, and for a time (1973–77) he also mounted productions in Lincoln Center.

In 1988, Papp announced his plan to produce the entire Shakespeare canon in six years in a Shakespeare Marathon. He began it at the Anspacher Theatre with *A Midsummer Night's Dream* directed by A. J. Antoon. And although set in the Brazilian jungle, it was "balanced, clear, and witty," with the plot of the young lovers being the best realized. Elizabeth McGovern as Helena "spoke the verse easily" and abandoned herself to the comic possibilities of the role. Al Pacino as Antony in *Julius Caesar*, the second play in the Marathon, also "spoke the verse thoughtfully, with full understanding of its meaning" (Hornby, pp. 340–42). In these instances, at least, the NYSF was not subjected, as it frequently was, to charges that its actors were unable to act in classics or to speak blank verse.

There have been triumphs in some of the less frequently performed plays, as well. Steven Berkoff's modern-dress *Coriolanus* (1989), with Christopher Walken as Coriolanus and Irene Worth as Volumnia, appealed to a contemporary urban audience, and *Pericles* (1991), directed by Michael Greif, with Campbell Scott as Pericles, was a surprising success.

Twelfth Night in 1989, however, glittered with a cast of movie stars, several of whom seemed to be reprising their latest film roles but to have little if any knowledge of what the play was about. Almost universally damned by the critics (who referred to Papp's program as "Shakespeare-with-Stars"), the production was the most popular in the Festival's history. John Simon wrote in his review that "It's a terrible delusion that you get free Shakespeare in Central Park" (quoted in Epstein, p. 440)—his point was that it wasn't Shakespeare at all.

A year later, not even the direction of Robin Phillips and the lead played by Denzel Washington could prevent an uneven production of *Richard III* (1990). In the same season, A. J. Antoon's *Taming of the Shrew*, with Tracey Ullman and Morgan Freeman, was characterized as a "spaghetti western," and much of the dialogue was found to be unintelligible because of the various and exaggerated regional dialects (Kramer, 1990). Yet despite all these complaints, it is well to keep in mind Robert Brustein's point that Papp was always willing to risk his reputation to keep the classics alive rather than stage complacent, unimaginative productions (1989, p. 30). And Kevin Kline brought to the NYSF considerable classical acting skills. Frank Rich of *The New York Times* thought that Kline and his director, Jane Howell (who had recently directed the *Henry VI–Richard III* tetralogy for the BBC), were outwitted by *Richard III* in Kline's 1983 Shakespearean debut with the NYSF (1983, p. C3), but *Much Ado about Nothing* (1988), directed by Gerald Freedman, with Kline playing Benedick as a *miles gloriosus* and Blythe Danner emphasizing Beatrice's disappointment in love rather than her merriness, was very well received by critics (such as Mimi Kramer of *The New Yorker*) and by the public.

When Kline played Hamlet in 1990 for the NYSF, he was doing so for the second time. Yet he did not please everyone, and Frank Rich wrote that in 1986 he had been directed "unassertively" by Liviu Ciulei, and that now, directing himself, despite his "intelligence, sardonic humor, verbal and physical virility," his production lacked "the spark that might make it deeply moving" (1990, p. C15). His Ophelia was Diane Venora, who had herself played Hamlet for the NYSF in a 1982–83 production that elicited more curiosity than praise. Shortly after the conclusion of his production, Kline co-directed it for a highly praised television version, an American *Hamlet* for posterity (Maher, p. 307).

Kline also played the Duke in a calypso *Measure for Measure* (the twenty-second production in the Shakespeare Marathon) directed by Michael Rudman in 1993 with a cast "essentially Caribbean black." Robert Brustein found it not only "terrific summer entertainment," but "distinguished overall by very confident classical acting." Kline's Duke was "the triumph of the evening," a figure so inept as the Friar that he didn't know how to make the sign of the cross and so little able to keep his mind on his own plans that he could be "vamped by an attractive whore," and who thus shocked everybody, "including himself, in the final recognition scene with his abrupt proposal to Isabella" (1993, p. 32).

George C. Wolfe's production of *The Tempest* (1995), set in the Caribbean, with Patrick Stewart as a "superbly human Prospero," "still enraged and resentful" about his deposition, might serve as a prime example of a New York Shakespeare Festival production. Many in the audience knew Stewart from his years as a leading actor (as Enobarbus and Shylock, among many other roles) with the Royal Shakespeare Company, but for most of the fans it was Stewart's fame from *Star Trek* that brought them to the Delacorte Theatre in Central Park and that enabled the production to go on to a later life in the commercial theatre after the summer run. But, as Margaret Loftus Ranald remarked, "Many of the actors needed voice work" (1995, p. 10), and Bill Irwin, as Trinculo, was inspired in his clowning, but not Shakespearean.

Other festivals have at least partly outgrown their Shakespeare-in-the-park beginnings and now stage some or all of their productions in indoor theatres, and charge admission to all productions. Some were never really populist. The organization of these companies varies greatly, as does the degree of professionalism and the quality of their productions.

The American Shakespeare Theatre, in Stratford, Connecticut, was not really a functioning theatre for all of its thirty years from 1955 to 1985. (See Appendix A for more information on the founding and early history of the American Shakespeare Theatre.) Its production history was spotty and erratic, with good early years under John Houseman, and a strong period under Michael Kahn from 1968 to 1976; the following season was canceled for lack of funds. But despite a resumption of production in 1978, the theatre never regained its strength, though Peter Coe's 1981 *Othello*, with James Earl Jones and Christopher Plummer, was a strong production that went on a national tour. Yet the very success of the production was a measure of what often seemed to be the weakness at the AST as a whole: a reliance on Broadway stars rather than the development of an ensemble. For the AST's last three years, productions were put on by John Houseman's Acting Company or Tina Packer's Shakespeare and Company from nearby Lenox, Massachusetts. When the insolvency of the American Shakespeare Festival "became official in 1985 there were claims that it had been artistically bankrupt years before" (Kennedy, *Looking at Shakespeare*, p. 231). The festival may be "developed" again as part of an international theatre center that would include a museum named for Katherine Hepburn, a Connecticut native, who played several roles there in the festival's early years.

The Oregon Shakespeare Festival in Ashland, founded in 1935 by Angus L. Bowmer, now has three theatres, the original outdoor Elizabethan Stage (remodeled in 1992), and two smaller indoor theatres, the Angus Bowmer (1970) and the Black Swan (1977). Remarkable continuity and stability have obtained in Ashland: When Bowmer retired in 1971, he was replaced by Jerry Turner, who served until 1991, when Henry Woronicz became artistic director. Libby Appel, whose last production as artistic director of the Indiana Repertory Theatre was a wonderfully effective *Tempest* with a cast of only seven actors, became only the fourth to lead the festival when she took over in the spring of 1996. Like her predecessors, she had had experience at the Oregon SF. In 1991, for example, she directed a controversial but nevertheless highly regarded modern-dress *Merchant of Venice* with no likable characters: The aggressive and vindictive Shylock disturbed the cool anti-Semitism of Christian Venice, and Portia was bored and self-centered.

The Alabama Shakespeare Festival, celebrating its twenty-fifth season in 1995–96, bills itself as the fifth largest Shakespeare Festival in the world. Like many others, it began as a summer festival a few weeks long, playing in a high-school auditorium. Founded in the small town of Anniston, Alabama, by Martin Platt, it moved to the state capital of Montgomery in 1985, thanks to the generosity of Winton M. Blount, whose gift of $21.5 million paid for the construction of the Carolyn Blount Theatre, named for his wife, a member of the board of directors. Plays are performed in either the 750-seat Festival theatre or the 225-seat Octagon. Usually three of the dozen or more plays produced each season are by Shakespeare. The thrust stage of the intimate Octagon was the site of a Victorian/Edwardian *All's Well That Ends Well* (1991) directed by Libby Appel, with a more than usually self-centered Bertram, played by Martin Kildare.

Among other notable festivals are the New Jersey Shakespeare Festival, founded by Paul Barry in 1963, and since 1972 housed at Drew University. Under Barry's direction, the festival completed the canon in 1986 with *The Two Noble Kinsmen*. The Utah Shakespeare Festival, founded in 1961 by Fred Adams, Professor of Theatre at Southern Utah University, has steadily improved its facilities and enlarged its audience throughout its more than three decades. The Colorado Shakespeare Festival has a long and distinguished record, as have Shakespeare at Santa Cruz, the Illinois Shakespeare Festival, The American Players Theatre in Wisconsin, and many others.

Non-Festival Theatres

Though technically not Shakespeare festivals, The Shakespeare Theatre in Washington, D.C., and Shakespeare Repertory in Chicago must be recognized for their focus on Shakespeare and for the high quality of their productions.

After twenty-two years at the Folger Shakespeare Library in Washington, D.C., The Shakespeare Theatre moved to the much more spacious quarters of the Lansburgh Theatre in 1992. Under the artistic direction of Michael Kahn since 1986, the theatre has prospered partly by casting film stars in leading roles and partly by supporting them with good direction. Kelly McGillis, for example, Kahn's former student at Juilliard, was highly praised for her Portia against Brian Bedford's Shylock in Michael Langham's 1988 *Merchant of Venice*; when she joined the company for the 1989–90 season, she was acclaimed in all her roles, but particularly for her Viola in a *Twelfth Night* that Kahn set in India during the Raj. A little tampering with the text eased the delightful production into the exotic setting without violating its spirit.

Generally speaking, Kahn is able to integrate the film stars into his productions, but occasionally there are problems. Kahn's "larger than life" *Richard III* (1990) with Stacy Keach was tension-filled and "unabashedly theatrical," but only Franchelle Stewart Dorn, as Queen Elizabeth, was "able to stand toe-to-toe with Keach" (Tocci, pp. 27–28). Keach met his equal in 1995, as well, when Helen Carey played his Lady in a production of *Macbeth*, directed by Joe Dowling on an abstract set, designed by Ming Cho Lee, dominated by a gaunt blood-red tree that served as the witches' perch. Tom Hulce lacked grandeur but was appealingly boyish and human as

Hamlet in Kahn's 1992 production. In short, in almost everything Kahn mounts, the high quality of the acting ensures balanced productions from what comes to seem like an ensemble company. An Edwardian *Love's Labor's Lost* in 1995, with the men as Cantabrigian scholars, made this feast of language fully intelligible with a cast composed largely of young and relatively unknown actors, thanks to the meticulous and imaginative direction of Laird Williamson.

Shakespeare Repertory in Chicago, founded in 1986 by Barbara Gaines, prides itself as being the only company in the United States devoted solely to Shakespeare year-round. Reviewing Gaines's 1993 *King Lear*, Justin Shaltz praised it as "typical of recent Shakespeare Repertory productions: imaginatively designed, faithful to the text, and featuring uniformly solid supporting performances" (p. 26). The text referred to is the First Folio, which Gaines regards as the "blueprint" for authentic Shakespearean production. But where in the First Folio text of *Othello* would she have found, for example, the African dancers and musicians or the Nazi–storm-trooper Iago of her 1995 production? Michael Pennington directed *Twelfth Night* in 1996, with Ronald Keaton playing Feste as an Irish clown, wearing tails, a shabby red sash, top hat, and red sneakers: As striking as was his appearance, Keaton was so understated and secure in his delivery that he exerted a presence at all times without dominating the production. Gaines has a penchant for doing the less popular plays and pleasing audiences while doing so: Her *Cymbeline* (1993 and 1995) and *Pericles* (1992) were highly regarded, as were her *Troilus and Cressida* (1989 and 1995) and *Measure for Measure* (1994).

Theatres not devoted to Shakespeare also do admirable work, of course. In Jon Jory's *Antony and Cleopatra* (1992) at the Actors Theatre of Louisville, Mercedes Ruehl as Cleopatra made defect perfection even as she acted the serpent of old Nile; Clancy Brown was a virile Antony, an imposing commander of men.

Romanian director Liviu Ciulei's 1989 production of *A Midsummer Night's Dream* at the Arena Stage in Washington, D.C., started with Hippolyta's being escorted in, stripped of her military black coveralls, and forcibly fitted with a white wedding gown. By the end of the scene, the mannequins that had provided several dress choices as they were positioned about the stage had become only so much litter on the floor; as she left, Hippolyta prompted a gasp from all her attendants and captors by walking on the train of the gown, which covered most of the stage. In Ciulei's Guthrie Theatre production (1985), Hippolyta's coveralls had been burned on a brazier. Like the famed Peter Brook production of 1970, Ciulei's was abstract, with basically white and shapeless costumes. There was no scenery except for a trapezoidal plexiglass platform suspended from the ceiling, underlit with fluorescent lights. Titania carried on her love scene with Bottom (to the disdain of the fairies, who were clearly embarrassed by Titania's infatuation) on this platform at floor level; from the elevated platform, Oberon and Puck observed the young lovers' confusion. The music by Philip Glass, whose work is usually monotonous and endlessly repetitious, was here exactly right in its abstractness.

Despite the more or less unisex costuming, this production was highly charged sexually, in a post-modern way. What came through most strongly in the forest scenes was the interchangeability of the young people. When one was not near the girl (or boy) one loved, one loved the girl (or boy) one was near. And there was an implied violence to the depicted sexuality: When Oberon anointed the eyes of Titania, he did so with a black blindfold, pressing it down forcefully, arousing in her the contortions of a nightmare; the same was true of the other anointings. Some of the details of Martin L. Platt's very good 1994 *Dream* at the Cincinnati Playhouse in the Park, set in Belle Epoque Argentina, seemed to derive from Ciulei's vision.

Ciulei said that he saw the play as fundamentally political. "It's a fight for power between Oberon and Titania, and it's a play about marriage and betrayal." Ciulei found in the four young lovers a commentary on "a hierarchical male society. As an example, the two ladies [who] are so vocal . . . . In the fifth act, when they marry, they don't get one line. That can be no accident" (quoted in Erstein, p. E5).

A not so happy but nevertheless important production was Peter Sellars's *Merchant of Venice* at Chicago's Goodman Theatre in 1994. Dubbed "The Merchant of Venice Beach" by some critics, it could be called post-modern in its esthetic. It lasted four hours, but a third or more of the audience did not know that, having abandoned it at the intermission, both during performances in Chicago and later during its tour of London and the continent. The production was a travesty of multicultural casting: blacks played the Jews, Asians played Portia and her household, and Latinos played the Venetians. Confusion reigned: Was Portia's black maid an oppressed black or an oppressed Jew? Nine television monitors cluttered the stage and the theatre, some of them showing the action on stage, some seemingly random scenes of a swimming pool being cleaned or of the Rodney King beating. The language was lost: Many of the actors were unable to speak their lines, and none seemed to want to. The voices were without character; projected over microphones in the ceiling, they lost all sense of locality: If a speaker was not shown on a television monitor, the audience was unable to guess who was speaking. For the trial scene, the Duke sat with his back to the audience, his mumbles inaudible to those few still remaining to listen.

In addition to the festival and individual theatre productions discussed above, several traveling companies deserve to be mentioned. Among these, probably the most important is ACTER (the Alliance for Creative Theatre, Education, and Research), founded in 1977 by Homer Swander of the University of California, Santa Barbara, in association with several members of the Royal Shakespeare Company, including Patrick Stewart. Annually since its founding, ACTER has sponsored five actors from the RSC and the London stage who tour universities and colleges, doing workshops with students, and, by doubling parts, performing complete Shakespeare plays with their cast of five.

The Acting Company has been touring the country with young actors at an early stage in their careers since its founding, in 1972 by John Houseman and Margot Harley, with the specific mission of bringing Shakespeare to small-town audiences who might otherwise never see a live Shakespearean production. Affiliated with the Juilliard School in New York City, it draws most, but not all, of its members from that school. Houseman served as director until his death in 1988, following which several directors succeeded him; but since 1994 Harley has been sole producing director.

The Shenandoah Shakespeare Express, billing itself as a "portable Shakespeare festival," offers a program of workshops and performances conducted by young actors. It is housed at James Madison University in Virginia.

SHAKESPEARE IN CANADA: THE STRATFORD FESTIVAL THEATRE

Certainly the most highly regarded Shakespearean theatre in North America is the Stratford Festival in Ontario, which has been doing work of consistently high quality since its founding in 1953. (For more on the Festival's early history see Appendix A.) Its strength from the beginning has been the development of a stable company—an ensemble—which nurtures young actors, along with the ability to attract actors of international stature who, on the whole, become full members of the company, even on occasion taking minor roles. Although Shakespeare's name disappeared from the title some time ago as the Festival broadened its offerings to attract visitors for longer stays in the small town, it is for Shakespeare that patrons return to Stratford annually. Since 1970, there have been five artistic directors: Robin Phillips (b. 1942), 1975–80; John Hirsch (1930–1989), 1981–85; John Neville (b. 1925), 1986–89; David William (b. 1926), 1990–93; and Richard Monette (b. 1944), 1994 to the present.

When Robin Phillips became artistic director, he introduced several innovations. He made the balcony on the Festival Stage removable, staged Shakespeare (*The Comedy of Errors*, set in the American West, and *The Two Gentlemen of Verona*, set in *la dolce vita* Italy—both 1975) for the first time in the Avon Theatre (a renovated movie theatre), and founded a Young Company. But his plans for instituting a theatre school were never realized.

Phillips immediately established a high standard. Setting *Measure for Measure* (1975) in Freud's Vienna, he cast William Hutt as the Duke, Brian Bedford as Angelo, Martha Henry as Isabella, and Kathleen Widdoes as Mariana. In the 1976 revival, Maggie Smith played Mistress Overdone. The production was stunningly effective, particularly in the final scene when Isabella refused the Duke's offer of marriage and took her novice's cap off before leaving the stage, signifying that though she was not yet ready for marriage, she had found that the convent was not for her. This touch Phillips owed to John Barton's RSC production of 1970.

Richard III and *As You Like It*, both of 1977 (the latter revived in 1978), were triumphs for Phillips and the company. Brian Bedford was a superb Richard, supported by three of the finest actresses in the world: Martha Henry as Lady Anne, Maggie Smith as Queen Elizabeth, and Margaret Tyzack as a fierce Queen Margaret. In *As You Like It*, Smith was a delightful Rosalind, ever on the brink of a new discovery, Bedford a wry Jaques, and Jack Wetherall a strikingly handsome Orlando. The costumes, by Robin Fraser Paye, were inspired by the watercolors of Thomas Rowlandson. Rarely had a comedy been given such exquisite attention to detail. Audiences were on their feet, crying, at the opening performances of both these plays, and probably on many other nights as well.

What these and other productions during Phillips's tenure illustrate was his ability not only to attract internationally renowned actors to Stratford, but to blend them into the company. In short, although the company during Phillips' years frequently enjoyed leading actors from England, and a few from the United States, it was nevertheless a largely Canadian company, with Canadian actors playing many leading roles. And it was an ensemble.

Michael Bogdanov's 1985 *Measure for Measure* was probably the best production during the tenure of John Hirsch as artistic director. It was certainly most controversial—indeed, many in the audience left in the middle of the performance. As is usual with Bogdanov, the production was set in the present. As the audience came into the Festival Theatre, the stage represented a disco, full of punks in leather, dancing to rock music. Alan Scarfe danced with Maria Ricossa until the lights went out during deafening music. When the lights came up the stage was cleared except for Scarfe, who was in the same spot, in character as the Duke.

At the moated grange, Mariana turned out to be Maria Ricossa. She listened to "Take, O, take those lips away" on a Walkman radio, belted out by three leather-clad transvestites on the balcony above. Angelo's charge that "her reputation was disvalued / In levity" was at least credible, if not proved. During the Duke's awkward couplets, while Mariana and Isabella conferred about the bed-trick, Scarfe's relishing of his cigar reeked of self-indulgent sensuality.

The final scene was staged as a press conference, another hallmark of a Bogdanov production. Vienna's public life was shown as being as corrupt as its underworld. Nicholas Pennell was a bitter Angelo, gracelessly accepting the wife forced upon him. When the lights went out at the end, Barbara March, an excellent Isabella, stood alone on the trapdoor from which Barnardine had emerged earlier; whether she would accept the Duke's proposal was not clear, but it seemed unlikely.

Although John Neville, appointed as the new artistic director in 1985, came with a reputation for being a good financial manager, he challenged conventional wisdom by devoting his first season, 1986, to the romances, *Pericles* (Richard Ouzounian, director), *Cymbeline* (in modern dress, Robin Phillips, director), and *The Winter's Tale* (David William, director). Sound productions all, they were moderately successful, filling forty to fifty-two percent of the large Festival Theatre. But pay the bills he did, partly by staging Broadway musicals on the Festival stage; when he ended his term in 1989, the Stratford Festival was financially sound once again, after having suffered large deficits during the early 1980s.

In 1987, Robin Phillips returned to direct the Young Company on The Third Stage in an excellent *Romeo and Juliet* and an even better *As You Like It*, a very sexy production in, paradoxically, Mennonite dress, with a tall and beautiful Nancy Palk as Rosalind and Albert Schultz as a witty and companionable Touchstone.

But across town in 1987, at the Avon Theatre, *Troilus and Cressida*, directed by David William, was not making many people happy. Like many of the productions in the Neville era, it was in modern dress. But the dress was extreme, to emphasize the play's decadence: The Greeks dressed in British khaki of World War II, the Trojans in oriental opulence. William Needles played Pandarus as a transvestite, and, in fact, a Trojan drag party was staged. But Neville at least prevented William from turning the killing of Hector into a homosexual rape by leather-clad bikers.

John Wood directed one of the finest productions of the Neville era in 1989, another modernized production on the Avon stage, setting *Henry V* in 1915, to great effect. Actors in sweat suits and jeans wandered on stage as if in a rehearsal room but snapped to attention with the playing of the national anthem. Then Geraint Wyn Davies handed a wreath to William Needles, a veteran of the original company of 1953, who, playing the Chorus and wearing the beret of the Canadian Legion, laid it against a bronze wall at the rear of the stage on which were (prematurely) inscribed the names that would be remembered on Crispin's Day. The allusion to the Vietnam Memorial was palpable. The Southampton scene was set in the Great Hall of Portchester Castle. There was dancing and "Onward, Christian Soldiers" and a bit of Gilbert and Sullivan were sung, as well as "After the Ball." Davies was a young and attractive Henry; his friends were equally as elegant in their Edwardian whites.

David William, also born in England, made his professional debut with the Old Vic and acted at the Shakespeare Memorial Theatre, as well as doing a considerable amount of directing. His first assignment at the Stratford Festival came in 1966, when he directed *Twelfth Night* at the request of Michael Langham. Several other assignments ensued, including an extraordinarily moving *King Lear* in 1972, with William Hutt in the title role. David William assumed the artistic directorship in 1990.

In 1991, under William's aegis, Michael Langham directed *Timon of Athens* at the Tom Patterson Theatre, the Third Stage newly renamed in honor of the Festival's founder. Langham's assistant director was Elliott Hayes, the Festival's literary manager and himself an excellent playwright. They interpolated scenes, cut others, and wrote some of their own lines. With Brian Bedford as Timon, the production, in modern dress, was a surprising success.

Joe Dowling directed an erotic *Midsummer Night's Dream* on the Festival Stage in 1993, with fairies violent, athletic, and catlike, as were Oberon and Titania, Colm Feore and Lucy Peacock. The young lovers, once in the forest, demonstrated the raw and indiscriminate sexuality just under the veneer of civilization. As Helena, Sheila McCarthy found her librarian's demeanor and her copy of *The Complete Works of William Shakespeare* unnecessary in that setting. Dowling had previously directed a similar but heavily multicultural *Dream* for the Acting Company, which toured the United States a couple of years earlier, and directed it again in 1993 for the Gate Theatre in Dublin.

Ming Cho Lee's minimal sets on the Avon stage, Brian Bedford's directing, and Scott Wentworth's petty Iago produced a great rarity in 1994, a good production of *Othello*. (With good reason, no one in Stratford likes to recall at least two earlier productions.) With Othello (Ron O'Neal, a film actor) modeled on General Benjamin Davis, the first black general in the U.S. Army and an advisor on race relations in Europe during World War II, the play worked, despite a lack of majesty in Othello. O'Neal had the bearing of a staff officer, not one who had spent his life in the "tented field," and the modernization of setting reduced his "Keep up your bright swords, for the dew will rust them" to "Hold your hands." The strikingly attractive Lucy Peacock innocently drew all male attention to her Desdemona, who was by turns—necessarily the wrong turns—tentative and self-confident. Wentworth had the stage at the end, shrinking physically against Ming Cho Lee's enormously tall white doors, his right arm hanging uselessly at his side, as it had been throughout the play, the bodily symbol of his defective moral sense.

Wentworth triumphed again the following year, in a production of *Macbeth* directed by Marti Maraden. He and his Lady, Seana McKenna, were thoroughly human. Exhausted and alone after the banquet, Macbeth gnawed on a crust of bread while Lady Macbeth tried to explain his irrational behavior with "You lack the season of all natures, sleep." When she rose to go off stage, she lifted her skirts, as if she were wading in blood. The gesture was unforgettable.

All of the Stratford Festival's recent artistic directors have been united in bewailing the government's small subsidy, about ten percent of the operating budget. Ticket prices continue to escalate, and the number of Shakespearean productions declines. For 1996, only three of eleven productions—*King Lear*,

As You Like It, and *The Merchant of Venice*—are by Shakespeare, and of these only *Lear* is on the Festival stage. *Amadeus* and *The Music Man* on that stage will pay the bills. The number and the ratio are typical of the nineties at Stratford.

FOREIGN SHAKESPEARE

In a recent collection of essays entitled *Foreign Shakespeare: Contemporary Performance*, the editor, Dennis Kennedy, addresses one of the chief questions with respect to the performance and appreciation of Shakespeare throughout the world in his "Introduction: Shakespeare Without His Language." Conceding that non-English speakers miss much of the linguistic pleasure that native speakers of English treasure in Shakespeare, Kennedy nevertheless argues that "some foreign performances may have a more direct access to the power of the plays" than we do because "it is common practice in the contemporary theatre to commission new translations for new productions, so that the language is not only colloquial but also becomes tied to the interpretation and the *mise en scène* of the particular performance" (p. 5). Kennedy cites the example of *Hamlet*, which "has long been read in England and America inside the romantic tradition, as the outcry of an individual tortured soul, focusing on the poetic insights of the central character." In eastern Europe, however, the play has frequently been seen as about rebellion, and has consequently been suppressed. He continues:

> In 1989, just before the collapse of the Stalinist government of the German Democratic Republic, I saw Siegfried Höchst's production at the Volksbühne in East Berlin, which treated Denmark as a literal prison from which almost everybody was trying to escape, just as almost everybody was trying to escape at that moment from East Germany. The stage was enclosed with three rows of wire fencing, and when Laertes was given permission to return to France in the second scene, he was handed a green document that looked suspiciously like the passports issued by West Germany. The audience howled with delight. (pp. 4–5)

An essentially similar political reading lay behind the Bulandra Theatre Company's *Hamlet*, which played for more than two hundred performances in Bucharest at about the same time. The production was directed by Alexandru Tocilescu, with Ion Caramitru playing Hamlet. "It would not be inappropriate," wrote Joan Montgomery Byles, "to ask what role the theatre played, if any, in the collapse of communism in Eastern Europe and whether this particular production of *Hamlet* played any part in the downfall of the Ceausescu regime" (p. 25). In the final scene, after Hamlet had killed Claudius/Ceausescu, Fortinbras arrives as the new military dictator.

> The dead Hamlet at his feet, Horatio rises to bear witness to these terrible events, to tell the truth of Hamlet's story, only to be surrounded by these securistii [Rosencrantz and Guildenstern] who, at the new tyrant's command, stab him to death in front of the now cowering court. The brutal knifing of Horatio by Fortinbras' sinister minions is an alarming killing of immense political import, for here is the final palace coup that wipes out everybody who can or will tell the truth. (p. 26)

Of a much different import was *Qui Est Là*, Peter Brook's adaptation of *Hamlet*, in his own theatre, Le Centre International De Créations Théâtrales, in Paris. Horatio delivered the play's first line, "Qui est là?" ("Who's there?"), and the many cuts in the play made room for the recitation by the actors of passages from "six theatre theorists: Meyerhold, Stanislavski, Gordon Craig, Brecht, Artaud, and Zeami (the last the author of *The Secret of Noh*). As the play progresses, passages are revived and extended, and Brook and his collaborators deliberate aloud on how to stage some of the most familiar moments of Shakespeare's play" (Schlueter, p. 20).

Peter Zadek, who fled Germany with his Jewish parents in 1933, grew up in England. He returned to Germany in 1958, where he has directed controversial productions of many of Shakespeare's plays. In his 1977 *Hamlet*, Gertrude, who was younger than Hamlet, had "red bull's eyes painted on her bare breasts," and costumes ranged from baroque to modern. "Zadek explained why his Hamlet was played like a clown and madman directing a circus of performers. Simply put, tragedies can be stupid and comedies serious. For Zadek, *Hamlet* was a serious comedy and Hamlet a character living in a chaotic world, a world of appearances, a character who plays roles while watching others playing roles" (Engle, p. 98).

Geraldo U. de Sousa gives another perspective on foreign Shakespeare in "*The Merchant of Venice*: Brazil and Cultural Icons," an article that reports on the growing importance and number of Shakespeare productions during the last decade in Brazil, a country with almost no theatrical tradition. The 1993 production of *The Merchant of Venice* by Limite: 151 Theatre Group was the first Brazilian production of the play. Because of Brazil's large black population, the production "downplayed racism" in the presentation of the suitors, concentrating instead on their personal eccentricities. "The Italian characters, like the Brazilian audience, set themselves apart as lovers of carnival," and "the *telenova* [soap opera] influence could clearly be detected in all the Italian characters" (p. 472). Much of the success of the Brazilian productions came from the translations by Bárbara Heliodora, which "are making literary history, recreating the rhythm, poetry, and flavor of Shakespeare's language while retaining a degree of archaism without becoming wooden and artificial" (p. 473). Whereas "populist directors like Roger Planchon in Lyon, Leopold Lindtberg in Vienna, and Giorgio Strehler in Milan, as well as [Manfred] Wekwerth, [Benno] Besson, and Friedo Solter in Berlin, struck a bargain with Shakespeare: He delivered a Renaissance classic text, they overlaid it with a postwar social text" (Kennedy, *Foreign Shakespeare*, p. 12), the Brazilians appear to have done something else: While being aware of and addressing contemporary social conditions, they have attempted to retain some of the linguistic values of the original Shakespearean text. The variety of approaches to Shakespearean performance, limited only by theatrical imagination, admits much latitude for debate, but to a degree the dispute is over matters of taste, not entirely over substance.

SHAKESPEARE ON FILM AND TELEVISION

The Shakespeare Plays on BBC-TV

In the past quarter-century, film has been not nearly so important to Shakespearean performance as has television. The chief reason for the prominence of television as the most common medium has been the filming of the entire canon by the British Broadcasting Corporation and the broadcast of these performances in both the United Kingdom and the United States. This dominance has been extended by the availability of these productions on videotape.

While filming James Barrie's *Little Minister* at Glamis Castle, BBC producer Cedric Messina had the thought that the setting would be excellent for *As You Like It*, and he proposed the idea to the British Broadcasting Corporation. He got BBC approval to do not just that play but the whole canon, a series which became *The Shakespeare Plays*, with Messina as producer for the first twelve plays (1978–1980). The plays were to be set in either the Elizabethan or their own historical period; an exception was eventually made for *Love's Labor's Lost*, which was set, rather elegantly, in the eighteenth century.

The plays were not presented in any particular order. Strict chronology would have inaugurated the series with the *Henry VI* plays and some of the lesser comedies and tragedies. The decision was made, therefore, to offer a variety of genres each season. The first season, 1978, consisted of *Romeo and Juliet*, *Richard II*, *As You Like It*, *Julius Caesar*, *Measure for Measure*, and *Henry VIII*. Of these, two were particularly strong productions: *Richard II* with Derek Jacobi as Richard, and *Measure for Measure*. The latter, directed by Desmond Davis, with Kate Nelligan as an attractive and vulnerable Isabella, Tim Pigott-Smith as a thoroughly credible Angelo, and John McEnery as a witty and intrusive Lucio, ranks among the best productions on stage as well as on film or television. But, paradoxically, the outdoor setting did not suit the pastoralism of *As You Like It*, and despite the excellent cast (Helen Mirren and Angharad Rees as Rosalind and Celia, Richard Pasco as Jaques), the production was among the least interesting. Pastoralism did not lend itself to realistic representation.

Obvious sequences were kept more or less together. David Giles, who had directed *Richard II*, was asked by Messina to complete the Lancastrian tetralogy for the second season. Jon Finch, the Bullingbrook of *Richard II*, continued as Henry IV, and other principals, once introduced in *1 Henry IV*—David Gwillim as a likeable Hal and Anthony Quayle as an ebullient Falstaff, for example—remained constant as well.

Messina was succeeded by Jonathan Miller for the next eleven plays (1980–1981). With a distinguished directing history himself, Miller brought in Jane Howell, Jack Gold, and Elijah Moshinsky. Though they sometimes lacked obvious qualifications (Gold had never done Shakespeare, and Moshinsky had never directed for television), they turned out to be excellent choices.

Jane Howell was appointed director of the *Henry VI–Richard III* sequence, which was conceived as a unit from the beginning. She formed what amounted to a repertory company. Actors doubled roles, and as a character disappeared from one play, the actor appeared in a later play in another role. Trevor Peacock, for example, after dying as Talbot in *1 Henry VI*, reappeared as Jack Cade in *2 Henry VI*. Ron Cook, in a variety of nameless roles in the earlier productions, blossomed into Richard of Gloucester and ultimately Richard III.

This First Tetralogy was highly acclaimed, and for good reason. Eschewing realism, Howell filmed all the plays in a thoroughly artificial setting, a warehouse with heavy wooden structures, such as ramps, suggesting a primitive fort as well as, at times, a playground, implying that the battles were the activities of superannuated boys. At the close of *Richard III*, Howell added a scene that she called a "reverse Pietà," with Margaret atop a pile of corpses, "cradling Richard's dead body and laughing in triumph" (Shenk, p. 33). The productions came across, given the setting, as theatrical plays rather than as realistic films.

Howell was also the director for the last play produced, *Titus Andronicus* (1985), with Trevor Peacock as Titus, Anna Calder-Marshall as Lavinia, and Hugh Quarshie as Aaron. She reordered some scenes and added the young, bespectacled Lucius as silent witness to several others, the spectacles intimating an intellectual and brooding detachment within a moving production.

There were objections that Miller himself as director, with a bias against grand tragedy, reduced *Othello* (1981) to domestic tragedy, partly by scaling down the soliloquies to intimate revelation. Miller also minimized Othello's blackness. Messina's choice for the part, the American James Earl Jones, had demonstrated his tragic potentiality on television as Lear in a 1973 PBS performance of Joseph Papp's Central Park production directed by Edwin Sherin. But British Equity denied Jones the role of Othello, and it was given to Anthony Hopkins.

Beginning in Miller's era and continuing under Shaun Sutton, his successor, the series became less populist. In a number of plays, the educated viewer would recognize the Vermeer interior, for example, in *The Taming of the Shrew* (1980), which Miller himself directed, or the lighting of Georges de La Tour in Moshinsky's production of *All's Well That Ends Well* (1980–1981). Probably the most painterly production was Moshinsky's *Love's Labor's Lost* (1984–85), heavily indebted to Watteau, done under Sutton and the only play set outside its own or Shakespeare's period. Such allusions did not exclude any viewers, but they enhanced the pleasure for those who recognized them. Miller wanted his viewers to be consciously aware of the artistic decisions made in producing the theatrical artifact and in defining its context (or the context of the people in the play).

Shaun Sutton produced the final fourteen plays of the series (1982–1985). During this period, Miller directed *King Lear*, his third essay at the play with the same cast. Having directed Michael Hordern as Lear and Frank Middlemass as the Fool at the Nottingham Playhouse in 1969, he used them again in the BBC's *Play of the Month* in 1975, a powerful two-hour production, and for the third time in the 1982 BBC version, essentially the same as the earlier two in costume and design (largely black-and-white), and even blocking (Willis, p. 127). When the Granada Television *King Lear* (1983, directed by Michael Elliott) was broadcast a few months later, with Olivier as Lear and Diana Rigg as Regan, most viewers preferred the BBC version, despite the presence of Olivier and the mythic Stonehenge setting. The Olivier/Elliott version seemed ineffective because, paradoxically, it had adhered too strictly to the text rather than relying on film resources. R. Alan Kimbrough found it "simply dated" in ignoring the comparatively recent shift from aural to visual emphasis (p. 120).

Macbeth, also produced in 1982 by Sutton, similarly provoked comparisons, not only with Polanski's 1971 film, but with a BBC production of 1975 produced by Messina and directed by John Gorrie, with Eric Porter and Janet Suzman. Jack Gold, who directed the 1982 BBC version, set his production among monoliths suggestive of Stonehenge in barbaric eleventh-century Scotland, but strove more for suggestion and atmosphere than for realism. Nicol Williamson dramatized the panting frenzy of a desperate Macbeth, but sometimes muffled the lines in doing so. Gold did not offer us any visions, but rather showed us Williamson seeing a dagger of the mind and Banquo's vacant stool. Jane Lapotaire, writhing on a bed of animal skins while invoking the spirits who tend on mortal thoughts to unsex her, gave exactly the opposite message as she clutched her woman's breasts. Suzman's Lady also exuded sexuality, and for some viewers more credibly. Though both were powerful productions, critical consensus favors the Gorrie production with Porter and Suzman, as being better cast and acted.

The British and American versions of the BBC Shakespeare differed because of differing television conventions. Whereas the BBC broadcast the plays with irregular timing periods as determined by the varying lengths of dramatic units, New York's WNET edited them into half-hour segments, the commercial television norm. Some plays were cut severely, most notably the *Henry VI* plays, from which seventy-seven minutes (largely battle scenes) were deleted to reduce their total length. *Troilus and Cressida* lost an entire scene in broadcast, but the scene remains on the Time/Life videotape (Willis, pp. 62–63).

For whom were the BBC productions intended? It seemed obvious to some that a series such as this should be conservative and traditional, to put in the bank, in a sense, interpretations that would stand the test of time. It was to be an archive that could be called on at will. And, in fact, there was an educational outreach program, complete with sound recordings, master sheets for duplicating plot summaries, and special introductions written for the texts to be used by students. But that program never realized the hopes of the devisers; it was heavily scaled down after the second season. Moreover, as soon as the first plays were shown, a protest arose that the productions were too conservative, that they broke no new ground, that they lacked distinctive directing styles.

Other Productions

Other videotaped performances deserve mention for the high quality of their interpretations. Two versions of *Othello* are particularly noteworthy: the 1989 RSC production directed by Trevor Nunn, noticed above (see page 1936), and that directed by Janet Suzman, a native of South Africa, at the Market Theatre in Johannesburg in 1987. The black South African John Kani is an Othello not overshadowed by the Iago of Richard Haines; Kani's dignified performance is complemented, not only by Haines's workmanlike Iago but by the Desdemona of the beautiful Joanna Weinberg. The whiteness of the lighting as well as of the setting for the final scene imparts the sense of pure sacrifice to the murder of Desdemona. To these should be added Trevor Nunn's *Antony and Cleopatra* (1974), derived from his RSC production of 1972. Janet Suzman plays a sensuous Cleopatra to the grizzled and generous Antony of Richard Johnson, with Corin Redgrave as a lean and begrudging Caesar. Patrick Stewart complements Antony perfectly in looks and values in one of his several incarnations as Enobarbus. Suzman's death scene is unparalleled in its majesty and dignity.

SHAKESPEARE ON FILM

Kenneth Branagh

Few films of Shakespeare's plays were made between Roman Polanski's *Macbeth* in 1971 and Kenneth Branagh's *Henry V* in 1989. Whatever the cause of this hiatus, some attribute the resumption of filming Shakespeare to the death of Sir Laurence Olivier in 1989. Olivier's *Henry V* (1944), *Hamlet* (1948), and *Richard III* (1955) had been regarded as definitive, and new film interpretations were thought not only commercially unfeasible but unnecessary. In 1989, however, the twenty-eight-year-old Kenneth Branagh produced a *Henry V* that not only challenged Olivier's dominance of the form, but spurred a revival of Shakespearean film-making.

As Olivier's version opened after a panoramic shot of London with the Chorus speaking from the stage of what purported to be the Globe Theatre, Branagh's version also called attention to its artificiality, opening on a sound stage, with Derek Jacobi as Chorus. Branagh's *Henry V* differs from Olivier's version chiefly in being less overtly heroic and patriotic, though it has its moments of glory: For example, the long sequence of Branagh carrying the dead boy off the battlefield at Agincourt to the strains of religious music. Rain and mud dominate the battle scenes so strongly that the film came to be called "Dirty Harry" by those working on it. And it is a film clearly influenced by other films, Vietnam War films as well as Shakespearean.

Much of Branagh's interpretation and many of the production details derive from Adrian Noble's antiheroic *Henry V* of 1984, in which Branagh had played Henry in his debut with the Royal Shakespeare Company. But Branagh has been charged with making the film less disturbing to a conservative and patriotic audience than Noble's version: His Henry enjoys the support of a sympathetic Chorus, whereas Noble's patriotic Chorus was often ironically undercut by the action of the play.

Branagh's joyful *Much Ado about Nothing* (1993), filmed in hot and fecund Tuscany and, according to Branagh, set indefinitely "anytime between 1700 and 1900," was a rousing popular success while remaining essentially faithful to Shakespeare. In a book about the film, Branagh cites several movie scenes which he used as models for scenes in *Much Ado*: Don Pedro's horsemen returning from defeating Don John, for example, is straight out of *The Magnificent Seven*. (And while they approach triumphantly, the expectant women, equally aroused, rush to bathe for the coming together of the sexes.) For Dogberry and his band of bumblers, the model was, partly, the Three Stooges.

With himself as Benedick and Emma Thompson as Beatrice, the film appealed to almost everyone, though some of the international casting seemed strange. No one objected to Denzel Washington as Don Pedro, though many found his acting wanting. The verbal tics and other comic bits that Michael Keaton used to characterize Dogberry were, however, out of harmony with the rest of the film. Robert Sean Leonard and Kate Beckinsale were attractive enough to keep the Claudio-Hero plot from being too much overshadowed.

In 1995, Branagh played Iago in Oliver Parker's film of *Othello*, with Laurence Fishburne in the title role, the first black to play the role on screen. The film was "helplessly Iagocentric," according to Terrence Rafferty in his *New Yorker* review; only Branagh had training in Shakespearean acting. As is typical of filmed Shakespeare, less than forty percent of Shakespeare's language survived the editing. And Rafferty noted that Parker's heavy cutting of soliloquies reduced "this stirring dramatic poem to a tattered collection of one-liners" (p. 127). Moreover Sam Crowl pointed out that "Parker's camera replaces Othello's text with his texture," presenting Fishburne's "young, powerful, sexy presence" visually (1996, p. 41).

Franco Zeffirelli

Franco Zeffirelli returned to Shakespearean filmmaking with Mel Gibson in the title role of *Hamlet* in 1990 in a film that managed to be a popular success without offending the critics. While watching the film, one gets easily caught up in its movement, seduced by the action and the professionalism. While the eyes are being filled, however, the lines are being cut, although on the whole intelligently. Zeffirelli retained only thirty-seven percent of *Hamlet*; the percentages for his *Shrew* (1966) and *Romeo and Juliet* (1968) were slightly less: thirty percent and thirty-five percent, respectively (Pilkington, p. 165). (For more information on Zeffirelli's earlier Shakespeare films, see Appendix A.)

What stays in the memory after seeing Zeffirelli's *Hamlet* is Glenn Close as Gertrude at the tomb of Hamlet's father (this opening scene replacing the scene on the battlements), the generally Elsinorish setting, including a scene or two outdoors—even Hamlet riding a horse on the beach—and a repeated shuffling and conflating and resetting of scenes. And yet all this tampering produces a good film, and the changes all make excellent sense as the viewer experiences them. The "To be or not to be" soliloquy seems proper enough in the crypt of Hamlet's father, for example, and some of the nunnery material is not out of place during the play-within-the-play.

But much is lacking, not least the restoration of order and the sense of something larger than the interesting adventures of an attractive man. Cutting the whole of the Fortinbras plot (as is often done) not only eliminates the "How all occasions do inform against me" soliloquy, but also lets the film end with no one to embrace rights of memory in the kingdom. For a contemporary film, there is a strange but not inappropriate minimum of music.

With respect to Shakespeare, Branagh is far more faithful than Zeffirelli to what is the heart of a Shakespearean production—the language—and Zeffirelli's equal in translating stage values into filmic terms. Branagh's *Hamlet*, about to be released, will provide another view of the play without diminishing Zeffirelli's achievement.

Other Film Productions

In addition to Branagh and Zeffirelli, others have recently produced Shakespearean films worthy of note in the post-Olivier era.

After playing the title role in Richard Eyre's *Richard III* at the Royal National Theatre in 1990 and then during a subsequent world tour, Ian McKellen decided to film the play. Because Eyre's commitments at the RNT precluded his continuing with the project, McKellen enlisted Richard Loncraine, an almost unknown film director, whose chief work had been anonymous commercials. Desiring a few internationally known film stars in the cast to attract audiences, producers willingly replaced several actors in the RNT production who had commitments to other productions.

McKellen wrote the screenplay, and because Loncraine tended to see the play largely in filmic, visual terms, he "tried to make sure that Shakespeare did not become overwhelmed and that the film would remain rooted in his words and intentions as I understood them" (McKellen and Loncraine, p. 10). Released in 1996, the 103-minute film was essentially Eyre's "icy fascist" production, set in the 1930s, jazzed up with motor cars and scenes set on location—St. Pancras Station serving as The Royal Palace.

Generally speaking, the tragedies and the histories seem to appeal most to producers and directors, and not often the comedies, despite a succession of *Shrews* (none since Zeffirelli's, however) with its potential for rowdiness, and Branagh's *Much Ado*. The only other recently filmed comedy is *As You Like It*, a contemporary version in which Christine Edzard set the Arden scenes among the homeless on a Rotherhithe building site in the Docklands at the east end of London. Suggestions of the City substitute for Duke Frederick's court milieu in this 1992 film, a film "perhaps not for all markets" (Crowl, 1993).

Despite the fears of many critics that Shakespeare is not fully adaptable to television, or, for that matter, to film, there is a long history of good Shakespearean film (and much bad as well) and, as recent years have shown, a growing body of good Shakespearean television. Yet these are visual media, and film directors in particular cut plays drastically, showing on the screen what is said or implied in the play, rather than remaining faithful to the text. Film and television productions must necessarily be judged on their own terms, as different in kind from stage performances. One overpowering advantage that these media provide, however, is easy and inexpensive access to the plays that otherwise would be denied to many viewers.

THE GLOBE THEATRE

In 1970, the expatriate American Sam Wanamaker established the Globe Playhouse Trust to reconstruct Shakespeare's Globe Theatre, which had been pulled down in 1644 after the Puritans had closed it two years earlier. A ground-breaking ceremony in 1987 on the approximate site of the Globe was followed in 1989 by two discoveries: in February, of some remains of the Rose Theatre (dating to 1587–88) and, in October, of the original Globe (1599; second Globe built on the same foundation immediately after the fire of 1613), about two hundred yards from the planned reconstruction. The site of the original Globe is covered by Anchor Terrace, an early nineteenth-century Georgian building protected as a Listed Building by English Heritage; English Heritage also protects the original Globe as a Scheduled Ancient Monument (Gurr, p. 147).

These discoveries have altered our conceptions of Elizabethan theatres, based so heavily on Arend van Buchell's copy of the drawing of the Swan Theatre by Johannes de Witt (c. 1596; see Plate 8) and on John Norden's view of London (1600), which shows the location of the Bankside playhouses. For one thing, Elizabethan theatres showed greater variety in design than had been thought: That is, they were not all configured like the Swan. Further, the Rose apparently was smaller than previous estimates had made it, with a diameter now estimated at about 72 feet, and the Globe was considerably larger (Foakes, pp. 10–13). New estimates for the Globe range from about 86 feet to about 100 feet.

The Globe reconstruction has been dogged with problems, with the result that the planned 1995 opening on 23 April, Shakespeare's putative birthday, has been continually delayed. Wanamaker died in December 1993, and Theo Crosby, the architect of the project, died the following summer. The tentative date for the official opening is now 1997, although *The Two Gentlemen of Verona* was mounted in a "Prologue Season" in August 1996. The target date for the opening of the entire Globe Theatre project, which will include the main theatre, an underground museum, the Inigo Jones Theatre, a restaurant and pub, and a library and flats, is 19 September 1999, about 400 years after the first recorded performance at Shakespeare's Globe.

The Globe itself will accommodate about 1,500 playgoers, approximately 1,000 seated and 500 standing, with a stage measuring 44 feet wide by 25 feet deep. The total cost is expected to be £30 million. Present plans call for a summer season of fifteen to twenty weeks, with performances to be given in the afternoon, in natural light, with occasional additional performances augmented by electric light in the evenings.

Two significant events in 1995 will have considerable influence on the use of the Globe. A conference held in London in April 1995, convened by the International Shakespeare Globe Centre, concluded with strong support for performances without intermissions, for performances to begin at 2 p.m., and for evening performances with artificial lights, a concession possibly allowed for monetary reasons. "The primacy of 'text as director' was unanimously endorsed," but just how that policy would be effected was not determined. "The practice of cutting, adjusting, or otherwise subverting sacrosanct text to serve contemporary audiences was discouraged." Authentic Elizabethan and Jacobean costumes were favored, and some all-male productions might be mounted (Nelsen, "Oaths and Oracles," p. 31).

The second event, during August and September 1995, consisted of several workshops held in the partially completed Globe, most of them concerned with testing the acoustics. In general, results showed that city noises were distracting, but that the "heavens," or canopy, over the stage and the tiring house behind it enhanced audibility. The function of the canopy is not entirely agreed upon among scholars, but a growing belief is that it served both as a sounding-board and as protection from the elements.

Two problems arose with respect to the canopy, however. The first presented a question of design authenticity. Stage historians generally agree that there were such canopies in Elizabethan theatres, but they do not agree on whether they covered the whole stage, or only part of it, as in the Swan drawing. "After a careful review of the evidence, a clear consensus [of theatre historians] endorsed the full canopy" (Nelsen, "The Heavens Must Wait," p. 37). The second problem was that many of the workshop performers were greatly dissatisfied with the pillars supporting the heavens and argued against including them at all, as a concession to authenticity made unnecessary by modern engineering. The dispute has been a major cause in delaying the opening of the Globe until 1997.

At the age of thirty-five, Mark Rylance was appointed the first artistic director of the Globe, to take over in January 1996. At the time of his appointment, Rylance was in rehearsal—both as director and as Macbeth—for what became known as the Hare Krishna *Macbeth*, in the Greenwich Theatre. When it opened in September 1995, it was universally panned. Lady Macbeth's urinating during the sleep-walking scene did not seem to upset the audiences so much as the verse-speaking in flat American accents and the whole Hare Krishna concept—bald heads, saffron robes, and sandals. Rylance has, nevertheless, a distinguished and varied transatlantic career, and will very likely prove a stimulating director of the Globe.

No one really believes that the reconstructed Globe Theatre will provide fully genuine Elizabethan or Jacobean productions. Yet the experience of working on a stage and in a building closely approximating Shakespeare's own has already revealed much of value to actors and audiences about the nature of Shakespearean production. As Proteus in the prologue season *Two Gentlemen of Verona* (directed by Jack Shepherd), Rylance effortlessly delivered monologues to the entire theatre. Audiences and actors alike are delighting in the intimate relationship they enjoy in the snug setting. At the very least, the Globe is stimulating great popular, as well as scholarly, interest in Shakespearean performance.

Public support for the arts in the United Kingdom, the United States, and Canada has been steadily declining in recent years, partly because of economic problems and also because of political considerations. Some theatre companies have been forced to cease operations, and others have had to rely on ever higher percentages of box-office receipts to pay their bills. And companies formerly devoting themselves primarily to Shakespeare have diversified their offerings—frequently staging musicals—to attract larger audiences.

Yet Shakespeare remains the most popular playwright of all time, and the number of productions of Shakespeare throughout the world continues to increase. For one thing, nation after nation comes to consider Shakespeare "our Shakespeare." And for another, new companies performing Shakespeare do not take customers away from the established companies and festivals: Rather, competition fosters increased interest in Shakespeare in performance, stimulating ever more productions on stage, film, and television. Kenneth Branagh, for example, in his forthcoming film of *Hamlet*, is no doubt building on his experience playing the title role in Adrian Noble's 1993 Royal Shakespeare Company production. As Olivier's 1948 *Hamlet* spurred audiences to seek out the real but nightly variable and partially unpredictable performance on stage, so did Zeffirelli's in 1990, and so will, we may hope, Branagh's.

Pilgrims will go to the reconstructed Globe Theatre out of historical curiosity, no doubt. Those who know the plays will be confirmed in their love of Shakespeare and of theatre. Others will join those legions as the fifth century of Shakespeare on stage confirms the performance of the plays as a rich tool for their teaching and analysis, and, more important, as one of life's fully rewarding pleasures. "'Tis true that a good play needs no epilogue."

WORKS CITED

Andrews, John F., ed. *William Shakespeare: His World, His Work, His Influence.* Vol. 3, *His Influence.* New York: Scribner's 1985. Containing Stanley Wells, "Shakespeare on the English Stage," 603–628, and Charles H. Shattuck, "Shakespeare in the Theatre: The United States and Canada," 629–661.

Bate, Jonathan, ed. *Titus Andronicus.* The Arden Shakespeare, Third Series. London: Routledge, 1995.

Bate, Jonathan, and Russell Jackson. *Shakespeare: An Illustrated Stage History.* Oxford: Oxford UP, 1996.

Bauman, Sally. *The Royal Shakespeare Company: A History of Ten Decades.* New York: Oxford UP, 1982.

Bedford, Kristina. *"Coriolanus" at the National.* London and Toronto: Associated UP, 1992.

Berkowitz, Gerald M. "Shakespeare in London, January-July 1987." *Shakespeare Quarterly* 38 (1987): 495–500.

Bevington, David, ed. *Antony and Cleopatra.* NCS. Cambridge: Cambridge UP, 1990.

Billington, Michael. "Gentle assault on acting's Everest." *Guardian Weekly* 6 June 1993: 25.

———. "On the throne of the spiderman." *Guardian* 2 May 1985: 10.

———. "The Reinvention of William Shakespeare." *World Press Review* July 1992: 24–25.

Bogdanov, Michael, and Michael Pennington. *The English Shakespeare Company: The Story of 'The Wars of the Roses,' 1986–1989.* London: Nick Hern, 1990.

Branagh, Kenneth. *Much Ado about Nothing,* by William Shakespeare. Screenplay, Introduction and Notes on the Making of the Movie. New York: Norton, 1993.

Brustein, Robert. "Fairy Tailspin." *The New Republic* 10 July 1989: 28–30.

———. "On Theatre: Travel Packages." *The New Republic* 23 & 30 Aug. 1993: 31–33.

Bulman, James C. "The BBC Shakespeare And 'House Style.'" *Shakespeare Quarterly* 35 (1984): 571–81.

Bulman, James C., and H.R. Coursen, eds. *Shakespeare on Television: An Anthology of Essays and Reviews.* Hanover: UP of New England, 1988.

Byles, Joan Montgomery. "Political Theatre: *Hamlet* in Romania." *Shakespeare Bulletin* 9.2 (1991): 25–26.

Coursen, H. R. *"Hamlet." Shakespeare Bulletin* 11.2 (1993): 24–26.

Colley, Scott. *Richard's Himself Again: A Stage History of* Richard III. NY: Greenwood, 1992.

Cooper, Roberta Krensky. *The American Shakespeare Theatre.* Washington: Folger, 1986.

Crowl, Samuel. "*As You Like It.*" *Shakespeare Bulletin* 11.3 (1993): 41.

———. "*Hamlet.*" *Shakespeare Bulletin* 13.1 (1995): 18–19.

———. "Hamlet 'Most Royal': An Interview with Kenneth Branagh." *Shakespeare Bulletin* 12.4 (1994): 5–8.

———. *Shakespeare Observed: Studies in Performance on Stage and Screen.* Athens: Ohio UP, 1992.

———. "*Othello.*" *Shakespeare Bulletin* 14.1 (1996): 41–42.

Cushman, Robert. "Royal Shakespeare Company advertising for help." *The Globe and Mail* [Toronto] 2 Oct. 1989: C9.

Davies, Anthony, and Stanley Wells. *Shakespeare and the Moving Image: The Plays on Film and Television.* Cambridge: Cambridge UP, 1994.

Dawson, Anthony B. *Hamlet. (Shakespeare in Performance.)* Manchester: Manchester UP, 1995.

De Sousa, Geraldo U. "*The Merchant of Venice:* Brazil and Cultural Icons." *Shakespeare Quarterly* 45 (1994): 469–474.

Engle, Ron. "Audience, style, and language in the Shakespeare of Peter Zadek." *Foreign Shakespeare: Contemporary Performance,* ed. Dennis Kennedy, Cambridge: Cambridge UP, 1993. 93–105.

Epstein, Helen. *Joseph Papp: An American Life.* New York: Little, 1994.

Erstein, Hap. "Romanian director's 'Dream' is dark vision." *The Washington Times* 28 Sept. 1989: E1+.

Fitter, Chris. "A Tale of Two Branaghs: *Henry V,* Ideology, and the Mekong Agincourt." *Shake-speare Left and Right,* ed. Ivo Kamps. New York: Routledge, 1991. 259–275.

Foakes, R.A. "Shakespeare's Elizabethan Stages." Bate and Jackson. *Shakespeare: An Illustrated Stage History.* Oxford: Oxford UP, 1996. 10–22.

Franks, Alan. "Hamlet's Hall of Fame." *The Times* [London] 2 Nov. 1994, Arts Section: 35.

Gardner, Helen. *In Defence of the Imagination.* Cambridge, MA: Harvard UP, 1982.

Geckle, George L. *A Midsummer Night's Dream. Shakespeare Bulletin* 11.2 (1993): 27–28.

Goodwin, John, ed. *Peter Hall's Diaries: The Story of a Dramatic Battle.* London: Hamish Hamilton, 1983.

Gross, John J. *Shylock: A Legend and its Legacy.* New York: Simon, 1992.

Gurr, Andrew. "Static scenes at the Globe and the Rose Elizabethan theatres." *Antiquity* 68 (1994): 146–47.

Gussow, Mel. "Actors Put a New Spin on the Old Bard at Stratford." *American Theatre* November 1994: 70–72.

Hayes, Elliott. "The Stratford Festival," *Stratford Festival 1992 Souvenir Magazine.* 34–53.

Hodgdon, Barbara. *Shakespeare in Performance: Henry IV, Part Two.* Manchester: Manchester UP, 1993.

Holland, Peter. "Shakespeare Performances in England 1990–1." *Shakespeare Survey* 45 (1992): 115–144.

Hornby, Richard. "Shakespeare in New York." *The Hudson Review* 41 (1988): 339–347.

Jamieson, Michael. "Shakespeare in Performance." *Shakespeare: A Bibliographical Guide.* Ed. Stanley Wells. New Edition. Oxford: Clarendon, 1990. 37–68.

Kennedy, Dennis, ed. *Foreign Shakespeare: Contemporary Performance.* Cambridge: Cambridge UP, 1993.

———. *Looking at Shakespeare: A Visual History of Twentieth-Century Performance.* Cambridge: Cambridge UP, 1993.

Kimbrough, R. Alan. "Olivier's *Lear* and the Limits of Video." Bulman and Coursen, *Shakespeare on Television* 115–122.

Kramer, Mimi. "Much Aplomb." *The New Yorker* 1 Aug 1988: 55–56.

———. "Spaghetti Western." *The New Yorker* 23 July 1990: 83.

Londre, Felicia. "Shakespeare Sans Sous." *American Theatre* December 1990: 54–55.

Maher, Mary Z. "At Last, An American Hamlet for Television." *Literature/Film Quarterly* 20.2 (1992): 301–07.

McKellen, Ian, and Richard Locraine. *Richard III:* A Screenplay. Excerpted in "From Hunch to Reality," *The Sunday Times* [London] 24 March 1996, Cinema Section: 8–10.

Mullin, Michael. "Shakespeare USA: The BBC Plays and American Education." *Shakespeare Quarterly* 35 (1984): 582–89.

———. *Theatre at Stratford-upon-Avon, First Supplement: A Catalog-Index to Productions of the Royal Shakespeare Company, 1979–1993.* Westport, CT. Greenwood, 1994.

Nelsen, Paul. "The Heavens Must Wait: Fallout from 'Workshop Season' Stymies Globe Progress." *Shakespeare Bulletin* 13.4 (1995): 37–38.

———. "Oaths and Oracles: Will the Globe Spin on an Axis of 'Authenticity'?" *Shakespeare Bulletin* 13.3 (1995): 27–32.

Pilkington, Ace G. "Zeffirelli's Shakespeare" in Davies and Wells: *Shakespeare and the Moving Image* 163–179.

Rafferty, Terrence. "Fidelity and Infidelity." *The New Yorker* 18 Dec. 1995: 124–127. [film rev. of "Sense and Sensibility" and of *Othello,* 126–127]

Ranald, Margaret Loftus. "*Henry V.*" *Shakespeare Bulletin* 11.3 (1993): 13–14.

———. "*The Tempest.*" *Shakespeare Bulletin* 13.4 (1995), 10–11.

Rich, Frank. "*Hamlet.*" *The New York Times* 9 May 1990, C15.

———. "*Richard III.*" *The New York Times* 15 July 1983, C3.

Richmond, Hugh M. *King Richard III.* (Shakespeare in Performance.) Manchester: Manchester UP, 1989.

Schlueter, June. "Qui Est Là." *Shakespeare Bulletin* 14.1 (1996): 20.

Shaltz, Justin. "*King Lear.*" *Shakespeare Bulletin* 11.3 (1993): 25–26.

Shenk, Linda. "Jane Howell and Subverting Shakespeare: Where Do We Draw the Line?" *Shakespeare Bulletin* 13.4 (1995): 33–35.

Skovmand, Michael. *Screen Shakespeare.* Aarhus, Denmark: Aarhus UP, 1994. Incl. Susanne Fabricius, "The Face of Honour. On Kenneth Branagh's Screen Adaptation of *Henry V,*" 87–98.

Smallwood, Robert. "Shakespeare at Stratford-upon-Avon, 1990." *Shakespeare Quarterly* 42 (1991): 345–59.

Tocci, Margaret M. "Shakespeare at the Folger: *Richard III.*" *Shakespeare Bulletin* 9.2 (1991): 27–28.

Warren, Roger. "Shakespeare on the twentieth-century stage." *The Cambridge Companion to Shakespeare Studies.* Ed. Stanley Wells. Cambridge: Cambridge UP, 1986. 257–272.

———. *Staging Shakespeare's Late Plays.* Oxford: Clarendon P, 1990.

Willis, Susan. *The BBC Shakespeare Plays: Making the Televised Canon.* Chapel Hill: U of North Carolina P, 1991.

I owe debts to many people in the writing of this essay, most of them acknowledged in the citations to their works. But in addition I wish to thank G. Blakemore Evans, the textual editor (Harvard University, retired), and J. J. M. Tobin (University of Massachusetts—Boston). Gordon Dennis (formerly of Westminster College, Oxford) continually provided valuable information and criticism as well as encouragement. As readers for Houghton Mifflin, James P. Lusardi (Lafayette College), Anthony B. Dawson (University of British Columbia), and Joyce Van Dyke (Harvard University) provided many constructive suggestions and caught several errors. John Rohweder, my research assistant, saved me countless hours of gathering information and fact-checking, and did so with marvelous efficiency as well as good will.

Appendix C

Records, Documents, and Allusions

G. Blakemore Evans

J. J. M. Tobin

The materials here collected illustrate various aspects of Shakespeare's life, career as a dramatist and poet, and reputation. They represent, of course, a selection only. For fuller collections the reader may consult: *Shakespeare's Centurie of Prayse*, ed. L. T. Smith, 2nd ed. (London, [1879]); *Some 300 Fresh Allusions to Shakspere*, ed. F. J. Furnivall (London, 1886); E. K. Chambers, *William Shakespeare* (Oxford, 1930), vol. II; and B. R. Lewis, *The Shakespeare Documents*, 2 vols. (Stanford, 1941).

Considerable care has been taken to present accurate texts (neither Chambers nor Lewis is always a safe guide in this respect). In all but five cases (Numbers 1, 15, 16, 21B, and 32) it has been possible to offer texts based on a fresh collation of the manuscripts (in facsimile or photostat) and the printed editions. In transcriptions from manuscripts the common abbreviated forms for *per*, *par*; *pre*, *pro*; final and medial *er* and *or* (or *our*); final *es*; and final *cion* (i.e. *tion*) have, in most cases, been silently expanded. Some more unusual abbreviations, particularly in Latin passages, have been expanded by inserting the inferred letters in italic. Angle brackets are used to indicate readings (letters, words, etc.) supplied at points where a manuscript has suffered damage; square brackets are used to indicate letters, words, or necessary punctuation omitted in the manuscript or printed text.

I. Life Records and Contemporary References

1. Shakespeare's Family

The following entries relating to the Shakespeare family are preserved in the parish records of Holy Trinity Church, Stratford-upon-Avon. For further information and discussion, see E. K. Chambers, *William Shakespeare*, II, 1–18, and B. R. Lewis, *The Shakespeare Documents*, vols. I and II, passim.

Christenings

1558, September 15. Ione Shakspere daughter to Iohn Shakspere
[John Shakespeare's first child, Joan, must have died by 1569, because another daughter was christened Joan in that year.]

1562, December 2. Margareta filia Iohannis Shakspere
[John Shakespeare's second child; buried April 30, 1563.]

1564, April 26. Gulielmus filius Iohannes Shakspere
[William Shakespeare was John Shakespeare's third child and eldest son, and, although not an old man when he died in 1616, he survived all his brothers and sisters except a second Joan (born 1569; died 1646). It should be noted that we do not know the exact date of Shakespeare's birth or death, only the dates of his christening and his burial (April 25, 1616). April 23 (St. George's Day) is the traditionally popular choice for both events, and that date as the day of his death has the strong support of the inscription on his monument in the Stratford parish church (see Number 6B, below). Since the monument is known to have been erected by 1623, it offers nearly contemporary evidence. No such evidence exists for April 23 as the date of his birth. The Second Prayer Book (1559) ordered that baptism be administered no later than the first Sunday or holy day following the day of birth. In 1564, April 23 was a Sunday and the feast day of St. Mark fell on April 25. Authorities believe that either April 22 or 23 is the

most likely date for Shakespeare's birthday, but that April 21 must also be considered as a possibility.]

1566, October 13. Gilbertus filius Iohannis Shakspere
[John Shakespeare's fourth child and second son; he died in 1612.]

1569, April 15. Ione the daughter of Iohn Shakspere
[John Shakespeare's fifth child and third daughter. She married William Hart, a hatter, but no record of the marriage appears in the parish records and nothing further is known about Hart. They had four children (see below); Hart died in 1616 and Joan in 1646. This is the only branch of Shakespeare's immediate family to survive past the seventeenth century; it continues to the present day.]

1571, September 28. Anna filia magistri Shakspere
[John Shakespeare's sixth child and fourth daughter; she died in 1579.]

1574, March 11. Richard sonne to Mr Iohn Shakspeer
[John Shakespeare's seventh child and third son; he died in 1613.]

1580, May 3. Edmund sonne to Mr Iohn Shakspere
[John Shakespeare's eighth and last child and fourth son. Edmund seems to have been an actor, although not associated with any known company. He was buried in Southwark at St. Saviour's Church on December 31, 1607. The church register records the burial of "Edmond Shakespeare a player in the Church". Someone, perhaps Shakespeare himself, paid twenty shillings on the same day for his burial and "a forenoone knell of the great bell".]

1583, May 26. Susanna daughter to William Shakespeare
[The first of Shakespeare's three children. She was married in 1607 to John Hall, a physician and resident of Stratford, but of obscure antecedents. They had one child (see below); Hall died in 1635 and Susanna in 1649.]

1585, February 2. Hamnet & Iudeth sonne & daughter to Williã Shakspere
[Twins, Hamnet and Judith, were Shakespeare's last children. Hamnet (of which name Hamlet is a variant form) died in 1596. Judith married Thomas Quiney, son of Richard Quiney and a resident of Stratford, in 1616, a few months before Shakespeare's death. They had three children (see below); Quiney died about 1655 and Judith in 1662.]

1600, August 28. Wilhelmus filius Wilhelmi Hart
[First child of Joan (Shakespeare) and William Hart; he died in 1639.]

1603, June 5. Maria filia Wilhelmi Hart
[Second child and first daughter of Joan (Shakespeare) and William Hart; she died in 1607.]

1605, July 24. Thomas fil. Wilhelmus Hart Hatter
[Third child and second son of Joan (Shakespeare) and William Hart. Thomas Hart married and had two sons, of whom the younger, George, who died in 1702, carried on the line; all present-day descendants of John Shakespeare are derived through this line.]

1608, February 21. Elizabeth dawghter to Iohn Hall geñ
[Shakespeare's first grandchild, the daughter and only child of Susanna (Shakespeare) and John Hall. Though twice married, Elizabeth died without issue, and her death (about 1670) marked the end of Shakespeare's direct line.]

1608, September 23. Mychaell sonne to Willyam Hart
[Fourth child and third son of Joan (Shakespeare) and William Hart; he died in 1618.]

1616, November 23. Shaksper fillius Thomas Quyny gent.
[Shakespeare's second grandchild, first son of Judith (Shakespeare) and Thomas Quiney, named in memory of his recently deceased grandfather; he died in 1617.]

1618, February 9. Richard fillius Thomas Quinee
[Shakespeare's third grandchild, second son of Judith (Shakespeare) and Thomas Quiney; he died without issue in 1639.]

1620, January 23. Thomas filius to Thomas Queeney
[Shakespeare's fourth and last grandchild, third son of Judith (Shakespeare) and Thomas Quiney; he died without issue in 1639.]

Marriages

1607, June 5. Iohn Hall gentlemã & Susanna Shaxspere

1616, February 10. Tho. Queeny tow Iudith Shakespeare
[Since this marriage took place without special license during a prohibited period (between Septuagesima Sunday and the Octave of Easter), both Quiney and his wife were called before the Consistory Court of Worcester, and, failing twice to appear, were excommunicated about May 11, 1616. By this period the sentence seems to have been little more than a formality. Their marriage may have been hastened by Shakespeare's final illness.]

Burials

1563, April 30. Margareta filia Iohannis Shakspere

1579, April 4. Anne daughter to Mr Iohn Shakspere

1596, August 11. Hamnet filius William Shakspere

1601, September 8. Mr Iohañes Shakspear⟨e⟩
[I.e. Shakespeare's father.]

1608, September 9. Mayry Shaxspere wydowe
[I.e. Shakespeare's mother, née Mary Arden.]

1612, February 3. Gilbertus Shakspere adolescens
[Since Gilbert Shakespeare died at the age of 45, "adolescens" is usually interpreted as meaning "bachelor." Malone interpreted the entry as referring to a son of Gilbert, but there is no record of his marriage or of the birth of a son.]

1613, February 4. Rich: Shakspeare

1616, April 17. Will Hartt hatter

1616, April 25. will Shakspere gent
[See the discussion under Shakespeare's christening entry.]

1617, May 8. Shakespere fillius Tho. Quyny, gent.

1618, November 1. Micael filius to Jone Harte, widowe

1623, August 8. Mrs Shakspeare.
[I.e. Shakespeare's wife, Anne.]

2. Shakespeare's Marriage

A. The License Entry (from the Bishop of Worcester's *Register*, Vol. XXXII, fol. 43v)

1582, November 27. Itm̃ eodem die s*imi*lis emanavit licen*cia* inter wm Shaxpere et Annã whateley de Temple grafton.

[This entry merely records that a license has been issued as of November 27, 1582. The license itself has not survived. It will be noticed that the maiden name of Shakespeare's wife is here given as Anne Whateley of Temple Grafton, whereas the Bond of Sureties (see below) gives it as Anne Hathwey (i.e. Hathaway) of Stratford, the traditional name first mentioned by Nicholas Rowe in 1709, who did not know either the license entry or the bond. This discrepancy has given rise to much theorizing, but the simplest and most widely accepted explanation is that the "Whateley" of the license entry is a clerical error for "Hathwey" and that the marriage did take place at Temple Grafton, a village about five miles from Stratford, although no Shakespeares or Hathaways seem to have had connections in Temple Grafton and it was customary for the bride to be married from her own parish. Research has shown that the Anne Hathwey named in the bond was fairly certainly the daughter of Richard Hathaway (died 1581) of Stratford. She was born c. 1556 (eight years before Shakespeare) and was buried August 8, 1623, seven years after Shakespeare's death.]

B. The Bond of Sureties, dated November 28, 1582 (from the Bishop of Worcester's registry)

N*o*verint uniuersi per pre*se*ntes nos ffulconẽ Sandells de Stratford in Comit*atu* warwic*ensi* agricolam et Ioh*ann*em Rychardson ib*ide*m agricola*m* teneri et firmiter obligari Ric*ardo* Cosin gen*er*oso et Rob*er*to warmstry notario pu*bli*co in quadraginta libris bone & legalis monete Anglie Soluend*is* eisdem Ric*ardo* et Rob*er*to hered*ibus* execut*oribus* vel assignatis suis ad quam quidem soluc*ion*em bene & fidel*iter* faciend*am* obligamus nos & vtru*mque* nos*tru*m per se pro toto & in solid*um* hered*es* executor*es* & admi*nis*trator*es* n*os*tros firmiter per pre*se*ntes Sigillis n*ost*ris sigillat*as* dat*um* 28 die nove*mbris* Anno Regni d*omi*ne n*ost*re Eliz*abethe* dei gratia Anglie ffranc*ie* & hib*ernie* Regine fidei defensoris &c 25° / [*Translation:* Know all men by these presents that we, Fulk Sandells of Stratford in the county of Warwick, yeoman, and John Richardson of the same place, yeoman, are held and firmly bound to Richard Cosin, gentleman, and Robert Warmstry, notary public, to pay forty pounds of good and lawful money of England to the same Richard and Robert, their heirs, executors, or assigns; to make which payment well and faithfully, we bind ourselves and each of us separately for the whole and total amount, our heirs, executors, and administrators firmly by these presents, sealed with our seals; given this 28th day of November in the twenty-fifth year of our Lady Elizabeth, by the grace of God Queen of England, France, and Ireland, Defender of the Faith, etc.]

The Condicion of this obligacion ys suche that if herafter there shall not appere any Lawfull Lett or impediment by reason of any precontract consan*gui*nitie affinitie or by any other lawfull meanes whatsoeuer but that willm̃ Shagspere one thone partie, and Anne hathwey of Stratford in the Dioces of worcester maiden may lawfully solennize m*atrim*ony together and in the same afterwardes remaine and continew like man and wiffe according vnto the lawes in that behalf prouided and moreouer if there be not at this present time any action sute quarrell or demaund moved or depending before any iudge eccl*es*iasticall or temporall for and concerning any suche lawfull lett or impediment. And moreouer if the said willm̃ Shagspere do not proceed to solennizacion of mariadg with the said Anne hathwey without the Consent of hir frindes. And also if the said willm̃ do vpon his owne proper Costes and expense defend & save harmles the right Reverend father in god Lord Iohñ bushop of worcester and his offycers for Licencing them the said willm̃ and Anne to be maried together with once asking of the bannes of m*atrim*ony betwene them and for all other causes wch may ensue by reason or occasion therof that then the said obligacion to be voyd and of none effect or els to stand & abide in full force and vertue [Below the last line is what appears to be a cross-mark, followed by a large capital S. It has been suggested that the cross is John Richardson's mark, the S, Fulk Sandells'.]

[A bond of sureties, involving other than the bridegroom himself, was required because Shakespeare was legally a minor (eighteen years old) at the time of the marriage. Worcester practice seems to have preferred sureties other than the father or close relatives. Nothing further is known of Fulk Sandells and John Richardson, presumably tenant farmers, except that their names appear, as supervisor and witness respectively, in the will (September 1, 1581) of Richard Hathaway, the father of Anne Hathaway. No particularly sensational significance should be placed on the fact that Shakespeare was married by license and "with once asking of the bannes." The more usual way was to have the banns called on three successive Sundays or saints' days; then no license was required. Since, however, Anne was already with child (Susanna was christened May 26, 1583) and the Advent season, one of several periods in the church calendar during which marriages were not permitted, began on December 2 in 1582 and ran to January 13, 1583, there was time for only one calling of the banns (St. Andrew's Day, November 30). To have delayed the marriage longer would only have caused unnecessary embarrassment for all the parties concerned. Moreover, there is a possibility that in common law Anne and Shakespeare were already husband and wife by a mutual expression of intent in the presence of witnesses, a procedure which was recognized as creating a valid marriage.

For further information, see E. K. Chambers, *William Shakespeare*, II, 41–52, and B. R. Lewis, *The Shakespeare Documents*, I, 160–77.]

3. Grant of Arms to John Shakespeare, October 20, 1596

The document here transcribed (Vincent MS. Article 24, in the College of Arms, London), believed to be a copy of an earlier extant draft (Vincent MS. Article 23), represents, it is assumed, an intermediate stage between that draft and the final "fair copy," properly sealed and witnessed, delivered to John Shakespeare (and now lost). Both the draft and the intermediate copy are in the same copyist's hand, though the substance of the grant was prepared by William Dethick, Garter Principal King-of-Arms. Shortly after this 1596 grant, John Shakespeare (probably at William's urging) applied to the College of Arms to have his newly acquired arms impaled with those of his wife, Mary Shakespeare (née Arden). A grant for this impalement was drawn up in 1599 by Dethick and the recently appointed (1597) Clarenceux King-of-Arms, William Camden (MS. R.21, in the College of Arms; transcribed by the same hand as the 1596 grant), but no official grant appears to have been issued. This is not quite the end of the story. In 1602 Ralph Brooke, York Herald, prepared charges against Dethick and Camden for having improperly granted arms to some twenty-three "mean" individuals, among them John Shakespeare (by then dead). In a manuscript volume now in the Folger Shakespeare Library (MS. 423.1, p. 28) Brooke made a sketch of the Shakespeare arms and below it sneeringly wrote "Shakespear ye Player / by Garter [i.e. Dethick]". The official outcome, if any, of these charges is not known, but apparently the original claim of John Shakespeare was upheld against Brooke, since William Shakespeare ("ye Player") continued to sign himself as "gentleman" to the time of his death.

Unfortunately, the intermediate copy of the grant has suffered considerable damage affecting the actual text of the document; in the present text (following E. K. Chambers' practice in *William Shakespeare*, II, 18–20) the resulting lacunae are partly supplied (in angle brackets) from Vincent MS. Article 23, the draft version—an admittedly dangerous procedure, since the two texts (the draft version and the intermediate version) are not always identical in other sections. Deletions in the manuscript are indicated by a line through the type words. Interlineations are reproduced in boldface type; a caret preceding indicates that the point of insertion is marked in the manuscript with a caret. For further information, see Chambers (cited above) and B. R. Lewis, *The Shakespeare Documents*, I, 208–17, 299–306; II, 336–46. The sketch (or "trick") of the arms at the head of the document is shown in the next column.

Shakespere
non sanz droict

To all and singuler Noble, and Gentilmen: of what Estate, degree, bearing Arms to whom these presentes shall come. *Willm̃ Dethick Garter* princip⟨all⟩ king of Arms sendethe greetinges. Knowe yee. that whereas by the authorite and auncyent pryveleges perteyning to my office from the Quenes most excellent Matie and by her highnesse most noble & victorious progenitors. I am to take generall notice & record for and too to make demonstracion **declaration** & testemonie for all causes of Arms and matters of Gent. [Gentrie *in draft*] thoroughe all her Ma^tes kingdoms, dominions, Principalites, Isles ⟨,⟩ and Provinces. To the'nd that as some men **manie gentilmẽ** by theyre auncyent names of families, kyndredes, & descentes have & enioye certeyne enseignes & cottes of Arms So it is v⟨erie⟩ expedient ∧ **in all tymes Ages** that some mẽ for theyr valeant factes, magnanimite, vertu, dignites & des⟨ertes⟩ maye have **vse** & beare suche tokens of honor and worthinesse.

Whereby theyre Name & good fame maye be the better knowen & divulged. and theyre Children & posterite (in all vertu to the syrvice of theyre Prynce & Contrie) encouraged: Wherefore being solicited, and by credible report ⟨info⟩rmed. That *Iohn. Shakespeare* of Stratford vppon Avon i⟨n⟩ the Count⟨e of⟩ warwik **Warwike** ⟨whose . . .⟩ parentes ⟨& late⟩ antecessors. **Grandfather** were for theyr **his** faithfull & va⟨leant service [was] advanced & reward⟩ed ⟨by the most Prudent⟩ Prince king *Henry* the seventhe of ⟨famous memorie sythence whiche tyme they have . . . . t⟩hose partes) continewed ∧ **in these partes being** of good reputacion ⟨& credit . . . . . And that the s⟩aid *Iohn* hathe maryed the daughter ⟨& one of the heyres of *Robert Arden* of Wilm^coote in the said⟩ Counte gent **esquire**. and for the encouragement of his posterite aforesaid to whom ∧ [*something illegible inserted above*]⟨. . . . . a⟩uncyent Custome of the Lawes of Arms maye descend. I have the said *G⟨arter* principall king⟩ of Arms have assigned, graunted, and by these presentes confirmed: This shie⟨ld or Cote o⟩f Arms. viz. *Gould*. on A Bend *Sables*. a Speare of the first steeled *argent*. And for his Creast or Cognizance a *falcon* his winges displayed *Argent*. standing on a wrethe of his Coullors. suppo⟨rting⟩ A *Speare Gould*. steeled as aforesaid sett vppon a helmett and **w^th** mantelles ∧ **& tasselles** as hathe ben accustomed and dothe more playnely appeare depicted on this margent:

Signefieing hereby ~~**hereby**~~ & by the authorite ~~**afore-said**~~ of my office aforesaid Ratefieing that it shalbe Lawfull for the said *Iohn Shakespeare.* gent. and for his cheldren yssue & posterite (at all tymes ∧ **& places** convenient) to beare and make demõnstracion of the said Blazon or Atchevment vppon theyre Shieldes, Targetes, escucheons, Cotes of Arms, ∧ ~~**Creastes or Cognizances**~~ pennons, Guydons. Seales, Ring⟨es⟩, ~~**Edefices**~~ **Edefices**, Buyldinges vtenseles, Lyueries, Tombes, or monumentes. or otherwise for all Lawfull warrlyke factes or Ciuile vse or exercises: according to the Lawes of Arms, and Customes that to gentillmen belongethe: wthout let or interruption of any **other** person or persons ∧ **for vse or** ~~**per**~~ bearing the same. In wittnesse & perpetuall remembrance hereof I have herevnto subscribed my name & fastened the Seale of my office endorzed wth the signett of my Arms. At the office of Arms London the xx. daye of October ~~**in**~~ the ~~**xxxix**~~ **xxxviijth** yeare of the reigne of our Soueraigne Lady *Elizabeth* by the grace of God Quene of England, ffrance and Irleland [*sic*] defender of the ffaythe etc. 1596.

This Iohn shoeth A patierne therof vnder *Clarent Cooks* hand.

~ paper. xx yeares past.

A Iustice of peace And [*written over* that] was Baylife ∧ ~~**Towne**~~ **officer & cheffe of the towne** of Stratford vppon Avon. xv or xvj years past.

That he hathe Landes & tene*men*tes. of good wealth. & Substance 500^{li}.

That he mar⟨ried a daughter and heyre of Arden, a gent. of worship.⟩

HEADING. **non sanz droict**: not without right. This is generally taken to represent the "word" or motto to be associated with the coat of arms, though not technically an official part of it. It may have been chosen, somewhat defensively perhaps, by John Shakespeare himself. In the manuscript the name and the motto are at the left, over the "trick" or sketch in outline of the proposed arms, marked with the first color (gold) and the second color (sable); see below, lines 41–48.
3–4. **Willm̃ Dethick . . . Arms.** Garter Principal King-of-Arms was the title of the chief officer of the College of Arms.
15. **enseignes:** badges of dignity or office.
17. **factes:** deeds, actions.
26–39. **whose . . . king.** The second half of these lines is almost entirely missing from the manuscript, and the beginning of the same lines has also suffered considerable loss. The material in angle brackets has been supplied from the earlier draft version (Vincent MS. Article 23), but in most cases the supplied material does not seem sufficient to account for the implied length of the truncated lines in the later copy. Thus, in line 26 "whose" does not adequately account for the presumed spacing of the manuscript before "parentes," and similar spacing difficulties occur in lines 31 and 33. In lines 26–27 the phrase "parentes ⟨& late⟩ antecessors. **Grandfather**" presents obvious difficulties in itself and later grammatically. The draft version reads "whose ∧ **parentes & late** antecessors" and this was what the present manuscript presumably read before the interlineation of "Grandfather" above "antecessors." Chambers, rightly perhaps, simply omits "antecessors." even though it is undeleted, but it is interesting that the 1599 Arden impalement document (MS. R.21) reads "whose parent ∧ **great Grandfather** and ∧ **late** Antecessor". In line 29, Chambers is followed in reading "reward⟩ed", the "ed" being barely legible in the MS; there is, however, part of another word following the detached "ed" (if indeed it is not "ede") which begins with an "h". Curiously, Lewis fails to transcribe anything at this point. In lines 37–38, Chambers fills the space here indicated between "whom" and "⟨a⟩uncyent" with the words "these achivmentes by the", the nearest approximation to which in the draft occurs in an added passage at the end: "To whom theyse achivments maie desend, by the auncient custom and lawes of Armes." The illegible word interlined above "whom" in line 37 is deciphered as "suche (?)" by Lewis.
41–42. **Gould. . . . Sables:** i.e. a shield with a gold field crossed from top right to bottom left (with relation to one behind the shield) by a dull black ("*Sables*") bar ("Bend"). A bend so placed is called a bend dexter.
42. **a Speare . . . argent:** i.e. a spear of gold ("of the first [color]") with a point ("steeled") of dull silver ("*argent*") to be placed in the bar, point up.
43. **Creast or Cognizance.** The two words mean the same thing and refer to the heraldic figure placed above the shield and helmet.
43–45. **a falcon . . . Coullors:** i.e. a dull silver ("*Argent*") falcon with outstretched ("displayed") wings standing (on its left foot) on a twisted wreath of the Shakespeare colors (i.e. gold and sable).
45–47. **suppo⟨rting⟩ . . . tasselles:** i.e. holding upright (in its right claw) a gold spear pointed with silver, as earlier detailed, set upon a helmet (of steel for a gentleman) and decorated with scroll effects ("mantelles ∧ **& tasselles**"). Perhaps some pictorial reference is intended here to the name "Shake-speare."
54. **Blazon or Atchevment.** Terms used to describe the whole coat of arms, both shield and crest.
55. **Targetes:** light round shields. **escucheons:** shields with armorial bearings.
57. **Guydons:** flags or pennants ("pennons"), broad at the end next the staff and forked or pointed at the other.
58. **Lyueries:** distinctive clothing worn by a person's servants.
62. **let:** hindrance. **other:** written above "of"; point of intended insertion not marked with a caret.
72–82. These lines appear to be independent notes and are not part of the actual grant; they do not appear in the draft version.
72. **shoeth A patierne.** The reading "shoeth" is uncertain; the present transcript follows Chambers; Lewis reads "sheweth (?)". A "patierne" is presumably a sketch (or "trick") of the arms such as that found near the beginning of this transcript.
72–73. **Clarent Cooks hand.** Robert Cook became Clarenceux King-of-Arms in 1567. As a deputy of the College of Arms, he visited Stratford in 1563, but this was before John Shakespeare had been made Bailiff (1568) and could claim any right to a coat of arms.
74. **~ paper.** According to Lewis, the tilde here stands for "in". **xx yeares past.** This would mean 1576.
77–78. **xv . . . past.** These figures are clearly incorrect, since John Shakespeare was Bailiff in 1568.
80. **500^{li}.** This is generally considered an impossibly high figure.
81–82. **mar⟨ried . . . worship,⟩.** The words in angle brackets are supplied (by Chambers) from a transcript of this passage made by Malone and printed in the Boswell-Malone *Shakespeare* (1821), II, 89; at some time after Malone saw it, the manuscript was mutilated at this point.

4. Richard Quiney's Letter to Shakespeare, October 25, 1598

The original letter is now preserved among the Wheler MSS at Shakespeare's birthplace, Stratford-on-Avon. Richard Quiney was a mercer of Stratford (whose son Thomas was in 1616 to marry Shakespeare's daughter Judith). This is the only personal letter written to Shakespeare that has survived, but, since it was found among Richard Quiney's own papers, it may never have come into Shakespeare's hands. For further information, see E. K. Chambers, *William Shakespeare*, II, 101–6, and B. R. Lewis, *The Shakespeare Documents*, I, 225–32.

Loveinge Contreyman I am bolde of yo^{w} as of a ffrende, craveinge yo^{wr} helpe wth xxx^{ll} vppon m^{r} Bushells & my securytee or m^{r} Myttons wth me[.] m^{r} Rosswell is nott come to London as yeate & I have especiall cawse, yo^{w} shall ffrende me muche in helpeing me out of all the debettes I owe in London I thancke god & muche quiet my mynde wch wolde nott be indebeted [.] I am nowe towardes the Cowrte in hope of answer for the dispatche of my Buysenes [.] yo^{w} shall nether loase creddytt nor monney by me the Lorde wyllinge & nowe butt perswade yo^{wr} selfe soe as I hope & yo^{w} shall nott need to feare butt wth all hartie thanckefullnes I wyll holde my tyme & content yo^{wr} ffrende & yf we Barg- / aine farther yo^{w} shalbe the paie m^{r} yo^{wr} selfe. my tyme biddes me hasten to an ende & soe I com̃itt thys [to] yo^{wr} care & hope of yo^{wr} helpe[.] I feare I shall nott be backe thys night ffrom the Cowrte. haste [.] the Lorde be wth yo^{w} & wth vs all amen [.] ffrom the Bell in Carter Lane the 25 octobr 1598 /

Yo^{wrs} in all kyndenes
Ryc. Quyney

[The letter is addressed on the verso:]

H

To my Loveinge good ffrend
& contreymann m^{r} w^{m}
Shackespere dlr thees /

[To the left of the address is a seal with the Quiney coat of arms, described as "or, on a bend sable, three trefoils slipped argent."]

LETTER. 1. **Contreyman:** i.e. fellow resident of Warwickshire. 2. **xxx^{ll}:** thirty pounds (a very substantial sum, worth several thousand dollars in terms of today's valuation).
13–14. **holde my tyme:** i.e. meet the date set for repayment.
15. **paie m^{r}:** paymaster.
17. **[to].** Accidentally omitted by Quiney.
20. **the Bell:** the inn in which Quiney was staying while in London.

ADDRESS. 1. **H.** This letter seems to be in a different hand from that of the letter and the rest of the address, which are both in Quiney's autograph. It has been interpreted to mean "Haste."
4. **dlr:** i.e. deliver. **thees.** Short for "these presents," i.e. the letter.

5. Shakespeare's Will

The original, dated March 25, 1616, formerly kept in the Principal Probate Registry at Somerset House, London, is now in the Public Record Office, London. Interlined insertions are here printed in boldface type, and the carets which in the original indicate most of the points of insertion are reproduced preceding the interlineations. Deleted words and passages are indicated by a line drawn through them. The only portions of the will in Shakespeare's autograph are the three signatures (one on each sheet) and "By me" preceding the third signature; these are reproduced on page 1790, above. Full information on the will may be found in E.K. Chambers, *William Shakespeare*, II 169–80, and B. R. Lewis, *The Shakespeare Documents*, II 471–507.

[*Sheet 1*]

Vicesimo Quinto die ~~Januarij~~ **martij** Anno Regni D*omi*ni n*ostr*i Jacobi nunc R*egis* Anglie &c decimo quarto & Scotie xlix° Annoq*ue* d*omi*ni 1616

T[*estamentum*]: w^{mj} Shackspeare /

R[*ecognoscatu*]r In the name of god Amen I Willm̃ Shackspeare of Stratford vpon Avon in the countie of warr gent in perfect health & memorie god be praysed doe make & Ordayne this my last will & testam^{t} in manner & forme followeing That ys to saye ffirst I Comend my Soule into the handes of god my Creator hoping & assuredlie beleeving through thonelie merittes of Iesus Christe my Saviour to be made partaker of lyfe everlastinge And my bodye to the Earth whereof yt ys made Itm̃ I Gyve & bequeath vnto my ~~sonne in L~~ daughter Iudyth One Hundred & ffyftie poundes of lawfull English money to be paied vnto her in manner & forme followeing That ys to saye One Hundred Poundes ∧ **in discharge of her marriage porcion** wthin one yeare after my deceas wth consideracion after the Rate of twoe shillinges in the pound for soe long tyme as the same shalbe vnpaied vnto her after my deceas & the ffyftie poundes Residewe thereof vpon her Surrendring ∧ **of** or gyving of such sufficient securitie as the overseers of this my will shall like of to Surrender or gra*u*nte All her estate & Right that shall discend or come vnto her after my deceas or ∧ **that shee** nowe hath of in or to one Copiehold ten*emen*te wth thappurten*au*nces lyeing & being in Stratford vpon Avon aforesaied in the saied countie of warr being parcell or holden of the mannour of Rowington vnto my daughter Susanna Hall & her heires for ever Itm̃ I Gyve & bequeath vnto my saied daughter Iudith One Hundred & ffyftie Poundes more if shee or Anie issue of her bodie be Lyvinge att thend of three Yeares next ensueing the daie of the date of this my will during wch tyme my executours to paie her consideracion from my deceas according to the Rate aforesaied And if she dye wthin the saied terme wthout issue of her bodye then my will ys & I doe gyve & bequeath One Hundred Poundes thereof to my Neece Elizabeth Hall & the ffiftie Poundes to be sett fourth by my executours during the lief of my Sister Iohane Harte & the vse & proffitt thereof Cominge shalbe payed to my saied Sister Ione & after her deceas the saied l^{li} shall Remaine Amongst the children of my saied Sister Equallie to be devided Amongst them But if my saied daughter Iudith be lyving att thend of the saied three Yeares or anie yssue of her bodye then my will ys & soe I devise & bequeath the saied Hundred & ffyftie poundes to be sett out ∧ **by my executours & overseers** for the best benefitt of her & her issue & ∧ **the stock** not **to be** paied vnto her soe long as she shalbe marryed & Covert Baron ~~by my executours & overseers~~ but my will ys that she shall have the consideracion yearelie paied vnto her during her lief & after her deceas the saied stock and consideracion to bee paied to her children if she have Anie & if not to her executours or assignes she lyving the saied terme after my deceas Provided that yf such husbond as she shall att thend of the saied three Yeares be marryed vnto or att anie [tyme] after doe sufficientlie Assure vnto her & thissue of her bodie landes Awnswereable to the porcion by this my will gyven vnto her & to be adiudged soe by my executours & overseers then my will ys that the saied Cl^{li} shalbe paied to such husbond as shall make such assurance to his owne vse Itm̃ I gyve & bequeath vnto my saied sister Ione xx^{li} & all my wearing Apparrell to be paied & deliuered wthin one yeare after my deceas And I doe will & devise vnto her ∧ **the house** wth thappurten*aun*ces in Stratford wherein she dwelleth for her naturall lief vnder the yearelie Rent of xij^{d} Itm̃ I gyve and bequeath

[*In left margin, damaged but generally legible*] William Shakspere

[Sheet 2]

vnto her three sonns Wellim̃ Harte [*a blank*] Hart & Michaell Harte ffyve poundes A peece to be payed wthin one Yeare after my deceas to be ~~sett out for her wthin one Yeare after my deceas by my executours wth thadvise & direccions of my overseers for her best proffitt vntill her Marriage and then the same with the increase thereof to be paied vnto~~ her Itm̃ I gyve & bequeath vnto her **the saied Elizabeth Hall** All my Plate ∧ **(except my brod silver & gilt bole)** that I now have att the date of this my will Itm̃ I gyve & bequeath vnto the Poore of Stratford aforesäied tenn poundes to m^{r} Thomas Combe my Sword to Thomas Russell Esquier ffyve poundes & to ffrauncis Collins of the Borough of warr in the countie of warr gent thirteene poundes Sixe shillinges & Eight pence to be paied wthin one Yeare after my deceas Itm̃ I gyve & bequeath to m^{r} ~~Richard Tyler thelder~~ **Hamlett Sadler** xxvj^{s} viij^{d} to buy him A Ringe ∧ **to Willm̃ Raynoldes gent xxvj^{s} viij^{d} to buy him A Ringe** to my godson Willm̃ Walker xx^{s} in gold to Anthonye Nashe gent xxvj^{s} viij^{d} & to Mr Iohn Nashe xxvj^{s} **viij^{d}** ~~in gold~~ ∧ **& to my ffellowes Iohn Hemynges Richard Burbage & Henry Cundell xxvj^{s} viij^{d} A peece to buy them Ringes** Itm̃ I Gyve Will bequeath & devise vnto my daughter Susanna Hall ∧ **for better enabling of her to performe this my will & towardes the performans thereof** All that Capitall Messuage or ten*emen*te wth thappurten*aun*ces ∧ **in Stratford aforesaied** Called the newe place wherein I nowe dwell & twoe messuages or ten*emen*tes wth thappurten*aun*ces scituat lyeing & being in Henley streete wthin the borough of Stratford aforesaied And all my barnes stables Orchardes gardens landes ten*emen*tes & heredita*men*tes whatsoever scituat lyeing & being or to be had Receyved perceyved or taken wthin the townes Hamlettes villages ffieldes & groundes of Stratford vpon Avon Oldstratford Bushopton & welcombe or in anie of them in the saied countie of warr And alsoe All that Messuage or ten*emen*te wth thappurten*aun*ces wherein one Iohn Robinson dwelleth scituat lyeing & being in the blackfriers in London nere the Wardrobe & all other my landes ten*emen*tes and heredita*men*tes whatsoeuer To Have & to hold All & sing*u*ler the saied premisses wth their Appurten*aun*ces vnto the saied Susanna Hall for & during the terme of her naturall lief & after her deceas to the first sonne of her bodie lawfullie yssueing & to the heires Males of the bodie of the saied first Sonne lawfullie yssueinge & for defalt of such issue to the second Sonne of her bodie lawfullie issueinge & so to the heires Males of the bodie of the saied Second Sonne lawfullie yssueinge & for defalt of such heires to the third Sonne of the bodie of the saied Susanna Lawfullie yssueing & of the heires Males of the bodie of the saied third sonne lawfullie yssueing And for defalt of such issue the same soe to be & Remaine to the ffourth ~~sonne~~ ffyfth sixte & Seaventh sonnes of her bodie lawfullie issueing one after Another & to the heires

2 Willm̃ Shakspere

[Sheet 3]

Males of the bodies of the saied ffourth fifth Sixte & Seaventh sonnes lawfullie yssueinge in such manner as yt ys before Lymitted to be & Remaine to the first second & third Sonns of her bodie & to their heires Males And for defalt of such issue the saied premisses to be & Remaine to my sayed Neece Hall & the heires Males of her bodie Lawfullie yssueing & for defa⟨lt o⟩f such issue to my daughter Iudith & the heires Males of her bodie lawfullie yssueinge And for defalt of such issue to the Right heires of me the saied Willm̃ Shackspere for ever ∧ **Itm̃ I gyve vnto my wief my second best bed wth the furniture** Itm̃ I gyve & bequeath to my saied daughter Iudith my broad silver gilt bole All the Rest of my goodes Chattels Leases plate Iewels & household stuffe whatsoever after my dettes and Legasies paied & my funerall expences discharged I gyve devise & bequeath to my Sonne in Lawe Iohn Hall gent & my daughter Susanna his wief whom I ordaine & make executours of this my Last will and testam^{t} And I doe intreat & Appoint ∧ **the saied** Thomas Russell Esquier & ffraunci⟨s⟩ Collins gent to be overseers hereof And doe Revoke All former wills & publishe this to be my last will and testam^{t} In Witnesse whereof I have herevnto put my ~~Seale~~ **hand** the daie & Yeare first aboue Written.

By me William Shakspeare

witnes to the publishing
hereof. Fra: Collyns
Iulyus Shawe
Iohn Robinson
Hamnet Sadler
Robert Whattcott

[*Endorsed*] Probatum cora*m* Mag*ist*ro Willm̃o Byrde legum doc*tore* Comissarū &cis xxij^{do} die mensis Iunij Anno d*omi*ni 1616. Juram*en*^{to} Iohannis Hall vnius ex̃ &cis Cui &cis de bene &cis Iurat.

Res*e*rvat p*otes*tate &cis Susanne Hall al*teri* ex̃ &cis cu*m* ven*e*rit &cis petitur.

In*ventoriu*m ex*hibitum*

1–3. **Vicesimo . . . 1616:** on the twenty-fifth day of March, in the fourteenth year of the reign of our lord King James now King of England, etc., and of Scotland the forty-ninth, in the year of our Lord 1616. The month has been altered from "Januarij" to "martij", a change that has been taken to mean that Shakespeare's will was first prepared for execution on January 25, set aside pending the forthcoming marriage of his daughter Judith to Thomas Quiney, which took place February 10, 1616, and the first sheet rewritten as of March 25 to allow for a bequest to his daughter as a married woman, the anomalous "Januarij" being a scribal error carried over from the original first sheet. Certainly Judith is treated as being already married in the will as it now stands (note the reference to her as unmarried in the deleted passage at the top of Sheet 2), and there is a cancelled reference in line 15 to Shakespeare's "sonne in L" (i.e. Thomas Quiney). 26. **her:** i.e. Susanna Hall.
46. **li:** fifty pounds. Cf. "Clli" (one hundred and fifty pounds) in line 66.
54. **Covert Baron:** under the protection of a husband.
62. **att anie [tyme].** The reading is disputed. Some (including Chambers) transcribe as "attaine"; others (including Lewis) "att anie" as here. The manuscript itself seems clearly to read "att anie", and, since the words fall at the end of a line, the scribal omission of some word like "tyme" at the beginning of the next line would represent a common enough type of error.
75–77. **vnto . . . deceas.** These lines appear to have been added at the top of Sheet 2 and are probably part of the text of the original Sheet 1 for which there was no room on the rewritten Sheet 1. The following words ("to be . . . paied vnto") have been deleted, since they refer to Judith Shakespeare as unmarried.
75–76. **[a blank] Hart.** Supply "Thomas". The failure to remember the child's first name is somewhat ironic, since it is only through the line of Thomas Hart that descendants of John Shakespeare survive today.
82. **her Itm̃.** "her" should have been deleted with the preceding cancelled matter.
87–99. **Thomas Combe . . . Ringes.** For information on the various individuals here named as legatees, see Chambers and Lewis. To students of Shakespeare the most interesting item is, of course, the bequests, to buy mourning rings, made to "my ffellowes" (i.e. fellow actors and members of the King's Men), Heminge, Burbage, and Condell, the first and third of whom were concerned in the publication of the First Folio (1623).
92. **Hamlett Sadler.** Note that the name appears as "Hamnet Sadler" among the list of witnesses (line 166).
141. **Neece Hall:** i.e. Elizabeth, Susanna Hall's daughter.
146. **wief my second best bed.** This is the only reference in the will to Shakespeare's wife, Anne, and much ink has been spilled needlessly by those who read into this inserted bequest Shakespeare's animosity against Anne. Actually no mention of Anne was necessary, since she was fully provided for, as his widow, by existing law, and a bed, with all its furnishings, was an item of considerable value, and in this case perhaps of sentiment.
168. **Probatum.** Probate was granted June 22, 1616.

6. Shakespeare's Epitaphs

A. The following epitaph is roughly inscribed on the flat stone that covers Shakespeare's grave in the chancel of Holy Trinity Church, Stratford. To the left, by the north wall, is the grave of Shakespeare's wife, Anne; to the right, the grave of Susanna Hall, Shakespeare's elder daughter. Tradition has it that Shakespeare himself composed this uninspired jingle and ordered it to be placed on his tombstone in an attempt to prevent the later removal of his bones to the charnel-house attached to the church—a common practice. Perhaps so. At any rate, Shakespeare's grave has never been opened for examination. Authorities differ as to whether the present stone is the original or a replacement made in the later eighteenth century. The fullest recent discussion of the inscription may be found in B. R. Lewis, *The Shakespeare Documents*, II, 527–30.

GOOD FREND FOR IESVS SAKE FORBEARE,
TO DIGG THE DVST ENCLOASED HEARE:
BLESTE BE Yᵉ MAN Yᵗ SPARES THES STONES,
AND CVRST BE HE Yᵗ MOVES MY BONES.

3. **Bleste.** This reading is disputed. Lewis, for example, declares for "Blese". "Yᵉ" and "Yᵗ" (also in line 4) are common abbreviated forms for "the" and "that," the "y" being a corruption of the Old English Þ (= th). "Yᵉ" (meaning "the") was never pronounced as "ye," despite popular misconceptions today.

B. The following epitaph appears on a monument, containing a bust of Shakespeare, placed on the north wall of the chancel in Holy Trinity Church. This monument had certainly been erected by 1623, since Leonard Digges refers to it in his elegy prefixed to the First Folio (see above, page 71), and is believed to be the work of Garret Janssen, who, by this date, owned a tombmaker's shop in Southwark, not far from the Globe Theatre. The author of the epitaph is unknown; probably he was one of Shakespeare's London friends. It has been suggested that Shakespeare's company, the King's Men, may have played an important part in having the monument erected. For a full discussion see B. R. Lewis, *The Shakespeare Documents*, II, 542–47.

IVDICIO PYLIVM, GENIO SOCRATEM, ARTE MARONEM,
TERRA TEGIT, POPVLVS MÆRET, OLYMPVS HABET

STAY PASSENGER, WHY GOEST THOV BY SO FAST?
READ IF THOV CANST, WHOM ENVIOVS DEATH HATH PLAST,
WITH IN THIS MONVMENT SHAKSPEARE: WITH WHOME,
QVICK NATVRE DIDE: WHOSE NAME DOTH DECK Yˢ TOMBE,
FAR MORE THEN COST: SIEH ALL, Yᵗ HE HATH WRITT,
LEAVES LIVING ART, BVT PAGE, TO SERVE HIS WITT.

OBIIT AÑO DOˡ 1616
ÆTATIS • 53 DIE 23 APᴿ •

1–2. **Iudicio . . . habet:** In judgment a Nestor [*Pylius* is a poetic form referring to Nestor], in wit a Socrates, in art a Virgil; the earth buries [him], the people mourn [him], Olympus possesses [him].
5. **with in this monument.** The writer evidently did not know that Shakespeare was not buried in the monument. This suggests a writer not immediately connected with Stratford.
6. **quick nature dide:** living nature died. **Yˢ:** this.
7. **more.** Possibly a comma follows this word. **cost:** i.e. costly ornamentation.
7–8. **Sieh . . . witt:** since all that he hath written leaves the work of living writers but as a page waiting on his wit. "Sieh" is an error for "Sith" (= since).
9–10. **Obiit . . . Apʳ:** he died in the year of our Lord 1616, at the age of 53, on the 23rd day of April. In the abbreviated final word, it is uncertain whether the letter above the "p" is indeed "r".

7. Shakespeare's Supposed Epitaph on John Combe

The connection of the following epitaph with Shakespeare is highly conjectural, though it depends on several independent attributions (the earliest being in 1634). The epitaph exists in several variant forms and is an adaptation of an earlier generalized epitaph on a usurer ("Ten in the hundred lies vnder this stone, / And a hundred to ten but to th' Devil he's gone.") published by H. P. in *The More the Merrier* (1608), sig. C2. There is even a tradition that it was at one time inscribed on Combe's funeral monument in the Stratford church; another that a two-line version was composed at Combe's request. At any rate, John Combe was a man of some wealth, according to tradition a money-lender, and generous in his benefactions. He died in 1614, leaving, among a large number of bequests, five pounds to William Shakespeare. It is difficult to believe that Shakespeare rewarded his generosity by composing some version of the epitaph after Combe's death. If he had any hand in it, it was most likely, as J. Q. Adams suggests, as part of some earlier light-hearted tavern competition.

The first version below appeared as early as 1619 in Patrick Hannay's *A Happy Husband* (sig. L2^{V}), containing a reissue, with additions, of Richard Brathwait's *Remains after Death* (1618), without attribution to Shakespeare:

An Epitaph Vpon one *Iohn Combe* of Stratford vpon *Auen*, a notable Vsurer, fastened vpon a Tombe that he had caused to be built in his life time.

Ten in the hundred must lie in his graue,
But a hundred to ten whether God will him haue?
Who then must be interr'd in this Tombe?
Oh (quoth the Diuell) my *Iohn a Combe.*

The second version is from a commonplace book written by Robert Dobyns (Folger Shakespeare Library, MS. 267.1, fol. 72):

In 1673 I Robert Dobyns being at Stratford vpon Avon & visiting the Church there transcribed these two Epitaphs, the first is on William Shakespeare's monument. the other is upon ye monument of a noted usurer [the Shakespeare epitaph follows; then]

Tenn in the hundred here lyeth engraued
A hundred to ten his Soule is new saued
If anny one ask: who lyeth in this Tomb
Oh ho quoth the Diuell tis my Iohn a Combe

Since my being at Stratford the heires of Mr Combe haue Caused these verses to be razed so y^{t} now they are not legible.

A version very close to this one appears in Nicholas Rowe's life of Shakespeare (1709).

Several other epitaphs have been attributed to Shakespeare; see J. Q. Adams, "Shakespeare as a Writer of Epitaphs" in *The Manly Anniversary Studies in Language and Literature* (Chicago, 1923), pp. 78–89. See also E. K. Chambers, *William Shakespeare*, II, 138–141, 246, 250–51, 253, and B. R. Lewis, *The Shakespeare Documents*, II, 325–29.

8. Robert Greene's Attack on Shakespeare

The following passage, from *Greenes, Groats-worth of witte, bought with a million of Repentance* (1592), sig. F1, contains the earliest printed allusion to Shakespeare and by the very bitterness of its language suggests that already in 1592 he was a person to reckon with in theatrical circles.

To those Gentlemen his Quondam acquaintance, that spend their wits in making plaies, R. G. *wisheth a better exercise, and wisdome to preuent his extremities. . . .*

Base minded men all three of you [Marlowe, Nashe, Peele], if by my miserie you be not warnd: for vnto none of you (like mee) sought those burres to cleaue: those Puppets (I meane) that spake from our mouths, those Anticks garnisht in our colours. Is it not strange, that I, to whom they all haue beene beholding: is it not like that you, to whome they all haue beene beholding, shall (were yee in that case as I am now) bee both at once of them forsaken? Yes trust them not: for there is an vpstart Crow, beautified with our feathers, that with his *Tygers hart wrapt in a Players hyde*, supposes he is as well able to bombast out a blanke verse as the best of you: and beeing an absolute *Iohannes fac totum*, is in his owne conceit the onely Shake-scene in a countrey. O that I might intreat your rare wits to be imploied in more profitable courses: & let those Apes imitate your past excellence, and neuer more acquaint them with your admired inuentions. I knowe the best husband of you all will neuer proue an Vsurer, and the kindest of them all will neuer proue a kind nurse: yet whilest you may, seeke you better Maisters; for it is pittie men of such rare wits, should be subiect to the pleasure of such rude groomes.

13–14. **vpstart Crow . . . feathers.** Although he is not actually mentioned by name, it is clear (from "*Tygers . . . hyde*" [lines 14–15] and "Shake-scene" [line 18]) that the "vpstart Crow" is Shakespeare. The meaning of "beautified with our feathers" has been much debated. Some interpret the phrase as an indictment of Shakespeare for plagiarism; others, as merely a reference to Shakespeare as an actor. There is evidence for both views and the matter must be considered unsettled.
14–15. **Tygers . . . hyde.** Parody of a line in *3 Henry VI*, I.iv.137 ("O tiger's heart wrapp'd in a woman's hide!").
15–16. **bombast . . . you:** stuff out (i.e. write) blank verse as well as the best of you (i.e. Marlowe, Nashe, Peele).
17. **Iohannes fac totum:** a John do-it-all or jack-of-all-trades. **conceit:** conception, imagination.
22. **best husband:** most thrifty one.

9. Henry Chettle's Apology to Shakespeare

Chettle, who was responsible for the publication of Greene's *Groats-worth of witte* in 1592, later in that year inserted in his own *Kind-Hartes Dreame* an epistle "To the Gentlemen Readers" which included the following passage.

. . . About three moneths since died *M. Robert Greene*, leauing many papers in sundry Booke sellers hands, among other his Groats-worth of wit, in which a letter written to diuers play-makers, is offensiuely by one or two of them taken, and because on the dead they cannot be auenged, they wilfully forge in their conceites a liuing Author: and after tossing it to and fro, no remedy, but it must light on me. How I haue all the time of my conuersing in printing hindred the bitter inueying against schollers, it hath been very well knowne, and how in that I dealt I can sufficiently prooue. With neither of them that take offence was I acquainted, and with one of them [Marlowe] I care not if I neuer be: The other [Shakespeare], whome at that time I did not so much spare, as since I wish I had, for that as I haue moderated the heate of liuing writers, and might haue vsde my owne discretion (especially in such a case) the Author beeing dead, that I did not, I am as sory, as if the originall fault had beene my fault, because my selfe haue seene his demeanor no lesse ciuill than he exelent in the qualitie he professes: Besides, diuers of worship haue reported, his vprightnes of dealing, which argues his honesty, and his facetious grace in writting, that aprooues his Art.

7. conceites: imaginations. **21. ciuill**: polite, gentle.
22. qualitie: profession.
22–23. diuers of worship: various men of high social position.
24. honesty: honorable character, integrity. **facetious**: urbane, polished (earliest use of the word in English and only example in this sense; usually means "witty, amusing" [*O.E.D.*]). **25. aprooues**: proves, demonstrates.

10. *Willobie His Avisa* (1594)

Although *Willobie His Avisa* is a poem of the *roman à clef* variety and affords many tantalizing mysteries (including the question whether its declared author, Henry Willobie, ever existed), critics until very recently were agreed that "H. W." stood for Henry Wriothesley, Earl of Southampton, Shakespeare's patron, and "W. S." for William Shakespeare, "the old player." In a new study (1970), however, B. N. De Luna, while not denying the identification of "W. S." with Shakespeare, argues for a double identity in "H. W.": (1) Robert Dudley, Earl of Leicester, and (2) Robert Devereux, Earl of Essex, both suitors of Queen Elizabeth (i.e. Avisa). The verse exchanges which follow the passage below (through Cant. LXXIIII) between "H. W.", "W. S.", and Avisa are more or less purely conventional, with "W. S." playing the role of the experienced but unsuccessful counsellor to the wooer. One couplet assigned to "W. S." ("She is no Saynt, She is no Nonne, / I thinke in tyme she may be wonne.") in Cant. XLVII is thought to echo *Titus Andronicus*, II.i.82–83. For fuller discussion see G. B. Harrison, ed., *Willobie His Avisa* (London, 1926), E. K. Chambers, *William Shakespeare*, I, 569–71, and B. N. De Luna, *The Queen Declined: An Interpretation of "Willobie His Avisa"* (Oxford, 1970).

Cant. XLIIII.

Henrico Willobego. Italo-Hispalensis.

H. W. being sodenly infected with the contagion of a fantasticall fit, at the first sight of *A*, pyneth a while in secret griefe, at length not able any longer to indure the burning heate of so feruent a humour, bewrayeth the secresy of his disease vnto his familiar frend W. S. who not long before had tryed the curtesy of the like passion, and was now newly recouered of the like infection; yet finding his frend let bloud in the same vaine, he took pleasure for a tyme to see him bleed, & in steed of stopping the issue, he inlargeth the wound, with the sharpe rasor of a willing conceit, perswading him that he thought it a matter very easy to be compassed, & no doubt with payne, diligence & some cost in time to be obtayned. Thus this miserable comforter comforting his frend with an impossibilitie, eyther for that he now would secretly laugh at his frends folly, that had giuen occasion not long before vnto others to laugh at his owne, or because he would see whether an other could play his part better then himselfe, & in vewing a far off the course of this louing Comedy, he determined to see whether it would sort to a happier end for this new actor, then it did for the old player. But at length this Comedy was like to haue growen to a Tragedy, by the weake & feeble estate that H. W. was brought vnto, by a desperate vewe of an impossibility of obtaining his purpose, til Time & Necessity, being his best Phisitions brought him a plaster, if not to heale, yet in part to ease his maladye. In all which discourse is liuely represented the vnrewly rage of unbrydeled fancy, hauing the raines to roue at liberty, with the dyuers & sundry changes of affections & temptations, which Will, set loose from Reason, can deuise. &c.

3. A: i.e. Avisa.
6–9. W. S. . . . infection. If "W. S." is accepted as William Shakespeare, the reference here would seem to be to the "story" of the sonnets.
9–10. let . . . vaine: i.e. suffering from the same disease (with reference to phlebotomy or bloodletting).
12. sharpe . . . conceit: i.e. an imagination willing to cut deeply. **26. estate**: state, condition.
29. plaster: a healing application. **32. fancy**: passion.

11. John Manningham, ["Richard the Third and William the Conqueror"]

The passage below is from Manningham's *Diary* (British Museum, Harleian MS. 5353, fol. 29^{v}). Manningham was a member of the Middle Temple and a barrister-at-law; he died in 1622. For another extract from the *Diary*, see Number 19, below.

[March 13, 1602] Vpon a tyme when Burbidge played Rich. 3. there was a citizen greue soe farr in liking wth him, that before shee went from the play shee appointed him to come that night vnto hir by the name of Ri: the 3. Shakespeare ouerhearing their conclusion, went before, was intertained, and at his game ere Burbidge came. Then message being brought that Rich. the 3^{d}. was at the dore, Shakespeare caused returne to be made that William the Conquerour was before Rich. the 3. Shakespeares name wthm *m^{a} Curle* /

11. m^{a} Curle: Master Curle (either Manningham's father-in-law, William, or his brother-in-law, Edward), Manningham's source for the anecdote.

II. Contemporary Notices of the Plays and Poems

12. [*I Henry VI*] Thomas Nashe, from *Pierce Penilesse his Supplication to the Diuell* (1592)

The following passage (sig. F3) refers to the so-called Talbot scenes in *1 Henry VI*, IV.ii–vii. Talbot is believed to have been acted by Richard Burbage, later the principal actor of the Chamberlain's Men.

How would it haue ioyed braue *Talbot* (the terror of the French) to thinke that after he had lyne two hundred yeares in his Tombe, hee should triumphe againe on the Stage, and haue his bones newe embalmed with the teares of ten thousand spectators at least, (at seuerall times) who in the Tragedian that represents his person, imagine they behold him fresh bleeding.

13. [*Richard III*, *Venus and Adonis*, *Lucrece*, *Romeo and Juliet*] The Parnassus Plays

The three so-called Parnassus plays (*The Pilgrimage to Parnassus* and *The Return from Parnassus, Parts 1* and *2*) were performed between Christmas 1598 and Christmas 1601 by the students at St. John's College, Cambridge. Only Part 2 of *The Return* received contemporary publication (1606); the two earlier plays were not published until the nineteenth century (ed. W. D. Macray, 1886). Aside from the several references to Shakespeare, these plays contain a number of interesting references to other contemporary writers. The standard modern edition is J. B. Leishman's (London, 1949). The present selections are based on the manuscript (Bodleian Library, Rawlinson D. 398, fols. 214^{v}–215^{r}, 216^{v}) for *The Return, Part 1*, and on the first of the two 1606 quartos for *The Return, Part 2*.

The Return from Parnassus, Part 1

III.i (lines 983–1033 in Leishman)

Gullio Pardon faire lady, thoughe sicke thoughted Gullio maks a maine vnto thee, & like a bould faced sutore gins to woo thee.

Ingen[ioso]: We shall haue nothinge but pure Shakspeare, and shreds of poetrie y^{t} he hath gathered at the theators.

Gullio Pardon mee moy mitressa, ast am a gentleman ye moone in comparison of thy bright hue a meere slutt, *Anthonies* Cleopatra a blacke browde milkmaide, Hellen a dowdie

Ingen: Marke Romeo, and Iuliet. o monstrous theft, I thinke he will runn throughe a whole booke of Samuell Daniells

Gullio Thrise fairer than my selfe, thus I began
the gods faire riches, sweete aboue compare
Staine to all Nimphes, [m]ore louely the[n] a man
More white and red than doues and roses are
Nature that made thee wth herselfe had strife,
saith that the worlde hath ending wth thy life.

Ingen: Sweete Mr Shakspeare. . . .

Ingen: My pen is youre bounden vassall to commande, but what vayne woulde it please you to haue them in.

Gullio Not in a vaine veine (prettie y faith) make mee them in two or three diuers vayns, in Chaucers, Gowers and Spencers and Mr Shakspeares, Marry I thinke I shall entertaine those verses wch run like these.

Even as the sunn wth purple coloured face
had tane his laste leaue on the weeping
morne. &c.

O sweet Mr Shakspeare, Ile haue his picture in my study at the courte.

IV.i (lines 1189–1210 in Leishman)

Gullio. . . . Let mee heare Mr Shakespears veyne.

Ingen: Faire Venus queene of beutie, and of loue
thy red cloth stayne the blushinge of the morne
thy snowie neck shameth the milke white doue
thy presence doth this naked worlde adorne
Gazinge on thee all other nymphes I scorne
when ere thou dyest slowe shine that satterday
Beutie and grace muste sleepe wth thee for aye.

Gullio Noe more[:] I am one that can iudge accordinge to the proverbe *bouem ex vnguibus*, ey marry S^{r} these haue some life in them, let this duncified worlde esteeme of Spencer and Chaucer, Ile worshipp sweet Mr Shakspeare, and to honoure him will lay his Venus, and Adonis vnder my pillowe, as wee reade of one (I do not well remember his name) but I am sure he was a kinge, slept wth Homer vnder his beds heade. Well Ile bestowe a frenche crowne in the faire writinge of them out, and then Ile instructe thee about the deliuery of them, meane while, Ile haue thee make an elegant description of my M^{ris}, liken the worste part of her to Cynthia[:] make also a familiar Dialogue betwixt her, and my selfe, Ile now in, and correct these verses. *Exit.*

III.i.1–3. **sicke thoughted . . . thee.** Adapted from *Venus and Adonis,* lines 5–6.
7. **ast am:** perhaps dialectal for "as I am".
8–9. **hue a.** Read probably "hue's a".
9–10. **Anthonies . . . dowdie.** Adapted from *Romeo and Juliet,* II.iv.39–43. Perhaps the peculiar jargon in line 7 above ("Pardon mee moy mitressa") was suggested by the immediately following lines: "Signior Romeo, *bon jour!* there's a French salutation to your French slop."
12–13. **booke . . . Daniells.** The reference is presumably principally to Daniel's sonnet sequence, *Delia.*
14–19. **Thrise . . . life.** Adapted from *Venus and Adonis,* lines 7–12.
16. **more . . . then.** MS corrected from *Venus and Adonis;* "then" = than. 27. **entertaine:** find most acceptable.
29–30. **Even . . . morne.** From *Venus and Adonis,* lines 1–2 (substituting "on" for "of").

IV.i.2–8. **Faire . . . aye.** Intended as a parody of Shakespeare's style in *Venus and Adonis,* though written in a stanza of seven rather than six lines.
10. **bouem ex vnguibus:** (one may know) the bull by his hooves; the proverb is properly "the lion is known by his claws."
15. **one:** Alexander the Great.

The Return from Parnassus, Part 2

I.ii (lines 300–304 in Leishman)

Ing[*enioso*]. . . . *William Shakespeare.*
Iud[*icio*]. Who loues [not *Adons* loue, or *Lucrece*] rape,
His sweeter verse contaynes hart robbing [lines],
Could but a grauer subiect him content,
Without loues foolish lazy languishment.

IV.iii (lines 1766–74 in Leishman)

Kemp. Few of the vniuersity men pen plaies well, they smell too much of that writer *Ouid,* and that writer *Metamorphosis,* and talke too much of *Proserpina* & *Iuppiter.* Why heres our fellow *Shakespeare* puts them all downe, I and *Ben Ionson* too. O that *Ben Ionson* is a pestilent fellow, he brought vp *Horace* giuing the Poets a pill, but our fellow *Shakespeare* hath giuen him a purge that made him beray his credit:

Bur[*bage*]. Its a shrewd fellow indeed: . . .

IV.iv (lines 1835–40 in Leishman)

Bur[*bage*]. I like your face, and the proportion of your body for *Richard* the 3. I pray M. *Phil.* let me see you act a little of it.

Phil[*omusus*]. Now is the winter of our discontent,
Made glorious summer by the sonne of Yorke,
[&c.]

I.ii.2–5. **Who . . . languishment.** The praise of Shakespeare, as well as the strong criticism of Jonson, in these plays must, as Leishman points out, be regarded as somewhat equivocal. Shakespeare is shown only in his role as a love poet.
2. **not . . . Lucrece.** The reading of the Halliwell-Phillipps MS (now in the Folger Shakespeare Library). Q1 reads *"Adonis* loue, or *Lucre's"*, omitting "not".
3. **lines.** The reading of the Halliwell-Phillipps MS. Q1 reads "life".

IV.iii.1 s.p. **Kemp.** William Kemp was a famous comedian who had been a member of the Chamberlain's Men, Shakespeare's company.
2. **smell too much of:** i.e. imitate and borrow too much from.
3. **writer Metamorphosis:** i.e. Ovid once more. Kemp is being made to show his ignorance as a mere actor by taking the name of Ovid's principal work as that of an author. We are meant then to evaluate the following praise of Shakespeare and the consequent unfavorable comment on Jonson in terms of its supposed source. 5. **I:** i.e. ay.
6–7. **Horace . . . pill.** A reference to Jonson's part in the War of the Theatres. In *Poetaster* (1601) Horace administers a "pill" to Crispinus (Marston) and causes him to vomit up what Jonson considered to be Marston's outlandish vocabulary.
7–8. **Shakespeare . . . credit.** A much-discussed passage. One view holds that the "purge" refers to Dekker's answer to *Poetaster, Satiro-Mastix* (1601), for which the author here wrongly supposes Shakespeare to have been at least partly responsible; the other view sees Shakespeare's "purge" in the character of Ajax in *Troilus and Cressida* (c. 1601–2).
8. **beray his credit:** dirty his reputation.
9 s.p. **Burbage:** i.e. Richard Burbage, the principal actor of the Chamberlain's Men and the creator of the role of Shakespeare's Richard III. **shrewd:** malignant, malicious, satirical.

IV.iv.4–5. **Now . . . Yorke:** the opening lines of *Richard III,* substituting "the" for "this" in line 2.
6. **&c.** Supplied from the Halliwell-Phillipps MS.

13A. [*Venus and Adonis, The Rape of Lucrece*] Richard Barnfield (1598)

Richard Barnfield, from his "A Remembrance of Some English Poets" in *Poems of Divers Humours,* itself part of a volume *The Encomium of Lady Pecunia* (1598). Barnfield is the author of at least two (Numbers 8 and 20) of the twenty poems contained in *The Passionate Pilgrim.* His sonnets show him to be a possible source for Shakespeare's own sonnets.

And *Shakespeare* thou, whose hony-flowing Vaine,
(Pleasing the World) thy praises doth obtaine.
Whose *Venus* and whose *Lucrece* (sweete, and chaste)
Thy name in fames immortall Booke haue plac't.
Live euer you, at least in Fame liue euer:
Well may the Bodye dye, but Fame dies neuer.
(E2v)

14. [*The Comedy of Errors*] From *Gesta Grayorum* (1594–95)

The following passages are from the first edition, London, 1688, pp. 43–44. It describes a portion of the revels that took place at Gray's Inn, one of the Inns of Court, during a period that began on December 20 (St. Thomas' Eve), 1594, and extended through Shrovetide, ending on Shrove Tuesday, March 4, 1595.

The next grand Night was intended to be upon *Innocents-Day* [December 28, 1594] at Night; at which time there was a great Presence of Lords, Ladies, and worshipful Personages, that did expect some notable Performance at that time; which, indeed, had been effected, if the multitude of Beholders had not been so exceeding great, that thereby there was no convenient room for those that were Actors; . . . Against which time, our Friend, the *Inner Temple,* determined to send their Ambassador to our Prince of State [the Prince of Purpoole], . . . The Ambassador came very gallantly appointed, and attended by a great number of brave Gentlemen, which arrived at our Court about Nine of the Clock at Night. . . . He was received very kindly of the Prince, and placed in a Chair besides His Highness, to the end that he might be Partaker of the Sports intended. . . . When the Ambassador was placed, as aforesaid, and that there was something to be performed for the Delight of the Beholders, there arose such a disordered Tumult and Crowd upon the Stage, that there was no Opportunity to effect that which was intended: There came so great a number of worshipful Personages upon the Stage, that might not be displaced; and Gentlewomen, whose Sex did privilege them from Violence, that when the Prince and his Officers had in vain, a good while, expected and endeavoured a Reformation, at length there was no hope of Redress for that present. The Lord Ambassador and his Train thought that they were not so kindly entertained, as was before expected, and thereupon would not stay any longer at that time, but, in a sort, discontented and displeased. After their Departure the Throngs and Tumults did somewhat cease, although so much of them continued, as was able to disorder and confound any good Inventions whatsoever. In regard whereof, as also for that the Sports intended were especially for the gracing of the *Templarians*, it was thought good not to offer any thing of Account, saving Dancing and Revelling with Gentlewomen; and after such Sports, a Comedy of Errors (like to *Plautus* his *Menechmus*) was played by the Players. So that Night was begun, and continued to the end, in nothing but Confusion and Errors; whereupon, it was ever afterwards called, *The Night of Errors*. . . . The next Night upon this Occasion, we preferred Judgments thick and threefold, which were read publickly by the Clerk of the Crown, being all against a Sorcerer or Conjurer that was supposed to be the Cause of that confused Inconvenience. Therein was contained, How he had caused the Stage to be built, and Scaffolds to be reared to the top of the House, to increase Expectation. . . . Also that he caused Throngs and Tumults, Crowds and Outrages, to disturb our whole Proceedings. And Lastly, that he had foisted a Company of base and common Fellows, to make up our Disorders with a Play of Errors and Confusions; and that that Night had gained to us Discredit, and it self a Nickname of Errors. All which were against the Crown and Dignity of our Sovereign Lord, the Prince of *Purpoole*.

. . . The next grand Night was upon *Twelfth-day* at Night [January 6, 1595]; . . . First, There came six Knights of the Helmet, with three that they led as Prisoners, and were attired like Monsters and Miscreants. The Knights gave the Prince to understand, that as they were returning from their Adventures out of *Russia*, wherein they aided the Emperor of *Russia*, against the *Tartars*, they surprized these three Persons, which were conspiring against His [i.e. the Prince of Purpoole's] Highness and Dignity: . . . Which [i.e. a masque] being done, the Trumpets were commanded to sound, and then the King at Arms came in before the Prince, and told His Honour, that there was arrived an Ambassador from the mighty Emperor of *Russia* and *Moscovy*, that had some Matters of Weight to make known to His Highness. So the Prince willed that he should be admitted into his Presence, who came in Attire of *Russia*, accompanied with two of his own Country, in like Habit.

9. **Inner Temple.** Another of the Inns of Court.
11. **Prince of state:** i.e. Prince of Purpoole (see lines 61–62), the Christmas Prince or Lord of Misrule, specially elected to serve for the duration of the revels.
33. **in a sort.** Supply some verb like "left" or "departed" before or after this phrase.
40. **any . . . Account.** This may be interpreted to suggest that *The Comedy of Errors* was not considered a very significant part of the planned revels.
57. **Company . . . Fellows:** i.e. the members of Shakespeare's company, who played *The Comedy of Errors*.
64–82. The supposed visit of the Russian ambassador to the Court of the Prince of Purpoole has been seen as suggesting to Shakespeare the masque of Muscovites in *Love's Labor's Lost*, V.ii.

15. [*Richard II*] Sir Edward Hoby's Letter to Sir Robert Cecil, December 7, 1595

Hoby's letter (Hatfield MS. XXXVI, fol. 60; ed. E. K. Chambers, *RES*, I [1925], 75–76) has often been considered important terminal evidence for the dating of Shakespeare's *Richard II*. Recent comment, however, is more cautious, since it is not clear from the context that the "K. Richard" referred to is a play or, if it is, that the play is necessarily Shakespeare's.

Sir, findinge that you wer not convenientlie to be at London to morrow night I am bold to send to knowe whether Teusdaie [December 9] may be anie more in your grace to visit poore Channon rowe where as late as it shal please you a gate for your supper shal be open: & K. Richard present him self to your vewe. Pardon my boldnes that ever love to be honored with your presence nether do I importune more then your occasions may willingly assent unto, in the meanetime & ever restinge At your command Edw. Hoby. [*Endorsed*] 7 Dec. 1595 readile [*this last word in another hand*].

4. **Channon rowe:** Canon Row, Westminster.
11. **readile:** readily, i.e. without delay.

15A. [*Richard III, Romeo and Juliet*] John Marston, *The Scourge of Villainie*

Marston (1598) parodies Richard's despairing cry in *Richard III*, V.iv.107, in the opening of *Satyre VII: A Cyniche Satyre* with the words "A Man, a man, a kingdome for a man" (F1ᵛ) and, in *Satyre X: Humours*, links *Romeo and Juliet* with the Curtain theatre, perhaps the London venue of the Lord Chamberlain's company between the reopening of the theatres in 1597 and the opening of the newly constructed Globe in 1599.

Luscus, what's playd today? faith now I know
I set thy lips abroach, from whence doth flow
Naught but pure *Iuliat* and *Romeo*.
Say, who acts best? *Drusus*, or *Roscio*?
Now I have him, that nere of ought did speak
But when of playes or Plaiers he did treate.
Hath made a common-place booke out of plaies
And speakes in print, at least what ere he sayes
Is warrented by Curtaine *plaudeties*,
If ere you heard him courting *Lesbias* eyes;
Say (Curteous Sir) speakes he not movingly
From out some new pathetique Tragedie?

(H4)

1ff. Davenport, in his standard edition (1961) based on the enlarged 1599 version, points out that this passage is the source for a scene in *The Return from Parnassus, Part 1*. See Appendix C, Number 13.
4. **Roscio.** Quintus Roscius, celebrated Roman actor and friend of Catullus and Cicero, to whom Edward Alleyn, leading man in the Lord Admiral's company, was often compared. If Alleyn is to be understood by Roscio, then it is likely Burbage is suggested by Drusus.
7. **made a common-place booke out of plaies.** Davenport, again, and Herford and Simpson point out that this was a common enough practice to have aroused the comment of Beaumont, and Fletcher and Massinger, in the prologues to

The Woman Hater (1607) and *The Custom of the Country* (c. 1620).
9. **Curtaine:** in Shoreditch, south of the Theatre. **plaudeties:** Either rounds of applause or the appeals for same.
10–12. G. B. Evans points out that "Apart from attesting to the popularity of *Romeo and Juliet* on the stage in 1598, Marston here appears to be linking it with 'some new pathetique Tragedie,' which Luscus pilfers in wooing his lady. No other known play which might have been considered 'new' in 1598 fits the description so well, and this suggests that *Romeo and Juliet* was comparatively new in 1598" (*Romeo and Juliet*, 1984, p. 2).

15B. [*Love's Labor's Lost*] Robert Tofte

Robert Tofte (d. 1620), poet and translator of works of Ariosto, Tasso, and Boiardo, wrote *Alba: The Month's Mind of a Melancholy Lover* (1598), a misogynistically tainted lament in three parts, the third of which refers to the poet's having seen a performance of *Love's Labor's Lost*, the first quarto of which was published in the same year of 1598.

Love's Labor Lost, I once did see a Play,
Ycleped so, so called to my paine,
Which I to heare to my small Ioy did stay,
Giuing attendance on my froward Dame.
My misgiuing minde presaging to me Ill,
Yet was I drawne to see it gainst my Will.

This *Play* no *Play* but Plague was unto me,
For there I lost the Loue I liked most;
And what to others seemede a iest to be,
I, that (in earnest) found vnto my cost.
To euery one (saue me) twas *Comicall*,
Whilst *Tragick* like to me it did befall.

Each Actor plaied in cunning wise his part,
But chiefly Those entrapt in *Cupids* snare;
Yet All was fained, twas not from the hart;
They seemede to grieue, but yet they felt no care.
'Twas I that Griefe (indeed) did beare in brest,
The others did but make a show in Iest.

Yet neither faining theirs, nor my meer Truth,
Could make her once so much as for to smile;
Whilst she (despite of pitie milde and ruth)
Did sit as skorning of my Woes the while.
Thus did she sit to see Loue lose his Loue,
Like hardned rock that force nor power can
move. (Sig. G5)

2. **ycleped:** called; the "ed" is stressed.
3. **stay:** stop.
4. **froward:** hostile.
5. **presaging:** forecasting.
7. **Plague.** A word of very great force in London in the 1590's.
13. **cunning:** skillful.
19. **meer:** absolute.
21. **ruth:** sorrow.

15C. [*Venus and Adonis, The Rape of Lucrece, Julius Caesar*] John Weever

(a) [From *Epigrammes in the oldest Cut, and newest Fashion* (1599), iv.22. Weever (1576–1632) was a poet and antiquary from Lancashire, where he enjoyed the patronage of a number of interconnected land-owning families (cf. E. A. J. Honigmann, *Shakespeare: The "Lost Years"* (1985), pp. 50–8).]

Ad Gulielmum Shakespeare.

Honie-tong'd *Shakespeare* when I saw thine issue
I swore *Apollo* got them and none other,
Their rosie-tainted features cloth'd in tissue,
Some heauen born goddesse said to be their
mother:
Rose-checkt *Adonis* with his amber tresses,
Faire fire-hot *Venus* charming him to loue her,
Chaste *Lucretia* virgine-like her dresses,
Prowd lust-stung *Tarquine* seeking still to proue
her:
Romea [,] *Richard*; more whose names I know not,
Their sugred tongues, and power attractive beuty
Say they are Saints althogh that Sts they shew not
For thousands vowes to them subiectiue dutie:
They burn in loue thy children *Shakespear* het
them,
Go, wo thy Muse more Nymphish brood beget
them.

3. **tissue:** a rich fabric, often interwoven with gold or silver threads.
8. **prove:** test or have experience of.
9. ***Romea*:** Probably a typographical error for *Romeo*.
11. **Sts:** saints.
12. **subiectiue:** submissive, obedient.
13. **het:** heated.
14. **wo:** woo, pay court to, make love.

(b) [From *The Mirror of Martyrs, or The Life and Death of Sir Iohn Oldcastle* (1601), St. 4. The dedication says that the book "some two yeares ago was made fit for the Print."]

The many-headed multitude were drawne
By *Brutus* speach, that *Caesar* was ambitious,
When eloquent *Mark Antonie* had showne
His vertues, who but *Brutus* then was vicious?

2. **Brutus speach.** Cf. *Julius Caesar*, III.ii.12–47. **ambitious.** Cf. *Julius Caesar*, III.ii.78.

16. [*Julius Caesar*] Thomas Platter

Platter, born at Basle in 1574, travelled in England from September 18 to October 20, 1599. He included the following record in his account of his travels (ed. by G. Binz in *Anglia*, XXII [1899], 458).

Den 21 Septembris [1599] nach dem Imbissessen, etwan vmb zwey vhren, bin ich mitt meiner geselschaft v̈ber dz wasser gefahren, haben in dem streüwinen Dachhaus die Tragedy vom ersten Keyser Iulio Caesare mitt ohngefahr 15 personen sehen gar artlich agieren, zu endt der Comedien dantzeten sie ihrem gebraucht nach gar v̈berausz zierlich, ye zwen in mannes vndt 2 in weiber kleideren angethan, wunderbahrlich mitt einanderen.

[*Translation:* On the 21st of September, after lunch, around two o'clock, I went with my companions over the water [i.e. the Thames], [and] in the strewed roof-house [i.e. the playhouse with the thatched roof] saw the tragedy of the first emperor Julius Caesar with nearly fifteen characters very well acted; at the end of the comedy, in conformity with their custom, they danced with all possible grace, two dressed in men's and two in women's clothes, marvellously with one another.]

17. [*Ur-Hamlet*] From Thomas Nashe's Preface to Robert Greene's *Menaphon* (1589)

The so-called *Ur-Hamlet*, to which Nashe is here (sig. **3) referring, is a lost play, probably by Thomas Kyd, which is generally believed to be the direct source for Shakespeare's *Hamlet*.

. . . But least I might seeme with these night crowes, *Nimis curiosus in aliena republica*. I'le turne backe to my first text, of studies of delight; and talke a little in friendship with a few of our triuiall translators. It is a common practise now a daies amongst a sort of shifting companions, that runne through euery arte and thriue by none, to leaue the trade of *Nouerint* whereto they were borne, and busie themselues with the indeuors of Art, that could scarcelie latinize their neck-verse if they should haue neede; yet English *Seneca* read by candle light yeeldes manie good sentences, as *Bloud is a begger*, and so foorth: and if you intreate him faire in a frostie morning, he will afford you whole *Hamlets*, I should say handfulls of tragical speaches. But ô griefe! *tempus edax rerum*, what's that will last alwaies? The sea exhaled by droppes will in continuance be drie, and *Seneca* let bloud line by line and page by page, at length must needes die to our stage: which makes his famisht followers to imitate the Kidde in *Aesop*, who enamoured with the Foxes newfangles, forsooke all hopes of life to leape into a newe occupation; and these men renowncing all possibilities of credit or estimation, to intermeddle with Italian translations: . . .

2. **Nimis . . . republica:** too meddlesome in a country foreign (to me); cf. Cicero, *De Officiis*, I, xxxiv, 127.
7. **Nouerint:** i.e. scrivener (to whom the name was applied because many legal documents began with "Noverint" = "know [all men by these presents]"). Thomas Kyd's father was a scrivener.
10. **neck-verse:** the opening of Psalm 51 (*Miserere mei*), used by criminals claiming benefit of clergy.
10–11. **English Seneca.** Probably a reference to a translation of the ten tragedies then attributed to Seneca edited by Thomas Newton (1581).
12. **Bloud . . . begger.** This "sentence" (i.e. aphorism) does not appear in Newton's *Seneca*.
13. **frostie morning.** Possibly a reference to the opening scene in the *Ur-Hamlet*; cf. Shakespeare's *Hamlet*, I.i.
15. **tempus edax rerum:** time the destroyer of all things.
20. **Kidde in Aesop.** The context here refers not to Aesop's *Fables* but to the May eclogue in Spenser's *Shepherd's Calendar*. Many critics see a direct reference to Thomas Kyd and to his recently published translation from Tasso called *The Householder's Philosophy* (1588); others deny any necessary application of the passage to Kyd.

18. [*Hamlet* (and *Venus and Adonis* and *Lucrece*)] Gabriel Harvey

The following manuscript note in Harvey's hand appears on fol. 394ᵛ in his copy of Speght's edition of Chaucer (1598). A facsimile of the page may be found in *Gabriel Harvey's Marginalia*, ed. G. C. Moore Smith (Stratford-upon-Avon, 1913). The note has been variously dated between 1598 and July 21, 1603, when Mountjoy (see line 14) was created Earl of Devonshire. Because the present tense is used of Essex (in line 10), opinion has favored a date before his execution, on February 25, 1601, but Leo Kirschbaum (*SP*, XXXIV [1937], 168–75) points out that Harvey may here be using the historical present, as he does elsewhere. For the idea that Harvey's praise of *Hamlet* involves an unconscious irony, in that Shakespeare incorporated words and themes from Harvey's own works in the tragedy, see J. J. M. Tobin, "Gabriel Harvey: 'Excellent Matter of Emulation'," *Hamlet Studies*, VII (1985), 94–100.

Heywoods prouerbs, with His, & Sir Thomas Mores Epigrams, may serue for sufficient supplies of manie of theis deuises. And now translated Petrarch, Ariosto, Tasso, & Bartas himself deserve curious comparison with Chaucer, Lidgate, & owre best Inglish, auncient & moderne. Amongst which, the Countesse of Pembrokes Arcadia, & the Faerie Queene ar now freshest in request: & Astrophil, & Amyntas ar none of the idlest pastimes of sum fine humanists. The Earle of Essex much commendes Albions England: and not vnworthily for diuerse notable pageants, before, & in the Chronicle. Sum Inglish, & other Histories nowhere more sensibly described, or more inwardly discouered. The Lord Mountioy makes the like account of Daniels peece of the Chronicle, touching the Vsurpation of Henrie of Bullingbrooke. Which in deede is a fine, sententious, & politique peece of Poetrie: as proffitable, as pleasurable. The younger sort takes much delight in Shakespeares Venus, & Adonis: but his Lucrece, & his tragedie of Hamlet, Prince of Denmarke, haue it in them, to please the wiser sort. Or such Poets: or better: or none.

Vilia miretur Vulgus: mihi flavus Apollo
Pocula Castaliae plena ministret aquae: quoth Sir Edward Dier, betwene iest, & earnest. Whose written deuises farr excell most of the sonets, and cantos in print. His Amaryllis, & Sir Walter Raleighs Cynthia, how fine & sweet inuentions? Excellent matter of emulation for Spencer, Constable, France, Watson, Daniel, Warner, Chapman, Siluester, Shakespeare, & the rest of owr florishing metricians. I looke for much, aswell in verse, as in prose, from mie two Oxford frends, Doctor Gager, & M. Hackluit: both rarely furnished for the purpose: & I haue a phansie to Owens new Epigrams, as pithie as elegant, as pleasant as sharp, & sumtime as weightie as breife: & amongst so manie gentle, noble, & royall spirits meethinkes I see sum heroical thing in the clowdes: mie soueraine hope. Axiophilus shall forgett himself, or will remember to leaue sum memorials behinde him: & to make an vse of so manie rhapsodies, cantos, hymnes, odes, epigrams, sonets, & discourses, as at idle howers, or at flowing fitts he hath compiled. God knows what is good for the world, & fitting for this age.

10. **Albions England.** By William Warner (1586, etc.).
15. **Daniels . . . Chronicle:** i.e. *The Civil Wars between the Two Houses of Lancaster and York* (1595). 22. **Or:** either.
24–25. **Vilia . . . aquae.** From Ovid's *Amores*, I, xv, 35–36;

"Let what is cheap excite the marvel of the crowd; for me may golden Apollo minister full cups from the Castalian fount" (Loeb trans.). The same lines appear on the title-page of Shakespeare's *Venus and Adonis* (1593).
31. **Watson.** Thomas Watson died in 1592 and was, therefore, not among "florishing metricians." If Harvey's note is dated after 1599, the same objection would apply to Spenser (mentioned earlier in line 30), who died in that year.
36. **Owens new Epigrams.** John Owen's *Epigrammata* were not published until 1606. Unless Harvey's note was written in 1606 or later, he must have known these epigrams in manuscript. 40. **Axiophilus.** Probably Harvey himself.

18A. [*Hamlet*] Anthony Scoloker

A relative of the more celebrated Anthony Scoloker (fl. 1548), Protestant printer and translator, he has been thought (on the basis of the word "Friendly") to have been acquainted with Shakespeare himself; he certainly was acquainted with *Hamlet* as it was performed, interpreting the protagonist's madness as actual rather than feigned. In his Epistle to the reader he implies the popularity of Hamlet and subsequently he refers to the hero's insanity: "Puts off his cloathes; his shirt he onely weares, / Much like mad-*Hamlet*; thus as Passion teares." (E2^{V})

[From *Epistle to Daiphantus, or the Passions of Love* (1604), sig. A2.]

It should be like the *Neuer-too-well read Arcadia*, where the *Prose* and *Verce* (*Matter* and *Words*) are like his *Mistresses* eyes, one still excelling another and without Coriuall: or to come home to the vulgars *Element*, like *Friendly Shakespeare's Tragedies*, where the *Commedian* rides, when the *Tragedian* stands on Tip-toe: Faith it should please all, like Prince *Hamlet*. But in sadnesse, then it were to be feared he would runne mad: Insooth I will not be moone-sicke, to please: nor out of my wits though I displeased all.

1. **Arcadia.** Sir Philip Sidney's prose romance (1590), the most considerable narrative work of the Elizabethan period.
4. **Coriuall:** competitor with an equal claim.
6. **on Tip-toe.** Suggests the elevated nature of tragedy by alluding to the ancient tragic actor's wearing of the buskin, or thick-soled boot.

19. [*Twelfth Night*] John Manningham

The following passage from Manningham's *Diary* (British Museum, Harleian MS. 5353) has been transcribed from a facsimile in J. O. Halliwell-Phillipps, *Outlines of the Life of Shakespeare* (10th ed., 1898), II, 82. It describes a festive occasion (Candlemas Day, February 2, 1602) at the Middle Temple. On Manningham, see the headnote to Number 11, above.

febr: 1601 [i.e. 1602 New Style] /

2. at our feast wee had a play called [*some letters crossed through*] Twelue night or what you will /./ much like the com̃edy of Errores / or Menechmi in plautus / but most like and neere to that in Italian called Inganni / a good practice in it to make the steward beleeue his Lady widdowe was in Loue wth him. by counterfeyting a letter / as from his lady in generall termes / telling him what shee liked best in him / and prescribing his gesture in smiling [,] his apparaile / etc. and then when he came to practise making him belieue they tooke him to be mad etc /

3. **com̃edy of Errores:** i.e. Shakespeare's play. **Menechmi.** The Plautine source of Shakespeare's *The Comedy of Errors.*
5. **Inganni.** There is a play of this name by Nicolo Secchi (1562) and one by Curzio Gonzaga (1592; contains the name Cesare), but Manningham may have meant *Ingannati* (1537), a play somewhat closer to Shakespeare's, containing a Fabio, a Malevolti, and a reference to Twelfth Night (Epiphany).
6. **Lady widdowe.** Olivia is not a widow in the text of *Twelfth Night* as we now have it, though she is so described in one of Shakespeare's principal sources for the play, Barnabe Rich's story of "Apolonius and Silla" in his *Farewell to Military Profession* (1581).
7. **lady.** The facsimile shows what looks like an "M" following "lady"; perhaps it should be taken as an abbreviation for "Mistress."

20. [*Macbeth, Cymbeline, The Winter's Tale*] Dr. Simon Forman

The following manuscript jottings by Dr. Simon Forman (1552–1611) are bound up as part (fols. 200–207^{v}) of a substantial volume (Bodleian Ashm. MS. 208), containing, in Forman's holograph, astrological, alchemical, and biographical materials. They record performances seen by Forman at the Globe in 1611 of *Macbeth, Cymbeline, Richard II* (not Shakespeare's), and *The Winter's Tale.* (The date 1610 assigned by Forman to the performance of *Macbeth* that he attended on Saturday, April 20, is presumably a slip for 1611, since April 20 fell on a Saturday in 1611 but not in 1610.) Some of his details are especially interesting because they suggest possible differences between the play as performed at the Globe and the text as preserved in F1. In the present text extra minim strokes in *m* and *n* have been silently regularized.

The Bocke of Plaies and Notes therof per formane for Common Pollicie

IN Mackbeth at the glod [Globe] 1610 [1611] the 20 of Aprill ♄ [Saturday]. ther was to be obserued firste howe Mackbeth and Bancko 2 noble mẽ of Scotland Ridinge thorowe a wod the[r] stode befor them 3 women feiries or Nimphes And Saluted Mackbeth sayinge .t. 3 tymes vnto him. haille mackbeth. king of Codon for thou shalt be a kinge but shalt beget No kinges &c. then said Bancko what all to mackbeth And nothing to me. yes said the nimphes haille to thee Banko thou shalt beget kinges. yet be no kinge And so they departed & cam to the Courte of Scotland to Dunkin king of Scotes and yt was in the dais of Edward the Confessor. And Dunkin bad them both kindly wellcom. And made Mackbeth forth with Prince of Northumberland. and sent him hom to his own castell and appointed mackbeth to prouid for him for he wold Sup wth him the next dai at night. & did soe. And mackebeth contrived to kill Dunkin. & thorow the persuasion of his wife did that night Murder the kinge in his own Castell beinge his guest And ther were many prodigies seen that night & the dai before. And when Mack Beth had murdred the kinge the blod on his handes could not be washed of by Any means. nor from his wiues handes wch handled the bluddi daggers in hiding them By wch means they became both much amazed & Affronted. the murder being knowen Dunkins 2 sonns fled the on to England the [other to] Walles to saue them selues. they beinge fled, they were supposed guilty of the murder of their father which was nothing soe Then was Mackbeth crowned kinge and then he for feare of Banko his old Companion that he should beget kinges but be no kinge him self. he contriued the death of Banko and caused him to be Murdred on the way as he Rode The next night beinge at supper wth his noble men whom he had bid to a feaste to the wch also Banco should haue com.) he began to speake of Noble Banco and to wish that he wer ther. And as he thus did standing vp to drincke a Carouse to him. the ghoste of Banco came and sate down in his cheier behind him. And he turninge About to sit down Again sawe the goste of banco which fronted him so. that he fell into a great passion of fear & fury. Vtteringe many wordes about his murder by wch when they hard that Banco was Murdred they Suspected Mackbet.

Then mack dove fled to England to the kinges sonn. And soe they Raised an Army And cam into scotland. and at dunston Anyse over thrue Mackbet. In the meantyme whille macdouee was in England Mackbet slewe mack doues wife & children. and after in the battelle mackdoue slewe Mackbet.

obserue Also howe Mackbetes quen did Rise in the night in her slepe & walke and talked and confessed all & the docter noted her wordes.

of Cimbalin king of England

Remember also the storri of Cymbalin king of England in Lucius tyme. howe Lucius Cam from octauus Cesar for Tribut and being denied. after sent Lucius wth a greate Arme [*or* Arnie] of Souldiars who landed at milford hauen. and After wer vanquished by Cimbalin and Lucius taken prisoner and all by means of 3 outlawes of the wch 2 of them were the sonns of Cimbelim token from him when they were but 2 yers old. by an old man whom Cymbalin banished. and he kept them as his own sonns 20 yers wth him in A cave. And howe of [*error for* one] of them slewe Clotan that was the quens sonn goinge To milford hauen to sek the loue of Innogen the kinges daughter whom he had banished also for louinge his daughter. and howe the Italiã that cam from her loue. conveied him selfe into A Cheste. and said yt was a chest of plate sent from her loue & others to be presented to the kinge. And in the depest of the night she being aslepe. he opened the cheste & cam forth of yt. And vewed her in her bed and the markes of her body. & toke a wai her braclet & after Accused her of adultery to her loue &c And in thend howe he came wth the Romains into England & was taken prisoner and after Reueled to Innogen. Who had turned her self into mans apparrell & fled to mete her loue at milford hauen. & chanchsed to fall on the Caue in the wodes wher her 2 brothers were & howe by eating a sleping Dram they thought she had bin deed & laid her in the wodes & the body of cloten by her. in her loues apparrell that he left behind him & howe she was found by lucius etc /

IN Richard the 2 At the glob 1611 the 30 of Aprill / ♂ [Tuesday]

Remember therin howe Iack strawe by his overmoch boldnes. not beinge pollitick nor supporting Anye thinge. was Soddenly at Smithfeld Bars stabbed by walworth the major of London & soe he and his wholle Army was over throwen Therfore in such a case or the like, never admit any party wthout a bar betwen. for A man Cannot be to wise, nor kepe him selfe to safe.

Also remember howe the duke of gloster. The Erell of Arundell oxford and others. crossing the kinge in his humor. about the duke of Erland and Bushy wer glad to fly and Raise an hoste of men. and beinge in his Castell. howe the d of Erland cam by nighte to betray him wth 300 men. but hauinge pryuie warninge ther of kept his gates faste And wold not suffer the Enimie to Enter, wch went back Again wth a flie in his eare. and after was slainte by the Erell of Arundell in the battell

Remember also. when the duke and Arundell cam to London wth their Army. kinge Richard came forth to them and met them and gaue them fair wordes. and promised them pardon and that all should be well yf they wold discharge their Army. vpon whose promises and faier Speaches they did yt and Affter the king byd them all to A banket and soe betraid them And cut of their heades &c because they had not his pardon vnder his hand & sealle before but his worde /

Remember therin Also howe the ducke of Lankaster pryuily contryued all villany. to set them all together by the ears and to make the nobilyty to Envy the kinge and mislyke of him and his gouernmentes by which means. he made his own sonn king which was henry Bullinbrocke

Remember also howe the duke of Lankaster asked A wise man, wher him selfe should ever be kinge And he told him no, but his sonn should be a kinge. And when he had told him, he hanged him vp for his Labor. because he should not brute yt abrod or speke ther of to others. This was a pollicie in the com̄on wealthes opinion But I sai yt was a villaines parte and a Iudas kisse to hange the man. for telling him the truth Beware by this Example of noble men / and of their fair wordes & sai lyttell to them, lest they doe the Like by thee for thy good will /

IN the Winters Talle at the glob 1611 the 15 of maye ☿ [Wednesday].

Obserue ther howe Lyontes the kinge of Cicillia was overcom wth Ielosy of his wife with the kinge of Bohemia his frind that came to see him. and howe he Contriued his death and wold haue had his cup berer to haue poisoned. who gaue the king of bohemia warning therof & fled with him to bohemia /

Reme*m*ber also howe he sent to the Orakell of appollo & the Aunswer of apollo. that she was giltles. and that the king was Ielouse &c and howe Except the child was found Again that was loste the kinge should die wthout yssue. for the child was caried into bohemia & ther laid in a forrest & brought vp by a sheppard And the kinge of bohemia his sonn maried that wentch & howe they fled into Cicillia to Leontes. and the sheppard hauing showed the letter of the noble man by whom Leontes sent a was [? *error for* away] that child and the Iewells found about her. she was knowen to be leontes daughter and was then 16 yers old

Remember also the Rog that cam in all tottered like coll pixci / . and howe he feyned him sicke & to haue bin Robbed of all that he had and howe he cosoned the por man of all his money. and after cam to the shep sher with a pedlers packe & ther cosoned them Again of all ther money And howe he changed apparrell wth the kinge of bomia his sonn. and then howe he turned Courtiar &c / beware of trustinge feined beggars or fawninge fellouse

7. **Codon:** error for "Codor" i.e. Cawdor.
14–15. **Mackbeth . . . Northumberland.** There seems to be confusion here in Forman's mind between Macbeth, who was made Thane of Cawdor, and Malcolm, who was made Prince of Cumberland. 24. **of:** off. 28. **on:** one.
68. **Innogen.** This is historically the correct form of the name and it has been suspected that the Fl form "Imogen" may be the result of compositorial (or scribal) misreading.
69. **whom . . . banished.** Cloten is not banished in the play.
88. **Richard the 2.** As noted above, this is not Shakespeare's play of that name, nor does it show any points of contact with the anonymous play *Woodstock* (c. 1591–95; sometimes called *1 Richard II*). The rebellion of Jack Straw is the subject of an anonymous play called *The Life and Death of Jack Straw* (c. 1590–93). 93. **major:** mayor.
156. **the Rog:** the rogue (Autolycus).
157. **coll pixci:** colt-pixie, a mischievous fairy.
160. **shep sher:** sheep shearing.
162. **bomia:** error for "Bohemia."

21. [*Henry VIII* and the Burning of the Globe]

A. Sir Henry Wotton, from a Letter to Sir Edmund Bacon, July 2, 1613

The burning of the Globe Theatre on June 29, 1613, during a performance (possibly the first) of *Henry VIII,* was a newsworthy event, of which several brief accounts survive. The earliest extant text of the one that follows is in *Letters of Sir Henry Wotton to Sir Edmund Bacon* (1661), p. 29.

. . . Now, to let matters of State sleep, I will entertain you at the present with what hath happened this week at the banks side. The Kings Players had a new Play, called *All is true*, representing some principall pieces of the raign of *Henry* 8. which was set forth with many extraordinary circumstances of Pomp and Majesty, even to the matting of the stage; the Knights of the Order, with their Georges and Garter, the Guards with their embroidered Coats, and the like: sufficient in truth within a while to make greatness very familiar, if not ridiculous. Now, King *Henry* making a Masque at the Cardinal *Wolsey*'s house, and certain Chambers being shot off at his entry, some of the paper, or other stuff wherewith one of them was stopped, did light on the thatch, where being thought at first but an idle smoak, and their eyes more attentive to the show, it kindled inwardly, and ran round like a train, consuming within less then an hour the whole house to the very grounds.

This was the fatal period of that vertuous fabrique; wherein yet nothing did perish, but wood and straw, and a few forsaken cloaks; only one man had his breeches set on fire, that would perhaps have broyled him, if he had not by the benefit of a provident wit put it out with bottle Ale. The rest when we meet: . . .

13. **Chambers:** small pieces of ordnance, used for firing salutes.
15. **thatch:** i.e. the thatched roofing of the galleries.

B. A Ballad on the Fire

Two ballads on the fire were entered on the Stationers' Register the day after it occurred. No copies of such printed ballads have survived, but it is possible that the following ballad was identical with one of the ballads then published. It was first printed in the *Gentleman's Magazine* (LXXXVI [1816], 114) by Joseph Hazlewood, "copied from an old manuscript volume of poems," and there is a nineteenth-century transcript in the Folger Shakespeare Library (Art Folio 271). Later Halliwell-Phillipps (*Outlines of the Life of Shakespeare*, 2nd ed., 1882, pp. 472–74) claimed to have printed his version ("Doubts having been suggested respecting the genuineness of this poem") from "an early seventeenth-century manuscript, of unquestionable authenticity, preserved in the library of Sir Mathew Wilson, Bart., of Eshton Hall, co. York." E. K. Chambers (*Elizabethan Stage*, 11, 420–22) notes that the Eshton collection had "recently been sold, with the verses, to Mr. G. D. Smith of New York." The present location of the manuscript (presumably the same as that referred to by Hazlewood) is unknown. The text below is based on that in Chambers, with a few adjustments in spelling from the earlier printings.

A Sonnett upon the pittifull burneing of the Globe playhowse in London.

Now sitt the downe, Melpomene,
  Wrapt in a sea-cole robe,
And tell the dolefull tragedie,
  That late was playd at Globe;
For noe man that can singe and saye
[But?] was scard on St. Peters daye.
    Oh sorrow, pittifull sorrow, and yett
      all this is true.

All yow that please to understand,
  Come listen to my storye,
To see Death with his rakeing brand
  Mongst such an auditorye;
Regarding neither Cardinalls might,
Nor yett the rugged face of Henry the Eight.
    Oh sorrow, &c.

This fearfull fire beganne above,
  A wonder strange and true,
And to the stage-howse did remove,
  As round as taylors clewe;
And burnt downe both beame and snagg,
And did not spare the silken flagg.
    Oh sorrow, &c.

Out runne the knightes, out runne the lordes,
  And there was great adoe;

Some lost their hattes, and some their swordes;
  Then out runne Burbidge too;
The reprobates, though druncke on Munday,
Prayd for the Foole and Henry Condye.
    Oh sorrow, &c.

The perrywigges and drumme-heades frye,
  Like to a butter firkin;
A wofull burneing did betide
  To many a good buffe jerkin.
Then with swolne eyes, like druncken
    Flemminges,
Distressed stood old stuttering Heminges.
    Oh sorrow, &c.

Noe shower his raine did there downe force
  In all that sunn-shine weather,
To save that great renowned howse;
  Nor thou, O ale-howse, neither.
Had itt begunne belowe, sans doubte,
Their wives for feare had pissed itt out.
    Oh sorrow, &c.

Bee warned, yow stage-strutters all,
  Least yow againe be catched,
And such a burneing doe befall,
  As to them whose howse was thatched;
Forbeare your whoreing, breeding biles,
And laye up that expence for tiles.
    Oh sorrow, &c.

Goe drawe yow a petition,
  And doe yow not abhorr itt,
And gett, with low submission,
  A licence to begg for itt
In churches, sans churchwardens checkes,
In Surrey and in Midlesex.
    Oh sorrow, pittifull sorrow, and yett
      all this is true.

2. **sea-cole:** black (like mineral coal), a proper robe for Melpomene, the muse of tragedy. Sea-coal fires are specifically associated with the theatre by Digges (see below, Number 26, line 54).
6. **[But?].** Some such addition seems necessary for the sense required.
7. **all . . . true.** This part of the refrain obviously reflects the title ("All is true") by which Sir Henry Wotton refers to the play we know as *Henry VIII.*
10. **rakeing:** fast-moving, roving. **brand:** knife, scythe.
13. **Eight:** eighth (note rhyme with *might*).
17. **stage-howse:** the theatre itself. **remove:** move, spread.
18. **round . . . clewe:** as round as a tailor's ball of thread (with special reference to both the general shape and name of the Globe Theatre).
19. **snagg:** angular beam support (?); *O.E.D.* offers no meaning that seems to fit the context.
20. **silken flagg:** the flag flown from the top of the theatre to show that a performance was in progress.
25, 27, 34. **Burbidge . . . Henry Condye . . . Heminges.** These men were all well-known actors belonging to Shakespeare's company, the King's Men. T. W. Baldwin (*The Organization and Personnel of the Shakespearean Company,* Princeton, 1927) suggests that Burbage took the part of Cardinal Wolsey, and Condell that of Buckingham. The reference to John Heminges is a little puzzling, since it is believed that he had retired from acting around 1611. The reference to "the Foole" in line 27 is also puzzling; no Fool's role seems called for in *Henry VIII.*
33. **eyes.** Hazlewood and the Folger transcript read "lipps" and "lips" respectively.
39. **ale-howse.** Another report (John Chamberlain to Sir Ralph Winwood, July 8, 1613) notes that "a dwelling-house adjoining" was also destroyed by the fire, perhaps the same as the ale-house here mentioned.
47. **biles:** boils, i.e. venereal sores.
48. **laye . . . tiles:** save up the money and spend it to roof your theatres with tiles (instead of thatch). Profiting by the hint, the rebuilt Globe (opened by June 30, 1614) appeared splendidly with tiled roofing.

21A. [*Titus Andronicus, The Winter's Tale, The Tempest*] Ben Jonson

In the Introduction to *Bartholomew Fair* (Herford and Simpson, volume VI, pp. 16–17), performed 1614, published 1631, Jonson writes disparagingly of old-fashioned taste in plays, linking *Titus Andronicus* to Kyd's *The Spanish Tragedy* (1592) as examples of outmoded drama. "Five and twenty, or thirty years" is presumably more an approximation then an exact recollection (see Frank Kermode's remarks on p. 1065). Jonson disapproves of the use of the unnatural in Shakespeare's late romances.

Hee that will sweare, *Ieronimo*, or *Andronicus* are the best playes, yet shall passe vnexcepted at, heere, as a man whose Iudgement shewes it is constant, and hath stood still, these fiue and twentie, or thirtie yeeres. Though it be an *Ignorance*, it is a vertuous and stay'd ignorance; . . . If there bee neuer a *Servant-monster* i'the *Fayre*; who can helpe it? he sayes; nor a nest of *Antiques*? Hee is loth to make Nature afraid in his *Playes*, like those that beget *Tales*, *Tempests*, and such like *Drolleries*, to mixe his head with other mens heeles, let the concupisence of *Iigges* and *Dances*, raigne as strong as it will amongst you: yet if the *Puppets* will please any body, they shall be entreated to come in.

1. **Ieronimo:** father of the murdered Horatio and vengeful protagonist of *The Spanish Tragedy.*
6. **Servant-monster.** Stephano and Trinculo refer to Caliban as "servant-monster" in *The Tempest,* at III.ii.3, 4, and 8.
7. **nest:** group. **Antiques:** antics; that is, clowns; perhaps referring to the twelve carters, shepherds, et al. who dance disguised as the punningly titled "Saltiers/Satyrs" in *The Winter's Tale,* IV.iv.
10. **concupisence:** extreme desire, lust. **of:** for.

III. Early Critical Comment on the Plays and Poems

22. Francis Meres, from *Palladis Tamia, Wits Treasury* (1598)

The following passages are from "A comparatiue discourse of our English Poets, with the Greeke, Latine, and Italian Poets" (fols. 279–87). The standard edition of this section of Meres's treatise is that of D. C. Allen (Urbana, Illinois, 1933).

As the Greeke tongue is made famous and eloquent by *Homer, Hesiod, Euripides, Aeschilus, Sophocles, Pindarus, Phocylides* and *Aristophanes;* and the Latine tongue by *Virgill, Ouid, Horace, Silius Italicus, Lucanus, Lucretius, Ausonius* and *Claudianus:* so the English tongue is mightily enriched, and gorgeouslie inuested in rare ornaments and resplendent abiliments by sir *Philip Sidney, Spencer, Daniel, Drayton, Warner, Shakespeare, Marlow* and *Chapman.* . . .

As the soule of *Euphorbus* was thought to liue in *Pythagoras:* so the sweete wittie soule of *Ouid* liues in mellifluous & hony-tongued *Shakespeare,* witnes his *Venus* and *Adonis,* his *Lucrece,* his sugred Sonnets among his priuate friends, &c.

As *Plautus* and *Seneca* are accounted the best for Comedy and Tragedy among the Latines: so *Shakespeare* among the English is the most excellent in both kinds for the stage; for Comedy, witnes his *Gentlemen of Verona,* his *Errors,* his *Loue labors lost,* his *Loue labours wonne,* his *Midsummers night dreame,* & his *Merchant of Venice:* for Tragedy his *Richard the 2. Richard the 3. Henry the 4. King Iohn, Titus Andronicus* and his *Romeo* and *Iuliet.*

As *Epius Stolo* said, that the Muses would speake with *Plautus* tongue, if they would speak Latin: so I say that the Muses would speak with *Shakespeares* fine filed phrase, if they would speake English. . . .

As *Ouid* saith of his worke; *Iamque opus exegi, quod Iouis ira, nec ignis, Nec poterit ferrum, nec edax abolere vetustas.* And as *Horace* saith of his; *Exegi monumentum aere perennius; Regalique situ pyramidum altius; Quod non imber edax; Non Aquilo impotens possit diruere; aut innumerabilis annorum series & fuga temporum:* so say I seuerally of sir *Philip Sidneys, Spencers, Daniels, Draytons, Shakespeares,* and *Warners workes;*

Non Iouis ira: imbres: Mars: ferrum: flamma, senectus,
Hoc opus vnda: lues: turbo: venena ruent. . . .

As *Pindarus, Anacreon* and *Callimachus* among the Greekes; and *Horace* and *Catullus* among the Latines are the best Lyrick Poets: so in this faculty the best among our Poets are *Spencer* (who excelleth in all kinds) *Daniel, Drayton, Shakespeare, Bretton.*

As these Tragicke Poets flourished in Greece, *Aeschylus, Euripides, Sophocles, Alexander Aetolus, Achaeus Erithriaeus, Astydamas Atheniensis, Apollodorus Tarsensis, Nicomachus Phrygius, Thespis Atticus,* and *Timon Apolloniates;* and these among the Latines, *Accius, M. Attilius, Pomponius Secundus* and *Seneca:* so these are our best for Tragedie, the Lorde *Buckhurst,* Doctor *Leg* of Cambridge, Doctor *Edes* of Oxforde, maister *Edward Ferris,* the Authour of the *Mirrour for Magistrates, Marlow, Peele, Watson, Kid, Shakespeare, Drayton, Chapman, Decker,* and *Beniamin Iohnson.* . . .

The best Poets for Comedy among the Greeks are these, *Menander, Aristophanes, Eupolis Atheniensis, Alexis Terius, Nicostratus, Amipsias Atheniensis, Anaxandrides Rhodius, Aristonymus, Archippus Atheniensis* and *Callias Atheniensis;* and among the Latines, *Plautus, Terence, Naeuius, Sext. Turpilius, Licinius Imbrex,* and *Virgilius Romanus:* so the best for Comedy amongst vs bee, *Edward* Earle of Oxforde, Doctor *Gager* of Oxforde, Maister *Rowley* once a rare Scholler of learned Pembrooke Hall in Cambridge, Maister *Edwardes* one of her Maiesties Chappell, eloquent and wittie *Iohn Lilly, Lodge, Gascoyne, Greene, Shakespeare, Thomas Nash, Thomas Heywood, Anthony Mundye* our best plotter, *Chapman, Porter, Wilson, Hathway,* and *Henry Chettle.* . . .

As these are famous among the Greeks for Elegie, *Melanthus, Mymnerus Colophonius, Olympius Mysius, Parthenius Nicaeus, Philetas Cous, Theogenes Megarensis,* and *Pigres Halicarnassaeus;* and these among the Latines, *Mecaenas, Ouid, Tibullus, Propertius, T. Valgius, Cassius Seuerus* & *Clodius Sabinus:* so these are the most passionate among vs to bewaile and bemoane the perplexities of Loue, *Henrie Howard* Earle of Surrey, sir *Thomas Wyat* the elder, sir *Francis Brian,* sir *Philip Sidney,* sir *Walter Rawley,* sir *Edward Dyer, Spencer, Daniel, Drayton, Shakespeare, Whetstone, Gascoyne, Samuell Page* sometimes fellowe of *Corpus Christi* Colledge in Oxford, *Churchyard, Bretton.*

20. **Loue labours wonne.** The play has not survived, at least under this name. It is now known, however, that a play with this title was among the printed stock of a bookseller in 1603, in whose catalogue it is listed immediately following Shakespeare's *Love's Labor's Lost* (see T. W. Baldwin, *Shakspere's "Love's Labor's Won"* [Carbondale, Illinois, 1957]).
28–30. **Iamque . . . vetustas.** From *Metamorphoses,* XV, 871–72: "And now my work is done, which neither the wrath of Jove, nor fire, nor sword, nor the gnawing tooth of time shall ever be able to undo" (Loeb trans.).
30–34. **Exegi . . . temporum.** From *Odes,* III, xxx, 1–5: "I have finished a monument more lasting than bronze and loftier than the Pyramids' royal pile, one that no wasting rain, no furious north wind can destroy, or the countless chain of years and the ages' flight" (Loeb trans.).
37–38. **Non . . . ruent.** Apparently Meres's imitation of the quotations above: "Not the wrath of Jove, nor storms of rain, nor war, nor sword, nor fire, nor age, nor flood, nor plague, nor whirlwind, nor poison shall bring this work to ruin."

22A. John Davies of Hereford

A poet and writing-master, Davies (1565?–1618) was a voluminous writer who mentioned Shakespeare and Burbage together in his lengthy treatise on physiological and psychological matters, *Microcosmos.* Two years later, he again linked them in what appear to be their frustrated dramatic efforts. Five years after that, he addressed to Shakespeare one of his more than three hundred epigrams, noting that Shakespeare, as an actor, sometimes played the part of the king.

(a) [From *Microcosmos* (1603), st. 627.]

Players, I loue yee, and your *Qualitie*,
As ye are Men, that pass time not abus'd:
And some I love for *painting, poesie* [*in margin, glossing* "some," W. S. R. B.],
And say fell *Fortune* cannot be excus'd,
That hath for better *uses* you refus'd:
Wit, Courage, good shape, good partes, and all *good*,
As long as all these *goods* are no *worse* us'd,
And though the *stage* doth staine pure gentle *blood*,
Yet generous yee are in *minde* and *moode*.

1. **Qualitie:** both "profession" and "skill."
3. **W. S.:** William Shakespeare. **R. B.:** Richard Burbage. The two are linked in terms of painting and poetry in the creating of the impresa of the Earl of Rutland in 1613.
4. **fell:** cruel.

(b) [From *The Civile Warres of Death and Fortune* (1605), st. 76.]

Some followed her by acting all mens parts [*in margin*, Stage plaiers],
These on a Stage she rais'd (in scorne) to fall:
And made them Mirrors, by their acting Arts,
Wherin men saw their faults, thogh ne'r so small:
Yet some she guerdond not, to their desarts [*in margin*, W. S. R. B.];
But, othersome, were but ill-Action all:
Who while they acted ill, ill staid behinde,
(By custom of their maners) in their minde.

5. **guerdond:** rewarded.

(c) [From *The Scourge of Folly* (1610), Epigram 159.]

To our English Terence, Mr. Will.
Shake-speare.

Some say (good *Will*) which I, in sport, do sing,
Had'st thou not plaid some Kingly parts in sport,
Thou hadst bin a companion for a *King*;
And, beene a King among the meaner sort.
Some others raile; but, raile as they thinke fit,
Thou hast no rayling, but, a raigning Wit:
And honesty *thou sow'st, which they do reape;*
So, to increase their Stocke *which they do keepe.*

23. Francis Beaumont, from "To M[r] B: J: [Ben Jonson]"

The poem in which the following lines appear was first printed complete by E. K. Chambers in *William Shakespeare*, II, 224, from the Holgate MS, fol. 110 (Pierpont Morgan Library). In line 17 the Holgate MS reads "deere" (so also in the copy in British Museum, Additional MS. 30982); "cleere" is Chambers' emendation. The poem was written about 1615. Its reference to Shakespeare is particularly interesting as being the earliest example of the *"lusus naturae"* view of him as one who wrote "naturally" without the help of "learning." Compare the quotations from Milton, below.

. . . here I would let slippe
(If I had any in mee) schollershippe,
And from all Learninge keepe these lines as [cl]eere
as Shakespeares best are, which our heires shall heare
Preachers apte to their auditors to showe
how farr sometimes a mortall man may goe
by the dimme light of Nature, . . .

24. William Basse, "On Mr. Wm. Shakespeare"

The following verses, written between 1616 and (probably) 1623, circulated widely in various manuscript versions (the Folger Shakespeare Library possesses at least seven); they are here reprinted from British Museum, Lansdowne MS. 777, fol. 67[v]. They were published among Donne's poems in 1633 (omitted in 1635 edition) and in *Poems: written by Wil. Shake-speare. Gent.* (1640, sig. K8[v]), where they are attributed to "W. B.".

On Mr. Wm. Shakespeare.
he dyed in Aprill 1616.

Renowned Spencer lye a thought more nye
To learned Chaucer, and rare Beaumond lye
A little neerer Spenser to make roome
For Shakespeare in your threefold fowerfold Tombe.
To lodge all fowre in one bed make a shift
Vntill Doomesday, for hardly will a fift
Betwixt this day and that by Fate be slayne
For whom your Curtaines may be drawn againe.
If your precedency in death doth barre
A fourth place in your sacred sepulcher,
Vnder this carued marble of thine owne
Sleepe rare Tragœdian Shakespeare, sleep alone,
Thy vnmolested peace, vnshared Caue,
Possesse as Lord not Tenant of thy Graue,
That vnto us & others it may be
Honor hereafter to be layde by thee.
Wm. Basse.

25. John Milton, "What neede my Shakespeare"

This poem appears among the preliminaries to the Shakespeare Second Folio (1632). It is dated 1630 in Milton's *Poems* (1645), and appears also in *Poems: written by Wil. Shakespeare. Gent.* (1640), sig. K8.

An Epitaph on the admirable Dramaticke Poet,
W. Shakespeare.

What neede my *Shakespeare* for his honour'd bones,
The labour of an Age, in piled stones
Or that his hallow'd Reliques should be hid
Vnder a starre-ypointing Pyramid?
Deare Sonne of Memory, great Heire of *Fame*,
What needst thou such dull witnesse of thy Name?
Thou in our wonder and astonishment
Hast built thy selfe a lasting Monument:
For whil'st to th' shame of slow-endevouring Art
Thy easie numbers flow, and that each part
Hath from the leaves of thy unvalued Booke,
Those Delphicke Lines with deepe Impression tooke
Then thou our fancy of her selfe bereaving,
Dost make us Marble with too much conceiving,
And so Sepulcher'd in such pompe dost lie
That Kings for such a Tombe would wish to die.

1. **neede.** The 1645 text reads "needs" and makes other changes as follows: "weak" for "dull" (line 6); "live-long" for "lasting" (line 8); "heart" for "part" (line 10); "it self" for "her selfe" (line 13).
9–14. **For . . . conceiving.** Milton again voices the contrast between "nature" and "art" in his reference to Shakespeare in "L'Allegro," lines 131–34:

> Then to the well-trod stage anon,
> If *Jonsons* learned Sock be on,
> Or sweetest *Shakespear* fancies childe,
> Warble his native Wood-notes wilde, . . .

Cf. Francis Beaumont's verses "To M^r^ B: J:", above.
11. **unvalued:** invaluable.

26. Leonard Digges, "Poets are borne not made"

The following commendatory poem is prefixed to *Poems: written by Wil. Shake-speare. Gent.* (1640), sigs. *3–4. Leonard Digges (1588–1635), poet and translator, scholar and traveller, was closely associated with Oxford University. Another poem by Digges appears among the preliminary matter to the Shakespeare First Folio; see above, p. 103.

Poets are borne not made, when I would prove
This truth, the glad rememberance I must love
Of never dying *Shakespeare*, who alone,
Is argument enough to make that one.
First, that he was a Poet none would doubt,
That heard th' applause of what he sees set out
Imprinted; where thou hast (I will not say
Reader his Workes for to contrive a Play:
To him twas none) the patterne of all wit,
Art without Art unparaleld as yet.
Next Nature onely helpt him, for looke thorow
This whole Booke, thou shalt find he doth not borrow,
One phrase from Greekes, nor Latines imitate,
Nor once from vulgar Languages Translate,
Nor Plagiari-like from others gleane,
Nor begges he from each witty friend a Scene
To peece his Acts with, all that he doth write,
Is pure his owne, plot, language exquisite,
But oh! what praise more powerfull can we give
The dead, than that by him the Kings men live,
His Players, which should they but have shar'd the Fate,
All else expir'd within the short Termes date;
How could the Globe have prospered, since through want
Of change, the Plaies and Poems had growne scant.
But happy Verse thou shalt be sung and heard,
When hungry quills shall be such honour bard.
Then vanish upstart Writers to each Stage,
You needy Poetasters of this Age,
Where *Shakespeare* liv'd or spake, Vermine forbeare,
Least with your froth you spot them, come not neere;
But if you needs must write, if poverty
So pinch, that otherwise you starve and die,
On Gods name may the Bull or Cockpit have
Your lame blancke Verse, to keepe you from the grave:
Or let new Fortunes younger brethren see,
What they can picke from your leane industry.
I doe not wonder when you offer at
Blacke-Friers, that you suffer: tis the fate
Of richer veines, prime judgements that have far'd
The worse, with this deceased man compar'd.
So have I seene, when Cesar would appeare,
And on the Stage at halfe-sword parley were,
Brutus and *Cassius*: oh how the Audience,
Were ravish'd, with what wonder they went thence,
When some new day they would not brooke a line,
Of tedious (though well laboured) *Catilines;*
Sejanus too was irkesome, they priz'de more
Honest *Iago*, or the jealous Moore.
And though the Fox and subtill Alchimist,
Long intermitted could not quite be mist,
Though these have sham'd all the Ancients, and might raise,
Their Authours merit with a crowne of Bayes.
Yet these sometimes, even at a friends desire
Acted, have scarce defrai'd the Seacoale fire
And doore-keepers: when let but *Falstaffe* come,
Hall, Poines, the rest you scarce shall have a roome
All is so pester'd: let but *Beatrice*
And *Benedicke* be seene, loe in a trice
The Cockpit Galleries, Boxes, all are full
To heare *Maluoglio* that crosse garter'd Gull.
Briefe, there is nothing in his wit fraught Booke,
Whose sound we would not heare; on whose worth looke
Like old coynd gold, whose lines, in every page,
Shall passe true currant to succeeding age.
But why doe I dead *Sheakspeares* praise recite,
Some second *Shakespeare* must of *Shakespeare* write;
For me tis needlesse, since an host of men
Will pay to clap his praise, to free my pen.

Leon. Digges.

1. **Poets . . . made.** A version of the anonymous Latin tag (perhaps adapted from Florus) *Poeta nascitur non fit*; a commonplace of the period.
7. **say.** The 1640 text wrongly reads "say)".
10–18. **Art without Art . . . exquisite.** Here again is the view of Shakespeare as Nature's child. Cf. the poems by Francis Beaumont and John Milton. The assertion of Shakespeare's complete originality is, of course, nonsense in the terms here defined. 20. **Kings men**: Shakespeare's company.
23. **the Globe**: the playhouse of the King's Men, rebuilt 1614.
33. **Bull or Cockpit**: the Red Bull and the Cockpit, two other theatres, described here as offering inferior plays and performances.
35. **new Fortunes.** A reference to the rebuilt Fortune Theatre of 1623.
38. **Blacke-Friers**: the Second Blackfriars Theatre, acquired by the King's Men in 1608 and used by them until 1642.
42. **halfe-sword parley.** A reference to the quarrel scene between Brutus and Cassius (*Julius Caesar*, IV.iii).
46–47. **Catilines; Sejanus.** Ben Jonson's two coldly received tragedies. The name of the first is *Catiline*; that "*Catilines*" is a misprint, not an inflected form, is shown by the preceding rhyme-word, "line".
48. **Honest . . . Moore.** In Shakespeare's *Othello*.
49. **the Fox . . . Alchimist.** Jonson's two most famous comedies ("the Fox" = *Volpone*; Subtle is the name of the title-role in *The Alchemist*).
55–56. **Falstaffe . . . Poines.** In Shakespeare's *1* and *2 Henry IV*. *Hall* = *Hal*.
57–58. **Beatrice And Benedicke.** In Shakespeare's *Much Ado about Nothing*.
59. **Cockpit**: i.e. the standing room around the raised stage.
60. **Maluoglio**: i.e. Malvolio, in Shakespeare's *Twelfth Night*.

27. Ben Jonson, from *Timber: or, Discoveries; Made upon Men and Matter*

With this extract (pp. 97–98 in *Works* [1640], sig. *N3*) compare the two sets of commendatory verses by Jonson in the preliminaries to the Shakespeare First Folio (pp. 58, 65–66, above). In his "Conversations with Drummond" (1619) Jonson tersely remarked "That Shaksperr wanted Arte."

De Shake-speare nostrat.

I remember, the Players have often mentioned it as an honour to *Shakespeare*, that in his writing, (whatsoever he penn'd) hee never blotted out line. My answer hath beene, would he had blotted a thousand. Which they thought a malevolent speech. I had not told posterity this, but for their ignorance, who choose that circumstance to commend their friend by, wherein he most faulted. And to justifie mine owne candor, (for I lov'd the man, and doe honour his memory (on this side Idolatry) as much as any.) Hee was (indeed) honest, and of an open, and free nature: had an excellent *Phantsie;* brave notions, and gentle expressions: wherein hee flow'd with that facility, that sometime it was necessary he should be stop'd: *Sufflaminandus erat;* as *Augustus* said of *Haterius*. *Augustus in Hat.* His wit was in his owne power; would the rule of it had beene so too. Many times hee fell into those things, could not escape laughter: As when hee said in the person of *Cæsar*, one speaking to him; *Cæsar thou dost me wrong*. Hee replyed: *Cæsar did never wrong, but with just cause:* and such like; which were ridiculous. But hee redeemed his vices, with his vertues. There was ever more in him to be praysed, then to be pardoned.

MARGINAL HEADING. **De Shakespeare nostrat.**: "Concerning our Shakespeare" ("*nostrat.*" being an abbreviated form for *nostrati*).
3–4. **hee . . . line.** Cf. Heminge and Condell's "To the great Variety of Readers," prefixed to the First Folio: "And what he thought, he vttered with that easinesse, that wee haue scarse receiued from him a blot in his papers." It has been suggested that Jonson may have aided Heminge and Condell in writing this preface. 12. **Phantsie**: imagination.
15. **Sufflaminandus erat**: "He needed the drag-chain" (adapted from Marcus Seneca's *Controversiae*, IV, preface). Quintus Haterius was a Roman rhetorician (died A.D. 26). The marginal heading means "Augustus on Hat[erius]."
19–22. **hee . . . cause.** For a full discussion of this passage, see *Ben Jonson*, ed. C. H. Herford and Percy and Evelyn Simpson (Oxford, 1952), XI, 231–33. Cf. *Julius Caesar*, III.i.47–48, "Know, Caesar doth not wrong, nor without cause / Will he be satisfied." It is possible that Jonson here quotes an earlier version of the passage.

28. Margaret Cavendish, Duchess of Newcastle, from *CCXI. Sociable Letters* (1664)

Margaret Cavendish was a bluestocking and, with her husband, William Cavendish, Duke of Newcastle, much interested in literature. She published extensively, if not always wisely, poems, plays, and the series of letters here drawn upon. In the following letter (No. CXXIII, pp. 244–48) she anticipates Dryden in being the first to give a general prose assessment of Shakespeare as dramatist.

Madam,

I Wonder how that Person you mention in your Letter, could either have the Conscience, or Confidence to Dispraise *Shakespear*'s Playes, as to say they were made up onely with Clowns, Fools, Watchmen, and the like; But to Answer that Person, though *Shakespear*'s Wit will Answer for himself, I say, that it seems by his Judging, or Censuring, he Understands not Playes, or Wit; for to Express Properly, Rightly, Usually, and Naturally, a Clown's, or Fool's Humour, Expressions, Phrases, Garbs, Manners, Actions, Words, and Course of Life, is as Witty, Wise, Judicious, Ingenious, and Observing, as to Write and Express the Expressions, Phrases, Garbs, Manners, Actions, Words, and Course of Life, of Kings and Princes; and to Express Naturally, to the Life, a Mean Country Wench, as a Great Lady, a Courtesan, as a Chast Woman, a Mad man, as a Man in his right Reason and Senses, a Drunkard, as a Sober man, a Knave, as an Honest man, and so a Clown, as a Well-bred man, and a Fool, as a Wise man; nay, it Expresses and Declares a Greater Wit, to Express, and Deliver to Posterity, the Extravagancies of Madness, the Subtilty of Knaves, the Ignorance of Clowns, and the Simplicity of Naturals, or the Craft of Feigned Fools, than to Express Regularities, Plain Honesty, Courtly Garbs, or Sensible Discourses, for 'tis harder to Express Nonsense than Sense, and Ordinary Conversations, than that which is Unusual; and 'tis Harder, and Requires more Wit to Express a Jester, than a Grave Statesman; yet *Shakespear* did not want Wit, to Express to the Life all Sorts of Persons, of what Quality, Profession, Degree, Breeding, or Birth soever; nor did he want Wit to Express the Divers, and Different Humours, or Natures, or Several Passions in Mankind; and so Well he hath Express'd in his Playes all Sorts of Persons, as one would think he had been Transformed into every one of those Persons he hath Described; and as sometimes one would think he was Really himself the Clown or Jester he Feigns, so one would think, he was also the King, and Privy Counsellor; also as one would think he were Really the Coward he Feigns, so one would think he were the most Valiant, and Experienced Souldier; Who would not think he had been such a man as his Sir *John Falstaff*? and who would not think he had been *Harry* the Fifth? & certainly *Julius Caesar*, *Augustus Caesar*, and *Antonius*, did never Really Act their parts Better, if so Well, as he hath Described them, and I believe that *Antonius* and *Brutus* did not Speak Better to the People, than he hath Feign'd them; nay, one would think that he had been Metamorphosed from a Man to a Woman, for who could Describe *Cleopatra* Better than he hath done, and many other Females of his own Creating, as *Nan Page*, Mrs. *Page*, Mrs. *Ford*, the Doctors Maid, *Bettrice*, Mrs. *Quickly*, *Doll Tearsheet*, and others, too many to Relate? and in his Tragick Vein, he Presents Passions so Naturally, and Misfortunes so Probably, as he Peirces the Souls of his Readers with such a True Sense and Feeling thereof, that it Forces Tears through their Eyes, and almost Perswades them, they are Really

Actors, or at least Present at those Tragedies. Who would not Swear he had been a Noble Lover, that could Woo so well? and there is not any person he hath Described in his Book, but his Readers might think they were Well acquainted with them; indeed *Shakespear* had a Clear Judgment, a Quick Wit, a Spreading Fancy, a Subtil Observation, a Deep Apprehension, and a most Eloquent Elocution; truly, he was a Natural Orator, as well as a Natural Poet, and he was not an Orator to Speak Well only on some Subjects, as Lawyers, who can make Eloquent Orations at the Bar, and Plead Subtilly and Wittily in Law-Cases, or Divines, that can Preach Eloquent Sermons, or Dispute Subtilly and Wittily in Theology, but take them from that, and put them to other Subjects, and they will be to seek; but *Shakespear*'s Wit and Eloquence was General, for, and upon all Subjects, he rather wanted Subjects for his Wit and Eloquence to Work on, for which he was Forced to take some of his Plots out of History, where he only took the Bare Designs, the Wit and Language being all his Own; and so much he had above others, that those, who Writ after him, were Forced to Borrow of him, or rather to Steal from him; I could mention Divers Places, that others of our Famous Poets have Borrow'd, or Stoln, but lest I should Discover the Persons, I will not Mention the Places, or Parts, but leave it to those that Read his Playes, and others, to find them out. I should not have needed to Write this to you, for his Works would have Declared the same Truth: But I believe, those that Dispraised his Playes, Dispraised them more out of Envy, than Simplicity or Ignorance, for those that could Read his Playes, could not be so Foolish to Condemn them, only the Excellency of them caused an Envy to them. By this we may perceive, Envy doth not Leave a man in the Grave, it Follows him after Death, unless a man be Buried in Oblivion, but if he Leave any thing to be Remembred, Envy and Malice will be still throwing Aspersion upon it, or striving to Pull it down by Detraction. But leaving *Shakespear*'s Works to their own Defence, and his Detractors to their Envy, and you to your better Imployments, than Reading my Letter, I rest,

Madam,

Your faithful Friend
and humble Servant.

4–6. Shakespear's Playes . . . like. A somewhat similar attitude toward Shakespeare's wit is found in William Cartwright's second poem to John Fletcher (lines 69–71): "*Shakespeare* to [i.e. compared to] thee was dull, whose best jest lyes / I'th Ladies questions, and the Fooles replyes; / Old Fashion'd wit, . . ." (*Plays and Poems*, ed. G. B. Evans, 1951, p. 521). In line 75 Cartwright adds: "Nature was all his Art," thus aligning himself with the views of Francis Beaumont, Milton, etc.
56–57. Doctors Maid, Bettrice, Mrs. Quickly. The Duchess seems to forget that Mrs. Quickly of *1* and *2 Henry IV* also appears as Dr. Caius' servant in *The Merry Wives of Windsor*. Bettrice is presumably the Beatrice of *Much Ado about Nothing*. **78. to seek:** at a loss.

29. John Dryden

A. From *An Essay of Dramatick Poesie* (1668), pp. 47–48

To begin then with *Shakespeare*; he was the man who of all Modern, and perhaps Ancient Poets, had the largest and most comprehensive soul. All the Images of Nature were still present to him, and he drew them not laboriously, but luckily: when he describes any thing, you more than see it, you feel it too. Those who accuse him to have wanted learning, give him the greater commendation: he was naturally learn'd; he needed not the spectacles of Books to read Nature; he look'd inwards, and found her there. I cannot say he is every where alike; were he so, I should do him injury to compare him with the greatest of Mankind. He is many times flat, insipid; his Comick wit degenerating into clenches, his serious swelling into Bombast. But he is always great, when some great occasion is presented to him: no man can say he ever had a fit subject for his wit, and did not then raise himself as high above the rest of Poets,

Quantum lenta solent inter viburna cupressi.

The consideration of this made Mr. *Hales* of *Eaton* say, That there was no subject of which any Poet ever writ, but he would produce it much better treated of in *Shakespeare*; and however others are now generally prefer'd before him, yet the Age wherein he liv'd, which had contemporaries with him, *Fletcher* and *Johnson*, never equall'd them to him in their esteem: And in the last Kings Court, when *Ben's* reputation was at highest, Sir *John Suckling*, and with him the greater part of the Courtiers, set our *Shakespeare* far above him.

B. From the Preface to *Troilus and Cressida* (1679), sigs. A4^v, b2, b3^v

. . . In the age of that Poet [Aeschylus], the *Greek* tongue was arriv'd to its full perfection; they had then amongst them an exact Standard of Writing, and of Speaking: The *English* Language is not capable of such a certainty; and we are at present so far from it, that we are wanting in the very Foundation of it, a perfect Grammar. Yet it must be allow'd to the present Age, that the tongue in general is so much refin'd since *Shakespear's* time, that many of his words, and more of his Phrases, are scarce intelligible. And of those which we understand some are ungrammatical, others course; and his whole stile is so pester'd with Figurative expressions, that it is as affected as it is obscure. 'Tis true, that in his later Plays he had worn off somewhat of the rust; but the Tragedy [*Troilus and Cressida*] which I have undertaken to correct, was, in all probability, one of his first endeavours on the Stage. . . .

If *Shakespear* be allow'd, as I think he must, to have made his Characters distinct, it will easily be infer'd that he understood the nature of the Passions: because it has been prov'd already, that confus'd passions make undistinguishable Characters: yet I cannot deny that he has his failings: but they are not so much in the passions themselves, as in his manner of expression: he often obscures his meaning by his words, and sometimes makes it unintelligible. I will not say of so great a Poet, that he distinguish'd not the blown puffy stile, from true sublimity; but I may venture to maintain that the fury of his fancy often transported him, beyond the bounds of Judgment, either in coyning of new words and phrases, or racking words which were in use, into the violence of a Catachresis: 'Tis not that I would explode the use of Metaphors from passions, for *Longinus* thinks 'em necessary to raise it; but to use 'em at every word, to say nothing without a Metaphor, a Simile, an Image, or description, is I doubt to smell a little too strongly of the Buskin. . . .

. . . If *Shakespear* were stript of all the Bombast in his passions, and dress'd in the most vulgar words, we should find the beauties of his thoughts remaining; if his embroideries were burnt down, there would still be silver at the bottom of the melting-pot: but I fear (at least, let me fear it for my self) that we who Ape his sounding words, have nothing of his thought, but are all out-side; there is not so much as a dwarf within our Giants cloaths. . . .

An Essay of Dramatick Poesie. 4–5. **he . . . luckily.** Dryden here picks up the view of Shakespeare, earlier encountered in the selections from Francis Beaumont, Milton, and Jonson, as Nature's child. As he says (line 8), "he was naturally learn'd."

14. **clenches:** puns, quibbles.
19. **Quantum . . . cupressi.** From Virgil, *Eclogues*, I, 25: "as cypresses oft do among the bending osiers" (Loeb trans.). The 1668 edition wrongly reads "*viberna*".
20–21. **Mr. Hales of Eaton:** John Hales (1584–1656), a Fellow of Eton College. Rowe, in his "Life of Shakespeare" (*Works*, 1709), tells us that "In a Conversation between Sir *John Suckling*, Sir *William D'Avenant*, *Endymion Porter*, Mr. *Hales* of *Eaton*, and *Ben Johnson*; Sir *John Suckling*, who was a profess'd Admirer of *Shakespear*, had undertaken his Defence against *Ben Johnson* with some warmth; Mr. *Hales*, who had sat still for some time, hearing *Ben* frequently reproaching him with the want of Learning, and Ignorance of the Antients, told him at last, *That if Mr.* Shakespear *had not read the Antients, he had likewise not stollen any thing from 'em*; (a Fault the other made no Conscience of) *and that if he would produce any one Topick finely treated by any of them, he would undertake to shew something upon the same Subject at least as well written by* Shakespear."

THE PREFACE TO *Troilus and Cressida*. 8–9. **the tongue . . . Shakespear's time.** Dryden here expresses the common attitude of Restoration writers toward the language of Shakespeare and other Elizabethan-Jacobean writers.
17–18. **one . . . stage.** Modern criticism would, of course, deny that *Troilus and Cressida* is one of Shakespeare's early plays; it is now generally dated 1601–2.
20. **distinct:** i.e. individual entities.
34. **Catachresis:** abuse of metaphor, misuse of words. **explode:** reject.
39. **Buskin:** the boot worn by actors in Greek tragedy; hence, here, the high style associated with tragedy.
41. **vulgar:** commonplace, everyday.
47–48. **dwarf . . . cloaths.** Cf. *Macbeth*, V.ii.21–22: ". . . like a giant's robe / Upon a dwarfish thief."

IV. Documents Relating to the Theatre

30. Contract for the Building of the Fortune Theatre, Drawn between Philip Henslowe, Edward Alleyn, and Peter Street, January 8, 1600

The original document is among the Alleyn Papers at Dulwich College (Muniment No. 22). Apart from its importance as the fullest physical description we possess of an Elizabethan public playhouse, it is of great interest for its frequent, if infuriatingly general, references to the Globe Theatre. The Fortune, built originally for the Admiral's Men, was situated in the Parish of St. Giles without Cripplegate. Henslowe's contract (dated August 29, 1613) for the Hope Theatre, with frequent references to the Swan as its model, also survives among the Alleyn Papers (Muniment No. 49); see Chambers, *The Elizabethan Stage* (1923), II, 466–68.

This Indenture made the Eighte daie of Ianuarye 1599 And in the Twoe and Fortyth yeare of the Reigne of our sovereigne Ladie Elizabeth by the grace of god Queene of Englande ffraunce and Irelande defender of the ffaythe &c Betwene Phillipp Henslowe and Edwarde Allen of the parishe of Ste Saviors in Southwark in the Countie of Surrey gentlemen on thone parte And Peeter Streete Cittizen and Carpenter of London on thother parte **witnesseth** That whereas the saide Phillipp Henslowe & Edward Allen the daie of the date hereof Haue bargayned Compounded & agreed wth the saide Peter Streete ffor the erectinge buildinge & settinge upp of a newe howse and Stadge, for a Plaiehowse in and vppon a certeine plott or parcell of grounde appoynted oute for that purpose Scytuate and beinge nere Goldinge lane in the parishe of Ste Giles wthoute Cripplegate of London To be by him the saide Peeter Streete or som̄e other sufficyent woorkmen of his provideinge and appoyntemte and att his propper Costes & Chardges for the consideracion hereafter in theis pre*sen*tes expressed Made erected, builded and sett upp In manner & forme followeinge (that is to saie) The frame of the saide howse to be sett square and to conteine ffowerscore foote of Lawfull assize everye waie square wthoute, and fiftie fiue foote of like assize square everye waie wthin, wth a good suer and stronge foundacion of pyles brick Lyme and sand, bothe wthoute & wthin, to be wroughte one foote of assize att the Leiste aboue the grounde And the saide fframe to conteine Three Stories in heighth The first or Lower Storie to Conteine Twelue foote of Lawfull assize in heighth The second Storie Eleaven foote of Lawfull assize in heigth And the Third or vpper Storie to conteine Nyne foote of Lawfull assize in height. **All which** Stories shall conteine Twelue foote and a half of lawfull assize in breadth througheoute besides a Iuttey forwardes in eyther of the saide Twoe vpper Stories of Tenne ynches of Lawfull assize, wth ffower convenient divisions for gentlemens roomes and other sufficient and convenient divisions for Twoe pennie roomes wth necessarie Seates to be placed and sett Aswell in those roomes as througheoute all the rest of the galleries of the saide howse and wth suche like steares Conveyances & divisions wthoute & wthin as are made & Contryved in and to the late erected Plaiehowse On the Banck in the saide parishe of Ste Savio^{rs} Called the Globe wth a Stadge and Tyreinge howse to be made erected & settupp wthin the saide fframe, wth a shadowe or cover over the saide Stadge, wch Stadge shalbe placed & sett As alsoe the stearecases of the saide fframe in suche sorte as is prefigured in a Plott thereof drawen And wch Stadge shall conteine in length ffortie and Three foote of lawfull assize and in breadth to extende to the middle of the yarde of the saide howse, The same Stadge to be paled in belowe wth good stronge and sufficyent newe oken bourdes And likewise the Lower Storie of the saide fframe wthinside, and the same lower storie to be alsoe laide over and fenced wth stronge yron pykes And the saide Stadge to be in all other proporcions Contryved and fashioned Like vnto the Stadge of the saide Plaiehowse Called the Globe, wth convenient windowes and lightes glazed to the saide Tyreinge howse And the saide fframe Stadge and Stearecases to be covered wth Tyle, and to haue a sufficient gutter of Lead to Carrie & convey the water frome the Coveringe of the saide Stadge to fall backwardes And alsoe all the saide fframe and the Staircases thereof to be sufficyently enclosed wthoute wth Lathe Lyme & haire and the gentlemens roomes and Twoe pennie roomes to be seeled wth Lathe Lyme & haire and all the fflowers of the saide Galleries Stories and Stadge to be bourded wth good & sufficyent newe deale bourdes of the whole thicknes wheare need shalbe. **And** the saide howse and other thinges beforemencioned to be made & doen To be in all other Contrivitions Conveyances fashions thinge and thinges effected finished and doen according to the manner and fashion of the saide howse Called the Globe Saveinge only that all the princypall and maine postes of the saide fframe and Stadge forwarde shalbe square and wroughte palasterwise wth carved proporcions Called Satiers to be placed and sett on the Topp of every of the same postes And saveinge alsoe that the said Peeter Streete shall not be chardged wth anie manner of pay⟨ntin⟩ge in or aboute the saide fframe howse or Stadge or anie parte thereof nor Rendringe the walls wthin Nor seelinge anie more or other roomes then the gentlemens roomes Twoe pennie roomes and Stadge before remembred / **nowe theiruppon** the saide Peeter Streete dothe covenante promise and graunte ffor himself his executo^{rs} and administrato^{rs} to and wth the saide Phillipp Henslowe and Edward Allen and either of them and thexecuto^{rs} and administrato^{rs} of them and either of them by theis pre*sen*tes In manner & forme followeinge (that is to saie) That he the saide Peeter Streete his executo^{rs} or assignes shall & will att his or their owne propper costes & Chardges well woorkmanlike & substancyallie make erect sett upp and fully finishe In and by all thinges accordinge to the true meaninge of theis pre*sen*tes wth good stronge and substancyall newe Tymber and other necessarie stuff All the saide fframe and other woorkes whatsoever In and vppon the saide plott or parcell of grounde (beinge not by anie aucthoretie Restrayned, and haveinge ingres egres & regres to doe the same) before the ffyue & Twentith daie of Iulie next Com̃einge after the date hereof **And shall alsoe** att his or theire like costes and Chardges Provide and finde All manner of woorkemen Tymber Ioystes Rafters boordes dores boltes hinges brick Tyle Lathe Lyme haire sande nailes Leede Iron Glasse woorkmanshipp and other thinges whatsoever wch shalbe needefull Convenyent & necessarie for the saide fframe & woorkes & everie parte thereof **And** shall alsoe make all the saide fframe in every poynte for Scantlinges Lardger and bigger in assize Then the Scantlinges of the Timber of the saide newe erected howse Called the Globe **And alsoe** that he the saide Peeter Streete shall furthwth aswell by himself As by suche other and soemanie woorkmen as shalbe Convenient & necessarie enter into and vppon the saide buildinges and woorkes And shall in reasonable manner proceede therein wthoute anie wilfull detraccion vntill the same shalbe fully effected and finished / **In consideracion** of all wch buildinges and of all stuff & woorkemanshipp thereto belonginge The saide Phillipp Henslowe & Edwarde Allen and either of them ffor themselues theire and either of theire executo^{rs} & administrato^{rs} doe Ioynctlie & seuerallie Covenante & graunte to & wth the saide Peeter Streete his executo^{rs} & administrato^{rs} by theis pre*sen*tes That they the saide Phillipp Henslowe & Edward Allen or one of them Or the executo^{rs} administrato^{rs} or assignes of them or one of them Shall & will well & truelie paie or Cawse to be paide vnto the saide Peeter Streete his executo^{rs} or assignes Att the place aforesaid appoynted for the erectinge of the saide fframe The full som̃e of ffower hundred & ffortie Poundes of lawfull money of Englande in manner & forme followeinge (that is to saie) Att suche tyme And when as the Tymber woork of the saide fframe shalbe rayzed & sett upp by the saide Peeter Streete his executo^{rs} or assignes, Or wthin Seaven daies then next followeinge Twoe hundred & Twentie poundes And att suche time and when as the saide fframe & woorkes shalbe fullie effected & ffynished as is aforesaide Or wthin Seaven daies then next followeinge, thother Twoe hundred and Twentie poundes wthoute fraude or Coven. **Prouided allwaies** and it is agreed betwene the saide parties That whatsoever som̃e or som̃es of money the saide Phillipp Henslowe & Edward Allen or either of them or thexecuto^{rs} or assignes of them or either of them shall lend or deliver vnto the saide Peter Streete his executo^{rs} or assignes or anie other by his appoyntem^{te} or consent ffor or concerninge the saide woorkes or anie parte thereof or anie stuff thereto belonginge before the raizeinge & settinge upp of the saide fframe, shalbe reputed accepted taken & accoumpted in parte of the firste paym^{te} aforesaid of the saide soñe of ffower hundred & ffortie poundes And all suche soñe or soñes of money as they or anie of them shall as aforesaid lend or deliver betwene the razeinge of the saide fframe & finishinge thereof and of all the rest of the saide woorkes. Shalbe reputed accepted taken & accoumpted in parte of the laste paym^{te} aforesaid of the same soñe of ffower hundred & ffortie poundes. Anie thinge abouesaid to the contrary notwthstandinge / **In witnes whereof** the parties abouesaid to theis pre*s*ente Indentures Interchaungeably haue sett their handes and Seales. Yeoven the daie and yeare ffirste abouewritten /

Sealed and deliuered by the saide Peter Streete in the presence of *me William Harris Pub Scr* And me *Fraunc*is *Smyth* appr to the said Scr /

[Endorsed:] Peater Streat ffor The Building of the ffortune /

1. **1599:** i.e. 1600 (New Style).
16–17. **Golding lane . . . London:** i.e. in the northwest suburbs, outside the jurisdiction of the London City Council.
20. **att.** Interlined, with a caret.
23–24. **frame . . . square.** The square structure of the Fortune distinguished it from the circular, or polygonal, form of most other London theatres, including the Globe. When it was rebuilt, after being destroyed by fire in 1621, it was converted to the more usual circular form.
41. **gentlemens roomes:** i.e. more expensive seating for the gentry.
49. **Tyreinge howse:** i.e. attiring house, where the actors dressed.
50–51. **shadowe or cover:** i.e. the "heavens," a roofing, supported by pillars, extending part way over the stage.
53. **Plott:** plan. The "Plott" has not survived.
55–56. **in breadth . . . yarde.** Given the inside measurement of 55 feet (line 26), this would mean a stage that extended out into the yard about 27 feet. 64. **lights:** panes.
72–73. **be seeled:** be ceiled, i.e. have their walls and roof lined; cf. line 89. 73. **fflowers:** floors.
78. **Contrivitions:** contrivances (?; not in *O.E.D.*).
83–84. **wroughte palasterwise:** i.e. finished decoratively in the fashion of pilasters.
84. **proporcions:** figures. **Satiers:** satyrs.
89. **Rendringe:** covering with a first coat of plaster (earliest citation in *O.E.D.* 1659).
118. **Scantlinges:** prescribed measurements (in thickness and breadth of a beam). 126: **detraccion:** detraction, delay.
152. **Coven:** covin, deceit. 161. **razeinge:** raising, erecting.
174. **Yeoven:** given.
177. **Pub Scr:** public scrivener. 178. **appr:** apprentice.

31. Royal Warrant for a Patent Instituting the Lord Chamberlain's Men as the King's Men, May 17, 1603

The original document is in the Public Record Office, London. This royal warrant was followed two days later (May 19) by the actual patent bearing the great seal as ordered. In wording it is essentially the same as the warrant, but is headed by "Commissio specialis pro Laurencio Fletcher & Willelmo Shackespeare et aliis." For further information see E. K. Chambers, *The Elizabethan Stage* (Oxford, 1923), II, 208–9; B. R. Lewis, *The Shakespeare Documents*, II, 363–66.

By the king

Right trusty and welbeloued Counsello^{r} we greete you well and will and Coñaund you y^{t} vnder o^{r} priuie Seale in yor Custody for the time being you Cause o^{r} l*ett*res to be directed to the keeper of o^{r} greate seale of England, Comaunding him y^{t} vnder o^{r} said greate Seale he cause o^{r} l*ett*res to be made patentes in forme following. *Iames* by the grace of God king of England Scotland ffraunce & Irland defendo^{r} of the faith &c. To all Iustices Maio^{rs} Sheriffes Constables Hedboroughes and other o^{r} officers and loving subiectes greeting. Know ye y^{t} we of o^{r} speciall grace certaine knowledge & meere motion, haue licenced and authorized & by these pre*s*entes doo licence & authorize these o^{r} seruantes Lawrence ffletcher, William Shakespeare Richard Burbage Augustine Phillippes Iohn Heminges Henry Condell william Sly Robt Armyn Richard Cowlye and the rest of their associates, freely to vse and exercise the Arte and facultie of playing Comedies Tragedies Histories Enterludes Moralles Pastoralles Stage plaies & such other like as they haue already studied or heerafter shall vse or studie aswell for the recreation of o^{r} loving subiect⟨es⟩ as for o^{r} solace and pleasure when we shall thinke good to see them during o pleasure. And the said Comedies Tragedies Histories Enterludes Moratt Pastoralles Stage plaies & such like To shew and exercise publiquely to their best Commoditie, when the infection of the plague shall decrease as well wthin their now vsuall howse called the Globe wthin o^{r} Countie of Surrey as also wthin any towne Halles or Mouthalles or other convenient places wthin the lib*er*ties and freedome of any other Cittie Vniversitie Towne or Borough whatsoeuer wthin o^{r} said Realmes and dominions. Willing and Comaunding you and euery of you as you tender o^{r} pleasure not only to permitt and suffer them heerin wthout any yor lettes hinderances or molestacions during o^{r} said pleasure, but also to be ayding and assisting to them yf any wrong be to them offered. And to allowe them such former Courtesies as hath bene giuen to men of their place and qualitie. And also what further fauo^{r} you shall shew to these o^{r} seruantes for o^{r} sake we shall take kindely at yor handes. In witnes wherof &c. And these o^{r} l*ett*res shall be yor sufficient warrant and discharge in this behalf. Giuen vnder o^{r} Signet at o^{r} Manno^{r} of Greenwiche the seavententh day of May in the first yeere of o^{r} raigne of England ffraunce and Irland, and of Scotland the six and thirtieth.

ex*pedi* per Lake

1. **Counsello^{r}:** i.e. Lord Cecil of Esingdon, Keeper of the Privy Seal "for the time being."
10. **Hedboroughes:** parish officers identical in function with the petty constable (*O.E.D.*).
12. **meere motion:** personal desire.
13. **these presentes:** the present document.
14. **Lawrence ffletcher.** The only name listed not earlier associated with the Chamberlain's Men. Fletcher had headed

English actors performing in Scotland and had thus become known to and favored by King James. Chambers considers it doubtful that he ever became an actor with the newly instituted King's Men.
20. **Moralles**: i.e. morality plays.
28. **Commoditie**: advantage, profit.
31. **Mouthalles**: i.e. moot halls, council chambers.
42. **qualitie**: profession.
50. **expedi per**: arrange through. **Lake.** Identity unknown.

32. An Epilogue by Shakespeare?

The following epilogue, now preserved in the University Library, Cambridge (MS.Dd. 5.75, fol. 46), has been claimed as possibly by Shakespeare (William A. Ringler and Steven W. May, "An Epilogue Possibly by Shakespeare," *MP*, LXX [1972], 138–39). The epilogue is contained in a commonplace book belonging to, and in the hand of, Henry Stanford, which seems to have been written between about 1581 and 1613. At the time the epilogue was written, Stanford was attached to the household of the second Baron Hunsdon, who became Lord Chamberlain in 1597, the year after he succeeded his father as the official patron of Shakespeare's company. The heading to the epilogue indicates that it was delivered before Queen Elizabeth (probably at court) and gives the date as 1598; and the epilogue itself makes clear (line 11) that the performance took place at Shrovetide, the three days (Quinquagesima Sunday and the following Monday and Tuesday) immediately preceding Lent. Since Lent never begins as late as March 25, and since Stanford throughout his volume uses Old Style dating (which begins the new year on March 25), the date here given as 1598 would be 1599 New Style. Two plays were performed at court at Shrovetide in 1599: one by the Admiral's Men on Quinquagesima Sunday (February 18) and a second, by the Chamberlain's Men, on Shrove Tuesday (February 20). Unfortunately, no record of the titles of the plays remains and the epilogue itself gives no hint. However, as Ringler and May point out, the ties of Stanford to the Hunsdon family would make it likely that the epilogue belongs to the play performed by the Chamberlain's Men. Coincidentally, Shakespeare refers to a "pancake for Shrove Tuesday" in *All's Well That Ends Well*, II.ii.24.

Ringler and May comment: "The epilogue's grammar is consistent throughout with Shakespeare's usage, and such forms as the uninflected genitive in line 16, 'father Quene', or the use of 'which' as a personal pronoun in line 9 occur in his printed texts. Each word in the epilogue occurs elsewhere in Shakespeare's works, with the exception of 'circuler' [line 4]." What may be considered a close parallel example of the uninflected genitive occurs in the F1 text of *Antony and Cleopatra*, II.vii.127–28: "Oh *Anthony*, you haue my Father house."

to ye Q. by ye players 1598.

As the diall hand tells ore/
ye same howers yt had before
still beginning in ye ending/
circuler account still lending
So most mightie Q. we pray/
like ye diall day by day
you may lead ye seasons on/
making new when old are gon.
that the babe wch now is yong/
& hathe yet no vse of tongue
many a shrouetyde here may bow/
to y^{t} empresse I doe now
that the children of these lordes/
sitting at your counsell bourdes
may be graue & aeged seene/
of her y^{t} was ther father Quene
once I wishe this wishe again/
heauen subscribe yt wth amen.

33. [*Othello* at Oxford, 1610] Supplement to Part II

In the *Times Literary Supplement* (July 20, 1933) Geoffrey Tillotson drew attention to a letter by Henry Jackson, a member of Corpus Christi College, Oxford, written in September 1610, in which he recorded performances given in Oxford by the King's Men of Ben Jonson's *The Alchemist* and Shakespeare's *Othello*. The letter is preserved only in some excerpts, made probably about fifty years later, by a friend of Jackson's, William Fulman, who was also connected with Corpus Christi College. The excerpts appear in Vol. X (fols. 83^{v}, 84^{r}) of the Fulman Papers (in the Library of Corpus Christi College). After discussing the infamous abuse of Holy Scripture in *The Alchemist*, Jackson continues:

> Habuerunt et Tragoedias, quas decorè, et aptè agebant. In quibus non solùm dicendo, sed etiam facièndo quaedam lachrymas movebant.—
> —At verò Desdemona illa apud nos a marito occisa, quanquam optimè semper causam egit, interfecta tamen magis movebat; cum in lecto decumbens spectantium misericordiam ipso vultu imploraret.
> —Sept. 1610.

[*Translation:* They also had tragedies, which they acted with propriety and fitness. In which (tragedies), not only through speaking but also through acting certain things, they moved (the audience) to tears. But truly the celebrated Desdemona, slain in our presence by her husband, although she pleaded her case very effectively throughout, yet moved (us) more after she was dead, when, lying on her bed, she entreated the pity of the spectators by her very countenance.]

Appendix D

Annals, 1552–1616

G. Blakemore Evans

J. J. M. Tobin

The following *Annals* for the period 1552–1616 are drawn from a variety of sources. The principal references are: Geoffrey Bullough, ed., *Narrative and Dramatic Sources of Shakespeare* (8 vols., London, 1957–75); Douglas Bush, *English Literature in the Earlier Seventeenth Century* (Oxford, 1945; rev. ed., 1962); E. K. Chambers, *William Shakespeare: A Study of Facts and Problems* (2 vols., Oxford, 1930) and *The Elizabethan Stage* (4 vols., Oxford, 1923); J. A. Froude, *History of England from the Fall of Wolsey to the Death of Elizabeth* (12 vols., London, 1856–70); S. R. Gardiner, *History of England, 1603–1616* (2 vols., London, 1863); [J. C. Ghosh], *Annals of English Literature, 1475–1925* (Oxford, 1935; rev. ed., 1936); Alfred Harbage, Samuel Schoenbaum, and Sylvia S. Wagonheim, eds., *Annals of English Drama, 975–1700* (rev. ed., London, 1989); W. L. Langer, ed., *An Encyclopedia of World History* (Boston, 5th ed., 1972); G. B. Harrison, ed., *The Elizabethan Journals, 1591–1603* (London, 1938) and *A Jacobean Journal, 1603–1606* (London, 1941); C. S. Lewis, *English Literature in the Sixteenth Century Excluding Drama* (Oxford, 1954); J. E. Neale, *Elizabeth I and Her Parliaments, 1559–1581* (London, 1953) and *Elizabeth I and Her Parliaments, 1584–1601* (London, 1957); F. P. Wilson, *The English Drama, 1485–1585* (Oxford, 1969).

The yearly listings for drama do not, except in cases of special interest, include (a) lost plays, (b) Latin school and college plays, (c) civic entertainments, or (d) masques. A single date in parentheses following a play title indicates the date of publication; where the date of composition is considered uncertain within a span of more than two years, as indicated by Harbage-Schoenbaum, the suggested limits are given first, followed by the date of publication. Starred entries refer to works known to have been used by Shakespeare and to analogues to the plays and poems; in most cases Shakespeare's particular indebtedness is indicated in a note following the entry.

	EVENTS	SHAKESPEARE
1552	Sixth year of Edward VI (reigned 1547–53). Forty-two Articles of the Church of England published by Archbishop Cranmer (1551). Publication of Second Prayer Book of Edward VI (the First in 1549). Christ's Hospital and thirty other grammar schools founded by royal order. BORN: Philemon Holland, Sir Walter Raleigh (?), Edmund Spenser. DIED: Alexander Barclay, John Leland.	John Shakespeare, Shakespeare's father, is fined a shilling (April 29) for accumulating an unauthorized dunghill in Henley Street, Stratford. (This is the first record of John Shakespeare as resident in Stratford, where he practiced the trade of a glover. His father, Richard Shakespeare, was a resident of nearby Snitterfield.)
1553	Death of Edward VI (July 6). Accession of Queen Mary (reigned 1553–58), after abortive attempt to place Lady Jane Grey on the throne as Edward VI's chosen successor (Lady Jane executed February 12, 1554). Roman Catholic bishops restored. Bishop Gardiner made chief minister and Cranmer thrown into prison. Sir Hugh Willoughby and Richard Chancellor sail for Cathay. Servetus (in Geneva) burned for denying the Trinity. BORN: Richard Hakluyt, Anthony Munday. DIED: François Rabelais.	
1554	Sir Thomas Wyatt's rebellion (to make Elizabeth queen) is crushed. Reginald Pole returns to England as Papal Legate. Mary marries Philip of Spain (July 25). Elizabeth committed to the Tower, but later removed to Woodstock. Parliament refuses Mary the right to change the succession (a move aimed against Elizabeth). Stationers' Register begins (runs to 1640). Trinity College (Oxford) founded. John Knox meets Calvin in Geneva. BORN: Stephen Gosson, Fulke Greville, Richard Hooker, John Lyly (1553?), Sir Philip Sidney.	
1555	The Act of Reconciliation passed and Roman Catholicism officially reestablished in England, but church lands are not restored. Persecution and burning of Protestants; John Rogers the first victim, then, among many others, Bishops Hopper, Latimer, and Ridley. Merchant Adventurers (the Muscovy Company) chartered. Religious Peace of Augsburg (Germany), allowing freedom of worship to Protestants. BORN: Lancelot Andrewes. DIED: Sir David Lindsay.	Anne Hathaway, Shakespeare's future wife, born 1555/6 (died 1623).
1556	More Protestants burned, among them Archbishop Cranmer. Dudley's plot (to dethrone Mary in favor of Elizabeth) is betrayed and the conspirators are executed. Glovers' Company incorporated. BORN: George Peele. DIED: Nicholas Udall.	Death of Robert Arden, Shakespeare's maternal grandfather.
1557	War with France; army dispatched under Earl of Pembroke; French defeated at battle of St. Quentin. Caius College (Cambridge) and St. John's College (Oxford) founded. Stationers' Company incorporated. BORN: Thomas Kyd (?), Thomas Watson.	John Shakespeare marries Mary Arden, eldest daughter of Robert Arden; is recorded as one of the four Stratford constables.
1558	Last two Protestants burned (November); during Mary's reign just under 300 were martyred. Death of	Joan, eldest of John Shakespeare's eight children, born (christened September 15; dead by 1569,

DRAMA AND THEATRE HISTORY	NON-DRAMATIC LITERATURE	
"Mr. S." (William Stevenson?), *Gammer Gurton's Needle* (possibly a few years later; 1575). Nicholas Udall, *Ralph Roister Doister* (c. 1567). [First English comedies to show strong influence of Latin drama.] EUROPEAN: Jodelle, *Cléopâtre* and *La Rencontre* (first French "classical" tragedy and comedy).	*Edward Hall, *The Union of the Two Noble and Illustre Families of Lancaster and York* (fifth ed. [first ed., 1542]; a principal source for Shakespeare's English history plays [*Richard II* to *Richard III*]). EUROPEAN: Ronsard, *Amours*, Vol. 1.	1552
Anon., *A New Enterlude for Children to Play, Named Jack Juggler* (possibly a few years later; c. 1562; significant as an adaptation of Plautus' *Amphitruo).* Anon. (Udall?), *Respublica* (MS).	Gavin Douglas (tr. of Virgil), *Aeneid.* Eden (tr. of Münster), *A Treatise of the New India* (i.e. America). *Sir Thomas Elyot, *The Book Named the Governor* (first ed. 1531; probable source for *The Two Gentlemen of Verona*; possible source for *2 Henry IV*; contains an analogue to *Julius Caesar*). Grimald (tr. of Cicero), *Three Books of Duties.* Sir Thomas More, *Dialogue of Comfort.* Paynell (tr. of Guido delle Colonne), *The Faithful and True Story of the Destruction of Troy.* *Thomas Wilson, *The Art of Rhetoric* (source for *Sonnets* and *Love's Labor's Lost*). EUROPEAN: *Lazarillo de Tormes* (first picaresque "novel"). Ronsard, *Odes.*	1553
Anon. (Udall? or William Hunnis?), *Jacob and Esau* (1568). Anon., *Wealth and Health* (1565).	*Gower, *Confessio Amantis* (first published 1493; source for *The Comedy of Errors* and *Pericles;* contains an analogue to *The Merchant of Venice*). Knox, *An Admonition . . . [to] Avoid God's Vengeance.* Lindsay, *Dialogue betwixt Experience and Ane Courtier.* EUROPEAN: *Bandello, *Novelle* (Vols. I–III; contains probable source for *Much Ado about Nothing*).	1554
First notice of the Earl of Worcester's Men; provincial until 1602; became Queen Anne's Men in 1604.	Baldwin (ed.), *Memorial of Such Princes as Have Been Unfortunate in the Realm of England* (suppressed first ed. of *A Mirror for Magistrates*; see 1559). Bourchier (Lord Berners), *History of Arthur of Little Britain.* Cheke, *De Pronuntiatione.* John Heywood, *Two Hundred Epigrams.* *Lydgate (tr. of Guido delle Colonne), *The Ancient History and Only True Chronicle of the Wars* [of Troy] (first published 1513; source for *Troilus and Cressida*). Anon., *Institution of a Gentleman.* EUROPEAN: Ramus, *Dialectique.*	1555
John Foxe, *Christus Triumphans* (1556).	Colville (tr. of Boethius), *The Book Called The Comfort of Philosophy.* John Heywood, *The Spider and the Fly.* Genevan *Metrical Psalter.* Record, *The Castle of Knowledge.*	1556
First record of the use of inn-yards for stage plays: Saracen's Head in Islington, Boar's Head at Aldgate. Anon., *The Sackful of News* (not extant), a burlesque performed at the Boar's Head Inn, Aldgate, and then suppressed.	*More, *Works, Written by Him in the English Tongue.* North (tr. of Guevara), *The Dial of Princes.* Record, *The Whetstone of Wit, Which Is the Second Part of Arithmetic* (the first part published 1542). Surrey (tr.), *Certain Books of Virgil's Aeneis.* *Tottel (ed.), *Songs and Sonnets* (i.e. *Tottel's Miscellany*). Tusser, *A Hundreth Good Points of Husbandry.* Anon., *Court of Venus, with Many Proper Ballads.* EUROPEAN: Inquisition issues first *Index Librorum Prohibitorum.*	1557
Jasper Heywood (tr. of Seneca), *Troas* (1559). Jane Lumley (tr.), *Iphigenia in Aulis* (MS; date	Bullein, *The Government of Health.* Knox, *The First Blast of the Trumpet against the Monstrous Regiment of*	1558

	EVENTS	SHAKESPEARE
1558 (cont.)	Queen Mary (November). Accession of Queen Elizabeth (reigned 1558–1603). Sir William Cecil (later Baron Burleigh) made Secretary of State. Protestantism restored. Calais lost to England (January 6), after 211 years of occupation. Mary, Queen of Scots, marries the Dauphin (later Francis II), promising to convert Scotland to Roman Catholicism. BORN: Robert Greene, Thomas Lodge.	when another daughter was named Joan). John Shakespeare fined fourpence for failing to keep his gutters clean.
1559	Peace with France. Elizabeth refuses an offer of marriage from Philip II. Elizabeth's first Parliament summoned. Acts of Uniformity (fine for non-attendance at church) and Supremacy (Elizabeth as head of the Anglican Church). All Marian bishops, except one, refuse to take the oath and are replaced. Edward VI's Second Prayer Book revised. Matthew Parker made Archbishop of Canterbury. Return of Protestant reformers from the continent. Knox stirs up the Reformation in Scotland. Mary assumes the title "Queen of England and Scotland." BORN: George Chapman (?).	John Shakespeare recorded as an "affeeror" or assessor of fines at the leet-court in Stratford.
1560	Treaty of Berwick (between Elizabeth and the Scottish reformers). Treaty of Edinburgh (French forces required to leave Scotland). Statute against destruction of church monuments. Reformation of the coinage. Elizabeth dissuaded from marriage with her favorite, Lord Robert Dudley, by popular feeling against him. Presbyterianism officially established in Scotland (the Confession of Faith). Publication of the Geneva ("Breeches") Bible in Geneva (the favorite Puritan translation; used, together with the "Bishops' Bible," 1568, by Shakespeare). Westminster School founded. BORN: Henry Chettle (?). DIED: Joachim du Bellay, Philipp Melanchthon.	
1561	Shane O'Neill raises a rebellion in Ireland. Mary, on the death of her husband, Francis II (1560), returns to Scotland and clashes with John Knox. St. Paul's steeple destroyed by lightning. The Merchant Taylors School (London) founded. BORN: Francis Bacon, Sir John Harington (?), Edwin Sandys, Robert Southwell.	Death of Shakespeare's grandfather, Richard Shakespeare. John Shakespeare elected a chamberlain of the Stratford Corporation; reelected 1562.
1562	Council of Trent (third session). Elizabeth ill with smallpox. Sir John Hawkins' voyages (1562–68), in part slave-trading ventures. Poor Laws first established. French civil wars (Catholics vs. Huguenots) begin with the Massacre of Vassy; Elizabeth aids the Huguenots (under Condé) by occupying Le Havre with an English force. BORN: Samuel Daniel, Lope de Vega.	Margaret, John Shakespeare's second daughter, born (christened December 2; died 1563).

very uncertain, between 1549 and 1577; important as probably the first English translation of Euripides). Lewis Wager, *The Life and Repentance of Mary Magdalene* (1566).

Women and *The Appellation of John Knox*. P. Morwyng (tr. of Joseph ben Gorion, pseudonym), *A Compendious History of the Jews' Commonweal*. Thomas Phaer (tr. of Virgil), *The Seven First Books of the Aeneidos* (nine bks., 1562; completed by Thomas Twyne, 1584). 1558 (cont.)

EUROPEAN: Du Bellay, *Antiquités de Rome* and *Poemata*. *Giovanni Fiorentino, *Il Pecorone* (probable source for *The Merchant of Venice*; contains an analogue to *The Merry Wives of Windsor*). Marguerite de Navarre, *Heptaméron*, Pt. I.

First mention of Lord Robert Dudley's Men (later known as the Earl of Leicester's Men).

William Wager, *The Longer Thou Livest the More Fool Thou Art* (c. 1566). Anon., *The Coronation of Queen Elizabeth* (1558/9; description of a London pageant).

Aylmer, *An Harbor . . . against the Late Blown Blast Concerning the Government of Women*. *Baldwin (ed.), *A Mirror for Magistrates* (see 1555; probable source for *Richard III*; possible source for *3 Henry VI*, *Richard II*, and *1 Henry IV*; contains analogues to *2 Henry VI* and *Henry V*). *Fabyan, *The Chronicle of Fabyan, Continued to the End of Queen Mary* (first published in English 1533 and 1542; source for *1 Henry VI*). 1559

EUROPEAN: Amyot (tr. of Plutarch), *Les Vies des Hommes Illustres Grecs et Romains* (basis of North's translation; see 1579). Du Bellay, *Regrets*. Minturno, *De Poeta*. Montemayor, *La Diana* (source for *The Two Gentlemen of Verona*).

Sir Thomas Benger appointed Master of the Revels (until 1572).

*Jasper Heywood (tr. of Seneca), *Thyestes* (1560; source for *Titus Andronicus*). Thomas Ingeland, *The Disobedient Child* (c. 1569). William Wager, *Enough Is as Good as a Feast* (1565–70). Anon., *Robin Hood* (c. 1560; popular May Games play). Anon., *Tom Tyler and His Wife* (date uncertain, 1558–63; 1661).

W. Barker (tr. of Xenophon), *The Discipline, School, and Education of Cyrus*. T. C. (tr. of Boccaccio), *A Pleasant and Delightful History of Gelesus, Cymon, and Iphigenia*. Copeland, *Gyl of Braintford's Testament*. *Googe (tr. of Palingenius), *The First Three Books of the Zodiac of Life* (next three, 1561; all twelve, 1565). John Heywood, *A Fourth Hundred of Epigrams*. Howell (tr.), *The Fable of Ovid Treating of Narcissus*. Knox, *An Answer to a Great Number of Blasphemous Cavillations*. Whitehorne (tr. of Machiavelli), *The Art of War*. *Anon., *Frederyke of Jennen* (first published 1518; source for *Cymbeline*). 1560

EUROPEAN: Ronsard, *Les Discours*.

Jasper Heywood (tr. of Seneca), *Hercules Furens* (1561). Thomas Preston, *A Lamentable Tragedy Mixed Full of Pleasant Mirth, Containing the Life of Cambises, King of Persia* (c. 1569). Anon., *The Pedlar's Prophecy* (1595). Anon., *Romeo and Juliet* (date uncertain, not extant; referred to by Arthur Brooke in his *Romeus and Juliet*, 1562). *Anon. (Udall?), *Thersites* (published about this year; probably dates from c. 1537; contains an analogue to *1 Henry IV*).

Wm. Baldwin, *A Marvellous Hystory Intituled Beware the Cat*. 1561
*Chaucer, *Works* (ed. Stow; see also Speght, 1598; "The Knight's Tale," source for Theseus plot in *A Midsummer Night's Dream* and for *The Two Noble Kinsmen*; "The Miller's Tale" for the obscenities in the Pyramus and Thisby episode of *A Midsummer Night's Dream*. *The Legend of Good Women*, probable source for *Lucrece*; *Troilus and Criseyde*, probable source for *Troilus and Cressida*). *Dolman (tr.), *Those Five Questions Which M. T. Cicero Disputed in His Manor of Tusculanum* (perhaps used for Ulysses' degree speech in *Troilus and Cressida*). Eden (tr. of Cortes), *The Art of Navigation*. Gilby (tr. of Cicero), *An Epistle . . . to His Brother Quintus*. *Hoby (tr. of Castiglione), *The Courtier* (probable source for *Much Ado*). Norton (tr. of Calvin), *The Institution of Christian Religion*.

EUROPEAN: Scaliger, *Poetices*.

The Earl of Warwick's Men first heard of in the provinces, in London by 1575; transferred to the Earl of Oxford's Men in 1580.

Alexander Neville (tr. of Seneca), *Oedipus* (1563). Norton and Sackville, *The Tragedy of Gorboduc* (1565, 1570; first English play in blank verse and first tragedy in English to show strong influence of Senecan form and matter).

*Arthur Brooke, *History of Romeus and Juliet* (source for *Romeo and Juliet* and *The Two Gentlemen of Verona*). Bullein, *Bulwark against All Sickness*. John Heywood, *Works* (i.e. Proverbs and Epigrams). Jewel, *Apologia Ecclesiae Anglicanae* (an anonymous English tr. appeared in the same year) and *An Apology of Private Mass* (with an answer by Thomas Cooper). Latimer, *XXVII Sermons*. *Sternhold and Hopkins (trs.), *The Whole Book of Psalms* (metrical; the first of some 270 editions down to 1640). 1562

EUROPEAN: Rabelais, *Pantagruel* (Bk. V, posth.; begun 1532).

	EVENTS	SHAKESPEARE
1563	Elizabeth's second Parliament summoned. Anglican Church finally established; adopts the Thirty-Nine Articles (replacing Cranmer's Forty-Two). Penal bill against Roman Catholics. English and Scottish statutes against witchcraft enacted. Plague in London and slight earthquakes in various parts of England. Potatoes introduced into England from America by Hawkins. BORN: John Bull, John Dowland, Michael Drayton, Joshua Sylvester. DIED: John Bale, Arthur Brooke.	Death of Margaret Shakespeare (buried April 30).
1564	Peace of Troyes (with France); England renounces claims on Calais for cash settlement. Flemish Protestant refugees come to England. Puritans persecuted and their form of worship attacked. Elizabeth visits Cambridge. Gipsies expelled from England. Captain Thomas Stukeley plunders Spanish ships in Ireland. BORN: Galileo, Christopher Marlowe, William Shakespeare. DIED: John Calvin, Michelangelo.	William Shakespeare, John Shakespeare's eldest son, born (christened April 26). John Shakespeare is listed among the "capital burgesses" of Stratford; he gives money for the relief of plague victims in Stratford.
1565	Mary, Queen of Scots, (against Elizabeth's express order) marries Henry Stuart, Lord Darnley, who is then declared king. Mary joins the Catholic Alliance. Pressure on Elizabeth to marry is increased; among her many suitors over the past seven years, who had included most of the crowned heads of Europe, Charles, Grand Duke of Austria, appears politically the most acceptable. Sir Henry Sidney made Elizabeth's Deputy in Ireland. Royal College of Surgeons permitted to dissect corpses. BORN: Francis Meres.	John Shakespeare appointed an alderman of Stratford.
1566	Elizabeth's third Parliament summoned. David Rizzio, Mary's secretary, murdered by order of Darnley. Birth of James (VI of Scotland, I of England), son of Mary and Darnley. Parliament presses for a settlement of the succession; Elizabeth refuses, but extricates herself by promising to marry. Elizabeth visits Oxford. BORN: Edward Alleyn; Robert Devereux, 2nd Earl of Essex. DIED: Bartolomé de Las Casas, Sir Thomas Hoby, Suleiman I (The Magnificent).	Gilbert, John Shakespeare's second son, born (christened October 13; died 1612).

DRAMA AND THEATRE HISTORY	NON-DRAMATIC LITERATURE	
First notice of first Lord Strange's Men, active in the provinces until 1570.	*Baldwin, *A Mirror for Magistrates* (third ed., enlarged to include Sackville's *Induction*). *Foxe, *Acts and Monuments* (known as the "Book of Martyrs"; rev. eds., 1570, 1583; a much shorter Latin version, *Commentarii Rerum in Ecclesia Gestarum*, was published in 1554 [Strassburg]; source for "miracle of St. Albans" in *2 Henry VI* and for Cranmer's trial in *Henry VIII*; probable source for *Sir Thomas More*; possible source for *King John*). Golding (tr.), *Histories of Justin*. Googe, *Eclogues, Epitaphs, and Sonnets*. *Grafton, *An Abridgment of the Chronicles of England*. John Hall, *A Poesy in Form of a Vision against Witchcraft*. Rainold, *Foundation of Rhetoric*. Winzet, *The Book of Fourscore-Three Questions*. EUROPEAN: *Index Librorum Prohibitorum*. Minturno, *Arte Poetica*.	1563
First notice of Lord Rich's Men. R. B. (Richard Bower?), *A New Tragical Comedy of Appius and Virginia*. John Jeffere (?), *The Bugbears* (MS; tr. of Grazzini's *La Spiritata*, 1561).	Anne Bacon (tr. of Jewel), *An Apology or Answer in Defense of the Church of England*. Bullein, *A Dialogue Both Pleasant and Pitiful against the Fever Pestilence*. Thomas Harding, *An Answer to Master Jewel's Challenge*. Scots *Prayerbook and Psalter*. EUROPEAN: *Belleforest, *Histoires Tragiques* (Vol. II, 1565; Vol. III, 1568 [possibly used in *Much Ado about Nothing*]; Vol. IV, 1570; Vol. V, 1570 [source for *Ur-Hamlet*, and possibly used by Shakespeare independently]; Vols. VI, VII, 1582). Wierus, *De Praestigiis Daemonum* (attacks belief in witchcraft).	1564
Richard Edwards, *The Excellent Comedy of Two Friends, Damon and Pithias* (1571; probable source for *The Two Gentlemen of Verona*). *John Studley (tr. of Seneca), *Agamemnon* (1566; source for *Macbeth*) and *Medea* (1566). Anon., *King Darius* (1565).	William Allen, *A Defense and Declaration Touching Purgatory*. *Awdeley, *The Fraternity of Vagabonds*. *Thomas Cooper, *Thesaurus Linguae Romanae et Britannicae* (fifth ed. 1587, the standard Latin-English dictionary). Bernard Garter, *The Tragical and True History Which Happened between Two English Lovers*. *Golding (tr.), *The First Four Books of P. Ovidius Naso's Work Entitled Metamorphosis* (Bks. I–XV published 1567; principal source for *Venus and Adonis*; source for *Titus Andronicus*, *The Winter's Tale*, and *The Tempest*; and *Sonnets*, esp. Bk. XV; probable source for horning of Falstaff in *The Merry Wives of Windsor* and for *Troilus and Cressida*). *Grafton, *A Manual of the Chronicles of England to This Year 1565*. John Hall, *The Court of Virtue: Containing Many Holy Songs, Sonnets, Psalms, and Ballets*. Jewel, *A Reply unto Master Harding's Answer*. More, *Opera*. Newton (tr. of Lemnius), *The Touchstone of Complexions*. Henry Parker (tr.), *The Triumphs of F. Petrarch* (*Virgil in His Epigrams of Cupid and Drunkenness*). Peend (tr. of Ovid), *The Pleasant Fable of Hermaphroditus and Salmacis*. *Stow, *A Summary of English Chronicles*. EUROPEAN: *Giraldi Cinthio, *Hecatommithi* (principal source for *Othello*; probable source for *Measure for Measure*). Palestrina, *Missa Papae Marcelli*. Ronsard, *Abrégé de l'Art Poétique*.	1565
Edwards, *Palamon and Arcite*, two parts (not extant; cf. *The Two Noble Kinsmen*). *George Gascoigne, *Supposes* (1573; tr. of Ariosto's *Il Suppositi*, 1509; first sustained use of prose in English comedy; source for *The Comedy of Errors* and *The Taming of the Shrew*). Gascoigne and Kinwelmershe, *Jocasta* (1573; parades as tr. of Euripides, actually from Dolce's *Giocasta*, 1549). Thomas Nuce (tr. of Seneca), *Octavia* (c. 1566). Lewis Wager, *A New Interlude . . . the Life and Repentance of Marie Magdalene*. Robert Wilmot and others, *Gismond of Salerne* (later revised by Wilmot as *Tancred and Gismunda*, 1591).	*Adlington (tr. of Apuleius), *The XI Books of the Golden Ass, with The Marriage of Cupido and Psyches* (ransacked by Shakespeare throughout the canon). *Alday (tr. of Boaistuau), *Theatrum Mundi, the Theatre or Rule of the World* (contains an analogue to *Timon of Athens*). Drant (tr.), *A Medicinable Moral, That Is, the Two Books of Horace His Satires*. Granthum (tr. of Boccaccio), *A Pleasant Disport of Divers Noble Personages Entitled Philocopo*. Lindsay, *Deploration of Death of Queen Magdalen*. *Painter (tr. of Boccaccio, Bandello, Belleforest), *The Palace of Pleasure* (Vol. I; Vol. II, 1567; contains Livy's story of Lucrece used in *The Rape of Lucrece*; the principal source for *All's Well That Ends Well* from Boccaccio; and an analogue to *Timon of Athens*). Underdowne, *The Excellent History of Theseus and Ariadne*. EUROPEAN: Luther, *Tischreden*.	1566

	EVENTS	SHAKESPEARE
1567	Revolt of the Netherlands against Spanish rule. Darnley murdered; Mary marries Earl of Bothwell (one of the murderers) and is forced to abdicate in favor of her son, James, who becomes James VI at the age of thirteen months; Earl of Moray becomes regent. Shane O'Neill finally defeated and killed; Ireland reduced to submission (the work of Sir Henry Sidney). Rugby School founded. BORN: William Alexander, Earl of Sterling (?), Richard Burbage, Thomas Campion, Thomas Nashe, St. Francis de Sales.	
1568	Mary flees to England and is detained in Bolton Castle by Elizabeth. A commission is set up to determine Mary's complicity in Darnley's murder; the incriminating "Casket Letters"; her guilt generally acknowledged, but a verdict of non-proven finally engineered. Publication of the "Bishops' Bible" (in great part the work of Matthew Parker, and the foundation of the King James 1611 version). The Roman Catholic English College founded at Douai. BORN: Henry Wotton. DIED: Roger Ascham, Miles Coverdale.	John Shakespeare elected Bailiff of Stratford, the highest town office. The Queen's Players and Worcester's Men play at Stratford.
1569	Mary removed to Tutbury Castle, under more rigorous guard. Failure of the rebellion of the Duke of Norfolk and the Northern Earls (in favor of Mary). BORN: Barnabe Barnes (?), John Davies.	Joan, John Shakespeare's third daughter, born (christened April 15; died 1646).
1570	Elizabeth excommunicated and "deposed" by Pope Pius V. Earl of Moray murdered by Bothwellhaugh; replaced by Earl of Lennox as regent. BORN: Guy Fawkes, Thomas Middleton, Samuel Rowlands (?).	
1571	Elizabeth's fourth Parliament summoned. The Treasons Bill passed; a bill limiting the clergy's necessary subscription only to doctrinal Articles of Faith also passed	Anne, John Shakespeare's fourth daughter, born (christened September 28; died 1579). He is at this time chief alderman.

DRAMA AND THEATRE HISTORY	NON-DRAMATIC LITERATURE	
First and only notice of the Red Lion Inn (Stepney parish) as a playing-place. John Pickering, *A New Enterlude of Vice Containing the History of Horestes, with the Cruel Revengement of His Father's Death upon His Own Natural Mother* (1667). William Wager (?), *The Trial of Treasure* (1567).	William Allen, *A Treatise Made in Defense of the Lawful Power of the Priesthood to Remit Sins.* Drant (tr.), *Horace His Art of Poetry, Pistles, and Satires Englished.* Sir Geoffrey Fenton (tr. of Bandello), *Certain Tragical Discourses.* Hake (tr. of Thomas à Kempis), *The Imitation or Following of Christ.* Harman, *A Caveat or Warening for Common Cursetors.* Jewel, *A Defense of the Apology of the Church of England.* Mulcaster (tr. of Fortescue), *A Learned Commendation of the Politic Laws of England.* Matthew Parker (tr. of Aelfric), *A Testimony of Antiquity.* Paynell (tr.), *The Treasury of Amadis of France.* James Sandford (tr.), *The Manual of Epictetus*; (tr. of Plutarch), *The Amorous and Tragical Tales* (contains also "The History of Cariclea and Theagines" [tr. of Heliodorus]). Turberville, *Epitaphs, Epigrams, Songs, and Sonnets*; (tr. of Ovid), *The Heroical Epistles*; (tr. of Mantuan), *The Eclogues.*	1567
Ulpian Fulwell, *Like Will to Like, Quod the Devil to the Collier* (perhaps as early as 1562; 1568). Anon., *The Marriage of Wit and Science* (1569).	Humphrey Baker, *The Well-Spring of Sciences* (i.e. arithmetic). *Grafton, *This [Chronicle of Britain] Beginning at William the Conqueror Endeth with . . . Elizabeth* (second ed., *A Chronicle at Large*, appeared in 1569; probable source for *2 Henry VI*). Thomas Howell, *The Arbor of Amity* and *Pleasant Sonnets and Pretty Pamphlets.* Lambard, *Archaionomia.* Lindsay, *Works.* North (tr. of Guevara), *The Dial of Princes* (new ed. with a fourth part, "The Favored Courtier"). Skelton, *Pithy, Pleasant, and Profitable Works.* Thomas Smith, *De Recta et Emendata Linguae Anglicae Scriptione.* Tilney, *A Brief and Pleasant Discourse of the Duties of Marriage.* Turberville (tr. of Mancinus), *A Plain Path to Perfect Virtue.*	1568
First notice of the Earl of Sussex's Men; intermittently active until 1594; Shakespeare may have had some connection with them in 1593. Thomas Garter, *The Most Virtuous and Godly Susanna* (perhaps as early as 1563; 1578).	Richard Day, *Christian Prayers and Meditations in English* (referred to as Queen Elizabeth's Prayerbook). Edward Fenton, *Certain Secret Wonders of Nature.* Sir John Hawkins, *A True Declaration of the Troublesome Voyage . . . to the Parties of Guiana and the West Indies.* Newton (tr. of Cicero), *Paradoxa Stoicorum* (with *Scipio's Dream*) and *The Worthy Book of Old Age.* Theodore Roest (tr. of Van der Noodt), *A Theatre for Worldlings* (contains Spenser's earliest published verse). James Sandford (tr. of Agrippa), *Of the Vanity of Arts and Sciences.* C. T. (tr. of Boccaccio), *A Notable History of Nastagio and Traversari.* Richard Tottel (tr. of Henry de Bracton), *On the Laws and Customs of England.* Underdowne (tr. of Heliodorus), *An Aethiopian History*; (tr.), *Ovid His Invective against Ibis.* EUROPEAN: Mercator, *Chronologia.* Baptista Porta, *Magia Naturalis.*	1569
*Anon. (Thomas Preston?), *The History of the Two Valiant Knights, Sir Clyomon and Clamydes* (possibly as late as 1583; 1599; probable source for *As You Like It*; possible source for *Cymbeline*).	Ascham. *The Schoolmaster, or Plain and Perfit Way of Teaching Children the Latin Tongue* and *A Report and Discourse of the Affairs of Germany.* Sir Geoffrey Fenton (tr.), *A Discourse of the Civil Wars in France.* Foxe, *The Ecclesiastical History* and *A Sermom of Christ Crucified.* Googe (tr. of Kirchmeyer), *The Popish Kingdom, or Reign of Anti-Christ.* Henryson (tr.), *The Moral Fables of Aesop.* North (tr. of Fables of Bidpai), *The Moral Philosophy of Doni.* Thomas Wilson (tr. of Demosthenes), *The Three Orations in Favor of the Olynthians with Four Orations against King Philip.* EUROPEAN: Castelvetro, *Poetica d'Aristotele.* Ortelius, *Theatrum Orbis Terrarum.* Palladio, *I Quatro Libri dell' Architettura.*	1570
Anon., *New Custom* (1573).	Grafton, *A Little Treatise Containing Many Proper Tables* (contains calendar, almanac, table of tides in English harbors, best days to be let blood, bathe, or purge,	1571

	EVENTS	SHAKESPEARE
1571 (cont.)	(a victory for Puritan consciences). Elizabeth's marriage with the Duke of Anjou (later Henry III) proposed; dropped before the end of the year, in favor of Anjou's younger brother, the Duke of Alençon. Ridolfi Plot (to depose Elizabeth and set Mary on the English throne). Lennox assassinated; replaced by Earl of Mar as regent. Battle of Lepanto won against the Turks. Slaves, captured from the Spanish, sold in Dover. Act for the incorporation of Oxford and Cambridge. Harrow School founded. BORN: Robert Cotton, Johannes Kepler. DIED: Benvenuto Cellini, John Jewel, Georgio Vasari.	
1572	Elizabeth's fifth Parliament summoned. Ridolfi Plot exposed; Norfolk and others executed. Massacre of St. Bartholomew (August 24). Treaty of Blois (Anglo-French defense league). Elizabeth begins long negotiations for marriage with Alençon. Mar dies (poisoned?); replaced by Earl of Morton as regent. George Buchanan publishes versions of the "Casket Letters" in his *De Maria Scotorum Regina*. The Vestmentarian Controversy begins. Actors not under the protection of a patron declared rogues and vagabonds. The Society of Antiquaries founded by Matthew Parker. BORN: Thomas Dekker (?), John Donne, Ben Jonson. DIED: John Knox, Peter Ramus (murdered).	Leicester's Men play at Stratford.
1573	Siege of La Rochelle (a Huguenot stronghold). Walter Devereux tries unsuccessfully to colonize Ulster with English settlers; English control of Ireland temporarily lost. Henry Wriothesley (later third Earl of Southampton), Shakespeare's patron, is born (October 6). Tycho Brahe announces the discovery of a new star. BORN: Inigo Jones, William Laud.	
1574	Treaty of Bristol signed, settling commercial disputes (between England and Spain). Roman Catholics persecuted in England. BORN: Richard Barnfield, Joseph Hall.	Richard, John Shakespeare's third son, born (christened March 11; died 1613). Warwick's and Worcester's Men play at Stratford.
1575	New Poor Law. Two Dutch Anabaptists burned in England. On death of Parker, Edmund Grindal made Archbishop. Elizabeth approached for aid against Spain by the Dutch provinces. Dudley (now Earl of Leicester, 1564) entertains Elizabeth at Kenilworth. BORN: Jacob Boehme, Thomas Heywood (?), Samuel Purchas (?), Cyril Tourneur (?), John Webster (?). DIED: Matthew Parker.	
1576	Elizabeth's sixth Parliament summoned. Sack of Antwerp by the Spanish; this produces the Treaty of Ghent, uniting the Dutch provinces against Spanish rule. Emergence	About this time, or perhaps earlier (1567), John Shakespeare seems to have applied to the College of Arms for a coat of arms, none was issued

principal fairs, highway distances from one town to another, etc.). Latimer, *Fruitful Sermons.* Matthew Parker (ed.), *Historia Major of Matthew Paris.* 1571 (cont.)

First notice of the Earl of Essex's Men; almost entirely provincial.

Gascoigne, *The Mask for Lord Montacute* (1573). Nathaniel Woodes, *The Conflict of Conscience, Containing the Most Lamentable History of the Desperation of Francis Spera* (possibly as late as 1581; 1581).

Buchanan, *De Maria Scotorum Regina* (attacking Mary and publishing a version of the "Casket Letters"). Churchyard (tr.), *The First Three Books of Ovid's De Tristibus.* Sir Geoffrey Fenton, *Monophylo, a Philosophical Discourse of Love.* Field and Wilcox, *An Admonition to the Parliament.* *R. H. (tr. of Lavater), *Of Ghosts and Spirits Walking by Night* (useful with reference to *Hamlet* and *Julius Caesar*). Higgins (ed.), *Huloet's Dictionary* (English, Latin, French). Latimer, *Seven Sermons Made upon the Lord's Prayer.* Matthew Parker, *De Antiquitate Britannicae Ecclesiae* (probably the first book privately printed in England). Pseudo-Cartwright, *A Second Admonition to the Parliament.* Tyndale, Frith, and Barnes, *The Whole Works.* Whitgift, *An Answer to a Certain Libel Intitled An Admonition to the Parliament.* Sir Thomas Wilson, *A Discourse upon Usury.* 1572

EUROPEAN: Camoëns, *Os Lusiados.* Henri Estienne, *Thesaurus Linguae Graecae.* Ronsard, *La Franciade* (Bks. I–IV).

Thomas Blagrave appointed acting Master of the Revels (until 1579).

Thomas Cartwright, *A Reply to an Answer Made of Master Doctor Whitgift.* Gascoigne, *A Hundreth Sundry Flowers, Bound up in One Small Posy.* Tusser, *Five Hundreth Points of Good Husbandry.* 1573

EUROPEAN: Bandello, *Novelle* (Vol. IV). Brahe, *De Nova Stella.* Desportes, *Diane, etc.* Du Bartas, *Judith.* Tasso, *Aminta.*

First notice of the Earl of Derby's Men.

Thomas Churchyard and J. Roberts, *The Queen's Entertainment at Bristow* (1575).

Thomas Cartwright (tr. of Travers), *A Full and Plain Declaration of Ecclesiastical Discipline.* Sir Geoffrey Fenton, *A Form of Christian Policy* (early attack on the players). Hellowes (tr.), *The Familiar Epistles of Sir Antony of Guevara.* *Higgins (ed.), *The First Part of the Mirror for Magistrates* (see 1559; source for *King Lear*). Matthew Parker (tr.), *The Life of the Seventieth Archbishop of Canterbury*; (tr. of Asser), *Aelfredi Regis Res Gestae.* Barnabe Rich, *A Right Excellent and Pleasant Dialogue, between Mercury and an English Soldier.* Reginald Scot, *A Perfit Platform of a Hop Garden.* Whitgift, *The Defense of the Answer to the Admonition.* 1574

First notices of the Bel Savage Inn (London) and the Bull Inn (London) as playing-places.

Gascoigne, *The Glass of Government*, "a tragicall comedie" (1575). Gascoigne, William Hunnis, and others, *The Princely Pleasures at Kenilworth* (1576). Gascoigne (?) and Sir Henry Lee (?), *The Queen's Entertainment at Woodstock* (1575). Arthur Golding (tr. of Beza), *Abraham's Sacrifice* (1577).

Breton, *A Small Handful of Fragrant Flowers.* Thomas Cartwright, *The Second Reply against Master Whitgift's Second Answer.* Churchyard, *The First Part of Churchyard's Chips.* Sir Geoffrey Fenton (tr. of Guevara), *Golden Epistles.* Gascoigne, *The Posies.* Laneham, *A Letter, Wherein Part of the Entertainment unto the Queen at Killingworth Castle Is Signified.* Rolland, *Ane Treatise Callit the Court of Venus.* Turberville, *The Book of Falconry or Hawking* and *The Noble Art of Venery or Hunting.* 1575

EUROPEAN: Ronsard, *Sonnets pour Hélène.* Tasso, *Gerusalemme Liberata* (rev. ed., 1581).

The Theatre (Shoreditch), the first regular playhouse in London, built by James Burbage on land leased for twenty-one years. The Children of the

Fleming (tr. of Cicero, Pliny the Younger, and others), *A Panoply of Epistles.* Fulwell, *The First Part of the Eighth Liberal Science Entitled Ars Adulandi.* Gascoigne, *The Steel* 1576

	EVENTS	SHAKESPEARE
1576 (cont.)	of William, Prince of Orange, as Protestant leader in the Dutch provinces. Martin Frobisher begins his voyage in search of a Northwest Passage. BORN: John Marston, St. Vincent de Paul. DIED: Earl of Bothwell, Cardan, Titian.	(see 1596), but he seems to have been sent some kind of preliminary sketch of the proposed blazon. Leicester's Men play at Stratford.
1577	Sir Francis Drake, in the *Pelican,* and with four other ships, begins his voyage around the world (returned 1580). After many earlier promises of aid, this expedition, by harrying Spanish shipping, was Elizabeth's principal contribution to the Protestant cause in the Dutch provinces. Edward Grindal "sequestered" from his archbishopric of Canterbury for failing to suppress the Puritan "prophesying" movement. BORN: Robert Burton, Thomas Coryat, Peter Paul Rubens. DIED: George Gascoigne, Sir Thomas Smith.	About this year John Shakespeare's fortunes begin to decline and he is increasingly cited for various debts.
1578	Elizabeth pursues a dangerous policy in the Dutch provinces by trying to play on both sides; finally breaks off all direct dealings with the Protestant group. Plans for her marriage with Alençon are revived. Battle of Alcazar and death of Captain Thomas Stukeley. The English College moves from Douai to Rheims. BORN: William Harvey, George Sandys. DIED: Don John of Austria.	Lord Strange's Men and Essex's Men play at Stratford.
1579	Union of Utrecht, uniting the northern provinces of Holland as Protestant. Simier visits England to treat with Elizabeth on the projected marriage with Alençon. Opposition to the marriage becomes strong, but the secret marriages of her favorites, Leicester and Hatton, drive Elizabeth to invite a visit from Alençon. John Stubbs's right hand struck off for writing *The Gaping Gulf,*	Death of Anne Shakespeare (buried April 4). Derby's Men play at Stratford.

1576 (cont.)

Chapel begin performances at the First Blackfriars Theatre (the first "private" house); joined by the Children of Paul's c. 1583; defunct by 1584. First notice of the Bell Inn (London) as a playing-place.

George Wapull, *The Tide Tarrieth No Man* (1576). Anon., *Common Conditions* (c. 1576).

Glass, a Satire, Together with the Complaint of Philomene, The Drum of Doomsday, A Delicate Diet for Dainty-Mouth'd Drunkards. Sir Humphrey Gilbert, *A Discourse of a Discovery for a New Passage to Cataia.* Kerton (tr. of Pope Innocent III), *The Mirror of Man's Life.* Lambard, *A Perambulation of Kent. The Paradise of Dainty Devices* (contains poems of Richard Edwards, Jasper Heywood, Lord Vaux, and others). Robert Peterson (tr. of della Casa), *Galateo, A Treatise of Manners.* *Pettie (tr.), *A Petite Palace of Pettie His Pleasure.* *Whetstone, *The Rock of Regard* (source for *Much Ado*).
EUROPEAN: Bodin, *La République.* Gentillet, *Discours sur les Moyens de Bien Gouverner . . . contre Nicolas Machiavel* (English tr., 1602).

1577

The Curtain Theatre (Moorfields, Shoreditch) opened. First notice of second Lord Strange's Men; amalgamated with the Admiral's Men about 1589.

Stephen Gosson, *Captain Mario* (acted 1581–82, not extant) and *Praise at Parting* (acted 1581–82, not extant). Thomas Lupton, *A Moral and Pitiful Comedy, Intituled, All for Money* (1578). *Anon., *The History of Error* (not extant; perhaps an adaptation of Plautus' *Menaechmi* and suggested as a possible source for *The Comedy of Errors*).

Breton, *The Works of a Young Wit Trussed Up with a Fardel of Pretty Fancies* and *A Flourish upon Fancy.* Thomas Cartwright, *The Rest of the Second Reply against Master Whitgift's Second Answer.* Eden (tr. of Peter Martyr), *The History of Travel in the West and East Indies* (see 1555). Gascoigne, *The Spoil of Antwerp.* Googe (tr. of Conrad Heresbach), *Four Books of Husbandry.* Grange, *The Golden Aphroditis* (including *Grange's Garden*). Gabriel Harvey, *Ciceronianus,* possible influence upon *Twelfth Night,* includes enthusiasm for capital letters and the linking of rhetoric and hair styling. Hellowes (tr. of Guevara), *A Chronicle Containing the Lives of Ten Emperors of Rome.* *Holinshed, *The First Volume of the Chronicles of England, Scotland, and Ireland* (includes William Harrison's *The Description of Britain*; see 1587 for ed. used by Shakespeare). Kendall, *Flowers of Epigrams.* Northbrooke, *A Treatise Wherein Dicing, Dancing, etc. Are Reproved.* Henry Peacham (the elder), *The Garden of Eloquence.* *Richard Robinson (tr.), *Gesta Romanorum* (no copy of this ed. extant; another ed. in 1595; probable source for the "casket story" in *The Merchant of Venice*).

1578

First notice of Lord Berkeley's Men; active until 1610 in the provinces.

Gosson, *Catiline's Conspiracies* (c. 1576–79; not extant). Sir Philip Sidney, *The Lady of May* (c. 1578–82; 1598). *George Whetstone, *The Right Excellent and Famous History of Promos and Cassandra, Divided into Two Comical Discourses* (adaptation of Giraldi Cinthio's *Hecatommithi*; source for *Measure for Measure*). *Anon., *The Jew* (c. 1576–79; not extant; possible source for *The Merchant of Venice*).

*W. B. (tr. of Appian), *An Ancient History and Exquisite Chronicle of the Romans' Wars, Both Civil and Foreign* (source for *Antony and Cleopatra*; possible source for *Julius Caesar*). George Best, *A True Discourse of the Late Voyages* [i.e. Frobisher's] *of Discovery.* *Blenerhasset (ed.), *The Second Part of the Mirror for Magistrates* (see 1559; source for *Cymbeline*). Churchyard, *A Lamentable and Pitiful Description of the Woeful Wars in Flanders* and *A Discourse of the Queen's Majesty's Entertainment in Suffolk and Norfolk.* Florio, *First Fruits, a Perfect Induction to the Italian and English Tongues.* Hellowes (tr. of Guevara), *A Book of the Invention of the Art of Navigation.* Hunnis, *A Hiveful of Honey* (metrical version of Genesis). *Lyly, *Euphues, the Anatomy of Wit* (contains an analogue to *The Two Gentlemen of Verona*). Thomas Proctor (ed.), *A Gorgeous Gallery of Gallant Inventions.* Barnabe Rich, *Alarm to England.* Rolland, *The Seven Sages, Translated Out of Prose in Scottish Metre.* Whetstone, *A Remembrance of the Well-Employed Life of George Gascoigne.* *Henry Wotton (tr. from French), *A Courtly Controversy of Cupid's Cautels* (contains an analogue to *The Two Gentlemen of Verona*).
EUROPEAN: Du Bartas, *La Semaine.* Mercator, *Tabulae Geographicae.* Ronsard, *Sonnets pour Hélène.*

1579

Edmund Tilney appointed Master of the Revels (until 1610). First notice of the Cross Keys Inn (London) as a playing-place.

Francis Merbury, *A Marriage between Wit and Wisdom* (date should perhaps be 1570).

Bowes (tr. of Gentillet), *An Apology or Defense for the Christians of France.* Churchyard, *The Misery of Flanders, Calamity of France, Misfortune of Portugal* and *A General Rehearsal of Wars.* Sir Geoffrey Fenton (tr. of Guicciardini), *The Wars of Italy.* Frampton (tr.), *The Most Noble and Famous Travels of Marcus Paulus* [Marco Polo]. Gosson, **The School of Abuse, Containing a Pleasant Invective*

	EVENTS	SHAKESPEARE
1579 (cont.)	an attack on the Alençon match. English College in Rome founded. BORN: John Fletcher. DIED: Nicholas Bacon, Thomas Gresham	
1580	Scottish General Assembly declares episcopacy unscriptural. Edmund Campion and Robert Parsons set up a Jesuit mission in England. Lord Grey de Wilton made Deputy in Ireland (Edmund Spenser his secretary); the Pope's secret attempt to regain Ireland for Roman Catholicism foiled. Drake returns from his voyage in triumph, having played havoc with Spanish shipping and taken tremendous booty. Elzevir Press founded in Amsterdam. DIED: Camoëns, John Heywood (?), Raphael Holinshed (?), Thomas Tusser.	Edmund, John Shakespeare's fourth son, born (christened May 3; died 1607). Lord Berkeley's Men play at Stratford.
1581	Elizabeth's seventh Parliament summoned. Recusancy laws enacted, but a secret recusant press established in Essex. Campion, with two other priests, executed for "treason," the first Roman Catholic priests to suffer death under Elizabeth. The marriage game with Alençon continues, now on, now off; he visits Elizabeth again. The Brownists or Independents become active. St. Paul's Cathedral damaged by small earthquake. William of Orange made hereditary Statthalter of the Dutch States. BORN: Franz Hals, Thomas Overbury, James Ussher.	Worcester's Men play at Stratford.
1582	Gregorian Calendar (i.e. New Style) promulgated by the Pope (Gregory XIII); not then adopted in Protestant countries (not adopted officially in England until 1752). The Gowrie Conspiracy (successful seizure of the young James by the Protestant Scottish lords). Attempted assassination of William of Orange. Publication of the Roman Catholic English translation of the New Testament at Rheims. Plague in London. London Bridge waterworks begun (to supply the City with water). Edinburgh University founded (with one professor). Jesuit mission to China begun. BORN: John Barclay, Phineas Fletcher, William Peter. DIED: George Buchanan, Sebastian Westcott.	Shakespeare marries Anne Hathaway; license issued November 27 (see Appendix C, Number 2). Lord Berkeley's Men play at Stratford.

1579 (cont.)

against Poets, Pipers, Players, Jesters, and Such Like Caterpillers of the Commonwealth and *The Ephemerides of Phialo* (contains *Apology for the School of Abuse*). Lodge, [Answer to Gosson]. Munday, *The Mirror of Mutability.* *North (tr. of Amyot's Plutarch), *The Lives of the Noble Grecians and Romans* (principal source for Shakespeare's Roman plays and *Timon of Athens*; source, in addition to Chaucer's "Knight's Tale," for the Theseus plot in *A Midsummer Night's Dream*; possible source for *Titus Andronicus*). *Spencer, *The Shepherd's Calendar.* John Stubbs, *The Discovery of a Gaping Gulf Whereinto England Is Like to Be Swallowed.* Twyne (tr. of Petrarch), *Physic against Fortune.*

1580

First notice of the theatre at Newington Butts (one mile southwest of London Bridge); possibly erected as early as 1576; associated briefly with the Admiral's and the Chamberlain's Men in 1594.

*Thomas Legge, *Richardus Tertius* (MS; a threepart Latin play possibly known to Shakespeare).

Buchanan, *De Jure Regni apud Scotos Dialogus.* William Bullokar, *Bullokar's Book at Large for the Amendment of Orthography for English Speech.* Churchyard, *A Light Bundle of Lively Discourses Called Churchyard's Charge.* Frampton, *A Discourse of Tartaria, Scythia, etc.* Humphrey Gifford, *A Posy of Gillyflowers.* P. Golding (tr. of Froissart), *An Epitome of Frossard, Compiled by J. Sleydan* (Lord Berners' tr. of Froissart appeared c. 1523–25). Gabriel Harvey (and Spenser), *Three Proper Letters* and *Two Other Letters.* Thomas Lupton, *Siuquila: Too Good to Be True.* Lyly, *Euphues and His England.* Munday, **Zelauto, the Fountain of Fame* (possible source for *The Merchant of Venice*) and *A Second and Third Blast of Retrait from Plays and Theatres.* Rogers (tr. of Thomas à Kempis), *Of the Imitation of Christ.* Saker, *Narbonus, the Labyrinth of Liberty.* *Stow, *The Chronicles of England . . . unto . . . 1580* (probable source for *Richard III* and *1 Henry IV*; possible source for *2 Henry IV*). EUROPEAN: Bodin, *Démonomanie des Sorciers,* Cervantes, *Galatea.* *Montaigne, *Essais* (Bks. I and II).

1581

George Peele, *The Arraignment of Paris* (c. 1581–84; 1584) . Thomas Watson (tr. of Sophocles, in Latin), *Antigone.* *Robert Wilson, *The Three Ladies of London* (1584; offers a possible analogue to *The Merchant of Venice*).
EUROPEAN: *Nicolo Secchi, *L'Interesse* (offers an analogue to *Twelfth Night*).

William Allen, *An Apology and True Declaration of the Institution of the Two English Colleges* (Rheims and Douai). *Arthur Hall (tr.), *Ten Books of Homer's Iliads.* Thomas Howell, *His Devices for His Own Exercise and His Friends' Pleasure.* Lambard, *Eirenarcha, or The Office of the Justices of Peace.* *Thomas Lupton, *The Second Part and Knitting Up of the Book Entitled Too Good to Be True* (contains an analogue to *Measure for Measure*). Mulcaster, *Positions Necessary for the Training Up of Children.* Munday, *A Courtly Controversy between Love and Learning.* *Newton, Jasper Heywood, and others (trs.), *Seneca His Ten Tragedies* (for earliest publication of each play, see under Drama). Pettie (tr. of Guazzo), *The Civil Conversation* (Bk. IV added by Young, 1586). Barnabe Rich, **His Farewell to Military Profession* (principal source for *Twelfth Night*; possible source for *The Merry Wives of Windsor*) and *The Strange and Wonderful Adventures of Don Simonides* (Vol. II, 1584). EUROPEAN: Tasso, *Gerusalemme Liberata.*

1582

*Richard Edes, *Caesar Interfectus* (only a description survives; analogue to *Julius Caesar*). *Anon. (Anthony Munday?), *The Rare Triumphs of Love and Fortune* (1589; source for *Cymbeline*).

William Allen, *A Brief History of the . . . Martyrdom of XII . . . Priests.* Breton, *The Toys of an Idle Head* (in second ed. of *A Flourish upon Fancy*). *Buchanan, *Rerum Scoticarum Historia* (probable source for *Macbeth*). Gosson, *Plays Confuted in Five Actions.* Hakluyt, *Divers Voyages Touching the Discovery of America.* Mulcaster, *The First Part of the Elementary Which Entreateth of Right Writing of Our English Tongue.* Munday, *A Discovery of Edmund Campion and His Confederates* and *The English Roman Life.* Robert Parsons, *The First Book of the Christian Exercise Appertaining to Resolution* (later called *A Christian Directory*). Barnabe Rich, *The True Report of a Late Practice Enterprised by a Papist.* Robinson (tr. of Leland), *A Learned and True Assertion of the Life of Prince Arthur.* Stanyhurst (tr.), *The First Four*

	EVENTS	SHAKESPEARE
1583	James VI appears to throw in his lot with Elizabeth and the Protestant cause. Getting out of Alençon marriage costs Elizabeth £650,000 to preserve peace with France. The Arden and Throgmorton Plots (against Elizabeth, in favor of Mary); some 11,000 Roman Catholics arrested as a result of the Throgmorton confessions. On death of Grindal, John Whitgift made Archbishop. Irish insurgents, under the Earl of Desmond, defeated. Sir Humphrey Gilbert claims Newfoundland in Elizabeth's name. Levant Company chartered. Galileo discovers the principle of the pendulum. BORN: Edward Herbert (of Cherbury), Orlando Gibbons, Hugo Grotius, Philip Massinger. DIED: Humphrey Gilbert.	Susanna, Shakespeare's elder daughter, born (christened May 26; died 1649). Essex's Men play at Stratford.
1584	Elizabeth's eighth Parliament summoned (lasted into 1585). Seven Jesuits executed. Spanish ambassador forced to leave England. War with Spain now considered inevitable. James VI tries to engage the Pope's aid against Elizabeth. Death of Alençon. Murder of William of Orange (by order of Spain). The Bond of Association formed, under Leicester's leadership, to protect Elizabeth. Mary removed again to Tutbury Castle, virtually a prisoner. Sir Walter Raleigh's expedition to inspect North America for colonization is a failure. Emmanuel College (Oxford) founded; Richard Hooker and John Harvard early members. BORN: John Beaumont (?), John Pym, John Selden.	
1585	Elizabeth refuses the sovereignty of the Dutch States. James VI sells out finally to Elizabeth and is cursed by his mother, Mary. Elizabeth sends an army, under Leicester, to the relief of the Dutch States. Drake's successes against Spain at Vigo, St. Domingo, Cartagena, etc. seriously affect Spanish morale. Parry Plot (to assassinate Elizabeth) revealed. Colonists sent to Roanoke Island, Virginia; return in 1586. New English settlements in Ireland. BORN: William Drummond, Giles Fletcher (the younger), Richelieu. DIED: "The Admirable" Crichton, Pierre de Ronsard, Thomas Tallis.	Hamnet and Judith, Shakespeare's twin son and daughter, born; christened February 2. Hamnet died 1596; Judith died 1662.
1586	Elizabeth's ninth Parliament summoned (lasted into 1587). Babington Plot (to assassinate Elizabeth); Mary condemned to death because of supposed complicity; she is removed to Fotheringay Castle. Leicester accepts the governorship of the Dutch States in the Queen's name, but against her command; after Battle of Zutphen, in which Sir Philip Sidney suffers fatal wounds, Leicester is recalled. The Pope, Sixtus V, offers Philip of Spain one million crowns for a successful invasion of England. Star Chamber decree requires prior approval by church authorities for all publications. Cavendish's first voyage to the South Seas. BORN: John Ford.	Shakespeare may have left Stratford about this year (or a year earlier). The tradition that he was forced to leave Stratford because of a deer-stealing episode is now not generally accepted. A contemporary of Shakespeare's, William Beeston, an actor, reported that he became a schoolmaster in the country, but nothing certain is known of Shakespeare's whereabouts until 1592, by which time he is in London. Queen Elizabeth's Men, Lord Stafford's Men, and Leicester's Men play at Stratford.

DRAMA AND THEATRE HISTORY	NON-DRAMATIC LITERATURE	
The Rose Theatre (Bankside) built by Philip Henslowe. Robert Greene, *Alphonsus, King of Aragon* (1599). *Thomas Kyd, *The Spanish Tragedy* (c. 1582–92; c. 1592). *Christopher Marlowe, *1 Tamburlaine the Great* (1590). Marlowe and Thomas Nashe, *Dido, Queen of Carthage* (c. 1587–93; 1594). Peele, *The Love of King David and Fair Bethsabe* (c. 1587–94; 1599).	John Bridges, *A Defense of the Government Established in the Church of England.* Churchyard, *The Worthiness of Wales.* Angel Day (tr. of Longus), *Daphnis and Chloe* (contains also *The Shepherds' Holiday*). Fraunce (tr. of Thomas Watson), *The Lamentations of Amyntas* (see 1585). George Gifford, *A Discourse of the Subtle Practices of Devils.* Greene, **Euphues His Censure to Philautus* and *Penelope's Web.* Grove, *The Most Famous and Tragical History of Pelops and Hippodamia* (contains also *Epigrams, Songs, and Sonnets*). *Higgins (ed.), *The Mirror for Magistrates* (three pts.; source for *King Lear* and *Cymbeline;* contains an analogue to *Julius Caesar*). *Holinshed, *Chronicles* (second ed.; see 1577; a principal source for Shakespeare's English history plays and for *Lear, Macbeth,* and *Cymbeline*), some parts suppressed by government for dealing with contemporary affairs and printing recent documents. Knox, [*The History of the Reformation of Religion within the Realm of Scotland*]. Kyffin, *The Blessedness of Britain* and *A Defense of the Honorable Sentence and Execution of the Queen of Scots.* Rankins, *The Mirror of Monsters, Wherein Is Described the Vices Caused by Sight of Plays.* Barnabe Rich, *A Pathway to Military Practice.* Sidney and Golding (trs. of De Mornay), *A Work Concerning the Trueness of the Christian Religion.* Turberville (tr. of Boccaccio), *Tragical Tales.* Whetstone, *The Censure of a Loyal Subject* and *Sir Philip Sidney, His Honorable Life.* Young (tr. of Boccaccio), *Amorous Fiametta.* EUROPEAN: Tasso, *Discorsi dell'Arte Poetica.*	1587
Thomas Hughes and others, *The Misfortunes of Arthur* (1588) . Thomas Lodge, *The Wounds of Civil War, Lively Set Forth in the True Tragedies of Marius and Scilla* (c. 1587–92). *Lyly, *Endymion, the Man in the Moon* (1594; possible source for the fairy episode in *The Merry Wives of Windsor*; influence on presentation of Armado and Moth in *Love's Labor's Lost*; analogue to *1 Henry IV*). *Marlowe, *2 Tamburlaine the Great* (1590). Henry Porter, *1 The Two Angry Women of Abingdon* (c. 1585–91; 1599). Robert Wilson, *The Three Lords and Three Ladies of London* (1590). *Anon. (Peele?), *The Troublesome Reign of John, King of England* (in two parts; 1591, principal source for Shakespeare's *King John*). Anon., *The Wars of Cyrus* (c. 1587–94; 1594; based on a play by Richard Farrant, c. 1578).	Robert Allen, *An Admonition to the Nobility and People of England and Ireland.* *Averell, *A Marvellous Combat of Contrarieties* (source for Menenius' fable in *Coriolanus*). Bigges, *A Summary and True Discourse of Sir Francis Drake's West Indian Voyage.* Bright, *Charactery, An Art of Short, Swift, and Secret Writing.* Byrd, *Psalms, Sonnets, and Songs of Sadness and Piety.* Fraunce, *The Arcadian Rhetoric.* Greene, **Pandosto, the Triumph of Time* (principal source for *The Winter's Tale*); *Perimedes the Blacksmith*; *Alcida, Greene's Metamorphosis.* Hariot, *A Brief and True Report of the New Found Land of Virginia.* "Martin Marprelate," *Oh Read over Dr. John Bridges.* Munday, *The Banquet of Dainty Conceits*; (tr.), *Palmerin d'Oliva* (second part, 1596). Rankins, *The English Ape, the Italian Imitation.* John Udall, *The State of the Church of England* (also called *Diotrephes*). Anon. (tr. of Theocritus), *Six Idillia.* EUROPEAN: *Montaigne, *Essais* (Bk. III).	1588
Master of the Revels given official authority for censoring and licensing all plays in London. Amalgamation of Strange's and the Admiral's Men, until 1594. Greene, *Friar Bacon and Friar Bungay* (c. 1589–92; 1594). *Kyd, *Hamlet* (c. 1582–89; not extant; usually considered as the most immediate source of Shakespeare's *Hamlet*). Lyly, **Midas* (1592; source for *The Comedy of Errors* and *The Two Gentlemen of Verona*) and *Mother Bombie* (1594). *Marlowe, *The Jew of Malta* (1633; source for *The Merchant of Venice*). Anthony Munday, *John a' Kent and John a' Cumber* (MS; c. 1587–90). Peele, *The Battle of Alcazar* (1594). *Anon., *The Taming of a Shrew* (c. 1588–93; 1594; may be a "bad" quarto of Shakespeare's *The Taming of the Shrew*, 1593–94).	Anti-Martin tracts (some perhaps by Nashe or Lyly): *An Almond for a Parrot; A Countercuff Given to Martin Junior by . . . Pasquil of England; Mar-Martin; Martin's Month's Mind, Pap with a Hatchet; The Return of the Renowned Cavaliero Pasquil; A Whip for an Ape; Rhymes against Martin Marprelate.* Byrd, *Songs of Sundry Natures.* Thomas Cooper, *An Admonition to the People of England.* Robert Devereux, *A True Copy of a Discourse Written by a Gentleman Employed in the Late Voyage of Spain and Portugal.* Greene, *Ciceronis Amor, Tully's Love*; *Menaphon, Camilla's Alarum to Slumbering Euphues* (see Appendix C, Number 17); *The Spanish Masquerado.* Hakluyt, *The Principal Navigations, Voyages, and Discoveries of the English Nation* (enlarged 1598, 1600). Ive, *The Practice of Fortification* (including *Instructions for the Wars* [tr. of Du Bellay]). *Lodge, *Scilla's Metamorphosis* (probable source for *Venus and Adonis*). "Martin Marprelate," *Certain Mineral and Metaphysical Schoolpoints*; *Ha' Ye Any Work for Cooper*; *Theses Martinianae*; *The Just Censure and Reproof of Martin Junior; The Protestation of Martin Marprelate*; *A Dialogue.* Nashe, *The Anatomy of Absurdity.* Peele, *A Farewell to . . .*	1589

	EVENTS	SHAKESPEARE
1590	Henry of Navarre wins a victory over the Roman Catholic Leaguers at the Battle of Ivry. James VI marries Anne of Denmark. Death of Sir Francis Walsingham, next to Burleigh Elizabeth's principal adviser. Scottish trials for witchcraft (James VI himself supervised the examinations). BORN: William Bradford, William Browne (?). DIED: G. Salluste du Bartas, George Puttenham.	Sometime between this year and 1596 (probably after 1593) Shakespeare is thought by some scholars to have written the "Countess scenes" in the anonymous play *Edward III.* *2 Henry VI* (1590–91); published 1623; "bad" quarto, *The First Part of the Contention betwixt the Two Famous Houses of York and Lancaster (1594).* *3 Henry VI* (1590–91); published 1623; "bad" quarto, *The True Tragedy of Richard Duke of York* (1595).
1591	Earl of Essex, with an army, sent to aid Henry of Navarre in Normandy. Sir John Norris sent as commander in Brittany. Hacket's Conspiracy (a Puritan fanatic, who declared himself King of Europe). Elizabeth entertained at Elvetham by the Earl of Hertford. Cavendish's second voyage. Fight and destruction of the *Revenge*, under Sir Richard Grenville, at Flores. Proclamation against recusants. Essex leads the English contingent at the Siege of Rouen. Trinity College (Dublin) founded. Tea first introduced into England. BORN: Robert Herrick. DIED: Christopher Hatton, St. John of the Cross, Luis Ponce de León, Henry Smith.	
1592	Presbyterian system established by Scottish Parliament. Drake sacks Corunna, but fails to capture Lisbon. Essex recalled from France. The Great Carrack (the *Madre de Dios*) captured; booty valued at £150,000. Elizabeth visits Oxford. Plague in London. Count Mompelgard (given the Order of the Garter as Duke of Württemberg in 1597) visits England. BORN: John Eliot, Nicholas Ferrar, Francis Quarles. DIED: Robert Greene, Michel de Montaigne, Thomas Watson.	Shakespeare attacked by Robert Greene in his *Groatsworth of Wit* (see Appendix C, Number 8), the earliest reference to Shakespeare as active in the theatre. John Shakespeare cited for failing to attend monthly church services, as the law required, for fear of being arrested for debt. *Richard III* (1592–93); published 1623; "bad" quarto 1597. *Venus and Adonis* (1592–93); published 1593. *The Comedy of Errors* (1592–94); published 1623.

1589 (cont.)

Sir John Norris and Sir Francis Drake (contains *A Tale of Troy*). Puttenham, *The Art of English Poesy.* EUROPEAN: Della Porta, *Magia Naturalis.* Lipsius, *Politicorum sive Civilis Doctrinae.*

1590

Greene, *The Scottish History of James IV* (1598) and *George a' Greene, the Pinner of Wakefield* (c. 1587–91; 1599; attributed to Greene). Greene and Lodge, *A Looking Glass for London and England* (c. 1587–91; 1594). *Mary Herbert, Countess of Pembroke (tr. of Garnier), *The Tragedy of Antonius* (1592; analogue to *Antony and Cleopatra*). Lyly, *Love's Metamorphosis* (c. 1588–90; 1601). *Thomas Nelson, *The Device of a Pageant . . . [for] the Right Honorable John Allot* (1590; contains an analogue to *2 Henry VI*). Peele, *The Old Wive's Tale* (c. 1588–94; 1595). Robert Wilson, *The Cobbler's Prophecy* (c. 1589–93; 1594). *Anon., *Edward III* (c. 1590–95; 1596; some parts of this play—the "Countess scenes"—have been attributed to Shakespeare). Anon. (Robert Wilson?), *Fair Em, the Miller's Daughter of Manchester, with the Love of William the Conqueror* (?1593; wrongly attributed to Shakespeare). *Anon., *The True Chronicle History of King Leir, and His Three Daughters, Gonorill, Ragan, and Cordella* (c. 1588–90; 1605; source for Shakespeare's *King Lear*). *Anon., *Mucedorus* (c. 1588–98; 1598; wrongly attributed to Shakespeare; possible source for *The Winter's Tale*). Anon. (Thomas Kyd?), *The Tragedy of Soliman and Perseda* (c. 1589–92; c. 1592).

Peter Bales, *Writing Schoolemaster.* Sir John Davies, *Epigrams and Elegies* (including Marlowe's *Ovid's Elegies*). Greene, *Never Too Late, or A Powder of Experience Sent to All Youthful Gentlemen*; *Greene's Mourning Garment*; (tr. of *La Bursa Reale*) *The Royal Exchange.* Richard Harvey, *Plain Percival, the Peace-Maker of England* and *A Theological Discourse of the Lamb of God.* Henry Holland, *A Treatise against Witchcraft.* *Lodge, *Rosalynde, Euphues' Golden Legacy* (principal source for *As You Like It*). "Martin Marprelate," *Mar Mar-Martin.* Munday (tr.), *The First Book of Amadis of Gaul* (Bk. II, 1595). Peele, *Polyhymnia.* *Sidney, *The Countess of Pembroke's Arcadia* (augmented 1593; source for the Gloucester subplot in *King Lear*; possible source for *Pericles*; contains an analogue to *The Two Gentlemen of Verona*). *Spencer, *The Faerie Queene* (Bks. I–III; Bks. IV–VI, 1596; "Mutabilitie Cantos," 1609; Bk. II a probable source for *Much Ado about Nothing* and *King Lear*). Sylvester (tr. of Du Bartas), *A Canticle of the Victory Obtained by Henry IV at Ivry.* *Tarlton, *Tarlton's News out of Purgatory: Only Such a Jest as His Jig* (possible source for *The Merry Wives of Windsor*). Vallans, *A Tale of Two Swans.* Thomas Watson, *Meliboeus* (Latin and English eds.) and *The First Set of Italian Madrigals Englished.* Edward Webbe, *The Rare and Most Wonderful Things Which Edward Webbe Hath Seen.*

1591

Restraint against acting on Sundays and Thursdays to allow for proper attendance at bear-baiting.

Nicholas Breton (and Lyly?), *The Honorable Entertainment Given to the Queen's Majesty in Progress, at Elvetham in Hampshire, by the Right Honorable the Earl of Hertford* (1591). Greene, *The History of Orlando Furioso, One of the Twelve Peers of France* (c. 1589–93; 1594; actor's "part" for Orlando preserved). Peele, *The Famous Chronicle of King Edward I* (c. 1590–93; 1593) and *Descensus Astraeae* (1591). W. S. (George Peele? or Robert Greene?), *The Lamentable Tragedy of Locrine, the Eldest Son of King Brutus* (1595; wrongly attributed to Shakespeare). Anon. (Thomas Kyd?), *The Lamentable and True Tragedy of Master Arden of Feversham in Kent* (c. 1585–92; 1592; probably the earliest of the so-called "domestic" tragedies; wrongly attributed to Shakespeare). *Anon., *The Life and Death of Jack Straw* (c. 1590–93; 1593; analogue to Cade's rebellion in *2 Henry VI*). *Anon., *The True Tragedy of Richard III* (c. 1588–94; 1594; probable source for Shakespeare's *Richard III*).

Breton, *Briton's Bower of Delights.* *John Clapham, *Narcissus* (a covert attack on Southampton; *Venus and Adonis* perhaps written as an answer). Drayton, *The Harmony of the Church.* Giles Fletcher (the elder), *Of the Russe Commonwealth.* Fraunce, *The Countess of Pembroke's Ivychurch* and *The Countess of Pembroke's Emanuel.* Greene, *Farewell to Folly*; *A Maiden's Dream*; *A Notable Discovery of Cosenage*; **The Second Part of Coney-Catching* (probable source for *The Winter's Tale*). *Harington (tr. of Ariosto), *Orlando Furioso in English Heroical Verse* (Bk. V a probable source for *Much Ado about Nothing*). James VI, *His Majesty's Poetical Exercises.* Lodge, *The Famous, True, and Historical Life of Robert Second Duke of Normandy, Surnamed Robin the Devil* and *Catharos, Diogenes in His Singularity.* William Perkins, *A Golden Chain, or The Description of Theology.* Raleigh, *A Report of the Truth of the Fight about the Isles of the Azores.* Henry Savile (tr.), *Four Books of the Histories of Cornelius Tacitus.* *Sidney, *Astrophel and Stella* (unauthorized ed.); Southwell, *Mary Magdalen's Funeral Tears.* *Spenser, *Complaints* (source for *Sonnets*) and *Daphnaida.* Anon., *News from Scotland* (account of the North Berwick witch trial). EUROPEAN: Bruno, *De Immenso et Innumerabilis seu de universo et mundis.*

1592

The Earl of Pembroke's Men formed; played until 1600. Philip Henslowe begins his *Diary* (continued until 1604; a major source of information about theatrical events, principally in connection with the Admiral's Men). London theatres essentially closed by the plague from June of this year until June of 1594; acting companies forced to tour the provinces.

Greene (?), *The First Part of the Tragical Reign of Selimus, Sometime Emperor of the Turks* (c. 1586–93; 1594; no second part known). Greene (?) (rev. by

Breton, *The Pilgrimage to Paradise, Joined with The Countess of Pembroke's Love.* Churchyard, *A Handful of Gladsome Verses Given to the Queen's Majesty at Woodstock.* *Constable, *Diana* (source for *Sonnets*, enlarged 1594), "Cuthbert Cony-Catcher," *The Defense of Cony-Catching.* *Daniel, *Delia, Containing Certain Sonnets* (includes *The Complaint of Rosamond*, source for *A Lover's Complaint*; an augmented ed., 1594). Greene, *The Third and Last Part of Coney-Catching*; *A Disputation between a He Coney-Catcher and a She Coney-Catcher*; *The Black Book's Messenger*; *A Quip for an Upstart Courtier*; *Philomela, the Lady Fitzwater's Nightingale*;

EVENTS | SHAKESPEARE

1593

Elizabeth's eleventh Parliament summoned. Church attendance ordained on pain of banishment. Further actions taken against recusants, and three Brownist leaders (Barrow, Penry, Greenwood) executed for writing seditious books. Henry of Navarre reverts to Roman Catholicism for political purposes. The Warboys witch trials (three "witches" executed). Plague continues with increasing severity in London.
BORN: George Herbert, Izaak Walton.
DIED: Christopher Marlowe, Philip Stubbes.

Shakespeare's dedication of *Venus and Adonis* to Henry Wriothesley, Earl of Southampton.

Sonnets (1593–99); published 1609.
The Rape of Lucrece (1593–94); published 1594.
Titus Andronicus (1593–94); published 1594.
The Taming of the Shrew (1593–94); published 1623; "bad" quarto (?), *The Taming of a Shrew* (1594).

1594

Henry of Navarre crowned (as Henry IV) at Chartres; an attempt is made to assassinate him. Dr. Lopez tried and executed for supposed intent to poison Elizabeth. Yorke's Plot (to assassinate Elizabeth) revealed. A son, Henry, is born to James VI. Sir John Norris captures Croyzon (Brittany). Hugh O'Neill, Earl of Tyrone, leads an uprising in Ulster. Sidney Sussex College (Cambridge) founded.
BORN: James Howell (?), Nicholas Poussin.
DIED: Martin Frobisher, Barnabe Googe, Thomas Kyd, Gerardus Mercator, William Painter, Giovanni da Palestrina, Ferdinando, Lord Strange, Earl of Derby.

Shakespeare's dedication of *The Rape of Lucrece* to Henry Wriothesley, Earl of Southampton. In *Willobie His Avisa* Shakespeare, under the initials "W. S.", is described as an unsuccessful counsellor in a love affair involving "H. W." (identified as either Henry Wriothesley or a composite of Leicester and Essex) and as having recently been involved in a similar affair himself (see Appendix C, Number 10).

The Two Gentlemen of Verona; published 1623.
Love's Labor's Lost (1594–95; revised 1597); published 1598.
Sir Thomas More (1590–93; revised 1594–95; for other proposed dates, see the introduction to the "Additions ascribed to Shakespeare," pp. 1775–79); published 1844.
King John (1594–96); published 1623.
The Comedy of Errors (?) performed December 28 at Gray's Inn.
The Taming of the Shrew (?) performed at Newington Butts in June; recorded by Henslowe in his *Diary*, probably erroneously, as *"A Shrowe."* See Chronology, p. 79.

1595

Sir John Norris (recalled from Brittany) fails to put down Tyrone's revolt; nevertheless Tyrone asks for a truce.

Shakespeare about this time living in St. Helen's parish, Bishopsgate (London). His name mentioned

DRAMA AND THEATRE HISTORY	NON-DRAMATIC LITERATURE	
Henry Chettle), *John of Bordeaux* (the MS of this play is an example of the kind of reported texts that served as copy-text for the Shakespeare "bad" quartos). Marlowe, *The Tragical History of Doctor Faustus* ("bad" quarto, 1604; full text, 1616) and **The Troublesome Reign and Lamentable Death of Edward II* (1594; strongly influenced Shakespeare's *Richard II*). Nashe, **Summer's Last Will and Testament* (1600; source for several plays involving transfer of power, including *Richard III, Julius Caesar,* and *Hamlet*). *William Warner (tr. of Plautus), *Menaechmi* (c. 1592–94; 1595; Shakespeare may have used this translation in *The Comedy of Errors*). *Anon., *1 Richard II*, or *Thomas of Woodstock* (MS; c. 1591–95; source for Shakespeare's *Richard II*; also influenced *1 Henry IV*).	*Greene's Vision, Written at the Instant of His Death*; *The Repentance of Robert Greene*; **Greene's Groatsworth of Wit, Bought with a Million of Repentance* (see Appendix C, Number 8). Gabriel Harvey, *Four Letters and Certain Sonnets Especially Touching Robert Greene.* Lodge, *Euphues' Shadow.* Nashe, **Pierce Penniless His Supplication to the Devil* (source for *Hamlet* and several other plays, see Appendix C, Number 12) and *Strange News of the Intercepting Certain Letters.* *Barnabe Rich, *The Adventures of Brusanus, Prince of Hungaria* (contains an analogue to *Measure for Measure*). Henry Smith, *Sermons.* Spenser (?) (tr. of pseudo-Plato), *Axiochus.* Stow, *The Annals of England* (various continuations down to 1631). Philip Stubbes, *A Perfect Pathway to Felicity.* EUROPEAN: Revised ed. of *Vulgate* (*Biblia Sacra*).	1592 (cont.)
George Attowell, *Attowell's Jig* (*Francis and Richard*) (c. 1590–95; c. 1595; an example of the sort of entertainment presented after a play). *Samuel Daniel, *Cleopatra* (1594; in 1599 ed., probable source for *Antony and Cleopatra*). Marlowe, *The Massacre at Paris* (c. 1594). *Anon., *The Jealous Comedy* (not extant; conjecturally suggested as a source for *The Merry Wives of Windsor*).	Barnabe Barnes, *Parthenophil and Parthenophe, Sonnets, Madrigals, Elegies, Odes.* *Chettle, *Kind Heart's Dream* (see Appendix C, Number 9). Churchyard, *Churchyard's Challenge.* Drayton, *Idea, the Shepherd's Garland.* Giles Fletcher (the elder), *Licia, or Poems of Love.* George Gifford, *A Dialogue Concerning Witches and Witchcrafts.* *Gabriel Harvey, *Pierce's Supererogation, or A New Praise of the Old Ass* (possible use in Hamlet) and *A New Letter of Notable Contents.* Richard Harvey, *Philadelphus, or A Defense of Brutes and the Brutan History.* Henryson, *The Testament of Cresseid* (published earlier among Chaucer's *Works*; analogue to *Troilus and Cressida*). *Lodge, *Phillis, Honored with Pastoral Sonnets* (contains *The Tragical Complaint of Elstred*, possible source of *A Lover's Complaint*) and *The Life and Death of William Longbeard.* Lok, *Sundry Christian Passions Contained in Two Hundred Sonnets.* Morley, *Canzonets, or Little Short Songs to Three Voices.* *Nashe, *Christ's Tears over Jerusalem* (source for several plays, esp. *Macbeth* with Miriam prefiguring Lady Macbeth). Norden, *Speculum Britanniae, the First Part, A Description of Middlesex.* Peele, *The Honor of the Garter.* Shakespeare, *Venus and Adonis.* *Sidney, *Arcadia* (augmented). Philip Stubbes, *A Motive to Good Works.* Thomas Watson, *The Tears of Fancy, or Love Disdained.* Anon. *The Phoenix Nest* (verse collection).	1593
Emergence of the Lord Chamberlain's (Lord Hunsdon's) Men, the company with which Shakespeare was associated until his death; became the King's Men in 1603. Both the Admiral's and the Chamberlain's Men performed at the theatre at Newington Butts in this year. *Francis Bacon, Thomas Campion, and others, *Gesta Grayorum* (1594–95; 1688; contains, among other entertainments, Campion's *Proteus and the Adamantine Rock*, considered the first extant example of the formal masque, which may also have suggested the mask of Muscovites in *Love's Labor's Lost*). Kyd (tr. of Garnier), *Cornelia* (1594; interesting as an example of neo-Senecan French tragedy). Munday, Thomas Dekker, Chettle, ?Thomas Heywood, ?Shakespeare, *Sir Thomas More* (MS; rev. of play first composed c. 1590–93; famous for the scene in Hand D, generally assigned to Shakespeare; see pp. 1775 ff.). Anon. (Munday? or Thomas Heywood?), *A Knack to Know an Honest Man* (1596). EUROPEAN: *Orlando Pescetti, *Il Cesare* (possible source for *Julius Caesar*).	*Barnfield, *The Affectionate Shepherd* (source for *Sonnets*) and (?) *Greene's Funerals.* Richard Carew (tr. of Tasso), *Godfrey of Bouloigne, or the Recovery of Hierusalem* (Cantos I–VI). Chapman, *The Shadow of Night.* John Davis, *The Seaman's Secrets.* Dickenson, *Arisbas, Euphues amidst His Slumbers.* Drayton, *Piers Gaveston; Matilda*; *Idea's Mirror, Amours in Quaterzains.* I. G. (tr.), *Di Grassi His True Art of Defense.* *Hooker, *Of the Laws of Ecclesiastical Polity* (Bks. I–IV; Bk. V, 1597). Morley, *Madrigals to Four Voices.* Munday (tr.), *The First Book of Primaleon of Greece* (Bk. II, 1596; Bk. III, 1619). *Nashe, *The Terrors of the Night, or A Discourse of Apparitions* (source for several plays, incl., for dream interpretation, *Romeo and Juliet* and *Julius Caesar*) and *The Unfortunate Traveler* (source for several plays, incl. *Hamlet* and *All's Well*). William Percy, *Sonnets to the Fairest Coelia.* *Sabie, *The Fisherman's Tale* (source for *The Winter's Tale*). Shakespeare, *The Rape of Lucrece.* Sylvester, *Monodia* (contains *The Triumph of Faith* [tr. of Du Bartas]). *Laurence Twine, *The Pattern of Painful Adventures* (source for *Pericles*). "Henry Willobie," *Willobie His Avisa* (see Appendix C, Number 10). Anon., *Zepheria.* EUROPEAN: Mercator, *Atlas.* Tasso, *Discorsi del Poema Eroico.*	1594
The Swan Theatre (Bankside) built; see the contemporary drawing (c. 1596) of the stage and interior by	Barnabe Barnes, *A Divine Century of Spiritual Sonnets.* Barnfield, *Cynthia, with Certain Sonnets and The Legend of*	1595

	EVENTS	SHAKESPEARE
1595 (cont.)	Raleigh sails on his voyage to Guiana; explores the Orinoco. Robert Southwell, the Jesuit, executed. Prentices riot in London; five hanged. Small Spanish contingent lands in Cornwall, burning several towns; rumors of another Spanish Armada being assembled at Lisbon. Drake and Hawkins sail on a voyage to the West Indies (both die, 1596, on the expedition). BORN: Thomas Carew, Thomas May (?). DIED: Torquato Tasso, George Turberville (?).	in connection with payments (March 15), for the performance of two comedies at court (December 26 and 28, 1594), to the newly re-formed Lord Chamberlain's company, in which he now appears to be a "sharer." There is a tradition, reported first by Rowe, that Southampton gave Shakespeare "a thousand Pounds to enable him to go through with a Purchase." The sum mentioned is unrealistically large, but J. D. Wilson suggests that perhaps Southampton aided Shakespeare in buying his "share" in the Chamberlain's Men. *Richard II* (1595); published 1597. *Romeo and Juliet* (1595–96); published 1599; "bad" quarto 1597. *A Midsummer Night's Dream* (1595–96); published 1600. *Richard III* or *Richard II* perhaps performed in December at Sir Edward Hoby's London house.
1596	Calais is taken by the Spanish, but the Spanish fleet at Cadiz is destroyed by an expedition under Essex and Howard. Treaty signed with France (against Spain). The Dunkirk pirates begin to harass English shipping. High price and scarcity of grain. Sir Thomas Egerton becomes Lord Keeper. A daughter, Elizabeth, is born to James VI. The Brownists publish their "True Confession." Lectures first given at Gresham College (London). Fabricius makes the first observation of a variable star. Mahomet III succeeds Murad III as Emperor of the Turks and has all his brothers killed. BORN: René Descartes, Henry Lawes, James Shirley. DIED: Jean Bodin; Henry, Lord Hundson; George Peele.	Grant of arms made to John Shakespeare (October 20; see Appendix C, Number 3), giving him the right to sign himself as "Gentleman." A writ of attachment to keep the peace issued against Shakespeare, Francis Langley, Dorothy Soer, and Anne Lee by William Wayte; Langley was owner of the recently built Swan Theatre, but the circumstances leading to the writ are unknown, as is the outcome. Death of Shakespeare's son, Hamnet (buried August 11). Death of Shakespeare's uncle, Henry Shakespeare. *The Merchant of Venice* (1596–97); published 1600. *1 Henry IV* (1596–97); published 1598.

the Dutchman Johannes de Witt (Plate 8).

Anon., *Caesar and Pompey, or Caesar's Revenge* (c. 1592–96; c. 1606; possible source for *Julius Caesar*). Anon., *Edmond Ironside, or War Hath Made All Friends* (MS; c. 1590–1600).

1595 (cont.)

Cassandra. Beddingfield (tr. of Machiavelli), *The Florentine History*. Breton, *Mary Magdalen's Love*. Campion, *Poemata, ad Thamesin*. Chapman, *Ovid's Banquet of Sense*. Chettle, *Piers Plainess' Seven Years' Prenticeship*. Churchyard, *A Musical Consort of Heavenly Harmony* (with *A Praise of Poetry*). Copley, *Wits, Fits, and Fancies, also Love's Owl*. *Daniel, *The Civil Wars between the Two Houses of Lancaster and York* (Bks. I–[V]; Bks. VI–VIII, 1609; probable source for *Richard II* and *1* and *2 Henry IV*; possible source for *Henry V*). John Davis, *The World's Hydrographical Description*. Drayton, *Endimion and Phoebe, Idea's Latmus*. Thomas Edwards, *Cephalus and Procris*. Emanuel Forde, *The Most Pleasant History of Ornatus and Artesia*. Gosson, *Quips for Upstart Newfangled Gentlewomen*. Lodge, *A Fig for Momus*. Gervase Markham, *The Most Honorable Tragedy of Sir Richard Grenville*. Morley, *The First Books of Ballets to Five Voices* and *The First Book of Canzonets to Two Voices*. William Perkins, *A Sick Man's Salve*. *Sabie, *Flora's Fortune, the Second Part of The Fisherman's Tale* (source for *The Winter's Tale*). *Saviolo, *His Practice, in Two Books* (on rapier and dagger and honorable quarrels; possibly used in *As You Like It*). *Sidney, *An Apology for Poetry* [or *The Defense of Poesy*] (2 eds.; source for Menenius' fable in *Coriolanus*). *Southwell, *Moeoniae*; *Saint Peter's Complaint* (written ten years before; probable source for *The Rape of Lucrece*); *The Triumphs over Death*. Spenser, *Colin Clout's Come Home Again* and *Amoretti and Epithalamion*. Anon., *Alcilia*. Anon. (tr. of Du Bartas), *The First Day of the World's Creation*.

EUROPEAN: *Montaigne, *Essais* (completed).

1596

George Chapman, *The Blind Beggar of Alexandria* (1598). Ben Jonson, *A Tale of a Tub* (1640; extant text represents a revision in 1633). Anon. (in part by Thomas Heywood?), *The Famous History of the Life and Death of Captain Thomas Stukeley* (1605).

Ralph Brooke, *A Discovery of Certain Errors in [Camden's] Britannia*. *Caxton (tr. of Le Fevre; rev. by W. Fiston), *The Ancient History of the Destruction of Troy* (first published c. 1475 as *Recuyell of the Histories of Troy*; source for *Troilus and Cressida*). Churchyard, *A Pleasant Discourse of Court and Wars*. Copley, *A Fig for Fortune*. Danett (tr.), *The History of Philip de Comines*. Sir John Davies, *Orchestra, or A Poem of Dancing*. Dickenson, *The Shepherd's Complaint*. Drayton, *Mortimeriados, the Lamentable Civil Wars of Edward II and the Barons* (rev. 1603) and *The Tragical Legend of Robert Duke of Normandy, with the Legend of Matilda the Chaste*. Griffin, *Fidessa, More Chaste Than Kind*. Harington, *A New Discourse of a Stale Subject Called the Metamorphosis of Ajax*; *An Anatomy of the Metamorphosed Ajax*; *Ulysses upon Ajax*; *An Apology, or Rather a Retraction*. Richard Johnson, *The Most Famous History of the Seven Champions of Christendom*. Keymis, *A Relation of the Second Voyage to Guiana* (contains Chapman's *Carmen Epicum*). Lodge, *The Devil Conjured*; *A Margarite of America*; *Wit's Misery and the World's Madness*; (?) *Prosopopeia, Containing The Tears of the Holy Mary*. Lynche, *Diella, Certain Sonnets, Adjoined to the Poem of Dom Diego and Ginevra*. Gervase Markham, *The Poem of Poems, or Sion's Muse*. Thomas Middleton, *The Wisdom of Solomon Paraphrased*. Munday (tr.), *The History of Palmerin of England*. *Nashe, *Have with You to Saffron Walden* (source for *Romeo and Juliet*, *Twelfth Night*, and other plays). *L. P. (Anthony Munday?) (tr. of Sylvain), *The Orator, Handling a Hundred Several Discourses in Form of Declamations* (contains analogues to the bond story in *The Merchant of Venice* and to the brothel scenes in *Pericles*). Raleigh, *The Discovery of the Large, Rich, and Beautiful Empire of Guiana*. William Smith, *Chloris, or The Complaint of the Passionate Despised Shepherd*. *Spenser, *The Faerie Queene* (Bks. I–VI [I–III revised]); *Prothalamion*; *Four Hymns*.

	EVENTS	SHAKESPEARE
1597	Elizabeth's twelfth Parliament summoned (lasted into 1598). Essex, Sir Francis Vere, Raleigh lead an unsuccessful sea expedition against Spain (the Islands Voyage). A second Spanish Armada is scattered by bad weather within two days' sail of Land's End. A proclamation against inordinate apparel (subjects must dress according to social position). DIED: Aldus Manutius (the younger).	Fine levied on Shakespeare's purchase of New Place in Stratford. Record of Shakespeare's failure to pay his subsidy taxes on his goods in St. Helen's parish (London); tax seems to have been paid by 1600. *The Merry Wives of Windsor* (1597; revised 1600–1); published 1623; "bad" quarto 1602.
1598	French civil wars end with the Edict of Nantes (granting French Protestants limited toleration and the right to hold elective office). Death of Philip II. Truce with Tyrone in Ireland expires; new rebellion. Elizabeth boxes Essex's ear in Council for incivility. Death of Burleigh, Elizabeth's principal counsellor from the beginning of her reign; succeeded in his position by his son, Robert Cecil. Sir Thomas Bodley endows the Bodleian Library.	Shakespeare, at Stratford, recorded (February 4) as holding ten quarters of malt during a period of corn shortage. Shakespeare's name listed first among the "principall Comoedians" in Jonson's *Every Man in His Humor.* Francis Meres, in *Palladis Tamia*, lists twelve plays (including *Loue labours wonne*) as by Shakespeare (see Appendix C, Number 22). *2 Henry IV*; published 1600. *Much Ado about Nothing* (1598–99); published 1600.
1599	Essex sent to Ireland as Lord Deputy with a large army; his efforts against Tyrone fail and he returns to England against Elizabeth's command, is disgraced, and detained in close custody. A Council order against publication of satires; certain books of satires publicly burned (all Gabriel Harvey's and Thomas Nashe's works proscribed). Threat of a third Spanish Armada.	Shakespeare about this time, or slightly earlier, living in the Clink on the Surrey Bankside. John Shakespeare applied to the College of Arms to have the Arden arms impaled on his; a grant was written up but probably not officially issued.

DRAMA AND THEATRE HISTORY	NON-DRAMATIC LITERATURE	

Second Blackfriars Theatre, a "private" theatre, constructed by James Burbage; not used, however, until 1600 (see 1600, 1608). Chamberlain's Men forced on provincial tour, until October, as the result of an inhibition against playing in London. Chamberlain's Men performed at the Curtain from late 1597 to 1599, while the Theatre was being torn down and the Globe being built; probably the Curtain was the "wooden O" referred to in *Henry V* (1599).

Chapman, *An Humorous Day's Mirth* (*The Comedy of Humors*) (1599; significant as anticipating many essentials of Jonson's "comedy of humors"). Jonson, *The Case Is Altered* (1609; extant text represents a later revision). Lyly, *The Woman in the Moone*. Nashe and Jonson, *The Isle of Dogs* (not extant).

Bacon, *Essays, Meditationes Sacrae, Colors of Good and Evil* (the *Essays* augmented 1612, 1625). Thomas Beard, *The Theatre of God's Judgments*. Breton, *Auspicante Jehova, Mary's Exercise; Wit's Trenchmore; The Will of Wit, Wit's Will, or Will's Wit;* (with others) *The Arbor of Amorous Devices*. John Dowland, *The First Book of Songs*. Drayton, *England's Heroical Epistles*. *Gerard, *The Herbal* (probable source for concluding song in *Love's Labor's Lost*). Joseph Hall, *Virgidemiarum* (Bks. I–III; Bks. IV–VI, 1598). (?) Gabriel Harvey, *The Trimming of Thomas Nashe, Gentleman*. James VI, *Demonology, in Form of a Dialogue*. Ling (ed.), *Politeuphuia, or Wit's Commonwealth*. Lok, *Ecclesiastes, Abridged and Dilated in English Poesy* (with *Sonnets of Christian Passions*). Christopher Middleton, *The Famous History of Chinon of England*. Montgomery, *The Cherry and the Slae*. E. S., *The Discovery of the Knights of the Post*. Tofte, *Laura, the Toys of a Traveler, or the Feast of Fancy*. Weelkes, *Madrigals to Three, Four, etc. Voices*. Anon., *Certain Worthy Manuscript Poems* (associated with Joseph Hall). 1597
EUROPEAN: Kepler, *Mysterium Cosmographicum*.

The Theatre (Shoreditch) torn down; materials used in the building of the Globe (Bankside).

William Haughton, *Englishmen for My Money* (1616). Jonson, *Every Man in His Humor* (1601; rev. version, 1616). Munday (rev. by Chettle), *The Downfall of Robert Earl of Huntingdon, Afterward Called Robin Hood of Merry Sherwood* (1601). Munday and Chettle, *The Death of Robert Earl of Huntingdon* (1601).

Barnfield, *The Combat between Conscience and Covetousness; The Complaint of Poetry for the Death of Liberality;* **The Encomium of Lady Pecunia* (source for *Sonnets*), *Poems in Divers Humors*. Bastard, *Chrestoleros, Seven Books of Epigrams*. Bernard (tr.), *Terence in English*. Breton, *A Solemn Passion of the Soul's Love*. *Chapman (tr. of Homer), *Seven Books of the Iliads* (Bks. I–II, VII–XI; complete *Iliad*, 1611; source for *Troilus and Cressida*) and *Achilles' Shield*; also continuation of Marlowe's *Hero and Leander*. Churchyard, *A Wished Reformation of Wicked Rebellion*. J. D. (tr.), *Aristotle's Politics*. Deloney, *The Gentle Craft* (Pts. I and II); *Jack of Newberry; Thomas of Reading* (dates of all uncertain; no early eds. have survived). Dickenson, *Greene in Conceit, New Raised from His Grave to Write the Tragic History of Fair Valeria of London*. Florio, A *World of Words, or Dictionary in Italian and English*. *Emanuel Forde, *Parismus, the Renowned Prince of Bohemia* (possible source for *Twelfth Night* and *The Winter's Tale*). *Greneway (tr.), *The Annals of Cornelius Tacitus* (Bk. I, enlarged, 1604; source for *Henry V*, particularly the king's nocturnal visit; possible source for *Julius Caesar*). Guilpin, *Skialetheia, or A Shadow of Truth*. James VI, *The True Law of Free Monarchies*. *Marlowe, *Hero and Leander*. Marston, *The Metamorphosis of Pygmalion's Image, and Certain Satires* and *The Scourge of Villainy* (augmented 1599). *Meres, *Palladis Tamia, Wit's Treasury* (see Appendix C, Number 22). Rankins, *Seven Satires Applied to the Week*. Samuel Rowlands, *The Betraying of Christ, Judas in Despair*. Southwell, *A Short Rule of Good Life*. *Speght (ed.), *Works of Chaucer* (see 1561). Stow, *A Survey of London*. Sylvester (tr. of Du Bartas), *The Second Week, or Childhood of the World*. Tofte, *Alba: The Month's Mind of a Melancholy Lover*, refers to *Love's Labor's Lost* (cf. Appendix C, Number 15C.); (tr. of Boiardo), *Orlando Inamorato* (Bks. I–III). Weelkes, *Ballets and Madrigals to Five Voices*. Wilby, *The First Set of English Madrigals*. *Bartholomew Young (tr. of Montemayor), *Diana* (source for *The Two Gentlemen of Verona*). 1598
EUROPEAN: Lope de Vega, *Arcadia*.

The Globe Theatre (Bankside) opened for the Chamberlain's Men; the theatre most commonly associated with Shakespeare's career.

*Chettle and Dekker, *Troilus and Cressida* (not extant; known only from a MS "plot" fragment; possible source for Shakespeare's play). Dekker, *The Pleasant*

Allott (ed.), *Wit's Theatre of the Little World*. Cutwode, *Caltha Poetarum, or The Bumble Bee*. *Daniel, *The Poetical Essays* (contains *Musophilus* and *Letter from Octavia to Marcus Antonius*, sources for *Julius Caesar*, and the latter possibly for *Antony and Cleopatra*). *Sir John Davies, *Nosce Teipsum* (source for *Julius Caesar*), *This Oracle Expounded in Two Elegies* and *Hymns of Astraea, in Acrostic Verse*. 1599

	EVENTS	SHAKESPEARE
1599 (cont.)	BORN: Oliver Cromwell, Anthony Van Dyck, Diego y Velasquez. DIED: Edmund Spenser.	*Henry V*; published 1623; "bad" quarto 1600. *Julius Caesar*; published 1623. *As You Like It*; published 1623. *Julius Caesar* performed December 21; seen by the Swiss traveler Thomas Platter. See Appendix C, Number 16.
1600	Lord Mountjoy sent as Lord Deputy to command English forces in Ireland. Essex tried for neglect of his duties, convicted and disgraced, but left at liberty. Victory at Nieuport (Flanders) against the Spanish. A second Gowrie Conspiracy (James VI narrowly escapes assassination). Will Kemp's morris-dance from London to Norwich. St. Helena claimed by England. East India Company chartered. A son, Charles (later Charles I, is born to James VI. Giordano Bruno burned at Rome for maintaining the plurality of inhabited worlds. BORN: Pedro Calderón, John Earle (?), Peter Heylyn, William Prynne (?), Charles Stuart, later Charles I. DIED: Thomas Deloney (?), Richard Hooker, Thomas Nashe (or 1601).	*Hamlet* (1600–1); published 1604; "bad" quarto 1603; possibly performed at Oxford. "Sir John Old Castell" acted March 6 at Lord Hundson's (the Lord Chamberlain's) London house. Probably *1* or *2 Henry IV.*
1601	Elizabeth's thirteenth Parliament summoned. Essex attempts rebellion; is tried and executed; Earl of Southampton also found guilty, but only imprisoned. Siege of Ostend; English reinforcements sent. Mountjoy defeats a Spanish attempt on Ireland. New Poor Law, throwing responsibility on the parish (basically unchanged until 1834). Virginio Orsino, Duke of Brachiano, received at court. Captain James Lancaster's voyage to the East Indies (returned 1603). BORN: Athanasius Kircher.	John Shakespeare's (?) "Spiritual Testament," six-leaf manuscript found in 1757 in the Shakespeare House on Henley Street, which indicates that the testator died a Roman Catholic. See James McManaway, "John Shakespeare's 'Spiritual Testament,'" *SQ*, XVIII (1967), 197–205. Death of John Shakespeare (buried September 8). Shortly before his death he was called upon by the Stratford Corporation to aid them with advice in a lawsuit. *Richard II* played at the Globe (February 7) at the instigation of Essex's party as an incentive to rebellion; a

1599 (cont.)

Comedy of Old Fortunatus (1600; reworking of an earlier play, perhaps by Greene) and *The Shoemakers' Holiday, or the Gentle Craft* (1600). *Michael Drayton, Richard Hathway, Munday, and Robert Wilson (rev. by Dekker), *The First Part of the True and Honorable History of the Life of Sir John Oldcastle, the Good Lord Cobham* (1600; a second part, not extant, was written in 1600; an answer to Shakespeare's treatment of Oldcastle-Falstaff in the *Henry IV* plays; wrongly attributed to Shakespeare). Thomas Heywood (?) and others (?), *1* and *2 Edward IV* (c. 1592–99; 1600). Jonson, *Every Man Out of His Humor* (1600). John Marston, *The History of Antonio and Mellida. The First Part* (1602) and *Histrio-Mastix, or the Player Whipt* (1610; rev. of an earlier play, c. 1589; Marston's presentation of Jonson as Chrisogonus is supposed to have paved the way for the War of the Theatres). Henry Porter, *Two Merry Women of Abingdon* (not extant). Anon., *A Larum for London, or The Siege of Antwerp* (1602). Anon. (Chettle? or Dekker?), *Look about You* (1600). Anon., *The Pilgrimage to Parnassus.* *Anon., *The Thracian Wonder* (c. 1590–1600; 1661; possible source for *The Winter's Tale).* Anon. (Thomas Heywood?), *A Warning for Fair Women* (1599). Anon., *The Wisdom of Doctor Dodypoll* (1600).

Greene, *Orpharion* (first extant ed.). Sir John Hayward, *The First Part of the Life and Reign of King Henry IV.* Alexander Hume, *Hymns, or Sacred Songs, and Certain Precepts.* William Jaggard (ed.), *The Passionate Pilgrim* (includes some poems by Shakespeare). James VI, *Basilikon Doron.* *Lewkenor (tr. of Contarini), *The Commonwealth and Government of Venice* (source for *Othello*). T. M., *Micro-cynicon, Six Snarling Satires.* Marlowe (tr. of Ovid) and Sir John Davies, *Epigrams and Elegies* (exact date uncertain). *Nashe, *Nashe's Lenten Stuff* (source material for several plays, incl. *Henry V, Julius Caesar,* and *Hamlet*). Silver, *Paradoxes of Defense.* Storer, *The Life and Death of Thomas Wolsey, Cardinal.* Weever, *Epigrams in the Oldest Cut and Newest Fashion.*

EUROPEAN: Mateo Alemán, *Guzmán de Alfarache* (picaresque novel, englished 1622 by J. Mabbe as *The Rogue*).

1600

The Fortune Theatre (St. Giles without Cripplegate) built by Edward Alleyn and Philip Henslowe for the Admiral's Men in competition to the Globe (see Appendix C, Number 30); used by various acting groups after 1603; demolished in 1662. The Children of the Chapel occupy the Second Blackfriars Theatre.

Chettle, John Day, and ?William Haughton, *1 The Blind Beggar of Bednal Green* (1659). Dekker, Chettle, and Haughton, *The Pleasant Comedy of Patient Grissil* (1603). Fulke Greville, *Alaham* (1633). Haughton, *Grim the Collier of Croydon* (*The Devil and His Dame*) (1662). Thomas Heywood, *The Four Prentices of London* (c. 1592–1600; 1615). Jonson, *The Fountain of Self-Love, or Cynthia's Revels* (1601). Marston, *Antonio's Revenge. The Second Part* (1602) and *Jack Drum's Entertainment, or the Comedy of Pasquil and Katherine* (1601). Anon. (perhaps Day, Dekker, and Haughton), *Lust's Dominion, or the Lascivious Queen* (1657). Anon. (Day? or Lyly?), *The Maid's Metamorphosis* (1600). Anon., *1 The Return from Parnassus* (see Appendix C, Number 13). Anon., *The True Chronicle of the Whole Life and Death of Thomas Lord Cromwell* (1602; wrongly attributed to Shakespeare). Anon. (Dekker?), *The Weakest Goeth to the Wall* (1600).

EUROPEAN: Alexandre Hardy, *Coriolan* (1625).

Allott (ed.), *England's Parnassus.* Bodenham (ed.), *England's Helicon* and *Belvedere, or The Garden of the Muses.* Breton, *The Strange Fortune of Two Excellent Princes*; *Melancholic Humors*; *Pasquil's Mad-Cap and Mad-Cap's Message*; *The Second Part of Pasquil's Mad-Cap, Entitled The Fool's Cap*; *Pasquil's Mistress*; *Pasquil's Pass and Passeth Not.* Cornwallis, *Essays* (augmented 1610). John Dowland, *The Second Book of Songs.* Fairfax (tr. of Tasso), *Godfrey of Bouloigne.* William Gilbert, *De Magnete.* Thomas Heywood (tr. of Ovid), *The Art of Love.* *Philemon Holland (tr. of Livy), *The Roman History* (probable source for *Coriolanus*). *Robert Jones, *The First Book of Songs and Airs* (source of some song snatches in *Twelfth Night*). William Kemp, *Kemp's Nine Days' Wonder, Performed in a Dance from London to Norwich.* F. L. (tr.), *Ovidius Naso His Remedy of Love.* Gervase Markham, *The Tears of the Beloved.* Marlowe (tr.), *Lucan's First Book* (*Pharsalia*). *Morley, *First Book of Airs, or Little Short Songs.* Samuel Rowlands, *The Letting of Humor's Blood in the Head-Vein.* Sir Anthony Sherley, *A True Report of Sir A. Sherley's Journey Overland to Venice.* Tourneur, *The Transformed Metamorphosis.* William Vaughan, *The Golden Grove, Moralized in Three Books.* Weelkes, *Madrigals of Five and Six Parts.* Anon., *Book of Merry Riddles.*

1601

The War of the Theatres, principally involving Jonson vs. Marston and Dekker, at its height.

Dekker, *Satiro-Mastix, or the Untrussing of the Humorous Poet* (1602; the concluding blow in the War of the Theatres). John (?) Dymock (tr.), *Il Pastor Fido, or The Faithful Shepherd* (1602; first English translation of Guarini's immensely influential pastoral tragicomedy). Jonson, *Poetaster, or The Arraignment* (1602; Jonson's attempt to silence Marston and Dekker in the War of the Theatres). Marston, *What You Will* (1607; part of the attack on Jonson). Anon.

Bacon, A *Declaration of the Practices and Treasons Committed by Robert Late Earl of Essex.* Breton, *A Divine Poem, Divided into Two Parts: The Ravished Soul and The Blessed Weeper*; *No Whipping nor Tripping*; *The Longing of a Blessed Heart.* Chamber, *A Treatise against Judicial Astrology.* *Chester, *Love's Martyr, or Rosalin's Complaint* (contains Shakespeare's "The Phoenix and Turtle"). Cornwallis, *Discourses upon Seneca the Tragedian.* Dent, *The Plain Man's Pathway to Heaven.* Dolman (tr. of La Primaudaye), *The Third Volume of the French Academy.* *Philemon Holland (tr. of Pliny), *The History of the World* (source for *Othello*).

	EVENTS	SHAKESPEARE
1601 (cont.)	DIED: Tycho Brahe, William Lambard, Sir Thomas North (?).	member of Shakespeare's company, Augustine Phillips, was questioned by the authorities but no charges were brought. "The Phoenix and Turtle" (c. 1601) in Chester's *Love's Martyr.* *Twelfth Night* (1601–2); published 1623. *Troilus and Cressida* (1601–2); published 1609.
1602	The Duke of Biron's plot against Henry IV revealed; Biron executed. Proclamation ordering Jesuits and secular priests to leave England. Captain Bartholomew Gosnold's voyage to New England. The Bodleian Library opened. BORN: William Chillingworth, Owen Feltham (?), William Lilly. DIED: William Perkins.	Conveyance of land (127 acres) to Shakespeare in Old Stratford (May 1) by John Combe for the sum of £320. Copyhold for a cottage in Chapel Lane (or Dead Lane), Rowington Manor, Stratford (September 28). Shakespeare's right to possess a coat of arms is attacked by Ralph Brooke, York Herald, but the original grant (1596) is sustained. *All's Well That Ends Well* (1602–3); published 1623. *Twelfth Night* performed February 2 at the Middle Temple. See Appendix C, Number 19.
1603	Death of Queen Elizabeth (March 24); her funeral on April 28. Accession of James I (VI of Scotland), as Elizabeth's choice, in preference to that of the legal heir, William Seymour. Tyrone surrenders to Mountjoy. The Millenary Petition (Puritan demands for reformation in the Anglican Church). The Watson Plot (to seize James's person). The Act of Uniformity reinforced. The Cobham Plot (to overthrow James in favor of Lady Arabella Stuart); Raleigh, implicated, is imprisoned until 1616. Plague rages in London (30,561 deaths). James sells knighthoods. Master Bartholomew Gilbert's voyage to Virginia. BORN: Sir Kenelm Digby, Shakerley Marmion. DIED: Thomas Cartwright, Pierre Charron, William Gilbert, Thomas Morley.	Shakespeare recorded as one of the "principall Tragoedians" in Jonson's *Sejanus*; last appearance of his name in Jonson's actors' lists. He may have visited Lady Pembroke at Wilton House (Wiltshire) between October and December in connection with a performance of *As You Like It* there put on for King James.
1604	Hampton Court Conference; a new translation of the Bible advocated and a committee of forty-seven appointed to prepare it. James's first Parliament summoned; asserts rights of election and the freedom of members from arrest. Proclamation banishing Jesuits and seminary priests; Robert Catesby plots revenge. A revised and somewhat more severe act against witchcraft passed. Peace declared with Spain. Ostend falls to the Spanish. On death of Whitgift, Richard Bancroft made Archbishop. A special tax laid on tobacco to restrain its use. Captain George Weymouth's voyage to New England, and Captain Charles Leigh's expedition to establish a colony in Guiana. DIED: Thomas Churchyard.	About this time Shakespeare sues Philip Rogers, apothecary, for debt in Stratford. As a member of the King's Men, Shakespeare is granted four yards of red cloth for James's procession through London (March 15). *Measure for Measure*; published 1623. *Othello*; published 1622. "A play of Robin goode-fellow," (?) *A Midsummer Night's Dream* performed January 1 at Court. "The Moor of Venis" performed November 1 at Whitehall. "A play of the Merry wives of Winsor" performed November 4 at Whitehall. "A play Caled Mesur for Mesur" performed December 26 at Whitehall.

1601 (cont.)

(Thomas Middleton?), *Blurt, Master Constable* (1602). Anon., *The Contention between Liberality and Prodigality* (1602). Anon. (Thomas Heywood? or Chettle?), *The Trial of Chivalry* (1605).

Robert Johnson, *Essays, or Rather Imperfect Offers.* Robert Jones, *The Second Book of Songs and Airs.* Morley, *Madrigals, the Triumphs of Oriana.* Rosseter, *A Book of Airs.* Thomas Wright, *The Passions of the Mind.*
EUROPEAN: Charron, *De la Sagesse.*

1602

Chapman, *Sir Giles Goosecap, Knight* (1606); *The Gentleman Usher* (*Vincentio and Margaret*) (c. 1602–4; 1606); *May-Day* (c. 1601–9; 1611). Chettle, *Hoffman, or A Revenge for a Father* (1631). Thomas Heywood (?), *How a Man May Choose a Good Wife from a Bad* (1602). Thomas Heywood, *The Royal King and the Loyal Subject* (1637). Thomas Middleton, *The Family of Love* (c. 1602–7; 1608). Anon. (Thomas Heywood?), *The Fair Maid of the Exchange* (c. 1594–1607; 1607). Anon. (Dekker?), *The Merry Devil of Edmonton* (1608; wrongly attributed to Shakespeare). *Anon., *Timon* (date debated, as is its exact relation to Shakespeare's *Timon of Athens*). Anon. (Samuel Rowley?), *Wily Beguil'd* (c. 1596–1606; 1606).

Basse, *Sword and Buckler, or Servingman's Defense* and *Three Pastoral Elegies, of Anander, Anetor, and Muridella.* Francis Beaumont (tr. of Ovid), *Salmacis and Hermaphroditus.* John Beaumont, *The Metamorphosis of Tobacco.* John Brereton, *A Brief and True Relation of the Discovery of the North Part of Virginia.* Breton, *The Soul's Harmony*; *The Mother's Blessing*; *Old Mad-Cap's New Gallimaufry*; *A True Description of Unthankfulness*; *Wonders Worth the Hearing*; *A Post with a Mad Packet of Letters*; *The Passion of a Discontented Mind.* Campion, *Observations in the Art of English Poesy.* John Davies, *Mirum in Modum, a Glimpse of God's Glory and the Soul's Shape.* Davison (ed.), *A Poetical Rhapsody.* Deloney, *Strange Histories, of Kings, Princes, Dukes, [etc.].* Lodge, *Paradoxes against Common Opinions*; (tr.), **The Famous and Memorable Works of Josephus* (contains an analogue to *Julius Caesar*). Patericke (tr. of Gentillet), *A Discourse upon the Means of Well Governing . . . Against Nicholas Machiavel the Florentine.* Samuel Rowlands, *'Tis Merry When Gossips Meet.* John Willis, *Art of Stenographie.*
EUROPEAN: Lope de Vega, *La Hermosura de Angelica.*

1603

Chamberlain's Men licensed by royal order as the King's Men (see Appendix C, Number 31). Admiral's Men become Prince Henry's Men; later (1613) became the Palsgrave's Men. Sir George Buck appointed as acting Master of the Revels (as Master, 1611, until 1622). Theatres closed because of plague the latter half of this year and until April 1604.

Thomas Heywood, *A Woman Kill'd with Kindness* (1607). Jonson, *Sejanus His Fall* (1605). Anon., *2 The Return from Parnassus* (1606; contains a reference to Shakespeare's supposed role in attacking Jonson in the recent War of the Theatres; see Appendix C, Number 13).

Bacon, *A Brief Discourse Touching the Happy Union of the Kingdoms of England and Scotland.* John Barclay, *Euphormionis Lusinini Satyricon* (Paris). Breton, *A Dialogue Full of Pith and Pleasure between Three Philosophers.* Chettle, *England's Mourning Garment.* Daniel, *A Panegyric Congratulatory to the King's Majesty* (contains the *Defense of Rhyme*). John Davies, *Microcosmos, the Discovery of the Little World.* Dekker, *The Wonderful Year, 1603.* John Dowland, *The Third and Last Book of Songs or Airs.* *Florio (tr. of Montaigne), *The Essays, or Moral, Politic Discourses* (used by Shakespeare in *Hamlet* [in MS], *King Lear,* and *The Tempest*). Fowldes (tr. of Homer), *Batrachomyomachia.* Joseph Hall, *The King's Prophecy, or Weeping Joy.* *Samuel Harsnett, *A Declaration of Egregious Popish Impostures* (source for *King Lear*). Philemon Holland (tr. of Plutarch), *The Philosophy, Commonly Called The Morals.* Knolles, *The General History of the Turks.* Lodge, *A Treatise of the Plague.* Norden, *A Pensive Soul's Delight.* Tofte (?) (tr.), *The Bachelor's Banquet.*

1604

Queen Anne's Men formed from Worcester's Men.

Chapman, *All Fools* (1605); *Bussy D'Ambois* (c. 1600–4; 1607); *Monsieur D'Olive* (1606). Daniel, *Philotas* (1605). John Day, *Law Tricks, or Who Would Have Thought It* (c. 1604–7; 1608). Dekker and Middleton, *1 The Honest Whore, with the Humors of the Patient Man and the Longing Wife* (1604). Dekker and John Webster, *The Famous History of Sir Thomas Wyatt* (c. 1602–7; 1607) and *Westward Hoe!* (1607). Thomas Heywood, *1 If You Know Not Me, You Know Nobody, or The Troubles of Queen Elizabeth* (1605) and *The Wise Woman of Hogsdon* (1638). Marston, *The Dutch Courtesan* (1605) and (with Induction by Webster) **The Malcontent* (1604; possible source for Gloucester's attempted suicide in *King Lear*). Middleton, *The Phoenix* (1607). *Samuel Rowley, *When*

Alexander, *Aurora* and *A Paraenesis to the Prince.* Bacon, *His Apology in Certain Imputations Concerning the Late Earl of Essex* and *Certain Considerations Touching the Better Pacification of the Church of England.* Bateson, *The First Set of English Madrigals.* Breton, *The Passionate Shepherd* and *Grimello's Fortunes.* Churchyard, *Churchyard's Good Will.* Dallington, *The View of France.* Dekker, *News from Gravesend Sent to Nobody.* John Dowland, *Lachrimae, or Seven Tears.* Drayton, *The Owl*; *Moses in a Map of His Miracles*; *A Paean Triumphal.* Michael East, *Madrigals . . . Apt for Viols and Voices.* Sir John Hayward, *The Sanctuary of a Troubled Soul* (Pt. II, 1607). James I, *A Counterblast to Tobacco.* Thomas Middleton, *Father Hubbard's Tales, or The Ant and the Nightingale* and *The Black Book.* Barnabe Rich, *A Soldier's Wish to Britain's Welfare* and *The Fruits of Long Experience.* Samuel Rowlands, *Look to It, for I'll Stab Ye.* Sir Anthony Sherley, *Wit's New Dial.* Wrednot (ed.), *Palladis*

	EVENTS	SHAKESPEARE
		"The plaie of Errors" performed December 28 at Whitehall *Love's Labor's Lost* (?) performed at the Earl of Southampton's London house.
1605	Strong action against Roman Catholics and Puritans is pressed by James. Episcopacy restored in Scotland by James's order; Presbyterians ejected. A daughter, Mary, is born to James. James visits Oxford. Catesby's Gunpowder Plot discovered (November 5); Catesby and Thomas Percy killed in being captured; Guido Fawkes (alias John Johnson) imprisoned (executed 1606). Amnesty granted to the Irish rebels (March 11). A catalogue of the Bodleian Library printed. BORN: Sir Thomas Browne, Thomas Randolph, Bulstrode Whitelocke. DIED: Theodore Beza, John Stow.	Shakespeare is left "a thirty shillings peece in gold" by the will (May 4) of his fellow actor Augustine Phillips. He purchases a half-interest in tithes in Old Stratford, Welcombe, and Bishopton (July 24). *King Lear*; published 1608. Between January 1 and 6, "A play of 'Loves Labours Lost'" performed at Whitehall. January 7 "was played the play of Henry the fift." "A play of the Marthant of Venis" performed February 10 and 12.
1606	Parliament balks at the proposed union of England and Scotland. Oath of Allegiance imposed. Henry Garnet, Provincial of the Jesuits, executed as a conspirator in the Gunpowder Plot; the Jesuit doctrine of equivocation much publicized. A new act against recusancy (heavy fines for failure to attend Anglican services and receive the sacrament). Virginia chartered between the London and Plymouth Companies; the plantation expedition, under Captain Christopher Newport, sails December 19. Sir Edward Coke made Chief Justice of the Common Pleas. Christian IV, King of Denmark and brother of Queen Anne, makes a state visit. BORN: Pierre Corneille, Sir William Davenant, Sir William Killigrew, Rembrandt van Rijn, Edmund Waller. DIED: Arthur Golding, John Lyly.	*Macbeth*; published 1623. *Antony and Cleopatra* (1606–7); published 1623. *King Lear*; performed at Whitehall on December 26.
1607	Controversy between ecclesiastical courts (headed by Archbishop Bancroft) and civil courts (headed by Coke) over their jurisdictional powers. Settlement by the Plymouth Company in northern Virginia; unsuccessful, and all return in 1608. Captain John Smith settles Jamestown. The Earls of Tyrone and Tyrconnel flee to the continent. Francis Bacon made Solicitor-General. BORN: Madame de Scudery. DIED: Henry Chettle, Sir Edward Dyer, Thomas Legge, Penelope Rich.	Susanna Shakespeare married (June 5) to John Hall (born 1575, died 1635) in Stratford. Death of Shakespeare's brother Edmund (buried December 31); described as "a player." *Hamlet* (September 5) and *Richard II* (September 30) acted on board Captain William Keeling's ship, the *Dragon*, off Sierra Leone, "which I permitt to keepe my people from idlenes and vnlawful games, or sleepe"; *Hamlet* repeated in 1608 (March 31). *Coriolanus* (1607–8); published 1623. *Timon of Athens* (1607–8); published 1623. *Pericles* (1607–8); published 1609.

DRAMA AND THEATRE HISTORY | NON-DRAMATIC LITERATURE

1604 (cont.)

You See Me, You Know Me, or The Famous Chronicle History of Henry VIII (1605; probable source for *Henry VIII*). Anon., *The Fair Maid of Bristow* (1605). *Anon. (Dekker?), *The London Prodigal* (1605; wrongly attributed to Shakespeare; may have influenced Edgar's use of dialect in *King Lear*). Anon., *The Wit of a Woman* (1604).

Palatium, Wisdom's Palace (the fourth part of *Wit's Commonwealth*).

1605

The Red Bull Theatre (St. James, Clerkenwell) built; occupied by Queen Anne's Men until 1617.

Chapman, *Caesar and Pompey* (c. 1599–1607; 1631) and *The Widow's Tears* (c. 1603–9; 1612). Chapman, Marston, and Jonson, *Eastward Hoe!* (1605). Daniel, *The Queen's Arcadia* (1606). Dekker, *2 The Honest Whore* (1630). *Matthew Gwinne, *Tres Sibyllae* (Oxford entertainment for James I; analogue to *Macbeth*). Thomas Heywood *2 If You Know Not Me, You Know Nobody* (1606). Jonson, *The Mask of Blackness* (c. 1608; Jonson's first masque for the court). Marston, *Parasitaster, or The Fawn* (1606) and *The Wonder of Women, or Sophonisba* (1606). Middleton, *A Trick to Catch the Old One* (c. 1604–7; 1608) and *Your Five Gallants* (c. 1604–7; 1608). Anon., *No-Body and Some-Body, with The True Chronicle History of Elydure* (c. 1603–6; c. 1606).

Bacon, *Of the Proficience and Advancement of Learning*. Breton, *The Soul's Immortal Crown, Divided into Seven Days' Works* and *The Honor of Valor*. *Camden, *Remains of a Greater Work Concerning Britain* (contains Richard Carew's *Excellency of the English Tongue*; Camden's work is a source for Menenius' fable in *Coriolanus*). Daniel, *Certain Small Poems*. John Davies, *Humor's Heaven on Earth* and *Wit's Pilgrimage, through a World of Amorous Sonnets*. Drayton, *Poems* (first collected ed.). Joseph Hall, *Mundus Alter et Idem* (see 1609) and *Meditations and Vows Divine and Moral*. Montgomery, *The Mind's Melody, Containing Certain Psalms*. Richard Rowlands (pseudonym, R. Verstegen), *A Restitution of Decayed Intelligence* (concerning English antiquities). Samuel Rowlands, *Hell's Broke Loose*. Sir Edwin Sandys, *A Relation of the State of Religion* (in the western parts of the world). Sylvester (tr.), *Du Bartas His Divine Weeks and Works*. Peter Woodhouse, *Democritus His Dream, or The Contention between the Elephant and the Flea*. EUROPEAN: Cervantes, *Don Quixote* (Pt. I). Fresnoye, *L'Art Poétique*.

1606

Act *To Restrain Abuses of Players* passed (against profanity and criticism of the establishment in plays).

Francis Beaumont and John Fletcher, *The Woman Hater* (1607). Day, *The Isle of Gulls* (1606). Dekker, *The Whore of Babylon* (1607). Jonson, *Volpone, or The Fox* (1607). Middleton, *A Mad World, My Masters* (c. 1604–7; 1608) and *Michaelmas Term* (c. 1604–6; 1607). Edward Sharpham, *The Fleer* (1607). George Wilkins, *The Miseries of Enforc'd Marriage* (1607). Anon. (Middleton?), *The Puritan, or The Widow of Watling Street* (1607; wrongly attributed to Shakespeare). Anon. (Tourneur? or Middleton?), *The Revenger's Tragedy* (1607). Anon. (Wilkins?), *A Yorkshire Tragedy* (c. 1605–8; 1608; wrongly attributed to Shakespeare).

John Barclay, *Sylvae*. Bryskett (tr. of Giraldi), *A Discourse of Civil Life*. William Burton (tr. of Erasmus), *Seven Dialogues Both Pithy and Profitable*. Dekker, *The Double P. P., a Papist in Arms*; *The Seven Deadly Sins of London*; *News from Hell, Brought by the Devil's Carrier*. Drayton, *Poems Lyric and Pastoral*. Joseph Hall, *The Art of Divine Meditation* and *Heaven upon Earth*. *Philemon Holland (tr. of Suetonius), *The History of Twelve Caesars* (contains an analogue to *Julius Caesar*). Knolles (tr. of Bodin), *The Six Books of a Commonweal*. Parrot, *The Mouse-Trap* (epigrams). Henry Peacham (the younger), *The Art of Drawing with the Pen and Limning in Water Colors*. William Perkins, *The Whole Treatise of the Cases of Conscience* (Pt. I, 1604). Barnabe Rich, *Faults, Faults, and Nothing Else but Faults*. Samuel Rowlands, *A Terrible Battle between Time and Death*. Southwell, *A Fourfold Meditation on the Four Last Things*. Richard West, *News from Bartholomew Fair*. Anon. (official), *A True and Perfect Relation of the Whole Proceedings against* [Henry] *Garnet, etc.* EUROPEAN: Joseph Scaliger, *Thesaurus Temporum*.

1607

William Alexander, *The Alexandraean Tragedy* (c. 1605–7; 1607) and *Julius Caesar* (1607). Barnabe Barnes, *The Devil's Charter, or Pope Alexander VI* (1607). Beaumont (and Fletcher?), *The Knight of the Burning Pestle* (1607–c. 1610; 1613). Day, William Rowley, and Wilkins, *The Travels of the Three English Brothers* (1607). Thomas Heywood, *The Rape of Lucrece, A True Roman Tragedy* (c. 1606–8; 1608). Lewis (?) Machin, *Every Woman in Her Humor* (c. 1603–8; 1609). John Mason, *The Turk* (*Mulleasses the Turk*) (1610). Sharpham, *Cupid's Whirligig* (1607). Anon., *Claudius Tiberius Nero* (1607). EUROPEAN: Monteverdi, *Orfeo*.

Cleland, *The Institution of a Young Noble Man*. Cowell, *The Interpreter: or Book Containing the Signification of Words*. John Davies, *Summa Totalis, or All in All*. Dekker, *A Knight's Conjuring, Done in Earnest, Discovered in Jest*; (with George Wilkins), *Jests to Make You Merry*. Drayton, *The Legend of Great Cromwell*. Grimestone (tr. of de Serres), *A General Inventory of the History of France*; (tr. of Goulart), **Admirable and Memorable Histories* (contains an analogue for the Sly framework in *The Taming of the Shrew*). Joseph Hall, *Holy Observations*. James I, *Triplici Nodo, Triplex Cuneus, or An Apology for the Oath of Allegiance*. Richard Johnson, *The Pleasant Conceits of Old Hobson, the Merry Londoner* and *The Pleasant Walks of Moorfields*. Robert Jones, *The First Set of Madrigals*. Lennard (tr. of Charron), *Of Wisdom, Three Books* (published between 1607 and 1612). Gervase Markham, *Cavelarice, or The English*

	EVENTS	SHAKESPEARE
1608	James's proposal for the union of England and Scotland rejected by Parliament; but all subjects born after his accession in 1603 (the "Postnati") are regarded at law as having a common nationality. James's levy of new impositions on merchants leads to the beginning of parliamentary debate on the "Great Contract" (a scheme by which Parliament would grant the King a settled yearly income in exchange for his surrender of certain feudal prerogatives). Formation of the Protestant Union, under Frederick IV, Elector Palatine, and Christian of Anhalt. John Brewster's Separatists emigrate to Holland. Champlain founds Quebec. BORN: Thomas Fuller, John Milton, Evangelista Torricelli. DIED: Sir Geoffrey Fenton, Thomas Sackville.	Birth of Shakespeare's granddaughter, Elizabeth Hall (christened February 21; died 1670; Shakespeare's last surviving descendant). Death of Shakespeare's mother, Mary (buried September 9). Shakespeare sues John Addenbrooke for debt in Stratford (December 17–June 7, 1609). Shakespeare becomes a one-seventh sharer in the Second Blackfriars Theatre, this year leased by the King's Men from Richard Burbage. *Pericles* (?) seen in London by French and Venetian ambassadors.
1609	Further controversy between Bancroft and Coke, in which Coke argues to restrain the King's power to remove a case from the civil courts to the ecclesiastical courts. Catholic League formed by Maximilian, Duke of Bavaria. Expulsion of the Moors from Spain. The Bermudas claimed for England by the Virginia Company (colonized 1612). Publication of the Roman Catholic English translation of the Old Testament at Douai (see 1582). Ambrosian Library (Milan) founded. Bank of Amsterdam founded. BORN: Edward Hyde, Sir John Suckling. DIED: Jacobus Arminius, Barnabe Barnes, J. J. Scaliger, William Warner.	Unauthorized publication of Shakespeare's *Sonnets*. *Cymbeline* (1609–10); published 1623.
1610	Parliament issues a Petition of Grievances and a Petition of Right and, dissatisfied with James's compromise answers, abandons the "Great Contract." James angrily dissolves his first Parliament (February 1611). Prince Henry created Prince of Wales. On Bancroft's death, George Abbot made Archbishop. England supports the Protestant Union. Chelsea College (theological) founded by James. Henry IV, after allying himself with the Protestant Union, assassinated by François Ravaillac. DIED: Robert Parsons, Matteo Ricci	Record of Shakespeare's holding a lease on a barn in Henley Street, Stratford, probably inherited from his father. About this year Shakespeare is believed to have returned to Stratford to live. *The Winter's Tale* (1610–11); published 1623. *Othello*, "L'histoire du More de Venise," performed on April 30 at the Globe. *Pericles* and *King Lear* performed at Candelmas in Gowthwaite, Yorkshire (with quartos as promptbooks). "One of the playes acted and played was Perocles prince of Tire, And the other was Kinge Lere."

DRAMA AND THEATRE HISTORY	NON-DRAMATIC LITERATURE	
	Horseman and *The English Arcadia, Alluding His Beginning from Sir Philip Sidney's Ending* (Pt. II, 1613). Niccols, *The Cuckoo.* John Owen, *Epigrammatum Libri Tres.* Peele, *Merry Conceited Jests of George Peele.* Samuel Rowlands, *Democritus, or Doctor Merry-Man His Medicines* and *Diogenes' Lanthorn.* Topsell (tr. of Gesner and others), *The History of Four-Footed Beasts.* Walkington, *The Optic Glass of Humors.* Richard West, *The Court of Conscience, or Dick Whipper's Sessions.* Anon., *Dobson's Dry Bobs.* EUROPEAN: D'urfé, *Astrée* (Pt. 1).	1607 (cont.)
The King's Men lease the Second Blackfriars as an indoor, "private" theatre. Robert Armin, *The Two Maids of More-Clacke* (1609). Lording Barry, *Ram Alley, or Merry Tricks* (1611). Chapman, *The Conspiracy and Tragedy of Charles Duke of Biron* (1608). Day, *Humor Out of Breath* (1608). Dekker and Middleton, *The Roaring Girl, or Moll Cutpurse* (c. 1604–10; 1611). Fletcher, *The Faithful Shepherdess* (c. 1609). Fletcher and Beaumont, *Cupid's Revenge* (c. 1607–12; 1615). Gervase Markham and Lewis Machin, *The Dumb Knight* (1608). William Rowley, *A Shoemaker a Gentleman* (c. 1607–9; 1638). William Rowley (and a collaborator), *The Birth of Merlin, or The Child Hath Found His Father* (c. 1597–1621; 1662; title-page wrongly names Shakespeare as the collaborator). John Sansbury, *Periander* (MS; included in *The Christmas Prince*, a dramatic festival at St. John's College, Oxford).	Armin, *A Nest of Ninnies.* Breton, *Divine Considerations of the Soul.* Dekker, *The Bellman of London; Lanthorn and Candlelight; The Dead Term, or Westminster's Complaint for Long Vacations; The Great Frost: Cold Doings in London.* Grimestone, *A General History of the Netherlands.* Joseph Hall, *Characters of Virtues and Vices, and Epistles* (Vol. III, 1611). *Thomas Heywood (tr. of Sallust), *The Two Most Worthy and Notable Histories, The Conspiracy of Catiline and The War with Jugurth Maintained* (contains an analogue to *Julius Caesar*). Robert Jones, *Ultimum Vale.* Parrot, *Epigrams.* Henry Peacham (the younger), *The More the Merrier.* William Perkins, *A Discourse of the Damned Art of Witchcraft.* Samuel Rowlands, *Humor's Looking-Glass.* John Smith, *A True Relation of Such Occurrences as Hath Happened in Virginia.* Tofte (tr.), *Ariosto's Satires.* Topsell, *The History of Serpents.* R. West, *Wit's A. B. C., or A Century of Epigrams.* *Wilkins, *The Painful Adventures of Pericles, Prince of Tyre* (based in part on Shakespeare's *Pericles* [as performed]). *Anon. (tr. of Belleforest), *The History of Hamlet* (earliest extant ed.; possible source for Shakespeare's *Hamlet*).	1608
The King's Men begin performances in the Second Blackfriars Theatre in the autumn; continued in use until 1642. Beaumont and Fletcher, *Philaster, or Love Lies A-Bleeding* (c. 1608–10; 1620). Nathan Field, *A Woman Is a Weathercock* (1612). Fletcher and Beaumont, *The Coxcomb* (c. 1608–10; 1647). Thomas Heywood and William Rowley, *Fortune by Land and Sea* (c. 1607–9; 1655). Jonson *Epicoene, or The Silent Woman* (1616) and *The Mask of Queens* (1609; first masque to employ the anti-masque device). Middleton, William Rowley, and Fletcher, *Wit at Several Weapons* (c. 1609–20; 1647). Cyril Tourneur, *The Atheist's Tragedy* (c. 1607–11; 1611).	Bacon, *De Sapientia Veterum Liber.* Chapman, *Euthymiae Raptus, or The Tears of Peace.* John Davies, *The Holy Rood, or Christ's Cross.* Dekker, *The Gull's Hornbook; Four Birds of Noah's Ark; Work for Armorers, or The Peace Is Broken; The Raven's Almanack, Foretelling of a Plague, Famine, and Civil War.* Healey (tr. of Joseph Hall), *The Discovery of a New World.* Thomas Heywood, *Troia Britannica, or Great Britain's Troy.* Philemon Holland (tr. of Ammianus Marcellinus), *The Roman History.* John Jewel, *Works.* Robert Jones, *A Musical Dream, or the Fourth Book of Airs.* W. M., *The Man in the Moon, or The English Fortune Teller.* Gervase Markham, *The Famous Whore or Noble Courtesan, Containing the Lamentable Complaint of Paulina, the Famous Roman Courtesan.* Barnabe Rich, *Room for a Gentleman, or the Second Part of Faults* (see 1606). Samuel Rowlands, *The Knave of Clubs* and *A Whole Crew of Kind Gossips.* J. T. (tr. of Boethius), *Five Books of Philosophical Comfort.* Wilby, *The Second Set of English Madrigals.* EUROPEAN: Grotius, *Mare Liberum.* Kepler, *Astronomia Nova.*	1609
Beaumont and Fletcher, *The Maid's Tragedy* (c. 1608–11; 1619). Chapman, *The Revenge of Bussy D'Ambois* (c. 1601–12; 1613). Robert Daborne, *A Christian Turn'd Turk* (c. 1609–12; 1612). Thomas Heywood, *1 The Fair Maid of the West, or A Girl Worth Gold* (c. 1597–1610; 1631) and *The Golden Age, or The Lives of Jupiter and Saturn* (c. 1609–11; 1611). Jonson, *The Alchemist* (1612). Marston and William Barksted, *The Insatiate Countess* (c. 1610–13; 1613).	Campion, *Two Books of Airs.* Donne, *Pseudo-Martyr.* Giles Fletcher (the younger), *Christ's Victory and Triumph.* Guillim, *A Display of Heraldry.* Healey (tr.), *St. Augustine of the City of God*; (tr.), *Epictetus His Manual*, and *Cebes His Table.* Heath, *Two Centuries of Epigrams.* Philemon Holland (tr. of Camden), *Britain, or A Chorographical Description of England, Scotland, and Ireland.* Robert Jones, *The Muses' Garden for Delights, or the Fifth Book of Airs.* *Jourdain, *A Discovery of the Bermudas, Otherwise Called the Isle of Devils* (source for *The Tempest*). Gervase Markham, *Markham's Masterpiece, or What Doth a Horseman Lack.* Barnabe Rich, *A New Description of Ireland.*	1610

	EVENTS	SHAKESPEARE
1611	A new plantation of Ulster undertaken by English and Scots. Baronets created as a new order of knighthood (hereditary); they were attained by purchase and intended to encourage the Ulster plantation. Lady Arabella Stuart imprisoned for marrying William Seymour. Robert Carr, James's favorite, created Viscount Rochester. Arminian Baptists (in London) publish their first Confession, including a statement favoring religious toleration. Gustavus Adolphus becomes King of Sweden. The King James (so-called "Authorized") version of the Bible published. Thomas Sherley rearrives in England as ambassador from the Shah of Persia, negotiates treaty. BORN: James Harrington, Henry Ireton, Thomas Urquhart. DIED: Giles Fletcher (the elder), Richard Mulcaster.	About this year Shakespeare is concerned, with others, to defend his Stratford tithes in the Court of Chancery. *The Tempest* acted at Court (Whitehall), "Hallomas night" (November 1); published 1623. *The Winter's Tale* ("ye winters nightes Tayle") acted at Court November 5; Simon Forman had seen a production at the Globe on May 15. *Macbeth* performed at the Globe April 20, according to Forman. See Appendix C, Number 20.
1612	Bartholomew Legate and Edward Wightman, Unitarians, burned for heresy (the last to be executed for purely religious beliefs in England). Trial and execution of the so-called Lancashire Witches. Death of the Earl of Salisbury (Robert Cecil), James's Lord Treasurer. Death of Prince Henry (November 6). Charterhouse School (London) founded. Tobacco cultivated in Virginia. BORN: Anne Bradstreet, Samuel Butler, Thomas Fairfax. DIED: Sir John Harington.	Shakespeare is a witness in a suit brought against Christopher Mountjoy by his son-in-law Stephen Belott, testifying that in 1604 he acted as intermediary for Mountjoy in arranging the marriage of Mary, Mountjoy's daughter, with Belott, but that he cannot now remember the exact terms then agreed to. Death of Shakespeare's brother Gilbert (buried February 3). *Henry VIII*, probably with Fletcher (1612–13); published 1623 (see Appendix C, Number 21). *Cardenio*, with Fletcher (1612–13); lost, but the basis of Lewis Theobald's *Double Falsehood* (1728).
1613	Princess Elizabeth married to Frederick V, Elector Palatine. Rochester (Robert Carr) created Earl of Somerset; he marries the Countess of Essex, whose divorce from the young Earl of Essex, forced by James's order, creates a national scandal. Just before the divorce, Sir Thomas Overbury, who had opposed the marriage, was poisoned	Shakespeare is left five pounds in the will of John Comber; see Appendix C, Number 7. Death of Shakespeare's brother Richard (buried February 4). He purchases Blackfriars Gatehouse (March 10). He is paid forty-four shillings (March 31) for furnishing an "impreso" (i.e. an emblem and motto) for

1610 (cont.)

Richard Rich, *News from Virginia, the Lost Flock Triumphant.* Selden, *The Duello, or Single Combat.* Roger Sharpe, *More Fools Yet.* *Strachey, *A True Reportory of the Wrack and Redemption of Sir Thomas Gates* (concerns the Bermudas; first published in *Purchas His Pilgrims,* 1625; source [in MS] for *The Tempest*). *[Virginia Council], *A True Declaration of the Estate of the Colony in Virginia* (source for *The Tempest*).

EUROPEAN: Bellarmine, *De potestate summis ponteficio in rebus temporalibus.* Galileo, *Siderius Nuncius.*

1611

Beaumont and Fletcher, *A King and No King* (1619). John Cooke, *Greene's Tu Quoque, or The City Gallant* (c. 1608–12; 1614). Dekker, *Match Me in London* (c. 1611–13; 1631). Dekker and ?Daborne, *If it Be Not Good, the Devil Is in It* (1612). Field, *Amends for Ladies* (1618). Fletcher (rev. by James Shirley), *The Night Walker, or The Little Thief* (1640). Fletcher, *The Woman's Prize, or The Tamer Tam'd* (c. 1604–17; 1647). Thomas Heywood, *The Brazen Age* (c. 1610–13; 1613) and *The Silver Age* (c. 1610–12; 1613). Jonson, *Catiline His Conspiracy* (1611). Middleton, *No Wit, No Help like a Woman's* (1611) and *A Chaste Maid in Cheapside* (c. 1611–13; 1630). Anon. (Middleton?), *The Second Maiden's Tragedy* (MS).

EUROPEAN: *Flaminio Scala, *Flavio Tradito* (in *Il Teatro delle Favole Rappresentative*; offers an analogue to *The Two Gentlemen of Verona*).

Brathwait, *The Golden Fleece* (including *Narcissus' Change* and *Aeson's Dotage*). Byrd, *Psalms, Songs, and Sonnets for Voices or Viols.* John Cartwright, *The Preacher's Travels* (to the East Indies). Coryate, *Coryate's Cramb, or His Colewort Twice Sodden; Coryate's Crudities, Hastily Gobbled up in Five Months' Travels; The Odcombian Banquet.* Cotgrave, *A Dictionary of the French and English Tongues.* John Davies, *The Scourge of Folly.* Donne, *An Anatomy of the World* (*First Anniversary*) and *Ignatius His Conclave* (also a Latin ed.). Roger Fenton, *A Treatise of Usury.* Florio, *Queen Anna's New World of Words.* John Speed, *The Theatre of the Empire of Great Britain* and *The History of Great Britain.*

1612

R. A. (Robert Armin? or Robert Anton?), *The Valiant Welshman, or The True Chronicle History of the Life and Valiant Deeds of Caradoc the Great, King of Cambria, Now Called Wales* (c. 1610–15; 1615). Fletcher and Beaumont, *The Captain* (c. 1609–12; 1647). Fletcher (and Beaumont? or Field?), *Four Plays or Moral Representations in One* (c. 1608–13; 1647). *Fletcher and Shakespeare, *Cardenio* (c. 1612–13; not extant; basis of Lewis Theobald's *Double Falsehood, or The Distress'd Lovers,* 1728). Thomas Heywood, *1* and *2 Iron Age* (1632). John Webster, *The White Devil, or The Tragedy of Paulo Giordano Ursini, Duke of Brachiano, with The Life and Death of Vittoria Corombona the Famous Venetian Courtesan* (c. 1609–12; 1612). Anon., *Thorney Abbey, or The London Maid* (c. 1606–14; 1662; shows strong influence of *Macbeth*).

Alexander, *An Elegy on the Death of Prince Henry.* Breton, *Wit's Private Wealth, Stored with Choice Commodities* and *Cornucopiae: Pasquil's Nightcap.* John Brinsley (the elder), *Ludus Literarius, or The Grammar School* and *Sententiae Pueriles, Translated Grammatically.* Campion, *The Third and Fourth Book of Airs.* Chapman (tr.), *Petrarch's Seven Penitential Psalms* and *An Epicede, or Funeral Song, on the Death of Henry Prince of Wales.* Cotta, *A Short Discovery of the Dangers of Ignorant Practicers of Physic.* Daniel, *The First Part of the History of England* (Pt. II, 1618). John Davies, *The Muse's Sacrifice, or Divine Meditations.* Sir John Davies, *A Discovery of the True Causes Why Ireland Was Never Entirely Subdued until His Majesty's Reign.* Donne, *Of the Progress of the Soul* (*Second Anniversary*). John Dowland, *A Pilgrim's Solace* (music book). Drayton, *Poly-Olbion, or A Chorographical Description of Great Britain* (Pt. II, 1622). Gibbons, *The First Set of Madrigals and Motets.* Joseph Hall, *Contemplations upon the Principal Passages of the Holy Story* (in eight vols., published between 1612 and 1626). Thomas Heywood, *An Apology for Actors.* Richard Hooker, *A Remedy against Sorrow and Fear.* Lok (with Eden; tr. of Peter Martyr), *De Novo Orbe, or The History of the West Indies.* Henry Peacham (the younger), *Minerva Britanna, or A Garden of Heroical Devices.* Samuel Rowlands, *The Knave of Hearts: Hail Fellow Well Met.* Shelton (tr. of Cervantes), *The History of Don Quixote* (Pt. II, 1620). John Smith, *A Map of Virginia.* Strachey, *For the Colony in Virginia Britannia: Laws Divine, Moral, and Martial.* Sylvester, *Lachrimae Lachrimarum.* Wither, *Prince Henry's Obsequies* and *Epithalamia, or Nuptial Poems.*

1613

The Globe Theatre burnt during a performance of Shakespeare and Fletcher's *Henry VIII* (see Appendix C, Number 21).

Beaumont, *Inner Temple and Gray's Inn Mask* (c. 1613; probable source for morris-dance in *The Two Noble Kinsmen*). Fletcher, *Bonduca* (c. 1611–14; 1647).

Lewis Bayly, *The Practice of Piety* (earliest ed. extant). William Browne, *Britannia's Pastorals* (Pt. II, 1616). Campion, *Songs of Mourning Bewailing the Death of Prince Henry.* Dallington, *Aphorisms, Civil and Military.* John Davies, *The Muse's Tears for the Loss of Henry Prince of Wales.* Dekker, *A Strange Horse-Race, at the End of Which*

	EVENTS	SHAKESPEARE
1613 (cont.)	in the Tower, by order of the Countess of Essex. Bacon made Attorney-General. Coke made Chief Justice. Wadham College (Oxford) founded. BORN: John Cleveland, Richard Crashaw, François de la Rochefoucauld, Jeremy Taylor. DIED: Sir Thomas Bodley, Henry Constable.	Lord Rutland on the occasion of the tilt in honor of the anniversary of the King's accession (March 24); Burbage is paid the same amount "for paynting and making yt." *The Two Noble Kinsmen*, with Fletcher; published 1634.
1614	James's second Parliament (nicknamed "The Addled") summoned; dissolved by James for refusing to grant impositions and resisting the imprisonment of some members. At Somerset's secret instigation, Diego Sarmiento (later Gondomar), Spanish ambassador, proposes a marriage between Prince Charles and the Infanta. Sir George Villiers, later (1617) Duke of Buckingham, emerges as Somerset's rival for James's favor. Fulke Greville made Chancellor of the Exchequer. United New Netherlands Company founded. John Napier introduces logarithms. BORN: Henry More. DIED: Sir William Cornwallis, El Greco.	Shakespeare is peripherally concerned in a suit to oppose the enclosure of certain lands in Welcombe to preserve his lease and tithes.
1615	Somerset and his wife tried and condemned for the murder of Overbury; later (1624) pardoned. Raleigh offends James by writing "The Prerogative of Parliaments." James visits Cambridge. Rosicrucian Order founded in Germany. BORN: Richard Baxter, John Denham. DIED: Robert Armin.	

DRAMA AND THEATRE HISTORY	NON-DRAMATIC LITERATURE	
Fletcher and Beaumont, *The Scornful Lady* (c. 1613–16; 1616). Fletcher (with Field? or Massinger? or Tourneur?), *The Honest Man's Fortune* (1647). John Stephens, *Cynthia's Revenge, or Maenander's Ecstasy* (1613). Robert Tailor, *The Hog Hath Lost His Pearl* (1614).	*Comes in the Catch-Poles' Masque.* John Dennys, *The Secrets of Angling.* Drummond, *Tears on the Death of Meliades.* Sir John Hayward, *The Lives of the Three Norman Kings of England.* Gervase Markham, *The English Husbandman* (Pt. II. 1614) and *Hobson's Horse-Load of Letters, or A President for Epistles.* Purchas, *Purchas His Pilgrimage.* Barnabe Rich, *Opinion Defied, Discovering the Engines, Traps, and Trains That Are Set to Catch Opinion* and *The Excellency of Good Women.* Samuel Rowlands, *More Knaves Yet? The Knaves of Spades and Diamonds.* Scoggin, *Scoggin His Jests* (earliest ed. extant; first published c. 1565). Sir Anthony Sherley, *His Relation of His Travels into Persia.* Spelman, *De Non Temerandis Ecclesiis, A Tract of the Rights and Respect Due unto Churches.* John Stephens, *Cynthia's Revenge, or Maenander's Ecstasy.* Alexander Whitaker, *Good News from Virginia.* Wither, *Abuses Stript and Whipt.*	1613 (cont.)
The Hope Theatre (Bankside) built by Philip Henslowe and Jacob Meade. The Globe Theatre reopened; finally demolished in 1644. Daniel, *Hymen's Triumph* (1615). Fletcher, *Valentinian* (1647) and *Wit without Money* (c. 1614–20; 1639). Jonson, *Bartholomew Fair* (1631). W. Smith, *The Hector of Germany, or The Palsgrave, Prime Elector* (1615). Webster *The Tragedy of the Duchess of Malfi* (1623). Anon. (Beaumont and Fletcher?), *The Faithful Friends* (MS).	Alexander, *Dooms-day.* Bacon, *The Charge of Sir Francis Bacon Touching Duels.* John Barclay, *Icon Animorum* (English tr. by Thomas May, 1631). Brathwait, *The Scholar's Medley, or An Intermixt Discourse upon Historical and Poetical Relations.* William Browne (and others), *The Shepherd's Pipe.* Chapman, *Andromeda Liberata*; (tr.), *Homer's Odysses* (completed 1615). Drummond, *Poems.* Gentleman, *England's Way to Win Wealth.* Gorges (tr.), *Lucan's Pharsalia.* Thomas Heywood, *The Life and Death of Hector* (from Lydgate). Lodge (tr.), *The Works of L. A. Seneca, Both Moral and Natural.* Napier, *Mirifici Logarithmorum Canonis Descriptio* (English tr. by E. Wright, 1616). Overbury, *The Wife* (with *Characters*; other *Characters* added 1615, many by Webster). Raleigh, *The History of the World.* Barnabe Rich, *The Honesty of This Age.* Selden, *Titles of Honor.* Sylvester (tr. of Bertaut), *The Parliament of Virtues Royal* (Pt. II, 1616).	1614
Fletcher, *Monsieur Thomas* (c. 1610–16; 1639). Phineas Fletcher, *Sicelides* (1631). Middleton, *More Dissemblers besides Women* (1657) and *The Witch* (MS; c. 1609–16). George Ruggle, *Ignoramus* (Latin; 1630). S. S., *The Honest Lawyer* (1616). Thomas Tomkis, *Albumazar* (1615; adapted from Della Porta's *L'Astrologo*). *Anon., *Romeus and Julietta* (MS fragment).	Thomas Adams, *Mystical Bedlam, or The World of Madmen.* John Andrewes, *The Anatomy of Baseness, or The Four Quarters of a Knave.* Brathwait, *A Strappado for the Devil: Epigrams and Satires.* Breton, *Characters upon Essays Moral and Divine.* Camden, *Annales Rerum Anglicarum et Hibernicarum Regnante Elizabetha* (Bk. IV, 1627; English tr. by A. Darcie, 1625, and R. Browne, 1629). Harington, *Epigrams Both Pleasant and Serious* (enlarged 1618). Gervase Markham, *Country Contentments* (Bk. I, *Of Riding Great Horses.* Bk. II, *The English Huswife*). Samuel Rowlands, *The Melancholy Knight.* George Sandys, *A Relation of a Journey Begun Anno Domini 1610.* Thomas Scot, *Philomythy or Philomythology, Wherein Outlandish Birds, Beasts, and Fishes Are Taught to Speak True English* (Pt. II, 1616). John Stephens, *Satirical Essays, Characters, and Others.* Joseph Swetnam, *The Arraignment of Lewd, Idle, Froward, and Unconstant Women.* Wither, *Fidelia* and *The Shepherd's Hunting.*	1615

	EVENTS	SHAKESPEARE
1616	The Cautionary Towns (Flushing, Brill) given to the Dutch for a small cash settlement. Coke, for his opposition to James, dismissed and disgraced. Bacon promised Lord Chancellorship. Lady Arabella Stuart dies in the Tower. Prince Charles created Prince of Wales. William Harvey first explains his theory of the circulation of the blood. First Independent "meeting house" erected. DIED: Francis Beaumont, Cervantes, Richard Hakluyt, Philip Henslowe, William Shakespeare.	Shakespeare's daughter Judith is married (February 10) to Thomas Quiney (born 1589, died 1655); their first son, named "Shaksper," christened November 23, died 1617 (buried May 8). Shakespeare makes his will (March 25; see Appendix C, Number 5) and dies April 23 (buried April 25). Death of Shakespeare's brother-in-law, William Hart (buried April 17).

J.C. Visscher's fine panoramic view of London (1616, or possibly a little earlier) is the best-known of the early seventeenth-century maps of the city. Visscher, however, seems to have had little if any firsthand knowledge of London, instead taking his topographical details from earlier maps, not always the best. The location of the Globe should be slightly farther south and east. In fact, what is here labelled as "The Globe" is, from its location, in all probability the Rose Theatre.

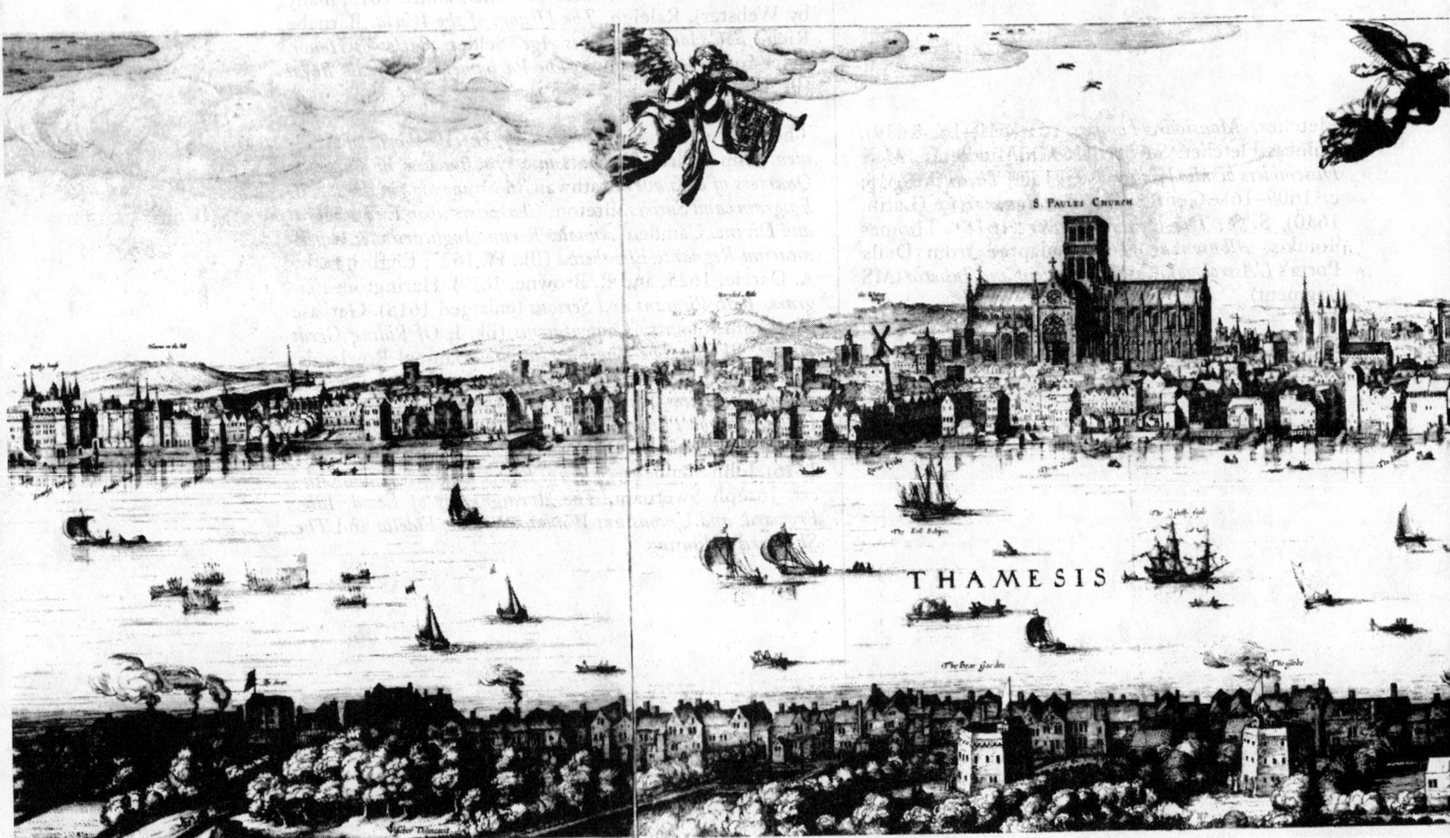

DRAMA AND THEATRE HISTORY

Fletcher (rev. by Middleton?), *The Nice Valor, or The Passionate Madman* (c. 1615–25; 1647). Fletcher and Beaumont, *Love's Pilgrimage* (1647). Jonson, *The Devil Is an Ass* (1631). Thomas May, *Julius Caesar* (Latin; not extant). Middleton, *The Widow* (c. 1615–17; 1652).

NON-DRAMATIC LITERATURE

Breton, *Crossing of Proverbs: Cross-Answers and Cross-Humors* and *The Good and the Bad, or Descriptions of the Worthies and Unworthies of This Age.* John Bullokar, *An English Expositor, Teaching the Interpretation of the Hardest Words.* Cornwallis, *Essays, or Rather Encomions* and *Essays of Certain Paradoxes.* Coryate, *T. Coryate, Traveller for the English Wits, Greeting from the Court of the Great Mogul.* Cotta, *The Trial of Witchcraft, Showing the True Method of the Discovery.* John Davies, *A Select Second Husband for Sir Thomas Overbury's Wife, Now a Matchless Widow.* Fortescue (ed. and tr. by Selden), *De Laudibus Legum Angliae.* Godfrey Goodman, *The Fall of Man.* Healey (tr. of Theophrastus), *Characters.* James I, *Works.* Jonson, *Works* (besides the early plays, contains *Epigrams* and *The Forest*). Gervase Markham, *Markham's Method or Epitome.* Niccols, *Sir Thomas Overbury's Vision* and *London's Artillery, Briefly Containing the Noble Practice of That Worthy Society.* John Smith, *A Description of New England.* 1616

The Swan Theatre may be seen farther west on the south bank. Panoramic views of London by John Norden (1600) of the first Globe (1599) and Wencelaus Hollar (1647) of the second Globe (1614) appear to show both theatres as structurally cylindrical, but the most recent research suggests that their framework was actually a twenty-sided polygon. See Plate 32 and Appendix C, No. 21. *(Copyright British Museum)*

Selected Bibliography

For more complete listings see:

Jaggard, William, *Shakespeare Bibliography* [1911]

Ebisch, Walther, and L. L. Schücking, *A Shakespeare Bibliography* (1931) and *Supplement for the Years 1930–35* (1937)

Smith, Gordon R., *A Classified Shakespeare Bibliography, 1936–1958* (1963)

Cambridge Bibliography of English Literature, ed. F. W. Bateson (1941), Vol. I, and Vol. V, Supplement, ed. George Watson (1957); *New Cambridge Bibliography of English Literature*, ed. George Watson, Vol. I (1974)

Berman, Ronald, *A Reader's Guide to Shakespeare's Plays: A Descriptive Bibliography* (1965; rev. ed., 1973)

Bevington, David, *Shakespeare* (Goldentree Bibliographies) (1978)

Garland Shakespeare Bibliographies, gen. ed. William Godshalk (1980–)

Champion, Larry, *The Essential Shakespeare: An Annotated Bibliography of Major Modern Studies* (1986)

Wells, Stanley, ed., *Shakespeare: A Bibliographical Guide, New Ed.*, (1990)

See also the annual *MLA International Bibliography* (subject, author) (1981–) and the annual surveys of Shakespeare studies in *Shakespeare Survey* and *The Year's Work in English Studies.*

Shakespeare periodicals:

Shakespeare-Jahrbuch (1864–)

Shakespeare-Jahrbuch (Weimar; 1964/65–)

Shakespeare Newsletter, eds., Louis Marder, J. W. Mahon, and T. A. Pendleton (1951–)

Shakespeare Quarterly, eds. J. G. McManaway, R. J. Schoeck, J. F. Andrews, and Barbara A. Mowat (1950–)

Shakespearean Research and Opportunities, ed. W. R. Elton (1965–)

Shakespeare Studies, ed. J. Leeds Barroll (1965–)

Shakespeare Studies (Tokyo) (1962–)

Shakespeare Survey, eds. Allardyce Nicoll, Kenneth Muir, and Stanley Wells (1948–)

The Upstart Crow: A Shakespeare Journal, ed. W. E. Bennet (1978–)

The following are useful compendiums of information:

Alexander, Marguerite, *A Reader's Guide to Shakespeare and His Contemporaries* (1979)

Andrews, John F., ed., *William Shakespeare: His World, His Work, His Influence* (3 vols., 1985)

Berger, T. L., and W. C. Bradford, *An Index of Characters in the English Printed Drama to the Restoration* (1975)

Bergeron, David M., and Geraldo U. de Sousa, *Shakespeare, A Study and Research Guide* (1975; 3rd ed., 1995)

Brown, J. R., *Discovering Shakespeare: A New Guide to the Plays* (1986)

Campbell, O. J., and E. G. Quinn, eds., *The Reader's Encyclopedia of Shakespeare* (1966)

Granville-Barker, Harley, and G. B. Harrison, eds., *A Companion to Shakespeare Studies* (1959)

Halliday, F. E., *A Shakespeare Companion, 1564–1964* (1964)

Holzknecht, K. J., *The Backgrounds of Shakespeare's Plays* (1950)

McDonald, Russ, *The Bedford Companion to Shakespeare: An Introduction with Documents* (1996)

Muir, Kenneth, and Samuel Schoenbaum, eds., *A New Companion to Shakespeare Studies* (1971)

Sugden, E. H., *A Topographical Dictionary to the Works of Shakespeare and His Fellow Dramatists* (1925)

Sutherland, James, and Joel Hurstfield, eds., *Shakespeare's World* (1964)

Thomson, W. H., *Shakespeare's Characters: A Historical Dictionary* (1951)

Wells, Stanley, ed., *The Cambridge Companion to Shakespeare Studies* (1987)

For glossaries, concordances, and the like, see under "Language and Imagery," below.

The most important annotated editions of Shakespeare are:

Plays and Poems, ed. James Boswell (the younger) and Edmond Malone (21 vols., 1821)

Cambridge Shakespeare, ed. W. G. Clark and W. A. Wright (9 vols., 1863–66; rev. ed., 1891–93). Very little annotation, but for many years the standard text.

New Variorum Shakespeare, ed. H. H. Furness et al. (1871–). The volumes beginning with S. B. Hemingway's edition of *1 Henry IV* (1936) are most valuable; the older volumes are to be used with caution. Thirteen of the latter have been reissued with new bibliographies (by Louis Marder); there is also a Supplement (ed. G. B. Evans) to *1 Henry IV.*

Arden Shakespeare, ed. W. J. Craig and R. H. Case (1899–1944)

New Arden Shakespeare, ed. Una M. Ellis-Fermor, H. F. Brooks, Harold Jenkins, and Brian Morris (1951–82)

Arden Shakespeare Third Series, eds. Richard Proudfoot, Ann Thompson, and David Kastan (1995–)

The New Penguin Shakespeare, eds. T. J. B Spencer and Stanley Wells (1967–)

The New Shakespeare (Cambridge), eds. A. T. Quiller-Couch, J. Dover Wilson, et al. (1921–67)

Sixteen Plays of Shakespeare, ed. G. L. Kittredge (1946)

The Oxford Shakespeare, eds. Stanley Wells, Gary Taylor, et al. (1982–)

The New Cambridge Shakespeare, eds. Philip Brockbank, Brian Gibbons, et al. (1984–)

TUDOR AND STUART SOCIETY

Akrigg, G. P. V., *Jacobean Pageant* (1962)

Bindoff, S. T., *Tudor England* (1959)

Black, J. B., *The Reign of Elizabeth, 1558–1603* (1936; 2nd ed., 1959)

Buxton, John, *Elizabethan Taste* (1963)

Bradbrook, M. C., *Artist and Society in Shakespeare's England* (1982)

Bray, Alan, *Homosexuality in Renaissance England* (1982, 2nd ed. 1988)

Briggs, Julia, *This Stage-Play World: English Literature and Its Background, 1580–1625* (1983)
Byrne, M. St. C., *The Elizabethan Home* (1930; enlarged ed., 1949)
———, *Elizabethan Life in Town and Country* (1925; 8th ed., 1961)
Camden, Carroll, *The Elizabethan Woman* (1952)
Chaudhuri, Sukanta, *Infirm Glory: Shakespeare and the Renaissance Image of Man* (1981)
Davies, Godfrey, *The Early Stuarts, 1603–1660* (1937; 2nd ed., 1959)
Dent, Alan, *World of Shakespeare: Sports and Pastimes* (1974)
Elton, G. R., *England under the Tudors* (1955)
Evans, G. B., *Elizabethan-Jacobean Drama: A New Mermaid Background Book* (1987)
Frye, R. M., *Shakespeare's Life and Times: A Pictorial Record* (1967)
Guy, John, ed., *The Reign of Elizabeth I: Court and Culture in the Last Decade* (1995)
Halliday, F. E., *Shakespeare in His Age* (1956)
Harrison, G. B., *England in Shakespeare's Day* (1928)
———, ed., *The Elizabethan Journals* (rev. ed., 1955)
———, ed., *A Jacobean Journal, 1603–1606* (1941); *A Second Jacobean Journal, 1607–1610* (1958)
Hurstfield, Joel, and A. G. R. Smith, eds., *Elizabethan People: State and Society* (1972)
Jordan, Constance, *Renaissance Feminism: Literary Texts and Political Models* (1990)
Kelso, Ruth, *Doctrine for the Lady of the Renaissance* (1956)
———, *The Doctrine of the English Gentleman in the Sixteenth Century* (1929)
Klein, Joan Larsen, *Daughters, Wives, and Widows: Writings by Men about Women and Marriage in England, 1500–1640* (1992)
Lee, Sidney, and C. T. Onions, eds., *Shakespeare's England* (2 vols., 1916)
Lewalski, Barbara Kiefer, *Writing Women in Jacobean England* (1993)
Lytle, Guy, and Stephen Orgel, eds., *Patronage in the Renaissance* (1981)
Nicoll, Allardyce, *The Elizabethans* (1957)
———, ed., *Shakespeare in His Own Age* (*Shakespeare Survey 17*, 1964)
Pearson, L. E., *Elizabethans at Home* (1957)
Rowse, A. L., *The England of Elizabeth: The Structure of Society* (1950; rev. ed., 1976)
Schoenbaum, Samuel, *Shakespeare: The Globe and the World* (1979)
Singman, Jeffery L., *Daily Life in Elizabethan England* (1995)
Stone, Lawrence, *The Crisis of the Aristocracy* (1965)
———, *The Family, Sex and Marriage in England, 1500–1800* (1977)
Wilson, J. Dover, *Life in Shakespeare's England* (1911; rev. ed., 1949)
Woodbridge, Linda, *Women and the English Renaissance: Literature and the Nature of Womankind, 1540–1620* (1986)
Wright, L. B., *Middle-Class Culture in Elizabethan England* (1959)

BIOGRAPHY

Chambers, E. K., *William Shakespeare: A Study of Facts and Problems* (2 vols., 1930). There is an abridgment of it by Charles Williams, *A Short Life of Shakespeare with the Sources* (1933)
Alexander, Peter, *Shakespeare's Life and Art* (1939, 1961)
Bentley, G. E., *Shakespeare: A Biographical Handbook* (1961)
Brinkworth, E. R. C., *Shakespeare and the Bawdy Court of Stratford* (1973)
Chute, Marchette, *Shakespeare of London* (1949)
Eccles, Mark, *Shakespeare in Warwickshire* (1961)
Fraser, Russell, *Young Shakespeare* (1988)
———, *Shakespeare, The Later Years* (1992)
Fripp, E. I., *Shakespeare, Man and Artist* (2 vols., 1938)
Halliday F. E., *The Life of Shakespeare* (1961)
Halliwell-Phillipps, J. O., *Outlines of the Life of Shakespeare* (2 vols., 1887)
Honigmann, E. A. J., *Shakespeare: The Lost Years* (1985)
Hotson, Leslie, *I, William Shakespeare, Do Appoint Thomas Russell, Esquire* (1937)
———, *Shakespeare versus Shallow* (1931)
Lewis, B. Roland, *The Shakespeare Documents* (2 vols., 1941)
McManaway, J. G., *The Authorship of Shakespeare* (1962)
Quennell, Peter, *Shakespeare* (1963)
Reese, M. M., *Shakespeare: His World and His Work* (1953)
Rowse, A. L., *William Shakespeare* (1963; new ed., 1973)
Schoenbaum, Samuel, *Shakespeare's Lives* (1970)
———, *William Shakespeare: A Documentary Life* (1975)
Sisson, C. J., "Studies in the Life and Environment of Shakespeare since 1900," *Shakespeare Survey 3* (1950), 1–12
Smart, J. S., *Shakespeare: Truth and Tradition* (1928; with memoir and preface, 1966)
Spencer, Hazelton, *The Art and Life of William Shakespeare* (1940)
Wilson, J. Dover, *The Essential Shakespeare* (1932)

THE TEXT

Facsimiles

First Folio
- Ed. Sidney Lee (1902). The best of the pre-Hinman facsimiles.
- Ed. H. Kökeritz and C. T. Prouty (1955)
- Methuen Facsimile (1910)
- Norton Facsimile, ed. Charlton Hinman. A "critical" edition inasmuch as it is printed entirely from the corrected state of each sheet.

Second, Third, and Fourth Folios
- Methuen Facsimiles (1909, 1905, 1904)
- Boydell and Brewer Facsimiles, ed. Marvin Spevack (3 vols., 1985)

Quartos of the plays
- Ed. F. J. Furnivall (43 vols., 1880–89). To be used with great caution.
- Oxford Quarto Facsimiles, ed. W. W. Greg (13 vols., 1939–66), continued by Charlton Hinman (3 vols. to date, 1975). The titles available are *King Lear, The Merchant of Venice, The Merry Wives of Windsor, Hamlet* (Q2) *Hamlet* (Q1), *Pericles, Romeo and Juliet* (Q2), *Troilus and Cressida, Henry V, Love's Labor's Lost, The True Tragedy of Richard Duke of York (3 Henry VI), Richard III, Richard II, 1 Henry IV, Much Ado about Nothing, Othello.*
- *Titus Andronicus*, ed. J. Q. Adams (1937)
- *Shakespeare's Plays in Quarto: A Facsimile Edition*, eds., Kenneth Muir and M. J. B. Allen (1981)
- Warren, Michael, ed., *The Complete "King Lear" 1608–1623: Texts and Parallel Texts in Photographic Facsimile Prepared by Michael Warren* (1989)

Poems
- Ed. Sidney Lee (1905)
- Ed. J. M. Osborn, L. L. Martz, E. M. Waith (1964)

Studies of Textual Problems

Black, M. W., and M. A. Shaaber, *Shakespeare's Seventeenth-Century Editors, 1632–1685* (1937)

Blayney, P. W. M., *The Texts of "King Lear" and Their Origins*, Vol. I (1982)
Bowers, F. T., *Bibliography and Textual Criticism* (1964)
———, *On Editing Shakespeare and the Elizabethan Dramatists* (1955; enlarged ed., 1966)
———, *Textual and Literary Criticism* (1959)
Dawson, G. E., and R. Kennedy-Skipton, *Elizabethan Handwriting 1500–1650: A Manual* (1966)
DeGrazia, Margreta, *Shakespeare Verbatim* (1990)
Gaskell, Philip, *A New Introduction to Bibliography* (1972)
Greg, W. W., *Two Elizabethan Stage Abridgments, "The Battle of Alcazar" and "Orlando Furioso": An Essay in Critical Bibliography* (1923). A basic study.
———, *The Editorial Problem in Shakespeare: A Survey of the Foundations of the Text* (1942; rev. ed., 1955)
———, "The Rationale of Copy-text," *Studies in Bibliography*, III (1950), 19–36
———, *The Shakespeare First Folio: Its Bibliography and Textual History* (1955)
Hart, Alfred, *Stolne and Surreptitious Copies: A Comparative Study of Shakespeare's Bad Quartos* (1943)
Hinman, Charlton, *The Printing and Proof-Reading of the First Folio of Shakespeare* (2 vols., 1963)
Honigmann, E. A. J., *The Stability of Shakespeare's Text* (1965)
———, *The Texts of Othello and Shakespearian Revision* (1996)
Hope, Jonathan, *The Authorship of Shakespeare's Plays: A Socio-Linguistic Study* (1994)
Howard-Hill, T. H., *Ralph Crane and Some Shakespeare First Folio Comedies* (1972)
———, ed., *Shakespearian Bibliography and Textual Criticism: A Bibliography* (1971)
———, *Compositors B and E in the Shakespeare First Folio and Some Recent Studies* (1976)
———, *A Reassessment of Compositors B and E in the First Folio Tragedies* (1977)
———, *Shakespeare and 'Sir Thomas More'—Essays on the Play and its Shakesperian Interest* (1989)
Ioppolo, Grace, *Revising Shakespeare* (1991)
Irace, Kathleen O., *Reforming the "Bad" Quartos: Performance and Provenance of Six Shakespearian First Editions* (1994)
Jarvis, Simon, *Scholars and Gentlemen: Shakespearian Textual Criticism and Representation of Scholarly Labour 1725–1765* (1995)
McGann, Jerome J., ed., *Textual Criticism and Literary Interpretation* (1985)
McKenzie, D. F., "Printers of the Mind: Some Notes on Bibliographical Theories and Printing-House Practices," *Studies in Bibliography*, XXII (1969), 1–75
McKerrow, R. B., *An Introduction to Bibliography for Literary Students* (1927; rev. impression, 1928)
———, *Prolegomena for the Oxford Shakespeare: A Study in Editorial Method* (1939)
Maguire, Laurie E., *Shakespearean Suspect Texts: The "Bad" Quartos and Their Contexts* (1996)
Nosworthy, J. M., *Shakespeare's Occasional Plays: Their Origin and Transmission* (1965)
Partridge, A. C., *Orthography in Shakespeare and Elizabethan Drama* (1964)
Pollard, A. W., *Shakespeare's Folios and Quartos* (1909)
———, *Shakespeare's Fight with the Pirates* (1920)
Prosser, Eleanor, *Shakespeare's Anonymous Editors: Scribe and Compositor in the Folio Text of "2 Henry IV"* (1981)
Sisson, C. J., *New Readings in Shakespeare* (2 vols., 1956)
Tanselle G. T., *Textual Criticism since Greg: A Chronicle, 1950–1985* (1988)
Taylor, Gary, and John Jowett, *Shakespeare Reshaped 1606–1623* (1993)
Walker, Alice, *Textual Problems of the First Folio* (1953)
Walton, J. K., *The Quarto Copy for the First Folio of Shakespeare* (1971)
Wells, Stanley, and Gary Taylor, *Modernizing Shakespeare's Spelling, with Three Studies in the Text of "Henry V"* (1979)
Wells, Stanley, *Re-Editing Shakespeare for the Modern Reader* (1984)
Wells, Stanley, Gary Taylor, John Jowett and William Montgomery, *William Shakespeare: A Textual Companion* [to the Oxford one volume *Complete Works* (1984) and Oxford one volume Original-Spelling *Complete Works* (1986)], 1987
Willoughby, E. E., *The Printing of the First Folio of Shakespeare* (1933)
Yamada, Akihiro, *Thomas Creede: Printer to Shakespeare and His Contemporaries* (1994)

For textual studies of the individual plays and poems used in this edition, see the "Note on the Text" following each of the plays or poems. For more recent articles on Shakespeare's text, see such journals as *The Library, Studies in Bibliography, Papers of the Bibliographical Society of America, Analytical & Enumerative Bibliography*, and *Text*.

LANGUAGE AND IMAGERY

Reference Works

Abbott, E. A., *A Shakespearian Grammar* (1869 and later eds.)
Cercignani, Fausto, *Shakespeare's Works and Elizabethan Pronunciation* (1981)
Dent, R. W., *Shakespeare's Proverbial Language: An Index* (1981)
Dobson, E. J., *English Pronunciation, 1500–1700* (2 vols., 1957; 2nd ed., 1968)
Franz, Wilhelm, *Die Sprache Shakespeares in Vers und Prosa* (4th ed., 1939)
Howard-Hill, T. H., *Oxford [Old-Spelling] Shakespeare Concordances* (1969– ; separate vol. for each play)
Kökeritz, Helge, *Shakespeare's Names: A Pronouncing Dictionary* (1959)
———, *Shakespeare's Pronunciation* (1953)
Nares, Robert, *A Glossary . . . of Shakespeare and His Contemporaries* (1822, rev. and enlarged by J. O. Halliwell and Thomas Wright, 2 vols., 1872)
Onions, C. T., *A Shakespeare Glossary* (1911; rev. ed., 1953; rev., with additions, by R. D. Eagleson, 1985)
Partridge, Eric, *Shakespeare's Bawdy* (1947; rev. ed., 1955)
Rubinstein, Frankie, *A Dictionary of Shakespeare's Sexual Puns and Their Significance* (1984, 2nd ed., 1989)
Schmidt, Alexander, *Shakespeare-Lexicon* (2 vols., 1874–75; 3rd ed. rev. G. Sarrazin, 1902)
Spevack, Marvin, *A Complete and Systematic Concordance to the Works of Shakespeare* (9 vols., 1968–80)
———, *The Harvard Concordance to Shakespeare* (1973)
———, *A Shakespeare Thesaurus* (1993)
Tilley, M. P., *A Dictionary of the Proverbs in England in the Sixteenth and Seventeenth Centuries* (1950) [with special references to Shakespeare]
Ule, Louis, *A Concordance to the Shakespeare Apocrypha, I–III* (1987)
Viëtor, Wilhelm, *A Shakespeare Phonology* (1906)

Criticism

Armstrong, E. A., *Shakespeare's Imagination* (1946; rev. ed., 1963)
Barton, John, *Playing Shakespeare* (1984)
Berry, Ralph, *The Shakespearean Metaphor: Studies in Language and Form* (1978)
Blake, N. F., *Shakespeare's Language: An Introduction* (1983)
Bradbrook, M. C., "Fifty Years of the Criticism of Shakespeare's Style: A Retrospect," *Shakespeare Survey* 7 (1954), 1–11
Burton, D. M., *Shakespeare's Grammatical Style* (1973)

Clemen, Wolfgang, *The Development of Shakespeare's Imagery* (1951)
Coleman, E. A. M., *The Dramatic Use of Bawdy in Shakespeare* (1974)
Crane, Milton, *Shakespeare's Prose* (1951)
Donaworth, Jane, *Shakespeare and the Sixteenth-Century Study of Language* (1984)
Ellis-Fermor, Una M., *The Frontiers of Drama* (1945; rev. ed., 1948)
Empson, William, *The Structure of Complex Words* (1951)
Evans, B. I., *The Language of Shakespeare's Plays* (1952)
Halliday, F. E., *The Poetry of Shakespeare's Plays* (1954)
Hankins, J. E., *Shakespeare's Derived Imagery* (1953)
Holmes, Elizabeth, *Aspects of Elizabethan Imagery* (1929)
Hulme, Hilda M., *Explorations in Shakespeare's Language* (1962)
Joseph, Sister Miriam, *Shakespeare's Use of the Arts of Language* (1947)
Mahood, M. M., *Shakespeare's Wordplay* (1957)
Ness, F. W., *The Use of Rhyme in Shakespeare's Plays* (1941)
Sherbo, Arthur, *The Birth of Shakespeare Studies: Commentators from Rowe (1709) to Boswell-Malone (1821)* (1986)
Sipe, Dorothy L., *Shakespeare's Metrics* (1968)
Spurgeon, Caroline F. E., *Shakespeare's Imagery and What It Tells Us* (1935)
Stauffer, D. A., *Shakespeare's World of Images: The Development of His Moral Ideas* (1949)
Trousdale, Marion, *Shakespeare and the Rhetoricians* (1982)
Vickers, Brian, *The Artistry of Shakespeare's Prose* (1968)
Whiter, Walter, *Specimen of a Commentary on Shakespeare* (1794)
Wilson, F. P., *Shakespeare and the Diction of Common Life* (1941; rev. version in *Shakespearian and Other Studies*, ed. Helen Gardner, 1969)
Wright, George T., *Shakespeare's Metrical Art* (1988)

SOURCES AND INFLUENCES

General Intellectual Background

Allen, D. C., *The Star-Crossed Renaissance* (1941)
Baker, Herschel, *The Dignity of Man: Studies in the Persistence of an Idea* (1947; reprinted as *The Image of Man*, 1961)
Baldwin, T. W., *William Shakspere's Petty School* (1943)
———, *William Shakspere's Small Latine & Lesse Greeke* (2 vols., 1944)
Braden, Gordon and William Kerrigan, *The Idea of the Renaissance* (1989)
Burt, Richard and John Michael Archer, eds., *Enclosure Acts: Sexuality, Property and Culture in Early Modern England* (1994)
Bush, Douglas, *The Renaissance and English Humanism* (1939)
Craig, Hardin, *The Enchanted Glass: The Elizabethan Mind in Literature* (1936)
Curry, W. C., *Shakespeare's Philosophical Patterns* (1937)
Curtius, E. R., *European Literature and the Latin Middle Ages* (trans. W. R. Trask 1953)
Draper, J. W., *The Humors and Shakespeare's Characters* (1945)
Driver, T. F., *The Sense of History in Greek and Shakespearean Drama* (1960)
Frye, R. M., *Shakespeare and Christian Doctrine* (1963)
Greenblatt, Stephen, *Renaissance Self-Fashioning: From More to Shakespeare* (1980)
Hall, Kim F., *Things of Darkness: Economies of Race and Gender in Early Modern England* (1996)
Harris, Victor, *All Coherence Gone* (1949)
Helgeson, Richard, *Forms of Nationhood: The Elizabethan Writing of England* (1992)
Hendricks, Margo, and Patricia Parker, eds., *Women, "Race," and Writing in the Early Modern Period* (1994)
Hoeniger, F. D., *Medicine and Shakespeare in the English Renaissance* (1992)
Hutton, Ronald, *The Rise and Fall of Merry England: The Ritual Year, 1400–1700* (1994)
Johnson, F. R., *Astronomical Thought in Renaissance England* (1937)
Jordan, Constance, *Renaissance Feminism: Literary Texts and Political Models* (1990)
Kantorowicz, E. H., *The King's Two Bodies: A Study in Medieval Political Theology* (1957)
Kinney, Arthur, *Humanist Poetics: English Thought, Rhetoric, and Fiction in the Sixteenth Century* (1986)
Kocher, P. H., *Science and Religion in Elizabethan England* (1953)
Manley, Lawrence, *Literature and Culture in Early Modern London* (1995)
Peck, Linda Levy, ed., *The Mental World of the Jacobean Court* (1991)
Shuger, Debora Kuller, *Habits of Thought in the English Renaissance: Religion, Politics, and the Dominant Culture* (1990)
Smith, Bruce R., *Homosexual Desire in Shakespeare's England: A Cultural Poetics* (1991, with new preface 1994)
Spencer, Theodore, *Shakespeare and the Nature of Man* (1942, rev., 1947)
Stapfer, Paul, *Shakespeare and Classical Antiquity* (1880)
Stevenson, D. L., ed., *The Elizabethan Age* (1966)
Thompson, J. A. K., *Shakespeare and the Classics* (1952)
Tillyard, E. M. W., *The Elizabethan World Picture* (1946)
Velz, J. W., *Shakespeare and the Classical Tradition* (1968)
Watson, C. B., *Shakespeare and the Renaissance Concept of Honor* (1960)

Primary Literary Sources

Boswell-Stone, W. G., ed., *Shakspere's Holinshed* (1896, 1907)
Bullough, Geoffrey, *Narrative and Dramatic Sources of Shakespeare* (8 vols., 1957–75)
Gollancz, Israel, gen. ed., *The Shakespeare Classics* (11 vols. by various eds., 1907–13)
Hazlitt, W. C., ed., *Shakespeare's Library* (6 vols., 1875)
Hosley, Richard, ed., *Shakespeare's Holinshed* (1968)
McCallum, M. W., *Shakespeare's Roman Plays and Their Background* (1910)
Muir, Kenneth, *Shakespeare's Sources* (Vol. I [Comedies and Tragedies], 1957; rev. to include the Histories and Romances as *The Sources of Shakespeare's Plays*, 1977)
Rouse, W. H. D., *Shakespeare's Ovid* (1904)
Skeat, W. W., ed., *Shakespeare's Plutarch* (1875)
Spencer, T. J. B., ed., *Elizabethan Love Stories* (1968) [sources of 8 plays]
———, ed., *Shakespeare's Plutarch* (1964)
See also the New Variorum series.

Special Literary Influences

Baker, Howard, *Induction to Tragedy: A Study in a Development of Form in "Gorboduc," "The Spanish Tragedy," and "Titus Andronicus"* (1939)
Baldwin, T. W., *William Shakspere's Five-Act Structure* (1947)
Bate, Jonathan, *Shakespeare and Ovid* (1993)
Bevington, David, *From "Mankind" to Marlowe* (1962)
———, *Tudor Drama and Politics: A Critical Approach to Topical Meaning* (1968)
Brower, R. A., *Hero and Saint: Shakespeare and the Graeco-Roman Heroic Tradition* (1972)
Chubb, Louise George, *Italian Drama in Shakespeare's Time* (1989)
Clemen, Wolfgang, *English Tragedy before Shakespeare* (1961)
Cole, H. C., *A Quest of Inquirie: Some Contexts of Tudor Literature* (1973)
Cunliffe, J. W., *The Influence of Seneca on Elizabethan Tragedy* (1893)

Dessen, Alan, *Shakespeare and the Late Moral Plays* (1986)
Donaldson, E. T., *The Swan at the Well: Shakespeare Reading Chaucer* (1985)
Doran, Madeleine, *Endeavors of Art: A Study of Form in Elizabethan Drama* (1954)
Eliot, T. S., "Seneca in Elizabethan Translation" (1927, repr. in *Selected Essays*, 1932)
Farnham, Willard, *The Medieval Heritage of Elizabethan Tragedy* (1936)
Gesner, Carol, *Shakespeare and the Greek Romance: A Study of Origins* (1970)
Herrick, M. T., *Comic Theory in the Sixteenth Century* (1950)
———, *Tragi-comedy: Its Origin and Development in Italy, France, and England* (1955)
Jones, Emrys, *The Origins of Shakespeare* (1979)
Kastner, L. E., and H. B. Charlton, Introduction to *Poetical Works of Sir William Alexander* (1925), Vol. I [for the influence of Seneca in England and on the Continent]
F. L. Lucas, *Seneca and Elizabethan Tragedy* (1922)
Mackenzie, W. R., *The English Moralities* (1914)
Martindale, Charles and Michelle, *Shakespeare and the Uses of Antiquity: An Introductory Essay on Shakespeare and Renaissance Classicism* (1990)
Miola, Robert S., *Shakespeare and the Classical Tradition: The Influence of Seneca* (1992)
———, *Shakespeare and Classical Comedy: The Influence of Plautus and Terence* (1994)
Noble, Richmond, *Shakespeare's Biblical Knowledge* (1935)
Riehle, Wolfgang, *Shakespeare, Plautus and the Humanist Tradition* (1990)
Ristine, Frank, *English Tragi-comedy* (1910)
Rossiter, A. P., *English Drama from Early Times to the Elizabethans* (1948)
Snuggs, H. L., *Shakespeare and Five Acts* (1960)
Thompson, Ann, *Shakespeare's Chaucer: A Study in Literary Origins* (1978)
Tobin, J. J. M., *Shakespeare's Favorite Novel: A Study of "The Golden Asse" as Prime Source* (1984)
Whitaker, V. K., *Shakespeare's Use of Learning: An Inquiry into the Growth of His Mind and Art* (1953)

THE THEATRE

The Contemporary Stage

Adams, J. C., *The Globe Playhouse* (1942; 2nd ed., 1961)
Adams, J. Q., *Shakespearean Playhouses* (1917)
Armstrong, W. A., *The Elizabethan Private Theatres: Facts and Problems* (1958)
Baldwin, T. W., *The Organization and Personnel of the Shakespearean Company* (1927)
Beckerman, Bernard, *Shakespeare at the Globe, 1599–1609* (1962)
Bentley, G. E., *The Jacobean and Caroline Stage* (7 vols., 1941–68)
———, *Shakespeare and His Theatre* (1964)
Berry, Herbert, ed., *The First Public Playhouse: The Theatre in Shoreditch (1576–1598)* (1979)
Bradbrook, M. C., *The Rise of the Common Player* (1962)
Chambers, E. K., *The Elizabethan Stage* (4 vols., 1923)
Cook, Ann J., *The Privileged Playgoers of Shakespeare's London, 1576–1642* (1985)
David, Richard, *Shakespeare in the Theatre* (1978)
Davies, W. R., *Shakespeare's Boy Actors* (1939)
Dessen, Alan C., *Recovering Shakespeare's Theatrical Vocabulary* (1995)
Evans, G. Blakemore, ed., *Elizabethan-Jacobean Drama: A New Mermaid Background Book* (1987)
Farley-Hills, David, *Shakespeare and the Rival Playwrights 1600–1606* (1990)
Foakes, R. A., and R. T. Rickert, eds., *Henslowe's Diary* (1961)
———, *Illustrations of the English Stage, 1580–1642* (1985)
Greg, W. W., ed., *Dramatic Documents from the Elizabethan Playhouses* (2 vols., 1931)
———, *Henslowe Papers* (1907)
———, *Henslowe's Diary* (2 vols., 1904, 1908)
Gurr, Andrew, *The Shakespearean Stage 1574–1642* (1970; 3rd ed., 1992)
———, *Playgoing in Shakespeare's London* (1987)
———, *The Shakespearian Playing Companies* (1996)
Harbage, Alfred, *Shakespeare and the Rival Traditions* (1952)
———, *Shakespeare's Audience* (1941)
———, *Theatre for Shakespeare* (1955)
———, and Samuel Schoenbaum, *Annals of English Drama, 975–1700* (rev. ed., 1964)
Hartnoll, Phyllis, ed., *Shakespeare in Music* (1964)
Hattaway, Michael, *Elizabethan Popular Theatre: Plays in Performance* (1982)
Hodges, C. W., *The Globe Restored* (1953; rev. ed., 1968)
———, *Shakespeare's Second Globe* (1973)
———, *Shakespeare and the Players* (1948)
———, et al., eds., *The Third Globe* (1981)
Holmes, Martin, *Shakespeare and His Players* (1972)
———, *Shakespeare's Public: The Touchstone of His Genius* (1960)
Hotson, Leslie, *Shakespeare's Wooden O* (1960)
Ingram, William, *The Business of Playing: The Beginnings of the Adult Professional Theater in Elizabethan London* (1992)
Joseph, B. L., *Elizabethan Acting* (2nd ed., 1964)
Kernan, Alvin, *The Playwright as Magician: Shakespeare's Image of the Poet in the English Public Theater* (1979)
———, *Shakespeare, the King's Playwright: Theater in the Stuart Court*, 1603–1613 (1995)
Kernodle, G. R., *From Art to Theatre: Form and Convention in the Renaissance* (1944)
King, T. J., *Shakespearean Staging, 1599–1642* (1971)
———, *Casting Shakespeare's Plays: London Actors and Their Roles, 1590–1642* (1992)
Knutson, Roslyn Lander, *The Repertory of Shakespeare's Company 1594–1613* (1991)
Lawrence, W. J., *The Physical Conditions of the Elizabethan Public Playhouse* (1927)
———, *Pre-Restoration Stage Studies* (1927)
Leacroft, Richard, *The Development of the English Playhouse* (1973)
Leech, Clifford, and T. W. Craik, eds., *The "Revels" History of the Drama in English: Vol. III, 1576–1613* (1975)
Linthicum, Marie C., *Costume in the Drama of Shakespeare and His Contemporaries* (1936)
Munkelt, Margarete, *Bühnenanweisung und Dramaturgie: Hinweise zu Interpretation und Inszenierung in Shakespeares "First Folio" und den Quartoversionen* (1981)
Nagler, A. M., *Shakespeare's Stage* (trans. Ralph Mannheim, 1958)
Nelson, Alan H., *Early Cambridge Theatres: College, University and Town Stages 1464–1720* (1994)
Orrell, John, *The Quest for Shakespeare's Globe* (1983)
Reynolds, G. F., *The Staging of Elizabethan Plays at the Red Bull Theater* (1940)
Seng, P. J., *The Vocal Songs in the Plays of Shakespeare: A Critical History* (1967)
Shakespeare Survey 1 (1948); *12* (1959) [largely devoted to Shakespeare's theatre]
Shapiro, I. A., "The Bankside Theatres: Early Engravings," *Shakespeare Survey 1* (1948), 25–37
———, "Robert Fludd's Stage-Illustration," *Shakespeare Studies*, II (1967), 192–209
Shapiro, Michael, *Children of the Revels: The Boy Companies of Shakespeare's Time and Their Plays* (1977)
———, *Gender in Play on the Shakespearian Stage: Boy Heroines and Female Pages* (1994)

Slater, A. P., *Shakespeare the Director* (1982)
Smith, Irwin, *Shakespeare's Blackfriars Playhouse* (1964)
———, *Shakespeare's Globe Playhouse* (1956)
Southern, Richard, *The Staging of Plays before Shakespeare* (1973)
Styan, J. L., *Shakespeare's Stagecraft* (1967)
Thompson, Peter, *Shakespeare's Theatre* (1983)
Venezky, Alice S., *Pageantry on the Shakespearean Stage* (1951)
Welsford, E., *The Court Masque* (1927)
Wickham, Glynne, *Early English Stages, 1300–1660* (2 vols. in 3, 1959, 1963, 1972)
———, *Shakespeare's Dramatic Heritage* (1969)
Withington, Robert, *English Pageantry* (2 vols., 1918–20)
Yates, Frances A., *Theatre of the World* (1969)

Stage History

Avery, E. L., C. B. Hogan, A. H. Scouten, G. W. Stone, Jr., W. Van Lennep, *The London Stage 1660–1800* (11 vols., 1965–68)
Ball, Robert H., *Shakespeare on Silent Film* (1968)
Barish, Jonas, *The Antitheatrical Prejudice* (1981)
Bartholomeusz, Dennis, *Macbeth and the Players* (1969)
Barton, John, *Playing Shakespeare* (1984)
Bate, Jonathan and Russell Jackson, eds., *Shakespeare: An Illustrated Stage History* (1996)
Bentley, G. E., *The Professions of Dramatist and Player in Shakespeare's Time* (1984)
Berry, Ralph, *Shakespeare and the Awareness of the Audience* (1985)
Bevington, David, *Action Is Eloquence: Shakespeare's Language of Gesture* (1984)
Branam, G. C., *Eighteenth-Century Adaptations of Shakespearean Tragedy* (1956)
Brown, J. R., *Shakespeare's Plays in Performance* (1966)
Buchman, Lorne, *Still in Movement: Shakespeare on Screen* (1991)
Bulman, James C., and Herbert Coursen, *Shakespeare on Television: An Anthology of Essays and Reviews* (1988)
Byrne, M. St. C., *A History of Shakespearean Production in England*, Part I, 1700–1800 (1948)
———, "Fifty Years of Shakespearian Production: 1898–1948," *Shakespeare Survey 2* (1949), 1–20
Carlisle, Carol J., *Shakespeare from the Greenroom* (1969)
Crosse, Gordon, *Fifty Years of Shakespearean Playgoing* (1941)
Davies, Anthony, *Filming Shakespeare's Plays: The Adaptations of Laurence Olivier, Orson Welles, Peter Brook and Akira Kurosawa* (1988)
Dessen, Alan, *Elizabethan Stage Conventions and Modern Interpreters* (1984)
Donohue, J. W., *Dramatic Character in the English Romantic Age* (1970)
Evans, G. B., *Shakespearean Prompt-Books of the 17th Century* (8 vols., 1960–96)
Genest, John, *Some Account of the English Stage, 1660–1830* (10 vols., 1832)
Goldman, Michael, *Acting and Action in Shakespearean Tragedy* (1985)
Halstead, W. P., *Shakespeare As Spoken: A Collection of 5000 Acting Editions and Promptbooks of Shakespeare* (13 vols., 1977–83)
Hogan, C. B., *Shakespeare in the Theatre, 1701–1800* (2 vols., 1952, 1957)
Hotson, Leslie, *The Commonwealth and Restoration Stage* (1928)
Jackson, Russell, Robert Smallwood, and Philip Brockbank, eds., *Players of Shakespeare*, 3 vols. (1986–93)
Joseph, B. L., *Acting Shakespeare* (1960)
———, *The Tragic Actor* (1969)
Kennedy, Dennis, ed., *Foreign Shakespeare: Contemporary Performance* (1993)
Long, John H., *Shakespeare's Use of Music*, 3 vols. (1963–67)
Manvell, Roger, *Shakespeare and the Film* (1971)
Nicoll, Allardyce, *Dryden as an Adapter of Shakespeare* (1922)
———, *A History of English Drama* (6 vols., rev. ed., 1955–59)
Odell, G. C. D., *Annals of the New York Stage* (15 vols., 1927–49)
———, *Shakespeare from Betterton to Irving* (2 vols., 1920)
Price, J. G., ed., *The Triple Bond: Plays, Mainly Shakespearean, in Performance* (1975)
Rosenberg, Marvin, *The Masks of "King Lear"* (1972)
———, *The Masks of "Othello"* (1961)
———, *The Masks of "Hamlet"* (1992)
Salgado, Gamini, *Eyewitnesses of Shakespeare* (1975)
Shakespeare Survey 39 (1986) [devoted largely to Shakespeare on film and radio]
Shattuck, C. H., *The Hamlet of Edwin Booth* (1969)
———, ed., *John Philip Kemble: Promptbooks* (11 vols. [first 9 vols. contain the Shakespearean productions], 1974)
———, *Shakespeare on the American Stage*, Vol. I (1976); Vol. II (1987)
———, *The Shakespeare Promptbooks: A Descriptive Catalogue* (1965)
———, *William Charles Macready's "King John"* (1962)
Southern, Richard, *Changeable Scenery* (1952)
Speaight, Robert, *Shakespeare on the Stage: An Illustrated History of Shakespearean Performance* (1973)
Spencer, Christopher, *Five Restoration Adaptations of Shakespeare* (1965)
Spencer, Hazelton, *Shakespeare Improved* (1927)
Sprague, A. C., *Shakespeare and the Actors: The Stage Business in His Plays, 1660–1905* (1944)
———, *Shakespeare and the Audience* (1935)
———, *Shakespeare's Histories, Plays for the Stage* (1964)
———, *Shakespearian Players and Performances* (1953)
———, and J. C. Trewin, *Shakespeare's Plays Today: Some Customs and Conventions of the Stage* (1972)
Styan, J. L., *The Shakespeare Revolution* (1977)
Thaler, Alwin, *Shakespeare to Sheridan* (1922)
Thomson, Peter, *Shakespeare's Professional Career* (1992)
Trewin, J. C., *Shakespeare on the English Stage, 1900–1964* (1964)
Weimann, Robert, *Shakespeare and the Popular Tradition in the Theater* (1978)
Williams, Harcourt, *Old Vic Saga* (1949)
Williamson, Audrey, *Old Vic Drama* (1948); *Old Vic Drama 2* (1957)
Winter, William, *Shakespeare on the Stage*, series 1, 2, 3 (1911, 1915, 1916)
For annual reviews of Shakespearean productions, see *Shakespeare Survey* and *Shakespeare Quarterly.*

GENERAL CRITICISM

Adelman, Janet, *Suffocating Mothers: Fantasies of Maternal Origin in Shakespeare's Plays* (1992)
Aers, Lesley, and Nigel Wheale, eds., *Shakespeare in the Changing Curriculum* (1991)
Alexander, Peter, ed., *Studies in Shakespeare* (1964) [selected British Academy Shakespeare lectures]
Allman, E. J., *Player King and Adversary: Two Faces of Play in Shakespeare* (1980)
Arthos, John, *The Art of Shakespeare* (1964)
———, *Shakespeare: The Early Writings* (1972)
———, *Shakespeare's Use of Dream and Vision* (1977)
Bamber, Marie, *Comic Women, Tragic Men: A Study of Gender and Genre in Shakespeare* (1982)
Barber, C. L., and Richard Wheeler, *The Whole Journey: Shakespeare's Power of Development* (1986)
Barton, Anne, *Essays, Mainly Shakespearian* (1994)

Bate, Jonathan, *Shakespeare and the English Romantic Imagination* (1989)
Baxter, John, *Shakespeare's Poetic Styles* (1980)
Berry, Francis, *The Shakespeare Inset: Word and Picture* (1965)
Bethell, S. L., *Shakespeare and the Popular Dramatic Tradition* (1944)
Birney, A. L., *Satiric Catharsis and Shakespeare: A Theory of Dramatic Structure* (1973)
Bloom, Allan, and H. V. Jaffe, *Shakespeare's Politics* (1964)
Bradbrook, M. C., *Shakespeare and Elizabethan Poetry* (1951)
———, *Shakespeare: The Poet in His World* (1978)
———, *Shakespeare the Craftsman* (1979)
Braden, Gordon, *Renaissance Tragedy and the Senecan Tradition: Anger's Privilege* (1985)
Bradshaw, Graham, *Shakespeare's Skepticism* (1987)
———, *Misrepresentations: Shakespeare and the Materialists* (1993)
Brennan, Anthony, *Shakespeare's Dramatic Structures* (1986)
Bristol, Michael D., *Shakespeare's America, America's Shakespeare* (1990)
Brown, J. R., *Shakespeare's Dramatic Style* (1970)
Brown, J. R., and Bernard Harris, eds., *Early Shakespeare* (Stratford-upon-Avon Studies 3, 1961)
———, *Later Shakespeare* (Stratford-upon-Avon Studies 8, 1966)
Bruster, Douglas, *Drama and the Market in the Age of Shakespeare* (1992)
Bush, Geoffrey, *Shakespeare and the Natural Condition* (1956)
Calderwood, J. L., *Shakespeare's Metadrama* (1971)
Campbell, O. J., *Shakespeare's Satire* (1943)
Carroll, William C., *Fat King Lean Beggar: Representations of Poverty in the Age of Shakespeare* (1996)
Cavell, Stanley, *Disowning Knowledge in Six Plays of Shakespeare* (1987)
Chambers, E. K., *Shakespeare: A Survey* (1925)
Charnes, Linda, *Notorious Identity: Materializing the Subject in Shakespeare* (1993)
Clemen, Wolfgang, *Shakespeare's Dramatic Art* (1972)
Coghill, Nevill, *Shakespeare's Professional Skills* (1964)
Coleridge, S. T., *Shakespearean Criticism*, ed. T. M. Raysor (2 vols., 1930); *Coleridge on Shakespeare*, ed. R. A. Foakes (1971)
Colie, Rosalie, *Shakespeare's Living Art* (1974)
Colman, E. A. M., *The Dramatic Use of Bawdy in Shakespeare* (1974)
Cook, Ann Jennalie, *Making a Match: Courtship in Shakespeare and His Society* (1991)
Council, Norman, *When Honour's at the Stake: Ideas of Honour in Shakespeare's Plays* (1973)
Coursen, H. R., *The Compensatory Psyche: A Jungian Approach to Shakespeare* (1986)
Craig, Hardin, *An Interpretation of Shakespeare* (1948)
Crane, Mary Thomas, *Framing Authority: Sayings, Self, and Society in Sixteenth-Century England* (1993)
Crane, Milton, ed., *Shakespeare's Art: Seven Essays* (1973)
Dash, I. G., *Wooing, Wedding, and Power: Women in Shakespeare* (1981)
Dawson, A. B., *Indirections: Shakespeare and the Art of Illusion* (1978)
Desmet, Christy, *Reading Shakespeare's Characters: Rhetoric, Ethics, and Identity* (1992)
Dillon, Janette, *Shakespeare and the Solitary Man* (1981)
Dollimore, Jonathan, *Radical Tragedy: Religion, Ideology, and Power in the Drama of Shakespeare and His Contemporaries* (1984)
Dowden, Edward, *Shakspere: A Critical Study of His Mind and Art* (1875)
Dreher, D. E., *Dominion and Defiance: Fathers and Daughters in Shakespeare* (1985)
Driscoll, J. P., *Identity in Shakespearean Drama* (1983)
Dusinberre, Juliet, *Shakespeare and the Nature of Women* (1979)
Eastman, Arthur M., *A Short History of Shakespearean Criticism* (1968)
Edwards, Philip, *Shakespeare and the Confines of Art* (1968)
———, *Shakespeare: A Writer's Progress* (1986)
Ellis-Fermor, Una M., *Shakespeare the Dramatist* (1961)
Empson, William, *Essays on Shakespeare* (1986)
Engle, Lars, *Shakespearean Pragmatism: Market of His Time* (1993)
Erickson, Peter, *Patriarchal Structures in Shakespeare's Plays* (1985)
Evans, G. B., ed., *Shakespeare: Aspects of Influence* (1976)
Evans, Maurice, *Signifying Nothing: Truth's True Contexts in Shakespeare's Text* (1986)
Faas, Ekbert, *Shakespeare's Poetics* (1986)
Faber, M. D., ed., *The Design Within: Psychoanalytic Approaches to Shakespeare* (1970)
Farnham, Willard, *The Shakespearean Grotesque* (1971)
Fergusson, Francis, *Shakespeare: The Pattern in His Carpet* (1970)
French, A. L., *Shakespeare and the Critics* (1972)
French, Marilyn, *Shakespeare's Division of Experience* (1983)
Frost, David L., *The School of Shakespeare: The Influence of Shakespeare on English Drama, 1600–42* (1968)
Frye, Northrop, *Anatomy of Criticism: Four Essays* (1957)
Frye, R. M., *Shakespeare: The Art of the Dramatist* (1970)
Garber, M. B., *Dream in Shakespeare: From Metaphor to Metamorphosis* (1974)
———, *Coming of Age in Shakespeare* (1981)
———, *Shakespeare's Ghost Writers: Literature as Uncanny Causality* (1987)
Gibbons, Brian, *Shakespeare and Multiplicity* (1993)
Gillies, John, *Shakespeare and the Geography of Difference* (1994)
Goddard, H. C., *The Meaning of Shakespeare* (1951)
Godshalk, W. L., *Patterning in Shakespearean Drama* (1973)
Goldman, Michael, *Shakespeare and the Energies of Drama* (1972)
Grady, Hugh, *The Modernist Shakespeare* (1991)
Granville-Barker, Harley, *Prefaces to Shakespeare* (2 vols., 1946–47)
———, *More Prefaces to Shakespeare* (1974)
Greenblatt, Stephen, *Shakespearean Negotiations: The Circulation of Social Energy in Renaissance England* (1988)
Greer, Germaine, *Shakespeare* (1986)
Grudin, Robert, *Mighty Opposites: Shakespeare and Renaissance Contrariety* (1979)
Hamilton, A. C., *The Early Shakespeare* (1967)
Harbage, Alfred, *William Shakespeare: A Reader's Guide* (1963)
———, *A Kind of Power: The Shakespeare-Dickens Analogy* (1975)
Hart, Jonathan, ed., *Reading the Renaissance: Culture, Poetics, and Drama* (1996)
Hartwig, Joan, *Shakespeare's Analogical Scene: Parody as Structural Syntax* (1983)
Hawkes, Terence, *Meaning by Shakespeare* (1992)
———, *Shakespeare's Talking Animals; Language and Drama in Society* (1973)
Hazlitt, William, *Characters of Shakespeare's Plays* (1817)
Hibbard, G. R., *The Making of Shakespeare's Dramatic Poetry* (1981)
Hillman, Richard, *Shakespearean Subversions: The Trickster and the Play-text* (1992)
Hirsh, J. E., *The Structure of Shakespearean Scenes* (1981)
Hobson, Alan, *Full Circle: Shakespeare and Moral Development* (1972)

Hoenselaars, A. J., *Images of Englishmen and Foreigners in the Drama of Shakespeare and His Contemporaries: A Study of Stage Characters and National Identity in English Renaissance Drama* (1992)
———, *Reclamations of Shakespeare* (1994)
Holderness, Graham, ed., *The Shakespeare Myth* (1988)
Holland, Norman, *Psychoanalysis and Shakespeare* (1966)
———, Sidney Homan, and Bernard J. Paris, eds., *Shakespeare's Personality* (1989)
Homan, Sidney, *When the Theater Turns to Itself: The Aesthetic Metaphor in Shakespeare* (1981)
———, *Shakespeare's Theater of Presence: Language, Spectacle, and the Audience* (1986)
Horwich, Richard, *Shakespeare's Dilemmas* (1988)
Howard, Jean E., and Marion F. O'Connor, eds., *Shakespeare Reproduced: The Text in History and Ideology* (1987)
Hudson, H. N., *Shakespeare: His Life, Art, and Character* (1872)
Hunter, G. K., *Dramatic Identities and Cultural Studies in Shakespeare and His Contemporaries* (1978)
Jardine, Lisa, *Still Harping on Daughters: Women and Drama in the Age of Shakespeare* (1983)
———, *Reading Shakespeare Historically* (1996)
Johnson, Samuel, Preface and notes to his edition of Shakespeare (1765); ed. Arthur Sherbo, Vols. VII and VIII of the Yale Edition of Johnson (1968)
Jones, Emrys, *Scenic Form in Shakespeare* (1971)
Kahn, Coppélia, *Man's Estate: Masculine Identity in Shakespeare* (1981)
Kastan, David Scott, and Peter Stallybrass, eds., *Staging the Renaissance: Reinterpretation of Elizabethan and Jacobean Drama* (1991)
Kermode, Frank, *Shakespeare, Spenser, Donne* (1971)
Kernan, Alvin, *The Cankered Muse: Satire of the English Renaissance* (1959)
Kiernan, Pauline, *Shakespeare's Theory of Drama* (1996)
Kirsch, Arthur, *Shakespeare and the Experience of Love* (1981)
Knapp, Robert S., *Shakespeare—The Theater and the Book* (1989)
Knights, L. C., *Drama and Society in the Age of Jonson* (1937)
———, *How Many Children Had Lady Macbeth? An Essay in the Theory and Practice of Shakespeare Criticism* (1933)
———, *Some Shakespearean Themes* (1959)
Kozintsev, Grigori, *Shakespeare: Time and Conscience* (1966)
Laroque, Francois, *Shakespeare's Festive World: Elizabethan Seasonal Entertainment and the Professional Stage* (tr. Janet Lloyd 1991)
Leavis, F. R., *The Common Pursuit* (1952)
Levin, Harry, *Shakespeare and the Revolution of the Times* (1976)
Levin, Richard, *New Readings vs. Old Plays: Recent Trends in the Re-interpretation of English Renaissance Drama* (1979)
Lukacher, Ned, *Daemonic Figures: Shakespeare and the Question of Conscience* (1994)
McAlindon, T., *Shakespeare and Decorum* (1974)
McDonald, Russ, *Shakespeare and Jonson/Jonson and Shakespeare* (1988)
McGuire, P. C., *Speechless Dialect: Shakespeare's Open Silences* (1985)
Mallin, Eric S., *Inscribing the Time: Shakespeare and the End of Elizabethan England* (1995)
Marder, Louis, *His Exits and His Entrances: The Story of Shakespeare's Reputation* (1963)
Marienstras, Richard, *New Perspectives on the Shakespearean World* (1985)
Maus, Katherine Eisman, *Inwardness and Theater in the English Renaissance* (1995)
Melchiori, Giorgio, *Shakespeare's Garter Plays: "Edward III" to "Merry Wives of Windsor"* (1994)
Milward, Peter, *Shakespeare's Religious Background* (1973)
Montrose, Louis, *The Purpose of Playing: Shakespeare and the Cultural Politics of the Elizabethan Theater* (1996)
Morris, Harry, *Last Things in Shakespeare* (1986)
Muir, Kenneth, "Fifty Years of Shakespearian Criticism: 1900–1950," *Shakespeare Survey 4* (1951), 1–25
———, *Shakespeare as Collaborator* (1960)
———, *Shakespeare the Professional, and Related Studies* (1973)
Neely, C. T., *Broken Nuptials in Shakespeare's Plays* (1985)
Newman, Karen, *Fashioning Femininity and English Renaissance Drama* (1991)
Novy, M. L., *Love's Argument: Gender Relations in Shakespeare* (1984)
Nutall, A. D., *A New Mimesis: Shakespeare and the Representation of Reality* (1983)
Parker, Barbara L., *Precious Seeing: Love and Reason in Shakespeare's Plays* (1987)
Parker, G. F., *Johnson's Shakespeare* (1989)
Parker, Patricia, *Literary Fat Ladies: Rhetoric, Gender, Property* (1987)
———, *Shakespeare from the Margins: Language, Culture, Context* (1996)
Paster, Gail, *The Idea of the City in the Age of Shakespeare* (1985)
Patterson, Annabel, *Shakespeare and the Popular Voice* (1989)
Pechter, Edward, *What Was Shakespeare? Renaissance Plays and Changing Critical Practice* (1995)
Phillips, O. H., *Shakespeare and the Lawyers* (1972)
Pinciss, G. M., *Literary Creations: Conventional Characters in the Drama of Shakespeare and His Contemporaries* (1988)
Pye, Christopher, *The Regal Phantasm: Shakespeare and the Politics of Spectacle* (1990)
Quinones, R. J., *The Renaissance Discovery of Time* (1972)
Rabkin, Norman, *Shakespeare and the Common Understanding* (1967)
———, *Shakespeare and the Problem of Meaning* (1981)
Ralli, A., *A History of Shakespearian Criticism* (2 vols., 1932)
Reed, Robert, *Crime and God's Judgement in Shakespeare* (1983)
Righter, Anne [Anne Barton], *Shakespeare and the Idea of the Play* (1962)
Roberts, Jeanne Addison, *The Shakespearean Wild: Geography, Genus, and Gender* (1991)
Rose, Mark, *Shakespearean Design* (1972)
Rose, Mary Beth, *The Expense of Spirit: Love and Sexuality in English Renaissance Drama* (1988)
Ryan, Kiernan, *Shakespeare—Harvester New Readings* (1989 2nd ed., 1995)
Salingar, Leo, *Dramatic Form in Shakespeare and the Jacobeans* (1986)
Salkeld, Duncan, *Madness and Drama in the Age of Shakespeare* (1993)
Sams, Eric, *The Real Shakespeare: Retrieving the Early Years, 1564-1594* (1995)
Sanders, Wilbur, *The Dramatist and the Received Idea: Studies in the Plays of Marlowe and Shakespeare* (1968)
Sandler, Robert, ed., *Northrop Frye on Shakespeare* (1986)
Schmidgall, Gary, *Shakespeare and the Courtly Aesthetic* (1981)
Schücking, L. L., *Character Problems in Shakespeare's Plays* (1922)
Sewell, Arthur, *Character and Society in Shakespeare* (1951)
Shapiro, James, *Rival Playwrights: Marlowe, Jonson, Shakespeare* (1991)
———, *Shakespeare and the Jews* (1996)
Siemon, J. R., *Shakespearean Iconoclasm* (1984)
Skura, Meredith, *Shakespeare the Actor and the Purposes of Playing* (1993)
Smith, Marion B., *Dualities in Shakespeare* (1966)
Soellner, Rolf, *Shakespeare's Patterns of Self-Knowledge* (1972)
Spivack, Bernard, *Shakespeare and the Allegory of Evil* (1958)

Stewart, J. I. M., *Character and Motive in Shakespeare* (1949)
Stoll, E. E., *Art and Artifice in Shakespeare* (1933)
———, *Shakespeare Studies* (1927)
Swinburne, A. C., *A Study of Shakespeare* (1880)
Talbert, E. W., *Elizabethan Drama and Shakespeare's Early Plays* (1963)
Taylor, Gary, *To Analyse Delight: A Hedonist Criticism of Shakespeare* (1985)
———, *Reinventing Shakespeare: A Cultural History, from the Restoration to the Present* (1989)
Traub, Valerie, *Desire and Anxiety: Circulations of Sexuality in Shakespearean Drama* (1992)
Traversi, Derek, *An Approach to Shakespeare* (3rd ed., 1969)
Truax, Elizabeth, *Metamorphosis in Shakespeare's Plays: A Pageant of Heroes, Gods, Maids and Monsters* (1992)
Turner, R. Y., *Shakespeare's Apprenticeship* (1974)
van den Berg, Kent T., *Playhouse and Cosmos: Shakespearean Theatre as Metaphor* (1985)
Van Doren, Mark, *Shakespeare* (1939)
Van Laan, T. F., *Role-playing in Shakespeare* (1985)
Vickers, Brian, *Appropriating Shakespeare: Contemporary Critical Quarrels* (1993)
Viswanathan, S., *The Shakespeare Play as Poem* (1980)
Waith, Eugene M., *Patterns and Perspectives in English Renaissance Drama* (1988)
Watson, R. N., *Shakespeare and the Hazards of Ambition* (1984)
Weiss, Theodore, *The Breath of Clowns and Kings: Shakespeare's Early Comedies and Histories* (1971)
Weitz, Margaret Collins, ed., *Shakespeare, Philosophy and Literature: Essays by Morris Weitz* (1996)
Williams, Gordon, *Shakespeare, Sex and the Print Revolution* (1996)
Wilson, F. P., *Shakespearian and Other Studies* (ed. Helen Gardner, 1969)
Wilson, Rawdon, *Shakespearean Narrative* (1995)
Woodbridge, Linda, *The Scythe of Saturn: Shakespeare and Magical Thinking* (1994)
Zeeveld, W. G., *The Temper of Shakespeare's Thought* (1974)
Zukofsky, Louis, *Bottom: On Shakespeare* (1986)

Anthologies of criticism

Barker, Deborah E. and Ivo Kamps., eds., *Shakespeare and Gender: A History* (1995)
Bevington, David, and Jay Halio, eds., *Shakespeare: Pattern of Excelling Nature* (1978)
Bradby, Anne, ed., *Shakespeare Criticism, 1919–1935* (1936); *Shakespeare Criticism, 1935–1960* (1963)
Calderwood, J. L., and H. E. Toliver, eds., *Essays in Shakespearean Criticism* (1970)
Dean, L. F., ed., *Shakespeare: Modern Essays in Criticism* (1957; rev. ed., 1967)
Dollimore, Jonathan, and Alan Sinfield, eds., *Political Shakespeare: New Essays in Cultural Materialism* (1985, 2nd ed., 1994)
Drakakis, John, ed., *Alternative Shakespeares* (1985)
———, ed., and intro., *Shakespearian Tragedy* (1992)
Edwards, Philip, ed., *Shakespeare's Styles* (1980)
Erickson, Peter, and Coppélia Kahn, eds., *Shakespeare's "Rough Magic": Renaissance Essays in Honor of C. L. Barber* (1985)
Garber, M. B., ed., *Cannibals, Witches, and Divorce: Estranging the Renaissance* (1987)
Halliday, F. E., ed., *Shakespeare and His Critics* (rev. ed., 1958)
Harris, L. L., and Mark Scott, eds., *Shakespearean Criticism* (1984–86)
Honigmann, E. A. J. (intro.), *British Academy Lectures 1980–89* (1993)
Kamps, Ivo, ed., *Shakespeare Left and Right* (1991)
———, *Materialist Shakespeare: A History* (1995).
Kermode, Frank, ed., *Four Centuries of Shakespearean Criticism* (1965)
Kernan, A. B., ed., *Modern Shakespearean Criticism* (1970)
Lenz, R. S. L., Gayle Greene, and C. T. Neely, eds., *The Women's Part: Feminist Criticism of Shakespeare* (1980)
McDonald, Russ, ed., *Shakespeare Reread: The Texts in New Contexts* (1994)
Mahon, John W. and Thomas A. Pendleton, eds., *"Fanned and Winnowed Opinions": Shakespearean Essays Presented to Harold Jenkins* (1987)
Muir, Kenneth, ed., *Interpretations of Shakespeare* (1985)
Parker, Patricia, and Geoffrey Hartman, eds., *Shakespeare and the Question of Theory* (1985)
Rabkin, Norman, ed., *Approaches to Shakespeare* (1964)
Sales, Roger, ed., *Shakespeare in Perspective* (2 vols., 1982, 1985)
Schwartz, Murray, and Coppélia Kahn, eds., *Representing Shakespeare: New Pychoanalytic Essays* (1982)
Siegel, P. N., ed., *His Infinite Variety* (1964)
Smith, D. Nichol, ed., *Shakespeare Criticism: A Selection [1623–1840]* (1916; rev. ed., 1963)
Vickers, Brian, ed., *Shakespeare: The Critical Heritage* (6 vols., 1974–81)
Wagner, B. M., ed., *The Appreciation of Shakespeare* (1949)
Wells, Stanley, ed., *Shakespeare in the Nineteenth Century* (1982)
———, ed., *Shakespeare in the Twentieth Century* (1984)
Woodbridge, Linda, and Edward Berry, eds., *True Rites and Maimed Rites: Ritual and Anti-Ritual in Shakespeare and His Age* (1992)

THE COMEDIES

Barber, C. L., *Shakespeare's Festive Comedy: A Study of Dramatic Form and Its Relation to Social Custom* (1959)
Berry, Edward, *Shakespeare's Comic Rites* (1985)
Berry, Ralph, *Shakespeare's Comedies: Explorations in Form* (1972)
Bonazzo, B. E., *Shakespeare's Early Comedies: A Structural Analysis* (1966)
Bradbrook, M. C., *The Growth and Structure of Elizabethan Comedy* (1955)
Brown, J. R., *Shakespeare and His Comedies* (2nd ed., 1962)
Bryant, J. A., *Shakespeare and the Uses of Comedy* (1986)
Carroll, W. C., *The Metamorphoses of Shakespearean Comedy* (1986)
Champion, L. S., *The Evolution of Shakespeare's Comedy* (1970)
Charlton, H. B., *Shakespearian Comedy* (1938)
Coghill, Nevill, "The Basis of Shakespearian Comedy," *Essays and Studies* (1950), pp. 1–28
Elam, Keir, *Shakespeare's Universe of Discourse: Language Games in the Comedies* (1984)
Evans, Bertrand, *Shakespeare's Comedies* (1960)
Foakes, R. A., *Shakespeare: The Dark Comedies to the Last Plays: From Satire to Celebration* (1971)
Freedman, Barbara, *Staging the Gaze: Postmodernism, Psychoanalysis, and Shakespearean Comedy* (1991)
Frye, Northrop, "The Argument of Comedy," *English Institute Essays 1948* (1949)
———, "Characterization in Shakespeare's Comedy," *Shakespeare Quarterly*, IV (1953), 271–77
———, *A Natural Perspective: The Development of Shakespearean Comedy and Romance* (1965)
———, *The Myth of Deliverance: Reflections on Shakespeare's Problem Comedies* (1983)
Goldsmith, R. H., *Wise Fools in Shakespeare* (1955)

Gordon, G. S., *Shakespearian Comedy and Other Studies* (1944)
Gross, John, *Shylock: A Legend and Its Legacy* (1992)
Hall, Jonathan, *Anxious Pleasures: Shakespearean Comedy and the Nation-State* (1995)
Hassel, R. C., *Faith and Folly in Shakespeare's Romantic Comedies* (1980)
Houston, J. D., *Shakespeare's Comedies of Play* (1981)
Hunter, G. K., *William Shakespeare: The Late Comedies* (1962)
Hunter, R. G., *Shakespeare and the Comedy of Forgiveness* (1965)
Jensen, Ejner J., *Shakespeare and the Ends of Comedy* (1991)
Lawrence, W. W., *Shakespeare's Problem Comedies* (1931)
Leggett, Alexander, *Shakespeare's Comedy of Love* (1974)
Levin, Harry, *Playboys and Killjoys: An Essay on the Theory and Practice of Comedy* (1987)
Levin, R. A., *Love and Society in Shakespearean Comedy: A Study of Dramatic Form and Content* (1985)
MacCary, W. T., *Friends and Lovers: The Phenomenology of Desire in Shakespearean Comedy* (1985)
Macdonald, Ronald R., *William Shakespeare: The Comedies* (1992)
McFarland, Thomas, *Shakespeare's Pastoral Comedy* (1972)
Mangan, Michael, *A Preface to Shakespeare's Comedies* (1996)
Martz, W. J., *Shakespeare's Universe of Comedy* (1971)
Muir, Kenneth, *Shakespeare's Comic Sequence* (1985)
Newman, Karen, *Shakespeare's Rhetoric of Comic Character: Dramatic Convention in Classical and Renaissance Comedy* (1985)
Nevo, Ruth, *Comic Transformations in Shakespeare* (1980)
Ornstein, Robert, *Shakespeare's Comedies: From Roman Farce to Romantic Mystery* (1986)
Palmer, D. J., and Malcolm Bradbury, eds., *Shakespearian Comedy*, Stratford-upon-Avon Studies 14 (1972)
Palmer, John, *Comic Characters of Shakespeare* (1946)
Parrott, T. M., *Shakespearean Comedy* (1949)
Pettet, E. C., *Shakespeare and the Romance Tradition* (1949)
Phialas, P. G., *Shakespeare's Romantic Comedies* (1966)
Reimer, A. P., *Antic Fables: Patterns of Evasion in Shakespeare's Comedies* (1980)
Richmond, Hugh, *Shakespeare's Sexual Comedy* (1971)
Salingar, Leo, *Shakespeare and the Tradition of Comedy* (1974)
Sen Gupta, S. C., *Shakespearian Comedy* (1950)
Shaheen, Naseeb, *Biblical References in Shakespeare's Comedies* (1993)
Shakespeare Survey 8 (1955); *22* (1969); *32* (1979); *37* (1984) [devoted largely to the comedies]
Smidt, Kristian, *Unconformities in Shakespeare's Early Comedies* (1986)
Spivack, Charlotte, *The Comedy of Evil and Shakespeare's Stage* (1979)
Stevenson, D., *The Love-Game Comedy* (1946)
Stoll, E. E., *Shakespeare's Young Lovers* (1937)
Swinden, Patrick, *An Introduction to Shakespeare's Comedies* (1973)
Teague, Francis, ed., *Acting Funny: Comic Theory and Practice in Shakespeare's Plays* (1994)
Thompson, K. M., "Shakespeare's Romantic Comedies," *PMLA*, LXVII (1952), 1079–93
Tillyard, E. M. W., *Shakespeare's Early Comedies* (1965)
———, *Shakespeare's Problem Plays* (1949)
Toole, W. B., *Shakespeare's Three Problem Plays* (1966)
Traversi, Derek, *William Shakespeare: The Early Comedies* (1960)
Ure, Peter, *William Shakespeare: The Problem Plays* (1961)
Vaughn, J. A., *Shakespeare's Comedies* (1980)
Westlund, Joseph, *Shakespeare's Reparative Comedies: A Psychoanalytic View of the Middle Plays* (1984)
Wheeler, Richard, *Shakespeare's Development and the Problem Comedies: Turn and Counter-Turn* (1981)
Williamson, M. L., *The Patriarchy of Shakespeare's Comedies* (1986)
Wilson, J. Dover, *Shakespeare's Happy Comedies* (1962)
Young, David, *The Heart's Forest: A Study of Shakespeare's Pastoral Plays* (1972)

Anthologies of criticism

Lerner, Laurence, ed., *Shakespeare's Comedies* (1967)
Muir, Kenneth, ed., *Shakespeare: The Comedies* (1965)
———, and Stanley Wells, eds., *Aspects of Shakespeare's Problem Plays* (1982)
Ornstein, Robert, ed., *Discussions of Shakespeare's Problem Comedies* (1961)
Palmer, D. J., ed., *Shakespeare's Later Comedies* (1971)
Waller, Gary, ed., *Shakespeare's Comedies* (1991)
Weil, Herbert, ed., *Discussions of Shakespeare's Romantic Comedy* (1966)

Studies of individual plays

Baldwin, T. W., *On the Compositional Genetics of "The Comedy of Errors"* (1965)
Bennett, Josephine W., *"Measure for Measure" as Royal Entertainment* (1966)
Briggs, K. M., *The Anatomy of Puck* (1959)
Campbell, O. J., *Comicall Satyre and Shakespeare's "Troilus and Cressida"* (1938)
Chambers, R. W., *The Jacobean Shakespeare and "Measure for Measure"* (1937)
Cole, Howard C., *The "All's Well" Story from Boccaccio to Shakespeare* (1981)
Green, William, *Shakespeare's "Merry Wives of Windsor"* (1962)
Hotson, Leslie, *The First Night of "Twelfth Night"* (1954)
Kimbrough, Robert, *Shakespeare's "Troilus and Cressida" and Its Setting* (1964)
Lascelles, Mary, *Shakespeare's "Measure for Measure"* (1953)
Leech, Clifford, *"Twelfth Night" and Shakespearian Comedy* (1965)
Mulryne, J. R., *Shakespeare: "Much Ado about Nothing"* (1965)
Presson, R. K., *Shakespeare's "Troilus and Cressida" and the Legends of Troy* (1953)
Price, J. G., *The Unfortunate Comedy: A Study of "All's Well That Ends Well" and its Critics* (1968)
Prouty, C. T., *The Sources of "Much Ado about Nothing"* (1950)
Rhoads, D. A., *Shakespeare's Defense of Poetry: "A Midsummer Night's Dream" and "The Tempest"* (1986)
Shell, Marc, *The End of Kinship: "Measure for Measure," Incest and the Ideal of Universal Siblinghood* (1988)
Stevenson, D. L., *The Achievement of "Measure for Measure"* (1966)
Young, David, *Something of Great Constancy: The Art of "A Midsummer Night's Dream"* (1966)
Wiles, David, *Shakespeare's Almanac: "A Midsummer Night's Dream," Marriage and the Elizabethan Calendar* (1993)

THE HISTORIES

Bacquet, Paul, *Les pièces historique de Shakespeare: La première tetralogie et "le Roi Jean"* (1978)
———, *Les pièces historique de Shakespeare: La deuxième tetralogie et "Henri VIII"* (1979)
Becker, G. J., *Shakespeare's Histories* (1977)
Berry, E. I., *Patterns of Decay: Shakespeare's Early Histories* (1975)
Blanpied, J. W., *Time and the Artist in Shakespeare's English Histories* (1983)
Boris, E. A., *Shakespeare's English Kings, the People and the Law* (1978)

Calderwood, J. L., *Metadrama in Shakespeare's Henriad: "Richard II" to "Henry V"* (1979)
Campbell, Lily B., *Shakespeare's "Histories": Mirrors of Elizabethan Policy* (1947)
Champion, Larry, *Perspectives in Shakespeare's English Histories* (1980)
Champion, Larry S., *"The Noise of Threatening Drum": Dramatic Strategy and Political Ideology in Shakespeare and the English Chronicle Plays* (1990)
Coursen, H. R., *The Leasing out of England: Shakespeare's Second Henriad* (1982)
Fleischer, M. H., *The Iconography of the English History Play* (1974)
Hart, Jonathan, *Theater and World: The Problematics of Shakespeare's History* (1992)
Hodgdon, Barbara, *The End Crowns All: Closure and Contradiction in Shakespeare's History* (1991)
Holderness, Graham, *Shakespeare's History* (1985)
Jorgensen, P. A., *Shakespeare's Military World* (1956)
Kastan, David, *Shakespeare and the Shapes of Time* (1982)
Kelly, H. A., *Divine Providence in the England of Shakespeare's Histories* (1970)
Knights, L. C., *William Shakespeare: The Histories* (1962)
Leech, Clifford, *William Shakespeare, The Chronicles* (1962)
Leggatt, Alexander, *Shakespeare's Political Drama: The History Plays and the Roman Plays* (1988)
Manheim, Michael, *The Weak King Dilemma in the Shakespearean History Play* (1973)
Ornstein, Robert, *A Kingdom for a Stage: The Achievement of Shakespeare's History Plays* (1972)
Palmer, John, *Political Characters of Shakespeare* (1945)
Patterson, Annabel, *Reading Holinshed's "Chronicles"* (1994)
Pearlman, E., *Shakespeare: The History Plays* (1992)
Pierce, R. B., *Shakespeare's History Plays: The Family and the State* (1971)
Porter, Joseph, *The Drama of Speech Acts: Shakespeare's Lancastrian Tetralogy* (1979)
Prior, M. E., *The Drama of Power: Studies in Shakespeare's History Plays* (1973)
Pugliatti, Paola, *Shakespeare the Historian* (1996)
Rackin, Phyllis, *Stages of History: Shakespeare's English Chronicles* (1990)
Reese, M. M., *The Cease of Majesty: A Study of Shakespeare's History Plays* (1961)
Ribner, Irving, *The English History Play in the Age of Shakespeare* (1957; rev. ed., 1965)
Richmond, H. M., *Shakespeare's Political Plays* (1967)
Rossiter, A. P., *"Angel with Horns" and Other Shakespeare Lectures*, ed., Graham Storey (1961)
Saccio, Peter, *Shakespeare's English Kings: History, Chronicle, and Drama* (1977)
Sen Gupta, S. C., *Shakespeare's Historical Plays* (1964)
Shaheen, Naseeb, *Biblical References in Shakespeare's History Plays* (1989)
Shakespeare Survey 6 (1953); *38* (1985) [devoted in good part to the histories]
Siegel, P. N., *Shakespeare's English and Roman History Plays: A Marxist Approach* (1986)
Smidt, Kristian, *Unconformities in Shakespeare's History Plays* (1982)
Stirling, Brents, *The Populace in Shakespeare* (1949)
Talbert, E. W., *The Problem of Order* (1962)
Thayer, C. G., *Shakespearean Politics: Government and Misgovernment in the Great Histories* (1983)
Tillyard, E. M. W., *Shakespeare's History Plays* (1944)
Traversi, Derek, *Shakespeare: From "Richard II" to "Henry V"* (1957)
Velz, John W., ed., *Shakespeare's English Histories: A Quest for Form and Genre* (1996)
Wikander, M. H., *The Play of Truth and State: Historical Drama from Shakespeare to Brecht* (1986)
Wilders, John, *The Lost Garden: A View of Shakespeare's English and Roman History Plays* (1978)
Winny, James, *The Player King: A Study of Shakespeare's Later History Plays* (1968)

Anthologies of criticism

Bloom, Harold, ed., *William Shakespeare: Histories and Poems* (1986)
Dorius, R. J., ed., *Discussions of Shakespeare's Histories: "Richard II" to "Henry V"* (1964)
Waith, E. M., ed., *Shakespeare: The Histories* (1965)

Studies of individual plays

Barber, C. L., "Rule and Misrule in *Henry IV*," *Shakespeare's Festive Comedy* (1959)
Churchill, G. B., *Richard the Third up to Shakespeare* (1900)
Clemen, W. H., *A Commentary on Shakespeare's "Richard III,"* trans. Jean Bonheim (1968)
Curren-Aquino, Deborah T., ed., *"King John": New Perspectives* (1989)
Hassel, R. C., *Songs of Death: Performance, Interpretation, and the Text of "Richard III"* (1984)
Humphreys, A. R., *Shakespeare: "Richard II"* (1967)
Jenkins, Harold, *The Structural Problem in Shakespeare's "Henry the Fourth"* (1956)
Morgann, Maurice, *Essay on the Dramatic Character of Sir John Falstaff* (1777; critical ed. by D. A. Fineman, 1972)
Price, H. T., *Construction in Shakespeare* (1951) [*Henry VI*]
Riggs, David, *Shakespeare's Heroical Histories: "Henry VI" and Its Literary Tradition* (1971)
Wilson, J. Dover, *The Fortunes of Falstaff* (1943)

THE TRAGEDIES

Barber, C. L., *Creating Elizabethan Tragedy: The Theater of Marlowe and Kyd* (1988)
Barroll, J. L., *Artificial Persons: The Formation of Character in the Tragedies of Shakespeare* (1974)
———, *Shakespearean Tragedy* (1984)
Bayley, John, *Shakespeare and Tragedy* (1981)
Belsey, Catherine, *The Subject of Tragedy: Identity and Difference in Renaissance Drama* (1985)
Bowers, F. T., *Elizabethan Revenge Tragedy, 1587–1642* (1940)
Bradley, A. C., *Shakespearean Tragedy* (1904). See also Katharine Cooke, *A. C. Bradley and His Influence in Twentieth-Century Criticism* (1972)
Brooke, Nicholas, *Shakespeare's Early Tragedies* (1968)
Brower, R. A., *Hero and Saint: Shakespeare and the Graeco-Roman Heroic Tradition* (1972)
Campbell, Lily B., *Shakespeare's Tragic Heroes: Slaves of Passion* (1930)
Cantor, P. A., *Shakespeare's Rome: Republic and Empire* (1976)
Charlton, H. B., *Shakespearian Tragedy* (1948)
Charney, Maurice, *Shakespeare's Roman Plays: The Function of Imagery in the Drama* (1961)
Coursen, R., *Christian Ritual and the World of Shakespeare's Tragedies* (1976)
Cunningham, J. V., *Woe or Wonder: The Emotional Effect of Shakespearean Tragedy* (1951)
Danson, Lawrence, *Tragic Alphabet: Shakespeare's Drama of Language* (1974)
Doran, Madeleine, *Shakespeare's Dramatic Language* (1976)
Enright, D. J., *Shakespeare and the Students* (1970)
Evans, Bertrand, *Shakespeare's Tragic Practice* (1979)
Everett, Barbara, *Young Hamlet: Essays on Shakespeare's Tragedies* (1989)

Farnham, Willard, *Young Hamlet: Essays on Shakespeare's Tragedies* (1989)
———, *Shakespeare's Tragic Frontier: The World of His Final Tragedies* (1936)
Felperin, Howard, *Shakespearean Representation: Mimesis and Modernity in Elizabethan Tragedy* (1977)
Foakes, R. A., *Hamlet versus Lear: Cultural Politics and Shakespeare's Art* (1993)
Foreman, W. C., *The Music of the Close: The Final Scenes of Shakespeare's Tragedies* (1978)
Frye, Northrop, *Fools of Time: Studies in Shakespearian Tragedy* (1967)
Hawkes, Terence, *Shakespeare and the Reason: A Study of the Tragedies and the Problem Plays* (1964)
Holloway, John, *The Story of the Night: Studies in Shakespeare's Major Tragedies* (1961)
Jorgensen, Paul A., *William Shakespeare: The Tragedies* (1985)
Kiefer, Frederick, *Fortune and Elizabethan Tragedy* (1983)
Kirsch, Arthur, *The Passions of Shakespeare's Tragic Heroes* (1990)
Knight, G. W., *The Imperial Theme* (1931)
———, *The Wheel of Fire* (1930)
Lawlor, John, *The Tragic Sense in Shakespeare* (1960)
Long, Michael, *The Unnatural Scene: A Study of Shakespeare's Tragedies* (1976)
MacCallum, M. W., *Shakespeare's Roman Plays and Their Background* (1910)
Mack, Maynard, *Everybody's Shakespeare: Reflections Chiefly on the Tragedies* (1993)
Mack, Maynard, Jr., *Killing the King: Three Studies in Shakespeare's Tragic Structure* (1973)
McAlindon, T., *English Renaissance Tragedy* (1986)
———, *Shakespeare's Tragic Cosmos* (1991)
McElroy, Bernard, *Shakespeare's Mature Tragedies* (1973)
Mangan, Michael, *A Preface to Shakespeare's Tragedies* (1991)
Mehl, Dieter, *Shakespeare's Tragedies; An Introduction* (1986)
Miles, Geoffrey, *Shakespeare and the Constant Romans* (1996)
Miola, R. S., *Shakespeare's Rome* (1983)
Morris, Ivor, *Shakespeare's God: The Role of Religion in the Tragedies* (1972)
Muir, Kenneth, *Shakespeare and the Tragic Pattern* (1958)
———, *William Shakespeare: The Great Tragedies* (1961)
Nevo, Ruth, *Tragic Form in Shakespeare* (1972)
Ornstein, Robert, *The Moral Vision of Jacobean Tragedy* (1960)
Palmer, John, *Political Characters of Shakespeare* (1945)
Payne, Michael, *Irony in Shakespeare's Roman Plays* (1974)
Phillips, J. E., *The State in Shakespeare's Greek and Roman Plays* (1940)
Proser, M. N., *The Heroic Image in Five Shakespearean Tragedies* (1965)
Rackin, Phyllis, *Shakespeare's Tragedies* (1978)
Ribner, Irving, *Patterns in Shakespearian Tragedy* (1960)
Rosen, William, *Shakespeare and the Craft of Tragedy* (1959)
Schanzer, Ernest, *The Problem Plays of Shakespeare: A Study of "Julius Caesar," "Measure for Measure," "Antony and Cleopatra"* (1963)
Shaheen, Naseeb, *Biblical References in Shakespeare's Tragedies* (1987)
Shakespeare Survey 10 (1957); *31* (1978) [devoted largely to the Roman plays]
Shakespeare Survey 27 (1974) [devoted to the early tragedies]
Siegel, P. N., *Shakespearean Tragedy and the Elizabethan Compromise* (1957)
Simmons, J. L., *Shakespeare's Pagan World: The Roman Tragedies* (1975)
Snyder, Susan, *The Comic Matrix of Shakespeare's Tragedies* (1979)
Spencer, T. J. B., *Shakespeare: The Roman Plays* (1963)
Spivack, Bernard, *Shakespeare and the Allegory of Evil* (1958)
Stampfer, Judah, *The Tragic Engagement: A Study of Shakespeare's Classical Tragedies* (1968)
Sternfeld, F. W., *Music in Shakespearean Tragedy* (1963)
Stirling, Brents, *Unity in Shakespearian Tragedy: The Interplay of Theme and Character* (1956)
Traversi, Derek, *Shakespeare: The Roman Plays* (1963)
Whitaker, V. K., *The Mirror up to Nature: The Technique of Shakespeare's Tragedies* (1965)
Wilson, H. S., *On the Design of Shakespearian Tragedy* (1957)
Young, David, *The Action to the Word: Structure and Style in Shakespearean Tragedy* (1990)

Anthologies of criticism

Charney, Maurice, ed., *Discussions of Shakespeare's Roman Plays* (1964)
Harbage, Alfred, ed., *Shakespeare: The Tragedies* (1964)
Lerner, Laurence, ed., *Shakespeare's Tragedies* (1957)
Rose, Mark, *Shakespeare's Early Tragedies* (1994)
Woodford, Susanne L., ed., *Shakespeare's Late Tragedies* (1996)
Young, David, *Shakespeare's Middle Tragedies* (1993)

Studies of individual plays

Adamson, Jane, *"Othello" as Tragedy* (1980)
Adelman, Janet, *The Common Liar: An Essay on "Antony and Cleopatra"* (1973)
Aldus, P. J., *Mousetrap: Structure and Meaning in "Hamlet"* (1977)
Alexander, Nigel, *Poison, Play, and Duel: A Study in "Hamlet"* (1971)
Alexander, Peter, *Hamlet: Father and Son* (1955)
Baker, Howard, *Induction to Tragedy* (1961) [*Titus Andronicus*]
Bayley, John, *The Characters of Love* (1961) [*Othello*]
Bonjour, Adrien, *The Structure of "Julius Caesar"* (1958)
Booth, Stephen, *"King Lear," "Macbeth": Indefinition and Tragedy* (1983)
Brown, J. R., and Bernard Harris, eds., *"Hamlet,"* Stratford-upon-Avon Studies 5 (1963)
Butler, Francelia, *The Strange Critical Fortunes of Shakespeare's "Timon of Athens"* (1966)
Calderwood, James L., *The Properties of "Othello"* (1989)
Cantor, Paul A., *Shakespeare: "Hamlet"* (1989)
Chambers, R. W., *"King Lear"* (1940)
Charney, Maurice, *Style in "Hamlet"* (1969)
Colie, Rosalie, and F. T. Flahiff, *Some Facets of "King Lear": Essays in Prismatic Criticism* (1974)
Cox, L. S., *Figurative Design in "Hamlet": The Significance of the Dumb Show* (1974)
Danby, J. F., *Poets on Fortune's Hill* (1952) [*King Lear; Antony and Cleopatra*]
———, *Shakespeare's Doctrine of Nature: A Study of "King Lear"* (1951)
Dodsworth, Martin, *Hamlet Closely Observed* (1985)
Elliott, G. R., *Dramatic Providence in "Macbeth"* (1958)
———, *Flaming Minister: A Study of "Othello" as a Tragedy of Love and Hate* (1953)
———, *Scourge and Minister: A Study of "Hamlet" as a Tragedy of Revengefulness and Justice* (1951)
Elliot, Martin, *Shakespeare's Invention of Othello: A Study in Early Modern English* (1988)
Elton, W. R., *"King Lear" and the Gods* (1966)
Fisch, Harold, *Hamlet and the Word: The Covenant Pattern in Shakespeare* (1971)
Fraser, Russell, *Shakespeare's Poetics in Relation to "King Lear"* (1962)
Gardner, Helen, *The Noble Moor* (1956)
Goldberg, E. L., *An Essay on "King Lear"* (1974)
Gottschalk, Paul, *The Meanings of "Hamlet": Modes of Literary Interpretation since Bradley* (1972)
Gurr, Andrew, *"Hamlet" and the Distracted Globe* (1978)

Halio, Jay L., ed., *Shakespeare's Romeo and Juliet": Texts, Contexts, and Interpretation* (1995)
Heilman, R. B., *Magic in the Web: Action and Language in "Othello"* (1956)
———, *This Great Stage: Image and Structure in "King Lear"* (1948)
Huffman, Clifford, *"Coriolanus" in Context* (1971)
James, D. G., *The Dream of Learning* (1951) [*Hamlet; King Lear*]
Jones, Ernest, *Hamlet and Oedipus* (1949; rev. of an essay first published in 1910)
Jorgensen, P. A., *Lear's Self-Discovery* (1967)
———, *Our Naked Frailties: Sensational Art and Meaning in "Macbeth"* (1971)
Joseph, Bertram, *Conscience and the King* (1953) [*Hamlet*]
Kerrigan, William, *Hamlet's Perfection* (1994)
Knights, L. C., *An Approach to "Hamlet"* (1960)
Levin, Harry, *The Question of Hamlet* (1959)
Lewis, Wyndham, *The Lion and the Fox* (1927) [*King Lear; Coriolanus*]
McGee, Arthur, *The Elizabethan "Hamlet"* (1987)
Mack, Maynard, *"King Lear" in Our Time* (1965)
Markels, Julian, *The Pillar of the World: "Antony and Cleopatra" in Shakespeare's Develcpment* (1968)
Moore, O. H., *The Legend of Romeo and Juliet* (1950)
Muir, Kenneth, *Shakespeare's "Hamlet"* (1963)
Paul, H. N., *The Royal Play of Macbeth* (1950)
Prosser, Eleanor, *Hamlet and Revenge* (1967; 2nd ed., 1971)
Ray, Robert H., *Approaches to Teaching Shakespeare's "King Lear"* (1986)
Reibetanz, John, *The "Lear" World: A Study of "King Lear" in Its Dramatic Context* (1977)
Seward, J. H., *Tragic Vision in "Romeo and Juliet"* (1973)
Shakespeare Survey, Five volumes are devoted largely to individual tragedies: *9* (1956) and *33* (1980) to *Hamlet; 13* (1960) to *King Lear; 19* (1966) to *Macbeth; 21* (1968) to *Othello.*
Soellner, Rolf, *"Timon of Athens": Shakespeare's Pessimistic Tragedy* (1979)
Taylor, Gary, and Michael Warren, eds., *The Division of the Kingdoms: Shakespeare's Revision of "King Lear"* (1983)
Urkowitz, Steven, *Shakespeare's Revision of "King Lear"* (1980)
Vaughan, Virginia Mason, *"Othello": A Contextual History* (1994)
Waith, E. M., *The Herculean Hero in Marlowe, Chapman, Shakespeare, and Dryden* (1963) [*Antony and Cleopatra; Coriolanus*]
Walker, Roy, *"The Time Is Free": A Study of "Macbeth"* (1949)
———, *"The Time Is Out of Joint": A Study of "Hamlet"* (1948)
Weitz, Morris, *"Hamlet" and the Philosophy of Literary Criticism* (1964)
William, C. C. H., comp., *Readings on the Character of Hamlet, 1661–1947* (1951)
Wilson, J. Dover, *What Happens in "Hamlet"* (1935)

THE ROMANCES

Bergeron, D. M., *Shakespeare's Romances and the Royal Family* (1985)
Bethell, S. L., *"The Winter's Tale": A Study* (1947)
Bieman, Elizabeth, *William Shakespeare: The Romances* (1990)
Bishop, T. G., *Shakespeare and the Theatre of Wonder* (1996)
Brown, J. R., and Bernard Harris, eds., *Later Shakespeare*, Stratford-upon-Avon Studies 9 (1966)
Danby, J. F., *Poets on Fortune's Hill* (1952)
Felperin, Howard, *Shakespearean Romance* (1972)
Foakes, R. A., *Shakespeare: From the Dark Comedies to the Last Plays: From Satire to Celebration* (1971)
Frye, Northrop, *A Natural Perspective: The Development of Shakespearean Comedy and Romance* (1965)
———, *The Secular Scripture: A Study of the Structure of Romance* (1976)
Gesner, Carol, *Shakespeare and the Greek Romance: A Study of Origins* (1970)
Hamilton, Donna B., *Virgil and* The Tempest (1990)
Hartwig, Joan, *Shakespeare's Tragicomic Vision* (1972)
Hunt, Maurice, *Approaches to Teaching Shakespeare's "The Tempest" and Other Late Romances* (1992)
Hunter, R. G., *Shakespeare and the Comedy of Forgiveness* (1965)
James, D. G., *The Dream of Prospero* (1967)
Kermode, Frank, *William Shakespeare: The Final Plays* (1963)
Knight, G. W., *The Crown of Life* (1947)
———, *The Shakespearian Tempest* (1932)
Mincoff, Marco, *Things Supernatural and Causeless: Shakespearean Romance* (1987, 1993)
Mowat, B. A., *The Dramaturgy of Shakespeare's Romances* (1976)
Nelson, T. A., *Shakespeare's Comic Theory: A Study of Art and Artifice in the Last Plays* (1973)
Peterson, D. L., *Time, Tide and Tempest: A Study of Shakespeare's Romances* (1973)
Pettet, E. C., *Shakespeare and the Romance Tradition* (1950)
Pyle, Fitzroy, *"The Winter's Tale": A Commentary on the Structure* (1969)
Shakespeare Survey 11 (1958); *29* (1976) [largely devoted to the romances]
Simmonds, Peggy Munoz, *Myth, Emblem, and Music in Shakespeare's "Cymbeline": An Iconographic Reconstruction* (1992)
Smith, Hallett, *Shakespeare's Romances: A Study of Some Ways of the Imagination* (1972)
Sokol, B. J., *Art and Illusion in "The Winter's Tale"* (1994)
Tillyard, E. M. W., *Shakespeare's Last Plays* (1938)
Traversi, Derek, *Shakespeare: The Last Phase* (1954)
Uphaus, Robert, *Beyond Tragedy: Structure and Experience in Shakespeare's Romances* (1981)
Vaughan, Alden T., and Virginia Mason Vaughan, *Shakespeare's Caliban: A Cultural History* (1991)
Velie, A. R., *Shakespeare's Repentance Plays: The Search for an Adequate Form* (1972)
Yates, Frances, *Shakespeare's Last Plays* (1975)

THE POEMS

Akrigg, G. P. V., *Shakespeare and the Earl of Southampton* (1968)
Baldwin, T. W., *On the Literary Genetics of Shakespere's Poems* (1950)
Booth, Stephen, *An Essay on Shakespeare's Sonnets* (1969)
Bush, Douglas, *Mythology and the Renaissance Tradition in English Poetry* (1932; rev. ed., 1963)
Calvert, Hugh, *Shakespeare's Sonnets and Problems of Autobiography* (1987)
Cruttwell, Patrick, *The Shakespearean Moment and Its Place in the Poetry of the Seventeenth Century* (1955)
Donow, H. S., *The Sonnet in England and America: A Bibliography of Criticism* (1982) [contains an index to criticism on each of Shakespeare's Sonnets]
Dubrow, Heather, *Captive Victors: Shakespeare's Narrative Poems and Sonnets* (1987)
———, *Echoes of Desire: Petrarchanism and Its Counterdiscourse* (1995)
Fineman, J., *Shakespeare's Perjured Eye: The Invention of Poetic Subjectivity in the Sonnets* (1987)
Foster, Donald W., *Elegy by W. S.: a Study in Attribution* (1989)

Hammond, Gerald, *The Reader and Shakespeare's Young Man Sonnets* (1981)
Herrnstein, Barbara, ed., *Discussions of Shakespeare's Sonnets* (1964)
Hubler, Edward, *The Sense of Shakespeare's Sonnets* (1952)
———, Northrop Frye, L. A. Fiedler, Stephen Spender, and R. P. Blackmur, *The Riddle of Shakespeare's Sonnets* (1962)
Jakobson, Roman, and Lawrence Jones, *Shakespeare's Verbal Art in "Th' Expense of Spirit"* (1970)
Knight, G. W., *The Mutual Flame: On Shakespeare's Sonnets and "The Phoenix and the Turtle"* (1955)
Krieger, Murray, *A Window to Criticism: Shakespeare's Sonnets and Modern Poetics* (1964)
Landry, Hilton, *Interpretations in Shakespeare's Sonnets* (1963)
———, ed., *New Essays on Shakespeare's Sonnets* (1976)
Leishman, J. B., *Themes and Variations in Shakespeare's Sonnets* (1961)
Lever, J. W., *The Elizabethan Love Sonnet* (1956)
Martin, Philip, *Shakespeare's Sonnets: Self, Love, and Art* (1972)
Matchett, W. H., *"The Phoenix and the Turtle": Shakespeare's Poem and Chester's "Loues Martyr"* (1965)
Melchiori, Giorgio, *Shakespeare's Dramatic Meditations: An Experiment in Criticism* (1976)
Ramsey, Paul, *The Fickle Glass: A Study of Shakespeare's Sonnets* (1979)
Shakespeare Survey 15 (1962) [devoted largely to Shakespeare's songs, sonnets, and other poems]
Smith, Hallett, *Elizabethan Poetry* (1952)
Stirling, Brents, *The Shakespeare Sonnet Order* (1968)
Wait, R. J. C., *The Background to Shakespeare's "Sonnets"* (1972)
Weiser, David K., *Shakespeare's Speaker in the Sonnets* (1987)
Wilson, J. Dover, *Shakespeare's Sonnets: An Introduction for Historians and Others* (1963)
Wilson, Katharine M., *Shakespeare's Sugared Sonnets* (1974)
Winny, James, *The Master-Mistress: A Study of Shakespeare's Sonnets* (1968)

A brothel. Frontispiece of Nicholas Goodman's *Holland's Leaguer* (1632). The brothel here shown was an especially notorious one in Southwark kept by a Mistress Holland (compare the Bawd in *Pericles* or Mistress Overdone in *Measure for Measure*). Situated on an island, it was outside regular legal jurisdiction and took extraordinary measures to protect its position. Observe the drawbridge, the guard (or pander) with a halberd, and the studded door with a special espial wicket. The garden is formally laid out for amorous strolling, with an arbor in one corner for more private entertainment. "Leaguer" may here be used in the sense of "military encampment" (i.e., for love's wars), but it may also perhaps have been a cant term for a brothel since "leaguer-lady" was a euphemistic name for a camp-follower.

Index to the Characters in the Plays

The act-scene reference indicates where a character first appears in each play.

Index to First Lines of the Sonnets

Index to First Lines of *The Passionate Pilgrim*

Index to First Lines of Songs and Song Snatches

Index to First Lines of Songs and Song Snatches

Selected Glossary

Most of the words selected for this Glossary are relatively common words in Shakespeare's vocabulary which are still current today but were often employed in Elizabethan times in senses differing from those in modern usage. The definitions do not usually include meanings in common use today, but the absence of a modern meaning from an entry must not be taken to imply that the entry word did not also carry that meaning in Elizabethan English. The context in which a word is used should generally make it clear whether the modern sense is applicable, or whether one of the earlier senses recorded in the Glossary is required to clarify the meaning. Where a word did not bear the usual modern meaning(s) in Shakespeare's time, the Glossary notes this limitation. Most of the words in the Glossary are defined in the footnotes to the plays but generally only on their first appearance in each play; hence readers may welcome a short glossary of the kind here offered.

The following sources were used in compiling the Glossary: (1) the glosses in the present edition; (2) the *Oxford English Dictionary*; (3) Alexander Schmidt, *Shakespeare-Lexicon* (2 vols., 4th ed. [revised, Gregor Sarrazin], Berlin, 1923); (4) C. T. Onions, *A Shakespeare Glossary* (2nd ed. revised, Oxford, 1953).

'a: *pron.* he

a': *prep.* of, on, at, in

absolute: *adj.* faultless, finished, perfect, positive, unconditional

abuse: *v.* deceive, disfigure, dishonor; *n.* deception, delusion

accent: *n.* language, speech, word

accident: *n.* event, occurrence

action: *n.* gesture; campaign

addition: *n.* mark of distinction, title, style of address

admiration: *n.* wonder; faculty of exciting wonder; marvel

admire: *v.* marvel, wonder at

advance: *v.* lift up, raise

advantage: *n.* chance, opportune time; interest (on money)

advice: *n.* deliberation, consultation; (with *on more*) reflection, consideration

affect: *v.* aim at, desire, imitate, love; *n.* affection, disposition, inclination

affection: *n.* bent of mind, disposition, inclination; wish, desire; love, passion; affectation

after: *prep.* in accordance with, at the rate of

again: *adv.* in return; on the other hand; moreover, besides

against: *prep.* in preparation for; just before; towards, to

agents: *n.* senses; organs

alarum (*or* **alarm**)**:** *n.* call to arms; attack

all: *n.* the whole, everything, everybody; *adj.* any, every; *adv.* entirely, only, quite, wholly; *conj.* although

along: *adv.* at full length, prostrate; onward, on; together; *prep.* throughout the length of

amaze: *v.* dismay, thoroughly confuse; *n.* extreme astonishment

amazement: *n.* bewilderment, distraction, frenzy

and: *conj.* if, though

and if: *conj.* if

angel: *n.* gold coin worth ten shillings

anon: *adv.* at once, immediately; soon

answer: *v.* answer for, satisfactorily account for; encounter; discharge, settle

appeal: *v.* accuse, impeach; refer to higher authority; *n.* accusation; plea to higher authority

appointment: *n.* accoutrement, equipment; resolution; direction

apprehend: *v.* arrest, seize; understand; imagine

apprehension: *n.* arrest; physical or mental perception, understanding; imagination

approve: *v.* prove, test; try, experience

apt: *adj.* fit, docile, natural, willing

argument: *n.* cause, immediate business, reason, subject, theme

as: *pron.* that; *conj.* as if, though, so that; *prep.* in the character of

aspect: *n.* look, glance, appearance; view; the relative position of the heavenly bodies as they appear to an observer on the earth's surface at a given time; also the influence of these positions on man (astrological term)

at: *prep.* in, for, at the cost of

atone: *v.* agree, reconcile

attach: *v.* arrest

attaint: *v.* convict; dishonor, stain; *n.* impeachment; infectious influence, dishonorable stain

attend: *v.* accompany, wait upon; be intent upon; guard, watch; await, expect

aunt: *n.* gossip; prostitute

avoid: *v.* be gone, leave, retire

aweful: *adj.* demanding reverence

bald: *adj.* meagre, trifling; bare-headed

bale: *n.* disaster, injury

band (*or* **bond**): *v.* to join in troops; *n.* moral obligation; legal bond; tie, fetter

bank: *v.* coast, skirt; *n.* sea-shore, shelving elevation in sea or river bed; bench

bare: *v.* shave; *adj.* paltry, worthless; threadbare

bate: *v.* abate, deduct, dispense with; weaken; flutter (the wings); *n.* strife

battle: *n.* army; single combat

bear: *v.* conduct, execute, sustain; contain

behind: *adv.* beyond, still to come

beholding: *past part., adj.* beholden, indebted

bestow: *v.* stow, place; employ; spend, lay out; grant, give

bill: *n.* spear or axe with a concave blade; note, list, label; advertisement

blank: *v.* blanch; *n.* target (i.e. white spot at the centre of); void; lottery ticket that fails to draw a prize

blood: *n.* full vigor, fleshly nature, passion, spirit, will; condition, descent

blow: *v.* foul, sully; swell; blossom, bloom; breathe

bond: *see* band

brave: *v.* challenge, defy; make splendid; *n.* bravado, defiant threat; *adj.* excellent, fine; finely clothed, splendid; haughty, saucy; fitting

break: *v.* crack (a joke); disclose, reveal; become bankrupt; make docile (as a horse); fall out, quarrel

break with: *v.* inform

breast: *n.* heart; singing voice

breath: *n.* speech, language, utterance; power of breathing

breathe: *v.* speak; exercise briskly; rest

brief: *n.* letter, abstract

briefly: *adv.* in a short time, quickly, soon

brook: *v.* endure; like, permit

busy: *v.* employ, keep engaged; *adj.* officious, meddling; active

but: *conj.* except, except that, if, only, otherwise than, unless, without

buy: be with (in the phrase *God buy you*)

by: *prep.* about, at the hands of, by reason of

by and by: at once, immediately; soon, shortly

caitiff: *n.* wretch

canker: *n.* ulcer; wild rose

capable: *adj.* having intelligence; impressionable, susceptible; (with *of*) open to, qualified to possess (legal)

capital: *adj.* chief, principal; deadly, fatal

captain: *n.* general; *adj.* chief

careful: *adj.* attentive, provident; burdened with sorrow

careless: *adj.* heedless, without concern for consequences

case: *n.* mask, suit; set

casual: *adj.* accidental, subject to chance

cause: *n.* case in dispute; affair, business

censure: *v.* judge, give an opinion on; *n.* judgment, sentence; blame

centre: *n.* the earth (in Ptolemaic astronomy)

character: *v.* engrave, inscribe; *n.* handwriting, lettering; (pl.) letters (of the alphabet)

charge: *v.* load, burden; level; order; *n.* command of troops; troop; load, burden; importance; cost, expense; order

charm: *v.* cast a spell, conjure; *n.* spell

clip: *v.* embrace; curtail, cut

close: *v.* agree, join (hands), meet, grapple; *n.* musical cadence; enclosure; close encounter, union; *adj.* secret, concealed; *adv.* tightly

closet: *n.* chamber, private room; cabinet

clown: *n.* country fellow, churl; buffoon, jester

coat: *n.* armor, coat of mail; coat of arms

cog: *v.* beguile, cheat, deceive

cold: *adj.* deliberate; chaste; faint (scent)

color: *v.* disguise, give a specious appearance to; *n.* appearance, character; excuse, pretext; (pl.) military standards, flags

comfortable: *adj.* cheerful, comforting

commodity: *n.* consignment of wares; convenience, advantage, profit; expediency

common: *v.* share, take part; talk, converse; *n.* common people; common land; *adj.* belonging equally to more than one or to the community; general; usual; characteristic of the common people

compass: *v.* bring to pass; *n.* circumference; limits, range, expanse; moderation

complete: *adj.* perfect, full; accomplished

complexion: *n.* appearance; temperament, constitution

composition: *n.* a whole formed from different ingredients; constitution; compact, accord; consistency (not used by Shakespeare to describe a literary or musical work)

conceit: *v.* form an idea or opinion; *n.* conception, idea, opinion, thought; imagination, invention, fancy

conceited: *past part., adj.* full of imagination or fancy, witty, ingenious; possessed of an opinion (modern sense not used by Shakespeare)

condition: *n.* contract; rank, social position; temper, mental disposition

confer: *v.* compare

confound: *v.* consume, destroy; mingle indistinguishably

confusion: *n.* overthrow, ruin; (pl.) commotions

conscience: *n.* consciousness, reflection; conscientiousness; good sense, judgment

contemn: *v.* despise, think hateful

continent: *n.* that which contains or encloses something; land (as enclosing rivers or seas); receptacle; summary, abstract, inventory; *adj.* restraining; temperate, chaste

control: *v.* overpower

convenient: *adj.* fit, proper, becoming, decent; easy, commodious

conversation: *n.* intercourse; behavior, deportment, conduct

convey: *v.* escort; steal
cope: *v.* encounter; (with *with*) match
corn: *n.* grain, wheat (never used for "maize")
countenance: *v.* be in keeping with; favor; *n.* bearing, face; favor, protection, patronage
cousin: *n.* kinsman; term of address from sovereign to sovereign
coz: *n.* cousin
craft: *v.* do a good piece of work; *n.* stratagem; (pl.) artisans (members of a trade or craft)
cross: *v.* meet, face; go counter to; *n.* coin (from the cross on one side); *adj.* going from one side to another; perverse; *adv.* athwart
crown: *n.* head, pate; coin worth five shillings
cry: *v.* extol; *n.* report; company, pack
cunning: *n.* ability, knowledge, skill; *adj.* clever, skillful
curious: *adj.* anxious; accurate, careful, elegant; fastidious, demanding care; *adv.* delicately, minutely
current: *n.* unimpeded course; *adj.* common; sterling, genuine
curst: *adj.* shrewish; savage, vicious
custom: *n.* habit
cut: *v.* carve, represent in stone; *n.* working horse; ornamental slash in a garment; (pl. with *draw*) lots

date: *n.* duration, end of a period of time
dear: *adj.* expensive, valuable; significant, successful; loving; dire, intense
defeat: *v.* destroy, ruin, disfigure; defraud; *n.* destruction, ruin
defend: *v.* forbid
defy: *v.* challenge; reject, renounce
deliver: *v.* exhibit, present, report; send; prove; speak
demand: *v.* question, ask; claim, request; *n.* question; request, suit
demerit: *n.* desert, merit; offenses, sins
depart: *v.* part; die; *n.* departure; death
despite: *v.* vex; *n.* contempt, scorn; malice; (with *in*) in defiance of
dial: *n.* clock, watch
diffidence: *n.* distrust, suspicion (not used in the sense of "self-distrust")
discover: *v.* betray, detect, discern, espy, reveal, show, tell, view
dismal: *adj.* disastrous; ill-boding, sinister
dispatch: *v.* kill, make away with; deprive (of); make haste; conclude, settle
division: *n.* arrangement; disunion, fraction, separation; (in music) embellishment, variation; definite portion of a battalion or squadron
doom: *v.* judge; *n.* judgment
doubt: *v.* hesitate to believe; distrust; fear, suspect; *n.* irresolution, uncertainty (of mind); apprehension, suspicion
doubtful: *adj.* fearful, suspicious; uncertain; breeding suspicion
dread: *v.* fear for; *n.* one specially revered; *adj.* held in awe; dreadful, terrible
dreadful: *adj.* filled with fear; held in awe; terrible
duty: *n.* dutiful respect, reverence; filial piety; (pl.) due merits; expression of submission or deference

eager: *adj.* ardent, impetuous; biting, keen, sharp, sour
ecstasy: *n.* excitement; madness, violent agitation of mind
edge: *n.* appetite, desire; sword
effect: *v.* give effect to; produce; *n.* (purposed) result; drift, tenor; manifestation; accomplishment, fulfillment
effeminate: *adj.* unmanly, womanish, self-indulgent; tender, gentle; capricious
element: *n.* constituent part (from the "four elements": earth, water, air, fire); atmosphere, sky, (pl.) heavens; natural habitation
engine: *n.* instrument; instrument of war or torture; bodily mechanism; contrivance, plot
entertain: *v.* assume; admit; receive, maintain, take into service; treat; pass (the time); *n.* reception
entertainment: *n.* reception, treatment; provision for the table
entreat: *v.* enter into negotiation; treat; pass (the time)
envy: *v.* show malice; *n.* enmity, malice, spite
estimate: *n.* value, repute, rank
even: *adj.* equal, uniform; precise; equable; *adv.* in exact agreement; equally, exactly; fully, quite
event: *n.* consequence, result, outcome
exclaim: *v.* rail at, protest against; *n.* loud outcry (so *exclamation*)
excrement: *n.* outgrowth (of hair); (pl.) nails
excursion: *n.* sally, sortie (not used in modern sense)
expedience: *n.* haste; expedition (not used pejoratively)
expedient: *adj.* proper, convenient; speedy, hasty; expeditious, quick (not used pejoratively)
expedition: *n.* speedy progress; haste, dispatch; warlike enterprise

face: *v.* show a false face; brave, bully; trim; *n.* pretense
fact: *n.* act, crime
factor: *n.* agent, a substitute in mercantile affairs
fair: *v.* beautify; *n.* one who is beautiful; beauty; *adj.* apt, just; courteous; *adv.* civilly, courteously (with *to speak*); honestly; fittingly; favorably, fortunately, successfully; gently, softly
fall: *v.* drop, let fall; shrink; happen, befall; *n.* shedding (of blood); downward stroke (with a sword); ebb (of the tide); musical cadence; wrestling bout; sin, fault
fame: *v.* report; make famous; *n.* common talk, rumor, report; reputation
fancy: *v.* like; love; *n.* imagination; image, conception; fantasticalness; taste, liking; love; love-song (impromptu)
fantasy: *n.* deluding imagination; imagination; caprice
fatal: *adj.* foreboding mischief and death; pernicious, deadly; instrumental to destiny
favor: *n.* countenance, face; appearance; beauty of form and feature; permission, pardon; attraction, charm; lenity; benefit; lover's gift
fear: *v.* frighten; fear for, worry about; doubt; *n.* concern; object of fear or dread, dread, dreadfulness
fearful: *adj.* filled with fear; frightened, timid; dreadful, terrible
fellow: *n.* servant; equal; comrade, companion; consort; one of a pair
fine: *v.* to bring to an end; punish; *n.* end; punishment, penalty; *adj.* delicate, nice, subtle; refined; splendidly

dressed; *adv.* delicately, subtly

flaw: *v.* damage, mar; *n.* crack; fragment; blemish; blast of wind, squall; snowflake

flesh: *v.* inure to bloodshed; inflame to ardor or rage by promise of success; plunge a weapon into flesh; gratify (lust); *n.* human nature (with its limitations); (with *in*) in healthy condition

fond: *adj.* doting, foolish; infatuated; having a strong affection for; trifling; eager (for), desirous (of)

for: *conj.* because; in order that; *prep.* as; despite; instead of; because of, on account of; for fear of; permitting

for and: and moreover

for because: because

for that: because

for why: because

form: *n.* image, portrait; good order; behavior, (pl.) manners

formal: *adj.* ceremonious, precise; stiff, rigid; dignified; normal in intellect, sane

frame: *v.* direct one's steps; cause, bring to pass; *n.* form, structure, logical structure; plan, system; the earth; the human body

frank: *adj.* open, undisguised; liberal, bountiful

free: *v.* (with *from*) secure; clear from blame, absolve; banish, get rid of; *adj.* generous, magnanimous; innocent, unconcealed; admitting no restraint

fret: *v.* vex; complain; fray, eat away; adorn with carved or embossed work; finger (a musical instrument); *n.* finger-stop (on a musical instrument)

from: *prep.* contrary to; apart from; remote from; out of; from among; otherwise than

front: *v.* march in the front rank; *n.* forehead; front line of battle; beginning

full: *adj.* complete; *adv.* very, exceedingly; fully, quite

furnish: *v.* endow, equip; dress; decorate

furniture: *n.* equipment; provision; harness, trappings

general: *n.* the whole; the people as a whole, the multitude

gentle: *v.* ennoble; *n* (pl.) gentlefolk; *adj.* of high birth, noble; tame

get: *v.* beget

glass: *n.* mirror; hourglass; eyeball

go: *v.* walk

gossip: *v.* make merry at a (christening) feast; *n.* sponsor at baptism; tattling, gossiping woman

grace: *v.* gratify, delight; *n.* favor; ornament; fortune, luck; sense of duty; mercy, pardon; God (as the source of grace)

gracious: *adj.* finding favor, acceptable; pious, virtuous; kind, benevolent; happy, fortunate; lovely, attractive

gripe: *v.* seize, grasp; grieve; *n.* grasp; vulture

habit: *n.* dress, clothes; demeanor

hair: *n.* kind, nature, character; figurative for something very small, jot, tittle, iota

halberd: *n.* combination of spear and battle-axe mounted on a long shaft; a soldier so armed

happily: *adv.* haply, perchance; fortunately, favorably

happy: *adj.* fortunate, propitious; apt, skilful; appropriate, fitting

hardly: *adv.* severely, harshly; with difficulty; scarcely

harness: *n.* body-armor

h'as: he has

h'ath: he hath

hateful: *adj.* full of hatred, hostile, malignant

head: *v.* behead; *n.* army, troop; antlers; source, origin; promontory

heart: *n.* courage, spirit; inclination; disposition, temperament; the organ of wisdom; term of endearment or commendation

heaviness: *n.* drowsiness; grief, melancholy, sadness

heavy: *adj.* sad, depressing, sorrowful; drowsy; dull, stupid; slow; heinous; weighty

helpless: *adj.* affording no help; unprofitable, unavailing

hint: *n.* occasion, opportunity

his: *pron.* its (the form *its* occurs only a few times in Shakespeare); form of genitive inflection = *'s*

ho: *interj.* used to call for attention or service; expression of mockery or rebuke; cry of exaltation (not used in the sense of "hold," "stop")

home: *adv.* to its right or proper place; exactly to the point aimed at (usually with ***strike*** or ***speak***)

honest: *adj.* honorable; true, genuine; chaste; seemly

honesty: *n.* honorable behavior, integrity; chastity

horse: *n.* cavalry; (coll. pl.) horses

hose: *n.* long stockings; breeches

host: *v.* lodge; *n.* army; innkeeper (cf. ***hostess***)

humor: *n.* one of the four fluids of the body (blood, choler, phlegm, melancholy), the preponderance of any one determining a man's temperament or complexion; temperament, disposition; mood, temper; fancy, whim; disease

how: *adv.* as; to what degree; what; however; (with *so* following) why; *interj.* used to express surprise

i': *prep.* in

idle: *adj.* useless, vain, futile; thoughtless, silly, absurd

idly (*or* **idlely**)**:** *adv.* foolishly; indifferently; carelessly

if: *conj.* even if

impudent: *adj.* shameless; saucy

incapable: *adj.* (with *of*) insensible; not admitting; lacking capacity or fitness (for)

indifferent: *adj.* average; somewhat; impartial; *adv.* fairly, tolerably

inform: *v.* inspire, imbue; instruct; (refl.) learn; report

innovation: *n.* rebellion, disturbance; change for the worse (used only pejoratively by Shakespeare)

innovator: *n.* revolutionary (used as above)

insensible: *adj.* imperceptible to the senses

instance: *n.* evidence, proof, token, sign; motive

instrument: *n.* bodily organ; agent; tool

insult: *v.* (with *over* or *on*) exult proudly or scornfully

intelligence: *n.* communication, intercourse; espionage (cf. *intelligencer*)

intend: *v.* purpose making; express, signify; pretend; incline

invest: *v.* endow; dress up

Jack (*or* **jack**)**:** *n.* ill-mannered fellow, knave; figure in a clock which strikes the hour; upright piece of wood fixed to the key-lever in a virginal; a small bowl used as the mark in the game of bowls; quarter pint measure

jar: *v.* to be out of tune; quarrel; *n.* discord; quarrel, contention, combat

jet: *v.* strut, swagger; (with *upon*) encroach

jealous (*or* **jealious**): *adj.* suspicious, apprehensive; mistrustful

joint: *n.* member, limb; hinge

just: *adj.* honest, trustworthy, faithful; *adv.* exactly, just so, right

justify: *v.* show to be right, vindicate; prove, verify

keep: *v.* guard; occupy; preserve, retain; pursue, continue to make; maintain; restrain (oneself); observe, practice; hold, have; dwell, live, stay; *n.* keeping, custody, guard

kind: *n.* natural disposition; general nature or the order of natural phenomena; manner, fashion; race, class; family stock; *adj.* natural; affectionate, friendly

knave: *n.* male servant; fellow; boy; villain, rogue

knavery: *n.* roguish or waggish tricks; underhand dealing

last: *n.* conclusion, end; last time; *adj.* late

law: *interj.* la

lay: *v.* bury; lay with traps; stake, wager; *n.* wager

lead: *v.* carry; undertake to begin a dance (with); go forward; *n.* bullets, shot

learn: *v.* teach; inform of

leave: *v.* abandon, forsake; stop, discontinue, cease; *n.* permission; permission to depart; leave-taking; liberty, license

leg: *n.* bow (drawing back one leg and bending the other)

let: *v.* hinder; *n.* hindrance

lewd: *adj.* bad, base, vile, worthless; vulgar

liberal: *adj.* bountiful, generous; gentleman-like in habit or character; gross, licentious

liberty: *n.* license; (pl.) privileges, rights

light: *v.* fall, descend; grow light; *adj.* unchaste, wanton; trivial

like: *v.* please; feel affection; (with *of*) be pleased with; liken, compare; *adj.* likely, probable; such; *adv.* equally, alike; likely, probably; likewise

list: *v.* please, choose, desire; *n.* limit, boundary; barriers of a tilting field; the field itself; desire, inclination; catalogue (of soldiers); outer edge or selvage of cloth

live: *adv.* lief, soon

look how: just as

look what: whatever

look when: just as when

lust: *v.* desire carnally; *n.* pleasure, delight; desire; carnal desire

lusty: *adj.* lively, active; stout, vigorous; merry; lustful

luxurious: *adj.* lascivious, lustful (always used pejoratively)

luxury: *n.* lust, lechery (used as above)

make: *v.* give (a dinner); muster (a force); shut, bar; do; have to do with (in phrase *meddle and make*); go; *n.* mate (husband or wife)

marry: *interj.* indeed, why, to be sure (a weakened oath, "by the Virgin Mary")

mass: *interj.* (also with *by the*) used with reference to the Roman Mass (a weakened oath)

may: *v.* can

mean: *n.* means, instrument, agency; medium, mediocrity; resource(s); opportunity; *adj.* common, lowly, vulgar

measure: *v.* judge, estimate; traverse; (with *swords*) fight; *n.* unit of capacity; carouse, toast; limit; moderation; stately dance; stately gait; tune, rhythm

meet: *adj.* proper, fit, decent

memory: *n.* memorial, memento

mere: *adj.* pure, perfect, absolute, utter; what something is and nothing more; *adv.* absolutely, entirely, purely; without any other quality than its bare self

metal: *n.* (fig.) stuff, material, substance; (fig.) gold; (fig.) sword (*metal* and *mettle* were interchangeable spellings in Elizabethan English)

mettle: *n.* quality of disposition or temperament; natural vigor or ardor (of a horse); spirit, courage

mind: *v.* remind; perceive, notice; be inclined; *n.* judgment, opinion; purpose, desire; intention towards

miss: *v.* do without; fail; be wanting; *n.* fault, offence; loss

modern: *adj.* commonplace, trite, ordinary (not used in "modern" sense)

modest: *adj.* moderate, becoming; unassuming; not impudent

modesty: *n.* moderation; decency, propriety

moe: *adj.* more (in number)

more: *adj.* greater (in degree or extent)

mortal: *adj.* deadly, fatal; subject to death; human

motion: *n.* bodily movement or exertion; instigation, urging; influence; motive, cause; offer, proposal; puppet-show

mould: *n.* model, pattern; bodily form; earth

mouth: *n.* testimony; voice (of hounds)

move: *v.* incite, instigate, arouse; make angry, exasperate; propose, suggest; be active, look alive

muse: *v.* marvel, wonder; complain

music: *n.* consort of musicians

mystery: *n.* secret, something difficult to understand; calling, trade, profession; skill

naked: *adj.* unarmed; unfurnished, destitute; exposed; bare

name: *n.* honor, credit; family stock

nature: *n.* natural affection; filial feeling

naught: *n.* wickedness, wrong; *adj.* worthless, useless; wicked; lost, ruined

naughty: *adj.* bad, wicked, good for nothing, worthless (not used in modern sense)

near: *adj. comp.* nearer; *adv.* intimately, closely

nerve: *n.* sinew, muscle

next: *adj.* nearest in relationship or place; quickest

nice: *adj.* delicate; fastidious, scrupulous; precise; petty, trifling; reluctant; wanton, lascivious; minute, subtle; accurate, exact (not used in the sense of "agreeable")

nothing: *adv.* not at all, in no way

number: *n.* the multitude; (pl.) verses

o': *prep.* of, on

obscene: *adj.* repulsive, loathsome, disgusting (Shakespeare, who first used the word, does not give it a sexual connotation)
occupation: *n.* handicraft, trade; workingmen
of: *prep.* from, away from, by, in, on, during; in respect of
of force: of necessity
offer: *v.* act offensively, make an attack; venture, presume
office: *n.* duty, function, service; (pl.) service quarters
on: *prep.* of, in, from, under, with; approaching
only: *adj.* sole; best; principal, chief
opinion: *n.* reputation, credit; renown; estimate of oneself (good or bad)
or: *conj.* before, sooner than; and
or ere: before
or . . . or: either . . . or
ordinance: *n.* decree of destiny; practice, rank, order; cannon, ordnance
organ: *n.* musical wind instrument (pipe); part of the body; instrument
out: *adj.* exhausted, empty; aloof; at variance; at a loss for words; *adv.* outside, abroad; fully
overlook: *v.* look down upon from above; survey; peruse; supervise, take care of; overtop
owe: *v.* own, possess

pack: *v.* go away in a hurry, be gone; conspire
pain: *n.* punishment, penalty; trouble, labor, effort; duty
painful: *adj.* laborious, toilsome
pale: *n.* pallor; fence, paling; fenced enclosure
parcel: *n.* part, portion; detail, item; party, set; (pl.) qualities
party: *n.* part; faction, side; ally
pass: *v.* die; experience, suffer; exceed; neglect, omit; transfer; give judgment; pledge; make a thrust (in swordplay); care; *n.* passage; predicament; thrust or lunge (in swordplay); fencing bout
passing: *adj.* excessive, surpassing, extreme; *adv.* exceedingly, surpassingly, extremely
passion: *v.* suffer grief, sorrow; *n.* emotion (painful or pleasing); grief, pain; feelings of love; lamentation
passionate: *adj.* disturbed, grieved, sorrowful
perdie (*or* **perdy**): *adv.* or *interj.* certainly, indeed, assuredly (a weakened oath, like French *pardieu*, originally "by God")
perdition: *n.* ruin; loss
perfect: *v.* accomplish; inform completely; *adj.* complete, finished; full, mature; sane, sound; correct; certain, accurate; contented
perforce: *adv.* by force or violence; of necessity
person: *n.* external appearance (of a man or woman)
pick: *v.* pitch, throw
plain: *adj.* even, level, smooth; clear, open, evident; simple; artless, frank, honest; mere, bare; *adv.* clearly; simply
plate: *v.* cover with metal plates (clothe in armor) (not used in modern sense)
poise: *v.* weigh, estimate; counterbalance; *n.* weight
pole: *n.* poll, number of heads; head; the pole-star
policy: *n.* prudent management; form of government; administration of public affairs; contrivance, crafty device, stratagem

politic: *adj.* relating to politics; versed in public affairs; prudent, wise; artful, cunning
pomp: *n.* ceremonial procession, pageant; splendor
pompous: *adj.* magnificent, splendid (not used in perjorative sense)
popular: *adj.* plebeian, vulgar (not used by Shakespeare in the sense of "admired or loved by people generally")
portly: *adj.* imposing, stately, dignified; corpulent
possess: *v.* take possession of, seize; inform, acquaint
post: *v.* hasten, speed; convey swiftly; *n.* messenger, courier; post-horse; *adv.* as fast as possible
post-haste: *n.* great haste; *adj.* expeditious; *adv.* as fast as possible
power: *n.* army, force, troops
practice: *v.* perform; plot; use artifice or stratagem; *n.* execution; stratagem, conspiracy, plot, scheme
pregnant: *adj.* apt; ready, prompt; receptive; artful; clear, obvious; probable
present: *adj.* immediate, instant
presently: *adv.* at once, now, directly
president: *n.* precedent; sign, token; original from which a copy has been made
press: *v.* oppress; crowd, throng; push; conscript; *n.* crowd, throng; warrant for conscripting
pretend: *v.* assert; allege falsely; intend, mean, import; present; claim (Shakespeare does not use in the sense of "make pretense" or "feign")
pretense: *n.* pretext; intention, purpose, design
prevent: *v.* anticipate, forestall; escape
pride: *n.* magnificence, pomp; height, prime; honor; sexual desire; mettle in a horse
profess: *v.* avow, declare, affirm; claim to have knowledge of
proof: *n.* test, trial; experience; result, issue; having the quality of impenetrability (usually with reference to armor); *adj.* impenetrable
proper: *adj.* (one's or its) own; characteristic, peculiar; excellent, fine (also ironic); honest; suitable, becoming; handsome, elegant; *adv.* appropriately
property: *v.* make a property or tool of; appropriate; *n.* particular or characteristic quality
protest: *v.* declare with solemnity; proclaim publicly; promise, vow; *n.* protestation (not used by Shakespeare in the sense of "object" or "remonstrate")
proud: *adj.* elated, pleased, exalted, splendid; lavish; spirited (of animals); swelling (of waters); sexually excited
prove: *v.* test, try; find out by experience; establish as true; become; turn out to be
purchase: *v.* acquire, obtain; acquire otherwise than by inheritance; buy; *n.* acquisition; spoil, booty
put: *v.* wager (on); foist a trick (on); lay blame (on); pass off news (on); urge, incite; oblige, force; assert

quaint: *adj.* skilled, clever; fine, dainty; elaborate; handsome, elegant
quality: *n.* character, disposition, nature; attainment; rank, position; profession, occupation; manner; skill
question: *v.* inquire into; debate, talk; *n.* (with *in*) on trial; conversation
quick: *adj.* living, alive; pregnant; perceptive; swift; nimble

quicken: *v.* make alive; stimulate, refresh

quit: *v.* acquit, clear; requite, repay, reward; set free; surrender one's claim to

race: *n.* lineage, generation (of men); breed (of animals); natural disposition; root (of ginger); running, course

rank: *adj.* gross, coarse; coarsely luxuriant; puffed up, swollen; offensively strong in smell; lustful; corrupt, foul

rate: *v.* estimate, value; chide; *n.* estimate; price

rather: *adv.* sooner, before, more; more properly or correctly speaking; on the contrary; more willingly, with better liking

reason: *v.* hold discussion, discourse, talk; question; argue; *n.* observation, remark, explanation (of something); cause, ground; reasonable speech or behavior; reasonable amount

regard: *v.* consider, take into account; hold in honor; *n.* look, glance; repute, account; heed; consideration, thoughtful attention

remember: *v.* remind; commemorate; consider

remorse: *n.* compassion, pity; compunction of conscience

reprove: *v.* disprove, refute; reprehend, blame

resolve: *v.* dissolve, melt; answer (a question); dispel (doubt); free from doubt or anxiety; determine; *n.* settled purpose

respect: *v.* regard, consider; heed; prize, value; *n.* consideration, regard; care, attention; opinion

revolution: *n.* alteration, change (produced by time) (not used in the sense of "rebellion")

right: *adj.* straight; *adv.* in a straight course; exactly, justly; (before adj. and adv.) highly, most, very

riot: *n.* dissipation, wild revelling

round: *v.* finish off; encircle; become spherical; whisper; *n.* circle, circlet; circular dance; *adj.* plain, straightforward; plainspoken

roundly: *adv.* bluntly, directly, freely; outspokenly

rub: *v.* (in bowls) strike against a small object (the jack); *n.* impediment (fig. from bowling)

ruin: *v.* demolish, destroy; *n.* decay; fall, destruction; perdition

sad: *adj.* grave, serious; melancholy

sadness: *n.* seriousness; (with *in*) in truth, seriously

safe: *v.* make safe; *adj.* sound, sane; harmless

scale: *v.* weigh, measure

scope: *n.* aim, object; intention

seat: *n.* throne; estate; saddle

secure: *v.* make careless or overconfident; make safe or guard from danger; *adj.* free from apprehension; careless, heedless, unsuspecting; free from danger, safe

self: *adj.* one's own; same, selfsame; (with *one*) one and the same

sense: *n.* one of the five senses or perception by those organs, feeling; mental perception, understanding; power of reasoning; rational meaning, reason; import; faculty of thinking; sensuality

sensible: *adj.* capable of, or endowed with, physical feeling or perception, sensitive; endowed with feelings or emotions; perceptible, tangible; judicious

sensibly: *adv.* feelingly, as of one having feeling

sentence: *n.* judicial decision; moral aphorism, axiom

service: *n.* place and office of a servant, servanthood; duty of a servant; religious worship; military duty; courses of a meal

several: *adj.* distinct, separate; various; different

shadow: *v.* shelter; conceal, hide; *n.* shade; darkness; image in a looking-glass; image, portrait; product of the imagination; anything unsubstantial or unreal

shape: *n.* form, figure; external appearance; something bodied forth by the imagination; disguise

shift: *v.* change; exchange; contrive, practice; *n.* device, stratagem, trick; change

should: sometimes used where modern idiom requires *would*

show: *n.* appearance; vision, sight; display, ostentation; spectacle, play

shrewd: *adj.* bad, malicious, harmful; sly, cunning; sharp, piercing (always pejorative in meaning)

siege: *n.* seat; status, position, rank

silly: *adj.* deserving of pity; helpless, defenseless (of women); harmless, innocent; plain, simple; witless, foolish

simple: *n.* medicinal herb; ingredient in a compound; *adj.* mere, pure; plain, average in quality, common; artless, harmless; silly, witless, weak in intellect

sith: *adv.*, *prep.*, *conj.* since

skill: *v.* (with *not*) makes no great difference, is no great matter; *n.* discernment, sagacity, wit; cunning, pretense; ability

skilless: *adj.* inexpert; ignorant

snuff: *n.* huff, resentment, taking offence; the burning wick of a candle

so: *adv.* in such a degree; in the same degree; in such a manner, thus, accordingly; in the same manner, also; *conj.* provided or on condition that; *interj.* expressing approval, good

soft: *interj.* not so fast, wait a bit, hold on

something: *adv.* somewhat, in some measure, rather

sometime(s): *adv.* from time to time; once; formerly

sooth: *n.* truth; flattery, cajoling

soothe (*or* sooth): *v.* humor; flatter

sore: *adj.* grievous, heavy, evil; *adv.* grievously; very

sort: *v.* choose with respect to fitness; find out, contrive; ordain; associate; be fit or proper; fall out, turn out; *n.* kind, species; order, quality, rank; class of people; way, manner, fashion; state, condition; company (in a derogatory sense), gang; lot

sound (*or* swoun, swound): *v.* swoon

sovereign: *adj.* most potent, efficacious; supreme; princely, royal

speculation: *n.* power of seeing; looking on; watcher, scout (not used in modern senses)

speed: *v.* fare (well or ill); succeed; hasten, dispatch; *n.* fortune, success

spite: *v.* vex; thwart malignantly; *n.* malice, ill-will; grief, vexation; outrage

spleen: *n.* the organ itself seen as the seat of emotions and passions; fiery temper; eagerness; hate, malice; impulse, fit (of anger or laughter); caprice

spurn: *v.* kick; treat with contempt; *n.* contemptuous thrust or stroke; kick

stain: *v.* discolor, spot; darken, make dim; disfigure, deface; soil, taint, corrupt; *n.* spot, tinge; taint of disgrace

stale: *v.* render stale, make common or worthless; *n.* decoy, bait; dupe, laughing-stock; urine (of horses); harlot; *adj.* no longer fresh, worn out by use

stand: *v.* withstand, resist; remain stationary, stop; make a stand, fight; remain, stay; (in imper.) hold, forbear, stop; *n.* station; stop, halt; resistance

start: *v.* make a sudden, involuntary motion; move suddenly, rise or spring up; alarm, startle; rouse; *n.* sudden, involuntary motion; hasty fit, capricious impulse; sudden setting out

state: *n.* body politic, commonwealth; governing body, government; estate, property; rank, status; grandeur, dignity; royalty, kingship; throne

stay: *v.* stand still, stop; delay, tarry; detain; prop, support; await, wait for; offer resistance to; *n.* check, hindrance; prop, support

stick: *v.* stab, pierce; fasten, attach; hesitate, scruple; stand out; be fixed

stiff: *adj.* stout; hard, strong; stubbornly borne; resistant

still: *adj.* silent; soft (of music); constant, continual; *adv.* always, forever, continually

stomach: *v.* be angry at, resent; *n.* appetite; inclination, disposition; anger, resentment; courage; pride, arrogance

stout: *adj.* valiant, brave; proud, haughty; strong; unyielding (not used in the sense of "fat," "corpulent")

straight: *adv.* immediately, at once, straightway; straight forward, in a direct line

strait: *n.* narrow passage; difficulty; *adj.* strict, tight; close-fisted

strangely: *adv.* as a foreigner; coldly, reservedly; extraordinarily, uncommonly; in a manner to cause wonder or surprise

subtle (*or* subtile): *adj.* cunning, crafty, sly; thin, fine, delicate

success: *n.* issue, result, outcome; good or bad fortune; succession

sudden: *adj.* unexpected; speedy; hasty, quick; rash; violent; performed immediately

suddenly: *adv.* unexpectedly, all at once; extempore; quickly; immediately, at once; soon

suffer: *v.* bear with patience; undergo with pain; be injured; be put to death; experience (in a good or bad sense)

sufferance: *n.* bearing with patience; pain, torment; suffering, distress; permission, allowance; endurance

suggest: *v.* insinuate; prompt; tempt, seduce (almost always used in a pejorative sense)

suggestion: *n.* prompting to evil, incitement; temptation, seduction (always used in a pejorative sense)

sweet: *n.* anything pleasant (especially to the taste); pleasure, delight; sweetheart; sweetness of smell, fragrance; *adj.* pleasing to any of the senses; delightful, lovely; kind, gentle; perfumed; dear; *adv.* in a manner agreeable to the senses; softly, gently

take: *v.* strike; strike with disease; charm, captivate; destroy; seize; make prisoner; bear, carry; catch (a disease); assume

tall: *adj.* goodly, fine; strong (in fight), valiant, brave; stately

tell: *v.* count, number; strike (the hour)

tend: *v.* attend, wait on, serve; await; guard; take care of; accompany

tender: *v.* offer, present; show, exhibit; regard with kindness, hold dear, take care of; *n.* offer for acceptance; thing offered; regard, care; *adj.* young, immature; gentle, kind; loving, fond; mild or soft (of air); finely sensitive (in a physical sense)

tent: *v.* to search or probe (a wound); cure; lodge; *n.* a roll of lint used to probe and cleanse a wound; pavilion

th': the; they; thou; thy

that: *conj.* in that, because; so that, provided that; in as much as

thought: *n.* anxiety, care; melancholy

throat: *n.* voice

through(ly): *adv.* thoroughly, completely

timeless: *adj.* untimely, premature; unseasonable

tire: *v.* to dress, adorn, attire; satiate, disgust; (with *upon*) seize and tear ravenously (used of birds of prey); *n.* head-dress

to: *prep.* in addition to, besides; against; in accordance with; in comparison with; with regard to, as to; as, for; of

touch: *v.* strike, injure; come near; come to shore; reach, attain; test by a touchstone, try; handle skilfully; concern; infect; move, rouse; make an impression on; fill with passion or feeling; *n.* affection, feeling; touchstone; test, proof; the fingering of a musical instrument; trait; dash or spice (of)

toward: *adj.* docile, compliant; bold, forward; *adv.* forthcoming, about to take place

train: *v.* entice, lure, educate, teach; *n.* tail of a peacock or meteor; retinue; troop, army; bait

translate: *v.* transform, change; interpret, explain

trash: *v.* check a dog that runs too fast by placing a weight on its neck (used figuratively)

troth: *n.* truth; faith

true: *adj.* honest, trustworthy; well-proportioned; *adv.* truly

truth: *n.* faith, honesty; fidelity, loyalty

try: *v.* purify, refine (as gold); prove or examine by test; inquire into; make an experiment

umbrage: *n.* shadow

undergo: *v.* undertake; carry the weight of, sustain; suffer; enjoy

unjust: *adj.* faithless, false; untrue; dishonorable

unkind: *adj.* unnatural; unrelenting; ungentle, rough

unless: *prep.* except, but for; *adv.* (with a clause) except if; if there be not

up: *adv.* on foot; going on, in action; aloft; in arms

upon: *prep.* in consequence of, on account of, because of; on the strength of; at or about (a time); against; over

use: *v.* make a practice of; do, make; treat; have, possess; be accustomed, be wont; put out at interest; *n.* advantage, profit; habitual practice, habit; necessity, exigency; interest paid for borrowed money

very: *adj.* veritable, true, real; complete, perfect; alone, mere

villain: *n.* serf, servant, slave; rascal (but most frequent in modern sense)

virtue: *n.* bravery, valor (Latin *virtus*); power; accomplishment, excellence, merit; very substance, essence

vulgar: *n.* the common people; the vernacular language; *adj.* common; low, mean; commonplace, ordinary; public; common to all

wait: *v.* attend, pay attendance; accompany; join, follow; await

want: *v.* be without, lack; need (not used in the sense "wish for" or "desire")

wanton: *v.* play, dally, trifle; *n.* person of unrestrained, sportive, or roguish behavior, a merry rogue; a spoiled boy; an effeminate person; a lascivious woman; *adj.* playful, frolicsome; capricious; loose, light, trifling; luxuriant, luxurious; effeminate; lustful, lascivious

waste: *v.* destroy, consume, spend; wear away; *n.* destruction, devastation; (= *vast*) boundless space

watch: *v.* stay awake; keep guard; be vigilant; look out for; keep a hawk awake (in order to tame it); catch in the act; *n.* state of being awake; vigilance, attention; sentinel(s), guard(s)

weed: *v.* uproot; *n.* dress, clothing, garb

what: *pron.* who; whatever; what kind of; *adv.* why, how

when as: when

which: *pron.* who

while: *n.* (preceded by *the*) at the present; *conj.* as long as; till, until

whiles: *conj.* whilst, during the time that; as long as; at the same time that

who: *pron.* which; (used for) whom

whom: *pron.* which; (used for) who

will: *v.* wish, desire; order, bid, require; *n.* intention, desire; command, authority; carnal desire, lust

wink: *v.* close both eyes; give a significant look; (with *at* or *upon*) seem not to see; sleep; *n.* a short moment; closing of the eyes (with reference to death); glimpse

wit: *v.* known; *n.* understanding, wisdom, judgment; imagination, invention

with: *prep.* by, at, on, against; by means of; at the summons of

withal: *prep.* with (used at the end of a clause); *adv.* with this, with it, therewith; at the same time, besides, moreover, also

wood: *adj.* mad

worship: *v.* honor, dignify; *n.* honor, dignity; title of honor

wreak: *v.* revenge; *n.* vengeance, revenge

'zounds (*or* **'swounds**)**:** *interj.* God's wounds (strong oath)